ROAD ATLAS

SUPER CLEAR SCALE

1.5 miles to 1 inch
1:100 000*

NO.1 BEST SELLER

NAVIGATOR® TRUCKER'S BRITAIN

NEW EDITION

CONTENTS

II Key to map symbols
III Restricted motorway junctions
IV Route planning maps
X Distances and journey times
1 Road maps of Britain
315 Urban approach maps

315 Bristol *approaches*	320 Glasgow *approaches*	327 Manchester *approaches*
316 Birmingham *approaches*	321 Leeds *approaches*	328 Newcastle *approaches*
318 Cardiff *approaches*	322 London *approaches*	329 Nottingham *approaches*
319 Edinburgh *approaches*	326 Liverpool *approaches*	330 Sheffield *approaches*

331 Town plans
331 Aberdeen, Aberystwyth, Ashford, Ayr, Bangor, Barrow-in-Furness, Bath, Berwick-upon-Tweed
332 Birmingham, Blackpool, Bournemouth, Bradford, Brighton, Bristol, Bury St Edmunds
333 Cambridge, Canterbury, Cardiff, Carlisle, Chelmsford, Cheltenham, Chester, Chichester, Colchester
334 Coventry, Derby, Dorchester, Dumfries, Dundee, Durham, Edinburgh, Exeter
335 Fort William, Glasgow, Gloucester, Grimsby, Hanley, Harrogate, Holyhead, Hull
336 Inverness, Ipswich, Kendal, King's Lynn, Leeds, Lancaster, Leicester, Lewes
337 Lincoln, Liverpool, Llandudno, Llanelli, Luton, Macclesfield, Manchester
338 London
340 Maidstone, Merthyr Tydfil, Middlesbrough, Milton Keynes, Newcastle, Newport, Newquay, Newtown, Northampton
341 Norwich, Nottingham, Oban, Oxford, Perth, Peterborough, Plymouth, Poole, Portsmouth
342 Preston, Reading, St Andrews, Salisbury, Scarborough, Shrewsbury, Sheffield, Southampton
343 Southend-on-Sea, Stirling, Stoke, Stratford-upon-Avon, Sunderland, Swansea, Swindon, Taunton, Telford
344 Torquay, Truro, Wick, Winchester, Windsor, Wolverhampton, Worcester, Wrexham, York
345 Index to town plans
361 Index to road maps of Britain
402 County and unitary authority boundaries

www.philips-maps.co.uk

First published in 2009 by Philip's
a division of Octopus Publishing Group Ltd
www.octopusbooks.co.uk
Carmelite House, 50 Victoria Embankment
London EC4Y 0DZ
An Hachette UK Company
www.hachette.co.uk

Eighth edition 2023
First impression 2023

ISBN 978-1-84907-612-8

Cartography by Philip's

Data for the caravan sites provided by The Camping and Caravanning Club.

Information for the selection of Wildlife Trust nature reserves provided by The Wildlife Trusts.

Information for National Parks, Areas of Outstanding Natural Beauty, National Trails and Country Parks in Wales supplied by the Countryside Council for Wales.

Information for National Parks, Areas of Outstanding Natural Beauty, National Trails and Country Parks in England supplied by Natural England. Data for Regional Parks, Long Distance Footpaths and Country Parks in Scotland provided by Scottish Natural Heritage.

Information for Forest Parks supplied by the Forestry Commission

Information for the RSPB reserves provided by the RSPB

Gaelic name forms used in the Western Isles provided by Comhairle nan Eilean.

Data for the National Nature Reserves in England provided by Natural England. Data for the National Nature Reserves in Wales provided by Countryside Council for Wales. Darparwyd data'n ymwneud â Gwarchodfeydd Natur Cenedlaethol Cymru gan Gyngor Cefn Gwlad Cymru.

Information on the location of National Nature Reserves in Scotland was provided by Scottish Natural Heritage.

Data for National Scenic Areas in Scotland provided by the Scottish Executive Office. Crown copyright material is reproduced with the permission of the Controller of HMSO and the Queen's Printer for Scotland. Licence number C02W0003960.

*Parts of Scotland at smaller scale

Printed in China

Road map symbols

Motorway

Motorway junctions – full access, restricted access

Toll motorway

Motorway service area

Motorway under construction

Primary route – dual, single carriageway, services
– under construction, narrow

Primary destination

Numbered junctions – full, restricted access

A road – dual, single carriageway
– under construction, narrow

B road – dual, single carriageway
– under construction, narrow

Minor road – dual, single carriageway

Drive or track

Urban side roads (height, weight and width restrictions not shown)

Height restriction, width restriction – feet and inches

Tunnel, weight restriction – tonnes

Distance in miles

Roundabout, multi-level junction,

Toll, steep gradient – points downhill

National trail – England and Wales

Long distance footpath – Scotland

Railway with station, level crossing, tunnel

Preserved railway with level crossing, station, tunnel

Tramway

National boundary

County or unitary authority boundary

Car ferry, catamaran

Passenger ferry, catamaran

Hovercraft

Internal ferry – car, passenger

Principal airport, other airport or airfield

Area of outstanding natural beauty, National Forest – England and Wales, Forest park, National park, National scenic area – Scotland, Regional park

Woodland

Beach – sand, shingle

Navigable river or canal

Lock, flight of locks, canal bridge number

Caravan or camping sites
– CCC* Club Site, Ready Camp Site, Camping in the Forest Site
– CCC Certificated Site, Listed Site

*Categories defined by The Camping and Caravanning Club of Great Britain

Viewpoint, park and ride, spot height – in metres

Linear antiquity

Adjoining page number, OS National Grid reference – see page 402

Tourist information

Example	Symbol
BYLAND ABBEY	Abbey or priory
WOODHENGE	Ancient monument
SEALIFE CENTRE	Aquarium or dolphinarium
CITY MUSEUM AND ART GALLERY	Art collection or museum
TATE ST IVES	Art gallery
1644	Battle site and date
ABBOTSBURY SWANNERY	Bird sanctuary or aviary
BAMBURGH CASTLE	Castle
YORK MINSTER	Cathedral
SANDHAM MEMORIAL CHAPEL	Church of interest
	Country park
SEVEN SISTERS	– England and Wales
LOCHORE MEADOWS	– Scotland
ROYAL BATH & WEST SHOWGROUND	County show ground
MONK PARK FARM	Farm park
HILLIER GARDENS AND ARBORETUM	Garden, arboretum
ST ANDREWS	Golf course – 18-hole
TYNTESFIELD	Historic house
SS GREAT BRITAIN	Historic ship
HATFIELD HOUSE	House and garden
CUMBERLAND PENCIL MUSEUM	Museum
MUSEUM OF DARTMOOR LIFE	– Local
NAT MARITIME MUSEUM	– Maritime or military
	Marina
SILVERSTONE	Motor racing circuit
	Nature reserves
HOLTON HEATH	– National nature reserve
BOYTON MARSHES	– RSPB reserve
DRAYCOTT SLEIGHTS	– Wildlife Trust reserve
	Picnic area
WEST SOMERSET RAILWAY	Preserved railway
THIRSK	Racecourse
LEAHILL TURRET	Roman antiquity
THRIGBY HALL	Safari park
FREEPORT BRAINTREE	Shopping village
MILLENNIUM STADIUM	Sports venue
ALTON TOWERS	Theme park
	Tourist information
NATIONAL RAILWAY MUSEUM	Transport collection
LEVANT MINE	World heritage site
HELMSLEY	Youth hostel
MARWELL	Zoo
SUTTON BANK VISITOR CENTRE / GLENFIDDICH DISTILLERY	Other place of interest

Approach map symbols

Motorway

Toll motorway

Motorway junction – full, restricted access

Service area

Under construction

Primary route – dual, single carriageway

Service area

Multi-level junction

roundabout

Under construction

A road – dual, single carriageway

B road – dual, single carriageway

Minor road – dual, single carriageway

Ring road

Height restriction, width restriction – feet and inches

Weight restriction – tonnes

Distance in miles

Railway with station

Tramway with station

Underground or metro station

Congestion charge area

Road map scale

1:100 000 • 1cm = 1km • 1 inch = 1.58 miles

0 1 2 3 4 5 km

0 1 2 3 miles

Road map scale (Isle of Man and parts of Scotland)

1: 200 000 • 1cm = 2km • 1 inch = 3.15 miles

0 1 2 3 4 5 6 7 8 9 10 km

0 1 2 3 4 5 6 miles

Load and vehicle restrictions – please read

Where a warning sign is displayed, any height obstructions, including but not limited to low bridges and overhead cables, are shown in the atlas where such obstructions cross navigable roads selected for inclusion.

While every effort has been made to include all relevant and accurate information, due to limitations of scale a single symbol may be used to indicate more than one feature, or when the restriction applies to a longer stretch of road. It is not possible to show restrictions on urban side roads.

Height restrictions lower than 16'6" and width restrictions narrower than 13 feet, are all shown in three-inch multiples and have been rounded down where necessary. Weight restrictions indicate weak bridges and the maximum gross weight which could be supported is shown in tonnes.

The information is believed to be correct at the time of printing. The publishers cannot be held responsible for any damage sustained as the result of using information in this atlas.

Any information on height, width and weight restrictions in the UK as noted on pages 1–330 of this atlas has been derived from the OS material used to compile this atlas.
Any information on height, width and weight restrictions on the Isle of Man has been derived from the relevant information as supplied by the Isle of Man Highways Department.

Restricted motorway junctions

M1	Northbound	Southbound
2	No exit	No access
4	No exit	No access
6A	No exit. Access from M25 only	No access. Exit to M25 only
7	No exit. Access from A414 only	No access. Exit to A414 only
17	No access. Exit to M45 only	No exit. Access from M45 only
19	No exit to A14	No access from A14
21A	No access	No exit
23A		Exit to A42 only
24A	No exit	No access
35A	No access	No exit
43	No access. Exit to M621 only	No exit. Access from M621 only
48	No exit to A1(M) southbound	

M3	Eastbound	Westbound
8	No exit	No access
10	No access	No exit
13	No access to M27 eastbound	
14	No exit	No access

M4	Eastbound	Westbound
1	Exit to A4 eastbound only	Access from A4 westbound only
2	Access from A4 eastbound only	Access to A4 westbound only
21	No exit	No access
23	No access	No exit
25	No exit	No access
25A	No exit	No access
29	No exit	No access
38		No access
39	No exit or access	No exit
42	Access from A483 only	Exit to A483 only

M5	Northbound	Southbound
10	No exit	No access
11A	No access from A417 eastbound	No exit to A417 westbound

M6	Northbound	Southbound
3A	No access.	No exit. Access from M6 eastbound only
4A	No exit. Access from M42 southbound only	No access. Exit to M42 only
5	No access	No exit
10A	No access. Exit to M54 only	No exit. Access from M54 only
11A	No exit. Access from M6 Toll only	No access. Exit to M6 Toll only
20	No exit to M56 eastbound	No access from M56 westbound
20A	No exit	No access
24	No exit	No access
25	No access	No exit
30	No exit. Access from M61 northbound only	No access. Exit to M61 southbound only
31A	No access	No exit
45	No access	No exit

M6 Toll	Northbound	Southbound
T1		No exit
T2	No exit, no access	No access
T5	No exit	No access
T7	No access	No exit
T8	No access	No exit

M8	Eastbound	Westbound
6	No exit	No access
6A	No access	No exit
7	No Access	No exit
7A	No exit. Access from A725 northbound only	No access. Exit to A725 southbound only
8	No exit to M73 northbound	No access from M73 southbound
9	No access	No exit
13	No exit southbound	Access from M73 southbound only
14	No access	No exit
16	No exit	No access
17	No exit	
18		No exit
19	No exit to A814 eastbound	No access from A814 westbound
20	No exit	No access
21	No access from M74	No exit
22	No exit. Access from M77 only	No access. Exit to M77 only
23	No exit	No access
25	Exit to A739 northbound only. Access from A739 southbound only	
25A	No exit	No access
28	No exit	No access
28A	No exit	No access
29A	No exit	No access

M9	Eastbound	Westbound
2	No access	No exit
3	No exit	No access
6	No access	No exit
8	No exit	No access

M11	Northbound	Southbound
4	No exit	No access
5	No access	No exit
8A	No access	No exit
9	No access	No exit
13	No access	No exit
14	No exit to A428 westbound	No exit. Access from A14 westbound only

M20	Eastbound	Westbound
2	No access	No exit
3	No exit Access from M26 eastbound only	No access Exit to M26 westbound only
10	No access	No exit
11A	No access	No exit

M23	Northbound	Southbound
7	No exit to A23 southbound	No access from A23 northbound
10A	No exit	No access

M25	Clockwise	Anticlockwise
5	No exit to M26 eastbound	No access from M26 westbound
19	No access	No exit
21	No exit to M1 southbound. Access from M1 southbound only	No exit to M1 southbound. Access from M1 southbound only
31	No exit	No access

M27	Eastbound	Westbound
10	No exit	No access
12	No access	No exit

M40	Eastbound	Westbound
3	No exit	No access
7	No exit	No access
8	No exit	No access
13	No exit	No access
14	No access	No exit
16	No access	No exit

M42	Northbound	Southbound
1	No exit	No access
7	No access Exit to M6 northbound only	No exit. Access from M6 northbound only
7A	No access. Exit to M6 southbound only	No exit
8	No exit. Access from M6 southbound only	Exit to M6 northbound only. Access from M6 southbound only

M45	Eastbound	Westbound
M1 J17	Access to M1 southbound only	No access from M1 southbound
With A45	No access	No exit

M48	Eastbound	Westbound
M4 J21	No exit to M4 westbound	No access from M4 eastbound
M4 J23	No access from M4 westbound	No exit to M4 eastbound

M49	Southbound	Northbound
18A	No exit to M5 northbound	No access from M5 southbound

M53	Northbound	Southbound
11	Exit to M56 eastbound only. Access from M56 westbound only	Exit to M56 eastbnd only. Access from M56 westbound only

M56	Eastbound	Westbound
2	No exit	No access
3	No access	No exit
4	No exit	No access
7		No access
8	No exit or access	No exit
9	No access from M6 northbound	No access to M6 southbound
15	No exit to M53	No access from M53 northbound

M57	Northbound	Southbound
3	No exit	No access
5	No exit	No access

M60	Clockwise	Anticlockwise
2	No exit	No access
3	No exit to A34 northbound	No exit to A34 northbound
4	No access from M56	No exit to M56
5	No exit to A5103 southbound	No exit to A5103 northbound
14	No exit	No access
16	No exit	No access
20	No access	No exit
22		No access
25	No access	
26		No exit or access
27	No exit	No access

M61	Northbound	Southbound
2	No access from A580 eastbound	No exit to A580 westbound
3	No access from A580 eastbound. No access from A666 southbound	No exit to A580 westbound
M6 J30	No exit to M6 southbound	No access from M6 northbound

M62	Eastbound	Westbound
23	No access	No exit

M65	Eastbound	Westbound
9	No access	No exit
11	No exit	No access

M66	Northbound	Southbound
1	No access	No exit

M67	Eastbound	Westbound
1A	No access	No exit
2	No exit	No access

M69	Northbound	Southbound
2	No exit	No access

M73	Northbound	Southbound
2	No access from M8 eastbound	No exit to M8 westbound

M74	Northbound	Southbound
3	No access	No exit
3A	No exit	No access
7	No exit	No access
9	No exit or access	No access
10		No exit
11	No exit	No access
12	No access	No exit

M77	Northbound	Southbound
4	No exit	No access
6	No exit	No access
7	No exit	
8	No access	No access

M80	Northbound	Southbound
4A	No access	No exit
6A	No exit	No access
8	Exit to M876 northbound only. No access	Access from M876 southbound only. No exit

M90	Northbound	Southbound
1	Access from A90 northbound only	No access. Exit to A90 southbound only
2A	No access	No exit
7	No exit	No access
8	No access	No exit
10	No access from A912	No exit to A912

M180	Eastbound	Westbound
1	No access	No exit

M621	Eastbound	Westbound
2A	No exit	No access
4	No exit	
5	No exit	No access
6	No access	No exit

M876	Northbound	Southbound
2	No access	No exit

A1(M)	Northbound	Southbound
2	No access	No exit
3		No access
5	No exit	No exit, no access
14	No exit	No access
40	No access	No exit
43	No exit. Access from M1 only	No access. Exit to M1 only
57	No access	No exit
65	No access	No exit

A3(M)	Northbound	Southbound
1	No exit	No access
4	No access	No exit

A38(M) with Victoria Rd, (Park Circus) Birmingham	
Northbound	No exit
Southbound	No access

M4 Junctions 25, 25A, 26

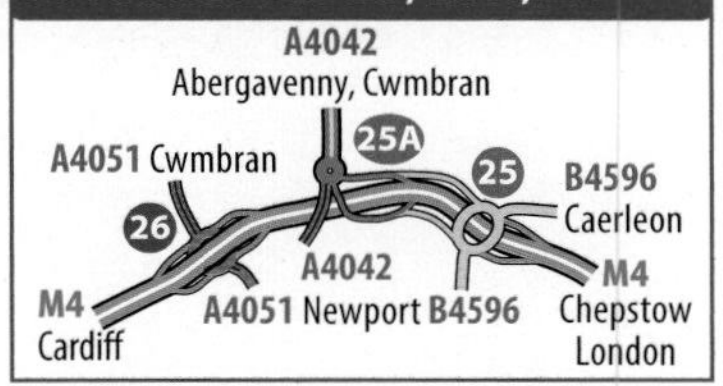

A4042 Abergavenny, Cwmbran
A4051 Cwmbran
25A
25
B4596 Caerleon
26
A4042
M4 Cardiff
A4051 Newport B4596
M4 Chepstow London

A48(M)	Northbound	Southbound
M4 Junc 29	Exit to M4 eastbound only	Access from M4 westbound only
29A	Access from A48 eastbound only	Exit to A48 westbound only

A57(M)	Eastbound	Westbound
With A5103	No access	No exit
With A34	No access	No exit

A58(M)	Southbound
With Park Lane and Westgate, Leeds	No access

A64(M)	Eastbound	Westbound
With A58 Clay Pit Lane, Leeds	No access from A58	No exit to A58

A74(M)	Northbound	Southbound
18	No access	No exit
22		No exit to A75

A194(M)	Northbound	Southbound
A1(M) J65 Gateshead Western Bypass	Access from A1(M) northbound only	Exit to A1(M) southbound only

M6 Junc 20 · M56 Junc 9

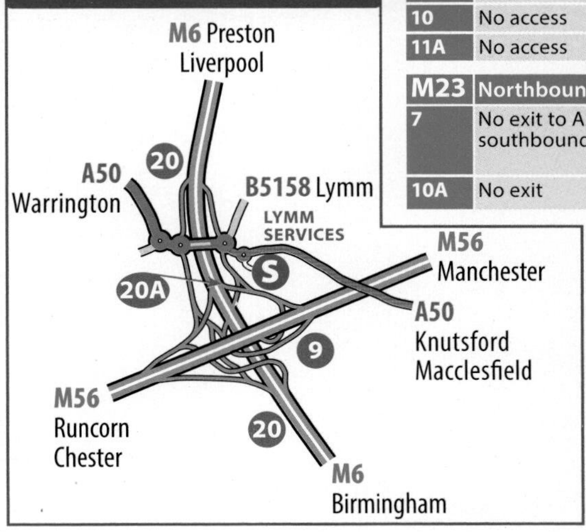

M6 Preston Liverpool
A50 Warrington
20
B5158 Lymm
LYMM SERVICES
S
M56 Manchester
20A
A50 Knutsford Macclesfield
9
M56 Runcorn Chester
20
M6 Birmingham

M3 Junctions 13, 14 · M27 Junction 4

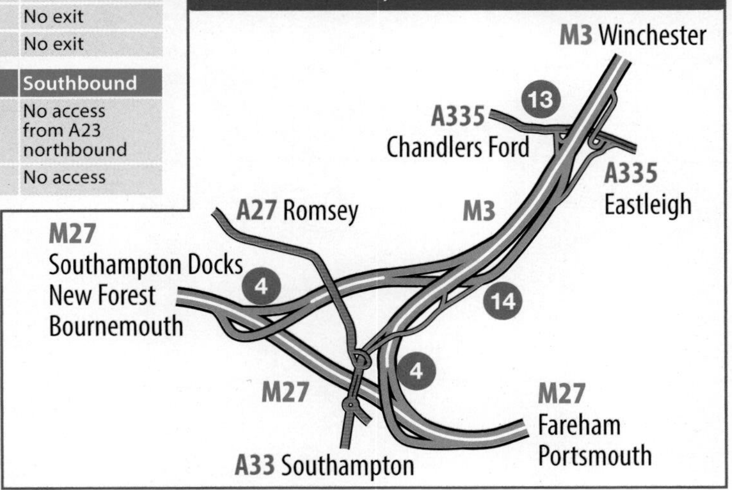

M3 Winchester
A335 Chandlers Ford
13
A335 Eastleigh
A27 Romsey
M3
M27 Southampton Docks New Forest Bournemouth
4
14
4
M27
M27 Fareham Portsmouth
A33 Southampton

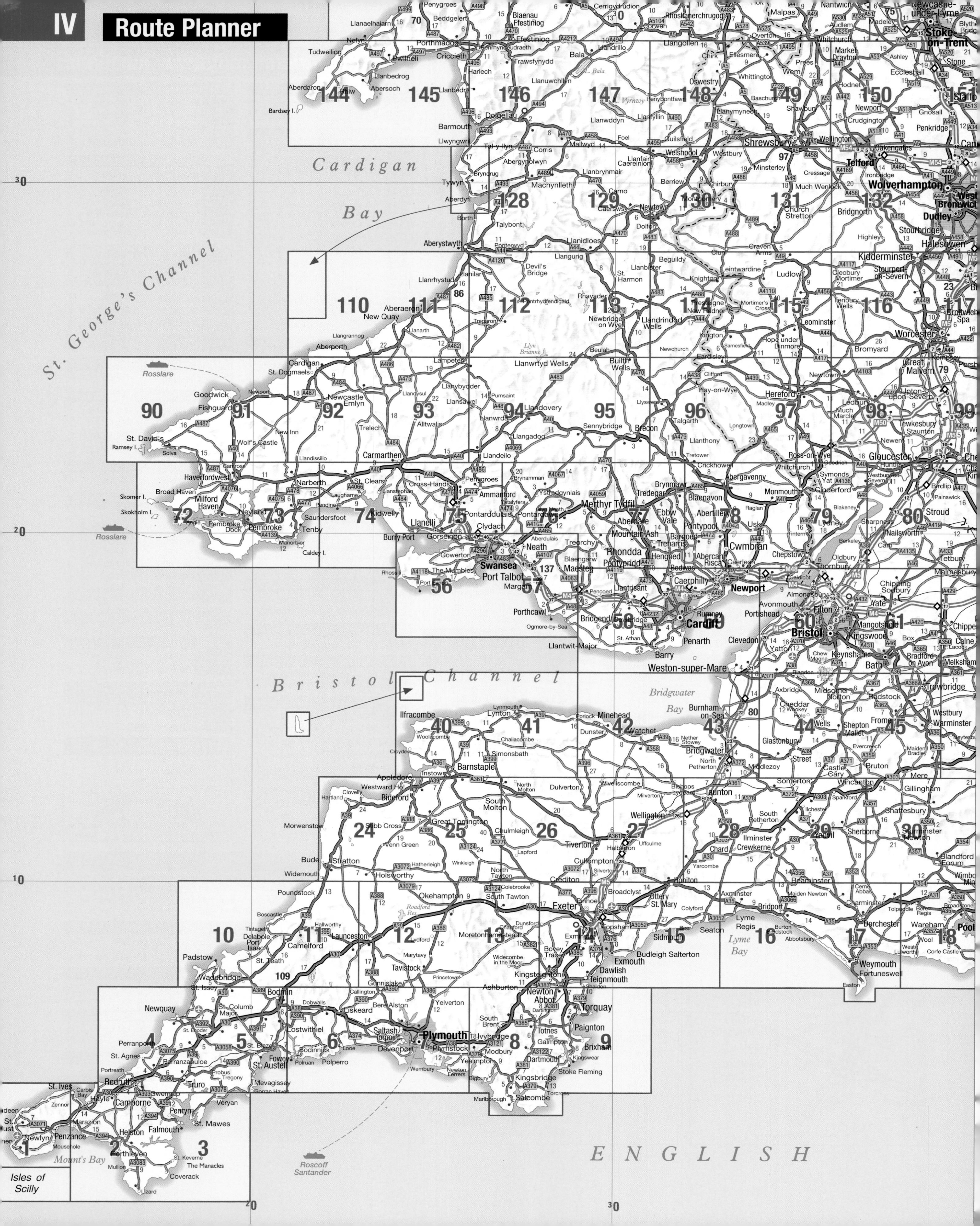
Cardigan
Bay
St. George's Channel
Bristol Channel
Bridgwater Bay
Lyme Bay
Mount's Bay
ENGLISH
Isles of Scilly
Rosslare
Roscoff Santander
Shrewsbury
Telford
Wolverhampton
Dudley
Kidderminster
Worcester
Hereford
Gloucester
Aberystwyth
Carmarthen
Swansea
Port Talbot
Newport
Cardiff
Bristol
Bath
Weston-super-Mare
Taunton
Exeter
Plymouth
Torquay
Barnstaple
Bridgwater
Yeovil
Dorchester
Weymouth
Truro
Penzance
St. Ives
Newquay
Bodmin

V
Motorway
junctions - full,restricted
Toll motorway
Services
Primary route
single/dual carriageway
A Road
B Road
Distances - in miles
major
minor
Railway
National boundary
Ferry route
Dieppe
Airport
Scale 1:1129000 1cm = 11.29km 1 inch = 17.82 miles
0 5 10 15 20 25 30 35 40 45 50 miles
0 10 20 30 40 50 60 70 80 km
CHANNEL
Strait of Dover
LONDON
BIRMINGHAM
Nottingham
Leicester
Coventry
Northampton
Peterborough
Cambridge
Norwich
Ipswich
Colchester
Oxford
Reading
Luton
Southampton
Portsmouth
Brighton
Dover
Calais
Boulogne-sur-Mer
Hoek van Holland
Dunkerque
Guernsey
Jersey
Cherbourg
St. Malo
Bilbao
Santander
Caen
Le Harve

254
255
256
257
258
259
260
261
262
263
266
267
268
269
270
271
272
273
244
245
246
247
248
249
250
251
236
237
238
239
240
241
228
229
230
231
232
219
220
221
222
223
210
211
212
213
192
202
203
204
193
194
195
178
179
180
181
182
183
184
162
163
164
165
166
167
168
North Channel
IRISH SEA
Isle of Man
Firth of Clyde
Solway Firth
Luce Bay
Morecambe Bay
Liverpool Bay
Anglesey
Arran
Edinburgh
Glasgow
Greenock
Paisley
Kilmarnock
Ayr
Prestwick
Troon
Irvine
Girvan
Stranraer
Newton Stewart
Dumfries
Carlisle
Hawick
Galashiels
Peebles
Moffat
Lockerbie
Campbeltown
Belfast
Larne
Bangor
Newtownards
Lisburn
Downpatrick
Newcastle
Douglas
Ramsey
Peel
Castletown
Port Erin
Workington
Whitehaven
Maryport
Cockermouth
Keswick
Penrith
Kendal
Windermere
Ambleside
Barrow-in-Furness
Lancaster
Morecambe
Fleetwood
Blackpool
Preston
Blackburn
Burnley
Southport
Liverpool
Birkenhead
St. Helens
Wigan
Bolton
Manchester
Salford
Stockport
Warrington
Chester
Wrexham
Crewe
Stoke-on-Trent
Holyhead
Bangor
Caernarfon
Llandudno
Colwyn Bay
Rhyl
Porthmadog
Pwllheli
Liverpool Douglas
Belfast
Dublin
Belfast Dublin

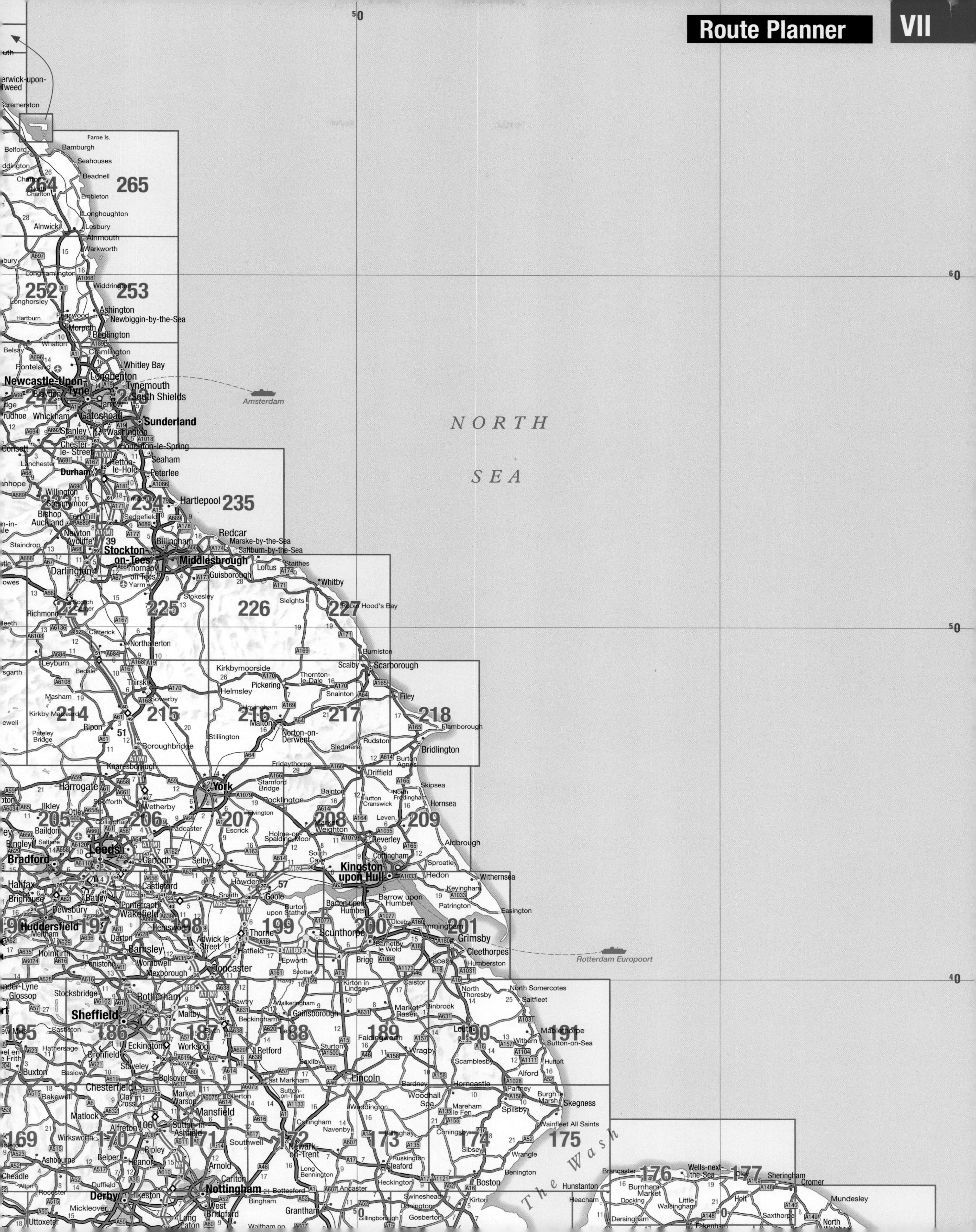
NORTH
SEA
Amsterdam
Rotterdam Europoort
The Wash
Farne Is.
Bamburgh
Seahouses
Beadnell
Embleton
Longhoughton
Lesbury
Alnwick
Alnmouth
Warkworth
Widdrington
Ashington
Newbiggin-by-the-Sea
Pegswood
Morpeth
Bedlington
Cramlington
Whitley Bay
Ponteland
Longbenton
Newcastle-Upon-Tyne
Tynemouth
South Shields
Blaydon
Whickham
Gateshead
Jarrow
Sunderland
Stanley
Washington
Chester-le-Street
Houghton-le-Spring
Consett
Seaham
Lanchester
Durham
Hetton-le-Hole
Peterlee
Willington
Hartlepool
Spennymoor
Bishop Auckland
Ferryhill
Sedgefield
Newton Aycliffe
Billingham
Redcar
Marske-by-the-Sea
Saltburn-by-the-Sea
Staindrop
Stockton-on-Tees
Middlesbrough
Thornaby on Tees
Darlington
Guisborough
Loftus
Staithes
Whitby
Yarm
Stokesley
Sleights
Robin Hood's Bay
Richmond
Scotch Corner
Catterick
Northallerton
Burniston
Leyburn
Bedale
Kirkbymoorside
Scalby
Scarborough
Thirsk
Helmsley
Pickering
Thornton-le-Dale
Snainton
Filey
Masham
Sowerby
Hovingham
Kirkby Malzeard
Ripon
Malton
Norton-on-Derwent
Flamborough
Pateley Bridge
Boroughbridge
Stillington
Rudston
Sledmere
Bridlington
Burton Agnes
Fridaythorpe
Knaresborough
Driffield
Harrogate
York
Stamford Bridge
Skipsea
Bainton
Hutton Cranswick
North Frodingham
Ilkley
Spofforth
Wetherby
Pocklington
Hornsea
Otley
Collingham
Elvington
Leven
Baildon
Tadcaster
Escrick
Market Weighton
Bingley
Saltaire
Holme-on-Spalding-Moor
Beverley
Aldbrough
Bradford
Leeds
Garforth
Selby
South Cave
Cottingham
Sproatley
Kingston upon Hull
Hedon
Withernsea
Halifax
Castleford
Howden
Keyingham
Brighouse
Batley
Pontefract
Snaith
Goole
Barton upon Humber
Barrow upon Humber
Patrington
Easington
Dewsbury
Wakefield
Burton upon Stather
Huddersfield
Hemsworth
Thorne
Scunthorpe
Immingham
Grimsby
Meltham
Darton
Adwick le Street
Barnetby le Wold
Holmfirth
Barnsley
Hatfield
Epworth
Cleethorpes
Penistone
Wombwell
Brigg
Laceby
Humberston
Mexborough
Doncaster
Scotter
Haxey
Caistor
Kirton in Lindsey
North Somercotes
North Thoresby
Saltfleet
Glossop
Stocksbridge
Rotherham
Bawtry
Walkeringham
Market Rasen
Binbrook
Sheffield
Maltby
Gainsborough
Louth
Mablethorpe
Castleton
Beckingham
Blyth
Hathersage
Eckington
Worksop
Retford
Sturton
Faldingworth
Withern
Sutton-on-Sea
Dronfield
Saxilby
Wragby
Scamblesby
Huttoft
Buxton
Baslow
Staveley
East Markham
Lincoln
Alford
Bolsover
Chesterfield
Bakewell
Clay Cross
Market Warsop
Ollerton
Sutton-on-Trent
Bardney
Horncastle
Partney
Burgh le Marsh
Skegness
Woodhall Spa
Matlock
Mansfield
Mareham le Fen
Spilsby
Waddington
Cuningham
Alfreton
Sutton-in-Ashfield
Navenby
Coningsby
Wainfleet All Saints
Wirksworth
Southwell
Newark-on-Trent
Billinghay
Sibsey
Ripley
Belper
Ashbourne
Heanor
Ruskington
Sleaford
Wrangle
Arnold
Long Bennington
Cheadle
Duffield
Carlton
Heckington
Benington
Boston
Brancaster
Hunstanton
Wells-next-the-Sea
Cley
Sheringham
Cromer
Burnham Market
Derby
Ilkeston
Nottingham
Bottesford
Ancaster
Swineshead
Donington
Heacham
Docking
Walsingham
Holt
Mundesley
Mickleover
West Bridgford
Bingham
Grantham
Billingborough
Gosberton
Kirton
Dersingham
Fakenham
Saxthorpe
North Walsham
Uttoxeter
Long Eaton
Waltham on
265
264
252
253
242
243
233
234
235
225
226
227
224
214
215
216
217
218
205
206
207
208
209
197
198
199
200
201
185
186
187
188
189
190
191
169
170
171
172
173
174
175
176
177
50
60
40

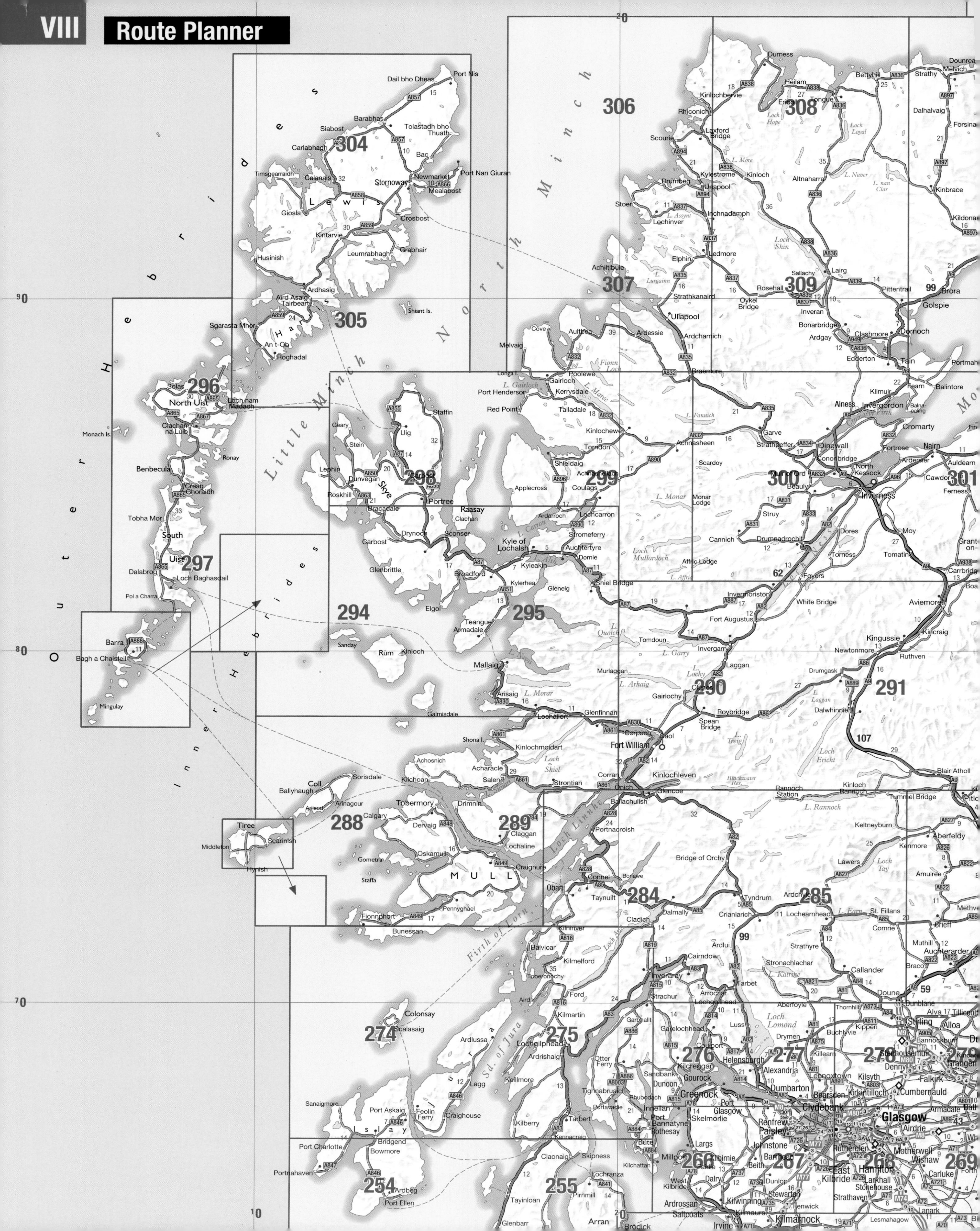
Outer Hebrides
Inner Hebrides
Little Minch
North Minch
304
305
306
307
308
309
296
297
298
299
300
301
294
295
290
291
288
289
284
285
274
275
276
277
278
279
254
255
266
267
268
269
Dail bho Dheas
Port Nis
Barabhas
Siabost
Tolastadh bho Thuath
Carlabhagh
Bac
Timsgearraidh
Calanais
Stornoway
Newmarket
Port Nan Giuran
Mealabost
Lewis
Giosla
Crosbost
Kintarvie
Leumrabhagh
Grabhair
Husinish
Ardhasig
Aird Asaig Tairbeart
Shiant Is.
Sgarasta Mhor
Harris
An t-Ob
Roghadal
Solas
North Uist
Loch nam Madadh
Clachan na Luib
Monach Is.
Ronay
Benbecula
Creag Ghoraidh
Tobha Mor
South Uist
Dalabrog
Loch Baghasdail
Pol a Charra
Barra
Bagh a Chaisteil
Mingulay
Durness
Bettyhill
Strathy
Dounreay
Melvich
Kinlochbervie
Heilam
Eriboll
Tongue
Rhiconich
Loch Hope
Loch Loyal
Dalhalvaig
Forsinard
Scourie
Laxford Bridge
L. More
Kylestrome
Kinloch
Altnaharra
L. Naver
Kinbrace
Drumbeg
Unapool
Stoer
Lochinver
Inchnadamph
Kildonan
Loch Shin
Ledmore
Elphin
Lairg
Achiltibuie
Sallachy
Rosehall
Pittentrail
Brora
Golspie
Strathkanaird
Oykel Bridge
Inveran
Ullapool
Bonarbridge
Clashmore
Dornoch
Ardgay
Cove
Aultbea
Ardessie
Ardcharnich
Edderton
Tain
Portmahomack
Melvaig
Fionn Loch
Braemore
Longa I.
Gairloch
Poolewe
L. Gairloch
Port Henderson
Kerrysdale
Loch Maree
Kilmuir
Fearn
Balintore
Red Point
Talladale
Alness
Invergordon
Cromarty Firth
Kinlochewe
Garve
Cromarty
Torridon
Achnasheen
Strathpeffer
Dingwall
Fortrose
Nairn
Conon Bridge
Ardersier
Auldearn
Shieldaig
Scardoy
Muir of Ord
North Kessock
Cawdor
Inverness
Ferness
Applecross
Coulags
L. Monar
Monar Lodge
Beauly
Lochcarron
Struy
Ardarroch
Stromeferry
Cannich
Drumnadrochit
Dores
Moy
Grantown-on-Spey
Kyle of Lochalsh
Auchtertyre
Dornie
Loch Mullardoch
Affric Lodge
Torness
Tomatin
Carrbridge
Kyleakin
Shiel Bridge
Foyers
Invermoriston
White Bridge
Aviemore
Fort Augustus
Kincraig
Kingussie
Newtonmore
Ruthven
Tomdoun
L. Garry
Invergarry
L. Quoich
Laggan
Drumgask
Murlaggan
L. Lochy
L. Arkaig
Gairlochy
Loch Laggan
Dalwhinnie
Spean Bridge
Roybridge
L. Treig
Loch Ericht
Blair Atholl
Staffin
Geary
Uig
Stein
Lephin
Dunvegan
Skye
Portree
Roskhill
Bracadale
Raasay
Clachan
Drynoch
Sconser
Carbost
Glenbrittle
Broadford
Kylerhea
Glenelg
Elgol
Teangue
Armadale
Sanday
Rum
Kinloch
Mallaig
Arisaig
L. Morar
Lochailort
Glenfinnan
Galmisdale
Corpach
Caol
Fort William
Shona I.
Kinlochmoidart
Loch Shiel
Achosnich
Acharacle
Kilchoan
Salen
Strontian
Corran
Kinlochleven
Onich
Glencoe
Ballachulish
Blackwater Res.
Rannoch Station
Kinloch Rannoch
L. Rannoch
Tummel Bridge
Pitlochry
Coll
Sorisdale
Ballyhaugh
Arinagour
Tobermory
Drimnin
Calgary
Dervaig
Claggan
Lochaline
Portnacroish
Tiree
Scarinish
Middleton
Hynish
Gometra
Oskamull
Staffa
MULL
Craignure
Loch Linnhe
Oban
Connel
Bonawe
Taynuilt
Bridge of Orchy
Keltneybury
Kenmore
Aberfeldy
Loch Tay
Lawers
Amulree
Tyndrum
Dalmally
Crianlarich
Lochearnhead
St. Fillans
Comrie
Crieff
Pennyghael
Fionnphort
Bunessan
Firth of Lorn
Cladich
Ardlui
Strathyre
Muthill
Auchterarder
Balvicar
Kilmelford
Cairndow
Stronachlachar
Loch Katrine
Callander
Braco
Toberonochy
Inveraray
Arrochar
Tarbet
Doune
Dunblane
Strachur
Lochgoilhead
Aberfoyle
Ford
Thornhill
Stirling
Alloa
Colonsay
Scalasaig
Kilmartin
Garbhallt
Loch Lomond
Drymen
Kippen
Buchlyvie
Luss
Garelochhead
Ardlussa
Lochgilphead
Ardrishaig
Coulport
Helensburgh
Alexandria
Killearn
Denny
Grangemouth
Kilcreggan
Jura
Sd. of Jura
Otter Ferry
Gourock
Dumbarton
Kilsyth
Falkirk
Lagg
Kellmore
Sandbank
Dunoon
Lennoxtown
Kirkintilloch
Cumbernauld
Sanaigmore
Tighnabruaich
Greenock
Port Glasgow
Clydebank
Port Askaig
Feolin Ferry
Craighouse
Portavadie
Rhubodach
Innellan
Bearsden
Glasgow
Airdrie
Islay
Kilberry
Tarbert
Port Bannatyne
Rothesay
Skelmorlie
Renfrew
Paisley
Rutherglen
Motherwell
Wishaw
Port Charlotte
Bridgend
Bowmore
Kennacraig
Bute
Johnstone
Barrhead
Largs
Claonaig
Skipness
Kilchattan
Millport
Kilbirnie
Beith
East Kilbride
Hamilton
Larkhall
Carluke
Portnahaven
Lochranza
Dalry
Dunlop
Stonehouse
Ardbeg
Port Ellen
Tayinloan
Pirnmill
West Kilbride
Ardrossan
Saltcoats
Stewarton
Kilwinning
Kilmaurs
Fenwick
Strathaven
Lanark
Glenbarr
Arran
Brodick
Irvine
Kilmarnock
Lesmahagow

Shetland Islands
Unst
Yell
Mainland
Fetlar
Baltasound
Haroldswick
Norwick
Cullivoe
Gutcher
Belmont
Mid Yell
Funzie
Burravoe
Ulsta
Isbister
Hillswick
St Magnus Bay
Brae
Voe
Vidlin
Whalsay
Symbister
Out Skerries
Sandness
Dale
Aith
Walls
Neap
Easter Skeld
Lerwick
I. of Noss
Foula
Scalloway
Hamnavoe
West Burra
Scousburgh
Northpunds
Boddam
Toab
Sumburgh
Aberdeen Kirkwall
Fair Isle
312
313
Orkney Islands
Westray
Pierowall
Midbea
Hollandstoun
N. Ronaldsay
The North Sound
Burness
Rapness
Calfsound
Overbister
Eday
Sanday
Stronsay
Wasbister
The Barony
Twatt
Dounby
Redland
Balfour
Stromness
Finstown
Kirkwall
Orphir
Gritley
St. Mary's
Copinsay
Scapa Flow
Hoy
Lyness
Flotta
Longhope
South Walls
St. Margaret's Hope
South Ronaldsay
Burwick
Pentland Firth
Stronsay Firth
Aberdeen Lerwick
314
John o' Groats
Mey
Dunnet
Castletown
Thurso
Scrabster
Sordale
Halkirk
Hastigrow
Nybster
Keiss
Reiss
Watten
Wick
Mybster
Thrumster
Ulbster
Achavanich
Lybster
Latheron
Dunbeath
Berriedale
Ousdale
Helmsdale
310
311
Lossiemouth
Burghead
Kinloss
Forres
Elgin
Findochty
Portknockie
Buckie
Portsoy
Banff
Macduff
Rosehearty
Fraserburgh
Inverallochy
New Aberdour
Strichen
Crimond
New Pitsligo
Mintlaw
Old Deer
Peterhead
Boddam
Keith
Huntly
Turriff
Fortrie
Dufftown
Rothes
Charlestown of Aberlour
Methlick
Tarves
Ellon
Cruden Bay
Newburgh
Oldmeldrum
Inverurie
Kemnay
Alford
Tomintoul
Newmachar
Kintore
Dyce
Balmedie
Bridge of Don
Aberdeen
Westhill
Cults
Peterculter
Portlethen
Newtonhill
Stonehaven
Banchory
Aboyne
Ballater
Braemar
Tarland
Torphins
Kirkwall Lerwick
302
303
292
293
Laurencekirk
Inverbervie
Johnshaven
Brechin
Montrose
Kirriemuir
Forfar
Arbroath
Carnoustie
Monifieth
Dundee
Blairgowrie
Coupar Angus
Perth
Newport-on-Tay
Tayport
Leuchars
St. Andrews
Cupar
Crail
Anstruther
St. Monance
Elie
Leven
Buckhaven
Kirkcaldy
Glenrothes
Kinross
Dunfermline
Burntisland
Firth of Forth
Firth of Tay
286
287
North Berwick
Dunbar
Edinburgh
Musselburgh
Prestonpans
Haddington
East Linton
Dalkeith
Livingston
Penicuik
Gorebridge
St. Abb's
Coldingham
Eyemouth
Duns
Berwick-upon-Tweed
Lauder
Peebles
Galashiels
Coldstream
Flodden
Bamburgh
Farne Is.
280
281
282
283
270
271
272
273

Distances and journey times

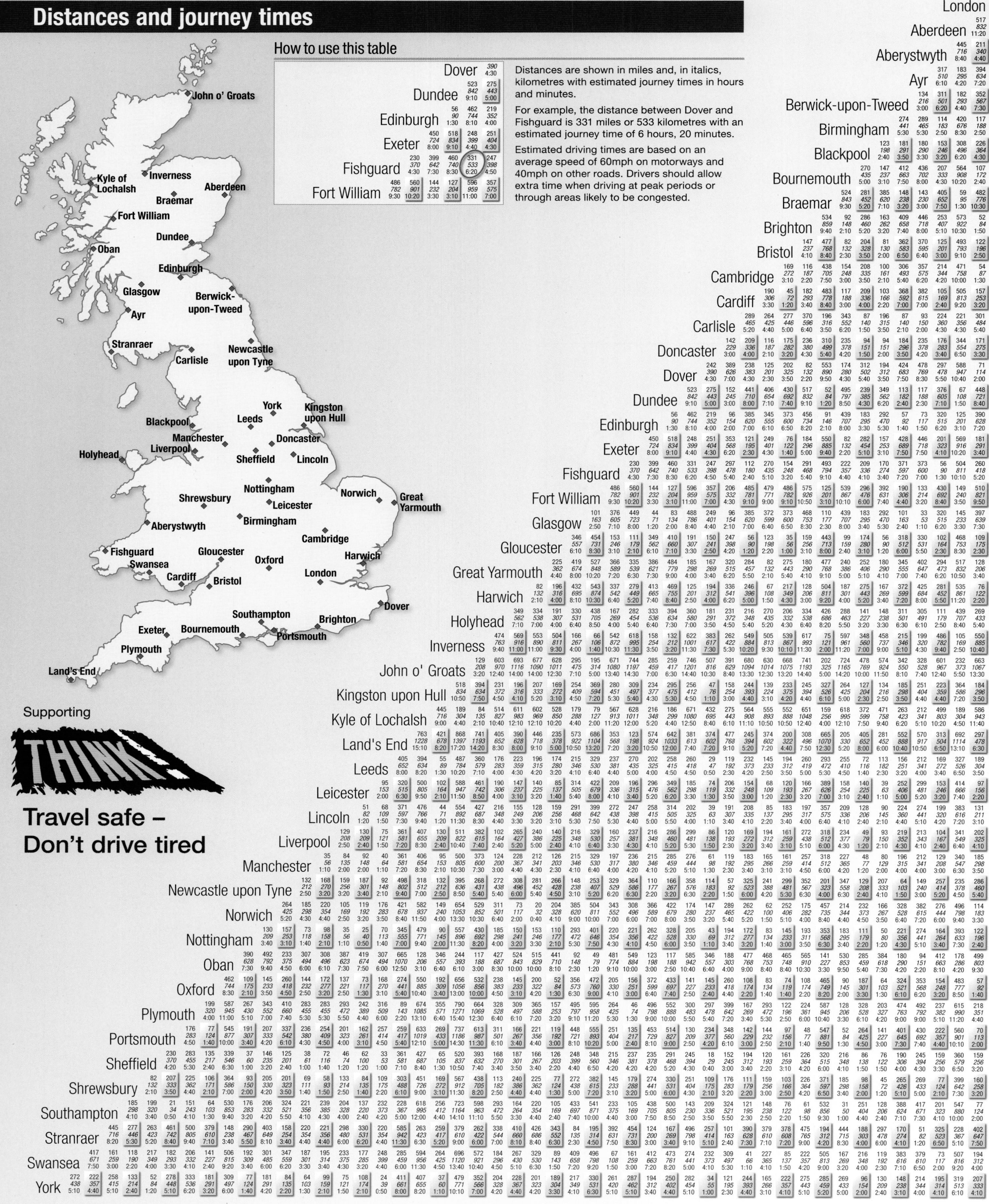

How to use this table

	Dover	Dundee	Edinburgh	Exeter	Fishguard
Dover					
Dundee	523 / 842 / 9:10				
Edinburgh	462 / 744 / 8:10	56 / 90 / 1:30			
Exeter	248 / 399 / 4:40	518 / 834 / 9:10	450 / 724 / 8:00		
Fishguard	331 / 533 / 6:20	460 / 740 / 8:30	399 / 642 / 7:30	230 / 370 / 4:30	
Fort William	596 / 959 / 11:00	127 / 204 / 3:10	144 / 232 / 3:30	560 / 901 / 10:20	486 / 782 / 9:30

(Also printed in the example: Dover–London 390 / 4:30; Dundee–Doncaster 275 / 443 / 5:00; Edinburgh–Doncaster 219 / 352 / 4:00; Exeter–Doncaster 251 / 404 / 4:30; Fishguard–Doncaster 247 / 398 / 4:50; Fort William–Doncaster 357 / 575 / 7:00.)

Distances are shown in miles and, in italics, kilometres with estimated journey times in hours and minutes.

For example, the distance between Dover and Fishguard is 331 miles or 533 kilometres with an estimated journey time of 6 hours, 20 minutes.

Estimated driving times are based on an average speed of 60mph on motorways and 40mph on other roads. Drivers should allow extra time when driving at peak periods or through areas likely to be congested.

Each cell: miles / *kilometres* / journey time (h:mm).

	London	Aberdeen	Aberystwyth	Ayr	Berwick-upon-Tweed	Birmingham	Blackpool	Bournemouth	Braemar	Brighton	Bristol	Cambridge	Cardiff	Carlisle	Doncaster	Dover	Dundee	Edinburgh	Exeter	Fishguard	Fort William	Glasgow	Gloucester	Great Yarmouth	Harwich	Holyhead	Inverness	John o' Groats	Kingston upon Hull	Kyle of Lochalsh	Land's End	Leeds	Leicester	Lincoln	Liverpool	Manchester	Newcastle upon Tyne	Norwich	Nottingham	Oban	Oxford	Plymouth	Portsmouth	Sheffield	Shrewsbury	Southampton	Stranraer	Swansea
Aberdeen	517 / 832 / 11:20
Aberystwyth	211 / 340 / 4:40	445 / 716 / 8:40
Ayr	394 / 634 / 7:20	183 / 295 / 4:20	317 / 510 / 6:10
Berwick-upon-Tweed	352 / 567 / 7:30	182 / 293 / 4:40	311 / 501 / 6:20	134 / 216 / 3:00
Birmingham	117 / 188 / 2:50	420 / 676 / 8:30	114 / 183 / 2:50	289 / 465 / 5:30	274 / 441 / 5:30
Blackpool	226 / 364 / 4:30	308 / 496 / 6:20	153 / 246 / 3:20	180 / 290 / 3:30	181 / 291 / 3:50	123 / 198 / 2:40
Bournemouth	107 / 172 / 2:40	564 / 908 / 10:20	207 / 333 / 4:30	436 / 702 / 8:00	412 / 663 / 7:50	147 / 237 / 3:10	270 / 435 / 5:00
Braemar	482 / 776 / 10:30	59 / 95 / 1:30	405 / 652 / 7:50	143 / 230 / 3:00	148 / 238 / 3:20	385 / 620 / 7:10	281 / 452 / 5:20	524 / 843 / 9:30
Brighton	52 / 84 / 1:50	573 / 922 / 10:30	253 / 407 / 5:10	446 / 718 / 8:00	409 / 658 / 7:40	163 / 262 / 3:20	286 / 460 / 5:20	92 / 148 / 2:10	534 / 859 / 9:40
Bristol	122 / 196 / 2:50	493 / 793 / 9:10	125 / 201 / 3:00	370 / 595 / 6:40	362 / 583 / 6:50	81 / 130 / 2:00	204 / 328 / 3:50	82 / 132 / 2:30	477 / 768 / 8:40	147 / 237 / 4:10
Cambridge	54 / 87 / 1:30	471 / 758 / 10:00	214 / 344 / 4:20	357 / 575 / 6:20	306 / 493 / 5:40	100 / 161 / 2:10	208 / 335 / 3:50	154 / 248 / 3:00	438 / 705 / 7:50	116 / 187 / 2:20	169 / 272 / 3:10
Cardiff	157 / 253 / 3:20	505 / 813 / 9:20	105 / 169 / 2:40	382 / 615 / 7:00	368 / 592 / 7:00	103 / 166 / 2:20	209 / 336 / 4:00	117 / 188 / 3:00	483 / 778 / 8:40	182 / 293 / 3:40	45 / 72 / 1:20	190 / 306 / 3:30
Carlisle	301 / 484 / 5:40	221 / 356 / 4:30	224 / 360 / 4:30	93 / 150 / 2:00	87 / 140 / 2:10	196 / 315 / 3:50	87 / 140 / 1:50	343 / 552 / 6:20	196 / 316 / 3:50	370 / 596 / 6:40	277 / 446 / 5:00	264 / 425 / 4:40	289 / 465 / 5:20
Doncaster	171 / 275 / 3:30	344 / 554 / 6:50	176 / 283 / 3:40	235 / 378 / 4:20	184 / 296 / 3:50	94 / 151 / 2:00	94 / 151 / 1:50	235 / 378 / 4:20	310 / 499 / 5:40	236 / 380 / 4:30	175 / 282 / 3:20	116 / 187 / 2:10	209 / 336 / 4:00	142 / 229 / 3:00
Dover	71 / 114 / 2:00	588 / 947 / 10:40	297 / 478 / 5:50	478 / 769 / 8:30	424 / 683 / 7:50	194 / 312 / 3:50	312 / 502 / 5:40	174 / 280 / 4:30	553 / 890 / 9:50	82 / 132 / 2:20	202 / 325 / 3:50	125 / 201 / 2:30	238 / 383 / 4:30	389 / 626 / 7:00	242 / 390 / 4:30
Dundee	448 / 721 / 8:40	67 / 108 / 1:50	376 / 605 / 7:10	117 / 188 / 2:30	113 / 182 / 2:40	349 / 562 / 6:20	239 / 385 / 4:30	495 / 797 / 8:50	52 / 84 / 1:20	517 / 832 / 9:10	430 / 692 / 7:40	406 / 654 / 7:10	441 / 710 / 8:00	152 / 245 / 3:00	275 / 443 / 5:00	523 / 842 / 9:10
Edinburgh	390 / 628 / 7:20	125 / 201 / 3:10	320 / 515 / 6:20	73 / 117 / 1:50	57 / 92 / 1:40	292 / 470 / 5:30	183 / 295 / 3:30	439 / 707 / 8:00	91 / 146 / 2:10	456 / 734 / 8:20	373 / 600 / 6:50	345 / 555 / 6:10	385 / 620 / 7:00	96 / 154 / 2:00	219 / 352 / 4:00	462 / 744 / 8:10	56 / 90 / 1:30
Exeter	181 / 291 / 3:40	569 / 916 / 10:20	201 / 323 / 4:10	446 / 718 / 7:50	428 / 689 / 7:50	157 / 253 / 3:10	282 / 454 / 5:10	82 / 132 / 2:20	550 / 885 / 9:40	184 / 296 / 5:00	76 / 122 / 1:40	249 / 401 / 4:30	121 / 195 / 2:30	353 / 568 / 6:20	251 / 404 / 4:30	248 / 399 / 4:40	518 / 834 / 9:10	450 / 724 / 8:00
Fishguard	260 / 418 / 5:20	504 / 811 / 10:10	56 / 90 / 1:30	373 / 600 / 7:00	371 / 597 / 7:20	170 / 274 / 3:40	209 / 336 / 4:10	222 / 357 / 4:40	493 / 794 / 9:10	291 / 468 / 5:40	154 / 248 / 3:20	270 / 435 / 5:10	112 / 180 / 2:40	297 / 478 / 5:40	247 / 398 / 4:50	331 / 533 / 6:20	460 / 740 / 8:30	399 / 642 / 7:30	230 / 370 / 4:30
Fort William	510 / 821 / 9:50	149 / 240 / 3:50	430 / 692 / 8:40	133 / 214 / 3:20	190 / 306 / 4:40	392 / 631 / 7:40	296 / 476 / 6:00	539 / 867 / 10:10	125 / 201 / 3:10	575 / 926 / 10:50	486 / 782 / 9:10	479 / 771 / 9:00	485 / 781 / 9:10	206 / 332 / 4:30	357 / 575 / 7:00	596 / 959 / 11:00	127 / 204 / 3:10	144 / 232 / 3:30	560 / 901 / 10:20	486 / 782 / 9:30
Glasgow	397 / 639 / 7:30	145 / 233 / 3:30	320 / 515 / 6:20	33 / 53 / 1:10	101 / 163 / 2:40	292 / 470 / 5:30	183 / 295 / 3:40	439 / 707 / 8:00	110 / 177 / 2:30	468 / 753 / 8:30	373 / 600 / 6:50	372 / 599 / 6:40	385 / 620 / 7:00	96 / 154 / 2:10	249 / 401 / 4:40	488 / 786 / 8:40	83 / 134 / 2:00	44 / 71 / 1:20	449 / 723 / 8:00	376 / 605 / 7:10	101 / 163 / 2:50
Gloucester	109 / 175 / 2:30	468 / 753 / 8:30	102 / 164 / 2:30	330 / 531 / 5:50	318 / 512 / 6:00	56 / 90 / 1:20	174 / 280 / 3:10	99 / 159 / 2:40	443 / 713 / 8:00	159 / 256 / 3:10	35 / 56 / 1:00	123 / 198 / 2:20	56 / 90 / 1:20	247 / 398 / 4:20	150 / 241 / 2:50	191 / 307 / 3:30	410 / 660 / 7:10	349 / 562 / 6:10	111 / 179 / 2:10	153 / 246 / 3:10	454 / 731 / 8:30	346 / 557 / 6:10
Great Yarmouth	128 / 206 / 3:40	517 / 832 / 10:50	294 / 473 / 6:20	402 / 647 / 7:40	345 / 555 / 7:00	180 / 290 / 4:10	252 / 406 / 5:10	240 / 386 / 5:00	477 / 768 / 9:10	180 / 290 / 4:10	275 / 443 / 5:40	82 / 132 / 2:10	284 / 457 / 5:50	320 / 515 / 6:20	167 / 269 / 3:40	185 / 298 / 4:00	484 / 779 / 9:00	386 / 621 / 7:30	335 / 539 / 6:30	366 / 589 / 7:20	527 / 848 / 10:20	419 / 674 / 8:00	225 / 362 / 4:40
Harwich	76 / 122 / 2:20	535 / 861 / 11:20	281 / 452 / 5:50	425 / 684 / 8:00	372 / 599 / 7:20	167 / 269 / 3:40	275 / 443 / 5:20	187 / 301 / 4:00	504 / 811 / 9:20	128 / 206 / 3:00	217 / 349 / 4:30	67 / 108 / 1:50	246 / 396 / 5:00	336 / 541 / 6:20	194 / 312 / 4:00	125 / 201 / 2:50	469 / 755 / 8:40	413 / 665 / 7:40	279 / 449 / 5:20	337 / 542 / 6:40	543 / 874 / 10:30	432 / 695 / 8:10	196 / 316 / 4:00	82 / 132 / 2:10
Holyhead	269 / 433 / 5:40	439 / 707 / 8:40	111 / 179 / 2:50	305 / 491 / 6:10	311 / 501 / 6:30	148 / 238 / 3:30	141 / 227 / 3:20	288 / 463 / 5:50	426 / 686 / 8:20	334 / 538 / 6:40	206 / 332 / 4:30	270 / 435 / 5:20	216 / 348 / 5:40	231 / 372 / 4:50	181 / 291 / 3:50	360 / 580 / 7:00	394 / 634 / 7:30	333 / 536 / 6:40	282 / 454 / 5:40	167 / 269 / 4:00	438 / 705 / 8:50	330 / 531 / 6:40	191 / 307 / 4:00	334 / 538 / 7:00	349 / 562 / 7:10
Inverness	550 / 885 / 10:40	105 / 169 / 2:50	486 / 782 / 9:40	199 / 320 / 4:30	215 / 346 / 5:10	458 / 737 / 9:00	348 / 560 / 7:00	597 / 961 / 11:20	75 / 121 / 2:00	617 / 993 / 11:30	539 / 867 / 10:10	505 / 813 / 9:30	549 / 884 / 10:20	262 / 422 / 5:30	383 / 617 / 7:30	622 / 1001 / 11:30	132 / 212 / 3:20	158 / 254 / 3:50	618 / 995 / 11:30	542 / 872 / 10:30	66 / 106 / 1:40	166 / 267 / 4:00	504 / 811 / 9:30	553 / 890 / 11:00	569 / 916 / 11:00	474 / 763 / 9:40
John o' Groats	663 / 1067 / 13:30	232 / 373 / 5:50	601 / 967 / 12:40	328 / 528 / 7:40	342 / 550 / 8:10	574 / 924 / 11:50	478 / 769 / 10:00	724 / 1165 / 14:20	202 / 325 / 5:00	741 / 1193 / 14:40	668 / 1075 / 13:20	630 / 1014 / 12:30	680 / 1094 / 13:30	391 / 629 / 8:40	507 / 816 / 10:30	746 / 1201 / 14:40	259 / 417 / 6:30	285 / 459 / 7:00	744 / 1197 / 14:30	671 / 1080 / 13:40	195 / 314 / 5:00	295 / 475 / 7:10	628 / 1011 / 12:30	677 / 1090 / 14:00	693 / 1116 / 14:00	603 / 970 / 12:40	129 / 208 / 3:20
Kingston upon Hull	184 / 296 / 3:50	364 / 586 / 7:20	223 / 359 / 4:40	251 / 404 / 4:40	185 / 298 / 3:50	134 / 216 / 2:50	127 / 204 / 2:30	264 / 425 / 5:00	327 / 526 / 6:10	245 / 394 / 4:40	233 / 375 / 4:20	139 / 224 / 3:10	244 / 393 / 4:40	158 / 254 / 3:00	47 / 76 / 1:10	256 / 412 / 4:50	295 / 475 / 5:30	234 / 377 / 4:30	309 / 497 / 5:40	280 / 451 / 5:30	369 / 594 / 7:20	254 / 409 / 4:50	169 / 272 / 3:10	207 / 333 / 5:20	196 / 316 / 4:10	231 / 372 / 4:50	394 / 634 / 7:50	518 / 834 / 10:50
Kyle of Lochalsh	586 / 943 / 11:40	189 / 304 / 4:50	499 / 803 / 10:20	212 / 341 / 5:10	263 / 423 / 6:20	471 / 758 / 9:40	372 / 599 / 7:50	618 / 995 / 12:10	159 / 256 / 4:00	651 / 1048 / 12:40	552 / 888 / 10:50	555 / 893 / 10:50	564 / 908 / 11:10	275 / 443 / 6:10	432 / 695 / 8:40	671 / 1080 / 12:50	186 / 299 / 4:40	216 / 348 / 5:20	628 / 1011 / 12:00	567 / 913 / 11:20	79 / 127 / 2:00	179 / 288 / 4:40	528 / 850 / 10:20	602 / 969 / 12:10	611 / 983 / 12:10	514 / 827 / 10:40	84 / 135 / 2:10	189 / 304 / 4:40	445 / 716 / 9:00
Land's End	297 / 478 / 6:30	692 / 1114 / 13:10	313 / 504 / 6:50	570 / 917 / 10:50	552 / 888 / 10:40	281 / 452 / 6:00	405 / 652 / 8:00	205 / 330 / 5:20	665 / 1070 / 12:30	308 / 496 / 7:50	200 / 322 / 4:40	374 / 602 / 7:20	245 / 394 / 5:20	477 / 768 / 9:10	374 / 602 / 7:20	381 / 613 / 7:40	642 / 1033 / 12:00	574 / 924 / 10:50	123 / 198 / 3:20	353 / 568 / 7:20	686 / 1104 / 13:20	573 / 922 / 10:50	235 / 378 / 5:00	446 / 718 / 9:10	390 / 628 / 8:00	405 / 652 / 8:30	741 / 1193 / 14:20	868 / 1397 / 17:20	421 / 678 / 8:20	763 / 1228 / 15:10
Leeds	189 / 304 / 3:50	327 / 526 / 6:50	169 / 272 / 3:40	212 / 341 / 4:00	156 / 251 / 3:20	113 / 182 / 2:30	72 / 116 / 1:40	255 / 410 / 4:50	293 / 472 / 5:30	260 / 419 / 5:00	194 / 312 / 3:50	145 / 233 / 2:50	232 / 373 / 4:20	119 / 192 / 2:30	29 / 47 / 0:50	260 / 418 / 4:50	258 / 415 / 4:50	202 / 325 / 4:00	270 / 435 / 5:00	237 / 381 / 4:40	329 / 530 / 6:40	215 / 346 / 4:10	174 / 280 / 3:20	196 / 315 / 4:20	223 / 359 / 4:30	176 / 283 / 4:00	360 / 579 / 7:10	487 / 784 / 10:20	55 / 89 / 1:30	394 / 634 / 8:20	405 / 652 / 8:00
Leicester	97 / 156 / 2:20	414 / 666 / 7:40	153 / 246 / 3:20	299 / 481 / 5:20	252 / 406 / 5:00	39 / 63 / 1:10	140 / 225 / 2:40	158 / 254 / 3:10	389 / 626 / 7:00	166 / 267 / 3:20	120 / 193 / 2:30	68 / 109 / 1:20	154 / 248 / 3:00	206 / 332 / 3:50	74 / 119 / 1:30	185 / 298 / 3:30	349 / 562 / 6:20	296 / 476 / 5:20	196 / 315 / 3:40	209 / 336 / 4:10	422 / 679 / 8:00	314 / 505 / 5:40	85 / 137 / 1:40	140 / 225 / 3:20	147 / 237 / 3:10	190 / 306 / 4:00	461 / 742 / 8:50	588 / 947 / 11:50	102 / 164 / 2:10	500 / 805 / 9:50	320 / 515 / 6:30	95 / 153 / 2:00
Lincoln	131 / 211 / 3:10	383 / 616 / 7:20	199 / 320 / 4:20	274 / 441 / 5:10	224 / 360 / 4:40	90 / 145 / 2:10	128 / 206 / 2:40	209 / 336 / 4:10	357 / 575 / 6:40	197 / 317 / 4:00	183 / 295 / 3:40	85 / 137 / 2:20	208 / 335 / 4:10	191 / 307 / 3:40	39 / 63 / 1:10	202 / 325 / 4:00	314 / 505 / 5:50	258 / 415 / 5:00	247 / 398 / 4:40	272 / 438 / 5:30	399 / 642 / 7:50	291 / 468 / 5:30	159 / 256 / 3:10	128 / 206 / 3:20	155 / 249 / 3:30	216 / 348 / 4:40	427 / 687 / 8:30	554 / 892 / 11:30	44 / 71 / 1:20	476 / 766 / 9:40	371 / 597 / 7:30	68 / 109 / 1:50	51 / 82 / 1:20
Liverpool	202 / 325 / 4:10	341 / 549 / 6:40	104 / 167 / 2:40	213 / 343 / 4:10	219 / 352 / 4:30	93 / 150 / 2:10	49 / 79 / 1:20	234 / 377 / 4:30	318 / 512 / 6:00	272 / 438 / 5:10	161 / 259 / 3:10	194 / 312 / 3:40	169 / 272 / 3:20	120 / 193 / 2:30	86 / 138 / 1:50	299 / 481 / 5:30	286 / 460 / 5:20	216 / 348 / 4:10	237 / 381 / 4:30	160 / 257 / 3:30	329 / 530 / 6:40	216 / 348 / 4:10	140 / 225 / 2:40	240 / 386 / 5:00	265 / 427 / 5:20	102 / 164 / 2:40	382 / 615 / 7:40	511 / 822 / 10:40	130 / 209 / 2:40	407 / 655 / 8:30	361 / 581 / 7:20	75 / 121 / 1:50	130 / 209 / 2:40	129 / 208 / 2:50
Manchester	185 / 298 / 3:50	340 / 547 / 6:30	129 / 208 / 3:00	212 / 341 / 4:00	196 / 315 / 4:00	80 / 129 / 2:00	48 / 77 / 1:20	227 / 365 / 4:20	318 / 512 / 6:00	257 / 414 / 4:50	161 / 259 / 3:10	165 / 266 / 3:10	183 / 295 / 3:40	119 / 192 / 2:30	61 / 98 / 1:30	276 / 444 / 5:10	285 / 459 / 5:20	215 / 346 / 4:10	236 / 380 / 4:20	197 / 317 / 4:00	329 / 530 / 6:40	215 / 346 / 4:10	126 / 203 / 2:30	212 / 341 / 4:30	228 / 367 / 4:40	124 / 200 / 3:00	373 / 600 / 7:30	500 / 805 / 10:30	95 / 153 / 2:10	406 / 654 / 8:30	361 / 581 / 7:20	40 / 64 / 1:10	92 / 148 / 2:00	84 / 135 / 2:00	35 / 56 / 1:10
Newcastle upon Tyne	286 / 460 / 5:40	235 / 378 / 4:50	257 / 414 / 5:20	149 / 240 / 3:00	64 / 103 / 1:50	207 / 333 / 4:10	129 / 208 / 2:40	347 / 558 / 6:30	201 / 323 / 4:00	352 / 567 / 6:30	299 / 481 / 5:30	241 / 388 / 4:20	325 / 523 / 6:00	57 / 92 / 1:50	114 / 183 / 2:20	358 / 576 / 6:30	166 / 267 / 3:20	110 / 177 / 2:20	364 / 586 / 6:30	329 / 529 / 6:20	253 / 407 / 5:20	148 / 238 / 3:10	266 / 428 / 4:50	281 / 452 / 5:40	308 / 496 / 6:00	272 / 438 / 5:40	268 / 431 / 5:40	395 / 636 / 8:50	132 / 212 / 2:50	318 / 512 / 7:00	498 / 802 / 9:40	92 / 148 / 2:10	187 / 301 / 3:40	159 / 256 / 3:20	168 / 270 / 3:20	132 / 212 / 2:50
Norwich	114 / 183 / 3:30	496 / 798 / 9:40	276 / 444 / 6:00	382 / 615 / 7:20	328 / 528 / 6:40	166 / 267 / 3:50	232 / 373 / 4:50	214 / 344 / 4:40	457 / 735 / 8:40	175 / 282 / 4:00	252 / 406 / 5:10	62 / 100 / 1:50	262 / 422 / 5:20	289 / 465 / 5:40	147 / 237 / 3:20	174 / 280 / 3:50	422 / 679 / 8:00	366 / 589 / 7:00	308 / 496 / 6:00	343 / 552 / 7:00	504 / 811 / 10:00	385 / 620 / 9:00	204 / 328 / 4:10	20 / 32 / 0:40	73 / 117 / 2:00	311 / 501 / 6:40	529 / 852 / 10:30	654 / 1053 / 13:30	149 / 240 / 4:00	582 / 937 / 11:50	421 / 678 / 8:40	176 / 283 / 3:50	119 / 192 / 3:20	105 / 169 / 2:50	220 / 354 / 4:40	185 / 298 / 4:30	264 / 425 / 5:20
Nottingham	122 / 196 / 2:40	393 / 633 / 7:30	164 / 264 / 3:40	274 / 441 / 5:10	221 / 356 / 4:30	50 / 80 / 1:20	111 / 179 / 2:20	183 / 295 / 3:40	353 / 568 / 6:30	193 / 311 / 3:50	145 / 233 / 3:00	83 / 134 / 1:40	172 / 277 / 3:20	194 / 312 / 3:40	43 / 69 / 1:10	205 / 330 / 3:50	328 / 528 / 6:00	262 / 422 / 4:50	221 / 356 / 4:10	220 / 354 / 4:30	401 / 646 / 7:50	293 / 472 / 5:30	110 / 177 / 2:10	153 / 246 / 3:30	150 / 241 / 3:20	185 / 298 / 4:00	430 / 692 / 8:20	557 / 896 / 11:30	90 / 145 / 2:00	479 / 771 / 9:40	345 / 555 / 7:00	70 / 113 / 1:40	25 / 40 / 0:50	35 / 56 / 1:10	98 / 158 / 2:10	73 / 118 / 1:40	157 / 253 / 3:10	130 / 209 / 3:40
Oban	499 / 803 / 9:30	178 / 286 / 4:20	412 / 663 / 8:10	94 / 151 / 2:20	180 / 290 / 4:20	384 / 618 / 7:30	285 / 459 / 5:40	530 / 853 / 9:50	141 / 227 / 3:30	565 / 910 / 10:30	465 / 748 / 8:40	468 / 753 / 8:40	477 / 768 / 9:00	188 / 303 / 4:00	346 / 557 / 6:40	585 / 942 / 10:40	117 / 188 / 2:50	123 / 198 / 3:00	549 / 884 / 10:00	481 / 774 / 9:10	49 / 79 / 1:20	92 / 148 / 2:30	441 / 710 / 8:10	515 / 829 / 10:00	524 / 843 / 10:00	427 / 687 / 8:30	117 / 188 / 3:00	244 / 393 / 6:10	346 / 557 / 6:40	128 / 206 / 3:10	665 / 1070 / 12:50	307 / 494 / 6:00	419 / 674 / 7:50	387 / 623 / 7:30	308 / 496 / 6:10	307 / 494 / 6:00	233 / 375 / 4:50	492 / 792 / 9:40	390 / 628 / 7:30
Oxford	57 / 92 / 1:40	483 / 777 / 8:50	154 / 248 / 3:20	353 / 568 / 6:20	324 / 521 / 6:10	64 / 103 / 1:30	187 / 301 / 3:30	90 / 145 / 2:00	465 / 749 / 8:20	108 / 174 / 2:20	74 / 119 / 1:40	83 / 134 / 1:40	108 / 174 / 2:20	260 / 418 / 4:40	145 / 233 / 2:40	141 / 227 / 2:50	433 / 697 / 7:40	372 / 599 / 6:40	156 / 251 / 3:00	205 / 330 / 4:10	472 / 760 / 9:00	356 / 573 / 6:30	52 / 84 / 1:30	200 / 322 / 4:20	145 / 233 / 3:10	238 / 383 / 4:50	532 / 856 / 10:00	656 / 1056 / 13:00	192 / 309 / 3:40	550 / 885 / 10:40	274 / 441 / 5:40	168 / 270 / 3:10	73 / 117 / 1:30	137 / 221 / 2:50	172 / 277 / 3:20	144 / 232 / 2:50	260 / 418 / 4:50	145 / 233 / 3:50	109 / 175 / 2:10	462 / 744 / 8:30
Plymouth	218 / 351 / 4:40	615 / 990 / 11:20	237 / 382 / 5:10	492 / 792 / 9:00	474 / 763 / 9:00	203 / 327 / 4:20	328 / 528 / 6:10	128 / 206 / 3:30	587 / 945 / 10:40	224 / 361 / 6:00	122 / 196 / 2:50	293 / 472 / 5:30	167 / 269 / 3:40	399 / 642 / 7:20	297 / 478 / 5:40	300 / 483 / 5:50	552 / 888 / 10:00	496 / 798 / 9:00	46 / 74 / 1:30	264 / 425 / 5:30	595 / 958 / 11:20	495 / 797 / 9:10	157 / 253 / 3:20	365 / 588 / 7:20	309 / 497 / 6:10	328 / 528 / 6:40	664 / 1069 / 12:30	790 / 1271 / 15:40	355 / 571 / 6:40	674 / 1085 / 13:10	89 / 143 / 2:20	316 / 509 / 6:00	242 / 389 / 4:40	293 / 472 / 5:50	283 / 455 / 5:30	283 / 455 / 5:30	410 / 660 / 7:40	343 / 552 / 7:00	267 / 430 / 5:10	587 / 945 / 11:00	199 / 320 / 4:00
Portsmouth	70 / 113 / 2:00	560 / 901 / 10:10	222 / 357 / 4:40	430 / 692 / 7:40	401 / 645 / 7:30	141 / 227 / 3:00	264 / 425 / 4:50	52 / 84 / 1:30	547 / 881 / 9:50	48 / 77 / 1:40	97 / 156 / 2:10	144 / 232 / 2:50	142 / 229 / 3:00	348 / 560 / 6:10	234 / 377 / 4:20	130 / 209 / 2:50	514 / 827 / 9:00	453 / 729 / 8:10	135 / 217 / 2:40	251 / 404 / 5:00	555 / 893 / 10:20	448 / 721 / 8:10	119 / 192 / 3:00	221 / 356 / 4:40	166 / 267 / 3:40	311 / 501 / 6:10	613 / 987 / 11:30	737 / 1186 / 14:30	269 / 433 / 5:00	633 / 1019 / 12:10	259 / 417 / 5:40	257 / 414 / 4:50	162 / 261 / 3:10	201 / 323 / 4:00	254 / 409 / 4:50	236 / 380 / 4:30	337 / 542 / 6:10	207 / 333 / 4:20	191 / 307 / 3:40	545 / 877 / 10:00	77 / 124 / 1:40	176 / 283 / 4:50
Sheffield	159 / 256 / 3:20	360 / 579 / 6:50	159 / 256 / 3:30	245 / 394 / 4:30	190 / 306 / 4:00	76 / 122 / 1:50	86 / 138 / 1:50	216 / 348 / 4:10	320 / 515 / 6:00	226 / 364 / 4:20	161 / 259 / 3:10	120 / 193 / 2:20	194 / 312 / 3:40	152 / 245 / 3:00	18 / 29 / 0:40	245 / 394 / 4:30	291 / 468 / 5:20	235 / 378 / 4:20	237 / 381 / 4:20	215 / 346 / 4:20	348 / 560 / 6:50	248 / 399 / 4:40	126 / 203 / 2:20	166 / 267 / 3:40	187 / 301 / 3:50	168 / 270 / 3:40	393 / 632 / 7:40	520 / 837 / 10:50	65 / 105 / 1:30	427 / 687 / 8:40	361 / 581 / 7:10	33 / 53 / 1:00	62 / 100 / 1:20	46 / 74 / 1:20	72 / 116 / 1:40	38 / 61 / 1:00	125 / 201 / 2:40	146 / 235 / 3:20	37 / 60 / 1:00	339 / 546 / 6:30	135 / 217 / 2:40	283 / 455 / 5:30	230 / 370 / 4:20
Shrewsbury	160 / 258 / 3:20	399 / 642 / 7:30	77 / 124 / 2:10	269 / 433 / 5:00	265 / 426 / 5:10	45 / 72 / 1:20	98 / 158 / 2:00	185 / 298 / 3:40	371 / 597 / 6:50	226 / 364 / 4:20	103 / 166 / 2:50	159 / 256 / 3:00	111 / 179 / 2:20	176 / 283 / 3:20	109 / 175 / 2:10	251 / 404 / 4:30	330 / 531 / 6:00	274 / 441 / 5:00	179 / 288 / 3:20	145 / 233 / 3:10	382 / 615 / 7:20	272 / 438 / 5:00	77 / 124 / 1:30	225 / 362 / 4:40	240 / 386 / 4:40	113 / 182 / 2:50	438 / 705 / 8:20	567 / 912 / 11:30	169 / 272 / 3:10	451 / 726 / 9:00	303 / 488 / 6:10	109 / 175 / 2:20	84 / 135 / 1:40	133 / 214 / 2:50	58 / 93 / 1:50	69 / 111 / 1:40	201 / 323 / 3:50	205 / 330 / 4:20	93 / 150 / 2:00	364 / 586 / 7:00	106 / 171 / 2:10	225 / 362 / 4:40	207 / 333 / 3:50	82 / 132 / 2:10
Southampton	77 / 124 / 2:00	547 / 880 / 10:00	201 / 323 / 4:10	417 / 671 / 7:30	388 / 624 / 7:10	128 / 206 / 2:40	251 / 404 / 4:40	31 / 50 / 1:00	532 / 856 / 9:30	61 / 98 / 1:50	76 / 122 / 2:20	148 / 238 / 2:50	121 / 195 / 2:30	324 / 521 / 5:50	209 / 336 / 3:50	143 / 230 / 2:50	500 / 805 / 8:50	438 / 705 / 7:50	105 / 169 / 3:00	233 / 375 / 4:40	541 / 871 / 10:00	433 / 697 / 7:40	105 / 169 / 2:40	220 / 354 / 4:40	164 / 264 / 3:30	293 / 472 / 5:50	598 / 963 / 11:10	723 / 1164 / 14:10	256 / 412 / 4:40	618 / 995 / 12:00	228 / 367 / 5:00	232 / 373 / 4:20	137 / 220 / 2:40	204 / 328 / 4:00	239 / 385 / 4:30	221 / 356 / 4:10	324 / 521 / 5:50	206 / 332 / 4:20	176 / 283 / 3:20	530 / 853 / 9:40	64 / 103 / 1:30	151 / 243 / 4:10	21 / 34 / 0:50	199 / 320 / 3:40	185 / 298 / 4:10
Stranraer	402 / 647 / 7:50	228 / 367 / 5:10	325 / 523 / 6:50	51 / 82 / 1:20	170 / 274 / 4:10	297 / 478 / 6:00	188 / 303 / 4:00	444 / 715 / 8:30	194 / 312 / 4:20	475 / 765 / 9:00	378 / 608 / 7:20	379 / 610 / 7:10	390 / 628 / 7:30	101 / 163 / 2:40	257 / 414 / 5:10	496 / 798 / 9:10	167 / 269 / 3:40	124 / 200 / 3:00	454 / 731 / 8:30	392 / 631 / 7:50	195 / 314 / 4:50	84 / 135 / 2:30	343 / 552 / 6:30	426 / 686 / 8:40	410 / 660 / 8:10	338 / 544 / 7:00	262 / 422 / 6:00	379 / 610 / 9:00	259 / 417 / 5:20	263 / 423 / 6:30	585 / 942 / 11:30	220 / 354 / 4:40	330 / 531 / 6:20	298 / 480 / 6:00	221 / 356 / 4:40	220 / 354 / 4:40	158 / 254 / 3:40	403 / 649 / 8:10	290 / 467 / 5:50	148 / 238 / 3:40	379 / 610 / 7:10	500 / 805 / 9:40	461 / 742 / 8:40	263 / 423 / 5:20	277 / 446 / 5:30	445 / 716 / 8:20
Swansea	194 / 312 / 4:00	507 / 816 / 9:20	73 / 117 / 2:00	379 / 610 / 6:50	383 / 616 / 7:10	119 / 192 / 2:30	216 / 348 / 4:00	167 / 269 / 3:20	505 / 813 / 9:00	222 / 357 / 4:20	85 / 137 / 1:50	227 / 365 / 4:10	41 / 66 / 1:10	309 / 497 / 5:30	232 / 373 / 4:10	274 / 441 / 5:00	473 / 761 / 8:20	412 / 663 / 7:20	161 / 259 / 3:00	67 / 108 / 1:50	496 / 798 / 9:20	409 / 658 / 7:20	89 / 143 / 1:50	329 / 530 / 6:30	267 / 430 / 5:10	184 / 296 / 4:50	572 / 921 / 10:40	696 / 1120 / 13:40	264 / 425 / 4:50	594 / 956 / 11:30	285 / 459 / 6:00	248 / 399 / 4:40	177 / 285 / 3:20	233 / 375 / 4:30	195 / 314 / 3:40	187 / 301 / 3:30	347 / 559 / 6:20	301 / 485 / 6:00	192 / 309 / 3:40	506 / 815 / 9:20	141 / 227 / 2:40	206 / 332 / 4:10	182 / 293 / 3:30	217 / 349 / 4:00	118 / 190 / 2:20	161 / 259 / 3:00	417 / 671 / 7:50
York	207 / 333 / 4:10	319 / 513 / 6:10	195 / 314 / 4:10	214 / 344 / 4:00	148 / 238 / 3:10	130 / 209 / 2:40	96 / 154 / 2:00	269 / 433 / 5:00	285 / 459 / 5:20	275 / 443 / 5:10	222 / 357 / 4:10	165 / 266 / 3:10	244 / 393 / 4:40	121 / 195 / 2:30	34 / 55 / 1:00	282 / 454 / 5:10	250 / 402 / 4:40	194 / 312 / 3:40	287 / 462 / 5:10	261 / 420 / 5:10	330 / 531 / 6:30	217 / 349 / 4:10	189 / 304 / 3:30	201 / 323 / 4:20	228 / 367 / 4:40	204 / 328 / 4:20	352 / 566 / 7:00	479 / 771 / 10:10	37 / 60 / 1:10	407 / 655 / 8:20	411 / 661 / 8:00	24 / 39 / 0:50	108 / 174 / 2:10	75 / 121 / 1:50	99 / 159 / 2:10	64 / 103 / 1:30	84 / 135 / 2:20	181 / 291 / 4:20	77 / 124 / 1:40	309 / 497 / 6:00	181 / 291 / 3:20	333 / 536 / 6:20	278 / 448 / 5:10	52 / 84 / 1:20	133 / 214 / 2:40	258 / 415 / 5:10	222 / 357 / 4:40	272 / 438 / 5:10

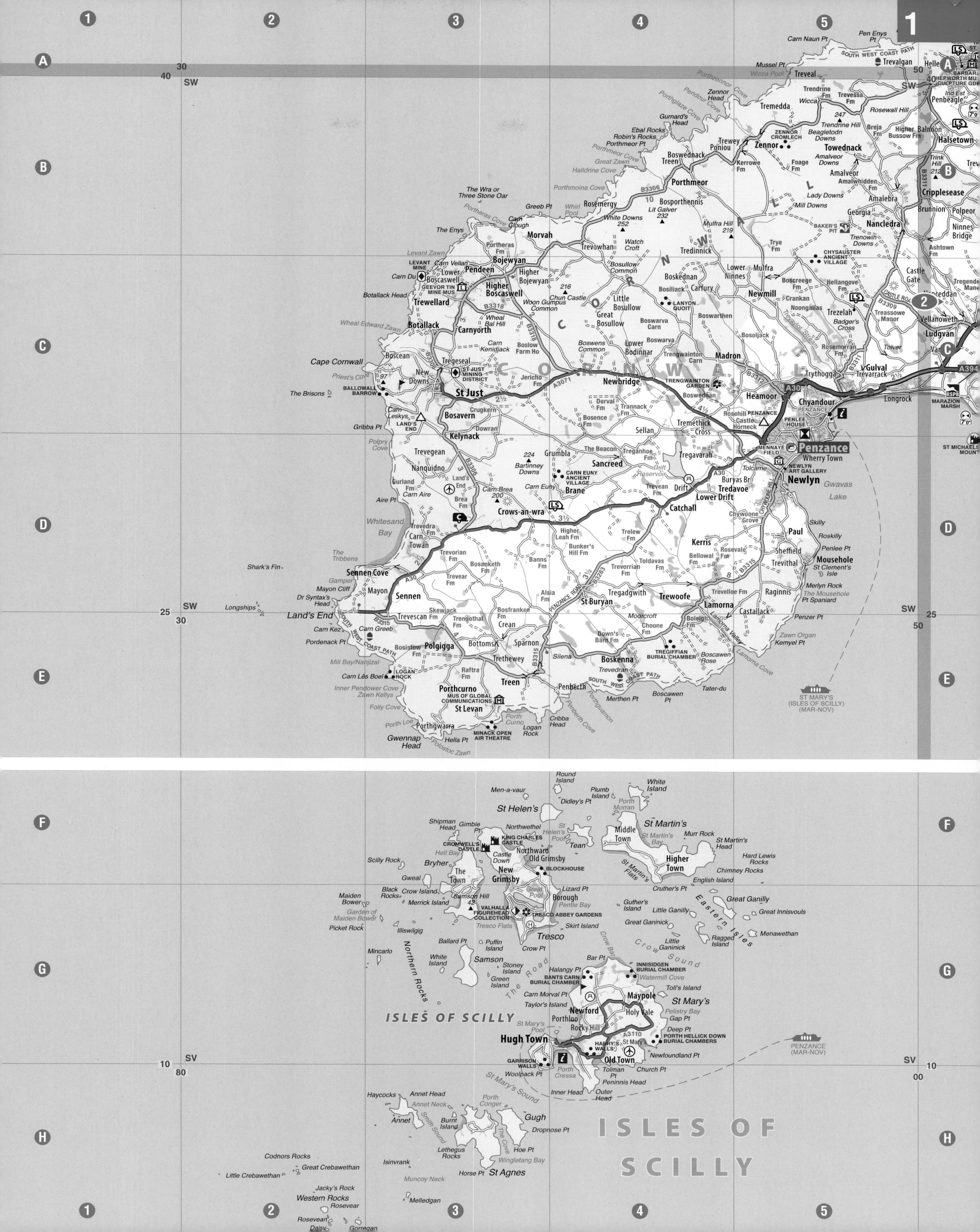
Carn Naun Pt
Pen Enys Pt
SOUTH WEST COAST PATH
Trevalgan
Mussel Pt
Wicca Pool
Treveal
Porthzennor Cove
Pendour Cove
Zennor Head
Porthglaze Cove
Gurnard's Head
Tremedda
Trendrine Fm
Wicca
Trevessa Fm
Rosewall Hill
Trendrine Hill
Beagletodn Downs
Breja Fm
Higher Bussow Fm
Balnoon
Halsetown
Penbeagle
Ebal Rocks
Robin's Rocks
Porthmeor Pt
Porthmeor Cove
Great Zawn
Halldrine Cove
Trewey
Poniou
Zennor
ZENNOR CROMLECH
Towednack
Boswednack
Treen
Kerrowe Fm
Foage Fm
Amalveor Downs
Amalveor
Amalwhidden
Amalebra
Cripplesease
Brunnion
Polpeor
Ninnes Bridge
Trink Hill
Porthmeor
Porthmoina Cove
B3306
Bosporthennis
Lit Galver 232
Lady Downs
Mill Downs
Georgia
Nancledra
The Wra or Three Stone Oar
Greeb Pt
Whirl Pool
Rosemergy
White Downs 252
Mulfra Hill 219
BAKER'S PIT
Trenowin Downs
Ashtown Fm
Portheras Cove
Carn Clough
The Enys
Morvah
Watch Croft
Trevowhan
Tredinnick
Trye Fm
CHYSAUSTER ANCIENT VILLAGE
Castle Gate
Tregenden Manor
Levant Zawn
Portheras Fm
LEVANT MINE
Carn Vellan
Lower Boscaswell
Pendeen
Bojewyan
Higher Bojewyan
Bosullow Common
Lower Ninnes
Mulfra
Boskednan
Boscreege Fm
Hellangove Fm
Carn Du
GEEVOR TIN MINE MUS
Higher Boscaswell
216
Chun Castle
Little Bosullow
Bosiliack
LANYON QUOIT
Carfury
Newmill
Crankan
Noongallas
Trezelah
Badger's Cross
Treassowe Manor
Vellanoweth
Ludgvan
Botallack Head
Trewellard
Woon Gumpus Common
Great Bosullow
Boswarva Carn
Boswarthen
Wheal Edward Zawn
Botallack
Carnyorth
Wheal Bal Hill
B3318
Bosoljack
Carn Kenidjack
Boslow Farm Ho
Bosvens Common
Lower Bodinnar
Boswarva
Trengwainton Carn
Madron
Rosemorran Fm
Gulval
Trevarrack
Tolver
Cape Cornwall
Boscean
Tregeseal
ST JUST MINING DISTRICT
Priest's Cove
New Downs
Jericho Fm
A3071
Newbridge
TRENGWAINTON GARDEN
B3312
Trythogga
Longrock
A394
MARAZION MARSH
The Brisons
BALLOWALL BARROW
St Just
Boswednan
Heamoor
A30
Chyandour
Carn Leskys
LAND'S END
Bosavern
Crugkern
Dorval Fm
Trannack Fm
Bosence Fm
Trenethick Cross
Rosehill
PENZANCE
Castle Horneck
PENLEE HOUSE
Gribba Pt
Kelynack
Dowran
Sellan
ST MICHAEL'S MOUNT
Polpry Cove
Trevegean
The Beacon
Treganhoe Fm
Tregavarah
MENNAYE FIELD
Penzance
Wherry Town
Nanquidno
224 Bartinney Downs
Grumbla
Sancreed
Drift Reservoir
Tolcarne
NEWLYN ART GALLERY
Gurland Fm
Carn Aire
Land's End
B3306
CARN EUNY ANCIENT VILLAGE
Carn Euny
Brane
Trevean Fm
Drift
Buryas Br
Tredavoe
Newlyn
Gwavas Lake
Brea Fm
Carn Brea 200
Lower Drift
Aire Pt
Crows-an-wra
Catchall
Chywoone Grove
Skilly
Whitesand Bay
Trevedra Fm
Carn Towan
Higher Leah Fm
Trelew Fm
Kerris
Paul
Roskilly
Penlee Pt
The Tribbens
Trevorian Fm
Bosanketh Fm
Banns Fm
Bunker's Hill Fm
Bellowal Fm
Rosevale Fm
Sheffield
Mousehole
Shark's Fin
Sennen Cove
Gamper
Mayon Cliff
Mayon
Trevear Fm
Trevorrian Fm
Toldavas Fm
Trevithal
St Clement's Isle
Merlyn Rock
The Mousehole
Pt Spaniard
Dr Syntax's Head
Longships
Sennen
Skewjack
Alsia Fm
PENZANCE ROAD
Tregadgwith
Trewoofe
Trevelloe Fm
Lamorna
Raginnis
Land's End
Trevescan Fm
Bosfranken Fm
Crean
St Buryan
Moorcroft
Castallack
Penzer Pt
Carn Kez
Carn Greeb
B3315
Trengothal Fm
Choone Fm
Boleigh Fm
Lamorna Valley
Zawn Organ
Kemyel Pt
Pordenack Pt
Bosistow Fm
Polgigga
Bottoms
Sparnon
Down's Barn Fm
Mill Bay/Nanjizal
Trethewey
Silena
Boskenna
TREGIFFIAN BURIAL CHAMBER
Boscawen Rose
Lamorna Cove
Carn Lês Boel
LOGAN ROCK
Raftra Fm
Treen
Trevedran
SOUTH WEST COAST PATH
Inner Pendower Cove
Zawn Kellys
Porthcurno
Penberth
Tater-du
MUS OF GLOBAL COMMUNICATIONS
Merthen Pt
Boscawen Pt
ST MARY'S (ISLES OF SCILLY) (MAR-NOV)
Folly Cove
St Levan
Porth Curno
Penberth Cove
Porth Loe
Porthgwarra
Cribba Head
Porthguarnon
Logan Rock
MINACK OPEN AIR THEATRE
Gwennap Head
Hella Pt
Polostoc Zawn
Round Island
White Island
Men-a-vaur
Plumb Island
Didley's Pt
Porth Morran
St Helen's
St Martin's
Shipman Head
Gimble Pt
Northwethel
St Helen's Pool
Middle Town
St Martin's Bay
Murr Rock
St Martin's Head
CROMWELL'S CASTLE
KING CHARLES CASTLE
Tean
Hell Bay
Castle Down
Northward
Old Grimsby
Higher Town
Hard Lewis Rocks
Scilly Rock
Bryher
St Martin's Flats
Chimney Rocks
The Town
New Grimsby
BLOCKHOUSE
English Island
Gweal
Maiden Bower
Black Rocks
Crow Island
Samson Hill 42
Great Pool
Lizard Pt
Crruther's Pt
Borough
Great Ganilly
Garden of Maiden Bower
Merrick Island
VALHALLA FIGUREHEAD COLLECTION
TRESCO ABBEY GARDENS
Pentle Bay
Guther's Island
Little Ganilly
Great Innisvouls
Picket Rock
Tresco Flats
Skirt Island
Eastern Isles
Illiswilgig
Great Ganinick
Menawethan
Ballard Pt
Puffin Island
Tresco
Crow Bar
Little Ganinick
Ragged Island
Mincarlo
Northern Rocks
White Island
Samson
Crow Pt
Crow Sound
Stoney Island
Bar Pt
INNISIDGEN BURIAL CHAMBER
Green Island
Halangy Pt
BANTS CARN BURIAL CHAMBER
Watermill Cove
The Road
Toll's Island
Carn Morval Pt
Maypole
St Mary's
Taylor's Island
Newford
Holy Vale
Pelistry Bay
ISLES OF SCILLY
St Mary's Pool
Porthloo
Gap Pt
Rocky Hill
Deep Pt
Hugh Town
A3110
PORTH HELLICK DOWN BURIAL CHAMBERS
HARRY'S WALLS
St Mary's
PENZANCE (MAR-NOV)
GARRISON WALLS
Old Town
Newfoundland Pt
Porth Cressa
Tolman Pt
Church Pt
Woolpack Pt
Peninnis Head
St Mary's Sound
Inner Head
Outer Head
Haycocks
Annet Head
Annet Neck
Porth Conger
Annet
Smith Sound
Burnt Island
Gugh
Dropnose Pt
ISLES OF SCILLY
The Cove
Lethegus Rocks
Hoe Pt
Codnors Rocks
Great Crebawethan
Isinvrank
Wingletang Bay
Little Crebawethan
Horse Pt
St Agnes
Muncoy Neck
Jacky's Rock
Western Rocks
Melledgan
Rosevear
Rosevean
Daisy
Gorregan
SW
SV
1
2
3
4
5
A
B
C
D
E
F
G
H

ST IVES BAY
MOUNT'S BAY
CORNWALL
Goonhilly Downs
St Ives
Carbis Bay
Lelant
Hayle
Copperhouse
Phillack
Gwithian
Camborne
Tuckingmill
Pool
Carnbrea
Roscroggan
Kehelland
Connor Downs
Roseworthy
Barripper
Praze-an-Beeble
Crowan
Leedstown
Townshend
Godolphin Cross
Releath
Nancegollan
Crowntown
Wendron
Porkellis
Burras
Carnkie
Four Lanes
Troon
Penmarth
Stithians
Lanner
Rame
Constantine
Gweek
Helston
Trewennack
Porthleven
Breage
Ashton
Germoe
Praa Sands
Rinsey
Sithney
Marazion
Perranuthnoe
Goldsithney
St Hilary
Relubbus
St Erth
Canon's Town
Crowlas
Ludgvan
Nancledra
Cripplesease
Halsetown
Gulval
Longrock
Mawgan
Garras
St Martin
Traboe
Cury
Gunwalloe
Berepper
Mullion
Mullion Cove
Penhale
Kuggar
Ruan Minor
Cadgwith
Grade
St Ruan
Lizard
Landewednack
Lizard Point
Church Cove
Cross Lanes
St Michaels Mount
Cudden Pt
Hoe Pt
Rinsey Head
Trewavas Head
Tye Rocks
Porthleven Sands
Gunwalloe Fishing Cove
Halzephron Cliff
Poldhu Pt
Predannack Head
Vellan Head
Soap Rock
Gull Rock
Lion Rock
Venton Hill Pt
Enoch Rock
Bass Pt
Hot Pt
Whale Rock
Kildown Pt
Cornish Seal Sanctuary
Culdrose Airfield
Flambards
Museum of Cornish Life
Godolphin House
Predannack Airfield
A30
A394
A3083
B3280
B3297
B3293
B3296
B3302
B3303
B3304
SW
50
10
0 1 2 3 miles
0 1 2 3 4 5 km
1 2 3 4 5 6
A B C D E F G H

3
VERYAN BAY
CARRICK ROADS
FALMOUTH BAY
Falmouth
Penryn
St Mawes
St Just in Roseland
Portscatho
Gerrans
Veryan
Portloe
Philleigh
Feock
Mylor Bridge
Flushing
Devoran
Playing Place
Carnon Downs
Perranarwothal
Budock Water
Mawnan Smith
Mawnan
Helford Passage
St Anthony-in-Meneage
Manaccan
Porthallow
Porthoustock
St Keverne
Coverack
Tregidden
Zoar
Penhallick
Ponsongath
Dodman Pt
Nare Head
Pendennis Castle
St Anthony Head
Zone Pt
Pennance Pt
Rosemullion Head
Nare Pt
Lowland Pt
Black Head
A B C D E F G H
7 8 9 10 11

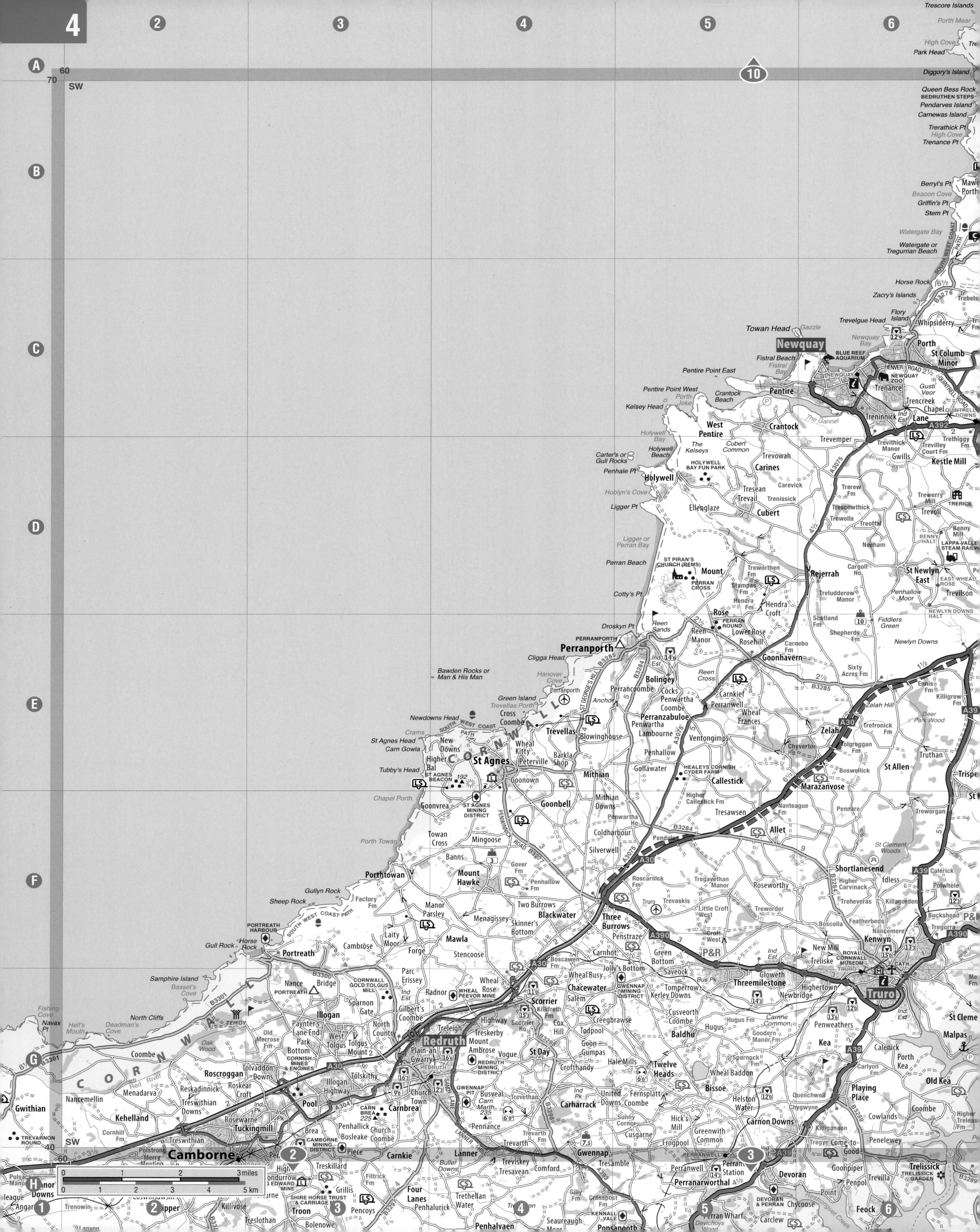

4
2
3
4
5
6
A
B
C
D
E
F
G
H
60
70
SW
10
Trescore Islands
Porth Mear
High Cove
Park Head
Diggory's Island
Queen Bess Rock
BEDRUTHEN STEPS
Pendarves Island
Carnewas Island
Trerathick Pt
High Cove
Trenance Pt
Berryl's Pt
Beacon Cove
Griffin's Pt
Stem Pt
Watergate Bay
Watergate or Tregurrian Beach
SOUTH WEST COAST PATH
Horse Rock
Zacry's Islands
Flory Island
Trevelgue Head
Whipsiderry
Towan Head
Gazzle
Newquay
Newquay Bay
Porth
St Columb Minor
BLUE REEF AQUARIUM
Fistral Beach
Fistral Bay
NEWQUAY
HENVER ROAD
NEWQUAY ZOO
QUINTRELL ROAD
Pentire Point East
Pentire Point West
Porth Joke
Crantock Beach
Pentire
Trenance
Gusti Veor
Trencreek
Chapel
Kelsey Head
Treninnick
Ind Est
Lane
QUINTRELL DOWNS
West Pentire
Crantock
The Gannel
Trevemper
A392
Holywell Bay
Holywell Beach
The Kelseys
Cubert Common
Trevithick Manor
Trevilley Court Fm
Trethiggy Fm
Gwills
River Gannel
Kestle Mill
Carter's or Gull Rocks
Penhale Pt
HOLYWELL BAY FUN PARK
Trevowah
Carines
Holywell
Hoblyn's Cove
Tresean
Trevail
Carevick
Trenissick
Trerew Fm
Trewerry Mill
TRERICE
Ligger Pt
Ellenglaze
Cubert
Trescowthick
Trewolla
Trevoll
A3075
Treoffal
Benny Mill
BENNY HALT
Neeham
LAPPA VALLEY STEAM RAILWAY
Ligger or Perran Bay
Perran Beach
ST PIRAN'S CHURCH (REMS)
PERRAN CROSS
Mount
Treworthen
Stampas Fm
Rejerrah
Cargoll Ho
St Newlyn East
EAST WHEAL ROSE
Cotty's Pt
Hendra Fm
Hendra Croft
Treludderow Manor
Penhallow Moor
Trevilson
NEWLYN DOWNS HALT
Reen Sands
Rose
PERRAN ROUND
Scotland Fm
Fiddlers Green
Droskyn Pt
Reen Manor
Lower Rose
Rosehill
Shepherds Fm
Newlyn Downs
PERRANPORTH
Perranporth
Cligga Head
B3285
Ind Est
Carnebo Fm
Goonhavern
Sixty Acres Fm
Bawden Rocks or Man & His Man
Hanover Cove
Perranporth
ST GEORGE'S HILL
Bolingey
Reen Cross
Ennis Fm
Killigrew Fm
Green Island
Trevellas Porth
Anchor
Perrancoombe
Cocks
Carnkief
Perranwell
Zelah Hill
A39
Newdowns Head
Cross Coombe
CORNWALL
Penwartha Coombe
Perranzabuloe
Wheal Frances
Deer Park Wood
Crams
SOUTH WEST COAST PATH
Trevellas
Blowinghouse
Penwartha
Lambourne
Ventongimps
Zelah
Trefronick Fm
St Agnes Head
Carn Gowla
New Downs
Wheal Kitty
Barkla Shop
Chyverton Ho
Tolgroggan Fm
Truthan
Tubby's Head
Higher Bal
St Agnes
Peterville
Penhallow
A30
Boswellick
St Allen
Trispe
ST AGNES BEACON 192
Goonown
Mithian
Gollawater
HEALEYS CORNISH CYDER FARM
Callestick
Marazanvose
Chapel Porth
Goonvrea
ST AGNES MINING DISTRICT
Goonbell
Mithian Downs
Higher Callestick Fm
Nanteague Fm
Tresawsen
Pennare
Treworgan
PENWINNICK ROAD
Penwartha Ho
B3284
Allet
Porth Towan
Towan Cross
Mingoose
Coldharbour
Pendeley
St Clement Woods
Banns
Silverwell
Porthtowan
Mount Hawke
Gover Fm
Penhallow Fm
Roscarnick
Tregavethan Manor
Roseworthy
Shortlanesend
Higher Carvinack
Idless
Calerick
Polwhele
Gullyn Rock
Sheep Rock
Factory Fm
Manor Parsley
Two Burrows
Truro
Trevaskis
Little Croft West
Treworder
Treheveras
Killagorden
Menagissey
Skinner's Bottom
Blackwater
Three Burrows
Boscolla
Featherbeds
Buckshead
P&R
PORTREATH HARBOUR
Laity Moor
Mawla
Penstraze
A390
Croft West
Kenwyn
Nancemere
Tregurra
Gull Rock
Horse Rock
Portreath
Cambrose
Forge
Stencoose
Carnhot
Green Bottom
Ind Est
New Mill
ROYAL CORNWALL MUSEUM
Parc Erissey
Boscawen Fm
Jolly's Bottom
P&R
Saveock
Treliske
CATH
Samphire Island
Basset's Cove
Nance
Bridge
CORNWALL GOLD TOLGUS MILL
Ind Est
Wheal Rose
Wheal Busy
GWENNAP MINING DISTRICT
Tomperrow
Gloweth
Threemilestone
Highertown
Truro
Fishing Cove
PORTREATH
Radnor
WHEAL PEEVOR MINE
Chacewater
Kerley Downs
Newbridge
Sparnon Gate
Scorrier
Salem
B3301
Navax Pt
Hell's Mouth
Deadman's Cove
North Cliffs
TEHIDY
Illogan
Gilbert's Coombe
Killifreth Fm
Creegbrawse
Cusveorth Coombe
Carrine Common
Penweathers
Ind Est
St Clement
Old Merrose Fm
Paynter's Lane End
North Country
Highway
Scorrier Ho
Cox Hill
Todpool
Hugus Fm
Goodern Manor Fm
Malpas
Oak Wood
Park Bottom
West Tolgus
Redruth
Treleigh
Treskerby
Mount Ambrose
Baldhu
Hugus
Kea
Calenick
Coombe
Tolgus Mount
Plain-an-Gwarry
Vogue
St Day
Goon Gumpas
Porth Kea
Carlyon Fm
CORNISH MINES & ENGINES
REDRUTH
REDRUTH MINING DISTRICT
Hale Mills
Twelve Heads
Sparnock Fm
Roscroggan
Tolvaddon Downs
Crofthandy
Wheal Baddon
Old Kea
CORNWALL
Red River
Menadarva
Reskadinnick
Roskear Croft
Tolskithy
SANDY LANE
Illogan Highway
Playing Place
Bissoe
Quenchwell
Nancemellin
Treswithian Downs
Pool
Church Town
GWENNAP PIT
Busveal
Carn Marth 235
Trevethan
Carharrack
Ind Pk
United Downs
Fernsplatt Coombe
Helston Water
Chygwyne
Cowlands
Gwithian
Kehelland
Rosewarne
Tuckingmill
A3047
Carnbrea
CARN BREA 225
Penhallick
Bosleake
Church Coombe
Sunny Corner
Hick's Mill
Carnon Downs
Carnon River
Killiganoon
Higher Trelease Fm
TREVARNON ROUND
Cornhill Fm
Brea
Pennance
Trevarth Fm
Cusgarne
Greenwith Common
Tregye
Come-to-Good
Penelewey
Treswithian
CAMBORNE MINING DISTRICT
Trevarth
Frogpool
Polstrong
Merry Meeting
Camborne
Piece
Carnkie
Lanner
Gwennap
PERRANWELL
Perranwell
Perran Station
Tresamble
Goonpiper
Penpol
Trevilla
Trelissick
TRELISSICK GARDEN
B3289
Pulsack Manor
Treskillard
Buller Downs
Treviskey
Tresavean
Comford
Filtrick Fm
Four Lanes
Trethellan Water
Gilly Fm
Crosspost Fm
Perranarworthal
Devoran
Point
Manor Downs
Trenowin
Londuurrow
SHIRE HORSE TRUST & CARRIAGE MUSEUM
Grillis
Troon
Pencoys
Penhalurick
KENNALL VALE
DEVORAN & PERRAN
Chycoose
Carclew
Feock
Restronguet Creek
Killivose
Treslothan
Bolenowe
Penhalvaen
Seureaugh Moor
Ponsanooth
Perran Wharf
Devichoys Wood
0
1
2
3 miles
0
1
2
3
4
5 km

5
Porthcothan
Trevethan
Treburrick
Little Petherick
Mellingey
St Issey
Trevance
Wadebridge
Royal Cornwall Showground
St Breock
Polmorla
Egloshayle
Clapper
Sladesbridge
Lower Croan
Croanford
Pencarrow House
Tredethy
Helland
Hellandbridge
Penrose
St Merryn Airfield (disused)
Treglinnick
Trenance
Treravel Fm
Tredinnick
St Ervan
Rumford
Tregona
Engollan
Trerair Fm
Trevisker Fm
Downhill
St Eval Airfield (disused)
St Eval
St Jidgey
Cannalidgey
Pawton Manor Fm
Camel Creek Adventure Park
Bear's Downs
Long Stone
Bogee Common
Trelow Downs
Scotland Corner
208
Longstone
Higher Cransworth
Lantuel
Rosenannon Downs
Burlawn
Pengelly Fm
Hay
Tredannick
Costislost
Bozion Fm
Polgeel Wood
Polbrock
Washaway
Lane-end
Mount Charles
Burlorne Tregoose
Brocton
Penaligon Downs
Great Grogley Downs
Boscarne Junction
Dunmere
Clerkenwater
St Petroc's Church
Museum
Cooksland
Long Downs
Trenance
Merlin Fm
Dayman's Fm
Denzell Downs
Prince's Common
CORNWALL
Trevarrian
Lower Denzell
Higher Denzell
Winnard's Perch
Cornish Birds of Prey Centre
Rosenannon
Rutherbridge
Newdowns Fm
Nanstallon
Bodmin
The Beacon 162
Bodmin General Bus Cen
Courtroom Experience
St Mawgan
Higher Tolcarne
Carloggas
Whitewater Fm
Rosedinnick
Retallack
Killeganogue Fm
Skewes
Treliver
Tregolls
Tregustick
Tregawne
Withielgoose Mills
Mulberry
Threewaters
St Lawrence
Treningle
Bodmin & Wenford Railway
Halgavor Moor
Carminow Cross
Turfdown
Fletchersbridge
Tregurrian
Talskiddy
Trevornick
Withiel
Withielgoose
Lower Woodley
Bodwannick
Cadwin
Lamorick
Trekillick Fm
Lidcutt Fm
Newquay Cornwall Airport
Lower Trenowth
Higher Trenowth
Trewan Hall
Gluvian
Little Halveor
Tresawle
Tregamere
St Wenn
Lanjew
Trenance
Tregurtha Fm
Tregonetha
Lancorla Fm
Hendra
Retire
Tremore
Tremorebridge
Rosehill
Lanivet
Tremeere Manor
Tregullon
St Columb Major
Ind Est
Demelza
Inchs
Retire Common
West Downs
Reperry Cross
Lanhydrock House
Cutmadoc
Newton
Trebyan
Bofarnel
Tregaswith
Trekenning
Tregatillian
Tresaddern
Dennis Fm
Castle Downs 214
Castle an Dinas
Castle Fm
Saddle Rock
Belowda Beacon 227
Bryn Mill
Brynn Hill
Lower Brynn
Redtye
St Inunger Fm
Lower Woon
Fenton Pits
Treisaac Fm
Trebarber
Trevithick
Rosesuggan
Quoit
Higher Trenowth
Belowda
Victoria
Mount Pleasant
Cornwall Services
Innis Downs
Rosevath Fm
Mena
Trebell Green
Bokiddick
Lesquite Fm
Logan Stone 209
Helman Tor
Creney Fm
Maudlin
Sweethouse
Restormel Castle
Colan
Trebudannon
Porth Reservoir
Springfields Fun Park & Pony Centre
Quoit Fm
Providence
Roche
Higher Town
Criggan Moors
Trescoll
Lockengate
Bokiddick Downs
Lowertown
Boslymon
Redmoor
Bosoughan
Lady Nance
Nankelly
Killaworgey
Ruthvoes
Screech Owl Sanctuary
Tregoss Moor
Tregoss
Victoria Rd
Roche
Trebilcock
Criggan
Bodwen
Corgee
Breney Fm
Rosenev Fm
Bodwen Fm
Hillhead
Quintrell Downs
Mountjoy
Pollawyn Fm
Trugo Fm
Black Cross
Trevarren
Goss Moor
Hallew
Bilberry
Higher Menadew
Tredinnick
Lostwithiel
Coswarth
White Cross
Toldish
Ind Est
St Columb Road
Indian Queens
Gaverigan Manor
Goss Moor
Enniscaven
Trerank Moor
Roche Rock
Woon
Carbis
Gracca
Trezaise
Molinnis
Bugle
Lower Menadue
Lavrean
Bodiggo
Luxulyan
Trenant Fm
Lanlivery
Puddle
Sandyway Wood
Castle
Tregonning
Dairyland Farm World
Retyn Fm
Perrose Fm
Fraddon
B3279
Domellick Fm
Carne
Gothers
Cleers
Coldvreath
Carbis Common
Carnsmerry
Roseveah
Bowling Green
Luxulyan
Bodanna Fm
Troan
Blue Anchor
Carsella Fm
St Dennis
Hendra
Ind Est
Whitemoor
312
Hensbarrow Beacon
Hensbarrow Downs
Rescorla
Bridges
Treskilling
Rosemelling
Luxulyan Valley
Penpillick
Milltown
Lantyan
Gummow's Shop
Penhale
St Enoder
Boswallow Fm
Trerice Manor Fm
Retew
Currian Vale
Stenalees
Treverbyn
Resugga Green
Knightor
Treverbyn
Trevanney Fm
Medros Fm
North Hill Wood
Tywardreath Highway
Ponts Mill
Carruggatt Wood
Tredinnick Fm
Penrose Manor
Trevessa Fm
Burthy Row Fm
Chytane Fm
Burthy Fm
Summercourt
Treviscoe Barton
Rostowrack Downs
Treviscoe
Nanpean
Greensplat
Wheal Martyn China Clay Country Pk & Mus
Carthew
Penwithick
Trethurgy
Carluddon
Little Carne Fm
Eden Project
St Blazey
Bodelva
Lanescot
Treesmill
Lawhibbet Fm
Torfrey
Golant
Chapel Town
Trenithon Fm
Resparva Fm
Mitchell
A30
Brighton
Melbur
Trethosa
Goonabarn
Foxhole
Carpalla
Carloggas
Trenance Downs
Screddal
Ind Est
Biscovillack Fm
Carclaze
Menear Fm
Garker
Kilhallon
Tywardreath
Trenython Manor
Kilgogue Fm
Carland Cross
Resurgance Fm
Arrallas Fm
Menna
A3058
Nankervis
Scarcewater
Terras
High Street
Hornick
Penisker Fm
Trethowel
Tregrehan Mills
St Blazey Gate
Tregrehan
Biscovey
Par
Polmear
Hendra Fm
Trelassick
Trelassick Ho
Trendeal
Gregan Gate
Penhale Fm
Trelion
St Stephen
Long Lane
Court Fm
Lanjeth
Gover Valley
Trewoon
St Austell
St Austell Brewery
Boscoppa
Bethel
Holmbush
Ind Est
Pine Lodge Gdns
Carlyon Bay
Ind Pk
A3082
Par Sands
Spit Pt
Polkerris
Passage
St Enoder Wood
Ladock Wood
Pollard's Fm
New Mills
Carnemough Fm
Woodland Valley Fm
Coombe
Bosithow Barn
St Mewan
Naphysick Barton
Tregandanel
Mount Charles
Charlestown
Shipwreck Treasure Mus
Gull Island
Landrion Pt
Charlestown Harbour
Fishing Pt
Killyvarder Rock
Menabilly
St Catherine's Castle
Readymoney
Ladock
Nansough Fm
Trobus Fm
Trewince Ho
Resparveth
Grampound Road
Trevan Wood
Garlenick Manor
Ventonwyn Fm
Dowgas Fm
A390
Trelowth
Polgooth
Trewhiddle
Tregorrick
Roseweek
Carrickowel Pt
Lower Porthpean
Robin's Rock
ST AUSTELL BAY
Kestle Fm
Tre-Knoll Fm
Trewinnow
Nantellan
Trevillick
Sticker
Hewas Water
Paramoor
Commerce Common
London Apprentice
Levalsa Meor
Higher Porthpean
Porthpean
Phoebe's Pt
Gwendra Pt
Castle Gotha Fm
Ropehaven
Southground Pt
Sandy Cove
Great Tregassow Wood
Treliane Wood
Cuskayne Fm
Tregoose
Trevolland
Grampound
Paramoor Wood
Shepherdshill Wood
Trencreek Fm
Penberlan Fm
Nunnery Hill
King's Wood
Trenarren
Porthtowan
Black Head
Drennick
Probus
A390
Parkengear
Trewithen
Creed
Gargus Fm
Lanhadron Fm
Pentewan
Gamas Pt
Tresillian
Green Mill
Trelowthas
West Trelowthas
Denas Water
Golden Mill
Tregonjohn Fm
Tregidgeo Fm
Pensagillas Fm
The Lost Gardens of Heligan
Peruppa Fm
Pentewan Beach
MEVAGISSEY BAY
Tresawle
Grogarth Fm
Carveth Wood
Carveth
St Ewe
Beacon Cross
Polmassick
Kestle
Penare Pt
Great Trewirgie
Killiow Fm
Tregony
Stepaside
Tregonhayne
Tregonan Fm
Trevithick Fm
Trelessick Fm
Trelewack Fm
Trelevean Fm
World of Model Railways
Mevagissey
Stuckumb Pt
Merther
Trevear
Trewarthenick
Ind Est
Ferder
Pencoose
Goviley Vean
Goviley Major
Trellssick
Methrose Fm
Portmellon
Polkirt Beach
Namprathic
Merther Lane
Tregenna
Penvose
Trethewey Fm
Treluckey
Hay Barton Fm
Treberrick
Trevennen Fm
Trevarrick
Gorran High Lanes
Chapel Pt
Colana Beach
Lamorran Wood
Ruan Lanihorne
Demain Fm
Castlezens Fm
Trevilveth
Tubbs Mill
Rescassa
Gorran Churchtown
Trewollock
Turbot Pt
Pabyer Pt
St Michael Penkevil
Lamorran
Ruan River
Trengrouse Fm
West Portholland
East Portholland
St Michael Caerhays
Caerhays Castle
Treveor
Trevesson Fm
Boswinger
Gorran Haven
Lamledra
Gwinges/Gwineas
Maenease Point/Pen-a-Maen
Tretheake Manor
Veryan Green
May's Rock
Porthluney Cove
Boswinger
Greeb Pt
Vault Beach or Bow
Treworga
Trethurbes
Trethennal Manor
South West Coast Path
Penare
Philleigh
Ruan Lanes
Trewartha
Hartriza Pt
Penveor Pt
High Pt
Lizard Pool
Dodman Pt
Shag Rock
VERYAN BAY
Crugsillick Manor
Melinsey
Veryan
Tregamenna Manor Fm
Portloe
Manare Pt
Treworthal
Lower Mill
Tregairewoon Fm
Treworlas
Carne
Gerrans
Rosen Cliff
SX
10
70
40

6
Cardinham Moor
Hard Head
Redhill Downs
Colliford Downs
Lord's Park Fm
Westerlake Fm
Sparretts Fm
THE HURLERS STONE CIRCLES
Craddock Moor
Minions
Dunslea
Upton Cross
CARADON MINING DISTRICT
Caradon Hill
Caradon Town
Downgate
Trewoodloe
Golberdon
Higher Carblake
Praze
Millpool
St Bellarmin's Tor
Maidenwell
Carburrow Tor
Letter Moor
Redhill Downs
Draynes Common
Siblyback Lake
Trekeivesteps
Gonamena
Tokenbury Manor
Pensilva
Racecourse Downs
Cardinham Downs
Fore Downs
Warleggan Down
Hobb's Hill
Wortha
Northwood
Carpuan
Draynes
GOLITHA FALLS
Commonmoor
Darite
KING DONIERT'S INSCRIBED STONE
Higher Tremarcoombe
TRETHEVY QUOIT
Tremar
Crow's Nest
Middlehill
Charaton Cross
Bicton Manor
Trevigro
Haye Fm
Cardinham
Milltown
Warleggan
Pantersbridge
Treslea Downs
Carne Wood
Tremaddock Fm
Berry Down
Trenant
Treworrick
Trecarne
St Cleer
Newton Fm
Rosecraddoc Manor
Wayland
Woolston
Appledore
Frogwell
Deviock Wood
Hurstocks Wood
Old Cardinham Castle
Mount
Lestow Fm
St Neot
Goonzion Downs
CARNGLAZE SLATE CAVERNS
Treverbyn Mill
Treverbyn
Lampretten Ho
Trethinnick Fm
Treleathick
St Ive
Gang
Merryhue
Thornton
Parkfield
St Ive Cross
Dunnerdake Fm
Durnaford Fm
Cooksland
Callabarrett Wood
Long Downs
Kingswood Downs
Pinsla Park
Tawna Downs
Higher Hill Fm
Welltown
Lower Hill
Trenay
Tredinnick
Ley
Carnglaze Caverns
Woodland Fm
Bokenna Wood
Ashford Wood
Venton Veor
Treworgey Manor
Woodhill Manor
Trengrove Fm
Venton Ho
Penhawger Fm
Hendrabridge
Ludcott Fm
Merrymeet
Westdown Wood
Vicarage Wood
Hammett
Crendle Down
Turfdown
COLESLOGGETT HALT
Fletchersbridge
Redrice Wood
Holtroad Downs
Cabilla Wood
Bear Wood
Drawbridge
Twelvewoods
Doublebois
East Tuelmenna
High Wood
Trembraze
Addington
Pengover Green
Stony Br
Quethiock
Bodmin Parkway
Penkestle Downs
Hall Downs
Draw Wood
Largin Wood
Bodithiel Fm
Dobwalls
Old Park
LISKEARD MUS
Liskeard
Looe Mills
Moorswater
Treburgie
Tregondale Fm
Goodmerry Fm
Hepwell Br
Leigh Fm
Pounda
Trehunist
Trebrown
LANHYDROCK HOUSE
Cutmadoc
Newton
Great Wood
Bofarnel
Bofarnel Downs
Newbridge Wood
West Taphouse
Tithe Hall Fm
Middle Taphouse
East Taphouse
Gelly Fm
Trevelmond
St Pinnock
Boduel
Camellion
COOMBE
LISKEARD
Tencreek Fm
Roseland
Tregrill
Trewint
Lambest
Penpoll
Bedwindle Fm
Cripstone Fm
Babbington
Connon
Lodge Hill
Menheniot
Bodway
Doddycross
Pathada Wood
Sweethouse
Fairy Cross
Trewindle
Braddock
Cliver Wood
Scawns Fm
Penfrane Manor
Trussel Br
Trethawle Fm
Lower Clicker
MENHENIOT
Coldrenick
Trehurst
Tilland
Molenick
Tideford Cross
RESTORMEL CASTLE
Druid's Hill
Crickapit Mill
Trevillis Wood
Wilton Fm
West Trevillies
St Keyne
Lametton Mill
Great Trethew
Roselyon
Deerpark Wood
Trenchway Wood
Herodsfoot
Lean Park Fm
Horningtops
Berry Fm
Cutmere
Hillhead
Sandylake
Brooks
Beara Fm
Woodlay Fm
Hollowpark
Bethany
Budge's Shop
Kernow Mill
Tideford
Lostwithiel
Millham Fm
Coombe Fm
Trebarret
Polmartin Fm
Bury Down
Trewidland
Fursdon
Bylane End
Trebrownbridge Wood
Catchfrench Manor
LOSTWITHIEL
Bridgend
Beacon Hill
Polpiece
Bawdoe Fm
Couch's Mill
Netherton
Pendruffle Wood
Black Down
Windsor Wood
CAUSELAND
Landlooe Br
Pensipple
Wilton Fm
Trerulefoot
Bake Manor
Castle
Botallick
Abovetown
Tremadart Wood
Landare Fm
Churchbridge
Polvean Cross
Polvean Wood
Duloe
Westnorth Fm
Wringworthy
Lower Trenode
Lydcott Wood
Bake Wood
Widegates
Newham Fm
St Winnow
Winnick
Bocaddon
Penquite Fm
Trefanny Hill
Gillhill Wood
Tredinnick
Tregarlandbridge
Tregarland
Bin Down
Shortacross
Hessenford
Milltown
Lantyan
Ribby Fm
Lerryn
Tregarrick Mill
Highercliff
SANDPLACE
Sandplace
Morval
Cleese Fm
Minard Fm
Polbathic
Great Wood
Lanreath
Trevollard
East Court Wood
Muchlarnick
Puffiland Fm
Trelowia
No Man's Land
Bokenver Wood
Carcoe Fm
Narkurs
Lantyan Wood
GOLANT
Wooda Fm
Treire Fm
Court Wood
Hall Wood
Snowden's Bridge
Keveral Wood
Penquite Cliff
Tregarrick Fm
Pelynt
Milcombe
Great Tree
Treesmill
Lawhibbet
Torfrey
St Veep
Haye Fm
Lancare Fm
Catherinepark Wood
Kiln Wood
Tan Acre Wood
Watergate
Trenant Wood
St Martin
MONKEY SANCTUARY
Penhale Fm
Seaton
Golant
Trefrawl
Trelay Fm
Trelawne Manor
Millendreath
Plaidy
Downderry
Tywardreath
Trenython Manor
Penpoll
Peakswater
Polveithan Fm
Bake Fm
Penkelly
Polean Fm
Barcelona
Trad Est
Shutta
East Looe
Bodigga Cliff
Colmer Rocks
SOUTH WEST COAST PATH
Trezare Fm
Penpoll Creek
Mixtow
Lanteglos Highway
Trenewan
Polmear
Whitecross
Trevedda Fm
Trethake Fm
Tremeer Fm
Great Tratford
West Watergate
POLPERRO ROAD
West Looe
Looe
LOOE MUSEUM
Looe Bay
Hannafore
Hannafore Pt
PASSAGE LANE
Bodinnick
Pont
Carneggan Fm
Frogmore Fm
Great Kellow Fm
Tencreek
Portlooe
Polkerris
Fowey
Lansallos
Carey Park
Porthallow
Talland
ST GEORGE'S ISLAND MARINE NATURE RESERVE
St George's or Looe Island
WHITSAND
Menabilly
Readymoney
Pont Pill
Churchtown Fm
CORNWALL
Crumplehorn
Brent
Talland Bay
Portnadler Bay
ST CATHERINE'S CASTLE
Polruan
West Coombe
Lantivet Bay
Hard Hd 132
HERITAGE MUS OF SMUGGLING & FISHING
Polperro
Downend Pt
Coombe Hawne
Washing Rocks
Blackbottle Rock
Lantic Bay
Pencarrow Head
Shag Rock
Chapel Cliff
Southground Pt
Sandy Cove
SX
0 1 2 3 miles
0 1 2 3 4 5 km

Kelly Bray
Monkscross
St Ann's Chapel
Gunnislake
TAMAR VALLEY MINING DISTRICT
Higher Walreddon
Grenofen
Fullamoor
Eggworthy
Cramber Tor
Whiteworks
Bowling Green
Callington
Harrowbarrow
Albaston
Drakewalls
Rising Sun
Silver Valley
Kit Hill
Earth Work
Mount Lodge
Dupath Well Chapel
Metherell
Norris Green
Cotehele
Calstock
Morwellham Quay
Hocklake Fm
Horrabridge
Walkhampton
Gnatham Barton
Dousland
Yennadon Down
Burrator Reservoir
Sheeps Tor
Combshead Tor
Down Tor
Leather Tor
Peek Hill
Horseyeatt
Higher Hittisham
Nun's Cross Fm
Haye
Coombe Fm
Rill Fm
Ashton
Newbridge
Viverdon Down
Morden Fm
St Dominick
Bohetherick
Trehill Fm
Tuckermarsh
Bere Alston
Buckland Monachorum
The Garden House
Buckland Abbey
Crapstone
Axtown
Harrowbeer
Yelverton
Meavy
Sheepstor
Ditsworthy Warren
Hartor Tors
Amy Down
Bealbury
Heathfield Fm
Crocadon Wood
Halton Barton
St Mellion
St Mellion Park
Hole's Hole
Halton Quay
Cotts
Weir Quay
Lockridge Fm
Woolacombe Fm
Milton Combe
Chub Tor
Olderwood Plantn
Hoo Meavy
Clearbrook
Lovaton
Catstor Down
Callisham Down
Ringmoor Down
Gutter Tor
Upper Plym Valley
Giant's Hill
Willings Walls Warren
Hentor Warren
Legis Tor
TAMAR VALLEY
DARTMOOR NATIONAL PARK
Trewashford Fm
Polborder
Paynter's Cross
Herod Wood
Pillaton
Kernock
Pillatonmill
South Sillaton
Crosspark Wood
Lopwell
Bere Ferrers
Thorn Pt
Blaxton Wood
Lower Upperton
North Wood
Trowlesworthy Tors
Cadover Br
Shell Top
Penn Moor
Penn Beacon
Shaugh Moor
DEVON
Leigh Fm
Cargreen
River Tamar
River Tavy
Shaden Moor
Shaugh Prior
Leigh
Roborough
Bickleigh
Collard Tor
Wotter
Lee Moor
Tolchmoor Gate
Rook Tor
Hatt
Rumbullion Fm
Botusfleming
Landulph
Weir Pt
Neal Pt
Kingsmill Lake
Warleigh Pt
Warleigh Point
North Coombe Fm
Widewell
Woolwell
Bickleigh Vale
Hartstone Fm
Faunstone Fm
Wotton
Trewandra
Landrake
Lantallack Cross
Notter
Carkeel
Skinham Pt
Warren Pt
Tamerton Foliot
Glenholt
Southway
Whitleigh
Great Shaugh Wood
Little Pethill Fm
Crownhill Down
Newpark Waste
Quick Br
Headon Down
Piall Br
Saltash Services
Tremayon
Trematon
Latchbrook
Saltash
Burraton
South Pill
Forder
Ernesettle
Crownhill Fort
Derriford
Estover
Cann Wood
Long Down
Drakeland Corner
Smallhanger
Dartmoor Zoological Park
Yondertown
Cornwood
Berry Hill
St Erney
Mary Newman's Cottage
Wearde
Riverside
St Budeaux
King's Tamerton
Honicknowle
Manadon
Crownhill
Leigham
Plym Valley Railway
Hemerdon Ball
Lutton
Sparkwell
Hemerdon
Burraton Coombe
Trehan
Trematon Castle
St Stephens
Churchtown Farm Community
Antony Passage
Barne Barton
Weston Mill Lake
Ham
Weston Mill
Pennycross
The Parkway
Eggbuckland
Longbridge
Woodford
Newnham Park
Lower Venton Fm
Mark's Br
Cadleigh Lodge
St Germans
Jupiter Pt
Antony House
Sheviock Wood
Erth Hill
Lynher River or St Germans
Wilcove
Hamoaze
Keyham
Ford
Peverell
Home Park
Compton
Efford
Crabtree
Chaddlewood
Plympton
Venton
Lee Mill
Berry Down
Maryfield
Bus Cen
Sheviock
VALLEY
Stoke
Mannamead
Mutley
Mount Gould
Laira
Saltram House
Underwood
River Plym
PLYMOUTH
Plymouth
Devonport
Stonehouse
Brickfields Rec. Gnd
The Box
Smithaleigh
Hunsdon Fm
Torpoint
Antony
Crafthole
Deadman's Pt
St John's Lake
Sango Island
Merchant's House
National Marine Aquarium
Royal Citadel
Langage
Blackpool
Billacombe
West Sherford
East Sherford
Southwood Wood
Popple's Br
Lotherton Br
Portwrinkle
Trethill Cliffs
Long Sands
St John
Hounster Hill
Cremyll
Devils Pt
Western King Pt
Mount Batten Pt
Cattedown
Oreston
Pomphlett
Plymstock
Elburton
Elburton Road
Efford Fm
Yeo Fm
Stonycross Fm
Worston
Tregantle Cliff
Sharrow Pt
Freathy
Insworke
Southdown
Millbrook
Millbrook Lake
Mount Edgcumbe
Drake's Island
Dunstone Pt
Jennycliff Bay
Turnchapel
Hooe
Combe
Brixton
Yealmpton
Yealmbridge
Dunstone
Butland Wood
BAY
Anderton
THE SOUND
Picklecombe Pt
South West Coast Path
Barn Fm
Coombe Fm
Spriddlestone
Spriddlestone Ho
Staddiscombe
Torr
Holbeton
Staddon Pt
Bovisand Bay
Bovisand Lodge
Down Thomas
Raneleigh Fm
Hollacombe Hill
Wembury Wood
Cofflete Creek
River Yealm
Ashcombe Fm
Creacombe Fm
Kingsand
Cawsand
Captain Blake's Pt
Pier Cellars
Rame
Polhawn Cove
Lillery's Cove
Penlee Pt
Rame Head
Roscoff Santander (Mar-Nov)
Manor Bourne
SOUTH DEVON
Knighton
Steer Pt
Collaton Fm
Luson
Borough Fm
Heybrook Bay
Wembury
Renney Rocks
Wembury Pt
Blackstone Rocks
Season Pt
Warren Pt
Mouthstone Pt
Newton Ferrers
Bridgend
Membland
Pool Mill Fm
Preston Fm
Alston Hall
Battisborough Cross
Haye Fm
Poole Fm
Mothecombe
St Anchorite's Rock
Erme Mouth
Noss Mayo
Worswell
Gara Pt
Netton Fm
Stoke Ho
Blackstone Pt
Hilsea Pt
Stoke Pt
Wadham Rocks
Blackaterry Pt
Butcher's Cove
Mary's Rocks
Beacon Pt
SX
60
70
40
A
B
C
D
E
F
G
H
7
8
9
10
11
12
13

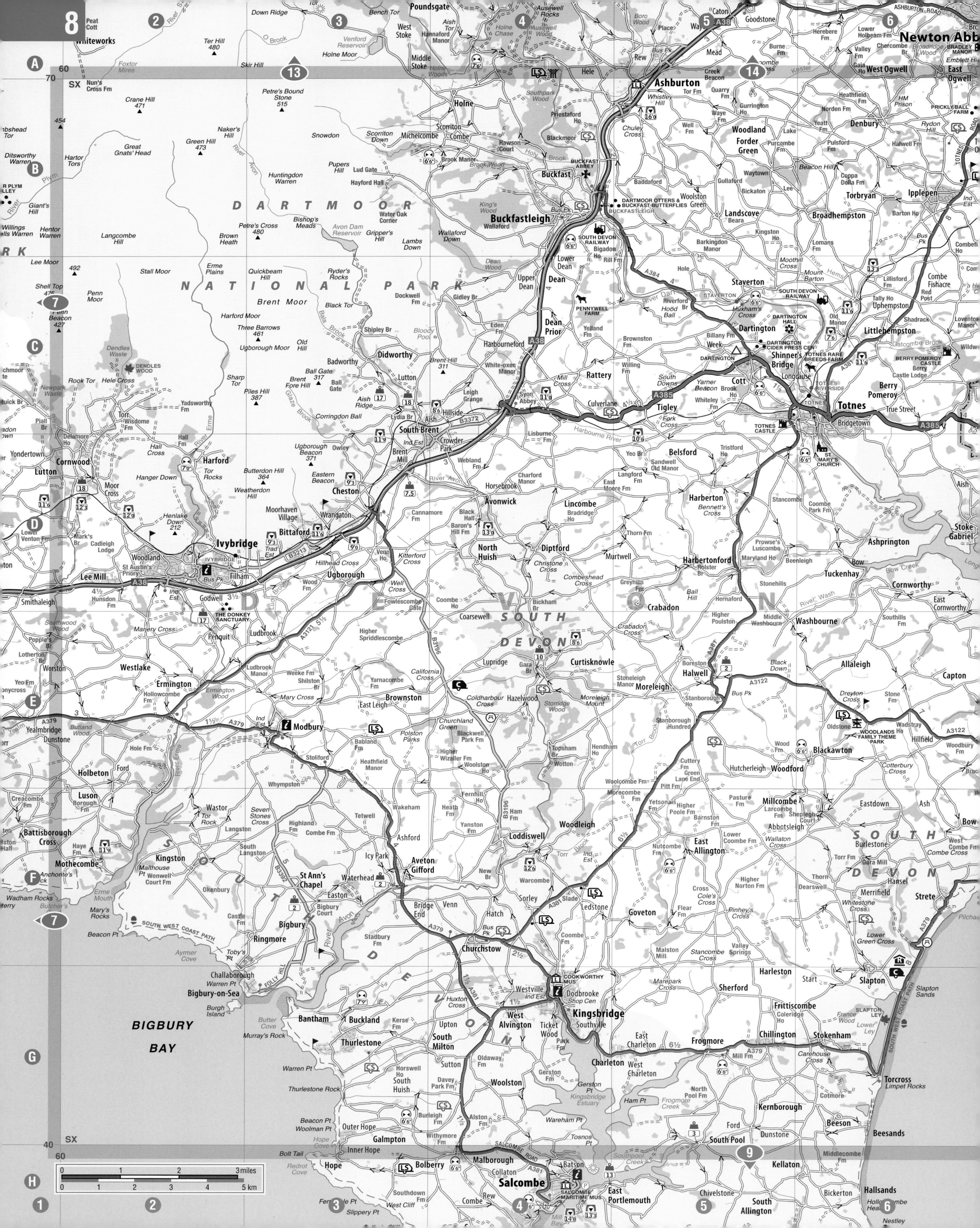
Peat Cott
Whiteworks
Down Ridge
Bench Tor
Poundsgate
Ausewell Rocks
Caton
Goodstone
Newton Abbot
Ter Hill 480
West Stoke
Hannaford Manor
Aish Tor
Holne Chase
Ausewell Wood
Boro Wood
Place
Mead
Rew
Bus Pk
Herebere Fm
Burne Fm
Lower Holbeam Fm
Valley Fm
Chercombe Br
Bradley Manor
Emblett Hill
Venford Reservoir
Holne Moor
Middle Stoke
Holne Woods
Foxtor Mires
Skir Hill
Hele
Ashburton
Creek Fm
West Ogwell
East Ogwell
SX
Nun's Cross Fm
Petre's Bound Stone 515
Crane Hill 471
Holne
Southpark Wood
Priestaford Ho
Whistley Hill
Tor Fm
Quarry Fm
Gurrington Ho
Heathfield Fm
HM Prison
Nordon Fm
Prickly Ball Farm
Denbury
Rydon Hill
Halwell Fm
Hobshead Tor
Ditsworthy Warren
Hartor Tors
Naker's Hill
Green Hill 473
Great Gnats' Head
Snowdon
Scorriton
Scorriton Down
Michelcombe
Combe
Rawson Court
Blackmoor
Chuley Cross
Well Fm
Waye Fm
Woodland
Forder Green
Purcombe Fm
Lake
Yeatt Fm
Pulsford Fm
Pupers Hill
Lud Gate
Hayford Hall
Huntingdon Warren
Brook Manor
Brook Wood
Holy Brook
Buckfast Abbey
Buckfast
Baddaford
Gullaford
Waytown
Bickaton
Lee
Woolston Green
Beacon Hill
Coppa Dolla Fm
Torbryan
Ipplepen
Giant's Hill
Dartmoor Otters & Buckfast Butterflies
Buckfastleigh
DARTMOOR
Water Oak Corner
Bishop's Meads
Avon Dam Reservoir
Gripper's Hill
Wallaford Down
King's Wood
Wallaford
Landscove
Beara
Broadhempston
Barton Ho
Willings Walls Warren
Hentor Warren
Langcombe Hill
Brown Heath
Petre's Cross 480
Lambs Down
South Devon Railway
Bigadon Ho
Rill Fm
Kingston Ho
Barkingdon Manor
Lomans Fm
Lee Moor
492
Stall Moor
Erme Plains
Quickbeam Hill
Ryder's Rocks
Dean Wood
Lower Dean
Dean
Upper Dean
Hole
Moothill Cross
Mount Barton
River Hems
Lillisford Fm
Combe Fishacre
Shell Top
Penn Beacon 427
Penn Moor
NATIONAL PARK
Brent Moor
Black Tor
Dockwell Fm
Gidley Br
Staverton
Riverford Br
Hood Ball
Pennywell Farm
South Devon Railway
Huxham's Cross
Dartington Hall
Old Manor
Tally Ho
Upphempston
Red Post
Harford Moor
Three Barrows 461
Ugborough Moor
Shipley Br
Bloody Pool
Eden Fm
Dean Prior
Yelland Fm
Brownston Fm
Billany Fm
Week
Dartington
Dartington Cider Press Cen
Shinner's Bridge
Totnes Rare Breeds Farm
Littlehempston
Shadrack
Loventon Manor
Berry Pomeroy Castle
Berry Castle Lodge
Dendles Waste
Dendles Wood
Old Hill
Badworthy
Didworthy
Brent Hill 311
Harbourneford
White-oxen Manor
Willing Fm
Rattery
South Downs
Longcause
Yarner Beacon
Brook Ho
Cott
Totnes Riverside
Berry Pomeroy
Rook Tor
Hele Cross
Sharp Tor
Piles Hill 387
Ball Gate 317
Brent Fore Hill
Ball Gate
Aish Ridge
Lutton
Leigh Grange
Mill Cross
Syon Abbey
Culverlane
Whiteley Fm
Tigley
Totnes
True Street
Bridgetown
Yadsworthy Fm
Torr
Wisdome
Corringdon Ball
Lydia Br
Aish
Hillside
South Brent
Lisburne Fm
Harbourne River
Fork Cross
Totnes Castle
Delamore
Yondertown
Cornwood
Lutton
Hall Cross
Hall Fm
Harford
Tor Rocks
Ugborough Beacon 371
Owley
Brent Mill
Ind Est
Crowder Park
Webland Fm
Charford Manor
Yeo Br
Sandwell Old Manor
Belsford
Tristford Ho
St Mary's Church
Moor Cross
Hanger Down
Butterdon Hill 364
Weatherdon Hill
Eastern Beacon
Cheston
Horsebrook
Langford Fm
East Moore Fm
Harberton
Bennett's Cross
Stancombe
Coombe Park Fm
Aish
Henlake Down 212
Moorhaven Village
Wrangaton
Cannamore Fm
Avonwick
Black Hall
Baron's Hill Fm
Lincombe
Bradridge Ho
Thorn Fm
Stoke Gabriel
Lower Venton Fm
Mark's Br
Cadleigh Lodge
Woodland
Ivybridge
Bittaford
Trad Est
Venn Ho
Kitterford Cross
North Huish
Diptford
Murtwell
Prowse's Luscombe
Maryland Ho
Harbertonford
Rolster Br
Beenleigh
Ashprington
St Austin's Priory
Lee Mill
Filham
Hillhead Cross
Ugborough
Wood Fm
Well Cross
Christone Cross
Combeshead Cross
Greyhills Fm
Bow
Bow Creek
Tuckenhay
Stonehills
Cornworthy
East Cornworthy
Smithaleigh
Hunsdon Fm
Ind Est
Godwell
The Donkey Sanctuary
Fowlescombe Gate
Coombe Ho
Bickham Br
Ball Hill
Hernaford
Crabadon
River Wash
Middle Washbourne
Washbourne
Southills Fm
Southwood Wood
Manery Cross
Penquit
Ludbrook
Coarsewell
SOUTH DEVON
Higher Poulston
Popple's Br
Higher Spriddlescombe
Crabadon Cross
Lotherton Br
Worston
Westlake
Ludbrook Manor
Weeke Fm
Shilston Br
California Cross
Lupridge
Gara Br
Curtisknowle
Stoneleigh Manor
Moreleigh
Boreston
Halwell
Black Down
Allaleigh
Capton
Yeo Fm
Ponycross
Ermington
Hollowcombe Fm
Ermington Wood
Yarnacombe Fm
Mary Cross
Brownston
East Leigh
Coldharbour Cross
Hazelwood
Storridge Wood
Moreleigh Mount
Stanborough Ho
Bus Pk
Dreyton Cross
Stone Fm
Yealmbridge
Dunstone
Butland Wood
Modbury
Churchland Green
Blackwell Park Fm
Polston Parks
Babland Fm
Stanborough Hundred
Oldstone
Woodlands Family Theme Park
Wadstray Ho
Hillfield
Woodbury Fm
Hole Fm
Stoliford
Heathfield Manor
Higher Wizaller Fm
Woolston Ho
Topsham Br
Wotton
Hendham Ho
Wood Fm
Blackawton
Cutterbury Cross
Holbeton
Ford
Whympston
Cuttery Fm
Green Lane End
Hutcherleigh
Woodford
Woolcombe Fm
Morecombe Fm
Pitt Fm
Pasture Fm
Millcombe
Larcombe Fm
Shepleigh Court
Eastdown
Ash
Luson
Creacombe Fm
Wastor
Tor Rock
Seven Stones Cross
Wakeham
Fernhill Ho
Heath Fm
Ham Fm
Yetsonais Fm
Higher Poole Fm
Barnston Fm
Abbotsleigh
Bow
Battisborough Cross
Langston
Highland Fm
Combe Fm
Tetwell
Yanston Fm
Woodleigh
Lower Coombe Fm
Wallaton Cross
SOUTH
Burlestone
West Combe Fm
Combe Cross
Haye Fm
Kingston
South Langston
Ashford
Loddiswell
Nutcombe Ho
East Allington
Torr Fm
Gara Mill
Mothecombe
Anchorite's Rock
Malthouse Pt
Wonwell Court Fm
St Ann's Chapel
Icy Park
Waterhead
Aveton Gifford
New Br
Warcombe
Higher Norton Fm
Thorn
Dearswell
DEVON
Hansel
Merrifield
Okenbury
Erme Mouth
Wadham Rocks
Butcher's Rocks
Mary's Rocks
Castle Fm
Easton
Bigbury Court
Bridge End
Venn
Sorley
Slade
Ledstone
Goveton
Cross Cole's Cross
Flear Fm
Pinhey's Cross
Whitestone Cross
Strete
Beacon Pt
South West Coast Path
Bigbury
Ringmore
Stadbury Fm
Hatch
Churchstow
Coombe Fm
Malston Mill
Stancombe Cross
Valley Springs
Lower Green Cross
Aymer Cove
Toby's Pt
Challaborough
Warren Pt
Bigbury-on-Sea
Folly Hill
Westville
Ind Est
Cookworthy Mus
Dodbrooke
Shop Cen
Marepark Cross
Sherford
Harleston
Start
Slapton
Slapton Sands
Burgh Island
BIGBURY BAY
Butter Cove
Murray's Rock
Bantham
Buckland
Kerse Fm
Huxton Cross
West Alvington
Ticket Wood
Kingsbridge
Southville
Frittiscombe
Coleridge Ho
France Wood
Slapton Ley
Lower Ley
East Charleton
Frogmore
Chillington
Stokenham
Upton
South Milton
Park Fm
Thurlestone
Oldaway Fm
Charleton
West Charleton
Mill Fm
Carehouse Cross
Warren Pt
Sutton
Horswell Ho
South Huish
Gerston Fm
Gerston Pt
Kingsbridge Estuary
Torcross
Limpet Rocks
Thurlestone Rock
Davey Park Fm
Woolston
Ham Pt
North Pool Fm
Frogmore Creek
Cotmore
Beacon Pt
Woolman Pt
Outer Hope
Burleigh Fm
Alston Fm
Wareham Pt
Kernborough
Beeson
Beesands
Hope Cove
Inner Hope
Galmpton
Withymore Fm
Tosnos Pt
South Pool
Ford
Dunstone
Bolt Tail
Redrot Cove
Hope
Bolberry
Malborough
Salcombe Road
Batson
Southpool Creek
Kellaton
Middlecombe Fm
Collaton
Salcombe
Salcombe Maritime Mus
East Portlemouth
Chivelstone
South Allington
Bickerton
Hallsands
Hallsands Head
Southdown Fm
Fern Hill Pt
Slippery Pt
West Cliff
Combe
Rew
Mill Bay
Nestley
3 miles
5 km

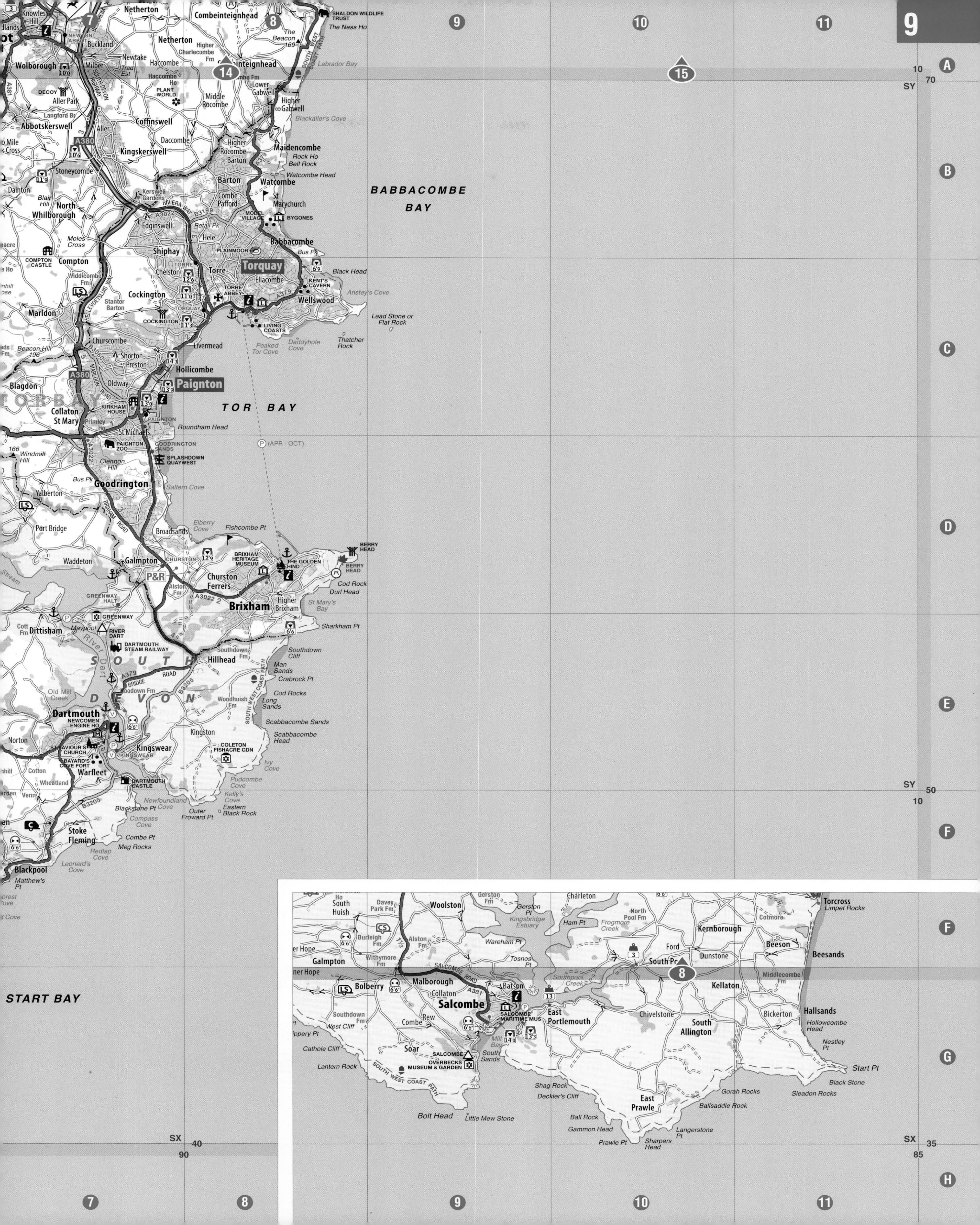

Padstow
Wadebridge
Padstow Bay
Port Isaac Bay
Trevose Head
Constantine Bay
Treyarnon
Porthcothan
St Merryn
Harlyn
Trevone
Crugmeer
Rock
Polzeath
New Polzeath
Trebetherick
St Minver
Pityme
Port Quin
Port Isaac
Port Gaverne
Trelights
St Endellion
Pendoggett
Trelill
St Kew
St Kew Highway
Chapel Amble
Little Petherick
St Issey
St Breock
Egloshayle
Burniere
Bodieve
Whitecross
St Ervan
Rumford
St Eval
St Jidgey
Washaway
Tintagel Head
Pentire Pt
Gulland Rock
Newland
The Mouls
Rumps Pt
River Camel
CORNWALL
SOUTH WEST COAST PATH
ROYAL CORNWALL SHOWGROUND
NATIONAL LOBSTER HATCHERY
PRIDEAUX PLACE
CAMEL CREEK ADVENTURE PARK
PENCARROW HOUSE
A39
A389
B3276
B3314
B3267
SW
0 1 2 3 miles
0 1 2 3 4 5 km

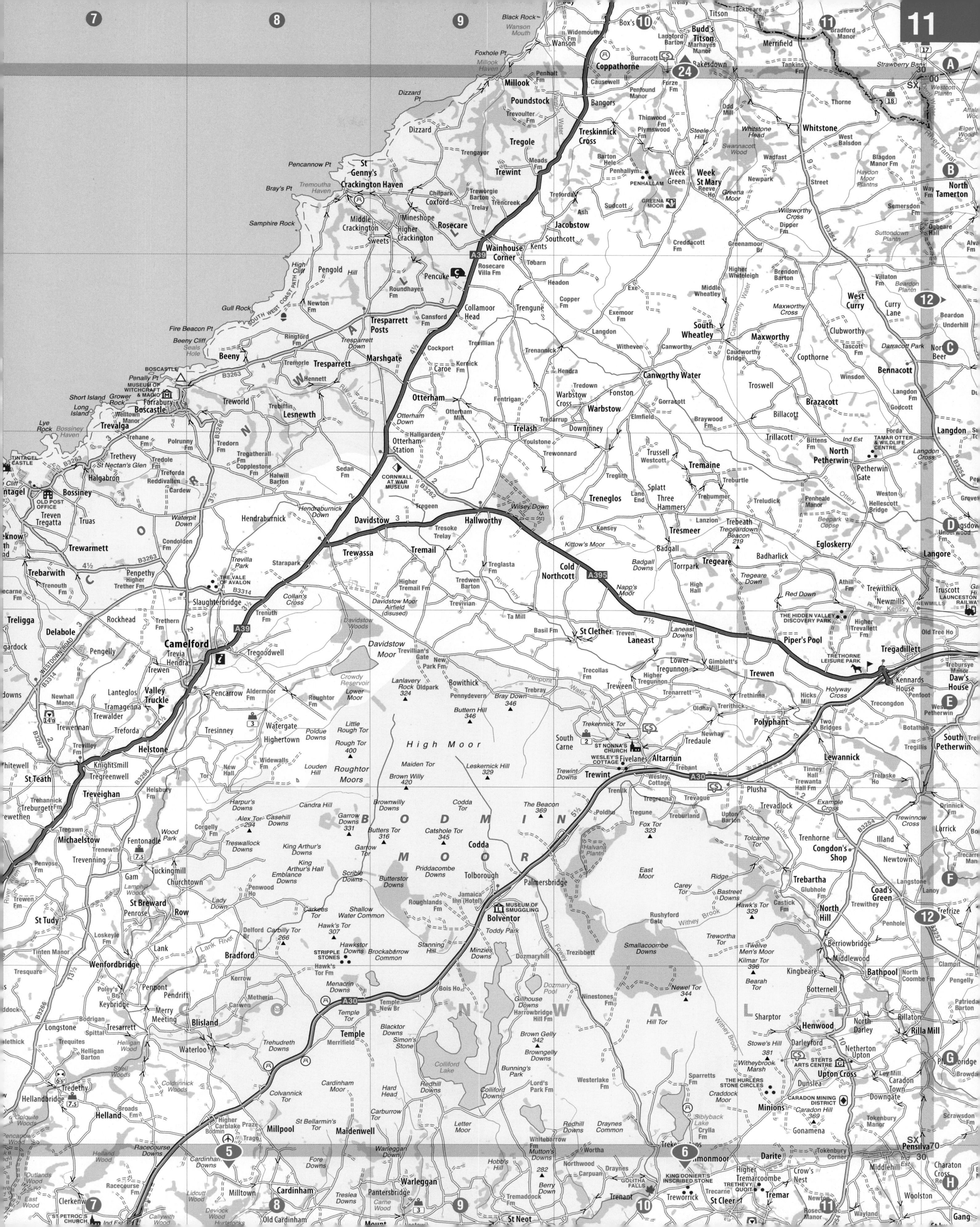
7
8
9
10
11
12
24
5
6
Black Rock
Wanson Mouth
Wanson
Widemouth
Box's
Budd's Titson
Titson
Merrifield
Bradford Manor
Foxhole Pt
Millook Haven
Millook
Coppathorne
Bakesdown
Burracott
Strawberry Bank
Penhalt Fm
Causewell
Penfound Manor
Furze Fm
Tankins Fm
Dizzard Pt
Dizzard
Poundstock
Treveulter Fm
Bangors
Odd Mill
Thorne
Treskinnick Cross
Thinwood Fm
Plymswood Fm
Steele Hill
Whitstone Head
Whitstone
West Balsdon
Tregole
Tamar Otter Water
River Tamar
Tremoutha Haven
Pencannow Pt
Bray's Pt
St Genny's
Crackington Haven
Tengayor
Meads Fm
Barton Hele
Penhallym
Penhallam
Week Green
Week St Mary
Reeve Ho
Swannacott Wood
Wadfast
Blagdon Manor Fm
Haydon Moor Plantns
North Tamerton
Trewint
Chilpark
Coxford
Treworgie Barton
Trencreek
Treforda
Sudcott
Greena Moor
Newpark
Street
Samphire Rock
Middle Crackington
Mineshope
Higher Crackington
Sweets
Rosecare
Trelay
Jacobstow
Ash
Willsworthy Cross
Dipper Fm
Semersdon Fm
Ogbeare Hall
Suttondown Plantn
Wainhouse Corner
Southcott
Kents
Creddacott Fm
Greenamoor Br
High Cliff
Pengold
Hill
Pencuke
Rosecare Villa Fm
Tobarn
Headon
Higher Whiteleigh
Brendon Barton
Villaton Fm
Beardon Plantn
Roundhayes Fm
Middle Wheatley
Gull Rock
South West Coast Path
Newton Fm
Collamoor Head
Trengune
Copper Fm
Exe
Exemoor Fm
Maxworthy Cross
West Curry
Curry Lane
Cansford Fm
Trespareett Posts
Langdon
South Wheatley
Maxworthy
Clubworthy
Fire Beacon Pt
Beeny Cliff
Seals Hole
Ringford Fm
Trespareett Down
Cockport
Trevillian
Trenannick
Withevan
Canworthy
Caudworthy Bridge
Caudworthy Water
Tascott Fm
Darracott Park
Copthorne
Beeny
Tremorle
Trespareett
Marshgate
Caroe
Kernick Fm
Hendra
Canworthy Water
Winsdon
Bennacott
Boscastle
Penally Pt
Museum of Witchcraft & Magic
Forrabury
B3263
Hennett
River Valency
Tredown
Fonston
Troswell
Short Island
Grower Rock
Long Island
Welltown Manor
Boscastle
Treworld
Trebiffin
Lesnewth
Otterham
Fentrigan
Warbstow Cross
Warbstow
Gorracott
Brazacott
Langdon Fm
Godcott
Lye Rock
Bossiney Haven
Trevalga
Otterham Down
Otterham Mill
Trelash
Tredarrup
Downinney
Elmfield
Billacott
Braywood Fm
Langdon
Trehane Fm
Polrunny Fm
Tredorn Fm
Hallgarden
Otterham Station
Youlstone
Trewonnard
Trussell
Westcott
Trillacott
Bittens Fm
Ind Est
North Petherwin
Forda
Tamar Otter & Wildlife Centre
Langdon Cross
Tintagel Castle
Trethevy
St Nectan's Glen
Tredole Fm
Tregatherall Fm
Copplestone Fm
Treforda
Reddivallen
Cardew
Halwill Barton
Sedan Fm
Cornwall at War Museum
B3262
Treglith
Tremaine
Petherwin Gate
Halgabron
Tintagel
Bossiney
Old Post Office
Treven
Tregatta
Truas
Hendraburnick Down
Tregeen
Wilsey Down
Lane End
Splatt
Three Hammers
Treburtle
Trehummer
Treludick
Penheale Manor
River Ottery
Weston
Hellescott Bridge
Hendraburnick
Waterpit Down
Davidstow
Tresoke
Trelay
Hallworthy
Treneglos
Lanzion
Trebeath
Tregeardown Beacon
Beepark Copse
Egloskerry
Trewarmett
Condolden Fm
Trewassa
Tremail
Kensey
Kittow's Moor
Tresmeer
Badgall
Badharlick
Langore
Trebarwith
B3263
Penpethy
Higher Trether Fm
Trevilla Park
The Vale of Avalon
Starapark
Treglasta Fm
Cold Northcott
A395
Badgall Downs
Torrpark
Tregeare
Tregeare Down
Athill Fm
Trewithick
Truscott
Trenouth Fm
Slaughterbridge
B3314
Collan's Cross
Higher Tremail Fm
Tredwen Barton
River Inny
Napp's Moor
High Hall
Red Down
Newmills
Launceston Railway
Treligga
Delabole
Rockhead
Trethern Fm
Trenuth Fm
Davidstow Moor Airfield (disused)
Trevivian
Ta Mill
The Hidden Valley Discovery Park
Higher Trevallett Fm
Old Tree Ho
Westdown Road
Pengelly
Camelford
Trevia
Hendra
Tregoodwell
Davidstow Woods
Davidstow Moor
Trevillian's Gate
Basil Fm
St Clether
Treven
Laneast
Laneast Downs
Piper's Pool
Trethorne Leisure Park
Tregadillett
Trewen
New Park Fm
Bowithick
Crowdy Reservoir
Lanlavery Rock
Oldpark
Pennydevern
Bray Down
Penpont Water
Trebray
Trecollas Fm
Lower Tregunnon
Higher Tregunnon
Gimblett's Mill
Treween
Trewen
Trenarrett
Trethinna
Hicks Mill
Holyway Cross
Trecongdon
Kennards House
Penfoot
Daw's House
West Petherwin
Newhall Manor
Lanteglos
Valley Truckle
Pencarrow
Aldermoor Fm
Roughtor Fm
Lower Moor
Buttern Hill
Oldhay
Trerithick
Polyphant
Two Bridges
Botathan
Trewalder
Tramagenna
Treforda
Tresinney
Watergate
Highertown
Poldue Downs
Little Rough Tor
Rough Tor
High Moor
Trekennick Tor
South Carne
St Nonna's Church
Newhay
Tredaule
South Petherwin
Tregillis
Trewennan
Trevilley Fm
Helstone
Knightsmill
Tregreenwell
B3266
New Hall
Widewalls Fm
Louden Hill
Roughtor Moors
Maiden Tor
Brown Willy
Leskernick Hill
Wesley's Cottage
Fivelanes
Altarnun
Trewint Downs
Trewint
Trebant
A30
Lewannick
Tinney Hall
Trewanta Hall Fm
Trelaske Ho
Whitewell
St Teath
Treveighan
Trehannick
Treburgett
Helsbury Fm
Harpur's Downs
Casehill Downs
Candra Hill
Brownwilly Downs
Codda Tor
The Beacon
Wesley Cottage
Plusha
Trerenna
Trevague
Tregune
Poldhu
Treburland
Upton Barton
River Lynher
Tredavlock
Example Cross
Orinnick Ho
Trewinnow Cross
Larrick
Trewethen
Tregawn
Michaelstow
Trenewth
Fentonadle
Wood Park
Corgelly Fm
Alex Tor
Garrow Downs
Bodmin Moor
Butters Tor
Catshole Tor
Codda
Halvana Plantn
Fox Tor
Tolcarne Tor
Trenhorne
Congdon's Shop
Illand
Newtown
Trevenning
Penvose Fm
Treswallock Downs
King Arthur's Downs
Garrow Tor
Priddacombe Downs
East Moor
Gam
Tuckingmill
Churchtown
King Arthur's Hall
Emblance Downs
Scribble Downs
Butterstor Downs
Tolborough
Palmersbridge
Carey Tor
Ridge
Bastreet Downs
Trebartha
Glubhole Fm
Coad's Green
Langstone
Lanoy
Lamphill Woods
Penwood Ho
Jamaica Inn (Hotel)
Museum of Smuggling
Bolventor
Hawk's Tor
North Hill
Trewithey
Trefrize
Treween Fm
St Breward
Penrose
Row
Lady Down
Carkees Tor
Shallow Water Common
Roughlands Fm
Rushyford Gate
Withey Brook
Castick Fm
Penhole
St Tudy
Loskeyle Fm
Delford Br
Carbilly Tor
Hawk's Tor
Toddy Park
River Fowey
Trezibbett
Smallacoombe Downs
Trewortha Tor
Twelve Men's Moor
Kilmar Tor
Berriowbridge
Middlewood
Clampit
Tinten Manor
Lank
Lank River
Stripple Stones
Hawkstor Downs
Brockabarrow Common
Stanning Hill
Minzies Downs
Dozmaryhill
Bearah Tor
Kingbeare
Bathpool
North Coombe Fm
Pengelly
Tresquare
Wenfordbridge
Bradford
Hawk's Tor Fm
Kerrow
Menacrin Downs
Bois Ho
Dozmary Pool
Newel Tor
Botternell
Poley's Br
Keybridge
Penpont
Pendrift
Metherin
Carwen
Temple New Br
Gillhouse Downs
Harrowbridge Hill Fm
Ninestones Fm
Hill Tor
Sharptor
Billaton
Patrieda Barton
Bodrigan
Longstone
Spittal
Tresarrett
Merry Meeting
Blisland
Temple Tor
Temple
Blacktor Downs
Simon's Stone
Brown Gelly
Browngelly Downs
Henwood
North Darley
Rilla Mill
Trequites
Helligan Barton
Helligan Wood
Waterloo
Trehudreth Downs
Merrifield
Colliford Lake
Witney Brook
Stowe's Hill
Darleyford
Netherton
Upton
Withey Brook Marsh
Sterts Arts Centre
Upton Cross
Caradon Town
Shell Woods
Coldrinnick Woods
Bunning's Park
Lord's Park Fm
Westerlake Fm
Sparretts Fm
The Hurlers Stone Circles
Dunslea
Ley Mill
Downgate
Tredethy
Hellandbridge
Cardinham Moor
Hard Head
Redhill Downs
Colliford Downs
Craddock Moor
Caradon Mining District
Caradon Hill
Colvannick Tor
Carburrow Tor
Siblyback Lake
Crylla Fm
Minions
Gonamena
Helland
Broads Fm
Colquite Woods
Higher Carblake
Bodmin
Praze
Tragg
Millpool
St Bellarmin's Tor
Maidenwell
Letter Moor
Redhill Downs
Draynes Common
Whitebarrow Fm
Tokenbury Manor
Scrawsdon Fm
Pensilva
Penca Wood
Helland Wood
Racecourse Downs
Cardinham Downs
Warleggan Down
Fore Downs
Hobb's Hill
Mutton's Downs
Wortha
Trekeivesteps
Commonmoor
Darite
Tokenbury Corner
Middlehill
Charaton Cross
Outlands Wood
Racecourse Fm
Milltown
Cardinham
Warleggan
Pantersbridge
Treslea Downs
Carne Wood
Northwood
Carpuan
Draynes
Golitha Falls
King Doniert's Inscribed Stone
Higher Tremarcoombe
Trethevy Quoit
Crow's Nest
Tremar
East Wood
Lidcutt Wood
Deviock Wood
Tremaddock Fm
Berry Down
Trenant
Treworrick
Trecarne
St Cleer
Woolston
Clerkenwater
St Petroc's Church
Old Cardinham
Callywith Wood
Mount
St Neot
Gang
Wayland

Leworthy
Brooks House
Parsonage Wood
Winscott Cross
Sillick Moor
Affalan Moor
North Down
Common
Claw Bridge
Halwill Moor Plantn
Lane End
Downs
Stonequarry Fm
Lease Fm
Whiddon Moor
Stewdon Moor
Northlew Manor
Landsend Fm
Rutleigh Ball Fm
Norley
South Yeo
Narracott
Marshford
Gribbleford Br
Clawmoor Fm
Cookworthy Moor Plantn
Langaford Moor
Forda Mill
Corfcott Green
Clawton
Buckhorn
Hunscott Fm
Haye Fm
East Down
Langaford
Halwill
Beaworthy
Crowden
Trew Fm
Northlew
Oak Cross
Westlake Fm
Homing Down
Heath Moor
East Kimber
Loveland Fm
Patchacott
Ashbury
Waytown
North Beer
Sandymoor Cross
Quoditch Cross
Rectory Fm
Halwill Mill
Stowford
Sixty Acre Moor
Mount Pleasant
South Moor
Blagdon Manor
North Tamerton
Raggott Hill
Commons Gate
Moortown
Swingate Cross
New Buildings
East Venn
Landhill
Quoditch
Westlake's Plantns
Broadmeads Plantn
Broadbury
Whiddon
Higher Prestacott
Foxhole
Beckett
Thorney Cross
Tetcott
Lana
Nethercott
Semersdon Fm
Tamerton Town
Tetcott Manor
Metherell Fm
Northcombe Plantn
Burden Fm
Venn Barton
Ashbury Plantations
Scobchester Down
Cruft Gate
Wadland Down Plantns
Coxwall
Ogbeare Hall
Alvacott Fm
Beardown Plantn
Lamanoor Plantn
Mount Lane
Larkworthy
Ashwater
Ashmill
North Thorne
Witherdon Wood
Luffincott
Henford
Henford Moor
Bradaford
Thorndon Ho
Moor
Eworthy
Brockscombe
Venn Down
Weeks-in-the-Moor
Maddaford
Villaton
Hornacott Barton
East Peeke
West Peeke
Ashwater Wood
Hole Fm
Lugworthy Cross
Germansweek
Blagrove Fm
Thorndon Cross
Thorndon Down
Risdon
Boasley Cross
Boasley
Curry Lane
Beardon
Underhill
Chapmans Well
Hollow Panson
Tillislow
Virginstow
Woodley Park
Westweekmoor
Seccombe Fm
Voulsdon Cross
Northcott
Newton Fm
Dubbs Cross
North Beer
East Panson
Coombeshead Park Fm
Norton Barton Manor
Willtown
Breazle Fm
Bratton Clovelly
Eversfield
Mendea
Hursdon Fm
Linnacombe
Sourton Cross Services
Cowsen Down
Bennacott
Boyton
Boyton Mill
Hele
West Panson
Scotland Fm
Venn Fm
Grinacombe Moor
Roadford Lake
South Hill
Week Fm
Forda
Langdon Fm
Godcott
Dunn's Fm
Carey Wood
Grove
Vennmoor Plantn
Upcott Wood
Headson Cross
Morson Fm
Ebsworthy Moor Fm
A30
Sourton
Prewley Moor
Sourton Tor
Langdon
Sutton Town
Bullapit
Pinslow Fm
St Giles on the Heath
Tower Hill
Downicary
Gaddacombe Cross
Eastlake Fm
Woolacott Fm
Langdon Cross
Tamar Otter & Wildlife Centre
Wilkie Down Fm
Polapit Tamar
Bridgetown
Gridley Corner
East Park
Downtown Fm
Thorne Moor
Broadwoodwidger
Slew Wood
Way Barton Fm
Trebick
Orchard Barton
Millaton Ho
Pool Cross
Collaven Manor
Bridestowe
East Tor
Tor Wood
Lake Down
Etherwin Gate
Peppershill
Eggbeare
Coombe Mill
Camp
Peter's Finger
East Druxton Fm
Kellacott
Rexon Cross
Rexon
Wortham
Venn Mill
Bidlake
Stone Fm
Leawood Ho
Lake
Southerly
Weston
Hellescott Bridge
Ladycross
Grovetown
Werrington
West Kitcham Fm
Boldford Bridge
Fernhill
Cross Green
Lower Mills
Wheatley Park Fm
Ashleigh Fm
Point
Combebow
Beara Down
Burley Wood
Gt Nodden 586
Southerly Down
Wringsdown
Underwood
Yeolmbridge
Ham Mill
Tipple Cross
Jays
Townleigh Fm
Alder Ho
Thrushelton
Lobhillcross
Stowford
Cannon Barn
Lewdown
Langore
Lowley Wood
Werrington Park
Nether Bridge
Colemans Cross
Carley
Wortham Manor
Higher Cookworthy
Lower Cookworthy
Dingle's Fairground Heritage Centre
Milford
Beechcombe
Burley Down
Shortacombe
Fernworthy Down
Vale Down
Nodden Gate
Little Links Tor
Beara
Smallacombe
Portgate
Cholwell Fm
Lewtrenchard
Cross Roads
Lew Mill
Galford Down
Brat Tor 460
Bray Tor
Trewithick
Newmills
Truscott
Gallows Hill
Launceston Steam Railway
Lanstephan
St Stephen's
Newport
Dutson
Liftondown
Welltown Fm
Lifton
Tinhay
Lew Wood
Dippertown
Eastcottdown Plantn
Lydford
High Down
Doeter Common
Danger area
Launceston
Launceston Castle
Old Tree Ho
Wooladon Fm
Lifton Park
Moonhouse Plantn
Blackdown Wood
Whiteley Fm
Hartly Wood
Sydenham Wood
Lowertown
Ford Fm
Longham Down
Lydford Castle
Lydford Gorge
White Hill 390
Tregadillett
Bus Pk
Retail Pk
Bulsworthy Fm
Treniffle
Carzantic
Gatherley Wood
Lake Fm
Lee Fm
Coryton
Lyd Valley Ho
Hall Fm
Henscott Plantns
Ger Tor
Kennards House
Trebursye Manor
Daw's House
Ind Est
Newton Fm
Hurdon Fm
Lawhitton Barton
Lawhitton
Gatherley
Warracott
Billacombe
Burns Hall
Liddaton
Bowden Hill
Langstone Manor
Wastor Fm
Black Down
Nat Tor
Lane End
Willsworthy
Penfoot
West Petherwin
Hall Fm
Meadwell
Chillaton Ho
Chillaton
Whitstone Fm
Rowden Fm
Botathan
South Petherwin
Trelinnoe
Tregillis
Tregada
Leburnick
Kelly
Kelly Ho
Borough
Week
West Blackdown
North Brentor
Gibbet Hill 353
Kingsett Down
Standon Fm
Brousentor Fm
Trelaske Ho
Trewarlett Cross
Little Comfort
Timbrelham
Bradstone
Pallastreet
Felldownhead
Holland
Tredown
Ramsdown Cross
Quither Common
Brent Tor
Blacknor Park
Kingsett
Horndon
Hill Bridge
Drinnick Fm
Landue
Penscombe
Hardstone Fm
Greystone
Dunterton
Milton Abbot
Milton Green
Edgecumbe
Longcross
The Beacon 294
Brinsabach Fm
Higher Fm
Mary Tavy
Midlands
Trewinnow Cross
Larrick
Bottonnet
Lezant
Trenute
Endsleigh
Endsleigh Gdns
Shortburn Fm
Willestrew Park
Wallabrook Fm
Cherrybrook House
Cudliptown
White Tor 465
Broadmoor Fm
Illand
Newtown
Trecarrell Manor
Trebullett
Trekenner
Nittings Down
Dunterue Wood
Wareham Wood
Great Haye Fm
Hurlditch Court
Chaddlehanger
Grendon Fm
Pitland Fm
Lower Godsworthy
Wedlake
Peter Tavy
Coad's Green
Langstone
Lanoy
Lower Trebullett
Treburley
Carthamartha
Rezare
Leigh Wood
Hardicott Fm
Collacombe Down
Collacombe Manor
Tamar Valley
Lamerton
Grammerby Wood
Higher Godsworthy
Danger area
Harford Br
Cox Tor 422
Roos Tor
Staple Tors 455
Trecarrell Br
Trefrize
Tregoiffe
Trerefters
Cornwall
Wooda Br
Bealsmill
Gunoak Wood
Ford Fm
Southcombe Fm
Portington
Belgrove Ho
Rushford
Venn Ho
Ind Est
Langford Fm
Hurdwick Fm
Wilminstone
Paisley Mead
Penhill
Kersbrook Cross
Tremollet Down
North Down
Kingston
Tutwell
Beera Fm
Sydenham Damerel
Cholwell
Nutley Fm
Kingford Fm
Kelly College
A386
Merrivale
Dennithorne
Pork Hill
Bathpool
North Coombe Fm
Clampit
Pengelly
Trevilla
Penpill Fm
Bray Shop
Duchy College
Venterdon
Stoke Climsland
Pempwell
Lidwell
Horsebridge
Townlake
Hartwell
Woodovis Ho
Hele Fm
Ottery
Chipshop
Ogbeare
Three Oaks
Millhill
Downhouse Fm
Tavistock
Tavistock Museum
Ind Est
Feather Tor
Vixen Tor
Moortown
Patrieda Barton
Trefinnick
Pitt Fm
Linkinhorne
Whiteford Fm
Alren Fm
Old Mill
Higher Land
Higher Hampt
Lower Hampt
Luckett
Latchley
Grenofen Wood
Lamerhooe
Hawkmoor House Fm
Blanchdown Wood
Artiscombe
Lumburn
Callington Road
Parswell
Whitchurch Down
Warren's Cross
Whitchurch
Pew Tor 320
Sampford Spiney
Rillaton
Rilla Mill
South Hill
Downgate
Coxpark
Gulworthy
Brook
Middlemoor
Plaster Down
By The Down
Ward Br
Plushabridge
Browda
Mornick
Launceston Road
Chilsworthy
Dimson
Hurlditch Horn
Birch Wood
Grenofen
Fullamoor
Caradon Town
Downgate
Trewoodloe
Maders
Kelly Bray
Kit Hill
Earth Work
Monkscross
St Ann's Chapel
Gunnislake
Tamar Valley Mining District
Morwelldown Plantns
Hartshole Fm
Higher Walreddon
West Down
Holewell Fm
Higher Ditisham
Golberdon
Scrawsdon Fm
Tokenbury Manor
Rising Sun
Silver Valley
Donkey Park
Morwell Wood
Dunridge
Bedford Br
Horseyeatt Welltown
Bowling Green
Harrowbarrow
Albaston
Drakewalls
Horrabridge
Trevigro
Haye
Callington
Metherell
Norris Green
Morwellham Quay
Maddacleave Wood
Hocklake Fm
Berra Tor
Uppaton
Walkhampton
Gnatham Barton
Middlehill
Woolston
Mount Lodge
Dupath Well Chapel
Corneal Fm
Cleave Fm
Cotehele
Calstock
Buckland Monachorum
The Garden House
Harrowbeer
Dousland
Yennadon Down
Gang
Merryhue
Frogwell
Coombe Fm
Rill Fm
Ashton
Morden Fm
St Dominick
Hatch Mill
Denham Br
Didham
0 1 2 3 miles
0 1 2 3 4 5 km

Broomford Manor
Stockbeare Fm
Langabeare Barton
Langabeer Moor
Teachmore Fm
A3072
Sampford Courtenay
Sampford Chapple
Trecott
Culm Cross
Newland Mill
North Tawton
Stone Fm
Nichols Nymett Cross
Hampson
Appledore Fm
Copplestone Ho
Knowle
Corner
Walson Barton
Ford Fm
Coleford
South Coombe
Coombe Ho
Hollacombe Cross
Penstone
Colebrooke
Halse Fm
de Bathe Fm
Broadnymett Moor
Glebe Ho
Chapple Moor
South Dornaford
Preston Moor
Lamerton Cross
Dornaford Park
Common Moor
Beacon Cross
Falcadon Fm
North Wood Moor
Cocktree Moor
Ham Fm
West Begbeer
Brownsland
Newcott
Hilldown
Brocks Cross
Stairhill Fm
Barn Fm
Neopardy
Yeoford
Gunstone Ho
Gunstone Mill
North Down
Okehampton
A386
Folly Gate
Padson
Elmead
Berrydown Plantn
Hill Barto
Wood Fm
Appledore Fm
Belstone Corner
Black Moor
Rowden
Itton
South Hill Fm
Itton Moor
Bowbeer
Grange Place
Hillerton
North Beer Fm
Wood Fm
Road Fm
Coltsfoot Fm
Ford Fm
Great Leigh Fm
Blackdown Fm
Abbeyford Woods
Brightley
Incott Fm
Halford Manor
Wyke Moor Cross
Heath
Heath Cross
Cullaford
Spreyton
Trehill Fm
Taw Green
Two Post Cross
Dragdown Hill
Spreyton Wood
Woodland Head
Chichacott
Webber Hill Fm
Narraton
Pudson Fm
Hilltown Fm
Church Hill Cross
Rat Combe
Wood Ho
Ball Hill Fm
Corscombe Down
Willey
Spitlar Cross
Hollycombe Moor
Nethercott
Croft
Westwood
Woodgreen Fm
Shortridge
Hittisleigh Barton
Crayford
Caddiford Fm
Collihill
Coombe Valley
Higher Berry
Hook Fm
Hittisleigh
Tillerton
Ind Est
B3260
Mus of Dartmoor Life
Okehampton
Fowley Cross
Whitehouse
Coombe Head
Greenhill Fm
Sticklepath
Moon's Cross
South Beer Fm
Fuidge Manor
Hittisleigh Mill
Wolfgar Fm
Hill Fm
Lewdon Fm
Medland Manor
Down Fm
Crosse Fm
Town Barton
Manor Ho
Castle
Okehampton Bracken Tor
East Hill 349
Tor Down
Cleave Ho
Skaigh
Finch Foundry
South Tawton
Oxenham Manor
Brandis Cross
Hollycombe Fm
Venbridge Ho
Withycombe Fm
Estrayer Park
Belstone
Skaigh Warren
South Zeal
A30
Forder Fm
Thorne Cross
Honeyford Fm
Cheriton Bishop
Coombe Fm
Okehampton Camp
436
Moorgate Fm
Scarey Tor
Cullever Steps 478
Ramsley
West Wyke
Fire Stone Cross
Grendon Fm
Hole Fm
Manor Fm
Melhulsh Barton
Middletown
Backworthy Brakes
Meldon
South Down
Meldon Reservoir
Black Down
Rowtor
East Week
Gooseford
Fairhaven Fm
Whiddon Down
Redlake Fm
Ford Ho
Puddicombe Ho
Veet Mill Fm
Crockernwell
Cheriton Cross
Haylake
Brook
Longstone Hill
West Mill Tor
East Okement Fm
Higher Tor
Cosdon Hill
Clannaborough Fm
Well Fm
Stone Fm
Drewsteignton
Coombe Hall
Lower Eggbeer Fm
Down
Corridge Fm
393
Homerton Hill
Okehampton Common
Yes Tor 619
New Bridge
East Mill Tor
Throwleigh
Shilstone Tor
Throwleigh Common
Rashleigh Fm
Spinsters Rock
France Hill
Cross Fm
Rectory Wood
Castle Drogo
Drewston Ho
Drewston Wood
Prestonbury Castle
Moor Fm
Transcombe's Loaf
Black Tor
High Willhays 621
Danger area
Black-a-Tor Copse
Oke Tor
Metheral Hill
Little Hound Tor
Kennon Hill 478
Moortown
Ensworthy
Aysh
Wonson
Thorne Fm
Way Fm
Sandypark
Whiddon Wood
Hanicombe Wood
Hore Wood
Butterdon Ball Wood
Cranbrook Castle
Wooston Castle
Hitchcombe Wood
Westacombe Fm
Bigport Fm
Upperton Fm
Zeal Fm
Butts
Dunsford
Slipper Stones
Dinger Tor
Steeperton Tor
Hound Tor
Rippator or Rival Tor
Buttern Hill 413
Thule
Murchington
Rushford Wood
B3206
Easton
Pinmoor Fm
River Teign
Bridford Wood
Logan Rock
Kitty Tor 585
Woodcock Hill
Lints Tor
Wild Tor
Okement Hill
Gidleigh Common
Scorhill Tor
Gidleigh
Holystreet Manor
Rushford Mill Fm
Chagford
Uppacott Fm
Bowden Fm
Smallridge Fm
Cod Wood
Steps Br
Dunsford
Leigh Fm
Heltor Rock
Ducksmoor Cottage
Windhill Gate
Gidleigh Tor
Teigncombe
Kestor
Chagford Ho
Great Weeke
Howton Fm
Coombe Court
Bleak Ho
Green Tor
Amicombe Hill
Gt Kneeset 568
Hangingstone Hill 604
Watern Tor
Hew Down
Kestor Rock 436
Thorn
Yeo Fm
Wayе Barton
Meldon Hall
Middlecott
Meacombe Fm
Sloncombe
Moretonhampstead
Doccombe
Cossick Fm
Furzelands
Ockerton Court
Hole Fm
Meldon Hill 390
Weddicott
DEVON
Chat Tor 541
Danger area
Black Ridge
Whitehorse Hill 601
Walla Brook Head
Stonetor Hill
Shovel Down
Frenchbeer
Collihole Fm
Higher Stiniel
Batworthy
Bughead Cross
Budleigh Fm
Pepperdon Fm
Blackingstone Rock
Laployd Plantn
Hole
DARTMOOR
Black Hill 584
Quintin's Man 552
Fernworthy Reservoir
Shapley
Jurston
Bovey Castle
Narramore Fm
Wray Barton
Kennick Reservoir
Lit.Kneeset 516
Danger area
Hurston
Lettaford
North Bovey
Bowden Fm
Gratnar Fm
Lewdons Fm
Higher Elsford Fm
Tottiford Reservoir
Trenchford Reservoir
Fur Tor 572
Sittaford Tor 537
Fernworthy Forest
Canna Park
Aller
Clapper Br
Waterm Oke
Cut Hill 604
The Meads
North West Passage
Winney's Down
NATIONAL
Chagford Common
Shapley Common
Moor Gate
Coombe Down
Easdon Tor 439
Langstone
Hunter's Tor
Assycombe Hill
White Ridge 504
Lower Hookner
Vogwell Fm
Easton
Bullaton Fm
Beadon Fm
Standon Hill
Walkham Head
Dartmoor Forest
Stannon Tor 462
Water Hill 489
Hookney Tor
King Tor
Heathercombe
Torhill Fm
Wingstone Fm
Lustleigh Cleave
Caseley Court
Slade Cross
Wreyland
Headland Warren
Warren House Inn
Grimspound (Earthwork)
Manaton
Water
Lustleigh
Lynch Tor 517
Danger area
Broad Down
Merripit Hill 449
Hameldown Tor 529
Heatree Ho
Cripdon Down
Hayne Down
Houndtor Wood
PARK
Rough Tor 546
Soussons Down
Soussons Fm
Becky Falls Woodland Park
Pullabrook Fm
Stone
Maiden Hill
Devil's Tor
Cocks Hill 501
Hartland Tor
Postbridge Information Centre
Postbridge
Runnage Fm
Penlee Fm
Pizwell Fm
Natsworthy Manor
Hamel Down
Hameldown Beacon 517
Hound Tor
Beckaford
Reddaford Water
East Dartmoor Woods & Heaths
Whitstone Ho
Southbrook Ho
Bovey Tracey Heritage Centre
Langstone Moor
Petertavy Great Common
Higher White Tor 525
Crow Tor
Lydford Tor
Arch Tor
Clapper Bridge
Grendon Fm
Blackaton Down
Chinkwell Tor 458
Greator Rocks
Smallacombe Rocks
Yarner Wood
Lower Down
Haytor Down
Black Dunghill 492
Beardown Tors 512
Wistman's Wood
Dury Fm
Bellever
Cator Common
Blackaton Manor
Hatchwell Fm
Wooder Manor
Bonehill Down
Haytor Rocks 454
Ullacombe Fm
Whisslewell Fm
Five Wyches Fm
Gt Mis Tor 539
Little Mis Tor
Powdermill
Littaford Tors
Bellever Tor 443
Riddon Ridge
Cator Court
Lower Cator
Bonehill
Widecombe in the Moor
B3387
Logan Stone
Top Tor
Haytor
Haytor Vale
Lewthorn Cross
Haytor Information Centre
Green Lane
Brimley
Ilsington
House of Marbles
Merrivale Prehistoric Settlement
Crockern Tor
Beardown Fm
Smith Hill
Dartmoor Expedition Centre
Dartmoor National Park
Wind Tor
Hemsworthy Gate 473
Rippon Tor
Blackslade Down
Liverton
Rundlestone
Parson's Cottage
Laughter Tor
Babeny
Bagtor Ho
Rora Wood
Two Bridges
Huccaby Tor
Dunnabridge Fm
Yar Tor
Corndon Tor 431
Corndon Ford Fm
Cold East Cross
Rora Ho
Blackpool
Yellowmeade Fm
HM Prison
North Hessary Tor 517
B3357
B3351
400
King's Tor
Princetown
National Park Visitor Centre
Moorlands Fm
Sherberton
Brimpts Fm
Dartmeet
Ponsworthy
Buckland in the Moor
Welstor
Sigford
Coombe Fm
Halshanger
Yeo Fm
Ingsdon Hill
Telegraph Hill
Devil's Bridge
South Hessary Tor
Royal Hill 407
Hexworthy
Sherberton Common
Sharp Tor
Bel Tor 354
Lower Town
Spitchwick Manor
Buckland Beacon
Auswell Cross
Whiddon Wood
Goodstone Woods
Bickington
Ingra Tor
Leeden Tor 389
Combestone Tor
Down Ridge
Bench Tor
Poundsgate
Auswell Rocks
Holne Chase
Boro Wood
Place
Caton
Goodstone
A38
Black Tor
Cramber Tor
445
Peat Cott
Whiteworks
Ter Hill 480
Venford Reservoir
Holne Moor
West Stoke
Aish Tor
Hannaford Manor
Wayе
Mead
Burne Fm
Herebere Fm
Leather Tor
Peek Hill 400
Foxtor Mires
Skir Hill
Middle Stoke
Holne Woods
Hele
Bus Pk
Rew
Coombe Cross
Creek Beacon
SX
70
80
Down Tor 366
Crane Hill 471
Petre's Bound Stone 515
Holne
Southpark Wood
Ashburton
Tor Fm
Quarry Fm
Lower Lowery
Burrator Reservoir
454
Sheeps Tor
Combshead Tor
Nakers Hill
Priestaford Ho
Whistley Hill
Waye Fm
Gurrington Ho
Heathfield
Sheepstor
Ditsworthy
Great Gnats' Head
Green Hill 473
Snowdon
Scorriton Down
Scorriton
Michelcombe
Combe
Blackmoor
Chuley Cross
Well Fm
Woodland
Forder Green
Purcombe Fm
Lake
Pulsford Fm
Hartor

Crediton
Shobrooke
Thorverton
Ellerhayes
Raddon
Efford
Shute
Nether Exe
Rewe
Columbjohn
Killerton Park
Budlake
Clyst Hydon
Clyst St Lawrence
Westwood
Sweetham
Hookway
Newton St Cyres
Brampford Speke
Nettacott
Stoke Canon
Upton Pyne
Half Moon Village
Venny Tedburn
Uton
Neopardy
Hollacombe
Salmonhutch
Fordton
Cowley
Poltimore
Broadclyst
Dog Village
Jack in the Green
Tedburn St Mary
Pathfinder Village
Whitestone
Exwick
Exeter
Polsloe
Whipton
Pinhoe
Monkerton
Clyst Honiton
Exeter International
Heavitree
Wonford
Sowton
Clyst St Mary
Farringdon
Aylesbeare
Wheatley
St Thomas
Longdown
Ide
Alphington
Countess Wear
Topsham
Clyst St George
Woodbury Salterton
Dunsford
Shillingford Abbot
Shillingford St George
Exminster
Ebford
Bridford
Bridfordmills
Doddiscombsleigh
Dunchideock
Clapham
Exton
Woodbury
Kennford
Kenn
Lympstone
Christow
Bennah
Higher Ashton
Lower Ashton
Powderham
Kenton
Starcross
Exmouth
Withycombe Raleigh
Littleham
Trusham
Teign Village
Hennock
Harcombe
Ashcombe
Cockwood
Dawlish Warren
Chudleigh
Bovey Tracey
Chudleigh Knighton
Ideford
Luton
Dawlish
Brimley
Heathfield
Liverton
Coldeast
Preston
Sandygate
Ashwell
Bishopsteignton
Holcombe
Teignmouth
Kingsteignton
Highweek
Newton Abbot
Shaldon
Combeinteignhead
Netherton
Stokeinteignhead
Wolborough
Milber
East Ogwell
West Ogwell
Abbotskerswell
Coffinswell
Maidencombe
Kingskerswell
River Exe
River Teign
M5
A30
A38
A377
A380
A376
A379
0 1 2 3 miles
0 1 2 3 4 5 km

Payhembury
Awliscombe
Raleigh
ALLHALLOWS MUSEUM
Northcote
Ham
Lower Ridge
Hawley Bottom
Higher Cheriton
Colestocks
Buckerell
Weston
Honiton
Littletown
Hamlet
Cleave
Wilmington
Dalwood
Smallridge
Weycroft
Millway Rise
Axminster
Millbrook
Talaton
Feniton
Fenny Bridges
Alfington
Gittisham
Offwell
Widworthy
Shute
Kilmington
AXE VALLEY WILDLIFE PARK
Gosford
Fairmile
Coombelake
Taleford
Woodford
Ottery St Mary
Blannicombe
Northleigh
Umborne
Tricombe
Farway
Church Green
Woodbridge
Seaton Junction
Whitford
Maidenhayne
Musbury
Wyke Green
West Hill
Broad Oak
Wiggaton
Fluxton
Metcombe
Venn Ottery
Tipton St John
Southerton
Harpford
Bowd
Sidbury
Cotford
Sidford
Harcombe
Southleigh
Colyton
Colyford
Holyford
Combpyne
Rousdon
Axmouth
Seaton
SEATON TRAMWAY
Beer
BEER QUARRY CAVES
Vicarage
Branscombe
Weston
Salcombe Regis
THE DONKEY SANCTUARY
Sid
Sidmouth
MUSEUM
Cotmaton
DORSET & EAST DEVON COAST
Newton Poppleford
Northmostown
Bulverton
Stowford
Hawkerland
Goosemoor
Colaton Raleigh
Kingston
Bicton College
BICTON PARK
OTTERTON MILL
North Star
Otterton
East Budleigh
Kersbrook
Knowle
Little Knowle
Budleigh Salterton
FAIRLYNCH ARTS CENTRE & MUSEUM
SEATON BAY
Beer Head
Culverhole Pt
Dowlands Cliffs and Landslips
Humble Pt
AXMOUTH TO LYME REGIS UNDERCLIFFS
Haven Cliff
Seaton Hole
SOUTH WEST COAST PATH
Chit Rocks
High Peak
Tortoiseshell Rocks
Big Picket Rock
Hern Point Rock
Ladram Bay
Smallstones Pt
Chiselbury Bay
Brandy Head
Black Head
Danger Pt
Weston Cliff
Dunscombe Cliff
Chapman's Rocks
Salcombe Hill Cliff
River Otter
River Sid
River Coly
River Axe
A30
A35
A3052
A375
B3174
B3176
B3172
EAST DEVON
27
28
16
A
B
C
D
E
F
G
H
7
8
9
10
11
SY
30
70

16
All Saints
Smallridge
Sart Fm
Waggs Plot
Wadbrook
Castle
Holditch
New House Fm
Tuckmill Fm
Elmore Fm
Easthay Fm
Sadborow
Trighay Fm
Tudhay
Brimley
Hawkchurch
Bagley Hill Fm
Coaxdon Hall
Tillworth
Gashay Fm
Home Fm
Birdsmoorgate
Marshalsea
Colmer Fm
Pilsdon Pen
Cockpit Hill
277
Swilletts Fm
Pilsdon Barn
Lewesdon Hill
272
Burstock Down
Laverstock Fm
Crabbs Hill
Redlands Yard
Waddon Hill
Buck's Head
Stoke Abbott
Gerrard's Hill
Stoke Water
Park Fm
Beaminster
Beaminster Museum
Shortmoor
Knowle Fm
Langdon Fm
Dirty Gate
Pipsford Fm
Storridge Hill
Marsh Fm
Toller Whelme
Rampisham Down
Burnt Bottom
Kingcombe Cross
28
29
Sisterhood
SY
Uphay Fm
Weycroft
Millway Rise
Ind Est
Axminster
Higher Lodge Fm
Chubb's Fm
Cuthayes Fm
Woodhouse Fm
Blackpool Corner
Millbrook
Sector
Pound House Fm
Lambert's Castle Hill
Marshwood
Lambert's Castle
Nash Fm
Marshwood Manor
Templeman's Ash
House Fm
Bettiscombe
Pilsdon Manor
Pilsdon
Yard Fm
Venn Fm
Blackney
Gilney Fm
South Bowood
North Bowood
Strode Manor
Lower Strode
Furleigh Cross
Whitecross
Netherbury
Hingsdon Fm
Silkhay Fm
Slape Manor
Crab Coppice
Mapperton Fm
South Warren Hill
Mapperton
Coltleigh Fm
Warren Hill
Hooke Park
Hooke
Mount Pleasant
Jack's Hill
Melplash
North Poorton
Loscombe
South Poorton
Gray's Fm
Poorton Hill
Wytherston Fm
Leigh Gate
Axminster
Lyme Road
Chard Road
B3261
Old Park Fm
Beaver Grange
Furzeleigh Ho
Furzeleigh
Bever Batch
Pound Fm
Wyld Warren
Dodpen Hill
Fishpond Bottom
Coombe
Gummershaye Fm
Baber's Fm
Higher Park Fm
Oakford Fm
Shave Cross
Monkwood
Lower Park Fm
Valehouse Fm
Lodgehouse Fm
Bluntshay
Stoke Mill Fm
New House Fm
Dunster Fm
Filford
Kingsland
Waytown
Oxbridge
Camesworth
Hincknowle
Elcombe Fm
Salwayash
Elwell Lodge
Lambrook
The Mount
Abbey Gate
Wyke Green
Raymond's Hill
Marsh Fm
Champernhayes Marsh
Coney's Castle
Prime Coppices
Monkton Wyld
Wylde Fm
Spence Fm
Champernhayes Fm
Wootton Fitzpaine
Abbott's Wootton Fm
Cards Mill Fm
Mandeville Stoke Fm
Dorset
Broad Oak
Purcombe Fm
Denhay Fm
Broadoak Fm
Moorbath
Salway Ash
Ash
Powerstock
West Milton
Pitcher's Hill
Merriott
Nettlecombe
Barrowland Fm
King's Fm
Luccas Fm
Trill
Yawl Hill
Harcombe Bottom
Penn
Westover Fm
Conegar Hill
Pitt Fm
Plenty Ho
Coppet Hill
Denhay Hill
Atrim
Dottery
Wooth
Mangerton
Corfe Fm
Marsh Fm
Park Fm
Trinity Hill
Whitty Hill
Yawl
Carswell Fm
Rhode Hill
Fern Hill
Catherston Leweston
Berne Fm
Whitchurch Canonicorum
Ryall
Hardown Hill
Morcombelake
North Chideock
Axen Fm
Old Warren Hill
Bilshay Fm
Pymore
Bradpole
Waddon Hill
Loders
Mappercombe Manor
Knowle Hill
Eggardon Hill
252
Eggardon Fm
Hart Grove Fm
Shapwick Hill
181
Holcombe
Uplyme
Sleech Wood
Dragon's Hill
Charmouth
River Char
A35
Chardown Hill
Norchard Fm
Chideock Manor
Miles Cross
Symondsbury
Court Orchard
Allington
Quarry Hill
Bridport
Coneygar
St Andrew's Well
Yondover
Uploders
Higher Buckland Fm
Combpyne Hill
Cannington Fm
Charmouth Heritage Coast Centre
South West Coast Path
Westhay Fm
Golden Cap
191
Langdon Hill
Chideock
Seatown
West Road
Eypy
Higher Eype
Vearse Fm
Trad Est
Skilling
Watton
Bridport Museum
Bothenhampton
Hyde
Walditch
Innsacre
Dorchester Road
Askerswell
Spyway
Askerswell Down
Shipton Hill
170
Nallers Fm
Combpyne
Shapwick Grange Fm
Dinosaurland
Lyme Regis
Ware
Virtle Rock
Pound Rock
Cobb
Aquarium
St Gabriel's Mouth
Wear Cliffs
Ridge Cliff
East Ebb Cove
Highlands
Lower Eype
Eype's Mouth
Pitfold Fm
Bennett's Hill Fm
Shipton Gorge
Lynch Fm
Higher Sturthill Fm
Lower Sturthill Fm
Hammiton
Chilcombe
Chilcombe Hill
Rousdon
A3052
Seven Rock Pt
Pinhay Bay
Dorset & East Devon Coast
Humble Pt
Axmouth to Lyme Regis Undercliffs
Dowlands Cliffs and Landslips
West Cliff
West Bay
Burton Road
B3157
East Cliff
Southover
Burton Cliff
Burton Bradstock
Bredy North Hill
Bredy Fm
Rudge Fm
Lower Coombe
Four Meads Fm
Litton Cheney
Common Lane
Cogden Fm
Modbury Fm
Beacon Knap
132
Golly Knapp Fm
Puncknowle
Swyre
The Knoll
181
Burton Mere
West Bexington
Dorset & East Devon Coast
Lyme Bay
A
B
C
D
E
F
G
H
15
1
2
3
4
5
6
SY
70
30
0
1
2
3 miles
0
1
2
3
4
5 km

Higher Wraxall
Wraxall
Lower Wraxall
Sandhills
Higher Chalmington
Chalmington
Castle Hill 183
Cattistock
Up Sydling
Peak End Hill 207
29
Cerne Abbas Giant
Cerne Abbas
Cerne Park
Weam Common Hill
Higher Down
Tenant's Hill
Higher Southcombe Fm
Plush
Plush Hill
Nettlecombe Fm
Lyscombe Fm
Thorncombe
30
Dole's Ash Fm
Manor Ho
East Hill
New Barn Fm
Newton Fm
Bramblecombe
Gallows Corner
Long Close Fm
Higher Kingcombe
Lower Kingcombe
Kingcombe Meadows Reserve
Lancombe Fm
Chilfrome
Grove Stall Fm
Whitesheet Hill
Lankham Bottom
Norden Hill
215 New Barn
Combe Bottom
Folly Hill
Peak End Hill
Cowdown Hill
Higher City Fm
Sydling St Nicholas
Huish Fm
Hill Barn
Smacam Down
Lower Barton Fm
Buck Hill 211
Green Hill
Pound Fm
Bow's Hill
Nether Cerne
East Hill
Piddletrenthide
Kingrove Bottom
College Down
Whitcombe Hill
Cheselbourne
Whitelands Downs
Cheselbourne West Down
Dole's Hill Plantn
Chebbard Fm
Lawn Barn Fm
Dewlish
Dewlish Parsonage Fm
Bagber Fm
Deverel Fm
Dorchester Road
Maiden Newton
Fore Hill
Toller Porcorum
Tollerford
Toller Fratrum
Frogmore Fm
Hog Cliff
Combe Hill
South Field Hill
Crete Hill
Bushes Barn
Magiston Hill
Magiston Fm
Godmanstone
White Lackington
Coombe Bottom
Heave Coppice
Piddlehinton
Bourne Fm
Druce Down
Druce Higher Barn
Puddletown Down
Park Hill
Lower Fm
Milborne Wood
Milborne Wood Fm
Milborne St Andrew
Weatherby Castle
Colesmoor Fm
Ferndown Fm
Wynford Wood
Manor Fm
Wynford Eagle
Chammen's Hill
Hog Cliff Hill
Cruxton
South Field Down
Magiston Fm
Fairmile Fm
Holcombe Bottom
New Buildings
Forston Barn
Forston
Little Puddle Bottom
Muston Fm
Little Puddle Hill
Peak Coppice
Hill's Copse
Basan Hill
Fryer's Br
Hill Barn
Ashley Barn
Roger Hill Fm
Shatcombe Fm
Wynford Ho
Round Hill Plantn
Crockway Fm
Frampton
Southover
Notton Hill Barn
Grimstone Down
Stratton Down
Haydon Hill
Charlton Higher Down
Wolfeton Clump
Laycock Fm
Waterston Manor
Druce Fm
Northbrook
Bardolf Manor
Devil's Brook
West Compton
Longlands Fm
Frampton Ho
Hog Hill
Grimstone
Charlton Down
Athelhampton
Burleston
Martyrs Museum
Tolpuddle
Tolpuddle Ball
Two Gates
Dorset
Compton Valence
New Littlewood Fm
Muckleford
Stratton
Ash Hill
Leap Gate
Hill Barn
Home Fm
Troy Town Fm
Puddletown
Yellowham Wood
Grey's Wood
Green Hill
Puddletown Forest
Athelhampton
Admiston Fm
Park Fm
South Ho
18
Affpuddle
Affpuddle Heath
Stancombe Fm
Hogleaze Fm
Town Hill Fm
Tout Hill
Bradford Peverell
Penn Hill
River Frome
Charminster
Higher Burton Fm
Silver's Lane
Higher Kingston Fm
Higher Bockhampton
Hardy's Cottage & Garden
Puddletown Heath
Castle Hill
Ilsington Wood
Southover Heath
Sares Wood
Marl Pits Wood
Tincleton
Clyffe Ho
Bryants Puddle Heath
Oakers Wood
Oakers Wood Ho
North Barn Fm
Kingston Russell
Dorchester Road
Wolfeton House
Burton
Old Crown Court
County Mus
Stinsford
Kingston Maurward
Kingston Maurward Animal Park & Gdns
Lower Bockhampton
Norris Mill Fm
Pine Lodge Fm
Snipe Moor
Pallington
Waddock Cross
Winterbourne Poor Lot Barrows
Martin's Down
Black Down
Winterbourne Abbas
Lower Skippet Fm
Combe Bottom
Bradford Down
Military Mus
Tutankhamun Mus
Dinosaur Museum
Litton Cheney
Long Bredy
Nine Stones
Lambert's Hill
North Hill
Winterbourne Steepleton
Poundbury
Dorchester
Frome Mead
White Mead
Woodsford
Hurst
Whatcombe Down
Maumbury Rings
Dorchester West
Dorchester South
Lower Lewell Fm
Hurst Heath
Moreton
Lower Fm
River Bride
Littlebredy
White Hill
Loscombe Fm
Rew Manor
Maiden Castle Fm
Max Gate
Frome Hill
West Stafford
Higher Woodsford
Park's Dairy Fm
Tenants Hill
Littlebredy Fm
Sheep Down
Martinstown or Winterbourne St Martin
Hog Hill
Maiden Castle
P&R
Conygar Hill
Stafford Fm
Lewell Lodge
Knighton Heath Wood
Crossways
Redbridge
Warmwell Road
West Lodge
Kingston Russell Stone Circle
Old Warren
Valley of Stones
Black Down
Goldcombe Fm
Winterborne Monkton
Winterborne Herrington
Winterborne Came
Whitcombe
Empool Heath
Holiday Pk
Bus Pk
Ashley Chase Ho
Gorwell Fm
Crow Hill
Hardy Monument
Shorn Hill
Great Hill
Ashton Fm
Monkton Hill
Herrington Fm
Whitcombe Manor
Cole Hill Wood
West Knighton
Outer Heath
Mill House Cider Museum
Whitcombe Vale
Abbotsbury Castle
Wears Fm
White Hill
South West Coast Path
Portesham Hill
Corton Down
Bayard Barn
Bayard Hill
Higher Came Fm
Cripton Cottage
Whitcombe Barn
Broadmayne
Warmwell Heath
Knap Fm
Tadnoll
Blacknoll
Lexington
Abbotsbury
Abbey (Rems)
Abbotsbury Plains
Portesham Fm
Portesham
Goose Hill
Coryates
Friar Waddon Hill
Came Down
Ridgeway Hill Tunnel
Warren Barn
Came Wood
Ridgeway Hill
Holcombe Bottom
Glebe Fm
Beech Fm
Brick Hill
Warmwell
Warmwell Down Barn
Owermoigne
Galton
West Fossil Fm
Portway
Abbotsbury Sub-Tropical Gardens
St Catherine's Chapel
Chapel Hill
Abbotsbury Children's Farm
Abbotsbury Swannery
Rodden Barn Fm
Merry Hill
Rodden
Rodden Ridge
Bramdon Lane
Upwey
Elwell
Upwey Manor
Hewish Fm
Broadwey
Bincombe Hill
Bincombe
White Horse Hill
White Horse
Green Hill
Water Supply
Sutton Poyntz
River Jordan
Poxwell Manor
Poxwell
Moigns Down
Grange Dairy
Holworth
Wareham Road
Winfrith Newburgh
Chaldon Herring or East Chaldon
Marley Wood
Chesters Hill
Wyke Wood
New Barn Fm
Hewish Hill
Holwell Fm
Lorton Ho
Lorton Meadows Nature Reserve
Littlemoor
Preston
White Horse Fm
Osmington Ho
Upton
Osmington
Manor Ho
Tatton Ho
Tatton Fm
Buckland Ripers
Nottington
Redlands
Corfe Hill
Overcombe
Jordan Hill Roman Temple
Osmington Mills
Spring Bottom Hill
South Down Fm
Burning Cliff
Chaldon Down
Langton Herring
Moor Fm
Coldharbour
Old Manor
Radipole
Lodmoor
Sea Life Centre
Bowleaze Cove
Dorset & East Devon Coast
Redcliff Pt
Black Head
England Coast Path
Ringstead Bay
Chideock Fm
Newlands Fm
West Fleet
Bagwell Fm
Weymouth Gateway Sculptures
Furzy Cliff
Melcombe Regis
Radipole Lake
Weymouth Bay
Chesil Beach
Gore Cove
Sea Barn Fm
Fleet
East Fleet
Chickerell
Putton
Southill
Swyre Head
St Oswald's Bay
Bat's Head
Bennetts Water Gardens
Charlestown
Westham
Retail Pk
Greenhill
Weymouth
Chickerell Road
Danger area
Deep Sea Adventure
Nothe Fort
East Fleet
Lanehouse
Rodwell
Dorset & East Devon Coast
Southlands
Wyke Regis
North Ship Channel
East Ship Channel
Small Mouth
Portland Harbour
Portland Castle
Nat. Sailing Academy
Balaclava Bay
Castletown
Portland
South Ship Channel
Fortuneswell
Bus Cen
HM Prison
Chiswell
Portland
Grove
HM YOI
Clay Ope
Ind Est
Easton
Shop Cen
Grove Cliff
Weston
Portland Museum
Church Ope Cove
Southwell
Freshwater Bay
Bill of Portland
SY
80
00
70
A
B
C
D
E
F
G
H
7
8
9
10
11

Milton Abbas
Higher Whatcombe
Whatcombe
Lower Whatcombe
Shapwick
Hound Hill
Tadden
Merry Field Hill
Pilford
Canford Bottom
Colehill
Chilbridge
Hillbutts
Winterborne Whitechurch
Charlton Down
Field Dairy
Sturminster Marshall
Wimborne Minster
Cowgrove
Leigh
Little Canford
Newton Peveril
Almer
East Almer Fm
Lion Lodge
Charborough Park
Henbury
Lambs' Green
Ashington
Oakley
Canford Magna
Merley
Sleight
East End
Winterborne Kingston
Winterborne Zelston
Mapperton
Huish
Marsh Br
Dullar Fm
Combe Almer
Corfe Mullen
Rushcombe Bottom
Milborne St Andrew
Anderson
Anderson Manor
Dairy Ho
Botany Bay Barn
Bere Down
Weatherby Castle
High Wood
Brock Hill
Green Fields Fm
Barrow Hill
Hill View
Broadstone
Bearwood
BOURNEMOUTH
Muddox Barrow Fm
East Field Fm
Bloxworth Down
West Park Fm
Lytchett Ho
Poor Common
Canford Heath
Roke Fm
Town's End
Bere Wood
West Morden
Morden
Dolman's Hill
Bartom's Hill
Lytchett Matravers
Upton Heath
Hillbourne
Waterloo
Tolpuddle
Tolpuddle Ball
Bere Regis
Shitterton
Black Hill
Woodbury Hill
Bloxworth Heath
Bloxworth
Newport
East Bloxworth
Whitefield
East Morden
Whitmore Bottom
Beacon Hill
Lytchett Heath
Upton Heath
Creekmoor
TOWER PARK LEISURE COMPLEX
MARTYRS MUSEUM
Turners Puddle
Hollow Oak
Throop
Dodding's Fm
Woodlake
Lower Woodbury Fm
Oak Hill
Black Heath
Sherford
Park Corner
Slepe
Post Green
Lytchett Minster
Upton
Newtown
Oakdale
Affpuddle
Affpuddle Heath
Briants Puddle
Chamberlayne's Fm
Lane End
Bere Heath
Sugar Hill
Wareham Forest
Morden Park
Sherford Br
FARMER PALMER'S
Organford
Pike's Fm
Hamworthy
Turlin Moor
Holes Bay
Stanley Green
Sterte
Longfleet
Branksome
Bryants Puddle Heath
Throop Heath
Chamberlayne's Heath
Warren
Phillliols Fm
Stroud Br
Decoy Heath
Gore Heath
Holton Heath
East Holton
Rockley Sands
Lake
Poole
Parkstone
Lilliput
Pallington
Tonerspuddle Heath
Warren Heath
Gallows Hill
CLOUDS HILL
Clouds Hill
DORSET
Trent Vale Fm
MORDEN BOG
Great Ovens Hill
Wood Bar Looe
SCAPLEN'S COURT MUS
Lower Hamworthy
Hurst
Moreton
Snelling Fm
Bovington Heath
Wool Heath
Longthorns Fm
MONKEY WORLD
South Heath
Budden's Fm
Trigon Hill
Cold Harbour
Carey Heath
Northport Heath
Sandford
Keysworth Fm
Keysworth Pt
Gold Pt
Patchins Pt
Poole Harbour
West Lodge
Cranes Moor
Bovington Camp
THE TANK MUSEUM
Woolbridge Heath
Stokeford Heath
Northport
Wareham
Swineham Pt
Arne Bay
Shipstal Pt
Maryland
The Villa
Brownsea Island
BROWNSEA ISLAND
Sandbanks
Whitcombe Vale
Broomhill Br
Tout Hill
East Burton
Wool
BINDON ABBEY (REMS)
Stokeford
Binnegar Hall
Binnegar
Worgret Heath
PRIORY OF LADY ST MARY
MUSEUM
ARNE
Arne
ARNE REEDBEDS
Fitzworth Pt
Furzey Island
North Haven Pt
Tadnoll
Blacknoll
Knighton Heath
Giddy Green
Braytown
Quarr Hill
Rushton
River Frome
East Stoke
Holmebridge
Holme Priory
Worgret
Ridge
Green Island
South Deep
Middlebere Fm
Cleavel Pt
Brand's Bay
Jerry's Pt
South Haven Pt
Shell Bay
West Burton Fm
Woodstreet Fm
New Buildings
Highwood Heath
East Holme
Stoborough
Slepe Fm
Hartland Moor
Newton Bay
Newton
Drove Island
West Fossil Fm
Portway
East Knighton
Highwood
West Holme
Danger area
Doreys Fm
Stoborough Green
PURBECK HEATHS
Hartland Stud
Wytch Fm
Wytch Heath
Oil Terminal
Goathorn Plantn
STUDLAND BEACH & NATURE RESERVE
Winfrith Newburgh
Coombe Wood
Coombe Keynes
Coombe Heath
West Holme Heath
Holme Heath
Creech Bottom
Grange Heath
Middlebere Heath
Rempstone Heath
Newton Heath
Greenlands Fm
Little Sea
Studland Bay
Chaldon Herring or East Chaldon
Vine's Down Bldgs
Marley Wood
Marley Wood House
Shaggs
Park Lodge
Hurst Mill
Povington Heath
Grange Heath
Creech
Creech Heath
Furzebrook
Norden Heath
Bushey
Lower Bushey Fm
Higher Bushey Fm
Redend Pt
Winfrith Hill
Belhuish Fm
Park Wood
Home Fm
Whiteway
East Creech
BLUE POOL
Norden
Knowle Hill
Rempstone Hall
Godlington Heath
THE AGGLESTONE
Black Down
Studland
Chideock Fm
LULWORTH CASTLE
Burngate Fm
East Lulworth
Stonehill Down
Barneston Manor
Cocknowle
CORFE CASTLE
MODEL VILLAGE & GARDEN
Rollington Fm
Corfe Castle
Woolgarston
Little Woolgarston
Ailwood Fm
Newlands Fm
Daggers Gate
Lulworth Camp
Povington Hill
West Creech Hill
Grange Arch
Purbeck Hills
ANIMAL SANCTUARY
Church Knowle
West Bucknowle Ho
Town's End
SWANAGE RAILWAY
Knitson Fm
New Buildings
Ulwell
Swyre Head
St Oswald's Bay
Dungy Head
HERITAGE CENTRE
Bat's Head
West Lulworth
LULWORTH COVE
Bindon Hill
Lulworth Cove
Mupe Bay
Worbarrow Bay
Whiteway Hill
Tyneham
Gad Cliff
Worbarrow
Steeple
Blackmanston Fm
Bradle Fm
West Orchard Fm
Blashenwell Fm
Lynch Fm
Harman's Cross
Godlington Manor
New Swanage
THE ETCHES COLLECTION
Kimmeridge
Brandy Bay
Smedmore Hill
Orchard Hill Fm
Kingston
Dunshay Manor
Swanage Bay
Swanage
New Barn
Herston
Langton Matravers
Peveril Pt
Hobarrow Bay
Kimmeridge Bay
Swyre Head
Swalland Fm
SOUTH WEST COAST PATH
Kimmeridge Ledges
Rope Lake Head
Coombe Bottom
Westhill Fm
Compact Fm
Acton
Eastington Fm
Durlston Bay
DURLSTON
Houns-tout Cliff
Renscombe Fm
Worth Matravers
California Fm
Durlston Head
Tilly Whim Caves
Egmont Pt
Chapman's Pool
Anvil Pt
Blackers Hole
Seacombe Cliff
DORSET & EAST DEVON COAST
St Aldhelm's or St Alban's Head
SY
80
70
0
1
2
3 miles
0
1
2
3
4
5 km

Uddens Plantn
Kingston
KINGSTON GREAT COMMON
Clayhill Bottom
Weirs
Ferndown
Trickett's Cross
Grange Estate
RINGWOOD RACEWAY
Matcham's Park
Bisterne
Sandford
Bisterne Common
Avon Water
Greenberry Br
Goatspen Plain
NAKED MAN
Wilverley Plain
Hinchesle Moor
South Weirs
Setley
STAPLEHILL ABBEY
KNOLL GARDENS
Foxbury Hill
Fir Grove Fm
Week Fm
Bisterne Manor
Upper Bisterne Fm
Ripley Wood
Dur Hill Down
Whitefield Hill
Whitten Bottom
Holmsley Ridge
Holmsley Lodge
Holmsley Inclosure
Wilverley Inclosure
Long Slade Bottom
Hincheslea Wood
Setthorns Cottage
Blackhamsley Ho
Setley Plain
Setley Common
Lower Bisterne Fm
Parley Common
East Parley Common
Hurn Forest
Week Common
Shirley Common
Thorney Hill
Wootton Coppice Inclosure
Set Thorns Inclosure
Widden Bottom
Battramsley
Dudsbury
West Parley
North Ripley
Martin's Copse
Hill Fm
Brownhill Inclosure
Broadley Inclosure
Durns Town
Longham
East Parley
BOURNEMOUTH
Avon
Ripley
Shirley
Forest Lodge
Ossemsley
HOLMSLEY ROAD
Wootton
Mead End
Sway
Birchy Hill
Shirley holms
Knighton
Parley Cross
Parley Green
Pithouse Fm
Sopley Common
Sopley
Bransgore
Bashley
Tiptoe
Broadley Ho
Arnewood Manor
Mount Pleasant
Merritown
ADVENTURE WONDERLAND
Hurn
North Bockhampton
Beech Ho
Bashley Park
Arnewood Court
Bear Cross
Berry Hill
West Hurn
Neacroft
Harrow Lodge
Ossemsley Manor
Bowling Green
Kinson
Ensbury
Red Hill
Northbourne
Muscliff
Blackwater
Dudmoor Fm
Town Common
Winkton
Middle Bockhampton
Waterditch
Godwinscroft
Hinton Park
Beckley
Beckley Fm
Hordle Grange
Buckland
East Howe
Mill Throop
Holdenhurst
South Bockhampton
SAMMY MILLER MOTORCYCLE MUSEUM
New Milton
Hordle
Ind Est
Winkton Common
Burton Common
Hinton
Hinton Ho
Ashley
Golden Hill
Arnewood Ho
ST BARBE MUS & GAL
Lymington
Turbary Common
Charminster
St Catherine's Hill
Jumpers Common
Burton
H A N T S
LYNDHURST ROAD
Ind Est
Wainsford Ho
Batchley Fm
Pennington
Moordown
Ensbury Park
Strouden
Ind Pk
Jumpers Green
Fairmile
HINTON ADMIRAL
Walkford
Hooper's Hill
APPLE COURT
Manor Ho
Everton
Wallisdown
Talbot Village
Winton
Highcliffe
Old Milton
Ashley Manor Fm
Leagreen
MILFORD ROAD
Rossmore
Bourne Valley
Talbot Woods
Queen's Park
Littledown
Iford
Purewell
Somerford
Bus Pk
Downton
CHRISTCHURCH ROAD
BRAXTON GARDENS
Talbot Heath
VITALITY STADIUM
POKESDOWN
Christchurch
Barton on Sea
Newlands Manor
Meyrick Park
Springbourne
Pokesdown
Southbourne
West
Tuckton
RED HOUSE
CASTLE & NORMAN HOUSE
Stanpit
Friars Cliff
HIGHCLIFFE CASTLE
Taddiford Fm
Lymore
BRANKSOME
BOURNEMOUTH Retail Pk
Boscombe
Wick
Christchurch Harbour
Mudeford
CHRISTCHURCH BAY
Westbourne
Bus Cen
Stanpit Marsh
Sandhills
Hordle Cliff
Milford on Sea
Sturt Pond
Keyhaven
West Cliff
RUSSELL-COTES MUSEUM
OCEANARIUM
Southbourne
Branksome Park
Bournemouth
VISITOR CENTRE
Hengistbury Head
Hurst Beach
Branksome Chine
POOLE BAY
Canford Cliffs
THE CHINES
Canford Cliffs Chine
Flag Head Chine
Poole Head
Totland Bay
Hatherwood Pt
CHAIR LIFT
Alum Bay
THE NEEDLES PARK
The Needles
THE NEEDLES OLD BATTERY
Warren Fm
Main Bench
Scratchell's Bay
Handfast Point or The Foreland
The Pinnacles
DORSET & EAST DEVON COAST
Ballard Pt
CHERBOURG
JERSEY GUERNSEY ST MALO
SZ
A
B
C
D
E
F
G
H
7
8
9
10
11
20
31
32

THE
H A N T S
I S L E O F W I G H T
Lymington
Newport
Cowes
East Cowes
Yarmouth
Totland
Freshwater
Freshwater Bay
Milford on Sea
Keyhaven
Pennington
Lower Pennington
Everton
Buckland
Walhampton
Waterford
Woodside
Boldre
Pilley
Portmore
Norleywood
South Baddesley
East End
Setley
Battramsley
East Boldre
Bucklers Hard
Exbury
Lepe
Blackfield
Langley
Calshot
West Common
Hill Head
Gurnard
Rew Street
Northwood
Whippingham
Hillis Corner
Porchfield
Parkhurst
Parkhurst Forest
Newtown
Hamstead
Cranmore
Ningwood Common
Ningwood
Shalfleet
Bouldnor
Thorley Street
Thorley
Wellow
Newbridge
Calbourne
Five Houses
Locksgreen
Carisbrooke
Gunville
Clatterford
Shide
Blackwater
Bowcombe
Gatcombe
Chillerton
Rookley
Godshill
Arreton
Horringford
Merstone
Staplers
Downend
Wootton Bridge
Wootton Common
Fairlee
Hunny Hill
Norton
Norton Green
Colwell
Weston Manor
Pound Green
Afton
Shalcombe
Brook
Hulverstone
Mottistone
Brighstone
Moortown
Limerstone
Shorwell
Yafford
Thorncross
Kingston
Little Atherfield
Atherfield Green
Pyle
Chale Green
Chale
Blackgang
Niton
Whitwell
Roud
St Lawrence
Wroxall
Southford
Nettlecombe
Bierley
Kingates
Brighstone Down 214
St Catherine's Hill 236
St Catherine's Down
Brighstone Bay
Compton Bay
Chale Bay
Totland Bay
Colwell Bay
Gurnard Bay
Thorness Bay
Newtown Bay
Osborne Bay
Cowes Roads
Needs Ore Pt
Hurst Beach
Hurst Castle
The Needles
Scratchell's Bay
St Catherine's Pt
Atherfield Pt
Hatherwood Pt
Warden Point
King's Quay
Old Castle Pt
Keyhaven & Pennington Marshes Nature Reserve
Forest Road
Calbourne Road
Newport Road
Military Road
Chale Street
Bowcombe Road
Newport Road
Whippingham Road
A3054
A3055
A3020
A3056
B3401
B3399
B3323
B3322
B3325
A337
32
33
19
SZ
70
30
A B C D E F G H
1 2 3 4 5 6
0 1 2 3 miles
0 1 2 3 4 5 km

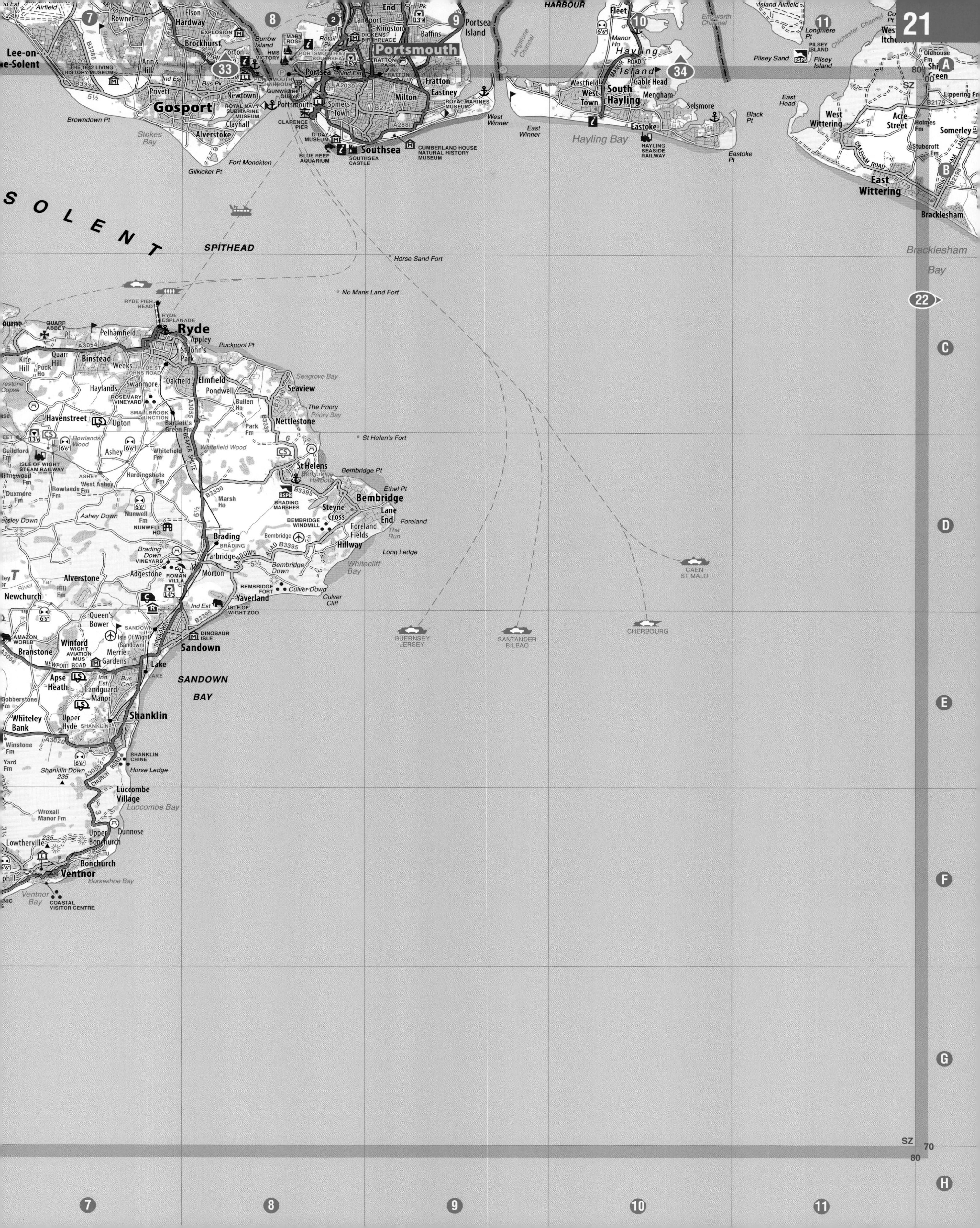

Lee-on-the-Solent
Rowner
Elson
Hardway
Brockhurst
Ann's Hill
THE 1642 LIVING HISTORY MUSEUM
Privett
Gosport
Newtown
ROYAL NAVY SUBMARINE MUSEUM
Clayhall
Alverstoke
Stokes Bay
Browndown Pt
Fort Monckton
Gilkicker Pt
Burrow Island
MARY ROSE
HMS VICTORY
Portsea
GUNWHARF QUAYS
Old Portsmouth
Somers Town
CLARENCE PIER
D-DAY MUSEUM
BLUE REEF AQUARIUM
Southsea
SOUTHSEA CASTLE
CUMBERLAND HOUSE NATURAL HISTORY MUSEUM
Landport
Kingston
DICKENS' BIRTHPLACE
Portsmouth
Baffins
Portsea Island
Fratton
Milton
Eastney
ROYAL MARINES MUSEUM
West Winner
East Winner
HARBOUR
Langstone Channel
Fleet
Manor Ho
Hayling Island
Westfield
West Town
South Hayling
Gable Head
Mengham
Selsmore
Eastoke
Hayling Bay
HAYLING SEASIDE RAILWAY
Black Pt
Eastoke Pt
Emsworth Channel
Chichester Channel
Longmere Pt
PILSEY ISLAND
Pilsey Sand
Pilsey Island
East Head
West Wittering
Acre Street
Holmes Fm
Somerley
Stubcroft Fm
East Wittering
Bracklesham
Bracklesham Bay
Lippering Fm
Oldhouse Fm
SOLENT
SPITHEAD
Horse Sand Fort
No Mans Land Fort
RYDE PIER HEAD
RYDE ESPLANADE
Ryde
QUARR ABBEY
Pelhamfield
Appley
St John's Park
Puckpool Pt
Kite Hill
Quarr Hill
Binstead
Weeks
Puck Ho
Haylands
Swanmore
ROSEMARY VINEYARD
Oakfield
Elmfield
Pondwell
Seagrove Bay
Seaview
SMALLBROOK JUNCTION
Bartlett's Green Fm
Bullen Ho
The Priory
Priory Bay
Havenstreet
Upton
Park Fm
Nettlestone
St Helen's Fort
Rowlands Wood
Ashey
Whitefield Wood
Whitefield Fm
Guildford Fm
ISLE OF WIGHT STEAM RAILWAY
Hardingshute Fm
St Helens
Bembridge Harbour
Bembridge Pt
West Ashey
Rowlands Fm
Duxmore Fm
BRADING MARSHES
Marsh Ho
Ethel Pt
Bembridge
Steyne Cross
Lane End
Foreland
Ashey Down
Nunwell Fm
NUNWELL HO
BEMBRIDGE WINDMILL
Foreland Fields
The Run
Brading
Hillway
Brading Down
VINEYARD
Yarbridge
SANDOWN ROAD
Long Ledge
Whitecliff Bay
Bembridge Down
Alverstone
Adgestone
ROMAN VILLA
Morton
BEMBRIDGE FORT
Culver Down
Culver Cliff
Newchurch
Yaverland
ISLE OF WIGHT ZOO
AMAZON WORLD
Queen's Bower
Winford
WIGHT AVIATION MUS
Merrie Gardens
DINOSAUR ISLE
Sandown
Branstone
NEWPORT ROAD
Lake
Apse Heath
Landguard Manor
SANDOWN BAY
Whiteley Bank
Upper Hyde
Shanklin
Winstone Fm
Yard Fm
SHANKLIN CHINE
Horse Ledge
Shanklin Down
235
CHURCH ROAD
Luccombe Village
Luccombe Bay
Wroxall Manor Fm
Dunnose
Upper Bonchurch
Lowtherville
Bonchurch
Ventnor
Horseshoe Bay
Ventnor Bay
COASTAL VISITOR CENTRE
CAEN ST MALO
GUERNSEY JERSEY
SANTANDER BILBAO
CHERBOURG
33
34
22
SZ
70
80
A
B
C
D
E
F
G
H
7
8
9
10
11

Rowlands Castle
Blendworth Common
Havant Thicket
Horsepasture Fm
Red Hill
Durrants
Stubbermere
Staunton
Dunsbury Hill Fm
Southleigh Forest
Havant
Leigh Park
Stockheath
Bedhampton
West Leigh
East Leigh Ho
Brockhampton
Denvilles
Warblington
Emsworth
New Brighton
Lumley
Langstone
North Binness Island
Long Island
South Binness Island
Broad Lake
LANGSTONE HARBOUR
Baker's Island
THE SPRING ARTS & HERITAGE CENTRE
Northney
North Hayling
Stoke
Tye
Fleet
Manor Ho
Hayling Island
Gable Head
Mengham
Westfield
West Town
South Hayling
Selsmore
Eastoke
Eastoke Pt
Hayling Bay
HAYLING SEASIDE RAILWAY
East Winner
Black Pt
Fowley Island
Wickor Pt
Marker Pt
Emsworth Channel
Sweare Deep
Great Deep
CHICHESTER HARBOUR
Thorney Island
Thorney Island Airfield
West Thorney
Thorney Channel
Pilsey Sand
PILSEY ISLAND
Pilsey Island
Longmere Pt
Chichester Channel
Cobnor Pt
Cobnor Fm
Chidham
Chidham Pt
Stanbury Pt
Prinsted Pt
Prinsted
Southbourne
Hermitage
Breach
Inlands
Nutbourne
Hambrook
Westbourne
Woodmancote
Funtington
Racton Monument
Racton Park Fm
Stanes Fm
Walderton
Walderton Down
Stoughton
West Ashling
East Ashling
Woodend
West Stoke
Stoke Down
Mid Lavant
East Lavant
Summersdale
Westerton
Strettington
Westhampnett
Goodwood
GOODWOOD HOUSE
Halnaker
BOXGROVE PRIORY
Boxgrove
Crockerhill
Eartham
Tangmere
MILITARY AVIATION MUSEUM
East Hampnett
Oving
Aldingbourne
Westergate
Norton
Nyton
Woodhorn Fm
Lidsey
Colworth
Elbridge
Shripney Manor
Merston
Runcton
North Mundham
Woldhurst
South Mundham
Lagness
Hunston
Chichester
Whyke
Portfield
Stockbridge
Apuldram
Fishbourne
Dell Quay
Bosham
Broadbridge
BOSHAM WALK CRAFT CENTRE
Bosham Hoe
West Itchenor
Shipton Green
Birdham
Birdham Pool
Donnington
Croucher's
Sidlesham Common
Street End
Chalder Fm
Highleigh
Sidlesham
Pagham Harbour
Pagham
Nyetimber
Rose Green
Aldwick
Bognor Regis
South Bersted
North Bersted
Barn Rocks
West Wittering
East Head
Acre Street
Somerley
Earnley
East Wittering
Bracklesham
Bracklesham Bay
Marsh Fm
WEST SUSSEX
Norton
Church Norton
Inner Owers
East Beach
Selsey
Selsey Bill
CAEN ST MALO
CHERBOURG
SANTANDER BILBAO
A3(M)
A27
A259
A286
A29
B2145
B2179
SO
SU
SZ
A B C D E F G H
1 2 3 4 5 6
33
34
21
0 1 2 3 miles
0 1 2 3 4 5 km

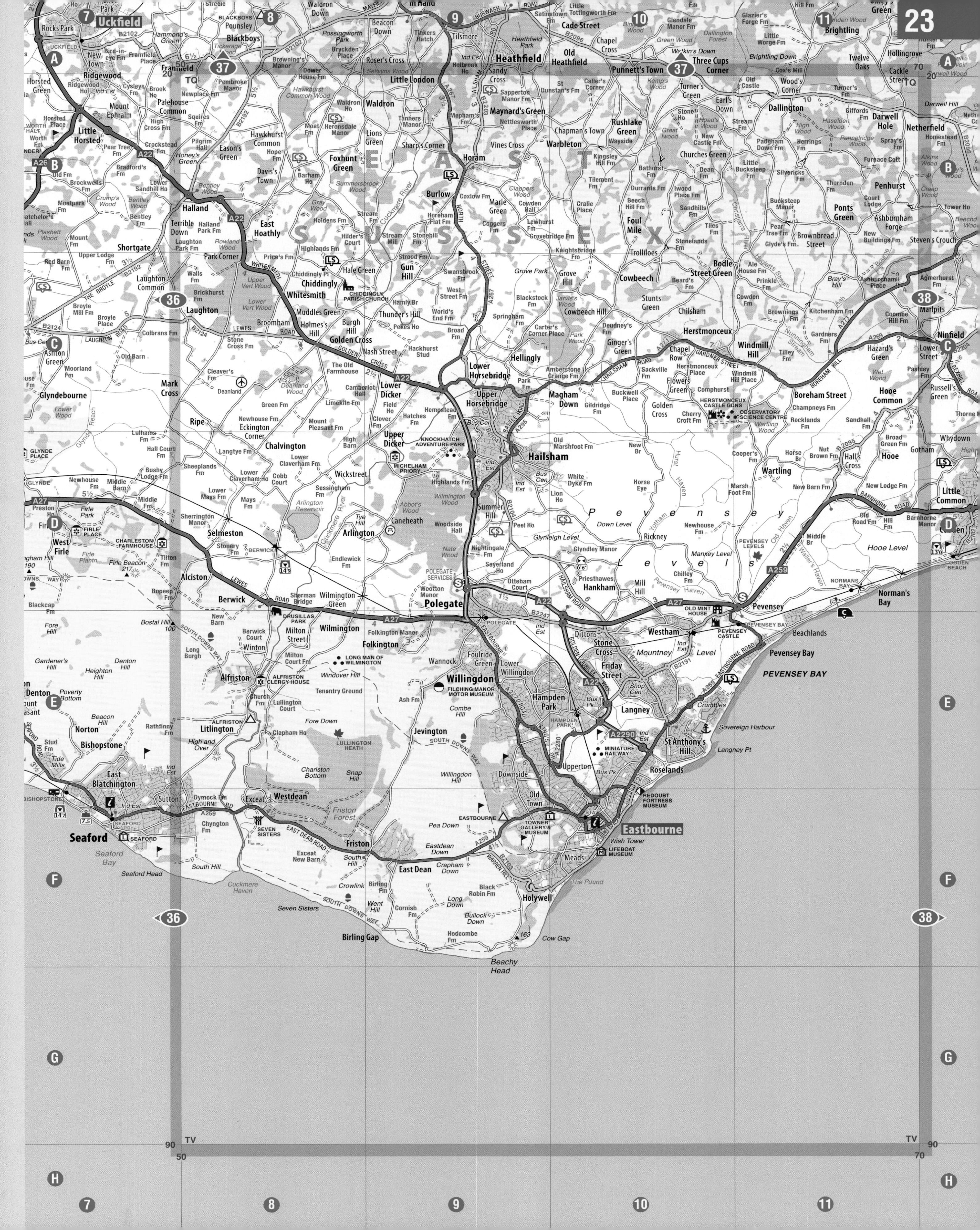

Uckfield
Rocks Park
Blackboys
Pounsley
Framfield
Ridgewood
Little Horsted
Horsted Green
Mount Ephraim
Palehouse Common
Hawkhurst Common
Eason's Green
Halland
Waldron
Little London
Heathfield
Old Heathfield
Cade Street
Punnett's Town
Three Cups Corner
Brightling
Hollingrove
Cackle Street
Dallington
Darwell Hole
Netherfield
Penhurst
Ponts Green
Ashburnham Forge
Brownbread Street
Steven's Crouch
Rushlake Green
Warbleton
Maynard's Green
Horam
Burlow
Foxhunt Green
Davis's Town
East Hoathly
Terrible Down
Shortgate
Laughton Common
Laughton
Whitesmith
Chiddingly
Gun Hill
Hale Green
Muddles Green
Golden Cross
Foul Mile
Trolliloes
Cowbeech
Bodle Street Green
Herstmonceux
Windmill Hill
Ninfield
Lower Street
Hellingly
Lower Horsebridge
Upper Horsebridge
Lower Dicker
Upper Dicker
Magham Down
Hailsham
Boreham Street
Hooe Common
Hooe
Wartling
Little Common
Cooden
Glyndebourne
Mark Cross
Ripe
Chalvington
Eckington Corner
Selmeston
Arlington
Caneheath
Summer Hill
Pevensey Levels
Rickney
Hankham
Mill Hill
Pevensey
Norman's Bay
West Firle
Alciston
Berwick
Polegate
Wilmington
Folkington
Westham
Stone Cross
Friday Street
Pevensey Bay
PEVENSEY BAY
Willingdon
Hampden Park
Langney
St Anthony's Hill
Sovereign Harbour
Langney Pt
Alfriston
Litlington
Jevington
Denton
Norton
Bishopstone
East Blatchington
Seaford
Seaford Bay
Seaford Head
Sutton
Exceat
Westdean
Friston
East Dean
Cuckmere Haven
Seven Sisters
Birling Gap
Upperton
Roselands
Eastbourne
Old Town
Meads
Holywell
Beachy Head
Cow Gap
E A S T S U S S E X
A22
A27
A259
A267
A271
A2290
36
37
38
TQ
TV
50
70
90
A
B
C
D
E
F
G
H
7
8
9
10
11

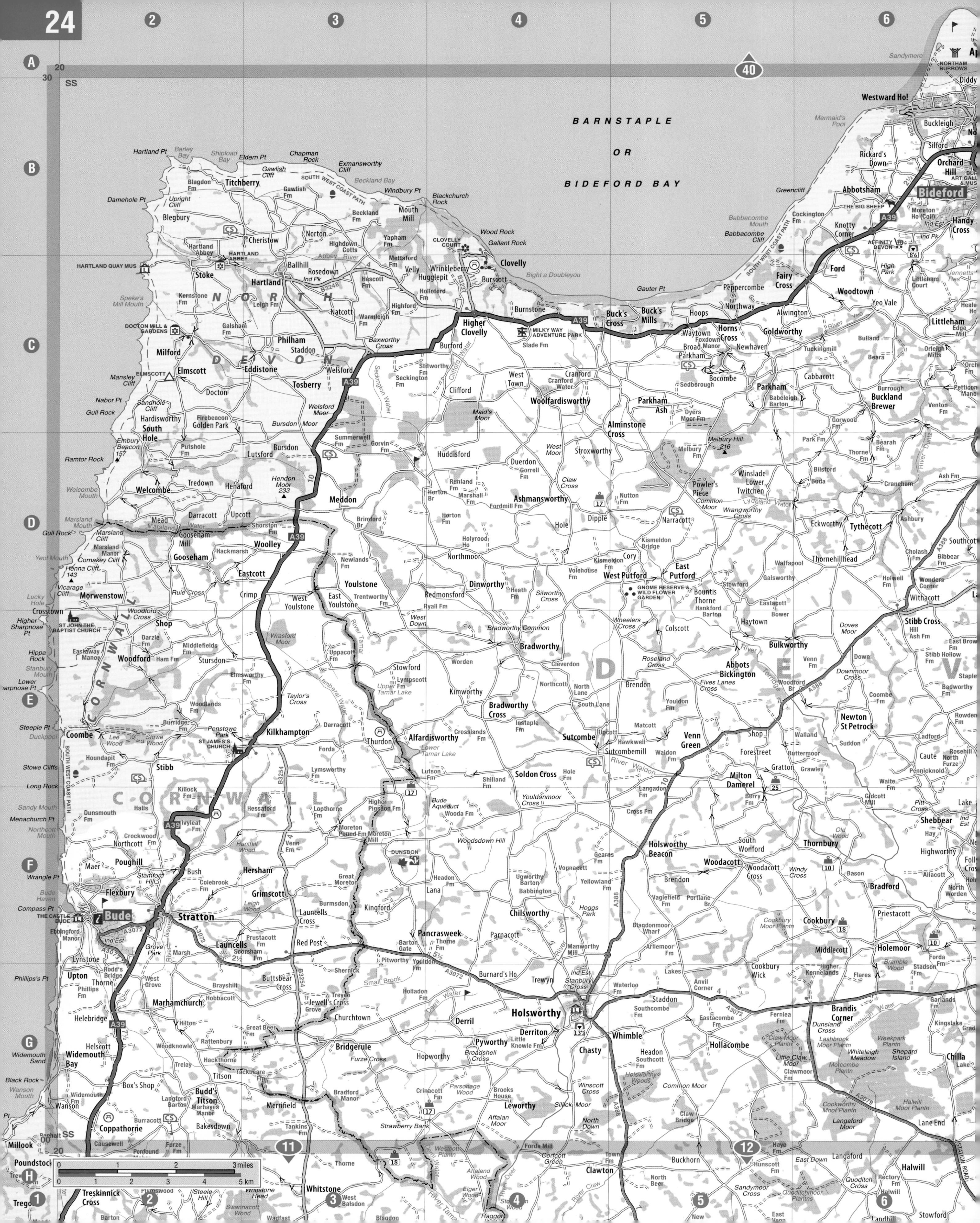
2
3
4
5
6
A
B
C
D
E
F
G
H
1
40
11
12
SS
BARNSTAPLE
OR
BIDEFORD BAY
Hartland Pt
Barley Bay
Shipload Bay
Eldern Pt
Chapman Rock
Exmansworthy Cliff
Gawlish Cliff
Beckland Bay
Windbury Pt
Blackchurch Rock
SOUTH WEST COAST PATH
Titchberry
Blagdon Fm
Gawlish Fm
Damehole Pt
Upright Cliff
Blegbury
Beckland Fm
Mouth Mill
Cheristow
Norton
Yapham Fm
Hartland Abbey
HARTLAND ABBEY
Highdown Cotts
CLOVELLY COURT
Wood Rock
Gallant Rock
HARTLAND QUAY MUS
Stoke
Hartland
Ballhill
Rosedown
Ind Pk
Mettaford Fm
Velly
Hugglepit
Wrinkleberry
Clovelly
Burscott
Bight a Doubleyou
Speke's Mill Mouth
Kernstone Fm
NORTH
Leigh Fm
Hescott Fm
Hollowford Fm
Natcott
Highford Fm
Warmleigh Fm
Burnstone
Higher Clovelly
MILKY WAY ADVENTURE PARK
Slade Fm
Buck's Cross
Buck's Mills
Gauter Pt
Peppercombe
Northway
Hoops
Waytown
Foxdown Manor
Broad Parkham
Horns Cross
Newhaven
Bocombe
Sedborough
DOCTON MILL & GARDENS
Galsham Fm
Milford
Philham
Staddon
Baxworthy Cross
Burford
Stitworthy Fm
Seckington Fm
DEVON
Elmscott
ELMSCOTT
Eddistone
Tosberry
Welsford
Mansley Cliff
Docton
Nabor Pt
Sandhole Cliff
Gull Rock
Hardisworthy
Firebeacon
Golden Park
South Hole
Embury Beacon 157
Welsford Moor
Bursdon Moor
Clifford
West Town
Cranford
Cranford Water
Woolfardisworthy
Parkham
Parkham Ash
Dyers Moor Fm
Maid's Moor
Alminstone Cross
Putshole Fm
Ramtor Rock
Lutsford
Bursdon
Summerwell Fm
Gorvin Fm
Huddisford
Duerdon
West Moor
Stroxworthy
Melbury Fm
Melbury Hill 216
Gorrell Fm
Welcombe Mouth
Welcombe
Tredown
Henaford
Hendon Moor 233
Runland Fm
Horton Br
Marshall Fm
Claw Cross
Ashmansworthy
Nutton Fm
Powler's Piece
Common Moor
Meddon
Fordmill Fm
Dipple
Narracott
Wrangworthy Cross
Marsland Mouth
Mead
Darracott
Upcott
Shorston Fm
Brimford Br
Horton Fm
Hole
Gull Rock
Marsland Cliff
Marsland Manor
Gooseham Mill
Holyrood Ho
Kismeldon Bridge
Yeol Mouth
Cornakey Cliff
Gooseham
Hackmarsh
Woolley
Northmoor
Cory
Kismeldon Fm
East Putford
Henna Cliff 143
Eastcott
Newlands Fm
Volehouse Fm
West Putford
GNOME RESERVE & WILD FLOWER GARDEN
Vicarage Cliff
Morwenstow
Rule Cross
Crimp
Youlstone
Trentworthy Fm
Redmonsford
Dinworthy
Heath Fm
Silworthy Cross
Bountis Thorne
Hankford Barton
Lucky Hole
Crosstown
ST JOHN THE BAPTIST CHURCH
West Youlstone
East Youlstone
Ryall Fm
West Down
Higher Sharpnose Pt
Woodford Cross
Shop
Wrasford Moor
Bradworthy Common
Wheelers Cross
Colscott
Bradworthy
Hippa Rock
Darzle Fm
Middlefields Fm
Uppacott Fm
River Tamar
Eastaway Manor
Woodford
Ham Fm
Sturdon
Stowford
Worden
Cleverdon
Roseland Cross
Stanbury Mouth
Lympscott Fm
Upper Tamar Lake
Northcott
Lower Sharpnose Pt
Elmsworthy Fm
Kimworthy
North Lane
Brendon
Fives Lanes Cross
Woodlands Fm
Taylor's Cross
Lamberal Water
Bradworthy Cross
South Lane
Youldon Fm
CORNWALL
Steeple Pt
Duckpool
Coombe
Lee Wood
Burridge Fm
Penstowe Park
Stowe Wood
Kilkhampton
Darracott
Thurdon
Alfardisworthy
Crosslands Fm
Instaple Fm
Sutcombe
Upcott
Matcott
Venn Green
ST JAMES'S CHURCH
Hawkwell
Sutcombemill
Waldon Fm
Houndapit Fm
Forda
Lower Tamar Lake
Stowe Cliffs
Stibb
Lymsworthy Fm
Lutson Fm
Soldon Cross
Hole Fm
River Waldon
Long Rock
Killock Fm
Shilland Fm
Langadon Fm
Sandy Mouth
Halls
Hessaford Fm
Lopthorne Fm
Higher Pigsdon Fm
Bude Aqueduct
Wooda Fm
Youldonmoor Cross
Cross Fm
Menachurch Pt
Dunsmouth Fm
Ivyleaf Fm
Moreton Pound Fm
Moreton Mill
Woodsdown Hill
Holsworthy Beacon
Northcott Mouth
Crockwood Fm
Northcott
Huntholl Wood
Venn Fm
DUNSDON
Gearns Fm
Maer
Poughill
Hersham
Vognacott
Wrangle Pt
Stamford Hill
Bush
Great Moreton
Headon Fm
Ugworthy Barton
Babbington
Yellowland Fm
Colebrook Fm
Lana
Flexbury
Grimscott
Bude Haven
Leigh Wood
Kingford
Chilsworthy
Hoggs Park
Compass Pt
THE CASTLE BUDE
Bude
Stratton
Burmsdon Fm
Launcells Cross
Pancrasweek
Parnacott
Ebbingford Manor
Ind Est
Prustacott Fm
Scorsham Fm
Red Post
Barton Gate
Thorne Fm
Manworthy Fm
Launcells
Grove Park
Marsh
Pitworthy Fm
Youldon Fm
Lynstone
Rodd's Bridge
Shernick
Small Brook
Burnard's Ho
Trewyn
Phillips's Pt
Upton
Thorne
West Grove
Buttsbear Cross
Ind Est
Stanbury Cross
Phillips
Brayshill
Hobbacott
Treyeo
Jewell's Cross
Holladon Fm
Derril Water
Holsworthy
Marhamchurch
Grove
Churchtown
Derril
Helebridge
Hilton
Great Beer Fm
Pyworthy
Derriton
Little Knowle Fm
Rattenbury
Bridgerule
Broadshell Cross
Helscott
Widemouth Sand
Woodknowle
Hackthorne
Furze Cross
Hopworthy
Widemouth Bay
Trelay
Tackbeare
Titson
Black Rock
Box's Shop
Budd's Titson
Marhayes Manor
Langford Barton
Bradford Manor
Crinacott Fm
Parsonage Wood
Brooks House
Lewortby
Merrifield
Wanson Mouth
Widemouth
Wanson
Burracott
Coppathorne
Bakesdown
Tankins Fm
Strawberry Bank
Affalan Moor
Millook
Causewell
Penfound
Furze Fm
Poundstock
Westcott Plantn
Forda Mill
Corfcott Green
Town Fm
Clawton
Thorne
Affaland Wood
Treskinnick Cross
Plymswood
Whitstone Head
Whitstone
West Balsdon
Elger Wood
River Tamar
River Deer
River Claw
North Beer
Trego
Swannacott Wood
Barton
Wadfast
Blagdon
Raggott
New
Staddon
Southcombe Fm
Waterloo Fm
Whimble
Chasty
Eastacombe Fm
Hollacombe
Headon
Southcott Fm
Holsworthy Woods
Winscott Cross
Common Moor
Sillick Moor
Claw Bridge
North Down
Buckhorn
Sandymoor Cross
Hunscott Fm
Hayes Fm
Langaford
East Down
Halwill
Quoditch Cross
Rectory Fm
Landhill
Stowford
Sandymere
NORTHAM BURROWS
Diddy
Westward Ho!
Mermaid's Pool
Buckleigh
Silford
Rickard's Down
Orchard Hill
Greencliff
Abbotsham
THE BIG SHEEP
Bideford
Babbacombe Mouth
Babbacombe Cliff
Cockington Fm
Knotty Corner
Moreton Ho (Coll)
Ind Est
Handy Cross
AFFINITY DEVON
Ford
High Park
Littleham Court
Fairy Cross
Woodtown
Yeo Vale
Alwington
Goldworthy
Littleham
Bulland
Beara
Tuckingmill
Orleigh Mills
Cabbacott
Babeleigh Barton
Buckland Brewer
Burrough Fm
Venton Fm
Gorwood Fm
Park Fm
Bearah Fm
Thorne Fm
Bilsford
Buda
Winslade
Lower Twitchen
Craneham
Lydeland Water
Ash Fm
Eckworthy
Tythecott
Ashbury
Southcott
Cholash Fm
Bibbear Fm
Thornehillhead
Waffapool
Galsworthy
Holwell Fm
Wonders Corner
Stowford
Eastacott
Bower
Withacott
Haytown
Doves Moor
Stibb Cross
Hill
Ash Fm
Bulkworthy
Abbots Bickington
Venn Fm
Down
Downmoor Cross
Stibb Hollow
Woodford Fm
Coombe Fm
Badworthy Fm
Newton St Petrock
Sudbon
Shop
Forestreet
Walland
Ladford
Buttermoor
Gratton
Grawley
Caute
North Furze
Pennicknold
Milton Damerel
Berry Fm
Waite Fm
Gidcott Mill
Pitt Cross
Lake
Shebbear
Hay
Old Wood
Thornbury
South Wonford
Woodacott
Woodacott Cross
Windy Cross
Highworthy
Bason
Allacott
Bradford
North Worden
Brendon
Vaglefield Fm
Portlane Br
Priestacott
Blagdonmoor Wharf
Cookbury
Cookbury Moor Plantn
Arliemoor Fm
Middlecott
Holemoor
Forda Fm
Cookbury Wick
Lakes
Higher Kennelands
Bramble Wood
Stadson Fm
Flares
Anvil Corner
Fernlea Fm
Brandis Corner
Garlands
Dunsland Cross
Kingslake
Claw Moor Plantn
Lashbrook Moor Plantn
Weekpark Plantn
Little Claw Moor
Whiteleigh Meadow
Shepard Island
Chilla
Clawmoor Fm
Motcombe Plantn
Cookworthy Moor Plantn
Halwill Moor Plantn
Langaford Moor
Lane End
STATION ROAD
A39
A388
A3072
A386
A3079
B3248
B3237
B3254
0 1 2 3 miles
0 1 2 3 4 5 km

25
Appledore
Instow
Bickleton
Newport
Landkey
Swimbridge Newland
Bishops Tawton
Tawstock
Swimbridge
West Buckland
Westleigh
Eastleigh
Horwood
Newton Tracey
Cobbaton
Chapelton
East Stowford
Chittlehampton
South Molton
Alverdiscott
Woodtown
Hiscott
Fishleigh Barton
Landcross
Weare Giffard
Yarnscombe
Atherington
Umberleigh
Warkleigh
Clapworthy
George Nympton
Satterleigh
Langridge Ford
Chittlehamholt
Monkleigh
Great Torrington
High Bullen
Sherwood Green
High Bickington
St Giles in the Wood
Kingscott
Frithelstock
Frithelstock Stone
Taddiport
Little Torrington
Roborough
King's Nympton
Burrington
Cadbury Barton
Elstone
Beaford
Cottwood
Riddlecombe
Chulmleigh
Ashreigney
Peters Marland
Winswell
Woollaton
Merton
Huish
Dolton
Ashley
Hollocombe
Eggesford Station
Petrockstow
Dowland
Wembworthy
Buckland Filleigh
Meeth
Iddesleigh
Winkleigh
Brushford
Coldridge
Sheepwash
Monkokehampton
Broadwood Kelly
Bondleigh
Black Torrington
Highampton
Hatherleigh
Honeychurch
Exbourne
North Tawton
Jacobstowe
Sampford Courtenay
Inwardleigh
Beaworthy
Northlew
Oak Cross
Patchacott
Ashbury
Itton
A39
A361
A377
A386
A3124
A3072
B3227
B3217
B3220

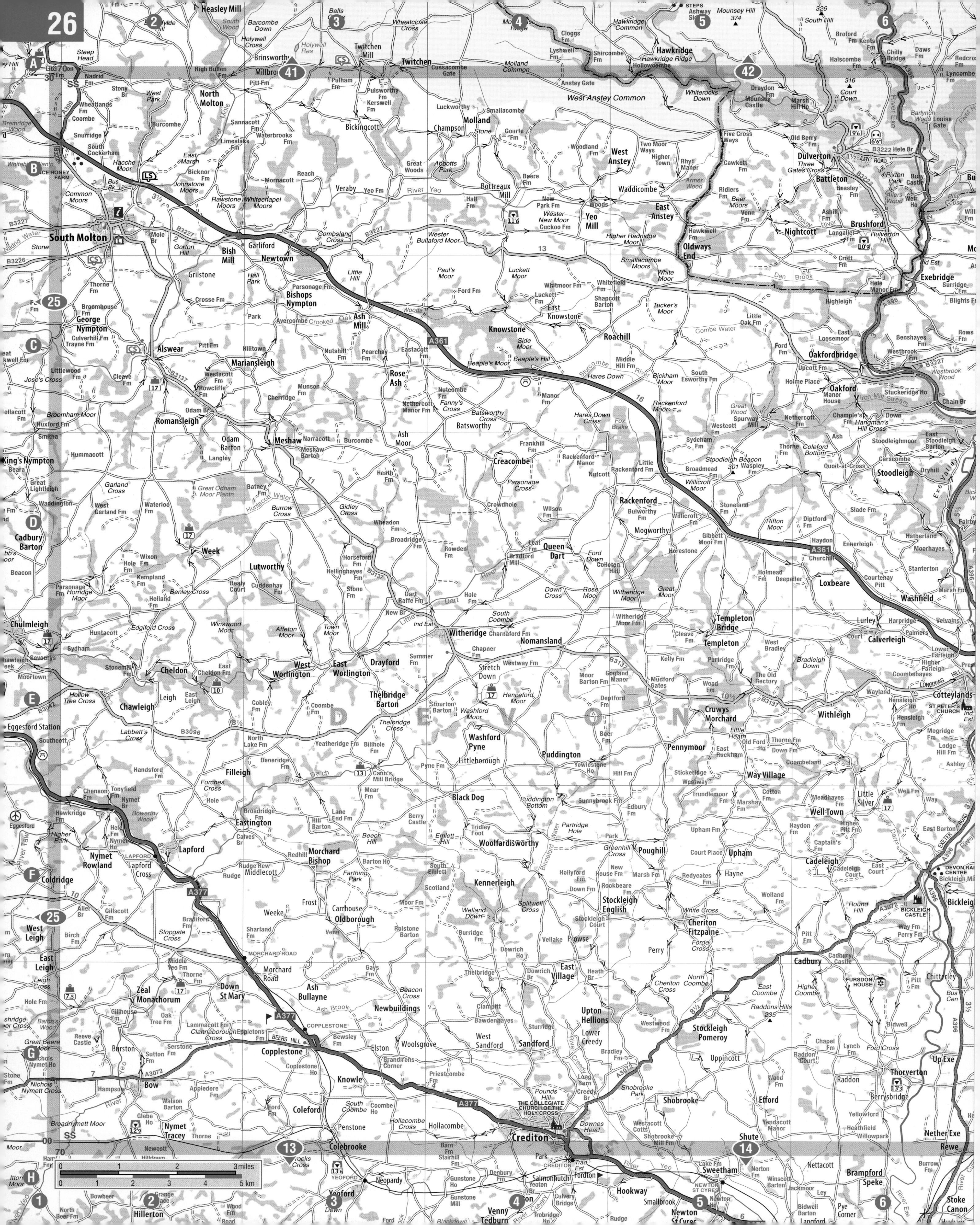
Heasley Mill
South Wood
Barcombe Down
Holywell Cross
Balls
Wheatclose Cross
Hawkridge Common
STEPS
Ashway
Mounsey Hill
374
326
South Hill
Broford Fm
Kents Fm
Chilly Bridge
Daws Fm
Redcross Fm
Steep Head
Holywell Res
Twitchen Mill
Brinsworthy
Twitchen
Cloggs Fm
Lyshwell Fm
Shircombe Fm
Hawkridge
Hawkridge Ridge
Hollowcombe
Halscombe Fm
Lyncombe Fm
High Bullen Fm
Millbrook
Pulham Fm
Cussacombe Gate
Molland Common
Anstey Gate
Whiterocks Down
Draydon Fm
Mounsey Castle
Marsh Hill Ho
316
Court Down
Nadrid Fm
Pitt Fm
Stony Br
West Park
North Molton
Pulsworthy Fm
Kerswell Fm
West Anstey Common
Luckworthy
Smallacombe
Molland
Stone
Gourte Fm
Wheatlands Fm
Coombe
Bremridge Wood
Snurridge
South Cockerham
Hacche Moor
Burcombe
Sannacott Fm
Limeslake Fm
River Mole
Waterbrooks Fm
Bickingcott
Champson
Woodland Fm
West Anstey
Two Moor Ways
Higher Town
Rhyll Manor
Five Cross Ways
Old Berry Fm
Dulverton
Hele Br
Three Gates Cross
Barlynch Wood
Louisa Gate
East Marsh
Bicknor Fm
Johnstone Moors
Mornacott
Reach
Great Woods
Abbotts Park
Beere Fm
Cawkett Fm
Armer Wood
Pixton Park
Bury Castle
Common Moors
Bus Pk
Rawstone Moors
Whitechapel Moors
Veraby
Yeo Fm
River Yeo
Bottreaux Mill
Hall Fm
New Park Fm
Woods
Waddicombe
Ridlers Fm
Beer Moors
Venn Fm
Battleton
Beasley Fm
Allers Wood
Weir Ho
B3227
South Molton
Mole Br
Gorton Hill
Bish Mill
Garliford
Combsland Cross
Wester Bullaford Moor
Wester New Moor
Cuckoo Fm
Yeo Mill
East Anstey
Higher Radnidge Moor
Hawkwell Fm
Oldways End
Nightcott
Ashill Fm
Langaller Fm
Brushford
Hulverton Hill
Nadrid Water
Stone
B3226
Newtown
Grilstone
Hall Park
Little Hill
Paul's Moor
Luckett Moor
Smallacombe Moors
White Moor
Den Brook
Croft Fm
Exebridge
Surridge Fm
Thorne Fm
Parsonage Fm
Bishops Nympton
Ford Fm
Whitmoor Fm
Luckett Fm
Whitefield Fm
Shapcott Barton
Tucker's Moor
Hele Manor Fm
Highleigh
Blights Fm
Broomhouse Fm
George Nympton
Culverhill Fm
Trayne Fm
Crosse Fm
Park
Avercombe
Crooked Oak
Woods
Ash Mill
East Knowstone
Knowstone
Roachill
Combe Water
Little Oak Fm
East Loosemoor
Benshayes Fm
Rows Fm
Littlewood Fm
Jose's Cross
Alswear
Pitt Fm
Hilltown
Mariansleigh
Nutshill Fm
Pearchay Fm
Eastacott Fm
A361
Side Moor
Beaple's Moor
Beaple's Hill
Middle Hill Fm
Ford Fm
Oakfordbridge
Westbrook Fm
Westbrook Wood
Cleave Fm
Westacott Fm
Rowcliffe Fm
B3137
Munson Fm
Cherridge
Rose Ash
Nutcombe Fm
Netherott Manor Fm
Fanny's Cross
Hares Down
Sturcombe
Bickham Moor
South Esworthy Fm
Holme Place
Oakford
Manor House
Stuckeridge Ho
Chain Br
Broomham Moor
Huxford Fm
Smitha
Romansleigh
Odam Br
Batsworthy Cross
Batsworthy
Manor Fm
Hares Down Cross
Fox Brake
Rackenford Moor
Great Wood
Spurway Mill
Westcott Fm
Netherott Fm
Chample's Fm
Hangman's Hill Cross
Down
Odam Barton
Meshaw
Narracott
Burcombe
Meshaw Barton
Ash Moor
Frankhill Fm
Sydeham Fm
Thorne Fm
Ash
Coleford Bottom
Stoodleighmoor
East Stoodleigh Barton
King's Nympton
Beara
Hummacott
Langley
Creacombe
Rackenford Manor
Little Rackenford Fm
Stoodleigh Beacon
301
Waspley Fm
Quoit-at-Cross
Carscombe
Stoodleigh
Dryhill
Great Lightleigh
Waddington
Garland Cross
Great Odham Moor Plantn
Batney Fm
Huntacott Water
Heath Fm
Nutcott
Broadmead Fm
Willicroft Moor
Exe Valley
West Garland Fm
Waterloo Fm
Burrow Cross
Gidley Cross
Parsonage Cross
Crowdhole
Rackenford
Bulworthy Fm
Stoneland Fm
Slade Fm
Cadbury Barton
Beacon
Wheadon Fm
Wilson Fm
Willicroft Fm
Rifton Moor
Diptford Fm
Broadridge Fm
Mogworthy
Gibbett Moor Fm
Hatherland
Haydon
Ennerleigh
Moorhayes
Week
Hole Fm
Wixon Fm
Lutworthy
Horseford Fm
Rowden Fm
Leat Fm
Bradford Mill
Queen Dart
Ford Down
Horestone
Churchill
Kempland Fm
Hellinghayes Fm
Colleton Hall
Holmead Fm
Deepaller
Loxbeare
Stanterton
Parsonage Fm
Horridge Moor
Bealy Court
Cuddenhay Fm
Benley Cross
Stone Fm
Courtenay Pitt
Holland Fm
Dart Raffe Fm
Hole Fm
Down Cross
Rose Moor
Witheridge Moor
Great Moor
Washfield
Marsh Fm
Chulmleigh
Huntacott
Edgiford Cross
Winswood Moor
Affeton Moor
Town Moor
New Br
Little Dart
Ind Est
South Coombe
Witheridge
Charnaford Fm
Witheridge Moor Fm
Templeton Bridge
Templeton
Lurley
Harpridge
Calverleigh
Velvains
Palmers
Sydham
Savourys
Moortown
Stonemill
Cheldon
East Cheldon Fm
West Worlington
East Worlington
Drayford
Summer Fm
Chapner Fm
Stretch Down
Westway Fm
Nomansland
Cleave Fm
Kelly Fm
Partridge Fm
West Bradley
Bradleigh Down
Court
Lower Farleigh
Higher Farleigh
Coombehayes
Chawleigh
Leigh
East Leigh
Cobley Fm
Coombe Fm
Thelbridge Barton
Stourton Barton
Henceford Moor
Moor Barton Fm
Gogland Manor
Mudford Gates
Wood Fm
The Old Rectory
Wayland
LONGDRAG HILL
Cotteylands
Hollow Tree Cross
B3042
Washford Moor
Deptford Fm
Cruwys Morchard
Withleigh
Hensleigh Ho
ST PETER'S CHURCH
Eggesford Station
Southcott
Labbett's Cross
B3096
Thelbridge Cross
Washford Pyne
Beer Fm
Little Heath
Old Ford Ho
Thorne Fm
Down Fm
Mogridge Fm
Lodge Hill Fm
North Lake Fm
Yeatheridge Fm
Billhole Fm
Littleborough
Puddington
Pennymoor
East Ruckham
Coombeland
Ashley
DEVON
Handsford Fm
Deneridge Fm
Filleigh
Cann's Mill Bridge
Pyne Fm
Yowlestone Ho
Hill Fm
Stickeridge
Westway
Way Village
Chenson Fm
Tonyfield Fm
Forches Cross
River Dalch
Mear Fm
Black Dog
Trundlemoor Fm
Cotton Fm
Meadhayes Fm
Little Silver
Well Fm
Nymet Br
Hole
Broadridge Fm
Puddington Bottom
Sunnybrook Fm
Marshay Fm
Well Town
Way
Hawkridge Fm
Bowerthy Wood
Eggesford
Heywood
Eastington
Lane End Fm
Berry Castle
Edbury Fm
Upham Fm
Haydon Fm
Higher Pitt Fm
East Barton
Higher Park
Nymet Ho
Lapford
Calves Br
Hill Barton
Beech Hill
Emlett Hill
Tridley Foot
Partridge Hole
Park
Captain's Fm
River Taw
Nymet Rowland
LAPFORD
Lapford Cross
Redhill
Morchard Bishop
Woolfardisworthy
Greenhill Cross
Poughill
Court Place
Upham
Cadeleigh
Cadeleigh Court
East Court
DEVON RAILWAY CENTRE
Bickleigh Mill
Coldridge
Rudge Rew Fm
Middlecott
Rudge
Barton Ho
Farthing Park
South Emlett
Kennerleigh
Hollyford Fm
New House Fm
Marsh Fm
Hayne
Down Fm
Rookbeare Fm
Redyeates Fm
Bickleigh
A377
Aller Br
Frost
Carrhouse
Oldborough
Scotland
Moor Fm
Welland Down
Splitwell Cross
Stockleigh English
Welland Fm
Round Hill
BICKLEIGH CASTLE
West Leigh
Gillscott Fm
Bradiford Fm
Weeke
Stockleigh Court
White Cross
Cheriton Fitzpaine
A3072
Way Fm
Perry Fm
Birch Fm
Stopgate Cross
Sharland Fm
Venn
Rolstone Barton
Burridge Fm
Vellake
Prowse
Forde Cross
Pitt Fm
Perry
Dowrich Ho
MORCHARD ROAD
Gays Fm
East Leigh
Middle Yeo Fm
Thorne Fm
Morchard Road
Knathorne Brook
Thelbridge Br
Dowrich Br
East Village
Heath Fm
North Coombe
Cadbury
Cadbury Castle
FURSDON HOUSE
Pitt Fm
Chitterley
Leigh Cross
Zeal Monachorum
Down St Mary
Ash Bullayne
Beacon Cross
Cheriton Cross
East Coombe
Higher Coombe
Bus Cen
Hole Fm
Gillhouse Fm
Oak Tree Fm
Newbuildings
Clampitt
Upton Hellions
Raddons Hills
235
A396
Lammacott Fm
Clannaborough
Eppletons Fm
Ash Brook
COPPLESTONE
Bawdenhayes
Sturridge
Lower Creedy
Westwood Fm
Stockleigh Pomeroy
Bidwell
Baron's Wood
Reeve Castle
Burston
Serstone Fm
Copplestone
Bewsley Fm
BEERS HILL
Elston
Woolsgrove
West Sandford
Sandford
River Creedy
Bradley Fm
Chapel Fm
Lynch Fm
Ford Cross
Great Beere Moor
Sutton Fm
Coplestone Ho
Brandirons Corner
Uppincott
Raddon Court
Up Exe
Nichols Nymet Ho
Nichols Nymett Cross
A3072
Bow
Hampson
Knowle
Priestcombe
Long Barn
Creedy
Shobrooke Park
Wood Fm
Raddon
Thorverton
Berrysbridge
Appledore Fm
Walson Barton
Ford Fm
Coleford
South Coombe
Coombe Ho
Pounds Hill
THE COLLEGIATE CHURCH OF THE HOLY CROSS
Shobrooke
Efford
Yellowford
Broadnymett Moor
Glebe Ho
Nymet Tracey
Thorne
Penstone
Hollacombe Cross
Hollacombe
Crediton
Downes Head
Westacott Cotts
Yendacott Manor
Heathfield
Willowpark
Moor
Newcott
Colebrooke
Barn Fm
Stairhill Fm
Shobrooke Mill Fm
Shute
Nether Exe
Rewe
Itton Moor
Crocks Cross
YEOFORD
Neopardy
Gunstone Ho
Denbury Fm
Salmonhutch
Fordton
Park
CREDITON
Lake Fm
Sweetham
Norton Fm
Winscott Barton
Nettacott
Brampford Speke
Burrow Fm
Bowbeer
Grange Place
Hillerton
North Beer Fm
Wood Fm
Yeoford
Gunstone Mill
Yeoton
Culvery Bridge
Hookway
Smallbrook
NEWTON ST CYRES
Newton St Cyres
Jackmoor
Ley
Bidwell Barton
Pye Corner
Stoke Canon
Venny Tedburn
Trobridge
Langford
Rudge
Ford
Blackdown
0 1 2 3 miles
0 1 2 3 4 5 km
SS
30
00
70

SOMERSET
DEVON
BLACKDOWN
HILLS
Brompton Regis
Hartford
Upton
Skilgate
Bampton
Clatworthy
Huish Champflower
Maundown
Chipstable
Raddington
Waterrow
Petton
Shillingford
Clayhanger
Ashbrittle
Wiveliscombe
Langley Marsh
Milverton
Langford Budville
Bathealton
Kittisford
Appley
Stawley
Tolland
Lydeard St Lawrence
Brompton Ralph
Handy Cross
Pyleigh
Combe Florey
East Combe
Cothelstone
Cushuish
Bishops Lydeard
Ash Priors
Halse
Fitzhead
Preston Bowyer
Heathfield
Hillcommon
Norton Fitzwarren
Oake
Hillfarance
Bradford-on-Tone
Nynehead
East Nynehead
Runnington
Wellington
Rockwell Green
Thorne St Margaret
Holywell Lake
Sampford Arundel
White Ball
Hockworthy
Huntsham
Holcombe Rogus
Whipcott
Westleigh
Burlescombe
Red Ball
Appledore
Sampford Peverell
Halberton
Tiverton
Cowleymoor
Bolham
Chettiscombe
Chevithorne
Uplowman
East Mere
Whitnage
Nicholashayne
Culmstock
Hemyock
Churchstanton
Stapley
Clayhidon
Rosemary Lane
Bolham Water
Churchinford
Smeatharpe
Upottery
Rawridge
Luppitt
Dunkeswell
Sheldon
Abbey
Blackborough
Kentisbeare
Cullompton
Uffculme
Craddock
Ashill
Smithincott
Willand
Ash Thomas
Butterleigh
Bradninch
Silverton
Hele
Dulford
Kerswell
Broadhembury
Plymtree
Payhembury
Awliscombe
Honiton
Combe Raleigh
Monkton
Cotleigh
Clyst Hydon
Clyst St Lawrence
Talaton
Feniton
Gittisham
Buckerell
Westwood
Budlake
Killerton House
Ellerhayes
Langford
Westcott
Mutterton
Colebrook
Wilmington
Offwell
Mount Pleasant
Beacon
Wick
Wolverstone
Upton
Tale
Wellington Monument
Tiverton Services
Cullompton Services
Taunton Deane Services
A361
A38
A373
A303
A30
A35
M5

43
44
15
16
27
Taunton
Taunton Deane Services
Bishop's Hull
Norton Fitzwarren
Staplegrove
Kingston St Mary
Cheddon Fitzpaine
Monkton Heathfield
Bathpool
Creech St Michael
Creech Heathfield
North Newton
Thurloxton
West Monkton
Durston
Lyng
West Lyng
Burrow-bridge
Athelney
Othery
Pathe
Stathe
Aller
High Ham
Low Ham
Langport
Huish Episcopi
Muchelney
Drayton
Curry Rivel
Stoke St Gregory
Meare Green
North Curry
Knapp
Ruishton
Henlade
Thornfalcon
Stoke St Mary
Wrantage
Fivehead
Curry Mallet
Isle Brewers
Isle Abbotts
Beercrocombe
Hatch Beauchamp
West Hatch
Hatch Green
Orchard Portman
Thurlbear
Staplehay
Trull
Pitminster
Blagdon Hill
Angersleigh
Staple Fitzpaine
Bickenhall
Curland
Windmill Hill
Ashill
Ilton
Puckington
Barrington
Stocklinch
Shepton Beauchamp
South Petherton
Kingsbury Episcopi
East Lambrook
West Lambrook
Westport
Hambridge
Broadway
Horton
Ilminster
Ashwell
Seavington St Michael
Seavington St Mary
Lopen
Donyatt
Kingstone
Dowlish Wake
Dinnington
Hinton St George
Crock Street
Buckland St Mary
Bishopswood
Churchstanton
Churchinford
Combe St Nicholas
Wadeford
Cricket Malherbie
Chillington
Chaffcombe
Cudworth
Chard
Cricket St Thomas
Whitestaunton
Howley
Yarcombe
Upottery
Rawridge
Marsh
Newcott
Smeatharpe
Whatley
Winsham
Wayford
Clapton
Seaborough
Drimpton
Forton
Tatworth
South Chard
Chardstock
Stockland
Furley
Millhayes
Membury
Churchill
Tytherleigh
Holditch
Thorncombe
Hawkchurch
Burstock
Broadwindsor
Marshalsea
Pilsdon
Bettiscombe
Blackney
Marshwood
Smallridge
Axminster
Weycroft
Dalwood
Wilmington
Offwell
Monkton
Cotleigh
Ham
Heathstock
Whitehorn
S O M E R S E T
D E V O N
B L A C K D O W N   H I L L S
D O R S E T
A38
A358
A378
A361
A303
A30
A35
A372
M5
B3170
B3168
B3162
B3165
0 1 2 3 miles
0 1 2 3 4 5 km

Somerton
Kingweston
Keinton Mandeville
Barton St David
West Lydford
Lydford-on-Fosse
Alford
Castle Cary
Lovington
Wheathill
Littleton
Hurcott
Charlton Mackerell
Charlton Adam
Babcary
Foddington
North Barrow
South Barrow
Galhampton
Shepton Montague
Bratton Seymour
Yarlington
Wincanton
Kingsdon
Long Sutton
Cary Fitzpaine
Lytes Cary Manor
Haynes International Motor Museum
Sparkford
North Cadbury
South Cadbury
Compton Pauncefoot
Blackford
Maperton
Holton
Lattiford
North Cheriton
South Cheriton
Podimore
Downhead
West Camel
Queen Camel
Sutton Montis
Little Weston
Weston Bampfylde
Bridgehampton
Yeovilton
Fleet Air Arm Mus
Speckington
Ilchester
Long Load
Little Load
Knole
Catsgore
Northover
Ilchester Mead
Limington
Chilton Cantelo
Draycott
Ashington
Marston Magna
Rimpton
Corton Denham
Charlton Horethorne
Stowell
Abbas Combe
Templecombe
Yenston
Henstridge Bowden
Sandford Orcas
Higher Sandford
Holway
Poyntington
Milborne Wick
Kingsbury Regis
Milborne Port
New Town
Stapleton
Ash
Highway
Martock
Hurst
Durnfield
Tintinhull
Chilthorne Domer
West Mudford
Mudford
Mudford Sock
Up Mudford
Adber
Gore
Trent
Nether Compton
Over Compton
Stallen
Sherborne
Oborne
Goathill
Purse Caundle
Haydon
Stourton Caundle
Yeovil Marsh
Vagg
Thorne Coffin
Houndstone
Hollands
Stoke sub Hamdon
West Stoke
East Stoke
Montacute
Norton sub Hamdon
Lufton
Lower Odcombe
Odcombe
Brympton
Alvington
Brympton D'Evercy
Preston Plucknett
Summerlands
Yeovil
New Town
Pen Mill
Chiselborough
Little Norton
Bradford Abbas
North Wootton
Alweston
Bishop's Caundle
Folke
Caundle Marsh
Bishop's Down
Longburton
Lillington
Thornford
West Chinnock
East Chinnock
Middle Chinnock
West Coker
Hardington Moor
North Coker
East Coker
Barwick
Stoford
Clifton Maybank
Beer Hackett
Knighton
Sutton Bingham
Hardington Mandeville
Pendomer
Hardington Marsh
Haselbury Plucknett
North Perrott
Closworth
Yetminster
Ryme Intrinseca
Leigh
Holnest
Holwell
Crouch Hill
Pleck
Pulham
West Pulham
Glanvilles Wootton
Netherstoke
Halstock
Higher Halstock Leigh
Lower Halstock Leigh
Melbury Osmond
Pimperne
Chetnole
Hamlet
Totnell
Three Gates
Hermitage
Middlemarsh
Tiley
Dunstish
Misterton
Crewkerne
South Perrott
Sockety
Winyard's Gap
Chedington
Corscombe
Weston
Norwood
West Chelborough
East Chelborough
Melbury Sampford
Melbury Bubb
Stockwood
Redford
Batcombe
Hilfield
Lyon's Gate
Buckland Newton
Henley
Evershot
Holywell
Minterne Magna
Minterne Parva
Beaminster
Buckham
Meerhay
Newtown
Toller Whelme
Rampisham
Uphall
Higher Wraxall
Wraxall
Lower Wraxall
Frome St Quintin
Higher Chalmington
Chalmington
Up Cerne
Up Sydling
Cerne Abbas
Alton Pancras
Piddletrenthide
Stoke Abbott
Netherbury
Melplash
North Poorton
Hooke
Higher Kingcombe
Lower Kingcombe
Chilfrome
Cattistock
Maiden Newton
Sydling St Nicholas
Nether Cerne
White Lackington
Toller
Loscombe
DORSET
A37
A30
A303
A359
A3088
A356
A352
A372
A371
B3151
B3153
B3148
B3145
B3146
B3163

Zeals
Lower Zeals
Mere
Charnage
Upton
Penselwood
Wolverton
Castle Ground Fm
Rook Street
Woodlands Manor
Southbrook
Limpers Hill
Bush Fm
Milton
The Green
Fonthill Gifford
Roundhill Grange
Brickhouse Fm
Pear Ash
Queen Oak
White Hill
Barrow Street
Underhill
Holloway
East Knoyle
Shalford
Leigh Common
Bourton
West Swainsford
Charlton Musgrove
Huntingford
Kinghay
Tisbury
Tuckingmill
Riding Gate
Silton
Bayford
West Bourton
Newtown
Pythouse
Stoke Trister
Milton on Stour
Sedgehill
East Hatch
Hatch
West Hill
Wincanton
Cucklington
Hale
Peacemarsh
Bowridge Hill
North End
Knapp Hill
Park Ho
West Hatch
Wardour
Childscourt School
Wyke
Gillingham
Semley
Lattiford
Gillingham Museum
Bay
Elm Hill
Sem Hill
Old Wardour Castle
Ham Common
North Cheriton
Langham
Ecliffe
Motcombe
Bittles Green
Barkers Hill
Donhead St Mary
Buckhorn Weston
Madjeston
South Cheriton
Rodgrove
Hartmoor
Bugley
Wincombe
Donhead St Andrew
Enmore Green
Horsington
Abbas Combe
Combe Throop
Kington Magna
Bowden
Ivy Cross
Milkwell
Birdbush
Brook Waters
Wilkinthroop
Templecombe
East Stour
East Stour Common
Duncliffe Hill
Shaftesbury
Gold Hill Museum
Ludwell
Charlton
New Town
West Stour
Alcester
St James
Higher Nyland
Lower Nyland
Fifehead Magdalen
Stour Provost
Stour Row
Cann
Cann Common
Yenston
Lower Marsh
Henstridge Marsh
Guy's Marsh
West Melbury
East Melbury
Melbury Abbas
Whitchurch
Henstridge Ash
Henstridge Bowden
Todber
Gannetts
Hains
Pillwell
Moorside
Kit Hill
Henstridge
Towns End
Marnhull
Mounters
Margaret Marsh
Twyford
Hartgrove
East Compton
Compton Abbas
Ashmore
Tollard Royal
Stalbridge
Pleck
Walton Elm
East Orchard
Woodbridge
Bedchester
Fontmell Magna
Purse Caundle
Stalbridge Weston
Stalbridge Common
Poolestown
Hinton St Mary
West Orchard
Manston
Sutton Waldron
Tollard Farnham
Stourton Caundle
Farrington
Iwerne Minster
Bishop's Caundle
Lydlinch
Sturminster Newton
Rixon
Hammoon
Fontmell Parva
Child Okeford
Iwerne Courtney or Shroton
Stubhampton
Tarrant Gunville
Holwell
Newton
The Bridge
Fiddleford
Gold Hill
Broad Oak
Sturminster Common
Hanford
Shillingstone
Tarrant Hinton
Crouch Hill
Pleck
Packers Hill
King's Stag
Fifehead Neville
Fifehead St Quintin
Okeford Fitzpaine
Ash
Kingston
Belchalwell
Belchalwell Street
Stourpaine
Pimperne
East Pulham
Woodrow
Pulham
Hazelbury Bryan
Pidney
Durweston
Blandford Camp
Tarrant Monkton
West Pulham
Wonston
Droop
Leigh
Ibberton
Park Gate
Turnworth
Bryanston
Tarrant Rawston
Duntish
Westfields
Woolland
Blandford Forum
Blandford St Mary
Langton Long Blandford
Mappowder
Stoke Wake
Tarrant Rushton
Buckland Newton
Henley
Bookham
Higher Ansty
Winterborne Houghton
Winterborne Stickland
Charlton Marshall
Tarrant Keyneston
Alton Pancras
Ansty Cross
Lower Ansty
Hilton
Winterborne Clenston
Thorncombe
Spetisbury
Tarrant Crawford
Melcombe Bingham
Higher Melcombe
Aller
Milton Abbas
Whatcombe
Plush
Bramblecombe
Winterborne Whitechurch
Piddletrenthide
Dewlish
Almer
Newton Peveril
White Lackington
Winterborne Kingston
Winterborne Zelston
DORSET
0 1 2 3 miles
0 1 2 3 4 5 km

Portash
Chilmark Common
Magna
Dinton
Dinton Park
Baverstock
Ditchampton
Fugglestone St Peter
Heath
Stratford Sub Castle
New Sarum
St Thomas's Bridge
Teffont Evias
Teffont Manor
Hindon Road
Barford St Martin
Ugford
Wilton
Westwood
Bishopdown
Queen Manor Fm
Lady Down
Lower Chicksgrove
Ley Fm
Bus Pk
Mill Fm
River Nadder
Hurdcott
Burcombe
Quidhampton
Wilton House
Bemerton
Laverstock
Burroughs Hill
Savage's Fm
Pitton Lodge
Chicksgrove
Fovant Wood
Compton Chamberlayne
Naishes Fm
Bulbridge
Wilton Park
Netherhampton
Salisbury
Churchfields
Milford
Ranger's Lodge Fm
King Manor Hill
Beechy Copse
Upper Chicksgrove
Haredene Wood
Great Ground Hill
Fir Hill
Fovant
Manor Fm
Burcombe Ivers
Hunt's Down
Home Fm
Netherhampton Road
West Harnham
Cathedral
Mompesson House
East Harnham
Ashley Hill
Long Copse
Withyslade Fm
Sutton Row
Sutton Mandeville
East Fm
Flamstone Fm
Hare Warren
Harnham
River Avon
Kennel Fm
Shute End
Britford
Clarendon Copse
Nightwood Copse
Swallowcliffe Wood
Compton Down
Hut Bottom
Hydon Hill
Little Down
Netton Down
Salisbury
Coombe Road
Bake Fm
Salisbury Road
Manor Fm
Hole Fm
Common Plantn
Walden Ho
Whitehouse Fm
Buxbury Fm
Sheep Well
Fovant Down
Down Barn
A354
Wellhouse Fm
Dogdean Fm
Lower Fm
Alderbury
Swallowcliffe
Ansty
Ansty Coombe
Sutton Down
Gurston Down
Wiltshire
The Pitts
Stratford Tony
Homington Down
Coombe Bissett
Longford Fm
Longford Park
Longford Castle
Whaddon
West Grimstead
Middle Down
Swallowcliffe Down
North Barn
Fifield Down
Knapp
Broad Chalke
Stoke Fm
Throope Manor Ho
River Ebble
Bishopstone
Homington
Odstock
Nunton
Bodenham
New Hall
Alderbury Ho
South Fm
Prescombe Down
Gurston Fm
Fifield Bavant
Mount Sorrel
Knighton Manor
Stoke Farthing
Croucheston
Throope Hill
Blandford Road
Matrimony Fm
Gallows Hill
West End
Church Bottom
Knighton Hill Fm
Mead End
Stratford Tony Down
Homington Down
Southdown Fm
Pennings Fm
Little Yews
Down Barn
Clearbury Ring
Clearbury Down
Charlton Manor Fm
The Giant's Grave
Witherington Fm
Witherington Down
Windmill Hill
Ebbesbourne Wake
Hill Fm
Rookhay Fm
Middleton Hill
Knowle Hill 197
Croucheston-Down Fm
Faulstone Down Fm
Jervoise Fm
Greenacres Fm
Yews Fm
The Highway
Charlton-All-Saints
Privett Fm
Alvediston
Cleeves Fm
Bowerchalke
Cranbourne Chase and
Great Yews
Barford Down Fm
Elcombe Fm
Trow Fm
Misselfore
Marleycombe Hill
Knighton Wood Fm
Lodge Fm
Knighton Wood
Toyd Clump
Black Hill
Round Clump
New Court Down
New Court Down Barn
New Court Fm
Barford Park Fm
Lower Bridmore Fm
243
Trow Down
East Combe Wood
Woodminton
Cow Down Hill
Verditch Chase
Chickengrove Bottom
Tenantry Fm
Whitsbury Down
Gallows Hill
Bus Cen
Wick
Downton
Templeman Fm
Lower Pensworth Fm
Manwood Copse
Chase Barn
East Chase Fm
Woodminton Down
Martin Drove End
Little Toyd Down
Cranway Fm
Toyd Fm
Botley's Fm
B3080
Morgan's Vale
Redlynch
Higher Bridmore Fm
Stonedown Wood
Middle Chase Fm
Cobley
St Brides Fm
Scotland Farm Cottage
Breamore Down
North Charford Down Fm
Lodge Farm Ho
Woodfalls
Lover
The Ridge
Rotherley Down
Chase Woods
West Chase Fm
West Woodyates Manor
Woodyates
West Wiltshire Downs
Martin Down
Martin
East Martin
Windmill Hill
Manor Ho
Dunberry Hill
Down Fm
Lower Fm
Down Fm
Breamore Wood
North Charford Manor Ho
Searchfield Fm
North Charford
Bohemia
Chase
Garston Wood
Tidpit
Damerham Knoll
Glebe Fm
Whitsbury
Breamore House
North Street
Hatchet Green
Hale
New Town
Martin Down
Hampshire
North Allenford Fm
Fordingbridge Road
Looseha Copse
Sandroyd School
Deanland
Bokerley Down
Oakley Fm
Rockbourne
Roundhill Fm
Outwick
Upper Street
South Charford Fm
Breamore
Woodgreen
Higherend Fm
Millersford Plantn
Oakley Down
Pentridge
Pentridge Hill
Knoll Fm
Rockstead Fm
Flood Street
Deanend
Woodcutts Common
New Barn
Kites Nest Fm
Blackheath Down
South Allenford Fm
Allen River
Radnall Wood
Minchington Down
Woodcutts
Penbury Knoll
Blagdon Fm
Roman Villa
Upper Burgate
Godshill Inclosure
Deadman Hill
Sixpenny Handley
Town Fm
Ackling Dyke
Crockerton Hill
Martin Wood
North End
Court Fm
Allen's Fm
Fryern Court
Burgate
Castle Hill
Millersford Bottom
Dean
Chapel Down Fm
Blackbush Down
Boulsbury Fm
Damerham
Wilkins's Coomb
Sandle Dairy Fm
Lower Burgate
Folds Fm
Brune's Purlieu
Stone Quarry Bottom
Black Gutter Bottom
New Town
Farnham
Dean Fm
Thorneyd Fm
Wyke Down
Bottlebush Down
Toby's Bottom
Stapleton Fm
South End
Ashley Park Fm
Boulsbury Wood
Lower Court Wood
Fordingbridge
B3078
Minchington
Gussage St Andrew
Canada Fm
Squirrel's Corner
Water Lake Bottom
Cranborne Fm
Boveridge
Boveridge Ho
Ashridge Copse
Sandleheath
Ind Est
Ashford
Alderholt Mill
Sandy Balls
Godshill
Newgrounds
Pitts Wood Inclosure
Coopers Hill
Goldfields Fm
Cashmoor
Gussage Hill
Wyke Fm
Harley Down
Monkton Up Wimborne
Creech Hill Ho
Manor Fm
Burwood
Biddlesgate Fm
Bratch Copse
Hyde Fm
Bull Hill Fm
Alderholt Park
Home Fm
Bus Pk
Criddlestyle
Ditchend Brook
Stuckton
Blissford
Hampton Ridge
Redbrook
Amberwood Inclosure
Cranborne
Ashes Fm
Holwell Fm
Crendell
Lower Daggons
Hart's Fm
Alderholt
Camel Green
Bickton
Frogham
Long Bottom
Latchmore Bottom
Alderhill Inclosure
Sloden Inclosure
Thickthorn Down
Tenantry Down
Manor Garden
Manor Ho
Lower Holwell
Rushmore Fm
Hare Lane
Daggons Road
Charing Cross
Daggons
Midgham Fm
Hyde
Hyde Common
Ogdens
Hungerford
Gussage St Michael
Wimborne St Giles
Lower Fm
Edmondsham Ho
Hare Lane Fm
Cripplestyle
Vale Acre Fm
Cranborne Common
Alderholt Common
Whitefield Bottom
Drove End Fm
Gorley Hill
Dorridge Hill
Furze Hill
Splash Br
Brockington Down
Gussage All Saints
Edmondsham
Smallbridge Fm
Telegraph Plantn
North Gorley
Bleak Hill
Harbridge Green
Ibsley Common
Broomy Lodge
High Corner Inn
Launceston Down
Higher Fm
Sovell Down
Knowlton Church & Earthworks
Brockington Fm
Amen Corner
Deer Park Fm
Dorset Heavy Horse Farm Park
Gotham
Pistle Down
North Fm
North Plumley Fm
Kent Hill
Harbridge
South Gorley
Long Crichel
Knowlton
Bowerswain Fm
Station Road
Sutton Holms
Birches Copse
Westworth Fm
Burrows Fm
Boveridge Heath
Turmer
Whitefield Plantn
Milkham Inclosure
Horse Down
Knowle Hill
Boys Wood
Whitmore Woodlands
B3081
Romford
Stephen's Castle
Verwood
Plumley Wood
Plumley Fm
Lower Turmer
Ibsley
Digden Bottom
Mockbeggar
Linwood
King's Garden
Moor Crichel
Cockroad Fm
Stanbridge Mill Fm
Bagman's Fm
Mount Pleasant Fm
Dewlands Common
Wild Church Bottom
Moon Hill
Harefield Plantn
Home Fm
Somerley Park
Ellingham
Moyles Court
Rockford Common
Appleslade Inclosure
Red Shoot Wood
Roe Inclosure
Buckherd Bottom
Bratley Plain
Little Down
Chetterwood
Horton Inn
North Fm
Woodlands Manor Fm
Woodlands Park
Woodlands Common
Moyles Court
Manswood
Dorset
Haythorne
Redman's Hill
Ebblake
Ringwood Forest
Rockford
Great Linford Inclosure
Pinnick Wood
Handy Cross
Rushton Hill
White Fm
New Town
Chalbury Fm
Horton
Manor Fm
Crab Orchard
Verwood Road
Blashford Lakes
Bigsburn Hill
Highwood
Little Linford Inclosure
Marrowbones Hill
Deans Leaze Fm
Witchampton
Chalbury
Wigbeth
Chalbury Common
Horton Tower
Fern Down Forest
Horton Heath
Clump Hill
Horton Common
Blashford
Goulding's Fm
North Poulner
Linford
Shobley
Ridley Plain
Backley Plain
Dean Fm
Uppington
High Lea Fm
Hinton Martell
Queen's Copse
Holt Wood
Mannington
Crooked Withies
Lower Common
Three Legged Cross
Moors Valley
Ringwood
Poulner
Hangersley
A31
Picket Post
Abbeycroft Down
Hemsworth
Bradford Fm
Clay Hill
Gaunt's Common
Lower Mannington
Little Forest
Lower Row
Ind Est
Bus Cen
Ashley Heath
Ashley
Watchmoor Wood
Picket Hill
Foulford
Picket Plain
Berry Wood
Hinton Mill Fm
Old Lawn Fm
Woodcutts Fm
Gaunt's Ho
Petersham Fm
Rosedale Fm
Higher Row
Holt Heath
Newman's Fm
Trad Est
Woolsbridge
Hightown
Liberty's Owl, Raptor & Reptile Centre
Vereley Hill
Hurn Fm
Hinton Parva
Stanbridge
Holt
Holt Heath
B3072
Moortown
Crow Hill
Burley Street
King Down Fm
Barnsley Fm
God's Blessing Green
White Sheet Plantn
West Moors Plantn
West Moors
Ringwood Road
St Ives
David's Hill
Avon Heath
Crow
Upper Kingston Fm
North Kingston
Castle Hill
Strodgemoor Bottom
Burley Beacon
Burley
Badbury Rings
Crab Fm
Lower Barnsley Fm
Clapgate
Pig Oak
Bothenwood Fm
Broom Hill
Garden Copse Fm
Ameysford
St Leonards
Avon Castle
Lakes Fm
Bagnum Fm
Cranes Moor
Blandford Road
Chilbridge Fm
Furzehill
Grange
Uddens
Uddens Plantn
Grange Estate
A338
Brixey's Fm
Kingston Great Common
Hound Hill
Merry Field Hill
Pilford
A31
Kingston
Wilkins Fm
Sandford
Bisterne Common
Kingston Lacy
Tadden
Deans Grove
Cannon Hill Plantn
Canford Bottom
Stapehill
Bus Pk
Trickett's Cross
Ringwood Raceway
Matcham's Ho
Bisterne
Upper Bisterne Fm
Dur Hill Down
New Barn Fm
Hillbutts
Chilbridge
Barford Fm
Wynne Copse
Minster
Walford Mill
Colehill
Stapehill Abbey
Foxbury Hill
Matcham's Park
Bisterne Manor
Bisley Wood
Whitefield Hill
Whitten Bottom
Holmsley Ridge
White Mill
Pamphill
Ind Est
Ferndown
Fir Grove Fm
Week Fm
B3347
Lower Bisterne Fm
Sturminster Marshall
Cowgrove
Deans Court
Wimborne Minster
Knoll Gardens
Parley Common
East Parley Common
Hurn Forest
Moors River
Shirley Common
North Ripley
Martin's Copse
Thorney Hill
Leigh
Stour
Little Canford
Canford School
Canford Magna
Hampreston
Ham Lane
A348
Dudsbury
West Parley
Avon
Ripley
Henbury
Mill St
Lambs Green
Ashington
Oakley
Sleight
East End
Merley Ho
Merley
Mootown Fm
Longham
Christchurch Road
East Parley
Bournemouth
Pithouse Fm
Sopley Common
Bransgore
Parley
SU
A
B
C
D
E
F
G
H
7
8
9
10
11
18
19
32
46
47

Pitton
West Winterslow
Sombourne
King's Somborne
Ashley
Sparsholt
Horsebridge
Bossington
West Tytherley
East Tytherley
Farley
East Grimstead
West Dean
Alderbury
Whaddon
West Grimstead
Lockerley
East Dean
Butt's Green
Mottisfont
Dunbridge
Kimbridge
Compton Brook
Lower Brook
Stonymarsh
Michelmersh
Braishfield
Pucknall
Standon
Hursley
Timsbury
Awbridge
Kent's Oak
Upper Ratley
Lower Ratley
Carter's Clay
Newtown
Whiteparish
Newton
Belbins
Abbotswood
Cupernham
Romsey
Ampfield
Knapp
Ratlake
Chandler's Ford
Eastleigh
Morgan's Vale
Redlynch
Lover
Woodfalls
North Charford
Hale
Landford
Plaitford
Sherfield English
East Wellow
West Wellow
Canada
Whitenap
North Baddesley
Chilworth
Toothill
Rownhams
Nursling
Ridge
Lee
Wigley
Ower
Nomansland
Bramshaw
Fritham
Brook
Cadnam
Newbridge
Copythorne
Calmore
Testwood
Totton
Netley Marsh
Winsor
Hillstreet
Stonyford
SOUTHAMPTON
Swaythling
Bassett
Portswood
Shirley
Millbrook
Freemantle
Southampton
Eling
Rushington
Woodlands
Ashurst
Marchwood
Pooksgreen
Hounsdown
Upper Canterton
Stoney Cross
Minstead
Newtown
Bartley
Lyndhurst
Emery Down
Bank
Clayhill
Broomy Lodge
Linwood
Burley Lodge
Burley Street
Burley
Bisterne Close
Brockenhurst
Balmerlawn
North Weirs
South Weirs
Setley
Beaulieu
Hatchet Gate
East Boldre
Dibden
Dibden Purlieu
Hythe
Hardley
Holbury
Hill Top
Bucklers Hard
Exbury
Woolston
Itchen
Northam
Ocean Village
Town Quay
Picket Post
Sway
Wootton
Pilley
Bull Hill
Sandy Down
Battramsley
Norleywood
THE NEW FOREST NATIONAL PARK
0 1 2 3 miles
0 1 2 3 4 5 km

33
Winchester
Weeke
Harestock
Winnall
Fulflood
Stanmore
St Giles's Hill
Chilcomb
Oliver's Battery
Compton
Shawford
Otterbourne
Twyford
Owslebury
Colden Common
Morestead
Allbrook
Bishopstoke
Fair Oak
Fisher's Pond
Crowdhill
Horton Heath
Durley
Upham
Lower Upham
Wintershill
Bishop's Waltham
Newtown
Hoe
Dean
Ashton
Northbrook
Swanmore
Upper Swanmore
Soberton
Soberton Heath
Droxford
Brockbridge
Meonstoke
Corhampton
Exton
Warnford
West Meon
East Meon
Langrish
Ramsdean
Privett
Froxfield Green
High Cross
Hinton Ampner
Kilmeston
Beauworth
Bramdean
Brockwood
Cheriton
New Cheriton
New Alresford
Tichborne
Ovington
Avington
Bishop's Sutton
Ropley
Ropley Dean
West Tisted
Monkwood
Easton
Hyde
No Man's Land
Lane End
Baybridge
Blackdown
Hensting
Highbridge
Brambridge
Nob's Crook
Stoke Common
Pylehill
West End
Hedge End
Botley
Curdridge
Waltham Chase
Shirrell Heath
Wickham
Shedfield
Kingsmead
Hoe Gate
Newtown
Hambleden
Denmead
Anthill Common
Hundred Acres
North Boarhunt
Boarhunt
Southwick
Waterlooville
Purbrook
Horndean
Clanfield
Catherington
Lovedean
Cowplain
Havant
Bedhampton
Leigh Park
Widley
Drayton
Farlington
Cosham
Wymering
Paulsgrove
Portchester
Fareham
Titchfield
Titchfield Common
Locks Heath
Warsash
Park Gate
Swanwick
Lower Swanwick
Bursledon
Hound
Netley
Old Netley
Hamble-le-Rice
Sholing
Bitterne
Thornhill
Hook
Newtown
Stubbington
Peel Common
Hill Head
Lee-on-the-Solent
Fleetlands
Bridgemary
Rowner
Hardway
Brockhurst
Elson
Gosport
Alverstoke
Clayhall
Portsmouth
Southsea
Fratton
Milton
Eastney
Baffins
Hilsea
North End
Portsea Island
PORTSMOUTH HARBOUR
LANGSTONE HARBOUR
Portsmouth
Fawley
Ashlett
Calshot
SOUTHAMPTON WATER
SOUTH DOWNS NATIONAL PARK
M3
M27
M275
A3(M)
A272
A32
A27
48
49
20
21
7
8
9
10
11
SU
A
B
C
D
E
F
G
H

49
50
33
21
22
Liphook
Liss
West Liss
East Liss
Liss Forest
Greatham
Longmoor Camp
Empshott
Hawkley
Colemore
Langley
Linchmere
Hammer
Kingsley Green
Fernhurst
Milland
Rake
Hill Brow
Steep
Steep Marsh
Petersfield
Sheet
Langrish
Stroud
Ramsdean
Rogate
Durleighmarsh
Trotton
Chithurst
Iping
Stedham
Woolbeding
Easebourne
Midhurst
Lodsworth
Henley
Lickfold
Lurgashall
Nursted
Buriton
Weston
South Harting
East Harting
Elsted
Treyford
Didling
Bepton
Cocking
Heyshott
Graffham
West Lavington
South Ambersham
Selham
Halfway Bridge
Clanfield
Chalton
Catherington
Horndean
Lovedean
Cowplain
Blendworth
Finchdean
Rowlands Castle
Forestside
Compton
West Marden
Up Marden
North Marden
East Marden
Chilgrove
West Dean
Singleton
Charlton
East Dean
Upwaltham
Stoughton
Walderton
Funtington
West Stoke
Mid Lavant
East Lavant
Westbourne
Woodmancote
West Ashling
East Ashling
Havant
Leigh Park
Bedhampton
Warblington
Emsworth
Southbourne
Hermitage
Nutbourne
Hambrook
Broadbridge
Bosham
Fishbourne
Chichester
Westhampnett
Boxgrove
Tangmere
Oving
Aldingbourne
Westergate
Woodgate
Halnaker
Strettington
Summersdale
Apuldram
Donnington
Hunston
North Mundham
Runcton
Merston
Colworth
Shripney
North Bersted
South Bersted
Bognor Regis
Langstone
North Hayling
Northney
Stoke
Fleet
Hayling Island
West Thorney
Thorney Island
Chidham
West Itchenor
Birdham
Bosham Hoe
Shipton Green
West Wittering
Somerley
Sidlesham
South Mundham
Nyetimber
Rose Green
Aldwick
Pagham
Highleigh
CHICHESTER HARBOUR
LANGSTONE HARBOUR
Hayling Bay
WEST SUSSEX
SOUTH DOWNS NATIONAL PARK
QUEEN ELIZABETH
UPPARK
STANSTED PARK
GOODWOOD
WEALD & DOWNLAND LIVING MUSEUM
WEST DEAN GARDENS
KINGLEY VALE
COWDRAY PARK
HOLLYCOMBE STEAM IN THE COUNTRY
THE SPRING ARTS & HERITAGE CENTRE
MILITARY AVIATION MUSEUM
BOSHAM WALK CRAFT CENTRE
BOXGROVE PRIORY
PALLANT HOUSE
ROMAN PALACE
PILSEY ISLAND
HAYLING SEASIDE RAILWAY
A3
A3(M)
A27
A272
A286
A259
A285
0 1 2 3 miles
0 1 2 3 4 5 km

Loxwood
Plaistow
Ifold
Slinfold
Park Street
Rapkyns
Broadbridge Heath
The Common
Horsham
The Haven
Itchingfield
Northchapel
Mackerel's Common
Roundstreet Common
Five Oaks
Two Mile Ash
Southwater Street
Mannings Heath
Ebernoe
Kirdford
Staples Hill
Great Common
Newpound Common
Barns Green
Monk's Gate
Balls Cross
Wisborough Green
Billingshurst
Southwater
Nuthurst
Strood Green
Parbrook
Brooks Green
Copsale
Coneyhurst
Dragons Green
Maplehurst
Gunter's Bridge
Adversane
Balls Green
Cowfold
Upperton
Tillington
Flathurst
Bedham
Coolham
Green Street
Shipley
Whitehall
West Grinstead
Petworth
Broadford Bridge
North Heath
Gay Street
Broomer's Corner
Byworth
Little Bognor
Codmore Hill
Dial Post
Littleworth
Fittleworth
Stopham
Nutbourne
West Chiltington
Goose Green
Partridge Green
Pulborough
Marehill
Coates
Hardham
Thakeham
Spear Hill
Duncton
West Chiltington Common
Wiggonholt
Coldwaltham
Barlavington
Warminghurst
Bines Green
West End
Ashurst
Smock Alley
Abingworth
Greatham
Watersfield
Ashington
Henfield
Sutton
Bignor
West Burton
Cootham
Storrington
Sullington Warren
Heath Common
Rock
Hole Street
Wiston
Bury
Rackham
Amberley
Sullington
Washington
Small Dole
Houghton
Steyning
Bramber
North Stoke
Upper Beeding
Madehurst
North End
South Stoke
Castle Town
Offham
Burpham
Findon
Botolphs
Slindon
Wepham
Nepcote
Coombes
Warningcamp
Patching
Arundel
Crossbush
High Salvington
Walberton
Binsted
Clapham
Findon Valley
North Lancing
Hammerpot
Poling Corner
Salvington
Lancing
Tortington
Poling
Durrington
Sompting
Barnham
Lyminster
Angmering
Broadwater
North End
Yapton
Ford
Wick
Toddington
Hangleton
East Worthing
South Lancing
Climping
East Kingston
Ferring
Littlehampton
East Preston
Goring-by-Sea
Worthing
Bilsham
Rustington
West Kingston
Kingston Gorse
West Worthing
Flansham
Brookpits
Ancton
Atherington
Elmer
Middleton-on-Sea
Felpham
A272
A24
A29
A283
A27
A259
A280
7
8
9
10
11
A
B
C
D
E
F
G
H

Horsham
Forest Grange
Springfield Fm
Leonard's Forest
Shelley Plain
Forest Row
Tilgate Forest Lodge
Highley Manor
Handcross Park
High Beeches
Wakehurst Place Gardens
Balcombe
Handcross
Nymans Garden
Ardingly
Highbrook
Chelwood Gate
Chelwood Common
Mannings Heath
Ashfold Crossways
Staplefield
Slaugham
Lower Beeding
Monk's Gate
Nuthurst
Warninglid
Crabtree
Slough Green
Whitemans Green
Cuckfield
Lindfield
Haywards Heath
Horsted Keynes
Danehill
Nutley
Bluebell Railway
Borde Hill Garden
Brook Street
Maplehurst
Bolney
Ansty
Chownes Mead
Bolnore
Scayne's Hill
Sheffield Green
Sheffield Park
Fletching
Cowfold
Crosspost
Kent Street
Wivelsfield
Wivelsfield Green
North Chailey
Chailey
Newick
Littleworth
Twineham
Twineham Green
Hickstead
Abbotsford
Burgess Hill
World's End
Wineham
Shermanbury
Partridge Green
Sayers Common
South Street
Spithurst
Ditchling Common
Henfield
West End
Blackstone
Albourne Green
Albourne
Hurstpierpoint
Hurst Wickham
Keymer
Hassocks
Ditchling
Plumpton Green
Plumpton
Chiltington
East Chiltington
Barcombe
Barcombe Cross
Woodmancote
Clayton
Westmeston
Streat
Cooksbridge
Hamsey
Small Dole
Poynings
Pyecombe
Saddlescombe
Fulking
Edburton
Offham
South Malling
Bramber
Upper Beeding
Wallands Park
Lewes
Castle Town
Botolphs
Patcham
Stanmer
Falmer
Kingston near Lewes
Southover
Brighton and Hove
Westdene
Withdean
Coldean
Mile Oak
Hangleton
West Blatchington
Moulsecoomb
Bevendean
Beddingham
Iford
Hove
Preston
Hollingdean
Woodingdean
Rodmell
Southease
Shoreham
Southwick
Kingston by Sea
Fishersgate
Aldrington
Portslade
Portslade-by-Sea
Shoreham-by-Sea
Lancing
South Lancing
Kemp Town
Whitehawk
Ovingdean
Telscombe
Piddinghoe
Brighton
Brighton Marina
Rottingdean
Saltdean
Telscombe Cliffs
Peacehaven
Newhaven
Peacehaven Heights
Harbour Heights
0 1 2 3 miles
0 1 2 3 4 5 km

Crowborough
Wadhurst
Durgates
Mark Cross
Rotherfield
Town Row
Jarvis Brook
Poundfield
Tidebrook
Riseden
Wallcrouch
Ticehurst
Three Leg Cross
Stonegate
Coggins Mill
Mayfield
Five Ashes
Butcher's Cross
Etchingham
Witherenden Hill
Burwash
Burwash Common
Burwash Weald
Broad Oak
Cross in Hand
Heathfield
Old Heathfield
Punnett's Town
Three Cups Corner
Brightling
Dallington
Netherfield
Darwell Hole
Penhurst
Ponts Green
Warbleton
Rushlake Green
Horam
Waldron
Little London
Maynard's Green
Vines Cross
Fairwarp
High Hurstwood
Maresfield
Duddleswell
Uckfield
Buxted
Hadlow Down
Pound Green
Framfield
Blackboys
Ridgewood
Little Horsted
Halland
East Hoathly
Chiddingly
Whitesmith
Gun Hill
Golden Cross
Laughton
Shortgate
Ripe
Chalvington
Upper Dicker
Lower Dicker
Hellingly
Upper Horsebridge
Lower Horsebridge
Hailsham
Magham Down
Herstmonceux
Windmill Hill
Cowbeech
Bodle Street Green
Boreham Street
Ninfield
Hooe
Wartling
Pevensey
Pevensey Levels
Westham
Polegate
Wilmington
Arlington
Berwick
Selmeston
Alciston
Firle
West Firle
Glyndebourne
Alfriston
Litlington
Jevington
Willingdon
Hampden Park
Langney
Stone Cross
Friday Street
St Anthony's Hill
Roselands
Eastbourne
Old Town
Westdean
Exceat
Friston
Seaford
East Blatchington
Bishopstone
Norton
Denton
South Heighton
Pevensey Bay
Norman's Bay
Sovereign Harbour
EAST SUSSEX
A

Flimwell
Hawkhurst
Gill's Green
Beal's Green
Woodsden
Iden Green
Broom Hill
Beacon Hill
West Cross
C M BOOTH COLLECTION OF HISTORIC VEHICLES
Rolvenden
Dingleden
Gun Green
Pipsden
Highgate
High Street
Slip Mill
Sisley Fm
Little Pix Hall Fm
Berner's Hill
Dale Hill
Leg Cross
Seacox Heath
Ringden Fm
Elm Hill Ho
Hensill Ho
Delmonden Ho
Four Throws
The Moor
Field Green
Sponden Ho
Standen Street
Springhill Fm
Kensham Fm
Great Maytham
Merrington Place
Cornhill
Rolvenden Layne
Wassall Ho
Great Job's Cross
Lowden Fm
Hillgate Fm
Friezingham Fm
Britcher Fm
Bulleign
Small Hythe
SMALLHYTHE PLACE
Reading Street
Barrowsland Fm
Appledore Heath
Pashley Manor
PASHLEY MANOR GDNS
Wardsbrook Fm
Chestnutfield Wood
Boarzell Wood
Brookgate Fm
Horns Corner
Hall Ho
Beeches Fm
Alderden Manor
Hope Ho
Sandhurst
Head's Fm
Hexden Fm
Linkhill
Lamberden
KENT & EAST SUSSEX RAILWAY
Mayham Fm
Potman's Heath
Peening Quarter
Plastre Court
Kingsgate Ho
Black Barn
Isle of Oxney
Stone
Ferry Fm
High House Fm
Chapel Bank
Swiftsden
London Barn Fm
Three Gates Fm
Conghurst Fm
Sandhurst Cross
Bourne Fm
Old Place Fm
Heronden Fm
Frogs Hill
Newenden
New Barn
Moon's Green
Maytham Wharf
Wittersham
Wittersham Manor
Wet Level
Methersham Fm
The Stocks
Holman's Fm
Catt Fm
Great Prawls Fm
Stone in Oxney
Cooper's Corner
Stone House Fm
New House Fm
Burgh Wood
Hurst Green
Brickhurst Wood
Boarsney Fm
Elms Fm
Etchingham
ETCHINGHAM
Burgh Hill
Little Iridge Fm
Haremere Hall
Iridge Place
Silver Hill
Clinsett's Fm
South Park
Lower Northlands Fm
Marsh Quarter Fm
Gate Ct
Brickhurst Wood
Rogers Wood
Blackbrook Fm
Ham Green
Tophill Fm
Newbridge Fm
Cliff Fm
Cliff Marsh Fm
Rother Levels
River Rother
Court Fm
March Fm
Underwood's Fm
Ockham Ho
Bugsell Mill Fm
Bush Barn
Beech House Fm
Bourne Fm
Bodiam
BODIAM CASTLE
Bodiam Br
Haiselman's Fm
New Ho
Moat Fm
Higham Ho
Dixter Wood
GREAT DIXTER
Northiam
FARM WORLD
Knelle Wood
Bellhurst Fm
Fontridge Manor
Willard's Hill
Northbridge Street
ROTHER VALLEY RLY CENTRE
ROBERTSBRIDGE
Salehurst
Squibs Fm
Snagshall
Quarry Fm
Ewhurst Green
Sogg's Ho
Sempstead Wood
Tufton Place
Spital Wood
Mill Corner
Glebe Ho
Goteley Manor
Woodgate Ho
Gooseley Fm
Four Oaks
Beckley
New House Fm
Moat Fm
Corkwood Fm
Baron's Grange
Bosney Fm
Boonshill
Flackley Ash
Old House Fm
Forstal Fm
Iden Wood
Iden
Socknersh Manor
Twish Hall
Robertsbridge
Brightling Hall
Glottenham Manor
Mill Wood
Walter's Fm
Park Fm
Fowlbrook Wood
Hollow Wall Fm
Collier's Green
Gate Barn
Watts Hill Fm
Lordine Court
Horns Cross
Clayhill
King's Bank
Stockhurst Fm
Weaver's Fm
Great Stent Fm
Peasmarsh
Mockbeggar
Houghton Green
Oxley's Green
Scalands Wood
Lordship Wood
Handsel Fm
Staplecross
Stockwood Fm
Tilebarn Fm
Gate Fm
Beckley Woods
Woodlands Fm
Peasmarsh Place
Rye Foreign
Lea Fm
Bowler's Town
Saltbarn Fm
Playden
East Guldeford
Mountfield Park Fm
Tunstall Fm
Taylor's Cott
Newpond Fm
Poppinghole Fm
Swaile's Green
The Grange
The Beacon
Maplestone Fm
Gate Cottage
Groves
Partridge Fm
Dew Fm
Clayton Fm
Leasam Ho
Rye
Black House Fm
EAST SUSSEX
Hollingrove
Cackle Street
Hunter's Fm
Darwell Reservoir
Darwell Wood
Baldwin's Fm
Mountfield Court
Mountfield
John's Cross
Vinehall Street
Barnes Wood
Cripp's Corner
Footland Fm
Footland Wood
Brede Green Cott
Chitcombe
Brede High Wood
Beckley Furnace
Conster Manor
Ludley Fm
Hayes Fm
Tillingham Fm
LAMB HOUSE
YPRES TOWER
HERITAGE CENTRE & TOWN MODEL
Darwell Hill
Darwell Hole
Netherfield
Netherfield Court
Crowhurst Fm
Crowhurst Wood
Woodmans Green
Great Sanders School
Jacob's Fm
Streetfield Wood
Powdermill Res
Goatham Green
Hurst Wood
Steephill Wood
Cackle Street
Broad Oak
Broadland Row
Great Sowdens Wood
Newman's Fm
Udimore
Gillshaw Fm
Codborough Fm
Watlands
Rye Harbour
RYE HARBOUR
CAMBER CASTLE
Spray's Fm
Homestead Fm
Eatenden Wood
Burnthouse Wood
Eastlands Fm
Wood's Place
Canadia
Whatlington
Sedlescombe
Brede Barn Fm
Brook Lodge Fm
BREDE STEAM GIANTS
Brede
Pickdick Fm
Little Park Wood
Great Park Wood
Court Fm
Stonelink Fm
Cock Marling
Float Fm
Rye Marsh Fm
WINCHELSEA
Ferry Br
Castle Fm
Nook Beach
Furnace Cott
Atkins Wood
High Wood
Spray's Wood
Netherfield Place
Kingswell Fm
Ashes Wood
Petley Wood
Sedlescombe Street
Pestalozzi Children's Village
Rocks Fm
Crowham Manor
Brede Level
Winchelsea
WINCHELSEA COURT HALL MUSEUM
Crutches Fm
Brook Fm
Penhurst
Creep Wood
Beech Fm
Le Rette Fm
Gate Fm
Bus Pk
Little Park Fm
Beanford Fm
Randall's Fm
Doleham Fm
Lidham Hill
Stocks Fm
Broad Street
Icklesham
Wickham Manor
Winchelsea Beach
Court Lodge
Tower Ho
Battle
Coarsebarn Fm
Marley Ho
Battle Barn Fm
Great Buckhurst Fm
Platnix Fm
Guestling Thorn
Manor Fm
Ashburnham Forge
Beechdown Wood
BATTLE ABBEY
1066
Great Wood
Kent Street
Yew Tree Ho
Oak Wood
Copshall
Knockbridge Fm
Elms Fm
Pett Level
New Buildings Fm
Steven's Crouch
Tellis Coppice
Tower Hill
Starr's Green
Branshill Fm
Norton's Fm
Ireland's Fm
Whiteland Wood
Westfield
Pannel
Great Park Fm
Telham
Little Hemingfold Fm
Claremont School
Lankhurst Fm
Rodger's Fm
Three Oaks
Pannel Fm
Ashburnham Place
Agmerhurst Ho
Parkgate Manor
Peppering Eye Fm
Loose Fm
Beauport Park
Eastlands Fm
Fraysland Fm
Church Fm
Guestling Wood
French Court Fm
Pett
Marlpits
Catsfield
Catsfield Manor
Millers Fm
Telham Hill
Pye's Fm
Telham Place
Breadsell Fm
Maplehurst Wood
Hole Fm
Coghurst Hall
HASTINGS
Guestling Green
New Barn Fm
Lunsford
Coombe Hill Fm
Ninfield
Catsfield Stream
FORE WOOD RSPB
CROWHURST
Baldslow
Bachelor's Bump
Friar's Hill
The Hall
Mallydams Wood
Cherry Garden Fm
Wakehams Fm
Cliff End
Hazard's Green
Lower Street
Catsfield Place
Crowhurst
Hurst Wood
Henley's Down
Nashes Fm
Park Fm
Ind Est
Hollington
Holmhurst St Mary
Hazel Ct
THE RIDGE
Ivy Ho
St Helen's
Ore
Fairlight
Stonelynk Fm
Fairlight Cove
Wet Wood
Pashley Fm
Sprays Wood
Watermill
Hill House Fm
Green Street
Lower Wilting Fm
Bus Pk
Ind Pk
Silverhill Park
St Helen's Wood
Broomsgrove
Clive Vale
Fairlight Pl
HASTINGS
Fire Hills
Hooe Common
Russell's Green
Potmans Place
Lunsford's Cross
Park Wood
Byne's Fm
Adam's Fm
Upper Wilting Fm
Silverhill
Bohemia
Blacklands
Belmont
Fairlight Glen
Covehurst Bay
Thorne Fm
Cole Wood
Acton's Fm
COMBE VALLEY COUNTRYSIDE PARK
Harley Shute
West Hill
ST CLEMENTS CAVE
Ecclesbourne Glen
Broad Green Fm
Whydown
Highwoods
The Highlands
Preston Hall
Worsham Fm
ST LEONARDS WARRIOR SQ
SHIPWRECK HERITAGE CENTRE
Gotham
Hooe
Sidley
Bulverhythe
WEST ST LEONARDS
BLUE REEF AQUARIUM
Hastings
Old Town
New Lodge Fm
Glenleigh Park
Old Town
Pebsham
West Marina
St Leonards
Little Common
KING OFFA WAY
Glyne Gap
Galley Hill
Barnhorne Manor
Cooden
COLLINGTON
COODEN DRIVE
MUS
BEXHILL
My Lord's Rock
Hooe Level
DE LA WARR PAVILION
Bexhill
COODEN BEACH
Norman's Bay
TQ
00
70
0 1 2 3 miles
0 1 2 3 4 5 km
A B C D E F G H
1 2 3 4 5 6
37 53 54

A
B
C
D
E
F
G
H
7
8
9
10
11
TR
20
30
00
54
55
Park Hill
Smith's Fm
Higham Fm
Thrift Cott
Bridge Fm
Johnson's Corner
Wey Street Fm
Will's Fm
Brooker Fm
Newchurch
Gammon's Fm
Forty Acre Cott
Burmarsh
Donkey Street
HORNE'S PLACE CHAPEL
The Dowels
Stockbridge Ho
Poplar Ho
Norwood Fm
Manor Ho
New Barn Fm
Chapel Cottage Fm
Orgarswick Fm
HYTHE ROAD
Dymchurch Wall
B2080
APPLEDORE
Bridge Fm
Ham Fm
Snave
R o m n e y
Lodgeland Fm
Willow Fm
Pickney Bush Fm
Blackmanstone Br
Sutton Fm
A259
DYMCHURCH MARTELLO TOWER
DYMCHURCH
Dymchurch
Whitehall Fm
Hope Fm
Brenzett Green
New House Fm
Moat Ho
M a r s h
Selinge Fm
ROMNEY, HYTHE & DYMCHURCH RAILWAY
Snargate
Poplar Fm
Spring Fm
North Fording Bungalow
St Mary in the Marsh
ST MARY'S BAY
St Mary's Bay
Priory Fm
A2070
Ivychurch
Melon Fm
Brodnyx
ROMNEY WARREN
Highknock Channel
CANAL
Fairfield Court
Brenzett Place
AERONAUTICAL MUSEUM
Blue House Fm
Honeychild Manor
Becket Barn Fm
Brenzett
Yoakes Court Fm
Beechcroft Fm
ROMNEY WARREN HALT
Fairfield
Brattle Ho
Old Hall Fm
Rheewall Fm
Sewer
ROMNEY MARSH
ROMNEY MARSH VISITOR CENTRE
DYMCHURCH ROAD
Poplar Hall
Bush Fm
New
Hope Fm
Warren Fm
Dean Court
A259
Brookland
Sycamore Fm
Old Romney
New Romney
NEW ROMNEY
Phoenix Caisson
B2071
New Buildings Fm
Whitehouse Fm
Hook Ho
Coldharbour Fm
Court Lodge
LYDD ROAD
Hammonds Corner
Littlestone-on-Sea
White Kemp Sewer
Blue House Fm
ROMNEY ROAD
Kemp's Hill
Romney Sands
GULDEFORD LANE
Old Cheyne Court
Midley Cotts
Hawthorn Corner
Coldicott Fm
Belgar Fm
Offen's Fm
W a l l a n d
Guldeford Lane Corner
Baynham Fm
Westbrook Fm
B2075
Footway Fm
Greatstone-on-Sea
Newland Fm
M a r s h
Kent Ditch
Little Cheyne Court
Little Scotney
Westbroke Ho
Jack's Court
ROMNEY SANDS
Lydd (London Ashford)
Barn Fm
Lydd
Red Ho
Pigwell
Lade
Scotney Court
Denge Marsh
Lydd-on-Sea
LYDD INTERNATIONAL RACEWAY
DUNGENESS
RSPB
Halfway Bush
Point Fm
Boulderwall Fm
Camber
Jury's Gap
Danger area
West Ripe
Holmstone
Lydd Ranges
Manor Fm
DUNGENESS
Broomhill Level
Danger area
Open Pits
Camber Sands
South Brooks
Brickwall Fm
Broomhill Sands
Danger area
RYE BAY
Dungeness Power Sta
DUNGENESS
THE OLD LIGHTHOUSE
Dungeness

56
56
SS
Lundy
Hen & Chickens
Seals' Rock
North West Pt
North East Pt
Gannets' Rock
Gannets' Bay
St James's Stone
Tibbetts Hill 138
LUNDY MARINE NATURE RESERVE
Tibbett's Pt
Jenny's Cove
Dead Cow Pt
Ackland's Moor 142
Lundy Roads
BIDEFORD (APRIL-OCT)
ILFRACOMBE (APRIL-OCT)
Halftide Rock
Beacon Hill
Castle Hill
Rat Island
Surf Pt
South West Pt
LUNDY (APRIL-OCT)
Capstone Pt
Samson's Bay
Water Mouth
WATERMOUTH CASTLE
Rawn's Rocks
Blackstone Pt
Elwill Bay
Trentishoe
Ilfracombe
Hele Bay
Hele
HELE CORN MILL
Hole Fm
Goosewell
Little Hangman 218
Gt Hangman 318
Hangman Pt
Holdstone Down 349
Trentishoe Down
Lester Cliff
Girt Fm
Girt Down
Holdstone Fm
Trentishoe Manor
Walner Fm
Heddon
Shag Pt
Flat Pt
Bull Pt
Pensport Rock
Lee Bay
MUSEUM
Chambercombe
CHAMBERCOMBE MANOR
Kitstone Hill
Berrynarbor
Lee
NORTH DEVON
Combe Martin
Verwill Fm
Tattiscombe Fm
Stony Corner
Knap Down Fm
Lee
Lincombe
Higher Slade
Rockham Bay
North Morte Fm
Higher Warcombe
Whitestone
Shaftsboro Fm
Campscott Fm
Slade Resrs
Lower Slade
Warmscombe Fm
Sterridge
Ruggaton Fm
Stoneditch Hill
Nutcombe Fm
Westleigh
Truckham Fm
Dean
Morte Pt
Mortehoe
Borough Cross
Oakridge Fm
Two Pots
Bowden Fm
Smython Fm
Henstridge
WILDLIFE & DINOSAUR PARK
Long Lane
Cowley Wood
Grunta Pool
Little Shelfin Fm
Ind Est
A3123
Ettiford Fm
Hempster Fm
River Umber
South Ley
Kentisbury
Higher Week Fm
Kentisbury Down
Woolacombe
Mill Rock
Manor Fm
Trimstone
Cheglinch
Hore Down Fm
Stapleton Fm
Berry Down
Berry Down Cross
Bugford
Stonecombe
Preston Ho
Bridwick Fm
Morte Bay
Ossaborough
Willingcott
Outer Narracott Fm
Ivycott
Roadway
Bradwell
Dean
Dean Cross
Hillcrest Fm
Cleave Fm
Highlands Fm
Patchole
Northcote Fm
Kentisbury Ford
Halls Cross
Wistlandpound Reservoir
Woolacombe Sand
Black Rock
Centery Fm
Higher Aylescott
Bittadon
Collacott Fm
Wigmore Fm
Ford Fm
Dingles Fm
Clifton
East Down
Arlington Beccott
Hallsdown Fm
Putsborough Sand
Pickwell Down
Spreacombe Manor
North Downs
West Down
Fullabrook
Burland Fm
Baggy Pt
SOUTH WEST COAST PATH
Pickwell
Castle Street Fm
Vention
Putsborough
Buckland Down
Stoneyard Wood
Fullabrook Down
Little Silver
Hewish Down
Bowden Corner
Churchill
Churchill Down
Arlington
Arlington Court
ARLINGTON COURT
Huckham Fm
Besshill Fm
Croyde Bay
Georgeham
North Buckland
Winsham Down Ho
Halsinger Down
Metcombe Down
Swindon Down
Whitefield Down
Okewill Cross
Garman's Down
Deerpark Wood
White Cawsey
Tidicombe Fm
Rye Park
Ora Hill
Croyde
Forda
Darracott
Nethercott
Upcott
Beara Down
Patsford
Gipsy Corner
Milltown
Viveham Fm
Plaistow Barton
Woolley Wood
South Woolley Fm
Loxhore
Cross
South Hole Fm
Incledon Fm
Halsinger
Winsham
Middle Marwood
Whiddon
Crockers
Higher Muddiford
Muddiford
The Warren
Chilbridge Fm
Loxhore Cott
CROYDE ROAD
SAUNTON ROAD
B3231
Buckland Manor
Lobb
Knowle
Boode
Beara
Marwood
Guineaford
Plaistow Mill
Shirwell Cross
Shirwell
Lower Loxhore
Saunton
Braunton
Pippacott
Whitehall
MARWOOD HILL
Kingsheanton
Town Fm
Sandy Lane Fm
Shop Cen
Luscott Barton
Waterlake
Prixford
BROOMHILL SCULPTURE GARDENS
Varley Fm
South Hill
Youlston Wood
Saunton Sands
Braunton Down
Knowl Water
Mainstone
Springfield Cross
Waytown Fm
Sepscott Fm
Bratton Cross
Heanton Punchardon
West Ashford
SHIRWELL ROAD
Brightlycott Fm
Chelfham
Horridge
Birch
Velator
Wrafton
A361
Ashford
Upcott Ho
Burridge
Hakeford
Stoke Rivers
Braunton Burrows
Braunton Marsh
Chivenor
Chivenor
Penhill Pt
Bradiford
Raleigh
Pitt Fm
Kingdon's Gardens
Snapper
Northleigh
Goodleigh
Middle Dean Fm
Horsey Island
Allen's Rock
Saltpill Duck Pond
Pilton
Pottington
River Yeo
Derby
Waytown
Youlden Ho
Hutcherton Down
Airy Pt
Danger area
Penhill
Ind Est
ST ANNE'S CHAPEL & MUSEUM
Barnstaple
MUSEUM OF BARNSTAPLE & NORTH DEVON
Coombe Fm
Willesleigh Fm
Dean Head
Gunn
Stone Cross
River Taw
Lower Yelland
Muddlebridge
BICKINGTON ROAD
Sticklepath
A3125
BARNSTAPLE
Bus Pk
Westacott
Birch
Accott
Broad Sands
Yelland
B3233
Fremington
Combrew
Bickington
Ind Est
Newport
Portmor
East Acland
Sandick
Crow Pt
Brake Plantns
Brynsworthy
Lake
P&R
A361
Landkey
Harford
Sandick Cross
Crow Rock
Instow Sands
N DEVON MARITIME MUSEUM
Bickleton
Myrtle Cott
A39
Roundswell
Rumsam
Landkey Newland
Swimbridge Newland
Hurscott
Yeoland Ho
Yarnacott
Riverton
Sandymere
NORTHAM BURROWS
Appledore
The Quay
Worlington
Collacott Fm
Upcott Fm
Hollamoor Clump
Bishops Tawton
Instow
Fullingcott Fm
SS
Diddywell
24
Huish
St John's Chapel
Eastacombe
Tawstock
25
Swimbridge
Kerscott
Huish Moor
Stonyland
A377
Hannaford
Bydown Ho
High Down
TAPELEY PARK GARDENS
Coombe Fm
Trayhill
Westleigh
Rushcott Fm
Prospect Corner
Uppacott
Downrew Ho
Horswell Fm
Hangman's Hill
Lane End Fm
Towner Fm
Northam
Holmacott
Eastleigh Manor
Halmpstone Manor
Silford
Horwood
0 1 2 3 miles
0 1 2 3 4 5 km

57
42
26
25
Foreland Pt
Countisbury Cove
Lynton
CLIFF RLY
Countisbury
LYN & EXMOOR MUSEUM
Lynmouth
Lynbridge
Wind Hill
Kipscombe Hill 343
Old Burrow Hill 345
Sugarloaf Hill
Woody Bay
Wringcliff Bay
Lee Bay
Crock Pt
Martinhoe
Dean
Caffyns Fm
WATERSMEET HOUSE
Wilsham
Coombe Fm
Leeford
Ashton Fm
Brendon
Malmsmead
Yenworthy Fm
Culbone Wood
Broomstreet Fm
CULBONE CHURCH
Gore Pt
Worthy
Porlock Bay
Hurlstone Pt
Selworthy Sand
Bossington
EXMOOR OWL & HAWK CENTRE
Kemacott
Martinhoe Common
East Ilkerton
Barbrook
West Lyn
Hillsford Br
Tippacott
Fellingscott
Oare
North Common
Lillycombe Ho
Yarner Fm
Porlock Weir
West Porlock
Porlockford
Lynch
Allerford
LYNTON & BARNSTAPLE RAILWAY
WOODY BAY
Killington
Stock Castle
Combe Park Ho
Bridge Ball
Rockford
Scob Hill
Slocombeslade
Cloud Fm
Oareford
Robber's Br
Westcott Brake
Porlock
Doverhay
KILLINGTON LANE
Beacon Castle
Bodley
Martinhoe Cross
West Ilkerton
Cheriton
Stock Common
Roborough Castle
Shilstone Hill 405
Tippacott Ridge
Malmsmead Hill 389
Great Black Hill
Weirwood Common
Porlock Common
Shillett Wood
HAWKCOMBE WOODS
Homebush Wood
Hawk Combe
Glen Lodge
Horner
Brandish Street
West Luccombe
Parracombe
Churchtown
Ilkerton Ridge
Shallowford
Furzehill
Dry Br
Withycombe Ridge
Stowey Ridge
Mill Hill
Doone Country
Parracombe Common
South Common
Cannon Hill
Furzehill Common
Cheriton Ridge
Pig Hill
Brendon Common 412
Black Hill
Tarr Ball Hill
Horner Wood
Rowley Down
Butter Hill
Saddle Gate
Exmoor
Hoaroak
Hoccombe Water
Badgworthy Hill
Manor Allotment
Kittuck Meads
Madacombe
Babe Hill
Luccombe Hill
Blackmoor Gate
Thorn Hill
Forest
Brendon Two Gates
Hoar Tor
Larkbarrow
Alderman's Barrow 447
Lucott Cross 465
The Mound 373
THE DUNKERY & HORNER WOOD
Robin How 428
Challacombe Common
Winaway
Hoaroak Hill
Exe Plain
Trout Hill
East Pinford
Swap Hill
Wilmersham Common
Higher Down
Challacombe Res
Pinkery Pond
The Chains 487
Blackpitts Gate
Swap Hill 444
Almsworthy Common
Dunkery Beacon 519
Friendship Fm
Stowford
Yelland Cross
Barton Gate
Swincombe
North Regis 417
Pinkery Fm
PINKERY CENTRE FOR OUTDOOR LEARNING
EXMOOR NATIONAL PARK
Warren Fm
Exford Common
Challacombe
NORTH LANE
Barton Town
Challacombe Mill
Old Close Bottom
Prayway Head
River Exe
Ashcombe Bottom
Hoar Moor
Codsend Moors
Dunkery Gate 387
Duredon Fm
Pitsworthy Fm
River Quarme
Leeham Ford Br
Shoulsbarrow Fm
Weirs Combe
Sloley Stone
Clovenrocks Br
Hill Fm
Kitnor Heath
Higher Ho
Codsend
Gallon Ho
Higher Riscombe Fm
Knightacott
Northland Corner
Wallover Down
Cornham Fm
Barle Water
Simonsbath
Honeymead Fm
Pennycombe Water
Edgcott
Coombe Fm
Larcombe Fm
Luckwell Bridge
Fullaford Down
Winstitchen Fm
White Water
Ashott Barton
Ley
Exford
CHURCH HILL
EXFORD
Horsecombe Fm
Leworthy
Rockley Fm
Bray Common
Squallacombe
Thornemead
White Cross
Chibbet Post
Little Bray Cross
Horcombe
Blue Gate
SOMERSET
Staddon Hill
Torre Fm
Hoe Fm
Berry Hill
Silkwood Top
North Court
Buckworthy
Emmett's Grange
Pickedstones
Staddon Fm
Wort Wood
Horsen Fm
Blackland Fm
Road Hill
Haxton Down
Down Fm
East Down Wood
Whitefield Down
Five Barrows Cross
Kinsford Gate
Wintershead Fm
Great Ferny Ball
Hillway Fm
ROOM HILL ROAD
Nethercote
Kemps
Benton
Mockham Down Gate
Lydcott Hall
Kinsford Water
Landacre Br
Withypool
Gravel Pit Cross
Long Holcombe
Horsen Hill 443
Lydcott
Mockham Down
Little Bray
Cross Gate
Holewater
Beara Hill Head
Poltimore Arms (PH)
Lydlicombe Bottom
Fyldon Common
Withycombe
Waterhouse Fm
Comer's Gate
Winn Brook
Barnacott Fm
Brayfordhill
Sherdon Fm
Woolcombe Allot
Withypool Common
Withypool Hill 398
Winsford Hill 426
Burrow Wood
Winsford
Edbrooke Ho
Kimbland Fm
Brayford
Hall
Yarde Gate Fm
North Radworthy
Woolcombe Fm
North Batsom
Great Bradley
West Howe
Slade Fm
High Bray
Fyldon
Shortacombe
Porchester's Post 388
The Allotment
Yellowcombe
Goodwells Head
The Old Rectory
Higher Molland
Molland Cross
Bentwichen
Long Wood
Darlick Moors
Withypool Cross
Halscombe Allot
West Water
Spire Cross
Charles
Popham
North Heasley
South Radworthy
Longstone Wells
Sportsman's Inn (PH)
Willingford Fm
Westwater
Westwater Allot
Liscombe
Summerway
Hudley Mill
Upcott Fm
Newtown Br
Hunnivins Fm
Radworthy Down
Tabor Hill
North Molton Ridge
Litton Water
Twitchen Ridge
Danes Brook
Hawkridge Plain
Hill Fm
TARR STEPS WOODLAND
Tarr Fm
Parsonage Fm
TARR STEPS
Draydon Knap
Little River
Spire
Old Ashway
Elwell
West Buckland School
East Buckland
Charles Bottom
Heasley Mill
Bampfylde Hill
Balls Cross
Wheatclose Cross
Moorhouse Ridge
Ashway Side
Mounsey Hill 374
326
South Hill
Macmillan Way West
South Wood
Barcombe Down
Holywell Cross
Hawkridge Common
Cloggs Fm
West Buckland
Huxtable Fm
Steep Head
Holywell Res
Twitchen Mill
Twitchen
Lyshwell Fm
Shircombe Fm
Hawkridge
Hawkridge Ridge
Hollowcombe
Brayley Hill
Brinsworthy
Molland Common
Litchadon Fm
High Bullen Fm
Millbrook
Pulham Fm
Cussacombe Gate
Park
A361
Leary Moors
Wheatlands Fm
West Park
North Molton
Pitt Fm
Pulsworthy Fm
Kerswell Fm
West Anstey Common
Whiterocks Down
Draydon Fm
Mounsey Castle
Marsh Hill Ho
Heddon
Oxford Down
Coombe
Burcombe
Sannacott Fm
Luckworthy
Smallacombe
Molland
Champson
Bickingcott
Challowford
Bremridge Wood
Snurridge
South Cockerham
Waterbrooks Fm
Limeslake Fm
River Mole
Stone
Woodland Fm
West
Two Moor Ways
Five Cross Ways
Old Berry Fm
Dulverton
Filleigh
A39
A399
B3358
B3223
B3224
SS
90
60
30
7
8
9
10
11
A
B
C
D
E
F
G
H

42
BRISTOL CHANNEL
58
41
26
27
Hurlstone Pt
Selworthy Sand
Selworthy Beacon 308
SOUTH WEST COAST PATH
Greenaleigh Pt
Bossington
EXMOOR OWL & HAWK CENTRE
Lynch
Memorial Hut
Porlock
Allerford
Selworthy
Wydon Fm
Woodcombe
Minehead
Madbrain Sands
Warren Pt
Higher Town
BUTLINS
Doverhay
Brandish Street
Holnicote
Hindon Fm
Bratton
Glen Lodge
West Luccombe
Horner
Blackford
Tivington
Troytes Fm
Periton
HOPCOTT ROAD
Alcombe
Great Headon Plantn
Dunster Beach
Ley Hill 317
Horner Wood
Luccombe
Knowle Top
Tivington Knowle
Periton Hill 295
Staunton Plantn
Penny Hill
Ellicombe
Marsh Street
Blue Anchor Bay
Quantock's Head
Huntscott
Wootton Courtenay
MINEHEAD
Knowle Hill
DOLL MUSEUM
Dunster
Luccombe Hill
Brockwell
DUNKERY VINEYARD
Aville Fm
DUNSTER WATERMILL
DUNSTER CASTLE GARDENS
Blue Anchor
HOME FARM
EASTBURY ROAD
Warren Bay
Watchet
St Audrie's Bay
Blue Ben
Black Rock
East Quantoxhead
Parkhouse Fm
Robin How 428
Cowbridge
Whits Wood
Carhampton
Marshwood Fm
Chapel Cleeve
Old Cleeve
Bye Fm
Kentsford Fm
St Decumans
Five Bells
Doniford
Rydon Fm
The Home Fm
Perry Fm
Higher Street
Townsend Fm
Kilve Court
Fairgarden Fm
Well Fm
Burrow
Timberscombe
Hur Wood
Broadwood Fm
Biddicott Fm
WEST SOMERSET RAILWAY
RAILWAY MUS
TROPIQUARIA ANIMAL & ADVENTURE PARK
Williton
Egrove Fm
West Quantoxhead
Amitabha Buddhist Centre
Pardlestone Fm
Dunkery Beacon 519
Elsworthy
Bickham
Aller Hill
Withycombe
Bilbrook
High Bridge
Wibble Fm
Staple
West Hill Beacon Hill 310
Pardlestone Hill
Dunkery Gate 387
Pitt Br
Croydon Ho
Gupworthy Fm
Combe Fm
Washford
CLEEVE ABBEY
Sampford Brett
Torweston Fm
Lower Weacombe
Weacombe
Longstone Hill
West Harwood Fm
Croydon Hill
Black Hill 353
Hungerford
Torre
Bicknoller Post
Ford Fm
Oaktrow Wood
EXMOOR
365
Lodge Fm
CIDER FARM
Fair Cross
Orchard Wyndham
Woolston
Bicknoller
Cutcombe
Stowey Fm
Well
381
Rodhuish Common
Rodhuish
Escott Fm
Beggearn Huish
Black Down Wood
Capton
Quantock Moor Fm
Chilcombe
Thorncombe Hill
NATIONAL PARK
Golsoncott
Lower Roadwater
Yarde
Croydon Hall
Wheddon Cross
Couple Cross
Nurcott Fm
Churchtown
Monkham Hill
Slowley Wood
Slowley Fm
Roadwater
Woodford
Yellow Wood Fm
Vellow
Newton
Thorncombe Ho
Luckwell Bridge
Kersham Hill 361
Luxborough
Kingsbridge
Tacker Street
Nettlecombe Court
Rowdon Fm
Escott Wayshill
Kingswood
Halsway Manor
Black Hill 358
Hoe Fm
Triscombe Fm
White Moor
Washford River
Monksilver
Coombe Cross
Catford Cott
Halsway
Crowcombe Park
SOMERSET
Honeywell Ho
Lype Hill 423
Colly Hill
Newcombe Fm
Langridge Wood
Woodadvent Fm
Birchanger Fm
Stogumber
Crowcombe Court
Crowcombe
Pooltown
Kemps
Great Cott
Quarme Hill 390
B3224
Chargot Ho
Langham Fm
Court Fm
Chapman's Fm
Stamborough
Leighland Chapel
Chidgley
Sticklepath
Bird's Hill
Wood Fm
Water Fm
Lawford
THE CHURCH HOUSE
South Quarme Fm
South Quarme Allotment
Kennisham Hill
Chargot Wood
Hook Hill Fm
Colton Fm
Pond Wood
Ashbeer
Leigh Cott
Lower Vexford
Withycombe
Luckyard Fm
Stone Lodge
Goosemoor
Langham Hill
Brendon Hills
Treborough Common
Treborough
Higher Vexford
Trisco
Flaxpool
Gupworthy
WITHIEL HILL
Elworthy
Heathfield Fm
Exton Hill 348
Weekfield Fm
Sminhays Corner
Eastern Wood
Hartrow Manor
Willett Ho
Rexton Fm
Winsford
Burrow Wood
Coppleham
Edbrooke Ho
West Howetown
Kendle Fm
Leigh Fm
Ford Fm
Eastcott Fm
Burrow Fm
Brendon Hill
Raleigh's Cross Inn
Holcombe Water Fm
Colwell Fm
Coleford Water
Crowcombe Heathfield
Rich's Holford
The Allotment
Yellowcombe
Exton
Withiel Fm
Brendon Hill Fm
Tone Fm
Tripp Bottom
Fryan Fm
Rook's Nest
Willett Hill
Willett
Coleford Fm
New Marsh
Coursley
Summerway
Combeshead Fm
Bridgetown
Howetown Fm
Hollam Fm
King's Brompton Fm
Blagdon Hill
Withiel Florey
Swansea Fm
Middle Bottom
Tripp Fm
Broadway Head Fm
Emble Fm
Whitmoor Fm
Westowe
Nethercott
Draydon Knap
Kings Brompton Forest
Cophole Fm
Middleton Court
Week Fm
Battin's Fm
Lydeard St Lawrence
Combe Wood
326
South Hill
Higher Foxhanger Fm
Brompton Regis
Rugg's Fm
East Withy Fm
Hele Fm
Brompton Ralph
Tolland
East Town
Broford Fm
Kents Fm
Hill Fm
Ditch Fm
Brown Fm
Clatworthy Reservoir
Bowden Fm
Manor Fm
Coortland Ho
Handy Cross
Halscombe Fm
Chilly Bridge
Daws Fm
Redcross Fm
Venne Cott
Rowes Fm
Clatworthy
Harwood Fm
Middle Stone Fm
Pitsford Hill
Pyleigh
Harewood Fm
Wimbleball Lake Res
West Withy Fm
White's Fm
Cording's Fm
Combe Bottom
Tarr
West Leigh
Pitpear Fm
316 Court
Lyncombe Fm
Perry Fm
Parsonage Fm
Moor Mill Fm
Homelea Fm
Ash Wood
SS
Draydon Fm
Hartford Bottom
Upton Fm
Hayne Fm
Bittescombe Manor
Coombe Fm
Huish Champflower
Whitefield
Hoccombe
Chapel Leigh
Mounsey Castle
West Hill Wood
Burrow Hill Fm
Northway
Sholford Fm
Shute Fm
Huish Moor
Langley
Langley Marsh
Brewers Fm
Upton
Maundown
Ford
Pond Close
Haddon Fm
Godhams Fm
Lotley Fm
Washbattle Br
Maundown Hill
Northgate
Croford Ho
Fitzhead
Halse
Old Berry Fm
Chapple Fm
Oxenleaze
Heydon Hill
Bulland
Challick
Castle
Dean Fm
Dulverton
Surridge Fm
Blindwell
B3222 Hele Br
Cross
0 1 2 3 miles
0 1 2 3 4 5 km

7
8
9
Weston-super-Mare
Tower Rock
Rudder Rock
Calf Rock
Steep Holm
59
Weston Bay
Clarence Park
Uphill
Uphill Manor
Oldmixon
Hutton
Locking
Elborough
Hillend
Banwell
Stonebridge
Knightcott
Banwell Castle
Wolvershill Manor
Woolvers Hill
Drove Fm
West End Fm
Lower Canada
Upper Canada
Hay Wood
Christon Plantn
Yarberry
Barleycombe Lodge
Bleadon Hill
Bleadon
Coombe Fm
Purn
Hellenge Hill
Hamwood
Wonderstone
Shiplate
South Hill
Christon
Oakes Fm
Barton
Loxton Hill
Shiplett House Fm
Loxton
Webbington
Crook Peak
Compton Bishop
Wavering Down
Fiddler's Pt
Brean Down
Black Pt
WALBOROUGH
The Grange
Brean Fm
Warren Fm
Brean
Diamond Fm
Ham Fm
Berrow Flats
North Farm Ho
Rhynemoor Fm
River Axe
Batch
Tarr's Fm
Wick Fm
Holm Fm
ANIMAL FARM ADVENTURE PARK
Northam Fm
BREAN THEME PARK
Lympsham
Poplar Fm
Eastertown
North Yeo Fm
Crab Hole
Rackley
Dunnett Fm
Cross
Lower Weare
Ford Common
Pitland Rhyne
East Rhyne
Wick
Lower Fm
Edingworth
Biddisham
Green Fm
44
A38
Berrow Manor
Bridge Fm
Sedgemoor Services
Weare
BRIDGWATER BAY
BRENT ROAD
Ham
BURTON ROW
Burton Row Fm
East Brent
Tarnock
Rooks Bridge
Badgworth
Badgworth Court
Berrow
Brent Knoll
Lake Ho
Stone Allerton
Allerton Moor
Chapel Allerton
New Homestead Fm
White Cross
Edithmead
Vole Fm
Vole
Plaish Fm
Ashton
Binham Moor
Burnham-on-Sea
Middle Burnham
Burnham Level
Somerset Court
Northwick
Wellfield Ho
Perry Fm
Blackford Moor
West Stoughton
Worston Ho
Dutch Court Fm
Mark Causeway
Mark
Sterl Island
Stert Flats
Stert Pt
Fenning Island
BRIDGWATER BAY
Highbridge
Alstone
HIGHBRIDGE & BURNHAM
Magnolia Ho
Walrow
MARK CAUSEWAY
Yarrow
Southwick
Totney Fm
Stook Ho
Little Moor
Westham
Watchfield
Southwick Fm
Lands End Fm
Hinkley Point Power Station
ENGLAND COAST PATH
Hinkley Point C under construction
Steart
Stockland Reach
Brent Fm
Huntspill
Malthouse Fm
Bason Bridge
Mark Moor
Stolford
Catsford Common
Whitewick Fm
Wall Common
Marsh Fm
The Island
Huntspill Level
SECRET WORLD WILDLIFE RESCUE
Hackness
East Huntspill
Cripp's Fm
Cripps River
Liberty Fm
Tealham Moor
River Brue
Park Fm
Lilstock
Wick Moor
Little Dowden's Fm
Chalcott Fm
Knighton
Burton
Shurton
Wick
Idson Fm
Woolstone Fm
WWT STEART MARSHES NATURE RESERVE
Bleak Br
West Huntspill
Withy Grove Fm
HUNTSPILL RIVER
Cote
Cote Corner
River Bridge
Burtle Hill
Kilton
Gunter's Grove
Cole Pool
Farringdon Hill Fm
Cock Fm
Stockland Bristol
Stockland Manor
Otterhampton
Dodds Fm
Stretcholt
Black Ditch
Withy Fm
Gold Corner
Chilton Moor
Hurst Fm
Burtle
Kilve
Higher Hill Fm
Great Plantn
Water Fm
Stogursey
Steyning Manor
Hill Ho
Pawlett
Huntspill River
Woolavington Level
South Drain
Stringston
Cockwood
Hill Fm
Gaunt's Fm
Pawlett Hams
Pawlett Hill
North Fm
Puriton Level
Catcott
Moor House Fm
Plud Fm
Fairfield Wood
Monkton Fm
Stockland Lovell Manor
Wrenmore Fm
Combwich
Combwich Reach
River Parrett
Dyche
Barnsworthy Fm
Holford
Durborough Fm
Stogursey Brook
Beere Manor Fm
Coultings
Putnell Fm
Hallicks Fm
Walpole
Puriton
Woolavington
Edington Heath
CATCOTT
Catcott Heath
Woodlands
Dodington
Peadon Fm
Perry Mill Fm
Roobies Fm
Pinnacle Hill
Bonson
Horn Hill
Rodway Fm
Down End
Dunball
Kings Sedgemoor Drain
Knowle Hall
Nidons
Woodlands Hill
Shervage Wood
Nether Stowey
Fiddington
Edbrook
Cannington Park
Dairy House Fm
Cossington
Grange
Chilton Polden
Edington
Catcott
Duke's Plantn
COLERIDGE COTTAGE
Whitnell
Knoll Green
Withiel Fm
CANNINGTON COLL
Rodway
Cannington
Horsey Pill
Groom House Fm
Crandon Br
Bawdrip
King's Fm
Bawdrip Level
Ford Fm
Dowsborough
Inwood Fm
Keenthorne
Padnoller Ho
Brymore School
Ashford Fm
Manor Fm
Perry Court Fm
Chilton Trinity
Knowle
Horsey
Peasy Fm
BATH ROAD
Kent Fm
Bincombe
Currypool Fm
The Grange
Perry Green
Bradney
Cock Hill
Stawell
Manor Fm
Robin Upright's Hill
Friarn
Over Stowey
Marsh Mills
Radlet
Bradley Green
Webndon Fm
Slape Cross
Pendon Hill
Quantock Combe
Adscombe
Seven Wells Wood
Aley
Pepper Hill
Rowdens Fm
Charlinch
Splatt
Charlynch
Gothelney Hall
B3339
Bridgwater
Newtown
East Bower
Sydenham
Parchey
Chedzoy
Ball Hill
Sutton Fm
Foxley
Tuxwell Fm
Four Forks
Crossmoor Fm
Gothelney Green
Clayhill Fm
Wembdon
Eastover
BRIDGWATER
Westfield Fm
West Moor
Fowler's Plot
Mount Close Batch
Fursland Fm
Moorlinch
Great Hill
Floorey Down
Plainsfield
Spaxton
Hawkridge Reservoir
Holmes Fm
Postridge Fm
Durleigh Reservoir
Northfield
BLAKE MUS
Sutton Mallet
Pit Hill
Great Wood
Round Hill
Pightley
Durleigh Brook
Rexworthy Fm
Durleigh
Hamp Brook
Hamp
Sharpham Hill
Greylake Fosse
Aisholt Wood
Hawkridge Common
Bare Ash
Troakes Fm
Wills Neck
Bagborough Hill
Durborough Fm
Aisholt
Lower Aisholt
Enmore Castle
Enmore
Willstock Fm
Dunwear
Westonzoyland
Liney
Penzoy Fm
Bussex
Burdenham Fm
GREYLAKE
RSPB
Briarwood Fm
Triscombe
Smokeham Fm
Lower Merridge
Merridge
Broomfield Hall
Andersfield
Goathurst
Bridgwater Services
Double Br
South Moor
Bishpool Fm
Good's Fm
Lydeard Hill
Rock Fm
Seven Ash
Bagborough Ho
West Bagborough
Gib Hill
Courtway
Wind Down
TEMPLE OF HARMONY
Higher Heathcombe Fm
Oakenford Fm
Rhode
Balls Fm
Compass
Huntworth
24
Andersea
Raymond's Fm
Weston Level
Langmead
Greylake Br
Overy Fm
Greylake
Ind Est
Heathfield
Park End
Twenty Acre Plantn
Rockhouse Fm
Huntstile
Woolmersdon
Gooding's Fm
North Petherton
Copse Fm
Linden Fm
Fordgate
WESTONZOYLAND PUMPING STATION
SOMERSET LEVELS
Shopnoller
Terhill
Buncombe Wood
Westleigh Fm
Lydeard Fm
Lydeard Cross
The Thickets
Rooks Castle Fm
Boomer
Melcombe
Shovel Ho
Petherton Park Fm
Yard
Cothelstone Hill
Cothelstone
Badger Copse
Ducks' Pool
FYNE COURT
Broomfield
Stream Fm
Stafford Fm
Northmoor Green or Moorland
Hoopers Elm Fm
Moorland House Fm
Thorngrove
Middlezoy
Nether Moor
Shride Fm
Charlton
Turn Hill
Ball Covert
Wort Wood
King's Cliff Wood
Langacre Rhyne
East Combe
Toulton
Ivyton Fm
Raswell Fm
Owl Hill Fm
Haddon Fm
Churchill Fm
Godfrey's Corner
Northmoor Main Drain
New House Fm
Saltmoor Fm
Othery
Pixford Fm
Beech Copse
Kingston Beacon
Ogshole Fm
Clavelshay
Shearston
North Newton
Middlemoor Br
West Yeo
Beer
Aller Wood
Cushuish
Volis Cross
Cheddon Down
Manor Ho
Thurloxton
St Michael Church
Maunsel Ho
Northmoor Corner
Lower Salt Moor
Pathe
Stanmoor Bridge
Hunter's Lodge
Breach Wood
Sandhill Park
East Lydeard
Portman Fm
27
Kingston St Mary
Quantock Fm
Burlinch
MAUNSEL LOCKS
BRIDGWATER & TAUNTON CANAL
Bankland
28
Burrow-bridge
Longstone
Aller Hill
Bishops Lydeard
Fennington
Yarde
Gadd's Bottom
Hill Fm
Coombe
Tuckerton
East Lyng
Ash Priors
Fennington Weir
Fulford
Volis Fm
Adsborough
West Newton
Hedging
Outwood
Lyng
Athelney Hill
Athelney
Stan Moor
Aller
Aller Court Fm
BISHOPS LYDEARD
Back Stream
Lower Portman Fm
Pickney
Nailsbourne
Mill Cross
Upper Cheddon
Hestercombe Fm
Primmore Corner
Lower Buckland Fm
Outwood Ho
Stathe
Greenway
Conquest Fm
Edgeborough Fm
Stonehouse Fm
HESTERCOMBE GARDENS
Gotton
Noah's Hill
West Monkton
Walford
Higher Durston
Durston
MAIN ROAD
Parsonage
Curload
Stathe Court
Sowy River
Middle Moor
Combe
Yarde
Goosenford
West Lyng
Hook Bridge
Holly
Court Langland's
Langland's
SOMERSET

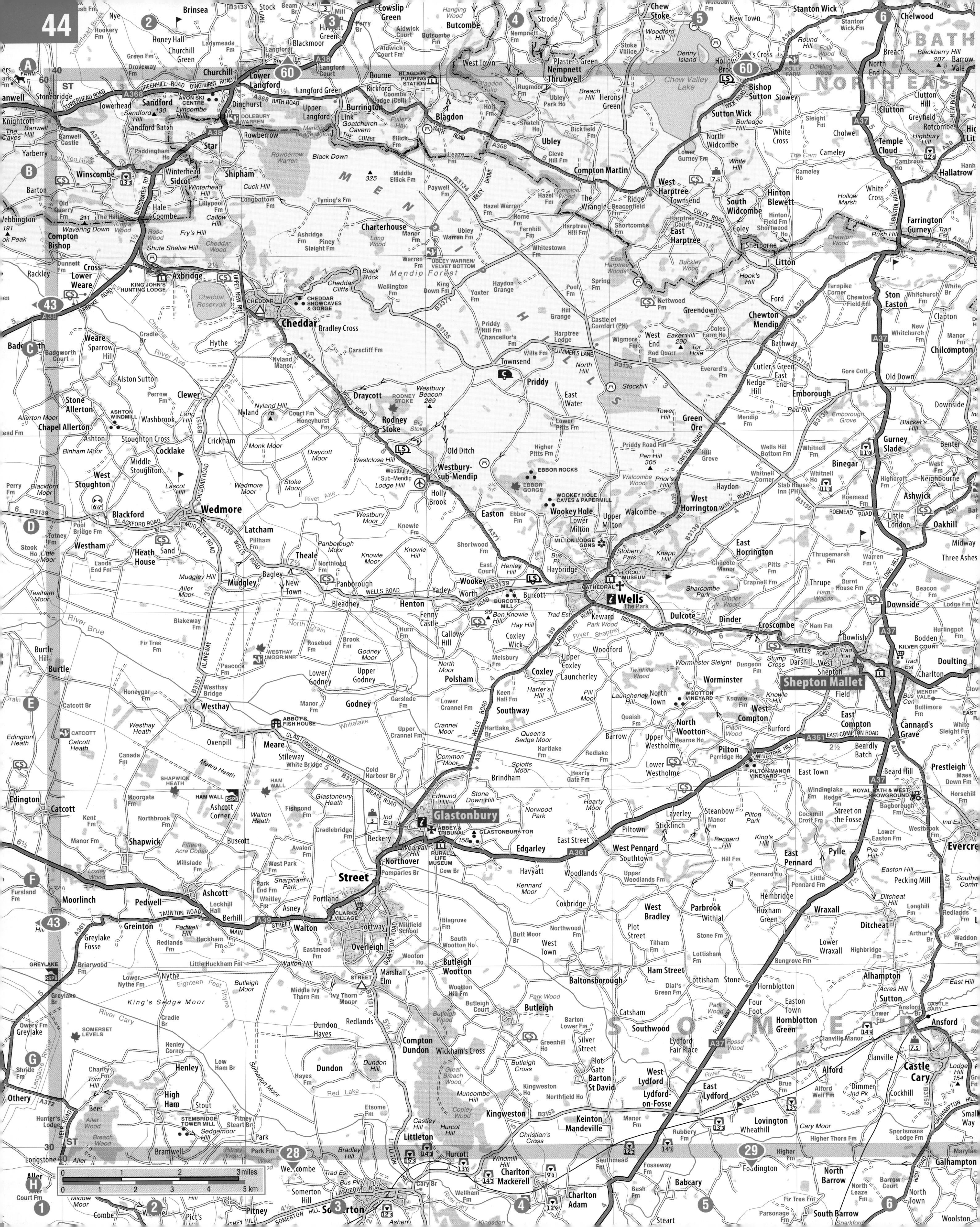

Brinsea
Nye
Honey Hall
Churchill Green
Churchill
Stock
Havyatt Green
Cowslip Green
Butcombe
Strode
Chew Stoke
Stanton Wick
Chelwood
BATH
Blackmoor
Langford
Lower Langford
Nempnett Thrubwell
West Town
Plaster's Green
Denny Island
Chew Valley Lake
Bishop Sutton
NORTH EAST
Stonebridge
Banwell
Towerhead
Sandford
AVON SKI CENTRE
Dinghurst
Langford Green
Rickford
Burrington
Blagdon
BLAGDON PUMPING STATION
Breach Hill
Herons Green
Ubley Park Ho
Stowey
Sutton Wick
Clutton
Knightcott
Sandford Batch
DOLEBURY WARREN
Rowberrow
Upper Langford
Link
Goatchurch Cavern
THE COMBE
Ubley
Compton Martin
North Widcombe
White Cross
Temple Cloud
Cameley
Hallatrow
Yarberry
Banwell Castle
Star
Black Down
Winscombe
Winterhead
Shipham
Sidcot
MENDIP
HILLS
Cuck Hill
Middle Ellick Fm
Paywell Fm
Hazel Warren Fm
West Harptree
Townsend
Ridge
Hinton Blewett
South Widcombe
Barton
Hale Coombe
Lillypool Fm
Callow Hill
Tyning's Fm
Charterhouse
Ubley Warren Fm
Home Fm
Fernhill Fm
Beaconfield Fm
The Wrangle
Harptree Court
East Harptree
Coley
Farrington Gurney
Compton Bishop
Wavering Down
The Hall
Rose Wood
Fry's Hill
Ashridge Fm
Piney Sleight Fm
Long Wood
Whitestown Fm
Harptree Hill Fm
Shortcombe Fm
Sherborne
Litton
Rush Hill
Shute Shelve Hill
Cheddar Wood
UBLEY WARREN/ VELVET BOTTOM
Rackley
Cross
Lower Weare
Axbridge
KING JOHN'S HUNTING LODGE
Cheddar Reservoir
Black Rock
Cheddar Cliffs
Wellington Fm
Mendip Forest
King Down Fm
Haydon Grange
Spring Fm
Pool Fm
Nettwood Fm
Hook's Hill
Ford
Turnpike Corner
Chewton Field Fm
Ston Easton
Whitchurch Fm
CHEDDAR SHOWCAVES & GORGE
Cheddar
Bradley Cross
Yoxter Fm
Priddy Hill Fm
Chancellor's Fm
Hill Grange
Castle of Comfort (PH)
Greendown
Chewton Mendip
Clapton
New Whitchurch Fm
Weare
Sparrow Hill
Badgworth
Badgworth Court
Cradle Br
River Axe
Hythe
Nyland Manor
Carscliff Fm
Townsend
Wills Fm
PLUMMER'S LANE
Harptree Lodge
West End
Wigmore Fm
Red Quarr Fm
Eaker Hill 290
Coles Farm Ho
Tor Hole
Bathway
Chilcompton
Alston Sutton
Clewer
Draycott
RODNEY STOKE
Westbury Beacon 269
Priddy
North Hill
Stockhill
Cutler's Green
East End
Everard's Fm
Nedge Hill
Gore Cott
Old Down
Stone Allerton
ASHTON WINDMILL
Chapel Allerton
Perrow Fm
Long Hill
Nyland
Nyland Hill 76
Court Fm
Honeyhurst Fm
Rodney Stoke
Big Stoke
East Water
Tower Hill
Green Ore
Mendip Fm
Red Hill
Emborough
Emborough Grove
Downside
Allerton Moor
Washbrook
Ashton
Stoughton Cross
Crickham
Monk Moor
Draycott Moor
Westclose Hill
Old Ditch
Lower Pitts Fm
Higher Pitts Fm
Priddy Road Fm
Pen Hill 305
Hill Grove
Wells Hill Bottom Fm
Whitnell Fm
Gurney Slade
Binegar
Blacker's Hill
Benter
Binham Moor
Cocklake
Middle Stoughton
West Stoughton
Lascot Hill
Wedmore Moor
Stoke Moor
Westbury-sub-Mendip
Westbury-Sub-Mendip Lodge Hill
EBBOR ROCKS
EBBOR GORGE
Walcombe Wood
Prior's Hill
Haydon
Whitnell Corner
Slab House Inn (PH)
Whitnell Fm
Neighbourne
Ashwick
Perry Fm
Blackford Moor
Blackford
BLACKFORD ROAD
Wedmore
Holly Brook
River Axe
WOOKEY HOLE CAVES & PAPERMILL
Wookey Hole
Walcombe
West Horrington
Roemead Fm
Little London
Oakhill
Pool Bridge Fm
Totney Fm
Westham
Latcham
Pillham Fm
Westbury Moor
Easton
Ebbor Fm
Lower Milton
Upper Milton
Knowle Fm
MILTON LODGE GDNS
East Horrington
Midway
Stook Ho
Little Moor
Heath House
Sand
Theale
Panborough Moor
Knowle Moor
Knowle Hill
Shortwood Fm
Stoberry Park
Knapp Hill
Thrupemarsh Fm
Warren Fm
Three Ashes
Lands End Fm
Mudgley Hill
Mudgley
Bagley
New Town
Northload Fm
Panborough
East Court Fm
Henley Hill
Haybridge
LOCAL MUSEUM
CATHEDRAL
Wells
The Park
Chilcote Manor
Pitts Fm
Crapnell Fm
Thrupe
Burnt House Fm
Beacon Fm
Lodge Fm
Tealham Moor
Aller Moor
Bleadney
Henton
Yarley
Wookey
Worth
WELLS ROAD
BURCOTT MILL
Burcott
Sharcombe Park
Ham Woods
Dinder Wood
Downside
Blakeway Fm
Fenny Castle
Ben Knowle Hill 99
Hay Hill
Trad Est
Keward
Park Wood
Dulcote
Dinder
Croscombe
Ham Fm
Bowlish
Bodden
Hurlingpot Fm
River Brue
North Drain
Hurn Fm
Callow Hill
Coxley Wick
River Sheppey
Woodford
KILVER COURT
Doulting
Burtle Hill
Fir Tree Fm
Rosebud Fm
Brook Fm
Godney Moor
Twinhills Wood
Worminster Sleight
Dungeon Fm
Stump Cross
Darshill
West Shepton
Charlton
Burtle
WESTHAY MOOR NNR
Peacock Fm
Lower Godney
Upper Godney
North Moor
Polsham
Melsbury Fm
Coxley
Upper Coxley
Launcherley
Worminster
Shepton Mallet
Honeygar Fm
Westhay Bridge
Westhay
Manor Fm
Godney
Garslade Fm
Keen Hill Fm
Harter's Hill
Pill Moor
North Town
WOOTTON VINEYARD
Knowle Fm
Knowle Hill
Field
MENDIP VALE
Bullimore Fm
Catcott Br
ABBOT'S FISH HOUSE
Whitelake
Lower Crannel Fm
Southway
Quaish Fm
West Compton
East Compton
Cannard's Grave
CATCOTT
Catcott Heath
Westhay Heath
Oxenpill
Meare
GLASTONBURY ROAD
Upper Crannel Fm
Crannel Moor
Hartlake Br
Queen's Sedge Moor
Barrow
North Wootton
Hearne Ho
Upper Westholme
Pilton
Perridge Ho
Burford
EAST COMPTON ROAD
Beardly Batch
Edington Heath
Canada Fm
Meare Heath
Stileway
White Bridge
Cold Harbour Br
Common Moor
Hartlake Fm
Redlake Fm
Lower Westholme
WHITSTONE HILL
PILTON MANOR VINEYARD
East Town
Prestleigh
Beard Hill
SHAPWICK HEATH
HAM WALL
HAM WALL
Glastonbury Heath
Splotts Moor
Brindham
Hearty Gate Fm
Windinglake Fm
Hedge Fm
ROYAL BATH & WEST SHOWGROUND
Bagborough Fm
Horsehill Fm
Edington
Catcott
Moorgate Fm
Ashcott Corner
Walton Heath
Fishpond Fm
Edmund Hill
Stone Down Hill
Glastonbury
ABBEY & TRIBUNAL
GLASTONBURY TOR
Norwood Park
Hearty Moor
Laverley
Sticklinch
Steanbow
Manor Fm
Pilton Park
Cockmill Croft Fm
Street on the Fosse
Kent Fm
Northbrook Fm
Cradlebridge Fm
Ind Est
Beckery
Wearyall Hill
RURAL LIFE MUSEUM
Edgarley
East Street
Piltown
West Pennard
Southtown
Pennard Hill
King's Hill
Lower Easton Fm
Westbrook Fm
Manor Fm
Shapwick
Fifteen Acre Copse
Buscott
Millslade Fm
Avalon Fm
Northover
Pomparles Br
Cow Br
Havyatt
Woodlands
Upper Woodlands Fm
Hill Fm
East Pennard
Pylle
Pye Hill
Easton Hill
Pecking Mill
Evercreech
Fursland Fm
Loxley Wood
West Park Fm
Sharpham Park
Park End Fm
Street
Kennard Moor
Pennard Ho
Little Pennard Fm
Moorlinch
Pedwell
Ashcott
Lockhill Hall
Whitley Fm
Asney
Portland
CLARKS VILLAGE
Coxbridge
West Bradley
Parbrook
Withial
Hembridge
Huxham Green
Wraxall
Ditcheat Hill
Longhill Fm
Redlands Fm
TAUNTON ROAD
Berhill
Greinton
Pedwell Hill
Walton
Portway
Millfield School
Blagrove Fm
Plot Street
Ditcheat
Arthur's Br
Waddon Fm
Greylake Fosse
Redlands Fm
Huckham Fm
Eastmead Fm
Overleigh
South Wootton Ho
Butt Moor Br
Northwood Fm
West Town
Tilham Fm
Stone Fm
Lower Wraxall
Highbridge Fm
GREYLAKE
Briarwood Fm
Little Huckham Fm
Walton Hill
Wootton Ho
Butleigh Wootton
Lottisham Fm
Bengrove Fm
Nythe
Lower Nythe Fm
Eighteen Feet Rhyne
Butleigh Moor
Marshall's Elm
Baltonsborough
Ham Street
Lottisham
Stone
Hornblotton
Alhampton
Acres Hill
East Hill
Greylake Br
King's Sedge Moor
Middle Ivy Thorn Fm
Ivy Thorn Manor
Wootton Hill Fm
Butleigh Court
Park Wood
Dial's Green Fm
Easton Town
Sutton
River Cary
Cradle Br
Redlands
Butleigh Wood
Butleigh
Barton Lower Fm
Catsham
Four Foot
Hornblotton Green
Lower Fm
Ansford
CASTLE CARY
Owery Fm
Greylake
SOMERSET LEVELS
Henley Corner
Dundon Hayes
Compton Dundon
Wickham's Cross
Greenhill Ho
Silver Street
Southwood
SOMERSET
Lydford Fair Place
Fosse Wood
Clanville Manor
Clanville
Castle Cary
Lodge Hill 154
Charity Fm
Turn Hill
Shride Fm
Henley
Low Ham Br
Dundon
Dundon Hill
Great Breach Wood
Butleigh Cross
Plot Gate
Barton St David
West Lydford
River Brue
Alford
Alford Well Fm
Dimmer Ind Pk
Cockhill
Othery
Hayes Fm
Red Lake
Kingweston Ho
Northfield Ho
Lydford-on-Fosse
East Lydford
Brue Fm
High Ham
Stout
Beer
Muncombe Hill
Kingweston
Keinton Mandeville
Manor Fm
Lovington
Wheathill
Cary Moor
GALHAMPTON ROAD
Small Way
Hunter's Lodge
Aller Wood
STEMBRIDGE TOWER MILL
Sedgemoor Hill
Pitney Steart Br
Etsome Fm
Copley Wood
Castley Hill
Hurcot Hill
Christian's Cross
Rubbery Fm
Sportsmans Lodge Fm
Higher Thorn Fm
Breach Wood
Park
Littleton
Higher Fm
Maryland
Longstone
Bramwell
Pitney Wood
Park Fm
Bradley Hill
Hurcott
Windmill Hill Fm
Charlton Mackerell
Southmead Fm
Fosseway Fm
Foddington
North Barrow
Galhampton
Aller
Aller Court Fm
Wellscombe
Trad Est
Somerton Hill
Bus Pk
LANGPORT ROAD
Cary Br
River Cary
Wellham Fm
Charlton Adam
Babcary
Bush Fm
Barrow Court
North Leaze Fm
North Town
Middle Moor
Combe
Pict's
Pitney
Somerton
Ashen
SOMERTON HILL
Steart
Fir Tree Fm
Parsonage Fm
South Barrow
Sparkford
Woolston
3 miles
5 km

SOMERSET
Bradford on-Avon
Holt
Trowbridge
Westbury
Warminster
Frome
Radstock
Midsomer Norton
Peasedown St John
Paulton
Timsbury
Farmborough
Priston
Inglesbatch
Southstoke
Combe Hay
Wellow
Dunkerton
Camerton
Clandown
Shoscombe
Writhlington
Kilmersdon
Stratton-on-the-Fosse
Holcombe
Coleford
Mells
Great Elm
Nunney
Buckland Dinham
Beckington
Rode
Norton St Philip
Woolverton
Laverton
Lullington
Tellisford
Farleigh Hungerford
Hinton Charterhouse
Freshford
Limpley Stoke
Westwood
Winsley
Turleigh
Wingfield
Southwick
North Bradley
Hilperton
Semington
Steeple Ashton
West Ashton
Heywood
Dilton Marsh
Chapmanslade
Corsley
Berkley
Standerwick
Upton Scudamore
Bishopstrow
Boreham
Norton Bavant
Sutton Veny
Longbridge Deverill
Horningsham
Maiden Bradley
Kilmington
Stourton
Mere
Zeals
Penselwood
Bourton
Wincanton
Bruton
Batcombe
Upton Noble
Witham Friary
Wanstrow
Leighton
East Cranmore
West Cranmore
Chesterblade
Evercreech
Milton Clevedon
North Brewham
South Brewham
Redlynch
Stoney Stoke
Shepton Montague
Bratton Seymour
Yarlington
Charlton Musgrove
Stoke Trister
Kingston Deverill
Brixton Deverill
Monkton Deverill
Chicklade
Hindon
West Knoyle
East Knoyle
The Green
Pertwood
CRANBOURNE CHASE AND WEST WILTSHIRE DOWNS
WILTSHIRE
Longleat Park
Longleat Safari Park
Stourhead
Alfred's Tower
Cley Hill
White Sheet Hill
A36
A361
A362
A366
A350
A303
A359
A371
B3092
B3098
B3099
B3081
46
61
29
30

Devizes
Sells Green
Bowerhill
Seend Cleeve
Seend
Semington
Littleton
Seend Head
The Stocks
Inmarsh
Poulshot
Nursteed
Etchilhampton
Stert
Beechingstoke
Woodborough
Bottlesford
Manningford Bruce
Patney
Potterne
Potterne Wick
Worton
Marston
Bulkington
Keevil
Great Hinton
Ashton Common
Bullenhill
Steeple Ashton
Little Marsh
The Strand
Cold Harbour
Bleet
Wedhampton
Urchfont
Chirton
Marden
Wilsford
Hilcott
North Newnton
Charlton
Rushall
Upavon
Conock
Eastcott
Easterton
Market Lavington
Littleton Panell
West Lavington
Little Cheverell
Great Cheverell
Erlestoke
Coulston
Edington
Bratton
Dunge
East Town
Gore Cross
Tilshead
Imber
Chitterne
Orcheston
Elston
Shrewton
Maddington
Rollestone
Larkhill
Durrington
West Chisenbury
East Chisenbury
Compton
Enford
Fifield
Netheravon
Salisbury Plain
Boreham
Bishopstrow
Norton Bavant
Heytesbury
Knook
Sutton Veny
Tytherington
Corton
Upton Lovell
Codford St Peter
Codford St Mary
Boyton
Sherrington
Stockton
Deptford
Fisherton de la Mere
Wylye
Steeple Langford
Hanging Langford
Little Langford
Winterbourne Stoke
Berwick St James
Stapleford
Serrington
Little Wishford
Great Wishford
Stoford
South Newton
West Amesbury
Stonehenge
Wilsford
Lake
Great Durnford
Upper Woodford
Middle Woodford
Lower Woodford
Little Durnford
Salterton
Pertwood
Higher Pertwood
Chicklade
Hindon
Berwick St Leonard
Fonthill Bishop
Fonthill Gifford
Ridge
Chilmark
Teffont Magna
Teffont Evias
Dinton
Baverstock
Barford St Martin
Burcombe
Wilton
Ditchampton
Chilhampton
Quidhampton
Bemerton
Netherhampton
Fugglestone St Peter
Stratford Sub Castle
Old Sarum
Salisbury
West Harnham
East Knoyle
Tisbury
Chicksgrove
Upper Chicksgrove
Sutton Mandeville
Fovant
Compton Chamberlayne
Cranbourne Chase and West Wiltshire Downs
Wiltshire
45
62
30
31
0 1 2 3 miles
0 1 2 3 4 5 km

Pewsey
Pewsey Wharf
Inlands Fm
Knowle
Kepnal
Fyfield
Little Salisbury
Milton Lilbourne
Southcott
Milkhouse Water
Littleworth
Westcourt
Conygre Fm
Easton
Eastcourt
Burbage
Marr Green
Kinwardstone Fm
West Grafton
East Grafton
Freewarren Fm
Suddene Park Fm
Wilton
Wilton Windmill
Wilton Common
Wilton Down
Marten
Marymere Fm
Rivar
Rivar Hill
Rivar Down
Starveall Fm
Botley Down
New Buildings
Town Fm
Grange Fm
Buttermere
Ballyack Ho
Sheepless Hill
Wright's Fm
Walbury Hill
Lower Fm
Manor Fm
Combe
Combe Hill
Woodhay Down
Pilot Hill
Hogs Hole
Jones' Fm
Goldenlands Fm
Easton Clump
Easton Hill
Southgrove Copse
Manor Fm
Grafton Fields
Lower Fm
Wexcombe
Noon's Fm
Manor Fm
Smay Down
Oxenwood
Pearce's Fm
Henley
Moordown Fm
Upper Horns Fm
Rockmoor Down
Combe Wood
Hart Hill Down
Milton Hill Clump
Fyfield Down
Pewsey Hill
Pewsey Hill Fm
Southgrove Fm
Crowdown Clump
Milton Hill Fm
Grafton Down
Tidcombe Down
Tidcombe
Beacon Fm
Fosbury Ho
Church Fm
Fosbury
Upper Row Fm
Winterside Fm
Manor Ho
Linkenholt
Faccombe
Curzon Street Fm
Privet Copse
Tow Barrow
Round Hill
Littledown Fm
Vernham Row
Netherton
Manor Fm
Ashmansworth
Everleigh Ashes
Down Fm
Spicey Buildings
Fairmile Down
Aughton Fm
Aughton Down
Inham Down
Aughton
Brunton
Silver Down
Down Barn
Fosbury Fm
258
Haydown Hill
Oakhill Wood
Box Fm
Vernham Bank
Vernham Street
Church Fm
Kimmer Fm
Lower Manor Fm
Alex Fm
Bruce Field Barn
Abbots Down
Grant's Firs
Cow Down
Summer Down
Thornhill Down
Collingbourne Kingston
Vernham Dean
Vernham Manor
Ankers Fm
Wister Copse
Faccombe Wood
Bohune Down
West Everleigh Down
Round Down
Cow Down
Rag Copse
Gammon's Fm
Chute Causeway
Little Down
Cleves Copse
Middle Conholt Fm
Upton Manor
Upton
Sidley Wood
Doyley Manor
Upavon Down
Upavon
Lower Everleigh
Lynden Down
Herridge Stud Fm
Mount Cowdown
Limmer Copse
New Barn
Conholt Ho
Conholt Park
Ambley Fm
Rushmore Down
NORTH WESSEX DOWNS
Sunton
Cadley
Dean Fm
Cathanger Wood
Hampshire Gate
Ibthorpe
The Dene
Lower Wyke Fm
Sladen Green
Lye Fm
Littlecott Down
Everleigh
Manor
East Everleigh
West Hill
Collingbourne Ducis
Hazelberry Plantn
Sunton Heath
Bauks Hill
Upper Chute
Lower Chute
Chute Standen
Chute Cadley
Whistler's Fm
Dowlands Fm
Pill Heath Fm
Hurstbourne Tarrant
Baden's Clump
Everleigh Down
Lower House Fm
Mount Orleans Fm
Collingbourne Wood
Honey Bottom
Jolly's Fm
Tangley Fm
Windmills
Hurstbourne Hill
Prior's Fm
Coombe Down
Hougoumont Fm
Wick Down
Coldridge Wood
Forest Ho
Tangley
Tangley Bottom
Blagden Copse
Blagden Ho
Doles Wood
Stoke
Baden Down Fm
Weather Hill Firs
Snail Down
Shaw Hill
Start Copse
Doles Fm
Bourne Park
Frenches Fm
Stokehill Fm
Weather Hill
Barrow Plantn
Widgerly Down
Crawlboys Fm
Coldridge Down
Longbottom Fm
Chute Lodge
Coombe Lane
Coombe Hill
Beach's Barn
Beach's Plantn
Castle Fm
Ludgershall Castle & Cross
Windmillhill Down
Biddesden Ho
Redhouse Fm
Roundaway Fm
Pigeon House Fm
Hatherden Ho
Goddards Fm
Wildhern
Rag Copse
Gang Br
Oak Tree Fm
Haxton Down
Haxton
224 Sidbury Hill
Pennings Barn
Pickpit Hill
Andover Road
Ludgershall
Bus Pk
Faberstown
Lambourne's Hill
Flinty Cott
Hatherden
Little London
Ridges Copse
Hackwood Copse
Middle Wyke Fm
Mile Ball
Netheravon
Chalkpit Hill
North Tidworth
Tidworth
Perham Down
South Park
Redenham
Tilly Down
Upper Enham
Enham Alamein
Woodhouse
Smannell
Airfield Camp Netheravon
Figheldean Down
Figheldean Field
Bourne Bottom
Lamb Down
Great Shoddesden
Little Shoddesden
Redenham Ho
Ragged Appleshaw
Clanville
Clanville Lodge
Penton Copse
Knights Enham
Finkley Ho
Finkley Manor Fm
Ablington Furze
Dunch Hill Plantn
Dunch Hill
Tidworth Camp
South Tidworth
Newdown Copse
Littleton Copse
Appleshaw
Chalk Croft Fm
Manor Fm
East Anton
Faulkner Down Fm
The Wig
Danger area
Ashdown Copse
Warren Hill
Ramridge Ho
Penton Mewsey
Figheldean
Ablington
Brigmerston Down
Tidworth Ho
Kimpton Down Fm
Kimpton Wood
Ramridge Cott
Penton Grafton
Foxcotte Retail Pk
Finkley Down Farm Park
Tinker's Hill
Picket Piece
Harewood Forest
Syrencot Ho
Silk Hill
The Belt
Home Fm
Kimpton
Fyfield
Weyhill
Weyhill Road
Penton Corner
Charlton
Bus Cen
Down Ho
London Road
Knighton Fm
Brigmerston Field
Milston Down
Pickford Hill
Ind Pk
Hackthorn Fm
Milston
Bulford Field
Brigmerston
The Cross Belt
Shipton Bellinger
Thruxton
Mullenspond
The Hawk Conservancy Trust
Andover
Andover Museum
Andover Down
Picket Twenty
Durrington
Nine Mile River
Snoddington Down Fm
East Cholderton
Trad Est
The Grange
Beacon Hill
Snoddington Manor
Racedown
Bush Fm
Piper's Hill
Little Park Fm
Bere Hill Fm
Middlecot Ho
Lains Fm
Amport
Monxton
Anna Valley
Cow Down
Balls Cotts
Bulford
Bulford Camp
Thruxton Fm
Cholderton Hill
Quarley
Amport Wood
Fox Fm
Amport Ho
Manor Fm
Abbotts Ann
Little Ann
Bury Hill
Upper Clatford
Cowdown Farm Ho
Augurs Hill Copse
Countess Road
Double Hedges
A3028
Cholderton Ho
Home Fm
Quarley Manor Fm
Sarson Wood
Great Wood
Eastover Fm
Ind Est Pachington Fm
Ratfyn
Countess
Beacon Hill Fm
Earl's Farm Down Barrows
Cholderton Rare Breeds Farm
Cholderton Lodge
Quarley Hill
Grateley
Golfard Fm
Monxton Fm
Eastover Copse
Home Fm
Goodworth Clatford
Upping Copse
Park Fm
Solstice Park
Bus Pk
Earl's Farm Down
Cholderton
Cholderton Road
Quarley Down Fm
Bus Pk
Grateley
Georgia Fm
Hurst Copse
Prospect Fm
Stonehanger Copse
Red Rice
Barrow Hill
New Barn
Longparish Road
Amesbury
Arundel Fm
Portway Fm
Three Corner Hat
Palestine
HAMPSHIRE
Salisbury Road
Romsey Road
Winchester Road
Wherwell
Bransbury Common
Newton Tony
Boar Knoll
Red Lodge Fm
Oklahoma Fm
Saxley Fm
Dipden Bottom
Flint Fm
Westover Fm
Gravel Hill
Newton Stacey
Salisbury Clumps
Boscombe Down Airfield
Allington
Wallop Road
Sunnyside Fm
Park Fm
Army Flying Museum
Clatford Oakcuts
Rowbury Fm
Fullerton Manor
Cottonworth
Chilbolton
Boscombe
Castle Fm
Station Road
Tunlands Fm
Hazel Down
Longstock Ho
Fullerton
West Down
Ivy Fm
Croft Fm
Over Wallop
Tower Hill
Middle Wallop
Down Fm
Charity Down Fm
Cleave Hill
Hazeldown Fm
Idmiston
Tidworth Road
Danebury Hill 143
Danebury Down
Leckford
Stonehill Park
Down Barn
Birdlymes Fm
Sudden Hill
Isle of Wight Hill
Jack's Bush Fm
Wallop Ho
Chattis Hill
Chattis Hill Ho
Longstock
Nether Wallop
Atners Towers
New Fm
High Post
Porton
Idmiston Down
Terstan
Leckford Lane
Downbarn West
Gomeldon
Roche Court Down
Hollom Down Fm
Beech Fm
Berry Court Fm
Fairview Fm
Sandydown Fm
Heath Ho
Dumper's Oak
Porton Down
Easton Down
Meon Hill
Houghton Down Fm
Stockbridge
Stockbridge Down
Long Copse
Windmill Hill
Winterbourne Dauntsey
Winterbourne Gunner
Lopcombe Corner
Darfield Fm
Battery Hill
Gutteridge Fm
Ashley's Copse
Nine Mile Water Fm
Homestead Fm
Steepleton Ho
North Park Fm
Winter Down Copse
Bushy Copse
Winterbourne Earls
Hurdcott
Roche Court
East Winterslow
Burrells Grove
Broughton Down Fm
Waterloo Fm
North Houghton
Marsh Court
North Park Wood
Rookley Manor
Old Sarum
Bracknell Croft
Winterbourne Down
New Manor Fm
Middle Winterslow
Warren Fm
Horseshoe Hill
Whiteshoot Hill
Manor Fm
Broughton
Eveley Fm
Houghton Lodge
All Saints Church
Little Somborne Ho
Ford
Firsdown
Hill Fm
Hampton Park
Stock Bottom
Dunstable Fm
The Common
Noad's Copse
Hoopers Fm
New Lease Fm
Little Somborne
Up Somborne
St Thomas's Bridge
Manor Fm
Bentleigh Fm
West Winterslow
Buckholt Fm
Houghton
Houghton Drayton
Yew Hill
Fussells Lodge Fm
Pitton
Woodgate Farm Ho
Hedgemoor Copse
Roake Fm
Wallop Brook
Queen Manor Fm
Savage's Fm
Carverel Copse
Picked Copse
King's Somborne
Ashley
Ashley Wood
Great Up Somborne Wood
Laverstock
Burroughs Hill
Pitton Lodge
Hound Wood
Norman Court
Broughton Hill
Queenwood Fm
Bossington
Horsebridge
Salisbury
Beechy Dean Copse
Bentley Wood
West Tytherley
Crown Fm
Stride's Fm
Pittleworth Fm
Forest of Bere Fm
Milford
Ranger's Lodge Fm
Manor Fm
Manor Hill
Coalpit Copse
Stony Batter
Furzedown
Ashley Hill
Ashley Down
Farley
Blackmoor Copse
Park Copse
Bentley Fm
Compton Manor
Humbers Wood
Mount Down 174
Long Copse
Barnridge Copse
Howe Copse
East Tytherley
The Green
Tytherley Common
Luke Copse
Parnholt Wood
Farley Down
Kennel Fm
River Avon
Britford
Shute End
Clarendon Ho
Nightwood Copse
Whitehouse Fm
East Grimstead
Keepers Cott
Dean Copse
Hawks Grove
Drove Farm Ho
Frenchmoor
Pug's Hole Fm
Lockerley Hall
Lain Copse
Spearywell Wood
Oakley
Compton
Brook
Lower Brook
Lower Eldon
Fishponds
Farley Fm
A338
A342
A343
A346
A303
A30
A345
A3057
A36
B3048
B3400
B3402
B3420
B3084
B3087
B3049
P&R
SU

Woolton Hill
East End
Penwood
Pound Street
Burghclere
Earlstone Common
Plastow Green
Tadley
Silchester
Axmansford
Baughurst
Wheat Hold
Wolverton Common
Pound Green
Browninghill Green
Pamber Green
Little London
Latchmere Green
Highclere
Whitway
Ecchinswell
Kingsclere
Wolverton
Towns End
Stony Heath
West Heath
Charter Alley
Pamber End
Ramsdell
Faccombe
Ashmansworth
Old Burghclere
Sydmonton
Crux Easton
Monk Sherborne
Sherborne St John
Cufaude
Hannington
Upper Wootton
Ibworth
North Oakley
Woodcott
Litchfield
Dunley
Binley
Hurstbourne Tarrant
Wootton St Lawrence
Popley
Oakridge
South View
Winklebury
Worting
Basingstoke
Eastrop
NORTH
WESSEX
DOWNS
Stoke
Swampton
Cole Henley
Quidhampton
Deane
Clarken Green
Church Oakley
Oakley
Newfound
Buckskin
South Ham
Kempshott
St Mary Bourne
Overton
Ashe
East Oakley
Brighton Hill
Cliddesden
Laverstoke
Whitchurch
Tufton
Freefolk
Southington
Steventon
North Waltham
Broadmere
Farleigh Wallop
Picket Piece
Andover Down
Hurstbourne Priors
Dummer
Ellisfield
Longparish
Middleton
Popham
Nutley
Lower Common
Forton
Axford
HAMPSHIRE
Bransbury
Woodmancott
Preston Candover
Bradley
Wherwell
Barton Stacey
Bullington
Upper Bullington
West Stratton
East Stratton
Chilton Candover
Lower Wield
Newton Stacey
Chilbolton
Sutton Scotney
Wonston
Stoke Charity
Micheldever
Brown Candover
Upper Wield
Northington
Swarraton
Hattingley
South Wonston
Crawley
Abbotstone
Old Alresford
Bighton
Kings Worthy
Headbourne Worthy
Martyr Worthy
Itchen Abbas
Itchen Stoke
Gundleton
Littleton
Easton
Avington
New Alresford
Bishop's Sutton
Up Somborne
Sparsholt
Ovington
Tichborne
Ropley Dean
Weeke
Winchester
Winnall
Fulflood
Chilcomb
Cheriton
New Cheriton
Bramdean
Stanmore
A34
A303
A30
A33
A339
A31
M3
B3400
B3047
B3046

Stratfield Saye
West End Green
Fair Oak Green
Heckfield
Eversley
Eversley Centre
Eversley Cross
Little Sandhurst
Sandhurst
College Town
Camberley
Bramshill
Yateley
Blackwater
York Town
Stratfield Turgis
Turgis Green
Hound Green
Hazeley
Hawley
Frimley
Sherfield on Loddon
Mattingley
Hartley Wintney
Hartfordbridge
Fox Lane
Chineham
Church End
Rotherwick
Lyde Green
West Green
Phoenix Green
Cove
Farnborough
Hook
Newnham
Winchfield
Pondtail
Old Basing
Daneshill
Hatch
Fleet
Church Crookham
Crookham Village
Dogmersfield
North Warnborough
Odiham
Up Nately
Mapledurwell
Greywell
Colt Hill
Mill Lane
Aldershot
Ash
Ash Vale
Tunworth
Upton Grey
Winslade
Ewshot
Crondall
Weston Corbett
Weston Patrick
South Warnborough
Long Sutton
Well
Farnham
Dippenhall
Compton
The Sands
Tongham
Badshot Lea
Runfold
Seale
Herriard
Southrope
Bagmore
Lower Froyle
Upper Froyle
Froyle
Bentley
Wrecclesham
Rowledge
The Bourne
Tilford
Elstead
Lasham
Shalden
Golden Pot
Holybourne
Binsted
Blacknest
Bucks Horn Oak
Frensham
Spreakley
Millbridge
Bentworth
Alton
Wilsom
Wyck
Wheatley
Kingsley
Thursley
Medstead
Beech
Chawton
East Worldham
West Worldham
Sleaford
Headley
Hindhead
Grayshott
Beacon Hill
Four Marks
Lower Farringdon
Upper Farringdon
Bordon
Lindford
Bordon Camp
Whitehill
Blackmoor
Selborne
Newton Valence
East Tisted
Conford
Liphook
Haslemere
Longmoor Camp
Greatham
Empshott
Colemore
Monkwood
West Tisted
Hawkley
Liss Forest
Langley
Fernhurst
SURREY

Chobham
Bagshot Heath
West End
Castle Green
Byfleet
West Byfleet
Cobham
Woking
Horsell
Cheapside
Sheerwater
Bisley
Knaphill
St John's
Frimley
Deepcut
Farnborough Green
Brookwood
Pyrford
Wisley
Downside
Stoke D'Abernon
Mytchett
Pirbright
Mayford
Old Woking
Kingfield
Ripley
Send
Send Marsh
Ockham
Leatherhead
Fetcham
Little Bookham
Great Bookham
Effingham
East Horsley
West Horsley
Worplesdon
Fox Corner
Sutton Green
Burntcommon
Ash Vale
Ash
Pitch Place
Jacobs Well
Slyfield
Burpham
West Clandon
East Clandon
Normandy
Wyke
Willey Green
Stoughton
Merrow
Guildford
Onslow Village
Flexford
Wanborough
Tongham
Newland's Corner
Gomshall
Shere
Albury
Chilworth
Puttenham
Compton
Littleton
Shalford
Blackheath
Westcott
Abinger Hammer
Wotton
Shackleford
Farncombe
Bramley
Wonersh
Brook
Farley Green
Peaslake
Sutton Abinger
Holmbury St Mary
Abinger Common
Coldharbour
Eashing
Godalming
Elstead
Milford
Shamley Green
SURREY HILLS
SURREY
Grafham
Tuesley
Forest Green
Thursley
Wheelerstreet
Hydestile
Hascombe
Rowly
Ewhurst
Cranleigh
Ewhurst Green
Walliswood
Oakwoodhill
Loxhill
Wormley
Sandhills
Hambledon
Brook
Dunsfold
Chiddingfold
Combe Common
Alfold Crossways
Alfold
Ellen's Green
Rudgwick
Rowhook
Grayswood
Haslemere
Ramsnest Common
Plaistow
Ifold
Loxwood
Bucks Green
Tisman's Common
Alfold Bars
Strood Green
Park Street
Slinfold
Itchingfield
Kingsley Green
Fisherstreet
Mackerel's Common
Roundstreet Common
Five Oaks
The Haven
49
66
34
35
0 1 2 3 miles
0 1 2 3 4 5 km

51
Epsom
Banstead
Coulsdon
Purley
Sanderstead
Ashtead
Leatherhead Common
Chipstead
Burgh Heath
Great Burgh
Tadworth
Kingswood
Walton on the Hill
Whyteleafe
Warlingham
Woldingham
Caterham
Chaldon
Old Coulsdon
Kenley
Hooley
Merstham
Limpsfield
Oxted
Titsey
Mickleham
Westhumble
Box Hill
SURREY HILLS
Reigate
Redhill
Buckland
Betchworth
Brockham
Pixham
Dorking
Nutfield
Bletchingley
Godstone
Tandridge
Earlswood
Salfords
Horley
Smallfield
Lingfield
Dormansland
North Holmwood
South Holmwood
Beare Green
Newdigate
Capel
Charlwood
Gatwick Airport
Burstow
Copthorne
Felbridge
East Grinstead
Crawley
Three Bridges
Ifield
Tilgate
Faygate
Rusper
Kingsfold
WEST SUSSEX
Colgate
Pease Pottage
Balcombe
Turners Hill
Sharpthorne
West Hoathly
Horsham
Handcross
Ardingly
Staplefield
Slaugham
Mannings Heath
M25
M23
A24
A25
A22
A23
A264
67
52
35
36

DOWNS
Leaves Green
Downe
Hazelwood
Badger's Mount
Halstead
Shoreham
Romney Street
Knatts Valley
Stansted
Vigo Village
Fairseat
Trottiscliffe
Knockholt Pound
Cudham
Biggin Hill
Knockholt
Otford
Kemsing
Heaverham
Wrotham
Fickleshole
Chelsham
Tatsfield
South Street
Chevening
Dunton Green
Seal
Borough Green
Platt
Chipstead
Riverhead
Ightham
Titsey
Westerham
Brasted
Sundridge
Sevenoaks
Kippington
Stone Street
Ivy Hatch
Crouch
Limpsfield
Oxted
Cross Keys
Plaxtol
Shipbourne
West Peckham
Ide Hill
Toy's Hill
Crockham Hill
Sevenoaks Weald
Oakhurst
KENT DOWNS
Hildenborough
Hadlow
Four Elms
Marlpit Hill
Edenbridge
Chiddingstone Causeway
Leigh
Tonbridge
Five Oak Green
Hever
Chiddingstone
Penshurst
KENT
Lingfield
Dormansland
Markbeech
Bidborough
Southborough
Tudeley
Capel
HIGH WEALD
Cowden
Speldhurst
Fordcombe
Rusthall
Pembury
East Grinstead
Hammerwood
Blackham
Ashurst
Langton Green
Royal Tunbridge Wells
Sunnyside
Ashurst Wood
Groombridge
Eridge Green
Bells Yew Green
Forest Row
Hartfield
Withyham
EAST SUSSEX
Frant
Coleman's Hatch
Lye Green
Danegate
Wych Cross
Crowborough
Mark Cross
Durgates
Wadhurst
Chelwood Gate
Ashdown Forest
Rotherfield
Town Row
Tidebrook
Jarvis Brook
Nutley
Duddleswell
0 1 2 3 miles
0 1 2 3 4 5 km

Snodland
Burham
Stockbury
Eccles
Kit's Coty
Westfield Sole
South Street
Birling
Ryarsh
Aylesford
Boxley
Bredgar
Addington
Leybourne
Larkfield
Ditton
Sandling
Detling
Thurnham
Hucking
Bicknor
Milstead
West Malling
Royal British Legion Village
East Malling
Penenden Heath
Wormshill
Frinsted
Offham
Maidstone
Bearsted
Hollingbourne
Kings Hill
East Barming
Roseacre
Teston
Wateringbury
Tovil
Otham
Leeds
Harrietsham
Lenham
West Farleigh
East Farleigh
Loose
Langley
Broomfield
Nettlestead
Coxheath
Boughton Monchelsea
Kingswood
Yalding
Linton
Chart Sutton
Sutton Valence
Ulcombe
Boughton Malherbe
Hunton
Laddingford
Chainhurst
Beltring
Paddock Wood
Marden
Headcorn
Collier Street
Staplehurst
Frittenden
Smarden
Brenchley
Horsmonden
Goudhurst
Cranbrook
Sissinghurst
Biddenden
High Halden
Lamberhurst
Kilndown
Hawkhurst
Benenden
Tenterden
Rolvenden
Flimwell
Ticehurst
Sandhurst
KENT
DOWNS
HIGH WEALD
Bewl Water
Bedgebury Forest
M20
M2
A229
A21
A262
A28
A26
A228

Faversham
Goodnestone
Ospringe
Preston
Davington
Dargate
Hernhill
Boughton Street
Dunkirk
Rough Common
Harbledown
Upper Harbledown
Staplestreet
Whitehill
Copton
Selgrove
Plumford
North Street
Sheldwich
South Street
Oversland
Selling
Chartham Hatch
Thanington
Rodmersham
Lynsted
Newbury
Kingsdown
Dungate
Erriottwood
Milstead
Bluetown
Newnham
Doddington
Eastling
Wichling
North Downs
Throwley
Hockley
Badlesmere
Leaveland
Shottenden
Chilham
Old Wives Lees
Chartham
Shalmsford Street
Bagham
Lenham
Warren Street
Stalisfield Green
Challock
Molash
Godmersham
Petham
Garlinge Green
KENT DOWNS
Charing
Charing Heath
Lenham Heath
Sandway
Eastwell Park
Westwell
Boughton Aluph
Boughton Lees
Bilting
Crundale
Waltham
Wye
Egerton
Pluckley
Pluckley Thorne
Little Chart
Hothfield
Kennington
Bybrook
Hastingleigh
Brook
Elmsted
Stelling Minnis
Ashford
South Ashford
Willesborough
Willesborough Lees
Great Chart
Sevington
Mersham
Smeeth
Brabourne
Brabourne Lees
Stowting
Postling
Sellindge
Stanford
Bethersden
Kingsnorth
Shadoxhurst
Stubbs Cross
Aldington
Bonnington
Court-at-Street
Lympne
West Hythe
Pedlinge
Newingreen
Westenhanger
Tenterden
High Halden
Woodchurch
Orlestone
Hamstreet
Ruckinge
Bilsington
Kenardington
Warehorne
Appledore
Appledore Heath
Reading Street
Small Hythe
Newchurch
Burmarsh
Dymchurch
Snave
Romney Marsh
Snargate
Brenzett
St Mary in the Marsh
Ivychurch
Palmarsh
Isle of Oxney
M2
M20
A20
A28
A251
A252
A2070
0 1 2 3 miles
0 1 2 3 4 5 km

SANDWICH BAY
Sandwich Flats
Richborough Port
Great Stonar
Sandwich
Sandwich Bay Estate
Westbere
Westbere Marshes
Stodmarsh
Grove
Preston
Elmstone
Westmarsh
Paramour Street
Ware
Lower Goldstone
Upper Goldstone
Ash Level
Sturry
Fordwich
Broad Oak
Canterbury
Littlebourne
Bekesbourne
Patrixbourne
Wickhambreaux
Ickham
Seaton
Wingham
Wingham Green
Wingham Well
Bramling
Hoaden
Shatterling
Durlock
Staple
Guilton
Ash
Cop Street
Weddington
Marshborough
Woodnesborough
Stone Cross
Worth
Lydden Valley
Eastry
Gore
Buttsole
Ham
Hacklinge
Finglesham
Betteshanger
Northbourne
Sholden
Deal
Upper Deal
Mill Hill
Walmer
Great Mongeham
Little Mongeham
Ripple
Sutton
East Studdal
Kingsdown
Ringwould
Oldstairs Bay
Nackington
Bridge
Bishopsbourne
Adisham
Aylesham
Goodnestone
Rowling
Knowlton
Chillenden
Nonington
Easole Street
Snowdown
Womenswold
Barham
Kingston
Elvington
Tilmanstone
Barfrestone
Eythorne
Woolage Green
Woolage Village
Frogham
Derringstone
Shepherdswell or Sibertswold
Coxhill
Coldred
Golgotha
KENT
Denton
Wootton
Lydden
Whitfield
Temple Ewell
West Langdon
East Langdon
Martin
Martin Mill
Guston
West Cliffe
St Margaret's at Cliffe
St Margaret's Bay
SOUTH FORELAND
Elham
Selsted
Swingfield Minnis
Swingfield Street
Ewell Minnis
Alkham
River
Kearsney
Crabble
Buckland
Dover
Maxton
Aycliff
Farthingloe
Drellingore
Densole
Hawkinge
Paddlesworth
Lyminge
Etchinghill
Capel-le-Ferne
West Hougham
Shakespeare Cliff
Channel Tunnel
CALAIS DUNKERQUE
Newington
Cheriton
Folkestone
Saltwood
Sandgate
Hythe
STRAIT OF DOVER

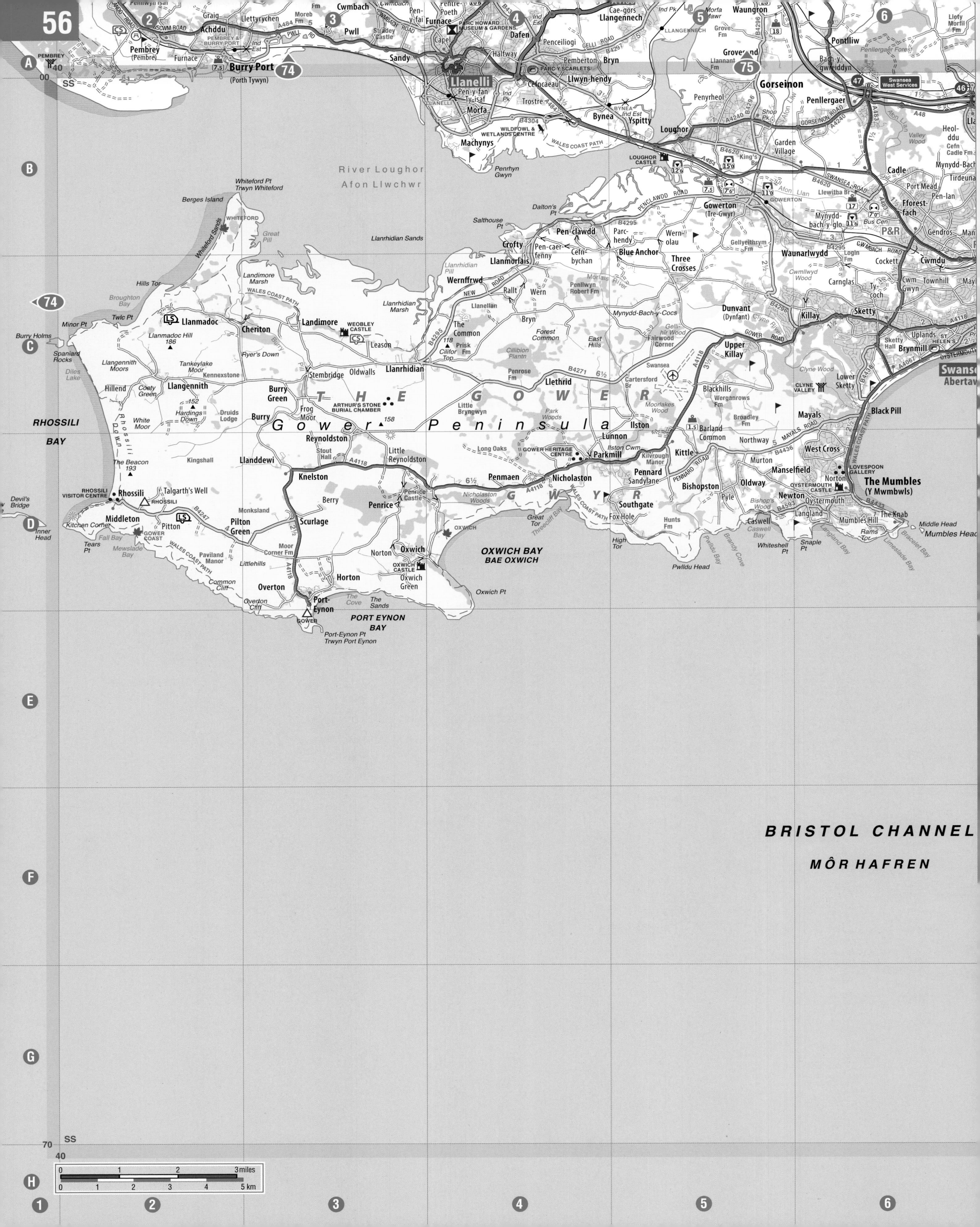

Pembrey
(Pembre)
Burry Port
(Porth Tywyn)
Achddu
Llettyrychen
Pwll
Furnace
Sandy
Cwmbach
Capel
Llanelli
Dafen
Penceiliogi
Halfway
Pemberton
Bryn
Llwyn-hendy
Llangennech
Waungron
Pontlliw
Gorseinon
Penllergaer
Penyrheol
Morfa
Trostre
Bynea
Yspitty
Machynys
Loughor
Garden Village
Cadle
Fforest-fach
Gendros
Penrhyn Gwyn
River Loughor
Afon Llwchwr
Whiteford Pt
Trwyn Whiteford
Berges Island
Whiteford Sands
Salthouse Pt
Dalton's Pt
Llanrhidian Sands
Gowerton
(Tre-Gwyr)
Pen-clawdd
Crofty
Llanmorlais
Blue Anchor
Three Crosses
Waunarlwydd
Cockett
Cwmdu
Landimore Marsh
Hills Tor
Broughton Bay
Twlc Pt
Minor Pt
Burry Holms
Llanmadoc
Cheriton
Landimore
Weobley Castle
Llanrhidian Marsh
Wernffrwd
Rallt
Wern
Llanellan
Bryn
The Common
Forest Common
Mynydd-Bach-y-Cocs
Dunvant
(Dynfant)
Killay
Sketty
Uplands
Brynmill
Swansea
Abertawe
Spaniard Rocks
Diles Lake
Llangennith Moors
Llanmadoc Hill
Tankeylake Moor
Kennexstone
Ryer's Down
Leason
Stembridge
Oldwalls
Llanrhidian
Cilifor Top
Prisk Fm
Cillibion Plantn
East Hills
Fairwood Corner
Upper Killay
Clyne Wood
Hillend
Coety Green
Llangennith
Burry Green
THE GOWER
Penrose Fm
Llethrid
Cartersford Br
Blackhills
Lower Sketty
Clyne Valley
RHOSSILI BAY
White Moor
Hardings Down
Druids Lodge
Burry
Frog Moor
Arthur's Stone Burial Chamber
Gower Peninsula
Little Bryngwyn
Park Woods
Moorlakes Wood
Werganrows Fm
Ilston
Barland Common
Broadley Fm
Mayals
Black Pill
Rhossili Down
Reynoldston
Lunnon
Northway
West Cross
Kingshall
Llanddewi
Stout Hall
Little Reynoldston
Long Oaks
Gower Heritage Centre
Parkmill
Ilston Cwm
Kilvrough Manor
Kittle
The Beacon 193
Knelston
Penmaen
Nicholaston
Pennard
Sandylane
Murton
Manselfield
Lovespoon Gallery
Bishopston
Oldway
Norton
The Mumbles
(Y Mwmbwls)
Rhossili Visitor Centre
Rhossili
Talgarth's Well
Berry
Penrice
Penrice Castle
Nicholaston Woods
Southgate
Newton
Oystermouth Castle
Oystermouth
Devil's Bridge
Middleton
Monksland
Pilton Green
Scurlage
Oxwich
Great Tor
Threecliff Bay
Fox Hole
Hunts Fm
Pyle
Bishop's Wood
Caswell
Langland
Mumbles Hill
The Knab
Middle Head
Mumbles Head
Kitchen Corner
Inner Head
Fall Bay
Tears Pt
Mewslade Bay
Pitton
Gower Coast
Paviland Manor
Moor Corner Fm
Littlehills
OXWICH BAY
BAE OXWICH
High Tor
Pwlldu Bay
Brandy Cove
Whiteshell Pt
Caswell Bay
Snaple Pt
Langland Bay
Rams Tor
Limeslade Bay
Bracelet Bay
Common Cliff
Overton
Horton
Norton
Oxwich Castle
Oxwich Green
Oxwich Pt
Pwlldu Head
Overton Cliff
Port-Eynon
The Cove
The Sands
PORT EYNON BAY
Port-Eynon Pt
Trwyn Port Eynon
Wales Coast Path
BRISTOL CHANNEL
MÔR HAFREN
0 1 2 3 miles
0 1 2 3 4 5 km

Clydach
Faerdre
Ynystawe
Gelliwastad Fm
Pant-lasau
Cwmrhydyceirw
Morriston (Treforys)
Tircanol
Heol-las
Birchgrove
Clase
Graig Trewyddfa
Treboeth
Landore
Llansamlet
Trallwn
Skewen
Lon-las
Tai'r-ysgol
Cwm
Bon-y-maen
Winsh-wen
Cefn-hengoed
Pentre-dwr
Coed Darcy
Llandarcy
Jersey Marine
Pentre-chwyth
Foxhole
Kilvey Hill
Port Tennant
St Thomas
Ty-draw
Crymlyn Burrows
Swansea Works
TENNANT CANAL
FABIAN WAY
THE NATIONAL WATERFRONT MUS
PLANTASIA
West Pier
CRYMLYN BOG & PANT-Y-SAIS
SWANSEA BAY
BAE ABERTAWE
Baglan Bay
Bae Baglan
River Neath
Witford Pt
Aberavon Sands
Sandfields
Aberavon
Port Talbot
PORT TALBOT PARKWAY
Harbourside Park under dev
Taibach
Margam
Margam Sands
Steel Works
Eglwys Nunydd Reservoir
Kenfig Sands
KENFIG POOL & DUNES
Kenfig Pool
Kenfig
VISITOR CENTRE
Sker Pt
Sker Court
Parc Newydd Fm
Flynnon-wen Rocks
Rest Bay
Nottage
Lock's Common
Hutchwns
Hutchwns Pt
Porthcawl
PORTHCAWL MUSEUM
Porthcawl Pt
CONEY BEACH
Sandy Bay
Rhych Pt
Trecco Bay
Newton Pt
Black Rocks
Clevis
Newton
WALES COAST PATH
Fforest Gôch
Banwen Fm
Erwsaethau Fm
Mynydd Drumau
Cefn-y-Garth
Glanbran Ho
Nant-y-Bran
Stanley Wood
Darran Wood
Mountain Wood
Bryn-coch
Cilfrew
Aberdulais
ABERDULAIS FALLS
Cadoxton-Juxta-Neath
Rhydding
Neath Abbey
Tonna (Tonnau)
THE GNOLL
Neath
Castell-Nedd
NEATH ABBEY
Melincryddan
Mount Pleasant
Cimla
NEATH CANAL
Briton Ferry (Llansawel)
Pant-Howel-Ddu
Baglan
Brynbryddan
Mynydd Dinas 258
Pantdu
Cwmafan
Corlannau
Caerhendy
Ynysygwas
Pen-y-cae
Goytre
Cwm Dyffryn
Ergyd Isaf
Brombil
Groes
MARGAM PARK
STONES
Gelli-gaer
Mynydd-y-Gaer 314
Bwlch
Pontrhydyfen
Foel Fynyddau 370
Pwll-y-glaw
Efail-fâch
Cerrig Llwydion
Cefn-Saeson
Baradychwallt
Cefn Morfudd 307
Mynydd Pen-Rhys 280
Rock
Cwm
Moel y Fen
Melincourt
Clyne
Wenallt Wood
Cwm Gwenffrwd
Mynydd Blaenafon
Cwm Blaenpelenna
Mynydd Fforch-Dwm
Tyle'r waun
Mynydd Nant-y-bar
Mynydd Rhiwgregen
Tonmawr
AFAN ARGOED
FOREST PARK
Cwm Afan
Duffryn
AFAN ARGOED
SOUTH WALES MINERS MUSEUM
Cwm yr Argoed
Mynydd Penhydd
Pen Disgwylfa
Carn Caca
Banwen Torybetel
Carn Caglau 493
Moel yr Hyrddod
Mynydd Corrwg Fechan
Mynydd Blaen-Nant-du
Glyncorrwg
Mynydd Ynyscorrwg 502
Mynydd Abergwynfi
Glyn Corrwg
Abercregan
Blaen-gwynfi
Coetgae Isaf
Nant y Fedw
Aber-gwynfi
Cymer
Foel Fawr 347
Croeserw
Brynheulog
Foely Dyffryn 366
Blaencaerau
Caerau
Mynydd Caerau
Craig Walter
Dyffryn
Rhiw Tor Cymry
Spelter
Mynydd Bach 433
Blaen Cwmdû
Blaengarw
Nantyffyllon
Bryn-Rhug Fm
Cwm Garw Fechan
Bryn
Mynydd Bychan
Cil-y-Gofid
Moel Gallt-y-cwm 272
Cwm Farteg
Mynydd Bach 319
Cwm Wernderi
Maesteg
Llwydarth
Garth
Garth Hill 257
Moel Cynhordy
Pontycymer
Cwm Sychbant
Cwm Nant-y-glo
Cwmfelin
Cwm y Garn
Margam Forest
Mynydd Margam 344
Cwm Cerdin
Moel Troed-y-rhiw
Pont Rhyd-y-cyff
Cynhordy Fm
Llangynwyd
Waun y Gilfach
Gadlys
Gilfach
Bryn-Cynan
BRIDGEND
PEN-Y-BONT AR OGWR
Craig Cwm Maelwg
Mynydd y Castell
Moel Ton-mawr 319
Cwm Cynffig
Craig yr Aber
Mynydd Baedan 251
Coytrahen
Ton Mawr Fm
Twyn-yr-hydd
Pentre Fm
Pen-y-bryn
Aberbaiden Fm
Ffordd-y-Gyfraith
Park Fm
PARC SLIP NATURE RESERVE
Fountain
Cwm-ffos
Kenfig House Fm
Caegarw
Kenfig Hill
BEDFORD
Cefn Cross
Llanmihangel
Pyle (Y Pil)
Pen-y-castell
Cefn Cribbwr
Mawdlam
North Cornelly
South Cornelly
Ty-Tanglwyst Fm
Ballas Fm
Stormy Down
Upper Park
Pant Fm
Court Colman
Ty'n-y-garn
Pen-y-fai
Llangewydd Court
Bryntirion
Cefn Glas
Laleston
The Grove
Newton Down
The Beacons
Manor Fm
Clement Fm
Tythegston
Whitney Fm
Wig Fach
CANDLESTON CASTLE
MERTHYR MAWR WARREN
Ton Fm
Merthyr Mawr
OGMORE CASTLE
Ogmore
Ogmore-by-Sea (Aberogwr)
Tusker Rock
Black Rocks
Groes Fm
Heol-y-mynydd
St Brides Major (Saint-y-Brid)
Pitcot
Penuchadre
Southerndown
GLAMORGAN HERITAGE COAST CENTRE
Dunraven Bay
Durval Fm
Old Castle Down
Castle-upon-Alun
Tondu
Brynmenyn
Bryncethin
Aberkenfig (Abercynffig)
Sarn
Pendre
Newcastle
Whiterock
Llangeinor
Bettws
Shwt
Bryngarw
Blaengarw
Pont-y-rhyl
Craig-yr-Hudol
Tylacoch
Mynydd Moelgeila
Pwll-y-garn
Cwm Gelli-wern
SS
90
00
70
7
8
9
10
11
75
76
77
58
A
B
C
D
E
F
G
H
Nash Pt

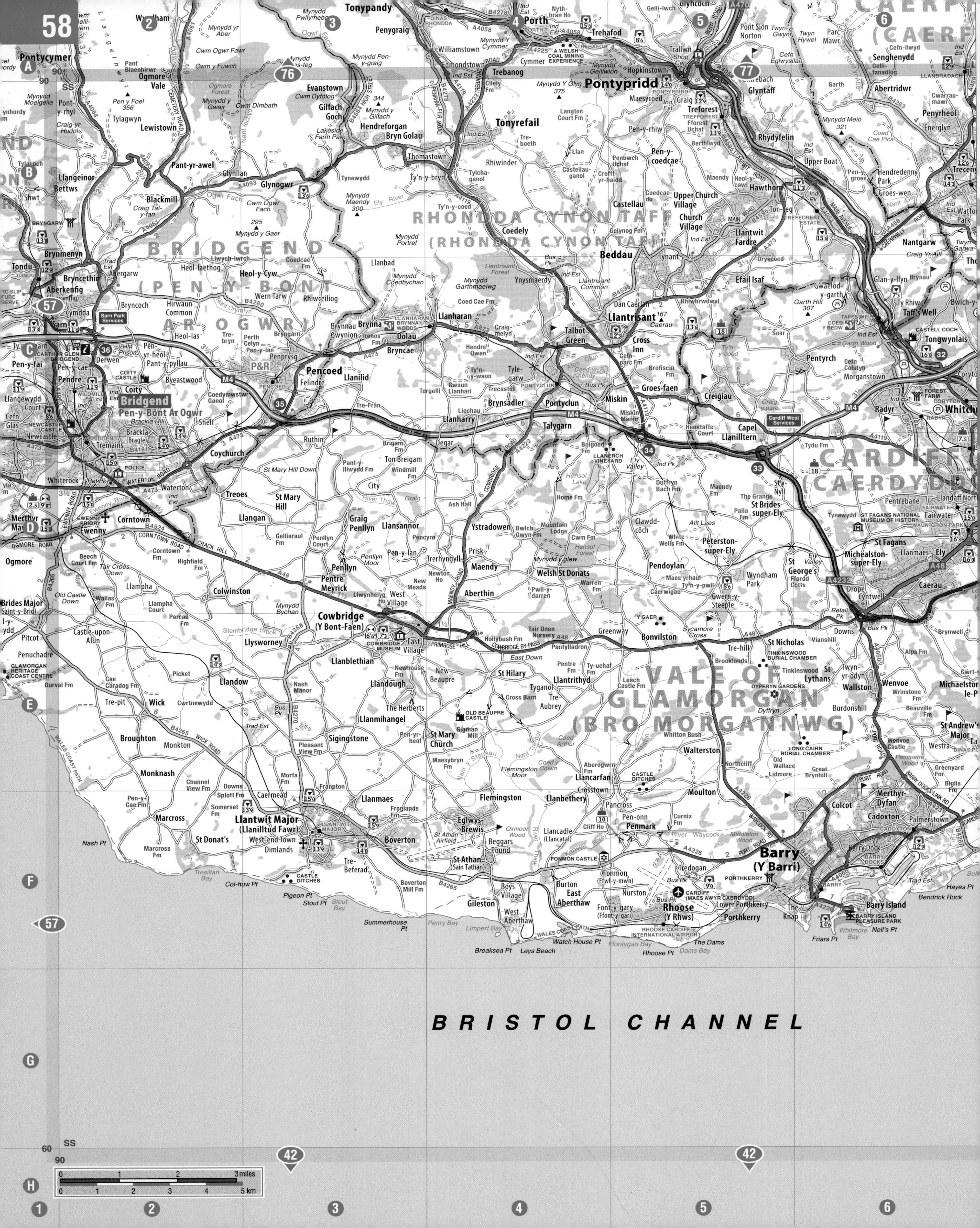

Tonypandy
Porth
Trehafod
Pontypridd
Trebanog
Tonyrefail
Pontycymer
Ogmore Vale
Evanstown
Gilfach Goch
Hendreforgan
Bryn Golau
Thomastown
Lewistown
Blackmill
Glynogwr
Pant-yr-awel
Llangeinor
Bettws
Brynmenyn
Tondu
Bryncethin
Aberkenfig
Heol-y-Cyw
Coedely
Beddau
Llantrisant
Talbot Green
Llanharan
Brynna
Dolau
Bryncae
Pencoed
Felindre
Llanilid
Pontyclun
Miskin
Groes-faen
Creigiau
Pentyrch
Tongwynlais
Radyr
Taff's Well
Nantgarw
Rhydyfelin
Treforest
Glyntaff
Upper Boat
Hawthorn
Church Village
Upper Church Village
Llantwit Fardre
Efail Isaf
Tynant
Castellau
Pen-y-coedcae
Hopkinstown
Maesycoed
Trallwn
Bridgend
Pen-y-Bont Ar Ogwr
Coity
Pen-y-fai
Pendre
Brackla
Tremains
Coychurch
Waterton
Treoes
Llangan
St Mary Hill
Ewenny
Corntown
Merthyr Mawr
Ogmore
Llanharry
Talygarn
Brynsadler
Ystradowen
Welsh St Donats
Pendoylan
Peterston-super-Ely
St Brides-super-Ely
St George's
Michaelston-super-Ely
St Fagans
Caerau
Ely
Capel Llanilltern
Cowbridge
(Y Bont-Faen)
Aberthin
Penllyn
Llansannor
Llanblethian
Llandough
Llysworney
Colwinston
Llampha
St Hilary
Llantrithyd
Bonvilston
St Nicholas
Tre-hill
Wenvoe
Wallston
Walterston
Llancarfan
Llanbethery
Moulton
Penmark
Flemingston
Eglwys-Brewis
St Athan
(Sain Tathan)
Gileston
Boverton
Llantwit Major
(Llanilltud Fawr)
St Donat's
Marcross
Monknash
Broughton
Wick
Llandow
Llanmaes
Rhoose
(Y Rhws)
Barry
(Y Barri)
Barry Island
Porthkerry
Cadoxton
Merthyr-Dyfan
Colcot
Palmerstown
East Aberthaw
West Aberthaw
Fonmon
Dyffryn
St Andrew's Major
RHONDDA CYNON TAF
(RHONDDA CYNON TAF)
BRIDGEND
(PEN-Y-BONT AR OGWR)
VALE OF GLAMORGAN
(BRO MORGANNWG)
CARDIFF
(CAERDYDD)
BRISTOL CHANNEL
M4
A48
A4226
A473
A4119
A4222
A4232
Cardiff West Services
Sarn Park Services
CARDIFF (MAES AWYR CAERDYDD)
RHOOSE CARDIFF INTERNATIONAL AIRPORT
BARRY ISLAND PLEASURE PARK
ST FAGANS NATIONAL MUSEUM OF HISTORY
DYFFRYN GARDENS
OLD BEAUPRE CASTLE
COWBRIDGE MUSEUM
GLAMORGAN HERITAGE COAST CENTRE
WALES COAST PATH
Nash Pt
Col-huw Pt
Summerhouse Pt
Breaksea Pt
Rhoose Pt
Friars Pt
Nell's Pt
76
77
57
42
0 1 2 3 miles
0 1 2 3 4 5 km

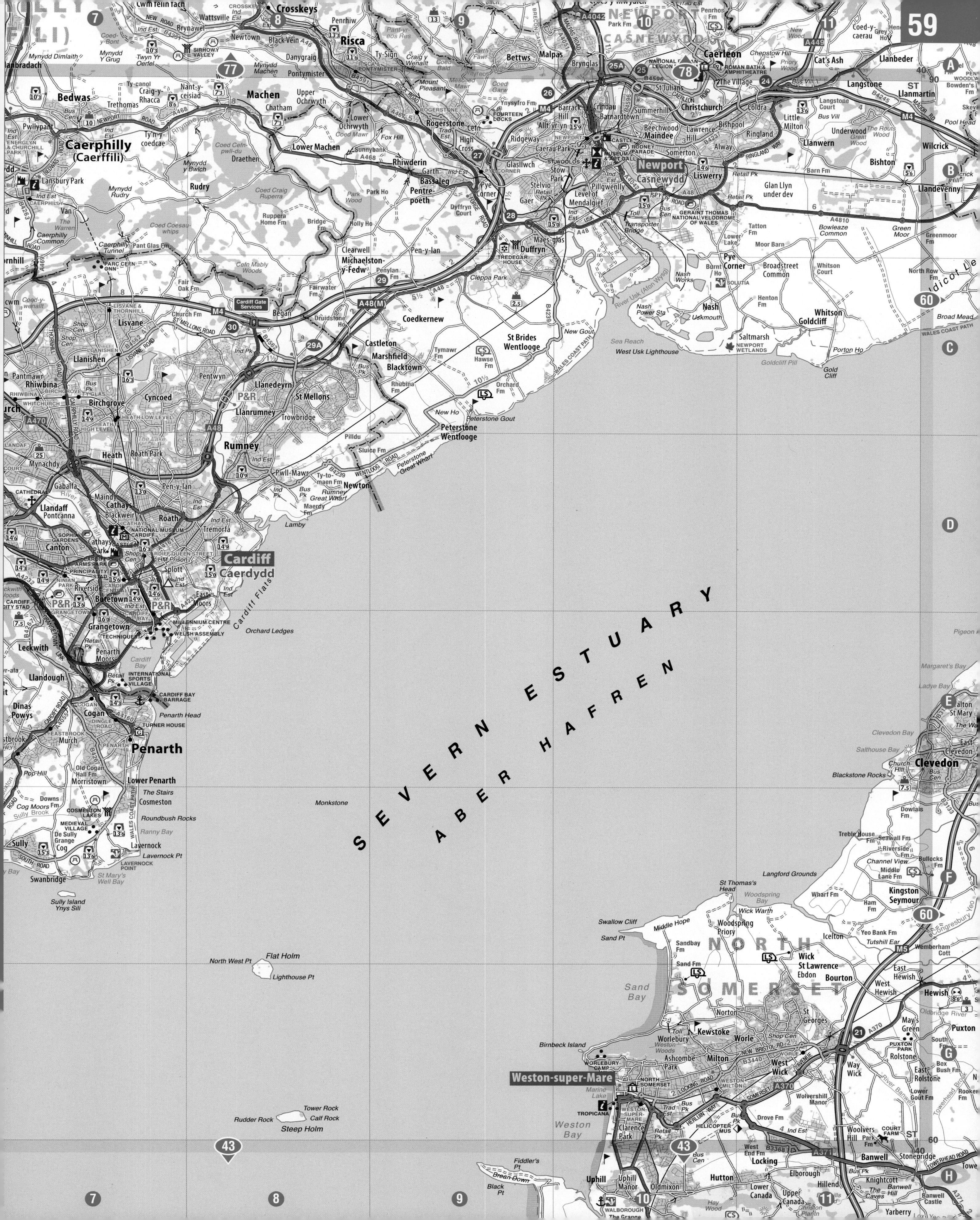

SEVERN ESTUARY
ABER HAFREN
NEWPORT
CASNEWYDD
NORTH
SOMERSET
Crosskeys
Risca
Wattsville
Brynawel
Newtown
Black Vein
Danygraig
Pontymister
Mynydd Dimlaith
Mynydd Machen
Bedwas
Trethomas
Machen
Upper Ochrwyth
Chatham
Caerphilly
(Caerffili)
Lansbury Park
Rudry
Draethen
Lower Machen
Rhiwderin
Bassaleg
Pentre-poeth
Rogerstone
High Cross
Bettws
Malpas
Brynglas
Caerleon
Cat's Ash
Llanbeder
Langstone
Llanmartin
Christchurch
St Julians
Summerhill
Beechwood
Maindee
Barnardtown
Crindau
Allt-yr-yn
Ridgeway
Glasllwch
Stow Park
Pillgwenlly
Level of Mendalgief
Gaer
Stelvio
Newport
Casnewydd
Lliswerry
Ringland
Llanwern
Bishton
Wilcrick
Llandevenny
Glan Llyn under dev
Duffryn
Maes-glas
Tredegar House
Pye Corner
Broadstreet Common
Nash
Whitson
Goldcliff
Saltmarsh
Newport Wetlands
West Usk Lighthouse
Sea Reach
Clearwell
Michaelston-y-Fedw
Pen-y-lan
Coedkernew
Castleton
Marshfield
Blacktown
St Brides Wentlooge
Peterstone Wentlooge
Began
Lisvane
Llanishen
Cyncoed
Pentwyn
Llanedeyrn
St Mellons
Llanrumney
Trowbridge
Rumney
Rhiwbina
Birchgrove
Heath
Roath Park
Mynachdy
Gabalfa
Llandaff
Pontcanna
Maindy
Cathays
Roath
Tremorfa
Pen-y-lan
Splott
Canton
Cathays Park
Riverside
Butetown
Grangetown
Cardiff
Caerdydd
Cardiff Flats
Orchard Ledges
Leckwith
Penarth Moors
Llandough
Cardiff Bay Barrage
Dinas Powys
Cogan
Penarth Head
Turner House
Murch
Penarth
Lower Penarth
The Stairs
Cosmeston
Roundbush Rocks
Ranny Bay
Lavernock
Lavernock Pt
Sully
Swanbridge
Sully Island
Ynys Sili
Monkstone
Flat Holm
North West Pt
Lighthouse Pt
Tower Rock
Rudder Rock
Calf Rock
Steep Holm
Clevedon
Clevedon Bay
Blackstone Rocks
Langford Grounds
St Thomas's Head
Woodspring Priory
Wick Warth
Middle Hope
Swallow Cliff
Sand Pt
Sand Bay
Kingston Seymour
Wick St Lawrence
Bourton
Hewish
Puxton
Kewstoke
Worle
Worlebury
Milton
Ashcombe Park
St Georges
West Wick
Birnbeck Island
Weston-super-Mare
Weston Bay
Locking
Hutton
Uphill
Oldmixon
Banwell
Brean Down
Fiddler's Pt
Black Pt
7
8
9
10
11
43
60
77
78
A
B
C
D
E
F
G
H

Parc-Seymour
Llanvaches
Discoed
Llandevaud
Penhow
Llanbeder
Chapel Fm
The Knoll
Carrow Hill
St Bride's Netherwent
Highmoor Hill
Llanmartin
Wilcrick
Bishton
Magor
Magor Services
Vinegar Hill
Rogiet
Llanfihangel Rogiet
Undy
Llandevenny
Causeway
Whitewall Common
Barecroft Common
Green Moor
Summerleaze
Redwick
Caldicot Level
Broad Mead
Porton Grounds
WALES COAST PATH
Welsh Grounds
Bedwin Sands
Caldicot
Deepweir
Portskewett
Sudbrook
CALDICOT CASTLE
SEVERN TUNNEL JUNCTION
Caerwent
Caerwent Brook
Crick
Mount Ballan
Leechpool
Mathern
Newton Green
Beachley
Severn Road Bridge
Prince of Wales Bridge
Severn Tunnel
Charston Sands
St Pierre Pill
Slimeroad Sand
Severn View Services
Aust
Old Passage
Littleton-on-Severn
Cowhill
Kington
Elberton
Olveston
Ingst
Tockington
Alveston
Alveston Down
Rudgeway
Thornbury
Morton
OLDOWN
New Passage
Redwick
Northwick
Awkley
Pilning
Severn Beach
SEVERN BEACH
Almondsbury
Marsh Common
Easter Compton
Over
Dyer's Common
Distribution Park
Avonmouth Works
Crook's Marsh
Gravel Banks
WILD PLACE PROJECT
Compton Greenfield
Elmington Manor Fm
CRIBBS CAUSEWAY
PLANET ICE
Catbrain
AEROSPACE BRISTOL MUS
Patchway
Little Stoke
Bradley Stoke
Stoke Gifford
Great Stoke
Winterbourne
Frogland Cross
Hallen
Berwick
Henbury
Brentry
Filton
Blaise Hamlet
Lawrence Weston
BLAISE CASTLE HOUSE
Southmead
Harry Stoke
Hambrook
Frenchay
Avonmouth
King Road
Shirehampton
Coombe Dingle
Westbury on Trym
Sea Mills
Henleaze
Horfield
Golden Hill
MEMORIAL STADIUM
CITY AND COUNTY OF BRISTOL
Fishponds
Stapleton
Broomhill
Stoke Bishop
Redland
Bishopston
HM Prison
Westbury Park
Sneyd Park
Eastville
Easton
Speedwell
Clifton
CLIFTON DOWN
Redland
Montpelier
CABOT CIRCUS
CABOT TOWER
SS GREAT BRITAIN
BRISTOL TEMPLE MEADS
St George
St Anne's Park
Conham
Hanham
Bristol
Arno's Vale
Bedminster
Knowle
Brislington
Broom Hill
Woodhill
Black Nore
West Hill
Portishead
Redcliff Bay
Hang Rock
Portishead Down
Sheepway
Middle Bridge
Gordano Services
Lodway
Pill
Easton-in-Gordano
Ham Green
Portbury
North Weston
Farley
Weston-in-Gordano
Clapton-in-Gordano
Walton-in-Gordano
GORDANO VALLEY
Walton Bay
Pigeon House Bay
Margaret's Bay
Ladye Bay
Charlcombe Bay
Abbots Leigh
Leigh Woods
NOAH'S ARK ZOO FARM
Lower Failand
Failand
Tyntesfield
TYNTESFIELD
Wraxall
ASHTON COURT ESTATE
Bower Ashton
Long Ashton
Ashton Vale
Walton St Mary
CLEVEDON COURT
Clevedon
Clevedon Bay
Clevedon Moor
Norton's Wood
CADBURY CAMP
Middletown
Tickenham
Stone-edge Batch
Nailsea
East End
Flax Bourton
Cambridge Batch
Backwell
Backwell Common
Farleigh
Yanley
Highridge
Bedminster Down
Headley Park
Novers Park
Filwood Park
Lower Knowle
Hengrove
Hengrove Park
Bishopsworth
Withywood
Hartcliffe
Whitchurch
Stockwood
Keynsham
Kenn
Kenn Moor
West End
Backwell West Town
NORTH
SOMERSET
Chelvey
Brockley
Barrow Gurney
Barrow Common
Dundry
East Dundry
Maes Knoll
Queen Charlton
Kingston Seymour
North End
Claverham
Yatton
Horsecastle
Cleeve
Lulsgate Bottom
BRISTOL INTERNATIONAL
Felton
Upper Town
Winford
North Wick
Norton Hawkfield
Norton Malreward
Belluton
Pensford
Congresbury
Hewish
West Hewish
Puxton
Wrington
Redhill
Ridgehill
Regil
Chew Magna
Stanton Drew
STANTON DREW STONE CIRCLES
Upper Stanton Drew
Stanton Wick
Chew Stoke
Brinsea
Churchill
Churchill Green
Cowslip Green
Havyatt Green
Butcombe
Nempnett Thrubwell
Strode
Chew Valley Lake
Denny Island
Bishop Sutton
Sutton Wick
Stowey
Clutton
Chelwood
BATH AND NORTH EAST SOMERSET
Lower Langford
Langford Green
Upper Langford
Rickford
Burrington
Blagdon
BLAGDON PUMPING STATION
Ubley
Rowberrow
Star
Banwell
Yarberry
Temple Cloud
Cholwell
M4
M5
M32
M48
M49
A38
A37
A369
A370
A4
A403
A4174
A368
B3130
B3128
B4055
Severn Road Bridge
Bristol International
0 1 2 3 miles
0 1 2 3 4 5 km
59
78
79
44
A B C D E F G H
1 2 3 4 5 6

Morton
Whitfield
Bibstone
Charfield
Kingswood
Tresham
Leighterton
Doughton
The Knapp
Cromhall
Churchend
Alderley
Burden Court Fm
Westonbirt Arboretum
Westonbirt
Shipton Moyne
Milbury Heath
Cromhall Common
Hillesley
Lower Kilcott
Upper Kilcott
Tytherington
Wickwar
Chase Hill
Oldbury on the Hill
Knockdown
Willesley
Easton Grey
Itchington
Bagstone
Hall End
Hawkesbury Upton
Hawkesbury
Starveall
Didmarton
Rangeworthy
Latteridge
Iron Acton
Horton
Little Badminton
Sopworth
Sherston
Pinkney
Foxley
Engine Common
Yate Rocks
Goose Green
Little Sodbury
Luckington
Norton
Frampton Cotterell
Nibley
Yate
Chipping Sodbury
Old Sodbury
Badminton
Alderton
Hullavington
Coalpit Heath
Mayshill
Rodford
Westerleigh Common
Acton Turville
Littleton Drew
Grittleton
Stanton St Quintin
Winterbourne Down
Westerleigh
Wapley
Dodington
Tormarton
Burton
Leigh Delamere
SOUTH
Codrington
Nettleton
WILTSHIRE
COTSWOLDS
Mangotsfield
Pucklechurch
Hinton
West Kington
Castle Combe
Kington St Michael
Staple Hill
Dyrham
Yatton Keynell
GLOUCESTERSHIRE
Siston
Abson
West Littleton
North Wraxall
Mountain Bower
Ford
Allington
Hardenhuish
Kingswood
Warmley
Doynton
Marshfield
Upper Wraxall
Slaughterford
Biddestone
Frogwell
Bridge Yate
Wick
Cold Ashton
Thickwood
Oldland
Colerne
Upper Pickwick
Corsham
Easton
Willsbridge
Bitton
Upton Cheyney
Langridge
St Catherine
Alcombe
Box
Hawthorn
Gastard
Notton
North Stoke
Woolley
Swainswick
Charlcombe
Northend
Batheaston
Neston
Kelston
Saltford
Bathford
Bathampton
Atworth
Whitley
Shaw
Beanacre
Corston
Weston
Bath
Monkton Farleigh
Burnett
Newton St Loe
Twerton
Claverton
South Wraxall
Norrington Common
Broughton Gifford
Melksham
Odd Down
Combe Down
Bradford Leigh
Stanton Prior
Englishcombe
Monkton Combe
Holt
Hunstrete
Marksbury
Inglesbatch
Southstoke
Bradford-on-Avon
Staverton
Farmborough
Priston
Midford
Limpley Stoke
Winsley
Turleigh
Semington
Hilperton
SOMERSET
Freshford
Avoncliff
Westwood
Dunkerton
Combe Hay
Twinhoe
Wellow
Peasedown St John
Carlingcott
Trowle Common
Trowbridge
M4
A46
A4
A36
A350
A420
A432

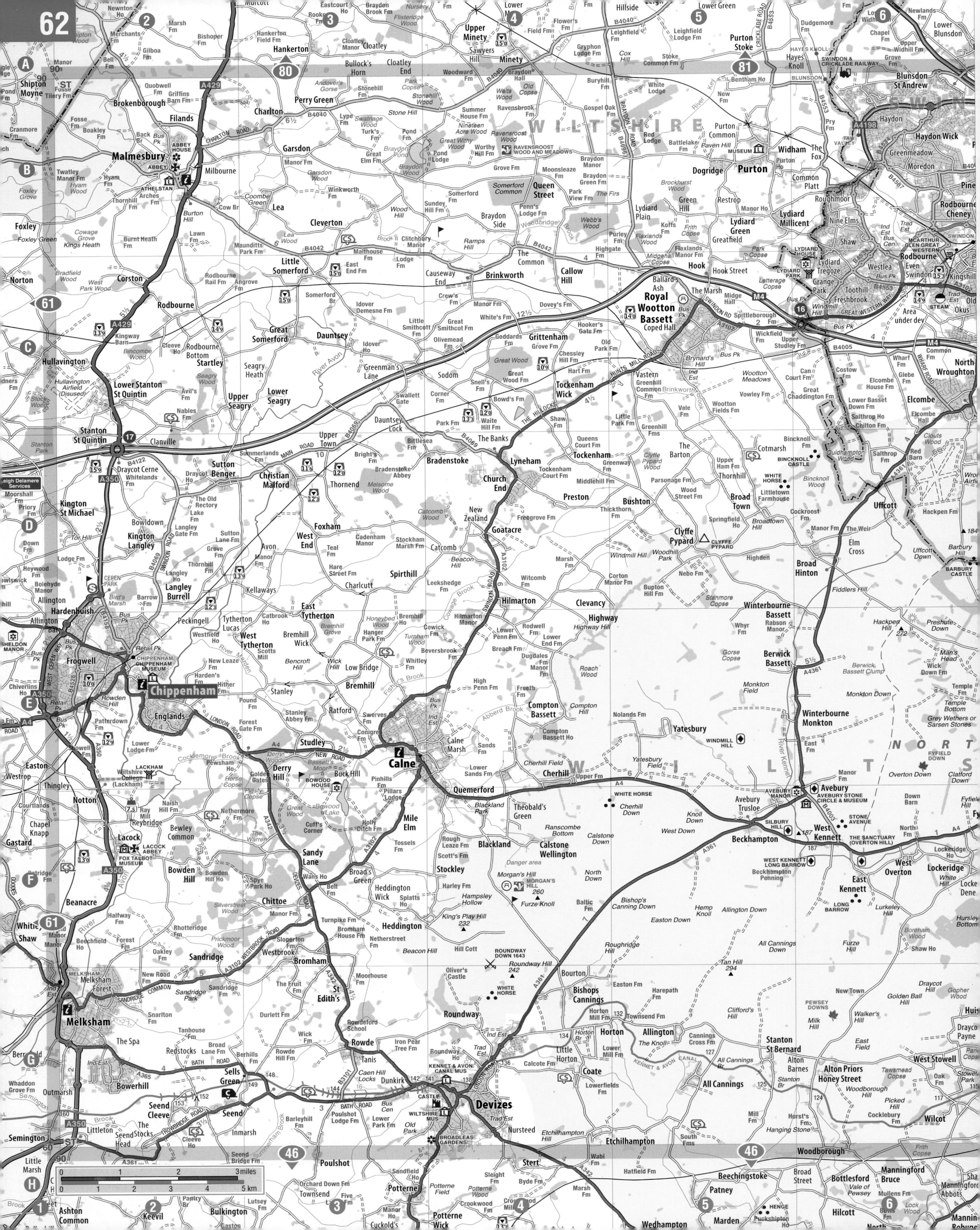

Malmesbury
Chippenham
Calne
Devizes
Melksham
Royal Wootton Bassett
Lyneham
Avebury
Purton
Minety
Upper Minety
Hankerton
Charlton
Garsdon
Lea
Cleverton
Brinkworth
Little Somerford
Great Somerford
Dauntsey
Hullavington
Lower Stanton St Quintin
Stanton St Quintin
Upper Seagry
Lower Seagry
Sutton Benger
Christian Malford
Kington St Michael
Kington Langley
Langley Burrell
Hardenhuish
Frogwell
Englands
Studley
Derry Hill
Quemerford
Cherhill
Yatesbury
Compton Bassett
Hilmarton
Goatacre
Bradenstoke
Tockenham
Tockenham Wick
Clyffe Pypard
Broad Hinton
Winterbourne Bassett
Berwick Bassett
Winterbourne Monkton
West Kennett
East Kennett
West Overton
Lockeridge
Beckhampton
Uffcott
Elcombe
Lydiard Millicent
Lydiard Green
Widham
Dogridge
Hook
Blunsdon St Andrew
Haydon Wick
Rodbourne Cheney
Wroughton
Lacock
Notton
Bowden Hill
Sandy Lane
Chittoe
Heddington
Bromham
Sandridge
Rowde
Roundway
Bishops Cannings
Horton
Allington
All Cannings
Etchilhampton
Stanton St Bernard
Alton Priors
Honey Street
West Stowell
Wilcot
Potterne
Poulshot
Seend
Seend Cleeve
Sells Green
Bowerhill
Semington
Beanacre
Whitley
Shaw
Keevil
Bulkington
Ashton Common
Marden
Patney
Beechingstoke
Manningford Bruce
Bottlesford
Woodborough
Stert
WILTSHIRE
SWINDON & CRICKLADE RAILWAY
KENNET & AVON CANAL
M4
A4
A429
A350
A3102
A342
A361
A4361
80
81
61
46

Swindon
Stratton St Margaret
Shrivenham
Watchfield
Longcot
Fernham
Baulking
Uffington
Woolstone
Kingston Lisle
Childrey
Sparsholt
West Challow
East Challow
Wantage
Letcombe Regis
Letcombe Bassett
Ashbury
Idstone
Bishopstone
Hinton Parva
Wanborough
Liddington
Chiseldon
Badbury
Wroughton
Lambourn
Upper Lambourn
Eastbury
East Garston
Great Shefford
Woodlands St Mary
Baydon
Aldbourne
Ramsbury
Ogbourne St George
Ogbourne St Andrew
Ogbourne Maizey
Marlborough
Mildenhall
Axford
Froxfield
Hungerford
Chilton Foliat
Kintbury
Inkpen
Great Bedwyn
Little Bedwyn
Shalbourne
Burbage
Pewsey
Wootton Rivers
Savernake Forest
Oxenwood
Buttermere
Ham
Combe
Faccombe
East Woodhay
Wickham
Welford
North Wessex Downs
Oxon
West Berkshire
Swindon
Wessex Downs
Wiltshire

Steventon
Milton Heights
Didcot
Wallingford
Crowmarsh Gifford
Wantage
Ardington
West Hendred
East Hendred
Harwell
Rowstock
Milton Hill
East Hagbourne
West Hagbourne
Upton
Blewbury
Chilton
South Moreton
North Moreton
Brightwell cum Sotwell
Aston Upthorpe
Aston Tirrold
Cholsey
Moulsford
North Stoke
South Stoke
Goring
Streatley
Woodcote
Ipsden
Letcombe Regis
Lockinge
West Ginge
East Ginge
West Ilsley
East Ilsley
Farnborough
Fawley
South Fawley
Catmore
Lilley
Brightwalton
Brightwalton Green
Chaddleworth
Leckhampstead
Leckhampstead Thicket
Peasemore
Beedon
Stanmore
Compton
Aldworth
Hampstead Norreys
Ashampstead
Upper Basildon
Lower Basildon
Whitchurch-on-Thames
Pangbourne
Quicks Green
Yattendon
Tidmarsh
Sulham
Chieveley
Downend
North Heath
Oare
Little Hungerford
Hermitage
Frilsham
Bradfield
Englefield
Theale
Welford
Weston
Wickham
Westbrook
Winterbourne
Boxford
Curridge
Longlane
Bucklebury
Stanford Dingley
Southend
Cold Ash
Upper Bucklebury
Thatcham
Newbury
Speen
Shaw
Donnington
Stockcross
Halfway
Marsh Benham
Bagnor
Midgham
Woolhampton
Aldermaston Wharf
Aldermaston
Padworth
Beenham
Brimpton
Wasing
Crookham
Greenham
Enborne
Hamstead Marshall
Wash Common
Newtown
Burghclere
Highclere
Headley
Kingsclere Woodlands
Ashford Hill
Heath End
Tadley
Baughurst
Pamber Heath
Silchester
Mortimer West End
Little London
Pamber Green
Wolverton
Ecchinswell
East Woodhay
West Woodhay
Inkpen Common
Ball Hill
Broad Laying
Woolton Hill
North End
NORTH WESSEX DOWNS
WEST BERKSHIRE
OXFORDSHIRE
M4
A34
A339
A4
A417
A329
A340
B4009
THE RIDGEWAY PATH
River Thames
River Kennet
River Lambourn
River Pang
River Enborne
KENNET & AVON CANAL
NEWBURY SHOWGROUND
Chieveley Services
DONNINGTON CASTLE
SNELSMORE COMMON
GREENHAM CONTROL TOWER VISITOR CENTRE
NEWBURY RACECOURSE
NEWBURY DISTRICT MUS
SANDHAM MEMORIAL CHAPEL
SILCHESTER ROMAN TOWN
BASILDON PARK
THE LIVING RAINFOREST
DIDCOT RAILWAY CENTRE
CHOLSEY & WALLINGFORD RAILWAY
VALE & DOWNLAND MUSEUM
82
83
63
48
SU
0 1 2 3 miles
0 1 2 3 4 5 km

Henley-on-Thames
Marlow
Maidenhead
Reading
Caversham
Tilehurst
Woodley
Earley
Whitley
Twyford
Wokingham
Bracknell
Crowthorne
Sandhurst
Camberley
Yateley
Bagshot
Frimley
Sonning
Shiplake
Wargrave
Binfield
Finchampstead
Arborfield
Shinfield
Spencers Wood
Swallowfield
Riseley
Eversley
Hawley
Cookham
Bourne End
Flackwell Heath
Loudwater
Nettlebed
Stoke Row
Checkendon
Sonning Common
Purley on Thames
Calcot
Burghfield
Mortimer
Stratfield Saye
Heckfield
Hartley Wintney
Hazeley
White Waltham
Waltham St Lawrence
Warfield
Winkfield
Ascot
Holyport
Bray
Taplow
Hambleden
Medmenham
Remenham
Hurley
Fawley
Turville
Fingest
Frieth
Stonor
Pishill
Bix
Highmoor Cross
Rotherfield Greys
Rotherfield Peppard
Kidmore End
Mapledurham
BUCKS
CHILTERNS
WINDSOR & MAIDENHEAD
WOKINGHAM
READING
BRACKNELL FOREST
River Thames

Beaconsfield
Loudwater
Chalfont St Peter
Northwood
Harrow
Flackwell Heath
Gerrards Cross
Denham
Ruislip
Eastcote
Rayners Lane
Hedgerley
Farnham Common
Stoke Poges
Uxbridge
Ickenham
Northolt
Burnham
Slough
Iver Heath
Iver
Hillingdon
Greenford
Yeading
Cookham
Taplow
George Green
Langley
Yiewsley
West Drayton
Hayes
Southall
Maidenhead Court
Cippenham
Richings Park
Harmondsworth
Heston
Bray
Dorney
Eton
Windsor
Datchet
Colnbrook
Poyle
Longford
Heathrow Airport
Hounslow
Cranford
Sipson
Harlington
Holyport
Fifield
Oakley Green
Old Windsor
Wraysbury
Stanwell
East Bedfont
Feltham
Twickenham
Winkfield
Cranbourne
Hythe End
Ashford
Hanworth
Egham
Englefield Green
Staines-upon-Thames
Sunbury-on-Thames
Hampton
Ascot
Sunninghill
Sunningdale
Virginia Water
Thorpe
Laleham
Littleton
Shepperton
West Molesey
East Molesey
Chertsey
Walton-on-Thames
Addlestone
Weybridge
Hersham
Esher
Bagshot
Windlesham
Lightwater
Chobham
Ottershaw
Woodham
New Haw
Byfleet
West Byfleet
Cobham
Woking
Pyrford
Wisley
Knaphill
Bisley
Stoke D'Abernon
WINDSOR & MAIDENHEAD
BUCKS
M4
M25
M40
M3
A4
A30
A40
A308
A316
A320
A322
A329
A330
A332
0 1 2 3 miles
0 1 2 3 4 5 km

Stanmore
Canons Park
Edgware
Finchley
Edmonton
Woodford
Belmont
Colindale
Hendon
Muswell Hill
Wood Green
Tottenham
Walthamstow
Wealdstone
Kenton
Kingsbury
Golders Green
Hornsey
Highgate
Greenhill
Harrow on the Hill
North Wembley
Wembley
Neasden
Cricklewood
Hampstead
Stoke Newington
Leyton
Leytonstone
Sudbury
Willesden
Islington
Hackney
Stratford
Alperton
Kilburn
Camden
Perivale
Harlesden
Shoreditch
Bethnal Green
West Ham
Ealing
Acton
Paddington
Finsbury
Holborn
City
Poplar
Shepherd's Bush
Mayfair
Westminster
Blackwall Tunnel
Hammersmith
Kensington
Southwark
Bermondsey
Chiswick
Chelsea
Lambeth
Deptford
Greenwich
Kew Br
Brentford
Fulham
Battersea
Camberwell
Peckham
Isleworth
Richmond
Mortlake
East Sheen
Putney
Clapham
Brixton
Lewisham
Wandsworth
Twickenham
Richmond Park
Balham
Dulwich
Catford
Ham
Teddington
Tooting
Wimbledon
Streatham
Sydenham
Kingston upon Thames
Merton
Mitcham
Penge
Beckenham
Bromley
New Malden
Morden
Norbury
South Norwood
Surbiton
Tolworth
Sutton
Carshalton
Croydon
Addiscombe
Shirley
Hook
Chessington
Cheam
Wallington
Ewell
Purley
Epsom
Banstead
Coulsdon
Ashtead
Chipstead
Whyteleafe
Warlingham
LONDON

Woodford
Woodford Bridge
Hainault
Fairlop
Fullwell Cross
Clayhall
Barkingside
Aldborough Hatch
Upper Walthamstow
South Woodford
Snaresbrook
Redbridge
Gants Hill
Cranbrook
Wanstead
Newbury Park
Seven Kings
Valentines Park
Leytonstone
Aldersbrook
Ilford
Goodmayes
Little Heath
Chadwell Heath
Marks Gate
Romford
Collier Row
Rise Park
Gidea Park
Harold Hill
Harold Wood
Harold Park
Gallows Corner
Ardleigh Green
Emerson Park
Tylers Common
Great Warley
Little Warley
Childerditch
Herongate
Thorndon Country Park
East Horndon
West Horndon
Cranham
Upminster
Hornchurch
Rush Green
Heath Park
Elm Park
Hacton
Corbets Tey
North Ockendon
South Ockendon
Bulphan
Orsett
Baker Street
Thurrock
Becontree
Dagenham
Barking
Loxford
Fair Cross
Little Ilford
Manor Park
Forest Gate
Plashet
Upton
Stratford
Plaistow
Upton Park
West Ham
East Ham
Wallend
Creekmouth
Barking Riverside
South Hornchurch
Rainham
Wennington
Aveley
North Stifford
Grangewaters Outdoor Centre
Beckton
Canning Town
Custom House
London
Barking Reach
Thames
Thamesmead
Crossness Pumping Station
Blackwall
Blackwall Tunnel
Royal Victoria Dock
Royal Albert Dock
London City
Silvertown
Thames Barrier
North Woolwich
Woolwich Ferry
Woolwich
New Charlton
Charlton
Greenwich
Plumstead
Plumstead Common
Abbey Wood
Erith Marshes
Belvedere
Erith
Erith Reach
Coldharbour
Aveley Marshes
Rainham Marshes
Wennington Marshes
Purfleet
Lakeside
West Thurrock
South Stifford
Grays
Chafford Hundred
Little Thurrock
Chadwell Place
Tilbury
Lessness Heath
East Wickham
West Heath
Northumberland Heath
North End
Crayford Ness
Crayford Marshes
Slade Green
Dartford Marshes
Long Reach
Dartford Tunnel
Dartford Crossing
Temple Hill
Blackheath
Kidbrooke
Shooters Hill
Eltham Park
Oxleas Wood
Welling
Bexleyheath
Falconwood
Danson House
Red House
Barnehurst
Crayford
Barnes Cray
Dartford
Stone
Greenhithe
Swanscombe Marshes
Northfleet
Rosherville
Gravesend
Knockhall
Swanscombe
Bluewater
Hither Green
Lee
Eltham
Eltham Palace
Avery Hill
Blackfen
Bexley
Old Bexley
Hall Place
Coldblow
Bowmans
New Eltham
Mottingham
Lamorbey Park
Longlands
Sidcup
Maypole
Heath Side
Fleet Downs
Darenth Wood
Bean
Stonewood
Perry Street
Grove Park
Downham
Chislehurst
Chislehurst West
Foxbury
North Cray
Foots Cray
Sundridge
Elmstead
Scadbury Park
Ruxley
Hextable
Puddledock
Hook Green
Wilmington
Hawley
Clement Street
Lane End
Darenth
Sutton at Home
South Darenth
Betsham
Southfleet
Northfleet Green
Istead Rise
Bromley
Bickley
Widmore
Shortlands
St Paul's Cray
Hockenden
Swanley
White Oak
Swanley Village
Horton Kirby
Longfield
New Barn
Hartley
Nash Street
Petts Wood
St Mary Cray
Derry Downs
Kevingtonn
Crockenhill
Farningham
Hartley Green
Southborough
Bromley Common
Hayes
Orpington
Ramsden
Goddington
Chelsfield
Eynsford
Lullingstone Roman Villa
Lullingstone Castle
Maplescombe
West Kingsdown
Fawkham Green
New Ash Green
Meopham Green
Keston
Keston Mark
Locksbottom
Farnborough
Green St Green
Maypole
Well Hill
Pratt's Bottom
Timberden Bottom
Shoreham
Badger's Mount
Halstead
Knatts Valley
Knockmill
Woodlands
Stansted
Fairseat
Vigo Village
Culverstone Green
Downe
Down House (Charles Darwin Mus)
Leaves Green
Biggin Hill
Cudham
Knockholt Pound
Knockholt
Otford
Kemsing
Heaverham
Crowdleham
Wrotham
Twitton
Fickleshole
Kent
Kent Downs
Thurrock

ESSEX
Burstead
Noak Hill
Crays Hill
Nevendon
Hockley
Hawkwell
Rochford
Rayleigh
Rayleigh Castle
Bullwood Hall
Mount Bovers
Stroud Green
London Southend Airport
Laindon
Lee Chapel
Pipps Hill
Basildon
Chalvedon
Pitsea
North Benfleet
Bowers Gifford
New Thundersley
Thundersley
Weir
Daws Heath
Eastwood
Great Berry
Langdon Hills
Kingswood
Vange
Tarpots
South Benfleet
Hadleigh
Southend-on-Sea
Prittlewell
Southchurch
Westley Heights
Dry Street
Pitsea Marsh
Hope's Green
Leigh-on-Sea
Chalkwell
Westcliff-on-Sea
Clifftown
Kursaal
Wat Tyler
Bowers Marshes
Vange Marshes
Benfleet
Hadleigh Castle
Hadleigh Marsh
Two Tree Island
Leigh
Leigh Sand
Great Malgraves
Wrens Park Fm
Horndon on the Hill
Arden Hall
Balstonia
Stanford le-Hope
Fobbing
Fobbing Marshes
Corringham
Northwick
Winter Gardens
Dutch Cottage Museum
Dutch Village
Canvey Island
Sunken Marsh
Canvey Pt
Chapman Sands
Marsh End Sand
Southend Pier
Pier Rly
Leigh Beck
Oozedam
Coryton
Shellhaven Pt
Hole Haven
Oil Storage Depot
Thorney Bay
Deadman's Pt
DP World London Gateway
Thames Haven
Coryton Wharves
Shell Haven
Mucking
Mucking Flats
Southfields
Thurrock Thameside Nature Reserve
River Thames
Blythe Sands
Mucking Marshes
Linford
East Tilbury
West Tilbury
Low Street
Coalhouse Fort
Tilbury Fort
England Coast Path
Egypt Bay
St Mary's Bay
West Pt
Lower Hope Pt
Cliffe Fleet
Cliffe Marshes
Halstow Marshes
St Mary's Marshes
Redham Mead
Cooling Marshes
Ryestreet Common
Allhallows-on-Sea
Allhallows Marshes
Cockleshell Beach
Roas Bank
Lees Marshes
Allhallows
Dagnam Fm
Decoy Fm
St Mary Hoo
Grain Marsh
The Flats
Isle of Grain
Grain
Cliffe
Cooling Street
Cooling
Bromhey Fm
High Halstow
Northward Hill
Cliffe Pools
West Street
Fenn Street
Lower Stoke
Middle Stoke
Stoke
Isle of Grain Power Sta
Garrison
Blue Town
Higham Saltings
Higham Marshes
Gravesend Reach
Milton
Denton
Shorne Marshes
Church Street
Higham
Dalham Fm
Parbrook Ho
Tunbridge Hill
Tudor Fm
Cooling Court Fm
Ducks Court
Sharnal Street
North Street
The Lappel
Queenborough Spit
Chalk
Lower Higham
Cliffe Woods
Great Chattenden Wood
Chattenden
Stoke Ooze
Elphinstone Pt
Sharp Ness
Stangate Spit
Deadmans Island
Riverview Park
Two Gates
Mockbeggar
Noke Street
Wainscott
Stonebridge
Broad Street
Hoo St Werburgh
Kingsnorth
Burntwick Island
Oakham Marsh
Oakham Ness Jetty
MEDWAY
River Medway
Queenborough
Singlewell
Shorne
Thong
Shorne Ridgeway
Gadshill
Lower Upnor
Upnor Castle
Upper Upnor
Hoo Salt Marsh
Bishop Spit
Bishop Ooze
Ham Ooze
Chetney Marshes
Rushenden
Shorne Wood
Frindsbury
St Mary's Island
Dickens World
Gillingham Reach
The Strand
Copperhouse Marshes
Nor Marsh
Milfordhope Marsh
Barksore Marshes
Bedlams Bottom
Ferry Marshes
Strood
Rochester
Cobham
Cobham Hall
Chatham Historic Dockyard
Brompton
Grange
Ham Green
Wetham Green
Horsham Marsh
Upchurch
Iwade
Sole Street
Lower Bush
Gillingham
Priestfield Stadium
Chatham
Troy Town
Luton
Lower Twydall
Twydall
Lower Rainham
Otterham Quay
Lower Halstow
Henley Street
Cuxton
Borstal
Rainham
Moor Street
Breach
KENT
Luddesdown
North Halling
Wayfield
Hale
Capstone
Newington
Bobbing
Milton Regis
Kemsley
Upper Halling
Halling
Wouldham
Hempstead
Wigmore
Medway Services
Hartlip
Lower Hartlip
Keycol
Key Street
Borden
DOWNS
Walderslade
Lords Wood
Farthing Corner
Chesley
Danaway
Sittingbourne
Paddlesworth
Snodland
Burham
Blue Bell Hill
Kit's Coty
Lidsing
Kemsley Street
Bredhurst
Yelsted
Hill Green
Stockbury
Oad Street
Harman's Corner
Hearts Delight
Tunstall
Highsted
Birling
Eccles
Westfield Sole
Dunn Street
Scragged Oak
South Street
Ryarsh
Leybourne Lakes
New Hythe
Lunsford
Aylesford
Pratling Street
Tyland Barn
Boxley
South Green
Bredgar
Woodstock
Addington
Leybourne
Larkfield
Little Preston
Forstal
Abbey Gate
Boxley Abbey
Kent Life Heritage Farm Park
Kent County Showground
White Horse Wood
Detling
Thurnham
Hucking
Bicknor
Swanton Street
Milstead
Ditton
Sandling
Harbourland
Allington
West Malling
New Town

Paglesham Eastend
Horseshoe Corner
Rugwood Fm
Eastwick Head
Island
Great Burwood Fm
Rugwood Head
Roper's Fm
Barling Marsh
Potton Island
Barling Hall Fm
Asplins Head
88
89
Fleet Head
New England Island
Bolts Fm
Barling
The Broomway
Butler's Fm
High Ho
Rushley Island
Shelford Head
Stonebridge
Little Wakering Wick
Havengore Island
Little Wakering
Oxenham Fm
Sharpness Head
Maplin Sands
Smither's Fm
Shopland Hall
Clay Street Fm
Oldbury Fm
Havengore Head
Haven Pt
Samuel's Corner
Great Wakering
Wakering Stairs
Bournes Green
Southchurch
North Shoebury
Black Grounds
Pig's Bay
Thorpe Bay
Kursaal
Cambridge Town
Shoeburyness
Sea Life Adventure
Eastern Esplanade
Thorpe Esplanade
Pier Rly
69
Southend Pier
Shoebury Ness
West Knock
East Knock
THAMES ESTUARY
Roas Bank
Grain Spit
The Flats
Grain
Garrison Pt
Jacob's Bank
Blue Town
Cheyney Rock
Sheerness
Scrapsgate
Mile Town
Marine Town
Minster Marshes
The Lappel
Queenborough Spit
West Minster
Halfway Houses
Abbey
Deadmans
West Swale
Queenborough Road
Minster Road
East End
Minster
Trouts
Warden Pt
Queenborough
Neats Court
Lower Road
Scocles Fm
Barnland Fm
Warden
Norwood Manor
Eastchurch
Rushenden
Neatscourt Marshes
Parsonage Fm
Leysdown Road
Bay View
Leysdown-on-Sea
Minster Marshes
Southlees Marshes
New Hook Fm
Old Hook Fm
Groves Fm
HM Prison
Old Rides Fm
Capel Hill Fm
Coastal Park
Isle of Sheppey
Stray Marshes
Muswell Manor
Leysdown Marshes
Ferry Marshes
The Dray
Ind Est
Swale
Elmley
Ridham Dock
Eastchurch Marshes
Harty Marshes
Tankerton Bay
Iwade
Elmley Island
Elmley Marshes
Kings Hill Fm
Elmley Marshes
Spitend Marshes
Shell Ness
Long Rock
Coldharbour Marshes
Dutchman's Island
Elliots Fm
The Swale
Whitstable
Swalecliffe
Isle of Harty
Tankerton
Lower Island
Chestfield & Swalecliffe
Shamfleet Creek
Pheasant Fm
The Lillies
The Swale
Peg Fleet
Spitend Pt
Mocketts
Whitstable Bay
Chestfield
Kemsley Down
Sayes Court
Kemsley
Sittingbourne & Kemsley Light Rly
Fowley Island
Conyer Creek
South Deep
The Ferry Inn
Horse Sands
Seasalter
The Oaze
Duncan Down
South Street
Milton Creek
Tonge Corner
Blacketts
South Oaze
Milton Regis
Court Hall Mus
Binny Cotts
Teynham Level
Conyer
Cleve Marshes
Graveney Marshes
Seasalter Level
Bogshole Fm
Radfall
Chalkwell
Murston
Teynham Street
Nagden Marshes
Clapham Hill
Sittingbourne
Teynham Court
Uplees
Poplar Hall
Court Lodge
Graveney Marshes
Fox's Cross
Burgess Fm
Clowes Wood
Snipeshill
Bax
Luddenham Court
Oare
Ham Marshes
Nagden
Broom Street
Graveney Hill
Monkshill Fm
Yorkletts
Pean Hill
Clowes Fm
Sittingbourne
Heritage Mus
Bapchild
Barrow Green
Deerton Street
Nash's Fm
Ham Fm
Highstreet
Red Lion Ho
Radfield
Haywood
Teynham
The Old Farm Ho
Four Oaks
Sandbanks
Graveney
Waterham
Dargate Common
Well Court
Frog Hall
Hearts Delight
Little Dully
Cellarhill
Shepherd Neame Brewery
Chart Gunpowder Mills
Culmers
Denstroude
Rodmersham
Dully Ho
Davington
Faversham
Langdon Court
Fostall
Honey Hill
Amery Court
Tunstall
Highsted
Rodmersham Green
Batteries Fm
Nouds Fm
Lewson Street
Beacon Hill
The Brents
Fleur de Lis Heritage Centre
Goodnestone
Dargate
Acorn Cott
Parsonage Fm
Tyler Hill
Grove End
Upper Rodmersham
Lynsted
Norton Ash
London Road
Ospringe
Ind Est
Ewell Fm
Hernhill
Fairbrook Fm
Blean Wood
Holly Hill
Blean Woods
Blean
Hothe Court Fm
Woodstock
Pitstock Fm
Judd's Hill
Maison Dieu
Perry Court
Loyterton
Preston
Staplestreet
North Bishopden Wood
Newbury
Lynsted Park
Nash Ct
Penfield
Kingsdown
Monk Fm
54
Mount Ephraim
Courte
Church Wood
Blean Woods
Bexon
Whitehill
Brenley Corner
Boughton Street
Dunkirk
Rough Common
Hanslett's Ho
Plumford
Copton
Brenley Ho
Boughton
Upper Harbledown
Homestall Wood
Hall Place
Bluetown
Churchman's Fm
Painter's Forstal
Selgrove
Sole Street Ho
Crouch
South Street
Hickmans Green
Boughton Bypass
Fishpond Wood
Canterbury West
Forester's Lodge Fm
Stock Wood
Sharsted Court
Champion Court
College Wood
Scooks Farm Ho
Littles
North
Owens Court
3 miles
5 km

NORTH SEA
Margate
Westgate on Sea
Birchington
Herne Bay
Reculver
Herne
Sturry
Fordwich
Canterbury
Broadstairs
Ramsgate
Minster
Monkton
Sarre
St Nicholas at Wade
Isle of Thanet
Cliftonville
Kingsgate
North Foreland
St Peters
Pegwell
Pegwell Bay
Sandwich
SANDWICH BAY
Richborough Port
Ash
Wingham
Preston
Stodmarsh
Grove
West Stourmouth
East Stourmouth
Westmarsh
Manston
Newington
St Lawrence
Westwood
Northdown
Garlinge
Hoath
Chislet
Upstreet
Hersden
Westbere
Calcott
Broad Oak
Herne Common
Greenhill
Beltinge
Hillborough
Bishopstone
Eddington
Hampton

ST BRIDES BAY
BAIE SAIN FFRAID
90
91
Newgale Sands
Maidenhall Pt
Rickets Head
Black Cliff
Madoc's Haven
Druidston Haven
Settling Nose
Black Pt
Sleek Stone
Broad Haven
(Aberllydan)
The Settlands
Little Haven
Goultrop Roads
Borough Head
Stack Rocks
Howney Stone
Ticklas Pt
Mill Haven
Halfway Rock
Wales Coast Path
Warey Haven
St Brides Haven
The Nab Head
Tower Pt
St Bride's
Garland Stone
Skomer Head
Skomer Island
North Haven
Little Sound
The Neck
Midland Island
Pigstone Bay
Skomer Island
Ynys Skomer
The Wick
Wooltack Pt
Trwyn Wooltack
Martin's Haven
Haven Pt
High Pt
Musselwick Sands
Musselwick Fm
Skomer Marine Nature Reserve Visitor Centre
Deadman's Bay
Marloes
Marloes Court
Marloes Sands
Rainy Rock
Albion Sands
Gateholm Stack
Gateholm Island
Ynys Gateholm
Marloes Sands
Red Cliff
Summer Only
Broad Sound
Skokholm Island
Little Bay Pt
Ynys Skokholm
Skokholm Island
The Stack
East Bay
Mad Bay
Long Pt
Hog Bay
Long Nose
Quarry Pt
The Head
Frank's Pt
Crab Rocks
Hooper's Pt
Westdale Bay
Great Castle Head
Iron Pt
Long Pt
Welshman's Bay
Little Castle Pt
Frenchman's Bay
Mill Bay
St Ann's Head
Pentir St Ann
Kete
Watwick Bay
Watwick Pt
West Blockhouse Pt
Castlebeach Bay
Dale Pt
Dale Roads
Dale
Townsend
Crabhall Fm
Little Marloes Fm
Windmill Park
Pearson Fm
Ripperston Fm
South Hill
Orlandon
Slatemill Bridge
Butterhill Fm
Slatehill Fm
Marles Fm
Musselwick
St Ishmael's
Watch House Pt
Lindsway Bay
Great Castle Head
Little Castle Head
Bicton
Sandy Haven
Herbrandston
Sandyhaven Pill
PEMBROKESHIRE COAST
NATIONAL PARK
Talbenny
Hasguard Cross
Hasguard Hall
Hasguard
Capeston
Walton West
Fenton
Walwyn's Castle
Moor Fm
Woodsend
Robeston West
Robeston Cross
Hooks
Tiers Cross
Anniket
Rose Cottage Fm
Oil Refinery
Thornton
Priory
Steynton
Lodge Fm
Liddeston
Hubberston
Milford Haven
Hakin
Pill
South Hook Pt
Stack Rock
Milford Haven
Aberdaugleddyf
Milford Haven
Aberdaugleddau
Venn Fm
Oil Refinery
Waterston
Leonardston
Llanstadwell
Honeyborough
Black Bridge
Wear Pt
Rosslare
Wood
Church Hill
Roch Gate
Roch
Ferny Glen
Cuffern
Dudwells
Robleston Hall
Haysford
Wolfsdale
Chapel Hill
Folly
Camrose Brook
Camrose
Cleddau Lodge
Cuttybridge
Knock Fm
Red Hill
Folkeston Hill
Simpson Cross
Keeston
Simpson
Nolton Haven
Nolton
Keeston Moor
Keeston Br
Knock Brook
Trapps Fm
Pelcomb Cross
Pelcomb
Dunston Grove
Pelcomb Bridge
Pelcomb Fm
Slade
Lambeston
Druidston
Haroldston West
Castle High
Rogeston
West Lambeston
Sutton Lodge
Cuckoo Grove
Sutton
Haverfordwest Town Mus
Albert Town
Haven Road
Corner Fm
Rosehill
Portfield Gate
Skerryford
Trad Est
Timber Hill
Hangstone Davey
Hill Fm
Dreenhill
Merlin's Bridge
Nattshook Fm
Broadway
West Denant
Denant
Ratford Bridge
Barn Fm
North Johnston Fm
Pope Hill
Johnston
Cranham
Deemshill
Rose Hill
Milford Road
Hayston Hall
Hayston Mill
Upper Scoveston
Scoveston
Scoveston Fort
Thorn Island
Chapel Bay
West Angle Bay
Angle
Angle Pt
Sawdern Pt
Popton Pt
Bullwell Bay
Oil Refinery
Angle Bay
Bae Angle
Rhoscrowther
Pwllcrochan
Pennar Mouth
Pembroke Power Sta
Lambeeth Fm
Rat Island
The Hall
Castles Bay
Sheep Island
Ynys y Defaid
Parsonsquarry Bay
Carters Green
East Pickard Bay
Kilpaison Burrows
Gravel Bay
Newton Corseside
Wallaston Green
Freshwater West
Gupton Fm
Corston
Great Furzenip
Castlemartin
Axton Hill
Frainslake Sands
Brownslade Burrows
Cold Comfort
Blucks Pool
Brownslade
Warren
Merrion
Merrion Cross
St Twynnells
Berry Slade
Wind Bay
Danger area
PEMBROKESHIRE
Artillery Range
COAST NATIONAL PARK
Linney Head
Pen-y-holt Bay
Bulliber Down
Mount Sion Down
Elegug Stacks
Flimston Bay
The Wash
Mewsford Pt
SM
SR
70
20
90
0 1 2 3 miles
0 1 2 3 4 5 km

Nantyreglwys
Garllegan Fawr
Cwm
Cefnmystrych
Ffynnon-ddrain
Pen-y-banc
Dyffryn
Marlais
Gellydogin
Pantygroes
Baily Mawr
Penback Fm
Bank y llain
Penlan
Llangarthginning
Rhosyn-coch
Drefach
Sarnau Fm
Bwlch Fm
Cwmduhen
Merthyr
Nantybwla
Trevaughan
Pentre'r hydd
Carmarthen
Caerfyrddin
Tanerdy
ROMAN AMPHITHEATRE
Bryn Myrddin
ABERGWILI JUNCTION
Abergwili
CARMARTHEN COUNTY MUSEUM
Blaencediw
Fynnonfoida
Llwyngwydd
Plascerdin
Pantyrhas
Cett
92
Meidrim
Hafod Fm
Derllys Court
Cwmau Bach
Trebersed
93
Llangunnor
CAPEL DEWI ROAD
Berthlwyd
Llangynin
Troedyrhiw
Esgair
B4299
B4298
Pantyderi
Pen-pontbren
Llethrach
Maes-y-Prior
Travellers Rest
LLYSONEN ROAD
Tre-gynwr
Nant
Pengwern
Penlan
Pentowin
MEIDRIM ROAD
Sarnau
UNITED COUNTIES SHOWGROUND
P&R
Johnstown
Ind Est
CARMARTHEN
Pensarn
mfelin
Penuwch
Blaenycoed
Pen-y-coed
Bron-y-gaer
Nantyrhebog
CORS GOCH LLANLLWCH
Llanllwch
Bolahaul Fm
Cilpost Fm
Aber
Llwynbychan
Whitland Abbey
Derry Hall
Wern Fm
Bancyfelin
Cwmcoch
Penplas
Wern Ddu
LLANSTEFFAN ROAD
B4312
Pibwrlwyd
A48
Beaulieu-fawr
The Grove
Llwyndewi
Pont-y-Fenni
13½
10½
Pwllygrafel
College Fm
Wernlaus
Cwmffrwd
Bwlchymynydd
THE GATE CRAFT CENTRE
Cowin Grove
Cwrt Malle
Ystradwalter
Oaklands
A40
Ind Est
Moor
Zabulon
Whitland
(Hendy-Gwyn)
Fforest Fm
WHITLAND
Pwll-trap
St Clears
Sanclêr
Asgood Fm
Llangynog
Maenllwyd
Ffynnon
Llaethdy
Dolaumeinion
Glasfryn
Glogue
Llangain
Croesyceiliog
Llwynfilltir
High Street
Trevaughan
Great Pale
Clog-y-fran
Dolerwydd
Backe
Ty'r Gate
Croes-y-ceilog
Moelfre
Waundas
Pistyll
Idole
Gelliddu
Rhydw
Llwyn-y-brain
Little Pale
River Taf Afon Taf
Lower Court
Ardderfin
Nantego
Llwyn-du
Penhen
Lan Ho
Old Pale
A477
Gelli
Coomb (Cheshire Home)
Bancycapel
B4306
B4309
Lowmead Fm
Brynamlwg
Brunant
Llanddowror
Moor Fm
Four Wheels
WALES COAST PATH
Penycoed
Gilfach
Towy Castle Fm
Parry's Castle
Cloigyn
B4328
73
aenwaun
205 Brandy Hill
Cnwce
Vaynor Fm
Cwmllyfri
Morfa Bach
A484
Pen-y-maes
Pencelli Fm
Gon Grove
Tre-hudion
Llwyngwcw
Llwyncelyn
Pontant
Cildywyll
New Mill
Halfpenny Furze
Hall Down
Whitehill Down
Cross Inn
Hendre
Lanmartin
Crugan-fawr
Ystradferthyr
West Rose
Woodhouse Fm
A4066
Llanybri
Lan Fm
Afon Tywi
CARMARTHENSHIRE
(SIR GAERFYRDDIN)
Cwm-celyn
Red Roses
Milton Fm
Glan-y-môr
Iscoed Home Fm
Clgadan Hall
Ystrad-fawr
Llandyfaelog
Hazel Grove
Windleway
Llandawke
Laugharne
(Talacharn)
DYLAN THOMAS BOATHOUSE
LAUGHARNE CASTLE
Black Scar
Pentowyn
Down Fm
Llansteffan
Ferry Fm
River Towy
Llancwm Fm
Manor Court
The Green
Pentre
West Pool
Syke
Colston Fm
Llansadurnen
B4314
Broadway
LLANSTEFFAN CASTLE
FERRYSIDE
Cilfeithy Fm
Wer
159 Marros Mountain
Brook
Lord's Park
St Anthony's Well
Ferryside
(Glan-y-Fferi)
East Pool
Tremoilet Fm
Castle Lloyd Fm
Westmead Fm
Plashett
River Taf Afon Taf
Wharley Pt
Broadlay
Wenallt
Mynydd y Garreg
4½
Allt-Cunedda
Marros
Pendine
(Pentywyn)
Llanmiloe
Hurst Ho
Pengay Fm
Broadway
Allt Fm
Penlan Uchaf
Rogerlay
Mynyddygarreg
HIRE COAST
AL PARK
Marros Beacon 123
Garness Fm
East Marsh
Longridge
East Ho
Ginst Pt
St Ishmael
Llansaint
Goitre
Glyn Abbey
Telpyn Fm
Dolwen Pt
West Marsh
Tanylan Fm
KIDWELLY CASTLE
Llangadog
Garreg Fm
Pont-newydd
Marros Sands
Gilman Pt
Laugharne Burrows
Salmon Point Scar
Penallt Fm
Telpyn Pt
Ragwen Pt
Pendine Sands
Danger area
Laugharne Sands
Kidwelly
(Cydweli)
Tywyn Pt
Gwendraeth
KIDWELLY
B4308
Cefn Sidan Sands
Danger area
Moat
Danger area
Ty Cornel Fm
CARMARTHEN BAY
BAE CAERFYRDDIN
Danger area
Pembrey Forest
WALES COAST PATH
PEMBREY
Waun y-clyn
Pinged
Bryndias Fm
Ty Mawr
FFRWD FARM MIRE
Penllwyn Uchaf
B4317
Penybedd
Penllwyn Isaf
Draenog
Cenrhos
Graig
GWSCWM ROAD
Achddu
PEMBREY & BURRY PORT
PEMBREY
Pembrey
(Pembre)
Furnace
Bu
(Por
Berges Island
Whiteford Sands
Hills Tor
Broughton Bay
Minor Pt
Twlc Pt
Llanmadoc
Burry Holms
Llanmadoc Hill 186
Spaniard Rocks
Llangennith Moors
Tankeylake Moor
Diles Lake
Kennexstone
Hillend
Coety Green
Llangennith
152 Hardings Down
Druids Lodge
Rhossili Down
White Moor
RHOSSILI BAY
56
The Beacon 193
Kingshall
RHOSSILI VISITOR CENTRE
Rhossili
Talgarth's Well
Blow Hole
Devil's Bridge
SN
20
SS
90
20
0 1 2 3 miles
0 1 2 3 4 5 km
A
B
C
D
E
F
G
H
1
2
3
4
5
6

Nantgaredig
Pont-ar-gothi
Llanegwad
Cilsan
Ffairfach
White Mill
Capel Dewi
Felindre
Dryslwyn
Dryslwyn Castle
Llanarthne
Golden Grove
Maerdy
Cwmgigfran
Paxton's Tower
The National Botanic Garden of Wales
Nantycaws
Penrhiwgoch
Trapp
Carreg Cennen Castle & Farm Centre
Derwydd
Milo
Temple Bar
Llanddarog
Maesybont
Carmel
Llandyfan
Black Mountain
Dre-fach
Porthyrhyd
Cwmisfael
Pentre-Gwenlais
Llandybie
Llangendeirne
Foel-gastell
Castell-y-rhingyll
Cefneithin
Gorslas
Blaenau
Brynamman
Upper Brynamman
Crwbin
Drefach
Cwm-y-glo
Cross Hands
Cae'r-bryn
Pen-y-groes
Morfa
Saron
Tir-y-dail
Garnant
Glanaman
Ammanford
(Rhydaman)
Betws
Pontamman
Bancffosfelen
Pontyberem
Tumble
(Y Tymbl)
Capel Hendre
Penybanc
Pantyffynnon
Gwaun-Cae-Gurwen
Pentre
Meinciau
Cwmgwili
Tycroes
Greynor
Cwmgors
Four Roads
Pont-Henri
Pontyates
(Pont-iets)
Llannon
Garnswllt
Bryndu
Llwyn-Têg
Pont Abraham Services
Cynheidre
Sylen
Llanedi
Carway
Horeb
Sardis
Five Roads
SWANSEA
(ABERTAWE)
Trimsaran
Pentrebach
Fforest
Hendy
Pontarddulais
Cwm-Dulais
Rhyd-y-gwin
Pontardawe
Trebanos
Felinfoel
Swiss Valley
Allt
Felindre
Rhyd-y-pandy
Craig-cefn-parc
Clydach
Llangennech
Waungron
Furnace
Dafen
Pwll
Bryn
Pontlliw
Grovesend
Sandy
Llanelli
Gorseinon
Penllergaer
Llwyn-hendy
Llangyfelach
Morriston
(Treforys)
Bynea
Yspitty
Loughor
Machynys
Garden Village
Cadle
Birchgrove
Llansamlet
River Loughor
Afon Llwchwr
Gowerton
(Tre-Gwyr)
Fforest-fach
Landore
Pen-clawdd
Crofty
Blue Anchor
Three Crosses
Waunarlwydd
Cockett
Cwmdu
Llanmorlais
Wernffrwd
Bon-y-maen
Pentre-chwyth
Foxhole
Port Tennant
St Thomas
Dunvant
(Dynfant)
Killay
Sketty
Landimore
Cheriton
Llanrhidian
Upper Killay
Brynmill
Swansea
Abertawe
Burry Green
THE GOWER
Gower Peninsula
Llethrid
Mayals
Black Pill
SWANSEA BAY
BAE ABERTAWE
Reynoldston
Ilston
Lunnon
Parkmill
Kittle
West Cross
Knelston
Penmaen
Nicholaston
Mumbles
The Mumbles
(Y Mwmbwls)
Newton
Oystermouth
Southgate
Penrice
Pennard
Mansel field

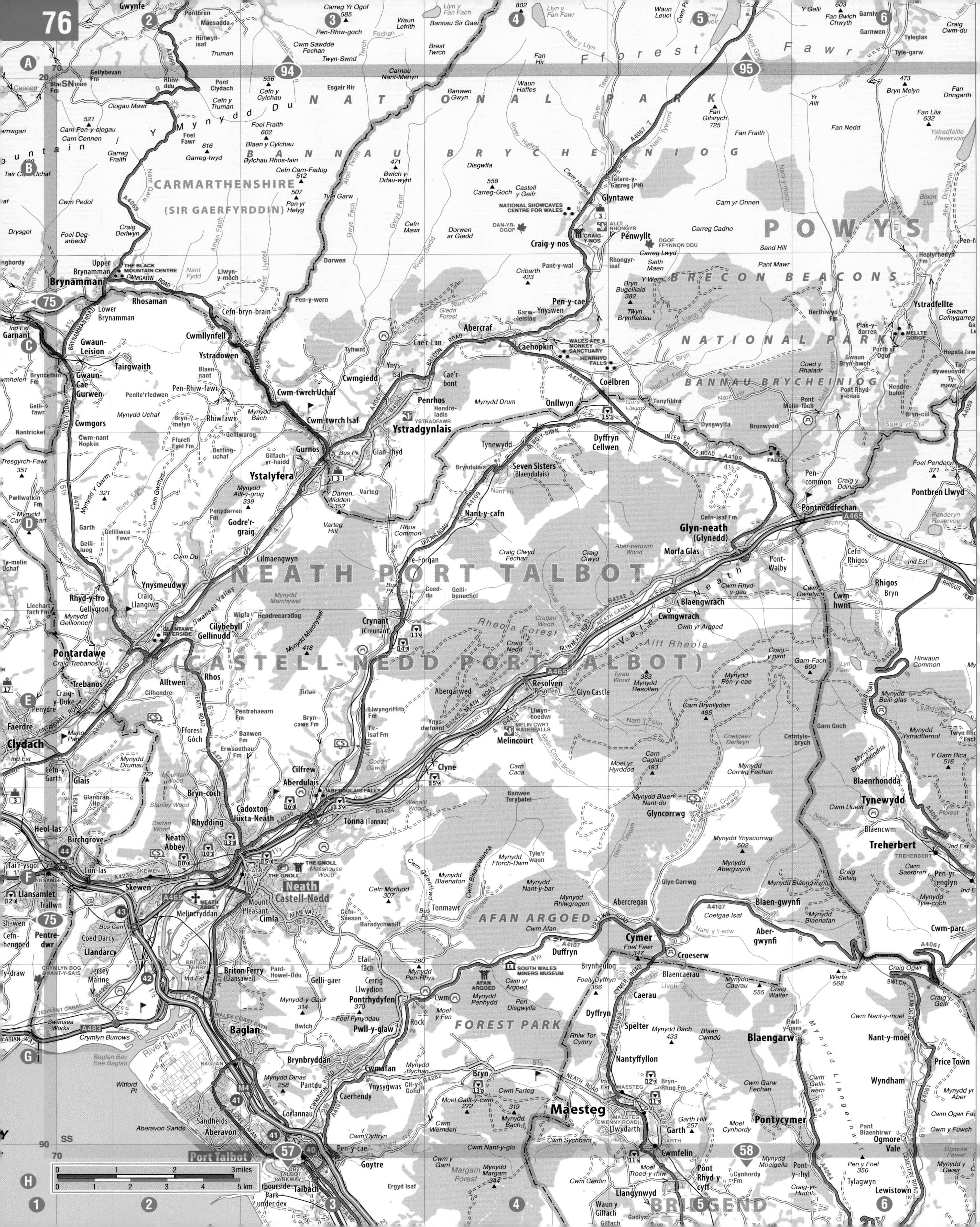

BANNAU BRYCHEINIOG NATIONAL PARK
Fforest Fawr
CARMARTHENSHIRE
(SIR GAERFYRDDIN)
POWYS
BRECON BEACONS NATIONAL PARK
BANNAU BRYCHEINIOG
NEATH PORT TALBOT
(CASTELL-NEDD PORT TALBOT)
AFAN ARGOED
FOREST PARK
BRIDGEND
Y Mynydd Du
Gwynfe
Brynamman
Upper Brynamman
Lower Brynamman
Rhosaman
Garnant
Gwaun-Leision
Tairgwaith
Gwaun-Cae-Gurwen
Cwmgors
Cwmllynfell
Ystradowen
Cwm-twrch Uchaf
Cwm-twrch Isaf
Gurnos
Ystradgynlais
Ystalyfera
Godre'r-graig
Abercraf
Caehopkin
Coelbren
Onllwyn
Glyntawe
Craig-y-nos
Pen-y-cae
Penwyllt
Dyffryn Cellwen
Seven Sisters
(Blaendulais)
Nant-y-cafn
Glyn-neath
(Glynedd)
Morfa Glas
Pontneddfechan
Ystradfellte
Pontbren Llwyd
Rhigos
Cwm-hwnt
Blaengwrach
Cwmgwrach
Resolven
(Resolfen)
Glyn Castle
Melincourt
Clyne
Tonna (Tonnau)
Aberdulais
Cilfrew
Crynant
(Creunant)
Pontardawe
Trebanos
Clydach
Alltwen
Rhos
Gellinudd
Cilybebyll
Ynysmeudwy
Rhyd-y-fro
Bryn-coch
Rhydding
Cadoxton-Juxta-Neath
Neath Abbey
Birchgrove
Llansamlet
Skewen
Neath
Castell-Nedd
Cimla
Melincryddan
Briton Ferry
(Llansawel)
Baglan
Port Talbot
Aberavon
Taibach
Cwmafan
Pontrhydyfen
Cymer
Duffryn
Glyncorrwg
Croeserw
Caerau
Maesteg
Nantyffyllon
Spelter
Blaengarw
Pontycymer
Garth
Cwmfelin
Llangynwyd
Treherbert
Tynewydd
Blaenrhondda
Blaen-gwynfi
Abergwynfi
Cwm-parc
Nant-y-moel
Price Town
Wyndham
Ogmore Vale
Lewistown
Swansea Bay
Baglan Bay
Aberavon Sands
Rheola Forest
Vale of Neath
0 1 2 3 miles
0 1 2 3 4 5 km

Brecon Beacons
MERTHYR TYDFIL
(MERTHYR TUDFUL)
RHONDDA CYNON TAFF
CAERPHILLY
(CAERFFILI)
BLAENAU GWENT
Merthyr Tydfil
Merthyr Tudful
Aberdare
(Aberdâr)
Mountain Ash
(Aberpennar)
Rhondda
Pontypridd
Caerphilly
Ebbw Vale
(Glyn Ebwy)
Tredegar
Rhymney
(Rhymni)
New Tredegar
(Tredegar Newydd)
Bargoed
(Bargod)
Blackwood
(Coed Duon)
Treharris
Abercynon
Nelson
Hengoed
Gelligaer
Ystrad Mynach
Hirwaun
Penderyn
Treorchy
(Treorci)
Ferndale
Tonypandy
Porth
Tonyrefail
Abercarn
Oakdale
Brynmawr
Nantyglo
Blaina
Beaufort
Llangynidr
Llangattock
Abercynafon
Dowlais
Aberfan
Troedyrhiw
Merthyr Vale
Pontsticill
Vaynor
Princetown
Pontlottyn
Fochriw
Tafarnau-bach
Dukestown
Trefil
Bedlinog
Cwmaman
Penrhiwceiber
Llwynypia
Ystrad
Ton-Pentre
Maerdy
Cilfynydd
Llanbradach
Bedwas
Senghenydd
Abertridwr
Trinant
Penywaun
Cwmbach
Aberaman
Nant-ddu
HEADS OF THE VALLEYS ROAD
A470
A465
A4059
A4054
A472
A469
A4048
A4233
A4058
A4060
B4560
95
96
78
58
59
77

BRECON BEACONS
NATIONAL PARK
BANNAU BRYCHEINIOG
MONMOUTHSHIRE
(SIR FYNWY)
BLAENAU GWENT
TORFAEN
(TOR-FAEN)
NEWPORT
CASNEWYDD
Abergavenny
Y Fenni
Crickhowell
(Crug Hywel)
Llangattock
Llangenny
Cwrt-y-gollen
Glangrwyney
Llanbedr
Gilwern
Llanelly
Govilon
Clydach
Blackrock
Llanelly Hill
Llanfoist
Llanellen
Nantyglo
Blaina
Coalbrookvale
Cwm-celyn
Forge Side
Blaenavon
Garn-yr-erw
Varteg
Cwmavon
Abersychan
Garndiffaith
Talywain
Abertillery
Blaenau-Gwent
Six Bells
Aberbeeg
Cwmtillery
East Bank
Llanhilleth
Brynithel
St Illtyd
Trinant
Pontypool
(Pont-y-pwl)
Trevethin
Griffithstown
Sebastopol
New Inn
Upper Cwmbran
Pontnewydd
Croesyceiliog
Cwmbran
Llanyrafon
Llantarnam
Oakfield
Henllys
Llanfrechfa
Crumlin
Oakdale
Newbridge
Lanfach
Abercarn
Cwmcarn
Pontywaun
Crosskeys
Risca
Rogerstone
Bettws
Malpas
Caerleon
Christchurch
Ponthir
Llanhennock
Usk
(Brynbuga)
Llanbadoc
Llangybi
Tredunnock
Newbridge-on-Usk
Raglan
Llandenny
Gwehelog
Monkswood
Little Mill
Goetre
Penperlleni
Llanover
Llanvihangel Gobion
Llanarth
Bettws Newydd
Kemeys Commander
Llanfair Kilgheddin
Nant-y-derry
Llantilio Pertholey
Mardy
Llanvetherine
Llantilio Crossenny
Llanvapley
Llandewi Rhydderch
Llandewi Skirrid
Llangattock Lingoed
Llanfihangel Crucorney
Bettws
Cross Ash
Bryngwyn
Tregare
Penrhos
Pen-yr-heol
Kingcoed
Twyn-y-Sheriff
Llangwm
Llanllowell
Coed-y-paen
Llanvaches
Parc-Seymour
Penhow
Llanbeder
Cat's Ash
Llanmartin
St Bride's Netherwent
Wilcrick
Machen
Lower Machen
M4
A40
A465
A4042
A449
A472
A467
A48
77
96
97
59
60
0 1 2 3 miles
0 1 2 3 4 5 km

Monmouth
Trefynwy
Chepstow
Cas-gwent
Coleford
Cinderford
Lydney
Thornbury
Caldicot
Berkeley
Mitcheldean
Newnham
Blakeney
Ross-on-Wye
Goodrich
Walford
Llangarron
Llancloudy
Welsh Newton
St Maughans
Rockfield
Dixton
Over Monnow
Wonastow
Mitchel Troy
Penallt
Redbrook
Newland
Staunton
Christchurch
Berry Hill
Five Acres
Joyford
Edge End
Mile End
Broadwell
Coalway
Milkwall
Ellwood
Parkend
Yorkley
Whitecroft
Bream
Pillowell
Viney Hill
St Briavels
Hewelsfield
Woolaston
Alvington
Aylburton
Tutshill
Sedbury
Beachley
Tintern Parva
Brockweir
Llandogo
Trellech
Whitebrook
Catbrook
Devauden
Shirenewton
Mathern
Caerwent
Crick
Portskewett
Aust
Oldbury-on-Severn
Shepperdine
Rockhampton
Falfield
Tortworth
Whitfield
Alveston
Elberton
Littleton-on-Severn
Ruardean
Drybrook
Lydbrook
Symonds Yat
Whitchurch
Ganarew
Longhope
Flaxley
Littledean
Ruspidge
Soudley
Awre
Purton
Sharpness
Newtown
Wanswell
Stone
Woodford
FOREST OF DEAN
FOREST PARK
GLOUCESTERSHIRE
SOUTH GLOUCESTERSHIRE
River Severn
River Wye
WYE VALLEY
Sheperdine Sands
Oldbury Sands
Severn Road Bridge
Severn View Services
Michaelwood Services

Gloucester
Taynton
Tibberton
Rudford
Maisemore
Twigworth
Innsworth
Parton
Bamfurlong
Benhall
Lansdown
Longford
Lassington
Highnam Green
Longlevens
Churchdown
Up Hatherley
Leckhampton
Glasshouse Hill
Huntley
Bulley
Highnam
Over
Kingsholm
Elmbridge
Badgeworth
Longhope
Little London
Birdwood
Churcham
Linton
National Waterways Museum
Wotton
Barnwood
Shurdington
Oakle Street
Minsterworth
Meadow Park
Barton
Coney Hill
Hucclecote
Blaisdon
Northwood Green
Elmore Back
Hempsted
St Paul's
Linden
Tredworth
Saintbridge
Abbeydale
Brockworth
Bentham
Little Shurdington
Flaxley
The Flat
Farleys End
Elmore
Podsmead
Lower Rea
Robins Wood Hill
Matson
Tuffley
Bondend
Watermead
Green Street
Little Witcombe
Barrow Wake
Shab Hill
Elton
Westbury-on-Severn
Chaxhill
Kenton Green
Lower Tuffley
Upton St Leonard's
Great Witcombe
Birdlip
Stockwell
Waterend
Quedgeley
Whaddon
Moorend
High Brotheridge
Nettleton
Stantway
Westbury Court Gdns
Gatwick
Boxbush
Longney
Hardwicke
Four Mile Elm
Brookthorpe
Cranham
Brimpsfield
Newnham
Broadoak
Strand
Cleeve
Rodley
River Severn
Painswick Hill
Paradise
Cotswold Commons & Beechwoods
Sheepscombe
Caudle Green
Arlingham
Milton End
Epney
Parkend
Haresfield
Colethrop
Harescombe
Painswick Rococo Garden
Jack's Green
Whiteway
Overton
Fretherne
Saul
Upper Framilode
Moreton Valence
Putloe
Little Haresfield
Stockend
Edge
Painswick
Longridge
Miserden
The Camp
Northington
Awre
Whitminster
Wheatenhurst
Standish
Haresfield Beacon
Pitchcombe
Wick Street
Lypiatt
Sudgrove
Throughame
Frampton on Severn
Fromebridge
Nupend
Arlebrook
Stroud Green
Whiteshill
Ruscombe
Randwick
Slad
Church End
Claypits
Chipmans Platt
Nastend
Oldend
Westrip
Bread Street
Puckshole
Uplands
Bisley
Battlescombe
Edgeworth
Frampton Sand
WWT Slimbridge Wetland Centre
Alkerton
Churchend
Millend
Eastington
Stonehouse
Cashes Green
Paganhill
Cainscross
Ebley
Stroud
Nashend
Waterlane
Purton
Shepherd's Patch
Middle Street
Cress Green
Bridgend
Ryeford
Stanley Downton
Dudbridge
Selsley
Rodborough
Bowbridge
Kitlye
Bournes Green
Tunley
Cambridge
Slimbridge
Leonard Stanley
King's Stanley
Butterrow
Lightpill
Kingscourt
Thrupp
Far Thrupp
Brimscombe
Eastcombe
Oakridge
Daneway
Bussage
Chalford
France Lynch
Frocester
Middleyard
Rooksmoor
Bagpath
Hinton
Halmore
Moorend
Woodchester
Houndscroft
Brownshill
Frampton Mansell
Gossington
Coaley
St Chloe
Littleworth
Minchinhampton Common
Burleigh
Hyde
Wanswell
Draycott
Silver Street
Woodchester Park
Amberley
Minchinhampton
Bubblewell
Burnt Ash
Breadstone
Berkeley Road
Upthorpe
Coaley Peak
Nympsfield
Windsoredge
Watledge
Hampton Green
Forest Green
Forwood
Box
Lower Cam
The Quarry
Cam
Upper Cam
Cockadilly
Nailsworth
Berkeley Heath
Tilsdown
Ashmead Green
Uley Long Barrow
The New Lawn
Newmarket
Shortwood
Ball's Green
Hampton Fields
Berkeley Castle
Stinchcombe
Heathfield
Kingshill
Owlpen
Rockness
Harleywood
Whiteway
Cherington
Rodmarton
Dursley
Uley
Downend
Horsley
Nag's Head
Avening
Woodmancote
Rockstowes
Shadwell
Bencombe
Barton End
Westfield
Highfields
Elcombe
Tiltups End
West End
Swanley
Nibley Green
Forthay
Millend
Pitt Court
Kingscote
Woodford
Lower Wick
Middle Wick
Stone
Michaelwood Services
North Nibley
Southend
Calcot Fm
Chavenage Green
Chavenage House
Tetbury Upton
Culkerton
Ashley
Damery
Howley
Bournstream
Wimley Hill
Bagpath
Newington Bagpath
Lasborough
Beverston Castle (rems of)
Beverston
Huntingford
Avening Green
Tortworth
Bradley Green
Bradley
Coombe
Ozleworth
Tetbury
Long Newnton
Chedglow
Wotton-under-Edge
Boxwell
Leyhill
Charfield Hill
Charfield Green
Bibstone
Charfield
Kingswood
Abbey Gatehouse
Little Bristol
Churchend
Tresham
Leighterton
Doughton
Townwell
Talbot's End
Cromhall
Wortley
Alderley
Westonbirt Arboretum
Heath End
Hillesley
Lower Kilcott
Westonbirt
Shipton Moyne
Brokenborough
Filands
Upper Kilcott
Oldbury on the Hill
Knockdown
Willesley
Easton Grey
Malmesbury
Abbey House
Ashworth Fm
Lower Woods Lodge
Inglestone Common
Splatt's Barn
Elmleaze Barn
0
1
2
3 miles
0
1
2
3
4
5 km
A
B
C
D
E
F
G
H
1
2
3
4
5
6
98
99
79
61
62

GLOUCESTERSHIRE
COTSWOLDS
WILTSHIRE
SWINDON
Cheltenham
Charlton Kings
Whittington
Sevenhampton
Syreford
Andoversford
Dowdeswell
Salperton
Notgrove
Cold Aston
Bourton-on-the-Water
Wyck Rissington
Upper Rissington
Little Rissington
Shipton
Shipton Solers
Shipton Oliffe
Hampen
Hazleton
Turkdean
Clapton-on-the-Hill
Great Rissington
Seven Springs
Coberley
Upper Coberley
Cowley
Compton Abdale
Withington
Cassey Compton
Hampnett
Northleach
Farmington
Sherborne
Great Barrington
Windrush
Little Barrington
Eastington
Yanworth
Stowell
Colesbourne
Elkstone
Chedworth
Fossebridge
Coln St Dennis
Calcot
Aldsworth
Syde
Winstone
Rendcomb
Foss Cross
Coln Rogers
Winson
Woodmancote
Calmsden
North Cerney
Duntisbourne Abbots
Duntisbourne Leer
Ablington
Arlington
Bibury
Bagendon
Duntisbourne Rouse
Middle Duntisbourne
Daglingworth
Barnsley
Coln St Aldwyns
Hatherop
Eastleach Turville
Eastleach Martin
Baunton
Ready Token
Quenington
Netherton
Fyfield
Stratton
Southrop
Cirencester
Ampney Crucis
Ampney St Mary
Ampney St Peter
Fairford
Milton End
Poulton
Coates
Chesterton
Preston
Harnhill
Siddington
Driffield
Meysey Hampton
Horcott
Whelford
Lechlade-on-Thames
Tarlton
Inglesham
Kemble
Ewen
Shorncote
South Cerney
Down Ampney
Marston Meysey
Dunfield
Kempsford
Poole Keynes
Kemble Wick
Somerford Keynes
Cerney Wick
Latton
Castle Eaton
Hannington Wick
Upper Inglesham
Chelworth
Oaksey
Ashton Keynes
Cricklade
Calcutt
Hannington
Highworth
Crudwell
Eastcourt
Leigh
Chelworth Upper Green
Chelworth Lower Green
Murcott
Hankerton
Upper Minety
Minety
Purton Stoke
Broad Blunsdon
Lower Blunsdon
Stanton Fitzwarren
Redlands
Sevenhampton
Cloatley
Charlton
Perry Green
Garsdon
Purton Common
Widham
Haydon Wick
Upper Stratton
South Marston
Penhill
Blunsdon St Andrew
Hayes Knoll
A40
A436
A417
A429
A419
A433
A435
A361
B4425
B4040
B4696
B4553
B4019
B4000
99
100
82
62
63
7
8
9
10
11
A
B
C
D
E
F
G
H

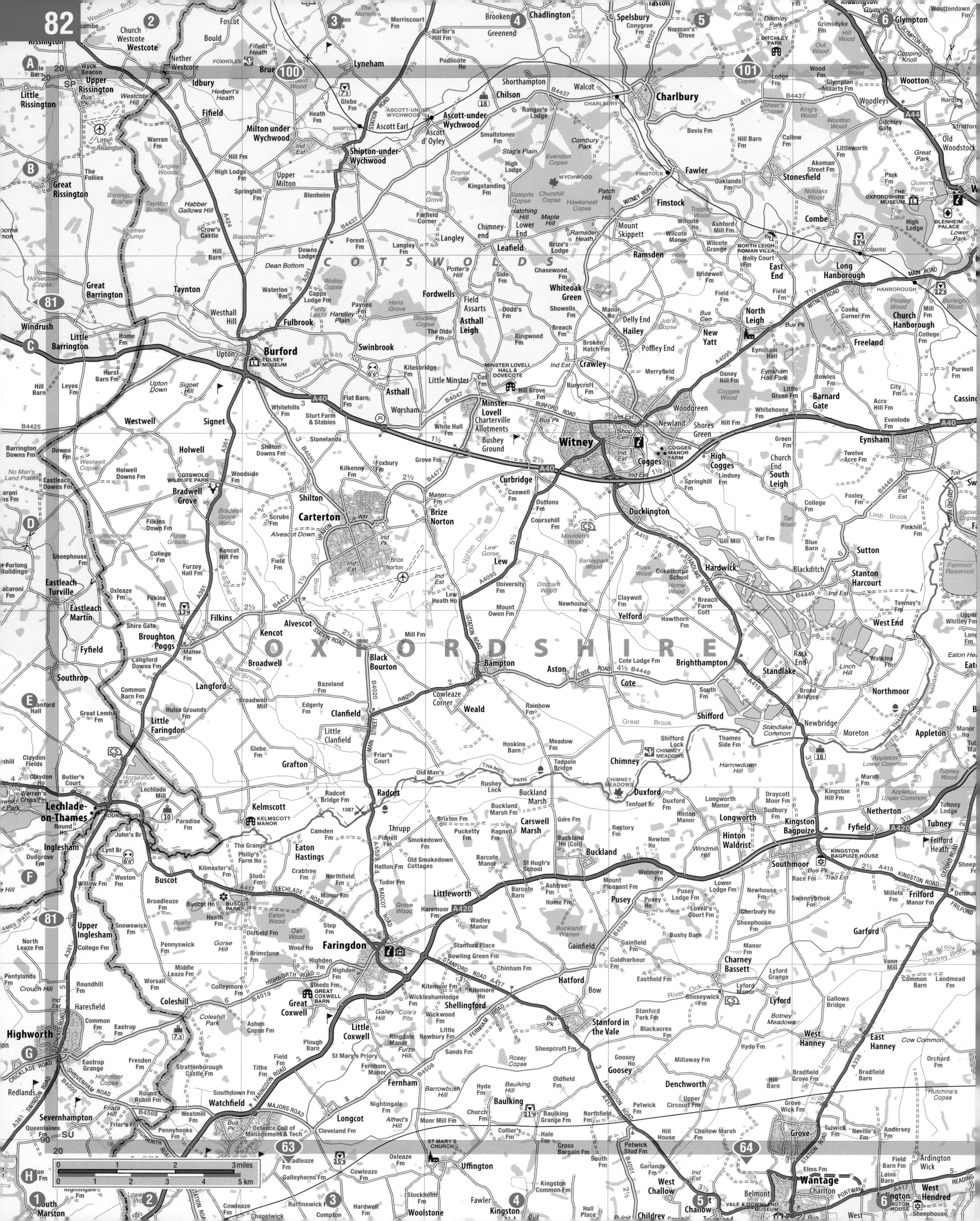

82
Church Westcote
Westcote
Nether Westcote
Idbury
Fifield
Little Rissington
Upper Rissington
Great Rissington
Milton under Wychwood
Shipton-under-Wychwood
Ascott-under-Wychwood
Ascott Earl
Lyneham
Chadlington
Spelsbury
Chilson
Shorthampton
Walcot
Charlbury
Glympton
Wootton
Woodleys
Old Woodstock
Fawler
Finstock
Stonesfield
Combe
Blenheim Palace
Cornbury Park
Wychwood
Leafield
Ramsden
Long Hanborough
Church Hanborough
Freeland
North Leigh
New Yatt
Hailey
Crawley
Whiteoak Green
Fordwells
Asthall Leigh
Swinbrook
Asthall
Worsham
Minster Lovell
Burford
Taynton
Fulbrook
Great Barrington
Little Barrington
Windrush
Westwell
Signet
Holwell
Bradwell Grove
Shilton
Carterton
Brize Norton
Curbridge
Witney
Cogges
Ducklington
Eynsham
Newland
Woodgreen
High Cogges
South Leigh
Hardwick
Sutton
Stanton Harcourt
Lew
Yelford
Alvescot
Kencot
Filkins
Broughton Poggs
Eastleach Turville
Eastleach Martin
Fyfield
Southrop
Langford
Broadwell
Black Bourton
Bampton
Aston
Cote
Brighthampton
Standlake
Northmoor
Weald
Clanfield
Little Clanfield
Little Faringdon
Grafton
Shifford
Chimney
Duxford
Radcot
Kelmscott
Lechlade-on-Thames
Inglesham
Buscot
Eaton Hastings
Thrupp
Carswell Marsh
Buckland
Longworth
Hinton Waldrist
Kingston Bagpuize
Southmoor
Fyfield
Tubney
Appleton
Netherton
Moreton
Frilford
Garford
Littleworth
Pusey
Faringdon
Upper Inglesham
Coleshill
Great Coxwell
Little Coxwell
Shellingford
Hatford
Gainfield
Charney Bassett
Lyford
Stanford in the Vale
Goosey
West Hanney
East Hanney
Denchworth
Highworth
Watchfield
Severnhampton
Longcot
Fernham
Baulking
Uffington
Woolstone
Kingston
Childrey
West Challow
Grove
Wantage
West Hendred
COTSWOLDS
OXFORDSHIRE
A40
A361
A420
A415
A417
A338
A4095
0 1 2 3 miles
0 1 2 3 4 5 km

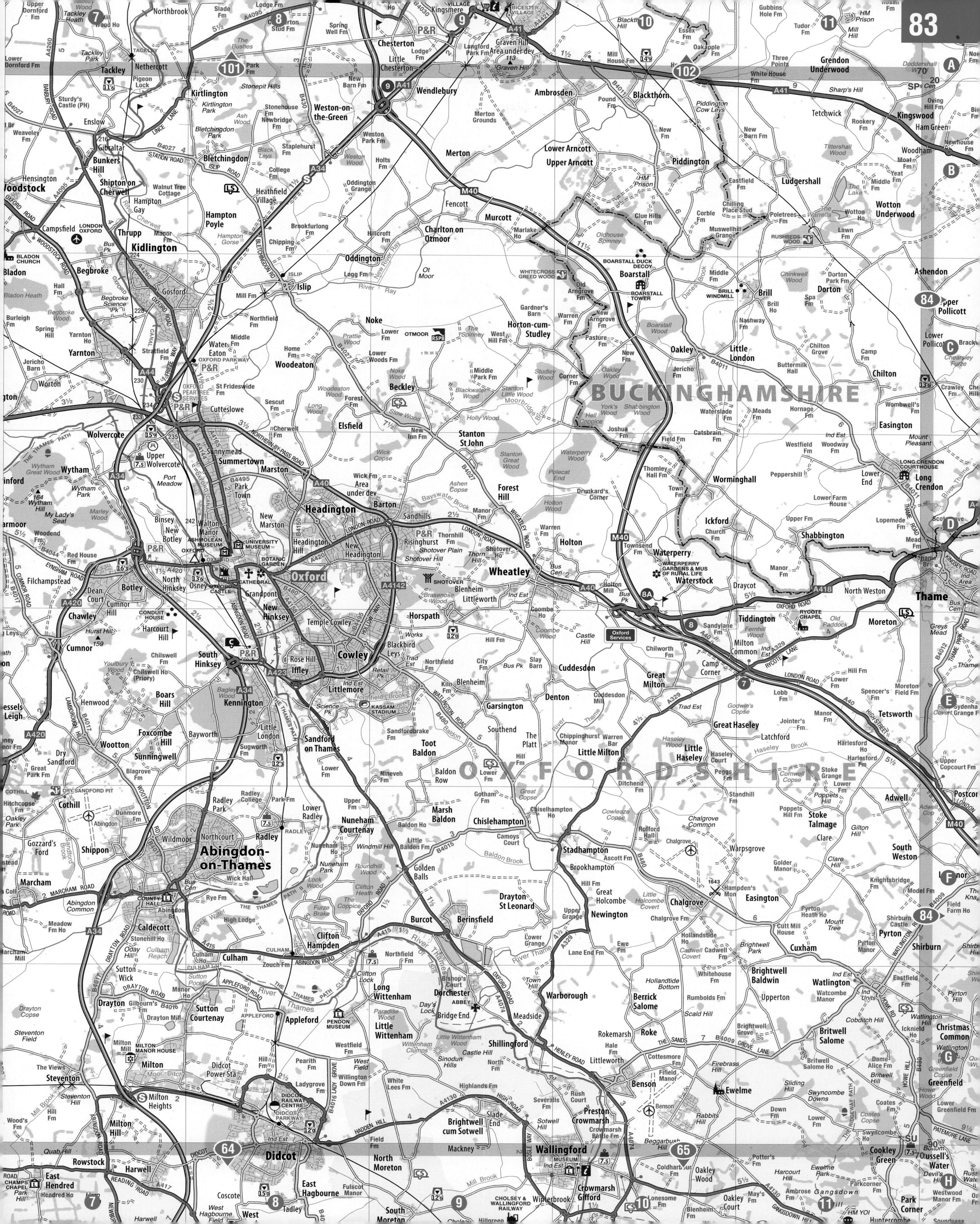
BUCKINGHAMSHIRE
OXFORDSHIRE
Oxford
Headington
Cowley
Kidlington
Abingdon-on-Thames
Didcot
Wallingford
Thame
Wheatley
Bicester Village
Chesterton
Wendlebury
Ambrosden
Blackthorn
Grendon Underwood
Kingswood
Tackley
Kirtlington
Weston-on-the-Green
Bletchingdon
Merton
Lower Arncott
Upper Arncott
Piddington
Ludgershall
Wotton Underwood
Woodstock
Shipton on Cherwell
Hampton Poyle
Thrupp
Charlton on Otmoor
Murcott
Fencott
Oddington
Islip
Boarstall
Brill
Dorton
Ashendon
Bladon
Begbroke
Yarnton
Noke
Horton-cum-Studley
Woodeaton
Beckley
Oakley
Little London
Chilton
Elsfield
Stanton St John
Easington
Wolvercote
Wytham
Summertown
Marston
Forest Hill
Worminghall
Long Crendon
Ickford
Shabbington
Holton
Waterperry
Waterstock
Botley
North Hinksey
Cumnor
Chawley
Horspath
Littleworth
Tiddington
North Weston
Moreton
Iffley
Littlemore
Kennington
South Hinksey
Garsington
Cuddesdon
Denton
Great Milton
Little Milton
Great Haseley
Little Haseley
Tetsworth
Sandford on Thames
Toot Baldon
Marsh Baldon
Chislehampton
Stadhampton
Radley
Nuneham Courtenay
Drayton St Leonard
Berinsfield
Chalgrove
Easington
Stoke Talmage
Adwell
South Weston
Pyrton
Shirburn
Watlington
Cuxham
Brightwell Baldwin
Berrick Salome
Warborough
Dorchester
Shillingford
Benson
Ewelme
Culham
Clifton Hampden
Long Wittenham
Little Wittenham
Appleford
Sutton Courtenay
Drayton
Milton
Steventon
Harwell
Rowstock
East Hendred
Brightwell cum Sotwell
North Moreton
South Moreton
Crowmarsh Gifford
Cholsey
Britwell Salome
Christmas Common
Greenfield
Cookley Green
M40
A34
A40
A41
A420
A329
A4074
A4130
A415
101
102
64
65
84

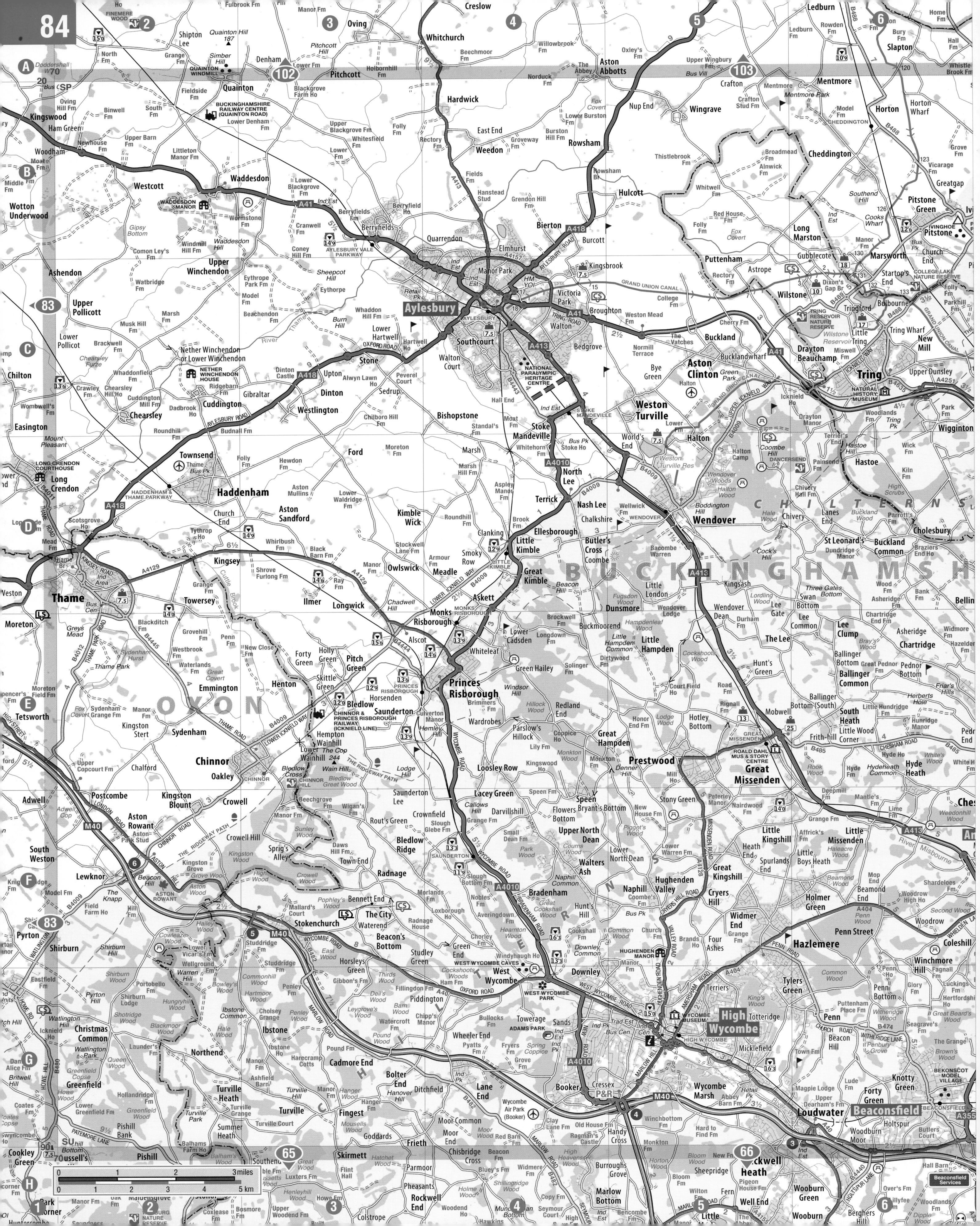
Creslow
Whitchurch
Oving
Quainton
Pitchcott
Hardwick
Aston Abbotts
Wingrave
Rowsham
Weedon
Waddesdon
Westcott
Kingswood
Woodham
Wotton Underwood
Ashendon
Upper Winchendon
Upper Pollicott
Lower Pollicott
Chilton
Easington
Long Crendon
Haddenham
Cuddington
Chearsley
Dinton
Westlington
Stone
Aylesbury
Southcourt
Walton
Bierton
Hulcott
Broughton
Buckland
Aston Clinton
Weston Turville
Halton
Wendover
Tring
Drayton Beauchamp
Wilstone
Long Marston
Puttenham
Marsworth
Cheddington
Mentmore
Ledburn
Slapton
Horton
Pitstone
Stoke Mandeville
Bishopstone
Ford
Kimble Wick
North Lee
Terrick
Ellesborough
Little Kimble
Great Kimble
Askett
Monks Risborough
Princes Risborough
Longwick
Ilmer
Owlswick
Meadle
Kingsey
Towersey
Thame
Moreton
Tetsworth
Emmington
Henton
Bledlow
Saunderton
Chinnor
Oakley
Sydenham
Aston Rowant
Crowell
Kingston Blount
Postcombe
Adwell
South Weston
Lewknor
Stokenchurch
Radnage
Bledlow Ridge
Piddington
West Wycombe
Downley
Hughenden Valley
Naphill
Walters Ash
Bradenham
Lacey Green
Speen
Prestwood
Great Missenden
Little Missenden
Great Kingshill
Hazlemere
High Wycombe
Booker
Cressex
Wycombe Marsh
Loudwater
Beaconsfield
Penn
Tylers Green
Holmer Green
Little Kingshill
Lee Common
Ballinger Common
Chartridge
Cholesbury
Buckland Common
St Leonard's
Lee Gate
Wendover Dean
Dunsmore
Little Hampden
Great Hampden
Little London
Kingsash
The Lee
Ibstone
Northend
Turville
Turville Heath
Fingest
Skirmett
Frieth
Lane End
Cadmore End
Bolter End
Christmas Common
Pishill
Shirburn
Pyrton
Watlington
Cookley Green
Flackwell Heath
Wooburn Green
Wooburn Moor
BUCKINGHAMSHIRE
OXON
CHILTERNS
HILLS
0 1 2 3 miles
0 1 2 3 4 5 km

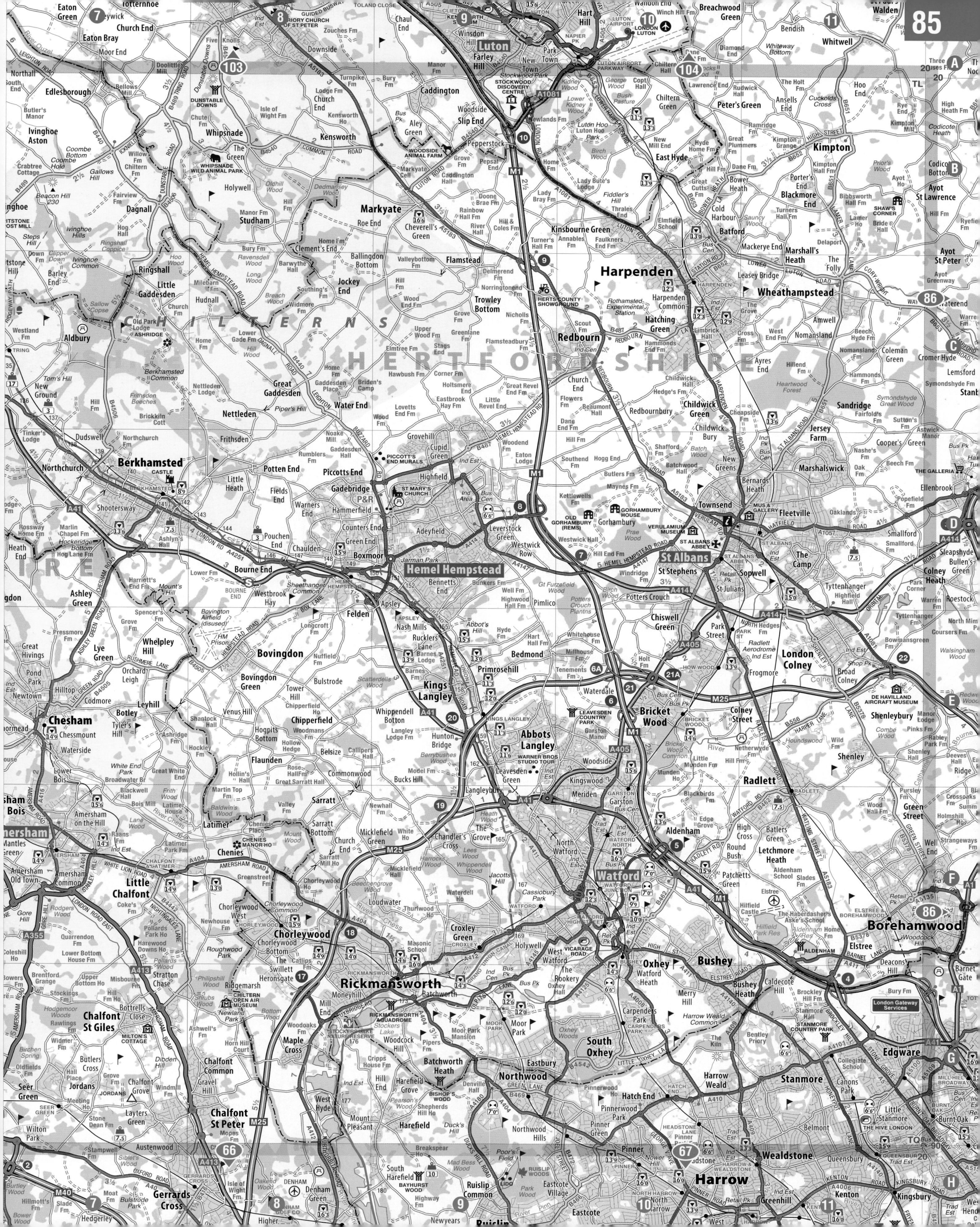
Luton
London Luton Airport
Harpenden
Kimpton
Wheathampstead
Redbourn
Markyate
Flamstead
Studham
Whipsnade
Dagnall
Ringshall
Little Gaddesden
Aldbury
Berkhamsted
Northchurch
CHILTERNS
HERTFORDSHIRE
Great Gaddesden
Nettleden
Water End
Hemel Hempstead
Boxmoor
Bourne End
Bovingdon
Chesham
St Albans
St Stephens
Sandridge
Marshalswick
Fleetville
Townsend
London Colney
Colney Heath
Park Street
Chiswell Green
Kings Langley
Abbots Langley
Bricket Wood
Radlett
Shenley
Watford
North Watford
Garston
Aldenham
Croxley Green
Rickmansworth
Chorleywood
Chenies
Little Chalfont
Amersham
Chalfont St Giles
Chalfont St Peter
Chalfont Common
Gerrards Cross
Jordans
Maple Cross
Harefield
Batchworth Heath
Northwood
South Oxhey
Oxhey
Bushey
Bushey Heath
Borehamwood
Elstree
Edgware
Stanmore
Harrow Weald
Hatch End
Pinner
Harrow
Wealdstone
Ruislip Common
Eastcote
M1
M25
A41
A405
A414
A5183
10
8
9
11
86
103
104
66
67

HERTFORDSHIRE
LONDON
ESSEX
Knebworth
Codicote
Welwyn
Welwyn Garden City
Hatfield
Hertford
Ware
Stevenage
Watton at Stone
Sacombe
High Cross
Wadesmill
Thundridge
Much Hadham
Hadham Cross
Widford
Hunsdon
Stanstead Abbotts
Great Amwell
St Margarets
Rye Park
Hoddesdon
Broxbourne
Roydon
Lower Nazeing
Nazeing
Wormley
Cheshunt
Turnford
Waltham Cross
Waltham Abbey
Cuffley
Goff's Oak
Brookmans Park
Welham Green
Potters Bar
South Mimms
Shenleybury
Borehamwood
Barnet
East Barnet
Cockfosters
Enfield
Enfield Chase
Ponders End
Edmonton
Southgate
Chingford
Buckhurst Hill
Loughton
Woodford
Woodford Bridge
Walthamstow
Tottenham
Wood Green
Hornsey
Finchley
Friern Barnet
Whetstone
Totteridge
Mill Hill
Edgware
Colindale
Kingsbury
Golders Green
Essendon
Bayford
Brickendon
Little Berkhamsted
Hertford Heath
Hertingfordbury
Cole Green
Letty Green
Bramfield
Stapleford
Tewin
Datchworth
Woolmer Green
Digswell
Panshanger
Lemsford
Stanborough
Hatfield Garden Village
Colney Heath
Northaw
Epping Green
Wildhill
Newgate Street
Hadley Wood
Monken Hadley
Arkley
Upshire
High Beach
Sewardstone
Epping Forest
Lee Valley Regional Park
M25
A1(M)
A10
A414
South Mimms Services
London Gateway Services
TL
TQ
miles
km

Bishop's Stortford
Great Dunmow
Little Dunmow
Takeley
Takeley Street
Great Hallingbury
Little Hallingbury
Thorley
Thorley Street
Spellbrook
Sawbridgeworth
High Wych
Hatfield Broad Oak
Hatfield Heath
Sheering
Harlow
Potter Street
Foster Street
Churchgate Street
Matching
Matching Tye
Matching Green
White Roding
Aythorpe Roding
Leaden Roding
High Roding
Great Canfield
High Easter
Pleshey
Good Easter
Margaret Roding
Abbess Roding
Beauchamp Roding
Mashbury
Chignall Smealy
Chignall St James
Great Waltham
Little Waltham
Broomfield
Felsted
Hartford End
Ford End
Howe Street
ESSEX
High Laver
Little Laver
Magdalen Laver
Moreton
Fyfield
Willingale
Roxwell
Writtle
Chelmsford
Moulsham
Widford
Shellow Bowells
Bobbingworth
Shelley
Chipping Ongar
High Ongar
North Weald Bassett
Epping
Coopersale Common
Theydon Bois
Theydon Mount
Abridge
Stapleford Tawney
Stapleford Abbotts
Stanford Rivers
Kelvedon Hatch
Navestock Heath
Navestock Side
Doddinghurst
Blackmore
Mountnessing
Ingatestone
Fryerning
Margaretting
Galleywood
Stock
Billericay
Great Burstead
Little Burstead
Hutton
Shenfield
Brentwood
Pilgrims Hatch
South Weald
Harold Hill
Harold Wood
Havering-atte-Bower
Noak Hill
Chigwell Row
Hainault
Collier Row
Romford
Gidea Park
Great Warley
Little Warley
Herongate
Ingrave
Dunton Wayletts
Laindon
West Horndon
Cranham
Upminster
Lambourne End
Norton Mandeville
Norton Heath
Toot Hill
Passingford Bridge
Crays Hill
M11
M25
A12
A127
A414
A1060
A120

Great Notley
Black Notley
Cressing
Tye Green
Coggeshall Hamlet
Feering
Kelvedon
Easthorpe
Messing
Tiptree
Layer Marney
Birch
Silver End
White Notley
Faulkbourne
Rivenhall
Rivenhall End
Fairstead
Terling
Great Leighs
Little Leighs
Chipping Hill
Witham
Great Braxted
Little Braxted
Tiptree Heath
Tolleshunt Knights
Paternoster Heath
Oxley Green
Great Totham
Little Totham
Tolleshunt Major
Tolleshunt D'Arcy
Wickham Bishops
Hatfield Peverel
Nounsley
Boreham
Broomfield
Springfield
Chelmer Village
Chelmsford
Little Baddow
Danbury
Woodham Walter
Langford
Heybridge
Heybridge Basin
Maldon
Osea Island
Northey Island
Goldhanger
Great Baddow
Sandon
Galleyend
Howe Green
Runsell Green
Woodham Mortimer
Hazeleigh
Rudley Green
Purleigh
Cock Clarks
Bicknacre
East Hanningfield
West Hanningfield
Hanningfield Reservoir
South Hanningfield
Rettendon
Rettendon Place
Woodham Ferrers
Stow Maries
Cold Norton
Latchingdon
Mundon
Steeple
Maylandsea
Mayland
Althorne
Ostend
North Fambridge
South Fambridge
South Woodham Ferrers
Creeksea
Burnham-on-Crouch
Hullbridge
Runwell
Ramsden Heath
Ramsden Bellhouse
Downham
Wickford
Shotgate
Rawreth
Canewdon
Ashingdon
Hockley
Hawkwell
Rochford
Great Stambridge
Paglesham Churchend
Paglesham Eastend
Ballards Gore
Crays Hill
Nevendon
North Benfleet
Rayleigh
Thundersley
Daws Heath
Eastwood
Pitsea
Barling
Little Wakering
South Green
Galleywood
Widford
Stock
Great Waltham
Little Waltham
Howe Street
Hartford End
Willows Green
Young's End
ESSEX
London Southend Airport
0 1 2 3 miles
0 1 2 3 4 5 km

Rowhedge
Alresford
Great Bentley
Weeley
Weeley Heath
Layer de la Haye
Malting Green
Abberton
Abberton Reservoir
Fingringhoe
South Green
Langenhoe
Fingringhoe Wick Nature Reserve
Thorrington
Aingers Green
Row Heath
South Heath
Hollybush Hill
St Osyth Heath
Little Clacton
Cook's Green
Great Holland
Clacton Village
Burrsville Park
Brightlingsea
Hurst Green
Peldon
Stafford's Corner
Little Wigborough
Great Wigborough
Copt Hall Marshes Nature Reserve
Mersea Island
East Mersea
Blue Row
Cudmore Grove
Colne Estuary
Mersea Flats
West Mersea
Mersea Island Mus
St Osyth Priory
St Osyth
Point Clear
Great Clacton
Clacton-on-Sea
Holland-on-Sea
Rush Green
Jaywick
Lee-over-Sands
St Osyth Beach
Colne Pt
Colne Bar
Brightlingsea Reach
Old Hall Marshes
Blackwater Estuary
Tollesbury
Tollesbury Wick Marshes
Cobmarsh Island
Virley Channel
The Nass
River Blackwater
English Coast Path
Sales Pt
Tip Head
St Peter's on the Wall
St Peter's Flat
Bradwell Waterside
East End
Bradwell on Sea
St Lawrence Bay
Ramsey Island
The Stone
Bradwell Marshes
Marshhouse Outfall
Dengie Flat
Dengie
St Lawrence
Tillingham
Tillingham Marshes
Asheldham
Southminster
Montsale
Deal Hall
Ray Sand
Burnham-on-Crouch
Holliwell Pt
Foulness Sands
Foulness Pt
River Crouch
Wallasea Island
Wallasea Wetlands
Churchend
Courtsend
Fishermans Head
Foulness Island
River Roach
Rugwood Head
Asplins Head
New England Island
Havengore Island
Shelford Head
Sharpness Head
Havengore Head
Haven Pt
Maplin Sands
TM
TR

IRISH SEA
MÔR IWERDDON
ST BRIDES BAY
BAIE SAIN FFRAID
72
PEMBROKESHIRE COAST
NATIONAL PARK
Ynys Deullyn
Trefin
(Trevine)
Porthgain
Penclegyr
Porth Dwfn
Porth Egr
Trwyn Llwyd
Aber Draw
Pwll Whiting
Pwll Llong
Pwll Olfa
Barry Island Fm
Felindre Ho
Binchurn Fm
Trwyncastell
Abereiddi Bay
Abereiddy
Portheiddy
Llanrhian
Llanon
Mesur-y-dorth
Aber-pwll
Aberdinas
Cwmwdig Water
Bank Ho
Porth Tre-wen
Tremynydd Fawr
Berea
Croes-goch
Trevigan
Trenewydd Fawr
Trefochlyd Fm
Dduallt
Penllechwen
Gesail-fawr
Porth-gwyn
Carn Treliwyd
Waun Beddau
Tretio
Tretio Common
Spite Moor
Carnhedryn Uchaf
Carn Treglemaes
Treglemais
Waun Fawr
Abernant
Treffynnon
Llechenhinen
St David's Head
Penmaen Dewi
Carn Llidi
181
ST DAVID'S
Carn Hen
Porthmelgan
Treleddyd-fawr
Carnhedryn
Llanhowel
Skyfog
Llanddinog
Rhodiad
Hendre
Porth Lleuog
Whitesands Bay
Porth-mawr
River Alun
Dowrog Common
Caerfarchell
Caerforiog
Paran
Mynydd du
Porthselau
Penarthur Fm
Treswny Moor
Tremaenhir
Point St John
Rhosson
BISHOP'S PALACE
CATHEDRAL
St David's
(Tyddewi)
Vachelich
Whitchurch
Middle Mill
Rickeston Hall
St Justinian
Nine Wells
Llandruidion
Morfa Common
Prendergast
Solva (Solfach)
Upper Solva
Lower Solva
Mount Fm
Brawdy Airfield (disused)
ST NON'S CHAPEL
Treginnis
St Non's Bay
Caerfai Bay
Caer Bwdy Bay
Porthlliski
Porth Clais
Porthlysgi Bay
Carreg Fran
Porthstinian
Summer only
North Bishop
Carreg Rhoson
Bishops and Clerks
Trwyn-Siôn-Owen
Trwyn-drain-du
Carnysgubor
Aber Mawr
RAMSEY ISLAND
Ramsey Island
Ynys Dewi
Rhod Isaf
136
RSPB
Aberfelin
Penrhyn Twll
Daufraich
South Bishop/Em-sger
Trwynmynachdy
Bay Dillyn
Meini Duon
Black Scar
Green Scar
Aber-west
Dinas Fawr
Dinas Fach
Porthmynawyd
Pointz Castle
Bus Pk
Pwll March
Newgale
Newgale Sands
PEMBROKESHIRE COAST PATH LLWYBR ARFORDIR PENFRO
WALES COAST PATH
A487
B4583
SM
60
50
20
0 1 2 3 miles
0 1 2 3 4 5 km
A B C D E F G H
1 2 3 4 5 6

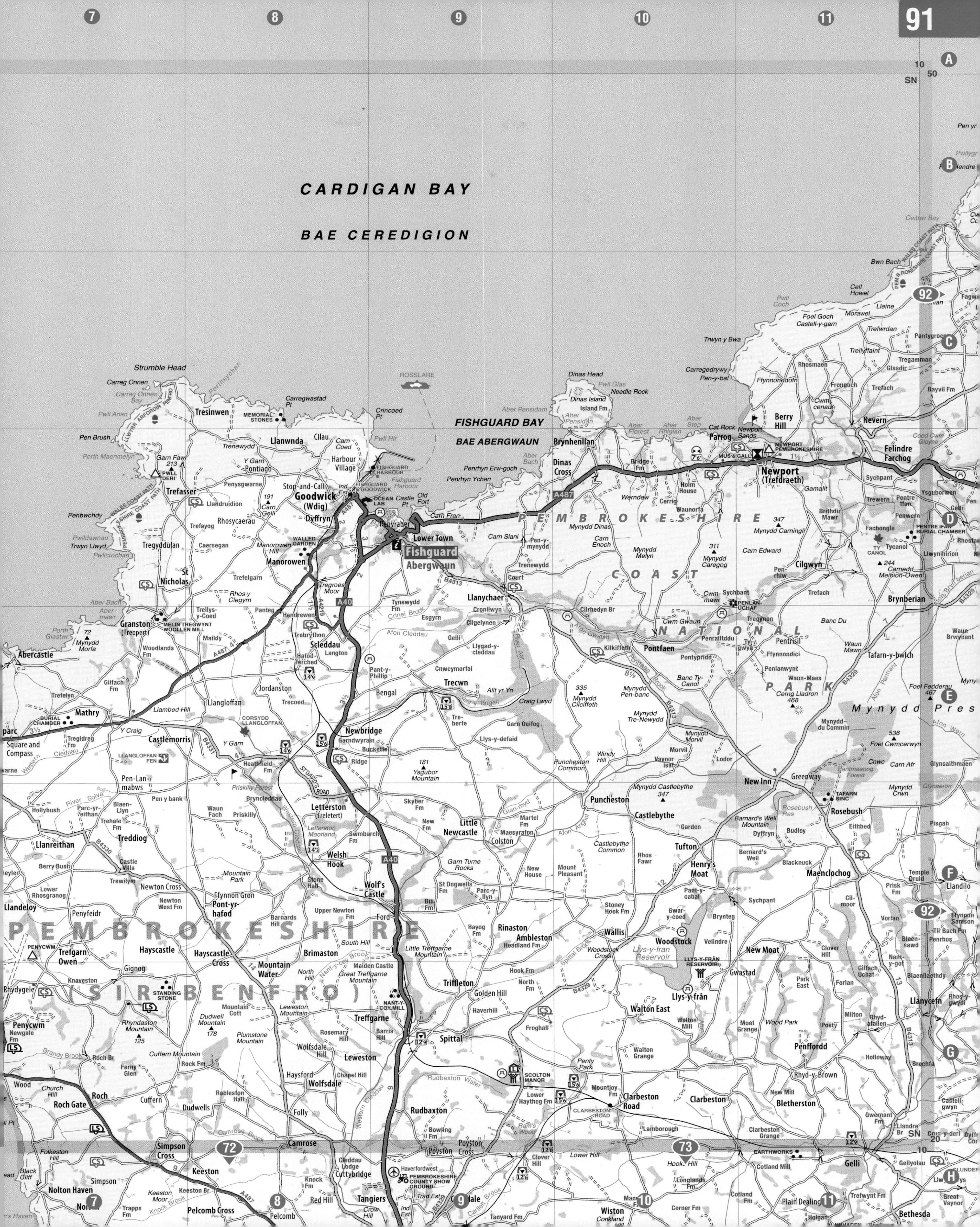
CARDIGAN BAY
BAE CEREDIGION
FISHGUARD BAY
BAE ABERGWAUN
PEMBROKESHIRE COAST NATIONAL PARK
PEMBROKESHIRE
(SIR BENFRO)
Mynydd Preseli
Strumble Head
Carreg Onnen
Pwll Arian
Pen Brush
Porth Maenmelyn
Tresinwen
Memorial Stones
Carregwastad Pt
Llanwnda
Cilau
Crincoed Pt
Rosslare
Garn Fawr
Trenewydd
Y Garn Pontiago
Harbour Village
Fishguard Harbour
Stop-and-Call
Goodwick (Wdig)
Ocean Lab
Castle Pt
Old Fort
Dyffryn
Penyraber
Lower Town
Fishguard
Abergwaun
Trefasser
Penysgwarne
Llandruidion
Carn Gelli
Rhosycaerau
Trefayog
Penbwchdy
Pwlldawnau
Trwyn Llwyd
Pwllcrochan
Tregyddulan
Caersegan
Manorowen Hill
Manorowen
Walled Garden
St Nicholas
Trefelgarn
Rhos-y Clegyrn
Tregroes Moor
Aber Bach
Abermawr
Porth Glastwr
Granston (Treopert)
Trellys-y-Coed
Melin Tregwynt Woollen Mill
Panteg
Hendrewen
Mynydd Morfa
Abercastle
Maildy
Woodlands Fm
Trebrython
Scleddau
Langton
Hafod-ferched
Pant-y-Phillip
Jordanston
Gilfach Fm
Trefelyn
Llangloffan
Trecoed
Bengal
Burial Chamber
Mathry
Lambed Hill
Corsydd Llangloffan
Y Craig
Tregidreg Fm
Square and Compass
Castlemorris
Y Garn
Llangloffan Fen
Heathfield Fm
Newbridge
Garndwyrain
Buckette
Ridge
Priskilly Forest
St David's Road
Pen-Lan-mabws
Pen y bank
Bryncleddau
Letterston (Treletert)
Letterston Moorland
River Solva
Hollybush
Parc-yr-eithan
Blaen-Llyn
Trehale Fm
Waun Fach
Priskilly
Llanreithan
Treddiog
Castle Villa
Berry Bush
Trewilym
Mountain Park
Newton Cross
Lower Rhosgranog
Newton West Fm
Ffynnon Gron
Pont-yr-hafod
Llandeloy
Penyfeidr
Stone Hall
Welsh Hook
Swmbarch Fm
Wolf's Castle
Ford
Upper Newton Fm
Barnards Hill
South Hill
Skyber Fm
New Fm
Little Newcastle
Colston
Maesyrafon
Martel Fm
Garn Turne Rocks
St Dogwells Fm
Parc-y-llyn
Bill Fm
Penycwm
Trefgarn Owen
Gignog
Hayscastle
Hayscastle Cross
Knaveston
Standing Stone
Brimaston
Mountain Water
North Hill
Nant-y-coy Brook
Maiden Castle
Great Treffgarne Mountain
Little Treffgarne Mountain
Nant-y-Coy Mill
Treffgarne
Rhydygele
Newgale
Rhyndaston Mountain
Mountain Cott
Dudwell Mountain
Plumstone Mountain
Leweston Mountain
Rosemary Hill
Barris Hill
Wolfsdale Hill
Leweston
Spittal
Brandy Brook
Roch Br
Cuffern Mountain
Rock Fm
Ferny Glen
Haysford
Chapel Hill
Wolfsdale
Wood
Church Hill
Roch Gate
Roch
Cuffern
Robleston Hall
Dudwells
Folly
Rudbaxton
Rudbaxton Water
Camrose
Camrose Brook
Simpston Cross
Keeston
Folkeston Hill
Black Cliff
Simpson
Nolton Haven
Keeston Moor
Keeston Br
Knock Brook
Trapps Fm
Pelcomb Cross
Pelcomb
Cleddau Lodge
Cuttybridge
Knock Fm
Red Hill
Tangiers
Crow Hill
Haverfordwest
Pembrokeshire County Show Ground
Trad Est
Ind Est
Bowling Fm
Poyston
Poyston Cross
Clover Hill
Tanyard Fm
Tregroes
Tynewydd Fm
Crinei Brook
Esgyrn
Afon Cleddau
Gelli
Cwcymorfol
Trecwn
Allt yr Yn
Nant y Bugail
Tre-berfe
Garn Deifog
Llys-y-defaid
Craig Lwyd
Ysgubor Mountain
Carn Fran
Carn Slani
Pen-y-mynydd
Trenewydd
Court
Llanychaer
Cronllwyn
Cilgelynen
Llygad-y-cleddau
Penrhyn Erw-goch
Penrhyn Ychen
Dinas Head
Pwll Glas
Needle Rock
Dinas Island
Island Fm
Aber Pensidan
Aber Bach
Brynhenllan
Dinas Cross
Bridge Fm
Werndew
Mynydd Dinas
Carn Enoch
Holm House
Cerrig
Waunorfa
Aber Fforest
Aber Rhigian
Aber Step
Cat Rock
Parrog
Newport Sands
Newport (Trefdraeth)
Mus & Gall
Newport Pembrokeshire
Gamallt
Mynydd Melyn
Mynydd Caregog
Mynydd Carningli
Carn Edward
Pen-rhiw
Cwm-mawr
Sychbant
Penlan-Uchaf
Cilrhedyn Br
Cwm Gwaun
Afon Gwaun
Kilkiffeth
Pontfaen
Penralltddu
Tycwgwyd
Pontypridd
Banc Ty-Canol
Mynydd Cilciffeth
Mynydd Pen-banc
Mynydd Tre-Newydd
Pontfaen Brook
Afon Cwmau
Mynydd Morvil
Morvil
Vaynor Isaf
Lodor
Puncheston Common
Windy Hill
Puncheston
Mynydd Castlebythe
Castlebythe
Garden
Glan-rhyd
Afon Anghof
Castlebythe Common
Rhos Fawr
New House
Mount Pleasant
Tufton
Henry's Moat
Pant-y-cabal
Gwar-y-coed
Stoney Hook Fm
Hayog Fm
Rinaston
Ambleston
Headland Fm
Wallis
Woodstock
Woodstock Cross
Llys-y-fran Reservoir
Llys-y-Frân Reservoir
Hook Fm
North Fm
Triffleton
Golden Hill
Haverhill
Froghall
Walton East
Walton Mill
Llys-y-frân
Gwastad
New Moat
Walton Grange
Penty Park
Scolton Manor
Mountjoy Fm
Lower Haythog Fm
Clarbeston Road
Clarbeston
Lamborough
Ram's Wood
Lower Hill
Hook Hill
Longlands Fm
Wiston
Conkland
Corner Fm
Cotland Fm
Cotland Mill
Earthworks
Clarbeston Grange
Gelli
Plain Dealing
Trefwynt Fm
Bethesda
Holgan
Pwll Coch
Trwyn y Bwa
Carregedrywy
Pen-y-bal
Berry Hill
Ffynnonddofn
Rhosmaen
Frongoch
Cwm-cenau
Trefach
Nevern
Felindre Farchog
Sychpant
Trewern
Pentre Ifan
Ysgubor-wen
Penwern
Brithdir Mawr
Fachongle
Pentre Ifan Burial Chamber
Ty Canol
Tycanol
Carnedd Meibion-Owen
Llwynihirion
Cilgwyn
Trefach
Banc Du
Brynberian
Tregynon
Pentrisil
Ffynnondici
Penlanwynt
Waun-Maes
Cerrig Lladron
Waun Mawr
Tafarn-y-bwlch
Waun Brwynant
Foel Feddau
Afon Pennant
Mynydd-du Commin
Foel Cwmcerwyn
Cnwc
Carn Afr
Pantmaenog Forest
Glynsaithmaen
Greenway
New Inn
Tafarn Sinc
Rosebush
Rosebush Res
Mynydd Crwn
Barnard's Well Mountain
Dyffryn
Budloy
Bernard's Well
Blacknuck
Maenclochog
Eithbed
Pisgah
Temple Druid
Prisk Fm
Llandilo
Sychpant
Cil-moor
Brynteg
Velindre
Vorlan
Blaen-sawd
Penrhos
Clover Hill
Gilfach Uchaf
Nant-y-gof
Blaenllaethdy
Park East
Forlan
Llanycefn
Rhos-y-gwydd
Milton
Moat Grange
Wood Park
Posty
Rhyd-afallen
Penffordd
Holloway
Brechfa
Rhyd-y-Brown
New Mill
Bletherston
Gwernant Fm
Llandre Br
Crug-y-deri
Gellyolau
Great Vaynor
Ceibwr Bay
Bwn Bach
Cell Howel
Foel Goch
Castell-y-garn
Morawel
Lleine
Trefwrdan
Trellyffaint
Pantygroes
Tregamman
Glasdir
Bayvil Fm
Pen yr
Pwllygranant
Felindre
Wales Coast Path
Pembrokeshire Coast Path
Llwybr Arfordir Penfro
Porthsychan
Pwll Hir
Pwll Deri
Mynydd Crwn
Penycwm
Rhosfach

Cardigan Island
Carreg Lydan
Pen Tew
Clos-y-graig
Ty Gwyn
Nantmawr
Aberporth
Tresaith
Penbryn
Ffynnon Berw
Maes-Y-Ffynnon
Nantycroy
Blaenplwyf
Parcllyn
Dyffryn
Dyffryn-bern
Sarnau
Brynhoffnant
Perthygopa
Allt-goch
North Fawr
Pwllglas
Rhippinllwyd
Pant-yr Holiad
Cemaes Head
Gwbert
Towyn Warren
Y Ferwig
Ffynoncyff
Login
Lleina
Tre-cefn
Felinwynt
Pen-rhiw
Trefere
Rhosygadair
Rhosygadair Fawr
Rhosygadair Newydd
Llwyn-coed
West Wales Airport, Aberporth
Cwmporthman
INTERNAL FIRE MUS OF POWER
Allt-y-goed
Penrhyn Castle
Poppit Sands
POPPIT SANDS
Pen yr Afr
Pengarn
Cippyn
Pwllygranant
Foel Hendre
Pantirion
Manian-fawr
Albro Castle
Clawddcam
St Dogmaels (Llandudoch)
Cwm Connell
Ceibwr Bay
ST DOGMAEL'S ABBEY
Bridgend
Cardigan
Aberteifi
CASTLE
TEIFI MARSHES NATURE RESERVE
Llangoedmor
Treforgan
Bronydd
Noyadd Wilym
WELSH WILDLIFE CENTRE
Forest
COEDMOR
Cilgerran
CILGERRAN CASTLE
Cwm Plysgog
Pen-lan
Castle Malgwyn Fm
Llechryd
Rockland
Tyhen
Tregibby Fm
Caemorgan New Mill
Banc-y-Warren
Cwrt Fm
Penparc
Tremain
Blaenannerch
Blaenporth
Glynarthen
Tan-y-groes
Glasgoed
Cwmcoednerth
Betws Ifan
Beulah
Brithdir
Felin-Wnda
Hawen
Pantgwyn
Dyffryn
Pantinker
Ffynnonciptil
Noyadd Trefawr
Allt-y-cadno
Trefaes-Fach
Ponthirwaun
Bryngwyn
Brongest
Troedyraur
Moylgrove
Hafod Grove
Monington
Bwn Bach
Fagwreinon
Penlan
Lleine
Llwyngwyddl
Trefigin
Rhydgaled
Penwaun
Pantygrwndy
Tredefaid
Pen-y-bryn
Croft
Felinganol
Bridell
Llantood
Glanrhyd
Trewenfron
Tregamman
Trefwrdan
Pantygroes
Pantgwyn Mawr
Parke
Penbanc
Crugiau
Pontgarreg
Pencelly
Nevern
Coed Cwm Gloyne
Felindre Farchog
Sychpant
PENGELLI FOREST
CASTELL HENLLYS IRON AGE FORT
Court
Blaengafren
Penycoed
Henllan
Eglwyswrw
Bwlchgarreg-lwyd
Penderi
Penlanfeigan
Pistyll Meigan
Dyffryn-Meigan
Trewern
Ysguborwen
Pen-y-benglog
Pantygarn
DYFFED SHIRE HORSE FARM
Eglwyswrw Common
Llanfair-Nant-Gwyn
Neuadd
Fachongle
PENTRE IFAN BURIAL CHAMBER
TY CANOL
Tycanol
Rhosfarced
Llwynihirion
Hendre
Temple Gate
Pontyglasier
Crosswell
Fountain Hill
Eglwyswen
Clover Hill
Blaenffos
Carnedd Meibion-Owen
Brynberian
Pensarn
Wern Ddu
Glynmaen
Pantyrodyn
Penygroes
Annedd Wen
Dyffryn Mawr
Gorsfraith
Cidigill
Tygwyn
Ty-canol
Fronlas
Rhydwen
Waun Brwynant
PEMBROKESHIRE
(SIR BENFRO)
Foel Drygarn
FORT
Crymych
Llainbanal
Crug-yr-hwch
Carn Goedog
Carn Bresab
Carn Bica
Mynydd-bach
Foel Fedderau
Carn Sian
Carnmenyn
Carn Gyfrwy
Tafarn-y-bwlch
Mynydd Preseli
Foel Cwmcerwyn
Craig Talfynydd
Caermeini
Carn Afr
Cnwc
Glynsaithmaen
Mynachlog-ddu
Pentre-galar
Rhos fach
Waun Isaf
Gors Fawr
Trefach
Pen-yr-allt
Fferm-y-Capel
Pentre Glas
Foel-Drych
Mynydd Crwn
Wern
Blaendyffryn
Pisgah
Allt-y-gog
Pont yr Haiarn
Ynysfawr
Carn Besi
Let-y-bwlch
Rhosfach
Llandre
Glandwr
Hebron
Temple Druid
Prisk Fm
Llandilo
Llangolman Common
Dandderwen
Llangolman
Gilfach-ddofn
Glandy Cross
Castell Garw
Maes-y-felin
Pant-y-Caws
Llwynyrebol
Vorlan
Ffynnon Samson
Tir Bach Fm
Penrhos
Blaen-sawd
Clyngwyn
Cilau-fawr
Efailwen
Blaenafon
Pantyrodyn
March-gwyn
Penrallt
Blaenllaethdy
Llanycefn
Rhos-y-gwydl
Marble Hall
Plas-y-bedw
Rhyd-afallen
Holloway
Brechfa
Bush Fm
Llandissilio
Castell-gwyn
Gwernant Fm
Llandre
Llanfallteg
Gellyc
Bethesda
Great Vaynor
Penpedwast
Gwarllwyn
Troedyrhiw
Nentydd
Nant-y-geifr-fawr
Glogue Fm
Glogue
Hermon
Llanfyrnach
Rhyd-y-gath
Tre fawr
Trehenry
Bryn-eithin
Graig
Pantygwyddel
Bribwll
Pant-y-gelli
Ffynnonau Dyfnant
Penlan
Rhydowen
Ffynonwen
Glyngarw
Dolwilym
Llanglydwen
Fron Fm
Llwynhugh
Maen-hir
Gwal y Filiast
Glyntaf
Trehir Uchaf
Cilhernin
Coynant
Fronhaul
Cefn-y-pant
Frowen
Canerw
Lan
Wernolau Fawr
Maesgwynne
Pensarn
Cilgynydd
Penlan
Cwmfelin Mynach
Wernberni
Llanboidy
Login
Ffynnonwen
Cross-hands
Cilowen
Blaencwmmau
Ffoswinau
Hafod
Cilanw
Pencnwc
Cwm-miles
Waunffrwd
Cilhengroes
Castell Draenog
Pantygroes
Gellydogin
Blaencediw
Dyffryn Marlais
Baily Mawr
Hiraeth
Gwarmacwydd
Henllan Amgoed
Lan
Wernlygoes
Rhydywrach
Blaenwernddu
Cwmfelin Boeth
Parciau
Sarnlas
Clipost Fm
Trewern
Whitland Abbey
Llanfallteg
Ffynnonfoida
Llwyngwyddd
Bank y llain
Pantyrhas
Penback Fm
Plascyrdin
Berthlwyd
Llangynin
Cethin Fm
Troedyrhiw
Pengwern
Esgair
Aber
Llwynybychan
The Grove
Blaencoed
Pen-y-coed
Penuwch
Pentowin
Penlan
Meidrim Road
Derry Hall
Wern Fm
Bancyfelin
Bron-y-gaer
Pantyderi
Pen-pontbren
Sarnau
Meidrim
Drefach
Sarnau Fm
Bwlch Fm
Hafod Fm
Cwmduhen
Rhosyn-coch
Corngafr
Garllegan Fawr
Llangarthginning
Nantyreglwys
Goetre Fawr
Caerlleon
Maen-coch
Goetre-uchaf
Penlan
Blaenwaun
Pilmawr
Trefach
Dyffryn Brodyn
Pencraig
Cwmbach
Llanwinio
Pwll-y-march
Panthowell
Cilfforch
Wernberni
Blaengelli
Pentrenrhiw
Llechclawdd
Ceifnau Fawr
Llwynau
Cilsant
Gellywen
Bwlchgwynt
Crugydeirne
Ty-hen
Cilhir-Uchaf
Eithin-duon-isaf
Felin-pandy
Eithin-duon-uchaf
Plas-y-parciau
Dyffryn
Plas-paun
Brynwl
Glandwr
Talfan Isaf
Cwm
Posty-isaf
Posty-Uchaf
Tal-y-fan-uchaf
Nant-y-bair
Pant-y-Cendy Hall
Abernant
Ffynnonwen
Penrallt Trawscoed
Fachddu
Pant-y-Grown
Talog
Pantyllyn
Blaengofer
Sychpant
Cwmgest
Brynmeini
Blaenbryn
Pencaerau Mawr
Castell Gorwyn
Llwyn-crwn
Pen-y-bont
Glasfryn
Penalltfangor
Blaendyfod
Clunpurfaith
Woodlands
Nantyrolchfa
Gilfachygestin
Pengraigfawr
Blaenparsel
Trenoeth
Fronlas
Glyn Dewi
Panteg
Cilevan
Berthlwyd
Gilfach-y-Bettws
Castell Mawry
Treparcau
Pantmelyn
Felindre
Cwm
Blaenpant
Rhyd-goch
Castell-mawr
Plasparcau
Elwyn
Pengraig
Gilfachwen Fm
Afon Cynin
Croes-llan
Llain-lwyd
Clynblewog Fm
Dinas
Trelech
Rhospwllygawnen
Clungarthen
Maniwan
Parcymynydd
Trafel-y-pwll
Nantcwmrhys
Llanwinio Common
Greenhall
Rhoscrugebolion
Carregwen
Nantycyw
Crugiwan
Bryn-Iwan
Waun-ceiliogau
Nantycerrig
Llwyncelyn-ian
Hen-feddau fawr
Pantgwyn-mawr
Nantyweirglodd
Blaengilfach
Cadifor Hall
Plasyrhafod
Maes-pwll
Highgate
Triol
Llwyn-yr-hwrdd
Tegryn
Coed-llwyd
Pantyrheddwch
Tyddyn
Clyn felin-fach
Dyffryn
Ty-mawr
Drysgol-goch
Hafod
Llwyndrain
Nant Neel
Nant-Ifan-fach
Pen-banc
Dolau-llannerch
Star
Frenni Fach
Frenni Fawr
Penlan-uchaf
Dolpwll
Dyffryn Cefn Faes
Bwlchygroes
Cwm Cneifa
Crynga
Pengribyn
Cwmorgan
Black-oak
Cil-waunydd Fawr
Cwmgelli Fm
Moelfre
Penrallt
Blaen Bran
Crugygorllwyn
Tanglwst
Maudland Ho
Penwaun Fm
Ddolwen
Cwmcych
Capel Iwan
Cwmpengraig
Blaenachddu
Pen y Garn
Rhydyfelin
Hendy
Pontgarreg
Lletty-clyd
Glyneithinog
CAWS CENARTH CHEESE
Lancych
Nantyrhawl
Penlangarreg
Pengwern
Tyhir
Cwmhiraeth
Clifforest Fm
Penrherber
Pen-y-bryn
Boncath
Penrally
Cilgwyn
Cilwendeg
Newchapel
CLYNFYW
Arleth
Werndddofn
Dolalau-isaf
Pen-bedw
Cilrhue Fach
Pentre
Cilast-uchaf
Cilast-isaf
Rhosygilwen
Ty-hen Fm
Rhos-hill
Mynydd Crogwy
Pen-cwm
Palle Fm
Maes-y-felin
Penwenallt Fm
Carreg-wen
Penparceithin
Abercych
Gelliorlas
Penlan-Cenarth
Cenarth
NATIONAL CORACLE CENTRE
Stradmore Mansion
Penfai
Penwernfawr
Alltybwla
Cwm-cou
Adpar
Cilgwyn
Newcastle Emlyn
(Castell Newydd Emlyn)
Aber-Arad
Pentrecagal
Llandyfriog
Berthyfedwen
Gilwen Fm
Blaenhalen
Allt Boeth
Penllwyn
Waung
Gillo Fm
Rhippinllwyd
Brongwyn
Cilfallen
Capel Tygwydd
Bryngwrog
Penrallt-Bie Fm
Penwernfach
Blaen-pant
Scotland Hill Fm
Llandygwydd
Llwynduris
Rhyd
Glanolmarch
Glanhelyg
Cafan Fm
Alltyresgob
Llwyn-yr-hal
Llwyncadfor
Wern Fach
Blaenswgwenllan Cross
Blaen-Cil-Llech
Pant-y-Bwla
Blaensyllyn
Bronwion
Wern Gadno
Cwrt Hen
Plas Troedyraur
Esgergraig
Pen-y-banc
Capel Gwnda
Coedperthi
Pantdaniel
Ffynnongog
Pencon Betws
Tyllwyd
Parcybwla
Fronlas
Lan
Rhosfawr
Cryngae Mawr
Ffynnon
Tynewydd
Wernynad
Blaenwenen
Parc-y-Gors
Rhos-wen
Nant-y-llan
Glaneirw
Maengwyn
Gilfach
Hendraws
Glandulas
College Mawr
Allt y corde
Blaen Waun
CEREDIGION
(SIR CEREDIGION)
CARMARTHENSHIRE
(SIR GAR)

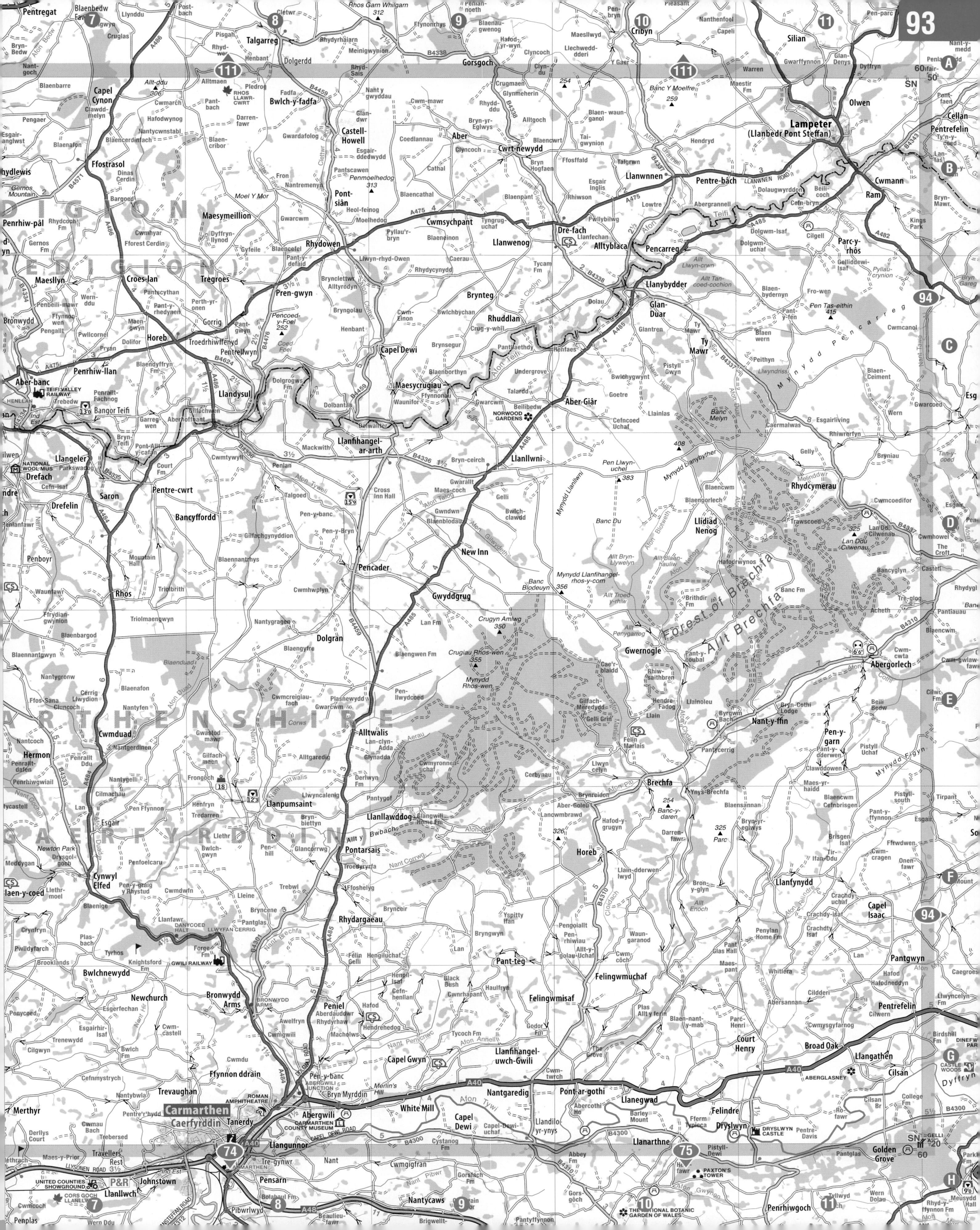
Pentregat
Talgarreg
Dolgerdd
Gorsgoch
Cribyn
Silian
Capel Cynon
Bwlch-y-fadfa
Castell-Howell
Aber
Cwrt-newydd
Lampeter
(Llanbedr Pont Steffan)
Olwen
Ffostrasol
Pont-siân
Llanwnnen
Pentre-bâch
Cwmann
Ram
Maesymeillion
Cwmsychpant
Dre-fach
Llanwenog
Alltyblaca
Pencarreg
Rhydowen
Maesllyn
Croes-lan
Tregroes
Pren-gwyn
Llanybydder
Brynteg
Rhuddlan
Glan-Duar
Horeb
Penrhiw-llan
Capel Dewi
Aber-banc
Llandysul
Maesycrugiau
Aber-Giâr
Llanfihangel-ar-arth
Llanllwni
Llangeler
Drefach
Saron
Pentre-cwrt
Drefelin
Bancyffordd
Rhydcymerau
Llidiad Nenog
Pencader
New Inn
Gwyddgrug
Rhos
Dolgran
Gwernogle
Abergorlech
Forest of Brechfa
Allt Brechfa
Mynydd Pencarreg
Alltwalis
Cwmduad
Hermon
Nant-y-ffin
Brechfa
Llanpumsaint
Llanllawddog
Pontarsais
Horeb
Cynwyl Elfed
Llanfynydd
Rhydargaeau
Capel Isaac
Pant-teg
Pantgwyn
Felingwmuchaf
Felingwmisaf
Bwlchnewydd
Newchurch
Bronwydd Arms
Peniel
Pentrefelin
Court Henry
Broad Oak
Llanfihangel-uwch-Gwili
Capel Gwyn
Llangathen
Cilsan
Ffynnon ddrain
Trevaughan
Carmarthen
Caerfyrddin
Tanerdy
Abergwili
White Mill
Capel Dewi
Nantgaredig
Pont-ar-gothi
Llanegwad
Felindre
Dryslwyn
Llanarthne
Golden Grove
Merthyr
Llangunnor
Johnstown
Llanllwch
Pensarn
Nantycaws
Penrhiwgoch
CEREDIGION
(CEREDIGION)
CARMARTHENSHIRE
(SIR GAERFYRDDIN)
A475
A485
A486
A484
A40
A48
B4459
B4338
B4337
B4336
B4310
B4300
TEIFI VALLEY RAILWAY
NATIONAL WOOL MUS
NORWOOD GARDENS
GWILI RAILWAY
ABERGLASNEY
DRYSLWYN CASTLE
PAXTON'S TOWER
THE NATIONAL BOTANIC GARDEN OF WALES
CARMARTHEN COUNTY MUSEUM
ROMAN AMPHITHEATRE
UNITED COUNTIES SHOWGROUND
CASTLE WOODS
Mynydd Llanybyther
Crugyn Amlwg 350
Crugiau Rhos-wen 355
Mynydd Rhos-wen
Pen Tas-eithin 415
111
74
75
94

112
112
93
93
75
76
A
B
C
D
E
F
G
H
1
2
3
4
5
6
CARMARTHENSHIRE
SIR GAERFYRDDIN
BRECON BEA
NATIONAL
BANNAU BRYCHE
Llanfair Clydogau
Bryn Glas
Tywi Forest
Allt y Wi
Cwmann
Pentrefelin
Cellan
Llanycrwys
Ffarmers
Ffaldybrenin
Harford
Pumsaint
DOLAUCOTHI GOLD MINES
Caio
Esgairdawe
Crugybar
Porthyrhyd
Cwrt-y-cadno
Llandre
Rhandirmwyn
Nant-y-Bai
Ystradffin
GWENFFRWD-DINAS
Cilycwm
Cynghordy
Divlyn
Siloh
Llansawel
TALLEY LAKES
Edwinsford
Abergorlech
Talley
TALLEY ABBEY
Cwm-byr
Llanwrda
Cwmdwr
Waunclunda
Llansadwrn
Felindre
Halfway
Cwmdu
Llandovery
Llanymddyfri
Myrtle Hill
Myddfai
Cilgwyn
Pentre-ty-gwyn
Babel
Halfway
Llangadog
Ashfield
Hermon
Felindre
Manordeilo
Tyle
Salem
Soar
Cwmifor
Dyffryn Ceidrych
Bethlehem
Y GAER HILLFORT
Pont-ar-llechau
Twynllanan
Llanddeusant
Talsarn
Rhosmaen
Pontbren Araeth
Pen-y-banc
Llandeilo
DINEFWR PARK
CASTLE WOODS
Dyffryn Tywi
Ffairfach
Capel Gwynfe
Pont Aber
Neuadd
CARREG CENNEN CASTLE & FARM CENTRE
Mynydd Du
Capel Isaac
Pantgwyn
Cilsan
Golden Grove
Usk Reservoir
Mynydd Myddfai
Llyn Brianne Reservoir
Bannau Brycheiniog 802
Bannau Sir Gaer
Carreg Yr Ogof 585
A40
A482
A483
A4069
B4302
B4337
B4310
B4300
B4343
0 1 2 3 miles
0 1 2 3 4 5 km

Cefn Crug
Beulah
Cilmery/Cilmeri
Rhosferig
SHOWGROUND
Oaklands
Builth Wells
Llanfair-ym-Muallt
Noyadd
Tynllwyn
Llanfaredd
Cwm Irfon
Garth
Llanfechan
Tyn-y-graig
Hendre
Erwhelm
Maes-y-cwm
Llanddewi'r Cwm
Aberedw
Alltmawr
Llanwrtyd
Llanwrtyd Wells
(Llanwrtud)
Llangammarch Wells
Maesmynis
Aberedw Rocks
Cefn-gorwydd
Drovers Arms
Drum-ddu
Llandeilo Graban
Tirabad
Mynydd Eppynt
Artillery Range
Pentre Dolau-Honddu
Gwenddwr
Erwood
Crickadarn
Upper Chapel
Sennybridge Training Area
Llaneglwys
Merthyr Cynog
Blaendyryn
Pont Rhyd-y-berry
Lower Chapel
Llandeilo'r Fan
Llanfihangel Nant Bran
Pont-faen
Pwllgloyw
Garthbrengy
Talachddu
Felinfach
Llandefaelog Fach
Llandefaelog
Sarnau
Battle
Cradoc
Llanddew
Pentre bach
Soar
POWYS
Llywel
Trecastle
Pentre'r-felin
Trallong
Aberbran
Aberyscir
Brecon
Aberhonddu
BRECON GAER ROMAN FORT
Sennybridge
(Pontsenni)
Defynnog
Penpont
Llanspyddid
Llanfaes
BRECON CATHEDRAL
BRECON CASTLE
REGIMENTAL MUS. OF THE ROYAL WELSH
BRECKNOCK MUSEUM (Y GAER)
Groesffordd
Llanywern
Llechfaen
Talyllyn
Tai'r-Bull
Libanus
NATIONAL PARK VISITOR CENTRE
Mynydd Illtud
Llanfrynach
Scethrog
Pencelli
Crai
Felin-Crai
Heol Senni
CRAIG CERRIG GLEISIAD A FAN FRYNYCH
BRECON BEACONS
Pen y Fan
Corn Du
Brecon Beacons
Cribin
Cross Oak
Talybont-on-Usk
Aber-Village
Cray Reservoir
Forest Fawr
Fan Gihirych
Fan Nedd
Fan Llia
Fan Fawr
Beacons Reservoir
Neuadd Reservoirs
Tor Glas
Talybont Forest
Brynmelyn

Hay-on-Wye
(Y Gelli Gandryll)
Talgarth
Bronllys
Glasbury
Clyro
Llowes
Painscastle
Llanbedr
Rhulen
Erwood
Crickadarn
Llyswen
Boughrood
Llanigon
Tregoyd
Velindre
Cusop
Clifford
Rhydspence
Whitney-on-Wye
Winforton
Willersley
Eardisley
Dorstone
Craswall
Llanthony
Longtown
Clodock
Walterstone
Pandy
Crickhowell
(Crug Hywel)
Bwlch
Llangors
Llangorse Lake
Tretower
Cwmdu
Llangattock
Talybont-on-Usk
Llansantffraed
Pencelli
Scethrog
Llanhamlach
Talyllyn
Felinfach
Llanfilo
Tredustan
Trefecca
Tredomen
Pengenffordd
Cathedine
Llangasty Talyllyn
The Black Mountains
Y Mynyddoedd Duon
BRECON BEACONS
NATIONAL PARK
BANNAU BRYCHEINIOG
P O W Y S
H E R E F
Lord Hereford's Knob or Twmpa
Hay Bluff 677
Waun Fach 811
Pen y Gadair Fawr 800
Black Hill 640
Sugar Loaf 596
Table Mountain 451
Castell Dinas 450
Capel-y-ffin
Vale of Ewyas
River Wye
River Usk
Offa's Dyke Path
A438
A470
A479
A4078
A40
B4350
B4348
B4351
B4594
B4560
B4558
A4079
A465
114
95
77
78
Llanfihangel-Crucorney
Tre-wyn
Bettws
Stanton
Forest Coal Pit
Michaelchurch Escley
Urishay Common
Llanveynoe
Snodhill
Bredwardine
Hardwicke
Merbach
Newchurch
Michaelchurch on Arrow
Brilley
Almeley
0 1 2 3miles
0 1 2 3 4 5 km

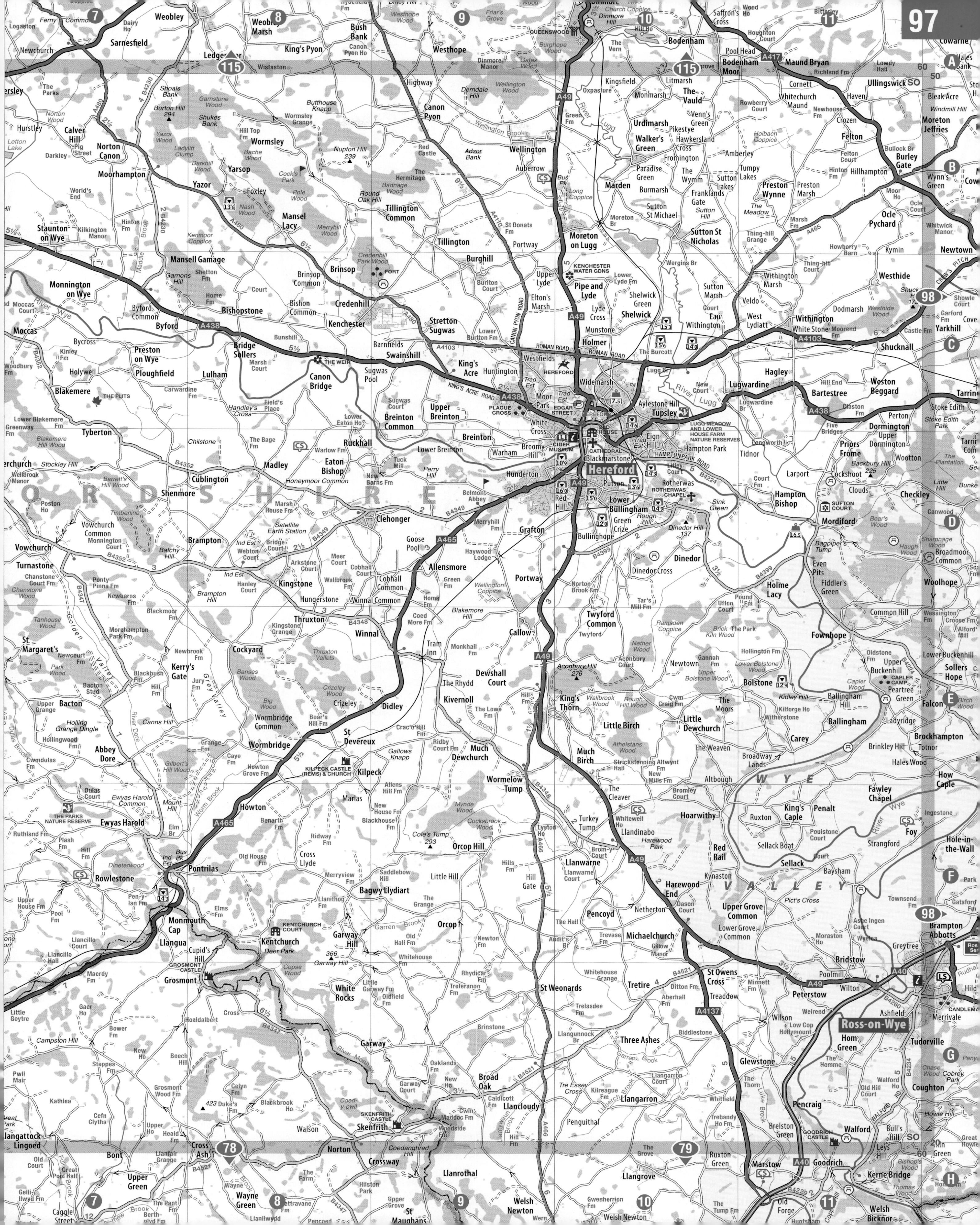
Weobley
Sarnesfield
Weobley Marsh
Bush Bank
King's Pyon
Westhope
Bodenham
Bodenham Moor
Maund Bryan
Ledgemoor
Wistaston
Dinmore Manor
Queenswood
Saffron's Cross
Ullingswick
Canon Pyon
Kingsfield
Monkmarsh
The Vauld
Whitechurch Maund
Cornett
Bleak Acre
Moreton Jeffries
Hurstley
Calver Hill
Norton Canon
Moorhampton
Wormsley
Yarsop
Yazor
Foxley
Mansel Lacy
Wellington
Auberrow
Marden
Urdimarsh
Walker's Green
Felton
Burley Gate
Preston Wynne
Staunton on Wye
Tillington Common
Tillington
Moreton on Lugg
Sutton St Michael
Sutton St Nicholas
Ocle Pychard
Newtown
Mansell Gamage
Brinsop
Burghill
Monnington on Wye
Byford
Bishopstone
Credenhill
Kenchester
Stretton Sugwas
Pipe and Lyde
Shelwick
Withington
Westhide
Moccas
Bridge Sollers
Swainshill
King's Acre
Holmer
Shucknall
Yarkhill
Preston on Wye
Ploughfield
Lulham
Canon Bridge
Blakemere
Hereford
Widemarsh
Lugwardine
Hagley
Bartestree
Weston Beggard
Tupsley
Aylestone Hill
Upper Breinton
Breinton Common
Breinton
Tyberton
Ruckhall
Eaton Bishop
Madley
Cublington
Shenmore
Hampton Bishop
Dormington
Priors Frome
Mordiford
Clehonger
Lower Bullingham
Grafton
Dinedor
Vowchurch
Turnastone
Brampton
Kingstone
Allensmore
Portway
Holme Lacy
Woolhope
Thruxton
Winnal
Twyford Common
Callow
Fownhope
St Margaret's
Cockyard
Kerry's Gate
Dewshall Court
Kivernoll
Bolstone
Sollers Hope
Bacton
Didley
King's Thorn
Little Dewchurch
Ballingham
Falcon
Abbey Dore
Wormbridge
St Devereux
Kilpeck
Much Dewchurch
Little Birch
Much Birch
Carey
Brockhampton
Wormelow Tump
How Caple
Howton
Ewyas Harold
Hoarwithy
King's Caple
Fawley Chapel
Penalt
Orcop Hill
Llanwarne
Foy
Rowlestone
Pontrilas
Sellack
Bagwy Llydiart
Harewood End
Upper Grove Common
Monmouth Cap
Llangua
Kentchurch
Garway Hill
Orcop
Pencoyd
Michaelchurch
Brampton Abbotts
Grosmont
White Rocks
St Weonards
Tretire
St Owens Cross
Bridstow
Peterstow
Ross-on-Wye
Garway
Three Ashes
Glewstone
Tudorville
Broad Oak
Llancloudy
Llangarron
Coughton
Pencraig
Skenfrith
Walford
Llangattock Lingoed
Bont
Cross Ash
Norton
Crossway
Marstow
Goodrich
Kerne Bridge
Upper Green
Llanrothal
Llangrove
Wayne Green
Welsh Newton
Welsh Bicknor
St Maughans
RIVER WYE
WYE VALLEY
HEREFORDSHIRE

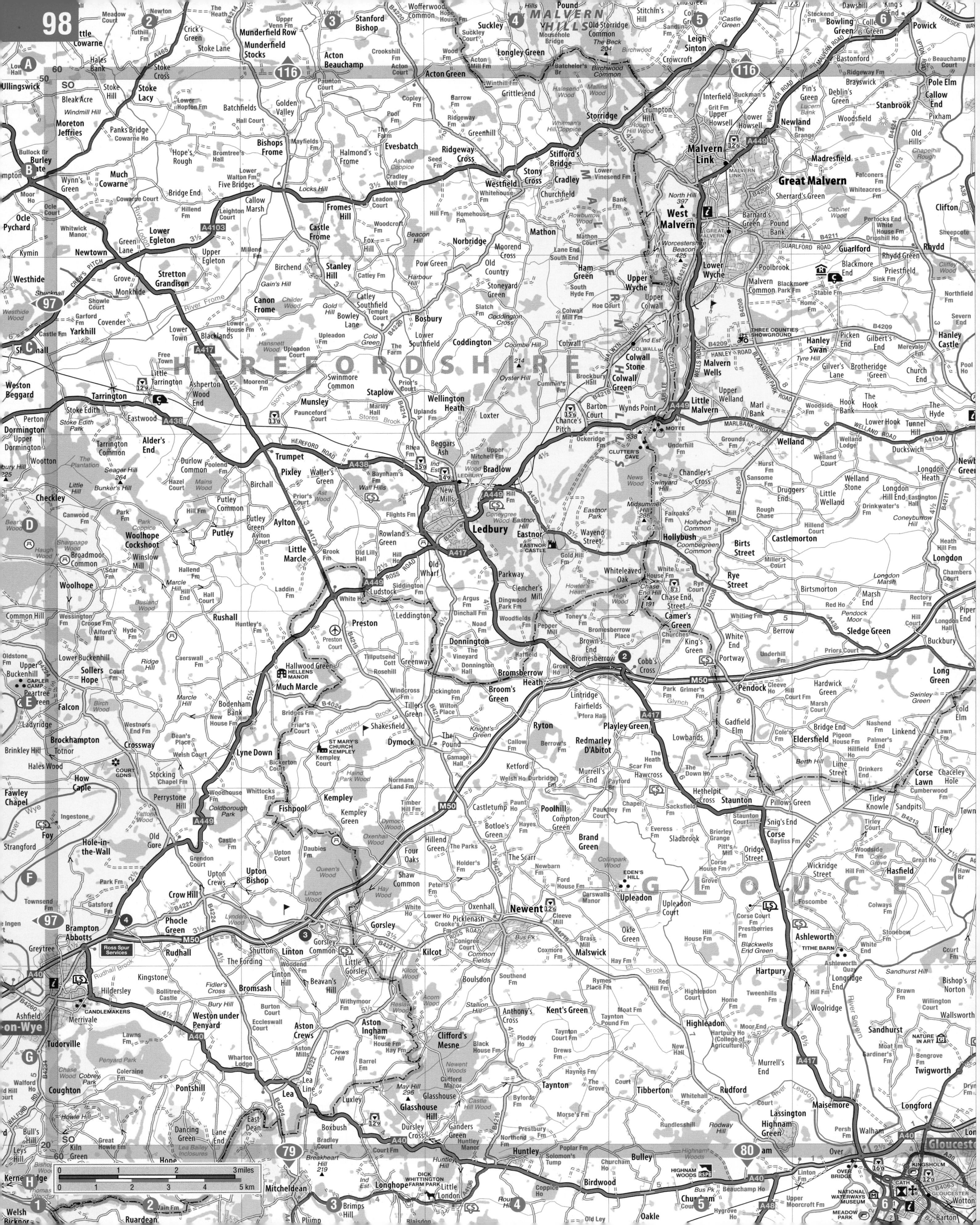
HEREFORDSHIRE
GLOUCES
MALVERN HILLS
116
97
79
80
Little Cowarne
Meadow Court
Newton
The Heath
Munderfield Row
Munderfield Stocks
Upper Venn Fm
Stanford Bishop
Acton Beauchamp
Wofferwood Common
Suckley
Longley Green
Pound
Old Storridge Common
The Beck 204
Stitchin's Hill
Leigh Sinton
Crowcroft
Castle Green
Stockend
Bowling Green
Dawshill
King's End
Powick
Bastonford
Ridgeway Fm
Pole Elm
Callow End
Pixham
Stanbrook
Newland
Acton Green
Crick's Green
Stoke Lane
Hales Bank
Stoke Cross
Stoke Lacy
Ullingswick
Bleak Acre
Windmill Hill
Moreton Jeffries
Panks Bridge
Cowarne Ho
Batchfields
Hall Court
Golden Valley
Paunton Court
Copley Fm
Barrow Fm
Grittlesend
Storridge
Crumpton Hill
Interfield
Upper Howsell
Lower Howsell
Bullock Br
Burley Gate
Wynn's Green
Much Cowarne
Hope's Rough
Bromtree's Hall
Bishops Frome
Mayfields Fm
Halmond's Frome
Evesbatch
Ashen Coppice
Ridgeway Cross
Stifford's Bridge
Stony Cross
Cradley
Westfield
Malvern Link
Madresfield
Great Malvern
Sherrard's Green
Clifton
Five Bridges
Locks Hill
Bridge End
Callow Marsh
Leighton Court
Fromes Hill
Castle Frome
Leadon Court
Woodcroft Fm
Beacon Hill
Norbridge
Mathon
North Hill 397
West Malvern
Barnard's Green
Pound Bank
Guarlford
Rhydd
Rhydd Green
Ocle Pychard
Whitwick Manor
Lower Egleton
Upper Egleton
Kymin
Newtown
Green Lane
Westhide
Shucknall
Grove
Monkhide
Stretton Grandison
Birchend
Stanley Hill
Catley Fm
Pow Green
Moorend Cross
Old Country
Ham Green
Upper Wyche
Lower Wyche
Worcestershire Beacon 425
Poolbrook
Blackmore End
Priestfield
Malvern Common
Canon Frome
Catley Southfield
Temple Court
Bowley Lane
Bosbury
Stoneyard Green
Coddington Cross
Colwall
Upper Colwall
Three Counties Showground
Hanley Swan
Picken End
Gilbert's End
Hanley Castle
Garford
Covender
Yarkhill
Lower Town
Blacklands
Upleadon Court
Lower Southfield
Coddington
Colwall Stone
Colwall Green
Malvern Wells
Gilver's Lane
Brotheridge Green
Church End
Free Town
Little Tarrington
Ashperton
Moorend Fm
Swinmore Common
Staplow
Munsley
Prior's Court
Wellington Heath
Loxter
Barton Court
Wynds Point
Little Malvern
Upper Welland
Marl Bank
Hook Bank
The Hook
The Hyde
Lower Hook
Tunnel Hill
Weston Beggard
Tarrington
Stoke Edith
Eastwood
Wood End
Pounceford Court
Stores Brook
Chance's Pitch
Welland
Duckswich
Dormington
Upper Dormington
Perton
Tarrington Common
Alder's End
Trumpet
Pixley
Waller's Green
Beggars Ash
Bradlow
Clutter's Cave
Chandler's Cross
Wootton
Seager Hill 264
Durlow Common
Hazel Court
Mains Wood
Birchall
Wall Hills
New Mills
Ledbury
Eastnor
Eastnor Castle
Wayend Street
Midsummer Hill
Hollybush
Welland Stone
Longdon Heath
Longdon Hill End
Little Welland
Druggers End
Checkley
Putley Common
Putley Green
Putley
Aylton
Flights Fm
Rowland's Green
Birts Street
Castlemorton
Woolhope Cockshoot
Broadmoor Common
Little Marcle
Old Lilly Hall
Hill Ho
Old Wharf
Gold Hill
Whiteleaved Oak
Longdon
Winslow Mill
Hallend
Woolhope
Marcle Hill
Ludstock
Siddington
Parkway
Clencher's Mill
Dingwood Park Fm
Chase End Hill 191
Chase End Street
Rye Street
Birtsmorton
Marsh End
Rushall
Preston
Leddington
Dinchall Fm
Camer's Green
Berrow
Sledge Green
Common Hill
Wessington
Alford's Mill
Hyde Fm
Preston Court
Donnington
The Vineyard
Bromesberrow Place
Bromesberrow
Brown's End
King's Green
White End
Portway
Buckbury
Upper Buckenhill
Lower Buckenhill
Sollers Hope
Hallwood Green
Hellens Manor
Much Marcle
Greenway
Bromsberrow Heath
Cobb's Cross
Pendock
Long Green
Hardwick Green
Falcon
Bodenham Bank
Windcross
Tillers Green
Brooms Green
Lintridge
Fairfields
Playley Green
Gadfield Elm
Eldersfield
Bridge End
Linkend
Brockhampton
Totnor
Crossway
Lyne Down
Friar's Court
Shakesfield
Dymock
The Pound
Ryton
Redmarley D'Abitot
Lowbands
Brinkley Hill
Hales Wood
How Caple
Court Gdns
Stocking
St Mary's Church Kempley
Kempley Court
Ketford
Murrell's End
Hawcross
Lime Street
Corse Lawn
Chaceley Hole
Fawley Chapel
Perrystone Hill
Whittocks End
Kempley
Kempley Green
Castletump
Poolhill
Compton Green
Hethelpit Cross
Staunton
Pillows Green
Tirley Knowle
Sandpits
Foy
Ingestone
Hole-in-the-Wall
Old Gore
Fishpool
Timber Hill Fm
Botloe's Green
Brand Green
Sladbrook
Snig's End
Corse
Tirley
Strangford
Upton Court
Daubies
Four Oaks
Holder's Fm
The Scarr
Eden's Hill
Oridge Street
Wickridge Street
Hasfield
Upton Crews
Upton Bishop
Queen's Wood
Shaw Common
Crow Hill
Phocle Green
Gatsford
Lyndors Wood
Linton Wood
Oxenhall
Newent
Upleadon
Upleadon Court
Foscombe
Ashleworth
Tithe Barn
Brampton Abbotts
Ross Spur Services
Rudhall
Shutton
Linton
Gorsley
Gorsley Common
Picklenash
Kilcot
Cleeve Mill
Malswick
Okle Green
Greytree
Kingstone
The Fording
Little Gorsley
Bus Pk
Coxmore
Hay Fm
Hartpury
Sandhurst Hill
Bishop's Norton
Hildersley
Candlemakers
Merrivale
Bromsash
Linton Hill
Beavan's Hill
Boulsdon
Southend Fm
Rymes Place Fm
Highleadon Court
Longridge End
Woolridge
Wallsworth
Weston under Penyard
Burton Court
Withymoor Fm
Acorn Wood
Anthony's Cross
Kent's Green
Highleadon
Sandhurst
Nature in Art
Ross-on-Wye
Tudorville
Aston Crews
Aston Ingham
Clifford's Mesne
Black House Fm
Taynton Court Fm
Murrell's End
Bengrove Fm
Twigworth
Walford
Coughton
Cobrey Park
Whatton Lodge
Coleraine
Pontshill
Lea Line
Lea
May Hill 296
Glasshouse
Glasshouse Hill
Byfords Fm
Taynton
The Grove
Tibberton
Whitehall Fm
Rudford
Maisemore
Longford
Lassington
Highnam Green
Walham
Bull's Hill
Great Howle Fm
Dancing Green
Lane End
East Dean
Boxbush
Bradley Court
Luxley
Dursley Cross
Ganders Green
Prestbury Fm
Rundleshill
Rodway Hill
Kiln Green
Hope
Mitcheldean
Breakheart Hill 219
Longhope
Dick Whittington Farm Park
Huntley
Little London
Northend Fm
Solomon's Tump
Birdwood
Bulley
Highnam Woods
Churcham
Over
Over Bridge
National Waterways Museum
Gloucester
Kingsholm
Wotton
Barton
Plump
Ruardean
Welsh Bicknor
Kerne Bridge
Brimps Hill
Blaisdon
Oakle
Old Ley
Upper Moorcroft Fm
Meadow Park
A465
A4103
A417
A438
A449
A4172
A4104
A40
A48
A38
M50
B4214
B4220
B4219
B4503
B4208
B4211
B4209
B4218
B4232
B4216
B4215
B4221
B4224
B4222
B4213
B4063
B4228
B4234
B4260
SO
0
1
2
3 miles
4
5 km

WORCESTERSHIRE
COTSWOLDS
Norton
Egdon
Peopleton
Bishampton
Ab Lench
Church Lench
Salford Priors
Marlcliff
Barton
Littleworth
Hatfield
Stoulton
Upper Wolverton
Lower Wolverton
Atch Lench
Abbots Salford
Kempsey
Stonebow
Throckmorton
Sheriff's Lench
Harvington Cross
Harvington
Cleeve Prior
Bickmarsh
Drake's Broughton
Pinvin
Wadborough
Pershore Airfield (disused)
Badger's Hill
Hill Furze
Wood Norton
Norton
Pirton
Wyre Piddle
Lower Moor
Fladbury Cross
Lenchwick
Chadbury
North Littleton
Middle Littleton
Pershore
Fladbury
Charlton
Twyford
Offenham
South Littleton
High Green
Besford
Wick
Greenhill
Evesham
Blackminster
Croome Park
Cropthorne
Aldington
Kinnersley
Dunstall Common
Defford
Little Comberton
Bricklehampton
Bengeworth
Bretforton
Earl's Croome
Birlingham
Hampton
Fairfield
Four Pools
Badsey
Holly Green
Baughton
Strensham Services North
Eckington
Great Comberton
Elmley Castle
Netherton
Upper Haselor
Wickhamford
Upton upon Severn
Lower Strensham
Strensham
Strensham Services South
Bredon Hill
Kersoe
Hinton on the Green
Hinton Cross
Vale of Evesham
Murcot
Naunton
Upper Strensham
Bredon's Norton
Childswickham
Willersey
Ripple
Westmancote
Ashton under Hill
Sedgeberrow
Aston Somerville
Twyning Green
Overbury
Conderton
Kemerton
Broadway
Queenhill
Twyning
Bredon
Lower Westmancote
Puckrup
Shuthonger
Beckford
Dumbleton
Wormington
Buckland
Laverton
Kinsham
Bushley
The Mythe
Northway
Aston Cross
Aston on Carrant
Teddington Hands
Great Washbourne
Little Beckford
Little Washbourne
Stanton
Snowshill
Mitton
Ashchurch
Alderton
Teddington
Toddington
Tewkesbury
Newtown
Homedowns
Natton
Pamington
Stanway
Forthampton
Walton Cardiff
Priors Park
Alstone
Frampton Court
Alderton Fields
Gretton Fields
Didbrook
Wood Stanway
Claydon
Oxenton
Dixton
Gretton
Taddington
Chaceley
Fiddington
Woolstone
Stanley Pontlarge
Greet
Hailes
Stumps Cross
Cutsdean
Tredington
Deerhurst
Gotherington
Prescott
Winchcombe
Ford
Farmcote
Apperley
Deerhurst Walton
Stoke Orchard
Bishop's Cleeve
Langley
Temple Guiting
Hardwicke
Woodmancote
Cleeve Hill
Postlip
Coombe Hill
Leigh
Elmstone Hardwicke
Southam
Kineton
Swindon
Boddington
Uckington
Barton
Charlton Abbots
Norton
Guiting Power
Prestbury
Staverton
Arle
Sandfields
Hawling
Down Hatherley
Golden Valley
Staverton Bridge
Battledown
Oakley
Brockhampton
Cheltenham
Sevenhampton
Parton
Charlton Kings
Whittington
Salperton
Syreford
Aylworth
Notgrove
Churchdown
Leckhampton
Up Hatherley
Lower Dowdeswell
Badgeworth
Dowdeswell
Upper Dowdeswell
Andoversford
Shipton Solers
Shipton
Shurdington
Barnwood
Foxcote
Kilkenny
Shipton Oliffe

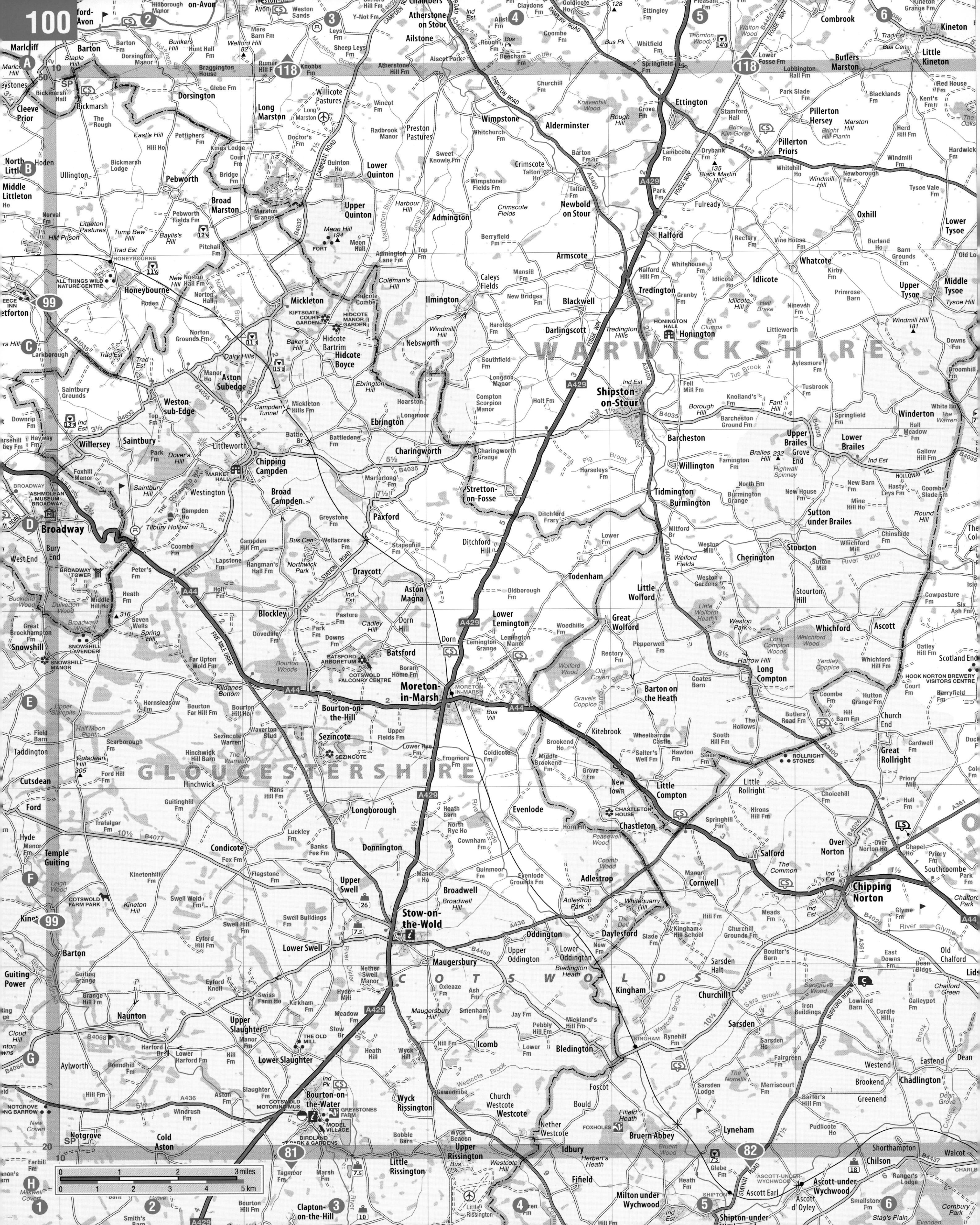

WARWICKSHIRE
GLOUCESTERSHIRE
COTSWOLDS
Marlcliff
Barton
Bickmarsh
Cleeve Prior
Dorsington
Long Marston
Welford Hill
Willicote Pastures
Atherstone on Stour
Ailstone
Alscot Park
Wimpstone
Alderminster
Ettington
Pillerton Hersey
Pillerton Priors
Butlers Marston
Kineton
Little Kineton
Combrook
North Littleton
Middle Littleton
Ullington
Pebworth
Broad Marston
Upper Quinton
Lower Quinton
Admington
Crimscote
Newbold on Stour
Halford
Fulready
Oxhill
Lower Tysoe
Middle Tysoe
Upper Tysoe
Whatcote
Idlicote
Honeybourne
HM Prison
ALL THINGS WILD NATURE CENTRE
Mickleton
KIFTSGATE COURT GARDEN
HIDCOTE MANOR GARDEN
Hidcote Bartrim
Hidcote Boyce
Ilmington
Nebsworth
Armscote
Blackwell
Tredington
Darlingscott
HONINGTON HALL
Honington
Shipston-on-Stour
Aston Subedge
Weston-sub-Edge
Saintbury
Willersey
Ebrington
Charingworth
Chipping Campden
MARKET HALL
Westington
Broad Campden
Paxford
Stretton-on-Fosse
Barcheston
Willington
Tidmington
Burmington
Upper Brailes
Lower Brailes
Winderton
Sutton under Brailes
Broadway
BROADWAY TOWER
ASHMOLEAN MUSEUM BROADWAY
Snowshill
SNOWSHILL MANOR
SNOWSHILL LAVENDER
Blockley
Draycott
Aston Magna
Todenham
Cherington
Stourton
Little Wolford
Great Wolford
Whichford
Ascott
Long Compton
Batsford
BATSFORD ARBORETUM
COTSWOLD FALCONRY CENTRE
Moreton-in-Marsh
Lower Lemington
Bourton-on-the-Hill
Sezincote
Barton on the Heath
Kitebrook
HOOK NORTON BREWERY VISITORS CENTRE
Great Rollright
ROLLRIGHT STONES
Little Rollright
Little Compton
Chastleton
CHASTLETON HOUSE
Evenlode
Longborough
Donnington
Condicote
Cutsdean
Ford
Temple Guiting
Hinchwick
Upper Swell
Lower Swell
Stow-on-the-Wold
Broadwell
Adlestrop
Daylesford
Oddington
Upper Oddington
Lower Oddington
Maugersbury
Salford
Over Norton
Chipping Norton
Cornwell
Kingham
Churchill
Sarsden
Guiting Power
Naunton
Upper Slaughter
Lower Slaughter
THE OLD MILL
Aylworth
Icomb
Bledington
Bourton-on-the-Water
COTSWOLD MOTORING MUS
MODEL VILLAGE
BIRDLAND PARK & GARDENS
Wyck Rissington
Church Westcote
Westcote
Nether Westcote
Foscot
Bould
Bruern Abbey
Lyneham
Chadlington
Notgrove
Cold Aston
Little Rissington
Upper Rissington
Idbury
Fifield
Milton under Wychwood
Ascott Earl
Ascott d'Oyley
Ascott-under-Wychwood
Chilson
Shorthampton
Walcot
Clapton-on-the-Hill
FIVE MILE DRIVE
CAMPDEN ROAD
SHIPSTON ROAD
BANBURY ROAD
FOSSE WAY
STATION ROAD
BURFORD ROAD
THE COTSWOLD WAY
A429
A44
A3400
A424
A436
A361
A422
B4035
B4632
B4081
B4479
B4077
B4450
B4068
B4026
B4437
0 1 2 3 miles
0 1 2 3 4 5 km

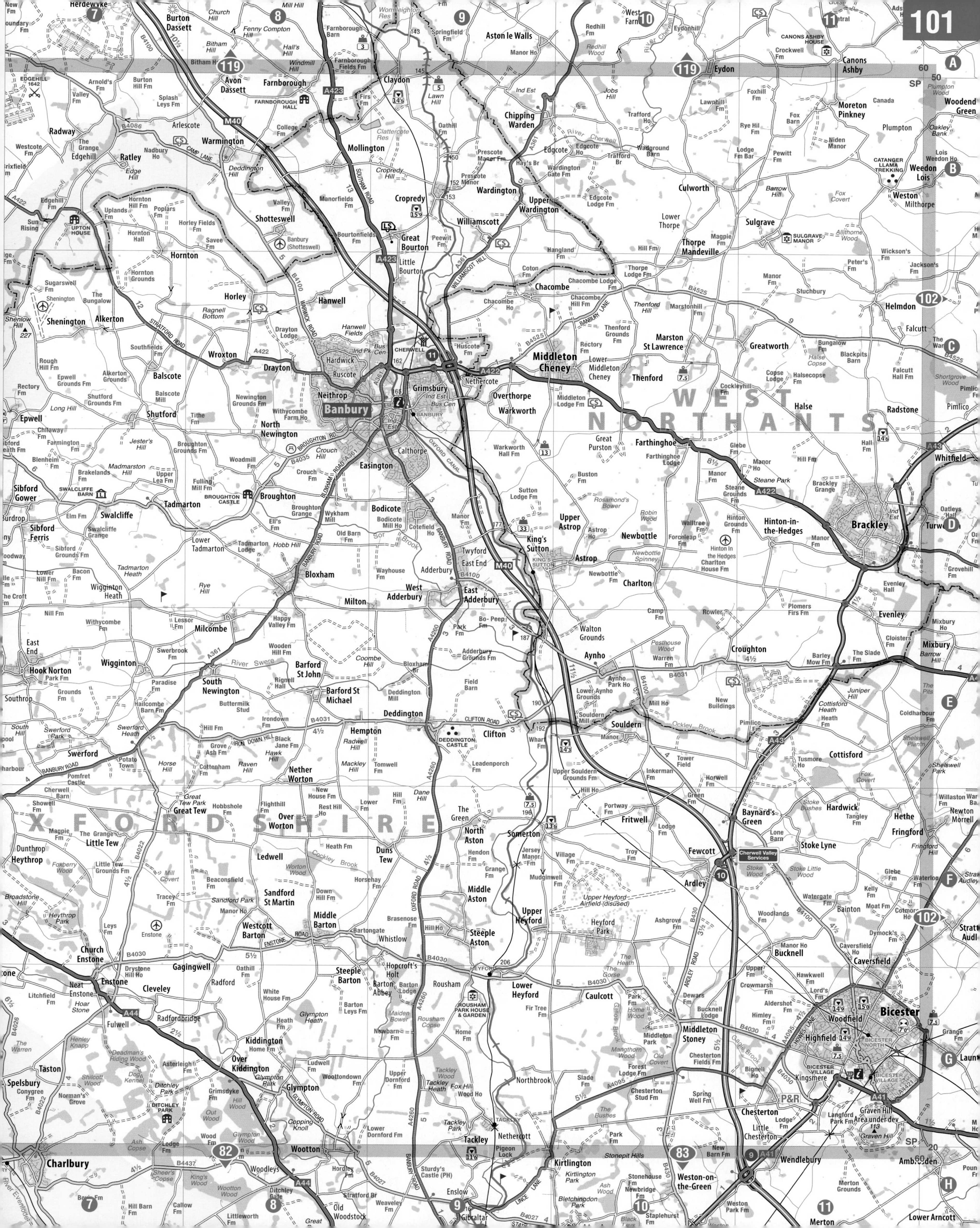
Herdewyke
Burton Dassett
Church Hill
Fenny Compton Hill
Mill Hill
Wormleighton Res
Farnborough Barn
Springfield Fm
Aston le Walls
Redhill Fm
West Farm
Eydonhill
Canons Ashby House
Canons Ashby
Bitham Hill
Hall's Hill
Windmill Hill
Manor Ho
Redhill Wood
Crockwell Fm
119
Avon Dassett
Farnborough
Farnborough Fields Fm
Claydon
Eydon
Edgehill 1642
Arnold's Fm
Burton Hill Fm
Farnborough Hall
Valley Fm
Splash Leys Fm
Firs Fm
Lawn Hill
Ind Est
Jobs Hill
Foxhill Fm
Lawnhill Fm
Moreton Pinkney
Canada
Woodend Green
Arlescote
Chipping Warden
Trafford Ho
Fox Barn
Rye Hill Fm
Plumpton
Oakley Bank
Radway
College Fm
Oathill Fm
Clattercote Res
River Cherwell
Niden Manor
Westcote Fm
The Grange
Edgehill
Warmington
Nadbury Ho
Camp Lane
Mollington
Prescote Manor Fm
Edgcote
Edgcote Ho
Trafford Br
Wadground Barn
Lodge Fm Bar
Pewitt Fm
Catanger Llama Trekking
Lois Weedon Ho
Weedon Lois
Ratley
Edge Hill
Deddington Hill
Cropredy Hill
Prescote Manor
Hay's Br
Wardington Gate Fm
Wardington
Culworth
Barrow Hill
Fox Covert
Weston
Milthorpe
Edgehill Fm
Hornton Hill Fm
Uplands Fm
Poplars Fm
Valley Fm
Manorfields Fm
Cropredy
Upper Wardington
Edgcote Lodge Fm
Lower Thorpe
Sulgrave
Sun Rising
Upton House
Horley Fields Fm
Shotteswell
Bourtonfields Fm
Williamscott
Sulgrave Manor
Allithorne Wood
Hornton Hall
Savee Fm
Banbury (Shotteswell)
Great Bourton
Peewit Fm
Magpie Fm
Thorpe Mandeville
Hill Fm
Hangland Fm
Wickson's Fm
Hornton
Little Bourton
Williamscot Hill
Coton Fm
Thorpe Lodge Fm
Peter's Fm
Jackson's Fm
Hornton Grounds
Manor Fm
Sugarswell Fm
The Bungalow
Chacombe
Chacombe Lodge Fm
Stuchbury
Shenington
Horley
Hanwell
Chacombe Ho
Chacombe Hill Fm
Banbury Lane
Thenford Hill
Marstonhill Fm
B4525
102
Helmdon
Shenlow Hill
Alkerton
Ragnell Bottom
Warwick Road
Hanwell Fields
Thenford Grounds Fm
Marston St Lawrence
Falcutt
Stratford Road
Drayton Lodge
Bus Cen
Cherwell
Huscote Fm
Rectory Fm
Greatworth
Bungalow Fm
Blackpits Barn
The Warren
Southfields Fm
Wroxton
Hardwick
Ind Pk
Middleton Cheney
Lower Middleton Cheney
Halse Copse
Halsecopse Fm
Falcutt Hall Fm
Rough Hill Fm
Alkerton Grounds
Balscote
Drayton
Ruscote
Nethercote
Thenford
Copse Lodge
Shortgrove Wood
Epwell Grounds Fm
Balscote Mill
Newington Grounds Fm
Neithrop
Grimsbury
Overthorpe
Cockleyhill Fm
Rectory Fm
Shutford Grounds Fm
Banbury
Ind Est
WEST NORTHANTS
Long Hill
Withycombe Farm Ho
Warkworth
Middleton Lodge Fm
Halse
Radstone
Pimlico
Epwell
Shutford
Tithe Fm
North Newington
Chilaway Fm
Jester's Hill
Broughton Rd
Oxford Canal
Great Purston
Farthinghoe
Glebe Fm
Hall Fm
Whitfield
Farmington Fm
Broughton Grounds Fm
Crouch Hill
Calthorpe
Warkworth Hall Fm
Farthinghoe Lodge
Manor Ho
Hill Fm
Blenheim Fm
Madmarston Hill
Woadmill Fm
Easington
Buston Fm
Steane Park
Brakelands Fm
Upper Lea Fm
Crouch Fm
Manor Fm
Brackley Grange
Sibford Gower
Swalcliffe Barn
Fulling Mill Fm
Broughton Castle
Broughton
Sutton Lodge Fm
Steane Grounds Fm
A422
Oatleys Hall
Tadmarton
Bodicote
Rosamond's Bower
Burdrop
Elm Fm
Swalcliffe
Broughton Grange
Wykham Mill
Bodicote Mill Ho
Cotefield Ho
Manor Fm
Upper Astrop
Robin Wood
Walltree Fm
Hinton Grounds Fm
Hinton-in-the-Hedges
Brackley
Turweston
Sibford Ferris
Swalcliffe Grange
Ell's Fm
Old Barn Fm
Sor Brook
King's Sutton
Astrop Ho
Newbottle
Forceleap Fm
Hinton in the Hedges
Manor Fm
Lower Tadmarton
Tadmarton Lodge
Hobb Hill
Twyford
East End
Astrop
Newbottle Spinney
Charlton House Fm
Sibford Grounds Fm
Bacon Fm
Adderbury
Grovehill Fm
Lower Nill Fm
Tadmarton Heath
Bloxham
Wayhouse Fm
Newbottle Fm
Charlton
Evenley Hall
Wigginton Heath
Rye Hill
West Adderbury
East Adderbury
Camp Fm
Plomers Firs Fm
The Croft
Milton
Rowler
Evenley
Nill Fm
Withycombe Fm
Lessor Fm
Happy Valley Fm
Bo-Peep Fm
Walton Grounds
Mixbury Ho
Milcombe
Park Fm
Cloisters Fm
Mixbury
East End
Swerbrook Fm
Wooden Hill Fm
Coombe Hill
Adderbury Grounds Fm
Pesthouse Wood
Croughton
The Slade Fm
Barrow Hill
Hook Norton
Wigginton
River Swere
Barford St John
Bloxham Br
Aynho
Warren Fm
Barley Mow Fm
Park Fm
South Newington
Rignell Hall
Field Barn
Aynho Park Ho
B4031
The Pits
Paradise Fm
Barford St Michael
Lower Aynho Grounds
Juniper Hill
Southrop
Grounds Fm
Buttermilk Stud
Deddington Mill
Mill Ho
New Buildings
Cottisford Heath
Coldharbour Fm
Hailcombe Barn Fm
Deddington
Souldern Mill
Souldern
Ockley Brook
South Hill
Swerford Park
Swerford Heath
Irondown Fm
Hempton
Clifton Road
Clifton
Pimlico Fm
Hill Fm
Iron Down Hill
Radwell Hill
Deddington Castle
Wharf Fm
Manor Ho
Heath Fm
Shelswell Plantn
Swerford
Grove Ash Fm
Black Jane Fm
Hawk Hill
Leadenporch Fm
Tower Field
Cottisford
Potato Town
Horse Hill
Raven Hill
Mackley Hill
Tomwell Fm
Upper Souldern Grounds Fm
Inkerman Fm
Tusmore Ho
Shelswell Park
Banbury Road
Pomfret Castle
Cottenham Fm
Nether Worton
Horwell Fm
Fox Covert
Cherwell Barn
Great Tew Park
New House Fm
Dane Hill
Hill Ho
Green Fm
Willaston Fm
Showell Fm
Great Tew
Hobbshole Fm
Flighthill Fm
Rest Hill Ho
Hill Fm
Lower Fm
The Green
Portway Fm
Baynard's Green
Stoke Bushes
Hardwick
Hethe
Newton Morrell
OXFORDSHIRE
Over Worton
North Aston
Fritwell
Lodge Fm
Lone Barn
Tangley Fm
Fringford
Magpie Fm
The Grange
Little Tew
Somerton
Heath Fm
Duns Tew
Stoke Lyne
Fringford Hill
Dunthrop
Heythrop
Hendon Fm
Jersey Manor Fm
Village Fm
Troy Fm
Fewcott
Cherwell Valley Services
Foxberry Wood
Little Tew Grounds Fm
Mill Covert
Ledwell
Worton Wood
Cockley Brook
Grange Fm
Mudginwell Fm
Stoke Wood
Stoke Little Wood
Glebe Fm
Waterloo Fm
Beaconsfield Fm
Horsehay Fm
Middle Aston
Upper Heyford Airfield (disused)
Ardley
Kelly Fm
Broadstone Hill
Tracey Fm
Sandford St Martin
Down Hill Fm
Watergate Fm
Moat Fm
Heythrop Park
Sandford Park
Middle Barton
Upper Heyford
Ashgrove Fm
Woodlands Fm
Bainton
Cotmore Ho
Manor Ho
Heyford Park
Leys Fm
Enstone
Westcott Barton
Brasenose Fm
Hill Ho
Steeple Aston
Dymock's Fm
Church Enstone
Enstone Road
Bartongate
Whistlow
The Heath
Manor Ho
Bucknell
Caversfield Ho
Drystone Hill Ho
Gagingwell
Oathill Fm
Steeple Barton
Hopcroft's Holt
Heyford
Lower Heyford
The Gorse
Caversfield
Enstone
Radford
Barton Abbey
Barton Lodge
Rousham
Caulcott
Upper Fm
Hawkwell Fm
Neat Enstone
Cleveley
Rousham Park House & Garden
Fir Tree Fm
Park Fm
Crowmarsh Fm
Lord's Fm
Litchfield Fm
Hoar Stone
White House Fm
Barton Leys Fm
Park Home Wood
Dewars Fm
Aldershot Fm
Bicester
Radfordbridge
Glympton Heath
Maiden Bower
Rousham Copse
Bucknell Lodge
Woodfield
Fulwell
Heath Fm
Newbarn Fm
Home Fm
Himley Fm
Highfield
Grange Fm
The Warren
Henley Knapp
Kiddington
Middleton Park
Middleton Stoney
Bicester North
Home Fm
Mangthorn Wood
Old Covert
Deadman's Riding Wood
Over Kiddington
Chesterton Fields Fm
Bicester Village
Kingsmere
Launton
Taston
Asterleigh Fm
Ludwell Fm
Upper Dornford Fm
Northbrook
Forest Lodge Fm
Bignell Ho
Shilcott Wood
Dog Kennel
Ditchley Park
Glympton Park
Wootton Fm
Tackley Wood
Tackley Heath
Fox Hill
Wood Ho
Slade Fm
Chesterton Stud Fm
Spring Well Fm
P&R
Spelsbury
Conygree Fm
Norman's Grove
Grimsdyke Fm
Hill Wood
Glympton
Glympton Road
The Bushes
Chesterton
Langford Park Fm
Graven Hill Area under dev
Ditchley Park
Out Wood
Copping Knoll
Lower Dornford Fm
Tackley Park
Tackley
Nethercott
Little Chesterton
Lodge Fm
Graven Hill
Ash Copse
Lodge Fm
Wood Fm
Glympton Wood
Park Fm
Charlbury
Wootton
Pigeon Lock
Kirtlington
Stonepit Hills
New Barn Fm
Wendlebury
Ambrosden
B4437
Sheer's Copse
King's Wood
Woodleys
Hordley Fm
Sturdy's Castle (PH)
Kirtlington Park
Stonehouse Fm
Newbridge Fm
Weston-on-the-Green
Merton Grounds
Pound Fm
River Evenlode
Bevin Fm
Hill Barn Fm
Callow Fm
Wootton Wood
Ditchley Gate
Stratford Br
Enslow
Ash Wood
Bletchingdon Park
Weston Park Fm
Littleworth Fm
Old Woodstock
Weaveley Fm
Gibraltar
Linch Lane
Staplehurst Fm
Merton
Lower Arncott
Great

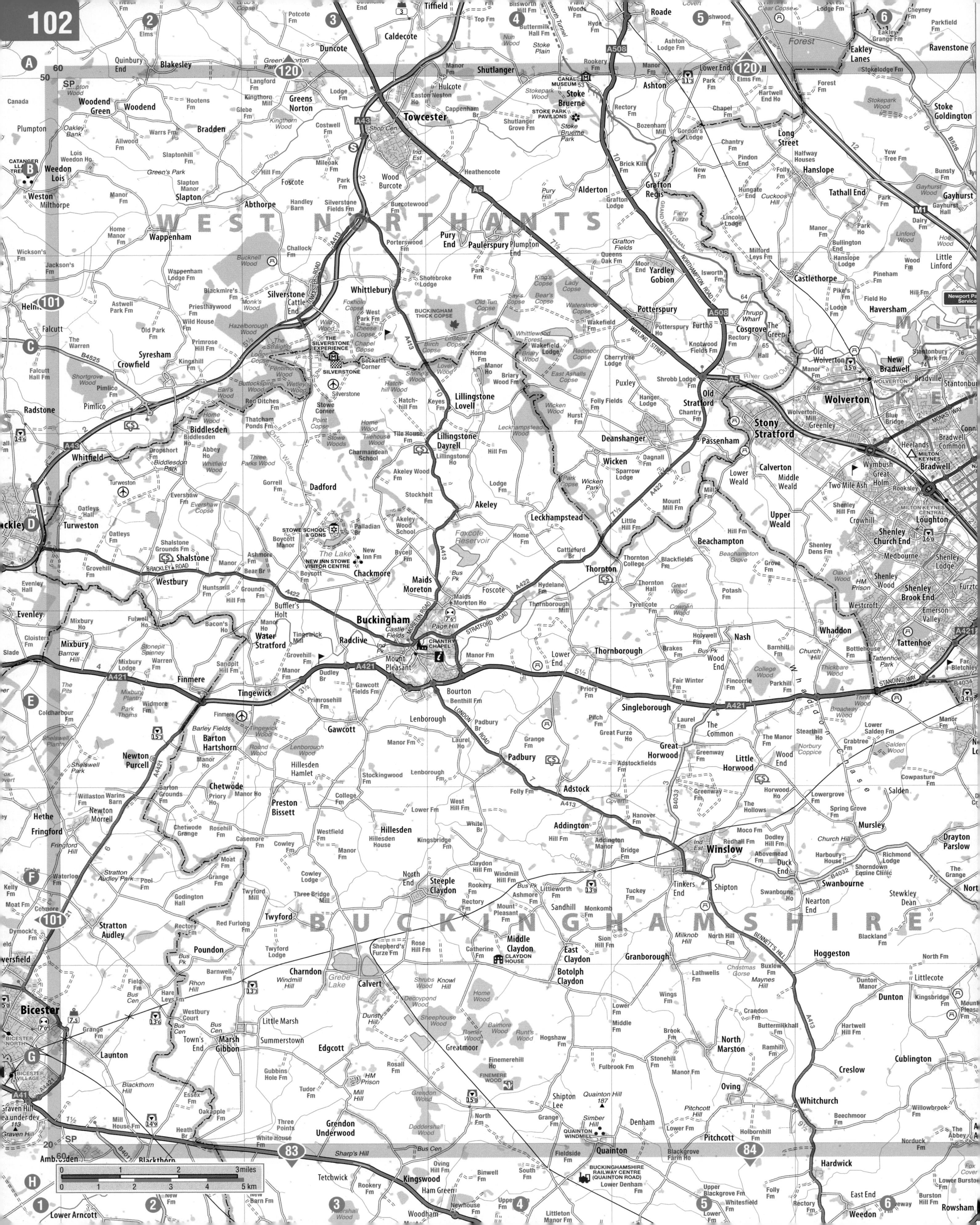

WEST NORTHANTS
BUCKINGHAMSHIRE
Tiffield
Caldecote
Duncote
Blakesley
Quinbury End
Roade
Ashton Lodge Fm
Ravenstone
Eakley Lanes
Forest
Top Fm
Buttermilk Hall Fm
Stoke Plain
Nun Wood
Shutlanger
Hulcote
Easton Neston Ho
Towcester
Canal Museum
Stoke Bruerne
Stoke Park Pavilions
Ashton
Stoke Goldington
Woodend Green
Woodend
Bradden
Hootens Fm
Greens Norton
Lodge Fm
Canada
Plumpton
Oakley Bank
Catanger Llama Trek
Weedon Lois
Weston
Milthorpe
Slapton
Slapton Manor
Abthorpe
Foscote
Wood Burcote
Heathencote
Alderton
Grafton Regis
Long Street
Hanslope
Tathall End
Gayhurst
Pury End
Paulerspury
Plumpton End
Wappenham
Yardley Gobion
Castlethorpe
Little Linford
Haversham
Whittlebury
Silverstone
Cattle End
Buckingham Thick Copse
Potterspury
Furtho
Cosgrove
The Green
Old Wolverton
New Bradwell
Bradville
Wolverton
Syresham
Crowfield
The Silverstone Experience
Silverstone
Radstone
Pimlico
Biddlesden
Lillingstone Lovell
Lillingstone Dayrell
Puxley
Old Stratford
Stony Stratford
Passenham
Deanshanger
Wicken
Calverton
Lower Weald
Middle Weald
Upper Weald
Two Mile Ash
Bradwell
Milton Keynes Central
Loughton
Whitfield
Turweston
Brackley
Dadford
Akeley
Leckhampstead
Stowe School & Gdns
New Inn Stowe Visitor Centre
Foxcote Reservoir
Chackmore
Maids Moreton
Foscote
Thornton
Beachampton
Shenley Church End
Medbourne
Shenley Brook End
Shalstone
Westbury
Evenley
Mixbury
Water Stratford
Buckingham
Radclive
Page Hill
Chantry Chapel
Thornborough
Nash
Whaddon
Tattenhoe
Finmere
Tingewick
Bourton
Lenborough
Gawcott
Padbury
Singleborough
Great Horwood
Little Horwood
Mursley
Salden
Newton Purcell
Barton Hartshorn
Hillesden Hamlet
Chetwode
Preston Bissett
Adstock
Addington
Winslow
Drayton Parslow
Hethe
Fringford
Hillesden
Steeple Claydon
North End
Swanbourne
Shipton
Tinkers End
Stratton Audley
Twyford
Poundon
Middle Claydon
Claydon House
East Claydon
Botolph Claydon
Granborough
Hoggeston
Charndon
Calvert
Dunton
Bicester
Launton
Marsh Gibbon
Little Marsh
Summerstown
Edgcott
North Marston
Creslow
Cublington
Oving
Whitchurch
Grendon Underwood
Pitchcott
Quainton
Buckinghamshire Railway Centre (Quainton Road)
Blackthorn
Kingswood
Hardwick
Weedon
Lower Arncott
Rowsham
A5
A43
A413
A421
A422
A508
A4421
A41
M1
B4525
B4032
B4033
Watling Street
Grand Union Canal
Monks Way
Standing Way
Bennett's Hill
120
101
83
84
0 1 2 3 miles
0 1 2 3 4 5 km

Olney
Weston Underwood
Clifton Reynes
Newton Blossomville
Bromham
Biddenham
Bedford
Goldington
Putnoe
Brickhill
Emberton
Great Denham
Queen's Park
Fenlake
Kempston
Elstow
Harrowden
Cardington
Cople
Shortstown
Stagsden
Astwood
Hardmead
Sherington
Chicheley
Tyringham
Filgrave
Lathbury
Newport Pagnell
North Crawley
Wootton
Kempston Hardwick
Wixams
Cotton End
Wilstead
Cranfield
Broad Green
Moulsoe
Willen
Marston Moretaine
Stewartby
Houghton Conquest
Haynes
Milton Keynes
Milton Keynes Village
Broughton
Woolstone
Salford
Lidlington
Millbrook
Ampthill
Maulden
Clophill
Brogborough
Wavendon
Woburn Sands
Aspley Guise
Ridgmont
Husborne Crawley
Steppingley
Flitton
Silsoe
Bletchley
Fenny Stratford
Walton
Simpson
Bow Brickhill
Aspley Heath
Flitwick
Greenfield
Pulloxhill
Woburn
Eversholt
Tingrith
Westoning
CENTRAL BEDFORDSHIRE
Little Brickhill
Great Brickhill
Harlington
Sharpenhoe
Barton-le-Clay
Hexton
Stoke Hammond
Potsgrove
Milton Bryan
Battlesden
Toddington
Streatley
CHILTERNS
Soulbury
Stewkley
Hockliffe
Tebworth
Wingfield
Chalgrave
Chalton
Upper Sundon
Lower Sundon
Leighton Buzzard
Linslade
Eggington
Stanbridge
Tilsworth
Houghton Regis
Sundon Park
Limbury
South End
Burcott
Billington
Dunstable
Leagrave
Luton
LUTON
Wing
Ledburn
Totternhoe
Eaton Bray
Caddington
Slapton
Edlesborough
Horton
Whipsnade
Kensworth
Wingrave
Cheddington
Ivinghoe Aston
Slip End
Pepperstock
M1
A5
A6
A421
A4146
A505
A509
A418
A4280
121
104
84
85

Great Barford
Blunham
Tempsford Rd
Everton
Gamlingay
Hatley St George
Arrington
Wimpole
New Wimpole
Willington
Moggerhanger
Girtford
Sandy
Potton
Cockayne Hatley
Croydon
Cardington
Cople
Beeston
Chapel End
Stratford
Sutton
Wrestlingworth
Tadlow
Wendy
Whaddon
Shingay
Thorncote Green
Northill
Ickwell Green
Upper Caldecote
Lower Caldecote
CENTRAL
BEDFORDSHIRE
Eyeworth
Abington Pigotts
Biggleswade
Old Warden
Shuttleworth Collection
Dunton
Guilden Morden
Bassingbourn
Holme
Haynes
Southill
Broom
Litlington
Steeple Morden
Stanford
Langford
Edworth
Hinxworth
Chicksands
Shefford
Clifton
Astwick
Ashwell
The Thrift
Beadlow
Campton
Henlow
Church End
Caldecote
Clophill
Newnham
Therfield
Stotfold
Arlesey
Slip End
Bygrave
Kelshall
Upper Gravenhurst
Meppershall
Upper Stondon
Lower Stondon
Radwell
Letchworth Garden City
Norton
Baldock
Sandon
Shillington
Clothall Common
Wallington
Roe Green
Higham Gobion
Holwell
Cadwell
Mill End
Barton-le-Clay
Pegsdon
Ickleford
Pirton
Clothall
Rushden
Willian
Hexton
Westmill
Walsworth
Weston
Throcking
CHILTERNS
Hitchin
Great Wymondley
Cottered
Little Offley
Charlton
Little Wymondley
Cromer
Graveley
Lilley
St Ippollytts
Great Offley
Gosmore
Ardeley
Walkern
Stevenage
Luton
Stopsley
Cockernhoe Green
King's Walden
Preston
Benington
Aston End
Shephall
Aston
Langley
St Paul's Walden
Broadwater
Hart Hill
Whitwell
Knebworth
Old Knebworth
Whempstead
Watton at Stone
Sacombe
Datchworth
Codicote
Kimpton
Woolmer Green
London Luton Airport
0 1 2 3 miles
0 1 2 3 4 5 km

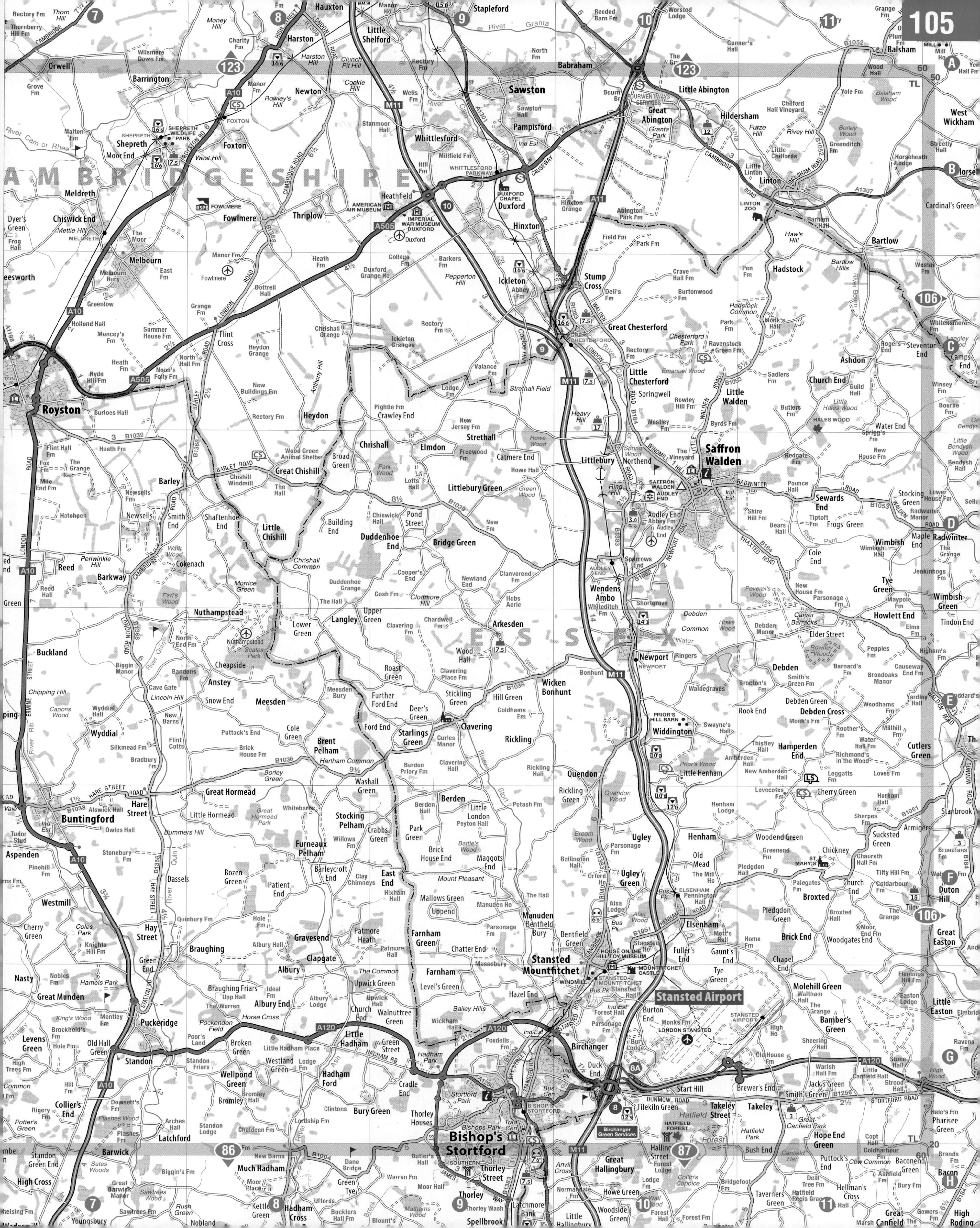
CAMBRIDGESHIRE
ESSEX
Royston
Saffron Walden
Bishop's Stortford
Stansted Airport
Buntingford
Sawston
Linton
Duxford
Great Chesterford
Little Chesterford
Great Abington
Little Abington
Hildersham
Babraham
Pampisford
Whittlesford
Harston
Hauxton
Little Shelford
Stapleford
Newton
Thriplow
Fowlmere
Foxton
Shepreth
Meldreth
Melbourn
Orwell
Barrington
Chiswick End
Heathfield
Hinxton
Ickleton
Stump Cross
Heydon
Chrishall
Great Chishill
Little Chishill
Elmdon
Strethall
Littlebury
Littlebury Green
Catmere End
Duddenhoe End
Bridge Green
Langley
Arkesden
Wendens Ambo
Newport
Wicken Bonhunt
Clavering
Rickling
Quendon
Ugley
Ugley Green
Widdington
Henham
Elsenham
Stansted Mountfitchet
Birchanger
Farnham
Manuden
Berden
Stocking Pelham
Furneaux Pelham
Brent Pelham
Meesden
Anstey
Nuthampstead
Barkway
Reed
Barley
Buckland
Wyddial
Westmill
Braughing
Puckeridge
Standon
Great Munden
Albury
Little Hadham
Hadham Ford
Much Hadham
Bury Green
Thorley
Great Hallingbury
Takeley
Little Canfield
Great Canfield
Broxted
Thaxted
Debden
Debden Green
Wimbish
Radwinter
Sewards End
Ashdon
Hadstock
Bartlow
Balsham
West Wickham
Little Walden
Great Easton
Little Easton
Molehill Green
Hatfield Forest
Imperial War Museum Duxford
American Air Museum
Shepreth Wildlife Park
Linton Zoo
Mountfitchet Castle
House on the Hill Toy Museum
Prior's Hall Barn
Audley End
Birchanger Green Services
M11
A10
A11
A120
A505
A1307
A1301
B1368
B1383
B1039
B1038
B184
B1051
B1052
B1053
B1256
B1004
123
86
87
106

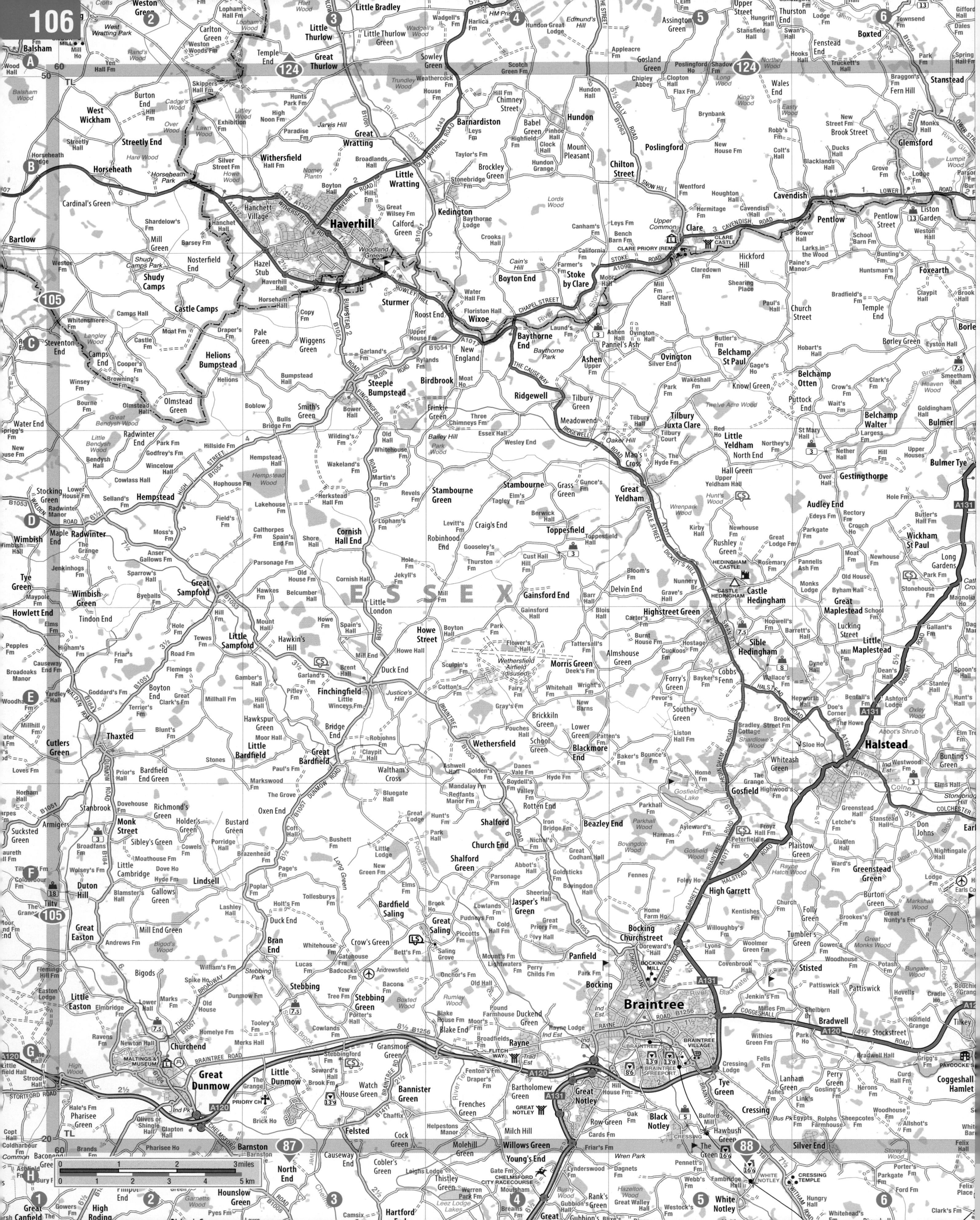

Balsham
Weston Green
Little Bradley
Little Thurlow
Great Thurlow
Little Thurlow Green
Wadgell's Fm
Hundon Great Lodge
Edmund's Hill
Assington Green
Upper Street
Thurston End
Boxted
Temple End
Sowley Green
West Wratting Park
Carlton Green
Weston Woods Fm
124
Gosland Green
Poslingford Ho
Stanstead
West Wickham
Burton End
Skippers Hall Fm
Hunts Park Fm
Chimney Street
Barnardiston
Hundon
Poslingford
Wales End
Glemsford
Streetly End
Withersfield
Great Wratting
Little Wratting
Babel Green
Mount Pleasant
Chilton Street
Brook Street
Horseheath
Horseheath Park
Brockley Green
Kedington
Haverhill
Hanchett Village
Calford Green
Cavendish
Pentlow
Pentlow Street
Liston Garden
Clare
Clare Castle
Clare Priory
Upper Common
Bartlow
Cardinal's Green
Shudy Camps
Shudy Camps Park
Hazel Stub
Boyton End
Stoke by Clare
Hickford Hill
Foxearth
Castle Camps
Sturmer
Wixoe
Roost End
Baythorne End
Ashen
Pannel's Ash
Ovington
Belchamp St Paul
Church Street
Temple End
Borley Green
105
Steventon End
Camps End
Pale Green
Wiggens Green
Helions Bumpstead
Steeple Bumpstead
Birdbrook
New England
Ridgewell
Belchamp Otten
Olmstead Green
Smith's Green
Frinkle Green
Tilbury Green
Meadowend
Tilbury Juxta Clare
Belchamp Walter
Bulmer
Water End
Radwinter End
Hempstead
Stambourne Green
Stambourne
Great Yeldham
Little Yeldham
Man's Cross
Gestingthorpe
Bulmer Tye
Stocking Green
Radwinter
Wimbish
Maple End
Cornish Hall End
Robinhood End
Craig's End
Toppesfield
Rushley Green
Audley End
Wickham St Paul
Long Gardens
Tye Green
Great Sampford
Wimbish Green
ESSEX
Little London
Gainsford End
Delvin End
Castle Hedingham
Highstreet Green
Great Maplestead
Howlett End
Tindon End
Little Sampford
Hawkin's Hill
Howe Street
Morris Green
Almshouse Green
Sible Hedingham
Little Maplestead
Lucking Street
Duck End
Finchingfield
Boyton End
Brickkiln Green
Cobbs Fenn
Forry's Green
Southey Green
Thaxted
Cutlers Green
Little Bardfield
Great Bardfield
Bridge End
Wethersfield
Blackmore End
School Green
Halstead
Waltham's Cross
Gosfield
Whiteash Green
Bunting's Green
Monk Street
Richmond's Green
Stanbrook
Oxen End
Shalford
Rotten End
Beazley End
Church End
Shalford Green
Sibley's Green
Little Cambridge
Lindsell
Duton Hill
Tilty
Great Easton
Mill End Green
Bardfield Saling
Great Saling
Jasper's Green
High Garrett
Greenstead Green
Bocking Churchstreet
Bran End
Crow's Green
Stebbing
Stebbing Green
Panfield
Bocking
Stisted
Pattiswick
Little Easton
Bigods
Churchend
Blake End
Duckend Green
Braintree
Bradwell
Stockstreet
Rayne
Great Dunmow
Little Dunmow
Bannister Green
Watch House Green
Bartholomew Green
Great Notley
Black Notley
Tye Green
Cressing
Coggeshall Hamlet
Pharisee Green
Felsted
Frenches Green
Milch Hill
Willows Green
Young's End
Silver End
Barnston
87
North End
Causeway End
Cobler's Green
Molehill Green
Thistley Green
88
White Notley
Hounslow Green
High Roding
Hartford End
Great Canfield
Chelmsford City Racecourse
Great Leighs

SUFFOLK
DEDHAM VALE
Shimpling
Alpheton
Preston St Mary
Kettlebaston
Hitcham
Wattisham Stone
Wattisham
Great Bricett
Ringshall Stocks
Barking Tye
Willisham Tye
Willisham
Little Blakenham
Bridge Street
Lavenham
Whelp Street
Bildeston
Nedging Tye
Naughton
Greenstreet Green
Offton
Nettlestead
Somersham
Brent Eleigh
Monks Eleigh
Chelsworth
Nedging
Milden
Swingleton Green
Chelsworth Common
Semer
Ash Street
Whatfield
Elmsett
Flowton
Long Melford
Acton Place
Humble Green
Little Waldingfield
Lindsey
Lindsey Tye
Drakestone Green
Aldham
Burstallhill
Acton
Cuckoo Tye
Great Waldingfield
Upsher Green
Priory Green
Parliament Heath
Rose Green
Burstall
Hintlesham
Chattisham
Washbrook
Rodbridge Corner
Newman's Green
Round Maple
Castling's Heath
Kersey Tye
Kersey Upland
Hadleigh
Sudbury
Chilton
Mill Green
Edwardstone
Broad Street
Gosling Green
William's Green
Hadleigh Heath
Coles Green
Copdock
Mace Green
Great Cornard
Cornard Tye
Newton
Groton
Sherbourne Street
Wicker Street Green
Horner's Green
Bower House Tye
Upper Layham
Layham
Ballingdon
Middleton
Boxford
Stone Street
Calais Street
Polstead Heath
Lower Layham
Sackers Green
Hagmore Green
Whitestreet Green
Little Cornard
Henny Street
Little Henny
Great Henny
Assington
Polstead
Shelley
Lower Raydon
Raydon
Little Wenham
Gipsy Row
Great Wenham
Capel St Mary
Workhouse Green
Harrow Street
Stoke-by-Nayland
Withermarsh Green
Holton St Mary
Twinstead Green
Twinstead
Lamarsh
Dorking Tye
Leavenheath
Honey Tye
Thorington Street
Higham
East Bergholt
Bentley
Lattinford Hill
Alphamstone
Bures Green
Nayland
Stratford St Mary
Brantham
Cripple Corner
Cross End
Pebmarsh
Bures
Boxted
Dedham
Cattawade
Mount Bures
Little Horkesley
Wormingford
Boxted Cross
Boxted Heath
Langham
Dedham Heath
Lawford
Manningtree
Countess Cross
Colne Engaine
Great Horkesley
Birchhall Corner
Ardleigh Heath
Ardleigh
Foxash Estate
White Colne
Wakes Colne
Wakes Colne Green
Janke's Green
Hemp's Green
Horkesley Heath
Little Bromley
Chappel
Fordham
West Bergholt
Mile End
Fox Street
Parson's Heath
Fordstreet
Great Tey
Gallows Green
Eight Ash Green
Braiswick
Welshwood Park
Crockleford Heath
Elmstead
Great Bromley
Aldham
Seven Star Green
Colchester
Elmstead Market
Hare Green
Balls Green
Marks Tey
Beacon End
Lexden
Stanway
Abbey Field
The Hythe
Little Tey
Copford
Copford Green
Stanway Green
Shrub End
Maypole Green
Old Heath
Wivenhoe Cross
Keelars Tye
Frating Green
Broad Green
Coggeshall
Easthorpe
Blackheath
Wivenhoe
Rowhedge
Alresford
Heckfordbridge
Hardy's Green
Feering
Birch
Layer de la Haye
Thorrington
Kelvedon
Gore Pit
Messing
Birch Green
Abberton
Langenhoe
Layer Breton
Layer Marney
Abberton Reservoir
Colchester Zoo
Beth Chatto Gardens
East Anglian Railway Museum
The Munnings Art Museum
Flatford Mill Visitor Centre
Jobserve Community Stadium
Fingringhoe Wick Nature Reserve
Wolves Wood
Melford Hall
Kentwell Hall
Gainsborough's House
Wattisham Station Heritage
St James's Chapel
Guildhall
Bourne Mill
St Botolph's Priory
High Woods
Firstsite
A134
A131
A1071
A1141
A12
A120
A133
A137
B1115
B1508
B1068
B1070
B1029
B1027
B1022
B1026
B1025
B1024
B1023
125
108
88
89

Ipswich
Felixstowe
Harwich
Dovercourt
Woodbridge
Walton-on-the-Naze
Frinton-on-Sea
Manningtree
Lawford
Mistley
Whitton
Westbourne
Kesgrave
Martlesham
Martlesham Heath
Rushmere St Andrew
Claydon
Great Blakenham
Little Blakenham
Bramford
Sproughton
Chantry
Stoke
Maidenhall
Gainsborough
Rose Hill
California
Priory Heath
Warren Heath
Belstead
Wherstead
Freston
Woolverstone
Chelmondiston
Pin Mill
Holbrook
Tattingstone
Bentley
Capel St Mary
Brantham
Cattawade
Stutton
Harkstead
Erwarton
Shotley
Shotley Gate
Nacton
Levington
Trimley St Martin
Trimley St Mary
Walton
Old Felixstowe
Felixstowe Ferry
Kirton
Falkenham
Bucklesham
Brightwell
Newbourne
Waldringfield
Hemley
Sutton
Shottisham
Bawdsey
Melton
Bromeswell
Great Bealings
Little Bealings
Playford
Culpho
Tuddenham St Martin
Westerfield
Witnesham
Henley
Akenham
Barham
Grundisburgh
Hasketon
Burgh
Parkeston
Wrabness
Bradfield
Ramsey
Little Oakley
Great Oakley
Wix
Horsley Cross
Tendring
Tendring Green
Beaumont
Thorpe-le-Soken
Kirby-le-Soken
Kirby Cross
Great Holland
Weeley
Weeley Heath
Great Bentley
Aingers Green
Thorrington
Little Clacton
Frating Green
Little Bentley
Hamford Water
River Orwell
River Stour
SUFFOLK
SUFFOLK COAST AND HEATHS
HOEK VAN HOLLAND
0 1 2 3 miles
0 1 2 3 4 5 km

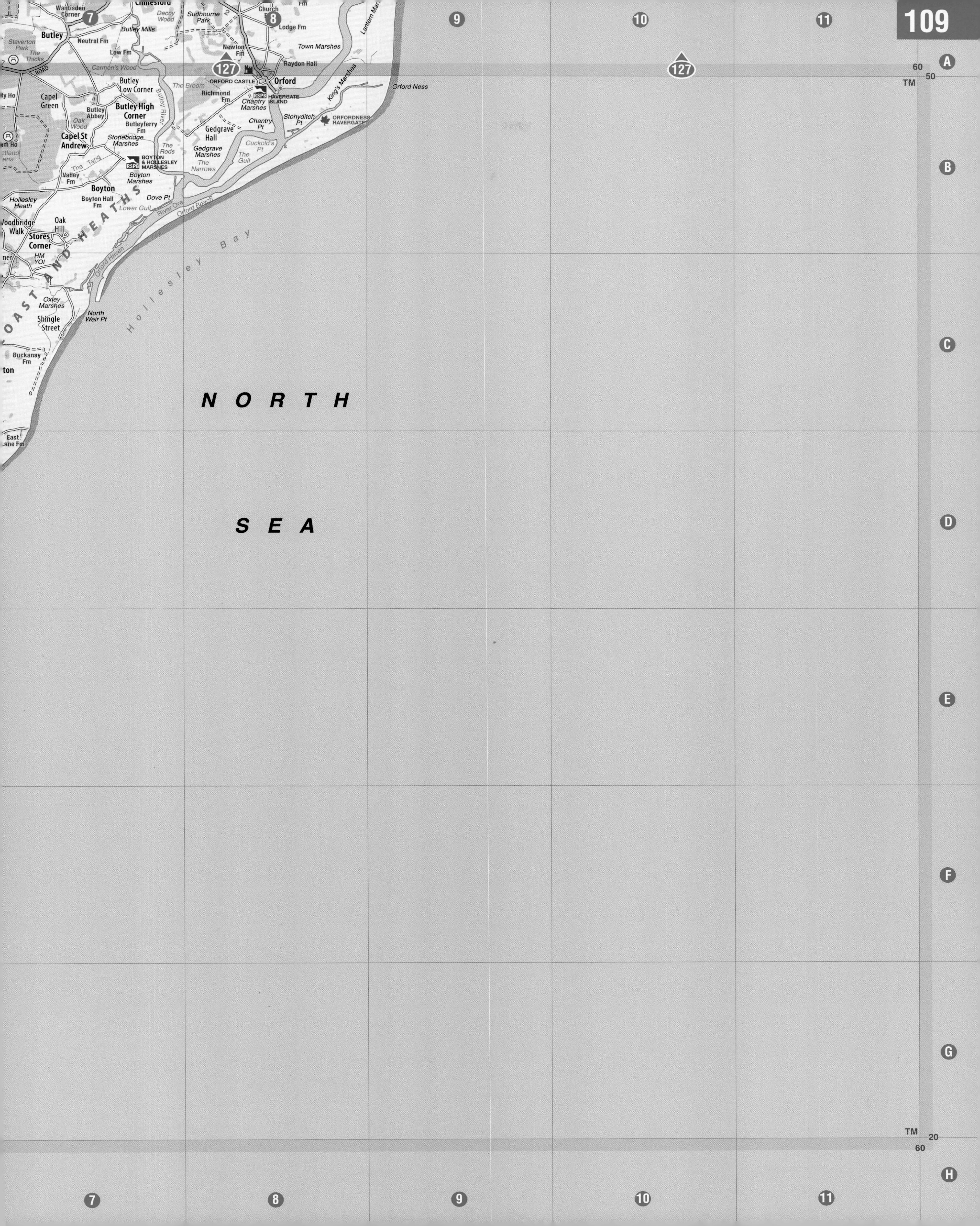

NORTH
SEA
Hollesley Bay
Orford
ORFORD CASTLE
HAVERGATE ISLAND
ORFORDNESS-HAVERGATE
Orford Ness
King's Marshes
Butley
Butley High Corner
Butley Low Corner
Capel St Andrew
Capel Green
Boyton
BOYTON & HOLLESLEY MARSHES
Gedgrave Hall
Sudbourne Park
Shingle Street
Stores Corner
Oak Hill
Woodbridge Walk
North Weir Pt
Orford Beach
River Ore
Butley River
127
TM

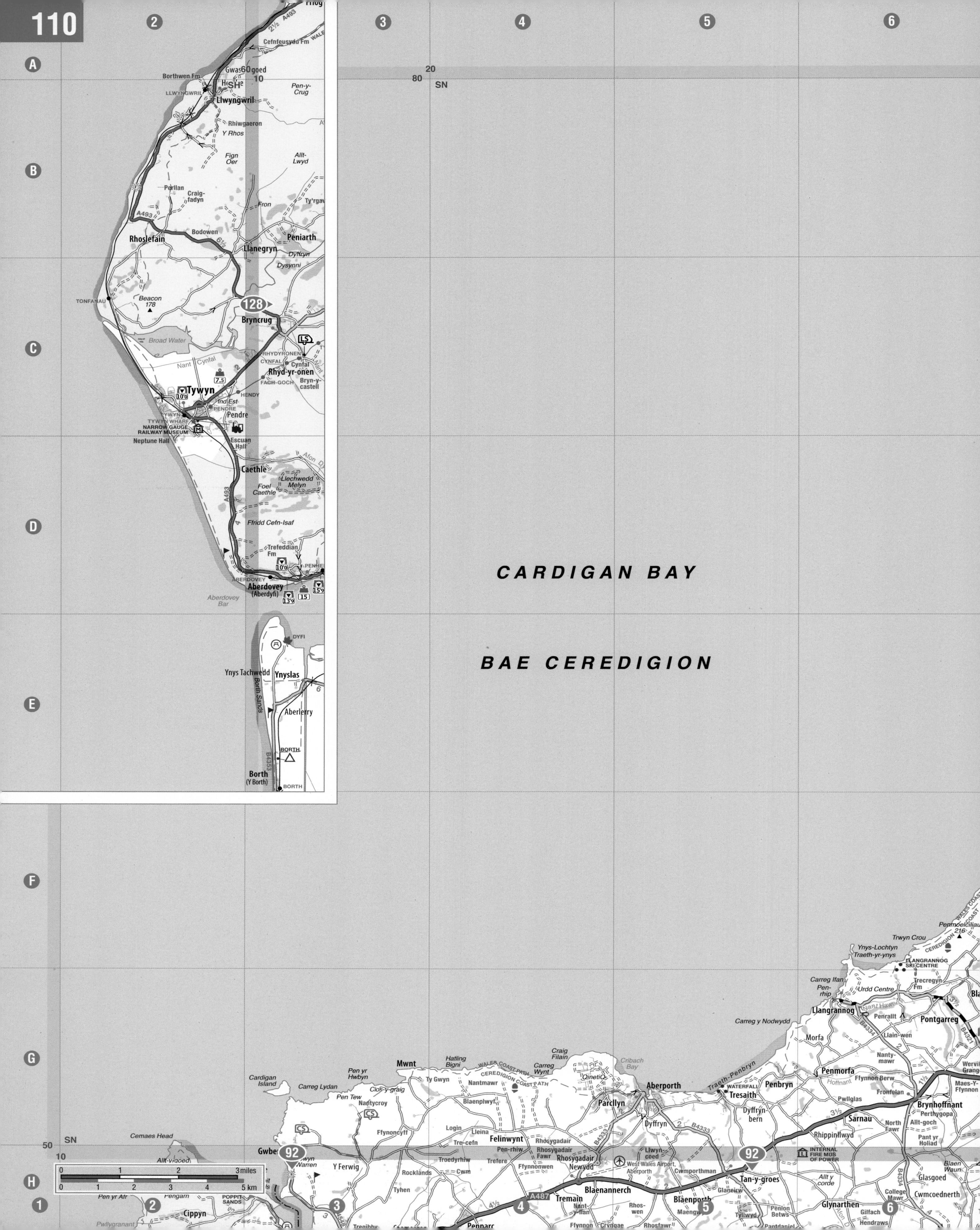
CARDIGAN BAY
BAE CEREDIGION
Llwyngwril
Rhoslefain
Llanegryn
Peniarth
Bryncrug
Tywyn
Rhyd-yr-onen
Pendre
Caethle
Aberdovey
(Aberdyfi)
Ynyslas
Ynys Tachwedd
Aberleffry
Borth
(Y Borth)
NARROW GAUGE RAILWAY MUSEUM
Neptune Hall
Broad Water
Borth Sands
Llangrannog
Pontgarreg
Penmorfa
Penbryn
Tresaith
Aberporth
Parcllyn
Mwnt
Felinwynt
Gwbert
Y Ferwig
Cippyn
Tremain
Blaenannerch
Blaenporth
Tan-y-groes
Sarnau
Brynhoffnant
Glynarthen
Cwmcoednerth
Cardigan Island
Cemaes Head
Dyffryn
Rhosygadair
Newydd
West Wales Airport
INTERNAL FIRE MUS OF POWER
LLANGRANNOG SKI CENTRE
WALES COAST PATH
CEREDIGION COAST PATH
A487
A493
B4333
B4334
B4353
128
92
0 1 2 3 miles
0 1 2 3 4 5 km

7
8
9
10
11
128
Aberystwyth
Trefechan
Penparcau
Southgate
Rhydyfelin
A487
Llanfarian
Chancery
(Rhydgaled)
Blaenplwyf
Aberbrwynen
Tan-y-graig
Trefedlin
Penrallt
Glan-rhos
ANTARON AVENUE
WALES COAST PATH
CEREDIGION COASTAL PATH
PENDERI CLIFFS
Cefngraigwen
Brynhir
Tyngwndwn
112
Ffos-y-bontbren
Carrog Fm
Aelybryn
Afon Carrog
Maenelin
Llanddeiniol
Plas Penbryn
Rhandir Uchaf
Bryngwyn
Ffynnonwen
Grip
Afon Wyre
Argoed
Chwc y Barcus
Tycam
Llangwyryfon
Llanrhystud
Cwm Wyre
Fferm Tynbeil
Treflys
Hafodlas
B4337
Ty-Newydd
Cwm Mabws
Mabws Hall
Fferm Trya
Afon Tryal
Gwarcaeau
Maes-crug
Trefenter
Hafod Ithel
361
Llansantffraed
FANTASY FARM PARK
Ffynnon Hywel
Rhyd-Rosser
Talwrn Hogfaen
Llanon
(Llan-non)
Digoed
Cwm Peris
Hafod-Peris
Glan Peris
Rhydlas
Talwrn-côch
Rhydfudr
Garnfach
Trawsnant
Tanlluest
Lluest-newydd
Pantanamlwg
Rhydydorth
Rhos-lwyd
Afon Cledan
Morfa Mawr Fm
Hafodwnog
Pantlleinau
Pantcynghorior
Penrhiw
Nebo
Ynys-hir
Gorswen Fm
Tygwyn
Rhos Haminiog
Rhydgaled
Rhos-maen
Cefn-gwyn
Aberarth
Cefngwrthafarn Uchaf
Cross Inn
Hafod
Drefaes
Waun-fawr
Glynhir
Lleust-mawr
Nantcoy
Gwarllyn
Tangarn
Aberaeron
B4577
Pennant
Frongoy
Llwynywen
Tyngwndwn
Pontsaeson
Dyffryn Arth
Bethania
Penuwch
Esgair-Arth
Caebislan Isaf
Afon Arth
Gors-ddalfa
Moelfryn
Clogfryn
Panteg
Pantyronen
Glwydgoch Fm
Monachty
Hafod-hir-isaf
Croes Wyntoedd
LAMPETER ROAD
Lloegr-ffch
Blaen Lluest
Cwm-march
Plas-y-Bryniau
Tangraig
Cefn-wig
Tan-banc
Henbant
Cilcert
Gilfach-yr-halen
Ffos-y-ffin
Henfynyw
Lletty Shon
Tynbedw
Ty'n-y-ffynnon
Coed
Hafodhir
Crynfryn
Hafod-y-gors
Rhiwlas
Lan-faelog
New Quay Head
New Quay
(Ceinewydd)
Birds Rock
Little Quay Bay
New Quay Bay
Oernant
Mwdwl Fm
Afon Aeron
LLANERCHAERON
Pen-wern
Trichrug
343
Dolau-couon
Tylau
Traethy Coubal
Penrhyn
Coed-y-Brenin
Tyglyn
Cilcennin
Brechfa Fawr
Cei-bach
Llwyncelyn
A482
Pen-rhiw
Llaethliw
Ty Mawr
Pilbach
Blaenfallen
Pen-cwm
Brechfafach
Maen-y-groes
Gilfachrheda
Llaingarreglwyd
Castell-y-geifr
Lluest
Neuadd-lwyd
Ciliau Aeron
Newbridge
Bwlch-y-graig
Blaencastell
Bronaeron
Byrlip
Pentrefelen
Afon Drywi
Bronfre
Allt y Fron
Bwlch-Llan
B4576
Capel Betws Lleucu
Cwmtydu
A486
Llwynderw
Neuadd
Pant Cefn
Cwm-mawr
Penlancwnlle Fan
Dolau Aeron
Penfoel
Penllwybr
Llanarth
Oakford
Rhiwbren Fawr
Ffynnondafalog
Trefran
Castell
Cross Inn
Motygido
Cefn Esgeronen
Nant-yr-efail
Ciliau-uchaf
Brynog
Tal-fan
Penbwich Mawr
Pensarnau
Goitre
Tegfan
Pemwern
Geneva
Pen-graig
Pantyrhen
Trefilan
Gartheli
Llwyn-y-groes
Frithwen
Nanternis
Blaenwern
Nant-y-gwrdy
Llwynrheol
Cil-Llwch
Bank Green Grove
Lluindain-fach
Afon Meurig
Brynbloda
Drefach Fm
Pen-cae
Capel Vicar
Moelfre
294
Tal-sarn
Abermeurig
Tre-fynor
Bwichwernen Fawr
Neuadd
Caerwedros
Pantyrhendy
Ffynnonmeredydd
Faenog Isaf
Dihewyd
Ystrad Aeron
Ty Hen
Llwyndafydd
Gelli
Llwynywernau
Gwynfryn
B4342
Ty'nyfron
Felinfach
Glanwern
Felindre
Berthlwyd Fawr
Gelligarneddau
Pwllglas
Cwmcynon
Hafodiwan
Pantgwyn
Mydroilyn
Castlehill
Lletlybowen
Gilfachyfrân
Synod Mill
CEREDIGION
Treberfedd
Wern-ddu
Temple Bar
Rhiwonnen
Llangybi Common
encelyn
Synod Inn
Gafriw
Feinog-uchaf
Cwm-cafn
Cilerwysg
Afon Ffynnon-Ddewi
Glanrhos
Rhosgoch-fach
Graigwen
Penbryn-Mawr
Bryn-gwyn
Blaen-waun
Nant-Sidyll
Caledrhydiau
Tryal Manor
Pensarnfawr
Bryn-goleu
Denmark Fm
Brynteilog
Clyngarw
Pant-sod
Gelli
Ffynnon-oer
(SIR CEREDIGION)
A487
Ffoshelyg-uchaf
Deri Lodge Wood
Llangybi
Pantgwyn
Esgair-wen
Rhydyfran
Cwmbychan
Rhydlydan
Gelli-gwenyn
Derry Ormond Park
Pentregat
Plwmp
Mynachlog
Rhos Garn Whilgarn
312
Penlan-noeth
Mount Pleasant
Blaenbedw Fawr
Post-bach
Cletwr
Pen-bryn
Betws Bledrws
Llynddu
Ffynonrhys
Pen-pare
Clyngwyn
Cruglas
Pisgah
Blaenau-gwenog
Nanthenfoel
Bryn-Bedw
Afon Bedw
Rhyd-wen
Talgarreg
Rhydyrhaiarn
Hafod-yr-wyn
Maesllwyd
Cribyn
Capeli
Silian
Long Wood
Nant-y-medd
Henbant
Dolgerdd
Meinigwynion
Clyncoch
Llechwedd-dderi
Y Gaer
Glan-Denys
Dyffryn
Penlanmedd
Nant-goch
Rhyd-Sais
B4338
Gorsgoch
Clyn-du
Gwarffynnon
Warren
Blaenbarre
Allt-ddu
306
Pledrog
93
Crugmaen
254
Ffrwd
Llanfair-clydogau
Capel Cynon
Cwmarch
RHOS LLAWR-CWRT
Fadfa
Bwlch-y-fadfa
B4459
Nant y gwyddau
Cwm-mawr
Glynmeherin
Banc Y
259
Maestir Fm
Olwen
Pont-faen
Clawdd-melyn
Pant-bach
Darren-fawr
Glan-dwr
Rhydd-ddu
Blaen-waun-ganol
Pengaer
Hafodwynog
Bryn-yr-Eglwys
Alltgoch
Lampeter
(Llanbedr Pont Steffan)
Pentrefelin
Nantycwnstabl
Castell-Howell
Coedlannau
Gwardafolog
Blaencwrt
Tai-gwynion
Hendryd
Blaenafon
Blaencerdinfach
Blaen-cribor
Clyncoch
Cwrt-newydd
Esgair-
A
B
C
D
E
F
G
H
SN
Mynydd

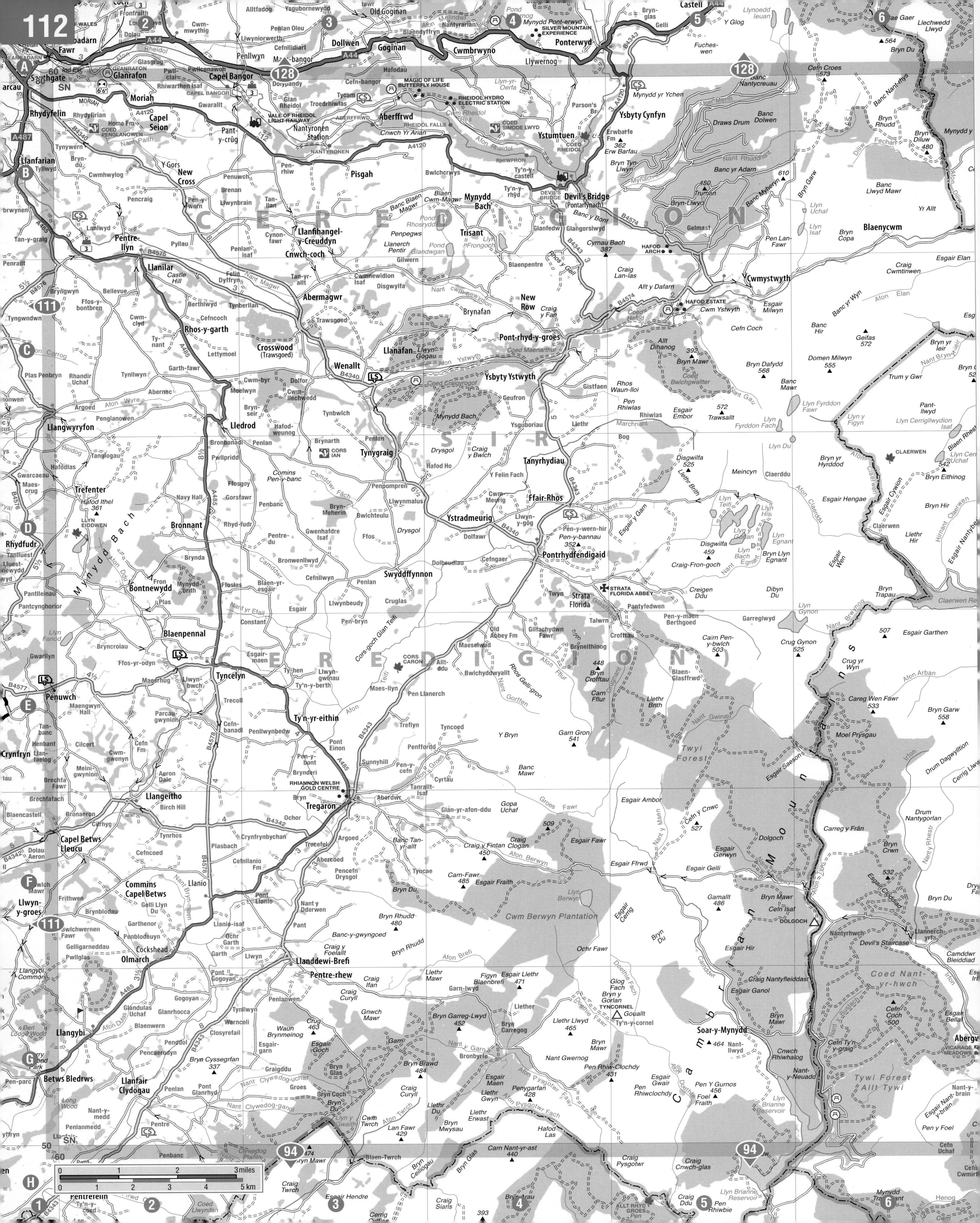

Fronfraith
Alltfadog
Ysguborhewydd
Old Goginan
Nantyrarian
Mynydd Pont-erwyd
SILVER MOUNTAIN EXPERIENCE
Castell
Bryn-glas
Gelli
Y Glog
Llynoedd Ieuan
Llechwedd Llwyd
Cwm-mwythig
Penlan Oleu
Llwyniorwerth
Cefnllidiart
Dollwen
Goginan
Blaendyffryn
Cwmbrwyno
Ponterwyd
Fuches-wen
564
Bryn Du
Llanbadarn Fawr
Penllwyn
Maes-bangor
Llywernog
Glasgrug
Pwllclai
Pwllcenawon
Capel Bangor
Hafodau
Dolypandy
Cefn-bangor
MAGIC OF LIFE BUTTERFLY HOUSE
Llyn-yr-Oerfa
Cefn Croes
573
Banc Nantycreuau
Banc Nant-rhys
Glanrafon
Rhiwarthen Isaf
Tycam
RHEIDOL HYDRO ELECTRIC STATION
Mynydd yr Ychen
Moriah
Gwarallt
Glan Rheidol
Troedrhiwlas
Parson's Br
Ysbyty Cynfyn
Rhydyfelin
VALE OF RHEIDOL LIGHT RAILWAY
Aberffrwd
Cwm Rheidol Res
Afon Merin
Home Fm
Capel Seion
Pant-y-crûg
Nantyronen Station
RHEIDOL FALLS
Cwnch Yr Arian
COED SIMDDE LWYD
Ystumtuen
Draws Drum
Banc Dolwen
Bryn Rhudd
Bryn Diluw
480
Mynydd y
COED PENGLANOWEN
Nant Paith
NANTYRONEN
COED RHEIDOL
Erwbarfe Fm
362
Erw Barfau
Llanfarian
Tynywern
Bryn-dû
Cwmhwylog
Y Gors
New Cross
Penuwch
Pen-rhiw
Pisgah
Bwlchcrwys
RHIWFRON
Ty'n-y-castell
Bryn Tyn-Llwyn
Banc yr Adarn
Nant Rhuddnant
Banc Llwyd Mawr
610
Mynach
Ty'n-y-rhyd
Devil's Bridge (Pontarfynach)
480
Truman
Bryn Garw
Yr Allt
Pencraig
Pen-y-wern
Brenan
Llwynbrain
Tan-llan
Banc Blaen Cwm-Magwr
Blaen Cwm-Magwr
Mynydd Bach
Banc y Bont
Bryn-Llwyd
Banc Myheryn
Llyn Uchaf
CEREDIGION
Llanlwyd
Pentre-llyn
Pyllau
Cynon-fawr
Llanfihangel-y-Creuddyn
Pond Rhosrydd
Penpegws
Trisant
Glanfedw
Glangorslwyd
Gelmast
Llyn Isaf
Bryn Copa
Blaenycwm
Tan-y-graig
Penllan isaf
Llanerch Pentir
Pond Glandwgan
Llyn Frongoch
Cyrnau Bach
387
Rhos y Gell
HAFOD ARCH
Pen Lan-Fawr
Penrallt
Llanilar
Castle Hill
Cnwch-coch
Gilwern
Blaenpentre
Craig Lan-las
Esgair Elan
Craig Cwmtinwen
Bryngwyn
Bellevue
Felin Dyffryn
Nant Magwr
Tan-yr-allt
Cwmnewidion Isaf
Disgwylfa
Allt y Dafarn
Cwmystwyth
Ffos-y-bontbren
Berthlwyd
Tynberllan
Abermagwr
Nant cwm-newydion
New Row
Craig y Fan
HAFOD ESTATE
Cwm Ystwyth
Esgair Milwyn
Afon Elan
Banc yr Wyn
Tyngwndwn
Cwm-clyd
Cefncoch
Rhos-y-garth
Trawsgoed
Brynafan
Coed Hafod
Banc Hir
Geifas
572
Cefn Coch
Afon Carrog
Ty-nant
Crosswood (Trawsgoed)
Lettymoel
Llanafan
Llwyn Gogau
Pont-rhyd-y-groes
Coed Maenarthur
Allt Dihanog
392
Bryn Mawr
Bryn Dafydd
568
Domen Milwyn
555
Bryn yr Ieir
Trum y Gwr
Plas Penbryn
Rhandir Uchaf
Tynllwyn
Garth-fawr
Wenallt
Afon Ystwyth
Coed Bwlchgwallter
Rhos Waun-lloi
Banc Mawr
Pant-llwyd
Cwm-byr
Dolfor
Ysbyty Ystwyth
Coed Craigyrogof
Gistfaen
Afon Gau
Llyn Fyrddon Fawr
Moelwyn
Abernac
Cwm-llechwedd
Geufron
Pen Rhiwlas
572
Trawsallt
Llyn y Figyn
Llyn Cerrigllwydion Isaf
Argoed
Afon Wyre
Bryn-seir
Tynbwlch
Mynydd Bach
Rhiwlas
Esgair Embor
Llyn Fyrddon Fach
Llangwyryfon
Penglanowen
Lledrod
Hafod-weunog
Penlan
Ysguboriau
Llethr
Marchnant
Bog
Llyn Du
Afon Beidog
Tanglogau
Bronbanadl
Penlan
Brynarth
CORS IAN
Tynygraig
SIR
Drysgol
Craig y Bwlch
Tanyrhydiau
Disgwylfa
525
Bryn yr Hyrddod
CLAERWEN
Llyn Cerrig Uchaf
542
Bryn Eithinog
Hafodlas
Pwllpridd
Comins Pen-y-banc
Camddwr Fach
Hafod Ho
Y Felin Fach
Llethr Brith
Meincyn
Claerddu
Gwarcaeau
Maes-crug
Trefenter
Ffosgoy
Penpompren
Cwm-Meurig
Ffair-Rhos
Afon Claerddu
Esgair Hengae
Esgair Cywion
Hafod Ithel
361
Navy Hall
Gorsfawr
Penbanc
Bryn-Meherin
Llwynmalus
Bwlchteulu
Ystradmeurig
Llwyn-y-gog
Llyn Teifi
Llyn Hir
Bryn Hir
LLYN EIDDWEN
Bronnant
Rhyd-fudr
Gwenhafdre Isaf
Drysgol
Dolfawr
Pen-y-wern-hir
Esgair y Garn
Llyn y Gorlan
Claerwen
Llethr Hir
Rhydfudr
Pentre-du
Ffos
Pen-y-bannau
352
Disgwylfa
459
Llyn Egnant
Esgair Wen
Mynydd Bach
Brynda
Bronwenllwyd
Dolbeudiau
Cefngaer
Pontrhydfendigaid
Llyn Bach
Bryn Llyn Egnant
Craig-Fron-goch
Afon Ddu
Fron
Bontnewydd
Mynydd-brith
Ffosias
Blaen-yr-esgair
Cefnllwyn
Penlan
Swyddffynnon
STRATA FLORIDA ABBEY
Creigen Ddu
Dibyn Du
Bryn Trapau
Pantlleinau
Pantcynghorior
Plas
Nant yr Efail
Esgair
Llwynbeudy
Cruglas
Twyn
Strata Florida
Glasffrwd
Pantyfedwen
Llyn Gynon
Claerwen Res
Blaenpennal
Constant
Pen-bryn
Talwrn
Pen-y-maen Berthgoed
Garreglwyd
Llyn Fanod
Bryncroiau
Cors-goch Glan Teifi
Old Abbey Fm
Gilfachydwn Fawr
Bryneithinog
Crofftau
Cairn Pen-y-bwlch
503
Crug Gynon
525
507
Esgair Garthen
Gwarllyn
Ffos-yr-odyn
Esgair-maen
CORS CARON
Maeselwad
Allt-ddu
448
Bryn Crofftau
Rhos Gelli-gron
Afon Fflur
Crug yr Wyn
Penuwch
Maesrhug
Llwyn-bwch
Tyncelyn
Ty-hen
Llwyn-gwinau
Ty'n-y-berth
Bwlchyddwyallt
Carn Fflur
Blaen-Glasffrwd
Afon Arban
Maengwyn Hall
Trecoll
Maes-llyn
Pen Llanerch
Nant Gorffen
Llethr Brith
Careg Wen Fawr
533
Bryn Garw
558
Tan-banc
Henbant
Cilcert
Parcau-gwynion
Ty'n-yr-eithin
Treflyn
Tyncoed
Y Bryn
Garn Gron
541
Nant Gwinau
Twyi Forest
Moel Prysgau
Crynfryn
Llan-faelog
Cwm-gwenyn
Cefn Fm
Cefn-banadl
Penllwynbedw
Pont Einon
Penffordd
Esgair Saeson
Drum Dagwyllion
Cerrig Llwyd
Meini-gwynion
Aeron Dale
Pen-y-bont
Brynderi
Sunnyhill
Pen-y-cefn
Cyrtau
Afon Groes
Banc Mawr
Brechfa Fawr
Brechfafach
Llangeitho
Birch Hill
RHIANNON WELSH GOLD CENTRE
Tanrallt-isaf
Bryn
Tregaron
Aberdwr
Gopa Uchaf
Esgair Ambor
Groes Fawr
Cambrian Mountains
Irfon
Drum Nantygorlan
Blaencastell
Bronaeron
Cilrhyg
Tynrhos
Ochor
Cwrynfrynbychan
Glan-yr-afon-ddu
509
Cefn y Cnwc
527
Dolgoch
Carreg y Frân
Capel Betws Lleucu
Cefncoed
Plasbach
Argoed
Trecefel
Banc Tan-yr-allt
Craig y Fintan
450
Craig Clogan
Esgair Fawr
Nant y Maen
Esgair Gerwyn
Bryn Crwn
Nant y Rhestr
Dolau Aeron
Cefnllanio Fm
Abercoed
Pencefn Drysgol
Tyncae
Afon Berwyn
Esgair Ffrwd
Esgair Gelli
532
Esgair Cloddiad
Commins Capel Betws
Gelli Llyn Du
Llanio
Pont Llanio
Carn-Fawr
485
Esgair Fraith
Llyn Berwyn
Gamallt
486
Bryn Mawr
Cefn Isaf
Bryn Du
Llwyn-y-groes
Frithwen
Brynblodau
Garthenor
Nant y Dderwen
Bryn Du
Bryn Rhudd
480
Cwm Berwyn Plantation
Esgair Cerrig
DOLGOCH
Nantyrhwch
Llannerch-yrfa
Gwlchwernen Fawr
Penblodeuyn
Llanio-isaf
Ochr Garth
Pant
Banc-y-gwyngoed
Bryn Du
Ochr Fawr
Esgair Hir
Devil's Staircase
Camddwr Bleiddiad
Gelligarneddau
Pwllglas
Cockshead
Olmarch
Garth
Llwyn
Craig y Foelallt
Llanddewi-Brefi
Bryn Rhudd
Afon Brefi
Craig Nantyfleiddiast
Coed Nant-yr-hwch
Llangybi Common
Pont Gogoyan
Pentre-rhew
Craig Ifan
Llethr Mawr
Figyn Blaenbrefi
Esgair Llethr
471
Garn-lwyd
Glog Fach
Bryn y Gorlan
TYNCORNEL
Doethie Fach
Esgair Ganol
Gogoyan
Penlanwen
Craig Curyll
Gnwch Mawr
Llether
Goualt
Ty'n-y-cornel
Bryn Mawr
Cefn-Coch
500
Glandulas Uchaf
Glanrhocca
Tynllwyn
Bryn Garreg-Lwyd
452
Bryn Carregog
Llethr Llwyd
465
Soar-y-Mynydd
464
Nant-llwyd
Esgair Bella
Llangybi
Long Wood
Blaenwern
Werncoli
Crug 463
Waun Brynmeinog
Garn
Nant y Garn
Bryn Mawr
Cnwch Rhiwhalog
Cefn Ty'n-y-graig
Abergwesyn
VICARAGE MEADOWS
Pendbol
Closyrefail
Esgair-garn
Esgair Goch
Bronbyrfe
Nant Gwernog
Pen Rhiw-Clochdy
431
Esgair Gwair
Nant-y-Neuadd
Betws Bledrws
Pencaerodyn
Bryn Cyssegrfan
337
Graigddu
Bryn Glas
Bryn Brawd
484
Esgair Maen
Penygarfan
428
Afon Pysgotwr
Pen Rhiwclochdy
Pen Y Gurnos
456
Foel Fraith
Tywi Forest
Allt Tywi
Llanfair Clydogau
Penlan
Pont Glanrhyd
Nant Clywedog-uchaf
Groes
Bryn Coch
Bryn Du
Craig Curyll
Llethr Gwyn
Afon Pysgotwr Fawr
Llyn Brianne Reservoir
Esgair Nant-y-brain
Nant-y-brain
Nant-y-medd
Penlanmedd
Pentre
Nant Clywedog-ganol
Afon Twrch
Cwm Twrch
Llethr Du
Llethr Erwast
Bryn Mwysau
Lan Fawr
429
Hafod Las
Pen y Foel
Penbanc
Blaen-Twrch
474
Bryn Mawr
Carn Nant-yr-ast
440
Bryn Glas
Craig Pysgotwr
Craig Cnwch-glas
Cefn Uchaf
Cefn Cwmirfon
Craig Twrch
Esgair Hendre
Bryn Cellioglog
Craig Siarls
393
Bryn-arau
ALLT RHYD Y GROES
Craig Ddu
Pen Rhiwbie
Llyn Brianne Reservoir
Mynydd Trawsnant
Henog
Pentrefelin
Ty'n-y-coed
Coed Llwynifan
0 1 2 3 miles
0 1 2 3 4 5 km

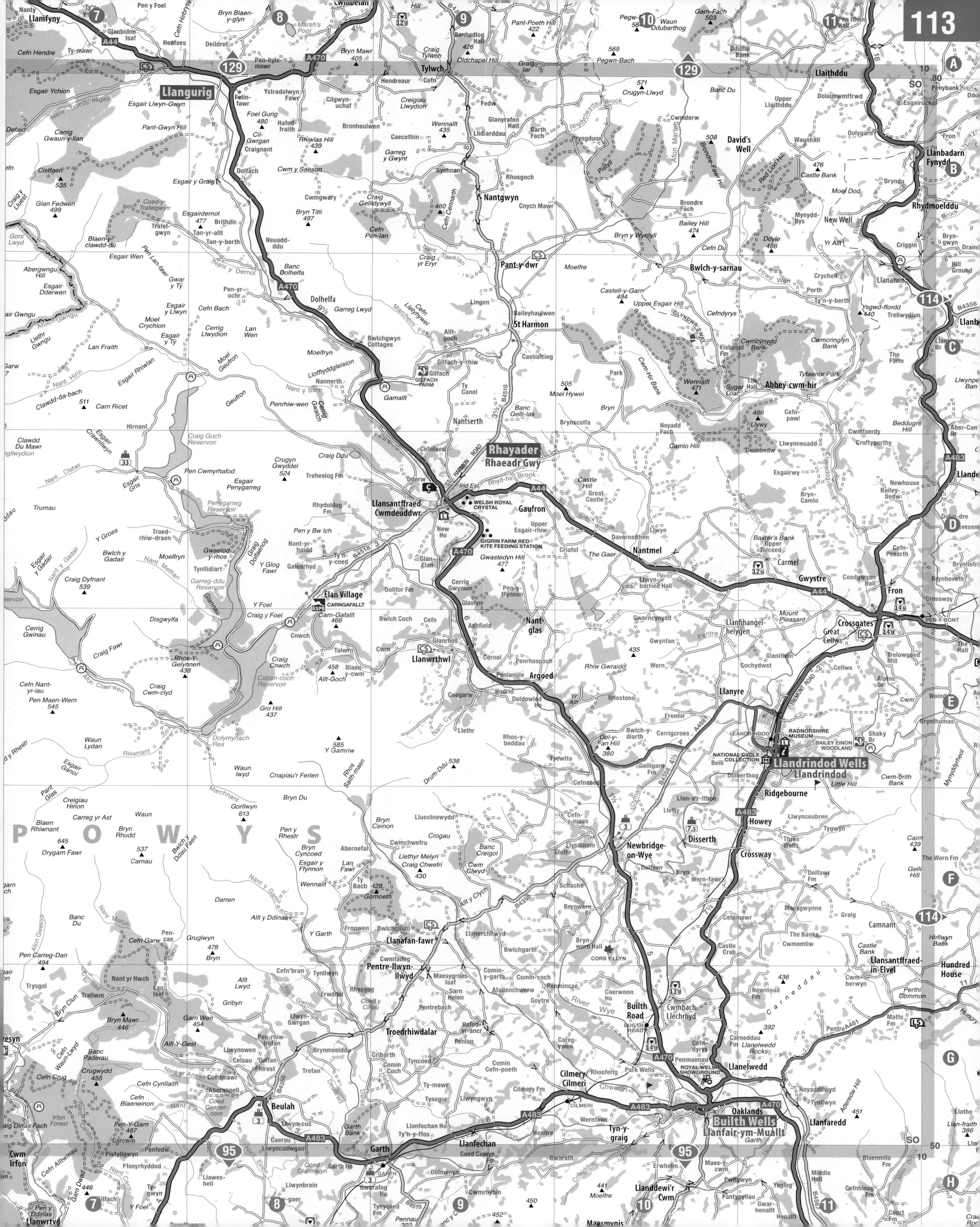
Llanifyny
Pen y Foel
Bryn Blaen-y-glyn
Marsh's Pool
Glanbidno Isaf
Henfaes
Deildref
Cefn Hendre
Ty-mawr
A44
129
Pen-hyle-mawr
A470
Bryn Mawr 405
Craig Tylwch
Banhadlog Hall 426
Oldchapel Hill
Pant-Poeth Hill 422
Graig Iar
569
Pegwn-Bach
Pegw-584
Waun Ddubarthog
Garn-Fach 503
Ddulluy Bank
Pen Ithon Hall
113
A
Tylwch
Hendreaur
Cefn
Nant Cyrtos
129
Llaithddu
SO
Penybank
Esgair Ychion
Llangurig
Esgair Llwyn-Gwyn
Felin-fawr
Ystradolwyn Fawr
Cilgwyn-uchaf
Creigiau Llwydion
Fedw
571 Crugyn-Llwyd
Banc Du
Upper Llaithddu
Dolauecwmffrwd
Esgairuchaf
Defaid
Cerrig Gwaun-y-llan
Foel Gurig 480
Hafod-fraith
Cil-Gwrgan
Craignant
Bronheulwen
Wennallt 435
Glanyrafon Halt
Llidiarddau
Garth Fach
Prysgduon
Cwmderw
508
Brondre-Fawr Hill
David's Well
Waunhall
Dolygarn
Fron
Pant-Gwyn Hill
Caecethin
Rhiwlas Hill 439
Garreg y Gwynt
Cwm y Saeson
Sychnant
Rhosgoch
Red Lion Hill
476
Castle Bank
Llanbadarn Fynydd
B
Cistfaen 535
Esgair y Graig
Dolfach
Cwmgwary
Craig Gellidywyll
Cefn Cennarth 460
Nantgwynn
Cnych Mawr
Brondre Fach
Mynydd-llys
Moel Dod
Bryndu
Rhydmoelddu
Glan Fedwen 499
Coed-y-Trafelgwyn
Esgairdernol 477
Brithdir
Bryn Titli 497
Cefn Pen-lan
Bailey Hill 474
New Well
Trafel-gwyn
Tan-yr-allt
Tan-y-berth
Neuadd-ddu
Bryn y Wyntyll
Ddyle 486
Yr Allt
Criggin
Bryn-gwyn
Gors Lwyd
Blaen-y-clawdd-du
Cefn Du
Esgair Wen
Pen Lan-fawr
Nant y Dernol
Craig yr Eryr
Nant Tawelan
Pant-y-dwr
Moelfre
Bwlch-y-sarnau
Hill Ground
Abergwngu Hill
Banc Dolhelfa
Esgair Dderwen
Gwar y Tŷ
A470
Crychell
Llananno
Pen-yr-ochr
Castell-y-Garn 494
Porth
Dolhelfa
Cefn Llethrhywel
Ty'n-y-berth
Ysgwd-ffordd 440
114
Trellwydion
Esgair y Llwyn
Cefn Bach
Garreg Lwyd
Lingen
Upper Esgair Hill
Cefndyrys
Glyndŵr's Way
Aton Gwngu
Moel Crychion
Baileyhaulwen
Llethr Gwngu
Cerrig Llwydion
Lan Wen
Bwlchgwyn Cottages
Allt-goch
St Harmon
Fishpool Fm
Cwmcynydd Bank
Cwmcringlyn Bank
C
Esgair y Tŷ
Lan Fraith
Moelfryn
Aton Gilfach-y-rhiw
Marteg
Caebalciog
The Farm
Moel Geufron
Esgair Rhiwlan
Llofftyddgleision
Gilfach
Gilfach Farm
Cwm-Hir Bank
Wennallt 471
Tyfaenor Park
Nant Hirin
Nannerth
Park
Ty Canol
505 Moel Hywel
Sugar Loaf
The Hall
Abbey-cwm-hir
Clawdd-da-bach
Nant y Sarn
Gamallt
B4518
511
Carn Ricet
Geufron
Penrhiw-wen
Cerrig Gwalch
Banc Gelli-las
Bryn
466 Llywy
Cefn-pawl
Hirnant
Nantserth
Brynscolfa
Noyadd Fach
Beddugre Hill
Cwmfaerdy
Clawdd Du Mawr
Esgair Crawnllwyn
Craig Goch Reservoir
Camlo Hill
Llwynneuadd
Croftyperthy
Cwmbedw
33
Crugyn Gwyddel 524
Craig Ddu
Cefnfaes
Harmon Road
Rhayader
Rhaeadr Gwy
Pen Cwmyrhafod
Treheslog Fm
Rhyd-hir Brook
Castle Hill
Esgairwy
Newhouse
Nant Clettwr
Esgair Gris
Esgair Penygarreg
Dderw
Ind Est
A44
Great Castle
Bailey-bedw
Bryn-Camlo
Penygarreg Reservoir
Llansantffraed Cwmdeuddwr
Welsh Royal Crystal
Gaufron
Trumau
Rhydoldog Fm
Upper Esgair-rhiw
Black Brook
Baxter's Bank
Upper Tolcoed
D
Y Groes
Troed-rhiw-draen
Craig Dolfaenog
Pen y Bw lch
New Ho
Gigrin Farm Red Kite Feeding Station
Daverneithen
Llwyn
Bwlch y Gadair
Nant-yr-haidd
B4518
Crizfol
The Gaer
Nantmel
Carmel
Cefn-Penarth
Gwaelod-y-rhos
Moelfryn
Ty'n-y-coed
Glan-Elan
A470
Gwastedyn Hill 477
Coedgwgan Hall
Esgair y Gadair
Nant y Gadair
Tynllidiart
Y Glog Fawr
Galedrhyd
Nant Methan
Garreg-ddu Reservoir
Pen-y-ffynnon
Llwyn barried Hall
River Dulas
Gwystre
Fron
Craig Dyfnant 539
Glannau
Elan Village
Carngafallt
Dolifor Fm
Cerrig Gwynion
A44
Crossway
Y Foel
Glaslyn
Nant-glas
Gwerncynydd
Mount Pleasant
Pen-y-bont
Disgwylfa
Craig y Foel
Carn-Gafallt 466
Bwlch Coch
Cefn
Ashfield
Llanfihangel-helygen
Crossgates
Great Cellws
Cerrig Gwinau
Cnwch
Pentre Brook
The Hall
Craig Fawr
Rhos-Y-Gelynnen 438
Craig Cnwch
Talwrn
Cwm
Glanrhos
Llanwrthwl
Cornel
Penrhosgoch
Gwynfan
435
Glanithon
Cellws
Trelowgoed Mill
Cefn Nant-yr-iau
Craig Cwm-clyd
458
Allt-Goch
Blaen-y-cwm
Penlanole
Argoed
Rhiw Gwraidd
Wern
Cochydwst
Alpine Br
Aton Claerwen
Caban-coch Reservoir
Pen Maen-Wern 545
Caegarw
Hodrid
Doldowlod Ho
Yr Allt
Rhostono
Llanyre
Cwm
Waind
E
Gro Hill 437
Nant Cymrun
Llethr
Fronhir
A4081
Brynthomas
Waun Lydan
Dolymynach Res
Rhos-y-beddau
Bwlch-y-diarth
Cerrigcroes
Llandrindod
Radnorshire Museum
Bailey Einon Woodland
Shaky Br
Esgair Ganol
Rhiwnant
585 Y Gamriw
Tyewtta
Dol-y-Fan Hill 380
National Cycle Collection
Beili
Llandrindod Wells
Cwm-brith Bank
Waun lwyd
Cnapiau'r Ferlen
Rhos Saith-maen
Drum-Ddu 538
Gelligarn Fm
B4358
Dolberthog
Llandrindod
Little Hill
Pant Glas
Marchnant
Cefncoed
Ridgebourne
Creigiau Hirion
Carreg yr Ast
Waun
Gorllwyn 613
Bryn Du
Llan-a'r-Ithon
Blaen Rhiwnant
Bryn Rhudd
Pen y Rhestr
Bryn Ceinon
Lluestnewydd
Estyn Brook
Cefn-y-maes
Lletty
A483
Howey
Llwynceubren
Tygwyn
P O W Y S
645
Drygarn Fawr
537 Carnau
Bwlch y Ddau Faen
Bryn Cyncoed
Abernefal
Crogau
Cwmchwefru
Llethyr Melyn
Banc Creigol
Llysdinam
Newbridge-on-Wye
Disserth
Three Wells
Cairn 439
Esgair y Ffynnon
Lan Fawr
Craig Chwefri 430
Cwm Clwyd
Dolfawr
Crossway
The Wern Fm
Nant y Garth
Wennallt
Ty Bach
Bryn
Wern-fawr
Dolfawr Fm
Gelli Hill
F
Darren
428 Gomoeth
Allt y Clych
B4358
Schache
Brynwern Br
Cefnmawr
Maesgwynne
Graig
Camnant Brook
Banc Du
Nant Melyn
Allt y Ddinas
Y Garth
Fronwen
Bwlchciliau
Llanerchllwyd
Dulas Brook
The Banks
114
Camnant
Cefn Garw
Pen-cae
Gruglwyn 478
Bryn
Llanafan-fawr
Bwlchgarth
Bryn-warn Hall
Cors y Llyn
Castle Crab
Cwmamliw
Castle Bank
Hirllwyn Bank
Pen Carreg-Dan 494
Cefn'bran
Cwmfadog
Pentre-llwyn-llwyd
Tynllwyn
Maesygroes Isaf
Comin-y-garth
Comin-coch
Llansantffraed-in-Elvel
Hundred House
Trysgol
Nant yr Hwch
Allt Lwyd
Rhysgog
Afallenchwerw
Penmincae
Caerwnon Ho
436
Newmead Fm
Cwm-berwyn
Trallwm
Lan Isaf
Erwddol
Coed y Cilliau
Sarn Helen
Goytre
River Wye
Builth Road
13.0
Perthi Common
Bryn Clun
Gribyn
Nant Gwnfel
Pentrebach
Hafod-yr-ancr
Cwmbach Llechrhyd
Carneddau
Pentre
A481
Matts Fm
Bryn Mawr 446
Garn Wen 454
Llwyn-Gwrgan
Troedrhiwdalar
Builth Road
392
Allt-Y-Gest
Pen-rhiw-trefan
Penlan
Caeg-ywen
Carneddau
Llanelwedd Rocks
Llwynowen
Brynmoelddu
14.0
Banc Paderau
Celsau
Doffan Fforest
Cribarth
Comin Coch
Tyncoed
Comin Cefn-poeth
Cefn-dyrys
G
Cefn Waun-Lwyd
Coedmawr
Trefan
A470
Penmaenau
Llanelwedd
Cefn Crug
Crugwydd 455
Aberannell
Ty-mawr
Cilmery/ Cilmeri
Rhosferig
Park Wells
Royal Welsh Showground
Cefn Cynllaith
Coed Caeper-corn
B4358
Tysegur
Llwyngwyn
Cilmery Fm
Chwefru
Noyaddlwyd
Cefn Blaeneinon
Nant Einon
Beulah
Dulas
A483
Cilmeri
A483
Oaklands
A470
Tynllwyn
Irfon Forest
Pen-Y-Garn 487
Llwyn-cus
Garth Bank
Llanfechan Ho
Ty'h-y-ffos
Wernfawr
Builth Wells
Llanfair-ym-Muallt
Aderow Hill
451
Llanfaredd
Llatho
Llan-fraith 386
Dinas Fach
Carcwm
A483
Llanfechan
Hendre
Tyn-y-graig
Garth
SO
Cwm Irfon
Pistyllgwyn
Penfedw
95
Caerau
Llwyncadwgan
Garth
Coed Cowyn Fm
Gwaralltt
95
Blaenmilo Fm
Middle Hall
Cefn Alltwinau
Fflosyrhyddod
Llawes-heli
Coed Clunmelyn
Garth Ho
Garth
Dolmenyn
Erwhelm
Maes-y-cwm
Pwllgwyn
Ysplog
Cefnhinog Fm
H
Garn Dwad
446
Gilfach
Ty-gwyn
Gwarafog Ho
Llwynbrain
Cwmrhybin
441 Moelfre
Llanddewi'r Cwm
Pantypyllau
Gwar-henallt
B4567
Y Foel
Tynycoed Fm
B4519
450
452
Maesmynis
Pen y Dinas
Llanwrtyd
Pennau
Henallt
Court Fm
7
8
9
10
11
7
8
9
10
11

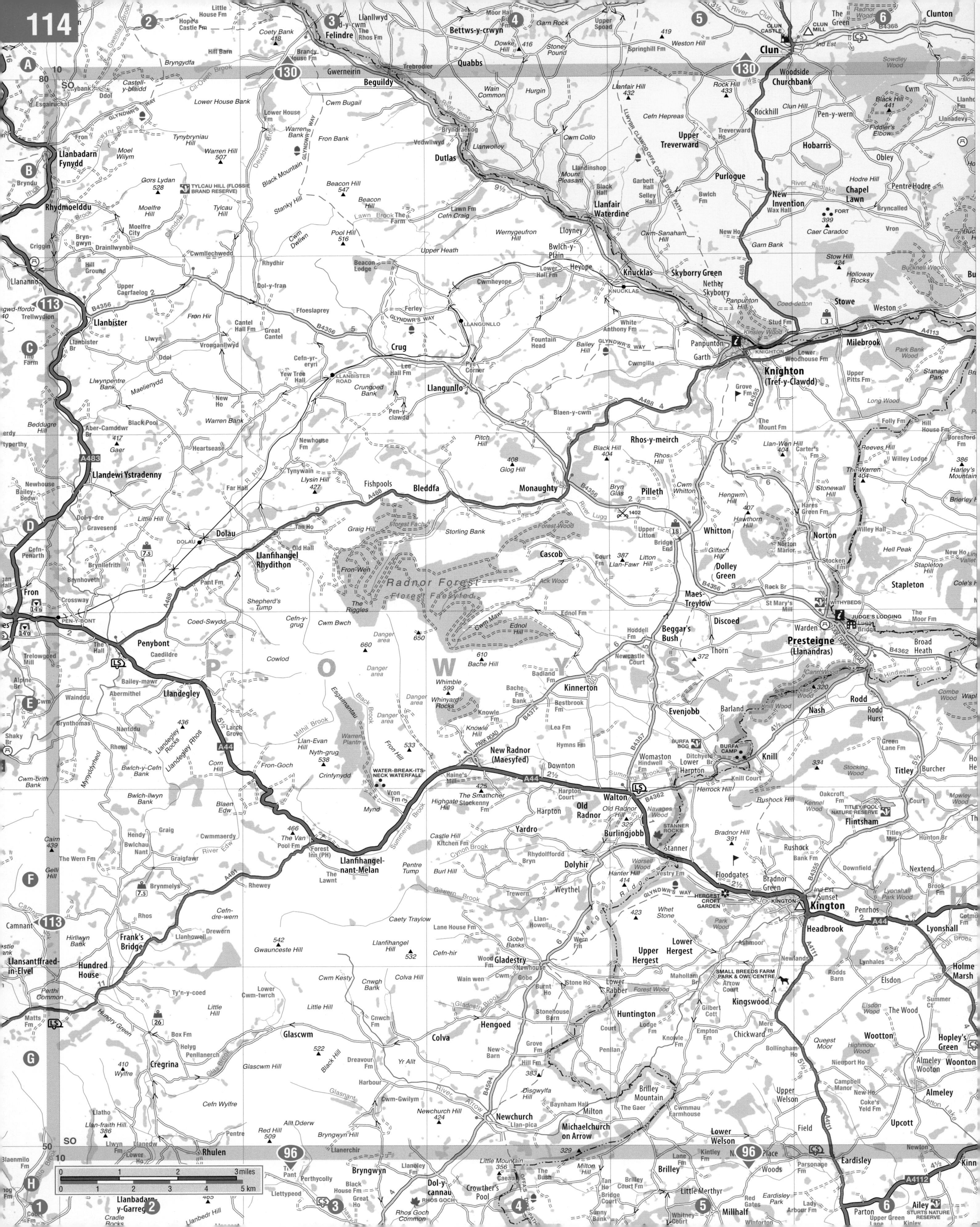
Felindre
Bettws-y-crwyn
Clun
Clunton
Beguildy
Quabbs
Gwerneirin
Trebrodier
Churchbank
Woodside
Rockhill
Pen-y-wern
Llanbadarn Fynydd
Dutlas
Upper Treverward
Hobarris
Obley
Purlogue
Chapel Lawn
New Invention
Caer Caradoc
Llanfair Waterdine
Rhydmoelddu
Knucklas
Skyborry Green
Heyope
Stowe
Weston
Llanbister
Crug
Llangunllo
Knighton (Tref-y-Clawdd)
Milebrook
Panpunton
Garth
Rhos-y-meirch
Llandewi Ystradenny
Bleddfa
Monaughty
Pilleth
Whitton
Norton
Dolau
Llanfihangel Rhydithon
Cascob
Dolley Green
Stapleton
Radnor Forest
Fforest Faesyfed
Fron
Penybont
Maes-Treylow
Discoed
Beggar's Bush
Presteigne (Llanandras)
Broad Heath
P O W Y S
Llandegley
Kinnerton
Evenjobb
Nash
Rodd
New Radnor (Maesyfed)
Knill
Titley
Walton
Old Radnor
Burlingjobb
Flintsham
Yardro
Llanfihangel-nant-Melan
Dolyhir
Kington
Headbrook
Lyonshall
Frank's Bridge
Hundred House
Llansantffraed-in-Elvel
Gladestry
Upper Hergest
Lower Hergest
Kingswood
Huntington
Hengoed
Colva
Glascwm
Cregrina
Wootton
Woonton
Almeley
Newchurch
Michaelchurch on Arrow
Upcott
Rhulen
Eardisley
Bryngwyn
Brilley
Lower Welson
Llanbadarn-y-Garreg
Millhalf
A44
A483
A488
A4113
A4111
A481
B4356
B4355
B4357
B4362
B4372
B4594
B4368
130
113
96
3 miles
5 km

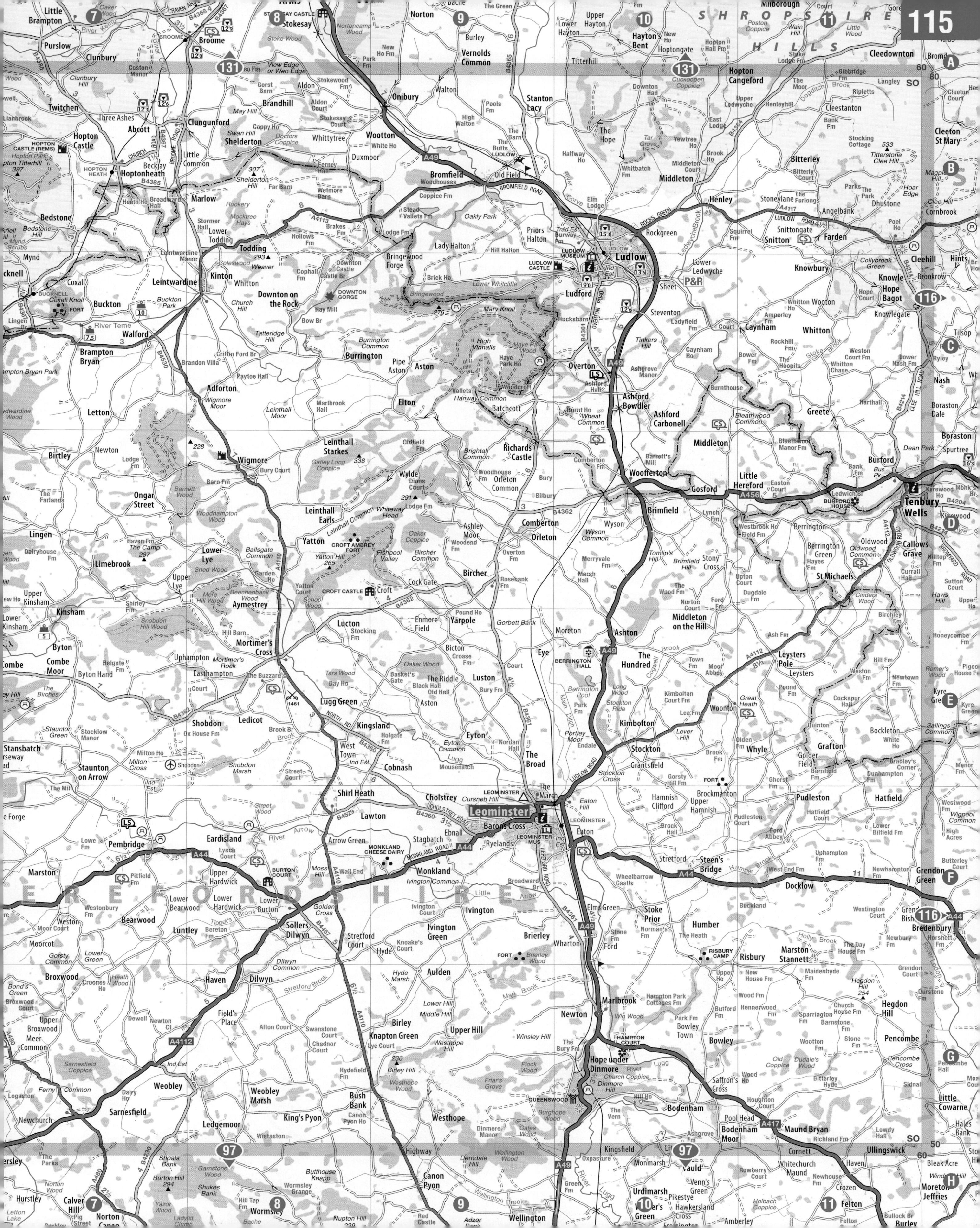

115
SHROPSHIRE HILLS
HEREFORDSHIRE
Little Brampton
Purslow
Clunbury
Twitchen
Abcott
Clungunford
Hopton Castle
Hoptonheath
Bedstone
Marlow
Leintwardine
Kinton
Todding
Buckton
Walford
Brampton Bryan
Adforton
Letton
Birtley
Wigmore
Lingen
Limebrook
Lower Lye
Aymestrey
Kinsham
Byton
Combe Moor
Mortimer's Cross
Shobdon
Ledicot
Staunton on Arrow
Pembridge
Eardisland
Marston
Bearwood
Luntley
Broxwood
Dilwyn
Sollers Dilwyn
Weobley
Sarnesfield
Ledgemoor
King's Pyon
Weobley Marsh
Broome
Stokesay
Onibury
Brandhill
Shelderton
Wootton
Bromfield
Burrington
Aston
Elton
Downton on the Rock
Leinthall Starkes
Leinthall Earls
Yatton
Lucton
Yarpole
Kingsland
Lugg Green
Cobnash
Shirl Heath
Lawton
Cholstrey
Monkland
Ivington
Ivington Green
Aulden
Birley
Knapton Green
Upper Hill
Westhope
Canon Pyon
Wellington
Norton
Vernolds Common
Stanton Lacy
Bitterley
Middleton
Henley
Ludlow
Ludford
Overton
Ashford Bowdler
Ashford Carbonell
Richards Castle
Orleton
Comberton
Bircher
Brimfield
Woofferton
Little Hereford
Gosford
Tenbury Wells
Middleton on the Hill
Ashton
Eye
The Hundred
Kimbolton
Stockton
Leominster
Barons Cross
Eaton
Steen's Bridge
Docklow
Pudleston
Hatfield
Stoke Prior
Humber
Risbury
Marston Stannett
Hegdon Hill
Pencombe
Newton
Marlbrook
Hope under Dinmore
Bodenham
Bodenham Moor
Maund Bryan
Ullingswick
Felton
Hopton Cangeford
Cleedownton
Cleeton St Mary
Caynham
Whitton
Greete
Burford
Knowbury
Cleehill
Leysters Pole
Grafton
Bredenbury
Little Cowarne
Grendon Green
131
97
116

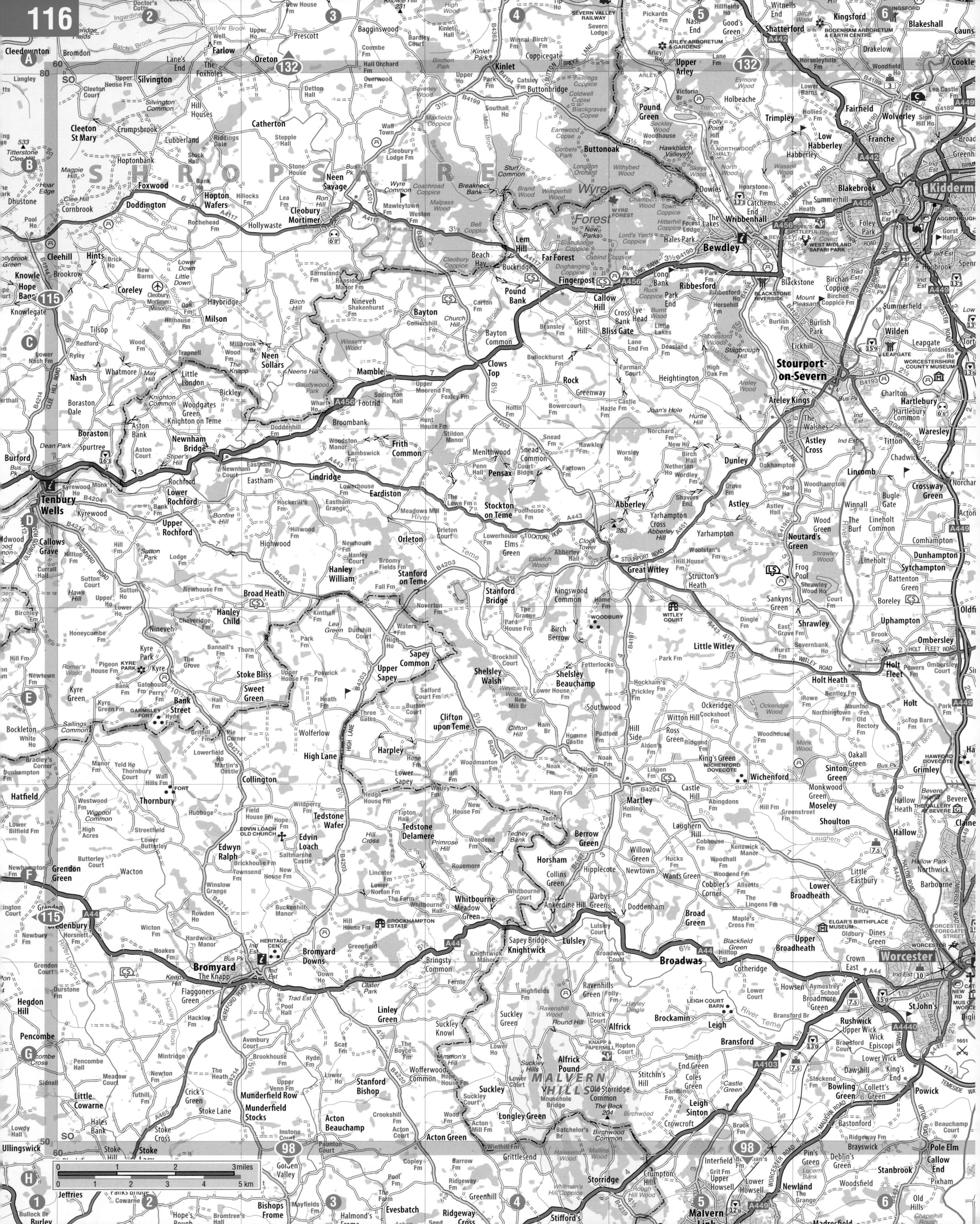
SHROPSHIRE
Farlow
Oreton
Kinlet
Upper Arley
Shatterford
Kingsford
Blakeshall
Silvington
Cleeton St Mary
Catherton
Buttonoak
Pound Green
Trimpley
Fairfield
Wolverley
Franche
Hoptonbank
Foxwood
Doddington
Hopton Wafers
Neen Savage
Cleobury Mortimer
Wyre Forest
Dowles
Wribbenhall
Blakebrook
Kidderminster
Bewdley
Far Forest
Fingerpost
Callow Hill
Bliss Gate
Ribbesford
Cleehill
Hints
Coreley
Milson
Neen Sollars
Bayton
Pound Bank
Nash
Whatmore
Little London
Mamble
Clows Top
Rock
Stourport-on-Severn
Areley Kings
Hartlebury
Boraston
Newnham Bridge
Frith Common
Lindridge
Eardiston
Pensax
Abberley
Astley Cross
Dunley
Astley
Lincomb
Tenbury Wells
Lower Rochford
Upper Rochford
Stockton on Teme
Great Witley
Orleton
Hanley William
Stanford on Teme
Stanford Bridge
Callows Grave
Broad Heath
Hanley Child
Kyre
Stoke Bliss
Sweet Green
Bank Street
Upper Sapey
Sapey Common
Shelsley Walsh
Shelsley Beauchamp
Little Witley
Holt Heath
Holt Fleet
Ombersley
Shrawley
Clifton upon Teme
Harpley
High Lane
Collington
Thornbury
Tedstone Wafer
Tedstone Delamere
Edvin Loach
Edwyn Ralph
Martley
Wichenford
Sinton Green
Grimley
Hallow
Berrow Green
Horsham
Grendon Green
Whitbourne
Ankerdine Hill
Knightwick
Lulsley
Broadwas
Lower Broadheath
Upper Broadheath
Worcester
Bredenbury
Bromyard
Bromyard Downs
Linley Green
Alfrick
Leigh
Brockamin
Bransford
Rushwick
St John's
Pencombe
Little Cowarne
Munderfield Row
Munderfield Stocks
Stanford Bishop
Suckley
Acton Beauchamp
Longley Green
Leigh Sinton
Powick
Acton Green
Stoke Lacy
Storridge
Malvern Link
MALVERN HILLS
0 1 2 3 miles
0 1 2 3 4 5 km

WORCESTERSHIRE
Hagley
West Hagley
Churchill
Blakedown
Clent
Romsley
Frankley
Bournville
Northfield
King's Norton
King's Heath
Longbridge
Rubery
Lickey
Cofton Hackett
Hopwood
Barnt Green
Alvechurch
Catshill
Fairfield
Wildmoor
Belbroughton
Bell End
Broome
Holy Cross
Drayton
Harvington
Stone
Mustow Green
Bluntington
Chaddesley Corbett
Shenstone
Dodford
Lickey End
Blackwell
Bromsgrove
Aston Fields
Sidemoor
Charford
Finstall
Tutnall
Tardebigge
Stoke Prior
Stoke Heath
Upton Warren
Wychbold
Hanbury
Woodgate
Bentley
Webheath
Redditch
Headless Cross
Crabbs Cross
Hunt End
Astwood Bank
Studley
Ipsley
Matchborough
Winyates
Beoley
Holt End
Portway
Hollywood
Wythall
Drakes Cross
Shirley
Solihull Lodge
Yardley Wood
Majors Green
Whitlock's End
Elmley Lovett
Cutnall Green
Hampton Lovett
Doverdale
Rushock
Elmbridge
Droitwich Spa
Salwarpe
Hadzor
Shernal Green
Feckenham
Bradley Green
Sambourne
Coughton
Alcester
Arrow
Oversley Green
Wixford
Broom
Bidford-on-Avon
Inkberrow
Stock Wood
Holberrow Green
Cookhill
Himbleton
Oddingley
Tibberton
Crowle
Warndon
Worcester
Spetchley
Whittington
Norton
Upton Snodsbury
Flyford Flavell
North Piddle
Naunton Beauchamp
Bishampton
Abberton
Kington
Rous Lench
Ab Lench
Church Lench
Atch Lench
Harvington
Salford Priors
Abbots Salford
Cleeve Prior
Dunnington
Iron Cross
Abbots Morton
Radford
Throckmorton
Pinvin
Peopleton
Grafton Flyford
White Ladies Aston
Churchill
Kempsey
Littleworth
Hatfield
Egdon
Wadborough
Drake's Broughton
Stonebow
Norton
Red Hill
Cherry Orchard
Ronkswood
Barbourne
Blackpole
Fernhill Heath
Hindlip
Martin Hussingtree
Dunhampstead
Saleway
Phepson
Shell
Goosehill Green
Broughton Green
Hanbury Hall
Woolmere Green
Webheath
Foxlydiate
Batchley
Enfield
Riverside
Smallwood
Southcrest
Lodge Park
Woodrow
Greenlands
Tynsall
M5
M42
A38
A44
A46
A422
A435
A441
A448
A449
A456
A491
A4538
133
118
99

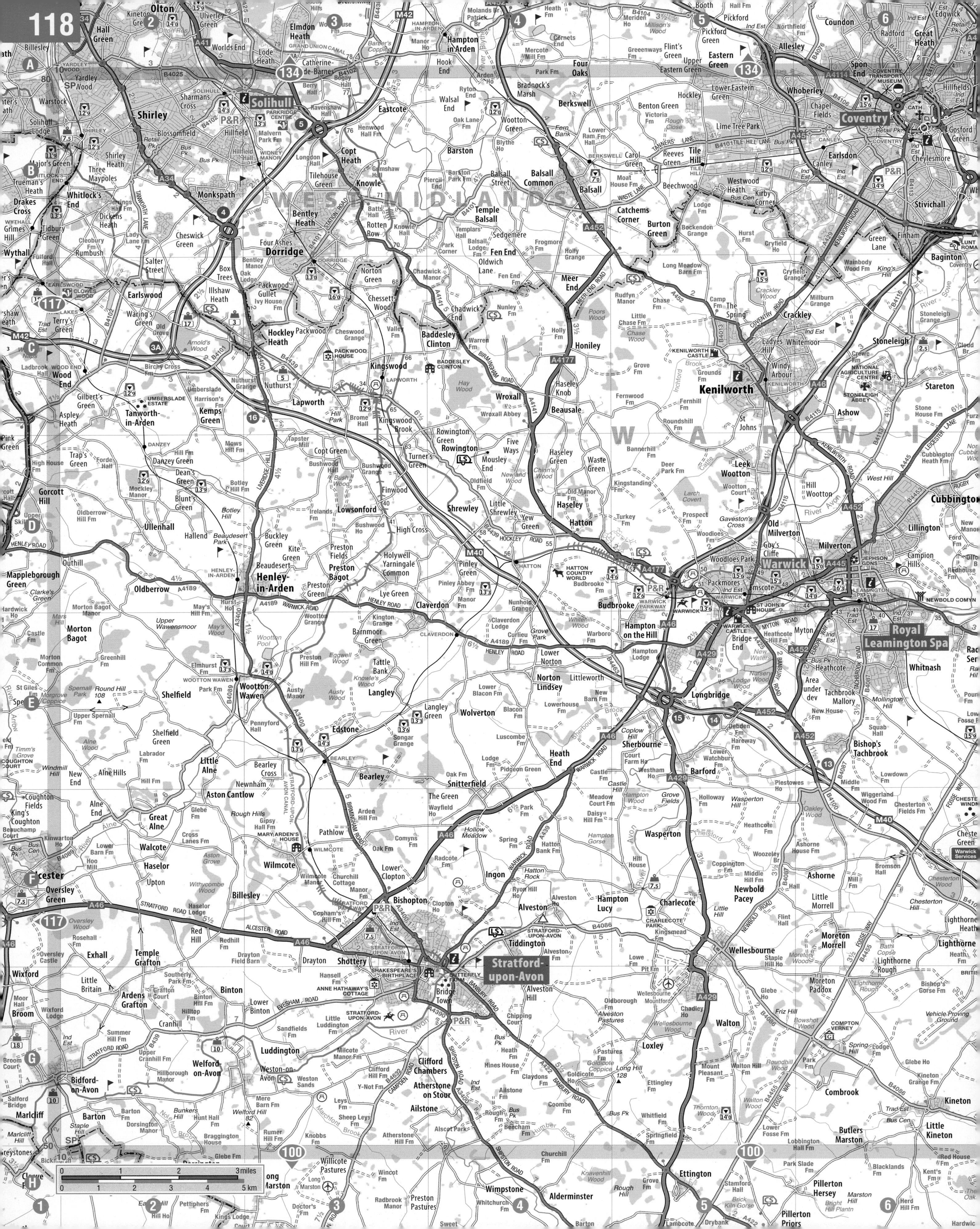

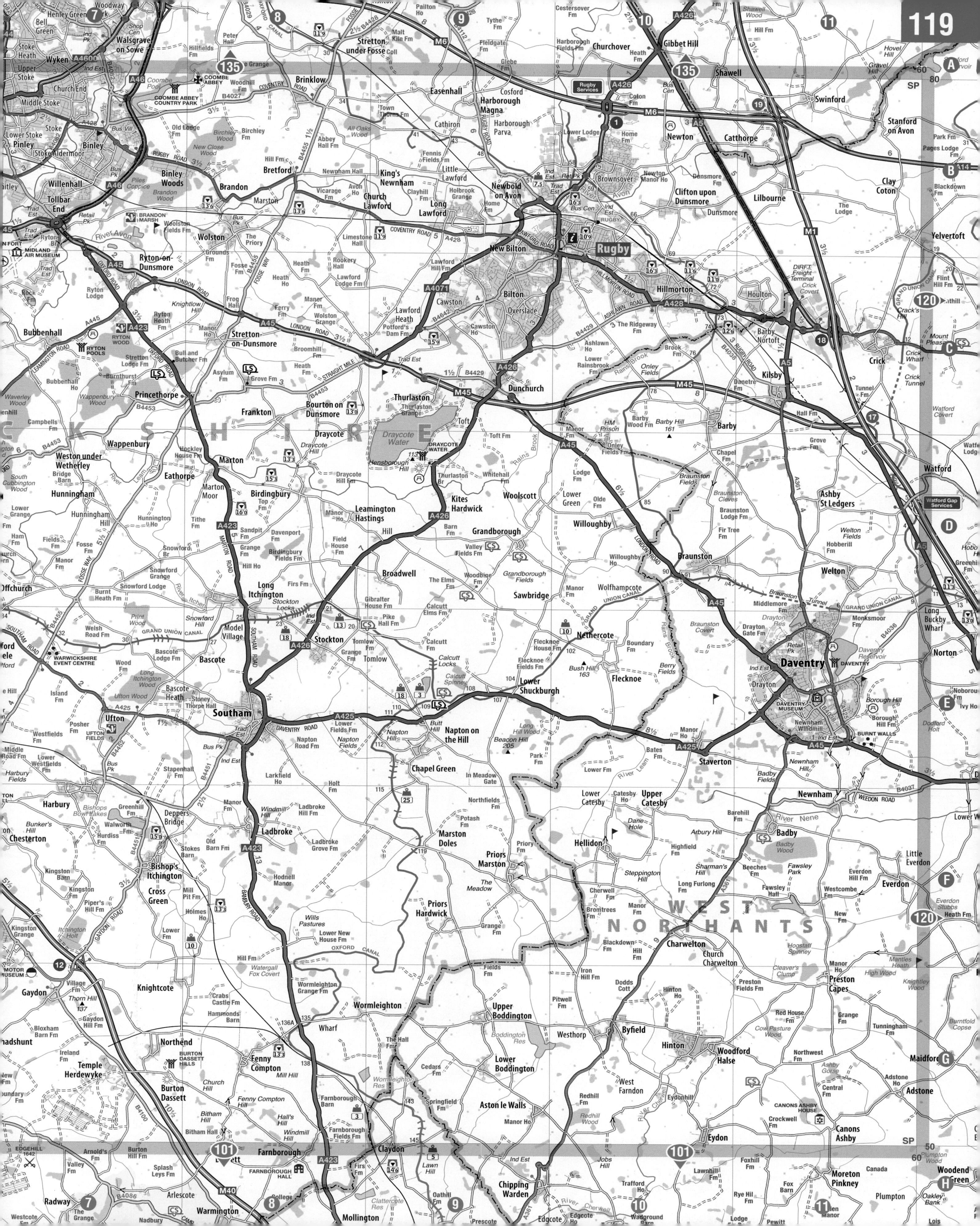
Henley Green
Woodway
Bell Green
Walsgrave on Sowe
Stoke Heath
Wyken
Upper Stoke
Church End
Middle Stoke
Lower Stoke
Stoke
Pinley
Stoke Aldermoor
Binley
Binley Woods
Willenhall
Tollbar End
Midland Air Museum
Coombe Abbey
Coombe Abbey Country Park
Brinklow
Stretton under Fosse
Easenhall
Cosford
Harborough Magna
Harborough Parva
Churchover
Gibbet Hill
Shawell
Swinford
Stanford on Avon
Rugby Services
Newton
Catthorpe
Clay Coton
Lilbourne
Yelvertoft
Clifton upon Dunsmore
Brownsover
Newbold on Avon
Little Lawford
King's Newnham
Church Lawford
Long Lawford
Bretford
Brandon
Marston
Wolston
Ryton-on-Dunsmore
Bubbenhall
Rugby
New Bilton
Bilton
Overslade
Hillmorton
Barby Nortoft
Crick
Kilsby
Dunchurch
Thurlaston
Draycote Water
Draycote
Toft
Frankton
Bourton on Dunsmore
Princethorpe
Stretton-on-Dunsmore
Wappenbury
Weston under Wetherley
Hunningham
Eathorpe
Marton
Birdingbury
Leamington Hastings
Kites Hardwick
Woolscott
Grandborough
Willoughby
Barby
Watford
Watford Gap Services
Ashby St Ledgers
Braunston
Welton
Long Itchington
Broadwell
Sawbridge
Wolfhampcote
Stockton
Nethercote
Flecknoe
Daventry
Drayton
Norton
Long Buckby Wharf
Bascote
Southam
Ufton
Lower Shuckburgh
Napton on the Hill
Chapel Green
Staverton
Newnham
Badby
Upper Catesby
Lower Catesby
Hellidon
Harbury
Ladbroke
Marston Doles
Priors Marston
Priors Hardwick
Bishop's Itchington
Cross Green
Chesterton
Charwelton
Church Charwelton
Everdon
Little Everdon
Preston Capes
Gaydon
Knightcote
Wormleighton
Upper Boddington
Lower Boddington
Westhorp
Byfield
Hinton
Woodford Halse
Northend
Temple Herdewyke
Fenny Compton
Burton Dassett
Aston le Walls
West Farndon
Eydon
Canons Ashby
Adstone
Maidford
Farnborough
Claydon
Chipping Warden
Moreton Pinkney
Woodend Green
Radway
Warmington
Mollington
Edgcote
WEST NORTHANTS
M6
M1
M45
M40
A45
A426
A423
A425
A428
A361
A5
A4071
135
101
120

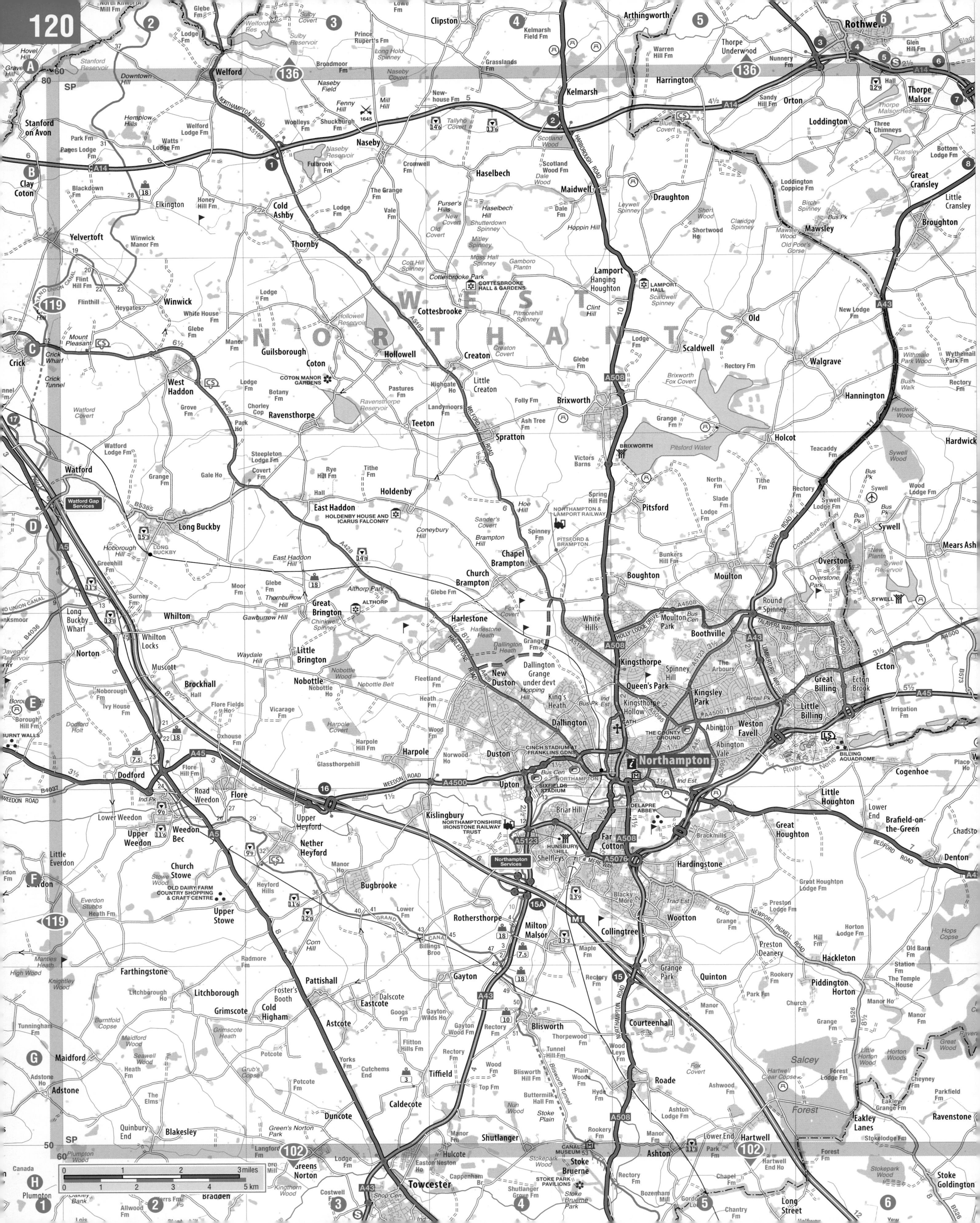
WEST NORTHANTS
Northampton
Welford
Clipston
Arthingworth
Rothwell
Naseby
Kelmarsh
Harrington
Orton
Thorpe Malsor
Loddington
Stanford on Avon
Haselbech
Maidwell
Draughton
Clay Coton
Elkington
Cold Ashby
Yelvertoft
Thornby
Mawsley
Broughton
Great Cransley
Little Cransley
Lamport
Hanging Houghton
Winwick
Cottesbrooke
COTTESBROOKE HALL & GARDENS
LAMPORT HALL
Old
Crick
Guilsborough
Coton
COTON MANOR GARDENS
Hollowell
Creaton
Little Creaton
Scaldwell
Walgrave
West Haddon
Ravensthorpe
Teeton
Brixworth
Hannington
Spratton
Holcot
Pitsford Water
Watford
Watford Gap Services
Holdenby
East Haddon
HOLDENBY HOUSE AND ICARUS FALCONRY
Pitsford
Long Buckby
Chapel Brampton
Church Brampton
NORTHAMPTON & LAMPORT RAILWAY
Sywell
Mears Ashby
Overstone
Boughton
Moulton
Great Brington
ALTHORP
Whilton
Harlestone
Long Buckby Wharf
Whilton Locks
Norton
Little Brington
Moulton Park
Boothville
Round Spinney
Kingsthorpe
Ecton
Muscott
Brockhall
Nobottle
New Duston
Dallington Grange under devt
Queen's Park
Kingsley Park
Great Billing
Little Billing
Weston Favell
Dallington
Abington
THE COUNTY GROUND
Abington Vale
CINCH STADIUM AT FRANKLINS GDNS
SIXFIELDS STADIUM
BILLING AQUADROME
Dodford
Harpole
Duston
Flore
Upton
Cogenhoe
Road Weedon
Kislingbury
Upper Weedon
Weedon Bec
Lower Weedon
Upper Heyford
Nether Heyford
NORTHAMPTONSHIRE IRONSTONE RAILWAY TRUST
Briar Hill
DELAPRE ABBEY
Far Cotton
Great Houghton
Little Houghton
Brafield-on-the-Green
Denton
Northampton Services
Shelfleys
Hunsbury Hill
Hardingstone
Little Everdon
Church Stowe
OLD DAIRY FARM COUNTRY SHOPPING & CRAFT CENTRE
Everdon
Upper Stowe
Bugbrooke
Rothersthorpe
Milton Malsor
Collingtree
Wootton
Preston Deanery
Hackleton
Grange Park
Quinton
Farthingstone
Pattishall
Gayton
Piddington
Horton
Litchborough
Grimscote
Cold Higham
Foster's Booth
Eastcote
Dalscote
Astcote
Blisworth
Courteenhall
Maidford
Tiffield
Roade
Salcey Forest
Adstone
Caldecote
Duncote
Blakesley
Shutlanger
Hartwell
Ravenstone
Eakley Lanes
Ashton
Stoke Bruerne
CANAL MUSEUM
STOKE PARK PAVILIONS
Greens Norton
Towcester
Hulcote
Stoke Goldington
Long Street
Plumpton
Blisworth Tunnel
GRAND UNION CANAL
River Nene
A14
A5199
A508
A43
A428
A4500
A45
A5
A5123
A5076
M1
A4508
B4036
B4037
B5385
B526
136
119
102
SP
0 1 2 3 miles
0 1 2 3 4 5 km

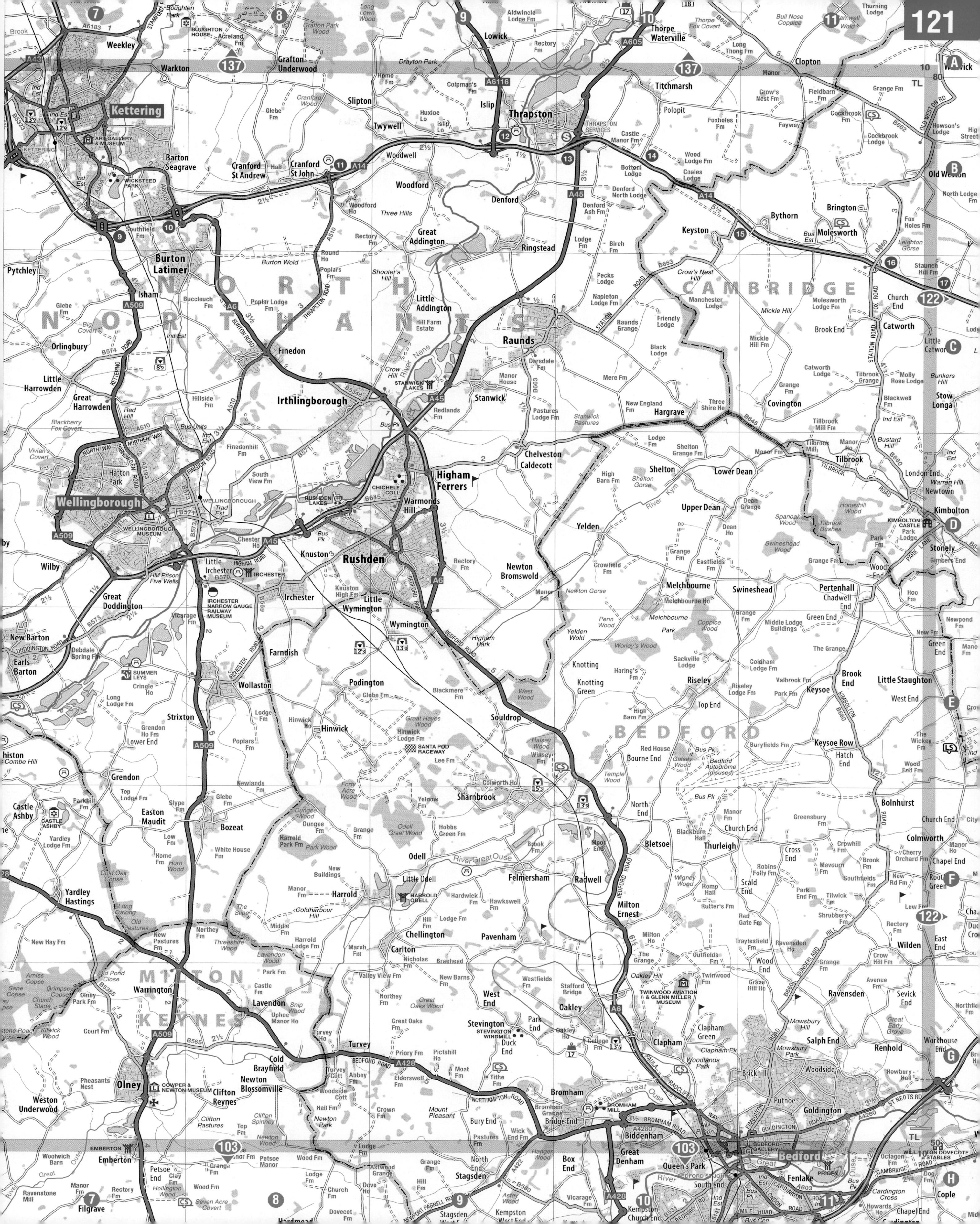
Weekley
Boughton Park
BOUGHTON HOUSE
Acreland Fm
Grafton Park Wood
Long Lown Wood
Lowick
Aldwincle Lodge Fm
Rectory Fm
Thorpe Waterville
Thorpe Fox Covert
Long Thong Fm
Bull Nose Coppice
Thurning Lodge
Clopton
Warkton
Grafton Underwood
Drayton Park
Home Fm
Colpman's Fm
Titchmarsh
Polopit
Crow's Nest Fm
Fieldbarn Fm
Grange Fm
Manor
Kettering
Cranford Wood
Slipton
Glebe Fm
Islip
Huxloe Lo
Islip Lo
Twywell
Thrapston
THRAPSTON SERVICES
Castle Manor Fm
Foxholes Fm
Fayway
Cockbrook Fm
Cockbrook Lodge
Howson's Lodge
ART GALLERY & MUSEUM
Barton Seagrave
Cranford St Andrew
Hall
Cranford St John
Woodwell
Wood Lodge Fm
Coales Lodge
Bottom Lodge
Old Weston
WICKSTEED PARK
Woodford
Denford
Denford North Lodge
Denford Ash Fm
North Lodge Fm
Woodford Ho
Three Hills
Brington
Bythorn
Keyston
Molesworth
Fox Holes Fm
Southfield Fm
Rectory Fm
Great Addington
Ringstead
Lodge Fm
Birch Fm
Leighton Gorse
Pytchley
Burton Latimer
Burton Wold
Round Ho
Poplars Fm
Shooter's Hill
Pecks Lodge
Crow's Nest Hill
Staunch Hill Fm
Isham
NORTHANTS
CAMBRIDGE
Glebe Fm
Buccleuch Fm
Poplar Lodge Fm
Little Addington
Napleton Lodge Fm
Manchester Lodge
Molesworth Lodge Fm
Mickle Hill
Church End
Big Covert
Hill Farm Estate
Raunds Grange
Friendly Lodge
Brook End
Catworth
Orlingbury
Finedon
Raunds
Black Lodge
Mickle Hill Fm
Little Catworth
Darsdale Fm
Little Harrowden
Crow Hill
River Nene
STANWICK LAKES
Manor House
Mere Fm
Catworth Lodge
Grange Fm
Tilbrook Grange
Molly Rose Lodge
Bunkers Hill
Great Harrowden
Hillside Fm
Irthlingborough
Stanwick
Redlands Fm
Pastures Lodge Fm
Stanwick Pastures
New England Fm
Hargrave
Three Shire Ho
Covington
Blackwell Fm
Stow Longa
Red Hill
Blackberry Fox Covert
Bus Units
Bus Pk
Ind Est
Tilbrook Mill Fm
Vivian's Covert
Hatton Park
Finedonhill Fm
Chelveston Caldecott
Lodge Fm
Shelton Grange Fm
Manor Fm
Tilbrook Mill
Bustard Hill
Tilbrook
Manor Ho
Wellingborough
WELLINGBOROUGH MUSEUM
South View Fm
Higham Ferrers
CHICHELE COLL
High Barn Fm
Shelton
Shelton Gorse
River Kym
Lower Dean
London End
Warren Hill
Newtown
RUSHDEN LAKES
Warmonds Hill
Dean Grange
Upper Dean
Honeyhill Wood
Kimbolton
KIMBOLTON CASTLE
Park Lodge
Spanoak Wood
Tilbrook Bushes
Wilby
Chester Ho
Knuston
Rushden
Yelden
Dean Ho
Swineshead Wood
Park Fm
Stonely
Gimbers End
HM Prison Five Wells
Little Irchester
IRCHESTER
Rectory Fm
Newton Bromswold
Crowfield Fm
Grange Fm
Eastfields Fm
Grange Fm
Wood End
Great Doddington
IRCHESTER NARROW GAUGE RAILWAY MUSEUM
Irchester
Knuston High Fm
Little Wymington
Manor Fm
Newton Gorse
Melchbourne
Melchbourne Ho
Swineshead
Pertenhall
Chadwell End
Hoo Fm
Vicarage Fm
Wymington
Melchbourne Park
Penn Wood
Grange Fm
Coppice Wood
Middle Lodge Buildings
Green End
Newpond Fm
New Barton
Earls Barton
Debdale Spring Fm
Farndish
Higham Park
Yelden Wold
Worley's Wood
The Grange
New Fm
Green End
SUMMER LEYS
Cringle Ho
Wollaston
Podington
Glebe Fm
Knotting
Knotting Green
Haring's Fm
Sackville Lodge
Coldham Lodge Fm
Riseley
Riseley Lodge Fm
Valbrook Fm
Brook End
Little Staughton
West End
Long Lodge Fm
Strixton
Grendon Ho Fm
Lower End
Lodge Fm
Hinwick Ho
Hinwick
Great Hayes Wood
Hinwick Lodge Fm
SANTA POD RACEWAY
Blackmere Fm
West Wood
Souldrop
High Barn Fm
Top End
Park Fm
Keysoe
BEDFORD
Poplars Fm
Lee Fm
Halsey Wood
Winsey Fm
Red House
Bourne End
Galsey Wood
Bus Pk
Bedford Autodrome (disused)
Temple Wood
Buryfields Fm
Keysoe Row
Hatch End
The Wickey Fm
Wood End Fm
Combe Hill
Grendon
Newlands Fm
Forty Acre Wood
Colworth Ho
Sharnbrook
North End
Bolnhurst
Castle Ashby
CASTLE ASHBY
Parkhill Fm
Top Lodge Fm
Easton Maudit
Glebe Fm
Slype Fm
Bozeat
Dungee Wood
Dungee Fm
Yelnow Fm
Grange Fm
Odell Great Wood
Hobbs Green Fm
Manor Ho
Church End
Blackburn Hall
Thurleigh
Greensbury Fm
Church End
Colmworth
Yardley Lodge Fm
Low Fm
Home Fm
Horn Wood
White House Fm
Harrold Park Fm
Park Wood
Odell
Brook Fm
Moor End
Bletsoe
Cross End
Crowhill Fm
Cherry Orchard Fm
Chapel End
Cold Oak Copse
River Great Ouse
Felmersham
Radwell
Robins Folly Fm
Mavourn Fm
Brook Fm
Southfields Fm
Rootham's Green
New Buildings
Little Odell
Wigney Wood
Romp Hall
Scald End
Yardley Hastings
Manor Fm
Harrold
HARROLD ODELL
Hardwick Fm
Hawkswell Fm
Milton Ernest
Park End Fm
Tilwick Fm
New Rd Fm
Low Fm
Coldharbour Hill
Rutter's Fm
Long Furlong
Old Pastures
The Slipe
Hill Fm
Lodge Fm
Shrubbery Fm
Middle Fm
Chellington
Pavenham
Red Gate Fm
Rectory Fm
New Hay Fm
New Pastures Fm
Northey Fm
Threeshire Wood
Harrold Lodge Fm
Marsh Fm
Carlton
Milton Ho
Traylesfield Fm
Ravensden Ho
Wilden
East End
Nicholas Fm
Brayhead
The Grange
Outfields Fm
Wood End
Grange Fm
Crow Hill Fm
Lavendon Wood
Amiss Copse
Old Pond Close
MILTON KEYNES
Park Fm
Castle Fm
Valley View Fm
New Barns Fm
Westfields Fm
Stafford Bridge
Oakley Hill
Twinwood Fm
Graze Hill Ho
Avenue Fm
Sane Copse
Grimpsey Copse
Church Slade
Olney Park Fm
Warrington
Lavendon
Northey Fm
Great Oaks Wood
West End
TWINWOOD AVIATION & GLENN MILLER MUSEUM
Ravensden
Sevick End
Kilwick Wood
Court Fm
Snip Wood
Uphoe Manor Ho
Great Oaks Fm
Stevington
STEVINGTON WINDMILL
Park End
Oakley
Oakley Ho
Duck End
Clapham
Clapham Green
Clapham Pk
Mowsbury Hill
Salph End
Renhold
Great Early Grove
Workhouse End
Stone Road Copse
Turvey Ho
Turvey
Priory Fm
Pictshill Ho
College Fm
Woodlands Park
Mowsbury Park
Brickhill
Woodside
Howbury Hall
Pheasants Nest
Cold Brayfield
Newton Blossomville
Turvey Cott
Abbey Fm
Elderswell Fm
Moat Fm
Tithe Fm
Bromham
Putnoe
Goldington
Olney
COWPER & NEWTON MUSEUM
Clifton Reynes
Woodside Cott
River Great Ouse
BROMHAM MILL
Bromham Grange
Bridge End
Weston Underwood
Clifton Pastures
Clifton Spinney
Top Fm
Hall Fm
Newton Park
Crown Fm
Mount Pleasant
Bury End
Pastures Fm
Wick End Fm
Biddenham
HM Prison
Bedford
BEDFORD GALLERY
Newton Wood
EMBERTON
Emberton
Petsoe Manor Fm
Petsoe Manor
Wood Fm
Lodge Fm
North End
Hanger Wood
Box End
Great Denham
Queen's Park
South End
Fenlake
PRIORY
Octagon Fm
DOVECOTE & STABLES
Cardington Cross
Cople
Woolwich Barn
Petsoe End
Clay Fm
Grange Fm
Astwood Grange
Grange Fm
Stagsden
Ravenstone Mill
Manor Fm
Rectory Fm
Hollington Wood
Wood Fm
Seven Acre Covert
Church Fm
Dove Ho
Hill Fm
Astey Wood
Vicarage Fm
Kempston Church End
Filgrave
Hardmead
Dovecot Fm
Stagsden West End
Kempston West End
Howards Fm
Chapel End

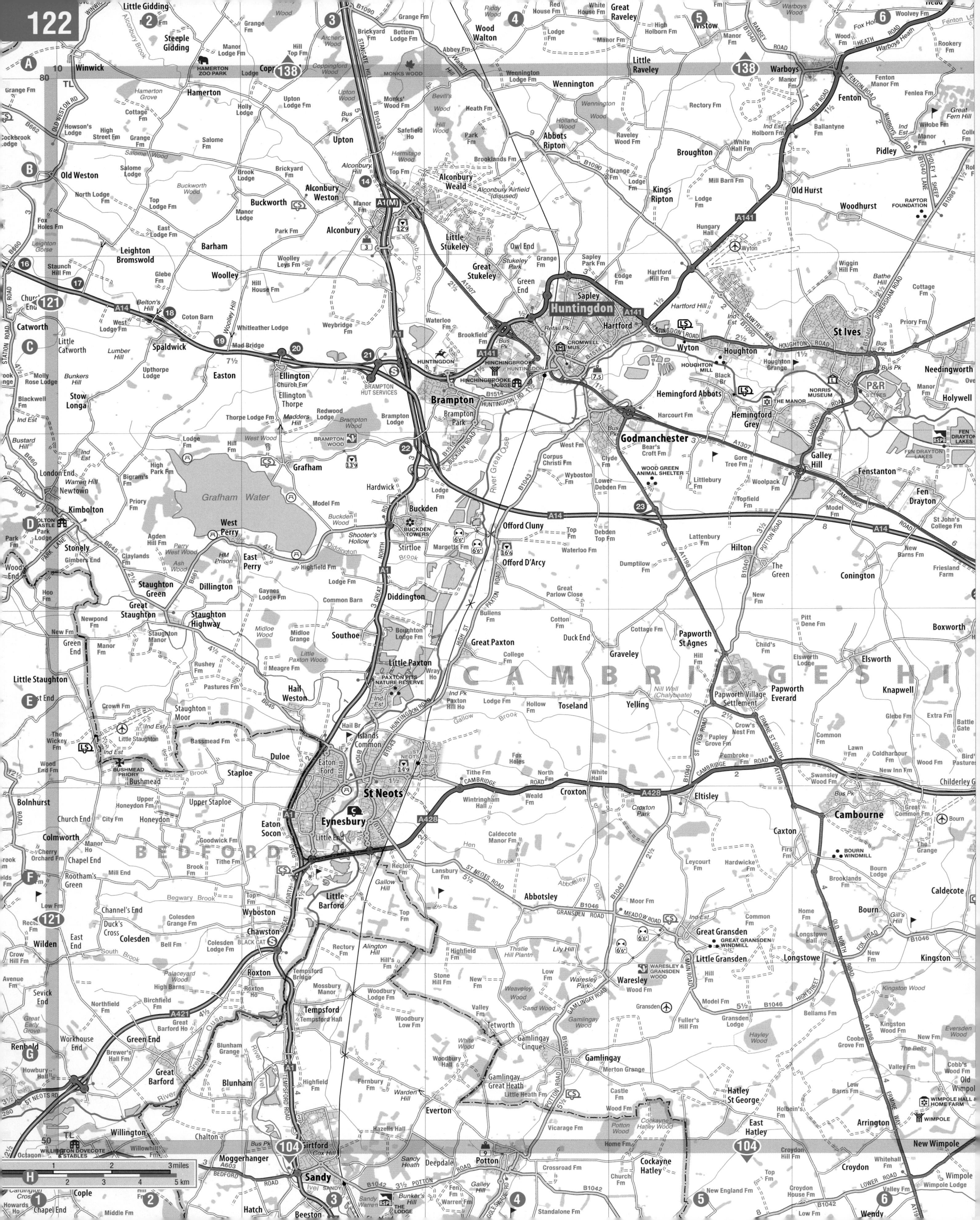
138
121
104
CAMBRIDGESHIRE
BEDFORD
Little Gidding
Steeple Gidding
Hamerton Zoo Park
Winwick
Hamerton
Wood Walton
Monks Wood
Great Raveley
Little Raveley
Wistow
Warboys
Fenton
Wennington
Upton
Old Weston
Alconbury Weston
Alconbury
Alconbury Weald
Alconbury Airfield (disused)
Buckworth
Barham
Abbots Ripton
Kings Ripton
Broughton
Old Hurst
Woodhurst
Pidley
Raptor Foundation
Leighton Bromswold
Woolley
Little Stukeley
Great Stukeley
Owl End
Stukeley Park
Sapley
Huntingdon
Hartford
Wyton
Houghton
St Ives
Hemingford Abbots
Hemingford Grey
Houghton Mill
Norris Museum
The Manor
Godmanchester
Wood Green Animal Shelter
Catworth
Little Catworth
Spaldwick
Easton
Ellington
Ellington Thorpe
Brampton
Brampton Park
Brampton Hut Services
Hinchingbrooke House
Cromwell Mus
Grafham
Grafham Water
Stow Longa
Kimbolton
Kimbolton Castle
Stonely
West Perry
East Perry
Perry West Wood
HM Prison
Buckden
Buckden Towers
Offord Cluny
Offord D'Arcy
Hardwick
Stirtloe
Diddington
Southoe
Dillington
Staughton Green
Great Staughton
Staughton Highway
Little Paxton
Great Paxton
Paxton Pits Nature Reserve
Graveley
Papworth St Agnes
Papworth Everard
Papworth Village Settlement
Toseland
Yelling
Hilton
Fenstanton
Fen Drayton
Fen Drayton Lakes
Conington
Elsworth
Knapwell
Boxworth
Needingworth
Holywell
Galley Hill
Little Staughton
Hail Weston
Bushmead
Bushmead Priory
Duloe
Staploe
Eaton Ford
Eaton Socon
St Neots
Eynesbury
Little End
Croxton
Eltisley
Cambourne
Caxton
Bourn
Bourn Windmill
Caldecote
Kingston
Longstowe
Little Gransden
Great Gransden
Great Gransden Windmill
Abbotsley
Waresley
Gamlingay
Gamlingay Cinques
Hatley St George
East Hatley
Arrington
Wimpole
Croydon
Cockayne Hatley
Potton
Everton
Tetworth
Sandy
Girtford
Beeston
Moggerhanger
Willington
Willington Dovecote & Stables
Blunham
Great Barford
Roxton
Tempsford
Chawston
Wyboston
Colesden
Wilden
Colmworth
Bolnhurst
Little Barford
Green End
Renhold
Chalton
Upper Staploe
Honeydon
Church End
Chapel End
Rootham's Green
Channel's End
Duck's Cross
Hatch
Cople
Howards
New Wimpole
Deepdale
A1(M)
A1
A14
A141
A1307
A1198
A428
A421
A603
B1040
B1043
B1046
B1042
B645
B660
B661
miles
km

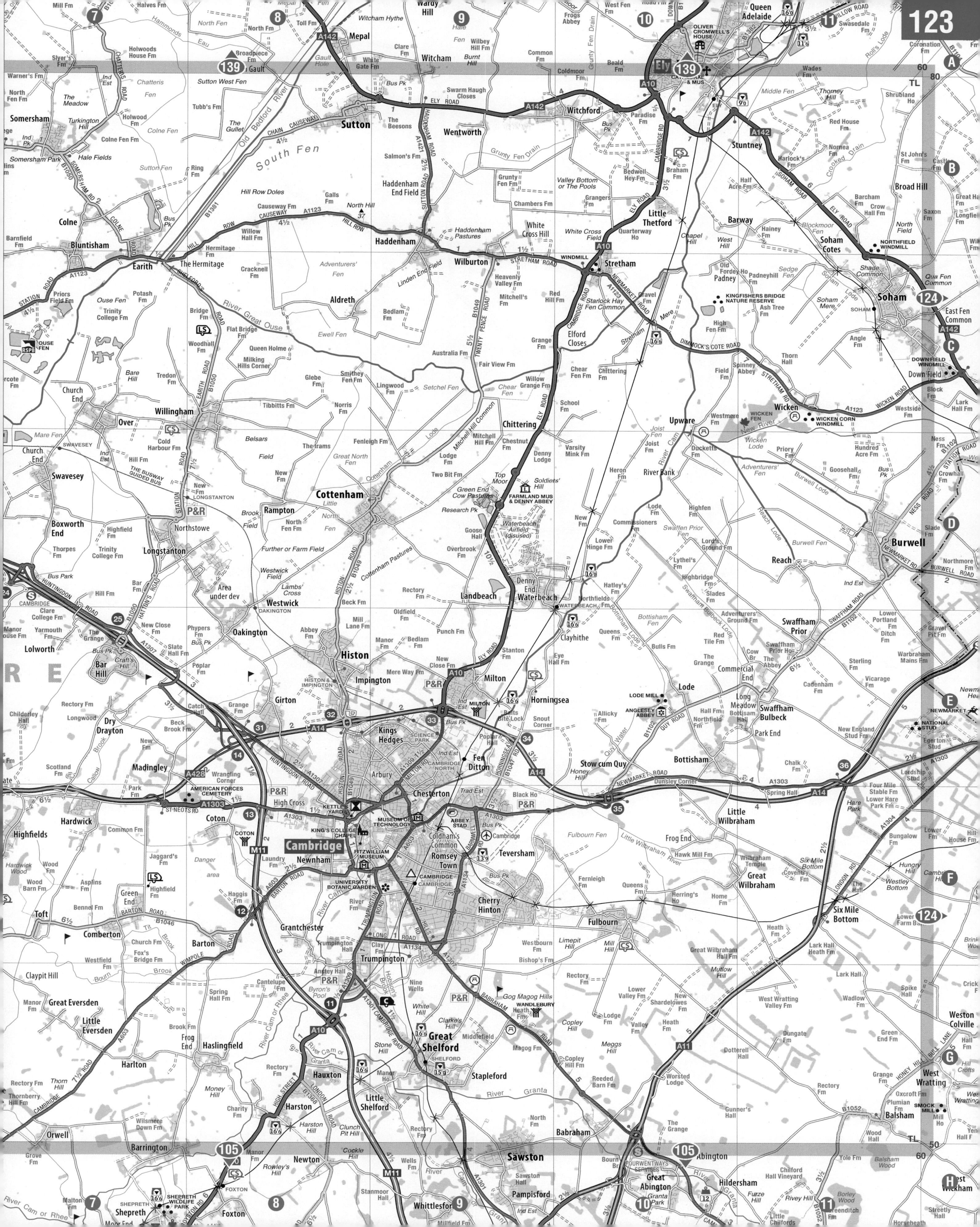
Mill Fm
Halves Fm
North Fen
North Fm
Toll Fm
Witcham Hythe
Wardy Hill
Mepal
Queen Adelaide
Swasedale Fm
Coronation Fm
Holwoods House Fm
Broadpiece Fm
Gault
Clare Fm
White Gate Fm
Witcham
Wilbey Hill Fm
Burnt Hill
Common Fm
Beald Fm
Ely
OLIVER CROMWELL'S HOUSE
CATHEDRAL & MUS
Wades Fm
Slyer's Fm
Warner's Fm
Ind Est
Chatteris Fen
Sutton West Fen
Coldmoor Fm
North Fen Fm
The Meadow
Bus Pk
Swarm Haugh Closes
ELY ROAD
Middle Fen
Thorney Hill
Shrubland Ho
Tubb's Fm
Holwood Fm
The Gullet
Sutton
The Beesons
Witchford
Paradise Fm
Red House Fm
Somersham
Turkington Hill
CHAIN CAUSEWAY
Colne Fen
Old Bedford River
Wentworth
Stuntney
Colne Fen Fm
Somersham Park
Hale Fields
South Fen
Salmon's Fm
Grunty Fen Drain
Braham Fm
Nornea Fm
Crooked Drain
St John's Fm
Castle Fm
Sutton Fen
Ring Fm
Bedwell Hey Fm
Harlock's Fm
Hill Row Doles
Haddenham End Field
Grunty Fen Fm
Valley Bottom or The Pools
Half Acre Fm
Broad Hill
Galls Fm
North Hill
Causeway Fm
Chambers Fm
Grangers Fm
Little Thetford
Barcham Fm
Crow Hall Fm
Great Hall
Colne
Willow Hall Fm
Haddenham Pastures
White Cross Hill
White Cross Field
Quarterway Ho
Barway
Hainey Fm
Blackmoor Fen
North Field
Saxon Fm
Longfield Fm
Barnfield Fm
Bluntisham
Hermitage Fm
Haddenham
Soham Cotes
NORTHFIELD WINDMILL
Earith
The Hermitage
Wilburton
STRETHAM ROAD
WINDMILL
Stretham
Chapel Hill
West Hill
Cracknell Fm
Adventurers' Fen
Linden End Field
Heavenly Valley Fm
Old Fordey Ho
Padney
Padneyhill Fm
Sedge Fen
Shade Common
Qua Fen Common
Priors Field Fm
Potash Fm
Ouse Fen
Trinity College Fm
Aldreth
Mitchell's Fm
Red Hill Fm
Starlock Hay Fen Common
Gravel Fm
KINGFISHERS BRIDGE NATURE RESERVE
Soham
Bridge Fm
Flat Bridge Fm
River Great Ouse
Bedlam Fm
Ewell Fen
Elford Closes
Ash Tree Fm
Soham Mere
East Fen Common
OUSE FEN
Woodhall Fm
Queen Holme
Grange Fm
High Fen Fm
DIMMOCK'S COTE ROAD
Angle Fm
Milking Hills Corner
Australia Fm
Thorn Hall
DOWNFIELD WINDMILL
Down Field
Bare Hill
Tredon Fm
Glebe Fm
Smithey Fen Fm
Fair View Fm
Chear Fen Fm
Chittering Fm
Field Fm
Spinney Abbey
Lingwood Fm
Setchel Fen
Chear Fen
Willow Grange Fm
Block Fm
Church End
Willingham
Tibbitts Fm
Norris Fm
School Fm
Wicken
WICKEN FEN
WICKEN CORN WINDMILL
Westside Fm
Lark Hall Fm
Over
Mare Fen
Belsars Field
The Irams
Fenleigh Fm
Mitchell Hill Fm
Chittering
Upware
Westmere Fm
New River
Swavesey
Cold Harbour Fm
Great North Fen
Chestnut Fm
Denny Lodge
Varsity Mink Fm
Joist Fen
Wicken Lode
Priory Fm
Hundred Acre Fm
Ness Fm
Church End
Hill Fm
Ind Est
THE BUSWAY GUIDED BUS
New Fm
Lodge Fm
Two Bit Fm
Top Moor
Soldiers' Hill
Heron Fm
River Bank
Ducketts Fm
Adventurers' Fen
Goosehall Fm
Bus Pk
Crowhall Fm
New Fm
LONGSTANTON
Cottenham
FARMLAND MUS & DENNY ABBEY
Green End Cow Pastures
Research Pk
Highfen Fm
Rampton
North Fen Fm
Boxworth End
Highfield Fm
Northstowe
Lode Fm
Commissioners Fm
Swaffen Prior Fen
Burwell
Slade Fm
Waterbeach Airfield (disused)
Goose Hall
Thorpes Fm
Trinity College Fm
Longstanton
Further or Farm Field
Overbrook Fm
Lower Hinge Fm
Lord's Ground Fm
Burwell Fen
Reach
Northmore Fm
BURWELL ROAD
Bus Park
Westwick Field
Lambs' Cross
Cottenham Pastures
Lythel's Fm
Highbridge Fm
Hill Fm
Bar Fm
Area under dev
Westwick
DAKINGTON
Rectory Fm
Landbeach
Denny End
Waterbeach
Hatley's Fm
Northfields Fm
Slades Fm
Ind Est
CAMBRIDGE
Clare College Fm
Beck Fm
Oldfield Fm
Adventurers' Ground Fm
Swaffham Prior
Lower Portland Fm
Manor House Fm
Yarmouth Fm
The Grange
New Close Fm
Phypers Fm
Oakington
Mill Lane Fm
Punch Fm
Bottisham Fen
Queens Fm
Ditch Fm
Gravel Pit Fm
Lolworth
Bus Pk
Slate Hall Fm
Abbey Fm
Manor Fm
Bedlam Fm
Clayhithe
Red Tile Fm
Bulls Fm
Bar Hill
Poplar Fm
Histon
New Close Fm
Stanton Fm
Eye Hall Fm
Cow Br
The Grange
Swaffham Prior Ho
The Abbey
Warbraham Mains Fm
Impington
Mere Way Fm
Milton
Commercial End
Sterling Fm
Vicarage Fm
HISTON & IMPINGTON
Horningsea
Lode
Cadenham Fm
Rectory Fm
Catch Hall
Girton
Ind Est
MILTON
LODE MILL
Long Meadow
Childerley Hall
Longwood
Grange Fm
Baits Bite Lock
Snout Corner
Allicky Fm
ANGLESEY ABBEY
Hall Fm
Bottisham Hall
Swaffham Bulbeck
NEWMARKET
Dry Drayton
Beck Brook Fm
Kings Hedges
SCIENCE PARK
Northfield Fm
Park End
New England Stud Fm
NATIONAL STUD
Egerton Stud
New Fm
Ind Est
CAMBRIDGE NORTH
Poplar Hall
Fen Ditton
Scotland Fm
Madingley
Wrangling Corner
Arbury
Stow cum Quy
Honey Hill
Bottisham
Chalk Fm
Lordship Stud
AMERICAN FORCES CEMETERY
Park Fm
Chesterton
Trad Est
NEWMARKET ROAD
Dunsley Corner
Spring Hall
Four Mile Stable Fm
Lower Hare Park Fm
Hare Park
ST NEOTS RD
High Cross
KETTLE'S YARD
Black Ho
Hardwick
Coton
MUSEUM OF TECHNOLOGY
ABBEY STAD
Little Wilbraham
Highfields
Common Fm
KING'S COLLEGE CHAPEL
Coldham's Common
Cambridge
Fulbourn Fen
Frog End
Bungalow Fm
Lower Fm
House Fm
Cambridge
FITZWILLIAM MUSEUM
Romsey Town
Teversham
Little Wilbraham River
Hawk Mill Fm
Jaggard's Fm
Danger area
Laundry Fm
Newnham
Wilbraham Temple
Six Mile Bottom
Hungry Hill
Hardwick Wood
Wood Fm
UNIVERSITY BOTANIC GARDEN
CAMBRIDGE
Fernleigh Fm
Queens Fm
Great Wilbraham
Coventry Fm
Westley Bottom
Wood Barn Fm
Asplins Fm
Highfield Fm
Green End
Haggis Fm
River Fm
Cherry Hinton
Herring's Fm
Home Fm
The Hall
Bennel Fm
BARTON ROAD
Grantchester
Fulbourn
Heath Fm
Six Mile Bottom
Lower Farm Barn
Toft
Comberton
Church Fm
Barton
LONG ROAD
Westbourn Fm
Limepit Hill
Mill Hill
Great Wilbraham Hall Fm
Lark Hall Heath Fm
Fox's Bridge Fm
Trumpington Hall
Clay Fm
Westfield Fm
Trumpington
Bishop's Fm
Mutlow Hill
Claypit Hill
WIMPOLE ROAD
Anstey Hall
Lark Hall
Spike Hall
Cantelupe Fm
Rectory Fm
Spring Hall Fm
Byron's Pool
Nine Wells
Gog Magog Hills
WANDLEBURY
Lower Valley Fm
New Shardelowes Fm
West Wratting Valley Fm
Wadlow Fm
Manor Fm
Great Eversden
White Hill
BABRAHAM ROAD
Little Eversden
Brook Fm
Clarke's Hill
Great Shelford
Middlefield
Lodge Fm
Copley Hill
Valley Fm
Heath Fm
Weston Colville
Field End
Haslingfield
River Cam or Rhee
Stone Hill
Magog Fm
Meggs Hill
Dungate Fm
Green End Fm
Harlton
Dotterell Hall
Hall Fm
Rectory Fm
Thorn Hill
Hauxton
SHELFORD
Manor Ho
Copley Hill Fm
Stapleford
Grange Fm
West Wratting
Hill Crofts
Rectory Fm
Thornberry Hill Fm
Money Hill
HIGH STREET
Little Shelford
River Granta
Reeded Barn Fm
Worsted Lodge
Rectory Fm
Oxcroft Fm
Plumian Fm
SMOCK MILL
Wilsmere Down Fm
Charity Fm
Harston
Harston Hill
Clunch Pit Hill
North Fm
Babraham
Gunner's Hall
The Grange
Balsham
Wood Hall
Mill Ho
Orwell
Barrington
Rectory Fm
Hill Fm
Grove Fm
Manor Fm
Newton
Cockle Hill
Wells Fm
Sawston
Bourn Br
FOURWENTWAYS SERVICES
Abington
Yole Fm
Balsham Wood
West Wickham
Rowley's Hill
River Cam
Sawston Hall
Great Abington
Granta Park
Hildersham
Chilford Hall Vineyard
Furze Hill
Rivey Hill
Malton Fm
Shepreth
SHEPRETH WILDLIFE PARK
FOXTON
Stanmoor Hall
Pampisford
Ind Est
Borley Wood
Whittlesford
Little Chilford
Streetly Hall
Moor End
Foxton
Millfield Fm
Horseheath
Cambridge
A10
A14
A11
M11
A142
A1123
A1303
A1307
A1309
A1134
A1301
A603
A428
B1049
B1050
B1047
B1102
B1052
139
105
124

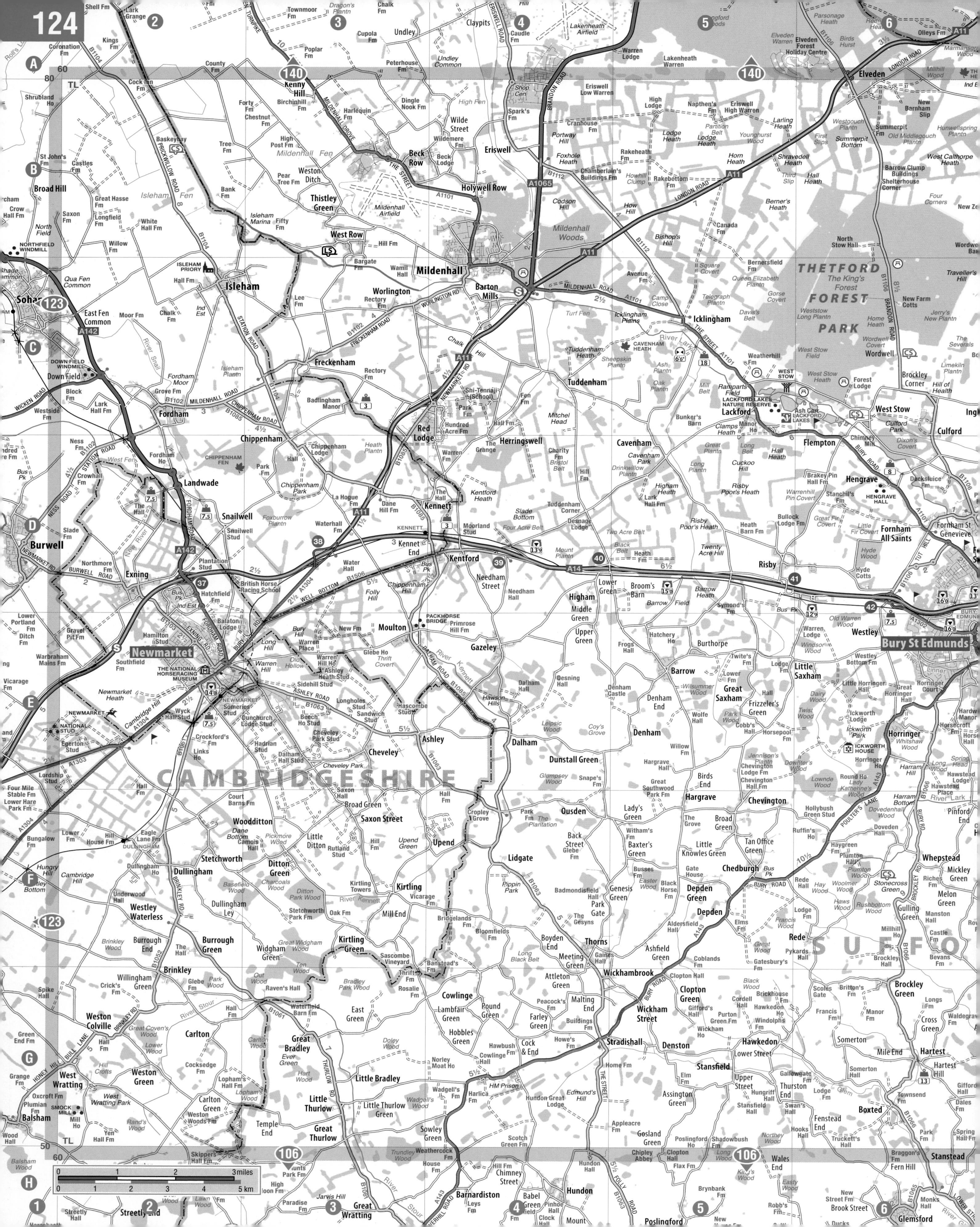

CAMBRIDGESHIRE
SUFFO
THETFORD
The King's Forest
FOREST
PARK
Mildenhall
Barton Mills
Worlington
Isleham
Soham
Freckenham
Fordham
Chippenham
Landwade
Snailwell
Burwell
Exning
Newmarket
Kennett
Kentford
Red Lodge
Herringswell
Tuddenham
Cavenham
Icklingham
Lackford
Flempton
Hengrave
Culford
West Stow
Elveden
Eriswell
Beck Row
Holywell Row
Thistley Green
West Row
Moulton
Gazeley
Higham
Barrow
Risby
Westley
Bury St Edmunds
Little Saxham
Great Saxham
Denham
Dalham
Ashley
Cheveley
Dunstall Green
Ousden
Hargrave
Chevington
Horringer
Saxon Street
Woodditton
Stetchworth
Dullingham
Ditton Green
Kirtling
Upend
Lidgate
Depden
Chedburgh
Rede
Whepstead
Kirtling Green
Burrough Green
Westley Waterless
Brinkley
Weston Colville
Carlton
Great Bradley
Little Bradley
Little Thurlow
Great Thurlow
Cowlinge
Wickhambrook
Wickham Street
Stradishall
Denston
Hawkedon
Stansfield
Clopton Green
Boxted
Hartest
Brockley Green
Stanstead
Glemsford
Hundon
Barnardiston
Great Wratting
Poslingford
Wales End
Chimney Street
Balsham
West Wratting
Weston Green
Skippers Hall Fm
Fornham All Saints
A11
A14
A142
A1065
A1101
A1304
A143
B1106
B1063
B1085
B1061
B1052
B1102
B1104
140
106
123
0 1 2 3 miles
0 1 2 3 4 5 km

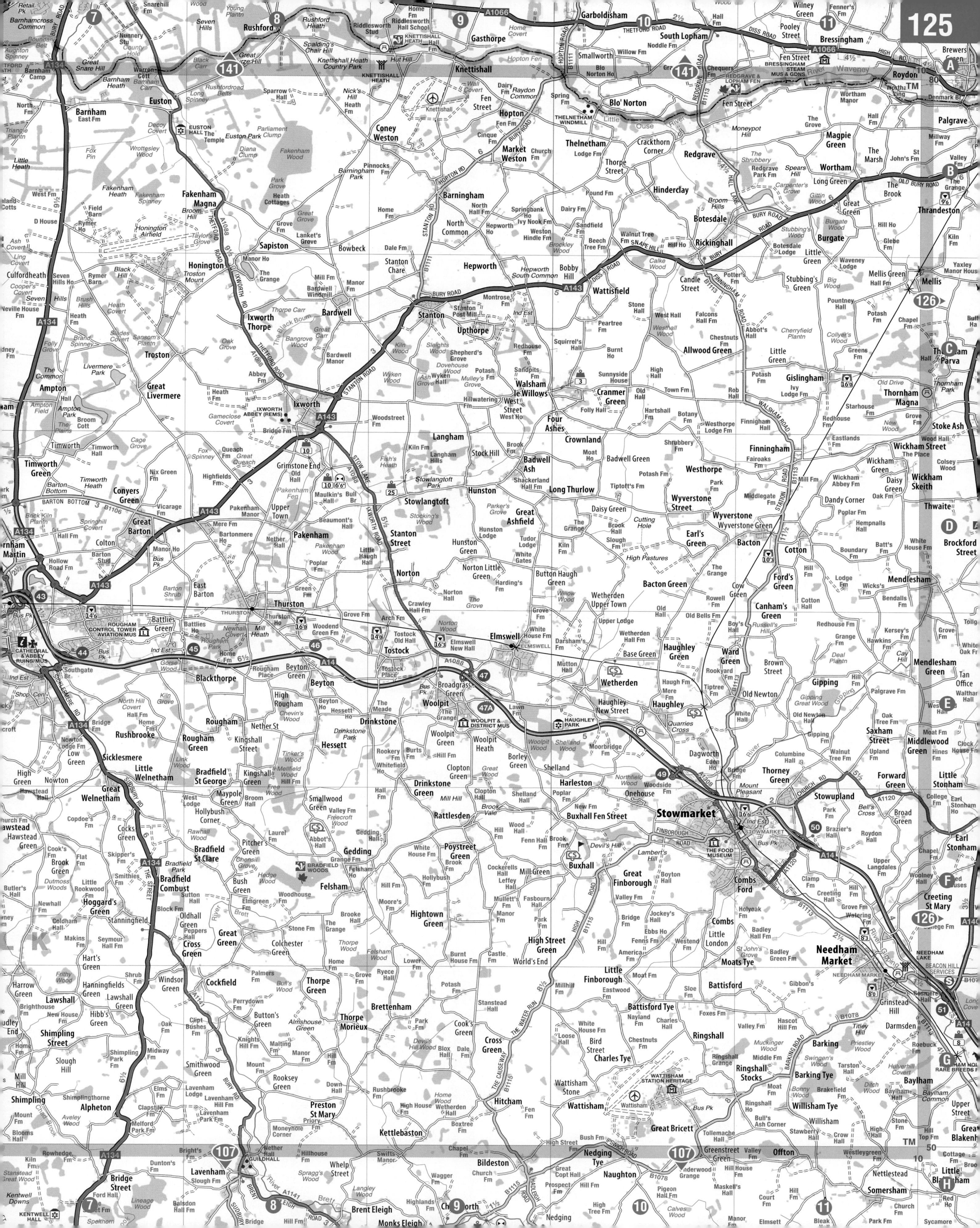

Rushford
Garboldisham
South Lopham
Bressingham
Roydon
Gasthorpe
Knettishall
Knettishall Heath Country Park
Euston
Barnham
Coney Weston
Hopton
Market Weston
Blo' Norton
Thelnetham
Redgrave
Palgrave
Wortham
Thorpe Street
Hinderclay
Botesdale
Rickinghall
Burgate
Mellis
Thrandeston
Fakenham Magna
Barningham
Sapiston
Honington
Hepworth
Wattisfield
Bardwell
Stanton
Upthorpe
Ixworth Thorpe
Troston
Allwood Green
Gislingham
Thornham Magna
Thornham Parva
Ampton
Great Livermere
Ixworth
Walsham le Willows
Cranmer Green
Four Ashes
Crownland
Langham
Badwell Ash
Finningham
Westhorpe
Wickham Skeith
Timworth Green
Conyers Green
Stowlangtoft
Hunston
Long Thurlow
Wyverstone Street
Great Barton
Pakenham
Great Ashfield
Bacton
Cotton
Brockford Street
Norton
Thurston
Elmswell
Bacton Green
Mendlesham
Tostock
Beyton
Woolpit
Haughley
Wetherden
Mendlesham Green
Rougham
Rougham Green
Drinkstone
Hessett
Gipping
Saxham Street
Sicklesmere
Little Welnetham
Great Welnetham
Bradfield St George
Drinkstone Green
Rattlesden
Harleston
Buxhall Fen Street
Stowmarket
Stowupland
Forward Green
Earl Stonham
Bradfield St Clare
Bradfield Combust
Gedding
Felsham
Buxhall
Great Finborough
Combs Ford
Creeting St Mary
Hoggard's Green
Cross Green
Hightown Green
High Street Green
Combs
Little London
Needham Market
Cockfield
Thorpe Green
Brettenham
Little Finborough
Battisford
Battisford Tye
Ringshall
Thorpe Morieux
Cross Green
Charles Tye
Ringshall Stocks
Barking
Barking Tye
Baylham
Lawshall
Shimpling Street
Alpheton
Shimpling
Preston St Mary
Kettlebaston
Hitcham
Wattisham
Great Bricett
Willisham Tye
Bridge Street
Lavenham
Bildeston
Nedging Tye
Naughton
Offton
Somersham
Little Blakenham
Brent Eleigh
Chelsworth
Monks Eleigh
Nedging
Stowmarket
Bury St Edmunds

Diss
Roydon
Walcot Green
Thelveton
Brewers Green
Frenze
Scole Common
Upper Street
Thorpe Abbotts
Brockdish
Needham
Weybread
Upper Weybread
Mendham Marshes
Withersdale Street
Metfield
St James South Elmham
Palgrave
Scole
Billingford
Billingford Windmill
Stuston Common
Oakley
Syleham
Fressingfield
Stuston
Great Green
Hoxne
Wingfield Green
Wingfield Castle
Wingfield Old College
Wingfield
Linstead Parva
Chediston
Thrandeston
Brome Street
Brome
Oakley Park
Cross Street
Heckfield Green
Battlesea Green
Pixey Green
Stradbroke
Chippenhall Green
Little Whittingham Green
Silverley's Green
Cratfield
Cookley
Swan Green
Mellis Green
Mellis
Yaxley
Langton Green
Eye
Denham
Ashfield Green
Hunting
Cranley
Braiseworth
Thornham Parva
Denham Street
Horham
Wootten Green
Russel's Green
Laxfield
Banyard's Green
Ubbeston Green
Heveningham
Thornham Magna
Occold
Redlingfield
Athelington
Wilby
Foals Green
Brundish Street
Stoke Ash
Wickham Street
Crown Corner
Stanway Green
Fingal Street
Brundish
Owl's Green
Thorndon
Rishangles
Dublin
Southolt
Bedingfield
Worlingworth
Badingham
Peasenhall
Wickham Skeith
Thwaite
Tannington
Maypole Green
Dennington
Brockford Street
Wetheringsett
Bedfield
Kenton
Bruisyard
Mendlesham
Blacksmith's Green
Aspall
Saxtead Little Green
Saxtead
Mid-Suffolk Light Railway & Mus
Monk Soham
Brabling Green
Cransford
Wetherup Street
Saxtead Green
Framlingham Castle
Framlingham
Sweffling
Mendlesham Green
Debenham
Ashfield
Earl Soham
Kettleburgh Lodge
Lampardbrook
Cole's Green
Great Glemham
Middlewood Green
Mickfield
Winston
Winston Green
Peats Corner
Brandeston
Cretingham
Kettleburgh
Parham
Stratford St. Andrew
Forward Green
Little Stonham
Stonham Aspal
Pettaugh
Framsden
Hacheston
Suffolk Owl Sanctuary
Earl Stonham
Monewden
Easton
Easton Farm Park
Marlesford
Little Glemham
Creeting Bottoms
Helmingham Hall Gardens
Helmingham
Letheringham
Creeting St Mary
Crowfield
Charsfield
Lower Hacheston
Campsey Ash
Wickham Market
Needham Lake
Coddenham Green
Gosbeck
Otley
Clopton Corner
Debach
Dallinghoo
Pettistree
Coddenham
Ashbocking
Hemingstone
Clopton
Bredfield
Rendlesham
Ufford
Baylham House Rare Breeds Farm
Baylham
Swilland
Burgh
Eyke
Barham
Henley
Witnesham
Grundisburgh
Hasketon
Melton
Bromeswell
Great Blakenham
Claydon
Rendlesham Forest
Culpho
Boot Street
Great Bealings
Mill Hills
Sutton Hoo
Woodbridge
Tuddenham
Tuddenham St Martin
Playford
Woodbridge Airfield (disused)
A140
A143
A1120
A12
A14
B1077
B1078
B1079
B1116
B1117
B1118
B1119
B1123
B1084
142
125
108
S
U
F
F
TM
0 1 2 3 miles
0 1 2 3 4 5 km

Covehithe
South Cove
Frostenden
Brampton
Stoven
Westhall
Mill Common
Rumburgh
Spexhall
Uggeshall
Clay Common
Cove Bottom
Wangford
Reydon
Reydon Smear
Southwold
SOUTHWOLD MUSEUM
Sole Bay
Gunhill Cliff
Easton Cliffs
The Warren
Green Heath
Wissett
Halesworth
HALESWORTH AIRFIELD MEM MUS
Holton
Upper Holton
Chediston Green
Walpole
Blyford
Wenhaston
Blythburgh
Blackheath
Walberswick
The Flats
Thorington
Bramfield
Sibton Green
Sibton
Hemp Green
Yoxford
Darsham
High Street
Westleton
Dunwich
DUNWICH MUSEUM
Grey Friars
Dunwich Cliffs
Minsmere Cliffs
MINSMERE RSPB
The Sluice
Middleton
Middleton Moor
Theberton
Eastbridge
Kelsale
North Green
Curlew Green
Carlton
Saxmundham
LEISTON ABBEY
Leiston
LONG SHOP MUSEUM
Sizewell
Knodishall
Benhall Green
Benhall Street
Sternfield
Coldfair Green
Aldringham
Friston
Farnham
Friday Street
Thorpe Ness
Thorpeness
Gromford
Snape
SNAPE MALTINGS
Blaxhall
NORTH WARREN RSPB
THE RED HOUSE
ALDEBURGH MUS
Aldeburgh
Fort Green
Slaughden
Aldeburgh Bay
Iken
Tunstall
Tunstall Forest
High Street
Sudbourne
Chillesford
Butley
Orford
Orford Ness
HAVERGATE ISLAND
ORFORDNESS-HAVERGATE
Capel Green
Butley High Corner
Gedgrave Hall
Bentwaters Airfield (disused)
SUFFOLK COAST AND HEATHS
SUFFOLK COAST
A12
A144
A145
A1094
A1095
B1119
B1121
B1122
B1125
B1126
B1127
B1069
B1078
B1084
B1123
B1124
B1353
B1387
143
109
TM
60
80
50
A
B
C
D
E
F
G
H
7
8
9
10
11

128
Friog
Braich Ddu
Mynydd Pencoed
Craig Cwm Amarch
Minffordd
Dol-ffanog
Mynydd Hafotty
Craig Hen-gae
Foel Crochan
Aberllefenni
Mynydd Cwmgerwyn
Mynydd Cwmcelli
Aberangell
Cefnfeusydd Fm
Pen y Garn 459
Trawsfynydd
Graig Lwyd
Craig Ysgiog
Llwyngwril
Pen-y-Crug
Esgair Berfa
Mynydd Pen-Rhiw
Mynydd Tyn-y-Fach
Foel Ddu
Tal-y-llyn
Mynydd Rugog
Corris Uchaf
Godre Fynydd
Cefn Llandybo
Rhiwgaeron
Y Rhos
Twllydarren
Llanfihangel-y-pennant
Castell y Bere
Foel Caer'berllan 380
Cedris Fm
Graig Goch 586
Mynydd-Ty'n-y-Ceunant
King Arthur's Labyrinth & Craft Centre
Mynydd Braich-Goch
Corris
Corris Railway
Fronfelen Hall
Moel Heulen
Mynydd Pen-Lan
Mynydd Du
Coed Pen-lan
Cefn Llwyd
Fign Oer
Allt-Lwyd
Meriafel
Abergynolwyn
Gamallt
Nant Gwernol
Graig Wen
Mynydd Cedris
Tarren Cadian
Corris Railway Museum
Ffridd Bwlch-Lluan
Foel
Dol-fôr
Cemmaes
Fron
Ty'rgawen
Birds' Rock (Craig yr Aderyn)
Ceinws
Ceinws Llanfechan 304
Mynydd Pant-Côch
Graig Ddu
Brynmelyn
Rhydygwiail
Gorwel Deg
Bodowen
Llanegryn
Peniarth
Abertrinant
Quarry Siding
Mynydd Pentre
Hendre
Foel Fawr
666
Cwm Cadian
Esgairgeiliog
Plas Llwyngwern
Centre for Alternative Technology
Mynydd Llwyn-Gwern
Mathafarn
Pen-y-gyrn
Commins Gwyn
Dysynni
Mynydd Tan-y-Coed 491
Foel Wyllt
Dolgoch
Mynydd Ty-Mawr
Tarrenhendre 633
Mynydd Rhyd-Galed 475
Foel y Geiff
Pantperthog
Gelli
Llanwrin
Cemmaes Road (Glantwymyn)
Talyllyn Railway
Tarrenbarcut
Mynydd Cefn-Caer
Mynydd Glandulas
Bryn-Coch 227
Bryncrug
Gwr-bach
Snowdonia National Park
Parc Cenedlaethol Eryri
Comins Bach
Cwm-Llywy-uchaf
Cefncoch-gwyllt
Commins Coch
Pandy
Tynllwyn-Hen
Pen Trum-Gwr
Esgair Uchaf
Foel-Goch
Foel-Y-Ffridd
Aber-Ffrydlan
River Dovey
Glyndŵr's Way
Hendreselfion
Rhosysilio 228
Berllan-dêg
Cefn Côch
Gwernbere
Rhyd-yr-onen
Tarren Cwm-Ffernol 550
Mynydd Esgairweddon
Pen-y-bont
Pwllglas
Abercegir
Darowen
Tywyn
Hendy
Trurn Gelli 535
Allt Nantygwenlli
Braich Ddu
Wales Coast Path
Braich y Golwydd
Pantlludw
Hafodty
Machynlleth
Bryn-Tudur
Warren Parc
Caen-hen
Fron-goch
Bryn Wg
Pendre
Escuan Hall
Corlan Fraith
Allt Gwyddgwion
Cynfal-Fawr
Cwrt
Pennal Towers
Pennal
Llugwy
Senedd-dy-Owain Glyndŵr
Cefn Dolgelynen
Ind Est
Newtown Road
Penegoes
Ffridd Wyllt
Tal-y-wern
Wenallt
Rhosywir
Caethle
Nantycynnog
Bryn Dinas
Caeceinach
Nant Cwm-sylwi
Derwenlas
Coed Llynlloedd
Forge
217
Copa Shôn
Allt Goch
Bryn-y-Brain
Rhiwgriafol
Tynewydd
Foel Caethle
Llechwedd Melyn
Happy Valley (Cwm Maethlon)
Mynydd y Llyn
Cors Dyfi
Dovey Junction
Llyn Glanmerin
Troed-y-rhiw
Afon Dulas
Afon Crewi
Groeslyn
Melinbyrhedyn
Moelfre 469
Dôl-Caradog
Tyddynbriddell Hill
Glaspwll
Pant-glâs
Ffridd Cefn-Isaf
Llyfnant Valley
Mynydd Eithaf
Craig Caerhedyn 286
Cefn Modfedd
Aberhosan
Trefeddian Fm
Penhelig
Aberdovey (Aberdyfi)
Glandyfi
Tarren Tyn-y-Maen
Ceniarth Fm
Cefnwyrygrug
Esgair Graflwyn 440
Banc y Cwn
Ynys-hir RSPB
Eglwys Fach
Cefn Coch Fm
Cwm-cemrhiw
Cwmydwrgi
Tarboudrain
Cleiriau
Nantyfyda
Esgair-Fochnant
Cefncyfritol
Rhosygarreg
Foel Fadian 564
Bryn y Fedwen
Aberdovey Bar
Afon Dyfi
Furnace
Foel Fawr
Moel Hyrddod
Mynachdy
Coed y Garth
Dyfi Furnace
Tyn-y-garth
Bwlch Einion
Pen Carreg-Gopa 447
388
Bwlch Corog
Pen Creigiau'r Llan 507
Rhiwgam
Hengwm-cyfeiliog
Ffridd Rhosygarreg
Uwch-y-coed
Dyfi
Penrhyn-gerwin
Badger Lodge
Artists Valley Cwm Einion
Llyn Penrhaeadr
Hafodwnog
Creigiau Bwlch-Hyddgen
Mawnog
Llechwedd Dillas 495
Glaslyn
Ynys Tachwedd
Ynyslas
Lodge Fm
Craig-y-penrhyn
Llyn Conach
Tarren Bwlch-gwyn
Foel Goch 479
Esgair Foel-Ddu
Llyn Dwfn
Llwyngwinau
Siambr Trawsfynydd
Llyn Cwm-byr
539
Bugeilyn
Cefn Llwyd 455
Borth Sands
Aberleri
Llancynfelyn
Plas y Gwynfryn
Tre'r-ddôl
Cwm Clettwr
Gwar-cwm
Afon Cetwr
Caer-arglwyddes
Moel-y-Llyn 521
Banc Bwlchygarreg
New Pool
Foel Grafiau
493 Mynydd Bychan
Llechwedd Crin
Cors Fochno
Moel y Garn 420
Castell 482
Bryn Moel 491
Croesau Hyddgen
Foel Uchaf 565
Carnfachbugeilyn 622
Borth (Y Borth)
Ynysycapel
Tre-Taliesin
Tynygraig Fm
Fronlas
Cwm Ceulan
Bryn Mawr 489
Llyn Nantycagl
Banc yr Wyn
566
Carn Hyddgen
Esgair Gorddi
Waun Lwyd
Llwyn-glas
Cerrig-tranau
Pentre-bach
Staylittle
Penpompren Hall
Tal-y-bont
Moel Fferm
423 Fynach Fawr
Bryn Gwyn
444
Banc Llechwedd-Mawr
Banc Lluestnewydd
Craig yr Eglwys
Pumlumon Cwmbiga 620
Fuches 510
Upper Borth
Pen-y-wern
Llyn-ysgubor-wen
Glanwern
Ceredigion
Wernddeg
Tynant
Carn Ower 482
Cefn yr Esgair
Maesnant
Pen Cerrig Tewion
Pen Pumlumon-Arwystli 741
Penybont
Lletyllwyd
Argoed-fawr
Bwlch-y-ddwyallt
Cwmere
Cyneiniog
Drosgol 550
Llyn Llygad Rheidol
Pumlumon Fach
Dôl-y-Bont
Glanfred
Tyn-y-parc
Taigwynion
Cynnull-mawr
Moel Golomen
Craig yr Allt-Ddu
Nant-y-moch Reservoir
Plynlimon / Pumlumon Fawr 752
Llandre
Ty'n-y-ffynnon
Dolgau Fm
Dole
Bryn-Hir
Banc Mynyddgorddu
Bont-goch (Elerch)
Llanerchclwydau
Mynydd Gorddu
Llyn Craigypistyll
Pen Cerrig
Bryn-Gwyn 443
Drum Peithnant
Pen Lluest-y-carn
Esgair y Maesnant
Wileirog
Ruel
Pen-y-cwm
Ty'n-rhos
Pen-y-garn
Pencefn
Llety-Ifan-Hên
(Sir Ceredigion)
Banc Lletty Ifan Hen
Disgwylfa Fawr 507
Esgair y Maen
506
Maenuwch
Ty'r Abby
Nantsiriol
Bow Street
Penrhyn-coch
Garth
Tynpynfarch
Coed Gruffydd
Syfydrin
Llyn Syfydrin
Bryn-Llwyd
Dyll Faen
Cripiau Eisteddfa-fach
Y Drum
546 Y Foel
Tir Gwyn
Fawnog y Bont
Clarach
Llangorwen
Salem
Pen-bont Rhydybeddau
Bryn-goleu
Llyn Pendam
Disgwylfa Fach 414
Eisteddfa Gurig
Ffynnon Caradog
Plas Gogerddan
Cefn Llwyd
Cwmsymlog
Llyn Blaenmelindwr
Hirnant
Drybedd
Foel Wyddon 535
Hirgoed-ddu
Llechwedd Hirgoed 535
Pont Rhydgaled
Camera Obscura & Cliff Railway
Frongoch Fm
Comins Coch
Fronfraith
Capel Dewi
Rhosgoch
Banc-y-Darren
Moelfryn
Cwmerfyn
Pen y Graig-ddu
Llyn Rhosgoch
Esgair Gorlan
Nant y Caerhedyn
Dinas Res
Bryn Glas 516
Cwmergyr
Peraidd Fynydd
Pant Mawr
National Library of Wales
Waun Fawr
Llanbadarn Fawr
Lovesgrove
Dolau
Cwm-mwythig
Nant-y-bwla
Alltfadog
Goginan-fawr
Ysguborenewydd
Old Goginan
Banc Creignant Mawr
Pond Llwernog
Mynydd Pont-erwyd
Silver Mountain Experience
Ceiro
Bryn-glas
Dyffryn Castell
Llynoedd Ieuan
Y Glog
Cae Gaer
Llechwedd Llwyd
Penlan Oleu
Llwyniorwerth
Cefnllidiart
Dollwen
Goginan
Blaendyffryn
Nantyrarian
Ponterwyd
Gelli
Fuches-wen
564
Bryn Du
Glanrafon
Penllwyn
Maes-bangor
Cwmbrwyno
Llywernog
Southgate
Pwllcenawon
Capel Bangor
Hafodau
Cefn-bangor
Magic of Life Butterfly House
Rheidol Hydro Electric Station
Parson's Br
Cefn Croes 573
Banc Nant-rhys
Penparcau
Rhiwarthen Isaf
Tycam
Troedrhiwlas
Cwm Rheidol Res
Mynydd yr Ychen
Ysbyty Cynfyn
Draws Drum
Banc Dolwen
Bryn Rhudd
Bryn Diluw 480
Mynydd
Rhyd
Vale of Rheidol Light Railway
Aberffrwd
Rheidol Falls
Coed Simdde Lwyd
Erwbarfe Fm
362 Erw Barfau
Tynywern
Penglanowen
Ty-crûg
Nantyronen Station
Cwmwch Yr Arian
Ystumtuen
Coed Rheidol
0 1 2 3 miles
0 1 2 3 4 5 km

Mallwyd
Mynydd Tatyglannau
Bryn Ysgwthan
Foel
Cefnau
Dolpebyll
Llangadfan
Blowty
Parc
Neuadd-wen
Hafan
Carnedd Wen 523
Ffridd Goch
Esgair Ddu
Cwm Tafolog
Llechwedd Mawr
Tafolog
Lletty-Mawr
Stone Ho
A458
Llanerfyl
Moel Bentyrch 338
Four Crosses
Cefndre
Llwydiarth
Tynrhos
Heniarth
Carnedd y Cylch
Waun Lwyd
Gwrachen
Nant Craigyfran
Mynydd Lluest Fach
Blaen-Tafolog
Bryn-uchel-isaf
Mynydd y Cemais
Ffridd Ganol
Pen Coed
Goetre
Goetre Fach
Plasynghraen
Diosg
Hirros Hall
Pentyrch
Hen-efail
New Road
Afon Einion
Dolgead Hall
Disgwylfa 386
Caerbwla
Glyn
Craig Fawr
Clegyrnant
Y Rhos
Dolwen
Moel Ddolwen
Sychtyn
Hirrhos Uchaf
Melin-y-grug
Maes-y-glydfa
Llanoddian Hall
Fron 412
Cannon
Llyn Gwyddior
Penylau Gwynion 450
Neinthirion
Dolau
Hafod
Belan Hall
Glaslyn
Gelli Gethin
Rhosaflo
Cwmllwyngog
Melin-y-ddôl
Ind Est
Waun-gau
Dôl Fawr
Mynydd Rhiw-Saeson
Cwm Pen Llydan
Waun y Sarn
Belan
Parc-y-rhiw
Rhiw-hiriaeth Isaf
Llanfair Caereinion
Pentre-Celyn
Llechwedd Du
Glyndŵr's Way
Mynydd Waun Fawr
Llyn Hir
Rhiw hirlaeth
Mount Pleasant
Moel Eiddew 453
Plas-rhiw-Saeson
Cors Fforchog
Cwmderwen
Bryn y Castell 368
Cross Fm
Tynllwyn
Fron-gôch
Waun Fawr
Pandy
Dol-y-garreg wen-isaf
Bryn y Lloi
Mynydd Lluest-y-graig
Plasiolyn
Bryn-moel
Waun
Gwern-y-bwlch
Brynaere
Cerrig y Tân
Esgair Priciau
Pant-y-milwyr
Ystrad Uchaf
Bryn-penarth
Esgair
Coed Ffridd-fawr
Pentremawr
Berth-las
Banc y Gorlan
Ffridd Fawr
Ffridd-Rhyd-Ddu 424
Pentre-lludw
Carreg-y-big
Foel Fawr
Lletty Gwilym Isaf
Tan-y-graig
Penarth
130
A470
Ty Pella
Llanbrynmair
Tafolwern
Bryn Gwyn
Twmpath Melyn 439
Nant Wythan
Gwaenydd
Frongoch Hall
Tyn-y-coed
Lawnt
Belan-deg
Maesprydd
Cwm Bustach
Tyn-y-coed
Corun-y-Ffridd 371
Cwmbychan-mawr
Dolfach
Moel Caetwpa
Braich-Odnant
B4518
Afon Iaen
Mynydd y Gribin
Cefn Coch
Llanllugan
Dwyrhiw
Gwernydd
Manafon
Cefn
Maesteg
Plas Esgair
Llan
Gelli
414 Y Foel
Gwaun-y-maglau
Ty Bach
Sychnant
Mynydd yr Hendre
Belan-ddu
Glan-yr-afon
Llanwyddelan
Old Hall
New Mills
Mynydd Ty'r-Sais 359
Pen Rhiw-Mwyn 388
Tawelfan
Bont-Dolgadfan
Newydd Fynyddog 412
Fron
Talerddig
Rhyd
Cwm Llwyd
Mynydd Pistyll-du
Mynydd Dwyriw
Pant
Adfa
Bryn Fm
Dolgair
Cefn-twlch
Cwm Ednant
Cae Madog
Brynbach
Cwmcalch Isaf
Ffridd yr Ystrad
Glanhanog
Brynderlwyn
Hendre
Dol-friog
Carneddau (ruin)
Castell-isaf
Mynydd Clogau 402
Trawsgelli
Argoed
Lower Fachwen
Dolymelinau
404 Banc Bronderwgoed
Mynydd Esgair
Cwncalch Uchaf 419
Derlwyn
Yr Allt
Y Glonc 461
Mynydd Cerriglwydion
Aberclawdd
Cochsidan
Tregynon
Pwllan
Esgair Geulan
Llannerch-yr-aur
Pennant
Wig
Sarnbigog
Rallt
Craigfryn
Lleustuchaf
The Heath
Bryn Du
Bechan Brook
Skew Br
Mynydd Penypistyll
Bryn Du
Bryn Amlwg 488
Pen y Pigyns
Pikins
Allt Fawr
Garreg-Hir 485
Gwgia
Brynheulog
Gregynog
Brithdir
Mynydd Cil-Cwm 527
Cilcwn
Creigiau Pennant
Hendre
Wylfa
Plas Llysyn
Bryn-côch
Tynyreithin
Carno
Sarn
Llyn y Tarw
Mynydd Llwytgoed
Cefn-llydan
Finger Post
Cwm-mawr
Pont Crugnant 449
Allt-Du
Pantle
Blaen-y-cwm
Bryn yr Aran
Pentre
Hafod
Plasnewydd
Parc-y-rhiw
Llyn Du
Llwydcoed
Ddifed
Gwern-y-pwll
New Ho
Cwm
Bwlch-y-ffridd
Highgate Hill
Trannon
Trawscoed
Wgi-fawr
Maesypandy
Bettws Hall
Bryn Moel
Dylife
P
O
W
Y
S
Bryn-yr-Oerfa 460
Bryn-Mawr 450
Waun Garno
396 Bryn y Gadair
Clatter
Mynydd Garth-Pwt
Penbedw
Garth Hill
Sowylfa Wood
Red Ho
Hirnant
Dolbachog
Esgair Hir
Blaencerniog
Gors Goch
Pontdolgoch
Alltwnnog
Llanwnog
Foel y Belan
Tyn sarn
Llwyn-y-gog
Rhydlydan
B4568
Fachwen Pool
Llechwedd Du
Rhiw
Fuches Dyfeity Fawr
Staylittle (Penffordd-Lâs)
Gamallt
Colwyn Brook
Hafod
Cefncoch
Cefn Gwyn
Ystradfaelog
Gwynfynydd
Bryn-y-pentre Wood
Point Fm
Tynyreithin Hall
Rhydyfelin
Newtown Y Drenewydd
Clywedog
Llwynygog
Yfridd Nantyrhafod 433
Mawnog Bryn-glas
Bryn Crugog 447
Cwm-gwernog
Oerle
Rhiwen
Wig Br
B4569
Caersws
Aberhafesp
Red Ho
Fedw-Ddu
Nant-yr-hafod
Waen-y-gittin
Y Gribyn
Felin Dyrnol
Llawr-y-glyn
Geseilfa
Long Hill
Waen
Gleiniant
Frydd
Argoed
Ddraenen Ddu
Carnedd
Long Length
A489
Bronfelin Hall
Milford
Oriel Davies Gallery
Braichyfedw
Gwernafon
The Hill 385
Cadwgan
Esgairieth
Derwllwydion
Cilhaul
Fforest
Bodaioch Hall
Trefeglwys
Afon Trannon
Cefn Carnedd 279
A470
Allt y Gaer
Frehafren
Glanhafren Hall
Maesyrhandir
Garth Owen
Lan 421
Llyn Clywedog
Dinas 445
B4518
Maesyblawd
Afon Cerist
Trewythen
Llandinam Hall
Cwmllwydion
Bryn-helyg
Pen-y-bryn
Stepaside
Cwmbiga
Banc-y-Groes 419
Nant-y-Gwrdu
Waun y Gadair
482 Bryn y Fan
Lluest-wen
Dolgwden
Cwmdylluan
Llyn Ebyr
Pen y Coed
Coedmawr
Hornby
Gwerneirin
Plas Dinam
Little London
Cefn-hir
Llyfnant Brook
Mochdre
Broneirion
Llandinam
Moel Lart 438
Cobblers Gate
Rhosfawr
Gelli Hir
Glascoed
Trawscoed
Hafod
Dolfor
Gendrum
470 Mynydd y Groes
Bryn-y-Tail 403
Llyn y Fan
Y Fan
Van
Croesllwyn
Tyddyn
Coed Mawr
Carreg
Court
Bryn Mawr
Bryntail
Garth
Cefngolleugoed
B4569
Gellilefrith
Oakley Park
Cefn
River Severn
Giant's Grave 516
Yr Allt
Mochdre Brook
Old Neuadd
Gwas
Cwm Deildre
Glyn
Penrallt
Morfodion
Bont-newydd
Lower Penrhuddlan
Pentre
130
Yr Esgair
Maenhinon 344
Cefnpenarth
Afon Clywedog
Allt Goch
Dolwen
Pencraig Rocks
Glôg Fm Glog
480
Black Gate
Tynyrwtra
Tan Hinon
Bronheulwen
Berth-lwyd Coppice
Allt y Moch
Panty-yr-esgair
Old Hall
Glan-y-nant
Old Market Hall
Llanidloes
Glyndfannau
Coed y Gaer
519 Waunlluestowain
Seven Wells
Glynhafren
Llwyn-derw
Caenfedw
Gorn Hill
Pen-y-banc
Y Foel Glyn-Feinion 435
Banc Cefnperfedd
Cider Ho
Foel-goch
Mount Severn
Bryn-côch
Glyn-Feinion
Craig Dugwin
Bryn Dadlau
Camnant
Fuches
Beili
Bryn Du Road
Newchapel
Tach
Dethenydd
Bryn Cwmrhiwdre
River Ithon
Neuadd-goch Bank
Castell-greidd
Banc Du
Glynbrochan
Ind Est
Brynddu
Moelfre 428
Blaenbythigion
Afon Brochan
Blaen Pathiog
Cwm
Blue Lins Brook
A483
Allt Pant-mawr
Pen Bwlch-y-Groes
Ffos y Ffwdan
368 Brynposteg Hill
The Cross
Waun
Graig
Nanty
Llanifyny
Ty'n-y-rhos
Pen y Foel
Cefn Hirbysg
Bryn Blaen-y-glyn
Cwmbelan
B4518
Pant-Poeth Hill 422
Pegw-Mawr 584
Waun Ddubarthog
Garn-Fach 503
Pen Ithon Hall
Garn
Glanbidno Isaf
Marsh's Pool
Cefn Hendre
Ty-mawr
A44
Henfaes
Deildref
Bryn Mawr 405
Banhadlog Hall
426 Oldchapel Hill
Craig Tylwch
569 Pegwn-Bach
Ddulluu Bank
Pen-hyle-mawr
A470
Tylwch
Graig-lar
Llaithddu
Llangurig
113
Esgair Ychion
Ystradolwyn Fawr
Hendreaur
Cefn
571 Crugyn-Llwyd
Banc Du
Dolauewmffrwd
Penybank
Esgair Llwyn-Gwyn
Felin-fawr
Cilgwyn-uchaf
Creigiau Llwydion
Upper Llaithddu
Esgairuchaf
Pant-Gwyn Hill
Foel Gurig 480
Hafod-wen
Fedw
Glanyrafon Hall
Cwmderw
Cerrig Gwaun-y-llan
Cil-Gwrgan
Bronheulwen
Wennallt 435
Lliadiarddau
Garth Fach
508
David's Well
Waunhall
Dolygarn
Llanbadarn
Craignant
Rhiwlas Hill 439
Caecethin
Garreg
Prysgduon
Marteg
Fron
SJ
SO
A
B
C
D
E
F
G
H
147
7
8
9
10
11

148
129
114
Welshpool
Y Trallwng
Newtown
Y Drenewydd
Llanfair Caereinion
Montgomery
(Trefaldwyn)
Bishop's Castle
Clun
Mathrafal
Tan-y-ffridd
Lower Hall Fm
Maesgwyn Uchaf
Tirnewydd
Groes-lwyd
Guilsfield
(Cegidfa)
Trewern
Winnington Green
Halfway House
Glyn Common
Marche Manor
Upper Hall
Llanerchbrochwel
Moel-y-garth
Brookland Hall
Trelydan
Cefn
Frochas
Brunant
Nelly Andrews Green
Mountain Fm
Vron Gate
Vennington
Lower Bryn-y-groes
Maesmawr Hall
Bryn-glas Hall
Cefnllwyd
Pentre
Henllan
The Glyn
Glascoed
Llangyniew
Heniarth
Cefn du uchaf
Y Figyn
Ty-brith
Cloddiau
Groespluan
Coed-y-wlad
Gungrog Hall
Buttington
Blackmore
Pen-y-Gaer
Frochas Fm
Moydog Fawr
Llanerchydol Hall
Cyfronydd
Welsh Harp Fm
Forest Fm
Whitton Grange
The Knapp
Caus Castle
Wallop Hall
Llanoddian Hall
Ind Est
Hengwm
Y Golfa
Golfa Fm
Raven Square
Powysland Mus
Hope
Haywood Fm
Mondaytown
Aston Hill
Hamptonhayes
Rhosfawr
Welshpool & Llanfair Light Railway
Sylfaen
Powis Castle
Cwm Dingle
Beacon Ring
Woodside Fm
Rowley Hill
Rowley
Aston Rogers
Aston Pigott
Little Worthen
Hampton Hall
Hampton Beech
Cil-haul
Dolarddyn
Castle Caereinion
Ty-n-y-pwll
Graig
Little Cwm
Cwm Fm
Spring Coppice
Belan Locks
Leighton
Walton Hill
Belan Bank
Tantree Bank
Mount Pleasant
Plasiolyn
Rhos Fawr Hill
Ashton
Y Byrwydd
Byrwydd
Pen-y-bryn
Pwll
Belan
Llyn Coed y Dinas
Cilcewydd
Leighton Hall
Fir Ho
Flying Dingle
Brockton
Binweston
Worthen
Bryn-penarth
Cefn-Crin
Yr Allt
Trefnant Hall
Mount Fm
Llwynderw
Trehelig
Mid-Wales
Fron
Ivy Ho
New Ho
The Stubb
Trelystan
Marton Hall
Leigh Hall
Leigh
Penarth
Maesprydd
Henllys
Pant-y-ffridd
Bank Fm
Bryn
Cross Lane Fm
Pen-y-Bank
Brithdir Hall
Edderton Hall
Red Ho
Court Ho
Kingswood
Gunley Wood
Stocktonwood
Marton
Marton Pool
Lower Wood
Betton
Whitsburn Hill
Knot Moor
Lady House Fm
Lord's Stone
Hopesgate
Manafon
Belan-deg
Cefn
Bank Hill
The Forest
Ty-Mawr Hill
Stingwern Hill
Penygoron
Felindre
Berriew
The Grove
Ackley Fm
Gunley Hall
Bromlow
Lyde
Pentirvin
Hope Park
Hope Valley
Hope
Bentlawnt
New Mills
Old Hall
Dolgair
Cefn-twlch
Ty-mawr
Bryncaemaeshir
Coed Tafol
Andrew Logan Museum of Sculpture
Pen-y-parc Wood
Vaynor Park
Glansevern Hall
Refail
Forden
Cwm Fm
Hem Fm
Hem Moor
Stockton
Rorrington Lodge
Meadowtown
Rorrington
Rorrington Hill
Hockleton Br
Wotherton
Hemford
Black Marsh
Gravelsbank
Nick Knolls
Cefngwernfa
Middle Ho
Cwmgwydd
Lower Fachwen
Dolymelinau
Pwllan
Upper Ho
Black Wood
Brooks
Garthmyl
Llifior Brook
Pied Ho
Salt Br
Shiregrove Br
Touchill
Crest Wood
Middleton Hall Fm
Middleton
Stapeley Hill
Mitchell's Fold
Gravels
Pennerley
Shelve
Tregynon
Red Ho
Cwm Harry
Pentre Llifior
Llandinier
Trwstllewelyn
Caerhowel Hall
Stalloe
Hendomen
Crankwell Fm
Chirbury
Bank
The Ridge Fm
New Ho
Weston House Fm
Mitchell's Fold Stone Circle
The Marsh
Grit Hill
Skew Br
Ty'n y Bryn
Brithdir
Glomen
Pen-y-coed Fm
Fron
Plas Meredydd
Abernant
Court Calmore
Ffridd Faldwyn
Montgomery Castle
Great Moat Fm
Marrington Hall
Priest Weston
White Grit
Squilver Fm
Berth Ho
Gregynog
Henfaes
Tanybryn
Clegodig
Rhydyware
Sutton
Lan Fawr
Cwmdulla Fm
Corndon Hill
Hyssington Marsh
Mucklewick Hill
Brook Ho Fm
Brooks Hill
Finger Post
Bettws Cedewain
Llwyn Coch
Ty'n-y-banadl
New Wells
Cwmdockin
Dolforwyn Hall
Green Lane
Cwminkin
Town Hill
Old Bell
Llwynobin
Dingle Br
Sidnal Fm
Corndon Fm
Woodgate Fm
Black Rhadley Hill
Highgate Hill
Bryncoch
Highgate
Glanbechan
Brynrorin
Pontyperchill
Dolforwyn Castle
Ffridd
Abermule
Brynderwen
Llandyssil
Fron
Little Mount
Upper Pentre
White Hall Fm
Rhiston
Alport
Old Church Stoke
Roundton Hill
Hurdley
Hyssington
Yewtree Fm
Linley Big Wood
Heath Mynd
Bettws Hill
Red Ho
Cwm
Cefn Mawr
Garn Wood
Aberbechan
The Court
Red Ho
Llwynmadoc Fm
Cwm Bromley
Pen-y-bryn Hall
Brompton Hall
Green
Churchstoke
Llanerch
Disgwylfa Hill
Tynyreithin Hall
Pont Fm
Rhydyfelin
Llanllwchaiarn
Pwll Penarth
Llenmerewig
Llanmerwig
Fron Faith Hall
New Ho
Pentreheyling
Mellington Fm
Simon's Castle
The Meadow
Pitcholds
Snead
More Fm
Bromleysmill
Oriel Davies Gallery
Pool Road
Penygelli
Penarth Tack
Treowen
Hodley
Goetre Hill
Upper Maenllwyd
Goitre
Gwern-y-go Wood
Bacheldre
Crow Wood
Lake Fm
Pentrenant Hall
Court Ho
Lower Cwm
Cwm Cae
Pentre
Aston Hall
Aston
Owlbury
Owlbury Hall
Owl's Lane
Lydham
Milford
Trehafren
Garth Owen
Maesyrhandir
Newtown
Dolfor Road
Bronyvastre
Dolforgan Hall
Glanmule
The Mule
Kerry
Sarn
Old Hall
Llancowrid
City
Hopton Uchaf
Pant Hill
Hopton Bank
Argoed
Cwm
Tan Ho
The Drewin
The Rolva
Caer Din
Dog & Duck Cott
Aston Hill
Lydham Manor
Lodge Fm
Bankshead
Castlegreen
Cabin
Pen-y-wern
Cefnperfa
The Forest
Penhempen
Graig
Brynllywarch
Penarron
Cwmydalfa
Black Hall
Drefor Fm
Cwm Earl
Bedran
Husky Hill
Lower Hill
Round Bank
Moat Hill
Edenhope Hill
Mainstone
Reilth Top
House on Crutches Mus
Lower Woodbatch Fm
Bus Pk
Wig
Carreg
Dolfor
Court
Cwm Mule
Radnorshire Gate
Kerry Hill
Block Wood
Stone Circle
Coed Nantyrhynau
Cefn Golog
Long Plantn
Ceri Forest
Cantlin Stone
Clun
Forest
Black Bank
Mason's Bank
Round Bank
Churchtown Hill
Churchtown
Cwm Ffrydd
Knuck Bank
Long Pike Hollow
Riddings
Colebatch Hill
Goat Ho
Colebatch
Hell Hole
Blakeridge Wood
Brampton Road
Cefn Einion
New Ho
Bryn Hill
Brockton
Acton Bank
Glôg Fm
Glog
Black Gate
Two Tumps
Rose Grove
Anchor
Cwm Moch
Bicton Brook Hill
Skeltons Bank
Hergan
Shadwell Hall
Three Gates
River Unk
Bryn
Acton
Lower Down
Walcot
Banc Cefnperfedd
Cider Ho
Source of River Teme
Bryn
Turgy
Kents Bank
Hall of the Forest
Folly Bank
Ale Oak
Mount Bank
Mardu
Llanhedrick
Argoed
Colstey Bank
Red Wood
Withins Wood
Sunnyhill
Neuadd-goch Bank
River Ithon
Cilfaesty Hill
Panty Hill
Cefn Vron Hill
Black Mountain
Badger Moor
Pentiken
Dingle-du-Bank
Caldy Bank
Graig Hill
Whitcott Keysett
Bicton
Banc Gorddwr
Cwm Gwyn
Blackmountain Fm
Castle Idris
Fron
Newcastle
Little Hall
Guilden Down
Steppleknoll
Clunton Hill
Carn Bryn-llwyd
Cwm-gwyn Hall
Hendre
Pound Gate Fm
Corkins Bank
Duffryn
Moor Hall
Guilfron
Garn Rock
Upper Spoad
River Clun
Clun Castle
Clun Mill
The Green
Radnor Wood
Clunton
Little House Fm
Hope's Castle Fm
Garn
Coety Bank
Llanllwyd
Rhyd-y-cwm
The Rhos Fm
Felindre
Bettws-y-crwyn
Dowke Hill
Stoney Pound
Weston Hill
Springhill Fm
Ind Est
Sowdley Wood
Hill Barn
Bryngydfa
Brandy House Fm
Trebrodier
Quabbs
Llwyn
Woodside
Castell-y-blaidd
Cil-Owen Brook
Gwerneirin
Beguildy
Wain Common
Hurgin
Llanfair Hill
Rock
Churchbank
Cwm
Black Hill
Clun Hill
Rockhill
Pen-y-wern
Lower House Fm
Cwm Bugail
Warren Bank
Cefn Hepreas
Upper Treverward
Treverward Ho
Cwm Collo
Llanwolley
Vedwllwyd
Bryndraenog
River Teme
Hobarris
Fiddler's Elbow
Esgair
Pennybank
Llanbadarn
Fron
Moel Wilym
Tynybryniau Hall
Warren Hill
Powys
3 miles
5 km

Preston
Hortonlane
Porthill
Kingsland
Belle Vue
Meole Brace
Cruckton
Emstrey
Norton
Uppington
Aston
Westbury
Yockleton
Stoney Stretton
Cruckmeole
Hanwood
Bayston Hill
Edge
Lea
Hinton
Farley
Hinwood
Atcham
Wroxeter
Donnington
Rushton
Asterley
Westley
Pontesbury
Pontesford
Pleatey
Great Lyth
Longden
Condover
Berrington
Longwood
Eaton Constantine
Dryton
Cantlop
Cound
Leighton
Minsterley
Habberley
Stapleton
Great Ryton
Pitchford
Cressage
Golding
Ploxgreen
Snailbeach
Church Pulverbatch
Pulverbatch
Dorrington
Acton Pigott
Acton Burnell
Frodesley
Harley
Crowsnest
Westcott
Longnor
Kenley
Ruckley
Stiperstones
Picklescott
Leebotwood
Woolstaston
Church Preen
Hughley
Stretton Westwood
Presthope
The Bog
Ratlinghope
Bridges
Plaish
Enchmarsh
All Stretton
Cardington
Gretton
Eastope
Bourton
Church Stretton
Longville in the Dale
East Wall
Brockton
Patton
Norbury
Wentnor
Wall Bank
Wall under Heywood
Hope Bowdler
Weston
Rushbury
Little Stretton
Shipton
Asterton
Minton
Ticklerton
Stanton Long
Derrington
Hatton
Marshbrook
Acton Scott
Eaton
Broadstone
Holdgate
Ditton Priors
Myndtown
Eaton
Lea
Whittingslow
Harton
Middlehope
Choulton
Eyton
Plowden
Horderley
Woolston
Alcaston
Westhope
Munslow
Aston Munslow
Tugford
Abdon
Edgton
Wistanstow
Strefford
Upper Affcot
Diddlebury
Boulden
Upper Heath
Corfton
Peaton
Clee St Margaret
Cheny Longville
Lower Dinchope
Halford
Sibdon Carwood
Newington
Hopesay
Kempton
Aston on Clun
Craven Arms
Culmington
Great Sutton
Stoke St Milborough
Little Brampton
Purslow
Clunbury
Broome
Stokesay
Norton
Vernolds Common
Hopton Cangeford
Cleedownton
Twitchen
Brandhill
Onibury
Stanton Lacy
Clungunford
Abcott
Shelderton
Wootton
Cleeton St Mary
SHROPSHIRE
SHROPSHIRE HILLS
The Long Mynd
Wenlock Edge
Corve Dale

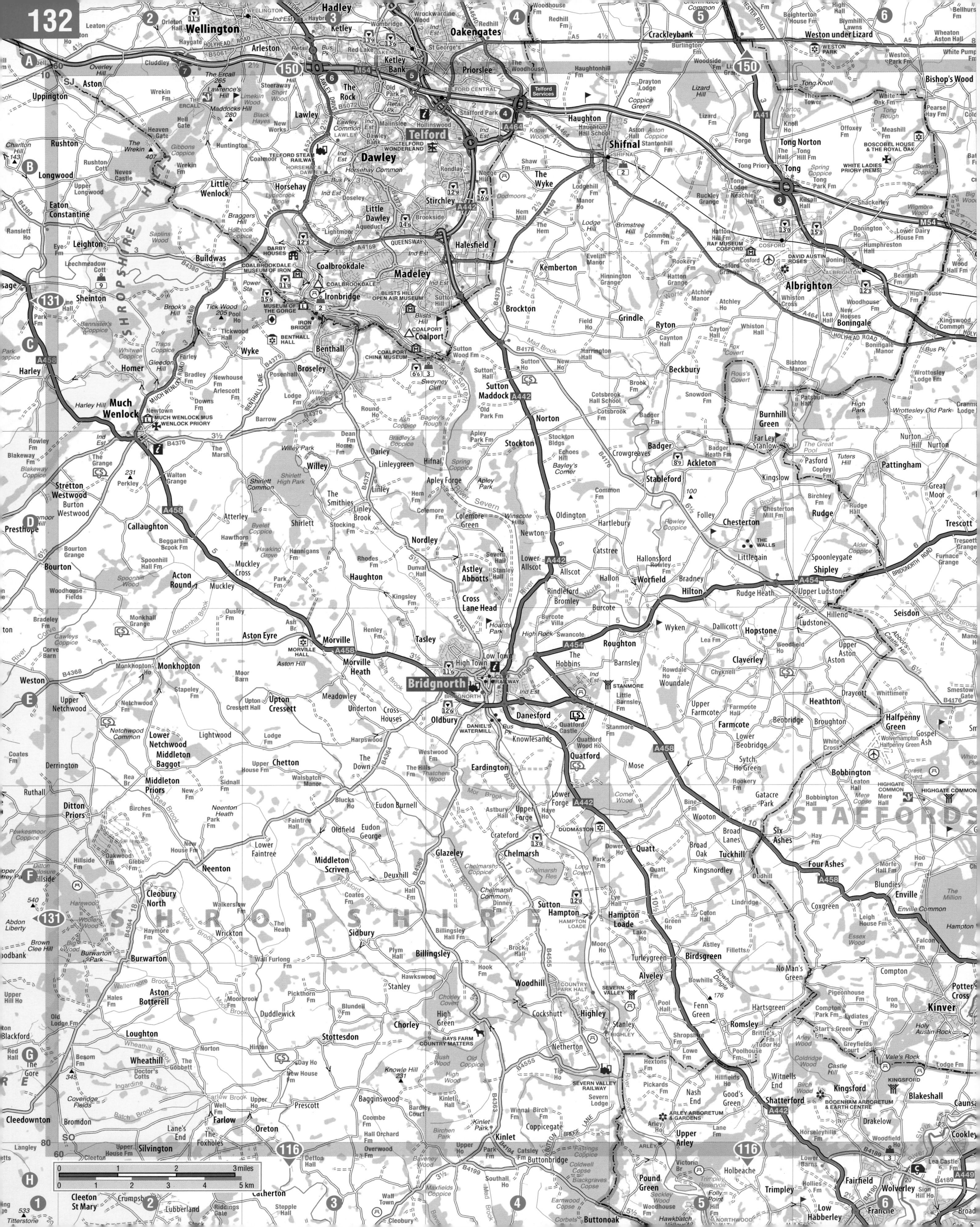

Wellington
Hadley
Ketley
Oakengates
Crackleybank
Weston under Lizard
Arleston
Ketley Bank
Priorslee
150
Telford
Dawley
Lawley
The Rock
Telford Services
Haughton
Shifnal
Tong Norton
Tong
Bishop's Wood
Uppington
Aston
Rushton
Longwood
Little Wenlock
Horsehay
Stirchley
The Wyke
Eaton Constantine
Leighton
Buildwas
Coalbrookdale
Madeley
Halesfield
Kemberton
Albrighton
Ironbridge
Sheinton
Brockton
Grindle
Ryton
Boningale
131
Coalport
Benthall
Broseley
Wyke
Beckbury
Harley
Homer
Much Wenlock
Sutton Maddock
Norton
Burnhill Green
Stockton
Badger
Ackleton
Pattingham
Willey
Stableford
Stretton Westwood
Burton Westwood
Chesterton
Rudge
Trescott
Presthope
Callaughton
Oldington
Nordley
Bourton
Acton Round
Astley Abbotts
Shipley
Muckley
Haughton
Cross Lane Head
Worfield
Hilton
Rudge Heath
Seisdon
Aston Eyre
Morville
Tasley
Roughton
Hopstone
Claverley
Monkhopton
Weston
Bridgnorth
Oldbury
Danesford
Upton Cressett
Heathton
Halfpenny Green
Quatford
Farmcote
Chetton
Eardington
Middleton Priors
Bobbington
Ditton Priors
Eudon Burnell
Lower Forge
STAFFORDS
Six Ashes
Glazeley
Chelmarsh
Quatt
Middleton Scriven
Tuckhill
Four Ashes
Neenton
Cleobury North
Enville
Sutton
Hampton Loade
SHROPSHIRE
Sidbury
Billingsley
Birdsgreen
Burwarton
Alveley
Woodhill
Aston Botterell
Highley
Kinver
Romsley
Chorley
Loughton
Stottesdon
Wheathill
Kingsford
Shatterford
Blakeshall
Farlow
Oreton
Cleedownton
Silvington
Kinlet
Upper Arley
116
Pound Green
Trimpley
Wolverley
Cleeton St Mary
Buttonoak

Stretton
Cannock Wood
Wimblebury
Gentleshaw
Farewell
Oldfallow
Hatherton
Heath Hayes
Chorley
Horsebrook
Cannock
Chase Terrace
Burntwood
Kiddemore Green
Brewood
Bridgtown
Norton East
Leomansley
Norton Canes
Chasetown
Hammerwich
Standeford
Churchbridge
Great Wyrley
Cheslyn Hay
Shareshill
Coven
Muckley Corner
Wall
Little Wyrley
Brownhills
Featherstone
Hobble End
Codsall Wood
Clayhanger
Shire Oak
Codsall
Essington
Springhill
Highbridge
Stonnall
Shenstone
Pelsall
Walsall Wood
Oaken
Fordhouses
Bushbury
Bloxwich
Shelfield
Vigo
Thornes
Lower Stonnall
Wood Hayes
Ashmore Park
New Invention
Short Heath
Leighswood
Footherley
Oxley
Harden
Rushall
Aldridge
Wergs
Wednesfield
Little Aston
Perton
Tettenhall Wood
Heath Town
Ashmore Lake
Bentley
Birchills
Wolverhampton
Willenhall
Walsall
Streetly
Four Oaks
Compton
Merry Hill
Bradmore
Blakenhall
Moseley
Priestfield
Bilston
Darlaston
Caldmore
Palfrey
Ettingshall
Lower Penn
Penn
Goldthorn Park
Colton Hills
Pheasey
Moxley
Bradley
Great Barr
New Oscott
Coseley
Wednesbury
Queslett
Kingstanding
Sedgley
Trysull
Wombourne
Tipton
Princes End
Ocker Hill
Hill Top
Grove Vale
Perry Beeches
Blakeley
Himley
Upper Gornal
The Black Country
Dudley
Tividale
Churchfield
West Bromwich
Hamstead
Perry Barr
Erdington
Swindon
Gornalwood
Oldbury
Handsworth
Aston
Gravelly Hill
Wall Heath
Kingswinford
Netherton
Rowley Regis
Smethwick
Bromley
Brierley Hill
West Midlands
Sandwell
Winson Green
Nechells
Wordsley
Cradley Heath
Old Hill
Blackheath
Bearwood
Birmingham
Amblecote
Quarry Bank
Stourton
Stourbridge
Lye
Halesowen
Quinton
Harborne
Edgbaston
Balsall Heath
Sparkhill
Moseley
Whittington
Wollescote
Hasbury
Selly Oak
Hall Green
Pedmore
Hagley
Woodgate
Bartley Green
Bournville
King's Heath
Churchill
Clent
Romsley
Northfield
King's Norton
Frankley
Cotteridge
Blakedown
Broome
Holy Cross
Solihull Lodge
Warstock

Lichfield
Edingale
Harlaston
Haunton
Chilcote
Measham
Clifton Campville
Appleby Magna
Elford
Streethay
Huddlesford
Whittington
Hademore
Leomansley
Wall
Thorpe Constantine
No Man's Heath
Newton Regis
Seckington
Appleby Parva
Austrey
Norton-Juxta-Twycross
Wigginton
STAFFS
Hopwas
Leyfields
Tamworth
Shuttington
Alvecote
Amington
Little Orton
Twycross
Shenstone
Weeford
Hints
Bonehill
Fazeley
Glascote
Polesworth
Warton
Orton-on-the-Hill
Little Hay
Footherley
Watford Gap
M6 TOLL
St Helena
Birchmoor
Dordon
Grendon
Sheepy Magna
Sheepy Parva
Wilnecote
Drayton Bassett
Dosthill
Pinwall
Little Aston
Hill Wood
Roughley
Streetly
Four Oaks
Hill
Whittington
Ratcliffe Culey
Grendon Common
Baddesley Ensor
Atherstone
Middleton
Wood End
Sutton Coldfield
Falcon Lodge
Kingsbury
Baxterley
Mancetter
Witherley
Fenny Drayton
Hurley
Bentley
Grove End
Bodymoor Heath
Marston
New Oscott
Boldmere
Wylde Green
Walmley
Wishaw
Over Green
Ridge Lane
Oldbury
Hartshill
Lea Marston
Erdington
Minworth
Curdworth
Whiteacre Heath
Nether Whitacre
Church End
Chapel End
Camp Hill
Galley Common
Tyburn
Water Orton
Castle Bromwich
Shustoke
Furnace End
Over Whitacre
Ansley
Stockingford
Coleshill
Old Arley
New Arley
Astley
WEST MIDLANDS
WARWICKSHIRE
Kitt's Green
Tile Cross
Maxstoke
Fillongley
Bedworth Heath
Birmingham
Yardley
Marston Green
Sheldon
Corley Ash
Corley
Corley Moor
Kinwalsey
Chapel Green
Ash Green
Keresley
Sparkhill
Moseley
Acock's Green
Elmdon
Little Packington
Butler's End
Meriden
Hawkes End
Olton
Bickenhill
Hampton in Arden
Coundon
Allesley
Great Heath
Radford
Springfield
Hall Green
Elmdon Heath
Eastern Green
Four Oaks
Berkswell
Whoberley
Coventry
Eastcote
Walsal End
Wootton Green
Hockley
Lime Tree Park
0 1 2 3 miles
0 1 2 3 4 5 km

LEICESTERSHIRE
THE NATIONAL FOREST
LEICESTERSHIRE
Ibstock
Ellistown
Stanton under Bardon
Markfield
Newtown Linford
Anstey
Cropston
Thurcaston
Wanlip
Birstall
Heather
Swepstone
Newton Burgoland
Battram
Bagworth
Thornton
Field Head
Groby
Ratby
Glenfield
Leicester
Belgrave
Nailstone
Odstone
Shackerstone
Barton in the Beans
Barlestone
Congerstone
Carlton
Bilstone
Osbaston
Newbold Verdon
Desford
Botcheston
Newtown Unthank
Kirby Muxloe
Kirby Fields
Leicester Forest East
Market Bosworth
Cadeby
Wellsborough
Shenton
Sutton Cheney
Peckleton
Kirby Mallory
Braunstone
Braunstone Town
New Lubbesthorpe
Aylestone
Knighton
Stoneygate
Clarendon Park
Upton
Stapleton
Dadlington
Thurlaston
Enderby
Glen Parva
Eyres Monsell
South Wigston
Blaby
Narborough
Huncote
Earl Shilton
Barwell
Normanton Turville
Stoke Golding
Higham on the Hill
Elmesthorpe
Potters Marston
Whetstone
Littlethorpe
Cosby
Countesthorpe
Kilby Bridge
Croft
Stoney Stanton
Sutton in the Elms
Hinckley
Burbage
Sketchley
Aston Flamville
Sapcote
Primethorpe
Broughton Astley
Willoughby Waterleys
Peatling Magna
Weddington
Nuneaton
St Nicolas Park
Attleborough
Whitestone
Burton Hastings
Smockington
Sharnford
Frolesworth
Leire
Dunton Bassett
Ashby Magna
Bruntingthorpe
Peatling Parva
Griff
Bedworth
Bramcote
Shelford
Wolvey
Copston Magna
Wibtoft
Claybrooke Magna
Claybrooke Parva
Ashby Parva
Ullesthorpe
Gilmorton
Walton
Bulkington
Ryton
Cloudesley Bush
Willey
Bitteswell
Lutterworth
Kimcote
Hawkesbury
Barnacle
Shilton
Hopsford
Withybrook
Ansty
Monks Kirby
Pailton
Little Walton
Cross in Hand
Misterton
Walcote
Foleshill
Potter's Green
Woodway Park
Henley Green
Walsgrave on Sowe
Wyken
Street Ashton
Stretton under Fosse
Churchover
Cotesbach
Gibbet Hill
South Kilworth
Shawell
Brinklow
Easenhall
Harborough Magna
Swinford
Stanford on Avon
Newton
Catthorpe
Binley
M1
M69
M6
A5
A46
A47
A426
A444
A4303
Leicester Forest East Services
Rugby Services
BOSWORTH FIELD 1485
COOMBE ABBEY COUNTRY PARK
BRADGATE PARK & SWITHLAND WOODS
BRADGATE HOUSE (RUINS)
NATIONAL SPACE SCIENCE CENTRE
BURBAGE COMMON & WOODS
FOSSE MEADOWS
153
136
119

Syston
Barsby Lodge
Barsby
Ashby Folville
Markham
Thorpe Satchville
Burrough Hill
Burrough on the Hill
Somerby
Cold Overton
Barleythorpe
Oakham
Wanlip
Birstall
Thurmaston
Barkby
Barkby Thorpe
South Croxton
Twyford
John O'Gaunt
Newbold
Owston
Knossington
Beeby
Hungarton
Marefield
Lowesby
Braunston-in-Rutland
Rushey Mead
Hamilton
Nether Hall
New Humberstone
Humberstone
Belgrave
Keyham
Cold Newton
Tilton on the Hill
Halstead
Scraptoft
Bushby
Thurnby
Evington
Crown Hills
North Evington
Highfields
LEICESTER CITY
Clarendon Park
Stoneygate
Knighton
South Knighton
Aylestone Park
Knighton Fields
Oadby
Stoughton
Houghton on the Hill
Billesdon
Skeffington
Tugby
East Norton
Loddington
Belton in Rutland
Allexton
Wardley
Ridlington
Gaulby
Frisby
King's Norton
Little Stretton
Great Stretton
Illston on the Hill
Rolleston
Noseley
Goadby
Wigston
Wigston Magna
South Wigston
Newton Harcourt
Great Glen
Scotland
Burton Overy
Carlton Curlieu
Shangton
Stockerston
Horninghold
Hallaton
Glooston
Blaston
Stonton Wyville
Cranoe
LEICESTERSHIRE
Kilby Bridge
Kilby
Wistow
The Woodlands
Kibworth Harcourt
Kibworth Beauchamp
Tur Langton
Church Langton
Slawston
Medbourne
Fleckney
Smeeton Westerby
Saddington
East Langton
Thorpe Langton
Welham
Weston by Welland
Drayton
Peatling Magna
Arnesby
Shearsby
Bruntingthorpe
Peatling Parva
Upper Bruntingthorpe
Mowsley
Knaptoft
Laughton
Gumley
Foxton
Ashley
Sutton Bassett
Middleton
East Carlton
Great Bowden
Wilbarston
Stoke Albany
Dingley
Brampton Ash
Carlton Purlieus
Walton
Lubenham
Market Harborough
Little Bowden
Theddingworth
Marston Trussell
East Farndon
Braybrooke
Pipewell
Husbands Bosworth
North Kilworth
Great Oxendon
Little Oxendon
Desborough
Rushton
South Kilworth
Sibbertoft
Clipston
Arthingworth
Rothwell
WEST NORTHANTS
Welford
Thorpe Underwood
Harrington
Kelmarsh
Orton
Thorpe Malsor
Naseby
Loddington
Stanford Reservoir
Welford Res
Sulby Reservoir
Saddington Reservoir
A6
A47
A563
A607
A427
A4304
A5199
A508
A14
B6047
B664
0 1 2 3 miles
0 1 2 3 4 5 km

Exton
Burley
RUTLAND FALCONRY & OWL CENTRE
LOSECOAT FIELD 1470
Tickencote Warren
Ryhall
Belmesthorpe
Greatford
Barholm
Stowe
Oakham
OAKHAM CASTLE
RUTLAND COUNTY MUSEUM
Barnsdale
Whitwell
Empingham
Tickencote
Great Casterton
Little Casterton
RUTLAND OPEN AIR THEATRE
Tallington
Uffington
Upper Hambleton
Rutland Water
Egleton
RUTLAND WATER
Vale of Catmose
The Grange
Northfields
BREWERY MUSEUM
Stamford
BURGHLEY HOUSE
Tinwell
Normanton
Edith Weston
Ketton
Aldgate
Geeston
Easton on the Hill
PRIEST'S HOUSE
Wothorpe
Burghley Park
Pilsgate
Bainton
Ashton
Barnack
BARNACK HILLS AND HOLES
Ufford
Brooke
Gunthorpe
River Gwash
Manton
Lyndon
North Luffenham
North Luffenham Airfield (disused)
Wing
Pilton
Preston
South Luffenham
Collyweston
Wittering
Southorpe
Ayston
Glaston
Morcott
Barrowden
Tixover
Duddington
COLLYWESTON GREAT WOOD & EASTON HORNSTOCKS
Thornhaugh
SACREWELL FARM & COUNTRY CENTRE
Upton
Uppingham
Bisbrooke
Seaton
Wakerley
River Welland
BEDFORD PURLIEUS
Wansford
Stibbington
Sutton
River Nene
Lyddington
LYDDINGTON BEDE HOUSE
Thorpe by Water
Harringworth
Shotley
Laxton
King's Cliffe
Yarwell
Sibson
Water Newton
Nassington
Apethorpe
Blatherwycke
Eyebrook Reservoir
Gretton
KIRBY HALL
Bulwick
Woodnewton
Elton
ELTON HALL
Fotheringhay
FOTHERINGHAY CASTLE
Caldecott
Deene
DEENE PARK
Deenethorpe
Southwick
SOUTHWICK HALL
Eaglethorpe
Rockingham
ROCKINGHAM CASTLE
Cotterstock
Tansor
Warmington
Glapthorn
Corby
Great Weldon
Little Weldon
Upper Benefield
Lower Benefield
Oundle
Ashton
Lutton
Polebrook
Stanion
Stoke Doyle
BARNWELL
Great Oakley
Little Oakley
Brigstock
LYVEDEN NEW BIELD
FERMYN WOODS
Armston
Hemington
NORTH NORTHANTS
Barnwell St Andrew
Barnwell
Barnwell All Saints
Pilton
Wadenhoe
Luddington in the Brook
Newton
Geddington
ELEANOR CROSS
Achurch
Thurning
Wigsthorpe
Sudborough
Aldwincle
BOUGHTON HOUSE
Weekley
Lowick
Thorpe Waterville
Clopton
Winwick
Warkton
Grafton Underwood
Kettering
ART GALLERY & MUSEUM
Slipton
Twywell
Islip
Thrapston
THRAPSTON SERVICES
Titchmarsh
Polopit
A1
A47
A43
A606
A6003
A6121
A427
A6116
A605
A6183
A1175
B1443

Market Deeping
Deeping St James
Towngate
Stowe
Deeping Gate
West Deeping
Maxey
Northborough
Etton
Glinton
Peakirk
Helpston
Bainton
Ashton
Ufford
Marholm
Crowland
Nene Terrace
Thorney
Thorney Toll
Newborough
Eye
Eye Green
PETERBOROUGH
Werrington
Gunthorpe
Paston
Walton
New England
Dogsthorpe
Millfield
Eastfield
Newark
Ravensthorpe
Bretton
Westwood
Longthorpe
Peterborough
Woodston
Fletton
Fengate
Stanground
Old Fletton
Orton Wistow
Orton Waterville
Orton Longueville
Orton Brimbles
Orton Malborne
Orton Goldhay
Orton Southgate
Hampton Hargate
Hampton Vale
Farcet
Yaxley
Norman Cross
Stilton
Folksworth
Morborne
Haddon
Alwalton
Chesterton
Water Newton
Castor
Ailsworth
Sutton
Stibbington
Upton
Elton
Over End
Whittlesey
Eastrea
Coates
Turves
Eldernell
Inham's End
North Side
Stone Bridge Corner
Bedford Level
North Level
Pondersbridge
CAMBRIDGESHIRE
Ramsey Mereside
Ramsey St Mary's
Ramsey Heights
Ramsey
Ramsey Forty Foot
Bury
Upwood
Great Raveley
Little Raveley
Wistow
Warboys
Fenton
Benwick
Holme
Conington
Glatton
Sawtry
Caldecote
Denton
Washingley
Lutton
Chapel End
Papley
Hemington
Luddington in the Brook
Great Gidding
Little Gidding
Steeple Gidding
Winwick
Coppingford
Hamerton
Wood Walton
Church End
Wennington
Abbots Ripton
Chapel Head
Gedney Hill
Shepeau Stow
Dowsdale
Peterborough Services
FERRY MEADOWS
NENE VALLEY RAILWAY
FLAG FEN ARCHAEOLOGY PARK
PETERBOROUGH MUSEUM
THE WESTON HOMES STADIUM
EAST OF ENGLAND SHOWGROUND
CROWN LAKES
CASTOR HANGLANDS
SACREWELL FARM & COUNTRY CENTRE
HOLME FEN
WOODWALTON FEN
UPWOOD MEADOWS
MONKS WOOD
HAMERTON ZOO PARK
RURAL MUSEUM
RAMSEY ABBEY GATEHOUSE
Upwood Airfield (disused)
Peterborough (Conington)
Peterborough (Sibson)
A1(M)
A1
A15
A16
A47
A605
A1139
A1260
A141
B1040
B1043
B1090
B1095
B1096
B1093
B660
156
137
122
0 1 2 3 miles
0 1 2 3 4 5 km

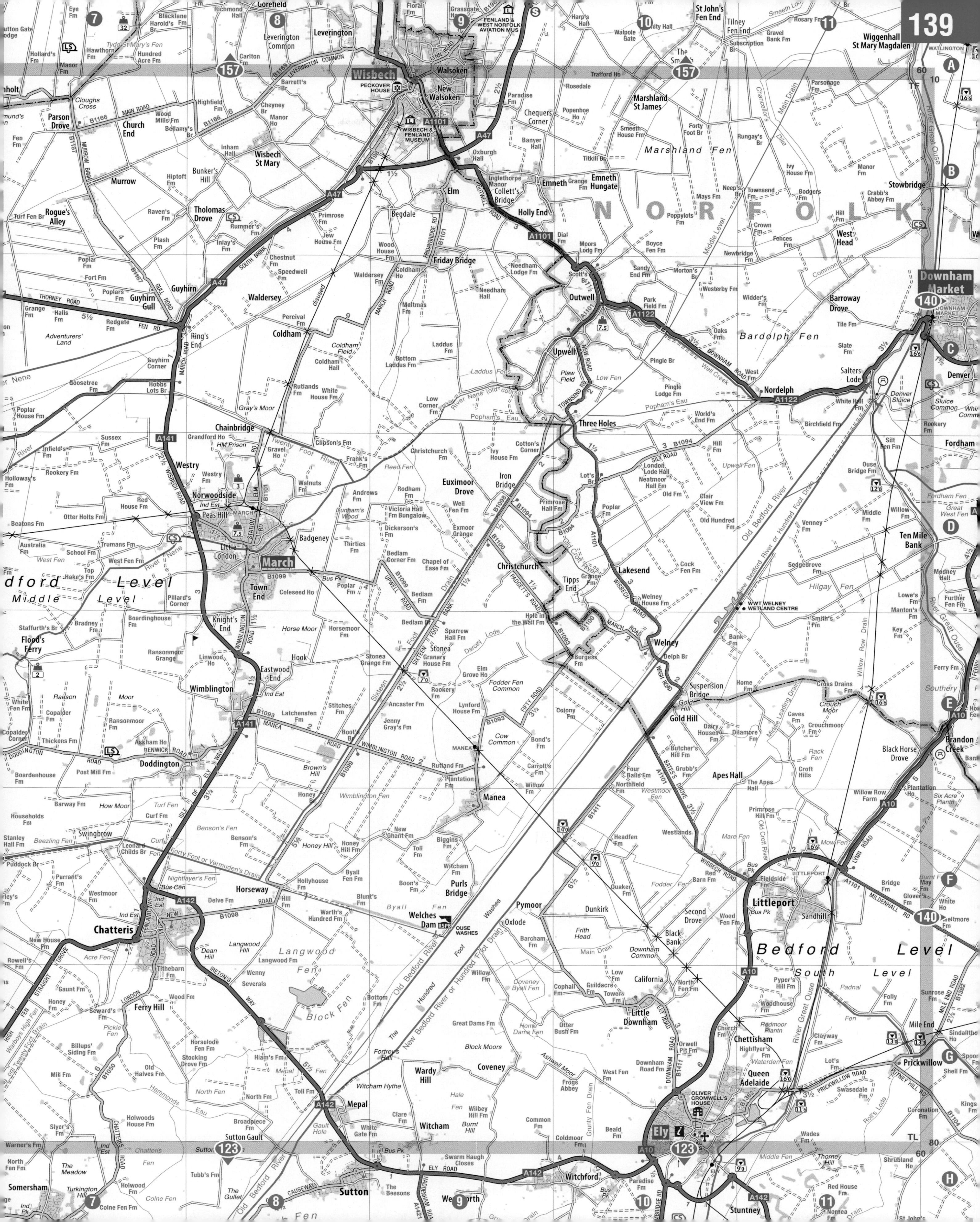
Wisbech
Walsoken
New Walsoken
Peckover House
Wisbech & Fenland Museum
Fenland & West Norfolk Aviation Mus
Leverington
Leverington Common
Gorefield
Wisbech St Mary
Parson Drove
Church End
Murrow
Tholomas Drove
Rogue's Alley
Guyhirn
Guyhirn Gull
Ring's End
Waldersey
Coldham
Elm
Friday Bridge
Begdale
Emneth
Emneth Hungate
Holly End
Outwell
Upwell
Marshland St James
Marshland Fen
St John's Fen End
Tilney Fen End
Wiggenhall St Mary Magdalen
Stowbridge
Downham Market
West Head
Barroway Drove
Bardolph Fen
Nordelph
Salters Lode
Denver
Denver Sluice
Fordham
NORFOLK
Three Holes
Welney
WWT Welney Wetland Centre
Lakesend
Christchurch
Euximoor Drove
Iron Bridge
Tipps End
Ten Mile Bank
Hilgay Fen
Chainbridge
Westry
Norwoodside
Peas Hill
March
Town End
Badgeney
Little London
Middle Level
Bedford Level
Knight's End
Wimblington
Eastwood End
Stonea
Hook
Doddington
Manea
Cow Common
Gold Hill
Suspension Bridge
Apes Hall
Southery
Brandon Creek
Black Horse Drove
Littleport
Sandhill
Bedford Level South Level
Chatteris
Horseway
Welches Dam
Ouse Washes
Purls Bridge
Pymoor
Oxlode
Langwood Fen
Block Fen
Ferry Hill
Mepal
Witcham
Wardy Hill
Coveney
Little Downham
California
Black Bank
Chettisham
Queen Adelaide
Prickwillow
Ely
Oliver Cromwell's House
Witchford
Sutton
Sutton Gault
Stuntney
Somersham
Old Bedford River
New Bedford River or Hundred Foot Drain
Forty Foot or Vermuden's Drain
Sixteen Foot Drain
Popham's Eau
River Nene
River Great Ouse
Flood's Ferry
Swingbrow
A47
A141
A142
A1101
A1122
A10
B1098
B1099
B1093
B1100
B1101
B1094
B1411
B1382
B1050
B1166
B1187
157
140
123
TF
TL

Downham Market
Swaffham
Watlington
Tottenhill
Wormegay
Marham
Shouldham
Runcton Holme
South Runcton
Shouldham Thorpe
Fincham
Barton Bendish
Beachamwell
Shingham
Cockley Cley
Stow Bardolph
Wimbotsham
Stradsett
Bexwell
Crimplesham
Broomhill
Denver
Wereham
Boughton
Oxborough
Gooderstone
West Dereham
Stoke Ferry
Whittington
Wretton
Fordham
Foulden
Hilborough
Bodney
Hilgay
Northwold
Didlington
Brookville
Methwold
Methwold Hythe
Cranwich
Mundford
Ickburgh
Southery
Feltwell
Weeting
Hockwold cum Wilton
Brandon
Santon Downham
Lakenheath
Brandon Creek
Brandon Bank
Little Ouse
Prickwillow
Mile End
Elveden
Eriswell
Undley
Claypits
West Tofts
Lynford
NORFOLK
SUFFOLK
THETFORD FOREST PARK
Breckland
Level
River Wissey
River Great Ouse
River Little Ouse
Ten Mile Bank
Stowbridge
158
139
124
0 1 2 3 miles
0 1 2 3 4 5 km

Little Fransham
Lyon's Green
Scarning
Toftwood
Clint Green
Mattishall Burgh
Mattishall
East Tuddenham
Colton
Necton
Ivy Todd
West End
Daffy Green
Yaxham
Westfield
Welborne
Holme Hale
Bradenham
High Green
Thorpe Row
Winburgh
Brandon Parva
Barford
North Pickenham
Shipdham
Garvestone
Thuxton
Runhall
Barnham Broom
Crowshill
Letton Green
Reymerston
Danemoor Green
Carleton Forehoe
Wramplingham
Ashill
Cranworth
Southburgh
Kimberley
Woodrising
Hardingham
Saham Hills
Crownthorpe
Wicklewood
Great Cressingham
Saham Toney
Ovington
Carbrooke
Frost Row
Hingham
Hackford
Wymondham
N O R F O L K
Watton
Scoulton
Deopham
Little Cressingham
Griston
Little Ellingham
Statland Common
Deopham Green
Morley St Botolph
Suton
Merton
Northacre
Caston
Rockland St Peter
Great Ellingham
Spooner Row
The Arms
Thompson
Stow Bedon
Rockland All Saints
Besthorpe
Tottington
Attleborough
Stanford
Breckles
Lower Stow Bedon
Mount Pleasant
Burgh Common
Shropham
Great Hockham
Puddledock
Old Buckenham
Church Green
Carleton Rode
Snetterton
Stonebridge
Illington
East Wretham
Wretham
Eccles Road
Stacksford
Wilby
New Buckenham
Larling
Harling Road
Hunt's Corner
Banham
Croxton
Quidenham
Bridgham
East Harling
Kenninghall
Dam Green
Winfarthing
Middle Harling
Kenninghall Heath
Brettenham
Shadwell
West Harling
North Lopham
Fersfield
Shelfanger
Thetford
Rushford
Garboldisham
South Lopham
Bressingham
Gasthorpe
Knettishall
Euston
Blo' Norton
Fen Street
Hopton
Coney Weston
Barnham
Thelnetham
Market
Roydon
A11
A1066
A1075
A134
B1108
B1077
B1111
B1113
B1135
159
125
142

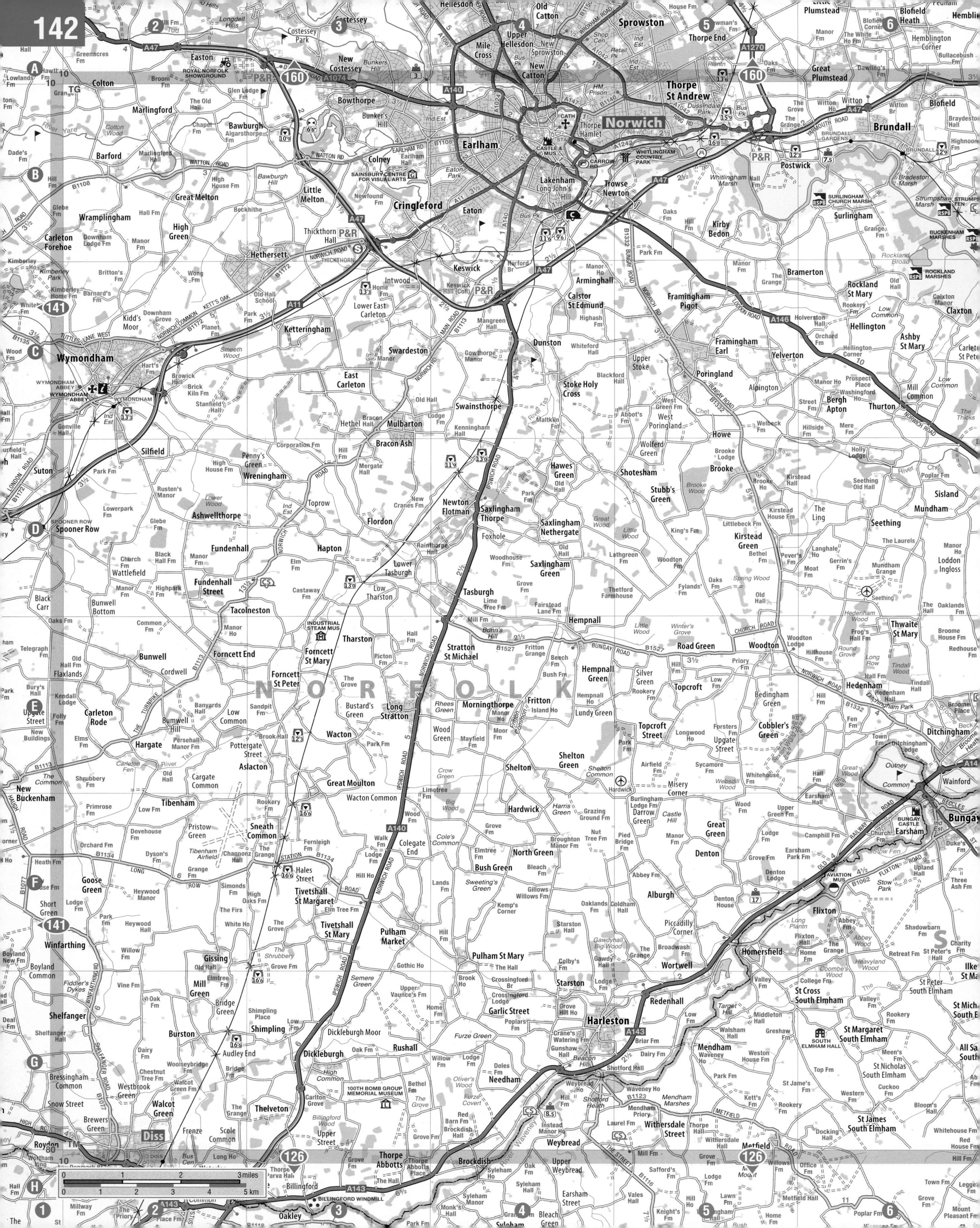

142
Hellesdon
Old Catton
Sprowston
Thorpe End
Little Plumstead
Blofield Heath
Costessey
Costessey Park
Easton
Royal Norfolk Showground
New Costessey
Mile Cross
Upper Hellesdon
New Sprowston
New Catton
Great Plumstead
Colton
Marlingford
Bowthorpe
Bawburgh
Earlham
Norwich
Thorpe St Andrew
Thorpe Hamlet
Brundall
Blofield
Barford
Colney
Sainsbury Centre for Visual Arts
Whitlingham Country Park
Postwick
Great Melton
Little Melton
Cringleford
Eaton
Lakenham
Trowse Newton
Surlingham
Wramplingham
High Green
Carleton Forehoe
Hethersett
Thickthorn Hall
Keswick
Kirby Bedon
Bramerton
Arminghall
Caistor St Edmund
Framingham Pigot
Rockland St Mary
Claxton
Intwood
Lower East Carleton
Ketteringham
Kidd's Moor
Wymondham
Wymondham Abbey
Swardeston
Dunston
Framingham Earl
Hellington
Ashby St Mary
Yelverton
East Carleton
Stoke Holy Cross
Upper Stoke
Poringland
Alpington
Bergh Apton
Thurton
Swainsthorpe
Mulbarton
Bracon Ash
Hethel
West Poringland
Howe
Silfield
Wreningham
Brooke
Suton
Hawes' Green
Shotesham
Stubb's Green
Sisland
Mundham
Spooner Row
Ashwellthorpe
Toprow
Flordon
Newton Flotman
Saxlingham Thorpe
Saxlingham Nethergate
Seething
Kirstead Green
Fundenhall
Hapton
Lower Tasburgh
Saxlingham Green
Loddon Ingloss
Wattlefield
Fundenhall Street
Tasburgh
Low Tharston
Tacolneston
Industrial Steam Mus
Tharston
Hempnall
Thwaite St Mary
Bunwell
Forncett End
Forncett St Mary
Stratton St Michael
Road Green
Woodton
Hedenham
Forncett St Peter
Hempnall Green
Topcroft
N O R F O L K
Carleton Rode
Long Stratton
Morningthorpe
Fritton
Bedingham Green
Ditchingham
Hargate
Wacton
Topcroft Street
Cobbler's Green
Aslacton
Shelton Green
Shelton
Great Moulton
Wacton Common
Wainford
New Buckenham
Tibenham
Hardwick
Bungay
Bungay Castle
Earsham
Sneath Common
Great Green
Denton
North Green
Goose Green
Hales Street
Tivetshall St Margaret
Bush Green
Alburgh
Flixton
Short Green
Tivetshall St Mary
Pulham Market
Winfarthing
Gissing
Pulham St Mary
Wortwell
Homersfield
Boyland Common
Mill Green
Starston
St Cross South Elmham
Shelfanger
Burston
Shimpling
Garlic Street
Harleston
Redenhall
Dickleburgh Moor
Rushall
St Margaret South Elmham
Audley End
Dickleburgh
Mendham
St Nicholas South Elmham
Bressingham Common
Westbrook Green
Needham
100th Bomb Group Memorial Museum
Walcot Green
Snow Street
Thelveton
Weybread
Withersdale Street
St James South Elmham
Brewers Green
Frenze
Scole Common
Upper Street
Diss
Roydon
Metfield
Thorpe Abbotts
Brockdish
Upper Weybread
Billingford
Billingford Windmill
Oakley
Earsham Street
Syleham
Norfolk
0 1 2 3 miles
0 1 2 3 4 5 km

Caister-on-Sea
Caister Pt
Acle
161
North Burlingham
Damgate
Stokesby
Runham
West End
West Caister
North Denes
Mautby
THRIGBY HALL WILDLIFE GARDENS
CAISTER CASTLE & MOTOR MUSEUM
Lingwood
Beighton
Moulton St Mary
Tunstall
South Burlingham
Halvergate
THE BROADS
Runham Vauxhall
Great Yarmouth
North Beach
The Beach
Cobholm Island
ELIZABETHAN HOUSE, LADY EVA & TOLHOUSE MUSEUMS
SEA LIFE CENTRE
PLEASURE BEACH
Southtown
Breydon Water
Buckenham
Hassingham
Freethorpe
Wickhampton
Southwood
BERNEY ARMS WINDMILL
BERNEY MARSHES & BREYDON WATER
BURGH CASTLE
Burgh Castle
Bradwell
South Denes
Cantley
Limpenhoe
Gorleston-on-Sea
Belton
Limpenhoe Hill
PETTITS ANIMAL ADVENTURE PARK
Reedham
Chedgrave Marshes
River Yare
River Waveney
Langley Street
Hardley Street
REDWINGS HORSE SANCTUARY (CALDECOTT)
Browston Green
Hopton on Sea
Nogdam End
Fritton
Chedgrave
Lower Thurlton
ST OLAVE'S PRIORY
St Olaves
The Dell
Lound
Loddon
Heckingham
Thurlton
Thorpe
Herringfleet
Blundeston
Corton
Hales
Raveningham
RAVENINGHAM GARDENS
HALES HALL BARN & GARDENS
Haddiscoe
Somerleyton
Three Cocked Hat
PLEASUREWOOD HILLS LEISURE PARK
Gunton
Brundish
Maypole Green
Toft Monks
Wheatacre Marshes
Burgh Marshes
Oulton
North Beach
Lowestoft Denes
LOWESTOFT MARITIME MUS
Kirby Cane
Stockton
Waterheath
Wheatacre
Normanston
Waterloo
Aldeby
Burgh St Peter
Lowestoft Ness
Oulton Broad
Lowestoft
Ellingham
Kirby Row
Geldeston
Gillingham
Dockeney
Dunburgh
Beccles Marshes
River Waveney
Castle Marsh
Claremont Pier
Kirkley
Beccles
BECCLES DISTRICT MUSEUM
Mettingham
Barsham
Shipmeadow
Worlingham
Barnby
Pakefield
EAST ANGLIA TRANSPORT MUS
Carlton Colville
North Cove
Gisleham
Ringsfield
Ringsfield Corner
Mutford
Hulver Street
Ilketshall St Andrew
Weston
Ellough
Rushmere
Kessingland
SUFFOLK
Henstead
AFRICA ALIVE!
Kessingland Beach
Shadingfield
Sotterley
Ilketshall St Lawrence
Redisham
Benacre
Benacre Ness
West End
Stone Street
Cox Common
Cuckold's Green
Wrentham
Mill Common
Brampton
Frostenden
Covehithe
Stoven
Westhall
South Cove
Rumburgh
Spexhall
Clay Common
Uggeshall
Cove Bottom
The Warren
127
Wissett
Broadway
Wangford
Upper Holton
Reydon
Reydon Smear
HALESWORTH AIRFIELD MEM MUS
Chediston Green

Morfa Nefyn
162
Nefyn
Edern
Groesffordd
Cwmistir
Penrhyn Cwmistir
Aber Geirch
Borth Wen
Porth Dinllaen
Trwyn Porth Dinllaen
Penrhyn Nefyn
Porth Nefyn
LLŶN MARITIME MUSEUM
Mynydd Nefyn
Moel Ty-Gwyn
Wern
Tir Bach
Tyddyn Uchaf
Bodeilias
Hendre Penprys
Garn Boduan 280
Tan-y-graig
Plasyngheidio
Glanrhyd
Moelypenmaen
Boduan
Tref-erwyn
Maesoglan
Glan-y-gors
Hendre
Coed Bodlel
CORS GEIRCH
Cors Geirch
Meillionen
Mochras
Traian
Mathan Isaf
Cefn Mine
Gallt y Beren
Tan-y-bryn
Rhyd-y-clafdy
Penrhos
Polish Home
Cefn Llanfair
Bryn Celyn Hall
Tyddyncaled
Wern Fawr
Afon Rhyd-hir
Rhos-y-llan
Porth Towyn
Porth Ysglaig
Towyn
Porth Ysgaden
Tudweiliog
Cefn Leisiog
Y Ddôl
Nyffryn
Brynodol
Tan-llan
Porth Gwylan
Penrallt
Gwyndy
Penllech Bach
Ty-mawr
Penrhyn Melyn
Cefntreuddyn
PwNgoed
Rhos-ddû
Dinas
Madryn Castle
Moel Caerau
371 Carn Fadryn
CARN FADRUN (FORT)
Garn Bach
Garnfadryn
Cefnamwlch
Ffridd-goch
Ffridd-wen
Penybryn
Tyn Llidiart
Myfyr
Tyn Simdda
Porth Colmon
Traeth Penllech
Porth Wen Bâch
Porth Ty-mawr
Berthaur
Porth Colmon
Morfa
Bryn Geinach
Penllech
Mynydd Cefnamwlch 182
Tregwm
Bryn-mawr
Llaniestyn
Penbodlas
Tynewydd
Carneddol
Pen-y-graig
WALES COAST PATH
Llangwnnadl
Porth Widlin
Porth Ferin
Penrhyn Mawr
Maen Mellt
Ty-mawr
Dinas
Porth Iago
Trwyn Glas
Porth Oer
Porth y Wrâch
Ty-hen
Methlem
Sarn Meyllteyrn
Trefaes
Cellar Fm
Bronphilip Fm
Inkermann Br
Rhedyn
Foel Bach
Foel Fawr
Henllys
Penarwel
Carreg y
Llanbedrog
Plas Glyn-y-weddw
Mynydd Tirycwmwd 132
Trwyn Llanbedrog
Pen-y-bryn
Lleiniau
Brynhunog Fawr
Llety'r Wym
Pant
Bryncroes
Tyn-y-coed
Coch-y-moel
Trygarn
Afon Soch
Nanhoron
Mynytho Common
Mynytho
Capel Newydd
G W Y N E D D
Pen-y-groeslon
Tocia
Hirwaun
Rhydlios
Botwnnog
Faerdre
Gelliwig
Llandegwning
Bryn Llewelyn
Coed-y-fron
Nant
Bodwi
Rhandir
Tan-y-mynydd
NEOLITHIC AXE FACTORY
304 Mynydd Rhiw
Tyddyn Corn Fm
Tyn-y-parc
Talsarn
Saithbont
Barach
Tyddyn Gwyn
Fach Fm
The Warren
Dinas Bâch
Dinas Fawr
Mynydd Carreg
Capel Carmel
Porthorion
Bryn-mawr
Carreg
Rhoshirwaun
Felin Uchaf
Meillionydd
Cruga Bach
Glangors
L L Ŷ N
Neigwl Ganol
Llawrdref Bellaf
Llangian
Glan Soch
WALES COAST PATH
PLAS-YN-RHIW
Ty Mawr
St Tudwal's Road
Penbennar
Abersoch
Angorfa St Tudwal
Morfa Gors
Braich Anelog
Anelog
Llanllawen
Porth Llanllawen
Mynydd Ystum
Hendre
Afon Daron
Penycaerau
Ty Cerrig
Rhiw
Ty Croes Mawr
Mynydd Graig
Trefollwyn
Punt Gwynedd
Towyn
Llanengan
Sarn Bach
Porth Tocyn
Penrhyn Du
Porth Bach
St Tudwal's Island East
Maen Du
Braich y Noddfa
Mynydd Mawr 160
Braich y Pwll
Gwyddel
Uwchmynydd
Aberdaron
Porth Simdde
Aberdaron Bay
Bryn Fm
Llanfaelrhys
MYNYDD-Y-CRAIG HEADLAND
PORTH NEIGWL OR HELL'S MOUTH
Tai-morfa
Newydd Fm
Bwlchtocyn
Marchroes
Cim
Porth Cadlan
Porth Ysgo
Trwyn Talfarach
Ogof Lwyd
Trwyn y Penrhyn
Ebolion
Porth Cloch
Trwyn Maen Melyn
Trwyn y Gwyddel
Bodermid
Porth Felen
Parwyd
Porth y Pistyll
Hen Borth
Ynys Gwylan-fawr
Ynys Gwylan-bâch
Pen y Cil
Nant Fm
Corn Fm
Nant-y-big
St Tudwal's Island West
Trwyn y Fulfran
MYNUDD CILAN
Trwyn Carreg-y-tir
Trwyn y Ffosle
Mynydd Gilan
Porth Ceiriad
Pared-mawr
Pistyll Cim
Trwyn yr Wylfa
Cilan Uchaf
Trwyn Llech-y-doll
Trwyn Cilan
Maen Bugail
Bardsey Sound
Swnt Enlli
Bae y Rhigol
Trwyn y Gorlech
Bae'r Nant
ST MARY'S ABBEY (RUINS)
OLD CROSSES
Maen Iau
Plas-bach
Carreg yr Honwy
YNYS ENLLI
Bardsey Island
Ynys Enlli
Porth Solfach
Cafn Enlli
Henllwyn
Ystwffwl Glas
Ogof Lladron
Ogof Diban
B4417
B4412
A497
B4354
B4415
B4413
A499
SH
10
40
0 1 2 3 miles
0 1 2 3 4 5 km

Penrhyn Llyn
Ysgubor Plas
Tyddyn Cestyll
Cefn Isaf
Llwyndyrys
Trallwyn Hall
Castell Gwgan
Maen-llwyd
Pencaenewydd
Talafon
Pentyrch isaf
Lôn-las
Llangybi
Maes Gwyn Uchaf
Penbryn
Rhosgyll
Fron-oleu
Bettws Bach
Rhoslan
Bryniau Ystumcegid
Bryn Hywel
Garnedd-hir
Garth Fm
Y Fedw 267
Prenteg
Pont Croesor
Bryn
Mynydd-mawr
Tyn Coed
Plas
162
Geufron
Ynysieci
Brynllefrith
Fetin Bencoed
Tyddyn-y-felin
Tyddyn cethin
Braich-y-saint
Tyddyn-lolyn
163
Penmorfa
Allt-wen
Tremadog
Coed Tremadog
Glan-y-morfa
Welsh Highland Heritage Railway
Welsh Highland Railway
Pen-y-Mount
Fron
Pentreuchaf
Rhos-fawr
Rhyd-y-gwystl
Pencraig
Bryngwdyn
Glyncoed
Llanarmon
Llwyn-dwyfog
Dynana
Pentrefelin
Wern
Moel-y-Gest 262
Bus Pk
Porthmadog
Y Garth
Penrhyn
Penrhyndeudraeth
Ty Du Isaf
Coed Rhos-fawr
Tyn-rhos-fawr
Y Ffôr
Cromlech
Pen-carth
Cabin Wood
Llanystumdwy
Trefan
Pen-y-Bryn
Railway Museum
Porthmadog Harbour
Minffordd
Bryn Rodyn
Llannerch
Brynaerau
Chwilog
Penarth Bach
Lloyd George Museum
Criccieth
Coed-y-llyn
Maritime Mus
Britannia Terr
Boston Lodge Halt
Rhosydd
Bryngoleu
Brynllaeth
Clogwyn
Penarth Fawr
Afon Wen
Bont Fechan
Muriau
Criccieth Castle
Morfa Bychan
Borth-y-Gest
Llandecwyn
Llannor
Tan-y-graig
Broom Hall
Abererch
Hafan y Mor
Penychain
Black Rock Sand
Wales Coast Path
Portmeirion
Brynhynog
Gorphwysfa
Efailnewydd
Pensarn Fm
Denio
Penrallt
Bryn-ynys
Allt Fawr
Ind Est
Pwllheli
Carreg yr Imbill
Penrhyn
Cerrig y Barcdy
Pen-ychain
Traeth Bach
Talsarnau
Afon y Glyn
Harlech Pt
Ynys
Tygwyn
Glan-y-wern
Glyn-cywarch
West End
Marian-y-mor
South Beach
Traeth Crugan
Morfa Harlech
Ty'n-yr-acrau
146
Coed Penmaen
Glyn Morfa
Moel Goedog
Merthyr Fm
Tremadog Bay
Bae Tremadog
Harlech
Foel Senigl
Harlech Castle
Maesyraelfor
Tyddyn Felin
Llanfair
Halod-yallyn
Llandanwg
Slate Caverns
Pen-y-bont
Pensarn
Coed Lletywalter
Pen-sarn
Llanbedr
Pentre Gwynfryn
Coed Aberartro
Shell Island
Taltreuddyn
Hendy
Llanbedr
Uwchlaw'r-coed
Pen-y-bryn
Morfa Dyffryn
Llwynion-fechan
Ynys-Gwrtheyrn
Coed Ystumgwern
Tal y fitnon
Waun Hir
Llanenddwyn
Dyffryn Burial Chamber
Meifod-uchaf
Cors-y-Gedol
Dyffryn Ardudwy
Llanddwywe
Tal-y-bont
Llecheiddior
Eithin-fynydd
Plas-canol
Llwyndu Fm
Llanaber
Barmouth (Abermaw)
RNLI Lifeboat Museum
Fairbourne Railway
Barmouth Bay
Bae Bermo
Golf Halt
Fairbourne
Cefnfeusydd Fm
Borthwen Fm
Gwastadgoed
Hendre
Llwyngwril
Rhiwgaeron
Y Rhos
A497
A499
A487
B4354
A496
A493
SH
60
10
A
B
C
D
E
F
G
H
7
8
9
10
11

Llanfrothen
Rhyd
Tan-y-bwlch
Maentwrog
Llan Ffestiniog
Pont yr Afon-Gam
Bont Newydd
Gellilydan
Penrhyndeudraeth
Minffordd
Portmeirion
Cilfor
Llandecwyn
Caerwych
Talsarnau
Soar
Ynys
Glan-y-wern
Eisingrug
Glyn-Cywarch
Llyn Trawsfynydd
Trawsfynydd
Pont Dolydd Prysor
Castell Prysor
Cwm Prysor
Y-Gors
Moel Llyfnant 751
Arenig Fawr
Foel Boeth 619
Bronaber
Buarthmeini
Rhinog Fawr
Rhinog 720
Rhinog Fach 712
Y Llethr 724
Diffwys 750
Pen-y-bont
Gwynfryn
Cors-y-Gedol
Dyffryn Ardudwy
Tal-y-bont
Llanaber
Barmouth (Abermaw)
Barmouth Bay
Bae Bermo
Fairbourne
Friog
Arthog
Ynysgyfflog
Cutiau
Caerdeon
Bontddu
Penmaenpool
Abergwynant
Llanelltyd
Dolgellau
Tabor
Brithdir
Bont Newydd
Rhydymain
Llanfachreth
Ganllwyd
Coed y Brenin Forest Park
Bed-y-coedwr
Pont Aber-Geirw
Cwm-hesgen
Capel Hermon
Rhobell Fawr 734
Dduallt 662
Pont Fronwydd
Snowdonia National Park
Parc Cenedlaethol Eryri
Cymer Abbey
Cadair Idris 893
Mynydd Moel 863
Minffordd
Dol-y-cae
Tal-y-llyn
Corris Uchaf
Corris
Aberllefenni
Aberangell
Dyfi Forest
Llanfihangel-y-pennant
Castell y Bere
Camlan
Cerist
Waun-Oer 670
Maen Du 674

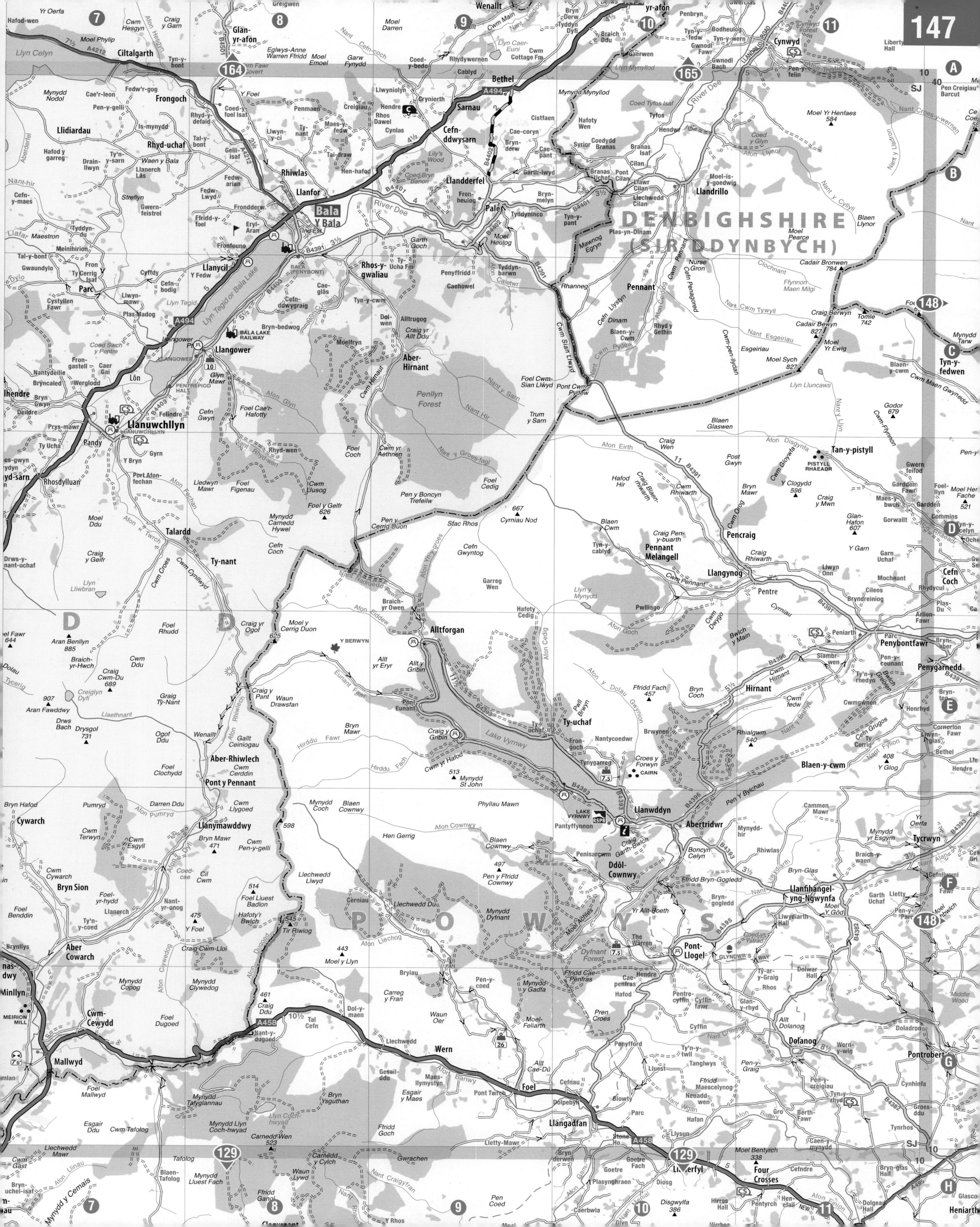
DENBIGHSHIRE
(SIR DDYNBYCH)
POWYS
Bala
Y Bala
Llyn Tegid or Bala Lake
Llyn Celyn
Ciltalgarth
Frongoch
Glan-yr-afon
Llidiardau
Rhyd-uchaf
Rhiwlas
Llanfor
Llandderfel
Sarnau
Bethel
Cefn-ddwysarn
Cynwyd
Llandrillo
Pale
Llanycil
Parc
Llangower
Llanuwchllyn
Pandy
Rhosdylluan
Talardd
Ty-nant
Rhos-y-gwaliau
Aber-Hirnant
Penllyn Forest
Cadair Berwyn 827
Cadair Bronwen 784
Moel Sych 827
Tomle 742
Tan-y-pistyll
Pistyll Rhaeadr
Pennant
Pencraig
Pennant Melangell
Llangynog
Pentre
Penybontfawr
Penygarnedd
Hirnant
Alltforgan
Y Berwyn
Lake Vyrnwy
Ty-uchaf
Llanwddyn
Abertridwr
Blaen-y-cwm
Ddôl-Cownwy
Llanfihangel-yng-Ngwynfa
Pont-Llogel
Dyfnant Forest
Aber-Rhiwlech
Pont y Pennant
Llanymawddwy
Cywarch
Bryn Sion
Aber Cowarch
Cwm-Cewydd
Mallwyd
Minllyn
Wern
Foel
Llangadfan
Llanerfyl
Four Crosses
Dolanog
Pontrobert
Tycrwyn
Heniarth
Aran Benllyn 885
Aran Fawddwy 907
A494
A4212
A458
B4391
B4393
B4396
B4395
B4382
B4401
B4402
B4403
B4501
164
165
148
129
SJ
10
40

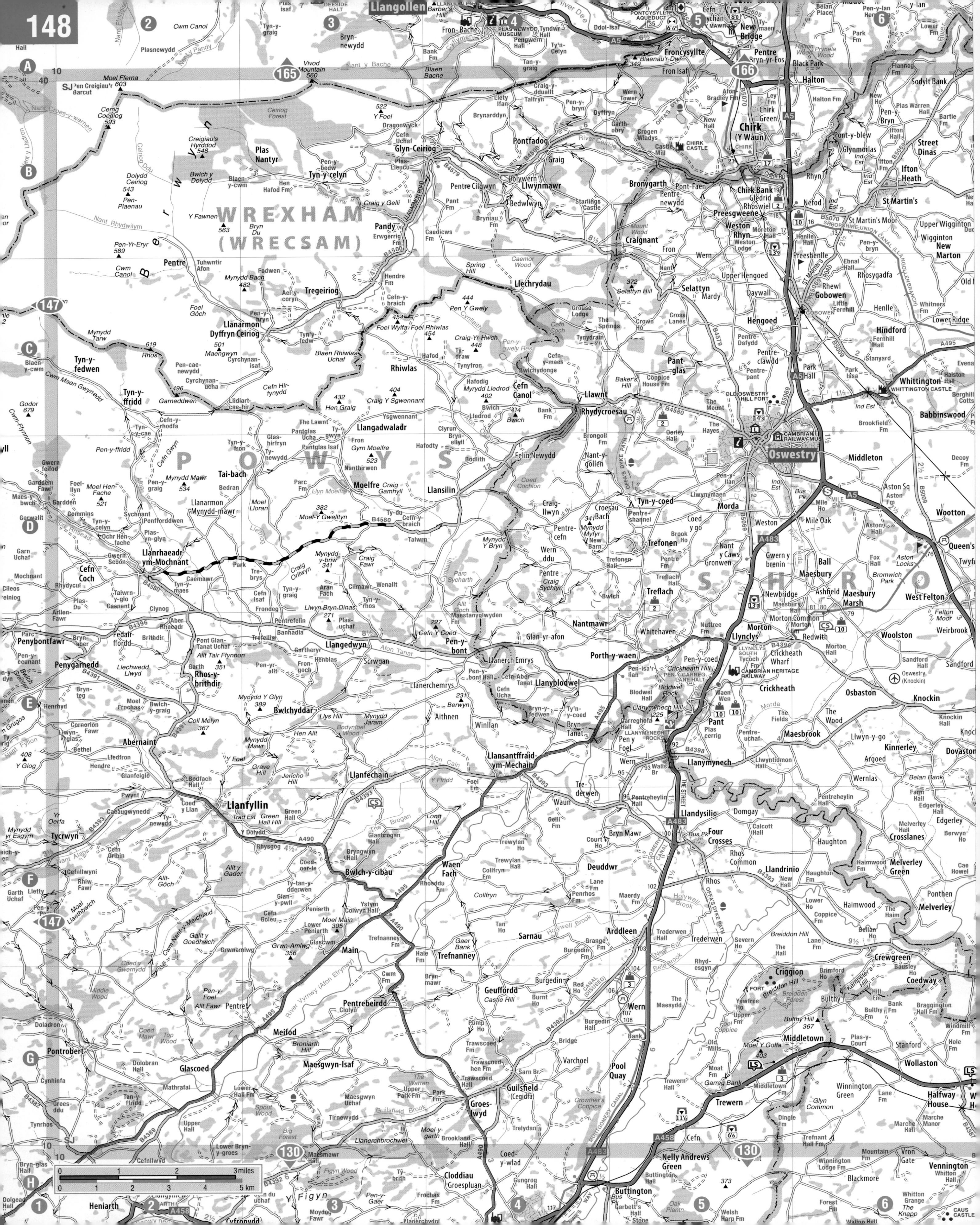

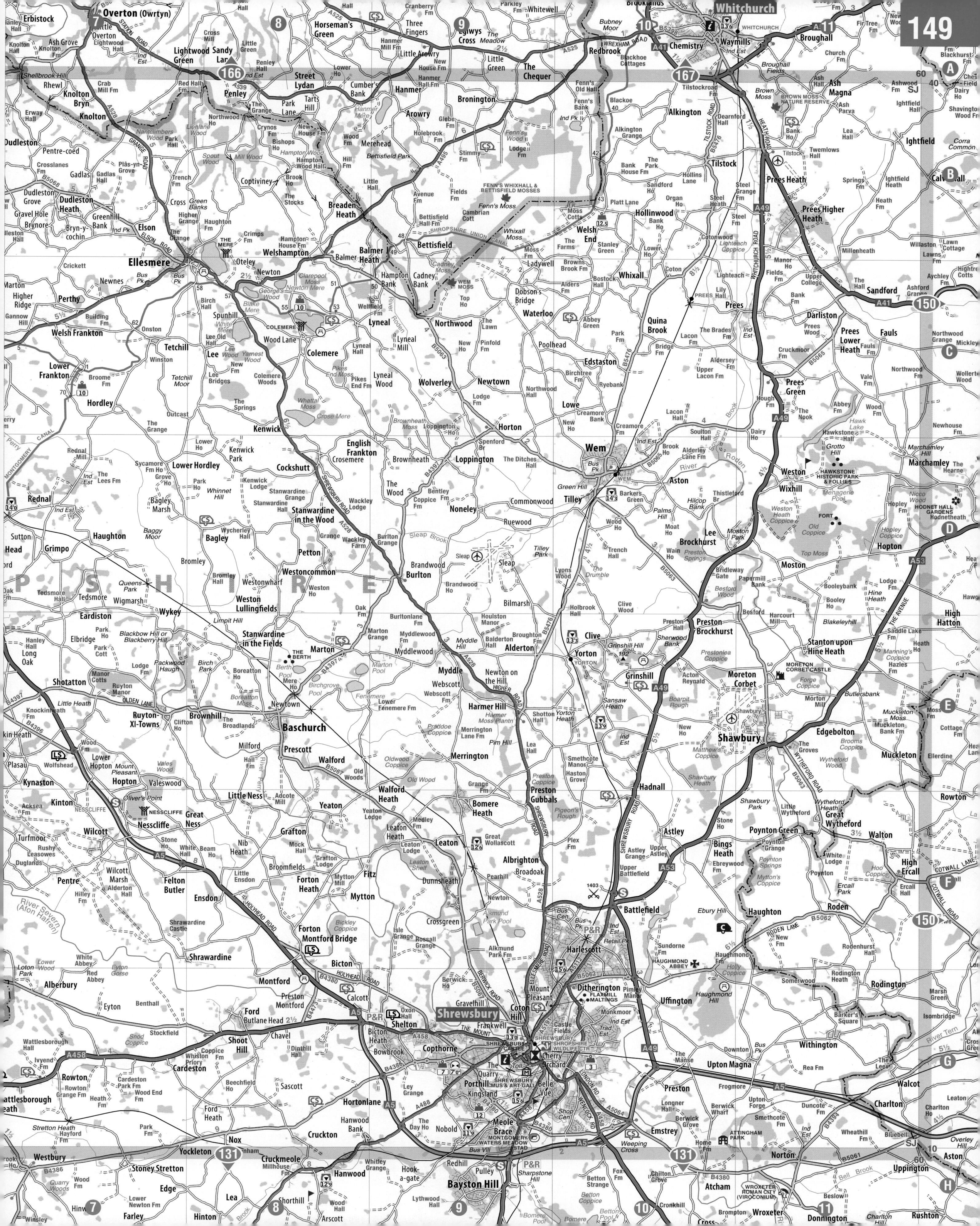
Whitchurch
Overton (Owrtyn)
Erbistock
Horseman's Green
Three Fingers
Eglwys Cross
Whitewell
Brooklands
Bubney Moor
Chemistry
Waymills
Broughall
Lightwood Green
Sandy Lane
Little Arowry
Redbrook
Little Green
The Chequer
Blackhoe Cottages
Broughall Fields
Ash Magna
Ash Parva
Brown Moss Nature Reserve
Tilstock Road
Knolton Bryn
Knolton
Penley
Street Lydan
Cumber's Bank
Hanmer
Bronington
Tarts Hill
Park Lane
Arowry
Fenn's Old Hall
Fenn's Bank
Blackoe
Alkington
Alkington Grange
Dearnford Hall
Heath Road
Ightfield
Tilstock
Prees Heath
Calverhall
Dudleston
Pentre-coed
Gadlas
Plas-yn-Grove
Dudleston Heath
Elson
Welshampton
Breaden Heath
Bettisfield
Fenn's Whixall & Bettisfield Mosses
Fenn's Moss
Cambrian Cott
Whixall Moss
Shropshire Union Canal
Platt Lane
Hollinwood
Welsh End
Prees Higher Heath
Ellesmere
The Mere
Balmer Heath
Hampton Bank
Cadney Bank
Ladywell
Whixall
Wem Moss
Dobson's Bridge
Waterloo
Quina Brook
Prees
Sandford
Darliston
Fauls
Prees Lower Heath
Perthy
Welsh Frankton
Spunhill
Colemere
Lyneal
Northwood
Wood Lane
Tetchill
Lee
Lower Frankton
Hordley
Newtown
Wolverley
Poolhead
Edstaston
Prees Green
Kenwick
Horton
Lowe
English Frankton
Loppington
Wem
Soulton
Marchamley
Weston
Wixhill
Hawkstone Historic Park & Follies
Hodnet Hall Gardens
Hodnethearth
Lower Hordley
Cockshutt
Noneley
Commonwood
Tilley
Aston
Lee Brockhurst
Rednal
Haughton
Bagley
Stanwardine in the Wood
Petton
Ruewood
Sleap
Hopton
Moston
Grimpo
Burlton
Weston Lullingfields
Westoncommon
Wykey
Bilmarsh
Preston Brockhurst
High Hatton
Eardiston
Tedsmore
Wigmarsh
Stanwardine in the Fields
Marton
Myddlewood
Alderton
Clive
Yorton
Grinshill
Moreton Corbet
Moreton Corbet Castle
Stanton upon Hine Heath
Shotatton
Myddle
Newton on the Hill
Ruyton-XI-Towns
Brownhill
Baschurch
Harmer Hill
Shawbury
Edgebolton
Knockin Heath
Kynaston
Prescott
Walford
Merrington
Muckleton
Hopton
Little Ness
Walford Heath
Preston Gubbals
Hadnall
Rowton
Kinton
Nesscliffe
Great Ness
Yeaton
Bomere Heath
Astley
Great Wytheford
Poynton Green
Wilcott
Grafton
Leaton
Bings Heath
Walton
Felton Butler
Fitz
Albrighton
Broadoak
High Ercall
Pentre
Ensdon
Forton Heath
Mytton
Battlefield
Haughton
Roden
Shrawardine
Montford Bridge
Crossgreen
Harlescott
Alberbury
Montford
Bicton
Dithering
Uffington
Rodington
Ford
Shelton
Coton Hill
Shrewsbury
Shoot Hill
Copthorne
Withington
Upton Magna
Rowton
Cardeston
Porthill
Kingsland
Belle Vue
Walcot
Charlton
Westbury
Yockleton
Nox
Cruckton
Meole Brace
Emstrey
Norton
Aston
Stoney Stretton
Edge
Cruckmeole
Hanwood
Bayston Hill
Atcham
Uppington
Lea
Farley
Hinton
Wroxeter
Rushton
Donnington

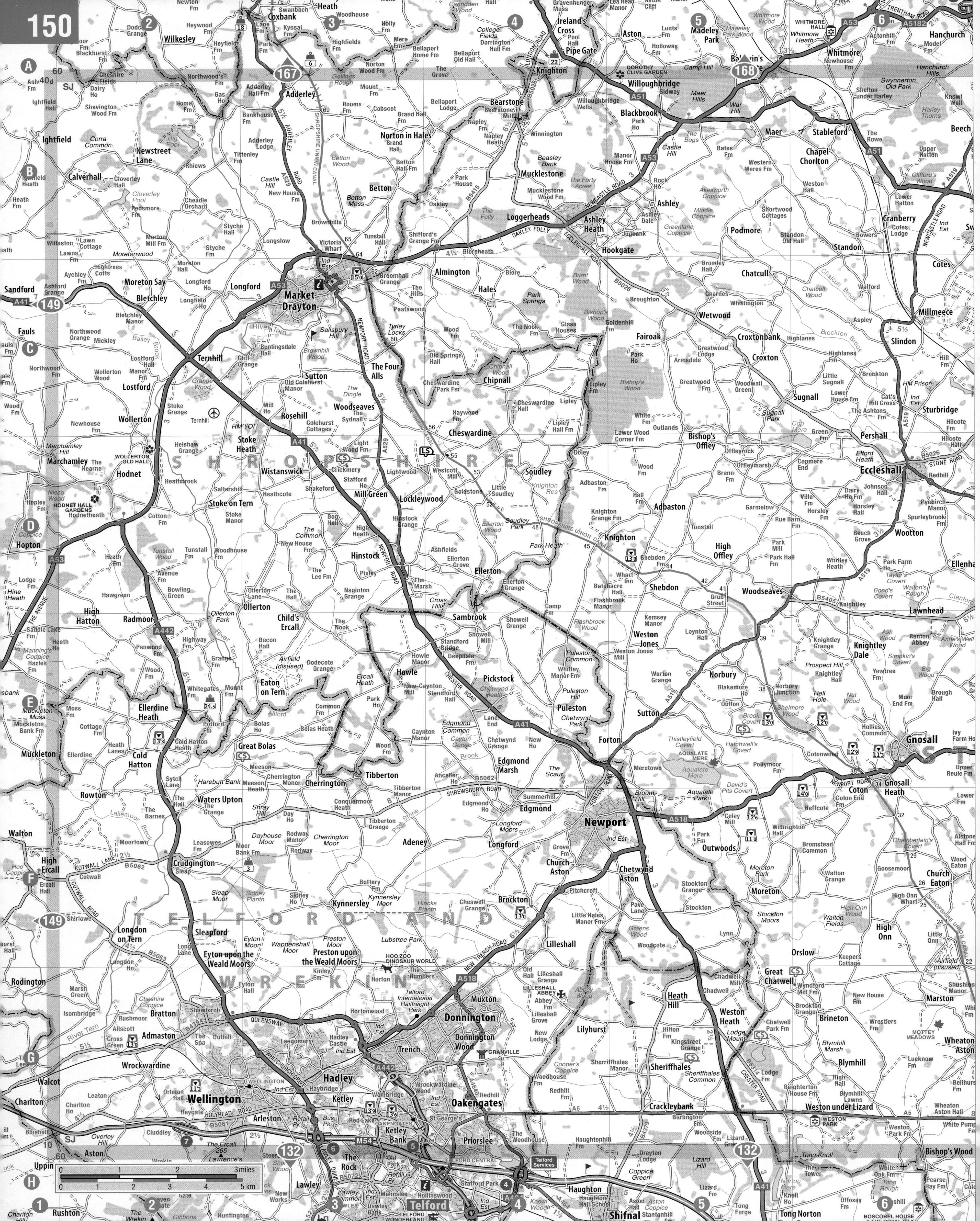

Coxbank
Wilkesley
Heath
Ireland's Cross
Pipe Gate
Knighton
Aston
Madeley Park
Baldwin's Gate
Whitmore
Hanchurch
167
168
Adderley
Willoughbridge
Dorothy Clive Garden
Bearstone
Blackbrook
Norton in Hales
Maer
Stableford
Chapel Chorlton
Ightfield
Newstreet Lane
Calverhall
Betton
Mucklestone
Loggerheads
Ashley
Ashley Heath
Hookgate
Podmore
Cranberry
Standon
Cotes
Almington
Hales
Chatcull
Market Drayton
Sandford
149
Moreton Say
Bletchley
Longford
Fauls
Ternhill
Lostford
Wollerton
Sutton
The Four Alls
Chipnall
Fairoak
Croxtonbank
Croxton
Wetwood
Millmeece
Slindon
Sugnall
Sturbridge
Rosehill
Woodseaves
Cheswardine
Pershall
Marchamley
Hodnet
Stoke Heath
Wistanswick
Soudley
Bishop's Offley
Eccleshall
SHROPSHIRE
Mill Green
Lockleywood
Stoke on Tern
Adbaston
Knighton
High Offley
Wootton
Hopton
Hinstock
Ellerton
Shebdon
Woodseaves
Lawnhead
High Hatton
Radmoor
Ollerton
Child's Ercall
Sambrook
Weston Jones
Knightley Dale
Howle
Pickstock
Norbury
Ellerdine Heath
Eaton on Tern
Puleston
Sutton
Muckleton
Cold Hatton
Great Bolas
Tibberton
Forton
Edgmond Marsh
Gnosall
Gnosall Heath
Coton
Rowton
Waters Upton
Cherrington
Edgmond
Newport
Walton
Adeney
Longford
Outwoods
High Ercall
Crudgington
Church Aston
Chetwynd Aston
Moreton
Church Eaton
Kynnersley
Brockton
High Onn
Longdon on Tern
Sleapford
TELFORD AND WREKIN
Lilleshall
Orslow
Eyton upon the Weald Moors
Preston upon the Weald Moors
Rodington
Great Chatwell
Marston
Donnington
Muxton
Heath Hill
Weston Heath
Bratton
Admaston
Lilyhurst
Brineton
Wheaton Aston
Wrockwardine
Trench
Donnington Wood
Sheriffhales
Blymhill
Hadley
Walcot
Charlton
Wellington
Ketley
Oakengates
Crackleybank
Weston under Lizard
Arleston
Ketley Bank
Priorslee
Aston
132
Uppin
The Rock
Lawley
Telford
Haughton
Shifnal
Tong Norton
Bishop's Wood
Rushton
Telford Services

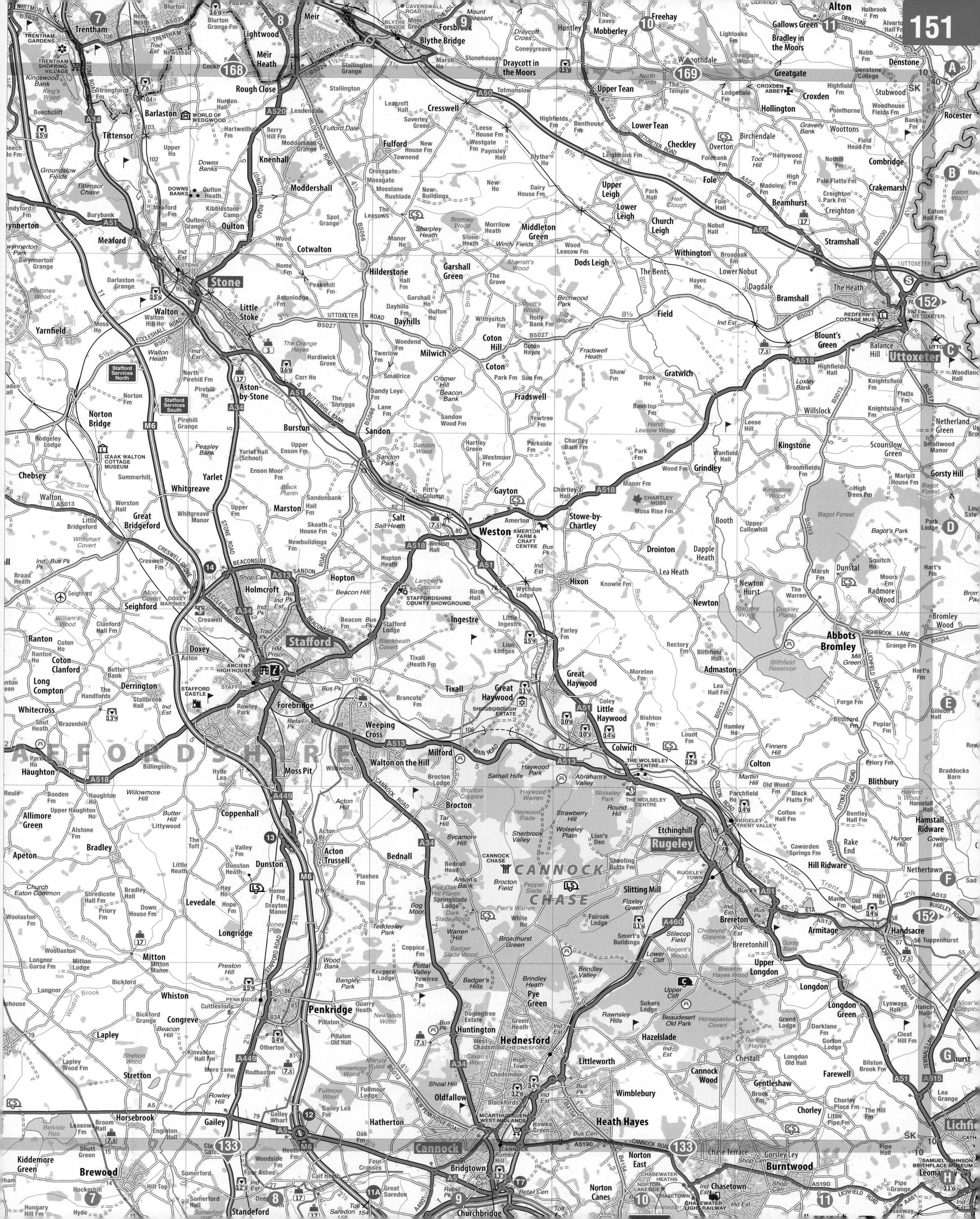
151
Trentham
Meir
Lightwood
Meir Heath
Blythe Bridge
Forsbrook
Draycott in the Moors
Freehay
Mobberley
Huntley
Alton
Gallows Green
Bradley in the Moors
Denstone
Greatgate
Rough Close
Barlaston
Tittensor
Knenhall
Fulford
Cresswell
Upper Tean
Lower Tean
Checkley
Croxden
Hollington
Rocester
Moddershall
Oulton
Meaford
Stone
Cotwalton
Hilderstone
Garshall Green
Middleton Green
Upper Leigh
Lower Leigh
Church Leigh
Withington
Dods Leigh
Fole
Beamhurst
Stramshall
Bramshall
Uttoxeter
Walton
Little Stoke
Yarnfield
Dayhills
Milwich
Coton Hill
Coton
Field
Blount's Green
Gratwich
Aston-by-Stone
Norton Bridge
Burston
Sandon
Fradswell
Kingstone
Chebsey
Yarlet
Whitgreave
Marston
Salt
Gayton
Weston
Stowe-by-Chartley
Grindley
Great Bridgeford
Seighford
Holmcroft
Hopton
Hixon
Drointon
Newton
Abbots Bromley
Stafford
Doxey
Ingestre
Tixall
Great Haywood
Little Haywood
Colwich
Ranton
Derrington
Forebridge
Weeping Cross
Milford
Walton on the Hill
Moss Pit
Haughton
Brocton
Coppenhall
Bradley
Dunston
Acton Trussell
Bednall
Cannock Chase
Rugeley
Etchinghill
Slitting Mill
Brereton
Armitage
Handsacre
Colton
Blithbury
Levedale
Longridge
Mitton
Whiston
Penkridge
Congreve
Lapley
Stretton
Pye Green
Huntington
Hednesford
Hazelslade
Littleworth
Cannock Wood
Gentleshaw
Longdon
Upper Longdon
Farewell
Chorley
Oldfallow
Gailey
Hatherton
Wimblebury
Heath Hayes
Horsebrook
Cannock
Norton East
Burntwood
Brewood
Kiddemore Green
Bridgtown
Norton Canes
Chasetown
Churchbridge
Standeford
STAFFORDSHIRE
CANNOCK CHASE

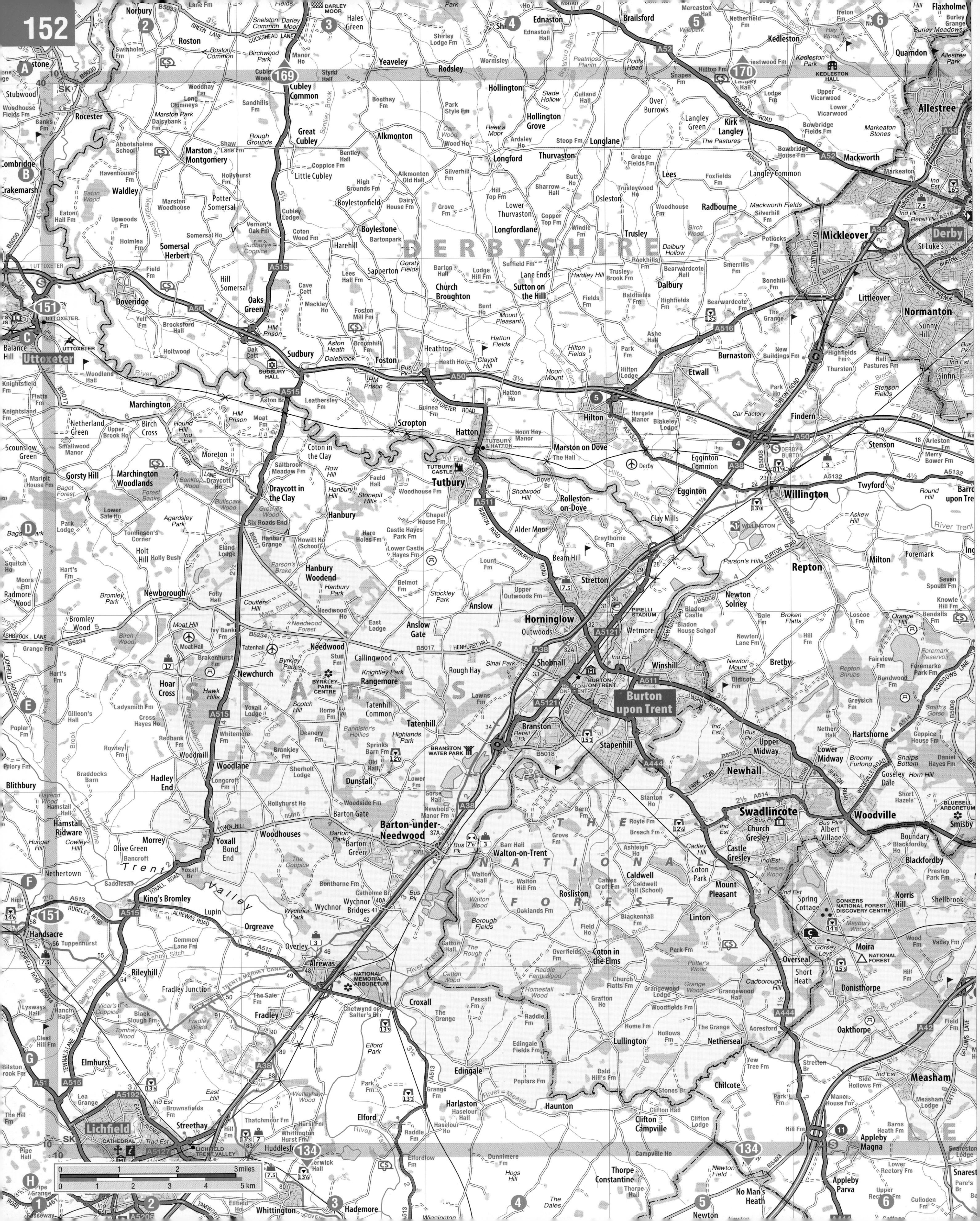

169
170
151
134
DERBYSHIRE
STAFFS
THE NATIONAL FOREST
Norbury
Roston
Darley Moor
Hales Green
Snelston Common
Ednaston
Brailsford
Mercaston
Kedleston
Quarndon
Flaxholme
Allestree
Kedleston Hall
Yeaveley
Rodsley
Cubley Common
Rocester
Hollington
Hollington Grove
Over Burrows
Kirk Langley
Langley Green
The Pastures
Great Cubley
Alkmonton
Longford
Thurvaston
Longlane
Mackworth
Markeaton Stones
Marston Montgomery
Little Cubley
Lees
Radbourne
Langley Common
Waldley
Boylestonfield
Osleston
Potter Somersal
Boylestone
Lower Thurvaston
Longfordlane
Trusley
Mickleover
Derby
St Luke's
Somersal Herbert
Harehill
Sapperton
Dalbury
Littleover
Normanton
Sunny Hill
Sutton on the Hill
Church Broughton
Hill Somersal
Doveridge
Oaks Green
Uttoxeter
Sudbury
Sudbury Hall
Foston
Heathtop
Burnaston
Etwall
Sinfin
Findern
Hilton
Marchington
Scropton
Hatton
Marston on Dove
Egginton
Stenson
Willington
Twyford
Tutbury
Tutbury Castle
Rolleston-on-Dove
Gorsty Hill
Marchington Woodlands
Draycott in the Clay
Hanbury
Alder Moor
Clay Mills
Repton
Milton
Foremark
Hanbury Woodend
Stretton
Newborough
Anslow
Anslow Gate
Horninglow
Newton Solney
Needwood
Rangemore
Winshill
Bretby
Shobnall
Burton upon Trent
Newchurch
Hoar Cross
Tatenhill
Branston
Stapenhill
Hartshorne
Upper Midway
Newhall
Swadlincote
Woodville
Smisby
Hadley End
Dunstall
Barton-under-Needwood
Walton-on-Trent
Church Gresley
Castle Gresley
Blackfordby
Hamstall Ridware
Yoxall
Morrey
Woodhouses
Rosliston
Caldwell
Mount Pleasant
King's Bromley
Wychnor
Orgreave
Linton
Coton in the Elms
Moira
Overseal
Handsacre
Alrewas
National Memorial Arboretum
Croxall
Rileyhill
Fradley
Donisthorpe
Oakthorpe
Lullington
Netherseal
Elmhurst
Edingale
Chilcote
Measham
Lichfield
Streethay
Harlaston
Elford
Haunton
Clifton Campville
Appleby Magna
Thorpe Constantine
No Man's Heath
Appleby Parva
Whittington
Hademore
Newton
Conkers National Forest Discovery Centre
Pirelli Stadium
Branston Water Park
Byrkley Park Centre
A52
A50
A38
A511
A515
A513
A444
A5121
A516
A5132
A514
A42
A51
A5192
A5127
A5206
B5020
B5017
B5234
B5008
B5016
B5018
0 1 2 3 miles
0 1 2 3 4 5 km

NOTTINGHAM
Nottingham
West Bridgford
Beeston
Stapleford
Long Eaton
Chilwell
Attenborough
Clifton
Ruddington
Sandiacre
Spondon
Chaddesden
DERBY CITY
Chellaston
Castle Donington
Kegworth
NOTTINGHAMSHIRE
East Leake
Melbourne
Loughborough
Shepshed
Coalville
Whitwick
Ibstock
Ashby-de-la-Zouch
Barrow upon Soar
Mountsorrel
Sileby
Birstall
Anstey
Markfield
Charnwood Forest
THE NATIONAL FOREST
LEICESTERSHIRE
Keyworth
Breedon on the Hill
Newton Burgoland

NOTTINGHAMSHIRE
LEICESTERSHIRE
Vale of Belvoir
Radcliffe on Trent
Bingham
Aslockton
Whatton
Bottesford
Elton
Orston
Easthorpe
Muston
Saxondale
Upper Saxondale
Harlequin
Holme Pierrepont
West Bridgford
Gamston
Bassingfield
Cropwell Butler
Cropwell Bishop
Tithby
Barnstone
Granby
Sutton
Langar
Redmile
Barkestone-le-Vale
Plungar
Belvoir
Woolsthorpe by Belvoir
Stenwith
Edwalton
Cotgrave
Tollerton
Owthorpe
Colston Bassett
Plumtree
Normanton-on-the-Wolds
Keyworth
Kinoulton
Harby
Stathern
Harston
Knipton
Stanton-on-the-Wolds
Hickling
Hose
Eaton
Eastwell
Branston
Croxton Kerrial
Widmerpool
Wysall
Long Clawson
Goadby Marwood
Willoughby-on-the-Wolds
Upper Broughton
Nether Broughton
Waltham on the Wolds
Wycomb
Scalford
Chadwell
Stonesby
Old Dalby
Wymeswold
Holwell
Ab Kettleby
Wartnaby
Grimston
Saxelbye
Burton on the Wolds
Six Hills
Shoby
Asfordby
Asfordby Hill
Thorpe Arnold
Freeby
Saxby
Garthorpe
Walton on the Wolds
Ragdale
Brentingby
Wyfordby
Melton Mowbray
Stapleford
Seagrave
Hoby
Frisby on the Wreake
Kirby Bellars
Rotherby
Burton Lazars
Thrussington
Sileby
Little Dalby
Whissendine
Ratcliffe on the Wreake
Rearsby
Great Dalby
Cossington
Gaddesby
East Goscote
Queniborough
Ashby Folville
Thorpe Satchville
Pickwell
Syston
Barsby
Burrough on the Hill
Somerby
Cold Overton
Barkby
South Croxton
Twyford
Barleythorpe
Oakham
John O'Gaunt
Marefield
Knossington
Beeby
Melton Carnegie Museum
A52
A46
A606
A607
A6006
B676
171
172
153
136
0 1 2 3 miles
0 1 2 3 4 5 km

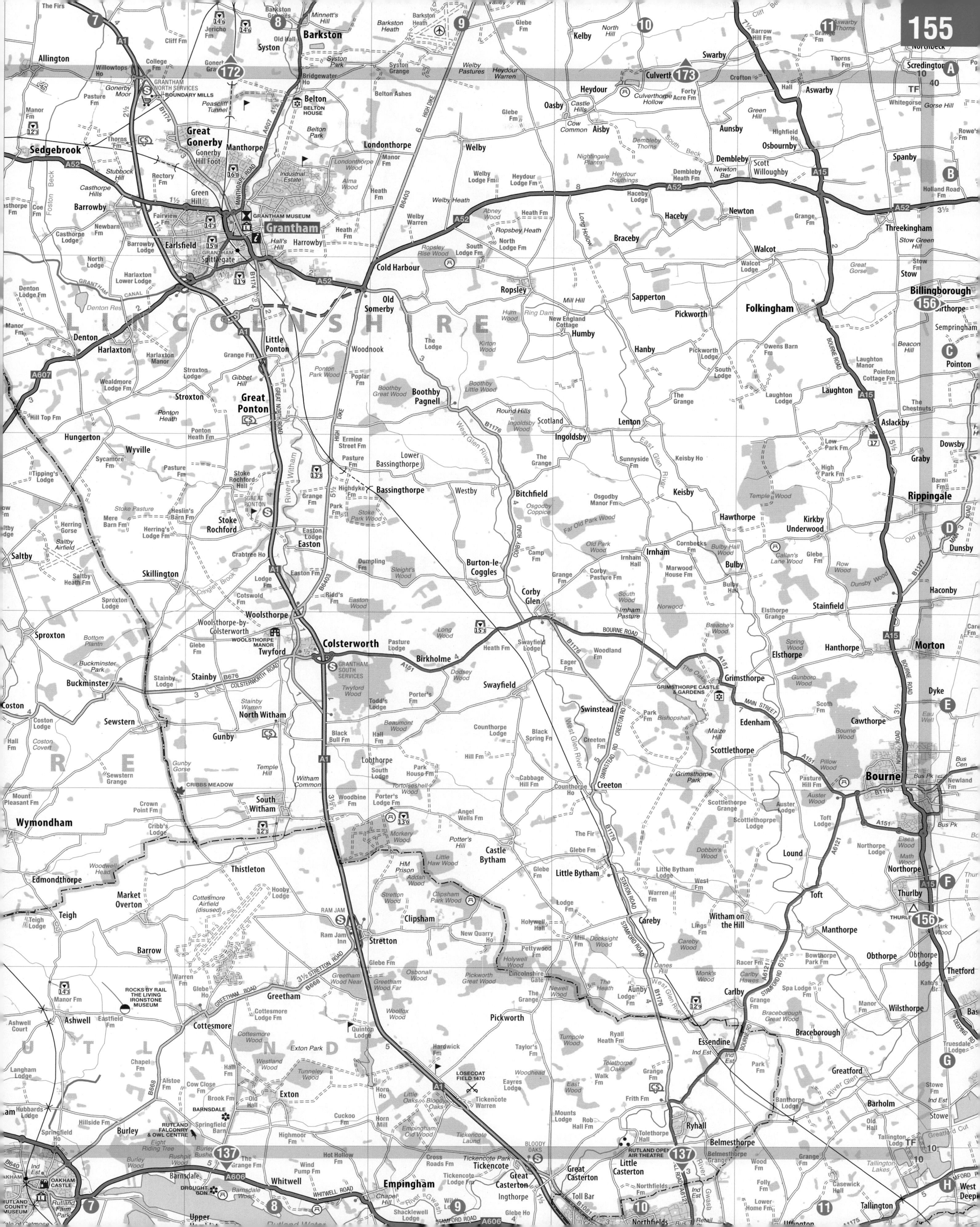

Barkston
Syston
Belton
Belton House
Allington
Sedgebrook
Great Gonerby
Manthorpe
Londonthorpe
Welby
Heydour
Oasby
Aisby
Culverthorpe Hollow
Culverth
Swarby
Aswarby
Aunsby
Dembleby
Osbournby
Scott Willoughby
Newton
Spanby
Scredington
Threekingham
Barrowby
Grantham
Grantham Museum
Earlsfield
Spittlegate
Harrowby
Cold Harbour
Haceby
Braceby
Walcot
Ropsley
Sapperton
Pickworth
Folkingham
Billingborough
Birthorpe
Sempringham
Pointon
Old Somerby
Humby
Hanby
Laughton
Denton
Harlaxton
Little Ponton
Great Ponton
Stroxton
Boothby Pagnell
Scotland
Lenton
Ingoldsby
Aslackby
Dowsby
Graby
Hungerton
Wyville
Lower Bassingthorpe
Bassingthorpe
Westby
Bitchfield
Keisby
Rippingale
Stoke Rochford
Hawthorpe
Kirkby Underwood
Dunsby
Saltby
Skillington
Easton
Burton-le-Coggles
Irnham
Bulby
Corby Glen
Stainfield
Haconby
Woolsthorpe
Woolsthorpe-by-Colsterworth
Woolsthorpe Manor
Sproxton
Colsterworth
Twyford
Birkholme
Grantham South Services
Buckminster
Stainby
Swayfield
Grimsthorpe
Grimsthorpe Castle & Gardens
Elsthorpe
Hanthorpe
Morton
Coston
Sewstern
North Witham
Gunby
Swinstead
Edenham
Scottlethorpe
Cawthorpe
Dyke
Bourne
Creeton
Cribbs Meadow
South Witham
Wymondham
Castle Bytham
Little Bytham
Lound
Northorpe
Thurlby
Thistleton
Edmondthorpe
Market Overton
Teigh
Clipsham
Ram Jam
Stretton
Careby
Witham on the Hill
Toft
Manthorpe
Obthorpe
Thetford
Barrow
Greetham
Carlby
Wilsthorpe
Rocks by Rail The Living Ironstone Museum
Ashwell
Cottesmore
Pickworth
Essendine
Braceborough
Exton
Greatford
Barnsdale
Rutland Falconry & Owl Centre
Burley
Ryhall
Barholm
Belmesthorpe
Stowe
Whitwell
Empingham
Tickencote
Great Casterton
Little Casterton
Rutland Open Air Theatre
Tolethorpe Hall
Oakham
Oakham Castle
Rutland County Museum
Tallington
Losecoat Field 1470
Lincolnshire
Rutland

Helpringham
Little Hale
Scredington
Thorpe Latimer
Swaton
Spanby
Threekingham
Horbling
Billingborough
Birthorpe
Sempringham
Pointon
Millthorpe
Little Wisbeach
Aslackby
Dowsby
Graby
Rippingale
Dunsby
Haconby
Morton
Dyke
Bourne
Northorpe
Thurlby
Obthorpe
Thetford
Wilsthorpe
Baston
Langtoft
Barholm
Stowe
Towngate
Market Deeping
Tallington
Frognall
Northborough
Maxey
Castle End
Twenty
Tongue End
Guthram Gowt
Pinchbeck Bars
Pinchbeck West
Pode Hole
Hop Pole
Deeping St Nicholas
Crowland
Cowbit
Peak Hill
Brotherhouse Bar
Spalding
Little London
Clay Lake
Fen End
Pinchbeck
Crossgate
Surfleet
Surfleet Seas End
Gosberton Clough
Risegate
Gosberton
Gosberton Cheal
Westhorpe
Quadring
Donington
Donington South Ing
Northgate
Northorpe
Bicker
Swineshead
North End
Drayton
Fenhouses
Blackjack
Asperton
Wigtoft
Sutterton
Algarkirk
Kirton
Kirton Holme
Frampton
Frampton West End
Kirton End
Wyberton
Sandholme
Skeldyke
Seadyke
Bucklegate
Fosdyke
Sutterton Dowdyke
Moulton
Moulton Chapel
Moulton Eaugate
Moulton Seas End
Weston
Weston Hills
Whaplode
Whaplode St Catherine
Whaplode Drove
Holbeach Drove
Holbeach Clough
Saracen's Head
Halesgate
Loosegate
Austendike
Low Fulney
Fulney
Shepeau Stow
Dowsdale
Gedney Hill
Throckenholt
Wykeham
Belnie
Wargate
Church End
Gosberton Clough
Spalding
Pinchbeck Engine Mus
Baytree Owl & Wildlife Centre
Springfields
Ayscoughfee Hall
Gordon Boswell Romany Museum
Jakemans Community Stadium
Moulton Mill
L I N C O L N S H I R E
A15
A151
A152
A16
A17
A52
A1175
B1397
B1180
B1165
B1166
155
173
174
138
0 1 2 3 miles
0 1 2 3 4 5 km

157
THE WASH
Scrane End
Freiston Low
Shore
Marsh Fm
HM Prison
The Scalp
River Witham
The Haven
Wyberton Marsh
Frampton Marsh
FRAMPTON MARSH
The Cots
Fosdyke Wash
Fleet Haven Outfall
Hospital Cotts
Lundy's Fm
Leadenhall Fm
Willow Tree Ho
Reckerby Fm
Thimbleby Ho
Lawyers Fm
Trevethoe Fm
Bingham Lodge
Holbeach St Matthew
Leaden Hall
Wards Fm
Sot's Hole
Christie Ho
Holbeach St Marks
Hartley Fm
Acre Ho
Browns Fm
Red House Fm
Dawsmere Ho
Wiles Fm
Dawsmere
Holbeach Marsh
Woodstoke Ho
Oldershaw Fm
Bleak House Fm
Dawsmere Creek
Keightley House Fm
Home Fm
Cardwell Ho
Gedney Marsh
Gedney Drove End
Middle Marsh Ho
Poplars Fm
Marsh Fm
Bertie Lodge
Crowmarsh Fm
Norfolk House Fm
Manor Fm
Onslow Fm
Red House Fm
The Grove
Fleet Haven
Black Barn
B1359
Red House Fm
Boat Mere Fm
Welby Ho
Clays Fm
Coney Garth Ho
Old White Ho
Brook House Fm
Sutton Corner
Lodge Fm
Lutton Leam
Crab's Hole
Holbeach Bank
Holbeach Hurn
Osbourne Ho
MARSH ROAD
Lutton Marsh
Penny Hill
Woodhouse Fm
Hurn Hall
Gedney Dyke
Lutton Grange
Leamlands
THE WASH
Cackle Hill
Hovenden Ho
Laurel Lodge Fm
Welby Ho
Lutton
Lutton Leam
Guy's Head
A17
Holbeach
WASHWAY ROAD
Old Leam Fm
Ind Est
B1515
Fleet Hargate
Lutton Gowts
Monmouth Ho
Lighthouse Fm
Kamarad Fm
Terrington Marsh
Admiral's Fm
Harrington Hall Fm
Chapelgate
King John Fm
Nene Lodge Fm
Walkers Marsh
Ongar Hill
Oak Lodge
Gedney
Maze Fm
Horseshoe Hole Fm
Pierrepont Fm
Fleet Lodge
Manor Ho
Stonegate Ho
GEDNEY RD
Little London
Common Fm
Avenue Fm
River Great Ouse
FEN ROAD
Fleet
Westmere House Fm
Balaclava Fm
Broadgate Ho
Manor Ho
New Ho
Nene Outfall Cut
Millbank Fm
Long Sutton
Bridge Fm
Weatherall Fm
Fern Fm
The Laurels Fm
Red House Fm
Garnsgate
Ind Est
Westmere Fm
Myrobella Fm
Bentinck Fm
Hurdletree Ho
Gedney Broadgate
Little Sutton
Port Sutton Bridge
Wingland Marsh
Wingland Grange
East Anglian Fm
Primrose Fm
Pulvertoft Hall Fm
Elder Lodge
White Ho Fm
Grove Fm
Sutton Bridge
Greenmarsh Fm
Rhoon Fm
Marsh Fm
Fen House Fm
Fen Fm
Onslow Fm
Bleak House Fm
Bellmount
ST JAMES ROAD
Old Gate
Sutton Crosses
Fields Fm
Orange Row
Saturday Br
Moorswood Fm
Home Fm
Emorsgate
Alma Lodge
Clenchwarton
West Lynn
TRUE'S YARD FISHERFOLK MUS
Clark's Hill
Red Ho
Foreman's Br
Poplar Ho
WISBECH RD
Petersppoint Fm
Poplar Tree Fm
South Green
Terrington St Clement
ST GEORGE'S GUILDHALL
Fleet Fen
South Holland Lodge
Hoe Fm
Margaretta Fm
CUSTOM HOUSE
Red House Br
Holland Ho
South Holland Ho
Willow Tree Fm
Kenwick Hall
KING'S LYNN
B1165
Sycamore Lodge
Wood Fm
Strawberry Hall
Tydd St Mary's Marsh
Gibbons Fm
Walpole Cross Keys
Lovell's Hall
Clifton's Br
Tydd St Mary
A1101
The Grange
Balsamfield Ho
Kenwick Fm
The Elms
Bell's Br
Sutton St James
DRAW DIKE
Gunthorpe Fm
Old Inclosed Marsh
Old Hall Fm
Tilney All Saints
White Cross Fm
Lowgate Ho
Tydd Gote
Corner Fm
Highenden Ho
Cherry Fm
Shepherd's Gate
Manor Fm
Walpole St Andrew
Hay Green
Merries Fm
Leedsgate Br
Manor Hill Fm
Tretton Manor Fm
Hannath Hall
Foul Anchor
Walpole Marsh
Bustards Fm
Jankinsfield Fm
Tilney High End
Manor Hill Corner
Trafford Ho
Flower Fm
Wash Dyke
Islington Lodge
Dunton Hall
Four Gotes
White House Fm
Broken Cross
White Ho Fm
Islington Hall Fm
Coy Br
Broadgate Ho
Cole Ho
Kirkgate Fm
Silverwood Fm
River Nene
Walpole St Peter
St Peter's Lodge
Duncan's Fm
Sandygate Fm
Tydd St Giles
Rose Hall
Bank Fm
Eau Brink
Saddle Bow
Hallgate Fm
Park Ho
Hornfield Ho
CHURCH LANE
Lodge Fm
Ingleborough Fm
Church End
Salgate Fm
Grangehill Ho
Ewings Fm
Oaktree Fm
North Level Main Drain
Marsh Fm
Ingleborough
NORFOLK
Aylmer Hall
White Hall Fm
Wiggenhall St Germans
Guanock Ho
Poplartree Fm
Honington House Fm
A47
Terrington St John
Wiggenhall St Mary the Virgin
Abbey Fm
Chestnut Ho
Lady Nun's Old Eau
B1165
Ferry Fm
Grange Fm
St John's Highway
Hirdling Ho
Mole Cove Fm
Sutton St Edmund
Newton
HIGH ROAD
Walpole Highway
Tilney St Lawrence
Thornton's Br
CAMBRIDGE
West Walton
Priory Fm
Faulkner Ho
Elm Tree Ho
Tilney cum Islington
Wiggenhall St Peter
Fenwick Fm
Poplartree Fm
A1101
Ratten Row
Guanock Fm
West Walton Highway
Black Ditch Level
Lordsbridge
Peter's Drove Br
Ivy Fm
Tree Fm
Holly Tree Fm
Barbers Fm
Oxfield Fm
Fitton End
Barrycott Lodge
West Drove Fm
White House Fm
Decoy Fm
Park Ho
Walton Highway
Green Lane Fm
Marshland
Magdalen Br
Eye Fm
Richmond Hall
Gorefield
Floral Fm
Grassgate Ho
FENLAND & WEST NORFOLK AVIATION MUS
Harp's Hall
Trinity Hall
St John's Fen End
Smeeth Lode
Rosary Fm
Blacklane Fm
Harold's Br
Leverington Common
Leverington
Walpole Gate
Tilney Fen End
Gravel Bank Fm
Wiggenhall St Mary Magdalen
Tydd St Mary's Fen
Subscription Br
WATLINGTON
Holland's Fm
Hawthorn Fm
Hundred Acre Fm
Carlton Fm
LYNN ROAD
The Smeeth
Manor Fm
LEVERINGTON COMMON
B1169
Wisbech
Walsoken
Trafford Ho
Clough's Cross
Barrett's Br
PECKOVER HOUSE
New Walsoken
Rosedale
Marshland St James
Parsonage Fm
Chancellor's Drove
Main Drain
Highfield Fm
Cheyney Br
Paradise Fm
Popenhoe Ho
Parson Drove
B1166
MAIN ROAD
Wood Mills Fm
Manor Ho
Chequers Corner
Forty Foot Br
Church End
Bellamy's Br
WISBECH & FENLAND MUSEUM
A1101
Banyer Hall
Smeeth House Fm
Rungay's Br
Dike
River Great Ouse
Fen Fm
B1187
Inham Hall
Wisbech
Oxburgh
Marshland Fen
Bull Dog Sand
Lynn Channel
174
175
158
139
139
158
166
166
166
32
TF
60
40
TF
10
60
A
B
C
D
E
F
G
H
7
8
9
10
11
7
8
9
10
11

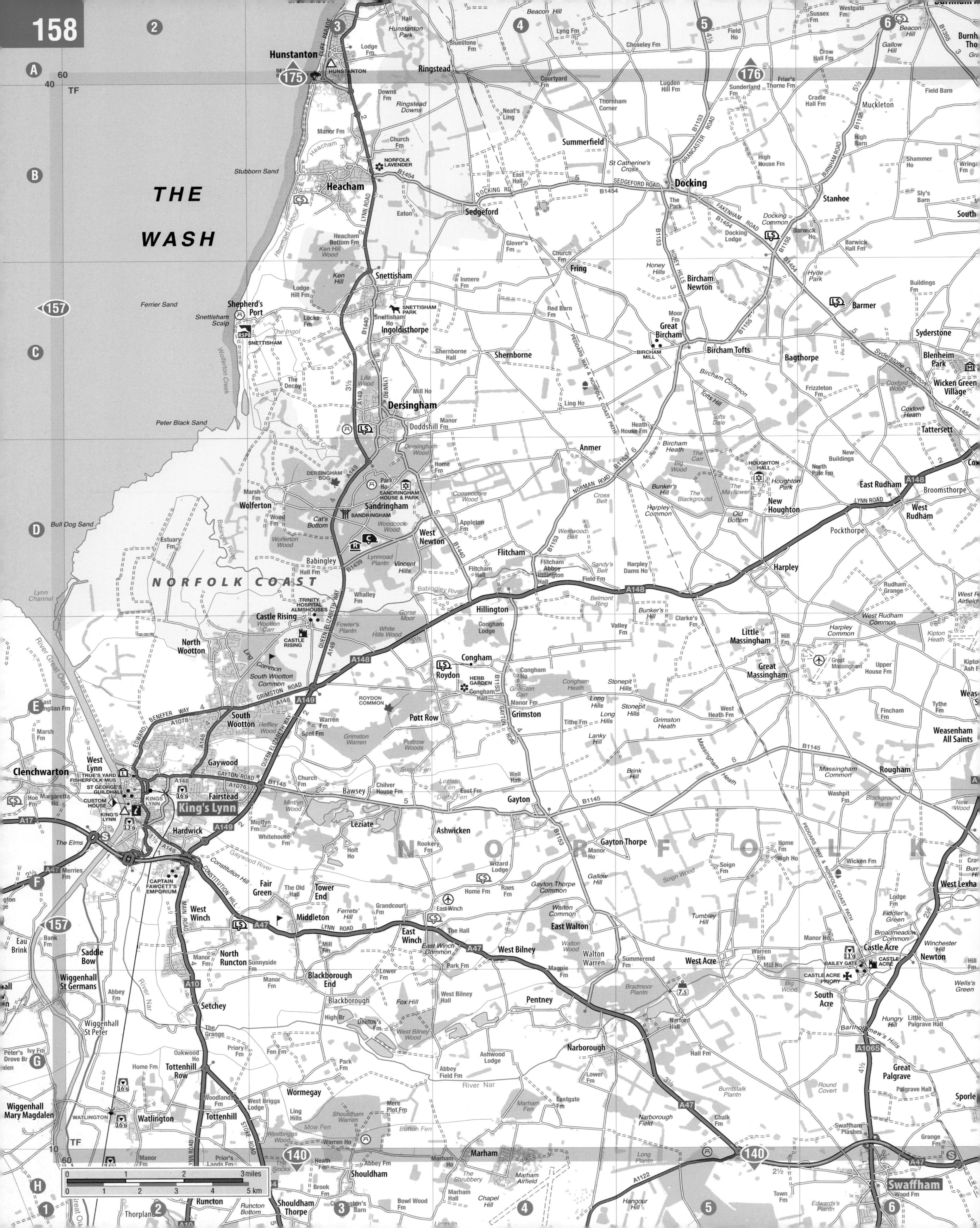
THE WASH
NORFOLK COAST
NORFOLK
Hunstanton
Ringstead
Heacham
Sedgeford
Docking
Stanhoe
Snettisham
Shepherd's Port
Ingoldisthorpe
Dersingham
Sandringham
Wolferton
West Newton
Babingley
Castle Rising
North Wootton
South Wootton
Gaywood
West Lynn
Clenchwarton
King's Lynn
Fairstead
Hardwick
Summerfield
Fring
Bircham Newton
Great Bircham
Birchain Tofts
Bagthorpe
Barmer
Syderstone
Shernborne
Anmer
Flitcham
Hillington
Congham
Roydon
Grimston
Pott Row
Harpley
Little Massingham
Great Massingham
New Houghton
East Rudham
West Rudham
Tattersett
Rougham
Weasenham All Saints
Gayton
Gayton Thorpe
Bawsey
Leziate
Ashwicken
East Winch
West Bilney
Middleton
Tower End
Fair Green
West Winch
North Runcton
Setchey
Saddle Bow
Wiggenhall St Germans
Wiggenhall St Peter
Wiggenhall Mary Magdalen
Tottenhill
Tottenhill Row
Watlington
Wormegay
Blackborough End
Pentney
Narborough
East Walton
West Acre
Castle Acre
South Acre
Newton
West Lexham
Great Palgrave
Sporle
Swaffham
Marham
Shouldham
Shouldham Thorpe
Runcton
Muckleton
Blenheim Park
Wicken Green Village
HUNSTANTON
NORFOLK LAVENDER
SNETTISHAM PARK
SANDRINGHAM HOUSE & PARK
DERSINGHAM BOG
TRINITY HOSPITAL ALMSHOUSES
CASTLE RISING
HOUGHTON HALL
TRUE'S YARD FISHERFOLK MUS
ST GEORGE'S GUILDHALL
CUSTOM HOUSE
CAPTAIN FAWCETT'S EMPORIUM
BAILEY GATE
CASTLE ACRE PRIORY
PEDDARS WAY & NORFOLK COAST PATH
A148
A149
A47
A10
A1065
A1078
A1076
A17
B1454
B1153
B1155
B1440
B1439
B1145
B1355
LYNN ROAD
GAYTON ROAD
GRIMSTON ROAD
CONSTITUTION HILL
MAIN ROAD
QUEEN ELIZABETH WAY
NORMAN ROAD
FAKENHAM ROAD
SEDGEFORD ROAD
DOCKING RD
175
176
157
140
0 1 2 3 miles
0 1 2 3 4 5 km

NORFOLK COAST
Temple
Manor Ho
Hill Wood
Old Common Plantn
Golden Gates
Gallow Hill
Warham St Mary Halt
Warham
Langham Lodge
Oulton Hill
Glandford
Swan Lodge
The Hangs
Branthill Fm
Branthill Lts
Wells & Walsingham Light Railway
Long Lane Fm
Short Lane Fm
Westgate
Langham
Summer House Hill
The Wing
Cley Park
Lawn Fm
Bayfield Hall
Scarboro' Wood
The Belt
Longlands Fm
176
177
Creake Abbey (Rems)
New Holkham
Abbey Fm
Blunt's Corner
Crabbe Castle Fm
Field Barn
Wighton Halt
Wighton
Setons Halt
Copy's Green
Old Barn Fm
Ellis Fm
Binham Priory & Wayside Cross
Binham
Saxlingham
Manor House Fm
Horse Hill
Smoker's Hole
Pereer's Hills
Letheringsett
Holt Hall (Coll)
The Gallery
Gresham's School
Holt
Kelling
Cromer Road
Holt Rd
Field Dalling
Breck Fm
Letheringsett Watermill
Little Thornage
Common Hill
Heath Fm
North Creake
Chantry Hills
Quarles Fm
Bunker's Hill
Edgar Fm
River Stiffkey
Field Ho
Abbot Fm
Foxburrow Fm
Little Marsh
Eastmoor Fm
Ingmote Hill
Thornage Road
Red Ho
High Hills
Shepherd's Hill
East Common
Haggard's Lodge
Egmere Fm
Egmere
Walsingham
Berry Hall
Great Walsingham Barns
Great Walsingham
County Fm
Clipstreet Fm
Bale Hall
Sharrington
Stowe Ollands
Hempstead
Little Walsingham
Walsingham Abbey Grounds & Shirehall Mus
Lower Green
Bale
Hill Ho
Heath Ho
Dam Hill
Creake
Waterden Fm
North Barsham Fm
Compton Hall
Waterden
Hall Fm
Hill House Fm
Grange Fm
Hindringham
Thornage
King's Hills
Edgefield Woods
Bloodgate Hill
Brinton
Bullfer Grove
Edgefield Hall
Lowes Fm
Bunker's Hill
The Dales
Pond Hills
Southgate
North Barsham
Houghton St Giles
Canister Hall Fm
Great Snoring
Vinepark Fm
Thursford Green
Thursford Collection
Frog Hall Fm
Hunworth
The Green
Hubbards Fm
The Gorse
West Barsham
Gunthorpe Park
Gunthorpe
Lobb's Valley
Burgh Stubbs
Stody
Starlings' Hill
Edgefield
Little Snoring
Thursford
Old Coach House
Pigg's Grave
Briningham
Leicester Square Fm
East Barsham
The Lings
Burgh Hall
Breck Fm
Little Wood
Cranmer Hall
Waterhouse Fm
Thorpland Hall
Wood Fm
Fakenham Road
White Ollands Fm
Edgefield Street
Fuel Fm
Old Covert
Park Fm
Melton Constable
Briston
Fir Patch
Manor Fm
Lodge Fm
Sculthorpe
Thorpland Lodge Fm
Little Snoring
Forty Acre Plantn
River Stiffkey
Barney
Neat's Close
Swanton Novers
Sculthorpe Airfield (disused)
Alethorpe Hall
Kettlestone
Melton Hall
Dairy Fm
The Grange
Grove Fm
Little Wood
Swanton Great Wood
Roper Fm
Dunton Patch
Fakenham
Croxton
Fulmodestone
Swanton Novers
Craymere Beck
Briston Common
Moor Hall
Holly Fm
Little London
Dunton
Manor Fm
Sculthorpe Moor
Heath Fm
Clipstone Ho
Brown's Covert
Common End
Tipples' Fm
The Lake
Wood Severals
Raw Hall
Holmes's Wood
Washpit Plantn
Rookery Fm
Blackwater Br
Gatesend Hill
Manor Ho
The Heath
Fakenham Common
Common Fm
Burnthouse Fm
Holly Heath Fm
Corpusty
Shereford
Hempton
Pensthorpe Natural Park
Pensthorpe Hall
Manor Fm
Park Fm
Hindolveston
Roundabout Fm
Doughton
Fakenham
Starmoor Wood
River Wensum
Fulmodeston Severals
Nethergate
Thurning
Hall Fm
Field Barn
Foundry Hill
Red Pits
Pynkney Hall
Tatterford
Manor Ho
Pudding Norton Hall
Little Ryburgh
Stibbard
Wood Norton
Hindolveston Wood
Black Water
Oak Grove
Cropton Hall
Southmill Fm
Toftrees
Highfield Fm
Clay Hill
Holly Hill
Ashcroft Fm
Abbey Fm
Page's Fm
Norton Corner
Pigs Pond Plantn
Canister Hall
Catchett's Fm
Manor Fm
Crome's Fm
Old Hall
Tyby
Wood Dalling
Crabgate
Heydon
Helhoughton Common
Lady Ferrers Wood
Great Ryburgh
Norton Hall
Foulsham
Guestwick
Wood Dalling Hall
Low Fm
Hill Fm
Raynham Park
Testerton Hall
Guist Bottom
Guist Hall
Painswhin Fm
Helhoughton
Beacon Hill
Colkirk
West Wood
Guist Hill
Upper Guist
Wakefield Fm
Guestwick Green
Fieldhouse Fm
Common End
Heath Fm
Littlemoor Fm
Forest Fm
Stinton Hall Fm
West Raynham
East Raynham
Oxwick
Hazelwood Fm
Gateley Hill
Hill Fm
Sennowe Park
High Wood
Guist
Norwich Road
Bexfield
Bates Moor Fm
Keeling Hall Fm
Primrose Fm
Gatehouse Fm
Green Fm
Manor Ho
Old Hall Fm
Manor Fm
Salle Moor Hall
Salle
Mill Covert
Vere Lodge
Webb's Covert
Pattesley Ho
Manor Fm
Dunham Hill
Bintree Mill
Foulsham
Kerdiston
South Raynham
Hamrow
Gateley
Broom Green
Twyford
Pockthorpe
Manor House Fm
Themelthorpe
Blue Tile Fm
River Wensum
Ash Fm
High Cross
Westfield Hall Fm
Brick Kiln Fm
Pettywell
Norman's Burrow Wood
Pear Tree Corner
Whissonsett
Heath Fm
Silverstone Fm
Swaffham Road
Uphouse Fm
Horningtoft
Harper's Green
Ling Plantn
Yarrow Ho
Field Barn Buildings
Bintree
Lizard Fm
Oaks Fm
Reepham
Wellingham
Godwick Moor
Malthouse Fm
Park Fm
Great Heath
Grange Fm
Bintree Hills
Bintree Woods
Tower Fm
Manor Fm
Foxley Wood
Wood Fm
Hackford Hall
Booton
Vale Fm
Whitwell Street
Peter
Manor Fm
Extreme Adventure
Godwick
Potthorpe
Park Ho
Fakenham Road
Reepham Road
Manorhouse Fm
Church Wood
Fox Covert
Dandy Fm
Tuttle Fm
Brisley
Morlice Hill
Elmham Road
Elmham Ho
North Elmham Saxon Cathedral (Rems)
Foxley
Woolfull Fm
Jordan Green
Whitwell Hall
Eves Hill
High Ho
Tittleshall
Eastfield Wood
Stanfield
Brisley Green
Ramsley Fm
High House Fm
Bawdeswell
Mill Fm
Manor Fm
High House Fm
Tittleshall Hill
Wicken Fm
Old Hall Fm
North Elmham
Billingford
Beck Hall
Billingford Road
Valley Fm
Whitwell Common
Fiddler's Hill
NORFOLK
Stanfield Road
Bawdeswell Heath
Sparham Ho
Manor Fm
Blackwater
Field Barn
Burwood Hall
Willow Grange
Great Wood
Worthing
Billingford Common
Elsing Lane Fm
Sparham
Great Witchingham
Litcham Heath
High House Fm
Mileham
Broom Hill
Spong Hill
Bylaugh Wood
Bylaugh Park
Sparham Hole
Fakenham Road
Clayhall Fm
River Fm
Lodge Fm
Grenstein Fm
Home Fm
East Bilney
Beetley Hall
Peacock Fm
Robertson Barracks
Swanton Morley Airfield (disused)
Waterfall Fm
Claypit Moor
Oaklands Fm
White House Fm
Litcham Road
Rawhall Wood
Horse Wood
Hungry Hill
Vale Fm
Old Hall
Old Hall Fm
Sparham Hall
Pockthorpe
Sparhamhill
Lenwade
Great Wood
Litcham
Lexham Road
The Warren
Bittering
Beetley
River Wensum
Castle Fm
Mill Street
Lyng
Norwich Road
Weston Ho
Easthaugh
Lexham Hall
Hulver Hill
Manor Ho
Gressenhall Farm & Workhouse
Swanton Morley Ho
Wensum Fm
Cadder's Hill
Dinosaur Adventure Park
East Lexham
River Nar
Punch Fm
Manor Fm
Dunfer Hole
Swanton Morley
Elsing
Collin Green Fm
Kempstone Lodge
Narrowgate Fm
Longham Hall
Gressenhall
Gorgate Hall
Hoe
Greengate
Peaseland Green
Weston Longville
Kempstone Manor Fm
Beeston
Dykewood Ho
Longham
Northall Green
Woodgate
Frog's Hall
Elsing Hall
Hall Fm
Primrose Green
Green Fm
Willows Fm
Greensgate
Tulip Hill
Church Fm
Canister Fm
Drury Square
Holly Fm
Sparrow Green
Dillington Hall
Brick Kiln Fm
Hoe Lodge
Willow Fm
Old Hall Fm
Whitehouse Fm
Heath Fm
Hockering Wood
Frans Green
Canister Fm
Great Dunham
Tuck's Fm
New Fm
High Green
Quebec Hall
Northall Green
Park Fm
Etling Green
Mowles Manor
Pound Fm
Hockering Heath
Fransgreen Fm
Weston Green
Croft Fm
Crane's Corner
Manor Ho
Bushy Common
Hill Fm
North Tuddenham
Ley's Fm
The Granary
Little Dunham
Dunham Lodge
Great Fransham
The Grange
Holly Fm
Crowe Hall
Hyde Hall
Wendling
Rush Meadow
Vale Fm
The Grange
Dereham
Quebec Rd
Old Hall Fm
Hawthorn Lodge
Whitford Br
Hockering
Poetsbree Hall Hills
Scarning Dale
Willow Fm
Ling's End
Lower Fm
White House Fm
Podmore
Scarning
Poplar Fm
Manor Fm
Dumpling Green
Whitehouse Fm
Stoneroad Fm
Clippings Green
Mattishall Burgh
Honingham
Grange Fm
Sporle Wood
Corbett's Lodge
Old Hall
Little Fransham
Lyon's Green
Park Fm
New Church Fm
Toftwood
Watering Fm
Clint Green
Old Hall Fm
Mattishall
Tollgate Fm
East Tuddenham
Old Hall
Greenacres Fm
Sparham Hall
Top Fm
Wood Fm
Necton Wood
Bradenham Hill
Broadway Fm
Old Hall Fm
Mid Norfolk Railway
Manor Fm
Shipdham Rd
Wolferton Ho
Lodge Fm
High Fm
Herne Hill Fm
High Ho
Yaxham
Yaxham
South Green
Lowlands Fm
Hawthorn Fm
Colton
Necton
Ivy Todd
Bradenham Hall
Bokenham Fm
Huntingfield Hall
Lawrence Fm
Daffy Green
Hedges Fm
Westfield
Brakefield Green
Welborne
Bickerstone Fm
141
Mona Fm
Vale Ho
West End
Manor Fm
Great Wood
Leys Fm
Brick Kiln Fm
The Park Fm
Winburgh
Holland's Hall
Welborne Common
Town Fm
Necton Common
River Wissey
Wyrley Fm
Dereham Road
Dereham Road
Whitehouse Fm
Bickeston Fm
River Yare
Colton Wood
Holme Hale Hall
Bradenham
Manor Fm
Thorpe Row
Park Fm
Upper Brandon Parva
Hill Ho
Dade's Fm
Holme
High
High
Rookery
Brandon Parva
Barford
A148
A1067
A1065
A47
B1105
B1355
B1110
B1156
B1146
B1145
B1354
B1149
B1535
160
TG

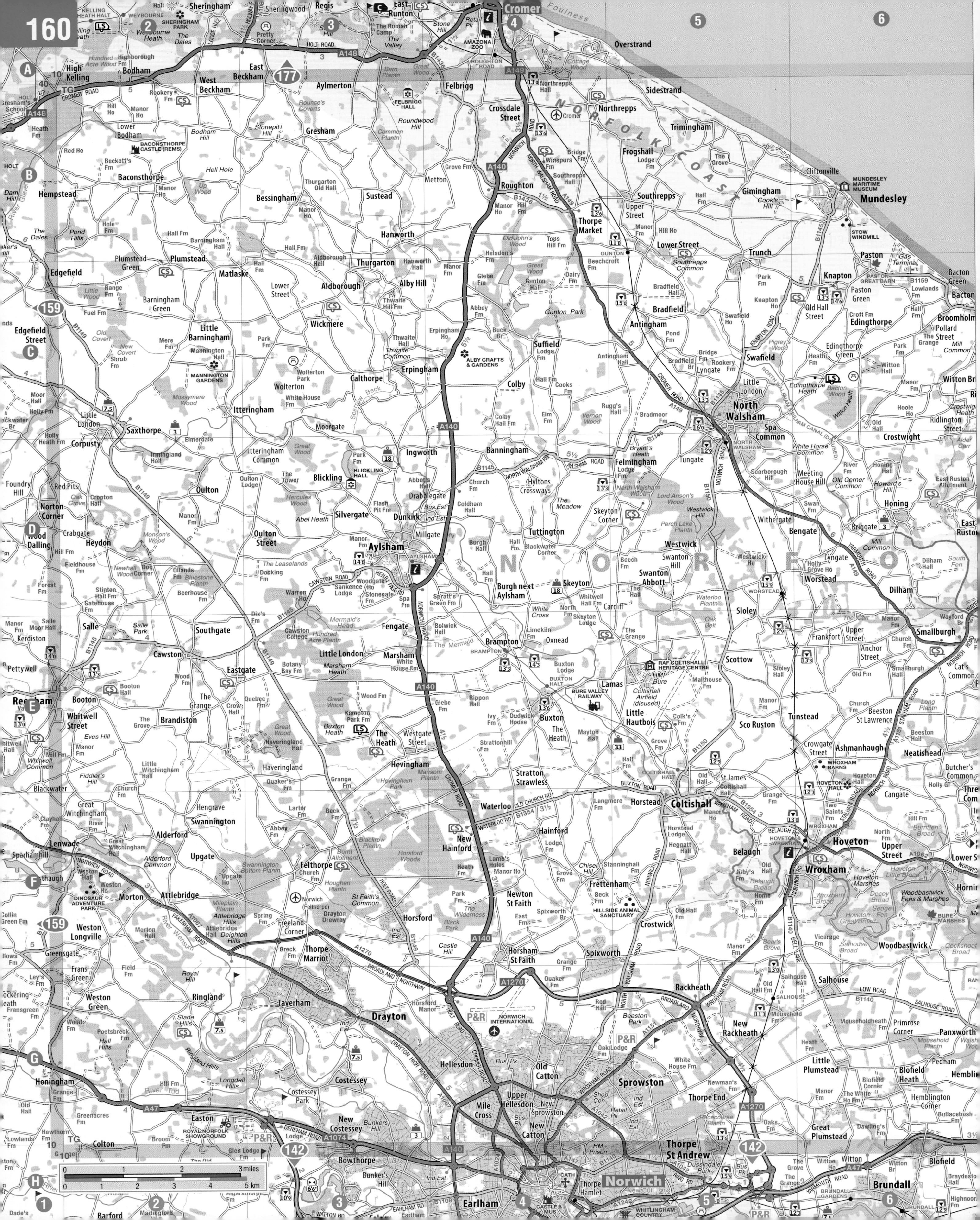
Sheringham
Cromer
Overstrand
High Kelling
Bodham
West Beckham
East Beckham
Aylmerton
Felbrigg
Crossdale Street
Northrepps
Sidestrand
Trimingham
Gresham
Lower Bodham
Baconsthorpe
Hempstead
Bessingham
Sustead
Metton
Roughton
Frogshall
Southrepps
Gimingham
Mundesley
Thorpe Market
Lower Street
Trunch
Paston
Knapton
Bacton
Edgefield
Plumstead
Matlaske
Thurgarton
Hanworth
Aldborough
Alby Hill
Bradfield
Antingham
Swafield
Edingthorpe
Little Barningham
Wickmere
Calthorpe
Erpingham
Suffield
Colby
Itteringham
Saxthorpe
Corpusty
North Walsham
Ingworth
Banningham
Felmingham
Blickling
Oulton
Aylsham
Tuttington
Westwick
Skeyton
Burgh next Aylsham
Swanton Abbott
Sloley
Worstead
Dilham
Smallburgh
Cawston
Salle
Southgate
Eastgate
Marsham
Brampton
Oxnead
Scottow
Buxton
Lamas
Little Hautbois
Tunstead
Reepham
Booton
Brandiston
Haveringland
Hevingham
Stratton Strawless
Coltishall
Horstead
Hoveton
Wroxham
Ashmanhaugh
Neatishead
Belaugh
Swannington
Alderford
Attlebridge
Morton
Lenwade
Felthorpe
Horsford
Newton St Faith
Frettenham
Crostwick
Spixworth
Horsham St Faith
Weston Longville
Ringland
Taverham
Drayton
Thorpe Marriot
Rackheath
Salhouse
Woodbastwick
Hellesdon
Old Catton
Sprowston
Thorpe End
Costessey
New Costessey
Easton
Honingham
Colton
Bowthorpe
Earlham
Norwich
Thorpe St Andrew
Brundall
Blofield
Great Plumstead
Little Plumstead
NORFOLK COAST
NORFOLK

161
7
8
9
10
11
A
B
C
D
E
F
G
H
TG
60
40
10
NORTH
SEA
Keswick
Walcott
Rookery Fm
Ostend
Walcott Ho
Walcott Hall
Happisburgh
Whimpwell Green
Eccles on Sea
Fox Hill
East Ruston Hall
B1159
Mill Fm
Bush Estate
Happisburgh Common
Grove Ho
EAST RUSTON OLD VICARAGE GDN
Manor Ho
Castle Fm
ENGLAND COAST PATH
Silcock's Fm
Lessingham
Hempstead
Manor Ho
High Hill
Brunstead Grange
Ingham Corner
Heath Fm
Hampstead Marshes
Sea Palling
Brunstead Hall
New Hall
The Hall
Brumstead Common
The Grove
Great Moss Fen
WAXHAM GREAT BARN
K
Manor Ho
Randall's Mill
Old Hall
Waxham
CALTHORPE BROAD
Ingham
Lound Fm
Brograve Fm
ROAD
Manor Ho
Stalham
Lambrigg Mill
Chapel Field
Stalham Green
Walnut Fm
MUSEUM OF THE BROADS
Whinmere Fm
Warren Fm
NORFOLK COAST
Sutton Hall
Hickling
Eastfield Fm
Horsey Corner
Berry Hall
Sutton
Hickling Green
Middle Marsh
Sutton Broad
Bray Fm
Longmoor Fm
Brayden Marshes
The Hall
HORSEY WINDMILL
Horsey
Barton Turf
Hickling Heath
Stubb
Hill Common
HICKLING BROAD NR
Stubb Mill
Horsey Mere
WINTERTON DUNES
Wood Fm
Wood Street
Hall Fm
Barton Broad
Heath Fm
HICKLING BROAD
Rush Hill
Blackfleet Broad
Hundred Stream
Winterton Holmes
Catfield
Catfield Common
Swim Coots
White Slea
Somerton Holmes
ANT BROADS & MARSHES
Catfield Hall
Meadow Dyke
THE BROADS
Sound Plantn
Heigham Sound
MARTHAM BROAD
Workhouse Common
Hall Fen
Burnley Hall
East Somerton
Irstead
Rookery Fm
Sharp Street
Hall Fm
Crome's Broad
Walton Hall
Potter Heigham
West Somerton
Winterton-on-Sea
How Hill
Damgate
HOW HILL
Ludham
River Thurne
Mustard Hyrn
Mill Fm
Neatishead Hall
High Barn Fm
Turf Fen
YARMOUTH ROAD
Thunder Hill
Blood Hills
River Ant
Fritton
White Gate Fm
7.5
Bastwick
Martham
Ludham
LUDHAM & POTTER HEIGHAM MARSHES
Ludham Hall
Cess
A1062
HIGH ROAD
Grange Fm
Johnson Street
Cold Harbour Fm
MILL RD
A149
Hemsby
Newport
Upper Street
Hundred Dike
Repps
Ormesby Broad
Decoy Fm
Dowe Hill
Sand Cliffs
Rollesby
MAIN ROAD
Scratby Hall
ST BENET'S ABBEY (REMS)
Thurne
Thurne Mouth
Ashby Hall
HEATH ROAD
B1152
Ranworth Broad
Ranworth Marshes
Ward Marsh
Ormesby St Michael
Ormesby St Margaret
Scratby
Boundary Ho
Clippesby
Narrowgate Corner
California
Fleet Dike
Ranworth
South Walsham Broad
Clippesby Ho
Burgh St Margaret (Flegburgh)
Lily Broad
Rollesby Broad
Manor Fm
River Bure
A1064
Low Fm
MAIN ROAD
FAIRHAVEN WOODLAND & WATER GARDEN
Pilson Green
Newgate Corner
Filby Broad
Filby
Nova Scotia Fm
South Walsham
Filby Heath
Tyegate Green
Upton
Billockby
Charity Fm
A1064
ROMAN TOWN
Town Green
Highfield Fm
Mill Hill Fm
Burgh Common
Mautby Lodge
NORWICH RD
Upton Green
Thrigby
Mautby
Caister Hall
Caister-on-Sea
NEWPORT ROAD
2 MAIN ROAD
THRIGBY HALL WILDLIFE GARDENS
CAISTER CASTLE & MOTOR MUSEUM
Muck Fleet
Lower Wood Fm
Watt's Hall Fm
Fishley
Whitegate Fm
Winsford Hall
Barn Fm
West End
West Caister
CAISTER BY-PASS
Caister Pt
Long Plantn
Burlingham Green
OLD ROAD
Woodlands Fm
Runham
Waters's Covert
Burlingham Ho
B1140
Stokesby
Gt Yarmouth North Denes
North Denes
YARMOUTH
Decoy Fm
Acle
Manor Fm
CAISTER ROAD
North Burlingham
NORWICH ROAD
The Hall
ACLE
Damgate
Mautby Marsh Fm
A47
143
A47
Lingwood Lodge
NEW ROAD
Ashtree Fm
NEW ROAD
Newtown
North Beach
Lingwood
15.3
Britannia Fm
Runham Vauxhall
Runham
Great Yarmouth
LINGWOOD
Staithe Fm
Beighton
Wood Fm
South
Moulton
Tunstall

CAERNARFON
BAY
BAE CAERNARFON
ISLE OF ANGLESEY
YNYS MÔN
Aberffraw
Llangadwaladr
Hermon
Bodorgan
Malltraeth
Llangaffo
Newborough
(Niwbwrch)
Pen-lon
Dwyran
Bethel
Trefdraeth
Capel Mawr
Llangwyfan-isaf
BARCLODIAD Y GAWRES BURIAL CHAMBER
TACLA TAID TRANSPORT MUSEUM
ANGLESEY MODEL VILLAGE
NEWBOROUGH WARREN & YNYS LLANDDWYN
Malltraeth Bay
Bae Malltraeth
Malltraeth Sands
Newborough Forest
Newborough Warren
Ynys Llanddwyn
WALES COAST PATH
Aber Ffraw Bay
Porth Cwyfan
Porth China
Penrhyn
Trefi
Bodowen
South Sands
Warren Fm
AIRWORLD AVIATION MUSEUM
Morfa Dinlle
Dinas Dinlle
Llandwrog
Pontllyfni
Aberdesach
Clynnog-fawr
Capel Uchaf
ST BEUNO'S WELL
Gyrn-goch
Bryn-yr-eryr
Trefor
Gwydir
Trwyn y Tâl
Trwyn y Gorlech
Llanaelhaearn
Yr Eifl 564
TRE'R-CEIRI (FORT)
Llithfaen
Pistyll
Morfa Nefyn
Nefyn
LLŶN MARITIME MUSEUM
Edern
Llwyndyrys
Pencaenewydd
Llangybi
Llanarmon
Chwilog
Fron
Rhos-fawr
Y Ffôr
Tan-y-graig
Garn Boduan 280
Carreg Ddu
Porth Dinllaen
Lleyn Peninsula
A4080
A499
A497
B4417
B4354
144
145
178
SH
0 1 2 3 miles
0 1 2 3 4 5 km

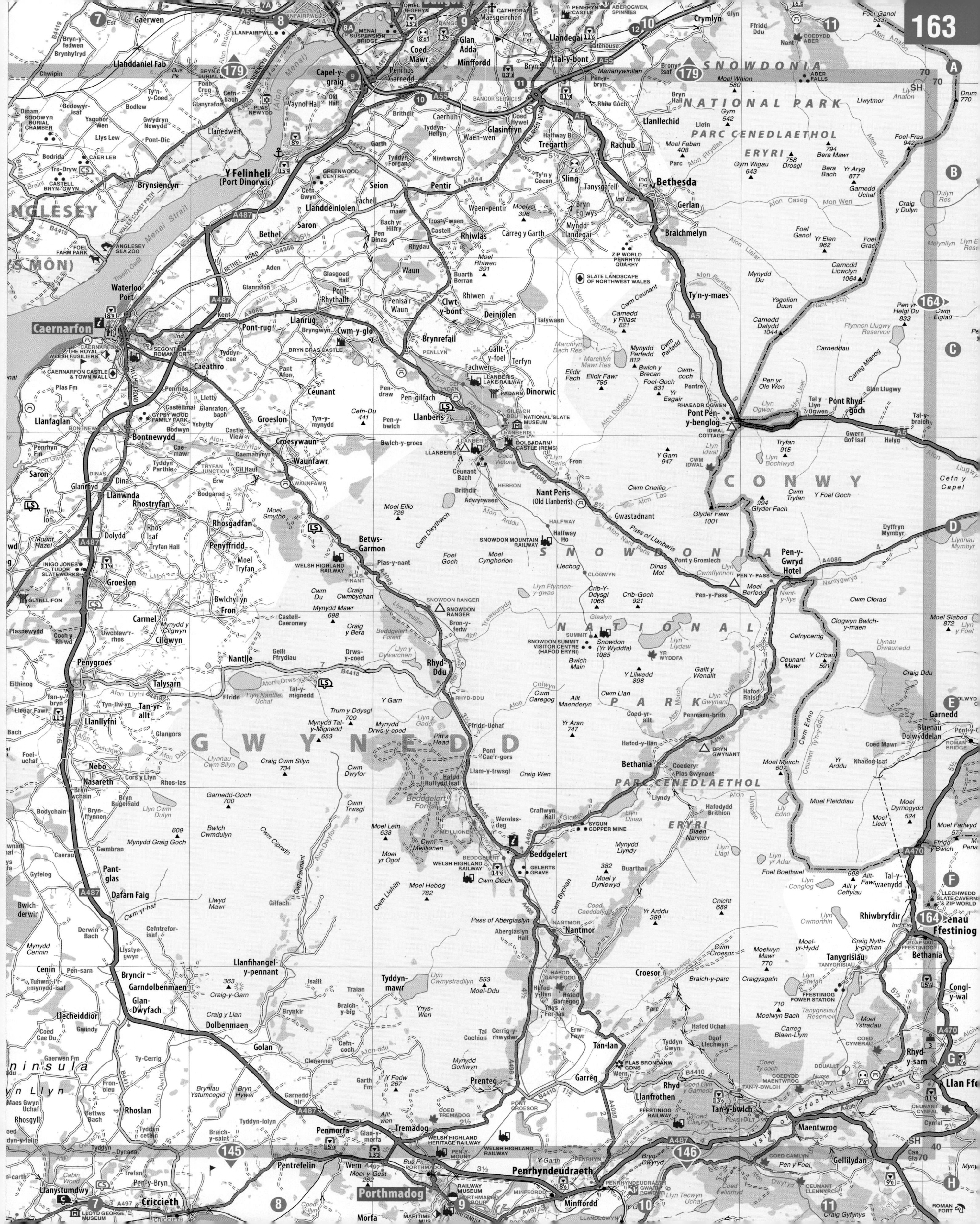

Gaerwen
Llanfairpwll
Menai Suspension Bridge
Bangor
Maesgeirchen
Penrhyn Castle
Llandegai
Crymlyn
Llanddaniel Fab
Snowdonia National Park
Parc Cenedlaethol Eryri
Aber Falls
Capel-y-graig
Glan Adda
Minffordd
Coed Mawr
Penrhos Garnedd
Tal-y-bont
Vaynol Hall
Llanllechid
Llanedwen
Glasinfryn
Tregarth
Rachub
Bodrida
Caer Leb
Brynsiencyn
Y Felinheli (Port Dinorwic)
Seion
Pentir
Sling
Bethesda
Gerlan
Anglesey
Llanddeiniolen
Saron
Bethel
Rhiwlas
Braichmelyn
Menai Strait
Anglesey Sea Zoo
Waun
Ty'n-y-maes
Waterloo Port
Caernarfon
Pont-rug
Llanrug
Cwm-y-glo
Clwt-y-bont
Deiniolen
Brynrefail
Caeathro
Ceunant
Dinorwic
Llanberis
Llanfaglan
Bontnewydd
Groeslon
Croesywaun
Waunfawr
Pont Pen-y-benglog
Pont Rhyd-goch
Tryfan
Glyder Fawr
Dinas
Llanwnda
Rhostryfan
Rhosgadfan
Nant Peris (Old Llanberis)
Betws-Garmon
Penyffridd
Snowdon Mountain Railway
Pass of Llanberis
Pen-y-Gwryd Hotel
Pen-y-Pass
Conwy
Fron
Carmel
Cilgwyn
Nantlle
Rhyd-Ddu
Snowdon (Yr Wyddfa) 1085
Penygroes
Talysarn
Llanllyfni
Gwynedd
Nebo
Nasareth
Bethania
Garnedd
Dolwyddelan
Beddgelert
Pant-glas
Dafarn Faig
Nantmor
Llanfihangel-y-pennant
Bryncir
Garndolbenmaen
Glan-Dwyfach
Dolbenmaen
Golan
Croesor
Rhiwbryfdir
Blaenau Ffestiniog
Tanygrisiau
Tan-lan
Garreg
Prenteg
Tremadog
Penmorfa
Llanfrothen
Tan-y-bwlch
Maentwrog
Gellilydan
Penrhyndeudraeth
Pentrefelin
Llanystumdwy
Criccieth
Porthmadog
Minffordd
Morfa
Llan Ffestiniog
Rhyd-y-sarn

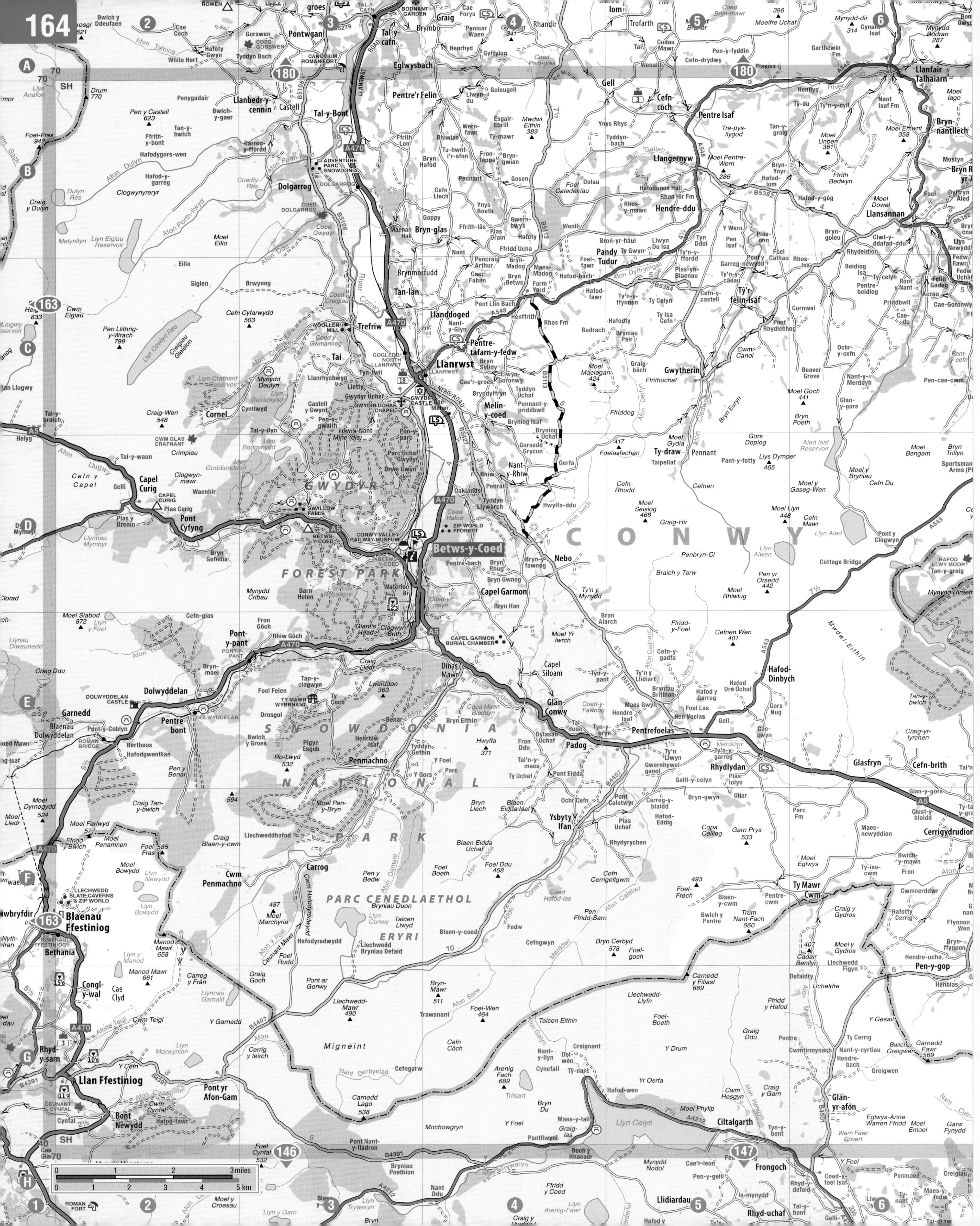

Rowen
groes
Tal-y-Cafn
Bodnant Garden
Graig
Cae Forys
Gyffin
Rhandir
Iom
Trofarth
Coed Bryn-mawr
396
Moelfre Uchaf
Mynydd-dir 314
Cynant Isaf
Bwlch y Ddeufaen
rosgl 621
Cae Coch
Gorswen
Coed Gorswen
Pontwgan
Tal-y-cafn
Brymbo
Penisar Waen
341
Hafoty Gwyn
Tyddyn Bach
White Hart
Canovium Roman Fort
Henrhyd
Gyffylog
Tail
Codau Mawr
Pen-y-fyddin
Plasisa
Cefn-drydwy
Garthewin Fm
Mynydd Bodran 287
Llyn Anafon
Drum 770
Eglwysbach
Coed Pant-glas
Wenallt
Gell
Cefn-coch
Llanfair Talhaiarn
Henllys
River Elwy
Moel Iago
Penygadair
Pen y Castell 623
Bwlch-y-gaer
Llanbedr-y-cennin
Castell
Tal-y-Bont
Pentre'r Felin
Llwyn-du
Goleugell
Ty-du
Ty'n-y-cyll
Nant Isaf Fm
Pentre Isaf
Bryn-nantllech
Ffrith-y-bont
Tan-y-bwlch
Wern-fawr
Esgair-Ebrill
Mwdwl Eithin 389
Ynys Rhys
Tre-pys-llygod
Tan-y-graig
Moel Unben 361
Moel Emwnt 358
Foel-Fras 942
Hafodygors-wen
Garreg-y-ffordd
Ffrith Lon
Rhiwlas
Ty-mawr
Tyddyn-bach
Afon Gallen
Llangernyw
Moel Pentre-Wern 286
Mostyn
Adventure Parc Snowdonia
Afon Dulyn
Tu-hwnt-i'r-afon
Fron-loppa
Bryn-gwian
Bryn Hafod
Coedty Res
Dolgarrog
Hafod-y-garreg
Clogwynyreryr
Dulyn Res
Craig y Dulyn
Cefn Llech
Pennant
Gosen
Foel Caledeiriau
Dolau
Hafodunos Hall
Rhan Hir Fm
Rhos-y-mawn
Hendre-ddu
Bryn-Ynyr
Ffrith Bedwyn
Hafod-lom
Hafod-y-gog
Moel Dowel
Llansannan
Dyffryn Aled
Coed Dolgarrog
Coed Gwydyr
Melynllyn
Llyn Eigiau Reservoir
Moel Eilio
Goppy
Maenan Hall
Bryn-glas
Ynys Boeth
Ffrith-lâs
Plas Drain
Gwern-bwys
Hafoty
Wenlli
Y Wern
Pen Isaf
Plas-onn
Bryn-goleu
Clwt-y-ddafad-ddu
Llys Newydd
Eilio
Afon Ddu
Nant
Ffridd Ucha
Bron-yr-haul
Pandy Tudur
Ty Gwyn
Llwyn Du Isa
Tyn Ddol
Ty'n-y-ffordd
Foel Cathau
Rhydeidion
Rhos-Isa
Siglen
Brwynog
River Conwy
Brynmorfudd
Pencraig Arthur
Bryn-Madog
Maes-Madog
Foel-fawr
Hafod-bach
Afon Dyffryn-gall
Plas-yn-Blaenau
Garreg-newydd
Ty'n-y-caeau
Beidiog Isa
Ty-celyn
Pont y Nant
Felin Gadeg
Heigl 833
Cwm Eigiau
Caer Faban
Bryn Betws
Farm Yard
Tan-lan
Coed Creigiau
B5384
Cefn-y-castell
Ty'r-felin-isaf
Pentre-beidiog
Acrau
Cae-Goronwy
Cefn Cyfarwydd 503
Pant Llin Bach
Hafod-fawr
Ty'n-y-ffynnon
Ty Celyn
Cornwal
Priddbwll
Cae-du
Llugwy Reservoir
Pen Llithrig-y-Wrach 799
Llyn Cowlyd Res
Creigiau Gleision
Woollen Mill
Trefriw
Coed y Gwmannog
Llanddoged
Nant-y-Glyn
Henffrith
Rhos Fm
Bodrach
Hafodty
Bryniau Pair
Ty Isa Cefn
Cwm Canol
Pont Rhydlechog
Ochr-y-cefn
Pant-y-cefn
Tai
Coed yr Allt
Gogledd North Llanrwst
Pentre-tafarn-y-fedw
Llanrwst
Bryn Syllty
Llwyn-Goronwy
Moel Maelogan 424
Graig-bach
Ffrithuchaf
Gwytherin
Beaver Grove
Nant-y-Merddyn
Pen-cae-cwm
Llan Llugwy
Llyn Crafnant Reservoir
Mynydd Deulyn
Llyn Geironydd
Llanrhychwyn
Tyn-llwyn
Lletty
Cae'r-groes
Bryndyffryn
Tyddyn Uchaf
Pennant-y-priddbwll
Melin-y-coed
Gwydyr Uchaf
Gwydir Uchaf Chapel
Gwydir Castle
Nebo Road
Ffriddog
Afon Derfyn
Afon Cledwen
Bryn Euryn
Moel Goch 441
Glan-y-gors
Tal-y-braich
Helyg
Craig-Wen 548
Cornel
Cyllwyd
Castell y Gwynt
Pen-y-gwaith
Hafna-Nant Mine (dis)
Pen-y-parc
Bryniog Isaf
Bryniog Uchaf
Gorsedd Grycun
Bryn Poeth
Cwm Glas Crafnant
Crimpiau
Tal-y-llyn
Llyn Bodgynydd
Parc Uchaf Gwydyr
417
Foelasfechan
Moel Gydia
Ty-draw
Taipellaf
Pennant
Gors Dopiog
Pant-y-fotty
Llys Dymper 465
Aled Isaf Reservoir
Moel Bengam
Bryn Trillyn
Tal-y-waun
Cefn y Capel
Gelli
Capel Curig
Clogwyn-mawr
Goddiondduon
Drws Gwyn
Rhiw
Nant-y-Rhiw
Oerfa
Cefn-Rhudd
Cefnen
Moel y Bryniau
Cefn Du
Moel y Gaseg-Wen
Sportsman Arms
Plas Curig
Waenhir
Gwydyr
Swallow Falls
Oaklands
Penrallt
Tyddyn Llywarch
Hwylfa-ddu
Afon Iwrch
Moel Seisiog 468
Graig-Hir
Moel Llyn 448
Cefn Mawr
Llyn Aled
Plas y Brenin
Pont Cyfyng
Mymbyr
Llynnau Mymbyr
Betws-y-Coed
Conwy Valley Railway Museum
Coed Hafod
Zip World Fforest
Conwy
Nebo
Penbryn-Ci
Llyn Alwen
Pont y Clogwyn
Hafod Elwy Moor
Tan-y-graig
Cottage Bridge
Bryn Gefeilia
Forest Park
Pentre-bach
Bryn Rhug
Bryn-y-fawnog
Bryn Gwnog
Capel Garmon
Braich y Tarw
Pen yr Orsedd 442
Mynydd Hiraeth
Clorad
Mynydd Cribau
Sarn Helen
Waterloo Br
Llyn Elsi Reservoir
Coed-y-celyn
Bryn Ifan
Ty'n y Mynydd
Moel Rhiwlug
Moel Siabod 872
Llyn y Foel
Cefn-glas
Fron Goch
Giant's Head
Clogwyn-Brith
Bron Alarch
Ffridd-y-Foel
Cefnen Wen 401
Mwdwl-Eithin
Llynau Diwaunedd
Pont-y-pant
Rhiw Goch
Capel Garmon Burial Chamber
Moel Yr Iwrch
Afon Ystumiau
Craig Lledr
Bryn-moel
Capel Siloam
Tyn-y-pant
Cefn-y-gadfa
Afon Cadnant
Nant y Foel
Ty'n y Llidiart
Hafod-Dinbych
Craig Ddu
Dolwyddelan
Tan-y-clogwyn
Lwerddon 363
Dinas Mawr
River Conwy
Foel Felen
Ty Mawr Wybrnant
Ty Coch
Coed Maen Bleddyn
Glan-Conwy
Coed-y-Fawnog
Maes Gwyn
Bryniau Brithion
Hafod y Garreg
Hafod Dre Uchaf
Tan-y-bwlch
Gors Nug
Dolwyddelan Castle
Garnedd
Pentre-bont
Drosgol
Benar
Afon Machno
Bryn Eithin
Hendre Isaf
Hen Voelas
Foel Las
Gell
Cae-gwyn
Blaenau Dolwyddelan
Pont-y-Coblyn
Roman Bridge
Bertheos
Snowdonia
Bwlch y Groes
Pigyn Esgob
Henrhiw Isaf
Tyddyn Gethin
Hwylfa 371
Fron Ddu
Dylasau Uchaf
Tai-duon
Tyn-y-bryn
Pentrefoelas
Merddwr
Craig-yr-lyrchen
Hafodgwenllian
Ro-Lwyd 532
Penmachno
Y Foel
Tai'n-y-maes
Padog
Ty'n Llwyn
Ty'n-y-garreg
Rhydlydan
Glasfryn
Cefn-brith
Pen y Benar
Y Gors
Parc
Ty Uchaf
Pont Eidda
Gwernhywel ganol
Gallt-y-celyn
Plas Iolyn
National
Moel Dyrnogydd 524
Craig Tan-y-bwlch
594
Moel Pen-y-Bryn
Bryn Llech
Blaen Eidda Isaf
Ochr Cefn
Pont Caletwyr
Carreg-y-blaidd
Bryn-gwyn
Glâr
Parc Fm
Glan-y-gors
Clust-y-blaidd
Moel Lledr
Moel Farlwyd 577
Ffridd y Bwlch
Moel Penamnen
Foel-Fras 585
Craig Blaen-y-cwm
Llechwedd-hafod
Park
Blaen Eidda Uchaf
Ysbyty Ifan
Plas Uchaf
Hafod-Eddig
Rhydyrchen
Copa Ceiliog
Garn Prys 533
Maes-newyddion
Cerrigydrudion
Moel Bowydd
Llyn Newydd
Carrog
Pen y Bedw
Foel Boeth
Foel Ddu 458
Afon Eidda
Cefn Cerrigellgwm
Moel Eglwys
Bwlch-y-mawn
Ty-isa-cwm
Fron
Llechwedd Slate Caverns & Zip World
Cwm Penmachno
Cwm Hafodyredwydd
Parc Cenedlaethol
Coed Hafod-las
Afon Caletwr
493
Foel-Frech
Blaen-y-cwm
Ty Mawr Cwm
Pentre-cwm
Cwmoerddwr
Llyn Bowydd
Blaenau Ffestiniog
487
Moel Marchyria
Bryniau Duon
Llyn Conwy
Talcen Llwyd
Pen Ffridd-Sarn
Bwlch y Pentre
Trum Nant-Fach 560
Craig y Gydros
Hafotty Cerrig
Ffynnon Wen
Bethania
Manod Mawr 658
Eryri
Hafodyredwydd
Afon y Foel
Ceunant Mawr
Llechwedd Bryniau Defaid
Blaen-y-coed
Fedw
Cefngwyn
Bryn Cerbyd 578
Foel-goch
407
Cadair Benllyn
Moel y Gydros
Llechwedd Figyn
Bryn-ffynnon
Hendre-ucha
Pen-y-gop
Llyn y Manod
Foel Rudd
Marddwr
Carnedd y Filiast 669
Defaidty
Henblas
Congl-y-wal
Cae Clyd
Manod Mawr 661
Carreg y Frân
Graig Goch
Pont ar Gonwy
Bryn-Mawr 511
Afon Serw
Llechwedd-Llyfn
Ffridd y Hafod
Ucheldre
Afon Mynach
Llynnau Gamallt
Llechwedd-Mawr 490
Trawsnant
Foel-Wen 464
Talcen Eithin
Foel-Boeth
Y Gesail
Cwm Teigl
Y Garnedd
Afon Teigl
Graig Ddu
Pentre
Ty Cerrig
Llyn Morwynion
Cerrig y leirch
Migneint
Cefn Côch
Nant-y-llyn
Craignant
Dol-wen
Y Drum
Cwmtirmynach
Nant-y-cyrtiau
Bwlch y Greigwen
Carnedd Fawr 569
Hendre-bach
Rhyd-y-sarn
Y Cefn
Llan Ffestiniog
Nant Derbyniad
Cefngarw
Arenig Fach 689
Cynefail
Tŷ-nant
Yr Oerfa
Greigwen
Pont yr Afon-Gam
Ceunant Cynfal
Afon Cynfal
Cwm Cynfal
Bont Newydd
Hafod-fawr
Carnedd Lago 538
Trinant
Bryn Du
Hafod-wen
Cwm Hesgyn
Craig y Garn
Afon Hesgyn
Glan-yr-afon
Cynfal
Mochowgryn
Y Foel
Maes-y-tail
Graig-las
Llyn Celyn
Moel Phylip
A4212
Ciltalgarth
Tyn-y-bont
Eglwys-Anne Warren Ffridd
Moel Emoel
Garw Fynydd
Wern Fawr Covert
Pont Nant-y-lladron
Pantllwyni
Foel Cynfal 532
B4391
Boch y Rhaeadr
Mynydd Nodol
Cae'r-leon
Pen-y-gelli
Frongoch
Y Foel
Coed-y-foel Isaf
Penmaen
Creiglau
Bryniau Poethion
Nant Ddu
Afon Tryweryn
Ffridd y Coed
Is-mynydd
Rhyd-y-defaid
Maes-y-fedw
Ty-nant
Moel y Croesau
Llyn y Garn
Llidiardau
Rhyd-uchaf
Tal-y-bont
Roman Fort
0 1 2 3 miles
0 1 2 3 4 5 km
SH
70
180
163
146
147
A470
A5
A548
A543
A4212
B4407
B4406
B5113
B5106
B5427
B5382
B4501
B4391

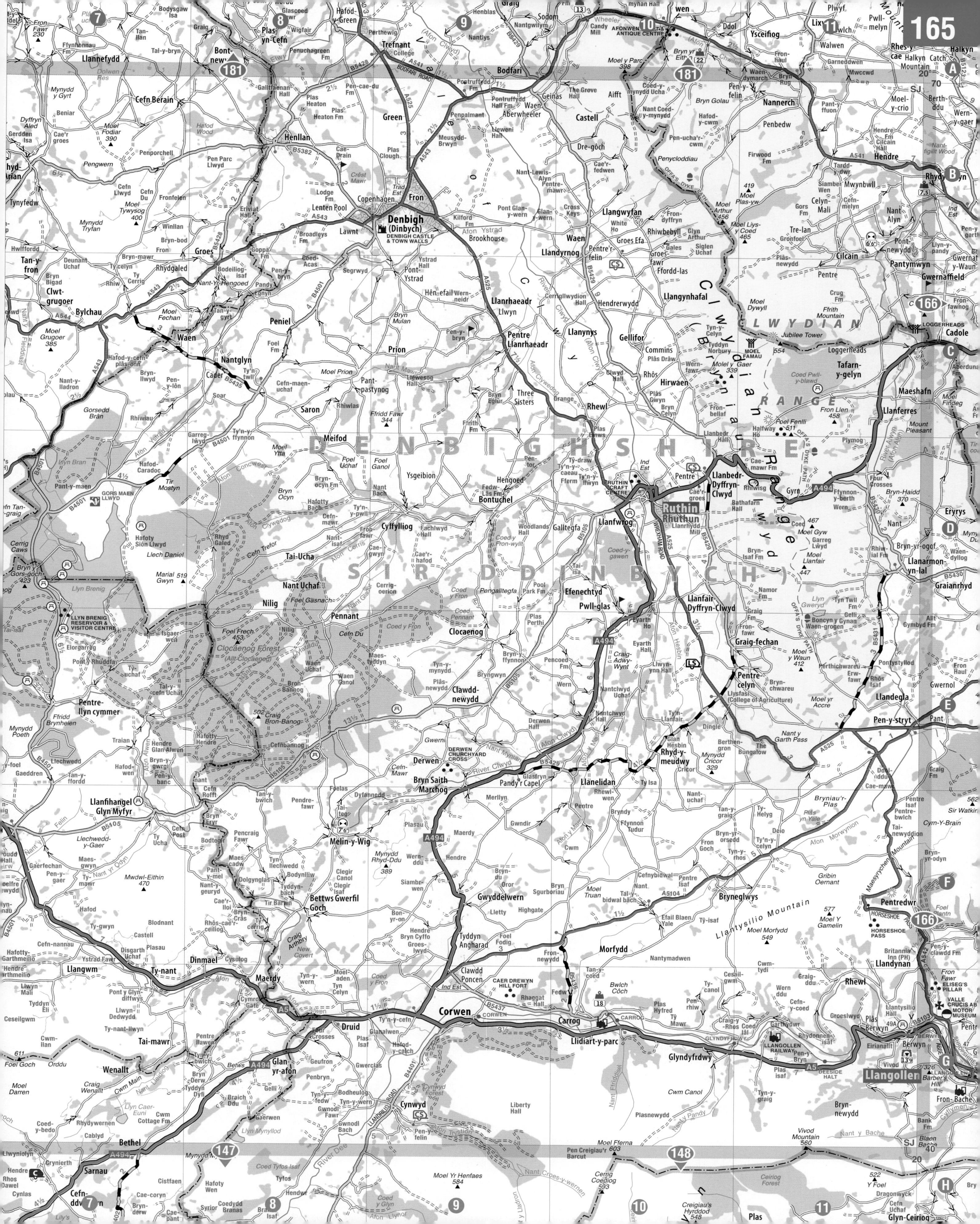
DENBIGHSHIRE
(SIR DDINBYCH)
CLWYDIAN RANGE
Clwydian Range (Bryniau Clwyd)
Vale of Clwyd
Denbigh (Dinbych)
DENBIGH CASTLE & TOWN WALLS
Ruthin Rhuthun
RUTHIN CRAFT CENTRE
Corwen
Llangollen
Trefnant
Bodfari
Henllan
Llannefydd
Cefn Berain
Bylchau
Waen
Nantglyn
Peniel
Prion
Saron
Meifod
Cyffylliog
Bontuchel
Llanfwrog
Llanrhaeadr
Pentre Llanrhaeadr
Llanynys
Rhewl
Gellifor
Hirwaen
Llangynhafal
Llandyrnog
Llangwyfan
Waen
Castell
Nannerch
Cilcain
Llanbedr-Dyffryn-Clwyd
Llanferres
Maeshafn
Loggerheads
Tafarn-y-gelyn
Llanarmon-yn-Ial
Eryrys
Graianrhyd
Llandegla
Pen-y-stryt
Efenechtyd
Pwll-glas
Llanfair-Dyffryn-Clwyd
Graig-fechan
Pentre-celyn
Clocaenog
Clawdd-newydd
Derwen
Bryn Saith Marchog
Melin-y-Wig
Llanelidan
Rhyd-y-meudwy
Gwyddelwern
Bryneglwys
Bettws Gwerfil Goch
Llanfihangel Glyn Myfyr
Pentre-llyn cymmer
Nant Uchaf
Nilig
Pennant
Tai-Ucha
Dinmael
Maerdy
Llangwm
Ty-nant
Druid
Glan-yr-afon
Cynwyd
Carrog
Llidiart-y-parc
Glyndyfrdwy
Morfydd
Rhewl
Llandynan
Pentredwr
Berwyn
Tai-mawr
Wenallt
Bethel
Sarnau
Clocaenog Forest
LLYN BRENIG RESERVOIR & VISITOR CENTRE
Llyn Brenig
GORS MAEN LLWYD
MOEL FAMAU
Jubilee Tower
Llantysilio Mountain
HORSESHOE PASS
ELISEG'S PILLAR
VALLE CRUCIS ABBEY
MOTOR MUSEUM
LLANGOLLEN RAILWAY
CAER DREWYN HILL FORT
DERWEN CHURCHYARD CROSS
AFONWEN CRAFT & ANTIQUE CENTRE
OFFA'S DYKE PATH
A525
A541
A543
A494
A5
A5104
B5105
B5429
B4501
181
166
147
148

FLINTSHIRE
(SIR Y FFLINT)
WREXHAM
(WRECSAM)
Chester
Wrexham
Wrecsam
Mold
Yr Wyddgrug
Queensferry
Llangollen
Connah's Quay
Shotton
Buckley
(Bwcle)
Hawarden
(Penarlâg)
Flint Mountain
(Mynydd Fflint)
Northop
(Llan-eurgain)
Oakenholt
Halkyn
Rhydymwyn
Soughton
(Sychdyn)
Ewloe
Ewloe Green
New Brighton
Alltami
Mynydd-isa
Leadmill
Gwernaffield
Pantymwyn
Cadole
Gwernymynydd
Maeshafn
Llanferres
Nercwys
Pontblyddyn
Leeswood
(Coed-Llai)
Treuddyn
Eryrys
Coed-Talon
Caergwrle
Hope
(Yr Hôb)
Penyffordd
Higher Kinnerton
Lower Kinnerton
Broughton
Bretton
Saltney
Lache
Handbridge
Balderton
Dodleston
Eccleston
Pulford
Rossett
Marford
Gresford
Llay
Cefn-y-bedd
Ffrith
Llanfynydd
Rhydtalog
Four Crosses
Bwlchgwyn
Gwynfryn
Minera
Coedpoeth
Brymbo
Gwersyllt
Rhosrobin
Garden Village
Acton
Rhosnesni
Rhosddu
Bersham
Rhostyllen
Marchwiel
Johnstown
Rhosllanerchrugog
Penycae
Ruabon
(Rhiwabon)
Cefn-mawr
Pont Cysyllte
Trevor
Garth
Chirk
(Y Waun)
Overton (Owrtyn)
Bangor-is-y-coed
Holt
Farndon
Churton
Aldford
Worthenbury
Threapwood
Penley
Erbistock
Halton
Llandegla
Pentredwr
Froncysyllte
Berwyn
Upton
Newton
Hoole
Rowton
Littleton
Vicarscross
Backford
Mollington
Saughall
Sealand
Garden City
Sandycroft
Mancot
Pen-y-stryt
Llandynan
Sir Watkin's Tower
Ruabon Mountain
Llandegla Forest
River Dee
Shropshire Union Canal
Llangollen Canal
Offa's Dyke Path
Wat's Dyke
0 1 2 3 miles
0 1 2 3 4 5 km

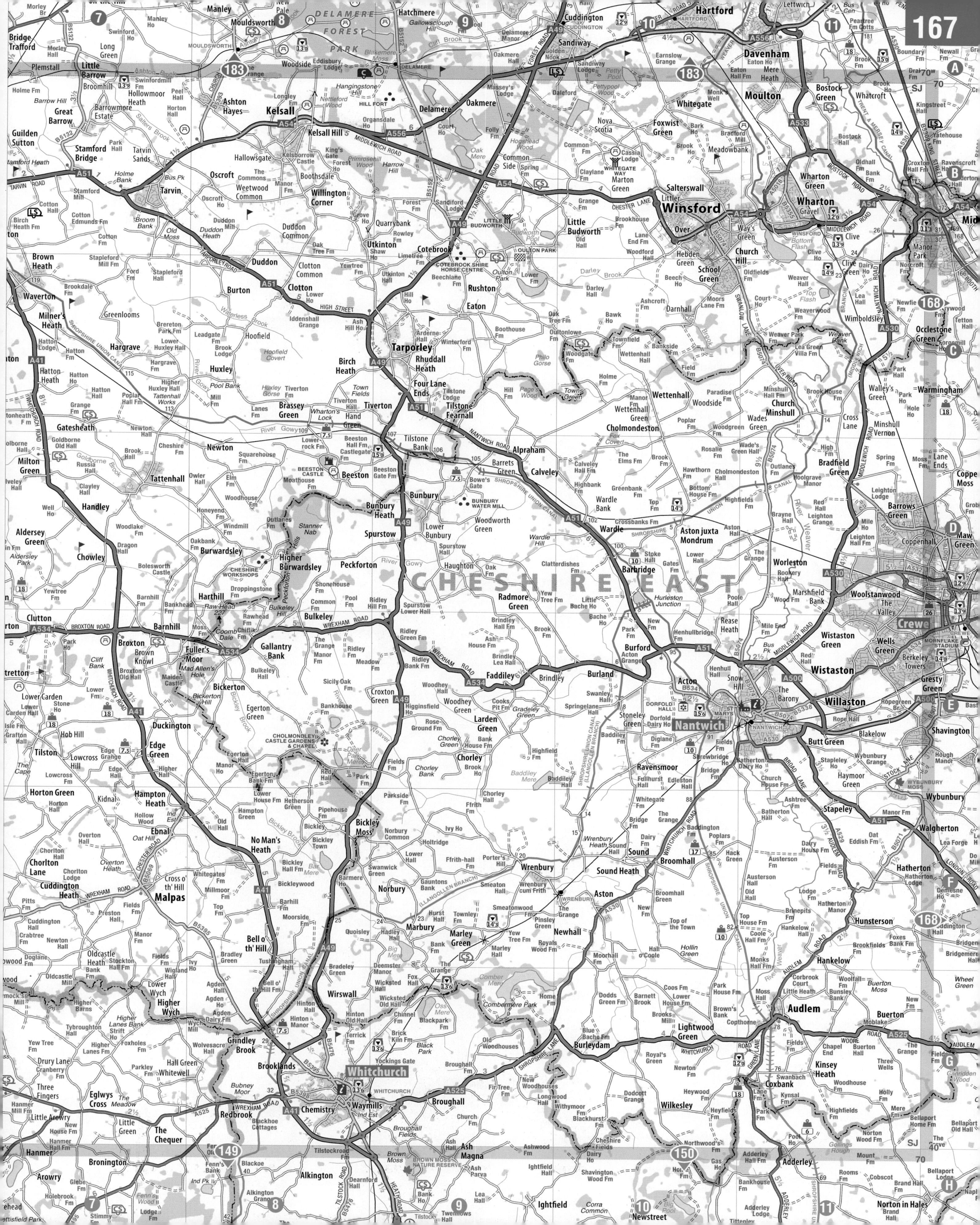
DELAMERE FOREST PARK
Manley
Mouldsworth
Hatchmere
Cuddington
Sandiway
Hartford
Davenham
Moulton
Bridge Trafford
Long Green
Little Barrow
Plemstall
Great Barrow
Barrowmore Estate
Guilden Sutton
Stamford Bridge
Tarvin Sands
Ashton Hayes
Kelsall
Kelsall Hill
Delamere
Oakmere
Whitegate
Foxwist Green
Nova Scotia
Common Side
Hallowsgate
Oscroft
Tarvin
Willington Corner
The Commons
Weetwood Common
Marton Green
Salterswall
Little Budworth
Winsford
Over
Wharton Green
Wharton
Bostock Green
Whatcroft
Utkinton
Cotebrook
Duddon
Clotton
Rushton
Eaton
Burton
Waverton
Milner's Heath
Hargrave
Tarporley
Birch Heath
Rhuddall Heath
Huxley
Four Lane Ends
Tiverton
Tilstone Fearnall
Brassey Green
Hand Green
Alpraham
Wettenhall
Woodside
Church Minshull
Cholmondeston
Warmingham
Gatesheath
Newton
Beeston
Beeston Castle
Calveley
Tattenhall
Milton Green
Bunbury
Bunbury Heath
Spurstow
Handley
Lower Bunbury
Woodworth Green
Wardle
Aston juxta Mondrum
Bradfield Green
Barrows Green
Coppenhall
Aldersey Green
Chowley
Burwardsley
Higher Burwardsley
Peckforton
CHESHIRE EAST
Haughton
Barbridge
Worleston
Radmore Green
Woolstanwood
The Valley
Crewe
Harthill
Bulkeley
Clutton
Barnhill
Broxton
Brown Knowl
Fuller's Moor
Gallantry Bank
Faddiley
Brindley
Burland
Burford
Acton
Wistaston
Wells Green
Willaston
Nantwich
Bickerton
Duckington
Edge Green
Tilston
Horton Green
Hampton Heath
Croxton Green
Larden Green
Chorley
Ravensmoor
Stapeley
Shavington
Wybunbury
Walgherton
No Man's Heath
Bickley Moss
Wrenbury
Sound
Broomhall
Sound Heath
Hatherton
Chorlton Lane
Cuddington Heath
Malpas
Norbury
Marbury
Marley Green
Aston
Newhall
Hunsterson
Hankelow
Bell o' th' Hill
Higher Wych
Wirswall
Audlem
Buerton
Grindley Brook
Burleydam
Lightwood Green
Brooklands
Whitchurch
Kinsey Heath
Coxbank
Eglwys Cross
Redbrook
Chemistry
Waymills
Broughall
Wilkesley
Little Arowry
The Chequer
Hanmer
Bronington
Ash Magna
Alkington
Adderley
Arowry
Ightfield
Newstreet
Norton in Hales
183
168
149
150
SJ
70

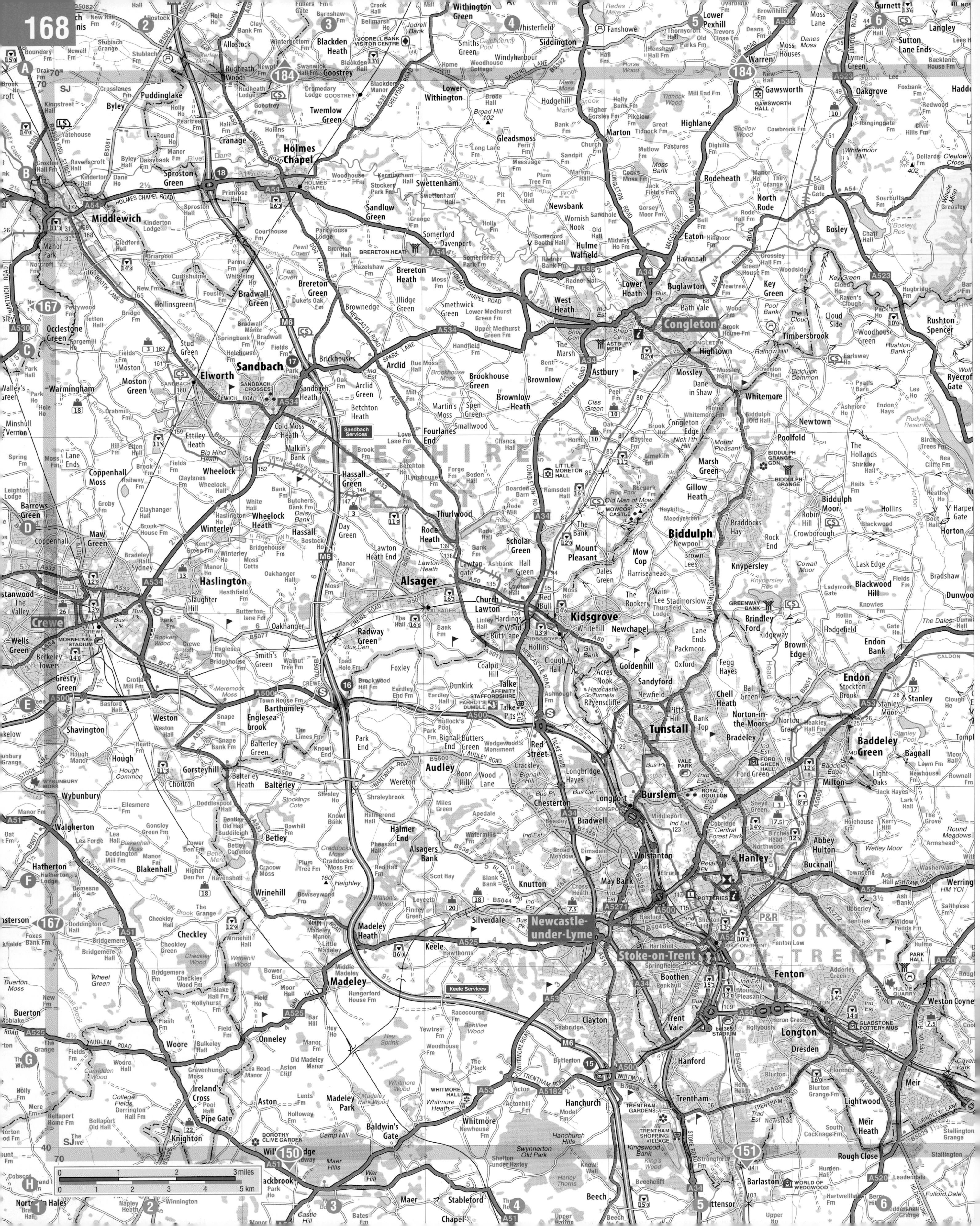
CHESHIRE EAST
STOKE-ON-TRENT
Holmes Chapel
Middlewich
Sandbach
Elworth
Congleton
Biddulph
Kidsgrove
Alsager
Haslington
Crewe
Tunstall
Burslem
Hanley
Stoke-on-Trent
Newcastle-under-Lyme
Longton
Fenton
Madeley
Audley
Goostrey
Byley
Cranage
Swettenham
Marton
Bosley
Rushton Spencer
Astbury
Mow Cop
Knypersley
Endon
Baddeley Green
Trentham
Barlaston
Meir
Keele
Silverdale
Chesterton
Wolstanton
Talke
Brereton Green
Wheelock
Winterley
Weston
Shavington
Wybunbury
Betley
Woore
Onneley
Whitmore
Hanchurch
Madeley Heath
Alsagers Bank
Knutton
Clayton
Trent Vale
Hanford
Dresden
Lightwood
Meir Heath
Stanley
Bucknall
Abbey Hulton
Milton
Bagnall
Kidsgrove
Red Street
Wereton
Betchton Heath
Hassall Green
Rode Heath
Scholar Green
Church Lawton
Sandbach Services
Keele Services
Congleton Edge
Timbersbrook
Gawsworth
Siddington
Withington Green
Lower Withington
Twemlow Green
Blackden Heath
Allostock
Warmingham
Coppenhall Moss
Wells Green
Gresty Green
Hough
Gorstyhill
Chorlton
Balterley
Barthomley
Englesea-brook
Walgherton
Hatherton
Checkley
Buerton
Knighton
Pipe Gate
Ireland's Cross
Aston
Madeley Park
Baldwin's Gate
Stableford
Maer
Chapel
Beech
Rough Close
Newchapel
Goldenhill
Sandyford
Packmoor
Brindley Ford
Brown Edge
Norton-in-the-Moors
Bradeley
Hollins
Warren
Oakgrove
Sutton Lane Ends
Langley
Lower Pexhill
Bosley
North Rode
Eaton
Buglawton
Hightown
Mossley
Whitemore
Key Green
Rodeheath
Highlane
Hulme Walfield
West Heath
Lower Heath
Newsbank
Brownlow Heath
Brookhouse Green
Smallwood
Arclid
Thurlwood
Mount Pleasant
Harriseahead
Biddulph Moor
Horton
Poolfold
Newtown
Marsh Green
Gillow Heath
Hodgefield
Ridgeway
0 1 2 3 miles
0 1 2 3 4 5 km

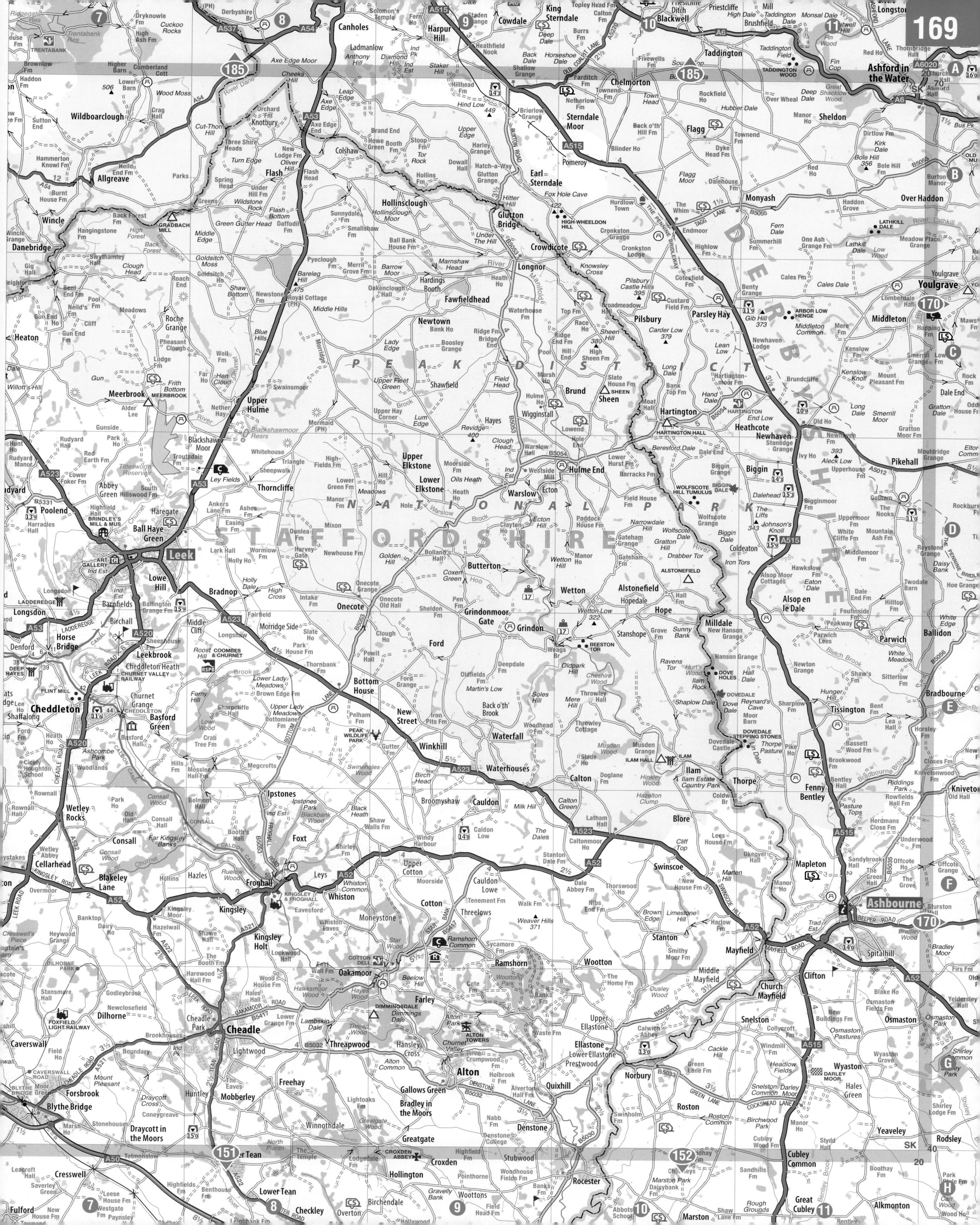
169
Canholes
Harpur Hill
Cowdale
King Sterndale
Blackwell
Taddington
Ashford in the Water
Chelmorton
Wildboarclough
Sterndale Moor
Flagg
Sheldon
Allgreave
Flash
Earl Sterndale
Monyash
Over Haddon
Wincle
Hollinsclough
Glutton Bridge
Danebridge
Crowdicote
Longnor
Fawfieldhead
Pilsbury
Parsley Hay
Youlgrave
Middleton
Heaton
Newtown
P E A K D I S T R I C T
D E R B Y S H I R E
Meerbrook
Upper Hulme
Brund
Sheen
Hartington
Heathcote
Newhaven
Pikehall
Upper Elkstone
Lower Elkstone
Hulme End
Warslow
Biggin
Thorncliffe
Poolend
Ball Haye Green
S T A F F O R D S H I R E
N A T I O N A L P A R K
Leek
Butterton
Lowe Hill
Bradnop
Onecote
Wetton
Alstonefield
Alsop en le Dale
Grindonmoor Gate
Grindon
Hope
Milldale
Ballidon
Parwich
Horse Bridge
Leekbrook
Ford
Cheddleton
Basford Green
Bottom House
New Street
Tissington
Bradbourne
Winkhill
Waterfall
Waterhouses
Calton
Ilam
Thorpe
Fenny Bentley
Ipstones
Cauldon
Blore
Wetley Rocks
Consall
Foxt
Cellarhead
Blakeley Lane
Froghall
Whiston
Swinscoe
Mapleton
Kingsley
Cotton
Ashbourne
Kingsley Holt
Stanton
Mayfield
Ramshorn
Oakamoor
Wootton
Clifton
Farley
Church Mayfield
Dilhorne
Cheadle
Threapwood
Snelston
Osmaston
Caverswall
Alton
Ellastone
Norbury
Wyaston
Forsbrook
Blythe Bridge
Mobberley
Freehay
Bradley in the Moors
Roston
Draycott in the Moors
Denstone
Yeaveley
Rodsley
Greatgate
Croxden
Hollington
Rocester
Cubley Common
Cresswell
Lower Tean
Checkley
Fulford
Great Cubley
Alkmonton
Marston
A53
A523
A520
A52
A515
A50
A522
A521
A54
A537
A6
B5053
B5054
B5032
B5417
185
151
152
170
SK

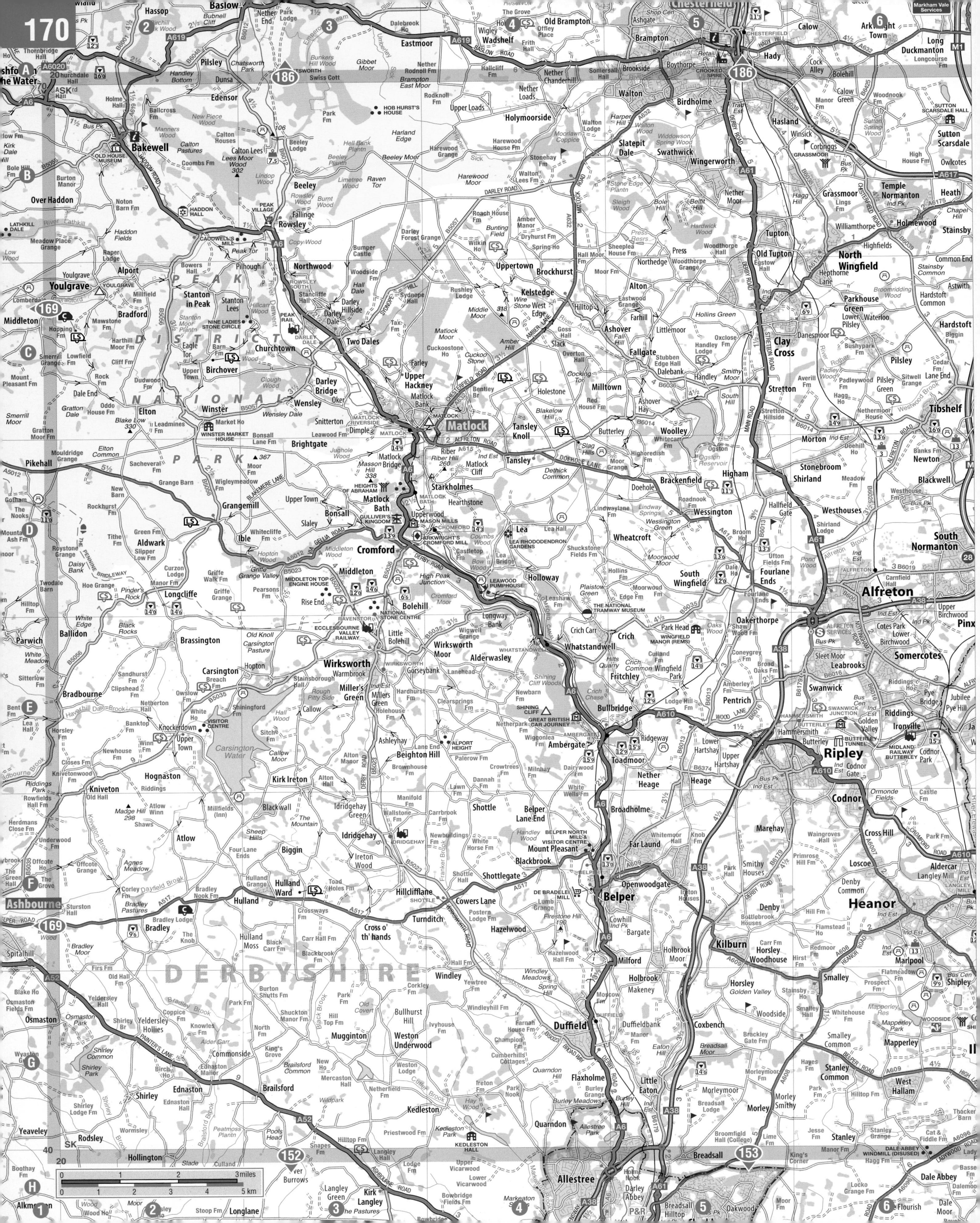

Baslow
Hassop
Chesterfield
Old Brampton
Brampton
Calow
Arkwright Town
Long Duckmanton
Markham Vale Services
Eastmoor
Wadshelf
Pilsley
Edensor
Bakewell
Hady
Walton
Birdholme
Holymoorside
Hasland
Sutton Scarsdale
Beeley
Slatepit Dale
Wingerworth
Grassmoor
Temple Normanton
Heath
Over Haddon
Rowsley
Holmewood
Tupton
Old Tupton
North Wingfield
Youlgrave
Alport
Northwood
Uppertown
Brockhurst
Kelstedge
Middleton
Stanton in Peak
Bradford
Darley Dale
Two Dales
Ashover
Clay Cross
Churchtown
Birchover
Upper Hackney
Fallgate
Milltown
Stretton
Tibshelf
Darley Bridge
Winster
Elton
Wensley
Matlock
Tansley Knoll
Woolley
Morton
Pikehall
Brightgate
Tansley
Matlock Bridge
Starkholmes
Higham
Shirland
Stonebroom
Blackwell
Newton
Grangemill
Matlock Bath
Bonsall
Upper Town
Brackenfield
Wessington
Westhouses
Aldwark
Ible
Cromford
Lea
Wheatcroft
South Normanton
Middleton
Holloway
South Wingfield
Fourlane Ends
Alfreton
Longcliffe
Bolehill
Ballidon
Brassington
Wirksworth
Wirksworth Moor
Alderwasley
Whatstandwell
Crich
Oakerthorpe
Somercotes
Carsington
Fritchley
Leabrooks
Swanwick
Bradbourne
Miller's Green
Bullbridge
Riddings
Ironville
Ambergate
Ripley
Knockerdown
Beighton Hill
Toadmoor
Heage
Nether Heage
Hognaston
Kniveton
Kirk Ireton
Shottle
Codnor
Belper Lane End
Broadholme
Atlow
Biggin
Idridgehay
Mount Pleasant
Far Laund
Blackbrook
Hulland Ward
Hulland
Belper
Heanor
Ashbourne
Bradley
Turnditch
Hazelwood
Kilburn
Milford
Marlpool
Osmaston
Windley
Holbrook
Smalley
Shipley
Duffield
Mugginton
Weston Underwood
Coxbench
Mapperley
Shirley
Ednaston
Brailsford
Flaxholme
Little Eaton
Stanley Common
West Hallam
Kedleston
Quarndon
Morley
Yeaveley
Rodsley
Stanley
Hollington
Allestree
Breadsall
Dale Abbey
Alkmonton
Longlane
Kirk Langley
Langley Green
DERBYSHIRE
PEAK DISTRICT NATIONAL PARK

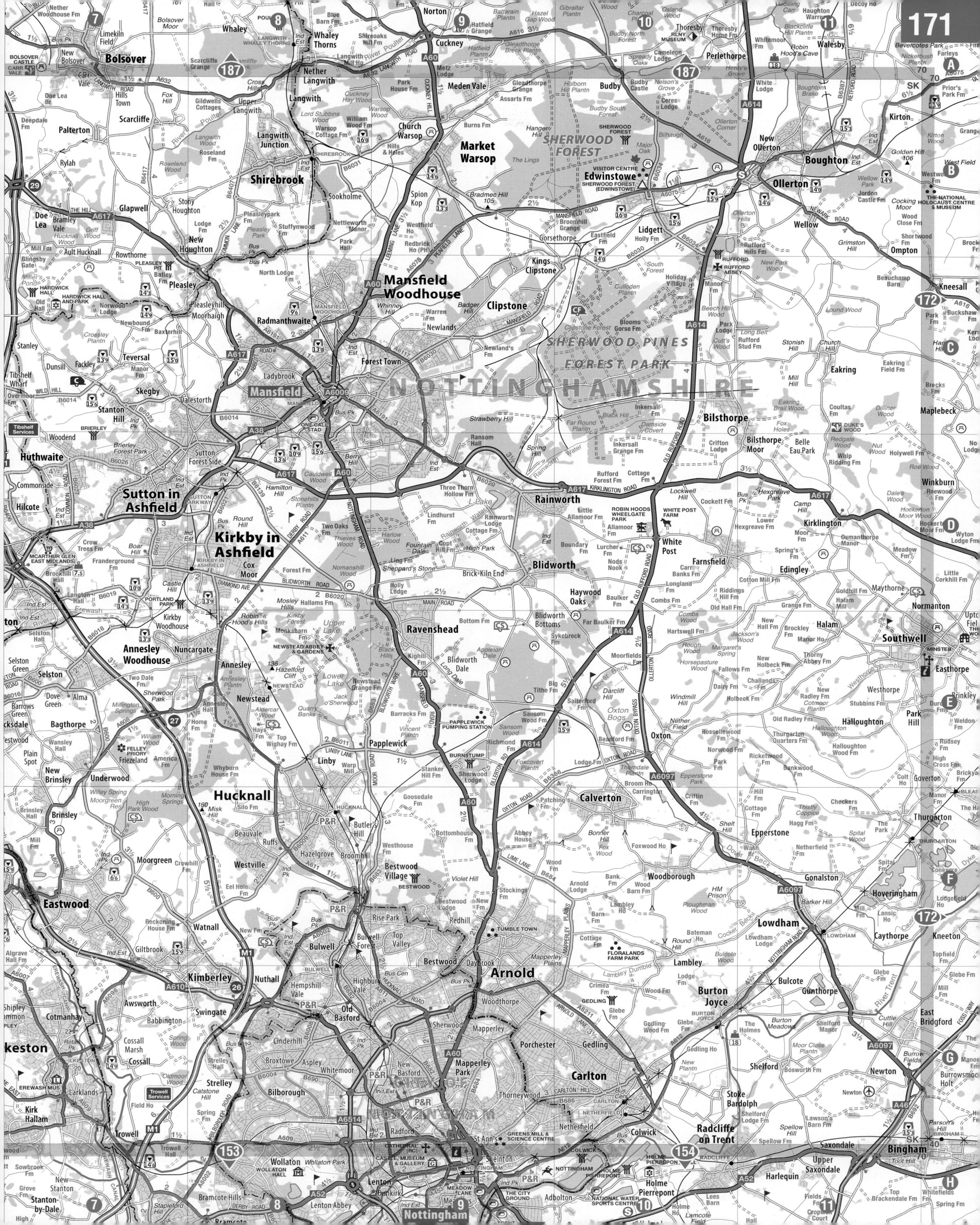
NOTTINGHAMSHIRE
SHERWOOD FOREST
SHERWOOD PINES FOREST PARK
Bolsover
Whaley
Whaley Thorns
Norton
Cuckney
Nether Langwith
Langwith
Meden Vale
Budby
Thoresby
Perlethorpe
Walesby
Scarcliffe
Palterton
Langwith Junction
Shirebrook
Church Warsop
Market Warsop
Edwinstowe
New Ollerton
Boughton
Ollerton
Wellow
Ompton
Kneesall
Glapwell
Doe Lea
Ault Hucknall
New Houghton
Pleasley
Rowthorne
Mansfield Woodhouse
Clipstone
Kings Clipstone
Lidgett
Radmanthwaite
Forest Town
Mansfield
Ladybrook
Teversal
Skegby
Stanton Hill
Huthwaite
Sutton in Ashfield
Kirkby in Ashfield
Rainworth
Bilsthorpe
Bilsthorpe Moor
Eakring
Maplebeck
Winkburn
Kirklington
Blidworth
White Post
Farnsfield
Edingley
Halam
Southwell
Normanton
Easthorpe
Ravenshead
Annesley Woodhouse
Annesley
Newstead
Papplewick
Linby
Hucknall
Calverton
Oxton
Epperstone
Halloughton
Thurgarton
Hoveringham
Gonalston
Lowdham
Caythorpe
Woodborough
Lambley
Arnold
Burton Joyce
Bulcote
Gunthorpe
East Bridgford
Eastwood
Underwood
Brinsley
Kimberley
Nuthall
Watnall
Bulwell
Bestwood
Bestwood Village
Mapperley
Porchester
Gedling
Carlton
Netherfield
Colwick
Shelford
Newton
Radcliffe on Trent
Bingham
Saxondale
Upper Saxondale
Holme Pierrepont
Adbolton
Ilkeston
Cossall
Strelley
Bilborough
Wollaton
Lenton
Nottingham
Kirk Hallam
Stanton-by-Dale
Trowell
Selston
Jacksdale
Bagthorpe
Cotmanhay
Awsworth
Old Basford
Sherwood
Mapperley Park
Arnold
Hempshill Vale
Cinderhill
Aspley
Radford
Stoke Bardolph
A60
A614
A617
A6097
A38
A610
A52
A46
M1
187
172
153
154
A
B
C
D
E
F
G
H
7
8
9
10
11
26
27
29
SK

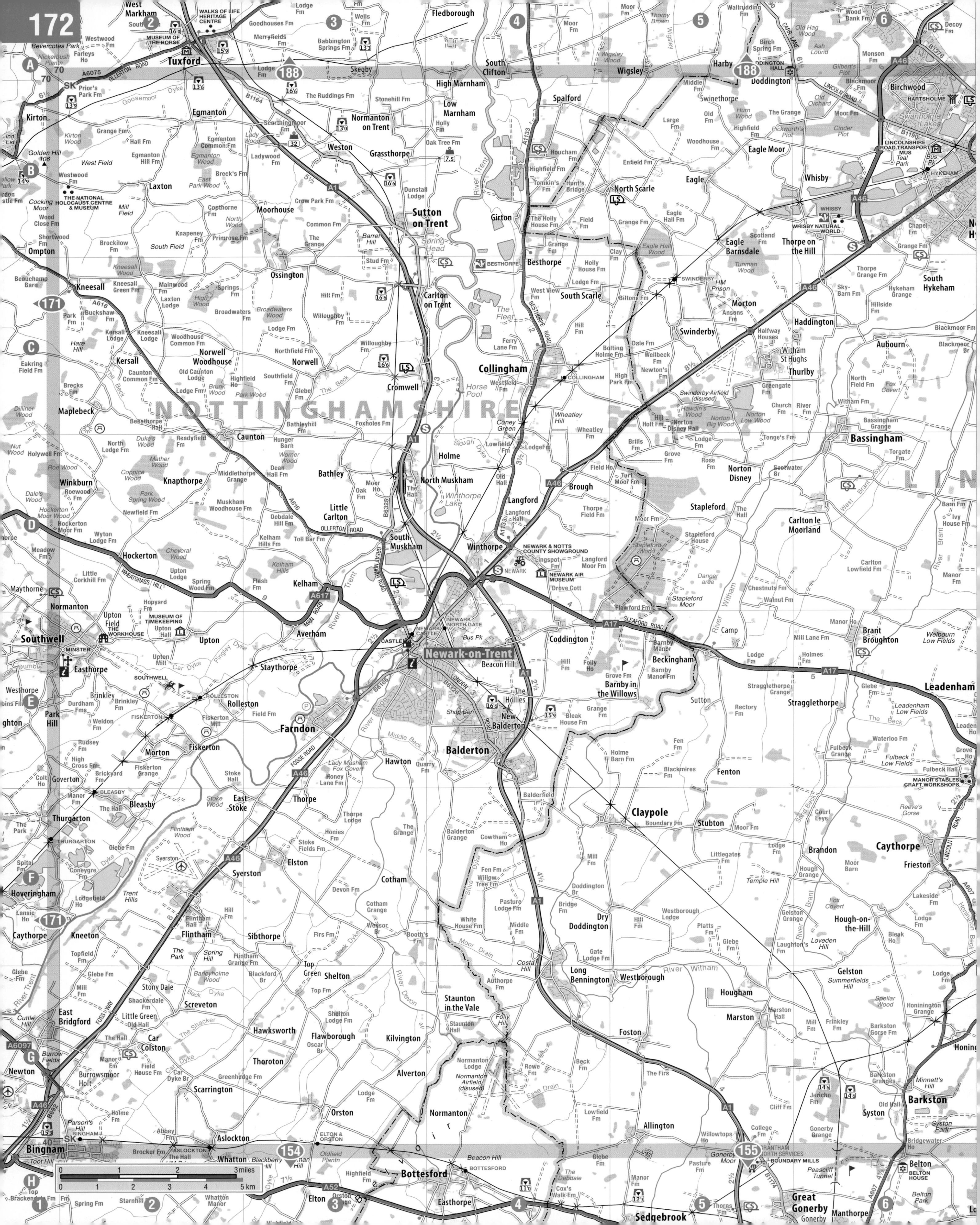
Tuxford
West Markham
Fledborough
Wigsley
Harby
Doddington
South Clifton
High Marnham
Low Marnham
Skegby
Egmanton
Kirton
Normanton on Trent
Weston
Grassthorpe
Spalford
Birchwood
Eagle Moor
Eagle
North Scarle
Whisby
Laxton
Moorhouse
Sutton on Trent
Girton
Besthorpe
Eagle Barnsdale
Thorpe on the Hill
South Hykeham
Ompton
Kneesall
Ossington
Carlton on Trent
South Scarle
Morton
Swinderby
Haddington
Aubourn
Kersall
Norwell Woodhouse
Norwell
Cromwell
Collingham
Witham St Hughs
Thurlby
Maplebeck
NOTTINGHAMSHIRE
Caunton
Bathley
Holme
North Muskham
Brough
Bassingham
Winkburn
Knapthorpe
Little Carlton
Langford
Stapleford
Norton Disney
Carlton le Moorland
South Muskham
Winthorpe
Hockerton
Kelham
Normanton
Southwell
Upton
Averham
Newark-on-Trent
Coddington
Beckingham
Brant Broughton
Barnby in the Willows
Leadenham
Easthorpe
Staythorpe
Rolleston
Farndon
New Balderton
Balderton
Stragglethorpe
Morton
Fiskerton
Hawton
Fenton
Thurgarton
Bleasby
East Stoke
Thorpe
Claypole
Stubton
Caythorpe
Brandon
Frieston
Syerston
Elston
Cotham
Hoveringham
Dry Doddington
Hough-on-the-Hill
Caythorpe
Kneeton
Flintham
Sibthorpe
Long Bennington
Westborough
Shelton
Hougham
Gelston
East Bridgford
Screveton
Staunton in the Vale
Marston
Hawksworth
Flawborough
Kilvington
Foston
Car Colston
Thoroton
Newton
Scarrington
Alverton
Barkston
Orston
Normanton
Allington
Syston
Aslockton
Bingham
Whatton
Bottesford
Belton
Great Gonerby
Elton
Easthorpe
Sedgebrook
Manthorpe
A1
A46
A17
A616
A617
A6075
A52
A607
A6097
A1133
B1164
B6166
B6326
188
171
154
155
NEWARK & NOTTS COUNTY SHOWGROUND
NEWARK AIR MUSEUM
MUSEUM OF TIMEKEEPING
THE WORKHOUSE
THE NATIONAL HOLOCAUST CENTRE & MUSEUM
WALKS OF LIFE HERITAGE CENTRE
MUSEUM OF THE HORSE
LINCOLNSHIRE ROAD TRANSPORT MUS
MANOR STABLES CRAFT WORKSHOPS
WHISBY NATURAL WORLD
BELTON HOUSE
0 1 2 3 miles
0 1 2 3 4 5 km

LINCOLN CASTLE
CATHEDRAL
LINCOLN ARBORETUM
BISHOP'S PALACE
Willingham Fen
NAVIGATION
FOSSDYKE
CANAL
River Witham
Boundary Fm
Old River Witham
Tile House Beck
Young Wood
Moat Ho
Great
Waddingworth
Austacre Wood
New Park Wood
Red Ho
Spotted Lodge
Hill Fm
New Boultham
Trad Est
Retail Pk
LNER STADIUM
GUILDHALL
B1308
LINCOLN
B1190
FEN ROAD
Shop Cen
Ind Est
Washingborough
Ings Fm
Heighington Fen
Branston Delph
Delph Fm
Branston Island
Abbey Fm
WRAGBY ROAD
Scotgrove Wood
Bardney Lock
Moor Fm
Grange Fm
Sand Nook Fm
Boultham
Canwick
INTERNATIONAL BOMBER COMMAND CTR
Manor Fm
Glebe Fm
Highfield Ho
Heighington
Branstone Fen
Branston Booths
Red House Fm
Bardney
Bardney Common
High Cell Ho
Birt Hill
Tupholme Hall Fm
Catchwater Drain
Bucknall
HORNCASTLE STREET
Edlington Scrubbs
Swallow Beck
Boultham Moor
Whitehall
Cliff Fm
Washingborough Top Fm
B1188
Third Hill Fm
Bracken Hill Fm
CAR DYKE (ROMAN CANAL)
BARDNEY RD
Poplars Fm
B1190
BRANSTON CAUSEWAY
Branston Lodge
Whitehouse Fm
B1202
Potterhanworth Booths
BARDNEY LIMEWOODS
Southrey Wood
Birch Wood
HORNCASTLE ROAD
Poplar Grove
Poplar Fm
BUCKNALL ROAD
Grange Fm
Horsington
Mapleton Fm
Firgrove Fm
Bracebridge
CANWICK
Canwick Manor Fm
LINCOLN ROAD
Ashfield Ho
Branston
Branston Moor
Campney Grange Fm
Horsington Wood
Poolham Fm
Darwood Fm
High Dar Wood
Bracebridge Heath
Manor Fm
Longhills Hall
Potterhanworth Wood
Abbey Warren Fm
Slixwold Wood
North Hykeham
River Witham
Bracebridge Low Fields
Grange Fm
Fox Covert
Ind Est
Potterhanworth
Southrey
Duckpool Br
Halstead Hall
STATION ROAD
B1178
Cherrystone Cott
Barff Fm
Neville Wood
Mere Hall
River Witham
Delph
Holmes Fm
Stixwould
Newstead Fm
Halstead Wood
Reeds Beck Fm
Reeds Beck
Moorside Fm
POTTERHANWORTH RD
SLEAFORD RD
Wasps Nest
Nocton
Ash House Fm
Potterhanworth Heath
Dunston Fen
Red Br
Waddington
East Mere Ho
Nocton Grange
Abbey Hill
Nocton
Sots Hole
Tanvats
Waterloo Fm
Bracken Wood
Lowfields Fm
Waddington
Beaufoe Manor
Highfield Fm
Nocton Heath
Fen Fm
Nocton Wood
Engine Fm
Metheringham
Willow Fm
Blankney Dales
Stixwould Grange
COTTAGE
B1191
Lincoln Lane Fm
Barn Fm
Dunston
Black Horse Fm
Roughton Moor
Woodhall Spa
Glebe Fm
Harmston Heath
Ram Fm
Glebe Fm
Metheringham Low Fields
Fenside Fm
Dales Head Dike
WITHAM ROAD
Landsdale Ho
Harmston
WHITE LANE
B1178
TOWER LANE
Coleby Lodge Fm
Hall Fm
Dunston Heath
Metheringham
Metheringham Barff Fm
CAR DYKE (ROMAN CANAL)
Glebe Fm
Kirkstead Br
Kirkstead Hall
Kirkstead
Harmston Field
Low Fields Fm
Heath Grange
LINCOLN RD
MOOR LANE
Barff Fm
Carr Dyke Fm
Martin Fen
Martin Dales
B1192
TATTERSHALL ROAD
Coleby Low Fields
Coleby
GRANTHAM ROAD
Hall Fm
Coleby Heath
Heath Ho
Boothby Heath Fm
METHERINGHAM HEATH LANE
Metheringham Lodge
Blankney Park
B1188
Blankney
North Moor Ho
Linwood Hall Fm
MARTIN SOUTH DROVE
B1191
Timberland Delph
Timberland Dales
Dales Br
Tonge Fm
Park Fm
HEATH LANE
B1202
Green Man Wood
Blankney Grange
Blankney Heath
Westmoor Fm
METHERINGHAM AIRFIELD VISITOR CENTRE
MOOR LANE
Martin
THORPE CAMP VISITOR CENTRE
Boothby Graffoe
Green Man Fm
Scopwick Low Field Fm
LINCOLNSHIRE
Scopwick Ho
Thorpe Tilney Fen
Thorpe Tilney Dales
Lodge Fm
Boothby Graffoe Low Fields
Navenby Heath
Scopwick Lodge Fm
Scopwick Heath
MAIN STREET
B1191
Timberland
Bank Fm
Navenby Low Fields
Navenby
Vine Ho
Temple High Grange Fm
HEATH ROAD
Scopwick
Kirkby Green
Evans' Fm
Thorpe Tilney
HIGH STREET
Walcott Hurn
Walcott Dales
Tattershall
TATTERSHALL CASTLE
Peacocks Fm
Heath Fm
Sheffield Ho
Wellingore
Highfield House Fm
Gorse Hill Covert
RAF DIGBY OPS ROOM MUSEUM
Rowston
Rowston Field Fm
Crown Fm
Walcott
Billinghay Hurn
Witham House Fm
Wellingore Low Fields
Glebe Fm
Ashby Hall
Rowston Grange
Field Fm
WALCOTT ROAD
B1189
Skirth
SLEAFORD
Tattershall Bridge
Wood Fm
Fox Covert
CLIFF ROAD
Heath Fm
Thompson's Bottom
Ashby Lodge
Ashby de la Launde
A153
Stennett's Fm
Dogdyke
Billinghay
Allens Fm
TATTERSHALL RD
Billinghay Dales
Glebe Fm
Griffin's Fm
Warren Houses
Slate House Fm
Digby
Digby Gorse
Home Fm
Grange Fm
North Kyme Common
Chapel Hill
Welbourn
Temple Fm
Springwell
Brook
Dorrington Grange
Digby Fen
Dorrington
Fen Ho
South Barn Fm
Temple Bruer
Peacock Lodge
Bloxholm
LINCOLN ROAD
Pitts Fm
Dike
Drove Fm
North Kyme Fen
Home Fm
Cocked Hat Plantn
Cocked Hat Fm
Moor Wood
Manor Fm
Hill Fm
NORTH INGS FARM MUSEUM
The Dales
Fendale Fm
North Kyme
High Dyke Fm
B1188
Dorrington
North Hills
Wong Fm
MAIN STREET
Vacherie Ho
Crossways Fm
Praie Grounds
River Slea
Cottage Fm
Moor Fm
Clayfields Fm
Decoy Ho
Reed Point
Hill Top Fms
Leadenham Heath
Stocks Heath Fm
New Homestead Fm
Dunsby House
Dale Fm
Roxholm Grange
Ind Est
Poplar Fm
Grange Fm
SLEAFORD ROAD
FERRY LANE
The Grange
Terry Booth Fm
Bus Pk
Reeves Plantn
Hall Fm
Roxholm Hall
Ruskington
RUSKINGTON
A153
Anwick
Park Ho
B1395
Lawn Hill Fm
Kyme Eau
Sheperds Fm
A17
RAF College Cranwell
CRANWELL AVENUE
B1429
Cranwell
Old Hall Fm
Moor Fm
Haverholme Priory
Cobbler's Lock
River Slea
Ewerby Waithe Common
WOOD LANE
River Slea
Kyme Eau
South Kyme
Heath Fm
Bleak House
Mill Fm
Cranwell
Westfield Wood
MOOR LANE
White Ho
Old River Slea
Fox Covert
Sycamore Ho
Maryland Ho
Caythorpe Heath
Barns Fm
Westfield Fm
Leasingham Moor
B1209
Leasingham
Pattingden Ho
Chestnut House Fm
Elms Fm
Frieston Heath Fm
Rauceby Grange
Heath Fm
CRANWELL AVIATION HERITAGE CENTRE
Ermine Street Fm
North Rauceby Heath
Moor Fm
Evedon Mill
Evedon
Ewerby
Ewerby Thorpe
CAR DYKE (ROMAN CANAL)
CLAY BANK
Fenmore Fm
Whitehouse Fm
Five Willow Wath Fm
Mill Green Fm
Normanton
Sparrow Gorse
Woodside Fm
High Wood
North Rauceby
Holdingham
Bus Pk
Galley Hill
Bargate Hill
Walks Fm
Howell Fen
Howell
Heckington Eau
Glebe Fm
Sadland Fm
Carlton Scroop
Sudbrook Hill Fm
Sudbrook Ho
HIGH DIKE
Crowland Fm
Lodge Fm
South Rauceby
Hall
Field Fm
Sleaford
Bouncing Hill
COGGLESFORD WATERMILL
SLEAFORD MUSEUM
NAT CENTRE FOR CRAFT & DESIGN
The Grange
Kirkby la Thorpe
Boughton
Wash Dike
Star Fen
Holme Ho
Six Hundreds Fm
Sudbrook
ANCASTER
Boiling Wells Fm
GRANTHAM RD
SLEAFORD
Mount Lane Fm
Bone's Fm
Asgarby
The Beck
Winkhill
SIDEBAR LANE
B1395
East Heckington
West Willoughby
Waterloo Fm
South Rauceby Lodge
Cliff Fm
RAUCEBY
B1517
Quarrington
Mareham Lane Fm
Sardesons Fm
Westfield
SLEAFORD RD
B1394
Heckington
Hall Fm
Mile Ho
Ancaster
TOWN END
A153
River Slea
Wilsford Warren
Grange Fm
Lodge Fm
Beacon Hill
Grange Fm
Lodge Fm
HECKINGTON WINDMILL
HECKINGTON
Poplar Ho
Hall Fm
WILLOUGHBY ROAD
High Field House
Slate House Fm
Wilsford
Silk Willoughby
Willoughby Gorse
Saltbox Fm
Bellhouse Fm
Burton Fm
Great Hale
Willoughby Heath
The Valley
Valley Fm
Kelby Fm
Cliff Beck
Burton Pedwardine
Hercocks Fm
Highfields Fm
Crow Lane Fm
White Ho
Barkston Heath
Glebe Fm
North Hill
Kelby
Barrow Hill Fm
Grange Fm
Aswarby Thorns
Burton Cliff
Burton Br
Little Hale
Willoughby Ho
Broadhurst Fm
Northbeck
MAIN ROAD
B1394
South Forty Foot Drain
Syston Grange
Welby Pastures
Heydour Warren
Swarby
Thorns Fm
Scredington
Poplar Fm
Helpringham
Glebe Fm
Park Ho
North Beck
Lowgrounds Fm
Crow Hall
Culverthorpe
Crofton
Hall
Aswarby
Culverthorpe Hollow
Forty Acre Fm
Oasby
Castle Hills
Whitegorse Fm
Gorse Hill
Thorpe Latimer
Poplartree Fm
Glebe Fm
Cow Common
Aisby
Green Hill
Aunsby
Highfield Ho
Rowe's Fm
Cow Bridge
Welby
South Beck
Osbournby
Swaton Common
Manor
Eau End
Nightingale
Dembleby
Spanby
HIGH DIKE
A607
A15
A17
B1191
B1189
B1188
B1517
B6403
189
174
155
156
TF
20
70
40

West Ashby
Bag Enderby
Harrington
Sutterby
Fordington
Claxby St Andrew
The Grange
Edlington
Thimbleby
Cottage Fm
Shearman's Wath Br
WOLDS WILDLIFE PARK
Low Toynton
High Toynton Lodge
Greetham Ho
Ashby Puerorum
Stainsby
Stockwith Mill Br
Aswardby
Langton
Dalby
Spotted Lodge
Woodbecks Fm
Hollow Yard
Hill Fm
Barsey Walk Fm
190
Horncastle
A158
HORNCASTLE STREET
SPILSBY ROAD
High Toynton
Scrafield
Greetham
Cliff Carr
Thunker Hollow
Hagworthingham Grange
Mount Pleasant
Hagworthingham
WINCEBY 1643
Highfield Fm
Gravel Pit Hill
PARTNEY ROAD
Sausthorpe
Gibbet Hill
Minster Fm
Thorpe Fm
Skendleby
Grebby
Skendleby Holme Fm
Edlington Scrubbs
Langton
Langton Hill
Manor Ho
Westfield Fm
BOSTON ROAD
Ind Est
Stonehill Fm
Mareham Grange
SNIPE DALES
Furze Fm
Windsor Fm
Aswardby Mill
Grange Fm
The Grange
Partney
Horsington
Mapleton Fm
Firgrove Fm
Poolham Hall
Old Woodhall
Thornton
Thornton Lodge Fm
Loxley Fm
Low Fm
Mareham on the Hill
Hall Fm
Winceby
SLASH LANE
Ivy Ho
Lusby
Northfield Fm
Raithby Br
Raithby by Spilsby
Vale Fm
Model Fm
Partney Br
LOWGATE ROAD
Darwood Fm
Ox Pasture Fm
Martin
Telegraph Ho
Hameringham
Asgarby
Eastfield Fm
Hundleby
Spilsby
Ashby by Partney
High Dar Wood
Redcap Fm
Hall Fm
Thornton Wood
Old River Bain
Scrivelsby
Glebe Fm
Long Fm
Hameringham Top
Mavis Enderby
Northorpe Fm
Moat Fm
Halton Holegate
Halstead Hall
Halstead Wood
Reeds Beck Fm
Moorside Fm
Highall Wood
Reeds Beck
Dalderby
Scrivelsby Grange
Holme Wood
The Grange
Stamford Ho
Hareby
Hareby Ho
Wheelabout Wood
Highfield Fm
Old Bolingbroke
BOLINGBROKE CASTLE
Glebe Fm
Eresby Ho
Monksthorpe
HOLE GATE
Halton Br
Sandhill Fm
NORTHCOTE HEAVY HORSE CENTRE
Waterloo Fm
Bracken Wood
Roughton
Roughton Moor
Glebe Fm
Wellsyke Fm
Cross Roads Fm
B1183
Holmwood Fm
Moorby
Hall Fm
Manor Fm
Kirkby Hill
High Barn
Manor Fm
Toynton All Saints
Great Steeping
COTTAGE MUS
173
Roughton Moor
Kirkby Moor
Haltham
Wood Enderby
The Grange
Haltham Wood
Haltham Beck
Dairy Fm
Miningsby
Miningsby Ho
West Keal
East Keal
Toynton St Peter
Halton Fenside
Woodhall Spa
Clement's Fm
Kirkby on Bain
Kirkstead Hall
Kirkstead
Ostler's Plantn
Fox Hill
Grange Fm
Riverslea Fm
Toft Hill
Hill Top Fm
Toft Grange
Enderby Hill Fm
Shirewood Fm
HIGHFIELD LANE
Revesby Abbey
Whaiff Ho
East Kirkby Ho
East Kirkby
Ind Est
Hagnaby
Laythorpe House Fm
A155
Hagnaby Priory
LINCOLNSHIRE AVIATION HERITAGE CENTRE
Manor Ho
Limes Fm
Woolham Fm
Toynton Fen Side
Hare Hills Fm
Fen Br
Little Steeping
LINCOLNSHIRE
Fox Covert
Fulsby Wood
Fulsby Wood Ho
Red House Fm
Mareham le Fen
Manor Ho
Revesby
The Grange
Revesby Bridge
SLEAFORD ROAD
Middle Fm
Ivy Ho
Manor
Kirkby Fenside
Keal Cotes
Sandleigh
Black Horse Br
Thorpe Dales
Kent's Br
TATTERSHALL ROAD
Park Fm
Tattershall Thorpe
THORPE CAMP VISITOR CENTRE
TUMBY LANE
Tumby
Nursery Fm
Birkwood Hall
St Helen's Wood
MAIN Bridge Ho
STREET
Bark Fm
Grange Fm
Grange Fm
Fen Fm
Poplar Tree Fm
Hagnaby Lock
Stickford Ho
The Grange
Stickford
Thorpe Br
Boston Corporation Fm
Royalty Fm East
Royalty Fm
Bellwater Fm
Bell Water Drain
Lodge Fm
Bank Fm
LEAGATE ROAD
Coningsby
Ind Est
Mareham Gate
Russell's Fm
West Fen Fm
Lapwater Fm
West Fen
Engine Fm
Hemholme Br
Drain Bank Plantn
Bethlem Fm
The Deeps
Tattershall
Walcott Dales
TATTERSHALL COLLEGE
TATTERSHALL CASTLE
BATTLE OF BRITAIN MEMORIAL FLIGHT
Witham House Fm
Hoplands Fm
Black Holt
Moor Side
Tumby Ho
Tumby Woodside
Newham Drain
Sheriff's Fm
New Bolingbroke
Fen Side
Fen Fm
Mexican Br
Dovecot Fm
Bell Water Drain
St Catherine's Fm
Pool Decoy
Blue Br
Mill Fm
Gaunt Ho
Bowsers Fm
West Fen Catchwater Drain
Catchwater
Poplars Fm
Dairy Farm Ho
Midville
New Leake
Eastville Fm
Fodder Dike
Coningsby
Langworth Grange
Reedham
Bridge Fm
Moorhouses
Slate House Fm
Fen Fm
Chapel Fm
Medlam Ho
Medlam Manor
Medlam Br
Stickney
A16
Midville House Fm
Waite's Fm
Eastville
Orchard Ho
Risdale Fm
Slated House Fm
LINCOLNSHIRE WILDLIFE PARK
Dickon Hills
Small End
SLEAFORD
Tattershall Bridge
A153
Hawthorn Hill
Ivy Ho
Stennett's Fm
Dogdyke
No Man's Friend Fm
Mill's Br
Medlam
Blacks Br
East Fen
Welsh's Fm
Manor Fm
Abbey Hills
Scrub Hill
Providence Ho
Catchwater
Bramley Fm
Carrington Ho
Stickney Grange
Wrangle Bank Fm
Claxy Ho
Dales
Glebe Fm
Packet House Fm
New York
Sandy Bank
Carrington Grange
Skirbeck Fm
West Houses
Lade Bank Br
Lade Bank
Wrangle Common
Gask's Fm
Chapel Hill
Bettinson's Fm
Hough Br
Wildmore Park
Bunker's Hill
Carrington
Bar Bridge Fm
Hunston House Fm
Rinders Fm
Hurn Br
Canada Fm
Hundle Houses
Dovecote Hall Fm
Henley Ho
Northlands
Simmon House Fm
Common Fm
Wrangle Bank
Greenfield Fm
Home Fm
Thornton Ho
Green Lane Cottage
Short's Corner
Hakerley Br
Bishop's Fm
Sibsey Fen Side
Star Fm
Wrangle Low Ground
Sigtoft Fm
Haven Bank
B1192
Waite's Fm
White House Fm
Leake Commonside
Manor Fm
Wrangle Lowgate
Light House Fm
Reed Point
Terry Booth Fm
River Witham
Castle
Champion Ho
Primrose Hill Fm
Riggalls Fm
Westville Fm
CARRINGTON
SIBSEY TRADER MILL
Mallow's Fm
Bank Fm
The Grange
New Fm
Leake Fold Hill
Toft Ho
Hermitage Fm
Castle Dike Fm
Newham
Home Fm
Black House Fm
Sibsey
Benington Br
Wrangle
Pelham's Lands Fm
BUBBLE CAR
Ash Tree Fm
CANISTER LANE
Frithville
HALE LANE
STATION ROAD
B1184
THE GRIDE
Old Leake
Joy Hill
Wrangle Hall
Hall End
Marsh Fm
Sheperds Fm
Holland Fen
Gipsey Bridge
B1184
Bank Fm
High Ferry
Ireland Fm
Green Fm
Leake
Dovecote Fm
Amber Fm
Poplars Fm
Beech House Fm
Laburnum Ho
Canister Hall
Peacock's Fm
Fishtoft Drove
Bank House Fm
Moulton Chantry Ho
Heronshaw Hall
Hampton House Fm
Moat Ho
Sailor's
Maryland Ho
Sycamore Ho
Langrick
Stone Bridge Fm
Pimlico Ho
Ivy House Fm
Hurn's End
Pattingden Ho
Chestnut House Fm
Vicarage Fm
Sellars Fm
Langrick Grange
Meer Booth Fm
Anton's Gowt
Field House Fm
Bank House Fm
Ings Fm
Leverton Highgate
Leverton Outgate
Leverton
Gill Br
Gill Syke
Sutterton Br
River Witham
Langrick Bridge
Reaches Marsh Fm
Cowbridge
Willows Fm
Hill Dyke
Butterwick Ings Fm
The Grange
Leverton Lucasgate
Mill Green Fm
Amber Hill
Sadland Fm
Two Hundreds Fm
Holland Fen
Hedgehog Bridge
Brothertoft
Redroof Fm
Boston West
Frith Bank
Kelsey Br
Boston Long Hedges
West End
Bay Hall
Benington
The Elms
Cowbridge Drain
Baker's Br
Haltoft End
A52
Benington Sea End
Glebe Fm
Glebe Fm
173
Spinney Fm
Barley Close
Boundary Fm
ST BOTOLPH'S CHURCH
Burton Corner
Willoughby Hills
Oak Ho
Round Ho
Six Hundreds Fm
Dovecote Fm
A52
WAINFLEET RD
Brand End
Butterwick
East Heckington
The Rakes
Great Fen
Wyberton Fen
MAUD FOSTER MILL
Boston
Freiston Br
HUBBERTS BRIDGE
BOARDSIDES
Boston
Ind Cen
White Loaf Hall
Butterwick Low
Swineshead Bridge
Aby House Fm
Hubbert's Bridge
SLEAFORD ROAD
Bus Pk
Ind Est
GUILDHALL
Freiston
A17
A1121
FEN DROVE
Baker's Br
A52
Chain Bridge
Skirbeck Quarter
Skirbeck
The Grange
Coupledyke Hall
Tamworth Green
FREISTON SHORE
Freiston Shore
Hall Fm
SWINESHEAD
Sykemouth Fm
SWINESHEAD ROAD
Fishtoft
Wood Fm
Freiston Low
New Hammond Beck
Old Hammond Beck
Scrane End
Brand End Fm
Bus Pk
High Br
Baythorpe
Hardwick Grange
Kirton Holme
Lilley's Br
Wyberton
Tytton Hall
JAKEMANS COMMUNITY STADIUM
Slippery Gowt Fm
Nunn' Br
North End
BOSTON ROAD
HOLMES LANE
Frampton West End
Wybert's Castle
Crawford's Fm
Swineshead
Fenhouses
Jubilee Fm
Kirton End
RALPHS LANE
Marsh Fm
HM
Abbey Fm
Crow Hall
Gauntlet Br
DONINGTON ROAD
Willoughby Ho
Frampton Ho
The Haven
157
The Scalp
BLACKJACK RO
156
Frampton
Lime Tree Fm
Marsh Fm
Wyberton Marsh
River Witham
Poplartree
Park's Fm
Roads Fm
Kirton
Manor Fm
Frampton Marsh
FRAMPTON MARSH
Fishmere
Golden Grove
0 1 2 3 miles
0 1 2 3 4 5 km

THE WASH
Skegness
Ingoldmells
Burgh le Marsh
Wainfleet All Saints
Wainfleet St Mary
Hunstanton
Old Hunstanton
Holme next the Sea
Ringstead
Friskney Flats
Wainfleet Sand
Wrangle Flats
Gibraltar Point
Seacroft
Croft
Friskney
Friskney Tofts
Thorpe St Peter
Irby in the Marsh
Firsby
Bratoft
Orby
Candlesby
Gunby
Welton le Marsh
Sloothby
Willoughby
Hogsthorpe
Addlethorpe
Seathorne
Winthorpe
Chapel St Leonards
191
157
158

HOLKHAM BAY
BRANCASTER BAY
SCOLT HEAD ISLAND
Holme next the Sea
Thornham
Titchwell
Brancaster
Brancaster Staithe
Burnham Deepdale
Burnham Norton
Burnham Overy Staithe
Burnham Overy Town
Holkham
Wells-next-the-Sea
NORFOLK COAST
Westgate
Burnham Market
Burnham Thorpe
Ringstead
Summerfield
Docking
Stanhoe
Muckleton
New Holkham
North Creake
South Creake
Sedgeford
Fring
Snettisham
Ingoldisthorpe
Bircham Newton
Great Bircham
Bircham Tofts
Bagthorpe
Barmer
Syderstone
Blenheim Park
Wicken Green Village
Sculthorpe
Tattersett
Dunton
Coxford
East Rudham
Waterden
North Barsham
West Barsham
East Barsham
Houghton St Giles
Great Snoring
Little Walsingham
Great Walsingham
Egmere
Warham
Wighton
Fakenham
Hempton
Shereford
Dersingham
Anmer
Shernborne
Broomsthorpe
WELLS & WALSINGHAM LIGHT RAILWAY
RAF SCULTHORPE HERITAGE CENTRE
CREAKE ABBEY (REMS)
HOLKHAM HALL
HOUGHTON HALL
SNETTISHAM PARK
TITCHWELL MARSH
HOLME BIRD OBSERVATORY

7
8
9
10
11
A
B
C
D
E
F
G
H
TG
Blakeney Pit
Warham Hole
West Sand
Cabbage Creek
Stiffkey Freshes
South Side
Pits Pt
The Marrams
BLAKENEY
Morston Salt Marshes
Great Barnett
New Cut
CLEY MILL
Stiffkey Salt Marshes
Stiffkey Greens
BLAKENEY GUILDHALL
CLEY MARSHES
PEDDARS WAY AND NORFOLK COAST PATH
Salthouse
Sheringham
HILLSIDE SHIRE HORSE SANCTUARY
Warborough Hill
Morston
Blakeney
Cley next the Sea
Newgate
MUCKLEBURGH COLLECTION
Weybourne
West Runton
Stiffkey
Cockthorpe Common
Joe's Hill
Wiveton
Wiveton Downs
Gravelpit Hill
Gallow Hill
SHERINGHAM ROAD
WEYBOURNE RD
Battledore Hill
Cockthorpe
Sparrow Hill
NORFOLK COAST
Kelling
Sheringham Hall
Upper Sheringham
Beeston Regis
East Runton
Langham Lodge
Oulton Hill
Glandford
Swan Lodge
Lowes Fm
The Hangs
NORTH NORFOLK RAILWAY (THE POPPY LINE)
KELLING HEATH HALT
Kelling Heath
SHERINGHAM PARK
Weybourne Heath
The Dales
Sheringwood
Pretty Corner
Stone Hill
The Roman Camp
The Valley
Long Lane Fm
Short Lane Fm
Westgate
Old Barn Fm
Langham
The Wing
Summer House Hill
Cley Park
Lawn Fm
Bayfield Hall
Hundred Acre Wood
Highborough Fm
High Kelling
Bodham
HOLT ROAD
West Beckham
East Beckham
Aylmerton
Felbrigg
BINHAM PRIORY & WAYSIDE CROSS
Binham
Saxlingham
Ellis Fm
Manor House Fm
Smoker's Hole
Horse Hill
Pereer's Hills
Holt Hall (Coll)
Gresham's School
CROMER ROAD
Rookery Fm
Hill Ho
Manor Ho
FELBRIGG HALL
Roundwood Hill
Field Dalling
Letheringsett
THE GALLERY
Abbot Fm
Foxburrow Fm
Field Ho
Little Marsh
Eastmoor Fm
Breck Fm
Little Thornage
LETHERINGSETT WATERMILL
Common Hill
Holt
Heath Fm
Lower Bodham
Red Ho
BACONSTHORPE CASTLE (REMS)
Bodham Hill
Stonepit Hill
Gresham
County Fm
Clipstreet Fm
Ingmote Hill
THORNAGE ROAD
HOLT
Beckett's Fm
Baconsthorpe
Hell Hole
Lower Green
Bale Hall
Bale
Sharrington
Stowe Ollands
Hill Ho
Heath Ho
Dam Hill
Hempstead
Manor Ho
Up Wood
Thurgarton Old Hall
Bessingham
Sustead
Metton
Hall Fm
Hill House Fm
Grange Fm
Hindringham
Thornage
King's Hills
Edgefield Woods
Manor Ho
160
Brinton
Bullfer Grove
Edgefield Hall
Lowes Fm
The Dales
Pond Hills
Hole Fm
Hall Fm
Barningham Hall
Hall Fm
Hanworth
Vinepark Fm
Thursford Green
THURSFORD COLLECTION
Frog Hall Fm
Gunthorpe Park
Gunthorpe
Lobb's Valley
Burgh Stubbs
Stody
The Green
Hunworth
Bunker's Hill
Starlings' Hill
Edgefield
Plumstead Green
Plumstead
Matlaske
Aldborough Hall
Thurgarton
Hanworth Hall
Manor Fm
Thursford
Old Coach House
Little Snoring
Pigg's Grave
Briningham
Burgh Hall
Little Wood
Range Fm
Barningham Green
Lower Street
Aldborough
Alby Hill
Thwaite Hill Fm
The Lings
Wood Fm
Breck Fm
White Ollands Fm
Fuel Fm
FAKENHAM ROAD
Edgefield Street
Little Barningham
Wickmere
Erpingham Ho
Neat's Close
Park Fm
Melton Constable
Briston
Fir Patch
Old Covert
New Covert
Shrub Fm
Mere Fm
Mannington Hall
MANNINGTON GARDENS
Park Fm
Thwaite Hall
Thwaite Common
ALBY & GARDENS
Forty Acre Plantn
River Stiffkey
Barney
Little Wood
Swanton Novers
Swanton Great Wood
Melton Hall
Dairy Fm
Bunker's Hill
Briston Common
Roper Fm
Wolterton Park
Wolterton
Erpingham
Calthorpe
Kettlestone
Craymere Beck
Moor Hall
Holly Fm
Mossymere Wood
White House Fm
Croxton
Fulmodestone
SWANTON NOVERS
Brown's Covert
The Lake
Holmes's Wood
Tipples' Fm
Wood Severals
Washpit Plantn
Rookery Fm
Blackwater Br
Little London
Itteringham
Saxthorpe
Moorgate
Clipstone Ho
Common End
Raw Hall
Common Fm
159
Hindolveston
Burnthouse Fm
Holly Heath Fm
Corpusty
Irmingland Hall
Itteringham Common
Great Wood
Park Fm
Ingworth
PENSTHORPE NATURAL PARK
Manor Fm
Park Fm
Nethergate
Roundabout Fm
Thurning
Thurning Hall Fm
Foundry Hill
Red Pits
Oulton Lodge
The Tower
Blickling
BLICKLING HALL
Pit Fm
Abbots Hall
Fulmodeston Severals
Field Barn
Hindolveston Wood
Oak Grove
Crompton Hall
Oulton
Hercules Wood
Flash Pit Fm
Little Ryburgh
Stibbard
Holly Hill
Wood Norton
Ashcroft Fm
Black Water
Norton Corner
Drabblegate
Coldham Hall

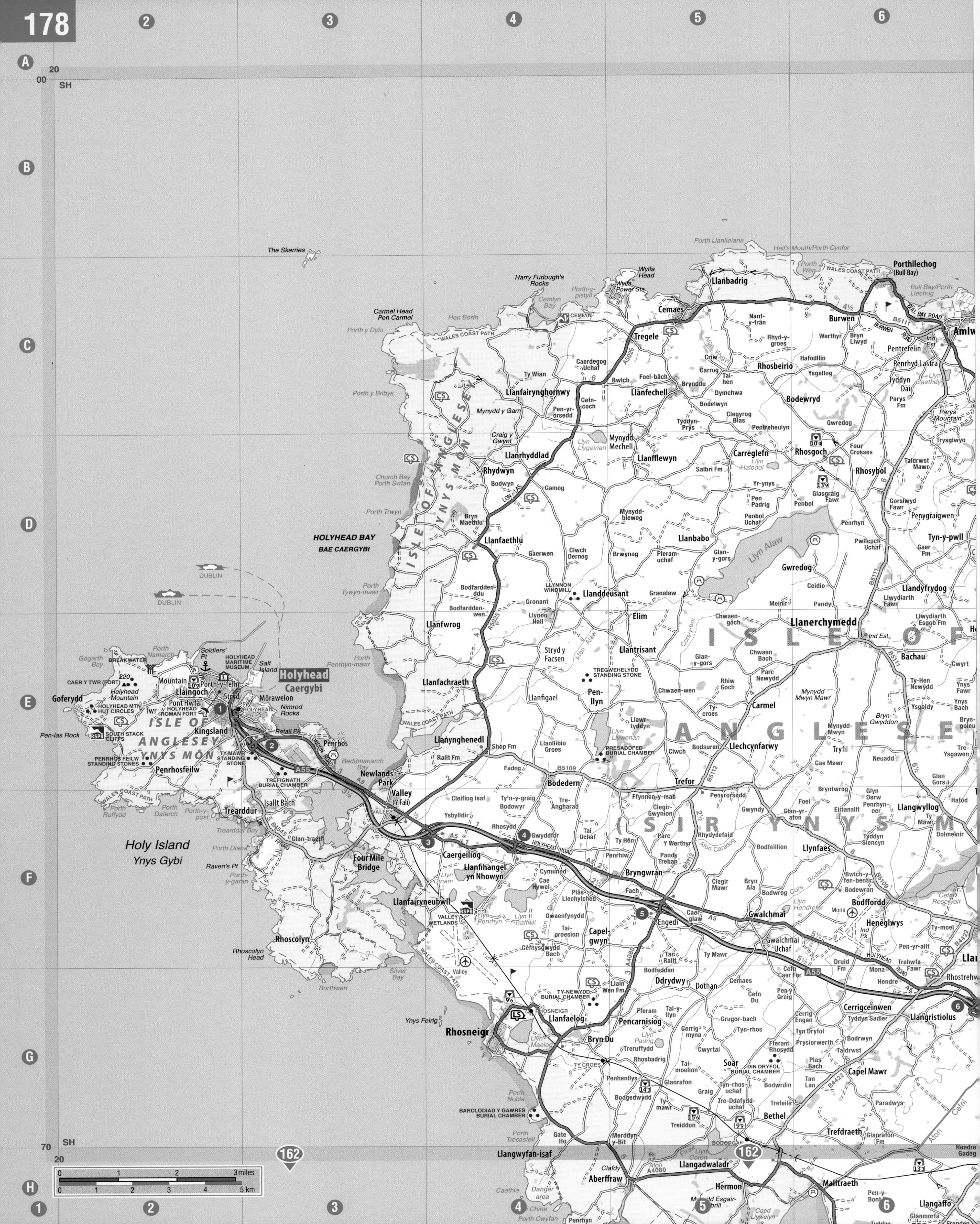
The Skerries
Porth Llanlleiana
Hell's Mouth/Porth Cynfor
Porthllechog (Bull Bay)
Harry Furlough's Rocks
Wylfa Head
Wylfa Power Sta
Llanbadrig
Cemaes
Carmel Head Pen Carmel
Cemlyn Bay
Hen Borth
Porth y Dyfn
WALES COAST PATH
Tregele
Burwen
Amlwch
Nant-y-frân
Rhyd-y-groes
Werthyr
Bryn Llwyd
Pentrefelin
Caerdegog Uchaf
Ty Wian
Bwlch
Foel-bâch
Llanfechell
Carrog
Rhosbeirio
Hafodllin
Ysgellog
Penrhyd Lastra
Tyddyn Dai
Llanfairynghornwy
Porth y Bribys
Mynydd y Garn
Cefn-coch
Pen-yr-orsedd
Brynddu
Dymchwa
Bodelwyn
Clegyrog Blas
Bodewryd
Parys Mountain
Parys Fm
Gwredog
Craig y Gwynt
Llanrhyddlad
Llyn Llygeirian
Mynydd Mechell
Tyddyn-Prys
Pentreheulyn
Rhosgoch
Trysglwyn
Four Crosses
Llanfflewyn
Carreglefn
Llyn Hafodol
Salbri Fm
Rhosybol
Taldrwst Mawr
Church Bay Porth Swtan
Rhydwyn
Bodwyn
Gamog
Yr-ynys
Glasgraig Fawr
Pen Padrig
Penbol
Gorslwyd Fawr
Penygraigwen
Porth Trwyn
Bryn Maethlu
Mynydd-blewog
Penbol Uchaf
Penrhyn
HOLYHEAD BAY
BAE CAERGYBI
Llanfaethlu
Llanbabo
Llyn Alaw
Pwllcoch Uchaf
Tyn-y-pwll
Gaerwen
Clwch Dernog
Brwynog
Fferam-uchaf
Glan-y-gors
Gwredog
Gaer Fm
ISLE OF ANGLESEY
YNYS MÔN
DUBLIN
Porth Tywyn-mawr
Bodfardden-ddu
LLYNNON WINDMILL
Llanddeusant
Granalaw
Ceidio
Llandyfrydog
Gronant
Pandy
Llwydiarth Fawr
Bodfardden-wen
Llynon Hall
Elim
Chwaen-gôch
Meinir
Llanerchymedd
Llwydiarth Esgob Fm
Llanfwrog
Ind Est
Porth Namarch
Soldiers' Pt
HOLYHEAD MARITIME MUSEUM
Salt Island
Gogarth Bay
BREAKWATER
Stryd y Facsen
Llantrisant
Chwaen Bach
Bachau
Cwyrt
Porth Penrhyn-mawr
Holyhead
Caergybi
CAER Y TWR (FORT)
Holyhead Mountain
Mountain
Llaingoch
Porth-y-felin
Stryd
TREGWEHELYDD STANDING STONE
Glan-y-gors
Parc Newydd
Llanfachraeth
Pen-Llyn
Rhiw Goch
Ty-Hen Newydd
Ynys Fawr
Goferydd
HOLYHEAD MTN HUT CIRCLES
Pont Hwfa
HOLYHEAD ROMAN FORT
Mômawelon
Nimrod Rocks
Llanfigael
Chwaen-wen
Mynydd Mwyn Mawr
Twr
Kingsland
Retail Pk
Llawr-tyddyn
Ty-croes
Carmel
Ysgoldy
Ynys Bach
Bryn-Gwyddon
Pen-las Rock
SOUTH STACK CLIFFS
Penrhos
Llyn Llywenan
Llanynghenedl
Shop Fm
Llanllibio Groes
PRESADDFED BURIAL CHAMBER
Bodsuran
Llechcynfarwy
Mynydd-Mwyn
Tryfil
Tre-Ysgawen
PENRHOS FEILW STANDING STONES
Penrhosfeilw
TY-MAWR STANDING STONE
Rallt Fm
Clwch
Cae Mawr
Neuadd
Beddmanarch Bay
Newlands Park
Fadog
Bodedern
Trefor
Glan Gors
TREFIGNATH BURIAL CHAMBER
Porth Ruffydd
Porth Dafarch
Porth-y-post
Trearddur
Valley (Y Fali)
Cleifiog Isaf
Ty'n-y-graig Bodowyr
Tre-Angharad
Ffynnon-y-mab
Clegir-Gwynion
Penyrorsedd
Bryntwrog
Glyn Derw Penrhyn-oer
Foel
Eirianallt
Llangwyllog
Hatod
Isallt Bach
Ysbylldir
Gwyndy
Glan-yr-afon
Ty Mawr
Holy Island
Ynys Gybi
Trearddur Bay
Glan-traeth
Rhosydd
Gwyddfor
Tai Uchaf
Ty Hên
Parc Y Werthyr
Rhydydefaid
Tyddyn Siencyn
Dolmeinir
Porth Diana
Raven's Pt
Porth-y-garan
Four Mile Bridge
Caergeiliog
HOLYHEAD ROAD
Penrhiw
Pandy Treban
Afon Caradog
Bodfeilion
Llynfaes
Llanfihangel yn Nhowyn
Llyn Dinam
Cymunod
Cae Hywel
Bryngwran
Clegir Mawr
Bryn Ala
Bwlch-y-fen-bentir
Bodewran
Llanfairyneubwll
Plâs Llechylched
Fach
Bodwrog
Llyn Hendref
Bodffordd
Cefni Reservoir
VALLEY WETLANDS
Llyn Penrhyn
Llyn Traffwll
Gwaenfynydd
Engedi
Caer glaw
Gwalchmai
Mona
Heneglwys
Tai-croesion
Capel-gwyn
Ind Pk
Ty-moel
Rhoscolyn
Gwalchmai Uchaf
Pen-yr-allt
Rhoscolyn Head
Cefnysgwydd Bach
Tan Rallt
Ty Mawr
Druid Fm
Trehwfa Fawr
Valley
Silver Bay
Bodfeddan
Ddrydwy
Dothan
Cemaes
Cefn Caer For
Mona
Hendre
Rhostrehwfa
Borthwen
TY-NEWYDD BURIAL CHAMBER
Llain Wen Fm
Cefn Du
Pen-y-Graig
Cerrigceinwen
Llangristiolus
Ynys Feirig
RHOSNEIGR
Llanfaelog
Fferam
Tal-y-llyn
Pencarnisiog
Grugor-bach
Cerrig Engan
Tyddyn Sadler
Rhosneigr
Llyn Maelog
Bryn Du
Llyn Padrig
Treruffydd
Cerrig-myna
Tyn-rhos
Tyn Dryfol
Bodrwyn
Prysiorwerth
Taldrwst
Cwyrtai
Fferam Rhosydd
TY CROES
Rhosbadrig
Tai-moelion
Soar
DIN DRYFOL BURIAL CHAMBER
Plas Bach
Capel Mawr
Penhenllys
Glanrafon
Tyn-rhos-uchaf
Bodwrdin
Tan Lan
Porth Nobla
Bodgedwydd
Graig
Trefeilir
Paradwys
Ty-mawr
Tre-Ddafydd-uchaf
BARCLODIAD Y GAWRES BURIAL CHAMBER
Treiddon
Bethel
Afon Cefni
Trefdraeth
Glanrafon Fm
Porth Trecastell
Gate Ho
Merddyn y-Bit
BODORGAN
Hendre Gadog
Llangwyfan-isaf
Llyn Coron
Clafdy
Llangadwaladr
Aberffraw
Caethle
Danger area
Hermon
Malltraeth
Pen-y-Bont
Llangaffo
China
Mynydd Esgair-brill
Coed Llywelyn
Porth Cwyfan
Penrhyn
Glanmorfa
Fronden
(SIR YNYS MÔN)
A55
A5
A5025
A4080
B4545
B5109
B5111
B5112
B4422
B5110
BULL BAY ROAD
BURWEN ROAD
LON LAS
LONDON ROAD
SH
00
20
70
162
0 1 2 3 miles
0 1 2 3 4 5 km

ISLE OF ANGLESEY
YNYS MÔN
CONWY BAY
BAE CONWY
Amlwch Port
Llaneilian
Pengorffwysfa
Penysarn
Nebo
Dulas
City Dulas
Brynrefail
Moelfre
MOELFRE SEAWATCH CENTRE
LLIGWY BURIAL CHAMBER
DIN LLIGWY
Llanallgo
Marianglas
Tynygongl
Benllech
Benllech Sand
Red Wharf Bay
Llanbedrgoch
Tan-y-graig
Pentraeth
Llanddyfnan
STONE SCIENCE
Talwrn
Pen-y-garnedd
Llansadwrn
Rhoscefnhir
Llanddona
Llangoed
Mariandyrys
Glan-yr-afon
Caim
Penmon
PENMON PRIORY
Puffin Island or Priestholm Ynys Seiriol
Lavan Sands
Llanfaes
BEAUMARIS CASTLE
GAOL & COURTHOUSE
Beaumaris
Gallows Point
Trwyn y Penrhyn
Llandegfan
Menai Bridge (Porthaethwy)
Llanfairpwll-gwyngyll
Bangor
Upper Bangor
Garth
Hirael
Maesgeirchen
PENRHYN CASTLE
Llandegai
Tal-y-bont
Abergwyngregyn
Llanfairfechan
Penmaenan
Garizim
Nant-y-pandy
Gorddinog
Glasinfryn
Tregarth
Rachub
Llanllechid
SNOWDONIA NATIONAL PARK
PARC CENEDLAETHOL ERYRI
Pentre Berw
Gaerwen
Llanddaniel Fab
Ceint
Penmynydd
Star
Coed Mawr
Glan Adda
Minffordd
Capel-y-graig
Vaynol Hall
Llanedwen
Rhosmeirch
Capel Coch
Maenaddwyn
Brynteg
Mynydd Bodafon
A55
A5
A5025
A5114
B5109
B5420
163
180

IRISH SEA
MÔR IWERDDON
Great Ormes Head
Pen-y-Gogarth
Hornby Cave
GREAT ORME
CABIN LIFT
GREAT ORME RAILWAY
GREAT ORME COPPER MINE
Toll
Llandudno Bay or Ormes Bay
Little Ormes Head
Cregiau Rhiwledyn
141
Llandudno
THE PARADE
COLWYN ROAD
Penrhynside
Penrhyn Bay (Bae Penrhyn)
Craig-y-don
Rhôs Pt
Rhôs-on-Sea
Llandrillo-yn-Rhos
Colwyn Bay (Bae Colwyn)
Conwy Sands
Llanrhos
Deganwy
Glanwydden
Bryn Pydew
Tywyn
Llandudno Junction (Cyffordd Llandudno)
Mochdre
Old Colwyn
Penmaen Rhôs
Llanddulas
Abergele
Dolwyd
Conwy
Gyffin
Dwygyfylchi
Penmaenmawr
Penmaenan
Capelulo
Llechwedd
Henryd
Llanfairfechan
Nant-y-pandy
Garizim
SNOWDONIA NATIONAL PARK
PARC CENEDLAETHOL ERYRI
CONWY
Bryn-rhys
Llansanffraid Glan Conwy
Pentrefelin
Bryn-y-maen
Llanelian-yn-Rhos
Llysfaen
Dolwen
Betws-yn-Rhos
Rowen
Ty'n-y-groes
Pontwgan
Tal-y-cafn
Graig
Eglwysbach
Pentre'r Felin
Tal-y-Bont
Gell
Cefn-coch
Pentre Isaf
Llanfair Talhaiarn
Bryn-nantllech
Dawn
Hafod-lom
Trofarth
Rhandir
Chwefford
River Conwy
A470
A55
A546
A547
A548
B5115
B5113
B5381
B5106
179
164
0 1 2 3 miles
0 1 2 3 4 5 km

7
8
9
10
11
A
B
C
D
E
F
G
H
SJ
182
165
Hilbre Island
Little Hilbre Island
RED ROCKS MARSH
MEOLS DRIVE
West Kirby
Marine Lake
Point of Ayr
(Yr Parlwr Du)
POINT OF AYR DEE ESTUARY
Talacre
Bus Pk
Wild Road
Tanlan Banks
Tanlan
Ffynnongroyw
Salisbury Middle
Mostyn Quay
Mostyn
Glan-y-don
Llannerch-y-môr
The Marsh
WALES COAST PATH
Rhyl
(Y Rhyl)
SEAQUARIUM
RHYL COAST ROAD
Y-Ffrith
VICTORIA ROAD
PRESTATYN ROAD
Prestatyn
Gronant
Gwespyr
Llanasa
Picton
Glasdir
Rhewl-fawr
Pen-y-ffordd
Garth
Glan-yr-afon
Kelston Fm
Meliden
(Gallt Melyd)
Gwaenysgor
Pydew Fm
Four Winds Fm
Tan-yr-allt
Gop Hill
251
Axton
Trelogan
Berthengam
Mynydd Mostyn
Wern Fm
Rhewl-Mostyn
Tre-Mostyn
Pentre-ffynnon Hall
Maes Pennant
Kinmel Bay
(Bae Cinmel)
Towyn
Ty-mawr
Pensarn
Belgrano
River Gele
Rhuddlan
Afon Clwyd
Retail Pk
Trad Est
Bryn Cwnin Fm
Llewerllyd
Pen-y-ffordd
Long Acre
Graig Fawr
DYSERTH WATERFALL
Dyserth
FORT
Moel Hiraddug
Bryniau
Mia Hall
Trelawnyd
Henfryn Hall
Marian
Pen-y-Cefn-isaf
Walwen
Sarn
MAEN ACHWYFAN
Bryn-coch
Whitford
(Chwitffordd)
BODRHYDDAN HALL
Ochr-y-foel
Cwm
Marian Cwm
Graig-Arthur
Plâs-mawr
Plas Captain
Llyn Helyg
Glol
Garreg
Per-ffordd-llân
Saith ffynnon
Lloc
Stokyn Hall
Greenfield
(Maes-Glas)
Mertyn Hall
Golch
Carmel
BASINGWERK ABBEY
GREENFIELD VALLEY HERITAGE PARK
Walwen
Whelston
DENBIGHSHIRE
(SIR DDINBYCH)
CLWYDIAN RANGE
OFFA'S DYKE PATH
ABERGELE ROAD
CASTLE
Abbey Fm
Pen-y-ffordd
Gofer
RHUDDLAN ROAD
Hendre bach
Bodoryn Fawr
Ty'n-y-llyn
Pengwern
Rhydyddauddwr Fm
Coed Cwm
Pant-y-dulath
Ffyddion Fm
Pant-y-Wacco
Gorsedd
Mwdwl-eithin
Pen-y-maes
Bryn Celyn
Holywell
(Treffynon)
Ffordd-las Bach Fm
St George
Bodelwyddan
Gwernigron Fm
Plas Coch Fm
Ty Isa Fm
Plas yn Cwm Hall
Rhuallt
Brynllithrig Hall
Cae Rhys Fm
Llwybr-h ir
Pen-y-cefn
Pantasaph
Pen-y-Ball Top
Smithy Gate
Naid-y-march
Tyn Twll Fm
Dinorben
Kinmel Hall
Moelfre
Glascoed
Bodelwyddan Park
GLASCOED RD
The Roe
CATHEDRAL
St Asaph
(Llanelwy)
Rhewl Fm
Moel Maenefa
290
Hartley Fm
FLINTSHIRE
(SIR Y FFLINT)
Pant
Calcoed
Brynford
Milwr
Talgrwn
Nant Meifod
Bryn-y-pin
Nant Bach
Groesffordd Marli
Hendy Fm
Bryn Asaph
Bryn-Polyn
Waen Goleugoed
Plas Coch
Bryntirion Fm
Tremeirchion
Bryngwyn Hall
Croes-wian
Caerwys Hall
Caerwys
Truly
Waen
Babell
Calcot Hall
Pwll-clai
Dolphin
Llongley
Tan-y-gaer
Pen-y-gribin
Bedd-y-cawr
Ty'n-y-ffordd
Glascoed Fawr
Eryl Hall
UPPER DENBIGH ROAD
Llannerch Hall
River Clwyd
Hafod-y-coed
Cefn Du
Lodge Fm
Maes-mynan Hall
Afon-wen
Ivy House
Mynydd-llan
Prysau
Pen-Uchar Plwyf
Halkyn Mountain
Pentre Halkyn
Bron-haul
Bodysgaw Isa
Plâs-uchaf Res
Tan-llan
Wigfair
Plas-yn-Cefn
Hafod-y-Green
Henblas
Graig
Sodom
Nantgwilym
Wheeler
Candy Mill
AFONWEN CRAFT & ANTIQUE CENTRE
Ddol
Ysceifiog
Lixwm
Bwlch
Pwll-melyn
Windmill
Old Hall
Halkyn
Fron Fawr
230
Ffynhonnau
Llannefydd
Tal-y-bryn
Bont-newydd
River Elwy
Penuchagreen Fm
Perthewig
Trefnant
College
Afon Clwyd
Nantlys
Moel y Parc
398
Bryn yr Eithin
Afon Chwiler
Fron-haul
Walwen
Garneddwen
Rhes-y-cae
Halkyn Mountain
Catch
Dolwen Res
BODFARI ROAD
Bodfari
Mwccwd
Bryn Rug
Waen-dymarch
Mynydd y Gyrt
Cefn Berain
Galltfaenan Hall
Pen-cae-du Fm
Pontruffydd Fm
Pontruffydd Hall Fm
Waen
Geinas
The Grove Hall
Aifft
Coed-y-mynydd Ucha
Pen-y-felin
Nannerch
Moel-y-crio
Berth-ddu
Wern-gaer
Pant-y-ffuon
Beniar
Plas Heaton
Plas Heaton Fm
Green
Penpalmant
Aberwheeler
Castell
Nant Coed-y-mynydd
Bryn Golau
Hafod-y-cwm
Penbedw
Hendre Fm
Cilcain Hall
Dyffryn Aled
Moel Fodiar
390
Cae'r groes
Hafod Wood
Gerdden Isa
Henllan
Meusyd Brwyn
Lleweni Hall
Dre-goch
Pen-ucha'r-cwm
Pennorchell
Nant-figillt Wood
A548
A547
A525
A5151
A5026
A541
A55
B5119
B5381
B5382
B5428
B5429
B5122
B5121
B5123
24
24A
25
26
27
27A
28
29
30
31
32
32A

193
181
166
LIVERPOOL
BAY
Crosby Channel
BELFAST
DOUGLAS
(NOV-MARCH)
DUBLIN
DOUGLAS
(MARCH-NOV)
ANTONY GORMLEY SCULPTURES
Little Crosby
Sefton
Lunt
Thornton
Netherton
Melling
Melling Mount
Blundellsands
Brighton le Sands
Great Crosby
Crosby
Buckley Hill
Aintree
Waterloo Park
Waterloo
Ford
Litherland
Orrell
Seaforth
Fazakerley
Gillmoss
Croxteth
Knowsley
Kirkby
Northwood
Westvale
Southdene
Tower Hill
Waddicar
Bootle
Walton
Norris Green
Dog & Gun
Kirkdale
Sandhills
Clubmoor
West Derby
Anfield
Tuebrook
Everton
Vauxhall
Stockbridge Village
Fincham
Woolfall Heath
Longview
Liverpool
Kensington
Knotty Ash
Dovecot
Page Moss
Roby
Huyton
Swanside
Old Swan
Broad Green
Edge Hill
Bowing Park
Childwall
Wavertree
Princes Park
Toxteth
Dingle
Sefton Park
Mossley Hill
Calderstones
Gateacre
Woolton
Belle Vale
Netherley
Aigburth
Allerton
Grassendale
Hunt's Cross
St Michael's Hamlet
Otterspool
Garston
Speke
Liverpool Airport
LIVERPOOL (JOHN LENNON)
MERSEYSIDE
New Brighton
Wallasey
Egremont
Liscard
Leasowe
Moreton
Poulton
Bidston
Bidston Hill
Seacombe
Claughton
Birkenhead
Upton
Noctorum
Oxton
Woodchurch
Arrowe Hill
Prenton
Tranmere
Rock Ferry
New Ferry
Hoylake
Meols
Dove Point
East Hoyle Bank
Saughall Massie
Greasby
Newton
West Kirby
Grange
Frankby
Caldy
Royden Park
Landican
Irby
Irby Hill
Thurstaston Common
Thurstaston
Thingwall
Storeton
Higher Bebington
Woodhey
Bebington
Bromborough Pool
Port Sunlight
Lower Bebington
Spital
Barnston
Brimstage
Pensby
Poll Hill
Heswall
The Dales
Dawpool Bank
Thornton Manor
Thornton Hough
Poulton Hall
Bromborough
Eastham Ferry
Eastham Sands
Eastham Locks
Eastham
Brookhurst
Raby Hall
Raby
Gayton
Gayton Sands
Parkgate
Hinderton
Willaston
Neston
Little Neston
Ness
NESS BOTANIC GARDENS
Hooton
Childer Thornton
Little Sutton
Overpool
Ellesmere Port
Stanlow
Stanlow Banks
Whitby
Great Sutton
Wolverham
Ledsham
Capenhurst
Burton
Puddington
Two Mills
Whitbyheath
Little Stanney
Thornton-le-Moors
Backford Cross
Backford
Dunkirk
Shotwick
Saughall
Mollington
Chester
Upton
Newton
Hoole Bank
Mickle Trafford
Wimbolds Trafford
Picton
Wervin
CHESHIRE WEST & CHESTER
River Mersey
Hilbre Island
Middle Hilbre Island
Marine Lake
Flint
(Y Fflint)
Flint Mountain
(Mynydd Fflint)
Holywell
(Treffynon)
Halkyn Mountain
Halkyn
Bagillt
Mount Pleasant
Pentre-Ffwrndan
Oakenholt
Rockcliffe
Kelsterton
Golftyn
Connah's Quay
Shotton
Garden City
Sealand
Walwen
Whelston
Greenfield
Milwr
Dolphin
Pwll-melyn
Rhes-y-cae
White Sands
Flint Marsh
The Marsh
Danger area
0 1 2 3 miles
0 1 2 3 4 5 km

Rainford
Billinge
Garswood
Bryn
Abram
Westleigh
Leigh
Tyldesley
Ashton-in Makerfield
Golborne
Lowton
Haydock
Newton-le-Willows
St Helens
Eccleston
Prescot
Huyton
Whiston
Rainhill
Sutton
Winwick
Croft
Culcheth
Glazebury
Risley
Birchwood
Cadishead
Glazebrook
WARRINGTON
Warrington
Great Sankey
Penketh
Latchford
Thelwall
Lymm
Widnes
Ditton
Hale
Runcorn
HALTON
Halton
Daresbury
Stretton
Moore
Appleton Thorn
Grappenhall
Stockton Heath
High Legh
Arley
Frodsham
Helsby
CHESHIRE WEST & CHESTER
Weaverham
Northwich
Barnton
Anderton
Hartford
Davenham
Moulton
Cuddington
Sandiway
Kelsall
Delamere
Oakmere
Mouldsworth
Manley
Alvanley
Kingsley
Crowton
Norley
Acton Bridge
Little Leigh
Comberbach
Great Budworth
Pickmere
Wincham
Rudheath
Lostock Gralam
Plumley
DELAMERE FOREST PARK
Chester Services
Burtonwood Services

Worsley
Swinton
Pendlebury
Kersal
Broughton Park
Moston
Failsworth
Hollinwood
Harpurhey
Newton Heath
Salford
Eccles
Manchester
Trafford Park
Stretford
Old Trafford
Hulme
Ardwick
Gorton
Droylsden
Denton
Ashton
Dukinfield
Irlam
Flixton
Urmston
Cadishead
Partington
Carrington
Sale
Chorlton-cum-Hardy
Withington
Didsbury
West Didsbury
Fallowfield
Rusholme
Levenshulme
Reddish
Heaton Moor
Stockport
Bredbury
Brooklands
Northenden
Timperley
Altrincham
Broadheath
Dunham Town
Bowdon
Hale
Wythenshawe
Gatley
Cheadle
Cheadle Hulme
Bramhall
Hazel Grove
Lymm
Manchester Airport
Ashley
Styal
Handforth
Woodford
Poynton
Rostherne
Mere
Tatton Park
Mobberley
Wilmslow
Knutsford
Over Tabley
Alderley Edge
Prestbury
Bollington
Macclesfield
Hurdsfield
Chelford
Over Peover
Plumley
Lower Withington
Goostrey
Holmes Chapel
Marton
Gawsworth
GREATER MANCHESTER
M60
M56
M6
M62
M602
A34
A6
A56
A555
A537
A523
195
196
183
168
A
B
C
D
E
F
G
H
1
2
3
4
5
6
0 1 2 3 miles
0 1 2 3 4 5 km

Stalybridge
Hazelhurst
Hyde
Newton
Godley
Mottram in Longdendale
Matley
Hattersley
Broadbottom
Tintwistle
Hadfield
Hollingworth
Padfield
Gamesley
Glossop
Old Glossop
Simmondley
Charlesworth
Chisworth
Compstall
Marple
Marple Bridge
Mellor
Strines
New Mills
Low Leighton
Newtown
Disley
High Lane
Hayfield
Little Hayfield
Birch Vale
Thornsett
Chinley Head
Chinley
Buxworth
Whaley Bridge
Furness Vale
Bridgemont
Horwich End
Chapel-en-le-Frith
Chapel Milton
Sparrowpit
Dove Holes
Peak Dale
Peak Forest
Combs
Fernilee
Kettleshulme
Taxal
Burbage
Buxton
Fairfield
Harpur Hill
King Sterndale
Cowdale
Blackwell
Taddington
Chelmorton
Sterndale Moor
Tideswell
Litton
Wardlow
Little Hucklow
Great Hucklow
Grindlow
Bradwell
Castleton
Hope
Aston
Bamford
Thornhill
Brough
Edale
Nether Booth
Upper Booth
Barber Booth
Crowden
Longdendale
Bleaklow
Howden Moors
Upper Derwent
Hope Forest
Kinder Scout
The Edge
High Peak
PEAK DISTRICT NATIONAL PARK
DERBYSHIRE
Vale of Edale
Macclesfield Forest
Wildboarclough
Sheldon
Ashford in the Water
Great Longstone
Little Longstone
Foolow
Eyam
Bretton
Abney
Miller's Dale
Wormhill
Tunstead
Wheston
Hargatewall
Snake Road
Pennine Way
Ladybower Reservoir
Derwent Reservoir
Howden Reservoir
Cowburn Tunnel
196
197
186
169
A628
A57
A6
A623
A624
A6013
A515
A5004
A537
A54
A53
A626
A6018
M67

Cubley
Oxspring
Roughbirchworth
Snowden Hill
Thurgoland
Crane Moor
Pilley
Upper Hoyland
Birdwell
Hoyland Common
Hoyland
Platts Common
Jump
Elsecar
Hemingfield
Brampton
Wath upon Dearne
West Melton
Langsett
Brock Holes
Upper Midhope
Midhopestones
Underbank Hall
Crimbles Fm
Hunshelf Hall
Green Moor
Wortley
Tankersley
Chapeltown
Upper Tankersley
Lane Royds Park
Rainborough Park
Newhill
Mickleden Edge
Bradshaw Hill
Barnside Moor
Ewden Height
Pike Lowe Stones
Pike Lowe
Fenny Common
Stocksbridge
Deepcar
Stone Moor
Finkle Street
Bromley
Howbrook
Westwood
Mortomley
Warren
Barrow
Harley
Wentworth
Cortworth
Hoober
Abdy
Whitwell Moor
Waldershaigh
Bolsterstone
Hollin Edge Height
Ewden Village
Cundy Hos
Hazelshaw Fm
Potter Hill
High Green
Charltonbrook
Lane End
Hood Hill
Spittal Houses
Wentworth Park
Nether Haugh
Upper Haugh
Ryecroft
Rawm
Upper Commons
Broomhead Hall
Broomhead Reservoir
Wharncliffe Chase
Wharncliffe Lodge
Wood Seats
Burncross
Barnes Hall
Thorpe Hesley
Scholes
Parkgate
Margery Hill
Stainery Clough
Broomhead Moor
Wigtwizzle
More Hall Res
Brightholmlee
Greno Woods
Wingfield
Greasbrough
Middle Moss
Featherbed Moss
Hobson Moss
PEAK
White Lee Fm
Spout House Hill
Wharncliffe Side
Wharncliffe Wood
Whitley
Ecclesfield
Keppel's Column
Dropping Well
Kimberworth Park
SOUTH
Hobson Moss Dike
Agden Bridge
Emlin Ridge
Wet Slack Ridge
Hill Ho
Foldrings
Oughtibridge
Grenoside
Thorn Hill
Kimberworth
Bradgate
Eastwood
East Dene
DISTRICT
High Bradfield
Holling Dale
Peat Pits Fm
Edge Mount
Bent Hills
Onesacre
Coumes Fm
Birley Edge
Beeley Wood
Blackburn Hill Top
Jordon
Rotherham
Clifton Park
Herringthorpe
Low Tor
Agden Reservoir
Holling Dale Plantn
Thornseat
Walker Ho
Low Bradfield
Prospect Fm
Worrall
Birley Carr
Parson Cross
Shiregreen
Masbrough
Clifton
Broom
Howden Moor
Howshaw Tor
NATIONAL
Back Tor
Brogging Moss
Bole Edge Plantn
Edgefield
Cliffe House Fm
Holdworth
Low Ash Fm
Middlewood
Wadsley Bridge
Longley Estate
Firth Park
Wincobank
Pismire Hill
Meadowhall
Magna Science Adventure Centre
Tinsley
Canklow
Tor Fm
Dale Dike Reservoir
Damflask Reservoir
Loxley Chase
Loxley Common
Wadsley
Hillsborough
Shirecliffe
Fir Vale
Moorgate
Deep Clough
Foulstone Moor
Strines Reservoir
Gibraltar Rocks
Ughill
Woodhouse Fm
Stacey Bank
Storrs Bridge
YORKSHIRE
Malinbridge
Owlerton
Parkwood Springs
Grimesthorpe
Carbrook
Brightside
Brinsworth
Dovestone Tor
Sugworth Hall
Platts Fm
Hall Broom
Dungworth
Hill Top
Storrs
Loxley
Crabtree Ponds
Pitsmoor
Utilita Arena
Dovestone Clough
Strines Edge
Bents Ho
Moor Lodge
Furnace Hill
Stannington
Attercliffe
Greenland
Ashes Fm
Derwent Moors
Rising Clough
Wheel Stones
Crawshaw Head Ho
Rod Moor
Load Brook
Hopwood Ho
Stopes
Walkley
Burngreave
Sheffield
Kelham Island Museum
Darnall
Catcliffe
Treeton
Waverley
Derwent Edge
Moscar Ho
Moscar Lodge
Hollow Meadows
Ronksley Fm
Under Tofts
Steel Bank
Cathedral
Park Hill
Whinstone Lee Tor
Cutthroat Br
Rails
Crookes
Crookesmoor
Orgreave
Handsworth
Ladybower Tor
Ashopton
Head Stone
Moscar Fields
Jarvis Clough
Rivelin Mill Br
Wyming Brook
Tapton Hill
Manor Park
Moscar Moor
High Lad Ridge
Ash Cabin Flat
Wyming Brook Fm
Rivelin Dams
Sandygate
Botanical Gardens
Ranmoor
Sheffield Park
Sheffield Services
Manor Estate
Richmond
Woodhouse Mill
Ladybower Reservoir
Ladybower Ho
Priddock Wood
Brown Edge
Fulwood
Highfield
Bramall Lane
Arbourthorne
Win Hill
Bamford Moor
High Neb
Stanage Edge
Fairthorn Lodge
Lodge Moor
Fulwood Hall
Greystones
Sharrow
Heeley City Farm
Woodhouse
Yorkshire Br
Redmires Reservoir
Brincliffe
Normanton Spring
Stanedge Lodge
Buck Stone
Rud Hill
Brown Edge Fm
Whiteley Wood
Ecclesall
Nether Edge
Heeley
Rollestone
Intake
Coisley Hill
Aston
White Stones
Bassett
Porter Clough
Carter Knowle
Meersbrook
Bishop's House
Bole Hill
Robin Hood's Cave
Ringinglow
Hollins End
Frecheville
Beighton
Bamford
Upper Hurst Fm
Greens Ho
Friar's Ridge
Cowper Stone
Sheephill Fm
Castle Dyke
Whirlow
Parkhead
Millhouses
Norton Woodseats
Gleadless Valley
Gleadless
Hackenthorpe
Drakehouse
Thornhill
Carr Bottom
Brookfield Manor
Kimber Court Fm
Lady Canning's Plantn
Barberfields Fm
Ecclesall Wood
Bolehill
Hemsworth
Charnock Hall
Moorhole
Owlthorpe
Waterthorpe
Sothall
Shatton
Bamford
Overstones Fm
Higger Tor
Moorside Fm
Abbeydale
Meadow Head
Norton
Lightwood
Carter Lodge
Highlane
Westfield
Holbrook
Elmore Hill Fm
Birley Fm
Toothill Fm
Mitchell Field
Burbage Moor
Houndkirk Moor
Fern Glen Fm
Brick Houses
Greenhill
Hazlebarrow
Hazlehurst Fm
Carterhall Fm
Ridgeway
Halfway
Shatton Edge
Old Lees Fm
Offerton Hall
Hathersage
Carl Wark
Over Owler Tor
Dore
Beauchief
Jordanthorpe
Ridgeway Moor
Mosborough
Hathersage Booths
Parson House
Hallfield Fm
Abbeydale Park
Totley Brook
Townhead
Bradway
Lowedges
Povey Fm
Plumbley
Oxclose
Over Dale
Abney Moor
Smelting Hill
Broadhay Fm
Leadmill
Kettle Ho
Fox House Inn
Blacka Moor
Bole Hill
Totley
Ockley Fm
Batemoor
Birleyhay
Ford
Eckington Hall
Reform Stone
Highlow Hall
Hazelford Hall
Holmley Common
Troway
Abney
Oaks Fm
Leam
Upper Padley
Longshaw
Longshaw Estate
Totley Moor
Totley Tunnel
New Totley
Mickley
Barnes Fm
Coal Aston
Bentleyhall Fm
Greenside
Bramley
Eckington
Boiley Fm
Bleak Knoll
Abney Clough
Bole Hill
Eyam Moor Stone Circle
Leam Hall
Brown Edge
Woodthorpe Hall
Dronfield Woodhouse
Snape Hill
Dronfield
Holmesdale
Summerley
Marsh Lane
Renishaw Hall Gdns
Renishaw Park
Birley Fm
Cockey Fm
Abney Grange
Bretton Clough
Eyam Moor
Sheriff Wood
Grindleford
Nether Padley
White Edge Moor
Flask Edge
Owler Bar
Moor Edge Fm
Old Hall
Gosforth Valley
Apperknowle
Middle Handley
Bretton
Stanage Ho
Sir William Hill
Fanshawe Gate
Holmesfield
Hallowes
Unstone Grange
Marsh Fm
Shepherd's Flat Fm
Highcliffe
Magclough Fm
Mag Clough
Grindleford
Bucka Hill
Lydgate
Cartledge
Cowley
Hill Top
Unstone
Hundall
West Handley
Red Lodge Fm
Eyam
Eyam Hall
Barbrook Reservoir
Holmesfield Common
Millthorpe
Bull Close Fm
Unstone Green
Nether Handley
White Lodge
Slittingmill
Foolow
Eyam View Fm
Froggatt Edge
Stoke Flat
White Edge
Big Moor
Smeekley Wood
Highlightley Fm
Brindwoodgate
Crowhole
DERBYSHIRE
Water Grove
Stoney Middleton
Froggatt
Foxlane Fm
Knowles Fm
Unthank
Revolution House Museum
New Whittington
Barrow Hill
Huggester
Burnt Heath
The Dale
Curbar Edge
Bradleylane Fm
Common Side
The Brushes
Netherthorpe
Staveley
Middleton Moor
High Fields
Calver Sough
Curbar
Warren Lodge
Ramsley Lodge
Baslow Edge
Moorhall
Wilday Green
Barlow
Sheepbridge
Old Whittington
Hollingwood
Woodthorpe
Coombs Dale
Calver
Cliff College
Grange Lumb Fm
Dunston Hole Fm
Dunston
Whittington Moor
New Brimington
Middlecroft
Poolsbrook
Longstone Moor
High Rake
Hassop Common
Peak Pasture
Nelson's Monument
Spitewinter Fm
Oxton Rakes
Bole Hill
Cutthorpe
Upper Newbold
Newbold
Technique Stadium
Stonegravels
Brimington
Brimington Common
Little Longstone
Rowland
Bubnell
Bridge End
Baslow
Baslow Hall
Over End
Nether End
Moorside Fm
Robin Hood
Freebirch
Barlow Grange
Hare Edge
Moorhay Fm
Overgreen
Linacre Wood
Linacre Reservoir
Loundsley Green
Tapton
Tapton Grove
West Wood
Inkersall Green
Inkersall
Duckmanton
Markham Vale Services
Great Longstone
Hassop
Bubnell Cliff
Birchill Bank Wood
Park Lodge
Dalebrook Ho
Eastmoor
Wigley
Wadshelf
Hollins
Old Brampton
Offley Place
The Grove
Frith Hall
Ashgate
Chesterfield
Calow
Arkwright Town
Long Duckmanton
Thornbridge Hall
Pilsley
Chatsworth Park
Bunkers Hill Wood
Gibbet Moor
Nether Rodnoll Fm
Brampton East Moor
Brampton
Boythorpe
Crooked Spire
Hady
Cock Alley
Bolehill
Ashford in the Water
Churchdale Hall
Ashford Hall
Handley Bottom
Dunsa
Chatsworth
Swiss Cott
Hallcliff Fm
Nether Chanderhill
Somersall Hall
Brookside
Walton
Birdholme
Calow Green
Woodnook Fm
Holme
Edensor
Hob Hurst's House
Park Fm
Rodknoll Fm
Upper Loads
Nether Loads
Holymoorside
Harper Hill Fm
Hasland
Manor Fm
Sutton Scarsdale Hall
Sutton Scarsdale
Pilsley
Bakewell
Calton Houses
Calton Pastures
Calton Lees
Beeley Lodge
Hell Bank Plantn
Harland Edge
Harewood Grange
Hare House
Walton Lodge
Slatepit Dale
Swathwick
Corbriggs
Winsick
Sutton Spring Wood
Kirk Dale
Bletton Fm
Bamford
Hathersage
Stanage Edge
0 1 2 3 miles
0 1 2 3 4 5 km

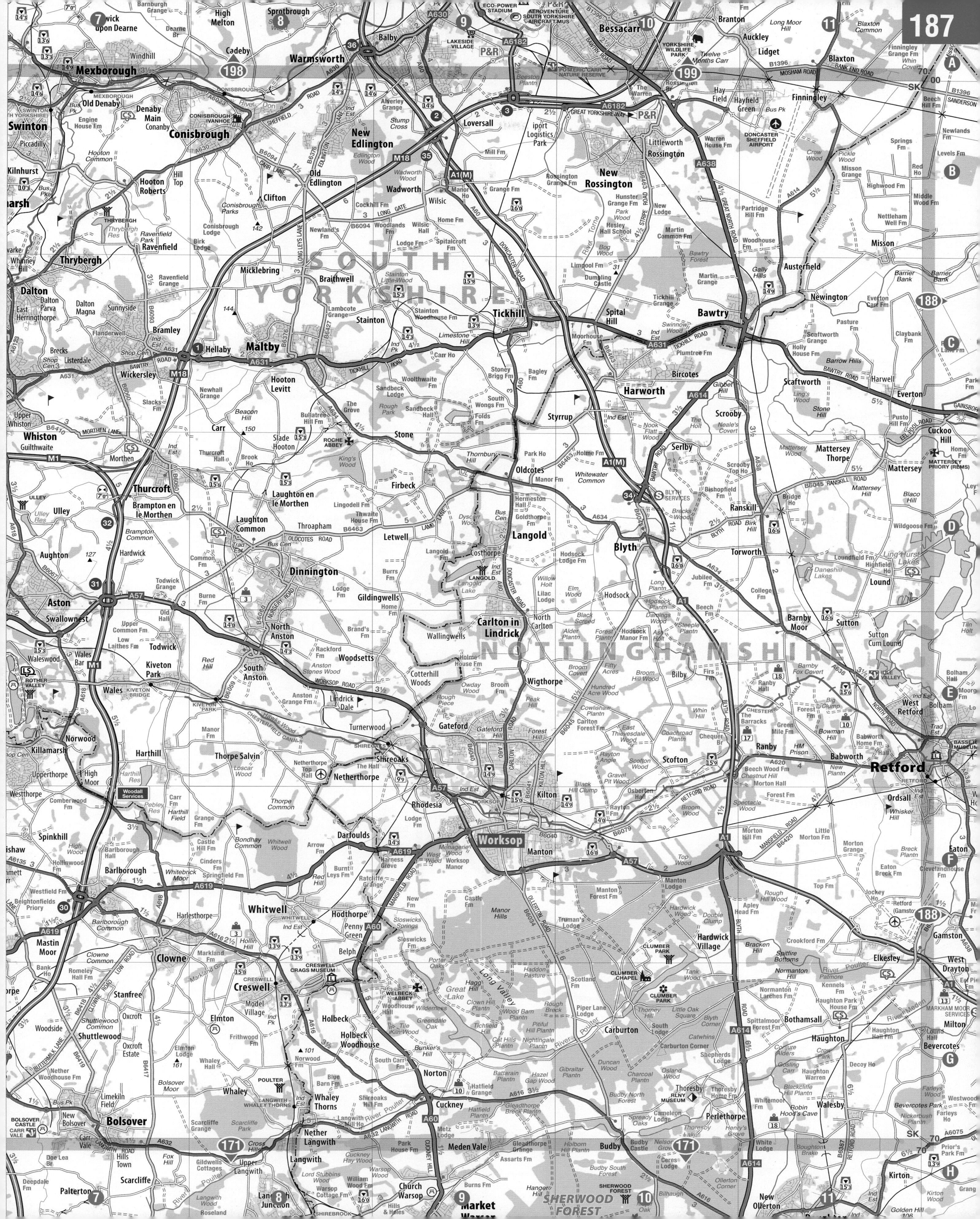
Mexborough
Swinton
Conisbrough
Denaby Main
Old Denaby
Warmsworth
Balby
Bessacarr
Branton
Auckley
Blaxton
Finningley
Loversall
New Edlington
Old Edlington
Wadworth
Wilsic
Hooton Roberts
Clifton
Ravenfield
Thrybergh
Dalton
Micklebring
Braithwell
Stainton
Tickhill
Maltby
Hellaby
Bramley
Wickersley
Hooton Levitt
Rossington
New Rossington
Harworth
Bircotes
Bawtry
Austerfield
Misson
Newington
Scrooby
Serlby
Styrrup
Oldcotes
Stone
Firbeck
Letwell
Langold
Blyth
Ranskill
Torworth
Everton
Harwell
Scaftworth
Mattersey
Mattersey Thorpe
Thurcroft
Laughton en le Morthen
Dinnington
Laughton Common
Aston
Swallownest
Aughton
Ulley
Whiston
Todwick
Kiveton Park
North Anston
South Anston
Gildingwells
Woodsetts
Carlton in Lindrick
Hodsock
Bilby
Wigthorpe
Barnby Moor
Sutton
Lound
Retford
West Retford
Ordsall
Babworth
Ranby
Gateford
Shireoaks
Netherthorpe
Rhodesia
Worksop
Manton
Kilton
Scofton
Osberton Hall
Harthill
Thorpe Salvin
Wales
Norwood
Killamarsh
Barlborough
Spinkhill
Whitwell
Clowne
Creswell
Darfoulds
Hodthorpe
Belph
Elmton
Holbeck
Norton
Cuckney
Whaley Thorns
Bolsover
Shuttlewood
Scarcliffe
Palterton
Langwith
Nether Langwith
Meden Vale
Budby
Carburton
Clumber Park
Perlethorpe
Walesby
Elkesley
Gamston
Haughton
Bothamsall
Milton
Kirton
Market Warsop
Church Warsop
SOUTH YORKSHIRE
NOTTINGHAMSHIRE
SHERWOOD FOREST
A1(M)
M18
M1
A57
A60
A614
A631
A634
A619
A616
A620
A638
198
199
188
171

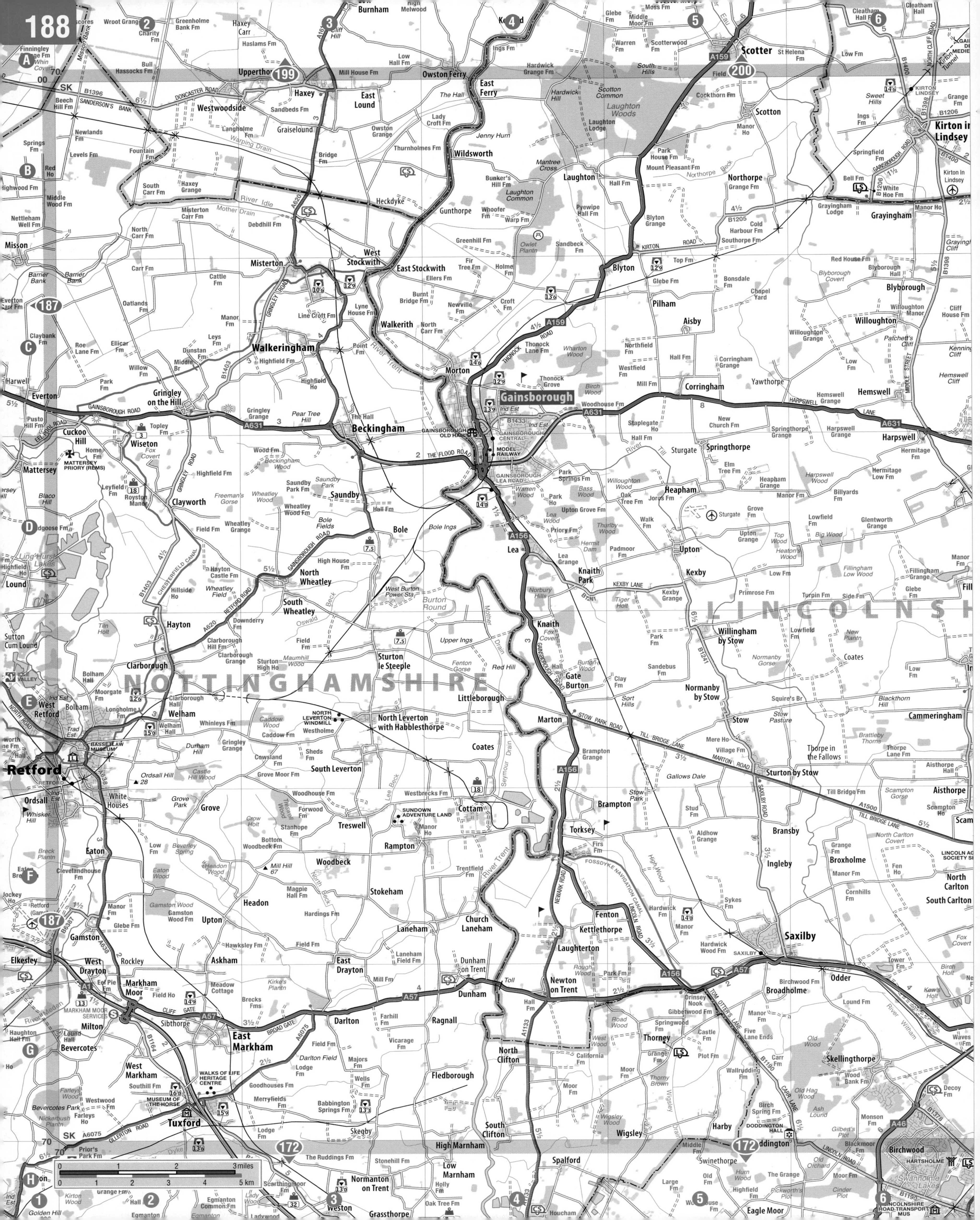
NOTTINGHAMSHIRE
LINCOLNSH
Gainsborough
Retford
Scotter
Kirton in Lindsey
Misterton
Walkeringham
Gringley on the Hill
Everton
Mattersey
Clayworth
Beckingham
Saundby
Bole
North Wheatley
South Wheatley
Hayton
Clarborough
Welham
West Retford
Ordsall
Eaton
Gamston
Elkesley
West Drayton
Markham Moor
Milton
Bevercotes
West Markham
Tuxford
East Markham
Darlton
Ragnall
Dunham
Fledborough
North Clifton
South Clifton
High Marnham
Low Marnham
Normanton on Trent
Skegby
Weston
Spalford
Wigsley
Harby
Doddington
Thorney
Skellingthorpe
Birchwood
Saxilby
Broadholme
Odder
Kettlethorpe
Fenton
Laughterton
Newton on Trent
Torksey
Brampton
Marton
Littleborough
Cottam
Rampton
Treswell
Woodbeck
Stokeham
Laneham
Church Laneham
East Drayton
Headon
Upton
Askham
Grove
South Leverton
North Leverton with Habblesthorpe
Sturton le Steeple
Coates
Gate Burton
Knaith
Knaith Park
Lea
Upton
Kexby
Heapham
Springthorpe
Sturgate
Corringham
Pilham
Aisby
Blyton
Laughton
Morton
Walkerith
East Stockwith
West Stockwith
Wildsworth
Gunthorpe
Owston Ferry
East Ferry
Haxey
Westwoodside
Graiseland
East Lound
Heckdyke
Misson
Scotton
Northorpe
Grayingham
Blyborough
Willoughton
Hemswell
Harpswell
Willingham by Stow
Normanby by Stow
Stow
Sturton by Stow
Bransby
Ingleby
Broxholme
North Carlton
South Carlton
Aisthorpe
Cammeringham
Thorpe in the Fallows
Burnham
Upperthorpe
A631
A620
A159
A156
A57
A1
A638
A1133
A46
B1403
B1241
B1190
B1398
B1400
B1205
B1396
Gainsborough Road
Stow Park Road
Till Bridge Lane
Fossdyke Navigation Canal
Chesterfield Canal
River Trent
River Idle
187
199
200
172

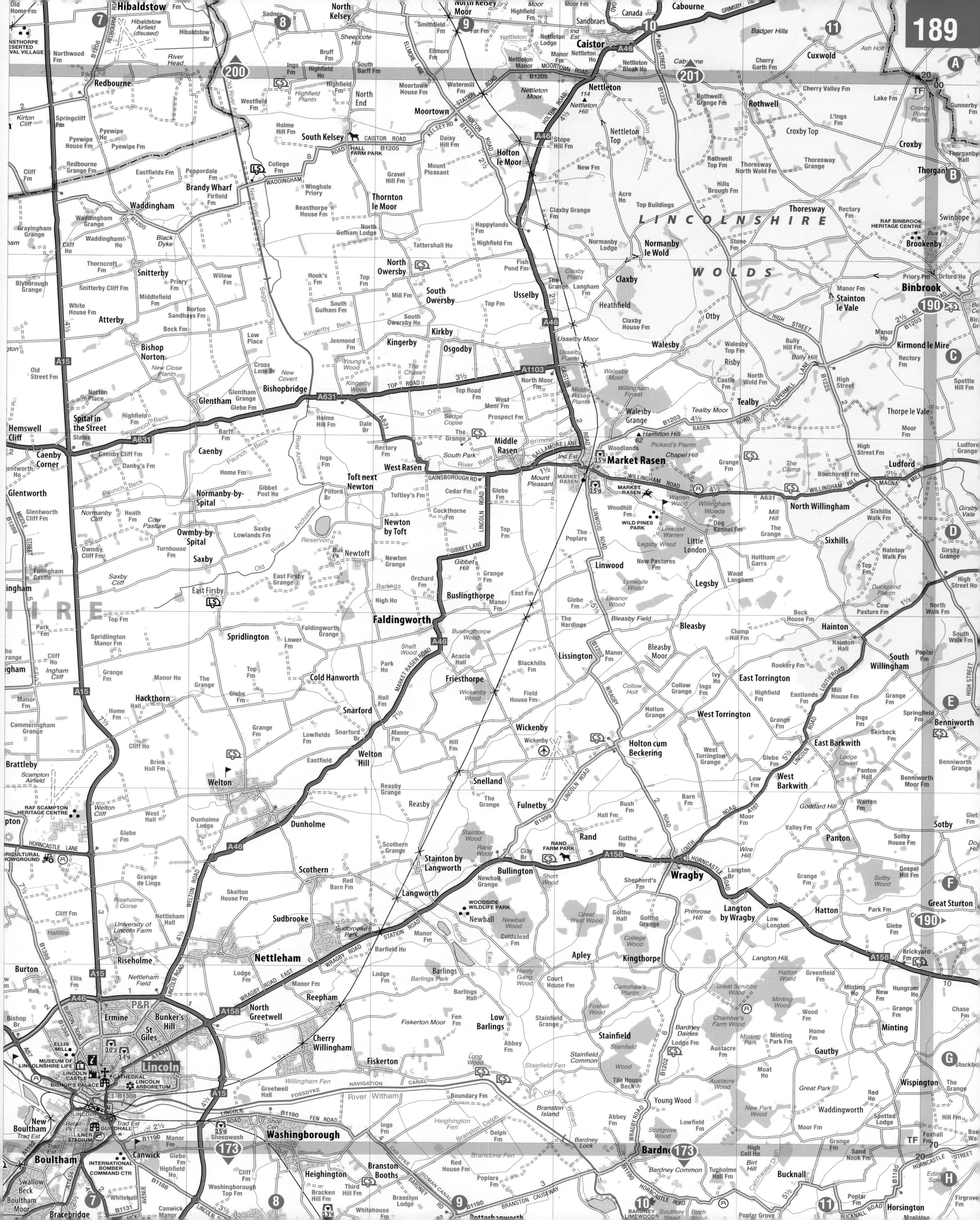

189
Hibaldstow
Sadney
North Kelsey
North Kelsey Moor
Canada
Cabourne
Sandbraes
Caistor
Cuxwold
Badger Hills
Redbourne
Hibaldstow Airfield (disused)
Northwood Fm
Bruff Fm
South Barff Fm
Nettleton
Nettleton Hill
Rothwell
Cherry Valley Fm
Lake Fm
Croxby Pond Plantn
Gunnerby Fm
Kirton Cliff
Springcliff Fm
Pyewipe Ho
Pyewipe House Fm
Pyewipe Fm
Highfield Plantn
North End
Moortown
South Kelsey
Holme Hill Fm
Holton le Moor
Nettleton Top
Croxby Top
Croxby
Thorganby Hall
Thorganby
Cliff Fm
Redbourne Grange Fm
Eastfields Fm
Pepperdale Fm
College Fm
Brandy Wharf
Firfield Ho
Waddingham
Winghale Priory
Gravel Hill Fm
Mount Pleasant
New Fm
Rothwell Top Fm
Thoresway North Wold Fm
Thoresway Grange
Hills Brough Fm
Thornton le Moor
Beasthorpe House Fm
Acre Ho
Top Buildings
Thoresway
Rectory Fm
Swinhope
Waddingham Grange
Grayingham Grange
Waddingham Ho
Black Dyke
Gulham Lodge
Happylands Fm
Highfield Fm
Claxby Grange Fm
LINCOLNSHIRE
WOLDS
RAF BINBROOK HERITAGE CENTRE
Brookenby
Cliff Ho
Tattershall Ho
Normanby Lodge
Normanby le Wold
Stone Fm
Thorncroft Fm
Snitterby
North Owersby
Fish Pond Fm
Claxby Platts
Claxby
Blyborough Grange
Snitterby Cliff Fm
Priory Fm
Willow Ho
Hook's Fm
Top Fm
South Owersby
The Grange
Langham Fm
Heathfield
Otby
Manor Fm
Stainton le Vale
Priory Fm
Orford Ho
Binbrook
White House Fm
Middlefield Fm
Norton Sandhays Fm
Atterby
South Gulham Fm
Mill Fm
Usselby
Top Fm
Claxby House Fm
Beck Fm
Low Place
Jesmond Fm
Kingerby
Kirkby
Osgodby
Usselby Moor
Walesby
Bully Hill Fm
Kirmond le Mire
Bishop Norton
New Close Plantn
Cross Lane Br
New Covert
Young's Wood
The Chase
Kingerby Wood
Usselby Plantn
Walesby Top Fm
Risby
Rectory Fm
Old Street Fm
Walesby Moor
Castle Fm
North Wold Fm
High Street
Spottle Hill Fm
Norton Place
Glentham Grange
Glentham
Bishopbridge
Top Road Fm
North Moor Fm
Willingham Forest
Tealby
Hemswell Cliff
Spital in the Street
Highfield Fm
Glebe Fm
Holme Hill Fm
Dale Br
West Moor Fm
Prospect Fm
Middle Rasen Plantn
Walesby Grange
Tealby Moor
Thorpe le Vale
Slates Fm
Barff Fm
Sedge Copse
The Grange
Middle Rasen
Hamilton Hill
Pickard's Plantn
Moor Fm
Caenby Corner
Caenby Cliff Fm
Caenby
Rectory Fm
South Park
Woodlands
Chapel Hill
High Street Fm
Ludford Grange
Danby's Fm
Ings Fm
Market Rasen
Grange Fm
The Clump
Ludford
Glentworth Ho
Home Fm
West Rasen
Toft next Newton
Mount Pleasant
Boucherett Fm
Glentworth
Normanby-by-Spital
Gibbet Post Ho
Pilford Br
Tottley's Fm
Cedar Fm
Glebe Fm
Warren Wood
Willingham Woods
North Willingham
Glentworth Cliff Fm
Normanby Cliff
Heath Fm
Cow Pasture
Cockthorne Fm
Woodhill Fm
WILD PINES PARK
Dog Kennel Fm
Mill Hill
Sixhills Walk Fm
Girsby Vale
Owmby-by-Spital
Saxby Lowlands Fm
Newton by Toft
Top Fm
The Poplars
Linwood Warren
Little London
The Grange
Sixhills
Girsby Grange
Owmby Cliff Fm
Turnhouse Fm
Reservoir
Newtoft
Legsby Wood
New Pastures Fm
Holtham Garrs
Hainton Walk Fm
Fillingham Castle
Saxby
Newton Grange
Gibbet Hill
Linwood
Top Fm
Saxby Cliff
East Firsby Grange
Orchard Fm
Grange Fm
Lynwode Wood
Wood Langham
Legsby
Duckpond Plantn
High Street Fm
East Firsby
Barlings Eau
Buslingthorpe
East Fm
Eleanor Wood
Cow Pasture Fm
North Walk Fm
Top Fm
High Ho
Manor Fm
Glebe Fm
Bleasby Field
Faldingworth
The Hardings
Beck House Fm
Bleasby
Hainton
Park Fm
Spridlington Manor Fm
Spridlington
Faldingworth Grange
Buslingthorpe Wood
Lower Fm
Clump Hill Fm
South Walk Fm
Hainton Hall
Cliff Ho
Ingham Cliff
Shaft Wood
Acacia Hall
Blackhills Fm
Lissington
Manor Fm
Bleasby Moor
Poplar Fm
South Willingham
Park Ho
Rookery Fm
Grange Fm
Manor Ho
The Grange
Top Fm
Cold Hanworth
Friesthorpe
Ivy Ho
East Torrington
Wickenby Wood
Field House Fm
Collow Holt
Collow Grange
Ings Fm
Highfield Fm
Eastlands Fm
Mill House Fm
Grange Fm
Manor Fm
Hackthorn
Glebe Fm
Hall Fm
Snarford
Holton Grange
West Torrington
Springfield Fm
Benniworth
Cammeringham Grange
Home Fm
Wickenby
Ings Fm
Grange Fm
Skirbeck Fm
Grange Fm
Lowfields Fm
Snarford Br
Manor Fm
Holton cum Beckering
East Barkwith
Brattleby
Scampton Airfield
Cliff Ho
Eastfield
Welton Hill
Hill Fm
West Torrington Grange
Glebe Fm
Lodge Covert
Benniworth Grange
Brink Hall Fm
Panton Hall
Welton
Snelland
Low Fm
West Barkwith
Benniworth Moor Fm
RAF SCAMPTON HERITAGE CENTRE
Reasby Grange
Reasby
The Grange
Fulnetby
Barn Fm
Goddard Hill
Warren Fm
Welton Cliff
West Hall
Dunholme Lodge
Dunholme
Stainton Wood
Bush Fm
Moor Fm
Valley Fm
Panton
Sotby
Glebe Fm
Hall Fm
Rand Wood
Rand
Goltho Ho
Sotby House Fm
AGRICULTURAL SHOWGROUND
Scothern Grange
Stainton by Langworth
Clay Br
RAND FARM PARK
Wire Hill
Gospel Hill Fm
Grange de Lings
Scothern
Bullington
Short Wood
Wragby
Grange Fm
Sotby Wood
Skelton House Fm
Red Barn Fm
Newball Grange
Shepherd's Fm
Langton Br
Great Sturton
Riseholme Gorse
Langworth
WOODSIDE WILDLIFE PARK
Langton by Wragby
Hatton
Cliff Fm
Nettleham Hall
Sudbrooke
Newball
Great West Wood
Goltho Hall
Goltho Grange
Primrose Hill
Low Langton
Park Fm
University of Lincoln Farm
Sudbrooke Park
Manor Fm
Newball Wood
Coldstead Fm
College Wood
Glebe Fm
Brickyard Fm
Hallifirs
Barfield Ho
Barlings
Apley
Kingthorpe
Langton Hill
Burton
Riseholme
Nettleham
Barlings Park
Hardy Gang Wood
Court House Fm
Hatton Wood
Greenfield Fm
Minting Ho
Hungram Ho
Ellis Fm
Nettleham Field
Lodge Fm
Lodge Fm
Manor Fm
Barlings Hall
Camshaw's Plantn
Great Scrubbs Wood
Minting Wood
New Fm
Grange Fm
Chase Fm
Bishop Br
P&R
Ermine
Bunker's Hill
St Giles
North Greetwell
Reepham
Low Barlings
Foxhall Wood
Stainfield Grange
Bardney Dairies
Chamber's Farm Wood
Wood Fm
Minting
ELLIS MILL
MUSEUM OF LINCOLNSHIRE LIFE
LINCOLN CASTLE
BISHOP'S PALACE
CATHEDRAL
LINCOLN ARBORETUM
Lincoln
Fiskerton Moor
Fen Fm
Abbey Fm
Cherry Willingham
Stainfield
Bardney Lodge Fm
Minting Park
Minting Park Fm
Home Fm
Fiskerton
Long Wood
Stainfield Common
Stainfield Fen
Austacre Fm
Gautby
Wispington
The Grange
Greetwell Hall
Willingham Fen
River Witham
Boundary Fm
Tile House Beck
Moat Ho
Austacre Wood
Great Park
Stockbo
Old River Witham
Red Ho
Waddingworth
New Boultham
Trad Est
LNER STADIUM
GUILDHALL
Washingborough
Shop Cen
Branston Island
Young Wood
Abbey Fm
Scotgrove Wood
Lowfield Fm
New Park Wood
Spotted Lodge
Hill Fm
Canwick
Sheepwash
Manor Fm
Heighington Fen
Branston Delph
Delph Fm
Ings Fm
Moor Fm
Foxhall Fm
Boultham
INTERNATIONAL BOMBER COMMAND CTR
Glebe Fm
Highfield Ho
Branstone Fen
Bardney Lock
Bardney
Grange Fm
High Cell Ho
Sand Nook Fm
Swallow Beck
Boultham Moor
Cliff Fm
Washingborough Top Fm
Whitehall
Heighington
Branston Booths
Red House Fm
Poplars Fm
Bardney Common
Tupholme Hall Fm
Birt Hill
Bucknall
Edlington Scrub
Bracken Hill Fm
Third Fm
Branston Lodge
Branston Causeway
Poplar Fm
Horsington
Bracebridge
Canwick Manor
Whitehouse Fm
Potterhanworth
Southrey Wood
Poplar Grove
Firgrove
A15
A46
A631
A1103
A158
A57
A1434
B1205
B1206
B1225
B1203
B1202
B1190
B1398
B1399
B1308
B1188
B1131
Old River Ancholme
New River Ancholme
River Rase
River Witham
Fossdyke Navigation

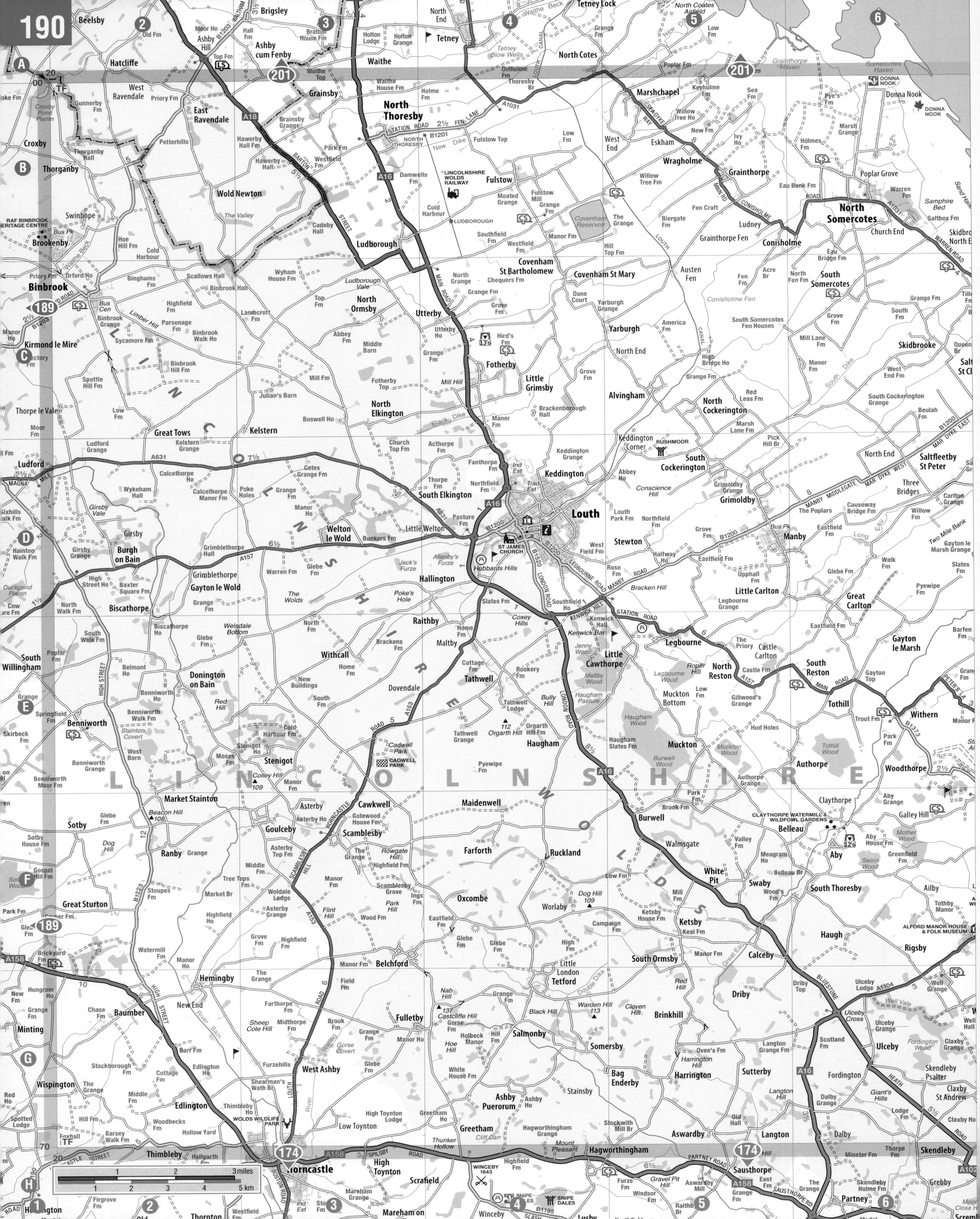
Beelsby
Brigsley
North End
Tetney Lock
North Coates Airfield
Moor Ho
Ashby Hill
Hall Fm
Ashby cum Fenby
Bratton House Fm
Holton Lodge
Holton Grange
Tetney
Tetney Blow Wells
Grange Fm
North Cotes
Low Fm
Hatcliffe
Waithe
Top Fm
201
Waithe Top
Waithe House Fm
Grainthorpe Haven
Poplar Fm
Somercotes Haven
West Ravendale
Priory Fm
Grainsby
Holme Fm
Thoresby Br
Marshchapel
Keyholme Fm
Sea Fm
Pye's Fm
Donna Nook
East Ravendale
North Thoresby
Willow Tree Ho
New Fm
Marsh Grange
Gunnerby Fm
Croxby Pond Plantn
Grainsby Grange
Station Road
Fen Lane
Fulstow Top
Low Fm
West End
Eskham
Ivy Ho
Holmes Fm
Croxby
Petterhills
Hawerby Hall Fm
Thorganby Hall
Thorganby
Hawerby Hall
Park Fm
Westfield Fm
New Dike
Wragholme
Grainthorpe
Poplar Grove
Barton Street
Damwells Fm
Lincolnshire Wolds Railway
Fulstow
Willow Tree Fm
Eau Bank Fm
Warren Fm
Samphire Bed
Saltbox Fm
Wold Newton
Moated Grange
Fulstow Mill
Grange Fm
Covenham Reservoir
The Grange
Fen Croft
Biergate Fm
Ludney
North Somercotes
Church End
Skidbrooke North End
RAF Binbrook Heritage Centre
Swinhope
The Valley
Cadeby Hall
Cold Harbour
Ludborough
Southfield Fm
Westfield Fm
Manor Fm
Grainthorpe Fen
Conisholme
Eau Bridge Fm
Brookenby
Hoe Hill Fm
Cold Harbour
Ludborough
Hill Top Fm
Austen Fen
Acre Br
North Fen Fm
South Somercotes
Priory Fm
Orford Ho
Binghams Fm
Scallows Hall
Wyham House Fm
Ludborough Vale
North Grange
Covenham St Bartholomew
Chequers Fm
Covenham St Mary
Fen Fm
Conisholme Fen
Binbrook
Binbrook Hall
Top Fm
North Ormsby
Grange Fm
Dane Court
Yarburgh Grange
Grange Fm
189
Highfield Fm
Bus Cen
Binbrook Grange
Lambcroft Fm
Utterby
Grove Fm
Yarburgh
America Fm
South Somercotes Fen Houses
South Fm
Grove Fm
Manor Ho
Limber Hill
Parsonage Fm
Abbey Fm
Utterby Ho
Hird's Fm
Kirmond le Mire
Sycamore Fm
Binbrook Walk Ho
Middle Barn
Grange Fm
Mill Lane Fm
Skidbrooke
Rectory Fm
Binbrook Hill Fm
Fotherby
North End
High Bridge Ho
Manor Fm
Spottle Hill Fm
Mill Fm
Fotherby Top
Mill Hill
Little Grimsby
Grove Fm
Grange Fm
West End Fm
Julian's Barn
Alvingham
Red Leas Fm
South Cockerington Grange
Thorpe le Vale
Low Fm
North Elkington
Brackenborough Hall
North Cockerington
Beulah Fm
Boswell Ho
Black Dike
Manor Fm
Marsh Lane Fm
Moor Fm
Great Tows
Kelstern
Kelstern Grange
Church Top Fm
Acthorpe Fm
Keddington Corner
Rushmoor
Pick Hill Br
North End
Saltfleetby St Peter
Ludford Grange
A631
Keddington Grange
Ludford
Calcethorpe Ho
Cotes Grange Fm
Fanthorpe Fm
Ind Est
Keddington
Abbey Ho
South Cockerington
Magna
Wykeham Hall
Calcethorpe Manor Fm
Poke Holes
Grange Fm
Thorpe Fm
South Elkington
Northfield Ho
Trad Est
Conscience Hill
Grimoldby Grange
Grimoldby
Three Bridges
Carlton Grange
Girsby Vale
Manor Ho
Louth
Louth Park Fm
Northfield Fm
Manby Middlegate
Mar Dyke West
The Poplars
Causeway Bridge Fm
Willow Fm
Girsby
Welton le Wold
Little Welton
Pasture Fm
St James Church
West Field Fm
Stewton
Grove Fm
Bus Pk
Manby
Eastfield Fm
Two Mile Bank
Hainton Walk Fm
Grimblethorpe Hall
Bunkers Fm
Allenby's Furze
Hubbards Hills
Halfway Ho
Gayton le Marsh Grange
Burgh on Bain
Girsby Grange
Glebe Fm
Jack's Furze
Warren Fm
Rose Fm
Eastfield Fm
Walk Fm
Slates Fm
Gimblethorpe
Hallington
Poke's Hole
Upphall Fm
Glebe Fm
Little Carlton
Pyewipe Fm
Duckpond Plantn
High Street Ho
Baxter Square Fm
Gayton le Wold
The Wolds
London Road
Legbourne Road
Manby Road
Bracken Hill
Great Carlton
Cow Pasture Fm
North Walk Fm
Biscathorpe
Grange Fm
Slates Fm
Southfield Ho
Kenwick Hill
Coxey Hills
Legbourne Grange
Eastfield Fm
Barfen Fm
Raithby
Station Road
Kenwick Hall
Kenwick Bar
South Walk Fm
Biscathorpe Ho
Welsdale Bottom
North Fm
Home Fm
Legbourne
The Priory
Castle Carlton
Gayton le Marsh
Poplar Fm
Glebe Ho
Brackens Fm
Maltby
Jenny Wood
Little Cawthorpe
South Willingham
Withcall
Cottage Fm
Roper Hill
North Reston
South Reston
Belmont Ho
Home Fm
Tathwell
Rookery Fm
Maltby Wood
Legbourne Wood
Castle Fm
Gayton Top
Donington on Bain
New Buildings
Dovendale
Bully Hill
Haugham Pasture
Muckton Bottom
Low Fm
Gillwood's Grange
Tothill
Grange Fm
Benniworth Ho
South Fm
Red Hill
Tathwell Lodge
Trout Fm
Withern
Springfield Fm
Benniworth
Benniworth Walk Fm
Stainton Covert
Cold Harbour Fm
Orgarth Hill
Orgarth Hill Fm
Haugham Wood
Hud Holes
Park Fm
Manor Fm
Skirbeck Fm
West Barn
River Bain
Stenigot Ho
Cadwell Park
Tathwell Grange
Haugham
Haugham Slates Fm
Muckton
Muckton Wood
Tothill Wood
Benniworth Grange
Moses Fm
Stenigot
Pyewipe Fm
Burwell Wood
Authorpe
Woodthorpe
Benniworth Moor Fm
Colley Hill
Manor Fm
L I N C O L N S H I R E
Authorpe Grange
Market Stainton
Asterby
Cawkwell
Maidenwell
Park Fm
Brook Fm
Claythorpe
Aby Grange
Galley Hill
Beacon Hill
Asterby Ho
Gatewood House Fm
Claythorpe Watermill & Wildfowl Gardens
Sotby
Glebe Fm
Goulceby
Scamblesby
Burwell
Belleau
Sotby House Fm
Dog Hill
Asterby Top Fm
The Grange
Rowgate Hill
Farforth
Ruckland
Walmsgate
Valley Fm
Aby House Fm
Mother Wood
Ranby
Grange
Highfield Fm
Meagram Ho
Aby
Greenfield Fm
Gospel Hill Fm
Middle Fm
Scamblesby Hill
White Pit
Swinn Wood
Tree Tops Fm
Manor Fm
Low Fm
Belleau Br
Swaby
Wood's Fm
South Thoresby
Ailby
Great Sturton
Stoupes Fm
Market Br
Woldale Lodge
Scamblesby Grove
Ings Fm
Oxcombe
Dog Hill
Mill Fm
Park Fm
Highfield Ho
Asterby Grange
Park Hill
Worlaby
Ketsby House Fm
Tothby Manor
Flint Hill
Wood Fm
Eastfield Fm
Ketsby
Keal Fm
Alford Manor House & Folk Museum
Grove Fm
Highfield Fm
Glebe Fm
Glebe Fm
Campaign Fm
High Fm
Haugh
Brickyard Fm
Watermill Fm
Manor Fm
Belchford
Little London
South Ormsby
Manor Fm
Calceby
Rigsby
Manor Ho
Field Fm
Tetford
Double Dike
Red Hill
Driby Top
Ulceby Lodge
Well Grange
Hemingby
The Grange
Hungram Ho
Nab Hill
Grange Fm
Driby
Well Vale
New Fm
Grange Fm
Baumber
Chase Fm
New End
Farthorpe Fm
Castcliffe Hill
Black Hill
Warden Hill
Cloven Hill
Brinkhill
Ulceby Cross
Ulceby Grange
Minting
River Bain
Sheep Cote Hill
Midthorpe Fm
Brook Fm
Fulletby
Gorse Fm
Hoe Hill
Holbeck Manor
Hill Fm
Salmonby
Somersby
Oven's Fm
Harrington Hall
Langton Grange Fm
Scotland Fm
Ulceby
Fordington Wood
Claxby Grange
Barr Fm
Grange Fm
Manor Ho
Gorse Covert
Stockborough Fm
Edlington Ho
Cottage Fm
Furzehills
West Ashby
Glebe Fm
White House Fm
Bag Enderby
Harrington
Sutterby
Fordington
Skendleby Psalter
Wispington
The Grange
Middle Fm
Shearman's Wath Br
Ashby Puerorum
Ashby Ho
Stainsby
Langton Hill
Giant's Hills
Claxby St Andrew
Red Ho
Edlington
Thimbleby Ho
Dalby Grange
Lodge Fm
Claxby Ho
Spotted Lodge
Hill Fm
Woodbecks Fm
Wolds Wildlife Park
High Toynton Lodge
Greetham Ho
Stockwith Mill Br
Old Hall
Hollow Yard
Low Toynton
Greetham
Cliff Carr
Hagworthingham Grange
Aswardby
Langton
Dalby
Foxhall
Barsey Walk Fm
Thunker Hollow
Mount Pleasant
Thimbleby
Hallgarth Fm
174
Horncastle
Spilsby Road
High Toynton
Hagworthingham
Partney Road
Minster Fm
Thorpe Fm
Skendleby
Sausthorpe
Winceby 1643
Highfield Fm
Furze Fm
Gravel Pit Hill
Aswardby Mill
East Fm
The Grange
Skendleby Holme Fm
Grebby
Scrafield
Mareham Grange
Windsor Fm
Grange Fm
Partney
Hagington
Firgrove Fm
Ind Est
Snipe Dales
Raithby Br
Mareham on the Hill
Winceby
Lusby
Thornton
Westfield Fm
3 miles
5 km

NORTH SEA
Saltfleet
Saltfleet Haven
Toby's Hill
Sea View Fm
Rimac
SALTFLEETBY THEDDLETHORPE DUNES
Saltfleetby All Saints
Lodge Fm
Theddlethorpe St Helen
Manor Ho
Hall Fm
Theddlethorpe All Saints
Gayton Engine
High Gate
Will Row
Gas Terminal
North End
THE SEAL SANCTUARY & WILDLIFE CENTRE
Meers Bridge
Westfield Fm
Stain Hill
Meers Bank
Mablethorpe Hall
FUN FAIR
Mablethorpe
Trusthorpe
Strubby Grange
Earl's Br
Poplar Fm
Grange Fm
Willow Fm
Bamber's Br
Strubby
Thorpe
Trusthorpe Hall
Maltby le Marsh
Manor Ho
Sutton on Sea
Sandilands
Poplar Lodge Fm
Mill Hill
Beesby
Abbey Fm
Hagnaby
Beesby Grange
Manor Fm
Washdyke Br
Hannah
Sea Bank Fm
Saleby
America Fm
Cob Hill
Saleby Manor
Glebe Fm
Markby
Priory Fm
The Grange
College Fm
Asserby Turn
Asserby
Willow Fm
Black House Fm
Thoresthorpe
Bilsby
Dryby Fm
Wold Sea Fm
Moat Ho
Manor Fm
Anderby Creek
Huttoft
The Manor
Alford
The Grange
Thurlby
Anderby
Bilsby Field
Farlesthorpe Fen
ON YOUR MARQUES
Wolla Bank
Langham Fm
Mumby
Manor Fm
Manor Ho
Chapel Six Marshes
Well Beck Fm
Farlesthorpe
School Fm
Mill Hill
Authorpe Row
Mawthorpe
Elsom Fm
Cumberworth
Cherry Fm
Mickleberry Hill
Chapman's Fm
Chapel Pt
Bonthorpe
Helsey
Croft Fm
Manor Fm
Chapel St Leonards
Listoft
Hogsthorpe
Willoughby
Poplar Fm
Willoughby High Drain
Burlands Beck
Claxby
Willoughby Wood
Hogsbeck Ho
Sloothby
Howlet Ho
Slackholme End
Hope Fm
Beeches Fm
Welton Low Wood
Welton High Wood
Thwaite Hall
Hasthorpe
Welbourne Fm
HARDY'S ANIMAL FARM
Highfield Fm
Habertoft
Addlethorpe
Ingoldmells
Candlesby Hill
Rookery Fm
Welton le Marsh
Boothby Hall
Boothby Grange
FANTASY ISLAND
Ingoldmells Pt
Manor Fm
Whitehouse
Corner Fm
MABLETHORPE RD
THEDDLETHORPE RD
ALFORD ROAD
SUTTON ROAD
ALFORD ROAD
HUTTOFT ROAD
SUTTON ROAD
MUMBY ROAD
LONG LANE
THURLBY ROAD
EAST ST
BEESBY ROAD
SALTFLEET ROAD
MAWTHORPE HILL ROAD
SKEGNESS ROAD
HANBY LANE
BAKER'S LANE
A1031
A1104
A157
A1111
A52
B1449
B1196
TF
70
00
175

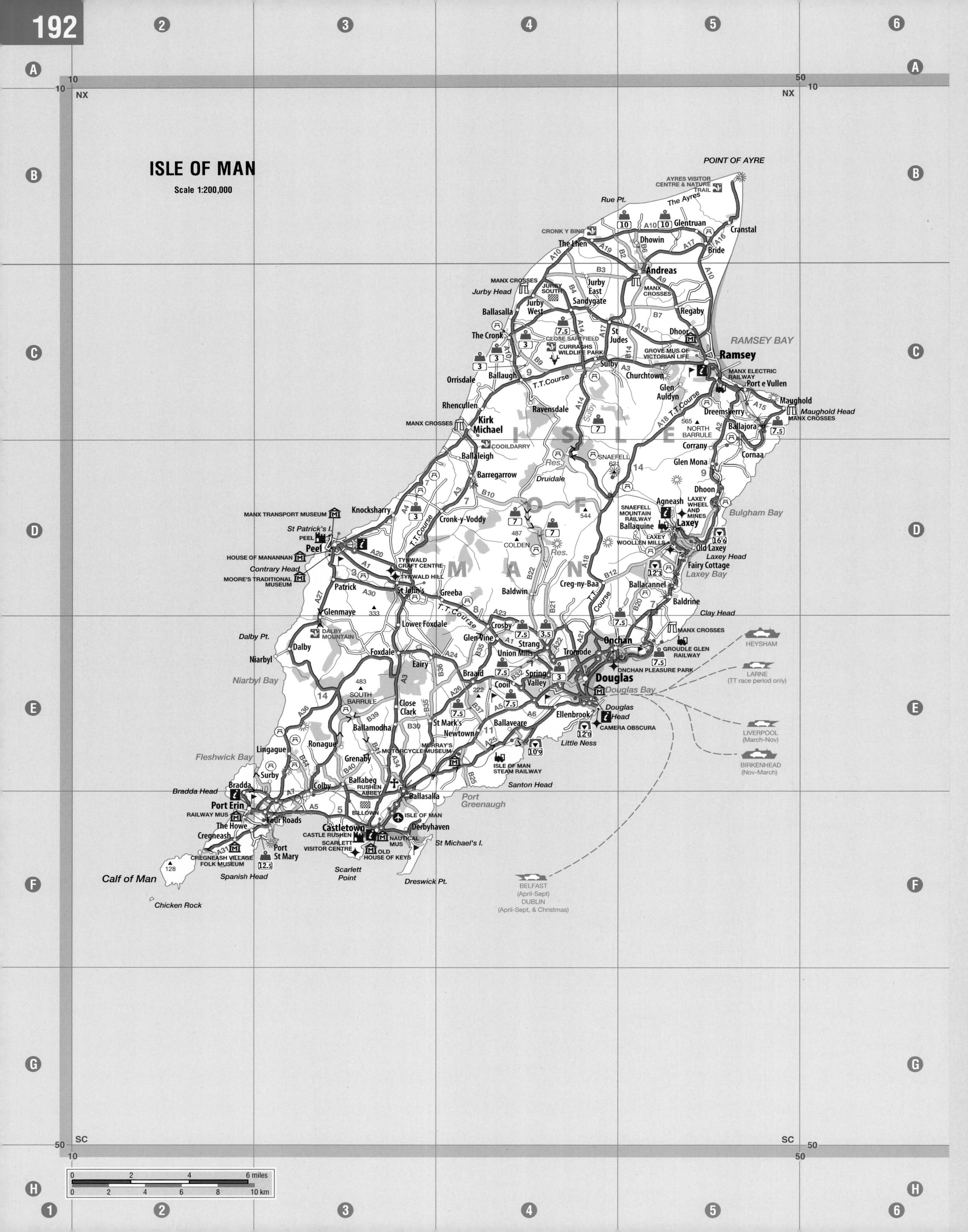
ISLE OF MAN
Scale 1:200,000
POINT OF AYRE
AYRES VISITOR CENTRE & NATURE TRAIL
The Ayres
Rue Pt.
Glentruan
Cranstal
CRONK Y BING
Dhowin
The Lhen
Bride
Andreas
MANX CROSSES
Jurby Head
Jurby East
Sandygate
MANX CROSSES
Jurby West
Ballasalla
Regaby
The Cronk
St Judes
Dhoor
CLOSE SARTFIELD
CURRAGHS WILDLIFE PARK
GROVE MUS OF VICTORIAN LIFE
RAMSEY BAY
Ramsey
Sulby
Churchtown
Orrisdale
Ballaugh
T.T.Course
MANX ELECTRIC RAILWAY
Port e Vullen
Glen Auldyn
Maughold
Maughold Head
MANX CROSSES
Rhencullen
Ravensdale
Dreemskerry
Kirk Michael
MANX CROSSES
NORTH BARRULE
Ballajora
COOILDARRY
Corrany
Ballaleigh
SNAEFELL
Cornaa
Res.
Glen Mona
Barregarrow
Druidale
Dhoon
MANX TRANSPORT MUSEUM
Knocksharry
Cronk-y-Voddy
Agneash
SNAEFELL MOUNTAIN RAILWAY
LAXEY WHEEL AND MINES
Bulgham Bay
St Patrick's I.
PEEL
Ballaquine
Laxey
Peel
COLDEN
LAXEY WOOLLEN MILLS
HOUSE OF MANANNAN
Old Laxey
Laxey Head
Contrary Head
TYNWALD CRAFT CENTRE
TYNWALD HILL
Fairy Cottage
Laxey Bay
MOORE'S TRADITIONAL MUSEUM
Patrick
St John's
Greeba
Baldwin
Creg-ny-Baa
Ballacannel
Baldrine
Glenmaye
Clay Head
Lower Foxdale
Crosby
DALBY MOUNTAIN
MANX CROSSES
Dalby Pt.
Glen Vine
Strang
Onchan
GROUDLE GLEN RAILWAY
Dalby
Union Mills
Tromode
Foxdale
Niarbyl
Eairy
ONCHAN PLEASURE PARK
Braaid
Spring Valley
Douglas
HEYSHAM
LARNE
(TT race period only)
Niarbyl Bay
SOUTH BARRULE
Cooil
Douglas Bay
Close Clark
Ellenbrook
Douglas Head
Ballamodha
St Mark's
Newtown
Ballaveare
CAMERA OBSCURA
Ronague
Little Ness
LIVERPOOL
(March-Nov)
Lingague
MURRAY'S MOTORCYCLE MUSEUM
Fleshwick Bay
Grenaby
ISLE OF MAN STEAM RAILWAY
BIRKENHEAD
(Nov-March)
Surby
Bradda
Ballabeg
RUSHEN ABBEY
Santon Head
Bradda Head
Colby
Ballasalla
Port Greenaugh
Port Erin
BILLOWN
ISLE OF MAN
RAILWAY MUS
Four Roads
Castletown
Derbyhaven
The Howe
CASTLE RUSHEN
NAUTICAL MUS
Cregneash
SCARLETT VISITOR CENTRE
St Michael's I.
Port St Mary
CREGNEASH VILLAGE FOLK MUSEUM
OLD HOUSE OF KEYS
Calf of Man
Spanish Head
Scarlett Point
Dreswick Pt.
BELFAST
(April-Sept)
DUBLIN
(April-Sept, & Christmas)
Chicken Rock
0 2 4 6 miles
0 2 4 6 8 10 km

Lytham St Anne's
St Annes
Fairhaven
Ansdell
Lytham
Warton
River Ribble
Southport
Crossens
Banks
Marshside
Churchtown
Birkdale
Hillside
Ainsdale
Ainsdale-on-Sea
Woodvale
Formby
Freshfield
Little Altcar
Great Altcar
Hightown
Ince Blundell
Little Crosby
Thornton
Sefton
Maghull
Lydiate
Halsall
Haskayne
Scarisbrick
Ormskirk
Aughton
Melling
Aintree
Netherton
Great Crosby
Blundellsands
Crosby
LANCS

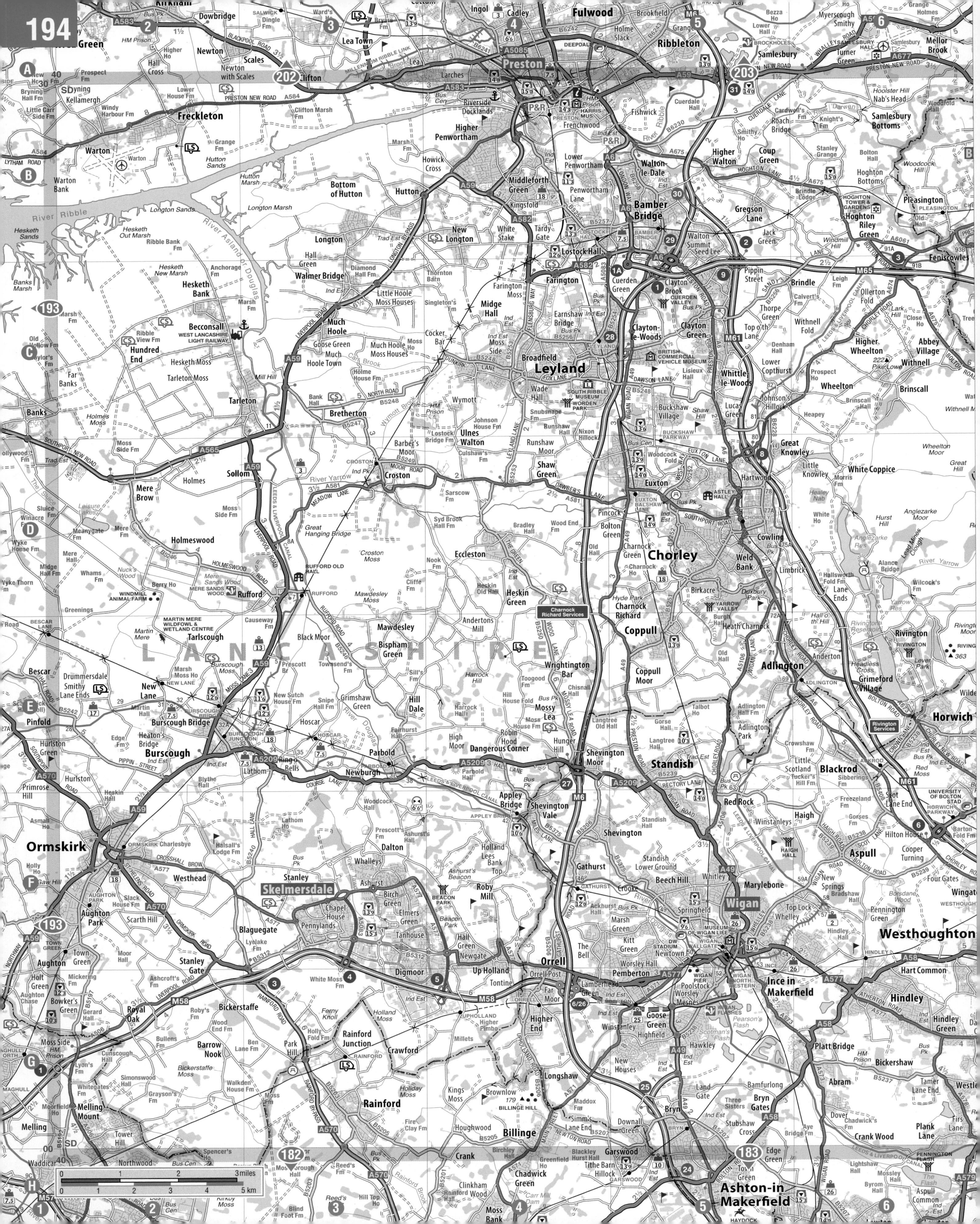
194
Preston
Fulwood
Ribbleton
Ingol
Cadley
Dowbridge
Lea Town
Newton
Scales
Newton with Scales
Clifton
Freckleton
Warton
Warton Bank
Kellamergh
River Ribble
Longton Sands
Longton Marsh
Hesketh Out Marsh
Hesketh Sands
Banks Marsh
Hesketh Bank
Becconsall
West Lancashire Light Railway
Hundred End
Hesketh Moss
Tarleton Moss
Tarleton
Banks
Bottom of Hutton
Hutton
Longton
Hall Green
Walmer Bridge
Much Hoole
Goose Green
Much Hoole Town
Much Hoole Moss Houses
Little Hoole Moss Houses
Bretherton
Croston
River Yarrow
Sollom
Mere Brow
Holmes
Holmeswood
Rufford
Rufford Old Hall
Martin Mere Wildfowl & Wetland Centre
Tarlscough
LANCASHIRE
Bescar
Drummersdale
New Lane
Burscough Bridge
Burscough
Pinfold
Ormskirk
Aughton Park
Aughton
Westhead
Scarth Hill
Stanley Gate
Bickerstaffe
Royal Oak
Melling
Melling Mount
Rainford
Rainford Junction
Crawford
Skelmersdale
Digmoor
Stanley
Ashurst
Dalton
Parbold
Newburgh
Lathom
Hoscar
Mawdesley
Bispham Green
Eccleston
Heskin Green
Charnock Richard
Charnock Richard Services
Coppull
Coppull Moor
Wrightington Bar
Mossy Lea
Dangerous Corner
High Moor
Shevington Moor
Shevington
Shevington Vale
Appley Bridge
Standish
Adlington
Chorley
Euxton
Leyland
Farington
Lostock Hall
Bamber Bridge
Walton-le-Dale
Higher Walton
Penwortham
Higher Penwortham
Middleforth Green
Kingsfold
New Longton
Midge Hill
Clayton-le-Woods
Clayton Green
Whittle-le-Woods
Buckshaw Village
Cuerden Green
Samlesbury
Mellor Brook
Hoghton
Brindle
Wheelton
Withnell
Brinscall
Abbey Village
Great Knowley
White Coppice
Rivington
Horwich
Blackrod
Haigh
Aspull
Westhoughton
Hindley
Ince in Makerfield
Wigan
Pemberton
Orrell
Up Holland
Billinge
Ashton-in Makerfield
Bryn
Bryn Gates
Abram
Platt Bridge
Winstanley
Goose Green
Garswood
Chadwick Green
Crank
Moss Bank
Kitt Green
Marsh Green
Newtown
Worsley Mesnes
Beech Hill
Marylebone
Springfield
Gathurst
Roby Mill
Red Rock
Lancaster Canal
Leeds & Liverpool Canal
M6
M61
M65
M58
A59
A6
A49
A58
A577
A5209
A570
A565
202
203
193
182
183
0 1 2 3 miles
0 1 2 3 4 5 km

Osbaldeston
Great Harwood
Clayton-le-Moors
Hapton
Rishton
Huncoat
Burnley
Rose Hill
Mereclough
Walk Mill
Pleckgate
Blackburn
Church
Accrington
Oswaldtwistle
Baxenden
Great Hameldon
Clow Bridge
Dunnockshaw
Love Clough
Goodshaw Chapel
Crawshawbooth
Water
Weir
Portsmouth
Cornholme
Holme Chapel
Forest of Rossendale
Darwen
Haslingden
Rawtenstall
Bacup
Whitworth
Helmshore
Edenfield
LANCASHIRE
BLACKBURN WITH DARWEN
Ramsbottom
Edgworth
Turton Bottoms
Belmont
Egerton
Tottington
Summerseat
Bury
Heywood
Rochdale
Milnrow
Royton
Bolton
Farnworth
Radcliffe
Whitefield
Prestwich
Middleton
Atherton
Tyldesley
Leigh
Little Hulton
Walkden
Worsley
Swinton
Pendlebury
Salford
Eccles
Failsworth
Droylsden
Moston
Blackley
Crumpsall
Chadderton
Astley
Westhoughton
Hindsford
Howe Bridge
Lostock
Kearsley
Ainsworth
Breightmet
Little Lever
Harwood
Bradshaw
Astley Bridge
Heaton
Deane
Daubhill
Great Lever
Rhodes
Birch
Alkrington Garden Village
Clifton
Manchester
GREATER MANCHESTER
M60
M61
M62
M65
M66
A56
A58
A666
A580
A6

Towneley
Gorple Reservoir
Heptonstall Moor
High Greenwood
Kid Stones
Hardcastle Crags
Winny Stone
Warley Moor Reservoir
Spa Head
Warley Moor
Ovenden Moor
Ogden
Causeway Foot
Raggalds
West Scholes
Clayton
Great Horton
Worsthorne Moor
Old Dolphin
Mountain
Queensbury
204
205
High Brown Knoll 444
Dean Head Resrs
Rocking Stone
Bradshaw
Clayton Heights
Buttershaw
Black Hameldon
Hoar Side Moor
Park
Shackleton
Pecket Well
Old Town
Sleepy Lowe
Brookhouse
Upper Brockholes
Ambler Thorn
Shibden Head
Pepper Hill
Stiperden Moor
Stiperden Bar Ho
Noah Dale
Rodmer Clough
High Gate
Midgehole
Dimmin Dale
Holdsworth
Illingworth
Catherine Slack
Shelf
Pearsons
Coal Clough Wind Fm
Stansfield Moor
Moorhall Fm
428
Colden
Jack Bridge
Slack
Heptonstall
Hebden Bridge
Chiserley
Crow Hill Nook 372
Luddenden Dean
Wainstalls
Moor End
Mixenden
Holmfield
Woodside
Stone Chair
Blackshaw Head
Booth
Ovenden Wood
Pule Hill
Coley
Coal Clough Fm
Hawks Stones
Shore
Pudsey
Bride Stones Moor
Keelam Heights
Staups Moor
Great Rock
Mytholm
Charlestown
Walkley Clogs
Midgley
Mount Tabor
Ovenden
Wheatley
Boothtown
Northowram
Priestley Green
Dean Fm
Portsmouth
Cornholme
Carr & Craggs Moor
Vale
Lower Moor
Greenhurst Hey
Great Ho
Edge End Fm
Eastwood
Erringden Grange
Erringden Moor
Mytholmroyd
Luddenden
Tower Hill
Highroad Well Moor
Bankfield Museum
Woodlands
Shibden Hall
Hipperholme
Lydgate
Hole Bottom
Castle Street
Edge End Moor
319
Hoo Hole
Hall Bank
Warley Town
Pellon
Beacon Hill 260
Halifax
Eureka!
Lightcliffe
Hove Edge
High Barn
Todmorden
Bell House Moor
Stoodley Pike Monument
Blackwood Common
Boulder Clough
Luddenden Foot
Friendly
Savile Park
Stoney Royd
Bank Top
Southowram
Sharneyford
Holden Gate
Bacup Road
Dobroyd Castle School
Mankinholes
Lumbutts
Withens Clough Reservoir
Pennine Way
Steep Lane
Sowerby
Sowerby Bridge
Norland Town
Siddal
Brookfoot
Clough Foot
Gorpley Reservoir
Stones
Shade
Knowl Wood
Walsden
Mary Towneley Loop
Horse Wood
Gaddings Dam
Withins Moor
Turley Holes Edge
Cragg Vale
Cock Hill
Crow Hill
Hubberton Green
Toot Hill
Clough Head
Pickwood Scar
Exley
Cromwell Bottom
Brighouse
Rastrick
Inchfield Moor
Lowers Reaps
Higher Hogshead
Britannia
Trough Gate
Freeholds Top
Ramsden Clough Res
Walsden Moor
Langfield Common
Warland Drain
Blake Moor
Triangle
Longley
Greetland Wall Nook
Lindwell
Greetland
Elland
Lower Edge
Upper Edge
Toothill
Fixby
Shawforth
Ramsden Wood
Bottomley
Warland Reservoir
Light Hazzles Res
Turvin Clough
Lumb
Cotton Stones
Mill Bank
Soyland Town
Kebroyd
West Vale
Rough Hill 434
Hades Hill 433
Noon Hill
Warland
Great Manshead Hill
Far Slack
Baitings Pasture
Ripponden
Barkisland
Holywell Green
Stainland
Jagger Green
Netheroyd Hill
263 Ainley Top
Millgate
Facit
Crook Hill
White Holme Res
Manshead End
Soyland Moor
Knave Holes Hill
Bottomley
Sowood Green
Cowcliffe
Birchencliffe
Fartown
Brown Wardle Hill
Turn Slack Clough
Calderbrook
Summit
Chelburn Resrs
Blackstone Edge Res
Rochdale Road
Baitings Res
Ryburn Res
Beacon Hill
Krumlin
Penny Hill
Sowood
Outlane
Lindley
Birkby
Whitworth
Watergrove Reservoir
Halifax Road
Cat Stones
Rishworth Moor
Dog Hill
Blackwood Common
Rishworth
Ringstone Edge Res
Pike End
Pike Law
Vicars Lot 347
Snow Lea
Nettleton Hill
Salendine Nook
Edgerton
Oakes
Quarmby
Marsh
Wardle
Shore Hall
Clough
Gale
Cowberry Hill
Blackstone Edge
Green Withens Res
Joiner Stones
Booth Wood
380 Wholestone Moor
Scapegoat Hill
Broadley
Rushy Hill
Shore
Caldermoor
Durn
Honresfeld
Littleborough
Blackstone Edge Fold
Clegg Moor
A672
M62
Scammonden Water
Saddleworth Road
Booth Wood Res
Pole Moor
Moorside Edge
Colne Valley Mus
Golcar
Leymoor
Paddock
Healey
Syke
Great Howarth
Smallbridge
HM Prison
Hurstead
Deerney
Greengate
Smithy Bridge
Cleggswood Hill
Hollingworth Lake
Hunger Hill
Deanhead Res
Town End
Lockwood
Crosland Hill
Huddersfield
Rochdale
Belfield
Firgrove
Little Clegg
Rakewood
Low House Moor
Windy Hill
Way Stone Edge
Buckstones Moss
New Hey Road
Deanhead
Slaithwaite Moor
Bradshaw
Wilberlee
Slaithwaite
Linthwaite
Newsome
Berry Brow
Armitage Bridge
Netherton
Spotland Bridge
Bib Knowl
Tunshill
Nicholas Pike
Norman Hill Res
Bleakedgate Moor
Buckstones Moss
Cupwith Hill
Drop Clough
Huddersfield Narrow Canal
Hill Top
Clough
Blackmoorfoot
Newbold
Milnrow
Lady House
Rough Bank
Ogden Res
Piethorne Res
Readycon Dean Res
Denshaw Moor
March Haigh Res
March Hill
Buckstones Ho
Stonepit Lee Clough
Stack End
Hey Green
Huck Hill
Lingards Wood
Black Moor
328
South Crosland
Scotgate
Honley
Stoneyfield
Lower Place
Turf Hill
Balderstone
Kirkholt
Castleton
Newhey
Haugh
Rooden Res
Crook Gate Res
Castleshaw Moor
Redbrook Clough
Close Moss
Marsden
Standedge Visitor Centre
Netherley
Pule Hill
Deer Hill Res
Meltham Grange
Crosland Edge
Honley Wood Bottom
Honley Moor
Brockholes
Bentgate
Whitefield Hall
Jubilee
Denshaw
Dowry Res
Broadhead Noddle
New Years Bridge Res
Standedge Tunnel
Binn Moor
Deer Hill Moss
Meltham
Meltham Mills
Wood Nook
Oldfield
Summit
Buersil Head
Burnedge
High Crompton
Gravel Hole
Crompton Moor
Crompton Fold
Old Tame
Dog Hill
Castleshaw Resrs
Bleak Hey Nook
Redbrook Res
Butterley Reservoir
Blakeley Res
Horseley Head Moss
Meltham Moor
Royd Edge
Wilshaw
Netherthong
Trub
Slattocks
Thornham Fold
Tandle Hill
Royton
Low Compton
Shaw
Fullwood
Clough
Besom Hill
Slackcote
Heights
Grains Bar
Harrop Dale
Swellands Res
Black Moss Res
Black Moss
Wessenden Res
West Nab 500
Wessenden Moor
Harden Moss
Harden Hill
Wolfstones Height
Upperthong
Holmfirth
Thorp
Cinder Hill Fm
Haggate
Heyside
Shaw Side
Sholver
Linfitts
Obelisk 375
Dale
Diggle
Broadstone Hill
South Clough
White Moss
Wessenden Head
Marsden Clough
Wood Cottage
Digley Res
Burnlee
Flush House
Hinchliffe Mill
Cartworth
Chadderton Fold
Holden Fold
Luzley Brook
Higginshaw
Roebuck Low
Delph
Thurston Clough
New Delph
Running Hill Head
Holmbridge
Washpit
Chadderton
Long Sight
Boundary Park
Acre
Watersheddings
Moorside
Strine Dale
Top o' th' Meadows
Wall Hill
Tame Water
Dobcross
Pobgreen
Dean Head Hill
Hey Clough
Dean Clough
Arrunden
Longley
Holme
Oldham Edge
Spring Hill
Uppermill
Saddleworth Mus & Gallery
Dick Hill
Upperwood Ho
Saddleworth Moor
Holme Clough
Wessenden Head Moor
Issue Edge 499
Bromlow Hill Res
White Gate
Busk
Greenacres
Clarksfield
Mumps
Austerlands
Burnedge
Bent Fm
Southhead
Grasscroft
Greenfield
Peak District
Ramsden Res
Riding Wood Res
Hade Edge
Middleton Road
Nimble Nook
Werneth
Moorhey
Glodwick
Oldham
Lees
Grotton
Springhead
Lydgate
Tunstead
Yeoman Hey Res
Dean Rocks
Ashway Stone
Middle Edge Moss
Round Hill
Dun Hill
Black Hill 582
Heyden Head
Kaye Edge
Holme Moss
Holme Woods
Yateholme Res
Crossley's Plantn
Daisy Lee Moor
Coppice
White Gate
Hathershaw
Pitses
Holts
Greater Manchester
Quick Edge
Roaches
Slate Pit Moss
Dove Stone Moss
Long Ridge Moss
Howels Head
Sliddens Moss
National Park
Ramsden Clough
Twizle Head Moss
Harden Clough
475
Hollins Road
Lime Side
Moston
Hollinwood
Failsworth
Woodhouses
Alt
Fitton Hill
Park Bridge
Park Bridge Heritage Centre
Alt Hill
Hartshead Pike
Brook Bottom
Alphin 469
White Gate
Dovestone Reservoir
Wimberry Moss
Chew Reservoir
Black Chew Head
Roundhill Moss
Crowden Meadows
Binns Moss
Britland Edge Hill 523
Great Grains Clough
Grains Moss
Winscar Reservoir
Knott Lanes
Daisy Nook
Bardsley
Limehurst
Smallshaw
Waterloo
Mossley
Hartshead Green
Luzley
Micklehurst
Buckton Moor
Hare Hill
Hoarstone Edge
Bowerclough Head
Laddow Rocks
Bareholme Moss
527 Westend Moss
Crowden Little Moor
Heyden
Moor
Cat Clough 499
Heyheads
Carrbrook
Hey Moss
Irontongue Hill
Windgate Edge
Featherbed Moss
Heyden Br
Hawthorn Clough
Gallows Moss
Daisy Nook
Taunton
Hurst
Hazelhurst
Buckton Vale
Slatepit Moor
Swineshaw Moor
Arnfield Flats
Rakes Moss
Black Tor
418
Oaksike Clough
372
Pikenaze Moor
Salter's Brook Br
Crowhill
Ashton-under-Lyne
184
185
Sun Green
Stalybridge
Boar Flat
Arnfield Moor
Robinson's Moss
Millstone Rocks
Highstone Rocks
Crowden
Smithy Clough
Ironbower Moss
Rose Clough
Round Hill 496
Millbrook
Brushes
Swineshaw Reservoir
Walkerwood Reservoir
Longdendale
Torside Reservoir
Lawrence Edge
Shining Clough
Black Moss
Far Black Clough
Featherbed Moss
Far Small Clough
Droylsden
Copley
Stalybridge
Fern Bank
Mottram
Rhodeswood Reservoir
Torside Naze
Middle Black Clough
Clayton
Ashley
0 1 2 3 miles
0 1 2 3 4 5 km

197
Bradford
West Bowling
Bowling
Bierley
Holme Wood
Tong
New Farnley
Beeston
Hunslet
Stourton
Swillington
Rothwell
Woodlesford
Oulton
Middleton
Robin Hood
Morley
Gildersome
Drighlington
Birkenshaw
Birstall
Gomersal
Cleckheaton
Batley
Heckmondwike
Liversedge
Dewsbury
Mirfield
Ossett
Horbury
Wakefield
Outwood
Stanley
Normanton
Altofts
Methley
Mickletown
Kippax
Great Preston
Whitwood
Ackton
Sharlston
Crofton
Walton
Wragby
Fitzwilliam
Kinsley
Havercroft
South Hiendley
Felkirk
Royston
Carlton
Shafton
Cudworth
Darton
Staincross
Barugh
Barnsley
Dodworth
Worsbrough
Kendray
Ardsley
Wombwell
Hoyland
Jump
Elsecar
Tankersley
Pilley
Birdwell
Wentworth
Thurgoland
Wortley
Oxspring
Penistone
Thurlstone
Millhouse Green
Stocksbridge
Langsett
Midhopestones
Silkstone
Cawthorne
Kexbrough
Hoylandswaine
Ingbirchworth
Denby Dale
Upper Cumberworth
Skelmanthorpe
Clayton West
High Hoyland
Shelley
Kirkburton
Emley
Flockton
Grange Moor
Lepton
Almondbury
Highburton
Farnley Tyas
Thurstonland
Shepley
Holmfirth
Hepworth
New Mill
Woolley
Notton
Crigglestone
Durkar
Sandal Magna
Hall Green
Netherton
Overton
Middlestown
Thornhill
Earlsheaton
Ravensthorpe
Kirkheaton
Upper Hopton
Dalton
Bradley
Brighouse
Hartshead
Wyke
Scholes
Oakenshaw
Low Moor
Thurlstone Moors
YORKSHIRE
SOUTH YORKSHIRE
M1
M62
M621
M606
A642
A635
A628
A629
A616
A61
A637
A636
Hartshead Moor Services
Woolley Edge Services
Leeds Skelton Lake Services
YORKSHIRE SCULPTURE PARK
NATIONAL COAL MINING MUSEUM FOR ENGLAND
EXPERIENCE BARNSLEY MUS
THWAITE MILLS INDUSTRIAL MUSEUM
MIDDLETON RAILWAY
MONK BRETTON PRIORY
CANNON HALL
ELSECAR HERITAGE RAILWAY
185
186
198
205
206

Micklefield
Roach Grange Fm
Peckfield Bar
Beacon Plantn
Steeton Hall
South Milford
STEETON HALL GATEWAY
Milford Lodge
Fryston Grange
Hagg Bush Fm
Owlet Hall
Thorpe Hall
Selby Dam
LEEDS ROAD
SELBY ABBEY
East Common
Newlands Fm
Goody Cross
Prestor
Kippax
Ledston Luck
Ledston Park
Peckfield Lodge
Lumby
MAIN ROAD
Hambleton
Thorpe Willoughby
Brayton
Ind Est
SE
Great Preston
Roman Ridge
Park House Fm
Ledsham
Monk Fryston
Brecks Fm
Hagg Ho
Gateforth Hall
Hambleton Hough
Burton Hall
Barlow Lodge
Commonside Fm
Ledston Hall
Ledston
Newfield Fm
Fairburn
Monk Fryston Lodge
Hillam
Bower's House Fm
Gateforth Wood
Gateforth
Top House Fm
Burn
Henwick Hall
Primrose Hill
Burn Airfield
Barlo
Beckfield Fm
Fairburn Ings
RSPB
Allerton Bywater
Burton Salmon
Burton Common Fm
Northfield Fm
Chestercourt Hall Fm
Common Ho
Lower Mickletown
Mickletown
New Fryston
Poole
Lodge Fm
Chestercourt House Fm
Methley
Willow Grove Fm
THE MEND-A-HOSE JUNGLE
Wheldale
Water Fryston
Park Ho
Birkin
West Haddlesey
Chapel Haddlesey
Eastfield House Fm
Quosquo Hall
Camblesforth
Methley Junction
Castleford
Airedale
Fryston Park
Brotherton
Byram Hall
Byram
Byram Fm
Beal
River Aire
NORTH
Temple Manor
Temple Hirst
Red Hill
Sutton
Kellington
Roall Manor Fm
Eggborough Power Stn (disused)
West Bank Ho
Whitwood
Cutsyke
Glasshoughton
FREEPORT CASTLEFORD
Ferrybridge
Kellingley
WEELAND ROAD
Thornfield Ho
Hut Green
Hirst Courtney
Carlton
Normanton
Loscoe
New Town
Knottingley
Eggborough
WHITLEY BRIDGE
Stubbs Br
Kellington Common
Hensall
Little Heck
Gowdall
Coates Hall Fm
SNAITH
Hopetown
North Featherstone
PONTEFRACT
PONTEFRACT CASTLE MUSEUM
Ferrybridge Services
Farpark Fm
Ind Est
Bus Pk
HENSALL
Woodhouse
Old Snydale
Ackton
PARK LANE
Pontefract
PONTEFRACT BAGHILL
Grove Town
Hodgewood Fm
Cridling Stubbs
Spring Lodge
High Eggborough
Whitley
Hollins Fm
Great Heck
Heck Hall Fm
AIRE & CALDER NAVIGATION
Gowdall Broach Fm
Hill Fm
West Cowick
Strawberry Hill
Park Lodge Fm
Chequerfield
Carleton
Darrington
Whitley Thorpe
Balne Moor Cross Roads
Balne Moor
Pollington
Animal Fm
Streethouse
FEATHERSTONE
Featherstone
Snydale
WAKEFIELD ROAD
Shop Cen
Scrombeck Fm
YORKSHIRE
North Hall Fm
Huntwick Grange Fm
Purston Jaglin
Ackworth Park Fm
Stapleton
Womersley
Womersley Park
Stocking Green Fm
Balne
Pollington Br
Pollington Grange
Park Fm
Southfield Reservoir
West Hardwick
Sharlston
Stapleton Park
Castle Fm
Dawland Fm
Drain
West End
Ash Tree Fm
Chapel Hill
Cross Hill
High Ackworth
East Hardwick
Cherry Tree Fm
Balne Lodge
Topham
Eskholme
Plaice Hills Fm
Foulby
Upper Lake
NOSTELL PRIORY
Acknorth Grange
Hessle
DONCASTER ROAD
Wentbridge
Little Smeaton
South End
River Went
Walden Stubbs
SELBY ROAD
Sykehouse
Wragby
Brakenhill
Ackworth School
Burnhill Ho
Low Ackworth
River Went
Ind Pk
Kirk Smeaton
Wentbank Ho
Stubbs Grange
Went Br
Went Fm
Fenwick
Fenwick Hall
Mawson Green
Santingley Grange
Moor Ho
Thorpe Audlin
Moat Hill Fm
Norton Common Fm
West End
FITZWILLIAM COUNTRY PARK
Fitzwilliam
Ackworth Moor Top
THORPE LANE
Thorpe Manor
Middle Field
BARNSDALE BAR SERVICES
Cliff Hill
Norton Priory
Norton
Fenwick Grange
Smallhedge Fm
Newstead
Hoyle Mill Dam
Lanes Fm
Badsworth
Rogerthorpe Manor
Ladythorpe Fm
Jett Hall
Moseley Grange
Westfield Ho
New House Fm
Fosterhouse
Ryhill
Kinsley
HEMSWORTH WATER PARK
Walton Wood Ho
Campsall
Campsmount Home Fm
CAMPSALL
Moss
COW LANE
Havercroft
Hemsworth
Royd Moor
Elm Leys Fm
Upton Beacon
Upton
Wrangbrook
Askern
Instoneville
Ind Est
Hawkhouse Green
Far Bank
South Hiendley
Vissitt Manor
North Elmsall
Hollins Fm
Rushy Moor
Haywood
SOUTH
Braithwaite
Skelbrooke
Robin Hood's Well
Burghwallis
Squirrel Wood
Sutton
Thorpe Grange
Wrancarr Ho
Trumfleet
Kirk Bramwith
South Bramwith
Shafton
Brierley
Moorthorpe
SOUTH ELMSALL
Burghwallis Grange
DONCASTER ROAD
Shirley Wood
YORKSHIRE
Stainforth
Shafton Two Gates
Grimethorpe Hall
Windmill Hill
Brierley Manor
MOORTHORPE
South Kirkby
South Elmsall
Moorhouse
Hampole
Skellow
Owston
Carcroft
Owston Wood
Thorpe in Balne
HATFIELD & STAINFORTH
Ling Ho
Upper Cudworth
ENGINE LANE
Belle Green
Moorhouse Common
Red Ho
Tilts Hills
Sixteen Acre Plantn
Tilts
Barnby Dun
Burntwood Hall
HOWELL WOOD
Hampole Grange
Cudworth
Grimethorpe
West Haigh Wood
Hooton Pagnell Wood
Hampole Wood
ADWICK
Shaftholme
Park Hill Grange
Warren Hill
Howell Ho
Wink Ho
Frickley Hall
Lound Hill
Adwick le Street
Hall Villa
Almholme
Dunsville
Houghton Lodge
Clayton
Hooton Pagnell
GREAT NORTH ROAD
Woodlands
Toll Bar
ASKERN ROAD
KIRK SANDALL
HIGH STREET
Cudworth Common
Pickburn
Brodsworth
Adwick Grange
Kirk Sandall
Windhill Fm
Great Houghton
Little Park
Bilham Grange
BRODSWORTH HALL
HIGHFIELDS
Highfields
Arksey
Green Lane Fm
Horse Carr Wood
Crook House Fm
Sandhill
Bilham House Fm
GREEN LANE
New Village
Long Sandall
THORNE ROAD
Edenthorpe
Edderthorpe
Thurnscoe East
THURNSCOE
LIDGET LANE
BARNSLEY ROAD
Scawthorpe
Sunnyfields
Ind Est
Bentley Common
Shaw Wood
West Moor Fm
Cranford Hall
Little Houghton
Thurnscoe
Hickleton
Marr
BARNSLEY ROAD
Bentley
WHEATLEY HALL ROAD
Wheatley Park
Armthorpe
West Moor Park
Middlecliffe
Bus Pk
Scawsby Hall
Scawsby
Cusworth
Bentley Rise
Wheatley Hills
Nutwell
Low Laithes
Millhouses
Billingley
Goldthorpe
Bella Wood
Marr Grange
CUSWORTH HALL MUSEUM
Wheatley
Intake
Low Fm
Snape Hill
Darfield
GOLDTHORPE
Ind Est
Highgate
CUSWORTH PARK
HM Prison DONCASTER
Doncaster
MUSEUM & ART GAL
Sandall Beat Wood
DONCASTER
Low Valley
Barnburgh
MELTON WOOD
Burntwood Grange
Smithley
Wombwell
Broomhill
Bolton upon Dearne
OLD MOOR
BOLTON-ON-DEARNE
Harlington
Toecroft Fm
Newton
Hyde Park
Cantley Common
Doncaster Common
Hexthorpe
Ind Est
ECO-POWER STADIUM
AEROVENTURE SOUTH YORKSHIRE AIRCRAFT MUS
Cantley
Bus Pk
Adwick upon Dearne
Barnburgh Grange
High Melton
Sprotbrough
Scabba Wood
Bessacarr
Hemingfield
Brampton
Dearne Br
Balby
LAKESIDE VILLAGE
YORKSHIRE WILDLIFE PARK
Twelve Months Carr
Elsecar
West Melton
Wath upon Dearne
Windhill
Cadeby
Warmsworth
Elsecar Heritage Railway
SE
Mexborough
POTTERIC CARR NATURE RESERVE
Coley Lane Fm
Newhill
Rossington Br
The Warren
Hay Field
MEXBOROUGH
CONISBROUGH
River Don
Old Denaby
Denaby Main
Conanby
Alverley Grange
Stump Cross
Loversall
GREAT YORKSHIRE WAY
Engine House Fm
CONISBROUGH IVANHOE
SHEFFIELD ROAD
iport Logistics Park
Swinton
SWINTON (SOUTH YORKSHIRE)
Conisbrough
New Edlington
Cortworth
Hoober
HOOBER LANE
Rossington
Warren House Fm
1
2
3 miles
1
2
3
4
5 km

EAST RIDING OF YORKSHIRE
NORTH LINCOLNSHIRE
Hemingbrough
Wressle
Newsholme
Brind
North Howden
Portington
Cavil
Eastrington
Newland
Hive
Sandholme
Gilberdyke
Scalby
Newport
Staddlethorpe
Bennetland
Walling Fen
Barmby on the Marsh
Long Drax
Asselby
Knedlington
Howden
Balkholme
Greenoak
Broomfleet
Drax
Boothferry
Kilpin Pike
Kilpin
Little Airmyn
Airmyn
Hook
Skelton
Laxton
Newland
Goole
Saltmarshe
Yokefleet
Blacktoft
Faxfleet
Whitton
Rawcliffe
Reedness
Little Reedness
Whitgift
Ousefleet
East Cowick
Rawcliffe Bridge
Old Goole
Swinefleet
Adlingfleet
Alkborough
Walcot
West Halton
Coleby
Garthorpe
Fockerby
Pincheon Green
Burton Stather
Burton upon Stather
Thealby
Luddington
Eastoft
Normanby
Moorends
Thorne Waste or Moors
Crowle Waste or Moors
Flixborough
Flixborough Stather
Dragonby
Amcotts
Fishlake
Thorne
Canal Side
Crowle
Crowle Park
Windsor
Wike Well End
Keadby
Gunness
Crosby
Frodingham
Scunthorpe
Brumby
Ealand
Hatfield
Althorpe
Burringham
Derrythorpe
Hatfield Woodhouse
West End
Sandtoft
Woodhouse
Westgate
Grey Green
Belton
Bracon
Beltoft
West Butterwick
East Butterwick
Yaddlethorpe
Bottesford
Ashby
Church Town
Isle of Axholme
Hatfield Moors
Messingham
Epworth
Wroot
Epworth Turbary
Low Burnham
Kelfield
Susworth
Scotterthorpe
Auckley
Lidget
Blaxton
Upperthorpe
Owston Ferry
Scotter
Finningley
Haxey
East Lound
East Ferry
Westwoodside
Graiselound
Wildsworth
Scotton
DONCASTER SHEFFIELD AIRPORT
Doncaster North Services
River Ouse
River Trent
River Don
Blacktoft Channel
Whitton Channel
Stainforth & Keadby Canal
M62
M18
M180
M181
207
208
200
187
188

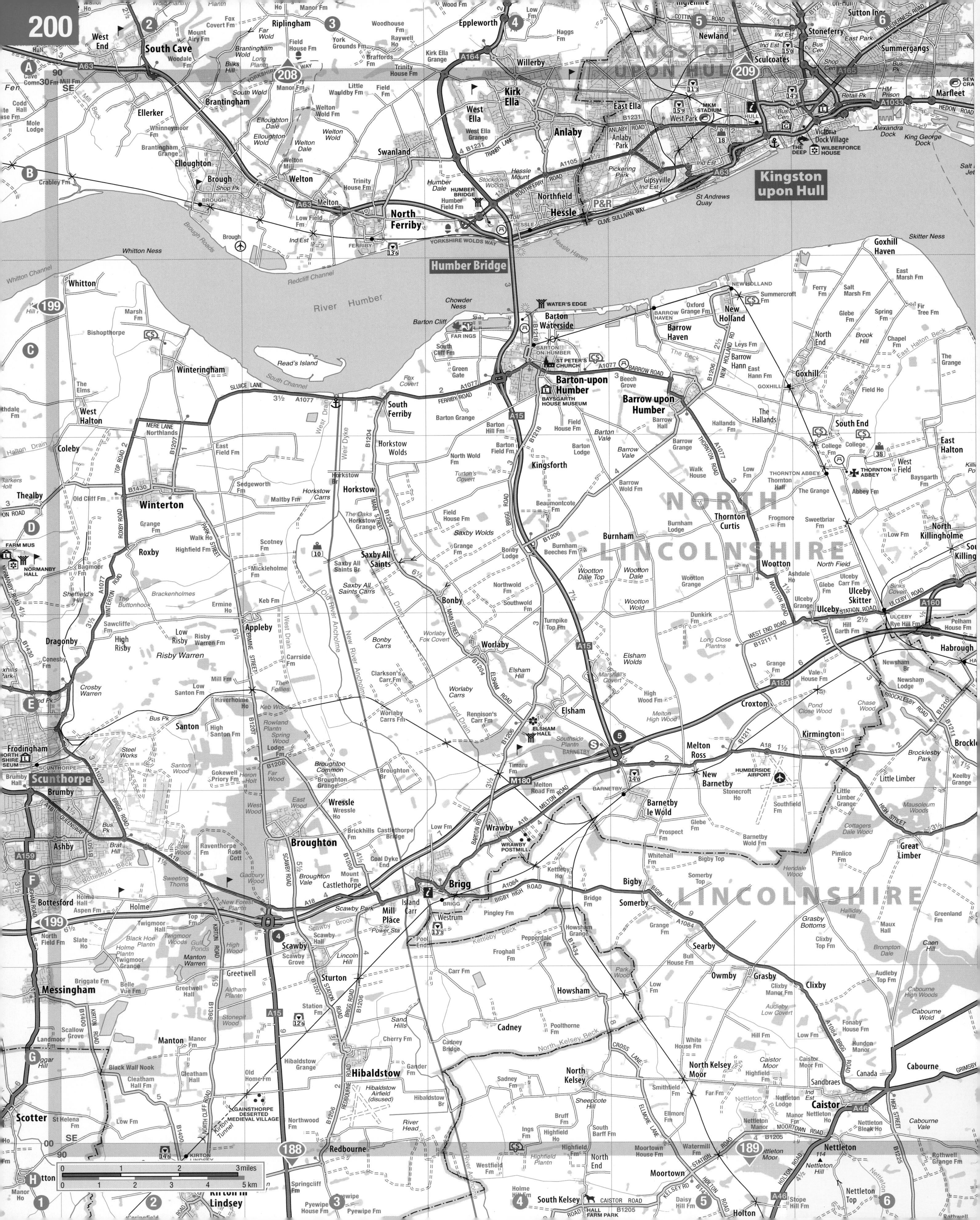
West End
South Cave
Riplingham
Eppleworth
Newland
Stoneferry
Sutton Ings
Summergangs
KINGSTON UPON HULL
Sculcoates
208
209
Brantingham
Ellerker
Willerby
Kirk Ella
West Ella
East Ella
Anlaby
Anlaby Park
West Park
Marfleet
Victoria Dock Village
Alexandra Dock
King George Dock
Elloughton
Brough
Welton
Swanland
Melton
North Ferriby
Hessle
Northfield
Gipsyville
Kingston upon Hull
Humber Bridge
River Humber
Whitton
Whitton Ness
Whitton Channel
Redcliff Channel
Read's Island
South Channel
Barton Cliff
Chowder Ness
Barton Waterside
Barton-upon Humber
Barrow Haven
New Holland
Barrow upon Humber
Goxhill
Goxhill Haven
Skitter Ness
Winteringham
West Halton
South Ferriby
Horkstow
Coleby
Thealby
Winterton
Roxby
NORTH LINCOLNSHIRE
Kingsforth
Burnham
Thornton Curtis
Thornton Abbey
South End
East Halton
North Killingholme
Saxby All Saints
Bonby
Worlaby
Wootton
Ulceby
Ulceby Skitter
Habrough
Appleby
Dragonby
Risby
Risby Warren
Santon
Elsham
Croxton
Kirmington
Melton Ross
New Barnetby
Barnetby le Wold
Humberside Airport
Frodingham
Scunthorpe
Brumby
Ashby
Bottesford
Broughton
Wressle
Wrawby
Brigg
Castlethorpe
Bigby
Somerby
Great Limber
Little Limber
Holme
Scawby
Sturton
Searby
Owmby
Grasby
Clixby
Howsham
Cadney
Messingham
Manton
Hibaldstow
North Kelsey
North Kelsey Moor
Caistor
Cabourne
Scotter
Redbourne
Kirton in Lindsey
Moortown
South Kelsey
Nettleton
Holton
LINCOLNSHIRE
199
188
189
0 1 2 3 miles
0 1 2 3 4 5 km

201
EAST RIDING OF YORKSHIRE
NORTH EAST LINCOLNSHIRE
River Humber
Mouth of the Humber
Grimsby Roads
Hedon
Withernsea
Patrington
Keyingham
Ottringham
Thorngumbald
Burstwick
Roos
Tunstall
Preston
Salt End
Paull
Halsam
Hollym
Holmpton
Welwick
Weeton
Skeffling
Easington
Kilnsea
Spurn Head
Sunk Island
Immingham
Stallingborough
Healing
Keelby
Grimsby
Cleethorpes
Humberston
New Waltham
Waltham
Holton le Clay
Tetney
North Thoresby
Laceby
Scartho
Aylesby
Riby
Irby upon Humber
Swallow
Cuxwold
Beelsby
Hatcliffe
Brigsley
Ashby cum Fenby
Barnoldby le Beck
Grainsby
Marshchapel
North Cotes
Tetney Lock
Rothwell
Croxby
East Ravendale
West Ravendale
Sunk Island Sands
Trinity Sands
Tetney High Sands
Foulholme Sands
Cherry Cobb Sands
Paull Holme Sands
Spurn Point Nature Reserve
Bull Sand Fort
Stony Binks
Humber Pilot Station
Spurn Discovery Centre
Cleethorpes Light Railway
The Jungle Zoo
Rotterdam

Heysham
Lower Heysham
Higher Heysham
Heysham Nuclear Power Sta
Half Moon Bay
DOUGLAS
Heysham Lake
Middleton Sands
Middleton
Overton
Heaton
Aldcliffe
Abraham Heights
CASTLE LANCASTER
ASHTON MEMORIAL
WILLIAMSON PARK & BUTTERFLY HOUSE
Scotforth
Bailrigg
Stodday
Quernmore
Sunderland Bank
Sunderland
Sunderland Point
Shoulder of Lune
Glasson
Conder Green
Galgate
Ellel
Thurnham
Lower Thurnham
Upper Thurnham
Smith Green
Hampson Green
Ortner
Cockersand Abbey Fm
Cockerham Sands
Cockerham
Pilling Sands
Preesall Sands
Braides
Sand Side
Forton
Hollins Lane
Bay Horse
Lancaster (Forton) Services
Street
Dolphinholme
Scorton
Cabus
Oakenclough
Calder Vale
North Wharf
Fleetwood
Knott End-on-Sea
Pilling Lane
Pilling
Stake Pool
Dam Side
Preesall
Preesall Park
Scronkey
Pilling Moss
Cockerham Moss
Winmarleigh
Winmarleigh Moss
Garstang
Nateby
Bonds
Bowgreave
Catterall
Churchtown
Stalmine
Stalmine Moss Side
Cold Row
Eagland Hill
Rossall School
Cleveleys
Burn Naze
Trunnah
Staynall
Hambleton
Thornton
Little Thornton
Anchorsholme
Little Bispham
Norbreck
Bispham
Out Rawcliffe
Little Eccleston
Great Eccleston
St Michael's on Wyre
Skippool
Poulton-Le-Fylde
Carleton
Warbreck
BLACKPOOL
Blackpool
Little Singleton
Singleton
Elswick
Thistleton
Inskip
Myerscough
Bilsborrow
Barton
Cuddy Hill
Catforth
Woodplumpton
Broughton
North Shore
Layton
Queenstown
BLACKPOOL TOWER & CIRCUS
SEA LIFE CENTRE
Central Pier
BLACKPOOL ZOO
Staining
Normoss
Esprick
Roseacre
Wharles
Greenhalgh
Corner Row
Great Marton
Weeton
Mythop
Little Marton
Hawes Side
Marton Moss Side
Mereside
BLACKPOOL PLEASURE BEACH
Common Edge
Peel Hill
Little Plumpton
Great Plumpton
Wesham
Kirkham
Treales
Higher Bartle
Lower Bartle
Sharoe Green
Fulwood
Cadley
Cottam
South Shore
Squires Gate
Great Marton Moss
Westby
Ribby
Wrea Green
Dowbridge
Newton
Scales
Newton with Scales
Lea Town
Clifton
Preston
Higher Ballam
Lower Ballam
Moss Side
Bryning
Kellamergh
Freckleton
Warton
Lytham St Anne's
Ansdell
Saltcotes
Crusader Bank
Higher Penwortham
Riverside Docklands
M55
M6
210
211
193
0 1 2 3 miles
0 1 2 3 4 5 km

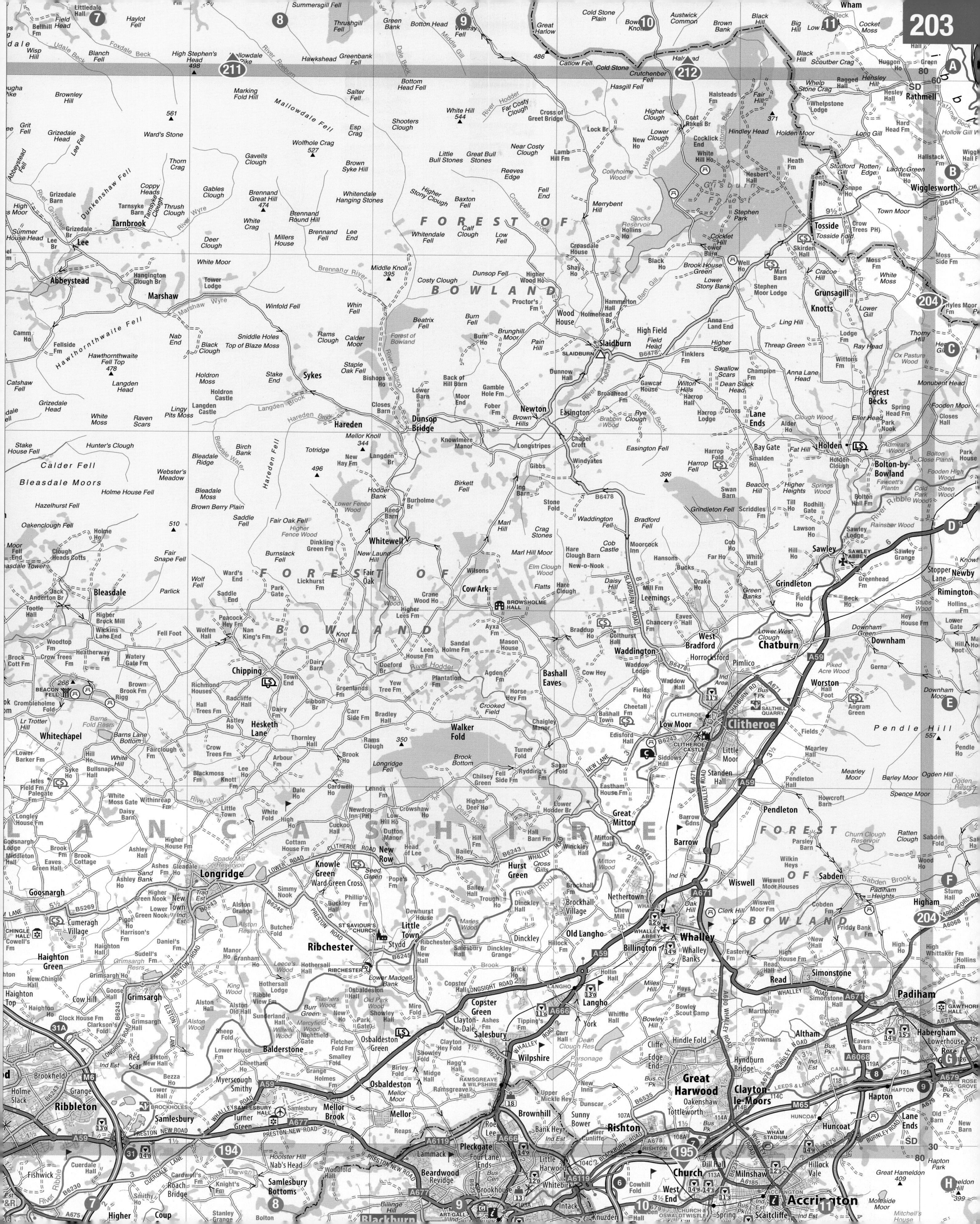
FOREST OF BOWLAND
FOREST OF BOWLAND
LANCASHIRE
FOREST OF BOWLAND
Abbeystead
Marshaw
Tarnbrook
Lee
Sykes
Hareden
Dunsop Bridge
Newton
Slaidburn
Easington
Wood House
Whitewell
Cow Ark
Bleasdale
Chipping
Hesketh Lane
Whitechapel
Walker Fold
Bashall Eaves
Waddington
West Bradford
Grindleton
Chatburn
Sawley
Holden
Bolton-by-Bowland
Tosside
Wigglesworth
Rathmell
Grunsagill
Knotts
Forest Becks
Lane Ends
Downham
Worston
Clitheroe
Low Moor
Pendleton
Pendle Hill
Great Mitton
Barrow
Longridge
Goosnargh
Knowle Green
Ribchester
Hurst Green
Whalley
Billington
Wiswell
Sabden
Higham
Padiham
Simonstone
Read
Langho
Copster Green
Salesbury
Wilpshire
Great Harwood
Clayton-le-Moors
Rishton
Accrington
Huncoat
Hapton
Altham
Church
Grimsargh
Haighton Green
Ribbleton
Samlesbury
Balderstone
Osbaldeston
Mellor
Mellor Brook
Pleckgate
Beardwood
Samlesbury Bottoms
Fishwick
Higher
Coup
Blackburn
Gisburn Forest
Stocks Reservoir
Calder Fell
Bleasdale Moors
Wolfhole Crag
Mellor Knoll
Whalley Abbey
Sawley Abbey
Browsholme Hall
Clitheroe Castle
Stonyhurst
A59
A671
A666
A677
A6119
A678
A680
A679
A6068
B6478
B6243
B6245
B6246
M6
M65
211
212
194
195
204

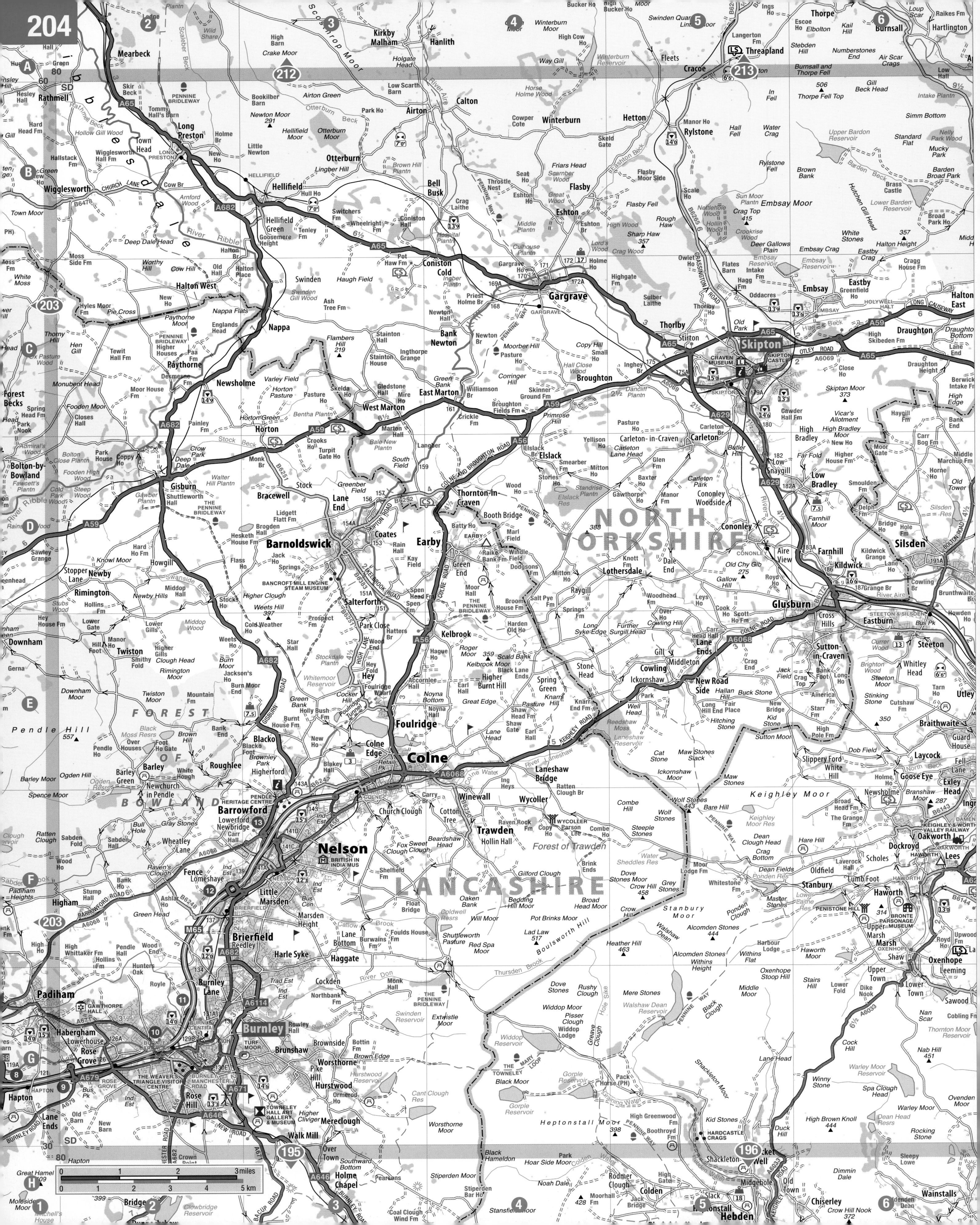

212
213
203
195
196
Mearbeck
Rathmell
Wigglesworth
Long Preston
Hellifield
Kirkby Malham
Hanlith
Airton
Calton
Otterburn
Winterburn
Hetton
Rylstone
Cracoe
Threapland
Burnsall
Thorpe
Hartlington
Embsay Moor
Bell Busk
Coniston Cold
Gargrave
Eshton
Flasby
Embsay
Eastby
Halton East
Draughton
Skipton
Thorlby
Stirton
Bank Newton
Broughton
East Marton
West Marton
Nappa
Paythorne
Newsholme
Halton West
Horton
Gisburn
Bolton-by-Bowland
Forest Becks
Bracewell
Barnoldswick
Coates
Earby
Lane End
Thornton-in-Craven
Elslack
Carleton-in-Craven
Carleton
Cononley
Farnhill
Kildwick
Silsden
Glusburn
Cross Hills
Eastburn
Steeton
Sutton-in-Craven
Lothersdale
Cowling
Middleton
Lane Ends
Kelbrook
Salterforth
Foulridge
Colne
Laneshaw Bridge
Wycoller
Trawden
Winewall
Nelson
Barrowford
Barley
Roughlee
Blacko
Higham
Padiham
Brierfield
Burnley
Harle Syke
Haggate
Worsthorne
Hurstwood
Brunshaw
Habergham
Hapton
Rose Hill
Mereclough
Walk Mill
Holme Chapel
Laycock
Goose Eye
Oakworth
Haworth
Stanbury
Oxenhope
Keighley Moor
Utley
Braithwaite
Hebden
Colden
Midgehole
Chiserley
Wainstalls
NORTH YORKSHIRE
LANCASHIRE
FOREST OF BOWLAND
Pendle Hill 557
Forest of Trawden
Boulsworth Hill
Heptonstall Moor
Stanbury Moor
PENNINE WAY
PENNINE BRIDLEWAY
River Ribble
River Aire
A65
A59
A682
A56
A6068
A629
A646
A671
A6114
A679
M65
0 1 2 3 miles
0 1 2 3 4 5 km

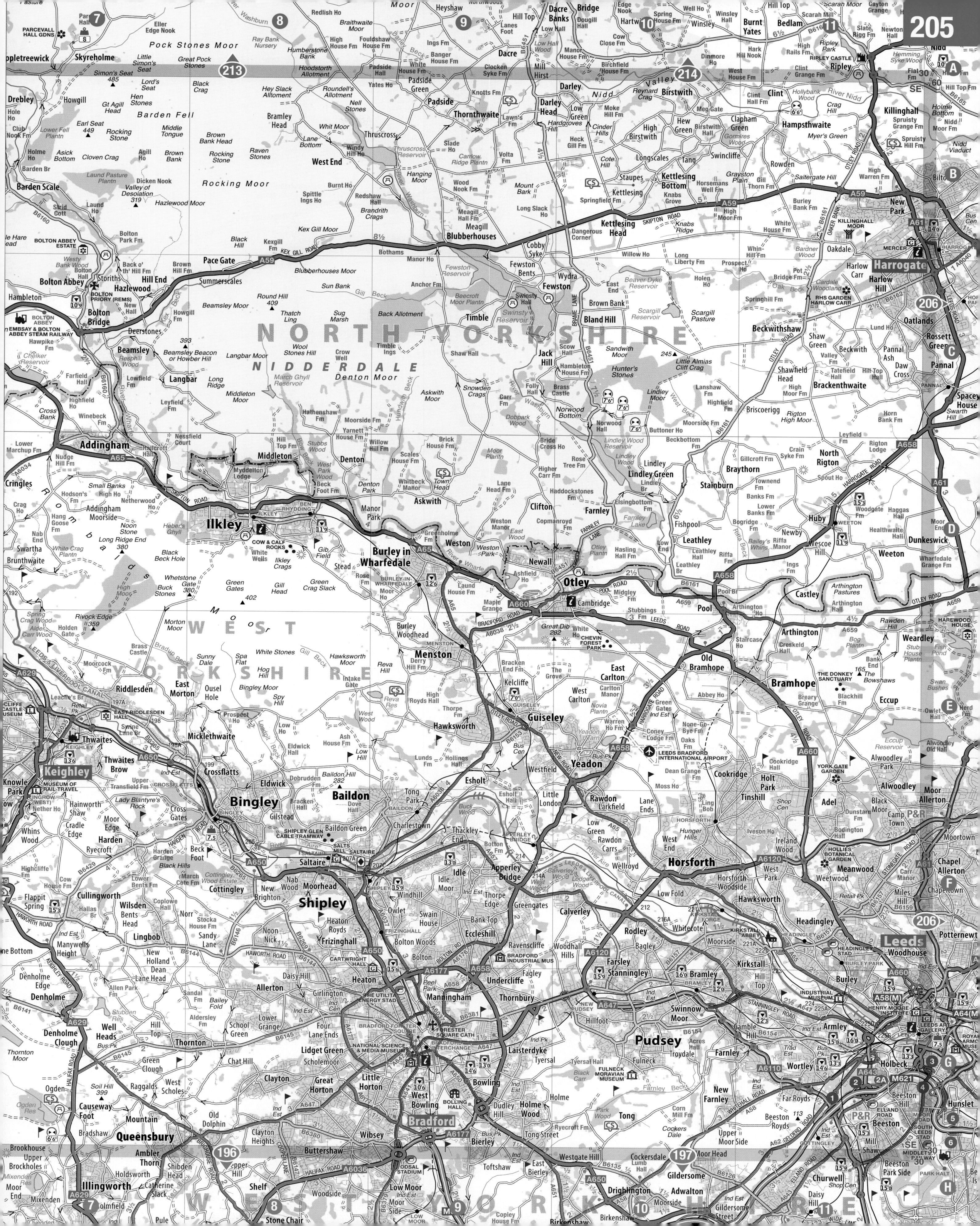
205
NORTH YORKSHIRE
NIDDERDALE
WEST YORKSHIRE
Rombalds Moor
Pock Stones Moor
Barden Fell
Rocking Moor
Denton Moor
Skyreholme
Dacre
Dacre Banks
Bridge
Darley
Darley Head
Birstwith
Clint
Bedlam
Burnt Yates
Ripley
Ripley Castle
Killinghall
Hampsthwaite
Thornthwaite
Padside
Thruscross
West End
Kettlesing
Kettlesing Head
Kettlesing Bottom
Blubberhouses
Pace Gate
Bolton Abbey
Hazlewood
Bolton Bridge
Hill End
Timble
Fewston
Bland Hill
Beckwithshaw
Harrogate
Harlow Hill
Oatlands
Pannal
Rossett Green
Brackenthwaite
Beamsley
Langbar
Jack Hill
Addingham
Middleton
Denton
Askwith
Ilkley
Burley in Wharfedale
Newall
Otley
Clifton
Farnley
Lindley Green
Braythorn
Stainburn
North Rigton
Huby
Leathley
Dunkeswick
Weeton
Castley
Pool
Arthington
Weardley
Bramhope
Old Bramhope
East Carlton
Menston
Guiseley
Yeadon
Hawksworth
Riddlesden
East Morton
Micklethwaite
Crossflatts
Bingley
Keighley
Thwaites
Thwaites Brow
Eldwick
Baildon
Esholt
Rawdon
Cookridge
Holt Park
Tinshill
Adel
Alwoodley
Moor Allerton
Saltaire
Shipley
Idle
Apperley Bridge
Horsforth
Calverley
Cottingley
Cullingworth
Wilsden
Harden
Lingbob
Eccleshill
Farsley
Rodley
Kirkstall
Headingley
Leeds
Woodhouse
Burley
Bramley
Stanningley
Heaton
Allerton
Manningham
Undercliffe
Thornbury
Denholme
Thornton
Clayton
Great Horton
Little Horton
Bradford
West Bowling
Bowling
Pudsey
Farnley
Armley
Holbeck
Wortley
Beeston
New Farnley
Queensbury
Mountain
Illingworth
Shelf
Wibsey
Buttershaw
Bierley
Tong
Gildersome
Adwalton
Drighlington
Churwell
Morley
Leeds Bradford International Airport
A59
A61
A65
A629
A650
A658
A660
A6120
A647
A6177
213
214
196
197
206

214
215
205
197
198
Knaresborough
Harrogate
Wetherby
Leeds
Tadcaster
Garforth
Rothwell
Sherburn in Elmet
Boston Spa
Collingham
Spofforth
Bramham
Linton-on-Ouse
Newton on Ouse
Beningbrough
Nun Monkton
Moor Monkton
Green Hammerton
Kirk Hammerton
Whixley
Great Ouseburn
Little Ouseburn
Thorpe Underwood
Tockwith
Marston Moor
Long Marston
Hutton Wandesley
Bilton in Ainsty
Rufforth
Askham Richard
Bilbrough
Catterton
Colton
Hessay
Angram
Healaugh
Newton Kyme
Thorp Arch
Clifford
Toulston
Stutton
Ulleskelf
Towton
Saxton
Barkston
Church Fenton
Little Fenton
Biggin
South Milford
Monk Fryston
Hillam
Lumby
Newthorpe
Fairburn
Ledsham
Ledston
Ledston Luck
Kippax
Great Preston
Little Preston
Swillington
Oulton
Methley
Micklefield
Old Micklefield
Garden Village
Aberford
Parlington
Barwick in Elmet
Scholes
Thorner
Shadwell
Scarcroft
Bardsey
East Rigton
East Keswick
Harewood
Weardley
Wike
Alwoodley
Moor Allerton
Chapel Allerton
Roundhay
Potternewton
Seacroft
Whitkirk
Halton
Colton
Manston
Austhorpe
Cross Gates
Harehills
Sheepscar
Burmantofts
Osmondthorpe
Hunslet
Beeston
Stourton
Swillington Common
Kirkby Overblow
Sicklinghall
Linton
Netherby
Dunkeswick
Weeton
Follifoot
Spacey Houses
Pannal
Rossett Green
Oatlands
Harlow Hill
Starbeck
Forest Moor
Woodlands
Scotton
Scriven
Farnham
Ferrensby
Brearton
Arkendale
Coneythorpe
Flaxby
Goldsborough
Allerton Mauleverer
Hopperton
Cattal
Hunsingore
Walshford
Little Ribston
Cowthorpe
Bickerton
North Deighton
Kirk Deighton
Ingmanthorpe
Walton
Wighill
Kirkby Wharfe
Bolton Percy
Killinghall
Bilton
New Park
Wetherby Services
York West Services
Leeds Skelton Lake Services
A1(M)
A59
A61
A58
A64
A659
A661
A658
A63
A162
A168
M1
M621
A6120
A642
A656
B1224
B1223
B1222
B1217
W E S T
Y O R K S H I R E
N O
0
1
2
3 miles
4
5 km

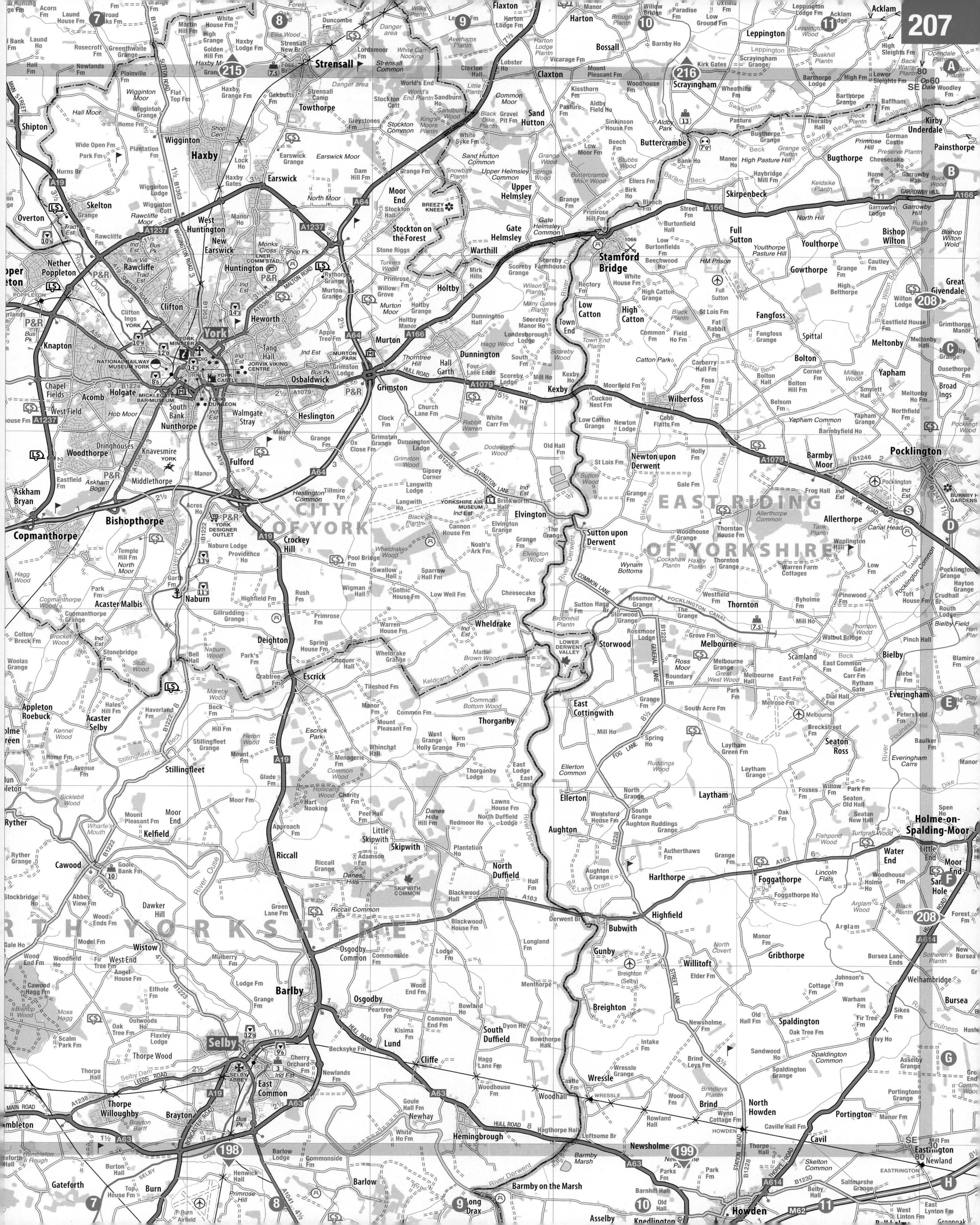

Strensall
Strensall Common
Towthorpe
Flaxton
Harton
Bossall
Claxton
Leppington
Scrayingham
Acklam
Kirby Underdale
Painsthorpe
Buttercrambe
Sand Hutton
Upper Helmsley
Gate Helmsley
Warthill
Stockton on the Forest
Moor End
Skirpenbeck
Bugthorpe
Stamford Bridge
Full Sutton
Youlthorpe
Gowthorpe
Bishop Wilton
Great Givendale
Fangfoss
Spittal
Meltonby
Yapham
Bolton
High Catton
Low Catton
Town End
Kexby
Wilberfoss
Dunnington
Holtby
Murton
Grimston
Osbaldwick
Heslington
Heworth
Huntington
Haxby
Wigginton
Earswick
New Earswick
West Huntington
Shipton
Skelton
Overton
Nether Poppleton
Rawcliffe
Clifton
York
Knapton
Acomb
Holgate
Chapel Fields
West Field
South Bank
Nunthorpe
Walmgate Stray
Fulford
Woodthorpe
Dringhouses
Middlethorpe
Askham Bryan
Bishopthorpe
Copmanthorpe
CITY OF YORK
Crockey Hill
Naburn
Acaster Malbis
Deighton
Wheldrake
Elvington
Sutton upon Derwent
Newton upon Derwent
Barmby Moor
Pocklington
Allerthorpe
EAST RIDING OF YORKSHIRE
Thornton
Melbourne
Storwood
Bielby
Scamland
Everingham
East Cottingwith
Thorganby
Escrick
Appleton Roebuck
Acaster Selby
Stillingfleet
Seaton Ross
Laytham
Ellerton
Aughton
Holme-on-Spalding-Moor
Ryther
Kelfield
Cawood
Riccall
Skipwith
North Duffield
Harlthorpe
Foggathorpe
Bubwith
Highfield
Gunby
Willitoft
Gribthorpe
Breighton
Spaldington
Wistow
Barlby
Osgodby
South Duffield
Lund
Cliffe
Selby
East Common
Thorpe Willoughby
Brayton
Hemingbrough
Wressle
Brind
North Howden
Portington
Newsholme
Cavil
Eastrington
Barmby on the Marsh
Barlow
Burn
Gateforth
Long Drax
Howden
Asselby
NORTH YORKSHIRE
A19
A64
A166
A1079
A1237
A163
A63
A614
B1228
B1222
B1223
B1363
208
198
199
215
216

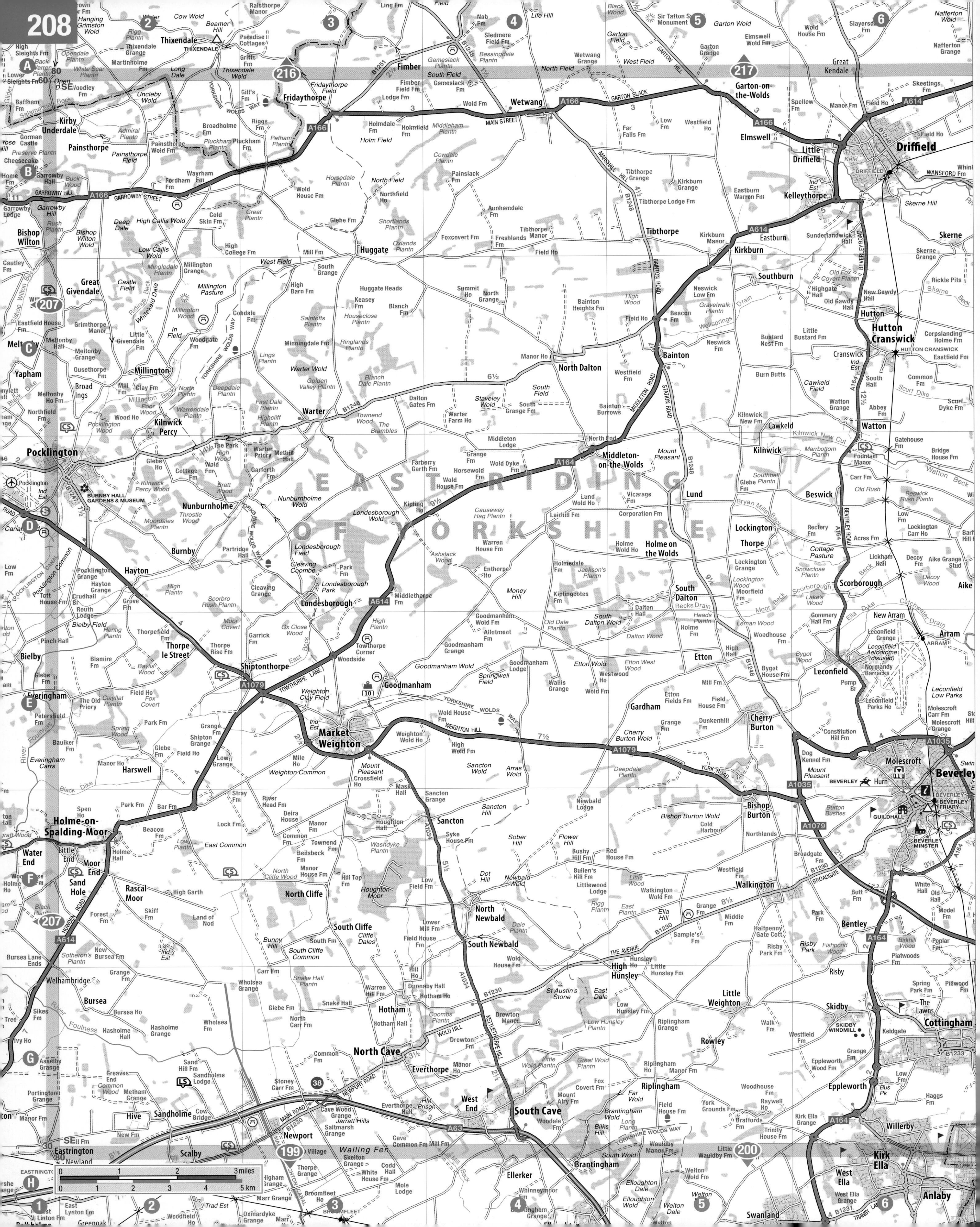
Thixendale
Fridaythorpe
Fimber
Wetwang
Garton-on-the-Wolds
Driffield
Kirby Underdale
Painsthorpe
Elmswell
Little Driffield
Kelleythorpe
Bishop Wilton
Huggate
Tibthorpe
Kirkburn
Eastburn
Skerne
Great Givendale
Southburn
Bainton
North Dalton
Hutton Cranswick
Yapham
Millington
Warter
Kilnwick Percy
Watton
Pocklington
Middleton-on-the-Wolds
Kilnwick
Nunburnholme
Lund
Beswick
EAST RIDING OF YORKSHIRE
Burnby
Holme on the Wolds
Lockington
Thorpe
Hayton
South Dalton
Scorborough
Londesborough
Arram
Bielby
Thorpe le Street
Shiptonthorpe
Etton
Leconfield
Everingham
Goodmanham
Gardham
Market Weighton
Cherry Burton
Harswell
Molescroft
Beverley
Holme-on-Spalding-Moor
Sancton
Bishop Burton
Water End
Moor End
Sand Hole
Rascal Moor
North Cliffe
Walkington
North Newbald
South Cliffe
Bentley
South Newbald
High Hunsley
Welhambridge
Bursea
Little Weighton
Hotham
Skidby
Cottingham
North Cave
Rowley
Everthorpe
Riplingham
Eppleworth
West End
South Cave
Hive
Sandholme
Willerby
Newport
Eastrington
Scalby
Kirk Ella
Ellerker
Brantingham
West Ella
Anlaby
Swanland
Yorkshire Wolds Way
A166
A614
A164
A1079
A1034
A1035
A63
B1246
B1248
B1230
216
217
207
199
200
3 miles
5 km

Ruston Parva
Harpham
Fraisthorpe
Nafferton
Lowthorpe
Gransmoor
Barmston
Barmston Sands
Great Kelk
Lissett
Ulrome
Ulrome Sands
Gembling
Wansford
Foston on the Wolds
Skipsea Castle
Skipsea
Skipsea Brough
Skipsea Sands
Beeford
Brigham
North Frodingham
Church End
Dunnington
Rotsea
Atwick
Atwick Sands
Hempholme
Bewholme
North Cliff
Burshill
Baswick Steer
Brandesburton
Hornsea
Hornsea Mere
Hornsea Bridge
Seaton
South Cliff
Leven
Catwick
Sigglesthorne
Rolston
Goxhill
Mappleton
Eske
Routh
Little Hatfield
Great Hatfield
Great Cowden
Tickton
Long Riston
Rise
Arnold
Withernwick
Weel
Meaux
Skirlaugh
New Ellerby
Marton
Aldbrough
Woodmansey
East Newton
Old Ellerby
West Newton
Thearne
Wawne
Flinton
Swine
Garton
Dunswell
Coniston
Grimston
Thirtleby
Sproatley
Humbleton
Fitling
Ganstead
Hilston
Bransholme
Bilton
Wyton
Sutton on Hull
Lelley
Owstwick
Inglemire
West Carr
Elstronwick
Burton Pidsea
Tunstall
Newland
Stoneferry
Sutton Ings
Kingston upon Hull
Sculcoates
Summergangs
Preston
Roos
Marfleet
Salt End
East Ella
West Park
Anlaby Park
Victoria Dock Village
Hedon
Haven Side
Burstwick
217
218
200
201
A165
A1035
A1033
A1079
B1242
B1244
B1238
B1249
B1240

Foldgate Fm
Corney Fell
Sele Bottom
Dunnerdale Fells
Scrithwaite Fm
Lind End
Bracelet Hall
Stable Harvey Moss
Sunny Bank
Thrang Crag Wood
Top o Selside
Bowkerstead Fm
Corney
Swallowhurst
Littlecell Bottom
Buck Barrow 549
Plough Fell
Frith Hall
Ulpha Park
Hesketh Hall
Woodland Grove
Pool Scar
Grass Paddocks
Long Crags
Brown Howe
Force Mills
Force Forge
Flatts
Corney Hall
Prior Park
Penn
Green Bank
Broughton Mills
Bridge End
Yew Bank
Tarn Riggs
Birk Knott
Bethecar Moor
Seaton Hall
Low Kinmont
Thwaites Fell
Rosthwaite
Lane End
Beacon Tarn
High Nibthwaite
Whitestock Hall
Ickenthwaite
Rusland
Crosslands
Hycemoor
Stoneside Hill 422
Mere Crags
Moss Side Fm
Woodland
Green Moor
Woodland Fell
Wool Knott
Greenholme Fm
Arklid Intake
Bootle
Bootle Fell
Lower Hawthwaite
Water Yeat
Arklid Fm
Stock Wood
Rusland Moss
Rushland Cross
Cross House
Fellgreen
Swinside Fell
Windy Slack
Bank End
Woodland Hall
Blawith Knott
Blawith
Furness Fells
Duddon Bridge
Manor Fm
Black Moss
Longfield Wood
Houkler Hall
Nibthwaite Grange
Park Wood
Side Ho
Skinner Pastures
Fellside
Broomhill
Broughton in Furness
Fell End
Birch Bank
Lin Crag Fm
Kirkthwaite Cottage
Low Hay Bridge
Stoupdale Crags 472
Gray Stones
Knott Hill
Greystone Ho
Ash House
Bandrake Head
Hill Park
Oxen Park
High Hay Bridge
Kiskin
Annaside
Little Fell
Buckman Brow
Eccle Riggs
Wreaks End
Fell Gate
Far Houses
Heathwaite Fm
Lowick Bridge
Sayles Fm
Burn Knott
Colton
Crook Fm
Barfield Tarn
Black Combe
Baystone Bank Res
Hazel Mount
Coal Gate
Kirkby Park Wood
Subberthwaite Common 298
Lowick
Bank Wood
Beckside Fm
Monk Foss Fm
Lady Hall
Duddon Mosses
White Moss
Ashlack Hall
Beck Stones
Great Burney
Stone Dykes
Lowick Hall
Esps Fm
Ridding Side Fm
Old Hall Fm
Bouth
Abbots Reading Fm
Lakeside
Haverthwaite
600
Fore Slack
Whicham Mill
Hallthwaites
Foxfield
Grizebeck
A5092
Wood Gate
Lowick Green
Ireland Moss
Causeway End
Hallbeck Ho
Mire Ho
The Green
Brockwood Hall
Arnaby
Bank End
Beanthwaite
Lowick Common
Beck Bottom
Spark Bridge
Tottlebank
A590
Haverthwaite
Dunningwell
Strands
Dove Bank
Gawthwaite
Hollow Oak
Gutterby Spa
Whitbeck
Green Road
Angerton Marsh
Chapels
Lowick High Common
Groffa Crag
Black Crags
Hill End
Whicham Valley
Kirkby Hall
Wall End
Brunt Riggs
England Coast Path
Woods
Kirkby-in-Furness
Broughton Beck
Penny Bridge
Legbarrow Pt
Whicham Hall
Millom Park
Park Ho
The Hill
Millom Marsh
Sand Side
Gill House Beck
Beck Side
Gunson Height
Moor Ho
Blade Moss
Greenodd
Mearness Fm
Mearness Point
Roudsea Wood
Whicham
Silecroft
Low Ho
Low Hall
Out Park
Well Ho
Hollowmire
Shooting House Hill
Mansriggs Hall
Bowstead Gates
Arrad Foot
Stribers Moss
Duddon Sands
Duddon Channel
Soutergate
Osmotherley Moor
Mansriggs
Nab Point
Roudsea Wood & Mosses
Kirksanton
Beck Wood
Borwick Rails Harbour
Heathem Hall Fm
Millom
Millom Heritage & Arts Centre
Bank House Moor
Higher Lath Fm
Newland Bottom
Plumpton Cottage Fm
Ashes Pt
Haverigg Pool
Ind Est
Borwick Rails
Dunnerholme
Marsh Grange
Harlock Res
Harlock Hill
Copse Hill
Old Hall Fm
Newland
Barrow Monument
Cumbria Crystal
Great Oath Hill 65
Hazelhurst Pt
HM Prison
Steel Green
RSPB
Hodbarrow
Pennington Res
Ulverston
Laurel & Hardy Mus
Leven Viaduct
Stewner Park Fm
Ewe Dale
Haverigg
Poaka Beck Res
Ghyll Fm
High Greaves
Stone Cross
South Ulverston
Plumpton Bight
Canal Foot
Hodbarrow Point
Haverigg Point
Wortbrig Scar
Askam in Furness
Ireleth
Tippin's Lane
Far Old Park Fm
Pennington Ho
Pennington
Outcast
Old Park Wood
Hammerside Pt
Marton
Loppergarth
Rowe Head
Swarthmoor Hall
Swarthmoor
Croftlands
Dragley Beck
Sandside
Cartmel Sands
Greenscoe Fm
High Haume Fm
Lindal Moor
Trinkeld Fm
Priory Road
Sand Gate Marsh
Chapel Island
Roanhead Fm
Mouzel Fm
Tytup Hall
Lindal in Furness
Sandscale Haws
Safari Zoo Cumbria
Flat Woods
Edge Hill
Conishead Priory & Manjushri Kadampa Meditation Centre
Lenibrick Point
Duddon Sands
Thwaite Flat
Great Urswick
Urswick Tarn
Bardsea
Wellhouse Fm
Cowpren Point
Lowsy Point
Dalton Castle
Dalton-in-Furness
Dalton
Skells Lodge
Holme Bank
Ulverston Sands
Scarth Channel
Scarth Bight
Park Road
Sinkfall
Bolton Heads
Little Urswick
Sunbrick
Sea Wood
Shope Tree Scar
North End Marsh
Ind Est
Billincoat Fm
Scales
Baycliff
North Walney
Walney Meetings
Hawcoat
Stainton with Adgarley
Newton
North Stank Fm
Mere Tarn
Wind Hill
Maskel Point
Ulverston Channel
Barrow (Walney Island)
Ormsgill
Bow Bridge
Furness Abbey
Gleaston Watermill
Gleaston
Colt Park
Aldingham
Walney Road
Crosslands Park
New Close Fm
Dendron
The Dunes Hotel Stadium
Newbarns
Beacon Hill
Stank
Barrow-in-Furness
Holbeck
Earnse Pt
North Walney
The Dock Mus
Hindpool
South Newbarns
Yarlside
Scarbarrow Hill
Newbiggin
Sea Mill
North Scale
Salthouse
Leece
Roosecote
Vickerstown
Moor Head Cottages
Barrow Island
Waterfront under dev
Page Bank Fm
Roosebeck
Peasholmes Fm
Water Garth Nook
Roosecote Sands
Rampside Road
Coast Road
Tummer Hill Marsh
Isle of Walney
Biggar Sands
Roosebeck Sands
Lancaster Sound
Westfield Point
Biggar
Rampside
Rampside Sands
South Channel
Long Rein Point
Roa Island
Piel Channel
Snab Sands
Wylock Marsh
Snab Pt
Sheep Island
Piel Island
Piel Castle
Foulney Island
Piel Harbour
South End
Scar End Point
Haws Point
South Walney
South East Point
Piel Bar
Douglas
220
202
A595
A5093
A593
A5084
B5281
A5087
A590
A5092
miles
km

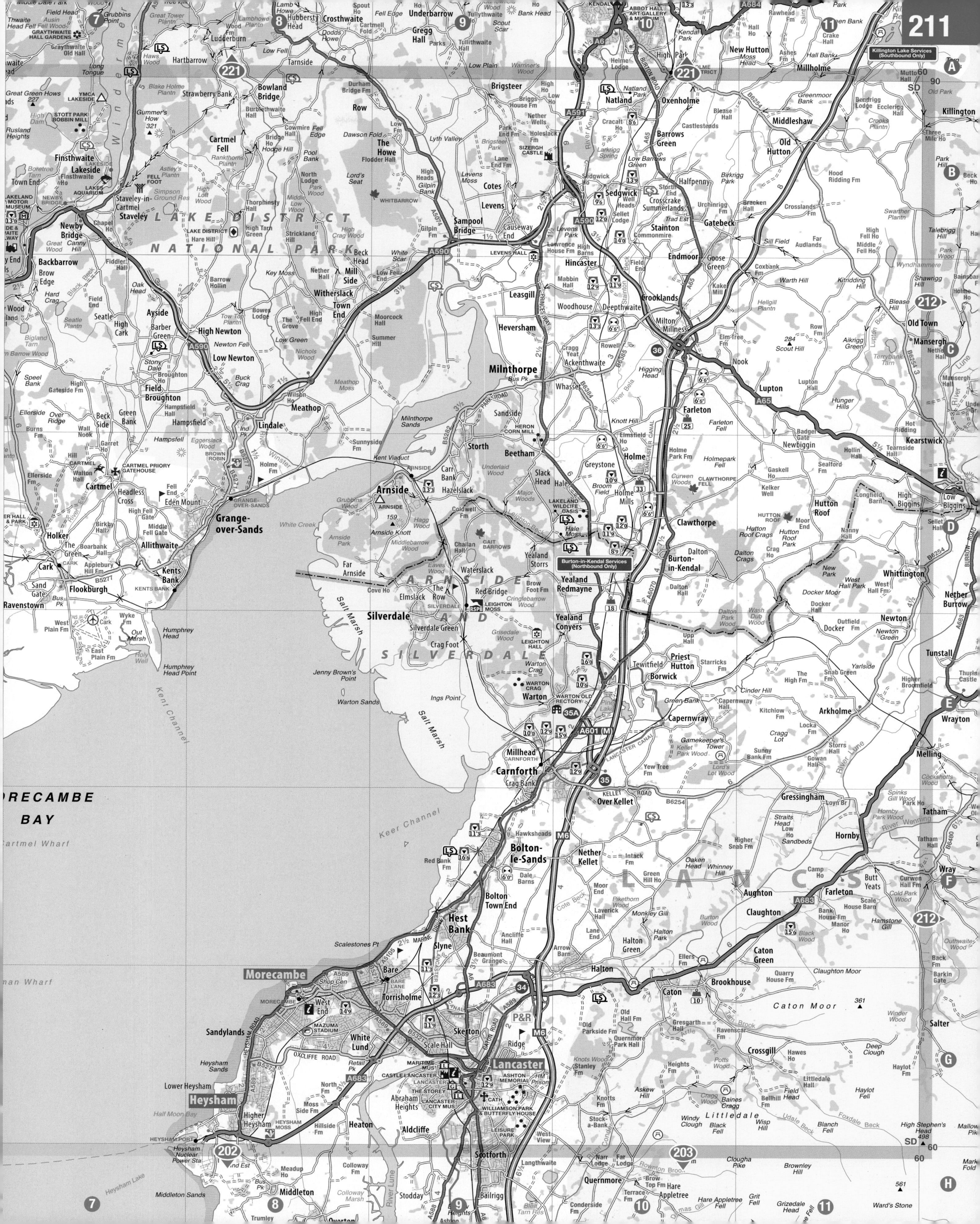
Killington Lake Services (Southbound Only)
Burton-in-Kendal Services (Northbound Only)
LAKE DISTRICT NATIONAL PARK
ARNSIDE AND SILVERDALE
MORECAMBE BAY
LANCS
Kendal
Natland
Oxenholme
New Hutton
Millholme
Killington
Middleshaw
Old Hutton
Barrows Green
Sedgwick
Halfpenny
Stainton
Gatebeck
Endmoor
Hincaster
Crooklands
Milton
Heversham
Milnthorpe
Lupton
Farleton
Kearstwick
Newbiggin
Holme
Beetham
Storth
Sandside
Arnside
Hutton Roof
Clawthorpe
Burton-in-Kendal
Whittington
Newton
Tunstall
Yealand Redmayne
Yealand Conyers
Silverdale
Priest Hutton
Borwick
Warton
Capernwray
Arkholme
Wrayton
Melling
Carnforth
Over Kellet
Gressingham
Hornby
Tatham
Wray
Bolton-le-Sands
Nether Kellet
Aughton
Farleton
Claughton
Caton Green
Hest Bank
Slyne
Halton
Brookhouse
Caton
Caton Moor
Morecambe
Bare
Torrisholme
Skerton
Sandylands
White Lund
Lancaster
Heysham
Lower Heysham
Aldcliffe
Scotforth
Quernmore
Middleton
Crossgill
Salter
Grange-over-Sands
Kents Bank
Allithwaite
Flookburgh
Cark
Holker
Cartmel
Lindale
Meathop
Field Broughton
Ayside
High Newton
Low Newton
Witherslack
Levens
Cotes
Sampool Bridge
Brigsteer
Underbarrow
Crosthwaite
Cartmel Fell
Bowland Bridge
Staveley-in-Cartmel
Newby Bridge
Lakeside
Finsthwaite
Backbarrow
Ravenstown
Humphrey Head
Kent Channel
Keer Channel
Salt Marsh
A590
A591
A65
A6
A601(M)
A683
A589
M6
221
212
202
203

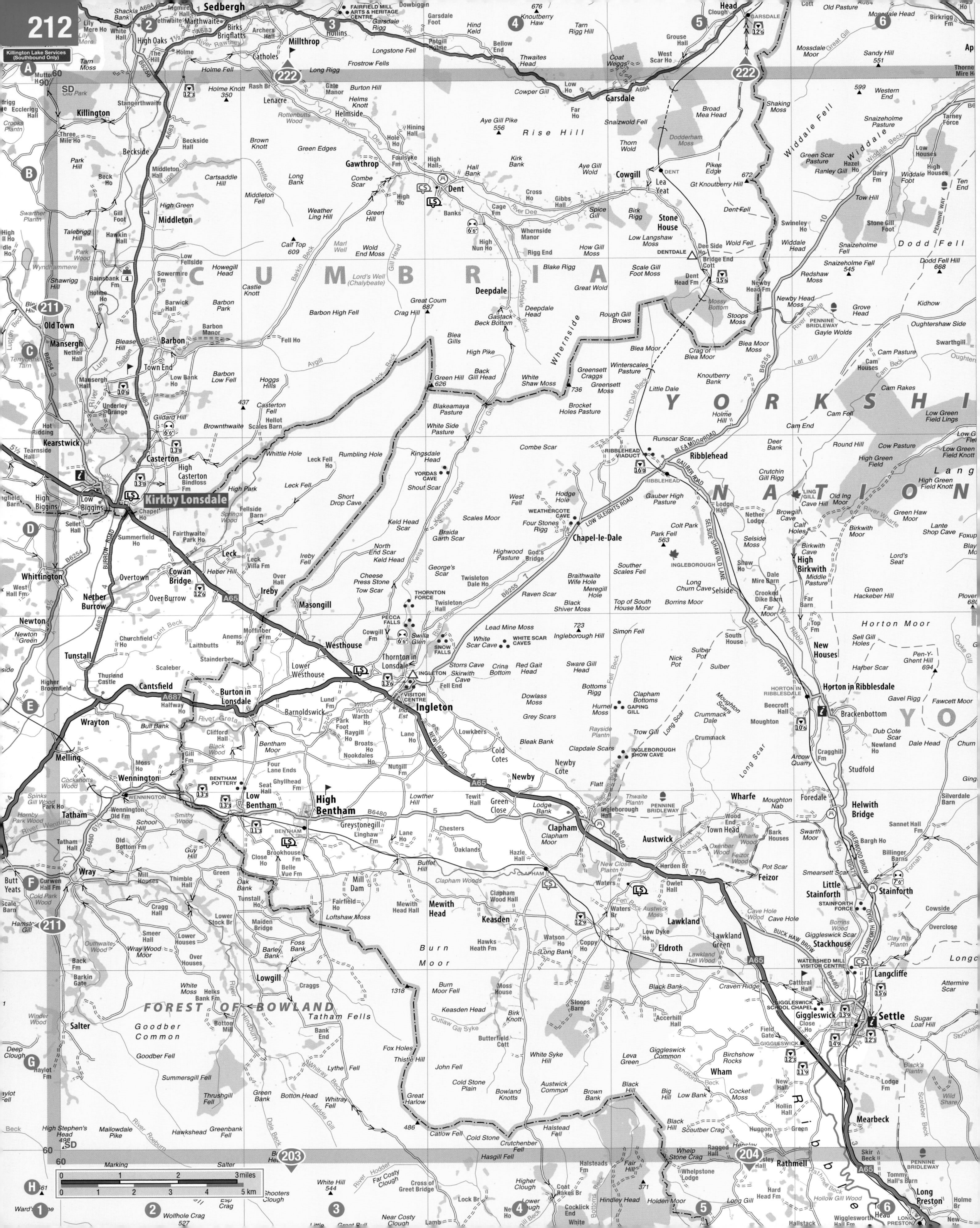
212
Killington Lake Services (Southbound Only)
Sedbergh
Shackla Bank
Marthwaite
Birks
Brigflatts
Archers Hall
Millthrop
Hollins
FAIRFIELD MILL ARTS & HERITAGE CENTRE
Dowbiggin
Garsdale Rigg
Garsdale Foot
Hind Keld
Knoutberry Haw
Tarn Rigg Hill
Head
Clough
GARSDALE
Old Pasture
Mossdale Head
Birkrigg Fm
High Oaks
Holme
Catholes
Longstone Fell
Potgill Holme
Bellow End
Thwaites Head
Coat Weggs
Grouse Hall
West Scar Ho
Mossdale Moor
Sandy Hill 551
Tarn Moss
Holme Fell
Frostrow Fells
Long Rigg
Holme Knott 350
Rash Br
Gate Manor
Burton Hill
Cowper Gill
Low Ho
Garsdale
Western End
Killington
Stangerthwaite
Lenacre
Helms Knott
Helmside
Rottenbutts Wood
Aye Gill Pike 556
Rise Hill
Far Ho
Snaizwold Fell
Broad Mea Head
Shaking Moss
Widdale Fell
Snaizeholme Pasture
Tarney Force
Three Mile Ho
Beckside Hall
Brown Knott
Green Edges
Hining Hall
Hole Ho
Thorn Wold
Dodderham Moss
Green Scar Pasture
Widdale
Beckside
Park Hill
Gawthrop
Foulsyke Fm
High Hall
Hall Bank
Kirk Bank
Aye Gill Wold
Cowgill
Pikes Edge
Ranley Gill
Hazel Ho
Low Houses
High Houses
Middleton Hall
Cartsaddle Hill
Long Bank
Combe Scar
Dent
Lea Yeat
Gt Knoutberry Hill
Dairy Fm
Widdale Foot
Ten End
Beck Ho
Middleton Fell
Weather Ling Hill
Green Hill
High Ho
Banks
Cross Ho
Gibbs Hall
Spice Gill
Birk Rigg
Stone House
Dent Fell
Tow Hill
High Green
Middleton
Cage Fm
River Dee
Swineley Ho
Stone Gill Foot
Gill Foot
Talebrigg Hill
Hawkin Hall
Calf Top 609
Marl Well
Wold End Moss
High Nun Ho
Whernside Manor
Low Langshaw Moss
Wold Fell
Widdale Head
Snaizeholme Fell
Dodd Fell
Park Wood
Low Fellside
Rigg End
How Gill Moss
DENTDALE
Dee Side Ho
Bridge End Cott
Snaizeholme Fell 545
Dodd Fell Hill 668
Shawrigg Hill
Bainsbank Fm
Sowermire Fm
Howegill Head
CUMBRIA
Lord's Well (Chalybeate)
Blake Rigg
Scale Gill Foot Moss
Dent Head Fm
Redshaw Moss
Holme Ho
Castle Knott
Deepdale
Great Wold
Newby Head Fm
Barwick Hall
Barbon Park
Great Coum 687
Crag Hill
Deepdale Head
Mossy Bottom
Newby Head Moss
Grove Head
Kidhow
Old Town
Mansergh
Barbon High Fell
Gastack Beck Bottom
Rough Gill Brows
Stoops Moss
PENNINE BRIDLEWAY
Gayle Wolds
Oughtershaw Side
Nether Hall
Blease Hill
Barbon Manor
Barbon
Fell Ho
Blea Gills
Whernside
Blea Moor
Crag of Blea Moor
Blea Moor Moss
Swarthgill
Town End
Aygill
High Pike
Cam Pasture
Cam Houses
Low Bank Ho
Barbon Low Fell
Hoggs Hills
Green Hill 626
Back Gill Head
White Shaw Moss
Greensett Craggs
Greensett Moss
Winterscales Pasture
Little Dale
Knoutberry Bank
Cam Rakes
Underley Grange
437
Casterton Fell
Blakeamaya Pasture
736
Brocket Holes Pasture
YORKSHIRE
Holme Hill
Cam Fell
Low Green Field Lings
Gildard Hill
Hellot Scales Barn
Hot Ridding
Brownthwaite
White Side Pasture
Cam End
Kearstwick
Casterton
Whittle Hole
Rumbling Hole
Kingsdale Head
Combe Scar
Runscar Scar
BLEA MOOR ROAD
RIBBLEHEAD VIADUCT
Ribblehead
Deer Bank
Round Hill
Cow Pasture
Low Green Field Knott
Leck Fell Ho
YORDAS CAVE
High Casterton
Bindloss Fm
Leck Fell
Shout Scar
RIBBLEHEAD
High Green Field
Crutchin Gill Rigg
High Green Field Knott
Low Biggins
High Biggins
Kirkby Lonsdale
Chapel Ho
High Park
Short Drop Cave
West Fell
Hodge Hole
WEATHERCOTE CAVE
Gauber High Pasture
LING GILL
Old Ing Moor
NATIONAL
Fellside Barn
Springs Wood
Scales Moor
Keld Head Scar
Four Stones Rigg
Lodge Hall
Nether Lodge
Browgill Cave
Green Haw Moor
Lante Shop Cave
Sellet Hall
Summerfield Ho
Fairthwaite Park Ho
Braida Garth Scar
LOW SLEIGHTS ROAD
Chapel-le-Dale
Colt Park
Calf Holes
Birkwith Moor
BURTON ROAD
North End Scar
Keld Head
Park Fell 563
Selside Moss
Birkwith Cave
Whittington
Leck
Leck Villa Fm
Ireby Fell
Highwood Pasture
God's Bridge
INGLEBOROUGH
SELSIDE SHAW OLD LANE
Lord's Seat
Overtown
Cowan Bridge
George's Scar
Shaw Ho
High Birkwith
Middle Pasture
West Hall Fm
Heber Hill
Over Hall
Cheese Press Stone
Tow Scar
Twisleton Dale Ho
Braithwaite Wife Hole
Meregill Hole
Southerscales Fell
Long Churn Cave
Dale Mire Barn
Selside
Green Hackeber Hill
Nether Burrow
Over Burrow
Ireby
THORNTON FORCE
Raven Scar
Black Shiver Moss
Top of South House Moor
Borrins Moor
Crooked Dike Barn
Far Barn
Masongill
Twisleton Hall
Far Moor
Horton Moor
Newton
Newton Green
PECCA FALLS
Lead Mine Moss
723
Ingleborough Hill
Simon Fell
Top Fm
Sell Gill Holes
Churchfield Ho
Anems Ho
Moffinber Fm
Cowgill Fm
Swilla Glen
SNOW FALLS
White Scar Cave
WHITE SCAR CAVES
South House
Sulber Pot
New Houses
Pen-Y-Ghent Hill 694
Laithbutts
Westhouse
Tunstall
Scaleber
Stainderber
Thornton in Lonsdale
Storrs Cave
Skirwith Cave
Crina Bottom
Red Gait Head
Sware Gill Head
Nick Pot
Sulber
Harber Scar
Thurland Castle
Lower Westhouse
INGLETON
VISITOR CENTRE
Fell End
Horton in Ribblesdale
Gavel Rigg
Fawcett Moor
Higher Broomfield
Cantsfield
Burton in Lonsdale
Lund Fm
Bottoms Rigg
Clapham Bottoms
GAPING GILL
Beecroft Hall
HORTON IN RIBBLESDALE
Halfway Ho
Barnoldswick
Ingleton
Dowlass Moss
Hurnel Moss
Brackenbottom
Wrayton
Bull Bank
River Greta
Park Foot
Wilson Wood
Warth Ho
Ind Est
Lowkbers
Grey Scars
Crummack Dale
Moughton
Dub Cote Scar
Newland Ho
Dale Head
Clifford Hall
Black Wood
Bentham Moor
Raygill Ho
Broats Ho
Nookdales Ho
Lane Ho
Cold Cotes
Bleak Bank
Rayside Plantn
Trow Gill
Long Scar
Crummack
Cragghill Fm
Melling
Moss Ho
Gill Fm
Four Lane Ends
Ghyllhead Fm
Nutgill Fm
Clapdale Scars
INGLEBOROUGH SHOW CAVE
Arcow Quarry
Studfold
Wennington
Cockshotts Wood
BENTHAM POTTERY
Seat Hall
Newby
Newby Cote
Flatt
Spinks Gill Wood
WENNINGTON
Low Bentham
High Bentham
Lowther Hill
Tewit Hall
Green Close
Lodge Bank
Thwaite Plantn
PENNINE BRIDLEWAY
Wharfe
Moughton Nab
Foredale
Silverdale Barn
Helwith Bridge
Hornby Park Wood
Park Ho
Tatham
Wennington Old Fm
Smithy Wood
School Hill
River Wenning
Greystonegill
BENTHAM
Chesters
Clapham
Ingleborough Hall
Wood End
Town Head
Wharfe Wood
Bark Houses
Austwick
Swarth Moor
Sannet Hall Fm
Tatham Hall
Old Bottom Fm
Linghaw Fm
Lane Ho
Oaklands
Clapham Moor
Hazle Hall
Oxenber Wood
Feizor Wood
Bargh Ho
Guy Hill
Close Ho
Brookhouse Fm
Belle Vue Fm
Buffet Hill
CLAPHAM
New Close Plantn
Harden Br
Pot Scar
Billinger Barns
Wray
Thimble Hall
Green
Mill Dam
Clapham Woods
Waters
Owlet Hall
Feizor
Smearsett Scar
Little Stainforth
Stainforth
Butt Yeats
Curwen Hall Fm
Cold Park Wood
Mill Houses
Oak Bank
Tunstall Ho
Fairfield Ho
Clapham Wood Hall
Mewith Head Hall
Mewith Head
Keasden
Waters Br
Austwick Moss
Lawkland
Cave Hole Wood
Cave Hole
STAINFORTH FORCE
Cowside
Cragg Hall
Lower Stock Br
Loftshaw Moss
Maiden Bridge
Hawks Heath Fm
Lawkland Green
Borrins Wood
Giggleswick Scar
Overclose
Smeer Hall
Lower Houses
Outhwaite Wood
Wray Wood Moor
Barley Bank
Foss Bank
Burn Moor
Watson Ho
Long Bank
Coppy Ho
Low Dyke Ho
Eldroth
Lawkland Hall Wood
BUCK HAW BROW
Stackhouse
Clay Pits Plantn
Over Houses
Back Fm
Barkin Gate
WATERSHED MILL VISITOR CENTRE
Langcliffe
White Moss
Helks Bank Fm
Lowgill
Craggs
1318
Burn Moor Fell
Moss House
Black Bank
Craven Ridge
Catteral Hall
Attermire Scar
FOREST OF BOWLAND
Tatham Fells
Keasden Head
Stoops Barn
Accerhill Hall
GIGGLESWICK SCHOOL CHAPEL
Giggleswick
Settle
Sugar Loaf Hill
Winder Wood
Salter
Goodber Common
Bottom Mill
Bank End
Outlaw Gill Syke
Birk Knott
Butterfield Cott
Field Gate
Close Ho
SETTLE
GIGGLESWICK
Deep Clough
Haylot Fm
Goodber Fell
Fox Holes
Thistle Hill
White Syke Hill
Leva Green
Giggleswick Common
Birchshow Rocks
Black's Plantn
Lythe Fell
John Fell
Wham
Lodge Fell
Summersgill Fell
Cold Stone Plain
Bowland Knotts
Austwick Common
Brown Bank
Black Hill
Big Hill
Low Bank
Cocket Moss
New Hall
Wild Share
Thrushgill Fell
Green Bank
Botton Head
Whitray Fell
Great Harlow
Hollin Hall
Mearbeck
High Stephen's Head 498
Mailowdale Pike
Hawkshead
Greenbank Fell
Dale Beck
486
Catlow Fell
Cold Stone
Halstead Fell
Black Hill
Scoutber Crag
Huggon Ho
Crutchenber Fell
Hasgill Fell
Whelp Stone Crag
Ragged Hall
Rathmell
Skir Beck
PENNINE BRIDLEWAY
Marking
Salter
White Hill 544
Far Costy Clough
Cross of Greet Bridge
Higher Clough
Halsteads Fm
Fair Hill
371
Whelpstone Lodge
Hard Head Fm
Tommy Hall's Barn
Long Preston
Shooters Clough
Esp Crag
Wolfhole Crag 527
Lock Br
Lower Clough
Coat Rakes Br
Cockiick End
Hindley Head
Holden Moor
Long Gill
Hollow Gill Wood
Wigglesworth Hall Fm
Near Costy Clough
Ribble
0 1 2 3 miles
0 1 2 3 4 5 km

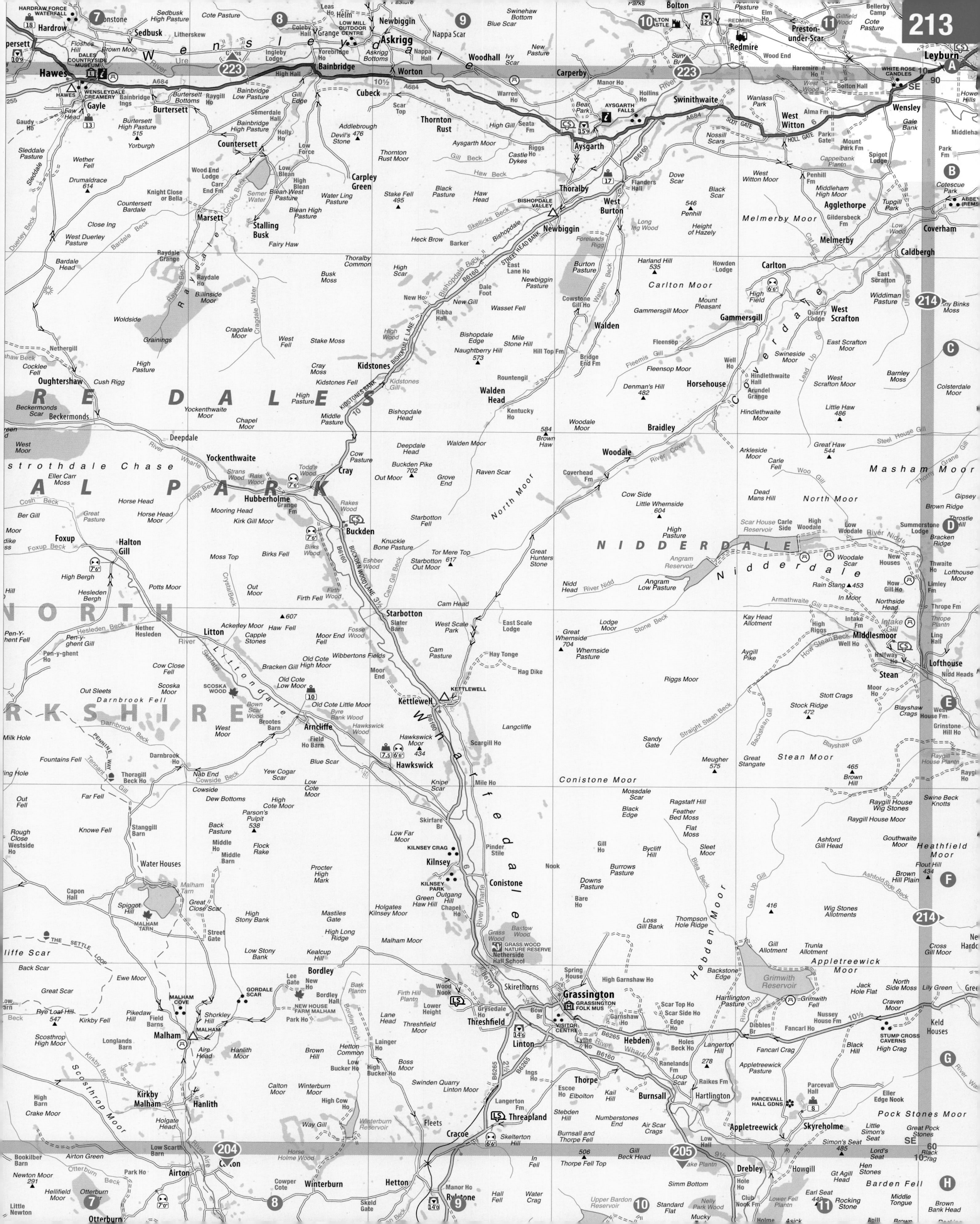
HARDRAW FORCE WATERFALL
Hardrow
Sedbusk
Sedbusk High Pasture
Cote Pasture
Litherskew
Helm
LOW MILL OUTDOOR CENTRE
Newbiggin
Askrigg
Nappa Scar
Swinehaw Bottom
Blue Scar
Bolton
Redmire
Preston-under-Scar
Bellerby Camp
Cote Pasture
Leyburn
Hawes
DALES COUNTRYSIDE MUSEUM
WENSLEYDALE CREAMERY
Gayle
Burtersett
Bainbridge
Bainbridge Ings
Bainbridge Low Pasture
Worton
Cubeck
Woodhall
Ivy Scar
New Pasture
Carperby
Manor Ho
Hollins Ho
Swinithwaite
Wanlass Park
West Witton
Wensley
WHITE ROSE CANDLES
Wensleydale
Ure
River Ure
A684
223
Semerdale Hall
Countersett
Addlebrough
476
Devil's Stone
Thornton Rust
High Gill
Seata Fm
Aysgarth
AYSGARTH FALLS
Bear Park
Nossill Scars
Alma Fm
Mount Park Fm
Spigot Lodge
Gale Bank
Thornton Rust Moor
Aysgarth Moor
Castle Dykes
Riggs Ho
Gill Beck
Haw Beck
B6160
Thoralby
Flanders Hall
Dove Scar
West Witton Moor
Penhill Fm
Middleham High Moor
Agglethorpe
Tupgill Park
Cotescue Park
Sleddale
Sleddale Pasture
Wether Fell
Drumaldrace
614
Knight Close or Bella
Countersett Bardale
Marsett
Semer Water
Stalling Busk
Carpley Green
Stake Fell
495
Black Pasture
Haw Head
BISHOPDALE VALLEY
West Burton
Newbiggin
Black Scar
546
Penhill
Height of Hazely
Melmerby Moor
Gildersbeck Fm
Melmerby
Coverham
Caldbergh
Close Ing
West Duerley Pasture
Bardale Beck
Fairy Haw
Heck Brow
Barker
Bishopdale
Forelands Rigg
Harland Hill
535
Howden Lodge
Carlton
Carlton Moor
Raydale Grange
Bardale Head
Raydale
Billinside Moor
Busk Moss
Thoralby Common
High Scar
Burton Pasture
East Lane Ho
Dale Foot
Newbiggin Pasture
New Ho
New Gill
Wasset Fell
Mount Pleasant
Gammersgill Moor
Gammersgill
High Field
East Scrafton
Widdiman Pasture
West Scrafton
Quarry Lodge
Woldside
Cragdale Moor
Grainings
Cragdale Water
West Fell
Stake Moss
Ribba Hall
High Wood
Bishopdale Edge
Mile Stone Hill
Naughtberry Hill
573
Hill Top Fm
Cowstone Gill Ho
Walden
Bridge End Fm
Fleensop
Fleensop Moor
Swineside Moor
Hindlethwaite Hall
Arundel Grange
Horsehouse
Coverdale
East Scrafton Moor
West Scrafton Moor
Barnley Moss
Colsterdale Moor
Nethergill
Cockle Fell
High Pasture
Cush Rigg
Oughtershaw
Cray Moss
Kidstones
Kidstones Fell
Rountengill
Walden Head
Denman's Hill
482
Little Haw
486
BECKERMONDS
Beckermonds Scar
Beckermonds
Yockenthwaite Moor
Chapel Moor
High Pasture
Middle Pasture
Bishopdale Head
Kentucky Ho
Woodale Moor
584
Brown Haw
Braidley
Hindlethwaite Moor
Deepdale
West Moor
Yockenthwaite
Deepdale Head
Walden Moor
Woodale
Arkleside Moor
Carle Fell
Great Haw
544
Langstrothdale Chase
Eller Carr Moss
Strans Wood
Rais Wood
Todd's Wood
Cow Pasture
Cray
Buckden Pike
702
Out Moor
Grove End
Raven Scar
Coverhead Fm
River Cover
Masham Moor
Cosh Beck
Hubberholme
Grange Fm
Horse Head
Horse Head Moor
Mooring Head
Kirk Gill Moor
Great Pasture
Ber Gill
Rakes Wood
Buckden
Starbotton Fell
North Moor
Cow Side
Little Whernside
604
Dead Mans Hill
North Moor
Ilton Moor
Gipsey
Brown Ridge
Foxup
Halton Gill
Foxup Beck
Moss Top
Birks Fell
Birks Wood
Knuckle Bone Pasture
Starbotton Out Moor
Tor Mere Top
617
Great Hunters Stone
High Pasture
NIDDERDALE
Angram Reservoir
Scar House Reservoir
Carle Side
High Woodale
Low Woodale
Woodale Scar
New Houses
Thwaite Ho
Lofthouse Moor
High Bergh
Hesleden Bergh
Potts Moor
Crystal Beck
Out Moor
Esher Wood
Cam Gill Beck
Firth Fell
Firth Wood
Nidd Head
River Nidd
Angram Low Pasture
Nidderdale
Rain Stang
453
In Moor
How Gill Ho
Limley Fm
NORTH
Pen-y-ghent Fell
Pen-y-ghent Gill
Pen-y-ghent Ho
Nether Hesleden
Hesleden Beck
Litton
Ackerley Moor
Haw Fell
607
Capple Stones
Moor End Fell
Fosse Wood
Starbotton
Slater Barn
Cam Head
West Scale Park
East Scale Lodge
Lodge Moor
Great Whernside
704
Whernside Pasture
Kay Head Allotment
Armathwaite Gill
Northside Head
Intake Fm
High Riggs
Middlesmoor
Thrope Fm
Ling Hall
Cow Close Fell
Scoska Moor
SCOSKA WOOD
Littondale
Bracken Gill
Old Cote High Moor
Wibbertons Fields
Cam Pasture
Hay Tonge
Hag Dike
Aygill Pike
How Stean Beck
Well Ho
Halfway Ho
Lofthouse
Stean
Nidd Heads
Out Sleets
Darnbrook Fell
YORKSHIRE
Old Cote Low Moor
Old Cote Little Moor
Byre Bank Wood
Moor End
Kettlewell
KETTLEWELL
Riggs Moor
Stott Crags
Stock Ridge
472
Blayshaw Crags
West House Fm
Grinstone Hill Ho
Milk Hole
Darnbrook Beck
West Moor
Brootes Barn
Arncliffe
Hawkswick Wood
Field Ho Barn
Hawkswick Moor
434
Scargill Ho
Langcliffe
Sandy Gate
Straight Stean Beck
Backstean Gill
Blayshaw Gill
Fountains Fell
PENNINE WAY
Darnbrook Ho
Tennant Gill
Thoragill Beck Ho
Nab End
Cowside Beck
Yew Cogar Scar
Blue Scar
Hawkswick
Knipe Scar
Mile Ho
Conistone Moor
Meugher
575
Great Stangate
Stean Moor
465
Brown Hill
Raygill House Plantn
Cowside
Dew Bottoms
Low Cote Moor
Out Fell
Far Fell
High Cote Moor
Parson's Pulpit
538
Mossdale Scar
Black Edge
Ragstaff Hill
Feather Bed Moss
Flat Moss
Raygill House Wig Stones
Raygill House Moor
Swine Beck Knotts
Rough Close Westside Ho
Knowe Fell
Stanggill Barn
Back Pasture
Middle Ho
Middle Barn
Flock Rake
Skirfare Br
Low Far Moor
KILNSEY CRAG
Kilnsey
Wharfedale
Pinder Stile
Nook
Gill Ho
Bycliff Hill
Sleet Moor
Ashford Gill Head
Gouthwaite Moor
Heathfield Moor
Water Houses
Procter High Mark
KILNSEY PARK
Burrows Pasture
Downs Pasture
Flout Hill
434
Brown Hill Plain
Ashfold Side Beck
Capon Hall
Malham Tarn
Spiggot Hill
MALHAM TARN
Great Close Scar
High Stony Bank
Mastiles Gate
Holgates Kilnsey Moor
Green Haw Hill
Outgang Hill
Chapel Ho
Conistone
River Wharfe
Bare Ho
Gate Up Gill
416
Loss Gill Bank
Thompson Hole Ridge
Hebden Moor
Wig Stones Allotments
THE SETTLE LOOP
Street Gate
High Long Ridge
Malham Moor
Grass Wood
Bastow Wood
GRASS WOOD NATURE RESERVE
Netherside Hall School
Gill Allotment
Trunla Allotment
Appletreewick Moor
Cross Gill Moor
Back Scar
Low Stony Bank
Kealcup Hill
Bordley
Ewe Moor
Lee Gate
New Ho
Bark Plantn
Wood Nook
Skirethorns
Spring House
High Garnshaw Ho
Backstone Edge
Grimwith Reservoir
Jack Hole Flat
North Side Moss
Lily Green
Great Scar
MALHAM COVE
GORDALE SCAR
Bordley Hall
NEW HOUSE FARM MALHAM
Firth Hill Plantn
Lower Height
Grysedale Ho
Grassington
GRASSINGTON FOLK MUS
Scar Top Ho
Scar Side Ho
Hartlington Pasture
Grimwith Fell
Nussey House Fm
Craven Moor
Rye Loaf Hill
547
Pikedaw Hill
Field Barns
Shorkley Hill
MALHAM
Park Ho
Lane Head
Threshfield Moor
Threshfield
Bow Br
VISITOR CENTRE
Garnshaw Ho
Edge Ho
Dibbles Br
Fancarl Ho
STUMP CROSS CAVERNS
Keld Houses
Kirkby Fell
Scosthrop High Moor
Longlands Barn
Malham
Aire Head
Hanlith Moor
Brown Hill
Hetton Common
Lainger Ho
Linton
B6265
Hebden
Holes Beck Ho
Langerton Hill
Fancarl Crag
Black Hill
High Crag
Kirkby Beck
Scosthrop Moor
Low Bucker Ho
High Bucker Ho
Boss Moor
Swinden Quarry
Linton Moor
Ings Ho
Thorpe
Ranelands Fm
Loup Scar
278
Raikes Fm
Appletreewick Pasture
High Barn
Kirkby Malham
Hanlith
Calton Moor
Winterburn Moor
High Cow Ho
Escoe Ho
Elbolton
Kail Hill
Burnsall
Hartlington
PARCEVALL HALL GDNS
Parcevall Hall
Eller Edge Nook
Crake Moor
Holgate Head
Way Gill
Winterburn Reservoir
Fleets
Langerton Fm
Threapland
Stebden Hill
Numberstones End
Air Scar Crags
Burnsall and Thorpe Fell
Appletreewick
Skyreholme
Little Simon's Seat
Pock Stones Moor
Great Pock Stones Moor
Simon's Seat
485
Bookilber Barn
Airton Green
Low Scarth Barn
Cracoe
Skelterton Hill
506
Thorpe Fell Top
Gill Beck Head
Low Hall
Lord's Seat
Black Crag
Newton Moor
291
Park Ho
Airton
Calton
River Aire
204
Horse Holme Wood
In Fell
205
Drebley
Howgill
Gt Agill Head
Hen Stones
Barden Fell
Hellifield Moor
Otterburn Beck
Otterburn
Cowper Cote
Winterburn
Hetton
Manor Ho
Rylstone
Hall Fell
Water Crag
Upper Bardon Reservoir
Standard Flat
Nelly Park Wood
Simm Bottom
Club Nook Fm
Lower Fell Plantn
Earl Seat
Rocking Stone
Middle Tongue
Brown Bank Head
Little Newton
Skeld Gate
Mucky
214
A
B
C
D
E
F
G
H
7
8
9
10
11

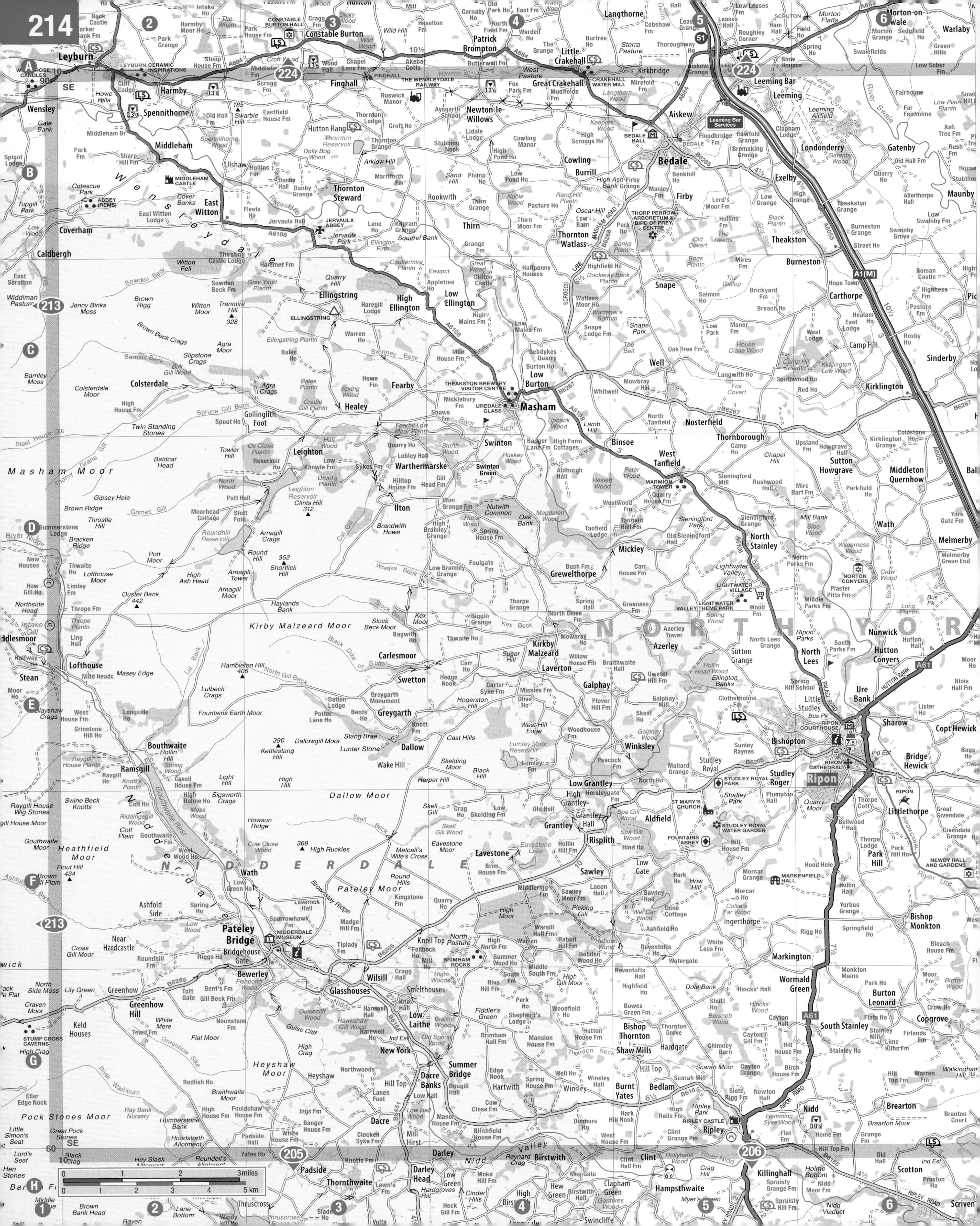

Leyburn
Constable Burton
Patrick Brompton
Langthorne
Morton-on-Swale
Warlaby
Harmby
Finghall
Great Crakehall
Little Crakehall
Kirkbridge
Leeming Bar
Leeming
Wensley
Spennithorne
Newton-le-Willows
Aiskew
Middleham
Thornton Steward
Bedale
Londonderry
Gatenby
Cowling
Burrill
Firby
Exelby
East Witton
Coverham
Rookwith
Thirn
Thornton Watlass
Theakston
Burneston
Caldbergh
Snape
Carthorpe
Ellingstring
High Ellington
Low Ellington
Sinderby
Colsterdale
Fearby
Healey
Masham
Low Burton
Well
Kirklington
Swinton
Nosterfield
Binsoe
West Tanfield
Thornborough
Leighton
Warthermarske
Sutton Howgrave
Middleton Quernhow
Masham Moor
Ilton
Wath
Melmerby
North Stainley
Mickley
Grewelthorpe
Kirby Malzeard Moor
Azerley
Nunwick
Hutton Conyers
North Lees
Kirkby Malzeard
Laverton
Carlesmoor
Swetton
Galphay
Lofthouse
Stean
Ure Bank
Sharow
Copt Hewick
Greygarth
Dallow
Winksley
Bishopton
Ripon
Bouthwaite
Ramsgill
Bridge Hewick
Studley Roger
Low Grantley
High Grantley
Grantley
Aldfield
Littlethorpe
Dallow Moor
Risplith
Sawley
Eavestone
Nidderdale
Wath
Pateley Moor
Bishop Monkton
Pateley Bridge
Markington
Wormald Green
Bewerley
Wilsill
Glasshouses
Greenhow
Greenhow Hill
Low Laithe
South Stainley
Copgrove
Burton Leonard
New York
Summer Bridge
Bishop Thornton
Shaw Mills
Heyshaw Moor
Dacre Banks
Hartwith
Winsley
Burnt Yates
Bedlam
Nidd
Brearton
Pock Stones Moor
Dacre
Ripley
Darley
Birstwith
Clint
Padside
Darley Head
Killinghall
Scotton
Thornthwaite
Hampsthwaite
Scriven
NORTH YOR
A1(M)
A61
A6108
A684
B6265
B6267
224
213
205
206
0 1 2 3 miles
0 1 2 3 4 5 km

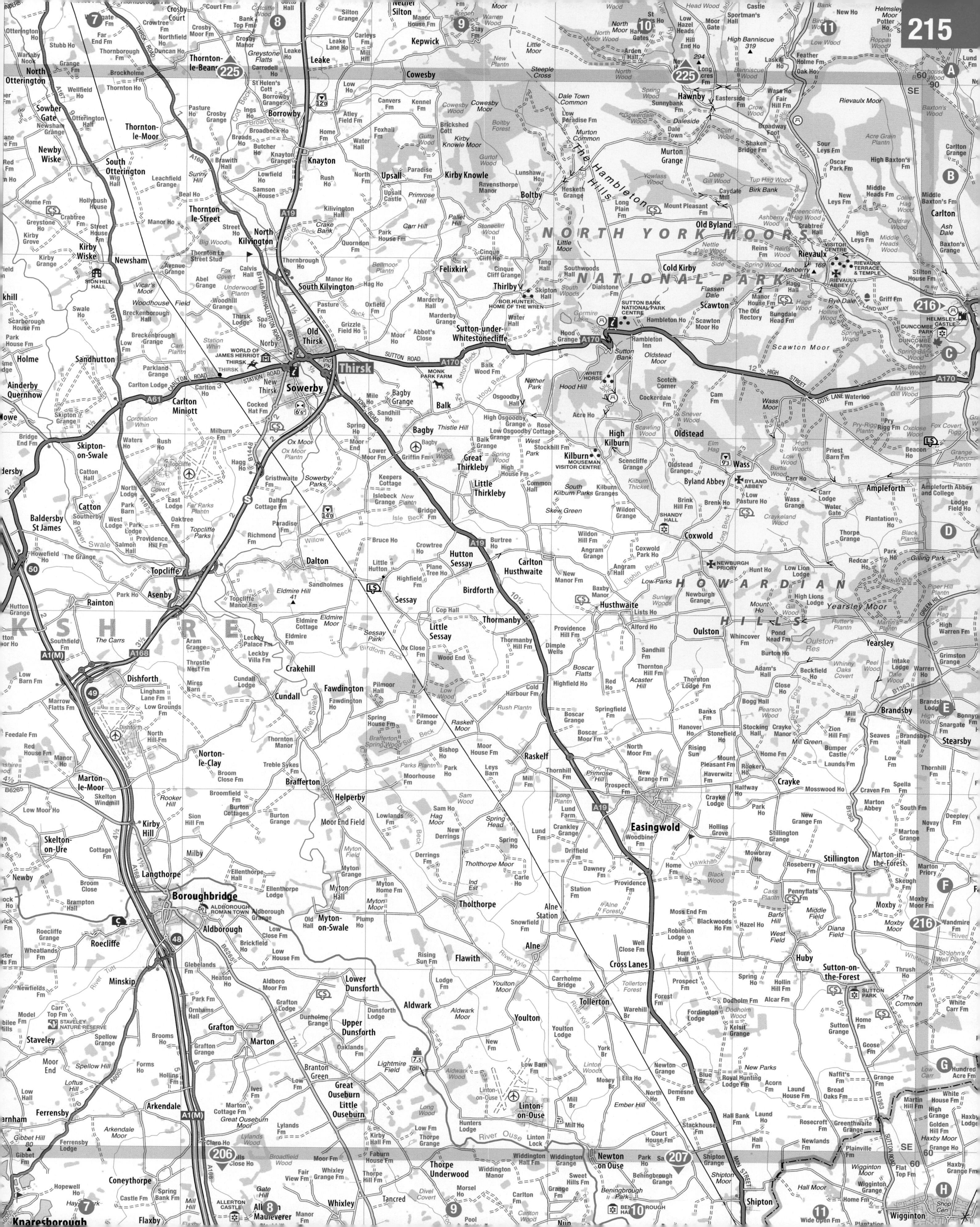
NORTH YORK MOORS
NATIONAL PARK
HOWARDIAN HILLS
The Hambleton Hills
YORKSHIRE
Thirsk
Sowerby
Old Thirsk
Easingwold
Boroughbridge
Aldborough
Thornton-le-Beans
North Otterington
South Otterington
Thornton-le-Moor
Thornton-le-Street
North Kilvington
South Kilvington
Newby Wiske
Kirby Wiske
Newsham
Sowber Gate
Sandhutton
Carlton Miniott
Skipton-on-Swale
Catton
Baldersby St James
Topcliffe
Asenby
Rainton
Dishforth
Cundall
Norton-le-Clay
Marton le Moor
Kirby Hill
Langthorpe
Milby
Roecliffe
Minskip
Staveley
Ferrensby
Arkendale
Grafton
Marton
Coneythorpe
Knaresborough
Flaxby
Allerton Mauleverer
Leake
Cowesby
Borrowby
Knayton
Kepwick
Upsall
Kirby Knowle
Boltby
Felixkirk
Thirlby
Sutton-under-Whitestonecliffe
Sutton Bank
Hawnby
Old Byland
Cold Kirby
Rievaulx
Scawton
Murton Grange
Oldstead
High Kilburn
Kilburn
Wass
Byland Abbey
Coxwold
Ampleforth
Husthwaite
Oulston
Yearsley
Brandsby
Stearsby
Crayke
Stillington
Marton-in-the-Forest
Moxby
Huby
Sutton-on-the-Forest
Carlton
Balk
Bagby
Great Thirkleby
Little Thirkleby
Dalton
Hutton Sessay
Sessay
Little Sessay
Carlton Husthwaite
Birdforth
Thormanby
Crakehill
Fawdington
Raskelf
Brafferton
Helperby
Myton-on-Swale
Tholthorpe
Alne
Alne Station
Flawith
Cross Lanes
Tollerton
Aldwark
Youlton
Lower Dunsforth
Upper Dunsforth
Great Ouseburn
Little Ouseburn
Branton Green
Linton-on-Ouse
Newton on Ouse
Thorpe Underwood
Whixley
Tancred
Shipton
Wigginton
River Swale
River Ouse
River Kyle
A1(M)
A19
A61
A168
A170
A167
B1448
B6265
B1363
B1257
SE
60
90
225
216
206
207
A
B
C
D
E
F
G
H
7
8
9
10
11

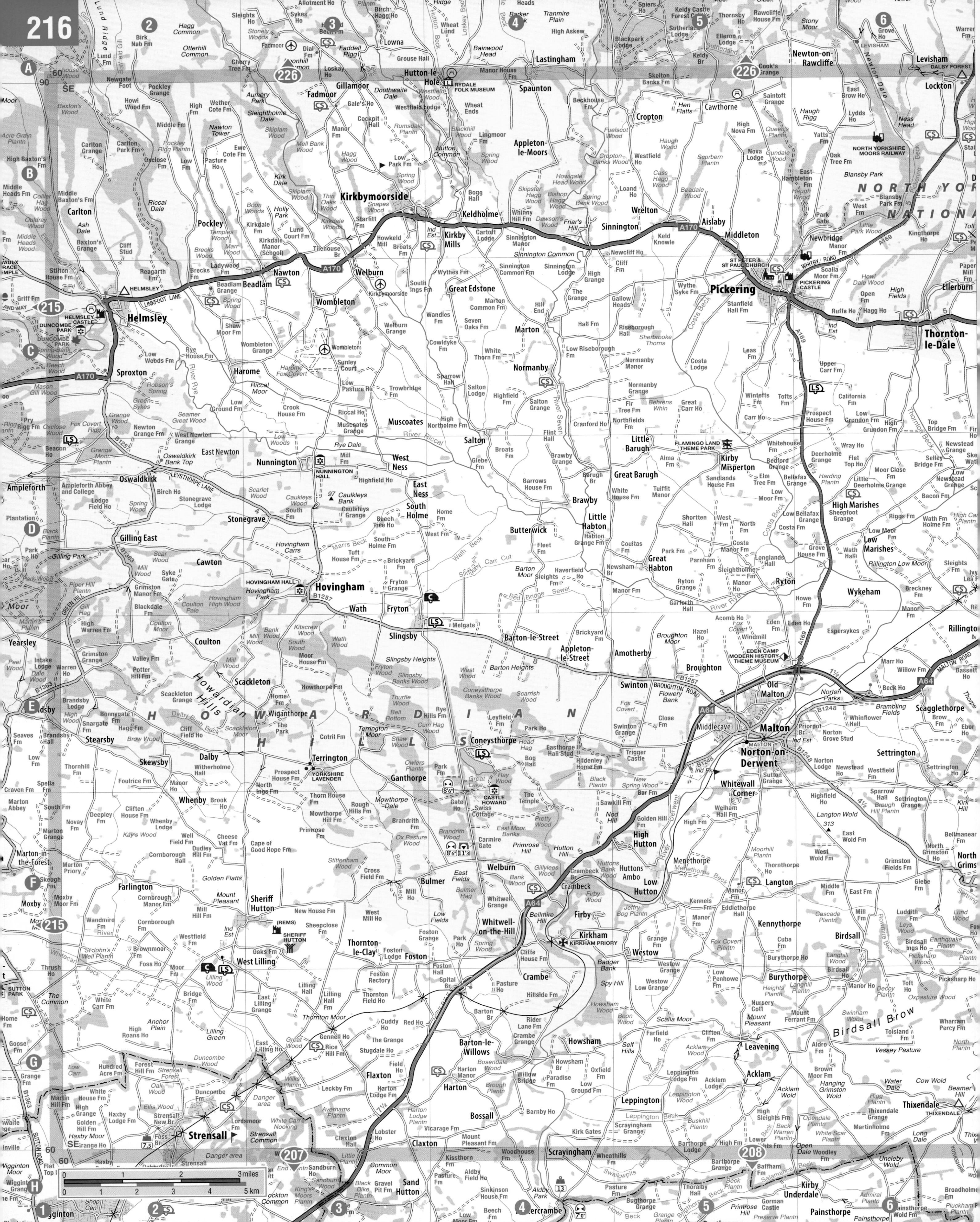

216
226
215
207
208
A170
A169
A64
B1257
B1363
B1248
B1251
Helmsley
Kirkbymoorside
Pickering
Thornton-le-Dale
Malton
Norton-on-Derwent
Old Malton
Hovingham
Strensall
Lastingham
Spaunton
Appleton-le-Moors
Cropton
Sinnington
Aislaby
Middleton
Levisham
Lockton
Newton-on-Rawcliffe
Hutton-le-Hole
RYDALE FOLK MUSEUM
Gillamoor
Fadmoor
Keldholme
Kirkby Mills
Nawton
Beadlam
Wombleton
Welburn
Great Edstone
Marton
Normanby
Salton
Muscoates
Harome
Sproxton
Pockley
Carlton
Oswaldkirk
Ampleforth
Ampleforth Abbey and College
Gilling East
Stonegrave
Nunnington
NUNNINGTON HALL
West Ness
East Ness
South Holme
Cawton
HOVINGHAM HALL
Wath
Fryton
Slingsby
Barton-le-Street
Appleton-le-Street
Amotherby
Swinton
Broughton
Butterwick
Brawby
Little Habton
Great Habton
Little Barugh
Great Barugh
Kirby Misperton
FLAMINGO LAND THEME PARK
High Marishes
Low Marishes
Ryton
Wykeham
Rillington
Scagglethorpe
Settrington
Coulton
Yearsley
Scackleton
Howardian Hills
Terrington
YORKSHIRE LAVENDER
Ganthorpe
Coneysthorpe
CASTLE HOWARD
Dalby
Skewsby
Stearsby
Whenby
Welburn
Bulmer
Sheriff Hutton
SHERIFF HUTTON
Farlington
Marton-in-the-Forest
Moxby
West Lilling
Thornton-le-Clay
Foston
Whitwell-on-the-Hill
Kirkham
KIRKHAM PRIORY
Crambe
Westow
Firby
High Hutton
Low Hutton
Huttons Ambo
Menethorpe
Langton
Kennythorpe
Birdsall
Burythorpe
Leavening
Acklam
Birdsall Brow
Thixendale
THIXENDALE
Howsham
Barton-le-Willows
Harton
Bossall
Flaxton
Claxton
Sand Hutton
Leppington
Scrayingham
Kirby Underdale
Painsthorpe
Whitewall Corner
EDEN CAMP MODERN HISTORY THEME MUSEUM
Middlecave
DUNCOMBE PARK
HELMSLEY CASTLE
ST PETER & ST PAUL CHURCH
PICKERING CASTLE
NORTH YORKSHIRE MOORS RAILWAY
NORTH YORK
NATIONA
DALBY FOREST
SUTTON PARK
0 1 2 3 miles
0 1 2 3 4 5 km

Scarborough
Scalby
Scalby Ness Rocks
West Head Coll
Newby
Scarborough
Sea Life Scarborough
Peasholm Park
Castle Cliff
Scarborough Castle
Rotunda Museum
Old & East Harbours
South Bay
South Sands
Black Rocks
White Nab
Cornelian Bay
Frank Cliff
Osgodby Pt
Cayton Cliff
Cayton Bay
Tenants' Cliff
Yons Nab
Lebberston Cliff
Gristhorpe Cliff
Cunstone Nab
The Wyke
Barrowcliff
Falsgrave
Scarborough Sports Village
Throxenby
Hackness
Suffield
Everley
Broxa
Langdale End
Low Dales
Binkleys Fm
Howden Hill
Keeper's Old Ho
Crosscliff Wood
Bickley Gate Fm
Toll Ho
Side Ho
High House Fm
Stain Dale
Low Pasture Fm
Green Dale
Peathead Rigg
Jingleby Ho
Ebberston Common Fm
Rock House Fm
Troutsdale Moor
Trouts Dale
Wrench Green
Cockrah Foot
Mount Misery
Brompton Moor Ho
Wykeham Forest
Dalby Forest
Thwaite Head
Swair Dale
High Dalby Ho
High Rigg Fm
Seive Dale
Snever Dale
Low Dalby
Broad Head Fm
Givendale Head Fm
Manor Ho
Hern Head Ho
North York Moors Forest Park
North York Moors National Park
Sheepwalk Plantn
Spiker's Hill
Scarwell Wood
Forge Valley Woods
Ruston Cliff Wood
Osborne Lodge
Iron Moor
Riggs Head Fm
East Ayton
West Ayton
The Honey Farm
Ayton Road
Racecourse Road
Weydale Fm
Moor House Fm
Falsgrave Moor Fm
Middle Deepdale
High Deepdale
Oliver's Mount
Irton
Irton Manor
Crossgates
Eastfield
Osgodby
Seamer
Cayton Low Road
Cayton
Mount Pleasant Fm
Redcliffe Fm
Lebberston
Main Street
Gristhorpe
Filey
Newbiggin
Filey Field
Beacon Hill
Lingholm
Killerby Grange
Playdale Farm Park
Lebberston Carr Fm
Magdalen Grange Fm
Carr Ho
Herdborough House Fm
Low Raincliffe Fm
Derwentdale Fm
Seamer Carr Fm
Star Carr Fm
Flixton Carr Plantn
Woodhouse Fm
Flixton
Folkton
Folkton Manor
Staxton
Spital Road
Muston
Muston Grange
Flotmanby Lane
West Flotmanby Wold Fm
Yorkshire Wolds Way
Royal Oak
Hunmanby
Stockendale Fm
Pilmoor Fm
Foxhill Fm
Folkton Ho
Folkton Wold Fm
Humble Bee Fm
Diamond Plantn
Flixton Wold
Willerby
Spital Ho
Staxton Brow
Staxton Wold Fm
Staxton Wold
Binnington Wold Fm
Willerby Wold Fm
Cotton Dale
Danebury Manor
The Camp
North Fordon Fm
High Fordon Fm
Prior Moor
Fordon
North Dale
Cans Dale
South Dale
Canndale Fm
Hunmanby Grange
Field House Fm
Howe Fm
Barf Fm
Vicarage Fm
Dale Fm
Hill Fm
Ganton
Ganton Wold Fm
Ganton Dale
Gantondale Ho
Windle Beck Fm
Bogg Hall
Hay Bridge Fm
River Hertford
Hertford Dale
Robin's Bottom Plantn
Ings Fm
Ings Br
New Ings Plantn
Ings Plantn
Charm Park
Wykeham
Wykeham Abbey
Swan Hill Fm
Wykeham Carr Fm
Ruston Carr Plantn
Gallows Hill
The Park
Scurf Carr Plantns
Hutton Buscel
Bedale Grange
Mount Pleasant
Ruston
Brompton
Brompton-by-Sawdon
Sawdon
Sawdon Dale
Sawdon Heights
Cockmoor Cott
East Moor Fm
Yederick Woods
Wykeham Moor Cotts
North Moor
Wykeham Grange
Kirkgate Lodge
Cote Head
Mount Pleasant Fm
Brompton Dale
Snainton
Ebberston
Allerston
Wilton
Wilton Grange
Pennistone Lane
Ebberston Ings
Carr Ho
White House Fm
Low Hall
Phoenix House Farm
Rye Topping Fm
Lowfield Fm
Derwent House
Woodlands Fm
Snainton Ings Ho
East Carr Ho
Wydale Hall
Mile Bush Fm
Hazel Hall Fm
Chafer Wood
Ebberston Hall
Netherby Dale
Moorsome Fm
Scamridge Fm
Kirk Dale
High Park Fm
Given Dale
Ox Dale
Warren Ho
Sand Dale
Stonygate Moor
Thornton Dale
Wilton Heights Plantn
Willow Grange
Carr House Fm
Rains Fm
Abbey Fm
Newstead Grange
Crake Hall
Marishes Lodge Fm
Yedingham
River Derwent
Whitehall Fm
Middle Flat
Lilac Fm
Field Ho
Yeddingham Cottage Fm
Yeddingham Grange Fm
East Heslerton Carr Ho
Sherburn Cut
East Heslerton Carr
Birch Plantn
Ings Fm
Malton Road
Wath House Fm
Knapton Lodge
Carr House Fm
Ochre Fm
Redcarr Plantn
West Fm
Poplar Fm
Middle Fm
Ochre Plantns
Sand Cotts
East Heslerton
Sherburn
Sherburn Lodge
Heslerton Grange
Westfield Fm
High Mill Fm
Potter Brompton
Brow Plantn
Crowsdale Wood
Westfield Wold
St Hildas Wold
Potter Brompton Wold
Scampston
Scampston Hall
Home Wood
East Knapton
West Knapton
Knapton Hall
West Heslerton
Rectory Fm
Knapton Grange
Plains Fm
Sands Wood
Wolds Way Lavender
Manor Wold Fm
Brow Plantn
Knapton Plantn
Wold Fm
West Fm
East Fm
West Heslerton Wold
Thorpe Bassett
Wintringham
Millbank Ho
Peacock Fm
Place Newton
Spring Fm
Scardale Plantn
Green Plantn
Ling Hall Fm
Whin Moor
East Heslerton Wold Fm
Sherburn Wold Fm
Sherburn Wold
Duggleby Wold Fm
Sunning Dale
Allison Wold Fm
Warren Ho
Wilson's Wold Fm
Foxholes Manor
Foxholes
Boythorpe Cott
Westfield Fm
Westfield Ho
Wold Newton
Wold Newton Field
Wold Newton Grange
Burton Fleming Grange
Burton Fleming
Hill Fm
Bartindale Fm
Gypsey Race
Willy Howe Fm
West Field Ho
Glebe Cott
Octon Grange
Maidensgrave Fm
Finley Hill
Refuge Fm
Thwing
Octon Manor
Ringlands Plantn
Highfield Fm
Octon Lodge
Octon
Swaythorpe Plantn
Rudston Grange
High Street
Springdale Fm
North Wold
Octon Cross Roads
Togdale Fm
Tog Dale
Broach Dale
Dotterill Park
Field Ho
Denby Ho
Rudston
Thorpe Hall
Field Ho
Raven Hill Fm
Kilham Grange Fm
South Side Mount
Wold Gate
Tufthill Fm
Thornholme Field
Burton Agnes Field
Thornholme
Burton Agnes Hall
Burton Agnes Manor House
Burton Agnes
Harpham Field
Harpham Grange
Quintin Bottom
Howe Covert
Harpham
Bracey Bridge
Fox Hill
Little Kelk Fm
Turtle Hill Fm
Lowthorpe
Airy Hill Fm
Wold Ho
Ruston Parva
Nafferton Wold
Nafferton Grange
Slayersdale Fm
Green Dikes Plantn
Cold Nab Plantn
Pockthorpe Hall
North Plantn
Kilham
Mount Pleasant
West End
Little Kilham Fm
Creyke Fm
Branton's Fm
Kilham West Field
Westfield Fm
Woodbine Cott
Langtoft
Wold Ho
Honey Hill
Langtoft Grange
Chalet Fm
Westfield Fm
Scarborough Road
Driffield Road
Field Ho
NORTH YORKSHIRE
EAST RIDING OF YORKSHIRE
The Wolds
Linton Wold
Linton Wold Fm
Rayslack Ho
Thirkleby Warren
Broom Fm
Haverdale Ho
High Barn
Weaverthorpe
Butterwick
Gara Fm
Weaverthorpe Slack
Manor Ho
Gypsey Race
Spaniel Fm
Helperthorpe
Rosemount Fm
Dikes Fields
Helperthorpe Pasture
Weaverthorpe Pasture
Ling Fm
Pasture Plantn
Summit Fm
Moor Fm
High Dale Fm
Wad Dale
Stac Hills
Settrington Beacon 651
Many Thorns Fm
Black Plantn
South Wold
Wold Ho
Yorkshire Wolds Way
High Mowthorpe Plantns
Kirby Wold Fm
Thirkleby Manor
East Lutton
West Lutton
South Plantn
Settrington Wood
Wood House Fm
High Mowthorpe Plantns
The Peak
Duggleby Wold
Mowthorpe Wold
Thirkleby Wold
High Field
Pasture Fm
Crake Dale
Little Pasture
Belle Vue Fm
Croom Dale Plantn
Kirby Grindalythe
Kirby Plantn
Duggleby
High Street
Crook Plantn
Croome Fm
Croome Wold
Burrow House Fm
Stonepit Balk
Low Mowthorpe Fm
Wharram Grange Fm
Wharram le Street
Crow Wood
Croome Ho
Bridlington Road
Cowlam Manor
Cottam Grange
Cottam
Cottam Ho
Wharram Percy
Bella Fm
Wold Fm
Wharram Percy Church & Deserted Medieval Village
Kirby Grange
Sledmere
Sledmere House
Wood Dale Plantn
Sledmere Castle
Avenue Wood
Towthorpe Plantn
Towthorpe Wold
Mill Fm
Deep Dale
North Plantn
Burdale Warren
Towthorpe
Towthorpe Field
Badger Wood
Woodhill Fm
Warren Fm
Sledmere Grange
Cottam Warren
Cottam Warren Fm
Ralsthorpe Manor
Ling Fm
Life Hill
Black Wood
Sir Tatton Sykes' Monument
Garton Wold
Elmswell Wold Fm
Wold House Fm
Great Kendale
Paradise Cottages
Nab Fm
Sledmere Field Fm
Bessingdale Plantn
Garton Field
Garton Grange
Wetwang Grange
West Field
North Field
Gamesiack Plantn
South Field
Fimber
Fimber Field Fm
Lodge Fm
Fridaythorpe
Fridaythorpe Field
Wold Fm
Wetwang
Main Street
Garton Slack
Garton Hill
Garton-on-the-Wolds
Holmdale Fm
Holmfield Fm
Middleham Plantn
Holm Field
Far Falls Fm
Low Fm
Westfield Ho
Elmswell
Spellow Fm
Manor Fm
Field Ho
Nafferton
Sleights Fm
Outgate Fm
Millingdale Fm
Great Kelk
Riggs Fm
Pefham Plantn
Cowdale
Little
Driffield
Field Ho

NORTH SEA
FILEY BAY
BRIDLINGTON BAY
EAST RIDING OF YORKSHIRE
Filey
Bridlington
Flamborough
Flamborough Head
Hunmanby
Reighton
Speeton
Bempton
Buckton
Sewerby
Grindale
Boynton
Carnaby
Bessingby
Hilderthorpe
Haisthorpe
Thornholme
Burton Agnes
Harpham
Fraisthorpe
Barmston
Gristhorpe
Muston
Primrose Valley
Reighton Gap
North Landing
South Landing
The Crofts
Burton Fleming
Great Kelk
Lissett
Filey Brigg
Bempton Cliffs
Speeton Cliffs
Buckton Cliffs
Thornwick Bay
Selwicks Bay
High Stacks
Flamborough Head Lighthouse
Sewerby Hall & Garden
Bondville Model Village
Bridlington Animal Park
Burton Agnes Hall
Burton Agnes Manor House
Danes Dyke
Flamborough Cliffs Nature Reserve
Fraisthorpe Sands
Barmston Sands
South Sands
North Sands
A165
A614
A1038
A1039
B1229
B1255
B1259
B1253
217
209

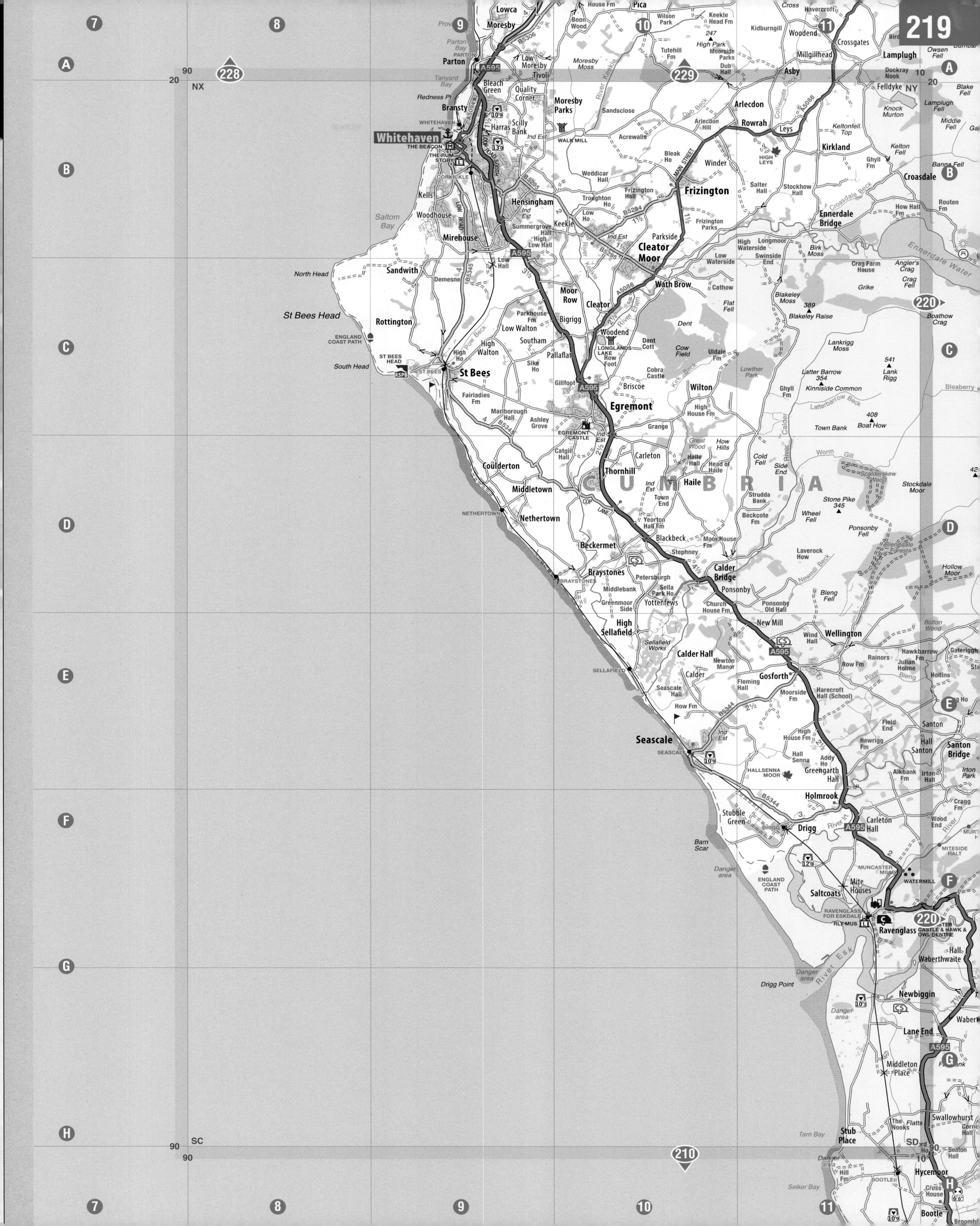
Lowca
Moresby
Pica
Parton
Low Moresby
Tivoli
Whitehaven
Bransty
Harras
Scilly Bank
Moresby Parks
Hensingham
Kells
Woodhouse
Mirehouse
Saltom Bay
North Head
Sandwith
St Bees Head
Rottington
St Bees
South Head
Egremont
Cleator Moor
Cleator
Frizington
Arlecdon
Rowrah
Asby
Lamplugh
Kirkland
Croasdale
Ennerdale Bridge
Ennerdale Water
Moor Row
Bigrigg
Woodend
Wath Brow
Wilton
CUMBRIA
Coulderton
Middletown
Nethertown
Thornhill
Haile
Beckermet
Braystones
Calder Bridge
Ponsonby
High Sellafield
Sellafield Works
Calder Hall
Gosforth
Wellington
Seascale
Holmrook
Drigg
Saltcoats
Ravenglass
Muncaster
Waberthwaite
Newbiggin
Lane End
Middleton Place
Stub Place
Hycemoor
Bootle
Santon Bridge
Irton
Drigg Point
River Esk
A595
A5086
B5345
B5344
B5295
220
228
229
210
NX
SC
NY
SD

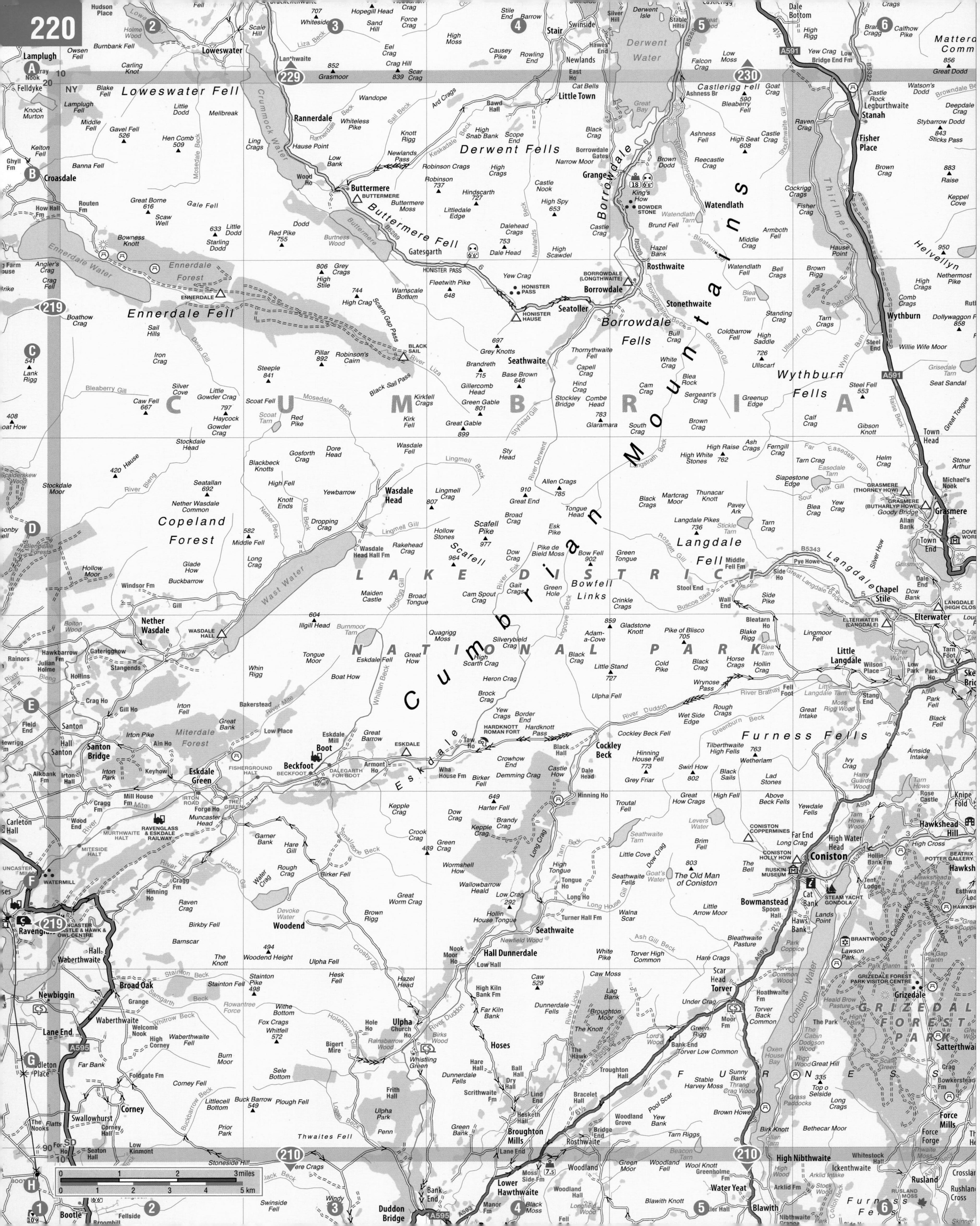
229
230
219
210
Lamplugh
Loweswater
Loweswater Fell
Crummock Water
Rannerdale
Derwent Water
Derwent Fells
Little Town
Stair
Swinside
Newlands
Castlerigg Fell
Croasdale
Buttermere
Buttermere Fell
Gatesgarth
Honister Pass
Ennerdale Water
Ennerdale Forest
Ennerdale Fell
Grange
Borrowdale
Watendlath
Rosthwaite
Seatoller
Stonethwaite
Borrowdale Fells
Stanah
Legburthwaite
Fisher Place
Thirlmere
Helvellyn
Wythburn
Wythburn Fells
Seathwaite
Great Gable
899
Pillar
892
Steeple
841
Haycock
797
Kirk Fell
Wasdale Head
Scafell Pike
977
Scafell
964
Copeland Forest
Wast Water
Nether Wasdale
Langdale Pikes
Langdale Fell
Bowfell Links
Chapel Stile
Elterwater
Grasmere
Little Langdale
Cumbrian Mountains
CUMBRIA
LAKE DISTRICT
NATIONAL PARK
Eskdale
Eskdale Green
Boot
Beckfoot
Santon Bridge
Miterdale Forest
Cockley Beck
Furness Fells
Hardknott Pass
Wrynose Pass
Coniston
The Old Man of Coniston
Seathwaite
Hall Dunnerdale
Ravenglass
Woodend
Broad Oak
Newbiggin
Waberthwaite
Lane End
Corney
Swallowhurst
Ulpha
Hoses
Broughton Mills
Torver
Coniston Water
Grizedale
GRIZEDALE FOREST PARK
Satterthwaite
Force Mills
High Nibthwaite
Lower Hawthwaite
Duddon Bridge
Bootle
Blawith
Rusland
Woodland
Water Yeat
A591
A593
A595
0 1 2 3 miles
0 1 2 3 4 5 km

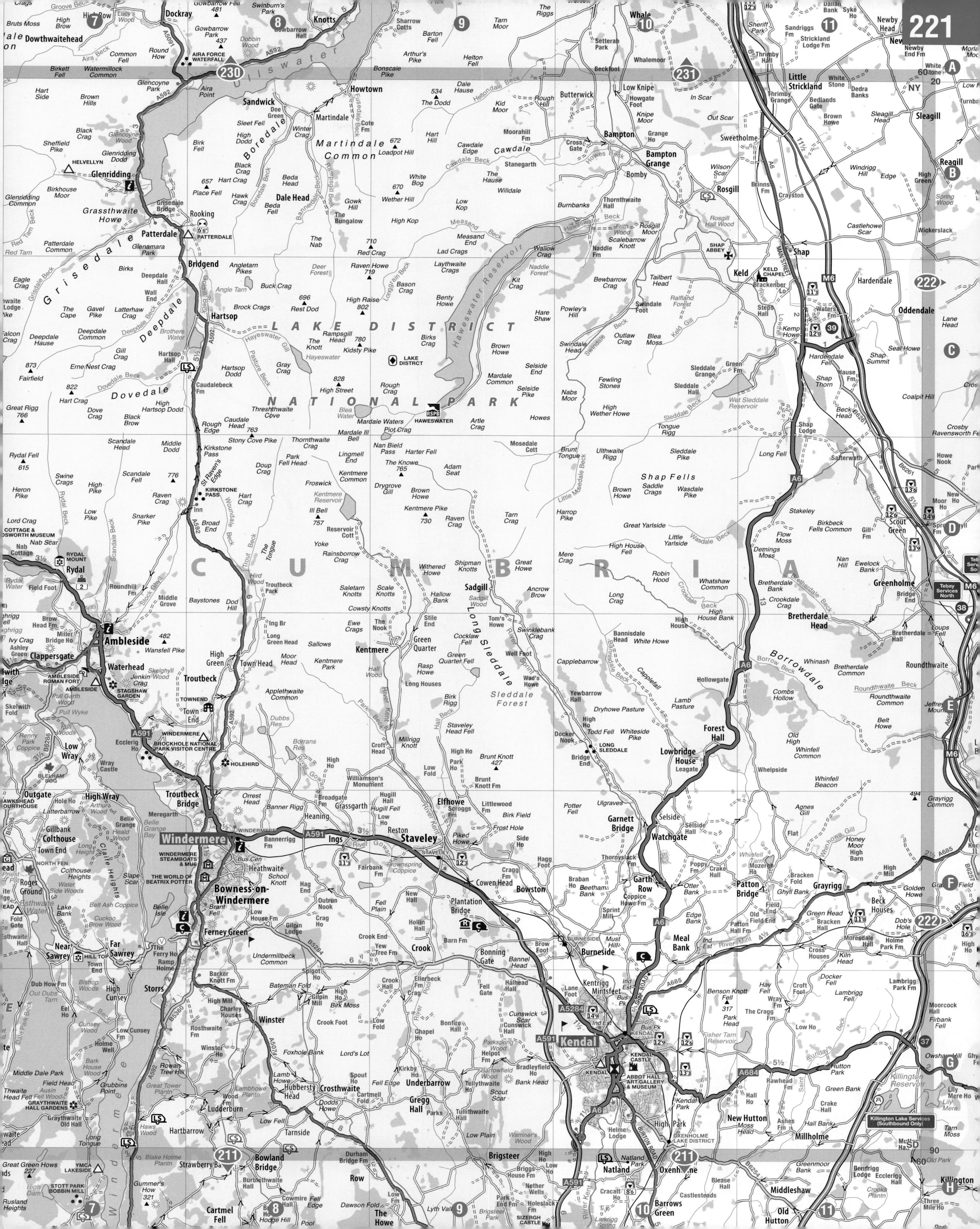
Dockray
Knotts
Whale
Newby Head
Little Strickland
Ullswater
Aira Force Waterfall
Howtown
Sandwick
Martindale
Martindale Common
Boredale
Butterwick
Low Knipe
Bampton
Bampton Grange
Sleagill
Reagill
Glenridding
Helvellyn
Dale Head
Rosgill
Grasmere Howe
Patterdale
Rooking
Grisedale
Bridgend
Haweswater Reservoir
Shap
Shap Abbey
Keld
Keld Chapel
Hardendale
Oddendale
Hartsop
Deepdale
Lake District National Park
High Street
Haweswater
Dovedale
Kirkstone Pass
Shap Fells
Cumbria
Rydal
Rydal Mount
Ambleside
Clappersgate
Waterhead
Stagshaw Garden
Troutbeck
Townend
Kentmere
Green Quarter
Sadgill
Long Sleddale
Sleddale Forest
Borrowdale
Bretherdale Head
Greenholme
Tebay Services North
Windermere
Brockhole National Park Visitor Centre
Holehird
Troutbeck Bridge
Staveley
Ings
Forest Hall
Lowbridge House
Garnett Bridge
Selside
Watchgate
Bowness-on-Windermere
The World of Beatrix Potter
Windermere Steamboats & Museum
Ferney Green
Far Sawrey
Near Sawrey
Hill Top
Crook
Burneside
Kendal
Kendal Castle
Abbot Hall Art Gallery & Museum
Patton Bridge
Grayrigg
Meal Bank
Beck Houses
Winster
Storrs
Crosthwaite
Underbarrow
Gregg Hall
Lyth Valley
Brigsteer
Bowland Bridge
Cartmel Fell
Natland
Oxenholme
Oxenholme Lake District
Barrows Green
New Hutton
Millholme
Middleshaw
Old Hutton
Killington
Killington Lake Services (Southbound Only)
Graythwaite Hall Gardens
Stott Park Bobbin Mill
YMCA Lakeside
Sizergh Castle
Windermere
Long Sleddale
Tarn Crag
Harter Fell
Kentmere Reservoir
Kentmere Pike
Ill Bell
Froswick
Thornthwaite Crag
Stony Cove Pike
Red Screes
Wansfell Pike
Grayrigg Common
Whinfell Beacon
Killington Reservoir

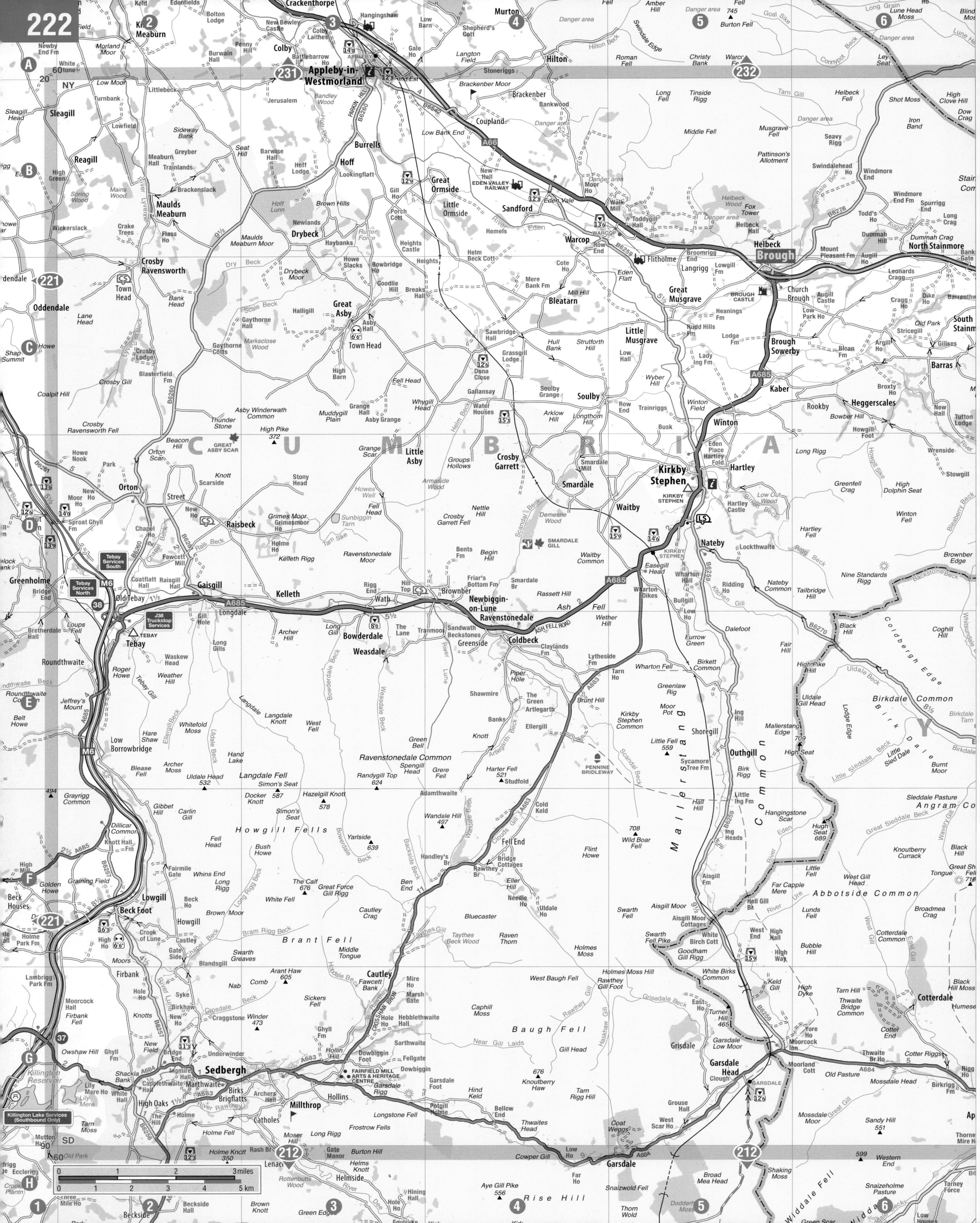
231
232
221
212
Appleby-in-Westmorland
Crackenthorpe
Hangingshaw
Murton
Colby
Battlebarrow
Burrells
Hoff
Drybeck
Great Asby
Great Ormside
Little Ormside
Sandford
Warcop
Hilton
Brackenber
Coupland
Flitholme
Great Musgrave
Little Musgrave
Brough
Church Brough
Brough Sowerby
Helbeck
North Stainmore
Kaber
Winton
Hartley
Kirkby Stephen
Nateby
Smardale
Waitby
Soulby
Bleatarn
Crosby Garrett
Little Asby
Orton
Raisbeck
Gaisgill
Kelleth
Tebay
Old Tebay
Longdale
Bowderdale
Weasdale
Newbiggin-on-Lune
Ravenstonedale
Coldbeck
Greenside
Brownber
Crosby Ravensworth
Maulds Meaburn
Kings Meaburn
Sleagill
Reagill
Oddendale
Greenholme
Roundthwaite
Lowgill
Beck Foot
Howgill
Sedbergh
Millthrop
Cautley
Garsdale
Garsdale Head
Cotterdale
Outhgill
Shoregill
Mallerstang
Mallerstang Common
Birkdale Common
Abbotside Common
Angram Common
Howgill Fells
Brant Fell
Baugh Fell
Ravenstonedale Common
Langdale Fell
Rise Hill
Widdale Fell
C U M B R I A
A66
A685
A683
A684
M6
B6259
B6260
B6261
B6257
B6542
B6276
B6270
Tebay Services South
Tebay Services North
J38 Truckstop Services
Killington Lake Services (Southbound Only)
Eden Valley Railway
Fairfield Mill Arts & Heritage Centre
Great Asby Scar
Smardale Gill
Pennine Bridleway
Brough Castle
Killington Reservoir
NY
SD
0 1 2 3 miles
0 1 2 3 4 5 km
1 2 3 4 5 6
A B C D E F G H

Long Grain Moss
Lane Head Fm
Arngill Ho
River Lune
Wemmergill Hall
Selset Reservoir
Grassholme
Grassholme Reservoir
Kelton
Hunter Ho
Harker Springs
West Pasture
Romaldkirk Moor
Hunderthwaite
Wildon Grange
Park House Fm
Howgill Grange
Hury
Gill Ho
Gill Field
West End
Wilden Beck
Doe Park
Thwaite Hall
Quarryhouse Fm
Rogermoor Fm
Kinninvie
Hawkesley Hill
Parrick Ho
Hedrick Grange
Shepherd's Lodge
Gawen Ho
Bolton Hill
Forthburn
Forthburn Plantn
Park Ho
High Garford
Streatlam Grange
High Ho
Snotterton Hall
Three Pikes
Hunderthwaite Moor
Soulgill Edge
Kelton Fell
Kelton Hill
Hill Gill Fm
Briar Dykes
River Balder
Balder Grange
Cotherstone
Stone Cross
Bluestone Grange
Streatlam Park
Great Wood
Broad Stone Rigg
Sheep Lair Hill
Black Hill
Corn Park
East Briscoe
Booze Wood
West Holme Ho
Cooper Ho
East Holme Ho
Ravensike Rigg
Mawk Hole Moss
Balder Head
Blackton Reservoir
Hury Reservoir
Willoughby Hall
Fiddler Ho
Crook Beck
Balderhead Reservoir
Hannah's Meadow
Clove Lodge
Pitcher Ho
Currack Rigg
Quarry Grange
Stainton
Westwick Moor
Ind Est
Caple Rigg
Mickleburnt Hill
Baldersdale
Water Knott
Hagworm Hall
Pennine Way
Yawd Sike
Scur Beck
Towler Hill
Pind Hill
Black Beck
Cotherstone Moor
Danger area
Lartington
Lartington Lane
Barnard Castle
Stell Plantn
East Town Pasture
Harton Crag
Round Hill
Balder Beck
Hunder Rigg
Gill Beck
Battle Hill
Osmond Flatt
Darlington Road
Hunder Hill
Hare Moss
Crag Hill 306
Cat Castle
Deepdale Wood
Startforth
HM YOI
Bowes Road
The Bowes Museum
Lowfield Garden
Hoy Ho
Arlaw Banks
Whorlton High Grange
Red Gill Moss
Slates Hill
Brown Rigg Moss
Deep Dale
Nabb Fm
North Field
Startforth Grange
Castle
Mount Eff
Westwick
Crawlaw Rigg
Caucabush Rigg
Great Allotment
Strand Foot
Levy Pool
Sledwich Cotts
Plucka Hill
Lartington High Moor
Fountain Head
Milestone Ho
River Tees
Grange Fm
Sledwich Hall
Great Knipe 515
Deepdale Beck
Flat Moss
Thorsgill Beck
Eggleston Abbey
Argill Beck
Green Sike Rigg
Tute Hill
Clint Ho
Boldron
Castle Fm
Colton Plantn
Rokeby Park
Rokeby Grange
Street Side Fm
Mortham Wood
Wycliffe
Thorpe
Beldoo Hill 477
Ravock Castle
Hulands Fm
Myre Keld Fm
West Hall
South Flats
Beldoo Moss
Bowes
Bowes Castle
Rovegill
Jock Ho
Kilmond Wood
The Street
Tutta Beck
Tutta Beck Fm
Birk Ho
Rokeby Park
Greta Bridge
Maiden Castle
Buzzard Hill
Gilmonby
Plover Hall
White Close Hill
Birk Hall
Fames Wood
Thorpe Fm
Black Riggs
Crag Green
Grey Scar Fm
Spital Grange
God's Br
West Charity Fm
Huggill Force
West Gates
Pry Rigg
Brignall
Wilson Ho
Eastwood Hall
Newsham Grange
Moudy Mea 522
River Greta
High Barn
Saunders Ho
Risp Howe
Round Table or Roper Castle
Wytham Moor
Trough Heads
Gilmonby Moor
Scargill Low Moor
Stone Close Ho
Green Gill
Hening Wood
North Wood
Crook's Ho
Dyson Ho
Ewebank Park
Bowes Moor
Collinson's Hill 434
Stainmore Forest
Seven Hills
Citron Seat 446
Thwaite Beck
Scargill
Gillbeck Br
Coronation Plantn
Newsham Lodge
Mill Hill
Early Lodge
Newsham
Causey Moss
Ay Gill
Sleightholme Farm
Eller Beck
Spanham
Low Swinston
Barningham
Barningham Park
Bog Moss
Sleightholme Beck
Gregory Beck
Bragg Ho
Woofergill
Great Black Hill
Scargill High Moor
Peak Hole
Haythwaite
Park Ho
Earby Hall
Dalton
Dry Gill
Bow Hills
White Crag
Scargill Crag Moss
Potter Sike
White Stone Gill
Kaber Fell
Polly Moss
Coney Seat Hill
Tarnhow Hill
Jinglepot Hole
The Stang
Barningham Moor
Dousgill Fm
Silver Hill Fm
Frumming Beck
Sleightholme Moor
Cleasby Hill 511
Faggergill Moss
Elsey Crag
Hope Edge
Carter Ho
Brownber
Taylor Rigg
Cocker
Mudbeck
Faggergill Moor
How Tallon 447
Newsham Moor
Low Ho
Byers Hill
Windsor Lodge
Crumma Ho
Back Gutter
Ease Gill
Tan Hill
Mirk Fell 571
William Gill
The Disputes
Hope Moor
Cocker Hill
Arndale Hill 515
Hoove
Long Green Gate
Long Green
Danger area
Dale Head
Hart Holes
Arndale Beck
Stonesdale Beck
Park Head
Shepherd's Lodge
Arkengarthdale Moor
Seal Houses Moor
Kexwith Moor
Arndale Hole
Lockey Wood
Holgate Moor
Rake Beck
Gayles Moor
Grass Moor
NORTH
Lad Gill
West Moor
Stonesdale Moor
Whaw
Low Moor
Moresdale Gill
Moresdale Ridge
West Ho
Holgate Pasture
Feldom Ranges
Kersey Green Scar
Slatepit Moss
Side Edge
Robert's Seat
East Gill Head
Water Crag
Wham Bottom
Great Punchard Gill
Great Punchard Head
Arkle Beck
Booze Moor
Shaw Moor
Hurst Moor
Hurst Peat Moss
Dicky Edge
Hog Hill
Ravenseat
Low Brown Hill
West Stonesdale Out Pasture
Rogan's Seat 672
Little Punchard Head
Whaw Edge
West Ho
Low Moor
YORKSHIRE DALES
583 Great Pinseat
Langthwaite
Washfold
Tongue Hill
Marske Beck
Tarn Moss
Close Hills
East Stonesdale
Gunnerside Moor
Friarfold Moor
Forefield Rake
Turf Moor
High Green
Booze
Fell End Moor
Storthwaite Hall
Hurst
Prys Ho
Munn End
Marske
West Stonesdale
Harker Ho
Arkle Town
Skelton Moor
Orgate
YORKSHIRE
Pry Hill
Park Br
West Wood
Crackpot Hall
Swinner Gill
Gunnerside Gill
Moor Ho
Reeth High Moor
Barras End
Owlands Fm
Stone Ho
River Swale
Keld Side
Keld
Thorns
Kisdon Force
Melbecks Moor
Winterings Edge
Moor Ho
Skelton
Jingle Pot
Clints
Great Sled Dale
Great Ash Gill
Ivelet Moor
Silver Hill
Mill Bottom
Calver Hill 487
Fremington Edge
Marrick Moor
Lower Stelling Fm
Cleaburn or Musgrove Pasture
Marske
Angram
Skeugh Head
Hooker Mill Scar
499
Black Hill
Feetham Pasture
Jingle Pot Edge
Whin Hall
Brownsey Moor
Thiernswood Hall
Town End Hall
Reeth
Copperthwaite Allotment
Fremington Edge
Hollins Fm
Deer Park Wood
Angram Lane
Birkbeck Wood
Kearton
Birk Park
Healaugh
Swaledale Museum
Fremington
Nun Cote Nook
Sour Nook
Bleaberry Head
Ivelet Wood
Elias's Stot Wood
Brownsey Ho
Blades
Wood End
Park Hall
Ivy Ho
Harkerside Place
Maiden Castle
Colt Park Wood
Garnless Scar
Marrick
High Park
Ellerton Lodge
Stock Dale
Moor Close
Thwaite Beck
Thwaite
Muker
Calvert Hos
Lodge Green
Low Row Pasture
Feetham
Drovers Ho
Low Whita
Horse Pasture Wood
Swale Hall
Grinton
Cogden Hall
Stainton Low Wood
Hartley Park
Black Bank
Thwaite Side
Straw Beck
Gunning Lane
Gunnerside
Ivelet
Satron
Haverdale Ho
Low Row
High Harker Hill
Harkerside Moor
Grinton Lodge
Stolerston Wood
Ellerton Abbey
Scar Spring Wood
Grainy Gill Moss
Cliff Beck
Hood Rigg
Muker Edge
Kearton's Wood
B6270
Spring End
Hag Wood
Bank Heads
Nettlebed Ho
Robson Ho
Hunt Ho
Kendell Bottom
Grinton Gill
Cogden Moor
Hags Gill Plantn
Stainton
Gill Head
Crackpot
Blea Barf 540
Ellerton Moor
Buttertubs Pass
Long Scar
NATIONAL PARK
Bloody Vale
Bents Ho
Gibbon Hill
High Carl
Greets Hill
Coal Pit Moor
Peat Fell
Fossdale Moss
Lovely Seat 675
Muker Common
Lover Gill Head
Oxnop Common
Oxnop Scar
Middle Tongue
Summer Lodge
Whitaside Moor
Greets Moss
Robin Cross Hill
Walburn Moor
Whity Gill
Tarn Rigg
Beldon Bottom
Golden Groves
Redmire Forest
Far Cranehow Bottom
411 Stainton Moor
Whit Fell
Bellerby Ranges
Turned Hill
Oxnop Beck Head
Pickerstone Ridge
East Bolton Moor
Apedale Beck
Preston Moor
Abbotside Common
Askrigg Common
Stags Fell
Whitfield Fell
West Bolton Moor
Apedale
Redmire Moor
Cranehow Bottom
Bellerby Moor
Clough Wood
Pike Hill
Sargill Beck
Stackhill Ho
Bull Scar
Bob Scar
Bolton Gill Plantn
Broomber Rigg
Fossdale
High Shaw
Sargill Parks
Beldon Peat Moor
Castle Bolton
Low Scar
Redmire Scar
Lang Scar
Layburn Moor
Bellerby
Washfold Fm
Hardraw Force Waterfall
Hardraw
Simonstone
Sedbusk High Pasture
Cote Pasture
Newbiggin Pasture
Ellerkin Scar
Swinehaw Bottom
Blue Scar
Bolton Parks
Redmire Pasture
Elm Ho
Gillfield Wood
Bellerby Camp
Cote Pasture
Rock Castle
Yarker Bank Fm
Sedbusk
Litherskew
Low Mill Outdoor Centre
Helm
Leas Ho
Newbiggin
Nappa Scar
Bolton Castle
Redmire
Preston-under-Scar
Fosdale
Hawes
Dales Countryside Museum
Brown Moor
Cams Ho
Ingleby Lodge
Yorebridge Ho
Grange
Askrigg
Askrigg Bottoms
Nappa Hall
Woodhall
Ivy Scar
New Pasture
Sunny Bank
Wood End
Leyburn
White Rose Candles
Wensleydale Creamery
Bainbridge
Worton
Carperby
Haremire Ho
Bolton Hall
Gayle
Bainbridge Ings
Burtersett Bottoms
Bainbridge Low Pasture
Raygill Ho
Gill Edge
Cubeck
Scar Top
Warren Ho
Manor Ho
Hollins Ho
Swinithwaite
Wanlass Park
Wensley
Howe Hills
Burtersett
Semerdale Hall
Bainbridge High Pasture
Aysgarth Falls
Alma Fm
West Witton
Gale Bank
Burtersett High Pasture 515
Addlebrough 476
Devil's Stone
Thornton Rust
High Gill
Seata Fm
Nossill Scars
Holl Gate
Mount Park Fm
Middleham
Countersett
Yorburgh
Low Force
Aysgarth Moor
Aysgarth
Sleddale
Gaudy Ho
A66
A67
A684
A688
B6270
B6277
B6278
B6279
Wensleydale
Swaledale
Arkengarthdale
DURHAM
NZ

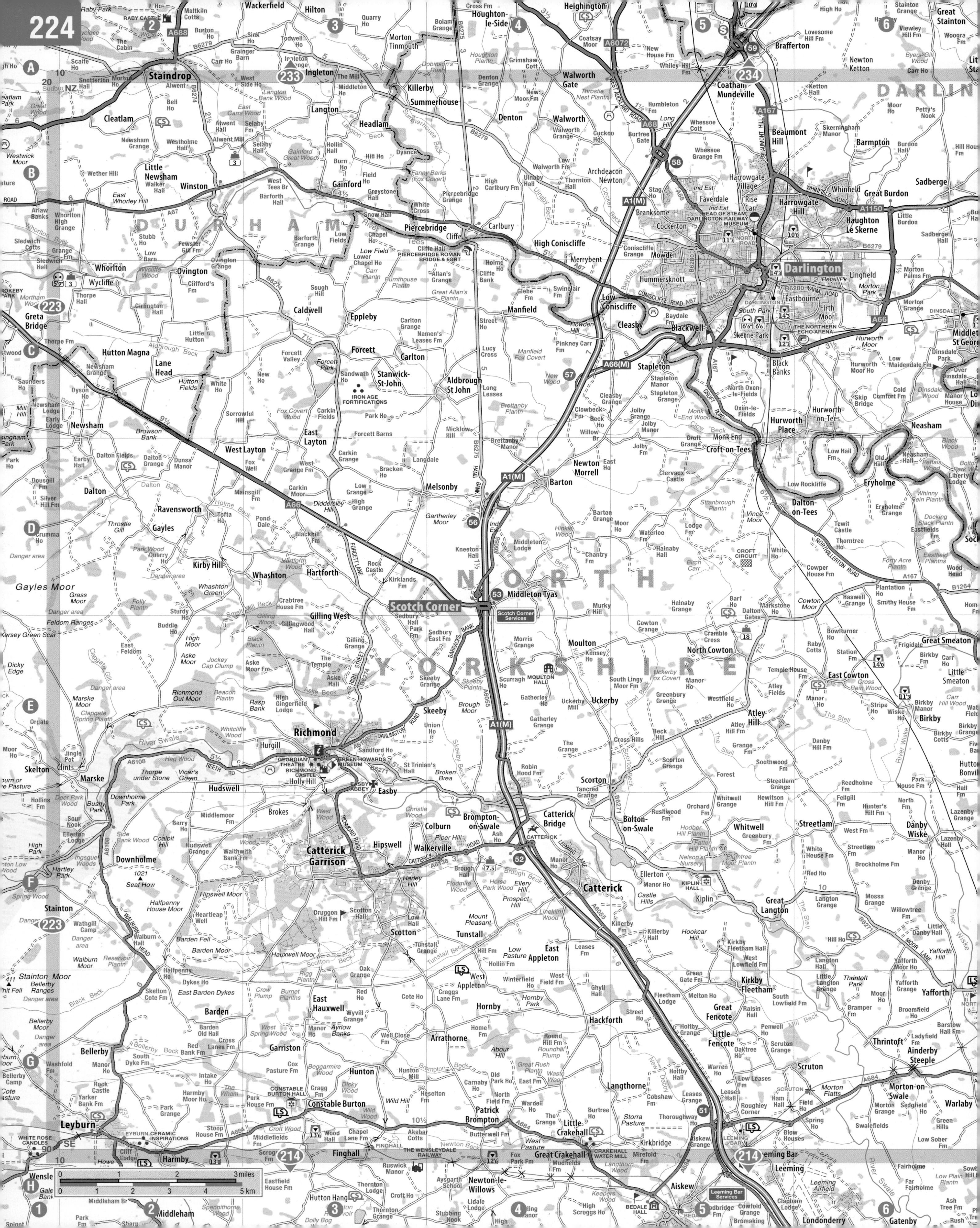

224
Raby Park
Raby Castle
Wackerfield
Hilton
Houghton-le-Side
Heighington
Staindrop
Ingleton
233
234
Killerby
Summerhouse
Denton
Walworth Gate
Walworth
Coatham Mundeville
Brafferton
Great Stainton
DARLIN
Cleatlam
Langton
Headlam
Beaumont Hill
Barmpton
Little Newsham
Winston
Gainford
Archdeacon Newton
Harrowgate Village
Harrowgate Hill
Whinfield
Great Burdon
Sadberge
D U R H A M
Piercebridge
Cliffe
Carlbury
High Coniscliffe
Merrybent
Branksome
Cockerton
Faverdale
Haughton Le Skerne
Darlington
Whorlton
Ovington
Wycliffe
Mowden
Hummersknott
Low Coniscliffe
Cleasby
Blackwell
Skerne Park
Eastbourne
Firth Moor
Lingfield
Greta Bridge
223
Caldwell
Eppleby
Manfield
Forcett
Carlton
Stanwick-St-John
Aldbrough St John
Stapleton
Hutton Magna
Lane Head
Newsham
East Layton
Hurworth-on-Tees
Hurworth Place
Neasham
Croft-on-Tees
West Layton
Newton Morrell
Barton
Melsonby
Dalton
Ravensworth
Gayles
Eryholme
Dalton-on-Tees
Kirby Hill
Whashton
Hartforth
N O R T H
Scotch Corner
Middleton Tyas
Gayles Moor
Gilling West
Moulton
North Cowton
Great Smeaton
East Cowton
Y O R K S H I R E
Skeeby
Uckerby
Atley Hill
Birkby
Richmond
Hurgill
Easby
Marske
Skelton
Hudswell
Brompton-on-Swale
Colburn
Catterick Bridge
Bolton-on-Swale
Scorton
Streetlam
Whitwell
Danby Wiske
Catterick Garrison
Hipswell
Walkerville
Catterick
Downholme
Kiplin
Great Langton
Stainton
Scotton
Tunstall
East Appleton
West Appleton
Kirkby Fleetham
Yafforth
East Hauxwell
Hornby
Barden
Hackforth
Great Fencote
Little Fencote
Bellerby
Garriston
Arrathorne
Thrintoft
Ainderby Steeple
Scruton
Hunton
Langthorne
Morton-on-Swale
Warlaby
Constable Burton
Patrick Brompton
Leyburn
Little Crakehall
Harmby
Finghall
Great Crakehall
214
Leeming Bar
Leeming
Newton-le-Willows
Aiskew
Bedale
Middleham
Londonderry
Gatenby
0 1 2 3 miles
0 1 2 3 4 5 km

Middlesbrough
Stockton-on-Tees
STOCKTON-ON-TEES
Thornaby on Tees
Grangetown
Eston
Ormesby
Acklam
Linthorpe
Marton
Nunthorpe
Hemlington
Coulby Newham
Guisborough
REDCAR AND CLEVELAND
MIDDLESBROUGH
Eaglescliffe
Egglescliffe
Yarm
Teesside International Airport
Longnewton
Elton
Hartburn
Fairfield
Bishopsgarth
Redmarshall
Bishopton
Carlton
Clarence
Billingham Beck
Transporter Bridge (Toll)
Riverside Stadium
South Bank
Lazenby
Wilton
Dunsdale
Normanby
Park End
Stainton
Thornton
Maltby
Newby
Hilton
Seamer
Tanton
Great Ayton
Langbaurgh
Newton under Roseberry
Roseberry Topping
Hutton Village
Hutton Gate
Captain Cook Schoolroom Mus.
Captain Cook's Monument
Little Ayton
Easby
Kildale
Battersby
Stokesley
Tame Bridge
Kirkleavington
Low Worsall
High Worsall
Middleton-on-Leven
Picton
Girsby
Crathorne
Rudby
Hutton Rudby
Enterpen
Sexhow
Potto
Goulton
Carlton in Cleveland
Faceby
Great Busby
Kirkby
Great Broughton
Ingleby Greenhow
Appleton Wiske
West Rounton
East Rounton
Hornby
Deighton
Welbury
Whorlton
Swainby
Heathwaite
Ingleby Arncliffe
Ingleby Cross
Cringle Moor
Cleveland Hills
Urra
Urra Moor
Chop Gate
Seave Green
Mount Grace Priory
Osmotherley
Osmotherley Moor
NORTH YORK MOORS NATIONAL PARK
East Harlsey
West Harlsey
Ellerbeck
Winton
Brompton
Northallerton
Romanby
Bullamoor
Kirby Sigston
Thimbleby
Over Silton
Nether Silton
Kepwick
Leake
Thornton-le-Beans
Cowesby
Borrowby
North Otterington
Thornton-le-Moor
Sowber Gate
Newby
Fangdale Beck
Bilsdale
Hawnby
Rievaulx Moor
Black Hambleton
Cleveland Way
A19
A172
A173
A174
A66
A67
A684
A167
B1257

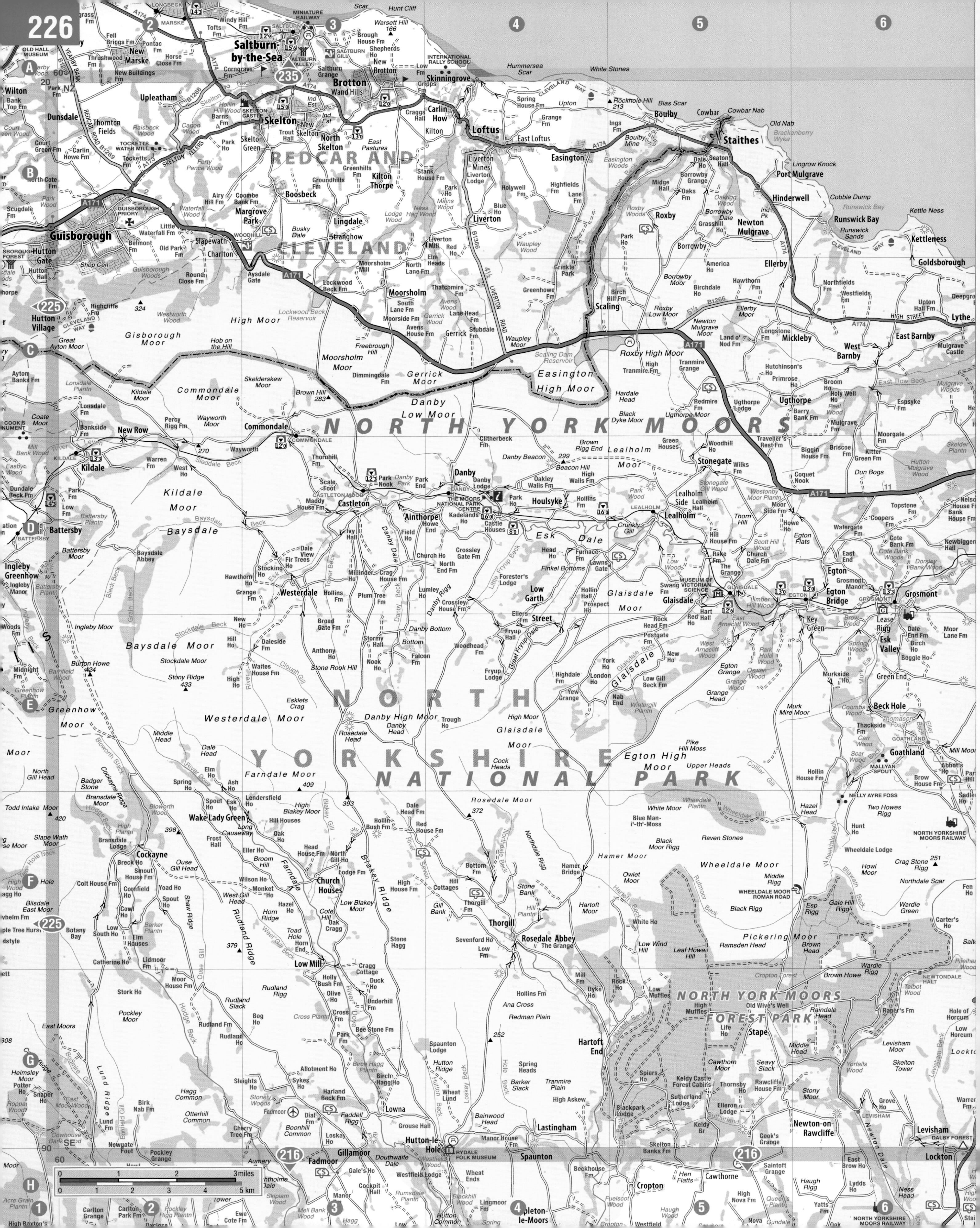
Saltburn-by-the-Sea
Brotton
Skinningrove
Skelton
North Skelton
Loftus
Easington
Boulby
Staithes
Port Mulgrave
Hinderwell
Runswick Bay
Kettleness
Goldsborough
Lythe
Guisborough
Hutton Gate
Hutton Village
REDCAR AND
CLEVELAND
Lingdale
Kilton Thorpe
Boosbeck
Margrove Park
Moorsholm
Liverton
Scaling
Roxby
Newton Mulgrave
Ellerby
Mickleby
East Barnby
West Barnby
Ugthorpe
NORTH YORK MOORS
Commondale
Kildale
Castleton
Danby
Ainthorpe
Houlsyke
Lealholm
Glaisdale
Egton
Egton Bridge
Grosmont
Westerdale
Battersby
Ingleby Greenhow
Baysdale
Low Garth
Street
Esk Dale
Beck Hole
Goathland
Esk Valley
NORTH
YORKSHIRE
NATIONAL PARK
Wake Lady Green
Cockayne
Church Houses
Farndale
Rosedale Abbey
Thorgill
Low Mill
Hartoft End
Stape
NORTH YORK MOORS
FOREST PARK
Lastingham
Hutton-le-Hole
Gillamoor
Fadmoor
Spaunton
Cropton
Cawthorne
Newton-on-Rawcliffe
Levisham
Lockton
Wheeldale Moor
Pickering Moor
Egton High Moor
Danby High Moor
Westerdale Moor
Baysdale Moor
Farndale Moor
Rosedale Moor
Glaisdale Moor
Blakey Ridge
Rudland Ridge
Lund Ridge
NORTH YORKSHIRE MOORS RAILWAY
RYDALE FOLK MUSEUM
A171
A174
235
225
216
0 1 2 3 miles
0 1 2 3 4 5 km

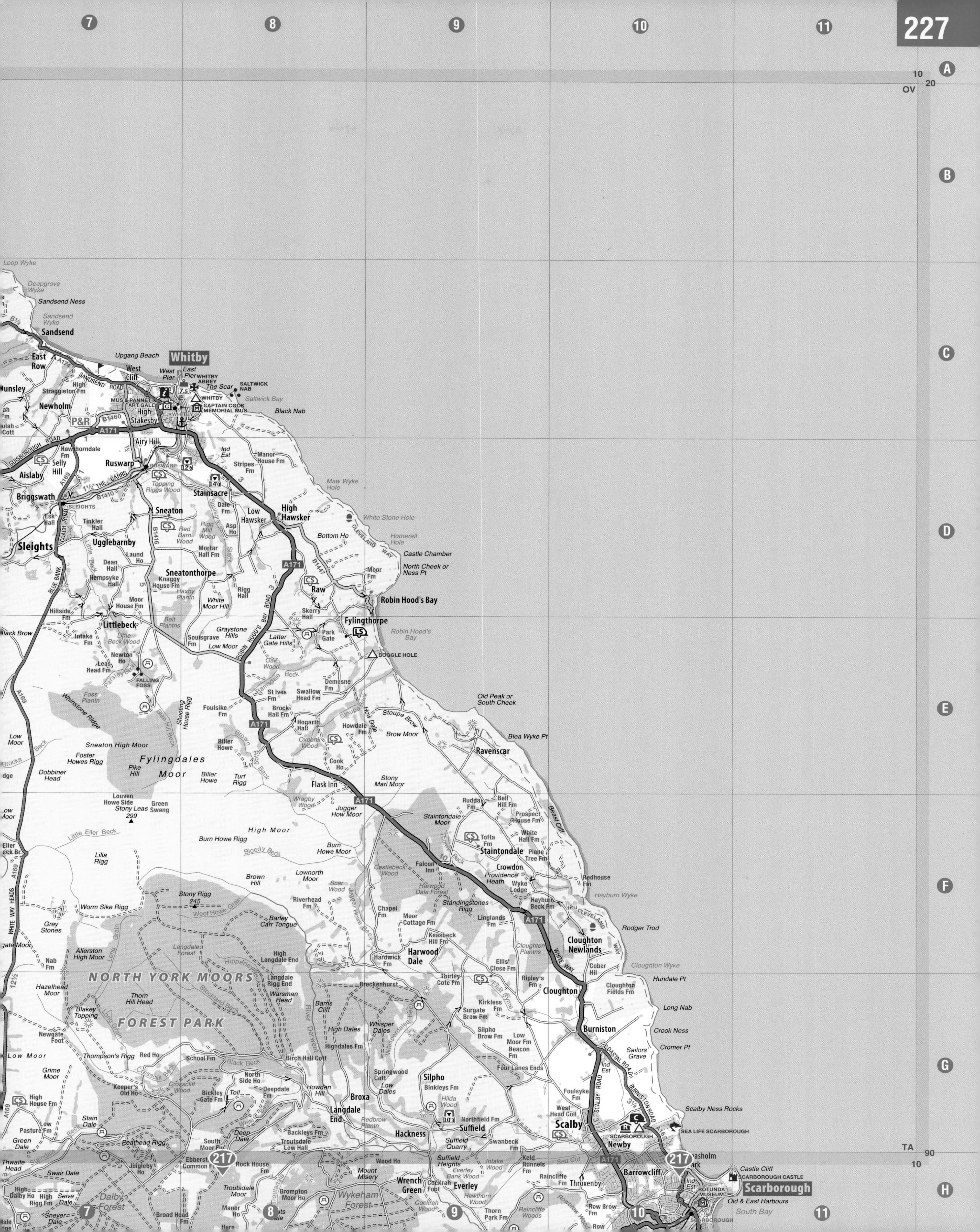
7
8
9
10
11
A
B
C
D
E
F
G
H
OV
TA
Loop Wyke
Deepgrove Wyke
Sandsend Ness
Sandsend Wyke
Sandsend
Upgang Beach
Whitby
East Row
West Cliff
West Pier
East Pier
WHITBY ABBEY
The Scar
SALTWICK NAB
Saltwick Bay
Black Nab
MUS & PANNETT ART GALL
WHITBY
CAPTAIN COOK MEMORIAL MUS
High Stakesby
Straggleton Fm
Newholm
P&R
B1460
A171
A174
SANDSEND ROAD
GUISBOROUGH ROAD
Airy Hill
Hawthorndale Fm
Selly Hill
Aislaby
Ruswarp
Ind Est
Manor House Fm
Stripes Fm
Maw Wyke Hole
THE CARRS
B1410
Briggswath
SLEIGHTS
Topping Riggs Wood
Stainsacre
Sneaton
Dale Fm
Low Hawsker
High Hawsker
White Stone Hole
Esk Hall
Tinkler Hall
Ugglebarnby
Red Barn Wood
Rigg Mill Wood
Asp Ho
Bottom Ho
CLEVELAND WAY
Homerell Hole
Castle Chamber
North Cheek or Ness Pt
Sleights
Laund Ho
Mortar Hall Fm
B1447
Dean Hall
Hempsyke Hall
Sneatonthorpe
Knaggy House Fm
Haxby Plantn
Rigg Hall
Moor Fm
Raw
Robin Hood's Bay
BLUE BANK
COACH ROAD
B1416
Moor House Fm
White Moor Hill
ROBIN HOOD'S BAY ROAD
Skerry Hall
Fylingthorpe
Hillside Fm
Littlebeck
Belt Plantns
Graystone Hills
Latter Gate Hills
Park Gate
Robin Hood's Bay
Black Brow
Intake Fm
Little Beck Wood
Soulsgrave Fm
Low Moor
BOGGLE HOLE
Newton Ho
Leas Head Fm
FALLING FOSS
Oak Wood
Ramsdale Beck
Demesne Fm
St Ives Fm
Swallow Head Fm
Foss Plantn
Whinstone Ridge
Foulsike Fm
Shooting House Rigg
Old Peak or South Cheek
Brock Hall Fm
Stoupe Brow
How Dale
A169
Hogarth Hall
Howdale Fm
Oxbank Wood
Brow Moor
Blea Wyke Pt
Low Moor
Sneaton High Moor
Biller Howe
Ravenscar
Foster Howes Rigg
Fylingdales
Pike Hill
Moor
Cook Ho
Dobbiner Head
Biller Howe
Turf Rigg
Stony Marl Moor
Flask Inn
Louven Howe Side
Green Swang
Stony Leas 299
Wragby Wood
Jugger How Moor
Rudda Fm
Bell Hill Fm
Prospect House Fm
Beast Cliff
Staintondale Moor
High Moor
Tofta Fm
White Hall Fm
Little Eller Beck
Burn Howe Rigg
Staintondale
Plane Tree Fm
Lilla Rigg
Bloody Beck
Burn Howe Moor
Falcon Inn
Crowdon
Brown Hill
Lownorth Moor
Castlebeck Wood
Providence Heath
Redhouse Fm
Scar Wood
Harwood Dale Forest
Wyke Lodge
Hayburn Wyke
Stony Rigg 245
Riverhead Fm
Hayburn Beck Fm
WHITE WAY HEADS
Worm Sike Rigg
Standingstones Rigg
Woof Howe Grain
Barley Carr Tongue
Chapel Fm
Moor Cottage Fm
Linglands Fm
Rodger Trod
Grey Stones
Keasbeck Hill Fm
Cloughton Newlands
Langdale Forest
Allerston High Moor
High Langdale End
Hardwick Fm
Harwood Dale
Cloughton Plantns
Ellis' Close Fm
WHITE WAY
Nab Fm
Cober Hill
Cloughton Wyke
NORTH YORK MOORS
Langdale Rigg End
Thirley Cote Fm
Ripley's Fm
Hundale Pt
Hazelhead Moor
Thorn Hill Head
Warsman Head
Breckenhurst
East Syme
Cloughton
Cloughton Fields Fm
Blakey Topping
FOREST PARK
Barns Cliff
Kirkless Fm
Surgate Brow Fm
Long Nab
Newgate Foot
River Derwent
High Dales
Whisper Dales
Silpho Brow Fm
Low Moor Fm
Beacon Fm
Burniston
Crook Ness
Cromer Pt
Low Moor
Thompson's Rigg
Red Ho
Highdales Fm
Sailors' Grave
COASTAL ROAD
School Fm
Black Beck
Birch Hall Cott
Four Lanes Ends
Ind Est
Grime Moor
Crosscliff Wood
North Side Ho
Springwood Cott
Silpho
Binkleys Fm
Low Dales
Keeper's Old Ho
Deepdale Fm
Howden Hill
Foulsyke Fm
High House Fm
Bickley Gate Fm
Toll
Broxa
Hilda Wood
SCALBY ROAD
BURNISTON ROAD
Scalby Ness Rocks
Langdale End
Redbrow Plantn
Northfield Fm
West Head Coll
Stain Dale
Scalby
SCARBOROUGH
Pasture Fm
Backleys Fm
Hackness
Suffield
SEA LIFE SCARBOROUGH
Green Dale
Deep Dale
Peathead Rigg
Troutsdale Low Hall
Suffield Quarry
Swanbeck Fm
Newby
South Moor Fm
Suffield Heights
Keld Runnels Fm
Sea Cut
217
Thwaite Head
Jingleby Ho
Elberst Common Fm
Rock House Fm
Wood Ho
Intake Wood
Everley Bank Wood
Barrowcliff
Castle Cliff
SCARBOROUGH CASTLE
Swair Dale
Mount Misery
Raincliffe Fm
Throxenby
Ind Est
High Dalby Ho
High Rigg Fm
Seive Dale
Dalby Forest
Troutsdale Moor
Wrench Green
Cockrah Foot
Everley
ROTUNDA MUSEUM
Scarborough
Brompton Moor Ho
Wykeham Forest
Hawthorn Wood
Old & East Harbours
Snever Dale
Broad Head Fm
Manor Ho
Cockrah Wood
Raincliffe Woods
Row Brow Fm
South Bay
Thorn Park Fm
Hern
Row
A171

EAST
STEWARTRY
COAST
Auchencairn
Auchencairn Bay
Auchencairn Ho
Drungans
Cairn Hill
Nether Hazelfield
Rascarrel
Rascarrel Bay
Airds Cott
Airds
Airds Pt
Balcary Bay
Balcary Pt
Castle Muir Pt
Barlocco Bay
Moyl
White Port
Almorness Pt
Hestan Island
237
238
219
Bank End
SENHOUSE ROMAN MUSEUM
LAKE DISTRICT COAST AQUARIUM
MARITIME MUS
Maryport
THE WAVE CENTRE
Netherton
Ewanrigg
Ellen
Risehow Fm
Risehow
Fothergill
Woodside
Flimby
St Helens
Standings
Camerton Grange
A596
Stud Fm
Siddick
Seaton
Camerton
Camerton Hall
Ribton Hall
North Side
Hawk Hill
Salmon Hall
Barepot
Stainburn Hall Fm
Great Clifton
Clifton Hall
WORKINGTON HALL
Stainburn
Workington
A66
HELENA THOMPSON MUSEUM
Close End
Moorclose
Schoose
Mossbay
Westfield
Moss Bay
East Town End Fm
Winscales
A595
Salterbeck
Harrington
High Harrington
Gale Ho
Lucy Close Fm
Wythemoor Ho
Lillyhall Industrial Estate
Distington Works
Grayson Green
West Ghyll End Fm
Harrington Parks
Kelmore Hill Fm
Wythemoor Head
Branthwaite Row Fm
Park Ho
Distington
Gilgarran
Cunning Pt
Barngill Ho
Common End
Lowca
High House Fm
Pica
Moresby
Boon Wood
Wilson Park
Keekle Head Fm
High Park
Providence Bay
Parton Bay
Parton
Low Moresby
Tivoli
Moresby Moss
Tutehill Fm
Dub Hall
Tanyard Bay
Redness Pt
Bransty
Moresby Parks
Sandsclose
Harras
Scilly Bank
Ind Est
WALK MILL
Arlecdon Hill
Acrewalls
Whitehaven
THE BEACON
THE RUM
Bleak
Moss Bay
England Coast Path
Main Road
B5306
A5094
River Keekle
Dub Beck
Lostrigg Beck
0 1 2 3 miles
0 1 2 3 4 5 km

Blitterlees
Heather Bank
Wolsty Hall
Dryholme
Parkhead
Flagstaff
Kingside Hill
Abbey Town
Raby Grange
Raby
High Ho
Wedholme Ho
Wedholme Hill
Corbet Houses
Middlemoor House
Moorhouse
Moorhouse Hall
Greyrigg Ho
Parton
Oulton Ho
Oulton
Dockrayrigg Ho
Dockray Hall
Lessonhall
Micklethwaite
Crofton
Bankend
Peluthe Gill
Wolsty
The Hill Fm
Kelsick
Dundraw
Moor Row
Beckfoot
Highlaws
Pelutho
Foulsyke Ho
Kelsickhouse Fm
Hunter's Cott
Waverbridge
Station Hill
Standingstone
Spittal Fm
Lowfield Ho
Aikhead
West End
Bridge Ho
Greenwood Ho
Hazel Head
Moorthwaite Lough
West Woodside
Ghyll Head Fm
West Ho
Grayson Ho
Aldoth
Southerfield Hall
Wheyrigg Fm
Dian Ho Fm
Waverbridge Mill
Western Bank
Wigton
Kirkland
Newtown
Lowsay Fm
East Fm
Weary Hall
Thornhill Moss & Meadow
Beck Fm
Hill Ho
Southerfield Ho
Crooklands
Blencogo
Glebelands
Low Houses
Highmoor
Syke Fm
Forest Hall
Tarns
Mereside
Holme
St Cuthbert
Tarns Dub
Mawbray
Common Moss
Croft Ho
Greenrigg Villa
Tewfit Moss
Thornby End
Parkgate
Waverton
Barugh
Brackenlands
High Longthwaite
Old Carlisle
Low Ling
Goodyhills
Jericho
Aikshaw
Clappers
Langrigg
Bromfield
New Mill
Barughsyke
Hawkrigg Ho
Gerrard Ho
Mire Cottages
Brackenthwaite
Dubmill Pt
Salta
Mealrigg
Greenah
Gill Ho
Woodlands Ho
Red Dial
Stoneraise Place
Raise Lodge
Low House Fm
Causa Grange
Edderside
Whinbank
Beechhill
High Scales
Crummock Bank
Waterside
Red Hall
Greenhill Fm
Watch Hill
New Cowper
Woodrow
Westward
Westnewton
Low Row
Crookdake Hall
Blaithwaite Ho
Crookdake Mill
Bolton Low Houses
Intack Fm
Islekirk Hall
Bolton New Houses
Bolton Wood Lane
High Hall
Westward Park
Park Wood
Lord's Close
Yearngill Pasture Ho
Carr Wood
Crookdake
Thackthwaite Hall
Brownrigg Hall Fm
Newton Field
Warwick Hall
Wellington Fm
Percy Hill
Studholmerigg Wood
Gill
Allonby
Bus Pk
Scalegill Wood
Fletchertown
Hazelsprings Fm
Brocklebank
Bowscale
Brayton Park
Watchhill
Bog Hall
Clea Hall
Allonby Bay
Aiglegill
Aspatria
Mealsgate
Town Head
Hilltop
Waverhead Fm
Hayton
Tilekiln Cott
Baggrow
Leesrig Fm
Harbybrow
Weary Hall
Quarry Hill Fm
Pow Bank
Harriston
Blennerhasset
Quarry Hill Ho
Angerton Bank
Bolton Park
Faulds Spring
Hazel Mount
Prospect
Hall Bank
Aspatria
Aldersceugh
Catlands Hill
Blue Dial
Oughterside
Arkleby Mill
Plumbland Mill
Kirkland Guards
Low Mill
Newbiggin Grange
Boltongate
Pow Heads
Faulds Brow
Brownrigg
Paddigill
Allerby
Westmoor End
Beech Hill
Ellenbank Hall
Oughterside Mill
Arkleby
Park Ho
Ellen Bank
Sandale
Seat
Crosscanonby
Crosby Villa
Arkleby Ho
Threapland
Overgates
West Ho
Torpenhow
Prior Hall
Newlands Fm
Thistlebottom
Whelpo
Moor Park
Parsonby
Plumbland
Bothel
New Park
Ireby
Dale Side
Croft House Fm
Snowhill
Parkend
Long Lea
Birkby Lodge
Crosby
Bullgill
Gilcrux
Grange Fm
Wharrels Hill
Borrowscale
Whitrigg
Aughertree
Uldale Mill Fm
Aughertree Fell
Clay Gap
Springwell Ho
High Flatt Fm
Threapland Lees
The Battery
Bird Ho
Birkby
Rosegill Mill
Greengill
Wardhall Common
High Houses
High Ireby
Green How
Green Head
Branthwaite
Fell Side
Row Hall
New Grange
Caer Mote
Bothel Craggs
Crosshow
Dearham
Grange Grassings
Uldale
Kirkborough
Row Brow
Low Ho
Hill Fm
Moota Hill
Threapland Moss
Whittas Park
Ruthwaite
Chapel House Fm
Mickle Rigg
Hay Knott
Deer Hills
Townhead
Tallentire Hill
Millstone Moor
Salkeld Cross
Sunderland Heads
Binsey
Scawthwaite Close
Longlands
Brae Fell
Caldbeck
Clints Crags
Over Water
Longlands Fell
Birk Moss
Tallentire
Sunderland
Harker Marsh
Craikhow Hall
West Ho
Blindcrake
Glebe Fm
Bewaldeth
Lowthwaite Fell
Shepherd Hall
Woodside Fm
Park Wood
Irton Ho
High Bewaldeth
Williamsgate
Low Barn
Iron Crag
Hennah Hall
Bank Head
Howgill Wood
Orthwaite
Great Sca Fell
Broughton Moor
Dovenby
Dovenby Mill
Redmain
Isel Hall
Isel
Long Close Fm
Horsemoor Hills
Meal Fell
Great Lingy Hill
Broughton Lodge
Bridekirk
Prospect Ho
Messengermire Wood
Great Cockup
Miller Moss
Hewthwaite Hall
Park Wood
Knott
Mountain View
Cumbria
Dovenby Craggs
Anns Hill
Wood Hall Fm
Forth Ho
Lake District Wildlife Park
Kestrel Lodge
Coomb Height
Little Broughton
Elva Hill
Kilnhill
North Row
Bassenthwaite
Melbecks
Dash Fm
Belle Vue
Hame's Hall
Park House Fm
Watch Hill
Setmurthy Common
Higham Hall
Ouse Bridge
Chapel
Great Broughton
Papcastle
Cockermouth Castle
Castlegate Ho
Wyndham Ho
Bully Ho
Dubwath
Barkbeth
Dead Crags
Great Calva
Skiddaw
Ribton Ho
Wordsworth House
Lambfoot
Embleton
Crag
Pheasant Inn
Scarness
High Side
Broad End
Bakestall
Brigham
Broughton Cross
Cockermouth
Westray
East Ho
Dyke Nook
Bassenthwaite Common
Skiddaw Forest
Tarn Bank
Scales Fm
Bouch Ho
Wythop Mill
Abbey
Sale Fell
Bassenthwaite Lake
Hare Crag
Nepgill
Espa Fm
Sand Hill
Skiddaw House
Mungrisdale Comm
Bridgefoot
Greysouthen
Tendley Hill
Dubbs Moss
Lake District National Park
Little Clifton
Rigging Gill
Eaglesfield
Shatton Lodge
Ling Fell
Mirehouse
Longside Edge
Sale How
Burnt Horse
Cloven Stone
Lamb Hill
Bent Houses
Shatton Hall
Low Fell
Wythop Moss
Wythop Hall
Lake District
Carl Side
Little Man
Olderfield Mill
Oldfield
Springfield Fm
Harrot
Empleton High Common
Broom Fell
Woodend
Redness Point
Dodd Wood
Grey Crags
Jenkin Hill
Lonscale Fell
Knowe Crags
Calva Hall
Deanscales
Galefield
High Dyke
Lorton
Graystones
Lord's Seat
Barf
Long Close Fm
Howgill Tongue
Blease Fell
Woodside
East Ho
Wood Fm
Brandlingill
Sandybeck Meadow
High Lorton
Oakfield House
Millbeck
Hollins Wood
Pardshaw Hall
Akebank Mill
Bank
Low Lorton
Scawgill Br
Thornthwaite
Applethwaite
Lonscale
Derwentfolds
Browtop
Dean
Leegate
Mosser Mains
Whin Fell
Whinfell Hall
Lorton Fells
Whinlatter
Thornthwaite Galleries
Ormathwaite
Branthwaite
Pardshaw
Fellside Fm
Lorton Vale
Whinlatter Forest Visitor Centre
Whinlatter Pass
Latrigg
Briery
Brundholme Wood
Branthwaite Edge
Mains
Mosser
Dodd Wood
Fellbarrow
Newhouse Fm
Forest Park
Bog Ho
How
Great Crosthwaite
Keswick
Burns Fm
Branthwaite Rigg
Crakeplace Hall
Ullock
Mosser Fell
Thackthwaite
Hopebeck
Hobcarton End
Hospital Plantn
Spring Bank
Braithwaite
Derwent Pencil Mus
High Hill
Castlerigg Stone Circle
Rigg Ho
Sourfoot Fell
Dodd
Portinscale
Brigham
Chestnut Hill
Row End
Mockerkin
Fangs Brow Fm
Miller Place
Grisedale Pike
Little Braithwaite
Ullock
Low Rigg
Mockerkin How
Waterend
Iredale Place
Darling Fell
Hobcarton Crag
Coledale Beck
Swinside
Castlerigg
Lingcroft
Dean Cross
Hudson Place
Low Fell
Brackenthwaite
Hopegill Head
Force Crag
Stile End
Barrow
Silver Hill
Derwent Isle
Stable Hills
Dale Bottom
Havercroft
Holme Wood
Loweswater
Whiteside
Sand Hill
Great Wood
Kidburngill
Woodend
Bird Dyke
Scale Hill
Stair
Swinside
High Rigg
High Moss
Derwent Water
Millgillhead
Crossgates
Burnbank Fell
Lamplugh
Owsen Fell
Loweswater
Liza Beck
Eel Crag
Causey Pike
Hawes End
Rowling End
Yew Crag
Low Bridge End Fm
Asby
Carling Knott
Lanthwaite
Grasmoor
Crag Hill
Scar Crag
Newlands
Falcon Crag
Low Moss
Dockray Nook
East Ho
Felldyke
Loweswater Fell
Wandope
Ard Crags
Cat Bells
Little Town
Castlerigg Fell
Goat Crag
Ashness Br
Bleaberry Fell
Knock Murton
Lamplugh Fell
Little Dodd
Mellbreak
Rannerdale
Bawd Hall
Great Bay
Middle Fell
Gavel Fell
Hen Comb
Whiteless Pike
Knott Rigg
High Snab Bank
Scope
Black Crag
Ashness
High Seat
Castle Crag
Raven Crag
Rowrah
Leys
Keltonfell Top
Kirkland
Kelton Fell
Ling Crags
Hause Point
Crummock Water
Newlands Pass
Derwent Fells
Borrowdale Gates
Solway Coast
Lake District National Park
England Coast Path
Solway

Baldwinholme
Nealhouse
Cardewlees
Moorend
Thursby
Dalston
Durdar
Brisco
Springfield Fm
Low Cotehill
Cotehill
Carlatton Mill
Moorthwaite Moss
Chapel Well
Hornsby
Micklethwaite
Crofton
West End
Evening Hill
West Curthwaite
Cardew
Cardew Lodge
Cumdivock
East Curthwaite
Chalkfoot
Green Head
Buckabank
Bridge End
Unthank
Sprunston
Stone Raise
Ratten Row
Pow Bank
Hillhouse Nook
Durdar Ho
Oakland Ho
Burthwaite Hill
Burthwaite
Newbiggin Hill
Carleton Hill
Park Ho
Wreay
Wreay Hall
Foulbridge
Bankdale Fm
Petteril Crook's Mill
Wragmire Moss
Wragmire Head
Ivy Cottage
Lowthian Gill
Stoney Wath Fm
Stand End
Warathwaite Head
Fishgarth Wood
Far Hornsby Gate
Gateshaw Mill
Holmwrangle
Broadbeck Mill
Lawson Hill
High Stand Plantn
Barrock Fell
Jacob's Gill
Broomfield
Hawksdale
Hawksdale Hall
Hawksdale Pasture
Raughton
Gaitsgill
Crown Inn (PH)
Longrigg Cott
Beck Ho
Ellerton Grange
Barrock Park
Low Hesket
Aiketgate
Hill Rigg
Nelson Hill
Armathwaite
Priory
Lockhills
Towngate
Ainstable
Forest Hall
Low Ling
Kirkstead
Brackenthwaite
Low House Fm
Rosleyrigg
Causa Grange
Rosley
River Wampool
Moss End
Rose Bank
Flat Bank
Warren Plantn
Raughton Head
Dobcross Hall
Skiprigg
Nether Welton
Park Ho
Mellguards
Southwaite Services
Southwaite
Southwaite Hill
Field Ho
Nunclose
Bank Ho
Bascodyke Foot
Bascodyke Head
Dale Mill
Westward Park
Intack Head
Grassgarth
Welton
Holm Ho
Stockdalewath
Knight's Lodge
Arnold Ho
Burble Fm
Sycamore Lodge
Broadfield Ho
High House Fm
Sewell Houses
Barrow Mill
Low Cotts
High Hesket
Coombs Wood
Longdales
Ruckcroft
Dale
Brothybeck
Borrans Hill
Sunny Vale
Lambfield Fm
Highbridge
Swathwaite Head
Beck Cotts
Harrington Ling Fm
Old Town
Nord Vue Fm
Baron Wood
Highfield
Gill
Hazelsprings Fm
Broad Moor
Sebergham Castle Fm
Town Head
Bulman Hill
Birks Hill
Jack Ho
Mirkbooths
High Head Castle
Ivegill
Sceugh Hill Fm
Inglewood Ho
Inglewood Cott
Blaze Fell
Baronwood Fm
Nunnery Ho
Chalkplains Wood
Waverhead Fm
New Ho
The Greens
Low Currigg
Raine Ho
The Ashes
Temsend
Low Braithwaite
Market Gate
Petterilgreen Cotts
Abbots Moss Fm
Low Plains
Faulds Spring
Kiln Gate
Sebergham
Lonning Head
Churchtown
Cockleythwaite
Middlesceugh
Low Grange
Bents Cotts
Wool Oaks Mill
Castlerigg Fm
Baronwood Park
Warnell Fell
Warnell Hall
Denton Side
Stockwell Hall
Sour Nook
Braithwaite Hall
Thiefside Cotts
Wood End Fm
Faulds Brow
Brownrigg
Parkhead
Ratten Row
Parson's Park
Starnmire
Middlesceugh Hall
Hurst
Inglewood
Hill Houses
Sceugh Dyke
Calthwaite
Thomas Close
Aik Bank Fm
Aikbank Common
Pears Ho
Bleaberry Hill
Crag Nook
Lazonby Hall
Paddigill
How-Gill
Oaker Lodge
Sowerby Row
Scales Hall
Bartons Fm
Scales Fm
Morton
Robinson Ho
Plumpton Foot
Knowe Fm
Lazonby & Kirkoswald
Townhead
Brackenbank
Faulds
Whelpo
Howk
Caldbeck
Throstle Hall
Newlands
The Nooks
Low Buildings
High Buildings
Southernby
Smallthwaite Ho
Hutton End
Brackenburgh Cotts
Low Grounds
Lazonby Fell
Upton
Parkend
Long Lea
Hesket Newmarket
Street Head
Banks Fm
Hall Field
Hewer Hill
Skelton Pasture
Skelton Wood End
Rediane End
Lower Dyke
Castlesteads
Scalehill
Clay Gap
Nether Row
Millhouse
Inglewood Edge
Holly Hill
Askrigg Hall
Parson's Park Wood
Newlands Hill
Forest
Pyeing Fm
Monks Ho
Scarfoot
Scratchmere Scar
Keld Fm
North Dykes
Braithwaite
Caldbeck
Fell Side
Potts Gill
Wood Hall
Low Moor Dyke
Haltcliff Hall
Whartonl Ho
Hutton Grange
Plumpton
Brockleymoor
Hay Knott
Deer Hills
Haltcliff Ho
Haltcliff Bridge
Sowerby Hall
Hole Ho
Starth Hill Fm
Pringle Ho
Hardrigg Hall
Unthank Ho
New Rent
Hutton-in-the-Forest
Fairbank Wood
Plumpton Old Hall
Wan Fell
Salkeld Dykes
Caldbeck Fells
West Fell
High Row
How Hill
Lamonby
Kirk Rigg
Skelton
Unthank
Unthank End
Rashmire Wood
Plumpton Hall
Plumpton Head
Burrell Green
Birk Moss
High Pike
Heggle Lane
Thwaite Hall
Town Head Fm
Lamonby Hall
Ellonby
Holme Head
Plumpton Head
Bowscar
Judge's Plantn
Carrock Beck
Bannest Hill
Stewart Hill
Millfield Lodge
Cumbria
The Tilery Fm
Kelbarrow Fm
Woodhead Fm
Foresthill
Great Sca Fell
Iron Crag
Miton Hill
Great Lingy Hill
Stone Ends
Hutton Roof
Scales
The Laithes
Johnby
Little Blencow
Laithes
Catterlen
Inglewood Bank
Inglewoodbank Cotts
Edenhall Grange
Round Knott
Carrock Fell
Greystoke Forest
Brown Hills
Blencow Hall
High Dyke
Low Dyke
Inglewood Inn Fm
Knott
Miller Moss
Coomb Height
Coomb
Grainsgill Beck
Swineside
Low Mill
Gillcambon
Great Blencow
Long Ashes
Milestone Ho
Greengill
Greengill Head
Wood Head
River Caldew
Mosedale
Caldew Wood
Newton Reigny
Catterlen Hall
Stagstones Fm
Beacon Hill
Tarn Crags
Murrah Hall
Greystoke Park
Mount Pleasant
Newton Rigg
Fair Hill
Great Calva
Lake District
Moss Dyke
Berrier Hill
Bunkers Hill
Pallet Hill
Bleak Ho
Scaws
Skiddaw Forest
Bowscale Fell
Raven Crags
Mungrisdale
Greystoke
Greenthwaite Hall
Tymparon Hall
Castletown
Thacka Beck
Penrith
The Tongue
Mungrisdale Common
Bannerdale Crags
Lake District
Eycott Hill
Berrier
Greystoke Moor
Old Riggs
Newbiggin
Penrith North Lakes
Penrith Castle
Pategill
Carleton
Skiddaw House
Cloven Stone
National Park
Sharp Edge
Nobles Fm
Berrier End
Greystoke Gill
Beckstones
Bell Mount
Brougham Castle
Eamont Bridge
Burnt Horse
Saddleback or Blencathra
Souther Fell
Blake Hills Fm
Whitbarrow Village
Beckside
Motherby
Penruddock Hall
Division Moor
Bus Pk
Flusco Pike
Hoghouse Hill
Redhills
Rheged
Sockbridge
Mayburgh Henge
Countess Pillar
Pembroke Ho
Roughten Gill
Hallsfell Top
Scales Fell
Askew Rigg Fm
Lofshaw Hill
Lisco Fm
Tarn Moss
Beckces
Penruddock
Stainton
Aldby Fm
Sockbridge Mill
Scales
Troutbeck
Highgate Fm
Hutton
Park Ho
Dalemain
Barton
Thorpe
Tirril
Glen Dowlin Fm
Clifton
Clifton Dykes
Blease Fell
Gategill Fell
Hall's Fell
Knowe Crags
Hutton Moor End
Red Syke Fm
Greta
Dacre
Dacre Beck
Blease Fm
Stoddah Fm
Sparket Mill
Hesket Fm
Dacre Lodge
Barton Ho
Lonscale
Derwentfolds
Guardhouse
Birkett Field
Spring Bank
Soulby Fell Fm
Soulby
Barton Hall
Buckholme Wood
Abbott Lodge
Threlkeld
Highgateclose
Rookin House Fm
Great Mell Fell
Routing Gill
Grovefoot Fm
Croft Head Fm
Low Moor
Brownrigg
Land Ends
Maiden Castle
Waterfoot
Pooley Bridge
High Hollows
Bus Cen
Threlkeld Common
Burns Fm
Birkett Mire
Little Mell Fell
Bell Grove
Elderbeck
Roehead
Skirsgill Hill
Askham
Lakeland Bird of Prey Centre
Lowther Castle
Lowther
Old Coach Road
Castlerigg Stone Circle
Row End
Threlkeld Knotts
Matterdale End
Moorend Fm
Old Park
Priest's Crag
Longthwaite
Wreay
Heughscar Hill
Lowther Park
Hackthorpe
Low Rigg
Lowthwaite Fm
Clough Head
Hollows
Cockley Moor
Ulcat Row
Watermillock
Park Foot
Waterside Ho
Askham Fell
Helton
Wanthwaite Crags
Wolf Crags
Gowbarrow Fell
Swinburn's Park
Barton Park
The Riggs
Dale Bottom
Groove Beck
Dockray
Knotts
Swarthbeck Cotts
Tarn Moor
Whale
High Rigg
Bram Cragg
Calfhow Pike
Bruts Moss
High Brow
High Row
Lucy's Wood
Gowbarrow Park
Gowbarrow Hall
Barton Fell
Setterah Park
Yew Crag
Bridge End
Low Fm
Matterdale Common
Dowthwaitehead
Dobbin Wood
Arthur's Pike
Helton Fell
Whalemoor
Great Dodd
Common Fell
Round How
Aira Force Waterfall
Ullswater
Bonscale Pike
Beckfoot
Birkett Fell
Watermillock Common
Watson's Dodd
Castle Rock
Glencoyne Park
Aira Point
Howtown
Dale Hause
Low Knipe
Butterwick
Rough Hill
Howgate Foot
Knipe Moor
In Scar
Brown Hills
Sandwick
Doe Green
Martindale
The Dodd
Kid Moor
Moorahill Fm
Out Scar
Sleet Fell
High Dodd
Winter Crag
Cote Fm
Hart Hill
Sticks Pass
Boredale
Birk Fell
Martindale Common
Loadpot Hill
Cawdale
Cross Gate
Bampton
Bampton Grange
Sheffield Pike
Glencoyne Wood
Fisher Place
High Seat
miles
km

NORTH PENNINES
Alston
Nenthead
Garrigill
Leadgate
Melmerby
Lazonby
Kirkoswald
Langwathby
Culgaith
Temple Sowerby
Long Marton
Dufton
Appleby-in-Westmorland
Murton
Hilton
Milburn
Knock
Kirkland
Skirwith
Ousby
Gamblesby
Renwick
Croglin
Newbiggin
Cumrew
Ayle
Blagill
Nenthall
Cross Fell 893
Great Dun Fell 848
Milburn Forest
Dufton Fell
Murton Fell
Hilton Fell
Alston Moor
Gilderdale Forest
Knarsdale Common
Moor House Upper Teesdale
High Cup Nick
Cauldron Snout Waterfall
Acorn Bank Garden
Long Meg & Her Daughters
Hartside Height
Nenthead Mines
South Tynedale Railway
Pennine Way
River Eden
River Tees
River South Tyne
A66
A686
A689
B6412
B6413
B6277
B6260
B6542
NY
80
50
20
A
B
C
D
E
F
G
H
7
8
9
10
11
240
241
232
221
222

232
NORTHUMBERLAND
NORTH PENNINES
DURHAM
Weardale
Teesdale
Sinderhope
Acton Moor
Broad Gate
Allendale Common
Hangman Hill
Pikeley Rigg
Stobbylee Burn
Hope Fell
Pennypie Ho
Pennypie Fell
Hotburn Hill
Ruffside Hall
Carterway Heads
Derwent Reservoir
Birkside Fell
Birkside
Reeding
Blanchland
Baybridge
Bridge End
Edmundbyers Common
Edmundbyers
Berry Bank
Derwent Br
Eddy's Bridge
Brownley Hill
533
Rye Close
Knock Shield
Sipton Shield
Harwoodshield Fell
427
Newbiggin Fell
Newbiggin
Kevelin Moor
Longwell Moor
Limestone Brae
Tedham Moss
Riddlehamhope Fell
Muggleswick
Muggleswick Park
Spartylea
Nookton Back Fell
Hunstanworth
High Townfield
Buckshott Fell
Black Cleugh
The Meres
Knockshield Moor
Elpha Green
Halleywell Fell
Western Meadows
439
Uzzles Hill
Cross Hill
375
Storeley Hill
West Cot Ho
Coal Gate
Birkhot
White Hill
Heatheryburn Moor
Boltshope Park
Ramshaw
Cross Rigg
Middle Rigg
Carrshield
Green Hill
White Ridge
506
Nookton Edge
Nookton West Fell
Ellers Hill
Sandyford
Harehope Hill
Byerhope Moss
Middles
Hisehope Reservoir
Smiddy Shaw Reservoir
Sikehead Dam
Boltshope
Black Hill
421
Muggleswick Common
Carrshield Moor
Swinhope Moor
Meadow Cott
Byerhope
Byerhope Reservoir
Quickcleugh Moss
Hunstanworth Moor
Smallburns Moor
The Dodd
Spring Ho
Dirt Pot
Edmondbyers Common
614
Allendale Common
West End
Bolt's Law
540
Hisehope Head
Coalcleugh
Allenheads
559
Redburn Edge
Cuthbert's Hill
Horseshoe Hill
519
Feldon Plain
409
Skaylock Hill
Middlehope Moor
Westend Moor
Allenheads Park
561
Redburn Common
Black Hill
Coalcleugh Moor
Kilhope Law
Rimey Law
Bell's Hill
Waskerley Reservoir
Steward Shield Meadow
Rookhope Chimney
Wolfcleugh Common
Cleugh Ho
Holy Well
Killhope Cross
A689
Bank Foot
Waskerley Park
Puddingthorn Moor
Bell's Hill
Bell's Bridge
Gold Hill
KILLHOPE - THE LEAD MINING MUSEUM
Wolf Cleugh Fm
Lintzgarth
Rookhope
Stanhope Common
Slit Foot
Mount Pleasant
Sedling Fell
Lintzgarth Common
Long Hill
512
Weatherhill Engine
Collier Law
516
Weather Law
Cowhorse Hill
Weardale Forest
Middlehope Moor
Smailsburn Common
Smailsburn
Millstone Rigg
Knoutberry Hill
Nag's Head
High Greenfield
Scarsike Head
539
Pasture Ho
Park Plantn
High Ho
Lanehead
Whitestone Ho
Cornriggs
Black Hill
604
White Edge
Wolsingham Park Moor
Cowshill
Copthill
Race Head
586
Middlehope Lodge
Hanging Wells
Ambling Gate
Mount Pleasant
Lamb's Head
648
Moss Moor
Halliwell Ho
Newhouse Moor
Northgate Fell
Crawleyside
Bents Head
Wearhead
Sunderland Fm
Ashy Bank
Stanhope
Hill Crest
Fatherley Hill
459
709
Dead Stones
White Edge
Middle Rigg
West Blackdene
Carr Brow Moor
DURHAM DALES CENTRE
Burnhope Reservoir
High Rigg
Ireshopeburn
New Meadows
White Hall
Rose Hill
Eastgate
White Ho
Aller Gill
STANHOPE
Burnhope Burn
Slack Ho
New Ho
East Blackdene
High Kitty Crag
Westgate
Park Ho
River Wear
Burnhope Moor
High House
St John's Chapel
Thimbleby Hill
Frosterley Cott
Intake Fm
Daddry Shield
Hawkwell Head
Ireshope Plains
Hill Hos
Brotherlee
Newlandside Fm
Rogerley Hall
Frosterley
Newlands Hall
Burnhope Seat
746
Glenwhelt
Littlewood Fm
Snape Gate
Snowhope Close
Bridge End
FROSTERLEY
Coves Ho
High Wood Meadows
New Close
Scaud Hill
Great Stony Hill
Catterick Moss
Ireshope Moor
Noon Hill
High Pike
586
Hill End
Ashgill Head
Harwood Common
Grass Hill Fm
Coldberry End
Causeway Hill
Harthope Moor
Chapel Fell
Swinside Ho
NORTH
Snowhope Moor
540
Bollihope Carrs
White Kirkley
Bollihope Ho
Harvey Hill
320
Harehope
Langdon Head
576
Black Hill
607
Snowhope Hill
Juniper Banks
Bollihope
Frog Hall
Grasshill Common
Three Pikes
Chapelfell Top
Swinhopehead Ho
Bollihope Common
Allotment Ho
Harthope Moss
Swinhope Moor
Westernhope Moor
Low Black Hill
Wager Head
Force Foot
Harwood
Langdon Fell
Langdon Common
696
Fendrith Hill
Dora's Seat
Swinhope Head
Five Pikes
478
Lingy Hill
PENNINES
Harnisha Hill
589
Raven Seat
Pawlaw Pike
488
Pikeston
Bleak Law
Low End
Church Bowers
Black Hill
Flushiemere Beck
Red Wing
White Mere
Newbiggin Common
Middleton Common
West Common
Binks Ho
Touting Hill
Peghorn Lodge
Valence Lodge
Langdon Beck
Pike Law
Flushiemere Ho
Carrs Hill
601
Hamsterley
Black Hill
393
Cow Green
Cow Green Reservoir
Widdybank Fell
Hunt Hall
New Ho
LANGDON BECK
Wool Pits Hill
High Beck Head
Watson's Br
White Hill
490
Sharnberry Flat
Widdy Bank Fm
Forest-in-Teesdale
Ettersgill
Moor Riggs
Broadley's Gate
Moor Ho
Red Grooves Ho
Coldberry
Hardberry Hill
529
492 Islington Hill
Middle End Plantn
Hamsterley Forest
CAULDRON SNOUT WATERFALL
Hill End
Cronkley
Ash Hill
Field Head
Club Gill
Monk's Moor
Neighbour Moor Ho
Thistle Green
White Well Green
HIGH FORCE
BOWLEES VISITOR CENTRE
Bowlees
Stable Edge
Hardberry Fm
Pennington Cott
Pennington Plantn
Grain Beck
PENNINE WAY
Hield Ho
Wynch Br
Newbiggin
Snaisgill
Raven Hills
521
Merrygill Moss
Danger area
Cronkley Fell
Noon Hill
Holwick Lodge
Eggleston Common
Holwick
Middle Side
Aukside
High Dyke
Stotley Grange
Cowlake
339
Knotts Plantn
Lang Hurst
Danger area
Holwick Fell
Holwick Scars
Swinket Mease Rigg
Green Fell End
Howden Moss
Dent Bank
Middleton-in-Teesdale
Blackton Head
Woodland Fell
Long Crag
Millstone How Hill
Park End Wood
Park End
Stotley Hall
Laverock Hall
Rotten Rigg
Crossthwaite Scars
Stone Houses
Mickle Fell
Crossthwaite Common
Step Ends
River Tees
Egglesburn
Hill Top
Hagworm Hill
Bink Moss
Buck Riggs
Harter Fell
481
Moor Rigg
Laithkirk
Ornella Fm
Bogg Ho
Danger area
Staple Moss
Bowbank
Mickleton
Eggleston
Stobgreen Plantn
Keekham Beck Head
Lune Moor
Low Bink Moss
Cote Ho
Stoop Hill
Icaron Lodge
EGGLESTON HALL
Folly Ho
White Ho
High Crag
Lune Forest
Cock Lake
520
East Park
Thringarth
Wythes Hill
Pallet Crag Ho
Hollin Side Wood
Paddock Wood
Philip Reed Moss
Close House Crags
Sleight Edge
Stake Hill
West Pasture
Bail Hill
Romaldkirk
Kinninvie
Close Ho
Fish Lake
High Plantn
Grassholme Reservoir
Rogermoor Fm
Lune Head Moss
Blindgill Moss
Forest Edge
Hargill Br
Wemmergill Hall
Grassholme
Harker Springs
Romaldkirk Moor
Great Wood
Hawkesley Hill
Long Grain Moss
Lane Head Fm
Danger area
Arngill Ho
Selset Reservoir
Hunderthwaite
Wildon Grange
Parrick Ho
Ley Seat
River Lune
Kelton Ho
Hunter Hill
Three Chimneys
Park House Fm
Wilden Beck
Doe Park
Thwaite Hall
Quarryhouse Fm
High Ho
High Garford
Soulgill Edge
Mickleton Moor
Howgill Grange
Hury
Gill Ho
Gill Field
West End
Helbeck
Sheep Lair Hill
Kelton Fell
Kelton Hill
Gill Fm
Briar Dykes
Balder Grange
Corn Park
Cotherstone
Stone Cross
Broad Stone Rigg
Black Hill
Hunderthwaite Moor
East Briscoe
Hury Reservoir
Booze Wood
Cooper Ho
West Holme Ho
Ravensike Rigg
Mawk Hole Moss
Balder Head
Blackton Reservoir
Willoughby Hall
Fiddler Ho
East Holme Ho
HANNAH'S MEADOW
Musgrave
Seavy Rigg
Caple Rigg
Clove Lodge
Pitcher Ho
Currack Rigg
Crook Beck
Towler Hill
Little Fell
Conrpot Beck
NY
241
242
231
222
223
3miles
5 km

Consett
Leadgate
Annfield Plain
Chester-le-Street
Allensford
Castleside
Knitsley
Delves
Lanchester
Burnhope
Sacriston
Edmondsley
Kimblesworth
Great Lumley
Waskerley
East Butsfield
Witton Gilbert
Langley Park
Pity Me
Framwellgate Moor
Aykley Heads
Satley
Cornsay
Cornsay Colliery
Quebec
Esh
Bearpark
Ushaw Moor
Broompark
Durham
Gilesgate
Sherburn
Esh Winning
Waterhouses
New Brancepeth
Shincliffe
High Shincliffe
High Stoop
East Hedleyhope
Brandon
Tow Law
Sunniside
Wolsingham North Moor
Bowburn
Wolsingham
Thornley
Billy Row
Brancepeth
Sunderland Bridge
Croxdale
Hett
Crook
Willington
Oakenshaw
Page Bank
Tudhoe
Mount Pleasant
Thinford
Fir Tree
Helmington Row
Sunnybrow
Byers Green
Spennymoor
Cornforth
Howden-le-Wear
Newfield
Middlestone Moor
Ferryhill
Ferryhill Station
Hunwick
High Grange
Binchester Blocks
Bedburn
Hamsterley
Witton-le-Wear
Westerton
Kirk Merrington
Redford
Middlestone
Chilton Lane
Witton Park
Toronto
Escomb
New Coundon
Coundon
Leasingthorne
Low Etherley
High Etherley
Bishop Auckland
Chilton
Rushyford
Toft Hill
Morley
St Helen Auckland
Eldon
Old Eldon
Shildon
Woodland
West Auckland
Newton Aycliffe
Copley
Butterknowle
Evenwood
Cockfield
Bildershaw
Royal Oak
Evenwood Gate
Redworth
Heighington
Aycliffe
Wackerfield
Hilton
Bolam
Houghton-le-Side
Staindrop
Ingleton
Langton
Killerby
Summerhouse
Walworth Gate
Coatham Mundeville
Brafferton
Cleatlam
Headlam
Denton
Walworth
Beaumont Hill
Durham Services
DURHAM
A68
A691
A690
A167
A688
A689
A6072
A1(M)
242
243
234
223
224

Houghton-Le-Spring
Seaham
Hetton-le-Hole
Murton
Easington
Easington Colliery
Peterlee
Horden
Blackhall Colliery
Thornley
Wheatley Hill
Wingate
Trimdon Colliery
Trimdon
Sherburn
Coxhoe
Cornforth
Ferryhill
Sedgefield
Bradbury
Wynyard Village
Hartlepool
Seaton Carew
Billingham
Middlesbrough
Stockton-on-Tees
Norton
Roseworth
Carlton
Bishopton
Great Stainton
Elstob
Stillington
Whitton
Thorpe Thewles
Aycliffe
Chilton
Bowburn
Shincliffe
Pittington
Littletown
Haswell
Shotton
Castle Eden
Hesleden
Hart
Elwick
Dalton Piercy
Greatham
Graythorp
Port Clarence
North Ormesby
South Bank
DURHAM
HARTLEPOOL
TYNE AND WEAR
DARLINGTON
STOCKTON-ON-TEES
North Sands
Seaton Sands
Hartlepool Bay
Featherbed Rocks
Horden Pt
Fox Holes
Shot Rock
Chourdon Pt
Nose's Pt
Liddle Stack
Parton Rocks
The Headland
Seal Sands
Teesmouth
Crimdon Park
Durham Coast

0 1 2 3 miles
0 1 2 3 4 5 km

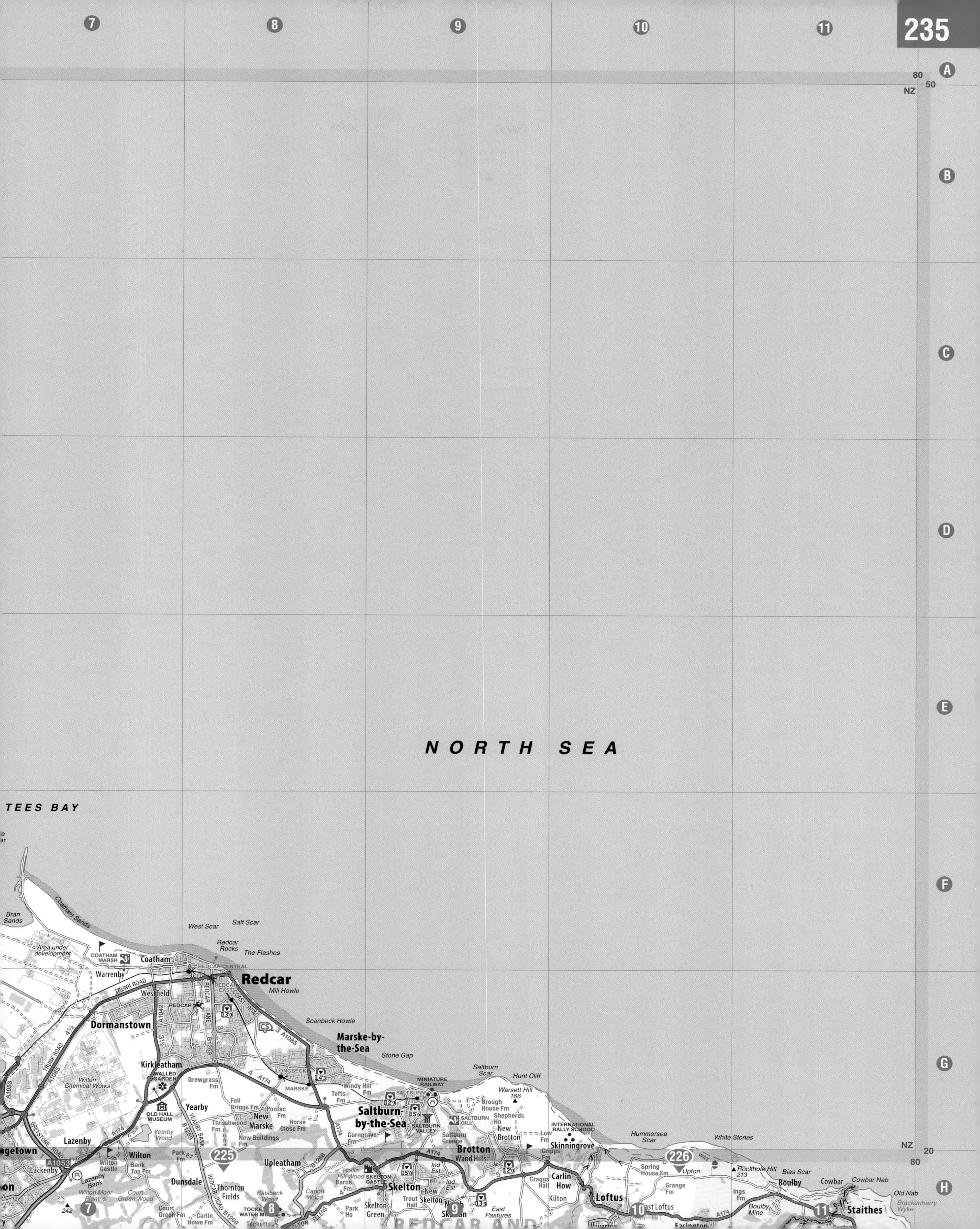
NORTH SEA
TEES BAY
Redcar
Coatham
Dormanstown
Kirkleatham
Marske-by-the-Sea
Saltburn-by-the-Sea
Brotton
Skinningrove
Carlin How
Loftus
Skelton
Staithes
Boulby
Upleatham
Yearby
New Marske
Wilton
Lazenby
Lackenby
Dunsdale
Warrenby
Westfield
Coatham Sands
Bran Sands
West Scar
Salt Scar
Redcar Rocks
The Flashes
Mill Howle
Scanbeck Howle
Stone Gap
Saltburn Scar
Hunt Cliff
Warsett Hill
166
Hummersea Scar
White Stones
Rockhole Hill
213
Bias Scar
Cowbar
Cowbar Nab
Old Nab
Brackenberry Wyke
A174
A1085
A1053
A1042
B1269
B1268
WILTON CHEMICAL WORKS
OLD HALL MUSEUM
WALLED GARDEN
MINIATURE RAILWAY
INTERNATIONAL RALLY SCHOOL
225
226
NZ
80
50
20

Ballantrae Bay
Ballantrae
Heronsford
Glen Tig
Water of Tig
Ballochmorrie
Black Clauchrie
Moan
Palgowan
Loch Enoch
Garleffin
Cosses
Balkissock
Barrhill
Laggan
Eldrick
Glentrool
Forest
Loch Valley
SILVER FLOWE
Downan Pt.
Downan
Glenapp Castle
Smyrt
Auchencrosh
Cairnlea
A714
Cairnderry
Glentrool Village
GLENTROOL VISITOR CENTRE
Glen Trool Lodge
BRUCE'S STONE
Gleanhead
Loch Trool
Loch Dee
NX
Arecleoch Forest
BENERAIRD
Drumlamford Loch
Dornal
Chirmorrie
Dalnaw
Bargrennan
LAMACHAN HILL
BELFAST
LARNE
Lagafater Lodge
Loch Dornal
Loch Ochiltree
Clachaneasy
Loch Middle
Kirroughtree Forest
Mark
Glen App
Milleur Pt.
Miltonise
Craig Airie Fell
Loch Maberry
Polbae
Loch Derry
Portencalzie
Barnhills
Mahaar
Corsewall
Kirkcolm
Loch Connell
LAGGANGAIRN STANDING STONES
Knowe
WOOD OF CREE
WILD GOAT PARK
Auchinleck
Cairnryan
Penwhirn Res.
Main Water of Luce
Cross Water of Luce
High Eldrig
Artfield Fell
B7027
Glenrazie
Penninghame Forest
Boreland
Cumloden
Penkiln Burn
A712
Palnure Burn
Ervie
Low Salchrie
The Wig
LOCH RYAN
Bankhead
Braid Fell
Balmurrie
Carseriggan
Barfad
Challoch
Minnigaff
Creebridge
Bargaly
KIRROUGHTREE VISITOR CENTRE
Newton Stewart
MINNIGAFF
Leswalt
Craigencross
New Luce
Auchmantle
Black Loch
Balminnoch
Loch Heron
Shennanton Ho.
Blackpark
Benfield
Stronord
Palnure
SOUTHERN UPLAND WAY
Loch Ronald
Airyligg
Shennanton
Drumphail
A75
Barraer
Carty Port
Innermessan
Lochinch Castle
B7043
A718
Glenstockadale
Auchnotteroch
CASTLE KENNEDY GARDENS
White Loch
Castle Kennedy
Stranraer
CASTLE OF ST JOHN VISITOR CENTRE
STRANRAER MUSEUM
Aird
Soulseat Loch
Knockglass
GLENWHAN GARDENS
Whitecairn
Balmesh
GLENLUCE ABBEY
Glenluce
Carscreugh
Dergoals
Tarf Water
Craighlaw Mains
Kirkcowan
B733
B735
Baltersan
Cree
Causeway End
Grange of Cree
Carsegowan
Creetown
Dernaglar Loch
Knock Moss
High Mindork
Spittal
Torhousemuir
TORHOUSE STONE CIRCLE
Bladnoch
Wigtown Sands
Dunragit
Mark
Lochans
Black Hd.
Dunskey Ho.
Droughduil
CASTLE OF PARK
Torrs Warren
Whitefield Loch
B7052
B7005
Wigtown
SCOTLAND'S BOOK TOWN
Carsluith
Pinminnoch
Colfin
B7077
B7084
Portpatrick
Awhirk
Stoneykirk
Luce Sands
Milton
Stairhaven
Auchenmalg
Fell Loch
Drumwalt
Castle Loch
Mochrum Loch
Culmazie
VISITOR CENTRE
Mains of Baldoon
Baldoon Sands
Braehead
Kirkinner
Port of Spittal Bay
Kildonan
B7042
A716
Auchenmalg Bay
Culshabbin
Airlies
Alticry
B7005
Loch Head
Barrachan
Whauphill
B7004
Culscadden
Cairngarroch
Cairngarroch Bay
KIRKMADRINE STONES
Sandhead
Sandhead Bay
Money Hd.
CHAPEL FINIAN
Elrig
Hole Stone Bay
Clachanmore
MOTE OF DRUCHTAG
Mochrum
Sorbie
Garlieston
Airyhassen
Milton Pt.
West Ardwell
Ardwell
Chapel Rossan Bay
Ardwell Mains
Ardwell Pt.
Drumtroddan
Drummoddie
GALLOWAY HOUSE GARDENS
DRUMTRODDAN STONES
Logan Mains
Port William
Monreith Mains
Moor of Ravenstone
Castlewigg
Cults
LOGAN BOTANIC GARDEN
Balgowan Pt.
LUCE BAY
Mull of Logan
LOGAN FISH POND MARINE LIFE CENTRE
Port Nessock or Port Logan Bay
Port Logan
Chapel Outon
Barsalloch Pt.
Monreith
Bishopton
PRIORY AND MUSEUM
Whithorn
Cairnywellan Hd.
B7065
Monreith Bay
WHITHORN TRUST DISCOVERY CENTRE
Clanyard Bay
Low Clanyard
Glasserton
FELL OF CARLETON
Laggantalluch Hd.
Kirkmaiden
Drummore
Cailliness Pt.
ST NINIAN'S CAVE
Kidsdale
Tonderghie
Isle of Whithorn
Damnaglaur
B7041
Port Castle Bay
Cutcloy
Crammag Hd.
Maryport
BURROW HEAD
Cairngaan
MULL OF GALLOWAY
Port Kemin
MULL OF GALLOWAY
0 2 4 6 miles
0 2 4 6 8 10 km

Dungeon
Earlstoun
Millquarter
Duchrae
Loch Urr
Sundaywell
Milton
Dunscore
Throughgate
Burnhead
ELLISLAND MUS & FARM
Duncow
Amisfield
Tinwald
Earlstoun Loch
St John's Town of Dalry
Corriedoo
Corriedoo Forest
Cairn Water
Gallaberry
Killylung
Kirkton
Drumbuie
Bogue
Garroch
Glenlee
Clatteringshaws Forest
Clatteringshaws Loch
Mid Garrary
Blackcraig
Knocklearn
Gibbshill
Balmaclellan
New Galloway
Newtonairds
Drumpark
Holywood
Locharbriggs
Heathhall
DUMFRIES AND GALLOWAY AVIATION MUS
Irongray
Newbridge
Lincluden
LINCLUDEN COLLEGE
The Grove
Craigencallie Ho.
Craignell
BRUCE'S STONE
Kenmure
Ironmacannie
Craig
Corsock
Glenkiln Res.
Margreig
Glenkiln
Glen
Shawhead
Terregles Banks
Dumfries
OLD BRIDGE HOUSE MUS
Maxwelltown
Greystone
BURNS HOUSE
ROBERT BURNS CENTRE
DUMFRIES MUSEUM & CAMERA OBSCURA
RAIDERS ROAD FOREST DRIVE
Bennan Forest
Loch Grannoch
Cairn Edward Hill
Loch Ken
Merkland
Glenlair
Urr Water
Crofts
Brooklands
Brae
Lochfoot
Lochrutton Loch
Cargenbridge
Kingholm Quay
FELL OF FLEET
Drumrash
Mossdale
Airds of Kells
Parton
Redcroft
Auchenreoch Loch
Crocketford or Ninemile Bar
Milton Loch
Milton
Islesteps
Mabie Forest
Mabie
Kelton
Stroan Loch
KEN-DEE MARSHES
Kirkpatrick Durham
Springholm
Beeswing
Loch Arthur
Lochaber Loch
KIRKCONNELL FLOW
Glencaple
Loch Skerrow
Woodhall Loch
CAIRNSMORE OF FLEET
Fleet Forest
Old Bridge of Urr
Crossmichael
DRUMCOLTRAN TOWER
Kirkconnell
Craig
Hardgate
Haugh of Urr
Kirkgunzeon
New Abbey
SWEETHEART ABBEY
Shearington
River Nith
Lochenbreck Loch
Townhead of Greenlaw
Clarebrand
Congeith
New Abbey Pow
NEW ABBEY CORN MILL
Bowhouse
Clints of Dromore
Dromore
Laurieston
Glenlochar
MOTE OF URR
Overton
Laurieston Forest
Loch Glentoo
THREAVE CASTLE
Leaths
LONG FELL
Loch Kindar
ESTUARY
Culcronchie
Loch Whinyeon
Castle Douglas
OLD BUITTLE TOWER
Barhill
Dalbeattie
Drumburn
Mark
Big Water of Fleet
Loch Mannoch
Glengap Forest
Loch Bargatton
THREAVE GARDEN & ESTATE
Carlingwark Loch
Boreland of Southwick
CRIFFELL
CARSTRAMON WOOD
BENGRAY
Glengap
Bridge of Dee
Rhonehouse or Kelton Hill
Gelston
Carsethorn
Glen
FLEET
Pulcree
Fleuchlang
Ringford
Dalbeattie Forest
Drumstinchall
Kirkbean
ARBIGLAND GARDENS
Caulkerbush
Prestonmill
Anwoth
CARDONESS CASTLE
Gatehouse of Fleet
Valleyfield
Airieland
Palnackie
Barnbarroch
CARSLUITH CASTLE
CAIRNHARROW
Lagganmullan
ORCHARDTON TOWER
Sandyhills
Mainsriddle
JOHN PAUL JONES COTTAGE MUSEUM
MERSEHEAD
CAIRNHOLY CAIRNS
VALLEY
Girthon
Twynholm
GALLOWAY HYDRO VISITOR CENTRE
Tongland
BENGAIRN
Kippford or Scaur
MOTE OF MARK
Rockcliffe
Colvend
Southerness
Barholm
Fleet Bay
BROUGHTON HOUSE AND GARDEN
EAST STEWARTRY COAST
ROUGH ISLAND
Rough I.
Portling
Mersehead Sands
Southerness Pt.
Ravenshall Pt.
Ringdoo Pt.
Rainton
Sandgreen
Barharrow
Whinnieliggate
Auchenleck
Craigshall
Castlehill Pt.
Carrick
STEWARTRY MUSEUM
Kirkcudbright
Culnaightrie
Auchencairn
Auchencairn Bay
Hestan I.
Islands of Fleet
Knockbrex
Bombie
Kirkcarswell
Auchencairn Ho
Balcary Pt.
St Mary's Isle
Mutehill
Borgue
Kirkandrews
Chapelton Row
Mill Hall
Dundrennan
Rascarrel
Rascarrel Bay
WIGTOWN BAY
Borness
Kirkcudbright Bay
The Lake
Townhead
Orroland
DUNDRENNAN ABBEY
Graplin
Ross
Balmae
Netherlaw
Port Mary
Borness Pt.
Abbey Hd.
Little Ross
SOLWAY FIRTH
MARYPORT MARITIME MUSEUM
Maryport
Flimby
Siddick
Seaton
Camerton
North Side
Workington
Stainburn
HELENA THOMPSON MUS
Westfield
Mossbay
Harrington
High Harrington
Distington
Lowca
Pica
Moresby
Keekle
Parton
Moresby Parks
Bransty
THE RUM STORY
Whitehaven
Hensingham
Saltom Bay
Mirehouse
Cleator Moor

DUMFRIES AND GALLOWAY
SOLWAY FIRTH
SOLWAY
NITH ESTUARY
Blackshaw Bank
Lockerbie
Lochmaben Castle
Heck
Hightae
Smallholm
Rammerscales
Woodlands
Torthorwald
Dumfries & Galloway Aviation Mus
The Grove
Greystone
Gasstown
Georgetown
Collin
Greenlea
Woodside
Elizafield
Racks
Brocklehirst
Cleughbrae
Mouswald
Langdyke
Carrutherstown
Dalton
Kirkwood
Middleshaw
Castlemilk
Kettleholm
Blackford
Burnswark
Burnswark Hill Fort
Middlebie
Ecclefechan
Thomas Carlyle's Birthplace
Hoddomcross
Hoddom Mains
Kirtlebridge
Eaglesfield
Brydekirk
Creca
Charlesfield
Annan
Welldale
Newbie
Shawhill
Watchill
Dornock
Cummertrees
Powfoot
Ruthwell
Savings Banks Museum
Clarencefield
Plans
Longbridgemuir
Horseholm
Bankend
Glencaple
Kelton
Shearington
Bowhouse
Blackshaw
Eastpark
Caerlaverock Castle
Caerlaverock
Wildfowl & Wetland Centre
Overton
Carsethorn
Arbigland Gardens
John Paul Jones Cottage Museum
Bowness-on-Solway
Campfield Marsh
Cardurnock
Anthorn
Whitrigg
Kirkbride
Newton Arlosh
Skinburness
Silloth
Greenrow
Causewayhead
Calvo
Seaville
Blitterlees
Abbey Town
Kingside Hill
Beckfoot
Pelutho
Highlaws
Newtown
Kelsick
Lessonhall
Dundraw
Waverbridge
Blencogo
Aldoth
A75
A74(M)
A701
A709
B725
B724
B7020
B7076
B5302
B5300
248
237
228
229
0 1 2 3 miles
0 1 2 3 4 5 km

Kirtleton
Crosslands
Springkell
Burnfoot
Chapelknowe
Newton
Kirkpatrick-Fleming
Hollee
Gretna Green
Gretna
Rigg
Old Graitney
Springfield
Browhouses
Redkirk Pt
Torduff Pt
Channel of River Esk
Rockcliffe Marsh
Burghmarsh Pt
Burgh Marsh
Drumburgh
Easton
Boustead Hill
Burgh by Sands
North End
Beaumont
Monkhill
Kirkandrews on Eden
Grinsdale
Fingland
Thurstonfield
Moorhouse
Kirkbampton
Oughterby
Little Bampton
Aikton
Wiggonby
Great Orton
Thornby
Baldwinholme
High Whinnow
Thursby
Mickelthwaite
Crofton
Wigton
West Curthwaite
Cardew
East Curthwaite
Dalston
Buckabank
Cummersdale
Newby West
Little Orton
Stainton
Kingstown
Houghton
Harker
Rockcliffe
Cargo
Blackford
Todhills
Westlinton
Sandysike
Longtown
Netherby
Canonbie
Evertown
Claygate
Hollows
Rowanburn
Woodhouselees
Moat
Carwinley
Easton
Catlowdy
Haggbeck
Stapleton
Roadhead
Baileyhead
Crossings
KIELDER FOREST PARK
Kirklinton
Hethersgill
Smithfield
Boltonfellend
Scalebyhill
Scaleby
Laversdale
Newtown
Irthington
Brunstock
Low Crosby
Linstock
Crosby-on-Eden
Walby
Houghton
Carlisle
Stanwix
Edentown
Botcherby
Harraby
Upperby
Morton
Carleton
Scotby
Wetheral
Great Corby
Warwick Bridge
Warwick on Eden
Heads Nook
Cumwhinton
Brisco
Durdar
Cotehill
Wreay
Burthwaite
Fenton
Faugh
Cumwhitton
C U M B R I A
SOLWAY MOSS 1542
Hadrian's Wall Path
Solway Aviation Mus
Carlisle Lake District Airport
A7
A74(M)
A75
M6
A6071
A689
A69
A595
A596
B5307
B5299
B6318
B6357
B7076
239
240
249
229
230
A
B
C
D
E
F
G
H

Kershope Forest
Bewcastle Fells
Blacklyne Ho
Cuddy's Hall
Kettle Hall
Sighty Crag 518
Horse Head
Gairs
Black Knowe 492
K I E L D E R
Rushy Knowe
Allerybank
Black Knors 248
Black Knors
Whiteyne Common
Long Bar
Smuggy's Pike
Long Crags
Hopehouse
Black Cleugh
Bailey Head
Baileyhead
Crookburn Hill
Black Stantling
Slaty Crag
Long Crag 456
The Shanks
Kielder Mires
Muckle Samuel's Crags
F O R E S T P A R K
Lowe Bush
Paddaburn
Clintburn
Little Dodd Hill
High Capon Edge
Claver Hill
The Flatt
Watch Rigg
Greyfell Common
Tarn Beck
Irthing Head
Blind Sike
Whitehill
Arthur Seat
Bailey Mill
Holmehead
Blackpool Gate
Crew Crag
Whiteside End
Gaylock Hill
Crew Moor
Canmock Rigg
Sheala Hill
Nook
Felecia Crags
Round Hill 310
Great Tongue Rigg
Round Top 325
Long Rigg
White Brae
Breakshaw Hill
Churnsike Lodge
Shank End
Wark Forest
West Cleugh
Haining
Crossings
Oakshaw Ford
Sleetbeck
Bankhead
Rawney
Grey Hill
Park Head
New Ho
Bullcleugh Gate
Blackrigg Foot
Wreay Hill
Butterburn Flow
Spy Rigg
N O R T H U M B
Great Watch Hill
Blue Hemmel
Shawhead
Brownhill
Heather Ho
Danger area
Hen Hill
Gowany Knowe
Nether Hill
Kinkry Hill
Roughsike
Ann's Hill
Peel o'Hill
Park
Bewcastle
Borderrigg
356
Barron's Pike
Leafy Rigg
Roadhead
Kirkbeckstown
Shopford
Gilbert's Hill
Greymare Hill
Butterburn
Lampert
N O
N A T I O
Roan Fm
Noblestown
Scotstown
Kilnstown
Kirk Beck
Whipper Slack
Black Fell
Grindon Green
Westfield Ho
239
High Parkfoot
Cocklett Rigg
Luke's Ho
Bushley Bank
Side Fell
Jock's Hill
Butterburn Hill
Cheeseburn Hill
Gowk Bank
Deer Hill
Hen Hill
Rough Sike
Lynecrook
Bellbank
Birk Bush
Kays Bank
Collin Bank
Green Knowe
Spadeadam Forest
Low King Hill
Jerrycalf Rigg
Berry Hill
Tip Hill
Gavelock Hill
Great Buckster
P A R
Selbystown
The Show
Low Park
The Beacon 310
Standingstone Rigg
Danger area
Hopealone
Harper Hill
Allergarth
White Rigg
Green Rigg
Crowrigg Sike
Wileysike Ho
Bell's Braes
Robinrock Flothers
Stapleton
Askerton Park
Gillalees Beacon
Spadeadam Fm
Kingturn Rigg
Rashbush Rigg
Middle Shield Rigg
Dumblar Rigg
Hugh's Hill
Burn Divot
Patties Hill
Low Park
Mollen Wood
Parkgate Cotts
Ash Moss
Peat Rigg
White Rigg
Rushey Hill
White Close
High Green Hill
Rinnion Hills
Forster's Hill
River Irthing
Long Moss
Highstead Ash
Black Rigg
Thirlwall Common (North Side)
Whiteside
Wall Shield
Benkshill
Kirkcambeck
Gallowberry
Palmer Hill
Waterhead Common
Jamie's Hill Sike
Watch Hill
Seed Rigg
Moss Peteral
Benks Hills
Ventners Hall
Edges Green
Swallow Crags
Cowburn Rigg
Bolton Fell
Popping Stone
Wardrew Fm
C U M B R I A
Lees Hill
Kingbridge Ford Br
West Hall
Tweedy Hill
Gilsland Spa
War Carr
Cairny Croft
Hangingshields Rigg
Chesters Pike
Cleughfoot
Sook Hill
Well Ho
Cocklet Hill
Leaps Rigg
Barns
B6318
Hill Ho
Spout Bank
Swaites
Park Nook
Craigsyke Ford
Miller Hill
Willowford Bridge Abutment
Midgeholme Moss
Birdoswald (Camboglanna) Roman Fort
Gilsland
Barron House
Burnt Walls
Low Old Shields
Hadrian's Wall
Hadrian's Wall (Course of)
Cawfields Milecastle
Pennine Way
Vallum (Course of)
Broomhill Moss
Walton Moss
Hainings Ho
White Hill
Walton Woodhead
Allieshaw Rigg
Leahill Turret
Harrow's Scar Milecastle
Poltross Burn Milecastle
Gap
Greenhead
Walltown
Cockmount Hill
Haltwhistle Common
Milestone Ho
Stanegate (Course of)
Walton Moss
Breaks Moss
Hill Head
Walton Wood
Craig Hill
High Ho
Denton Mains
Birdoswald
Thrup
Wardoughan
Fell End
Edge Hill
Lees Hall
Low Rigg
Walton
Garthside
Hadrian's Wall Path
Bank's East Turret
Banks
Hare Hill
Mains Rigg
Upper Denton
Gapshield
The College Fm
Blenkinsopp Hall
Haltwhistle
Hollin Crags
Town Foot
Common Ho
Low House Fm
Melkridge
Morrell Hill
Low Wall
Howgill
Lanercost
Banks Ho
Nook
Trywell Lodge
Thirlwall Common (South Side)
Todholes
Blenkinsopp Common
A69
Heads Wood
Kylesyke Hill
Kellwood
Burtholme
Lanercost Priory
St Mary's Vale
Denton Hall
Low Broom Hill
Lodges
Low Row
Hill Head
Hole Ho
Cross Bank
Bellister Castle
Plenmeller
Unthank Hall
East Unthank
Newtown
The Beck Fm
River Irthing
Cotehill Fm
Naworth Park
Denton Foot
Birch Craig
Black Rigg
Wain Rigg
Featherstone Common
Wydon Eals
Sandyford Rigg
Broomhouse
Howden Burn
Irthington
Kirby Moor
Quarrybeck Ho
Denton Ho
Cleugh Head
Denton Fell
Glencune Burn
Hartleyburn Common (North Side)
Bridge End
Park Village
Warren Ho
Broomhouse Common
Bridle Green
Blackcleugh Rigg
Red Hills
Old Church Fm
Brampton
Ind Est
Scarrow Hill
Low Houses
Whamoss Rigg
Greentarn Rigg
Cross Rigg
Peat Gate
Plenmeller Common
Middle Fm
Miltonrigg Wood
Milton Hill
Back Dike
Cocklit Hill
Cairn End
Beanlands Park
Rulehome Br
A689
Aaron's Town
Milton Hall
Milton
Kirkhouse
Moss Hill
Greenside Rigg
Follysyke Cotts
Byers Hall
Rowfoot
Ramshaw Fell
Park Barns
Wood's Hill
Low Geltbridge
Hallbankgate
Tarnhouse Rigg
Tindale
Haining Ho
Hill Ho
Clover Hill
Lambley Fm
Wood Houses
Coanwood
Hargill Ho
Todhillwood
Peat Hill
Gelt Ho
Edmond Castle
Talkin Tarn
Farlam
Boon Hill
Highfell Clesketts
Geltsdale
Bishop Hill
Midgeholme
Halton Lea Gate
Pennine Road
Lambley
Burn Ho
Garbutt Hill
Wolf Hills
Stonehouse
Western Ridge
Hayton
Street Ho
Talkin
Forest Head
Bruthwaite Forest
Tindale Fells
Whinney Fell
Hag Wood
Byers Fell
Lambley Common
Tows Bank
Quarry Ho
Coanwood Common
Laws Fell
Hayton Castle
Hayton Hill
How
Cote Hill
Greenwell
Chapel Ho
Turkey Hall
Talkin Head Fm
Talkin Fell 381
Brown Fell
458
Byers Pike
Hartleyburn Common (South Side)
Haltonlea Fell
Whitwham
Wallace's Crags
Ashholme Common
Brown Rigg
Parkhead Fell
Allenwood
Stockdale Hall
Fenton
Ring Gate
Kelky Fell
Butt of Blackburn
Glendue Burn
Eals
Dun Hill
Heads Nook
Fenton Lane Head
Whin Hill
Castle Carrock
Garth Head
Simmerson Hill
Cold Fell 621
Blackburn Head
Larchet Hill
Knowe Head
Eals Fell
Blaeberry
Glencairn Mill
Faugh
Tarn Lodge
Moss Knowe
Park Ho
Oaktree Hall
Long Dyke
Knotts Wood
Castle Carrock Fell
Tarnmonath Fell
Glendue Fell
Side Ho
Knarsdale Hall
The Bog
Snope Common
Pike Rigg
Mainsrigg Fell
Great Blacklaw Hill 595
Faugh Cleugh
Thinhope Burn
Knarsdale
Whitfield Moor
Nixon Head
Geltsdale Ho
Binney Bank
King's Forest of Geltsdale
P E N N I N E
Town Green
Williamston Common
Low Bradshaw Hill
Whitfield Law
Longdyke Fm
Morley Hill
Whitehead Hill
Black Dub
Albyfield
482
Cardunneth Pike
Black Hill
Knarsdale Forest
Slaggyford
Moreyhill Fell
Cumwhitton
Turnberry Ho
West Dun Hill
Aules Hill
Barhaugh Common
Dewley Fell
Carlatton Mill
Middle Top
Shawhead
Moorthwaite Moss
Chapel Well
Cumrew Fell
Geltsdale Middle
Three Pikes 585
Hartchyside
Bertram Hill
Far Ho
Dewley Field
Willyshaw Rigg
Eden Banks
New Water
Knarsdale Common
Lintley
Ayle Common
497
Long Cross
Cumrew
Hornsby
Butt Hill
Gelt Burn
Far Town
NY
Far Hornsby Gate
Gateshaw Mill
230
Newbiggin Fell
Blotting Raise 591
Thornhope Fell
231
Kirkhaugh
Ayle
Claraghyll Hall
Green Hill
Newbiggin
Croglin Fell
Castle Nook
High Shield
Whitley Castle
Kirkside Wood
South Tynedale Railway
White Ho
Newshield Moss
The Combs
Broad Mea
Knar Burn
Cairnhead Fm
Lawson Hill
Croglin
Grey Nag
0 1 2 3 miles
0 1 2 3 4 5 km

Redesmouth
Countesspark Wood
Ealinghamrigg Common
Ealingham Rigg
Watson's Walls
Dun's Pike
Shitlington Common
Shitlington Crags
Shitlington Hall
Cairnglastenhope
Pundershaw
Pundershaw Burn
Stone Ho
Bridge Ho
Esp Hill
Esp Mill
Brier Hill
Blackaburn
Camstone Rigg
Watergate Moor
Leadgate
Horneystead
Birk Hill
230
Harelaw
White Hill
Whygate
Stonehaugh
Coldcotes
Coldcotes Hill
Willowbog
Broadpool Common
Standard Hill
Middleburn
Coalcleugh
Black Rigg
Shepherdshield
N O R T H U M B E R L A N D
Haggle Rigg
Black Law
Long Edge
Bell Crags
Byreshaw Hill
Bellcrag Flow
Haughton Common
Townshield Bank
Simonburn Common
Stooprigg
Crow Crags
Halleypike Lough
Hemmel Rigg
Long Rigg
Well Rigg
Banno Crags
Long Crag
Sweet Rigg
Stonefolds
Queen's Crags
Teppermoor
Greenhaugh
Uppertown
Sharpley
Cockplay
Hadrian's Wall (course of)
Vallum (course of)
Hadrian's Wall Path
Carrawburgh Temple of Mithras
Black Carts Turret
Sewingshields Wall Turrets & Milecastle
Old Repeater Station
Brown Moor
Greenlee Lough
Broomlee Lough
Bonnyrigg Hall
Hotbank Crags
Housestead's (Vercovicium) Roman Fort & Museum
Howden Hill
Middle Ho
Cowey Sike
Settlingstones
Grindon Hill
Grindon Mill Hills
Grindon Lough
Crag Lough
Winshields Milecastle
Steel Rigg
Bradley Hall
Grandy's Knowe
Muckle Moss
Honeycrook Burn
The Sill at Hadrian's Wall
Long Stone
Thorngrafton Common
Thorngrafton
Whinnetley Moss
Hindshield
Haydon Fell
Fell Cott
Chesterholm (Vindolanda) Roman Fort & Museum
Westend Town
Birkshaw
Bardon Mill
Brown Rigg
Henshaw
Tow House
Whitechapel Hill
Prior Ho
Westley Bank
Chesterwood
Haydon Bridge
Lipwood Hall
Lipwood Well
Hill Ho
South Tyne
Redburn
Crow Hall
Ridley
Beltingham
High Barns
High Barn
Haughstrother Wood
Wool Ho
Burn Ho
Allen Banks & Staward Gorge
Vauce Wood
Farrow Shields
Ridley Common
Plankey Mill
Hag Bank
Harlow Field
Kingswood Common
Kingswood Rigg
Staward Manor
Haining Hall
Crag Head
Beacon Hill
337
Fellhouse Fell
Fell Ho
Dingbell Hill
Whitfield
Bearsbridge
Emley
Whitfield Hall
Park Head
Quarry Ho
Monk Cott
Keenley
Chapel Ho
Pia Troon
Parmentley Hall
Gate Ho
Morley Hill
Parmentley Cott
Mount Pleasant
Ninebanks
Middle Edge
Ouston
Round Hill
Herd's Ho
Drybum Moor
Black Hill
Hawkuplee
Ninebanks
Spartywell
Farneyside
Greenleycleugh
Ouston Fell
Acton Moor
Brownley Hill
533
White Hill
Mohope Head
Park Ho
Broadlee
Kevelin Moor
Mohope Moor
The Nook
Limestone Brae
Halley Moor
Broad Meadows
New Ho
The Meres
Black Cleugh
Hesleywell
546
Longwell Moor
Knockshield Moor
Elpha Green
Spartylea
Tedham Moss
Halleywell Fell
Western Meadows
Heatheryburn Moor
Nookton Back Fell
Riddlehamhope Fell
Hunstanworth
High Ho
Cross Hill
Townfield
Boltshope
Buckshott Fell
Anton Hill
Lee Hall Fm
Lee Hall
High Carry Ho
Low Carry Ho
River North Tyne
Manor Fm
Warksfield Head
Crossridge
Longstrother
South Fm
Birtley
Gold Island
The Ash
Pasture Ho
The Barnes
Woodley Shield
Wark
Warks Haugh
Comogan Fm
Threpwood Hill
Parkhouse Fm
Dinley Hill
High Moralee
Low Moralee
Sadbury Hill
Bleaklaw
Park End
Lyndhurst
Allgood Fm
Burn Ho
Simonburn
Hall Barns
Fairshaw Fm
Nunwick Mill
Burnmouth Cotts
Blackhill Fm
Steward's Ho
Short Moor
Pit Ho
Mallowburn Cottages
Rouchester Fell
Gunnerton Fell
Rubbingstob Hill
Pitland Hills
Lowshield Green
Rushey Law
Tone Hall
Low Fm
Waterfalls
Green Rigg
Lough Hill
Cowstand Hill
White Ho
Birney Hill
Carrycoats Hall
Colt Crag Reservoir
Colt Crag
Folly Moss
Sweethope Crags
Great Bavington
Quarry Ho
Newonstead Fm
Thockrington
Thockrington Crags
Little Bavington
Short Knowes
Little Swinburne
Barrasford Park
Great Swinburne
Swinburne Castle
Gunnerton
Green's Fell
Colwell
Liddell Hall
Fell Ho
Hallington Reservoir
Whiteside Law
Hallington
Bavington Hill Head
Bavington Hall
Moss Barns
Bavington Mount
Kirkheaton Wind Farm
Hallington High Fm
Hallington New Ho
Moatlaw
White Ho
Fell Lane Fm
Wood Hall Fm
Barrasford
Barrasford Green
Ellwood Ho
Edge Ho
Middle Fm
Haughton Castle
Wester Hall
Haughton Pasture
Haughton Mains
Chollerton
Beaumont Ho
Low Errington
Errington Red Ho
Bingfield
Bingfield East Quarter
New Bingfield
Bingfield Eastside
Well Ho
High Well Ho
Dere Street
Todridge Fell
Todridge
Shellbraes
Ryal
Rye Hill
Lincoln Hill
Chollerford
Walwick
Humshaugh
Cocklaw
Keepwick Fm
Beukley
Rose's Bower
The Whiggs
Great Whittington
Walwick Fell
Torney's Fell
Chesters Museum
Chesters (Cilurnum) Roman Fort
Low Brunton
Brunton Bank
Brunton Turret
Planetrees Roman Wall
Wall
Hill Head
Grottington Fm
Errington Hill Head
Little Whittington
Halton Red House
217
Lane Ho
Frankham Fell
Newbrough Lodge
Frankham
Stonecroft Ho
Newbrough
Fourstones
Written Crag
Codlaw Hill
Wall Fen Fm
Port Gate
Stagshaw Bank
Halton
Carr Houses
East Wood
Stagshaw High Ho
Fern Hill Fm
Carr Hill
Black Hill
Holly Hall
Stagshaw
Chantry Fm
Aydon Castle
Aydon
High Warden
Nether Warden
Warden
Wharmley
Greenshaw Plain
Woodshield Fm
Allerwash Hall
High Ho
East Mill Hills
Bridge End
Broom Park
Ind Est
Salmonswell Fm
Acomb
The Riding
Oakwood
Beaufront Hill Head
Beaufront Castle
Sandhoe
Shawwell Ho
Hampstead
Anick
Anick Grange
Bush Fm
Glendue
Wood Hall
Hackford Fm
High Wood
Hexham
Hexham Abbey
Tyne Green
Bridge End
Tyne Green
Corstopitum Roman Station
Wide Haugh
Corbridge
Thornbrough
Lowe's Fell
Ellfoot Ho
Elrington
Low Gate
Bagraw Fm
Breckon Hill
Moot Hall
Border History Mus
Delegate Hall
Cook Wood
Dilston Park
Dilston Physic Gdn
Dilston
Howden Dene
Corbridge
West Land Ends
Threepwood
Blackhall Plantns
Yellow Rigg
Benson's Fell
Oakerland
Swallowship Hill
High Town
West Fell
Prospect Hill
Grey Court
Riding Mill
Langley
Nilston Rigg
Plover Hill
227
Black Ho
Sunnyside
Kinnels
98
Temperley Grange
Blackhill Fm
Hexham
Peterel Field
Red Ho
Hole Ho
Birks
Lamb Shield
Beauclerc
The Paise
Stublick Hill
Stublick Moor
Greenridge
Loadman
West Dipton Burn
Diptonmill
Dipton Wood
Broomhaugh
Channel Well
Dotland Park
Red Hemmels
High Plains
Broomley Pit Ho
Catton Beacon
337
Emertley Hill
Rebel Hill
Greenrigg Moor
Anchey Sike
Edge Ho
Lord's Lot
Spitalshield Moor
Ordley
Lee
Linnel Wood
Todburn Steel
Highfield Fm
White Ho
Bulman's Rigg
Cook's Ho
Juniper
Black Hall
Hirst Hill
185
Marley Cote Walls
Eastwood Ho
Old Town
Catton
Gaterley Hill
Lough Hill
Moss Well
Raven Currick Rigg
Reeds Rigg
Low Lane Ho
Barker Ho
Hamburn Hall
Dalton
Whitley Mill
Dye House
Finechambers Mill
Shield Hall
Steel
Low Ho
Peel Flatt
Slaley
Healey Mill
Burnt Ho
Hindley Hall
Lea Hall
Stone Hall
Eshells Moor
Whapweasel Burn
Springwell Ho
Whitley Chapel
Mire Ho
Dukesfield
Ridley Halls
Strothers Dale
Hill Top
Healey Hall
Thornley Gate
High Oustley
Broadwood Halls
Moorhouse Gate
Allendale Town
Wentworth Place
Finney Hill
Crawberry Hill
Burntridge Moor
Burnt Ridge
Salmon Field
Rawgreen
Holly Hill
White Ho
Steel Hall
Leadpipe Hill
Fell Plantn
Rowley Head
Stotsfold Fm
Stotsfold Hall
Rennys Barn
Spring Ho
Trygill
Colpitts Grange
Fell Cotts
Kellas
Wager Ho
Glen Hill
Scotch Halls
Herds Law
King's Law
357
Slaley Forest
Espershields Fm
Round Hill
Park Gill
Nettle Hill
Haggburn Gate
Studdon Park
Green Hill
Hexhamshire Common
White Hall
Broadwell Ho
Park Ho
Acton Fell
Embley Fell
War Law
315
Pithouse Fell
Wall Ho
Park
Green Dike
Garrets Hill
Newfold Ho
Sinderhope Gate
Ladle Well
Lilswood Grange
Grouse Ho
Loaning Ho
Burntshield Haugh
Burntshieldhaugh Fell
413
Blanchland Moor
Cowbyers Fell
Derwent Reservoir
Dean Rigg
Hotburn Hill
Pennypie Ho
Pennypie Fell
Hangman Hill
Sinderhope
Allendale Common
Broad Gate
Pikeley Rigg
Steelcrags Wood
Hope Fell
Birkside Fell
Birkside
Reeding
427
Newbiggin Fell
Blanchland
Baybridge
Newbiggin
Harwoodshield Fell
Rye Close
Knock Shield
Slipton Shield
Ruffside Hall
Ruffside Moor
Edmundbyers Common
Berry Bank
Harehope Hall

252
241
232
233
NZ
NORTHUMBERLAND
DURHAM
Capheaton
Harnham
Belsay
Belsay Hall, Castle & Gardens
Ogle
Shilvington
Saltwick
Stannington
Kirkheaton
Wallridge
Black Heddon
West Newham
Higham Dykes
Milbourne
Hallington
Ingoe
Ryal
Heugh
Fenwick
Matfen
Stamfordham
Dalton
Ponteland
Prestwick
Newcastle International Airport
Darras Hall
High Callerton
Black Callerton
Woolsington
Great Whittington
Ouston
Eachwick
Medburn
Harlow Hill
Halton Shields
Halton
Aydon
Newton Hall
Newton
Heddon-on-the-Wall
Throckley
Newburn
Walbottle
Westerhope
North Walbottle
Horsley
Wylam
Clara Vale
Ryton
Crawcrook
Ovingham
Ovington
Prudhoe
West Wylam
Eltringham
Mickley Square
Stocksfield
Riding Mill
Broomhaugh
Broomley
Painshawfield
New Ridley
Hedley on the Hill
Blaydon
Winlaton
Whickham
Greenside
Coalburns
Barlow
High Spen
Rowlands Gill
Chopwell
Blackhall Mill
Hamsterley
High Westwood
Ebchester
Medomsley
Burnopfield
Leazes
Hobson
Tanfield
Tantobie
Dipton
Annfield Plain
Stanley
Beamish
Leadgate
Consett
Shotley Bridge
Benfieldside
Bridgehill
Carterway Heads
Edmundbyers
Muggleswick
Healey
Whittonstall
Newlands
Kiln Pit Hill
Shotleyfield
Allensford
Templetown
Iveston
Castleside
Knitsley
Delves
Burnhope
Craghead
Kenton
Gosforth
Fenham
Scotswood
Dunston
Sunniside
Marley Hill
Byermoor
Causey
Brenkley
Seaton Burn
Dinnington
Brunswick Village
Hazlerigg
Shotton
Hadrian's Wall (course of)
Vallum (course of)
0 1 2 3 miles
0 1 2 3 4 5 km

Blyth
Cowpen
Newsham
South Beach
New Delaval
East Hartford
South Newsham
Shankhouse
Nelson Village
Cramlington
East Cramlington
Seaton Sluice
New Hartley
Seaton
Seaton Delaval Hall
Hartley
St Mary's Lighthouse
Seaton Terrace
Seaton Delaval
Holywell
Annitsford
Seghill
Fordley
Dudley
East Holywell
West Holywell
Whitley Sands
Spanish City
Whitley Bay
Burradon
Backworth
Earsdon
Monkseaton
Camperdown
Killingworth
Killingworth Village
West Monkseaton
Shiremoor
Murton
Preston Grange
Marden
Cullercoats
Tynemouth Aquarium
West Moor
Palmersville
New York
West Allotment
Forest Hall
Preston
Tynemouth
Castle & Priory
Rising Sun
Stephenson Railway Mus
Billy Mill
Longbenton
Battle Hill
North Shields
Amsterdam
Chirton
West Chirton
Holy Cross
Percy Main
Arbeia Roman Fort & Museum
Ocean Beach Pleasure Park
The Lawe
Newcastle upon Tyne
Wallsend
Willington
Howdon
Royal Quays
South Shields
Jesmond
Heaton
Rosehill
East Howdon
Howdon Pans
Frenchman's Bay
Segedunum Roman Fort
Tyne Tunnel
Jarrow
Jarrow Hall
St Paul's Monastery
Westoe
Hebburn Colliery
Tyne Dock
West Park
Horsley Hill
The Leas & Marsden Rock
Byker
Walker
Hebburn New Town
Hebburn
Harton
Marsden
West Harton
Simonside
Souter Lighthouse
Millennium Bridge
Gateshead
Felling Shore
Gateshead International Stadium
Monkton
Primrose
Biddick Hall
Cleadon Park
Cleadon Hills Fm
Lizards Fm
St Anthony's
Old Fold
Bill Quay
Pelaw
Hedworth
Whiteleas
Cleadon Grange
Cleadon
Whitburn Colliery
Whitburn
Mount Pleasant
Felling
Heworth
Wardley
Fellgate
Boldon Colliery
West Boldon
East Boldon
Deckham
Carr Hill
Windy Nook
Sheriff Hill
Leam Lane
Boldon
South Bents
Whitburn Bay
Beacon Lough
Whitehills
Low Fell
Wrekenton
Follingsby
Downhill
Witherwack
Carley Hill
Seaburn
Fulwell
Harlow Green
Springwell
North East Land, Sea & Air Mus
Usworth Hall
North Moor Fm
Hylton Red House
Marley Pots
Southwick
Roker
Eighton Banks
Usworth
Donwell
Hylton Castle
Castletown
Monkwearmouth
Low Eighton
Bowes Railway
Concord
Sulgrave
Stadium of Light
Deptford
Ayres Quay
National Glass Centre
St Peter's
Angel of the North
Albany
Washington
Pallion
Millfield
Bishopwearmouth
Birtley
Blackfell
Washington Village
Glebe Village
Barmston
North Hylton
Sunderland
Washington Old Hall
Wildfowl & Wetland Trust
South Hylton
Oxclose
Washington Services
Columbia
Pennywell
High Barnes
Humbledon
Hendon
Portobello
Biddick
Ayton
Offerton
Lambton
Grindon
Springwell
Hillview
Grangetown
Barley Mow
Ouston
Fatfield
Harraton
Penshaw Monument
Herrington Country Park
Hasting Hill
Thorney Close
Rickleton
Middle Herrington
Farringdon
New Silksworth
Pelton
Penshaw
West Herrington
New Herrington
East Herrington
Doxford Park
Tunstall
Ryhope
South Pelaw
Pelton Fell
Shiney Row
Philadelphia
Ryhope Engines Museum
Stony Gate
The Ankers
Chester-le-Street
Bournmoor
Newbottle
Grasswell
Thistley House Fm
Burdon
Seaham Grange
Down at the Farm
New Lambton
Sunniside
Emirates Riverside
Burnside
Warden Law
Old Burdon
Lumley Thicks
Fence Houses
Seaton
Northlea
Chester Moor
Great Lumley
Houghton-Le-Spring
Seaham
Lumley Grange
Dubmire
Colliery Row
Rainton Bridge
New Town
Hetton Downs
Seaton Moor Ho
Seaton Bank Top
West Lea
Deneside
Chilton Moor
Rainton Meadows Nat Res
Haverley Ho
Dalton Moor
Liddle Stack
Plawsworth
Charles Pit Cotts
Great Eppleton
Hetton-le-Hole
Slingley Hill
Dawdon
Dalton-le-Dale
Nose's Pt

256
256
236
236
NS
NX
FIRTH OF CLYDE
Culzean Bay
Culzean Castle
Culzean
Glasson Rock
Barwhin Pt
Maidenhead Bay
Morriston
Balvaird
Birniehill
Port Murray
Castle Port
Maidens
Kirkoswald
Turnberry Pt
Turnberry
Minnybae
Broadshean
Milton Burn
Turnberry Bay
Turnberry
Brest Rocks
High Park
Hallowshean
Glenhead
Chapelton Burn
Balkenna Isle
Littleton Fm
Macawston Fm
Chapelton
High McGownston
Townhead
Braehead
Drummuck
Dowhill
Lady Burn
Blair
Ladybank
Wright's Island
Dipple
Bargany Mains
High Craighead
Burnside Fm
A77
Ladywell
Barneil
B741
Burnhead
Chaperdonan
Ind Est
Macrindlestone
Robstone
Old Dailly
Girvan Mains
Camregan
B734
Penkill
Girvan
Houdston
Camregan Hill
Tralorg Hill
Saugh Hill
High Tralorg
Penwhapple Burn
Glendoune
Doune Hill
Horse Rock
Troweir Hill
High Troweir
Woodland Bay
A714
Dow Hill
Byne Hill
Laggan Hill
Tormitchell
Ardmillan Castle
Ardwell
Pinminnoch
Dalfask Hill
Pinmacher
Kilranny
Fell Hill
Cairn Hill
Benan Hill
Kirkland Hill
Kennedy's Pass
297
Grey Hill
Byne Burn
Laigh Letterpin
Daldowie Hill
Kirkland
Pinbain Hill
Knocklaugh Lodge
Pinmore
Merkland
Pinbain Burn
Knocklaugh
Water of Lendal
Currarie
Carleton Bay
Straid
Cundry Mains
Lendal Lodge
Fell Hill
Aldons Hill
Pinmore Mains
Lendalfoot
Carleton Castle
Holmhead
Whilk Isle
Balsalloch Hill
Knockdaw Hill
Breaker Hill
Bargain Hill
River Stinchar
Games Loup
Balcreuchan Port
Glake
Troax
Lochton Hill
Craig Hill
Glessal Hill
Little Bennane
Balcreuchan Burn
Pinwherry
Port Vad
South Ballaird
Craig Fm
Poundland
Bellamore
Bennane Head
Littleton Hill
Balhamie Hill
Clauchanton Hill
Kirkhill Ho
Craig Ho
Spencestone
Garleffin Hill
Bennane Lea
Colmonell
Alticane
Liglartrie
Belhamie
A77
Bougang Fm
Knockdolian
Dalreoch Hill
Milwharran Hill
Pinwherry Hill
Sixpence
Barbae Hill
Craigcarnochie Hill
B734
Glenduisk
265
Corseclays Fm
Polcardoch
Craigneil Hill
Ford Hill
Reuchal
Drumskeoch
Craigbrae
Ballochmorrie
Balig Fm
Cairn Hill
Knockdhu
Bents
Park End
Laggan Ho
Heronsford
Farden Hill
Glenwhask
Mains Road
Kildonan
Ballantrae
Water of Tig
Scaurhead White Cairn
Barrhill
Cosses
Craig Wood
Balkissock
Shiel Hill
Garleffin
Little Fell
Leffin Donald Hill
Eldridge Hill
Loch Hill
Cairnlea
Sgavoch Rock
Glenapp Castle
Altercannoch
Downan Pt
Balkissock Hill
Millmore
Altercannoch
Downan
Smyrton
Arecleoch Forest
Auchencrosh
Eyes
Smyrton Hill
Strawarren Fell
Wee Fell
Beneraird 439
Kilmoray
Knockshin
Currarie Fm
Auchencrosh Hill
Benaw
Swine Cave
338
Foreland Pt
RSPB
Ailsa Craig
Stranny Pt
Ailsa Craig
0 1 2 3 miles
0 1 2 3 4 5 km

EAST AYRSHIRE
SOUTH AYRSHIRE
Carrick
GALLOWAY FOREST PARK
DUMFRIES AND GALLOWAY
Maybole
Whitefaulds
Kirkmichael
Aitkenhead
Crosshill
Kirkoswald
Straiton
Patna
Polnessan
Burnfoot
Waterside
Dalmellington
Bellsbank
Dailly
Wallacetown
Ruglen
Kilkerran
Barr
Alton Albany Fm
Auchensoul
South Balloch
Pinvalley
Tallaminnoch
Stinchar Br
Waterhead on Minnoch
Craigmalloch
Loch Doon
Loch Head
Loch Bradan Reservoir
Loch Finlas
Knockdon
Glentrool Village
Glen Trool Lodge
Glenhead
Palgowan
Cairnderry
Eldrick
Black Clauchrie
Merrick 843
Kirriereoch Hill 786
Shalloch on Minnoch
Tarfessock 697
Benyellary 719
Mullwharchar 692
Corserine 814
Craiglee 523
Macaterick 499
Craigmasheenie 539
Shalloch 545
Polmaddie Hill
Craigenreoch 565
Pinbreck Hill 549
Eldrick Hill 486
Dunamoddie 355
Craig Dhu 415
Big Hill of The Baing 362
Big Hill of Glenmount 382
Back Fell 425
Hadyard Hill 324
Benquhat Hill 435
Benbeoch 463
Auchenroy Hill 367
Turgeny 356
Kildoach Hill 354
Dersalloch Hill 360
Blairquhan Castle
Crossraguel Abbey
Collegiate Church
Loch Doon Castle
Scottish Industrial Railway Centre
Dalmellington Road
Glentrool Visitor Centre
Bruce's Stone
Southern Upland Way
Silver Flowe
Rhinns Of Kells
Water of Girvan
River Stinchar
River Cree
Water of Minnoch
A77
A713
A714
B741
B7045
B7023
B734
257
246
236
A
B
C
D
E
F
G
H
7
8
9
10
11
NS
NX
50
10
80

Lingie Hill
Little Rigend Hill
Sunnyside
Laight Fm
Park Fm
Burnt Hill
Kelloside
Kirkconnel
Kelloholm
Lanehead
Burnside
Dalhanna Hill
Dalhanna Fm
High Cairn 553
McCrierick's Cairn 556
White Hill
White Knowe
Libry Moor
Upper Beoch
Peat Hill 385
Dalleagles
Straid Fm
Brockloch
Blarene Hill 358
Knocknide Hill 344
Lochbrowan Hill
575
Polnagrie Hill
NS
Benbain
Nith Lodge
Rigg Hill
Ashmark Hill
Hare Hill
Mynwhirr Hill 418
Corserig Hill 395
Glengape
Chang Hill 463
Benty Cowan Hill 477
Laglass Hill
Quintin Knowe 554
527
Dun Rig
Hog Hill
Brunt Rig
Barr Moor
463
Benbeoch
Maneight Hill
Barbeys Hill 468
Ewe Hill 437
Boltcraig Hill
EAST AYRSHIRE
High Chang Hill 534
Meikle Hill 441
564
Mid Hill
Bank Hill 530
Black Hill
Meikle Hill
Clawfin Hill
Enoch Hill 569
Auchincally Hill 506
Yarngallows Knowe 476
Blackcraig Hill 700
Benzien Craig
Cockclay
Monquhill
568
Strandlud Hill 531
Milray Hill 526
Struther's Brae 540
Euchanhead
559
Graystone Hill 539
Wham Rig
Whiteside Hill 516
Cruffel 557
Cloud Hill 451
Chair Hill
Benbrack 495
Prickeny Hill
Stony Knowes Hill
Hillend Hill
576
598
593 Magheuchan Rig
Afton Reservoir
Rough Naze
SOUTHERN UPLAND WAY
Snabb
Mossdale
Harthorn Hill
Dun Hill Moss
Gallow Rig Moss
White Knowes 541
Black Hill
Windy Standard 537
Craignane 501
Cannock Hill
Blacklorg Hill 681
Black Shoulder
Corse Hill 580
Polgown
Glenmuck Craig
Birny Hill
White Hill
Moor
Dun Hill
Lamb Hill
Wedder Hill 597
Carnine
Dalgonar
White Knowe 463
Ox Hill 472
Todden Hill
Brownhill
Meaul
Petillery Hill
Polwhat Rig
Jedburgh Knees
Millaneoch Hill
Alwhat 628
Campbells Hill
Carsphairn Forest
Brockloch Rig 518
Trostan Hill 698
Windy Standard
Brown Hill
Lorg Hill
Polskeoch
Countam 476
Wether Hill 486
Sunkhead Moss
Swarе Brae
Muckle Eriff Hill
Benbrack 448
Black Rig
Fortypenny Hill 466
Allan's Cairn 497
Herd Naze 476
Blackcraig Hill 500
Polnaskie Br
Dodd Hill
Waterhead Hill 539
Upper Hill
Hog Hill
Blue Stones
Ewe Hill
Altry Hill
Little Eriff Hill
Allan's Cairn
Ox Hill 505
Big Meaul
Mid Hill of Glenhead 531
High Countam
Eriff
Lamford
Darnscaw
Meadowhead
Waterhead
Wee Meaul
Currie Rig
Keoch Rig
Troston Hill
Loch Doon
Nether Holm of Dalquhairn
Coranbae Hill
568
Colt Hill 598
Lamgarroch 573
Scaur Law
Hard Knowe 458
Gairy of Cairnsmore
Moorbrock Hill 650
Dodd Hill 496
Black Hill
Blackcraig Hill 555
Lamford Hill 399
Laggeran Hill
Craigythorn
Cairn Hill
Croglin Craig
797 Cairnsmore of Carsphairn
Corlae
Cullendoch Hill
Brockloch Craig
Green Hill
Beninner 710
Meikle Dibbin Hill
Conrick Hill
Mullwhanny 535
Markreach Hill
Black Shoulder 688
Dodd Hill
580 Benbrack
Glenhead Rig
Craigencolon
Lamloch
Dunool 541
Cormunnoch Hill 507
Little Dibbin Hill
Blairoch
Benbuie
Brockloch
503 Martour Hill
Bail Hill 517
528 Black Craig
Woodhead
Holm Hill
Willieanna
498 Knockwirn
Craigengillan Hill
Auchrae Hill
Eldrick
Manquhill Hill 421
Corlae Hill
Glenskelly Hill
Green Well of Scotland
Craig of Knockgray 383
Quantans Hill
Craigengillan
Manquhill
Wether Hill
Cornharrow Shoulder
Garryhorn Rig 335
Holm of Daltallochan
330 Castle Hill
Knockower
623 Coran of Portmark
Knockgray
Marbrack
Furmiston Craig
Round Craigs
Dunnans Craig
Cornharrow Hill
Corriedow Hill 442
Garryhorn
Carsphairn
Lagwyne
Cornharrow
Ewe Craig
Shieldykes Hill
Shillingland Hill
Bow
Craighit
CAIRN AVEL
Carnavel
Burnfoot
Marscalloch Hill 381
Stroanfreggan Craig
Carroch Hill 405
Castle Craig
Craiglinan Craig
Auchenstroan
Cairnsgarroch 659
Bennan
330 Bardennoch Hill
Bardennoch
Muirdrochwood
Stroanfreggan Bridge
Carroch
Auchenstroan Craig
Woodhead Hill
Craigdarroch
695 Meaul
Craigenwallie
Marscalloch
Knowehead
Culmark Moss
Carroch
DUMFRIES AND GALLOWAY
GALLOWAY FOREST PARK
Shiel of Castlemaddie (Bothy)
Gairy Craig
Kendoon Loch
Carminnows
Bennan
Fingland Hill
Troston Hill
Neis Hill
Craigchessie
Goat Craigs
Castlemaddy
Polquhanity
Dundeugh Hill 271
Shiel Hill
Culmark Hill
Lochwhinnie Hill
Lochlee Hill 352
Troston
Bennan Knocksting 346
Minnygryle Hill 364
417 Big Morton Hill
Midlover Plantation
Torrs
Craignelder
Dalshangan
Barlae Hill
KENDOON
Mackilston Hill 294
Butterhole Bridge
Meikle Bennan 344
Knocksting Loch
Pointfoot Hill
Brown Hill 350
Glencrosh Hill
Carlin's Cairn
Craigrine
Dundeugh
Glenhoul
Kendoon
Craig Knuckle
Polmaddy
Glenshimmeroch Hill
Kilnair Hill
387 Lawglass
Polmaddy Gairy
814 Corserine
Craigencorr Hill
323 Greentop of Margree
Wether Hill
Castlefairn
Loch Harrow
Forrest Lodge
Strongassel
Nether Cleugh
Mackilston
Glenshimmeroch
Barlaes Hill 248
Hog Hill
Ewe Hill
North Gairy Top
Bennan Hill
Loch Minnoch
Scabbed Craigs
Divot Hill
Stroan Hill 344
Holmhead
Blackmark
Stroan Hill
Lochinvar
Regland Loch
Craigmuie Moor
Penneilly Wood
Millfire 716
Burnhead
Knockreoch Fm
Strongassel Hill
Barlaes Cott
Lochinvar Lodge
Largvey Hill
245 Stranfasket Hill
Tods Hill
Earlstoun
Loch Hill
Ardoch Hill
Duchrae
417 Fell Hill
Mid Hill
Shinmount
Polharrow Bridge
Loch Dungeon
Hannayston Hill
Barskeoch Mains
Milquarter
Blawquhairn Fm
Knockman Hill
Milnmark Hill
Loch Skae
Benneeve 358
Monybuie Hill
Waterhead
Tops of Craigeazle
Meikle Millyea 746
Clints of Clenrie
Rig of Clenrie
Barskeoch Hill
Earlstoun Loch
The Glenkens
Loch Howie
Blackcraig Hill
Straverron Hill
Snab Hill
Waterside Hill
Bogue Fell
Corriedoo
Corriedoo Forest
Monybuie
Drumbuie
Rig of Drumbuie 262
Garrock Hill
Tower
Bogue
Rhinns Of Kells
Little Millyea 578
Drumbuie Hill
Dunveoch Hill
Garroch
Waterside
St John's Town of Dalry
Barscobe Loch
Troquhain Hill
Ree Hill
Mc Whanns Stone
Darrou
Eldrick Hill
Glenlee Mains
Boat Knowe
Grennan Mill
Holme Mill
Barscobe Hill 257
Glen Knowe
Blackcraig
Green Top of Greenwhirn
NX
Benbrack
Glenlee
Low Benbrack
Holme Fm
Scroggie Hall
Glenlee Hill
Shiel Hill
Meikle Isle
Balmaclellan
Long Wood
Garcrogo Hill
Barmark Hill
Knocklearn
Upper Craigenbay
Maggot Hill
Gallows Knowe
Flintloch Hill
Hill
Bartaggart Hill
Caldow Moor
Gibbshill
Craigencallie
Ken Br
0 1 2 3 miles
0 1 2 3 4 5 km

Sanquhar
Crawick
Sanquhar Post Office
Tollbooth Museum
Mennock
Mennock Pass
Eliock Grange
Southern Upland Way
Lowther Hill 725
Durisdeermill
Durisdeer
Durisdeer Parish Church
Dalveen Pass
Enterkinfoot
Enoch
Holestane
Drumlanrig Castle & Gardens
Morton Castle
Carronbridge
Thornhill
Penpont
Tynron
Tynron Doon Fort
Keir Mill
Cample
Closeburn
Park
Kirkpatrick
Moniaive
Kirkland
Straith
Wallaceton
Glenmidge
Auldgirth
Dalswinton
Dunscore
Throughgate
Ellisland Mus & Farm
Burnhead
Duncow
Auchencairn
Amisfield
Gallaberry
Locharbriggs
Heathhall
Holywood
Newtonairds
Drumpark
Irongray
Newbridge
Lincluden College
Dumfries & Galloway Aviation Mus
The Grove
Tinwald
Kirkton
Ae Village
Forest of Ae
Burnfoot
Mitchellslacks
Locherben
Queensberry 697
Daer Reservoir
Dalmacallan Forest
Lochurr
Sundaywell
Milton
West Skelston
Auchenbrack
Auchenbainzie
Glenesslin
Nithsdale
A76
A702
A701
B729
B797
B740
259
248
237

A74(M)
Ericstane
Swatte Fell 728
Peat Hill 488
Carrifran
Ferny Hill
Black Knowe Head
Black Knowe
Blue Cairn
Black Craig
Bodesbeck Law 665
Broadgairhill
Phawnhope Hill 503
Mid Hill 521
Campland Hill 478
Greenhill Dod
Auldhousehill Br
Archie's Hill
Braefoot Wood
260
Granton Ho
Granton
Stot Knowe
Capplegill
Hang Gill
White Hill
Bughtrig
Bushie Law
Bloodhope Head
Nether Craig
Mosshope Bank 521
Type Knowes
Howslack
Greygill Head 474
Auldton Fell 501
Roundstonefoot
Shortwoodend
White Shank
Pot Law
Birnie Brae
Blue Cairn Hill
Mitchell Hill
Pentland Hill
Hods Hill
Beld Knowe
Mount Joe
Shiel Hill
Bught Knowe
Greskine Forest
Blacklaw Hill
Hind Hill
Merecleuch Hill
Sailfoot Law
Graham's Law
Ettrick Pen
Dobs Craig
Ewe Rig
Eastside
Mosshope Fell
SOUTHERN UPLAND WAY
Craig Hill
Rivox Moor
Gill Knowe
Rivox Fell
Craik's Craigs Plantn
Gallow Hill
Auldton Hill
Craigieburn Hill
Moffat Dale
Selcoth
Capel Fell
Hopetoun Craig 632
Ettrick Head
White Shank
Stell Bush Edge
Eastside Knowe
Wind Fell
Longbedholm Hill
Coatsgate
Chapel Fm
Moffat
MOFFAT MUSEUM
Hunterheck Hill
CRAIGIEBURN
Crofthead Hill
Croft Head 637
Bear Craig
White Knowe
Great Brow
Lamb Craig
Watch Craig 342
Whiteside Hill 554
Hangingshaw Hill
Coats Hill
Langshawbush Ho
Wait Hill
Gateshaw Rig
Loch Fell
Cauld Law
Blaeberry Hill
Cassock Hill
Nether Cassock
Annant Hill
Tarnis Head
Cairn Hill
Neath Hill
Lawesknowe
Dyke
Oakrigg
Dumcrieff
Craig Fell
Big Hill
Yadburgh Hill 474
Cowan Fell 564
Dun Moss
Big Strushel Burn
Thickside
Dumfedling
Cowley Head
Gatet Hill
Newmills
Oakriggside
Scaw'd Fell
Garroqill
Ewelairs Hill
Jock's Shoulder
Spots Law
Wetwood Hill 366
Belt Knowe
Davington
Craighoar Hill
Beattock Hill 259
Beattock
Easter Earshaig
Harestanes Height 566
Peat Hill
Kinnelhead
Mount Glass
Holms Bankend
Craigielandshill
Glengap Head
Wintergill Head
Ruegill Hill 496
Pot Hill
Mid Height 418
Eskdalemuir Forest
Ashy Bank
Stell Knowe
Beldcraig Wood
Craig Fell
Marchhouse
Milton
Upper Murthat
Brock Hill
Broken Back 397
Black Hill 474
Wet Slack
Peat Hill 374
Tates Hill
Bught Knowes
Lochan Burn
Lamb Hill
Lonnachie Rig
Queensberry
Meikle Hill
Cauldholm
Mid Murthat
Rispie Hill
Broadfield Height
Kirk Hill
Haregrain Rig
Mucklehead Knowe
Hen Knowes
Southerly Ridge
The Strip
Turf Hill
Laverhay Height
Inner Mid Hill
Whirl Rig
Dinnings Heights
Dinnings Hill
Long Knowe
Blue Cairn 333
Mount Haul
Knockilsine Hill
League Hill
Stockholm
Dundoran
Laverhay
Finniegill
Ramshaw Rig
A701
Cogrie Moor
Lochwood Plantn
Milne Fell
Milne Height
Three Mullach Hill
Macmaw Edge
Cairn Knowe
Black Esk Reservoir
Minnygap Height
Minnygap
Cairn Hill
Hillhead
Edwardsrig Plantn
Lochwood
Lochwood Moss
Lochwood Mains
Cogries Fm
Leithenhall
Broomhills
Pumplaburn
Wamphraygate
Hillhouse
Howgill Fell
Muir Hill
Branrigg
Grey Mare
Barnhimpen
Barns
Oldshields Wood
Riggheads Fm
Woodend
Newton
Annanbank Dairy
Plantationfoot
Sembletree Knowe
Scoop Hill
Macmaw Hill
Heckney Hill
Three Knowes
Hog Knowes
Castle Hill
Bog Shaw
Holehouse Hill
Mollin Moor
Raehills
Hazelbank Plantn
Tippet's Belt
Gateside
Blaze Hill
Fingland Fell
Loft Shaws
Waterhead
Dunscore Hill
Sergeant Knowe
Greengate Head
Sandyford
Castle O'er Forest
Black Esk
Forest of Ae
Whitefauld Hill
Mollin
St Ann's
Moss Plantn
Kirkhill
Dalmakethar
Langside
Matthew's Hill
Brunt Hill
Peat Hill
Dryfe Lodge
Fenton Heights
Shankend
Black Edge
Carterton Knowes
The Knock
Holehouse
Tawnaze Hill
Pumro Fell
Johnstonebridge
Springwells
Annandale Water Services
Cacrabank Hill
Gillesbie
Boreland Ho
Pikestone Hill
Great Hill
Thiellinn Knowe
Brownmoor Hill
Pheasantfield
Kirkland Hill
Chapelhill
A74(M)
Dinwoodie Mains
Broomhillbank Hill
Ravenscleugh
Berryscaur
Boreland
Millriggs
Little Millriggs
Witchshaw Rig
Fauld Hill
Horse Knowe
Downey Hill
Knockespen
Minister's Moss
Blackacre
Courance
Kerse Moor
Chapel Wood
Longerhallis Hill
Dinwoodie Lodge
Kirkslight Hill
Kirkmichael Fell
Heathfield Moor
Hangingshaw
Newbigging
Heithatpark
Carterton
Hallhills Loch
Hart Fell
Wood Hill
Wood Fm
Ae Village
Relic Hill
Wester Parkgate
Garrel Hill
Ross Mains
Greyrigg
Dinwoodie Green
Auchenroddan Forest
Gayfield Type
Mid Hill
White Hill
Burnfoot Cottage
Woodhill Edge
Dungairy Knowe
Whitcastles Hill
Lakehead Fm
Kirkmichael Mains
Parkgate
Nethermill
Gillrigg
Redhall Moss
Sibbaldbie
Firtree Hill
Heithat
Jardine Hall Mains
Claydaubing Br
Hogg Hill
Whitcastles
Barony Agricultural College
Third
Little Whitriggs
Gamerigg Plantn
Milngate
Cumleys
Redhall
Fourmerkland
Chipknowe
Balgray Home Fm
Balgray Ho
Bow Hill
Ae Bridgend
Dalruscan
Fulton
Templand
Comrue
Brieryhill
Nethercleuch
Corrie Common
Craighousestead Hill
Johnfield Moss
Millhousebridge
Newfield Moor
Hillside
Gillenbie
Penlaw
Corriehalls
Corrielea
Pike Knowe
Kinnel Br
Millbank
Broomhills
St Michael's Walls
Croftheads Hill
Pyatshaws Rig
Pearsby Hall
Shieldhill
Hazliebrae
Elshieshields
Todhillmuir
Riggheads
Pinnacle Wood
Chapelcroft
Bridgemuir
Muirhouse
Sandbed
Sloda Hill
Slodahill
Old Craighouse
Craighouse
Corriehills
Hightown Hill 250
Bankhead Glen
Bow Hill
Hightown
Bruntshields
Mill Loch
Broomhill
Applegarthtown
Dryfeholm Fm
Lockerbie Manor
South Corrielaw
Catlins
Sheepknowes
Meikle Whitriggs
Paddockhole
Crawth Hill
Hazelrig Fm
White Hill
Watchill
Marjoriebanks
Lochmaben
Torwood Plantn
Torwood Lodge
The Hass
Ind Est
Watscales
Halldykes
Corriemains
Whitstonehill
Wyliehole
Grange of Tundergarth
Seven Brethren
Standburn
Back Hill
Halleaths
Burnside
Priesthead
Ladyward
Lockerbie
Quhytewoollen
Rosebank
Raggiewhate
Bankshill
Northburn
Shaw's Hill
Long Plantn
Gall Moss
Kirk Loch
Castle Loch
Blackrig
Millhill
Mounthoolie
Grange Fell
Cullivait
Tinwald
Parkfoot
Whitelaird
LOCHMABEN CASTLE
Priestdykes
Scroggs
The Linns
Millantae
Tundergarth Mains
Birrens Hill
Tinwald Parks
Tinwald Ho
Hempland Hill
Branetrigg
Rye Muir
Hightae Mill Loch
Castle Mains
A709
South Turnmuir Plantn
Blackford
Westwood
Powhaffet
Risp Hill
Heck
Well Springs Plantn
Carruthers
Mossgrove
Parkend
Greenhill
Courstein
Torbeckhill Res
Crossbank
Heathhall
The Broom
Corsegreen
Millriggs
Skairfield
Hallmuir
BURNSWARK HILL FORT
Burnswark
Howat's Hill
Hartwood Hill
Muirfield
Hightae
Pilmuir Common
Stockbridge
Darlawhill
Gilmartin
Mossburn
Blackmoss Plantn
Gimmenbie
Grainhall
Dockenflat
The Grove
Tortorwald
Ind Est
Lochar
238
247
NT
NY
3 miles
5 km

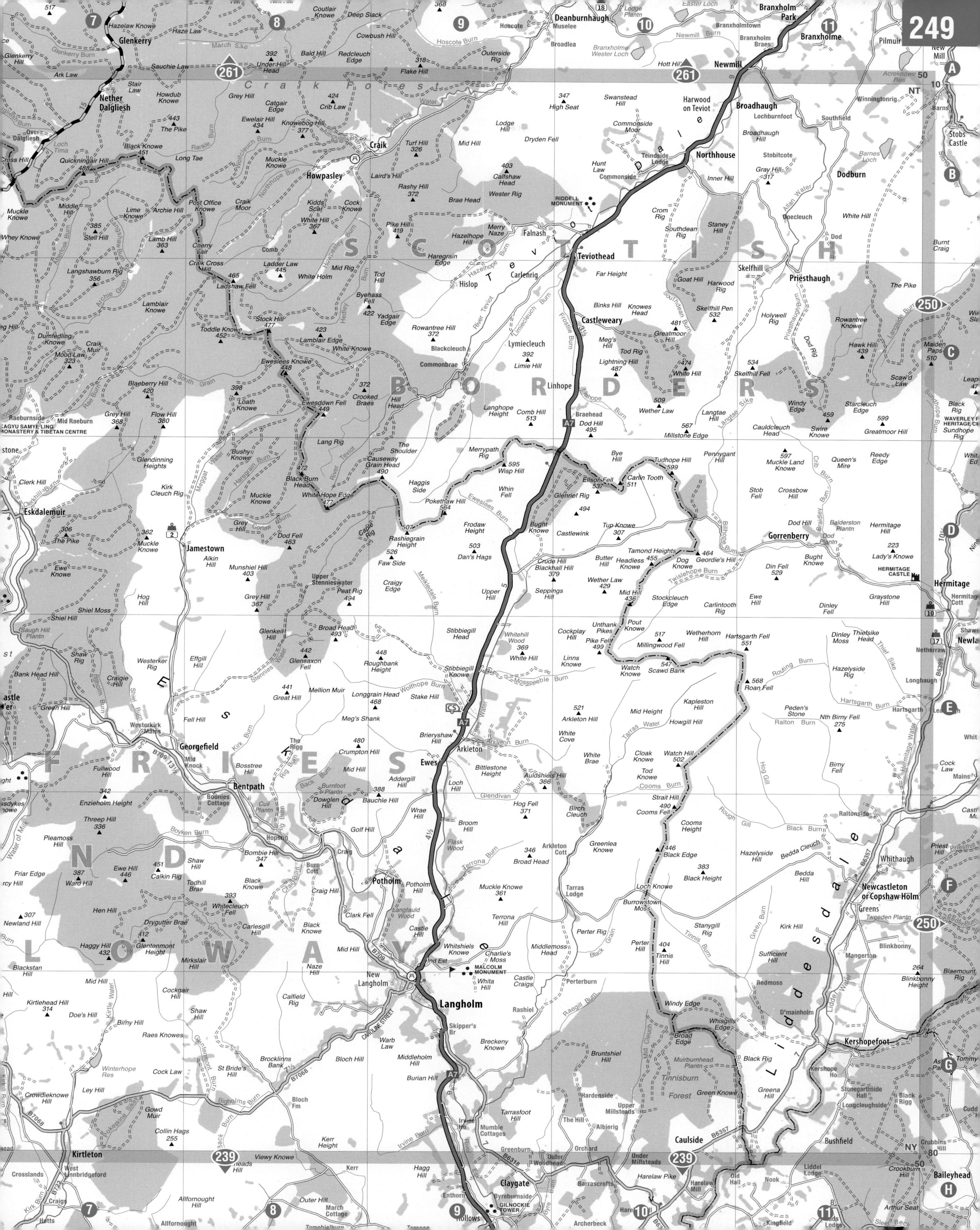
Glenkerry
Hazelaw Knowe
Haze Law
Coutlair Knowe
Deep Slack
Cowbush Hill
Deanburnhaugh
Muselee
Hoscote
Broadlea
Lodge Plantn
Easter Loch
Branxholm Park
Branxholmtown
Newmill Burn
Branxholm Braes
Branxholme
Pilmuir
New Mill
Glenkerry Hill
Glenkerry Burn
March Sike
Sauchie Law
392 Under Hill Head
Bald Hill
Redcleuch Edge
318 Flake Hill
Outerside Rig
Hoscote Burn
Branxholme Wester Loch
Hott Hill
Newmill
261
Ark Law
Stair Law
Nether Dalgliesh
Craik Forest
Howdub Knowe
Grey Hill
424 Crib Law
Catgair Edge
443 The Pike
Ewelair Hill 434
Knowebog Hill 377
Craik
347 High Seat
Swanstead Hill
Harwood on Teviot
Broadhaugh
Lochburnfoot
Winningtonrig
Acreknowe Res
Southfield
Barns
Stobs Castle
Lodge Hill
Mid Hill
Dryden Fell
Commonside Moor
Broadhaugh Hill
Stobitcote
Barnes Loch
Dalgliesh
Loch Tima
Cross Hill
Quickningair Hill 488
Black Knowe 451
Long Tae
Muckle Knowe
Turf Hill 326
Howpasley
Laird's Hill
403 Calfshaw Head
Hunt Law
Commonside
Teindside Lodge
Northhouse
Gray Hill 317
Inner Hill
Dodburn
Middle Hill
Muckle Knowe
Lime Knowe
Archie Hill
Post Office Knowe
Craik Moor
Kidds Scar
Cock Knowe
Rashy Hill 372
Brae Head
Wester Rig
Riddell Monument
Crom Rig
Allan Water
Doecleuch
White Hill
Whey Knowe
385 Stell Hill
Lamb Hill 363
White Hill 367
Pike Hill 419
Hazelhope Hill
Merry Naze
Falnash
Southdean Rig
Staney Hill
Dod
Burnt Craig
Cherry Lair
Comb
Ladder Law
Mid Rig
Tod Hill
Haregrain Edge
Teviothead
Skelfhill
Priesthaugh
Craik Cross Hill
Langshawburn Rig 356
465 Ladshaw Fell
White Holm
Hislop
Carlenrig
Far Height
Goat Hill
Harwood Rig
The Pike
Scottish Borders
Byehass Fell 422
Yadgair Edge
Lamblair Knowe
Binks Hill
Knowes Head
Skelfhill Pen 532
Castleweary
Holywell Rig
Rowantree Knowe
Stock Hill 477
Toddle Knowe 452
423 Lamblair Edge
White Knowe
Rowantree Hill 372
Blackcleuch
Lymiecleuch
Meg's Hill
481 Greatmoor Hill
Tod Rig
Dod Rig
Hawk Hill 439
Maiden Paps 510
Dumfedling Knowe
Craik Muir
Mood Law 323
Eweslees Knowe 448
Commonbrae
392 Limie Hill
Lightning Hill 487
474 White Hill
534 Skelfhill Fell
Scaw'd Law
Blaeberry Hill 420
398 Loath Knowe
372 Crooked Braes
Hill Head
Linhope
Raeburnside
Mid Raeburn
Kagyu Samye Ling Monastery & Tibetan Centre
Grey Hill 368
Flow Hill 380
Ewesdown Fell 449
Langhope Height
Comb Hill 513
Braehead
Dod Hill 495
509 Wether Law
Langtae Hill
Windy Edge
459
Starcleuch Edge
Black Rig
Waverley Heritage Centre
Sundhope Rig
567 Millstone Edge
Cauldcleuch Head
Swire Knowe
599 Greatmoor Hill
Lang Rig
The Shoulder
Merrypath Rig
595 Wisp Hill
Bye Hill
Tudhope Hill 599
Pennygant Hill
597 Muckle Land Knowe
Queen's Mire
Reedy Edge
Glendinning Heights
Bushy Knowe
Causeway Grain Head 490
Haggis Side
Ellson Fell 537
Carlin Tooth 511
Clerk Hill
Kirk Cleuch Rig
472 Black Burn Head
Whin Fell
Glenrief Rig
Stob Fell
Crossbow Hill
Eskdalemuir
Muckle Knowe
White Hope Edge 477
Pokethaw Hill 564
494
Dod Hill
Balderston Plantn
Hermitage Hill
Grey Hill
Dod Fell 463
Caple Rig
507
Frodaw Height
Bught Knowe
Castlewink
Tup Knowe 307
Gorrenberry
Dod Plantn
223 Lady's Knowe
362 Muckle Knowe
306 The Pike
Jamestown
Alkin Hill
Rashiegrain Height
526 Faw Side
503 Dan's Hags
Crude Hill
Blackhall Hill 379
Butter Hill
Tamond Heights
Headless Knowe 455
Dog Knowe
464 Geordie's Hill
Twislehope Burn
Din Fell 529
Bught Knowe
Hermitage Castle
Hermitage
Ewe Knowe
Munshiel Hill 403
Upper Stenniesewater
Craigy Edge
Upper Hill
Seppings Hill
Wether Law 429
Mid Hill 436
Stockcleuch Edge
Ewe Hill
Carlintooth Rig
Dinley Fell
Graystone Hill
Hog Hill
Grey Hill 367
Peat Rig 494
Shiel Moss
Shiel Hill
Saugh Hill Plantn
Glenkell Hill
Broad Head 493
Stibbiegill Head
Whitehill Wood
369 White Hill
Cockplay Hill
Unthank Pikes
Pout Knowe
Pike Fell 499
517 Millingwood Fell
Wetherhorn Hill
Hartsgarth Fell 551
Dinley Moss
Thiefsike Head
Netherraw
Shaw Rig
Westerker Rig
Effgill Hill
442 Glensaxon Fell
448 Roughbank Height
Stibbiegill Knowe
Linns Knowe
Watch Knowe
547 Scawd Bank
Hazelyside Rig
Bank Head Hill
Craigie Hill
441 Great Hill
Mellion Muir
Longgrain Head 468
Stake Hill
Mosspeeble Burn
568 Roan Fell
Longhaugh
Hartsgarth
Green Hill
Fell Hill
Meg's Shank
521 Arkleton Hill
Mid Height
Kapleston Hill
Howgill Hill
Peden's Stone
Nth Birny Fell 275
Westerkirk Mains
The Rigg
Brieryshaw Hill
Arkleton
White Cove
Ralton Burn
Georgefield
480 Crumpton Hill
Ewes
Bittlestone Height
White Brae
Cloak Knowe
Watch Hill 502
Birny Fell
Cock Law
Fullwood Hill
Mid Knock
Bosstree Hill
Mid Hill
Auldshiels Hill 366
Tod Knowe
Bentpath
Boonies Cottage
Addergill Hill
Loch Hill
Cooms Burn
Strait Hill 490 Cooms Fell
Raltonside
342 Enzieholm Height
Dowglen Hill
388 Bauchle Hill
Glendivan
Hog Fell 371
Birch Cleuch
Threep Hill 336
Cuil Plantn
Golf Hill
Wrae Hill
Broom Hill
Cooms Height
Pleamoss Hill
Boyken Burn
Hopsrig
Flask Wood
Arkleton Cott
Greenlea Knowe
Priest Hill
Whithaugh
Shaw Hill
Bombie Hill 347
Craig
346 Broad Head
446 Black Edge
Hazelyside Hill
Bedda Cleuch
Friar Edge
387 Ward Hill
Ewe Hill 446
451 Calkin Rig
Burn Cott
Tarras Lodge
383 Black Height
Bedda Hill
Tod Hill Brae
Black Knowe
Craig Hill
Potholm
Potholm Hill
Muckle Knowe 361
Loch Knowe
Newcastleton or Copshaw Holm
Greens
393 Whitecleuch Fell
Burrowstown Moss
307 Newland Hill
Hen Hill
Drygutter Brae
Carlesgill Hill
Clark Fell
Langfauld Wood
Terrona Hill
Tweeden Plantn
Stanygill Rig
Kirk Hill
412 Glentenmont Height
Castle Hill
Black Knowe
Perter Rig
Perter Hill
404 Tinnis Hill
Sufficient Hill
Blinkbonny
Haggy Hill 432
Mirkslair Hill
Mid Hill
Whitshiels Knowe
Charlie's Moss
Middlemoss Head
Mangerton
Blackstan Hill
Naze Hill
Malcolm Monument
Castle Craigs
Whita Hill
Redmoss
264 Blinkbonny Height
Blaemount Rig
Mid Hill
Cockgair Hill
New Langholm
Langholm
Perterburn
Kirtlehead Hill 314
Doe's Hill
Calfield Rig
Shaw Hill
Rashiel
Windy Edge
D'mainholm
Birny Hill
Raes Knowes
Skipper's Br
Whisgills Edge
Warb Law
Breckeny Knowe
Broad Edge
Bruntshiel Hill
Black Rig
Kershopefoot
Winterhope Res
Cock Law
St Bride's Hill
Brocklinns Bank
Bloch Hill
Middleholm Hill
Burian Hill
Muirburnhead Plantn
Tinnisburn Forest
Kershope Ho
Ley Hill
Crowdieknowe Hill
Bloch Fm
Hardenside
Upper Millsteads
Green Knowe
Greena Hill
Stonegarthside Hall
Black Rigg
Longcleughside
Gowd Muir
Collin Hags 255
Irvine Ho
Mumble Cottages
Tarrasfoot Hill
The Hill
Albierig
Kerr Height
Caulside
Bushfield
Crubbins Hill
Kirtleton
239
Heads Hill
Viewy Knowe
Greenburn
Outer Woodhead
Orchard
Under Millsteads
Crosslands
West Linnbridgeford
Kerr
Hagg Hill
Claygate
Barrascrofts
Harelaw Pike
Harelaw Mill
Old Hall
Nook
Liddel Lodge
Crookburn Hill
Baileyhead
Allfornought Hill
Outer Hill
March Cottage
Enthorn
Byreburnside
Gilnockie Tower
Craigs
Hollows
Arthur Seat
Hetts
Allfornought
Archerbeck
Kingfield
Dumfries and Galloway
Eskdale
Liddesdale
Teviot Dale

Coliforthill
Colislinn
Adderston Lee
Birneyknowe
Bonchester Bridge
Bonchester Hill
Hobkirk
Cleuch Head
Mackside
Doorpool Hill
Belling Hill
Mervins Law
Edgerston Rig
Falside
Roughlee
Stotfield Hill
Moor Head
Philip Law 414
Scaw'd Law 367
New Mill
Hoggfield Hill
Highend
Crown Plantn
Chesters
Southdean Mill
Bught Knowe
405
White Hill
Hareshaw Knowe
Hophills Nob 359
329
Knock Hills
Ephope Law
Barns
Stonedge
Folly Plantn
Spar Plantn
Wolflee Hill 393
Law Plantn
Southdean
Southdean Lodge
Croft Plantn
Lethem
Shaw Burn
Stobs Castle
Cogsmill
Stonedge Forest
Stonedge Hill
Peat Law
Wauchope Fm
Cribs Hole
Highlee Hill
Weasel Hill
Steele Knowe
Crink Law
Huntford
Deerlee Knowe
Lamblair Edge
Leithope Forest
Berryfell Fm
Berryfell Hill
Sim's Knowe
Hell's Hole
Crag Bank
CRAGBANK WOOD
Flush Plantn
Peden's Cleuch
Charlie's Knowe
Martinlee Plantn
Bught Knowe
REDESMIRE FRAY 1575
Arks Edge
Fairwood Fell
Leap Hill 471
Catcleugh Shin 544
Pike Fell 400
Templehall Hill
Wauchope Common
Black Hill
Millmoor Rig
Black Burn
Burns
Green Law
Tamshiel Rig
Scaw'd Law
Black Cleuch
Whitelee
Lumsdon Law 475
Lumsdon Burn
Shankend Fm
Burnt Craig
Harwood Moss
Brown's Hill
Brockie Law
Wellcleuch Plantn
Meadow Cleuch
Ramshope Lodge
Echo Crags
The Pike
Shankend Hill
Langburnshiels
Cooper's Cleuch
Wyndburgh Hill 507
Wauchope Forest
Green Law
Hardlee Flow
Dun Knowe
Bateinghope Burn
WHITELEE MOOR
Catcleugh
Windy Slack
Wigg Knowe
Black Cleuch
Fanna Hill 514
Dog Knowe
Note o' the Gate
Rushy Rig
Scrathy Holes
Dun Tae
Knox Knowe 500
Carter Fell 556
Cross Cleugh
Catcleugh Reservoir
Maiden Paps 510
Outer Knowe Head 415
Kiln Knowe
Whitegrain Fell
East Hill
Needs Law 444
Wheeling Head 448
Hartshorn Pike 545
551
Carry Burn
Limestone Knowe 551
Chattlehope Crag
Redesdale Forest
Scaw'd Law
Leap Hill 472
Sandy Edge
Lime Kiln Edge
430
Lamblair Hill 498
Singdean
Coomb Edge
Haggie Knowe
White Crags
Girdle Fell
Black Rig
Whitrope Cottages
WAVERLEY ROUTE HERITAGE CENTRE
Sundhope Rig
Mid Hill
Coopercleuch Knowe
Dod Fell
Heather Knowe
Craigy Knowe
Upper Stony Holes
Grey Mares Knowe 516
KIELDERHEAD
Kielderhead Moor
599
Greatmoor Hill
Peel Fell 602
Cairn Cleugh
Reedy Edge
Whitrope Edge
White Knowe
Caddroun Rig
West Kielder Moor
Kielder Head
Wool Meath
Woolmeath Edge
Woody Crags
Long Crag
Stitchel Hill 318
Saughtree Fell
Myredykes Plantn
Rushy Knowe
Mid Fell
KIELDER
East Kielder Moor
Blakehope Nick
Blackman's Law
Whitropefoot
Riccarton Junction
Nine Stane Rig
Bell Hill
Hob Knowe
Windy Knowe
Deadwater
Scaup Pikes
Scaup
Bran's Walls
Street Head
Berrymoor Edge 459
223
Lady's Knowe
Blackwood Hill
Shiel Knowe
Saughtree
Thorlieshope
Thorlieshope Pike 360
Wirchet
Deadwater Fell 569
Greyhound Law
Ewe Hill
Wether Lair
Smallhope Rigg
Long Crag
HERMITAGE CASTLE
Hermitage
Hermitage Cott
Bught Knowe
Burnmouth Fm
Thorlieshope Heights
Bells Moor
Ravenshill Moor
FOREST PARK
Ridge End Burn
Graystone Hill
Arnton Fell
SCOTTISH
Yarrow Knowe 295
Three Pikes
Hogswood Moor
Monk Side 513
Round Law
Emblehope Moor
Shaws
Newlands
Netherraw
Larriston
Larriston Rigg
Larriston Burn
Foulmire Heights
Hirst Craig
Crag Head
Greys Pike 445
Hawk Knowe
Burn Grange
BORDERS
403
Loch Knowe
Kielder
Mount Common
Butteryhaugh
KIELDER CASTLE VISITOR CENTRE
Harper Crag
Longhaugh
The Steele
Steele Road
Steeleroad-end
Hewisbridge Cott
Black Fell
Bewshaugh
Cat Cairn
Devil's Lapful
Wainhope
Rain's Hill
Larriston Fells
Millstone Crag
Earl's Seat
The Dodd 353
Leahaugh
512
Buckside Knowe
Gowanburn
Dinlabyre
Whitehaugh
Kirndean
Black Knowe
Bellingburn
Pithouse Crags
Rabbit Crag
Highfield
Cock Law
Mains
Ewe Knowe
Hobb's Flow
Coal Grain
Buck Fell
Bellingburn Head
Kielder Forest
The Cross
Old Castleton
Castleton Muir
Harden Moss
Flight Moss
Watch Knowe
Wilson's Pike
Akenshawburn
Ferny Knowe
Wellhaugh
Pope's Hill
Hawkhope
Wind Hill
The Forks
Rushy Knowe
Priest Hill
Harden Hill
Stell Knowe
Dinmontlair Knowe
Scotch Knowe
Caplestone Fell
Eliott's Pike
Greenside
KIELDER WATER BIRDS OF PREY CENTRE
Kielder Water
Hawkhope Hill
Green Eyes Crags
Whithaugh
Newcastleton or Copshaw Holm
Black Knowe
Newcastleton Forest
Lazy Knowe
Scald Pike
Falstone
Yarrow
Bullcrag Edge
TOWER KNOWE VISITOR CENTRE
Yarrow Moor
Stannersburn
Stokoe
Long Knowe
Kershopehead
Glendhu Hill 514
Dove Crags
High Long Ho
Kateshaw Hill
Lishaw Rigg
Rough Pike
Stower Hill
Low Cranecleugh
White Side
Ridge End
River North Tyne
Blinkbonny
Geordy's Pike
Muckle Knowe
Broomy Hill
Drove Rigg
264
Blinkbonny Height
Blaemount Rig
Long Rigg
Robbie's Rigg
Will's Knowe
Broomylinn
Jock's Pike
Dings Rigg
Smalesmouth
English Kershope
CUMBRIA
Black Hill
Lishaw Burn
Skelton Pike
Reamy Rigg
Gill Pike
The Rigg
Kyloe Crags
Archy's Rigg
Roughside Moor
Beckhead Crag
Stot Crags
Byreshield Hill
Black Crags
Tommy's Fell
Ash Park
Christianbury Crag 487
Blacklyne Common
Long Crags
Burnt Tom Crags
Christy's Crags
Bolts Law 395
Kershope Forest
Blacklyne Ho
Bewcastle Fells
Story's Gairs
KIELDER
Allerybank
Rushy Knowe
Black Rigg
Cuddy's Hall
Kettle Hall
Sighty Crag 518
Horse Head
Black Knowe 492
Black Cleugh
Crubbins Hill
Bailey Head
Black Knors 248
Long Bar
Whitelyne Common
Smuggy's Pike
Long Crags
Greenmeam Sike
Hopehouse
Chirdon Burn
Clave Hill
Crookburn Hill
Black Knors
Black Stantling
Slaty Crag
Long Crag 456
The Shanks
KIELDER MIRES
FOREST PARK
Clintburn
Watch Rigg
The Flatt
Greyfell Common
Tarn Beck
Lowe Bush
Paddaburn
Muckle Samuel's Crags
High Caporn Edge
Holmehead
Crew Crag
Gaylock Hill
Irthing Head
Whitehill
Little Dodd Hill
The Cheviot Hills
Liddesdale
0 1 2 3 miles
0 1 2 3 4 5 km

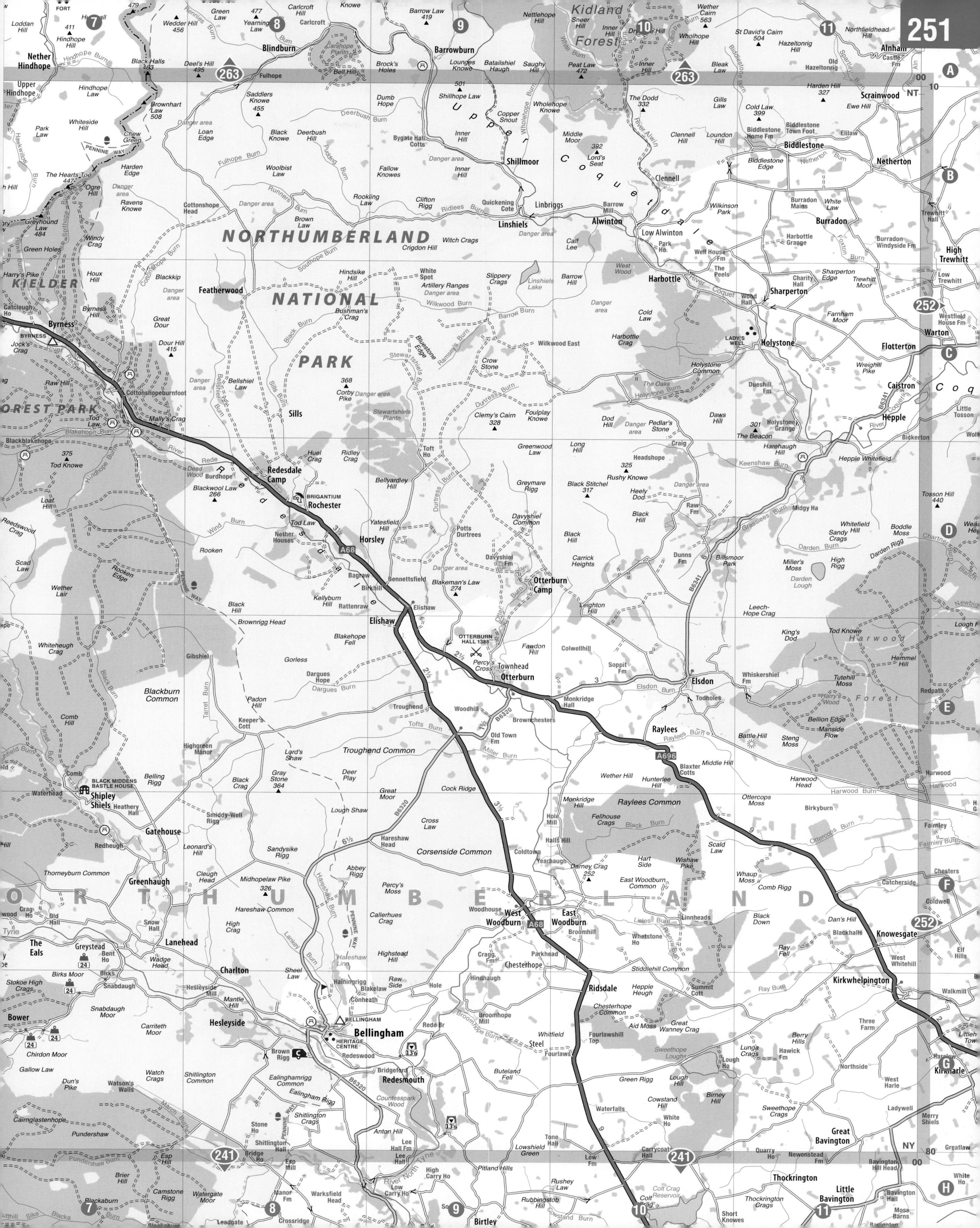
NORTHUMBERLAND NATIONAL PARK
KIELDER FOREST PARK
NORTHUMBERLAND
Upper Coquetdale
Kidland Forest
Redesdale
Nether Hindhope
Upper Hindhope
Blindburn
Barrowburn
Fulhope
Shillmoor
Linbriggs
Linshiels
Alwinton
Low Alwinton
Clennell
Biddlestone
Netherton
Burradon
High Trewhitt
Harbottle
Sharperton
Holystone
Lady's Well
Warton
Flotterton
Caistron
Hepple
Byrness
Cottonshopeburnfoot
Featherwood
Sills
Redesdale Camp
Rochester
Brigantium
Horsley
Elishaw
Otterburn Camp
Otterburn
Townhead
Otterburn Hall 1388
Percy's Cross
Elsdon
Raylees
Monkridge Hall
Troughend Common
Raylees Common
Corsenside Common
Blackburn Common
Shipley Shiels
Black Middens Bastle House
Gatehouse
Greenhaugh
Lanehead
Charlton
Hesleyside
Bellingham
Heritage Centre
Redesmouth
West Woodburn
East Woodburn
Ridsdale
Knowesgate
Kirkwhelpington
Kirkharle
Great Bavington
Little Bavington
Thockrington
Birtley
Greystead
The Eals
Bower
Pennine Way
A68
A696
B6320
B6341
263
252
241
NT
NY

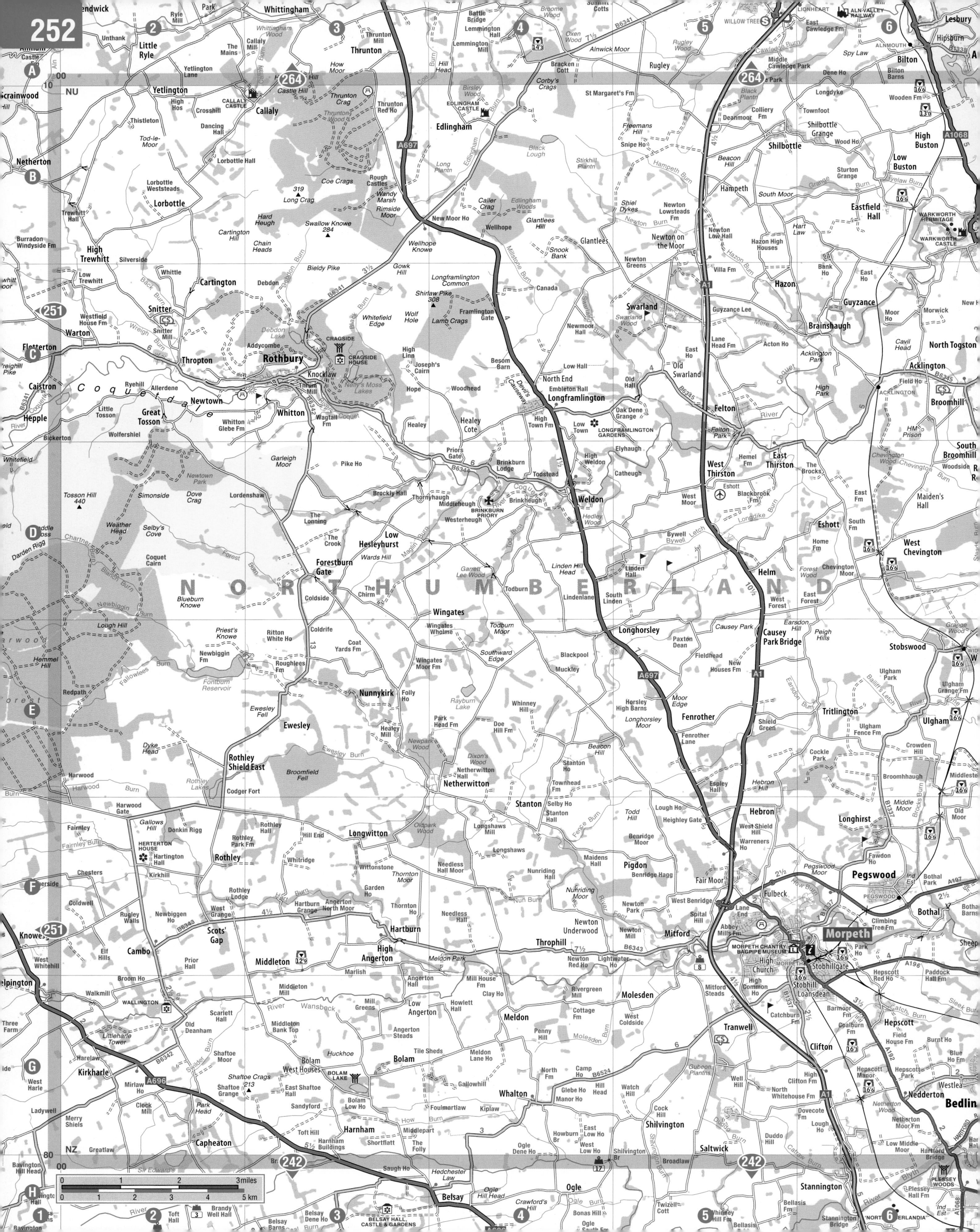
NORTHUMBERLAND
Whittingham
Thrunton
Little Ryle
Unthank
Yetlington
Callaly
Callaly Castle
Edlingham
Edlingham Castle
Lemmington Hall
Battle Bridge
Rugley
Alnwick Moor
Bracken Cott
Corby's Crags
St Margaret's Fm
Lesbury
Hipsburn
Bilton
Alnmouth
Spy Law
Dene Ho
Longdyke
Townfoot
Shilbottle
Shilbottle Grange
High Buston
Low Buston
Netherton
Scrainwood
Thistleton
Tod-le-Moor
Lorbottle Hall
Lorbottle
Lorbottle Weststeads
Coe Crags
319 Long Crag
Rough Castles
Wandy Marsh
Rimside Moor
New Moor Ho
Caller Crag
Edlingham Woods
Wellhope
Glantlees Hill
Glantlees
Freemans Hill
Snipe Ho
Beacon Hill
Hampeth
South Moor
Sturton Grange
Eastfield Hall
Warkworth Hermitage
Warkworth Castle
Trewhitt Hall
High Trewhitt
Low Trewhitt
Burradon
Windyside Fm
Silverside
Cartington
Cartington Hill
Hard Heugh
Chain Heads
Swallow Knowe 284
Bieldy Pike
Wellhope Knowe
Gowk Hill
Longframlington Common
Shirlaw Pike 308
Framlington Gate
Lamb Crags
Snook Bank
Canada
Newton Lowsteads Fm
Newton on the Moor
Newton Greens
Newton Low Hall
Hazon High Houses
Hazon
Guyzance
Guyzance Lee
Villa Fm
Bank Ho
East Ho
Moor Ho
Morwick
Brainshaugh
Snitter
Snitter Mill
Warton
Westfield House Fm
Flotterton
Thropton
Addycombe
Debdon
Rothbury
Cragside
Cragside House
Whitefield Edge
Wolf Hole
Knocklaw
Thrum Mill
Nelly's Moss Lakes
High Linn
Joseph's Cairn
Besom Barn
Swarland
Swarland Wood
Newmoor Hall
Low Hall
North End
Embleton Hall
Longframlington
Old Swarland
Old Hall
East Ho
Lane Head Fm
Acton Ho
Acklington Park
High Park
Cavil Head
North Togston
Acklington
Field Ho
Broomhill
Caistron
Hepple
Coquetdale
Allerdene
Ryehill
Newtown
Little Tosson
Great Tosson
Whitton
Whitton Glebe Fm
Wagtail Fm
Hope
Woodhead
Healey
Healey Cote
Devil's Causeway
High Town Fm
Low Town
Oak Dene Grange
Longframlington Gardens
Felton
Felton Park
HM Prison
Bickerton
Wolfershiel
Garleigh Moor
Pike Ho
Priors Gate
Brinkburn Lodge
Todstead
High Weldon
Elyhaugh
Catheugh
West Thirston
Hemel Fm
East Thirston
The Brocks
Chevington Wood
South Broomhill
Woodside
Tosson Hill 440
Simonside
Dove Crag
Lordenshaw
Brockly Hall
Thornyhaugh
Middleheugh
Brinkburn Priory
Brinkheugh
Weldon
Hedley Wood
Eshott
Blackbrook Fm
West Moor
Longdike Burn
East Fm
Maiden's Hall
South Fm
Eshott
Weather Head
Selby's Cove
The Lonning
The Crook
Low Hesleyhurst
Wards Hill
Westerheugh
Bywell
Home Fm
West Chevington
Chevington Moor
Forest Wood
Darden Rigg
Coquet Cairn
Forestburn Gate
Garrett Lee Wood
Linden Hill Head
Linden Hall
Helm
Blueburn Knowe
Coldside
The Chirm
Todburn
Lindenlane
South Linden
West Forest
East Forest
Wingates
Lough Hill
Priest's Knowe
Ritton White Ho
Coldrife
Coat Yards Fm
Wingates Wholme
Todburn Moor
Longhorsley
Paxton Dean
Causey Park
Causey Park Bridge
Earsdon Hill
Peigh Hills
Stobswood
Hemmel Hill
Newbiggin Fm
Roughlees Fm
Wingates Moor Fm
Southward Edge
Blackpool
Muckley
Fieldhead
New Houses Fm
Ulgham Park
Ulgham Grange Fm
Fontburn Reservoir
Redpath
Nunnykirk
Folly Ho
Rayburn Lake
Whinney Hill
Horsley High Barns
Longhorsley Moor
Moor Edge
Fenrother
Shield Green
Tritlington
Ulgham
Ewesley Fell
Ewesley
Heatley Mill
Park Head Fm
Doe Hill Fm
Fenrother Lane
Ulgham Fence Fm
Crowden Hill
Dyke Head
Newpark Wood
Dixon's Wood
Beacon Hill
Cockle Park
Rothley Shield East
Broomfield Fell
Netherwitton Hall
Netherwitton
Stanton Hill
Townhead Fm
Broomhaugh
Harwood
Codger Fort
Stanton
Selby Ho
Stanton Hall
Espley Hall
Hebron Hill
Middle Moor
Middleston
Harwood Gate
Gallows Hill
Donkin Rigg
Rothley Hall
Longwitton
Oldpark Wood
Longshaws Mill
Todd Hill
Lough Ho
Heighley Gate
Hebron
West Shield Hill
Warreners Ho
Longhirst
Old Moor
Fairnley
Herterton House
Hartington Hall
Rothley Park Fm
Rothley
Hill End
Whitridge
Longshaws
Needless Hall Moor
Maidens Hall
Benridge Moor
Pigdon
Benridge Hagg
Fawdon Ho
Chesters
Kirkhill
Wittonstone
Thornton Moor
Nunriding Hall
Nunriding Moor
Fair Moor
Pegswood Moor
Pegswood
Bothal Park
Coldwell
Rothley Lodge
Garden Ho
Hartburn Grange
Angerton North Moor
Thornton Ho
Needless Hall
Newton Park
West Benridge
Fulbeck
Lane End
Spital Hill
Bothal
Climbing Tree Fm
Rugley Walls
Newbiggen Ho
West Grange
Scots' Gap
Hartburn
Newton Underwood
Newton Mill
Mitford
Abbey Mills Fm
Morpeth
Morpeth Chantry Bagpipe Museum
Knowesgate
Cambo
Elf Hills
Prior Hall
Middleton
High Angerton
Meldon Park
Throphill
Newton Red Ho
Lightwater Ho
High Church
Stobhillgate
Park Ho
Hepscott Red Ho
Paddock Hall Fm
West Whitehill
Marlish
Angerton Hall
Mill House Fm
Clay Ho
Rivergreen Mill
Molesden
Mitford Steads
High Common Ho
Stobhill
Loansdean
Kirkwhelpington
Broom Ho
Walkmill
Wallington
Middleton Mill
Mill Greens
Low Angerton
Howlett Hall
Meldon
Cottage Fm
West Coldside
Catchburn Fm
Barmoor Fm
Coalburn Fm
Hepscott
Three Farm
Littleharle Tower
Scarlett Hall
Old Deanham
Middleton Bank Top
Angerton Steads
Penny Hill
Tranwell
Clifton
Field House Fm
Burnt Ho
Blue Ho Fm
Harelaw
Kirkharle
West Harle
Shaftoe Moor
Huckhoe
Bolam
Bolam West Houses
Bolam Lake
Tile Sheds
Meldon Lane Ho
North Fm
Camp Ho
Glebe Ho
Manor Ho
Hill Head
Watch Hill
Gubeon Plantn
West Hill
High Clifton Fm
North Whitehouse Fm
Hepscott Manor
Hepscott Park
Westlea
Nedderton
Bedlington
Mirlaw Ho
Clock Mill
Shaftoe Crags 213
Shaftoe Grange
East Shaftoe Hall
Sandyford
Bolam Low Ho
Gallowhill
Whalton
Foulmartlaw
Kiplaw
Netherton Wood
Netherton Moor Fm
Dovecote Fm
Ladywell
Merry Shiels
Park Head
Toft Hill
Harnham
Harnham Buildings
Middlepart
Shortflatt
The Folly
Howburn Br
East Low Ho
West Low Ho
Ogle Dene Ho
Cock Hill
Shilvington
Duddo Hill
Lough Ho
Low Middle Moor
Hartford Bridge
Capheaton
Greatlaw
Saltwick
Bavington Hill Head
Saugh Ho
Hedchester Law
Shilvington Br
Broadlaw
Stannington
Plessey Woods
Plessey Hall Fm
Belsay
Ogle Hill Head
Crawford's Hill
Ogle
Bonas Hill
Twizell Cott
Whinney Hill Fm
Bellasis
Stannington Bridge
Toft Hall
Brandy Well Hall
Belsay Dene Ho
Belsay Barns
Belsay Hall, Castle & Gardens
A697
A1
A1068
A696
A192
A197
A196
B6341
B6342
B6344
B6345
B6343
B6524
B1337
B1338
NU
NZ
0 1 2 3 miles
0 1 2 3 4 5 km

NORTH
SEA
Marden Rocks
Alnmouth Bay
Birling
Warkworth
Warkworth Harbour
Pan Pt
Wellhaugh Pt
Coquet Island
Gloster Hill
Amble
Moorhouse Fm
High Hauxley
Togston Hall
Radcliffe
Low Hauxley
HAUXLEY
Togston Barns
A1068
Togston East Fm
Danger area
Ladyburn Lake
Hadston
DRURIDGE BAY
Druridge Bay
Whitefield Ho
Chibburn Fm
High Chibburn
Widdrington
Hemscott Hill
Highthorn
Cresswell
Warkworthlane Cott
Hagg House
Ellington
Cresswell Home Fm
Lynemouth
Linton
East Moor Fm
Potland Fm
Works
Woodhorn
QUEEN ELIZABETH II
WOODHORN MUS
A189
Bus Cen
Woodbridge
Ashington
Newbiggin-by-the-Sea
Newbiggin Bay
Hirst
North Seaton
WANSBECK
Stakeford
North Seaton Colliery
West Sleekburn
Guide Post
Scotland Gate
Bomarsund
Bus Cen
Cambois
East Sleekburn
Choppington
Bedlington Station
Mount Pleasant Fm
North Blyth
Bebside
Cowpen
Blyth
Humford Mill
BEDLINGTON
Isabella Pit
East Hartford
Low Horton Fm
New Delaval
South Beach
Laverock Hall
South Newsham
Gloucester Lodge Fm
Shankhouse
Lysdon Fm
Stickley Fm
Meggie's Burn
NU
NZ

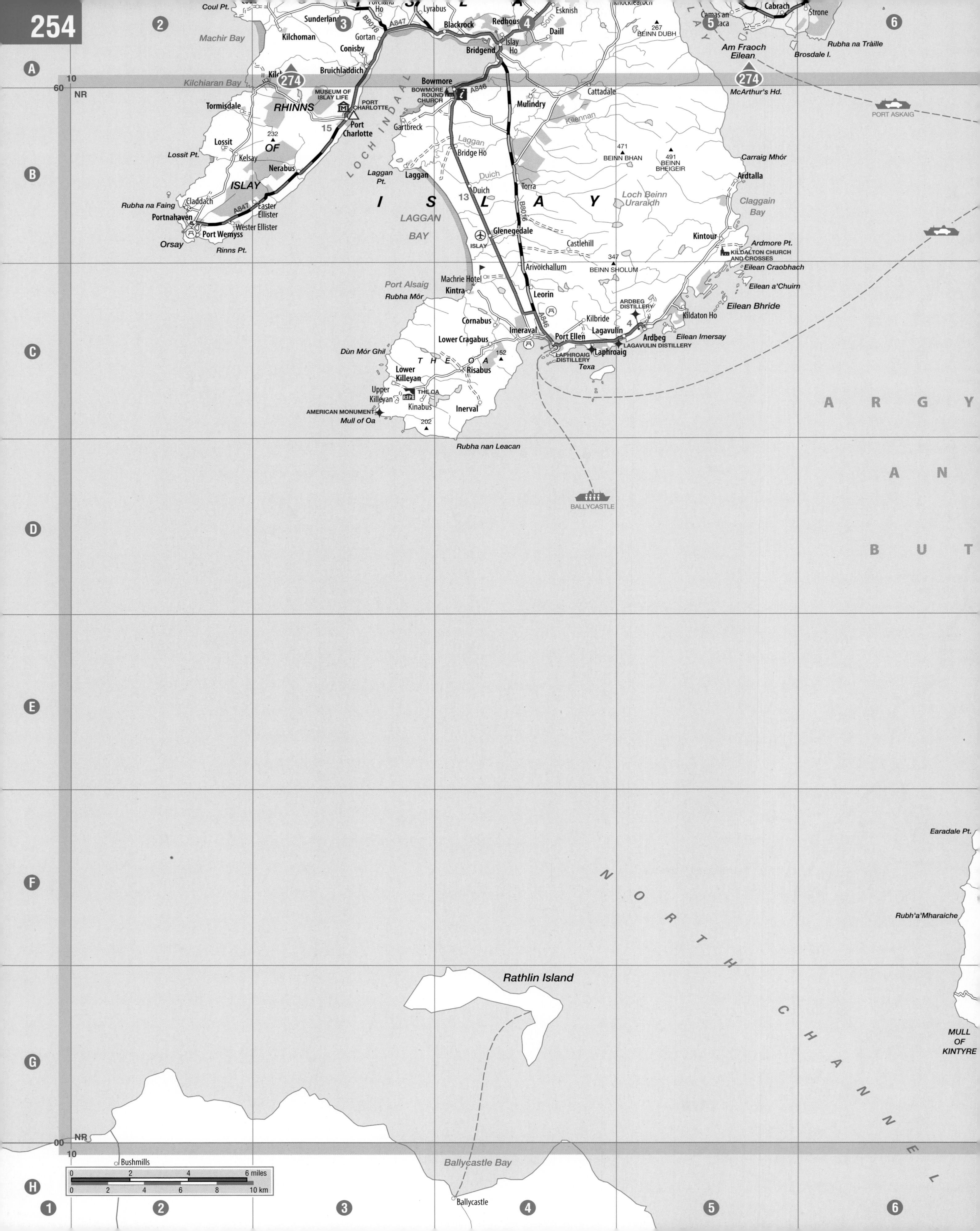

Coul Pt.
Machir Bay
Kilchoman
Sunderland
Conisby
Gortan
Bruichladdich
Lyrabus
Blackrock
Redhouse
Bridgend
Islay Ho
Esknish
Daill
267
BEINN DUBH
Camas an Staca
Cabrach
Strone
Rubha na Tràille
Brosdale I.
Am Fraoch Eilean
McArthur's Hd.
PORT ASKAIG
Kilchiaran Bay
274
NR
60
10
Bowmore
BOWMORE ROUND CHURCH
MUSEUM OF ISLAY LIFE
PORT CHARLOTTE
Port Charlotte
Tormisdale
RHINNS
OF
ISLAY
232
Lossit
Lossit Pt.
Kelsay
Nerabus
Claddach
Rubha na Faing
Portnahaven
Port Wemyss
Orsay
Rinns Pt.
Easter Ellister
Wester Ellister
A847
A846
B8018
B8016
LOCH INDAAL
Gartbreck
Laggan
Bridge Ho
Laggan Pt.
Mulindry
Cattadale
Kilennan
Duich
Torra
471
BEINN BHAN
491
BEINN BHEIGEIR
Carraig Mhór
Ardtalla
Claggain Bay
Loch Beinn Uraraidh
I S L A Y
LAGGAN BAY
Glenegedale
ISLAY
Castlehill
347
BEINN SHOLUM
Kintour
Ardmore Pt.
KILDALTON CHURCH AND CROSSES
Eilean Craobhach
Eilean a'Chuirn
Arivoichallum
Port Alsaig
Rubha Mòr
Machrie Hotel
Kintra
Leorin
ARDBEG DISTILLERY
Eilean Bhride
Kildaton Ho
Kilbride
Cornabus
Imeraval
Port Ellen
Lagavulin
Ardbeg
Eilean Imersay
LAGAVULIN DISTILLERY
Lower Cragabus
Dùn Mòr Ghil
THE OA
152
LAPHROAIG DISTILLERY
Laphroaig
Texa
Lower Killeyan
Risabus
Upper Killeyan
THE OA
Kinabus
AMERICAN MONUMENT
Mull of Oa
202
Inerval
Rubha nan Leacan
BALLYCASTLE
ARGYLL AND BUTE
Earadale Pt.
NORTH CHANNEL
Rubh'a'Mharaiche
Rathlin Island
MULL OF KINTYRE
Bushmills
Ballycastle Bay
Ballycastle
0 2 4 6 miles
0 2 4 6 8 10 km
A B C D E F G H
1 2 3 4 5 6

Kilberry
SCULPTURED STONES
Kennacraig
Redhouse
Carse Ho.
Dunmore
WEST LOCH TARBERT
CNOC A'BHAILESHIOS
Ardlamont Pt.
Ardroscadale
Rothesay
Straad
Loch Fad
Woodend Ho
Rubha Leathan
Loch Storn
275
Ardpatrick
Kilchamaig
Whitehouse
Northpark
Midpark
Inchmarnock
Loch Quien
Scoulag
MOUNT STUART HOUSE AND GARDENS
Ardpatrick Ho.
Gartnagrenach
Glenreasdell Mains
Skipness
SKIPNESS CASTLE
Skipness Pt.
Skipness Bay
Scalpsie
ISLAND OF BUTE
Piperhall
Ardpatrick Pt.
Portachoillan
Eilean Traighe
Claonaig
Claonaig Bay
Ardscalpsie Pt.
Scalpsie Bay
Stravanan Bay
Kingarth
Kilchattan
Kilchattan Bay
Ronachan Pt.
Ronachan Ho
A83
Clachan
CRUACH NAM FIADH
Loch Ciaran
TARBET (Oct-Mar)
SOUND OF BUTE
Eilean Garbh
West Tarbert Bay
East Tarbert Bay
(April-Oct)
ST BLANE'S CHAPEL
Tarbert
Ardailly
Gigha Island
Druimyeon More
Balochroy
Crossaig Glen
Crossaig
Loch Garasdale
Cock of Arran
LOCHRANZA CASTLE
Lochranza
Loch Ranza
Garroch Hd.
Little Cumbrae Island
Millstone Pt.
CRUACH MHIC GOUGAN
Ardminish
Ardminish Bay
Ardlamey
ACHAMORE GARDENS
Rhunahaorine
Gortinanane
Cour Bay
Cour
Catacol Bay
Catacol
Fairhaven
ISLE OF ARRAN DISTILLERY
266
BEINN BHREAC
MEALL NAN DAMH
Thundergay
Tayinloan
CNOC NAN CRAOBH
Gigalum Island
Cara Island
Braids
Killean
CRUACH MHIC-AN T-SAOIR
Auchenbreck
Carradale Water
Grogport
Pirnmill
NORTH
Loch Tanna
Sannox
Sannox Bay
Glen Sannox
Beacharr
CRUACH NAN GABHAR
Achaglass
Clachaig Water
Brackley
Whitefarland
BEINN BHARRAIN
CIR MHÒR
BEINN TARSUINN
GOAT FELL
Corrie
NORTH AYRSHIRE
Muasdale
Imachar
Balliekine
ISLE OF ARRAN
Merkland
ARDROSSAN
Rhonadale
Carradale
Port Righ
BRODICK
Glenrosa
BRODICK CASTLE
Glen Rosa
Amod
BEINN BHREAC
Glenacardoch Pt.
Belloch
Bridgend
Dougarie
Glen Iorsa
Glenbarr
CLAN MACALISTER CENTRE
Barr Water
Killegruer
Waterfoot
Torrisdale-Square
Torrisdale Castle
BEINN AN TUIRC
Carradale Pt.
Carradale Bay
Auchencar
Machrie Water
ISLE OF ARRAN HERITAGE MUSEUM
Brodick Bay
Brodick
Strathwhillan
North Corriegills
Auchagallon
Machrie
Glenloig
A'CHRUACH
Glen Cloy
South Corriegills
Cleongart
Saddell Glen
Machrie Bay
Bellochantuy Bay
Saddell
SADDELL ABBEY
Saddell Ho
Bellochantuy
Tormore
MACHRIE MOOR STANDING STONES
Clauchlands Pt.
CAMPBELTOWN (May-Sept Sat only)
A'CHRUACH
Saddell Bay
KILBRANNAN SOUND
KING'S CAVE
Balmichael
Blairbeg
Margnaheglish
Lamlash
Lamlash Bay
Cordon
Holy Island
Killocraw
Corrylach
Lussa Loch
Torbeg
Drumadoon Pt.
Shiskine
Birchburn
North Feorline
SGREADAN HILL
Ugadale
Tangy Loch
Kingscross Pt.
Kingscross
Auchencairn
TIGHVEIN
Blackwaterfoot
Drumadoon Bay
Kilpatrick
KILPATRICK DUN
Tangy
Skeroblingarry
Glenlussa Ho
Kilkeddan
Black Bay
Sliddery Water
Knockenkelly
Whiting Bay
North Kiscadale
South Kiscadale
Westport
Kilchenzie
Glenlussa Water
Peninver
Glenree
Corriecravie Moor
Corriecravie
Auchareoch
Clachaig
GLENASHDALE FALLS
Largymore
Largymeanoch
Ardnacross Bay
Brown Hd.
CARN BAN
Kilmory Water
Largybeg
West Darlochan
Kilmichael
Sliddery
Dippin
256
Machrihanish Bay
CAMPBELTOWN
Low Smerby
Lagg
Shannochie
Levencorroch
Dippin Head
Drumore
CAMPBELTOWN HERITAGE CENTRE
Machrihanish
Trodigal
Campbeltown
Campbeltown Loch
Island Davaar
DAVAAR ISLAND CAVE PAINTING
Kilmory
Bennan
Kildonan
TORRYLINN CAIRN
Bennan Hd.
Sound of Pladda
Moy
Drumlemble
B843
Stewarton
CAMPBELTOWN BUNKHOUSE
Kilkerran
Kildalloig
Pladda
Ballygroggan
Knocknaha
ARDROSSAN (May-Sept)
BRODICK (May-Sept, Sat only)
High Tirfergus
Achinhoan Hd.
BEINN GHUILEAN
THE SLATE
Lochorodale
Woodbank
CNOC MOY
Largiebaan
BALLYCASTLE
Feochaig
Glen Breackerie
CNOC ODHAR
Conie Glen
Johnston's Pt.
244
Knockstapplemore
Strone
North Carrine
Keprigan
Polliwilline
Polliwilline Bay
Strone Glen
Machariоch
Mill Park
Southend
Carskiey
Brunerican Bay
Cove Pt.
Port Mean
Rubha Chlachan
Sheep I.
Sanda Island
Ailsa Craig
NS

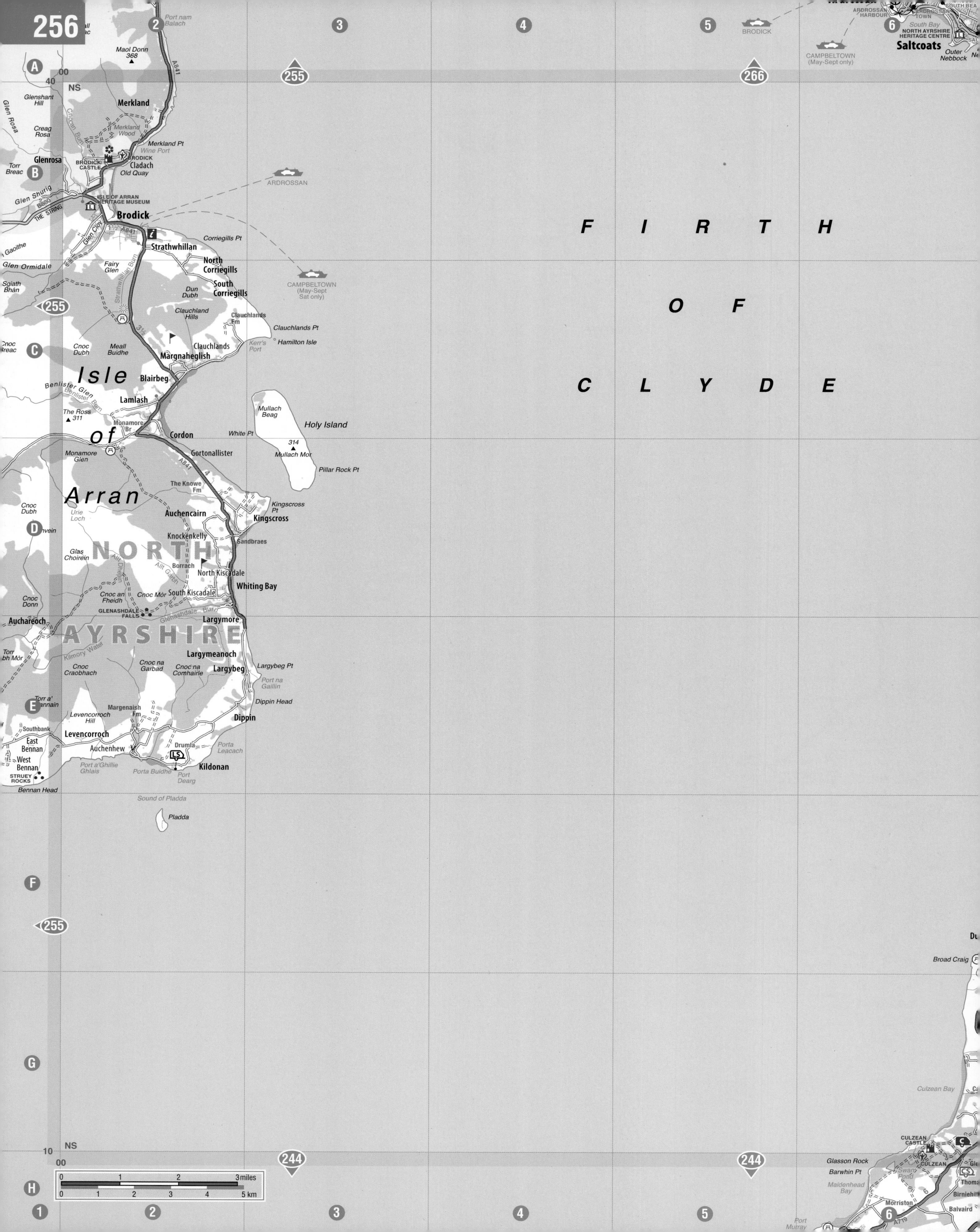
FIRTH OF CLYDE
Isle of Arran
NORTH AYRSHIRE
Merkland
Glenrosa
Brodick
Cladach
Old Quay
Merkland Pt
Wine Port
BRODICK CASTLE
ISLE OF ARRAN HERITAGE MUSEUM
Maol Donn 368
Port nam Balach
Glen Shurig
Glen Rosa
Glen Cloy
Glen Ormidale
Strathwhillan
Corriegills Pt
North Corriegills
South Corriegills
Dun Dubh
Fairy Glen
Clauchland Hills
Clauchlands Fm
Clauchlands Pt
Hamilton Isle
Kerr's Port
Clauchlands
Margnaheglish
Blairbeg
Lamlash
Cnoc Dubh
Meall Buidhe
The Ross 311
Monamore Br
Monamore Glen
Cordon
White Pt
Holy Island
Mullach Beag
Mullach Mor 314
Pillar Rock Pt
Gortonallister
The Knowe Fm
Kingscross Pt
Kingscross
Auchencairn
Urie Loch
Knockenkelly
Sandbraes
Glas Choirein
Borrach
North Kiscadale
Whiting Bay
South Kiscadale
Cnoc Mòr
Cnoc an Fheidh
Cnoc Donn
GLENASHDALE FALLS
Largymore
Auchareoch
Kilmory Water
Largymeanoch
Largybeg
Largybeg Pt
Cnoc Craobhach
Cnoc na Garbad
Cnoc na Comhairle
Port na Gaillin
Dippin Head
Dippin
Margenaish Fm
Levencorroch Hill
Levencorroch
Southbank
East Bennan
West Bennan
STRUEY ROCKS
Bennan Head
Auchenhew
Drumla
Porta Leacach
Kildonan
Port a'Ghillie Ghlais
Porta Buidhe
Port Dearg
Sound of Pladda
Pladda
ARDROSSAN
CAMPBELTOWN (May-Sept Sat only)
BRODICK
CAMPBELTOWN (May-Sept only)
ARDROSSAN HARBOUR
ARDROSSAN TOWN
South Bay
NORTH AYRSHIRE HERITAGE CENTRE
Saltcoats
Outer Nebbock
Broad Craig
Culzean Bay
CULZEAN CASTLE
CULZEAN
Glasson Rock
Barwhin Pt
Maidenhead Bay
Morriston
Balvaird
Port Murray
NS
255
266
244
0 1 2 3 miles
0 1 2 3 4 5 km

Irvine
Kilmarnock
Troon
Prestwick
Ayr
Maybole
Patna
Mauchline
Galston
Tarbolton
Dreghorn
Kilmaurs
Riccarton
Monkton
Drongan
Dalrymple
Alloway
EAST AYRSHIRE
SOUTH AYRSHIRE
Irvine Bay
Lady Isle
GLASGOW PRESTWICK INTERNATIONAL AIRPORT
266
267
258
245

Sneddon Law
Cowans Law
Thrashy Knowe
Pley Moss
Long Green
Braidley Moss
Mossmulloch
Caldermill
Laigh Crewburn
Hill Fm
Hall of Kype
Little Kype
Burnfoot Fm
Calder Moss
Hookhead
Midlinbank Fm
Hazliebank
High Hazliebank
Newmains
High Dyke
Little Kype West
Muirside
Wallacegill Muir
Coldwakning
Hallfield
Gilmourton
267
268
Alton Muirhouse
High Bowhill
Mount
Stobieside
Westertoun Fm
Middle Rig
Kypewa
NS
Little Glen
Harelea Hill
West Dykehead Fm
Drumclog
A71
Brownhill
West Newton
Crawlaw
Hungryhill
Wraes
Gateside
Bankhead
Loudoun Mains
West Heads
Cronan
East Heads
Foulpapple
Gamesland
Knevocklaw
Templehill
Howletburn
Drumboy Fm
Loudoun Hill 316
Rench Fm
Torfoot Fm
Syde Fm
High Dykes
Willochsheuch Moss
Martinside
Kype Lodge
Newmilns
Darvel
Waterside
Greenholm
Darvel Road
River Irvine
Allanton Newlands
Bransfield Fm
Windy
Wizen
Lochgate
North Halls
B745
Side Hill
Feeshie Moss
Rough Moss
Berry Moss
Dunside Res
Galston
Strath
Lanfine Home Fm
High Greenbank Fm
Gorsebraehead
Auchenbart
High Newton
Cairnsaigh
Peelhill
Overhouse
Halls Burn
B743
Harting Rig
Dunside Rig
Stonyhall
Windyhill
Molemount Fm
Sparnelbank
Clinchyard
Millands
Bellisle
Changue Hill
Tulloch Hill 300
King's Moss
Auchengilloch 462
Grouse Hill
Logan Fm
Middlefield
Eastfield Fm
Sornhill
Milrig
Drumdroch
Cairnhill
Newfield
Greenfield
Brow Hill
Mule Hill
Main Castle
Mill Rig
Laigh Plewland
High Plewland
Glengavel Reservoir
Dungavel Hill 457
Goodbush Hill 475
Spirebush Hill 469
Nutberry Hill 522
257
West Burnhead
Langside
Lawdyke
Mean Muir
Logan Moss
Distinkhorn 386
Anderside Hill
Black Loch Moss
Bankend Rig
Regal Hill
Whitehill Fm
Burn
Bogend
Wynds
Brown's Muir
Flacket Hill
Avon Head
Laird Knowe
Little Hartmidden
Twopenny Knowe
Bibblon Hill 431
Dippal Rig
Starpet Rig 451
Priesthill Height 493
Craig
Bruntwood Mains
Tongue
Rodinghead Ho
Low Holehouse
Meadowhead
Crofthead
Grange Muir
Hart Hill
Burnt Hill
Meanlour Hill
Head of Greenock Water
Hare Craig
Roughdyke Fm
Boghead
Auchmannoch
Knockdon
Wedder Hill 434
Middlefield Law 466
Priesthill
South Auchenbrain
Barboigh
Weitshaw Muir
Reppoch Knowe
Craigs Hill
Sclanor Hill
A76
Barwheys
Auchmillan
Darnhay
Weitshaw
Pepper Knowe
Auchenlongford Hill
Stony Hill
Dun Rig
Greenock Bridge
Black Hill
Auchmillanhill
Blackbriggs
Oxenshaw
Upper Hall
Glenbu
Brigland
Wealth of Waters
Heath Cottage
Meath Hill
Aikencleugh
Netherwood
Laigh Hall
Lightshaw
Garfield
Redgate
Sorn Mains
Greenock Water
Tardoes
Mauchline Mains
Tincorn Hill
Limmerhaugh Muir
Greenock Mains
Marchouse Hill
Burnfoot Moor
Muirkirk
Crossflatt
Earl Hill
Mauchline
Blindburn
Welton
Grassmillees
Sorn Castle
Sorn
Dalgain
Daldilling
Nethershield
River Ayr
Smallburn
Smallburn Road
Auldhouseburn
Brack Hill
Hawk Hill
Kames
Catrine Mains
Haugh
Catrine
Whiteflat
Barrshouse
Upper Heilar
Midwellwood Fm
A70
Kingencleugh Ho
Logan
Gilmilnscroft
EAST
Little Cairn Table 517
High Wood
The Steel
Barskimming Mains
Syke
High Clews
Catrineshaw
Kenstey
Bogend
B705
Brackenhill
Roundshaw Fm
Airds Moss
Boghead Lane
Wood Hill
Cairn Table 593
AYRSHIRE
Little Heateth
Drumfork
Meikle Heateth
Glensham Rock Fm
Cairn Hill
Fingland Hill 462
Slatehole
Treeshill
Townhead
Darnlaw
Knagshill
Back Rogerton
Common
Cronberry
Knockbreck
Dalfad Moss
Whiteyards
Wardlaw Hill 497
Panbreck Hill
Mid Hill
Steelpark
Blackfauldhead
Knowe
Auchinleck
Commondyke Fm
Muirkirk Road
Barony Road
Dykes Fm
Lugar
Wallaceton
Penmore
Ochiltree
Thirdpart
Boswell Mausoleum
Holmhead
Stony Hill 562
Carston
Lugar Water
Gass Water
Low Moss
Logan
Glenmuir Water
Dornal Moss
Glenmuir Hill
Connor Hill
Drummond's Knowe
White Hill 480
Laigh Tarbeg
Mote Toll
Ochiltree Mains
Grimgrew
Dumfries House
Cumnock
Kier Hardie Statue
Barshare
Little Auchengibbert
Crosslar
Garleffan Fm
High Dalblair
East Foredibban Hill
Nether Black Law
Black Law
Back o' Hill
Orchardton
Netherthird
Holm Burn
Dalblair
Rottenrow
High Carston
Crosshill
Knockshinnock
Barmickhill
Horsecleugh Fm
Craigens
Borland Mains
Avisyard Hill 330
Roughhill Moss
Whiteholm
Benalt 382
Black Hill 431
Auchtitench Hill 467
Earl Hill
Burnock Mill
Skares
Garlaff
Greenside
Dumfries Road
Crawford Hill
Airds Hill
Over Guelt
Shiel Rig
Crook Brae 385
Clocklowie Hill 442
Dennigall Hill
Auchlin
Mossback
High Burnside
Borland
Glaisnock
Cairnscadden Hill 314
Edge Hill 345
Calton Fm
Auchencloigh
The Muir
High Polqueys
Millstone Knowe
Halfmerk Hill 453
Kirkland Hill 507
Black Loch
Carnivan Hill 324
White Knowe
Benston Fm
Creoch Loch
Lochhill
Rottenyard
Roughside
Craigdullyeart Hill
Nivison Hill 460
Lethans Hill
Todholes Hill 481
Auchlin Rig
Burnockhead
High Mount 365
Carsgailoch Hill
Hall of Auchincross
Loch o' th' Lowes
Pathhead
Polqueys
Hall of Mansfield
Corsencon Hill 475
Glenwharrie
Lagrae
Kirkland
Guffock Hill
Greenhill
Black Hill
Fordmouth
North Boig
New Cumnock
Mansfield
Mansfield Mains
Corsencon
Todholes
Stannery Knowe 363
Woodend
Connel Park
East Polquhirter
Meikle Westland
Glen Hall
Laigh Cairn
Kirkland Planth
Tappet Hill
Dalricket Mill
Dalgig
Bankglen
West Polquhirter
Over Cairn
River Nith
Brown Hill
Mid Hill
Hungry Hill
Burnfoot Road
West Park Fm
High Park
Burntonhill
High Cairn
Rigg Fm
Nether Cairn
Kelloside
Kirkconnel
Kelloholm
Over Hill
Lingie Hill
Little Rigend Hill
Laight Fm
Burnt Hill
Sunnyside
Lanehead
Burnside
Brockloch
Dalhanna Hill
Dalhanna Fm
Lochbrowan Hill
High Cairn 553
McCrierick's Cairn 556
White Hill 406
White Knowe
Libry Moor
Upper Beoch
NS
Peat Hill 385
Strait Fm
Dalleagles
Blarene Hill 358
Knocknide Hill 344
Ashmark Hill
Hare Hill
Polnagrie Hill
246
Corserig Hill 395
Glengape
Benbain
Nith
Headmark Moss
Chang Hill 463
Benty Cowan Hill 477
Ewe Hill 437
Pollach Burn
Laglass Hill
Quintin Knowe 554
Polstacher Burn
Kello Water
Hog Hill
Brunt Rig
Barr Moor
0 1 2 3 miles
0 1 2 3 4 5 km

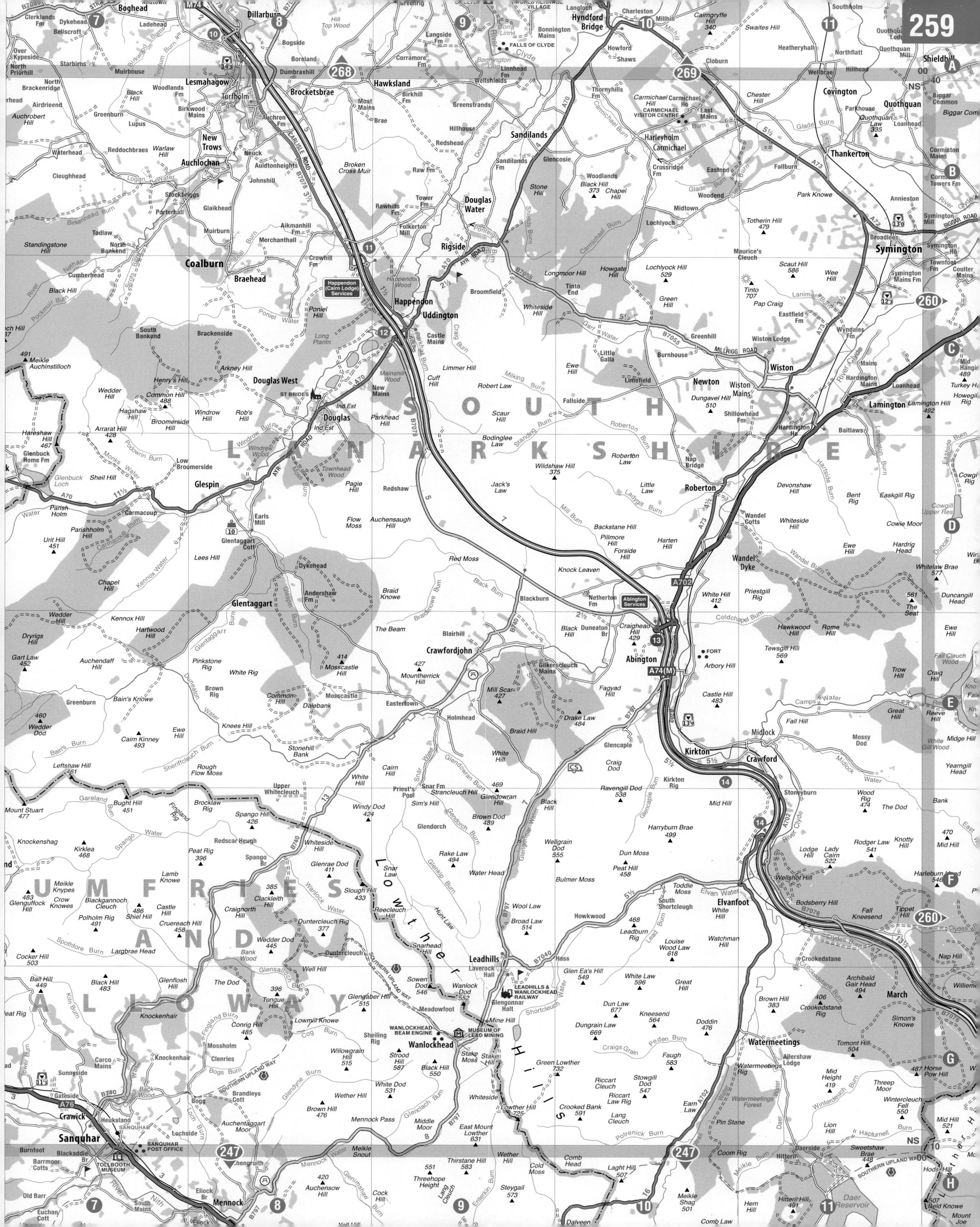

259
268
269
260
247
SOUTH LANARKSHIRE
DUMFRIES AND GALLOWAY
Lowther Hills
Boghead
Dillarburn
Hyndford Bridge
Charleston
Falls of Clyde
New Lanark World Heritage Village
Lesmahagow
Turfholm
Brocketsbrae
Hawksland
Carmichael
Carmichael Visitor Centre
Covington
Quothquan
Thankerton
Biggar Road
New Trows
Auchlochan
Sandilands
Harleyholm
Douglas Water
Rigside
Coalburn
Braehead
Happendon (Cairn Lodge) Services
Happendon
Uddington
Symington
Tinto 707
Wiston
Newton
Lamington
Douglas West
Douglas
St Brides
Glespin
Roberton
Wandel Dyke
Abington Services
Abington
Crawfordjohn
Glentaggart
Leadhills
Leadhills & Wanlockhead Railway
Wanlockhead
Museum of Lead Mining
Wanlockhead Beam Engine
Green Lowther 732
Lowther Hill 725
Elvanfoot
Kirkton
Crawford
Watermeetings
Daer Reservoir
March
Crawick
Sanquhar
Sanquhar Post Office
Tollbooth Museum
Mennock
Eliock
Southern Upland Way
Carlisle Road
Ayr Road
Millrigg Road
A70
A73
A72
A702
A74(M)
A76
B7078
B7055
B740
B797
B7040
B7076
M74

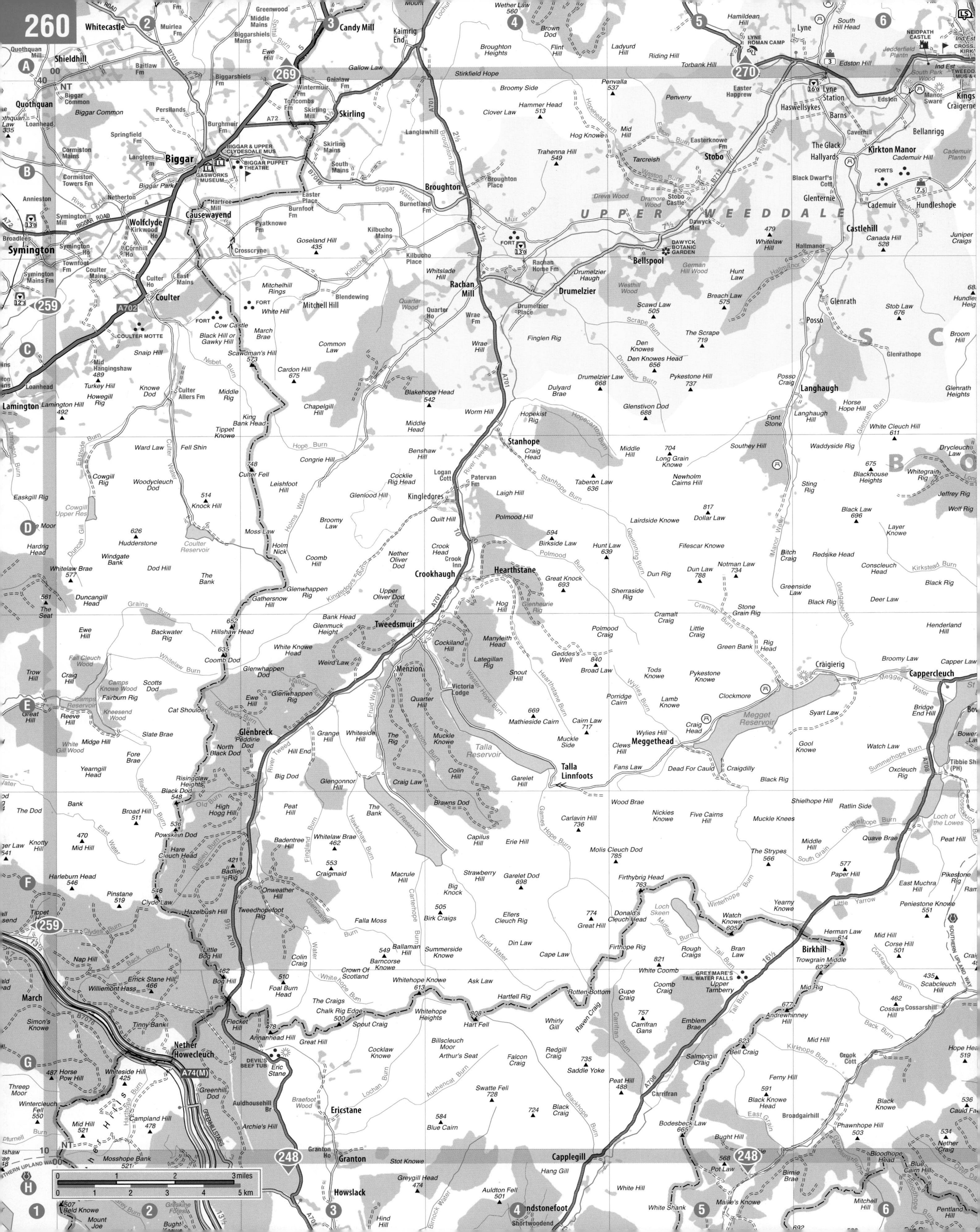

262
Colmslie
Langshaw
Over Langshaw
Bluecairn
Chapel on Leader
Kedslie
Birkenside
Legerwood Hill
West Morriston
East Morriston
Huntshaw Hill
Fans
Fans Hill
Darlingfield
Falsidehill
Hume
Hume Crags
Hardiesmill Place
Whitehill Ho
Lurgie Craigs
Sweethope Hill
Stichill
Stichill Home Fm
Stichill Eastfield
Harpertoun
Hassington East Mains
Hassington West Mains
Blue Houses
Kaimflat
Caldronbrae
Mosshouses
Cairneymount
Leadervale Ho
Earlston Mains
Earlston
Craigsford Mains
Ind Est
Cowdenknowes Mains
White Hill
Mellerstain House
Sheep Covert
Blinkbonny
Parkend
Ladhope Moor
Chatto Craigs
Glendearg
Buckholm Hill
Darling's Hill
Easter Housebyres
Halliburton
Galashiels
Langlee Mains
Langlee
Wester Housebyres
Easter Langlee
Ferny Hill
Faw Plantn
Packman's Burn
Sorrowlessfield Mains
Redpath Hill
The Park
Redpath
Brotherstone Moor
Brotherstone Hill
Brotherstone
Rachelfield
Girnick
Hundy Mundy
Girrick
Nenthorn
Nenthorn Ho
Old Nenthorn
Spotsmains
Courthill
Smailholm
East Third
West Third
Smailholm Mains
Mien's Plantn
Easter Muirdean
Edenbank
Berryhill
Kelso
Ednam
Ednam Hill
Newtonlees
Newton Don
Hendersyde Fm
Hendersyde Park
Kaimknowe
Queen's Ho
Floors Home Fm
Floors Castle
Salmon Fishing Museum
Gala Hill
Lowood
Tweedbank
Gattonside
Gattonside Mains
Pavilion Fm
Gattonside Ho
Priorwood Gardens
Melrose Abbey
Main Street
EILDON AND
Leaderfoot
Halidean Mill
Craighouse
Bettyfield
Smailholm Tower
Whitrighill
Haymount
Abbotsford House
Darnick
Melrose
Dingleton
The Three Hills Roman Heritage Centre
Newstead
Bemersyde
Bemersyde Moss
Butchercote
Fox Covert
Maidenhall
Sucklawridge
Kay Brae
Border Union Showground
Springwood
Wallacenick
Kelso Abbey
Maxwellheugh
Wooden Ho
Touting Birk's Hill
Boleside
Abbotsmoss
Huntlyburn Ho
Eildon
Monksford
Faldonside
Cauldshiels Loch
Rhymer's Glen
LEADFOOT
Eildon Hills
Clintmains
Dryburgh
Mertoun Br
Mertoun Gardens
Magdalene Hall
Dalcove Mains
Manorhill
Trows
Roxburgh Barns
Maisondieu
Spylaw
Newtown St Boswells
Greenwells
Whiterigg
Dryburgh Abbey
Lessudden Bank
Rutherford Lodge
River Tweed
Cauldshiels Hill
Bowden Moor
Lindean
Faughill Moor
Longleefoot
Faughill
Bowden
Whitelee
St Boswells
Fens
Benrig
Littledean
Rutherford Mains
Roxburgh Newtown
Roxburgh Mill
Heiton Mill
Heiton
Ladyrig
Over Whitlaw Fm
Lindean Moor
Mainhill
Camieston
Charlesfield
Maxton
Riddletonhill
Ploughlands
Rutherford
Big Wood
Roxburgh
Roxburgh Moor
Roxburgh Mains
Sunlaws Mill
Greenhead
Whitlaw Mosses
Bell Hill
Prieston
Old Prieston
Kippilaw Mains
Eastfield
Kippilaw
Northfield
Thornielaw
Elliston
Fox Covert
Forest Lodge
Morridgehall
Muirhouselaw
Steelmoor Plantn
Upper Nisbet Moor
Duke's Strip
Graham's Law
Grahamslaw Plantn
Bowmont Forest
Midlem
Whitmuir Hall
Midlem Mill
Milrighall
Clarilaw
Alerigg
Greenend
Longnewton
Longnewton Forest
Ancrum Moor 1545
Upper Nisbet
Blackrig Plantn
Kalemouth
Ormiston Mains
Caverton Hillhead
Old Caverton
SCOTTISH
Shawburn
Toftbarns
Chesterknowes
Alewater Ho
Chapel Fm
Cavers Carre
Bewlie Mains
Bewlie
Belses Mill Fm
Palacehill
Lilliardsedge Park
Down Law
Peniel Heugh
Waterloo Monument
Ploughlands
Mosstower
Eckford
Eckfordmoss
Marlefield
Playknowe Plantn
Lilliesleaf
Clerklands
Riddell
West Middles
Craggs
Old Belses
Belses
Pinnacle
Woodhead Fm
Ancrum
Howden
Woodside
Nisbet
Nisbetmill
Kirkmains
Crailing
Crailing Tofts
Crailing Ho
Wooden Hill
Rocky Covert
Wooden Loch
North Synton
Newhouse
Bowismiln
Hermiston
Harelaw
Netherraw
Firth
Catshawhill
Greenhouse
Rawflat
Bloomfield
Whitehouse
Belses Muir
Troneyhill
Ancrum Craig
Broom Covert
Copland
Ancrum West Mains
Harestanes Countryside Visitor Centre
Shortacres
Mounthooly
Baittens
Littledeanlees
Blakeman's Crag
Castle Knowe
Cessford
Droveroad Plantn
Minto Kames
North Lodge
Teviot Dale
Grange Banks
Chesters Grange
Chesters
Lanton Mill
Bonjedward
Bonjedward Ho
Mount Ulston
Langdales
Bank Hill
Black Craig
Huntlaw Burn
Newlands
Barnhills Moor Plantn
Barnhills Fm
Lanton
Lanton Moor
Ulston Moor
Crailinghall
Marchcleuch
Hassendean Common
Minto Hills
Lambslair Plantn
Cleuchhead
Newton
Gospel Hall Fm
Lanton Hill
Mary Queen of Scots House
Crouchie Wood
Wildcat Gate
Overwells Cott
Old Hall
Samieston
Cappuck Br
Rennieston
Upper Samieston
Faw Laws
Hassendean
Dearly Burn
Minto
Menslaws
Deanfoot
Spittal-on-Rule
Jedburgh
Jedburgh Abbey
Jedburgh Castle Jail Mus
Howden
Harden Mains
Shibden Hill
Whitton Loch
Hallywell Hill
Horsleyhill
Melgund Glen
River Teviot
Jedburgh Road
Hassendean Bank
Dunion Hill
Todlaw
Hunthill
Hardenpeel
Crook Knowes
Knowetownhead
Clarilaw
Teviot Bank
Denholm
Bedrule Mill
Hundalee
Hag Plantn
Scraesburgh
Oxnam
Towncfoot Hill
Bloodylaws Hill
Cunzierton Fm
East Boonraw
Newton
Appletreehall
Midshiels
Ashybank
Denholm Dean
Bedrule
Black Law
Ferniehirst Castle
Glendouglas
Langlee
Kersheugh
Oxnamrow Hill
Spital Tower
BORDERS
Stirches Mains
Gala Law
Burnhead
Bucklands
Cavers Mains
Mill Court
Midgard
Denholmhill
Gilboa Wood
Watch Knowe
Swinnie
Oxnam Sawmill
Mossburnford
Swinside Hall
Harkers Hill
Bus Pk
Burnfoot
Hawick
Midgard
Effledge
Whitriggs
Fort
Rubers Law
West Lees
Billerwell
Swinnie Plantn
Gilliestongues
Bairnkine
Mossburnford Bank
Newbigging
Heip Hill
Wilton
Weensland
Ind Est
Cauldmill
Deanbrae
Cavers Knowes
Nether Tofts
Old Fodderlee
Easter Fodderlee
Willowford Burn
Woodhouse
Dolphinston
Peg Law
Hawick Museum
Cauld
Drumlanrig's Tower
Parkdaill
Lynnwood
Ormiston
Kirkton
Hallrule
Wester Fodderlee
Faw Hill
Jed Water
Newbigging Burn
Camptown
Falla
North Riccalton
Kaimend
Burnt Plantn
Hallrule Mill
Weens Ho
Abbotrule
Ruletownhead
Mervinslaw
Lawsuit Law
Dod Hill
Vertish Hill
White Hill
Kirkton Hill
Weensmoor Fm
Bonchester Bridge
Bonchester Hill
Belling Hill
Mervins Law
Stotfield Hill
Moor Head
Scaw'd Law
Birneyknowe
Coliforthill
Colislinn
Adderston Lee
Pilmuir
New Mill
Hoggfield Hill
Hobkirk
Fodderlee Burn
Doorpool Hill
Falside
Roughlee
Edgerston
Edgerston Rig
Philip Law
Acreknowe Res
Highend
Cleuch Head
Crown Plantn
Mackside
Chesters
Southdean Mill
Bught Knowe
White
Stonedge
Folly Plantn
Spar Plantn
Law Plantn
Croft Plantn
White Hill
Haresha Knowe
Knock Hills
Hophills Nob
Ephope Law
Southdean
Southdean Lodge
Stobs Castle
Cogsmill
Stonedge Hill
Wauchope Fm
Wolfiee Hill
Cribs Hole
Highlee Hill
Weasel Hill
Steele Knowe
Crink Law
Letham
Huntford
Deerlee Knowe
Leithope Forest
Lamblair Edge
3miles
5 km

263
Coldstream
Cornhill-on-Tweed
Birgham
Carham
Wark
West Learmouth
East Learmouth
Branxton
Crookham
Etal
Ford
Ford Forge
Flodden
Milfield
Kimmerston
Doddington
Nesbit
Fenton Town
Newtown
Coupland
Lanton
Kilham
Westnewton
Kirknewton
Akeld
Wooler
Humbleton
Earle
Middleton Hall
North Middleton
South Middleton
Ilderton
Langleeford
Greensidehill
Ingram
Prendwick
Alnham
Scrainwood
Netherton
Biddlestone
Barrowburn
Blindburn
Sourhope
Mowhaugh
Cliftoncote
Linton
Crookhouse
Morebattle
Town Yetholm
Kirk Yetholm
Frogden
Whitton
Hownam
Chatto
Nether Hindhope
Upper Hindhope
Sprouston
Kerchesters
Hadden
Holefield
Pressen
Mindrum
Pawston
Shotton
Downham
Howtel
Lempitlaw
Hoselaw
Blakelaw
Windywalls
Eccles
Lennel
Melkington
Hethpool
The Cheviot
Windy Gyle
Kidland Forest
NORTHUMBERLAND
NORTHUMBERLAND NATIONAL PARK
The Cheviot Hills
PENNINE WAY
River Tweed
Bowmont Water
River Glen
Upper Coquetdale
A697
A698
B6352
B6351
B6396
B6401
B6350
B6353
B6354
B6348
B6525
272
273
264
251

NORTH SEA
Embleton Bay
Castle Pt
BUNSTANBURGH CASTLE
Queen Margaret's Cove
Craster
Cullernose Pt
Howick
Rumbling Kern
Red Stead
Howick Haven
Sugar Sands
Low Stead
Howdiemont Sands
Red Ends
Boulmer
Boulmer Haven
Field Ho
Seaton Pt
Marden Rocks
Alnmouth Bay
NU
50
40
10

253
253

FIRTH OF CLYDE
INVERCLYDE
CLYDE-MUIRSHIEL REGIONAL PARK
NORTH AYRSHIRE
Island of Bute
Great Cumbrae Island
Little Cumbrae Island
Inverkip
Wemyss Bay
Skelmorlie
Upper Skelmorlie
Meigle
Routenburn
Largs
Fairlie
Millport
Innellan
Toward
Castle Toward
Port Lamont
Knockdow
Ardbeg
Craigmore
Montford
Ascog
Kerrycroy
Scoulag
Piperhall
Meikle Kilchattan Butts
Kingarth
Kilchattan Bay
Portencross
Ardneil
Thirdpart
West Kilbride
Seamill
Ardrossan
Saltcoats
Stevenston
Kilwinning
Irvine
Dalry
Blairland
Kilbirnie
Glengarnock
Beith
Longbar
Lochwinnoch
Highfield
Drakemyre
Giffordland
Dalgarven
Chapelhill
Dykesmains
Auchenharvie
Garvock
Shielhill
Dreghorn
Fullarton
Girdle Toll
Kilchattan Bay
Fairlie Roads
Downcraig Ferry
Hunterston Sands
Hunterston Power Sta
Farland Head
Bell Stane
Horse Isle
Brodick
Campbeltown (May-Sept only)
Museum of the Cumbraes
The Marine Station & David Robertson Mus
Mount Stuart
Victorian Fernery
Ardencraig Gardens
St Blane's Chapel
Kelburn Country Centre
Haylie Chambered Tomb
Old Kirk
Muirshiel
Ayrshire Museum of Country Life & Costume
North Ayrshire Heritage Centre
Scottish Maritime Museum
Ardrossan Castle
Eglinton Castle
Kilwinning Abbey
Hill of Stake 522
Misty Law 510
Burnt Hill 486
Blacklaw 466
Creuch Hill 441
Hannah Law 396
Auchenbourach 360
Buachailean 346
Hardridge Hill 258
A78
A760
A737
B780
B714
B781
B782
B896
B899
B881
A844
276
275
255
256
257
NS
0 1 2 3 miles
0 1 2 3 4 5 km

277
268
257
258
RENFREWSHIRE
CITY OF GLASGOW
EAST RENFREWSHIRE
EAST AYRSHIRE
Bearsden
Kilmacolm
Bishopton
Erskine
Dalmuir
Clydebank
Drumchapel
Kessington
Bishopbriggs
Inchinnan
Renfrew
Yoker
Scotstoun
Knightswood
Jordanhill
Anniesland
Maryhill
Kelvindale
Springburn
Houston
Crosslee
Craigends
Bridge of Weir
Ranfurly
Linwood
Partick
Kelvinside
Port Dundas
Royston
Whiteinch
Govan
Shieldhall
Hillington
Cardonald
Craigton
Mosspark
Glasgow
Pollokshields
Gorbals
Brookfield
Kilbarchan
Johnstone
Millarston
Elderslie
Paisley
Castlehead
Blackhall
Charleston
Thornly Park
Pollok
Govanhill
Oatlands
Polmadie
Rutherglen
Millikenpark
Glenburn
Foxbar
Hurlet
Priesthill
Shawlands
Langside
Cathcart
Newlands
Nitshill
Mansewood
Muirend
Howwood
Waterside
Crossmill
Dovecothall
Carnwadric
Thornliebank
Giffnock
Netherlee
Castlemilk
Barrhead
Arden
Auchenback
Stamperland
Gateside
Springhill
Sheddens
Neilston
Crookfur
Clarkston
Busby
Newton Mearns
Broom
Kirkhill
Uplawmoor
Mearns
Waterfoot
Thorntonhall
Peel Park
Netherton
Hairmyres
Newlandsmuir
Gateside
Lugton
Halket
Eaglesham
Barrmill
Greenhills
Burnhouse
Gabroc Hill
Fullwood
Dunlop
Kingsford
Auchentiber
Stewarton
Fenwick
Laigh Fenwick
Waterside
Cunninghamhead
Kilmaurs
Onthank
Moscow
Springside
Knockentiber
Crosshouse
Knockinlaw
Kilmarnock

Bathgate
Armadale
Livingston
Blackburn
Whitburn
Harthill
Fauldhouse
Shotts
West Calder
Forth
Carluke
Lanark
Carnwath
Carstairs
Carstairs Junction
Uphall
Pumpherston
Mid Calder
Addiewell
Breich
Wilsontown
Auchengray
Tarbrax
Dunsyre
Newbigging
Walston
Dolphinton
Elsrickle
Libberton
Pettinain
Covington
Quothquan
Thankerton
Skirling
Kirkfieldbank
New Lanark
Hyndford Bridge
Sandilands
Kilncadzow
Yieldshields
Braehead
Cleghorn
Ravenstruther
M8
A70
A71
A706
A721
A73
A702

EDINBURGH
PENTLAND HILLS REGIONAL PARK
Pentland Hills
SCOTTISH BORDERS
MIDLOTHIAN
TWEED VALLEY FOREST PARK
Moorfoot
Penicuik
Peebles
Dalkeith
Bonnyrigg and Lasswade
Loanhead
Roslin
Currie
Balerno
West Linton
Carlops
Leadburn
Eddleston
Kirkurd
Melbourne
Dolphinton
Blyth Bridge
Romannobridge
Lyne
Kings Muir
Cardrona
280
269
260
261

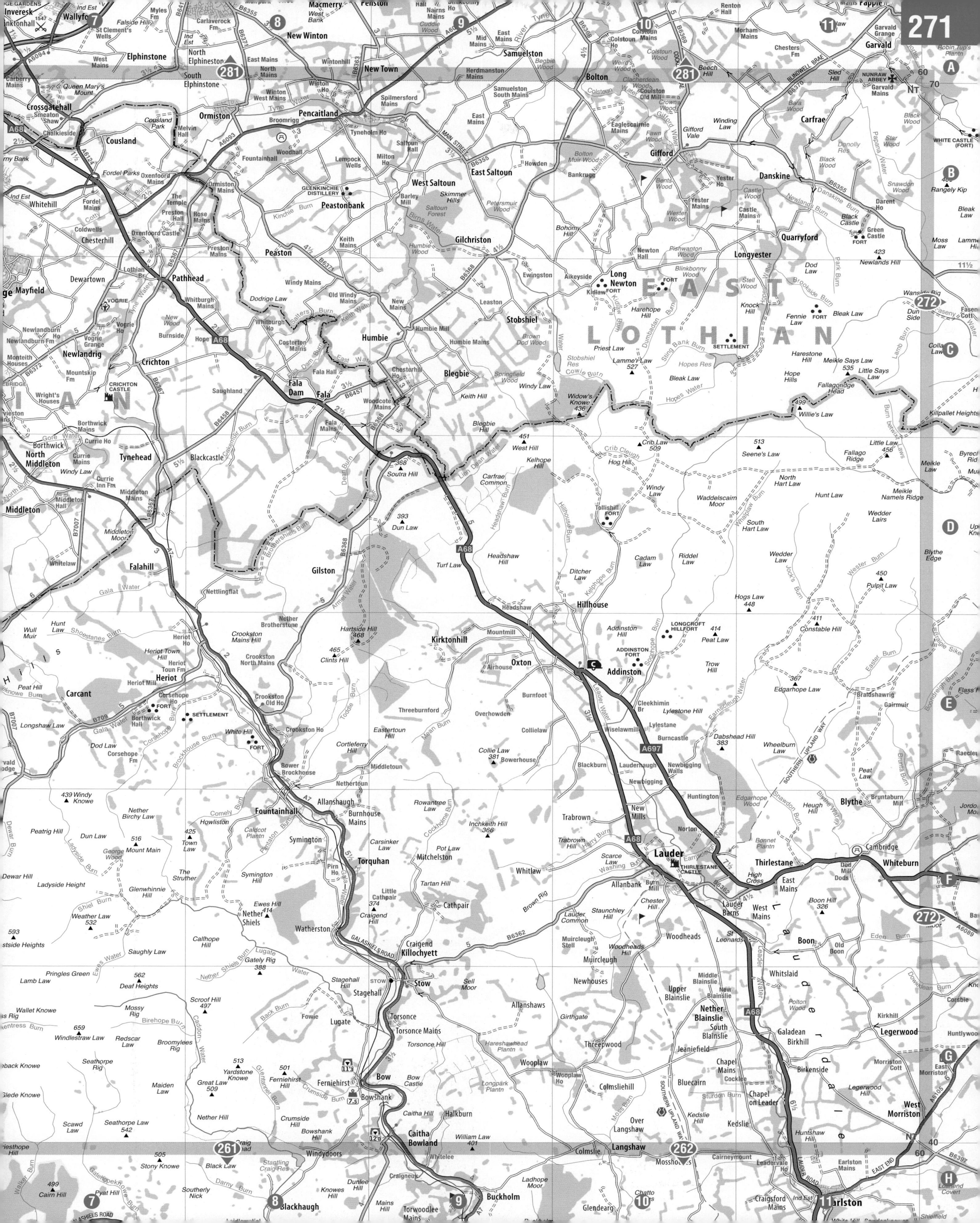

Inveresk
Wallyford
St Clement's Wells
Macmerry
West Bank
Penston
New Winton
Elphinstone
North Elphinstone
South Elphinstone
New Town
Samuelston
Bolton
Garvald
Nunraw Abbey
Crossgatehall
Smeaton Shaw
Chalkieside
Cousland
Ormiston
Pencaitland
Tyneholm Ho
Fountainhall
Woodhall
Lempock Wells
Saltoun Hall
East Saltoun
Howden
Gifford
Gifford Vale
Carfrae
Danskine
White Castle (Fort)
Fordel Parks
Oxenfoord Mains
Whitehill
Fordel Mains
Ormiston Mains
Glenkinchie Distillery
Peastonbank
West Saltoun
Skimmer Hills
Saltoun Forest
Bankrugg
Yester Ho
Yester Mains
Castle Mains
Black Castle
Green Castle
Rangely Kip
Bleak Law
Chesterhill
Oxenfoord Castle
Preston Hall
Rose Mains
Peaston
Keith Mains
Gilchriston
Bothomy Hill
Newton Hall
Longyester
Quarryford
Newlands Hill
Dewartown
Mayfield
Pathhead
Windy Mains
Ewingston
Aikeyside
Long Newton
Fort
East
Lothian
Vogrie
Whitburgh Mains
Dodridge Law
Old Windy Mains
New Mains
Leaston
Stobshiel
Harehope Hill
Knock Hill
Fennie Law
Bleak Law
Dun Side
Newlandburn
Newlandburn Fm
Vogrie Grange
Burnside
Hope
Whitburgh Ho
Costerton Mains
Humbie
Humbie Mill
Humbie Mains
Brown Dod Wood
Priest Law
Settlement
Newlandrig
Monteith Houses
Crichton
Mountskip Fm
Fala Hall
Chesterhill
Blegbie
Stobshiel Res
Lammer Law 527
Harestone Hill
Meikle Says Law
Little Says Law 535
Hope Hills
Crichton Castle
Wright's Houses
Saughland
Fala Dam
Fala
Woodcote Mains
Keith Hill
Springfield Wood
Windy Law
Bleak Law
Hopes Res
Fallagoridge Head
Widow's Knowe 436
Willie's Law 499
Borthwick Mains
Currie Ho
Borthwick
North Middleton
Fala Mains
Blegbie Hill
451 West Hill
Crib Law 509
Seene's Law 513
Little Law 456
Fallago Ridge
Currie Mains
Tynehead
Blackcastle
Soutra Hill 368
Kelhope Hill
Hog Hill
North Hart Law
Hunt Law
Meikle Namels Ridge
Windy Law
Carfrae Common
Currie Inn Fm
Middleton
Middleton Hall
Middleton Mains
Middleton Moor
Windy Law
Waddelscairn Moor
Tollishill Fort
South Hart Law
Wedder Lairs
393 Dun Law
Headshaw Hill
Cadam Law
Riddel Law
Wedder Law
Blythe Edge
Whitelaw
Falahill
Gilston
Turf Law
Ditcher Law
Pulpit Law 450
Nettlingflat
Hillhouse
Hogs Law 448
Headshaw
Nether Brotherstone
Longcroft Hillfort
Wull Muir
Hunt Law
Heriot Ho
Crookston Mains Hill
Hartside Hill 468
Kirktonhill
Mountmill
Addinston Hill
414 Peat Law
Constable Hill 411
Heriot Town Hill
Heriot Toun Fm
Crookston North Mains
465 Clints Hill
Oxton
Airhouse
Addinston Fort
Addinston
Trow Hill
Heriot
Heriot Mill
Peat Hill
Carcant
Corsehope Ho
Fort
Settlement
Crookston Old Ho
Burnfoot
Cleekhimin Br
Lylestone Hill
367 Edgarhope Law
Bradshawrig
Gairmuir
Borthwick Hall
Longshaw Law
Threeburnford
Overhowden
Lylestone
Collielaw
Crookston Ho
Eastertoun Hill
Wiselawmill
Burncastle
Dabshead Hill 383
Wheelburn Law
Dod Law
Corsehope Fm
White Hill
Fort
Cortleferry Hill
Collie Law 381
Bowerhouse
Southern Upland Way
Bower
Brockhouse
Middletoun
Blackburn
Lauderhaugh
Newbigging Walls
Peat Law
Nethertoun
Newbigging
Huntington
Edgarhope Wood
439 Windy Knowe
Nether Birchy Law
Allanshaugh
Burnhouse Mains
Rowantree Law
New Mills
Heugh Hill
Blythe
Bruntaburn Mill
Fountainhall
Howliston
Inchkeith Hill 366
Trabrown
Norton
Peatrig Hill
Dun Law
516 Mount Main
425 Town Law
Caldcot Plantn
Symington
Carsinker Law
Pot Law
Trabrown Hill
Bonnet Plantn
Cambridge
George Wood
Mitchelston
Scarce Law
Lauder
Thirlestane Castle
Thirlestane
Whiteburn
Dewar Hill
Ladyside Height
The Struther
Symington Hill
Torquhan
Pirn Ho
Tartan Hill
Whitlaw
Allanbank
Burn Mill
High Cross
East Mains
Dod Mill
Dods
Glenwhinnie Hill
Little Cathpair
374 Craigend Hill
Cathpair
Brown Rig
Chester Hill
Lauder Barns
West Mains
Boon Hill 326
Weather Law 532
Ewes Hill 414
Nether Shiels
Watherston
Lauder Common
Stanchley Hill
Woodheads
St Leonards
Boon
Old Boon
593
Saughly Law
Calfhope Hill
Craigend
Killochyett
Muircleugh Steil
Woodheads Hill
Muircleugh
Whitslaid
Lauderdale
Pringles Green
Gately Rig 388
Stagehall Hill
Stow
Sell Moor
Newhouses
Middle Blainslie
New Blainslie
Upper Blainslie
Lamb Law
562 Deaf Heights
Stagehall
Polton Wood
Wallet Knowe
Mossy Rig
Scroof Hill 497
Allanshaws
Nether Blainslie
South Blainslie
Kirkhill
Legerwood
Corsbie
Fowie
Lugate
Torsonce
Torsonce Mains
Girthgate
Galadean
Birkhill
Huntlywood
659 Windlestraw Law
Redscar Law
Broomylees Rig
Torsonce Hill
Hareshawhead Plantn
Threepwood
Jeaniefield
Seathorpe Rig
513 Yardstone Knowe
501 Ferniehirst Hill
Bow
Wooplaw
Chapel Mains
Cocklee
Bluecairn
Birkenside
Morriston Cott
East Morriston
Maiden Law
Great Law 509
Ferniehirst
Bowshank
Bow Castle
Wooplaw Ho
Longpark Plantn
Colmsliehill
Chapel on Leader
Legerwood Hill
West Morriston
Glede Knowe
Nether Hill
Crumside Hill
Caitha Hill
Halkburn
Over Langshaw
Kedslie Hill
Kedslie
Scawd Law
Seathorpe Law 542
Bowshank Hill
Caitha Bowland
William Law 401
Huntshaw Hill
Craig Head
Windydoors
Whitelee
Colmslie
Langshaw
Mosshouses
Cairneymount
505 Stony Knowe
Black Law
Stantling Craig Res
Leadervale Ho
Earlston Mains
Earlston
East End
Lauder Road
Cairn Hill 499
Pyat Hill
Southerly Nick
Knowes Hill
Dunlee Hill
Blackhaugh
Craigneuk
Ladhope Moor
Buckholm
Glendearg
Craigsford Mains
Ind Est
Mains Hill
Torwoodlee Mains
Chatto
Lochend Covert
Galashiels Road
Blindwell Brae
Main Street
Tyne Water
Gala Water
Leader Water
A68
A7
A697
A6093
A6124
A6105
A6089
B6355
B6368
B6371
B6367
B6372
B6458
B6457
B6362
B7007
B709
B6369
B6370
B6363
B6397
281
272
262
261
NT 70
NT 40
60
A
B
C
D
E
F
G
H
7
8
9
10
11
12

EAST LOTHIAN
SCOTTISH BORDERS
Lammermuir
Merse
Cockburnspath
Cove
Oldhamstocks
Old Cambus
Grantshouse
Ecclaw
Nether Monynut
Abbey St Bathans
Ellemford
Cranshaws
Longformacus
Preston
Lintlaw
Blanerne
Cumledge
Edrom
Buxley
Duns
Clockmill
Cheeklaw
Gavinton
Choicelee
Polwarth
Blackadder West
Sinclair's Hill
Bogend
Fogo
Fogorig
Sisterpath
Swinton
Swintonmill
Greenlaw
Westruther
Wedderlie
Halliburton
Thornydykes
Houndslow
Whiteburn
Legerwood
Huntlywood
Gordon
Middlethird
Easter Howlaws
Lambden
Leitholm
Orange Lane
Eccles
Hume
Falsidehill
Fans
West Morriston
Stichill
Coldstream
Birgham
Carham
Dunbar Common
Spartleton Edge
Monynut Edge
Whiteadder Reservoir
Watch Water Reservoir
Twin Law 447
Southern Upland Way
Jim Clarke Motorsport Mus
Manderston
Edinshall Broch
Green Knowe Tower
The Hirsel
Swinton Kirk
Edrom Church
Dunglass Collegiate Church
A1
A697
A6105
A6112
A1107
A698
B6456
B6355
B6365
B6437
B6460
B6461
B6364
B6438
271
282
262
263
0 1 2 3 miles
0 1 2 3 4 5 km

Holy Island (Lindisfarne)
Goswick Sands
Snook Pt
Snipe Pt
Keel Head
Emmanuel Head
Beal Pt
Causeway
LINDISFARNE
Beal Sands
Holy Island Sands
LINDISFARNE HERITAGE CENTRE
Holy Island
LINDISFARNE CASTLE
LINDISFARNE PRIORY
Castle Pt
Granary Pt
Hole Mouth
Burrows Hole
Fenham
Guile Pt
Lowmoor Pt
Ross Pt
Tealhole Pt
Buckton
Ross Back Sands
Fast Castle Head
Wheat Stack
Telegraph Hill
FAST CASTLE
Oatlee Hill
Lumsdaine
Lumsdaine Moor
Cross Law
SETTLEMENT
Coldingham Loch
Mire Loch
St Abb's Head
ST ABB'S HEAD
Horsecastle Bay
Bell Hill
Starney Bay
Northfield
St Abbs
St Abb's Haven
Coldingham Bay
Yellow Craig
Buskinburn Ho
Coldingham Moor
Huxton
Temple Hall
PRIORY
Coldingham
Press Castle
Abbey Park
Press Mains
Three Burn Grange
Grange Plantn
Gallows Law
Callercove Pt
Hairy Ness
EYEMOUTH MUSEUM
Hallydown
Eyemouth
Scout Pt
Horse Head
Fancove Head
Blackhill
Cairncross
North Wood
Heugh Head
Howburn
Reston
East Reston Mill
Littledean Fm
Aytonwood Ho
Fox Covert
Breeches Rock
Ayton Mains
Loanside
Auchencrow
AYTON CASTLE
Ayton
Burnmouth
Ross
Ross Pt
Berrybank
Peelwalls Ho
Cocklaw
Ayton Hill 199
Chester Hill
Peelwalls Fm
Prenderguest
Millerton Hill
Hilton Bay
Causeway Bank
Horn Burn
Lamberton Moor
Lamberton Beach
Meg's Dub
Oldcastles
Foulden Hill
Greenfield Plantns
Edington Covert
Westmains Moor
North Crowlea Plantn
Hag Wood
Deans Hill
Witches' Knowe
Lamberton
Chirnside
Lazybeds Plantn
Kilbann
Mordington Holdings
Marshall Meadows Bay
Marshall Meadows
Foulden New Mains
FOULDEN TITHE BARN
Mordington Ho
St John's Haven
Chirnsidebridge
Nether Mains
West Foulden
Foulden Bastle
Foulden
Clappers
West Edge Fm
Stuartslaw
Mains
Whiteadder Water
Edrington Ho
Bus Pk
Allanton
Hutton Hall Barns
Broadmeadows Ho
Clarabad Mill
Edrington Mains
DUNS ROAD
1333
Halidon Hill
Highfields
Sharper's Head
Bucket Rocks
Hutton
Meadow House Mains
Paxton North Mains
Baldersbury Hill
Berwick-upon-Tweed
BERWICK BARRACKS & MAIN GUARD
BERWICK BOROUGH MUS
BERWICK
Broomdykes
Hutton Mains
Spital Mains
Paxton
New Mills
Grangeburn Mill Fm
Mill Fm
Tweedmouth
Blackadder Mount
Blackadder Bank
Sunwick Fm
SHIELFIELD PARK
Sandstell Pt
Spittal
Highcliffe
Doons Law
Winfield
PAXTON HOUSE
River Tweed
East Ord
Bear's Head
Fishwick
UNION SUSPENSION BRIDGE
Loanend
Ord Mains
Prior Park
Whitsome
Hilton
Jardinefield
Redshin Cove
Fishwick Mains
Horncliffe
Longridge Towers
Tweedmouthmoor
Borewell Fm
Whitsomehill
East Newton
Horndean
Green Hill
Horncliffe Mains
Fellow Hills
Norham East Mains
Velvet Hall
Ewe Hill
Murton
Scremerston
Saltpan Rocks
Norham West Mains
Thornton Park
Murton White Ho
Unthank Fm
Unthank Blue Ho
Old Town Covert
New Ladykirk
Ladykirk
NORHAM CASTLE
Emerick Fm
Royalty Fm
Thornton Cottage
Thornton Mains
Allerdean Mill
Scremerston Hill
Scremerston Town Fm
Cheswick Black Rocks
Greenside Cotts
Norham
Morris Hall
Thornton
Allerdeanmill Burn
Camphouses
Cheswick Sands
Fox Covert
Shoreswood
Shoreswood Hall
Shoresdean
West Allerdean
Cheswick Ho
Cheswick
Simprim Mains
East Newbiggin
Battle Moor
Grievestead Moor
Allerdean Grange
Allerdean Greens
Coal Burn
Cheswick Buildings
Ladykirk House
Windmill Hill
Goswick
Milne Graden East Mains
Groat Haugh
Ancroft Northmoor
Ancroft
Simprim
Wideopen Plantn
Grindon
Ancroft Mill
Goswick Sands
Holy Island (Lindisfarne)
Milne Graden West Mains
Tillmouth Fm
NORTHUMBERLAND
Ancroft Southmoor
Bridge Mill
Haggerston
Snook Pt
Westmoor Plantn
Felkington
Haydon Dean
Berrington Law
Berrington Ho
Brockmill Fm
Beal Pt
Toft Hill
Mattilees Hill
Berrington
New Haggerston
Tweedmill
Shellacres
Brick Kiln Plantn
Berrington Lough
Bowsden Moor
Beal
Causeway
LINDISFARNE
Twizel Mill
Fadden Hill
Duddo
Mattilees Cott
Jacks Law
Lickar Dean
Beal Sands
Holy Island Sands
Common Plantn
Castle Heaton
Duddo Hill
Bowsden
West Mains Inn
Donaldson's Lodge
Black Bank
Tindal Ho
Woodside Fm
Low Wood
Bowsden West Fm
Old Dryburn
Lowick Mill
Mount Hooley
Granary Pt
Melkington
Syning Hill
Hazely Hill
High Wood
Barmoor Hill
Dry Burn
Hunting Hall
Fenham
Heaton Moor
New Heaton
Peter's Plantn
Barleymill Bank
Rhodes Hill
Black Heddon
West Kyloe
Fenwick
Barmoor Castle
Barmoor Lane End
Lowick
East Kyloe
Lowmoor Pt
Cornhill-on-Tweed
Heaton Covert
ETAL CASTLE
Etal
Etal Rhodes
Etal Moor
Barmoor Ridge
Moss Hall
Fenwick Wood
Pallinsburn Ho
HEATHERSLAW LIGHT RAILWAY
HEATHERSLAW CORNMILL
Letham Hill
Ford Forge
Ford Common Cott
Moss Wood
Kyloe Hills
Tealhole Pt
Cookstead
Kyloe Wood
Bareless
Crookham Westfield
Crookham
HEATHERSLAW
Hay Fm
LADY WATERFORD HALL
Ford Common
FORT
Barmoor South Moor
Redhouse Moor
Moorhouse
202 Shepherdskirk Hill
Buckton
Campfield
Branxton
Windy Law
Barmore
Shiellow
Buckton Moor
283
263
264

288
289
254
254

Lochbuie Ho
Laggan Lodge
405 DRUIM FADA
Laggan
Deer Forest
LORD LOVAT'S CAVE
FIRTH OF LORN
289
Insh I.
Frank Lockwood's Island
Sound of Insh
Ardencaple Ho
CLACHAN BRIDGE
Clachan-Seil
Clachan
Seil
Easdale
AN CALA GARDENS
EASDALE ISLAND FOLK MUSEUM
Balvicar
Acha
Cuan
Dubh-fheith
Ferry
Torsa
Seil Sound
Cullipool
Bardrishaig
Garbh Eileach
Garvellachs
Luing
Sound of Luing
Ardinamir
Achafolla
SCARBA, LUNGA AND THE GARVELLACHS
Eilean Dubh Mor
Eileach an Naoimh
Toberonochy
Shuna Sound
Shuna Ho
Shuna
Lunga
Shuna Pt.
CRUACH SCARBA 449
Kilmory Lodge
Rubha Aird Luing
Scarba
Gulf of Corryvreckan
Am Buth
Dunach
Ardentallen
Glen Feochan
Knipoch
Kilninver
Barochreal
Raera
Glen Euchar
Scammadale
368 A'CHRUACH
Bragleenmore
Loch Scamadale
438 CARN DEARG
267 CRUACH RAREY
Caddleton
Braes of Lorn
Blaran
Innie
Loch Tralaig
Melfort
Ardanstur
Kilchoan
Kilmelford
Loch Melfort
Glenmore
ARDUAINE GARDEN
Arduaine
Kames
Lagalochan
491 CARN DUCHARA
365
Garraron
Turnalt
Barbreck
Craobh Haven
Barravullin
Lunga
Barbreck Ho
Kintraw
350 CRUACH AN EACHLAICH
Torran
Lerigoligan
Ardfern
Craignish Castle
Kirkton
227 CREAG MHOR
Eilean Righ
CARNASSARIE CASTLE
Aird
Loch Craignish
Rèisa an t-Sruith
Craignish Pt.
Island Macaskin
Kilmartin
GLEBE CAIRN
KILMARTIN HOUSE MUSEUM
319
KILMARTIN SCULPTURED STONES
RI CRUIN CAIRN
Slockavullin
Poltalloch
Loch Crinan
Duntrune Castle
Crinan
Kilmahumaig
Crinan Ferry
Dunadd
Add
MOINE MHOR
Mòine Mhòr
CAIRNBAAN CUP & RING MARKS
Bellanoch
Dounie
Dunans
Cairnbaan
Kilbride
Leckuary
231 DUN DUBH
CUP AND RING MARKS
Kilmichael Glassary
Bridgend
Achnasnelloch
ROCK MARKINGS
Achnabreck
Kinuachdrachd
296 CRUACH NA SEILCHEIG
Kinuachdrachd Harbour
Glengarrisdale Bay
ARGYLL
365 BEN GARRISDALE
Lealt Burn
Lussa
Lealt
JURA
Ardlussa
Ardlussa Bay
Inverlussa
Lussagiven
Glenn Aoistail
A846
Tarbert
265
Gallachoille
KNAPDALE
Carsaig
Tayvallich
Kintallan
Cam Loch
Crinan Canal
Lochgilphead
Achanamara
Kilmichael of Inverlussa
360
Ardrishaig
Ashfield
Barrahormid
TAYNISH
Taynish
Loch Sween
466 CRUACH LUSACH
Achabraid
Loch Gilp
A83
KEILLS CHAPEL
Keillmore
Dunrostan
New Ulva
CASTLE SWEEN
Island of Danna
Loch na Cille
Inverneill
Stronachullin Lodge
Lochead
241 ST COLUMBA'S CAVE
Danna na Cloiche
Achahoish
477
Eilean Mòr
ST CORMAC'S CHAPEL
CHAPEL
Kilmory
Kilmory Bay
Ellary
Clachbreck
Erines
Baile Boidheach
562 STOB ODHAR
Loch Caolisport
Ormsary
Pt. of Knap
SOUND OF JURA
Druimdrishaig
Loch Chaorain
329
305
Loch nan Torran
Miller's Bay
Cretshengan
CRUACH LAGAIN 264
Coulaghailtro
Kilberry Hd.
SCULPTURED STONES
Kilberry
Torinturk
Rhu
Carse Ho.
Dunmore
Loch Stornoway
Ardpatrick
Kilchamaig
255
Ardpatrick Ho.
Ardpatrick Pt.
Portachoillan
Eilean Traighe
Ronachan Pt.
Clachan
269 CRUACH NAM FIADH
Claonaig
Claonaig Bay
Tarbert
Barfad
East Loch Tarbert
Dubhchladach
West Tarbert
Corranbuie
WEST LOCH TARBERT
Kennacraig
Redhouse
Whitehouse
422 CNOC A'BHAILESHIOS
Gartnagrenach
Glenreasdell Mains
Skipness
SKIPNESS CASTLE
Skipness Pt.
Skipness Bay
LOCHRANZA (Oct-Mar)
254
Kilbride
Midi
Musdale
Sior Loch
Kilchrenan
Annat
Lower Achachenna
North Port
Ardanaiseig
Cladich Steading
Cladich
Portsonachan
South Port
284
515 BEINN CHAPULL
Fineglen
ARGYLL AND BUTE
Inverinan
Ballimeanoch
Allt Beochlich
Tullich
550 BEINN GHLAS
Erigbeag
Glen Aray
Lochavich Ho
Drissaig
Kilmun
Loch Avich
Barnaline
Dalavich
Blarghour
589 CRUACH MHOR
Ardchonnell
ARDCHONNELL CASTLE
Portinnisherrich
Three Bridges
Maam
Dubh Loch
Carloonan
BELL TOWER
INVERARAY CASTLE
Inverliever Forest
Kilmaha
Eredine
LOCH AWE
Durran
Braevallich
INVERARAY JAIL
Inveraray
Newtown
514 AN SUIDHE
Douglas Water
Dalchenna
Arichamish
Inverliever Lodge
Eredine Forest
482 BEINN DEARG
Ardnagowan
Ford
Finchairn
FINCHAIRN CASTLE
Ederline
Loch Leacann
Auchindrain
AUCHINDRAIN OPEN AIR MUSEUM
Kenmore
Creggans
Clachan Strachur
458 CRUACH MHIC FHIONNLAICH
Brenchoillie
Strachur Bay
Strachurmore
Stroneskar
Loch Gaineamhach
Furnace
Mid Letter
Barmolloch
Sandhole
Cumlodden
Glen Sluain
420
Crarae
CRARAE GLEN GARDENS
Newton
Gleann Airigh
Minard
Invernoad
Glenbranter
Leanach
Glenbranter Forest
Garbhallt
LACHLAN CASTLE
Tullochgorm
Birdfield
Lachlan Bay
Minard Castle
618 BEINN BHEAG
Loch Glashan
Strathlachlan Forest
493
Caol Ghleann
LOCH ECK
Lephinmore
Kilbridemore
Asknish
Bernice
Lochgair
Lephinchapel
Dunans
741 BEINN MHOR
LOCH FYNE
Middle Kames
Conchra
Garrachra
Carrick
CRUACH CHUILCEACHAN 435
Glendaruel Forest
Glenmassan
Achanelid
Largiemore
Port Ann
KILMORY CASTLE GARDENS
KILMORY WOODLAND PARK
Achnaba
Otter Ferry
Camquhart
601 SGORACH MOR
Glen Massan
Castleton
Eilean Mòr
432 CRUACH NAN CUILEAN
Balliemore
Loch Tarsan
276
Benmore
Clachan of Glendaruel
KILMODAN SCULPTURED STONES
Glendaruel
Craigendive
Ballimore
Bealach Maim
Auchnagarron
Ardtaraig
Glen Lean
Dalinlongart
Auchnaha
Lochead
Auchenbreck
Clachaig
Glen Kin
Kilfinan Bay
458 CRUACH NAN CAORACH
405
Loch Riddon
611 CRUACH NAN CAPULL
Glenstriven
Kilfinan
Otter Ho
Ormidale Lodge
Springfield
Acharossan
454 BEINN BHREAC
Drum
KYLES OF BUTE
506 BEINN BHREAC
Braingortan
522 BLACK CRAIG
Melldalloch
Glachavoil
Ardentraive
Colintraive
Inverchaolain
LOCH STRIVEN
Auchalick Bay
266
Rhubodach
Algaltraig
Couston
418 CORLARACH HILL
Port Driseach
Tighnabruaich
Ardmarnock Bay
Barmore I.
Stonefield Castle Hotel
Auchenlochan
Kames
Kilmichael
Crispie
Asgog Loch
Glenan Bay
Portavadie
Millhouse
Kyles of Bute
227
Glen More
WINDY HILL 278
Glenmore
Knockdow
Corlarach Forest
Glen Fyne
Port Lamont
Newton Park
Castle Toward
Blair's Ferry
Gecknabae
Ettrickdale
Ardamaleish
Ardyne Pt.
266
Craig Lodge
Kames B.
Port Bannatyne
St Colmac
Asgog Bay
Kilbride Bay
Carry
Kildavanan
ROTHESAY CASTLE
Rothesay Bay
Ettrick Bay
Westland
Craigmore
Ardlamont Ho.
Upper Ardroscadale
Rothesay
Montford
VICTORIAN FERNERY
Ardlamont Pt.
Greenan
Loch Fad
Townhead
Ascog
Straad
Woodend Ho
Kerrycroy
ISLAND OF BUTE
Rubha Leathan
60 Northpark
Midpark
Loch Quien
Scoulag
MOUNT STUART HOUSE AND GARDENS
255
Inchmarnock
Scalpsie
Piperhall
Ardscalpsie Pt.
Scalpsie Bay
Kingarth
Stravanan Bay
Kilchattan
SOUND OF BUTE

ARGYLL FOREST PARK
ARGYLL AND BUTE
INVERCLYDE
Lochgoilhead
Drimsynie
Corrow
Lettermay
Blairlomond
Coilessan
Morelaggan
Creagan
Beinn Tharsuinn 619
Cruach na Cioba
Tom Nan Gamhna
Cnoc Coinnich 761
Coilessan Glen
Garbh
The Steeple
Carn Glas
Dùn Mòr 502
Inverlounin
Beinn Reithe 653
Tullich Hill 632
Beinn Bhreac 681
Firkin
Tullich Fm
Doune
Stob Gobhlach
INVERBEG GALLERY
Inverbeg
Glen Douglas
Douglas Water
Glen Sluain
Creag Dhubh
465 Beinn Lagan
Carnach Mòr
Curra Lochain
779 Beinn Bheula
767 Creag Sgoilte
Cruach nam Miseag
Loch Goil
Lettermay Burn
Cormonachan Glen
Beach
The Saddle
Tom Molach
Rubha na Beithe
Craggan Hill
Sròn Mallanach
Cona Ghleann
Doune Hill 734
Beinn Lochain
Mid Hill
642 Beinn Dubh
Meall Reamhar
Glenbranter
Glenshellish Fm
Invernoaden
Beinn Dubhain
Lochain nan Cnaimh
Cnoc na Tricriche
Glen Branter
Glenbranter Forest
Coire Ealt
Sgurr a' Choinnich
Beannan
Glenmallan
Tom Buidhe
Beinn Bhreac
Cruach an t-Sidhein
703 Beinn Eich
Glen Mollochan
Edentaggart
Luss Water
Craigbrack
Dornoch Point
Island
Stuck
Whistlefield
Carrick Castle
CARRICK CASTLE
Beinn Bhreac
Cruacha Bhuic 635
Carraig na Maraig
Toll nam Muc
Meall Daraich
Carraig nan Ròn
Portincaple
Whistlefield
Beinn a Mhanaich 709
Maol an Fheidh
Gleann na Caorainn
The Strone
Beinn Chaorach 713
Coire Coinghil
Coille-eughain Hill
Sron an Laoigh Burn
Shelling Burn
656 Beinn Tharsuinn
657 Creag an Leinibh
Beinn Ruisg 595
Auchengaich Burn
Auchengavin Burn
530
618 Beinn Bheag
Meall Breac
Bernice Glen
Bernice
Rubha Barbh
Cnoc Madaidh
Cnoc Fraorach
Cruach an Draghair
Creachan Mor 657
Knap Burn
Toll a' Bhuic
Loch Long
Garelochhead
GARELOCHHEAD
Cnoc na h-Airighe
Balenock 638
Coire Cuinne
Auchengaich Hill
Creachan Hill 536
Beinn Mhor 741
Meall Dubh
Meall an t-Sith
Coire an t-Sith
Garrachra Glen
Sligrachan
Sligrachan Hill
Castle Craig
Allt Coille Mheadhanaich
Rockville
Mambeg
Port an Lochain
Lochan Ghlas Laoigh
Strone House
Auchengaich
Faslane Bay
Faslane Port
A817
Glen Fruin
Fruin Water
Finlas Water
Shemore
Paper Cave
Clach Bheinn 643
Capull Cloiche 577
Creachan Mor 571
Garrachra
Glenmassan
664 Beinn Ruadh
Drynain
Drynain Glen
Barnacabber
Shepherd's Pt
Stronvochlan
Finart Bay
Carraig Mhaol
Carnban Pt
Creachan Beag 547
Creag Liath
Cnap Rheamhar
Ardentinny
Coulport
Garelochhead Forest
Rahane
Gare Loch
Shantron Hill
Duchlage
Stronlonag
Stonefield
Glen Massan
Creag Dhonnaiche
River Massan
Inverchapel Burn
Meall Dubh
Stronchullin Hill
Maol Riabhach
Little Rahane
ROSNEATH ROAD
Shandon
West Kilbride
Bailymenoch
Blairglas
580 An Creachan
Benmore Home Fm
BENMORE BOTANIC GARDENS
Eckford Ho
Ardpeaton
Airlig
Blairvadach
East Kilbride
Inverlauren
Dumfad
601 Sgorach Mor
Corarsik
Corarsik Burn
Benmore
Uig
Creag Mhòr
Gairletter
Gairletter Pt
Hattonburn
Clynder
Highlandman's Wood
Daligan
Dumfin
Glenlean
Glen Lean
432 Meall an Fhamhair
Ballochyle Hill
Puck's Glen
Blairmore Hill
Cnoc a'Mhadaidh
Rashfield
Ardbeg
Bellcairn
Knockderry Fm
Stroul
Stroul Bay
Rhu
GLENARN GARDEN
THE HILL HOUSE
LUSS ROAD
A818
Bannachra Muir
Clachaig Hill 521
Allt Coire Cheathaich
Inverecк
Kilmun Hill
Blairmore
Rosneath
Cairndhu Pt
HELENSBURGH UPPER
HELENSBURGH CENTRAL
SINCLAIR STREET
313 Ben Bowie
Ballochyle
Dalinlongart
KILMUN ARBORETUM
MIDGE LANE
SHORE ROAD
Blairmore
Garelochhead Forest
Clachan Fm
Rosneath Bay
Castle Pt
THE ROWAN GALLERY
WEST CLYDE ST
Helensburgh
EAST CLYDE ST
Townhead
Camis Eskan Fm
B836
Clachaig
Little Eachaig River
Holy Loch
Kilmun
Graham's Pt
Cove
Lindowan Res
Rosneath Home Fm
Robert Ness
Craigendoran
CRAIGENDORAN
Camis Eskan Ho
Killoeter
Sandhaven
Meall Criche
Meall Buidhe
Dalinlongart Hill
Gibb's Pt
Strone
Strone Pt
Barons Pt
Gallow Hill
Culwatty Bay
Perch Rock
Rosneath Pt
CARDROSS ROAD
Mid Hill
Blackoch Burn
Glen Kin
Sandbank
Finbracken Hill
Lazaretto Pt
Ardnadam
Kilcreggan
Portkil
Portkil Bay
Portkil Pt
Colgrain
Cruach nan Capull 611
Stronsaul
Bus Pk Ind Est
Black Craig 568
Leacann nan Gall
Hunter's Quay
Lyleston Fm
Ardmore
Glenstriven
Giant's Knowe 504
Bishop's Seat
Kirn
ALEXANDRA PARADE
KEMPOCK STONE
Kempock Pt
Fort Matilda
Gourock
GOUROCK
Gourock Bay
West Bay
Ashton
Greenock Ocean Terminal
McLEAN MUS & ART GALLERY
Greenock West
Greenock
River Clyde
Kelhurn
Geilston
CARDROSS
Glenkin Burn
Balgaidh Burn
Horse Seat
ST JOHN'S CHURCH
Dunoon
East Bay
HIGHLAND MARY'S STATUE
McInroy's Pt
CLOCH ROAD
Midton
Levan
Ind Est
Cloch Pt
CLOCH LIGHTHOUSE
Larkfield
Central
GREENOCK CENTRAL
Cartsdyke
Garvel Pt
Pillar Bank
522 Black Craig
Berry Burn
West Bay
Kilbride Hill
Burneven Hill
Braeside
Branchton
Ravenscraig
DRUMFROCHAR
Spango
Overton
Whinhill
Strone Farm
Bridgend
Strone
Gibshill
CARTSDYKE
Ladyburn
Port Glasgow
GREENOCK ROAD
Lilybank
PORT GLASGOW
Inverchaolain
Glen Chaolain
472 Blar Buidhe
Corlarach Hill 391
Bullwood
BULLWOOD ROAD
Bull Rock
Lunderston
IBM
INVERKIP ROAD
New Yetts Res
Whinhill Res
Burnhead Moor
Whitelees Moor
Devol
Harelaw Res
NEWARK CASTLE
Broadfield
Mid Auchinlech
Bardrainney
Blairbuie
Brackley Pt
Colarach Hill 419
Garrowchorran Hill
Lunderston Bay
Ardgowan
Greenock Cut
395 Kilmarnock Hill
Corlarach Forest
Bankfoot
Compensation Res
Loch Thom
Darndaff Moor
Corlick Hill
Devol Moor
Ardgowan Pt
Beinn Ruadh 323
Inverkip Bay
Inverkip
Dunrod Hill
Shielhill
Cunston Cott
Cnoc a' Mhadaidh
Everton
Crawhin Hill
Gryfe Reservoirs
Dykefoot
Priestside Fm
Glen Fyne
Finnock Bog Fm
Daff Res
Leapmoor Forest
Crawhin Res
Garvock
Gryfe Water
Auchenbothie Mains
Buachailean 346
Innellan Hill
Innellan
Colaouse Hill
Port Lamont
Knockdow
Achafour Fm
Newton Park
SHORE ROAD
Wemyss Pt
High Finnock Penin
Wemyss Bay
Forbes Place
Blood Moss
Wenchly Top
Cairncurran Hill
Jock's Craig
Garvock Hill
Berry Hill
Rottenburn Br
Little Creuch Hill
Creuch Hill 441
Laverock Stone
Balrossie School
White Hill
WEMYSS BAY
Ferret of Keith Moor
Red Burn
Lockminwood Hill
Burnbank Water
Hardridge Hill 258
Lairds
East Green
Ardyne
Castle Toward
Toward Fm
Upper Skelmorlie
Green Water
0 1 2 3 miles
0 1 2 3 4 5 km
284
275
266
A815
A814
A880
A78
A770
A8
B833
B788
B786
B832
NS

QUEEN ELIZABETH
FOREST PARK
STIRLING
LOCH LOMOND AND
THE TROSSACHS NATIONAL PARK
WEST
DUNBARTONSHIRE
EAST
DUNBARTONSHIRE
Ben Lomond
Tom Fithich
Beinn Bhan 569
Mill of Chon
Loch Ard
Milton
DAVID MARSHALL LODGE VISITOR CENTRE
Aberfoyle
Arntamie
Nether Glenny
Port of Menteith
Ptarmigan Lodge
Tom Dubh nan Caorach
Eilean Gorm
Couligartan
Sron Aonaich 577
Moin Eich
Bad Dearg
Innis Ard
Kirkton
Stonefield
Malling
INCHMAHOME PRIORY
Lake of Menteith
Blairhoyle
Rowardennan
BEN LOMOND BUNKHOUSE
Coille Mhor Hill
Duchray Castle
Garbeg Hill
Deer Craig
Balleich
Windygate
Shannochill
Loch Macanrie
Cardross Moss
Lochend Ho
Beinne Uird 597
Maol an Iaruinn
Drumore Wood
Loch Ard Forest
Arndrum
Cobleland
FOREST WALKS
Drum Wood
Big Wood
Gartur
Dykehead
Drum of Clashmore
Gartmore Ho
Gartmore
Fir Hill
Barbadoes
Gartrenich Moss
Collymoon Moss
Parks of Garden
Binnean Nan Gobhar
Beinn Bhreac 577
Kelty Water
Lime Hill
Borland Fm
Borland Water
Dalmary
East Gartfarran
Ross Wood
Ross Point
Camas an Losgainn
Rowardennan Forest
High Corrie
Corrie
Flanders Moss
Wester Offerance
Blackhouse
Newburn
Middleton
Gartentruach
Anchorage Cottage
461 Gualann
Ward
Turner
Woodend
Kepdowrie
Easter Mye
Wester Mye
Arnprior
Garchell
Gartclach
Rhu Wood
Inchlonaig
Tom a' Mhorair
FOREST WALKS
Park of Auchentroig
Crotlevane
Gartachoil
Auchentroig
Buchlyvie
Ballochneck
Cashley
Arngibbon
Luss
Strathcashell Point
Milarrochy
Moor Park
Bad Ochainaich
Badivow
Hoish
Douchlage
Upper Balwill
Gowston
Thirds
Easter Culbowie
Townhead
Camstraddan
Inchconnachan
358 Conic Hill
WEST HIGHLAND WAY
Arrochymore Point
Muir Park Reservoir
Bàt a' Charchel
Wester Culbowie
Whiteleys
Badenkep
Inchtavannach
Inchcruin
Inchfad
Auchmar
Balmaha
Milton of Buchanan
Buchlyvie Muir
LOCH LOMOND
Inchcailloch
Clairinsh
Garadhban Forest
Spittal Ballat
Glenfoot
Gaisland
Tombrake
Knockingalloch
Balgair Muir
Inchmoan
Gartfairn
Loaninghead
Templelea
STIRLING ROAD
Cairnhall
Shian
Camoquhill
Loch Lomond
Rossdhu Ho
Torrinch
Endrick Mouth
Creinch
High Mains
Mid Shandon
Buchanan Smithy
Ballindalloch Muir
Harvieston
Balfron Station
Balfron
Buchanan Old Ho
Drymen
Buchanan Castle
Clachanry
Endrick Br
Dalfoil
Ballochearn
Endrick Water
Ross Park
Inchmurrin
Mains Fm
Ross Priory
Gartochraggan
Kilmaronock Ho
Drymen Br
Drumhead
Ballochruin
Drumtian
Boquhan Old Ho
Nether Glinns Fm
Killearn Br
Carbeth Ho
Boquhan
Clayland
Ballikinrain
Overton
Fintry
Badshalloch
Catter Ho
Parkhill
Drumquhassle
Drumore
Head of Balglass
Millstone Wood
Mount
Auchentullich
Gartness
The Firs
BALFRON ROAD
Heron's Court
Boquhan Glen
Sir Archibald's Plantn
Garadhban Forest
LOCH LOMOND & THE TROSSACHS
Gartocharn
Bent
Third
Gartlinbantrick
Tullycross
Croftamie
Spittal
Dunmore
Lorn
Tullochan
Duncryne 142
Burnbrae
Cambusmoon
Little Finnery
Cattermuir Lodge
Dalmair Ho
Finnich Blair
Auchenibert
Kilmorie
Killearn
Ballikinrain Muir
Dechrode
Nether Ross
Blairlinnans
High Duncryne
Blairennich
Caldarvan
Mavie Mill
Finnich Glen
Laighparks
Westerton
High Lettre
Allanrowie
Arden
Boturich Castle
Blairlusk
Little Blairlusk
Graystonelea
Killearn Ho
Shanacles
Lochend Cott
Caldarvan Loch
Craighat
Earl's Seat 578
Garloch Hill 543
Ledrishmore
Blairnyle
Duck Bay
Over Balloch
BALLOCH CASTLE
Old Kirk
Ballagan
Gallangad Fm
Cameron Muir
Aucheneck Ho
Blaneswell
Dumgoyne
GLENGOYNE DISTILLERY
SEA LIFE LOCH LOMOND AQUARIUM
Balloch
Westerton
Merkins Fm
Cameron Wood
LOCH LOMOND SHORES
BIRD OF PREY CENTRE
Blairquhomrie
Gallangad Muir
Stockiemuir
Owsen Hill
Hog Hill
Hart
Dumbain
Mill of Haldane
Auchencarroch
Blairquhomrie Muir
Stockie Muir
Strathblane Hills
Tullichewan Fm
Dumbreck 508
Blairquhosh
Fin Glen
Almeel Burn
Alexandria
LOCH LOMOND OUTLET CENTRE
Jamestown
Ind Est
Quinloch Muir
Dumgoyach Fm
Duntreath Castle
303 Bromley Muir
Auchineden Hill 357
Campsie Dene
Knocknair
Northfield Cott
257 Pappert Hill
Arlehaven
Overton Muir
Nobleston Wood
Auchenreoch Muir
Dumbarton Muir
Burncrooks Reservoir
Thief's Hill
Netherton
Ballagan Ho
Clachan of Campsie
Asker Fm
Bonhill
Carbeth Ho
Blanefield
Strathblane
STRATHBLANE ROAD
Carman Res
Shop Cen
Meikle White Hill 353
Craigallian Loch
Ballagan Fm
Balcorrach
Carman Muir
Renton
Ind Est
Auchenreoch
Mains
Dunglass
Craigend Fm
Kilmahew Fm
Doughnot Hill 374
Fyn Loch
401
Kilmannan Reservoir
Tomibeg
Craigton Burn
Dumbrock Loch
Craigend Castle
Mugdock Loch
Loch Ardinning
Craigend Muir
Dalmoak Ho
Maryland
Kipperoch Fm
Bellsmyre
Black Linn Res
Kilpatrick Hills
Cochno Loch
MUGDOCK
Mugdock
Craigmaddie Ho
Ardoch
Townend
Lang Craigs
Brown Hill
Fynloch Hill
Loch Humphrey
Carneddans Wood
Craigmaddie Muir
Blairskaith Muir
Castlehill
Overtoun Ho
Mugdock Reservoir
Craigash
Blochairn
CARDROSS ROAD
Dalreoch
DALREOCH
Dumbarton
Cochno Hill
Jaw Res
Maidens Paps
Barraston Fm
Langshot Fm
Dennystown
DUMBARTON CENTRAL
Silverton
The Slacks
Greenside Reservoir
Craigmaddie Reservoir
Blairskaith
Brucehill
Kirktonhill
DUMBARTON EAST
C & G SYSTEMS STADIUM
Muirhouses
Fluchter
CASTLE
Milton
Hill of Dun
DUMBARTON ROAD
Edinbarnet
Douglas Muir
MILNGAVIE
LILLIE ART GALLERY
Dowan Fm
Back o' Hill
Bardowie Loch
Bowling
BOWLING
GREAT WESTERN ROAD
Cochno
Whitehill Fm
Milngavie
Duntiglennan Fm
Duntocher
Faifley
Shop Cen
Bardowie
Balmore
MAIN ROAD
FINLAYSTONE COUNTRY ESTATE
LANGBANK
Langbank
Old Kilpatrick
GLASGOW ROAD
Hardgate
Lawmuir
ROMAN BATH HOUSE
Temple of Boclair
Buchley
Cadder
Erskine Bridge
KILPATRICK
East Langbank
Ferryhill Plantn
GREENOCK ROAD
ANTONINE WALL
Bearsden
BEARSDEN
HILLFOOT
Achendores Fell
North Glen Fm
Whitemoss Fm
Mountblow
Parkhall
Radnor Park
Kessington
ANTONINE WALL (COURSE OF)
FORTH & CLYDE CANAL
Wilderness Plantn
Jellyhill
Bishopton
West Porton
Bargarran
Dalmuir
Formakin
Gatehead
Dargavel Village
Rashielee
Rossland
Shop Cen
SINGER
Kilbowie
Retail Pk
DRUMRY
Drumchapel
DRUMCHAPEL
WESTERTON
Blackhill
Summerston
Possil Loch
Mid Glen
Meiklefield
West Glenshinnoch
BISHOPTON
Erskine
Park Mains
Newshot Island
CLYDEBANK MUSEUM
CLYDEBANK
Bishopbriggs
Old Hall
Elphinstone Wood
Kilmacolm
Freeland
Clydebank
Whitecrook
Knightswood
Temple
Maryhill
Dawsholm Park
SUMMERSTON
Lambhill
Milton
Colston
Lawfield Fm
CROSS
Dargavel Ho
Nether Southbar
Inchinnan
YOKER
Yoker
GARSCADDEN
KELVINDALE
Kelvindale
POSSILPARK
PARKHOUSE
ASHFIELD
Kirkton Fm
Barochan Ho
Wellees Fm
Chapel Fm
Scotstoun
Jordanhill
Anniesland
ANNIESLAND
SCOTSTOUNHILL
JORDANHILL
FIRHILL STADIUM
Springburn
Knapps Loch
East Fulwood
New Mains
Town of Inchinnan
Blythswood
Renfrew
Brownsfield
285
278
267
277

Ruskie
Brae of Boquhapple
Boquhapple
Thornhill
Deanston
Doune
Doune Castle
Dunblane
Cath
Bridge of Allan
Blair Drummond
Blair Drummond Safari Park
Blair Drummond Moss
Flanders Moss
Dykehead
Parks of Garden
Arnprior
Cauldhame
Kippen
Glentirranmuir
Old Leckie
Gargunnock
Gargunnock House
Raploch
Stirling
Smith Art Gall & Mus
Old Town Jail
Cambuskenneth
Cambuskenneth Abbey
Riverside
Forthbank Stadium
Causewayhead
Cornton
The National Wallace Mon
Airthrey Castle
Blairlogie
Craigmill
Badgergate
Sunnylaw
Dumyat
418
Cambusbarron
Torbrex
Braehead
Battle of Bannockburn Visitor Centre
St Ninians
Bannockburn
Fallin
Whins of Milton
Stirling Services
Plean
Cowie
Craigend
Carleatheran
485
Gargunnock Hills
Touch Hills
Lees Hill
411
Stronend
511
Fintry Hills
Culcreuch Castle
Fintry
Harvieston
Ballochearn
Earl's Hill
441
Easter Cringate
Cairnoch Hill
413
Loch Walton
Carron Valley Reservoir
Carron Valley Forest
Kilsyth Hills
Meikle Bin
570
Tomtain
453
Garrel Hill
459
Campsie Fells
Lecket Hill
547
Cort-ma Law
531
Holehead
551
Dungoil
424
Muirmill
Carron Bridge
Denny
Dunipace
Fankerton
Stoneywood
Head of Muir
Bonnybridge
Dennyloanhead
Antonine Wall
Banknock
Longcroft
Haggs
Castlecary
Greenhill
High Bonnybridge
Kilsyth
Colzium House
Queenzieburn
Lennoxtown
Balgrochan
Clachan of Campsie
Milton of Campsie
Birdston
Twechar
Croy
Dullatur
Cumbernauld Village
Old Inns Services
Abronhill
Cumbernauld
Balloch
Kirkintilloch
Auld Kirk Mus
Waterside
Condorrat
Westfield
Luggiebank
Palacerigg
Lenzie
Bishopbriggs
Cadder
Jellyhill
Torrance
Bardowie
Balmore
Mollinsburn
Moodiesburn
Chryston
Muirhead
Gartcosh
Glenboig
Greenfoot
Riggend
Wattston
Greengairs
Longriggend
Caldercruix
Jawcraig
Stand
Springburn
Lumloch
Auchinloch
Stirling
East Dunbartonshire
North Lanarkshire
Falkirk
285
286
277
268
0 1 2 3 miles
0 1 2 3 4 5 km

CLACKMANNANSHIRE
FIFE
Alva
Tillicoultry
Dollar
Castle Campbell
Dollar Glen
Yetts o' Muckhart
Pool of Muckhart
Rumbling Bridge
Crook of Devon
Drum
Coldrain
Powmill
Cleish
Cleish Hills
Hardiston
Blairingone
Devonside
Coalsnaughton
Fishcross
Sauchie
Tullibody
Cambus
Alloa
Alloa Tower
Clackmannan
Clackmannan Tower
Forest Mill
Saline
Steelend
Knockhill
Kennet
Kilbagie
South Alloa
Dunmore
Airth
The Pineapple
Kincardine
Kincardine Bridge
Tulliallan Castle (College)
Culross
Culross Palace
Blairhall
Comrie
Oakley
Carnock
Gowkhall
Milesmark
Cowstrandburn
High Valleyfield
Low Valleyfield
Newmills
Cairneyhill
Low Torry
Torryburn
Crombie
Charlestown
Limekilns
Rosyth
Crossford
Dunfermline Abbey
Townhill
Wellwood
Letham
Stenhousemuir
Antonshill
Carronshore
Skinflats
Grangemouth
Bo'ness
Grangepans
Carriden
Muirhouses
Blackness
Blackness Castle
The Kelpies Sculpture
The Helix
Falkirk
Falkirk Wheel
Camelon
Laurieston
Grahamston
Callendar House
Polmont
Redding
Westquarter
Reddingmuirhead
Brightons
Rumford
Wallacestone
Maddiston
Shieldhill
California
Linlithgow
Linlithgow Bridge
Linlithgow Palace
Linlithgow Loch
Philpstoun
Old Philpstoun
Queensferry
Queensferry Crossing
Hopetoun House
House of The Binns
Winchburgh
Threemiletown
Bridgend
Kingscavil
Beecraigs
Cockleroy 278
Torphichen
Torphichen Preceptory
Ecclesmachan
Broxburn
Uphall
Uphall Station
Dechmont
Wester Dechmont
Pumpherston
Bathgate
Bennie Museum
Slamannan
Avonbridge
Westfield
Armadale
Blawhorn Moss
Livingston
Kirkliston
Newbridge
Burnside
Wilkieston
River Forth
Union Canal
Antonine Wall (course of)
M9
M8
M876
A91
A977
A907
A985
A706
A803
A904
286
280
269
Ben Cleuch 721
The Law 638
King's Seat Hill 648
Tarmangie Hill 645
Knock Hill 364

Kinross
Loch Leven
Loch Leven Castle
St Serf's Island
286
Scotlandwell
Auchmuirbridge
Leslie
Glenrothes
Markinch
Milton of Balgonie
Balcurvie
Windygates
Cameron Bridge
Caskieberran
Pitteuchar
Coaltown of Balgonie
Stenton
Kinglassie
Thornton
Gairney Bank
Cleish
Ballingry
Lochore
Lochran
Fife Regional Park
Crosshill
Woodend
Auchterderran
Bowhill
Cluny
East Wemyss
Coaltown of Wemyss
West Wemyss
Kelty
Glencraig
Cardenden
Dundonald
Dunnikier
Chapel
Gallatown
Sinclairtown
Dysart
Blair
Boreland
Templehall
Pathhead
Hayfield
Newliston
Kirkcaldy
Ravenscraig Castle
Panhall
Port Brae
Lochgelly
Lumphinnans
Cowdenbeath
Lassodie
279
Auchtertool
Linktown
Kirkcaldy Sands
Bowershall
Kingseat
Hill of Beath
Townhill
Wellwood
Kingseathill
Halbeath
Crossgates
Donibristle
Fordell
Balmule
Orrock
Grange
Kinghorn
Pettycur
Dunfermline
Pitcorthie
Duloch
Aberdour
Burntisland
Kirkton
Rosyth
Inverkeithing
Hillend
Dalgety Bay
Limekilns
Pattiesmuir
St Colm's Abbey
Inchcolm
Inchkeith
Firth of Forth
Cow & Calves
Inchmickery
North Queensferry
Queensferry Crossing
Forth Road Bridge
Forth Bridge
Port Edgar
Queensferry
Dalmeny
Dalmeny House
Cramond Island
Newton
Newbigging
Cramond
Silverknowes
Davidson's Mains
Muirhouse
Granton
Pilton
Trinity
Newhaven
Leith
Barnton
Cramond Bridge
Drylaw
Inverleith
Warriston
Broughton
Pilrig
Craigentinny
Restalrig
Edinburgh
Portobello
Joppa
Musselburgh
Kirkliston
Turnhouse
Clermiston
Blackhall
Craigleith
Lochend
Abbeyhill
Meadowbank
Newbridge
Corstorphine
Murrayfield
Ravelston
Dean
New Town
Old Town
Duddingston
Northfield
Bingham
Brunstane
Newhailes
Gogar
Ratho Station
Burnside
South Gyle
Stenhouse
Gorgie
Merchiston
Newington
Prestonfield
Craigmillar
Niddrie
Newcraighall
Sighthill
Saughton
Slateford
Longstone
Morningside
Craiglockhart
Ratho
Hermiston
Wester Hailes
Kingsknowe
Braid
Liberton
Danderhall
Millerhill
Juniper Green
Colinton
Oxgangs
Comiston
Fairmilehead
Gracemount
Gilmerton
Kaimes
Swanston
Bonaly
Burnwynd
Torphin
270
0 1 2 3 miles
0 1 2 3 4 5 km

Kennoway
Silverburn Park
Scoonie
Ind Est
Leven Links
Leven
Kirkland Dam
Kirkland
Bayview Stadium
Innerleven
Methilhill
Crossroads
Methil Heritage Centre
Methil
Denbeath
Buckhaven
Largo Bay
287
Mount Pleasant
Fife Coastal Path
West Muircambus
Kilconquhar Loch
St Ford
Broomlees
Ruddons Pt
St Ford Links
Grange
Shell Bay
Kincraig Pt
Earlsferry
Chapel Ness
Elie
Wood Haven
Elie Ness
Sauchar Pt
Ardross
Souterrain
St Monans
St Monan's Windmill
St Monan's Chapel
Fife Coastal Path
282
Bass Rock
Fidra
Brigs of Fidra
Craigleith
Lamb
Law Rocks
Eyebroughy
Weaklaw Rocks
Longskelly Rocks
Longskelly Pt
Broad Sands
Cowton Rocks
North Berwick Bay
Scottish Seabird Centre
Milsey Bay
Leckmoram Ness
Canty Bay
Gin Head
Tantallon Castle
Car Rocks
Auldhame
Eldbotle Wood
Yellow Craig Plantn
Duncan's Plantn
New Mains
West Links
Black Rocks
Broad Wood
Dirleton
Dirleton Castle & Garden
Dirleton Road
North Berwick
The Glen
Ind Est
Heugh Fm
North Berwick Law
Blackdykes
Gullane Bay
Hummell Rocks
Gullane Pt
Gullane Links
Main Street
Gullane
Saltcoats
Gullane Sands
Gala Law
Luffness Links
West Fenton
Craighead Cott
Fenton Barns
East Fenton
New Mains
Mill Burn
Kingston Ho
Kingston
Carperstane
Balgone Ho
Sheriff Hall
Craigmoor Wood
East Craig
Wamphray
Scoughall
Whitekirk Covert
New Mains
Whitekirk
Whitekirk Br
Aberlady Bay
Aberlady Pt
Craigielaw Pt
Craigielaw
Aberlady
Park Hills
Congalton Cotts
Congalton Gardens
Stonelaws
Howden
Binning Wood
Muirton
Prora
Drem
East Fortune
Ashfield Ho
Oak Wood
Luffness Mains
Myreton Motor Mus
Gosford Sands
Gosford Bay
Gosford House
West Fortune
Dingleton
East Fortune Airfield
Fortoun Bank
Tyninghame
Smeaton Ho
Preston Mains
National Museum of Flight
Gilmerton Ho
Ballencrieff Mains
Ballencrieff
The Chesters Fort
Preston
Preston Mill & Phantassie Doocot
Phantassie
Ferny Ness
Spittal
Garleton Fm
Camptoun
Kilduff Hill
Kilduff Ho
Athelstaneford
Markle Mains
Markle
East Linton
Howmuir
Longniddry
Pencraig Wood
Pencraig Brae
Beanston Mains
East
Cockenzie and Port Seton
Seton Sands
Hopetoun Mon
Barney Mains
Setonhill
West Garleton Ho
Garleton Hills
Abbey Mains
Bangly Hill
Links Road
Seton Collegiate Church
Seton Mains
Edinburgh Road
Ind Est
Seton West Mains
Seton
Wheatrig
Amisfield Mains
Sandy's Mill
Hailes Castle
Hairy Craig
Traprain
Grangemuir
Southfield Fm
Alderston Mains
Abbeymill Fm
Mackie Rocks
Prestonpans
Cuthill Rocks
High Street
Preston
Cuthill
Elvingston
Merryhatton
Huntington
Alderston
Haddington
Stevenson Mains
Traprain Law
Ruchlaw Mains
Luggate Burn
Whittinghame Mains
Meadowmill
Ind Est
Prestonpans
Preston Grange Industrial Heritage Mus
Levenhall
Dolphingstone
Tranent Mains
Tranent
Adniston
Hoprig Mains
Gladsmuir
Back Burn
Bus Pk
Ind Est
Letham Ho
St Mary's Collegiate Church
Monkmains Cott
West Beanston
Coldale
Beanford Burn
Lothian
Whittinghame
Kingslaw
Pinkie Braes
P&R
Wallyford
Ind Est
Muirpark
Macmerry
West Bank
Ind Est
Penston
Lamblair Wood
Letham Mains
Clerkington Mains
Lennoxlove
Mitchell Hall
Lawhead Plantn
West Mains
Papple
Liberty Hall
Nairns Mains
Blinkbonny Ho
Renton Hall
Myles Fm
Falside Hill
St Clement's Wells
Carlaverock Fm
Cuddie Wood
Whitelaw Hill
Garvald Grange
Stoneypath Tower
Birks Plantn
Robin Tup's Plantn
Garvald
New Winton
River Tyne
East Mains
Mid Mains
Colstoun Mains
Colstoun Ho
Morham Mains
Chesters Fm
Ind Est
North Elphinstone
Elphinstone
West Mains
East Mains
North Mains
Wintonhill
New Town
Samuelston
Begbie Wood
Colstoun Wood
Weird's Wood
Beech Hill
Sled Hill
Blindwell Brae
Nunraw Abbey
Garvald Mains
South Elphinstone
Queen Mary's Mount
Winton Ho
Winton West Mains
Herdmanston Mains
Samuelston South Mains
Bolton
Clacherdean Wood
Colstoun
Coulston Old Mill
271
Crossgatehall
Smeaton Shaw
Chalkieside
Cousland
Cousland Park
Melvin Hall
Ormiston
Broomrigg
Tyne Water
Pencaitland
Spilmersford Mains
Tyneholm Ho
Saltoun Hall
East Mains
Eaglescairnie Mains
Crown Wood
Fawn Wood
Gifford Water
Gifford Vale
Gifford
Winding Law
Carfrae
Bara Wood
Black Wood
Star Wood
White Castle (Fort)
Woodhall
Milton
Fountainhall
Bolton Muir
Donolly Res
Papana
60
NT
00
70

North Ness
ISLE OF MAY
Isle of May
South Ness
Bass Rock
NORTH SEA
Tantallon Castle
Auldhame
Scoughall
Whitekirk
Tyninghame
Preston
Dunbar
Belhaven
West Barns
Broxburn
East Barns
Skateraw
Thorntonloch
Innerwick
Spott
Pitcox
Stenton
Traprain
Luggate Burn
Garvald
Oldhamstocks
Cockburnspath
Coye
Old Cambus
Ecclaw
EAST LOTHIAN
John Muir's Birthplace
The Chesters (Fort)
Dunglass Collegiate Church
Preston Mill & Phantassie Doocot
Nunraw Abbey
Dunbar Cement Works
Torness Pt
Barns Ness
Meikle Pinkerton
Halls
Siccar Pt
Greenheugh Pt
Meikle Poo Craig
Hirst Rocks
3 miles
5 km

7
8
9
10
11
A
B
C
D
E
F
G
H
10
00
NT
NT
70
10
Fast Castle Head
Wheat Stack
Telegraph Hill
FAST CASTLE
Oatlee Hill
Dowlaw Burn
Lumsdaine
Lumsdaine Moor
Coldingham Loch
SETTLEMENT
Mire Loch
St Abb's Head
ST ABB'S HEAD
Horsecastle Bay
Bell Hill
Starney Bay
273
273

LOCH RANNOCH AND GLEN LYON
LOCH LOMOND AND THE TROSSACHS NATIONAL PARK
STIRLING
QUEEN ELIZABETH FOREST PARK
RANNOCH MOOR
TAY FOREST
Rannoch Station
Black Corries Lodge
Loch Eigheach
Loch Laidon
Loch Rannoch
Bridge of Ericht
Killichonan
Craiganor Lodge
Kinloch Rannoch
Dunalastair
Tummel Bridge
Tressait
Carie
Inverhadden
Crossmount
Tullochroisk
Finnart
Bridge of Gaur
Camghouran
Black Wood of Rannoch
SCHIEHALLION
Glengoulandie
Loch Kinardochy
Foss
Garth
Keltneyburn
Camserney
Dull
CASTLE MENZIES
Fortingall
Bridge of Lyon
Taymouth Castle
Kenmore
Croftmoraig
Fearnan
SCOTTISH CRANNOG CENTRE
Acharn
Falls of Acharn
Remony
Ardradnaig
Innerwick
Camusvrachan
Invervar
Carnbahn
Balnahanaid
Bridge of Balgie
Meggernie Castle
Gallin
Pubil
Cashlie
Loch Lyon
Stronuich Reservoir
Glen Lyon
BEN LAWERS
Loch na Lairige
MEALL NAN TARMACHAN
Lawers
Carie
Loch Tay
Ardtalnaig
Claggan
Milton Morenish
Kiltyrie
Morenish
Ardeonaig
Kenknock
Glen Lochay
Duncroisk
FALLS OF LOCHAY AND FISH LIFT
Boreland
MOIRLANICH LONGHOUSE
Finlarig
Killin
Monemore
Achmore
FALLS OF DOCHART
Bovain
Breadalbane
Achallader
Auch
Clifton
Tyndrum
Auchtertyre
Dalrigh
Strath Fillan
Crianlarich
Inverherive
Lochdochart House
Auchessan
GLEN DOCHART
Ledcharrie
Auchlyne
Ardchyle
Wester Lix
Lix Toll
Glen Ogle
Benmore
Portnellan
BEN MORE
STOB BINNEIN
Derrydaroch
Glen Falloch
Falls of Falloch
Lochearnhead
Craggan
Edinchip
Edinample
EDINAMPLE FALLS
Dalveich
Ardveich
Derry
Loch Earn
St Fillans
Ardvorlich
Ardtrostan
Dundurn
River Earn
Dunira
MELVILLE MONUMENT
Comrie
Dalchonzie
Tullybannocher
EARTHQUAKE HOUSE
Aberuchill Castle
Ross
Dalginross
Lawers
Ochtertyre
Quoig
Lochlane
Glascorrie
Loch Lednock Reservoir
Glen Lednock
Invergeldie
Funtullich
Carroglen
BEN CHONZIE
Loch Turret Reservoir
Balquhidder
ROB ROY'S GRAVE
Auchtubh
Balquhidder Station
Glenample
Braes of Balquhidder
Monachylemore
Craigruie
Stronvar
Loch Doine
Loch Voil
Inverlochlarig
Ballimore
Strathyre
Strathyre Forest
Immervoulin
BEN VORLICH
Forest of Glenartney
Glen Artney
Dalchruin
Tigh-na-Blair
Auchinner
Auchnashelloch
Culloch
Torlum Wood
Ochtermuthill
BEN CLACH
Langside
Glenlichorn
Braco Castle
ARDOCH ROMAN CAMP
Western Feddal
Ardlui
Inverarnan
BEN A'CHROIN
STOB A'CHOIN
BEN EACH
Ardchullarie More
Loch Lubnaig
BENVANE
BEINN BHREAC
Portnellan
Strath Gartney
Glen Finglas Res.
UAMH BHEAG
Drumardoch
Anie
Pass of Leny
Brenachoile Lodge
Stronachlachar
ROB ROY'S CAVE
Garrison
Inversnaid
Inversnaid Hotel
LOCH KATRINE
Loch Arklet
THE GREAT TROSSACHS FOREST
The Trossachs
BEN LEDI
Coireachrombe
FALLS OF LENY
Leny Ho.
ROB ROY AND TROSSACHS VISITOR CENTRE
BRACKLINN FALLS
Kilmahog
Bochastle
Callander
Easter Brackland
Auchenlaich
Drumloist
Braes of Doune
TROSSACHS PIER COMPLEX
SS SIR WALTER SCOTT
Trossachs Hotel
Brig o'Turk
Coilantogle
Callandrode
Loch Ard Forest
Frenich
BEN VENUE
Loch Achray
THE TROSSACHS
Duncraggan
Lendrick Lodge
Invertrossachs
Loch Venachar
Loch Drunkie
Menteith Hills
Achray Forest
Loch Chon
Cailness
Tarbet
LOCH PARK
LOMOND
Craig Rostan
BEN LOMOND
Kinlochard
Altskeith
Drumlean
D. MARSHALL LODGE VISITOR CENTRE
Stronmachair
Mill of Chon
Couligartan
Loch Ard
Milton
Aberfoyle
Kirkton
Balleich
Cobleland
Ptarmigan Lodge
Firkin
Rowardennan
BEN LOMOND BUNKHOUSE
Inverbeg
INVERBEG GALLERY
Rowardennan Forest
Duchray Water
Gartmore
Gartmore Ho
Dalmary
Port of Menteith
Lake of Menteith
INCHMAHOME PRIORY
Malling
Gartur
Lochend Ho
Dykehead
Torrie Forest
Loch Rusky
Brae of Boquhapple
Bigram
Ruskie
Goodie Water
Thornhill
FLANDERS MOSS
Flanders Moss
Blairdrummond Moss
Drumvaich
Lanrick
Deanston
Burn of Cambus
Doune
Blair Drummond
Easter Row
BLAIR DRUMMOND SAFARI PARK
The Bows
Dalbrack
Lerrocks
Kilbryde Castle
Kinbuck
Ashfield
CATHEDRAL
Dunblane
LEIGHTON LIBRARY
Sunnylaw
Bridge of Allan
Blairlogie
Causeway
Sheriff Muir 1715

Easter Lednathie
Redheugh
Glenogil
Auchnacree
Deuchar
Menmuir
Tigerton
Balnamoon
Lochty
Belliehill
Balrownie
Newtonmill
Little Brechin
West Muir
Keithock
Trinity
Brechin
Craigo
Lochside
St Cyrus
Morphie
Logie
North Craigo
Pathhead
Hillside
Kirkhill
Maltings
Milton Ness
Glenquiech
Ogil
Fern
Noranside
Careston
Mains of Balhall
Horniehaugh
Dykehead
CAPTAIN SCOTT & DR WILSON CAIRN
CAT LAW
Pearsie
Cortachy
Memus
Careston Castle
Tannadice
Cadger Path
Noran Water
South Esk
BRECHIN CASTLE CENTRE
CATHEDRAL & ROUND TOWER
CALEDONIAN RAILWAY
HOUSE OF DUN
Bridge of Dun
Montrose Basin
Montrose
MUSEUM AND ART GALLERY
Scurdie Ness
WILLIAM LAMB MEMORIAL STUDIO
MONTROSE BASIN VISITOR CENTRE
Inchbraoch
Ferryden
Kirkton of Craig
Barnhead
Kinnaird Castle
Farnell
Bonnyton
Carcary
Maryton
Dunninald
Long Craig
Fishtown of Usan
Boddin Pt.
Balloch
Inverquharity
Murthill
Finavon
Oathlaw
Shielhill
Aldbar Castle
Netherton
Mains of Melgund
Middle Drums
MILE HILL
Kirkton of Kingoldrum
Kinnordy
Northmuir
Kirriemuir
BARRIE'S BIRTHPLACE
LOCH OF KINNORDY NATURE RESERVE
Crosston
ABERLEMNO SCULPTURED STONES
Aberlemno
Montreathmont Forest
Montreathmont Moor
Pitkennedy
Carse Gray
Blackgate
Turin
RESTENNETH PRIORY
Rescobie
Lunanhead
Reswallie
Rossie Moor
Westerton
Renmure
Braehead of Lunan
Lunan
LUNAN BAY
Redcastle
Westmuir
GATEWAY TO THE GLENS MUS
Maryton
Mosside
Mains of Ballindarg
Padanaram
FORFAR LOCH
Forfar
THE MEFFAN GALL & MUS
Kirkton of Airlie
Airlie
Craigton
Roundyhill
Drumgley
Leys of Cossans
ST ORLAND'S STONE
Dean Water
Kingsmuir
Burnside
Dunnichen
Letham
Balgavies
Milldens
Dubton
Glasterlaw
Guthrie
Kinnell
Pitmuies
PITMUIES GARDEN
Friockheim
Bolshan
Boysack
Lunan Water
Inverkeilor
Inchock
Lang Craig
Ethie Mains
Red Head
Ethie Castle
Ruthven House
EASSIE SCULPTURED STONE
GLAMIS CASTLE
Glamis
Caldhame
Lowrie Moor
Bowriefauld
Idvies
Chapelton
Leysmill
Cauldcots
Drunkendub
Castleton
Charleston
Douglastown
Thornton
Kirkton
Craichie
Lour
Tulloes
Cononsyth
Balkeerie
Eassie
Kirkinch
Milton
Foffarty
Gateside
Inverarity
Whigstreet
Mosston
Colliston
Letham Grange
Auchmithie
Meg's Craig
Wester Denoon
ARK HILL
Nether Handwick
Kirkbuddo
Greystone
Redford
St Vigeans
ST VIGEANS STONES & MUSEUM
Maryville
Woodville Feus
Gallowfauld
Carrot
Hayhillock
Carmyllie
Denhead of Arbilot
Hayshead
Cliffburn
The Deil's Heid
ARBROATH ABBEY
Arbroath
SIGNAL TOWER MUSEUM
Coldstream
Bonnyton
Balkemback
Kirkton of Auchterhouse
Tealing
Todhill
Husbandtown
CROMBIE
Fauldiehill
Arbirlot
Balmirmer
Easter Knox
Elliot
Auchterhouse
North Dronley
Leoch
Muir of Pert
Newbigging
Inveraldie
East March
Bucklerheads
Wellbank
Monikie
Kirkton of Monikie
Craigton
Monikie Burn
CARLUNGIE SOUTERRAIN
Salmond's Muir
Hatton
Muirdrum
East Haven
Dronley
Muirhead
Birkhill
Bridgefoot
Burnside of Duntrune
Kellas
Drumsturdy
Newbigging
Clayholes
BARRY MILL
Panbride
Carnoustie
Fowlis
CAMPERDOWN AND TEMPLETON WOODS
CLATTO
Downfield
Fintry
SOUTERRAIN ARDESTIE
Baldovie
Mains of Ardestie
Barry
CARNOUSTIE
Barry Links
Liff
Denhead of Gray
Benvie
VERDANT WORKS
Lochee
MILLS OBSERVATORY
MUS AND ART GALL
MUS OF TRANSPORT
Craigie
Douglas & Angus
West Ferry
Monifieth
Stannergate
Broughty Ferry
BROUGHTY CASTLE MUSEUM
Barnhill
Buddon Ness
Longforgan
Invergowrie
Dundee
V&A DUNDEE
Tay Bridge
DISCOVERY POINT
Tayport
TENTSMUIR
Castle Huntly
Kingoodie
UNIVERSITY BOTANIC GARDENS
Newport-on-Tay
Scotscraig
Woodhaven
Tay Rail Bridge
Wormit
Shanwell
Tentsmuir Forest
Fetterdale
Balmerino
BALMERINO ABBEY
Kirkton
Bottomcraig
Gauldry
Pickletillem
Coultra
Hazelton Walls
Kilmany
Lucklawhill
Rhynd
Carrick
Leuchars
LEUCHARS NORMAN CHURCH
Creich
Brunton
Rathillet
Logie
Balmullo
Milton
Eden Mouth
Luthrie
Muirhead
Guardbridge
EDEN ESTUARY CENTRE
ST ANDREWS BAY
Moonzie
Dairsie or Osnaburgh
Kincaple
ST ANDREWS
ST ANDREWS AQUARIUM
Lindifferon
MOUNT HILL
Kilmaron Castle
Foodieash
WORLD GOLF MUS
St Andrews
CATH & ST RULE'S TOWER
Strathkinness
Clatto
Newpark
Fernie
Cupar
Kemback
Blebocraigs
Balone
CRAIGTOUN
ST ANDREWS BOTANIC GARDEN
Brownhills
Buddo Ness
Boarhills
Babbet Ness
Bow of Fife
Cupar Muir
Denhead
SCOTTISH DEER CENTRE
HILL OF TARVIT
Pitscottie
Prior Muir
Kingsbarns
Cambo Ness
CAMBO GARDENS
Carr Brigs
Tullybothy Craigs
Springfield
Bridgend
Ceres
Baldinnie
Cameron Res.
Cameron Burn
Stravithie
Dunino
Beleybridge
Ladybank
SCOTSTARVIT TOWER
Craigrothie
FIFE FOLK MUSEUM
Pitlessie
Cults
Chance Inn
Struthers
Peat Inn
Balcomie
Craighead
Wormiston Ho
Fife Ness
CRAIL TOLBOOTH
Kingskettle
Balmalcolm
Burnturk
Kettlehill
Falfield
Radernie
Lathones
Kingsmuir
Lochty
SCOTLAND'S SECRET BUNKER
Crail
CRAIL MUSEUM AND HERITAGE CENTRE
West Ness
Woodside
New Gilston
Montrave
Kame
Largoward
Carnbee
Pitcorthie
Pitkierie
Kilrenny
Rameldry Mill Bank
Wester Newburn
Lathallan Mill
KELLIE CASTLE AND GARDEN
FIFE COASTAL PATH
Langdyke
Baintown
Arncroach
Newton of Balcormo
Grangemuir
Anstruther Easter
SCOTTISH FISHERIES MUSEUM
Star
Bonnybank
Kirkton of Largo
Lundin Links
Drumeldrie
Colinsburgh
Abercrombie
Kilconquhar
Pittenweem
Anstruther Wester
Kennoway
Scoonie
ROBINSON CRUSOE STATUE
Lower Largo
Balchrystie
ST FILLAN'S CAVE
ST MONAN'S WINDMILL
Balgonie Castle
Balcurvie
SILVERBURN PARK
Ardross
St Monans
ST MONAN'S CHURCH
LETHAM GLEN
Leven
Largo Bay
Ruddons Pt.
Grange
Elie
Milton of Balgonie
Windygates
Innerleven
Earlsferry
Chapel Ness
Sauchar Pt.
ISLE OF MAY
Isle of May
Methil
MUSEUM
Buckhaven
Coaltown of Balgonie
East Wemyss
Coaltown of Wemyss
NO

COLL
TIREE
Muck
Gometra
Ulva
Iona
Staffa
Lunga
Treshnish Isles
Bac Mor
Little Colonsay
Inch Kenneth
Erisgeir
Erraid
ROSS OF MULL
LOCH TUATH
LOCH NA KEAL
LOCH SCRIDAIN
ARDMEANACH
SOUND OF EIGG
Arinagour
Tobermory
Dervaig
Calgary
Fionnphort
Bunessan
Scarinish
Sorisdale
Bousd
Cornaigmore
Gallanach
Arnabost
Grishipoll
Clabhach
Ballyhaugh
Totronald
Arileod
Uig
Acha
Breachacha Castle
Friesland
Caolas
Salum
Vaul
Kirkapol
Ruaig
Gott
Kenovay
Cornaigbeg
Heanish
Baugh
Crossapol
Balinoe
Balemartine
Mannal
Hynish
West Hynish
Heylipol
Moss
Kilmoluaig
Balephuil
Barrapol
Middleton
Kilkenneth
Balevullin
Hough
Sraid Ruadh
Sanna
Achnaha
Portuairk
Achosnich
Ormsaigmore
Ormsaigbeg
Kilchoan Bay
Point of Ardnamurchan
ARDNAMURCHAN LIGHTHOUSE
Glengorm Castle
MULL MUSEUM
Sunipol
Croig
Penmore Mill
Achnadrish
Ensay
Haunn
Burg
Kilninian
Achleck
Fanmore
Ballygown
Lagganulva
Oskamull
Ulva House
Balnahard
Tiroran
Kintra
Aridhglas
Fidden
Tiraghoil
Knockvologan
Ardalanish
Ardchiavaig
Uisken
Scoor
Torrans
Baile Mor
IONA ABBEY AND CATHEDRAL
MACLEAN'S CROSS
IONA HERITAGE CENTRE
FINGAL'S CAVE
CASTLEBAY (Apr - Oct, Wed only)
OBAN

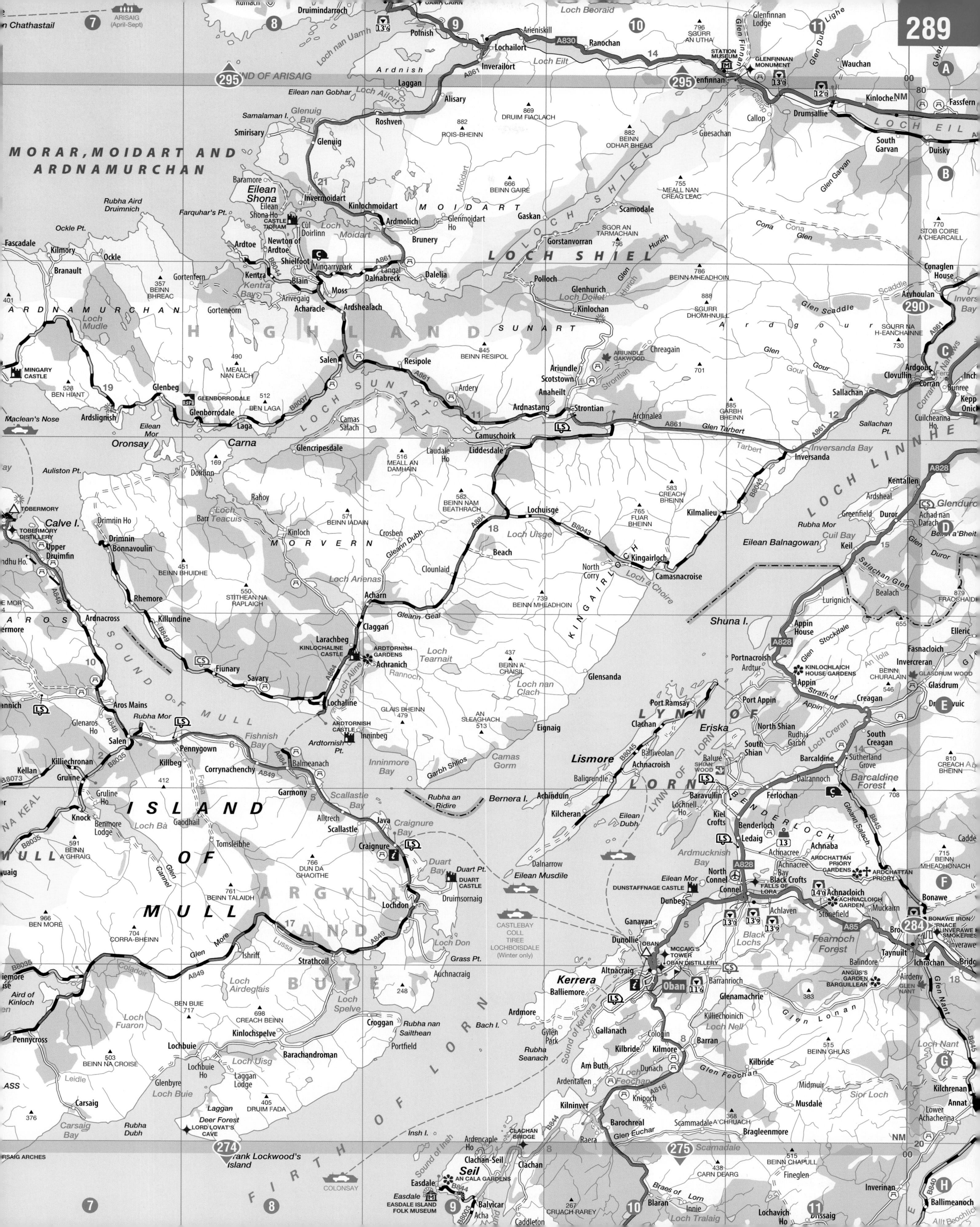
MORAR, MOIDART AND ARDNAMURCHAN
SOUND OF ARISAIG
MOIDART
LOCH SHIEL
ARDNAMURCHAN
HIGHLAND
SUNART
Ardgour
LOCH SUNART
MORVERN
SOUND OF MULL
ISLAND OF MULL
ARGYLL AND BUTE
LYNN OF LORN
BENDERLOCH
FIRTH OF LORN
LOCH LINNHE
LOCH EIL
Loch Beoraid
Loch Eilt
Loch nan Uamh
Loch Ailort
Loch Moidart
Loch Mudle
Loch Doilet
Loch Teacuis
Loch Arienas
Loch Uisge
Loch Aline
Loch Teàrnait
Loch nan Clach
Loch a' Choire
Loch Creran
Loch Nell
Loch Feochan
Loch Spelve
Loch Uisg
Loch Buie
Loch Bà
Loch Don
Loch Tralaig
Loch Nant
Druimindarroch
Polnish
Arieniskill
Lochailort
Inverailort
Ranochan
Glenfinnan Lodge
Glenfinnan
STATION MUSEUM
GLENFINNAN MONUMENT
Wauchan
Kinlocheil
Fassfern
Drumsallie
Callop
Guesachan
South Garvan
Duisky
Laggan
Alisary
Roshven
Glenuig
Smirisary
Samalaman I.
Eilean nan Gobhar
Ardnish
Eilean Shona
Baramore
Invermoidart
Kinlochmoidart
Ardmolich
Glenmoidart Ho
Brunery
Gaskan
Scamodale
Gorstanvorran
CASTLE TIORAM
Cùl Doirlinn
Newton of Ardtoe
Ardtoe
Shielfoot
Mingarrypark
Langal
Dalnabreck
Dalelia
Kentra
Blain
Moss
Acharacle
Arivegaig
Ardshealach
Gortenfern
Gorteneorn
Kilmory
Ockle
Fascadale
Branault
Polloch
Glenhurich
Kinlochan
Salen
Resipole
Ardery
Ariundle
ARIUNDLE OAKWOOD
Scotstown
Anaheilt
Strontian
Ardnastang
Chreagain
MINGARY CASTLE
Glenbeg
GLENBORRODALE
Glenborrodale
Laga
Ardslignish
Maclean's Nose
Eilean Mor
Camas Salach
Camuschoirk
Liddesdale
Archnalea
Glen Tarbert
Inversanda
Inversanda Bay
Sallachan
Clovullin
Ardgour
Corran
Conaglen House
Aryhoulan
Glen Scaddle
Oronsay
Carna
Glencripesdale
Laudale Ho
Dorlinn
Auliston Pt.
Rahoy
Drimnin Ho
Drimnin
Bonnavoulin
Kinloch
Crosben
Lochuisge
Kingairloch
Camasnacroise
North Corry
Kilmalieu
Kentallen
Ardsheal
Duror
Keil
Eilean Balnagowan
Cuil Bay
Beach
Clounlaid
Acharn
Claggan
Larachbeg
KINLOCHALINE CASTLE
ARDTORNISH GARDENS
Achranich
Rhemore
Killundine
Ardnacross
Fiunary
Savary
Lochaline
Glensanda
Eignaig
Inninbeg
ARDTORNISH CASTLE
Ardtornish Pt.
TOBERMORY
TOBERMORY DISTILLERY
Calve I.
Upper Druimfin
Aros Mains
Rubha Mor
Salen
Pennygown
Killbeg
Corrynachenchy
Balmeanach
Garmony
Glenaros Ho
Killiechronan
Gruline
Kellan
Knock
Benmore Lodge
Gaodhail
Tomsleibhe
Alltrech
Scallastle
Scallastle Bay
Java
Craignure
Duart Bay
DUART CASTLE
Druimsornaig
Lochdon
Strathcoil
Auchnacraig
Ishriff
Glen More
Kinlochspelve
Croggan
Portfield
Barachandroman
Lochbuie
Laggan Lodge
Lochbuie Ho
Pennycross
Carsaig
Carsaig Bay
Rubha Dubh
LORD LOVAT'S CAVE
Frank Lockwood's Island
Shuna I.
Appin House
Portnacroish
KINLOCHLAICH HOUSE GARDENS
Appin
Port Appin
Port Ramsay
Clachan
Lismore
Eriska
North Shian
South Shian
Balure
Baravullin
Achnacroish
Baligrundle
Achinduin
Kilcheran
Bernera I.
Creagan
South Creagan
Barcaldine
Ferlochan
Benderloch
Ledaig
Achnaba
ARDCHATTAN PRIORY GARDENS
ARDCHATTAN PRIORY
North Connel
Connel
Black Crofts
FALLS OF LORA
Achnacloich
Dunbeg
DUNSTAFFNAGE CASTLE
Eilean Musdile
Dalnarrow
Ganavan
Dunollie
Oban
MCCAIG'S TOWER
OBAN DISTILLERY
Barranrioch
Glenamachrie
Kerrera
Balliemore
Ardmore
Gallanach
Kilbride
Kilmore
Barran
Dunach
Am Buth
Ardentallen
Kilninver
Knipoch
Raera
Barochreal
Scammadale
Bragleenmore
Musdale
Kilchrenan
Annat
Taynuilt
Bonawe
Ichrachan
Glen Nant
Glen Lonan
Glen Feochan
Glen Euchar
Clachan-Seil
CLACHAN BRIDGE
Seil
AN CALA GARDENS
Easdale
EASDALE ISLAND FOLK MUSEUM
Balvicar
Blaran
Inverinan
Lochavich
CASTLEBAY COLL TIREE LOCHBOISDALE (Winter only)
COLONSAY
ARISAIG (April-Sept)

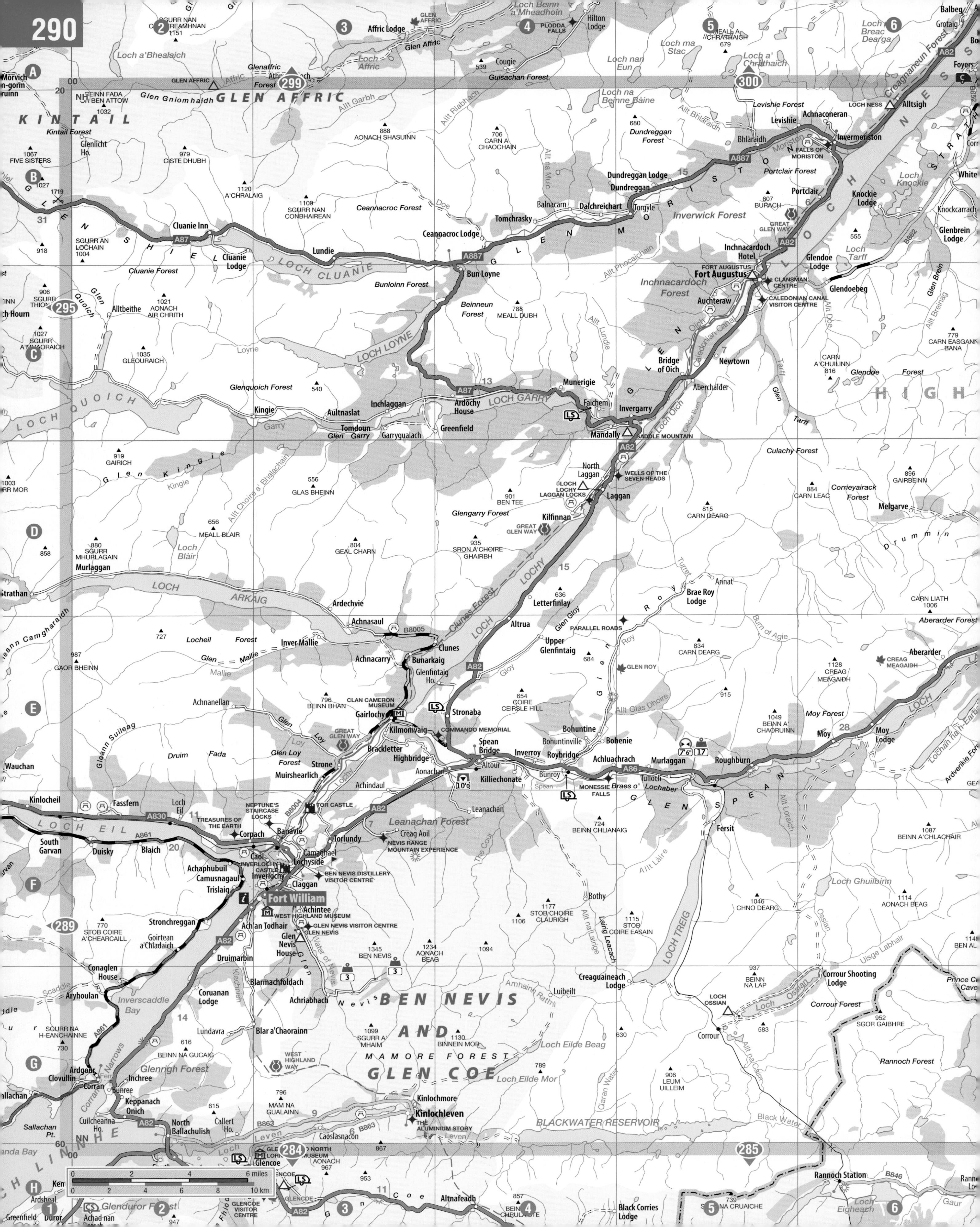

Affric Lodge
Glen Affric
Loch a'Bhealaich
Plodda Falls
Hilton Lodge
Loch Beinn a'Mheadhoin
Meall a' Chrathaich 679
Loch ma Stac
Loch nan Eun
Loch a' Chràthaich
Loch Breac Dearga
Balbeg
Grotaig
Foyers
Cougie
Guisachan Forest
Glenaffric Forest
GLEN AFFRIC
299
300
Morvich
KINTAIL
Kintail Forest
Glenlicht Ho.
1067 FIVE SISTERS
979 CISTE DHUBH
888 AONACH SHASUINN
706 CARN A' CHAOCHAIN
Loch na Beinne Bàine
680
Dundreggan Forest
Levishie Forest
Levishie
Achnaconeran
Bhlaraidh
Invermoriston
Falls of Moriston
Portclair Forest
Portclair
Loch Ness
Alltsigh
Creag nan Eun Forest
A82
A887
Dundreggan Lodge
Dundreggan
Torgyle
Dalchreichart
Balnacarn
Tomchrasky
Ceannacroc Lodge
Ceannacroc Forest
1120 A'CHRALAIG
1109 SGURR NAN CONBHAIREAN
Cluanie Inn
Cluanie Lodge
Lundie
LOCH CLUANIE
A87
Glen Shiel
SGURR AN LOCHAIN 1004
Cluanie Forest
Bun Loyne
Bunloinn Forest
Beinneun Forest
788 MEALL DUBH
GLEN MORISTON
Inverwick Forest
607 BURACH
Great Glen Way
Knockie Lodge
Loch Knockie
Knockcarrach
Glenbrein Lodge
555
Loch Tarff
Inchnacardoch Hotel
Fort Augustus
Inchnacardoch Forest
Clansman Centre
Caledonian Canal Visitor Centre
Glendoe Lodge
Glendoebeg
Auchteraw
Glen Quoich
Alltbeithe
1021 AONACH AIR CHRITH
295
1027 SGURR A'MHAORAICH
1035 GLEOURAICH
LOCH LOYNE
Glenquoich Forest
540
LOCH QUOICH
Kingie
Aultnaslat
Inchlaggan
Tomdoun
Glen Garry
Garrygualach
Ardochy House
LOCH GARRY
Greenfield
Munerigie
Faichem
Invergarry
Mandally
Saddle Mountain
Bridge of Oich
Caledonian Canal
Newtown
Aberchalder
Loch Oich
779 CARN EASGANN BANA
CARN A'CHUILINN 816
Glendoe Forest
HIGH
919 GAIRICH
Glen Kingie
556 GLAS BHEINN
901 BEN TEE
North Laggan
Loch Lochy
Laggan Locks
Wells of the Seven Heads
Laggan
Culachy Forest
884 CARN LEAC
Corrieyairack Forest
896 GAIRBEINN
Melgarve
815 CARN DEARG
Glengarry Forest
Kilfinnan
656 MEALL BLAIR
880 SGURR MHURLAGAN
858
Murlaggan
Loch Blàir
804 GEAL CHARN
935 SRON A'CHOIRE GHAIRBH
Drummin
LOCH ARKAIG
Strathan
Ardechvie
636
Letterfinlay
Brae Roy Lodge
Annat
CARN LIATH 1006
Aberarder Forest
Achnasaul
B8005
Clunes
Clunes Forest
LOCH LOCHY
Altrua
Parallel Roads
Glen Gloy
Glen Roy
Upper Glenfintaig
684
834 CARN DEARG
1128 CREAG MEAGAIDH
Creag Meagaidh
Aberarder
727
Locheil Forest
Inver Mallie
Glen Mallie
987 GAOR BHEINN
Achnacarry
Bunarkaig
Glenfintaig Ho.
A82
915
654 COIRE CEIRSLE HILL
Achnanellan
796 BEINN BHAN
Clan Cameron Museum
Gairlochy
Stronaba
Commando Memorial
Kilmonivaig
Great Glen Way
Bohuntine
Bohuntinville
Bohenie
1049 BEINN A' CHAORUINN
Moy Forest
Moy
Moy Lodge
LOCH LAGGAN
Gleann Suileag
Druim Fada
Glen Loy
Glen Loy Forest
Brackletter
Highbridge
Spean Bridge
Inverroy
Roybridge
Achluachrach
Murlaggan
Roughburn
Wauchan
Strone
Muirshearlich
Aonachan
Altour
Killiechonate
Bunroy
A86
Monessie Falls
Tulloch
Braes o' Lochaber
Achindaul
Kinlocheil
Fassfern
Loch Eil
Neptune's Staircase Locks
Tor Castle
A830
Treasures of the Earth
Corpach
Banavie
B8004
Leanachan
Leanachan Forest
Creag Aoil
Nevis Range Mountain Experience
724 BEINN CHLIANAIG
GLEN SPEAN
Fersit
1087 BEINN A'CHLACHAIR
LOCH EIL
South Garvan
Duisky
Blaich
A861
Torlundy
Caol
Camaghael
Lochyside
Inverlochy Castle
Inverlochy
Achaphubuil
Camusnagaul
Trislaig
Ben Nevis Distillery Visitor Centre
Claggan
Fort William
Achintee
West Highland Museum
Glen Nevis Visitor Centre
Glen Nevis
Glen Nevis House
Allt Làire
Bothy
Loch Ghuilbinn
1046 CHNO DEARG
1114 AONACH BEAG
289
770 STOB COIRE A'CHEARCAILL
Stronchreggan
Goirtean a'Chladaich
Ach'an Todhair
1177 STOB CHOIRE CLAURIGH
1106
1115 STOB COIRE EASAIN
1234 AONACH BEAG
1345 BEN NEVIS
1094
Laire Leacach
LOCH TREIG
Conaglen House
Druimarbin
Blarmachfoldach
Aryhoulan
Inverscaddle Bay
Coruanan Lodge
Achriabhach
BEN NEVIS AND GLEN COE
Amhainn Rath
Luibeilt
Creaguaineach Lodge
937 BEINN NA LAP
Loch Ossian
Corrour Shooting Lodge
Corrour Forest
Corrour
583
952 SGOR GAIBHRE
Lundavra
Blar a'Chaorainn
SGURR NA H-EANCHAINNE 730
616 BEINN NA GUCAIG
1099 SGURR A'MHAIM
1130 BINNEIN MOR
Loch Eilde Beag
630
Mamore Forest
Glenrigh Forest
West Highland Way
789
Loch Eilde Mor
906 LEUM UILLEIM
Rannoch Forest
Ardgour
Clovullin
Corran
Corran Narrows
Inchree
Bunree
Keppanach
Onich
796 MAM NA GUALAINN
Kinlochmore
Kinlochleven
The Aluminium Story
615
Callert Ho.
North Ballachulish
Cuilcheanna Ho.
Sallachan Pt.
B863
Caolasnacon
BLACKWATER RESERVOIR
Black Water
Loch Leven
867
284
285
Glencoe
Glencoe North Lorn Museum
967
953
Glencoe Visitor Centre
Rannoch Station
B846
Loch Eigheach
739 SRON NA CRUAICHE
857 BEINN CHRULAISTE
Black Corries Lodge
Altnafeadh
Glen Coe
Glenduror Forest
Achad nan
947
Ardsheal
Greenfield
Duror
Gaur
0 2 4 6 miles
0 2 4 6 8 10 km

291
300
301
292
285
286
MONADHLIATH MOUNTAINS
CAIRNGORM NATIONAL PARK
CAIRNGORM MOUNTAINS
THE CAIRNGORM MOUNTAINS
GRAMPIAN MTS.
FOREST OF ATHOLL
GLEN GARRY
GLEN ERROCHTY
LOCH TUMMEL
LOCH RANNOCH
PERTH AND KINROSS
GAICK FOREST
BADENOCH
Inverfarigaig
Farigaig Forest
Foyers
Errogie
Aultnagoire
Farraline
Dunmaglass Lodge
Garbole
Corrievorrie
Knockandoo
Dalmigavie Lodge
Dalmigavie
Coignascallan
Glen Mazeran
Findhorn
Slochd
Carrbridge
Landmark Forest Adventure Park
Duthil
Lochanhully
Sluggan
Ellan
Feith Mhor
Dalnahaitnach
Tullochgribban
Skye of Curr
Speyside Centre
Balnacruie
Broomhill
Aultmore
Nethy Bridge
Dell Lodge
Drumuillie
Cullachie
Birchfield
Deishar
Boat of Garten
East Croftmore
Loch Garten
Abernethy Forest
Chapelton
Kinveachy
Wester Dalvoult
Street of Kincardine
Aundorach
Avielochan
Strathspey Railway
Auchgourish Gdns
Speyside Way
Auchgourish
Easter Tulloch
Lochgarthside
Loch Mhor
Wester Aberchalder
Easter Aberchalder
Lyne of Gorthleck
Bailebeag
Garthbeg
Coignafearn Lodge
Coignafearn Forest
Dalbeg
Eskin
Garrogie Lodge
Killin Lodge
Loch Killin
Glen Markie
Stronelairg Lodge
Allt Cam Ban
Eil
Caggan
Gramsh
Dalfaber
Pityoulish
Glenmore Forest Park
The Queen's Forest
Aviemore
Craigellachie
The Aviemore Ski Centre
Cairngorm Whisky Centre
Coylumbridge
Lynwilg
Inverdruie
Loch Alvie
Doune
Polchar
Rothiemurchus Estate Visitor Centre
Glenmore Visitor Centre
Cairngorm Reindeer Centre
Glenmore Lodge
Alvie
Delfour
Whitewell
Loch Morlich
Rothiemurchus
Rothiemurchus Lodge
Loch an Eilein
Loch an Eilein Visitor Centre
Inshriach Forest
Speybank
Kincraig
Invereshie House
Feshiebridge
Lagganlia
Highland Wildlife Park
Loch Insh
Farr
Balavil
Insh
Ballintean
Lynchat
Kingussie
Insh Marshes
Inveruglass
Balachroick
Pitmain
Clan McPherson Mus
Strone
Newtonmore
Highland Folk Museum
Ruthven
Torcroy
Drumguish
Tolvah
Invereshie & Inshriach
Loch Einich
Glen Banchor
Calder
Allt Madagain
Ralia Lodge
Cairngorms Adventure Centre
Achlean
Glentromie Lodge
Glen Tromie
Glen Feshie
Greagdhubh Lodge
Glentruim House
Gergask
Balgowan
Crathie
Garvamore
Laggan
Cluny Castle
Drumgask
Catlodge
Crubenbeg
Etteridge
Glenfeshie Lodge
Glenfeshie Forest
Glenshero Lodge
Strath Mashie
Strathmashie House
Crubenmore Lodge
Loch Crunachdan
Aberarder Lodge
Cromra
Feagour
Kinloch Laggan
Gallovie
Loch Caoldair
Ardverikie
Cuaich
Loch Cuaich
Loch an t-Seilich
Dalwhinnie
Dalwhinnie Distillery
Gaick Lodge
Loch Bhrodainn
Loch an Duin
Loch Ericht Forest
Loch Pattack
Ben Alder Lodge
Balsporran Cottages
North Drumachter Lodge
Cama Choire
Sronphadruig Lodge
Dail-na-Mine Forest
Glen Bruar
Bruar Lodge
Forest Lodge
Culra Lodge
Ben Alder Forest
Loch Ericht
Loch a' Bhealaich Bheithe
Dalnaspidal Lodge
Dalnaspidal Forest
Dalnacardoch Forest
Dalnacardoch Lodge
Dalnamein Lodge
Corrievarkie Lodge
Edendon Water
Glen Tilt
Glen Dirich
Tarf Water
Geldie Burn
Bynack Burn
Loch Loch
Talla Bheith Forest
Duinish
Loch Con
Loch Errochty
Trinafour
Dalchalloch
Auchleeks Ho.
Falls of the Bruar
Clan Donnachaidh Museum
Pitagowan
Calvine
Struan
Old Struan
Blair Castle
Old Blair
Tirinie
Old Bridge of Tilt
Lude House
Blair Atholl
Blair Atholl Mill
Ballentoul
Tulach Hill
Atholl Country Life
Aldclune
Killiecrankie
Killiecrankie Visitor Centre
Lettoch
Glen Girnaig
Fincastle Ho.
Bonskeid House
Tenandry
Loch Bhac
Tummel Forest
Balavoulin
Queen's View
Tressait
Tummel Bridge
Dunalastair
Dunalastair Water
Kinloch Rannoch
Killichonan
Carie
Inverhadden
Crossmount
Tullochroisk
Camghouran
Finnart
Black Wood of Rannoch
Foss
Lick
Falls of Tummel
Linn of Tummel
Loch Faskally
Balmore
Explorer's Garden
Moulin
Kinnaird
Pitlochry
Edradour Distillery
Milton of Edradour
Blair Athol Distillery Visitor Centre
Dalnavaid
Glen Brerachan
Ben Vrackie
Creag Dubh
Ben Vuirich
Carn Liath
Beinn a' Ghlo
Cairngorm Chairlift & Ski Centre
Cairn Gorm 1245
Braeriach 1296
Ben Macdui 1309
Sgoran Dubh Mor 1111
Carn Eilrig
Carn Ban Mor 1052
Mullach Clach a' Bhlair 1019
Beinn Bhrotain 1157
Derry Cairngorm 1155
Carn Ealar 994
An Sgarsoch 1006
Beinn Dearg 1008
Braigh Sron Ghorm 879
Sron a' Chleirich 816
A' Chailleach 930
Carn Ban 942
Geal Charn 925
Marg na Craige 832
Carn Dearg Mor 857
Meallach Mhor 768
Garbh-mheall Mor 592
Uchd a' Chlarsair 788
Carn na Caim 941
Creagan Mor 774
A' Bhuidheanach Bheag 936
The Sow of Atholl 803
Beinn Udlamain
Meall na Leitreach 775
Beinn Mholach 841
Beinn a' Chuallaich 891
Sron Bheag 515
Beinn Eilde 674
Carn Sgulain 812
Carn an Fhreiceadain 878
Calpa Mor 814
Carn na Laraiche Maoile 809
Carn na Saobhaidhe 811
Carn Coire na Creiche 826
Burrach Mor 828
Carn Odhar 802
Beinn Bhreac Mhor 807
Carn na Saobhaidh 714
Carn Coire na h-Easgainn 790
Cnoc Fraing 745
Geal Charn Mor 824
Carn Sleamhuinn 677
An Suidhe 541
Meall na h-Aisre 862
A9
A86
A889
A95
A924
B9152
B970
B9150
B847
B846
B8019
B8079
B862

REVACK ESTATE
SPEYSIDE WAY
Lynemore
722 CREGGAN A'CHAISE
Inverlochy
CARN DAIMH
Auchnarrow
Knockandhu
Achdregnie
Livet
B9002
ST MARY'S CHURCH
721 THE BUCK
632 HILL OF THREE STONES
Clova
SCOTTISH SCULPTURE WORKSHOP
Lumsden
Broomhill
Aultmore
Nethy Bridge
Blairgorm
Dirdhu
Bridge of Brown
301
Burn of Lochy
Glenlivet Forest
Strathavon Lo.
Fodderletter
Croughly
Braes of Glenlivet
Clashnoir
Chapeltown
302
Birchfield
Dell Lodge
Dell
Lettoch
Clachaig
East Croftmore
LOCH GARTEN
A939
Bridge of Avon
TOMINTOUL & GLENLIVET DISCOVERY CENTRE
Tomintoul
Milton
TOMINTOUL
588
Scalan
568 BADDOCH
Dorback Lodge
Delnabo
ABERNETHY CENTRE
Larg
Forest Lodge
Abernethy Forest
Audorach
588 CARN MEADHONACH
Conglass Water
804 CARN MOR
LADDER HILLS
Glenbuchat Lodge
Badenyon
Water of Buchat
658
Belnacraig
Rinmore
Kildrummy
KILDRUMMY CASTLE & GARDEN
Milltown of Kildrummy
Mossat
A97
Don
Easter Tulloch
ABERNETHY
Braes of Abernethy
Dorback Burn
688
Water of Ailnack
Blairnamarrow
Water of Nochty
Kirkton of Glenbuchat
Glenbuchat Castle
MORAY
LECHT SKI CENTRE
718 THE SOCACH
Shiel
Glen Ernan
Ernan Water
Bellabeg
Edinglassie Ho.
Forbestown
Strathdon
Glenkindie
Towie
Sinnahard
Milltown of Towie
Balnakel
MEALL A'BHUACHAILLE
810
821 GEAL CHARN
Avon
Dalestie
792 CARN EALASAID
Inverernan Ho.
Waterside
Candacraig Ho.
Heugh head
Boultenstone
Deskryshiel
Tornashean Forest
GLENMORE VISITOR CENTRE
CAIRNGORM REINDEER CENTRE
Glenmore Lodge
Water of Caiplich
Burn of Loin
711
673
Milltown
Colnabaichin
Don
Hillockhead
531 CRAIG OF BUNZEACH
619
GLENMORE
742
291
742 BIG GARVOUN
Inchrory
Allt Tuileach
Delnadamph
Cock Bridge
Corgarff
Tornahaish
Deskry Water
Easter Davoch
CORGARFF CASTLE
Migvie
Coynach
Dounes
CAIRNGORM CHAIRLIFT & SKI CENTRE
1090 BYNACK MORE
Faindouran Lodge
GLEN AVON
CAIRNGORM
A939
749
Balgrennie
17
715 THE BRUACH
Forest of Glenavon
Logie Coldstone
Tarland
CAIRNGORM
1245
CAIRN GORM 1245
Loch Builg
823 BROWN COW HILL
744
Morven Lodge
871 MORVEN
Bridgefoot
Leys
TOMNAVERIE STONE CIRCLE
Loch Avon
1107
1171 BEN AVON
10
Glen Fenzie
Milton of Logie
Glendavan Ho.
Ordie
MOUNTAINS
1082 BEINN A'CHAORRUINN
NATIONAL
Gairnshiel Lodge
12
Gairn
MUIR OF DINNET
604
299 SCAR HILL
Loch Etchachan
BENIMACDUI 1309
Lary
BURN O VAT
Loch Davan
Loch Kinord
THE CAIRNGORM MOUNTAINS
1089 CARN EAS
900 CULARDOCH
B976
743 GEALLAIG HILL
MTS.
Glen Gairn
Bridge of Gairn
Milton of Tullich
Clarack
A93
B9119
Dinnet
11
1155 DERRY CAIRNGORM
931 BEINN BHREAC
Bush Crathie
Coilacriech
8
Culsh
Muir of Dinnet
B976
Deecastle
Glascorrie
CRATHIE CHURCH
Crathie
Dee
Littlemill
Ballater
Greystone
Glen Tanar House
Derry Burn
CARN NA DROCHAIDE 818
PARK
BALMORAL CASTLE AND GARDENS
House of Glenmuick
Bridge of Muick
529
Derry Lodge
BRAEMAR CASTLE
Inver
Invergelder
Easter Balmoral
ROYAL LOCHNAGAR DISTILLERY VISITOR CENTRE
Khantore
Birkhall
Girnock Burn
Mill of Sterin
Glen Tanar
Water of Tanar
GLEN TANAR
Lui Water
GRAMPIAN
BRAEMAR
Invercauld House
Glen Lui
Allanaquoich
Braemar
KINDROCHIT CASTLE
BRAEMAR
9
Glen Gelder
601
Aucholzie
CLACHAN YELL 526
Forest of Glen Tanar
Mar Lodge
Forest of Mar
Claybokie
INVEREY
MAR LODGE ESTATE
Tomintoul
Ballochbuie Forest
LINN OF MUICK WATERFALL
LINN OF DEE
Muir
Inverey
Balintuim
Auchallater
DEESIDE AND LOCHNAGAR
Muick
Glen Muick
727 COCK CAIRN
742 HILL OF CAT
Dee
Geldie Burn
BALMORAL FOREST
674
818 CARN LIATH
Glen Ey
Ey Burn
Allt Connie
Callater Burn
1150 LOCHNAGAR
850 CONACHCRAIG
Allt-na-giubhsaich
SPITTAL OF GLENMUICK VISITOR CENTRE
Spittal of Glenmuick
939 MOUNT KEEN
721 FASHEILACH
Burn of Branny
Water of Tarf
Bynack Burn
Lochcallater Lodge
Loch Callater
Glen Callater
A93
834
Baddoch
Dubh Loch
Glas-allt Shiel
Glen Mark
Water of Mark
Glenmark
920 CARN BHAC
1012 CAIRN BANNOCH
998 BROAD CAIRN
Loch Muick
Glen Lee
696 MONAWEE
Invermark Lodge
Auchronie
Milton
Tarfside
939 AN SOCACH
14
1019 CARN AN TUIRC
958 TOLMOUNT
1048 BEINN IUTHARN MHOR
Cluni Water
Loch Vrotachan
GLENSHEE SKI CENTRE
Water of Unich
Loch Lee
Inchgrundle
Drumgreen
Tilt
Loch nan Eun
933 THE CAIRNWELL
832 LAIR OF ALDARARIE
Moulzie
Glen Doll
Glendoll Lodge
MUCKLE CAIRN 826
Glen Effock
PERTH
Devil's Elbow
1068 GLAS MAOL
Caenlochan Forest
Braedownie
Glendoll Forest
Loch Brandy
CRUYS 741
Water of Saughs
Loch Loch
1051 GLAS TULAICHEAN
905 FINALTY HILL
CORRIE FEE
691 WEST KNOCK
Isla
947 DRIESH
Glenlocksie Lodge
BEN GULABIN 806
Tulchan Lodge
758
Clova
778 WHITE HILL
1120 BEINN A'GHLO
291
Waterhead
Hunthill Lodge
AND
Glenlochsie
808 MONAMEANACH
Linns
B955
Wheen
ANGUS
903 BEN VUIRICH
Spittal of Glenshee
756 FINBRACKS
Gleann Fearnach
801 BEN EARB
Glenshee Lodge
Loch Beanie
Auchavan
Delnamer
Old Craig
Glenprosen Lodge
Kilburn
Rottal
Dalhenzean
740 BADENDUN HILL
Glen Prosen
Balnaboth
PROSEN
Glenprosen Village
794 MEALL UAINE
A93
Corrydon
702 DUCHRAY HILL
15
545 AULD DARKNEY
KINROSS
Glen Shee
512
Clachnabrain
Glen Clova
Dalnaglar Castle
Meikle Forter
Glenisla Forest
611
South Esk
Glenmoy
Dalnavaid
Tarvie
19
Straloch
Glen Brerachan
Enochdhu
STRATH
Cray
Lair
Folda
Glenmarkie Lodge
B955
Redheugh
Auchnacree
Glenogil
Deuchar
B951
744 MOUNT BLAIR
Brewlands Bridge
Backwater Res.
Glenhead Farm
Easter Lednathie
Glenquiech
Ogil
Fern
Ashintully Castle
Longdrum
Horniehaugh
Noranside
A924
641 NO'REAG DHUBH
Freuchies
668 CAT LAW
CAPTAIN SCOTT & DR WILSON CAIRN
Dykehead
Newmill of Inshewan
Kirkmichael
Blacklunans
Kirkton of Glenisla
24
Middle Balnald
286
13
520 CAIRN GIBBS
Bellaty
497 CREIGH HILL
Balintore
Pearsie
287
Memus
Tannadice
Edradour
EDRADOUR DISTILLERY
Milton of Edradour
BLAIR ATHOL DISTILLERY VISITOR CENTRE
534 MEALL REAMHAR
BALMYLE
444
Forest of Alyth
Dykends
Balloch
Inverquharity
Murthill
Shielhill
Finavon
Oathlaw
409 MILE HILL
B951
Kirkton of Kingoldrum
Kinnordy
Northmuir
0 2 4 6 miles
0 2 4 6 8 10 km
A B C D E F G H
1 2 3 4 5 6

Knockespock Ho.
Auchleven
Chapel of Garioch
Lethenty
Kirkton of Bourtie
Hattoncrook
Pettymuick
Culterculen
Foveran
Coldwells Croft
Bogs
Whitehaugh Forest
Lickleyhead Castle
BENNACHIE 528
Pittodrie
Newbigging
BATTLE OF HARLAW MEMORIAL
Mains of Blackhall
Inveramsay
Thalgardy
BRANDSBUTT STONE
Burgh Muir
Hillbrae
Whiterashes
Affleck
Woodlands
Udny Station
Tillycorthie
Tillygreig
Minnes
Rashierieve
Hatterseat
Muckletown
GARIOCH
Inverurie
Keith Hall
Hillhead
Nether Crimond
Tillykerrie
Ardo Ho.
Straloch
Delfrigs
ABERDEENSHIRE
Tullynessle
Terpersie Castle
Keig
Castle Forbes
Upper Woodend
Bograxie
Manar Ho.
Port Elphinstone
KINKELL CHURCH
Kinmuck
Middleton
Balbithan Ho.
Newmachar
Reisque
Middlemuir
Craigie
Causeyend
Drumhead
Bridge of Alford
Montgarrie
HAUGHTON
Rorandle
Pitfichie Forest
Burnhervie
Westerton
Lower Woodend
Don
Overton
Aquhythie
Blairdaff
Dalmadilly
Clovenstone
Burgh Muir
Balbithan
Wester Fintray
Cairnpark
Blackbraes
Kinmundy
Whitecairns
Belhelvie
BALMEDIE
Balmedie
GRAMPIAN TRANSPORT MUS
Alford
Gateside
Auchintoul
Muir of Alford
Asloun
Kingsford
HERITAGE MUSEUM
Whitehouse
Pitmunie
Pitfichie
Grantlodge
Upper Coullie
Kemnay
Cottown
Kintore
Hatton of Fintray
OLD CHURCH
Cothall
Drumligair
Potterton
Blackdog
Todlachie
Monymusk
Craigearn
Leschangie
Leylodge
Woodlands
Overton
Dyce
ABERDEEN
Parkhill Ho.
Corby Loch
Mundurno
Ley
Torries
Kirkton of Tough
Little Lynturk
Moor of Balvack
Causeyton
Cluny Castle
Lauchintilly
CASTLE FRASER
Letter
Glasgoforest
Muir of Kinellar
Blackburn
Muir of Fowlis
Bridgend
Tillyfourie
Ordhead
Sauchen
Lyne of Skene
Blackchambers
Haughs of Clinterty
ABERDEEN CITY
Stoneywood
Bankhead
Denmore
Milton of Cushnie
Tillyfour
Correnie Moor
Corrennie Forest
Achath
Bogentory
Chapel of Stoneywood
East Auchronie
Hayton
Bridge of Don
CRUICKSHANK BOTANIC GARDEN
Leochel Cushnie
CRAIGIEVAR CASTLE
Kintocher
Milton of Corsindae
Old Kinnernie
Dunecht
Skene Ho.
Newhills
Bucksburn
BRIG O' BALGOWNIE
ST MACHAR'S CATHEDRAL
Whiteknowes
Bankhead
Corsindae
Kirkton of Skene
Woodside
Old Aberdeen
KIRKWALL LERWICK
494 BENAQUHALLIE
Loch of Skene
Westhill
Kittybrewster
KING'S COLLEGE VISITOR CENTRE
Tillylo.
Tullochvenus
Midmar
STONE CIRCLE
Culfosie
Easter Culfosie
Northfield
Mastrick
Aberdeen
Altdargue
Comers
Tillybirloch
Marionburgh
Echt
Elrick
Kingswells
ABERDEEN SCIENCE CENTRE
Craskins
CULSH SOUTERRAIN
Perkhill
Tornaveen
Lurg
South Kirkton
Garlogie
Cairnie
Wester Ord
Easter Ord
GORDON HIGHLANDERS MUSEUM
Ferryhill
Girdle Ness
Wartle
Knowehead
Lumphanan
Findrack Ho.
Drumlasie
Midmar Forest
Redhill
Mannofield
Nigg Bay
Greg Ness
DAVID WELCH WINTER GARDENS
Torry
Kincorth
PEEL RING OF LUMPHANAN
Milton of Auchinhove
HILL OF FARE 433
Landerberry
Northton
Benthoul
Blacktop
Contlaw
Milton of Murtle
Cults
Bieldside
Ruthrieston
Garthdee
DOONIES FARM
Coull
Oldtown
Auchlossan
Burn of Corrichie
West Cullery
Holemill
Craigton
Banchory-Devenick
Nigg
Cove Bay
Torphins
SLUG OF DESS FALLS
Milton of Campfield
Milton of Cullerlie
Hardgate
Milltimber
Charlestown
Balnagowan
Mid Beltie
Hattonburn
Hirn
DRUM CASTLE
Peterculter
Coalford
Heathcot
Auchlunies
Aboyne
Kincardine O'Neil
Tillydrine
Brathens
Myrebird
Brucklebog
Drumoak
Mains of Drum
Kirkton of Maryculter
Burnhead
Hare Ness
Maryfield
Blainacraig Ho
Backhill of Trustach
Bridge of Canny
East Mains
Upper Lochton
The Neuk
CRATHES CASTLE AND GARDENS
Schoolhill
Hillside
Marywell
Findon Ness
Birsemore
Potarch
BANCHORY MUSEUM
Woodside of Arbeadie
Crathes
Badentoy Park
Findon
Portlethen Village
Birse
Ballogie
Marywell
Blackhall
Stranog
Muirskie
Auchlee
Portlethen
Burn of Cattie
Blackhall Forest
Arbeadie
Banchory
ROYAL DEESIDE RLY
Kirkton of Durris
Woodlands
Denside
Upper Burnhaugh
Downies
Cammachmore Bay
TOM'S CAIRN 310
Deebank
Auchattie
Bridge of Feugh
Crossroads
Cammachmore
Chapelton of Elsick
525 CARNFERG
Finzean Ho
Glencat
Tillygarmond
Belts of Collonach
Durris Forest
Borrowfield
Cookney
Newtonhill
Finzean
Boghead
Strachan
Blackness
Blairdryne
Netherley
Percie
Whitestone
Lochton
CAIRN MON EARN 378
Muchalls
Forest of Birse
Backburn
RAEDYKES ROMAN CAMP
Bridge of Muchalls
Water of Feugh
Union Cottage
Garrol Hill
376 MONGOUR
617
Water of Aven
Water of Dye
Burn of Sheeoch
Mergie
Rickarton
Garron Pt.
MOUNT SHADE 507
534 KERLOCH
Cowie Water
Cowie
Kirktown of Fetteresso
Glendye Lodge
Bridge of Dye
TOLBOOTH MUSEUM
Tewel
Fetteresso Forest
Stonehaven
Burn of Tennet
778 MOUNT BATTOCK
Glen Dye
Tannachie
Carmont
New Mill
Castle Haven
DUNNOTTAR CASTLE
Thornyhive Bay
Drumtochty Forest
464
Mains of Dellavaird
525 MELUNCART
BURNS FAMILY MEMORIALS
Glenfarquhar Lodge
Fiddes
Drumlithie
FOWLSHEUGH
Blackcraigs
Drumtochty Castle
Glenbervie
Barras
Mill of Uras
Crawton
Cairn o' Mount
Pitforthie
THE RETREAT GLEN ESK FOLK MUS
Millden Lodge
Strath Finella
Monboddo House
Mondynes
Roadside of Catterline
Crawton Bay
Dalhastnie
Clatterin Bridge
Glensaugh
Auchenblae
Cocketty
Catterline
Braidon Bay
Holmhead
Brownmuir
Todhead Point
East Cairnbeg
Roadside of Kinneff
North Esk
Fordoun
Parkneuk
Arbuthnott
Auchmull
Mains of Balnakettle
Thainston
Craigmoston
GRASSIC GIBBON CENTRE
ARBUTHNOTT CHURCH
Kinneff
FETTERCAIRN DISTILLERY VISITOR CENTRE
Howe of the Mearns
Davo Mains
ARBUTHNOTT HOUSE GARDENS
Mains of Allardice
678 HILL OF WIRREN
Fettercairn
Scotston
Little John's Haven
Balbegno Castle
West Burnside
Bent
Haulkerton
Inverbervie
Mains of Thornton
Tulloch
Bervie Bay
Dalbog
Meikle Strath
Laurencekirk
Inch of Arnhall
Garvock
Gannochy
Witton
Sauchieburn
Garvock Hill
Redford
Gourdon
Craigendowie
EDZELL CASTLE AND GARDENS
Johnstone Mains
Benholm
Bridgend
Balfield
Edzell
Luthermuir
Luther Water
Dykelands
West Water
Dunlappie
440
Johnshaven
Ilyarblet
North Water Bridge
Mains of Kirktonhill
Bush
Rome
North Esk
Marykirk
Milton of Mathers
Ledmore
Inchbare
Pert
Ecclesgreig
West Mathers
Kirkton of Menmuir
Tigerton
Newtonmill
Craigo
Lochside
St Cyrus
Milton Ness
Balrownie
Logie Pert
Logie
Morphie
Balnamoon
Keithock
Muirton of Ballochy
North Craigo
Mains of Balhall
Lochty
Belliehill
Little Brechin
Pathhead
ST CYRUS
West Muir
Trinity
Hillside
Careston
Brechin
Kirkhill
HOUSE OF DUN
Maltings
BRECHIN CASTLE CENTRE
Dun
CALEDONIAN RAILWAY
Careston Castle
CATHEDRAL ROUND TOWER
South Esk
Bridge of Dun
Montrose Basin
Montrose
Aldbar Castle
Barnhead
MUSEUM AND ART GALLERY
Netherton
Kinnaird Castle
Inchbraoch
Scurdie Ness
Mains of Melgund
Middle Drums
MONTROSE BASIN VISITOR CENTRE
WILLIAM LAMB MEMORIAL STUDIO
Crosston
ABERLEMNO SCULPTURED STONES
Aberlemno
Farnell
Bolshan
Maryton
Ferryden
Kirkton of Craig

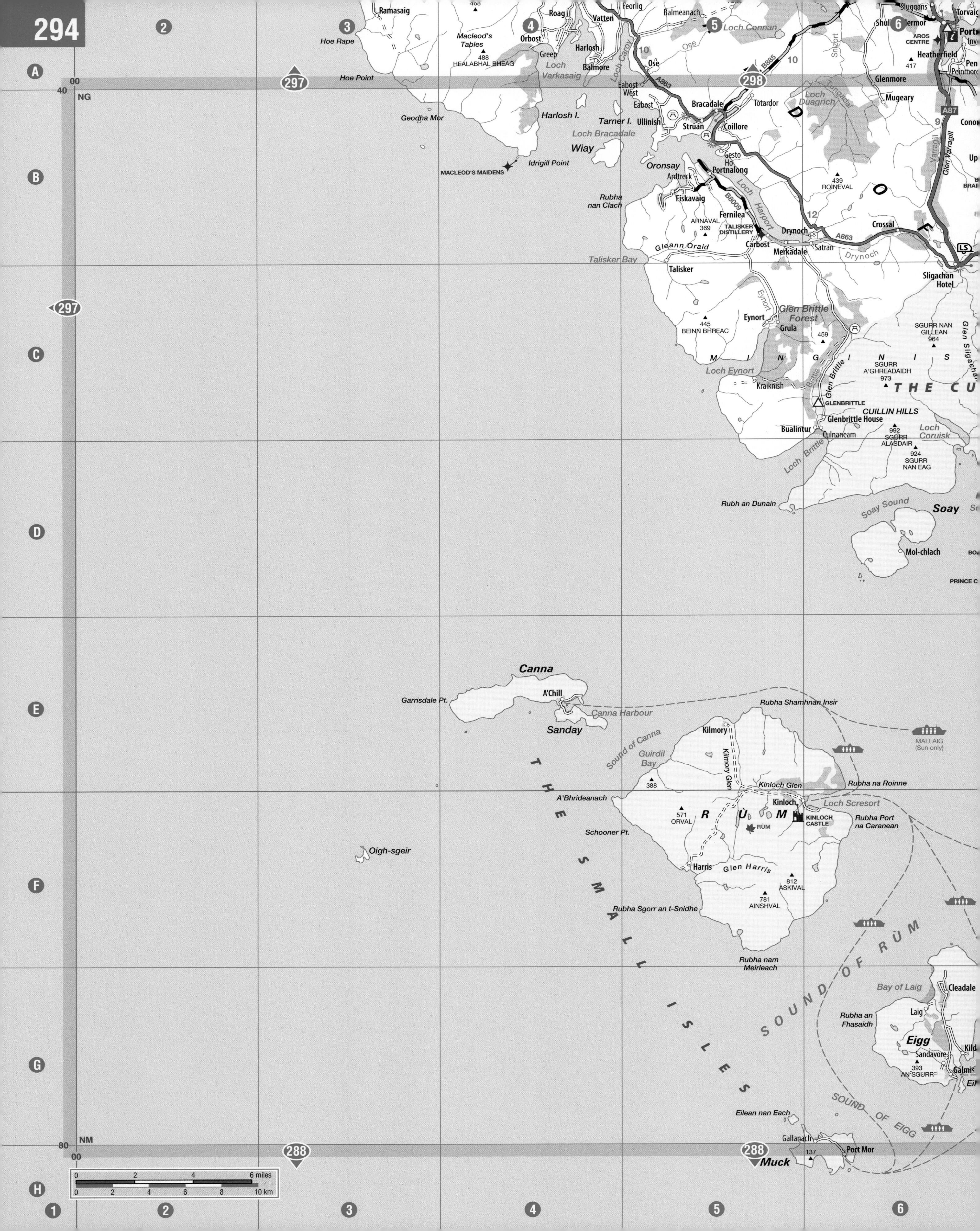
Ramasaig
Hoe Rape
Hoe Point
Macleod's Tables
488
HEALABHAL BHEAG
Roag
Orbost
Greep
Loch Varkasaig
Harlosh
Balmore
Vatten
Feorlig
Balmeanach
Loch Connan
Loch Caroy
Ose
Eabost West
Eabost
A863
B885
Bracadale
Totardor
Loch Duagrich
Tungadal
Glenmore
Mugeary
Heatherfield
Sluggans
Torvaig
Portree
AROS CENTRE
417
Peinmore
A87
Glen Varragill
Varragill
Geodha Mor
Harlosh I.
Tarner I.
Ullinish
Struan
Coillore
Loch Bracadale
Wiay
Idrigill Point
MACLEOD'S MAIDENS
Oronsay
Gesto Ho
Portnalong
Ardtreck
Fiskavaig
Loch Harport
B8009
Rubha nan Clach
439
ROINEVAL
Fernilea
ARNAVAL
369
TALISKER DISTILLERY
Carbost
Drynoch
Crossal
Merkadale
Satran
Drynoch
Gleann Oraid
Talisker Bay
Talisker
Sligachan Hotel
Eynort
Glen Brittle Forest
Grula
445
BEINN BHREAC
459
SGURR NAN GILLEAN
964
Glen Sligachan
SGURR A'GHREADAIDH
973
M I N G I N I S
THE CU
Loch Eynort
Kraiknish
Glen Brittle
GLENBRITTLE
CUILLIN HILLS
Glenbrittle House
Bualintur
Culnaneam
992
SGURR ALASDAIR
924
SGURR NAN EAG
Loch Coruisk
Loch Brittle
Rubh an Dunain
Soay Sound
Soay
Mol-chlach
PRINCE C
Canna
A'Chill
Garrisdale Pt.
Canna Harbour
Sanday
Rubha Shamhnan Insir
MALLAIG (Sun only)
Kilmory
Sound of Canna
Guirdil Bay
Kilmory Glen
388
Kinloch Glen
Rubha na Roinne
A'Bhrideanach
Kinloch
Loch Scresort
571
ORVAL
R Ù M
RÙM
KINLOCH CASTLE
Rubha Port na Caranean
Schooner Pt.
Oigh-sgeir
Harris
Glen Harris
812
ASKIVAL
781
AINSHVAL
Rubha Sgorr an t-Snidhe
THE SMALL ISLES
Rubha nam Meirleach
SOUND OF RÙM
Bay of Laig
Cleadale
Laig
Rubha an Fhasaidh
Eigg
Sandavore
393
AN SGURR
Galmisdale
SOUND OF EIGG
Eilean nan Each
Gallanach
137
Port Mor
Muck
NG
NM
297
298
288
0 2 4 6 miles
0 2 4 6 8 10 km
A B C D E F G H
1 2 3 4 5 6

ISLAND OF RAASAY
INNER SOUND
Glame
Balmeanach
Balachuirn
Holoman Bay
Camastianavaig
Tianavaig Bay
Oskaig
Lower Ollach
Raasay Ho.
Clachan
RAASAY OUTDOOR CENTRE
Ollach
The Braes
Narrows of Raasay
Inverarish
North Fearns
East Suisnish
Eyre Point
Eyre
Caol Mór
Balmeanach
Peinchorran
Loch Sligachan
Sconser
GLAMAIG 775
Moll
Scalpay
Corran a Chan Uachdaraich
Scalpay Ho.
Loch Ainort
Luib
Dunan
Caolas Scalpay
Guillamon I.
Pabay
Longay
Crowlin Islands
Eilean Mór
Caolas Mór
Eilean na Bà
Rubha na'Leac
DUN CAAN
443
385
Applecross
Milton
Camusteel
Camusterrach
Ard-dhubh
Culduie
Ardban
Toscaig
Uags
BEALACH NA BA
MEALL GORM 710
BEINN BHAN 896
Couldoran
Rassal
Tornapress
Sanachan
Russel
Glen Mor
Slumbay
Lochcarron
Kirkton
Tullich
New Kelso
Strathcarron
Achintee
Attadale Ho. GARDEN
Attadale
Ardarroch
Achintraid
Loch Kishorn
Kishorn I.
Reraig Cot
STROME CASTLE
Stromemore
Ardnarff
Ardaneaskan
Stromeferry
LOCH CARRON
An Dubh-aird
Plockton
Achmore
Braeintra
Port Cam
Duirinish
Drumbuie
Achnandarach
Erbusaig
Badicaul
Black Is.
Kyle of Lochalsh
Kyleakin
CASTLE MOIL
BRIGHT WATER VISITOR CENTRE
Balmacara Square
Balmacara
LOCHALSH WOODLAND GARDEN
Reraig
Kirkton
Auchertyre
Nostie
Ardelve
Avernish
Glas Eilean
LOCH ALSH
Dornie
EILEAN DONAN CASTLE
Totaig
Ardintoul Pt.
Ardintoul
Letterfearn
Keppoch
Conchra
Bundalloch
Carndu
Allt-nan-sugh
Sallachy
Gleann Udalain
Loch Long
Camas-luinie
Killilan
Faddonch
Glen Elchaig
Loch nan Eun
SGUMAN COINNTICH 879
CARN NAN IOMAIREAN 486
Loch an Iasaich
Attadale Forest
Bendronaig Lodge
Carnach
Loch na Leitreach
FALLS OF GLOMACH
Skye
RED HILLS
Broadford Bay
Waterloo
Ashaig
Lower Breakish
Upper Breakish
Corry
Broadford
Harrapool
Old Corry
INTERNATIONAL OTTER SURVIVAL FUND
Skulamus
GLAS BHEINN MHOR 570
BLA BHEINN 928
Loch na Crèitheach
Torrin
Suardal
Kilbride
Faoilean
Strathaird
Kirkibost
Kilmarie
BEN MEABOST 346
Loch Slapin
Strath
Heast
Suisnish
Rubha Suisnish
Elgol
Glasnakille
Loch Eishort
Ord
DUNSCAITH CASTLE
Tokavaig
Rubha na h-Easgainne
Tarskavaig
Tarskavaig Pt.
Achnacloich
SGURR NA COINNICH 739
KYLERHEA OTTER HAVEN
Glen Arroch
Allt Mór
Kylerhea
Kyle Rhea
BEN ASLAK 610
Kinloch
Drumfearn
Loch na Dal
Duisdalemore
Duisdalebeg
Camuscross
Isleornsay
Ornsay
Sandaig Is.
Teangue
Sasaig
KNOCK CASTLE
Knock Bay
Ferindonald
Kilbeg
Kilmore
Armadale Castle
Glen Meadhonach
CLAN DONALD CENTRE
ARMADALE GARDENS
Armadale Bay
Calligarry
Ardvasar
Rubha Charn nan Cearc
Aird of Sleat
Tormore
Ard Thurinish
Point of Sleat
SLEAT
SOUND OF SLEAT
Bernera
Galltair
Glenelg
BERNERA BARRACKS
Glenelg Bay
Scallasaig
Còsag
Eilanreach
GLENELG BROCHS
Cnoc Fhionn
Glen More
Balvraid
Abhainn a' Ghlinne Bhig
Upper Sandaig
BEINN A' CHAPAILL 742
BEINN SGRITHEALL 974
BEINN NAN CAORACH 774
Arnisdale
Glen Arnisdale
Corran
LOCH HOURN
BEINN A' CHUIRN 603
SGURR AN AIRGID 841
Inverinate
Loch Duich
Dorusduain
Ruarach
Morvich
Carn-gorm
Ault a'chruinn
Ratagan
Invershiel
Shiel Bridge
KINTAIL
Kintail Forest
Glenlicht Ho.
FIVE SISTERS 1067
BEINN FADA OR BEN ATTOW 1032
GLEN SHIEL
Glenshiel Forest
THE SADDLE 1010
SGURR AN LOCHAIN 1004
Kinlochhourn Forest
DRUIM FADA 713
BUIDHE BHEINN 879
SGURR THIONAIL 906
Kinloch Hourn
Glen Quoich
Alltbeithe
HIGHLAND
KNOYDART
Rubha Ard Slisneach
Inverguseran
BEINN NA CAILLICH 785
Barrisdale Bay
Airor
Glen Barrisdale
SGURR A' MHAORAICH 1027
LADHAR BHEINN 1020
Gleann na Guiserein
Abhainn Chosaidh
LOCH QUOICH
Sandaig
Sandaig Bay
Scottas
LUINNE BHEINN 939
Gleann an Dubh-Lochain
Inverie
Inverie Bay
Rubha Raonuill
GAIRICH 919
MEALL BUIDHE 946
MALLAIG HERITAGE CENTRE
Mallaig
Mallaig Bheag
CANNA (Sun only)
LOCHBOISDALE
BEINN BHUIDHE 855
SGURR MOR 1003
Camusrory
Carnach
SGURR NA CICHE 1040
Glasnacardoch
LOCH NEVIS
Kylesknoydart
Beoraidbeg
Stoul
Bracara
Bracorina
Tarbet
Kylesmorar
North Morar
Morar
Glenancross
Garamor
Brinacory
Swordland
Glen Dessarry
SGURR MHURLAGAIN 880
Meallaggan
Strathan
Kinlochmorar
CARN MOR 829
Glen Pean
Traigh Ho.
Scamadale
LOCH MORAR
Portnaluchaig
Lettermorar
Oban
AN STAC 718
Bunacaimb
Eilean Ighe
Back of Keppoch
South Morar
Gortenacullish
Kinloid
Meoble
Luinga Bheag
Luinga Mhor
Arisaig
Loch nan Ceall
SIDHEAN MOR 599
MEITH BHEINN 710
SGURR NAN COIREACHAN 965
SGURR THUILM 963
Gleann Camgharaidh
GAOR BHEINN 987
Rumach
Druimindarroch
LOCH NAN UAMH CAIRN
Loch Beoraid
Kinlochbeoraid
Glenfinnan Lodge
Glen Dubh Lighe
Gleann Suileag
Chathastail
(April-Sept)
Loch nan Uamh
Polnish
Arieniskill
SGURR AN UTHA 796
MORAR, MOIDART AND ARDNAMURCHAN
SOUND OF ARISAIG
Lochailort
Ranochan
Loch Eilt
STATION MUSEUM
GLENFINNAN MONUMENT
Wauchan
Ardnish
Inverailort
Glenfinnan
Kinlocheil
Fassfern
Eilean nan Gobhar
Laggan
Loch Ailort
Alisary
DRUIM FIACLACH 869
Callop
Drumsallie
LOCH EIL
Samalaman I.
Glenuig Bay
Roshven
ROIS-BHEINN 882
BEINN ODHAR BHEAG 882
Smirisary
Glenuig
Guesachan
South Garvan
Duisky
A87
A851
A830
A861
A890
A896
B8083
B8008
B883
298
299
289
290
NG
NM

SOUTH LEWIS, HARRIS AND NORTH UIST
NA HEARADH (HARRIS)
UIBHIST A TUATH (NORTH UIST)
BEINN NA FAOGHLA (BENBECULA)
CAOLAS NA HEARADH
AN CAOLAS MHONACH
LOCH DUNVEGAN
ST KILDA
St Kilda or Hirta (Hiort)
Boreray
Soay
Tarasaigh (Taransay)
Pabaidh (Pabbay)
Eilean Bhearnaraigh (Berneray)
Baile Sear (Baleshare)
Na h-eileanan Monach (Heisker or Monach Islands)
Griomasaigh (Grimsay)
Loch nam Madadh (Lochmaddy)
Tairbeart (Tarbert)
An t-Ob (Leverburgh)
Kirkibost Island
Haskeir I.
Haskeir Eagach
Shillay
Little Shillay
Vallay
Oronsay
Ensay
Killegray
Ronay
Hermetray
Coppay
Stockinish I.
Lingarabay I.
A859
A865
A867
B893
305
298
UIG

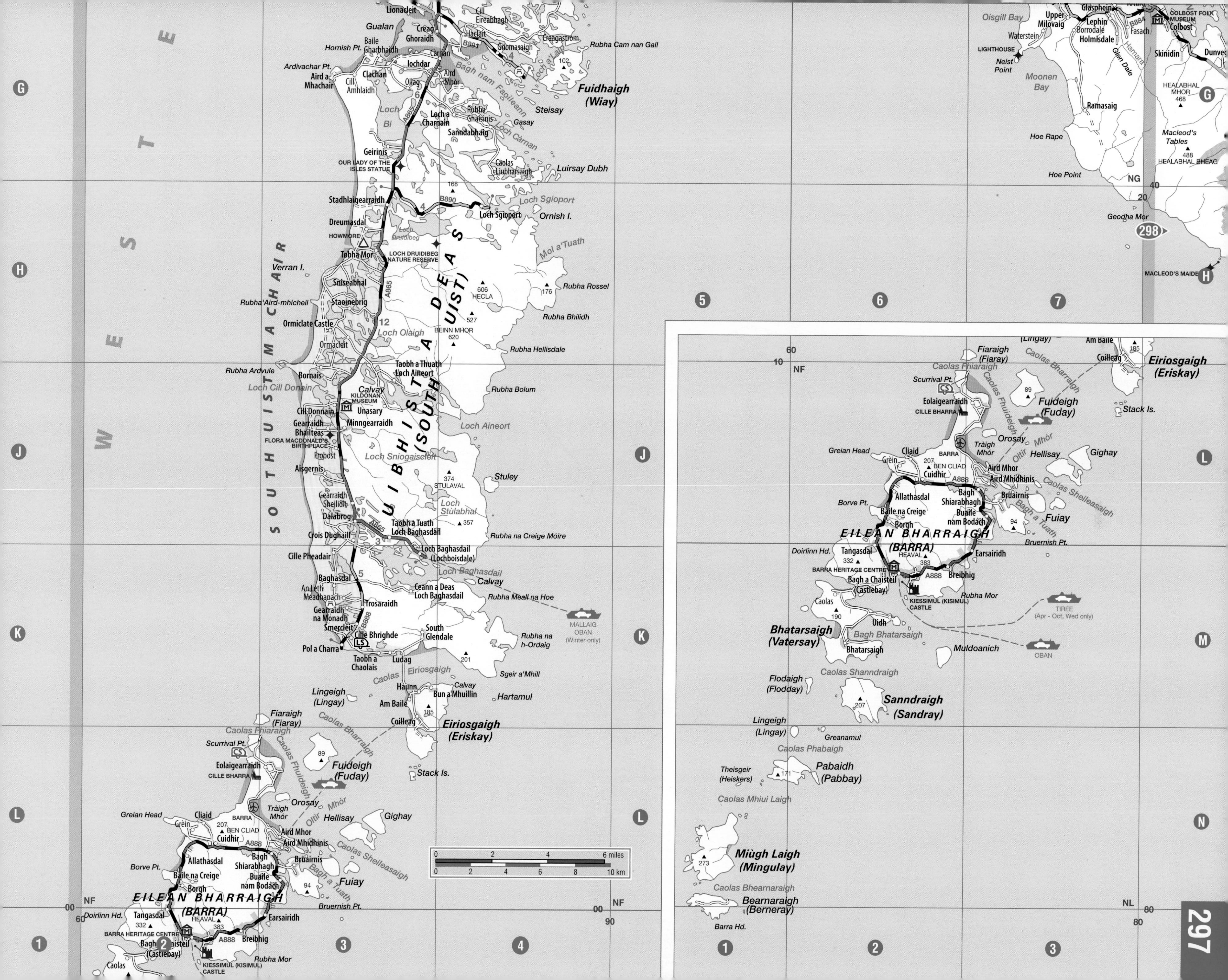

UIBHIST A DEAS (SOUTH UIST)
SOUTH UIST MACHAIR
WEST
Lionacleit
Gualan
Creag Ghoraidh
Cill Eireabhagh
Haclait
Gramasaigh
Creagastrom
Rubha Cam nan Gall
Hornish Pt.
Baile Gharbhaidh
Iochdar
Carnan
Ardivachar Pt.
Aird a Mhachair
Clachan
Cill Amhlaidh
Olaig
Aird Mhor
Bagh nam Faoileann
Fuidhaigh (Wiay)
Steisay
Loch Bi
Loch a Charnain
Rubha Ghaisinis
Gasay
Sanndabhaig
Loch Carnan
Geirinis
OUR LADY OF THE ISLES STATUE
Caolas Luibharsaigh
Luirsay Dubh
Stadhlaigearraidh
Loch Sgioport
Ornish I.
Dreumasdal
HOWMORE
Tobha Mor
LOCH DRUIDIBEG NATURE RESERVE
Mol a'Tuath
Verran I.
Snìseabhal
HECLA
Rubha Rossel
Rubha'Aird-mhicheil
Staoinebrig
Rubha Bhilidh
Ormiclate Castle
Loch Olaigh
BEINN MHOR
Ormacleit
Rubha Hellisdale
Rubha Ardvule
Bornais
Taobh a Thuath Loch Aineort
Loch Cill Donain
Calvay
KILDONAN MUSEUM
Rubha Bolum
Cill Donnain
Unasary
Gearraidh Bhailteas
Minngearraidh
Loch Aineort
FLORA MACDONALD'S BIRTHPLACE
Frobost
Loch Sniogaisceit
Aisgernis
Stuley
STULAVAL
Gearraidh Sheilidh
Loch Stùlabhal
Dalabrog
Taobh a Tuath Loch Baghasdail
Crois Dughaill
Rubha na Creige Móire
Cille Pheadair
Loch Baghasdail (Lochboisdale)
Loch Baghasdail
Calvay
Baghasdal
An Leth Meadhanach
Ceann a Deas Loch Baghasdail
Rubha Meall na Hoe
Gearraidh na Monadh
Trosaraidh
Smercleit
MALLAIG OBAN (Winter only)
Cille Bhrighde
South Glendale
Rubha na h-Ordaig
Pol a Charra
Taobh a Chaolais
Ludag
Sgeir a'Mhill
Caolas Eiriosgaigh
Lingeigh (Lingay)
Haunn
Calvay
Bun a'Mhuillin
Hartamul
Am Baile
Coilleag
Eiriosgaigh (Eriskay)
Fiaraigh (Fiaray)
Caolas Fhiaraigh
Caolas Bharraigh
Scurrival Pt.
Eolaigearraidh
CILLE BHARRA
Caolas Fhuideigh
Fuideigh (Fuday)
Stack Is.
Orosay
Tràigh Mhór
Oitir Mhór
Greian Head
Cliaid
Grein
BARRA
BEN CLIAD
Cuidhir
Hellisay
Gighay
Aird Mhor
Aird Mhidhinis
Caolas Sheileasaigh
Allathasdal
Bagh Shiarabhagh
Bruairnis
Borve Pt.
Baile na Creige
Buaile nam Bodach
Borgh
Bagh a Tuath
Fuiay
EILEAN BHARRAIGH (BARRA)
Bruernish Pt.
Dorlinn Hd.
Tangasdal
HEAVAL
Earsairidh
BARRA HERITAGE CENTRE
Bagh a Chaisteil (Castlebay)
Breibhig
Rubha Mor
Caolas
KIESSIMUL (KISIMUL) CASTLE
Oisgill Bay
Upper Milovaig
Glaspheìn
Lephin
Borrodale
Holmisdale
Fasach
COLBOST FOLK MUSEUM
Colbost
Skinidin
Dunvegan
LIGHTHOUSE
Waterstein
Neist Point
Glen Dale
Hamara
Moonen Bay
HEALABHAL MHOR
Ramasaig
Hoe Rape
Macleod's Tables
HEALABHAL BHEAG
Hoe Point
Geodha Mor
298
MACLEOD'S MAIDENS
TIREE (Apr - Oct, Wed only)
OBAN
Uidh
Bhatarsaigh (Vatersay)
Bagh Bhatarsaigh
Bhatarsaigh
Muldoanich
Caolas Shanndraigh
Flodaigh (Flodday)
Sanndraigh (Sandray)
Lingeigh (Lingay)
Greanamul
Caolas Phabaigh
Theisgeir (Heiskers)
Pabaidh (Pabbay)
Caolas Mhiui Laigh
Miùgh Laigh (Mingulay)
Caolas Bhearnaraigh
Bearnaraigh (Berneray)
Barra Hd.
0 2 4 6 miles
0 2 4 6 8 10 km

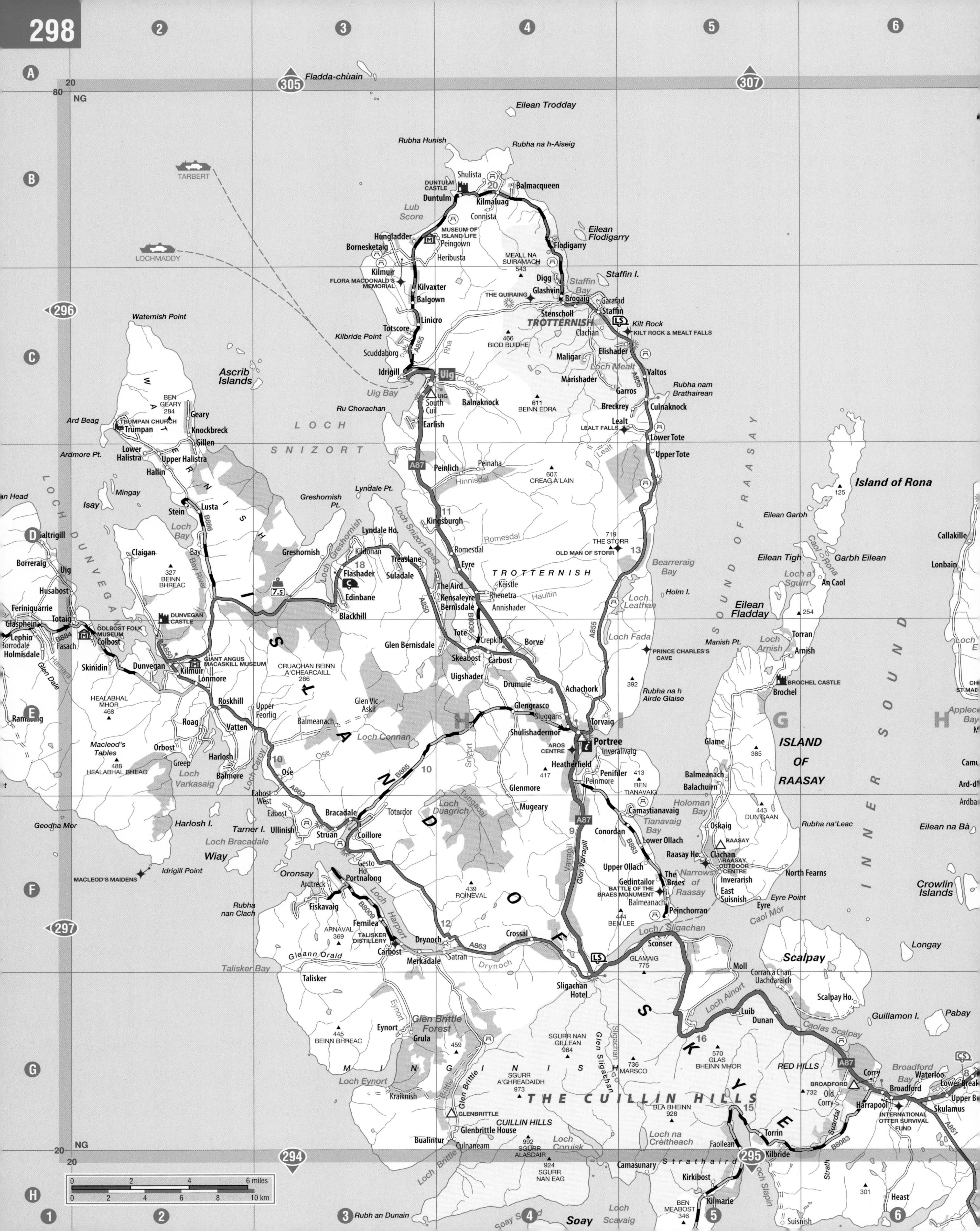

Fladda-chùain
Eilean Trodday
Rubha Hunish
Rubha na h-Aiseig
TARBERT
Shulista
DUNTULM CASTLE
Duntulm
Balmacqueen
Kilmaluag
Lub Score
Connista
Eilean Flodigarry
Hungladder
MUSEUM OF ISLAND LIFE
Peingown
Borneskeitaig
Flodigarry
LOCHMADDY
Heribusta
MEALL NA SUIRAMACH 543
Kilmuir
FLORA MACDONALD'S MEMORIAL
Staffin I.
Kilvaxter
Digg
Staffin Bay
Balgown
THE QUIRAING
Glashvin
Brogaig
Garafad
Staffin
Stenscholl
Waternish Point
TROTTERNISH
Linicro
Kilt Rock
Totscore
KILT ROCK & MEALT FALLS
Clachan
Kilbride Point
466 BIOD BUIDHE
Scuddaborg
Elishader
Maligar
Loch Mealt
Ascrib Islands
Idrigill
Uig
Conon
Valtos
Marishader
Uig Bay
South Cuil
Garros
Rubha nam Brathairean
BEN GEARY 284
Geary
Balnaknock
611 BEINN EDRA
Ru Chorachan
Breckrey
Culnaknock
Ard Beag
TRUMPAN CHURCH
Trumpan
Knockbreck
Earlish
LOCH
Lealt
LEALT FALLS
Lower Tote
Gillen
Lower Halistra
Upper Halistra
SNIZORT
Ardmore Pt.
Upper Tote
Hallin
Peinlich
Peinaha
Hinnisdal
607 CREAG A' LAIN
Mingay
Lyndale Pt.
Island of Rona
Greshornish Pt.
Isay
Stein
Lusta
Loch Bay
Kingsburgh
Eilean Garbh
Lyndale Ho.
Galtrigill
Claigan
Greshornish
Kildonan
Romesdal
719 THE STORR
OLD MAN OF STORR
Callakille
Treaslane
Bay
Borreraig
Uig
327 BEINN BHREAC
Flashader
Suladale
Eyre
TROTTERNISH
Bearreraig Bay
Eilean Tigh
Garbh Eilean
Lonbain
Loch a' Sguirr
An Caol
Husabost
Edinbane
The Aird
Keistle
Kensaleyre
Rhenetra
Haultin
Holm I.
Feriniquarrie
DUNVEGAN CASTLE
Blackhill
Bernisdale
Annishader
Loch Leathan
Eilean Fladday
Totaig
Glasphein
COLBOST FOLK MUSEUM
Colbost
Lephin
Fasach
Borrodale
Holmisdale
Glen Bernisdale
Tote
Crepkill
Borve
Loch Fada
Manish Pt.
Torran
Loch Arnish
Arnish
GIANT ANGUS MACASKILL MUSEUM
Skeabost
Carbost
PRINCE CHARLES'S CAVE
Glen Dale
Skinidin
Dunvegan
Kilmuir
Lonmore
CRUACHAN BEINN A'CHEARCAILL 266
Uigshader
Drumuie
392
BROCHEL CASTLE
Brochel
Achachork
Rubha na h Airde Glaise
HEALABHAL MHOR 468
Roskhill
Upper Feorlig
Glen Vic Askil
Glengrasco
Sluggans
Ramasaig
Roag
Vatten
Balmeanach
Loch Connan
Shulishadermor
Torvaig
Portree
Glame
ISLAND OF RAASAY
AROS CENTRE
Inveralivaig
Macleod's Tables
Orbost
385
488 HEALABHAL BHEAG
Greep
Harlosh
Ose
Heatherfield
Penifiler
413 BEN TIANAVAIG
Balmeanach
Balachuirn
Loch Varkasaig
Balmore
417
Peinmore
Glenmore
Eabost West
Eabost
Holoman Bay
443 DUN CAAN
Loch Duagrich
Mugeary
Camastianavaig
Rubha na'Leac
Harlosh I.
Tarner I.
Ullinish
Bracadale
Totardor
Tianavaig Bay
Geodha Mor
Eilean na Bà
Struan
Coillore
Conordan
Oskaig
Loch Bracadale
Lower Ollach
RAASAY
Wiay
Raasay Ho.
Clachan
Gesto Ho.
RAASAY OUTDOOR CENTRE
MACLEOD'S MAIDENS
Idrigill Point
Oronsay
Portnalong
Upper Ollach
The Braes
North Fearns
Ardtreck
Gedintailor
BATTLE OF THE BRAES MONUMENT
Narrows of Raasay
Inverarish
Crowlin Islands
439 ROINEVAL
East Suisnish
Fiskavaig
Balmeanach
Eyre
Eyre Point
Rubha nan Clach
Fernilea
444 BEN LEE
Peinchorran
Caol Mòr
ARNAVAL 369
TALISKER DISTILLERY
Loch Harport
Drynoch
Crossal
Loch Sligachan
Sconser
Longay
Gleann Oraid
Carbost
Satran
Merkadale
Drynoch
GLAMAIG 775
Scalpay
Talisker Bay
Moll
Corran a Chan Uachdaraich
Talisker
Sligachan Hotel
Loch Ainort
Scalpay Ho.
Glen Brittle Forest
Eynort
Luib
Dunan
Guillamon I.
Pabay
445 BEINN BHREAC
Grula
SGURR NAN GILLEAN 964
Glen Sligachan
Caolas Scalpay
459
570 GLAS BHEINN MHOR
736 MARSCO
RED HILLS
Broadford Bay
Corry
Waterloo
Lower Breakish
Loch Eynort
SGURR A'GHREADAIDH 973
THE CUILLIN HILLS
BROADFORD
Broadford
732
Old Corry
Upper Breakish
Kraiknish
Glen Brittle
BLA BHEINN 928
Harrapool
Skulamus
GLENBRITTLE
INTERNATIONAL OTTER SURVIVAL FUND
CUILLIN HILLS
Loch na Crèitheach
Glenbrittle House
Suardal
Torrin
Bualintur
Loch Coruisk
Faoilean
Culnaneam
992 SGURR ALASDAIR
Strathaird
Kilbride
924 SGURR NAN EAG
Camasunary
Loch Brittle
Kirkibost
Loch Slapin
Strath
301
Heast
BEN MEABOST 346
Kilmarie
Rubh an Dunain
Soay Sound
Soay
Loch Scavaig
Suisnish
INNER SOUND
SOUND OF RAASAY
LOCH DUNVEGAN
WATERNISH
ISLAND OF SKYE
MINGINISH
A87
A855
A850
A863
B885
B886
B884
B8036
B883
B8009
B8083
A851
305
307
296
297
294
295
0 2 4 6 miles
0 2 4 6 8 10 km

WESTER ROSS
Poolewe
Gairloch
GAIRLOCH MUSEUM
LOCH GAIRLOCH
Charlestown
Port Henderson
Badachro
Opinan
South Erradale
Redpoint
Shieldaig
Kerrysdale
Londubh
INVEREWE GARDEN
Naast
Tournaig
Brae
Rubha 'Ard na Bà
Aird Dubh
North Erradale
Big Sand
Port Erradale
Rubha Bàn
Longa Island
Caolas Beag
CARN DEARG
Lonemore
Smithstown
Mial
Strath
Loch Bad a' Chreamh
Loch Kernsary
Kernsary
Inveran
Loch Tollaidh
MEALL AN DOIREAN 420
Ardlair
791 BEINN AIRIGH CHARR
FIONN LOCH
Dubh Loch
LOCH MAREE
LOCH MAREE ISLANDS
Eilean Subhainn
Letterewe
Letterewe Forest
Furnace
Talladale
VICTORIA FALLS
Loch Bad an Sgalaig
Dubh Loch
Loch Clàir
Kerry
Erradale
Abhainn Braigh-horrisdale
Loch Gaineamhach
Flowerdale
Forest
875 BAOSBHEINN Forest
Loch na h-Oidhche
Shieldaig
624 BEINN BHREAC
Loch a' Bhealaich
Craig
Glen Grudie
Loch Garbhaig
980 SLIOCH
Lochan Fada
1019 MULLACH COIRE MHIC FHEARCHAIR
860 BEINN LAIR
680 BEINN A'CHAISGEIN BEAG
Fisherfield Forest
908 BEINN DEARG MHOR
914 BEINN A' CHLAIDHEIMH
Strath na Sealga
Loch na Sealga
Dundonnell
Achneigie
Forest
Fain
Auchindrean
Braemore
CORRIESHALLOCH GORGE
Inverbroom
Auchlunachan
Clachan
Braemore Forest
Loch a'Bhraoin
934
1110 SGURR MOR
999 A'CHAILLEACH
748 GROBAN
807
949 MEALL GORM
Fannich
Forest
Abhainn a'Chadh'Bhuidhe
BEINN NAN RAMH 711
LOCH FANNICH
Fannich Lodge
Strath Chrombuill
Lochrosque Forest
Kinlochewe Forest
Heights of Kinlochewe
Leckie
692
Taagan
Anancaun
Incheril
Kinlochewe
Cromasaig
Glen Docherty
Badavanich
Achnasheen
Dosmuckeran
ROSS
933 FIONN BHEINN
Abhainn Bruachaig
878
Kinlochewe Forest
BEINN EIGHE
1010 BEINN EIGHE
985 BEINN ALLIGIN
Rubha na Fearn
Fearnmore
Fearnbeg
Arinacrinachd
Reaulay
Cuaig
Kenmore
Loch a' Chracaich
Loch Torridon
Lower Diabaig
Upper Diabaig
Alligin Shuas
Rechullin
Inveralligin
Torridon Ho.
Torridon Forest
1054 LIATHACH
Glen Torridon
Fasag
TORRIDON
Torridon VISITOR CENTRE
Annat
Balgy
Ardheslaig
Loch Shieldaig
Upper Loch Torridon
Shieldaig
Abhainn Thrail
Loch Clair
Coulin Lodge
Loch Coulin
782 SGURR DUBH
Coulin
Coulin Forest
Abhainn Dubh
Loch a'Chroisg
Ledgowan Forest
Ledgowan
Loch Gowan
550 CARN-BEAG
538 CARN MHARTUIN
Abhainn Chuaig
Allt na h-Eirigh
Loch Gaineamhach
493 CROIC-BHEINN
Abhainn Dubh
Ben-damph Forest
BEN SHIELDAIG 439
Loch Damh
Loch an Eoin
678 CARN BREAC
Glen Carron
Loch Sgamhain
Scardroy
Loch Beannacharain
626 BEINN A'CHLACHAIN
Glenshieldaig Forest
Loch Lundie
513
902 BEINN DAMH
993 MAOL CHEAN-DEARG
907
Ashnashellach Lodge
Craig
Glencarron Lodge
928
Glencarron and Glenuig Forest
Glenuaig Lodge
Glen Fhiodhaig
849 BAC AN EICH
Loch a Caoidhe
HARTFIELD HOUSE
Hartfield
Applecross Ho.
Applecross Forest
Applecross
Camusterrach
Culduie
BEALACH NA BA
710 MEALL GORM
896 BEINN BHAN
Couldoran
Kinloch Damph
Loch Coultrie
Abhainn Dearg
Lair
Achnashellach Forest
Loch Dughaill
Balnacra
Coulags
Arineckaig
862
1053
1007 MAOILE LUNNDAIDH
814
Tullich
New Kelso
Strathcarron
Achintee
Kirkton
Rassal
Tornapress
Russel
Sanachan
Glen Mor
Slumbay
Lochcarron
Ardarroch
Achintraid
Loch Kishorn
Kishorn I.
Toscaig
Reraig
Cot
STROME CASTLE
Stromemore
Ardaneaskan
LOCH CARRON
Stromeferry
Ardnarff
Attadale Ho. GARDEN
Attadale
594
Bendronaig Lodge
Loch Calavie
West Monar Forest
Loch an Laoigh
LURG MHOR 986
Loch Monar
Monar Lodge
East Monar Forest
An Gead Loch
Loch an Tachdaidh
Uisge Misgeach
Attadale Forest
Loch Cruoshie
Loch an Iasaich
706 AN CRUACHAN
1086 AN RIABHACHAN
1150 SGURR NA LAPAICH
Killilan Forest
AONACH BUIDHE 899
1069
East Benula Forest
Loch Mullardoch
Glen Cannich
Uags
Caolas Mòr
An Dubh-aird
Plockton
Achmore
486 CARN NAN IOMAIREAN
Braeintra
Port Cam
Duirinish
Drumbuie
Achnandarach
Gleann Udalain
Sallachy
Allt-nan-sùgh
Killilan
SGUMAN COINNTICH 879
Black Is.
Erbusaig
Badicaul
Balmacara Square
Kyle of Lochalsh
CASTLE MOIL
BRIGHT WATER VISITOR CENTRE
Kyleakin
Balmacara
LOCHALSH WOODLAND GARDEN
Reraig
Kirkton
Auchtertyre
Nostie
Conchra
Loch Long
Camas-luinie
Faddonch
Iron Lo.
Carnach
Glen Elchaig
Allt na Doire Gairbhe
Loch na Leitreach
FALLS OF GLOMACH
Gleann Sithidh
West Benula Forest
Gleann A'Chòilich
1005
1053 TOLL CREAGACH
1111 TOM A CHOINICH
1183 CARN EIGE
Gleann nam Fiadh
Affric Lodge
GLEN AFFRIC
Glen Affric
Bundalloch
Ardelve
Dornie
EILEAN DONAN CASTLE
Carndu
634
Loch nan Eun
Elchaig
LOCH ALSH
Avernish
Glas Eilean
Ardintoul Pt.
Ardintoul
Totaig
Keppoch
Letterfearn
SGURR AN AIRGID 841
SGURR NAN CEATHREAMHNAN 1151
Inverinate
Dorusduain
Loch Duich
Ruarach
Loch a'Bhealaich
Morvich
Carn-gorm
Ault a'chruinn
Glenaffric Forest
Athnamulloch
Loch Affric
Glen Affric
539
SGURR NA COINNICH 739
KYLERHEA OTTER HAVEN
Kyle Rhea
Glen Arroch
Allt Mòr
Ferry
Bernera
Galltair
Kylerhea
603 BEINN A'CHUIRN
Glenelg
BARRACKS
Scallasaig
Cnoc Fhionn
RATAGAN
Ratagan
Invershiel
Shiel Bridge
BEINN FADA OR BEN ATTOW 1032
Glen Gniomh
GLEN AFFRIC
Allt Garbh
Allt Riabhach
610 BEN ASLAK
Glenelg Bay
Eilanreach
Mosag
GLENELG BROCHS
Glen More
Balvraid
Abhainn a' Ghlinne Bhig
779
KINTAIL
Kintail Forest
Glenlicht Ho.
1067 FIVE SISTERS
979 SGURR A'BHEALAICH DHEIRG
888 AONACH SHASUINN
706 CARN A' CHOACHAN
A832
A896
A890
A87
B8021
B8056
B8057
NH
80
20
A
B
C
D
E
F
G
H
7
8
9
10
11
300
307
295
290

Deanich Lodge
Diebidale
Forest
Loch a'Chairn
Meikle Gluich
Aultnamain Inn
Gleann Beag
Crom Loch
BEINN THARSUINN
Glen Diebidale
CARN CHUINNEAG
Auchmarean
BEINN DEARG
Strath More
309
Loch a'Chaorainn
BEINN A'CHAISTEIL
CORRIESHALLOCH GORGE
MEALL LEACACHAIN
Lubachlaggan
Loch Vaich
MEALL A' GHRIANAIN
Inchbae Forest
Kildermorie Forest
Kildermorie Lodge
Braeantra
BEINN THARSUINN
Strath Rory
Strath Rusdale
Black Water
Baldoon
Strathy
CNOC CORR GUINIE
Kinhriv
Braemore Forest
Dirrie More
Abhainn Droma
Lochdrum
Loch Droma
Strathvaich Forest
Strathvaich Lodge
Strath Vaich
Strathrannoch
Strath Rannoch
BEINN NAN EUN
Loch Morie
Inchlumpie
Loanreoch
Ardross
Ardross Forest
Easter Ardross
Stittenham
Dalnavie
Loch Glascarnoch
A835
Wyvis Lodge
Loch Glass
QUEEN'S CAIRN
Boath
Ardross Castle
Wester Lealty
Badachonacher
Achandunie
Newmore
SGURR MOR
BEINN LIATH MHOR A 'GHIUBHAIS LI
Aultguish Inn
Culzie Lodge
Nonikiln
Mossfield
Alness
Achnacarry
FYRISH MONUMENT
Moultavie
Kinlochluichart Forest
MEALL GORM
MEALL MHIC IOMHAIR
Inchbae Lodge
Garbat Forest
Garbat
BEN WYVIS
Glen Glass
Eileanach Lodge
Novar House
Dalmore
DALMORE DISTILLERY
Fannich Forest
299
Fannich Lodge
LOCH FANNICH
Aultdearg
Corriemoillie Forest
Black Water
Allt nan Caorach
Assynt Ho.
Redburn
Culcairn
Evanton
Alness Bay
Ferryton
Resolis
Swordale
Drummond
Alnessferry
Newhall
LITTLE WYVIS
Strathgarve Forest
Foulis Castle
Clach Liath Forest
Cullicudden
Newmills
Springfield
AN CABAR
Corriemoillie
Lochluichart
Gorstan
Grudie
Achanalt
Strathgarve Lodge
CIOCH MHOR
Ardullie
STOREHOUSE OF FOULIS
Easter Brae
Wester Brae
Kinbeachie
Shoreton
Millbuie
Dosmuckeran
A832
Strath Bran
Loch Luichart
Garve
Loch Achanalt
Loch Garve
Heights of Brae
Woodlands
Mountgerald
Tulloch Castle
Findon Mains
Culbo
Bottacks
Fodderty
Dingwall
Braefindon
Loch Bhad Ghaineamhaich
SGURR MARCASAIDH
ROGIE FALLS
Auchterneed
HIGHLAND MUS OF CHILDHOOD
Knockfarrel
Culbokie
MOUNT EAGLE
Killen
Glenmarksie
Tarvie
Craigdarroch
Strathpeffer
Loch Ussie
MACDONALD MONUMENT
Urquhart
Wester Strath
Little Scatwell
Loch Achilty
Comrie
Lochussie
Tollie
Alcaig
Belmaduthy
Loch Meig
Torrachilty Wood
Jamestown
Maryburgh
Corntown
Duncanston
Rosehaugh Mains
SGURR A'MHUILINN
Milton
Porin
Dalnacroich
Curin
Scatwell Ho
Contin
Knockbain
Suddie
Gowan
Achlorachan
Bridgend
STRATHCONON
TORR ACHILTY DAM FISH LIFT
Conon Bridge
Conon House
Easter Kinkell
Leanaig
Roskill House
CARN MHARTUIN
Gleann Meinich
Loch Achonachie
Muirton Mains
Marybank
Bishop Kinkell
A835
Bennetsfield
STRATH CONON
Glenmeanie
Fairburn House
Urray
Muckernich
Munlochy
Munlochy Bay
Scardroy
Muir of Fairburn
Newmore
Tore
Allangrange Mains
Loch Beannacharain
GLEN ORD DISTILLERY
Balvaird
Drynie Park
Kilcoy
Fettes
Glackmore
Bogallan
Drumderfit
Carnoch
Inverchoran
CARN NA COINNICH
Cabaan Forest
Auchmore
Muir of Ord
Arpafeelie
Drumsmittal
Kilmuir
FOREST
Orrin Reservoir
Ardnagrask
Redcastle
Craigrory
Craigton
BAC AN EICH
Corriehallie Forest
Loch nan Eun
Corry of Ardnagrask
Aultvaich
Windhill
Tomich House
Milton
Charlestown
North Kessock
Glen Orrin
Gleann Goibhre
CNOC EILLE MOR
Loch nam Bonnach
Clashandorran
Dunmore
BEAULY FIRTH
Loch na Caoidhe
Ruilick
BEAULY PRIORY
Lovat
Groam
Bunchrew
South Kessock
Drumindorsair
Beauly
Kirkhill
HIGHLAND
Balblair
Inchmore
Lentran
CRAIG PHADRIG FORT
BALNAIN HOUSE
Leachkin
FLORAL HALL & VISITOR CENTRE
CASTLE GARRISON ENCOUNTER
Culcabock
Inverness
Kilmorack
Balchraggan
Drumchardine
BEINN A'BHA'ACH ARD
Breakachy
AIGAS DAM FISH LADDER
Easter Moniack
Newtonhill
Dunain Ho.
East Monar Forest
Erchless Forest
Crask of Aigas
Beaufort Castle
Cabrich
PRINGLE WEAVERS
Castle Leys
SGURR A'CHOIRE GHLAIS
Neaty Burn
Erchless Castle
Aigas Forest
Culburnie
Kiltarlity
THE AIRD
South Clunes
Dochgarroch
Caledonian Canal
Leys Castle
Culligran Falls
Inchmore
Craigdhu
AN LEACAINN
Ness
Scaniport
Monar Lodge
GLEN
Struy
Mid Main
Camault Muir
Glaichbea
Dochfour Ho.
Braulen Lodge
Glen Strathfarrar
Farrar
Eskadale
Druimkinnerras
Boblainy
Strath Dores
Essich
Loch Beannacharan
STRATHFARRAR
Mauld
Ardendrain
Lochend
Lairgmore
Glenstrathfarrar Forest
Ardchuilk
Struy Forest
Boblainy Forest
Loch a'Mhuillidh
Loch Bruicheach
Cragganvallie
GREAT GLEN WAY
Drumashie Moor
SGOR NA DIOLLAID
Carnoch
Glen Convinth
Aldourie Castle
Dalveallan
CAIRN GORM
Abriachan
ABRIACHAN GARDEN NURSERY
Balnafoich
Glassburn
MEALL NAN CAORACH
Balchraggan
Dores
Loch Ashie
Glencannich Forest
Muchrachd
Balmore
STRATHGLASS
Dunlichity Lodge
Liatrie
CARN NAM BAD
Mullardoch House
Cannich
LOCH NESS CENTRE & EXHIBITION
MEALL NA H-EILRIG
STRATHNAIRN
Loch Duntelchaig
Glen Urquhart
Balbeg
Uppertown
Balnagrantach
Potmaily
Balnain
Buntait
Braefield
Fasnakyle Forest
Loch Mullardoch
Glen Cannich
Corrimony
CAIRN
Milton
Achnabat
STAC NA CATHAIG
Mains of Flichity
Shenval
Rychraggan
Drumnadrochit
BCC LOCH NESS
CORRIMONY
Loch Meiklie
Lochletter
Enrick
Lewiston
Urquhart Bay
DOG FALLS
Tullich
Brinmore
TOLL CREAGACH
Fasnakyle Ho
Glenurquhart Forest
Strone
Affric
Tomich
Guisachan
Divach
Upper Lenie
Lower Lenie
URQUHART CASTLE
COBB MEMORIAL
Torness
Loch Ruthven
East Croachy
Balmacaan Forest
LOCH RUTHVEN
Aberarder House
Balcladaich
TOM A' CHOINICH
Abhainn Deabhag
Coiltie
Bunloit
Balbeg
Ancarraig
Balchraggan
Loch Beinn a'Mheadhoin
Hilton Lodge
PLODDA FALLS
GLEN AFFRIC
Affric Lodge
Glen Affric
MEALL A' CHRATHAICH
Loch nam Breac Dearga
Grotaig
Inverfarigaig
Aultnagoire
Errogie
FARIGAIG FOREST CENTRE
Easter Boleskine
CARN NA SAOBHAIDH
Loch ma Stac
Loch a' Chrathaich
Creagnaneun Forest
Farigaig Forest
Dunmaglass Lodge
Lyne of Gorthleck
Farraline
Loch nan Eun
Cougie
Guisachan Forest
Foyers
Easter Aberchalder
Wester Aberchalder
Allt Uisg an t-Sidhein
Loch na Beinne Baine
290
Levishie Forest
LOCH NESS
Alltsigh
Lochgarthside
BEINN BHREAC MHOR
291
Levishie
Achnaconeran
Loch Mhor
Glendoebeg Forest
Bhlaraidh
Invermoriston
FALLS OF MORISTON
Bailebeag
Corriegarth Lodge
Garthbeg
Abercalder Burn
CARN ODHAR
CHAOCHAIN
A887
Moriston
STRATHERRICK
A82
A831
A862
A9
A832
B862
B852
B851
B9169
B9163
B9176
NH
0 2 4 6 miles
0 2 4 6 8 10 km

Tarbat Discovery Centre
Bindal
Portmahomack
Glenmorangie Distillery
Aldie Watermill
St Duthus's Chapel
Tain Through Time Visitor Centre
Tarlogie
Morangie
Tain
Tain Tolbooth
Upper Bogrow
Quarryhill
Arthurville
Aldie
Hilton
Balcherry
Balnagall
Lochslin
Inver
Arboll
Wester Arboll
Seafield
Rockfield
Tarrel
Toulvaddie
Morangie Forest
Lower Pitkerrie
Geanies House
Rhynie
Kingscauseway
Loandhu
Fearn Station
East Lamington
Hartmount
Hill of Fearn
Fearn
Fearn Abbey
Cadboll
Lamington
Newfield
Marybank
Logie Hill
Hilton of Cadboll
Torran
Scotsburn
Pithmaduthy
Arabella
Loans of Tullich
Broomton
Balintore
Shandwick Stone
Shandwick
Kildary
Tullich Muir
Milton
Tarbat Ho.
Ankerville
Chapelhill
Nigg Bay
Kilmuir
Pitcalnie
Port an Righ
Barbaraville
Nigg
Northfield
Sands of Nigg
Mount Canisp
King's Cave
Balintraid
Balnapaling
Balnabruaich
Saltburn
Castlecraig
Invergordon
Nigg Ferry
Ferry
Cromarty Court House
Newhall Point
Cromarty
Sutors of Cromarty
Cromarty Bay
Hugh Miller's Birthplace Cottage & Museum
Udale Bay
Newton
Shore Mill
Jemimaville
Davidston
Poyntzfield
Navity
Muirton
Glenurquhart
Upper Eathie
Craighead
Whitebog
Balmungie
M O R A Y   F I R T H
Groam House Museum and Pictish Centre
Rosemarkie
Fortrose Cathedral
Fort George
Fortrose
Heritage Exhibition
Avoch
Avoch Bay
Chanonry Pt.
Kirkton
Baddock
The Highlanders' Mus
Ardersier
Whiteness Head
Nairn Literary Institute Museum
Nairn Museum
Culbin Sands
Nairn
Tradespark
Kingsteps
Druim
Boath Dovecote
Auldearn
Moss-side
Househill
Gollanfield
Milton of Gollanfield
Muir of the Clans
Geddes House
Fisherton
Inverness
Lochside
Rosefield
Castle Stuart
Clephanton
Cawdor
Regoul
Piperhill
Alturlie Pt.
Tornagrain
Croy
Kilravock Castle
Cawdor Castle and Gardens
Culcharry
Moraybhill
Newton
Easter Galcantray
Achindown
Culloden
Balloch
Cantraywood
Culloden Forest
Western Galgantray
Cantraydoune
Smithton
Newlands
Cantraybruich
Culloden Battlefield
Clava Cairns
Assich Forest
Westhill
Castletown
Mains of Daltulich
House of Daviot
Daviot
Craggie
Auchnahillin
Kirkton of Barevan
Mains of Clunas
Balmore
Fornesfield
Laiken Forest
Littlemill
Mid Urchany
Achavraat
Achavelgin
Redburn
Newlands of Fleenas Wood
Ardclach Tower
Ardclach
Ferness
Glenferness House
Dulsie
Banchor
Carn Sgumain
Drynachan Lodge
Daless
Beinn Bhuidhe Mhor
Beinn Bhreac
Carn nan Tri-Tighearnan
Moy Burn
Meall a'Bhreacraibh
Ballachrochin
Meall Mor
Moy Hall
Loch Moy
Moy
Strathdearn Forest
Ruthven
Carn na h-Easgainn
Upper Inverbrough
Balvraid
Carn an t-Sean-Liathanaich
Corrybrough
Tomatin Distillery
Tomatin
Raigbeg
Carn a'Choire Mhoir
Carn Glas-Choire
Findhorn Bridge
Beinn Bhreac
Glen Kyllachy
Kyllachy House
Clune
Knockandoo
Corrievorrie
Slochd
Garbole
Dalmigavie Lodge
Glen Mazeran
Sluggan
Carrbridge
Landmark Forest Adventure Park
Ellan
Feith Mhor
Dalnahaitnach
Dalmigavie
Coignascallan
Eil
Caggan
Chapelton
Kinveachy
Avielochan
Deishar
Boat of Garten
Wester Dalvoult
Strathspey Railway
Street of Kincardine
Loch Garten
Loch Garten Abernethy
Abernethy Forest
Aundorach
Auchgourish
Drumuillie
Cullachie
Balnacruie
Broomhill
Nethy Bridge
Birchfield
East Croftmore
Lower Dell
Dell Lodge
Lettoch
Clachaig
Larg
Forest Lodge
Abernethy Centre
Blairgorm
Dorback Lodge
Baddoch
Braes of
Carn Meadhonach
Tomintoul & Glenlivet Discovery Centre
Tomintoul
Delnabo
Bridge of Avon
Milton
Bridge of Brown
Dirdhu
Conglass Water
Cairngorms National Park
Speyside Way
Revack Estate
Speyside Centre
Skye of Curr
Tulloch-gribban
Dulnain Bridge
Duthil
Lochanhully
Clan Grant Mausoleum & Church
Achnahannet
Beinn Mhor
Craggan
Glenbeg
Dreggie
Grantown Museum
Grantown-on-Spey
Anagach
Speybridge
Congash
Lynemore
Creggan a'Chaise
Cromdale
Auchroisk
Haughs of Cromdale
Hills of Cromdale
Inverlochy
Burn of Lochy
Strathavon Lo.
Fodderletter
Croughly
Braes
Chapeltown
Clashnoir
Knockandhu
Auchnarrow
Glenlivet Forest
Carn Daimh
Tomnavoulin
Ballcorach
Castleton
Glenlivet Distillery
Glenlivet
Shenval
Auchbreck
Downan
Drumin
Camerory
Cottartown
Upper Port
Glaschoil
Lynmore
Delliefure
Dalriach
Mains of Dalvey
Upper Derraid
Auchnagallin
Wester Auchnagallin
Lettoch
Carn na Loine
Advie
Cragganmore Distillery
Craggenmore
Bridge of Avon
Dalchirach
Haugh of Kilnmaichlie
Craggan
Strath Spey
Lochindorb
Lochindorb Castle
Lochindorb Lodge
Carn-Ruigh Charrach
Hill of Aitnoch
Aitnoch
Dava
Larig Hill
Allt a' Ghealladh
Burn of Tulchan
Carn Kitty
Shenvault
Divie
Milltown
Dorback Burn
Marypark
Bellehiglash
Glenfarclas Distillery
Speyside Way
Daugh of Kinermony
Carron
Knockando
Knockando Ho.
Speyside Way
Upper Knockando
Cardhu Distillery
Cardow
Archiestown
Elchies Forest
Carn na Cailliche
Burn of Rothes
Lossie
Loch Dallas
M O R A Y
Beachans
Glenernie
Relugas
Mount
Coulmony Ho.
Logie
Logie Steading Visitor Centre
Drumine Forest
Fornighty
Lethen Ho.
Clune
Wester Milton
Darnaway Forest
Blackhills
Easter Milton
Conicavel
Whitemire
Darnaway Castle
Earlsmill
Brodie Castle
Brodie
Maviston
Cloddymoss
Kintessack
Culbin Forest
The Bar
Kincorth Ho.
Moy Ho.
Dyke
Forres
Sueno's Stone
Springfield
Nelson Tower
Kinloss Abbey
Kinloss
Grange Hall
Findhorn
Findhorn Bay
Blervie Castle
Califer
Dallas Dhu Distillery
Mundale
Rafford
Altyre Ho.
Moor of Granary
Damhead
Altyre Woods
Findhorn
Briach
Phorp
Newtyle Forest
Branchill
Dallas Lodge
Dallas
Craigroy
Mill Buie
Ballachraggan
Cairn Uish
Hatton
Dallas Forest
Glenlatterach
Kellas
Barnhill
Stoneyfield
Foresterseat
Pluscarden Abbey
Monaughty Forest
Mains of Burgie
Muir of Miltonduff
Miltonduff
Auchtertyre
Birnie Church
Thomshill
Upper Bogside
Cloves
East Grange
Miltonhill
Coltfield
Alves
Ardgye
Lower Hempriggs
Roseisle Forest
Burghead Bay
Burghead
Burghead Visitor Centre
Hopeman
Cummingston
Roseisle
College of Roseisle
Duffus
Old Duffus
Gordonstoun
Duffus Castle
Palace of Spynie
Covesea
Covesea Skerries
Lossiemouth Fisheries & Community Museum
Stotfield
Quarrywood
Rosebrae
Newton
Laverackloch
Bishopmill
Elgin
Elgin Museum
Elgin Cathedral
Old Mills
Moray Motor Museum
New Elgin
Pittendreich
Mayne Ho.
Glassgreen
Paddockhaugh
Spynie

311
NJ
Halliman Skerries
Covesea Skerries
LOSSIEMOUTH FISHERIES & COMMUNITY MUSEUM
Branderburgh
Lossiemouth
Stotfield
Covesea
Duffus
Gordonstoun
Old Duffus
301
DUFFUS CASTLE
PALACE OF SPYNIE
Spynie
Loch Spynie
Lossie Forest
SPEY BAY
Quarrywood
Laverackloch
Elgin
Bishopmill
ELGIN MUSEUM
ELGIN CATHEDRAL
CASHMERE VISITOR CENTRE
OLD MILLS
MORAY MOTOR MUSEUM
New Elgin
Pittendreich
Miltonduff
Muir of Miltonduff
Mayne Ho.
Glassgreen
Moss of Barmuckity
COXTON TOWER
Auchtertyre
Paddockhaugh
BIRNIE CHURCH
Thomshill
Longmorn
Fogwatt
Clackmarras
Blackhills
Upper Bogside
Coleburn
MILLBUIES
Teindland Forest
Glenlatterach
338
365 CAIRN UISH
Glen of Rothes
Auchinroath
Newlands
Rothes
GLEN GRANT DISTILLERY
Burn of Rothes
Elchies Forest
404 CARN NA CAILLICHE
369
Whiteacen
MACALLAN DISTILLERY
Archiestown
CARDHU DISTILLERY
Cardow
Upper Knockando
Knockando
Knockando Ho.
Carron
Daugh of Kinermony
Robertstown
SPEYSIDE VISITOR CENTRE
Ringorm
Speyview
Glenallachie
Charlestown of Aberlour
Milltown of Edinvillie
SPEYSIDE COOPERAGE VISITOR CENTRE
Craigellachie
Dandaleith
Arndilly Ho.
471 BEN AIGAN
Aikenway
SPEYSIDE WAY
Stonewells
Lochhill
Leuchars Ho.
Moss of Meft
Urquhart
Darkland
Lhanbryde
Burniestrype
Lochs Crofts
Mosstodloch
Dipple
Orbliston
Altonside
Westerton
Inchberry
Ordiequish
Wood of Ordiequish
MORAY
Mains of Cairnty
Shalloch
Balnabreich
Mulben
Rosarie Forest
Belnagarrow
Kingston
SCOTTISH DOLPHIN CENTRE
Garmouth
TUGNET ICE HOUSE
Spey Bay
Porttanachy
Nether Dallachy
Upper Dallachy
Bogmoor
BAXTERS HIGHLAND VILLAGE
Auchenhalrig
Newlands of Tynet
FOCHABERS FOLK MUSEUM HERITAGE CENTRE
Fochabers
Braes of Enzie
Speymouth Forest
Forgie
Aultmore
Newmill
Buckie
Buckpool
Gordonsburgh
Portgordon
Slackhead
Broadley
Cairnfield Ho.
Preshome
ST. GREGORY'S CHAPEL
Clochan
Drybridge
Slate Haugh
Shiel Muir
Findochty
Portknockie
Portessie
Rathven
Bauds of Cullen
Connage
Cullen
Cullen Bay
Logie Hd.
Old Cullen
Lintmill
FINDLATER CASTLE
Sandend
Sandend Bay
Redhythe Pt.
Portsoy
Seatown
Boyne Bay
Knock Hd.
Boyndie Bay
Whitehills
Macduff
Banff
DUFF HOUSE
Inverboyndie
Boyndie
Auds
Easter Whyntie
Birkenbog
Bogtown
JOINER'S WORKSHOP
Fordyce
Milton
Kirktown of Deskford
DESKFORD CHURCH
Ardiecow
Berryhillock
Drochedlie
Tillynaught
Brodiesord
Little Toux
Mickle Toux
Newmills of Boyne
Craibstone
301 MILLSTONE HILL
Goukstone
Deerhill
Grange Crossroads
Broadrashes
Garralburn
Glen of Newmill
Mains of Edingight
Edingight Ho.
KNOCK HILL
Whitehill
Sillyearn
Cranoch
Bracobrae
Davoch of Grange
Knock
Drumnagorrach
Farmtown
Nethermills
Gordonstown
Ordiqhill
Grantown
Cornhill
Culphin
Weachyburn
Finnygaud
Blacklaw
Knowes of Elrick
Knowehead
Ramsburn
Crombie Castle
Old Crombie
Aberchirder
Cranna
Bogton
Marnoch
Clunie
Carnousie
Knauchland
Moss-side
Rothiemay Crossroads
Tarryblake Ho.
Fife Keith
Keith
STRATHISLA DISTILLERY
Mains of Auchoynanie
Balloch Wood
Blackhillock
North Whiteley
Edintore
KEITH AND DUFFTOWN RLY
Poolside
Rosarie
Towiemore
Maggieknockater
Kininvie Ho.
Drummuir Castle
Drummuir
Slogan
Glack of Midthird
Midtown of Buchromb
Balvenie
BALVENIE CASTLE
GLENFIDDICH DISTILLERY
Dufftown
Milltown of Auchindoun
Midtown of Glass
Little Pitlurg
Coachford
Glen of Coachford
Cairnie
313 THE BIN
The Bin Forest
Haddoch
Ruthven
Milltown of Rothiemay
Midplaugh
344 FOURMAN HILL
Bogniebrae
Yonder Bognie
Mains of Mayen
Hillbrae
Inverkeithny
Auchininna
Milburn
Corse of Kinnoir
NORDIC SKI CENTRE
HUNTLY CASTLE
Huntly
Drumdelgie
Daugh of Cairnborrow
Cairnborrow
Westerton
Torry
Haugh of Glass
Deveron
Terryhorn
Wellheads
STRATHBOGIE
Bailiesward
Bridgend
Tillathrowie
Succoth
Mill of Lynebain
Tomnaven
Coynachie
Clashindarroch Forest
Clashindarroch
Mytice
Kirkney
Gartly
Culdrain
Kirkstile
Shanquhar
Corncatterach
Blackburn
Wester Mosshead
Brideswell
Slioch
Lessendrum
Drumblade
Forgue
Cobairdy
Pitfancy
GLENDRONACH DISTILLERY
Drumblair
Fortrie
Carlincraig
Brownhill
Denmoss
Balgaveny
Largue
Aucharnie
Corse
Drumdollo
Denend
Thomastown
Hillhead
Ythanwells
Logie Newton
Badenscoth
Redhill
Greystone
Bainshole
Fisherford
Glens of Foudland
467 HILL OF FOUDLAND
Kirkton of Culsalmond
Rothmaise
Colpy
Cairnhill
Largie
Upper Boddam
Wrangham
Bonnyton
Knockenbaird
Aulton
Insch
Newton Ho.
Old Rayne
Pitmachie
Ardoyne
Westhall
Kirkton
Oyne
Kirkton of Oyne
Auchleven
Lickleyhead Castle
528 BENNACHIE
GARIOCH
Newbigging
Cults
434 KNOCKANDY HILL
LEITH HALL
Wraes
The Shevock
Smithston
Kennethmont
Oldtown
Ardlair
Towie
Milton of Noth
Milton of Lesmore
Rhynie
Cottown
Belhinnie
Clatt
Duncanstone
Leslie
Auchmenzie
Knockespock Ho.
Wheedlemont
Craig Castle
B9002 ST MARY'S CHURCH
Bogs
Whitehaugh Forest
Coldwells Croft
Muckletown
Clova
SCOTTISH SCULPTURE WORKSHOP
Lumsden
CORREEN HILLS
ABERDEEN
Glenton
Keig
Castle Forbes
Upper Woodend
Lower Woodend
Tullynessle
Terpersie Castle
518 LORD ARTHUR'S CAIRN
Mossat
Kildrummy
KILDRUMMY CASTLE & GARDEN
Milltown of Kildrummy
Don
Bridge of Alford
Montgarrie
HAUGHTON
GRAMPIAN TRANSPORT MUS
Alford
Muir of Alford
Auchintoul
Rorandle
Pitfichie Forest
Pitfichie
Pitmunie
Gateside
MONYMUSK ARTS CENTRE
Auchindoun Castle
487 THE SCALP
Kirktown of Mortlach
Lettoch
Sheandow
MEIKLE CONVAL 569
Glen Rinnes
Dullan Water
840 BEN RINNES
Favillar
Kirkhill
Glenfiddich Lodge
Glen Fiddich
Ballochford
Bridgend
Glenfiddich Forest
Inverharroch
Ardwell
Black Water
Blackwater Lodge
Auchmair
Cabrach
595
571 ROUND HILL
Aldivalloch
Aldunie
Blackwater Forest
742
732 CARN AN T-SUIDHE
721 THE BUCK
632 HILL OF THREE STONES
Badenyon
Glenbuchat Lodge
Water of Buchat
Water of Nochty
Belnacraig
Glenbuchat Castle
Kirkton of Glenbuchat
Rinmore
292
293
Marypark
GLENFARCLAS DISTILLERY
Bellehiglash
Craggenmore
Bridge of Avon
Dalchirach
Haugh of Glenmaichlie
Craggan
Drumin
Downan
GLENLIVET DISTILLERY
Glenlivet
Castleton
Shenval
Auchbreck
Badeach
Tomnavoulin
CARN DAIMH
Knockandhu
Achdregnie
Auchnarrow
Glenlivet Forest
Livet
Croughly
Clashnoir
Braes of Glenlivet
Chapeltown
Scalan
Milton
TOMIN
Conglass Water
0 2 4 6 miles
0 2 4 6 8 10 km

Fraserburgh
Peterhead
Rosehearty
Inverallochy
Crimond
Boddam
Cruden Bay
Ellon
Oldmeldrum
Inverurie
Newmachar
Turriff
New Pitsligo
Strichen
Mintlaw
New Deer
Maud
Fyvie
Newburgh
Balmedie
Kintore
Kemnay
B U C H A N
F O R M A R T I N E
Fraserburgh Bay
Peterhead Bay
Sandford Bay
Bay of Cruden
Loch of Strathbeg
Newburgh Bar
Kinnaird Head
Rattray Head
Buchan Ness
Troup Hd.
Pennan Hd.
Head of Garness
Forest of Deer
Moss of Cruden
Sands of Forvie
NK

RUBHA ROBHANAIS (BUTT OF LEWIS)
CHURCH OF ST MOULAG
Cunndal
Coig Peighinnean
Eoropaidh
HARBOUR VIEW GALLERY
Port Nis
Adabroc
Sgiogarstaigh
Lìonal
Tabost
Suainebost
Cros
Dail bho Thuath
Dail bho Dheas
Cross Sands
Aird Dhail
Glen Cross
Dail
Cuiashader
Cellar Head
Tolsta Head
Tolastadh bho Thuath
Bail' Ur Tholastaidh
Gleann Tholàstaidh
Port Bun a'Ghlinne
Creag Fhraoch
Vatisker Pt.
BROAD BAY OR LOCH A TUATH
Rubha an t-Siumpain
Port Mholair
Aird
Port Nan Giùran
Cnoc Amhlaigh
Seisiadar
Sulaisiadar
EYE PENINSULA
Pabail Uarach
Pabail Iarach
Bàgh Phabail
Garrabost
An Cnoc
Suardail
A'Chearc
Aiginis
ST COLUMBA'S
Breibhig
Bac
Griais
Cnoc an t-Solais
Col
Col Uarach
Coll Sands
Aird Thunga
Tunga
Sròn Ruadh
STORNOWAY
Mealabost
Stornoway
Newmarket
Lacasdal
Sanndabhaig
Tolm
Airinis
Holm I.
ULLAPOOL
Gabhsann bho Thuath
Gabhsann bho Dheas
Mealabost Bhuirgh
Bail Àrd Bhuirgh
Coig Peighinnean Bhuirgh
Siadar
Siadar Iarach
Siadar Uarach
Baile an Truiseil
TRUSHAL STONE
Rubha Leathann
Aird Barvas
Barabhas Uarach
Barabhas
Barabhas Iarach
Brù
Arnol
BLACK HOUSE MUSEUM
LOCH NA MUILNE
Bragar
Labost
Siabost bho Thuath
Siabost bho Dheas
SHAWBOST NORSE MILL
SHAWBOST MUSEUM
Pairc Shiaboist
Bàgh Dhail Beag
Dail Beag
Dail Mor
GEARRANNAN BLACKHOUSE VILLAGE
GARENIN
Na Gearrannan
Borghastan
Carlabhagh
Ciribhig
Loch Chàrlabhaigh
DUN CARLOWAY BROCH
Dun Charlabhaigh
MUIRNEAG
248
Gleann Mòr Barvas
Glen Bragar
Gleann Bhruthadail
261
BEINN BRAGAR
292
BEINN MHOLACH
Loch Langabhat
Gabhsann bho Dheas
Borgh
Loch Mòr Shanndabhat
Abhainn Ghearadha
Loch Sgeireach Mor
Griais
Lacasdal
Loch Urghag
Loch Breibhat
Loch Scarabhat Mhòr
Loch Mòr an Stàirr
Loch nan Stearnag
Loch Urabhal
Lacasdail
ISLE OF LEWIS (LEODHAIS)
Grianan
An Gleann Ur
Cnoc Mairi
LEWS CASTLE & MUS NAN EILEAN
LEWIS LOOM CENTRE
AN LANNTAIR GALLERY
Arnish Moor
Loch Orasaigh
Griomsidar
Ben Casgro
Raerinish Pt.
Liurbost
Ranais
Crosbost
Barkin Is.
Tabhaidh Mhor
Eilean Chaluim Chille
Eilean Orasaidh
Crobeag
Cromor
Eilean Thoraidh
Ceos
Eireasort
Gearraidh Bhaird
Lacasaidh
Baile Ailein
Soval Lodge
Loch Trealabhal
Laxay
Loch Tobhta Bridein
Loch nam Falcag
Loch Airigh na h-Airde
ACHMORE STONE CIRCLE
Acha Mor
223
Loch a' Ghainmhich
Gearraidh na h-Aibhne
CALANAIS VISITOR CENTRE
CALANAIS SMALL STONE CIRCLES
Calanais
CALANAIS STANDING STONES
Linsiadar
Breascleit
Loch Lacsabhat Ard
Loch Smuaisebhal
Tolastadh a Chaolais
Keava
Eilean Kearstay
Loch Ròg an Ear
Little Bernera
Crothair
Breacleit
NORSE MILL
Great Bernera
BERNERA
Bhalasaigh
Circebost
Barraglom
Tobhtarol
Crulabhig
Iarsiadar
Tacleit
Vuia Mòr
Vuia Beag
Bostadh
IRON AGE HOUSE
Tobson
Vacsay
Pabay Mor
Campay
Floday
Harsgeir
AN CAOLAS
An Galan Uigeach
Bhaltos
Cnip
Uigen
Riof
Loch Rog
Floday
Geisiadar
Ungisiadar
256
Loch Tungabhat
Loch Rog
Scaliscro
Giosla
Loch Morsgail
Loch Coirigerod
Einacleite
Loch Fuaroil
397
BEINN MHEADHONACH
Loidse Mhorsgail
Loch Cro Criosdaig
Cliobh
Miabhig
Cairisiadar
SUAINAVAL
429
Loch Suaineabhal
Loch Grunabhat
Loch Chaolartan
Aird Uig
205
Bàgh Fhiabhaig
Eadar Dha Fhadhail
Timsgearraidh
Cradhlastadh
Càrnais
574
MEALISVAL
Islibhig
Breanais
Mangurstadh
Ard More Mangersta
Aird Fenish
Aird Brenish
Mealasta
Caolas an E
a Island
Tamanabhagh
B8014
B8013
B8015
B895
A857
A858
A866
B897
B8011
B8059
A859
306
307
NB
00
60
70
A
B
C
D
E
F
1
2
3
4
5
6
7
8
10
12
14
15
16
19
20

HIGHLAND
SOUTH LEWIS
HARRIS AND
CEANN A TUATH NA HEARADH
NA HEARADH (HARRIS)
NORTH UIST
LOCH A SIAR
CAOLAS NAN EILEAN
CAOLAS NA HEARADH
PARK OR PAIRC
LOCH LANGABHAT
Forest of Harris
South Harris Forest
TROTTERNISH
Eilean Scalpaigh (Scalpay)
Na h-Eileanan Mòra (Shiant Islands)
Eilean Mhuire
Eilean an Tighe
Garbh Eilean
Eilean Iubhard
Tarasaigh (Taransay)
Scarp
Kearstay
Killegray
Ensay
Hermetray
Fladda-chuain
Eilean Trodday
Eilean Flodigarry
Staffin I.
Stockinish I.
Lingarabay I.
Soay Mòr
Soay Beag
Gilsay
Lingay
Scaravay
Langay
Groay
Opsay
Groatay
Sursay
Tahay
Tairbeart (Tarbert)
An t-Ob (Leverburgh)
Seilebost
Horgabost
Borve Lodge
Sgarasta Mhor
Taobh Tuath
Roghadal
Fionnsbhagh
Miabhag
Urgha
Scalpay
Maraig
Aline Lodge
Seaforth I.
Ceann Tarabhaigh
Aird a' Mhulaidh
Huisinis
Cliasmol
Abhainn Suidhe
Aird Asaig
Kebock Head
Marbhig
Calbost
Grabhair
Leumrabhagh
Orasaigh
Eisgean
Tabost
Kershader
Ceann Shiphoirt
Rubha Hunish
Duntulm
Balmacqueen
Kilmaluag
Flodigarry
Digg
Glashvin
Brogaig
Stenscholl
Staffin
Kilt Rock
Kilvaxter
Balgown
Linicro
Totscore
Kilmuir
Hungladder
Borneskeitaig
Shulista
Peingown
Heribusta
Connista
The Quiraing
Meall na Suiramach 543
Waternish Point
Toe Head
Rubha Sgeirigin
Taransay Glorigs
Hushinish Pt.
Renish Pt.
Weaver's Pt.
Madadh Gruamach
UIG
A859
B8060
B887
307
298
296
NG
70
60
00
6 miles
10 km

CAPE WRATH
Kearvaig
Geodha Ruadh na Fola
Bay of Keisgaig
Geodha Ruadh
Loch Keisgaig
371 SGRIBHIS-BHEINN
Inshore
308
457 FASHVEN
Achier
Am Balg
423 BEINN DEARG
Sandwood Loch
485 CREAG RIABHACH
Strath Shinary
Rubh'an Fhir Léithe
Loch na Gainimh
Grudie
332 GHLAS BHEINN
Sheigra
Balchrick
Blairmore
Droman
Oldshore Beg
Oldshoremore
Eilean Roin Mor
521 FARRMHEALL
A838
Rhig
19
Gualin Ho.
Loch Clash
Kinlochbervie
B801
Badcall
Inshegra
Achriesgill
Bagh Loch an Roin
Loch Inchard
Rhiviche
9
Achlyness
L. na Claise Carnaich
Loch Dughaill
Ardmore Pt.
Ceathramh Garbh
Rhiconich
Rubha Ruadh
Ardmore
Portlevorchy
Skerricha
GANU MOR 908
Foinaven
Fanagmore
Tarbet
NORTH-WEST SUTHERLAND
Handa Island
Loch Laxford
Loch a'Garbh-bhaid Mòr
Foindle
Sound of Handa
Loch nam Brac
A894
Laxford Bridge
Badnabay
Loch an Easa Uaine
787 ARKLE
Scourie Bay
Laxford
Scourie More
Scourie
Gorm Loch
Lochstack Lodge
Rubh'Aird an t-Sionnaich
Upper Badcall
Lower Badcall
719 BEN STACK
Stack
Airdachuilinn
Badcall Bay
18
BEINN AUSKAIRD 386
Strath Stack
Eil. a'Bhreitheimh
Duartbeg
Loch Crocach
REAY FOREST
Achfary
332
Rubha a'Mhucard
Lochmore Lodge
Loch More
Meall Mòr
Calbha Mòr
Duartmore Bridge
Loch na Creige Duibhe
Eddrachillis Bay
Calbha Beag
Duartmore Forest
Loch an Leathaid Bhuain
Point of Stoer
Oldany Island
Loch a'Chairn Bhain
Kylestrome
547
Forest
Cirean Geardail
R. nan Còsan
161
Eilean Chrona
Culkein Drumbeg
Loch Nedd
Ardvar
Kylesku
Glendhu
Rubha Stoer
Culkein
Clashnessie Bay
Oldany
B869
Unapool
Loch Glendhu
Gleann
Dubh
Cluas Deas
Achnacarnin
Drumbeg
Nedd
8
530 BEINN AIRD DA LOCH
566
Clashmore
Loch Poll
Glenleraig
Newton
Loch Glencoul
NB
NC
70
80
30
1
2
3
4
5
6
7
8
A
B
C
D
E
F

Rienachait
Stoer
Rubh'a' Mhill Dheirg
Bay of Stoer
Clachtoll
R. Leumair
Achmelvich Bay
Rhicarn
Achmelvich
ACHMELVICH BEACH
Rubha Rodha
Baddidarach
Lochinver
Brackloch
Glencanisp Lodge
Soyea I.
Loch Inver
Kirkaig Pt.
Badnaban
Strathan
A'Chleit
ASSYNT-
COIGACH
Loch Kirkaig
Inverkirkaig
Rubha na Breige
Eilean Mór
Rubha Coigeach
ENARD BAY
Rhegreanoch
Falls
Rubh'a' Choin
Inverpolly Lodge
Camas Eilean Ghlais
Rubha Mor
Reiff
Brae of Achnahaird
Altandhu
SUMMER ISLES SMOKEHOUSE
Loch Vatachan
Eilean Mullagrach
Isle Ristol
Polbain
Glas-leac Mór
Aird of Coigach
Loch Osgaig
Loch Sionascaig
Polly
Inverpolly Forest
613
STAC POLLAIDH
849
CUL MOR
Drumrunie Forest
Loch an Doire Dhuibh
Linneraineach
769
CUL BEAG
Loch Lurgainn
Achiltibuie
Loch Bad a'Ghaill
Tanera Beg
Badentarbat Bay
Polglass
Badenscallie
ACHININVER
BEN MOR COIGACH
Summer Isles
Tanera Mór
Horse Sound
Horse I.
Glas-leac Beag
Culnacraig
743
BEINN MOR COIGACH
Achduart
Priest I.
Eilean Dubh
Bottle I.
Carn nan Sgeir
Loch an Leothaid
808
QUINAG
Loch Beannach
Lochassynt Lodge
LOCH ASSYNT
Little Assynt
Loch Feith an Leothaid
540
Skiag Bridge
ARDVRECK CASTLE
Inchnadamph
Inchnadamph Forest
EAS COUL AULIN WATERFALL
776
BEINN UIDHE
740
Gorm Loch Mór
792
BEINN LEOID
Loch an Eircill
Glencanisp
SUILVEN
731
Forest
Fionn Loch
Loch na Gainimh
846
CANISP
Stronchrubie
998
BEN MORE ASSYNT
718
BREABAG
MEALL AN AONAICH
715
Loch Awe
Cam Loch
Loch Veyatie
Ledbeg
Ledmore
Altnacealgach Hotel
Loch Ailsh
Benmore Lodge
Elphin
Knockan
Loch Urigill
KNOCKAN CRAG
CROMALT HILLS
517
HIGHLAND
Oykel
364
AN STUC
Loch Craggie
Drumrunie
COIGACH
Langwell Lodge
Rappach
Strath nan Lon
578
MEALL AN FHUARAIN
Strathcanaird
Kanaird
Blughasary
Runie
Camas Mór
Strath Kanaird
Keonchulish
Loch Kanaird
Isle Martin
STORNOWAY
415
Allt Beinn Donuill
Rappach Water
Duag Bridge
Ardmair
ISLE MARTIN MICRO MUSEUM
Rhue
Annat Bay
Rhidorroch Forest
548
Greenstone Point
Calleach Hd.
Rubha Beag
Opinan
Rubha Mór
Stattic Pt.
LITTLE LOCH BROOM
Scoraig
Carnach
Rireavach
Morefield
Ullapool
ULLAPOOL MUSEUM
Loch Achall
Rhidorroch Ho.
Loch an Daimh
Cormulzie Lodge
Mellon Udrigle
Gruinard I.
635
BEINN GHOBHLACH
ULLAPOOL
Glen Achall
Rhidorroch
East Rhidorroch Lodge
Strath Mulzie
Srón a' Gheodha Dhuibh
Eilean Furadh Mór
Achgarve
Mungasdale
Badluarach
Camas Mór
Rubha Reidh
155
Laide
Gruinard Bay
Gruinard House
Durnamuck
Badcaul
Allt na h-Airbhe
Braes of Ullapool
558
BEINN EILIDEACH
LECKMELM SHRUBBERY AND ARBORETUM
Leckmelm
Badrallach
Loch an Draing
Cove
Mellon Charles
Ormiscaig
Bualnaluib
Sand
Second Coast
First Coast
Inchina
Badbea
Blarnalearoch
LOCH BROOM
642
MEALL DUBH
677
MEALL NAM BRADHAN
Loch a'Choire Mhoir
Freevater
296
AN CUAIDH
Mellangaun
Isle of Ewe
Firemore
Tighnafiline
Aultbea
Drumchork
Little Gruinard
302
Gruinard
Camusnagaul
Ardessie
767
SAIL MHOR
29
Dundonnell Hotel
Dundonnell
Rhiroy
Ardindrean
Ardcharnich
Douchary
927
SEANA BHRAIGH
845
CARN BAN
Loch Sguod
Melvaig
Aultgrishan
Inverasdale
Midtown
LOCH EWE
Loch a'Bhaid-luachraich
Loch Fada
Little Gruinard
Strath Beag
Eilean Darach
Letters
12
Inverlael Forest
Seana Chamas
Brae
Rubha 'Ard na Bà
14
Dundonnell House
Strathnasheallag Forest
AN TEALLACH
1062
Inverlael
LAEL FOREST GARDEN
Lael Forest
Peterburn
B8021
B8057
Naast
Tournaig
Aird Dubh
Clachan Inverbroom
735
Gleann Beag
Port Erradale
Loch Bad a'Chreamh
INVEREWE GARDEN
Londubh
680
BEINN A'CHAISGEIN BEAG
Loch na Sealga
Auchlunachan
Broom
Lael
928
9
North Erradale
Poolewe
Loch Kernsary
Fisherfield Forest
Dundonnell
Forest
Auchindrean
889
1084
BEINN DEARG
628
Tollomuick Forest
NG
NH
80
70
30
954
Rubha Bàn
Big Sand
299
908
BEINN DEARG MHOR
Strath na Sealga
Achneigie
Fain
Braemore
Strath More
Longa Island
Caolas Beag
CARN DEARG
Lonemore
Mial
Strath
Smithstown
GAIRLOCH MUSEUM
Gairloch
Inveran
Kernsary
Loch Tollaidh
FIONN LOCH
MEALL AN DOIRFAN
Dubh Loch
914
BEINN A'
Dundonnell
Abhainn Cuileig
CORRIESHALLOCH GORGE
MEALL LEACACH
618
A894
A837
A835
A832
B869
Inver
Kirkaig
Loanan
Abhainn
304
305
309
10
8
13
5
17
G
H
J
K
L
1
2
3
4
5
6
7
8
0
2
4
6 miles
0
2
4
6
8
10 km

CAPE WRATH
Kearvaig
Geodha Ruadh na Fola
Bay of Keisgaig
Geodha Ruadh
Am Balg
Sandwood Loch
Loch Keisgaig
Strath Shinary
Sheigra
Balchrick
Blairmore
Droman
Oldshore Beg
Oldshoremore
Kinlochbervie
Loch Clash
Badcall
Inshegra
Achriesgill
Rhivichie
Loch Inchard
Achlyness
Ceathramh Garbh
Ardmore Pt.
Ardmore
Portlevorchy
Skerricha
Fanagmore
Foindle
Loch Laxford
Badnabay
Laxford Bridge
Scourie
Lower Badcall
Calbha Mòr
Duartmore Bridge
Duartmore Forest
Ardvar
Kylestrome
Kylesku
Unapool
Newton
Loch Glencoul
Loch Glendhu
Glendhu
Inshore
Achiemore
Keoldale
Sangomore
Balnakeil
Balnakeil Bay
BALNAKEIL CHURCH
BALNAKEIL CRAFT VILLAGE
Durness
DURNESS SMOO
SMOO CAVE
Leirinmore
Sangobeg
Faraid Head
Kyle of Durness
Sarsgrum
Loch Airigh na Beinne
Grudie
Rhigolter
Gualin Ho.
FARRMHEALL
Strath Dionard
Loch Dionard
L. na Claise Carnaich
Rhiconich
GANU MOR
Foinaven
NORTH-WEST SUTHERLAND
Loch a' Garbh-bhaid Mòr
Loch an Easain Uaine
ARKLE
Lochstack Lodge
Loch Stack
BEN STACK
Strath Stack
Achfary
Airdachuilinn
REAY FOREST
Lochmore Lodge
Loch More
Loch na Creige Duibhe
Loch an Leathaid Bhuain
Aultanrynie
Kinloch
West Merkland
Loch Merkland
BEINN AUSKAIRD
BEINN AIRD DA LOCH
Gorm Loch
MEALL MEADHONACH
LOCH ERIBOLL
Portnancon
Eilean Choraidh
Eriboll
Polla
Strath Beag
BEINN SPIONNAIDH
CRANSTACKIE
Rispond
Eilean Hoan
Eilean Clùimhrig
Geodh'a' Bhrideoin
Whiten Head
Heilam
Hope
Lochside
Kempie
Loch Hope
AN LEAN-CHARN
BEN HOPE
Loch Crocach
FEINNE-BHEINN MOR
Strathmore
Alltnacaillich
DUN DORNAIGIL BROCH
Glen Golly
Gobernuisgach Lodge
Allt a' Chraois
Loch Coire na Saidhe Duibhe
BEN HEE
Loch a' Ghorm-choire
A'Mhoine
Druim nan Cliar
KYLE OF TONGUE
Loch na Seilg
Loch a' Ghobha-Dhuibh
Loch Meadie
Meadie Burn
Mudale
Rubha Thormaid
BEN HUTIG
Achininver
West Strathan
Strathan
Portvasgo
Port Vasgo
Midfield
Lubinvullin
Achinahuagh
Talmine
Skinnet
Midtown
Achuvoldrach
Kyle of Tongue
CASTLE VARRICH
TONGUE
Kirkiboll
Tongue
Ribigill
Kinloch Lodge
Loch an Dherue
Loch Haluim
BEN LOYAL
Loch Loyal Lodge
CNOC NAN CULLEAN
Loch Coulside
Inchkinloch
Altnaharra
Rabbit Is.
Tongue Bay
Coldbackie
Blandy
Dallcharn
Skullomie
Strathan Skerray
Skerray
Caol Raineach
Eilean nan Ron
Neave I. or Coombe I.
Clashedy
Achtoty
Airdtorrisdale
Torrisdale
Torrisdale Bay
Borgie
Borgie Forest
Loch Craggie
BEINN STUMANADH
Loch Loyal
Loch Syre
Loch Eileanach
POLE HILL
Grumbeg
Loch Naver
Achadh an Eas
Mallart
Clebrig
BEN KLIBRECK
Loch Choire Lodge
Farr Pt.
Farr
STRATHNAVER MUSEUM
Crask
Bettyhill
Achina
Invernaver
Leckfurin
Swordly
Kirtomy
Kirtomy Pt.
Clachan Burn
ACHANLOCHY CLEARANCE VILLAGE
Skelpick
Skelpick Burn
Achagary
STRATHNAVER
Carnachy
Rhifail
Rough Haugh
BEINN RIFA-GIL
Skail
Langdale
Syre
Dalvina Lo.
ROSAL CLEARANCE TRAIL
Naver Forest
Loch Rimsdale
Loch Truderscaig
Rimsdale Burn
Loch Meadie
Loch Buidhe Mor
Loch Mor na Caorach
Loch nan Clach
Loch Strathy
Loch nan Clàr
Loch Badanloch
Badanloch Lodge
Loch an Alltan Fhearna
Badanloch Forest
Garvault Hotel
BEN GRIAM MORE
BEN GRIAM BEG
Loch Druim a'Chliabhain
Loch Crocach
Loch na Saobhaidhe
Armadale
Armadale Bay
Armadale Burn
Ardmore Pt.
Brawl
Aultiphurst
Lednagullin
Strathy Forest
Strathy Bay
Totegan
Strathy Point
Bowside
Loch Meala
The Uair
HIGHLAND
Helmsdale
Arichlinie
NM
NC

309
LOCH SHIN
BEN ARMINE FOREST
EASTER ROSS
DORNOCH FIRTH
ASSYNT-COIGACH
CROMALT HILLS
Lairg
Bonar Bridge
Dornoch
Tain
Golspie
Embo
Edderton
Ardgay
Invershin
Rosehall
Oykel Bridge
Ledmore
Inchnadamph
Skiag Bridge
Lochassynt Lodge
Little Assynt
Elphin
Knockan
Drumrunie
Leckmelm
Inverlael
Crask Inn
Overscaig Hotel
Merkland Lodge
Altnacealgach Hotel
Strath Oykel
Strath Tirry
Glen Cassley
Strath Fleet
Strath Brora
Rogart
Dalchork Wood
Shin Forest
Oykel Forest
Amat Forest
Croich
The Craigs
Deanich Lodge
Alladale Lodge
Glencalvie Lodge
Carbisdale Castle
Falls of Shin Visitor Centre
Skibo Castle
Dornoch Cathedral
Ardvreck Castle
Eas Coul Aulin Waterfall
Leckmelm Shrubbery and Arboretum
Lael Forest Garden
Corrieshalloch Gorge
Loch Broom
Morangie Forest
Glenmorangie Distillery
Tain Through Time Visitor Centre
A836
A837
A838
A839
A949
A9
A835
B9176
B9168

314
308
ST MARGARETS HOPE
BURWICK (May-Sept)
STROMNESS
Island of Stroma
Nethertown
Uppertown
Langaton Point
Red Head
Mell Head
DUNCANSBY HEAD
Stacks of Duncansby
Boars of Duncansby
John o' Groats
Huna
Kirkstyle
Canisbay
Gills Bay
Gills
St John's Pt.
Men of Mey
East Mey
CASTLE OF MEY
Harrow
Mey
Scarfskerry Pt.
Scarfskerry
Ham
Rattar
Barrock
Inkstack
St John's Loch
Corsback
Dunnet
DUNNET HEAD
Briga Hd.
Brough
Hunspow
MARY ANN'S COTTAGE
The Thirl
NATURAL HISTORY VISITOR CENTRE
DUNNET BAY
FLAGSTONE INTERPRETATIVE TRAIL
Castlehill
Clardon Hd.
Clardon
Murkle
Castletown
CASTLETOWN
Holborn Hd.
Thurso Bay
Scrabster
THURSO CASTLE
Thurso
Thurso East
Haimer
Millbank
Janetstown
Newlands of Geise
Glengolly
Geise
Spear Hd.
Brims Castle
Brims Ness
ST MARY'S CHAPEL
Crosskirk
Bridge of Forss
Lythmore
Achreamie
Buldoo
Dounreay
Upper Dounreay
CNOC FREKEDAIN CHAMBERED CAIRN
Sandside Bay
Sandside Ho.
Fresgoe
Isauld
Reay
Achvarasdal
Red Pt.
Melvich Bay
Portskerra
Bighouse
Melvich
Baligill
Strathy
Strathy Bay
Strathy Point
Totegan
Aultivullin
Aultiphurst
Brawl
Armadale
Armadale Bay
Lednagullin
Golval
Bowside Lodge
Strathy Forest
Loch Meala
Achiemore
Upper Bighouse
Craigtown
Dalhalvaig
Croick
Trantlemore
Trantlebeg
STRATH HALLADALE
Forsinain
Forsinard
Forsinard Station
FORSINARD FLOWS
Loch nam Breac
The Uair
Loch Akran
Loch na Seilge
Westfield
Shebster
Achnavast
Lieurary
Broubster
Loch Calder
Shurrery
Shurrery Lodge
Brawlbin
Dorrery
Loch Olginey
Scotscalder Station
Olgrinmore
Buckies
Calder Mains
Halkirk
Sordale
Braal Castle
Weydale
Achingills
Stemster
Knockdee
Roadside
Clayock
Banniskirk Mains
Banniskirk Ho.
Achalone
Harpsdale
Strathcoul
Spittal
Westerdale
Braehour
Mybster
Backlass
Loch of Toftingall
Acharole
Watten
Loch Watten
Wester Watten
Oldhall Ho
South Dunn
Quoynee
Catchory
Mains of Watten
North Watten
Gillock
Halcro
Bower
Bowertower
Stemster Ho.
Hastigrow
Kirk
Myrelandhorn
Killimster
Olrig Ho.
Hilliclay
Durran
Greenland
Greenland Mains
Tain
Loch Heilen
Syster
Lochend
Reaster
Bowermadden
Lyth
LYTH ARTS CENTRE
Sortat
Barrock Ho.
Howe
Alterwall
Slickly
Brabster
Gill Burn
Upper Gills
Stroupster
Freswick
Freswick Bay
Skirza
Skirza Head
Tofts
Ness Head
BUCHOLLY CASTLE
CAITHNESS BROCH CENTRE
Auckengill
Nybster
Brough Head
Keiss
KEISS CASTLE
Stain
Mireland
SINCLAIR'S BAY
Reiss
Winless
Sibster
CASTLE SINCLAIR
CASTLE GIRNIGOE
Noss Head
Ackergill
Noss
Sealky Head
Staxigoe
WICK HERITAGE MUS
Papigoe
Wick
Broadhaven
Wick Bay
Haster
Milton
Stirkoke Ho.
Bilbster
Strath
Old Wick
South Hd.
CASTLE OF OLD WICK
Gote O'Tram
Newton
Whiterow
Hempriggs House
Loch Hempriggs
Helman Hd.
Blingery
Tannach
Badlipster
Kensary
Munsary Cottage
GREY CAIRNS OF CAMSTER
Camster
HILL OF OLICLETT
Thrumster
Gansclet
Borrowston
Sarclet
Sarclet Hd.
South Yarrows
Loch of Yarrows
Ulbster
Mains of Ulbster
CAIRN OF GET
Whaligoe
East Clyth
HILL O' MANY STANES
Mid Clyth
Bruan
West Clyth
Lybster
Invershore
Upper Lybster
Roster
Rumster Forest
Crofts of Benachielt
Rangag
Achavanich
STEMSTER HILL
Loch Rangag
Braehungie
Forse Ho.
Swiney
Forse
Burrigill
CLAN GUNN HERITAGE CENTRE
Latheron
Latheronwheel
Latheronwheel Ho.
Buoltach
Houstry
Smerral
WAG OF FORSE
Badnagie
Knockinnon
LAIDHAY CROFT MUSEUM
Balcraggie Lodge
Braemore
Dunbeath Water
Berriedale Water
Burn of Houstry
CNOCAN CONACHREAG
Little River
Strathmore Lodge
Loch Ruard
Loch Thulachan
Backlass
Loch Sand
Loch More
Lochmore Cottage
Loch Eileanach
Loch Gaineimh
Loch Meadie
Loch Dubh nan Geodh
Altnabreac Station
Lochdhu
Sleach Water
Dalnawillan Lodge
Dalganachan
Loch a' Mhuilinn
BEN ALISKY
Loch Breac
Loch Dubh
Glutt Lodge
Glutt Water
CNOC LOCH MHADADH
Gobernuisgeach
Loch Sletill
SLETILL HILL
BEINN NAM BAD MOR
Loch Tuim Ghlais
Loch Caluim
Torran Water
Loch Scye
Loch Shurrery
Loch Saorach
Loch Thormaid
Achvarasdal Burn
Forss Water
Sandside Burn
Knockfin Heights
Rumsdale Water
Achentoul Forest
Achentoul
Lochside
Loch an Ruathair
Strath Beg
Kinbrace
Loch Arichlinie
Greamchary
Allt Airigh-dhamh
BEN GRIAM BEG
Loch Druim a'Chliabhain
Loch Crocach
Loch na Saobhaidhe
Garvault Hotel
BEN GRIAM MORE
Badanloch Forest
Badanloch Lodge
Loch Badanloch
Loch an Clàr
Loch Strathy
Loch nan Clach
Loch Mor na Caorach
Loch Meadie
Helmsdale
HIGHLAND

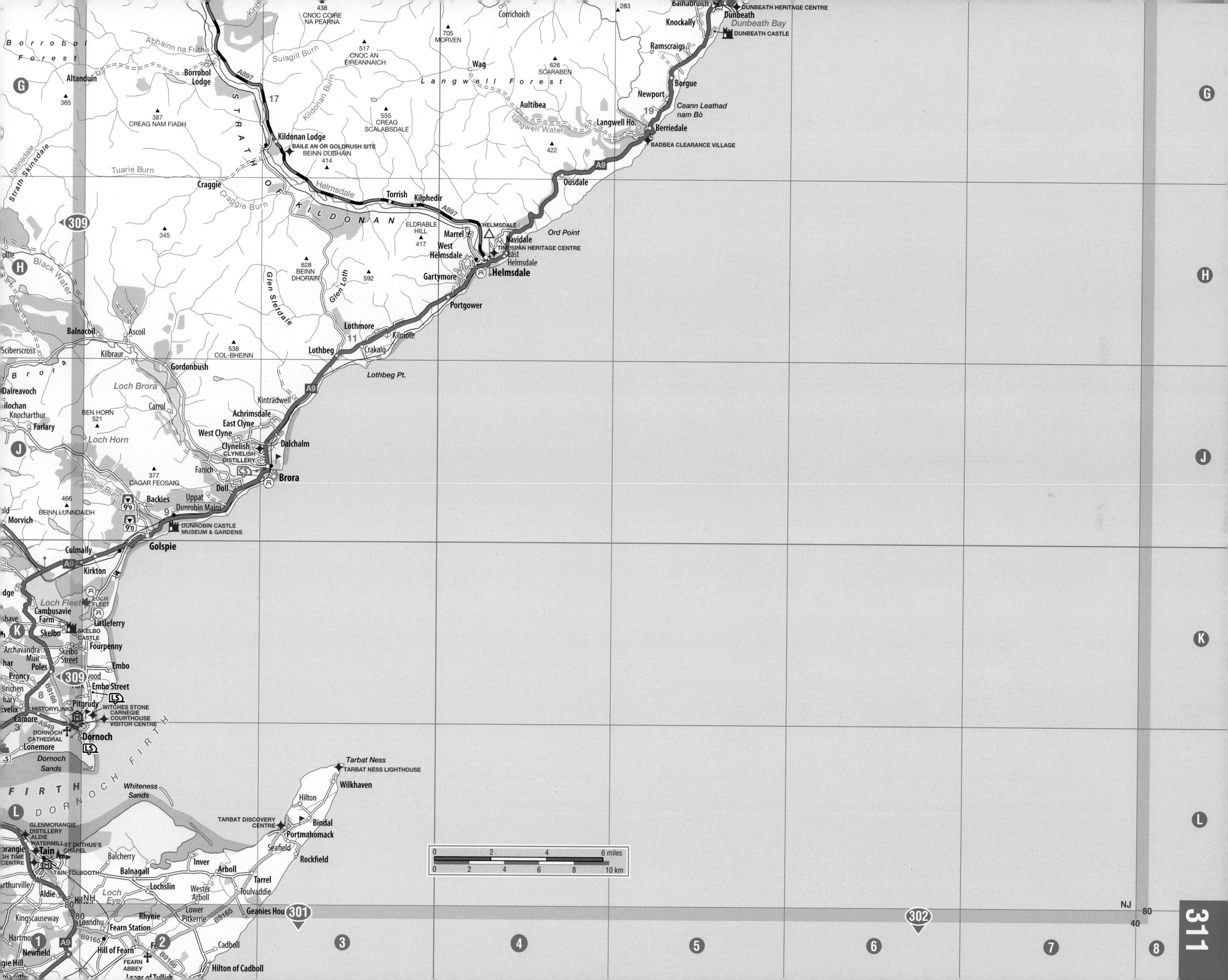
Dunbeath
DUNBEATH HERITAGE CENTRE
Dunbeath Bay
DUNBEATH CASTLE
Knockally
Ramscraigs
Borgue
Newport
Ceann Leathad nam Bò
Berriedale
BADBEA CLEARANCE VILLAGE
Langwell Ho.
Langwell Water
Aultibea
Langwell Forest
626 SCARABEN
422
Wag
705 MORVEN
Corrichoich
283
438 CNOC COIRE NA PEARNA
517 CNOC AN EIREANNAICH
555 CREAG SCALABSDALE
Suisgill Burn
Kildonan Burn
Abhainn na Frithe
Borrobol Forest
Borrobol Lodge
Altanduin
365
387 CREAG NAM FIADH
A897
17
STRATH OF KILDONAN
Kildonan Lodge
BAILE AN ÒR GOLDRUSH SITE
BEINN DUBHAIN
414
Strath Skinsdale
Skinsdale
Tuarie Burn
Craggie
Craggie Burn
Helmsdale
Torrish
Kilphedir
A897
ELDRABLE HILL
417
Marrel
West Helmsdale
HELMSDALE
Navidale
TIMESPAN HERITAGE CENTRE
East Helmsdale
Helmsdale
Ord Point
Ousdale
A9
309
345
Black Water
628 BEINN DHORAIN
Glen Loth
592
Gartymore
Portgower
Glen Sletdale
Lothmore
11
Kilmote
Crakaig
Lothbeg
Lothbeg Pt.
538 COL-BHEINN
Balnacoil
Ascoil
Sciberscross
Kilbraur
Gordonbush
Brora
Loch Brora
Dalreavoch
Knocharthur
Farlary
BEN HORN 521
Loch Horn
Carrol
Kintradwell
Achrimsdale
East Clyne
West Clyne
Clynelish
CLYNELISH DISTILLERY
Dalchalm
Fanich
Brora
377 CAGAR FEOSAIG
Golspie Burn
Doll
Backies
Uppat
Dunrobin Mains
466 BEINN LUNNDAIDH
Morvich
9
DUNROBIN CASTLE MUSEUM & GARDENS
Golspie
Culmaily
Kirkton
Loch Fleet
LOCH FLEET
Cambusavie Farm
Littleferry
Skelbo
SKELBO CASTLE
Skelbo Street
Fourpenny
Archavandra Muir
Poles
Embo
Proncy
309
Embo Street
B9168
HISTORYLINKS
Pitgrudy
WITCHES STONE
CARNEGIE COURTHOUSE
VISITOR CENTRE
A949
DORNOCH CATHEDRAL
Dornoch
Lonemore
Dornoch Sands
DORNOCH FIRTH
Whiteness Sands
Tarbat Ness
TARBAT NESS LIGHTHOUSE
Wilkhaven
Hilton
TARBAT DISCOVERY CENTRE
Bindal
Portmahomack
Seafield
Rockfield
GLENMORANGIE DISTILLERY
ALDIE WATERMILL
ST DUTHUS'S CHAPEL
Tain
TAIN TOLBOOTH
Balcherry
Balnagall
Inver
Arboll
Tarrel
Loch Eye
Lochslin
Wester Arboll
Toulvaddie
Aldie
Hill
Kingscauseway
Loandhu
Rhynie
Lower Pitkerrie
B9165
Geanies Hou
301
Fearn Station
Hill of Fearn
FEARN ABBEY
B9166
Cadboll
Hilton of Cadboll
Newfield
302
0 2 4 6 miles
0 2 4 6 8 10 km
NJ
80
40
G
H
J
K
L
1
2
3
4
5
6
7
8

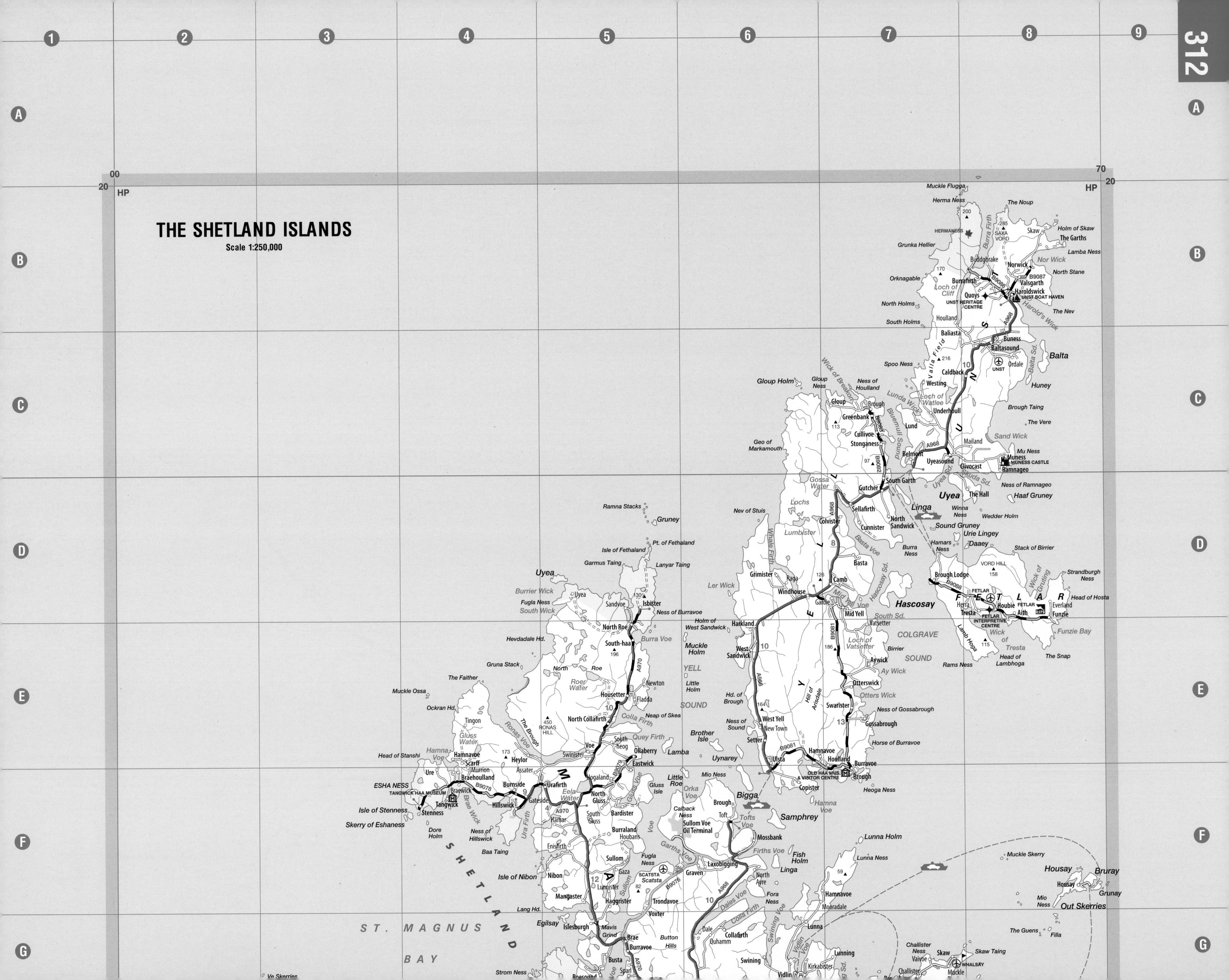
THE SHETLAND ISLANDS
Scale 1:250,000
HP
Unst
Yell
Fetlar
Mainland
Muckle Flugga
Herma Ness
Hermaness
Burra Firth
Saxa Vord
Skaw
Holm of Skaw
The Garths
Lamba Ness
Norwick
Nor Wick
North Stane
Valsgarth
Haroldswick
Unst Boat Haven
Buddabrake
Burrafirth
Quoys
Unst Heritage Centre
Loch of Cliff
Harold's Wick
The Nev
Grunka Hellier
Orknagable
North Holms
South Holms
Houlland
Baliasta
Buness
Baltasound
Balta
Balta Sd.
Ordale
Valla Field
Caldback
Westing
Huney
Spoo Ness
Loch of Watlee
Underhoull
Brough Taing
The Vere
Lund
Sand Wick
Mailand
Mu Ness
Muness
Muness Castle
Ramnageo
Belmont
Uyeasound
Clivocast
Uyea
Uyea Sd.
Skuda Sd.
Ness of Ramnageo
Haaf Gruney
The Hall
Linga
Winna Ness
Wedder Holm
Sound Gruney
Urie Lingey
Daaey
Hamars Ness
Stack of Birrier
Brough Lodge
Vord Hill
Wick of Gruting
Strandburgh Ness
Head of Hosta
Houbie
Aith
Everland
Funzie
Funzie Bay
Herra
Tresta
Fetlar Interpretive Centre
Wick of Tresta
Lamb Hoga
Head of Lambhoga
The Snap
Rams Ness
Gloup Holm
Gloup Ness
Wick of Breakon
Ness of Houlland
Gloup
Brough
Greenbank
Cullivoe
Stonganess
Bluemull Sound
Geo of Markamouth
South Garth
Gutcher
Gossa Water
Sellafirth
Cunnister
North Sandwick
Burra Ness
Basta Voe
Basta
Nev of Stuis
Lochs of Lumbister
Colvister
Whale Firth
Grimister
Raga
Windhouse
Camb
Gardie
Mid Yell
Mid Yell Voe
Hascosay
Hascosay Sd.
South Sd.
Ler Wick
Vatsetter
Loch of Vatsetter
COLGRAVE SOUND
Birrier
Aywick
Ay Wick
Harkland
West Sandwick
Hill of Arisdale
Otterswick
Otters Wick
Ness of Gossabrough
Gossabrough
Horse of Burravoe
Swarister
West Yell
New Town
Setter
Hd. of Brough
Ness of Sound
Ulsta
Hamnavoe
Houlland
Burravoe
Old Haa Mus & Visitor Centre
Copister
Heoga Ness
Hamna Voe
Holm of West Sandwick
Muckle Holm
YELL SOUND
Little Holm
Brother Isle
Uynarey
Ramna Stacks
Gruney
Pt. of Fethaland
Isle of Fethaland
Lanyar Taing
Garmus Taing
Isbister
Ness of Burravoe
Sandvoe
North Roe
Burra Voe
South-haa
Uyea
Burrier Wick
Fugla Ness
South Wick
Hevdadale Hd.
Gruna Stack
Roer Water
Newton
Housetter
Fladda
Colla Firth
Neap of Skea
North Collafirth
Ronas Hill
Voe
Quey Firth
South Heog
Ollaberry
Eastwick
Lamba
Mio Ness
Little Roe
Gluss Isle
The Faither
Muckle Ossa
Ockran Hd.
Tingon
Gluss Water
Hamna Voe
Hamnavoe
Scarff
Heylor
Head of Stanshi
Ure
Braehoulland
Burnside
Assater
Swinister
Hogaland
ESHA NESS
Tangwick Haa Museum
Braewick
Tangwick
Stenness
Isle of Stenness
Skerry of Eshaness
Brae Wick
Dore Holm
Ness of Hillswick
Hillswick
Urafirth
Eela Water
Gateside
Ura Firth
North Gluss
Bardister
South Gluss
Hamar
Orka Voe
Calback Ness
Sullom Voe Oil Terminal
Brough
Toft
Tofts Voe
Bigga
Samphrey
Burraland
Houbans
Ensirth
Sullom
Fugla Ness
Scatsta
Graven
Garths Voe
Mossbank
Firths Voe
Fish Holm
Linga
Laxobigging
North Ayre
Fora Ness
Lunna Holm
Lunna Ness
Baa Taing
Isle of Nibon
Nibon
Lunnister
Mangaster
Haggrister
Trondavoe
Voxter
Dales Voe
Colla Firth
Swining Voe
Hamnavoe
Mooradale
Lang Hd.
Egilsay
Islesburgh
Mavis Grind
Brae
Burravoe
Busta
Button Hills
Dale
Collafirth
Quhamm
Lunna
Vidlin Voe
Vidlin
Lunning
Swining
Kirkabister
ST. MAGNUS BAY
SHETLAND
Strom Ness
Ve Skerries
Muckle Skerry
Housay
Bruray
Grunay
Mio Ness
Out Skerries
The Guens
Filla
Challister Ness
Vaivoe
Skaw
Skaw Taing
Whalsay
Challister

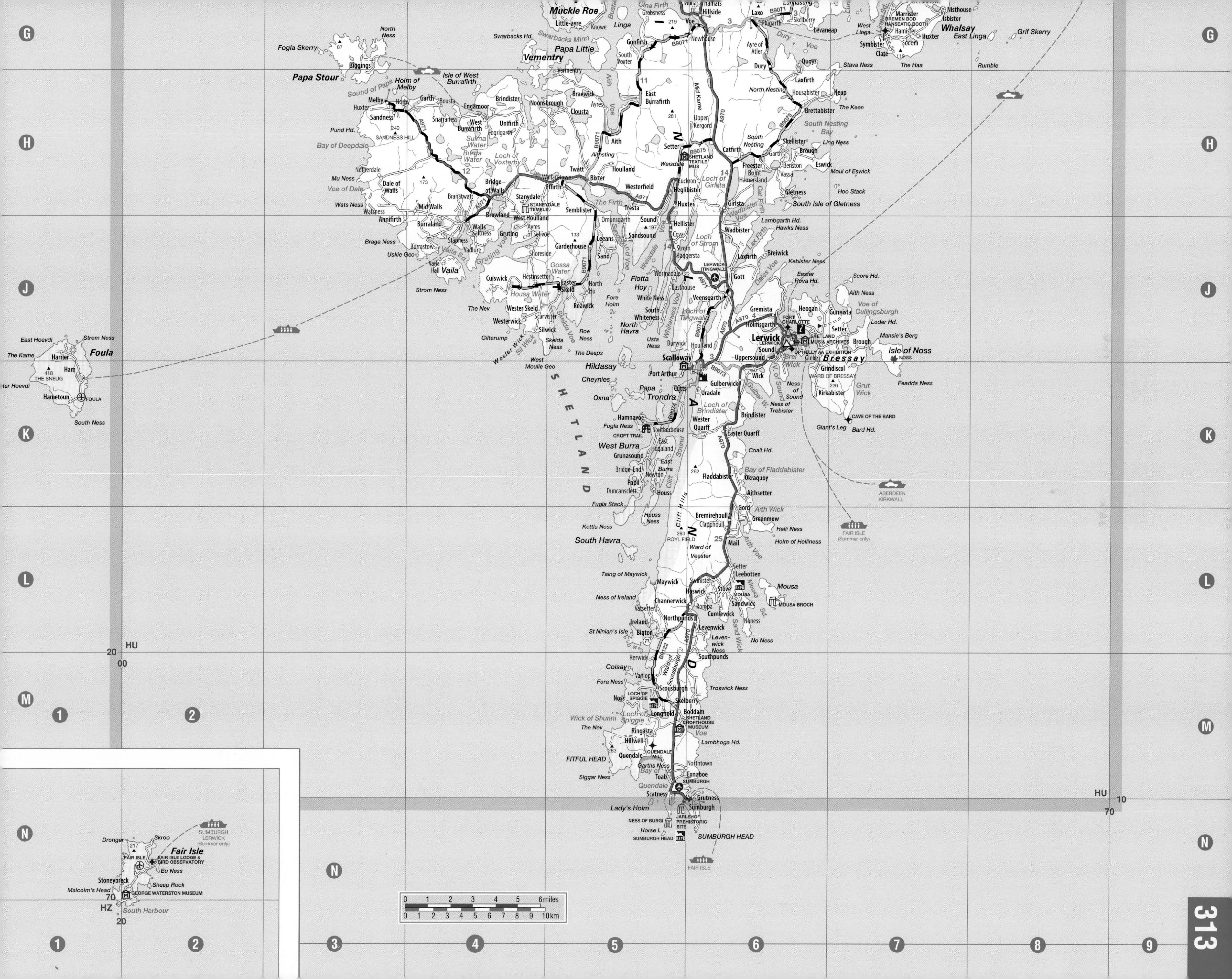
SHETLAND
Lerwick
Bressay
Isle of Noss
Mousa
Scalloway
Trondra
West Burra
East Burra
Hildasay
Papa Stour
Vementry
Papa Little
Muckle Roe
Whalsay
Vaila
South Havra
Foula
Fair Isle
Sumburgh
Sumburgh Head
Fitful Head
Lady's Holm
Aith
Walls
Sandness
Melby
Bixter
Tresta
Weisdale
Gott
Girlsta
Catfirth
Sandwick
Levenwick
Bigton
Boddam
Quendale
Toab
Grutness
Voe
Laxo
Symbister
A970
A971
B9074
Fair Isle (Summer only)
Aberdeen Kirkwall
Sumburgh Lerwick (Summer only)
HU
HZ
0 1 2 3 4 5 6 miles
0 1 2 3 4 5 6 7 8 9 10 km

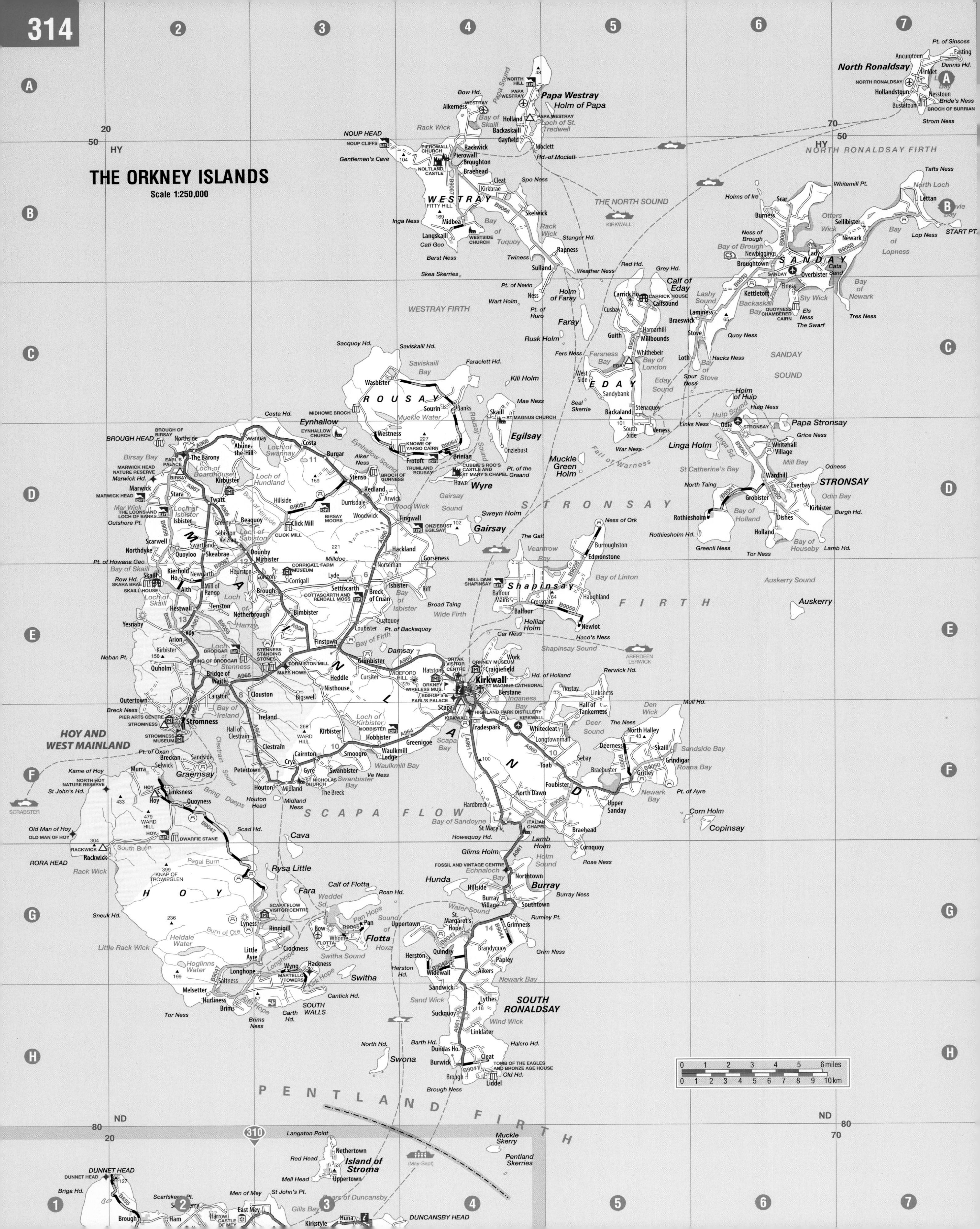
314
THE ORKNEY ISLANDS
Scale 1:250,000
HY
ND
North Ronaldsay
Pt. of Sinsoss
Ancumtoun
Easting
Dennis Hd.
Linklet
Hollandstoun
Nesstoun
Bride's Ness
Bustatoun
BROCH OF BURRIAN
Strom Ness
NORTH RONALDSAY FIRTH
Papa Westray
Holm of Papa
Holland
Loch of St. Tredwell
Backaskaill
Gayfield
Moclett
Hd. of Moclett
Papa Sound
Bow Hd.
Aikerness
Bay of Skaill
Rack Wick
NOUP HEAD
NOUP CLIFFS
Gentlemen's Cave
PIEROWALL CHURCH
Rackwick
Pierowall
Broughton
Braehead
NOLTLAND CASTLE
WESTRAY
FITTY HILL
Midbea
Cleat
Kirkbrae
Spo Ness
Skelwick
Rack Wick
Inga Ness
Langskaill
WESTSIDE CHURCH
Bay of Tuquoy
Cati Geo
Stanger Hd.
Rapness
Berst Ness
Twiness
Sulland
Skea Skerries
Weather Ness
THE NORTH SOUND
KIRKWALL
Tafts Ness
North Loch
Whitemill Pt.
Holms of Ire
Scar
Lettan
Burness
Otters Wick
Sellibister
Newark
Bay of Lopness
Lop Ness
START PT.
Ness of Brough
Bay of Brough
Newbiggings
Broughtown
Lady
SANDAY
Overbister
Cata Sand
Kettletoft
Elness
Sty Wick
Bay of Newark
Tres Ness
Lashy Sound
Backaskaill Bay
QUOYNESS CHAMBERED CAIRN
Els Ness
The Swarf
Red Hd.
Grey Hd.
Calf of Eday
Carrick Ho.
CARRICK HOUSE
Calfsound
Braeswick
Laminess
Stove
Quoy Ness
Hacks Ness
Pt. of Nevin
Ness
Holm of Faray
Wart Holm
Pt. of Huro
WESTRAY FIRTH
Faray
Rusk Holm
Cusbay
Guith
Hamarhill
Millbounds
Whitebeir
Fersness Bay
Bay of London
Fers Ness
EDAY
West Side
Sandybank
Eday Sound
Loth
Bay of Stove
Spur Ness
SANDAY SOUND
Seal Skerrie
Backaland
South Side
Stenaquoy
Veness
Holm of Huip
Huip Sound
Huip Ness
Links Ness
Odie
Papa Stronsay
Grice Ness
Linga Holm
Whitehall Village
Mill Bay
Linga Sd.
St Catherine's Bay
Odness
Wardhill
North Taing
STRONSAY
Everbay
Odin Bay
Grobister
Kirbister
Burgh Hd.
Bay of Holland
Rothiesholm
Dishes
Holland
Rothiesholm Hd.
Bay of Houseby
Lamb Hd.
Greenli Ness
Tor Ness
Sacquoy Hd.
Saviskaill Hd.
Saviskaill Bay
Faraclett Hd.
Kili Holm
Wasbister
ROUSAY
Mae Ness
Sourin
Banks
Skaill
ST MAGNUS CHURCH
Egilsay
Muckle Water
Rousay Sound
Westness
KNOWE OF YARSO CAIRN
Frotoft
TRUMLAND ROUSAY
Brinian
Onziebust
Muckle Green Holm
Fall of Warness
War Ness
Costa Hd.
MIDHOWE BROCH
Eynhallow
EYNHALLOW CHURCH
Eynhallow Sound
Aiker Ness
BROCH OF GURNESS
CUBBIE'S ROO'S CASTLE AND ST MARY'S CHAPEL
Hawn
Wyre
Pt. of the Graand
Gairsay Sound
Wood Wick
Sweyn Holm
Gairsay
STRONSAY
Ness of Ork
BROUGH OF BIRSAY
Northside
Swannay
BROUGH HEAD
Abune the Hill
Loch of Swannay
Costa
Burgar
Birsay Bay
The Barony
EARL'S PALACE
BIRSAY
MARWICK HEAD NATURE RESERVE
Marwick Hd.
Loch of Boardhouse
Loch of Hundland
Kirbuster
Tingwall
ONZIEBUST EGILSAY
Marwick
MARWICK HEAD
Stara
Twatt
Hillside
Durrisdale
Arwick
Woodwick
Mar Wick
THE LOONS AND LOCH OF BANKS
Loch of Isbister
Outshore Pt.
Isbister
Greeny
Beaquoy
Click Mill
CLICK MILL
BIRSAY MOORS
Sebiston
Velzian
Loch of Sabiston
Scarwell
Northdyke
Swartland
Quoyloo
Skeabrae
Dounby
Mirbister
Milldoe
Hackland
Gorseness
The Galt
Burroughston
Edmonstone
Veantrow Bay
Pt. of Howana Geo
Bay of Skaill
Row Hd.
SKARA BRAE
SKAILL HOUSE
Skaill
Kierfiold Ho
Newgarth
Hourston
CORRIGALL FARM MUSEUM
Corrigall
Norseman
Lyde
Settiscarth
Isbister
Riff
Broad Taing
Wide Firth
MILL DAM SHAPINSAY
Balfour Mains
Shapinsay
Crossgate
Haughland
Bay of Linton
Auskerry Sound
Auskerry
FIRTH
Aith
Mill of Rango
Brough
COTTASCARTH AND RENDALL MOSS
Breck of Cruan
Bay of Isbister
Balfour
Helliar Holm
Newlot
Haco's Ness
Loch of Skaill
Hestwall
Tenston
Netherbrough
Bimbister
Quatquoy
Coubister
Pt. of Backaquoy
Yesnaby
Harray
Voy
Finstown
Bay of Firth
Car Ness
Arion
Loch of Stenness
Damsay
Shapinsay Sound
ABERDEEN LERWICK
Neban Pt.
Kirbister
BRODGAR
STENNESS STANDING STONES
RING OF BRODGAR
Grimbister
ORKNEY MUSEUM
Work
Rerwick Hd.
Quholm
TORMISTON MILL
MAES HOWE
Heddle
Cursiter
WIDEFORD HILL
ORKNEY WIRELESS MUS.
Hatston
ORTAK VISITOR CENTRE
Craigiefield
Kirkwall
ST MAGNUS CATHEDRAL
Berstane
Hd. of Holland
Bridge of Waith
Nisthouse
BISHOP'S & EARL'S PALACE
Inganess Bay
Yinstay
Linksness
Mull Hd.
Outertown
Cairston
Clouston
Bigswell
Scapa
HIGHLAND PARK DISTILLERY
Hall of Tankerness
Den Wick
Breck Ness
PIER ARTS CENTRE
STROMNESS
Stromness
Bay of Ireland
Ireland
Loch of Kirbister
HOBBISTER
Tradespark
Whitecleat
Deer Sound
The Ness
North Halley
HOY AND WEST MAINLAND
STROMNESS MUSEUM
Hall of Clestrain
WARD HILL
Kirbister
Hobbister
Longtownmail
Skaill
Sandside Bay
Grindigar
Pt. of Oxan
Clestrain
Greenigoe
Scapa Bay
Deerness
Roana Bay
Breckan
Sandside
Selwick
Graemsay
Clestrain Sound
Cairnston
Smoogro
Waulkmill Lodge
Waulkmill Bay
Toab
Sebay
Braebuster
Gritley
Kame of Hoy
Murra
NORTH HOY NATURE RESERVE
St John's Hd.
Linksness
Hoy
Bring Deeps
Quoyness
Petertown
Crya
Gyre
Swanbister
ST NICHOLAS CHURCH
Swanbister Bay
Ve Ness
Foubister
Newark Bay
Pt. of Ayre
SCRABSTER
Houton
Midland
The Breck
Houton Head
Midland Ness
North Dawn
Upper Sanday
Corn Holm
SCAPA FLOW
Hardbreck
Bay of Sandoyne
St Mary's
ITALIAN CHAPEL
Braehead
Copinsay
Old Man of Hoy
OLD MAN OF HOY
WARD HILL
Scad Hd.
HOY
DWARFIE STANE
Cava
Howequoy Hd.
Lamb Holm
Cornquoy
RACKWICK
Rackwick
RORA HEAD
South Burn
Glims Holm
Rose Ness
Rack Wick
Pegal Burn
Rysa Little
FOSSIL AND VINTAGE CENTRE
Echnaloch Bay
Holm Sound
Northtown
KNAP OF TROWIEGLEN
Hunda
Burray
Calf of Flotta
Fara
Roan Hd.
Hillside
Burray Village
Burray Ness
Weddel Sd.
Southtown
Sneuk Hd.
SCAPA FLOW VISITOR CENTRE
Pan Hope
Water Sound
Rumley Pt.
Lyness
Rinnigill
Pan
Sound of Hoxa
Uppertown
St. Margaret's Hope
Grimness
Heldale Water
Burn of Ore
Bow
FLOTTA
Whome
Flotta
Little Rack Wick
Little Ayre
Crockness
Switha Sound
Herston
Quindry
Brandyquoy
Grim Ness
Hoglinns Water
Longhope
Hackness
Wyng
MARTELLO TOWERS
Herston Hd.
Widewall
Papley
Aikers
Saltness
Switha
Newark Bay
Melsetter
Hurliness
Brims
Aith Hope
Kirk Hope
SOUTH WALLS
Cantick Hd.
Sandwick
Lythes
SOUTH RONALDSAY
Sand Wick
Tor Ness
Brims Ness
Garth Hd.
Suckquoy
Wind Wick
Linklater
North Hd.
Barth Hd.
Halcro Hd.
Swona
Dundas Ho.
Burwick
Cleat
TOMB OF THE EAGLES AND BRONZE AGE HOUSE
Old Hd.
Brough
Liddel
Brough Ness
PENTLAND FIRTH
Langaton Point
310
Muckle Skerry
Nethertown
Red Head
Island of Stroma
Pentland Skerries
Mell Head
Uppertown
(May-Sept)
DUNNET HEAD
Briga Hd.
Scarfskerry Pt.
Men of Mey
St John's Pt.
Bay of Duncansby
Gills Bay
East Mey
Harrow
CASTLE OF MEY
Brough
Ham
Kirkstyle
Huna
DUNCANSBY HEAD
0 1 2 3 4 5 6 miles
0 1 2 3 4 5 6 7 8 9 10 km

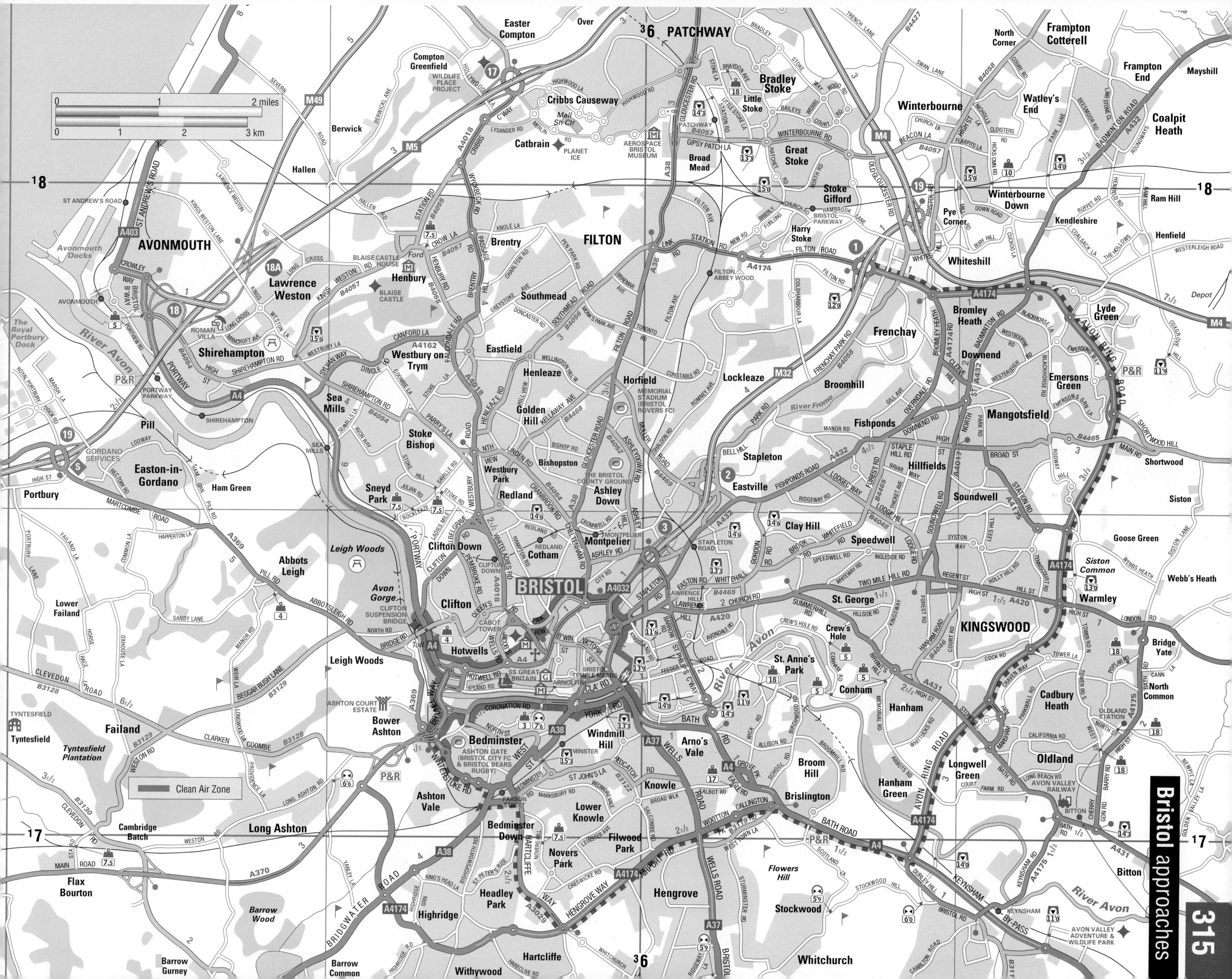
PATCHWAY
Easter Compton
Over
Compton Greenfield
WILDLIFE PLACE PROJECT
Cribbs Causeway
Mall Sh Ctr
Catbrain
PLANET ICE
AEROSPACE BRISTOL MUSEUM
Bradley Stoke
Little Stoke
Great Stoke
Broad Mead
Stoke Gifford
Harry Stoke
BRISTOL PARKWAY
Berwick
Hallen
AVONMOUTH
Avonmouth Docks
The Royal Portbury Dock
Lawrence Weston
Henbury
BLAISE CASTLE
Brentry
FILTON
Southmead
Shirehampton
ROMAN VILLA
Westbury on Trym
Eastfield
Henleaze
Horfield
MEMORIAL STADIUM (BRISTOL ROVERS FC)
Lockleaze
Broomhill
Frenchay
Winterbourne
Watley's End
North Corner
Frampton Cotterell
Frampton End
Mayshill
Coalpit Heath
Winterbourne Down
Pye Corner
Kendleshire
Ram Hill
Henfield
Whiteshill
Bromley Heath
Downend
Lyde Green
Emersons Green
Mangotsfield
Depot
Shortwood
Siston
Goose Green
Siston Common
Webb's Heath
Warmley
Sea Mills
Stoke Bishop
Golden Hill
Bishopston
THE BRISTOL COUNTY GROUND
Ashley Down
Westbury Park
Redland
Fishponds
Stapleton
Eastville
Hillfields
Soundwell
Pill
GORDANO SERVICES
Easton-in-Gordano
Ham Green
Portbury
Sneyd Park
Clifton Down
Cotham
Montpelier
Clay Hill
Speedwell
Leigh Woods
Abbots Leigh
Avon Gorge
CLIFTON SUSPENSION BRIDGE
Clifton
BRISTOL
Hotwells
SS GREAT BRITAIN
BRISTOL TEMPLE MEADS
St. George
KINGSWOOD
Lower Failand
Crew's Hole
St. Anne's Park
Conham
Bridge Yate
North Common
Cadbury Heath
Oldland
OLDLAND STATION
AVON VALLEY RAILWAY
Failand
Tyntesfield
Tyntesfield Plantation
ASHTON COURT ESTATE
Bower Ashton
Bedminster
ASHTON GATE (BRISTOL CITY FC & BRISTOL BEARS RUGBY)
Windmill Hill
Arno's Vale
River Avon
Hanham
Broom Hill
Hanham Green
Longwell Green
Clean Air Zone
Ashton Vale
Long Ashton
Cambridge Batch
Knowle
Lower Knowle
Brislington
Bedminster Down
Novers Park
Filwood Park
Flowers Hill
Bitton
Flax Bourton
Barrow Wood
Headley Park
Hengrove
Stockwood
Keynsham
AVON VALLEY ADVENTURE & WILDLIFE PARK
Highridge
Barrow Gurney
Barrow Common
Withywood
Hartcliffe
Whitchurch
2 miles
3 km
M4
M5
M32
M49
A4
A38
A37
A369
A4174
A4018
AVON RING ROAD
P&R

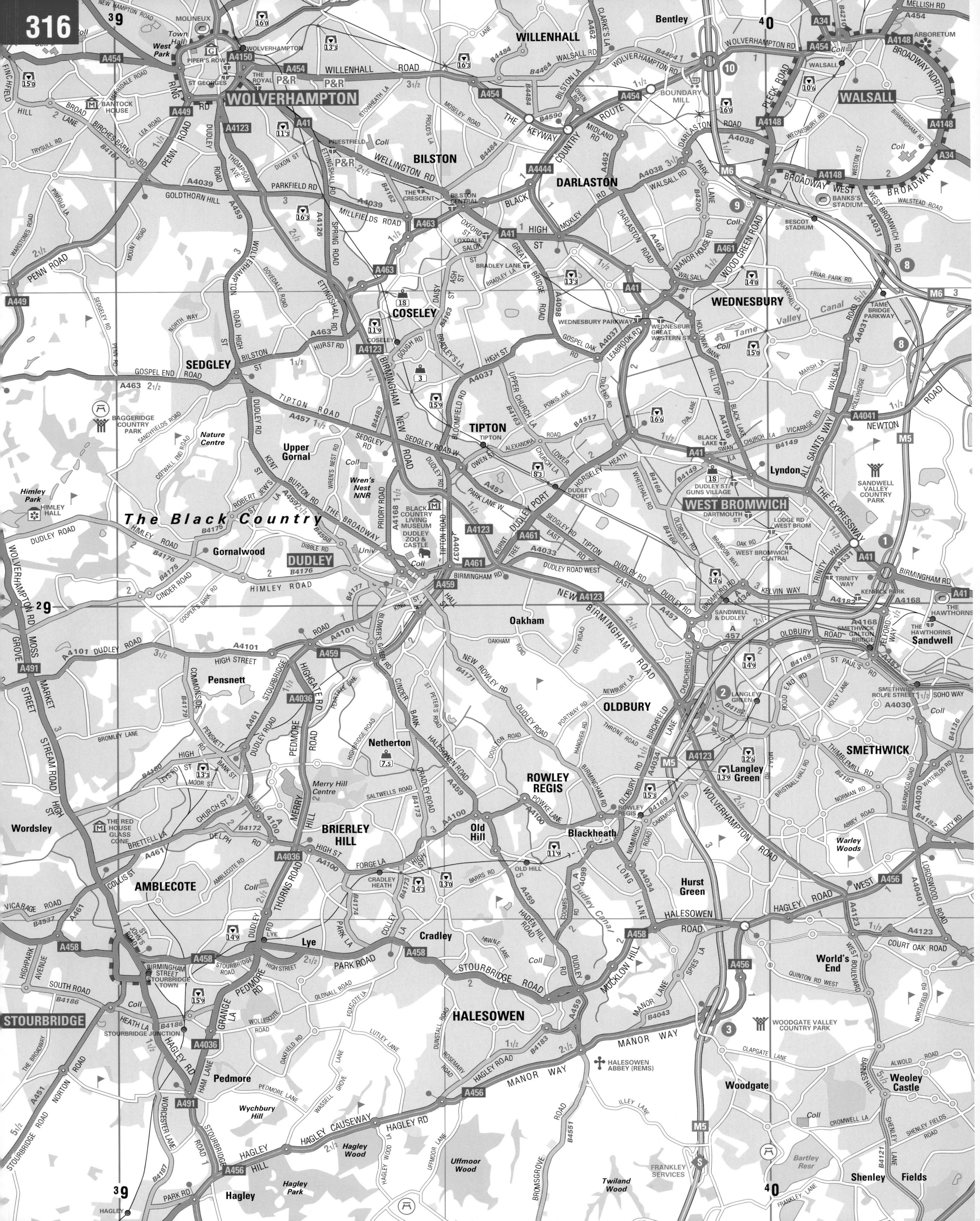

WOLVERHAMPTON
WALSALL
WEST BROMWICH
DUDLEY
STOURBRIDGE
The Black Country
Bentley
WILLENHALL
BILSTON
DARLASTON
WEDNESBURY
COSELEY
SEDGLEY
TIPTON
Upper Gornal
Gornalwood
Lyndon
Newton
Oakham
Pensnett
OLDBURY
SMETHWICK
Sandwell
Netherton
ROWLEY REGIS
Langley Green
Wordsley
BRIERLEY HILL
Old Hill
Blackheath
AMBLECOTE
Hurst Green
Lye
Cradley
HALESOWEN
World's End
Pedmore
Woodgate
Weoley Castle
Wychbury Hill
Hagley Wood
Uffmoor Wood
Twiland Wood
Hagley Park
Hagley
Shenley Fields
Bartley Resr
Warley Woods
Merry Hill Centre
Wren's Nest NNR
Nature Centre
Himley Park
HIMLEY HALL
BAGGERIDGE COUNTRY PARK
BANTOCK HOUSE
BLACK COUNTRY LIVING MUSEUM
DUDLEY ZOO & CASTLE
SANDWELL VALLEY COUNTRY PARK
WOODGATE VALLEY COUNTRY PARK
THE RED HOUSE GLASS CONE
HALESOWEN ABBEY (REMS)
FRANKLEY SERVICES
BESCOT STADIUM
BANKS'S STADIUM
ARBORETUM
THE HAWTHORNS
BOUNDARY MILL
Tame Valley Canal
Dudley Canal

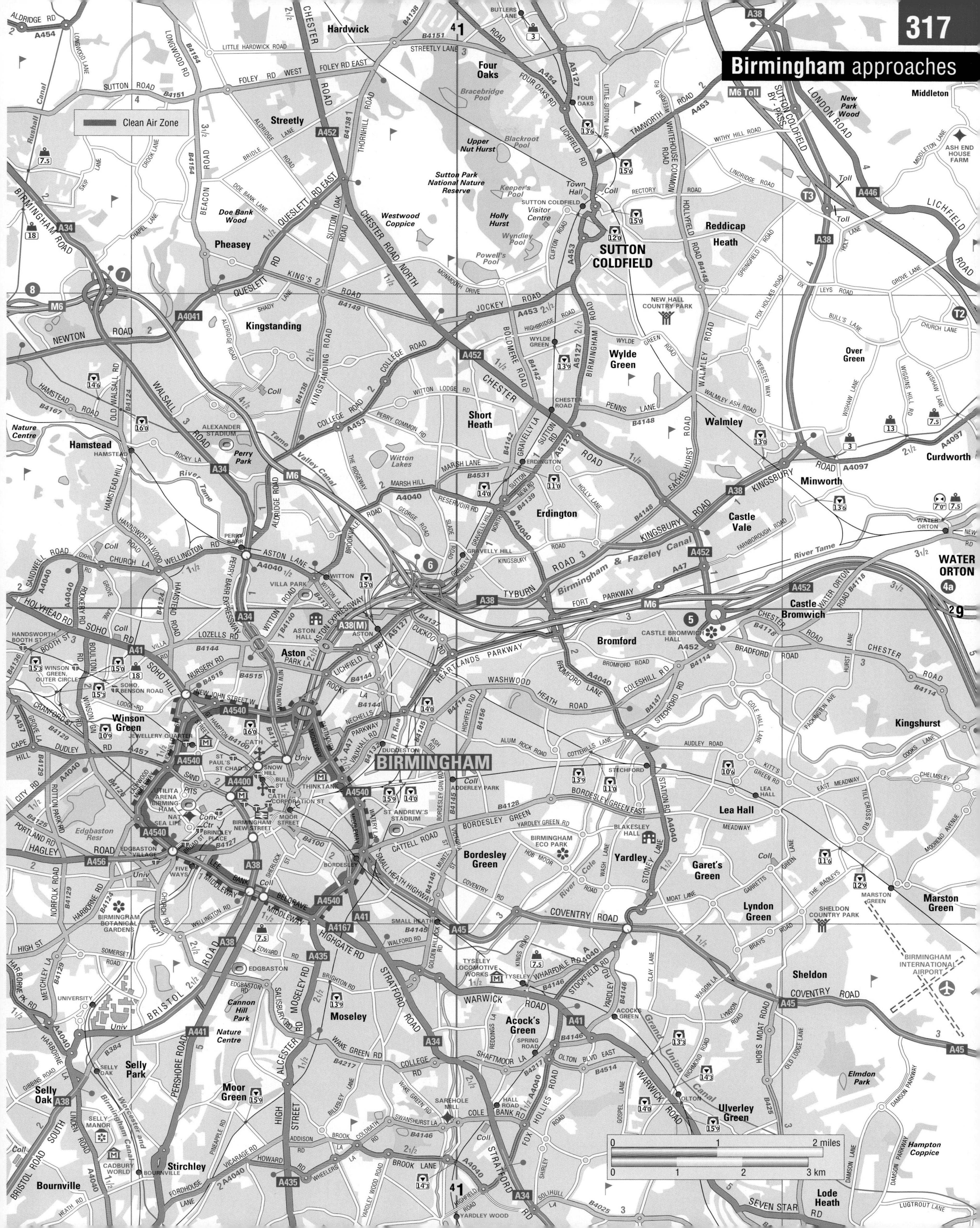
Clean Air Zone
Hardwick
Four Oaks
Bracebridge Pool
Streetly
Upper Nut Hurst
Blackroot Pool
Sutton Park National Nature Reserve
Keeper's Pool
Middleton
New Park Wood
Ash End House Farm
Doe Bank Wood
Westwood Coppice
Holly Hurst
Wyndley Pool
Powell's Pool
Pheasey
SUTTON COLDFIELD
Reddicap Heath
New Hall Country Park
Kingstanding
Wylde Green
Over Green
Short Heath
Walmley
Nature Centre
Hamstead
Alexander Stadium
Perry Park
Witton Lakes
Curdworth
Minworth
Erdington
Castle Vale
Water Orton
WATER ORTON
Villa Park
Birmingham & Fazeley Canal
River Tame
Castle Bromwich
Bromford
Castle Bromwich Hall
Aston
Aston Hall
Winson Green
Kingshurst
Jewellery Quarter
BIRMINGHAM
Thinktank
St Andrew's Stadium
Utilita Arena Birmingham
Lea Hall
Edgbaston Resr
Bordesley Green
Birmingham Eco Park
Yardley
Garet's Green
Marston Green
Lyndon Green
Sheldon Country Park
Birmingham Botanical Gardens
Sheldon
Birmingham International Airport
Edgbaston
Tyseley Locomotive Works
Cannon Hill Park
Moseley
Acock's Green
Nature Centre
Selly Park
Selly Oak
Moor Green
Sarehole Mill
Ulverley Green
Elmdon Park
Hampton Coppice
Selly Manor
Cadbury World
Stirchley
Bournville
Lode Heath
Grand Union Canal
Worcester and Birmingham Canal
0 1 2 miles
0 1 2 3 km

CARDIFF
(CAERDYDD)
CAERPHILLY
(CAERFFILI)
Marshfield
Castleton
Blacktown
Peterstone Wentlooge
(Llanbedr Gwynllŵg)
Michaelston-y-Fedw
St. Mellons
(Llaneirwg)
Trowbridge
Newton
Began
Rumney
(Rhymni)
Pwll-Mawr
Llanrumney
Llanedeyrn
Pentwyn
Tremorfa
Lisvane
(Llys Faen)
Cyncoed
Roath Park
Roath
Splott
Cathays
Maindy
Heath
Llanishen
Thornhill
Birchgrove
Rhiwbina
Pantmawr
Whitchurch
Llandaff North
Gabalfa
Llandaff
(Llandaf)
Pontcanna
Canton
Riverside
Grangetown
Butetown
Saltmead
Llandough
Leckwith
Michaelston-le-Pit
Fairwater
Ely
(Tre-lai)
Caerau
Michaelston-super-Ely
St Fagans
(Sain Ffagan)
Radyr
Morganstown
Taff's Well
(Ffynnon-Taf)
Tongwynlais
Nantgarw
Glan-y-llyn
Groes-wen
Pentyrch
Gwaelod-y-garth
Culverhouse Cross
Wenvoe
(Gwenfo)
Wallston
Twyn-yr-odyn
Downs
St Lythans
St Nicholas
(Sain Nicolas)
Drope
St George's
St Brides-super-Ely
(Llansanffraid-ar-Elai)
Church Village
Soar
Watford
Van
Rudry
Garth
Llwyncelyn
Park Wood
Cefn Mably Woods
Coed Craig Ruperra
Coed Coesau-Whips
Coed Parc-y-Van
Caerphilly Common
The Warren
Coed-y-Wenallt
Garth Wood
Coed y Gedrys
Grath Hill
Taff vale
River Taff
River Ely
Rhymney River
The Lake
Llanishen Reservoir
Cardiff Bay Barrage
Cardiff Gate Retail Park
Valegate Retail Park
CARDIFF INTERNATIONAL WHITE WATER
CARDIFF INTERNATIONAL POOL
ICE ARENA
WALES MILLENNIUM CENTRE
NATIONAL ASSEMBLY
BBC ROATH LOCK STUDIOS
TECHNIQUEST
CARDIFF CASTLE
NATIONAL MUSEUM CARDIFF
SOPHIA GARDENS STAD
CARDIFF ARMS PARK
PRINCIPALITY STADIUM
ST FAGANS NATIONAL MUSEUM OF HISTORY
CARDIFF INTERNATIONAL SPORTS STAD
CARDIFF CITY STAD
LLANDAFF CATHEDRAL
TINKINSWOOD BURIAL CHAMBER
CARDIFF WEST SERVICES
CARDIFF GATE SERVICES
M4
A48(M)
A48
A470
A469
A4232
A4119
A4054
A4160
A4050
A4055
0
1
2 miles
0
1
2
3 km

EDINBURGH
Leith
Newhaven
Granton
Wardie
Drylaw
Craigleith
Blackhall
Murrayfield
Corstophine
Clermiston
Cramond
Cammo
Cramond Bridge
Craigiehall
South Gyle
Longstone
Colinton
Bonaly
Torphin
Currie
Hermiston
Baberton
Craiglockhart
Merchiston
Churchill
Comiston
Liberton
Nether Liberton
Alnwickhill
Braid Hills
Prestonfield
The Inch
Moredun
Gilmerton
Danderhall
Niddrie
Bingham
Northfield
Craigentinny
Portobello
Joppa
Stoneybank
Old Craighall
Easter Millerhill
MUSSELBURGH
Inveresk
DALKEITH
Eskbank
BONNYRIGG
LOANHEAD
Muirhouse
Eskgrove
Easthouses
Holyrood Park
Arthur's Seat
Dunsapie Loch
Duddingston Loch
Leith Links
Middle Craigs
Eastern Craigs
Granton Harbour
Cramond Island
Drum Sands
Fisherrow Sands
Pentland Hills
THE CITY OF EDINBURGH BY-PASS
Edinburgh Airport
Calton Hill
Meadow Park
Royal Observatory
Royal Botanic Garden
Palace of Holyroodhouse
Scottish Parliament
RZSS Edinburgh Zoo
Dalmeny House
Malleny Garden
Bonaly Country Park
Hillend Country Park
Midlothian Snowsports Centre
Dreghorn Services
Edinburgh Services
Dalkeith Park
Inveresk Lodge Gardens
Craigmillar Castle
Lauriston Castle
Burnshot Wood
Glenpunty Wood
Long Green
Torduff Resr
Bonaly Resr
Clubbiedean Resr
Harlaw Resr
Breakwater
2 miles
3 km
32
33
67

GLASGOW
Drumchapel
Kessington
BISHOPBRIGGS
Auchinloch
Moodiesburn
Chryston
MUIRHEAD
Gartcosh
STEPPS
Robroyston
Balornock
Springburn
Milton
Knightswood
Kelvinside
Jordanhill
Firhill
Partick
Craigend
Riddrie
Easterhouse
Dennistoun
Govan
Ibrox
Carntyne
Springboig
Swinton
Bargeddie
Hillington
Gallowgate
Pollokshields
Muirhead
Crookston
Mont Vernon
Braidfauld
Broomhouse
Clyde Gateway East
Birkenshaw
Crossmyloof
Govanhill
Langside
RUTHERGLEN
CAMBUSLANG
Westburn
Newton
UDDINGSTON
Priesthill
Nitshill
Hillpark
Cathcart
Croftfoot
Muirend
Castlemilk
Flemington
Orchard Park
Giffnock
Netherlee
Williamwood
CLARKSTON
Carmunnock
Crookfur
Blantyre
Dechmont Hill
River Clyde
Forth and Clyde Canal
Wilderness Plantation
Nature Reserve
Dawsholm Park
Victoria Park
Braehead Shopping Centre
Alexandra Park
Glasgow Green
Tollcross Park
Richmond Park
Queen's Park
Bellahouston Park
Pollok Country Park
Silverburn Shopping Centre
Nature Trail Linn Park
Rouken Glen Park
Cathkin Braes Country Park
Waulkmill Glen Reservoir
0 1 2 miles
0 1 2 3 km

EAST BARNET
FRIERN BARNET
Osidge
Whetstone
North Finchley
FINCHLEY
Muswell Hill
Fortis Green
East Finchley
Highgate
Hampstead Heath
HAMPSTEAD
Parliament Hill
Gospel Oak
Dartmouth Park
Belsize Park
Swiss Cottage
Primrose Hill
Regents Park
MARYLEBONE
St. John's Wood
Maida Vale
West Hampstead
Kilburn
Westbourne Park
Hampstead Garden Suburb
Golders Green
Temple Fortune
Golders Hill Park
Child's Hill
Woodside Park
West Finchley
Totteridge
Underhill
Church End
Mill Hill East
Mill Hill
HENDON
Henlys Corner
Brent Cross
Cricklewood
Dollis Hill
WILLESDEN
Gladstone Park
Brondesbury
Kensal Rise
Harlesden
Neasden
Old Oak Common
Wormwood Scrubs Park
East Acton
Stonebridge
Park Royal
West Acton
Gipsy Corner
Arkley
Barnet Gate
Stirling Corner
Five Ways Corner
West Hendon
Colindale
Grahame Park
Burnt Oak
Brent Reservoir (Welsh Harp)
Kingsbury
Wembley Park
Barn Hill
EDGWARE
Edgware Bury
Queensbury
Little Stanmore
Canons Park
Elstree
Brockley Hill
STANMORE
Belmont
KENTON
Preston Road
North Wembley
WEMBLEY
Sudbury
Alperton
Hanger Lane
EALING
Perivale
Northwick Park
Stanmore Common
Bushey Heath
Harrow Weald
Wealdstone
Greenhill
HARROW
Harrow on the Hill
South Harrow
Roxeth
Headstone
West Harrow
BUSHEY
Headstone Lane
North Harrow
GREENFORD
Hatch End
OXHEY
PINNER
Rayners Lane
Eastcote
South Ruislip
NORTHOLT
Yeading
South Oxhey
Oxhey Woods
Eastcote Village
Ruislip Manor

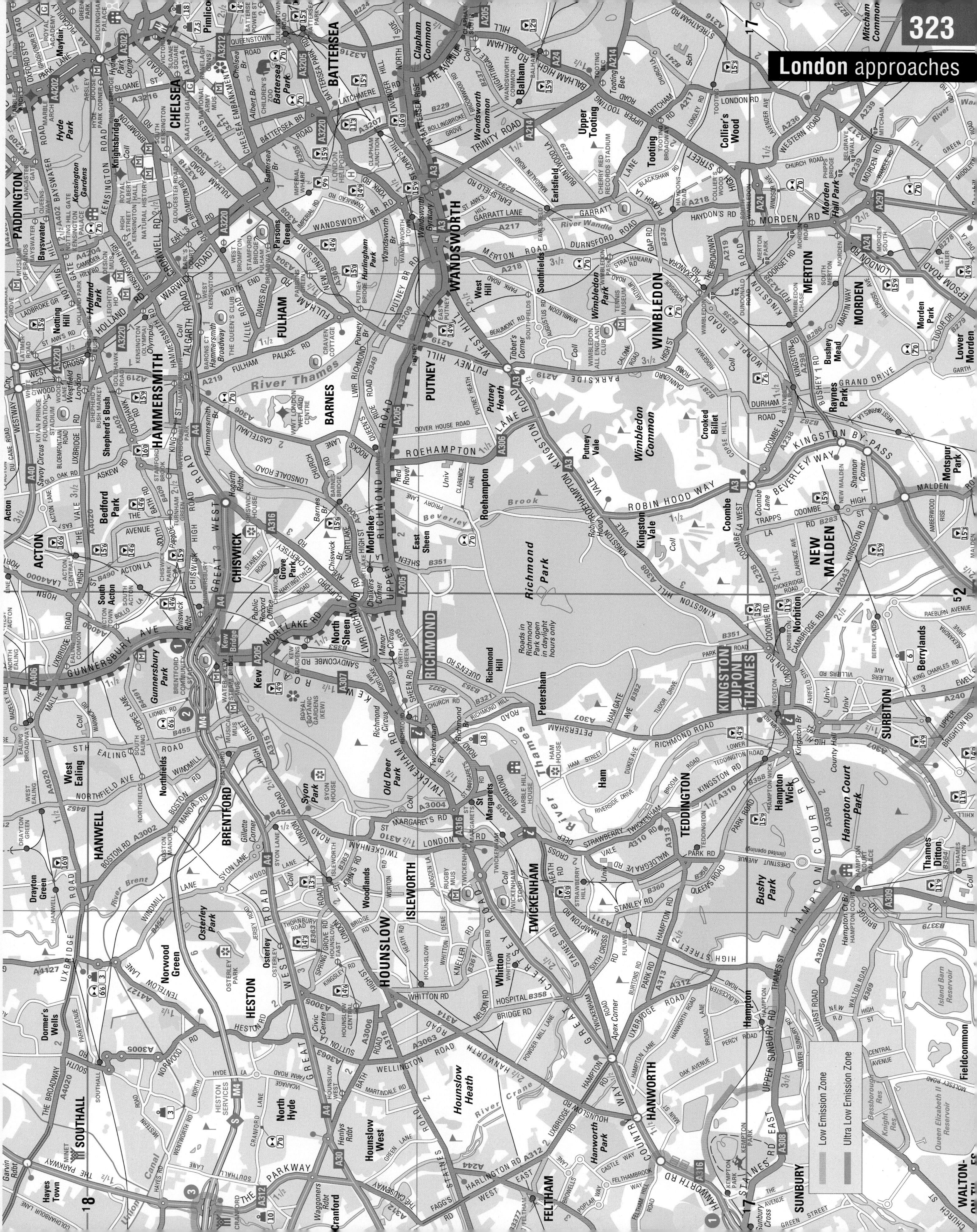
PADDINGTON
Kensington Gardens
Hyde Park
Mayfair
Knightsbridge
CHELSEA
Pimlico
BATTERSEA
Battersea Park
Clapham Common
Balham
Wandsworth Common
Upper Tooting
Tooting
Collier's Wood
Mitcham Common
Notting Hill
Holland Park
Shepherd's Bush
HAMMERSMITH
FULHAM
Parsons Green
Hurlingham Park
WANDSWORTH
Earlsfield
Southfields
Wimbledon Park
WIMBLEDON
MERTON
MORDEN
Morden Hall Park
Morden Park
Lower Morden
River Thames
BARNES
PUTNEY
Putney Heath
Wimbledon Common
Raynes Park
Bushey Mead
ACTON
South Acton
Bedford Park
CHISWICK
Mortlake
East Sheen
Roehampton
Putney Vale
Kingston Vale
Coombe
NEW MALDEN
Motspur Park
Richmond Park
Roads in Richmond Park open in daylight hours only
RICHMOND
Richmond Hill
North Sheen
Kew
Royal Botanic Gardens (Kew)
Gunnersbury Park
Petersham
KINGSTON UPON THAMES
Norbiton
Berrylands
SURBITON
West Ealing
HANWELL
Northfields
BRENTFORD
Syon Park
Old Deer Park
St Margarets
Ham
TEDDINGTON
Hampton Wick
Hampton Court Park
Thames Ditton
Drayton Green
Osterley Park
Norwood Green
ISLEWORTH
Woodlands
HOUNSLOW
TWICKENHAM
Whitton
Bushy Park
Hampton
HESTON
Dormer's Wells
SOUTHALL
North Hyde
Hounslow West
Hounslow Heath
HANWORTH
Hanworth Park
FELTHAM
SUNBURY
Fieldcommon
WALTON-ON-THAMES
Hayes Town
Cranford
Island Barn Reservoir
Queen Elizabeth II Reservoir
Low Emission Zone
Ultra Low Emission Zone

Low Emission Zone
Ultra Low Emission Zone
2 miles
3 km
Cockfosters
Oakwood
Grange Park
Bush Hill Park
Ponders End
Sewardstonebury
LOUGHTON
SOUTHGATE
Winchmore Hill
CHINGFORD
Osidge
Palmers Green
Lower Edmonton
Friday Hill
Buckhurst Hill
CHIGWELL
Arnos Grove
Woodford Wells
Chingford Hatch
Grange Hill
FRIERN BARNET
EDMONTON
Highams Park
Hale End
WOODFORD
Colney Hatch
Bowes Park
WOOD GREEN
Woodford Bridge
Woodford Green
Higham Hill
Fullwell Cross
Clayhall
Muswell Hill
TOTTENHAM
Tottenham Hale
WALTHAMSTOW
Snaresbrook
Barkingside
Redbridge
Newbury Park
Gants Hill
HORNSEY
Crouch End
South Tottenham
WANSTEAD
Seven Kings
Highgate
Stamford Hill
Finsbury Park
Upper Clapton
Cranbrook
Hampstead
Archway
STOKE NEWINGTON
Clapton
Leytonstone
Dartmouth Park
Lea Bridge
LEYTON
ILFORD
HAMPSTEAD
Gospel Oak
Tufnell Park
Highbury
Shacklewell
Clapton Park
Manor Park
Loxford
Belsize Park
Kentish Town
Canonbury
Temple Mills
Forest Gate
Little Ilford
Fair Cross
Swiss Cottage
Dalston
HACKNEY
STRATFORD
Plashet
BARKING
CAMDEN TOWN
Victoria Park
Upton
Upton Park
ISLINGTON
SHOREDITCH
Old Ford
WEST HAM
Wallend
Regents Park
BOW
Plaistow
EAST HAM
FINSBURY
BETHNAL GREEN
Bromley
MARYLEBONE
Spitalfields
Holborn
Stepney
Beckton

River Thames
North Woolwich
Woolwich Ferry
WOOLWICH
Plumstead
Shooters Hill
Falconwood
Oxleas Wood
East Wickham
New Eltham
Avery Hill
Longlands
CHISLEHURST
Chislehurst Common
Petts Wood
ELTHAM
Eltham Common
Eltham Palace
SIDCUP
Elmstead Wood
Elmstead
Widmore
Bickley
Southborough
Custom House
Silvertown
Thames Barrier
Charlton
Kidbrooke
Mottingham
Grove Park
Sundridge Park
BROMLEY
Bromley
Canning Town
Blackwall Tunnel
North Greenwich
GREENWICH
Greenwich Park
BLACKHEATH
Blackheath Park
LEWISHAM
Hither Green
Lee
Plaistow
Downham
Shortlands
Hayes
POPLAR
Canary Wharf
ISLE OF DOGS
Millwall
CATFORD
Bellingham
Bell Green
Beckenham Place Park
BECKENHAM
Eden Park
Brockley
Ladywell
Limehouse
Rotherhithe
DEPTFORD
New Cross
Nunhead
Honor Oak
Forest Hill
PENGE
Elmers End
Wapping
BERMONDSEY
Peckham
Peckham Rye Park
East Dulwich
Dulwich
Anerley
Woodside
Aldgate
CAMBERWELL
Elephant & Castle
Walworth
Kennington
Camberwell Green
Dulwich Park
West Dulwich
South Norwood
Selhurst
LAMBETH
BRIXTON
Brockwell Park
Tulse Hill
STREATHAM
Norbury
Thornton Heath
Vauxhall
Streatham Common
Streatham Vale
Mitcham Common
CLAPHAM
Clapham Common
BATTERSEA
Battersea Park
Pimlico
CHELSEA
Mayfair
Green Park
Hyde Park
Grange Mills
Tooting Bec Common
Furzedown
Balham
Tooting Bec
Upper Tooting
Wandsworth Common
Collier's Wood
MITCHAM

Great Crosby
CROSBY
ANTONY GORMLEY SCULPTURES - ANOTHER PLACE
Waterloo
Town Hall
RIMROSE VALLEY COUNTRY PARK
LITHERLAND
Seaforth
SEAFORTH & LITHERLAND
Docks
Ferries to Belfast, Douglas & Dublin
BOOTLE
BOOTLE NEW STRAND
BOOTLE ORIEL ROAD
Melling
Kirkby Park
KIRKBY
Westvale
AINTREE
AINTREE RACE COURSE
OLD ROAN
FAZAKERLEY
Fazakerley
Croxteth
Knowsley
Walton
West Derby
CROXTETH COUNTRY PARK
Stockbridge Village
Anfield
Stanley Park
GOODISON PARK
Newsham Park
Huyton with Roby
Roby
HUYTON
Broad Green
BROAD GREEN
WAVERTREE TECHNOLOGY PARK
Wavertree Park
Edge Hill
Wavertree
Childwall
New Brighton
NEW BRIGHTON
WALLASEY
Kingsway
Queensway
BIRKENHEAD NORTH
Birkenhead Park
BIRKENHEAD
HAMILTON SQUARE
CONWAY PARK
BIRKENHEAD CENTRAL
MUS OF LIVERPOOL
MARITIME MUSEUM
TATE LIVERPOOL
Royal Albert Dock
BEATLES STORY
M&S BANK ARENA
LIVERPOOL
MOORFIELDS
LIME STREET
JAMES STREET
CENTRAL
Toxteth
Sefton Park
Dingle
Otterspool
Aigburth
SUDLEY HOUSE
MOSSLEY HILL
CALDERSTONES PARK
MENDIPS
Allerton
WEST ALLERTON
Woolton
HALEWOOD COUNTRY PARK
HUNTS CROSS
Hunt's Cross
LIVERPOOL SOUTH PARKWAY
CRESSINGTON
GARSTON
SPEKE
SPEKE HALL
LIVERPOOL JOHN LENNON AIRPORT
Terminal Building
LIVERPOOL AIRPORT
River Mersey
Oxton
Tranmere
PRENTON PARK
ROCK FERRY
GREEN LANE
BEBINGTON
LADY LEVER ART GALLERY
PORT SUNLIGHT MUS
PORT SUNLIGHT
Port Sunlight
Spital
SPITAL
Brimstage
Bromborough
BROMBOROUGH RAKE
Eastham Ferry
EASTHAM COUNTRY PARK
Locks
0 1 2 miles
0 1 2 3 km

River Irwell
Outwood
Whitefield
Besses o' th' Barn
Middleton
Simister
Rhodes
Alkrington Garden Village
Ringley
Park Lane
Heaton Park
Heaton Park Resr
Higher Blackley
Clifton Country Park
Prestwich
Charlestown
Clifton Green
Newtown
Prestwich Forest Park
Crumpsall
Boggart Hole Clough
New Moston
Hollinwood
Swinton
Broughton Park
Kersal
Moston
Pendlebury
Harpurhey
Westwood Park
Ellesmere Park
Strangeways
Newton Heath
Miles Platting
Little Bolton
Seedley
Salford
Patricroft
Clayton
Eccles
Manchester
Barton upon Irwell
Manchester Ship Canal
Openshaw
Hulme
Ardwick
Trafford Park
The Trafford Centre
Gorton
Old Trafford
Moss Side
Rusholme
Ryder Brow
Firswood
Stretford
Longford Park
Whalley Range
Levenshulme
North Reddish
Reddish
Chorlton-cum-Hardy
Ashton upon Mersey
Withington
River Mersey
Sale Water Park
Barlow Moor
Chorlton Water Park
West Didsbury
Burnage
South Reddish
Sale
Woodhouses
Brooklands
Heaton Mersey
Heaton Norris
Northern Moor
Fletcher Moss
Stockport
Timperley
Roundthorn
Gatley
Cheadle
Wythenshawe
Altrincham
Newall Green
Cheadle Hulme
M60
M62
M602
M56
A57(M)
0 1 2 miles
0 1 2 3 km

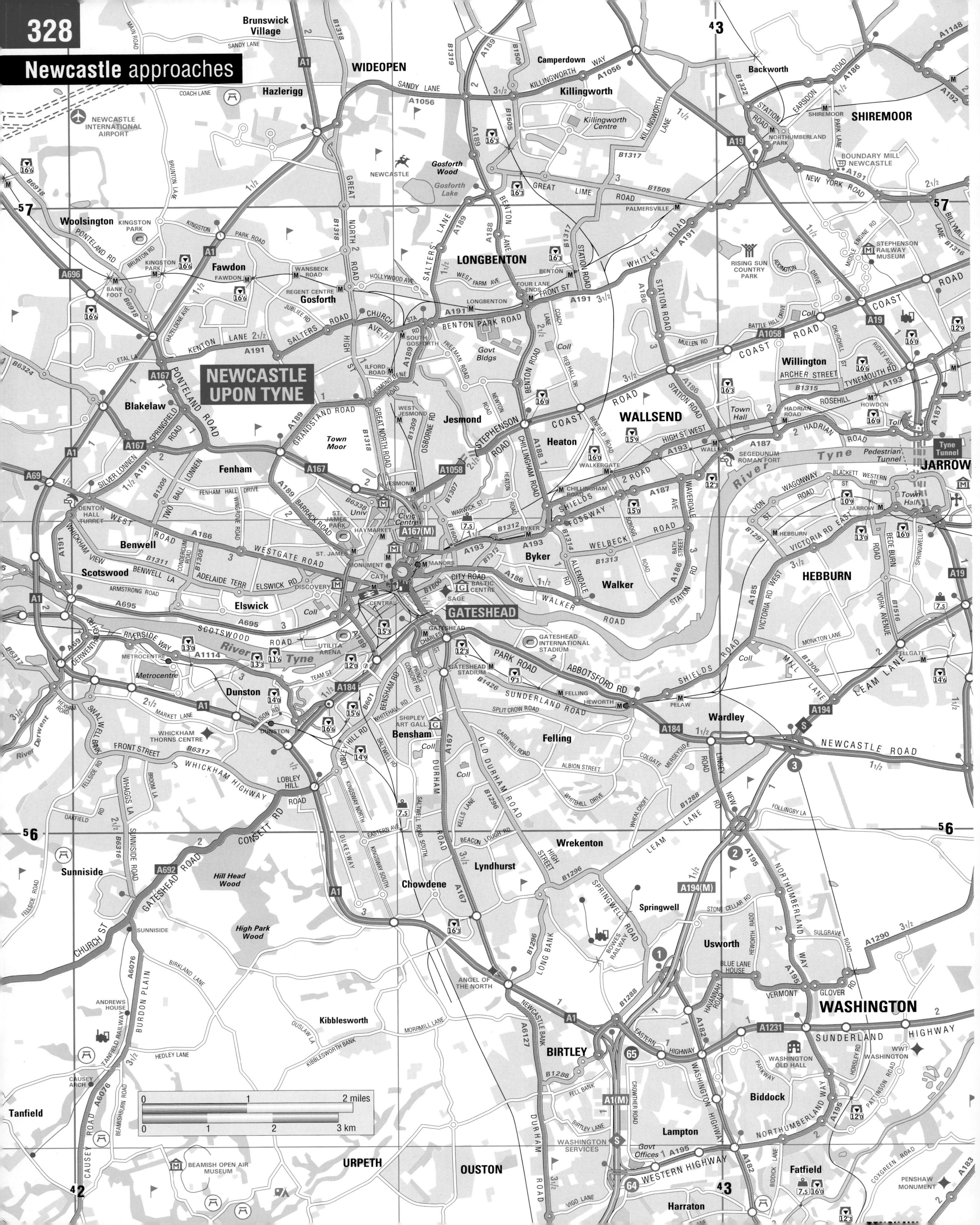
Brunswick Village
WIDEOPEN
Hazlerigg
Camperdown
Killingworth
Killingworth Centre
Backworth
SHIREMOOR
NORTHUMBERLAND PARK
BOUNDARY MILL NEWCASTLE
NEWCASTLE INTERNATIONAL AIRPORT
Gosforth Wood
Gosforth Lake
NEWCASTLE
Woolsington
KINGSTON PARK
Fawdon
Gosforth
LONGBENTON
PALMERSVILLE
RISING SUN COUNTRY PARK
STEPHENSON RAILWAY MUSEUM
Govt Bldgs
NEWCASTLE UPON TYNE
Blakelaw
Jesmond
Heaton
WALLSEND
Willington
Town Hall
Town Moor
Fenham
DENTON HALL TURRET
SEGEDUNUM ROMAN FORT
Pedestrian Tunnel
Tyne Tunnel
JARROW
Benwell
Scotswood
Elswick
Byker
Walker
HEBBURN
DISCOVERY
BALTIC CENTRE
SAGE
GATESHEAD
GATESHEAD INTERNATIONAL STADIUM
River Tyne
UTILITA ARENA
METROCENTRE
Metrocentre
Dunston
GATESHEAD STADIUM
SHIPLEY ART GALL.
Bensham
Felling
Wardley
WHICKHAM THORNS CENTRE
LOBLEY HILL
River Derwent
Wrekenton
Lyndhurst
Sunniside
Hill Head Wood
High Park Wood
Chowdene
Springwell
Usworth
BOWES RAILWAY
ANGEL OF THE NORTH
WASHINGTON
VERMONT
GLOVER
Kibblesworth
ANDREWS HOUSE
BIRTLEY
WWT WASHINGTON
WASHINGTON OLD HALL
Biddock
CAUSEY ARCH
Tanfield
Lampton
WASHINGTON SERVICES
Govt Offices
URPETH
OUSTON
BEAMISH OPEN AIR MUSEUM
Fatfield
PENSHAW MONUMENT
Harraton
0 1 2 miles
0 1 2 3 km

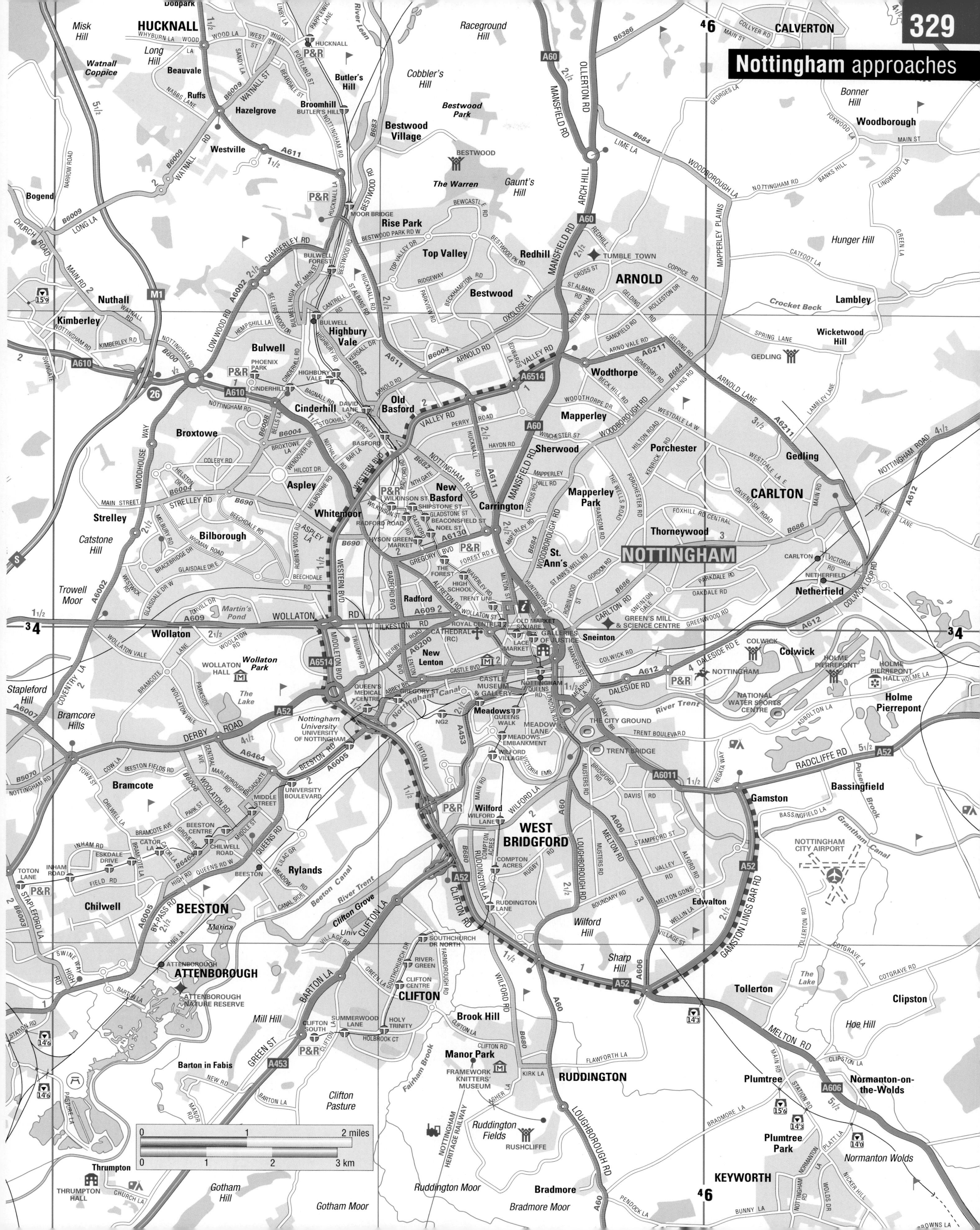

ROTHERHAM
SHEFFIELD
ECCLESFIELD
GRENOSIDE
HILLSBOROUGH
Wharncliffe Wood
Oughtibridge
Beeley Wood
Birley Edge
Birley Carr
Worrall
Wadsley
Wadsley Bridge
Parson Cross
Longley Estate
Shiregreen
Concord Park
Pismire Hill
Firth Park
Fir Vale
Shirecliffe
Owlerton
Loxley
Parkwood Springs
Pitsmoor
Grimesthorpe
Brightside
Carbrook
Wincobank
Blackburn
Dropping Well
Kimberworth Park
Kimberworth
Bradgate
Greasbrough
Masbrough
Eastwood
Clifton Park
Broom
Herringthorpe
Dalton
Dalton Parva
Dalton Magna
Sunnyside
Whinney Hill
Brecks
Listerdale
Wickersley
Moorgate
Canklow
Tinsley
Jordan
Brinsworth
Whiston
Morthen
Upper Whiston
Guilthwaite
Brampton en le Morthen
Ulley
Treeton
Catcliffe
Tinsley Park
Greenland
Attercliffe
Darnall
Waverley
Dore House Industrial Estate
Handsworth
Aughton
Orgreave
Woodhouse Mill
Fence
Richmond
Woodhouse
Swallownest
Aston
Knowle Top
Malinbridge
Walkley
Burngreave
Steel Bank
Crookesmoor
Crookes
Tapton Hill
Sandygate
Ranmoor
Greystones
Fulwood
Sharrow
Manor Park
Sheffield Park
Manor Estate
Arbourthorne
Lowfield
Heeley
Brincliffe
Ecclesall
Nether Edge
Carter Knowle
Meersbrook
Newfield Green
Intake
Hollins End
Gleadless
Normanton Spring
Hackenthorpe
Drakehouse
Beighton
Frecheville
Birley
Hemsworth
Gleadless Valley
Norton Woodseats
Backmoor
Millhouses
Parkhead
Whirlow
Ecclesall Wood
Abbeydale
Meadow Head
Norton
Jordanthorpe
Greenhill
Lowedges
Abbeydale Park
Totley Rise
Totley Bents
Lightwood
Highlane
Moorhole
Owlthorpe
Waterthorpe
Holbrook
Westfield
Halfway
Plumbley
Ridgeway
Ridgeway Moor
Ford
Sothall
Rother Valley Lake
Wales
Killamarsh
Norwood
Woodall
Upperthorpe
River Rivelin
River Rother
River Sheaf
Limb Brook
The Moss
R. Don
Sheffield to Keadby Canal
M1
A57
A61
A630
A631
A618
A6102
A6135
A621
A625
2 miles
3 km

Town plan symbols

- Motorway
- Primary route – dual, single carriageway
- A road – dual, single carriageway
- B road – dual, single carriageway
- Minor through road
- One-way street
- Pedestrian roads
- Shopping streets
- Railway with station
- Tramway with station
- Underground or Metro station
- Hospital
- Parking
- Police, Post Office
- Shopmobility
- Youth hostel
- Bus or railway station building
- Shopping precinct or retail park
- Park
- Congestion charge zone
- Abbey or cathedral
- Ancient monument
- Aquarium
- Art gallery
- Bird collection or aviary
- Building of interest
- Castle
- Church of interest
- Cinema
- Garden
- Historic ship
- House
- House and garden
- Museum
- Preserved railway
- Roman antiquity
- Safari park
- Theatre
- Tourist information
- Zoo
- Other place of interest

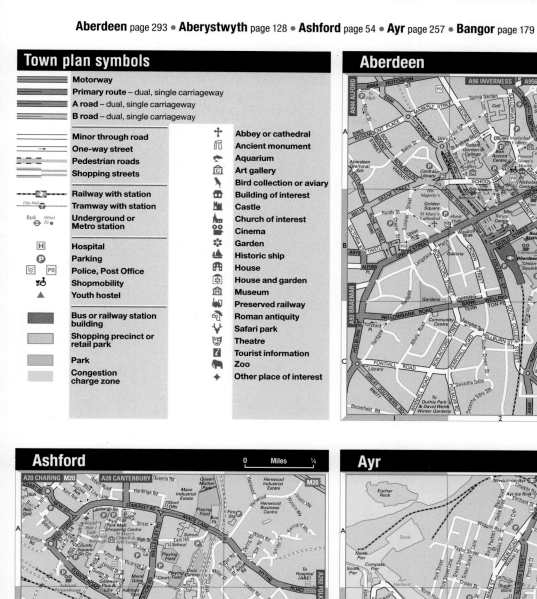

Aberdeen

0 Miles ¼

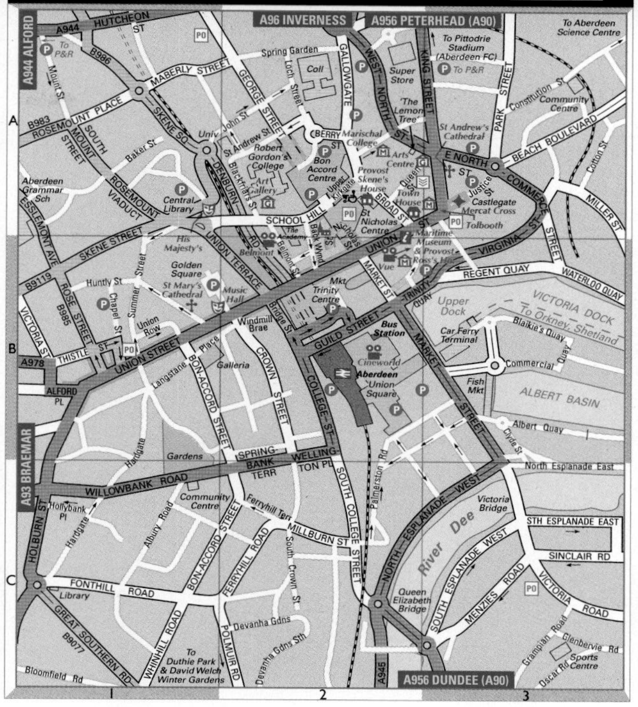

A96 INVERNESS · A956 PETERHEAD (A90) · A944 ALFORD · A93 BRAEMAR · A956 DUNDEE (A90)

Aberystwyth

0 Miles ¼

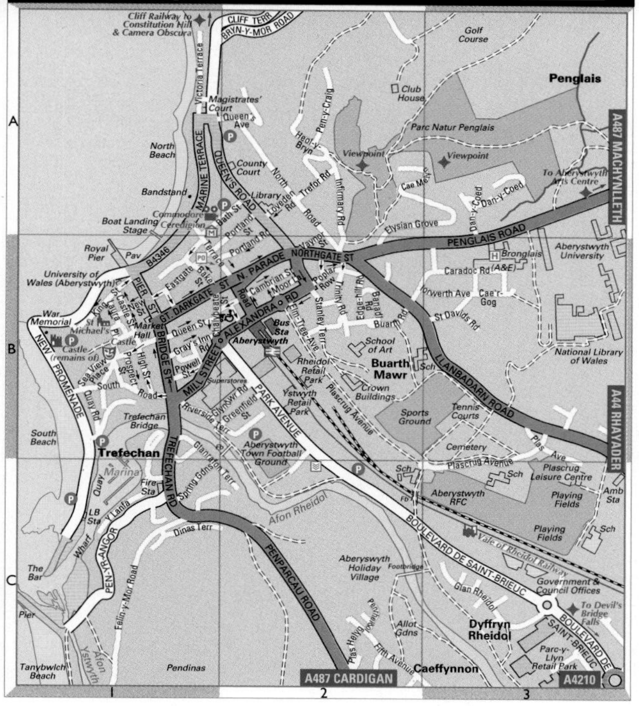

A487 MACHYNLLETH · A44 RHAYADER · A487 CARDIGAN · A4210

Ashford

0 Miles ¼

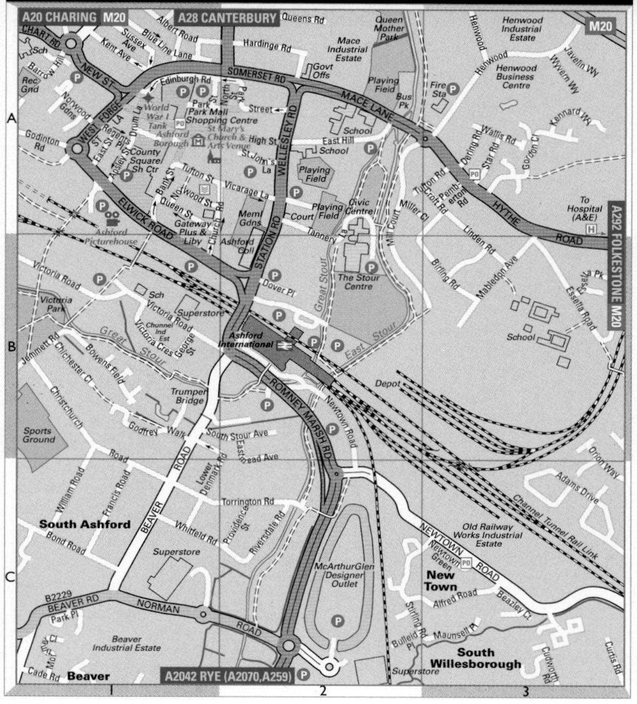

A20 CHARING M20 · A28 CANTERBURY · M20 · A292 FOLKESTONE M20 · A2042 RYE (A2070,A259)

Ayr

0 Miles ¼

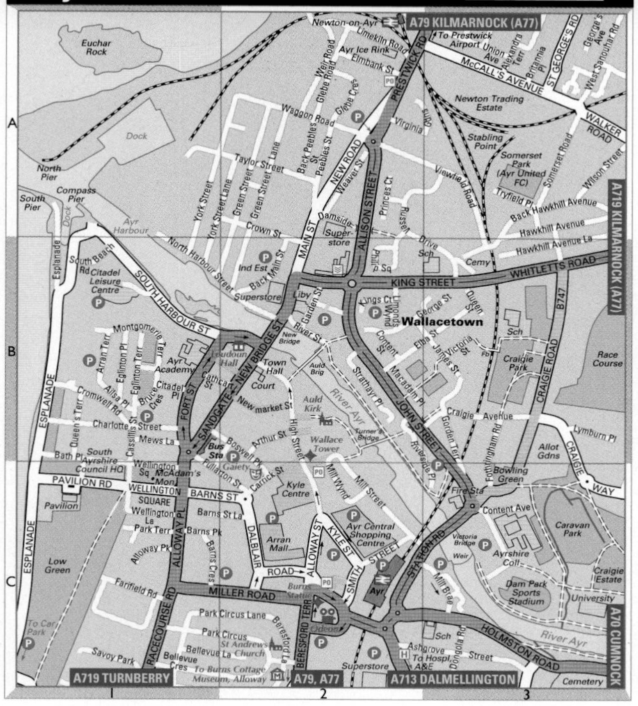

A79 KILMARNOCK (A77) · A719 KILMARNOCK (A77) · A719 TURNBERRY · A79, A77 · A713 DALMELLINGTON · A70 CUMNOCK

Bangor

0 Miles ¼

A5 BETWS-Y-COED, A55 CONWY · A5 HOLYHEAD (A55) · A4087 CAERNARFON (A487)

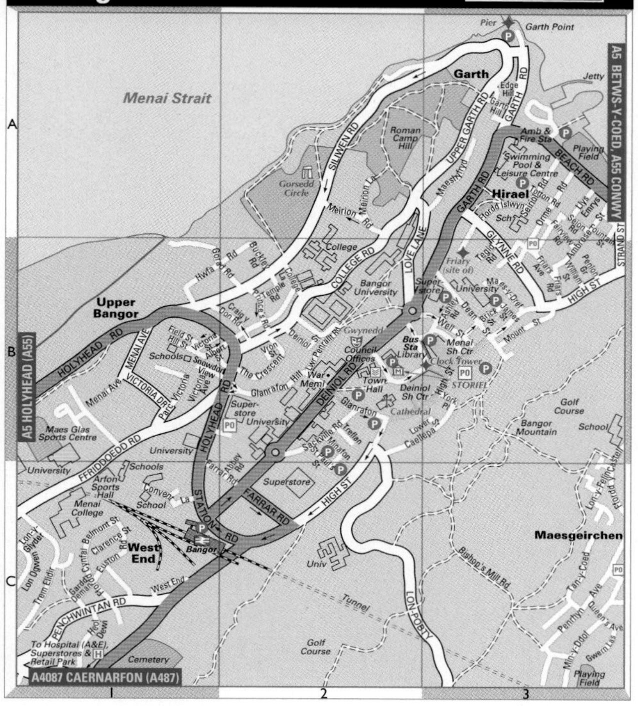

Barrow-in-Furness

0 Miles ¼

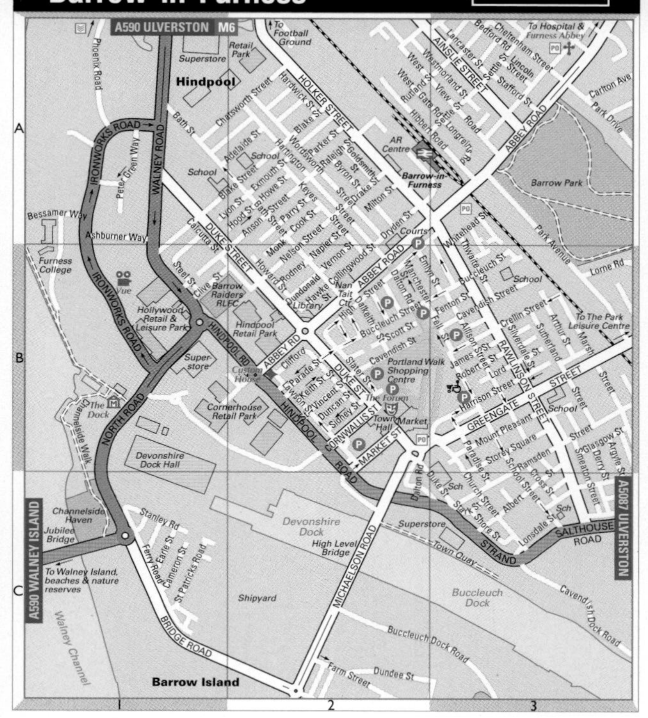

Bath

0 Miles ¼

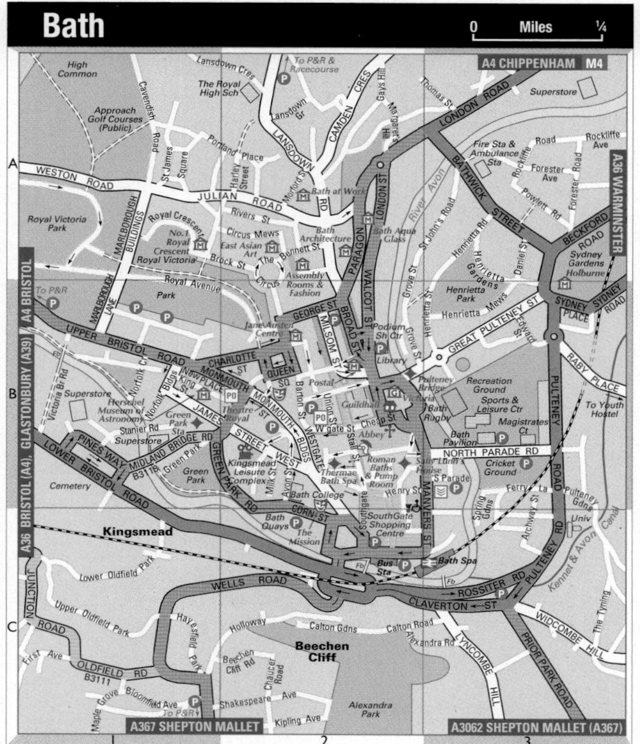

Berwick-upon-Tweed

0 Miles ¼

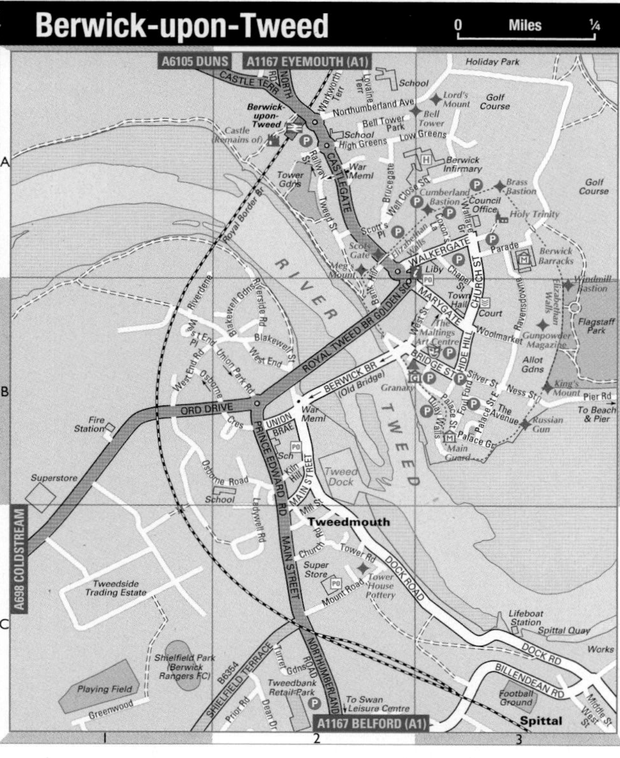

Birmingham
0 Miles ¼
A4040 OUTER RING ROAD
A41 WOLVERHAMPTON M5
A34 WALSALL M6
A38(M) TO M6
A5127 SUTTON COLDFIELD
A47 CASTLE BROMWICH M6
A457 DUDLEY
A456 KIDDERMINSTER M5
A4540 RING ROAD
A38 BROMSGROVE
A441 REDDITCH
A41 STRATFORD-UPON-AVON (A34, A3400) M42
A45 COVENTRY, AIRPORT & NEC M42
GIB HEATH
WINSON GREEN
ASTON
NEW TOWN
BROOKFIELDS
DUDDESTON
LADYWOOD
BORDESLEY
Edgbaston Reservoir

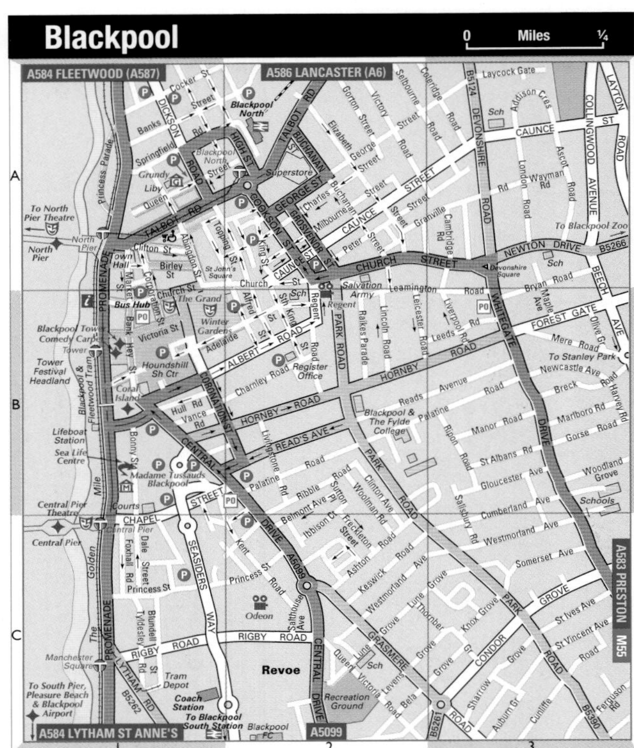
Blackpool
0 Miles ¼
A584 FLEETWOOD (A587)
A586 LANCASTER (A6)
A583 PRESTON M55
A584 LYTHAM ST ANNE'S
A5099
Revoe

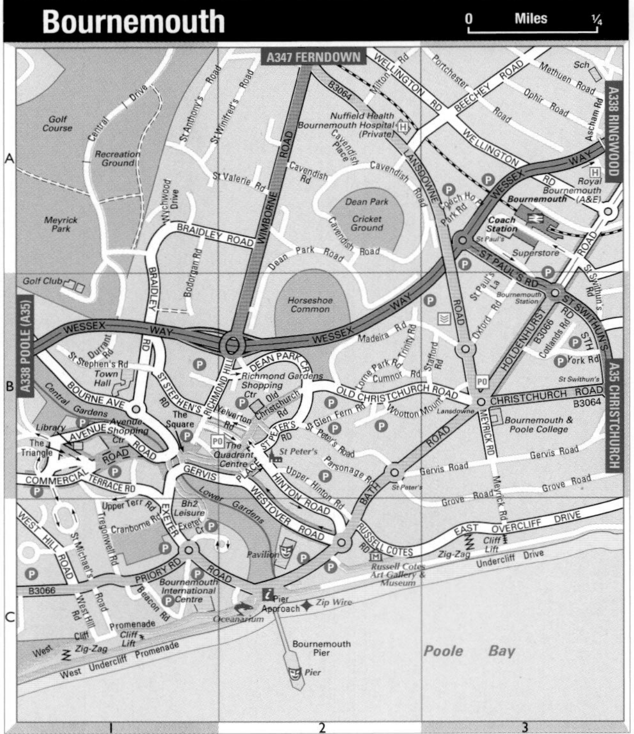
Bournemouth
0 Miles ¼
A347 FERNDOWN
A338 RINGWOOD
A338 POOLE (A35)
A35 CHRISTCHURCH
Meyrick Park
Dean Park Cricket Ground
Horseshoe Common
Poole Bay

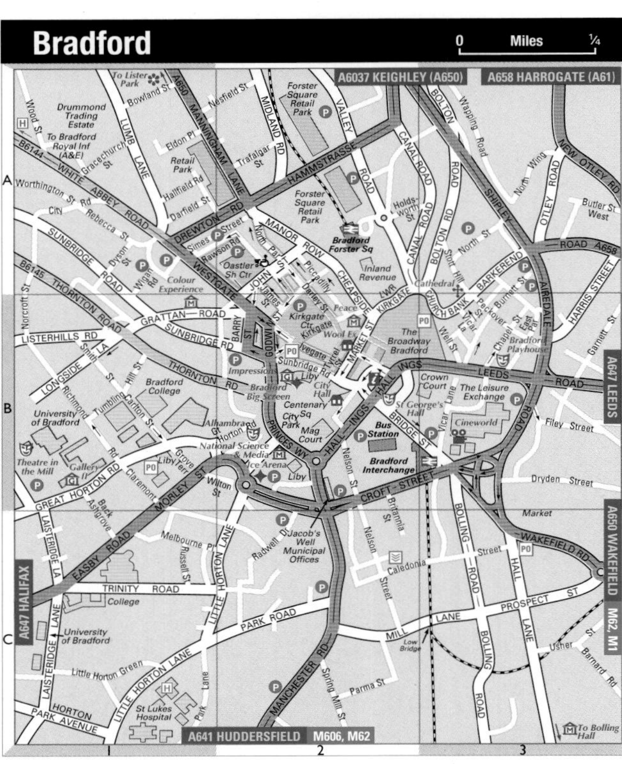
Bradford
0 Miles ¼
A6037 KEIGHLEY (A650)
A658 HARROGATE (A61)
A647 LEEDS
A650 WAKEFIELD M62, M1
A647 HALIFAX
A641 HUDDERSFIELD M606, M62

Brighton
0 Miles ¼
A23 CRAWLEY M23
A270 WORTHING (A27)
A270 LEWES (A27)
A259 WORTHING
A259 NEWHAVEN

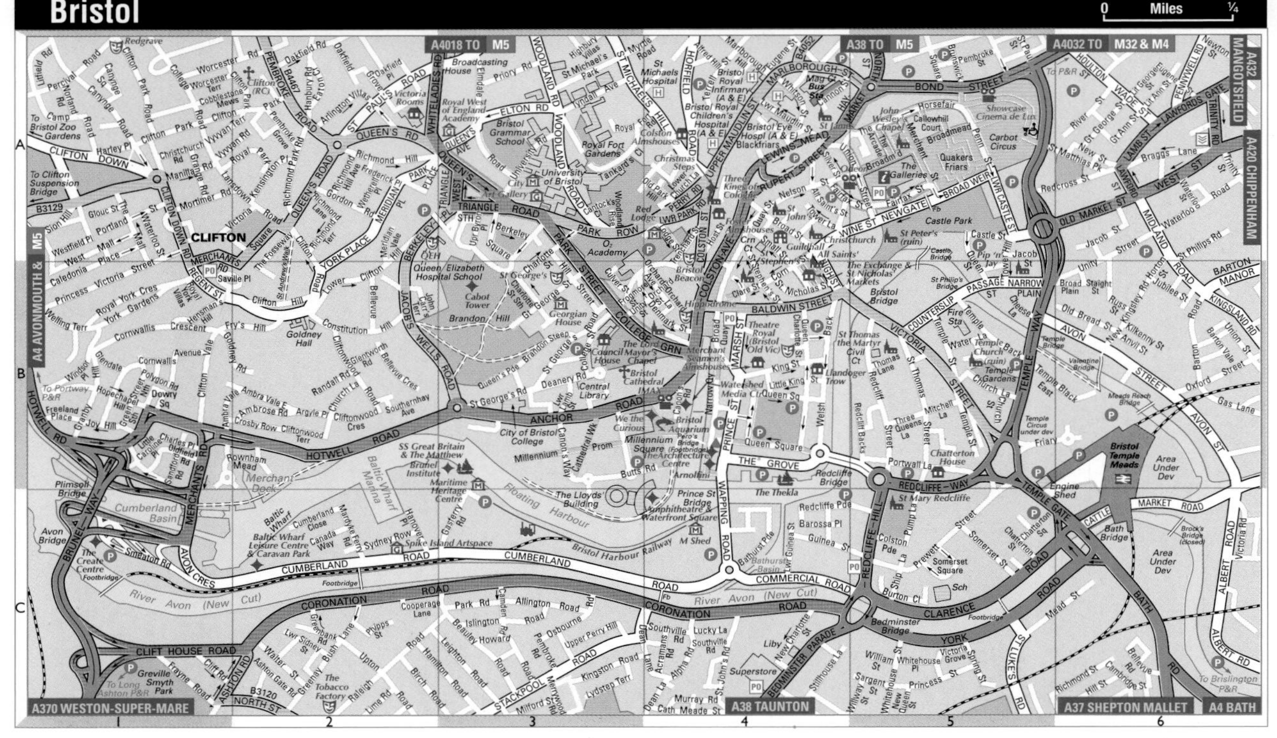
Bristol
0 Miles ¼
A4018 TO M5
A38 TO M5
A4032 TO M32 & M4
A432 MANGOTSFIELD
A420 CHIPPENHAM
A4 AVONMOUTH & M5
A370 WESTON-SUPER-MARE
A38 TAUNTON
A37 SHEPTON MALLET
A4 BATH
CLIFTON

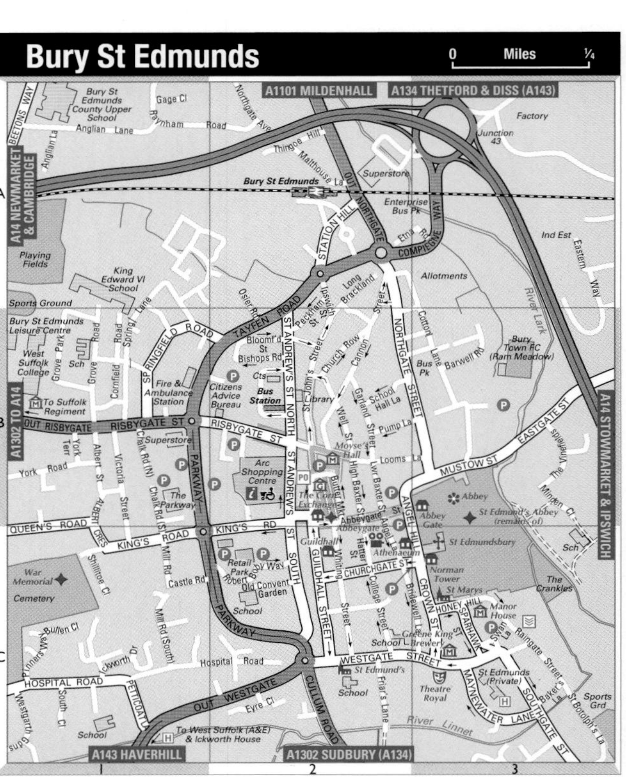
Bury St Edmunds
0 Miles ¼
A1101 MILDENHALL
A134 THETFORD & DISS (A143)
A14 NEWMARKET & CAMBRIDGE
A1302 TO A14
A14 STOWMARKET & IPSWICH
A143 HAVERHILL
A1302 SUDBURY (A134)

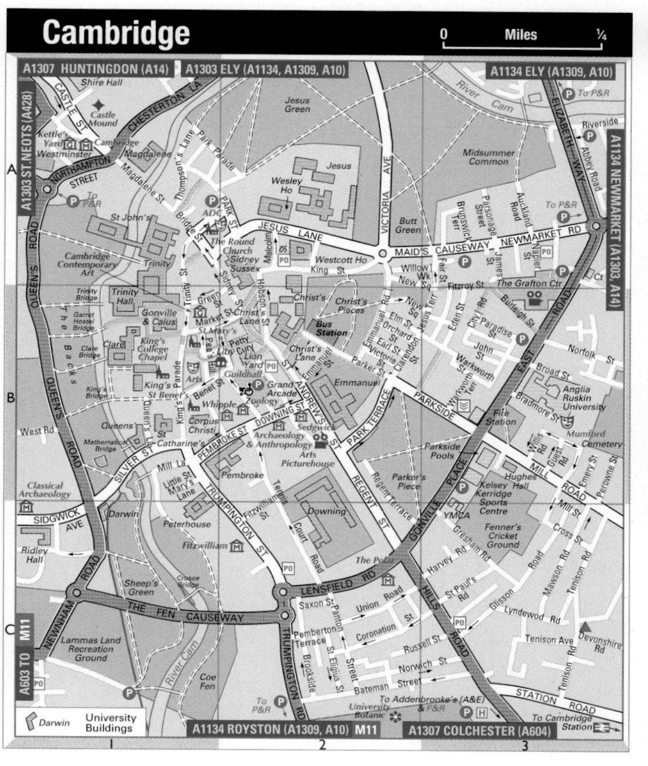
Cambridge
0 Miles ¼
A1307 HUNTINGDON (A14)
A1303 ELY (A1134, A1309, A10)
A1134 ELY (A1309, A10)
A1134 NEWMARKET (A1303, A14)
A1303 ST NEOTS (A428)
A603 TO M11
A1134 ROYSTON (A1309, A10) M11
A1307 COLCHESTER (A604)
University Buildings

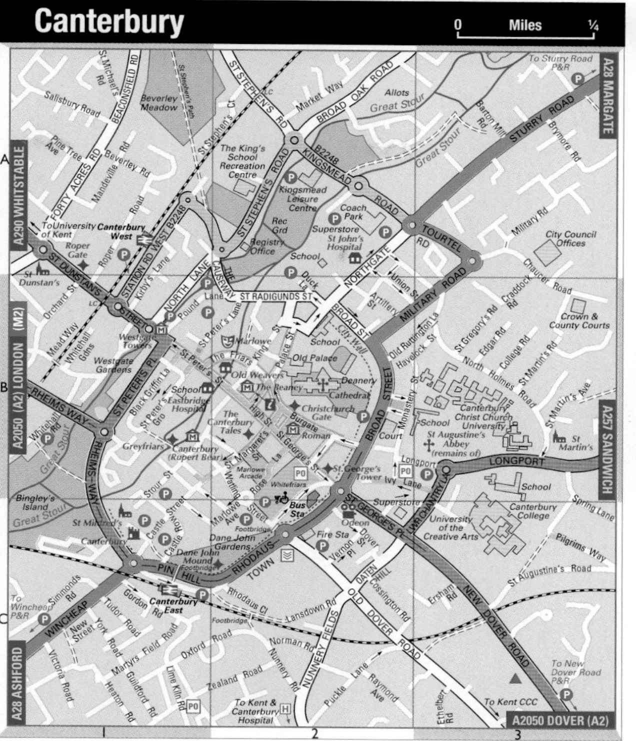
Canterbury
0 Miles ¼
A28 MARGATE
A290 WHITSTABLE
A2050 (A2) LONDON (M2)
A257 SANDWICH
A28 ASHFORD
A2050 DOVER (A2)

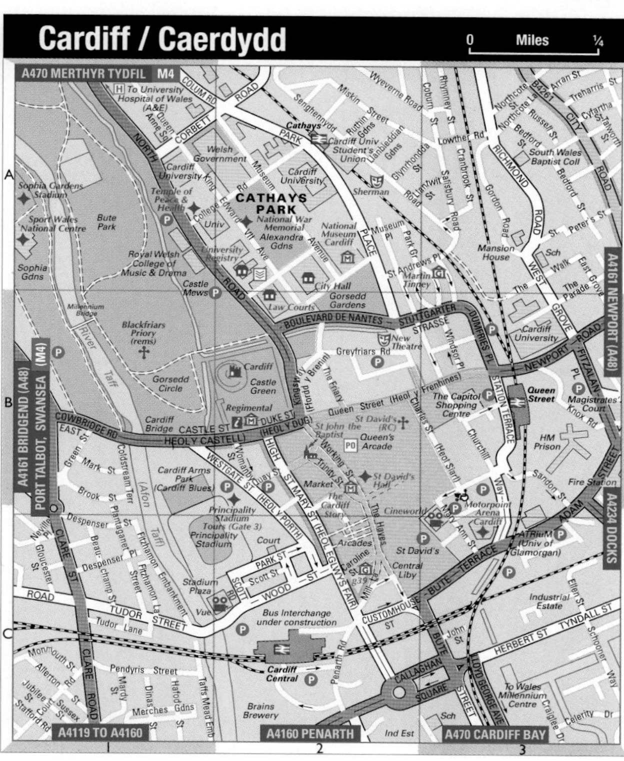
Cardiff / Caerdydd
0 Miles ¼
A470 MERTHYR TYDFIL M4
A4161 NEWPORT (A48)
A4161 BRIDGEND (A48) PORT TALBOT, SWANSEA (M4)
A4234 DOCKS
A4119 TO A4160
A4160 PENARTH
A470 CARDIFF BAY

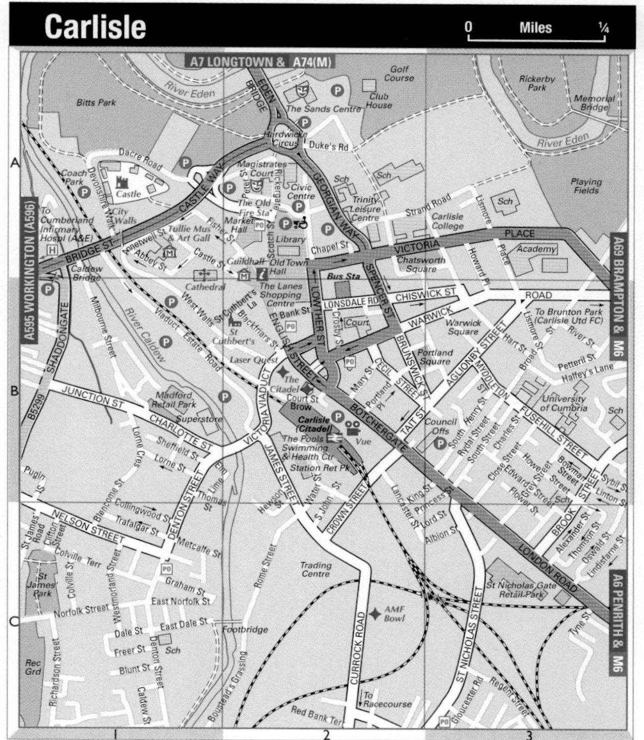
Carlisle
0 Miles ¼
A7 LONGTOWN & A74(M)
A595 WORKINGTON (A596)
A69 BRAMPTON & M6
A6 PENRITH & M6

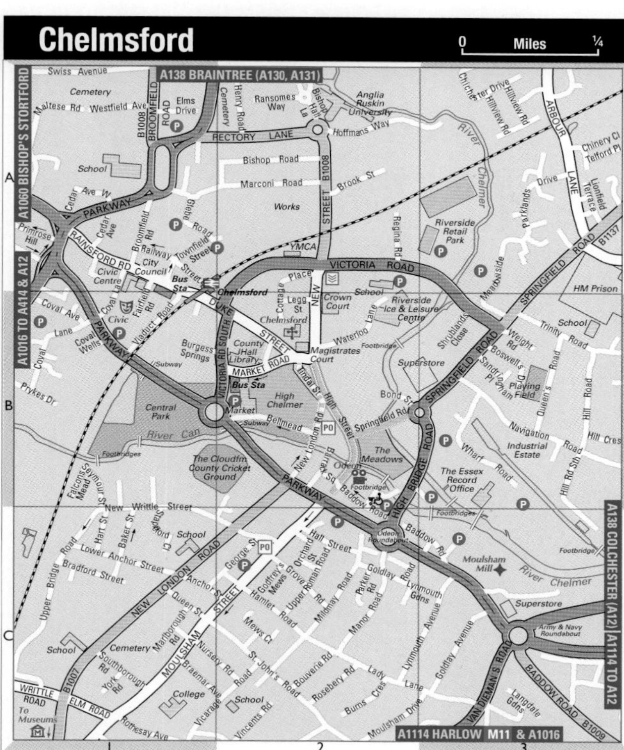
Chelmsford
0 Miles ¼
A138 BRAINTREE (A130, A131)
A1060 BISHOP'S STORTFORD
A1016 TO A414 & A12
A138 COLCHESTER (A12) A1114 TO A12
A1114 HARLOW M11 & A1016

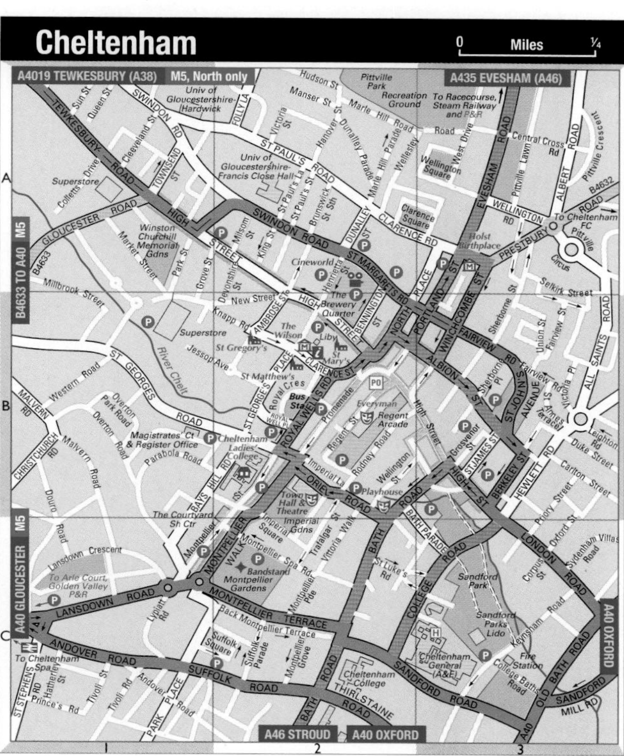
Cheltenham
0 Miles ¼
A4019 TEWKESBURY (A38) M5, North only
A435 EVESHAM (A46)
B4633 TO A40 M5
A40 GLOUCESTER M5
A40 OXFORD
A46 STROUD
A40 OXFORD

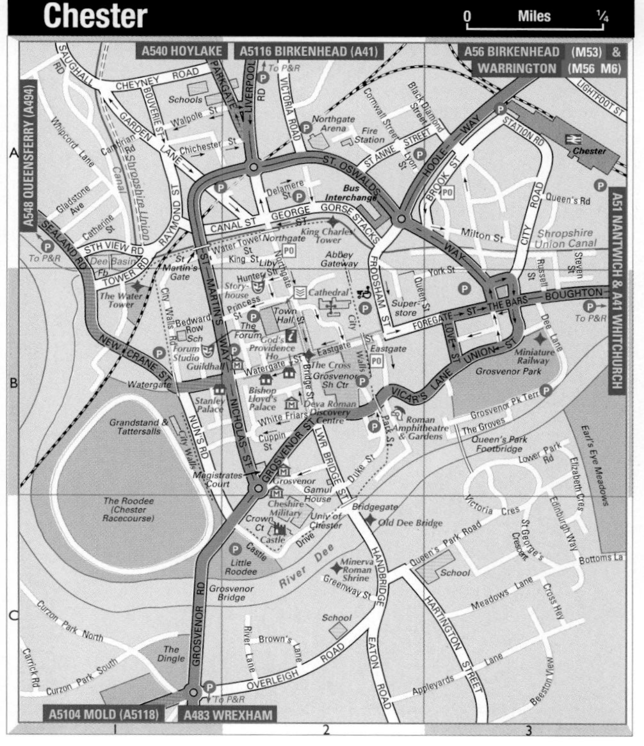
Chester
0 Miles ¼
A540 HOYLAKE
A5116 BIRKENHEAD (A41)
A56 BIRKENHEAD (M53) & WARRINGTON (M56 M6)
A548 QUEENSFERRY (A494)
A51 NANTWICH & A41 WHITCHURCH
A5104 MOLD (A5118)
A483 WREXHAM

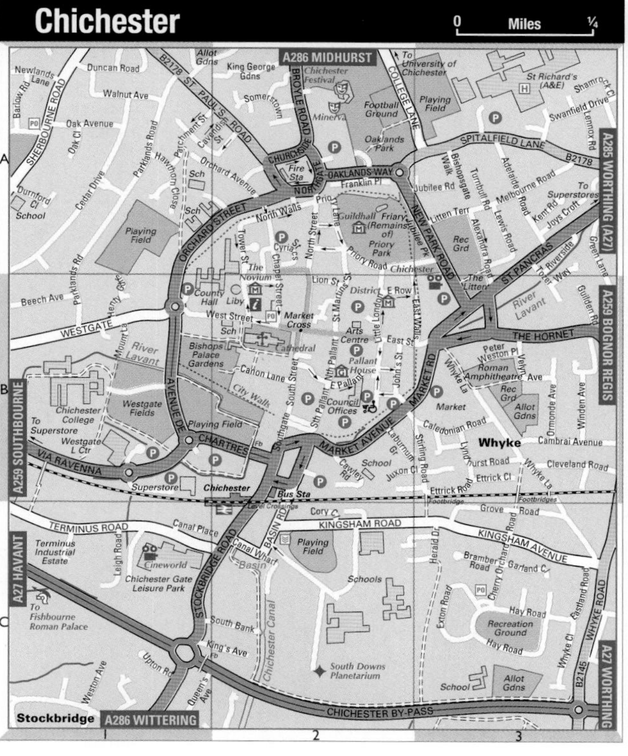
Chichester
0 Miles ¼
A286 MIDHURST
A285 WORTHING (A27)
A259 BOGNOR REGIS
A259 SOUTHBOURNE
A27 HAVANT
A27 WORTHING
Stockbridge
A286 WITTERING
CHICHESTER BY-PASS

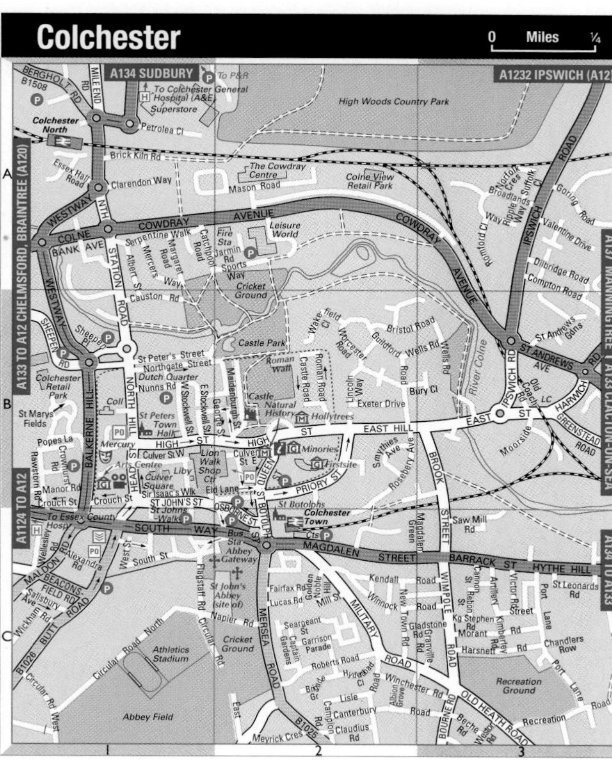
Colchester
0 Miles ¼
A134 SUDBURY
A1232 IPSWICH (A12)
A133 TO A12 CHELMSFORD BRAINTREE (A120)
A137 MANNINGTREE
A133 CLACTON-ON-SEA
A1124 TO A12
A134 TO A133
High Woods Country Park

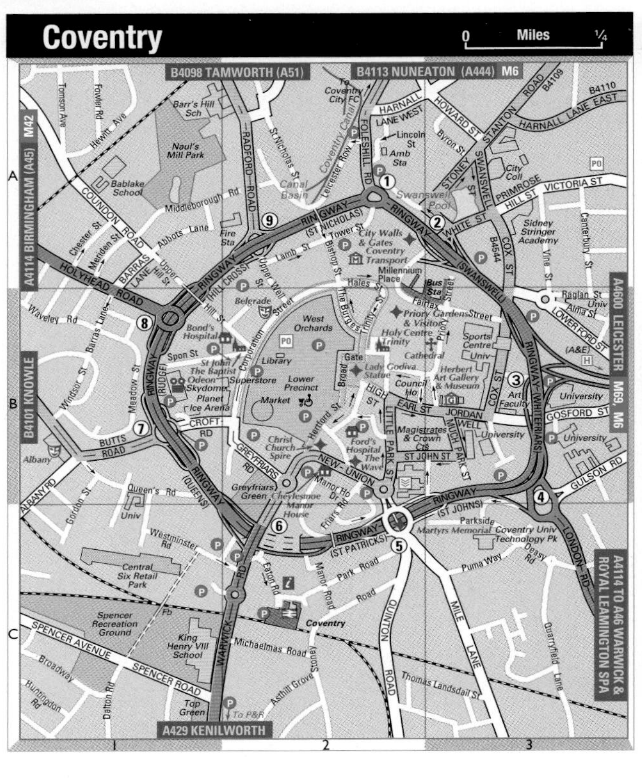
Coventry
0 Miles ¼
B4098 TAMWORTH (A51)
B4113 NUNEATON (A444) M6
A4114 BIRMINGHAM (A45) M42
B4101 KNOWLE
A4600 LEICESTER M69 M6
A4114 TO A46 WARWICK & ROYAL LEAMINGTON SPA
A429 KENILWORTH

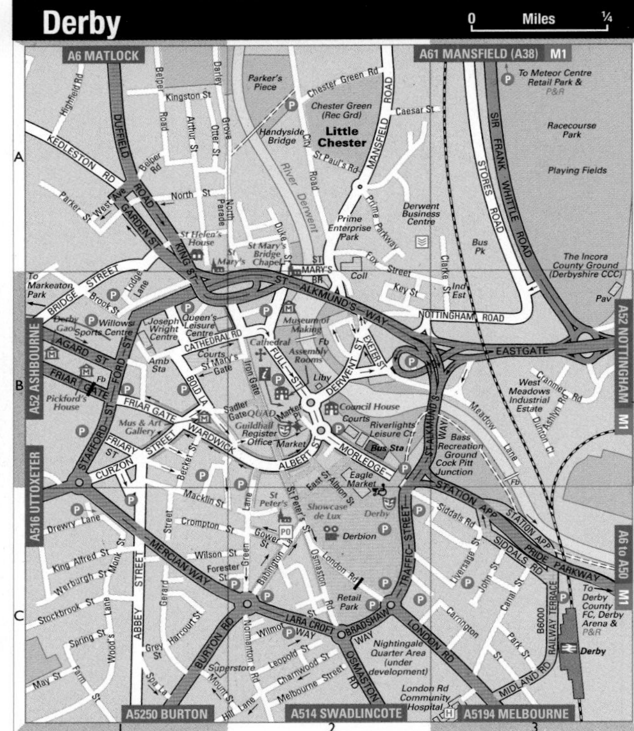
Derby
0 Miles ¼
A6 MATLOCK
A61 MANSFIELD (A38) M1
A52 ASHBOURNE
A516 UTTOXETER
A52 NOTTINGHAM M1
A6 to A50 M1
A5250 BURTON
A514 SWADLINCOTE
A5194 MELBOURNE

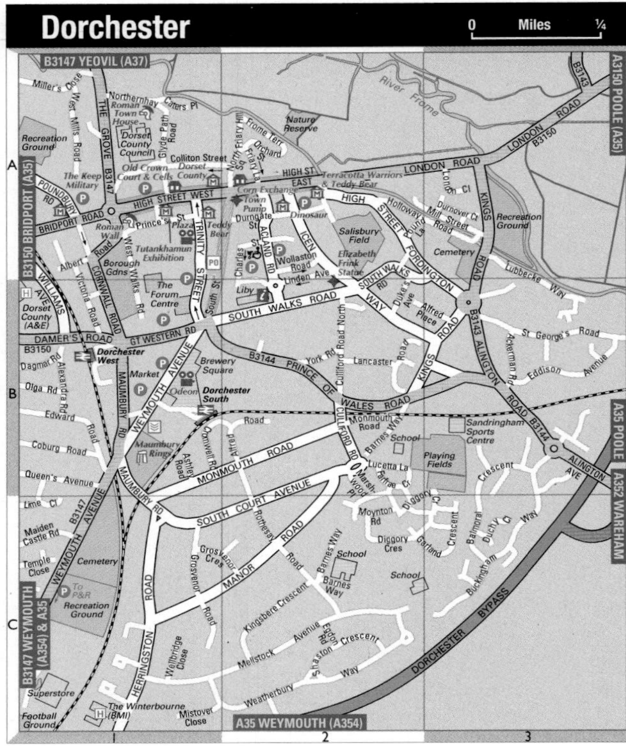
Dorchester
0 Miles ¼
B3147 YEOVIL (A37)
A3150 POOLE (A35)
B3150 BRIDPORT (A35)
B3147 WEYMOUTH (A354) & A35
A35 WEYMOUTH (A354)
A35 POOLE A352 WAREHAM

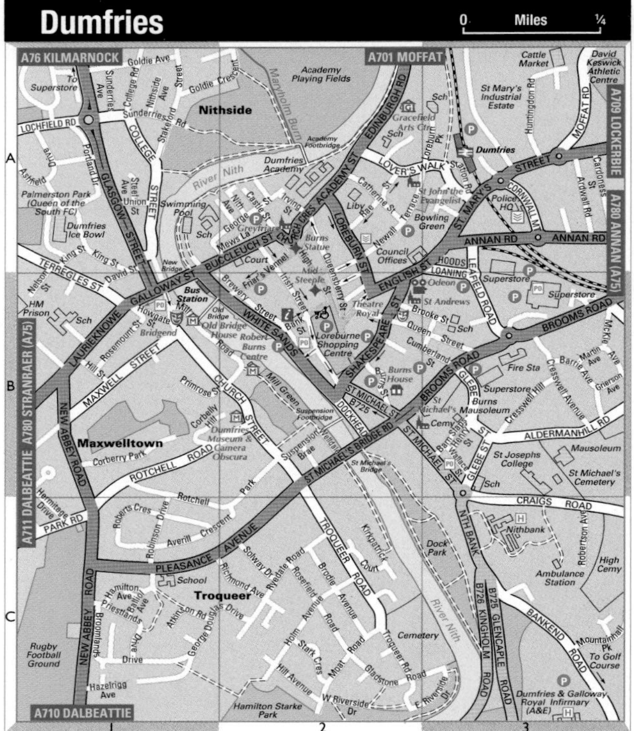
Dumfries
0 Miles ¼
A76 KILMARNOCK
A701 MOFFAT
A709 LOCKERBIE
A780 ANNAN (A75)
A711 DALBEATTIE A780 STRANRAER (A75)
A710 DALBEATTIE

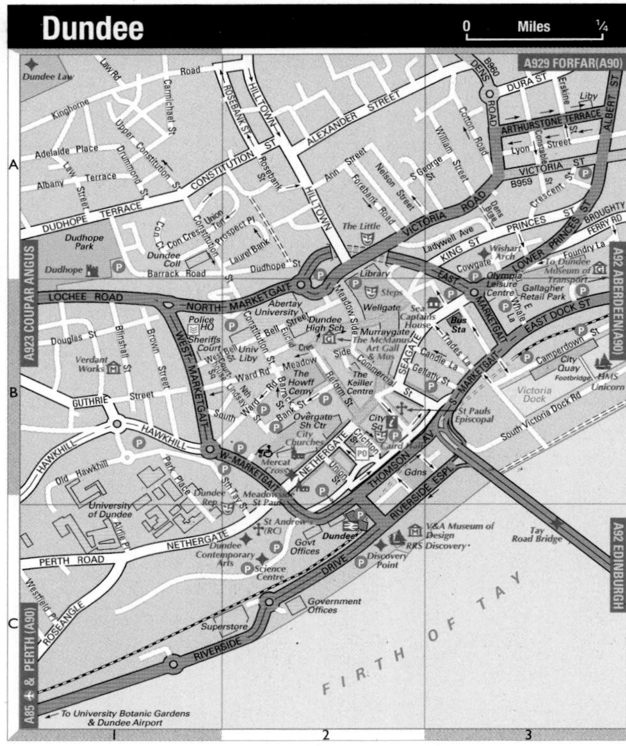
Dundee
0 Miles ¼
A929 FORFAR (A90)
A923 COUPAR ANGUS
A92 ABERDEEN (A90)
A92 EDINBURGH
FIRTH OF TAY
To University Botanic Gardens & Dundee Airport

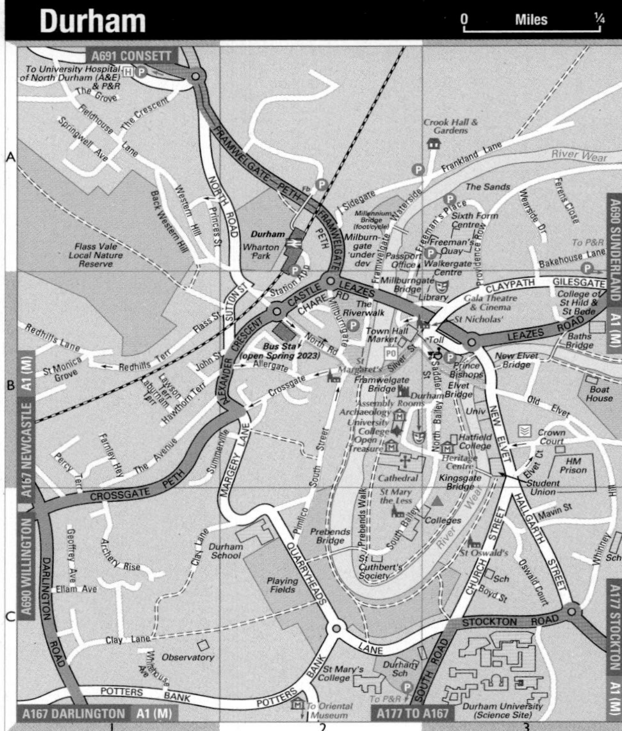
Durham
0 Miles ¼
A691 CONSETT
A690 SUNDERLAND
A1 (M)
A167 NEWCASTLE A1 (M)
A690 WILLINGTON
A177 STOCKTON A1 (M)
A167 DARLINGTON A1 (M)
A177 TO A167

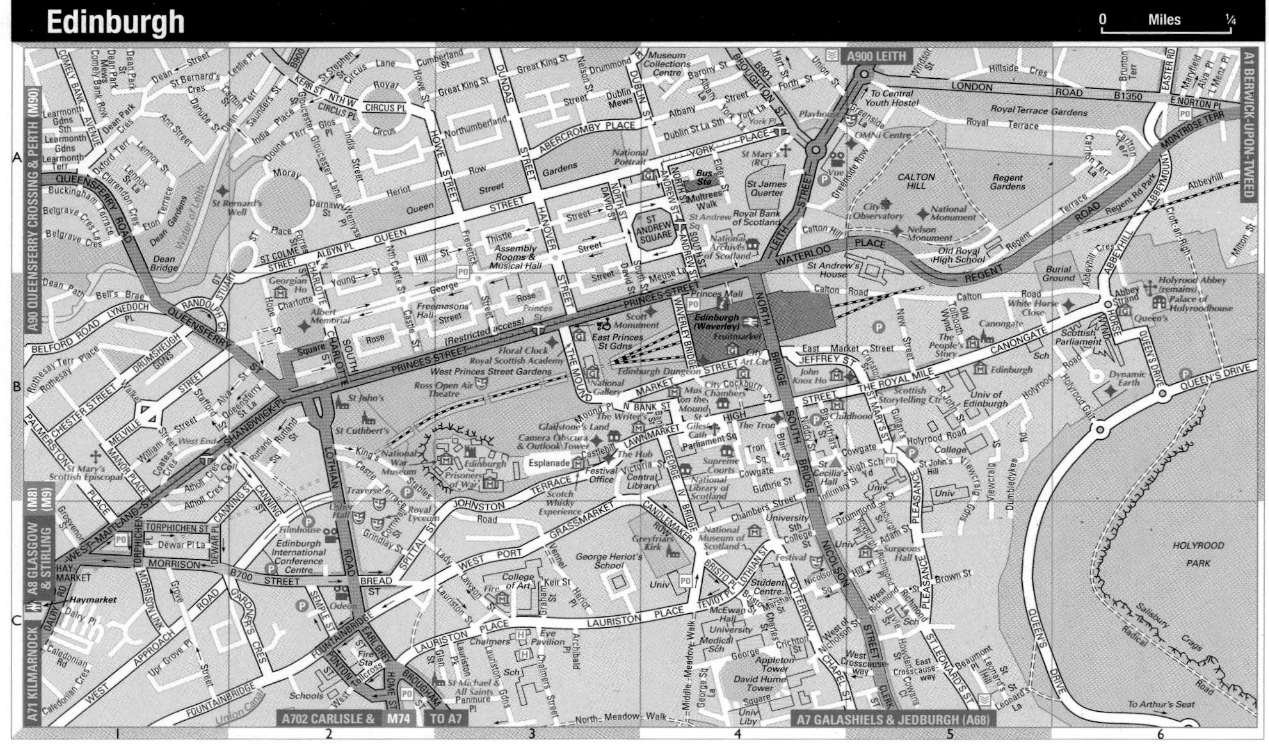
Edinburgh
0 Miles ¼
A900 LEITH
A1 BERWICK-UPON-TWEED
A90 QUEENSFERRY CROSSING & PERTH (M90)
A8 GLASGOW & STIRLING (M8) (M9)
A71 KILMARNOCK
A702 CARLISLE & M74
TO A7
A7 GALASHIELS & JEDBURGH (A68)

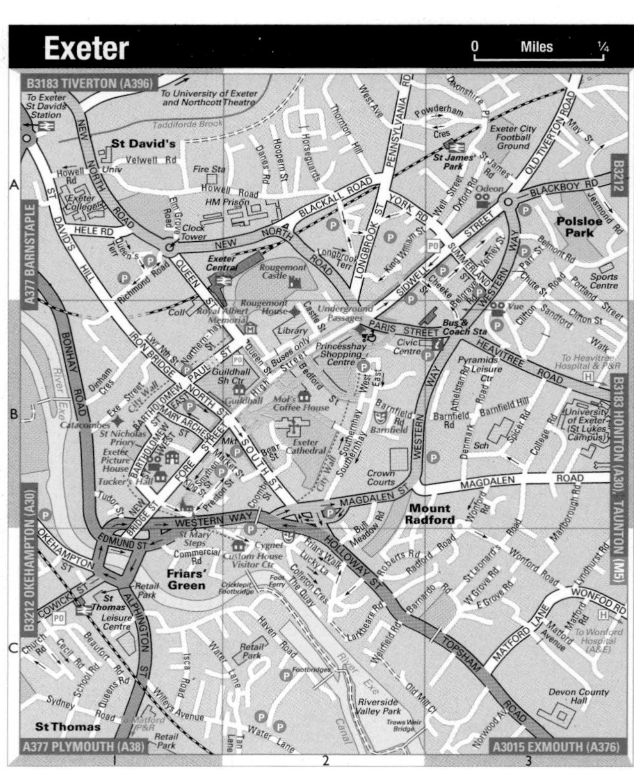
Exeter
0 Miles ¼
B3183 TIVERTON (A396)
A377 BARNSTAPLE
B3212 OKEHAMPTON (A30)
B3183 HONITON (A30), TAUNTON (M5)
A377 PLYMOUTH (A38)
A3015 EXMOUTH (A376)

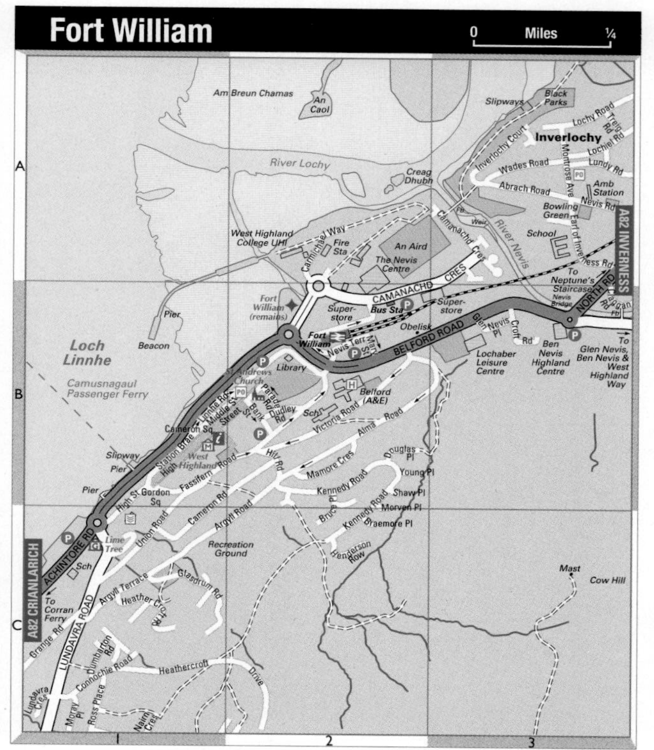
Fort William
Miles
Inverlochy
River Lochy
Loch Linnhe
A82 INVERNESS
A82 CRIANLARICH
Belford Road
Camusnagaul Passenger Ferry
Lochaber Leisure Centre
Belford (A&E)
Cow Hill

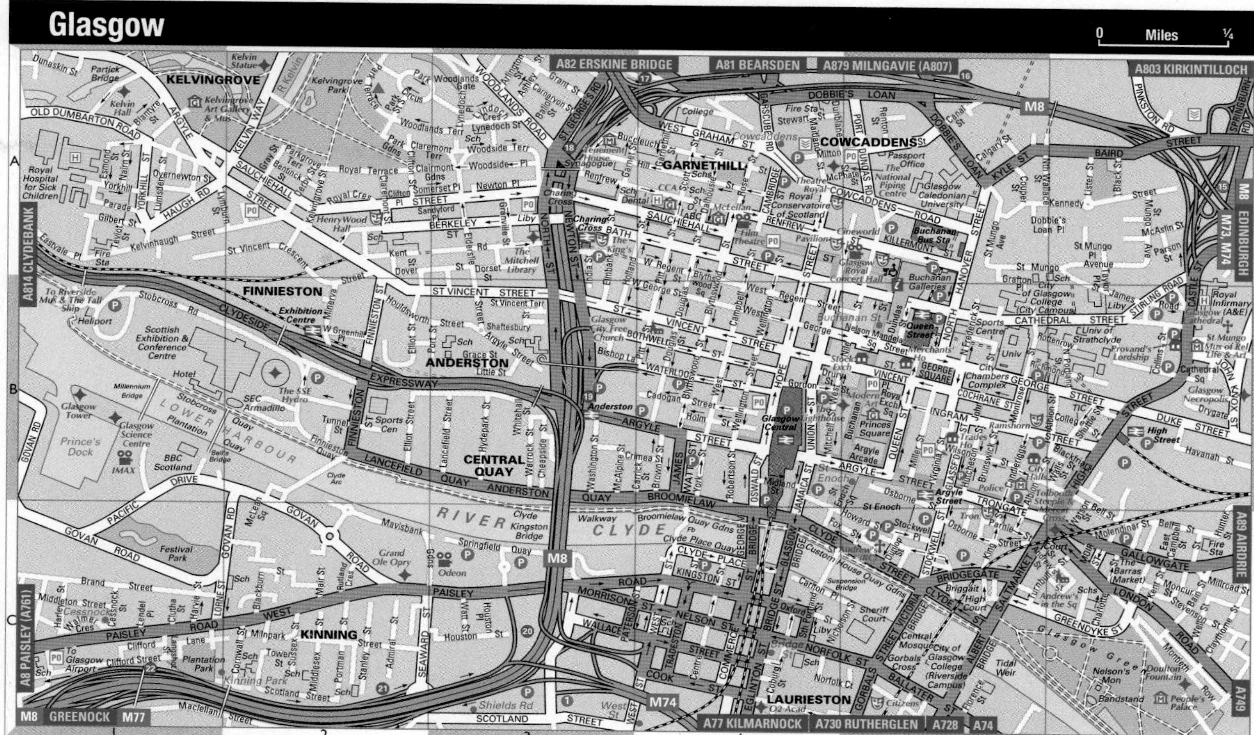
Glasgow
Miles
A82 ERSKINE BRIDGE
A81 BEARSDEN
A879 MILNGAVIE (A807)
A803 KIRKINTILLOCH
KELVINGROVE
COWCADDENS
GARNETHILL
FINNIESTON
ANDERSTON
CENTRAL QUAY
KINNING
LAURIESTON
RIVER CLYDE
A814 CLYDEBANK
A8 PAISLEY (A761)
M8 GREENOCK
M77
A77 KILMARNOCK
A730 RUTHERGLEN
A728
A74
A749
A89 AIRDRIE
M8 EDINBURGH
M73, M74

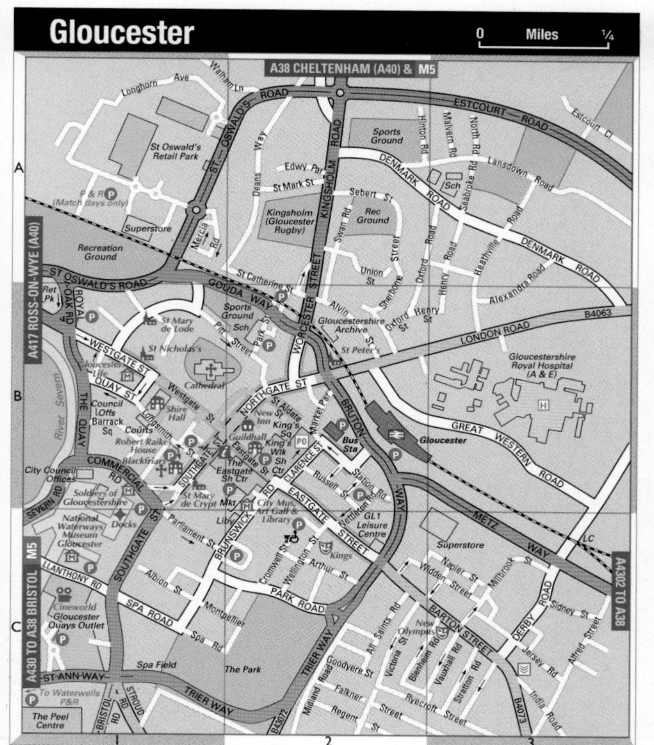
Gloucester
Miles
A38 CHELTENHAM (A40) & M5
A417 ROSS-ON-WYE (A40)
A430 TO A38 BRISTOL M5
A4302 TO A38
Gloucestershire Royal Hospital (A & E)
Cathedral
The Park
Spa Field

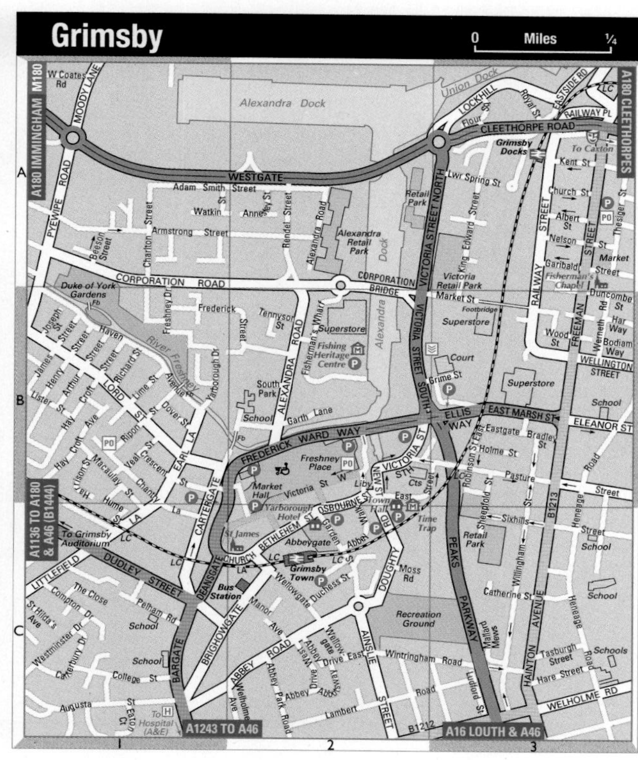
Grimsby
Miles
Alexandra Dock
A180 IMMINGHAM M180
A180 CLEETHORPES
A1136 TO A180 & A46 (B1444)
A1243 TO A46
A16 LOUTH & A46
Grimsby Town
Recreation Ground

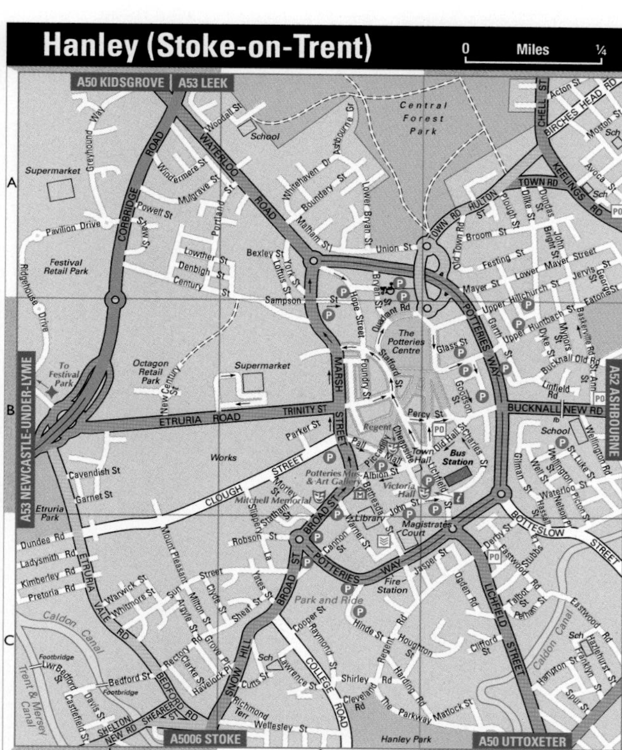
Hanley (Stoke-on-Trent)
Miles
A50 KIDSGROVE
A53 LEEK
A52 ASHBOURNE
A53 NEWCASTLE-UNDER-LYME
A5006 STOKE
A50 UTTOXETER
Central Forest Park
Festival Retail Park
Caldon Canal
Trent & Mersey Canal

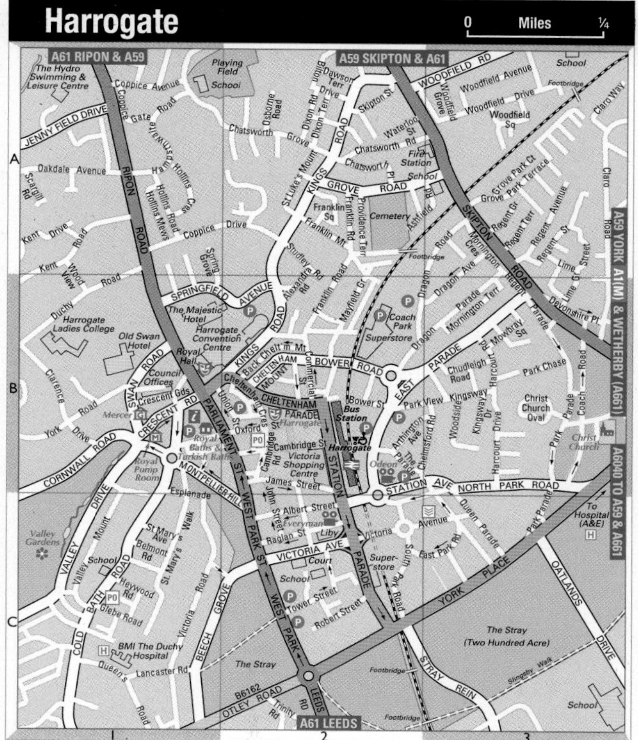
Harrogate
Miles
A61 RIPON & A59
A59 SKIPTON & A61
A59 YORK A1(M) & WETHERBY (A661)
A6040 TO A59 & A661
A61 LEEDS
The Stray (Two Hundred Acre)
Valley Gardens

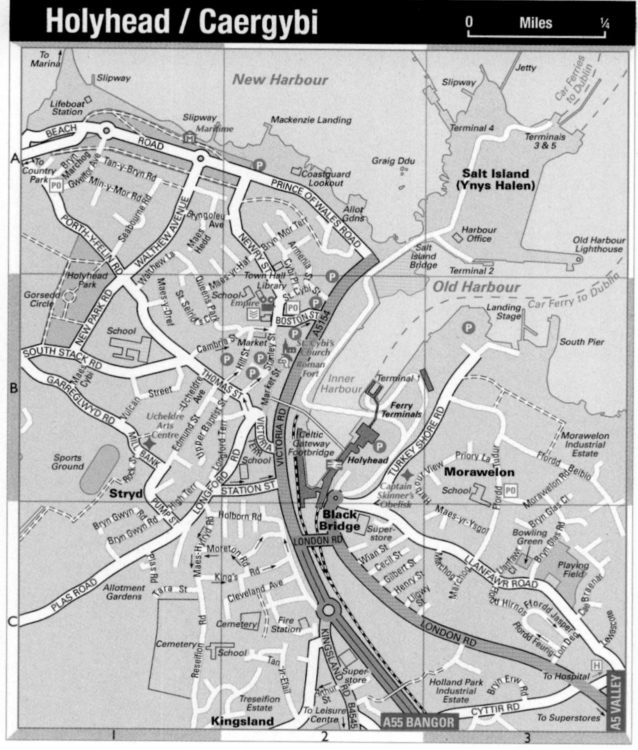
Holyhead / Caergybi
Miles
New Harbour
Salt Island (Ynys Halen)
Old Harbour
Morawelon
Stryd
Black Bridge
Kingsland
A55 BANGOR
A5 VALLEY

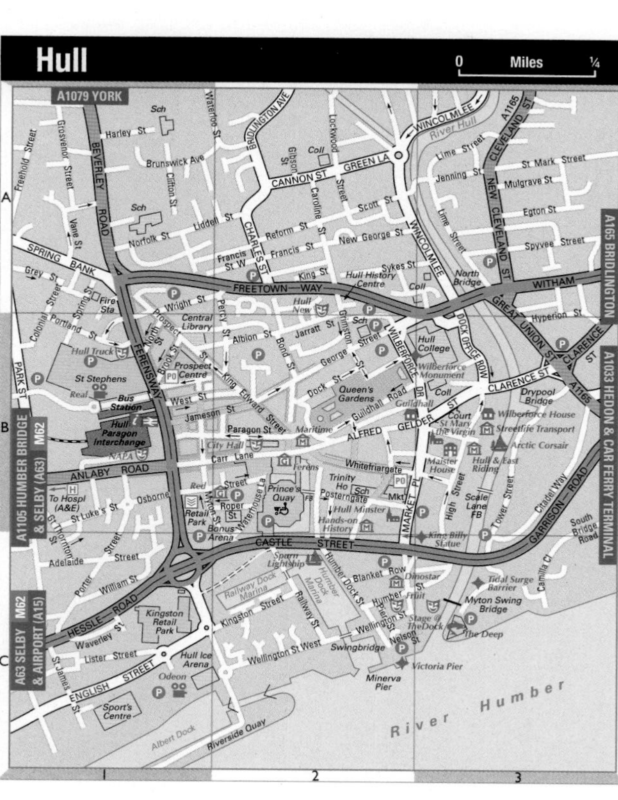
Hull
Miles
A1079 YORK
A165 BRIDLINGTON
A1033 HEDON & CAR FERRY TERMINAL
A1105 HUMBER BRIDGE & SELBY (A63) M62
A63 SELBY & AIRPORT (A15) M62
River Humber
River Hull
Hull Paragon Interchange

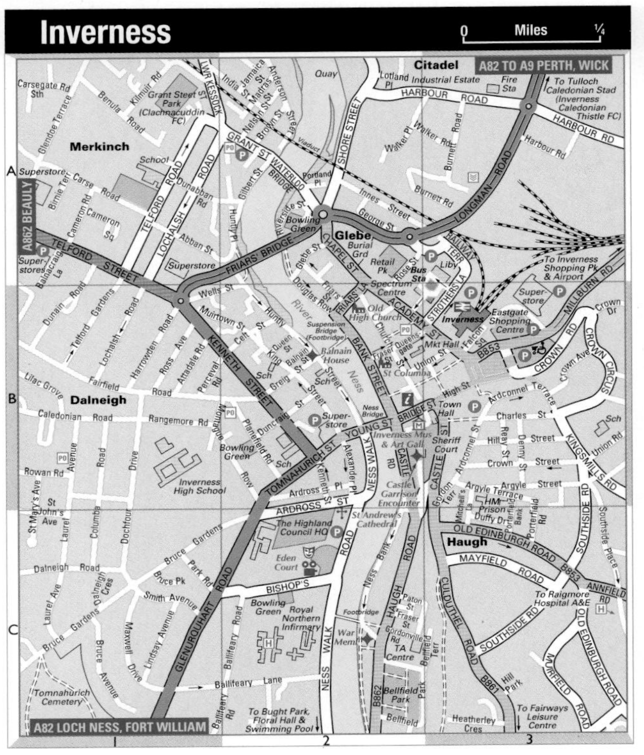
Inverness
0 Miles ¼
A82 TO A9 PERTH, WICK
A862 BEAULY
A82 LOCH NESS, FORT WILLIAM
Merkinch
Dalneigh
Citadel
Glebe
Haugh

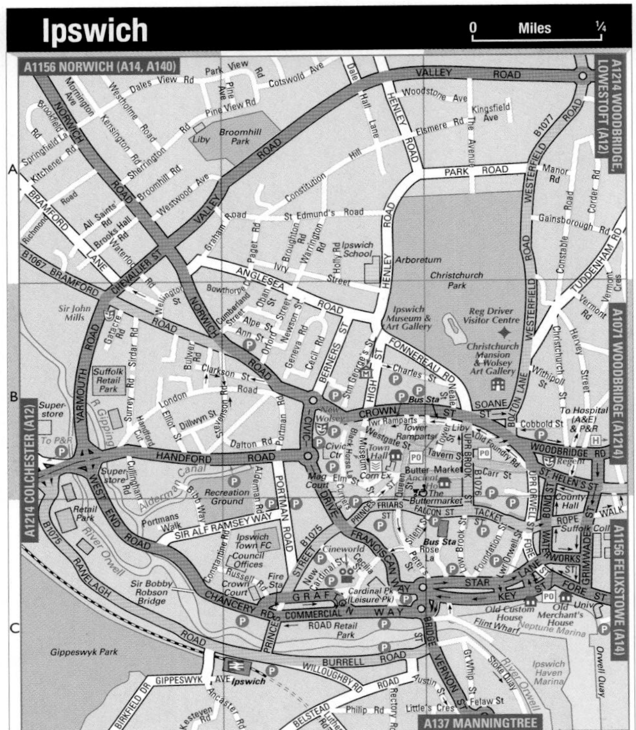
Ipswich
0 Miles ¼
A1156 NORWICH (A14, A140)
A1214 WOODBRIDGE LOWESTOFT (A12)
A1071 WOODBRIDGE
A1156 FELIXSTOWE (A14)
A1214 COLCHESTER (A12)
A137 MANNINGTREE

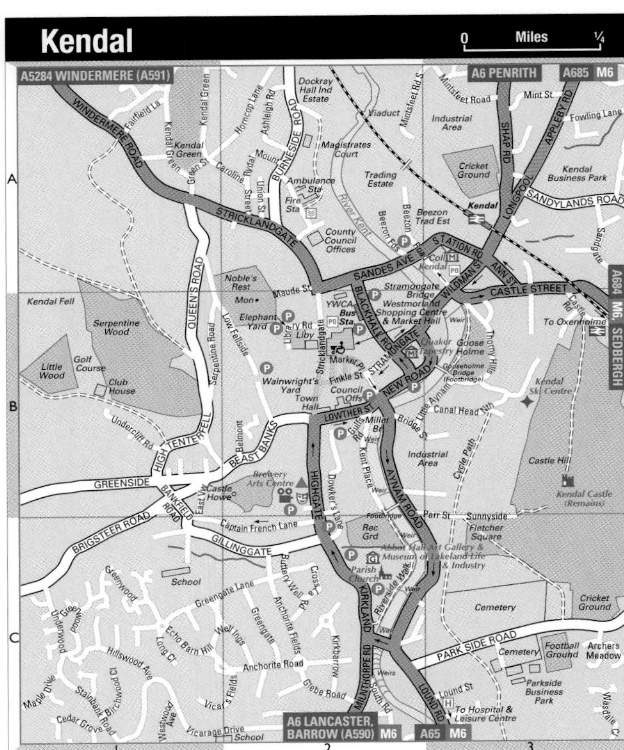
Kendal
0 Miles ¼
A5284 WINDERMERE (A591)
A6 PENRITH
A685 M6
A684 M6 SEDBERGH
A6 LANCASTER, BARROW (A590) M6
A65 M6

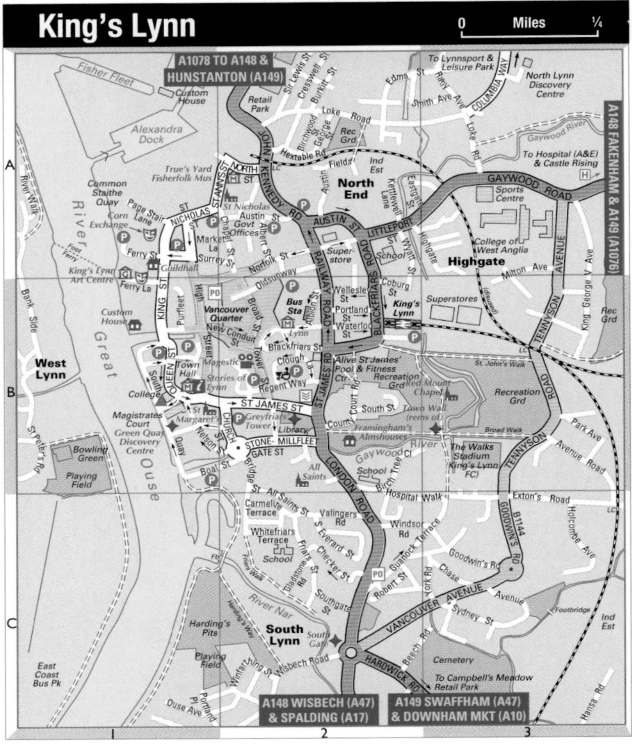
King's Lynn
0 Miles ¼
A1078 TO A148 & HUNSTANTON (A149)
A148 FAKENHAM & A149 (A1076)
A148 WISBECH (A47) & SPALDING (A17)
A149 SWAFFHAM (A47) & DOWNHAM MKT (A10)
West Lynn
North End
Highgate
South Lynn

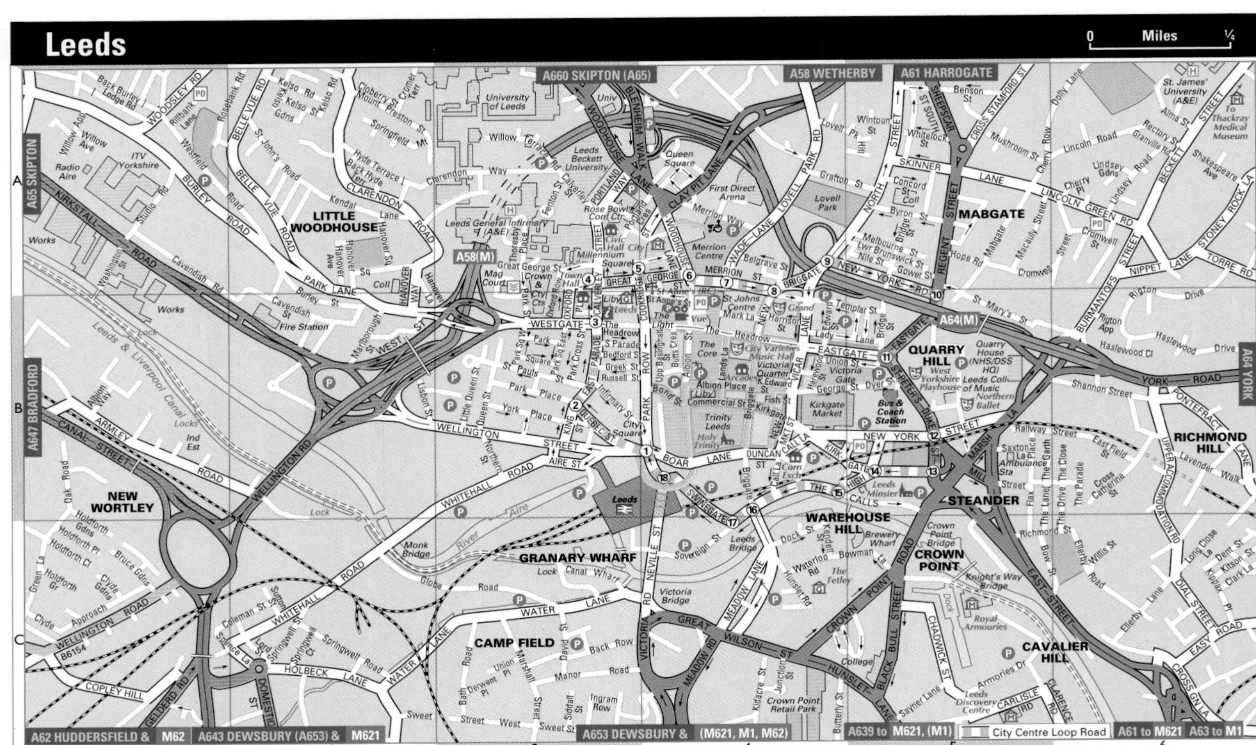
Leeds
0 Miles ¼
A660 SKIPTON (A65)
A58 WETHERBY
A61 HARROGATE
A65 SKIPTON
A647 BRADFORD
A64 YORK
A62 HUDDERSFIELD & M62
A643 DEWSBURY (A653) & M621
A653 DEWSBURY & (M621, M1, M62)
A639 to M621, (M1)
City Centre Loop Road
A61 to M621
A63 to M1
LITTLE WOODHOUSE
MABGATE
QUARRY HILL
RICHMOND HILL
NEW WORTLEY
GRANARY WHARF
WAREHOUSE HILL
STEANDER
CROWN POINT
CAMP FIELD
CAVALIER HILL

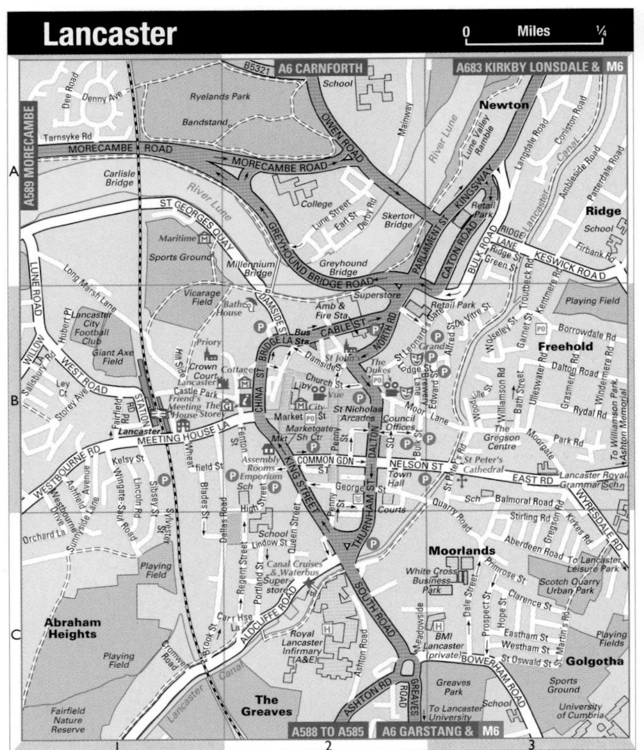
Lancaster
0 Miles ¼
A6 CARNFORTH
A683 KIRKBY LONSDALE & M6
A589 MORECAMBE
A588 TO A585
A6 GARSTANG & M6
Newton
Ridge
Freehold
Moorlands
Abraham Heights
The Greaves
Golgotha

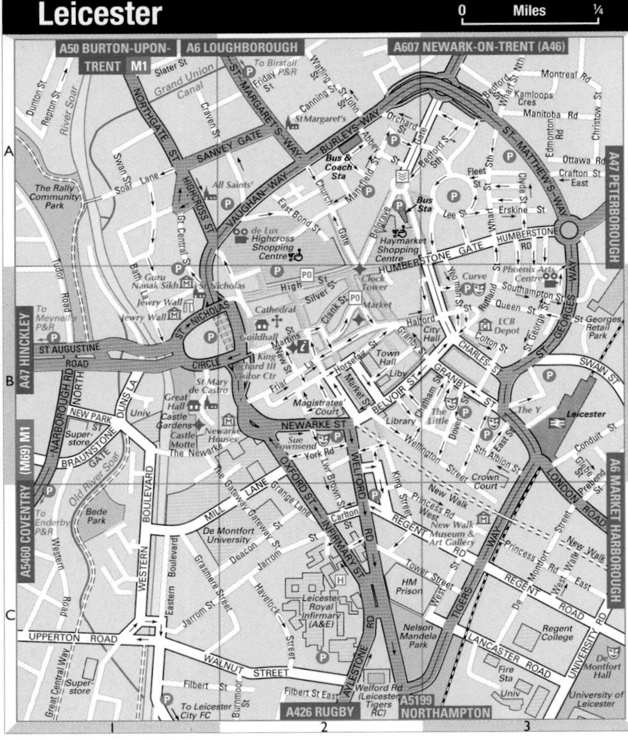
Leicester
0 Miles ¼
A50 BURTON-UPON-TRENT M1
A6 LOUGHBOROUGH
A607 NEWARK-ON-TRENT (A46)
A47 PETERBOROUGH
A47 HINCKLEY
A5460 COVENTRY (M69) M1
A6 MARKET HARBOROUGH
A426 RUGBY
A5199 NORTHAMPTON

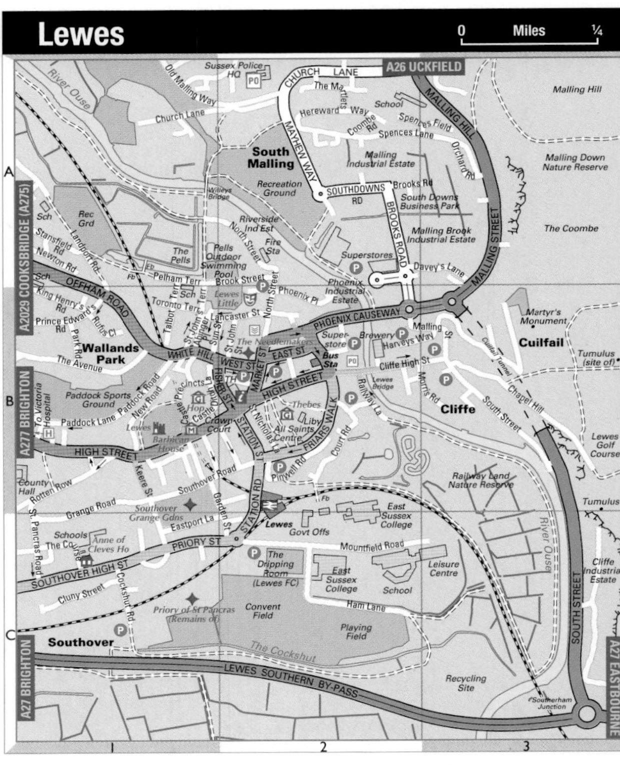
Lewes
0 Miles ¼
A26 UCKFIELD
A2029 COOKSBRIDGE (A275)
A277 BRIGHTON
A27 BRIGHTON
A27 EASTBOURNE
South Malling
Wallands Park
Cuilfail
Cliffe
Southover

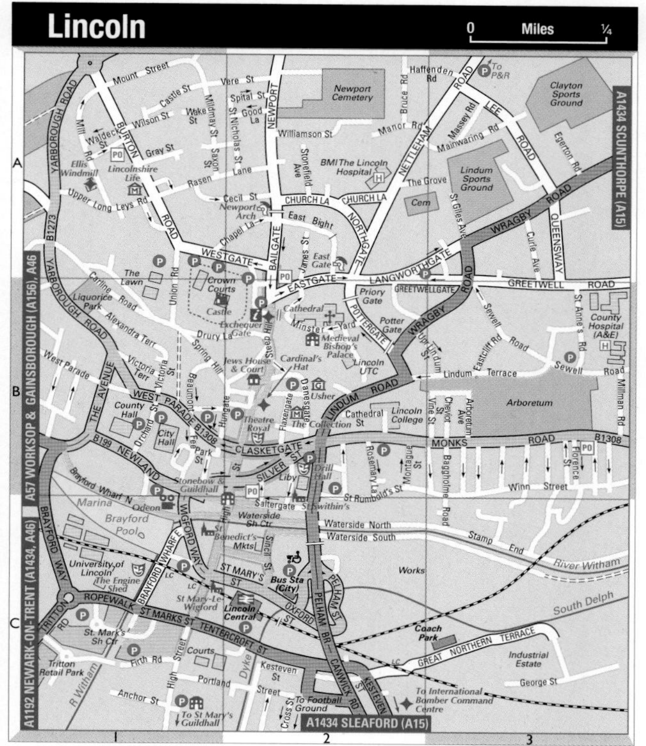
Lincoln
0 Miles ¼
A1434 SCUNTHORPE (A15)
A156 GAINSBOROUGH (A156), A46
A57 WORKSOP & GAINSBOROUGH
A1192 NEWARK-ON-TRENT (A1434, A46)
A1434 SLEAFORD (A15)
Newport Cemetery
Clayton Sports Ground
Lindum Sports Ground
County Hospital (A&E)
Arboretum
Lincoln UTC
Brayford Pool
University of Lincoln
Lincoln Central
River Witham
South Delph
Works
Industrial Estate
Tritton Retail Park
WESTGATE
EASTGATE
GREETWELL ROAD
MONKS ROAD
WRAGBY ROAD
LINDUM ROAD
Waterside North
Waterside South
ST MARY'S ST
GREAT NORTHERN TERRACE
To International Bomber Command Centre
To St Mary's Guildhall
To Football Ground

Liverpool
0 Miles ¼
A5036 TO A565
A565 SOUTHPORT
A5038 KIRKDALE
A59 PRESTON
M57 & M58 & KINGSWAY TUNNEL
A580 TO A59
A5049 WEST DERBY
A57 WARRINGTON
A5047 TO M62 & MANCHESTER
A5036 TO A562
A561 GARSTON
A5038 TO A561
A5039 TO A562
A5048 TO A562
Princes Half Tide Dock
Princes Jetty
Princes Dock
RIVER MERSEY
Lime Street
Moorfields
James St
Liverpool Central
Liverpool ONE
Queen Square Bus Sta
Royal Liverpool University Hospital (A&E)
Metropolitan Cathedral (RC)
Cathedral
University of Liverpool
Liverpool John Moores University
Albert Dock
Tate Liverpool
Queensway Tunnel Docks Exit
Passenger Ferry to Woodside
Passenger Ferry to Seacombe
Car Ferry to Douglas & Dublin
Mersey Rail Tunnel
QUEENSWAY (Birkenhead Tunnel)
M&S Bank Arena & Convention Centre
DALE STREET
HANOVER STREET
DUKE STREET
LONDON ROAD
HARDMAN ST
SCOTLAND RD
WEST DERBY ROAD
PRESCOT STREET
UPPER DUKE STREET

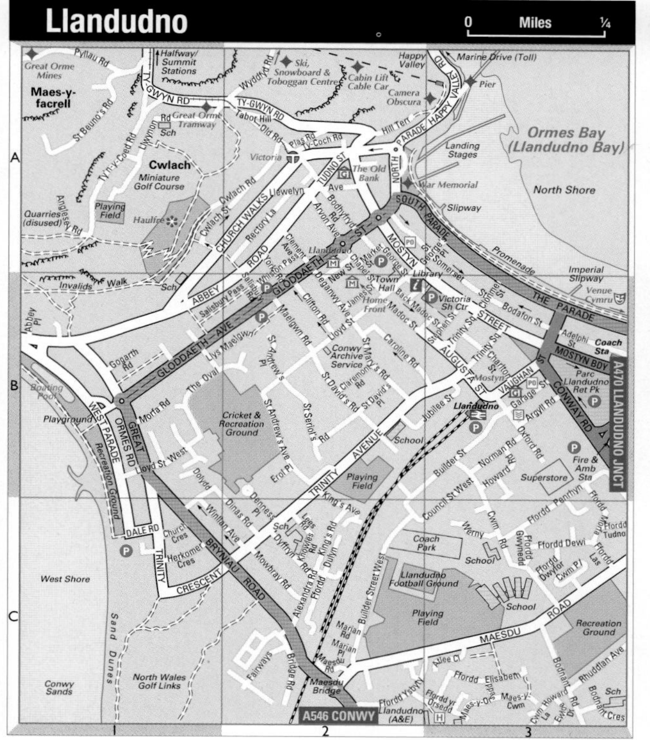
Llandudno
0 Miles ¼
A470 LLANDUDNO JUNCT
A546 CONWY
Great Orme Mines
Maes-y-facrell
Halfway/Summit Stations
Great Orme Tramway
Cwlach
Miniature Golf Course
Ormes Bay (Llandudno Bay)
North Shore
Pier
Marine Drive (Toll)
Llandudno
Cricket & Recreation Ground
Playing Field
Coach Park
Llandudno Football Ground
Recreation Ground
West Shore
Conwy Sands
North Wales Golf Links
Sand Dunes
MOSTYN ST
THE PARADE
GLODDAETH AVE
TRINITY AVENUE
MAESDU
Llandudno (A&E)

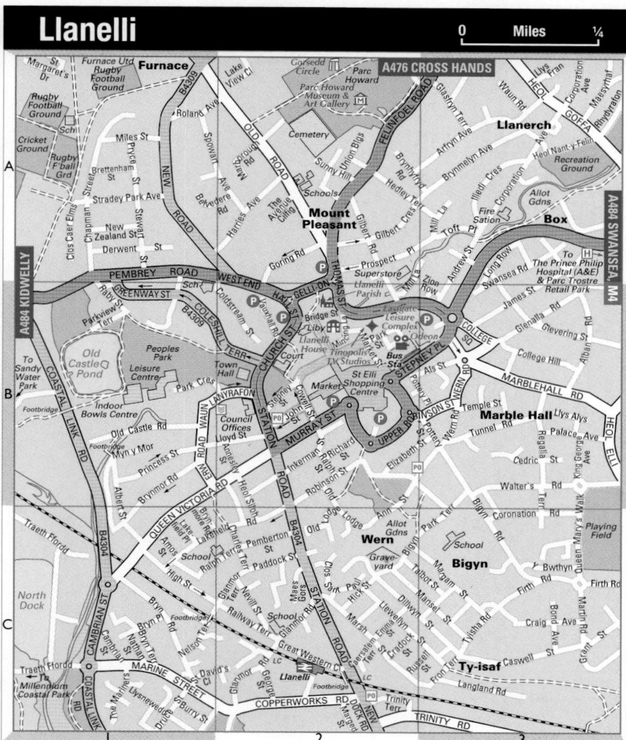
Llanelli
0 Miles ¼
A476 CROSS HANDS
A484 SWANSEA, M4
A484 KIDWELLY
Furnace
Llanerch
Mount Pleasant
Box
Marble Hall
Wern
Bigyn
Ty-isaf
Old Castle Pond
Peoples Park
North Dock
Millennium Coastal Park
Llanelli
Cemetery
The Prince Philip Hospital (A&E) & Parc Trostre Retail Park
Recreation Ground
Playing Field
PEMBREY ROAD
QUEEN VICTORIA RD
MARINE STREET
COPPERWORKS RD
TRINITY RD
FELINFOEL ROAD

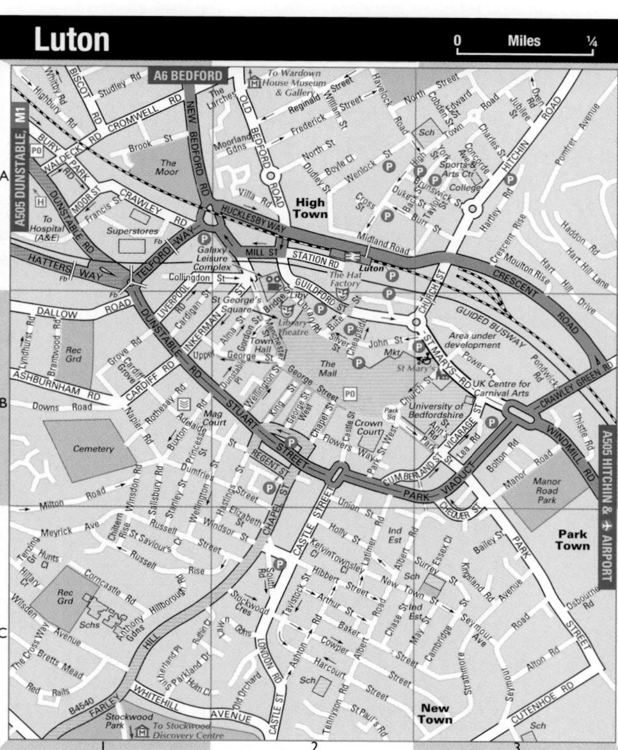
Luton
0 Miles ¼
A6 BEDFORD
M1
A505 DUNSTABLE
A505 HITCHIN & AIRPORT
High Town
Luton
The Moor
To Wardown House Museum & Gallery
Galaxy Leisure Complex
The Mall
St George's Square
Cemetery
Rec Grd
University of Bedfordshire
Crown Court
Manor Road Park
Park Town
New Town
UK Centre for Carnival Arts
To Stockwood Discovery Centre
GUIDED BUSWAY
HATTERS WAY
DALLOW
ASHBURNHAM RD
CRESCENT
WHITEHILL AVENUE

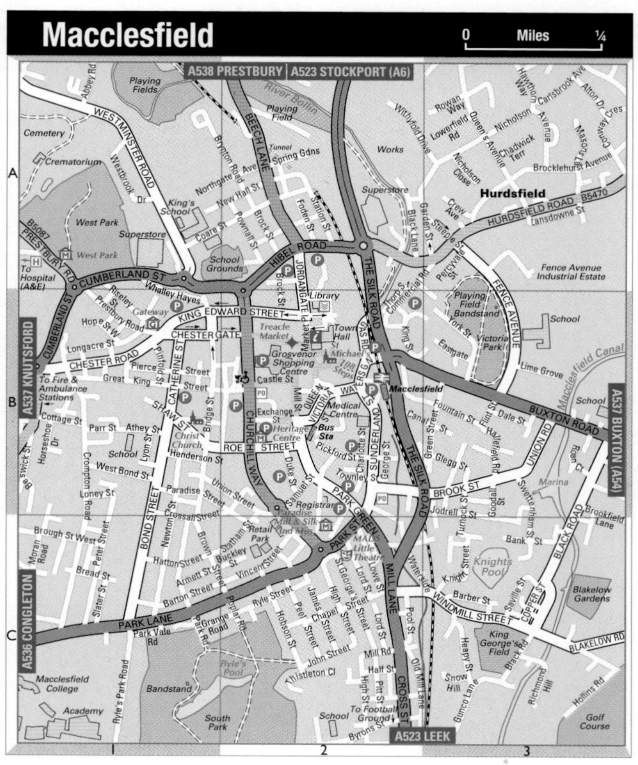
Macclesfield
0 Miles ¼
A538 PRESTBURY
A523 STOCKPORT (A6)
A537 KNUTSFORD
A537 BUXTON (A54)
A536 CONGLETON
A523 LEEK
Playing Fields
Cemetery
Crematorium
West Park
Hurdsfield
Fence Avenue Industrial Estate
Macclesfield
Knights Pool
Blakelow Gardens
King George's Field
Golf Course
South Park
Macclesfield College
Academy
Bandstand
CUMBERLAND ST
HURDSFIELD ROAD
KING EDWARD STREET
CHESTERGATE
PARK LANE
BUXTON ROAD
BROOK ST
Macclesfield Canal
River Bollin

Manchester
0 Miles ¼
A6042 TO A56
A56 BURY
A665 TO A56
A664 ROCHDALE
A62 OLDHAM
A6 PRESTON
M6
A662 DROYLSDEN
A635 ASHTON-u-Lyne
A57 WARRINGTON
M602
A5065 TO A56
M60
A56 ALTRINCHAM
A6144 STRETFORD
A5103 MANCHESTER AIRPORT (M56)
A34 CONGLETON
A6 STOCKPORT
A57 DENTON
A57(M)
MANCUNIAN WAY
Victoria
Piccadilly
Deansgate
Oxford Road
Salford Central
Manchester Arndale
Town Hall
Manchester Central Convention Complex
Science & Industry Museum (MOSI)
Regent Retail Park
University of Manchester (North Campus)
Manchester Metropolitan University (MMU)
New Islington Marina
Rochdale Canal
River Irwell
River Medlock
Manchester Ship Canal
Bridgewater Canal
Ashton Canal
CHAPEL STREET
LIVERPOOL ROAD
REGENT ROAD
PETER STREET
QUAY STREET
WHITWORTH ST WEST
GREAT ANCOATS STREET
ARDWICK GREEN ST
HYDE RD
CHESTER ROAD

ST. JOHN'S WOOD
REGENT'S PARK
SOMERS TOWN
LISSON GREEN
FITZROVIA
BLOOMSBURY
PADDINGTON
SOHO
MAYFAIR
ST JAMES'S
HYDE PARK
GREEN PARK
KENSINGTON GARDENS
KNIGHTSBRIDGE
BROMPTON
WESTMINSTER
PIMLICO

HOXTON
FINSBURY
SHOREDITCH
CLERKENWELL
HOLBORN
THE CITY
SOUTHWARK
SOUTH BANK
LAMBETH
NEWINGTON
BERMONDSEY
PENTONVILLE ROAD
CITY ROAD
OLD STREET
CLERKENWELL ROAD
THEOBALDS ROAD
HIGH HOLBORN
HOLBORN VIADUCT
LONDON WALL
FLEET STREET
STRAND
ALDWYCH
VICTORIA EMBANKMENT
UPPER THAMES STREET
LOWER THAMES STREET
QUEEN VICTORIA STREET
CANNON STREET
CHEAPSIDE
THREADNEEDLE STREET
LEADENHALL STREET
FENCHURCH STREET
EASTCHEAP
BISHOPSGATE
COMMERCIAL STREET
WHITECHAPEL HIGH ST
TOWER HILL
TOWER BRIDGE
LONDON BRIDGE
SOUTHWARK STREET
BOROUGH HIGH STREET
TOOLEY STREET
WATERLOO ROAD
WESTMINSTER BRIDGE
LAMBETH ROAD
KENNINGTON ROAD
NEW KENT ROAD
WALWORTH ROAD
OLD KENT ROAD
RIVER THAMES
St Paul's Cathedral
Barbican
Tate Modern
The Tower of London
Waterloo
Liverpool Street
Imperial War Museum
Lambeth Palace
Miles
0
½
5
6
7
8
B
C
D
E
F

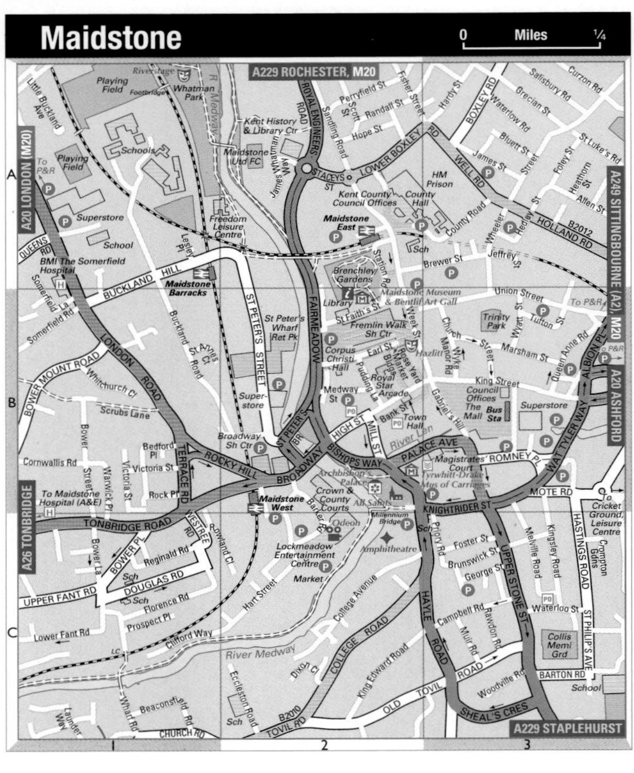
Maidstone
0 Miles ¼
A229 ROCHESTER, M20
A249 SITTINGBOURNE (A2, M20)
A20 LONDON (M20)
A20 ASHFORD
A26 TONBRIDGE
A229 STAPLEHURST
Maidstone East
Maidstone Barracks
Maidstone West
River Medway
Mote Rd
Tonbridge Road
Upper Fant Rd

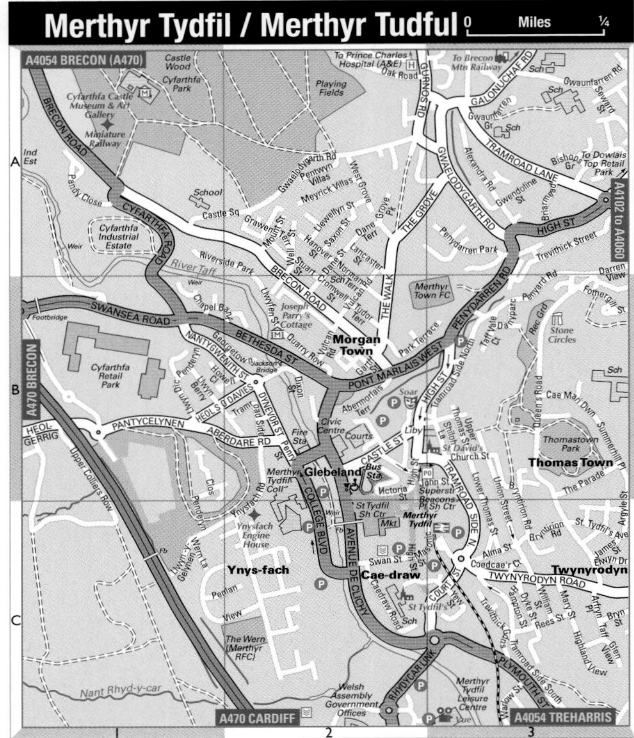
Merthyr Tydfil / Merthyr Tudful
0 Miles ¼
A4054 BRECON (A470)
A470 BRECON
A4102 to A4060
A470 CARDIFF
A4054 TREHARRIS
Morgan Town
Thomas Town
Georgetown
Ynys-fach
Cae-draw
Twynyrodyn
Swansea Road
Pont Marlais Way

Middlesbrough
0 Miles ¼
A1046
A1046 STOCKTON-ON-TEES
A178 HARTLEPOOL
A1046 STOCKTON-ON-TEES
A1032 BILLINGHAM (A19)
A19 SUNDERLAND
A66 STOCKTON-ON-TEES
A19 THIRSK
A1032 HEMLINGTON & A19
A172 STOKESLEY & THIRSK (A19)
A66 REDCAR (A1085)
A1085 REDCAR
River Tees
Transporter Bridge (Toll)
Middlesbrough
Ayresome Street
Park Road North
Park Road South
Albert Park

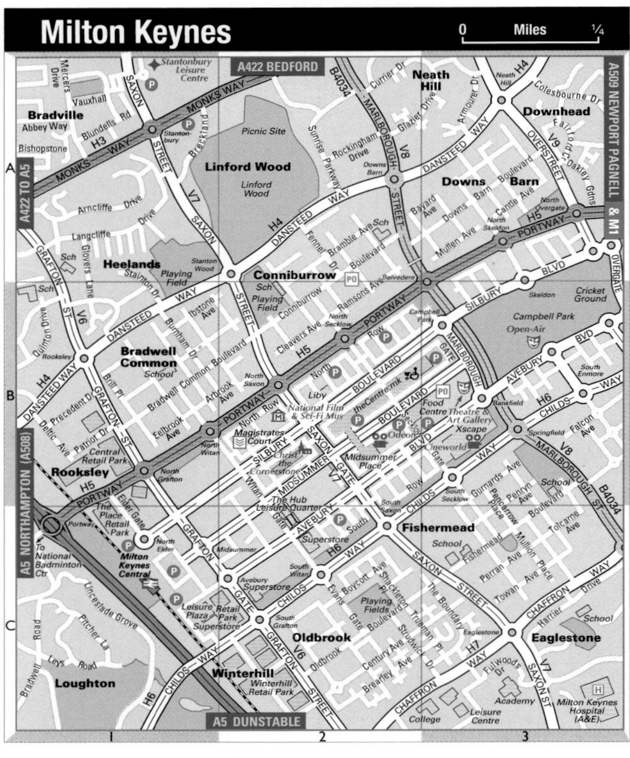
Milton Keynes
0 Miles ¼
A422 BEDFORD
A509 NEWPORT PAGNELL & M1
A422 to A5
A5 NORTHAMPTON (A508)
A5 DUNSTABLE
Bradville
Neath Hill
Downhead
Linford Wood
Downs Barn
Heelands
Conniburrow
Bradwell Common
Rooksley
Fishermead
Oldbrook
Eaglestone
Winterhill
Loughton
Portway
Dansteed Way

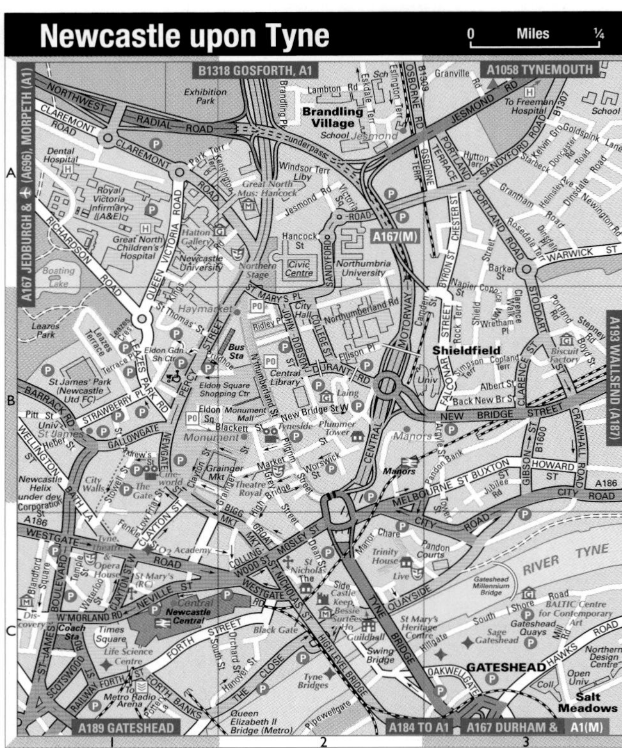
Newcastle upon Tyne
0 Miles ¼
B1318 GOSFORTH, A1
A1058 TYNEMOUTH
A167 JEDBURGH & (A696), MORPETH (A1)
A193 WALLSEND (A187)
A189 GATESHEAD
A184 TO A1
A167 DURHAM & A1(M)
Brandling Village
Shieldfield
GATESHEAD
River Tyne
Salt Meadows
New Bridge Street

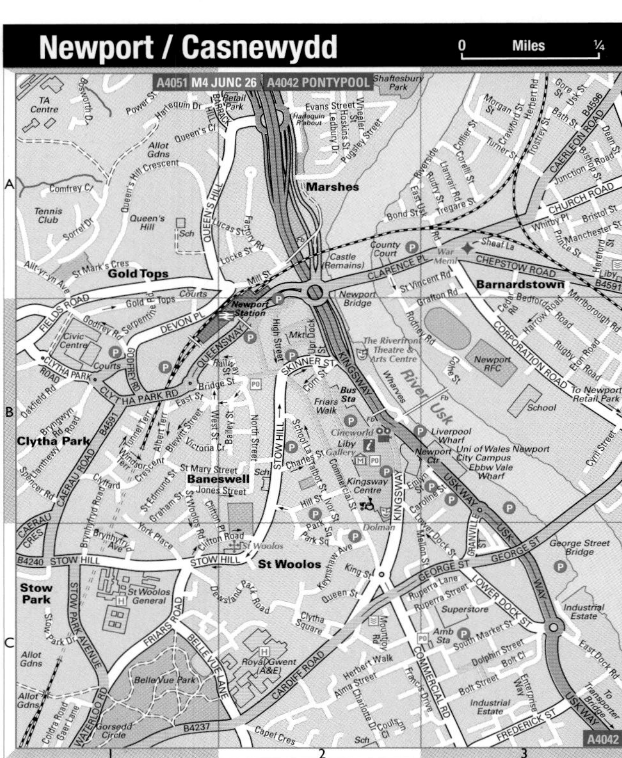
Newport / Casnewydd
0 Miles ¼
A4051 M4 JUNC 26
A4042 PONTYPOOL
A4042
Marshes
Gold Tops
Barnardstown
Clytha Park
Baneswell
Stow Park
St Woolos
River Usk
Stow Hill

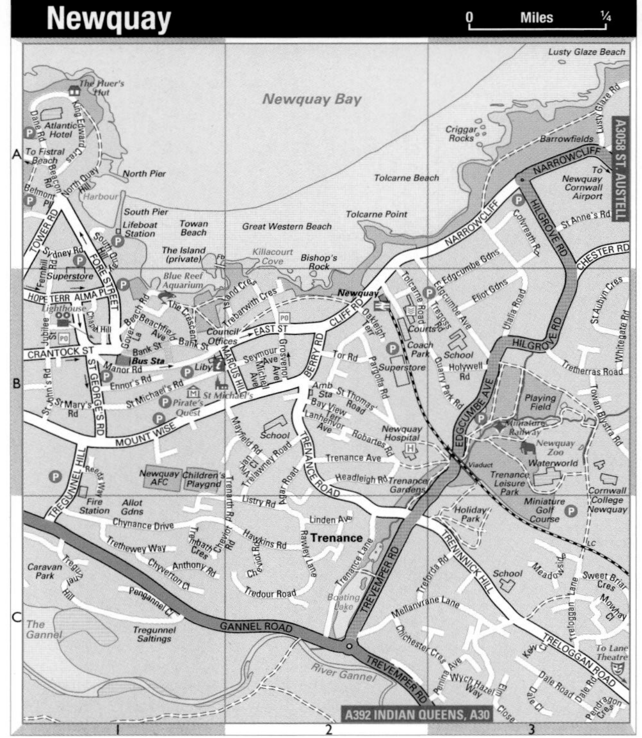
Newquay
0 Miles ¼
Newquay Bay
A3058 ST. AUSTELL
A392 INDIAN QUEENS, A30
Towan Beach
Tolcarne Beach
Newquay
Trenance
Gannel Road
River Gannel
Mount Wise
Narrowcliff

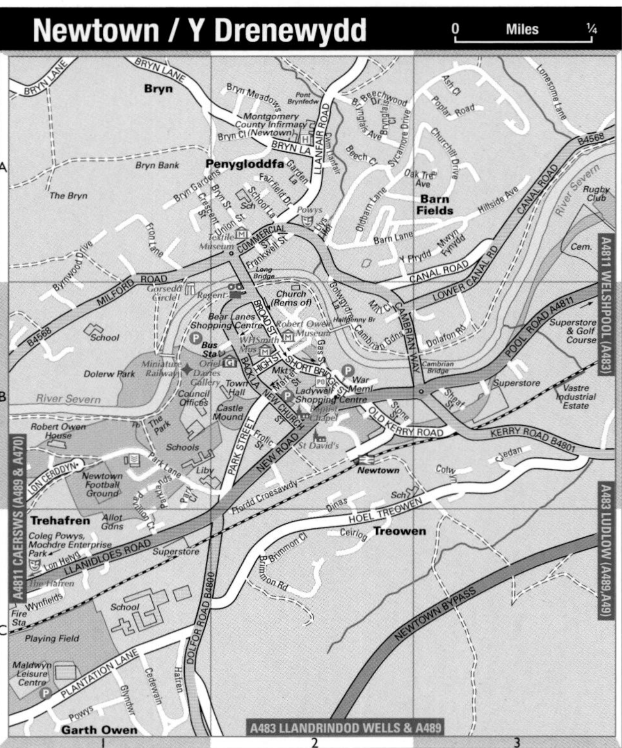
Newtown / Y Drenewydd
0 Miles ¼
Bryn
Penygloddfa
Barn Fields
River Severn
A483 WELSHPOOL (A490)
A483 LUDLOW (A489, A49)
A4811 CAERSWS (A489 & A470)
A483 LLANDRINDOD WELLS & A489
Trehafren
Treowen
Garth Owen
Newtown

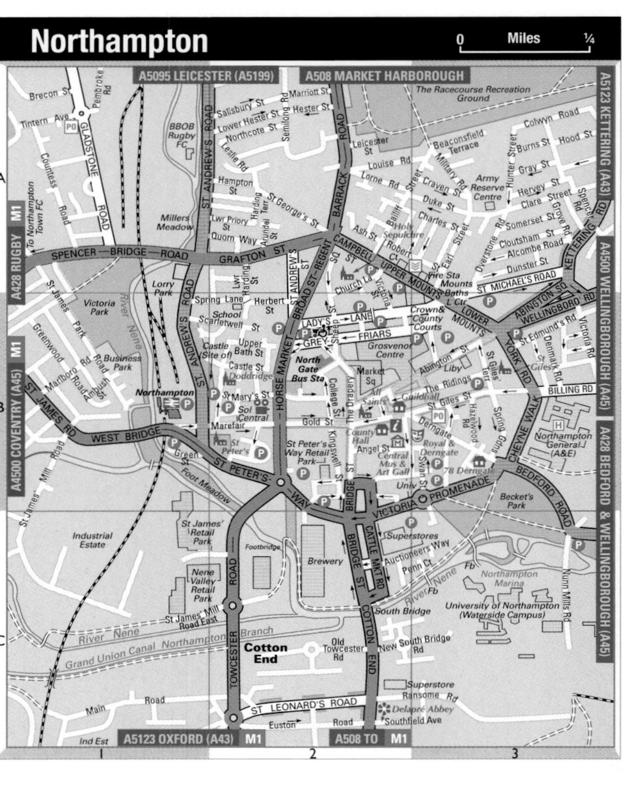
Northampton
0 Miles ¼
A5095 LEICESTER (A5199)
A508 MARKET HARBOROUGH
A5123 KETTERING (A43) (A6)
A4500 WELLINGBOROUGH (A45)
A428 BEDFORD & WELLINGBOROUGH (A45)
A428 RUGBY M1
A4500 COVENTRY (A45) M1
A5123 OXFORD (A43) M1
A508 TO M1
Spencer Bridge Road
Grafton St
Victoria Park
Cotton End
River Nene
St Leonard's Road

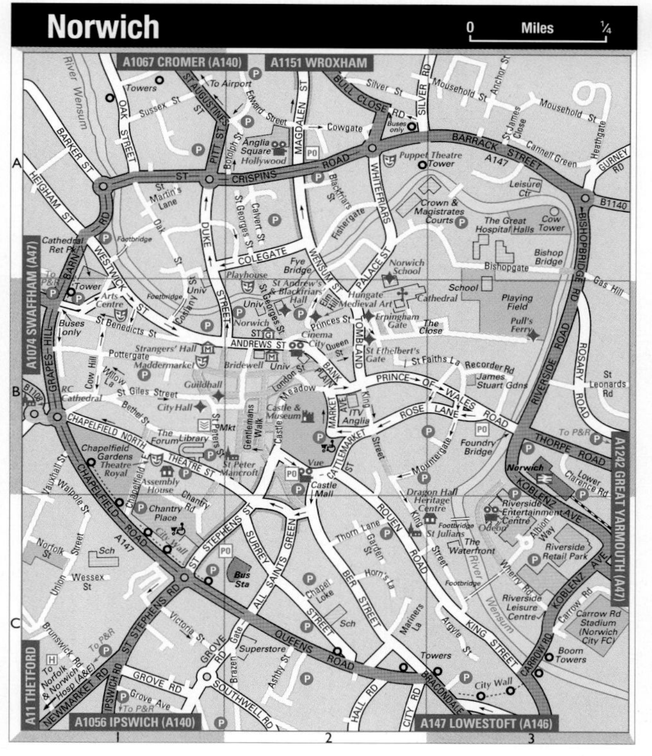
Norwich
0 Miles ¼

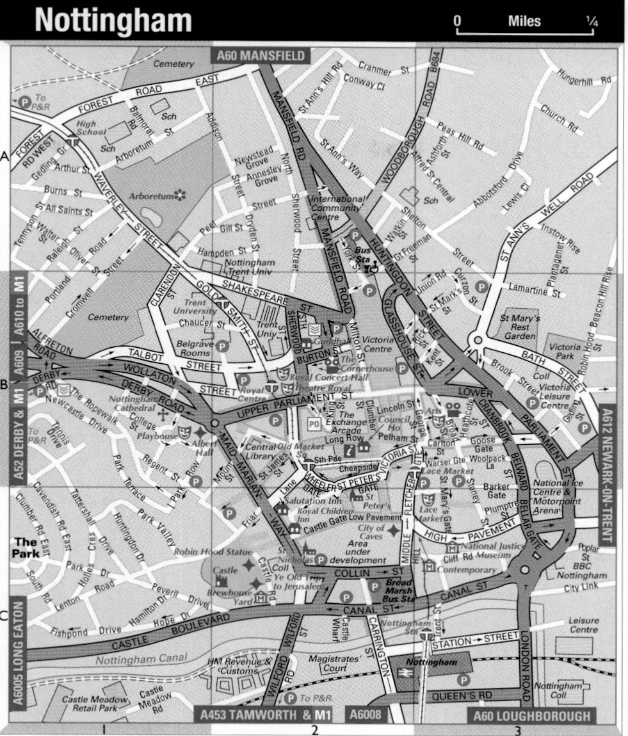
Nottingham
0 Miles ¼

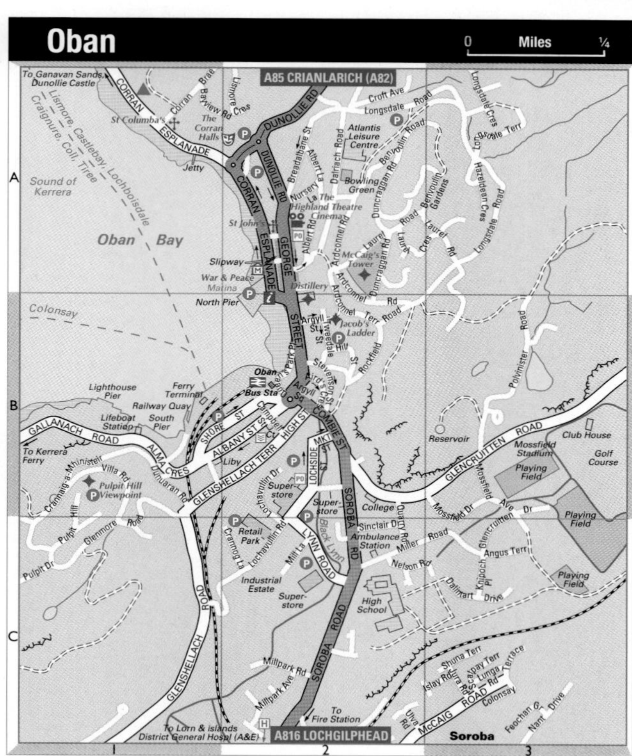
Oban
0 Miles ¼

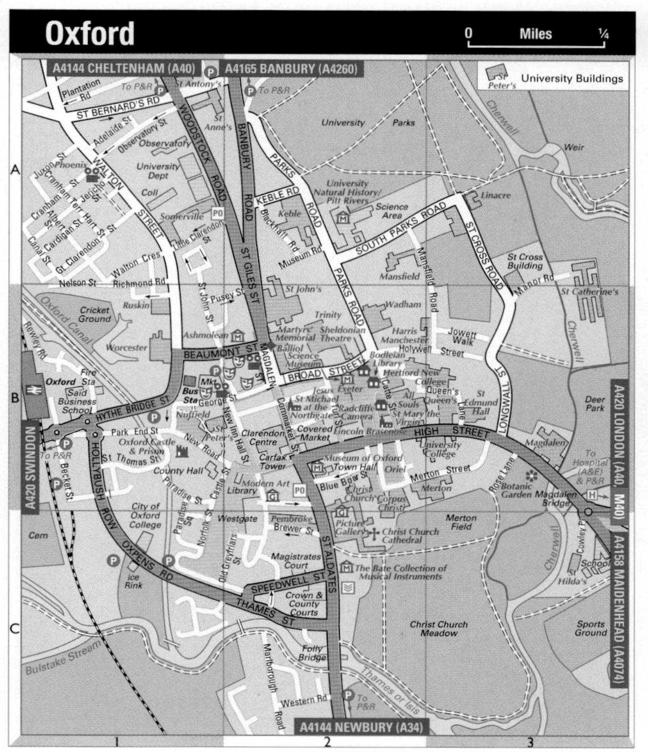
Oxford
0 Miles ¼

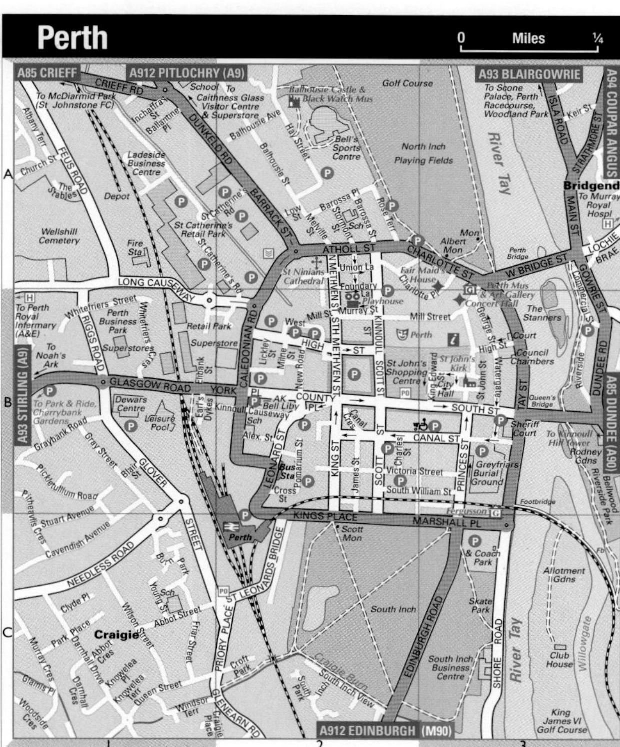
Perth
0 Miles ¼

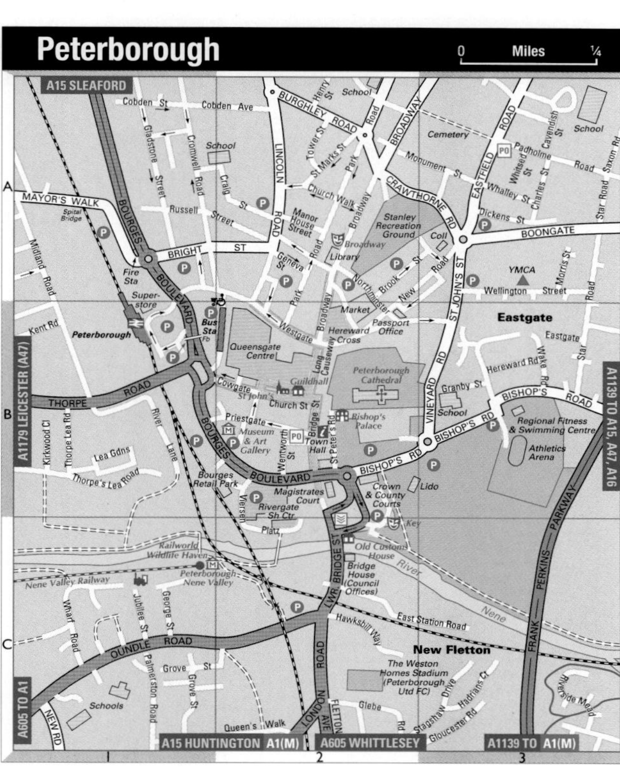
Peterborough
0 Miles ¼

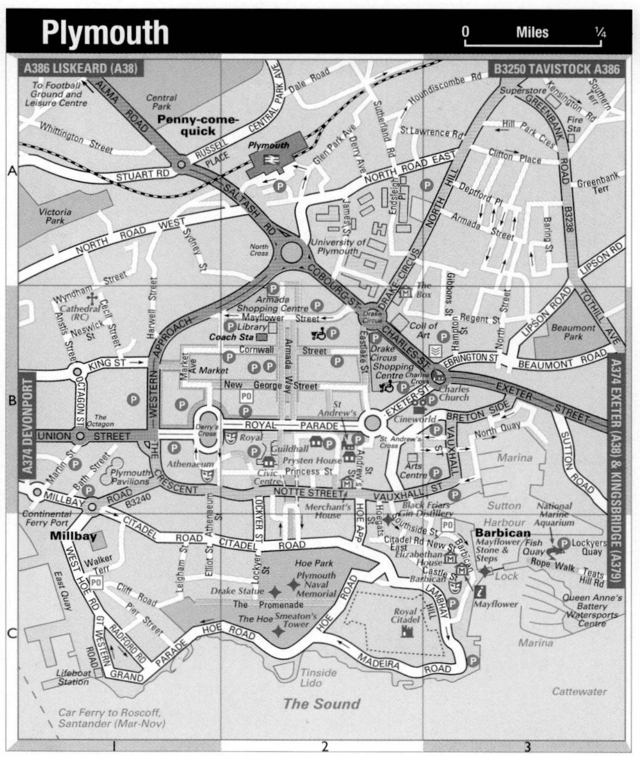
Plymouth
0 Miles ¼

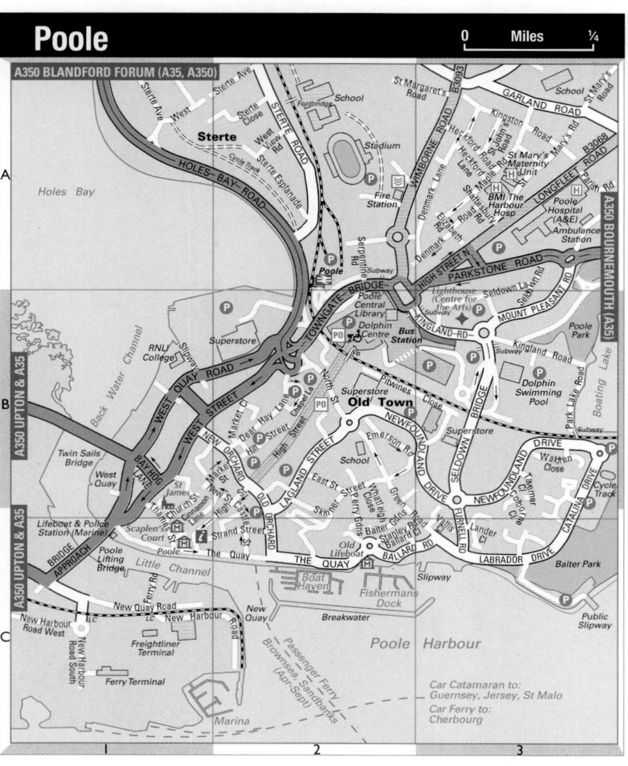
Poole
0 Miles ¼

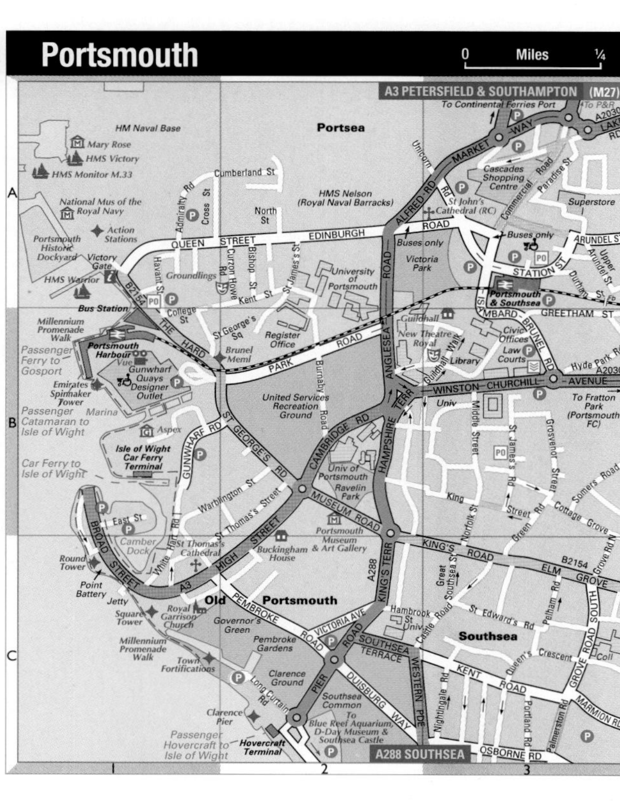
Portsmouth
0 Miles ¼

Preston

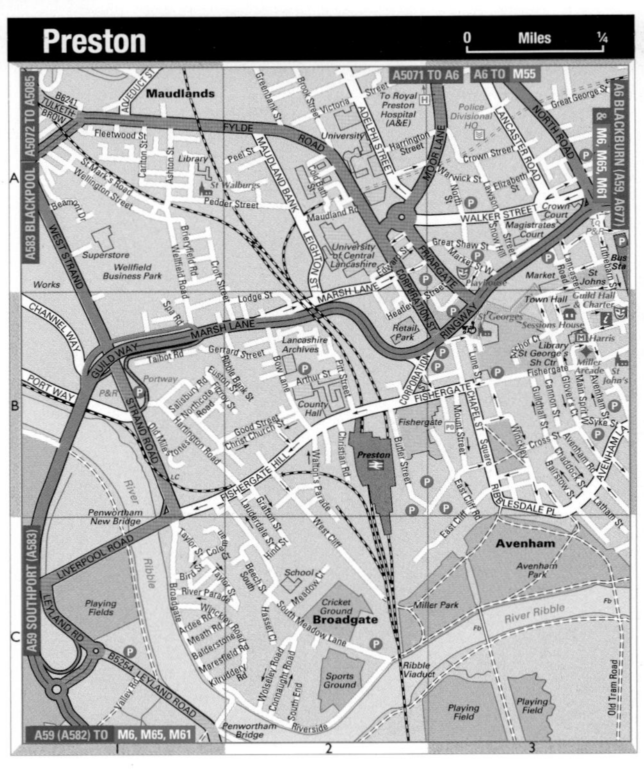

Reading

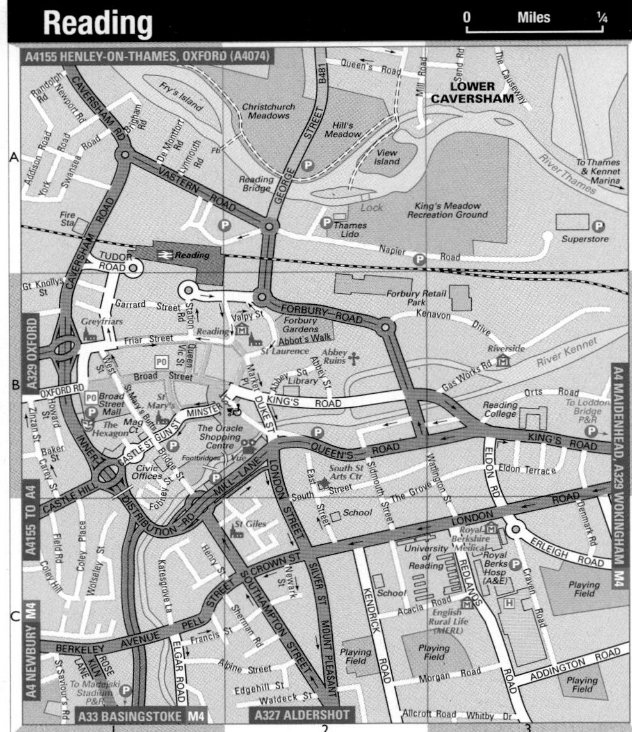

St Andrews

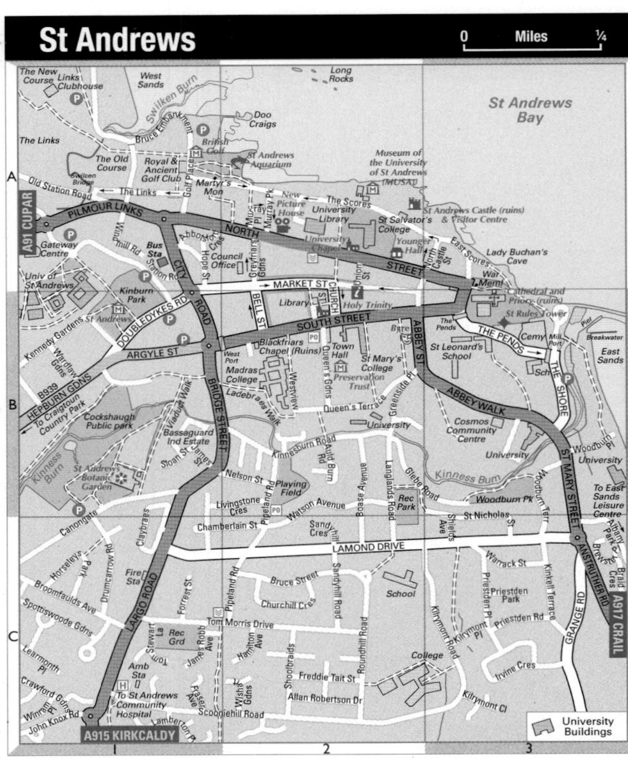

Salisbury

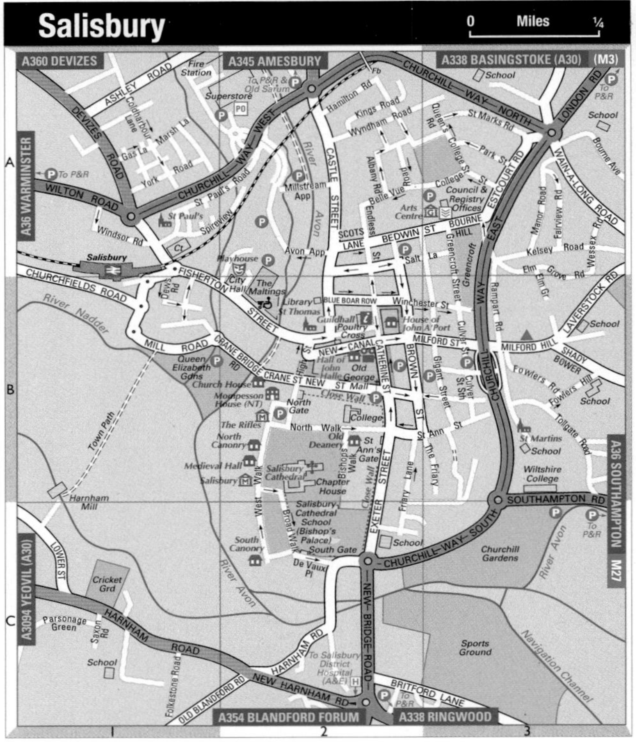

Scarborough

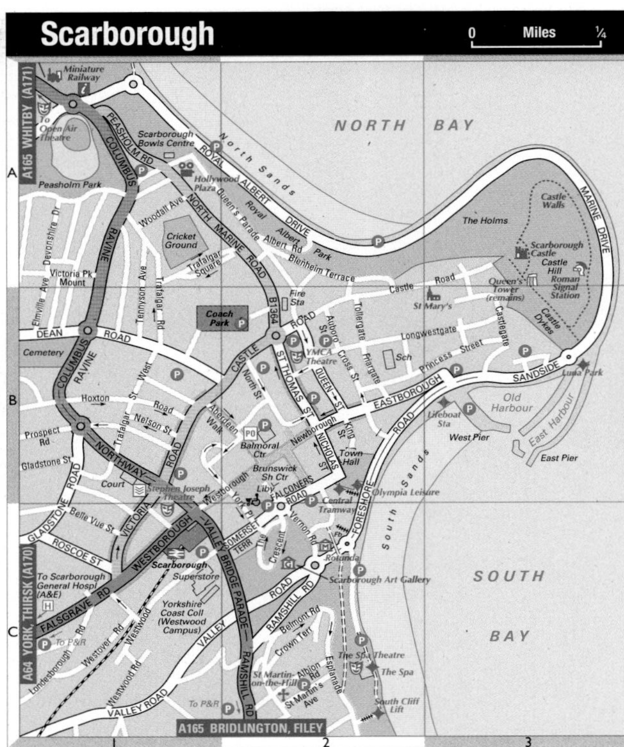

Shrewsbury

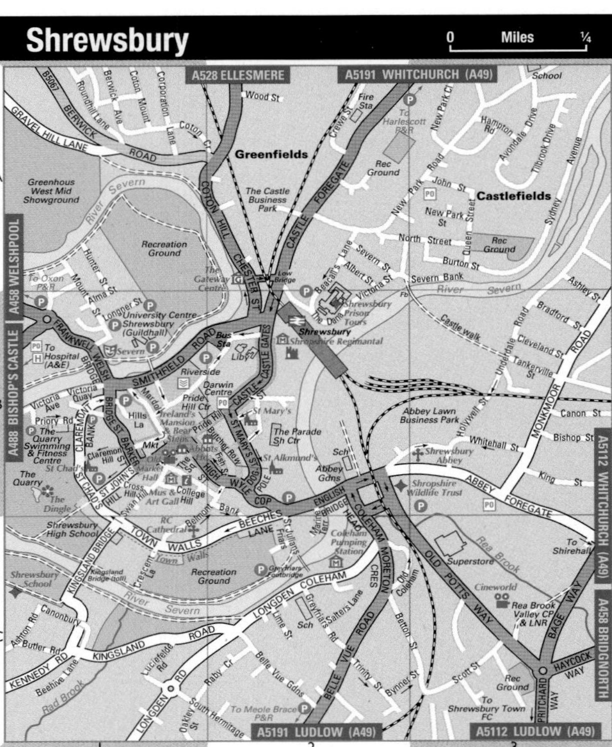

Sheffield

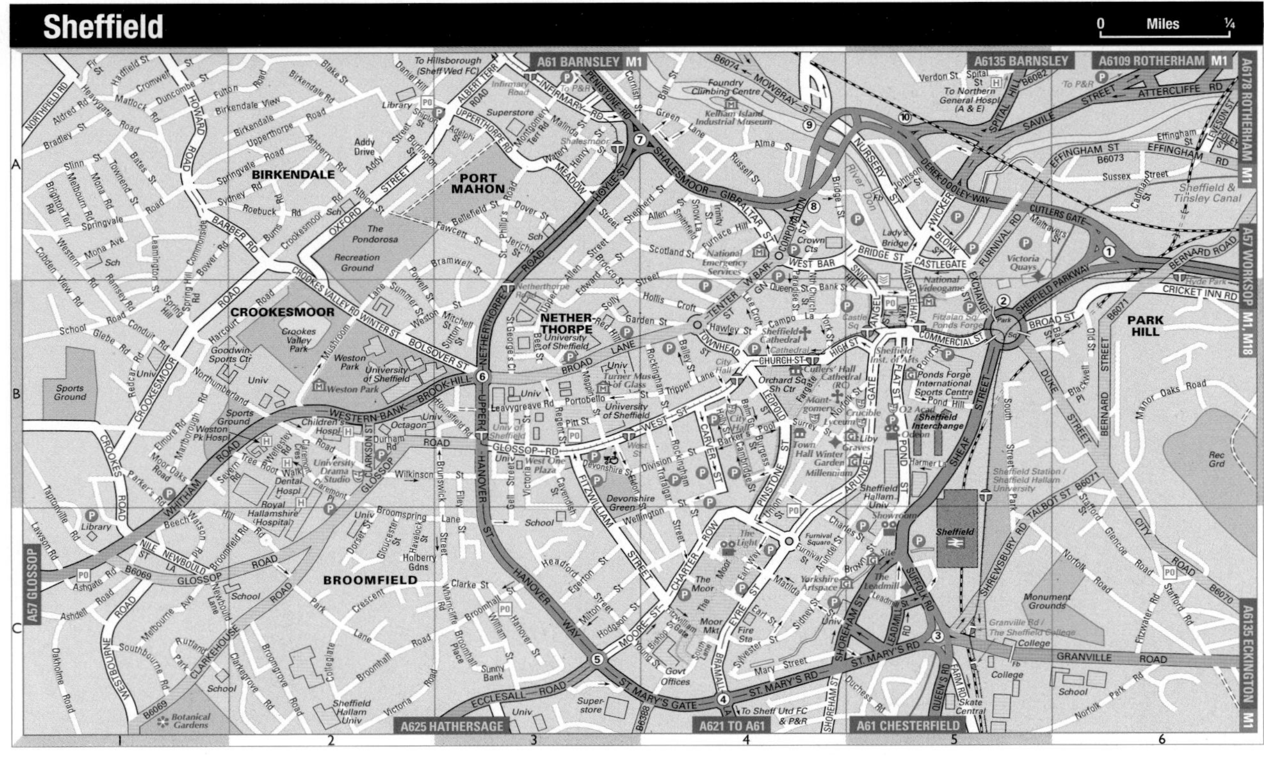

Southampton

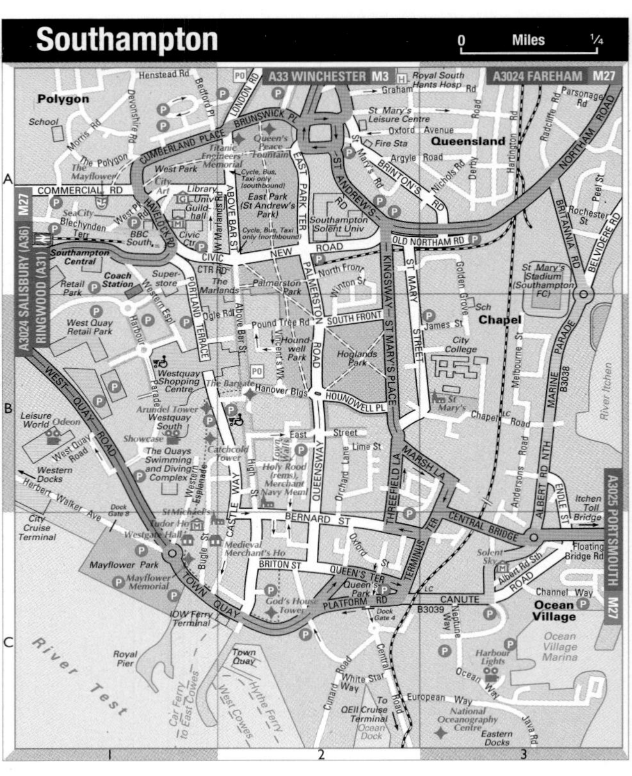

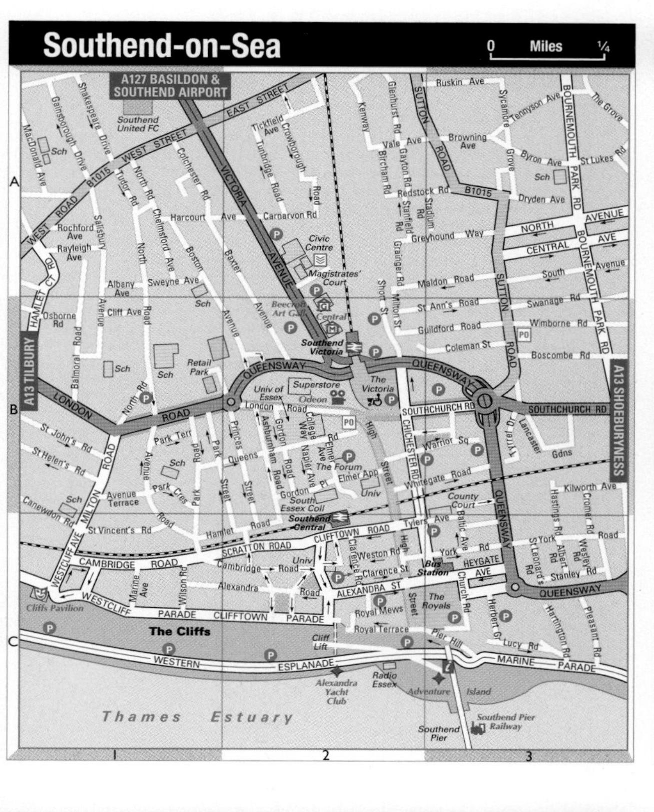
Southend-on-Sea
0 Miles ¼
A127 BASILDON & SOUTHEND AIRPORT
A13 TILBURY
A13 SHOEBURYNESS
Thames Estuary
The Cliffs

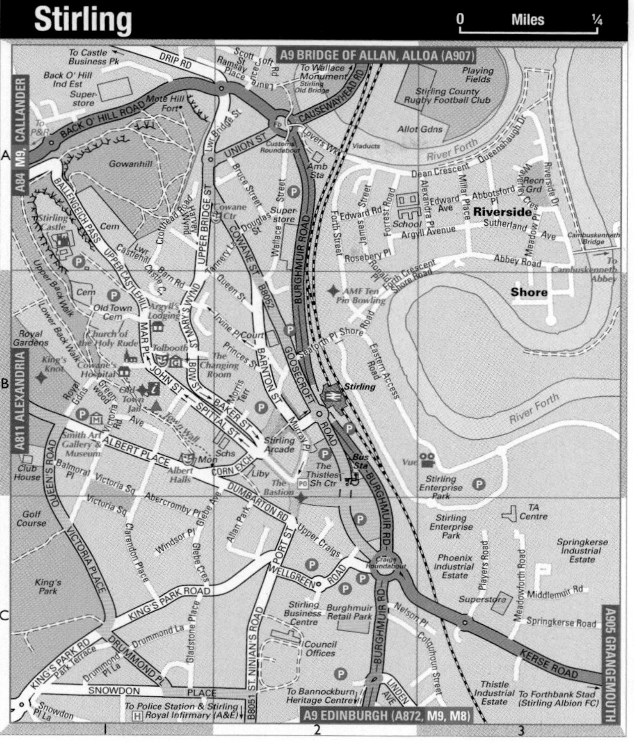
Stirling
0 Miles ¼
A9 BRIDGE OF ALLAN, ALLOA (A907)
A84 M9 CALLANDER
A811 ALEXANDRIA
A9 EDINBURGH (A872, M9, M8)
A905 GRANGEMOUTH
Riverside
Shore

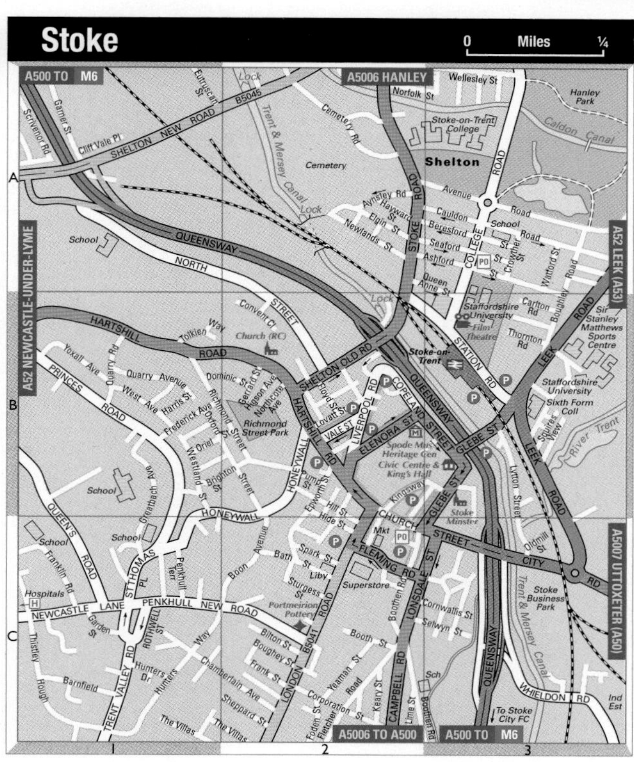
Stoke
0 Miles ¼
A500 TO M6
A5006 HANLEY
A52 NEWCASTLE-UNDER-LYME
A52 LEEK (A53)
A5007 UTTOXETER (A50)
A5006 TO A500
A500 TO M6
Shelton

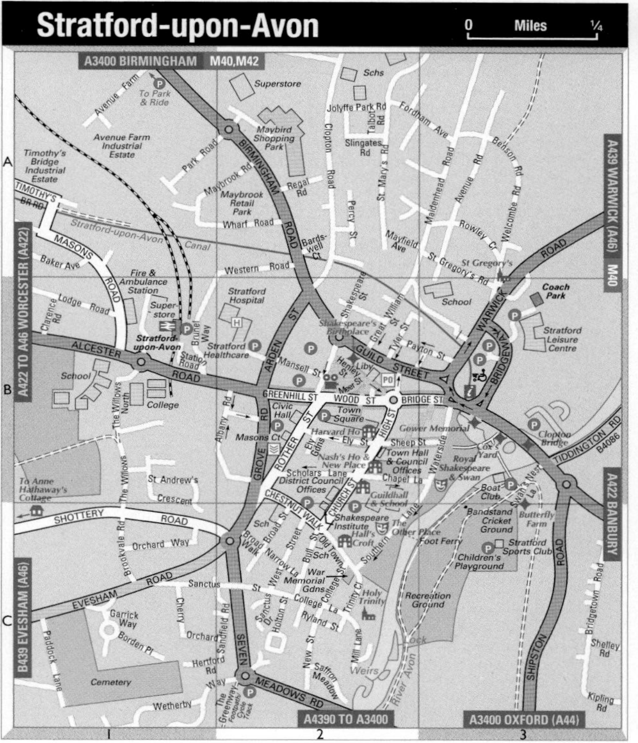
Stratford-upon-Avon
0 Miles ¼
A3400 BIRMINGHAM M40,M42
A439 WARWICK (A46) M40
A422 TO A46 WORCESTER (A422)
A422 BANBURY
B439 EVESHAM (A46)
A4390 TO A3400
A3400 OXFORD (A44)

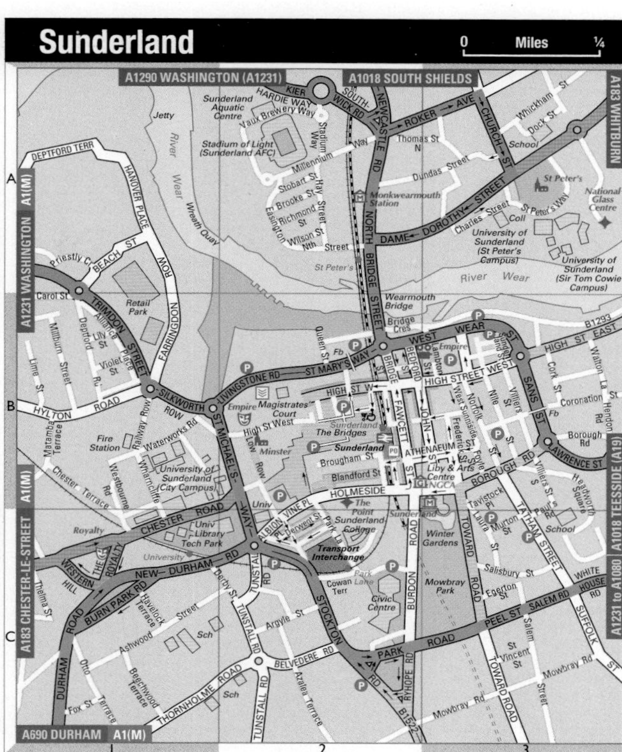
Sunderland
0 Miles ¼
A1290 WASHINGTON (A1231)
A1018 SOUTH SHIELDS
A183 WHITBURN
A1231 WASHINGTON A1(M)
A183 CHESTER-LE-STREET A1(M)
A1018 TEESSIDE (A19)
A1231 to A1080
A690 DURHAM A1(M)

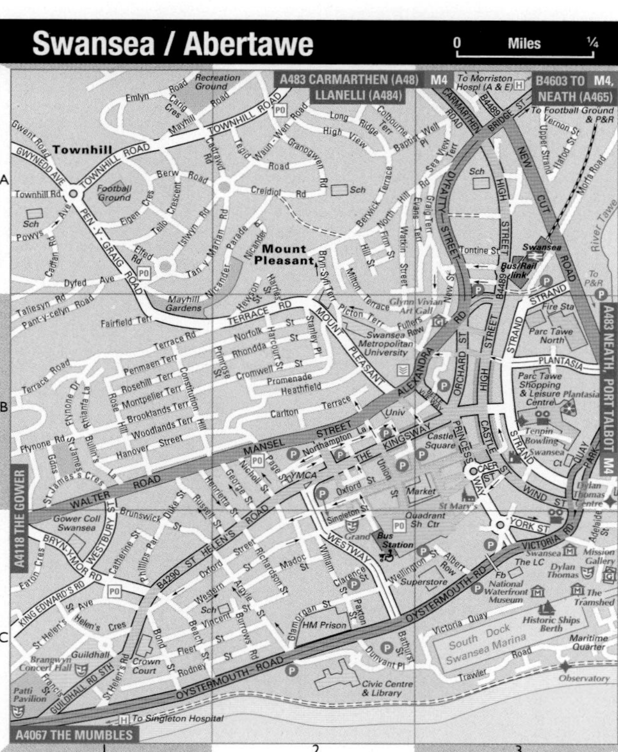
Swansea / Abertawe
0 Miles ¼
A483 CARMARTHEN (A48) M4 LLANELLI (A484)
B4603 TO M4, NEATH (A465)
A483 NEATH, PORT TALBOT M4
A4118 THE GOWER
A4067 THE MUMBLES
Townhill
Mount Pleasant

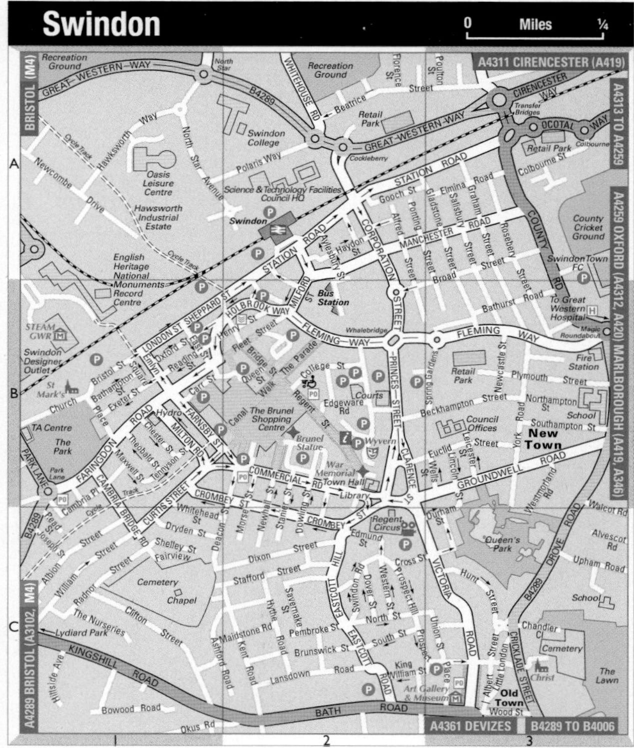
Swindon
0 Miles ¼
BRISTOL (M4)
A4311 CIRENCESTER (A419)
A3102 TO A4259
A4259 OXFORD (A4312, A420) MARLBOROUGH (A419, A346)
A4289 BRISTOL (A3102, M4)
A4361 DEVIZES
B4289 TO B4006
New Town
Old Town

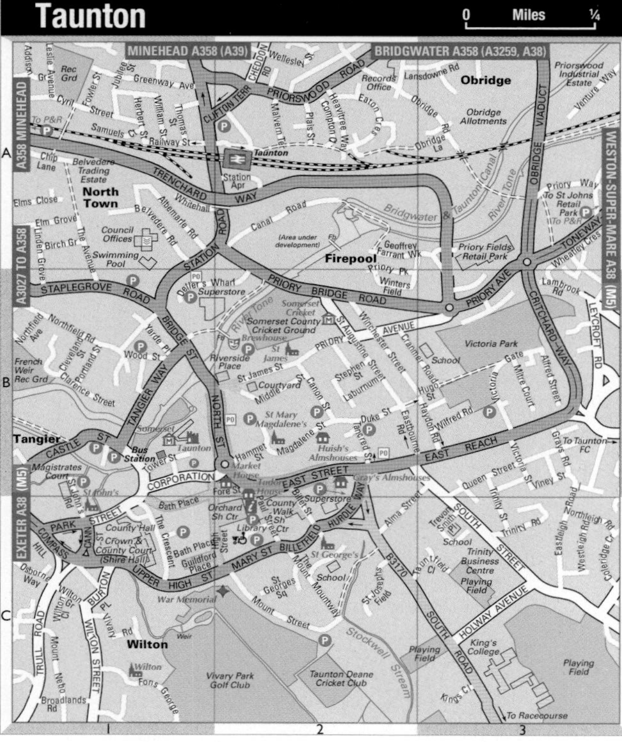
Taunton
0 Miles ¼
MINEHEAD A358 (A39)
BRIDGWATER A358 (A3259, A38)
A358 MINEHEAD
A3027 TO A358
WESTON-SUPER-MARE A38 (M5)
EXETER A38 (M5)
Obridge
North Town
Firepool
Tangier
Wilton

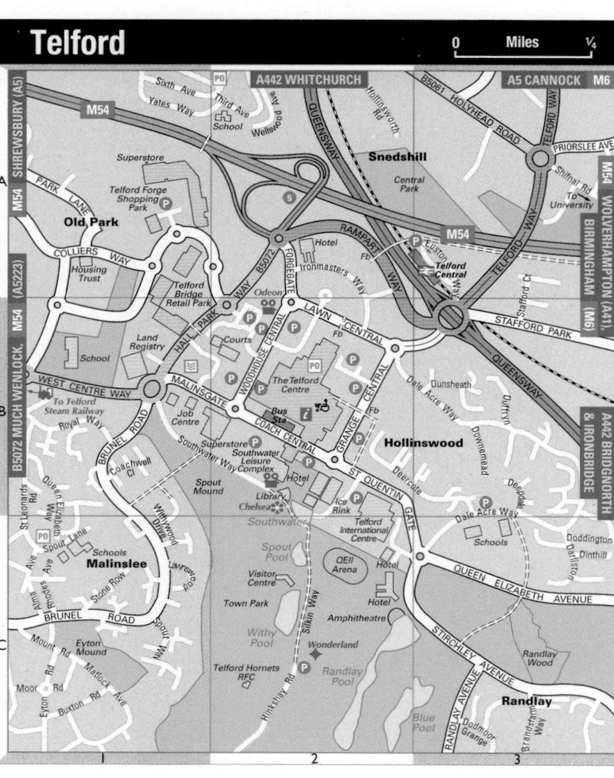
Telford
0 Miles ¼
A442 WHITCHURCH
A5 CANNOCK M6
M54 SHREWSBURY (A5)
M54 (A5223)
B5072 MUCH WENLOCK
M54 WOLVERHAMPTON (A41), BIRMINGHAM (M6)
A442 BRIDGNORTH & IRONBRIDGE
Snedshill
Old Park
Hollinswood
Malinslee
Randlay

Torquay

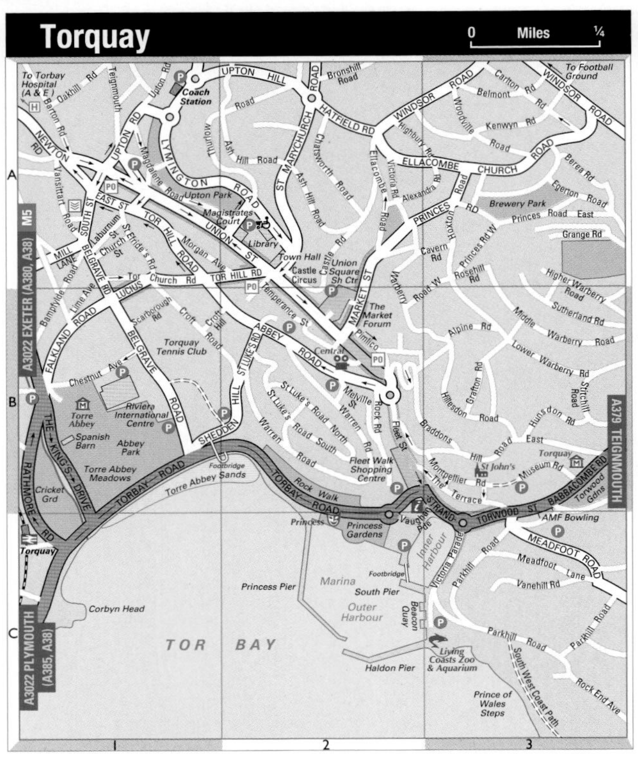

Truro

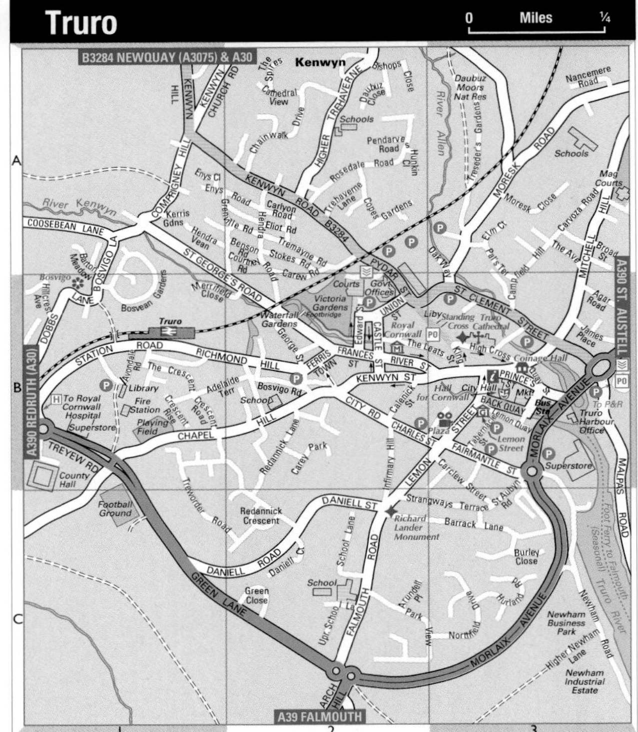

Wick

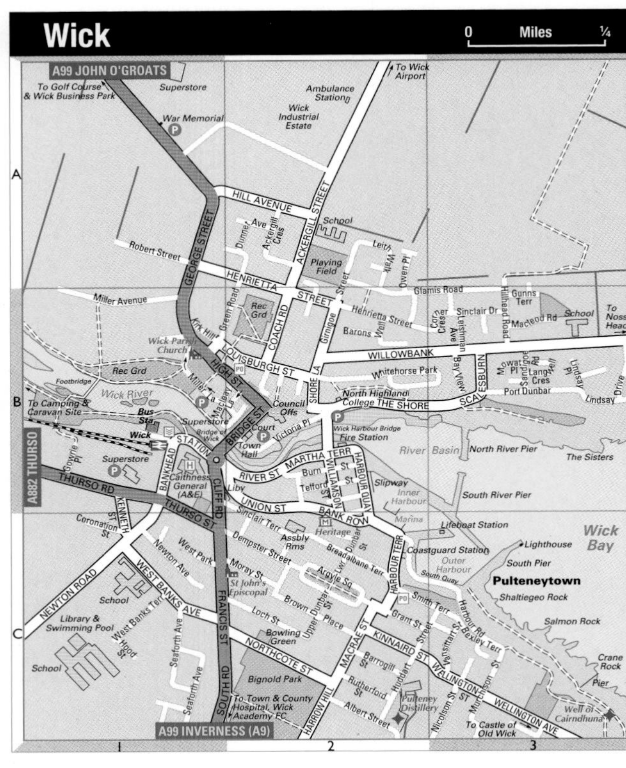

Winchester

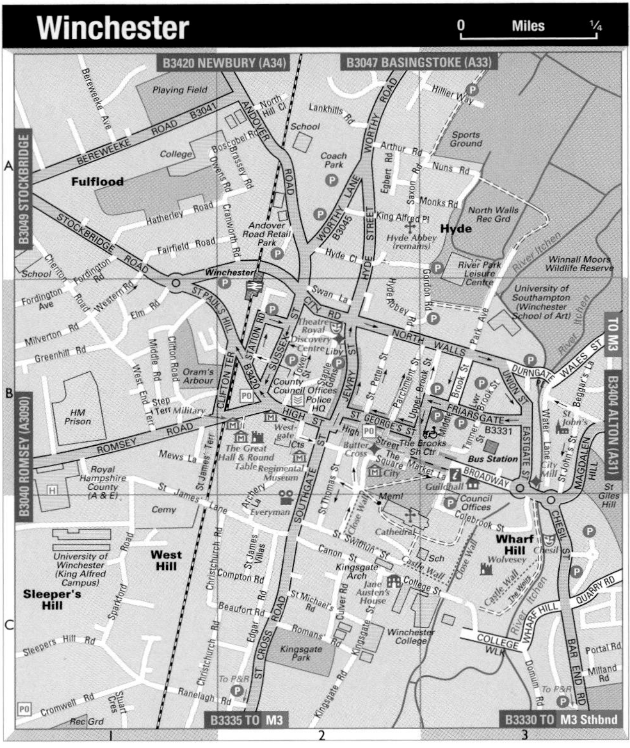

Windsor

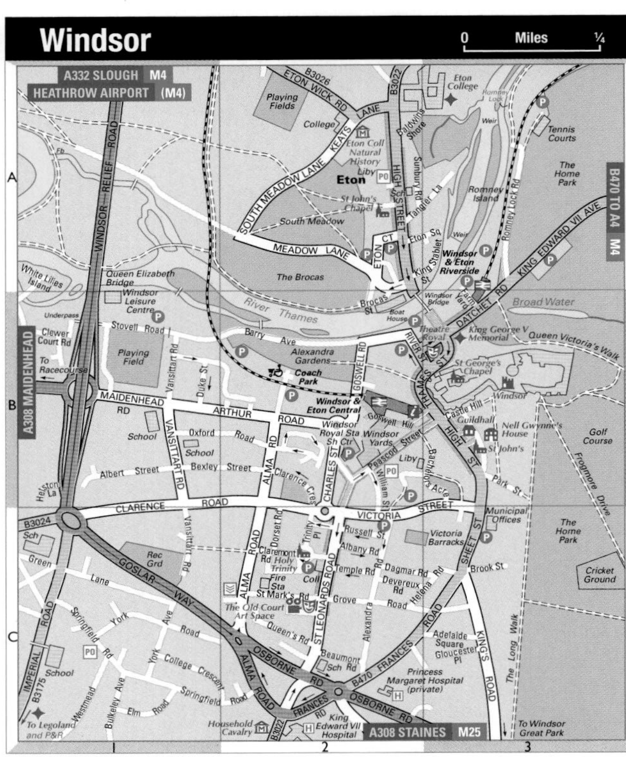

Wolverhampton

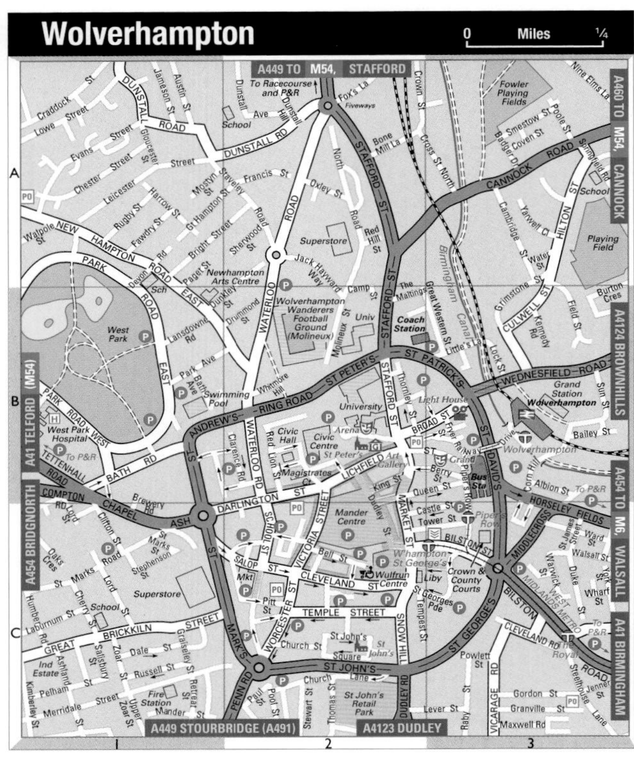

Worcester

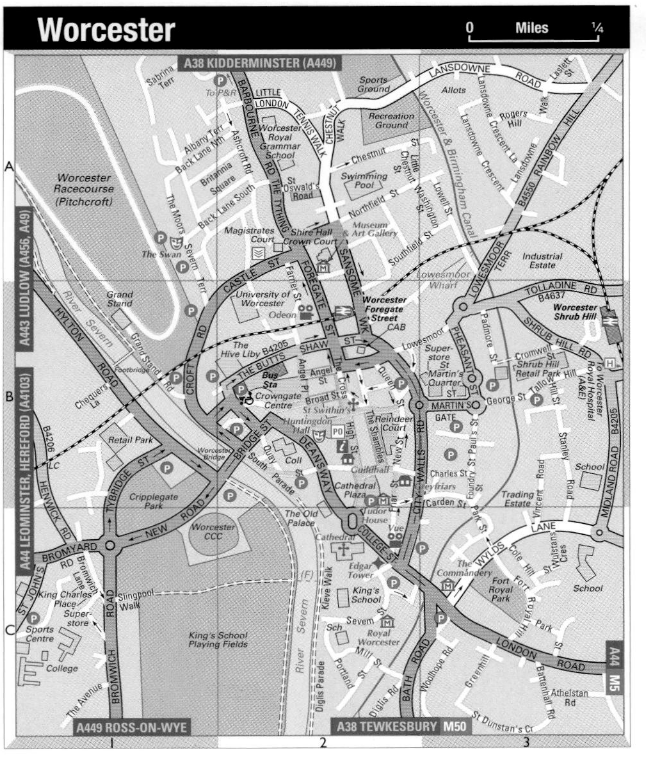

Wrexham / Wrecsam

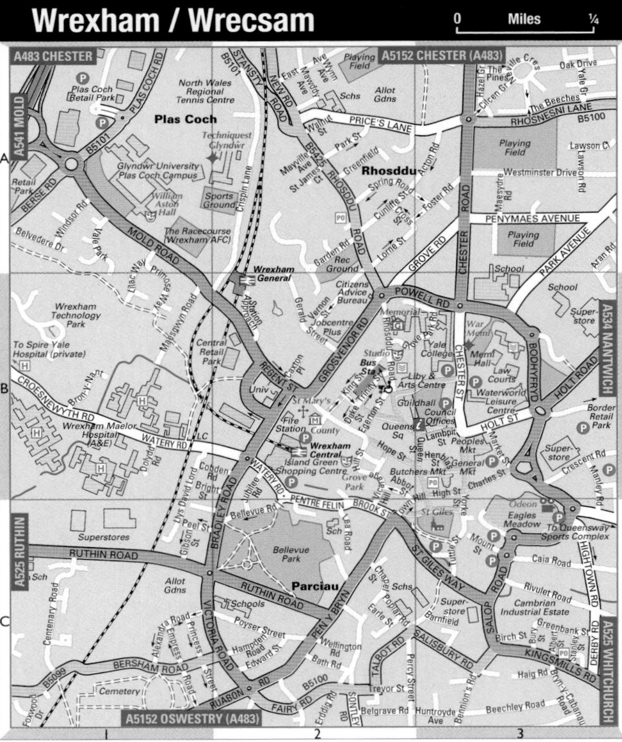

York

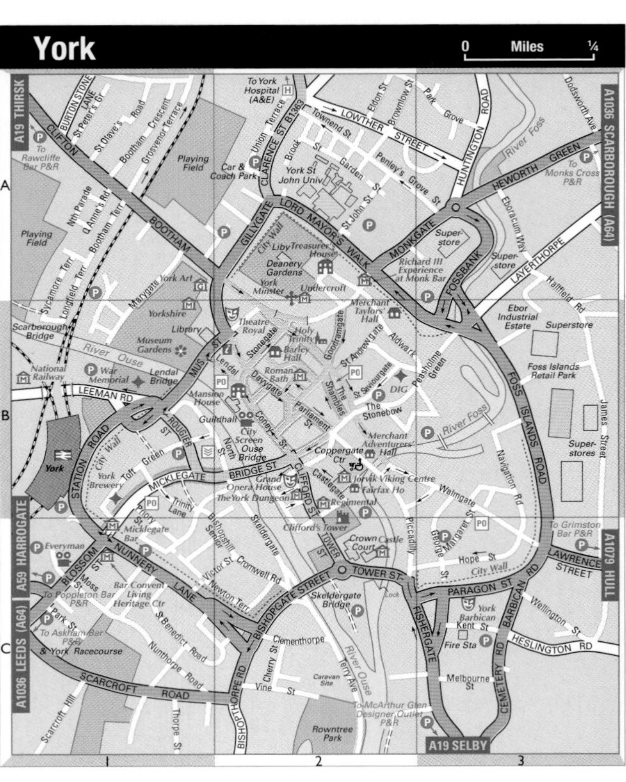

Town plan indexes

Aberdeen 331
Aberdeen B2
Aberdeen Grammar School A1
Academy, The B2
Albert Basin B3
Albert Quay B3
Albury Rd C1
Alford Place B1
Art Gallery A2
Arts Centre A2
Back Wynd A2
Baker St A1
Beach Boulevard A3
Belmont B2
Belmont St B2
Berry St A2
Blackfriars St A2
Blaikie's Quay B3
Bloomfield Rd C1
Bon Accord Centre A2
Bon-Accord St B1/C1
Bridge St B2
Broad St A2
Bus Station B2
Car Ferry Terminal B3
Castlegate A3
Central Library A1
Chapel St B1
Cineworld B2
Clyde St B3
College A2
College St B2
Commerce St A3
Commercial Quay B3
Community Centre A3/C1
Constitution St A3
Cotton St A3
Crown St B2
Denburn Rd A2
Devanha Gardens C2
Devanha Gdns South C2
East North St A3
Esslemont Avenue A1
Ferryhill Rd C2
Ferryhill Terrace C2
Fish Market B3
Fonthill Rd C1
Galleria B1
Gallowgate A2
George St A2
Glenbervie Rd C3
Golden Square B1
Grampian Rd C3
Great Southern Rd C1
Guild St B2
Hardgate B1/C1
His Majesty's Theatre A1
Holburn St C1
Hollybank Place C1
Huntly St B1
Hutcheon St A1
Information Centre B2
John St A2
Justice St A3
King St A2
Langstane Place B1
Lemon Tree, The A2
Library C1
Loch St A2
Maberly St A1
Marischal College A2
Maritime Mus & Provost Ross's House B2
Market B2
Market St B2/B3
Menzies Rd C3
Mercat Cross ✦ A3
Millburn St C2
Miller St A3
Mount St A1
Music Hall B1
North Esp East C3
North Esp West C2
Oscar Rd C3
Palmerston Rd C2
Park St A3
Police Station A2
Polmuir Rd C2
Post Office A1/A2/A3/B1/C3
Provost Skene's Ho A2
Queen Elizabeth Br C2
Queen St A2
Regent Quay B3
Regent Road B3
Robert Gordon's Coll. A2
Rose St B1
Rosemount Place A1
Rosemount Viaduct A1
St Andrew St A2
St Andrew's Cath † A3
St Mary's Cathedral † B1
St Nicholas Centre A2
St Nicholas St A2
School Hill A2
Sinclair Rd C3
Skene Square A1
Skene St B1
South College St C2
South Crown St C2
South Esp East C3
South Esp West C3
South Mount St A1
Sports Centre C3
Spring Garden A2
Springbank Terrace C2
Summer St B1
Superstore A2
Thistle St B1
Tolbooth A3
Town House A2
Trinity Centre B2
Union Row B1
Union Square B2
Union St B1/B2
University A2
Upper Dock B3
Upper Kirkgate A2
Victoria Bridge C3
Victoria Dock B3
Victoria Rd C3
Victoria St B2
Virginia St A3
Vue B2
Waterloo Quay B3
Wellington Place B2
West North St A2
Whinhill Rd C1
Willowbank Rd C1
Windmill Brae B2

Aberystwyth 331
Aberystwyth Holiday Village C2
Aberystwyth Library and Ceredigion Archives A2
Aberystwyth RFC C3
Aberystwyth Sta B2
Aberystwyth Town Football Ground B2
Aberystwyth Univ. B3
Alexandra Rd B2
Ambulance Station C3
Baker St B1
Banadl Rd B2
Bandstand A1
Bar, The C1
Bath St A2
Boat Landing Stage A1
Bvd de Saint-Brieuc C3
Bridge St B1
Bronglais Hospital B3
Bryn-y-Mor Rd A2
Buarth Rd B2
Bus Station B2
Cae Melyn A2
Cae'r-Gog B3
Cambrian St B2
Caradoc Rd B3
Caravan Site C2
Castle Theatre B1
Castle (remains of) B1
Castle St B1
Cemetery B3
Ceredigion Mus A1
Chalybeate St B1
Cliff Terrace A2
Club House A2
Commodore A1
County Court A2
Crown Buildings B2
Dan-y-Coed A3
Dinas Terrace C1
Eastgate B1
Edge-hill Rd B2
Elm Tree Avenue B2
Elysian Grove A2
Felin-y-Mor Rd C1
Fifth Avenue C2
Fire Station C1
Glanrafon Terrace B1
Glan Rheidol C3
Glyndwr Rd B2
Golf Course A3
Government & Council Offices C3
Gray's Inn Rd B1
Great Darkgate St B1
Greenfield St B2
Heol-y-Bryn A2
High St B1
Infirmary Rd A2
Iorwerth Avenue B3
King St B1
Lauraplace B1
Lifeboat Station C1
Llanbadarn Rd B3
Loveden Rd A2
Magistrates Court A1
Marina C1
Marine Terrace A1
Market Hall B1
Mill St B1
Moor Lane B2
National Lbry of Wales B3
New Promenade B1
New St B1
North Beach A1
North Parade B2
North Rd A2
Northgate St B2
Parc Natur Penglais A3
Parc-y-Llyn Retail Pk C3
Park Avenue B2
Pavillion B1
Pen-y-Craig A2
Pen-yr-angor C1
Pendinas C1
Penglais Rd B3
Penrheidol C2
Pier St B1
Plas Avenue B3
Plas Helyg C2
Plascrug Avenue B2/C3
Plascrug Leisure Ctr C3
Police Station C2
Poplar Row B2
Portland Rd B2
Portland St A2
Post Office B1
Powell St B1
Prospect St B1
Quay Rd B1
Queen St B1
Queen's Avenue A2
Queen's Rd A2
Rheidol Retail Park B2
Riverside Terrace B1
St Davids Rd B3
St Michael's B1
School of Art B2
Seaview Place B1
Shopmobility B2
South Beach B1
South Rd B1
Sports Ground B2
Spring Gardens C1
Stanley Terrace B2
Superstore B1/B2
Superstore B2/C3
Swimming Pool & Leisure Centre C3
Tanybwlch Beach C1
Tennis Courts B3
Terrace Rd B1
Trefechan Bridge B1
Trefechan Rd C2
Trefor Rd A2
Trinity Rd B2
University of Wales (Aberystwyth) B1
Vale of Rheidol Railway C3
Vaynor St B2
Victoria Terrace A1
Viewpoint ✦ A2
Viewpoint ✦ A3
War Memorial B1
Wharf Quay C1
Y Lanfa C1
Ystwyth Retail Park B2

Ashford 331
Adams Drive C3
Albert Rd A1
Alfred Rd C3
Apsley St A1
Ashford Borough Museum A1
Ashford College B2
Ashford International Station B2
Ashford Picturehouse A1
Bank St A1
Barrowhill Gardens A1
Beaver Industrial Est C1
Beaver Rd C1
Beazley Court C3
Birling Rd B3
Blue Line Lane A1
Bond Rd C1
Bowens Field B1
Bulleid Place C2
Business Park A2
Cade Rd C1
Chart Rd A1
Chichester Close B1
Christchurch Rd B1
Chunnel Industrial Est B1
Church Rd A1
Civic Centre A2
County Square Shopping Centre A1
Croft Rd A3
Cudworth Rd C3
Curtis Rd C3
Dering Rd A3
Dover Place B2
Drum Lane A1
East Hill A2
East St A1
Eastmead Avenue B2
Edinburgh Rd A1
Elwick Rd A1
Essella Park B3
Essella Rd B3
Fire Station A3
Forge Lane A1
Francis Rd C1
Gateway Plus and Liby A1
George St B1
Godfrey Walk B1
Gordon Close A3
Government Offices A2
Hardinge Rd A2
Henwood A3
Henwood Bsns Centre A3
Henwood Ind Est A3
High St A2
Hythe Rd A3
Javelin Way A3
Jemmett Rd B1
Kennard Way A3
Kent Avenue A1
Linden Rd B3
Lower Denmark Rd C1
Mabledon Avenue B3
Mace Industrial Est A2
Mace Lane A2
Maunsell Place C3
McArthurGlen Designer Outlet C2
Memorial Gardens A2
Mill Court A2
Miller Close A2
Mortimer Close C1
New St A1
Newtown Green C3
Newtown Rd B2/C3
Norman Rd C1
North St A2
Norwood Gardens A1
Norwood St A1
Old Railway Works Industrial Estate C3
Orion Way C3
Pk Mall Shopping Ctr A1
Park Place A1
Park St A1/A2
Pemberton Rd A3
Police Station A1
Post Office A1
Providence St C2
Queen St A1
Queens Rd A2
Regents Place A1
Riversdale Rd C2
Romney Marsh Rd B2
St John's Lane A2
St Mary's Church & Arts Venue A1
Somerset Rd A2
South Stour Avenue B2
Star Rd A3
Station Rd B2
Stirling Rd C2
Stour Centre, The B2
Superstore B1
Sussex Avenue A1
Tannery Lane A2
Torrington Rd C2
Trumper Bridge B1
Tufton Rd A3
Tufton St A1
Vicarage Lane A2
Victoria Crescent B1
Victoria Park B1
Victoria Rd B1
Wallis Rd A3
Wellesley Rd A2
West St A1
Whitfield Rd C1
William Rd C1
World War I Tank ✦ A1
Wyvern Way A3

Ayr 331
Ailsa Place B1
Alexandra Terrace A3
Allison St B2
Alloway Park C1
Alloway Place C1
Alloway St C2
Arran Mall C2
Arran Terrace B1
Arthur St B2
Ashgrove St C2
Auld Brig B2
Auld Kirk B2
Ayr C2
Ayr Academy B1
Ayr Central Shopping Centre C2
Ayr Harbour A1
Ayr Ice Rink A2
Ayrshire College C3
Back Hawkhill Avenue A3
Back Main St B2
Back Peebles St A2
Barns Crescent C1
Barns Park C1
Barns St C1
Barns Street Lane C1
Bath Place B1
Bellevue Crescent C1
Bellevue Lane C1
Beresford Lane C2
Beresford Terrace C2
Boswell Park B2
Britannia Place A3
Bruce Crescent B1
Burns Statue ✦ C2
Bus Station B1
Carrick St C2
Cassillis St B1
Cathcart St B1
Charlotte St B1
Citadel Leisure Ctr B1
Citadel Place B1
Compass Pier A1
Content Avenue C3
Content St B2
Craigie Avenue B3
Craigie Rd B3
Craigie Way B3
Cromwell Rd B1
Crown St A2
Dalblair Rd C2
Dam Park Sports Stadium C3
Damside A2
Dongola Rd C3
Eglinton Place B1
Eglinton Terrace B1
Elba St B2
Elmbank St A2
Esplanade B1
Euchar Rock A1
Farifield Rd C1
Fort St B1
Fothringham Rd C3
Fullarton St C1
Gaiety C2
Garden St B2
George St B2
George's Avenue A3
Glebe Crescent A2
Glebe Rd A2
Gorden Terrace B3
Green St A2
Green Street Lane A2
Hawkhill Avenue A3
Hawkhill Avenue Lane B3
High St B2
Holmston Rd C3
James St B3
John St B2
King St B2
Kings Court B2
Kyle Centre C2
Kyle St C2
Library B2
Limekiln Rd A2
Limonds Wynd B2
Loudoun Hall B2
Lymburn Place B3
Macadam Place B2
Main St B2
Mcadam's Monument C1
Mccall's Avenue A3
Mews Lane B1
Mill Brae C3
Mill St C2
Mill Wynd C2
Miller Rd C1
Montgomerie Terrace B1
New Bridge B2
New Bridge St B2
New Rd B2
Newmarket St B2
Newton-on-Ayr Sta A2
North Harbour St B1
North Pier A1
Odeon C2
Park Circus C1
Park Circus Lane C1
Park Terrace C1
Pavilion Rd C1
Peebles St A2
Philip Square B2
Police Station B2
Prestwick Rd B1
Princes Court A2
Queen St B3
Queen's Terrace B1
Racecourse Rd C1
River St B2
Riverside Place B2
Russell Drive A2
St Andrews Church C2
St George's Rd A3
Sandgate B1
Savoy Park C1
Smith St C2
Somerset Park (Ayr United FC) A3
Somerset Rd A3
South Beach Rd B1
South Harbour St B1
South Pier A1
Station Rd C2
Strathayr Place B2
Superstore A2/B2
Taylor St A2
Town Hall B2
Tryfield Place A3
Turner's Bridge B2
Union Avenue A3
Victoria Bridge C3
Victoria St B3
Viewfield Rd A3
Virginia Gardens A2
Waggon Rd A2
Walker Rd A3
Wallace Tower ✦ B2
Weaver St A2
Weir Rd A2
Wellington Lane C1
Wellington Square C1
West Sanouhar Rd A3
Whitletts Rd B3
Wilson St A3
York St A1
York Street Lane B1

Bangor 331
Abbey Rd C2
Albert St B1
Ambrose St A3
Ambulance Station A3
Arfon Sports Hall C1
Ashley Rd B3
Bangor Mountain B3
Bangor Station C1
Bangor University B2
Beach Rd A3
Belmont St C1
Bishop's Mill Rd C3
Brick St B3
Buckley Rd B2
Bus Station B3
Caellepa B2
Caernarfon Rd C1
Cathedral † B2
Cemetery C1
Clarence St C1
Clock Tower ✦ B3
College B2
College Lane B2
College Rd B2
Convent Lane C1
Council Offices B2
Craig y Don Rd B2
Crescent, The B2
Dean St B3
Deiniol Rd B2
Deiniol Shopping Ctr B2
Deiniol St B2
Edge Hill A3
Euston Rd C1
Fairview Rd A3
Farrar Rd C2
Ffordd Cynfal C1
Ffordd Islwyn A3
Ffordd y Castell C3
Ffriddoedd Rd B1
Field St B1
Fountain St A3
Friars Avenue B3
Friars Rd B3
Friary (Site of) ✦ B3
Gardd Deman C1
Garth Hill A3
Garth Point A3
Garth Rd A3
Glanrafon B2
Glanrafon Hill B2
Glynne Rd B3
Golf Course B3
Golf Course C2
Gorad Rd B1
Gorsedd Circle A2
Gwern Las C3
Heol Dewi C1
High St B3/C2
Hill St B1
Holyhead Rd B1
Hwfa Rd B1
James St B3
Library B2
Llys Emrys A3
Lon Ogwen C1
Lon-Pobty C2
Lon-y-Felin C3
Lon-y-Glyder C1
Love Lane B2
Lower Penrallt Rd B2
Lower St B2
Maes Glas Sports Ctr B1
Maes-y-Dref B3
Maeshyfryd A3
Meirion Lane A2
Meirion Rd A2
Menai Avenue B1
Menai College C1
Menai Shopping Ctr B3
Min-y-Ddol C3
Minafon B2
Mount St B3
Orme Rd A3
Parc Victoria B1
Penchwintan Rd C1
Penlon Grove B3
Penrhyn Avenue C3
Pier ✦ A3
Police Station B2
Post Office B2/B3/C3
Prince's Rd B2
Queen's Avenue C3
Sackville Rd B2
St Paul's St B2
Seion Rd A3
Seiriol Rd A3
Siliwen Rd A2
Snowdon View B1
Station Rd C1
STORIEL B2
Strand St B3
Superstore B3/C2
Swimming Pool and Leisure Centre A3
Tan-y-Coed C3
Tegid Rd B3
Temple Rd B2
Theatr Gwynedd B2
Totton Rd A3
Town Hall B2
Treflan B2
Trem Elidir C1
University B2
Upper Garth Rd A3
Victoria Avenue B1
Victoria Drive B1
Victoria St B1
Vron St B2
Well St B3
West End C1
William St B3
York Place B3

Barrow-in-Furness 331
Abbey Rd A3/B2
Adelaide St A2
Ainslie St A3
Albert St C3
Allison St B3
Anson St A2
AR Centre B2
Argyle St B3
Arthur St B3
Ashburner Way A1
Barrow Park A3
Barrow Raiders RLFC B1
Barrow-in-Furness Station A2
Bath St A1/B2
Bedford Rd A3
Bessamer Way A1
Blake St A1/A2
Bridge Rd C1
Buccleuch Dock C3
Buccleuch Dock Rd C2/C3
Buccleuch St B2/B3
Byron St A2
Calcutta St A1
Cameron St C1
Carlton Avenue A3
Cavendish Dock Rd C3
Cavendish St B2/B3
Channelside Haven C1
Channelside Walk B1
Chatsworth St A2
Cheltenham St A3
Church St C3
Clifford St B2
Clive St B1
Collingwood St B2
Cook St A2
Cornerhouse Retail Pk B2
Cornwallis St B2
Courts A2
Crellin St B3
Cross St C3
Custom House ✦ B2
Dalkeith St B2
Dalton Rd B2/C2
Derby St B3
Devonshire Dock C2
Devonshire Dock Hall B1
Dock Museum, The B1
Drake St A2
Dryden St A2
Duke St A1/B2/C3
Duncan St B2
Dundee St C2
Dundonald St B2
Earle St C1
Emlyn St B2
Exmouth St A2
Farm St C2
Fell St B3
Fenton St B3
Ferry Rd C1
Forum, The B2
Furness College B1
Glasgow St B3
Goldsmith St A2
Greengate St B3
Hardwick St A2
Harrison St B2
Hartington St A2
Hawke St B2
Hibbert Rd A2
High Level Bridge C2
High St B2
Hindpool Rd B2
Hindpool Retail Park B2
Holker St A2
Hollywood Retail & Leisure Park B1
Hood St A2
Howard St B2
Howe St A2
Ironworks Rd A1/B1
James St B3
Jubilee Bridge C1
Keith St B2
Keyes St A2
Lancaster St A3
Lawson St B2
Library B2
Lincoln St A3
Longreins Rd A3
Lonsdale St C3
Lord St B3
Lorne Rd B3
Lyon St A2
Manchester St B2
Market B2
Market St B2
Marsh St B3
Michaelson Rd C2
Milton St A2
Monk St B2
Mount Pleasant B3
Nan Tait Centre B2
Napier St B2
Nelson St B2
North Rd B1
Open Market B2
Parade St B2
Paradise St B3
Park Avenue A3
Park Drive A3
Parker St A2
Parry St A2
Peter Green Way A1
Phoenix Rd A1
Police Station B2
Portland Walk Shopping Centre B2
Raleigh St A2
Ramsden St B3
Rawlinson St B3
Robert St B3
Rodney St B2
Rutland St A2
St Patricks Rd C1
St Vincent St B2
Salthouse Rd C3
School St B2
Scott St B2
Settle St A3
Shore St C3
Sidney St B2
Silverdale St B3
Slater St B2
Smeaton St B3
Stafford St A3
Stanley Rd C1
Stark St C3
Steel St B1
Storey Square B3
Strand C3
Superstore A1/B1/C3
Sutherland St B3
Thwaite St B3
Town Hall B2
Town Quay C3
Vernon St B2
Vue Cinema B2
Walney Rd A1
West Gate Rd A2
West View Rd A3
Westmorland St A3
Whitehead St A3
Wordsworth St A2

Bath 331
Alexandra Park C2
Alexandra Rd C2
Ambulance Station A3
Approach Golf Courses (Public) A1
Archway St C3
Assembly Rooms & Fashion Museum A2
Avon St B2
Barton St B2
Bath Abbey † B2
Bath Aqua Glass A2
Bath at Work Mus A2
Bath College B2
Bath Rugby (The Rec) B3
Bath Spa Station C3
Bathwick St A3
Beckford Road A3
Beechen Cliff Rd C2
Bennett St A2
Bloomfield Avenue C1
Broad Quay C2
Broad St B2
Brock St A1
Bus Station C2
Calton Gardens C2
Calton Rd C2
Camden Crescent A2
Cavendish Rd A1
Cemetery B1
Charlotte St B2
Chaucer Rd C2
Cheap St B2
Circus Mews A2
Claverton St C2
Corn St C2
Cricket Ground B3
Daniel St A3
East Asian Art Mus A2
Edward St B3
Ferry Lane B3
Fire Station A3
First Avenue C1
Forester Avenue A3
Forester Rd A3
Gays Hill A2
George St B2
Great Pulteney St B3
Green Park B1
Green Park Rd B2
Green Park Station ✦ B1
Grove St B2
Guildhall B2
Harley St A2
Hayesfield Park C1
Henrietta Gardens A3
Henrietta Mews B3
Henrietta Park B3
Henrietta Rd A3
Henrietta St B3
Henry St B2
Herschel Museum of Astronomy B1
High Common A1
Holburne Museum B3
Holloway C2
James St West B1/B2
Jane Austen Centre B2
Julian Rd A1
Junction Rd C1
Kingsmead Leisure Complex B2
Kipling Avenue C2
Lansdown Crescent A1
Lansdown Grove A2
Lansdown Rd A2
Library B2
London Rd A3
London St A2
Lower Bristol Rd B1
Lower Oldfield Park C1
Lyncombe Hill C3
Magistrates' Court B3
Manvers St B3
Maple Grove C1
Margaret's Hill A2
Marlborough Bldgs A1
Marlborough Lane B1
Midland Bridge Rd B1
Milk St B2
Milsom St B2
Mission The B2
Monmouth St B2
Morford St A2
Museum of Bath Architecture, The A2
New King St B1
No 1 Royal Cres A1
Norfolk Buildings B1
Norfolk Crescent B1
North Parade Rd B3
Oldfield Rd C1
Paragon A2
Pines Way B1
Podium Shopping Ctr B2
Police Station B3
Portland Place A2
Post Office B2/C2
Postal Museum B2
Powlett Rd A3
Prior Park Rd C3
Pulteney Bridge ✦ B2
Pulteney Gardens B3
Pulteney Rd B3/C3
Queen Square B2
Raby Place B3
Recreation Ground B3
Rivers St A2
Rockliffe Avenue A3
Rockliffe Rd A3
Roman Baths & Pump Room B2
Rossiter Rd C3
Royal Avenue A1
Royal Crescent A1
Royal High School, The A2
Royal Victoria Park A1
St James Square A1
St John's Rd A3
Sally Lunn's House ✦ B2
Shakespeare Avenue C2
Shopmobility B2
South Parade B3
SouthGate Shopping Centre C2
Sports & Leisure Ctr B3
Spring Gardens C3
Stall St B2
Stanier Rd B1
Superstore A3/B1
Sydney Gardens A3
Sydney Place B3
Sydney Rd B3
Theatre Royal B2
Thermae Bath Spa ✦ B2
Thomas St A3
Tyning, The C3
Union St B2
University C3
Upper Bristol Rd B1
Upper Oldfield Park C1
Victoria Art Gallery B2
Victoria Bridge Rd B1
Walcot St B2
Wells Rd C1
Westgate Buildings B2
Westgate St B2
Weston Rd A1
Widcombe Hill C3

Berwick-upon-Tweed 331
Avenue, The B3
Bank Hill B2
Bell Tower ✦ A3
Bell Tower Park A2
Berwick Barracks A3
Berwick Br B2
Berwick Infirmary A3
Berwick-upon-Tweed A2
Billendean Rd C3
Blakewell Gardens B2
Blakewell St B2
Brass Bastion ✦ A3
Bridge St B3
Brucegate St A2
Castle (Remains of) A2
Castle Terrace A2
Castlegate A2
Chapel St A3
Church Rd C2
Church St B3
Council Office A3
Court B3
Coxon's Lane A3
Cumberland Bastion ✦ A3
Dean Drive C2
Dock Rd C2/C3
Elizabethan Walls A2/B3
Fire Station B1
Flagstaff Park B3
Football Ground C3
Foul Ford B3
Golden Square B2
Golf Course A3
Granary ✦ B3
Greenwood C1
Gunpowder Magazine ✦ B3
Hide Hill B3
High Greens A2
Holy Trinity A3
Information Centre A2
Kiln Hill B2
King's Mount ✦ B3
Ladywell Rd C2
Library A3
Lifeboat Station C3
Lord's Mount ✦ A3
Lovaine Terrace A2
Low Greens A3
Main Guard B3
Main St B2/C2
Maltings Art Centre, The ✦ B3
Marygate B3
Meg's Mount ✦ A2
Middle St C3
Mill St C2
Mount Rd C2
Museum B3
Ness St B3
North Rd A2
Northumberland Ave. A2
Northumberland Rd C2
Ord Drive B1
Osborne Crescent B2
Osborne Rd B1
Palace Grove B3
Palace St B3
Palace St East B3
Parade A3
Pier Rd B3
Playing Field C1
Police Station C1
Post Office B2/B3
Prince Edward Rd B2
Prior Rd C2
Quay Walls B3
Railway St A2
Ravensdowne B3
Riverdene B1
Riverside Rd B2
Royal Border Br A2
Royal Tweed Br B2
Russian Gun ✦ B3
Scots Gate ✦ A2
Scott's Place A2
Shielfield Park (Berwick Rangers FC) C1
Shielfield Terrace C2
Silver St B3
Spittal Quay C3
Superstore B1/C1/C2
Tower Gardens A2
Tower Ho Pottery ✦ C2
Tower Rd C2
Town Hall B3
Turret Gardens C2
Tweedbank Retail Pk C2
Tweed Dock B2
Tweed St A2
Tweedside Trading Est C1
Union Brae B2
Union Park Rd B2
Walkergate A3
Wallace Grove A3
War Memorial A2
War Memorial B2
Warkworth Terrace A2
Well Close Square A2
West End B2
West End Place B1
West End Rd B1
West St B3
West St C3
Windmill Bastion ✦ B3
Woolmarket B3
Works C3

Birmingham 332
Abbey St A2
Aberdeen St A1
Acorn Grove B2
Adams St A5
Adderley St C5
Albert St B4
Albion St B2
Alcester St C5
Aldgate Grove A3
All Saint's St A2
All Saints Rd A2
Allcock St C5
Allesley St A4
Allison St C4
Alma Crescent B6
Alston Rd C1
Arcadian Centre C4
Arthur St C6
Assay Office B3
Ashted Circus B5
Aston Expressway A5
Aston St B4

Aston University B4/B5
Avenue Rd A5
Bacchus Rd A1
Bagot St B4
Banbury St B5
Barford Rd B1
Barford St C4
Barn St C5
Barnwell Rd C6
Barr St A3
Barrack St B5
Barwick St B4
Bath Row C3
Beaufort Rd C1
Belmont Row B5
Benson Rd A1
Berkley St C3
Bexhill Grove C3
Birchall St C5
Birmingham City FC C6
Birmingham City Hospital (A&E) A1
Birmingham City Univ B3
Birmingham Wheels Park B6
Bishopsgate St C3
Blews St A4
Bloomsbury St A6
Blucher St C3
Bordesley St C4
Bowyer St C5
Bradburne Way A5
Bradford St C5
Branston St A3
Brearley St A4
Brewery St A4
Bridge St C3
Bridge St West A4
Brindley Drive B3
Brindley Place C3
Broad St C3
Broad St Cineworld C2
Broadway Plaza C2
Bromley St C5
Bromsgrove St C4
Brookfield Rd A2
Browning St C2
Bryant St A1
BT Tower B3
Buckingham St A3
Bull St B4
Bull St B4
Bullring C4
Cambridge St C3
Camden Drive B3
Camden St B2
Cannon St C4
Cardigan St B5
Carlisle St A1
Carlyle Rd C1
Caroline St B3
Carver St B2
Cato St A6
Cattell Rd C6
Cattells Grove A6
Cawdor Crescent C1
Cecil St B4
Cemetery A2/B2
Cemetery Lane A2
Centenary Square C3
Ctr Link Industrial Est A6
Charlotte St B3
Cheapside C4
Chester St A5
Children's Hospital (A&E) B4
Church St B4
Claremont Rd A2
Clarendon Rd C1
Clark St C1
Clement St B3
Clissold St B2
Cliveland St B4
Coach Station C5
College St B2
Colmore Circus B4
Colmore Row B4
Commercial St C3
Constitution Hill B3
Convention Ctr, The C3
Cope St B2
Coplow St B1
Corporation St C4
Council House B3
County Court B4
Coveley Grove A2
Coventry Rd C6
Coventry St C5
Cox St B3
Crabtree Rd A2
Cregoe St C3
Crescent Avenue A2
Crescent Theatre C3
Crescent, The A2
Cromwell St A6
Cromwell St B3
Cube, The C3
Curzon Circle B5
Curzon St B5
Custard Factory C5
Cuthbert Rd B1
Dale End B4
Dart St C6
Dartmouth Circus A4
Dartmouth Middleway A5
Dental Hospital B4
Deritend C5
Devon St A6
Devonshire St A1
Digbeth High St C4
Dolman St B6
Dover St A1
Duchess Rd C2
Duddeston B6
Duddeston Manor Rd B5
Duddeston Mill Rd B6
Duddeston Mill Trading Estate B6
Dudley Rd B1
Edgbaston Village C2
Edmund St B3
Edward St B3
Elkington St A4
Ellen St B2
Ellis St C3
Erskine St B6
Essex St C4
Everyman C3
Eyre St B2
Farm Croft A3
Farm St A3
Fazeley St B4/C5
Felstead Way B5
Finstall Close B5
Five Ways C2
Five Ways C2
Fiveway Shopping Ctr C2
Fleet St B3
Floodgate St C5
Ford St A2
Fore St C4
Forster St B5
Francis Rd C2
Francis St B5
Frankfort St A4
Frederick St B3
Freeth St C1
Freightliner Terminal B6
Garrison Circus C5
Garrison Lane C6
Garrison St B6
Gas St C3
Geach St A4
George St B3
George St West B2
Gibb St C5
Gilby Rd C2
Gillott Rd B1
Glover St C5
Goode Avenue A2
Goodrick Way A6
Gordon St B6
Graham St B3
Grand Central Shopping Centre C4
Granville St C3
Gray St C6
Great Barr St C5
Great Charles St Queensway B3
Great Francis St B6
Great Hampton Row A3
Great Hampton St A3
Great King St A3
Great King St North A3
Great Lister St A5
Great Tindal St C2
Green Lane C6
Green St C5
Greenway St C6
Grosvenor St West C2
Guest Grove A3
Guild Close C2
Guildford Drive A4
Guthrie Close A3
Hagley Rd C1
Hall St B3
Hampton St A3
Handsworth New Rd A1
Hanley St B4
Harford St A3
Harmer Rd A2
Harold Rd C1
Hatchett St A4
Heath Mill Lane C5
Heath St B1
Heaton St A2
Heneage St B5
Henrietta St B4
Herbert Rd C6
High St C4
High St C5
Hilden Rd B5
Hill St C3/C4
Hindlow Close B6
Hingeston St B2
Hippodrome Theatre C4
HM Prison A1
Hockley Circus A2
Hockley Hill A3
Hockley St A3
Holliday St C3
Holloway Circus C4
Holloway Head C3
Holt St B5
Horse Fair C4
Hospital St A4
Howard St B3
Howe St B5
Hubert St A5
Hunters Rd A2
Hunters Vale A3
Huntly Rd C2
Hurst St C4
Icknield Port Rd B1
Icknield Square B2
Icknield St A2/B2
IKON C3
Inge St C4
Irving St C3
James Watt Queensway B4
Jennens Rd B5
Jewellery Quarter A3
Jewellery Quarter A3
Jewellery Quarter Museum B3
John Bright St C4
Keeley St C6
Kellett Rd B5
Kent St C4
Kenyon St B3
Key Hill A3
Key Hill Circus A2
Kilby Avenue C2
King Edwards Rd B2
King Edwards Rd C3
Kingston Rd C6
Kirby Rd A1
Ladywood Arts & Leisure Centre B1
Ladywood Circus C1
Ladywood Middleway C2/C3
Ladywood Rd C1
Lancaster St B4
Landor St B6
Law Courts B4
Lawley Middleway B5
Ledbury Close C2
Ledsam St B2
Lees St A1
Legge Lane B3
Lennox St A3
Library A6/C3
Library C3
Lighthorne Avenue B2
Link Rd B1
Lionel St B3
Lister St B5
Little Ann St C5
Little Hall Rd A6
Liverpool St C5
Livery St B3/B4
Lodge Rd A1
Lord St A5
Love Lane A5
Loveday St B4
Lower Dartmouth St C6
Lower Loveday St B4
Lower Tower St A4
Lower Trinity St C5
Lucus Circus A3
Ludgate Hill B3
Mailbox Centre & BBC C3
Margaret St B3
Markby Rd A1
Marroway St B1
Maxstoke St C6
Melvina Rd A6
Meriden St C4
Midland St B6
Milk St C5
Mill St A5
Millennium Point B5
Miller St A4
Milton St A4
Moat Lane C4
Montague Rd C1
Montague St C5
Monument Rd C1
Moor St Queensway C4
Moor Street C4
Moorsom St A4
Morville St C2
Mosborough Cres A3
Moseley St C4
Mott St B3
Mus & Art Gallery B3
Musgrave Rd A1
National Sea Life Centre C3
Navigation St C3
Nechell's Park Rd A6
Nechells Parkway B5
Nechells Place A6
New Alexandra C3
New Bartholomew St C4
New Canal St C5
New John St West A3
New Spring St B2
New St C4
New Street C4
New Summer St A4
New Town Row A4
Newhall Hill B3
Newhall St B3
Newton St B4
Newtown A4
Noel Rd C1
Norman St A1
Northbrook St B1
Northwood St B3
Norton St A2
Odeon C2
Old Crown House C5
Old Rep Theatre, The C4
Old Snow Hill B4
Oliver Rd C1
Oliver St A5
Osler St C1
Oxford St C5
Palmer St C5
Paradise Circus Queensway C3
Paradise St C3
Park Rd A2
Park St C4
Pavilions C4
Paxton Rd A2
Peel St A1
Pershore St C4
Phillips St A4
Pickford St C5
Pinfold St C4
Pitsford St A2
Plough & Harrow Rd C1
Police Station A4/B4/C2/C4
Pope St B2
Portland Rd C1
Post Office A5/B1/B3/B5/C3/C5
Preston Rd A1
Price St B4
Princip St B4
Printing House St B4
Priory Queensway B4
Pritchett St A4
Proctor St A5
Radnor St A2
Rea St C4
Regent Place B3
Register Office C3
Repertory Theatre C3
Reservoir Rd C1
Richard St A5
River St C5
Rocky Lane A5/A6
Rodney Close C2
Roseberry St B2
Rotton Park St B1
Royal Birmingham Conservatoire B5
Rupert St A5
Ruston St C2
Ryland St C2
St Andrew's Ind Est C6
St Andrew's Rd C6
St Andrew's St C6
St Bolton St C6
St Chads B4
St Chad's Cath (RC) B4
St Chads Queensway B4
St Clements Rd A6
St George's St A3
St James Place B5
St Marks Crescent B2
St Martin's C4
St Paul's B3
St Paul's B3
St Paul's Square B3
St Philip's B4
St Stephen's St A4
St Thomas' Peace Garden C3
St Vincent St C2
Saltley Rd A6
Sand Pits Parade B3
Severn St C3
Shadwell St B4
Sheepcote St C2
Shefford Rd A4
Sherborne St C2
Shylton's Croft C2
Skipton Rd C2
Smallbrook Queensway C4
Smith St A3
Snow Hill B4
Snow Hill Queensway B4
Soho, Benson Rd A1
South Rd A2
Spencer St B3
Spring Hill B2
Staniforth St B4
Station St C4
Steelhouse Lane B4
Stephenson St C4
Steward St B2
Stirling Rd C1
Stour St B2
Suffolk St Queensway C3
Summer Hill Rd B2
Summer Hill St B2
Summer Hill Terrace B2
Summer Lane A4
Summer Row B3
Summerfield Cres B1
Summerfield Park B1
Superstore B2
Sutton St C3
Swallow St C3
Sydney Rd C6
Symphony Hall C3
Talbot St A1
Temple Row C4
Temple St C4
Templefield St C6
Tenby St B3
Tenby St North B2
Tennant St C2/C3
Thimble Mill Lane A6
Thinktank (Science & Discovery) B5
Thomas St A4
Thorpe St C4
Tilton Rd C6
Tower St A4
Town Hall C3
Town Hall C3
Trent St C5
Turner's Buildings A1
Unett St A3
Union Terrace B5
Upper Trinity St C5
Utilita Arena C2
Uxbridge St A3
Vauxhall Grove B5
Vauxhall Rd B5
Vernon Rd C1
Vesey St B4
Viaduct St B5
Victoria Square C3
Villa St A3
Vittoria St B3
Vyse St B3
Walter St A6
Wardlow Rd A5
Warstone Lane B2
Washington St C3
Water St B3
Waterworks Rd C1
Watery Lane C5
Western Rd B1
Wharf St A2
Wheeler St A3
Whitehouse St A5
Whitmore St A2
Whittall St B4
Wholesale Market C4
Wiggin St B1
Willes Rd A1
Windsor Industrial Est A5
Windsor St A5
Windsor St B5
Winson Green Rd A1
Witton St C6
Wolseley St C6
Woodcock St B5

Blackpool 332

Abingdon St A1
Addison Crescent A3
Adelaide St B1
Albert Rd B2
Alfred St B2
Ascot Rd A3
Ashton Rd C2
Auburn Grove C3
Bank Hey St B1
Banks St A1
Beech Avenue A3
Bela Grove C2
Belmont Avenue B2
Birley St A1
Blackpool & Fleetwood Tram B1
Blackpool & the Fylde College B2
Blackpool FC C2
Blackpool North A2
Blackpool North A2
Blackpool Tower B1
Blundell St C1
Bonny St B1
Breck Rd B3
Bryan Rd A3
Buchanan St A2
Bus Hub B1
Cambridge Rd A3
Caunce St A2/A3
Central Drive B1/C2
Central Pier C1
Central Pier C1
Central Pier Theatre C1
Chapel St C1
Charles St A2
Charnley Rd B2
Church St A1/A2
Clinton Avenue B2
Coach Station A2/C1
Cocker St A1
Coleridge Rd A3
Collingwood Avenue A3
Comedy Carpet B1
Condor Grove C3
Cookson St A2
Coronation St B1
Corporation St A1
Courts B1
Cumberland Avenue B3
Cunliffe Rd C3
Dale St C1
Devonshire Rd A3
Devonshire Square A3
Dickson Rd A1
Elizabeth St A2
Ferguson Rd C3
Forest Gate B3
Foxhall Rd C1
Freckleton St C2
George St A2
Gloucester Avenue B3
Golden Mile, The C1
Gorse Rd B3
Gorton St A2
Grand Theatre, The B1
Granville Rd A2
Grasmere Rd C2
Grosvenor St A2
Grundy Art Gallery A1
Harvey Rd B3
Hornby Rd B2
Houndshill Shopping Centre B1
Hull Rd B1
Ibbison Court C2
Kent Rd C2
Keswick Rd C2
King St A2
Knox Grove C3
Laycock Gate A3
Layton Rd A3
Leamington Rd B2
Leeds Rd B3
Leicester Rd B2
Levens Grove C2
Library A1
Lifeboat Station B1
Lincoln Rd B2
Liverpool Rd B3
Livingstone Rd B2
London Rd A3
Lune Grove C2
Lytham Rd C1
Madame Tussaud's Blackpool B1
Manchester Square C1
Manor Rd B3
Maple Avenue B3
Market St A1
Marlboro Rd B3
Mere Rd B3
Milbourne St A2
Newcastle Avenue B3
Newton Drive A3
North Pier A1
North Pier A1
North Pier Theatre A1
Odeon C2
Olive Grove B3
Palatine Rd B2
Park Rd B2/C3
Peter St A2
Post Office B1/B2/B3
Princess Parade A1
Princess St C1/C2
Promenade A1/C1
Queen St A1
Queen Victoria Rd C2
Raikes Parade B2
Reads Avenue B2
Regent Cinema B2
Regent Rd B2
Register Office B2
Ribble Rd B2
Rigby Rd C1/C2
Ripon Rd B3
St Albans Rd B3
St Ives Avenue C3
St John's Square A1
St Vincent Avenue C3
Salisbury Rd B3
Salthouse Avenue C2
Salvation Army Ctr A2
Sands Way C2
Sea Life Centre B1
Seasiders Way C1
Selbourne Rd A2
Sharrow Grove C3
Somerset Avenue C3
South King St B2
Springfield Rd A1
Sutton Place B2
Talbot Rd A1/A2
Thornber Grove C2
Topping St A1
Tower B1
Town Hall A1
Tram Depot C1
Tyldesley Rd C1
Vance Rd B1
Victoria St B1
Victory Rd A2
Wayman Rd A3
Westmorland Ave C2/C3
Whitegate Drive B3
Winter Gardens Theatre B1
Woodland Grove B3
Woolman Rd B2

Bournemouth 332

Ascham Rd A3
Avenue Rd B1
Ave Shopping Centre B1
Bath Rd C2
Beacon Rd C1
Beechey Rd A3
Bodorgan Rd B1
Bourne Avenue B1
Bournemouth A3
Bh2 Leisure C1
Bournemouth & Poole College B3
Bournemouth International Centre C1
Bournemouth Pier C2
Bournemouth Sta B3
Braidley Rd A1
Cavendish Place A2
Cavendish Rd A2
Central Drive A1
Central Gardens B1
Christchurch Rd B3
Cliff Lift C1/C3
Coach House Place A3
Coach Station A3
Commercial Rd B1
Cotlands Rd B3
Cranborne Rd C1
Cricket Ground A2
Cumnor Rd B2
Dean Park A2
Dean Park Crescent B2
Dean Park Rd A2
Durrant Rd B1
East Overcliff Drive C3
Exeter Crescent C1
Exeter Rd C1
Gervis Place B1
Gervis Rd B3
Glen Fern Rd B2
Golf Club B1
Grove Rd B3
Hinton Rd C2
Holdenhurst Rd B3
Horseshoe Common B2
Information Centre C2
Lansdowne B3
Lansdowne Rd A2
Lorne Park Rd B2
Lower Gardens B1/C2
Madeira Rd B2
Methuen Rd A3
Meyrick Park A1
Meyrick Rd B3
Milton Rd A2
Nuffield Health Bournemouth Hospital (private) A2
Oceanarium C2
Old Christchurch Rd B2
Ophir Rd A3
Oxford Rd B3
Park Rd A3
Parsonage Rd B2
Pavilion C2
Pier Approach C2
Pier Theatre C2
Police Station A3/B3
Portchester Rd A3
Post Office B1/B3
Priory Rd C1
Quadrant, The B2
Recreation Ground A1
Richmond Gardens Shopping Centre B2
Richmond Hill Rd B1
Russell-Cotes Art Gallery & Museum C2
Russell Cotes Rd C2
St Anthony's Rd A1
St Michael's Rd C1
St Paul's A3
St Paul's Lane B3
St Paul's Rd A3
St Peter's B2
St Peter's B2
St Peter's Rd B2
St Stephen's Rd B1/B2
St Swithun's B3
St Swithun's Rd B3
St Swithun's Rd South B3
St Valerie Rd A2
St Winifred's Rd A2
Square, The B1
Stafford Rd B3
Terrace Rd B1
Town Hall B1
Tregonwell Rd C1
Triangle, The B1
Trinity Rd B2
Undercliff Drive C3
Upper Hinton Rd B2
Upper Terrace Rd C1
Wellington Rd A2/A3
Wessex Way A3/B1/B2
West Cliff Promenade C1
West Hill Rd C1
West Undercliff Prom C1
Westover Rd B2
Wimborne Rd A2
Wootton Mount B2
Wychwood Drive A1
Yelverton Rd B2
York Rd B3
Zig-Zag Walks C1/C3
Zip Wire C2

Bradford 332

Alhambra B2
Back Ashgrove B1
Barkerend Rd A3
Barnard Rd C3
Barry St B2
Bolling Rd C3
Bolton Rd A3
Bowland St A1
Bradford Big Screen B2
Bradford College B1
Bradford Forster Square A2
Bradford Interchange B3
Bradford Playhouse B3
Bridge St B2
Britannia St B2
Broadway Bradford, The B2
Burnett St B3
Bus Station B2
Butler St West A3
Caledonia St C2
Canal Rd A2
Carlton St B1
Cathedral A3
Centenary Square B2
Chapel St B3
Cheapside A2
Church Bank B3
Cineworld B3
City Hall B2
City Rd A1
Claremont B1
Colour Experience B1
Croft St B2
Crown Court B3
Darfield St A1
Darley St A2
Drewton Rd A1
Drummond Trading Estate A1
Dryden St B3
Dyson St A1
Easby Rd C1
East Parade B3
Eldon Place A1
Filey St B3
Forster Sq Retail Pk A2
Gallery II B1
Garnett St B3
Godwin St B2
Gracechurch St A1
Grattan Rd B1
Great Horton Rd B1/B2
Grove Terrace B1
Hall Ings B2
Hall Lane C3
Hallfield Rd A1
Hammstrasse A2
Harris St B3
Holdsworth St A2
Ice Arena B2
Impressions B2
Information Centre B2
Inland Revenue A2
Ivegate B2
Jacob's Well Municipal Offices B2
James St A2
John St A2
Kirkgate B2
Kirkgate Centre B2
Laisteridge Lane C1
Leeds Rd B3
Leisure Exchange, The B3
Library B1/B2
Listerhills Rd B1
Little Horton Green C1
Little Horton Lane C1
Longside Lane B1
Lower Kirkgate B2
Lumb Lane A1
Magistrates Court B2
Manchester Rd C2
Manningham Lane A1
Manor Row A2
Market C3
Market St B2
Melbourne Place C1
Midland Rd A2
Mill Lane C2
Morley St B1
National Science and Media Museum B2
Nelson St B2/C2
Nesfield St A2
New Otley Rd A3
Norcroft St B1
North Parade A2
North St A3
North Wing A3
Oastler Shopping Ctr A2
Otley Rd A3
Park Avenue C1
Park Lane C1
Park Rd C2
Parma St C2
Peace Museum B2
Peckover St B3
Piccadilly A2
Police Station C2
Post Office B1/B2/B3/C3
Princes Way B2
Prospect St C3
Radwell Drive C2
Rawson Rd A1
Rebecca St A1
Richmond Rd B1
Russell St C1
St George's Hall B2
St Lukes Hospital C1
Shipley Airedale Rd A3/B3
Shopmobility A2
Simes St A1
Smith St B1
Spring Mill St C2
Stott Hill A3
Sunbridge Rd A1/B1/B2
Theatre in the Mill B1
Thornton Rd A1/B1
Trafalgar St A2
Trinity Rd C1
Tumbling Hill St B1
Tyrrel St B2
Univ of Bradford B1/C1
Usher St C3
Valley Rd A2
Vicar Lane B3
Wakefield Rd C3
Wapping Rd A3
Well St B3
Westgate A1
White Abbey Rd A1
Wigan Rd A1
Wilton St B1
Wood St A1
Wool Exchange B2
Worthington St A1

Brighton 332

Addison Rd A1
Albert Rd B2
Albion Hill B3
Albion St B3
Ann St A3
Baker St A3
Black Lion St C2
Brighton A2
Brighton Centre C2
Brighton Fishing Museum C2
Brighton Pier (Palace Pier) C3
Brighton Zip Wire C3
British Airways i360 Tower C1
Broad St C3
Buckingham Place A2
Buckingham Rd B2
Cannon Place C1
Carlton Hill B3
Chatham Place A1
Cheapside A3
Church St B2
Churchill Square Shopping Centre B2
Clifton Hill B1
Clifton Place B1
Clifton Rd B1
Clifton St A2
Clifton Terrace B1
Clyde Rd A3
Coach Station C3
Compton Avenue A2
Davigdor Rd A1
Denmark Terrace B1
Ditchling Rd A3
Dome B2
Duke St B2
Duke's Lane C2
Dyke Rd A1/B2
East St C2
Edward St B3
Elmore Rd B3
Fleet St A2
Frederick St B2
Gardner St B2
Gloucester Place B3
Gloucester Rd B2
Goldsmid Rd A1
Grand Junction Rd C2
Grand Parade B3
Grove Hill B3
Guildford St A2
Hampton Place B1
Hanover Terrace A3
High St C3
Highdown Rd A1
Information Centre C2
John St B3
Jubilee Clock Tower B2
Kemp St B2
Kensington Place B2
Kings Rd C1
Lanes, The C2
Law Courts B3
Lewes Rd A3
Library B2
London Rd A3
Madeira Drive C3
Marine Parade C3
Middle St C2
Montpelier Place B1
Montpelier Rd B1
Montpelier St B1
Mus & Art Gallery B3
New England Rd A2
New England St A2
New Rd B2
Nizells Avenue A1
Norfolk Rd B1
Norfolk Terrace B1
North Rd B2
North St B2
Odeon C2
Old Shoreham Rd A1
Old Steine C3
Osmond Rd A1
Over St B2
Oxford St A3
Park Crescent Terrace A3
Phoenix Brighton B3
Phoenix Rise A3
Police Station B3
Post Office A1/A3/C3
Preston Rd A2
Preston St B1
Prestonville Rd A1
Queen's Rd B2
Queen Square B2
Regency Square C1
Regent St B2
Richmond Place B3
Richmond St B3
Richmond Terrace A3
Rose Hill Terrace A3
Royal Pavilion B2
St Bartholomew's A3
St James's St C3
St Nicholas Rd B2
St Nicholas' B2
St Peter's A3
Sea Life Brighton C3
Shaftesbury Rd A3
Ship St C2
Sillwood Rd B1
Sillwood St B1
Southover St A3
Spring Gardens B2
Stanford Rd A1
Stanley Rd A3
Surrey St B2
Sussex St B3
Swimming Pool B3
Sydney St B3
Temple Gardens B1
Terminus Rd A2
Theatre Royal B2
Tidy St B2
Town Hall C2
Toy & Model Mus A2
Trafalgar St B2
Union Rd A3
University of Brighton B3
Upper Lewes Rd A3
Upper North St B1
Viaduct Rd A3
Victoria Gardens B3
Victoria Rd B1
Volk's Electric Railway C3
West Pier (derelict) C1
West St C2
Western Rd B1
Whitecross St B2
YHA C3
York Place B3
York Rd B1

Bristol 332

Acramans Rd C4
Albert Rd C6
Alfred Hill A4
All Saint's St A4
All Saints' B4
Allington Rd C3
Alpha Rd C4
Ambra Vale B1
Ambra Vale East B2
Ambrose Rd B2
Amphitheatre & Waterfront Square C4
Anchor Rd B3
Anvil St B6
Arcade, The A5
Architecture Centre, The B4
Argyle Place B2
Arlington Villas A2
Arnolfini B4
Art Gallery A3
Ashton Gate Rd C2
Ashton Rd C1
Avon Bridge C1
Avon Crescent C1
Avon St B6
Baldwin St B4
Baltic Wharf C2
Baltic Wharf Leisure Ctr & Caravan Park C2
Baltic Wharf Marina C2
Barossa Place C4
Barton Manor B6
Barton Rd B6
Barton Vale B6
Bath Rd C6
Bathurst Basin C4
Bathurst Parade C4
Beauley Rd C3
Bedminster Bridge C5
Bedminster Parade C4
Bellevue B2
Bellevue Crescent B2
Bellevue Rd C6
Berkeley Place A2
Berkeley Square A3
Birch Rd C2
Blackfriars A4
Bond St A5
Braggs Lane A6
Brandon Hill B3
Brandon Steep B3
Bristol Aquarium B4
Bristol Beacon B4
Bristol Bridge B5
Bristol Cath (CE) B3
Bristol Eye Hospital (A&E) A4
Bristol Grammar School A3
Bristol Harbour Railway C3
Bristol Royal Children's Hospital A4
Bristol Royal Infirmary (A&E) A4
Bristol Temple Meads Station B6
Broad Plain B6
Broad Quay B4
Broad St A4
Broad Weir A5
Broadcasting House A3
Broadmead A5

Brunel Institute ✦ B3
Brunel Way C1
Brunswick Square A5
Burton Close C5
Bus Station A4
Butts Rd B3
Cabot Circus A5
Cabot Tower ✦ B3
Caledonia Place B1
Callowhill Court A5
Cambridge St C6
Camden Rd C3
Camp Rd A1
Canada Way C2
Cannon St A4
Canon's Way B3
Cantock's Close A3
Canynge Rd A1
Canynge Square A1
Castle Park A5
Castle St A5
Cathedral Walk B3
Catherine Meade St C4
Cattle Market Rd C6
Central Library B3
Charles Place B1
Charlotte St B3
Charlotte St South B3
Chatterton House 🏛 B5
Chatterton Square C5
Chatterton St C5
Cheese Lane B5
Christchurch ⛪ A4
Christchurch Rd A1
Christmas Steps ✦ A4
Church Lane B2/B5
Church St B5
City Museum 🏛 A3
City of Bristol College B3
Civil and Family Justice Centre B5
Clare St B4
Clarence Rd C5
Cliff Rd C1
Clift House Rd C1
Clifton Cath (RC) ✝ A2
Clifton Down A1
Clifton Down Rd A1
Clifton Hill B2
Clifton Park A1/A2
Clifton Park Rd A1
Clifton Rd A2
Clifton Vale B1
Cliftonwood Crescent B2
Cliftonwood Rd B2
Cliftonwood Terrace B2
Cobblestone Mews A1
College Green B3
College Rd A1
College St B3
Colston Almshouses 🏛 A4
Colston Avenue B4
Colston Parade C5
Colston St A4
Commercial Rd C4
Constitution Hill B2
Cooperage Lane C2
Corn St B4
Cornwallis Avenue B1
Cornwallis Crescent B1
Coronation Rd C2/C4
Council House 🏛 B3
Counterslip B5
Create Centre, The ✦ C1
Crosby Row B2
Crown Court A4
Culver St B3
Cumberland Basin C1
Cumberland Close C2
Cumberland Rd C2/C3
Dean Lane C4
Deanery Rd B3
Denmark St B4
Dowry Square B1
Eaton Crescent A2
Elmdale Rd A3
Elton Rd A3
Eugene St A4/A6
Exchange and St Nicholas' Markets, The 🏛 B4
Fairfax St A4
Fire Station B5
Floating Harbour C3
Fosseway, The A2
Foster Almshouses 🏛 A4
Frayne Rd C1
Frederick Place A2
Freeland Place B1
Friary B5
Frogmore St B3
Fry's Hill B2
Galleries shopping centre, The A5
Gas Lane B6
Gasferry Rd C3
Georgian House 🏛 B3
Glendale B1
Glentworth Rd B2
Gloucester St A1
Goldney Hall B2
Goldney Rd B1
Gordon Rd A2
Granby Hill B1
Grange Rd A1
Great Ann St A6
Great George Rd B3
Great George St A6/B3
Green St North B1
Green St South B1
Greenay Bush Lane C2
Greenbank Rd C2
Greville Smyth Park C1
Grove, The B4
Guildhall 🏛 A4
Guinea St C4
Hamilton Rd C3
Hanbury Rd A2
Hanover Place C2
Harley Place A1
Haymarket A5
Hensman's Hill B1
High St B4
Highbury Villas A3
Hill St B3
Hill St C6
Hippodrome 🎭 B4
Hopechapel Hill B1
Horfield Rd A4
Horsefair, The A5
Horton St B6
Host St A4
Hotwell Rd B1/B2
Houlton St A6
Howard Rd C3
IMAX Cinema 🎬 B4
Islington Rd C3
Jacob St A5/A6
Jacob's Wells Rd B2
John Carr's Terrace B2
John Wesley's Chapel ⛪ A5
Joy Hill B1
Jubilee St B6
Kensington Place A2
Kilkenny St B6
King St B4
Kingsland Rd B6
Kingston Rd C3
Lamb St A6
Lansdown Rd A2
Lawford St A6
Lawfords Gate A6
Leighton Rd C3
Lewins Mead A4
Lime Rd C2
Litfield Rd A1
Little Ann St A6
Little Caroline Place B1
Little George St A6
Little King St B4
Llandoger Trow 🏛 B4
Lloyds' Building, The C3
Lodge St A4
Lord Mayor's Chapel, The ⛪ B4
Lower Castle St A5
Lower Church Lane A4
Lower Clifton Hill B2
Lower Guinea St C4
Lower Lamb St B3
Lower Maudlin St A4
Lower Park Rd A4
Lower Sidney St C2
Lucky Lane C4
Lydstep Terrace C3
M Shed 🏛 C4
Magistrates' Court A4
Manilla Rd A1
Mardyke Ferry Rd C2
Maritime Heritage Centre 🏛 B3
Marlborough Hill A4
Marlborough St A4
Marsh St B4
Mead St C5
Merchant Dock B2
Merchant Seamen's Almshouses 🏛 B4
Merchant St A5
Merchants Rd A1
Merchants Rd C1
Meridian Place A2
Meridian Vale A2
Merrywood Rd C3
Midland Rd A6
Milford St C3
Millennium Promenade B3
Millennium Square B3
Mitchell Lane B5
Mortimer Rd A1
Murray Rd C4
Myrtle Rd A3
Narrow Plain B5
Narrow Quay B4
Nelson St A4
New Charlotte St C4
New Kingsley Rd B6
New Queen St C5
New St A6
Newgate A5
Newton St A6
Norland Rd A1
North St C2
O2 Academy B3
Oakfield Grove A2
Oakfield Place A2
Oakfield Rd A2
Old Bread St B6
Old Market St A6
Old Park Hill A4
Oldfield Rd B1
Orchard Avenue B4
Orchard Lane B4
Orchard St B4
Osbourne Rd C3
Oxford St B6
Park Place A2
Park Rd C3
Park Row A3
Park St A3
Passage St B5
Pembroke Grove A2
Pembroke Rd A2
Pembroke Rd C3
Pembroke St A5
Penn St A5
Pennywell Rd A6
Percival Rd A1
Pero's Bridge B4
Perry Rd A4
Phipps St C2
Pip 'n' Jay ⛪ B5
Plimsoll Bridge B1
Polygon Rd B1
Portland St A1
Portwall Lane B5
Post Office 📮 A1/A3/A5/ B1/B4/C4/C5
Prewett St C5
Prince St B4
Prince St Bridge C4
Princess St C5
Princess Victoria St B1
Priory Rd A3
Pump Lane C5
QEH Theatre 🎭 A2
Quakers Friars A5
Quay St A4
Queen Charlotte St B4
Queen Elizabeth Hospital School B2
Queen Square B4
Queen St A5
Queen's Avenue A3
Queen's Parade B3
Queen's Rd A2/A3
Raleigh Rd C2
Randall Rd B2
Red Lodge 🏛 A4
Redcliffe Backs B5
Redcliffe Bridge B4
Redcliffe Hill C5
Redcliffe Parade C4
Redcliffe St B5
Redcliffe Way B5
Redcross St A6
Redgrave Theatre 🎭 A1
Regent St B1
Richmond Hill A2
Richmond Hill Avenue A2
Richmond Lane A2
Richmond Park Rd A2
Richmond St C6
Richmond Terrace A2
River St A6
Rownham Mead B2
Royal Fort Rd A3
Royal Park A2
Royal West of England Academy 🏛 A3
Royal York Crescent B1
Royal York Villas B1
Rupert St A4
Russ St B6
St Andrew's Walk B2
St George's 🎭 B3
St George's Rd B3
St James ⛪ A4
St John's ⛪ A4
St John's Rd C4
St Luke's Rd C5
St Mary Redcliffe ⛪ C5
St Matthias Park A6
St Michael's Hill A3
St Michael's Hosp 🏥 A4
St Michael's Park A3
St Nicholas St B4
St Paul St A5
St Paul's Rd A2
St Peter's (ruin) ⛪ A5
St Philip's Bridge B5
St Philips Rd A6
St Stephen's ⛪ B4
St Stephen's St B4
St Thomas St B5
St Thomas the Martyr ⛪ B5
Sandford Rd B1
Sargent St C5
Saville Place B1
Ship Lane C5
Shopmobility A5
Showcase Cinema de Lux 🎬 A5
Silver St A4
Sion Hill A1
Small St A4
Smeaton Rd C1
Somerset Square C5
Somerset St C5
Southernhay Avenue B2
Southville Rd C4
Spike Island Artspace 🏛 C2
Spring St C5
Superstore C4
SS Great Britain and the Matthew ⛴ B2
Stackpool Rd C3
Staight St B6
Stillhouse Lane C4
Sydney Row C2
Tankard's Close A3
Temple Back B5
Temple Back East B5
Temple Bridge B5
Temple Church ⛪ B5
Temple Circus B5
Temple Gate C5
Temple St B5
Temple Way B5
Terrell St A4
Theatre Royal (Bristol Old Vic) 🎭 B4
Thekla ⛴ B4
Thomas Lane B5
Three Kings of Cologne ⛪ A4
Three Queens Lane B5
Tobacco Factory, The 🎭 C2
Tower Hill B5
Tower Lane A4
Trenchard St A4
Triangle South A3
Triangle West A3
Trinity Rd A6
Trinity St A6
Tyndall Avenue A3
Union St A5
Union St B6
Unity St A6
Unity St B3
University of Bristol A3
University Rd A3
Upper Byron Place A3
Upper Maudlin St A4
Upper Perry Hill C3
Upton Rd C2
Valentine Bridge B6
Victoria Grove C5
Victoria Rd C6
Victoria Rooms 🏛 A2
Victoria Square A2
Victoria St B5
Vyvyan Rd A1
Vyvyan Terrace A1
Wade St A6
Walter St C2
Wapping Rd C4
Water Lane B5
Waterloo Rd A6
Waterloo St A1
Waterloo St A6
Watershed Media Centre ✦ B4
We the Curious ✦ B3
Welling Terrace B1
Welsh Back B4
West Mall A1
West St A6
Westfield Place A1
Wetherell Place A2
Whitehouse Place C5
Whitehouse St C5
Whiteladies Rd A2
Whitson St A4
William St C5
Willway St C5
Windsor Place B1
Wine St A4
Woodland Rd A3
Woodland Rise A3
Worcester Rd A1
Worcester Terrace A1
YHA ▲ B4
York Gardens B1
York Place A2
York Rd C5

Bury St Edmunds 332

Abbey Gardens ✿ B3
Abbey Gate 🏛 B3
Abbeygate 🎬 B2
Abbeygate St B2
Albert Crescent B1
Albert St B1
Angel Hill B2
Angel Lane B2
Anglian Lane A1
Arc Shopping Centre B2
Athenaeum 🏛 C2
Baker's Lane C3
Barwell Rd B3
Beetons Way A1
Bishops Rd B2
Bloomfield St B2
Bridewell Lane C2
Bullen Close C1
Bury St Edmunds ⇌ A2
Bury St Edmunds County Upper Sch A1
Bury St Edmunds Leisure Centre B1
Bury Town FC (Ram Meadow) B3
Bus Station B2
Business Park B3
Butter Market B2
Cannon St B2
Castle Rd C1
Cemetery C1
Chalk Rd (N) B1
Chalk Rd (S) B1
Church Row B2
Churchgate St C2
Citizens Advice Bureau B2
College St C2
Compiegne Way A3
Corn Exchange, The 🏛 B2
Cornfield Rd B1
Cotton Lane B3
Courts B2
Covent Garden C2
Crown St C3
Cullum Rd C2
Eastern Way A3
Eastgate St B3
Enterprise Bsns Park A2
Etna Rd A2
Eyre Close C2
Fire & Ambulance Sta B1
Friar's Lane C2
Gage Close A1
Garland St B2
Greene King Brewery 🏛 C3
Grove Park B1
Grove Rd B1
Guildhall 🏛 C2
Guildhall St C2
Hatter St C2
High Baxter St B2
Honey Hill C3
Hospital Rd C1/C2
Ickworth Drive C1
Industrial Estate A3
Information Centre ℹ B2
Ipswich St A2
King Edward VI Sch A1
King's Rd C1/B2
Library B2
Long Brackland A2
Looms Lane B2
Lwr Baxter St B2
Malthouse Lane A2
Manor House 🏛 C3
Maynewater Lane C3
Mill Rd C1
Mill Rd (South) C1
Minden Close B3
Moyse's Hall 🏛 B2
Mustow St B3
Norman Tower 🏛 C3
Northgate Avenue A2
Northgate St B2
Osier Rd A2
Out Northgate A2
Out Risbygate B1
Out Westgate C2
Parkway B1/C2
Parkway, The B1
Peckham St B2
Petticoat Lane C1
Phoenix Day Hosp 🏥 C1
Pinners Way C1
Police Station 🏛 C3
Post Office 📮 B2
Pump Lane B2
Queen's Rd B1
Raingate St C3
Raynham Rd A1
Retail Park C2
Risbygate St B1/B2
Robert Boby Way C2
St Andrew's St North B2
St Andrew's St South B2
St Botolph's Lane C3
St Edmund's ⛪ C2
St Edmund's Abbey (Remains) ✦ B3
St Edmunds Hospital (Private) 🏥 C3
St Edmundsbury ✝ C3
St John's St B2
St Marys ⛪ C3
School Hall Lane B2
Shillitoe Close C1
South Close C1
Southgate St C3
Sparhawk St C3
Spring Lane B1
Springfield Rd B1
Station Hill A2
Swan Lane C3
Tayfen Rd B2
Theatre Royal 🎭 C3
Thingoe Hill A2
Victoria St B1
Vinefields, The B3
War Memorial ✦ C1
Well St B2
West Suffolk College B1
Westgarth Gardens C1
Westgate St C2
Whiting St C2
York Rd B1
York Terrace B1

Cambridge 333

Abbey Rd A3
ADC 🎭 A2
Anglia Ruskin Univ B3
Archaeology & Anthropology 🏛 B2
Arts Picturehouse 🎬 B2
Arts Theatre 🎭 B1
Auckland Rd A3
Backs, The B1
Bateman St C2
Benet St B1
Bradmore St B3
Bridge St A1
Broad St B3
Brookside C2
Brunswick Terrace A3
Burleigh St B3
Bus Station B2
Butt Green A2
Cambridge Contemporary Art Gallery 🏛 B1
Castle Mound ✦ A1
Castle St A1
Cemetery B3
Chesterton Lane A1
Christ's (College) B2
Christ's Lane B2
Christ's Pieces B2
City Rd B3
Clare Bridge B1
Clare (College) B1
Clarendon St B2
Coe Fen C2
Coronation St C2
Corpus Christi (Coll) B1
Court A3
Cross St C3
Crusoe Bridge C1
Darwin (College) C1
Devonshire Rd C3
Downing (College) C2
Downing St B2
Earl St B2
East Rd B3
Eden St B3
Elizabeth Way A3
Elm St B2
Emery St B3
Emmanuel (College) B2
Emmanuel Rd B2
Emmanuel St B2
Fair St A3
Fen Causeway, The C1
Fenner's Cricket Gd C3
Fire Station B3
Fitzroy St A3
Fitzwilliam Mus 🏛 C2
Fitzwilliam St C2
Garrett Hostel Bridge B1
Glisson Rd C3
Gonville & Caius (Coll) B1
Gonville Place C2
Grafton Centre, The A3
Grand Arcade B2
Green St B1
Gresham Rd C3
Guest Rd B3
Guildhall 🏛 B2
Harvey Rd C3
Hills Rd C3
Hobson St B2
Hughes Hall (College) B3
James St A3
Jesus (College) A2
Jesus Green A2
Jesus Lane A2
Jesus Terrace B3
John St B3
Kelsey Kerridge Sports Centre B3
Kettle's Yard 🏛 A1
King's Bridge B1
King St A2
King's (College) B1
King's Coll Chapel ⛪ B1
King's Parade B1
Lammas Land Rec Gd C1
Lensfield Rd C2
Library B2
Lion Yard B2
Little St Mary's Lane B1
Lyndewod Rd C3
Magdalene (College) A1
Magdalene St A1
Maid's Causeway A3
Malcolm St A2
Market St B1
Mathematical Bridge B1
Mawson Rd C3
Midsummer Common A3
Mill Lane B1
Mill Rd B3
Mill St C3
Mumford 🎭 B3
Mus of Cambridge 🏛 A1
Museum of Classical Archaeology 🏛 C1
Napier St A3
New Square A2
Newmarket Rd A3
Newnham Rd C1
Norfolk St B3
Northampton St A1
Norwich St C2
Orchard St B2
Panton St C2
Paradise St B3
Park Parade A1
Park St A2
Park Terrace B2
Parker St B2
Parker's Piece B2
Parkside B3
Parkside Pools B3
Parsonage St A3
Pea's Hill B1
Pemberton Terrace C2
Pembroke (College) B2
Pembroke St B1
Perowne St B3
Peterhouse (College) C1
Petty Cury B2
Polar Museum, The 🏛 C2
Police Station 🏛 B3
Post Office 📮 A3/B2/C1/C2/C3
Queen's Lane B1
Queen's Rd B1
Queens' (College) B1
Regent St B2
Regent Terrace B2
Ridley Hall (College) C1
Riverside A3
Round Church, The ⛪ A1
Russell St C2
St Andrew's St B2
St Benet's ⛪ B1
St Catharine's (Coll) B1
St Eligius St C2
St John's (College) A1
St Mary's ⛪ B1
St Paul's Rd C3
Saxon St C2
Sedgwick Museum 🏛 B2
Sheep's Green C1
Shire Hall A1
Sidgwick Avenue C1
Sidney St A2
Sidney Sussex (Coll) A2
Silver St B1
Station Rd C3
Tenison Avenue C3
Tenison Rd C3
Tennis Court Rd B2
Thompson's Lane A1
Trinity (College) A1
Trinity Bridge B1
Trinity Hall (College) B1
Trinity St B1
Trumpington Rd C2
Trumpington St B1
Union Rd C2
University Botanic Gardens ✿ C2
Victoria Avenue A2
Victoria St B2
Warkworth St B3
Warkworth Terrace B3
Wesley House (Coll) A2
West Rd B1
Westcott House (Coll) A2
Westminster (Coll) A1
Whipple 🏛 B2
Willis Rd B3
Willow Walk A2
YMCA C3
Zoology 🏛 B2

Canterbury 333

Artillery St B2
Barton Mill Rd A3
Beaconsfield Rd A1
Beaney, The 🏛 B2
Beverley Meadow A1
Beverley Rd A1
Bingley's Island B1
Black Griffin Lane B1
Broad Oak Rd A2
Broad St B2
Brymore Rd A3
Burgate B2
Bus Station C2
Canterbury Castle 🏰 C1
Canterbury Christ Church University B3
Canterbury College C3
Canterbury East ⇌ C1
Canterbury Tales, The ✦ B2
Canterbury West ⇌ A1
Castle Row C1
Castle St C1
Cathedral ✝ B2
Causeway, The A2
Chaucer Rd A3
Christchurch Gate ✦ B2
City Council Offices A3
City Wall B2
Coach park A2
College Rd B3
Cossington Rd C2
Court B2
Craddock Rd A3
Crown & County Courts B3
Dane John Gardens C2
Dane John Mound ✦ C1
Deanery B2
Dover St C2
Duck Lane B2
Eastbridge Hosp 🏛 B1
Edgar Rd B3
Ersham Rd C3
Ethelbert Rd C3
Fire Station C2
Forty Acres Rd A1
Friars, The B2
Gordon Rd C1
Greyfriars ✦ B1
Guildford Rd C1
Havelock St B2
Heaton Rd C1
High St B2
Information Ctr ℹ A2/B2
Ivy Lane B2
New St C1
King St B2
King's School B2/B3
King's School Recreation Ctr, The A2
Kingsmead Leisure Ctr A2
Kingsmead Rd A2
Kirby's Lane B1
Lansdown Rd C2
Lime Kiln Rd C1
Longport B3
Lower Chantry Lane C3
Mandeville Rd A1
Market Way A2
Marlowe Arcade B2
Marlowe Avenue C2
Marlowe Theatre 🎭 B2
Martyrs Field Rd C1
Mead Way B1
Military Rd B2
Monastery St B2
Museum of Canterbury (Rupert Bear Mus) 🏛 B1
New Dover Rd C3
New St C1
Norman Rd C2
North Holmes Rd B3
North Lane B1
Northgate A2
Nunnery Fields C2
Nunnery Rd C2
Oaten Hill C2
Odeon Cinema 🎬 C2
Old Dover Rd C2
Old Palace B2
Old Ruttington Lane B2
Old Weavers 🏛 B2
Orchard St B1
Oxford Rd C1
Palace St B2
Pilgrims Way C3
Pin Hill C1
Pine Tree Avenue A1
Police Station 🏛 C2
Post Office B2, C1
Pound Lane B1
Puckle Lane C2
Raymond Avenue C2
Recreation Ground A2
Registry Office A2
Rheims Way B1
Rhodaus Close C2
Rhodaus Town C2
Roman Museum 🏛 B2
Roper Gateway A1
Roper Rd A1
Rose Lane B2
Shopmobility B2
St Augustine's Abbey (remains) ✝ B3
St Augustine's Rd C3
St Dunstan's ⛪ A1
St Dunstan's St A1
St George's Place C2
St George's St B2
St George's Tower ✦ B2
St Gregory's Rd B3
St John's Hospital 🏛 A2
St Margaret's St B2
St Martin's ⛪ B3
St Martin's Avenue B3
St Martin's Rd B3
St Michael's Rd A1
St Mildred's ⛪ C1
St Peter's Grove B1
St Peter's Lane B2
St Peter's Place B1
St Peter's St B1
St Radigunds St B2
St Stephen's Court A1
St Stephen's Path A1
St Stephen's Rd A2
Salisbury Rd A1
Simmonds Rd C1
Spring Lane C3
Station Rd West B1
Stour St B1
Sturry Rd A3
Tourtel Rd A3
Tudor Rd C1
Union St B2
University for the Creative Arts C3
Vernon Place C2
Victoria Rd C1
Watling St B2
Westgate Gardens B1
Westgate Towers 🏛 B1
Whitefriars B2
Whitehall Gardens B1
Whitehall Rd B1
Wincheap C1
York Rd C1
Zealand Rd C2

Cardiff Caerdydd 333

Adam St B3
Alexandra Gardens A2
Allerton St C1
Arran St A3
ATRiuM (University of Glamorgan) C3
Beauchamp St C1
Bedford St A3
Blackfriars Priory (rems) ✝ B1
Boulevard De Nantes B2
Brains Brewery C2
Brook St B1
Bute Park A1
Bute St C2
Bute Terrace C3
Callaghan Square C2/C3
Capitol Shopping Centre, The B3
Cardiff Arms Park (Cardiff Blues) B1
Cardiff Bridge B1
Cardiff Castle 🏰 B2
Cardiff Central Sta ⇌ C2
Cardiff Story, The 🏛 B2
Cardiff Univ A1/A2/B3
Cardiff University Student's Union A2
Caroline St C2
Castle Green B2
Castle Mews A1
Castle St (Heol y Castell) B1
Cathays Station ⇌ A2
Celerity Drive C3
Central Library C2
Charles St (Heol Siarl) B3
Churchill Way B3
City Hall 🏛 A2
City Rd A3
Clare Rd C1
Clare St C1
Coburn St A3
Coldstream Terrace B1
College Rd A1
Colum Rd A1
Court C2
Court Rd C1
Craiglee Drive C3
Cranbrook St A3
Customhouse St C2
Cyfartha St A3
Despenser Place C1
Despenser St C1
Dinas St C1
Duke St (Heol y Dug) B2
Dumfries Place B3
East Grove A3
Ellen St C3
Fire Station B3
Fitzalan Place B3
Fitzhamon Emb C1
Fitzhamon Lane C1
Friary, The B2
g39 🏛 B2
Gloucester St C1
Glynrhondda St A2
Gordon Rd A3
Gorsedd Gardens B2
Green St B1
Greyfriars Rd B2
Hafod St C1
Hayes, The B2
Herbert St C3
High St B2
HM Prison B3
Industrial Estate C3
Information Centre ℹ B2
John St C3
Jubilee St C1
King Edward VII Ave A1
Kingsway (Ffordd y Brenin) B2
Knox Rd B3
Law Courts B2
Llanbleddian Gdns A2
Llantwit St A2
Lloyd George Avenue C3
Lower Cathedral Rd B1
Lowther Rd A3
Magistrates Court B3
Mansion House A3
Mardy St C1
Mark St B1
Market B2
Mary Ann St C3
Merches Gardens C1
Mill Lane C2
Millennium Bridge B1
Miskin St A2
Monmouth St C1
Motorpoint Arena Cardiff ✦ C3
Museum Avenue A2
Museum Place A2
National Museum Cardiff 🏛 A2
National War Meml ✦ A2
Neville Place C1
New Theatre 🎭 B2
Newport Rd B3
Northcote Lane A3
Northcote St A3
Parade, The A3
Park Grove A4
Park Place A2
Park St C2
Penarth Rd C2
Pendyris St C1
Plantaganet St C1
Post Office B2
Principality Stadium C1
Principality Stadium Tours (Gate 3) ✦ B2
Quay St B2
Queen's Arcade B2
Queen Anne Square A1
Queen St (Heol y Frenhines) B2
Queen St Station ⇌ B3
Regimental Museums 🏛 B2
Rhymney St A3
Richmond Rd A3
Royal Welsh College of Music and Drama A1
Russell St A3
Ruthin Gardens A2
St Andrews Place A2
St David's B2/C2
St David's ✝ B2
St David's Hall ✦ B2
St John the Baptist ⛪ B2
St Mary St (Heol Eglwys Fair) B2
St Peter's St A3
Salisbury Rd A3
Sandon St B3
Schooner Way C3
Scott Rd C2
Scott St C2
Senghennydd Rd A2
Sherman Theatre 🎭 A2
Sophia Gardens A1
Sophia Gardens Stadium ✦ A1
South Wales Baptist College A3
Sport Wales National Centre ✦ A1
Stafford Rd C1
Stadium Plaza C1
Station Terrace B3
Stuttgarter Strasse B2
Sussex St C1
Taffs Mead Embankment C1
Talworth St A3
Temple of Peace & Health ✦ A1
Treharris St A3
Trinity St B2
Tudor Lane C1
Tudor St C1
Tyndall St C3
Vue 🎬 C1
Walk, The A3
Welsh Government A1
West Grove A3
Westgate St (Heol y Porth) B2
Windsor Place B3
Womanby St B2
Wood St C2
Working St B2
Wyeverne Rd A2

Carlisle 333

Abbey St A1
Aglionby St B3
Albion St C3
Alexander St C3
AMF Bowl ✦ C2
Annetwell St A1
Bank St B2
Bitts Park A1
Blackfriars St B2
Blencome St C1
Blunt St C1
Botchergate B2
Boustead's Grassing C2
Bowman St B3
Bridge St A1
Broad St B3
Brook St C3
Brunswick St B2
Bus Station B2
Caldew Bridge A1
Caldew St C1
Carlisle (Citadel) Station ⇌ B2
Carlisle College A2
Castle 🏰 A1
Castle St A1
Castle Way A1
Cathedral ✝ A1
Cecil St B2
Chapel St A2
Charles St B3
Charlotte St B1
Chatsworth Square A2
Chiswick St B2
Citadel, The ✦ B2
City Walls A1
Civic Centre A2
Clifton St C1
Close St B3
Collingwood St C1
Colville St C1
Colville Terrace C1
Council Offices B3
Court B2
Court St Brow B2
Crosby St B2
Crown St C2
Currock Rd C2
Dacre Rd A1

Dale St C1
Denton St C1
Devonshire Walk A1
Duke's Rd A2
East Dale St C1
East Norfolk St C1
Eden Bridge A2
Edward St B3
Elm St B1
English St B2
Fire Station A2
Fisher St A1
Flower St B3
Freer St C1
Fusehill St B3
Georgian Way A2
Gloucester Rd C3
Golf Course A2
Graham St C1
Grey St B3
Guildhall Museum A2
Halfey's Lane B3
Hardwicke Circus A2
Hart St B3
Hewson St C2
Howard Place A3
Howe St B3
Information Centre A2
James St B2
Junction St B1
King St B2
Lancaster St B2
Lanes Shopping Centre, The B2
Laser Quest B2
Library A2
Lime St B1
Lindisfarne St C3
Linton St B3
Lismore Place A3
Lismore St B3
London Rd C3
Lonsdale Rd B2
Lord St C3
Lorne Crescent B1
Lorne St B1
Lowther St B2
Madford Retail Park B1
Magistrates' Court A2
Market Hall A2
Mary St B2
Memorial Bridge A3
Metcalfe St C1
Milbourne St B1
Myddleton St B3
Nelson St C1
Norfolk St C1
Old Fire Sta, The A2
Old Town Hall A2
Oswald St C3
Peter St A2
Petteril St B3
Pools B2
Portland Place B2
Portland Square B2
Post Office A2/B2/C1/C3
Princess St C2
Pugin St B1
Red Bank Terrace C2
Regent St C3
Richardson St C1
Rickerby Park A3
Rickergate A2
River St B3
Rome St C2
Rydal St B3
St Cuthbert's B2
St Cuthbert's Lane B2
St James' Park C1
St James' Rd C1
St Nicholas Gate Retail Park C3
St Nicholas St C3
Sands Centre, The A2
Scotch St A2
Shaddongate B1
Sheffield St B1
Shopmobility A2
South Henry St B3
South John St C2
South St B3
Spencer St B2
Station Retail Park B2
Strand Rd A2
Superstore B1
Sybil St B3
Tait St B2
Thomas St B1
Thomson St C3
Trafalgar St C1
Trinity Leisure Centre A2
Tullie Museum & Art Gallery A1
Tyne St C3
University of Cumbria B3
Viaduct Estate Rd B1
Victoria Place A2
Victoria Viaduct B2
Vue B2
Warwick Rd B2
Warwick Square B3
Water St B2
West Walls B1
Westmorland St C1

Chelmsford 333

Anchor St C1
Anglia Ruskin Univ A2
Arbour Lane A3
Baddow Rd B2/C3
Baker St C1
Barrack Square B2
Bellmead B2
Bishop Hall Lane A2
Bishop Rd A2
Bond St B2
Boswells Drive B3
Bouverie Rd C2
Bradford St C1
Braemar Avenue C1
Brook St A2
Broomfield Rd A1
Burgess Springs B1
Burns Crescent C2
Bus Station B1/B2
Cedar Avenue A1
Cedar Avenue West A1
Cemetery A1
Cemetery A2
Cemetery C1
Central Park B1
Chelmsford B2
Chelmsford A1
Chichester Drive A3
Chinery Close A3
City Council A1
Civic Centre A1
Civic Theatre B1
Cloudfm County Cricket Ground, The B2
College C1
Cottage Place A2
County Hall B2
Coval Avenue B1
Coval Lane B1
Coval Wells B1
Crown Court B2
Duke St B2
Elm Rd C1
Elms Drive A1
Essex Record Office, The B3
Fairfield Rd B1
Falcons Mead B1
George St C2
Glebe Rd A1
Godfrey's Mews C2
Goldlay Avenue C3
Goldlay Rd C2
Grove Rd C2
Hall St C2
Hamlet Rd C2
Hart St C1
Henry Rd A2
High Bridge Rd B2
High Chelmer Shopping Centre B2
High St B2
Hill Crescent B3
Hill Rd B3
Hill Rd Sth B3
Hillview Rd A3
HM Prison A3
Hoffmans Way A2
Hospital B2
Lady Lane C2
Langdale Gardens C3
Legg St B2
Library B2
Lionfield Terrace A3
Lower Anchor St C1
Lynmouth Avenue C2
Lynmouth Gardens C3
Magistrates Court B2
Maltese Rd A1
Manor Rd C2
Marconi Rd A2
Market A2
Market Rd B2
Marlborough Rd C1
Meadows Shopping Centre, The B2
Meadowside A3
Mews Court C2
Mildmay Rd C2
Moulsham Drive C2
Moulsham Mill C3
Moulsham St C1/C2
Navigation Rd B3
New London Rd B2/C1
New St A2/B2
New Writtle St C1
Nursery Rd C2
Orchard St C2
Odeon B2
Parker Rd C2
Parklands Drive A3
Parkway A1/B1/B2
Police Station A2
Post Office B2/C2
Primrose Hill A1
Prykes Drive B1
Queen St C1
Queen's Rd B3
Railway St A1
Rainsford Rd A1
Ransomes Way A2
Rectory Lane A2
Regina Rd A2
Riverside Ice & Leisure Centre B2
Riverside Retail Park A3
Rosebery Rd C2
Rothesay Avenue C1
St John's Rd C2
Sandringham Place B3
Seymour St B1
Shopmobility B2
Shrublands Close B3
Southborough Rd C1
Springfield Rd A3/B2/B3
Stapleford Close C1
Superstore B2/C3
Swiss Avenue A1
Telford Place A3
Tindal St B2
Townfield St A1
Trinity Rd B3
University B1
Upper Bridge Rd C1
Upper Roman Rd C2
Van Dieman's Rd C3
Viaduct Rd B1
Vicarage Rd C1
Victoria Rd A2
Victoria Rd South B2
Vincents Rd C2
Waterloo Lane B2
Weight Rd B3
Westfield Avenue A1
Wharf Rd B3
Writtle Rd C1
YMCA A2
York Rd C1

Cheltenham 333

Albert Rd A3
Albion St B3
All Saints Rd B3
Ambrose St B2
Andover Rd C1
Back Montpellier Terr C2
Bandstand C2
Bath Parade B2
Bath Rd C2
Bays Hill Rd C1
Bennington St B2
Berkeley St B3
Brewery Quarter, The A2
Brunswick St South A2
Bus Station B2
Carlton St B3
Central Cross Road A3
Cheltenham College C2
Cheltenham FC A3
Cheltenham General (A&E) C3
Cheltenham Ladies' College B2
Christchurch Rd B1
Cineworld A2
Clarence Rd A2
Clarence Square A2
Clarence St B2
Cleeveland St A1
College Baths Road C3
College Rd C2
Colletts Drive A1
Corpus St C3
Devonshire St A2
Douro Rd B1
Duke St B3
Dunalley Parade A2
Dunalley St A2
Everyman B2
Evesham Rd A3
Fairview Rd B3
Fairview St B3
Fire Station C3
Folly Lane A2
Gloucester Rd A1
Grosvenor St B3
Grove St A1
Hanover St A2
Hatherley St C1
Henrietta St A2
Hewlett Rd B3
High St B2/B3
Holst Birthplace Museum A3
Hudson St A2
Imperial Gardens C2
Imperial Lane B2
Imperial Square C2
Information Centre B2
Keynsham Rd C3
King St A2
Knapp Rd B2
Lansdown Crescent C1
Lansdown Rd C1
Leighton Rd B3
Library B2
London Rd C3
Lypiatt Rd C1
Malvern Rd B1
Manser St A2
Market St A1
Marle Hill Parade A2
Marle Hill Rd A2
Millbrook St A1
Milsom St A2
Montpellier Gardens C2
Montpellier Grove C2
Montpellier Parade C2
Montpellier Spa Rd C2
Montpellier St C1
Montpellier Terrace C2
Montpellier Walk C2
New St B2
North Place B2
Old Bath Rd C3
Oriel Rd B2
Overton Park Rd B1
Overton Rd B1
Oxford St C3
Parabola Rd B1
Park Place C1
Park St A1
Pittville Circus A3
Pittville Crescent A3
Pittville Lawn A3
Pittville Park A2
Playhouse B2
Portland St B3
Prestbury Rd A3
Prince's Rd C1
Priory St B3
Promenade B2
Queen St A1
Recreation Ground A2
Regent Arcade B2
Regent St B2
Rodney Rd B2
Royal Crescent B2
Royal Well Place B2
Royal Wells Rd B2
St George's Place B2
St Georges Rd B1
St Gregory's B2
St James St B3
St John's Avenue B3
St Luke's Rd C2
St Margarets Rd A2
St Mary's B2
St Matthew's B2
St Paul's Lane A2
St Paul's Rd A2
St Paul's St A2
St Stephen's Rd C1
Sandford Parks Lido C3
Sandford Mill Road C3
Sandford Park C3
Sandford Rd C2
Selkirk St A3
Sherborne Place B3
Sherborne St B3
Suffolk Parade C2
Suffolk Rd C1
Suffolk Square C1
Sun St A1
Swindon Rd B2
Sydenham Villas Rd C3
Tewkesbury Rd A1
The Courtyard B1
Thirlstaine Rd C2
Tivoli Rd C1
Tivoli St C1
Town Hall & Theatre B2
Townsend St A1
Trafalgar St C2
Union St B3
Univ of Gloucestershire (Francis Close Hall) A2
Univ of Gloucestershire (Hardwick) A1
Victoria Place B3
Victoria St A2
Vittoria Walk C2
Wellesley Rd A2
Wellington Rd A3
Wellington Square A3
Wellington St B2
West Drive A3
Western Rd B1
Wilson, The B2
Winchcombe St B3
Winston Churchill Memorial Gardens A1

Chester 333

Abbey Gateway A2
Appleyards Lane C3
Bars, The B3
Bedward Row B1
Beeston View C3
Bishop Lloyd's Palace B2
Black Diamond St A2
Bottoms Lane C3
Boughton B3
Bouverie St A1
Bus Interchange A2
Bridge St B2
Bridgegate C2
Brook St A3
Brown's Lane C2
Cambrian Rd A1
Canal St A2
Carrick Rd C1
Castle C2
Castle Drive C2
Cathedral B2
Catherine St A1
Cheshire Military Museum C2
Chester A3
Cheyney Rd A1
Chichester St A1
City Rd A3
City Walls B1/B2
City Walls Rd B1
Cornwall St A2
Cross Hey C3
Cross, The B2
Crown Court C2
Cuppin St B2
Curzon Park North C1
Curzon Park South C1
Dee Basin A1
Dee Lane B3
Delamere St A2
Deva Roman Discovery Centre B2
Dingle, The C1
Duke St B2
Eastgate B2
Eastgate St B2
Eaton Rd C2
Edinburgh Way C3
Elizabeth Crescent B3
Fire Station A2
Foregate St B2
Forum Studio B2
Forum, The B2
Frodsham St B2
Gamul House B2
Garden Lane A1
George St A2
Gladstone Avenue A1
God's Providence House B2
Gorse Stacks A2
Greenway St C2
Grosvenor Bridge C1
Grosvenor Museum B2
Grosvenor Park B3
Grosvenor Park Terrace C1
Grosvenor Shopping Centre B2
Grosvenor St B2
Groves Rd B3
Groves, The B3
Guildhall Museum B1
Handbridge C2
Hartington St C3
Hoole Way A2
Hunter St B2
Information Centre B2
King Charles' Tower A2
King St A2
Library B2
Lightfoot St A3
Little Roodee C2
Liverpool Rd A2
Love St B3
Lower Bridge St B2
Lower Park Rd B3
Lyon St A2
Magistrates Court B2
Meadows Lane C3
Meadows, The B3
Milton St A3
Minerva Roman Shrine C2
Miniature Railway B3
New Crane St B1
Nicholas St B2
Northgate A2
Northgate Arena A2
Northgate St A2
Nun's Rd B1
Old Dee Bridge C2
Overleigh Rd C2
Park St B2
Police Station B2
Post Office A2/A3
Princess St B2
Queen St B2
Queen's Park Rd C3
Queen's Rd A3
Race Course B1
Raymond St A1
River Lane C2
Roman Amphitheatre & Gardens B2
Roodee (Chester Racecourse), The B1
Russell St A3
St Anne St A2
St George's Crescent C3
St Martin's Gate A1
St Martin's Way B1
St Oswalds Way A2
Saughall Rd A1
Sealand Rd A1
South View Rd A1
Stanley Palace B1
Station Rd A3
Steven St A3
Storyhouse B2
Superstore B2
Tower Rd B1
Town Hall B2
Union St B3
University of Chester C2
Vicar's Lane B2
Victoria Crescent C3
Victoria Rd A2
Walpole St A1
Water Tower St A1
Water Tower, The B1
Watergate B1
Watergate St B2
Whipcord Lane A1
White Friars B2
York St B3

Chichester 333

Adelaide Rd A3
Alexandra Rd A3
Arts Centre B2
Ave de Chartres B1/B2
Barlow Rd A1
Basin Rd C2
Beech Avenue B1
Bishops Palace Gardens B2
Bishopsgate Walk A3
Bramber Rd C3
Broyle Rd A2
Bus Station B2
Caledonian Rd B3
Cambrai Avenue B3
Canal Place C1
Canal Wharf C2
Canon Lane B2
Cathedral B2
Cavendish St A1
Cawley Rd B2
Cedar Drive A1
Chapel St A2
Cherry Orchard Rd C3
Chichester B2
Chichester By-Pass C2/C3
Chichester College B1
Chichester Cinema B3
Chichester Festival A2
Chichester Gate Leisure Park C1
Churchside A2
Cineworld C1
City Walls B2
Cleveland Rd B3
College Lane A2
Cory Close C2
Council Offices B2
County Hall B2
District B2
Duncan Rd A1
Durnford Close A1
East Pallant B2
East Row B2
East St B2
East Walls B3
Eastland Rd C3
Ettrick Close B3
Ettrick Rd B3
Exton Rd C3
Fire Station A2
Football Ground A2
Franklin Place A2
Friary (Rems of) A2
Garland Close C3
Green Lane A3
Grove Rd C3
Guilden Rd B3
Guildhall A2
Hawthorn Close A1
Hay Rd C3
Henty Gardens B1
Herald Drive C3
Hornet, The B3
Information Centre B2
John's St B3
Joys Croft A3
Jubilee Park A3
Jubilee Rd A3
Juxon Close B2
Kent Rd A3
King George Gardens A2
King's Avenue C2
Kingsham Avenue C3
Kingsham Rd C2
Laburnum Grove B2
Leigh Rd C1
Lennox Rd A3
Lewis Rd A3
Library B2
Lion St B2
Litten Terrace A3
Litten, The A3
Little London B2
Lyndhurst Rd B3
Market B3
Market Avenue B2
Market Cross B2
Market Rd B3
Melbourne Rd A3
Minerva A2
Mount Lane B1
New Park Rd A3
Newlands Lane A1
North Pallant B2
North St A2
North Walls A2
Northgate A2
Novium, The B2
Oak Avenue A1
Oak Close A1
Oaklands Park A2
Oaklands Way A2
Orchard Avenue A1
Orchard St A1
Ormonde Avenue B3
Pallant House B2
Parchment St A1
Parklands Rd A1/B1
Peter Weston Place B3
Police Station C2
Post Office A1/B2/C3
Priory Lane A2
Priory Park A2
Priory Rd A2
Queen's Avenue C1
Riverside A3
Roman Amphitheatre B3
St Cyriacs A2
St Martins' St B2
St Pancras A3
St Paul's Rd A2
St Richard's Hospital (A&E) A3
Shamrock Close A3
Sherbourne Rd A1
Somerstown A2
South Bank C2
South Downs Planetarium C2
South Pallant B2
South St B2
Southgate B2
Spitalfield Lane A3
Stirling Rd B3
Stockbridge Rd C1/C2
Swanfield Drive A3
Terminus Ind Est C1
Tower St A2
Tozer Way A3
Turnbull Rd A3
Upton Rd C1
Velyn Avenue B3
Via Ravenna B1
Walnut Avenue A1
West St B2
Westgate B1
Westgate Fields B1
Westgate Leisure Ctr B1
Weston Avenue C1
Whyke Close C3
Whyke Lane B3
Whyke Rd C3
Winden Avenue B3

Colchester 333

Abbey Gateway C2
Albert St A1
Albion Grove C2
Alexandra Rd C1
Artillery St C3
Arts Centre B1
Balkerne Hill B1
Barrack St C3
Beaconsfield Rd C1
Beche Rd C3
Bergholt Rd A1
Bourne Rd C3
Brick Kiln Rd A1
Brigade Grove C2
Bristol Rd B2
Broadlands Way A3
Brook St B3
Bury Close B2
Bus Station B2
Butt Rd C1
Campion Rd C2
Cannon St C3
Canterbury Rd C2
Captain Gardens C2
Castle B2
Castle Park B2
Castle Rd B2
Catchpool Rd A1
Causton Rd B1
Chandlers Row C3
Circular Rd East C2
Circular Rd North C1
Circular Rd West C1
Clarendon Way A1
Claudius Rd C2
Colchester A1
Colchester Camp Abbey Field C1
Colchester Retail Park B1
Colchester Town C2
Colne Bank Avenue A1
Colne View Retail Park A2
Compton Rd A3
Cowdray Avenue A1/A2
Cowdray Centre, The A2
Crouch St B1
Crowhurst Rd B1
Culver Square Shopping Centre B1
Culver St East B2
Culver St West B1
Dilbridge Rd A3
East Hill B2
East St B3
East Stockwell St B1
Eld Lane B1
Essex Hall Rd A1
Exeter Drive B2
Fairfax Rd C2
Fire Station A2
Firstsite B2
Flagstaff Rd C1
Garrison Parade C2
George St B2
Gladstone Rd C2
Golden Noble Hill C2
Goring Rd A3
Granville Rd C3
Greenstead Rd B3
Guildford Rd B2
Harsnett Rd C3
Harwich Rd B3
Head St B1
High St B1/B2
High Woods Country Park A2
Hollytrees B2
Hyderabad Close C2
Hythe Hill C3
Information Centre B2
Jarmin Rd A2
Kendall Rd C2
Kimberley Rd C3
King Stephen Rd C3
Leisure World A2
Library B1
Lincoln Way B2
Lion Walk Shopping Centre B1
Lisle Rd C2
Lucas Rd C2
Magdalen Green C3
Magdalen St C2
Maidenburgh St B2
Maldon Rd C1
Manor Rd B1
Margaret Rd A1
Mason Rd A2
Mercers Way A1
Mercury B1
Mersea Rd C2
Meyrick Crescent C2
Mile End Rd A1
Military Rd C2
Mill St C2
Minories B2
Moorside B3
Morant Rd C3
Napier Rd C2
Natural History B2
New Town Rd C2
Norfolk Crescent A3
North Hill B1
North Station Rd A1
Northgate St B1
Nunns Rd B1
Odeon B1
Old Coach Rd B3
Old Heath Rd C3
Osborne St B2
Petrolea Close A1
Police Station C1
Popes Lane B1
Port Lane C3
Post Office B2/C1
Priory St B2
Queen St B2
Rawstorn Rd B1
Rebon St C3
Recreation Rd C3
Ripple Way A3
Roberts Rd C2
Roman Rd B2
Roman Wall B2
Romford Close A3
Rosebery Avenue B2
St Andrews Avenue B3
St Andrews Gardens B3
St Botolph St B2
St Botolphs B2
St John's Abbey (site of) C2
St John's St B1
St Johns Walk Shopping Centre B1
St Leonards Rd C3
St Marys Fields B1
St Peter's St B1
St Peters B1
Salisbury Avenue C1
Saw Mill Rd C3
Sergeant St C2
Serpentine Walk A1
Sheepen Place B1
Sheepen Rd B1
Sir Isaac's Walk B1
Smythies Avenue B2
South St C1
South Way C1
Sports Way A2
Suffolk Close A3
Superstore A1
Town Hall B1
Valentine Drive A3
Victor Rd C3
Wakefield Close B2
Wellesley Rd C1
Wells Rd B2/B3
West St C1
West Stockwell St B1
Weston Rd C3
Westway A1
Wickham Rd C1
Wimpole Rd C3
Winchester Rd C2
Winnock Rd C2
Worcester Rd B2

Coventry 334

Abbots Lane A1
Albany B1
Albany Rd B1
Alma St B3
Ambulance Station A2
Art Faculty B3
Asthill Grove C2
Bablake School A1
Barras Lane A1/B1
Barr's Hill School A1
Belgrade B2
Bishop St A2
Bond's Hospital B1
Broad Gate B2
Broadway C1
Burges, The B2
Bus Station A3
Butts Radial B1
Byron St A3
Canterbury St A3
Cathedral B3
Central Six Retail Park C1
Chester St A1
Cheylesmore Manor House B2
Christ Church Spire B2
City College A3
City Walls & Gates A2
Corporation St B2
Council House B2
Coundon Rd A1
Coventry Station C2
Coventry Transport Museum A2
Coventry University Technology Park C3
Cox St A3
Croft Rd B1
Dalton Rd C1
Deasy Rd C3
Earl St B2
Eaton Rd C2
Fairfax St B2
Fire Station A2
Foleshill Rd A2
Ford's Hospital B2
Fowler Rd A1
Friars Rd C2
Gordon St C1
Gosford St B3
Greyfriars Green B2
Greyfriars Rd B2
Gulson Rd B3
Hales St A2
Harnall Lane East A3
Harnall Lane West A2
Herbert Art Gallery & Museum B3
Hertford St B2
Hewitt Avenue A1
High St B2
Hill St B1
Holy Trinity B2
Holyhead Rd A1
Howard St A3
Huntingdon Rd C1
Information Centre B3
Jordan Well B3
King Henry VIII Sch C1
Lady Godiva Statue B2
Lamb St A2
Leicester Row A2
Library B2
Lincoln St A2
Little Park St B2
London Rd C3
Lower Ford St B3
Lower Precinct Shopping Centre B2
Magistrates & Crown Courts B2
Manor House Drive B2
Manor Rd C2
Market B2
Martyrs Memorial C2
Meadow St B1
Meriden St A1
Michaelmas Rd C2
Middleborough Rd A1
Mile Lane C3
Millennium Place A2
Much Park St B3
Naul's Mill Park A1
New Union B2
Odeon B1
Park Rd C2
Parkside C3
Planet Ice Arena B1
Post Office A3,B2
Primrose Hill St A3
Priory Gardens & Visitor Centre B2
Priory St B3
Puma Way C3
Quarryfield Lane C3
Queen's Rd B1
Quinton Rd C2
Radford Rd A2
Raglan St B3
Ringway (Hill Cross) A1
Ringway (Queens) B1
Ringway (Rudge) B1
Ringway (St Johns) B3
Ringway (St Nicholas) A2
Ringway (St Patricks) C2
Ringway (Swanswell) A2
Ringway (Whitefriars) B3
St John the Baptist B2
St Nicholas St A2
Sidney Stringer Acad A3
Skydome B1
Spencer Avenue C1
Spencer Rec Gnd C1
Spencer Rd C1
Spon St B1
Sports Centre B3
Stoney Rd C2
Stoney Stanton Rd A3
Superstore B2
Swanswell Pool A3
Thomas Landsdail St C2
Tomson Avenue A1
Top Green C1
Tower St A2
Trinity St B2
University B3
University Sports Ctr B3
Upper Hill St A1
Upper Well St A2
Victoria St A3
Vine St A3
Wave, The B2
Warwick Rd C2
Waveley Rd B1
West Orchards Shopping Centre B2
Westminster Rd C1
White St A3
Windsor St B1

Derby 334

Abbey St C1
Agard St B1
Albert St B2
Albion St B2
Ambulance Station B1
Arthur St A1
Ashlyn Rd B3
Assembly Rooms B2
Babington Lane C2
Bass Recreation Gd B3
Becket St B1
Belper Rd A1
Bold Lane B1
Bradshaw Way C2
Bradshaw Way Retail Park C2
Bridge St B1
Brook St B1
Burton Rd C1
Bus Station B2
Business Park A3
Caesar St A2
Canal St C3
Carrington St C3
Cathedral B2
Cathedral Rd B1
Charnwood St C2
Chester Green Rd A2
City Rd A2
Clarke St A3
Cock Pitt Junction B3
Council House B2
Courts B1
Cranmer Rd B3
Crompton St C1
Crown & County Courts B2
Curzon St B1
Darley Grove A1
Derbion C2
Derby C3
Derby C2
Derby Gaol B1
Derwent Bsns Centre A2
Derwent St B2
Drewry Lane C1
Duffield Rd A1
Duke St A2
Dunton Close B3
Eagle Market C2
East St B2
Eastgate B3
Exeter St B2
Farm St C1
Ford St B1
Forester St C1
Fox St A2
Friar Gate B1
Friary St B1
Full St B2
Garden St A1
Gerard St C1
Gower St C2
Green Lane C2
Grey St C1
Guildhall B2
Handyside Bridge A2
Harcourt St C1
Highfield Rd A1
Hill Lane C2
Incora County Ground (Derbyshire CCC), The B3
Information Centre B2
Iron Gate B2
John St C3
Joseph Wright Centre B1
Kedleston Rd A1
Key St B2
King Alfred St C1
King St A1
Kingston St A1
Lara Croft Way C2
Leopold St C2
Liversage St C3
Lodge Lane B1
London Rd C2
London Rd Community Hospital C2
Macklin St C1
Mansfield Rd A2
Market B2
Market Place B2
May St C1
Meadow Lane B3
Melbourne St C2
Mercian Way C1
Midland Rd C3
Monk St C1
Morledge B2
Mount St C1
Mus & Art Gallery B1

Museum of Making .B2
North Parade .A1
North St .A1
Nottingham Rd .B3
Osmaston Rd .C2
Otter St .A1
Park St .C3
Parker St .A1
Pickford's House .B1
Police Station .A2, B2
Post Office .A1/A2/B1/C2/C3
Pride Parkway .C3
Prime Enterprise Park A2
Prime Parkway .A2
QUAD ✦ .B2
Queens Leisure Ctr .B1
Racecourse Park .A3
Railway Terrace .C3
Register Office .B2
Riverlights Leisure Ctr B2
Sadler Gate .B1
St Alkmund's Way .B1/B2
St Helens House ✦ .A1
St Mary's .A1
St Mary's Bridge .A2
St Mary's Bridge Chapel .A2
St Mary's Gate .B1
St Paul's Rd .A2
St Peter's .C2
St Peter's St .C2
Showcase De Lux .C2
Siddals Rd .C3
Sir Frank Whittle Rd .A3
Spa Lane .C1
Spring St .C1
Stafford St .B1
Station Approach .C3
Stockbrook St .C1
Stores Rd .A3
Traffic St .C2
Wardwick .B1
Werburgh St .C1
West Avenue .A1
West Meadows Ind Est B3
Wharf Rd .A2
Wilmot St .C2
Wilson St .C1
Wood's Lane .C1

Dorchester 334

Ackerman Rd .B3
Acland Rd .A2
Albert Rd .A1
Alexandra Rd .B1
Alfred Place .B3
Alfred Rd .B2
Alington Avenue .B3
Alington Rd .B3
Ashley Rd .B1
Balmoral Crescent .C3
Barnes Way .B2/C2
Borough Gardens .A1
Brewery Square .B1
Bridport Rd .A1
Buckingham Way .C3
Caters Place .A1
Cemetery .A3/C1
Charles St .A2
Coburg Rd .B1
Colliton St .A1
Cornwall Rd .A1
Cromwell Rd .B1
Culliford Rd .B2
Culliford Rd North .B2
Dagmar Rd .B1
Damer's Rd .B1
Diggory Crescent .C2
Dinosaur Museum .A2
Dorchester Bypass .C2
Dorchester South Station .B1
Dorchester West Station .B1
Dorset County (A&E) .B1
Dorset County Council Offices .A1
Dorset County Mus .A1
Duchy Close .C3
Duke's Avenue .B2
Durngate St .A2
Durnover Court .A3
Eddison Avenue .B3
Edward Rd .B1
Egdon Rd .C2
Elizabeth Frink Statue ✦ .B2
Farfrae Crescent .B2
Forum Centre, The .B1
Friary Hill .A2
Friary Lane .A2
Frome Terrace .A2
Garland Crescent .C3
Glyde Path Rd .A1
Grosvenor Crescent .C1
Grosvenor Rd .C1
Grove, The .A1
Gt Western Rd .B1
Herrington Rd .C1
High St East .A2
High St Fordington .A2
High Street West .A1
Holloway Rd .A2
Icen Way .A2
Information Centre .B2
Keep Military Museum, The .A1
Kings Rd .A3/B3
Kingsbere Crescent .C2
Lancaster Rd .B2
Library .A1
Lime Close .C1
Linden Avenue .B2
London Close .A3
London Rd .A2/A3
Lubbecke Way .A3
Lucetta Lane .B2
Maiden Castle Rd .C1
Manor Rd .C2
Market .B1
Marshwood Place .B2
Maumbury Rd .B1
Maumbury Rings .B1
Mellstock Avenue .C2
Mill St .A3
Miller's Close .A1
Mistover Close .C1
Monmouth Rd .B1/B2
Moynton Rd .C2
Nature Reserve .A2
North Square .A2
Northernhay .A1
Odeon .B1
Old Crown Court & Cells .A1
Olga Rd .B1
Orchard St .A2
Plaza .B1
Police Station .B1
Post Office .A1
Pound Lane .A2
Poundbury Rd .A1
Prince of Wales Rd .B2
Prince's St .A1
Queen's Avenue .B1
Roman Town House .A1
Roman Wall .A1
Rothesay Rd .C2
St George's Rd .B3
Salisbury Field .A2
Sandringham Sports Centre .B3
Shaston Crescent .C2
Smokey Hole Lane .B3
South Court Avenue .C1
South St .B1
South Walks Rd .B2
Superstore .C3
Teddy Bear Mus .A1
Temple Close .C1
Terracotta Warriors & Teddy Bear Mus .A2
Town Hall .A2
Town Pump ✦ .A2
Trinity St .A1
Tutankhamun Exhibition .A1
Victoria Rd .B1
Weatherbury Way .C2
Wellbridge Close .C1
West Mills Rd .A1
West Walks Rd .A1
Weymouth Avenue .C1
Williams Avenue .B1
Winterbourne (BMI) .C1
Wollaston Rd .A2
York Rd .B2

Dumfries 334

Academy St .A2
Aldermanhill Rd .B3
Ambulance Station .C3
Annan Rd .A3
Ardwall Rd .A3
Ashfield Drive .A1
Atkinson Rd .C1
Averill Crescent .C1
Balliol Avenue .C1
Bank St .B2
Bankend Rd .C3
Barn Slaps .B3
Barrie Avenue .B3
Beech Avenue .A1
Bowling Green .A3
Brewery St .B1
Bridgend Theatre .B1
Brodie Avenue .C2
Brooke St .B2
Broomlands Drive .C1
Brooms Rd .B3
Buccleuch St .A2
Burns House .B2
Burns Mausoleum .B3
Burns St .B2
Burns Statue ✦ .A2
Bus Station .B1
Cardoness St .A3
Castle St .A2
Catherine St .A2
Cattle Market .A3
Cemetery .B3
Cemetery .C2
Church Crescent .A2
Church St .B2
College Rd .A1
College St .A1
Corbelly Hill .B1
Corberry Park .B1
Cornwall Mt .A3
Council Offices .A2
Court .A2
Craigs Rd .C3
Cresswell Avenue .B3
Cresswell Hill .B3
Cumberland St .B3
David Keswick Athletic Centre .A3
David St .B1
Dock Park .C3
Dockhead .B2
Dumfries .A3
Dumfries Academy .A2
Dumfries Ice Bowl .A1
Dumfries Museum & Camera Obscura .B2
Dumfries & Galloway Royal Infirmary (A&E) .C3
East Riverside Drive .C3
Edinburgh Rd .A2
English St .B2
Fire Station .B3
Friar's Vennel .A2
Galloway St .B1
George Douglas Drive .C1
George St .A2
Gladstone Rd .C2
Glasgow St .A1
Glebe St .B3
Glencaple Rd .C3
Goldie Avenue .A1
Goldie Crescent .A1
Golf Course .C3
Gracefield Arts Ctr .A2
Greyfriars .A2
Grierson Avenue .B3
Hamilton Avenue .C1
Hamilton Starke Park .C2
Hazelrigg Avenue .C1
Henry St .B3
Hermitage Drive .C1
High Cemetery .C3
High St .A2
Hill Avenue .C2
Hill St .B1
HM Prison .B1
Holm Avenue .C2
Hoods Loaning .A3
Howgate St .B1
Huntingdon Rd .A3
Information Centre .B2
Irish St .B2
Irving St .A2
King St .A1
Kingholm Rd .C3
Kirkpatrick Court .C2
Laurieknowe .B1
Leafield Rd .B3
Library .A2
Lochfield Rd .A1
Loreburn Park .A3
Loreburn St .A2
Loreburne Shopping Centre .B2
Lover's Walk .A2
Martin Avenue .B3
Mausoleum .B3
Maxwell St .B1
McKie Avenue .B3
Mews Lane .A2
Mid Steeple ✦ .B2
Mill Green .B2
Mill Rd .B1
Moat Rd .C2
Moffat Rd .A3
Mountainhall Park .C3
Nelson St .B1
New Abbey Rd .B1/C1
New Bridge .B1
Newall Terrace .A2
Nith Avenue .A2
Nith Bank .C3
Nithbank Hospital .C3
Nithside Avenue .A1
Odeon .B2
Old Bridge .B1
Old Bridge House .B1
Palmerston Park (Queen of the South FC) .A1
Park Rd .C1
Pleasance Avenue .C1
Police Headquarters .A3
Police Station .A2/A3
Portland Drive .A1
Post Office .B1/B2/B3
Priestlands Drive .C1
Primrose St .B1
Queen St .B3
Queensberry St .A2
Rae St .A2
Richmond Avenue .C2
Robert Burns Ctr .B2
Roberts Crescent .C1
Robertson Avenue .C3
Robinson Drive .C1
Rosefield Rd .C2
Rosemount St .B1
Rotchell Park .C1
Rotchell Rd .B1
Rugby Football Gd .C1
Ryedale Rd .C2
St Andrews .B2
St John the Evangelist .A2
St Josephs College .B3
St Mary's Ind Est .A3
St Mary's St .A3
St Michael St .B2
St Michael's .B2
St Michael's Bridge .B2
St Michael's Bridge Rd B2
St Michael's Cemetery B3
Shakespeare St .B2
Solway Drive .C2
Stakeford St .A1
Stark Crescent .C2
Station Rd .A3
Steel Avenue .A1
Sunderries Avenue .A1
Sunderries Rd .A1
Superstore .B3
Suspension Brae .B2
Swimming Pool .A1
Terregles St .B1
Theatre Royal .B2
Troqueer Rd .C2
Union St .A1
Wallace St .B3
Welldale .B2
West Riverside Drive .C2
White Sands .B2

Dundee 334

Abertay University .B2
Adelaide Place .A1
Airlie Place .C1
Albany Terrace .A1
Albert St .A3
Alexander St .A2
Ann St .A2
Arthurstone Terrace .A3
Bank St .B2
Barrack Rd .A1
Barrack St .B2
Bell St .B2
Blinshall St .B1
Broughty Ferry Rd .A3
Brown St .B1
Bus Station .B3
Caird Hall .B2
Camperdown St .B3
Candle Lane .B3
Carmichael St .A1
City Churches .B2
City Quay .B3
City Square .B2
Commercial St .B2
Constable St .A3
Constitution Crescent .A1
Constitution Court .A1
Constitution St .A1/B2
Cotton Rd .A3
Courthouse Square .B1
Cowgate .A3
Crescent St .A3
Crichton St .B2
Dens Brae .A3
Dens Rd .A3
Discovery Point ✦ .C2
Douglas St .B1
Drummond St .A1
Dudhope Castle .A1
Dudhope St .A2
Dudhope Terrace .A1
Dundee .C2
Dundee Contemporary Arts ✦ .C2
Dundee High School .B2
Dundee Law ✦ .A1
Dundee Rep .C2
Dunhope Park .A1
Dura St .A3
East Dock St .B3
East Marketgait .B3
East Whale Lane .B3
Erskine St .A3
Euclid Crescent .B2
Forebank Rd .A2
Foundry Lane .A3
Gallagher Retail Park .B3
Gellatly St .B3
Government Offices .C2
Guthrie St .B1
Hawkhill .B1
Hilltown .A2
HMS Unicorn ✦ .B3
Howff Cemetery, The .B2
Information Centre .B2
Keiller Shopping Centre .B2
Keiller Centre, The .B2
King St .A3
Kinghorne Rd .A1
Ladywell Avenue .A3
Laurel Bank .A2
Law Rd .A1
Law St .A1
Library .A2/A3
Library and Steps Theatre .A2
Little Theatre, The .A2
Lochee Rd .B1
Lower Princes St .A3
Lyon St .A3
McManus Art Gallery & Museum, The .B2
Meadow Side .B2
Meadowside St Pauls .B2
Mercat Cross ✦ .B2
Murraygate .B2
Nelson St .A2
Nethergate .B2/C1
North Lindsay St .B2
North Marketgait .B2
Old Hawkhill .B1
Olympia Leisure Centre .B3
Overgate Shopping Centre .B2
Park Place .B1
Perth Rd .C1
Police Station .B1
Post Office .B2
Princes St .A3
Prospect Place .A2
Reform St .B2
Riverside Drive .C2
Riverside Esplanade .C2
Roseangle .C1
Rosebank St .A2
RRS Discovery .C2
St Andrew's .C2
St Pauls Episcopal .B3
Science Centre ✦ .C2
Seagate .B2
Sheriffs Court .B1
Shopmobility .B2
South George St .A2
South Marketgait .B3
South Tay St .B2
South Victoria Dock Road .B3
South Ward Rd .B2
Tay Road Bridge ✦ .C3
Thomson Avenue .B2
Trades Lane .B3
Union St .B2
Union Terrace .A1
University Library .B2
University of Dundee .B1
Upper Constitution Street .A1
Verdant Works ✦ .B1
V&A Museum of Design .C2
Victoria Dock .B3
Victoria Rd .A2
Victoria St .A3
Ward Rd .B1
Wellgate .B2
West Bell St .B1
West Marketgait .B1/B2
Westfield Place .C1
William St .A3
Wishart Arch ✦ .A3

Durham 334

Alexander Crescent .B2
Allergate .B2
Archery Rise .C1
Assembly Rooms .B2
Avenue, The .B1
Back Western Hill .A1
Bakehouse Lane .A3
Baths Bridge .B3
Boat House .B3
Boyd St .C3
Bus Station .B2
Castle Chare .B2
Cathedral .B2
Church St .C3
Clay Lane .C1
Claypath .B3
College of St Hild & St Bede .B3
County Hospital .B1
Crescent, The .A1
Crook Hall & Gardens .A3
Crossgate .B2
Crossgate Peth .C1
Crown Court .B3
Darlington Rd .C1
Durham .A2
Durham Castle .B2
Durham School .C2
Durham University (Science Site) .C3
Ellam Avenue .C1
Elvet Bridge .B3
Elvet Court .B3
Farnley Hey .B1
Ferens Close .A3
Fieldhouse Lane .A1
Flass St .B1
Flass Vale Local Nature Reserve .A1
Framwelgate Bridge .B2
Framwelgate .A2
Framwelgate Peth .A2
Framwelgate Waterside .A2
Frankland Lane .A3
Freeman's Place .A3
Freeman's Quay Leisure Centre .A3
Gala Theatre & Cinema .B3
Geoffrey Avenue .C1
Gilesgate .B3
Grey College .C3
Grove, The .A1
Hallgarth St .C3
Hatfield College .B3
Hawthorn Terrace .B1
Heritage Centre .B3
HM Prison .B3
John St .B1
Kingsgate Bridge .B3
Laburnum Terrace .B1
Lawson Terrace .B1
Leazes Rd .B2/B3
Library .B2
Margery Lane .B2
Market .B2
Mavin St .C3
Millburngate .B2
Millburngate Bridge .B2
Millennium Bridge (foot/cycle) .A2
Mountjoy Research Centre .C3
Mus of Archaeology .B2
New Elvet .B3
New Elvet Bridge .B3
North Bailey .B3
North End .A1
Observatory .C1
Old Elvet .B3
Open Treasure .B2
Oriental Museum .C2
Oswald Court .C3
Passport Office .A2
Percy Terrace .B1
Pimlico .C2
Police Station .B3
Post Office .A1/B2
Potters Bank .C1/C2
Prebends Bridge .C2
Prebends Walk .C2
Prince Bishops Shopping Centre .B3
Princes St .A1
Providence Row .A3
Quarryheads Lane .C2
Redhills Lane .B1
Redhills Terrace .B1
Riverwalk, The .B2
Saddler St .B3
St Cuthbert's Society .C2
St Margaret's .B2
St Mary the Less .C2
St Mary's College .C2
St Monica Grove .B1
St Nicholas' .B3
St Oswald's .C3
Sands, The .A3
Shopmobility .B3
Sidegate .A2
Silver St .B2
Sixth Form College .A3
South Bailey .C2
South Rd .C3
South St .B2
Springwell Avenue .A1
Station Approach .B2
Stockton Rd .C3
Student Union .B3
Summerville .B1
Sutton St .B2
Town Hall .B2
University Arts Block .B3
University College ✦ .B2
Walkergate Centre .A3
Wearside Drive .A3
Western Hill .A1
Wharton Park .A2
Whinney Hill .C3
Whitehouse Avenue .C1
YHA .C3

Edinburgh 334

Abbey Strand .B6
Abbeyhill .A6
Abbeyhill Crescent .B6
Abbeymount .A6
Abercromby Place .A3
Adam St .C5
Albany Lane .A4
Albany St .A4
Albert Memorial ✦ .B2
Albyn Place .A2
Alva Place .A6
Alva St .B1
Ann St .A1
Appleton Tower .C4
Archibald Place .C3
Assembly Rooms & Musical Hall .A3
Atholl Crescent .B1
Atholl Crescent Lane .C1
Bank St .B4
Barony St .A4
Beaumont Place .C5
Belford Rd .B1
Belgrave Crescent .A1
Belgrave Cres Lane .A1
Bell's Brae .B1
Blackfriars St .B4
Blair St .B4
Bread St .C2
Bristo Place .C4
Bristo St .C4
Brougham St .C2
Broughton St .A4
Brown St .C5
Brunton Terrace .A6
Buckingham Terrace .A1
Burial Ground .A6
Bus Station .A4
Caledonian Crescent .C1
Caledonian Rd .C1
Calton Hill .A4
Calton Hill .A5
Calton Rd .B4
Camera Obscura & Outlook Tower ✦ .B3
Candlemaker Row .C4
Canning St .B2
Canongate .B5
Canongate .B5
Carlton St .A1
Carlton Terrace .A6
Carlton Terrace Lane .A6
Castle St .B2
Castle Terrace .B2
Castlehill .B3
Central Library .B4
Chalmers Hospital .C3
Chalmers St .C3
Chambers St .C4
Chapel St .C4
Charles St .C4
Charlotte Square .B2
Chester St .B1
Circus Lane .A2
Circus Place .A2
City Art Centre .B4
City Chambers .B4
City Observatory ✦ .A5
Clarendon Crescent .A1
Clerk St .C5
Coates Crescent .B1
Cockburn St .B4
College of Art .C3
Comely Bank Avenue .A1
Comely Bank Row .A1
Cornwall St .C2
Cowans Close .C5
Cowgate .B4
Cranston St .B5
Crichton St .C4
Croft-An-Righ .A6
Cumberland St .A2
Dalry Place .C1
Dalry Rd .C1
Danube St .A1
Darnawy St .A2
David Hume Tower .C4
Davie St .C5
Dean Bridge .A1
Dean Gardens .A1
Dean Park Crescent .A1
Dean Park Mews .A1
Dean Park St .A1
Dean Path .B1
Dean St .A1
Dean Terrace .A1
Dewar Place .C1
Dewar Place Lane .C1
Doune Terrace .A2
Drummond Place .A3
Drummond St .C5
Drumsheugh Gardens .B1
Dublin Mews .A3
Dublin St .A4
Dublin St Lane South .A4
Dumbiedykes Rd .B5
Dundas St .A3
Dynamic Earth ✦ .B6
Earl Grey St .C2
East Crosscauseway .C5
East Market St .B4
East Norton Place .A6
East Princes St Gdns .B3
Easter Rd .A6
Edinburgh (Waverley) .B4
Edinburgh Castle .B3
Edinburgh Dungeon ✦ B4
Edinburgh International Conference Centre .C2
Elder St .A4
Esplanade .B3
Eton Terrace .A1
Eye Pavilion .C3
Festival Office .B3
Festival Theatre Edinburgh .C4
Filmhouse .C2
Fire Station .C2
Floral Clock ✦ .B3
Forres St .A2
Forth St .A4
Fountainbridge .C2
Frederick St .A3
Freemasons' Hall .B3
Fruitmarket .B4
Gardner's Crescent .C2
George Heriot's School .C3
George IV Bridge .B4
George Square .C4
George Square Lane .C4
George St .B3
Georgian House .B2
Gladstone's Land .B3
Glen St .C3
Gloucester Lane .A2
Gloucester Place .A2
Gloucester St .A2
Graham St .C3
Grassmarket .C3
Great King St .A3
Great Stuart .B1
Greenside Lane .A5
Greenside Row .A5
Greyfriars Kirk .C4
Grindlay St .C2
Grosvenor St .C1
Grove St .C1
Gullan's Close .B5
Guthrie St .B4
Hanover St .A3
Hart St .A4
Haymarket .C1
Haymarket Station .C1
Heriot Place .C3
Heriot Row .A2
High School Yard .B5
High St .B4
Hill Place .C5
Hill St .A2
Hillside Crescent .A5
Holyrood Abbey (Remains) .A6
Holyrood Gait .B6
Holyrood Park .C6
Holyrood Rd .B5
Home St .C2
Hope St .B2
Horse Wynd .B6
Howden St .C5
Howe St .A2
Hub, The ✦ .B3
India Place .A2
India St .A2
Infirmary St .B4
Information Centre .B4
Jeffrey St .B4
John Knox House .B4
Johnston Terrace .C3
Keir St .C3
Kerr St .A2
King's Stables Rd .B2
Lady Lawson St .C3
Lauriston Gardens .C3
Lauriston Park .C3
Lauriston Place .C3
Lauriston St .C3
Lawnmarket .B3
Learmonth Gardens .A1
Learmonth Terrace .A1
Leith St .A4
Lennox St .A1
Lennox St Lane .A1
Leslie Place .A2
London Rd .A5
Lothian Rd .B2
Lothian St .C4
Lower Menz Place .A6
Lynedoch Place .B1
Manor Place .B1
Market St .B4
Marshall St .C4
Maryfield .A6
McEwan Hall .C4
Medical School .C4
Melville St .B1
Meuse Lane .B4
Middle Meadow Walk .C4
Milton St .A6
Montrose Terrace .A6
Moray Place .A2
Morrison Link .C1
Morrison St .C1
Mound Place .B3
Mound, The .B3
Multrees Walk .A4
Mus Collections Ctr .A4
Mus of Childhood .B5
Mus of Edinburgh .B5
Museum of Fire .C3
Mus on the Mound .B4
National Archives of Scotland .A4
National Museum of Scotland .C4
National Gallery .B3
National Library of Scotland .B4
National Monument ✦ A5
National Portrait Gallery .B4
National War Mus .B3
Nelson Monument ✦ .A5
Nelson St .A3
New St .B5
Nicolson Square .C4
Nicolson St .C4
Niddry St .B4
North Bank St .B3
North Bridge .B4
North Castle St .A2
North Charlotte St .A2
North Meadow Walk .C3
North St Andrew St .A4
North St David St .A3
North West Circus Pl .A2
Northumberland St .A3
Odeon .C2
Old Royal High School .A5
Old Tolbooth Wynd .B5
OMNi Centre ✦ .A4
Oxford Terrace .A1
Palace of Holyroodhouse .B6
Palmerston Place .B1
Panmure Place .C3
Parliament Square .B4
People's Story, The B5
Playhouse Theatre .A4
Pleasance .C5
Police Station .A4
Ponton St .C2
Post Office .A3/B4/B5/C1/C2/C4
Potterrow .C4
Princes Mall .B4
Princes St .B3
Princes St .B3
Prisoners of War .B3
Queen's Gallery .B6
Queen St .A2
Queen Street Gardens .A3
Queen's Drive .B6/C6
Queensferry Rd .A1
Queensferry St .B1
Queensferry Street La .B2
Radical Rd .C6
Randolph Crescent .B1
Regent Gardens .A5
Regent Rd .B5
Regent Rd Park .A6
Regent Terrace .A5
Richmond Lane .C5
Richmond Place .C5
Rose St .B2
Ross Open Air Theatre .B3
Rothesay Place .B1
Rothesay Terrace .B1
Roxburgh Place .C5
Roxburgh St .C5
Royal Bank of Scotland .A4
Royal Circus .A2
Royal Lyceum .C2
Royal Mile, The .B5
Royal Scottish Acad B3
Royal Terrace .A5
Royal Terrace Gdns .A5
Rutland Square .B2
Rutland St .B2
St Andrew Square .A4
St Andrew Square .A4
St Andrew's House .A4
St Bernard's Cres .A1
St Bernard's Well ✦ .A1
St Cecilia's Hall .B4
St Colme St .A2
St Cuthbert's .B2
St Giles' .B4
St James Quarter Shopping Centre .A4
St John St .B5
St John's .B2
St John's Hill .B5
St Leonard's Hill .C5
St Leonard's Lane .C5
St Leonard's St .C5
St Mary's .A4
St Mary's Scottish Episcopal .B1
St Mary's St .B5
St Michael & All Saints .C3
St Stephen St .A2
Salisbury Crags .C6
Saunders St .A2
Scotch Whisky Experience ✦ .B3
Scott Monument ✦ .B4
Scottish Parliament .B6
Scottish Storytelling Centre ✦ .B5
Semple St .C2
Shandwick Place .B2
South Bridge .B4
South Charlotte St .B2
South College St .C4
South Learmonth Gardens .A1
South St Andrew St .A4
South St David St .A3
Spittal St .C2
Stafford St .B1
Student Centre .C4
Surgeons' Hall .C5
Supreme Courts .B4
Teviot Place .C4
Thistle St .A3
Torphichen Place .C1
Torphichen St .C1
Traverse Theatre .B2
Tron Square .B4
Tron, The ✦ .B4
Union St .A4
University .C4
University Library .C4
Univ of Edinburgh .B5
Upper Grove Place .C1
Usher Hall .C2
Vennel .C3
Victoria St .B3
Viewcraig Gardens .B5
Viewcraig St .B5
Vue .A4
Walker St .B1
Waterloo Place .A4
Waverley Bridge .B4
Wemyss Place .B2
West Approach Rd .C1
West Crosscauseway .C5
West End .B1
West Maitland St .C1
West of Nicholson St .C4
West Port .C3
West Princes St Gdns .B3
West Richmond St .C5
West Tollcross .C2
White Horse Close ✦ .B6
William St .B1
Windsor St .A5
Writer's Mus, The .B4
York Lane .A4
York Place .A4
York Place .A4
Young St .B2

Exeter 334

Alphington St .C1
Athelstan Rd .B3
Barnardo Rd .C3
Barnfield Hill .B3
Barnfield Rd .B2/B3
Barnfield Theatre .B2
Bartholomew St East .B1
Bartholomew St West .B1
Bear St .B2
Beaufort Rd .C1
Bedford St .B2
Belgrave Rd .A3
Belmont Rd .A3
Blackall Rd .A2
Blackboy Rd .A3
Bonhay Rd .B1
Bull Meadow Rd .C2
Bus & Coach Station .B3
Castle St .B2
Catacombes ✦ .B1
Cecil Rd .C1
Cheeke St .A3
Church Rd .C1
Chute St .A3
City Wall .B1/B2
Civic Centre .B2
Clifton Rd .B3
Clifton St .B3
Clock Tower .A1
College Rd .B3
Colleton Crescent .C2
Commercial Rd .C1
Coombe St .B2
Cowick St .C1
Crown Courts .B2
Custom House Visitor Centre .C2
Cygnet Theatre .C2
Danes' Rd .A2
Denmark Rd .B3
Devon County Hall .C3
Devonshire Place .A3
Dinham Crescent .B1
East Grove Rd .C3
Edmund St .C1
Elm Grove Rd .A1
Exe St .B1
Exeter Cathedral .B2
Exeter Central Sta .A1
Exeter City Football Ground .A3
Exeter College .A1
Exeter Picture Ho .B1
Fire Station .A1
Fore St .B1
Friars Walk .C2
Guildhall .B2
Guildhall Shopping Ctr B2
Haven Rd .C2
Heavitree Rd .B3
Hele Rd .A1
High St .B2
HM Prison .A2
Holloway St .C2
Hoopern St .A2
Horseguards .A2
Howell Rd .A1
Information Centre .B3
Iron Bridge .B1
Isca Rd .C1
Jesmond Rd .A3
King St .B1
King William St .A2
Larkbeare Rd .C2
Leisure Centre .C1
Library .B2
Longbrook St .A2
Longbrook Terrace .A2
Lower North St .B1
Lucky Lane .C2
Lyndhurst Rd .C3
Magdalen Rd .B3
Magdalen St .B2
Market .B2
Market St .B2
Marlborough Rd .C3
Mary Arches St .B1
Matford Avenue .C3
Matford Lane .C3
Matford Rd .C3
May St .A3
Mol's Coffee House B2
New Bridge St .B1
New North Rd .A1/A2
North St .B1
Northernhay St .B1
Norwood Avenue .C3
Odeon .A3
Okehampton St .C1
Old Mill Close .C2
Old Tiverton Rd .A3
Oxford Rd .A3
Paris St .B2
Parr St .A3
Paul St .B1
Pennsylvania Rd .A2
Portland Street .A3
Post Office .A3/B2/C1
Powderham Crescent .A3
Preston St .B1
Princesshay Shopping Centre .B2
Pyramids Leisure Ctr .B3
Quay, The .C2
Queen St .A1
Queen's Terrace .A1
Queens Rd .C1

Radford Rd C2
Richmond Rd A1
Roberts Rd C2
Rougemont Castle A2
Rougemont House ✦ B2
Royal Albert Memorial Museum B2
St David's Hill A1
St James' Pk Sta A3
St James' Rd A3
St Leonard's Rd C3
St Mary Steps C1
St Nicholas Priory B1
St Thomas Station C1
Sandford Walk B3
School Rd C1
Sidwell St A2
Smythen St B1
South St B2
Southernhay East B2
Southernhay West B2
Spicer Rd B3
Sports Centre A3
Summerland St A3
Sydney Rd C1
Tan Lane C2
Thornton Hill A2
Topsham Rd C3
Tucker's Hall B1
Tudor St B1
Underground Passages ✦ B2
University of Exeter (St Luke's Campus) B3
Velwell Rd A1
Verney St A3
Vue B3
Water Lane C1/C2
Weirfield Rd C2
Well St A3
West Avenue A2
West Grove Rd C3
Western Way A3/B1/B2
Willeys Avenue C1
Wonford Rd B3/C3
York Rd A2

Fort William 335

Abrach Rd A3
Achintore Rd C1
Alma Rd B2
Am Breun Chamas A2
Ambulance Station A3
An Aird A2
Argyll Rd C1
Argyll Terrace C1
Bank St B2
Belford Hospital B2
Ben Nevis Highland Centre B3
Black Parks A3
Braemore Place C2
Bruce Place C2
Bus Station B2
Camanachd Cres A3/B2
Cameron Rd C1
Cameron Square B1
Carmichael Way A2
Claggan Rd B3
Connochie Rd C1
Cow Hill C3
Creag Dhubh A2
Croft Rd B3
Douglas Place B2
Dudley Rd B2
Dumbarton Rd C1
Earl of Inverness Rd A3
Fassifern Rd B1
Fire Station A2
Fort William B2
Fort William (Remains) ✦ B2
Glasdrum Rd C1
Glen Nevis Place B3
Gordon Square B1
Grange Rd C1
Heathercroft Drive C1
Heather Croft Rd C1
Henderson Row C2
High St B1
Hill Rd B2
Information Centre A3
Inverlochy Court A3
Kennedy Rd B2/C2
Library B2
Lime Tree Gallery ✦ C1
Linnhe Rd B1
Lochaber Leisure Ctr B3
Lochiel Rd A3
Lochy Rd A3
Lundavra Crescent C1
Lundavra Rd C1
Lundy Rd A3
Mamore Crescent B2
Mary St B2
Middle St B1
Montrose Avenue A3
Moray Place C1
Morven Place C2
Nairn Crescent C1
Nevis Bridge B3
Nevis Centre, The A2
Nevis Rd A3
Nevis Terrace B2
North Rd B3
Obelisk B2
Parade Rd B2
Police Station C1
Post Office A3/B2
Ross Place C1
St Andrews B2
Shaw Place B2
Station Brae B1
Superstore B3
Treig Rd A3
Union Rd C1
Victoria Rd B2
Wades Rd A3
West Highland B1
West Highland College UHI A2
Young Place B2

Glasgow 335

Admiral St C2
Albert Bridge C5
Albion St B5
Anderston B3
Anderston Quay B3
Argyle Arcade B5
Argyle St A1/A2/B3/B4/B5
Argyle Street B5
Arlington St A3
Arts Centre B3
Ashley St A3
Bain St C6
Baird St A6
Baliol St A3
Ballater St C5
Barras (Market), The C6
Bath St A3
BBC Scotland B1
Bell St C6
Bell's Bridge B1
Bentinck St A2
Berkeley St A3
Bishop Lane B3
Black St A6
Blackburn St C2
Blackfriars St B6
Blantyre St A1
Blythswood Square A4
Blythswood St B4
Bothwell St B4
Brand St C1
Breadalbane St A2
Bridge St C4
Bridge St C4
Bridgegate C5
Briggait C5
Broomielaw B4
Broomielaw Quay Gardens B3
Brown St B4
Brunswick St B5
Buccleuch St A3
Buchanan Bus Station A5
Buchanan Galleries A5
Buchanan St B5
Buchanan St B5
Cadogan St B4
Caledonian University A5
Calgary St A5
Cambridge St A4
Canal St A5
Candleriggs B5
Carlton Place C4
Carnarvon St A3
Carrick St B4
Castle St B6
Cathedral Square B6
Cathedral St B5
Central Mosque C5
Ctr for Contemporary Arts A4
Centre St C4
Cessnock C1
Cessnock St C1
Charing Cross A3
Charlotte St C6
Cheapside St B3
Cineworld A5
Citizens' Theatre C5
City Chambers Complex B5
City Halls B5
City of Glasgow College (City Campus) B5
City of Glasgow College (Riverside Campus) C5
Clairmont Gardens A2
Claremont St A2
Claremont Terrace A2
Claythorne St C6
Cleveland St A3
Clifford Lane C1
Clifford St C1
Clifton Place A2
Clifton St A2
Clutha St C1
Clyde Arcade B2
Clyde Place C4
Clyde Place Quay C4
Clyde St C5
Clyde Walkway C3
Clydeside Expressway B2
Coburg St C4
Cochrane St B5
College St B6
Collins St B6
Commerce St C4
Cook St C4
Cornwall St C2
Couper St A5
Cowcaddens A4
Cowcaddens Rd A4
Crimea St B3
Custom Ho Quay Gdns C4
Dalhousie St A4
Dental Hospital A4
Derby St A2
Dobbie's Loan A4/A5
Dobbie's Loan Place A5
Dorset St A3
Douglas St B4
Doulton Fountain ✦ C6
Dover St A2
Drury St B4
Drygate B6
Duke St B6
Dunaskin St A1
Dunblane St A4
Dundas St B5
Dunlop St C5
East Campbell St C6
Eastvale Place A1
Eglinton St C4
Elderslie St A3
Elliot St B2
Elmbank St A3
Esmond St A1
Exhibition Centre B2
Festival Park C1
Film Theatre ✦ A4
Finnieston Quay B2
Finnieston St B2
Fire Station C6
Florence St C5
Fox St C5
Gallowgate C6
Garnet St A3
Garnethill St A4
Garscube Rd A4
George Square B5
George St B5
George V Bridge C4
Gilbert St A1
Glasgow Bridge C4
Glasgow Cathedral ✝ B6
Glasgow Central B4
Glasgow City Free Church B4
Glasgow Green C6
Glasgow Necropolis ✦ B6
Glasgow Royal Concert Hall A5
Glasgow Science Centre ✦ B1
Glasgow Tower ✦ B1
Glassford St B5
Glebe St A6
Gorbals Cross C5
Gorbals St C5
Gordon St B4
Govan Rd B1/C1/C2
Grace St B3
Grafton Place A5
Grand Ole Opry ✦ C2
Grant St A3
Granville St A3
Gray St A2
Greendyke St C6
Grey Eagle St B7
Harley St C1
Harvie St C1
Haugh Rd A1
Havanah St B6
Heliport B1
Henry Wood Hall A2
High Court C5
High St B6
High Street B6
Hill St A3
Holland St A3
Holm St B4
Hope St A5
Houldsworth St B2
Houston Place C3
Houston St C3
Howard St C5
Hunter St C6
Hutcheson St B5
Hydepark St B3
Imax Cinema B1
India St A3
Information Centre B5
Ingram St B5
Jamaica St B4
James Watt St B4
John Knox St B6
John St B5
Kelvin Hall ✦ A1
Kelvin Statue ✦ A2
Kelvin Way A2
Kelvingrove Art Gallery & Museum A1
Kelvingrove Park A2
Kelvingrove St A2
Kelvinhaugh St A1
Kennedy St A6
Kent Rd A2
Killermont St A5
King St B5
King's, The A3
Kingston Bridge C3
Kingston St C4
Kinning Park C2
Kyle St A5
Lancefield Quay B2
Lancefield St B3
Langshot St C1
Lendel Place C1
Lighthouse, The ✦ B4
Lister St A6
Little St B3
London Rd C6
Lorne St C1
Lower Harbour B1
Lumsden St A1
Lymburn St A1
Lyndoch Crescent A3
Lynedoch Place A3
Lynedoch St A3
Maclellan St C1
Mair St C2
Maitland St A4
Mansell St C7
Mavisbank Gardens C2
Mcalpine St B3
Mcaslin St A6
McLean Square C2
McLellan Gallery A4
McPhater St A4
Merchants' House B5
Middlesex St C2
Middleton St C1
Midland St B4
Miller St B5
Millennium Bridge B1
Millroad St C6
Milnpark St C2
Milton St A4
Minerva St B2
Mitchell St West B4
Mitchell Liby, The ✦ A3
Modern Art Gallery B5
Moir St C6
Molendinar St C6
Moncur St C6
Montieth Row C6
Montrose St B5
Morrison St C3
Nairn St A1
National Piping Centre, The ✦ A5
Nelson Mandela Sq B5
Nelson St C4
Nelson's Monument C6
Newton Place A3
Newton St A3
Nicholson St C4
Nile St B5
Norfolk Court C4
Norfolk St C4
North Frederick St B5
North Hanover St B5
North Portland St B6
North St A3
North Wallace St A5
O2 ABC A4
O2 Academy ✦ C4
Odeon C3
Old Dumbarton Rd A1
Osborne St B5/C5
Oswald St B4
Overnewton St A1
Oxford St C4
Pacific Drive B1
Paisley Rd C3
Paisley Rd West C1
Park Circus A2
Park Gardens A2
Park St South A2
Park Terrace A2
Parkgrove Terrace A2
Parnie St C5
Parson St A6
Partick Bridge A1
Passport Office A5
Pavilion Theatre A4
Pembroke St A3
People's Palace C6
Pitt St A4/B4
Plantation Park C1
Plantation Quay B1
Police Museum B5
Police Station A4/A6
Port Dundas Rd A5
Port St B2
Portman St C2
Prince's Dock B1
Princes Square B5
Provand's Lordship B6
Queen St B5
Queen Street B5
Ramshorn B5
Renfrew St A3/A4
Renton St A5
Richmond St B5
Robertson St B4
Rose St A4
Rottenrow B5
Royal Concert Hall A5
Royal Conservatoire of Scotland A4
Royal Crescent A2
Royal Exchange Sq B5
Royal Highland Fusiliers Museum A3
West Glasgow Ambulatory Care A1
Royal Infirmary B6
Royal Terrace A2
Rutland Crescent C2
St Andrew's in the Square C6
St Andrew's (RC) ✝ C5
St Andrew's St C5
St Enoch B5
St Enoch Shopping Ctr B5
St Enoch Square B4
St George's Rd A3
St James Rd B6
St Kent St C6
St Mungo Avenue A5/A6
St Mungo Museum of Religious Life & Art B6
St Mungo Place A6
St Vincent Crescent A2
St Vincent Place B5
St Vincent St B3/B4
St Vincent Terrace B3
Saltmarket C5
Sandyford Place A3
Sauchiehall St A2/A4
SEC Armadillo B2
School of Art A4
Sclater St B7
Scotland St C2
Scott St A4
Scottish Exhibition & Conference Centre B1
Seaward St C2
Shaftesbury St B3
Sheriff Court C5
Shields Rd C3
Shopmobility A5
Shuttle St B6
Somerset Place A2
South Portland St C4
Springburn Rd A6
Springfield Quay C3
SSE Hydro The B2
Stanley St C2
Stevenson St C6
Stewart St A4
Stirling Rd B6
Stobcross Quay B1
Stobcross Rd B1
Stock Exchange B5
Stockwell Place C5
Stockwell St B5
Stow College A4
Sussex St C2
Synagogue A3
Taylor Place A6
Tenement House A3
Teviot St A1
Theatre Royal A4
Tolbooth Steeple & Mercat Cross ✦ C6
Tower St C2
Trades House B5
Tradeston St C4
Transport Museum A1
Tron C5
Trongate B5
Tunnel St B2
Turnbull St C5
Union St B4
Univ of Strathclyde B6
Victoria Bridge C5
Virginia St B5
Wallace St C3
Walls St B6
Walmer Crescent C1
Warrock St B3
Washington St B3
Waterloo St B4
Watson St B6
Watt St C3
Wellington St B4
West Campbell St B4
West George St B4
West Graham St A4
West Greenhill Place B2
West Regent St A4
West Regent St B4
West St C4
West St C4
Whitehall St B3
Wilkes St C7
Wilson St B5
Woodlands Gate A3
Woodlands Rd A3
Woodlands Terrace A2
Woodside Place A3
Woodside Terrace A3
York St B4
Yorkhill Parade A1
Yorkhill St A1

Gloucester 335

Albion St C1
Alexandra Rd B3
Alfred St C3
All Saints Rd C2
Alvin St B2
Arthur St C2
Barrack Square B1
Barton St C2
Blackfriars ✝ B1
Blenheim Rd C2
Bristol Rd C1
Brunswick Rd C2
Bruton Way B2
Bus Station B2
Cineworld C1
City Council Offices B1
City Museum, Art Gallery & Library B2
Clarence St B2
Commercial Rd B1
Council Offices B1
Courts B1
Cromwell St C2
Deans Way A2
Denmark Rd A3
Derby Rd C3
Docks ✦ C1
Eastgate St B2
Eastgate, The B1
Edwy Parade A2
Estcourt Close A3
Estcourt Rd A3
Falkner St C2
GL1 Leisure Centre C2
Gloucester Cath ✝ B1
Gloucester Life B1
Gloucester Quays Outlet C1
Gloucester Station B2
Gloucestershire Archive B2
Gloucestershire Royal Hospital (A&E) B3
Goodyere St C2
Gouda Way A1
Great Western Rd B3
Guildhall B2
Heathville Rd A3
Henry Rd B3
Henry St B2
Hinton Rd A2
India Rd C3
Information Centre B1
Jersey Rd C3
King's C2
King's Walk Shopping Centre B2
Kingsholm (Gloucester Rugby) A2
Kingsholm Rd A2
Lansdown Rd A3
Library C2
Llanthony Rd C1
London Rd B3
Longhorn Avenue A1
Longsmith St B1
Malvern Rd A3
Market B2
Market Parade B2
Mercia Rd A1
Metz Way C3
Midland Rd C2
Millbrook St C3
Montpellier C1
Napier St C3
National Waterways Mus Gloucester C1
Nettleton Rd C2
New Inn B2
New Olympus C3
North Rd A3
Northgate St B2
Oxford Rd A2
Oxford St B2
Park & Ride Gloucester A1
Park Rd C2
Park St B2
Park, The C2
Parliament St C1
Peel Centre, The C1
Pitt St B1
Police Station C3
Post Office B2
Quay St B1
Quay, The B1
Recreation Ground A1/A2
Regent St C2
Robert Raikes Ho B1
Royal Oak Rd B1
Russell St B2
Ryecroft St C2
St Aldate St B2
St Ann Way C1
St Catherine St A2
St Mark St A2
St Mary de Crypt B1
St Mary de Lode B1
St Nicholas's B1
St Oswald's Rd A1
St Oswald's Retail Pk A1
St Peter's B2
Seabroke Rd A3
Sebert St A2
Severn Rd C1
Sherborne St B2
Shire Hall B1
Sidney St C3
Soldiers of Gloucestershire B1
Southgate St B1/C1
Spa Field C1
Spa Rd C1
Sports Ground A2/B2
Station Rd B2
Stratton Rd C3
Stroud Rd C1
Superstore A1
Swan Rd A2
Trier Way C1/C2
Union St A2
Vauxhall Rd C3
Victoria St C2
Walham Lane A1
Wellington St C2
Westgate Retail Park B1
Westgate St B1
Widden St C2
Worcester St B2

Grimsby 335

Abbey Drive East C2
Abbey Drive West C2
Abbey Park Rd C2
Abbey Rd C2
Abbey Walk C2
Abbeygate Shopping Centre C2
Abbotsway C2
Adam Smith St A1/A2
Ainslie St C2
Albert St A3
Alexandra Dock A2/B2
Alexandra Rd A2/B2
Alexandra Retail Park A2
Annesley St A2
Armstrong St A1
Arthur St B1
Augusta St C1
Bargate C1
Beeson St A1
Bethlehem St C2
Bodiam Way B3
Bradley St B3
Brighowgate C1/C2
Bus Station C2
Canterbury Drive C1
Cartergate B1/C1
Catherine St C3
Chantry Lane B1
Charlton St A1
Church Lane C2
Church St A3
Cleethorpe Rd A3
Close, The C1
College St C1
Compton Drive C1
Corporation Bridge A2
Corporation Rd A1
Court B2/B3
Crescent St B1
Deansgate C1
Doughty Rd C2
Dover St B1
Duchess St C2
Dudley St C1
Duke of York Gardens B1
Duncombe St B3
Earl Lane B1
East Marsh St B3
East St B2
Eastgate B3
Eastside Rd A3
Eaton Court C1
Eleanor St B3
Ellis Way B3
Fisherman's Chapel A3
Fisherman's Wharf B2
Fishing Heritage Centre B2
Flour Square A3
Frederick St B3
Frederick Ward Way B2
Freeman St A3/B3
Freshney Drive B1
Freshney Place B2
Garden St C2
Garibaldi St A3
Garth Lane B2
Grime St B3
Grimsby Docks Sta A3
Grimsby Town Sta C2
Hainton Avenue C3
Har Way B3
Hare St C3
Harrison St B1
Haven Avenue B1
Hay Croft Avenue B1
Hay Croft St B1
Heneage Rd B3/C3
Henry St B1
Holme St B3
Hume St C1
James St B1
Joseph St B1
Kent St A3
King Edward St A3
Lambert Rd C2
Library B2
Lime St B1
Lister St B1
Littlefield Lane C1
Lockhill A3
Lord St B1
Lower Spring St A3
Ludford St C3
Macaulay St B1
Mallard Mews C3
Manor Avenue C2
Market A3
Market Hall B2
Market St B3
Moody Lane A3
Moss Rd C2
Nelson St A3
New St B2
Osbourne St B2
Pasture St B3
Peaks Parkway C3
Pelham Rd C1
Police Station B3
Post Office B1/B2
Pyewipe Rd A1
Railway Place A3
Railway St A3
Recreation Ground C2
Rendel St A2
Retail Park A2/B3
Richard St B1
Ripon St B1
Robinson St East B3
Royal St A3
St Hilda's Avenue C1
St James B2
Sheepfold St B3/C3
Shopmobility B2
Sixhills St C3
South Park B2
Superstore B3/B2
Tasburgh St C3
Tennyson St B2
Thesiger St A3
Time Trap C2
Town Hall B2
Veal St B1
Victoria Retail Park A3
Victoria St North A2
Victoria St South B2
Victoria St West B2
Watkin St A1
Welholme Avenue C2
Welholme Rd C3
Wellington St B3
Wellowgate C2
Werneth Rd B3
West Coates Rd A1
Westgate A2
Westminster Drive C1
Willingham St C3
Wintringham Rd C2
Wood St B3
Yarborough Drive B1
Yarborough Hotel C2

Hanley 335

Acton St A3
Albion St B2
Argyle St C1
Ashbourne Grove A2
Avoca St A3
Baskerville Rd B3
Bedford Rd C1
Bedford St C1
Bethesda St B2
Bexley St A2
Birches Head Rd A3
Botteslow St C3
Boundary St A2
Broad St C2
Broom St A3
Bryan St A2
Bucknall New Rd B3
Bucknall Old Rd B3
Bus Station C3
Cannon St C2
Castlefield St C1
Cavendish St B1
Central Forest Park A2
Century Retail Park B1
Charles St B3
Cheapside B2
Chell St A3
Clarke St C1
Cleveland Rd C2
Clifford St C3
Clough St B2
Clough St East B2
Clyde St C1
College Rd C2
Cooper St C2
Corbridge Rd A1
Cutts St C2
Davis St C1
Denbigh St A1
Derby St C3
Dilke St A3
Dudson Ctr, The A2
Dundas St A3
Dundee Rd C1
Dyke St B3
Eastwood Rd C3
Eaton St A3
Etruria Park B1
Etruria Rd B1
Etruria Vale Rd C1
Festing St A3
Festival Heights Retail Park A1
Festival Retail Park A1
Fire Station C2
Foundry St B2
Franklyn St C3
Garnet St B1
Garth St B3
George St A3
Gilman St B3
Glass St B3
Goodson St B3
Greyhound Way A1
Grove Place C1
Hampton St C3
Hanley Park C2
Hanley Park C2
Harding Rd C2
Hassall St B3
Havelock Place C1
Hazlehurst St C3
Hinde St C2
Hope St B2
Houghton St C2
Hulton St A3
Information Centre B2
Jasper St C2
Jervis St A3
John Bright St A3
John St B2
Keelings Rd A3
Kimberley Rd C1
Ladysmith Rd C1
Lawrence St C2
Leek Rd C3
Library C2
Lichfield St C3
Linfield Rd B3
Loftus St A2
Lower Bedford St C1
Lower Bryan St A2
Lower Mayer St A3
Lowther St A1
Magistrates Court C2
Malham St A2
Marsh St B2
Matlock St C3
Mayer St A3
Milton St C1
Mitchell Arts Centre B2
Moston St A3
Mount Pleasant C1
Mulgrave St A1
Mynors St B3
Nelson Place B3
New Century St B1
Octagon Retail Park B1
Ogden Rd C3
Old Hall St B3
Old Town Rd A3
Pall Mall B2
Palmerston St C3
Park and Ride C2
Parkway, The C2
Pavilion Drive A1
Pelham St C3
Percy St B2
Piccadilly B2
Picton St B3
Plough St A3
Police Station C2
Portland St A1
Post Office A3/B2
Potteries Centre, The B2
Potteries Museum & Art Gallery B2
Potteries Way B1
Powell St A1
Pretoria Rd C1
Quadrant Rd B2
Ranelagh St C2
Raymond St C2
Rectory Rd C1
Regent Rd C2
Regent Theatre B2
Richmond Terrace C2
Ridgehouse Drive A1
Robson St C2
St Ann St B3
St Luke St B3
Sampson St B2
Shaw St A1
Sheaf St C2
Shearer St C1
Shelton New Rd C1
Shirley Rd C2
Slippery Lane B2
Shopmobility B3
Snow Hill C2
Spur St C3
Stafford St B2
Stubbs Lane C3
Sun St C1
Supermarket A1/B2
Superstore B2
Talbot St C3
Town Hall B2
Town Rd A3
Trinity St B2
Union St A2
Upper Hillchurch St A3
Upper Huntbach St B3
Victoria Hall B3
Warner St C2
Warwick St C1
Waterloo Rd A1
Waterloo St B3
Well St B3
Wellesley St C2
Wellington Rd B3
Wellington St B3
Whitehaven Drive A2
Whitmore St C1
Windermere St A1
Woodall St A1
Yates St C2
York St A2

Harrogate 335

Albert St C2
Alexandra Rd B2
Arthington Avenue B2
Ashfield Rd A2
Back Cheltenham Mount B2
Beech Grove C1
Belmont Rd C1
Bilton Drive A2
BMI The Duchy Hospital C1
Bower Rd B2
Bower St B2
Bus Station B2
Cambridge Rd B2
Cambridge St B2
Cemetery A2
Chatsworth Grove A2
Chatsworth Place A2
Chatsworth Rd A2
Chelmsford Rd B3
Cheltenham Cres B2
Cheltenham Mt B2
Cheltenham Parade B2
Christ Church B3
Christ Church Oval B3
Chudleigh Rd B3
Clarence Drive B1
Claro Rd A3
Claro Way A3
Coach Park B2
Coach Rd B3
Cold Bath Rd C1
Commercial St B2
Coppice Avenue A1
Coppice Drive A1
Coppice Gate A1
Cornwall Rd B1
Council Offices B1
Crescent Gardens B1
Crescent Rd B1
Dawson Terrace A2
Devonshire Place B3
Dixon Rd A2
Dixon Terrace A2
Dragon Avenue B3
Dragon Parade B2
Dragon Rd B2
Duchy Rd B1
East Parade B2
East Park Rd C3
Esplanade B1
Everyman C2
Fire Station A2
Franklin Mount A2
Franklin Rd B2
Franklin Square A2
Glebe Rd C1
Grove Park Court A3
Grove Park Terrace A3
Grove Rd A2
Hampswaite Rd A1
Harcourt Drive B3
Harcourt Rd B3
Harrogate B2
Harrogate Convention Centre B1
Harrogate Justice Centre (Magistrates' and County Courts) C2
Harrogate Ladies Coll B1
Harrogate Theatre B2
Heywood Rd C1
Hollins Crescent A1
Hollins Mews A1
Hollins Rd A1
Hydro Leisure Ctr, The A1
Information Centre B1
James St B2
Jenny Field Drive A1
John St B2
Kent Drive A1
Kent Rd A1
Kings Rd A2
Kingsway B3
Kingsway Drive B3
Lancaster Rd C1
Leeds Rd C2
Lime Grove B3
Lime St A3
Mayfield Grove B2
Mercer B1
Montpellier Hill B1
Mornington Crescent A3
Mornington Terrace B3
Mowbray Square B3
North Park Rd B3
Oakdale Avenue A1
Oatlands Drive C3
Odeon B2
Osborne Rd A2
Otley Rd C2
Oxford St B2
Parade, The B2
Park Chase B3
Park Parade B3
Park View B2
Parliament St B1
Police Station C3
Post Office B2/C1
Providence Terrace A2
Queen Parade C3
Queen's Rd C1
Raglan St C2
Regent Avenue A3
Regent Grove A3
Regent Parade A3
Regent St A3
Regent Terrace A3
Ripon Rd A1
Robert St C2
Royal Baths & Turkish Baths B1
Royal Pump Room B1
St Luke's Mount A2
St Mary's Avenue C1
St Mary's Walk C1
Scargill Rd A1
Skipton Rd A3

Skipton St A2
Slingsby Walk C3
South Park Rd C2
Spring Grove A1
Springfield Avenue B1
Station Avenue B2
Station Parade B2
Stray Rein C3
Stray, The C2/C3
Studley Rd A2
Superstore B2/C1
Swan Rd B1
Tower St C2
Trinity Rd C2
Union St B2
Valley Drive C1
Valley Gardens C1
Valley Mount C1
Victoria Avenue C2
Victoria Rd C1
Victoria Shopping Ctr B2
Waterloo St A2
West Park C2
West Park St C2
Wood View A1
Woodfield Avenue A3
Woodfield Drive A3
Woodfield Grove A3
Woodfield Rd A3
Woodfield Square A3
Woodside B3
York Place C3
York Rd B1

Holyhead Caergybi 335

Armenia St A2
Arthur St C2
Beach Rd A1
Boston St B2
Bowling Green C3
Bryn Erw Rd C3
Bryn Glas Close C3
Bryn Glas Rd C3
Bryn Gwyn Rd C1
Bryn Marchog A1
Bryn Mor Terrace A2
Bryngoleu Avenue A1
Cae Braenar C3
Cambria St B1
Captain Skinner's Obelisk ✦ B2
Cecil St C2
Celtic Gateway Footbridge B2
Cemetery C1/C2
Cleveland Avenue C2
Coastguard Lookout A2
Court B2
Cybi Place A2
Cyttir Rd C3
Edmund St B1
Empire B2
Ferry Terminals B2
Ffordd Beibio B3
Ffordd Feurig C3
Ffordd Hirnos C3
Ffordd Jasper C3
Ffordd Tudur B3
Fire Station C2
Garreglwyd Rd B1
Gilbert St C2
Gorsedd Circle B1
Gwelfor Avenue A1
Harbour Office A3
Harbour View B3
Henry St C2
High Terrace C1
Hill St B2
Holborn Rd C2
Holland Park Ind Est C3
Holyhead Park B1
Holyhead Station B2
King's Rd C2
Kingsland Rd C2
Lewascote C3
Library B2
Lifeboat Station A1
Llanfawr Close C3
Llanfawr Rd C3
Lligwy St C2
Lon Deg C3
London Rd C3
Longford Rd B1
Longford Terrace B1
Maes Cybi B1
Maes Hedd A1
Maes-Hyfryd Rd C1
Maes-y-Dref B1
Maes-yr-Haf A2/B1
Maes-yr-Ysgol C3
Marchog C3
Marina A1
Maritime Museum A1
Market B2
Market St B2
Mill Bank B1
Min-y-Mor Rd A1
Morawelon Ind Est B3
Morawelon Rd B3
Moreton Rd C1
New Park Rd B1
Newry St A2
Old Harbour Lighthouse A3
Plas Rd C1
Police Station B2
Porth-y-Felin Rd A1
Post Office A1/B2/B3
Prince of Wales Rd A2
Priory Lane B3
Pump St C1
Queens Park B1
Reseifion Rd C1
Rock St B1
Roman Fort B2
St Cybi St B2
St Cybi's Church B2
St Seiriol's Close B1
Salt Island Bridge A2
Seabourne Rd A1
South Stack Rd B1
Sports Ground B1
Stanley St B2
Station St B2
Superstore C2
Tan-y-Bryn Rd A1
Tan-yr-Efail C2
Tara St C1
Thomas St B1
Town Hall A2
Treseifion Estate C2
Turkey Shore Rd B2
Ucheldre Arts Ctr ✦ B1
Ucheldre Avenue B1
Upper Baptist St B1
Victoria Rd B2
Victoria Terrace B2
Vulcan St B1
Walthew Avenue A1
Walthew Lane A1
Wian St C2

Hull 335

Adelaide St C1
Albert Dock C1
Albion St B2
Alfred Gelder St B2
Anlaby Rd B1
Arctic Corsair ✦ B3
Beverley Rd A1
Blanket Row C2
Bond St B2
Bonus Arena B2
Bridlington Avenue A2
Brook St B1
Brunswick Avenue A1
Bus Station B1
Camilla Close C3
Cannon St A2
Caroline St A2
Carr Lane B2
Castle St C2
Central Library B1
Charles St A2
Citadel Way B3
Clarence St B3
Cleveland St A3
Clifton St A1
Colonial St B1
Court B2
Deep, The C3
Dinostar C2
Dock Office Row B3
Dock St B2
Drypool Bridge B3
Egton St A3
English St C1
Ferens Gallery B2
Ferensway B1
Fire Station A1
Francis St A2
Francis St West A2
Freehold St A1
Freetown Way A2
Früit Theatre C2
Garrison Rd B3
George St B2
Gibson St A2
Great Thornton St B1
Great Union St A3
Green Lane A2
Grey St A1
Grimston St B2
Grosvenor St A1
Guildhall B2
Guildhall Rd B2
Hands-on History B2
Harley St A1
Hessle Rd C1
High St B3
Hull Minster B2
Hull Paragon Interchange Sta B1
Hull & East Riding Museum B3
Hull Ice Arena C1
Hull City Hall B2
Hull College B3
Hull History Centre A2
Hull New Theatre A2
Hull Truck Theatre B1
Humber Dock Marina C2
Humber Dock St C2
Humber St C2
Hyperion St A3
Information Centre B1
Jameson St B1
Jarratt St B2
Jenning St A3
King Billy Statue ✦ C2
King Edward St B2
King St A2
Kingston Retail Park C1
Kingston St C2
Liddell St A1
Lime St A3
Lister St C1
Lockwood St A2
Maister House B3
Maritime Museum B2
Market B2
Market Place B2
Minerva Pier C2
Mulgrave St A3
Myton Swing Bridge C3
Myton St B1
NAPA (Northern Acad of Performing Arts) B1
Nelson St C2
New Cleveland St A3
New George St A2
Norfolk St A1
North Bridge A3
North St B1
Odeon C1
Old Harbour C3
Osborne St B1
Paragon St B2
Park St B1
Percy St A2
Pier St C2
Police Station B1
Porter St C1
Portland St B1
Post Office B1/B2
Posterngate B2
Prince's Quay B2
Prospect Centre B1
Prospect St B1
Queen's Gardens B2
Railway Dock Marina C2
Railway St C2
Real B1
Red Gallery B1
Reform St A2
Retail Park B1
Riverside Quay C2
Roper St B2
St James St C1
St Luke's St B1
St Mark St A3
St Mary the Virgin B3
St Stephens Shopping Centre B1
Scale Lane Footbridge B3
Scott St A2
South Bridge Rd B3
Sport's Centre C1
Spring Bank A1
Spring St B1
Spurn Lightship C2
Spyvee St A3
Stage @TheDock C3
Sykes St A2
Tidal Surge Barrier ✦ C3
Tower St B3
Trinity House B2
Vane St A1
Victoria Pier ✦ C2
Waterhouse Lane B2
Waterloo St A1
Waverley St C1
Wellington St C2
Wellington St West C2
West St B1
Whitefriargate B2
Wilberforce Drive B2
Wilberforce House B3
Wilberforce Monument ✦ B3
William St C1
Wincolmlee A3
Witham A3
Wright St A1

Inverness 336

Abban St A1
Academy St B2
Alexander Place B2
Anderson St A2
Annfield Rd C3
Ardconnel St B3
Ardconnel Terrace B3
Ardross Place B2
Ardross St B2
Argyle St B3
Argyle Terrace B3
Attadale Rd B1
Ballifeary Lane C2
Ballifeary Rd C1/C2
Balnacraig Lane A1
Balnain House ✦ B2
Balnain St B2
Bank St B2
Bellfield Park C2
Bellfield Terrace C3
Benula Rd A1
Birnie Terrace A1
Bishop's Rd C2
Bowling Green B2
Bridge St B2
Brown St A2
Bruce Avenue C1
Bruce Gardens C1
Bruce Park C1
Burial Ground A2
Burnett Rd A3
Bus Station B3
Caledonian Rd B1
Cameron Rd A1
Cameron Square A1
Carse Rd A1
Carsegate Rd Sth A1
Castle Garrison Encounter ✦ B2
Castle Rd B2
Castle St B3
Celt St B2
Chapel St A2
Charles St B3
Church St B2
Columba Rd B1/C1
Crown Avenue B3
Crown Circus B3
Crown Drive B3
Crown Rd B3
Crown St B3
Culduthel Rd C3
Dalneigh Crescent C1
Dalneigh Rd C1
Denny St B3
Dochfour Drive B1/C1
Douglas Row B2
Duffy Drive C3
Dunabban Rd A1
Dunain Rd B1
Duncraig St B2
Eastgate Shopping Ctr B3
Eden Court C2
Fairfield Rd B1
Falcon Square B3
Fire Station A3
Fraser St B2
Fraser St C2
Friars' Bridge A2
Friars' Lane B2
Friars' St A2
George St A2
Gilbert St A2
Glebe St A2
Glendoe Terrace A1
Glenurquhart Rd C1
Gordon Terrace B3
Gordonville Rd C2
Grant St A2
Grant Street Park (Clachnacuddin FC) A1
Greig St B2
Harbour Rd A3
Harrowden Rd B1
Haugh Rd C2
Heatherley Crescent C3
High St B3
Highland Council Headquarters, The C2
Hill Park C3
Hill St B3
HM Prison B3
Huntly Place A2
Huntly St B2
India St A2
Industrial Estate A3
Information Centre B2
Innes St A2
Inverness B3
Inverness High Sch B1
Inverness Museum & Art Gallery B2
Jamaica St A2
Kenneth St B2
Kilmuir Rd A1
King St B2
Kingsmills Rd B3
Laurel Avenue B1/C1
Library A3
Lilac Grove B1
Lindsay Avenue C1
Lochalsh Rd A1/B1
Longman Rd A3
Lotland Place A2
Lower Kessock St A1
Madras St A2
Maxwell Drive C1
Mayfield Rd C3
Millburn Rd B3
Mitchell's Lane C3
Montague Row B2
Muirfield Rd C3
Muirtown St B1
Nelson St A2
Ness Bank C2
Ness Bridge B2
Ness Walk B2/C2
Old Edinburgh Rd C3
Old High Church B2
Park Rd C1
Paton St C2
Perceval Rd B1
Planefield Rd B2
Police Station A3
Porterfield Bank C3
Porterfield Rd C3
Portland Place A2
Post Office A2/B1/B2
Queen St B2
Queensgate B2
Railway Terrace A3
Rangemore Rd B1
Reay St B3
Riverside St A2
Rose St A2
Ross Avenue B1
Rowan Rd B1
Royal Northern Infirmary C2
St Andrew's Cath C2
St Columba B2
St John's Avenue C1
St Mary's Avenue C1
Sheriff Court B3
Shore St A2
Smith Avenue C1
Southside Place C3
Southside Rd C3
Spectrum Centre B2
Strothers Lane B3
Superstore A1/B2
TA Centre C2
Telford Gardens B1
Telford Rd A1
Telford St A1
Tomnahurich Cemetery C1
Tomnahurich St B2
Town Hall B3
Union Rd B3
Union St B3
Victorian Market B3
Walker Place A2
Walker Rd A3
War Memorial ✦ C2
Waterloo Bridge A2
Wells St B1
Young St B2

Ipswich 336

Alderman Rd B2
All Saints' Rd A1
Alpe St B2
Ancaster Rd C1
Ancient House B3
Anglesea Rd B2
Ann St B2
Arboretum A2
Austin St C2
Avenue, The A3
Belstead Rd C2
Berners St B2
Bibb Way B1
Birkfield Drive C1
Black Horse Lane B2
Bolton Lane B3
Bond St C3
Bowthorpe Close B2
Bramford Lane A1
Bramford Rd A1
Bridge St C2
Brookfield Rd A1
Brooks Hall Rd A1
Broomhill Park A2
Broomhill Rd A1
Broughton Rd A2
Bulwer Rd B1
Burrell Rd C2
Bus Station B3
Butter Market B2
Buttermarket Shopping Centre, The B3
Cardinal Pk Leisure Pk C2
Carr St B3
Cecil Rd B2
Cecilia St C2
Chancery Rd C2
Charles St B2
Chevallier St A1
Christchurch Mansion & Wolsey Art Gallery B3
Christchurch Park A3
Christchurch St B3
Cineworld C2
Civic Centre B2
Civic Drive B2
Clarkson St B1
Cobbold St B3
Commercial Rd C2
Constable Rd A3
Constantine Rd C1
Constitution Hill A2
Corder Rd A3
Corn Exchange B2
Cotswold Avenue A2
Council Offices C2
County Hall B3
Crown Court C2
Crown St B2
Cullingham Rd B1
Cumberland St B2
Curriers Lane B2
Dale Hall Lane A2
Dales View Rd A1
Dalton Rd B2
Dillwyn St B1
Elliot St B1
Elm St B2
Elsmere Rd A3
Falcon St C2
Felaw St C3
Flint Wharf C3
Fonnereau Rd B2
Fore St C3
Foundation St C3
Franciscan Way C2
Friars St C2
Gainsborough Rd A3
Gatacre Rd B1
Geneva Rd B2
Gippeswyk Avenue C1
Gippeswyk Park C1
Grafton Way C2
Graham Rd A1
Great Whip St C3
Grimwade St C3
Handford Cut B1
Handford Rd B1
Henley Rd A2
Hervey St B3
High St B2
Holly Rd A2
Ipswich Haven Marina ✦ C3
Ipswich Museum & Art Gallery B2
Ipswich School A2
Ipswich Station C2
Ipswich Town FC (Portman Road) C2
Ivry St A2
Kensington Rd A1
Kesteven Rd C1
Key St C3
Kingsfield Avenue A3
Kitchener Rd A1
Library A1
Little's Crescent C2
London Rd B1
Low Brook St C3
Lower Orwell St C3
Luther Rd C2
Magistrates Court B2
Manor Rd A3
Mornington Avenue A1
Museum St B2
Neale St B3
New Cardinal St C2
New Cut East C3
New Wolsey B2
Newson St B2
Norwich Rd A1/B1
Oban St B2
Old Custom House C3
Old Foundry Rd B3
Old Merchant's Ho C3
Orford St B2
Paget Rd A2
Park Rd A3
Park View Rd A2
Peter's St C2
Philip Rd C2
Pine Avenue A2
Pine View Rd A2
Police Station B2
Portman Rd B2
Portmans Walk C1
Post Office B2
Princes St C2
Prospect St B1
Queen St B2
Ranelagh Rd C1
Recreation Ground B1
Rectory Rd C2
Regent Theatre B3
Reg Driver Visitor Centre ✦ B3
Retail Park C1
Retail Park C2
Richmond Rd A1
Rope Walk C3
Rose Lane C2
Russell Rd C2
St Edmund's Rd A2
St George's St B2
St Helen's St B3
Sherrington Rd A1
Shopmobility B2
Silent St C2
Sir Alf Ramsey Way C1
Sir Bobby Robson Bridge C1
Sirdar Rd B1
Sir John Mills Theatre B1
Soane St B3
Springfield Lane A1
Star Lane C3
Stevenson Rd B1
Stoke Quay C3
Suffolk College C3
Suffolk Retail Park B1
Superstore B1
Surrey Rd B1
Tacket St C3
Tavern St B3
Tower Ramparts B2
Tower Ramparts Shopping Centre B2
Tower St B3
Town Hall B2
Tuddenham Rd A3
University C3
Upper Brook St B3
Upper Orwell St B3
Valley Rd A2
Vermont Crescent B3
Vermont Rd B3
Vernon St C3
Warrington Rd A2
Waterloo Rd A1
Waterworks St C3
Wellington St B1
West End Rd B1
Westerfield Rd A3
Westgate St B2
Westholme Rd A1
Westwood Avenue A1
Willoughby Rd C2
Withipoll St B3
Woodbridge Rd B3
Woodstone Avenue A3
Yarmouth Rd B1

Kendal 336

Abbot Hall Art Gallery & Museum of Lakeland Life & Industry C2
Ambulance Station A2
Anchorite Fields C2
Anchorite Rd C2
Ann St A3
Appleby Rd A3
Archers Meadow C3
Ashleigh Rd A2
Aynam Rd B2
Bankfield Rd B1
Beast Banks B2
Beezon Fields A2
Beezon Rd A2
Beezon Trad Estate A3
Belmont B2
Birchwood Close C1
Blackhall Rd B2
Brewery Arts Ctr B2
Bridge St B2
Brigsteer Rd C1
Burneside Rd A2
Bus Station B2
Buttery Well Rd C2
Canal Head North B3
Captain French Lane C2
Caroline St A2
Castle Hill B3
Castle Howe B2
Castle Rd B3
Castle St A3/B3
Cedar Grove C1
Council Offices B2
County Council Offices A2
Cricket Ground A3
Cricket Ground C3
Cross Lane C2
Dockray Hall Ind Est A2
Dowker's Lane B2
East View B1
Echo Barn Hill C1
Elephant Yard B2
Fairfield Lane A1
Finkle St B2
Fire Station A2
Fletcher Square C3
Football Ground C3
Fowling Lane A3
Gillinggate C2
Glebe Rd C2
Golf Course B1
Goose Holme B3
Gooseholme Bridge B3
Green St A1
Greengate C2
Greengate Lane C1/C2
Greenside B1
Greenwood C1
Gulfs Rd B2
High Tenterfell B1
Highgate B2
Hillswood Avenue C1
Horncop Lane A2
Kendal A3
Kendal Business Park A3
Kendal Castle (Remains) B3
Kendal Fell B1
Kendal Green A1
Kendal Ski Centre ✦ B3
Kendal Station A3
Kent Place B2
Kirkbarrow C2
Kirkland C2
Library B2
Library Rd B2
Little Aynam B3
Little Wood B1
Long Close C1
Longpool A3
Lound Rd C3
Lound St C3
Low Fellside B2
Lowther St B2
Magistrates Court A2
Maple Drive C1
Market Place B2
Maude St B2
Miller Bridge B2
Milnthorpe Rd C2
Mint St A3
Mintsfeet Rd A3
Mintsfeet Rd South A2
New Rd B2
Noble's Rest B2
Parish Church C2
Park Side Rd C3
Parkside Bsns Park C3
Parr St B3
Police Station A2
Post Office A3/B2
Quaker Tapestry ✦ B2
Queen's Rd B1
Riverside Walk C2
Rydal Mount A2
Sandes Avenue A2
Sandgate A3
Sandylands Rd A3
Serpentine Rd B1
Serpentine Wood B1
Shap Rd A3
South Rd C2
Stainbank Rd C1
Station Rd A3
Stramongate B2
Stramongate Bridge B2
Stricklandgate A2/B2
Sunnyside C3
Thorny Hills B3
Town Hall B2
Undercliff Rd B1
Underwood C1
Union St A2
Vicar's Fields C2
Vicarage Drive C1/C2
Wainwright's Yard B2
Wasdale Close C3
Well Ings C2
Westmorland Shopping Centre & Market Hall B2
Westwood Avenue C1
Wildman St A3
Windermere Rd A1
YHA B2
YWCA B2

King's Lynn 336

Albert St A2
Albion St B2
Alive St James' Swimming Pool B2
All Saints B2
All Saints St B2
Austin Fields A2
Austin St A2
Avenue Rd B3
Bank Side B1
Beech Rd C2
Birch Tree Close B2
Birchwood St A2
Blackfriars Rd B2
Blackfriars St B2
Boal St B1
Bridge St B2
Broad St B2
Broad Walk B3
Burkitt St A2
Bus Station B2
Carmelite Terrace C2
Chapel St A2
Chase Avenue C3
Checker St C2
Church St B2
Clough Lane B2
Coburg St B2
College of West Anglia A3
Columbia Way A3
Common Staithe Quay A1
Corn Exchange A1
County Court Rd B2
Cresswell St A2
Custom House A1
East Coast Business Park C1
Eastgate St A2
Edma St A2
Exton's Rd C3
Ferry Lane B1
Ferry St A1
Framingham's Almshouses B2
Friars St C2
Friars Walk C2
Gaywood Rd A3
George St A2
Gladstone Rd C2
Goodwin's Rd C3
Green Quay Discovery Centre ✦ B1
Greyfriars' Tower ✦ B2
Guanock Terrace C2
Guildhall A1
Hansa Rd C3
Harding's Way C2
Hardwick Rd C2
Hextable Rd A2
High St B1
Holcombe Avenue C3
Hospital Walk C2
Information Centre B1
John Kennedy Rd A2
Kettlewell Lane A2
King George V Avenue B3
King St B1
King's Lynn Art Centre A1
King's Lynn Station B2
Library B2
Littleport St A2
Loke Rd A2
London Rd B2
Lynn Museum B2
Magistrates Court B1
Majestic B2
Market Lane A1
Millfleet B2
Milton Avenue A3
Nar Valley Walk C2
Nelson St B1
New Conduit St B2
Norfolk St A2
North Lynn Discovery Centre ✦ A3
North St A2
Oldsunway B2
Ouse Avenue C1
Page Stair Lane A1
Park Avenue B3
Police Station B2
Portland Place C1
Portland St B2
Purfleet B1
Queen St B1
Raby Avenue A3
Railway Rd A2
Red Mount Chapel B3
Regent Way B2
River Walk A1
Robert St C2
Shopmobility B2
St Ann's St A1
St James St B2
St James' Rd B2
St John's Walk B3
St Margaret's B1
St Nicholas A2
St Nicholas St A1
St Peter's Rd B1
Sir Lewis St A2
Smith Avenue A3
South Everard St C2
South Gate ✦ C2
South Quay B1
South St B2
Southgate St C2
Stonegate St B2
Stories of Lynn B1
Surrey St A1
Sydney St C3
Tennyson Avenue B3
Tennyson Rd B3
The Walks Stadium (King's Lynn FC) B3
Tower St B2
Town Hall B1
Town Wall (Remains) ✦ B3
True's Yard Fisherfolk Museum A2
Valingers Rd C2
Vancouver Avenue C2
Vancouver Quarter B2
Waterloo St B2
Wellesley St B2
Whitefriars Terrace C2
Windsor Rd C2
Winfarthing St C2
Wisbech Road C2
Wyatt St A2
York Rd C3

Lancaster 336

Aberdeen Rd C3
Aldcliffe Rd C2
Alfred St B3
Ambleside Rd A3
Ambulance & Fire Station B2
Ashfield Avenue B1
Ashton Rd C2
Assembly Rooms Emporium B2
Balmoral Rd B3
Bath House B2
Bath St B3
Blades St B1
BMI Lancaster (private) C3
Borrowdale Rd B3
Bowerham Rd C3
Brewery Lane B2
Bridge Lane B2
Brook St C1
Bulk Rd A3
Bulk St B2
Bus Station B2
Cable St B2
Canal Cruises & Waterbus ✦ C2
Carlisle Bridge A1
Carr House Lane C2
Castle B1
Castle Park B1
Caton Rd A3
China St B2
Church St B2
City Museum B2
Clarence St C3
Common Garden St B2
Coniston Rd A3
Cottage Museum B2
Council Offices B2
Courts B2
Cromwell Rd C1
Crown Court B1
Dale St C3
Dallas Rd B1/C1
Dalton Rd B3
Dalton Square B2
Damside St B2
De Vitre St B3
Dee Rd A1
Denny Avenue A1
Derby Rd A2
Dukes, The B2
Earl St A2
East Rd B3
Eastham St C3
Edward St B3
Fairfield Nature Reserve C1
Fairfield Rd B1
Fenton St B2
Firbank Rd A3
Friend's Meeting House B1
Garnet St B3
George St B2
Giant Axe Field B1
Grand B2
Grasmere Rd B3
Greaves Park C3
Greaves Rd C2
Green St A3
Gregson Centre, The B3
Gregson Rd C3
Greyhound Bridge A2
Greyhound Bridge Rd A2
High St B2
Hill Side B1
Hope St C3
Hubert Place B1
Information Centre B2
Kelsy St B1
Kentmere Rd B3
Keswick Road A3
King St B2
Kingsway A3
Kirkes Rd C3
Lancaster City Football Club B1
Lancaster Royal Grammar School B3
Lancaster Station B1
Langdale Rd A3
Ley Court B1
Library B2
Lincoln Rd B1
Lindow St C2
Lodge St B2
Long Marsh Lane B1
Lune Rd A1
Lune St A2
Lune Valley Ramble A3
Mainway A2
Maritime Museum A1
Marketgate Shopping Centre B2
Market St B2
Meadowside C2
Meeting House Lane B1
Millennium Bridge A2
Moor Lane B2
Moorgate B3
Morecambe Rd A1/A2
Nelson St B2
North Rd B2
Orchard Lane C1
Owen Rd A2
Park Rd B3
Parliament St A3
Patterdale Rd A3
Penny St B2
Police Station B2
Portland St C2
Post Office B2/B3
Primrose St C3
Priory B1
Prospect St C3
Quarry Rd B3
Queen St C2
Regent St C2
Ridge Lane A3
Ridge St A3
Royal Lancaster Infirmary (A&E) C2
Rydal Rd B3
Ryelands Park A1
St Georges Quay A1
St John's B2
St Leonard's Gate B2
St Martin's Rd C3
St Nicholas Arcades Shopping Centre B2
St Oswald St C3
St Peter's B3
St Peter's Rd B3
Salisbury Rd B1
Scotch Quarry Urban Park C3
Sibsey St B1
Skerton Bridge A2
South Rd C2
Station Rd B1
Stirling Rd C3
Storey Avenue B1
Storey, The B2
Sunnyside Lane C1
Sylvester St C1
Tarnsyke Rd A1
Thurnham St C2
Town Hall B2
Troutbeck Rd B3
Ulleswater Rd B3
University of Cumbria C3
Vicarage Field B1
Vue B2
West Rd B1
Westbourne Drive C1
Westbourne Rd B1
Westham St C3
Wheatfield St B1
White Cross Business Park C2
Williamson Rd B3
Willow Lane B1
Windermere Rd B3
Wingate-Saul Rd B1
Wolseley St B3
Woodville St B3
Wyresdale Rd C3

Leeds 336

Aire St B3
Albion Place B4
Albion St B4
Albion Way B1
Alma St A6
Ambulance Station B5
Arcades B4
Armley Rd B1
Armories Drive C5
Back Burley Lodge Rd A1
Back Hyde Terrace A2
Back Row C3
Bath Rd C3
Beckett St A6
Bedford St B3
Belgrave St A4
Belle Vue Rd A2
Benson St A5
Black Bull St C5
Blenheim Walk A3
Boar Lane B4
Bond St B4
Bow St C5
Bowman Lane C4
Brewery C4
Brewery Wharf C5
Bridge St A5/B5
Briggate B4
Bruce Gardens C1
Burley Rd A1
Burley St B1
Burmantofts St B6
Bus & Coach Station B5
Butterly St C4
Butts Crescent B4
Byron St A5
Call Lane B4
Calls, The B5
Calverley St A3/B3
Canal St B1
Canal Wharf C3
Carlisle Rd C5
Cavendish Rd A1
Cavendish St A2
Chadwick St C5
Cherry Place A6
Cherry Row A5
City Museum A4
City Varieties Music Hall B4
City Square B3
Civic Hall A3
Clarence Road C5
Clarendon Rd A2
Clarendon Way A3
Clark Lane C6
Clay Pit Lane A4
Cloberry St A2
Close, The B6
Clyde Approach C1
Clyde Gardens C1
Coleman St C2
Commercial St B4
Concord St A5
Cookridge St A4
Copley Hill C1
Core, The B4
Corn Exchange B4
Cromer Terrace A2
Cromwell St A5
Cross Catherine St B6
Cross Green Lane C6
Cross Stamford St A5
Crown & County Courts A3
Crown Point Bridge C5
Crown Point Rd C4
Crown Point Retail Pk C4
David St C3
Dent St C6
Derwent Place C3
Dial St C6
Dock St C4
Dolly Lane A6
Domestic St C2
Drive, The B6
Duke St B5
Duncan St B4
Dyer St B5
East Field St B6
East Parade B3
East St C5
Eastgate B5
Easy Rd C6
Edward St B4
Ellerby Lane C6
Ellerby Rd C6
Fenton St A3
Fire Station B2
First Direct Arena A4
Fish St B4
Flax Place B5
Garth, The B5
Gelderd Rd C1
George St B4
Globe Rd C2
Gower St A5
Grafton St A4
Grand Theatre B4
Granville Rd A6
Great George St A3
Great Wilson St C4
Greek St B3
Green Lane C1
Hanover Avenue A2
Hanover Lane A2
Hanover Square A2
Hanover Way A2
Harewood St B4
Harrison St B4
Haslewood Close B6
Haslewood Drive B6
Headrow, The B3/B4
High Court B5
Holbeck Lane C2
Holdforth Close C1
Holdforth Gardens B1
Holdforth Grove C1
Holdforth Place C1
Holy Trinity B4
Hope Rd A5
Hunslet Lane C4
Hunslet Rd C4
Hyde Terrace A2
Infirmary St B3
Information Centre B3
Ingram Row C3
ITV Yorkshire A1
Junction St C4
Kelso Gardens A2
Kelso Rd A2
Kelso St A2
Kendal Lane A2
Kendell St C4
Kidacre St C4
King Edward St B4
King St B3
Kippax Place C6
Kirkgate B4
Kirkgate Market B4
Kirkstall Rd A1
Kitson St C6
Knight's Way Bridge C5
Lady Lane B4
Lands Lane B4
Lane, The B5
Lavender Walk B6
Leeds Art Gallery B3
Leeds Beckett Univ A3
Leeds Bridge C4
Leeds Coll of Music B5
Leeds Discovery Ctr C5
Leeds General Infirmary (A&E) A3
Leeds Minster B5
Leeds Station B3
Library B3/B4
Light, The B4
Lincoln Green Rd A6
Lincoln Rd A6
Lindsey Gardens A6
Lindsey Rd A6
Lisbon St B3
Little Queen St B3
Long Close Lane C6
Lord St C2
Lovell Park A4
Lovell Park Hill A4
Lovell Park Rd A4
Lower Brunswick St A5
Mabgate A5
Macauly St A5
Magistrates Court A3
Manor Rd C3
Mark Lane B4
Marlborough St B2
Marsh Lane B5
Marshall St C3
Meadow Lane C4
Meadow Rd C4
Melbourne St A5
Merrion Centre A4
Merrion St A4
Merrion Way A4
Mill St B5
Millennium Square A3
Monk Bridge C2
Mount Preston St A2
Mushroom St A5
Neville St C4
New Briggate A4/B4
New Market St B4
New York Rd A5
New York St B5
Nile St A5
Nippet Lane A6
North St A4
Northern Ballet B5
Northern St B3
Oak Rd B1
Oxford Place B3
Oxford Row A3
Parade, The B6
Park Cross St B3
Park Lane A2
Park Place B3
Park Row B4
Park Square B3
Park Square East B3
Park Square West B3
Park St B3
Police Station A3
Pontefract Lane B6
Portland Crescent A3
Portland Way A3
Post Office B4/B5
Quarry House (NHS/DSS Headquarters) B5
Quebec St B3
Queen St B3
Radio Aire A1
Railway St B5
Rectory St A6
Regent St A5
Richmond St C5
Rigton Approach B6
Rigton Drive B6
Rillbank Lane A1
Rosebank Rd A1
Rose Bowl Conference Centre A3
Royal Armouries C5
Russell St B3
St Anne's Cath (RC) A4
St Anne's St B4
St James' Hospital A6
St John's Rd A2
St Johns Centre B4
St Mary's St B5
St Pauls St B3
Saxton Lane B5
Sayner Lane C5
Shakespeare Avenue A6
Shannon St B6
Sheepscar St South A5
Siddall St C3
Skinner Lane A5
South Parade B3
Sovereign St C4
Spence Lane C2
Springfield Mount A2
Springwell Court C2
Springwell Rd C2
Springwell St C2
Stoney Rock Lane A6
Studio Rd A1
Sutton St C2
Sweet St C3
Sweet St West C3
Swinegate B4
Templar St B5
Tetley, The C4
Thoresby Place A3
Torre Rd A6
Town Hall A3
Trinity Leeds B4
Union Place C3
Union St B5
University of Leeds A3
Upper Accommodation Rd B6
Upper Basinghall St B4
Vicar Lane B4
Victoria Bridge C4
Victoria Gate B4
Victoria Quarter B4
Victoria Rd C4
Vue B4
Wade Lane A4
Washington St A1
Water Lane C3
Waterloo Rd C4
Wellington Rd B2/C1
Wellington St B3
West St B2
West Yorkshire Playhouse B5
Westfield Rd A1
Westgate B3
Whitehall Rd B3/C2
Whitelock St A5
Willis St C6
Willow Approach A1
Willow Avenue A1
Willow Terrace Rd A3
Wintoun St A5
Woodhouse Lane A3/A4
Woodsley Rd A1
York Place B3
York Rd B6

Leicester 336

Abbey St A2
All Saints' A1
Aylestone Rd C2
Bath Lane A1
Bede Park C1
Bedford St A3
Bedford St South A3
Belgrave Gate A2
Belvoir St B2
Braunstone Gate B1
Burleys Way A2
Burnmoor St C2
Bus & Coach Station A2
Canning St A2
Carlton St C2
Castle Motte B1
Castle Gardens B1
Cathedral B2
Charles St B3
Chatham St B2
Christow St A3
Church Gate A2
City Hall B3
Clank St B2
Clock Tower B2
Clyde St A3
Colton St B3
Conduit St B3
Crafton St East A3
Craven St A1
Crown Courts B3
Curve B3
De Lux A2
De Montfort Hall C3
De Montfort St C3
De Montfort Univ C1
Deacon St C2
Dover St B3
Duns Lane B1
Dunton St A1
East St B3
East Bond Street A2
Eastern Boulevard C1
Edmonton Rd A3
Erskine St A3
Filbert St C1
Filbert St East C2
Fire Station C3
Fleet St A3
Friar Lane B2
Friday St A2
Gateway St C2
Gateway, The C2
Glebe St B3
Granby St B3
Grange Lane C2
Grasmere St C1
Great Central St A1
Great Hall B1
Guildhall B2
Guru Nanak Sikh Museum B1
Halford St B2
Havelock St C2
Haymarket Shopping Centre A2
High St A2
Highcross Shopping Centre A2
Highcross St A1
HM Prison C2
Horsefair St B2
Humberstone Gate B2
Humberstone Rd A3
Infirmary St C2
Information Centre B2
Jarrom St C2
Jewry Wall B1
Kamloops Crescent A3
King Richard III Visitor Centre B2
King St B2
Lancaster Rd C3
LCB Depot B3
Lee St A3
Leicester Royal Infirmary (A&E) C2
Leicester Station B3
Library B2
London Rd C3
Lower Brown St B2
Magistrates' Court B2
Manitoba Rd A3
Mansfield St A2
Market B2
Market St B2
Mill Lane C2
Montreal Rd A3
Narborough Rd North B1
Nelson Mandela Park C2
New Park St B1
New St B2
New Walk C3
New Walk Museum & Art Gallery C3
Newarke Houses B2
Newarke St B2
Newarke, The B1
Northgate St A1
Orchard St A2
Ottawa Rd A3
Oxford St C2
Phoenix Arts Centre B3
Police Station A3
Post Office B2
Prebend St C3
Princess Rd East C3
Princess Rd West C3
Queen St B3
Rally Community Park, The A2
Regent College C3
Regent Rd C2/C3
Repton St A1
Rutland St B3
St Augustine Rd B1
St Georges Retail Park B3
St George St B3
St Georges Way B3
St John St A2
St Margaret's A2
St Margaret's Way A2
St Martins B2
St Mary de Castro B1
St Matthew's Way A3
St Nicholas B1
St Nicholas Circle B1
Sanvey Gate A2
Silver St B2
Slater St A1
Soar Lane A1
South Albion St B3
Southampton St B3
Sue Townsend Theatre B2
Swain St B3
Swan St A1
Tigers Way C3
Tower St C3
Town Hall B2
Tudor Rd B1
University of Leicester C3
University Rd C3
Upperton Rd C1
Vaughan Way A2
Walnut St C2
Watling St A2
Welford Rd B2
Welford Rd (Leicester Tigers RC) C2
Wellington St B2
West St C3
West Walk C3
Western Boulevard C1
Western Rd C1
Wharf St North A3
Wharf St South A3
Y Theatre, The B3
Yeoman St B3
York Rd B2

Lewes 336

Abinger Place B1
All Saints Centre B2
Anne of Cleves Ho C1
Avenue, The B1
Barbican Ho Mus B1
Brewery B2
Brook St A2
Brooks Rd A2
Bus Station B2
Castle Ditch Lane B1
Castle Precincts B1
Chapel Hill B3
Church Lane A1/A2
Cliffe High St B2
Cliffe Industrial Est C3
Cluny St C1
Cockshut Rd C1
Convent Field C2
Coombe Rd A2
County Hall B1
Course, The C1
Court Rd B2
Crown Court B2
Cuilfail Tunnel B3
Davey's Lane A3
Dripping Room, The (Lewes FC) C2
East St B2
East Sussex College C2
Eastport Lane C1
Fire Station A2
Fisher St B2
Friars Walk B2
Garden St B1
Government Offices C2
Grange Rd B1
Ham Lane C2
Harveys Way B2
Hereward Way A2
High St B1/B2
Hop Gallery B2
Information Centre B2
Keere St B1
King Henry's Rd B1
Lancaster St B2
Landport Rd A1
Leisure Centre C3
Lewes Bridge B2
Lewes Castle B1
Lewes Golf Course B3
Lewes Southern By-Pass C2
Lewes Station B2
Library B2
Malling Brook Ind Est A3
Malling Down Nature Reserve A3
Malling Hill A3
Malling Industrial Est A2
Malling St A3/B3
Market St B2
Martlets, The A2
Martyr's Monument B3
Mayhew Way A2
Morris Rd B3
Mountfield Rd C2
Needlemakers, The B2
New Rd B1
Newton Rd A1
North St A2/B2
Offham Rd B1
Old Malling Way A1
Orchard Rd A3
Paddock Lane B1
Paddock Rd B1
Paddock Sports Gd B1
Park Rd B1
Pelham Terrace A1
Pells Outdoor Swimming Pool A1
Pells, The A1
Phoenix Causeway B2
Phoenix Industrial Est B2
Phoenix Place B2
Pinwell Rd B2
Police Station B2
Post Office B2
Prince Edward's Rd B1
Priory of St Pancras (remains of) C1
Priory St C1
Railway Lane B2
Railway Land Nature Reserve B3
Rotten Row B1
Riverside Ind Est A2
Rufus Close B1
St John St B2
St John's Terrace B1
St Nicholas Lane B2
St Pancras Rd C1
Sewage Works C3
South Downs Bsns Pk A3
South St B3/C3
Southdowns Rd A2
Southerham Junction C3
Southover Grange Gardens B1
Southover High St C1
Southover Rd B1
Spences Field A3
Spences Lane A2
Stansfield Rd A1
Station Rd B2
Station St B2
Sun St B1
Superstore A2/B2
Sussex Police HQ A2
Talbot Terrace B1
Thebes Gallery B2
Toronto Terrace B1
Town Hall B2
West St B2
White Hill B1
Willeys Bridge A1

Lincoln 337

Alexandra Terrace B1
Anchor St C1
Arboretum B3
Arboretum Avenue B3
Avenue, The B1
Baggholme Rd B3
Bailgate A2
Beaumont Fee B1
BMI The Lincoln Hospital A2
Brayford Way C1
Brayford Wharf East C1
Brayford Wharf North B1
Bruce Rd A2
Burton Rd A1
Bus Station (City) C2
Canwick Rd C2
Cardinal's Hat B2
Carline Rd B1
Castle B1
Castle St A1
Cathedral B2
Cathedral St B2
Cecil St A2
Chapel Lane A2
Cheviot St B3
Church Lane A2
City Hall B1
Clasketgate B2
Clayton Sports Gd A3
Coach Park C2
Collection, The B2
County Hospital (A&E) B3
County Hall B1
Courts C1
Cross St C2
Crown Courts B1
Curle Avenue A3
Danesgate B2
Drill Hall B2
Drury Lane B1
East Bight A2
East Gate A2
Eastcliff Rd B3
Eastgate B2
Egerton Rd A3
Ellis Windmill A1
Engine Shed, The C1
Exchequer Gate B2
Firth Rd C1
Flaxengate B2
Florence St B3
George St C3
Good Lane A2
Gray St A1
Great Northern Terrace C3
Greetwell Rd B3
Greetwellgate B3
Grove, The A3
Haffenden Rd A2
High St B2/C1
Hungate B2
James St A2
Jews House & Court B2
Kesteven St C2
Langworthgate A2
Lawn, The B1
Lee Rd A3
Library B2
Lincoln Central Station C2
Lincoln College B2
Lincolnshire Life A1
Lincoln University Technical Coll (UTC) B2
Lindum Rd B2
Lindum Sports Ground A3
Lindum Terrace B3
Liquorice Park B1
Mainwaring Rd A3
Manor Rd A2
Market C2
Massey Rd A3
Medieval Bishop's Palace B2
Mildmay St A1
Mill Rd A1
Millman Rd B3
Minster Yard B2
Monks Rd B3
Montague St B2
Mount St A1
Nettleham Rd A2
Newland B1
Newport A2
Newport Arch A2
Newport Cemetery A2
Northgate A2
Odeon C1
Orchard St B1
Oxford St C2
Park St B1
Pelham Bridge C2
Pelham St C2
Portland St C2
Post Office A1/B2/B3
Potter Gate B2
Priory Gate B2
Queensway A3
Rasen Lane A1
Ropewalk C1
Rosemary Lane B2
St Anne's Rd B3
St Benedict's C1
St Giles Avenue A3
St Mark's Shopping Centre C1
St Marks St C1
St Mary-le-Wigford C1
St Mary's St C2
St Nicholas St A2
St Rumbold's St B2
St Swithin's B2
Saltergate C1
Saxon St A1
Sewell Rd B3
Silver St B2
Sincil St C2
Spital St A2
Spring Hill B1
Stamp End C3
Steep Hill B2
Stonebow & Guildhall C2
Stonefield Avenue A2
Tentercroft St C1
Theatre Royal B2
Tritton Rd C1
Tritton Retail Park C1
Union Rd B1
University of Lincoln C1
Upper Lindum St B3
Upper Long Leys Rd A1
Usher B2
Vere St A2
Victoria St B1
Victoria Terrace B1
Vine St B3
Wake St A1
Waldeck St A1
Waterside North C2
Waterside Shopping Centre C2
Waterside South C2
West Parade B1
Westgate A2
Wigford Way C1
Williamson St A2
Wilson St A1
Winn St B3
Wragby Rd A3
Yarborough Rd A1

Liverpool 337

Abercromby Square C5
Addison St A3
Adelaide Rd B6
Ainsworth St B4
Albany Rd B6
Albert Edward Rd B6
Angela St C6
Anson St B4
Argyle St C3
Arrad St C4
Ashton St B5
Audley St A4
Back Leeds St A2
Basnett St B3
Bath St A1
Beacon, The B3
Beatles Story, The C2
Beckwith St C3
Bedford Close C5
Bedford St North C5
Bedford St South C5
Benson St C4
Berry St C4
Birkett St A4
Bixteth St B2
Blackburne Place C4
Bluecoat B3
Bold Place C4
Bold St C4
Bolton St B3
Bridport St B4
Bronte St B4
Brook St A1
Brownlow Hill B4/B5
Brownlow St B5
Brunswick Rd A5
Brunswick St B1
Bus Station C2
Butler Crescent A6
Byrom St A3
Caledonia St C4
Cambridge St C5
Camden St A4
Canada Boulevard B1
Canning Dock C2
Canterbury St A4
Cardwell St C6
Carver St A4
Cases St B3
Castle St B2
Catherine St C5
Cavern Club B3
Central Library A3
Chapel St B2
Charlotte St B3
Chatham Place C6
Chatham St C5
Cheapside B2
Chavasse Park C2
Chestnut St C5
Christian St A3
Church St B3
Clarence St B4
Clayton Square Shopping Centre B3
Coach Station A4
Cobden St A5
Cockspur St A2
College St C3
College St North A5
College St South A5
Colquitt St C4
Comus St A3
Concert St C3
Connaught Rd B6
Cook St B2
Copperas Hill B4
Cornwallis St C3
Covent Garden B2
Craven St A4
Cropper St B3
Crown St B5/C6
Cumberland St B2
Cunard Building B1
Dale St B2
Dansie St B4
Daulby St B5
Dawson St B3
Dental Hospital B5
Derby Square B2
Drury Lane B2
Duckinfield St B4
Duke St C3
Earle St A2
East St A2
Eaton St A2
Edgar St A3
Edge Lane B6
Edinburgh Rd A6
Edmund St B2
Elizabeth St B5
Elliot St B3
Empire Theatre B4
Empress Rd B6
Epstein Theatre B3
Epworth St A5
Erskine St A5
Everyman Theatre C5
Exchange St East B2
FACT C4
Falkland St A5
Falkner St C5/C6
Farnworth St A6
Fenwick St B2
Fielding St A6
Fire Station A4
Fleet St C3
Fraser St A4
Freemasons Row A2
Gardner Row A3
Gascoyne St A2
George St B2
Gibraltar Road A1
Gilbert St C3
Gildart St A4
Gill St B4
Goree B2
Gower St C2
Gradwell St C3
Great Crosshall St A3
Great George St C4
Great Howard St A1
Great Newton St B4
Greek St B4
Green Lane B4
Greenside A5
Greetham St C3
Gregson St A5
Grenville St C3
Grinfield St C6
Grove St C5
Guelph St A6
Hackins Hey B2
Haigh St A4
Hall Lane B6
Hanover St B3
Harbord St C6
Hardman St C4
Harker St A4
Hart St B4
Hatton Garden A2
Hawke St B4
Helsby St B6
Henry St C3
Highfield St A2
Highgate St B6
Hilbre St B4
Hope Place C4
Hope St C4
Hope University A5
Houghton St B3
Hunter St A3
Hutchinson St A6
Information Ctr B4/C2
Institute for the Performing Arts C4
International Slavery Museum C2
Irvine St B6
Irwell St B2
Islington A4
James St B2
James St Station B2
Jenkinson St A4
John Moores University A2/A3/A4/B4/C4
Johnson St A3
Jubilee Drive B6
Kempston St A4
Kensington A6
Kensington Gardens B6
Kensington St A6
Kent St C3
King Edward St A1
Kinglake St B6
Knight St C4
Lace St A3
Langsdale St A4
Law Courts C2
Leece St C4
Leeds St A2
Leopold Rd B6
Lime St B3
Lime St Station B4
Liver St C2
Liverpool Central Station B3
Liverpool Landing Stage B1
Liverpool Institute for Performing Arts (LIPA) C4
Liverpool ONE C2
Liverpool Wheel, The C2
London Rd A4/B4
Lord Nelson St B4
Lord St B2
Lovat St C6
Low Hill A5
Low Wood St A6
Lydia Ann St C3
M&S Bank Arena C2
Mansfield St A4
Marmaduke St B6
Marsden St A6
Martensen St B6
Marybone A3
Maryland St C4
Mason St B6
Mathew St B2
May St B4
Melville Place C6
Merseyside Maritime Museum C2
Metquarter B3
Metropolitan Cathedral (RC) B5
Midghall St A2
Molyneux Rd A6
Moor Place B4
Moorfields B2
Moorfields Station B2
Moss St A5
Mount Pleasant B4/B5
Mount St C4
Mount Vernon B6
Mulberry St C5
Municipal Buildings B2
Mus of Liverpool C2
Myrtle St C5
Naylor St A2
Nelson St C4
New Islington A4
New Quay B1
Newington St C3
North John St B2
North St A3
North View B6
Norton St A4
O2 Academy B4
Oakes St B5
Odeon B2
Old Hall St A1
Old Leeds St A2
Oldham Place C4
Oldham St C4
Olive St C6
Open Eye Gallery C2
Oriel St A2
Ormond St B2
Orphan St C6
Overbury St C6
Overton St B6
Oxford St C5
Paisley St A1
Pall Mall A2
Paradise St C3
Park Lane C3
Parker St B3
Parr St C3
Peach St B5
Pembroke Place B4
Pembroke St B5
Philharmonic Hall C5
Phythian Park A6
Pickop St A2
Pilgrim St C4
Pitt St C3
Playhouse Theatre B3
Pleasant St B4
Police HQ C2
Police Sta A4/A6/B4
Pomona St B4
Port of Liverpool Building B2
Post Office A2/A4/A5/B2/B3/B4/C4
Pownall St C2
Prescot St A5
Preston St B3
Princes Dock A1
Princes Gardens A2
Princes Jetty A1
Princes Parade B1
Princes St B2
Pythian St A6
Queen Square Bus Station B3
Queensland St C6
Queensway Tunnel (Docks exit) B1
Queensway Tunnel (Entrance) B3
Radio City B2
Ranelagh St B3
Redcross St B2
Renfrew St B6
Renshaw St B4
Richmond Row A4
Richmond St B3
Rigby St A2
Roberts St A1
Rock St B4
Rodney St C4
Rokeby St A4
Romily St A6
Roscoe Lane C4
Roscoe St C4
Rose Hill A3
Royal Albert Dock C2
Royal Court Theatre B3
Royal Liver Building B1
Royal Liverpool Hospital (A&E) B5
Royal Mail St B4
Rumford Place B2
Rumford St B2
Russell St B4
St Andrew St B4
St Anne St A4
St Georges Hall B3
St John's Centre B3
St John's Gardens B3
St John's Lane B3
St Joseph's Crescent A4
St Minishull St B5
St Nicholas Place B1
St Paul's Square A2
Salisbury St A4
Salthouse Dock C2
Salthouse Quay C2
Sandon St C5
Saxony Rd B6
Schomberg St A6
School Lane B2
Seel St C3
Seymour St B4
Shaw St A5
Shopmobility C2
Sidney Place C6
Sir Thomas St B3
Skelhorne St B4
Slater St C3
Smithdown Lane B6
Soho Square A4
Soho St A4
South John St B2
Springfield A4
Stafford St A4
Standish St A3
Stanley St B2
Strand St C2
Strand, The B2
Suffolk St C3
Sydney Jones Library C5
Tabley St C3
Tarleton St B3
Tate Liverpool Gallery C2
Teck St B6
Temple St B2
Titanic Memorial B1
Tithebarn St B2
Town Hall B2
Trowbridge St B4
Trueman St A3
Union St B2
Unity Theatre C4
University C5
University of Liverpool B5
Upper Baker St A6
Upper Duke St C4
Upper Frederick St C3
Vauxhall Rd A2
Vernon St B2
Victoria Gallery & Museum B5
Victoria St B2
Vine St C5
Wakefield St A4

Walker Art Gallery 🏛 A3
Walker St A6
Wapping C2
Water St B1/B2
Waterloo Rd A1
Wavertree Rd B6
West Derby Rd A6
West Derby St B5
Western Approaches War Museum 🏛 B2
Whitechapel B3
Whitley Gardens A5
William Brown St B3
William Henry St A4
Williamson Square B3
Williamson St B3
Williamson's Tunnels Heritage Centre ✦ C6
Women's Hospital Ⓗ C6
Wood St B3
World Museum, Liverpool 🏛 A3
York St C3

Llandudno 337

Abbey Place B1
Abbey Rd B1
Adelphi St B3
Alexandra Rd C2
Anglesey Rd A1
Argyll Rd B3
Arvon Avenue A2
Atlee Close C3
Augusta St B3
Back Madoc St B2
Bodafon St B3
Bodhyfryd Rd A2
Bodnant Crescent C3
Bodnant Rd C3
Bridge Rd C2
Bryniau Rd C1
Builder St B3
Builder St West C2
Cabin Lift Cable Car ✦ A2
Camera Obscura ✦ A3
Caroline Rd B2
Chapel St A2
Charlton St B3
Church Crescent C1
Church Walks A2
Claremont Rd B2
Clement Avenue A2
Clifton Rd B2
Clonmel St B3
Coach Station B3
Conway Rd B3
Conwy Archive Service B2
Council St West C3
Cricket and Rec Gd B2
Cwlach Rd A2
Cwlach St A1
Cwm Howard Lane C3
Cwm Place C3
Cwm Rd C3
Dale Rd C1
Deganwy Avenue B2
Denness Place C2
Dinas Rd C2
Dolydd B1
Erol Place B2
Ewloe Drive C3
Fairways C2
Ffordd Dewi C3
Ffordd Dulyn C2
Ffordd Dwyfor C3
Ffordd Elisabeth C3
Ffordd Gwynedd C3
Ffordd Las C3
Ffordd Morfa C3
Ffordd Penrhyn C3
Ffordd Tudno C3
Ffordd yr Orsedd C3
Ffordd Ysbyty C2
Fire & Ambulance Sta B3
Garage St B3
George St A2
Gloddaeth Avenue B1
Gloddaeth St B2
Gogarth Rd B1
Great Orme Mines ✦ A1
Great Ormes Rd B1
Great Orme Tramway ✦ A2
Happy Valley A2
Happy Valley Rd A3
Haulfre Gardens ✿ A1
Herkomer Crescent C1
Hill Terrace A2
Home Front Mus 🏛 B2
Hospice B1
Howard Rd B3
Information Centre ℹ B2
Invalids' Walk B1
James St B2
Jubilee St B3
King's Avenue C2
King's Rd C2
Knowles Rd C2
Lees Rd C2
Library B2
Llandudno 🏛 A2
Llandudno (A&E) Ⓗ C2
Llandudno Station ≋ B3
Llandudno Football Gd C2
Llewelyn Avenue A2
Lloyd St B2
Lloyd St West B1
Llwynon Rd A1
Llys Maelgwn B1
Madoc St B2
Maelgwn Rd B2
Maes-y-Cwm C3
Maes-y-Orsedd C3
Maesdu Bridge C2
Maesdu Rd C2/C3
Marian Place C2
Marian Rd C2
Marine Drive (Toll) A3
Market St A2
Miniature Golf Course A1
Morfa Rd B1
Mostyn 🏛 B3
Mostyn Broadway B3
Mostyn St B3
Mowbray Rd C2
New St A2
Norman Rd B3
North Parade A2
North Wales Golf Links C1
Old Bank, The 🏛 A2
Old Rd A2
Oval, The B1
Oxford Rd B3
Parade, The B3
Parc Llandudno Retail Park B3
Pier ✦ A3
Plas Rd A2
Police Station ▣ B3
Post Office ✉ A2/B3
Promenade A3
Pyllau Rd A1
Rectory Lane A2
Rhuddlan Avenue C3
St Andrew's Avenue B2
St Andrew's Place B2
St Beuno's Rd A1
St David's Place B2
St David's Rd B2
St George's Place A3
St Mary's Rd B2
St Seriol's Rd B2
Salisbury Pass B1
Salisbury Rd B2
Somerset St B3
South Parade A2
Stephen St B3
Tabor Hill A2
Town Hall B2
Trinity Avenue B1
Trinity Crescent C1
Trinity Square B3
Tudno St A2
Ty-Coch Rd A2
Ty-Gwyn Rd A1/A2
Ty'n-y-Coed Rd A1
Vaughan St B3
Victoria Shopping Centre B3
Victoria 🚋 A2
War Memorial ✦ A2
Werny Wylan C3
West Parade B1
Whiston Pass A2
Winllan Avenue C2
Wyddfyd Rd A2
York Rd A2

Llanelli 337

Alban Rd B3
Albert St B1
Als St B3
Amos St C1
Andrew St A3
Ann St C2
Annesley St B2
Arfryn Avenue A3
Avenue Cilfig, The A2
Belvedere Rd A1
Bigyn Park Terrace C3
Bigyn Rd C3
Bond Avenue C3
Brettenham St A1
Bridge St B2
Bryn Place C1
Bryn Rd C1
Bryn Terrace C1
Bryn-More Rd C1
Brynhyfryd Rd A2
Brynmelyn Avenue A3
Brynmor Rd B1
Burry St C1
Bus Station B2
Caersalem Terrace C2
Cambrian St C1
Caswell St C3
Cedric St B3
Cemetery A2
Chapman St A1
Charles Terrace C2
Church St B2
Clos Caer Elms A1
Clos Sant Paul C2
Coastal Link Rd B1/C1
Coldstream St B2
Coleshill Terrace B1
College Hill B3
College Square B3
Copperworks Rd C2
Coronation Rd C3
Corporation Avenue A3
Council Offices B2
Court B2
Cowell St B2
Cradock St C2
Craig Avenue C3
Cricket Ground A1
Derwent St A1
Dillwyn St C2
Druce St C1
Eastgate Leisure Complex ✦ B2
Elizabeth St B2
Emma St C2
Erw Rd B1
Felinfoel Rd A2
Fire Station A3
Firth Rd C3
Fron Terrace C3
Furnace United Rugby Football Ground A1
Gelli-On B2
George St C2
Gilbert Crescent A2
Gilbert Rd A2
Glanmor Rd C2
Glanmor Terrace C2
Glasfryn Terrace A3
Glenalla Rd B3
Glevering St B3
Goring Rd A2
Gorsedd Circle 🏛 A2
Grant St C3
Graveyard C2
Great Western Close C2
Greenway St B1
Hall St B2
Harries Avenue A2
Hedley Terrace A2
Heol Elli B3
Heol Goffa A3
Heol Nant-y-Felin A3
Heol Siloh B2
Hick St C2
High St C1
Indoor Bowls Centre B1
Inkerman St B2
Island Place B2
James St B3
John St B2
King George Avenue B3
Lake View Close A2
Lakefield Place C1
Lakefield Rd C1
Langland Rd C3
Leisure Centre B1
Library B2
Llanelli House ⌂ B2
Llanelli Parish Church ⛪ B2
Llanelli Station ≋ C2
Llewellyn St C2
Lliedi Crescent A3
Lloyd St B2
Llys Alys B3
Llys Fran A3
Llysnewedd C1
Long Row A3
Maes Gors C2
Maesyrhaf A3
Mansel St C3
Marblehall Rd B3
Marborough Rd A2
Margam St C3
Marged St C2
Marine St C1
Mariners, The C1
Market B2
Market St B2
Marsh St C2
Martin Rd C3
Miles St A1
Mill Lane A3/B2
Mincing Lane B2
Murray St B2
Myn y Mor B1
Nathan St C1
Nelson Terrace C1
Nevill St C2
New Dock Rd C2
New Rd A1
New Zealand St A1
Odeon 🎦 B2
Old Lodge C2
Old Rd A2
Paddock St C2
Palace Avenue B3
Parc Howard A2
Parc Howard Museum & Art Gallery 🏛 A2
Park Crescent B1
Park St B2
Parkview Terrace B1
Pemberton St C2
Pembrey Rd A1
Peoples Park B1
Police Station ▣ B2
Post Office ✉ B2/C2
Pottery Place B3
Pottery St B3
Princess St B1
Prospect Place A2
Pryce St A1
Queen Mary's Walk C3
Queen Victoria Rd C1
Raby St B1
Railway Terrace C2
Ralph St B2
Ralph Terrace C1
Regalia Terrace B3
Rhydyrafon A3
Richard St B2
Robinson St B2
Roland Avenue A1
Russell St C3
St David's Close C1
St Elli Shopping Ctr B2
St Margaret's Drive A1
Spowart Avenue A1
Station Rd B2/C2
Stepney Place B2
Stepney St B2
Stewart St A1
Stradey Park Avenue A1
Sunny Hill A2
Superstore A2
Swansea Rd A3
Talbot St C3
Temple St B3
Thomas St A2
Tinopolos TV Studios ✦ B2
Toft Place A3
Town Hall B2
Traeth Ffordd C1
Trinity Rd C3
Trinity Terrace C2
Tunnel Rd B3
Tysha Rd C3
Union Blgs A2
Upper Robinson St B2
Vauxhall Rd B2
Walter's Rd B3
Waun Lanyrafon B2
Waun Rd A3
Wern Rd B3
West End A2
Y Bwthyn C3
Zion Row B3

London 338

Abbey Orchard St E4
Abbey St E8
Abchurch Lane D7
Abingdon St E5
Achilles Way D3
Acton St B5
Addington St E5
Air St D4
Albany St B3
Albemarle St D4
Albert Embankment F5
Alberta St F6
Aldenham St A4
Alderney St F3
Aldersgate St C7
Aldford St D3
Aldgate ⊖ C8
Aldgate High St C8
Aldwych C5
Allsop Place B2
Alscot Rd E8
Amwell St B6
Angel ⊖ A6
Appold St C8
Argyle Square B5
Argyle St B5
Argyll St C4
Arnold Circus B8
Artillery Lane C8
Artillery Row E4
Ashbridge St B2
Association of Photographers Gallery 🏛 B7
Baker St ⊖ B2
Baker St B2
Balaclava Rd F8
Balcombe St B2
Baldwin's Gardens C6
Balfour St F7
Baltic St B7
Bank ⊖ C7
Bank Museum 🏛 C7
Bank of England C7
Bankside D7
Bankside Gallery 🏛 D6
Banner St B7
Barbican ≋⊖ C7
Barbican Centre for Arts, The C7
Barbican Gallery 🏛 C7
Basil St E2
Bastwick St B7
Bateman's Row B8
Bath St B7
Bath Terrace E7
Bayley St C4
Baylis Rd E6
Bayswater Rd D2
Beak St D4
Beauchamp Place E2
Bedford Row C5
Bedford Square C4
Bedford St D5
Bedford Way B4
Beech St C7
Belgrave Place E3
Belgrave Rd F4
Belgrave Square E3
Bell Lane C8
Belvedere Rd E5
Berkeley Square D3
Berkeley St D3
Bermondsey St E8
Bernard St B5
Berners Place C4
Berners St C4
Berwick St C4
Bessborough St F4
Bethnal Green Rd B8
Bevenden St B7
Bevis Marks C8
BFI (British Film Institute) 🎦 D5
BFI London IMAX Cinema 🎦 D6
Bidborough St B5
Binney St C3
Birdcage Walk E4
Bishopsgate C8
Black Prince Rd F5
Blackfriars ≋⊖ D6
Blackfriars Bridge D6
Blackfriars Rd E6
Blackfriars Passage D6
Blandford St C2
Blomfield St C7
Bloomsbury St C4
Bloomsbury Way C5
Bolton St D3
Bond St ⊖ C3
Borough ⊖ E7
Borough High St E7
Borough Rd E6
Boswell St C5
Bourne St F3
Bow St C5
Bowling Green Lane B6
Brad St D6
Brandon St F7
Bressenden Place E4
Brewer St D4
Brick St D3
Bridge St E5
Britannia Walk B7
British Film Institute (BFI) 🎦 D5
British Library ⌂ B4
British Museum 🏛 C5
Britton St B6
Broad Sanctuary E4
Broadley St C2
Broadway E4
Brompton Rd E2
Brompton Square E2
Brook Drive F6
Brook St D3
Brown St C2
Brunswick Place B7
Brunswick Shopping Centre, The B5
Brunswick Square B5
Brushfield St C8
Bruton St D3
Bryanston St C2
BT Centre C7
Buckingham Gate E4
Buckingham Palace ⌂ E4
Buckingham Palace Rd F3
Bunhill Row B7
Byward St D8
Cabinet War Rooms & Churchill Museum 🏛 E4
Cadogan Lane E3
Cadogan Place E2
Cadogan Square F2
Cadogan St F2
Cale St F2
Caledonian Rd A5
Calshot St A5
Calthorpe St B5
Calvert Avenue B8
Cambridge Circus C4
Cambridge Square C2
Cambridge St F3
Camomile St C8
Cannon St D7
Cannon St ≋⊖ D7
Capel Manor College B3
Capland St B1
Carey St C5
Carlisle Lane E5
Carlisle Place E4
Carlton House Terrace D4
Carmelite St D6
Carnaby St C4
Carter Lane C6
Carthusian St C7
Cartwright Gardens B5
Castle Baynard St D6
Cavendish Place C3
Cavendish Square C3
Caxton Hall E4
Caxton St E4
Central St B7
Chalton St B4
Chancery Lane ⊖ C6
Chapel St C2
Chapel St E3
Charing Cross ≋⊖ D5
Charing Cross Rd C4
Charles II St D4
Charles Dickens Museum, The 🏛 B5
Charles Square B7
Charles St D3
Charlotte Rd B8
Charlotte St C4
Chart St B7
Charterhouse Square C6
Charterhouse St C6
Chatham St F7
Cheapside C7
Chenies St C4
Chesham St E3
Chester Square F3
Chester Way F6
Chesterfield Hill D3
Cheval Place E2
Chiltern St C3
Chiswell St C7
Church St B2
City Garden Row A6
City Rd B7
City Thameslink ≋ C6
City University, The B6
Claremont Square A6
Clarendon St F3
Clarges St D3
Clerkenwell Close B6
Clerkenwell Green B6
Clerkenwell Rd B6
Cleveland St C4
Clifford St D4
Clink Prison Mus 🏛 D7
Cliveden Place F3
Clock Museum 🏛 C7
Club Row B8
Cockspur St D4
Coleman St C7
Columbia Rd B8
Commercial Rd C9
Commercial St C8
Compton St B6
Conduit St D3
Congreve St F8
Connaught Square C2
Connaught St C2
Constitution Hill E3
Copperfield St E6
Coptic St C5
Cornhill C7
Cornwall Rd D6
Coronet St B8
County St E7
Courtauld Gallery 🏛 D5
Courtenay St F6
Covent Garden ⊖ D5
Covent Garden ✦ D5
Cowcross St C6
Cowper St B7
Crampton St F7
Cranbourn St D4
Craven St D5
Crawford Place C2
Crawford St C2
Creechurch Lane C8
Cricket Museum 🏛 B1
Cromer St B5
Cromwell Rd F1
Crosby Row E7
Crucifix Lane E8
Cumberland Gate D2
Cumberland St F3
Cumberland Terrace A3
Cuming Museum 🏛 F7
Curtain Rd B8
Curzon St D3
Cut, The E6
D'arblay St C4
Dante Rd F6
Davies St C3
Dean St C4
Deluxe Gallery 🏛 B8
Denbigh Place F4
Denmark St C4
Dering St C3
Devonshire St C3
Diana, Princess of Wales Memorial Fountain ✦ D1
Diana, Princess of Wales Memorial Walk E4
Dingley Rd B7
Dorset St C2
Doughty St B5
Douglas St F4
Dover St D3
Downing St E5
Draycott Avenue F2
Draycott Place F2
Druid St E8
Drummond St B4
Drury Lane C5
Drysdale St B8
Duchess St C3
Dufferin St B7
Duke of Wellington Pl E3
Duke St C3/D3
Duke St Hill D7
Duke's Place C8
Duncannon St D5
Dunton Rd F8
East Rd B7
East St F7
Eastcastle St C4
Eastcheap D8
Eastman Dental Hospital Ⓗ B5
Eaton Gate F3
Eaton Place E3
Eaton Square E3
Eaton Terrace F3
Ebury Bridge F3
Ebury Bridge Rd F3
Eccleston Bridge F3
Eccleston Square F3
Eccleston St E3
Edgware Rd C2
Edgware Rd ⊖ C2
Egerton Gardens E2
Eldon St C7
Elephant & Castle ≋ F7
Elephant and Castle ≋⊖ E6
Elephant Rd F7
Elizabeth Bridge F3
Elizabeth St F3
Elm Tree Rd B1
Elystan Place F2
Elystan St F2
Embankment ⊖ D5
Endell St C5
Endsleigh Place B4
Enid St E8
Ennismore Gardens E2
Erasmus St F4
Euston ≋⊖ B4
Euston Rd B4
Euston Square ⊖ B4
Evelina Children's Hospital E5
Eversholt St A4
Exhibition Rd E1
Exmouth Market B6
Fair St E8
Falmouth Rd E7
Fann St B7
Farringdon ≋⊖ C6
Farringdon Rd C6
Farringdon St C6
Featherstone St B7
Fenchurch St D8
Fenchurch St ≋ D8
Fetter Lane C6
Finsbury Circus C7
Finsbury Pavement C7
Finsbury Square B7
Fitzalan St F6
Fitzmaurice Place D3
Fleet St C6
Fleming Lab. Mus 🏛 C1
Floral St D5
Florence Nightingale Museum 🏛 E5
Folgate St C8
Fore St C7
Foster Lane C7
Foundling Mus, The 🏛 B5
Francis St F4
Frazier St E6
Freemason's Hall C5
Friday St C7
Fulham Rd F1
Gainsford St E8
Garden Row E6
Gee St B7
Geological Museum 🏛 E1
George Row E9
George St C2
Gerrard St D4
Gibson Rd F5
Giltspur St C6
Glasshouse St D4
Glasshouse Walk F5
Gloucester Place C2
Gloucester Square C1
Gloucester St F4
Golden Hinde ⛵ D7
Golden Lane B7
Golden Square D4
Goodge St ⊖ C4
Goodge St C4
Gordon Hospital Ⓗ F4
Gordon Square B4
Goswell Rd B6
Gough St B5
Goulston St C8
Gower St B4
Gracechurch St D7
Grafton Way B4
Graham Terrace F3
Grange Rd E8
Grange Walk E8
Gray's Inn Rd B5
Great College St E5
Great Cumberland Pl C2
Great Dover St E7
Great Eastern St B8
Great Guildford St D7
Great Marlborough St C4
Great Ormond St B5
Great Ormond Street Children's Hosp Ⓗ B5
Great Percy St B5
Great Peter St E4
Great Portland St ⊖ B3
Great Portland St C3
Great Queen St C5
Great Russell St C4
Great Scotland Yard D5
Great Smith St E4
Great Suffolk St D6/E6
Great Titchfield St C4
Great Tower St D8
Great Windmill St D4
Greek St C4
Green Park ⊖ D4
Green St D3
Greencoat Place F4
Gresham St C7
Greville St B5/C6
Greycoat Hospital Sch E4
Greycoat Place E4
Grosvenor Crescent E3
Grosvenor Gardens E3
Grosvenor Place E3
Grosvenor Square D3
Grosvenor St D3
Grove End Rd B1
Guards Museum and Chapel 🏛 E4
Guildhall Art Gallery 🏛 C7
Guilford St B5
Guy's Hospital Ⓗ D7
Haberdasher St B7
Hackney Rd B8
Half Moon St D3
Halkin St E3
Hall PL B1
Hall St B6
Hallam St C3
Hamilton Close B1
Hampstead Rd B4
Hanover Square C3
Hans Crescent E2
Hans Rd E2
Hanway St C4
Hardwick St B6
Harewood Avenue B2
Harley St C3
Harper Rd E6
Harrington Rd F1
Harrison St B5
Harrowby St C2
Hasker St F2
Hastings St B5
Hatfields D5
Hay's Galleria D8
Hay's Mews D3
Hayles St F6
Haymarket D4
Hayward Gallery 🏛 D5
Helmet Row B7
Herbrand St B5
Hercules Rd E5
Hertford St D3
Heygate St F7
High Holborn C5
Hill St D3
HMS Belfast ⛵ D8
Hobart Place E3
Holborn ⊖ C5
Holborn C6
Holborn Viaduct C6
Holland St D6
Holmes Museum 🏛 B2
Holywell Lane B8
Horse Guards' Rd D4
Horseferry Rd F4
Houndsditch C8
Houses of Parliament ⌂ E5
Howland St C4
Hoxton Square B8
Hoxton St B8
Hugh St F3
Hunter St B5
Hunterian Museum 🏛 C5
Hyde Park D2
Hyde Park Corner ⊖ E3
Hyde Park Crescent C2
Hyde Park St C2
Imperial Coll London E1
Imperial College Rd E1
Imperial War Mus 🏛 E6
Information Centre ℹ D4, F3, C7
Inner Circle B3
Ironmonger Row B7
Jacob St E9
Jamaica Rd E8
James St C3
James St D5
Jermyn St D4
Jockey's Fields C5
John Carpenter St D6
John Fisher St D9
John Islip St F4
John St B5
Johnathan St F5
Judd St B5
Kennings Way F6
Kennington ⊖ F6
Kennington Lane F6
Kennington Park Rd F6
Kennington Rd E6/F6
Kensington Gardens D1
Kensington Gore E1
Kensington Rd E1
Keyworth St E6
King Charles St E5
King St D5
King William St C7
King's College London D5
King's Cross ≋ A5
King's Cross Rd B5
King's Cross St Pancras ⊖ A5
King's Rd F2
Kingley St C4
Kingsland Rd B8
Kingsway C5
Kinnerton St E3
Kipling St E7
Knightsbridge ⊖ E2
Lamb St C8
Lamb's Conduit St C5
Lambeth Bridge F5
Lambeth High St F5
Lambeth North ⊖ E6
Lambeth Palace ⌂ E5
Lambeth Palace Rd E5
Lambeth Rd E6
Lambeth Walk F5
Lancaster Gate ⊖ D1
Lancaster Place D5
Lancaster St E6
Lancaster Terrace D1
Langham Place C3
Lant St E7
Leadenhall St C8
Leake St E5
Leather Lane C6
Leathermarket St E8
Leicester Square ⊖ D4
Leicester St D4
Leonard St B7
Leroy St E8
Lever St B7
Lexington St D4
Lidlington Place A4
Lime St D8
Lincoln's Inn Fields C5
Lindsey St C6
Lisle St D4
Lisson Grove B1
Lisson St C2
Liverpool St C8
Liverpool St ≋⊖ C8
Lloyd Baker St B6
Lloyd Square B6
Lodge Rd B2
Lollard St F6
Lombard St C7
London Aquarium 🐟 E5
London Bridge ≋⊖ D7
London Bridge Hospital Ⓗ D7
London City Hall ⌂ D8
London Dungeon 🏛 E5
London Guildhall Univ C7
London Rd E6
London St C1
London Transport Museum 🏛 D5
London Wall C7
London Eye ✦ E5
Long Acre D5
Long Lane C6
Long Lane E7
Longford St B3
Lord's Cricket Gd (MCC & Middlesex CCC) B1
Lower Belgrave St E3
Lower Grosvenor Pl E3
Lower Marsh E6
Lower Sloane St F3
Lower Thames St D7
Lowndes St E3
Ludgate Circus C6
Ludgate Hill C6
Lupus St F4
Luxborough St C3
Lyall St E3
Macclesfield Rd B7
Madame Tussaud's ✦ B3
Maddox St D3
Malet St C4
Mall, The E4
Maltby St E8
Manchester Square C3
Manchester St C3
Manciple St E7
Mandela Way F8
Mandeville Place C3
Mansell St D8
Mansion House ⌂ C7
Mansion House ⊖ D7
Maple St C4
Marble Arch ⊖ C2
Marble Arch D2
Marchmont St B5
Margaret St C4
Margery St B6
Mark Lane D8
Marlborough Rd D4
Marshall St C4
Marshalsea Rd E7
Marsham St E4
Marylebone ≋⊖ B2
Marylebone High St C3
Marylebone Lane C3
Marylebone Rd B3/C2
Marylebone St C3
Mecklenburgh Square B5
Middle Temple Lane C6
Middlesex St (Petticoat Lane) C8
Midland Rd A4
Millbank F5
Milner St F2
Minories C8
Monck St E4
Monkton St F6
Monmouth St C5
Montagu Place C2
Montagu Square C2
Montagu St C5
Montague Place C4
Montpelier St E2
Montpelier Walk E2
Monument ⊖ D7
Monument St D7
Monument, The ✦ D7
Moor Lane C7
Moorfields C7
Moorfields Eye Hospital Ⓗ B7
Moorgate C7
Moorgate ≋⊖ C7
Moreland St B6
Morley St E6
Mortimer St C4
Mossop St F2
Mount Pleasant B6
Mount St D3
Murray Grove A7
Mus of Gdn History 🏛 E5
Museum of London 🏛 C7
Museum St C5
Myddelton Square B6
Myddelton St B6
National Gallery 🏛 D4
National Hospital Ⓗ B5
National Portrait Gallery 🏛 D4
Natural History Museum 🏛 E1
Neal St C5
Nelson's Column ✦ D5
Neville St F1
New Bond St C3/D3
New Bridge St C6
New Cavendish St C3
New Change C7
New Fetter Lane C6
New Inn Yard B8
New Kent Rd F7
New North Rd A7
New Oxford St C4
New Scotland Yard E5
New Square C5
Newburn St F5
Newgate St C6
Newington Butts F6
Newington Causeway E7
Newton St C5
Nile St B7
Noble St C7
Noel St C4
Norfolk Crescent C2
Norfolk Square C1
North Audley St D3
North Carriage Drive D2
North Crescent C4
North Ride D2
North Row D3
North Wharf Rd C1
Northampton Square B6
Northington St B5
Northumberland Ave D5
Norton Folgate C8
Nottingham Place C3
Old Bailey C6
Old Broad St C7
Old Brompton Rd F1
Old Compton St C4
Old County Hall E5
Old Gloucester St C5
Old Jamaica Rd E9
Old Kent Rd F8
Old King Edward St C7
Old Marylebone Rd C2
Old Montague St C9
Old Nichol St B8
Old Paradise St F5
Old Spitalfields Mkt C8
Old St B7
Old St ≋⊖ B7
Old Vic 🎭 E6
Onslow Gardens F1
Onslow Square F1
Ontario St E6
Open Air Theatre 🎭 B3
Operating Theatre Museum 🏛 D7
Orange St D4
Orchard St C3
Ossulston St A4
Outer Circle B2
Ovington Square E2
Oxford Circus ⊖ C4
Oxford St C3/C4
Paddington ≋⊖ C1
Paddington St C3
Page's Walk E8
Palace St E4
Pall Mall D4
Pall Mall East D4
Pancras Rd A5
Panton St D4
Paris Garden D6
Park Crescent B3
Park Lane D3
Park Rd B2
Park St D3
Park St D7
Parker St C5
Parliament Square E5
Parliament St E5
Paternoster Square C6
Paul St B7
Pear Tree St B6
Pelham Crescent F2
Pelham St F1
Penfold St C2
Penton Place F6
Penton Rise B5
Penton St A6
Pentonville Rd A5/A6
Percival St B6
Petticoat Lane (Middlesex St) C8
Petty France E4
Phoenix Place B5
Phoenix Rd A4
Photo Gallery 🏛 D4
Piccadilly D3
Piccadilly Circus ⊖ D4
Pilgrimage St E7
Pimlico ⊖ F4
Pimlico Rd F3

Pitfield St B8
Pollock's Toy Mus C4
Polygon Rd A4
Pont St E2
Porchester Place C2
Portland Place C3
Portman Mews C3
Portman Square C3
Portman St C2
Portugal St C5
Postal Mus, The B5
Poultry C7
Praed St C1
Primrose St C8
Prince Consort Rd E1
Prince's Gardens E1
Princes St C7
Procter St C5
Provost St B7
Quaker St B8
Queen Anne St C3
Queen Elizabeth Hall D5
Queen Elizabeth St E8
Queen Square B5
Queen St D7
Queen Street Place D7
Queen Victoria St D6
Queens Gallery E4
Queensberry Place F1
Quilter St B9
Radnor St B7
Rathbone Place C4
Rawlings St F2
Rawstorne St B6
Red Lion Square C5
Red Lion St C5
Redchurch St B8
Redcross Way D7
Reedworth St F6
Regency St F4
Regent Square B5
Regent St C4
Regent's Park B3
Richmond Terrace E5
Ridgmount St C4
Riley Rd E8
Rivington St B8
Robert St B3
Rochester Row F4
Rockingham St E7
Rodney Rd F7
Rolls Rd F8
Ropemaker St C7
Rosebery Avenue B6
Rossmore Rd B2
Rothsay St E8
Rotten Row E2
Roupell St D6
Royal Acad of Arts D4
Royal Academy of Dramatic Art (RADA) B4
Royal Acad of Music B3
Royal Albert Hall E1
Royal Artillery Memorial E2
Royal Brompton Hospital F1/F2
Royal Coll of Nursing C3
Royal Coll of Surgeons C5
Royal Festival Hall D5
Royal London Hospital for Integrated Medicine C5
Royal Marsden Hosp F1
Royal National Theatre D6
Royal National Throat, Nose and Ear Hosp B5
Royal Opera House D5
Rushworth St E6
Russell Square B4
Russell Square B5
Rutland Gate E2
Saatchi Gall F2
Sackville St D4
Sadlers Wells B6
Saffron Hill C6
St Alban's St D4
St Andrew St C6
St Barnabas St F3
St Bartholomew's Hospital C6
St Botolph St C8
St Bride St C6
St George's Circus E6
St George's Drive F4
St George's Rd E6
St George's Square F4
St Giles High St C4
St James's Palace D4
St James's Park E4
St James's St D4
St John St B6
St John's Wood Rd B1
St Margaret St E5
St Mark's Hospital B6
St Martin's Lane D5
St Martin's Le Grand C7
St Mary Axe C8
St Mary's Hospital C1
St Pancras International A5
St Paul's C7
St Paul's Cathedral C7
St Paul's Churchyard C6
St Thomas St D7
St Thomas' Hospital E5
Sale Place C2
Sancroft St F5
Savile Row D4
Savoy Place D5
Savoy St D5
School of Hygiene & Tropical Medicine C4
Science Museum E1
Scrutton St B8
Sekforde St B6
Serpentine Gallery E1
Serpentine Rd D2
Seven Dials C5
Seward St B6
Seymour Place C2
Seymour St C2
Shad Thames D8/E8
Shaftesbury Avenue D4
Shakespeare's Globe Theatre D7
Shepherd Market D3
Sherwood St D4
Shoe Lane C6
Shoreditch High St B8
Shoreditch High St B8
Shorts Gardens C5
Shouldham St C2
Shrek's Adventure E5
Sidmouth St B5
Silk St C7
Sir John Soane's Museum C5
Skinner St B6
Sloane Avenue F2
Sloane Square F2
Sloane Square F3
Sloane St E2
Snow Hill C6
Soho Square C4
Somerset House D5
South Audley St D3
South Carriage Drive E2
South Eaton Place F3
South Kensington F1
South Molton St C3
South Parade F1
South Place C7
South St D3
South Terrace F2
South Wharf Rd C1
Southampton Row C5
Southampton St D5
Southwark D6
Southwark Bridge D7
Southwark Bridge Rd D7
Southwark Cath D7
Southwark Park Rd F8
Southwark St D7
Spa Rd E8
Speakers' Corner D2
Spencer St B6
Spital Square C8
Spring St C1
Stamford St D6
Stanhope St B4
Stanhope Terrace D1
Stephenson Way B4
Stock Exchange C6
Stoney St D7
Strand C5
Strathearn Place D2
Stratton St D3
Sumner St D6
Sussex Gardens C1
Sussex Place C1
Sussex Square D1
Sussex St F3
Sutton's Way B7
Swan St E7
Swanfield St B8
Swinton St B5
Sydney Place F1
Sydney St F2
Tabard St E7
Tabernacle St B7
Tachbrook St F4
Tanner St E8
Tate Britain F5
Tate Modern D7
Tavistock Place B5
Tavistock Square B4
Tea & Coffee Mus D7
Temple D6
Temple Avenue D6
Temple Place D5
Terminus Place E3
Thayer St C3
Theobald's Rd C5
Thorney St F5
Threadneedle St C7
Throgmorton St C7
Thurloe Place F1
Thurloe Square F2
Tonbridge St B5
Tooley St D8
Torrington Place B4
Tothill St E4
Tottenham Court Rd B4
Tottenham Ct Rd C4
Tottenham St C4
Tower Bridge D8
Tower Bridge App D8
Tower Bridge Rd E8
Tower Hill D8
Tower Hill D8
Tower of London, The D8
Toynbee St C8
Trafalgar Square D4
Trinity Square D8
Trinity St E7
Trocadero Centre D4
Tudor St D6
Turin St B9
Turnmill St C6
Tyers St F5
Ufford St E6
Union St D6
University Coll Hosp B4
University College London (UCL) B4
University of London C4
Univ of Westminster C3
University St B4
Upper Belgrave St E3
Upper Berkeley St C2
Upper Brook St D3
Upper Grosvenor St D3
Upper Ground D6
Upper Montague St C2
Upper St Martin's La D5
Upper Thames St D7
Upper Wimpole St C3
Upper Woburn Place B4
Vauxhall Bridge Rd F4
Vauxhall St F5
Vere St C3
Vernon Place C5
Vestry St B7
Victoria E3
Victoria and Albert Museum E1
Victoria Coach Station F3
Victoria Embankment D5
Victoria Place Shopping Centre F3
Victoria St E4
Villiers St D5
Vincent Square F4
Vinopolis City of Wine D7
Virginia Rd B8
Wakley St B6
Walbrook C7
Walcot Square F6
Wallace Collection C3
Walnut Tree Walk F6
Walton St F2
Walworth Rd F7
Wardour St C4/D4
Warner St B6
Warren St B4
Warren St B4
Warwick Square F4
Warwick Way F4
Waterloo E6
Waterloo Bridge D5
Waterloo East D6
Waterloo Rd E6
Watling St C7
Webber St E6
Welbeck St C3
Wellington Arch E3
Wellington Mus E3
Wellington Rd B2
Wellington Row B9
Wells St C4
Wenlock St A7
Wentworth St C8
West Carriage Drive D2
West Smithfield C6
West Square E6
Westbourne St D1
Westbourne Terrace C1
Westminster E5
Westminster Abbey E5
Westminster Bridge E5
Westminster Bridge Rd E6
Westminster Cathedral (RC) E4
Westminster City Hall E4
Westminster Hall E5
Weymouth St C3
Wharf Rd A7
Wharton St B5
Whitcomb St D4
White Cube B8
White Lion Hill D6
White Lion St A6
Whitechapel Rd C9
Whitecross St B7
Whitefriars St C6
Whitehall D5
Whitehall Place D5
Wigmore Hall C3
Wigmore St C3
William IV St D5
Willow Walk F8
Wilmington Square B6
Wilson St C7
Wilton Crescent E3
Wilton Rd F4
Wimpole St C3
Winchester St F3
Wincott St F6
Windmill Walk D6
Woburn Place B5
Woburn Square B4
Wood St C7
Woodbridge St B6
Wootton St D6
Wormwood St C8
Worship St B7
Wren St B5
Wynyatt St B6
Young Vic E6
York Rd E5
York St C2
York Terrace East B3
York Terrace West B3
York Way A5

Luton 337

Adelaide St B1
Albert Rd C2
Alma St B2
Alton Rd C3
Anthony Gardens C1
Arthur St C2
Ashburnham Rd B1
Ashton Rd C2
Back St A2
Bailey St C3
Baker St C2
Biscot Rd A1
Bolton Rd B3
Boyle Close A2
Brantwood Rd B1
Bretts Mead C1
Bridge St B2
Brook St A1
Brunswick St A3
Burr St A3
Bury Park Rd A1
Bute St B2
Buxton Rd B2
Cambridge St C3
Cardiff Grove B1
Cardiff Rd B1
Cardigan St A2
Castle St B2/C2
Chapel St C2
Charles St A3
Chase St C2
Cheapside B2
Chequer St C3
Chiltern Rise C1
Church St B2/B3
Cinema A2
Cobden St A3
College A3
Collingdon St A1
Concorde Avenue A3
Corncastle Rd C1
Cowper St C2
Crawley Green Rd B3
Crawley Rd A1
Crescent Rd A3
Crescent Rise A3
Cromwell Rd A1
Cross St A2
Cross Way, The C1
Crown Court B2
Cumberland St B2
Cutenhoe Rd C3
Dallow Rd B1
Downs Rd B1
Dudley St A2
Duke St A2
Dumfries St B1
Dunstable Place B2
Dunstable Rd A1/B1
Edward St A3
Elizabeth St C2
Essex Close C3
Farley Hill C1
Flowers Way B2
Francis St A1
Frederick St A2
Galaxy Leisure Complex A2
George St B2
George St West B2
Gordon St B2
Grove Rd B1
Guildford St A2
Haddon Rd A3
Harcourt St C2
Hart Hill Drive A3
Hart Hill Lane A3
Hartley Rd A3
Hastings St B2
Hat Factory, The B2
Hatters Way A1
Havelock Rd A2
Hibbert St C2
High Town Rd A3
Highbury Rd A1
Hightown Community Sports & Arts Centre A3
Hillary Crescent C1
Hillborough Rd C1
Hitchin Rd A3
Holly St C2
Holm C1
Hucklesby Way A2
Hunts Close C1
Inkerman St A2
John St B2
Jubilee St A3
Kelvin Close C2
King St B2
Kingsland Rd C3
Larches, The A2
Latimer Rd C2
Lawn Gardens C2
Lea Rd B3
Library B2
Library Rd B2
Library Theatre B2
Liverpool Rd B1
London Rd C2
Luton Station A2
Lyndhurst Rd B1
Magistrates Court B2
Mall, The B2
Manchester St B2
Manor Rd B3
Manor Road Park B3
May St C3
Meyrick Avenue C1
Midland Rd A2
Mill St A2
Milton Rd B1
Moor St A1
Moor, The A1
Moorland Gardens A2
Moulton Rise A3
Napier Rd B1
New Bedford Rd A1
New Town St C2
North St A3
Old Bedford Rd A2
Old Orchard C2
Osbourne Rd C3
Oxen Rd A3
Park Square B2
Park St B3/C3
Park St West B2
Park Viaduct B3
Parkland Drive C1
Police Station B1
Pomfret Avenue A3
Pondwicks Rd B3
Post Office A1/B2
Power Court B3
Princess St B1
Red Rails C1
Regent St B2
Reginald St A2
Rothesay Rd B1
Russell Rise C1
Russell St C1
Ruthin Close C1
St Ann's Rd B3
St George's Square B2
St Mary's B3
St Marys Rd B3
St Paul's Rd C2
St Saviour's Crescent C1
Salisbury Rd B1
Seymour Avenue C3
Seymour Rd C3
Silver St B2
South Rd C2
Stanley St B1
Station Rd A2
Stockwood Crescent C2
Stockwood Park C1
Strathmore Avenue C2
Stuart St B2
Studley Rd A1
Surrey St C3
Sutherland Place C1
Tavistock St C2
Taylor St A3
Telford Way A1
Tennyson Rd C2
Tenzing Grove C1
Thistle Rd B3
Town Hall B2
Townsley Close C2
UK Centre for Carnival Arts B3
Union St B2
Univ of Bedfordshire B3
Upper George St B2
Vicarage St B3
Villa Rd A2
Waldeck Rd A1
Wardown House Mus & Gallery A2
Wellington St B1/B2
Wenlock St A2
Whitby Rd A1
Whitehill Avenue C1
William St A2
Wilsden Avenue C1
Windmill Rd B3
Windsor St C2
Winsdon Rd B1
York St A3

Macclesfield 337

108 Steps B2
Abbey Rd A1
Alton Drive A3
Armett St C1
Athey St B1
Bank St C3
Barber St C3
Barton St C1
Beech Lane A2
Beswick St B1
Black Lane A2
Black Rd C3
Blakelow Gardens C3
Blakelow Rd C3
Bond St B1/C1
Bread St C1
Bridge St B1
Brock St A2
Brocklehurst Avenue A3
Brook St B3
Brookfield Lane B3
Brough St West C1
Brown St C1
Brynton Rd A2
Buckley St C2
Bus Station B2
Buxton Rd B3
Byrons St C2
Canal St B3
Carlsbrook Avenue A3
Castle St B2
Catherine St B1
Cemetery A1
Chadwick Terrace A3
Chapel St C2
Charlotte St B2
Chester Rd B1
Chestergate B1
Christ Church B1
Churchill Way B2
Coare St A1
Commercial Rd B2
Conway Crescent A3
Copper St C3
Cottage St B1
Crematorium A1
Crew Avenue A3
Crompton Rd B1/C1
Cross St C2
Crossall St C1
Cumberland St A1/B1
Dale St B3
Duke St B2
Eastgate B3
Exchange St B2
Fence Avenue B3
Fence Ave Ind Est A3
Flint St B3
Foden St A2
Fountain St B3
Garden St A3
Gas Rd B2
Gateway Gallery B1
George St B2
Glegg St B3
Golf Course C3
Goodall St B3
Grange Rd C1
Great King St B1
Green St B3
Grosvenor Shopping Centre B2
Gunco Lane C3
Half St C2
Hallefield Rd B3
Hatton St C1
Hawthorn Way A3
Heapy St C3
Henderson St B1
Heritage Centre B2
Hibel Rd A2
High St C2
Hobson St C2
Hollins Rd C3
Horseshoe Drive B1
Hurdsfield Rd A3
Information Centre B2
James St C2
Jodrell St B3
John St C2
Jordangate A2
King Edward St B2
King George's Field C3
King St B2
King's School A1
Knight Pool C3
Knight St C3
Lansdowne St A3
Library B2
Lime Grove B3
Loney St B1
Longacre St B1
Lord St C2
Lowe St C2
Lowerfield Rd A3
Lyon St B1
Macclesfield College C1
Macclesfield Sta B2
MADS Little Theatre C2
Marina B3
Market B2
Market Place B2
Masons Lane A3
Mill Lane C2
Mill Rd C2
Mill St B2
Moran Rd C1
New Hall St A2
Newton St C1
Nicholson Avenue A3
Nicholson Close A3
Northgate Avenue A2
Old Mill Lane C2
Paradise Mill C2
Paradise St B1
Park Green B2
Park Lane C1
Park Rd C1
Park St C2
Park Vale Rd C1
Parr St B1
Peel St C2
Percyvale St A3
Peter St C1
Pickford St B2
Pierce St B1
Pinfold St B1
Pitt St C2
Police Station B2
Pool St C2
Poplar Rd C2
Post Office B2
Pownall St A2
Prestbury Rd A1/B1
Queen Victoria St B2
Queen's Avenue A3
Registrar B2
Retail Park C2
Richmond Hill C3
Riseley St B1
Roan Court B3
Roe St B2
Rowan Way A3
Ryle St C2
Ryle's Park Rd C1
St George's St C2
St Michael's B2
Samuel St B2
Saville St C3
Shaw St B1
Silk Rd, The A2/B2
Slater St C1
Snow Hill C3
South Park C1
Spring Gardens A2
Statham St C2
Station St A2
Steeple St A3
Sunderland St B2
Superstore A1/A2/C2
Swettenham St B3
Thistleton Close C2
Thorp St B2
Town Hall B2
Townley St B2
Treacle Market B2
Turnock St C3
Union Rd B3
Union St B2
Victoria Park B3
Vincent St C2
Waters Green B2
Waterside C2
West Bond St B1
West Park A1
West Park Museum A1
Westbrook Drive A1
Westminster Rd A1
Whalley Hayes B1
Windmill St C3
Withyfold Drive A2
York St B3

Maidstone 340

Albion Place B3
All Saints B2
Allen St A3
Amphitheatre C2
Archbishop's Palace B2
Bank St B2
Barker Rd C2
Barton Rd C3
Beaconsfield Rd C1
Bedford Place B1
Bishops Way B2
Bluett St A3
BMI The Somerfield Hospital A1
Bower Lane C1
Bower Mount Rd B1
Bower Place C1
Bower St B1
Boxley Rd A3
Brenchley Gardens A2
Brewer St A3
Broadway B2
Broadway Shopping Centre B2
Brunswick St C3
Buckland Hill A1
Buckland Rd B1
Bus Station B3
Campbell Rd C3
Church Rd C1
Church St B3
Cinema C2
Clifford Way C1/C2
College Avenue C2
College Rd C2
Collis Memorial Gdn C3
Cornwallis Rd B1
Corpus Christi Hall B2
Council Offices B3
County Hall A2
County Rd A3
Crompton Gardens C3
Crown & County Courts B2
Curzon Rd A3
Dixon Close C2
Douglas Rd C1
Earl St B2
Eccleston Rd C2
Fairmeadow B2
Fisher St A2
Florence Rd C1
Foley St A3
Foster St C3
Freedom Leisure Centre A1/A2
Fremlin Walk Shopping Centre B2
Gabriel's Hill B3
George St C3
Grecian St A3
Hardy St A3
Hart St C2
Hastings Rd C3
Hayle Rd C3
Hazlitt B2
Heathorn St A3
Hedley St A3
High St B2
HM Prison A3
Holland Rd A3
Hope St A2
Information Centre B2
James St A3
James Whatman Way A2
Jeffrey St A3
Kent County Council Offices A2
Kent History & Liby Ctr A2
King Edward Rd C2
King St B3
Kingsley Rd C3
Knightrider St B3
Launder Way C1
Lesley Place A1
Library B2
Little Buckland Ave A1
Lockmeadow Leisure Complex C2
London Rd B1
Lower Boxley Rd A2
Lower Fant Rd C1
Magistrates Court B3
Maidstone Barracks Station A1
Maidstone East Sta A2
Maidstone Museum & Bentlif Art Gall B2
Maidstone Utd FC A2
Maidstone West Sta B2
Mall, The B3
Market C2
Market Buildings B2
Marsham St B3
Medway St B2
Melville Rd C3
Mill St B2
Millennium Bridge C2
Mote Rd B3
Muir Rd C3
Old Tovil Rd C3
Palace Avenue B3
Perryfield St A2
Police Station B3
Post Office B2/C3
Priory Rd C3
Prospect Place C1
Pudding Lane B2
Queen Anne Rd B3
Queens Rd A1
Randall St A2
Rawdon Rd C3
Reginald Rd C1
Riverstage A1
Rock Place B1
Rocky Hill B1
Romney Place B3
Rose Yard B2
Rowland Close C1
Royal Engineers' Rd A2
Royal Star Arcade B2
St Annes Court B1
St Faith's St B2
St Luke's Rd A3
St Peter St B2
St Peter's Bridge B2
St Peter's Wharf Retail Park B2
St Philip's Avenue C3
Salisbury Rd A3
Sandling Rd A2
Scott St A2
Scrubs Lane B1
Sheal's Crescent C3
Somerfield Lane B1
Somerfield Rd B1
Staceys St A2
Station Rd A2
Superstore A1/B2/B3
Terrace Rd B1
Tonbridge Rd C1
Tovil Rd C2
Town Hall B2
Trinity Park B3
Tufton St B3
Tyrwhitt-Drake Museum of Carriages B2
Union St B3
Upper Fant Rd C1
Upper Stone St C3
Victoria St B1
Warwick Place B1
Wat Tyler Way B3
Waterloo St C3
Waterlow Rd A3
Week St B2
Well Rd A3
Westree Rd C1
Wharf Rd C1
Whatman Park A1
Wheeler St A3
Whitchurch Close B1
Woodville Rd C3
Wyatt St B3
Wyke Manor Rd B3

Manchester 337

Adair St B6
Addington St A5
Adelphi St A1
Advent Way B6
Albert Square B3
Albion St C3
Ancoats Grove B6
Ancoats Grove North B6
Angela St C2
Aquatics Centre C4
Ardwick Green North C5
Ardwick Green Park C5
Ardwick Green South C5
Arlington St A2
Artillery St B3
Arundel St C2
Atherton St B2
Atkinson St B3
Aytoun St B4
Back Piccadilly A4
Baird St B5
Balloon St A4
Bank Place A1
Baring St B5
Barrack St C1
Barrow St A1
Bendix St A5
Bengal St A5
Berry St C5
Blackfriars Rd A3
Blackfriars St A3
Blantyre St C2
Bloom St B4
Blossom St A5
Boad St B5
Bombay St B4
Booth St A3
Booth St B4
Bootle St B3
Brazennose St B3
Brewer St A5
Bridge St A3
Bridgewater Hall B3
Bridgewater Place A4
Bridgewater St B2
Brook St C4
Brotherton Drive A2
Brown St A3
Brown St B4
Brunswick St C6
Brydon Avenue C6
Buddhist Centre A4
Bury St A2
Bus & Coach Station B4
Bus Station B4
Butler St A6
Buxton St C5
Byrom St B3
Cable St A5
Cambridge St C3/C4
Camp St B3
Canal St B4
Cannon St A1
Cardroom Rd A6
Carruthers St A6
Castle St C2
Castlefield Arena B2
Cateaton St A3
Cathedral A3
Cathedral St A3
Cavendish St C4
Chapel St A1/A3
Chapeltown St B5
Charles St C4
Charlotte St B4
Chatham St B4
Chepstow St B3
Chester Rd C1/C2
Chester St C4
Chetham's School of Music A3
China Lane B5
Chippenham Rd A6
Chorlton Rd C2
Chorlton St B4
Church St A2
Church St A4
City Park A4
City Rd East C3
Civil Justice Centre B2
Cleminson St A2
Clowes St A3
College Land A3
Collier St B2
Commercial St C3
Conference Centre C4
Cooper St B4
Copperas St A4
Corn Exchange, The A4
Cornbrook C1
Cornell St A5
Corporation St A4
Cotter St C6
Cotton St A5
Cow Lane B1
Cross St B3
Crown Court B4
Crown St C2
Dalberg St C6
Dale St A4/B5
Dancehouse, The C4
Dantzic St A4
Dark Lane C6
Dawson St C2
Dean St A5
Deansgate A3/B3/C2
Deansgate Castlefield C3
Deansgate Station C3
Dolphin St C6
Downing St C5
Ducie St B5
Duke Place B2
Duke St B2
Durling St C6
East Ordsall Lane A2/B1
Edge St A4
Egerton St C2
Ellesmere St C1
Everard St C1
Everyman B2
Every St B6
Exchange Square A4
Factory, The B2
Fairfield St B5
Faulkner St B4
Fennel St A3
Fire Station A5
Ford St A2
Ford St C6
Fountain St B4
Frederick St A2
Gartside St B2
Gaythorne St A1
George Leigh St A5
George St B4
Gore St A2
Goulden St A5
Granby Row B4
Gravel Lane A3
Great St B6
Great Ancoats St A5
Great Bridgewater St B3
Great George St A1
Great Jackson St C2
Great Marlborough St C4
Great Northern Leisure Complex B3
Greengate A3
Grosvenor St C5
Gun St A5
Hall St B3
Hampson St B1
Hanover St A4
Hanworth Close C5
Hardman St B3
Harkness St C6
Harrison St B6
Hart St B4
Helmet St B6
Henry St A5
Heyrod St B6
High St A4
Higher Ardwick C6
Hilton St A4/A5
Holland St A6
HOME Entertainment Complex C3
Hood St A5
Hope St B1
Hope St B4
Houldsworth St A5
Hoyle St C6
Hulme Hall Rd C1
Hulme St A1
Hulme St C3
Hyde Rd C6
Islington Way A1
Information Centre B4
Irwell St A2
Jackson Crescent C2
Jackson's Row B3
James St A1
Jenner Close C2
Jersey St A5
John Dalton St B3
John Ryland's Liby B3
John St A2
Kennedy St B3
Kincardine Rd C5
King St A3
King St West A3
Law Courts B3
Laystall St B5
Lever St A5
Library B3
Linby St C2
Little Lever St A4
Liverpool Rd B2
Liverpool St B1
Lloyd St B3
Lockton Close C5
London Rd B5
Long Millgate A3
Longacre St B6
Loom St A5
Lower Byrom St B2
Lower Mosley St B3
Lower Moss Lane C2
Lower Ormond St C4
Loxford Lane C4
Luna St A5
Major St B4
Mamucium B2
Manchester Arndale A4
Manchester Art Gallery B4
Manchester Central Convention Complex B3
Manchester Metropolitan University (MMU) B4/C4
Manchester Piccadilly Station B5
Manchester Technology Centre C4
Mancunian Way C3

Manor St C5
Marble St A4
Market St A2
Market St A4
Market St A4
Marsden St A3
Marshall St A5
Mayan Avenue A2
Medlock St C3
Middlewood St B1
Miller St A4
Minshull St B4
Mosley St A4
Mount St B3
Mulberry St B3
Murray St A5
Museum of Science & Industry (MOSI) B2
Nathan Drive A2
National Football Museum A4
Naval St A5
New Bailey St A2
New Elm Rd B2
New Islington A6
New Islington Sta B6
New Quay St B2
New Union St A6
Newton St A5
Nicholas St B4
North Western St C6
Oak St A4
Odeon A4/B3
Old Mill St A6
Oldfield Rd A1/C1
Oldham Rd A5
Oldham St A4
Opera House B3
Ordsall Lane C1
Oxford Rd C4
Oxford Rd C4
Oxford St B4
Paddock St C6
Palace Theatre B4
Pall Mall A3
Palmerston St B6
Parker St B4
Peak St B5
Penfield Close C5
Peoples' History Museum B2
Peru St A1
Peter St B3
Piccadilly A4
Piccadilly B5
Piccadilly Gardens B4
Piercy St A6
Poland St A5
Police Museum A5
Police Station B3/B5
Pollard St B6
Port St A5
Portland St B4
Portugal St East B5
Post Office A2/A4/A5/B3/B4/C4
Potato Wharf B2
Princess St B3/C4
Quay St A2
Quay St B2
Queen St B3
Radium St A5
Redhill St A5
Regent Retail Park B1
Regent Rd B1
Rice St B2
Richmond St B4
River St C3
Roby St B5
Rodney St A6
Rosamond St A2
Royal Exchange A3
Sackville St B4
St Andrew's St B6
St Ann St A3
St Ann's A3
St George's Avenue C1
St James St B4
St John St B3
St John's Cath (RC) A2
St Mary's A3
St Mary's Gate A3
St Mary's Parsonage A3
St Peter's Square B3
St Stephen St A2
Salford Approach A3
Salford Central A2
Sheffield St B5
Sherratt St A5
Shopmobility A4
Shudehill A4
Shudehill A4
Sidney St C4
Silk St A5
Silver St B4
Skerry Close C5
Snell St B6
South King St B3
Sparkle St B5
Spear St A4
Spring Gardens A4
Stanley St B2
Store St B5
Superstore B1
Swan St A4
Tariff St B5
Tatton St C1
Temperance St B6/C6
Thirsk St C6
Thomas St A4
Thompson St A5
Tib Lane B3
Tib St A4
Town Hall (Manchester) B3
Town Hall (Salford) A2
Trafford St C3
Travis St B5
Trinity Way A2
Turner St A4
Union St C6
University of Manchester (North Campus) C5
University of Salford A1
Upper Brook St C5
Upper Cleminson St A1
Upper Wharf St A1
Urban Exchange A5
Vesta St B6
Victoria A4
Victoria Station A4
Wadesdon Rd C5
Water St B2
Watson St B3
West Fleet St B1
West King St A2
West Mosley St B4
Weybridge Rd A6
Whitworth St B4
Whitworth St West C3
William St A2
William St C6
Wilmott St C3
Windmill St B3
Windsor Crescent A1
Withy Grove A4
Woden St C1
Wood St B3
Woodward St A6
Worrall St C1
Worsley St C2
York St B4
York St C2
York St C4

Merthyr Tydfil
Merthyr Tudful 340

Aberdare Rd B2
Abermorlais Terrace B2
Alexandra Rd A3
Alma St C3
Arfryn Place C3
Argyle St C3
Avenue De Clichy C2
Beacons Place Shopping Centre C2
Bethesda St B2
Bishops Grove A3
Brecon Rd A1/B2
Briarmead A3
Bryn St C3
Bryntirion Rd B3/C3
Bus Station B2
Cae Mari Dwn B3
Caedraw Rd C2
Castle Square A1
Castle St B2
Chapel C2
Chapel Bank B1
Church St B3
Civic Centre B2
Clos Penderyn B1
Coedcae'r Court C3
College Boulevard C2
County and Crown Courts B2
Court St C3
Cromwell St B2
Cyfarthfa Castle, Mus and Art Gallery A1
Cyfarthfa Ind Est A1
Cyfarthfa Park A1
Cyfarthfa Retail Park B1
Cyfarthfa Rd A1
Dane St A2
Dane Terrace A2
Danyparc B3
Darren View A3
Dixon St B2
Dyke St C3
Dynevor St B2
Elwyn Drive C3
Fire Station B2
Fothergill St B3
Galonuchaf Rd A3
Garth St B2
Georgetown B2
Grawen Terrace A2
Grove Park A2
Grove, The A2
Gurnos Rd A2
Gwaelodygarth Rd A2/A3
Gwaunfarren Grove A3
Gwaunfarren Rd A3
Gwendoline St A3
Hampton St C3
Hanover St A2
Heol S O Davies B1
Heol-Gerrig B1
High St A3/B2/B3/C2
Highland View C3
Howell Close B1
Jackson's Bridge B2
James St C3
John St B3
Joseph Parry's Cott B2
Lancaster St A2
Library B2
Llewellyn St A2
Llwyfen St B2
Llwyn Berry B1
Llwyn Dic Penderyn B1
Llwyn-y-Gelynen C1
Lower Thomas St B3
Market C2
Mary St C3
Masonic St C2
Merthyr Tydfil College B2
Merthyr Town FC B3
Merthyr Tydfil Leisure Centre C3
Merthyr Tydfil Sta C3
Meyrick Villas A2
Miniature Railway A1
Mount St A2
Nantygwenith St B1
Norman Terrace B2
Oak Rd A2
Old Cemetery B3
Pandy Close A1
Pantycelynen B1
Parade, The B3
Park Terrace B2
Penlan View C2
Penry St B2
Pentwyn Villas A2
Penyard Rd B3
Penydarren Park A3
Penydarren Rd B3
Plymouth St C3
Police Station C2
Pont Marlais West B2
Post Office B2
Quarry Row B2
Queen's Rd B3
Rees St C3
Rhydycar Link C2
Riverside Park A1
St David's B3
St Tydfil's C2
St Tydfil's Avenue C3
St Tydfil's Square Shopping Centre C2
Saxon St A2
School of Nursing A2
Seward St A3
Shiloh Lane B3
Stone Circles B3
Stuart St A2
Summerhill Place B3
Superstore B3
Swan St C2
Swansea Rd B1
Taff Glen View C3
Taff Vale Court B3
Theatre Soar B2
Thomastown Park B3
Tramroad Lane A3
Tramroad Side B2
Tramroad Side North B3
Tramroad Side South C3
Trevithick Gardens C3
Trevithick St A3
Tudor Terrace B2
Twynyrodyn Rd C3
Union St B3
Upper Colliers Row B1
Upper Thomas St B3
Victoria St B2
Vue C3
Vulcan Rd B2
Walk, The B2
Warlow St C3
Well St A2
Welsh Assembly Government Offices C2
Wern Lane C1
Wern, The (Merthyr RFC) C2
West Grove A2
William St C3
Yew St C3
Ynysfach Engine Ho C2
Ynysfach Rd C2

Middlesbrough
340

Abingdon Rd C3
Acklam Rd C1
Albert Park C3
Albert Rd B2
Albert Terrace C2
Ambulance Station C1
Aubrey St C3
Avenue, The C2
Ayresome Gardens C2
Ayresome Green Lane C1
Ayresome St C2
Barton Rd A1
Bilsdale Rd C3
Bishopton Rd C3
Borough Rd B2/B3
Bowes Rd A2
Breckon Hill Rd B3
Bridge St West B2
Brighouse Rd A1
Burlam Rd C1
Bus Station B2
Cannon Park B1
Cannon Park Way B2
Cannon St B1
Captain Cook Square B2
Carlow St C1
Castle Way C3
Chipchase Rd C2
Cineworld B3
Cleveland Centre B2
Clive Rd C2
Commercial St A2
Corporation Rd B2
Costa St C2
Council Offices B3
Crescent Rd C2
Crescent, The C2
Cumberland Rd C2
Depot Rd A2
Derwent St B2
Devonshire Rd C2
Diamond Rd B2
Dock St B3
Dorman Museum C2
Douglas St B3
Eastbourne Rd C2
Eden Rd C3
Fire Station A3
Forty Foot Rd A2
Gilkes St B2
Gosford St A2
Grange Rd B2
Gresham Rd B2
Harehills Rd C1
Harford St C2
Hartington Rd B2
Haverton Hill Rd A1
Hey Wood St B1
Highfield Rd C3
Hillstreet Centre B2
Holwick Rd B1
Hutton Rd C3
Ironmasters Way B1
Lambton Rd C3
Lancaster Rd C2
Lansdowne Rd C3
Latham Rd C2
Law Courts B2/B3
Lees Rd B2
Leeway B3
Library B2/C2
Linthorpe Cemetery C1
Linthorpe Rd B2
Lloyd St B2
Longford St C2
Longlands Rd C3
Lower East St A3
Lower Lake C3
Macmillan Academy C1
Maldon Rd C1
Manor St B2
Marsh St B2
Marton Rd B3
Middlesbrough By-Pass B2/C1
Middlesbrough Coll B3
Middlesbrough Dock B3
Middlesbrough Leisure Park B3
Middlesbrough Sta B2
Middletown Park C2
MIMA B3
Mulgrave Rd C2
Newport Bridge B1
Newport Bridge Approach Rd B1
Newport Rd B2
North Ormesby Rd B3
North Rd B2
Northern Rd C1
Outram St B2
Oxford Rd C2
Park Lane C2
Park Rd North C2
Park Rd South C2
Park Vale Rd C3
Parliament Rd B1
Police Station A2
Port Clarence Rd A3
Portman St B2
Post Office B3/C1/C2
Princes Rd B2
Python A2
Riverside Park Rd A1
Riverside Stadium (Middlesbrough FC) B3
Rockliffe Rd C2
Romaldkirk Rd B1
Roman Rd C2
Roseberry Rd C3
St Barnabas' Rd C2
St Paul's Rd B2
Saltwells Rd B3
Scott's Rd A3
Seaton Carew Rd A3
Shepherdson Way B3
Shopmobility B2
Snowdon Rd A2
South West Ironmasters Park B1
Southfield Rd B2
Southwell Rd C2
Springfield Rd C1
Startforth Rd A2
Stockton Rd C1
Stockton St A2
Superstore B2
Surrey St C2
Sycamore Rd C2
Tax Offices B3
Tees Viaduct C1
Teessaurus Park A2
Teesside Tertiary Coll C3
Temenos B3
Thornfield Rd C1
Town Hall B2
Transporter Bridge (Toll) A3
Union St B2
University of Teesside B2
Upper Lake C2
Valley Rd C3
Ventnor Rd C2
Victoria Rd B2
Vulcan St A2
Warwick St C2
Wellesley Rd B3
West Lane C1
West Lane Hospital C1
Westminster Rd C2
Wilson St B2
Windward Way B3
Woodlands Rd B2
York Rd C3

Milton Keynes
340

Abbey Way A1
Arbrook Avenue B1
Armourer Drive A3
Arncliffe Drive A1
Avebury C2
Avebury Boulevard C2
Bankfield B3
Bayard Avenue A2
Belvedere A2
Bishopstone A1
Blundells Rd A1
Boundary, The C3
Boycott Avenue C2
Bradwell Common Bvd B1
Bradwell Rd C1
Bramble Avenue A2
Brearley Avenue C2
Breckland A1
Brill Place B1
Burnham Drive B1
Campbell Park B3
Cantle Avenue A3
Central Retail Park C1
Century Avenue C2
Chaffron Way C3
Childs Way C1
Christ the Cornerstone B2
Cineworld B2
Civic Offices B2
Cleavers Avenue B2
Colesbourne Drive A3
Conniburrow Bvd B2
Currier Drive A2
Dansteed Way A2/A3/B1
Deltic Avenue B1
Downs Barn A2
Downs Barn Bvd A3
Eaglestone C3
Eelbrook Avenue B1
Elder Gate B1
Evans Gate C2
Fairford Crescent A3
Falcon Avenue B3
Fennel Drive A2
Fishermead Boulevard C3
Food Centre B3
Fulwoods Drive C3
Glazier Drive A2
Glovers Lane A1
Grafton Gate C1
Grafton St A1/C2
Gurnards Avenue B3
Harrier Drive C3
The Hub Leisure Quarter B2/C2
Ibstone Avenue B1
Langcliffe Drive A1
Leisure Centre C3
Leisure Plaza C1
Leys Rd C1
Library B2
Linceslade Grove C1
Linford Wood A2
Magistrates Court B2
Marlborough Gate B3
Marlborough St A2/B3
Mercers Drive A1
Midsummer C2
Midsummer Boulevard B2
Midsummer Place B2
Milton Keynes Central C1
Milton Keynes Hospital (A&E) C3
Monks Way A1
Mullen Avenue A3
Mullion Place C3
National Film & Sci-Fi Museum B2
Neath Hill A3
North Elder C1
North Grafton B1
North Overgate A3
North Row B2
North Saxon B2
North Secklow B2
North Skeldon A3
North Witan B1
Oakley Gardens A3
Odeon B2
Oldbrook Boulevard C2
Open-Air Theatre B3
Overgate A3
Overstreet A3
Patriot Drive B1
Pencarrow Place B3
Penryn Avenue B3
Perran Avenue C3
Pitcher Lane C1
Place Retail Park, The C1
Police Station B2
Portway B2
Post Office A2/B2/B3
Precedent Drive B1
Quinton Drive B1
Ramsons Avenue B2
Retail Park C2
Rockingham Drive A2
Rooksley B1
Saxon Gate B2
Saxon St A1/C3
Secklow Gate B2
Shackleton Place C2
Shopmobility B2
Silbury Boulevard B2
Skeldon A3
South Enmore B3
South Grafton C2
South Row C2
South Saxon C2
South Secklow B3
South Witan C2
Springfield B3
Stainton Drive A1/B1
Stanton Wood A1
Stantonbury A1
Stantonbury Leisure Centre A1
Strudwick Drive C2
Sunrise Parkway A2
Superstore C1/C2
Theatre & Art Gallery B3
theCentre:mk B2
Tolcarne Avenue C3
Towan Avenue C3
Trueman Place C2
Vauxhall A1
Winterhill Retail Park C2
Witan Gate B2
Xscape B3

Newcastle upon Tyne
340

Albert St B3
Argyle St B3
Back New Bridge St B3
BALTIC Centre for Contemporary Art C3
Barker St A3
Barrack Rd B1
Bath Lane B1
Bessie Surtees House C2
Bigg Market C2
Biscuit Factory B3
Black Gate C2
Blackett St B2
Blandford Square C1
Boating Lake A1
Boyd St B3
Brandling Park A2
Bus Station B2
Buxton St B3
Byron St A3
Camden St B2
Castle Keep C2
Central C1
Central Library B2
Central Motorway B2
Chester St A3
Cineworld B1
City Hall B2
City Rd B3/C3
City Walls C1
Civic Centre A2
Claremont Rd A1
Clarence St B3
Clarence Walk B3
Clayton St C1/B1
Clayton St West C1
Close, The C2
Coach Station C1
College St B2
Collingwood St C2
Copland Terrace B3
Coppice Way B3
Corporation St B1
Courts C3
Crawhall Rd B3
Dean St C2
Dental Hospital A1
Dinsdale Place A3
Dinsdale Rd A3
Discovery C1
Doncaster Rd A3
Durant Rd B2
Eldon Square B1
Eldon Square Shopping Centre B2
Ellison Place B2
Eskdale Terrace A2
Eslington Terrace A2
Exhibition Park A1
Falconar St B3
Fenkle St C1
Forth Banks C1
Forth St C1
Gallowgate B1
Gate, The B1
Gateshead Millennium Bridge C3
Gateshead Quays C3
Gibson St B3
Goldspink Lane A3
Grainger Market B2
Grainger St B2
Grantham Rd A3
Granville Rd A3
Great North Children's Hospital A1
Great North Museum: Hancock A2
Grey St B2
Groat Market C2
Guildhall C2
Hancock St A2
Hanover St C2
Hatton Gallery A1
Hawks Rd C3
Haymarket B2
Heber St B1
Helmsley Rd A3
High Bridge B2
High Level Bridge C2
Hillgate C3
Howard St B3
Hutton Terrace A3
Jesmond A2
Jesmond Rd A2/A3
John Dobson St B2
Jubilee Rd B3
Kelvin Grove A3
Kensington Terrace A2
Laing Gallery B2
Lambton Rd A2
Leazes Crescent B1
Leazes Lane B1
Leazes Park B1
Leazes Park Rd B1
Leazes Terrace B1
Library A2
Life Science Centre C1
Live C2
Low Friar St C1
Manor Chare C2
Manors B2
Manors Station B2
Market St B2
Melbourne St B2
Mill Rd C3
Monument B2
Monument Mall Shopping Centre B2
Morpeth St A2
Mosley St C2
Napier St A3
New Bridge St West B2/B3
Newcastle Central Station C1
Newcastle University A1
Newgate St B1
Newington Rd A3
Northern Design Centre C3
Northern Stage Theatre A2
Northumberland Rd B2
Northumberland St B2
Northumbria University A2
Northwest Radial Rd A1
O2 Academy C1
Oakwellgate C3
Open University C3
Orchard St C2
Osborne Rd A2
Osborne Terrace A3
Pandon C3
Pandon Bank B3
Park Terrace A1
Percy St B1
Pilgrim St B2
Pipewellgate C2
Pitt St B1
Plummer Tower A2
Police Station C1
Portland Rd A3/B3
Portland Terrace A3
Post Office B1/B2
Pottery Lane C1
Prudhoe Place B1
Prudhoe St B1
Quayside C2
Queen Elizabeth II Bridge C2
Queen Victoria Rd A1
Richardson Rd A1
Ridley Place B2
Rock Terrace B3
Rosedale Terrace A3
Royal Victoria Infirmary A1
Sage Gateshead C3
St Andrew's St B1
St James B1
St James' Boulevard C1
St James' Park (Newcastle Utd FC) B1
St Mary's Heritage Centre C3
St Mary's (RC) C1
St Mary's Place B2
St Nicholas C2
St Nicholas St C2
St Thomas' St B1
Sandyford Rd A2/A3
Shield St B3
Shieldfield B3
Shopmobility B1
Side, The C2
Simpson Terrace B3
South Shore Rd C3
South St C1
Starbeck Avenue A3
Stepney Rd B3
Stoddart St B3
Stowell St B1
Strawberry Place B1
Swing Bridge C2
Temple St C1
Terrace Place B1
Theatre Royal B2
Times Square C1
Tower St B3
Trinity House C2
Tyne Bridge C2
Tyne Bridges C2
Tyne Theatre & Opera House C1
Tyneside B2
Victoria Square A2
Warwick St A3
Waterloo St C1
Wellington St B1
Westgate Rd C1/C2
Windsor Terrace A2
Worswick St B2
Wretham Place B3

Newport
Casnewydd 340

Albert Terrace B1
Allt-yr-Yn Avenue A1
Alma St C2
Ambulance Station C3
Bailey St B2
Barrack Hill A2
Bath St A3
Bedford Rd B3
Belle Vue Lane C1
Belle Vue Park C1
Bishop St A3
Blewitt St B1
Bolt Close C3
Bolt St C3
Bond St A2
Bosworth Drive A1
Bridge St B1
Bristol St A3
Bryngwyn Rd B1
Brynhyfryd Avenue C1
Brynhyfryd Rd C1
Bus Station B2
Caerau Crescent C1
Caerau Rd B1
Caerleon Rd A3
Capel Crescent C2
Cardiff Rd C2
Caroline St B3
Castle (Remains) A2
Cedar Rd B3
Charles St B2
Charlotte Drive C2
Chepstow Rd A3
Church Rd A3
Cineworld B2
Civic Centre B1
Clarence Place A2
Clifton Place B1
Clifton Rd C1
Clyffard Crescent B1
Clytha Park Rd B1
Clytha Square C2
Coldra Rd C1
Collier St A3
Colne St B3
Comfrey Close A1
Commercial Rd C3
Commercial St B2
Corelli St A3
Corn St B2
Corporation Rd B3
Coulson Close C2
County Court A2
Courts A1, B1
Crawford St A3
Cyril St B3
Dean St A3
Devon Place B1
Dewsland Park Rd C2
Dolman B2
Dolphin St C3
East Dock Rd C3
East St B1
East Usk Rd A3
Ebbw Vale Wharf B3
Emlyn St B2
Enterprise Way C3
Eton Rd B3
Evans St A2
Factory Rd A2
Fields Rd B1
Francis Drive C2
Frederick St C3
Friars Rd C1
Friars Walk B2
Gaer Lane C1
George St C3
George Street Bridge C3
Godfrey Rd B1
Gold Tops B1
Gore St A3
Gorsedd Circle C1
Grafton Rd A3
Graham St B1
Granville St C3
Harlequin Drive A1
Harrow Rd B3
Herbert Rd A3
Herbert Walk C2
Hereford St A3
High St B2
Hill St B2
Hoskins St A2
Information Centre B2
Ivor St B2
Jones St B1
Junction Rd A3
Keynshaw Avenue C2
King St C2
Kingsway B2
Kingsway Centre B2
Ledbury Drive A2
Library A3
Library, Museum & Art Gallery B2
Liverpool Wharf B3
Llanthewy Rd B1
Llanvair Rd A3
Locke St A2
Lower Dock St C3
Lucas St A2
Manchester St A3
Market B2
Marlborough Rd B3
Mellon St C3
Mill St A2
Morgan St A3
Mountjoy Rd C2
Newport Bridge A2
Newport Centre B2
Newport RFC B3
Newport Station B2
North St B2
Oakfield Rd B1
Park Square C2
Police Station A3/C2
Post Office B2/C3
Power St A1
Prince St A3
Pugsley St A2
Queen St C2
Queen's Close A1
Queen's Hill A1
Queen's Hill Crescent A1
Queensway B2
Railway St B2
Riverfront Theatre & Arts Centre, The B2
Riverside A3
Rodney Rd B2
Royal Gwent (A&E) C2
Rudry St A3
Rugby Rd B3
Ruperra Lane C3
Ruperra St C3
St Edmund St B1
St Mark's Crescent A1
St Mary St B1
St Vincent Rd A3
St Woolos C2
St Woolos General (no A&E) C1
St Woolos Rd B1
School Lane B2
Serpentine Rd B1
Shaftesbury Park A2
Sheaf Lane A3
Skinner St B2
Sorrel Drive A1
South Market St C3
Spencer Rd B1
Stow Hill B2/C1/C2
Stow Park Avenue C1
Stow Park Drive C1
TA Centre A1
Talbot St B2
Tennis Club A1
Tregare St A3
Trostrey St A3
Tunnel Terrace B1
Turner St A3
University of Wales Newport City Campus B3
Upper Dock St B2
Usk St A3
Usk Way B3/C3
Victoria Crescent B1
War Memorial A3
Waterloo Rd C1
West St B1
Wharves B2
Wheeler St A2
Whitby Place A3
Windsor Terrace B1
York Place C1

Newquay
340

Agar Rd B2
Alma Place B1
Ambulance Station B2
Anthony Rd C1
Atlantic Hotel A1
Bank St B1
Barrowfields A3
Bay View Terrace B2
Beach Rd B1
Beachfield Avenue B1
Beacon Rd A1
Belmont Place A1
Berry Rd B2
Blue Reef Aquarium B1
Boating Lake C2
Bus Station B1
Chapel Hill B1
Chester Rd A3
Cheviot Rd C1/C2
Chichester Crescent C2
Chynance Drive C1
Chyverton Close C1
Cliff Rd B2
Coach Park B2
Colvreath Rd A3
Cornwall College Newquay B3
Council Offices B1
Crantock St B1
Crescent, The B1
Criggar Rocks A3
Dale Close C3
Dale Rd C3
Dane Rd A1
East St B2
Edgcumbe Avenue B3
Edgcumbe Gardens B3
Eliot Gardens B3
Elm Close C3
Ennor's Rd B1
Fernhill Rd B1
Fire Station B1
Fore St B1
Gannel Rd C2
Golf Driving Range B3
Gover Lane B1
Great Western Beach A2
Grosvenor Avenue B2
Harbour A1
Hawkins Rd C2
Headleigh Rd B2
Hilgrove Rd A3/B3
Holywell Rd B3
Hope Terrace B1
Huer's Hut, The A1
Information Centre B1
Island Crescent B2
Jubilee St B1
Kew Close C3
Killacourt Cove A2
King Edward Crescent A1
Lanhenvor Avenue B2
Library B1
Lifeboat Station A1
Lighthouse B1
Linden Avenue C2
Listry Rd C2
Lusty Glaze Beach A3
Lusty Glaze Rd A3
Manor Rd B1
Marcus Hill B2
Mayfield Rd B2
Meadowside C3
Mellanvrane Lane C2
Michell Avenue B2
Miniature Golf Course C3
Miniature Railway B3
Mount Wise B1
Mowhay Close C3
Narrowcliff A3
Newquay B2
Newquay Hospital B2
Newquay Town Football Ground B1
Newquay Zoo B3
North Pier A1
North Quay Hill A1
Oakleigh Terrace B2
Pargolla Rd B2
Pendragon Crescent C3
Pengannel Close C1
Penina Avenue C3
Pirate's Quest B1
Police Sta & Courts B2
Post Office B1/B2
Quarry Park Rd B3
Rawley Lane C2
Reeds Way B1
Robartes Rd B2
St Anne's Rd A3
St Aubyn Crescent B3
St George's Rd B1
St John's Rd B1
St Mary's Rd B1
St Michael's B1
St Michael's Rd B1
St Thomas' Rd B2
Seymour Avenue B2
South Pier A1
South Quay Hill A1
Superstore B2
Sweet Briar Crescent C3
Sydney Rd A1
Tolcarne Beach A2
Tolcarne Point A2
Tolcarne Rd B2
Tor Rd B2
Towan Beach A1
Towan Blystra Rd B3
Tower Rd A1
Trebarwith Crescent B2
Tredour Rd C2
Treforda Rd C3
Tregoss Rd B3
Tregunnel Hill B1/C1
Tregunnel Saltings C1
Trelawney Rd B2
Treloggan Lane C3

Treloggan Rd C3
Trembath Crescent C1
Trenance Avenue B2
Trenance Gardens B2
Trenance Lane C2
Trenance Leisure Park B3
Trenance Rd B2
Trenarth Rd B2
Treninnick Hill C3
Tretherras Rd B3
Trethewey Way C1
Trevemper Rd C2
Ulalia Rd B3
Vivian Close B2
Waterworld B3
Whitegate Rd B3
Wych Hazel Way C3

Newtown
Y Drenewydd 340

Ash Close A3
Back Lane B2
Baptist Chapel B2
Barn Lane A2
Bear Lanes Shopping Centre B2
Beech Close A2
Beechwood Drive A2
Brimmon Close C2
Brimmon Rd C2
Broad St B2
Bryn Bank A1
Bryn Close A2
Bryn Gardens A1
Bryn Lane A1/A2
Bryn Meadows A2
Bryn St A2
Bryn, The A1
Brynglais Avenue A2
Brynglais Close A2
Bus Station B2
Byrnwood Drive A1
Cambrian Bridge B3
Cambrian Gardens B2
Cambrian Way B2
Canal Rd A3
Castle Mound B2
Cedewain C1
Ceiriog A1
Cemetery A3
Church (Remains of) B2
Churchill Drive A3
Cledan B3
Colwyn B3
Commercial St A2
Council Offices B1
Crescent St A1
Cwm Llanfair A2
Dinas B2
Dolafon Rd B3
Dolerw Park B1
Dolfor Rd C1
Fairfield Drive A2
Ffordd Croesawdy B2
Fire Station C1
Frankwell St A2
Frolic St B2
Fron Lane A1
Garden Lane A2
Gas St B2
Glyndwr C1
Golwgydre Lane B2
Gorsedd Circle B1
Hafren C1
Halfpenny Bridge B2
High St B2
Hillside Avenue A3
Hoel Treowen C2
Kerry Rd B3
Ladywell Shopping Ctr B2
Library B1
Llanfair Rd A2
Llanidloes Rd C1
Llys Ifor A2
Lon Cerddyn B1
Lon Helyg C1
Lonesome Lane A3
Long Bridge A2
Lower Canal Rd B3
Maldwyn Leisure Ctr C1
Market B2
Market St B2
Milford Rd B1
Mill Close B2
Miniature Railway B1
Montgomery County Infirmary (Newtown) A2
Mwyn Fynydd A3
New Church St B2
New Rd B2
Newtown Bypass C3
Newtown Football Gd B1
Newtown Station B2
Oak Tree Avenue A3
Old Kerry Rd B2
Oldbarn Lane A2
Oriel Davies Gallery B2
Park Close B1
Park Lane B1
Park St B2
Park, The B1
Parklands B1
Pavillion Court C1
Plantation Lane C1
Police Station B1
Pont Brynfedw A2
Pool Rd B3
Poplar Rd A3
Post Office B2
Powys C1
Powys Theatre A2
Regent B2
Robert Owen House B1
Robert Owen Mus B2
Rugby Club A3
St David's B2
School Lane A2
Sheaf St B3
Short Bridge St B2
Stone St B2
Superstore B3/C1
Sycamore Drive A2
Textile Museum A2
Town Hall B2
Union St A2
Vastre Industrial Est B3
War Memorial B2
WHSmith Museum B2
Wynfields C1
Y Ffrydd A3

Northampton 340

78 Derngate B3
Abington Square B3
Abington St B3
Alcombe St A3
All Saints' B2
Ambush St B1
Angel St B2
Army Reserve Centre A3
Arundel St A2
Ash St A2
Auctioneers Way C2
Bailiff St A2
Barrack Rd A2
BBOB Rugby FC A1
Beaconsfield Terrace A3
Becket's Park C3
Bedford Rd B3
Billing Rd B3
Brecon St A1
Brewery C2
Bridge St C2
Broad St B2
Burns St A3
Bus Station B2
Campbell St A2
Castle (Site of) B2
Castle St B2
Cattle Market Rd C2
Central Museum & Art Gallery B2
Charles St A3
Cheyne Walk B3
Church Lane A2
Clare St A3
Cloutsham St A3
College St B2
Colwyn Rd A3
Cotton End C2
Countess Rd A1
County Hall B2
Court A2
Craven St A3
Crown & County Courts B3
Denmark Rd B3
Derngate B3
Doddridge Church B2
Drapery, The B2
Duke St A3
Dunster St A3
Earl St A3
Euston Rd C2
Fire Station A3
Foot Meadow B2
Gladstone Rd A1
Gold St B2
Grafton St A2
Gray St A3
Green St B1
Greenwood Rd B1
Greyfriars B2
Grosvenor Centre B2
Grove Rd A3
Guildhall B2
Hampton St A2
Harding Terrace A2
Hazelwood Rd B3
Herbert St B2
Hervey St A3
Hester St A2
Holy Sepulchre A2
Hood St A3
Horse Market B2
Hunter St A3
Information Centre B2
Kettering Rd A3
Kingswell St B2
Lady's Lane B2
Leicester St A2
Leslie Rd A2
Library B3
Lorne Rd A2
Lorry Park A1
Louise Rd A2
Lower Harding St A2
Lower Hester St A2
Lower Mounts B3
Lower Priory St A2
Main Rd C1
Marefair B2
Market Square B2
Marlboro Rd B1
Marriott St A2
Millers Meadow A1
Military Rd A3
Mounts Baths Leisure Centre A3
Nene Valley Retail Pk C1
New South Bridge Rd C2
Northampton General Hospital (A&E) B3
Northampton Marina C3
Northampton Sta B1
Northcote St A2
Nunn Mills Rd C3
Old Towcester Rd C2
Overstone Rd A3
Pembroke Rd A1
Penn Court C2
Police Station B3
Post Office A1/B3
Quorn Way A2
Ransome Rd C3
Regent Square A2
Ridings, The B3
Robert St A2
Royal & Derngate Theatres B3
St Andrew's Rd B1
St Andrew's St A2
St Edmund's Rd B3
St George's St A2
St Giles B3
St Giles St B3
St Giles' Terrace B3
St James Park Rd B1
St James Rd B1
St James Retail Park C1
St James' Mill Rd B1
St James' Mill Rd East C1
St Leonard's Rd C2
St Mary's St B2
St Michael's Rd A3
St Peter's B2
St Peter's Way Shopping Precinct B2
St Peter's Way B2
Salisbury St A2
Scarletwell St B2
Semilong Rd A2
Sheep St B2
Sol Central (Leisure Centre) B2
Somerset St A3
South Bridge C2
Southfield Avenue C2
Spencer Bridge Rd A1
Spencer Rd A3
Spring Gardens B3
Spring Lane B2
Superstore C2
Swan St B3
Tintern Avenue A1
Towcester Rd C2
Univ of Northampton (Waterside Campus) C3
Upper Bath St B2
Upper Mounts A2
Victoria Park A1
Victoria Promenade B2
Victoria Rd B3
Victoria St A2
Wellingborough Rd B3
West Bridge B1
York Rd B3

Norwich 341

Albion Way C3
All Saints Green C2
Anchor St A3
Anglia Square A2
Argyle St C3
Arts Centre B1
Ashby St C2
Assembly House B1
Bank Plain B2
Barker St A1
Barn Rd A1
Barrack St A3
Ber St C2
Bethel St B1
Bishop Bridge A3
Bishopbridge Rd A3
Bishopgate A3
Blackfriars St A2
Botolph St A2
Bracondale C3
Brazen Gate C2
Bridewell Museum B2
Brunswick Rd C1
Bull Close Rd A2
Bus Station C2
Calvert St A2
Cannell Green A3
Carrow Rd C3
Castle & Museum B2
Castle Mall B2
Castle Meadow B2
Cathedral B2
Cathedral (RC) B1
Cathedral Retail Park A1
Cattlemarket St B2
Chantry Place C1
Chantry Rd C1
Chapel Loke C2
Chapelfield East B1
Chapelfield Gardens B1
Chapelfield North B1
Chapelfield Rd B1
Cinema City B2
City Hall B1
City Rd C2
City Wall C1/C3
Close, The B2/B3
Colegate A2
Coslany St B1
Cow Hill B1
Cow Tower A3
Cowgate A2
Crown & Magistrates' Courts A2
Dragon Hall Heritage Centre C3
Duke St A1
Edward St A2
Elm Hill B2
Erpingham Gate B2
Fishergate A2
Forum, The B1
Foundry Bridge B3
Fye Bridge A2
Garden St C2
Gas Hill B3
Gentlemans Walk B2
Grapes Hill B1
Great Hospital Halls, The A3
Grove Avenue C1
Grove Rd C1
Guildhall B1
Gurney Rd A3
Hall Rd C2
Heathgate A3
Heigham St A1
Hollywood A2
Horn's Lane C2
Hungate Medieval Art B2
Ipswich Rd C1
ITV Anglia C3
James Stuart Gdns B3
King St B2
King St C3
Koblenz Avenue C3
Leisure Centre A3
Library B1
London St B2
Lower Clarence Rd B3
Maddermarket B1
Magdalen St A2
Mariners Lane C2
Market B2
Market Avenue B2
Mountergate B3
Mousehold St A3
Newmarket Rd C1
Norfolk St C1
Norwich City FC C3
Norwich Gallery B2
Norwich School B2
Norwich Station B3
Oak St A1
Odeon C3
Palace St A2
Pitt St A1
Playhouse B2
Police Station B1
Post Office A2/B2/B3/C1
Pottergate B1
Prince of Wales Rd B2
Princes St B2
Pull's Ferry B3
Puppet Theatre A2
Queen St B2
Queens Rd C2
Recorder Rd B3
Riverside Entertainment Centre C3
Riverside Leisure Ctr C3
Riverside Rd B3
Riverside Retail Park C3
Rosary Rd B3
Rose Lane B2
Rouen Rd C2
St Andrews St B2
St Augustines St A1
St Benedicts St B1
St Crispins Road A1
St Ethelbert's Gate B2
St Faiths Lane B3
St Georges St A2
St Giles St B1
St James Close A3
St Julians C2
St Leonards Rd B3
St Martin's Lane A1
St Peter Mancroft B2
St Peters St B1
St Stephens Rd C1
St Stephens St C1
Shopmobility C1
Silver Rd A2
Silver St A2
Southwell Rd C2
St. Andrew's & Blackfriars' Hall B2
Strangers' Hall B1
Superstore C2
Surrey St C2
Sussex St A1
Theatre Royal B1
Theatre St B1
Thorn Lane C2
Thorpe Rd B3
Tombland B2
Union St C1
Vauxhall St B1
Victoria St C1
Vue B2
Walpole St B1
Waterfront, The C3
Wensum St A2
Wessex St C1
Westwick St A1
Wherry Rd C3
Whitefriars A2
Willow Lane B1

Nottingham 341

Abbotsford Drive A3
Addison St A1
Albert Hall B1
Alfred St Central A3
Alfreton Rd B1
All Saints St A1
Annesley Grove A2
Arboretum A1
Arboretum St A1
Arthur St A1
Arts Theatre B3
Ashforth St A3
Balmoral Rd A1
Barker Gate B3
Bath St B3
BBC Nottingham C3
Beacon Hill Rise B3
Belgrave Rooms B1
Bellar Gate B3
Belward St B3
Brewhouse Yard C2
Broad Marsh Bus Sta C2
Broad St B3
Brook St B3
Burns St A1
Burton St B2
Bus Station A2
Canal St C2
Carlton St B3
Carrington St C2
Castle C2
Castle Boulevard C1
Castle Gate C2
Castle Meadow Rd C1
Castle Meadow Retail Pk C1
Castle Rd C2
Castle Wharf C2
Cavendish Rd East C1
Cemetery A1/B1
Chaucer St B1
Cheapside B2
Church Rd A3
City Link C3
City of Caves C2
Clarendon St B1
Cliff Rd C3
Clumber Rd East C1
Clumber St B2
College St B1
Collin St C2
Contemporary C3
Conway Close A2
Cornerhouse, The B2
Council House B2
Cranbrook St B3
Cranmer St A2
Cromwell St B1
Curzon St B3
Derby Rd B1
Dryden St A2
Exchange Centre, The B2
Fishpond Drive C1
Fletcher Gate B3
Forest Rd East A1
Forest Rd West A1
Friar Lane C2
Gedling Grove A1
Gedling St B3
George St B3
Gill St A2
Glasshouse St B2
Goldsmith St B2
Goose Gate B3
Great Freeman St A2
Guildhall B2
Hamilton Drive C1
Hampden St A1
Heathcote St B3
High Pavement C3
High School A1
HM Revenue & Customs C2
Holles Crescent C1
Hope Drive C1
Hungerhill Rd A3
Huntingdon Drive C1
Huntingdon St A2
Information Centre B2
Instow Rise A3
International Community Centre A2
Kent St B3
King St B2
Lace Market B3
Lace Mkt Theatre C3
Lamartine St B3
Leisure Centre C3
Lenton Rd C1
Lewis Close A3
Lincoln St B2
London Rd C3
Long Row B2
Low Pavement C2
Lower Parliament St B3
Magistrates' Court C2
Maid Marian Way B2
Mansfield Rd A2/B2
Middle Hill C2
Milton St B2
Mount St B2
National Ice Centre & Motorpoint Arena C3
National Justice Museum C3
Newcastle Drive B1
Newstead Grove A2
North Sherwood St A2
Nottingham Arena C3
Nottingham Cath B2
Nottingham College C3
Nottingham Station C3
Nottingham Trent University A2/B2
Old Market Square B2
Oliver St A1
Park Drive C1
Park Row C1
Park Terrace B1
Park Valley C1
Park, The C1
Peas Hill Rd A3
Peel St A1
Pelham St B2
Peveril Drive C1
Plantagenet St A3
Playhouse Theatre B1
Plumptre St C3
Police Station B1/B2
Poplar St C3
Portland Rd B1
Post Office B2
Queen's Rd C3
Raleigh St A1
Regent St B1
Rick St B3
Robin Hood St B3
Robin Hood Statue C2
Ropewalk, The B1
Royal Centre B2
Royal Children Inn C2
Royal Concert Hall B2
St Ann's Hill Rd A2
St Ann's Way A2
St Ann's Well Rd A3
St James' St B2
St Mark's St B3
St Mary's Rest Garden B3
St Mary's Gate B3
St Nicholas C2
St Peter's C2
St Peter's Gate B2
Salutation Inn C2
Shakespeare St B2
Shelton St A2
Shopmobility A2
South Parade B2
South Rd C1
South Sherwood St B2
Station Street C3
Stoney St B3
Talbot St B1
Tattershall Drive C1
Tennis Drive B1
Tennyson St A1
Theatre Royal B2
Trent St C3
Trent University B2
Union Rd B3
Upper Parliament St B2
Victoria Centre B2
Victoria Leisure Ctr B3
Victoria Park B3
Victoria St B2
Walter St A1
Warser Gate B3
Watkin St A2
Waverley St A1
Wheeler Gate B2
Wilford Rd C2
Wilford St C2
Wollaton St B1
Woodborough Rd A2
Woolpack Lane B3
Ye Old Trip to Jerusalem C2
York St A2

Oban 341

Aird's Crescent B2
Albany St B2
Albert Lane A2
Albert Rd A2
Alma Crescent B1
Ambulance Station C2
Angus Terrace C3
Ardconnel Rd A2
Ardconnel Terrace B2
Argyll Square B2
Argyll St B2
Atlantis Leisure Ctr A2
Bayview Rd A1
Benvoulin Rd A2
Bowling Green A2
Breadalbane St A2
Bus Station B2
Campbell St B2
College B2
Colonsay Terrace C3
Combie St B2
Corran Brae A1
Corran Esplanade A1/A2
Corran Halls, The A2
Court B2
Crannaig-a-Mhinisteir B1
Crannog Lane C2
Croft Avenue A2
Dalintart Drive C3
Dalriach Rd A2
Distillery B2
Drummore Rd C2
Duncraggan Rd A2
Dunollie Rd A2
Dunuaran Rd B1
Feochan Grove C3
Ferry Terminal B1
Gallanach Rd B1
George St A2
Glencruitten Drive C3
Glencruitten Rd B3
Glenmore Rd C1
Glenshellach Rd C1
Glenshellach Terrace B2
Hazeldean Crescent A3
High St B2
Hill St B2
Industrial Estate C2
Information Centre B2
Islay Rd C3
Jacob's Ladder B2
Jura Rd C3
Knipoch Place C3
Laurel Crescent A2
Laurel Rd A2/A3
Library B1
Lifeboat Station B1
Lighthouse Pier B1
Lismore Crescent A2
Lochavullin Drive B2
Lochavullin Rd C2
Lochside St B2
Longsdale Crescent A3
Longsdale Rd A2/A3
Longsdale Terrace A3
Lunga Rd C3
Lynn Rd C2
Market St B2
McCaig Rd C3
McCaig's Tower A2
Mill Lane C2
Miller Rd C2
Millpark Avenue C2
Millpark Rd C2
Mossfield Avenue B3
Mossfield Drive B3
Mossfield Stadium B3
Nant Drive C3
Nelson Rd C2
North Pier B2
Nursery Lane A2
Oban B2
Oban Phoenix A2
Police Station B2
Polvinister Rd B3
Post Office A2/B2
Pulpit Drive C1
Pulpit Hill C1
Pulpit Hill Viewpoint B1
Quarry Rd C2
Queen's Park Place B2
Railway Quay B1
Retail Park B1
Rockfield Rd B2
St Columba's A1
St John's A2
Scalpay Terrace C3
Shore St B1
Shuna Terrace C3
Sinclair Drive C2
Soroba Rd B2/C2
South Pier B2
Stevenson St B2
Tweedale St B2
Ulva Rd C2
Villa Rd B1
War & Peace A2

Oxford 341

Adelaide St A1
Albert St A1
All Souls (College) B2
Ashmolean Mus B2
Balliol (College) B2
Banbury Rd A2
Bate Collection of Musical Instruments C2
Beaumont St B1
Becket St B1
Blackhall Rd A2
Blue Boar St B2
Bodleian Library B2
Botanic Garden B3
Brasenose (College) B2
Brewer St C2
Broad St B2
Burton-Taylor Theatre B2
Bus Station B1
Canal St A1
Cardigan St A1
Carfax Tower B2
Castle B1
Castle St B1
Catte St B2
Cemetery C1
Christ Church (Coll) B2
Christ Church Cath C2
Christ Church Mdw C2
City of Oxford College C1
Clarendon Centre B2
Cornmarket St B2
Corpus Christi (Coll) B2
County Hall B1
Covered Market B2
Cowley Place C3
Cranham St A1
Cranham Terrace A1
Cricket Ground B1
Crown & County Courts C2
Deer Park B3
Exeter (College) B2
Fire Station B1
Folly Bridge C2
George St B1
Great Clarendon St A1
Harris Manchester (College) B2
Hart St A1
Hertford (College) B2
High St B3
Hollybush Row B1
Holywell St B2
Hythe Bridge St B1
Ice Rink C1
Jericho St A1
Jesus (College) B2
Jowett Walk B3
Juxon St A1
Keble (College) A2
Keble Rd A2
Library B2
Linacre (College) A3
Lincoln (College) B2
Little Clarendon St A1
Longwall St B3
Magdalen (College) B3
Magdalen Bridge B2
Magdalen St B2
Magistrate's Court C2
Manor Rd B3
Mansfield (College) A2
Mansfield Rd A3
Market B1
Marlborough Rd C2
Martyrs' Memorial B2
Merton (College) B3
Merton Field B3
Merton St B2
Mus of Modern Art B2
Museum of Oxford B2
Museum Rd A2
New College (College) B3
New Inn Hall St B2
New Rd B1
New Theatre B2
Norfolk St C1
Nuffield (College) B1
Observatory A1
Observatory St A1
Odeon B1/B2
Old Fire Station B1
Old Greyfriars St C2
Oriel (College) B2
Oxford Castle & Prison B1
Oxford Station B1
Oxford University Research Centres A1
Oxpens Rd C1
Paradise Square C1
Paradise St B1
Park End St B1
Parks Rd A2/B2
Pembroke (College) C2
Phoenix A1
Picture Gallery C2
Plantation Rd A1
Playhouse B2
Police Station C2
Post Office A1/B2
Pusey St B1
Queen's (College) B3
Queen's Lane B3
Radcliffe Camera B2
Rewley Rd B1
Richmond Rd A1
Rose Lane B3
Ruskin (College) B1
Said Business School B1
St Aldates C2
St Anne's (College) A1
St Antony's (College) A1
St Bernard's Rd A1
St Catherine's (Coll) B3
St Cross Building A3
St Cross Rd A3
St Edmund Hall (Coll) B3
St Giles St A2
St Hilda's (College) C3
St John St B2
St John's (College) B2
St Mary the Virgin B2
St Michael at the Northgate B2
St Peter's (College) B1
St Thomas St B1
Science Area A2
Science Museum B2
Sheldonian Theatre B2
Somerville (College) A1
South Parks Rd A2
Speedwell St C2
Sports Ground C3
Thames St C2
Town Hall B2
Trinity (College) B2
Turl St B2
University Coll (Coll) B3
Univ Natural History Mus & Pitt Rivers Mus A2
University Parks A2
Wadham (College) B2
Walton Crescent A1
Walton St A1
Western Rd C2
Westgate C2
Woodstock Rd A1
Worcester (College) B1

Perth 341

AK Bell Library B2
Abbot Crescent C1
Abbot St C1
Albany Terrace A1
Albert Monument A3
Alexandra St B2
Atholl St A2
Balhousie Avenue A2
Balhousie Castle & Black Watch Museum A2
Balhousie St A2
Ballantine Place A1
Barossa Place A2
Barossa St A2
Barrack St A2
Bell's Sports Centre A2
Bellwood B3
Blair St B1
Burn Park C1
Bus Station B2
Caledonian Rd B2
Canal Crescent B2
Canal St B3
Cavendish Avenue C1
Charles St B2
Charlotte Place A2
Charlotte St A3
Church St A1
City Hall B3
Club House C3
Clyde Place C1
Coach Park C3
Commercial St A3
Concert Hall B3
Council Chambers B3
County Place B2
Court B3
Craigie Place C2
Crieff Rd A1
Croft Park C2
Cross St B2
Darnhall Crescent C1
Darnhall Drive C1
Dewars Centre B1
Dundee Rd B3
Dunkeld Rd A1
Earl's Dykes B1
Edinburgh Rd C3
Elibank St B1
Fair Maid's House A3
Fergusson B3
Feus Rd A1
Fire Station A1
Foundary Lane A2
Friar St C1
George St B3
Glamis Place C1
Glasgow Rd B1
Glenearn Rd C2
Glover St B1/C1
Golf Course A2
Gowrie St A3
Gray St B1
Graybank Rd B1
Greyfriars Burial Gd B3
Hay St A2
High St B2/B3
Inchaffray St A1
Industrial/Retail Park B1
Information Centre B2
Isla Rd A3
James St B2
Keir St A3
King Edward St B3
King James VI Golf Course C3
King St B2
Kings Place C2
Kinnoull Causeway B2
Kinnoull St B2
Knowelea Place C1
Knowelea Terrace C1
Ladeside Bsns Centre A1
Leisure Pool B1
Leonard St B2
Lickley St B2
Lochie Brae A3
Long Causeway A1
Low St A2
Main St A3
Marshall Place C3
Melville St A2
Mill St B3
Milne St B2
Murray Crescent C1
Murray St B2
Needless Rd C1
New Rd B2
North Inch A3
North Methven St A2
Park Place C1
Perth B2
Perth Bridge A3
Perth Business Park B1
Perth Museum & Art Gallery B3
Perth Station C2
Pickletulllum Rd B1
Pitheavlis Crescent C1
Playhouse B2
Police Station A2
Pomarium St B2
Post Office B2/C2
Princes St B3
Priory Place C2
Queen St C1
Queen's Bridge B3
Riggs Rd B1
Riverside B3
Riverside Park B3
Rodney Gardens B3
Rose Terrace A2
St Catherine's Rd A1/A2
St Catherine's Retail Park A1
St John St B3
St John's Kirk B3
St John's Shopping Ctr B2
St Leonards Bridge C2
St Ninians Cathedral A2
Scott Monument C2
Scott St B2
Sheriff Court B3
Shore Rd C3
Skate Park C3
South Inch C2
South Inch Bsns Ctr C3
South Inch Park C2
South Inch View C2
South Methven St B2
South St B3
South William St B2
Stables, The A1
Stanners, The B3
Stormont St A2
Strathmore St A3
Stuart Avenue C1
Superstore B1/B2
Tay St B3
Union Lane A2
Victoria St B2
Watergate B3
Wellshill Cemetery A1
West Bridge St A3
West Mill St B2
Whitefriers Crescent B1
Whitefriers St B1
Wilson St C1
Windsor Terrace C1
Woodside Crescent C1
York Place B2
Young St C1

Peterborough 341

Athletics Arena B3
Bishop's Palace B2
Bishop's Rd B2/B3
Boongate A3
Bourges Boulevard A1
Bourges Retail Pk B1/B2
Bridge House (Council Offices) C2
Bridge St B2
Bright St A1
Broadway A2
Broadway A2
Brook St A2
Burghley Rd A2
Bus Station B2
Cavendish St A3
Charles St A3
Church St B2
Church Walk A2
Cobden Avenue A1
Cobden St A1
Cowgate B2
Craig St A2
Crawthorne Rd A2
Cromwell Rd A1
Dickens St A3
Eastfield Rd A3
Eastgate B3
East Station Road C2
Fire Station A1
Fletton Avenue C2
Frank Perkins Parkway C3
Geneva St A2
George St C1
Gladstone St A1
Glebe Rd C2
Gloucester Rd C3
Granby St B3
Grove St C1
Guildhall B2
Hadrians Court C3
Hawksbill Way C2
Henry St A2
Hereward Cross (shopping) B2

Hereward Rd B3
Information Centre B2
Jubilee St C1
Kent Rd B1
Key Theatre C2
Kirkwood Close B1
Lea Gardens B1
Library A2
Lincoln Rd A2
London Rd C2
Long Causeway B2
Lower Bridge St C2
Magistrates Court B2
Manor House St A2
Mayor's Walk A1
Midland Rd A1
Monument St A2
Morris St A3
Mus & Art Gallery B2
Nene Valley Railway C1
New Rd A2
New Rd C1
Northminster A2
Old Customs House C2
Oundle Rd C1
Padholme Rd A3
Palmerston Rd C1
Park Rd A2
Passport Office B2
Peterborough Cath B2
Peterborough Nene Valley C1
Peterborough Sta B1
Police Station B2
Post Office A3/B2
Priestgate B2
Queen's Walk C2
Queensgate Centre B2
Railworld Wildlife Haven C1
Regional Fitness & Swimming Centre B3
River Lane B1
Rivergate Shopping Centre B2
Riverside Mead C3
Russell St A1
St John's B2
St John's St A3
St Marks St A2
St Peter's Rd B2
Saxon Rd A3
Spital Bridge A1
Stagshaw Drive C3
Star Rd B3
Superstore B1
Thorpe Lea Rd B1
Thorpe Rd B1
Thorpe's Lea Rd B1
Tower St A2
Town Hall B2
Viersen Platz B2
Vineyard Rd B3
Wake Rd B3
Wellington St A3
Wentworth St B2
Westgate B2
Weston Homes Stadium (Peterborough United FC) The C2
Whalley St A3
Wharf Rd C1
Whitsed St A3
YMCA A3

Plymouth 341

Alma Rd A1
Anstis St B1
Armada Shopping Ctr B2
Armada St A3
Armada Way B2
Arts Centre B2
Athenaeum B1
Athenaeum St C1
Barbican C3
Barbican C3
Baring St A3
Bath St B1
Beaumont Park B3
Beaumont Rd B3
Black Friars Gin Distillery C2
Box, The A2
Breton Side B3
Coach Station A2
Castle St C3
Cathedral (RC) B1
Cecil St B1
Central Park A1
Central Park Avenue A2
Charles Church B3
Charles Cross B3
Charles St B2
Cineworld B2
Citadel Rd C2
Citadel Rd East C2
Civic Centre B2
Cliff Rd C1
Clifton Place A3
Cobourg St A2
College of Art B2
Continental Ferry Port B1
Cornwall St B2
Crescent, The B1
Dale Rd A2
Deptford Place A3
Derry Avenue A2
Derry's Cross B1
Drake Circus B2
Drake Circus Shopping Centre B2
Drake Statue C2
Eastlake St B2
Ebrington St B3
Elizabethan House C3
Elliot St C1
Endsleigh Place A2
Exeter St B3
Fire Station A3
Fish Quay C3
Gibbons St A3
Glen Park Avenue A2
Grand Parade C1
Great Western Rd C1
Greenbank Rd A3
Greenbank Terrace A3
Guildhall B2
Hampton St B3
Harwell St B1
Hill Park Crescent A3
Hoe Approach B2
Hoe Rd C2
Hoe, The C2
Hoegate St C2
Houndiscombe Rd A2
Information Centre C3
James St A2
Kensington Rd A3
King St B1
Lambhay Hill C3
Leigham St C1
Library B2
Lipson Rd A3/B3
Lockyer St C2
Lockyers Quay C3
Madeira Rd C2
Marina B3
Market B1
Market Avenue B1
Martin St B1
Mayflower St B2
Mayflower Stone & Steps C3
Mayflower C3
Merchant's House B2
Millbay Rd B1
National Marine Aquarium C3
Neswick St B1
New George St B2
New St C3
North Cross A2
North Hill A3
North Quay B2
North Rd East A2
North Rd West A1
North St B3
Notte St B2
Octagon, The B1
Octagon St B1
Pennycomequick A1
Pier St C1
Plymouth Naval Memorial C2
Plymouth Pavilions B1
Plymouth Station A2
Police Station B3
Post Office B2,C1,C3
Princess St B2
Promenade, The C2
Prysten House B2
Queen Anne's Battery Watersports Centre C3
Radford Rd C1
Regent St B3
Rope Walk C3
Royal Citadel C2
Royal Parade B2
Royal Theatre B2
Russell Place A1
St Andrew's B2
St Andrew's Cross B2
St Andrew's St B2
St Lawrence Rd A2
Saltash Rd A2
Shopmobility B2
Smeaton's Tower C2
Southern Terrace A3
Southside St C2
Stuart Rd A1
Sutherland Rd A2
Sutton Rd B3
Sydney St A1
Teats Hill Rd C3
Tothill Avenue B3
Union St B1
Univ of Plymouth A2
Vauxhall St B2/3
Victoria Park A1
Walker Terrace C1
West Hoe Rd C1
Western Approach B1
Whittington St A1
Wyndham St B1

Poole 341

Ambulance Station A3
Baiater Gardens C2
Baiter Park C3
Ballard Close C2
Ballard Rd C2
Bay Hog Lane B1
BMI The Harbour Hospital A3
Bridge Approach C1
Bus Station B2
Castle St B2
Catalina Drive B3
Chapel Lane B2
Church St B1
Cinnamon Lane B1
Colborne Close B3
Dear Hay Lane B2
Denmark Lane A3
Denmark Rd A3
Dolphin Centre B2
East St B2
Elizabeth Rd A3
Emerson Rd B2
Ferry Rd C1
Ferry Terminal C1
Fire Station A2
Freightliner Terminal C1
Furnell Rd B3
Garland Rd A3
Green Rd B2
Heckford Lane A3
Heckford Rd A3
High St B2
High St North A3
Hill St B2
Holes Bay Rd A1
Hospital (A&E) A3
Information Centre C2
Kingland Rd B3
Kingston Rd A3
Labrador Drive C3
Lagland St B2
Lander Close C3
Lighthouse, Poole Centre for the Arts B3
Longfleet Rd A3
Maple Rd A3
Market Close B2
Market St B2
Mount Pleasant Rd B3
New Harbour Rd C1
New Harbour Rd South C1
New Harbour Rd West C1
New Orchard B1
New Quay Rd C1
New St B2
Newfoundland Drive B2
North St B2
Old Lifeboat C2
Old Orchard B2
Parish Rd A3
Park Lake Rd B3
Parkstone Rd A3
Perry Gardens B2
Pitwines Close B2
Police Station A2
Poole Central Library B2
Poole Lifting Bridge C1
Poole Park B2
Poole Station A2
Poole Museum C1
Post Office B2
Quay, The C2
RNLI College B1
St John's Rd A3
St Margaret's Rd A2
St Mary's Maternity Unit A3
St Mary's Rd A3
Seldown Bridge B3
Seldown Lane B3
Seldown Rd B3
Serpentine Rd A2
Scaplen's Court C1
Shaftesbury Rd A3
Skinner St B2
Slipway B1
Stanley Rd C2
Sterte Avenue A2
Sterte Avenue West A1
Sterte Close A2
Sterte Esplanade A2
Sterte Rd A2
Strand St C2
Superstore B3
Swimming Pool B3
Taverner Close B3
Thames St B1
Towngate Bridge B2
Twin Sails Bridge B1
Vallis Close C3
Waldren Close B3
West Quay B1
West Quay Rd B1
West St B1
West View Rd A2
Whatleigh Close B2
Wimborne Rd A3

Portsmouth 341

Action Stations C1
Admiralty Rd A1
Alfred Rd A2
Anglesea Rd A2
Arundel St B3
Aspex B1
Bishop St A2
Broad St C1
Buckingham House C2
Burnaby Rd B2
Bus Station B1
Camber Dock C1
Cambridge Rd B2
Car Ferry to Isle of Wight B1
Cascades Shopping Centre A3
Castle Rd C3
Civic Offices B3
Clarence Pier C2
College St B1
Commercial Rd A3
Cottage Grove B3
Cross St A1
Cumberland St A2
Duisburg Way C2
Durham St A3
East St B1
Edinburgh Rd A2
Elm Grove C3
Emirates Spinnaker Tower B1
Governor's Grn C1
Great Southsea St C3
Green Rd B3
Greetham St B3
Grosvenor St B3
Groundlings A2
Grove Rd North C3
Grove Rd South C3
Guildhall B3
Guildhall Walk B3
Gunwharf Quays Designer Outlet B1
Gunwharf Rd B1
Hambrook St C2
Hampshire Terrace B2
Hanover St A1
Hard, The B1
High St C2
HM Naval Base A1
HMS Nelson (Royal Naval Barracks) A2
HMS Monitor M.33 A1
HMS Victory A1
HMS Warrior A1
Hovercraft Terminal C2
Hyde Park Rd B3
Information Ctr A1/B3
Isambard Brunel Rd B3
Isle of Wight Car Ferry Terminal B1
Kent Rd C3
Kent St A2
King St B3
King's Rd C3
King's Terrace C2
Lake Rd A3
Law Courts B3
Library B3
Long Curtain Rd C2
Marina B1
Market Way A3
Marmion Rd C3
Mary Rose A1
Middle St B3
Millennium Promenade Walk B1/C1
Museum Rd B2
National Museum of the Royal Navy A1
Naval Recreation Gd C2
Nightingale Rd C3
Norfolk St B3
North St A2
Osborne Rd C3
Paradise St A3
Park Rd B2
Passenger Catamaran to Isle of Wight B1
Passenger Ferry to Gosport B1
Pelham Rd C3
Pembroke Gardens C2
Pier Rd C2
Point Battery C1
Police Station B3
Portsmouth & Southsea Station A3
Portsmouth Harbour Station B1
Portsmouth Historic Dockyard A1
Portsmouth Museum & Art Gallery B2
Post Office A1/A3/B3
Queen St A1
Queen's Crescent C3
Ravelin Park B2
Register Office B2
Round Tower C1
Royal Garrison Church C1
St Edward's Rd C3
St George's Rd B2
St George's Square B1
St George's Way B2
St James's Rd B3
St James's St A2
St John's Cath (RC) A3
St Thomas's Cath C1
St Thomas's St B2
Shopmobility A3/B1
Somers Rd B3
Southsea Common C2
Southsea Terrace C2
Square Tower C1
Station St A3
Town Fortifications C1
Unicorn Rd A2
United Services Recreation Ground B2
University of Portsmouth A2/B2
Univ of Portsmouth B3
Upper Arundel St A3
Victoria Avenue C2
Victoria Park A2
Victory Gate A1
Vue B1
Warblington St B1
Western Parade C2
White Hart Rd C1
Winston Churchill Ave B3

Preston 342

Adelphi St A2
Anchor Court B3
Aqueduct St A1
Ardee Rd C1
Arthur St B2
Ashton St A1
Avenham Lane B3
Avenham Park C3
Avenham Rd B3
Avenham St B3
Bairstow St B3
Balderstone Rd C1
Beamont Drive A1
Beech St South C2
Bird St C1
Bow Lane B2
Brieryfield Rd A1
Broadgate C1
Brook St A2
Bus Station A3
Butler St B2
Cannon St B3
Carlton St A1
Chaddock St B3
Channel Way B1
Chapel St B3
Christ Church St B2
Christian Rd B2
Cold Bath St A2
Coleman Court C1
Connaught Rd C2
Corporation St A2/B2
County Hall B2
Cricket Ground C2
Croft St A1
Cross St B3
Crown Court A3
Crown St A3
East Cliff C3
East Cliff Rd B3
Edward St A3
Elizabeth St A3
Euston St B1
Fishergate B2/B3
Fishergate Hill B2
Fishergate Shopping Centre B2
Fitzroy St B1
Fleetwood St A1
Friargate A3
Fylde Rd A1/A2
Gerrard St B2
Glover's Court B3
Good St B2
Grafton St B2
Great George St A3
Great Shaw St A3
Greenbank St A2
Guild Way B1
Guild Hall & Charter B3
Guildhall St B3
Harrington St A2
Harris Museum B3
Hartington Rd B1
Hasset Close C2
Heatley St B2
Hind St C2
Information Centre B3
Kilruddery Rd C1
Lancashire Archives B2
Lancaster Rd A3/B3
Latham St B3
Lauderdale St C2
Lawson St A3
Leighton St A2
Leyland Rd C1
Library A1
Library B3
Liverpool Rd C1
Lodge St B2
Lune St B3
Magistrate's Court A3
Main Sprit West B3
Maresfield Rd C1
Market St West A3
Marsh Lane B1/B2
Maudland Bank A2
Maudland Rd A2
Meadow Court C2
Meath Rd C1
Miller Arcade B3
Miller Park C3
Moor Lane A3
Mount St B3
North Rd A3
North St A3
Northcote Rd B1
Old Milestones B1
Old Tram Rd C3
Pedder St A1/A2
Peel St A2
Penwortham Bridge C2
Penwortham New Bridge C1
Pitt St B2
Playhouse A3
Police Station A3
Portway B1
Post Office B3
Preston Station B2
Retail Park B2
Ribble Bank St B2
Ribble Viaduct C2
Ribblesdale Place B3
Ringway B3
River Parade C1
Riverside C2
St George's Shopping Centre B3
St Georges B3
St John's Minster B3
St Johns Shopping Ctr A3
St Mark's Rd A1
St Walburges A1
Salisbury Rd B1
Sessions House B3
Snow Hill A3
South End C2
South Meadow Lane C2
Spa Rd B1
Sports Ground C2
Strand Rd B1
Syke St B3
Talbot Rd B1
Taylor St C1
Tithebarn St A3
Town Hall B3
Tulketh Brow A1
University of Central Lancashire A2
Valley Rd C1
Victoria St A2
Walker St A3
Walton's Parade B2
Warwick St A3
Wellfield Bsns Park A1
Wellfield Rd A1
Wellington St A1
West Cliff C2
West Strand A1
Winckley Rd C1
Winckley Square B3
Wolseley Rd C2

Reading 342

Abbey Ruins B2
Abbey Square B2
Abbey St B2
Abbot's Walk B2
Acacia Rd C2
Addington Rd C3
Addison Rd A1
Allcroft Rd C3
Alpine St C2
Baker St B1
Berkeley Avenue C1
Bridge St B2
Brigham Rd A1
Broad St B1
Broad Street Mall B1
Carey St B1
Castle Hill C1
Castle St B1
Causeway, The A3
Caversham Rd A1
Christchurch Meadows A2
Civic Offices B1
Coley Hill C1
Coley Place C1
Craven Rd C3
Crown St C2
De Montfort Rd A1
Denmark Rd C3
Duke St B2
East St B2
Edgehill St C2
Eldon Rd B3
Eldon Terrace B3
Elgar Rd C1
Erleigh Rd C3
Field Rd C1
Fire Station A1
Fobney St B1
Forbury Gardens B2
Forbury Rd B2
Forbury Retail Park B2
Francis St C1
Friar St B1
Garrard St B1
Gas Works Rd B3
George St A2
Great Knollys St B1
Greyfriars B1
Grove, The B2
Gun St B1
Henry St C1
Hexagon Theatre, The B1
Hill's Meadow A2
Howard St B1
Inner Distribution Rd B1
Katesgrove Lane C1
Kenavon Drive B2
Kendrick Rd C2
King's Mdw Rec Gd A2
King's Rd B2
Library B2
London Rd C3
London St B2
Lynmouth Rd A1
Magistrate's Court B1
Market Place B2
Mill Lane B2
Mill Rd A2
Minster St B1
Morgan Rd C3
Mount Pleasant C2
Museum of English Rural Life (MERL) C3
Napier Rd A2
Newark St C2
Newport Rd A1
Oracle Shopping Centre, The B1
Orts Rd B3
Oxford Road B1
Pell St C1
Post Office B1
Queen Victoria St B1
Queen's Rd A2
Queen's Rd B2
Randolph Rd A1
Reading Bridge A2
Reading College B3
Reading Station A1
Redlands Rd C3
Riverside Museum B3
Rose Kiln Lane C1
Royal Berkshire Medical Museum C3
Royal Berks Hospital (A&E) C3
St Giles C2
St Laurence B2
St Mary's B1
St Mary's Butts B1
St Saviour's Rd C1
Send Rd A3
Sherman Rd C2
Sidmouth St B2
Silver St C2
South St B2
South St Arts Ctr B2
Southampton St C2
Station Rd B1
Superstore A3
Swansea Rd A1
Thames Lido A2
Tudor Road A1
University of Reading C3
Valpy St B2
Vastern Rd A1
Vue B2
Waldeck St C2
Watlington St B3
West St B1
Whitby Drive C3
Wolseley St C1
York Rd A1
Zinzan St B1

St Andrews 342

Abbey St B2
Abbey Walk B3
Abbotsford Crescent A1
Albany Park C3
Allan Robertson Drive C2
Ambulance Station C1
Anstruther Rd C3
Argyle St B1
Auld Burn Rd B2
Bassaguard Ind Est B1
Bell St B2
Blackfriars Chapel (Ruins) B2
Boase Avenue B2
Braid Crescent C3
Brewster Place C3
Bridge St B1
British Golf Mus A1
Broomfaulds Avenue C1
Bruce Embankment A1
Bruce St C2
Bus Station A1
Byre Theatre B2
Canongate C1
Cathedral and Priory (Ruins) B3
Cemetery B1
Chamberlain St C1
Church St B2
Churchill Crescent C2
City Rd A1
Claybraes C1
Cockshaugh Public Park B1
Cosmos Community Centre B3
Council Office A2
Crawford Gardens C1
Doubledykes Rd B1
Drumcarrow Rd C1
East Sands B3
East Scores A3
Fire Station C1
Forrest St C1
Fraser Avenue C1
Freddie Tait St C2
Gateway Centre A1
Glebe Rd B2
Golf Place A1
Grange Rd C3
Greenside Place B2
Greyfriars Gardens A2
Hamilton Avenue C2
Hepburn Gardens B1
Holy Trinity B2
Horseleys Park C1
Information Centre B2
Irvine Crescent C3
James Robb Avenue C1
James St B1
John Knox Rd C1
Kennedy Gardens B1
Kilrymont Close C3
Kilrymont Place C3
Kilrymont Rd C3
Kinburn Park B1
Kinkell Terrace C3
Kinnesburn Rd B2
Ladebraes Walk B2
Lady Buchan's Cave A3
Lamberton Place C1
Lamond Drive C2
Langlands Rd B2
Largo Rd C1
Learmonth Place C1
Library B2
Links Clubhouse A1
Links, The A1
Livingstone Crescent B2
Long Rocks A2
Madras College B2
Market St A2
Martyr's Monument A1
Murray Park A2
Murray Place A2
Mus of the Univ of St Andrews (MUSA) A2
Nelson St B2
New Course, The A1
New Picture House A2
North Castle St A3
North St A2
Old Course, The A1
Old Station Rd A1
Pends, The B3
Pilmour Links A1
Pipeland Rd B2/C2
Police Station A2/C1
Post Office B2
Preservation Trust B2
Priestden Park C3
Priestden Place C3
Priestden Rd C3
Queen's Gardens B2
Queen's Terrace B2
Roundhill Rd C2
Royal & Ancient Golf Club A1
St Andrews B1
St Andrews Aquarium A2
St Andrews Botanic Garden B1
St Andrews Castle (Ruins) & Visitor Centre A2
St Leonard's School B3
St Mary St B3
St Mary's College B2
St Nicholas St C3
St Rules Tower B3
St Salvator's College A2
Sandyhill Crescent C2
Sandyhill Rd C2
Scooniehill Rd C2
Scores, The A2
Shields Avenue C3
Shoolbraids C2
Shore, The B3
Sloan St B1
South St B2
Spottiswoode Gdns C1
Station Rd A1
Swilcen Bridge A1
Tom Morris Drive C2
Tom Stewart Lane C1
Town Hall B2
Union St A2
University Chapel A2
University Library A2
University of St Andrews A1
Viaduct Walk B1
War Memorial A3
Wardlaw Gardens B1
Warrack St C3
Watson Avenue B2
West Port B2
West Sands A1
Westview B2
Windmill Rd A1
Winram Place C1
Wishart Gardens C2
Woodburn Park B3
Woodburn Place B3
Woodburn Terrace B3
Younger Hall A2

Salisbury 342

Albany Rd A2
Arts Centre A3
Ashley Rd A1
Avon Approach A2
Ayleswade Rd C2
Bedwin St A2
Belle Vue A2
Bishops Walk B2
Blue Boar Row B2
Bourne Avenue A3
Bourne Hill A3
Britford Lane C2
Broad Walk C2
Brown St B2
Castle St A2
Catherine St B2
Chapter House B2
Church House B2
Churchfields Rd B1
Churchill Gardens C3
Churchill Way East B3
Churchill Way North A3
Churchill Way South C2
Churchill Way West A1
City Hall B2
Close Wall B2
Coldharbour Lane A1
College St A3
Council and Registry Offices A3
Court A1
Crane Bridge Rd B2
Crane St B2
Cricket Ground C1
Culver St South B3
De Vaux Place C2
Devizes Rd A1
Dews Rd B1
Elm Grove B3
Elm Grove Rd A3
Endless St A2
Estcourt Rd A3
Exeter St C2
Fairview Rd A3
Fire Station A1
Fisherton St A1
Folkestone Rd C1
Fowlers Hill B3
Fowlers Rd B3
Friary Lane B2
Friary, The B3
Gas Lane A1
Gigant St B3
Greencroft B3
Greencroft St A3
Guildhall B2
Hall of John Halle B2
Hamilton Rd A2
Harnham Mill B1
Harnham Rd C1/C2
High St B2
Ho of John A'Port B2
Information Centre B2
Kelsey Rd A3
King's Rd A2
Laverstock Rd B3
Library B2
London Rd A3
Lower St C1
Maltings, The B2
Manor Rd A3
Marsh Lane A1
Medieval Hall B2
Milford Hill B3
Milford St B3
Mill Rd B1
Mill Stream Approach A2
Mompesson House B2
New Bridge Rd C2
New Canal B2
New Harnham Rd C2
New St B2
North Canonry B2
North Gate B2
North Walk B2
Old Blandford Rd C1
Old Deanery B2
Old George Hall B2
Park St A3
Parsonage Green C1
Playhouse Theatre A2
Police Station A3
Post Office A2/B2
Poultry Cross B2
Queen Elizabeth Gdns B1
Queen's Rd A3
Rampart Rd B3
Rifles, The B2
St Ann St B2
St Ann's Gate B2
St Marks Rd A3
St Martins B3
St Paul's A1
St Paul's Rd A1
St Thomas B2
Salisbury Cathedral B2
Salisbury Cathedral Sch (Bishop's Palace) C2
Salisbury Mus, The B2
Salisbury Station A1
Salt Lane A3
Saxon Rd C1
Scots Lane A2
Shady Bower B3
Shopmobility B2
South Canonry C2
South Gate C2
Southampton Rd B2
Spire View A1
Sports Ground C3
Tollgate Rd B3
Town Path B1
Wain-a-Long Rd A3
Wessex Rd A3
West Walk C2
Wilton Rd A1
Wiltshire College B3
Winchester St B3
Windsor Rd A1
Wyndham Rd A2
YHA B3
York Rd A1

Scarborough 342

Aberdeen Walk B2
Albert Rd A2
Albion Rd C2
Auborough St B2
Balmoral Centre B2
Belle Vue St C1
Belmont Rd C2
Blenheim Terrace A2
Brunswick Shopping Centre B2
Castle Dykes B3
Castle Hill A3
Castle Rd B2
Castle Walls A3
Castlegate B3
Cemetery B1
Central Tramway B2
Coach Park B1
Columbus Ravine A1
Court B1
Crescent, The C2
Cricket Ground A1
Cross St B2
Crown Terrace C2
Dean Rd B1
Devonshire Drive A1
East Harbour B3
East Pier B3
Eastborough B2
Elmville Avenue B1
Esplanade C2
Falconers Rd B2
Falsgrave Rd C1
Fire Station B2
Foreshore Rd B2
Friargate B2
Gladstone Rd B1
Gladstone St B1
Hollywood Plaza A1
Holms, The A3
Hoxton Rd B1
King St B2
Library B2
Lifeboat Station B3
Londesborough Rd C1
Longwestgate B3
Marine Drive A3
Luna Park B3
Miniature Railway A1
Nelson St B1
Newborough B2
Nicolas St B2
North Marine Rd A1
North St B2
Northway B1
Old Harbour B3
Olympia Leisure B2
Peasholm Park A1
Peasholm Rd A1
Police Station B1
Post Office B2
Princess St B3
Prospect Rd B1
Queen St B2
Queen's Parade A2
Queen's Tower (Remains) A3
Ramshill Rd C2
Roman Signal Sta A3
Roscoe St C1
Rotunda Museum C2
Royal Albert Drive A2
Royal Albert Park A2
St Martin-on-the-Hill C2
St Martin's Avenue C2
St Mary's B3
St Thomas St B2
Sandside B3
Scarborough C1
Scarborough Art Gallery C2
Scarborough Bowls Centre A1
Scarborough Castle A3
Shopmobility C2
Somerset Terrace C2
South Cliff Lift C2
Spa Theatre, The C2
Spa, The C2
Stephen Joseph Theatre C1
Tennyson Avenue B1
Tollergate B2
Town Hall B2
Trafalgar Rd B1
Trafalgar Square A1
Trafalgar St West B1
Valley Bridge Parade C2
Valley Rd C1
Vernon Rd C2
Victoria Park Mount A1
Victoria Rd B1
West Pier B3
Westborough C1
Westover Rd C1
Westwood C1
Woodall Avenue A1
YMCA Theatre B2
York Place B2
Yorkshire Coast College (Westwood Campus) C1

Sheffield 342

Addy Drive A2
Addy St A2
Adelphi St A3
Albert Terrace Rd A3
Albion St A2
Aldred Rd A1
Allen St A4
Alma St A4
Angel St B5
Arundel Gate B5
Arundel St C4
Ashberry Rd A2
Ashdell Rd C1
Ashgate Rd C1
Athletics Centre B2
Attercliffe Rd A6
Bailey St B4
Ball St A4
Balm Green B4
Bank St B4
Barber Rd A2
Bard St B5
Barker's Pool B4
Bates St A1
Beech Hill Rd C1
Beet St B3
Bellefield St A3
Bernard Rd A6
Bernard St B6
Birkendale A2
Birkendale Rd A2
Birkendale View A1
Bishop St C4
Blackwell Place B6
Blake St A2
Blonk St A5
Bolsover St B2
Botanical Gardens C1
Bower Rd A1
Bradley St A1
Bramall Lane C4
Bramwell St A3
Bridge St A4/A5
Brighton Terrace Rd A1
Broad Lane B3
Broad St B6
Brocco St A3
Brook Hill B3
Broomfield Rd C1
Broomgrove Rd C2
Broomhall Place C3
Broomhall Rd C2
Broomhall St C3
Broomspring Lane C2
Brown St C5
Brunswick St B3
Burgess St B4
Burlington St A2
Burns Rd A2
Cadman St A6
Cambridge St B4
Campo Lane B4
Carver St B4
Castle Square B5
Castlegate A5
Cathedral B4
Cathedral (RC) ✝ B4
Cavendish St B3
Charles St C4
Charter Row C4
Children's Hospital B2
Church St B4
City Hall B4
City Hall B4
City Rd C6
Claremont Crescent B2
Claremont Place B2
Clarke St C3
Clarkegrove Rd C2
Clarkehouse Rd C1
Clarkson St B2
Cobden View Rd A1
Collegiate Crescent C2
Commercial St B5
Commonside A1
Conduit Rd B1
Cornish St A3
Corporation St A4
Cricket Inn Rd B6
Cromwell St A1
Crookes Rd B1
Crookes Valley Park B2
Crookes Valley Rd B2
Crookesmoor Rd A2
Crown Court A4
Crucible Theatre B5
Cutlers' Hall B4
Cutlers Gate A6
Daniel Hill A2
Dental Hospital B2
Derek Dooley Way A5
Devonshire Green B3
Devonshire St B3
Division St B4
Dorset St C2
Dover St A3
Duchess Rd C5
Duke St B5
Duncombe St A1
Durham Rd B2
Earl St C4
Earl Way C4
Ecclesall Rd C3
Edward St B3
Effingham Rd A6
Effingham St A6
Egerton St C3
Eldon St B3
Elmore Rd B1
Exchange St B5
Eyre St C4
Fargate B4
Farm Rd C5
Fawcett St A3
Filey St B3
Fir St A1
Fire Station C4
Fitzalan Square/ Ponds Forge B5
Fitzwater Rd C6
Fitzwilliam Gate C4
Fitzwilliam St B3
Flat St B5
Foley St A6
Foundry Climbing Ctr A4
Fulton Rd A1
Furnace Hill A4
Furnival Rd A5
Furnival Square C4
Furnival St C4
Garden St B3
Gell St B3
Gibraltar St A4
Glebe Rd B1
Glencoe Rd C6
Glossop Rd B2/B3/C1
Gloucester St C2
Government Offices C4
Granville Rd C6
Granville Rd / The Sheffield College C5
Graves Gallery B5
Green Lane A4
Hadfield St A1
Hanover St C3
Hanover Way C3
Harcourt Rd B1
Harmer Lane B5
Havelock St C2
Hawley St B4
Haymarket B5
Headford St C3
Heavygate Rd A1
Henry St A3
High St B4
Hodgson St C3
Holberry Gardens C2
Hollis Croft B4
Holly St B4
Hounsfield Rd B3
Howard Rd A1
Hoyle St A3
Hyde Park A6
Infirmary Rd A3
Infirmary Rd A3
Jericho St A3
Johnson St A5
Kelham Island Industrial Museum A4
Lawson Rd C1
Leadmill Rd C5
Leadmill St C5
Leadmill, The ✦ C5
Leamington St A1
Leavygreave Rd B3
Lee Croft B4
Leopold St B4
Leveson St A6
Library A2/B5/C1
Light, The C4
Lyceum Theatre B5
Malinda St A3
Maltravers St A5
Manor Oaks Rd B6
Mappin St B3
Marlborough Rd B1
Mary St C4
Matilda St C4
Matlock Rd A1
Meadow St A3
Melbourn Rd A1
Melbourne Avenue C1
Millennium Galleries B5
Milton St C3
Mitchell St B3
Mona Avenue A1
Mona Rd A1
Montgomery Terr Rd A3
Montgomery Theatre B4
Monument Grounds C6
Moor Oaks Rd B1
Moor, The C4
Moor Market C4
Moore St C3
Mowbray St A4
Mushroom Lane B2
National Emergency Service A4
National Videogame B5
Netherthorpe Rd B3
Netherthorpe Rd B3
Newbould Lane C1
Nile St C1
Norfolk Park Rd C6
Norfolk Rd C6
Norfolk St B4
North Church St B4
Northfield Rd A1
Northumberland Rd B1
Nursery St A5
O2 Academy B5
Oakholme Rd C1
Octagon B2
Odeon B5
Old St B6
Orch Sq Shopping Ctr B4
Oxford St A2
Paradise St B4
Park Lane C2
Park Square B5
Parker's Rd B1
Pearson Building (University) C2
Penistone Rd A3
Pinstone St B4
Pitt St B3
Police Station B5
Pond Hill B5
Pondorosa, The A2
Pond St B5
Ponds Forge International Sports Centre B5
Portobello St B3
Post Office A2/B3/B5/ C1/C3/C4/C6
Powell St A2
Queen St B4
Queen's Rd C5
Ramsey Rd B1
Red Hill B3
Redcar Rd B1
Regent St B3
Rockingham St B4
Roebuck Rd A2
Royal Hallamshire Hospital C2
Russell St A4
Rutland Park C1
St George's Close B3
St Mary's Gate C3
St Mary's Rd C4/C5
St Philip's Rd A3
Savile St A5
School Rd B1
Scotland St A4
Severn Rd B1
Shalesmoor A4
Shalesmoor A3
Sheaf St B5
Sheffield Cathedral ✝ B4
Sheffield Hallam Univ B5
Sheffield Ice Sports Ctr – Skate Central C5
Sheffield Institute of Arts B5
Sheffield Interchange B5
Sheffield Parkway A6
Sheffield Station C5
Sheffield Sta/ Sheffield Hallam Univ B5
Sheffield University B2
Shepherd St A3
Shipton St A2
Shopmobility B3
Shoreham St C4
Showroom C5
Shrewsbury Rd C5
Sidney St C4
Site Gallery C5
Slinn St A1
Smithfield A4
Snig Hill A5
Snow Lane A4
Solly St B3
South Lane C4
South Street Park B5
Southbourne Rd C1
Spital Hill A5
Spital St A5
Spring Hill B1
Spring Hill Rd B1
Springvale Rd A1
Stafford Rd C6
Stafford St B6
Suffolk Rd C5
Summer St B2
Sunny Bank C3
Superstore A3/C3
Surrey St B4
Sussex St A6
Sutton St B3
Sydney Rd A2
Sylvester St C4
Talbot St B5
Taptonville Rd B1
Tenter St B4
Town Hall B4
Townend St A1
Townhead St B4
Trafalgar St B4
Tree Root Walk B2
Trinity St A4
Trippet Lane B4
Turner Mus of Glass B3
Union St B4
Univ Drama Studio B2
Univ of Sheffield B3
Upper Allen St A3
Upper Hanover St B3
Upperthorpe Rd A2/A3
Verdon St A5
Victoria Rd C2
Victoria St B3
Waingate B5
Watery St A3
Watson Rd C1
Wellesley Rd B2
Wellington St C3
West Bar A4
West Bar Green A4
West One Plaza B3
West St B3
West St B3
Westbourne Rd C1
Western Bank B2
Western Rd A1
Weston Park B2
Weston Park Hosp B2
Weston Park Mus B2
Weston St A2
Wharncliffe Rd C3
Whitham Rd B1
Wicker A5
Wilkinson St B2
William St C3
Winter Garden ✦ B4
Winter St B2
York St B4
Yorkshire Artspace C5
Young St C4

Shrewsbury 342

Abbey Foregate B3
Abbey Gardens B2
Abbey Lawn Bsns Park B3
Abbots House B2
Albert St A2
Alma St B1
Ashley St A3
Ashton Rd C1
Avondale Drive A3
Bage Way C3
Barker St B1
Beacall's Lane A2
Beeches Lane C2
Beehive Lane C1
Belle Vue Gardens C2
Belle Vue Rd C2
Belmont Bank C1
Berwick Avenue A1
Berwick Rd A1
Betton St C2
Bishop St B3
Bradford St B3
Bridge St B1
Burton St A3
Bus Station B2
Butcher Row B2
Butler Rd C1
Bynner St C2
Canon St B3
Canonbury C1
Castle Bsns Park, The A2
Castle Foregate A2
Castle Gates B2
Castle Walk B3
Castle St B2
Cathedral (RC) ✝ C1
Chester St A2
Cineworld C3
Claremont Bank B1
Claremont Hill B1
Cleveland St B3
Coleham Head B2
Coleham Pumping Station C2
College Hill B1
Corporation Lane A1
Coton Crescent A1
Coton Hill A2
Coton Mount A1
Crescent Lane C1
Crewe St A2
Cross Hill B1
Dana, The B2
Darwin Centre B2
Dingle, The B1
Dogpole B2
English Bridge B2
Fish St B2
Frankwell B1
Gateway Ctr, The A2
Gravel Hill Lane A1
Greenhous West Mid Showground A1
Greyfriars Rd C2
Hampton Rd A3
Haycock Way C3
High St B1
Hills Lane B1
Holywell St B3
Hunter St A1
Information Centre B1
Ireland's Mansion & Bear Steps B1
John St A3
Kennedy Rd C1
King St B3
Kingsland Bridge C1
Kingsland Bridge (toll) C1
Kingsland Rd C1
Library B2
Lime St C2
Longden Coleham C2
Longden Rd C1
Longner St B1
Luciefelde Rd C1
Mardol B1
Marine Terrace C2
Market B1
Monkmoor Rd B3
Moreton Crescent C2
Mount St A1
New Park Close A3
New Park Rd A2
New Park St A3
North St A2
Oakley St C1
Old Coleham C2
Old Market Hall B1
Old Potts Way C3
Par Shopping Ctr, The B2
Police Station B1
Post Office B1/B2/B3
Pride Hill B1
Pride Hill Centre B1
Priory Rd B1
Pritchard Way C3
Quarry Swimming & Fitness Centre, The B1
Queen St A3
Raby Crescent C2
Rad Brook C1
Rea Brook C3
Rea Brook Valley Country Park & Local Nature Reserve C3
Riverside B1
Roundhill Lane A1
St Alkmund's B2
St Chad's B1
St Chad's Terrace B1
St John's Hill B1
St Julians Friars C2
St Mary's B2
St Mary's St B2
Salters Lane C2
Scott St C3
Severn Theatre B1
Severn Bank A3
Severn St A2
Shrewsbury A2
Shrewsbury Abbey B3
Shrewsbury High School C1
Shrewsbury Museum & Art Gall B1
Shrewsbury Prison Tours ✦ B2
Shrewsbury School ✦ C1
Shropshire Regimental Museum B2
Shropshire Wildlife Trust ✦ B3
Smithfield Rd B1
South Hermitage C1
Square, The B1
Superstore C3
Swan Hill B1
Sydney Avenue A3
Tankerville St B3
Tilbrook Drive A3
Town Walls C1
Trinity St C2
Underdale Rd B3
University Centre Shrewsbury (Guildhall) B1
Victoria Avenue B1
Victoria Quay B1
Victoria St B2
Welsh Bridge B1
Whitehall St B3
Wood St A2
Wyle Cop B2

Southampton 342

Above Bar St A2
Albert Rd North B3
Albert Rd South C3
Andersons Rd B3
Argyle Rd A2
Arundel Tower ✦ B1
Bargate, The ✦ B2
BBC South A1
Bedford Place A1
Belvidere Rd A3
Bernard St C2
Blechynden Terrace A1
Brinton's Rd A2
Britannia Rd A3
Briton St C2
Brunswick Place A2
Bugle St C1
Canute Rd C3
Castle Way C2
Catchcold Tower ✦ B1
Central Bridge C3
Central Rd C2
Channel Way C3
Chapel Rd B3
City Art Gallery A1
City College B3
City Cruise Terminal C1
Civic Centre A1
Civic Centre Rd A1
Coach Station B1
Commercial Rd A1
Cumberland Place A1
Cunard Rd C2
Derby Rd A3
Devonshire Rd A1
Dock Gate 4 C2
Dock Gate 8 B1
East Park (Andrew's Park) A2
East Park Terrace A2
East St B2
Endle St B3
European Way C2
Fire Station A2
Floating Bridge Rd C3
God's House Tower ✦ C2
Golden Grove A3
Graham Rd A2
Guildhall A1
Hanover Buildings B2
Harbour Lights C3
Harbour Parade B1
Hartington Rd A3
Havelock Rd A1
Henstead Rd A1
Herbert Walker Ave B1
High St B2
Hoglands Park B2
Holy Rood (Rems), Merchant Navy Memorial B2
Houndwell Park B2
Houndwell Place B2
Hythe Ferry C2
Isle of Wight Ferry Terminal C1
James St B3
Kingsway A2
Leisure World B1
Library A1
Lime St B2
London Rd A2
Marine Parade B3
Marlands Shopping Centre, The A1
Marsh Lane B2
Mayflower Meml ✦ C1
Mayflower Park C1
Mayflower Theatre, The A1
Medieval Merchant's House C1
Melbourne St B3
Morris Rd A1
National Oceanography Centre ✦ C3
Neptune Way C3
New Rd A2
Nichols Rd A3
North Front A2
Northam Rd A3
Ocean Dock C2
Ocean Village Marina C3
Ocean Way C3
Odeon B1
Ogle Rd B1
Old Northam Rd A2
Orchard Lane B2
Oxford Avenue A2
Oxford St C2
Palmerston Park A2
Palmerston Rd A2
Parsonage Rd A3
Peel St A3
Platform Rd C2
Polygon, The A1
Portland Terrace B1
Post Office B2
Pound Tree Rd B2
Quays Swimming & Diving Complex, The B1
Queen's Park C2
Queen's Peace Fountain ✦ A2
Queen's Terrace C2
Queensway B2
Radcliffe Rd A3
Rochester St A3
Royal Pier C1
Royal South Hants Hospital A2
St Andrew's Rd A2
St Mary's B3
St Mary St A2
St Mary's Leisure Ctr A2
St Mary's Place B2
St Mary's Rd A2
St Mary's Stadium (Southampton FC) A3
St Michael's C1
SeaCity Museum A1
Showcase Cinema de Lux B1
Solent Sky C3
South Front B2
Southampton Central Station A1
Southampton Solent University A2
Terminus Terrace C2
Threefield Lane B2
Titanic Engineers' Memorial ✦ A2
Town Quay C1
Town Walls B2
Tudor House C1
Vincent's Walk B2
Westgate Hall C1
West Marlands Rd A1
West Park A1
West Park Rd A1
West Quay Rd B1
West Quay Retail Park B1
Western Esplanade B1
Westquay Shopping Centre B1
Westquay South B1
White Star Way C2
Winton St A2

Southend-on-Sea 343

Adventure Island ✦ C3
Albany Avenue A1
Albert Rd C3
Alexandra Rd C2
Alexandra St C2
Alexandra Yacht Club ✦ C2
Ashburnham Rd B2
Avenue Rd B1
Avenue Terrace B1
Balmoral Rd B1
Baltic Avenue B3
Baxter Avenue A2/B2
Beecroft Art Gallery B2
Bircham Rd A2
Boscombe Rd B3
Boston Avenue A1/B2
Bournemouth Park Rd A3
Browning Avenue A3
Bus Station C3
Byron Avenue A3
Cambridge Rd C1/C2
Canewdon Rd B1
Carnarvon Rd A2
Central Avenue A3
Central Museum B2
Chelmsford Avenue A1
Chichester Rd B2
Church Rd C3
Civic Centre A2
Clarence Rd C2
Clarence St C2
Cliff Avenue B1
Cliffs Pavilion C1
Clifftown Parade C2
Clifftown Rd C2
Colchester Rd A1
Coleman St B3
College Way B2
County Court B3
Cromer Rd B3
Crowborough Rd A2
Dryden Avenue A3
East St A2
Elmer Approach B2
Elmer Avenue B2
Forum, The B2
Gainsborough Drive A1
Gayton Rd A2
Glenhurst Rd A2
Gordon Place B2
Gordon Rd B2
Grainger Rd A2
Greyhound Way A3
Grove, The A3
Guildford Rd B3
Hamlet Court Rd B1
Hamlet Rd C1
Harcourt Avenue A1
Hartington Rd C3
Hastings Rd B3
Herbert Grove C3
Heygate Avenue C3
High St B2/C2
Information Centre C3
Kenway A2
Kilworth Avenue B3
Lancaster Gardens B3
London Rd B1
Lucy Rd C3
MacDonald Avenue A1
Magistrates' Court A2
Maldon Rd A2
Marine Avenue C1
Marine Parade C3
Marine Rd C1
Milton Rd B1
Milton St B2
Napier Avenue B2
North Avenue A3
North Rd A1/B1
Odeon B2
Osborne Rd B1
Park Crescent B1
Park Rd B1
Park St B1
Park Terrace B1
Pier Hill C3
Pleasant Rd C3
Police Station A2
Post Office B2/B3
Princes St B2
Queens Rd B2
Queensway B2/B3/C3
Radio Essex C2
Rayleigh Avenue A1
Redstock Rd A2
Rochford Avenue A1
Royal Mews C2
Royal Terrace C2
Royals Shopping Centre, The C3
Ruskin Avenue A3
St Ann's Rd B3
St Helen's Rd B1
St John's Rd B1
St Leonard's Rd C3
St Lukes Rd A3
St Vincent's Rd C1
Salisbury Avenue A1/B1
Scratton Rd C2
Shakespeare Drive A1
Shopmobility B2
Short St A2
South Avenue A3
Southchurch Rd B3
Southend Central B2
Southend Pier Railway C3
Southend United FC A1
Southend Victoria B2
Stanfield Rd A2
Stanley Rd C3
Sutton Rd A3/B3
Swanage Rd B3
Sweyne Avenue A1
Sycamore Grove A3
Tennyson Avenue A3
Tickfield Avenue A2
Tudor Rd A1
Tunbridge Rd A2
Tylers Avenue B3
Tyrrel Drive B3
University of Essex B2/C2
Vale Avenue A2
Victoria Avenue A2
Victoria Shopping Centre, The B2
Warrior Square B3
Wesley Rd C3
West Rd A1
West St A1
Westcliff Avenue C1
Westcliff Parade C1
Western Esplanade C1
Weston Rd C2
Whitegate Rd B3
Wilson Rd C1
Wimborne Rd B3
York Rd C3

Stirling 343

Abbey Rd A3
Abbotsford Place A3
Abercromby Place C1
Albert Halls B1
Albert Place B1
Alexandra Place A3
Allan Park C2
Ambulance Station A2
AMF Ten Pin Bowling ✦ B2
Argyll Avenue A3
Argyll's Lodging ✦ B1
Back O' Hill Ind Est A1
Back O' Hill Rd A1
Baker St B2
Ballengeich Pass A1
Balmoral Place B1
Barn Rd B1
Barnton St B2
Bastion, The ✦ C2
Bow St B1
Bruce St A2
Burghmuir Retail Park C2
Burghmuir Rd A2/B2/C2
Bus Station B2
Cambuskenneth Bridge A3
Castle Court B1
Causewayhead Rd A2
Cemetery A1
Changing Room, The B1
Church of the Holy Rude B1
Clarendon Place C1
Club House B1
Colquhoun St C3
Corn Exchange B2
Council Offices C2
Court B2
Cowane Centre A2
Cowane St A2
Cowane's Hospital B1
Crofthead Rd A1
Dean Crescent A3
Douglas St A2
Drip Rd A1
Drummond Lane C1
Drummond Place C1
Drummond Place Lane C1
Dumbarton Rd C2
Eastern Access Rd B2
Edward Avenue A3
Edward Rd A2
Forrest Rd A2
Fort A1
Forth Crescent B2
Forth St A2
Gladstone Place C1
Glebe Avenue C1
Glebe Crescent C1
Golf Course C1
Goosecroft Rd B2
Gowanhill A1
Greenwood Avenue B1
Harvey Wynd A1
Information Centre B1
Irvine Place B2
James St A2
John St B1
Kerse Rd C3
King's Knot ✦ B1
King's Park C1
King's Park Rd C1
Laurencecroft Rd A2
Leisure Pool B2
Library B2
Linden Avenue C2
Lovers Wk A2
Lower Back Walk B1
Lower Bridge St A2
Lower Castlehill A1
Mar Place B1
Meadow Place A3
Meadowforth Rd C3
Middlemuir Rd C3
Millar Place A3
Morris Terrace B2
Mote Hill A1
Murray Place B2
Nelson Place C2
Old Town Cemetery B1
Old Town Jail ✦ B1
Park Terrace C1
Phoenix Industrial Est C3
Players Rd C3
Port St C2
Post Office B2
Princes St B2
Queen St B2
Queen's Rd B1
Queenshaugh Drive A3
Ramsay Place A2
Riverside Drive A3
Ronald Place A1
Rosebery Place A2
Royal Gardens B1
Royal Gardens B1
St Mary's Wynd B1
St Ninian's Rd C2
Scott St A2
Seaforth Place B2
Shore Rd B2
Smith Art Gallery & Museum B1
Snowdon Place C1
Snowdon Place Lane C1
Spittal St B2
Springkerse Ind Est C3
Springkerse Rd C3
Stirling Arcade B2
Stirling Bsns Centre C2
Stirling Castle A1
Stirling County Rugby Football Club A3
Stirling Enterprise Pk B3
Stirling Old Bridge A2
Stirling Station B2
Superstore A1/A2
Sutherland Avenue A3
TA Centre C3
Tannery Lane A2
Thistle Industrial Est C3
Thistles Shopping Centre, The B2
Tolbooth ✦ B1
Town Wall B1
Union St A2
Upper Back Walk B1
Upper Bridge St A1
Upper Castlehill B1
Upper Craigs C2
Victoria Place C1
Victoria Rd B1
Victoria Square B1/C1
Vue B2
Wallace St A2
Waverley Crescent A3
Wellgreen Rd C2
Windsor Place C1
YHA B1

Stoke 343

Ashford St A3
Avenue Rd A3
Aynsley Rd A2
Barnfield C1
Bath St C2
Beresford St A3
Bilton St C2
Boon Avenue C2
Booth St C2
Boothen Rd C2/C3
Boughey St C2
Boughley Rd B3
Brighton St B1
Campbell Rd C2
Carlton Rd B2
Cauldon Rd A3
Cemetery A2
Cemetery Rd A2
Chamberlain Avenue C1
Church (RC) B2
Church St C2
City Rd C3
Civic Centre & King's Hall B3
Cliff Vale Place A1
College Rd A2
Convent Close B2
Copeland St B2
Cornwallis St C3
Corporation St C2
Crowther St A3
Dominic St B1
Elenora St B2
Elgin St B2
Epworth St A3
Etruscan St A1
Film Theatre B3
Fleming Rd C2
Fletcher Rd C2
Floyd St B2
Foden St C2
Frank St C2
Franklin Rd C1
Frederick Avenue B1
Garden St C1
Garner St A1
Gerrard St B2
Glebe St B3
Greatbach Avenue B1
Hanley Park A3
Harris St B1
Hartshill Rd B1
Hayward St A2
Hide St B2
Higson Avenue B2
Hill St B2
Honeywall B2
Hunters Drive C1
Hunters Way C1
Keary St C2
Kingsway B2
Leek Rd B3
Library C2
Lime St C2
Liverpool Rd B2
London Rd C2
Lonsdale St C2
Lovatt St B2
Lytton St B3
Market C2
Newcastle Lane C1
Newlands St A2
Norfolk St A2
North St A1/B2
Northcote Avenue B2
Oldmill St C3
Oriel St B1
Oxford St B1
Penkhull New Rd C1
Penkhull St C1
Portmeirion Pottery ✦ C2
Post Office A3
Princes Rd B1
Pump St B2
Quarry Avenue B1
Quarry Rd B1
Queen Anne St A3
Queen's Rd C1
Queensway A1/B2/C3
Richmond St B1
Richmond St Park B1
Rothwell St C1
St Peter's B3
St Thomas Place C1
Scrivenor Rd A1
Seaford St A3
Selwyn St C3
Shelton New Rd A1
Shelton Old Rd B2
Sheppard St C2
Sir Stanley Matthews Sports Centre B3
Spark St C2
Spencer Rd B3
Spode Museum Heritage Centre B2
Spode St C2
Squires View B3
Staffordshire Univ B3
Station Rd B3
Stoke Business Park C3
Stoke Rd A2
Stoke-on-Trent Coll A3
Stoke-on-Trent Sta B3
Sturgess St C2
Thistley Hough C1
Thornton Rd B3
Tolkien Way B1
Trent Valley Rd C1
Vale St B2
Villas, The C1
Watford St A3
Wellesley St A3
West Avenue B1
Westland St B1
Yeaman St C2
Yoxall Avenue B1

Stratford-upon-Avon 343

Albany Rd B1
Alcester Rd B1
Ambulance Station B1
Arden St B2
Avenue Farm A1
Ave Farm Ind Est A1
Avenue Rd A3
Baker Avenue A1
Bandstand C3
Benson Rd A3
Birmingham Rd A2
Boat Club B3
Borden Place C1
Bridge St B2
Bridgetown Rd C3
Bridgeway B3
Broad St C2
Broad Walk C2
Brookvale Rd C1
Brunel Way B1
Bull St C2
Butterfly Farm ✦ C3
Cemetery C1
Chapel Lane B2
Cherry Orchard C1
Chestnut Walk B2
Children's Playground C3
Church St C2
Civic Hall B2
Clarence Rd B1
Clopton Bridge ✦ B3

Clopton Rd A2
College B1
College Lane C2
College St C2
Community Sports Ctr B1
Council Offices (District) B2
Courtyard, The C2
Cox's Yard B3
Cricket Ground C3
Ely Gardens B2
Ely St B2
Evesham Rd C1
Fire Station B1
Foot Ferry C3
Fordham Avenue A2
Garrick Way C1
Gower Memorial B3
Great William St B2
Greenhill St B2
Greenway, The C2
Grove Rd B2
Guild St B2
Guildhall & School B2
Hall's Croft C2
Harvard House B2
Henley St B2
Hertford Rd C1
High St B2
Holton St C2
Holy Trinity C2
Information Centre B3
Jolyffe Park Rd A2
Kipling Rd C3
Library B2
Lodge Rd B1
Maidenhead Rd A3
Mansell St B2
Masons Court B2
Masons Rd A1
Maybird Shopping Pk A2
Maybrook Retail Park A2
Maybrook Rd A1
Mayfield Avenue A2
Meer St B2
Mill Lane C2
Moat House Hotel B3
Narrow Lane C2
Nash's Ho & New Pl B2
New St C2
Old Town C2
Orchard Way C1
Other Place, The C2
Paddock Lane C1
Park Rd A1
Payton St B2
Percy St A2
Police Station B2
Post Office B2
Recreation Ground C2
Regal Road A2
Rother St B2
Rowley Crescent A3
Royal Shakespeare Theatre B3
Ryland St C2
Saffron Meadow C2
St Andrew's Crescent B1
St Gregory's A3
St Gregory's Rd A3
St Mary's Rd A2
Sanctus Drive C2
Sanctus St C1
Sandfield Rd C2
Scholars Lane B2
Seven Meadows Rd C2
Shakespeare Institute C2
Shakespeare St B2
Shakespeare's Birthplace B2
Sheep St B2
Shelley Rd C3
Shipston Rd C3
Shottery Rd C1
Slingates Rd A2
Southern Lane C2
Station Rd B1
Stratford Healthcare B2
Stratford Hospital B2
Stratford Leisure Ctr B3
Stratford Sports Club B1
Stratford-upon-Avon Station B1
Swan Theatre B3
Swan's Nest Lane B3
Talbot Rd A2
Tiddington Rd B3
Timothy's Bridge Industrial Estate A1
Timothy's Bridge Rd A1
Town Hall & Council Offices B2
Town Square B2
Trinity Close C2
Tyler St B2
War Memorial Gdns B3
Warwick Rd B3
Waterside B3
Welcombe Rd A3
West St C2
Western Rd A2
Wharf Rd A2
Willows North, The B1
Willows, The B1
Wood St B2

Sunderland 343

Albion Place C2
Alliance Place B1
Argyle St C2
Ashwood St C1
Athenaeum St B2
Azalea Terrace C2
Beach St A1
Bedford St B2
Beechwood Terrace C1
Belvedere Rd C2
Blandford St B2
Borough Rd B3
Bridge Crescent B2
Bridge St B2
Bridges, The B2
Brooke St A2
Brougham St B2
Burdon Rd C2
Burn Park C1
Burn Park Rd C1
Burn Park Tech Park C1
Carol St B1
Charles St A3
Chester Rd C1
Chester Terrace B1
Church St A3
Civic Centre C2
Cork St B3
Coronation St B3
Cowan Terrace C2
Dame Dorothy St A2
Deptford Rd B1
Deptford Terrace A1
Derby St C2
Derwent St C2
Dock St A3
Dundas St A2
Durham Rd C1
Easington St A2
Egerton St C3
Empire B3
Empire Theatre B2
Farringdon Row B1
Fawcett St B2
Fire Station B1
Fox St C1
Foyle St B3
Frederick St B3
Hanover Place A1
Havelock Terrace C1
Hay St A2
Headworth Square B3
Hendon Rd B3
High St East B3
High St West B2/B3
Holmeside B2
Hylton Rd B1
John St B3
Kier Hardie Way A2
Lambton St B3
Laura St C3
Lawrence St B3
Library & Arts Centre B3
Lily St B1
Lime St B1
Livingstone Rd B2
Low Row B2
Magistrates' Court B2
Matamba Terrace B1
Millburn St B1
Millennium Way A2
Minster B2
Monkwearmouth Station Museum A2
Mowbray Park C3
Mowbray Rd C3
Murton St C3
National Glass Ctr A3
New Durham Rd C1
Newcastle Rd A2
Nile St B3
Norfolk St B3
North Bridge St A2
Northern Gallery for Contemporary Art (NGCA) B3
Otto Terrace C1
Park Lane C2
Park Lane C2
Park Rd C2
Paul's Rd B3
Peel St C3
Point, The B2
Police Station B2
Priestly Crescent A1
Queen St B2
Railway Row B1
Retail Park B1
Richmond St A2
Roker Avenue A2
Royalty Theatre C1
Royalty, The C1
Ryhope Rd C2
St Mary's Way B2
St Michael's Way B2
St Peter's A3
St Peter's A2
St Peter's Way A3
St Vincent St C3
Salem Rd C3
Salem St C3
Salisbury St C3
Sans St B3
Shopmobility B2
Silkworth Row B1
Southwick Rd A2
Stadium of Light (Sunderland AFC) A2
Stadium Way A2
Stobart St A2
Stockton Rd C2
Suffolk St C3
Sunderland A2
Sunderland Aquatic Centre A2
Sunderland College C2
Sunderland Mus B3
Sunderland St B3
Sunderland Station B2
Tatham St C3
Tavistock Place B3
Thelma St C1
Thomas St North A2
Thornholme Rd C1
Toward Rd C3
Transport Interchange C2
Trimdon St Way B1
Tunstall Rd C2
University C1
University Library C1
University of Sunderland (City Campus) B1
University of Sunderland (St Peter's Campus) A3
Univ of Sunderland (Sir Tom Cowie Campus) A3
Vaux Brewery Way A2
Villiers St B3
Villiers St South B3
Vine Place C2
Violet St B1
Walton Lane B3
Waterworks Rd B1
Wearmouth Bridge B2
West Sunniside B3
West Wear St B3
Westbourne Rd B1
Western Hill C1
Wharncliffe B1
Whickham St A3
White House Rd C3
Wilson St North A2
Winter Gardens C3
Wreath Quay A1

Swansea Abertawe 343

Adelaide St C3
Albert Row C3
Alexandra Rd B3
Argyle St C1
Baptist Well Place A2
Beach St C1
Belle Vue Way B3
Berw Rd A1
Berwick Terrace A2
Bond St C1
Brangwyn Concert Hall C1
Bridge St A3
Brooklands Terrace B1
Brunswick St C1
Bryn-Syfi Terrace A2
Bryn-y-Mor Rd C1
Bullins Lane B1
Burrows Rd C1
Bus Station C2
Bus/Rail link A3
Cadfan Rd A1
Cadrawd Rd A1
Caer St B3
Carig Crescent A1
Carlton Terrace B2
Carmarthen Rd A3
Castle Square B3
Castle St B3
Catherine St C1
Cinema C3
Civic Centre & Library C2
Clarence St C2
Colbourne Terrace A2
Constitution Hill B1
Court B3
Creidiol Rd A2
Cromwell St B2
Crown Courts C1
Duke St B1
Dunvant Place C2
Dyfatty Park A3
Dyfatty St A3
Dyfed Avenue A1
Dylan Thomas Ctr B3
Dylan Thomas Theatre C3
Eaton Crescent C1
Eigen Crescent A1
Elfed Rd A1
Emlyn Rd A1
Evans Terrace A3
Fairfield Terrace B1
Ffynone Drive B1
Ffynone Rd B1
Fire Station B3
Firm St A2
Fleet St C1
Francis St C1
Fullers Row B2
George St B2
Glamorgan St C2
Glynn Vivian Art Gallery B3
Gower Coll Swansea C1
Graig Terrace A3
Grand Theatre C2
Granogwen Rd A2
Guildhall C1
Guildhall Rd South C1
Gwent Rd A1
Gwynedd Avenue A1
Hafod St A3
Hanover St B1
Harcourt St B2
Harries St A2
Heathfield B2
Henrietta St B1
Hewson St B2
High St A3/B3
High View A2
Hill St A2
Historic Ships Berth C3
HM Prison C2
Islwyn Rd A1
King Edward's Rd C1
Kingsway, The B2
LC, The C3
Long Ridge A2
Madoc St C2
Mansel St B2
Maritime Quarter C3
Market B3
Mayhill Gardens B1
Mayhill Rd A1
Milton Terrace A2
Mission Gallery C3
Montpelier Terrace B1
Morfa Rd A3
Mount Pleasant B2
National Waterfront Museum C3
New Cut Rd A3
New St A3
Nicander Parade A2
Nicander Place A2
Nicholl St B2
Norfolk St B2
North Hill Rd A2
Northampton Lane B2
Observatory C3
Orchard St B3
Oxford St B2
Oystermouth Rd C1
Page St B2
Pant-y-Celyn Rd B1
Parc Tawe North B3
Parc Tawe Shopping & Leisure Centre B3
Patti Pavilion C1
Paxton St C2
Pen-y-Graig Rd A1
Penmaen Terrace B1
Phillips Parade C1
Picton Terrace B2
Plantasia B3
Plantasia B3
Police Station B2
Post Office A1/A2/C1/C2
Powys Avenue A1
Primrose St B2
Princess Way B3
Promenade B2
Pryder Gardens A1
Quadrant Shopping Centre C2
Quay Park B3
Rhianfa Lane B1
Rhondda St B2
Richardson St C2
Rodney St C1
Rose Hill B1
Rosehill Terrace B1
Russell St B1
St Helen's Avenue C1
St Helen's Crescent C1
St Helen's Rd C1
St James Gardens B1
St James's Crescent B1
St Mary's B3
Sea View Terrace A3
Singleton St C2
South Dock C3
Stanley Place B2
Strand B3
Swansea Castle B3
Swansea Metropolitan University B2
Swansea Museum C3
Swansea Station A3
Taliesyn Rd B1
Tan y Marian Rd A1
Tegid Rd A2
Teilo Crescent A1
Tenpin Bowling B3
Terrace Rd B1/B2
Tontine St A3
Townhill Rd A1
Tramshed, The C3
Trawler Rd C3
Union St B2
Upper Strand A3
Vernon St A3
Victoria Quay C3
Victoria Rd B3
Vincent St C1
Walter Rd B1
Watkin St A2
Waun-Wen Rd A2
Wellington St C2
Westbury St C1
Western St C1
Westway C2
William St C2
Wind St B3
Woodlands Terrace B1
YMCA B2
York St C3

Swindon 343

Albert St C3
Albion St C1
Alfred St A2
Alvescot Rd C3
Art Gallery & Mus C3
Ashford Rd C1
Aylesbury St A2
Bath Rd C2
Bathampton St B1
Bathurst Rd B3
Beatrice St A2
Beckhampton St B3
Bowood Rd C1
Bristol St B1
Broad St A3
Brunel Shopping Centre, The B2
Brunel Statue B2
Brunswick St C2
Bus Station B2
Cambria Bridge Rd B1
Cambria Place B1
Canal Walk B2
Carr St B1
Cemetery C1/C3
Chandler Close C3
Chapel C1
Chester St B1
Christ Church C3
Church Place B1
Cirencester Way A3
Clarence St B2
Clifton St C1
Cockleberry A2
Colbourne A3
Colbourne St A3
College St B2
Commercial Rd B2
Corporation St A2
Council Offices B3
County Cricket Gd A3
County Rd A3
Courts B2
Cricklade Street C3
Crombey St B1/C2
Cross St C2
Curtis St B1
Deacon St C1
Designer Outlet (Great Western) B1
Dixon St C2
Dover St C2
Dowling St C2
Drove Rd C3
Dryden St C1
Durham St C3
East St B1
Eastcott Hill C2
Eastcott Rd C2
Edgeware Rd B2
Edmund St C2
Elmina Rd A3
Emlyn Square B1
English Heritage National Monuments Record Centre B1
Euclid St B3
Exeter St B1
Fairview C1
Faringdon Rd B1
Farnsby St B1
Fire Station B3
Fleet St B2
Fleming Way B2/B3
Florence St A2
Gladstone St A3
Gooch St A2
Graham St A3
Great Western Way A1/A2
Groundwell Rd B3
Hawksworth Way A1
Haydon St A2
Henry St B2
Hillside Avenue C1
Holbrook Way B2
Hunt St C3
Hydro B1
Hythe Rd C2
Information Centre B2
Joseph St C1
Kent Rd C2
King William St C2
Kingshill Rd C1
Lansdown Rd C2
Lawn, The C3
Leicester St B3
Library B2
Lincoln St B3
Little London C3
London St B1
Magic B3
Maidstone Rd C2
Manchester Rd A3
Maxwell St B1
Milford St B2
Milton Rd B1
Morse St C2
Newcastle St B3
Newcombe Drive A1
Hawsworth Ind Est A1
Newhall St C2
North St C2
North Star A1
North Star Avenue A1
Northampton St B3
Nurseries, The C1
Oasis Leisure Centre A1
Ocotal Way A3
Okus Rd C1
Old Town C3
Oxford St B1
Parade, The B2
Park Lane B1
Park Lane B1
Park, The B1
Pembroke St C2
Plymouth St B3
Polaris Way A2
Police Station B2
Ponting St A2
Post Office B1/B2/C3
Poulton St A3
Princes St B2
Prospect Hill C2
Prospect Place C2
Queen St B2
Queen's Park C3
Radnor St C1
Read St C1
Reading St B1
Regent Circus C2
Regent St B2
Retail Park A2/A3/B3
Rosebery St A3
St Mark's B1
Salisbury St A3
Savernake St C2
Science & Technology Facilities Council HQ A2
Shelley St C1
Sheppard St B1
Shopmobility B2
South St C2
Southampton St B3
Spring Gardens B3
Stafford Street C2
Stanier St C2
Station Road A2
STEAM GWR B1
Swindon College A2
Swindon Rd C2
Swindon Station A2
Swindon Town Football Club A3
TA Centre B1
Tennyson St B1
Theobald St B1
Town Hall B2
Transfer Bridges A3
Union St C2
Upham Rd C3
Victoria Rd C3
Walcot Rd B3
War Memorial B2
Wells St B3
Western St C2
Westmorland Rd B3
Whalebridge B2
Whitehead St C1
Whitehouse Rd A2
William St C1
Wood St C3
Wyvern Theatre & Arts Centre B2
York Rd B3

Taunton 343

Addison Grove A1
Albemarle Rd A1
Alfred St B3
Alma St C2
Avenue, The A1
Bath Place C1
Belvedere Rd A1
Billet St B2
Billetfield C2
Birch Grove A1
Brewhouse Theatre B2
Bridge St B1
Bridgwater & Taunton Canal A2
Broadlands Rd C1
Burton Place C1
Bus Station B1
Canal Rd A2
Cann St C1
Canon St B2
Castle St B1
Cheddon Rd A2
Chip Lane A1
Clarence St B1
Cleveland St B1
Clifton Terrace A2
Coleridge Crescent C3
Compass Hill C1
Compton Close A2
Corporation St B1
Council Offices A1
County Walk Shopping Centre C2
Courtyard B2
Cranmer Rd B2
Crescent, The C1
Critchard Way B3
Cyril St A1
Deller's Wharf B1
Duke St B2
East Reach B3
East St B3
Eastbourne Rd B2
Eastleigh Rd C3
Eaton Crescent A2
Elm Grove A1
Elms Close A1
Fons George C1
Fore St B2
Fowler St A1
French Weir Rec Grd B1
Geoffrey Farrant Walk A2
Gray's Almshouses B2
Grays Rd B3
Greenway Avenue A1
Guildford Place C1
Hammet St B2
Haydon Rd B3
Heavitree Way A2
Herbert St A1
High St C2
Holway Avenue C3
Hugo St B3
Huish's Almshouses B2
Hurdle Way C2
Information Centre C2
Jubilee St A1
King's College C3
Kings Close C3
Laburnum St B2
Lambrook Rd B3
Lansdowne Rd A3
Leslie Avenue A1
Leycroft Rd B3
Library C2
Linden Grove A1
Magdalene St B2
Magistrates Court B1
Malvern Terrace A2
Market House B2
Mary St C2
Middle St B2
Mitre Court B3
Mount Nebo C1
Mount St C2
Mount, The C2
Mountway C2
Mus of Somerset B1
North St B2
Northfield Avenue B1
Northfield Rd B1
Northleigh Rd C3
Obridge Allotments A3
Obridge Lane A3
Obridge Rd A3
Obridge Viaduct A3
Orchard Shopping Ctr C2
Osborne Way C1
Park St C1
Paul St C2
Plais St A2
Playing Field C3
Police Station A1
Portland St B1
Post Office B1/B2
Priorswood Ind Est A3
Priorswood Rd A2
Priory Avenue B2
Priory Bridge Rd B2
Priory Fields Retail Pk A3
Priory Park A2
Priory Way A3
Queen St B3
Railway St A1
Records Office A2
Recreation Ground A1
Riverside Place B2
St Augustine St B2
St George's C2
St Georges Square C2
St James B2
St James St B2
St John's C1
St John's Rd B1
St Josephs Field C2
St Mary Magdalene's B2
Samuels Court A1
Shire Hall & Law Courts C1
Somerset County Cricket Ground B2
Somerset County Hall C1
Somerset Cricket B2
South Rd C3
South St C3
Staplegrove Rd B1
Station Approach A2
Station Rd A1
Stephen St B2
Superstore C2
Swimming Pool A1
Tancred St B2
Tangier Way B1
Tauntfield Close C3
Taunton Castle B1
Taunton Deane Cricket Club C2
Taunton Station A2
Thomas St A1
Toneway A3
Tower St B1
Trenchard Way A2
Trevor Smith Place C3
Trinity Bsns Centre C3
Trinity Rd C3
Trinity St B3
Trull Rd C1
Tudor House B2
Upper High St C1
Venture Way A3
Victoria Gate B3
Victoria Park B3
Victoria St B3
Viney St B3
Vivary Park Golf Club C2
Vivary Rd C1
War Memorial C1
Wellesley St A2
Wheatley Crescent A3
Whitehall A1
Wilfred Rd B3
William St A1
Wilton Church C1
Wilton Close C1
Wilton Grove C1
Wilton St C1
Winchester St B2
Winters Field B2
Wood St B1
Yarde Place B1

Telford 343

Alma Avenue C1
Amphitheatre C2
Bowling Alley B2
Brandsfarm Way C3
Brunel Rd B1
Bus Station B2
Buxton Rd C1
Central Park A2
Chelsea Gardens B2
Coach Central B2
Coachwell Close B1
Colliers Way A1
Courts B2
Dale Acre Way B3
Darliston C3
Deepdale B3
Deercote B2
Dinthill C3
Doddington C3
Dodmoor Grange C3
Downemead B3
Duffryn B3
Dunsheath B3
Euston Way A3
Eyton Mound C1
Eyton Rd C1
Forgegate A2
Grange Central B2
Hall Park Way B1
Hinkshay Rd C2
Hollinsworth Rd A2
Holyhead Rd A3
Housing Trust A1
Ice Rink B2
Information Centre B2
Ironmasters Way A2
Job Centre B1
Land Registry B1
Lawn Central B2
Lawnswood C1
Library B2
Malinsgate B1
Matlock Avenue C1
Moor Rd C1
Mount Rd C1
Odeon B2
Park Lane A1
Police Station B1
Post Office A2/B2/C1
Priorslee Avenue A3
Queen Elizabeth Ave C3
Queen Elizabeth Way B1
Queensway A2/B3
QEII Arena C2
Rampart Way A2
Randlay Avenue C3
Randlay Wood C3
Rhodes Avenue C1
Royal Way B1
St Leonards Rd B1
St Quentin Gate B2
Shifnal Rd A3
Silkin Way C2
Sixth Avenue A1
Southwater Leisure Complex B2
Southwater Way B1
Spout Lane C1
Spout Mound B1
Spout Way C1
Stafford Court B3
Stafford Park B3
Stirchley Avenue C3
Stone Row C1
Superstoore B1
Telford Bridge Retail Park A1
Telford Central Sta A3
Telford Centre, The B2
Telford Forge Shopping Park A1
Telford Hornets RFC C2
Telford International Centre C2
Telford Way A3
Third Avenue A2
Town Park C2
Town Park Visitor Ctr B2
Wellswood Avenue A2
West Centre Way B1
Withywood Drive C1
Wonderland C2
Woodhouse Central B2
Yates Way A1

Torquay 344

Abbey Rd B2
Alexandra Rd A2
Alpine Rd B3
AMF Bowling C3
Ash Hill Rd A2
Babbacombe Rd B3
Bampfylde Rd B1
Barton Rd A1
Beacon Quay C2
Belgrave Rd A1/B1
Belmont Rd A3
Berea Rd A3
Braddons Hill Rd East B3
Brewery Park A3
Bronshill Rd A2
Carlton Rd A3
Castle Circus A2
Castle Rd A2
Cavern Rd A3
Central B2
Chatsworth Rd A2
Chestnut Avenue B1
Church St A1
Coach Station A1
Corbyn Head C1
Croft Hill B1
Croft Rd B1
East St A1
Egerton Rd A3
Ellacombe Church Rd A3
Ellacombe Rd A2
Falkland Rd B1
Fleet St B2
Fleet Walk Shopping Centre B2
Grafton Rd B3
Grange Rd A3
Haldon Pier C2
Hatfield Rd A2
Highbury Rd A2
Higher Warberry Rd A3
Hillesdon Rd B3
Hoxton Rd A3
Hunsdon Rd B3
Information Centre B2
Inner Harbour C3
Kenwyn Rd A3
King's Drive, The B1
Laburnum St A1
Law Courts A2
Library A2
Lime Avenue B1
Living Coasts C3
Lower Warberry Rd B3
Lucius St B1
Lymington Rd A1
Magdalene Rd A1
Marina C2
Market Forum, The B2
Market St B2
Meadfoot Lane C3
Meadfoot Rd C3
Melville St B2
Middle Warberry Rd B3
Mill Lane A1
Montpellier Rd B3
Morgan Avenue A1
Museum Rd B3
Newton Rd A1
Oakhill Rd A1
Outer Harbour C2
Parkhill Rd C3
Pimlico B2
Police Station A1
Post Office A1/B2
Prince of Wales Steps C3
Princes Rd A3
Princes Rd East A3
Princes Rd West A3
Princess Gardens C2
Princess Pier C2
Princess Theatre C2
Rathmore Rd B1
Recreation Grd B1
Riviera International Centre B1
Rock End Avenue C3
Rock Rd B2
Rock Walk B2
Rosehill Rd A3
South West Coast Path C3
St Efride's Rd A1
St John's B3
St Luke's Rd B2
St Luke's Rd North B2
St Luke's Rd South B2
St Marychurch Rd A2
Scarborough Rd B1
Shedden Hill B2
South Pier C2
South St A1
Spanish Barn B1
Stitchill Rd B3
Strand B3
Sutherland Rd B3
Teignmouth Rd A1
Temperance St B2
Terrace, The B3
Thurlow Rd A1
Tor Bay B1
Tor Church Rd A1
Tor Hill Rd A1
Torbay Rd B2
Torquay Museum B3
Torquay Station C1
Torquay Tennis Club B1
Torre Abbey B1
Torre Abbey Meadows B1
Torre Abbey Sands B1
Torwood Gardens B3
Torwood St C3
Town Hall A2
Union Square Shopping Centre A2
Union St A1
Upton Hill A2
Upton Park A1
Upton Rd A1
Vanehill Rd C3
Vansittart Rd A1
Vaughan Parade C2
Victoria Parade C3
Victoria Rd A2
Warberry Rd West B2
Warren Rd B2
Windsor Rd A2/A3
Woodville Rd A3

Truro 344

Adelaide Ter B1
Agar Rd B3
Arch Hill C2
Arundell Place C2
Avenue, The A3
Avondale Rd B1
Back Quay B3
Barrack Lane C3
Barton Meadow A1
Benson Rd A2
Bishops Close A2
Bosvean Gardens B1
Bosvigo Gardens B1
Bosvigo Lane A1
Bosvigo Rd B2
Broad St A3
Burley Close C3
Bus Station B3
Calenick St B2
Campfield Hill B3
Carclew St B3
Carew Rd A2
Carey Park B2
Carlyon Rd A2
Carvoza Rd A3
Castle St B2
Cathedral View A2
Chainwalk Drive A2
Chapel Hill B1
Charles St B2
City Hall B3
City Rd B2
Coinage Hall B3
Comprigney Hill A1
Coosebean Lane A1
Copes Gardens A2
County Hall B1
Courtney Rd A2
Crescent Rd B1
Crescent Rise B1
Crescent, The B1
Daniell Court C2
Daniell Rd C2
Daniell St C2
Daubuz Close A2
Daubuz Moors Nature Reserve A3
Dobbs Lane B1
Edward St B2
Eliot Rd A2
Elm Court A3
Enys Close A1
Enys Rd A1
Fairmantle St B3
Falmouth Rd C2
Ferris Town B2
Fire Station B1
Frances St B2
George St B2
Green Close C2
Green Lane C1
Grenville Rd A2
Hall For Cornwall B3
Hendra Rd A2
Hendra Vean A1
High Cross B3
Higher Newham Lane C3
Higher Trehaverne A2
Hillcrest Avenue B1
Hospital B2
Hunkin Close A2
Hurland Rd C3
Infirmary Hill B2
James Place B3
Kenwyn Church Rd A1
Kenwyn Hill A1
Kenwyn Rd A2
Kenwyn St B2
Kerris Gardens A1
King St B3
Leats, The B2
Lemon Quay B3
Lemon St Gallery B3
Library B1/B3
Malpas Rd B3
Magistrates Court A3
Market B3
Merrifield Close B1
Mitchell Hill A3

Moresk Close A3
Moresk Rd A3
Morlaix Avenue C3
Nancemere Rd A3
Newham Bsns Park C3
Newham Industrial Est C3
Newham Rd C3
Northfield Drive C3
Oak Way A3
Palace's Terrace A3
Park View C2
Pendarves Rd A2
Plaza Cinema B3
Police Station A2/B3
Post Office B3
Prince's St B3
Pydar St A2
Quay St B3
Redannick Crescent C2
Redannick Lane B2
Richard Lander Monument ✦ C2
Richmond Hill B1
River St B2
Rosedale Rd A2
Royal Cornwall Mus B2
St Aubyn Rd C3
St Clement St B3
St George's Rd A1
Standing Cross ✦ B3
School Lane C2
Spires, The A2
Station Rd B1
Stokes Rd A2
Strangways Terrace C3
Tabernacle St B3
Trehaverne Lane A2
Tremayne Rd A2
Treseder's Gardens A3
Treworder Rd B1
Treyew Rd B1
Truro Cathedral ✝ B3
Truro Harbour Office B3
Truro Station B3
Union St B3
Upper School Lane C2
Victoria Gardens B2
Waterfall Gardens B2

Wick 344

Ackergill Crescent A2
Ackergill St A2
Albert St C2
Ambulance Station A2
Argyle Square C2
Assembly Rooms C2
Bank Row C2
Bankhead B1
Barons Well B2
Barrogill St C2
Bay View B3
Bexley Terrace C3
Bignold Park C2
Bowling Green C2
Breadalbane Terrace C2
Bridge of Wick B1
Bridge St B2
Brown Place C2
Burn St B2
Bus Station B1
Caithness General Hospital (A&E) B1
Cliff Rd B1
Coach Rd B2
Coastguard Station C3
Corner Crescent B3
Coronation St C1
Council Offices B2
Court B2
Crane Rock C3
Dempster St C2
Dunnet Avenue A2
Fire Station B2
Francis St C1
George St A1
Girnigoe St B2
Glamis Rd B2
Gowrie Place B1
Grant St C2
Green Rd B2
Gunns Terrace B3
Harbour Quay B2
Harbour Rd C3
Harbour Terrace C2
Harrow Hill C2
Henrietta St A2/B2
Heritage Museum C2
High St B2
Hill Avenue A2
Hillhead Rd B3
Hood St C1
Huddart St C2
Kenneth St C1
Kinnaird St C2
Kirk Hill B1
Langwell Crescent B3
Leishman Avenue B3
Leith Walk A2
Library B2
Liby & Swimming Pool C1
Lifeboat Station C3
Lighthouse C3
Lindsay Drive B3
Lindsay Place B3
Loch St C2
Louisburgh St B2
Lower Dunbar St C2
Macleay Lane B1
Macleod Rd B3
MacRae St C2
Martha Terrace B2
Miller Avenue B1
Miller Lane B1
Moray St C2
Mowat Place B3
Murchison St C3
Newton Avenue C1
Newton Rd C1
Nicolson St C3
North Highland Coll. B2
North River Pier B3
Northcote St C2
Owen Place A2
Police Station B1
Port Dunbar B3
Post Office B2/C2
Pulteney Distillery ✦ C2
River St B2
Robert St A1
Rutherford St C2
St John's Episcopal C2
Sandigoe Rd B3
Scalesburn B3
Seaforth Avenue C1
Shore Lane B2
Shore, The B2
Sinclair Drive B3
Sinclair Terrace C2
Smith Terrace C3
South Pier C3
South Quay C3
South Rd C1
South River Pier B3
Station Rd B1
Superstore A1/B1
Telford St B2
Thurso Rd B1
Thurso St B1
Town Hall B2
Union St B2
Upper Dunbar St C2
Vansittart St C3
Victoria Place B2
War Memorial A1
Well of Cairndhuna ✦ C3
Wellington Avenue C3
Wellington St C3
West Banks Avenue C1
West Banks Terrace C1
West Park C1
Whitehorse Park B2
Wick Harbour Bridge B2
Wick Industrial Estate A2
Wick Parish Church B1
Wick Station B1
Williamson St B2
Willowbank B2

Winchester 344

Andover Rd A2
Andover Rd Retail Pk A2
Archery Lane C2
Arthur Rd A2
Bar End Rd C3
Beaufort Rd C2
Beggar's Lane B3
Bereweeke Avenue A1
Bereweeke Rd A1
Boscobel Rd A2
Brassey Rd A2
Broadway B3
Brooks Shopping Centre, The B3
Bus Station B3
Butter Cross ✦ B2
Canon St C2
Castle Wall C2/C3
Cathedral ✝ C2
Cheriton Rd A1
Chesil St C3
Chesil Theatre C3
Christchurch Rd C1
City Mill ✦ B3
City Museum B2
City Rd B2
Clifton Rd B1
Clifton Terrace B2
Close Wall C2/C3
Coach Park A2
Colebrook St C3
College St C2
College Walk C3
Compton Rd C2
Council Offices C3
County Council Offices B2
Cranworth Rd A2
Cromwell Rd C1
Culver Rd C2
Discovery Centre ✦ B2
Domum Rd C3
Durngate Place B3
Eastgate St B3
East Hill C3
Edgar Rd C2
Egbert Rd A2
Elm Rd B1
Everyman C2
Fairfield Rd A1
Fire Station B3
Fordington Avenue B1
Fordington Rd A1
Friarsgate B3
Gordon Rd B3
Great Hall & Round Table, The B2
Greenhill Rd B1
Guildhall B3
Hatherley Rd A1
High St B2
Hillier Way A3
HM Prison B1
Hyde Abbey (Remains) ✝ A2
Hyde Abbey Rd B2
Hyde Close A2
Hyde St A2
Information Centre B3
Jane Austen's Ho C2
Jewry St B2
King Alfred Place A2
Kingsgate Arch C2
Kingsgate Park C2
Kingsgate Rd C2
Kingsgate St C2
Lankhills Rd A2
Law Courts B2
Library B2
Lower Brook St B3
Magdalen Hill B3
Market Lane B2
Mews Lane B1
Middle Brook St B3
Middle Rd B1
Military Museums B2
Milland Rd C3
Milverton Rd B1
Monks Rd A3
North Hill Close A2
North Walls B2
North Walls Rec Gnd A3
Nuns Rd A3
Oram's Arbour B1
Owens Rd A2
Parchment St B2
Park & Ride C3
Park Avenue B3
Playing Field A1
Police HQ B1
Portal Rd C3
Post Office B2/C1
Ranelagh Rd C1
Regimental Mus B2
River Park Leisure Ctr B3
Romans' Rd C2
Romsey Rd B1
Royal Hampshire County Hospital (A&E) B1
St Cross Rd C2
St George's St B2
St Giles Hill C3
St James Villas C2
St James' Lane B1
St James' Terrace B1
St John's B3
St John's St B3
St Michael's Rd C2
St Paul's Hill B1
St Peter St B2
St Swithun St C2
St Thomas St C2
Saxon Rd A2
School of Art B3
Sleepers Hill Rd C1
Southgate St B2
Sparkford Rd C1
Square, The B2
Staple Gardens B2
Station Rd B2
Step Terrace B1
Stockbridge Rd A1
Stuart Crescent C1
Sussex St B2
Swan Lane B2
Tanner St B3
Theatre Royal B2
Tower St B2
Union St B3
Univ of Southampton (Winchester School of Art) B3
Univ of Winchester (King Alfred Campus) C1
Upper Brook St B2
Wales St B3
Water Lane B3
Weirs, The C3
West End Terrace B1
Western Rd B1
Westgate B2
Wharf Hill C3
Winchester Station A2
Winnall Moors Wildlife Reserve A3
Wolvesey Castle C3
Worthy Lane A2
Worthy Rd A2

Windsor 344

Adelaide Square C3
Albany Rd C2
Albert St B1
Alexandra Gardens B2
Alexandra Rd C2
Alma Rd B2
Arthur Rd B2
Bachelors Acre B3
Barry Avenue B2
Beaumont Rd C2
Bexley St B1
Boat House B2
Brocas St B2
Brocas, The A2
Brook St C3
Bulkeley Avenue C1
Castle Hill B3
Charles St B2
Claremont Rd C2
Clarence Crescent B2
Clarence Rd B1
Clewer Court Rd B1
Coach Park B2
College Crescent C1
Cricket Ground C3
Dagmar Rd C2
Datchet Rd B3
Devereux Rd C2
Dorset Rd C2
Duke St B1
Elm Rd C1
Eton College ✦ A3
Eton College Natural History Museum A2
Eton Court A2
Eton Square A2
Eton Wick Rd A2
Farm Yard B3
Fire Station C2
Frances Rd C2
Frogmore Drive B3
Gloucester Place C3
Goslar Way C1
Goswell Hill B2
Goswell Rd B2
Green Lane C1
Grove Rd C2
Guildhall B3
Helena Rd C2
Helston Lane B1
High St A2/B3
Holy Trinity C2
Home Park, The A3/C3
Household Cavalry C2
Imperial Rd C1
Information Centre B2
Keats Lane A2
King Edward VII Ave A3
King Edward VII Hospital C2
King George V Memorial ✦ B3
King Stable St A2
King's Rd C3
Library A2/B2
Long Walk, The C3
Maidenhead Rd B1
Meadow Lane A2
Municipal Offices C3
Nell Gwynne's Ho B3
Osborne Rd C2
Oxford Rd B1
Park St B3
Peascod St B2
Police Station C2
Post Office A2/C1
Princess Margaret Hospital (private) C2
Old Court Art Space, The C2
Queen Elizabeth Bridge A1
Queen Victoria's Walk B3
Queen's Rd C2
River St B2
Romney Island A3
Romney Lock A3
Romney Lock Rd A3
Russell St C2
St George's Chapel B3
St John's B3
St John's Chapel A2
St Leonards Rd C2
St Mark's Rd C2
Sheet St C3
Shopmobility B2
South Meadow A2
South Meadow Lane A2
Springfield Rd C1
Stovell Rd B1
Sunbury Rd A2
Tangier Lane A2
Temple Rd C2
Thames St B3
Theatre Royal B3
Trinity Place C2
Vansittart Rd B1/C1
Victoria Barracks C2
Victoria St C2
Westmead C1
White Lilies Island A1
William St B2
Windsor & Eton Central B2
Windsor & Eton Riverside A3
Windsor Bridge B3
Windsor Castle B3
Windsor Leisure Ctr B1
Windsor Relief Rd A1
Windsor Royal Station Shopping Centre B2
Windsor Yards B2
York Avenue C1
York Rd C1

Wolverhampton 344

Albion St B3
Arena B2
Art Gallery B2
Ashland St C1
Austin St A1
Badger Drive A3
Bailey St B3
Bath Avenue B1
Bath Rd B1
Bell St C2
Berry St B3
Bilston Rd C3
Bilston St C3
Birmingham Canal A3
Bone Mill Lane A2
Brewery Rd B1
Bright St A1
Burton Crescent B3
Bus Station B3
Cambridge St A3
Camp St B2
Cannock Rd A3
Castle St C2
Chapel Ash C1
Cherry St C1
Chester St A1
Church Lane C2
Church St C2
Civic Centre B2
Civic Hall B2
Clarence Rd B2
Cleveland St C2
Clifton St C1
Coach Station B2
Compton Rd B1
Corn Hill B3
Coven St A3
Craddock St A1
Cross St North A2
Crown & County Courts C3
Crown St A2
Culwell St B3
Dale St C1
Darlington St C1
Devon Rd A1
Drummond St B2
Dudley Rd C2
Dudley St B2
Duke St C3
Dunkley St B1
Dunstall Avenue A2
Dunstall Hill A2
Dunstall Rd A1/A2
Evans St A1
Fawdry St A1
Field St B3
Fire Station C1
Fiveways A2
Fowler Playing Fields A3
Fox's Lane A2
Francis St A2
Fryer St B3
Gloucester St A1
Gordon St C3
Graiseley St C1
Grand B3
Grand Station B3
Granville St C3
Great Brickkiln St C1
Great Hampton St A1
Great Western St A2
Grimstone St B3
Harrow St A1
Hilton St A3
Hive Library The B2
Horseley Fields C3
Humber Rd C1
Jack Hayward Way A2
Jameson St A1
Jenner St C3
Kennedy Rd B3
Kimberley St C1
King St B2
Laburnum St C1
Lansdowne Rd B1
Leicester St A1
Lever St C3
Library C3
Lichfield St B2
Light House B3
Little's Lane B3
Lock St B3
Lord St C1
Lowe St A1
Maltings, The B2
Mander Centre C2
Mander St C1
Market C2
Market St B2
Maxwell Rd C3
Merridale St C1
Middlecross C3
Molineux St B2
Mostyn St A1
Newhampton Arts Centre B1
New Hampton Rd East A1
Nine Elms Lane A3
North Rd A2
Oaks Crescent C1
Oxley St A2
Paget St A1
Park Avenue B1
Park Road East A1
Park Road West B1
Paul St C2
Pelham St C1
Penn Rd C2
Piper's Row B3
Piper's Row C3
Pitt St C2
Police Station C3
Pool St C2
Poole St A3
Post Office A1/B2/B2/C2/C3
Powlett St C3
Queen St B2
Raby St C3
Railway Drive B3
Red Hill St A2
Red Lion St B2
Retreat St C1
Ring Rd B2
Royal, The C3
Rugby St A1
Russell St C1
St Andrew's B1
St David's B3
St George's C3
St George's Parade C2
St James St C3
St John's C2
St John's C2
St John's Retail Park C2
St John's Square C2
St Mark's C1
St Marks Rd C1
St Marks St C1
St Patrick's B2
St Peter's B2
St Peter's B2
Salisbury St C1
Salop St C2
School St C2
Sherwood St A2
Smestow St A3
Snow Hill C2
Springfield Rd A3
Stafford St A2/B2
Staveley Rd A1
Steelhouse Lane C3
Stephenson St C1
Stewart St C2
Sun St B3
Tempest St C2
Temple St C2
Tettenhall Rd B1
Thomas St C2
Thornley St B2
Tower St C2
University B2
Upper Zoar St C1
Vicarage Rd C3
Victoria St C2
Walpole St A1
Walsall St C3
Ward St C3
Warwick St C3
Water St A3
Waterloo Rd B2
Wednesfield Rd B3
West Park (not A&E) B1
West Park Swimming Pool B1
Wharf St C3
Whitmore Hill B2
Wolverhampton B3
Wolverhampton B3
Wolverhampton St George's C2
Wolverhampton Wanderers Football Gnd (Molineux) B2
Worcester St C2
Wulfrun Centre C2
Yarwell Close A3
York St C3
Zoar St C1

Worcester 344

Albany Terrace A1
Angel Place B2
Angel St B2
Ashcroft Rd A2
Athelstan Rd C3
Avenue, The C1
Back Lane North A1
Back Lane South A1
Barbourne Rd A2
Bath Rd C2
Battenhall Rd C3
Bridge St B2
Britannia Square A1
Broad St B2
Bromwich Lane C1
Bromwich Rd C1
Bromyard Rd C1
Bus Station B2
Butts, The B2
Carden St B3
Castle St A2
Cathedral ✝ C2
Cathedral Plaza B2
Charles St B3
Chequers Lane B1
Chestnut St A2
Chestnut Walk A2
Citizens' Advice Bureau B2
City Walls Rd B2
Cole Hill C3
College St C2
Commandery, The C3
Cripplegate Park B1
Croft Rd B1
Cromwell St B3
Cross, The B2
Crowngate Centre B2
Deansway B2
Diglis Parade C2
Diglis Rd C2
Edgar Tower ✦ C2
Farrier St A2
Foregate St B2
Fort Royal Hill C3
Fort Royal Park C3
Foundry St B3
Friar St C2
George St B3
Grand Stand Rd B1
Greenhill C3
Greyfriars B2
Guildhall B2
Henwick Rd B1
High St B2
Hill St B3
Hive, The B2
Huntingdon Hall B2
Hylton Rd B1
Information Centre B2
King Charles Place Shopping Centre C1
King's School C2
King's School Playing Field C2
Kleve Walk C2
Lansdowne Crescent A3
Lansdowne Rd A3
Lansdowne Walk A3
Laslett St A3
Little Chestnut St A2
Little London A2
London Rd C3
Lowell St A3
Lowesmoor B2
Lowesmoor Terrace A3
Lowesmoor Wharf A3
Magistrates Court A2
Midland Rd B3
Mill St C2
Moors Severn Terrace, The A1
Mus & Art Gallery A2
Museum of Royal Worcester C2
New Rd C1
New St B2
Northfield St A2
Odeon B2
Old Palace The C2
Padmore St B3
Park St C3
Pheasant St B3
Pitchcroft Racecourse A1
Police Station A2
Portland St C2
Post Office B2
Quay St B2
Queen St B2
Rainbow Hill A3
Recreation Ground A2
Reindeer Court B2
Rogers Hill A3
Sabrina Terrace A1
St Dunstan's Cre C3
St John's C1
St Martin's Gate B3
St Martin's Quarter B3
St Oswald's Rd A2
St Paul's St B3
St Swithin's Church B2
St Wulstans Crescent C3
Sansome Walk A2
Severn St C2
Shambles, The B2
Shaw St B2
Shire Hall Crown Ct A2
Shrub Hill Rd B3
Shrub Hill Retail Park B3
Slingpool Walk C1
South Parade B2
Southfield St A2
Sports Centre A3
Stanley Rd B3
Swan, The A1
Swimming Pool A2
Tallow Hill B3
Tennis Walk A2
Tolladine Rd B3
Tudor House B2
Tybridge St B1
Tything, The A2
Univ of Worcester B2
Vincent Rd B3
Vue C2
Washington St A3
Woolhope Rd C3
Worcester Bridge B2
Worcester County Cricket Club C1
Worcester Foregate Street B2
Worcester Shrub Hill B3
Worcester Royal Grammar School A2
Wylds Lane C3

Wrexham Wrecsam 344

Abbot St B2
Acton Rd A3
Albert St C3
Alexandra Rd C1
Aran Rd A3
Barnfield C3
Bath Rd C2
Beeches, The A3
Beechley Rd C3
Belgrave Rd C2
Bellevue Park C2
Bellevue Rd C2
Belvedere Drive A1
Bennion's Rd C3
Berse Rd A1
Bersham Rd C1
Birch St C3
Bodhyfryd B3
Border Retail Park B3
Bradley Rd C2
Bright St B1
Bron-y-Nant B1
Brook St C2
Bryn-y-Cabanau Rd C3
Bury St C3
Bus Station B2
Butchers Market B3
Caia Rd C3
Cambrian Ind Est C3
Caxton Place B2
Cemetery C1
Centenary Rd C1
Central Retail Park B2
Chapel St C2
Charles St B3
Chester Rd A3
Chester St B3
Cilcen Grove A3
Citizens Advice Bureau B2
Cobden Rd B1
Council Offices B3
County B2
Crescent Rd B3
Crispin Lane A2
Croesnewyth Rd B1
Cross St A2
Cunliffe St A2
Derby Rd C3
Dolydd Rd B1
Duke St B2
Eagles Meadow C3
Earle St C2
East Avenue A2
Edward St C2
Egerton St B2
Empress Rd C1
Erddig Rd C2
Fairy Rd C2
Fire Station B2
Foster Rd A3
Foxwood Drive C1
Garden Rd A2
General Market B3
Gerald St B2
Gibson St C1
Glyndwr University Plas Coch Campus A1
Greenbank St C3
Greenfield A2
Grosvenor Rd B2
Grove Park B2
Grove Park Rd B3
Grove Rd A3
Guildhall B2
Haig Rd C3
Hampden Rd C2
Hazel Grove A3
Henblas St B3
High St B3
Hightown Rd C3
Hill St B2
Holt Rd B3
Holt St B3
Hope St B2
Huntroyde Avenue C3
Information Centre B3
Island Green Shopping Centre B2
Jobcentre Plus B2
Jubilee Rd B2
King St B2
Kingsmills Rd C3
Lambpit St B3
Law Courts B3
Lawson Close A3
Lawson Rd A3
Lea Rd C2
Library & Arts Centre B2
Lilac Way B1
Llys David Lord B1
Lorne St A2
Maesgwyn Rd B1
Maesydre Rd A3
Manley Rd B3
Market St B3
Mawddy Avenue A2
Mayville Avenue A2
Memorial Gallery B2
Memorial Hall B3
Mold Rd A1
Mount St C3
Neville Crescent A3
New Rd A2
North Wales Regional Tennis Centre A1
Oak Drive A3
Odeon C3
Park Avenue A3
Park St A2
Peel St C1
Pen y Bryn C2
Pentre Felin C2
Penymaes Avenue A3
Peoples Market B3
Percy St C2
Pines, The A3
Plas Coch Rd A1
Plas Coch Retail Park A1
Police Station B3
Poplar Rd C2
Post Office A2/B3/C3
Powell Rd B3
Poyser St C2
Price's Lane A2
Primose Way B1
Princess St C1
Queen St B3
Queens Square B2
Regent St B2
Rhosddu Rd A2/B2
Rhosnesni Lane A3
Rivulet Rd C3
Ruabon Rd C2
Ruthin Rd C1/C2
St Giles C3
St Giles Way C3
St James Court A2
St Mary's ✝ B2
Salisbury Rd C3
Salop Rd C3
Sontley Rd C2
Spring Rd A2
Stanley St C3
Stansty Rd A2
Station Approach B2
Studio B2
Superstore B3/C1
Talbot Rd C2
Techniquest Glyndwr ✦ A2
Town Hill C2
Trevor St C2
Trinity St B2
Tuttle St C3
Vale Park A1
Vernon St B2
Vicarage Hill B2
Victoria Rd C2
Walnut St A2
War Memorial ✦ B3
Waterworld Leisure Centre ✦ B3
Watery Rd B1/B2
Wellington Rd C2
Westminster Drive A3
William Aston Hall A1
Windsor Rd A1
Wrecsam
Wrexham AFC A1
Wrexham Central B2
Wrexham General B2
Wrexham Maelor Hospital (A&E) B1
Wrexham Technology Park B1
Wynn Avenue A2
Yale College B3
Yale Grove A3
Yorke St C3

York 344

Aldwark B2
Barbican Rd C3
Bar Convent Living Heritage Centre ✦ C1
Barley Hall B2
Bishopgate St C2
Bishopshill Senior C2
Bishopthorpe Rd C2
Blossom St C1
Bootham A1
Bootham Crescent A1
Bootham Terrace A1
Bridge St B2
Brook St A2
Brownlow St A2
Burton Stone Lane A1
Castle Museum C2
Castlegate B2
Cemetery Rd C3
Cherry St C2
City Screen B2
City Wall A2/B1/C3
Clarence St A2
Clementhorpe C2
Clifford St B2
Clifford's Tower B2
Clifton A1
Coach park A2
Coney St B2
Coppergate Centre B2
Cromwell Rd C2
Crown Court C2
Davygate B2
Deanery Gardens A2
DIG ✦ B2
Dodsworth Avenue A3
Eboracum Way A3
Ebor Industrial Estate B3
Eldon St A2
Everyman C1
Fairfax House B2
Fire Station C3
Fishergate C3
Foss Islands Rd B3
Foss Islands Retail Pk B3
Fossbank A3
Garden St A2
George St C3
Gillygate A2
Goodramgate B2
Grand Opera House B2
Grosvenor Terrace A1
Guildhall B2
Hallfield Rd A3
Heslington Rd C3
Heworth Green A3
Holy Trinity B2
Hope St C3
Huntington Rd A3
Information Centre B2
James St B3
Jorvik Viking Ctr B2
Kent St C3
Lawrence St C3
Layerthorpe A3
Leeman Rd B1
Lendal B2
Lendal Bridge B1
Library A2/B1
Longfield Terrace A1
Lord Mayor's Walk A2
Lowther St A2
Mansion House B2
Margaret St C3
Marygate A1
Melbourne St C3
Merchant Adventurers' Hall B2
Merchant Taylors' Hall B2
Micklegate B1
Micklegate Bar C1
Monkgate A2
Moss St C1
Museum Gdns B1
Museum St B1
National Railway Museum B1
Navigation Rd B3
Newton Terrace C2
North Parade A1
North St B2
Nunnery Lane C1
Nunthorpe Rd C1
Ouse Bridge B2
Paragon St C3
Park Grove A3
Park St C1
Parliament St B2
Peasholme Green B3
Penley's Grove St A2
Piccadilly B2
Police Station B2
Post Office B1/B2/C3
Priory St B1
Queen Anne's Rd A1
Regimental Mus B2
Richard III Experience at Monk Bar A2
Roman Bath B2
Rowntree Park C2
St Andrewgate B2
St Benedict Rd C1
St John St A2
St Olave's Rd A1
St Peter's Grove A1
St Saviourgate B2
Scarcroft Hill C1
Scarcroft Rd C1
Shambles, The B2
Shopmobility B2
Skeldergate C2
Skeldergate Bridge C2
Station Rd B1
Stonebow, The B2
Stonegate B2
Superstore A3
Sycamore Terrace A1
Terry Avenue C2
Theatre Royal B2
Thorpe St C1
Toft Green B1
Tower St C2
Townend St A2
Treasurer's House A2
Trinity Lane B1
Undercroft Mus A2
Union Terrace A2
Victor St C2
Vine St C2
Walmgate B3
War Memorial ✦ B1
Wellington St C3
York Art Gallery A1
York Barbican C3
York Brewery ✦ B1
York Dungeon, The B2
York Minster ✝ A2
York St John Univ A1
York Station B1

Index to road maps of Britain

Abbreviations used in the index

Aberdeen	Aberdeen City
Aberds	Aberdeenshire
Ald	Alderney
Anglesey	Isle of Anglesey
Angus	Angus
Argyll	Argyll and Bute
Bath	Bath and North East Somerset
BCP	Bournemouth, Christchurch and Poole
Bedford	Bedford
Blackburn	Blackburn with Darwen
Blackpool	Blackpool
Bl Gwent	Blaenau Gwent
Borders	Scottish Borders
Brack	Bracknell
Bridgend	Bridgend
Brighton	City of Brighton and Hove
Bristol	City and County of Bristol
Bucks	Buckinghamshire
Caerph	Caerphilly
Cambs	Cambridgeshire
Cardiff	Cardiff
Carms	Carmarthenshire
C Beds	Central Bedfordshire
Ceredig	Ceredigion
Ches E	Cheshire East
Ches W	Cheshire West and Chester
Clack	Clackmannanshire
Conwy	Conwy
Corn	Cornwall
Cumb	Cumbria
Darl	Darlington
Denb	Denbighshire
Derby	City of Derby
Derbys	Derbyshire
Devon	Devon
Dorset	Dorset
Dumfries	Dumfries and Galloway
Dundee	Dundee City
Durham	Durham
E Ayrs	East Ayrshire
Edin	City of Edinburgh
E Dunb	East Dunbartonshire
E Loth	East Lothian
E Renf	East Renfrewshire
Essex	Essex
E Sus	East Sussex
E Yorks	East Riding of Yorkshire
Falk	Falkirk
Fife	Fife
Flint	Flintshire
Glasgow	City of Glasgow
Glos	Gloucestershire
Gtr Man	Greater Manchester
Guern	Guernsey
Gwyn	Gwynedd
Halton	Halton
Hants	Hampshire
Hereford	Herefordshire
Herts	Hertfordshire
Highld	Highland
Hrtlpl	Hartlepool
Hull	Hull
Invclyd	Inverclyde
IoM	Isle of Man
IoW	Isle of Wight
Jersey	Jersey
Kent	Kent
Lancs	Lancashire
Leicester	City of Leicester
Leics	Leicestershire
Lincs	Lincolnshire
London	Greater London
Luton	Luton
Mbro	Middlesbrough
Medway	Medway
Mers	Merseyside
Midloth	Midlothian
M Keynes	Milton Keynes
Mon	Monmouthshire
Moray	Moray
M Tydf	Merthyr Tydfil
N Ayrs	North Ayrshire
Neath	Neath Port Talbot
NE Lincs	North East Lincolnshire
Newport	City and County of Newport
N Lanark	North Lanarkshire
N Lincs	North Lincolnshire
N Nhants	North Northamptonshire
Norf	Norfolk
Northumb	Northumberland
Nottingham	City of Nottingham
Notts	Nottinghamshire
N Som	North Somerset
N Yorks	North Yorkshire
Orkney	Orkney
Oxon	Oxfordshire
Pboro	Peterborough
Pembs	Pembrokeshire
Perth	Perth and Kinross
Plym	Plymouth
Powys	Powys
Ptsmth	Portsmouth
Reading	Reading
Redcar	Redcar and Cleveland
Renfs	Renfrewshire
Rhondda	Rhondda Cynon Taff
Rutland	Rutland
S Ayrs	South Ayrshire
Scilly	Scilly
S Glos	South Gloucestershire
Shetland	Shetland
Shrops	Shropshire
S Lanark	South Lanarkshire
Slough	Slough
Som	Somerset
Soton	Southampton
Southend	Southend-on-Sea
Staffs	Staffordshire
Stirling	Stirling
Stockton	Stockton-on-Tees
Stoke	Stoke-on-Trent
Suff	Suffolk
Sur	Surrey
Swansea	Swansea
Swindon	Swindon
S Yorks	South Yorkshire
T&W	Tyne and Wear
Telford	Telford and Wrekin
Thurrock	Thurrock
Torbay	Torbay
Torf	Torfaen
V Glam	The Vale of Glamorgan
Warks	Warwickshire
Warr	Warrington
W Berks	West Berkshire
W Dunb	West Dunbartonshire
Wilts	Wiltshire
Windsor	Windsor and Maidenhead
W Isles	Western Isles
W Loth	West Lothian
W Mid	West Midlands
W Nhants	West Northamptonshire
Wokingham	Wokingham
Worcs	Worcestershire
Wrex	Wrexham
W Sus	West Sussex
W Yorks	West Yorkshire
York	City of York

How to use the index

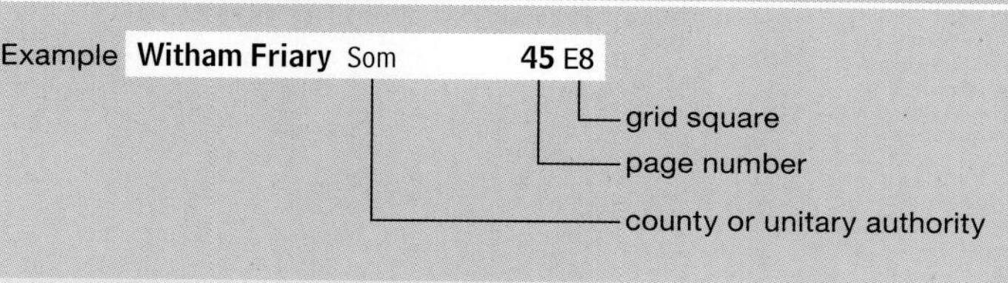

A

Aaron's Hill Sur 50 E3
Aaron's Town Cumb 240 E2
Abbas Combe Som 30 C2
Abberley Worcs 116 D5
Abberton Essex 89 B8
Worcs 117 G9
Abberwick Northumb 264 G4
Abbess End Essex 87 C9
Abbess Roding Essex 87 C9
Abbey Devon 27 E10
Abbeycwmhir Powys 113 C11
Abbey-cwm-hir Powys 113 C11
Abbeydale Glos 80 B5
S Yorks 186 E4
Abbeydale Park S Yorks 186 E4
Abbey Dore Hereford 97 E7
Abbey Field Essex 107 G9
Abbey Gate Kent 53 B9
Abbey Green Shrops 149 C10
Staffs 169 D7
Abbey Hey Gtr Man 184 B5
Abbeyhill Edin 280 G5
Abbey Hulton Stoke 168 F6
Abbey Mead Sur 66 F4
Abbey St Bathans
Borders 272 C5
Abbeystead Lancs 203 C7
Abbey Town Cumb 238 G5
Abbey Village Lancs 194 C6
Abbey Wood London 68 D3
Abbots Bickington Devon 24 E5
Abbots Bromley Staffs 151 E11
Abbotsbury Dorset 17 D7
Abbotsford W Sus 36 C4
Abbotsham Devon 24 B6
Abbotskerswell Devon 9 B7
Abbots Langley Herts 85 E9
Abbotsleigh Devon 8 F6
Abbots Leigh N Som 60 E4
Abbotsley Cambs 122 F4
Abbot's Meads Ches W 166 B5
Abbots Morton Worcs 117 F10
Abbots Ripton Cambs 122 B4
Abbots Salford Warks 117 G11
Abbotstone Hants 48 G5
Abbotswood Hants 32 C5
Sur 50 C4
Abbots Worthy Hants 48 G3
Abbotts Ann Hants 47 E10
Abcott Shrops 115 B7
Abdon Shrops 131 F11
Abdy S Yorks 186 B6
Aber Ceredig 93 B9
Aberaeron Ceredig 111 E9
Aberaman Rhondda 77 E8
Aberangell Gwyn 146 G6
Aber-Arad Carms 92 D6
Aberarder Highld 290 E6
Aberarder House Highld 300 G6
Aberarder Lodge Highld 291 E7
Aberargie Perth 286 F5
Aberarth Ceredig 111 E9
Aberavon Neath 57 C8
Aber-banc Ceredig 93 C7
Aberbargoed Caerph 77 E11
Aberbechan Powys 130 E2
Aberbeeg Bl Gwent 78 E2
Aberbran Powys 95 F9
Abercanaid M Tydf 77 E9
Abercarn Caerph 78 G2
Abercastle Pembs 91 E7
Abercegir Powys 128 C6
Aberchalder Highld 290 C5
Aberchirder Aberds 302 D6
Abercorn W Loth 279 F11
Aber Cowarch Gwyn 147 F7
Abercraf Powys 76 C4
Abercregan Neath 57 B11
Abercrombie Fife 287 G9
Abercwmboi Rhondda 77 F8
Abercych Pembs 92 C4
Abercynafon Powys 77 B9
Abercynffig *=Aberkenfig*
Bridgend 57 E11
Abercynon Rhondda 77 F9
Aberdalgie Perth 286 E4
Aberdâr *=Aberdare*
Rhondda 77 E7
Aberdare *=Aberdâr*
Rhondda 77 E7
Aberdaron Gwyn 144 D3
Aberdeen Aberdeen 293 C11
Aberdesach Gwyn 162 E6
Aberdour Fife 280 D3
Aberdovey *=Aberdyfi*
Gwyn 128 D2
Aberdulais Neath 76 E3
Aberdyfi *=Aberdovey*
Gwyn 128 D2
Aberedw Powys 95 B11
Abereiddy Pembs 90 E5
Abererch Gwyn 145 B7
Aberfan M Tydf 77 E9
Aberfeldy Perth 286 C2
Aberffraw Anglesey 162 B5
Aberffrwd Ceredig 112 B3
Mon 78 D5
Aberford W Yorks 206 F4
Aberfoyle Stirlinging 285 G9
Abergarw Bridgend 58 C2
Abergarwed Neath 76 E4
Abergavenny Mon 78 C3
Abergele Conwy 180 F6
Aber-Giâr Carms 93 C10
Abergorlech Carms 93 E11
Abergwaun *=Fishguard*
Pembs 91 D9
Abergwesyn Powys 113 G7
Abergwili Carms 93 G8
Abergwynant Gwyn 146 F3
Abergwynfi Neath 57 B11
Aber-gwynfi Neath 57 B11
Abergwyngregyn Gwyn 179 G11
Abergynolwyn Gwyn 128 B3
Aber-Hirnant Gwyn 147 C9
Aberhosan Powys 128 D6
Aberkenfig *=Abercynffig*
Bridgend 57 E11
Aberlady E Loth 281 E9
Aberlemno Angus 287 B9
Aberlerry Ceredig 128 E2
Aberllefenni Gwyn 128 B5
Aberllydan *=Broad Haven*
Pembs 72 C5
Aberllynfi *=Three Cocks*
Powys 96 D3
Abermagwr Ceredig 112 C3
Abermaw *=Barmouth*
Gwyn 146 F2
Abermeurig Ceredig 111 F11
Aber miwl *=Abermule*
Powys 130 E3
Abermorddu Flint 166 D4
Abermule *=Aber-miwl*
Powys 130 E3
Abernaint Powys 148 E2
Abernant Carms 92 G6
Powys 130 D3
Aber-nant Rhondda 77 E8
Abernethy Perth 286 F5
Abernyte Perth 286 D6
Aber-oer Wrex 166 F3
Aberogwr *=Ogmore by Sea*
V Glam 57 F11
Aberpennar *=Mountain Ash*
Rhondda 77 F8
Aberporth Ceredig 110 G5
Aber-Rhiwlech Gwyn 147 E8
Aberriw *=Berriew*
Powys 130 C3
Abersoch Gwyn 144 D6
Abersychan Torf 78 E3
Abertawe *=Swansea*
Swansea 56 C6
Aberteifi *=Cardigan*
Ceredig 92 B3
Aberthin V Glam 58 D4
Abertillery Bl Gwent 78 E2
Abertridwr Caerph 58 B6
Powys 147 F10
Abertrinant Gwyn 128 B2
Abertysswg Caerph 77 D10
Aberuchill Castle
Perth 285 E11
Aberuthven Perth 286 F3
Aber-Village Powys 96 G2
Aberyscir Powys 95 F9
Aberystwyth Ceredig 111 A11
Abhainn Suidhe
W Isles 305 H2
Abingdon-on-Thames
Oxon 83 F7
Abinger Common Sur 50 D6
Abinger Hammer Sur 50 D5
Abington S Lanark 259 E10
W Nhants 120 E5
Abington Pigotts Cambs 104 C6
Abington Vale
W Nhants 120 E5
Abingworth W Sus 35 D10
Ab Kettleby Leics 154 E4
Ab Lench Worcs 117 G10
Ablington Glos 81 D10
Wilts 47 D7
Abney Derbys 185 F11
Aboyne Aberds 293 D7
Abraham Heights Lancs 211 G9
Abram Gtr Man 194 G6
Abriachan Highld 300 F5
Abridge Essex 87 F7
Abronhill N Lanark 278 F5
Abshot Hants 33 F8
Abson S Glos 61 E8
Abthorpe W Nhants 102 B2
Abune-the-Hill Orkney 314 D2
Aby Lincs 190 F6
Acaster Malbis York 207 D7
Acaster Selby N Yorks 207 E7
Accrington Lancs 195 B9
Acha Argyll 275 B8
Argyll 288 D3
Achabraid Argyll 275 E9
Achachork Highld 298 E4
Achadh an Eas Highld 308 F6
Achad nan Darach
Highld 284 B4
Achadunan Argyll 284 F5
Achafolla Argyll 275 B8
Achagary Highld 308 D7
Achaglass Argyll 255 C8
Achahoish Argyll 275 F8
Achalader Perth 286 C5
Achallader Argyll 285 C7
Achalone Highld 310 D5
Acha Mor W Isles 304 F5
Achanalt Highld 300 C2
Achanamara Argyll 275 E8
Achandunie Highld 300 B6
Achanelid Argyll 275 E11
Ach'an Todhair Highld 290 F2
Achany Highld 309 J5
Achaphubuil Highld 290 F2
Acharacle Highld 289 C8
Acharn Highld 289 D9
Perth 285 C11
Acharole Highld 310 D6
Acharossan Argyll 275 F10
Acharry Muir Highld 309 K6
Achath Aberds 293 B9
Achavanich Highld 310 E5
Achavelgin Highld 301 D9
Achavraat Highld 301 E9
Achddu Carms 74 E6
Achdregnie Moray 302 G2
Achduart Highld 307 J5
Achentoul Highld 310 F2
Achfary Highld 306 F7
Achfrish Highld 309 H5
Achgarve Highld 307 K3
Achiemore Highld 308 C3
Highld 310 D2
A'Chill Highld 294 E4
Achiltibuie Highld 307 J5
Achina Highld 308 C7
Achinahuagh Highld 308 C5
Achindaul Highld 290 E3
Achindown Highld 301 E8
Achinduich Highld 309 J5
Achinduin Argyll 289 F10
Achingills Highld 310 C5
Achininver Highld 308 C5
Achintee Highld 290 F3
Highld 299 E9
Achintraid Highld 295 B10
Achlaven Argyll 289 F11
Achlean Highld 291 D10
Achleck Argyll 288 E6
Achlorachan Highld 300 D3
Achluachrach Highld 290 E4
Achlyness Highld 306 D7
Achmelvich Highld 307 G5
Achmore Highld 295 B10
Stirlinging 285 D9
Achnaba Argyll 275 E10
Argyll 289 F11
Achnabat Highld 300 F5
Achnabreck Argyll 275 D9
Achnacarnin Highld 306 F5
Achnacarry Highld 290 E3
Achnacloich Argyll 289 F11
Highld 295 E7
Achnaconeran Highld 290 B6
Achnacraig Argyll 288 E6
Achnacree Argyll 289 F11
Achnacree Bay Argyll 289 F11
Achnacroish Argyll 289 E10
Achnadrish Argyll 288 D6
Achnafalnich Argyll 284 E6
Achnagarron Highld 300 C6
Achnaha Highld 288 C6
Achnahanat Highld 309 K5
Achnahannet Highld 301 G9
Achnahard Argyll 288 G5
Achnairn Highld 309 H5
Achnaluachrach Highld 309 J6
Achnandarach Highld 295 B10
Achnanellan Highld 290 E2
Achnasaul Highld 290 E3
Achnasheen Highld 299 D11
Achnashelloch Argyll 275 D9
Achnavast Highld 310 C4
Achneigie Highld 299 B10
Achormlarie Highld 309 K6
Achorn Highld 310 F5
Achosnich Highld 288 C6
Achranich Highld 289 E9
Achreamie Highld 310 C4
Achriabhach Highld 290 G3
Achriesgill Highld 306 D7
Achrimsdale Highld 311 J3
Achtoty Highld 308 C6
Achurch N Nhants 137 G10
Achuvoldrach Highld 308 D5
Achvaich Highld 309 K7
Achvarasdal Highld 310 C3
Ackenthwaite Cumb 211 C10
Ackergill Highld 310 D7
Acklam Mbro 225 B9
N Yorks 216 G5
Ackleton Shrops 132 D5
Acklington Northumb 252 C6
Ackton W Yorks 198 C2
Ackworth Moor Top
W Yorks 198 D2
Acle Norf 161 G8
Acock's Green W Mid 134 G2
Acol Kent 71 F10
Acomb Northumb 241 D10
York 207 C7
Acre Gtr Man 196 F2
Lancs 195 C9
Acrefair Wrex 166 G3
Acres Nook Staffs 168 E4
Acre Street W Sus 21 B11
Acton Ches E 167 E10
Dorset 18 F5
London 67 C8
Shrops 130 G6
Staffs 168 G4
Suff 107 C7
Worcs 116 D6
Wrex 166 E4
Acton Beauchamp
Hereford 116 G3
Acton Bridge Ches W 183 F9
Acton Burnell Shrops 131 C10
Acton Green Hereford 116 G3
London 67 D8
Acton Pigott Shrops 131 C10
Acton Place Suff 107 B7
Acton Reynald Shrops 149 E10
Acton Round Shrops 132 D2
Acton Scott Shrops 131 F9
Acton Trussell Staffs 151 F8
Acton Turville S Glos 61 C10
Adabroc W Isles 304 B7
Adambrae W Loth 269 A10
Adam's Green Dorset 29 F8
Adbaston Staffs 150 D5
Adber Dorset 29 C9
Adbolton Notts 154 B2
Adderbury Oxon 101 D9
Adderley Shrops 150 B3
Adderley Green Stoke 168 G6
Adderstone Northumb 264 C4
Addiewell W Loth 269 C9
Addingham W Yorks 205 D7
Addingham Moorside
W Yorks 205 D7
Addington Bucks 102 F4
Corn 6 B5
Kent 53 B7
London 67 G11
Addinston Borders 271 E10
Addiscombe London 67 F10
Addlestone Sur 66 G5
Addlestonemoor Sur 66 F4
Addlethorpe Lincs 175 B8
Adel W Yorks 205 F11
Adeney Telford 150 F4
Adeyfield Herts 85 D9
Adfa Powys 129 C11
Adforton Hereford 115 C8
Adgestone IoW 21 D7
Adisham Kent 55 C8
Adlestrop Glos 100 F4
Adlingfleet E Yorks 199 C10
Adlington Ches E 184 E6
Lancs 194 E6
Adlington Park Lancs 194 E5
Admaston Staffs 151 E10
Telford 150 G2
Admington Warks 100 B4
Adpar Ceredig 92 C6
Adsborough Som 28 B3
Adscombe Som 43 F7
Adstock Bucks 102 E4
Adstone W Nhants 119 G11
Adswood Gtr Man 184 D5
Adversane W Sus 35 C9
Advie Highld 301 F11
Adwalton W Yorks 197 B8
Adwell Oxon 83 F11
Adwick le Street
S Yorks 198 F4
Adwick upon Dearne
S Yorks 198 G3
Adziel Aberds 303 D9
Ae Dumfries 247 F11
Ae Village Dumfries 247 F11
Affetside Gtr Man 195 E9
Affleck Aberds 303 G8
Affpuddle Dorset 18 C2
Affric Lodge Highld 299 G11
Afon Eitha Wrex 166 F3
Afon-wen Flint 181 G10
Afon Wen Gwyn 145 B8
Afton IoW 20 D2
Agar Nook Leics 153 G9
Agbrigg W Yorks 197 D10
Aggborough Worcs 116 B6
Agglethorpe N Yorks 213 B11
Aglionby Cumb 239 F10
Agneash IoM 192 D5
Aifft Denb 165 B10
Aigburth Mers 182 D5
Aiginis W Isles 304 E6
Aike E Yorks 209 D7
Aikenway Moray 302 E2
Aikerness Orkney 314 A4
Aikers Orkney 314 G4
Aiketgate Cumb 230 B5
Aikton Cumb 239 G7
Ailby Lincs 190 F6
Ailey Hereford 96 B6
Ailstone Warks 118 G4
Ailsworth Pboro 138 D2
Aimes Green Essex 86 E5
Ainderby Quernhow
N Yorks 215 C7
Ainderby Steeple
N Yorks 224 G6
Aingers Green Essex 108 G2
Ainley Top W Yorks 196 D6
Ainsdale Mers 193 E10
Ainsdale-on-Sea Mers 193 E9
Ainstable Cumb 230 B6
Ainsworth Gtr Man 195 E9
Ainthorpe N Yorks 226 D4
Aintree Mers 182 B5
Aird Argyll 275 C8
Dumfries 236 C2
Highld 299 B7
W Isles 296 F3
W Isles 304 E7
Airdachuilinn Highld 306 E7
Aird a Mhachair
W Isles 297 G3
Aird a' Mhulaidh
W Isles 305 G3
Aird Asaig W Isles 305 H3
Aird Dhail W Isles 304 B6
Airdens Highld 309 K6
Airdeny Argyll 289 G11
Aird Mhidhinis W Isles 297 L3
Aird Mhighe W Isles 296 C6
W Isles 305 J3
Aird Mhòr W Isles 297 G4
Aird Mhor W Isles 297 L3
Aird of Sleat Highld 295 E7
Airdrie N Lanark 268 B5
Airds of Kells Dumfries 237 B8
Aird Thunga W Isles 304 E6
Airdtorrisdale Highld 308 C6
Aird Uig W Isles 304 E2
Airedale W Yorks 198 B3
Aire View N Yorks 204 D5
Airidh a Bhruaich
W Isles 305 G4
Airieland Dumfries 237 D9
Airinis W Isles 304 E6
Airlie Angus 287 B7
Airlies Dumfries 236 D5
Airmyn E Yorks 199 B8
Airntully Perth 286 D4
Airor Highld 295 E9
Airth Falk 279 D7
Airthrey Castle
Stirlinging 278 B6
Airton N Yorks 204 B4
Airyhassen Dumfries 236 E5
Airy Hill N Yorks 227 D7
Airyligg Dumfries 236 C4
Aisby Lincs 155 B10
Lincs 188 C5
Aisgernis W Isles 297 J3
Aish Devon 8 C3
Devon 8 D6
Aisholt Som 43 F7
Aiskew N Yorks 214 B5
Aislaby N Yorks 216 B5
N Yorks 227 D7
Stockton 225 C8
Aisthorpe Lincs 188 E6
Aith Orkney 314 E2
Shetland 312 D8
Shetland 313 H5
Aithnen Powys 148 E4
Aithsetter Shetland 313 K6
Aitkenhead S Ayrs 245 B8
Aitnoch Highld 301 F9
Akeld Northumb 263 D11
Akeley Bucks 102 D4
Akenham Suff 108 B2
Albany T&W 243 F7
Albaston Corn 12 G4
Alberbury Shrops 149 G7
Albert Town Pembs 72 B6
Albert Village Leics 152 F6
Albourne W Sus 36 D3
Albourne Green W Sus 36 D3
Albrighton Shrops 132 C6
Shrops 149 F9
Albro Castle Ceredig 92 B3
Alburgh Norf 142 F5
Albury Herts 105 G8
Sur 50 D5
Albury End Herts 105 G8
Albury Heath Sur 50 D5
Albyfield Cumb 240 G2
Alby Hill Norf 160 C3
Alcaig Highld 300 D5
Alcaston Shrops 131 F9
Alcester Dorset 30 C5
Warks 117 F11
Alcester Lane's End
W Mid 133 G11
Alciston E Sus 23 D8
Alcombe Som 42 D3
Wilts 61 F10
Alconbury Cambs 122 B3
Alconbury Weald
Cambs 122 B4
Alconbury Weston
Cambs 122 B3
Aldbar Castle Angus 287 B9
Aldborough Norf 160 C3
N Yorks 215 F8
Aldborough Hatch
London 68 B3
Aldbourne Wilts 63 D9
Aldbrough E Yorks 209 F10
Aldbrough St John
N Yorks 224 C4
Aldbury Herts 85 C7
Aldcliffe Lancs 211 G9
Aldclune Perth 291 G11
Aldeburgh Suff 127 F9
Aldeby Norf 143 E8
Aldenham Herts 85 F10
Alderbrook E Sus 37 B8
Alderbury Wilts 31 B11
Aldercar Derbys 170 F6
Alderford Norf 160 F2
Alder Forest Gtr Man 184 B3
Alderholt Dorset 31 E10
Alderley Glos 80 G3
Alderley Edge Ches E 184 F4
Alderman's Green
W Mid 135 G7
Aldermaston W Berks 64 F5
Aldermaston Soke
W Berks 64 G6
Aldermaston Wharf
W Berks 64 F6
Alderminster Warks 100 B4
Aldermoor Soton 32 D5
Alder Moor Staffs 152 D4
Alderney BCP 18 C6
Alder Row Som 45 E9
Aldersbrook London 68 B2
Alder's End Hereford 98 C2
Aldersey Green Ches W 167 D7
Aldershawe Staffs 134 B2
Aldershot Hants 49 C11
Alderton Glos 99 E10
Shrops 149 E9
Suff 108 C6
Wilts 61 C10
W Nhants 102 B4
Alderton Fields Glos 99 E10
Alderwasley Derbys 170 E4
Aldfield N Yorks 214 F5
Aldford Ches W 166 D6
Aldgate Rutland 137 C9
Aldham Essex 107 F8
Suff 107 B10
Aldie Highld 309 L7
Aldingbourne W Sus 22 B6
Aldingham Cumb 210 E5
Aldington Kent 54 F5
Worcs 99 C11
Aldington Frith Kent 54 F4
Aldivalloch Moray 302 G3
Aldochlay Argyll 277 C7
Aldon Shrops 115 B8
Aldoth Cumb 229 B8
Aldourie Castle Highld 300 F6
Aldreth Cambs 123 C8
Aldridge W Mid 133 C11
Aldringham Suff 127 E8
Aldrington Brighton 36 F3
Aldsworth Glos 81 C11
Aldunie Moray 302 G3
Aldwark Derbys 170 D2
N Yorks 215 G9
Aldwarke S Yorks 186 C6
Aldwick W Sus 22 D6
Aldwincle N Nhants 137 G10
Aldworth W Berks 64 D5
Alehouseburn Aberds 302 C6
Alehousehill Aberds 303 G10
Ale Oak Shrops 130 G4
Alexandria W Dunb 277 F7
Aley Som 43 F7
Aley Green C Beds 85 B9
Alfardisworthy Devon 24 E3
Alfington Devon 15 B8
Alfold Sur 50 G4
Alfold Bars W Sus 50 G4
Alfold Crossways Sur 50 F4
Alford Aberds 293 B7
Lincs 191 F7
Som 44 G6
Alfred's Well Worcs 117 C8
Alfreton Derbys 170 D6
Alfrick Worcs 116 G4
Alfrick Pound Worcs 116 G4
Alfriston E Sus 23 E8
Algakirk Lincs 156 B5
Algaltraig Argyll 275 F11
Algarkirk Lincs 156 B5
Alhampton Som 44 G6
Aline Lodge W Isles 305 G3
Alisary Highld 289 B9
Alkborough N Lincs 199 C11
Alkerton Glos 80 D3
Oxon 101 C7
Alkham Kent 55 E9
Alkington Shrops 149 B10
Alkmonton Derbys 152 B3
Alkrington Garden Village
Gtr Man 195 G11
Alladale Lodge Highld 309 L4
Allaleigh Devon 8 E6
Allanaquoich Aberds 292 D3
Allanbank Borders 271 F10
N Lanark 268 D6
Allangrange Mains
Highld 300 D6
Allanshaugh Borders 271 F8
Allanshaws Borders 271 G9
Allanton Borders 273 E7
N Lanark 269 D7
S Lanark 268 E4
Allaston Glos 79 E10
Allathasdal W Isles 297 L2
Allbrook Hants 33 C7
All Cannings Wilts 62 G5
Allendale Town
Northumb 241 F8
Allen End Warks 134 D3
Allenheads Northumb 232 B3
Allensford Durham 242 G3
Allens Green Herts 87 B7
Allensmore Hereford 97 D9
Allenton Derby 153 C7
Allenwood Cumb 239 F11
Aller Devon 9 B7
Devon 27 F9
Dorset 30 G3
Som 28 B6
Allerby Cumb 229 D7
Allerford Som 27 B11
Som 42 D2
Aller Park Devon 9 B7
Allerston N Yorks 217 C7
Allerthorpe E Yorks 207 D11
Allerton Mers 182 D6
W Yorks 205 G8
Allerton Bywater
W Yorks 198 B2
Allerton Mauleverer
N Yorks 206 B4
Allesley W Mid 134 G6
Allestree Derby 152 B6
Allet Corn 4 F5
Allexton Leics 136 C6
Allgreave Ches E 169 B7
Allhallows Medway 69 D10
Allhallows-on-Sea
Medway 69 D10
Alligin Shuas Highld 299 D8
Allimore Green Staffs 151 F7
Allington Kent 53 B8
Lincs 172 G5
Wilts 47 F8
Wilts 61 D11
Wilts 62 G5
Allington Bar Wilts 61 E11
Allithwaite Cumb 211 D7
Alloa Clack 279 C7
Allonby Cumb 229 C7
Allostock Ches W 184 G2
Alloway S Ayrs 257 F8
Allowenshay Som 28 E5
All Saints Devon 28 G4
All Saints South Elmham
Suff 142 G6
Allscot Shrops 132 D4
Allscott Telford 150 G2
All Stretton Shrops 131 D9
Allt Carms 75 E9
Alltami Flint 166 B3
Alltbeithe Highld 290 C2
Alltchaorunn Highld 284 B5
Alltforgan Powys 147 E9
Alltmawr Powys 95 B11
Alltnacaillich Highld 308 E4
Allt-na-giubhsaich
Aberds 292 E4
Allt na h-Airbhe Highld 307 K6
Allt-nan-sùgh Highld 295 C11
Alltrech Argyll 289 F8
Alltsigh Highld 290 B6
Alltwalis Carms 93 E8
Alltwen Neath 76 E2
Alltyblaca Ceredig 93 B10
Allt-yr-yn Newport 59 B9

Allwood Green Suff 125 C10
Alma Notts 171 E7
Almagill Dumfries 238 B3
Almeley Hereford 114 G6
Almeley Wooton Hereford 114 G6
Almer Dorset 18 B4
Almholme S Yorks 198 F5
Almington Staffs 150 C4
Alminstone Cross Devon 24 C4
Almondbank Perth 286 E4
Almondbury W Yorks 197 D7
Almondsbury S Glos 60 C6
Almondvale W Loth 269 B11
Almshouse Green Essex 106 E5
Alne N Yorks 215 F9
Alne End Warks 118 F2
Alne Hills Warks 118 E2
Alness Highld 300 C6
Alnessferry Highld 300 C6
Alne Station N Yorks 215 F10
Alnham Northumb 263 G11
Alnmouth Northumb 264 G6
Alnwick Northumb 264 G5
Alperton London 67 C7
Alphamstone Essex 107 D7
Alpheton Suff 125 G7
Alphington Devon 14 C4
Alpington Norf 142 C5
Alport Derbys 170 C2
Powys 130 D5
Alpraham Ches E 167 D9
Alresford Essex 107 G11
Alrewas Staffs 152 F3
Alsager Ches E 168 D3
Alsagers Bank Staffs 168 F4
Alscot Bucks 84 E4
Alsop en le Dale Derbys 169 D11
Alston Cumb 231 B10
Devon 28 G4
Alstone Glos 99 E9
Glos 99 G8
Som 43 D10
Alstonefield Staffs 169 D10
Alston Sutton Som 44 C2
Alswear Devon 26 C2
Alt Gtr Man 196 G2
Altandhu Highld 307 H4
Altanduin Highld 311 G2
Altarnun Corn 11 E10
Altass Highld 309 J4
Altbough Hereford 97 E10
Altdargue Aberds 293 C7
Alterwall Highld 310 C6
Altham Lancs 203 G11
Alt Hill Gtr Man 196 G2
Althorne Essex 88 F6
Althorpe N Lincs 199 F10
Alticane S Ayrs 244 F6
Alticry Dumfries 236 D4
Altmore Windsor 65 D11
Altnabreac Station Highld 310 E4
Altnacealgach Hotel Highld 307 H7
Altnacraig Argyll 289 G10
Altnafeadh Highld 284 B6
Altnaharra Highld 308 F5
Altofts W Yorks 197 C11
Alton Derbys 170 C5
Hants 49 F8
Staffs 169 G9
Wilts 47 D7
Alton Barnes Wilts 62 G6
Altonhill E Ayrs 257 B10
Alton Pancras Dorset 30 G2
Alton Priors Wilts 62 G6
Altonside Moray 302 D2
Altour Highld 290 E4
Altrincham Gtr Man 184 D3
Altrua Highld 290 E4
Altskeith Stirling 285 G8
Altyre Ho Moray 301 D10
Alum Rock W Mid 134 F2
Alva Clack 279 B7
Alvanley Ches W 183 G7
Alvaston Derby 153 C7
Alvechurch Worcs 117 C10
Alvecote Warks 134 C4
Alvediston Wilts 31 C7
Alveley Shrops 132 G5
Alverdiscott Devon 25 B8
Alverstoke Hants 21 B8
Alverstone IoW 21 D7
Alverthorpe W Yorks 197 C10
Alverton Notts 172 G3
Alves Moray 301 C11
Alvescot Oxon 82 E3
Alveston S Glos 60 B6
Warks 118 F4
Alveston Down S Glos 60 B6
Alveston Hill Warks 118 G4
Alvie Highld 291 C10
Alvingham Lincs 190 C5
Alvington Glos 79 E10
Som 29 D8
Alwalton Cambs 138 D2
Alway Newport 59 B10
Alweston Dorset 29 E11
Alwington Devon 24 C6
Alwinton Northumb 251 B10
Alwoodley W Yorks 205 E11
Alwoodley Gates W Yorks 206 E2
Alwoodley Park W Yorks 205 E11
Alyth Perth 286 C6
Amalebra Corn 1 B5
Amalveor Corn 1 B5
Amatnatua Highld 309 K4
Am Baile W Isles 297 K3
Ambaston Derbys 153 C8
Ambergate Derbys 170 E4
Amber Hill Lincs 174 F2
Amberley Glos 80 E5
Hereford 97 B10
W Sus 35 E8
Amble Northumb 253 C7
Amblecote W Mid 133 F7
Ambler Thorn W Yorks 196 B5
Ambleside Cumb 221 E7
Ambleston Pembs 91 F10
Ambrosden Oxon 83 B10
Am Buth Argyll 289 G10
Amcotts N Lincs 199 E11
Amen Corner Brack 65 F10
Amersham Bucks 85 F7
Amersham Common Bucks 85 F7
Amersham Old Town Bucks 85 F7
Amersham on the Hill Bucks 85 F7
Amerton Staffs 151 D9
Amesbury Bath 45 B7
Wilts 47 E7
Ameysford Dorset 31 G9
Amington Staffs 134 C4
Amisfield Dumfries 247 G11
Amlwch Anglesey 178 C6
Amlwch Port Anglesey 179 C7
Ammanford = *Rhydaman* Carms 75 C10
Ammerham Som 28 F5
Amod Argyll 255 D8
Amotherby N Yorks 216 E4
Ampfield Hants 32 C6
Ampleforth N Yorks 215 D11
Ampney Crucis Glos 81 E9
Ampney St Mary Glos 81 E9
Ampney St Peter Glos 81 E9
Amport Hants 47 E9
Ampthill C Beds 103 D10
Ampton Suff 125 C7
Amroth Pembs 73 D11
Amulree Perth 286 D2
Amwell Herts 85 C11
Anagach Highld 301 G10
Anaheilt Highld 289 C10
Anancaun Highld 299 C10
An Caol Highld 298 D6
Ancarraig Highld 300 G4
Ancaster Lincs 173 G7
Anchor Shrops 130 G3
Anchorage Park Ptsmth 33 G11
Anchor Corner Norf 141 D10
Anchorsholme Blackpool 202 E2
Anchor Street Norf 160 E6
An Cnoc W Isles 304 E6
Ancoats Gtr Man 184 B5
Ancroft Northumb 273 F9
Ancroft Northmoor Northumb 273 F9
Ancrum Borders 262 E4
Ancton W Sus 35 G7
Ancumtoun Orkney 314 A7
Anderby Lincs 191 F8
Anderby Creek Lincs 191 F8
Andersea Som 43 G10
Andersfield Som 43 G8
Anderson Dorset 18 B3
Anderton Ches W 183 F10
Corn 7 E8
Lancs 194 E6
Andertons Mill Lancs 194 E4
Andover Hants 47 D11
Andover Down Hants 47 D11
Andoversford Glos 81 B8
Andreas IoM 192 C5
Andwell Hants 49 C7
Anelog Gwyn 144 D3
Anerley London 67 F10
Anfield Mers 182 C5
Angarrack Corn 2 B3
Angarrick Corn 3 B7
Angelbank Shrops 115 B11
Angersleigh Som 27 D11
Angerton Cumb 238 F6
Angle Pembs 72 E5
An Gleann Ur W Isles 304 E6
Angmering W Sus 35 G9
Angram N Yorks 206 D6
N Yorks 223 F7
Anick Northumb 241 D11
Anie Stirling 285 F9
Ankerdine Hill Worcs 116 F4
Ankerville Highld 301 B8
Anlaby E Yorks 200 B4
Anlaby Park Hull 200 B5
An Leth Meadhanach W Isles 297 K3
Anmer Norf 158 D4
Anmore Hants 33 E11
Annan Dumfries 238 D5
Annaside Cumb 210 B1
Annat Argyll 284 E4
Highld 290 D5
Highld 299 D8
Anna Valley Hants 47 E10
Annbank S Ayrs 257 E10
Annesley Notts 171 E8
Annesley Woodhouse Notts 171 E7
Annfield Plain Durham 242 G5
Anniesland Glasgow 267 B10
Annifirth Shetland 313 J3
Annishader Highld 298 D4
Annis Hill Suff 143 F7
Annitsford T&W 243 C7
Annscroft Shrops 131 B9
Ann's Hill Hants 33 G9
Annwell Place Derbys 152 F6
Ansdell Lancs 193 B10
Ansells End Herts 85 B11
Ansford Som 44 G6
Ansley Warks 134 E5
Ansley Common Warks 134 E6
Anslow Staffs 152 D4
Anslow Gate Staffs 152 D3
Ansteadbrook Sur 50 G2
Anstey Herts 105 E8
Leics 135 B10
Anstruther Easter Fife 287 G9
Anstruther Wester Fife 287 G9
Ansty Hants 49 E8
Warks 135 G7
Wilts 31 B7
W Sus 36 C3
Ansty Coombe Wilts 31 B7
Ansty Cross Dorset 30 G3
Anthill Common Hants 33 E10
Anthony Corn 7 E7
Anthony's Cross Glos 98 G4
Anthorn Cumb 238 F5
Antingham Norf 160 C5
An t-Ob W Isles 296 C6
Anton's Gowt Lincs 174 F3
Antonshill Falk 279 E7
Antony Corn 7 E7
Antony Passage Corn 7 D8
Antrobus Ches W 183 F10
Anvil Green Kent 54 D6
Anvilles W Berks 63 F10
Anwick Lincs 173 E10
Anwoth Dumfries 237 D7
Aonachan Highld 290 E4
Aoradh Argyll 274 G3
Apedale Staffs 168 F4
Aperfield London 52 B2
Apes Dale Worcs 117 C9
Apes Hall Cambs 139 E11
Apethorpe N Nhants 137 D10
Apeton Staffs 151 F7
Apley Lincs 189 F10
Apley Forge Shrops 132 D4
Apperknowle Derbys 186 F5
Apperley Glos 99 F7
Apperley Bridge W Yorks 205 F9
Apperley Dene Northumb 242 F3
Appersett N Yorks 223 G7
Appin Argyll 289 E11
Appin House Argyll 289 E11
Appleby N Lincs 200 E3
Appleby-in-Westmorland Cumb 231 G9
Appleby Magna Leics 134 B6
Appleby Parva Leics 134 B6
Applecross Highld 299 E7
Applecross Ho Highld 299 E7
Appledore Devon 27 E9
Devon 40 G3
Kent 39 B7
Appledore Heath Kent 54 G3
Appleford Oxon 83 G8
Applegarthtown Dumfries 248 G4
Applehouse Hill Windsor 65 C10
Applemore Hants 32 F5
Appleshaw Hants 47 D10
Applethwaite Cumb 229 F11
Appleton Halton 183 D8
Oxon 82 E6
Appleton-le-Moors N Yorks 216 B4
Appleton-le-Street N Yorks 216 E4
Appleton Park Warr 183 E10
Appleton Roebuck N Yorks 207 E7
Appleton Thorn Warr 183 E10
Appleton Wiske N Yorks 225 E7
Appletreehall Borders 262 F2
Appletreewick N Yorks 213 G11
Appley IoW 21 C8
Som 27 C9
Appley Bridge Lancs 194 F4
Apse Heath IoW 21 E7
Apsey Green Suff 126 E5
Apsley Herts 85 D9
Apsley End C Beds 104 E2
Apuldram W Sus 22 C4
Aqueduct Telford 132 B3
Aquhythie Aberds 293 B9
Arabella Highld 301 B8
Arbeadie Aberds 293 D8
Arberth = *Narberth* Pembs 73 C10
Arbirlot Angus 287 C10
Arboll Highld 311 L2
Arborfield Wokingham 65 F9
Arborfield Cross Wokingham 65 F9
Arborfield Garrison Wokingham 65 F9
Arbourthorne S Yorks 186 D5
Arbroath Angus 287 C10
Arbury Cambs 123 E8
Arbuthnott Aberds 293 F9
Archavandra Muir Highld 309 K7
Archdeacon Newton Darl 224 B5
Archenfield Hereford 96 C5
Archiestown Moray 302 E2
Archnalea Highld 289 C10
Arclid Ches E 168 C3
Arclid Green Ches E 168 C3
Ardachu Highld 309 J6
Ardailly Argyll 255 B7
Ardalanish Argyll 274 B4
Ardallie Aberds 303 F10
Ardalum Ho Argyll 288 F6
Ardamaleish Argyll 275 G11
Ardanaiseig Argyll 284 E4
Ardaneaskan Highld 295 B10
Ardanstur Argyll 275 B9
Ardargie House Hotel Perth 286 F4
Ardarroch Highld 295 B10
Ardban Highld 295 B9
Ardbeg Argyll 254 C5
Argyll 276 E3
Ardcharnich Highld 307 L6
Ardchiavaig Argyll 274 B4
Ardchonnell Argyll 275 B10
Ardchronie Highld 309 L6
Ardchuilk Highld 300 F2
Ardchullarie More Stirling 285 F9
Ardchyle Stirling 285 E9
Ardclach Highld 301 E9
Ard-dhubh Highld 299 E7
Arddleen Powys 148 F5
Ardechvie Highld 290 D3
Ardeley Herts 104 F6
Ardelve Highld 295 C10
Arden Argyll 277 E7
E Renf 267 D10
Ardencaple Ho Argyll 275 B8
Ardendrain Highld 300 F5
Arden Park Gtr Man 184 C6
Ardens Grafton Warks 118 G2
Ardentallen Argyll 289 G10
Ardentinny Argyll 276 D3
Ardentraive Argyll 275 F11
Ardeonaig Stirling 285 D10
Ardersier Highld 301 D7
Ardery Highld 289 C9
Ardessie Highld 307 L5
Ardfern Argyll 275 C9
Ardfernal Argyll 274 F6
Ardgartan Argyll 284 G6
Ardgay Highld 309 K5
Ardglassie Aberds 303 C10
Ardgour Highld 290 G2
Ardgye Moray 301 C11
Ardheslaig Highld 299 D7
Ardiecow Moray 302 C5
Ardinamir Argyll 275 B8
Ardindrean Highld 307 L6
Ardingly W Sus 36 B4
Ardington Oxon 64 B2
Ardington Wick Oxon 64 B2
Ardintoul Highld 295 C10
Ardlair Aberds 302 G5
Highld 299 B9
Ardlamey Argyll 255 C7
Ardlamont Ho Argyll 275 G10
Ardlawhill Aberds 303 C8
Ardleigh Essex 107 F11
Ardleigh Green London 68 B4
Ardleigh Heath Essex 107 E10
Ardler Perth 286 C6
Ardley Oxon 101 F10
Ardley End Essex 87 C8
Ardlui Argyll 285 F7
Ardlussa Argyll 275 E7
Ardmair Highld 307 K6
Ardmay Argyll 284 G6
Ardmenish Argyll 274 F6
Ardminish Argyll 255 C7
Ardmolich Highld 289 B9
Ardmore Argyll 289 G9
Highld 306 D7
Highld 309 L7
Ardnacross Argyll 289 E7
Ardnadam Argyll 276 F3
Ardnagowan Argyll 284 G4
Ardnagrask Highld 300 E5
Ardnarff Highld 295 B10
Ardnastang Highld 289 C10
Ardnave Argyll 274 F3
Ardneil N Ayrs 266 F3
Ardno Argyll 284 G5
Ardo Aberds 303 F8
Ardoch Argyll 277 F7
Perth 286 D4
Ardoch *continued* Stirling 285 F9
Ardochy House Highld 290 C4
Ardo Ho Aberds 303 G9
Ardoyne Aberds 302 G6
Ardpatrick Argyll 275 G8
Ardpatrick Ho Argyll 255 B8
Ardpeaton Argyll 276 D4
Ardradnaig Perth 285 C11
Ardrishaig Argyll 275 E9
Ardross Fife 287 G9
Highld 300 B6
Ardrossan N Ayrs 266 G4
Ardross Castle Highld 300 B6
Ardshave Highld 309 K7
Ardsheal Highld 289 D11
Ardshealach Highld 289 C8
Ardskenish Argyll 274 D4
Ardsley S Yorks 197 F11
Ardslignish Highld 289 C7
Ardtalla Argyll 254 B5
Ardtalnaig Perth 285 D11
Ardtaraig Argyll 275 E11
Ardtoe Highld 289 B8
Ardtreck Highld 294 B5
Ardtrostan Perth 285 E10
Ardtur Argyll 289 E11
Arduaine Argyll 275 B8
Ardullie Highld 300 C5
Ardvannie Highld 309 L6
Ardvar Highld 306 F6
Ardvasar Highld 295 E8
Ardveich Stirling 285 E10
Ardverikie Highld 291 E7
Ardvorlich Perth 285 E10
Ardwell Dumfries 236 E3
Moray 302 F3
S Ayrs 244 E5
Ardwell Mains Dumfries 236 E3
Ardwick Gtr Man 184 B5
Areley Kings Worcs 116 C6
Arford Hants 49 F10
Argoed Caerph 77 F11
Powys 113 E9
Powys 130 E5
Shrops 130 G6
Shrops 148 E6
Argos Hill E Sus 37 B9
Arichamish Argyll 275 C10
Arichastlich Argyll 284 D6
Aridhglas Argyll 288 G5
Arieniskill Highld 295 G9
Arileod Argyll 288 D3
Arinacrinachd Highld 299 D7
Arinagour Argyll 288 D4
Arineckaig Highld 299 E9
Arion Orkney 314 E2
Arisaig Highld 295 G8
Ariundle Highld 289 C10
Arivegaig Highld 289 C8
Arivoichallum Argyll 254 C4
Arkendale N Yorks 215 G7
Arkesden Essex 105 E9
Arkholme Lancs 211 E11
Arkleby Cumb 229 D8
Arkleton Dumfries 249 E9
Arkle Town N Yorks 223 E10
Arkley London 86 F2
Arksey S Yorks 198 F5
Arkwright Town Derbys 186 G6
Arle Glos 99 G8
Arlebrook Glos 80 D4
Arlecdon Cumb 219 B10
Arlescote Warks 101 B7
Arlesey C Beds 104 D3
Arleston Telford 150 G3
Arley Ches E 183 E11
Arley Green Ches E 183 E11
Arlingham Glos 80 C2
Arlington Devon 40 E6
E Sus 23 D8
Glos 81 D10
Arlington Beccott Devon 40 E6
Armadale Highld 308 C7
W Loth 269 B8
Armadale Castle Highld 295 E8
Armathwaite Cumb 230 B6
Armigers Essex 105 F11
Arminghall Norf 142 C5
Armitage Staffs 151 F11
Armitage Bridge W Yorks 196 E6
Armley W Yorks 205 G11
Armscote Warks 100 C4
Armsdale Staffs 150 C5
Armshead Staffs 168 F6
Armston N Nhants 137 F11
Armthorpe S Yorks 198 F6
Arnabost Argyll 288 D4
Arnaby Cumb 210 C3
Arncliffe N Yorks 213 E8
Arncroach Fife 287 G9
Arndilly Ho Moray 302 E2
Arne Dorset 18 D5
Arnesby Leics 136 E2
Arngask Perth 286 F5
Arnisdale Highld 295 D10
Arnish Highld 298 E5
Arniston Midloth 270 C6
Arnol W Isles 304 D5
Arnold E Yorks 209 E8
Notts 171 F9
Arno's Vale Bristol 60 E6
Arnprior Stirling 278 C2
Arnside Cumb 211 D9
Aros Mains Argyll 289 E7
Arowry Wrex 149 B9
Arpafeelie Highld 300 D6
Arpinge Kent 55 F7
Arrad Foot Cumb 210 C6
Arram E Yorks 208 E6
Arrathorne N Yorks 224 G4
Arreton IoW 20 D6
Arrington Cambs 122 G6
Arrivain Argyll 284 D6
Arrochar Argyll 284 G6
Arrow Warks 117 F11
Arrowe Hill Mers 182 D3
Arrowfield Top Worcs 117 C10
Arrow Green Hereford 115 F8
Arrunden W Yorks 196 F6
Arscaig Highld 309 H5
Arscott Shrops 131 B8
Arthill Ches E 184 D2
Arthington W Yorks 205 E11
Arthingworth W Nhants 136 G5
Arthog Gwyn 146 G2
Arthrath Aberds 303 F9
Arthursdale W Yorks 206 F3
Arthurstone Perth 286 C6
Arthurville Highld 309 L7
Artington Sur 50 D3
Artrochie Aberds 303 F10
Arundel W Sus 35 F8
Arwick Orkney 314 D3
Aryhoulan Highld 290 G2
Asby Cumb 229 G7
Ascog Argyll 266 C2
Ascoil Highld 311 H2
Ascot Windsor 66 F2
Ascott Warks 100 E6
Ascott d'Oyley Oxon 82 B4
Ascott Earl Oxon 82 B3
Ascott-under-Wychwood Oxon 82 B4
Asenby N Yorks 215 D7
Asfordby Leics 154 F4
Asfordby Hill Leics 154 F4
Asgarby Lincs 173 F10
Lincs 174 B4
Ash Devon 8 F6
Dorset 30 E5
Kent 55 B9
Kent 68 G5
Som 28 C3
Som 29 C7
Sur 49 C11
Ashaig Highld 295 C8
Ashampstead W Berks 64 D5
Ashampstead Green W Berks 64 D5
Ashansworth Hants 48 B2
Ashbank Kent 53 C10
Ash Bank Staffs 168 F6
Ashbeer Som 42 F5
Ashbocking Suff 126 G3
Ashbourne Derbys 169 F11
Ashbrittle Som 27 C9
Ashbrook Shrops 131 E9
Ash Bullayne Devon 26 G3
Ashburnham Forge E Sus 23 B11
Ashburton Devon 8 B5
Ashbury Devon 12 B6
Oxon 63 C9
Ashby N Lincs 200 F2
Ashby by Partney Lincs 174 B6
Ashby cum Fenby NE Lincs 201 G9
Ashby de la Launde Lincs 173 D9
Ashby-de-la-Zouch Leics 153 F7
Ashby Folville Leics 154 G4
Ashby Hill NE Lincs 201 G8
Ashby Magna Leics 135 E11
Ashby Parva Leics 135 F10
Ashby Puerorum Lincs 190 G4
Ashby St Ledgers W Nhants 119 D11
Ashby St Mary Norf 142 C6
Ashchurch Glos 99 E8
Ashcombe Devon 14 F4
Ashcombe Park N Som 59 G10
Ashcott Som 44 F2
Ashcott Corner Som 44 F2
Ashculme Devon 27 E10
Ashdon Essex 105 C11
Ashe Hants 48 D4
Asheldham Essex 89 E7
Ashen Essex 106 C4
Ashendon Bucks 84 C2
Asheridge Bucks 84 E6
Ashey IoW 21 D7
Ashfield Argyll 275 E8
Carms 94 F3
Hants 32 D5
Hereford 97 G11
Shrops 148 D6
Stirling 285 G11
Suff 126 E4
Ashfield Cum Thorpe Suff 126 E4
Ashfield Green Suff 124 F5
Suff 126 C5
Ashfields Shrops 150 D4
Ashfold Crossways W Sus 36 B2
Ashfold Side N Yorks 214 F2
Ashford Devon 8 F3
Devon 40 F4
Hants 31 E10
Kent 54 E4
Sur 66 E5
Ashford Bowdler Shrops 115 C10
Ashford Carbonell Shrops 115 C10
Ashford Common Sur 66 E5
Ashford Hill Hants 64 G5
Ashford in the Water Derbys 185 G11
Ashgate Derbys 186 G5
Ashgill S Lanark 268 F5
Ash Green Sur 50 D2
Warks 134 F6
Ashgrove Bath 45 B8
Ash Grove Wrex 166 G5
Ash Hill Devon 14 G4
Ashiestiel Borders 261 B10
Ashill Devon 27 E9
Norf 141 C7
Som 28 D4
Ashingdon Essex 88 G5
Ashington BCP 18 B6
Northumb 253 F7
Som 29 C9
W Sus 35 D10
Ashington End Lincs 175 B8
Ashintully Castle Perth 292 G3
Ashkirk Borders 261 E11
Ashlett Hants 33 G7
Ashleworth Glos 98 F6
Ashley Cambs 124 E3
Ches E 184 E3
Devon 25 E10
Dorset 31 G10
Glos 80 G6
Hants 19 B11
Hants 47 G11
Kent 55 D10
N Nhants 136 E5
Staffs 150 B5
Wilts 61 F10
Ashley Dale Staffs 150 B5
Ashley Down Bristol 60 D5
Ashley Green Bucks 85 D7
Ashleyhay Derbys 170 E3
Ashley Heath Ches E 184 D3
Dorset 31 G10
Staffs 150 B4
Ashley Moor Hereford 115 D9
Ashley Park Sur 66 F6
Ash Magna Shrops 149 B11
Ashmanhaugh Norf 160 E6
Ashmansworth Hants 48 B2
Ashmansworthy Devon 24 D4
Ashmead Green Glos 80 F3
Ashmill Devon 12 B3
Ash Mill Devon 26 C3
Ash Moor Devon 26 D3
Ashmore Dorset 30 D6
Ashmore Green W Berks 64 F4
Ashmore Lake W Mid 133 D9
Ashmore Park W Mid 133 C9
Ashnashellach Lodge Highld 299 E10
Ashopton Derbys 185 D11
Ashorne Warks 118 F6
Ashover Derbys 170 C4
Ashover Hay Derbys 170 C5
Ashow Warks 118 C6
Ash Parva Shrops 149 B11
Ashperton Hereford 98 C2
Ashprington Devon 8 D6
Ash Priors Som 27 B11
Ashreigney Devon 25 E10
Ashridge Court Devon 25 G11
Ash Street Suff 107 B10
Ashtead Sur 51 B7
Ash Thomas Devon 27 E8
Ashton Corn 2 D4
Hants 33 D9
Hereford 115 E10
Invclyd 276 F4
N Nhants 137 F11
Pboro 138 B2
Som 44 D2
W Nhants 102 B5
Ashton Common Wilts 45 B11
Ashton Gate Bristol 60 E5
Ashton Green E Sus 23 C7
Ashton Hayes Ches W 167 B8
Ashton Heath Halton 183 F9
Ashton-in-Makerfield Gtr Man 183 B9
Ashton Keynes Wilts 81 G8
Ashton under Hill Worcs 99 D9
Ashton-under-Lyne Gtr Man 184 B6
Ashton upon Mersey Gtr Man 184 C3
Ashton Vale Bristol 60 E5
Ashurst Hants 32 E4
Kent 52 F4
Lancs 194 F3
W Sus 35 D11
Ashurst Bridge Hants 32 E4
Ashurst Wood W Sus 52 F2
Ashvale Bl Gwent 77 C10
Ash Vale Sur 49 C11
Ashwater Devon 12 B3
Ashwell Devon 14 G3
Herts 104 D5
Rutland 155 G7
Som 28 D5
Ashwell End Herts 104 C5
Ashwellthorpe Norf 142 D2
Ashwick Som 44 D6
Ashwicken Norf 158 F4
Ashwood Staffs 133 F7
Ashybank Borders 262 F2
Askam in Furness Cumb 210 D4
Askern S Yorks 198 E5
Askerswell Dorset 16 C6
Askerton Hill Lincs 172 F4
Askett Bucks 84 D4
Askham Cumb 230 G6
Notts 188 G2
Askham Bryan York 207 D7
Askham Richard York 206 D6
Asknish Argyll 275 D10
Askrigg N Yorks 223 G8
Askwith N Yorks 205 D9
Aslackby Lincs 155 C11
Aslacton Norf 142 E3
Aslockton Notts 154 B4
Asloun Aberds 293 B7
Asney Som 44 F3
Aspall Suff 126 D3
Aspatria Cumb 229 C8
Aspenden Herts 105 F7
Asperton Lincs 156 B5
Aspley Nottingham 171 G8
Staffs 150 C6
Aspley Guise C Beds 103 D8
Aspley Heath C Beds 103 D8
Warks 117 C11
Aspull Gtr Man 194 F6
Aspult Common Gtr Man 183 B10
Assater Shetland 312 F4
Asselby E Yorks 199 B8
Asserby Lincs 191 F7
Asserby Turn Lincs 191 F7
Assington Suff 107 D8
Assington Green Suff 124 G5
Assynt Ho Highld 300 C5
Astbury Ches E 168 C4
Astcote W Nhants 120 G3
Asterby Lincs 190 F3
Asterley Shrops 131 B7
Asterton Shrops 131 E7
Asthall Oxon 82 C3
Asthall Leigh Oxon 82 C4
Astle Ches E 184 G4
Highld 309 K7
Astley Gtr Man 195 G8
Shrops 149 F10
Warks 134 F6
Worcs 116 D5
Astley Abbotts Shrops 132 D4
Astley Bridge Gtr Man 195 E8
Astley Cross Worcs 116 D6
Astley Green Gtr Man 184 B2
Astmoor Halton 183 E8
Aston Ches E 167 F10
Ches W 183 F9
Derbys 152 C3
Derbys 185 E11
Flint 166 B4
Hereford 115 C9
Hereford 115 E9
Herts 104 G5
Oxon 82 E4
Powys 130 E5
Shrops 132 E6
Shrops 149 D10
Staffs 151 E7
Staffs 168 G3
S Yorks 187 D7
Telford 132 B2
W Mid 133 F11
Wokingham 65 C9
Aston Abbotts Bucks 102 G6
Aston Bank Worcs 116 C2
Aston Botterell Shrops 132 G2
Aston-by-Stone Staffs 151 C8
Aston Cantlow Warks 118 F2
Aston Clinton Bucks 84 C5
Aston Crews Hereford 98 G3
Aston Cross Glos 99 E8
Aston End Herts 104 G5
Aston Eyre Shrops 132 E3
Aston Fields Worcs 117 D9
Aston Flamville Leics 135 E9
Aston Ingham Hereford 98 G3
Aston juxta Mondrum Ches E 167 D11
Aston le Walls W Nhants 119 G9
Aston Magna Glos 100 D3
Aston Munslow Shrops 131 F10
Aston on Carrant Glos 99 E8
Aston on Clun Shrops 131 G7
Aston-on-Trent Derbys 153 D8
Aston Pigott Shrops 130 B6
Aston Rogers Shrops 130 B6
Aston Rowant Oxon 84 F2
Aston Sandford Bucks 84 D3
Aston Somerville Worcs 99 D10
Aston Square Shrops 148 D6
Aston Subedge Glos 100 C2
Aston Tirrold Oxon 64 B5
Aston Upthorpe Oxon 64 B5
Astrop W Nhants 101 D10
Astrope Herts 84 C5
Astwick C Beds 104 D4
Astwith Derbys 170 C6
Astwood M Keynes 103 B9
Worcs 117 D8
Worcs 117 F7
Astwood Bank Worcs 117 E10
Aswarby Lincs 173 G9
Aswardby Lincs 190 G5
Atcham Shrops 131 B10
Atch Lench Worcs 117 G10
Athelhampton Dorset 17 C11
Athelington Suff 126 C4
Athelney Som 28 B4
Athelstaneford E Loth 281 F10
Atherfield Green IoW 20 F5
Atherington Devon 25 C9
W Sus 35 G8
Athersley North S Yorks 197 F11
Athersley South S Yorks 197 F11
Atherstone Som 28 D5
Warks 134 D6
Atherstone on Stour Warks 118 G4
Atherton Gtr Man 195 G7
Athnamulloch Highld 299 G11
Athron Hall Perth 286 G4
Atley Hill N Yorks 224 E5
Atlow Derbys 170 F2
Attadale Highld 295 B11
Attadale Ho Highld 295 B11
Attenborough Notts 153 B10
Atterbury M Keynes 103 D7
Atterby Lincs 189 C7
Attercliffe S Yorks 186 D5
Atterley Shrops 132 D2
Atterton Leics 135 D7
Attleborough Norf 141 D10
Warks 135 E7
Attlebridge Norf 160 F2
Attleton Green Suff 124 G4
Atwick E Yorks 209 C9
Atworth Wilts 61 F11
Auberrow Hereford 97 B9
Aubourn Lincs 172 C6
Auch Argyll 285 D7
Auchagallon N Ayrs 255 D9
Auchallater Aberds 292 E3
Auchareoch N Ayrs 255 E10
Aucharnie Aberds 302 E6
Auchattie Aberds 293 D8
Auchavan Angus 292 G3
Auchbreck Moray 302 G2
Auchenback E Renf 267 D10
Auchenbainzie Dumfries 247 D8
Auchenblae Aberds 293 F9
Auchenbrack Dumfries 247 D7
Auchenbreck Argyll 255 C8
Argyll 275 E11
Auchencairn Dumfries 237 D9
Dumfries 247 G11
N Ayrs 256 D2
Auchencairn Ho Dumfries 237 D10
Auchencar N Ayrs 255 D9
Auchencarroch W Dunb 277 E8
Auchencrosh S Ayrs 236 B3
Auchencrow Borders 273 C7
Auchendinny Midloth 270 C5
Auchengray S Lanark 269 E9
Auchenhalrig Moray 302 C3
Auchenharvie N Ayrs 266 G5
Auchenheath S Lanark 268 G6
Auchenhew N Ayrs 256 E2
Auchenlaich Stirling 285 G10
Auchenleck Dumfries 237 D9
Auchenlochan Argyll 275 F10
Auchenmalg Dumfries 236 D4
Auchenreoch E Dunb 278 F3
Auchensoul S Ayrs 245 E7
Auchentibber S Lanark 268 E3
Auchentiber N Ayrs 267 F7
Auchertyre Highld 295 C10
Auchessan Stirling 285 E8
Auchgourish Highld 291 B11
Auchinairn E Dunb 268 B2
Auchindrain Argyll 284 G4
Auchindrean Highld 307 L6
Auchininna Aberds 302 E6
Auchinleck Dumfries 236 B6
E Ayrs 258 E3
Auchinloch N Lanark 278 G3
Auchinner Perth 285 F10
Auchinraith S Lanark 268 D3
Auchinroath Moray 302 D2
Auchinstarry N Lanark 278 F4
Auchintoul Aberds 293 B7
Highld 309 K5
Auchiries Aberds 303 F10
Auchlee Aberds 293 D10
Auchleeks Ho Perth 291 G9
Auchleven Aberds 302 G6
Auchlinn Aberds 303 D7
Auchlochan S Lanark 259 B8
Auchlossan Aberds 293 C7
Auchlunachan Highld 307 L6
Auchlunies Aberds 293 D10
Auchlyne Stirling 285 E9
Auchmacoy Aberds 303 F9
Auchmair Moray 302 G3
Auchmantle Dumfries 236 C3
Auchmenzie Aberds 302 G5
Auchmillan E Ayrs 258 D2
Auchmithie Angus 287 C10
Auchmore Highld 300 D4
Auchmuirbridge Fife 286 G6
Auchmull Angus 293 F7
Auchnacraig Argyll 289 G9
Auchnacree Angus 292 G6
Auchnafree Perth 286 D2
Auchnagallin Highld 301 F10
Auchnagarron Argyll 275 E11
Auchnagatt Aberds 303 E9
Auchnaha Argyll 275 E10
Auchnahillin Highld 301 F7
Auchnarrow Moray 302 G2
Auchnashelloch Perth 285 F11
Auchnotteroch Dumfries 236 C1
Aucholzie Aberds 292 D5
Auchrannie Angus 286 B6
Auchroisk Highld 301 G10
Auchronie Angus 292 E6
Auchterarder Perth 286 F3
Auchteraw Highld 290 C5
Auchterderran Fife 280 B4
Auchterhouse Angus 287 D7
Auchtermuchty Fife 286 F6
Auchterneed Highld 300 D4
Auchtertool Fife 280 C4
Auchtertyre Moray 301 D11
Stirling 285 E7
Auchtubh Stirling 285 E9
Auckengill Highld 310 C7
Auckley S Yorks 199 G7
Audenshaw Gtr Man 184 B6
Audlem Ches E 167 G11
Audley Staffs 168 E3
Audley End Essex 105 D10
Essex 106 D6
Norf 142 G2
Suff 125 G7
Auds Aberds 302 C6
Aughertree Cumb 229 D11
Aughton E Yorks 207 F10
Lancs 193 F11
Lancs 211 F10
S Yorks 187 D7
Wilts 47 B8
Aughton Park Lancs 194 F2
Aukside Durham 232 F4
Auldearn Highld 301 D9
Aulden Hereford 115 G9
Auldgirth Dumfries 247 F10
Auldhame E Loth 281 E11
Auldhouse S Lanark 268 E2
Auldtown of Carnoustie Aberds 302 E6
Ault a'chruinn Highld 295 C11
Aultanrynie Highld 308 F3
Aultbea Highld 307 L3
Aultdearg Highld 300 C2
Aultgrishan Highld 307 L2
Aultguish Inn Highld 300 B3
Ault Hucknall Derbys 171 B7
Aultibea Highld 311 G4
Aultiphurst Highld 310 C2
Aultivullin Highld 310 C2
Aultmore Highld 301 G10
Moray 302 D4
Aultnagoire Highld 300 G5
Aultnamain Inn Highld 309 L6
Aultnaslat Highld 290 C3
Aulton Aberds 302 G6
Aulton of Atherb Aberds 303 E9
Aultvaich Highld 300 E5
Aunby Lincs 155 G10
Aundorach Highld 291 B11
Aunk Devon 27 G8
Aunsby Lincs 155 B10
Auquhorthies Aberds 303 G8
Aust S Glos 60 B5
Austendike Lincs 156 E5
Austen Fen Lincs 190 C5
Austenwood Bucks 66 B3
Austerfield S Yorks 187 C11
Austerlands Gtr Man 196 F3
Austhorpe W Yorks 206 G3
Austrey Warks 134 B5
Austwick N Yorks 212 F5
Authorpe Lincs 190 E6
Authorpe Row Lincs 191 G8
Avebury Wilts 62 F6
Avebury Trusloe Wilts 62 F5
Aveley Thurrock 68 C5
Avening Glos 80 F5
Avening Green S Glos 80 G2
Averham Notts 172 E3
Avernish Highld 295 C10
Avery Hill London 68 E2
Aveton Gifford Devon 8 F3
Avielochan Highld 291 B11
Aviemore Highld 291 B10
Avington Hants 48 G4
W Berks 63 F11
Avoch Highld 301 D7
Avon Hants 19 B8
Wilts 62 D3
Avonbridge Falk 279 G8
Avoncliff Wilts 45 B10
Avon Dassett Warks 101 B8
Avonmouth Bristol 60 D4
Avonwick Devon 8 D4
Awbridge Hants 32 C4
Awhirk Dumfries 236 D2
Awkley S Glos 60 B5
Awliscombe Devon 27 G10
Awre Glos 80 D2
Awsworth Notts 171 G7
Axbridge Som 44 C2
Axford Hants 48 E6
Wilts 63 F8
Axmansford Hants 64 G5
Axminster Devon 15 B11
Axmouth Devon 15 C11
Axton Flint 181 E10
Axtown Devon 7 B10
Axwell Park T&W 242 E5
Aycliff Kent 55 E10
Aycliffe Durham 233 G11
Aydon Northumb 242 D2
Aykley Heads Durham 233 C11
Aylburton Glos 79 E10
Aylburton Common Glos 79 E10
Ayle Northumb 231 B10
Aylesbeare Devon 14 C6
Aylesbury Bucks 84 C4
Aylesby NE Lincs 201 F8
Aylesford Kent 53 B8
Aylesham Kent 55 C8
Aylestone Leicester 135 C11
Aylestone Hill Hereford 97 C10
Aylestone Park Leicester 135 C11
Aylmerton Norf 160 B3
Aylsham Norf 160 D3
Aylton Hereford 98 D3
Aylworth Glos 100 G2
Aymestrey Hereford 115 D8
Aynho W Nhants 101 E10
Ayot Green Herts 86 C2
Ayot St Lawrence Herts 85 B11
Ayot St Peter Herts 86 B2
Ayr S Ayrs 257 E8
Ayre of Atler Shetland 313 G6
Ayres Shetland 313 H5
Ayres End Herts 85 C11
Ayres of Selivoe Shetland 313 J4
Ayres Quay T&W 243 F9
Aysgarth N Yorks 213 B10
Ayshford Devon 27 D8
Ayside Cumb 211 C7
Ayston Rutland 137 C7
Aythorpe Roding Essex 87 B9
Ayton Borders 273 C8
T&W 243 F7
Ayton Castle Borders 273 C8
Aywick Shetland 312 E7
Azerley N Yorks 214 E5

B

Babbacombe Torbay 9 B8
Babbington Notts 171 G7
Babbinswood Shrops 148 C6
Babbs Green Herts 86 B5
Babcary Som 29 B9
Babel Carms 94 D6
Babel Green Suff 106 B4
Babell Flint 181 G11
Babeny Devon 13 F9
Babingley Norf 158 D3
Babraham Cambs 123 G10
Babworth Notts 187 E11
Bac W Isles 304 D6

Bachau Anglesey 178 E6
Bache Shrops 131 G9
Bacheldre Powys 130 E4
Bachelor's Bump E Sus 38 E4
Bache Mill Shrops 131 F10
Bach-y-gwreiddyn Swansea 75 E10
Backaland Orkney 314 C5
Backaskaill Orkney 314 A4
Backbarrow Cumb 211 C7
Backbower Gtr Man 185 C7
Backburn Aberds 293 D10
Backe Carms 74 B3
Backfolds Aberds 303 D10
Backford Ches W 182 G6
Backford Cross Ches W 182 G5
Backhill Aberds 303 F7
Aberds 303 F10
Backhill of Clackriach Aberds 303 E9
Backhill of Fortree Aberds 303 E9
Backhill of Trustach Aberds 293 D8
Backies Highld 311 J2
Backlass Highld 310 D6
Highld 310 E4
Back Muir Fife 279 D11
Back of Keppoch Highld 295 G8
Back o' th' Brook Staffs 169 E9
Back Rogerton E Ayrs 258 E3
Back Street Suff 124 F4
Backwell N Som 60 F3
Backwell Common N Som 60 F3
Backwell Green N Som 60 F3
Backworth T&W 243 C8
Bacon End Essex 87 B10
Baconend Green Essex 87 B10
Bacon's End W Mid 134 F3
Baconsthorpe Norf 160 B2
Bacton Hereford 97 E7
Norf 160 C6
Suff 125 D11
Bacton Green Norf 160 C6
Suff 125 D10
Bacup Lancs 195 C11
Badachonacher Highld 300 B6
Badachro Highld 299 B7
Badanloch Lodge Highld 308 F7
Badarach Highld 309 K5
Badavanich Highld 299 D11
Badbea Highld 307 K5
Badbury Swindon 63 C7
Badbury Wick Swindon 63 C7
Badby W Nhants 119 F11
Badcall Highld 306 D7
Badcaul Highld 307 K5
Baddeley Edge Stoke 168 E6
Baddeley Green Stoke 168 E6
Baddesley Clinton Warks 118 C4
Baddesley Ensor Warks 134 D5
Baddidarach Highld 307 G5
Baddoch Aberds 292 E3
Baddock Highld 301 D7
Baddow Park Essex 88 E2
Badeach Moray 302 F2
Badenscallie Highld 307 J5
Badenscoth Aberds 303 F7
Badentoy Park Aberds 293 D11
Badenyon Aberds 292 B5
Badgall Corn 11 D10
Badgeney Cambs 139 D8
Badger Shrops 132 D5
Badgergate Stirling 278 B5
Badger's Hill Worcs 99 B10
Badger's Mount Kent 68 G3
Badger Street Som 28 D3
Badgeworth Glos 80 B6
Badgworth Som 43 C11
Badharlick Corn 11 D11
Badicaul Highld 295 C9
Badingham Suff 126 D6
Badintagairt Highld 309 H4
Badlesmere Kent 54 C4
Badlipster Highld 310 E6
Badluarach Highld 307 K4
Badminton S Glos 61 C10
Badnaban Highld 307 G5
Badnabay Highld 306 E7
Badnagie Highld 310 F5
Badninish Highld 309 K7
Badrallach Highld 307 K5
Badsey Worcs 99 C11
Badshalloch W Dunb 277 D9
Badshot Lea Sur 49 D11
Badsworth W Yorks 198 E3
Badwell Ash Suff 125 D9
Badwell Green Suff 125 D10
Badworthy Devon 8 C3
Bae Cinmel *=Kinmel Bay* Conwy 181 E7
Bae Colwyn *=Colwyn Bay* Conwy 180 F4
Bae Penrhyn *=Penrhyn Bay* Conwy 180 E4
Baffins Ptsmth 33 G11
Bagber Dorset 30 E3
Bagby N Yorks 215 C9
Bagby Grange N Yorks 215 C9
Bag Enderby Lincs 190 G5
Bagendon Glos 81 D8
Bagginswood Shrops 132 G3
Baggrow Cumb 229 C9
Bàgha Chàise W Isles 296 D5
Bagh a Chaisteil W Isles 297 M2
Bagham Kent 54 C5
Baghasdal W Isles 297 K3
Bagh Mor W Isles 296 F4
Bagh Shiarabhagh W Isles 297 L3
Bagillt Flint 182 F2
Baginton Warks 118 C6
Baglan Neath 57 C8
Bagley Shrops 149 D8
Som 44 D3
W Yorks 205 F10
Bagley Green Som 27 D10
Bagley Marsh Shrops 149 D7
Bagmore Hants 49 E7
Bagnall Staffs 168 E6
Bagnor W Berks 64 F3
Bagpath Glos 80 E5
Glos 80 G4
Bagshaw Derbys 185 E9
Bagshot Sur 66 G2
Wilts 63 F10
Bagshot Heath Sur 66 G2
Bagslate Moor Gtr Man 195 E11
Bagstone S Glos 61 B7
Bagthorpe Norf 158 C5
Notts 171 E7
Baguley Gtr Man 184 D4
Bagworth Leics 135 B8
Bagwyllydiart Hereford 97 F8
Bagwy Llydiart Hereford 97 F8
Bail Àrd Bhuirgh W Isles 304 C6
Bailbrook Bath 61 F9
Baildon W Yorks 205 F9
Baildon Green W Yorks 205 F8
Baile W Isles 296 C5
Baile Ailein W Isles 304 F4
Baile a Mhanaich W Isles 296 F3
Baile an Truiseil W Isles 304 C5
Bailebeag Highld 291 B7
Baile Boidheach Argyll 275 F8
Baile Gharbhaidh W Isles 297 G3
Baile Glas W Isles 296 F4
Baile Mhartainn W Isles 296 D3
Baile Mhic Phail W Isles 296 D4
Baile Mor Argyll 288 G4
W Isles 296 E3
Baile na Creige W Isles 297 L2
Baile nan Cailleach W Isles 296 F3
Baile Raghaill W Isles 296 D3
Bailey Green Hants 33 B11
Baileyhead Cumb 240 B2
Bailiesward Aberds 302 F4
Bailiff Bridge W Yorks 196 C6
Baillieston Glasgow 268 C3
Bail' Iochdrach W Isles 296 F4
Bailrigg Lancs 202 B5
Bail Uachdraich W Isles 296 E4
Bail' Ur Tholastaidh W Isles 304 D7
Bainbridge N Yorks 223 G8
Bainsford Falk 279 E7
Bainshole Aberds 302 F6
Bainton E Yorks 208 C5
Oxon 101 F11
Pboro 137 B11
Baintown Fife 287 G7
Bairnkine Borders 262 F5
Baker's Cross Kent 53 F9
Bakers End Herts 86 B5
Baker's Hill Glos 79 C9
Baker Street Thurrock 68 C6
Baker's Wood Bucks 66 B4
Bakesdown Corn 24 G2
Bakestone Moor Derbys 187 F8
Bakewell Derbys 170 B2
Bala *=Y Bala* Gwyn 147 B8
Balachroick Highld 291 C10
Balachuirn Highld 298 E5
Balance Hill Staffs 151 C11
Balavil Highld 291 C9
Balavoulin Perth 291 G10
Balbeg Highld 300 F4
Highld 300 G4
Balbeggie Perth 286 E5
Balbegno Castle Aberds 293 F8
Balbithan Aberds 293 B9
Balbithan Ho Aberds 293 B10
Balblair Highld 300 E5
Highld 301 C7
Highld 309 K5
Balby S Yorks 198 G5
Balcherry Highld 311 L2
Balchladich Highld 306 F5
Balchraggan Highld 300 E5
Highld 300 F5
Highld 300 G5
Balchrick Highld 306 D6
Balchrystie Fife 287 G8
Balcladaich Highld 300 G2
Balcombe W Sus 51 G10
Balcombe Lane W Sus 51 G10
Balcomie Fife 287 F10
Balcraggie Lodge Highld 310 F5
Balcurvie Fife 287 G7
Baldersby N Yorks 215 D7
Baldersby St James N Yorks 215 D7
Balderstone Gtr Man 196 E2
Lancs 203 G8
Balderton Ches W 166 C5
Notts 172 E4
Baldhu Corn 4 G5
Baldingstone Gtr Man 195 E10
Baldinnie Fife 287 F8
Baldock Herts 104 E4
Baldon Row Oxon 83 E9
Baldoon Highld 300 B6
Baldovie Dundee 287 D8
Baldrine IoM 192 D5
Baldslow E Sus 38 E3
Baldwin IoM 192 D4
Baldwinholme Cumb 239 G8
Baldwin's Gate Staffs 168 G3
Baldwins Hill W Sus 51 F11
Bale Norf 159 B10
Balearn Aberds 303 D10
Balemartine Argyll 288 E1
Balephuil Argyll 288 E1
Balerno Edin 270 B3
Balerominhor Argyll 274 D4
Balevullin Argyll 288 E1
Balfield Angus 293 G7
Balfour Orkney 314 E4
Balfour Mains Orkney 314 E4
Balfron Stirling 277 D10
Balfron Station Stirling 277 D10
Balgaveny Aberds 302 E6
Balgavies Angus 287 B9
Balgonar Fife 279 C10
Balgove Aberds 303 F8
Balgowan Highld 291 D8
Perth 286 E3
Balgown Highld 298 C3
Balgrennie Aberds 292 C6
Balgrochan E Dunb 278 F2
Balgy Highld 299 D8
Balhaldie Stirling 286 G2
Balhalgardy Aberds 303 G7
Balham London 67 E9
Balhary Perth 286 C6
Baliasta Shetland 312 C8
Baligill Highld 310 C2
Baligortan Argyll 288 E5
Baligrundle Argyll 289 E10
Balindore Argyll 289 F11
Balinoe Argyll 288 E1
Balintore Angus 286 B6
Highld 301 B8
Balintraid Highld 301 B7
Balintuim Aberds 292 E3
Balk N Yorks 215 C9
Balkeerie Angus 287 C7
Balkemback Angus 287 D7
Balk Field Notts 188 E2
Balkholme E Yorks 199 B9
Balkissock S Ayrs 244 G4
Ball Corn 10 G6
Shrops 148 D6
Ballabeg IoM 192 E3
Ballacannel IoM 192 D5
Ballachraggan Moray 301 E11
Ballachrochin Highld 301 F8
Ballachulish Highld 284 B4
Balladen Lancs 195 C10
Ballajora IoM 192 C5
Ballaleigh IoM 192 D4
Ballamodha IoM 192 E3
Ballantrae S Ayrs 244 G3
Ballaquine IoM 192 D5
Ballard's Ash Wilts 62 C5
Ballards Gore Essex 88 G6
Ballard's Green Warks 134 E5
Ballasalla IoM 192 C4
IoM 192 E3
Ballater Aberds 292 D5
Ballathie Perth 286 D5
Ballaugh IoM 192 C4
Ballaveare IoM 192 E4
Ballcorach Moray 301 G11
Ballechin Perth 286 B3
Balleich Stirling 277 B10
Balleigh Highld 309 L7
Ballencrieff E Loth 281 F9
Ballencrieff Toll W Loth 279 G9
Ballentoul Perth 291 G10
Ball Green Stoke 168 E5
Ball Haye Green Staffs 169 D7
Ballhill Devon 24 C3
Ball Hill Hants 64 G2
Ballidon Derbys 170 E2
Balliekine N Ayrs 255 D9
Balliemore Argyll 275 E11
Argyll 289 G10
Ballikinrain Stirling 277 D11
Ballimeanoch Argyll 284 F4
Ballimore Argyll 275 E10
Stirling 285 F9
Ballinaby Argyll 274 G3
Ballinbreich Fife 286 E6
Ballindean Perth 286 E6
Ballingdon Suff 107 C7
Ballingdon Bottom Herts 85 C8
Ballinger Bottom Bucks 84 E6
Ballinger Bottom (South) Bucks 84 E6
Ballinger Common Bucks 84 E6
Ballingham Hereford 97 E11
Ballingham Hill Hereford 97 E11
Ballingry Fife 280 B3
Ballinlick Perth 286 C3
Ballinluig Perth 286 B3
Ballintean Highld 291 C10
Ballintuim Perth 286 B5
Balliveolan Argyll 289 E10
Balloch Angus 287 B7
Highld 301 E7
N Lanark 278 G4
W Dunb 277 E7
Ballochan Aberds 293 D7
Ballochearn Stirling 277 D11
Ballochford Moray 302 F3
Ballochmorrie S Ayrs 244 G6
Ball o'Ditton Halton 183 D7
Ballogie Aberds 293 D7
Balls Cross W Sus 35 B7
Balls Green Essex 107 G11
E Sus 52 F3
W Sus 35 C10
Ball's Green Glos 80 F5
Balls Hill W Mid 133 E9
Ballygown Argyll 288 E6
Ballygrant Argyll 274 G4
Ballygroggan Argyll 255 F7
Ballyhaugh Argyll 288 D3
Balmacara Highld 295 C10
Balmacara Square Highld 295 C10
Balmaclellan Dumfries 237 B8
Balmacneil Perth 286 B3
Balmacqueen Highld 298 B4
Balmae Dumfries 237 E8
Balmaha Stirling 277 C8
Balmalcolm Fife 287 G7
Balmalloch N Lanark 278 F4
Balmeanach Argyll 288 F6
Argyll 289 E8
Highld 295 B7
Highld 298 E3
Highld 298 E5
Balmedie Aberds 293 B11
Balmer Shrops 149 C8
Balmer Heath Shrops 149 C8
Balmerino Fife 287 E7
Balmerlawn Hants 32 G4
Balmesh Dumfries 236 D3
Balmichael N Ayrs 255 D10
Balminnoch Dumfries 236 C4
Balmirmer Angus 287 D9
Balmoral Borders 261 B11
Balmore E Dunb 278 G2
Highld 298 E2
Highld 300 F3
Highld 301 E8
Perth 286 B3
Balmule Fife 280 D4
Balmullo Fife 287 E8
Balmungie Highld 301 D7
Balmurrie Dumfries 236 C4
Balnaboth Angus 292 G5
Balnabreich Moray 302 D3
Balnabruaich Highld 301 C7
Balnabruich Highld 311 G5
Balnacarn Highld 290 B4
Balnacoil Highld 311 H2
Balnacra Highld 299 E9
Balnacruie Highld 301 G9
Balnafoich Highld 300 F6
Balnagall Highld 311 L2
Balnagowan Aberds 293 C7
Balnagrantach Highld 300 F4
Balnaguard Perth 286 B3
Balnahanaid Perth 285 C10
Balnahard Argyll 274 D5
Argyll 288 F6
Balnain Highld 300 F4
Balnakeil Highld 308 C3
Balnakelly Aberds 293 B7
Balnaknock Highld 298 C4
Balnamoon Aberds 303 D9
Angus 293 G7
Balnapaling Highld 301 C7
Balne N Yorks 198 D5
Balnoon Corn 2 B2
Balochroy Argyll 255 B8
Balole Argyll 274 G4
Balone Fife 287 F8
Balornock Glasgow 268 B2
Balquharn Perth 286 D4
Balquhidder Stirling 285 E9
Balquhidder Station Stirling 285 E9
Balquhindachy Aberds 303 E8
Balrownie Angus 293 G7
Balsall W Mid 118 B4
Balsall Common W Mid 118 B4
Balsall Heath W Mid 133 G11
Balsall Street W Mid 118 B4
Balsam Cambs 123 G11
Balscote Oxon 101 C7
Balscott Oxon 101 C7
Balsham Cambs 123 G11
Balsporran Cottages Highld 291 F8
Balstonia Thurrock 69 C7
Baltasound Shetland 312 C8
Balterley Staffs 168 E3
Balterley Green Staffs 168 E3
Balterley Heath Staffs 168 E2
Baltersan Dumfries 236 C6
Balthangie Aberds 303 D8
Balthayock Perth 286 E5
Baltonsborough Som 44 G4
Balure Argyll 289 E11
Balvaird Highld 300 D5
Balvenie Moray 302 E3
Balvicar Argyll 275 B8
Balvraid Highld 295 D10
Highld 301 F8
Balwest Corn 2 C3
Bamber Bridge Lancs 194 B5
Bamber's Green Essex 105 G11
Bamburgh Northumb 264 C5
Bamff Perth 286 B6
Bamford Derbys 186 E2
Gtr Man 195 E11
Bamfurlong Glos 99 G8
Gtr Man 194 G5
Bampton Cumb 221 B10
Devon 27 C7
Oxon 82 E4
Bampton Grange Cumb 221 B10
Banavie Highld 290 F3
Banbury Oxon 101 C9
Bancffosfelen Carms 75 C7
Banchor Highld 301 E9
Banchory Aberds 293 D8
Banchory-Devenick Aberds 293 C11
Bancycapel Carms 74 B6
Banc-y-Darren Ceredig 128 G3
Bancyfelin Carms 74 B4
Bancyffordd Carms 93 D8
Bandirran Perth 286 D6
Bandonhill London 67 G9
Bandrake Head Cumb 210 B6
Banff Aberds 302 C6
Bangor Gwyn 179 G9
Bangor is y coed *=Bangor on Dee* Wrex 166 F5
Bangor on Dee *=Bangor-is-y-coed* Wrex 166 F5
Bangors Corn 11 B10
Bangor Teifi Ceredig 93 C7
Banham Norf 141 F11
Bank Hants 32 F3
Bankend Dumfries 238 D2
Bank End Cumb 210 B3
Cumb 228 D6
Bank Fold Blackburn 195 C8
Bankfoot Perth 286 D4
Bankglen E Ayrs 258 G4
Bankhead Aberdeen 293 B10
Aberds 293 C8
Dumfries 236 C2
Falk 278 E6
S Lanark 269 G7
Bank Hey Blackburn 203 G9
Bank Houses Lancs 202 C4
Bankland Som 28 B4
Bank Lane Gtr Man 195 D9
Bank Newton N Yorks 204 C4
Banknock Falk 278 F5
Banks Cumb 240 E3
Lancs 193 C11
Orkney 314 C4
Bank's Green Worcs 117 D9
Bankshead Shrops 130 F6
Bankshill Dumfries 248 G5
Bankside Falk 279 E7
Bank Street Worcs 116 E2
Bank Top Gtr Man 195 E8
Lancs 194 F4
Stoke 168 E5
T&W 242 D4
W Yorks 196 C6
W Yorks 205 F9
Banners Gate W Mid 133 D11
Banningham Norf 160 D4
Banniskirk Ho Highld 310 D5
Banniskirk Mains Highld 310 D5
Bannister Green Essex 106 G3
Bannockburn Stirling 278 C5
Banns Corn 4 F4
Banstead Sur 51 B8
Bantam Grove W Yorks 197 B9
Bantaskin Falk 279 F7
Bantham Devon 8 G3
Banton N Lanark 278 F5
Banwell N Som 43 B11
Banyard's Green Suff 126 C5
Bapchild Kent 70 G2
Baptist End W Mid 133 F8
Bapton Wilts 46 F3
Barabhas W Isles 304 D5
Barabhas Iarach W Isles 304 D5
Barabhas Uarach W Isles 304 C5
Barachandroman Argyll 289 G8
Baramore Highld 289 B8
Barassie S Ayrs 257 C8
Baravullin Argyll 289 F10
Barbadoes Stirling 277 B11
Barbaraville Highld 301 B7
Barbauchlaw W Loth 269 B8
Barber Booth Derbys 185 E10
Barber Green Cumb 211 C7
Barber's Moor Lancs 194 D3
Barbican Plym 7 E9
Barbieston S Ayrs 257 F10
Barbon Cumb 212 C2
Barbourne Worcs 116 F6
Barbreck Ho Argyll 275 C9
Barbridge Ches E 167 D10
Barbrook Devon 41 D8
Barby W Nhants 119 C10
Barby Nortoft W Nhants 119 C11
Barcaldine Argyll 289 E11
Barcelona Corn 6 E4
Barcheston Warks 100 D5
Barclose Cumb 239 E10
Barcombe E Sus 36 E6
Barcombe Cross E Sus 36 D6
Barcroft W Yorks 204 F6
Barden N Yorks 224 G2
Bardennoch Dumfries 246 E3
Barden Park Kent 52 D5
Barden Scale N Yorks 205 B7
Bardfield End Green Essex 106 E2
Bardfield Saling Essex 106 F3
Bardister Shetland 312 F5
Bardnabeinne Highld 309 K7
Bardney Lincs 173 B10
Bardon Leics 153 G8
Bardon Mill Northumb 241 E7
Bardowie E Dunb 277 G11
Bardown E Sus 37 B11
Bardrainney Invclyd 276 G6
Bardrishaig Argyll 275 B8
Bardsea Cumb 210 E6
Bardsey W Yorks 206 E3
Bardsley Gtr Man 196 G2
Bardwell Suff 125 C8
Bare Lancs 211 G9
Bare Ash Som 43 F9
Bareless Northumb 263 B9
Bar End Hants 33 B7
Barepot Cumb 228 F6
Bareppa Corn 3 D7
Barfad Argyll 275 G9
Dumfries 236 C5
Barford Norf 142 B2
Sur 49 F11
Warks 118 E5
Barford St John Oxon 101 E8
Barford St Martin Wilts 46 G5
Barford St Michael Oxon 101 E8
Barfrestone Kent 55 C9
Bargaly Dumfries 236 C6
Bargarran Renfs 277 G9
Bargate Derbys 170 F5
Bargeddie N Lanark 268 C4
Bargoed Caerph 77 F10
Bargrennan Dumfries 236 B5
Barham Cambs 122 B2
Kent 55 C8
Suff 126 G2
Barharrow Dumfries 237 D8
Barhill Dumfries 237 C10
Bar Hill Cambs 123 E7
Staffs 168 G3
Barholm Dumfries 237 D7
Lincs 155 G11
Barkby Leics 136 B2
Barkby Thorpe Leics 136 B2
Barkers Green Shrops 149 D10
Barkers Hill Wilts 30 B6
Barkestone-le-Vale Leics 154 C5
Barkham Wokingham 65 F9
Barking London 68 C2
Suff 125 G11
Barking Riverside London 68 C3
Barkingside London 68 B2
Barking Tye Suff 125 G11
Barkisland W Yorks 196 D5
Barkla Shop Corn 4 E4
Barkston Lincs 172 G6
N Yorks 206 F5
Barkston Ash N Yorks 206 F5
Barkway Herts 105 D7
Barlake Som 45 D7
Barlanark Glasgow 268 C3
Barland Powys 114 E5
Barland Common Swansea 56 D5
Barlaston Staffs 151 B7
Barlavington W Sus 35 D7
Barlborough Derbys 187 F7
Barlby N Yorks 207 G8
Barlestone Leics 135 B8
Barley Herts 105 D7
Lancs 204 E2
Barleycroft End Herts 105 F8
Barley End Bucks 85 C7
Barley Green Lancs 204 E2
Barley Mow T&W 243 G7
Barleythorpe Rutland 136 B6
Barling Essex 70 B2
Barlings Lincs 189 G9
Barlow Derbys 186 G4
N Yorks 198 B6
T&W 242 E5
Barlow Moor Gtr Man 184 C4
Barmby Moor E Yorks 207 D11
Barmby on the Marsh E Yorks 199 B7
Barmer Norf 158 C6
Barming Heath Kent 53 B8
Barmolloch Argyll 275 D9
Bar Moor T&W 242 E4
Barmoor Castle Northumb 263 B11
Barmoor Lane End Northumb 264 B2
Barmouth *=Abermaw* Gwyn 146 F2
Barmpton Darl 224 B6
Barmston E Yorks 209 B9
T&W 243 F8
Barmulloch Glasgow 268 B2
Barnaby Green Suff 127 B9
Barnacabber Argyll 276 D3
Barnack Pboro 137 B11
Barnacle Warks 135 G7
Barnaline Argyll 275 B10
Barnard Castle Durham 223 B11
Barnard Gate Oxon 82 C6
Barnardiston Suff 106 B4
Barnard's Green Worcs 98 B5
Barnardtown Newport 59 B10
Barnbarroch Dumfries 237 D10
Barnbow Carr W Yorks 206 F3
Barnburgh S Yorks 198 G3
Barnby Suff 143 F9
Barnby Dun S Yorks 198 F6
Barnby in the Willows Notts 172 E5
Barnby Moor Notts 187 E11
Barncluith S Lanark 268 E4
Barndennoch Dumfries 247 F9
Barne Barton Plym 7 D8
Barnehurst London 68 D4
Barnes Cray London 68 D4
Barnes Hall S Yorks 186 B4
Barnes Street Kent 52 D6
Barnet London 86 F2
Barnetby le Wold N Lincs 200 F5
Barnet Gate London 86 F2
Barnettbrook Worcs 117 B7
Barnett Brook Ches E 167 G10
Barney Norf 159 C9
Barnfield Kent 54 D2
Barnfields Hereford 97 C9
Staffs 169 D7
Barnham Suff 125 B7
W Sus 35 G7
Barnham Broom Norf 141 B11
Barnhead Angus 287 B10
Barnhill Ches W 167 E7
Dundee 287 D8
Moray 301 D11
Barnhills Dumfries 236 B1
Barningham Durham 223 C11
Suff 125 B9
Barningham Green Norf 160 C2
Barnmoor Green Warks 118 E3
Barnoldby le Beck NE Lincs 201 G8
Barnoldswick Lancs 204 D3
N Yorks 212 E3
Barns Borders 260 B6
Barnsbury London 67 C10
Barnsdale Rutland 137 B8
Barns Green W Sus 35 B10
Barnside W Yorks 197 F7
Barnsley Glos 81 D9
Shrops 132 E5
S Yorks 197 F10
Barnsole Kent 55 B9
Barnstaple Devon 40 G5
Barnston Essex 87 B10
Mers 182 E3
Barnstone Notts 154 B4
Barnt Green Worcs 117 C10
Barnton Ches W 183 F10
Edin 280 F3
Barnwell N Nhants 137 G10
Barnwell All Saints N Nhants 137 G10
Barnwell St Andrew N Nhants 137 F10
Barnwood Glos 80 B5
Barochreal Argyll 289 G10
Barons Cross Hereford 115 F9
Barr Highld 289 D8
S Ayrs 245 E7
Som 27 C11
Barra Castle Aberds 303 G7
Barrachan Dumfries 236 E5
Barrachnie Glasgow 268 C3
Barrack Aberds 303 E8
Barrack Hill Newport 59 B10
Barraer Dumfries 236 C5
Barraglom W Isles 304 E3
Barrahormid Argyll 275 E8
Barran Argyll 289 G10
Barranrioch Argyll 289 G10
Barrapol Argyll 288 E1
Barras Aberds 293 E10
Cumb 222 C6
Barrasford Northumb 241 C10
Barravullin Argyll 275 C9
Barr Common W Mid 133 D11
Barregarrow IoM 192 D4
Barrets Green Ches E 167 D9
Barrhead E Renf 267 D9
Barrhill S Ayrs 244 G6
Barrington Cambs 105 B7
Som 28 D5
Barripper Corn 2 B4
Barrmill N Ayrs 267 E7
Barrock Highld 310 B6
Barrock Ho Highld 310 C6
Barrow Glos 99 G7
Lancs 203 F10
Rutland 155 F7
Shrops 132 C3
Som 44 E5
Suff 124 E5
S Yorks 186 B5
Barroway Drove Norf 139 C11
Barrow Bridge Gtr Man 195 E7
Barrowburn Northumb 263 G9
Barrow Burn Northumb 263 G9
Barrowby Lincs 155 B7
Barrowcliff N Yorks 217 B10
Barrow Common N Som 60 F4
Barrowden Rutland 137 C8
Barrowford Lancs 204 F3
Barrow Green Kent 70 G3
Barrow Gurney N Som 60 F4
Barrow Hann N Lincs 200 C5
Barrow Haven N Lincs 200 C5
Barrowhill Kent 54 F6
Barrow Hill Derbys 186 F6
Dorset 18 B5
Barrow-in-Furness Cumb 210 F4
Barrow Island Cumb 210 F3
Barrowmore Estate Ches W 167 B7
Barrow Nook Lancs 194 G2
Barrows Green Ches E 167 D11
Cumb 211 B10
Notts 171 E7
Barrow's Green Mers 183 D8
Barrow Street Wilts 45 G10
Barrow upon Humber N Lincs 200 C5
Barrow upon Soar Leics 153 F11
Barrow upon Trent Derbys 153 D7
Barrow Vale Bath 60 G6
Barrow Wake Glos 80 B6
Barry Angus 287 D9
V Glam 58 F6
Barry Dock V Glam 58 F6
Barry Island V Glam 58 F6
Barsby Leics 154 G3
Barsham Suff 143 F7
Barshare E Ayrs 258 F3
Barstable Essex 69 B8
Barston W Mid 118 B4
Bartestree Hereford 97 C11
Barthol Chapel Aberds 303 F8
Bartholomew Green Essex 106 G4
Barthomley Ches E 168 E3
Bartington Ches W 183 F10
Bartley Hants 32 E4
Bartley Green W Mid 133 G10
Bartlow Cambs 105 B11
Barton Cambs 123 F8
Ches W 166 E6
Glos 80 B4
Glos 99 F11
IoW 20 D6
Lancs 193 F11
Lancs 202 F6
N Som 43 B11
N Yorks 224 D4
Oxon 83 D9
Torbay 9 B8
Warks 118 G2
Barton Abbey Oxon 101 G9
Barton Bendish Norf 140 B4
Barton Court Hereford 98 C4
Barton End Glos 80 F4
Barton Gate Devon 41 E7
Staffs 152 F3
Barton Green Staffs 152 F3
Barton Hartshorn Bucks 102 E2
Barton Hill Bristol 60 E6
N Yorks 216 G4
Barton in Fabis Notts 153 C10
Barton in the Beans Leics 135 B7
Barton-le-Clay C Beds 103 E11
Barton-le-Street N Yorks 216 E4
Barton-le-Willows N Yorks 216 G4
Barton Mills Suff 124 C4
Barton on Sea Hants 19 C10
Barton on the Heath Warks 100 E5
Barton St David Som 44 G4
Barton Seagrave N Nhants 121 B7
Bartonsham Hereford 97 D10
Barton Stacey Hants 48 E2
Barton Town Devon 41 E7
Barton Turf Norf 161 E7
Barton Turn Staffs 152 F4
Barton-under-Needwood Staffs 152 F3
Barton-upon-Humber N Lincs 200 C4
Barton Upon Irwell Gtr Man 184 B3
Barton Waterside N Lincs 200 C4
Barugh S Yorks 197 F10
Barugh Green S Yorks 197 F10
Barway Cambs 123 B10
Barwell Leics 135 D8
London 67 G7
Barwick Devon 25 F9
Herts 86 B5
Som 29 E9
Barwick in Elmet W Yorks 206 F3
Baschurch Shrops 149 E8
Bascote Warks 119 E8
Bascote Heath Warks 119 E7
Base Green Suff 125 E10
Basford Shrops 131 F7
Staffs 168 F5
Basford Green Staffs 169 E7
Bashall Eaves Lancs 203 E9
Bashley Hants 19 B10
Bashley Park Hants 19 B10
Basildon Essex 69 B8
Basingstoke Hants 48 C6
Baslow Derbys 186 G3
Bason Bridge Som 43 D10
Bassaleg Newport 59 B9
Bassenthwaite Cumb 229 E10
Bassett Soton 32 D6
S Yorks 186 E3
Bassett Green Soton 32 D6
Bassingbourn Cambs 104 C6
Bassingfield Notts 154 B2
Bassingham Lincs 172 C6
Bassingthorpe Lincs 155 D9
Bassus Green Herts 104 F6
Basta Shetland 312 D7
Basted Kent 52 B6
Baston Lincs 156 G2
Bastonford Worcs 116 G6
Bastwick Norf 161 F8
Baswich Staffs 151 E8
Baswick Steer E Yorks 209 D7
Batavaime Stirling 285 D8
Batch Som 43 B10
Batchcott Shrops 115 C9
Batchfields Hereford 98 B3
Batchley Worcs 117 D10
Batchworth Herts 85 G9
Batchworth Heath Herts 85 G9
Batcombe Dorset 29 G10
Som 45 F7
Bate Heath Ches E 183 F11
Bateman's Green Worcs 117 B11
Bateman's Hill Pembs 73 E8
Batemoor S Yorks 186 E5
Batford Herts 85 B10
Bath Bath 61 F8
Bathampton Bath 61 F9
Bathealton Som 27 C9
Batheaston Bath 61 F9
Bathford Bath 61 F9
Bathgate W Loth 269 B9
Bathley Notts 172 D3
Bathpool Corn 11 G11
Som 28 B3
Bath Side Essex 108 E5
Bath Vale Ches E 168 C5
Bathville W Loth 269 B8
Bathway Som 44 C5
Bathwick Bath 61 F9
Batlers Green Herts 85 F11
Batley W Yorks 197 C8
Batley Carr W Yorks 197 C8
Batsford Glos 100 E3
Batson Devon 9 G9
Batsworthy Devon 26 D4
Batten's Green Som 28 D3
Battenton Green Worcs 116 D6
Battersby N Yorks 225 D11
Battersea London 67 D9
Battisborough Cross Devon 7 F11
Battisford Suff 125 G11
Battisford Tye Suff 125 G10
Battle E Sus 38 D2
Powys 95 E10
Battledown Glos 99 G9
Battledown Cross Devon 25 F7
Battlefield Shrops 149 F10
Battle Hill T&W 243 D8
Battlesbridge Essex 88 G3
Battlescombe Glos 80 D6
Battlesden C Beds 103 F9
Battlesea Green Suff 126 B4
Battleton Som 26 B6
Battlies Green Suff 125 E7
Battram Leics 135 B8
Battramsley Hants 20 B2
Battramsley Cross Hants 20 B2
Batt's Corner Hants 49 E10
Battyeford W Yorks 197 C7
Batworthy Devon 13 D10
Bauds of Cullen Moray 302 C4
Baugh Argyll 288 E2
Baughton Worcs 99 C7
Baughurst Hants 48 B5
Baulking Oxon 82 G4
Baumber Lincs 190 G2
Baunton Glos 81 E8
Baverstock Wilts 46 G4
Bawburgh Norf 142 B3
Bawdeswell Norf 159 E10
Bawdrip Som 43 F10
Bawdsey Suff 108 C6
Bawsey Norf 158 F3
Bawtry S Yorks 187 C11
Baxenden Lancs 195 B9
Baxterley Warks 134 D5
Baxter's Green Suff 124 F5
Bay Dorset 30 B4
Highld 298 D2
Baybridge Hants 33 C8
Northumb 241 G11
Baycliff Cumb 210 E5
Baydon Wilts 63 D9
Bayford Herts 86 D4
Som 30 B2
Bay Gate Lancs 203 D11
Bay Horse Lancs 202 C5
Bayles Cumb 231 C10
Bayley's Hill Kent 52 C4
Baylham Suff 126 G2
Baylis Green Worcs 117 C11
Baynard's Green Oxon 101 F10
Baynhall Worcs 99 B7
Baysham Hereford 97 F11
Bayston Hill Shrops 131 B9
Bayswater London 67 C9
Baythorne End Essex 106 C4
Baythorpe Lincs 174 G2
Bayton Worcs 116 C3
Bayton Common Worcs 116 C4
Bay View Kent 70 E4
Bayworth Oxon 83 E8
Beach Highld 289 D9
S Glos 61 E8
Beachampton Bucks 102 D5
Beachamwell Norf 140 B5
Beachans Moray 301 E10
Beacharr Argyll 255 C7
Beachborough Kent 55 F7
Beach Hay Worcs 116 C4
Beachlands E Sus 23 E11
Beachley Glos 79 G9
Beacon Corn 2 B5
Devon 27 F11
Devon 28 F2
Beacon Down E Sus 37 C9
Beacon End Essex 107 G9
Beaconhill Northumb 243 B7
Beacon Hill Bath 61 F9
Bucks 84 G6
Cumb 210 E4
Dorset 18 C5
Essex 88 C5
Kent 53 G10
Notts 172 E4
Suff 108 B4
Sur 49 F11
Beacon Lough T&W 243 F7
Beacon's Bottom Bucks 84 F3
Beaconsfield Bucks 66 B2
Beaconside Staffs 151 E8
Beacrabhaic W Isles 305 J3
Beadlam N Yorks 216 C3
Beadlow C Beds 104 D2
Beadnell Northumb 264 D6
Beaford Devon 25 E9
Beal Northumb 273 G11
N Yorks 198 B4
Bealach Highld 289 D11
Bealach Maim Argyll 275 E10
Bealbury Corn 7 B7
Beal's Green Kent 53 G9
Bealsmill Corn 12 F3
Beambridge Shrops 131 F10
Beam Bridge Som 27 D10
Beam Hill Staffs 152 D4
Beamhurst Staffs 151 B11
Beamhurst Lane Staffs 151 B11
Beaminster Dorset 29 G7
Beamish Durham 242 G6
Beamond End Bucks 84 F6
Beamsley N Yorks 205 C7
Bean Kent 68 E5
Beanacre Wilts 62 F2
Beancross Falk 279 F8
Beanhill M Keynes 103 D7
Beanley Northumb 264 F3
Beansburn E Ayrs 257 B10
Beanthwaite Cumb 210 C4
Beaquoy Orkney 314 D3
Bear Cross BCP 19 B7
Beard Hill Som 44 E6
Beardly Batch Som 44 E6
Beardwood Blackburn 195 B7
Beare Devon 27 G7
Beare Green Sur 51 E7
Bearley Warks 118 E3
Bearley Cross Warks 118 E3
Bearnus Argyll 288 E5
Bearpark Durham 233 C10
Bearsbridge Northumb 241 F7
Bearsden E Dunb 277 G10
Bearsted Kent 53 B9
Bearstone Shrops 150 B4
Bearwood BCP 18 B6
Hereford 115 F7
W Mid 133 F10
Beasley Staffs 168 F4
Beattock Dumfries 248 C3
Beauchamp Roding Essex 87 C9
Beauchief S Yorks 186 E4
Beauclerc Northumb 242 E2
Beaudesert Warks 118 D3
Beaufort Bl Gwent 77 C11
Beaufort Castle Highld 300 E5
Beaulieu Hants 32 G5
Beaulieu Park Essex 88 C2
Beaulieu Wood Dorset 30 F2
Beauly Highld 300 E5
Beaumaris Anglesey 179 F10
Beaumont Cumb 239 F8
Essex 108 G3
Windsor 66 E3
Beaumont Hill Darl 224 B5
Beaumont Leys Leicester 135 B11
Beausale Warks 118 C4
Beauvale Notts 171 F8
Beauworth Hants 33 B9
Beavan's Hill Hereford 98 G3
Beaworthy Devon 12 B5
Beazley End Essex 106 F4
Bebington Mers 182 E4
Bebside Northumb 253 G7
Beccles Suff 143 E8
Becconsall Lancs 194 C2
Beck Bottom Cumb 210 C5
W Yorks 197 C10
Beckbury Shrops 132 C5
Beckces Cumb 230 F4
Beckenham London 67 F11
Beckermet Cumb 219 D10
Beckermonds N Yorks 213 C7
Beckery Som 44 F3
Beckett End Norf 140 D5
Beckfoot Cumb 220 E3
Cumb 229 B7
Beck Foot Cumb 222 F2
W Yorks 205 F8
Beckford Worcs 99 D9
Beckhampton Wilts 62 F5
Beck Head Cumb 211 C8
Beck Hole N Yorks 226 E6
Beck Houses Cumb 221 F11
Beckingham Lincs 172 E5
Notts 188 D3
Beckington Som 45 C10
Beckjay Shrops 115 B7
Beckley E Sus 38 C5
Hants 19 B10
Oxon 83 C9
Beckley Furnace E Sus 38 C4
Beck Row Suff 124 B3
Beckside Cumb 212 B2
Beck Side Cumb 210 C4
Cumb 211 C7
Beckton London 68 C2
Beckwith N Yorks 205 C11
Beckwithshaw N Yorks 205 C11
Becontree London 68 B3
Bedale N Yorks 214 B5
Bedburn Durham 233 E8
Bedchester Dorset 30 D5
Beddau Rhondda 58 B5
Beddgelert Gwyn 163 F9
Beddingham E Sus 36 F6
Beddington London 67 G10
Beddington Corner London 67 F9
Bedfield Suff 126 D4
Bedford Bedford 121 G11
Gtr Man 183 B11
Bedford Park London 67 D8
Bedgebury Cross Kent 53 G8
Bedgrove Bucks 84 C4
Bedham W Sus 35 C8
Bedhampton Hants 22 B2

Bedingfield Suff 126 D3
Bedingham Green Norf 142 E5
Bedlam N Yorks 214 G5
Som 45 D9
Bedlam Street W Sus 36 D3
Bedlar's Green Essex 105 G10
Bedlington Northumb 253 G7
Bedlington Station
Northumb 253 G7
Bedlinog M Tydf 77 E9
Bedminster Bristol 60 E5
Bedminster Down Bristol 60 F5
Bedmond Herts 85 E9
Bednall Staffs 151 F9
Bednall Head Staffs 151 F9
Bedrule Borders 262 F4
Bedstone Shrops 115 B7
Bedwas Caerph 59 B7
Bedwell Herts 104 G4
Wrex 166 F5
Bedwellty Caerph 77 E11
Bedwellty Pits Bl Gwent 77 D11
Bedwlwyn Wrex 148 B4
Bedworth Warks 135 F7
Bedworth Heath Warks 134 F6
Bedworth Woodlands
Warks 134 F6
Bed-y-coedwr Gwyn 146 D4
Beeby Leics 136 B3
Beech Hants 49 F7
Staffs 151 B7
Beechcliff Staffs 151 B7
Beechcliffe W Yorks 205 E7
Beechen Cliff Bath 61 G9
Beech Hill Gtr Man 194 F5
W Berks 65 G7
Beechingstoke Wilts 46 B5
Beech Lanes W Mid 133 F10
Beechwood Halton 183 E8
Newport 59 B10
W Mid 118 B5
W Yorks 206 F2
Beecroft C Beds 103 G10
Beedon W Berks 64 D3
Beedon Hill W Berks 64 D3
Beeford E Yorks 209 C8
Beeley Derbys 170 B3
Beelsby NE Lincs 201 G8
Beenham W Berks 64 F5
Beenham's Heath
Windsor 65 D10
Beenham Stocks
W Berks 64 F5
Beeny Corn 11 C8
Beer Devon 15 D10
Som 44 G2
Beercrocombe Som 28 C4
Beer Hackett Dorset 29 E9
Beesands Devon 8 G6
Beesby Lincs 191 E7
Beeslack Midloth 270 C4
Beeson Devon 8 G6
Beeston C Beds 104 B3
Ches W 167 D8
Norf 159 F8
Notts 153 B10
W Yorks 205 G11
Beeston Hill W Yorks 205 G11
Beeston Park Side
W Yorks 197 B9
Beeston Regis Norf 177 E11
Beeston Royds
W Yorks 205 G11
Beeston St Lawrence
Norf 160 E6
Beeswing Dumfries 237 C10
Beetham Cumb 211 D9
Som 28 E3
Beetley Norf 159 F9
Beffcote Staffs 150 F6
Began Cardiff 59 C8
Begbroke Oxon 83 C7
Begdale Cambs 139 B9
Begelly Pembs 73 D10
Beggar Hill Essex 87 E10
Beggarington Hill
W Yorks 197 C9
Beggars Ash Hereford 98 D4
Beggars Bush W Sus 35 F11
Beggar's Bush Powys 114 E5
Beggars Pound V Glam 58 F4
Beggearn Huish Som 42 F4
Beguildy Powys 114 B3
Beighton Norf 143 B7
S Yorks 186 E6
Beighton Hill Derbys 170 E3
Beili-glas Mon 78 C4
Beitearsaig W Isles 305 G1
Beith N Ayrs 266 E6
Bekesbourne Kent 55 B7
Bekesbourne Hill Kent 55 B7
Belah Cumb 239 F9
Belan Powys 130 C4
Belaugh Norf 160 F5
Belbins Hants 32 C5
Belbroughton Worcs 117 B8
Belchalwell Dorset 30 F3
Belchalwell Street Dorset 30 F3
Belchamp Otten Essex 106 C6
Belchamp St Paul Essex 106 C5
Belchamp Walter Essex 106 C6
Belcher's Bar Leics 135 B8
Belchford Lincs 190 F3
Beleybridge Fife 287 F9
Belfield Gtr Man 196 E2
Belford Northumb 264 C4
Belgrano Conwy 181 F7
Belgrave Ches W 166 C5
Leicester 135 B11
Staffs 134 C4
Belgravia London 67 D9
Belhaven E Loth 282 F3
Belhelvie Aberds 293 B11
Belhinnie Aberds 302 G4
Bellabeg Aberds 292 B5
Bellamore S Ayrs 244 F6
Bellanoch Argyll 275 D8
Bellanrigg Borders 260 B6
Bellasize E Yorks 199 B10
Bellaty Angus 286 B6
Bell Bar Herts 86 D3
Bell Busk N Yorks 204 B4
Bell Common Essex 86 E6
Belleau Lincs 190 F6
Belle Eau Park Notts 171 D11
Belle Green S Yorks 197 F11
Bellehiglash Moray 301 F11
Belle Isle W Yorks 197 B10
Bell End Worcs 117 B8
Bellerby N Yorks 224 G2
Belle Vale Mers 182 D6
W Mid 133 G9
Bellever Devon 13 F9
Bellevue Worcs 117 C9
Belle Vue Cumb 229 E8
Cumb 239 F9
Gtr Man 184 B5
Shrops 149 G9
S Yorks 198 G5
Belle Vue *continued*
W Yorks 197 D10
Bellfield E Ayrs 257 B10
Bellfields Sur 50 C3
Bell Green London 67 E11
W Mid 135 G7
Bell Heath Worcs 117 B9
Bell Hill Hants 34 C2
Belliehill Angus 293 G7
Bellingdon Bucks 84 D6
Bellingham London 67 E11
Northumb 251 G8
Bellmount Norf 157 E10
Belloch Argyll 255 D7
Bellochantuy Argyll 255 D7
Bell o' th' Hill Ches W 167 F8
Bellsbank E Ayrs 245 C11
Bell's Close T&W 242 E5
Bell's Corner Suff 107 D9
Bellshill N Lanark 268 C4
Northumb 264 C4
Bellside N Lanark 268 D6
Bellsmyre W Dunb 277 F8
Bellspool Borders 260 B5
Bellsquarry W Loth 269 C10
Bells Yew Green E Sus 52 F6
Belluton Bath 60 G6
Bellyeoman Fife 280 D2
Belmaduthy Highld 300 D6
Belmesthorpe Rutland 155 G10
Belmont Blackburn 195 D7
Durham 234 C2
E Sus 38 E4
London 67 G9
London 85 G11
Oxon 63 B11
S Ayrs 257 E8
Shetland 312 C7
Belnacraig Aberds 292 B5
Belnagarrow Moray 302 E3
Belnie Lincs 156 C5
Belowda Corn 5 C9
Belper Derbys 170 F4
Belper Lane End Derbys 170 F4
Belph Derbys 187 F8
Belsay Northumb 242 B4
Belses Borders 262 D3
Belsford Devon 8 D5
Belsize Herts 85 E8
Belstead Suff 108 C2
Belston S Ayrs 257 E9
Belstone Devon 13 C8
Belstone Corner Devon 13 B8
Belthorn Blackburn 195 C8
Beltinge Kent 71 F7
Beltingham Northumb 241 E7
Beltoft N Lincs 199 F10
Belton Leics 153 E8
Lincs 155 B8
N Lincs 199 F9
Norf 143 C9
Belton in Rutland
Rutland 136 C6
Beltring Kent 53 D7
Belts of Collonach
Aberds 293 D8
Belvedere London 68 D3
W Loth 269 B9
Belvoir Leics 154 C6
Bembridge IoW 21 D8
Bemersyde Borders 262 C3
Bemerton Wilts 46 G6
Bemerton Heath Wilts 46 G6
Bempton E Yorks 218 E3
Benacre Suff 143 G10
Ben Alder Lodge Highld 291 F7
Ben Armine Lodge
Highld 309 H7
Benbuie Dumfries 246 D6
Ben Casgro W Isles 304 F6
Benchill Gtr Man 184 D4
Bencombe Glos 80 F3
Benderloch Argyll 289 F11
Bendish Herts 104 G3
Bendronaig Lodge
Highld 299 F10
Benenden Kent 53 G10
Benfield Dumfries 236 C5
Benfieldside Durham 242 G3
Bengal Pembs 91 E9
Bengate Norf 160 D6
Bengeo Herts 86 C4
Bengeworth Worcs 99 C10
Bengrove Glos 99 E9
Benhall Glos 99 G8
Benhall Green Suff 127 E7
Benhall Street Suff 127 E7
Benhilton London 67 F9
Benholm Aberds 293 G10
Beningbrough N Yorks 206 B6
Benington Herts 104 G5
Lincs 174 F5
Benington Sea End
Lincs 174 F6
Benllech Anglesey 179 E8
Benmore Argyll 276 E2
Stirling 285 E8
Benmore Lodge Argyll 289 F7
Highld 309 H3
Bennacott Corn 11 C11
Bennah Devon 14 E2
Bennan N Ayrs 255 E10
Bennane Lea S Ayrs 244 F3
Bennetland E Yorks 199 B10
Bennetsfield Highld 300 D6
Bennett End Bucks 84 F3
Bennetts End Herts 85 D9
Benniworth Lincs 190 E2
Benover Kent 53 D8
Ben Rhydding W Yorks 205 D8
Bensham T&W 242 E6
Benslie N Ayrs 266 G6
Benson Oxon 83 G10
Benston Shetland 313 H6
Bent Aberds 293 F8
Benter Som 44 D6
Bentfield Bury Essex 105 F9
Bentfield Green Essex 105 F10
Bentgate Gtr Man 196 E2
Bent Gate Lancs 195 C9
Benthall Northumb 264 D6
Shrops 132 C3
Bentham Glos 80 B6
Benthoul Aberdeen 293 C10
Bentilee Stoke 168 F6
Bentlass Pembs 73 E7
Bentlawnt Shrops 130 C6
Bentley Essex 87 F9
E Yorks 208 F6
Hants 49 E9
Suff 108 D2
S Yorks 198 F5
Warks 134 D5
W Mid 133 D9
Worcs 117 D9
Bentley Common Warks 134 D5
Bentley Heath Herts 86 F2
W Mid 118 B3
Bentley Rise S Yorks 198 G5
Benton Devon 41 F7
Benton Green W Mid 118 B5
Bentpath Dumfries 249 E8
Bents W Loth 269 C9
Bents Head W Yorks 205 F7
Bentwichen Devon 41 G8
Bentworth Hants 49 E7
Benvie Dundee 287 D7
Benville Dorset 29 G8
Benwell T&W 242 E6
Benwick Cambs 138 E6
Beobridge Shrops 132 E5
Beoley Worcs 117 D11
Beoraidbeg Highld 295 F8
Bepton W Sus 34 D5
Berden Essex 105 F9
Bere Alston Devon 7 B8
Berechurch Essex 107 G9
Bere Ferrers Devon 7 C9
Berefold Aberds 303 F9
Berepper Corn 2 E5
Bere Regis Dorset 18 C2
Bergh Apton Norf 142 C6
Berghers Hill Bucks 66 B2
Berhill Som 44 F2
Berinsfield Oxon 83 F9
Berkeley Glos 79 F11
Berkeley Heath Glos 79 F11
Berkeley Road Glos 80 E2
Berkeley Towers
Ches E 167 E11
Berkhamsted Herts 85 D7
Berkley Som 45 D10
Berkley Down Som 45 D9
Berkley Marsh Som 45 D10
Berkswell W Mid 118 B4
Bermondsey London 67 D10
Bermuda Warks 135 F7
Bernards Heath Herts 85 D11
Bernera Highld 295 C10
Berner's Cross Devon 25 F10
Berner's Hill E Sus 53 G8
Berners Roding Essex 87 D10
Bernice Argyll 276 C2
Bernisdale Highld 298 D4
Berrick Salome Oxon 83 G10
Berriedale Highld 311 G5
Berrier Cumb 230 F3
Berriew = *Aberriw*
Powys 130 C3
Berrington Northumb 273 G10
Shrops 131 B10
Worcs 115 D11
Berrington Green
Worcs 115 D11
Berriowbridge Corn 11 F11
Berrow Som 43 C10
Worcs 98 E5
Berrow Green Worcs 116 F4
Berry Swansea 56 D3
Berry Brow W Yorks 196 E6
Berry Cross Devon 25 E7
Berry Down Cross Devon 40 E5
Berryfield Wilts 61 G11
Berryfields Oxon 84 B3
Berrygate Hill E Yorks 201 C8
Berry Hill Glos 79 C9
Pembs 91 C11
Stoke 168 F6
Worcs 117 E7
Berryhillock Moray 302 C5
Berrylands London 67 F7
Berry Moor S Yorks 197 G9
Berrynarbor Devon 40 D5
Berry Pomeroy Devon 8 C6
Berrysbridge Devon 26 G6
Berry's Green London 52 B2
Bersham Wrex 166 F4
Berstane Orkney 314 E4
Berth-ddu Flint 166 B2
Berthengam Flint 181 F10
Berwick E Sus 23 D8
Kent 54 F6
S Glos 60 C5
Berwick Bassett Wilts 62 E5
Berwick Hill Northumb 242 B5
Berwick Hills Mbro 225 B10
Berwick St James Wilts 46 F5
Berwick St John Wilts 30 C6
Berwick St Leonard
Wilts 46 G2
Berwick-upon-Tweed
Northumb 273 E9
Berwick Wharf Shrops 149 G10
Berwyn Denb 165 G11
Bescaby Leics 154 D6
Bescar Lancs 193 E11
Bescot W Mid 133 D10
Besford Shrops 149 E11
Worcs 99 C8
Bessacarr S Yorks 198 G6
Bessels Green Kent 52 B4
Bessels Leigh Oxon 83 E7
Besses o' th' Barn
Gtr Man 195 F10
Bessingby E Yorks 218 F3
Bessingham Norf 160 B3
Best Beech Hill E Sus 52 G6
Besthorpe Norf 141 D11
Notts 172 C4
Bestwood Nottingham 171 G9
Bestwood Village Notts 171 F9
Beswick E Yorks 208 D6
Gtr Man 184 B5
Betchcott Shrops 131 D8
Betchton Heath Ches E 168 C3
Betchworth Sur 51 D8
Bethania Ceredig 111 E11
Gwyn 163 E10
Gwyn 164 F2
Bethany Corn 6 D6
Bethel Anglesey 178 G5
Corn 5 E10
Gwyn 147 B9
Gwyn 163 B8
Bethelnie Aberds 303 F7
Bethersden Kent 54 E2
Bethesda Gwyn 163 B10
Pembs 73 B9
Bethlehem Carms 94 F3
Bethnal Green London 67 C10
Betley Staffs 168 F3
Betley Common Staffs 168 F2
Betsham Kent 68 E6
Betteshanger Kent 55 C10
Bettiscombe Dorset 16 B3
Bettisfield Wrex 149 B9
Betton Shrops 130 C6
Shrops 150 B3
Betton Strange Shrops 131 B10
Bettws Bridgend 58 B2
Mon 78 B3
Newport 78 G3
Bettws Cedewain Powys 130 D2
Bettws Gwerfil Goch
Denb 165 F8
Bettws Ifan Ceredig 92 B6
Bettws Newydd Mon 78 D5
Bettws-y-crwyn Shrops 130 G4
Bettyhill Highld 308 C7
Betws Bridgend 57 D11
Carms 75 C10
Betws Bledrws Ceredig 111 G11
Betws-Garmon Gwyn 163 D8
Betws Ifan Ceredig 92 B6
Betws-y-Coed Conwy 164 D4
Betws-yn-Rhos Conwy 180 G6
Beulah Ceredig 92 B5
Powys 113 G8
Bevendean Brighton 36 F4
Bevercotes Notts 187 G11
Bevere Worcs 116 F6
Beverley E Yorks 208 F6
Beverston Glos 80 G5
Bevington Glos 79 F11
Bewaldeth Cumb 229 E10
Bewbush W Sus 51 F8
Bewcastle Cumb 240 C3
Bewdley Worcs 116 B5
Bewerley N Yorks 214 G3
Bewholme E Yorks 209 C9
Bewley Common Wilts 62 F2
Bewlie Borders 262 D3
Bewlie Mains Borders 262 D3
Bewsey Warr 183 D9
Bexfield Norf 159 D10
Bexhill E Sus 38 F2
Bexley London 68 E3
Bexleyheath London 68 D3
Bexleyhill W Sus 34 B6
Bexon Kent 53 B11
Bexwell Norf 140 C2
Beyton Suff 125 E8
Beyton Green Suff 125 E8
Bhalasaigh W Isles 304 E3
Bhaltos W Isles 304 E2
Bhatarsaigh W Isles 297 M2
Bhlàraidh Highld 290 B5
Bibstone S Glos 79 G11
Bibury Glos 81 D10
Bicester Oxon 101 G11
Bickenhall Som 28 D3
Bickenhill W Mid 134 G3
Bicker Lincs 156 B4
Bicker Bar Lincs 156 B4
Bicker Gauntlet Lincs 156 B4
Bickershaw Gtr Man 194 G6
Bickerstaffe Lancs 194 G2
Bickerton Ches E 167 E8
Devon 9 G11
N Yorks 206 C5
Bickford Staffs 151 G7
Bickham Som 42 E3
Bickingcott Devon 26 B3
Bickington Devon 13 G11
Devon 40 G4
Bickleigh Devon 7 C10
Devon 26 F6
Bickleton Devon 40 G4
Bickley Ches W 167 F8
London 68 F2
Worcs 116 C2
Bickley Moss Ches W 167 F8
Bickley Town Ches W 167 F8
Bickleywood Ches W 167 F8
Bickmarsh Warks 100 B2
Bicknacre Essex 88 E3
Bicknoller Som 42 F6
Bicknor Kent 53 B11
Bickton Hants 31 E11
Bicton Hereford 115 E9
Pembs 72 D4
Shrops 130 G5
Shrops 149 F8
Bicton Heath Shrops 149 G9
Bidborough Kent 52 E5
Bidden Hants 49 D8
Biddenden Kent 53 F11
Biddenden Green Kent 53 E11
Biddenham Bedford 103 B10
Biddestone Wilts 61 E11
Biddick T&W 243 F8
Biddick Hall T&W 243 E9
Biddisham Som 43 C11
Biddlesden Bucks 102 C2
Biddlestone Northumb 251 B11
Biddulph Staffs 168 D5
Biddulph Moor Staffs 168 D6
Bideford Devon 25 B7
Bidford-on-Avon Warks 118 G2
Bidlake Devon 12 D5
Bidston Mers 182 C3
Bidston Hill Mers 182 D3
Bidwell C Beds 103 G10
Bielby E Yorks 207 E11
Bieldside Aberdeen 293 C10
Bierley IoW 20 F6
W Yorks 205 G9
Bierton Bucks 84 B4
Bigbury Devon 8 F3
Bigbury-on-Sea Devon 8 G3
Bigby Lincs 200 F5
Bigfrith Windsor 65 C11
Biggar Cumb 210 F3
S Lanark 260 B2
Biggar Road N Lanark 268 C5
Biggin Derbys 169 D11
Derbys 170 F3
N Yorks 206 F6
Thurrock 69 D7
Biggings Shetland 313 G3
Biggin Hill London 52 B2
Biggleswade C Beds 104 C3
Bighouse Highld 310 C2
Bighton Hants 48 G6
Biglands Cumb 239 G7
Big Mancot Flint 166 B4
Bignall End Staffs 168 E4
Bignor W Sus 35 E7
Bigods Essex 106 G2
Bigram Stirling 285 G10
Bigrigg Cumb 219 C10
Big Sand Highld 299 B7
Bigswell Orkney 314 E3
Bigton Shetland 313 L5
Bilberry Corn 5 C10
Bilborough Nottingham 171 G8
Bilbrook Som 42 E4
Staffs 133 C7
Bilbrough N Yorks 206 D6
Bilbster Highld 310 D6
Bilby Notts 187 E10
Bildershaw Durham 233 G10
Bildeston Suff 107 B9
Billacombe Plym 7 E10
Billacott Corn 11 C11
Billericay Essex 87 G11
Billesdon Leics 136 C4
Billesley Warks 118 F2
W Mid 133 G11
Billesley Common
W Mid 133 G11
Billingborough Lincs 156 C2
Billinge Mers 194 G4
Billingford Norf 126 B3
Norf 159 E10
Billingham Stockton 234 G5
Billinghay Lincs 173 E11
Billingley S Yorks 198 G2
Billingshurst W Sus 35 B9
Billingsley Shrops 132 F4
Billington C Beds 103 G8
Lancs 203 F10
Staffs 151 E7
Billockby Norf 161 G8
Bill Quay T&W 243 E7
Billy Mill T&W 243 D8
Billy Row Durham 233 D9
Bilmarsh Shrops 149 D9
Bilsborrow Lancs 202 F6
Bilsby Lincs 191 F7
Bilsby Field Lincs 191 F7
Bilsdon Devon 14 C2
Bilsham W Sus 35 G7
Bilsington Kent 54 G4
Bilson Green Glos 79 C11
Bilsthorpe Notts 171 C10
Bilsthorpe Moor Notts 171 D11
Bilston Midloth 270 C5
W Mid 133 D9
Bilstone Leics 135 B7
Bilting Kent 54 D5
Bilton E Yorks 209 G9
Northumb 264 G6
N Yorks 206 B2
Warks 119 C9
Bilton Haggs N Yorks 206 D5
Bilton in Ainsty N Yorks 206 D5
Bimbister Orkney 314 E3
Binbrook Lincs 190 C2
Binchester Blocks
Durham 233 E10
Bincombe Dorset 17 E9
Som 43 F7
Bindal Highld 311 L3
Bindon Som 27 C10
Binegar Som 44 D6
Bines Green W Sus 35 D11
Binfield Brack 65 E10
Binfield Heath Oxon 65 D8
Bingfield Northumb 241 C11
Bingham Edin 280 G6
Notts 154 B4
Bingley W Yorks 205 F8
Bings Heath Shrops 149 F10
Binham Norf 159 B9
Binley Hants 48 C2
W Mid 119 B7
Binley Woods Warks 119 B7
Binnegar Dorset 18 D3
Binniehill Falk 279 G7
Binscombe Sur 50 D3
Binsey Oxon 83 D7
Binsoe N Yorks 214 D4
Binstead Hants 49 E9
IoW 21 C7
Binsted Hants 49 E9
W Sus 35 F7
Binton Warks 118 G2
Bintree Norf 159 E10
Binweston Shrops 130 C6
Birch Essex 88 B6
Gtr Man 195 F11
Birch Acre Worcs 117 C11
Birchall Hereford 98 D3
Staffs 169 E7
Bircham Newton Norf 158 C5
Bircham Tofts Norf 158 C5
Birchan Coppice Worcs 116 C6
Birchanger Essex 105 G10
Birch Berrow Worcs 116 E4
Birchburn N Ayrs 255 E10
Birch Cross Staffs 152 C2
Birchden E Sus 52 F4
Birchencliffe W Yorks 196 D6
Birchend Hereford 98 C3
Birchendale Staffs 151 B11
Bircher Hereford 115 D9
Birches Green W Mid 134 E2
Birches Head Stoke 168 F5
Birchett's Green E Sus 53 G7
Birchfield Highld 301 G9
W Mid 133 E11
Birch Green Essex 88 B6
Herts 86 C3
Lancs 194 F3
Worcs 99 B7
Birchgrove Cardiff 59 D7
E Sus 36 B6
Swansea 57 B8
Birchhall Corner Essex 107 E10
Birch Heath Ches W 167 C8
Birch Hill Brack 65 F11
Ches W 183 G8
Birchill Devon 28 G4
Birchills W Mid 133 D10
Birchington Kent 71 F9
Birchley Heath Warks 134 E5
Birchmoor Warks 134 C5
Birchmoor Green
C Beds 103 E8
Bircholt Forstal Kent 54 E5
Birchover Derbys 170 C2
Birch Vale Derbys 185 D8
Birchwood Herts 86 D2
Lincs 172 B6
Som 28 E2
Warr 183 C10
Birchy Hill Hants 19 B11
Bircotes Notts 187 C10
Birdbrook Essex 106 C4
Birdbush Wilts 30 C6
Birdfield Argyll 275 D10
Birdforth N Yorks 215 D9
Birdham W Sus 22 D4
Birdholme Derbys 170 B5
Birdingbury Warks 119 D8
Birdlip Glos 80 C6
Birdsall N Yorks 216 F6
Birds Edge W Yorks 197 F8
Birds End Suff 124 E5
Birdsgreen Shrops 132 F5
Birds Green Essex 87 D9
Birdsmoorgate Dorset 28 G5
Birdston E Dunb 278 F3
Bird Street Suff 125 G10
Birdwell S Yorks 197 G10
Birdwood Glos 80 B2
Birgham Borders 263 B7
Birichen Highld 309 K7
Birkacre Lancs 194 D5
Birkby Cumb 229 D7
N Yorks 224 E6
W Yorks 196 D6
Birkdale Mers 193 D10
Birkenbog Aberds 302 C5
Birkenhead Mers 182 D4
Birkenhills Aberds 303 E7
Birkenshaw N Lanark 268 C3
S Lanark 268 F5
W Yorks 197 B8
Birkenshaw Bottoms
W Yorks 197 B8
Birkenside Borders 271 G11
Birkett Mire Cumb 230 G2
Birkhall Aberds 292 D5
Birkhill Angus 287 D7
Borders 260 F6
Borders 271 G11
Birkholme Lincs 155 E9
Birkhouse W Yorks 197 C7
Birkin N Yorks 198 B4
Birks Cumb 222 G3
W Yorks 197 B9
Birkshaw Northumb 241 D7
Birley Hereford 115 G9
Birley Carr S Yorks 186 C4
Birley Edge S Yorks 186 C4
Birleyhay Derbys 186 E5
Birling Kent 69 G7
Northumb 252 B6
Birling Gap E Sus 23 F9
Birlingham Worcs 99 C8
Birmingham W Mid 133 F11
Birnam Perth 286 C4
Birniehill S Lanark 268 E2
Birse Aberds 293 D7
Birsemore Aberds 293 D7
Birstall Leics 135 B11
W Yorks 197 B8
Birstall Smithies
W Yorks 197 B8
Birstwith N Yorks 205 B10
Birthorpe Lincs 156 C2
Birtle Gtr Man 195 E10
Birtley Hereford 115 D7
Northumb 241 B9
Shrops 131 E9
T&W 243 F7
Birtley Green Sur 50 E4
Birtsmorton Worcs 98 D6
Birts Street Worcs 98 D5
Bisbrooke Rutland 137 D7
Biscathorpe Lincs 190 D2
Biscombe Som 27 E11
Biscot Luton 103 G11
Biscovey Corn 5 E11
Bisham Windsor 65 C10
Bishampton Worcs 117 G9
Bish Mill Devon 26 B2
Bishon Common Hereford 97 C8
Bishop Auckland
Durham 233 F10
Bishopbridge Lincs 189 C8
Bishopbriggs E Dunb 278 G2
Bishop Burton E Yorks 208 F5
Bishopdown Wilts 47 G7
Bishop Kinkell Highld 300 D5
Bishop Middleham
Durham 234 E2
Bishopmill Moray 302 C2
Bishop Monkton
N Yorks 214 F6
Bishop Norton Lincs 189 C7
Bishopsbourne Kent 55 C7
Bishops Cannings Wilts 62 G4
Bishop's Castle Shrops 130 F6
Bishop's Caundle Dorset 29 E11
Bishop's Cleeve Glos 99 F9
Bishop's Down Dorset 29 E11
Bishops Frome Hereford 98 B3
Bishopsgarth Stockton 234 G4
Bishopsgate Sur 66 E3
Bishops Green Essex 87 B5
Bishop's Green W Berks 64 G4
Bishop's Hull Som 28 C2
Bishop's Itchington
Warks 119 F7
Bishops Lydeard Som 27 B11
Bishop's Norton Glos 98 G6
Bishops Nympton Devon 26 C3
Bishop's Offley Staffs 150 D5
Bishop's Quay Corn 2 D6
Bishop's Stortford
Herts 105 G9
Bishop's Sutton Hants 48 G6
Bishop's Tachbrook
Warks 118 E6
Bishops Tawton Devon 40 G5
Bishopsteignton Devon 14 G4
Bishopstoke Hants 33 D7
Bishopston Bristol 60 D5
Swansea 56 D5
Bishopstone Bucks 84 C4
E Sus 23 E7
Hereford 97 C8
Kent 71 F8
Swindon 63 C8
Wilts 31 B9
Bishopstrow Wilts 45 E11
Bishop Sutton Bath 44 B5
Bishop's Waltham Hants 33 D9
Bishopswood Som 28 E3
Bishop's Wood Staffs 132 B6
Bishopsworth Bristol 60 F5
Bishop Thornton
N Yorks 214 G5
Bishopthorpe York 207 D7
Bishopton Darl 234 G3
Dumfries 236 E6
N Yorks 214 E6
Renfs 277 G8
Warks 118 F3
Bishopwearmouth T&W 243 F9
Bishop Wilton E Yorks 207 B11
Bishpool Newport 59 B10
Bishton Newport 59 B11
Staffs 151 E10
Bisley Glos 80 D6
Sur 50 B3
Bisley Camp Sur 50 B2
Bispham Blackpool 202 E2
Bispham Green Lancs 194 E3
Bissoe Corn 4 G5
Bissom Corn 3 C7
Bisterne Hants 31 G10
Bisterne Close Hants 32 G2
Bitchet Green Kent 52 C5
Bitchfield Lincs 155 D9
Bittadon Devon 40 E4
Bittaford Devon 8 D3
Bittering Norf 159 F8
Bitterley Shrops 115 B11
Bitterne Soton 33 E7
Bitterne Park Soton 32 E6
Bitterscote Staffs 134 C4
Bitteswell Leics 135 F10
Bittles Green Dorset 30 C5
Bitton S Glos 61 F7
Bix Oxon 65 B8
Bixter Shetland 313 H5
Blaby Leics 135 D11
Blackacre Dumfries 248 E2
Blackadder West
Borders 272 E6
Blackawton Devon 8 E6
Black Bank Cambs 139 F10
Warks 135 F7
Black Banks Darl 224 C5
Black Barn Lincs 157 D8
Blackbeck Cumb 219 D10
Blackbird Leys Oxon 83 E9
Blackborough Devon 27 F9
Norf 158 G3
Blackborough End Norf 158 G3
Black Bourton Oxon 82 E3
Blackboys E Sus 37 C8
Blackbraes Aberds 293 B10
Blackbrook Derbys 170 F4
Derbys 185 E9
Mers 183 B8
Staffs 150 B5
Sur 51 D7
Blackburn Aberds 293 B10
Aberds 302 F5
Blackburn 195 B7
Blackburn *continued*
S Yorks 186 C5
W Loth 269 B9
Black Callerton T&W 242 D5
Black Carr Norf 141 D11
Blackcastle Midloth 271 D8
Blackchambers Aberds 293 B9
Black Clauchrie S Ayrs 245 G7
Black Corner W Sus 51 F9
Black Corries Lodge
Highld 284 B6
Blackcraig Dumfries 246 G6
Blackcraigs Angus 293 E7
Black Crofts Argyll 289 F11
Black Cross Corn 5 C8
Black Dam Hants 48 C6
Blackden Heath Ches E 184 G3
Blackditch Oxon 82 D6
Blackdog Aberds 293 B11
Black Dog Devon 26 F4
Blackdown Dorset 28 G5
Hants 33 C8
Warks 118 D6
Blackdyke Cumb 238 G4
Blackdykes E Loth 281 E11
Blacker Hill S Yorks 197 G11
Blacketts Kent 70 F2
Blackfell T&W 243 F7
Blackfen London 68 E3
Blackfield Hants 32 G6
Blackford Cumb 239 E9
Dumfries 248 G4
Perth 286 G2
Shrops 131 G11
Som 29 B11
Som 42 D2
Som 44 D2
Blackford Bridge
Gtr Man 195 F10
Blackfordby Leics 152 F6
Blackfords Staffs 151 G9
Blackgang IoW 20 F5
Blackgate Angus 287 B8
Blackhall Aberds 293 D8
Edin 280 G4
Renfs 267 C9
Blackhall Colliery
Durham 234 D5
Blackhall Mill T&W 242 F4
Blackhall Rocks Durham 234 D5
Blackham E Sus 52 F3
Blackhaugh Borders 261 B10
Blackheath Essex 107 G10
London 67 D11
Suff 127 C8
Sur 50 D4
W Mid 133 F9
Blackheath Park London 68 D2
Black Heddon Northumb 242 B3
Blackhill Aberds 303 D10
Aberds 303 E10
Aberds 303 F10
Durham 242 G3
Hants 32 D4
Highld 298 D3
Black Hill W Yorks 204 E6
Blackhillock Moray 302 E4
Blackhills Highld 301 D9
Moray 302 D2
Swansea 56 C5
Blackhorse Devon 14 C5
S Glos 61 D7
Black Horse Drove
Cambs 139 E11
Blackjack Lincs 156 B5
Black Lake W Mid 133 E9
Blackland Wilts 62 F4
Blacklands E Sus 38 E4
Hereford 98 C2
Black Lane Gtr Man 195 F9
Blacklaw Aberds 302 D6
Blackleach Lancs 202 G5
Blackley Gtr Man 195 G11
W Yorks 196 D6
Blacklunans Perth 292 G3
Black Marsh Shrops 130 D6
Blackmarstone Hereford 97 D10
Blackmill Bridgend 58 B2
Blackminster Worcs 99 C11
Blackmoor Bath 60 G5
Gtr Man 195 G7
Hants 49 G9
N Som 60 G3
Som 27 D11
Black Moor Lancs 194 E3
W Yorks 205 F11
Blackmoorfoot W Yorks 196 E5
Blackmoor Gate Devon 41 E7
Blackmore Essex 87 E10
Shrops 130 B6
Blackmore End Essex 106 E4
Herts 85 B11
Worcs 98 C6
Black Mount Argyll 284 C6
Blackness Aberds 293 D8
E Sus 52 G4
Falk 279 F11
Blacknest Hants 49 E9
Windsor 66 F3
Blacknoll Dorset 18 D2
Black Notley Essex 106 G5
Blacko Lancs 204 E3
Blackoe Shrops 149 B10
Blackpark Dumfries 236 C5
Black Park Wrex 166 G4
Black Pill Swansea 56 C6
Blackpole Worcs 117 F7
Black Pole Lancs 202 F5
Blackpool Blackpool 202 F2
Devon 7 E11
Devon 9 F7
Devon 14 G2
Pembs 73 C9
Blackpool Gate Cumb 240 B2
Blackridge W Loth 269 B7
Blackrock Argyll 274 G4
Bath 60 F6
Mon 78 C2
Black Rock Brighton 36 G4
Corn 2 C5
Blackrod Gtr Man 194 E6
Blackshaw Dumfries 238 D2
Blackshaw Head
W Yorks 196 B3
Blackshaw Moor Staffs 169 D8
Blacksmith's Corner
Suff 108 C2
Blacksmith's Green Suff 126 D2
Blacksnape Blackburn 195 C8
Blackstone Worcs 116 C5
W Sus 36 D2
Black Street Suff 143 F10
Black Tar Pembs 73 D7
Blackthorn Oxon 83 B10
Blackthorpe Suff 125 E8
Blacktoft E Yorks 199 C10
Blacktop Aberdeen 293 C10
Black Torrington Devon 25 F7
Blacktown Newport 59 C9
Black Vein Caerph 78 G2
Blackwall Derbys 170 F3
Blackwall *continued*
London 67 C11
Blackwall Tunnel
London 67 C11
Blackwater BCP 19 B8
Corn 4 F4
Hants 49 B11
IoW 20 D6
Norf 159 E11
Som 28 D3
Blackwaterfoot N Ayrs 255 E9
Blackwater Lodge
Moray 302 G3
Blackweir Cardiff 59 D7
Blackwell Cumb 239 G10
Darl 224 C5
Derbys 170 D6
Derbys 185 G10
Devon 27 B8
Warks 100 C4
Worcs 117 C9
W Sus 51 F11
Blackwood Caerph 77 F11
S Lanark 268 G5
Warr 183 C10
Blackwood Hill Staffs 168 D6
Blacon Ches W 166 B5
Bladbean Kent 55 D7
Blades N Yorks 223 F9
Bladnoch Dumfries 236 D6
Bladon Oxon 82 C6
Blaenannerch Ceredig 92 B4
Blaenau Carms 75 C10
Flint 166 D2
Blaenau Dolwyddelan
Conwy 164 E2
Blaenau Ffestiniog
Gwyn 164 F2
Blaenau-Gwent Bl Gwent 78 E2
Blaenavon Torf 78 D3
Blaenbedw Fawr
Ceredig 111 G7
Blaencaerau Bridgend 57 C11
Blaencelyn Ceredig 111 G7
Blaen-Cil-Llech Ceredig 92 C6
Blaen Clydach Rhondda 77 G7
Blaencwm Rhondda 76 F6
Blaendulais = *Seven Sisters*
Neath 76 D4
Blaendyryn Powys 95 D8
Blaenffos Pembs 92 D3
Blaengarw Bridgend 76 G6
Blaengwrach Neath 76 D5
Blaengwynfi Neath 57 B11
Blaen-gwynfi Neath 57 B11
Blaenllechau Rhondda 77 F8
Blaen-pant Ceredig 92 C5
Blaenpennal Ceredig 112 E2
Blaenplwyf Ceredig 111 B11
Blaenporth Ceredig 92 B5
Blaenrhondda Rhondda 76 E6
Blaenwaun Carms 92 F4
Blaen-waun Carms 92 F4
Ceredig 111 G7
Blaen-y-coed Carms 92 F6
Blaenycwm Ceredig 112 B6
Blaen-y-cwm Bl Gwent 77 C10
Denb 147 C10
Gwyn 146 E4
Powys 147 E11
Blagdon N Som 44 B4
Torbay 9 C7
Blagdon Hill Som 28 D2
Blagill Cumb 231 B10
Blaguegate Lancs 194 F3
Blaich Highld 290 F2
Blain Highld 289 C8
Blaina Bl Gwent 78 E2
Blainacraig Ho Aberds 293 D7
Blair Fife 280 C6
Blair Atholl Perth 291 G10
Blairbeg N Ayrs 256 C2
Blairburn Fife 279 D9
Blairdaff Aberds 293 B8
Blair Drummond Stirling 278 B4
Blairdryne Aberds 293 D9
Blairglas Argyll 276 D6
Blairgorm Highld 301 G10
Blairgowrie Perth 286 C5
Blairhall Fife 279 D10
Blairhill N Lanark 268 B4
Blairingone Perth 279 B9
Blairland N Ayrs 266 F6
Blairlinn N Lanark 278 G5
Blairlogie Stirling 278 B6
Blairlomond Argyll 276 B3
Blairmore Argyll 276 E3
Highld 306 D6
Blairnamarrow Moray 292 B4
Blairquhosh Stirling 277 E10
Blair's Ferry Argyll 275 G10
Blairskaith E Dunb 277 F11
Blaisdon Glos 80 B2
Blaise Hamlet Bristol 60 D5
Blakebrook Worcs 116 B6
Blakedown Worcs 117 B7
Blake End Essex 106 G4
Blakelands M Keynes 103 C7
Blakelaw Borders 263 C7
T&W 242 D6
Blakeley Staffs 133 E7
Blakeley Lane Staffs 169 F7
Blakelow Ches E 167 E11
Blakemere Hereford 97 C7
Blakenall Heath
W Mid 133 C10
Blakeney Glos 79 D11
Norf 177 E8
Blakenhall Ches E 168 F2
W Mid 133 D8
Blakeshall Worcs 132 G6
Blakesley W Nhants 120 G2
Blanchland Northumb 241 G11
Blandford Camp Dorset 30 F6
Blandford Forum Dorset 30 F5
Blandford St Mary Dorset 30 F5
Bland Hill N Yorks 205 C10
Blandy Highld 308 D6
Blanefield Stirling 277 F11
Blanerne Borders 272 D6
Blank Bank Staffs 168 F4
Blankney Lincs 173 C9
Blantyre S Lanark 268 D3
Blar a'Chaorainn Highld 290 G3
Blaran Argyll 275 B9
Blarghour Argyll 275 B10
Blarmachfoldach Highld 290 G2
Blarnalearoch Highld 307 K6
Blasford Hill Essex 88 C2
Blashford Hants 31 F11
Blaston Leics 136 D6
Blatchbridge Som 45 D9
Blatherwycke N Nhants 137 D9
Blawith Cumb 210 B5
Blaxhall Suff 127 F7
Blaxton S Yorks 199 G7
Blaydon T&W 242 E5
Blaydon Burn T&W 242 E5
Blaydon Haughs T&W 242 E5
Bleach Green Cumb 219 B9
Suff 126 B4

Bleadney Som 44 D3
Bleadon N Som 43 B10
Bleak Acre Hereford 98 B2
Bleak Hall M Keynes 103 D7
Bleak Hey Nook
Gtr Man 196 F4
Bleak Hill Hants 31 E10
Blean Kent 70 G6
Bleasby Lincs 189 E10
Notts 172 F2
Bleasby Moor Lincs 189 E10
Bleasdale Lancs 203 D7
Bleatarn Cumb 222 C4
Blebocraigs Fife 287 F8
Bleddfa Powys 114 D4
Bledington Glos 100 G4
Bledlow Bucks 84 E3
Bledlow Ridge Bucks 84 F3
Bleet Wilts 45 B11
Blegbie E Loth 271 C9
Blegbury Devon 24 B2
Blencarn Cumb 231 E8
Blencogo Cumb 229 B9
Blendworth Hants 34 E2
Blenheim Oxon 83 D9
Oxon 83 E9
Blenheim Park Norf 158 C6
Blenkinsopp Hall
Northumb 240 E5
Blennerhasset Cumb 229 C9
Blervie Castle Moray 301 D10
Bletchingdon Oxon 83 B8
Bletchingley Sur 51 C10
Bletchley M Keynes 103 E7
Shrops 150 C2
Bletherston Pembs 91 G11
Bletsoe Bedford 121 F10
Blewbury Oxon 64 B4
Bliby Kent 54 F4
Blickling Norf 160 D3
Blidworth Notts 171 D9
Blidworth Bottoms
Notts 171 E9
Blidworth Dale Notts 171 E9
Blindburn Northumb 263 G8
Blindcrake Cumb 229 E8
Blindley Heath Sur 51 D11
Blindmoor Som 28 E3
Blingery Highld 310 E7
Blisland Corn 11 G8
Blissford Hants 31 E11
Bliss Gate Worcs 116 C4
Blisworth W Nhants 120 G4
Blithbury Staffs 151 E11
Blitterlees Cumb 238 G4
Blockley Glos 100 D3
Blofield Norf 142 B6
Blofield Heath Norf 160 G6
Blo' Norton Norf 125 B10
Bloodman's Corner
Suff 143 D10
Bloomfield Bath 45 B7
Bath 61 G8
Borders 262 E3
W Mid 133 E9
Bloomsbury London 67 C10
Blore Staffs 150 C4
Staffs 169 F10
Bloreheath Staffs 150 B4
Blossomfield W Mid 118 B2
Blount's Green Staffs 151 C11
Blowick Mers 193 D11
Blowinghouse Corn 4 E4
Bloxham Oxon 101 D8
Bloxholm Lincs 173 E9
Bloxwich W Mid 133 C9
Bloxworth Dorset 18 C3
Blubberhouses N Yorks 205 B9
Blue Anchor Corn 5 D8
Som 42 E4
Swansea 56 B4
Bluebell Telford 149 G11
Blue Bell Hill Kent 69 G8
Bluecairn Borders 271 G10
Blue Hill Herts 104 G5
Blue Row Essex 89 C8
Bluetown Kent 54 B2
Blue Town Kent 70 D2
Blue Vein Wilts 61 F10
Bluewater Kent 68 E5
Blughasary Highld 307 J6
Blundellsands Mers 182 B4
Blundeston Suff 143 D10
Blundies Staffs 132 F6
Blunham C Beds 122 G3
Blunsdon St Andrew
Swindon 62 B6
Bluntington Worcs 117 C7
Bluntisham Cambs 123 C7
Blunts Corn 6 C6
Blunt's Green Warks 118 D2
Blurton Stoke 168 G5
Blyborough Lincs 188 C6
Blyford Suff 127 B8
Blymhill Staffs 150 G6
Blymhill Lawns Staffs 150 G6
Blyth Borders 270 F2
Northumb 253 G8
Notts 187 D10
Blyth Bridge Borders 270 F2
Blythburgh Suff 127 B9
Blythe Borders 271 F11
Blythe Bridge Staffs 169 G7
Blythe Marsh Staffs 169 G7
Blyth End Warks 134 E4
Blythswood Renfs 267 B10
Blyton Lincs 188 C5
Boarhills Fife 287 F9
Boarhunt Hants 33 F10
Boarsgreave Lancs 195 C10
Boarshead E Sus 52 G4
Boars Hill Oxon 83 E7
Boarstall Bucks 83 C10
Boasley Cross Devon 12 C5
Boath Highld 300 B5
Boat of Garten Highld 291 B11
Bobbing Kent 69 F11
Bobbington Staffs 132 E6
Bobbingworth Essex 87 D8
Bobby Hill Suff 125 C10
Boblainy Highld 300 F4
Bocaddon Corn 6 D3
Bochastle Stirling 285 G10
Bockhanger Kent 54 E4
Bocking Essex 106 G5
Bocking Churchstreet
Essex 106 F5
Bocking's Elm Essex 89 B11
Bockleton Worcs 115 E11
Bockmer End Bucks 65 B10
Bocombe Devon 24 C5
Bodantionail Highld 299 B7
Boddam Aberds 303 E11
Shetland 313 M5
Bodden Som 44 E6
Boddington Glos 99 F7
Bodedern Anglesey 178 E4
Bodellick Corn 10 G5
Bodelva Corn 5 E11
Bodelwyddan Denb 181 F8
Bodenham Hereford 115 G10
Bodenham *continued*
Wilts 31 B11
Bodenham Bank Hereford 98 E2
Bodenham Moor
Hereford 115 G10
Bodermid Gwyn 144 D3
Bodewryd Anglesey 178 C5
Bodfari Denb 181 G9
Bodffordd Anglesey 178 F6
Bodham Norf 177 E10
Bodiam E Sus 38 B3
Bodicote Oxon 101 D9
Bodiechell Aberds 303 E7
Bodieve Corn 10 G5
Bodiggo Corn 5 D10
Bodilly Corn 2 C5
Bodinnick Corn 6 E2
Bodle Street Green
E Sus 23 C11
Bodley Devon 41 D7
Bodmin Corn 5 B11
Bodmiscombe Devon 27 F10
Bodney Norf 140 D6
Bodorgan Anglesey 162 B5
Bodsham Kent 54 D6
Boduan Gwyn 144 B6
Boduel Corn 6 C4
Bodwen Corn 5 C10
Bodymoor Heath Warks 134 D4
Bofarnel Corn 6 C2
Bogallan Highld 300 D6
Bogbrae Aberds 303 F10
Bogend Borders 272 F5
Notts 171 F7
S Ayrs 257 C9
Bogentory Aberds 293 C9
Boghall Midloth 270 B4
W Loth 269 B9
Boghead Aberds 293 D8
S Lanark 268 G5
Bogmoor Moray 302 C3
Bogniebrae Aberds 302 E5
Aberds 302 E6
Bognor Regis W Sus 22 D6
Bograxie Aberds 293 B9
Bogs Aberds 302 G5
Bogs Bank Borders 270 E3
Bogside N Lanark 268 E6
Bogthorn W Yorks 204 F6
Bogton Aberds 302 D6
Bogtown Aberds 302 C5
Bogue Dumfries 246 G4
Bohemia E Sus 38 E4
Wilts 32 D2
Bohenie Highld 290 E4
Bohetherick Corn 7 B8
Bohortha Corn 3 C9
Bohuntine Highld 290 E4
Bohuntinville Highld 290 E4
Boirseam W Isles 296 C6
Bojewyan Corn 1 C3
Bokiddick Corn 5 C11
Bolahaul Fm Carms 74 B6
Bolam Durham 233 G9
Northumb 252 G3
Bolam West Houses
Northumb 252 G3
Bolas Heath Telford 150 E3
Bolberry Devon 9 G8
Bold Heath Mers 183 D8
Boldmere W Mid 134 E2
Boldon T&W 243 E9
Boldon Colliery T&W 243 E8
Boldre Hants 20 B2
Boldron Durham 223 C10
Bole Notts 188 D3
Bolehall Staffs 134 C4
Bolehill Derbys 170 E3
Derbys 186 G6
S Yorks 186 E5
Bole Hill Derbys 186 G4
Bolenowe Corn 2 B5
Boleside Borders 261 C11
Boley Park Staffs 134 B2
Bolham Devon 27 E7
Notts 188 E2
Bolham Water Devon 27 E11
Bolholt Gtr Man 195 E9
Bolingey Corn 4 E5
Bolitho Corn 2 C5
Bollihope Durham 232 E6
Bollington Ches E 184 F6
Bollington Cross Ches E 184 F6
Bolney W Sus 36 C3
Bolnhurst Bedford 121 F11
Bolnore W Sus 36 C4
Bolshan Angus 287 B10
Bolsover Derbys 187 G7
Bolsterstone S Yorks 186 B3
Bolstone Hereford 97 E11
Boltby N Yorks 215 B9
Bolter End Bucks 84 G3
Bolton Cumb 231 G8
E Loth 281 G10
E Yorks 207 C11
Gtr Man 195 F8
Northumb 264 G4
W Yorks 205 F9
Bolton Abbey N Yorks 205 C7
Bolton Bridge N Yorks 205 C7
Bolton-by-Bowland
Lancs 203 D11
Boltonfellend Cumb 239 D11
Boltongate Cumb 229 C10
Bolton Green Lancs 194 D5
Bolton Houses Lancs 202 G4
Bolton-le-Sands Lancs 211 F9
Bolton Low Houses
Cumb 229 C10
Bolton New Houses
Cumb 229 C10
Bolton-on-Swale
N Yorks 224 F5
Bolton Percy N Yorks 206 E6
Bolton Town End Lancs 211 F9
Bolton upon Dearne
S Yorks 198 G3
Bolton Wood Lane
Cumb 229 C11
Bolton Woods W Yorks 205 F9
Boltshope Park Durham 232 B4
Bolventor Corn 11 F9
Bomarsund Northumb 253 G7
Bombie Dumfries 237 D9
Bomby Cumb 221 B10
Bomere Heath Shrops 149 F9
Bonaly Edin 270 B4
Bonar Bridge Highld 309 K6
Bonawe Argyll 284 D4
Bonby N Lincs 200 D4
Boncath Pembs 92 D4
Bonchester Bridge
Borders 262 G3
Bonchurch IoW 21 F7
Bondend Glos 80 B5
Bond End Staffs 152 F2
Bondleigh Devon 25 G11
Bondman Hays Leics 135 B9
Bonds Lancs 202 E5
Bondstones Devon 25 F9
Bonehill Devon 13 F10
Bonehill *continued*
Staffs 134 C3
Bo'ness Falk 279 E9
Bonhill W Dunb 277 F7
Boningale Shrops 132 C6
Bonjedward Borders 262 E5
Bonkle N Lanark 268 D6
Bonnavoulin Highld 289 D7
Bonning Gate Cumb 221 F9
Bonnington Borders 261 B7
Edin 270 B2
Kent 54 F5
Bonnybank Fife 287 G7
Bonnybridge Falk 278 E6
Bonnykelly Aberds 303 D8
Bonnyrigg and Lasswade
Midloth 270 B6
Bonnyton Aberds 302 F6
Angus 287 B10
Angus 287 D7
E Ayrs 257 B10
Bonsall Derbys 170 D3
Bonskeid House Perth 291 G10
Bonson Som 43 E8
Bont Mon 78 B5
Bontddu Gwyn 146 F3
Bont-Dolgadfan Powys 129 C7
Bont Fawr Carms 94 F4
Bont goch *= Elerch*
Ceredig 128 F3
Bonthorpe Lincs 191 G7
Bontnewydd Ceredig 112 D2
Gwyn 163 D7
Bont-newydd Conwy 181 G8
Bont Newydd Gwyn 146 E5
Gwyn 164 G2
Bontuchel Denb 165 D9
Bonvilston *= Tresimwn*
V Glam 58 E5
Bon-y-maen Swansea 57 B7
Boode Devon 40 F4
Booker Bucks 84 G4
Bookham Dorset 30 G2
Booleybank Shrops 149 D11
Boon Borders 271 F11
Boon Hill Staffs 168 E4
Boorley Green Hants 33 E8
Boosbeck Redcar 226 B3
Boose's Green Essex 106 E6
Boot Cumb 220 E3
Booth Staffs 151 D10
W Yorks 196 B4
Booth Bank Ches E 184 D2
Booth Bridge Lancs 204 D4
Boothby Graffoe Lincs 173 D7
Boothby Pagnell Lincs 155 C9
Boothen Stoke 168 G5
Boothferry E Yorks 199 B8
Boothgate Derbys 170 F5
Booth Green Ches E 184 E6
Boothroyd W Yorks 197 C8
Boothsdale Ches W 167 B8
Boothstown Gtr Man 195 G8
Boothtown W Yorks 196 B5
Boothville W Nhants 120 E5
Booth Wood W Yorks 196 D4
Bootle Cumb 210 B2
Mers 182 B4
Booton Norf 160 E2
Boots Green Ches W 184 G3
Boot Street Suff 108 B4
Booze N Yorks 223 E10
Boquhan Stirling 277 D10
Boquio Corn 2 C5
Boraston Shrops 116 D2
Boraston Dale Shrops 116 C2
Borden Kent 69 G11
W Sus 34 C4
Border Cumb 238 G5
Bordesley W Mid 133 F11
Bordesley Green W Mid 134 F2
Bordlands Borders 270 F3
Bordley N Yorks 213 G8
Bordon Hants 49 F10
Bordon Camp Hants 49 F9
Boreham Essex 88 D3
Wilts 45 E11
Boreham Street E Sus 23 C11
Borehamwood Herts 85 F11
Boreland Dumfries 236 C5
Dumfries 248 E5
Fife 280 C6
Stirling 285 D9
Boreland of Southwick
Dumfries 237 C11
Boreley Worcs 116 D6
Borestone Stirling 278 C5
Borgh W Isles 296 C5
W Isles 297 L2
Borghasdal W Isles 296 C6
Borghastan W Isles 304 D4
Borgie Highld 308 D6
Borgue Dumfries 237 E8
Highld 311 G5
Borley Essex 106 C6
Borley Green Essex 106 C6
Suff 125 E9
Bornais W Isles 297 J3
Bornesketaig Highld 298 B3
Borness Dumfries 237 E8
Borough Scilly 1 G3
Boroughbridge N Yorks 215 F7
Borough Green Kent 52 B6
Borough Marsh
Wokingham 65 D9
Borough Park Staffs 134 B4
Borough Post Som 28 C4
Borras Wrex 166 E4
Borras Head Wrex 166 E5
Borreraig Highld 296 F7
Borrobol Lodge Highld 311 G2
Borrodale Highld 297 G7
Borrohill Aberds 303 D9
Borrowash Derbys 153 C8
Borrowby N Yorks 215 B8
N Yorks 226 B5
Borrowdale Cumb 220 C5
Borrowfield Aberds 293 D10
Borrowston Highld 310 E7
Borrowstoun Mains
Falk 279 E9
Borstal Medway 69 F8
Borth *= Y Borth* Ceredig 128 E2
Borthwick Midloth 271 D7
Borthwickbrae Borders 261 G10
Borthwickshiels
Borders 261 F10
Borth-y-Gest Gwyn 145 B11
Borve Highld 298 E4
Borve Lodge W Isles 305 J2
Borwick Lancs 211 E10
Borwick Rails Cumb 210 D3
Bosavern Corn 1 C3
Bosbury Hereford 98 C3
Boscadjack Corn 2 C5
Boscastle Corn 11 C8
Boscean Corn 1 C3
Boscombe BCP 19 C8
Wilts 47 F8
Boscomoor Staffs 151 G8
Boscoppa Corn 5 E10
Boscreege Corn 2 C3
Bosham W Sus 22 C4
Bosham Hoe W Sus 22 C4
Bosherston Pembs 73 G7
Boskednan Corn 1 C4
Boskenna Corn 1 E4
Bosleake Corn 4 G3
Bosley Ches E 168 B6
Boslowick Corn 3 C7
Boslymon Corn 5 C11
Bosoughan Corn 5 C7
Bosporthennis Corn 1 B4
Bossall N Yorks 216 G4
Bossiney Corn 11 D7
Bossingham Kent 54 D6
Bossington Hants 47 G10
Kent 55 B8
Som 41 D11
Bostadh W Isles 304 D3
Bostock Green Ches W 167 B11
Boston Lincs 174 G4
Boston Long Hedges
Lincs 174 F5
Boston Spa W Yorks 206 D4
Boston West Lincs 174 F3
Boswednack Corn 1 B4
Boswin Corn 2 C5
Boswinger Corn 5 G9
Boswyn Corn 2 B5
Botallack Corn 1 C3
Botany Bay London 86 F3
Mon 79 E8
Botcherby Cumb 239 F10
Botcheston Leics 135 B9
Botesdale Suff 125 B10
Bothal Northumb 252 F6
Bothampstead W Berks 64 D4
Bothamsall Notts 187 G11
Bothel Cumb 229 D9
Bothenhampton Dorset 16 C5
Bothwell S Lanark 268 D4
Bothy Highld 290 F4
Botley Bucks 85 E7
Hants 33 E8
Oxon 83 D7
Botloe's Green Glos 98 F4
Botolph Claydon Bucks 102 G4
Botolphs W Sus 35 F11
Bottacks Highld 300 C4
Botternell Corn 11 G11
Bottesford Leics 154 B6
N Lincs 199 F11
Bottisham Cambs 123 E10
Bottlesford Wilts 46 B6
Bottom Boat W Yorks 197 C11
Bottomcraig Fife 287 E7
Bottom House Staffs 169 E8
Bottomley W Yorks 196 D5
Bottom of Hutton Lancs 194 B3
Bottom o' th' Moor
Gtr Man 195 E7
Bottom Pond Kent 53 B11
Bottoms Corn 1 E3
Bottreaux Mill Devon 26 B4
Bottrells Close Bucks 85 G7
Botts Green Warks 134 E4
Botusfleming Corn 7 C8
Botwnnog Gwyn 144 C5
Bough Beech Kent 52 D3
Boughrood Powys 96 D2
Boughrood Brest Powys 96 D2
Boughspring Glos 79 F9
Boughton Ches W 166 B6
Lincs 173 F10
Norf 140 C3
Notts 171 B11
W Nhants 120 D5
Boughton Aluph Kent 54 D4
Boughton Corner Kent 54 D4
Boughton Green Kent 53 C9
Boughton Heath
Ches W 166 B6
Boughton Lees Kent 54 D4
Boughton Malherbe
Kent 53 D11
Boughton Monchelsea
Kent 53 C9
Boughton Street Kent 54 B5
Bougton End C Beds 103 D9
Boulby Redcar 226 B5
Bould Oxon 100 G4
Boulden Shrops 131 F10
Boulder Clough
W Yorks 196 C4
Bouldnor IoW 20 D3
Bouldon Shrops 131 F10
Boulmer Northumb 265 G7
Boulsdon Glos 98 G4
Boulston Pembs 73 C7
Boultenstone Aberds 292 B6
Boultham Lincs 173 B7
Boultham Moor Lincs 173 B7
Boulton Derbys 153 C7
Boulton Moor Derbys 153 C7
Boundary Leics 152 F6
Staffs 169 G7
Boundstone Sur 49 E10
Bountis Thorne Devon 24 D5
Bourn Cambs 122 F6
Bournbrook W Mid 133 G10
Bourne Lincs 155 E11
N Som 44 B3
Bourne End Bedford 121 E10
Bucks 65 B11
C Beds 103 C9
Herts 85 D8
Bournemouth BCP 19 C7
Bournes Green Glos 80 E6
Southend 70 B2
Worcs 117 C8
Bourne Vale W Mid 133 D11
Bourne Valley BCP 19 C7
Bournheath Worcs 117 C9
Bournmoor Durham 243 G8
Bournside Glos 99 G8
Bournstream Glos 80 G2
Bournville W Mid 133 G10
Bourton Bucks 102 E4
Dorset 45 G9
N Som 59 G11
Oxon 63 B8
Shrops 131 D11
Wilts 62 G4
Bourton on Dunsmore
Warks 119 C8
Bourton-on-the-Hill
Glos 100 E3
Bourton-on-the-Water
Glos 100 G3
Bourtreehill N Ayrs 257 B8
Bousd Argyll 288 C4
Bousta Shetland 313 H4
Boustead Hill Cumb 239 F7
Bouth Cumb 210 B6
Bouthwaite N Yorks 214 E2
Bouts Worcs 117 F10
Bovain Stirling 285 D9
Boveney Bucks 66 D2
Boveridge Dorset 31 E9
Boverton V Glam 58 F3
Bovey Tracey Devon 14 F2
Bovingdon Herts 85 E8
Bovingdon Green Bucks 65 B10
Herts 85 E8
Bovinger Essex 87 D8
Bovington Camp Dorset 18 D2
Bow Borders 271 G9
Devon 8 D6
Devon 26 G2
Orkney 314 G3
Oxon 82 G4
Bowbank Durham 232 G4
Bowbeck Suff 125 B8
Bow Brickhill M Keynes 103 E8
Bowbridge Glos 80 E5
Bowbrook Shrops 149 G9
Bow Broom S Yorks 187 B7
Bowburn Durham 234 D2
Bowcombe IoW 20 D5
Bow Common London 67 C11
Bowd Devon 15 C8
Bowden Borders 262 C3
Devon 8 F6
Dorset 30 C3
Bowden Hill Wilts 62 F2
Bowdens Som 28 B6
Bowderdale Cumb 222 E3
Bowdon Gtr Man 184 D3
Bower Highld 310 C6
Northumb 251 G7
Bower Ashton Bristol 60 E5
Bowerchalke Wilts 31 C8
Bower Heath Herts 85 B10
Bowerhill Wilts 62 G2
Bower Hinton Som 29 D7
Bowerhope Borders 261 E7
Bower House Tye Suff 107 C9
Bowermadden Highld 310 C6
Bowers Staffs 150 B6
Bowers Gifford Essex 69 B9
Bowershall Fife 279 C11
Bowertower Highld 310 C6
Bowes Durham 223 C9
Bowes Park London 86 G4
Bowgreave Lancs 202 E5
Bowgreen Gtr Man 184 D3
Bowhill Borders 261 D10
Fife 280 B4
Bowhouse Dumfries 238 D2
Bowhousebog or Liquo
N Lanark 269 D7
Bowing Park Mers 182 D6
Bowismiln Borders 262 E2
Bowithick Corn 11 E9
Bowker's Green Lancs 194 G2
Bowland Bridge Cumb 211 B8
Bowldown Wilts 62 D2
Bowlee Gtr Man 195 F10
Bowlees Durham 232 F4
Bowler's Town E Sus 38 C6
Bowley Hereford 115 G10
Bowley Lane Hereford 98 C3
Bowley Town Hereford 115 G10
Bowlhead Green Sur 50 F2
Bowling W Dunb 277 G9
W Yorks 205 G9
Bowling Alley Hants 49 D9
Bowling Bank Wrex 166 F5
Bowling Green Corn 5 D10
Corn 12 G3
Glos 81 E8
Hants 19 B11
Shrops 150 D2
W Mid 133 F8
Worcs 116 G6
Bowlish Som 44 E6
Bowmans Kent 68 E4
Bowmanstead Cumb 220 F6
Bowmore Argyll 254 B4
Bowness-on-Solway
Cumb 238 E6
Bowness-on-Windermere
Cumb 221 F8
Bow of Fife Fife 287 F7
Bowridge Hill Dorset 30 B4
Bowrie-fauld Angus 287 C9
Bowsden Northumb 273 G9
Bowsey Hill Windsor 65 C10
Bowshank Borders 271 G9
Bowside Lodge Highld 310 C2
Bowston Cumb 221 F9
Bow Street Ceredig 128 G2
Norf 141 D10
Bowthorpe Norf 142 B3
Bowyer's Common Hants 34 B3
Box Glos 80 E5
Wilts 61 F10
Boxbush Glos 80 C2
Glos 98 G3
Box End Bedford 103 B10
Boxford Suff 107 C9
W Berks 64 E2
Boxgrove W Sus 22 B6
Box Hill Sur 51 C7
Wilts 61 F10
Boxley Kent 53 B9
Boxmoor Herts 85 D9
Box's Shop Corn 24 G2
Boxted Essex 107 E9
Suff 124 G6
Boxted Cross Essex 107 E10
Boxted Heath Essex 107 E10
Box Trees W Mid 118 C2
Boxwell Glos 80 G4
Boxworth Cambs 122 E6
Boxworth End Cambs 123 D7
Boyatt Wood Hants 32 C6
Boyden End Suff 124 F4
Boyden Gate Kent 71 F8
Boyland Common Norf 141 G11
Boylestone Derbys 152 B3
Boylestonfield Derbys 152 B3
Boyndie Aberds 302 C6
Boyn Hill Windsor 65 C11
Boynton E Yorks 218 F2
Boysack Angus 287 C9
Angus 287 C10
Boys Hill Dorset 29 E11
Boys Village V Glam 58 F4
Boythorpe Derbys 186 G5
Boyton Corn 12 C2
Suff 109 B7
Wilts 46 F3
Boyton Cross Essex 87 D10
Boyton End Essex 106 E2
Suff 106 C4
Bozeat N Nhants 121 F8
Bozen Green Herts 105 F8
Braaid IoM 192 E4
Braal Castle Highld 310 C5
Brabling Green Suff 126 E5
Brabourne Kent 54 E5
Brabourne Lees Kent 54 E5
Brabster Highld 310 C7
Bracadale Highld 294 B5
Bracara Highld 295 F9
Braceborough Lincs 155 G11
Bracebridge Lincs 173 B7
Bracebridge Heath
Lincs 173 B7
Bracebridge Low Fields
Lincs 173 B7
Braceby Lincs 155 B10
Bracewell Lancs 204 D3
Bracken Bank W Yorks 204 F6
Brackenber Cumb 222 B4
Brackenbottom N Yorks 212 E6
Brackenfield Derbys 170 D5
Brackenhall W Yorks 197 D7
Bracken Hill W Yorks 197 C7
Brackenlands Cumb 229 B11
Bracken Park W Yorks 206 E3
Brackenthwaite Cumb 229 B11
Cumb 229 G9
N Yorks 205 C11
Brackla *= Bragle*
Bridgend 58 D2
Bracklamore Aberds 303 D8
Bracklesham W Sus 22 D4
Brackletter Highld 290 E3
Brackley Argyll 255 C8
W Nhants 101 D11
Brackloch Highld 307 G6
Bracknell Brack 65 F11
Braco Perth 286 G2
Bracobrae Moray 302 D5
Braco Castle Perth 286 F2
Bracon N Lincs 199 F9
Bracon Ash Norf 142 D3
Braco Park Aberds 303 C9
Bracorina Highld 295 F9
Bradaford Devon 12 C3
Bradbourne Derbys 170 E2
Bradbury Durham 234 F2
Bradda IoM 192 F2
Bradden W Nhants 102 B2
Braddock Corn 6 C3
Braddocks Hay Staffs 168 D5
Bradeley Stoke 168 E5
Bradeley Green Ches E 167 G8
Bradenham Bucks 84 F4
Norf 141 B8
Bradenstoke Wilts 62 D4
Brades Village W Mid 133 E9
Bradfield Devon 27 F9
Essex 108 E2
Norf 160 C5
W Berks 64 E6
Bradfield Combust Suff 125 F7
Bradfield Green
Ches E 167 D11
Bradfield Heath Essex 108 F2
Bradfield St Clare Suff 125 F8
Bradfield St George
Suff 125 E8
Bradford Corn 11 F8
Derbys 170 C2
Devon 24 F6
Gtr Man 184 B5
Northumb 264 C5
W Yorks 205 G9
Bradford Abbas Dorset 29 E9
Bradford Leigh Wilts 61 G10
Bradford-on-Avon
Wilts 61 G10
Bradford-on-Tone Som 27 C11
Bradford Peverell Dorset 17 C9
Bradgate S Yorks 186 C6
Bradiford Devon 40 G5
Brading IoW 21 D8
Bradley Derbys 170 F2
Glos 80 G3
Hants 48 E6
NE Lincs 201 F8
Staffs 151 F7
W Mid 133 D8
Wrex 166 E4
W Yorks 197 C7
Bradley Cross Som 44 C3
Bradley Fold Gtr Man 195 F9
Bradley Green Ches W 167 F8
Glos 80 G2
Som 43 F9
Warks 134 C5
Worcs 117 E9
Bradley in the Moors
Staffs 169 G9
Bradley Mills W Yorks 197 D7
Bradley Mount Ches E 184 F6
Bradley Stoke S Glos 60 C6
Bradlow Hereford 98 D4
Bradmore Notts 153 C11
W Mid 133 D7
Bradney Shrops 132 D5
Som 43 F10
Bradninch Devon 27 G8
Bradnock's Marsh
W Mid 118 B4
Bradnop Staffs 169 D8
Bradnor Green Hereford 114 F5
Bradpole Dorset 16 C5
Bradshaw Gtr Man 195 E8
Staffs 168 D6
W Yorks 196 E5
W Yorks 205 G7
Bradstone Devon 12 E3
Bradville M Keynes 102 C6
Bradwall Green Ches E 168 C3
Bradway S Yorks 186 E4
Bradwell Derbys 185 E11
Devon 40 E3
Essex 106 G6
M Keynes 102 D6
Norf 143 C10
Staffs 168 F4
Bradwell Common
M Keynes 102 D6
Bradwell Grove Oxon 82 D2
Bradwell Hills Derbys 185 E11
Bradwell on Sea Essex 89 D8
Bradwell Waterside
Essex 89 D7
Bradworthy Devon 24 E4
Bradworthy Cross Devon 24 E4
Brae Dumfries 237 B10
Highld 307 L3
Highld 309 J4
Shetland 312 G5
Braeantra Highld 300 B5
Braebuster Orkney 314 F5
Braedownie Angus 292 F4
Braeface Falk 278 E5
Braefield Highld 300 F4
Braefindon Highld 300 D6
Braegrum Perth 286 E4
Braehead Dumfries 236 D6
Orkney 314 B4
Orkney 314 F5
S Ayrs 257 E8
S Lanark 259 C8
S Lanark 267 D11
S Lanark 269 E9
Stirling 278 C6
Braehead of Lunan
Angus 287 B10
Braehoulland Shetland 312 F4
Braehour Highld 310 D4
Braehungie Highld 310 F5
Braeintra Highld 295 B10
Braelangwell Lodge
Highld 309 K5
Braemar Aberds 292 D3
Braemore Highld 299 B11
Braemore *continued*
Highld 310 F4
Brae of Achnahaird
Highld 307 H5
Brae of Boquhapple
Stirling 285 G10
Braepark Edin 280 F3
Brae Roy Lodge Highld 290 D5
Braeside Invclyd 276 F4
Braes of Enzie Moray 302 D3
Braes of Ullapool Highld 307 K6
Braeswick Orkney 314 C6
Braevallich Argyll 275 C10
Braewick Shetland 312 F4
Shetland 313 H5
Brafferton Darl 233 G11
N Yorks 215 E8
Brafield-on-the-Green
W Nhants 120 F6
Bragar W Isles 304 D4
Bragbury End Herts 104 G5
Bragenham Bucks 103 F8
Bragle *= Brackla*
Bridgend 58 D2
Bragleenmore Argyll 289 G11
Braichmelyn Gwyn 163 B10
Braichyfedw Powys 129 E7
Braid Edin 280 G4
Braides Lancs 202 C4
Braidfauld Glasgow 268 C2
Braidley N Yorks 213 C10
Braids Argyll 255 C8
Braidwood S Lanark 268 F6
Braigh Chalasaigh
W Isles 296 D5
Braigo Argyll 274 G3
Brailsford Derbys 170 G3
Brailsford Green Derbys 170 G3
Braingortan Argyll 275 F11
Brain's Green Glos 79 D11
Brainshaugh Northumb 252 C6
Braintree Essex 106 G5
Braiseworth Suff 126 C2
Braishfield Hants 32 B5
Braiswick Essex 107 F9
Braithwaite Cumb 229 G10
S Yorks 198 E6
W Yorks 204 E6
Braithwell S Yorks 187 C8
Brakefield Green Norf 141 B10
Brakenhill W Yorks 198 D2
Bramber W Sus 35 E11
Bramblecombe Dorset 30 G3
Brambridge Hants 33 C7
Bramcote Notts 153 B10
Warks 135 F8
Bramcote Hills Notts 153 B10
Bramcote Mains Warks 135 F8
Bramdean Hants 33 B10
Bramerton Norf 142 C5
Bramfield Herts 86 B3
Suff 127 C7
Bramford Suff 108 B2
W Mid 133 E8
Bramhall Gtr Man 184 D5
Bramhall Moor Gtr Man 184 D6
Bramhall Park Gtr Man 184 D5
Bramham W Yorks 206 E4
Bramhope W Yorks 205 E11
Bramley Derbys 186 F6
Hants 48 B6
Sur 50 D4
S Yorks 187 C7
W Yorks 205 F10
Bramley Corner Hants 48 B6
Bramley Green Hants 49 B7
Bramley Head N Yorks 205 B8
Bramley Vale Derbys 171 B7
Bramling Kent 55 B8
Brampford Speke Devon 14 B4
Brampton Cambs 122 C4
Cumb 231 G9
Cumb 240 E2
Derbys 186 G5
Hereford 97 D8
Lincs 188 F4
Norf 160 E4
Suff 143 G8
S Yorks 198 G2
Brampton Abbotts
Hereford 98 F2
Brampton Ash N Nhants 136 F5
Brampton Bryan
Hereford 115 C7
Brampton en le Morthen
S Yorks 187 D7
Brampton Park Cambs 122 C4
Brampton Street Suff 143 G8
Bramshall Staffs 151 C11
Bramshaw Hants 32 D3
Bramshill Hants 65 G8
Bramshott Hants 49 G10
Bramwell Som 28 B6
Branatwatt Shetland 313 H4
Branault Highld 289 C7
Branbridges Kent 53 D7
Brancaster Norf 176 E3
Brancaster Staithe Norf 176 E3
Brancepeth Durham 233 D10
Branch End Northumb 242 E3
Branchill Moray 301 D10
Branchton Invclyd 276 F4
Brand End Lincs 174 F5
Branderburgh Moray 302 B2
Brandesburton E Yorks 209 D8
Brandeston Suff 126 E4
Brand Green Glos 98 F4
Hereford 98 C5
Brandhill Shrops 115 B8
Brandis Corner Devon 24 G6
Brandish Street Som 42 D2
Brandiston Norf 160 E2
Brandlingill Cumb 229 F8
Brandon Durham 233 D10
Lincs 172 F6
Northumb 264 F2
Suff 140 F5
Warks 119 B8
Brandon Bank Cambs 140 F2
Brandon Creek Norf 140 E2
Brandon Parva Norf 141 B11
Brandsby N Yorks 215 E11
Brands Hill Windsor 66 D4
Brandwood Shrops 149 D9
Brandwood End
W Mid 117 B11
Brandy Carr W Yorks 197 C10
Brandy Hole Essex 88 F4
Brandyquoy Orkney 314 G4
Brandy Wharf Lincs 189 B8
Brane Corn 1 D4
Bran End Essex 106 F3
Branksome BCP 18 C6
Darl 224 B5
Branksome Park BCP 19 C7
Bransbury Hants 48 E2
Bransby Lincs 188 F5
Branscombe Devon 15 D9
Bransford Worcs 116 G5
Bransgore Hants 19 B9
Branshill Clack 279 C7
Bransholme Hull 209 G8
Branson's Cross Worcs 117 C11
Branston Leics 154 D6
Lincs 173 B8
Staffs 152 E4
Branston Booths Lincs 173 B9
Branstone IoW 21 E7
Bransty Cumb 219 B9
Brant Broughton Lincs 172 E6
Brantham Suff 108 E2
Branthwaite Cumb 229 D11
Cumb 229 G7
Branthwaite Edge Cumb 229 G7
Brantingham E Yorks 200 B2
Branton Northumb 264 F2
S Yorks 198 G6
Branton Green N Yorks 215 G8
Branxholme Borders 261 G11
Branxholm Park
Borders 261 G11
Branxton Northumb 263 B9
Brascote Leics 135 C8
Brassey Green Ches W 167 C8
Brassington Derbys 170 E2
Brasted Kent 52 C3
Brasted Chart Kent 52 C3
Brathens Aberds 293 D8
Bratoft Lincs 175 B7
Brattle Kent 54 G2
Brattleby Lincs 188 E6
Bratton Som 42 D2
Telford 150 G2
Wilts 46 C2
Bratton Clovelly Devon 12 C5
Bratton Fleming Devon 40 F6
Bratton Seymour Som 29 B11
Braughing Herts 105 F7
Braughing Friars Herts 105 G8
Braulen Lodge Highld 300 F2
Braunston W Nhants 119 D10
Braunstone Leics 135 C11
Braunstone Town
Leicester 135 C11
Braunston-in-Rutland
Rutland 136 B6
Braunton Devon 40 F3
Brawby N Yorks 216 D4
Brawith N Yorks 225 D10
Brawl Highld 310 C2
Brawlbin Highld 310 D4
Bray Windsor 66 D2
Braybrooke N Nhants 136 G5
Braydon Side Wilts 62 B4
Brayford Devon 41 G7
Brayfordhill Devon 41 G7
Brays Grove Essex 87 D7
Bray Shop Corn 12 G2
Braystones Cumb 219 D10
Brayswick Worcs 98 B6
Braythorn N Yorks 205 D10
Brayton N Yorks 207 G8
Braytown Dorset 18 D2
Bray Wick Windsor 65 D11
Braywoodside Windsor 65 D11
Brazacott Corn 11 C11
Brazenhill Staffs 151 E7
Brea Corn 4 G3
Breach Bath 60 G6
Kent 69 F10
W Sus 22 B3
Breachacha Castle
Argyll 288 D3
Breachwood Green
Herts 104 G2
Breacleit W Isles 304 E3
Breaden Heath Shrops 149 B8
Breadsall Derbys 153 B7
Breadsall Hilltop Derby 153 B7
Breadstone Glos 80 E2
Bread Street Glos 80 D4
Breage Corn 2 D4
Breakachy Highld 300 E4
Brealeys Devon 25 D8
Bream Glos 79 D10
Breamore Hants 31 D11
Bream's Meend Glos 79 D9
Brean Som 43 B9
Breanais W Isles 304 F1
Brearley W Yorks 196 B4
Brearton N Yorks 214 G6
Breascleit W Isles 304 E4
Breaston Derbys 153 C9
Brechfa Carms 93 E10
Brechin Angus 293 G7
Breckan Orkney 314 F2
Breckles Norf 141 E9
Breck of Cruan Orkney 314 E3
Breckrey Highld 298 C5
Brecks S Yorks 187 C7
Brecon Powys 95 F10
Bredbury Gtr Man 184 C6
Bredbury Green
Gtr Man 184 C6
Brede E Sus 38 D4
Bredenbury Hereford 116 F2
Bredfield Suff 126 G5
Bredgar Kent 69 G11
Bredhurst Kent 69 G9
Bredicot Worcs 117 G8
Bredon Worcs 99 D8
Bredon's Hardwick
Worcs 99 D8
Bredon's Norton Worcs 99 D8
Bredwardine Hereford 96 C6
Breedon on the Hill
Leics 153 E8
Breeds Essex 87 C11
Breedy Butts Lancs 202 E2
Breibhig W Isles 297 M2
W Isles 304 E6
Breich W Loth 269 C9
Breightmet Gtr Man 195 F8
Breighton E Yorks 207 G10
Breinton Hereford 97 D9
Breinton Common
Hereford 97 C9
Breiwick Shetland 313 J6
Brelston Green Hereford 97 G11
Bremhill Wilts 62 E3
Bremhill Wick Wilts 62 E3
Bremirehoull Shetland 313 L6
Brenachoile Lodge
Stirling 285 G8
Brenchley Kent 53 E7
Brenchoillie Argyll 284 G4
Brendon Devon 24 E5
Devon 24 F5
Devon 41 D9
Brenkley T&W 242 B6
Brent Corn 6 E4
Brent Cross London 67 B8
Brent Eleigh Suff 107 B8
Brentford London 67 D7
Brentford End London 67 D7
Brentingby Leics 154 F5
Brent Knoll Som 43 C10
Brent Mill Devon 8 D3
Brent Pelham Herts 105 E8
Brentry Bristol 60 D5

Brentwood Essex 87 G9
Brenzett Kent 39 B8
Brenzett Green Kent 39 B8
Brereton Staffs 151 F11
Brereton Cross Staffs 151 F11
Brereton Green Ches E 168 C3
Brereton Heath Ches E 168 C4
Breretonhill Staffs 151 F11
Bressingham Norf 141 G11
Bressingham Common
Norf 141 G11
Bretby Derbys 152 E5
Bretford Warks 119 B8
Bretforton Worcs 99 C11
Bretherdale Head
Cumb 221 E11
Bretherton Lancs 194 C3
Brettabister Shetland 313 H6
Brettenham Norf 141 G8
Suff 125 G9
Bretton Derbys 186 F2
Flint 166 C5
Pboro 138 C3
Brewer's End Essex 105 G11
Brewers Green Norf 142 G2
Brewer Street Sur 51 C10
Brewlands Bridge
Angus 292 G3
Brewood Staffs 133 B7
Briach Moray 301 D10
Briants Puddle Dorset 18 C2
Briar Hill W Nhants 120 F4
Brick End Essex 105 F11
Brickendon Herts 86 D4
Bricket Wood Herts 85 E10
Brickfields Worcs 117 F7
Brickhill Bedford 121 G11
Brick Hill Sur 66 G3
Brick House End Essex 105 F9
Brickhouses Ches E 168 C3
Brick Houses S Yorks 186 E4
Brick-kiln End Notts 171 D9
Brickkiln Green Essex 106 E4
Bricklehampton Worcs 99 C9
Bride IoM 192 B5
Bridekirk Cumb 229 E8
Bridell Pembs 92 C3
Bridestowe Devon 12 D6
Brideswell Aberds 302 F5
Bridford Devon 14 D2
Bridfordmills Devon 14 D2
Bridge Corn 2 D6
Corn 4 G3
Kent 55 C7
Som 28 F5
Bridge Ball Devon 41 D8
Bridge End Bedford 121 G10
Cumb 230 B3
Devon 8 F3
Durham 232 D6
Essex 106 E3
Flint 166 D4
Hereford 98 B2
Lincs 156 B2
Northumb 241 D10
Northumb 241 E10
Oxon 83 G9
Bridge-End Shetland 313 K5
Bridge End Sur 50 B5
Warks 118 E5
Worcs 98 E6
Bridgefoot Aberds 292 C6
Angus 287 D7
Cumb 229 F7
Bridge Green Essex 105 D9
Norf 142 G2
Bridgehampton Som 29 C9
Bridge Hewick N Yorks 214 E6
Bridgehill Durham 242 G3
Bridge Ho Argyll 254 B4
Bridgeholm Green
Derbys 185 E8
Bridgehouse Gate
N Yorks 214 F3
Bridgelands Borders 261 C11
Bridgemary Hants 33 G9
Bridgemere Ches E 168 F2
Bridgemont Derbys 185 E8
Bridgend Aberds 293 B7
Aberds 302 F5
Angus 293 G7
Argyll 255 D8
Argyll 274 G4
Argyll 275 D9
Corn 6 D2
Cumb 221 C7
Devon 7 F11
Fife 287 F7
Glos 80 E4
Highld 300 D3
Invclyd 276 F5
Moray 302 F3
N Lanark 278 G3
Pembs 92 B3
W Loth 279 F10
Bridgend = Pen-y-Bont ar-ogwr Bridgend 58 C2
Bridgend of Lintrathen
Angus 286 B6
Bridgeness Falk 279 E10
Bridge of Alford Aberds 293 B7
Bridge of Allan Stirling 278 B5
Bridge of Avon Moray 301 F11
Moray 301 G11
Bridge of Awe Argyll 284 E4
Bridge of Balgie Perth 285 C9
Bridge of Cally Perth 286 B5
Bridge of Canny Aberds 293 D8
Bridge of Craigisla
Angus 286 B6
Bridge of Dee Dumfries 237 D9
Bridge of Don
Aberdeen 293 B11
Bridge of Dun Angus 287 B10
Bridge of Dye Aberds 293 E8
Bridge of Earn Perth 286 F5
Bridge of Ericht Perth 285 B9
Bridge of Feugh Aberds 293 D9
Bridge of Forss Highld 310 C4
Bridge of Gairn Aberds 292 D5
Bridge of Gaur Perth 285 B9
Bridge of Lyon Perth 285 C11
Bridge of Muchalls
Aberds 293 D10
Bridge of Muick Aberds 292 D5
Bridge of Oich Highld 290 C5
Bridge of Orchy Argyll 284 D6
Bridge of Waith Orkney 314 E2
Bridge of Walls
Shetland 313 H4
Bridge of Weir Renfs 267 B7
Bridge Reeve Devon 25 E11
Bridgerule Devon 24 G3
Bridges Corn 5 D10
Shrops 131 D7
Bridge Sollers Hereford 97 C8
Bridge Street Suff 107 B7
Bridgeton Glasgow 268 C2
Bridgetown Corn 12 D2
Bridgetown *continued*
Devon 8 C6
Som 42 G2
Staffs 133 B9
Bridge Town Warks 118 G4
Bridge Trafford Ches W 183 G7
Bridge Yate S Glos 61 E7
Bridgham Norf 141 F9
Bridgnorth Shrops 132 E4
Bridgtown Staffs 133 B9
Bridgwater Som 43 F10
Bridlington E Yorks 218 F3
Bridport Dorset 16 C5
Bridstow Hereford 97 G11
Brierfield Lancs 204 F2
Brierholme Carr
S Yorks 199 E7
Brierley Glos 79 B10
Hereford 115 F9
S Yorks 198 E2
Brierley Hill W Mid 133 F8
Brierton Hrtlpl 234 E5
Briery Cumb 229 G11
Briery Hill Bl Gwent 77 D11
Briestfield W Yorks 197 D8
Brigflatts Cumb 222 G2
Brigg N Lincs 200 F3
N Lincs 200 F4
Briggate Norf 160 D6
Briggswath N Yorks 227 D7
Brigham Cumb 229 E7
Cumb 229 G11
E Yorks 209 C7
Brighouse W Yorks 196 C6
Brighstone IoW 20 E4
Brightgate Derbys 170 D3
Brighthampton Oxon 82 E5
Brightholmlee S Yorks 186 B3
Brightley Devon 13 B7
Brightling E Sus 37 C11
Brightlingsea Essex 89 B9
Brighton Brighton 36 G4
Corn 5 E8
Brighton Hill Hants 48 D6
Brighton le Sands Mers 182 B4
Brightons Falk 279 F8
Brightside S Yorks 186 D5
Brightwalton W Berks 64 D2
Brightwalton Green
W Berks 64 D2
Brightwalton Holt
W Berks 64 D2
Brightwell Suff 108 C4
Brightwell Baldwin
Oxon 83 F11
Brightwell cum Sotwell
Oxon 83 G9
Brigmerston Wilts 47 D7
Brignall Durham 223 C11
Brig o'Turk Stirling 285 G9
Brigsley NE Lincs 201 G9
Brigsteer Cumb 211 B9
Brigstock N Nhants 137 F8
Brill Bucks 83 C11
Corn 2 D6
Brilley Hereford 96 B5
Brilley Mountain Powys 114 G5
Brimaston Pembs 91 G8
Brimfield Hereford 115 D10
Brimington Derbys 186 G6
Brimington Common
Derbys 186 G6
Brimley Devon 13 F11
Devon 28 G4
Brimpsfield Glos 80 C6
Brimps Hill Glos 79 B11
Brimpton W Berks 64 G5
Brimpton Common
W Berks 64 G5
Brims Orkney 314 H2
Brims Castle Highld 310 B4
Brimscombe Glos 80 E5
Brimsdown London 86 F5
Brimstage Mers 182 E4
Brinacory Highld 295 F9
Brincliffe S Yorks 186 D4
Brind E Yorks 207 G10
Brindham Som 44 E4
Brindister Shetland 313 H4
Shetland 313 K6
Brindle Lancs 194 C6
Brindle Heath Gtr Man 195 G10
Brindley Ches E 167 E9
Brindley Ford Stoke 168 E5
Brindwoodgate Derbys 186 F4
Brineton Staffs 150 G6
Bringewood Forge
Hereford 115 C9
Bringhurst Leics 136 E6
Bringsty Common
Hereford 116 F4
Brington Cambs 121 B11
Brinian Orkney 314 D4
Briningham Norf 159 C10
Brinkhill Lincs 190 G5
Brinkley Cambs 124 G2
Notts 172 E2
Brinkley Hill Hereford 97 E11
Brinklow M Keynes 103 D8
Warks 119 B8
Brinkworth Wilts 62 C4
Brinmore Highld 300 G6
Brinnington Gtr Man 184 C6
Brinscall Lancs 194 C6
Brinsea N Som 60 G2
Brinsford Staffs 133 B8
Brinsley Notts 171 F7
Brinsop Hereford 97 C8
Brinsop Common
Hereford 97 C8
Brinsworth S Yorks 186 D6
Brinsworthy Devon 41 G9
Brinton Norf 159 B10
Brisco Cumb 239 G10
Briscoe Cumb 219 C10
Briscoerigg N Yorks 205 C11
Brisley Norf 159 E8
Brislington Bristol 60 E6
Brissenden Green Kent 54 F2
Bristnall Fields W Mid 133 F9
Bristol Bristol 60 E5
Briston Norf 159 C11
Britain Bottom S Glos 61 B9
Britannia Lancs 195 C11
Britford Wilts 31 B11
Brithdir Caerph 77 E11
Ceredig 92 B6
Gwyn 146 F5
British Torf 78 E3
Briton Ferry = Llansawel
Neath 57 C8
Britten's Bath 45 B7
Britwell Slough 66 C3
Britwell Salome Oxon 83 G11
Brixham Torbay 9 D8
Brixton Devon 7 E11
London 67 D10
Brixton Deverill Wilts 45 F11
Brixworth W Nhants 120 C4
Brize Norton Oxon 82 D4
Broad Alley Worcs 117 D7
Broad Blunsdon
Swindon 81 G11
Broadbottom Gtr Man 185 C7
Broadbridge W Sus 22 B4
Broadbridge Heath
W Sus 50 G6
Broadbury Devon 12 B5
Broadbush Swindon 81 G11
Broad Campden Glos 100 D3
Broad Carr W Yorks 196 D5
Broad Chalke Wilts 31 B8
Broad Clough Lancs 195 C11
Broadclyst Devon 14 B5
Broad Colney Herts 85 E11
Broad Common Worcs 117 D7
Broadfield Gtr Man 195 E10
Invclyd 276 G6
Lancs 194 C4
Lancs 195 B8
Pembs 73 E10
W Sus 51 G9
Broadford Highld 295 C8
Sur 50 D3
Broad Ford Kent 53 F8
Broadford Bridge W Sus 35 C9
Broadgate Hants 32 C6
Broadgrass Green Suff 125 E9
Broad Green Cambs 124 F3
C Beds 103 C9
Essex 105 D8
Essex 107 G7
London 67 F10
Mers 182 C6
Suff 124 F5
Suff 125 F11
Worcs 116 F5
Worcs 117 C9
Broadgreen Wood Herts 86 D4
Broadhalgh Gtr Man 195 E11
Broadham Green Sur 51 C11
Broadhaugh Borders 249 B10
Broadhaven Highld 310 D7
Broad Haven = Aberllydan
Pembs 72 C5
Broadheath Gtr Man 184 D3
Broad Heath Powys 114 E6
Staffs 151 D7
Worcs 116 D3
Broadhembury Devon 27 G10
Broadhempston Devon 8 B6
Broad Hill Cambs 123 B11
Broad Hinton Wilts 62 D6
Broadholm Derbys 170 F4
Broadholme Derbys 170 F5
Lincs 188 G5
Broad Ings E Yorks 208 C2
Broadland Row E Sus 38 D4
Broadlands Devon 14 G3
Broadlane Corn 2 C4
Broad Lane Corn 4 G3
Broad Lanes Shrops 132 F5
Broadlay Carms 74 D5
Broad Laying Hants 64 G2
Broad Layings Hants 64 G2
Broadley Lancs 195 D11
Moray 302 C3
Broadley Common Essex 86 D6
Broadleys Aberds 303 C8
Broad Marston Worcs 100 B2
Broadmayne Dorset 17 D10
Broad Meadow Staffs 168 F4
Broadmeadows
Borders 261 C10
Broadmere Hants 48 D6
Broadmoor Pembs 73 D9
Sur 50 D6
Broadmoor Common
Hereford 98 D2
Broadmore Green
Worcs 116 G6
Broadoak Dorset 16 B4
Glos 80 C2
Hants 33 E8
Shrops 149 F9
Wrex 166 D5
Broad Oak Carms 93 G11
Cumb 220 G2
Dorset 30 E3
E Sus 37 C10
E Sus 38 D4
Hants 49 C9
Hereford 97 G9
Kent 54 F4
Kent 71 G7
Mers 183 B8
Shrops 132 F5
Broadoak End Herts 86 C4
Broadoak Park Gtr Man 195 G9
Broad Parkham Devon 24 C5
Broadplat Oxon 65 C8
Broadrashes Moray 302 D4
Broadrock Glos 79 F8
Broadsands Torbay 9 D7
Broadsea Aberds 303 C9
Broad's Green Essex 87 C11
Wilts 62 F3
Broadshard Som 28 E6
Broadstairs Kent 71 F11
Broadstone BCP 18 B6
Kent 53 D11
Mon 79 E8
Shrops 131 F10
Broad Street E Sus 38 D5
Kent 53 B10
Kent 54 E6
Kent 55 E7
Medway 69 E9
Suff 107 C9
Wilts 46 B6
Broadstreet Common
Newport 59 C11
Broad Street Green
Essex 88 D5
Broad Tenterden Kent 53 G11
Broad Town Wilts 62 D5
Broadwas Worcs 116 F5
Broadwater Herts 104 G4
W Sus 35 G11
Broadwater Down Kent 52 F5
Broadwaters Worcs 116 B6
Broadwath Cumb 239 F11
Broadway Carms 74 D3
Carms 74 D5
Pembs 72 C5
Som 28 D4
Suff 127 B7
Worcs 99 D11
Broadway Lands
Hereford 97 E11
Broadwell Glos 79 C9
Glos 100 F4
Oxon 82 E3
Warks 119 D9
Broadwey Dorset 17 E9
Broadwindsor Dorset 28 G6
Broadwood Kelly Devon 25 F10
Broadwoodwidger Devon 12 D4
Brobury Hereford 96 C6
Brochel Highld 298 E5
Brochroy Argyll 284 D4
Brock Lancs 202 E6
Brockamin Worcs 116 G5
Brockbridge Hants 33 D10
Brockdish Norf 126 B4
Brockencote Worcs 117 C7
Brockenhurst Hants 32 G4
Brocketsbrae S Lanark 259 B8
Brockfield Devon 28 F4
Brockford Green Suff 126 D2
Brockford Street Suff 126 D2
Brockhall W Nhants 120 E2
Brockhall Village
Lancs 203 F10
Brockham Sur 51 D7
Brockham End Bath 61 F8
Brockham Park Sur 51 D8
Brockhampton Glos 99 F8
Glos 99 G10
Hants 22 B2
Hereford 97 E11
Brockhampton Green
Dorset 30 F2
Brockhill Borders 261 E9
Brock Hill Essex 88 F2
Brockholes W Yorks 197 E7
Brockhollands Glos 79 D10
Brockhurst Derbys 170 C4
Hants 33 G10
Warks 135 G9
Brocklebank Cumb 230 C2
Brocklehirst Dumfries 238 C3
Brocklesby Lincs 200 E6
Brockley London 67 E11
N Som 60 F3
Brockley Corner Suff 124 C6
Brockley Green Suff 106 B4
Suff 124 G6
Brockleymoor Cumb 230 D5
Brockloch Dumfries 246 D2
Brockmanton Hereford 115 F10
Brockmoor W Mid 133 F8
Brockscombe Devon 12 C5
Brock's Green Hants 64 G4
Brock's Watering Norf 142 E2
Brockton Shrops 130 C6
Shrops 130 F6
Shrops 131 E11
Shrops 132 C4
Staffs 150 C6
Telford 150 F4
Brockweir Glos 79 E8
Brockwell Som 42 E2
Brockwood Hants 33 B10
Brockworth Glos 80 B5
Brocton Corn 5 B10
Staffs 151 F9
Brodick N Ayrs 256 B2
Brodie Moray 301 D9
Brodiesord Aberds 302 C5
Brodsworth S Yorks 198 F4
Brogaig Highld 298 C4
Brogborough C Beds 103 D9
Broke Hall Suff 108 C3
Brokenborough Wilts 62 B2
Broken Cross Ches E 184 G5
Ches W 183 G11
Broken Green Herts 105 G8
Brokerswood Wilts 45 C10
Brokes N Yorks 224 F3
Brombil Neath 57 D9
Bromborough Mers 182 E4
Bromborough Pool
Mers 182 E4
Bromdon Shrops 132 G2
Brome Suff 126 B2
Bromesberrow Glos 98 E4
Bromesberrow Heath
Glos 98 E4
Brome Street Suff 126 B3
Bromeswell Suff 126 G6
Bromfield Cumb 229 B9
Shrops 115 B9
Bromford W Mid 134 E2
Bromham Bedford 121 G10
Wilts 62 F3
Bromley Herts 105 G8
London 67 C11
London 68 F2
Shrops 132 D4
Shrops 149 D8
S Yorks 186 B4
W Mid 133 F8
Bromley Common London 68 F2
Bromley Cross Essex 107 F11
Gtr Man 195 E8
Bromley Green Kent 54 F3
Bromley Hall Staffs 150 C5
Bromley Heath S Glos 61 D7
Bromley Park London 67 F11
Bromley Wood Staffs 152 E2
Bromlow Shrops 130 C6
Brompton London 67 D9
Medway 69 F9
N Yorks 217 C8
N Yorks 225 F7
Shrops 131 B10
Brompton-by-Sawdon
N Yorks 217 C8
Brompton-on-Swale
N Yorks 224 F4
Brompton Ralph Som 42 G5
Brompton Regis Som 42 G3
Bromsash Hereford 98 G2
Bromsberrow Heath Glos 98 E4
Bromsgrove Worcs 117 C9
Bromstead Common
Staffs 150 F6
Bromstead Heath Staffs 150 F6
Bromstone Kent 71 F11
Bromyard Hereford 116 G3
Bromyard Downs
Hereford 116 F3
Bronaber Gwyn 146 C4
Broncroft Shrops 131 F10
Brondesbury London 67 C8
Brondesbury Park London 67 C8
Broneirion Powys 129 F10
Brongest Ceredig 92 B6
Brongwyn Ceredig 92 C5
Bronington Wrex 149 B9
Bronllys Powys 96 D2
Bronnant Ceredig 112 D2
Bronwydd Ceredig 93 C7
Bronwydd Arms Carms 93 G8
Bronydd Powys 96 B4
Bronygarth Shrops 148 B5
Brook Carms 74 D3
Devon 12 G5
Devon 14 C2
Hants 32 B4
Hants 32 E3
IoW 20 E3
Kent 54 E5
Sur 50 D5
Sur 50 F2
Brook Bottom Gtr Man 185 D7
Gtr Man 196 G3
Lancs 202 E6
Brooke Norf 142 D5
Rutland 136 B6
Brookenby Lincs 190 B2
Brookend Glos 79 E11
Glos 79 F9
Oxon 100 G6
Brook End Bedford 121 E11
Cambs 121 C11
C Beds 104 B3
Herts 104 F6
M Keynes 103 C8
Wilts 61 C10
Worcs 99 B7
Brookfield Derbys 185 B8
Lancs 203 G7
Mbro 225 B9
Renfs 267 C8
Brookfoot W Yorks 196 C6
Brookgreen IoW 20 E3
Brook Green London 67 D8
Suff 125 F7
Brookhampton Oxon 83 F10
Shrops 131 E11
Som 29 B10
Brook Hill Hants 32 E3
Notts 153 C11
Brookhouse Blackburn 195 B7
Ches E 184 F6
Denb 165 B9
Lancs 211 G10
S Yorks 187 D8
W Yorks 196 B5
Brookhouse Green
Ches E 168 C4
Brookhouses Derbys 185 D8
Staffs 169 G7
Brookhurst Mers 182 E4
Brookland Kent 39 B7
Brooklands Dumfries 237 B10
Gtr Man 184 C3
Shrops 167 G8
Sur 66 G5
W Yorks 206 F2
Brookleigh Devon 14 B5
Brookmans Park Herts 86 E2
Brookpits W Sus 35 G8
Brook Place Sur 66 G3
Brookrow Shrops 116 C2
Brooks Corn 6 C3
Powys 130 D2
Brooksbottoms Gtr Man 195 D9
Brooksby Leics 154 F3
Brooks End Kent 71 F9
Brooks Green W Sus 35 C10
Brookside Brack 66 E2
Derbys 186 G5
Telford 132 B3
Brook Street Essex 87 G9
Kent 52 D5
Kent 54 G2
Suff 106 B6
W Sus 36 B4
Brookthorpe Glos 80 C4
Brookvale Halton 183 E8
Brookville Norf 140 D4
Brook Waters Wilts 30 C6
Brookwood Sur 50 B2
Broom C Beds 104 C3
Cumb 231 G9
Devon 28 G4
E Renf 267 D10
Pembs 73 D10
S Yorks 186 C5
Warks 117 G11
Broombank Worcs 116 C3
Broome Norf 143 E7
Shrops 131 D10
Shrops 131 G8
Worcs 117 B8
Broomedge Warr 184 D2
Broome Park Northumb 264 G4
Broomer's Corner
W Sus 35 C10
Broomershill W Sus 35 D9
Broomfield Aberds 303 F9
Cumb 230 B2
Essex 88 D2
Kent 53 C10
Kent 71 F7
Som 43 G8
Wilts 61 D11
Broomfields Shrops 149 F8
Broomfleet E Yorks 199 B11
Broom Green Norf 159 E9
Broomhall Ches E 167 F10
Windsor 66 F3
Broomhall Green
Ches E 167 F10
Broomham E Sus 23 C8
Broomhaugh Northumb 242 E2
Broomhill Borders 261 D11
Bristol 60 D6
Ches W 167 B7
Highld 301 G9
Kent 55 B8
Norf 140 C2
Northumb 252 C6
Notts 171 F8
S Yorks 198 G2
Broom Hill Bristol 60 E6
Dorset 31 G8
Durham 242 G4
London 68 F3
Suff 108 B5
Worcs 117 B8
Broomhill Bank Kent 52 E5
Broomholm Norf 160 C6
Broomhouse Glasgow 268 C3
Broomlands N Ayrs 257 B8
Broomley Northumb 242 E2
Broompark Durham 233 C10
Broomridge Stirling 278 C6
Broom's Barn Suff 124 D5
Broom's Green Glos 98 E4
Broomsgrove E Sus 38 E4
Broomsthorpe Norf 158 D6
Broom Street Kent 70 G4
Broomton Highld 301 B8
Broomy Hill Hereford 97 D9
Broomy Lodge Hants 32 E2
Broomyshaw Staffs 169 F9
Brora Highld 311 J3
Broseley Shrops 132 C3
Brotherhouse Bar Lincs 156 G5
Brotheridge Green
Worcs 98 C6
Brotherlee Durham 232 D4
Brotherstone Borders 262 B4
Brothertoft Lincs 174 F3
Brotherton N Yorks 198 B3
Brothybeck Cumb 230 C2
Brotton Redcar 226 B3
Broubster Highld 310 C4
Brough Cumb 222 C5
Derbys 185 E11
E Yorks 200 B2
Highld 310 B6
Notts 172 D4
Orkney 314 E3
Orkney 314 H4
Shetland 312 C7
Shetland 312 F6
Shetland 312 F7
Shetland 313 G7
Brough *continued*
Shetland 313 H6
Shetland 313 J7
Broughall Shrops 167 G9
Brough Lodge Shetland 312 D7
Brough Sowerby Cumb 222 C5
Broughton Borders 260 B4
Bucks 84 C4
Cambs 122 B5
Edin 280 F5
Flint 166 C4
Hants 47 G10
Lancs 202 F6
M Keynes 103 C7
N Lincs 200 F3
N Nhants 120 B6
N Yorks 204 C4
N Yorks 216 E5
Orkney 314 B4
Oxon 101 D8
Shrops 132 E6
Staffs 150 C5
V Glam 58 E2
Broughton Astley Leics 135 E10
Broughton Beck Cumb 210 C5
Broughton Common
N Lincs 200 E3
Wilts 61 G11
Broughton Cross Cumb 229 E7
Broughton Gifford Wilts 61 G11
Broughton Green Worcs 117 E9
Broughton Hackett
Worcs 117 G8
Broughton in Furness
Cumb 210 B4
Broughton Lodges Leics 154 E4
Broughton Mills Cumb 220 G4
Broughton Moor Cumb 228 E6
Broughton Park
Gtr Man 195 G10
Broughton Poggs Oxon 82 E2
Broughtown Orkney 314 B6
Broughty Ferry Dundee 287 D8
Brow Edge Cumb 211 C7
Browhouses Dumfries 239 D7
Browland Shetland 313 H4
Brown Bank N Yorks 205 C10
Brownber Cumb 222 D4
Brownbread Street
E Sus 23 B11
Brown Candover Hants 48 F5
Brownedge Ches E 168 C3
Brown Edge Lancs 193 E11
Mers 183 C8
Staffs 168 E6
Brownheath Devon 27 D10
Shrops 149 D9
Brown Heath Ches W 167 B7
Hants 33 D8
Brownheath Common
Worcs 117 E7
Brownhill Aberds 302 E6
Aberds 303 E8
Blackburn 203 G9
Shrops 149 E8
Brownhills Fife 287 F9
Shrops 150 B3
W Mid 133 B10
Brownieside Northumb 264 E5
Browninghill Green
Hants 48 B5
Brown Knowl Ches W 167 E7
Brown Lees Staffs 168 D5
Brownlow Ches E 168 C4
Mers 194 G4
Brownlow Fold Gtr Man 195 E8
Brownlow Heath
Ches E 168 C4
Brown Moor W Yorks 206 G3
Brownmuir Aberds 293 F9
Brown's Bank Ches E 167 G10
Brown's End Glos 98 E4
Brown's Green W Mid 133 E10
Brownshill Glos 80 E5
Brownshill Green
W Mid 134 G6
Brownside Lancs 204 G3
Brownsover Warks 119 B10
Brownston Devon 8 E3
Brown Street Suff 125 E11
Browns Wood M Keynes 103 D8
Browsburn N Lanark 268 C5
Browston Green Norf 143 C9
Browtop Cumb 229 G7
Broxa N Yorks 227 G8
Broxbourne Herts 86 D5
Broxburn E Loth 282 F3
W Loth 279 G11
Broxfield Northumb 264 F6
Broxholme Lincs 188 F6
Broxted Essex 105 F11
Broxton Ches W 167 E7
Broxtowe Nottingham 171 G8
Broxwood Hereford 115 G7
Broyle Side E Sus 23 C7
Brù W Isles 304 D5
Bruairnis W Isles 297 L3
Bruan Highld 310 F7
Bruar Lodge Perth 291 F10
Brucefield Fife 280 D2
Brucehill W Dunb 277 F7
Bruche Warr 183 D10
Brucklebog Aberds 293 D9
Bruera Ches W 166 C6
Bruern Abbey Oxon 100 G5
Bruichladdich Argyll 274 G3
Bruisyard Suff 126 D6
Brumby N Lincs 199 F11
Brunant Powys 130 B5
Brund Staffs 169 C10
Brundall Norf 142 B6
Brundish Norf 143 D7
Suff 126 D5
Brundish Street Suff 126 C5
Brundon Suff 107 C7
Brunery Highld 289 B9
Brunnion Corn 2 B2
Brunshaw Lancs 204 G3
Brunstane Edin 280 G6
Brunstock Cumb 239 F10
Brunswick Gtr Man 184 B4
Brunswick Park London 86 G3
Brunswick Village T&W 242 C6
Bruntcliffe W Yorks 197 B9
Brunt Hamersland
Shetland 313 H6
Brunthwaite W Yorks 205 D7
Bruntingthorpe Leics 136 F2
Brunton Fife 287 E7
Northumb 264 E6
Wilts 47 B8
Brushes Gtr Man 185 B7
Brushfield Derbys 185 G11
Brushford Devon 25 F11
Som 26 B6
Bruton Som 45 G7
Bryans Midloth 270 C6
Bryan's Green Worcs 117 D7
Bryanston Dorset 30 F5
Bryant's Bottom Bucks 84 F5
Brydekirk Dumfries 238 C5
Bryher Scilly 1 G3
Brymbo Conwy 180 G4
Wrex 166 E3
Brympton Som 29 D8
Brympton D'Evercy Som 29 D8
Bryn Caerph 77 F11
Carms 75 E8
Ches W 183 G10
Gtr Man 194 G5
Gwyn 179 G9
Neath 57 C10
Powys 130 C3
Rhondda 76 D6
Shrops 130 F5
Swansea 56 C4
Brynafan Ceredig 112 C4
Brynamman Carms 76 C2
Brynawel Caerph 77 G11
Brynberian Pembs 92 D2
Brynbryddan Neath 57 C9
Neath 57 C9
Bryn Bwbach Gwyn 146 B2
Bryncae Rhondda 58 C3
Rhondda 58 C3
Bryn Celyn Anglesey 179 F10
Flint 181 F11
Bryncethin Bridgend 58 C2
Bridgend 58 C2
Bryncir Gwyn 163 G7
Bryncoch Bridgend 58 C2
Bryn-coch Neath 57 B8
Bryn Common Flint 166 D3
Bryncroes Gwyn 144 C4
Bryncrug Gwyn 128 C2
Brynderwen Powys 130 D3
Bryndu Carms 75 D8
Bryn Du Anglesey 178 G4
Bryn Dulas Conwy 180 F6
Bryneglwys Denb 165 F10
Bryn Eglwys Gwyn 163 B10
Brynford Flint 181 G11
Bryn Gates Gtr Man 194 G5
Brynglas Newport 59 B10
Bryn-glas Conwy 164 B4
Brynglas Sta Gwyn 128 C2
Bryn Golau Rhondda 58 B3
Bryngwran Anglesey 178 F4
Bryngwyn Ceredig 92 B5
Mon 78 D5
Powys 96 B3
Brynhenllan Pembs 91 D10
Bryn-henllan Pembs 91 D10
Brynheulog Bridgend 57 C11
Brynhoffnant Ceredig 110 G6
Bryniau Denb 181 E9
Bryning Lancs 194 B2
Brynithel Bl Gwent 78 E2
Bryn-Iwan Carms 92 E6
Brynllywarch Powys 130 F3
Brynmawr Bl Gwent 77 C11
Bryn-mawr Gwyn 144 C4
Bryn Mawr Powys 148 F5
Brynmenyn Bridgend 58 B2
Brynmill Swansea 56 C6
Brynmorfudd Conwy 164 C4
Bryn Myrddin Carms 93 G8
Brynna Rhondda 58 C3
Bryn-nantllech Conwy 164 B6
Brynnau Gwynion
Rhondda 58 C3
Bryn-newydd Denb 165 G11
Bryn Offa Wrex 166 F4
Brynore Shrops 149 B7
Bryn-penarth Powys 130 C2
Bryn Pen-y-lan Wrex 166 G4
Bryn Pydew Conwy 180 F4
Brynrefail Anglesey 179 D7
Gwyn 163 C9
Bryn Rhyd-yr-Arian
Conwy 165 B7
Bryn-rhys Conwy 180 F4
Brynsadler Rhondda 58 C4
Bryn Saith Marchog
Denb 165 E9
Brynsiencyn Anglesey 163 B7
Bryn Sion Gwyn 147 F7
Brynsworthy Devon 40 G4
Bryn Tanat Powys 148 E4
Brynteg Anglesey 179 E7
Ceredig 93 C9
Wrex 166 E4
Bryntirion Bridgend 57 E11
Bryn-y-cochin Shrops 149 B7
Bryn-y-gwenin Mon 78 B4
Bryn-y-maen Conwy 180 F4
Bryn-yr-Eos Wrex 166 G3
Bryn-yr-eryr Gwyn 162 F5
Bryn-yr-ogof Denb 165 D11
Buaile nam Bodach
W Isles 297 L3
Bualintur Highld 294 C6
Bualnaluib Highld 307 K3
Buarthmeini Gwyn 146 C6
Bubbenhall Warks 119 C7
Bubblewell Glos 80 E5
Bubnell Derbys 186 G2
Bubwith E Yorks 207 F10
Buccleuch Borders 261 G8
Buchanan Smithy
Stirling 277 D9
Buchanhaven Aberds 303 E11
Buchan Hill W Sus 51 G9
Buchanty Perth 286 E3
Buchley E Dunb 277 G11
Buchlyvie Stirling 277 C11
Buckabank Cumb 230 B3
Buckbury Worcs 98 E6
Buckden Cambs 122 D3
N Yorks 213 D8
Buckenham Norf 143 B7
Buckerell Devon 27 G10
Bucket Corner Hants 32 C6
Buckfast Devon 8 B4
Buckfastleigh Devon 8 B4
Buckham Dorset 29 G7
Buckhaven Fife 281 B7
Buck Hill Wilts 62 E3
Buckholm Borders 261 B11
Buckholt Mon 79 B8
Buckhorn Devon 12 B3
Buckhorn Weston Dorset 30 C3
Buckhurst Kent 53 E10
Buckhurst Hill Essex 86 G6
Buckie Moray 302 C4
Buckies Highld 310 C5
Buckingham Bucks 102 E3
Buckland Bucks 84 C5
Devon 8 G3
Devon 14 G3
Glos 99 D11
Hants 20 B2
Herts 105 E7
Kent 55 E10
Oxon 82 F4
Sur 51 C8
Buckland Brewer Devon 24 C6
Buckland Common Bucks 84 D6
Buckland Dinham Som 45 C9
Buckland Down Som 45 C8
Buckland End W Mid 134 F2
Buckland Filleigh Devon 25 F7
Buckland in the Moor
Devon 13 G10
Buckland Marsh Oxon 82 F4
Buckland Monachorum
Devon 7 B9
Buckland Newton
Dorset 29 F11
Buckland Ripers Dorset 17 E8
Bucklands Borders 262 F2
Buckland St Mary Som 28 E3
Buckland Valley Kent 55 E10
Bucklandwharf Bucks 84 C5
Bucklebury W Berks 64 E5
Bucklebury Alley
W Berks 64 E4
Bucklegate Lincs 156 B6
Buckleigh Devon 24 B6
Bucklerheads Angus 287 D8
Bucklers Hard Hants 20 B4
Bucklesham Suff 108 C4
Buckley = *Bwcle* Flint 166 C3
Buckley Green Warks 118 D3
Buckley Hill Mers 182 B4
Bucklow Hill Ches E 184 E2
Buckminster Leics 155 E7
Buckmoorend Bucks 84 E4
Bucknall Lincs 173 B11
Stoke 168 F6
Bucknell Oxon 101 F11
Shrops 115 C7
Buckoak Ches W 183 G8
Buckover S Glos 79 G11
Buckpool Moray 302 C4
W Mid 133 F7
Buckridge Worcs 116 C4
Bucksburn Aberdeen 293 C10
Buck's Cross Devon 24 C4
Bucks Green W Sus 50 G5
Buckshaw Village Lancs 194 C5
Bucks Hill Herts 85 E9
Bucks Horn Oak Hants 49 E10
Buckskin Hants 48 C6
Buck's Mills Devon 24 C5
Buckton E Yorks 218 E3
Hereford 115 C7
Northumb 264 B3
Buckton Vale Gtr Man 196 G3
Buckworth Cambs 122 B2
Budbrooke Warks 118 D5
Budby Notts 171 B10
Buddgbrake Shetland 312 B8
Buddileigh Staffs 168 F3
Budd's Titson Corn 24 G2
Bude Corn 24 F2
Budge's Shop Corn 6 D6
Budlake Devon 14 B5
Budle Northumb 264 B5
Budleigh Som 27 D11
Budleigh Salterton Devon 15 E7
Budlett's Common E Sus 37 C7
Budock Water Corn 3 C7
Budworth Heath
Ches W 183 F11
Buersil Head Gtr Man 196 E2
Buerton Ches E 167 G11
Buffler's Holt Bucks 102 D3
Bufton Leics 135 B8
Bugbrooke W Nhants 120 F3
Bugford Devon 40 E6
Bughtlin Edin 280 G3
Buglawton Ches E 168 C5
Bugle Corn 5 D10
Bugle Gate Worcs 116 D6
Bugley Dorset 30 C3
Wilts 45 E11
Bugthorpe E Yorks 207 B11
Building End Essex 105 D8
Buildwas Shrops 132 C2
Builth Road Powys 113 G10
Builth Wells Powys 113 G10
Buirgh W Isles 305 J2
Bulbourne Herts 84 C6
Bulbridge Wilts 46 G5
Bulby Lincs 155 D11
Bulcote Notts 171 G11
Buldoo Highld 310 C3
Bulford Wilts 47 E7
Bulford Camp Wilts 47 E7
Bulkeley Ches E 167 E8
Bulkeley Hall Shrops 168 G2
Bulkington Warks 135 F7
Wilts 46 B2
Bulkworthy Devon 24 E5
Bullamoor N Yorks 225 G7
Bull Bay = *Porthllechog*
Anglesey 178 C6
Bullbridge Derbys 170 E5
Bullbrook Brack 65 F11
Bulleign Kent 53 G11
Bullenhill Wilts 45 B11
Bullen's Green Herts 86 D2
Bulley Glos 80 B3
Bullgill Cumb 229 D7
Bull Hill Hants 20 B2
Bullhurst Hill Derbys 170 G3
Bullinghope Hereford 97 D10
Bullington Hants 48 E3
Lincs 189 F9
Bullo Glos 79 D11
Bullock's Horn Wilts 81 G7
Bullockstone Kent 71 F7
Bulls Cross London 86 F4
Bulls Green Som 45 D8
Bull's Green Herts 86 B3
Norf 143 E8
Bull's Hill Hereford 97 G11
Bullwood Argyll 276 G3
Bullyhole Bottom Mon 79 F7
Bulmer Essex 106 C6
N Yorks 216 F3
Bulmer Tye Essex 106 D6
Bulphan Thurrock 68 B6
Bulstrode Herts 85 E8
Bulthy Shrops 148 G6
Bulverhythe E Sus 38 F3
Bulwark Aberds 303 E9
Mon 79 G8
Bulwell Nottingham 171 F8
Bulwell Forest
Nottingham 171 F8
Bulwick Leics 136 E3
N Nhants 137 E9
Bumble's Green Essex 86 D6
Bumwell Hill Norf 142 E2
Bun Abhainn Eadarra
W Isles 305 H3
Bunacaimb Highld 295 G8
Bun a'Mhuillin W Isles 297 K3
Bunarkaig Highld 290 E3
Bunbury Ches E 167 D9
Bunbury Heath Ches E 167 D9
Bunce Common Sur 51 D8
Bunchrew Highld 300 E6
Bundalloch Highld 295 C10
Buness Shetland 312 C8
Bunessan Argyll 288 G5
Bungay Suff 142 F6
Bunkers Hill Gtr Man 184 D6
Oxon 83 B7
Bunker's Hill Cambs 139 B8
Lincs 174 E3

Bunker's Hill *continued*
Lincs 189 G7
Norf 142 B3
Suff 143 C10
Bunloit Highld 300 G5
Bun Loyne Highld 290 C4
Bunnahabhain Argyll 274 F5
Bunny Notts 153 D11
Bunny Hill Notts 153 D11
Bunree Highld 290 G2
Bunroy Highld 290 E4
Bunsley Bank Ches E 167 G11
Bunstead Hants 32 C6
Buntait Highld 300 F3
Buntingford Herts 105 F7
Bunting's Green Essex 106 E6
Bunwell Norf 142 E2
Bunwell Bottom Norf 142 D2
Buoltach Highld 310 F5
Burbage Derbys 185 G8
Leics 135 E8
Wilts 63 G8
Burcher Hereford 114 E6
Burchett's Green
Windsor 65 C10
Burcombe Wilts 46 G5
Burcot Oxon 83 F9
Worcs 117 C9
Burcote Shrops 132 D4
Burcott Bucks 84 B4
Bucks 103 G7
Som 44 D4
Burdiehouse Edin 270 B5
Burdon T&W 243 G9
Burdonshill V Glam 58 E6
Burdrop Oxon 101 D7
Bures Suff 107 E8
Bures Green Suff 107 D8
Burford Ches E 167 E10
Devon 24 C4
Oxon 82 C3
Shrops 115 D11
Som 44 E5
Burg Argyll 288 E5
Argyll 288 G6
Burgar Orkney 314 D3
Burgate Hants 31 D11
Suff 125 B11
Burgates Hants 34 B3
Burgedin Powys 148 G4
Burge End Herts 104 E2
Burgess Hill W Sus 36 D4
Burgh Suff 126 G4
Burgh by Sands Cumb 239 F8
Burgh Castle Norf 143 B9
Burghclere Hants 64 G3
Burghclere Common
Hants 64 G3
Burgh Common Norf 141 E11
Burghead Moray 301 C11
Burghfield W Berks 65 F7
Burghfield Common
W Berks 64 F6
Burghfield Hill W Berks 65 F7
Burgh Heath Sur 51 B8
Burgh Hill E Sus 23 C8
E Sus 38 B2
Burghill Hereford 97 C9
Burgh le Marsh Lincs 175 B8
Burgh Muir Aberds 293 B9
Aberds 303 G7
Burgh next Aylsham
Norf 160 D4
Burgh on Bain Lincs 190 D2
Burgh St Margaret
= *Fleggburgh* Norf 161 G8
Burgh St Peter Norf 143 E9
Burgh Stubbs Norf 159 C10
Burghwallis S Yorks 198 E4
Burgois Corn 10 G4
Burham Kent 69 G8
Burham Court Kent 69 G8
Buriton Hants 34 C2
Burland Ches E 167 E10
Burlawn Corn 10 G5
Burleigh Brack 65 E11
Glos 80 E5
Burlescombe Devon 27 D9
Burleston Dorset 17 C11
Burlestone Devon 8 F6
Burley Hants 32 G2
Rutland 155 G7
Shrops 131 G9
W Yorks 205 G11
Burley Beacon Hants 32 G2
Burleydam Ches E 167 G10
Burley Gate Hereford 97 B11
Burley in Wharfedale
W Yorks 205 D9
Burley Lawn Hants 32 G2
Burley Lodge Hants 32 F2
Burley Street Hants 32 G2
Burley Woodhead
W Yorks 205 E9
Burlinch Som 28 B3
Burlingham Green Norf 161 G7
Burlingjobb Powys 114 F5
Burlish Park Worcs 116 C6
Burlorne Tregoose Corn 5 B10
Burlow E Sus 23 B9
Burlton Shrops 149 D9
Burmantofts W Yorks 206 G2
Burmarsh Hereford 97 B10
Kent 54 G5
Burmington Warks 100 D5
Burn N Yorks 198 B5
Burnage Gtr Man 184 C5
Burnard's Ho Devon 24 G4
Burnaston Derbys 152 C5
Burnbank S Lanark 268 D4
Burn Bridge N Yorks 206 C2
Burnby E Yorks 208 D2
Burncross S Yorks 186 B4
Burndell W Sus 35 G7
Burnden Gtr Man 195 F8
Burnedge Gtr Man 196 E2
Burnend Aberds 303 E8
Burneside Cumb 221 F10
Burness Orkney 314 B6
Burneston N Yorks 214 B6
Burnett Bath 61 F7
Burnfoot Borders 261 G10
Borders 262 F2
Dumfries 239 C7
Dumfries 247 E11
E Ayrs 245 B10
N Lanark 268 B5
Perth 286 G3
Burngreave S Yorks 186 D5
Burnham Bucks 66 C2
N Lincs 200 D5
Burnham Deepdale
Norf 176 E4
Burnham Green Herts 86 B3
Burnham Market Norf 176 E4
Burnham Norton Norf 176 E4
Burnham-on-Crouch
Essex 88 F6
Burnham-on-Sea Som 43 D10
Burnham Overy Staithe
Norf 176 E4
Burnham Overy Town
Norf 176 E4
Burnham Thorpe Norf 176 E5
Burnhead Aberds 293 D10
Borders 262 F2
Dumfries 247 D9
Dumfries 247 G10
S Ayrs 244 C6
Burnhervie Aberds 293 B9
Burnhill Green Staffs 132 C5
Burnhope Durham 233 B9
Burnhouse N Ayrs 267 E7
Burnhouse Mains
Borders 271 F8
Burniere Corn 10 G5
Burniestrype Moray 302 C3
Burniston N Yorks 227 G10
Burnlee W Yorks 196 F6
Burnley Lancs 204 G2
Burnley Lane Lancs 204 G2
Burnley Wood Lancs 204 G2
Burnmouth Borders 273 C9
Burn Naze Lancs 202 E2
Burn of Cambus
Stirling 285 G11
Burnopfield Durham 242 F5
Burnrigg Cumb 239 F11
Burnsall N Yorks 213 G10
Burn's Green Herts 104 G6
Burnside Aberds 303 E8
Angus 287 B9
E Ayrs 258 G3
Fife 286 G5
Perth 286 E4
Shetland 312 F4
S Lanark 268 C2
T&W 243 G8
W Loth 279 G11
Burnside of Duntrune
Angus 287 D8
Burnstone Devon 24 C4
Burnswark Dumfries 238 B5
Burnt Ash Glos 80 E5
Burntcommon Sur 50 C4
Burntheath Derbys 152 C4
Burnt Heath Derbys 186 F2
Essex 107 F11
Burnt Hill W Berks 64 E5
Burnthouse Corn 3 B7
Burnt Houses Durham 233 G8
Burntisland Fife 280 D4
Burnt Mills Essex 88 G2
Burnt Oak E Sus 37 B8
London 86 G2
Burnton E Ayrs 245 B11
Burnt Tree W Mid 133 E9
Burntturk Fife 287 G7
Burntwood Staffs 133 B11
Burntwood Green
Staffs 133 B11
Burntwood Pentre Flint 166 C3
Burnt Yates N Yorks 214 G5
Burnworthy Som 27 D11
Burnwynd Edin 270 B2
Burpham Sur 50 C4
W Sus 35 F8
Burradon Northumb 251 B11
T&W 243 C7
Burrafirth Shetland 312 B8
Burraland Shetland 312 F5
Shetland 313 J4
Burras Corn 2 C5
Burrastow Shetland 313 J4
Burraton Corn 7 D8
Burraton Coombe Corn 7 D8
Burravoe Shetland 312 F7
Shetland 312 G5
Burray Village Orkney 314 G4
Burrelldales Aberds 303 F7
Burrells Cumb 222 B3
Burrelton Perth 286 D6
Burridge Devon 28 F4
Devon 40 F5
Hants 33 E8
Burrigill Highld 310 F6
Burrill N Yorks 214 B4
Burringham N Lincs 199 F10
Burrington Devon 25 D10
Hereford 115 C8
N Som 44 B3
Burrough End Cambs 124 F2
Burrough Green Cambs 124 F2
Burrough on the Hill
Leics 154 G5
Burroughs Grove Bucks 65 B11
Burroughston Orkney 314 D5
Burrow Devon 14 B5
Som 28 C6
Som 42 E2
Burrowbridge Som 43 G11
Burrow-bridge Som 28 B5
Burrowhill Sur 66 G3
Burrows Cross Sur 50 D5
Burrowsmoor Holt
Notts 172 G2
Burrsville Park Essex 89 B11
Burrswood Kent 52 F4
Burry Swansea 56 C3
Burry Green Swansea 56 C3
Burry Port = *Porth Tywyn*
Carms 74 E6
Burscott Devon 24 C4
Burscough Lancs 194 E2
Burscough Bridge Lancs 194 E2
Bursdon Devon 24 D3
Bursea E Yorks 208 G2
Burshill E Yorks 209 D7
Bursledon Hants 33 F7
Burslem Stoke 168 F5
Burstall Suff 107 C11
Burstallhill Suff 107 B11
Burstock Dorset 28 G6
Burston Devon 26 G2
Norf 142 G2
Staffs 151 C8
Burstow Sur 51 E10
Burstwick E Yorks 201 B8
Burtersett N Yorks 213 B7
Burtholme Cumb 240 E2
Burthorpe Suff 124 E5
Burthwaite Cumb 230 B4
Burtle Som 43 E11
Burtle Hill Som 43 E11
Burtoft Lincs 156 B5
Burton BCP 17 C9
BCP 19 C9
Ches W 167 C8
Ches W 182 G4
Lincs 189 G7
Northumb 264 C5
Pembs 73 D7
Som 29 E8
Som 43 E7
V Glam 58 F4
Wilts 45 G10
Wilts 61 D10
Wrex 166 D5
Burton Agnes E Yorks 218 G2
Burton Bradstock Dorset 16 D5
Burton Corner Lincs 174 F4
Burton Dassett Warks 119 G7
Burton End Cambs 106 B2
Essex 105 G10
Burton Ferry Pembs 73 D7
Burton Fleming
E Yorks 217 E11
Burton Green Essex 106 F6
W Mid 118 B5
Wrex 166 D4
Burton Hastings Warks 135 E8
Burton-in-Kendal
Cumb 211 D10
Burton in Lonsdale
N Yorks 212 E3
Burton Joyce Notts 171 G10
Burton Latimer
N Nhants 121 C8
Burton Lazars Leics 154 F5
Burton-le-Coggles
Lincs 155 D9
Burton Leonard
N Yorks 214 G6
Burton Manor Staffs 151 E8
Burton on the Wolds
Leics 153 E11
Burton Overy Leics 136 D3
Burton Pedwardine
Lincs 173 G10
Burton Pidsea E Yorks 209 G10
Burton Salmon N Yorks 198 B3
Burton Stather N Lincs 199 D11
Burton upon Stather
N Lincs 199 D11
Burton upon Trent
Staffs 152 E5
Burton Westwood
Shrops 132 D2
Burtonwood Warr 183 C9
Burwardsley Ches W 167 D8
Burwarton Shrops 132 F2
Burwash E Sus 37 C11
Burwash Common
E Sus 37 C10
Burwash Weald E Sus 37 C10
Burwell Cambs 123 D11
Lincs 190 F5
Burwen Anglesey 178 C6
Burwick Orkney 314 H4
Shetland 313 J5
Burwood Shrops 131 F9
Burwood Park Sur 66 G6
Bury Cambs 138 G5
Gtr Man 195 E10
Som 26 B6
W Sus 35 E8
Buryas Br Corn 1 D4
Burybank Staffs 151 B7
Bury End Bedford 121 G9
C Beds 104 E2
Worcs 99 D11
Bury Green Herts 86 E4
Herts 105 G8
Bury Hollow W Sus 35 E8
Bury Park Luton 103 G11
Bury St Edmunds Suff 125 E7
Bury's Bank W Berks 64 F3
Burythorpe N Yorks 216 G5
Busbiehill N Ayrs 257 B9
Busbridge Sur 50 E3
Busby E Renf 267 D11
Buscot Oxon 82 F2
Buscott Som 44 F2
Bush Aberds 293 G9
Corn 24 F2
Bush Bank Hereford 115 G9
Bushbury Sur 51 D7
W Mid 133 C8
Bushby Leics 136 C3
Bush Crathie Aberds 292 D4
Bush End Essex 87 B9
Bush Estate Norf 161 D8
Bushey Dorset 18 E5
Herts 85 G10
Bushey Ground Oxon 82 D4
Bushey Heath Herts 85 G11
Bushey Mead London 67 F8
Bushfield Cumb 249 G11
Bush Green Norf 141 D10
Norf 142 F4
Suff 125 F8
Bush Hill Park London 86 F4
Bushley Worcs 99 E7
Bushley Green Worcs 99 E7
Bushmead Bedford 122 E2
Bushmoor Shrops 131 F8
Bushton Wilts 62 D5
Bushy Common Norf 159 G9
Bushy Hill Sur 50 C4
Busk Cumb 231 C8
Gtr Man 196 F2
Buslingthorpe Lincs 189 D9
Bussage Glos 80 E5
Bussex Som 43 F11
Busta Shetland 312 G5
Bustard Green Essex 106 F2
Bustard's Green Norf 142 E3
Bustatoun Orkney 314 A7
Busveal Corn 4 G4
Butcher's Common Norf 160 E6
Butcher's Cross E Sus 37 B9
Butcombe N Som 60 G4
Butetown Cardiff 59 D7
Bute Town Caerph 77 D10
Butlane Head Shrops 149 G8
Butleigh Som 44 G4
Butleigh Wootton Som 44 G4
Butlersbank Shrops 149 E11
Butlers Cross Bucks 85 G7
Butler's Cross Bucks 84 D4
Butler's End Warks 134 G4
Butler's Hill Notts 171 F8
Butlers Marston Warks 118 G6
Butley Suff 127 G7
Butley High Corner Suff 109 B7
Butley Low Corner Suff 109 B7
Butley Town Ches E 184 F6
Butlocks Heath Hants 33 F7
Butter Bank Staffs 151 E7
Butterburn Cumb 240 C5
Buttercrambe N Yorks 207 B10
Butteriss Gate Corn 2 C6
Butterknowle Durham 233 F8
Butterleigh Devon 27 F7
Butterley Derbys 170 C4
Derbys 170 E6
Buttermere Cumb 220 B3
Wilts 63 G10
Butterrow Glos 80 E5
Butters Green Staffs 168 E4
Buttershaw W Yorks 196 B6
Butterstone Perth 286 C4
Butterton Staffs 168 G4
Staffs 169 D9
Butterwick Cumb 221 B10
Durham 234 F3
Lincs 174 G5
N Yorks 216 D4
N Yorks 217 E9
Butteryhaugh Northumb 250 E4
Butt Green Ches E 167 E11
Buttington Powys 130 B5
Butt Lane Staffs 168 E4
Buttonbridge Shrops 116 B4
Button Haugh Green
Suff 125 D9
Buttonoak Worcs 116 B5
Button's Green Suff 125 G8
Butts Devon 14 D2
Buttsash Hants 32 F6
Buttsbear Cross Corn 24 G3
Buttsbury Essex 87 F11
Butts Green Essex 105 E9
Butt's Green Essex 88 E3
Hants 32 B4
Buttsole Kent 55 C10
Butt Yeats Lancs 211 F11
Buxhall Suff 125 F10
Buxhall Fen Street
Suff 125 F10
Buxley Borders 272 E6
Buxted E Sus 37 C7
Buxton Derbys 185 G9
Norf 160 E4
Buxworth Derbys 185 E8
Bwcle = *Buckley* Flint 166 C3
Bwlch Flint 181 G11
Powys 96 G2
Bwlch-derwin Gwyn 163 F7
Bwlchgwyn Wrex 166 E3
Bwlch-Llan Ceredig 111 F11
Bwlchnewydd Carms 93 G7
Bwlch-newydd Carms 93 G7
Bwlchtocyn Gwyn 144 D6
Bwlch-y-cibau Powys 148 F3
Bwlch-y-cwm Cardiff 58 C6
Bwlchyddar Powys 148 E3
Bwlch-y-fadfa Ceredig 93 B8
Bwlch-y-ffridd Powys 129 D11
Bwlchygroes Pembs 92 D4
Bwlchyllyn Gwyn 163 D8
Bwlch-y-Plain Powys 114 B4
Bwlch-y-sarnau Powys 113 C10
Bybrook Kent 54 E4
Bycross Hereford 97 C7
Byeastwood Bridgend 58 C2
Byebush Aberds 303 F7
Bye Green Bucks 84 C5
Byerhope Northumb 232 B3
Byermoor T&W 242 F5
Byers Green Durham 233 E10
Byfield W Nhants 119 G10
Byfleet Sur 66 G5
Byford Hereford 97 C7
Byford Common Hereford 97 C7
Bygrave Herts 104 D5
Byker T&W 243 E7
Byland Abbey N Yorks 215 D10
Bylchau Conwy 165 C7
Byley Ches W 168 B2
Bynea Carms 56 B4
Byram N Yorks 198 B3
Byrness Northumb 251 C7
Bythorn Cambs 121 B11
Byton Hereford 115 E7
Byton Hand Hereford 115 E7
Bywell Northumb 242 E2
Byworth W Sus 35 C7

C

Cabbacott Devon 24 C6
Cabbage Hill Brack 65 E11
Cabharstadh W Isles 304 F5
Cabin Shrops 130 F6
Cablea Perth 286 D3
Cabourne Lincs 200 G6
Cabrach Argyll 274 G5
Moray 302 G3
Cabrich Highld 300 E5
Cabus Lancs 202 D5
Cackle Hill Lincs 157 D7
Cackleshaw W Yorks 204 F6
Cackle Street E Sus 23 B11
E Sus 37 B7
E Sus 38 D4
Cadboll Highld 301 B8
Cadbury Devon 26 G6
Cadbury Barton Devon 25 D11
Cadbury Heath S Glos 61 E7
Cadder E Dunb 278 G2
Cadderlie Argyll 284 D4
Caddington C Beds 85 B9
Caddleton Argyll 275 B8
Caddonfoot Borders 261 C10
Caddonlee Borders 261 B10
Cadeby Leics 135 C8
S Yorks 198 G4
Cadeleigh Devon 26 F6
Cademuir Borders 260 B6
Cader Denb 165 C8
Cade Street E Sus 37 C10
Cadger Path Angus 287 B8
Cad Green Som 28 D4
Cadgwith Corn 2 G6
Cadham Fife 286 G6
Cadishead Gtr Man 184 C2
Cadle Swansea 56 B6
Cadley Lancs 202 G6
Wilts 47 C8
Wilts 63 F8
Cadmore End Bucks 84 G3
Cadnam Hants 32 E3
Cadney N Lincs 200 G4
Cadney Bank Wrex 149 C9
Cadole Flint 166 C2
Cadoxton V Glam 58 F6
Cadoxton-Juxta-Neath
Neath 57 B9
Cadshaw Blackburn 195 D8
Cadwell Herts 104 E3
Cadzow S Lanark 268 E4
Caeathro Gwyn 163 C7
Cae Clyd Gwyn 164 G2
Cae-gors Carms 75 E9
Caehopkin Powys 76 C4
Caemorgan Ceredig 92 B3
Caenby Lincs 189 D8
Caenby Corner Lincs 189 D7
Caerau Bridgend 57 C11
Cardiff 58 D6
Caerau Park Newport 59 B9
Cae'r-bont Powys 76 C4
Cae'r-bryn Carms 75 C9
Caerdeon Gwyn 146 F2
Caer-Estyn Wrex 166 D4
Caer-Farchell Pembs 90 F5
Caerffili = *Caerphilly*
Caerph 59 B7
Caerfyrddin = *Carmarthen*
Carms 93 G8
Caergeiliog Anglesey 178 F4
Caergwrle Flint 166 D4
Caergybi = *Holyhead*
Anglesey 178 E2
Caerhendy Neath 57 C9
Caerhun Gwyn 163 B9
Cae'r-Lan Powys 76 C4
Caerleon Newport 78 G4
Caer Llan Mon 79 D7
Caermead V Glam 58 F3
Caermeini Pembs 92 E2
Caernarfon Gwyn 163 C7
Caerphilly = *Caerffili*
Caerph 59 B7
Caersws Powys 129 E10
Caerwedros Ceredig 111 F7
Caerwent Mon 79 G7
Caerwent Brook Mon 60 B3
Caerwych Gwyn 146 B2
Caerwys Flint 181 G10
Caethle Gwyn 128 D2
Cage Green Kent 52 D5
Caggan Highld 291 B10
Caggle Street Mon 78 B5
Cailness Stirling 285 G7
Caim Anglesey 179 E10
Cainscross Glos 80 D4
Caio Carms 94 D3
Cairinis W Isles 296 E4
Cairisiadar W Isles 304 E2
Cairminis W Isles 296 C6
Cairnbaan Argyll 275 D9
Cairnbanno Ho Aberds 303 E8
Cairnborrow Aberds 302 E4
Cairnbrogie Aberds 303 G8
Cairnbulg Castle
Aberds 303 C10
Cairncross Angus 292 F6
Borders 273 C7
Cairnderry Dumfries 236 B5
Cairndow Argyll 284 F5
Cairness Aberds 303 C10
Cairneyhill Fife 279 D10
Cairnfield Ho Moray 302 C4
Cairngaan Dumfries 236 F3
Cairngarroch Dumfries 236 E2
Cairnhill Aberds 302 F6
Aberds 303 D7
N Lanark 268 C5
Cairnie Aberds 293 C10
Aberds 302 E4
Cairnlea S Ayrs 244 G6
Cairnleith Crofts Aberds 303 F9
Cairnmore Aberds 303 C9
Cairnorrie Aberds 303 E8
Cairnpark Aberds 293 B10
Dumfries 247 D9
Cairnryan Dumfries 236 C2
Cairnton Orkney 314 F3
Cairston Orkney 314 E2
Caister-on-Sea Norf 161 G10
Caistor Lincs 200 G6
Caistor St Edmund Norf 142 C4
Caistron Northumb 251 C11
Caitha Bowland Borders 271 G9
Cakebole Worcs 117 C7
Calais Street Suff 107 D9
Calanais W Isles 304 E4
Calbost W Isles 305 G6
Calbourne IoW 20 D4
Calceby Lincs 190 F5
Calcoed Flint 181 G11
Calcot Glos 81 C9
W Berks 65 E7
Calcot Row W Berks 65 E7
Calcott Kent 71 G7
Shrops 149 G8
Calcott's Green Glos 80 B3
Calcutt N Yorks 206 B2
Wilts 81 G10
Caldback Shetland 312 C8
Caldbeck Cumb 230 D2
Caldbergh N Yorks 213 B11
Caldecote Cambs 122 F6
Cambs 138 F2
Herts 104 D4
Warks 135 E7
W Nhants 120 G3
Caldecote Hill Herts 85 G11
Caldecott N Nhants 121 D9
Oxon 83 F7
Rutland 137 E7
Caldecotte M Keynes 103 D7
Calder Cumb 219 E10
Calderbank N Lanark 268 C5
Calder Bridge Cumb 219 D10
Calderbrook Gtr Man 196 D2
Caldercruix N Lanark 268 B6
Calder Grove W Yorks 197 D10
Calder Hall Cumb 219 E10
Calder Mains Highld 310 D4
Caldermill S Lanark 268 G3
Caldermoor Gtr Man 196 D2
Calderstones Mers 182 D6
Calder Vale Lancs 202 D6
Calderwood S Lanark 268 D2
Caldhame Angus 287 C8
Caldicot = *Cil-y-coed*
Mon 60 B3
Caldmore W Mid 133 D10
Caldwell Derbys 152 F5
N Yorks 224 C3
Caldy Mers 182 D2
Caledrhydiau Ceredig 111 G9
Cale Green Gtr Man 184 D5
Calenick Corn 4 G6
Caleys Fields Worcs 100 C4
Calf Heath Staffs 133 B8
Calford Green Suff 106 B3
Calfsound Orkney 314 C5
Calgary Argyll 288 D5
Caliach Argyll 288 D5
Califer Moray 301 D10
California Cambs 139 G10
Falk 279 F8
Norf 161 G10
Suff 108 C3
W Mid 133 G10
Calke Derbys 153 E7
Callakille Highld 298 D6
Callaly Northumb 252 B3
Callander Stirling 285 G10
Callandrode Stirling 285 G10
Callands Warr 183 C9
Callaughton Shrops 132 D2
Callendar Park Falk 279 F7
Callert Ho Highld 290 G2
Callerton T&W 242 D5
Callerton Lane End
T&W 242 D5
Callestick Corn 4 E5
Calligarry Highld 295 E8
Callington Corn 7 B7
Callingwood Staffs 152 E3
Calloose Corn 2 B3
Callop Highld 289 B11
Callow Derbys 170 E3
Hereford 97 E9
Callow End Worcs 98 B6
Callow Hill Mon 79 B8
Som 44 E4
Wilts 62 C4
Worcs 116 C4
Callow Marsh Hereford 98 B3
Callows Grave Worcs 115 D11
Calmore Hants 32 E4
Calmsden Glos 81 D8
Calne Wilts 62 E4
Calne Marsh Wilts 62 E4
Calow Derbys 186 G6
Calow Green Derbys 170 B6
Calrofold Ches E 184 G6
Calshot Hants 33 G7
Calstock Corn 7 B8
Calstone Wellington
Wilts 62 F4
Calthorpe Norf 160 C3
Oxon 101 D9
Calthwaite Cumb 230 C5
Calton Glasgow 268 C2
N Yorks 204 B4
Staffs 169 E10
Calton Lees Derbys 170 B3
Calvadnack Corn 2 B5
Calveley Ches E 167 D9
Calver Derbys 186 G2
Calverhall Shrops 150 B2
Calver Hill Hereford 97 B7
Calverleigh Devon 26 E6
Calverley W Yorks 205 F10
Calver Sough Derbys 186 F2
Calvert Bucks 102 G3
Calverton M Keynes 102 D5
Notts 171 F10
Calvine Perth 291 G10
Calvo Cumb 238 G4
Cam Glos 80 F3
Camaghael Highld 290 F3
Camas an Staca Argyll 274 G5
Camas-luinie Highld 295 C11
Camasnacroise Highld 289 D10
Camas Salach Highld 289 C8
Camastianavaig Highld 295 B7
Camasunary Highld 295 D7
Camault Muir Highld 300 E5
Camb Shetland 312 D7
Camber E Sus 39 D7
Camberley Sur 65 G11
Camberwell London 67 D10
Camblesforth N Yorks 199 B7
Cambo Northumb 252 F2
Cambois Northumb 253 G8
Camborne Corn 4 G3
Cambourne Cambs 122 F6
Cambridge Borders 271 F11
Cambs 123 F9
Glos 80 E3
W Yorks 205 D10
Cambridge Batch N Som 60 F4
Cambridge Town
Southend 70 C2
Cambrose Corn 4 F3
Cambus Clack 279 C7
Cambusavie Farm
Highld 309 K7
Cambusbarron Stirling 278 C5
Cambusdrenny Stirling 278 C5
Cambuskenneth Stirling 278 C6
Cambuslang S Lanark 268 D2
Cambusmore Lodge
Highld 309 K7
Cambusnethan
N Lanark 268 D6
Camden London 67 C9
Camden Hill Kent 53 F9
Camden Park Kent 52 F5
Cameley Bath 44 B6
Camelford Corn 11 E8
Camel Green Dorset 31 E10
Camelon Falk 279 E7
Camelsdale Sur 49 G11
Camer Kent 69 F7
Cameron Fife 280 B6
Cameron Bridge Fife 280 B6
Camerory Highld 301 F10
Camer's Green Worcs 98 D5
Camerton Bath 45 B7
Cumb 228 E6
E Yorks 201 B8
Camghouran Perth 285 B9
Cammachmore Aberds 293 D11
Cammeringham Lincs 188 E6
Camnant Powys 113 F11
Camoquhill Stirling 277 D10
Camore Highld 309 K7
Camp Lincs 172 E5
Campbeltown Argyll 255 E8
Camp Corner Oxon 83 E10
Camperdown T&W 243 C7
Camphill Derbys 185 F11
Camp Hill N Yorks 214 C6
Pembs 73 C10
Warks 134 E6
W Yorks 196 D5
Campion Hills Warks 118 D6
Campions Essex 87 C7
Cample Dumfries 247 E9
Campmuir Perth 286 D6
Campsall S Yorks 198 E4
Campsea Ashe Suff 126 F6
Camps End Cambs 106 C2
Campsey Ash Suff 126 F6
Campsfield Oxon 83 B7
Camps Heath Suff 143 E10
Campton C Beds 104 D2
Camptoun E Loth 281 F10
Camptown Borders 262 G5
Camp Town W Yorks 206 F2
Camquhart Argyll 275 E10
Camrose Pembs 91 G8
Camserney Perth 286 C2
Camster Highld 310 E6
Camuschoirk Highld 289 C9
Camuscross Highld 295 D8
Camusnagaul Highld 290 F2
Highld 307 L5
Camusrory Highld 295 F10
Camusteel Highld 299 E7
Camusterrach Highld 299 E7
Camusvrachan Perth 285 C10
Canada Hants 32 D3
Lincs 200 G6
Canadia E Sus 38 D2
Canal Foot Cumb 210 D6
Canal Side S Yorks 199 E7
Canbus Clack 279 C7
Candacraig Ho Aberds 292 B5
Candlesby Lincs 175 B7
Candle Street Suff 125 C10
Candy Mill S Lanark 269 G11
Cane End Oxon 65 D7
Caneheath E Sus 23 D9
Canewdon Essex 88 G5
Canford Bottom Dorset 31 G8
Canford Cliffs BCP 19 D7
Canford Heath BCP 18 C6
Canford Magna BCP 18 B6
Cangate Norf 160 F6
Canham's Green Suff 125 D11
Canholes Derbys 185 G8
Canisbay Highld 310 B7
Canklow S Yorks 186 C6
Canley W Mid 118 B6
Cann Dorset 30 C5
Cannalidgey Corn 5 B8
Cannard's Grave Som 44 E6
Cann Common Dorset 30 C5
Cannich Highld 300 F3
Cannington Som 43 F9
Canning Town London 68 C2
Cannock Staffs 133 B9
Cannock Wood Staffs 151 G10
Cannon's Green Essex 87 D9
Cannop Glos 79 C10
Canonbie Dumfries 239 B9
Canon Bridge Hereford 97 C8
Canonbury London 67 C10
Canon Frome Hereford 98 C3
Canon Pyon Hereford 97 B9
Canons Ashby
W Nhants 119 G11
Canonsgrove Som 28 C2
Canons Park London 85 G11
Canon's Town Corn 2 B2
Canterbury Kent 54 B6
Cantley Norf 143 C7
S Yorks 198 G6
Cantlop Shrops 131 B10
Canton Cardiff 59 D7
Cantraybruich Highld 301 E7
Cantraydoune Highld 301 E7
Cantraywood Highld 301 E7
Cantsfield Lancs 212 E2
Canvey Island Essex 69 C9
Canwick Lincs 173 B7
Canworthy Water Corn 11 C10
Caol Highld 290 F3
Caolas Argyll 288 E2
W Isles 297 M2
Caolas Fhlodaigh
W Isles 296 F4
Caolas Liubharsaigh
W Isles 297 G4
Caolas Scalpaigh
W Isles 305 J4
Caolas Stocinis W Isles 305 J3
Caol Ila Argyll 274 F5
Caoslasnacon Highld 290 G3
Capel Carms 75 E8
Kent 52 E6
Sur 51 E7
Capel Bangor Ceredig 128 G3
Capel Betws Lleucu
Ceredig 112 F2
Capel Carmel Gwyn 144 D3
Capel Coch Anglesey 179 E7
Capel Cross Kent 53 E8
Capel Curig Conwy 164 D2
Capel Cynon Ceredig 93 B7
Capel Dewi Carms 93 G9
Ceredig 93 C9
Ceredig 128 G2
Capel Garmon Conwy 164 D4
Capel Green Suff 109 B7
Capel-gwyn Anglesey 178 F4
Capel Gwyn Carms 93 G9
Capel Gwynfe Carms 94 G4
Capel Hendre Carms 75 C9
Capel Hermon Gwyn 146 D4
Capel Isaac Carms 93 F11
Capel Iwan Carms 92 D5
Capel-le-Ferne Kent 55 F8
Capel Llanilltern Cardiff 58 C5
Capel Mawr Anglesey 178 G6
Capel Newydd = *Newchapel*
Pembs 92 D4
Capel Parc Anglesey 178 D6
Capel St Andrew Suff 109 B7
Capel St Mary Suff 107 D11
Capel Seion Carms 75 C8
Ceredig 112 B2
Capel Siloam Conwy 164 E4
Capel Tygwydd Ceredig 92 C5
Capel Uchaf Gwyn 162 F6
Capelulo Conwy 180 F2
Capel-y-ffin Powys 96 E5
Capel-y-graig Gwyn 163 B8
Capenhurst Ches W 182 G5
Capernwray Lancs 211 E10
Capheaton Northumb 252 G2
Capland Som 28 D4
Cappercleuch Borders 260 E6
Capplegill Dumfries 248 B4
Capstone Medway 69 F9
Captain Fold Gtr Man 195 E11
Capton Devon 8 E6
Som 42 F5
Caputh Perth 286 D4
Caradon Town Corn 11 G11
Carbis Corn 5 D10
Carbis Bay Corn 2 B2
Carbost Highld 294 B5
Highld 298 E4
Carbrain N Lanark 278 G5
Carbrook S Yorks 186 D5
Carbrooke Norf 141 C9
Carburton Notts 187 G10
Carcant Borders 271 E7
Carcary Angus 287 B10
Carclaze Corn 5 E10
Carclew Corn 3 B7
Car Colston Notts 172 G2
Carcroft S Yorks 198 E4
Cardenden Fife 280 C4
Cardeston Shrops 149 G7
Cardew Cumb 230 B2
Cardewlees Cumb 239 G8
Cardiff Cardiff 59 D7
Cardigan = *Aberteifi*
Ceredig 92 B3
Cardinal's Green Cambs 106 B2
Cardington Bedford 103 B11
Shrops 131 D10
Cardinham Corn 6 B2
Cardonald Glasgow 267 C10
Cardow Moray 301 E11
Cardrona Borders 261 B8
Cardross Argyll 276 F6
Cardurnock Cumb 238 F5
Careby Lincs 155 F10
Careston Angus 293 G7
Careston Castle Angus 287 B9
Care Village Leics 136 D4
Carew Pembs 73 E8
Carew Cheriton Pembs 73 E8
Carew Newton Pembs 73 E8
Carey Hereford 97 E11
Carey Park Corn 6 E4
Carfin N Lanark 268 D5
Carfrae E Loth 271 B11
Carfury Corn 1 C4
Cargate Common Norf 142 E2
Cargenbridge Dumfries 237 B11
Cargill Perth 286 D5
Cargo Cumb 239 F9
Cargo Fleet Mbro 234 G6
Cargreen Corn 7 C8
Carham Northumb 263 B8
Carhampton Som 42 E4
Carharrack Corn 4 G4
Carie Perth 285 B10
Perth 285 D10
Carines Corn 4 D5
Carisbrooke IoW 20 D5
Cark Cumb 211 D7
Carkeel Corn 7 C8
Carlabhagh W Isles 304 D4
Carland Cross Corn 5 E7
Carlbury N Yorks 224 B4
Carlby Lincs 155 G11
Carlecotes S Yorks 197 G7
Carleen Corn 2 C4
Carlenrig Borders 249 C9
Carlesmoor N Yorks 214 E3
Carleton Cumb 219 D10
Cumb 230 F6
Cumb 239 G10
Lancs 202 F2
N Yorks 204 D5
W Yorks 198 C3
Carleton Forehoe Norf 141 B11
Carleton Hall Cumb 219 F11
Carleton-in-Craven
N Yorks 204 D5
Carleton Rode Norf 142 E2
Carleton St Peter Norf 142 C6
Carley Hill T&W 243 F9
Carlidnack Corn 3 D7
Carlincraig Aberds 302 E6
Carlingcott Bath 45 B7
Carlinghow W Yorks 197 C8
Carlingwark Devon 27 E11
Carlin How Redcar 226 B4
Carlisle Cumb 239 F10
Carloggas Corn 5 B7
Corn 5 E9
Carloonan Argyll 284 F4
Carlops Borders 270 D3
Carlton Bedford 121 F9
Cambs 124 G2
Leics 135 C7
Notts 171 G10
N Yorks 198 C6
N Yorks 213 C11
N Yorks 216 B2
N Yorks 224 C3
Stockton 234 G3
Suff 127 E7
S Yorks 197 E11
W Yorks 197 B10
Carlton Colville Suff 143 F10
Carlton Curlieu Leics 136 D3
Carlton Green Cambs 124 G2
Carlton Husthwaite
N Yorks 215 D9
Carlton in Cleveland
N Yorks 225 E10
Carlton in Lindrick
Notts 187 E9
Carlton le Moorland
Lincs 172 D6
Carlton Miniott N Yorks 215 C7
Carlton on Trent Notts 172 C3
Carlton Purlieus
N Nhants 136 F6
Carlton Scroop Lincs 172 G6
Carluddon Corn 5 D10
Carluke S Lanark 268 E6
Carlyon Bay Corn 5 E11
Carmarthen = *Caerfyrddin*
Carms 93 G8
Carmel Anglesey 178 E5
Carms 75 B9
Flint 181 F11
Gwyn 163 E7
Powys 113 D11
Carmichael S Lanark 259 B10
Carminow Cross Corn 5 B11
Carmont Aberds 293 E10
Carmunnock Glasgow 268 D2
Carmyle Glasgow 268 C2
Carmyllie Angus 287 C9
Carnaby E Yorks 218 F2
Carnach Highld 299 G10
Highld 307 K5
W Isles 305 J4
Carnachy Highld 308 D7
Càrnais W Isles 304 E2
Càrnan W Isles 297 G3
Carn Arthen Corn 2 B5
Carnbahn Perth 285 C10
Carnbee Fife 287 G9
Carnbo Perth 286 G4
Carnbrea Corn 4 G3
Carn Brea Village Corn 4 G3
Carnbroe N Lanark 268 C4
Carndu Highld 295 C10
Carnduff S Lanark 268 F3
Carnduncan Argyll 274 G3
Carne Corn 3 B10
Corn 3 E7
Corn 5 D9
Carnebone Corn 2 C6
Carnedd Powys 129 E10
Carnetown Rhondda 77 G9
Carnforth Lancs 211 E10
Carnglas Swansea 56 C6
Carn-gorm Highld 295 C11
Carnhedryn Pembs 90 F6
Carnhedryn Uchaf Pembs 90 F5
Carnhell Green Corn 2 B4
Carnhot Corn 4 F4
Carnkie Corn 2 B5
Corn 2 C6
Carnkief Corn 4 E5
Carno Powys 129 D9
Carnoch Highld 300 D2
Highld 300 F3
Carnock Fife 279 D10
Carnon Downs Corn 4 G5
Carnousie Aberds 302 D6
Carnoustie Angus 287 D9
Carnsmerry Corn 5 D10
Carn Towan Corn 1 D3
Carntyne Glasgow 268 B2
Carnwadric E Renf 267 D10
Carnwath S Lanark 269 F9
Carnyorth Corn 1 C3
Caroe Corn 11 C9
Carol Green W Mid 118 B5
Carpalla Corn 5 E9
Carpenders Park Herts 85 G10
Carpenter's Hill Worcs 117 C11
Carperby N Yorks 213 B10
Carpley Green N Yorks 213 B8
Carr Gtr Man 195 D9
S Yorks 187 C8
Carradale Argyll 255 D9
Carragraich W Isles 305 J3
Carr Bank Cumb 211 D9
Carrbridge Highld 301 G9
Carrbrook Gtr Man 196 G3
Carr Cross Lancs 193 E11
Carreglefn Anglesey 178 D5
Carreg-wen Pembs 92 C4
Carreg y garth Gwyn 163 B9
Carr Gate W Yorks 197 C10
Carr Green Gtr Man 184 D2
Carr Hill T&W 243 E7
Carrhouse Devon 26 F3
Carr Houses Mers 193 G10
Carrick Argyll 275 E10
Dumfries 237 D7
Fife 287 E8
Carrick Castle Argyll 276 C3
Carrick Ho Orkney 314 C5
Carriden Falk 279 E10
Carrington Gtr Man 184 C2
Lincs 174 E4
Midloth 270 C6
Nottingham 171 G9
Carroch Dumfries 246 E5

Carrog Conwy 164 F3
Denb 165 G10
Carroglen Perth 285 E11
Carrol Highld 311 J2
Carron Falk 279 E7
Moray 302 E2
Carronbridge Dumfries 247 D9
Carron Bridge Stirling 278 E4
Carronshore Falk 279 E7
Carrot Angus 287 C8
Carroway Head Staffs 134 D3
Carrow Hill Mon 78 G6
Carrshield Northumb 232 B2
Carrutherstown Dumfries 238 C4
Carr Vale Derbys 171 B7
Carrville Durham 234 C2
Carry Argyll 275 G10
Carsaig Argyll 275 E8
Argyll 289 G7
Carscreugh Dumfries 236 D4
Carsegowan Dumfries 236 D6
Carse Gray Angus 287 B8
Carse Ho Argyll 275 G8
Carseriggan Dumfries 236 C5
Carsethorn Dumfries 237 D11
Carshalton London 67 G9
Carshalton Beeches London 67 G9
Carshalton on the Hill London 67 G9
Carsington Derbys 170 E3
Carskiey Argyll 255 G7
Carsluith Dumfries 236 D6
Carsphairn Dumfries 246 E3
Carstairs S Lanark 269 F8
Carstairs Junction S Lanark 269 F9
Carswell Marsh Oxon 82 F4
Cartbridge Sur 50 B4
Carterhaugh Borders 261 D10
Carter Knowle S Yorks 186 E4
Carter's Clay Hants 32 C4
Carter's Green Essex 87 C8
Carter's Hill Wokingham 65 F9
Carterspiece Glos 79 C9
Carterton Oxon 82 D3
Carterway Heads Northumb 242 G2
Carthamartha Corn 12 F3
Carthew Corn 2 B5
Corn 5 D10
Carthorpe N Yorks 214 C6
Cartington Northumb 252 C2
Cartland S Lanark 269 F7
Cartledge Derbys 186 F4
Cartmel Cumb 211 D7
Cartmel Fell Cumb 211 B8
Cartsdyke Invclyd 276 F5
Cartworth W Yorks 196 F6
Carty Port Dumfries 236 C6
Carway Carms 75 D7
Carwinley Cumb 239 C10
Carwynnen Corn 2 B5
Cary Fitzpaine Som 29 B9
Carzantic Corn 12 E3
Carzield Dumfries 247 G11
Carzise Corn 2 C3
Cascob Powys 114 D4
Cashes Green Glos 80 D4
Cashlie Perth 285 C8
Cashmoor Dorset 31 E7
Cas Mael = Puncheston Pembs 91 F10
Cassey Compton Glos 81 C9
Cassington Oxon 83 C7
Cassop Durham 234 D2
Castallack Corn 1 D5
Castell Conwy 164 B3
Denb 165 B10
Castellau Rhondda 58 B5
Castell-Howell Ceredig 93 B8
Castell nedd = Neath Neath 57 B8
Castell Newydd Emlyn = Newcastle Emlyn Carms 92 C6
Castell-y-bwch Torf 78 G3
Castell-y-rhingyll Carms 75 C9
Casterton Cumb 212 D2
Castle Devon 28 G4
Som 27 B9
Castle Acre Norf 158 F6
Castle Ashby W Nhants 121 F7
Castle Bolton N Yorks 223 G10
Castle Bromwich W Mid 134 F2
Castle Bytham Lincs 155 F9
Castlebythe Pembs 91 F10
Castle Caereinion Powys 130 B3
Castle Camps Cambs 106 C2
Castle Carlton Lincs 190 E5
Castle Carrock Cumb 240 F2
Castlecary N Lanark 278 F5
Castle Cary Som 44 G6
Castle Combe Wilts 61 D10
Castlecraig Highld 301 C8
Castle Craig Borders 270 G2
Castlecroft Staffs 133 D7
Castle Donington Leics 153 D8
Castle Douglas Dumfries 237 C9
Castle Eaton Swindon 81 F10
Castle Eden Durham 234 D4
Castle End Pboro 138 B2
Castlefairn Dumfries 246 F6
Castlefields Halton 183 E8
Castle Fields Shrops 149 G10
Castle Forbes Aberds 293 B8
Castleford W Yorks 198 B2
Castle Frome Hereford 98 B3
Castle Gate Corn 1 C5
Castlegreen Shrops 130 F6
Castle Green London 68 C3
Sur 66 G3
S Yorks 197 G9
Castle Gresley Derbys 152 F5
Castlehead Renfs 267 C9
Castle Heaton Northumb 273 G8
Castle Hedingham Essex 106 D5
Castlehill Argyll 254 B4
Borders 260 B6
Highld 310 C5
S Ayrs 257 E9
W Dunb 277 F7
Castle Hill E Sus 37 B9
Gtr Man 184 C6
Kent 53 E7
Suff 108 B3
Worcs 116 F5
Castle Huntly Perth 287 E7
Castle Kennedy Dumfries 236 D3
Castlemaddy Dumfries 246 F3
Castlemartin Pembs 72 F6
Castlemilk Dumfries 238 B5
Glasgow 268 D2
Castlemorris Pembs 91 E8
Castlemorton Worcs 98 D5
Castle O'er Dumfries 248 E6
Castlerigg Cumb 229 G11
Castle Rising Norf 158 E3
Castleside Durham 233 B7
Castle Street W Yorks 196 C3
Castle Stuart Highld 301 E7
Castlethorpe M Keynes 102 C6
N Lincs 200 F3
Castleton Angus 287 C7
Argyll 275 E9
Derbys 185 E11
Gtr Man 195 E11
Moray 301 G11
Newport 59 C9
N Yorks 226 D3
Castleton Village Highld 300 E6
Castle Toward Argyll 266 B2
Castletown Ches W 166 E6
Cumb 230 E6
Dorset 17 G9
Highld 301 E7
Highld 310 C5
IoM 192 F3
Staffs 151 E8
T&W 243 F9
Castle Town W Sus 36 E2
Castletump Glos 98 F4
Castle-upon-Alun V Glam 58 E2
Castle Vale W Mid 134 E2
Castleweary Borders 249 C10
Castlewigg Dumfries 236 E6
Castley N Yorks 205 D11
Castling's Heath Suff 107 C9
Caston Norf 141 D9
Castor Pboro 138 D2
Caswell Swansea 56 D5
Catacol N Ayrs 255 C10
Cat Bank Cumb 220 F6
Catbrain S Glos 60 C5
Catbrook Mon 79 E8
Catch Flint 182 G2
Catchall Corn 1 D4
Catchems Corner W Mid 118 B4
Catchems End Worcs 116 B5
Catchgate Durham 242 G5
Catchory Highld 310 D6
Catcleugh Northumb 250 C6
Catcliffe S Yorks 186 D6
Catcomb Wilts 62 D4
Catcott Som 43 F11
Caterham Sur 51 B10
Catfield Norf 161 E7
Catfirth Shetland 313 H6
Catford London 67 E11
Catforth Lancs 202 F5
Cathays Cardiff 59 D7
Cathays Park Cardiff 59 D7
Cathcart Glasgow 267 C11
Cathedine Powys 96 F2
Catherine-de-Barnes W Mid 134 G3
Catherine Slack W Yorks 196 B5
Catherington Hants 33 E11
Catherton Shrops 116 B3
Cat Hill S Yorks 197 F8
Cathiron Warks 119 B9
Catholes Cumb 222 G3
Cathpair Borders 271 F9
Catisfield Hants 33 F8
Catley Lane Head Gtr Man 195 D11
Catley Southfield Hereford 98 C3
Catlodge Highld 291 D8
Catlowdy Cumb 239 B11
Catmere End Essex 105 D9
Catmore W Berks 64 C3
Caton Devon 13 G11
Lancs 211 G10
Caton Green Lancs 211 F10
Catrine E Ayrs 258 D2
Cat's Ash Newport 78 G5
Cat's Common Norf 160 E6
Cats Edge Staffs 169 E7
Catsfield E Sus 38 E2
Catsfield Stream E Sus 38 E2
Catsgore Som 29 B8
Catsham Som 44 G5
Catshaw S Yorks 197 G8
Catshill W Mid 133 B11
Worcs 117 C9
Cat's Hill Cross Staffs 150 C6
Catslackburn Borders 261 D8
Catslip Oxon 65 B8
Catstree Shrops 132 D4
Cattadale Argyll 274 G4
Cattal N Yorks 206 C4
Cattawade Suff 108 E2
Cattedown Plym 7 E9
Catterall Lancs 202 E5
Catterick N Yorks 224 F4
Catterick Bridge N Yorks 224 F4
Catterick Garrison N Yorks 224 F3
Catterlen Cumb 230 E5
Catterline Aberds 293 F10
Catterton N Yorks 206 D6
Catteshall Sur 50 E3
Catthorpe Leics 119 B11
Cattistock Dorset 17 B7
Cattle End W Nhants 102 C3
Catton Northumb 241 F8
N Yorks 215 D7
Catwick E Yorks 209 D8
Catworth Cambs 121 C11
Caudle Green Glos 80 C6
Caudlesprings Norf 141 C8
Caulcott C Beds 103 C9
Oxon 101 G10
Cauld Borders 261 G11
Cauldcoats Holdings Falk 279 F10
Cauldcots Angus 287 C10
Cauldhame Stirling 278 C2
Cauldmill Borders 262 G2
Cauldon Staffs 169 F9
Cauldon Lowe Staffs 169 F9
Cauldwells Aberds 303 D7
Caulkerbush Dumfries 237 D11
Caulside Dumfries 249 G10
Caundle Marsh Dorset 29 E11
Caunsall Worcs 132 G6
Caunton Notts 172 D2
Causeway Hants 33 E11
Hants 34 C2
Mon 60 B2
Causewayend S Lanark 260 B2
Causeway End Cumb 211 C8
Cumb 211 B9
Dumfries 236 C6
Essex 87 B11
Wilts 62 C4
Causeway Foot W Yorks 197 E7
W Yorks 205 G7
Causeway Green W Mid 133 F9
Causewayhead Cumb 238 G4
Stirling 278 B6
Causewaywood Shrops 131 D10
Causey Durham 242 F6
Causeyend Aberds 293 B11
Causey Park Bridge Northumb 252 E5
Causeyton Aberds 293 B8
Caute Devon 24 E6
Cautley Cumb 222 G3
Cavendish Suff 106 B6
Cavendish Bridge Leics 153 D8
Cavenham Suff 124 D5
Cavers Carre Borders 262 D3
Caversfield Oxon 101 F11
Caversham Reading 65 E8
Caversham Heights Reading 65 D8
Caverswall Staffs 169 G7
Cavil E Yorks 207 G11
Cawdor Highld 301 D8
Cawkeld E Yorks 208 C5
Cawkwell Lincs 190 F3
Cawood N Yorks 207 F7
Cawsand Corn 7 E8
Cawston Norf 160 E2
Warks 119 C9
Cawthorne N Yorks 216 B5
S Yorks 197 F9
Cawthorpe Lincs 155 E11
Cawton N Yorks 216 D2
Caxton Cambs 122 F6
Caynham Shrops 115 C11
Caythorpe Lincs 172 F6
Notts 171 F11
Cayton N Yorks 217 C11
Ceallan W Isles 296 F4
Ceann a Bhaigh W Isles 296 E3
Ceann a Bhàigh W Isles 305 J4
Ceannacroc Lodge Highld 290 B4
Ceann a Deas Loch Baghasdail W Isles 297 K3
Ceann Shiphoirt W Isles 305 G4
Ceann Tarabhaigh W Isles 305 G4
Cearsiadair W Isles 304 F5
Ceathramh Meadhanach W Isles 296 D4
Cefn Newport 59 B9
Powys 148 G5
Cefn Berain Conwy 165 B7
Cefn-brith Conwy 164 E6
Cefn-bryn-brain Carms 76 C2
Cefn-bychan Swansea 56 B4
Wrex 166 G3
Cefncaeau Carms 56 B4
Cefn Canol Powys 148 C4
Cefn-coch Conwy 164 B5
Cefn Coch Powys 129 C10
Powys 148 D2
Cefn-coed-y-cymmer M Tydf 77 D9
Cefn Cribbwr Bridgend 57 E11
Cefn Cross Bridgend 57 E11
Cefn-ddwysarn Gwyn 147 B9
Cefn Einion Shrops 130 F5
Cefneithin Carms 75 C9
Cefn-eurgain Flint 166 B2
Cefn Fforest Caerph 77 F11
Cefn Glas Bridgend 57 E11
Cefn Golau Bl Gwent 77 D10
Cefn-gorwydd Powys 95 B8
Cefn Hengoed Caerph 77 F10
Cefn-hengoed Swansea 57 B7
Cefn Llwyd Ceredig 128 G2
Cefn-mawr Wrex 166 G3
Cefnpennar Rhondda 77 E8
Cefn Rhigos Rhondda 76 D6
Cefn-y-bedd Flint 166 D4
Cefn-y-Crib Torf 78 F2
Cefn-y-Garth Swansea 76 E2
Cefn-y-pant Carms 92 F3
Cegidfa = Guilsfield Powys 148 G4
Cei-bach Ceredig 111 F8
Ceinewydd = New Quay Ceredig 111 F7
Ceint Anglesey 179 F7
Ceinws Powys 128 B5
Cellan Ceredig 94 B2
Cellarhead Staffs 169 F7
Cellarhill Kent 70 G3
Celyn-Mali Flint 165 B11
Cemaes Anglesey 178 C5
Cemmaes Powys 128 B6
Cemmaes Road = Glantwymyn Powys 128 C6
Cenarth Carms 92 C5
Cenin Gwyn 163 F7
Central Invclyd 276 F5
Central Milton Keynes M Keynes 102 D6
Ceos W Isles 304 F5
Ceres Fife 287 F8
Ceri = Kerry Powys 130 F2
Cerne Abbas Dorset 29 G11
Cerney Wick Glos 81 F9
Cerrigceinwen Anglesey 178 G6
Cerrig Llwydion Neath 57 C9
Cerrig-mân Anglesey 179 C7
Cerrigydrudion Conwy 165 F7
Cess Norf 161 F8
Cessford Borders 262 E6
Ceunant Gwyn 163 C8
Chaceley Glos 99 E7
Chaceley Hole Glos 98 E6
Chaceley Stock Glos 99 F7
Chacewater Corn 4 G4
Chackmore Bucks 102 D3
Chacombe W Nhants 101 C9
Chadbury Worcs 99 B10
Chadderton Gtr Man 196 F2
Chadderton Fold Gtr Man 195 F11
Chaddesden Derby 153 B7
Chaddesley Corbett Worcs 117 C7
Chaddlehanger Devon 12 F5
Chaddlewood Plym 7 D11
Chaddleworth W Berks 64 D2
Chadkirk Gtr Man 184 D6
Chadlington Oxon 100 G6
Chadshunt Warks 118 G6
Chadsmoor Staffs 151 G9
Chadstone W Nhants 121 F7
Chad Valley W Mid 133 F10
Chadwell Leics 154 E5
Shrops 150 G5
Chadwell End Bedford 121 D11
Chadwell Heath London 68 B3
Chadwell St Mary Thurrock 68 D6
Chadwick Worcs 116 D6
Chadwick End W Mid 118 C4
Chadwick Green Mers 183 B8
Chaffcombe Som 28 E5
Chafford Hundred Thurrock 68 D5
Chagford Devon 13 D10
Chailey E Sus 36 D5
Chainbridge Cambs 139 C8
Chain Bridge Lincs 174 G4
Chainhurst Kent 53 D8
Chalbury Dorset 31 F8
Chalbury Common Dorset 31 F8
Chaldon Sur 51 B10
Chaldon Herring or East Chaldon Dorset 17 E11
Chale IoW 20 F5
Chale Green IoW 20 F5
Chalfont Common Bucks 85 G8
Chalfont Grove Bucks 85 G7
Chalfont St Giles Bucks 85 G7
Chalfont St Peter Bucks 85 G8
Chalford Glos 80 E5
Oxon 84 E2
Wilts 45 C11
Chalford Hill Glos 80 E5
Chalgrave C Beds 103 F10
Chalgrove Oxon 83 F10
Chalk Kent 69 E7
Chalk End Essex 87 C10
Chalkfoot Cumb 230 B2
Chalkhill Norf 141 C7
Chalkhouse Green Oxon 65 D8
Chalkshire Bucks 84 D4
Chalksole Kent 55 E9
Chalkway Som 28 F5
Chalkwell Kent 69 G11
Southend 69 B11
Challaborough Devon 8 G3
Challacombe Devon 41 E7
Challister Shetland 312 G7
Challoch Dumfries 236 C5
Challock Kent 54 C4
Chalmington Dorset 29 G9
Chalton C Beds 103 F10
Hants 34 D2
Chalvedon Essex 69 B8
Chalvey Slough 66 D3
Chalvington E Sus 23 D8
Chambercombe Devon 40 D4
Chamber's Green Kent 54 E2
Champson Devon 26 B4
Chance Inn Fife 287 F7
Chancery = Rhydgaled Ceredig 111 B11
Chance's Pitch Hereford 98 C4
Chandler's Cross Herts 85 F9
Worcs 98 D5
Chandler's Ford Hants 32 C6
Chandlers Green Hants 49 B8
Channel's End Bedford 122 F2
Channel Tunnel Kent 55 F7
Channerwick Shetland 313 L6
Chantry Devon 25 C9
Som 45 D8
Suff 108 C2
Chapel Corn 4 C6
Cumb 229 E10
Fife 280 C5
Chapel Allerton Som 44 C2
W Yorks 206 F2
Chapel Amble Corn 10 F5
Chapel Brampton W Nhants 120 D4
Chapel Chorlton Staffs 150 B6
Chapel Cleeve Som 42 E4
Chapel Cross E Sus 37 C10
Chapel End Bedford 103 B11
Bedford 122 F2
Cambs 138 G2
C Beds 103 C11
Ches E 167 G11
Essex 105 G11
N Nhants 138 F2
Warks 134 E6
Chapel-en-le-Frith Derbys 185 E9
Chapel Field Gtr Man 195 F9
Norf 161 E7
Chapel Fields W Mid 118 B6
York 207 C7
Chapelgate Lincs 157 E8
Chapel Green Herts 104 D6
Warks 119 E9
Warks 134 F5
Chapel Haddlesey N Yorks 198 B5
Chapelhall N Lanark 268 C5
Chapel Head Cambs 138 G6
Chapelhill Dumfries 248 E3
Highld 301 B8
N Ayrs 266 G4
Perth 286 D4
Perth 286 E3
Perth 286 E6
Chapel Hill Aberds 303 F10
Glos 79 E10
Lincs 174 E2
Mon 79 F8
N Yorks 206 D2
Chapel House Lancs 194 F3
Chapel Knapp Wilts 61 F11
Chapelknowe Dumfries 239 C8
Chapel Lawn Shrops 114 B6
Chapel-le-Dale N Yorks 212 D4
Chapel Leigh Som 27 B10
Chapel Mains Borders 271 G11
Chapel Milton Derbys 185 E9
Chapel of Garioch Aberds 303 G7
Chapel of Stoneywood Aberdeen 293 B10
Chapel on Leader Borders 271 G11
Chapel Outon Dumfries 236 E6
Chapel Plaister Wilts 61 F10
Chapel Row Essex 88 E3
E Sus 23 C10
W Berks 64 F5
Chapels Blackburn 195 C7
Cumb 210 C4
Chapel St Leonards Lincs 191 G9
Chapel Stile Cumb 220 D6
Chapelthorpe W Yorks 197 D10
Chapelton Angus 287 C10
Devon 25 B9
Highld 291 B11
S Lanark 268 F3
Chapelton Row Dumfries 237 E8
Chapeltown Blackburn 195 D8
Moray 302 G2
S Yorks 186 B5
W Yorks 206 F2
Chapel Town Corn 5 D7
Chapman's Hill Worcs 117 B9
Chapmanslade Wilts 45 D10
Chapman's Town E Sus 23 B10
Chapmans Well Devon 12 C3
Chapmore End Herts 86 B4
Chappel Essex 107 F7
Charaton Cross Corn 6 B6
Charcott Kent 52 D4
Chard Som 28 F4
Chard Junction Dorset 28 G4
Chardleigh Green Som 28 E4
Chardstock Devon 28 G4
Charfield S Glos 80 G2
Charfield Green S Glos 80 G2
Charfield Hill S Glos 80 G2
Charford Worcs 117 D9
Chargrove Glos 80 B6
Charing Kent 54 D3
Charing Cross Dorset 31 E10
Charing Heath Kent 54 D2
Charing Hill Kent 54 C3
Charingworth Glos 100 D4
Charlbury Oxon 82 B5
Charlcombe Bath 61 F8
Charlcutt Wilts 62 D3
Charlecote Warks 118 F5
Charlemont W Mid 133 E10
Charles Devon 41 G7
Charles Bottom Devon 41 G7
Charlesfield Borders 262 D3
Dumfries 238 D5
Charleshill Sur 49 E11
Charleston Angus 287 C7
Renfs 267 C9
Charlestown Aberdeen 293 C11
Corn 5 E10
Derbys 185 C8
Dorset 17 F9
Fife 279 E11
Gtr Man 195 G10
Gtr Man 195 G11
Highld 299 B8
Highld 300 E6
W Yorks 196 B3
W Yorks 205 F9
Charlestown of Aberlour Moray 302 E2
Charles Tye Suff 125 G10
Charlesworth Derbys 185 C8
Charleton Devon 8 G5
Charlinch Som 43 F8
Charlottetown Fife 286 F6
Charlton Hants 47 D11
Herts 104 F3
London 68 D2
Northumb 251 F8
Oxon 64 B2
Redcar 226 B2
Som 28 B3
Som 44 E6
Som 45 C7
Sur 66 F5
Telford 149 G11
Wilts 30 C6
Wilts 46 B6
Wilts 62 B3
W Nhants 101 D10
Worcs 99 B10
Worcs 116 C6
W Sus 34 E5
Charlton Abbots Glos 99 G10
Charlton Adam Som 29 B8
Charlton-All-Saints Wilts 31 C11
Charltonbrook S Yorks 186 B4
Charlton Down Dorset 17 C9
Charlton Horethorne Som 29 C11
Charlton Kings Glos 99 G9
Charlton Mackrell Som 29 B8
Charlton Marshall Dorset 30 G5
Charlton Musgrove Som 30 B2
Charlton on Otmoor Oxon 83 B9
Charlton on the Hill Dorset 30 G5
Charlton Park Glos 99 G9
Charlton St Peter Wilts 46 B6
Charlwood E Sus 51 G11
Hants 49 G7
Sur 51 E8
Charlynch Som 43 F8
Charminster BCP 19 C8
Dorset 17 C9
Charmouth Dorset 16 C3
Charnage Wilts 45 G10
Charndon Bucks 102 G3
Charnes Staffs 150 C5
Charney Bassett Oxon 82 G5
Charnock Green Lancs 194 D5
Charnock Hall S Yorks 186 E5
Charnock Richard Lancs 194 D5
Charsfield Suff 126 F5
Chart Corner Kent 53 C9
Charter Alley Hants 48 B5
Charterhouse Som 44 B3
Chartershall Stirling 278 C6
Charterville Allotments Oxon 82 C4
Chartham Kent 54 C6
Chartham Hatch Kent 54 B6
Chart Hill Kent 53 D9
Chartridge Bucks 84 E6
Chart Sutton Kent 53 D10
Charvil Wokingham 65 D9
Charwelton W Nhants 119 F10
Chase Cross London 87 G8
Chase End Street Worcs 98 D5
Chase Hill S Glos 61 B8
Chase Terrace Staffs 133 B10
Chasetown Staffs 133 B10
Chastleton Oxon 100 F4
Chasty Devon 24 G4
Chatburn Lancs 203 E11
Chatcull Staffs 150 C5
Chatford Shrops 131 B9
Chatham Caerph 59 B8
Medway 69 F9
Chatham Green Essex 88 B2
Chathill Northumb 264 D5
Chat Hill W Yorks 205 G8
Chatley Worcs 117 E7
Chattenden Medway 69 E9
Chatter End Essex 105 F9
Chatteris Cambs 139 F7
Chatterley Staffs 168 E4
Chattern Hill Sur 66 E5
Chatterton Lancs 195 D9
Chattisham Suff 107 C11
Chattle Hill Warks 134 E3
Chatto Borders 263 F7
Chatton Northumb 264 D3
Chaulden Herts 85 D8
Chaul End C Beds 103 G11
Chavel Shrops 149 G8
Chavenage Green Glos 80 F5
Chavey Down Brack 65 F11
Chawleigh Devon 26 E2
Chawley Oxon 83 E7
Chawson Worcs 117 E7
Chawston Bedford 122 F3
Chawton Hants 49 F8
Chaxhill Glos 80 C2
Chazey Heath Oxon 65 D7
Cheadle Gtr Man 184 D5
Staffs 169 G8
Cheadle Heath Gtr Man 184 D5
Cheadle Hulme Gtr Man 184 D5
Cheadle Park Staffs 169 G8
Cheam London 67 G8
Cheapside Herts 105 E8
Sur 50 B4
Windsor 66 F2
Chearsley Bucks 84 C2
Chebsey Staffs 151 D7
Checkendon Oxon 65 C7
Checkley Ches E 168 F2
Hereford 97 D11
Staffs 151 B10
Checkley Green Ches E 168 F2
Chedburgh Suff 124 F5
Cheddar Som 44 C3
Cheddington Bucks 84 B6
Cheddleton Staffs 169 E7
Cheddleton Heath Staffs 169 E7
Cheddon Fitzpaine Som 28 B2
Chedglow Wilts 80 G6
Chedgrave Norf 143 D7
Chedington Dorset 29 F7
Chediston Suff 127 B7
Chediston Green Suff 127 B7
Chedworth Glos 81 C9
Chedworth Laines Glos 81 C8
Chedzoy Som 43 F10
Cheeklaw Borders 272 E5
Cheeseman's Green Kent 54 F4
Cheetam Hill Gtr Man 195 G10
Cheglinch Devon 40 E4
Chegworth Kent 53 C10
Cheldon Devon 26 E2
Chelfham Devon 40 F6
Chelford Ches E 184 G4
Chellaston Derby 153 C7
Chell Heath Stoke 168 E5
Chellington Bedford 121 F9
Chells Herts 104 F5
Chelmarsh Shrops 132 F4
Chelmer Village Essex 88 D2
Chelmick Shrops 131 E9
Chelmondiston Suff 108 D4
Chelmorton Derbys 169 B10
Chelmsford Essex 88 D2
Chelmsine Som 27 D11
Chelmsley Wood W Mid 134 F3
Chelsea London 67 D9
Chelsfield London 68 G3
Chelsham Sur 51 B11
Chelston Som 27 C11
Torbay 9 C7
Chelston Heathfield Som 27 C11
Chelsworth Suff 107 B9
Chelsworth Common Suff 107 B9
Cheltenham Glos 99 G8
Chelveston N Nhants 121 D9
Chelvey N Som 60 F3
Chelvey Batch N Som 60 F3
Chelwood Bath 60 G6
Chelwood Common E Sus 36 B6
Chelwood Gate E Sus 36 B6
Chelworth Wilts 81 G7
Chelworth Lower Green Wilts 81 G9
Chelworth Upper Green Wilts 81 G9
Chelynch Som 45 E7
Chemistry Shrops 167 G8
Cheney Longville Shrops 131 G8
Chenhalls Corn 2 B3
Chenies Bucks 85 F8
Cheny Longville Shrops 131 G8
Chepstow Mon 79 G8
Chequerbent Gtr Man 195 F7
Chequerfield W Yorks 198 C3
Chequers Corner Norf 139 B9
Chequertree Kent 54 F4
Cherhill Wilts 62 E4
Cherington Glos 80 F6
Warks 100 D5
Cheristow Devon 24 B3
Cheriton Devon 41 D8
Hants 33 B9
Kent 55 F7
Swansea 56 C3
Cheriton Bishop Devon 13 C11
Cheriton Cross Devon 13 C11
Cheriton Fitzpaine Devon 26 F5
Cheriton or Stackpole Elidor Pembs 73 F7
Cherrington Telford 150 E3
Cherrybank Perth 286 E5
Cherry Burton E Yorks 208 E5
Cherry Green Essex 105 F11
Herts 105 F7
Cherry Hinton Cambs 123 F9
Cherry Orchard Shrops 149 G9
Worcs 117 G7
Cherry Tree Blackburn 195 B7
Gtr Man 185 C7
Cherrytree Hill Derby 153 B7
Cherry Willingham Lincs 189 G8
Chertsey Sur 66 F4
Chertsey Meads Sur 66 F5
Cheselbourne Dorset 17 B11
Chesham Bucks 85 E7
Gtr Man 195 E10
Chesham Bois Bucks 85 F7
Cheshunt Herts 86 E5
Chesley Kent 69 G11
Cheslyn Hay Staffs 133 B9
Chessetts Wood Warks 118 C3
Chessington London 67 G7
Chessmount Bucks 85 E7
Chestall Staffs 151 G11
Chester Ches W 166 B6
Chesterblade Som 45 E7
Chesterfield Derbys 186 G5
Staffs 134 B2
Chesterhill Midloth 271 B7
Chesterhope Northumb 251 F9
Chesterknowes Borders 262 D2
Chester-le-Street Durham 243 G7
Chester Moor Durham 233 B11
Chesters Borders 262 E4
Borders 262 G4
Chesterton Cambs 123 E9
Cambs 138 D2
Glos 81 E8
Oxon 101 G11
Shrops 132 D5
Staffs 168 F4
Warks 118 E6
Chesterton Green Warks 118 F6
Chesterwood Northumb 241 D8
Chestfield Kent 70 F6
Chestnut Hill Cumb 229 G11
Chestnut Street Kent 69 G11
Cheston Devon 8 D3
Cheswardine Shrops 150 D4
Cheswell Telford 150 F4
Cheswick Northumb 273 F10
Cheswick Buildings Northumb 273 F10
Cheswick Green W Mid 118 B2
Chetnole Dorset 29 F10
Chettiscombe Devon 27 E7
Chettisham Cambs 139 G10
Chettle Dorset 31 E7
Chetton Shrops 132 E3
Chetwode Bucks 102 F2
Chetwynd Aston Telford 150 F5
Cheveley Cambs 124 E3
Chevening Kent 52 B3
Cheverell's Green Herts 85 B9
Chevin End W Yorks 205 E9
Chevington Suff 124 F5
Chevithorne Devon 27 D7
Chew Magna Bath 60 G5
Chew Moor Gtr Man 195 F7
Chew Stoke Bath 60 G5
Chewton Keynsham Bath 61 F7
Chewton Mendip Som 44 C5
Cheylesmore W Mid 118 B6
Chichacott Devon 13 B8
Chicheley M Keynes 103 B8
Chichester W Sus 22 C5
Chickenley W Yorks 197 C9
Chickerell Dorset 17 E8
Chicklade Wilts 46 G2
Chickney Essex 105 F11
Chicksands C Beds 104 D2
Chicksgrove Wilts 46 G3
Chickward Hereford 114 G5
Chidden Hants 33 D11
Chiddingfold Sur 50 F3
Chiddingly E Sus 23 C8
Chiddingstone Kent 52 D3
Chiddingstone Causeway Kent 52 D4
Chiddingstone Hoath Kent 52 E3
Chideock Dorset 16 C4
Chidgley Som 42 F4
Chidham W Sus 22 C3
Chidswell W Yorks 197 C9
Chieveley W Berks 64 E3
Chignall St James Essex 87 D11
Chignall Smealy Essex 87 C11
Chigwell Essex 86 G6
Chigwell Row Essex 87 G7
Chilbolton Hants 47 F11
Chilbolton Down Hants 48 F2
Chilbridge Dorset 31 G7
Chilcomb Hants 33 B8
Chilcombe Dorset 16 C6
Som 42 F6
Chilcompton Som 44 C6
Chilcote Leics 152 G5
Childerditch Essex 68 B6
Childerley Gate Cambs 123 F7
Childer Thornton Ches W 182 F5
Child Okeford Dorset 30 E4
Childrey Oxon 63 B11
Childsbridge Kent 52 B5
Child's Ercall Shrops 150 E3
Child's Hill London 67 B8
Childswickham Worcs 99 D11
Childwall Mers 182 D6
Childwick Bury Herts 85 C10
Childwick Green Herts 85 C10
Chilfrome Dorset 17 B7
Chilgrove W Sus 34 E4
Chilham Kent 54 C5
Chilhampton Wilts 46 G5
Chilla Devon 24 G6
Chillaton Devon 12 E4
Chillenden Kent 55 C9
Chillerton IoW 20 E5
Chillesford Suff 127 G7
Chillingham Northumb 264 D3
Chillington Devon 8 G5
Som 28 E5
Chillmill Kent 53 E7
Chilmark Wilts 46 G3
Chilmington Green Kent 54 E3
Chilsham E Sus 23 C10
Chilson Oxon 82 B4
Som 28 G4
Chilson Common Som 28 G4
Chilsworthy Corn 12 G4
Devon 24 F4
Chiltern Green C Beds 85 B10
Chilthorne Domer Som 29 D8
Chiltington E Sus 36 D5
Chilton Bucks 83 C11
Durham 233 F11
Kent 71 G11
Oxon 64 B3
Suff 107 C7
Chilton Candover Hants 48 E5
Chilton Cantelo Som 29 C9
Chilton Foliat Wilts 63 E10
Chilton Lane Durham 234 E2
Chilton Moor T&W 234 B2
Chilton Polden Som 43 F11
Chilton Street Suff 106 B5
Chilton Trinity Som 43 F9
Chilvers Coton Warks 135 E7
Chilwell Notts 153 B10
Chilworth Hants 32 D6
Sur 50 D4
Chilworth Old Village Hants 32 D6
Chimney Oxon 82 E5
Chimney-end Oxon 82 B4
Chimney Street Suff 106 B4
Chineham Hants 49 C7
Chingford London 86 G5
Chingford Green London 86 G5
Chingford Hatch London 86 G5
Chinley Derbys 185 E8
Chinley Head Derbys 185 E9
Chinnor Oxon 84 E3
Chipley Som 27 C10
Chipmans Platt Glos 80 D3
Chipnall Shrops 150 C4
Chippenhall Green Suff 126 B5
Chippenham Cambs 124 D3
Wilts 62 E2
Chipperfield Herts 85 E8
Chipping Herts 105 E7
Lancs 203 E8
Chipping Barnet London 86 F2
Chipping Campden Glos 100 D3
Chipping Hill Essex 88 B4
Chipping Norton Oxon 100 F6
Chipping Ongar Essex 87 E8
Chipping Sodbury S Glos 61 C8
Chipping Warden W Nhants 101 B9
Chipstable Som 27 B8
Chipstead Kent 52 B3
Sur 51 B9
Chirbury Shrops 130 D5
Chirk = Y Waun Wrex 148 B5
Chirk Bank Shrops 148 B5
Chirk Green Wrex 148 B5
Chirmorrie S Ayrs 236 B4
Chirnside Borders 273 D7
Chirnsidebridge Borders 273 D7
Chirton T&W 243 D8
Wilts 46 B5
Chisbridge Cross Bucks 65 B10
Chisbury Wilts 63 F9
Chiselborough Som 29 E7
Chiseldon Swindon 63 D7
Chiserley W Yorks 196 B4
Chislehampton Oxon 83 F9
Chislehurst London 68 E2
Chislehurst West London 68 E2
Chislet Kent 71 G8
Chislet Forstal Kent 71 G8
Chiswell Dorset 17 G9
Chiswell Green Herts 85 E10
Chiswick London 67 D8
Chiswick End Cambs 105 B7
Chisworth Derbys 185 C7
Chitcombe E Sus 38 C4
Chithurst W Sus 34 C4
Chittering Cambs 123 C9
Chitterley Devon 26 G6
Chitterne Wilts 46 E3
Chittlehamholt Devon 25 C11
Chittlehampton Devon 25 B10
Chittoe Wilts 62 F3
Chitts Hills Essex 107 F9
Chitty Kent 71 G8
Chivelstone Devon 9 G10
Chivenor Devon 40 G4
Chivery Bucks 84 D6
Chobham Sur 66 G3
Choicelee Borders 272 E4
Cholderton Wilts 47 E8
Cholesbury Bucks 84 D6
Chollerford Northumb 241 C10
Chollerton Northumb 241 C10
Cholmondeston Ches E 167 C10
Cholsey Oxon 64 B5
Cholstrey Hereford 115 F9
Cholwell Bath 44 B6
Chop Gate N Yorks 225 F11
Choppington Northumb 253 G7
Chopwell T&W 242 F4
Chorley Ches E 167 E9
Lancs 194 D5
Shrops 132 G3
Staffs 151 G11
Chorley Common W Sus 34 B4
Chorleywood Herts 85 F8
Chorleywood Bottom Herts 85 F8
Chorleywood West Herts 85 F8
Chorlton Ches E 168 E2
Chorlton-cum-Hardy Gtr Man 184 C4
Chorlton Lane Ches W 167 F7
Choulton Shrops 131 F7
Chowdene T&W 243 F7
Chowley Ches W 167 D7
Chownes Mead W Sus 36 C4
Chreagain Highld 289 C10
Chrishall Essex 105 D8
Christchurch BCP 19 C9
Cambs 139 D9
Glos 79 C9
Newport 59 B10
Christian Malford Wilts 62 D3
Christleton Ches W 166 B6
Christmas Common Oxon 84 G2
Christon N Som 43 B11
Christon Bank Northumb 264 E6
Christow Devon 14 D2
Chryston N Lanark 278 G3
Chub Tor Devon 7 B10
Chuck Hatch E Sus 52 G3
Chudleigh Devon 14 F3
Chudleigh Knighton Devon 14 F2
Chulmleigh Devon 25 E11
Chunal Derbys 185 C8
Church Lancs 195 B8
Churcham Glos 80 B3
Church Aston Telford 150 F4
Churchbank Shrops 114 B6
Church Brampton W Nhants 120 D4
Churchbridge Corn 6 D4
Staffs 133 B9
Church Brough Cumb 222 C5
Church Broughton Derbys 152 C4
Church Charwelton W Nhants 119 F10
Church Clough Lancs 204 F3
Church Common Hants 34 B2
Church Coombe Corn 4 G3
Church Cove Corn 2 G6
Church Crookham Hants 49 C10
Churchdown Glos 80 B5
Church Eaton Staffs 150 F6
Churchend Essex 89 G8
Essex 106 G2
Glos 80 D3
Glos 80 F2
Reading 65 E7
S Glos 80 G2
Church End Bedford 122 F2
Bucks 84 B6
Bucks 84 D2
Cambs 121 C11
Cambs 123 C7
Cambs 123 D7
Cambs 123 D8
Cambs 139 B7
C Beds 85 B8
C Beds 103 E9
C Beds 103 G9
C Beds 104 D3
C Beds 122 G3
Essex 88 B2
Essex 105 C11
Essex 105 F11
Essex 106 F4
E Yorks 209 C7
Glos 80 D2
Glos 99 D7
Hants 49 B7
Herts 85 C10
Herts 85 F8
Herts 104 E5
Herts 105 G8
Lincs 156 C4
Lincs 190 B6
London 67 C8
London 86 G2
Norf 157 F10
Oxon 82 D5
Oxon 100 E6
Suff 108 D4
Sur 50 B5
Warks 134 E4
Warks 134 E5
Wilts 62 D4
W Mid 119 B7
Worcs 99 B7
Church Enstone Oxon 101 G7
Churches Green E Sus 23 B10
Church Fenton N Yorks 206 F6
Churchfield Hereford 98 B4
W Mid 133 E10
Churchfields Wilts 31 B10
Churchgate Herts 86 E4
Churchgate Street Essex 87 C7
Church Green Devon 15 B9

Church Green *continued*
Norf 141 E11
Church Gresley Derbys 152 F5
Church Hanborough
Oxon 82 C6
Church Hill Ches W 167 C10
Pembs 73 C7
Staffs 151 G10
W Mid 133 D9
Worcs 117 D11
Church Hougham Kent 55 E9
Church Houses N Yorks 226 F3
Churchill Devon 28 G4
Devon 40 E5
N Som 44 B2
Oxon 100 G5
Worcs 117 B7
Worcs 117 G8
Churchill Green N Som 60 G2
Churchinford Som 28 E2
Church Knowle Dorset 18 E4
Church Laneham Notts 188 F4
Church Langton Leics 136 E4
Church Lawford Warks 119 B8
Church Lawton Ches E 168 D4
Church Leigh Staffs 151 B10
Church Lench Worcs 117 G10
Church Mayfield Staffs 169 G11
Church Minshull
Ches E 167 C11
Churchmoor Rough
Shrops 131 F8
Church Norton W Sus 22 D5
Church Oakley Hants 48 C5
Churchover Warks 135 G10
Church Preen Shrops 131 D10
Church Pulverbatch
Shrops 131 C8
Churchstanton Som 27 E11
Churchstoke Powys 130 E5
Churchstow Devon 8 F4
Church Stowe W Nhants 120 F2
Church Street Essex 106 C5
Kent 69 E8
Church Stretton Shrops 131 E9
Churchton Pembs 73 D10
Churchtown Corn 11 F7
Cumb 230 C3
Derbys 170 C3
Devon 24 G3
Devon 41 E7
IoM 192 C5
Lancs 202 E5
Mers 193 D11
Shrops 130 F5
Som 42 F3
Church Town Corn 4 G3
Leics 153 F7
N Lincs 199 F9
Sur 51 C11
Church Village Rhondda 58 B5
Church Warsop Notts 171 B9
Church Westcote Glos 100 G4
Church Whitfield Kent 55 D10
Church Wilne Derbys 153 C8
Churchwood W Sus 35 D8
Churnet Grange Staffs 169 E7
Churnsike Lodge
Northumb 240 B5
Churscombe Torbay 9 C7
Churston Ferrers Torbay 9 D8
Churt Sur 49 F11
Churton Ches W 166 D6
Churwell W Yorks 197 B9
Chute Cadley Wilts 47 C10
Chute Standen Wilts 47 C10
Chwefforrdd Conwy 180 G4
Chwilog Gwyn 145 B8
Chwitffordd =*Whitford*
Flint 181 F10
Chyandour Corn 1 C5
Chyanvounder Corn 2 E5
Chycoose Corn 3 B8
Chynhale Corn 2 C4
Chynoweth Corn 2 C2
Chyvarloe Corn 2 E5
Cicelyford Mon 79 E8
Cilan Uchaf Gwyn 144 E5
Cilau Pembs 91 D8
Cilcain Flint 165 B11
Cilcennin Ceredig 111 E10
Cilcewydd Powys 130 C4
Cilfor Gwyn 146 B2
Cilfrew Neath 76 E3
Cilfynydd Rhondda 77 G9
Cilgerran Pembs 92 C3
Cilgwyn Carms 94 F4
Ceredig 92 C6
Gwyn 163 E7
Pembs 91 D11
Ciliau Aeron Ceredig 111 F9
Cill Amhlaidh W Isles 297 G3
Cill Donnain W Isles 297 J3
Cille Bhrighde W Isles 297 K3
Cill Eireabhagh W Isles 297 G4
Cille Pheadair W Isles 297 K3
Cilmaengwyn Neath 76 D2
Cilmery Powys 113 G10
Cilsan Carms 93 G11
Ciltalgarth Gwyn 164 G5
Ciltwrch Powys 96 C3
Cilybebyll Neath 76 E2
Cil y coed =*Caldicot*
Mon 60 B3
Cilycwm Carms 94 D5
Cimla Neath 57 B9
Cinderford Glos 79 C11
Cinderhill Derbys 170 F5
Nottingham 171 G8
Cinder Hill Gtr Man 195 F9
Kent 52 D4
W Mid 133 E8
W Sus 36 B5
Cinnamon Brow Warr 183 C10
Cippenham Slough 66 C2
Cippyn Pembs 92 B2
Circebost W Isles 304 E3
Cirencester Glos 81 E8
Ciribhig W Isles 304 D3
City London 67 C10
Powys 130 F4
V Glam 58 D3
City Dulas Anglesey 179 D7
Clabhach Argyll 288 D3
Clachaig Argyll 276 E2
Highld 292 B2
N Ayrs 255 E10
Clachan Argyll 255 B8
Argyll 275 B8
Argyll 284 F5
Argyll 289 E10
Highld 295 B7
Highld 298 C4
Highld 307 G3
W Isles 297 G3
Clachaneasy Dumfries 236 B5
Clachanmore Dumfries 236 E2
Clachan na Luib
W Isles 296 E4
Clachan of Campsie
E Dunb 278 F2
Clachan of Glendaruel
Argyll 275 E10
Clachan-Seil Argyll 275 B8
Clachan Strachur Argyll 284 G4
Clachbreck Argyll 275 F8
Clachnabrain Angus 292 G5
Clachtoll Highld 307 G5
Clackmannan Clack 279 C8
Clackmarras Moray 302 D2
Clacton-on-Sea Essex 89 B11
Cladach N Ayrs 256 B2
Cladach Chairinis
W Isles 296 F4
Cladach Chireboist
W Isles 296 E3
Claddach Argyll 254 B2
Claddach-knockline
W Isles 296 E3
Cladich Argyll 284 E4
Cladich Steading Argyll 284 E4
Cladswell Worcs 117 F10
Claggan Highld 289 E8
Highld 290 F3
Perth 285 D11
Claigan Highld 298 D2
Claines Worcs 117 F7
Clandown Bath 45 B7
Clanfield Hants 33 D11
Oxon 82 E3
Clanking Bucks 84 D4
Clanville Hants 47 D10
Som 44 G6
Wilts 62 D2
Claonaig Argyll 255 B9
Claonel Highld 309 J5
Clapgate Dorset 31 G8
Herts 105 G8
Clapham Bedford 121 G10
Devon 14 D3
London 67 D9
N Yorks 212 F4
W Sus 35 F9
Clapham Green
Bedford 121 G10
N Yorks 205 B10
Clapham Hill Kent 70 G6
Clapham Park London 67 E9
Clap Hill Kent 54 F5
Clapper Corn 10 G6
Clapper Hill Kent 53 F10
Clappers Borders 273 D8
Clappersgate Cumb 221 E7
Clapphoull Shetland 313 L6
Clapton Som 28 F6
Som 44 C6
W Berks 63 E11
Clapton in Gordano
N Som 60 E3
Clapton-on-the-Hill
Glos 81 B11
Clapton Park London 67 B11
Clapworthy Devon 25 C11
Clarach Ceredig 128 G2
Clarack Aberds 292 D6
Clara Vale T&W 242 E4
Clarbeston Pembs 91 G10
Clarbeston Road Pembs 91 G10
Clarborough Notts 188 E2
Clardon Highld 310 C5
Clare Oxon 83 F11
Suff 106 B5
Clarebrand Dumfries 237 C9
Claregate W Mid 133 C7
Claremont Park Sur 66 G6
Claremount W Yorks 196 B5
Clarencefield Dumfries 238 D3
Clarence Park N Som 59 G10
Clarendon Park
Leicester 135 C11
Clareston Pembs 73 C7
Clarilaw Borders 262 D3
Borders 262 F2
Clarken Green Hants 48 C5
Clark Green Ches E 184 F6
Clarksfield Gtr Man 196 G2
Clark's Green Sur 51 F7
Clark's Hill Lincs 157 E7
Clarkston E Renf 267 D11
N Lanark 268 B5
Clase Swansea 57 B7
Clashandorran Highld 300 E5
Clashcoig Highld 309 K6
Clasheddy Highld 308 C6
Clashgour Argyll 284 C6
Clashindarroch Aberds 302 F4
Clashmore Highld 306 F5
Highld 309 L7
Clashnessie Highld 306 F5
Clashnoir Moray 302 G2
Clate Shetland 313 G7
Clatford Wilts 63 F7
Clatford Oakcuts Hants 47 F10
Clathy Perth 286 F3
Clatt Aberds 302 G5
Clatter Powys 129 E9
Clatterford IoW 20 D5
Clatterford End Essex 87 C10
Essex 87 D9
Essex 87 E8
Clatterin Bridge Aberds 293 F8
Clatto Fife 287 F8
Clatworthy Som 42 G5
Clauchlands N Ayrs 256 C2
Claughton Lancs 202 E6
Lancs 211 F11
Mers 182 D4
Clavelshay Som 43 G9
Claverdon Warks 118 E3
Claverham N Som 60 F2
Claverhambury Essex 86 E6
Clavering Essex 105 E9
Claverley Shrops 132 E5
Claverton Bath 61 G9
Claverton Down Bath 61 G9
Clawdd-côch V Glam 58 D5
Clawdd-newydd Denb 165 E9
Clawdd Poncen Denb 165 G9
Clawthorpe Cumb 211 D10
Clawton Devon 12 B3
Claxby Lincs 189 C10
Lincs 191 G7
Claxby St Andrew Lincs 191 G7
Claxton Norf 142 C6
N Yorks 216 G3
Claybokie Aberds 292 D2
Claybrooke Magna Leics 135 F9
Claybrooke Parva Leics 135 F9
Clay Common Suff 143 G9
Clay Coton W Nhants 119 B11
Clay Cross Derbys 170 C5
Claydon Glos 99 E8
Oxon 119 G9
Suff 126 G2
Clay End Herts 104 F6
Claygate Dumfries 239 B9
Kent 52 C6
Kent 53 E8
Sur 67 G7
Claygate Cross Kent 52 B6
Clayhall Hants 21 B8
London 86 G6
Clayhanger Devon 27 C8
Som 28 E4
W Mid 133 C10
Clayhidon Devon 27 D11
Clayhill E Sus 38 C4
Hants 32 F4
Clay Hill Bristol 60 E6
London 86 F4
W Berks 64 E5
Clayhithe Cambs 123 E10
Clayholes Angus 287 D9
Clay Lake Lincs 156 E5
Clayland Stirling 277 D11
Clay Mills Derbys 152 D5
Clayock Highld 310 D5
Claypit Hill Cambs 123 G7
Claypits Devon 27 B7
Glos 80 D3
Kent 55 B9
Suff 140 G4
Claypole Lincs 172 F5
Clays End Bath 61 G8
Claythorpe Lincs 190 F6
Clayton Gtr Man 184 B5
Staffs 168 G5
S Yorks 198 F3
W Sus 36 E3
W Yorks 205 G8
Clayton Brook Lancs 194 C5
Clayton Green Lancs 194 C5
Clayton Heights
W Yorks 205 G8
Clayton-le-Dale Lancs 203 G9
Clayton-le-Moors
Lancs 203 G10
Clayton-le-Woods
Lancs 194 C5
Clayton West W Yorks 197 E9
Clayworth Notts 188 D2
Cleadale Highld 294 G6
Cleadon T&W 243 E9
Cleadon Park T&W 243 E9
Clearbrook Devon 7 B10
Clearwell Glos 79 D9
Newport 59 B9
Clearwood Wilts 45 D10
Cleasby N Yorks 224 C5
Cleat Orkney 314 B4
Orkney 314 H4
Cleatlam Durham 224 B2
Cleator Cumb 219 C10
Cleator Moor Cumb 219 B10
Cleave Devon 28 G2
Clebrig Highld 308 F5
Cleckheaton W Yorks 197 B7
Cleddon Mon 79 E8
Cleedownton Shrops 131 G11
Cleehill Shrops 115 B11
Cleekhimin N Lanark 268 D5
Cleemarsh Shrops 131 G11
Clee St Margaret
Shrops 131 G11
Cleestanton Shrops 115 B11
Cleethorpes NE Lincs 201 F10
Cleeton St Mary Shrops 116 B2
Cleeve Glos 80 C2
N Som 60 F3
Oxon 64 C6
Cleeve Hill Glos 99 F9
Cleeve Prior Worcs 99 B11
Cleghorn S Lanark 269 F8
Clegyrnant Powys 129 B8
Clehonger Hereford 97 D9
Cleirwy =*Clyro* Powys 96 C4
Cleish Perth 279 B11
Cleland N Lanark 268 D5
Clements End Glos 79 D9
Clement's End C Beds 85 B8
Clement Street Kent 68 E4
Clench Wilts 63 G7
Clench Common Wilts 63 F7
Clencher's Mill Hereford 98 D4
Clenchwarton Norf 157 E11
Clennell Northumb 251 B10
Clent Worcs 117 B8
Cleobury Mortimer
Shrops 116 B3
Cleobury North Shrops 132 F2
Cleongart Argyll 255 D7
Clephanton Highld 301 D8
Clerkenwater Corn 5 B11
Clerkenwell London 67 C10
Clerk Green W Yorks 197 C8
Clerklands Borders 262 E2
Clermiston Edin 280 G3
Clestrain Orkney 314 F3
Cleuch Head Borders 262 G3
Cleughbrae Dumfries 238 C3
Clevancy Wilts 62 D5
Clevans Renfs 267 B7
Clevedon N Som 60 E2
Cleveley Oxon 101 G7
Cleveleys Lancs 202 E2
Cleverton Wilts 62 B3
Clevis Bridgend 57 F10
Clewer Som 44 C2
Clewer Green Windsor 66 D2
Clewer New Town
Windsor 66 D3
Clewer Village Windsor 66 D3
Cley next the Sea Norf 177 E8
Cliaid W Isles 297 L2
Cliasmol W Isles 305 H2
Cliburn Cumb 231 G7
Click Mill Orkney 314 D3
Cliddesden Hants 48 D6
Cliff Derbys 185 D8
Warks 134 D4
Cliffburn Angus 287 C10
Cliffe Lancs 203 G10
Medway 69 D8
N Yorks 207 G9
N Yorks 224 B4
Cliff End E Sus 38 E5
W Yorks 196 D6
Cliffe Woods Medway 69 E8
Clifford Devon 24 C4
Hereford 96 B4
W Yorks 206 E4
Clifford Chambers
Warks 118 G3
Clifford's Mesne Glos 98 G4
Cliffs End Kent 71 G10
Clifftown Southend 69 B11
Clifton Bristol 60 E5
C Beds 104 D3
Ches W 183 F8
Cumb 230 F6
Derbys 169 G11
Devon 40 E5
Gtr Man 195 G9
Lancs 202 G5
Northumb 252 G6
Nottingham 153 C11
N Yorks 205 D9
Oxon 101 E9
Stirling 285 D7
S Yorks 186 C6
S Yorks 187 B8
Worcs 98 B6
W Yorks 197 C7
Clifton *continued*
York 207 C7
Clifton Campville Staffs 152 G5
Cliftoncote Borders 263 E8
Clifton Green Gtr Man 195 G9
Clifton Hampden Oxon 83 F8
Clifton Junction
Gtr Man 195 G9
Clifton Manor C Beds 104 D3
Clifton Maybank Dorset 29 E9
Clifton Moor York 207 B7
Clifton Reynes
M Keynes 121 G8
Clifton upon Dunsmore
Warks 119 B10
Clifton upon Teme
Worcs 116 E4
Cliftonville Kent 71 E11
N Lanark 268 B4
Norf 160 B6
Climping W Sus 35 G8
Climpy S Lanark 269 D8
Clink Som 45 D9
Clinkham Wood Mers 183 B8
Clint N Yorks 205 B11
Clint Green Norf 159 G10
Clintmains Borders 262 C4
Clints N Yorks 224 E2
Cliobh W Isles 304 E2
Clipiau Gwyn 146 G6
Clippesby Norf 161 G8
Clippings Green Norf 159 G10
Clipsham Rutland 155 F9
Clipston Notts 154 C2
W Nhants 136 G4
Clipstone C Beds 103 F8
Clitheroe Lancs 203 E10
Cliuthar W Isles 305 J3
Clive Ches W 167 B11
Shrops 149 E10
Clive Green Ches W 167 C11
Clive Vale E Sus 38 E4
Clivocast Shetland 312 C8
Clixby Lincs 200 G6
Cloatley Wilts 81 G7
Cloatley End Wilts 81 G7
Clocaenog Denb 165 E9
Clochan Aberds 303 E9
Moray 302 C4
Clock Face Mers 183 C8
Clock House London 67 G9
Clockmill Borders 272 E5
Clock Mills Hereford 96 B5
Cloddiau Powys 130 B4
Cloddymoss Moray 301 D9
Clodock Hereford 96 F6
Cloford Som 45 E8
Cloford Common Som 45 E8
Cloigyn Carms 74 C6
Clola Aberds 303 E10
Clophill C Beds 103 D11
Clopton N Nhants 137 G11
Suff 126 G4
Clopton Corner Suff 126 G4
Clopton Green Suff 124 G5
Suff 125 E9
Closeburn Dumfries 247 E9
Close Clark IoM 192 E3
Close House Durham 233 F10
Closworth Som 29 E9
Clothall Herts 104 E5
Clothall Common Herts 104 E5
Clotton Ches W 167 C8
Clotton Common
Ches W 167 C8
Cloudesley Bush Warks 135 F9
Clouds Hereford 97 D11
Cloud Side Staffs 168 C6
Clough Gtr Man 196 D2
Gtr Man 196 F2
W Yorks 196 E5
Clough Dene Durham 242 F5
Cloughfold Lancs 195 C10
Clough Foot W Yorks 196 C2
Clough Hall Staffs 168 E4
Clough Head W Yorks 196 C5
Cloughton N Yorks 227 G10
Cloughton Newlands
N Yorks 227 F10
Clounlaid Highld 289 D9
Clousta Shetland 313 H5
Clouston Orkney 314 E2
Clova Aberds 302 G4
Angus 292 F5
Clovelly Devon 24 C4
Clove Lodge Durham 223 B8
Clovenfords Borders 261 B10
Clovenstone Aberds 293 B9
Cloves Moray 301 C11
Clovullin Highld 290 G2
Clowance Wood Corn 2 C4
Clow Bridge Lancs 195 B10
Clowne Derbys 187 F7
Clows Top Worcs 116 C4
Cloy Wrex 166 G5
Cluanie Inn Highld 290 B2
Cluanie Lodge Highld 290 B2
Clubmoor Mers 182 C5
Clubworthy Corn 11 C11
Cluddley Telford 150 G2
Clun Shrops 130 G6
Clunbury Shrops 131 G7
Clunderwen Carms 73 B10
Clune Highld 301 D9
Highld 301 G7
Clunes Highld 290 E4
Clungunford Shrops 115 B7
Clunie Aberds 302 D6
Perth 286 C5
Clunton Shrops 130 G6
Cluny Fife 280 B4
Cluny Castle Aberds 293 B8
Highld 291 D8
Clutton Bath 44 B6
Ches W 167 E7
Clutton Hill Bath 44 B6
Clwt-grugoer Conwy 165 C7
Clwt-y-bont Gwyn 163 C9
Clwydyfagwyr M Tydf 77 D8
Clydach Mon 78 C2
Swansea 75 E11
Clydach Terrace Powys 77 C11
Clydach Vale Rhondda 77 G7
Clydebank W Dunb 277 G9
Clyffe Pypard Wilts 62 D5
Clynder Argyll 276 E4
Clyne Neath 76 E4
Clynelish Highld 311 J2
Clynnog-fawr Gwyn 162 F6
Clyro =*Cleirwy* Powys 96 C4
Clyst Honiton Devon 14 C5
Clyst Hydon Devon 27 G8
Clyst St George Devon 14 D5
Clyst St Lawrence Devon 27 G8
Clyst St Mary Devon 14 C5
Cnìp W Isles 304 E2
Cnoc Amhlaigh W Isles 304 E7
Cnoc an t-Solais
W Isles 304 D6
Cnocbreac Argyll 274 F5
Cnoc Fhionn Highld 295 D10
Cnoc Màiri W Isles 304 E6
Cnoc Rolum W Isles 296 F3
Cnwch-coch Ceredig 112 B3
Coachford Aberds 302 E4
Coad's Green Corn 11 F11
Coal Aston Derbys 186 F5
Coal Bank Darl 234 G3
Coalbrookdale Telford 132 C3
Coalbrookvale Bl Gwent 77 D11
Coalburn S Lanark 259 C8
Coalburns T&W 242 E4
Coalcleugh Northumb 232 B2
Coaley Glos 80 E3
Coaley Peak Glos 80 E3
Coalford Aberds 293 D10
Coalhall E Ayrs 257 F10
Coalhill Essex 88 F3
Coalmoor Telford 132 B3
Coalpit Field Warks 135 F7
Coalpit Heath S Glos 61 C7
Coalpit Hill Staffs 168 E4
Coal Pool W Mid 133 C10
Coalport Telford 132 C3
Coalsnaughton Clack 279 B8
Coaltown of Balgonie
Fife 280 B5
Coaltown of Wemyss
Fife 280 B6
Coalville Leics 153 G8
Coalway Glos 79 C9
Coanwood Northumb 240 F5
Coarsewell Devon 8 E4
Coat Som 29 C7
Coatbridge N Lanark 268 C4
Coatdyke N Lanark 268 C5
Coate Swindon 63 C7
Wilts 62 G4
Coates Cambs 138 D6
Glos 81 E7
Lancs 204 D3
Lincs 188 E6
Midloth 270 C4
Notts 188 E4
W Sus 35 D7
Coatham Redcar 235 F7
Coatham Mundeville
Darl 233 G11
Coatsgate Dumfries 248 B3
Cobairdy Aberds 302 E5
Cobbaton Devon 25 B10
Cobbler's Corner Worcs 116 F5
Cobbler's Green Norf 142 E5
Cobbler's Plain Mon 79 E7
Cobbs Warr 183 D10
Cobb's Cross Glos 98 E5
Cobbs Fenn Essex 106 E5
Cobby Syke N Yorks 205 B9
Coberley Glos 81 B7
Cobhall Common
Hereford 97 D9
Cobham Kent 69 F7
Sur 66 G6
Cobleland Stirling 277 B10
Cobler's Green Essex 87 B11
Cobley Dorset 31 C8
Cobley Hill Worcs 117 C10
Cobnash Hereford 115 E9
Cobridge Stoke 168 F5
Cobscot Shrops 150 B3
Coburty Aberds 303 C9
Cockadilly Glos 80 E4
Cock Alley Derbys 186 G6
Cock and End Suff 124 G4
Cockayne N Yorks 226 F2
Cockayne Hatley
C Beds 104 B5
Cock Bank Wrex 166 F5
Cock Bevington Warks 117 G11
Cock Bridge Aberds 292 C4
Cockburnspath Borders 282 G5
Cock Clarks Essex 88 E4
Cockden Lancs 204 G3
Cockenzie and Port Seton
E Loth 281 F8
Cocker Bar Lancs 194 C4
Cockerham Lancs 202 C5
Cockermouth Cumb 229 E8
Cockernhoe Herts 104 G2
Cockernhoe Green
Herts 104 G2
Cockersdale W Yorks 197 B8
Cockerton Darl 224 B5
Cockett Swansea 56 C6
Cocketty Aberds 293 F9
Cockfield Durham 233 G8
Suff 125 G8
Cockfosters London 86 F3
Cock Gate Hereford 115 D9
Cock Green Essex 87 B11
Cockhill Som 44 G6
Cock Hill N Yorks 206 B6
Cocking W Sus 34 D5
Cocking Causeway
W Sus 34 D5
Cockington Torbay 9 C7
Cocklake Som 44 D2
Cocklaw Northumb 241 C10
Cockleford Glos 81 C7
Cockley Beck Cumb 220 E4
Cockley Cley Norf 140 C5
Cockley Hill W Yorks 197 D7
Cock Marling E Sus 38 D5
Cocknowle Dorset 18 E4
Cockpole Green
Wokingham 65 C9
Cocks Corn 4 E5
Cocks Green Suff 125 F7
Cockshead Ceredig 112 F2
Cockshoot Hereford 97 D11
Cockshutford Shrops 131 F11
Cockshutt Shrops 132 G4
Shrops 149 D8
Cock Street Kent 53 C9
Suff 107 D9
Cockthorpe Norf 177 E7
Cockwells Corn 2 C2
Cockwood Devon 14 E5
Som 43 E8
Cockyard Derbys 185 F8
Hereford 97 E8
Codda Corn 11 F9
Coddenham Suff 126 G2
Coddenham Green Suff 126 F2
Coddington Ches W 167 D7
Hereford 98 C4
Notts 172 E4
Codford St Mary Wilts 46 F3
Codford St Peter Wilts 46 F3
Codicote Herts 86 B2
Codicote Bottom Herts 86 B2
Codmore Bucks 85 E7
Codmore Hill W Sus 35 C9
Codnor Derbys 170 F6
Codnor Breach Derbys 170 F6
Codnor Gate Derbys 170 E6
Codnor Park Derbys 170 E6
Codrington S Glos 61 D8
Codsall Staffs 133 C7
Codsall Wood Staffs 132 B6
Codsend Som 41 F11
Coedcae Bl Gwent 77 D11
Coedcae *continued*
Torf 78 D3
Coed Cwnwr Mon 78 F6
Coed Darcy Neath 76 F2
Coedely Rhondda 58 B4
Coed Eva Torf 78 G3
Coedkernew Newport 59 C9
Coed Llai =*Leeswood*
Flint 166 D3
Coed Mawr Gwyn 179 G9
Coed Morgan Mon 78 C5
Coedpoeth Wrex 166 E3
Coed-Talon Flint 166 D3
Coedway Powys 148 G6
Coed-y-bryn Ceredig 93 C7
Coed-y-caerau Newport 78 G5
Coed-y-fedw Mon 78 D6
Coed y Garth Ceredig 128 E3
Coed y go Shrops 148 D5
Coed-y-paen Mon 78 F4
Coed-y-parc Gwyn 163 B10
Coed-yr-ynys Powys 96 G3
Coed Ystumgwern
Gwyn 145 E11
Coed-y-wlad Powys 130 B4
Coelbren Powys 76 C4
Coffee Hall M Keynes 103 D7
Coffinswell Devon 9 B7
Cofton Devon 14 E5
Cofton Common
W Mid 117 B10
Cofton Hackett Worcs 117 B10
Cog V Glam 59 F7
Cogan V Glam 59 E7
Cogenhoe W Nhants 120 E6
Cogges Oxon 82 D5
Coggeshall Essex 106 G6
Coggeshall Hamlet
Essex 107 G7
Coggins Mill E Sus 37 B9
Coignafearn Lodge
Highld 291 B8
Coignascallan Highld 291 B9
Coig Peighinnean
W Isles 304 B7
Coig Peighinnean Bhuirgh
W Isles 304 C6
Coilacriech Aberds 292 D5
Coilantogle Stirling 285 G9
Coilessan Argyll 284 G6
Coilleag W Isles 297 K3
Coillemore Highld 300 B6
Coillore Highld 294 B5
Coirea-chrombe Stirling 285 G9
Coisley Hill S Yorks 186 E6
Coity Bridgend 58 C2
Cokenach Herts 105 D7
Cokhay Green Derbys 152 D5
Col W Isles 304 D6
Colaboll Highld 309 H5
Colan Corn 5 C7
Colaton Raleigh Devon 15 D7
Colbost Highld 298 E2
Colburn N Yorks 224 F3
Colby Cumb 231 G9
IoM 192 E3
Norf 160 C4
Colchester Essex 107 F10
Colchester Green Suff 125 F8
Colcot V Glam 58 F6
Cold Ash W Berks 64 F4
Cold Ashby W Nhants 120 B3
Cold Ash Hill Hants 49 G10
Cold Ashton S Glos 61 E9
Cold Aston Glos 81 B10
Coldbackie Highld 308 D6
Coldbeck Cumb 222 E4
Coldblow London 68 E4
Cold Blow Pembs 73 C10
Cold Brayfield
M Keynes 121 G8
Coldbrook Powys 96 D3
Cold Christmas Herts 86 B5
Cold Cotes N Yorks 212 E4
Coldean Brighton 36 F4
Coldeast Devon 14 G2
Coldeaton Derbys 169 D10
Cold Elm Glos 98 E6
Colden W Yorks 196 B3
Colden Common Hants 33 C7
Coldfair Green Suff 127 E8
Coldham Cambs 139 C8
Staffs 133 B7
Coldham's Common
Cambs 123 F9
Cold Hanworth Lincs 189 E8
Coldharbour Corn 4 F5
Devon 27 E9
Dorset 17 E9
Glos 79 E9
Kent 52 C5
London 68 D4
Sur 50 E6
Cold Harbour Dorset 18 D4
Herts 85 B10
Kent 69 G11
Lincs 155 C9
Oxon 64 D6
Wilts 45 B11
Wilts 45 D11
Windsor 65 D10
Cold Hatton Telford 150 E2
Cold Hatton Heath
Telford 150 E2
Cold Hesledon Durham 234 B4
Cold Hiendley W Yorks 197 E11
Cold Higham W Nhants 120 G3
Coldingham Borders 273 B8
Cold Inn Pembs 73 D10
Cold Kirby N Yorks 215 C10
Coldmeece Staffs 151 C7
Cold Moss Heath
Ches E 168 C3
Cold Newton Leics 136 B4
Cold Northcott Corn 11 D10
Cold Norton Essex 88 E4
Coldoch Stirling 278 B3
Cold Overton Leics 154 G6
Coldra Newport 59 B11
Coldrain Perth 286 G4
Coldred Kent 55 D9
Coldridge Devon 25 F11
Cold Row Lancs 202 E3
Coldstream Angus 287 D7
Borders 263 B8
Coldvreath Corn 5 D9
Coldwaltham W Sus 35 D8
Cold Well Staffs 151 G11
Coldwells Aberds 303 E11
Coldwells Croft Aberds 302 G5
Cole Som 45 G7
Colebatch Shrops 130 F6
Colebrook Devon 27 F8
Colebrooke Devon 13 B11
Coleburn Moray 302 D2
Coleby Lincs 173 C7
N Lincs 199 D11
Cole End Essex 105 D11
Warks 134 F3
Coleford Devon 26 G3
Glos 79 C9
Coleford *continued*
Som 45 D7
Coleford Water Som 42 G6
Colegate End Norf 142 F3
Cole Green Herts 86 C3
Herts 105 E8
Colehall W Mid 134 F2
Cole Henley Hants 48 C3
Colehill Dorset 31 G8
Coleman Green Herts 85 C11
Coleman's Hatch E Sus 52 G3
Colemere Shrops 149 C8
Colemore Hants 49 G8
Colemore Green Shrops 132 D4
Coleorton Leics 153 F8
Coleorton Moor Leics 153 F8
Cole Park London 67 E7
Colerne Wilts 61 E10
Colesbourne Glos 81 C7
Colesbrook Dorset 30 B4
Cole's Cross Dorset 28 G5
Colesden Bedford 122 F2
Coles Green Suff 107 C11
Worcs 116 G5
Cole's Green Suff 126 E5
Coleshill Bucks 85 F7
Oxon 82 G2
Warks 134 F4
Coles Meads Sur 51 C9
Colestocks Devon 27 G9
Colethrop Glos 80 C4
Coley Bath 44 B5
Reading 65 E8
W Yorks 196 B6
Colfin Dumfries 236 D2
Colgate W Sus 51 G8
Colgrain Argyll 276 E6
Colham Green London 66 C5
Colindale London 67 B8
Colinsburgh Fife 287 G8
Colinton Edin 270 B4
Colintraive Argyll 275 F11
Colkirk Norf 159 D8
Collace Perth 286 D6
Collafield Glos 79 C11
Collafirth Shetland 312 G6
Collam W Isles 305 J3
Collamoor Head Corn 11 C9
Collaton Devon 9 G9
Collaton St Mary Torbay 9 D7
College Milton S Lanark 268 D2
College of Roseisle
Moray 301 C11
College Park London 67 C8
College Town Brack 65 G11
Collennan S Ayrs 257 C8
Collessie Fife 286 F6
Colleton Mills Devon 25 D11
Collett's Br Norf 139 B9
Collett's Green Worcs 116 G6
Collier Row London 87 G8
Collier's End Herts 105 G7
Collier's Green E Sus 38 C3
Kent 53 F9
Colliers Hatch Essex 87 E8
Collier Street Kent 53 D8
Collier's Wood London 67 E9
Colliery Row T&W 234 B2
Collieston Aberds 303 G10
Collin Dumfries 238 B2
Collingbourne Ducis
Wilts 47 C8
Collingbourne Kingston
Wilts 47 B8
Collingham Notts 172 C4
W Yorks 206 D3
Collington Hereford 116 E2
Collingtree W Nhants 120 F5
Collingwood Northumb 243 B7
Collins End Oxon 65 D7
Collins Green Warr 183 C9
Worcs 116 F4
Colliperiest Devon 27 E7
Colliston Angus 287 C10
Colliton Devon 27 G9
Collycroft Warks 135 F7
Collyhurst Gtr Man 195 G11
Collynie Aberds 303 F8
Collyweston N Nhants 137 C9
Colmonell S Ayrs 244 F4
Colmslie Borders 262 B2
Colmsliehill Borders 271 G10
Colmworth Bedford 122 F2
Colnabaichin Aberds 292 C4
Colnbrook Slough 66 D4
Colne Cambs 123 B7
Lancs 204 E3
Colne Bridge W Yorks 197 C7
Colne Edge Lancs 204 E3
Colne Engaine Essex 107 E7
Colnefields Cambs 123 B7
Colney Norf 142 B3
Colney Hatch London 86 G3
Colney Heath Herts 86 D2
Colney Street Herts 85 E11
Coln Rogers Glos 81 D9
Coln St Aldwyns Glos 81 D10
Coln St Dennis Glos 81 C9
Cologin Argyll 289 G10
Colpitts Grange
Northumb 241 F11
Colpy Aberds 302 F6
Colquhar Borders 270 G6
Colscott Devon 24 E5
Colshaw Staffs 169 B8
Colsterdale N Yorks 214 C2
Colsterworth Lincs 155 E8
Colston E Dunb 268 B2
Pembs 91 F9
Colston Bassett Notts 154 C3
Colstrope Bucks 65 B9
Coltfield Moray 301 C11
Colt Hill Hants 49 C8
Colthouse Cumb 221 F7
Colthrop W Berks 64 F4
Coltishall Norf 160 F5
Coltness N Lanark 268 D6
Colton
Cumb 210 B6
Norf 142 B2
N Yorks 206 E6
Staffs 151 E11
Suff 125 D7
W Yorks 206 G3
Colton Hills Staffs 133 D8
Colt Park Cumb 210 E5
Colt's Green S Glos 61 C8
Colt's Hill Kent 52 E6
Col Uarach W Isles 304 E6
Columbia T&W 243 F8
Columbjohn Devon 14 B5
Colva Powys 114 G4
Colvend Dumfries 237 D10
Colvister Shetland 312 D7
Colwall Hereford 98 C4
Colwall Green Hereford 98 C4
Colwall Stone Hereford 98 C5
Colwell IoW 20 D2
Northumb 241 B11
Colwich Staffs 151 E10
Colwick Notts 171 G10
Colwinston =*Tregolwyn*
V Glam 58 D2
Colworth W Sus 22 C6
Colwyn Bay =*Bae Colwyn*
Conwy 180 F4
Colychurch Bridgend 58 D2
Colyford Devon 15 C10
Colyton Devon 15 C10
Colzie Fife 286 F6
Combe Devon 7 E10
Devon 8 B4
Devon 9 G9
E Sus 37 B10
Hereford 114 E6
Oxon 82 B6
Som 28 B6
W Berks 63 G11
Combe Almer Dorset 18 B5
Combebow Devon 12 D5
Combe Common Sur 50 F3
Combe Down Bath 61 G9
Combe Fishacre Devon 8 C6
Combe Florey Som 43 G7
Combe Hay Bath 45 B8
Combeinteignhead
Devon 14 G4
Combe Martin Devon 40 D5
Combe Moor Hereford 115 E7
Combe Pafford Torbay 9 B8
Combe Raleigh Devon 27 G11
Comberbach Ches W 183 F10
Comberford Staffs 134 B3
Comberton Cambs 123 F7
Hereford 115 D9
Combe St Nicholas Som 28 E4
Combe Throop Som 30 C2
Combpyne Devon 15 C11
Combrew Devon 40 G4
Combridge Staffs 151 B11
Combrook Warks 118 G6
Combs Derbys 185 F8
Suff 125 F10
W Yorks 197 D8
Combs Ford Suff 125 F11
Combwich Som 43 E9
Comers Aberds 293 C8
Come-to-Good Corn 4 G6
Comeytrowe Som 28 C2
Comford Corn 2 B6
Comfort Corn 2 D6
Comhampton Worcs 116 D6
Comins Coch Ceredig 128 G2
Comiston Edin 270 B4
Comley Shrops 131 D9
Commercial End
Cambs 123 E11
Commins Denb 165 C10
Commins Capel Betws
Ceredig 112 F2
Commins Coch Powys 128 C6
Common Cefn-llwyn
Mon 78 G4
Commondale N Yorks 226 C3
Common Edge Blackpool 202 G2
Common End Cumb 228 G6
Derbys 170 C6
Common Hill Hereford 97 E11
Commonmoor Corn 6 B4
Common Moor Corn 6 B4
Common Platt Wilts 62 B6
Commonside Ches W 183 G8
Derbys 170 G2
Notts 171 D7
Common Side Ches W 167 B9
Derbys 170 F6
Derbys 186 F4
Commonwood Herts 85 E8
Shrops 149 D9
Wrex 166 E5
Common-y-coed Mon 60 B2
Comp Kent 52 B6
Compass Som 43 G9
Compstall Gtr Man 185 C7
Compton Derbys 169 F11
Devon 9 C7
Hants 32 B4
Hants 33 B7
Plym 7 D9
Staffs 132 G6
Sur 49 D11
Sur 50 D3
W Berks 64 D4
Wilts 46 C6
W Mid 133 D7
W Sus 34 E3
W Yorks 206 E3
Compton Abbas Dorset 30 D5
Compton Abdale Glos 81 B9
Compton Bassett Wilts 62 E4
Compton Beauchamp
Oxon 63 B9
Compton Bishop Som 43 B11
Compton Chamberlayne
Wilts 31 B8
Compton Common Bath 60 G6
Compton Dando Bath 60 G6
Compton Dundon Som 44 G3
Compton Durville Som 28 D6
Compton End Hants 33 B7
Compton Green Glos 98 F4
Compton Greenfield
S Glos 60 C5
Compton Martin Bath 44 B4
Compton Pauncefoot
Som 29 B10
Compton Valence Dorset 17 C7
Comrie Fife 279 D10
Highld 300 D4
Perth 285 C11
Perth 285 E11
Comrue Dumfries 248 F3
Conaglen House Highld 290 G2
Conanby S Yorks 187 B7
Conchra Argyll 275 E11
Highld 295 C10
Concord T&W 243 F8
Concraig Perth 286 F2
Concraigie Perth 286 C5
Conder Green Lancs 202 B5
Conderton Worcs 99 D9
Condicote Glos 100 F3
Condorrat N Lanark 278 G4
Condover Shrops 131 B9
Coney Hall London 67 G11
Coney Hill Glos 80 B5
Coneyhurst W Sus 35 C10
Coneysthorpe N Yorks 216 E4
Coneythorpe N Yorks 206 B3
Coney Weston Suff 125 B9
Conford Hants 49 G10
Congash Highld 301 G10
Congdon's Shop Corn 11 F11
Congeith Dumfries 237 C10
Congelow Kent 53 D7
Congerstone Leics 135 B7
Congham Norf 158 E4
Congleton Ches E 168 C5
Congleton Edge Ches E 168 C5
Congl-y-wal Gwyn 164 G2

Congresbury N Som 60 G2
Congreve Staffs 151 G8
Conham Bristol 60 E6
Conicavel Moray 301 D9
Coningsby Lincs 174 D2
Conington Cambs 122 D6
Cambs 138 F3
Conisbrough S Yorks 187 B8
Conisby Argyll 274 G3
Conisholme Lincs 190 B6
Coniston Cumb 220 F6
E Yorks 209 F9
Coniston Cold N Yorks 204 B4
Conistone N Yorks 213 F9
Conkwell Wilts 61 G9
Connage Moray 302 C4
Connah's Quay Flint 166 B3
Connel Argyll 289 F11
Connel Park E Ayrs 258 G4
Conniburrow M Keynes 103 D7
Connista Highld 298 B4
Connon Corn 6 C3
Connor Downs Corn 2 B3
Conock Wilts 46 B5
Conon Bridge Highld 300 D5
Conon House Highld 300 D5
Cononish Stirling 285 E7
Cononley N Yorks 204 D5
Cononley Woodside
N Yorks 204 D5
Cononsyth Angus 287 C9
Conordan Highld 295 B7
Conquermoor Heath
Telford 150 F3
Consall Staffs 169 F7
Consett Durham 242 G4
Constable Burton
N Yorks 224 G3
Constable Lee Lancs 195 C10
Constantine Corn 2 D6
Constantine Bay Corn 10 G3
Contin Highld 300 D4
Contlaw Aberdeen 293 C10
Conwy Conwy 180 F3
Conyer Kent 70 G3
Conyers Green Suff 125 D7
Cooden E Sus 38 F2
Cooil IoM 192 E4
Cookbury Devon 24 F6
Cookbury Wick Devon 24 F5
Cookham Windsor 65 B11
Cookham Dean Windsor 65 C11
Cookham Rise Windsor 65 C11
Cookhill Worcs 117 F11
Cookley Suff 126 B6
Worcs 132 G6
Cookley Green Oxon 83 G11
Cookney Aberds 293 D10
Cookridge W Yorks 205 E11
Cooksbridge E Sus 36 E6
Cooksey Corner Worcs 117 D8
Cooksey Green Worcs 117 D8
Cook's Green Essex 89 B11
Suff 125 G9
Cookshill Staffs 168 G6
Cooksland Corn 5 B11
Cooksmill Green Essex 87 D10
Cooksongreen Ches W 183 G9
Coolham W Sus 35 C10
Cooling Medway 69 D9
Coolinge Kent 55 F8
Cooling Street Medway 69 E8
Coombe Bucks 84 D4
Corn 4 G2
Corn 4 G5
Corn 4 G6
Corn 5 E9
Corn 6 C4
Corn 24 E2
Devon 14 G4
Devon 27 D8
Glos 80 G3
Hants 33 C11
Kent 55 B9
London 67 E8
Som 28 B3
Som 28 F6
Wilts 30 C5
Wilts 47 C7
Coombe Bissett Wilts 31 B10
Coombe Dingle Bristol 60 D5
Coombe Hill Glos 99 F7
Coombe Keynes Dorset 18 E2
Coombes W Sus 35 F11
Coombesdale Staffs 150 B6
Coombeswood W Mid 133 F9
Coomb Hill Kent 69 G7
Coombs End S Glos 61 C9
Coombses Som 28 F4
Coopersale Common
Essex 87 E7
Coopersale Street Essex 87 E7
Cooper's Corner Kent 52 D3
Cooper's Green E Sus 37 C7
Herts 85 D11
Cooper's Hill C Beds 103 D10
Sur 66 E3
Cooper Street Kent 55 B10
Cooper Turning
Gtr Man 194 F6
Cootham W Sus 35 E9
Copcut Worcs 117 E7
Copdock Suff 108 C2
Coped Hall Wilts 62 C5
Copenhagen Denb 165 B8
Copford Essex 107 G8
Copford Green Essex 107 G8
Copgrove N Yorks 214 G6
Copister Shetland 312 F6
Cople C Beds 104 B2
Copley Durham 233 F7
Gtr Man 185 B7
W Yorks 196 C5
Copley Hill W Yorks 197 B8
Coplow Dale Derbys 185 F11
Copmanthorpe York 207 D7
Copmere End Staffs 150 D6
Copnor Ptsmth 33 G11
Copp Lancs 202 F4
Coppathorne Corn 24 G2
Coppenhall Ches E 168 D2
Staffs 151 F8
Coppenhall Moss
Ches E 168 D2
Copperhouse Corn 2 B3
Coppice Gtr Man 196 G2
Coppicegate Shrops 132 G4
Coppingford Cambs 138 G3
Coppins Corner Kent 54 D2
Coppleham Som 42 G2
Copplestone Devon 26 G3
Coppull Lancs 194 E5
Coppull Moor Lancs 194 E5
Copsale W Sus 35 C11
Copse Hill London 67 E8
Copster Green Lancs 203 G9
Copster Hill Gtr Man 196 G2
Copston Magna Warks 135 F9
Cop Street Kent 55 B9
Copt Green Warks 118 D3
Copthall Green Essex 86 E6
Copt Heath W Mid 118 B3
Copt Hewick N Yorks 214 E6
Copthill Durham 232 C3
Copthorne Ches E 167 G11
Corn 11 C11
Shrops 149 G9
Sur 51 F10
Coptiviney Shrops 149 B8
Copt Oak Leics 153 G9
Copton Kent 54 B4
Copy's Green Norf 159 B8
Copythorne Hants 32 E4
Corbets Tey London 68 B5
Corbridge Northumb 241 E11
Corbriggs Derbys 170 B6
Corby N Nhants 137 F7
Corby Glen Lincs 155 E9
Corby Hill Cumb 239 F11
Cordon N Ayrs 256 C2
Cordwell Norf 142 E2
Coreley Shrops 116 C2
Cores End Bucks 66 B2
Corfe Som 28 D2
Corfe Castle Dorset 18 E5
Corfe Mullen Dorset 18 B5
Corfton Shrops 131 F9
Corfton Bache Shrops 131 F9
Corgarff Aberds 292 C4
Corgee Corn 5 C10
Corhampton Hants 33 C10
Corlae Dumfries 246 D5
Corlannau Neath 57 C9
Corley Warks 134 F6
Corley Ash Warks 134 F5
Corley Moor Warks 134 F5
Cornaa IoM 192 D5
Cornabus Argyll 254 C4
Cornaigbeg Argyll 288 E1
Cornaigmore Argyll 288 C4
Argyll 288 E1
Cornard Tye Suff 107 C8
Cornbank Midloth 270 C4
Cornbrook Shrops 116 B2
Corncatterach Aberds 302 F5
Cornel Conwy 164 C2
Corner Row Lancs 202 F4
Cornett Hereford 97 B11
Corney Cumb 220 G2
Cornforth Durham 234 E2
Cornharrow Dumfries 246 E5
Cornhill Aberds 302 D5
Powys 96 C2
Stoke 168 E5
Cornhill-on-Tweed
Northumb 263 B9
Cornholme W Yorks 196 B2
Cornish Hall End Essex 106 D3
Cornquoy Orkney 314 G5
Cornriggs Durham 232 C2
Cornsay Durham 233 C8
Cornsay Colliery
Durham 233 C9
Cornton Stirling 278 B5
Corntown Highld 300 D5
V Glam 58 D2
Cornwell Oxon 100 F5
Cornwood Devon 8 D2
Cornworthy Devon 8 D6
Corpach Highld 290 F2
Corpusty Norf 160 C2
Corran Highld 290 G2
Highld 295 E10
Corran a Chan Uachdaraich
Highld 295 C7
Corranbuie Argyll 275 G9
Corrany IoM 192 D5
Corrichoich Highld 311 G4
Corrie N Ayrs 255 C11
Corrie Common
Dumfries 248 F6
Corriecravie N Ayrs 255 E10
Corriecravie Moor
N Ayrs 255 E10
Corriedoo Dumfries 246 G5
Corriegarth Lodge
Highld 291 B7
Corriemoillie Highld 300 C3
Corriemulzie Lodge
Highld 309 K3
Corrievarkie Lodge
Perth 291 F7
Corrievorrie Highld 301 G7
Corrigall Orkney 314 E3
Corrimony Highld 300 F3
Corringham Lincs 188 C5
Thurrock 69 C8
Corris Gwyn 128 B5
Corris Uchaf Gwyn 128 B4
Corrour Highld 290 G5
Corrour Shooting Lodge
Highld 290 G6
Corrow Argyll 284 G5
Corry Highld 295 C8
Corrybrough Highld 301 G8
Corrydon Perth 292 G3
Corryghoil Argyll 284 E5
Corrykinloch Highld 309 G3
Corrylach Argyll 255 D8
Corrymuckloch Perth 286 D2
Corrynachenchy Argyll 289 E8
Corry of Ardnagrask
Highld 300 E5
Corsback Highld 310 B6
Corscombe Dorset 29 F8
Corse Aberds 302 E6
Glos 98 F5
Corse Lawn Worcs 98 E6
Corse of Kinnoir Aberds 302 E5
Corsewall Dumfries 236 C2
Corsham Wilts 61 E11
Corsindae Aberds 293 C8
Corsley Wilts 45 D10
Corsley Heath Wilts 45 D10
Corsock Dumfries 237 B9
Corston Bath 61 F7
Orkney 314 E3
Wilts 62 C2
Corstorphine Edin 280 G3
Cors-y-Gedol Gwyn 145 E11
Cortachy Angus 287 B7
Corton Suff 143 D10
Wilts 46 E2
Corton Denham Som 29 C10
Cortworth S Yorks 186 B6
Coruanan Lodge Highld 290 G2
Corunna W Isles 296 E4
Corvast Highld 309 K5
Corwen Denb 165 G9
Cory Devon 24 D5
Coryates Dorset 17 D8
Coryton Cardiff 58 C6
Devon 12 E5
Thurrock 69 C8
Còsag Highld 295 D10
Cosby Leics 135 E10
Coscote Oxon 64 B4
Coseley W Mid 133 E8
Cosford Warks 119 B9
Cosgrove W Nhants 102 C5
Cosham Ptsmth 33 F11
Cosheston Pembs 73 E8
Cosmeston V Glam 59 F7
Cosmore Dorset 29 F11
Cossall Notts 171 G7
Cossall Marsh Notts 171 G7
Cosses S Ayrs 244 G4
Cossington Leics 154 G2
Som 43 E11
Costa Orkney 314 D3
Costessey Norf 160 G3
Costessey Park Norf 160 G3
Costhorpe Notts 187 D9
Costislost Corn 10 G6
Costock Notts 153 D11
Coston Leics 154 E6
Norf 141 B11
Coswinsawsin Corn 2 B4
Cote Oxon 82 E4
Som 43 E10
W Sus 35 F10
Cotebrook Ches W 167 B9
Cotehill Cumb 239 G11
Cotes Cumb 211 B9
Leics 153 E11
Staffs 150 C6
Cotesbach Leics 135 G10
Cotes Heath Staffs 150 C6
Cotes Park Derbys 170 E6
Cotford St Lukes Som 27 B11
Cotgrave Notts 154 B2
Cothall Aberds 293 B10
Cotham Bristol 60 E5
Notts 172 F3
Cothelstone Som 43 G7
Cotheridge Worcs 116 G5
Cotherstone Durham 223 B10
Cothill Oxon 83 F7
Cotland Mon 79 E8
Cotleigh Devon 28 G2
Cotmanhay Derbys 171 G7
Cotmarsh Wilts 62 D5
Cotmaton Devon 15 D8
Coton Cambs 123 F8
Shrops 149 C10
Staffs 134 B3
Staffs 150 E6
Staffs 151 C9
W Nhants 120 C3
Coton Clanford Staffs 151 E7
Coton Hayes Staffs 151 C9
Coton Hill Shrops 149 G9
Staffs 151 C9
Coton in the Clay Staffs 152 D3
Coton in the Elms
Derbys 152 F4
Coton Park Derbys 152 F5
Cotonwood Shrops 149 B10
Staffs 150 E6
Cotswold Community
Wilts 81 F8
Cott Devon 8 C5
Cottam E Yorks 217 F9
Lancs 202 G6
Notts 188 F4
Cottartown Highld 301 F10
Cottenham Cambs 123 D8
Cottenham Park London 67 F8
Cotterdale N Yorks 222 G6
Cottered Herts 104 F6
Cotterhill Woods
S Yorks 187 E9
Cotteridge W Mid 117 B10
Cotterstock N Nhants 137 E10
Cottesbrooke W Nhants 120 C4
Cottesmore Rutland 155 G8
Cotteylands Devon 26 E6
Cottingham E Yorks 208 G6
N Nhants 136 E6
Cottingley W Yorks 205 F8
Cottisford Oxon 101 E11
Cotton Staffs 169 F9
Suff 125 D11
Cotton End Bedford 103 B11
W Nhants 120 F5
Cotton Stones W Yorks 196 C4
Cotton Tree Lancs 204 F4
Cottonworth Hants 47 F11
Cottown Aberds 293 B9
Aberds 302 G5
Aberds 303 E8
Cotts Devon 7 B8
Cottwood Devon 25 E10
Cotwall Telford 150 F2
Cotwalton Staffs 151 B8
Coubister Orkney 314 E3
Couch Green Hants 48 G4
Couch's Mill Corn 6 D2
Coughton Hereford 97 G11
Warks 117 E11
Coughton Fields Warks 117 F11
Cougie Highld 300 G2
Coulaghailtro Argyll 275 G8
Coulags Highld 299 E9
Coulby Newham Mbro 225 B10
Coulderton Cumb 219 D9
Couldoran Highld 299 E8
Couligartan Stirling 285 G8
Coulin Highld 299 D10
Coulin Lodge Highld 299 D10
Coull Aberds 293 C7
Argyll 274 G3
Coulmony Ho Highld 301 E9
Coulport Argyll 276 D4
Coulsdon London 51 B9
Coulshill Perth 286 G3
Coulston Wilts 46 C3
Coulter S Lanark 260 C2
Coultings Som 43 E8
Coulton N Yorks 216 E2
Coultra Fife 287 E7
Cound Shrops 131 C11
Coundlane Shrops 131 B11
Coundmoor Shrops 131 C11
Coundon Durham 233 F10
W Mid 134 G6
Coundongate Durham 233 F10
Coundon Grange
Durham 233 F10
Counters End Herts 85 D8
Countersett N Yorks 213 B8
Countess Wilts 47 E7
Countess Cross Essex 107 E7
Countess Wear Devon 14 D4
Countesthorpe Leics 135 D11
Countisbury Devon 41 D8
County Oak W Sus 51 F9
Coupar Angus Perth 286 C6
Coup Green Lancs 194 B5
Coupland Cumb 222 B4
Northumb 263 C10
Cour Argyll 255 C9
Courance Dumfries 248 E3
Coursley Som 42 G6
Court-at-Street Kent 54 F5
Court Barton Devon 14 D2
Court Colman Bridgend 57 E11
Court Corner Hants 48 B6
Courteenhall W Nhants 120 G5
Court Henry Carms 93 G11
Courthill Perth 286 C5
Court House Green
W Mid 135 G7
Courtsend Essex 89 G8
Courtway Som 43 G8
Cousland Midloth 271 B7
Cousley Wood E Sus 53 G7
Couston Argyll 275 F11
Cova Shetland 313 J5
Cove Argyll 276 E4
Borders 282 G5
Devon 27 D7
Hants 49 B11
Highld 307 K3
Cove Bay Aberdeen 293 C11
Cove Bottom Suff 127 B9
Covehithe Suff 143 G10
Coven Staffs 133 B8
Covender Hereford 98 C2
Coveney Cambs 139 G9
Covenham St Bartholomew
Lincs 190 C4
Covenham St Mary
Lincs 190 C4
Coven Heath Staffs 133 C8
Coven Lawn Staffs 133 B8
Coventry W Mid 118 B6
Coverack Corn 3 F7
Coverack Bridges Corn 2 C5
Coverham N Yorks 214 B2
Covesea Moray 301 B11
Covingham Swindon 63 B7
Covington Cambs 121 C11
S Lanark 259 B11
Cowan Bridge Lancs 212 D2
Cow Ark Lancs 203 D9
Cowbar Redcar 226 B5
Cowbeech E Sus 23 C10
Cowbeech Hill E Sus 23 C10
Cowbit Lincs 156 F5
Cowbog Aberds 303 D8
Cowbridge Lincs 174 F4
Som 42 E3
Cowbridge = Y Bont-Faen
V Glam 58 E3
Cowcliffe W Yorks 196 D6
Cowdale Derbys 185 G9
Cowden Kent 52 E3
Cowdenbeath Fife 280 C3
Cowdenburn Borders 270 E4
Cowen Head Cumb 221 F9
Cowers Lane Derbys 170 F4
Cowes IoW 20 B5
Cowesby N Yorks 215 B9
Cowesfield Green Wilts 32 C3
Cowfold W Sus 36 C2
Cowgill Cumb 212 B5
Cow Green Suff 125 D11
Cowgrove Dorset 18 B5
Cowhill Derbys 170 F5
S Glos 79 G10
Cow Hill Lancs 203 G7
Cowhorn Hill S Glos 61 E7
Cowie Aberds 293 E10
Stirling 278 D6
Cowlands Corn 4 G6
Cowleaze Corner Oxon 82 E4
Cowley Derbys 186 F4
Devon 14 B4
Glos 81 C7
London 66 C5
Oxon 83 E8
Cowleymoor Devon 27 E7
Cowley Peachy London 66 C5
Cowling Lancs 194 D5
N Yorks 204 E5
N Yorks 214 B4
Cowlinge Suff 124 G4
Cowlow Derbys 185 G9
Cowmes W Yorks 197 D7
Cowpe Lancs 195 C10
Cowpen Northumb 253 G7
Cowpen Bewley
Stockton 234 G5
Cowplain Hants 33 E11
Cow Roast Herts 85 C7
Cowshill Durham 232 C3
Cowslip Green N Som 60 G3
Cowstrandburn Fife 279 C10
Cowthorpe N Yorks 206 C4
Coxall Hereford 115 C7
Coxbank Ches E 167 G11
Coxbench Derbys 170 G5
Coxbridge Som 44 F4
Cox Common Suff 143 G8
Coxford Corn 11 B9
Norf 158 D6
Soton 32 D5
Coxgreen Staffs 132 F6
Cox Green Gtr Man 195 E8
Sur 50 G5
Windsor 65 D11
Coxheath Kent 53 C8
Coxhill Kent 55 D8
Cox Hill Corn 4 G4
Coxhoe Durham 234 D2
Coxley Som 44 E4
W Yorks 197 D9
Coxley Wick Som 44 E4
Coxlodge T&W 242 D6
Cox Moor Notts 171 D8
Coxpark Corn 12 G4
Coxtie Green Essex 87 F9
Coxwold N Yorks 215 D10
Coychurch Bridgend 58 D2
Coylton S Ayrs 257 E10
Coylumbridge Highld 291 B11
Coynach Aberds 292 C6
Coynachie Aberds 302 F4
Coytrahen Bridgend 57 D11
CoytrahÛn Bridgend 57 D11
Crabadon Devon 8 E5
Crabbet Park W Sus 51 F10
Crabble Kent 55 E9
Crabbs Cross Worcs 117 E10
Crabbs Green Herts 105 F9
Crabgate Norf 159 D11
Crab Orchard Dorset 31 F9
Crabtree Plym 7 D10
W Sus 36 B2
Crabtree Green Wrex 166 G4
Crackaig Argyll 274 G6
Crackenedge W Yorks 197 C8
Crackenthorpe Cumb 231 G9
Crackington Haven Corn 11 B8
Crackley Staffs 168 E4
Warks 118 C5
Crackleybank Shrops 150 G5
Crackpot N Yorks 223 F9
Crackthorn Corner
Suff 125 B10
Cracoe N Yorks 213 G9
Cracow Moss Ches E 168 F2
Staffs 168 F3
Craddock Devon 27 E9
Cradhlastadh W Isles 304 E2
Cradle Edge W Yorks 205 F7
Cradle End Herts 105 G9
Cradley Hereford 98 B4
W Mid 133 G8
Cradley Heath W Mid 133 F8
Cradoc Powys 95 E10
Crafthole Corn 7 E7
Crafton Bucks 84 B5
Crag Bank Lancs 211 E9
Crag Foot Lancs 211 E9
Craggan Highld 301 G10
Moray 301 F11
Stirling 285 E9
Cragganvallie Highld 300 F5
Craggenmore Moray 301 F11
Cragg Hill W Yorks 205 F10
Craggie Highld 301 F7
Highld 311 H2
Craggiemore Highld 309 J7
Cragg Vale W Yorks 196 C4
Craghead Durham 242 G6
Crahan Corn 2 C5
Crai Powys 95 G7
Craibstone Moray 302 D4
Craichie Angus 287 C9
Craig Dumfries 237 B8
Dumfries 237 C8
Highld 299 E10
Craiganor Lodge Perth 285 B10
Craig Berthlwyd M Tydf 77 F9
Craig Castle Aberds 302 G4
Craig-cefn-parc
Swansea 75 E11
Craigdallie Perth 286 E6
Craigdam Aberds 303 F8
Craigdarroch Dumfries 246 E6
Highld 300 D4
Craigdhu Highld 300 E4
Craig Douglas Borders 261 E7
Craigearn Aberds 293 B9
Craigellachie Moray 302 E2
Craigencallie Ho
Dumfries 237 B7
Craigencross Dumfries 236 C2
Craigend Borders 271 F9
Glasgow 268 B3
Perth 286 E3
Perth 286 E5
Stirling 278 D5
Craigendive Argyll 275 E11
Craigendoran Argyll 276 E6
Craigendowie Angus 293 G7
Craigends Renfs 267 B8
Craigens Argyll 274 G3
E Ayrs 258 F3
Craigentinny Edin 280 G5
Craigerne Borders 261 B7
Craighall Perth 286 C5
Craighat Stirling 277 E9
Craighead Fife 287 G10
Highld 301 C7
Craighill Aberds 303 E7
Craighlaw Mains
Dumfries 236 C5
Craighouse Argyll 274 G6
Craigie Aberds 293 B11
Dundee 287 D8
Perth 286 C5
Perth 286 E5
S Ayrs 257 C10
S Ayrs 257 E8
Craigiefield Orkney 314 E4
Craigiehall Edin 280 F3
Craigielaw E Loth 281 F9
Craigierig Borders 260 E6
Craigleith Edin 280 G4
Craig Llangiwg Neath 76 D2
Craig-llwyn Shrops 148 D4
Craiglockhart Edin 280 G4
Craig Lodge Argyll 275 G10
Craigmalloch E Ayrs 245 E11
Craigmaud Aberds 303 D8
Craigmill Stirling 278 B6
Craigmillar Edin 280 G5
Craigmore Argyll 266 B2
Craig-moston Aberds 293 F8
Craignant Shrops 148 B5
Craignell Dumfries 237 B7
Craigneuk N Lanark 268 C5
N Lanark 268 D5
Craignish Castle Argyll 275 C8
Craignure Argyll 289 F9
Craigo Angus 293 G8
Craigow Perth 286 G4
Craig Penllyn V Glam 58 D3
Craigrory Highld 300 E6
Craigrothie Fife 287 F7
Craigroy Moray 301 D11
Craigruie Stirling 285 E8
Craig's End Essex 106 D4
Craigsford Mains
Borders 262 B3
Craigshall Dumfries 237 D10
Craigshill W Loth 269 B11
Craigside Durham 233 D8
Craigston Castle Aberds 303 D7
Craigton Aberdeen 293 C10
Angus 287 B7
Angus 287 D9
Glasgow 267 C10
Highld 300 E6
Highld 309 H6
Highld 309 K6
Craigtown Highld 310 D2
Craig-y-don Conwy 180 E3
Craig-y-Duke Swansea 76 E2
Craig-y-nos Powys 76 B4
Craig-y-penrhyn
Ceredig 128 E3
Craig-y-Rhacca Caerph 59 B7
Craik Borders 249 B8
Crail Fife 287 G10
Crailing Borders 262 E5
Crailinghall Borders 262 E5
Crakaig Highld 311 H3
Crakehill N Yorks 215 E8
Crakemarsh Staffs 151 B11
Crambe N Yorks 216 G4
Crambeck N Yorks 216 F4
Cramhurst Sur 50 E2
Cramlington Northumb 243 B7
Cramond Edin 280 F3
Cramond Bridge Edin 280 F3
Crampmoor Hants 32 C5
Cranage Ches E 168 B3
Cranberry Staffs 150 B6
Cranborne Dorset 31 E9
Cranbourne Brack 66 E2
Hants 48 C6
Cranbrook Devon 14 B6
Kent 53 F9
London 68 B2
Cranbrook Common Kent 53 F9
Crane Moor S Yorks 197 G10
Crane's Corner Norf 159 G8
Cranfield C Beds 103 C9
Cranford Devon 24 C4
London 66 D6
Cranford St Andrew
N Nhants 121 B8
Cranford St John
N Nhants 121 B8
Cranham Glos 80 C5
London 68 B5
Cranhill Glasgow 268 B2
Warks 118 G2
Crank Mers 183 B8
Crank Wood Gtr Man 194 G6
Cranleigh Sur 50 F5
Cranley Suff 126 C3
Cranley Gardens London 67 B9
Cranmer Green Suff 125 C10
Cranmore IoW 20 D3
Som 45 E7
Cranna Aberds 302 D6
Crannich Argyll 289 E7
Crannoch Moray 302 D4
Cranoe Leics 136 D5
Cransford Suff 126 E6
Cranshaws Borders 272 C3
Cranstal IoM 192 B5
Cranswick E Yorks 208 C6
Crantock Corn 4 C5
Cranwell Lincs 173 F8
Cranwich Norf 140 E5
Cranworth Norf 141 C9
Craobh Haven Argyll 275 C8
Crapstone Devon 7 B10
Crarae Argyll 275 D10
Crask Highld 308 C7
Crask Inn Highld 309 G5
Craskins Aberds 293 C7
Crask of Aigas Highld 300 E4
Craster Northumb 265 F7
Craswall Hereford 96 D5
Crateford Shrops 132 F4
Staffs 133 B8
Cratfield Suff 126 B6
Crathes Aberds 293 D9
Crathie Aberds 292 D4
Highld 291 D7
Crathorne N Yorks 225 D8
Craven Arms Shrops 131 G8
Crawcrook T&W 242 E4
Crawford Lancs 194 G3
S Lanark 259 E11
Crawfordsyke S Lanark 269 F7
Crawfordjohn S Lanark 259 E9
Crawick Dumfries 259 G7
Crawley Devon 28 F3
Hants 48 G2
Oxon 82 C4
W Sus 51 F9
Crawley Down W Sus 51 F10
Crawley End Essex 105 C8
Crawley Hill Sur 65 G11
Crawleyside Durham 232 C5
Crawshaw W Yorks 197 E8
Crawshawbooth Lancs 195 B10
Crawton Aberds 293 F10
Cray N Yorks 213 D8
Perth 292 G3
Crayford London 68 E4
Crayke N Yorks 215 E11
Craymere Beck Norf 159 C11
Crays Hill Essex 88 G2
Cray's Pond Oxon 64 C6
Crazies Hill Wokingham 65 C9
Creacombe Devon 26 D4
Creagan Argyll 289 E11
Creagan Sithe Argyll 284 G6
Creag Aoil Highld 290 F3
Creagastrom W Isles 297 G4
Creag Ghoraidh
W Isles 297 G3
Creaguaineach Lodge
Highld 290 G5
Creaksea Essex 88 F6
Creamore Bank Shrops 149 C10
Crean Corn 1 E3
Creaton W Nhants 120 C4
Creca Dumfries 238 C6
Credenhill Hereford 97 C9
Crediton Devon 26 G4
Creebridge Dumfries 236 C6
Creech Dorset 18 E4
Creech Bottom Dorset 18 E4
Creech Heathfield Som 28 B3
Creech St Michael Som 28 B3
Creed Corn 5 F8
Creediknowe Shetland 312 G7
Creegbrawse Corn 4 G4
Creekmoor BCP 18 C6
Creekmouth London 68 C3
Creeksea Essex 88 F6
Creeting Bottoms Suff 126 F2
Creeting St Mary Suff 125 F11
Creeton Lincs 155 E10
Creetown Dumfries 236 D6
Creggans Argyll 284 G4
Cregneash IoM 192 F2
Creg-ny-Baa IoM 192 D4
Cregrina Powys 114 G2
Creich Fife 287 E7
Creigau Mon 79 F7
Creighton Staffs 151 B11
Creigiau Cardiff 58 C5
Crelly Corn 2 C5
Cremyll Corn 7 E9
Crendell Dorset 31 E9
Crepkill Highld 298 E4
Creslow Bucks 102 G6
Cressage Shrops 131 C11
Cressbrook Derbys 185 G11
Cresselly Pembs 73 D9
Cressex Bucks 84 G4
Cress Green Glos 80 E3
Cressing Essex 106 G5
Cresswell Northumb 253 E7
Staffs 151 B9
Cresswell Quay Pembs 73 D9
Creswell Derbys 187 G8
Staffs 151 D7
Staffs 151 D8
Creswell Green Staffs 151 G11
Cretingham Suff 126 E4
Cretshengan Argyll 275 G8
Creunant = Crynant
Neath 76 E3
Crewe Ches E 168 D2
Ches W 166 E6
Crewe-by-Farndon
Ches W 166 E6
Crewgarth Cumb 231 E8
Crewgreen Powys 148 F6
Crewkerne Som 28 F6
Crews Hill London 86 F4
Crew's Hole Bristol 60 E6
Crewton Derby 153 C7
Crianlarich Stirling 285 E7
Cribbs Causeway S Glos 60 C5
Cribden Side Lancs 195 C9
Cribyn Ceredig 111 G10
Criccieth Gwyn 145 B9
Crich Derbys 170 E5
Crich Carr Derbys 170 E4
Crichie Aberds 303 E9
Crichton Midloth 271 C7
Crick Mon 79 G7
W Nhants 119 C11
Crickadarn Powys 95 C11
Cricket Hill Hants 65 G10
Cricket Malherbie Som 28 E5
Cricket St Thomas Som 28 F5
Crickham Som 44 D2
Crickheath Shrops 148 E5
Crickheath Wharf
Shrops 148 E5
Crickhowell Powys 78 B2
Cricklade Wilts 81 G10
Cricklewood London 67 B8
Crickmery Shrops 150 D3
Crick's Green Hereford 116 G2
Criddlestyle Hants 31 E11
Cridling Stubbs N Yorks 198 C4
Cridmore IoW 20 E5
Crieff Perth 286 E2
Criggan Corn 5 C10
Criggion Powys 148 F5
Crigglestone W Yorks 197 D10
Crimble Gtr Man 195 E11
Crimchard Som 28 F4
Crimdon Park Durham 234 D5
Crimond Aberds 303 D10
Crimonmogate Aberds 303 D10
Crimp Corn 24 D3
Crimplesham Norf 140 C3
Crimscote Warks 100 B4
Crinan Argyll 275 D8
Crinan Ferry Argyll 275 D8
Crindau Newport 59 B10
Crindledyke N Lanark 268 D6
Cringleford Norf 142 B3
Cringles W Yorks 204 D6
Cringletie Borders 270 G4
Crinow Pembs 73 C10
Cripple Corner Essex 107 E7
Cripplesease Corn 2 B2
Cripplestyle Dorset 31 E9
Cripp's Corner E Sus 38 C3
Crispie Argyll 275 F10
Crist Derbys 185 E8
Critchell's Green Hants 32 B3
Critchill Som 45 D9
Critchmere Sur 49 G11
Crit Hall Kent 53 G9
Crizeley Hereford 97 E8
Croanford Corn 10 G6
Croasdale Cumb 219 B11
Crobeag W Isles 304 F5
Crockenhill Kent 68 F4
Crocker End Oxon 65 B8
Crockerhill Hants 33 F9
W Sus 22 B6
Crockernwell Devon 13 C11
Crockers Devon 40 F5
Crocker's Ash Hereford 79 B8
Crockerton Wilts 45 E11
Crockerton Green Wilts 45 E11
Crocketford or Ninemile Bar
Dumfries 237 B10
Crockey Hill York 207 D8
Crockham Heath
W Berks 64 G2
Crockham Hill Kent 52 C2
Crockhurst Street Kent 52 E6
Crockleford Heath
Essex 107 F10
Crockleford Hill Essex 107 F10
Crockness Orkney 314 G3
Crock Street Som 28 E4
Croesau Bach Shrops 148 D4
Croeserw Neath 57 B11
Croes-goch Pembs 87 E11
Croes-Hywel Mon 78 C4
Croes-lan Ceredig 93 C7
Croes Llanfair Mon 78 D4
Croesor Gwyn 163 G10
Croespenmaen Caerph 77 F11
Croes-wian Flint 181 G10
Croesyceiliog Carms 74 B6
Torf 78 F4
Croes-y-mwyalch Torf 78 G4
Croes y pant Mon 78 E4
Croesywaun Gwyn 163 D8
Croft Hereford 115 D9
Leics 135 D10
Lincs 175 C8
Pembs 92 C3
Warr 183 C10
Croftamie Stirling 277 D9
Croftfoot S Lanark 268 C2
Crofthandy Corn 4 G4
Croftlands Cumb 210 D5
Croftmalloch W Loth 269 C8
Croft Mitchell Corn 2 B5
Croftmoraig Perth 285 C11
Croft of Tillymaud
Aberds 303 F11
Crofton Cumb 239 G8
London 68 F2
Wilts 63 G9
W Yorks 197 D11
Croft-on-Tees N Yorks 224 D5
Crofts Dumfries 237 B9
Crofts Bank Gtr Man 184 B3
Crofts of Benachielt
Highld 310 F5
Crofts of Haddo Aberds 303 F8
Crofts of Inverthernie
Aberds 303 E7
Crofts of Meikle Ardo
Aberds 303 E8
Crofty Swansea 56 B4
Croggan Argyll 289 G9
Croglin Cumb 231 B7
Croich Highld 309 K4
Croick Highld 310 D2
Croig Argyll 288 D5
Crois Dughaill W Isles 297 J3
Cromarty Highld 301 C7
Cromasaig Highld 299 C10
Crombie Fife 279 D10
Crombie Castle Aberds 302 D5
Cromblet Aberds 303 F7
Cromdale Highld 301 G10
Cromer Herts 104 F5
Norf 160 A4
Cromer-Hyde Herts 86 C2
Cromford Derbys 170 D3
Cromhall S Glos 79 G11
Cromhall Common
S Glos 61 B7
Cromor W Isles 304 F6
Crompton Fold Gtr Man 196 F2
Cromra Highld 291 D7
Cromwell Notts 172 C3
Cromwell Bottom
W Yorks 196 C6
Cronberry E Ayrs 258 E4
Crondall Hants 49 D9
Cronk-y-Voddy IoM 192 D4
Cronton Mers 183 D7
Crook Cumb 221 G9
Devon 27 G11
Durham 233 D9
Crookdake Cumb 229 C9
Crooke Gtr Man 194 F5
Crooked Billet London 67 E8
Crookedholm E Ayrs 257 B11
Crooked Soley Wilts 63 E10
Crooked Withies Dorset 31 F9
Crookes S Yorks 186 D4
Crookesmoor S Yorks 186 D4
Crookfur E Renf 267 D10
Crookgate Bank Durham 242 F5
Crookhall Durham 242 G4
Crookham Northumb 263 B10
W Berks 64 G4
Crookham Village Hants 49 C9
Crookhaugh Borders 260 D4
Crookhill T&W 242 E5
Crookhouse Borders 263 D7
Crooklands Cumb 211 C10
Crook of Devon Perth 286 G4
Crookston Glasgow 267 C10
Cropredy Oxon 101 B9
Cropston Leics 153 G11
Cropthorne Worcs 99 C9
Cropton N Yorks 216 B5
Cropwell Bishop Notts 154 B3
Cropwell Butler Notts 154 B3
Cros W Isles 304 B7
Crosben Highld 289 D9
Crosbost W Isles 304 F5
Crosby Cumb 229 D7
IoM 192 E4
Mers 182 B4
N Lincs 199 E11
Crosby Court N Yorks 225 G7
Crosby Garrett Cumb 222 D4
Crosby-on-Eden Cumb 239 F11
Crosby Ravensworth
Cumb 222 C2
Crosby Villa Cumb 229 D7
Croscombe Som 44 E5
Crosemere Shrops 149 D8
Crosland Edge W Yorks 196 E6
Crosland Hill W Yorks 196 E6
Crosland Moor W Yorks 196 D6
Croslands Park Cumb 210 E4
Cross Devon 40 F3
Devon 40 G6
Shrops 149 B7
Som 44 C2
Crossaig Argyll 255 B9
Crossal Highld 294 B6
Crossapol Argyll 288 E1
Cross Ash Mon 78 B6
Cross-at-Hand Kent 53 D9
Cross Bank Worcs 116 C4
Crossbrae Aberds 302 D6
Crossburn Falk 279 G7
Crossbush W Sus 35 F8
Crosscanonby Cumb 229 D7
Cross Coombe Corn 4 E4
Crosscrake Cumb 211 B10
Crossdale Street Norf 160 B4
Cross End Bedford 121 F11
Essex 107 E7
M Keynes 103 D8
Crossens Mers 193 D11
Crossflatts W Yorks 205 E8
Crossford Fife 279 D11
S Lanark 268 F6
Crossgate Lincs 156 D4
Orkney 314 E4
Staffs 151 B8
Cross Gate W Sus 35 E8
Crossgatehall E Loth 271 B7
Crossgates Cumb 229 G7
Fife 280 D2
N Yorks 217 C10
Powys 113 E11
Cross Gates W Yorks 206 G3
Crossgill Cumb 231 C10
Lancs 211 G11
Crossgreen Shrops 149 F9
Cross Green Devon 12 D3
Staffs 133 B8
Suff 124 G6
Suff 125 F7
Suff 125 G9
Telford 150 G2
Warks 119 F7
W Yorks 206 G2
Crosshands Carms 92 G3
Cross Hands Carms 75 C9
Cross-hands Carms 92 G3
Cross Hands Pembs 73 C9
Cross Heath Staffs 168 F4
Crosshill E Ayrs 257 E11
Fife 280 B3
S Ayrs 245 B8
Cross Hill Corn 10 G6
Derbys 170 F6
Glos 79 F9
Cross Hills N Yorks 204 E6
Cross Holme N Yorks 225 F11
Crosshouse E Ayrs 257 B9
Cross Houses Shrops 131 B10
Shrops 132 E3
Crossings Cumb 240 B2
Cross in Hand E Sus 37 C9
Leics 135 G10
Cross Inn Carms 74 C3
Ceredig 111 E10
Ceredig 111 F7
Rhondda 58 C5
Crosskeys Caerph 78 G2
Cross Keys Kent 52 C4
Wilts 61 E11
Crosskirk Highld 310 B4
Crosslands Cumb 210 B6
Cross Lane Ches E 167 C11
Cross Lane Head Shrops 132 D4
Crosslanes Shrops 148 F6
Cross Lanes Corn 2 E5
Dorset 30 G3
N Yorks 215 F10
Oxon 65 D7
Wrex 166 F5
Crosslee Borders 261 F8
Renfs 267 B8
Crossley Hall W Yorks 205 G8
Cross Llyde Hereford 97 F8
Crossmichael Dumfries 237 C9
Crossmill E Renf 267 D10
Crossmoor Lancs 202 F4
Crossmount Perth 285 B11
Cross Oak Powys 96 G2
Cross of Jackston
Aberds 303 F7
Cross o' th' hands
Derbys 170 F3
Cross o' th' Hill Ches W 167 F7
Crosspost W Sus 36 C3
Crossroads Aberds 293 D9
E Ayrs 257 C11
Fife 281 B7
Cross Roads Devon 12 D5
W Yorks 204 F6
Cross Stone Aberds 303 G9
Cross Street Suff 126 B3
Crosston Angus 287 B9
Crosstown Corn 24 D2
V Glam 58 F4
Cross Town Ches E 184 F3
Crosswater Sur 49 F11
Crossway Hereford 98 E2
Mon 78 B6
Powys 113 F11
Crossway Green Mon 79 G8
Worcs 116 D6
Crossways Dorset 17 D11
Kent 68 D5
Mon 96 G6
S Glos 79 G11
Sur 49 F11

Crosswell =*Ffynnongroes*
Pembs 92 D2
Crosswood Ceredig 112 C3
Crosthwaite Cumb 221 G8
Croston Lancs 194 D3
Crostwick Norf 160 F5
Crostwight Norf 160 D6
Crothair W Isles 304 E3
Crouch Kent 52 B6
Kent 54 B5
Crouch End London 67 B9
Crouchers W Sus 22 C4
Croucheston Wilts 31 B9
Crouch Hill Dorset 30 E2
Crouch House Green
Kent 52 D2
Croughly Moray 301 G11
Croughton W Nhants 101 E10
Crovie Aberds 303 C8
Crow Hants 31 G11
Crowan Corn 2 C4
Crowborough E Sus 52 G4
Staffs 168 D6
Crowborough Warren
E Sus 52 G4
Crowcombe Som 42 F6
Crowcroft Worcs 116 G5
Crowden Derbys 185 B9
Devon 12 B5
Crowder Park Devon 8 D4
Crowdhill Hants 33 C7
Crowdicote Derbys 169 B10
Crowdleham Kent 52 B5
Crowdon N Yorks 227 F9
Crow Edge S Yorks 197 G7
Crowell Oxon 84 F2
Crowell Hill Oxon 84 F3
Crowfield Suff 126 F2
W Nhants 102 C2
Crowgate Street Norf 160 E6
Crowgreaves Shrops 132 D4
Crow Green Essex 87 F9
Crowhill Gtr Man 184 B6
M Keynes 102 D6
Crow Hill Hereford 98 F2
Crowhole Derbys 186 F4
Crowhurst E Sus 38 E3
Sur 51 D11
Crowhurst Lane End
Sur 51 D11
Crowland Lincs 156 G4
Crowlas Corn 2 C2
Crowle N Lincs 199 E9
Worcs 117 F8
Crowle Green Worcs 117 F8
Crowle Hill N Lincs 199 E9
Crowle Park N Lincs 199 E9
Crowmarsh Gifford Oxon 64 B6
Crown Corner Suff 126 C5
Crown East Worcs 116 G6
Crow Nest W Yorks 205 F8
Crownfield Bucks 84 F4
Crownhill Plym 7 D9
Crown Hills Leicester 136 C2
Crownland Suff 125 D10
Crownpits Sur 50 E3
Crownthorpe Norf 141 C11
Crowntown Corn 2 C4
Crown Wood Brack 65 F11
Crows-an-wra Corn 1 D3
Crow's Green Essex 106 F3
Crowshill Norf 141 B8
Crowsley Oxon 65 D8
Crowsnest Shrops 131 C7
Crow's Nest Corn 6 B5
Crowther's Pool Powys 96 B4
Crowthorne Brack 65 G10
Crowton Ches W 183 G9
Crow Wood Halton 183 D8
Croxall Staffs 152 G3
Croxby Lincs 189 B11
Croxby Top Lincs 189 B11
Croxdale Durham 233 D11
Croxden Staffs 151 B11
Croxley Green Herts 85 F9
Croxteth Mers 182 B6
Croxton Cambs 122 E4
N Lincs 200 E5
Norf 141 F7
Norf 159 C9
Staffs 150 C5
Croxtonbank Staffs 150 C5
Croxton Green Ches E 167 E8
Croxton Kerrial Leics 154 D6
Croy Highld 301 E7
N Lanark 278 F4
Croyde Devon 40 F2
Croyde Bay Devon 40 F2
Croydon Cambs 104 B6
London 67 F10
Crozen Hereford 97 B11
Crubenbeg Highld 291 D8
Crubenmore Lodge
Highld 291 D8
Cruckmeole Shrops 131 B8
Cruckton Shrops 149 G8
Cruden Bay Aberds 303 F10
Crudgington Telford 150 F2
Crudie Aberds 303 D7
Crudwell Wilts 81 G7
Crug Powys 114 C3
Crugmeer Corn 10 F4
Crugybar Carms 94 D3
Cruise Hill Worcs 117 E10
Crulabhig W Isles 304 E3
Crumlin Caerph 78 F2
Crumplehorn Corn 6 E4
Crumpsall Gtr Man 195 G10
Crumpsbrook Shrops 116 B2
Crumpton Hill Worcs 98 B5
Crundale Kent 54 D5
Pembs 73 B7
Cruwys Morchard Devon 26 E5
Crux Easton Hants 48 B2
Cruxton Dorset 17 B8
Crwbin Carms 75 C7
Crya Orkney 314 F3
Cryers Hill Bucks 84 F5
Crymlyn Gwyn 179 G10
Crymych Pembs 92 E3
Crynant =*Creunant*
Neath 76 E3
Crynfryn Ceredig 111 E11
Cuaich Highld 291 E8
Cuaig Highld 299 D7
Cuan Argyll 275 B8
Cubbington Warks 118 D6
Cubeck N Yorks 213 B9
Cubert Corn 4 D5
Cubitt Town London 67 D11
Cubley S Yorks 197 G8
Cubley Common Derbys 152 B3
Cublington Bucks 102 G6
Hereford 97 D8
Cuckfield W Sus 36 B4
Cucklington Som 30 B3
Cuckney Notts 187 G9
Cuckold's Green Suff 143 G9
Wilts 46 B3
Cuckoo Green Suff 143 D10
Cuckoo Hill Notts 188 C2
Cuckoo's Corner Hants 49 E8
Wilts 46 B4
Cuckoo's Knob Wilts 63 G7
Cuckoo Tye Suff 107 C7
Cuckron Shetland 313 H6
Cucumber Corner Norf 143 B7
Cuddesdon Oxon 83 E10
Cuddington Bucks 84 C2
Ches W 183 G10
Cuddington Heath
Ches W 167 F7
Cuddy Hill Lancs 202 F5
Cudham London 52 B2
Cudlipptown Devon 12 F6
Cudliptown Devon 12 F6
Cudworth Som 28 E5
Sur 51 E8
S Yorks 197 F11
Cudworth Common
S Yorks 197 F11
Cuerden Green Lancs 194 C5
Cuerdley Cross Warr 183 D8
Cufaude Hants 48 B6
Cuffern Pembs 91 G7
Cuffley Herts 86 E4
Cuiashader W Isles 304 C7
Cuidhir W Isles 297 L2
Cuidhtinis W Isles 296 C6
Cuiken Midloth 270 C4
Cuilcheanna Ho Highld 290 G2
Cuin Argyll 288 D6
Culbo Highld 300 C6
Culbokie Highld 300 D6
Culburnie Highld 300 E4
Culcabock Highld 300 E6
Culcairn Highld 300 C6
Culcharry Highld 301 D8
Culcheth Warr 183 B11
Culcronchie Dumfries 237 C7
Cùl Doirlinn Highld 289 B8
Culdrain Aberds 302 F5
Culduie Highld 299 E7
Culeave Highld 309 K5
Culford Suff 124 D6
Culfordheath Suff 125 C7
Culfosie Aberds 293 C9
Culgaith Cumb 231 F8
Culham Oxon 83 F8
Culkein Highld 306 F5
Culkein Drumbeg Highld 306 F6
Culkerton Glos 80 F6
Cullachie Highld 301 G9
Cullen Moray 302 C5
Cullercoats T&W 243 C9
Cullicudden Highld 300 C6
Cullingworth W Yorks 205 F7
Cullipool Argyll 275 B8
Cullivoe Shetland 312 C7
Culloch Perth 285 F11
Culloden Highld 301 E7
Cullompton Devon 27 F8
Culmaily Highld 311 K2
Culmazie Dumfries 236 D5
Culm Davy Devon 27 D10
Culmer Sur 50 F2
Culmers Kent 70 G5
Culmington Shrops 131 G9
Culmore Stirling 278 B3
Culmstock Devon 27 E10
Culnacraig Highld 307 J5
Cul na h-Aird W Isles 305 H3
Culnaightrie Dumfries 237 D9
Culnaknock Highld 298 C5
Culnaneam Highld 294 C6
Culpho Suff 108 B4
Culrain Highld 309 K5
Culra Lodge Highld 291 F7
Culross Fife 279 D9
Culroy S Ayrs 257 G8
Culscadden Dumfries 236 E6
Culsh Aberds 292 D5
Aberds 303 E8
Culshabbin Dumfries 236 D5
Culswick Shetland 313 J4
Cultercullen Aberds 303 G9
Cults Aberdeen 293 C10
Aberds 302 F5
Dumfries 236 E6
Fife 287 G7
Culverlane Devon 8 C4
Culverstone Green Kent 68 G6
Culverthorpe Lincs 173 G8
Culworth W Nhants 101 B10
Culzie Lodge Highld 300 B5
Cumberlow Green Herts 104 E6
Cumbernauld N Lanark 278 G5
Cumbernauld Village
N Lanark 278 F5
Cumber's Bank Wrex 149 B8
Cumberworth Lincs 191 G8
Cumdivock Cumb 230 B2
Cumeragh Village Lancs 203 F7
Cuminestown Aberds 303 D8
Cumledge Borders 272 D5
Cumlewick Shetland 313 L6
Cumlodden Argyll 275 D11
Cumloden Dumfries 236 C6
Cummersdale Cumb 239 G9
Cummerton Aberds 303 C8
Cummertrees Dumfries 238 D4
Cummingston Moray 301 C11
Cumnock E Ayrs 258 E3
Cumnor Oxon 83 E7
Cumnor Hill Oxon 83 D7
Cumrew Cumb 240 G2
Cumwhinton Cumb 239 G10
Cumwhitton Cumb 240 G2
Cundall N Yorks 215 E8
Cundy Cross S Yorks 197 F11
Cundy Hos S Yorks 186 B4
Cunninghamhead
N Ayrs 267 G7
Cunnister Shetland 312 D7
Cupar Fife 287 F7
Cupar Muir Fife 287 F7
Cupernham Hants 32 C5
Cupid Green Herts 85 D9
Cupid's Hill Mon 97 F8
Curbar Derbys 186 G3
Curborough Staffs 152 G2
Curbridge Hants 33 E8
Oxon 82 D4
Curdridge Hants 33 E8
Curdworth Warks 134 E3
Curgurrell Corn 3 B9
Curin Highld 300 D3
Curland Som 28 D3
Curland Common Som 28 D3
Curlew Green Suff 127 D7
Curling Tye Green Essex 88 D4
Curload Som 28 B4
Currarie S Ayrs 244 E5
Currian Vale Corn 5 D9
Curridge W Berks 64 E3
Currie Edin 270 B3
Currock Cumb 239 G10
Curry Lane Corn 11 C11
Curry Mallet Som 28 C4
Curry Rivel Som 28 B5
Cursiter Orkney 314 E3
Curteis' Corner Kent 53 F11
Curtisden Green Kent 53 E8
Curtisknowle Devon 8 E4
Curtismill Green Essex 87 F8
Cury Corn 2 E5
Cusbay Orkney 314 C5
Cusgarne Corn 4 G5
Cushnie Aberds 303 C7
Cushuish Som 43 G7
Cusop Hereford 96 C4
Custards Hants 32 F3
Custom House London 68 C2
Cusveorth Coombe Corn 4 G5
Cusworth S Yorks 198 G4
Cutcloy Dumfries 236 F6
Cutcombe Som 42 F2
Cutgate Gtr Man 195 E11
Cuthill E Loth 281 G7
Cutiau Gwyn 146 F2
Cutlers Green Essex 105 E11
Cutler's Green Som 44 C5
Cutmadoc Corn 5 C11
Cutmere Corn 6 C6
Cutnall Green Worcs 117 D7
Cutsdean Glos 99 E11
Cutsyke W Yorks 198 C2
Cutteslowe Oxon 83 C8
Cutthorpe Derbys 186 G4
Cuttiford's Door Som 28 E4
Cutts Shetland 313 K6
Cuttybridge Pembs 72 B6
Cuttyhill Aberds 303 D10
Cuxham Oxon 83 F11
Cuxton Medway 69 F8
Cuxwold Lincs 201 G7
Cwm Bl Gwent 77 D11
Denb 181 F9
Neath 57 C10
Powys 129 D11
Powys 130 E5
Shrops 114 B6
Swansea 57 B7
Cwmafan Neath 57 C9
Cwmaman Rhondda 77 F8
Cwmann Carms 93 B11
Cwmavon Torf 78 D3
Cwmbach Carms 75 E7
Carms 92 F5
Powys 96 D3
Rhondda 77 E8
Cwmbâch Rhondda 77 E8
Cwmbach Llechrhyd
Powys 113 G10
Cwmbelan Powys 129 G8
Cwmbran Torf 78 G3
Cwmbrwyno Ceredig 128 G4
Cwm-byr Carms 94 E2
Cwm Capel Carms 75 E7
Cwmcarn Caerph 78 G2
Cwmcarvan Mon 79 D7
Cwm-celyn Bl Gwent 78 D2
Cwm-Cewydd Gwyn 147 G7
Cwmcoednerth Ceredig 92 B6
Cwm-cou Ceredig 92 C5
Cwmcrawnon Powys 77 B10
Cwmcych Carms 92 D5
Cwmdare Rhondda 77 E7
Cwm Dows Caerph 78 F2
Cwmdu Carms 94 E2
Powys 96 G3
Swansea 56 C6
Cwmduad Carms 93 E7
Cwm-Dulais Swansea 75 E10
Cwmdwr Carms 94 E4
Cwmerfyn Ceredig 128 G3
Cwmfelin Bridgend 57 D11
M Tydf 77 E9
Cwmfelin Boeth Carms 73 B11
Cwm felin fach Caerph 77 G11
Cwmfelin Mynach Carms 92 G4
Cwmffrwd Carms 74 B6
Cwm Ffrwd-oer Torf 78 E3
Cwm-Fields Torf 78 E3
Cwm Gelli Caerph 77 F11
Cwmgiedd Powys 76 C3
Cwmgors Neath 76 C2
Cwmgwili Carms 75 C9
Cwmgwrach Neath 76 E5
Cwm Gwyn Swansea 56 C6
Cwm Head Shrops 131 F8
Cwm-hesgen Gwyn 146 D5
Cwmhiraeth Carms 92 D6
Cwm-hwnt Rhondda 76 D6
Cwmifor Carms 94 F3
Cwm Irfon Powys 95 B7
Cwmisfael Carms 75 B7
Cwm-Llinau Powys 128 B6
Cwmllynfell Neath 76 C2
Cwm-mawr Carms 75 C8
Cwm-miles Carms 92 G3
Cwm Nant-gam
Bl Gwent 78 C2
Cwmnantyrodyn
Caerph 77 F11
Cwmorgan Pembs 92 E5
Cwmparc Rhondda 77 F7
Cwm-parc Rhondda 77 F7
Cwmpengraig Carms 92 D6
Cwm Penmachno
Conwy 164 F3
Cwmpennar Rhondda 77 E8
Cwm Plysgog Ceredig 92 C3
Cwmrhos Powys 96 G3
Cwmrhydyceirw
Swansea 57 B7
Cwmsychpant Ceredig 93 B9
Cwmsyfiog Caerph 77 E11
Cwmsymlog Ceredig 128 G4
Cwmtillery Bl Gwent 78 D2
Cwm-twrch Isaf Powys 76 C3
Cwm-twrch Uchaf
Powys 76 C3
Cwmwdig Water Pembs 90 E6
Cwmwysg Powys 95 F7
Cwm-y-glo Carms 75 C9
Gwyn 163 C8
Cwmynyscoy Torf 78 F3
Cwmyoy Mon 96 G5
Cwmystwyth Ceredig 112 C5
Cwrt Gwyn 128 C3
Cwrt-newydd Ceredig 93 B9
Cwrt-y-cadno Carms 94 C3
Cwrt-y-gollen Powys 78 B2
Cydweli =*Kidwelly*
Carms 74 D6
Cyffordd Llandudno
=*Llandudno Junction*
Conwy 180 F3
Cyffylliog Denb 165 D9
Cyfronydd Powys 130 B2
Cymau Flint 166 D3
Cymdda Bridgend 58 C2
Cymer Neath 57 B11
Cymmer Rhondda 77 G8
Cyncoed Cardiff 59 C7
Cynghordy Carms 94 C6
Cynheidre Carms 75 D7
Cynonville Neath 57 B10
Cyntwell Cardiff 58 D6
Cynwyd Denb 165 G9
Cynwyl Elfed Carms 93 F7
Cywarch Gwyn 147 F7

D

Daccombe Devon 9 B8
Dacre Cumb 230 F5
N Yorks 214 G3
Dacre Banks N Yorks 214 G3
Daddry Shield Durham 232 D3
Dadford Bucks 102 D3
Dadlington Leics 135 D8
Dafarn Faig Gwyn 163 F7
Dafen Carms 75 E8
Daffy Green Norf 141 B9
Dagdale Staffs 151 C11
Dagenham London 68 C3
Daggons Dorset 31 E10
Daglingworth Glos 81 D7
Dagnall Bucks 85 B7
Dagtail End Worcs 117 E10
Dagworth Suff 125 E10
Dail Beag W Isles 304 D4
Dail bho Dheas W Isles 304 B6
Dail bho Thuath
W Isles 304 B6
Daill Argyll 274 G4
Dailly S Ayrs 245 C7
Dail Mor W Isles 304 D4
Dainton Devon 9 B7
Dairsie or Osnaburgh
Fife 287 F8
Daisy Green Suff 125 D10
Suff 125 D11
Daisy Hill Gtr Man 195 G7
W Yorks 197 B9
W Yorks 205 G8
Daisy Nook Gtr Man 196 G2
Dalabrog W Isles 297 J3
Dalavich Argyll 275 B10
Dalbeattie Dumfries 237 C10
Dalbeg Highld 291 B8
Dalblair E Ayrs 258 F4
Dalbog Angus 293 F7
Dalbrack Stirling 285 G11
Dalbury Derbys 152 C5
Dalby IoM 192 E3
Lincs 190 G6
N Yorks 216 E2
Dalchalloch Perth 291 G9
Dalchalm Highld 311 J3
Dalchenna Argyll 284 G4
Dalchirach Moray 301 F11
Dalchonzie Perth 285 E11
Dalchork Highld 309 H5
Dalchreichart Highld 290 B4
Dalchruin Perth 285 F11
Dalderby Lincs 174 B2
Dale Cumb 230 C6
Gtr Man 196 F3
Pembs 72 D4
Shetland 312 G6
Dale Abbey Derbys 153 B8
Dalebank Derbys 170 C5
Dale Bottom Cumb 229 G11
Dale Brow Ches E 184 F6
Dale End Derbys 170 C2
N Yorks 204 D5
Dale Head Cumb 221 B8
Dale Hill E Sus 53 G7
E Sus 53 G8
Dalelia Highld 289 C9
Dale Moor Derbys 153 B8
Dale of Walls Shetland 313 H3
Dales Brow Gtr Man 195 G9
Dales Green Staffs 168 D5
Daless Highld 301 F8
Dalestie Moray 292 B3
Dalestorth Notts 171 C8
Dalfaber Highld 291 B11
Dalfoil Stirling 277 D11
Dalganachan Highld 310 E4
Dalgarven N Ayrs 266 F5
Dalgety Bay Fife 280 E3
Dalginross Perth 285 E11
Dalguise Perth 286 C3
Dalhalvaig Highld 310 D2
Dalham Suff 124 E4
Dalhastnie Angus 293 F7
Dalhenzean Perth 292 G3
Dalinlongart Argyll 276 E2
Dalkeith Midloth 270 B6
Dallam Warr 183 C9
Dallas Moray 301 D11
Dallas Lodge Moray 301 D11
Dallcharn Highld 308 D6
Dalleagles E Ayrs 258 G3
Dallicott Shrops 132 E5
Dallimores IoW 20 C6
Dallinghoo Suff 126 G5
Dallington E Sus 23 B11
W Nhants 120 E4
Dallow N Yorks 214 E3
Dalmadilly Aberds 293 B9
Dalmally Argyll 284 E5
Dalmarnock Glasgow 268 C2
Perth 286 C3
Dalmary Stirling 277 B10
Dalmellington E Ayrs 245 B11
Dalmeny Edin 280 F2
Dalmigavie Highld 291 B9
Dalmigavie Lodge
Highld 301 G7
Dalmilling S Ayrs 257 E9
Dalmore Highld 300 C6
Dalmuir W Dunb 277 G9
Dalnabreck Highld 289 C8
Dalnacardoch Lodge
Perth 291 F9
Dalnacroich Highld 300 D3
Dalnaglar Castle Perth 292 G3
Dalnahaitnach Highld 301 G8
Dalnamein Lodge Perth 291 G9
Dalnarrow Argyll 289 F9
Dalnaspidal Lodge
Perth 291 F8
Dalnavaid Perth 292 G2
Dalnavie Highld 300 B6
Dalnaw Dumfries 236 B5
Dalnawillan Lodge
Highld 310 E4
Dalness Highld 284 B5
Dalnessie Highld 309 H6
Dalphaid Highld 309 H3
Dalqueich Perth 286 G4
Dalrannoch Argyll 289 E11
Dalreavoch Highld 309 J7
Dalriach Highld 301 F10
Dalrigh Stirling 285 E7
Dalry Edin 280 G4
N Ayrs 266 F5
Dalrymple E Ayrs 257 G9
Dalscote W Nhants 120 G3
Dalserf S Lanark 268 E6
Dalshannon N Lanark 278 G4
Dalston Cumb 239 G9
London 67 C10
Dalswinton Dumfries 247 F10
Dalton Cumb 211 D10
Dumfries 238 C4
Lancs 194 F3
Northumb 241 F10
Northumb 242 C4
Dalton *continued*
N Yorks 215 D8
N Yorks 224 D2
S Lanark 268 D3
S Yorks 187 C7
W Yorks 197 D7
Dalton-in-Furness
Cumb 210 E4
Dalton-le-Dale Durham 234 B4
Dalton Magna S Yorks 187 C7
Dalton-on-Tees
N Yorks 224 D5
Dalton Parva S Yorks 187 C7
Dalton Piercy Hrtlpl 234 E5
Dalveallan Highld 300 F6
Dalveich Stirling 285 E10
Dalvina Lo Highld 308 E6
Dalwey Telford 132 B3
Dalwhinnie Highld 291 E8
Dalwood Devon 28 G3
Dalwyne S Ayrs 245 D8
Damask Green Herts 104 F5
Damems W Yorks 204 F6
Damerham Hants 31 D10
Damery Glos 80 G2
Damgate Norf 143 B8
Norf 161 F9
Dam Green Norf 141 F11
Damhead Moray 301 D10
Dam Head W Yorks 196 B6
Damhead Holdings
Midloth 270 B5
Dam Mill Staffs 133 C7
Damnaglaur Dumfries 236 F3
Dam of Quoiggs Perth 286 G2
Damside Borders 270 F3
Dam Side Lancs 202 D4
Danaway Kent 69 G11
Danbury Essex 88 E3
Danbury Common Essex 88 E3
Danby N Yorks 226 D4
Danby Wiske N Yorks 224 F6
Dan Caerlan Rhondda 58 C5
Dancers Hill Herts 86 F2
Dancing Green Hereford 98 G2
Dandaleith Moray 302 E2
Danderhall Midloth 270 B6
Dandy Corner Suff 125 D11
Danebank Ches E 185 E7
Dane Bank Gtr Man 184 B6
Danebridge Ches E 169 B7
Dane End Herts 104 G6
Danegate E Sus 52 G5
Danehill E Sus 36 B6
Dane in Shaw Ches E 168 C5
Danemoor Green Norf 141 B11
Danesbury Herts 86 B2
Danesfield Bucks 65 C10
Danesford Shrops 132 E4
Daneshill Hants 49 C7
Danesmoor Derbys 170 C6
Danes Moss Ches E 184 G6
Dane Street Kent 54 C5
Daneway Glos 80 E6
Dangerous Corner
Gtr Man 195 G7
Lancs 194 E4
Daniel's Water Kent 54 E3
Danna na Cloiche Argyll 275 F7
Dannonchapel Corn 10 E6
Danskine E Loth 271 B11
Danthorpe E Yorks 209 G10
Danygraig Caerph 78 G2
Danzey Green Warks 118 D2
Dapple Heath Staffs 151 D10
Darby End W Mid 133 F9
Darby Green Hants 65 G10
Darbys Green Worcs 116 F4
Darby's Hill W Mid 133 F9
Darcy Lever Gtr Man 195 F8
Dardy Powys 78 B2
Darenth Kent 68 E5
Daresbury Halton 183 E9
Daresbury Delph Halton 183 E9
Darfield S Yorks 198 G2
Darfoulds Notts 187 F9
Dargate Kent 70 G5
Dargate Common Kent 70 G5
Dargavel Village Renfs 277 G8
Darite Corn 6 B5
Darkland Moray 302 C2
Darland Wrex 166 D5
Darlaston W Mid 133 D9
Darlaston Green W Mid 133 D9
Darley N Yorks 205 B10
Shrops 132 D3
Darley Abbey Derby 153 B7
Darley Bridge Derbys 170 C3
Darley Dale Derbys 170 C3
Darleyford Corn 11 G11
Darley Green Warks 118 C3
Darleyhall Herts 104 G2
Darley Head N Yorks 205 B9
Darley Hillside Derbys 170 C3
Darlingscott Warks 100 C4
Darlington Darl 224 C5
Darliston Shrops 149 C11
Darlton Notts 188 G3
Darmsden Suff 125 G11
Darnall S Yorks 186 D5
Darnaway Castle Moray 301 D9
Darnford Staffs 134 B2
Darnhall Ches W 167 C10
Darnhall Mains Borders 270 F4
Darn Hill Gtr Man 195 E10
Darnick Borders 262 C2
Darowen Powys 128 C6
Darra Aberds 303 E7
Darracott Devon 24 D2
Devon 40 F3
Darras Hall Northumb 242 C5
Darrington W Yorks 198 D3
Darrow Green Norf 142 F5
Darsham Suff 127 D8
Darshill Som 44 E6
Dartford Kent 68 E4
Dartford Crossing Kent 68 D5
Dartington Devon 8 C5
Dartmeet Devon 13 G9
Dartmouth Devon 9 E7
Dartmouth Park London 67 B9
Darton S Yorks 197 F10
Darvel E Ayrs 258 B3
Darvillshill Bucks 84 F4
Darwell Hole E Sus 23 B11
Darwen Blackburn 195 C7
Dassels Herts 105 F7
Datchet Windsor 66 D3
Datchet Common
Windsor 66 D3
Datchworth Herts 86 B3
Datchworth Green Herts 86 B3
Daubhill Gtr Man 195 F8
Daugh of Kinermony
Moray 302 E2
Dauntsey Wilts 62 C3
Dauntsey Lock Wilts 62 C3
Dava Moray 301 F10
Davenham Ches W 183 G11
Davenport Ches E 168 B4
Gtr Man 184 D5
Davenport Green
Ches E 184 F4
Gtr Man 184 D4
Daventry W Nhants 119 E11
Davidson's Mains Edin 280 F4
Davidston Highld 301 C7
Davidstow Corn 11 D9
David Street Kent 68 G6
David's Well Powys 113 B11
Davington Dumfries 248 C6
Kent 70 G4
Daviot Aberds 303 G7
Highld 301 F7
Davis's Town E Sus 23 B8
Davoch of Grange
Moray 302 D4
Davo Mains Aberds 293 F9
Davyhulme Gtr Man 184 B3
Daw Cross N Yorks 205 C11
Dawdon Durham 234 B4
Daw End W Mid 133 C10
Dawesgreen Sur 51 D8
Dawker Hill N Yorks 207 F7
Dawley Telford 132 B3
Dawley Bank Telford 132 B3
Dawlish Devon 14 F5
Dawlish Warren Devon 14 F5
Dawn Conwy 180 G5
Daw's Cross Essex 107 E7
Daw's Green Som 27 C11
Daws Heath Essex 69 B10
Dawshill Worcs 116 G6
Daw's House Corn 12 E2
Dawsmere Lincs 157 C8
Daybrook Notts 171 F9
Day Green Ches E 168 D3
Dayhills Staffs 151 C9
Dayhouse Bank Worcs 117 B9
Daylesford Glos 100 F4
Daywall Shrops 148 C5
Ddol Flint 181 G10
Ddôl Cownwy Powys 147 F10
Ddrydwy Anglesey 178 G5
Deacons Hill Herts 85 F11
Deadman's Cross
C Beds 104 C2
Deadman's Green
Staffs 151 B10
Deadwater Hants 49 F10
Northumb 250 D4
Deaf Hill Durham 234 D3
Deal Hall Essex 89 F8
Kent 55 C11
Dean Cumb 229 F7
Devon 8 C4
Devon 40 D6
Devon 40 E4
Devon 41 D8
Dorset 31 D7
Edin 280 G4
Hants 33 D9
Hants 48 G2
Lancs 195 B11
Oxon 100 G6
Som 45 E7
Dean Bank Durham 233 E11
Deanburnhaugh
Borders 261 G9
Dean Court Oxon 83 D7
Dean Cross Devon 40 E4
Deane Gtr Man 195 F7
Hants 48 C4
Deanend Dorset 31 D7
Dean Head S Yorks 197 G9
Deanich Lodge Highld 309 L3
Deanland Dorset 31 D7
Deanlane End W Sus 34 E2
Dean Lane Head
W Yorks 205 G7
Dean Park Renfs 267 B10
Dean Prior Devon 8 C4
Dean Row Ches E 184 E5
Deans W Loth 269 B10
Deans Bottom Kent 69 G11
Deanscales Cumb 229 F7
Deansgreen Ches E 183 D11
Dean's Green Warks 118 D2
Deanshanger W Nhants 102 D5
Deans Hill Kent 69 G11
Deanston Stirling 285 G11
Dean Street Kent 53 C8
Dearham Cumb 229 D7
Dearnley Gtr Man 196 D2
Debach Suff 126 G4
Debdale Gtr Man 184 B5
Debden Essex 86 F6
Essex 105 E11
Debden Cross Essex 105 E11
Debden Green Essex 86 F6
Essex 105 E11
De Beauvoir Town
London 67 C10
Debenham Suff 126 E3
Deblin's Green Worcs 98 B6
Dechmont W Loth 279 G10
Deckham T&W 243 E7
Deddington Oxon 101 E9
Dedham Essex 107 E11
Dedham Heath Essex 107 E11
Dedridge W Loth 269 B11
Dedworth Windsor 66 D2
Deebank Aberds 293 D8
Deecastle Aberds 292 D6
Deene N Nhants 137 E8
Deenethorpe N Nhants 137 E9
Deepcar S Yorks 186 B3
Deepclough Derbys 185 B8
Deepcut Sur 50 B2
Deepdale C Beds 104 B4
Cumb 212 C4
N Yorks 213 D7
Deepdene Sur 51 D7
Deepfields W Mid 133 E8
Deeping Gate Lincs 138 B2
Deeping St James Lincs 138 B3
Deeping St Nicholas
Lincs 156 F4
Deepthwaite Cumb 211 C10
Deepweir Mon 60 B3
Deerhill Moray 302 D4
Deerhurst Glos 99 F7
Deerhurst Walton Glos 99 F7
Deerland Pembs 73 C7
Deerness Orkney 314 F5
Deer's Green Essex 105 E9
Deerstones N Yorks 205 C7
Deerton Street Kent 70 G3
Defford Worcs 99 C8
Defynnog Powys 95 F8
Deganwy Conwy 180 F3
Degar V Glam 58 D4
Degibna Corn 2 D5
Deighton N Yorks 225 E7
W Yorks 197 D7
York 207 E8
Deiniolen Gwyn 163 C9
Deishar Highld 291 B11
Delabole Corn 11 E7
Delamere Ches W 167 B9
Delfour Highld 291 C10
Delfrigs Aberds 303 G9
Delliefure Highld 301 F10
Dell Lodge Highld 292 B2
Dell Quay W Sus 22 C4
Delly End Oxon 82 C5
Delnabo Moray 292 B3
Delnadamph Aberds 292 C4
Delnamer Angus 292 G3
Delph Gtr Man 196 F3
Delves Durham 233 B8
Delvine Perth 286 C5
Delvin End Essex 106 D5
Dembleby Lincs 155 B10
Demelza Corn 5 C9
Denaby Main S Yorks 187 B7
Denbeath Fife 281 B7
Denbigh Denb 165 B9
Denbury Devon 8 B6
Denby Derbys 170 F5
Denby Bottles Derbys 170 F5
Denby Common Derbys 170 F6
Denby Dale W Yorks 197 F8
Denchworth Oxon 82 G5
Dendron Cumb 210 E4
Denel End C Beds 103 D10
Denend Aberds 302 F6
Dene Park Kent 52 C5
Deneside Durham 234 B4
Denford N Nhants 121 B9
Staffs 169 E7
Dengie Essex 89 E7
Denham Bucks 66 B4
Bucks 102 G5
Suff 124 E5
Suff 126 C3
Denham Corner Suff 126 C3
Denham End Suff 124 E5
Denham Green Bucks 66 B4
Denham Street Suff 126 C3
Denhead Aberds 303 D9
Fife 287 F8
Denhead of Arbilot
Angus 287 C9
Denhead of Gray
Dundee 287 D7
Denholm Borders 262 F3
Denholme W Yorks 205 G7
Denholme Clough
W Yorks 205 G7
Denholme Edge
W Yorks 205 G7
Denholme Gate
W Yorks 205 G7
Denholmhill Borders 262 F3
Denio Gwyn 145 B7
Denmead Hants 33 E11
Denmore Aberdeen 293 B11
Denmoss Aberds 302 E6
Dennington Suff 126 D5
Dennington Corner Suff 126 D5
Dennington Hall Suff 126 D5
Denny Falk 278 E6
Denny Bottom Kent 52 F5
Denny End Cambs 123 D9
Dennyloanhead Falk 278 E6
Denny Lodge Hants 32 F4
Dennystown W Dunb 277 F7
Denshaw Gtr Man 196 E3
Denside Aberds 293 D10
Densole Kent 55 E8
Denston Suff 124 G5
Denstone Staffs 169 G9
Denstroude Kent 70 G6
Dent Cumb 212 B4
Dent Bank Durham 232 F4
Denton Cambs 138 F2
Darl 224 B4
E Sus 23 E7
Gtr Man 184 B6
Kent 55 D8
Kent 69 E7
Lincs 155 C7
Norf 142 F5
N Yorks 205 D8
Oxon 83 E9
W Nhants 120 F6
Denton Burn T&W 242 D5
Denton Holme Cumb 239 G10
Denton's Green Mers 183 B7
Denver Norf 140 C2
Denvilles Hants 22 B2
Denwick Northumb 264 G6
Deopham Norf 141 C11
Deopham Green Norf 141 D10
Deopham Stalland
Norf 141 D10
Depden Suff 124 F5
Depden Green Suff 124 F5
Deppers Bridge Warks 119 F7
Deptford London 67 D11
T&W 243 F9
Wilts 46 F4
Derby Derbys 153 B7
Devon 40 G5
Derbyhaven IoM 192 F3
Derbyshire Hill Mers 183 C8
Dereham Norf 159 G9
Dergoals Dumfries 236 D4
Deri Caerph 77 E10
Derriford Plym 7 D9
Derril Devon 24 G4
Derringstone Kent 55 D8
Derrington Shrops 132 E2
Staffs 151 E7
Derriton Devon 24 G4
Derry Stirling 285 E10
Derrydaroch Stirling 285 E7
Derry Downs London 68 F3
Derry Fields Wilts 81 G8
Derryguaig Argyll 288 F6
Derry Hill Wilts 62 E3
Derry Lodge Aberds 292 D2
Derrythorpe N Lincs 199 F10
Dersingham Norf 158 C3
Dertfords Wilts 45 D10
Dervaig Argyll 288 D6
Derwen Bridgend 58 C2
Denb 165 E9
Derwenlas Powys 128 D4
Derwydd Carms 75 B10
Desborough N Nhants 136 G6
Desford Leics 135 C9
Deskryshiel Aberds 292 B6
Detchant Northumb 264 B3
Detling Kent 53 B9
Deuchar Angus 292 G6
Deuddwr Powys 148 F4
Deuxhill Shrops 132 F3
Devauden Mon 79 F7
Deveral Corn 2 B3
Devil's Bridge
=*Pontarfynach*
Ceredig 112 B4
Devitts Green Warks 134 E5
Devizes Wilts 62 G4
Devol Invclyd 276 G6
Devonport Plym 7 E9
Devonside Clack 279 B8
Devon Village Clack 279 B8
Devoran Corn 3 B7
Dewar Borders 270 F6
Dewartown Midloth 271 C7
Dewes Green Essex 105 E9
Dewlands Common
Dorset 31 F9
Dewlish Dorset 17 B11
Dewsbury W Yorks 197 C8
Dewsbury Moor
W Yorks 197 C8
Dewshall Court Hereford 97 E9
Dhoon IoM 192 D5
Dhoor IoM 192 C5
Dhowin IoM 192 B5
Dhustone Shrops 115 B11
Dial Green W Sus 34 B6
Dial Post W Sus 35 D11
Dibberford Dorset 29 G7
Dibden Hants 32 F6
Dibden Purlieu Hants 32 F6
Dickens Heath W Mid 118 B2
Dickleburgh Norf 142 G3
Dickleburgh Moor Norf 142 G3
Dickon Hills Lincs 174 D6
Didbrook Glos 99 E11
Didcot Oxon 64 B4
Diddington Cambs 122 D3
Diddlebury Shrops 131 F10
Diddywell Devon 25 B7
Didley Hereford 97 E9
Didling W Sus 34 D4
Didlington Norf 140 D5
Didmarton Glos 61 B10
Didsbury Gtr Man 184 C4
Didworthy Devon 8 C3
Diebidale Highld 309 L4
Digbeth W Mid 133 F11
Digby Lincs 173 E9
Digg Highld 298 C4
Diggle Gtr Man 196 F4
Diglis Worcs 116 G6
Digmoor Lancs 194 F3
Digswell Herts 86 B3
Digswell Park Herts 86 C2
Digswell Water Herts 86 C3
Dihewyd Ceredig 111 F9
Dilham Norf 160 D6
Dilhorne Staffs 169 G7
Dillarburn S Lanark 268 G6
Dill Hall Lancs 195 B8
Dillington Cambs 122 D2
Som 28 D5
Dilston Northumb 241 E11
Dilton Marsh Wilts 45 D11
Dilwyn Hereford 115 G8
Dimlands V Glam 58 F3
Dimmer Som 44 G6
Dimple Derbys 170 C3
Gtr Man 195 D8
Dimsdale Staffs 168 F4
Dimson Corn 12 G4
Dinas Carms 92 E5
Corn 10 G4
Gwyn 144 B5
Gwyn 163 D7
Dinas Cross Pembs 91 D10
Dinas Dinlle Gwyn 162 D6
Dinas-Mawddwy Gwyn 147 G7
Dinas Mawr Conwy 164 E4
Dinas Powys V Glam 59 E7
Dinbych y Pysgod =*Tenby*
Pembs 73 E10
Dinckley Lancs 203 F9
Dinder Som 44 E5
Dinedor Hereford 97 D10
Dinedor Cross Hereford 97 D10
Dines Green Worcs 116 F6
Dingestow Mon 79 C7
Dinghurst N Som 44 B2
Dingle Mers 182 D5
Dingleden Kent 53 G10
Dingleton Borders 262 C2
Dingley N Nhants 136 F5
Dingwall Highld 300 D5
Dinlabyre Borders 250 E2
Dinmael Conwy 165 G8
Dinnet Aberds 292 D6
Dinnington Som 28 E6
S Yorks 187 D8
T&W 242 C6
Dinorwic Gwyn 163 C9
Dinton Bucks 84 C3
Wilts 46 G4
Dinwoodie Mains
Dumfries 248 E4
Dinworthy Devon 24 D4
Dipford Som 28 C2
Dipley Hants 49 B8
Dippenhall Sur 49 D10
Dippertown Devon 12 E4
Dippin N Ayrs 256 E2
Dipple Devon 24 D4
Moray 302 D3
S Ayrs 244 C6
Diptford Devon 8 D4
Dipton Durham 242 G5
Diptonmill Northumb 241 E10
Dirdhu Highld 301 G10
Direcleit W Isles 305 J3
Dirleton E Loth 281 E10
Dirt Pot Northumb 232 B3
Discoed Powys 114 E5
Discove Som 45 G7
Diseworth Leics 153 E9
Dishes Orkney 314 D6
Dishforth N Yorks 215 E7
Dishley Leics 153 E10
Disley Ches E 185 E7
Diss Norf 126 B2
Disserth Powys 113 F10
Distington Cumb 228 G6
Ditchampton Wilts 46 G5
Ditcheat Som 44 F6
Ditchfield Bucks 84 G4
Ditchford Hill Worcs 100 D4
Ditchingham Norf 142 E6
Ditchling E Sus 36 D4
Ditherington Shrops 149 G10
Ditteridge Wilts 61 F10
Dittisham Devon 9 E7
Ditton Halton 183 D7
Kent 53 B8
Ditton Green Cambs 124 F3
Ditton Priors Shrops 132 F2
Dittons E Sus 23 E10
Divach Highld 300 G4
Divlyn Carms 94 D5
Dixton Glos 99 E9
Mon 79 C8
Dizzard Corn 11 B9
Dobcross Gtr Man 196 F3
Dobs Hill Flint 166 C4
Dobson's Bridge Shrops 149 C9
Dobwalls Corn 6 C4
Doccombe Devon 13 D11
Dochfour Ho Highld 300 F6
Dochgarroch Highld 300 E6
Dockeney Norf 143 E7
Dockenfield Sur 49 E10
Docker Lancs 211 E11
Docking Norf 158 B5
Docklow Hereford 115 F11

Dockray Cumb 230 G3
Dockroyd W Yorks 204 F6
Doc Penfro = Pembroke Dock Pembs 73 E7
Docton Devon 24 C2
Dodbrooke Devon 8 G4
Dodburn Borders 249 B11
Doddenham Worcs 116 F5
Doddinghurst Essex 87 F9
Doddington Cambs 139 E7
Kent 54 B2
Lincs 188 G6
Northumb 263 C11
Shrops 116 B2
Doddiscombsleigh Devon 14 D3
Doddshill Norf 158 C3
Doddycross Corn 6 C6
Dodford W Nhants 120 E2
Worcs 117 C8
Dodington S Glos 61 C9
Som 43 E7
Dodleston Ches W 166 C5
Dodmarsh Hereford 97 C11
Dodscott Devon 25 D8
Dods Leigh Staffs 151 C10
Dodworth S Yorks 197 F10
Dodworth Bottom S Yorks 197 G10
Dodworth Green S Yorks 197 G10
Doe Bank W Mid 134 D2
Doe Green Warr 183 D9
Doehole Derbys 170 D5
Doe Lea Derbys 171 B7
Doffcocker Gtr Man 195 E7
Dogdyke Lincs 174 D2
Dog & Gun Mers 182 B5
Dog Hill Gtr Man 196 F3
Dogingtree Estate Staffs 151 G9
Dogley Lane W Yorks 197 E7
Dogmersfield Hants 49 C9
Dogridge Wilts 62 B5
Dogsthorpe Pboro 138 C3
Dog Village Devon 14 B5
Doirlinn Highld 289 D8
Dolanog Powys 147 G11
Dolau Powys 114 D2
Rhondda 58 C3
Dolbenmaen Gwyn 163 G8
Dole Ceredig 128 F2
Dolemeads Bath 61 G9
Doley Staffs 150 D4
Dolfach Powys 129 C8
Dol-ffanog Gwyn 146 G4
Dolfor Powys 130 F2
Dol-fôr Powys 128 B6
Dolgarrog Conwy 164 B3
Dolgellau Gwyn 146 F4
Dolgerdd Ceredig 111 G8
Dolgoch Gwyn 128 C3
Dolgran Carms 93 E8
Dolhelfa Powys 113 C8
Dolhendre Gwyn 147 C7
Doll Highld 311 J2
Dollar Clack 279 B9
Dolley Green Powys 114 D5
Dollis Hill London 67 B8
Dollwen Ceredig 128 G3
Dolphin Flint 181 G11
Dolphingstone E Loth 281 G7
Dolphinholme Lancs 202 C6
Dolphinston Borders 262 F5
Dolphinton S Lanark 270 F2
Dolton Devon 25 E9
Dolwen Conwy 180 G5
Powys 129 B9
Dolwyd Conwy 180 F4
Dolwyddelan Conwy 164 E2
Dôl-y-Bont Ceredig 128 F2
Dol-y-cannau Powys 96 B3
Dolydd Gwyn 163 D7
Dolyhir Powys 114 F4
Dolymelinau Powys 129 D11
Dolywern Wrex 148 B4
Domewood Sur 51 E10
Domgay Powys 148 F5
Dommett Som 28 E3
Doncaster S Yorks 198 G5
Doncaster Common S Yorks 198 G6
Dones Green Ches W 183 F10
Donhead St Andrew Wilts 30 C6
Donhead St Mary Wilts 30 C6
Donibristle Fife 280 D3
Doniford Som 42 E5
Donington Lincs 156 B4
Shrops 132 C6
Donington Eaudike Lincs 156 B4
Donington le Heath Leics 153 G8
Donington on Bain Lincs 190 E2
Donington South Ing Lincs 156 C4
Donisthorpe Leics 152 G6
Don Johns Essex 106 F6
Donkey Street Kent 54 G6
Donkey Town Sur 66 G2
Donna Nook Lincs 190 B6
Donnington Glos 100 F3
Hereford 98 E4
Shrops 131 B11
Telford 150 G4
W Berks 64 F3
W Sus 22 C5
Donnington Wood Telford 150 G4
Donwell T&W 243 F7
Donyatt Som 28 E4
Doomsday Green W Sus 35 B11
Doonfoot S Ayrs 257 F8
Dora's Green Hants 49 D10
Dorback Lodge Highld 292 B2
Dorcan Swindon 63 C7
Dorchester Dorset 17 C9
Oxon 83 G9
Dordale Worcs 117 C8
Dordon Warks 134 C5
Dore S Yorks 186 E4
Dores Highld 300 F5
Dorking Sur 51 D7
Dorking Tye Suff 107 D8
Dorley's Corner Suff 127 D7
Dormansland Sur 52 E2
Dormans Park Sur 51 E11
Dormanstown Redcar 235 G7
Dormer's Wells London 66 C6
Dormington Hereford 97 C11
Dormston Worcs 117 F9
Dorn Glos 100 E4
Dornal S Ayrs 236 B4
Dorney Bucks 66 D2
Dorney Reach Bucks 66 D2
Dorn Hill Worcs 100 E3
Dornie Highld 295 C10
Dornoch Highld 309 L7
Dornock Dumfries 238 D6
Dorrery Highld 310 D4
Dorridge W Mid 118 B3
Dorrington Lincs 173 E9
Shrops 131 C9
Dorsington Warks 100 B2
Dorstone Hereford 96 C6
Dorton Bucks 83 C11
Dorusduain Highld 295 C11
Doseley Telford 132 B3
Dosmuckeran Highld 300 C2
Dosthill Staffs 134 C4
Staffs 134 D4
Dothan Anglesey 178 G5
Dothill Telford 150 G2
Dottery Dorset 16 B5
Doublebois Corn 6 C3
Double Hill Bath 45 B8
Dougarie N Ayrs 255 D9
Doughton Glos 80 G5
Norf 159 D7
Douglas IoM 192 E4
S Lanark 259 C8
Douglas & Angus Dundee 287 D8
Douglastown Angus 287 C8
Douglas Water S Lanark 259 B9
Douglas West S Lanark 259 C8
Doulting Som 44 E6
Dounby Orkney 314 D2
Doune Highld 291 C10
Highld 309 J4
Stirling 285 G11
Doune Park Aberds 303 C7
Douneside Aberds 292 C6
Dounie Argyll 275 D8
Highld 309 K5
Highld 309 L6
Dounreay Highld 310 C3
Doura N Ayrs 266 G6
Dousland Devon 7 B10
Dovaston Shrops 149 E7
Dovecot Mers 182 C6
Dovecothall Glasgow 267 D10
Dove Green Notts 171 E7
Dove Holes Derbys 185 F9
Dovenby Cumb 229 E7
Dovendale Lincs 190 E4
Dove Point Mers 182 C2
Dover Gtr Man 194 G6
Kent 55 E10
Dovercourt Essex 108 E5
Doverdale Worcs 117 D7
Doverhay Som 41 D11
Doveridge Derbys 152 C2
Doversgreen Sur 51 D9
Dowally Perth 286 C4
Dowanhill Glasgow 267 B11
Dowbridge Lancs 202 G4
Dowdeswell Glos 81 B7
Dowe Hill Norf 161 F10
Dowlais M Tydf 77 D10
Dowlais Top M Tydf 77 D9
Dowland Devon 25 E9
Dowles Worcs 116 B5
Dowlesgreen Wokingham 65 F10
Dowlish Ford Som 28 E5
Dowlish Wake Som 28 E5
Downall Green Gtr Man 194 G5
Down Ampney Glos 81 F10
Downan Moray 301 F11
S Ayrs 244 G3
Downcraig Ferry N Ayrs 266 D3
Downderry Corn 6 E6
Downe London 68 G2
Downend Glos 80 F4
IoW 20 D6
S Glos 60 D6
W Berks 64 D3
Down End Som 43 E10
Downfield Dundee 287 D7
Down Field Cambs 124 C2
Downgate Corn 11 G11
Corn 12 G3
Down Hall Cumb 239 G7
Downham Essex 88 F2
Lancs 203 E11
London 67 E11
Northumb 263 C9
Downham Market Norf 140 C2
Down Hatherley Glos 99 G7
Downhead Som 29 B9
Som 45 D7
Downhead Park M Keynes 103 C7
Downhill Corn 5 B7
Perth 286 D4
T&W 243 F9
Downholland Cross Lancs 193 F11
Downholme N Yorks 224 F2
Downicary Devon 12 C3
Downies Aberds 293 D11
Downinney Corn 11 C10
Downley Bucks 84 G4
Down Park W Sus 51 F10
Downs V Glam 58 E6
Down St Mary Devon 26 G2
Downside C Beds 103 G10
E Sus 23 E9
N Som 60 F3
Som 44 D6
Sur 50 B6
Sur 51 B7
Down Street E Sus 36 C6
Down Thomas Devon 7 E10
Downton Hants 19 C11
Powys 114 E4
Shrops 149 G10
Wilts 31 C11
Downton on the Rock Hereford 115 C8
Dowsby Lincs 156 D2
Dowsdale Lincs 156 G5
Dowslands Som 28 C2
Dowthwaitehead Cumb 230 G3
Doxey Staffs 151 E8
Doxford Park T&W 243 G9
Doynton S Glos 61 E8
Drabblegate Norf 160 D4
Draethen Newport 59 B8
Draffan S Lanark 268 F5
Dragley Beck Cumb 210 D5
Dragonby N Lincs 200 E2
Dragons Green W Sus 35 C10
Drakehouse S Yorks 186 E6
Drakeland Corner Devon 7 D11
Drakelow Worcs 132 G6
Drakemyre Aberds 303 F9
N Ayrs 266 E5
Drake's Broughton Worcs 99 B8
Drakes Cross Worcs 117 B11
Drakestone Green Suff 107 B9
Drakewalls Corn 12 G4
Draughton N Yorks 204 C6
W Nhants 120 B5
Drawbridge Corn 6 B3
Drax N Yorks 199 B7
Draycot Oxon 83 D10
Draycot Cerne Wilts 62 D2
Draycote Warks 119 C8
Draycot Fitz Payne Wilts 62 G6
Draycot Foliat Swindon 63 D7
Draycott Derbys 153 C8
Glos 80 E2
Glos 100 D3
Shrops 132 E6
Som 29 C8
Som 44 C3
Worcs 99 B7
Draycott in the Clay Staffs 152 D3
Draycott in the Moors Staffs 169 G7
Drayford Devon 26 E3
Drayton Leics 136 E6
Lincs 156 B4
Norf 160 G3
Oxon 83 G7
Oxon 101 C8
Ptsmth 33 F11
Som 28 C6
Som 29 D7
Warks 118 F3
W Nhants 119 E11
Worcs 117 B8
Drayton Bassett Staffs 134 C3
Drayton Beauchamp Bucks 84 C6
Drayton Parslow Bucks 102 F6
Drayton St Leonard Oxon 83 F10
Drebley N Yorks 205 B7
Dreemskerry IoM 192 C5
Dreenhill Pembs 72 C6
Drefach Carms 75 C8
Carms 92 G5
Carms 93 D7
Dre-fach Carms 75 B11
Ceredig 93 B10
Drefelin Carms 93 D7
Dreggie Highld 301 G10
Dreghorn Edin 270 B4
N Ayrs 257 B9
Dre-gôch Denb 165 B10
Drellingore Kent 55 E8
Drem E Loth 281 F10
Dresden Stoke 168 G6
Dreumasdal W Isles 297 H3
Drewsteignton Devon 13 C10
Driby Lincs 190 G5
Driffield E Yorks 208 B6
Glos 81 F9
Drift Corn 1 D4
Drigg Cumb 219 F11
Drighlington W Yorks 197 B8
Drimnin Highld 289 D7
Drimnin Ho Highld 289 D7
Drimpton Dorset 28 F6
Drimsynie Argyll 284 G5
Dringhoe E Yorks 209 C9
Dringhouses York 207 D7
Drinisiadar W Isles 305 J3
Drinkstone Suff 125 E9
Drinkstone Green Suff 125 E9
Drishaig Argyll 284 F5
Drissaig Argyll 275 B10
Drive End Dorset 29 F9
Driver's End Herts 86 B2
Drochedlie Aberds 302 C5
Drochil Borders 270 G3
Drointon Staffs 151 D10
Droitwich Spa Worcs 117 E7
Droman Highld 306 D6
Dromore Dumfries 237 C7
Dron Perth 286 F5
Dronfield Derbys 186 F5
Dronfield Woodhouse Derbys 186 F4
Drongan E Ayrs 257 F10
Dronley Angus 287 D7
Droop Dorset 30 F3
Drope Cardiff 58 D6
Dropping Well S Yorks 186 C5
Droughduil Dumfries 236 D3
Droxford Hants 33 D10
Droylsden Gtr Man 184 B6
Drub W Yorks 197 B7
Druggers End Worcs 98 D5
Druid Denb 165 G8
Druidston Pembs 72 B5
Druim Highld 301 D9
Druimarbin Highld 290 F2
Druimavuic Argyll 284 C4
Druimdrishaig Argyll 275 F8
Druimindarroch Highld 295 G8
Druimkinnerras Highld 300 F4
Druimnacroish Argyll 288 E6
Druimsornaig Argyll 289 F9
Druimyeon More Argyll 255 B7
Drum Argyll 275 F10
Edin 270 B6
Perth 286 G4
Drumardoch Stirling 285 F10
Drumbeg Highld 306 F6
Drumblade Aberds 302 E5
Drumblair Aberds 302 E6
Drumbuie Dumfries 246 G3
Highld 295 B9
Drumburgh Cumb 239 F7
Drumburn Dumfries 237 C11
Drumchapel Glasgow 277 G10
Drumchardine Highld 300 E5
Drumchork Highld 307 L3
Drumclog S Lanark 258 B4
Drumdelgie Aberds 302 E4
Drumderfit Highld 300 D6
Drumdollo Aberds 302 F6
Drumeldrie Fife 287 G8
Drumelzier Borders 260 C4
Drumfearn Highld 295 D8
Drumgask Highld 291 D8
Drumgelloch N Lanark 268 B5
Drumgley Angus 287 B8
Drumgreen Angus 292 F6
Drumguish Highld 291 D9
Drumhead Aberds 293 B11
Drumin Moray 301 F11
Drumindorsair Highld 300 E4
Drumlasie Aberds 293 C8
Drumlean Stirling 285 G8
Drumlemble Argyll 255 F7
Drumliah Highld 309 K6
Drumligair Aberds 293 B11
Drumlithie Aberds 293 E9
Drumloist Stirling 285 G10
Drummersdale Lancs 193 E11
Drummick Perth 286 E3
Drummoddie Dumfries 236 E5
Drummond Highld 300 C6
Drummore Dumfries 236 F3
Drummuir Moray 302 E3
Drummuir Castle Moray 302 E3
Drumnadrochit Highld 300 G5
Drumnagorrach Moray 302 D5
Drumness Perth 286 F2
Drumoak Aberds 293 D9
Drumore Argyll 255 E8
Drumpark Dumfries 247 G9
Drumpellier N Lanark 268 B4
Drumphail Dumfries 236 C4
Drumrash Dumfries 237 B8
Drumrunie Highld 307 J6
Drumry W Dunb 277 G10
Drums Aberds 303 G9
Drumsallie Highld 289 B11
Drumsmittal Highld 300 E6
Drumstinchall Dumfries 237 D10
Drumsturdy Angus 287 D8
Drumtochty Castle Aberds 293 F8
Drumtroddan Dumfries 236 E5
Drumuie Highld 298 E4
Drumuillie Highld 301 G9
Drumvaich Stirling 285 G10
Drumwalt Dumfries 236 D5
Drumwhindle Aberds 303 F9
Drunkendub Angus 287 C10
Drury Flint 166 C3
Drurylane Norf 141 C8
Drury Lane Wrex 167 G7
Drury Square Norf 159 F8
Drybeck Cumb 222 B3
Drybridge Moray 302 C4
N Ayrs 257 B9
Drybrook Glos 79 B10
Dryburgh Borders 262 C3
Dryden Borders 261 E11
Dry Doddington Lincs 172 F4
Dry Drayton Cambs 123 E7
Dryhill Kent 52 B3
Dry Hill Hants 49 F7
Dryhope Borders 261 E7
Drylaw Edin 280 F4
Drym Corn 2 C4
Drymen Stirling 277 D9
Drymere Norf 140 B5
Drymuir Aberds 303 E9
Drynachan Lodge Highld 301 F8
Drynain Argyll 276 D3
Drynham Wilts 45 B11
Drynie Park Highld 300 D5
Drynoch Highld 294 B6
Dry Sandford Oxon 83 E7
Dryslwyn Carms 93 G11
Dry Street Essex 69 B7
Dryton Shrops 131 B11
Drywells Aberds 302 D6
Duag Bridge Highld 309 K3
Duartbeg Highld 306 F6
Duartmore Bridge Highld 306 F6
Dubbs Cross Devon 12 C3
Dubford Aberds 303 C8
Dubhchladach Argyll 275 G9
Dublin Suff 126 D3
Dubton Angus 287 B9
Dubwath Cumb 229 E9
Duchally Highld 309 H3
Duchlage Argyll 276 D6
Duchrae Dumfries 246 G5
Duck Corner Suff 109 C7
Duck End Bedford 103 C11
Bedford 121 G9
Bucks 102 F5
Cambs 122 E4
Essex 105 G10
Essex 106 E3
Essex 106 F3
Duckend Green Essex 106 G4
Duckhole S Glos 79 G10
Duckington Ches W 167 E7
Ducklington Oxon 82 D5
Duckmanton Derbys 186 G6
Duck's Cross Bedford 122 F2
Ducks Island London 86 F2
Duckswich Worcs 98 D6
Dudbridge Glos 80 E4
Dudden Hill London 67 B8
Duddenhoe End Essex 105 D9
Duddingston Edin 280 G5
Duddington N Nhants 137 C9
Duddlestone Som 28 C2
Duddleswell E Sus 37 B7
Duddlewick Shrops 132 G3
Duddo Northumb 273 G8
Duddon Ches W 167 C8
Duddon Bridge Cumb 210 B3
Duddon Common Ches W 167 B8
Dudleston Shrops 148 B6
Dudleston Grove Shrops 149 B7
Dudleston Heath (Criftins) Shrops 149 B7
Dudley T&W 243 C7
W Mid 133 E8
Dudley Hill W Yorks 205 G9
Dudley Port W Mid 133 E9
Dudley's Fields W Mid 133 C9
Dudley Wood W Mid 133 F8
Dudlows Green Warr 183 E10
Dudsbury Dorset 19 B7
Dudswell Herts 85 D7
Dudwells Pembs 91 G8
Duerdon Devon 24 D4
Duffield Derbys 170 G4
Duffieldbank Derbys 170 G5
Duffryn Neath 57 B10
Newport 59 B9
Shrops 130 G4
Dufftown Moray 302 F3
Duffus Moray 301 C11
Dufton Cumb 231 F9
Duggleby N Yorks 217 F7
Duich Argyll 254 B4
Duiletter Argyll 284 D5
Duinish Perth 291 G8
Duirinish Highld 295 B9
Duisdalebeg Highld 295 D8
Duisdalemore Highld 295 D9
Duisky Highld 290 F2
Duke End Warks 134 F4
Dukesfield Northumb 241 F10
Dukestown Bl Gwent 77 C10
Dukinfield Gtr Man 184 B6
Dulas Anglesey 179 D7
Dulcote Som 44 E5
Dulford Devon 27 F9
Dull Perth 286 C2
Dullatur N Lanark 278 F4
Dullingham Cambs 124 F2
Dullingham Ley Cambs 124 F2
Dulnain Bridge Highld 301 G9
Duloch Fife 280 D2
Duloe Bedford 122 E3
Corn 6 D4
Dulsie Highld 301 E9
Dulverton Som 26 B6
Dulwich London 67 E10
Dulwich Village London 67 E10
Dumbarton W Dunb 277 F7
Dumbleton Glos 99 D10
Dumcrieff Dumfries 248 C4
Dumfries Dumfries 237 B11
Dumgoyne Stirling 277 E10
Dummer Hants 48 D5
Dumpford W Sus 34 C4
Dumpinghill Devon 24 F6
Dumpling Green Norf 159 G10
Dumplington Gtr Man 184 B3
Dumpton Kent 71 F11
Dun Angus 287 B10
Dunach Argyll 289 G10
Dunadd Argyll 275 D9
Dunain Ho Highld 300 E6
Dunalastair Perth 285 B11
Dunan Highld 295 C7
Dunans Argyll 275 D9
Argyll 275 D11
Dunball Som 43 E10
Dunbar E Loth 282 F3
Dunbeath Highld 311 G5
Dunbeg Argyll 289 F10
Dunblane Stirling 285 G11
Dunbog Fife 286 F6
Dunbridge Hants 32 B4
Duncansclett Shetland 313 K5
Duncanston Highld 300 D5
Duncanstone Aberds 302 G5
Dun Charlabhaigh W Isles 304 D3
Dunchideock Devon 14 D3
Dunchurch Warks 119 C9
Duncombe Lancs 202 F6
Duncote W Nhants 120 G3
Duncow Dumfries 247 G11
Duncraggan Stirling 285 G9
Duncrievie Perth 286 G5
Duncroisk Stirling 285 D9
Duncton W Sus 35 D7
Dundas Ho Orkney 314 H4
Dundee Dundee 287 D8
Dundeugh Dumfries 246 F3
Dundon Som 44 G3
Dundonald Fife 280 C4
S Ayrs 257 C9
Dundon Hayes Som 44 G3
Dundonnell Highld 307 L5
Dundonnell Hotel Highld 307 L5
Dundonnell House Highld 307 L6
Dundraw Cumb 229 B10
Dundreggan Highld 290 B5
Dundreggan Lodge Highld 290 B5
Dundrennan Dumfries 237 E9
Dundridge Hants 33 D9
Dundry N Som 60 F5
Dundurn Perth 285 E11
Dundyvan N Lanark 268 C4
Dunecht Aberds 293 C9
Dunfermline Fife 279 D11
Dunfield Glos 81 F10
Dunford Bridge S Yorks 197 G7
Dungate Kent 54 B2
Dunge Wilts 45 C11
Dungeness Kent 39 D9
Dungworth S Yorks 186 D3
Dunham Notts 188 G4
Dunham-on-the-Hill Ches W 183 G7
Dunham on Trent Notts 188 G4
Dunhampstead Worcs 117 E8
Dunhampton Worcs 116 D6
Dunham Town Gtr Man 184 D2
Dunham Woodhouses Gtr Man 184 D2
Dunholme Lincs 189 F8
Dunino Fife 287 F9
Dunipace Falk 278 E6
Dunira Perth 285 E11
Dunkeld Perth 286 C4
Dunkerton Bath 45 B8
Dunkeswell Devon 27 F10
Dunkeswick N Yorks 206 D2
Dunkirk Cambs 139 F10
Ches W 182 G5
Kent 54 B5
Norf 160 D4
Nottingham 153 B11
S Glos 61 B9
Staffs 168 E4
Wilts 62 G3
Dunk's Green Kent 52 C6
Dunlappie Angus 293 G7
Dunley Hants 48 C3
Worcs 116 D5
Dunlichity Lodge Highld 300 F6
Dunlop E Ayrs 267 F8
Dunmaglass Lodge Highld 300 G5
Dunmere Corn 5 B10
Dunmore Argyll 275 G8
Falk 279 D7
Highld 300 E5
Dunnerholme Cumb 210 D4
Dunnet Highld 310 B6
Dunnichen Angus 287 C9
Dunnikier Fife 280 C5
Dunninald Angus 287 B11
Dunning Perth 286 F4
Dunnington E Yorks 209 C9
Warks 117 G11
York 207 C9
Dunningwell Cumb 210 C3
Dunnockshaw Lancs 195 B10
Dunnose IoW 21 F7
Dunnsheath Shrops 149 F9
Dunn Street Kent 54 D3
Kent 69 G9
Dunollie Argyll 289 F10
Dunoon Argyll 276 F3
Dunragit Dumfries 236 D3
Dunrobin Mains Highld 311 J2
Dunrostan Argyll 275 E8
Duns Borders 272 E5
Dunsa Derbys 186 G2
Dunsby Lincs 156 D2
Dunscar Gtr Man 195 E8
Dunscore Dumfries 247 G9
Dunscroft S Yorks 199 F7
Dunsdale Redcar 226 B2
Dunsden Green Oxon 65 D8
Dunsfold Sur 50 F4
Dunsfold Common Sur 50 F4
Dunsfold Green Sur 50 F4
Dunsford Devon 14 D2
Sur 50 F4
Dunshalt Fife 286 F6
Dunshillock Aberds 303 E9
Dunsill Notts 171 C7
Dunsinnan Perth 286 D5
Dunskey Ho Dumfries 236 D2
Dunslea Corn 11 G11
Dunsley N Yorks 227 C7
Staffs 133 G7
Dunsmore Bucks 84 D5
Warks 119 B10
Dunsop Bridge Lancs 203 C9
Dunstable C Beds 103 G10
Dunstal Staffs 151 D11
Dunstall Staffs 152 E3
Dunstall Common Worcs 99 C7
Dunstall Green Suff 124 E4
Dunstall Hill W Mid 133 C8
Dunstan Northumb 265 F7
Dunstan Steads Northumb 264 E6
Dunster Som 42 E3
Duns Tew Oxon 101 F9
Dunston Derbys 186 G5
Dunston *continued*
Lincs 173 C9
Norf 142 C4
Staffs 151 F8
T&W 242 E6
Dunstone Devon 7 E11
Devon 8 G5
Dunston Heath Staffs 151 F8
Dunston Hill T&W 242 E6
Dunsville S Yorks 198 F6
Dunswell E Yorks 209 F7
Dunsyre S Lanark 269 F11
Dunterton Devon 12 F3
Dunthrop Oxon 101 F7
Duntisbourne Abbots Glos 81 D7
Duntisbourne Leer Glos 81 D7
Duntisbourne Rouse Glos 81 D7
Duntish Dorset 29 F11
Duntocher W Dunb 277 G9
Dunton Bucks 102 G6
C Beds 104 C4
Norf 159 C7
Dunton Bassett Leics 135 E10
Dunton Green Kent 52 B4
Dunton Patch Norf 159 C7
Dunton Wayletts Essex 87 G11
Duntrune Castle Argyll 275 D8
Duntulm Highld 298 B4
Dunure S Ayrs 257 F7
Dunvant = Dynfant Swansea 56 C5
Dunvegan Highld 298 E2
Dunveth Corn 10 G5
Dunwear Som 43 F10
Dunwich Suff 127 C9
Dunwood Staffs 168 D6
Dupplin Castle Perth 286 F4
Durdar Cumb 239 G10
Durgan Corn 3 D7
Durgates E Sus 52 G6
Durham Durham 233 C11
Durisdeer Dumfries 247 C9
Durisdeermill Dumfries 247 C9
Durkar W Yorks 197 D10
Durleigh Som 43 F9
Durleighmarsh W Sus 34 C3
Durley Hants 33 D8
Wilts 63 G8
Durley Street Hants 33 D8
Durlock Kent 55 B9
Durlow Common Hereford 98 D2
Durn Gtr Man 196 D2
Durnamuck Highld 307 K5
Durness Highld 308 C4
Durnfield Som 29 C7
Durno Aberds 303 G7
Durns Town Hants 19 B11
Duror Highld 289 D11
Durran Argyll 275 C10
Highld 310 C5
Durrant Green Kent 53 F11
Durrants Hants 22 B2
Durrington Wilts 47 E7
W Sus 35 F10
Durrisdale Orkney 314 D3
Dursley Glos 80 F3
Wilts 45 C11
Dursley Cross Glos 98 G3
Durston Som 28 B3
Durweston Dorset 30 F5
Dury Shetland 313 G6
Duryard Devon 14 C4
Duston W Nhants 120 E4
Dutch Village Essex 69 C9
Duthil Highld 301 G9
Dutlas Powys 114 B4
Duton Hill Essex 106 F2
Dutson Corn 12 D2
Dutton Ches W 183 F9
Duxford Cambs 105 B9
Oxon 82 F5
Duxmoor Shrops 115 B8
Dwygyfylchi Conwy 180 F2
Dwyran Anglesey 162 B6
Dwyrhiw Powys 129 C11
Dyce Aberdeen 293 B10
Dyche Som 43 E7
Dye House Northumb 241 F10
Dyer's Common S Glos 60 C5
Dyer's Green Cambs 105 B7
Dyffryn Bridgend 57 C11
Carms 92 G6
Ceredig 110 G5
Pembs 91 D8
Dyffryn Ardudwy Gwyn 145 E11
Dyffryn-bern Ceredig 110 G5
Dyffryn Castell Ceredig 128 G5
Dyffryn Ceidrych Carms 94 F4
Dyffryn Cellwen Neath 76 D5
Dyke Lincs 156 E2
Moray 301 D9
Dykehead Angus 292 G5
N Lanark 269 D7
Stirling 277 B11
Dykelands Aberds 293 G9
Dykends Angus 286 B6
Dykeside Aberds 303 E7
Dykesmains N Ayrs 266 G5
Dylife Powys 129 E7
Dymchurch Kent 39 B9
Dymock Glos 98 E4
Dynfant = Dunvant Swansea 56 C5
Dyrham S Glos 61 D8
Dysart Fife 280 C6
Dyserth Denb 181 F9

E

Eabost Highld 294 B5
Eabost West Highld 298 E3
Each End Kent 55 B10
Eachway Worcs 117 B9
Eachwick Northumb 242 C4
Eadar Dha Fhadhail W Isles 304 E2
Eagland Hill Lancs 202 D4
Eagle Lincs 172 B5
Eagle Barnsdale Lincs 172 B5
Eagle Moor Lincs 172 B5
Eaglesfield Cumb 229 F7
Dumfries 238 C6
Eaglesham E Renf 267 E11
Eaglestone M Keynes 103 D7
Eaglethorpe N Nhants 137 E11
Eagle Tor Derbys 170 C2
Eagley Gtr Man 195 E8
Eairy IoM 192 E3
Eakley Lanes M Keynes 120 G6
Eakring Notts 171 C11
Ealand N Lincs 199 E9
Ealing London 67 C7
Eals Northumb 240 F5
Eamont Bridge Cumb 230 F6
Earby Lancs 204 D3
Earcroft Blackburn 195 C7
Eardington Shrops 132 E4
Eardisland Hereford 115 F8
Eardisley Hereford 96 B6
Eardiston Shrops 149 D7
Worcs 116 D3
Earith Cambs 123 C7
Earle Northumb 263 D11
Earlestown Mers 183 B9
Earley Wokingham 65 E9
Earlham Norf 142 B4
Earlish Highld 298 C3
Earls Barton N Nhants 121 E7
Earls Colne Essex 107 F7
Earl's Common Worcs 117 F9
Earl's Court London 67 D9
Earl's Croome Worcs 99 C7
Earlsdon W Mid 118 B6
Earl's Down E Sus 23 B10
Earlsferry Fife 281 B9
Earlsfield Lincs 155 B8
London 67 E9
Earlsford Aberds 303 F8
Earl's Green Suff 125 D10
Earlsheaton W Yorks 197 C9
Earl Shilton Leics 135 D9
Earlsmill Moray 301 D9
Earl Soham Suff 126 E4
Earl Sterndale Derbys 169 B9
Earlston Borders 262 B3
E Ayrs 257 B10
Earlstone Common Hants 64 G3
Earl Stoneham Suff 126 F2
Earl Stonham Suff 126 F2
Earlstoun Dumfries 246 G4
Earlswood Mon 79 F7
Sur 51 D9
Warks 118 C2
Earnley W Sus 22 D4
Earnock S Lanark 268 E3
Earnshaw Bridge Lancs 194 C4
Earsairidh W Isles 297 M3
Earsdon T&W 243 C8
Earsham Norf 142 F6
Earsham Street Suff 126 B4
Earswick York 207 B8
Eartham W Sus 22 B6
Earthcott Green S Glos 61 B7
Easby N Yorks 224 E3
N Yorks 225 D11
Easdale Argyll 275 B8
Easebourne W Sus 34 C5
Easenhall Warks 119 B9
Eashing Sur 50 E2
Easington Bucks 83 C11
Durham 234 C4
E Yorks 201 D11
Lancs 203 C10
Northumb 264 C4
Oxon 83 F11
Oxon 101 D9
Redcar 226 B4
Easington Colliery Durham 234 C4
Easington Lane T&W 234 B3
Easingwold N Yorks 215 F10
Easole Street Kent 55 C9
Eason's Green E Sus 23 B8
Eassie Angus 287 C7
East Aberthaw V Glam 58 F4
Eastacombe Devon 25 B8
Devon 25 C9
Eastacott Devon 25 C10
East Acton London 67 C8
East Adderbury Oxon 101 D9
East Allington Devon 8 F5
East Amat Highld 309 K4
East Anstey Devon 26 B5
East Anton Hants 47 D11
East Appleton N Yorks 224 F4
East Ardsley W Yorks 197 B10
East Ashling W Sus 22 B4
East Aston Hants 48 D2
East Auchronie Aberds 293 C10
East Ayton N Yorks 217 B9
East Bank Bl Gwent 78 D2
East Barkwith Lincs 189 E11
East Barming Kent 53 C8
East Barnby N Yorks 226 C6
East Barnet London 86 F3
East Barns E Loth 282 F4
East Barsham Norf 159 C8
East Barton Suff 125 D8
East Beach W Sus 22 E5
East Beckham Norf 177 E11
East Bedfont London 66 E5
East Bergholt Suff 107 D11
East Bierley W Yorks 197 B7
East Bilney Norf 159 F9
East Blackdene Durham 232 D3
East Blatchington E Sus 23 E7
East Bloxworth Dorset 18 C3
East Boldon T&W 243 E9
East Boldre Hants 32 G5
East Bonhard Perth 286 E5
Eastbourne Darl 224 C6
E Sus 23 F10
East Bower Som 43 F10
East Brent Som 43 C11
Eastbridge Suff 127 D9
East Bridgford Notts 171 G11
East Briscoe Durham 223 B9
Eastbrook Som 28 C2
V Glam 59 E7
East Buckland Devon 41 G7
East Budleigh Devon 15 E7
Eastburn E Yorks 208 B5
W Yorks 204 E6
Eastburn Br W Yorks 204 E6
East Burnham Bucks 66 C3
East Burrafirth Shetland 313 H5
East Burton Dorset 18 D2
Eastbury London 85 G9
W Berks 63 D10
East Butsfield Durham 233 B8
East Butterleigh Devon 27 F7
East Butterwick N Lincs 199 F10
Eastby N Yorks 204 C6
East Cairnbeg Aberds 293 F9
East Calder W Loth 269 B11
East Carleton Norf 142 C3
East Carlton N Nhants 136 F6
W Yorks 205 E10
East Chaldon or Chaldon Herring Dorset 17 E11
East Challow Oxon 63 B11
East Charleton Devon 8 G5
East Chelborough Dorset 29 F9
East Chiltington E Sus 36 D5
East Chinnock Som 29 E7
East Chisenbury Wilts 46 C6
East Cholderton Hants 47 D9
Eastchurch Kent 70 E3
East Clandon Sur 50 C5
East Claydon Bucks 102 F4
East Clevedon N Som 60 E2
East Clyne Highld 311 J3
East Clyth Highld 310 F7
East Coker Som 29 E8
Eastcombe Glos 80 E5
East Combe Som 43 G7
East Common N Yorks 207 G8
East Compton Dorset 30 D5
Som 44 E6
East Cornworthy Devon 8 D6
Eastcote London 66 B6
W Mid 118 B3
W Nhants 120 G3
Eastcote Village London 66 B6
Eastcott Corn 24 D3
Wilts 46 B4
East Cottingwith E Yorks 207 E10
Eastcotts Bedford 103 B11
Eastcourt Wilts 63 G8
Wilts 81 G7
East Cowes IoW 20 B6
East Cowick E Yorks 199 C7
East Cowton N Yorks 224 E6
East Cramlington Northumb 243 B7
East Cranmore Som 45 E7
East Creech Dorset 18 E4
East Croachy Highld 300 G6
East Croftmore Highld 291 B11
East Curthwaite Cumb 230 B2
East Dean E Sus 23 F9
Glos 98 G3
Hants 32 B3
W Sus 34 E6
East Dene S Yorks 186 C6
East Denton T&W 242 D6
East Didsbury Gtr Man 184 C5
Eastdon Devon 14 F5
Eastdown Devon 8 F6
East Down Devon 40 E6
East Drayton Notts 188 F3
East Dulwich London 67 E10
East Dundry N Som 60 F5
East Ella Hull 200 B5
East End Bedford 122 F2
Bucks 84 B4
C Beds 103 C9
Dorset 18 B5
Essex 89 D8
E Yorks 201 B9
E Yorks 209 B9
E Yorks 209 G9
Glos 81 E11
Hants 20 B3
Hants 33 C11
Hants 64 G2
Herts 105 F9
Kent 53 E11
Kent 53 F10
Kent 70 E3
M Keynes 103 C8
N Som 60 E3
Oxon 82 C5
Oxon 101 D9
Oxon 101 E7
S Glos 61 E9
Som 29 B10
Som 44 C5
Som 45 D7
Suff 108 E2
Suff 126 F3
East End Green Herts 86 C3
Easter Aberchalder Highld 291 B7
Easter Ardross Highld 300 B6
Easter Balgedie Perth 286 G5
Easter Balmoral Aberds 292 D4
Easter Boleskine Highld 300 G5
Easter Brackland Stirling 285 G10
Easter Brae Highld 300 C6
Easter Cardno Aberds 303 C9
Easter Compton S Glos 60 C5
Easter Cringate Stirling 278 D4
Easter Culfosie Aberds 293 C9
Easter Davoch Aberds 292 C6
Easter Earshaig Dumfries 248 C2
Easter Ellister Argyll 254 B3
Easter Fearn Highld 309 L6
Easter Galcantray Highld 301 E8
Eastergate W Sus 22 B6
Easterhouse Glasgow 268 B3
Easter Housebyres Borders 262 B2
Easter Howgate Midloth 270 C4
Easter Howlaws Borders 272 G4
Easter Kinkell Highld 300 D5
Easter Knox Angus 287 D9
Easter Langlee Borders 262 B2
Easter Lednathie Angus 292 G5
Easter Milton Highld 301 D9
Easter Moniack Highld 300 E5
Eastern Green W Mid 134 G5
Easter Ord Aberdeen 293 C10
Easter Quarff Shetland 313 K6
Easter Rhynd Perth 286 F5
Easter Row Stirling 278 B5
Easterside Mbro 225 B10
Easter Silverford Aberds 303 C7
Easter Skeld Shetland 313 J5
Easter Softlaw Borders 263 C7
Easterton Wilts 46 C4
Easterton of Lenabo Aberds 303 E10
Easterton Sands Wilts 46 B4
Eastertown Som 43 C10
Eastertown of Auchleuchries Aberds 303 F10
Easter Tulloch Highld 291 B11
Easter Whyntie Aberds 302 C6
East Everleigh Wilts 47 C8
East Ewell Sur 67 G8
East Farleigh Kent 53 C8
East Farndon W Nhants 136 F4
East Fen Common Cambs 124 C2
East Ferry Lincs 188 B4
Eastfield Borders 262 D2
Bristol 60 D5
N Lanark 269 C7
N Lanark 278 G4
Northumb 243 B7
N Yorks 217 C10
Pboro 138 D4
S Lanark 268 C2
S Yorks 197 G9
Eastfield Hall Northumb 252 B6
East Fields W Berks 64 F3
East Finchley London 67 B9
East Finglassie Fife 280 B5
East Firsby Lincs 189 D8
East Fleet Dorset 17 E8
East Fortune E Loth 281 F10
East Garforth W Yorks 206 G4
East Garston W Berks 63 D11
Eastgate Durham 232 D5
Norf 160 E2
Pboro 138 D4
East Gateshead T&W 243 E7
East Ginge Oxon 64 B2
East Gores Essex 107 G7
East Goscote Leics 154 G2

East Grafton Wilts 63 G9
East Grange Moray. 301 C10
East Green Hants 49 E9
Suff. 124 G3
Suff. 127 D8
East Grimstead Wilts 32 B2
East Grinstead W Sus 51 F11
East Guldeford E Sus. 38 C6
East Haddon W Nhants . . 120 D3
East Hagbourne Oxon. 64 B4
Easthall Herts 104 G3
East Halton N Lincs. 200 D6
Eastham Mers. 182 E5
Worcs 116 D3
East Ham London. 68 C2
Eastham Ferry Mers 182 E5
East Hampnett W Sus 22 B6
Easthampstead Brack. . . . 65 F11
Easthampton Hereford . . . 115 E8
East Hanney Oxon 82 G6
East Hanningfield Essex . .88 E3
East Hardwick W Yorks . . 198 D3
East Harling Norf. 141 F9
East Harlsey N Yorks 225 F8
East Harnham Wilts 31 B10
East Harptree Bath 44 B5
East Hartford Northumb . 243 B7
East Harting W Sus 34 D3
East Hatch Wilts. 30 B6
East Hatley Cambs 122 G5
Easthaugh Norf. 159 F11
East Hauxwell N Yorks . . . 224 G3
East Haven Angus. 287 D9
Eastheath Wokingham 65 F10
East Heckington Lincs . 173 G11
East Hedleyhope
Durham. 233 C9
East Helmsdale Highld . . 311 H4
East Hendred Oxon 64 B3
East Herringthorpe
S Yorks 187 C7
East Herrington T&W . . . 243 G9
East Heslerton N Yorks . . 217 D8
East Hewish N Som. 59 G11
East Hill Kent 68 G5
East Hoathly E Sus 23 B8
East Hogaland Shetland . 313 K5
East Holme Dorset 18 D3
East Holton Dorset. 18 C5
East Holywell Northumb . 243 C8
Easthope Shrops 131 D11
Easthopewood Shrops . 131 D11
East Horndon Essex 68 B6
Easthorpe Essex. 107 G8
Leics 154 B6
Notts. 172 E2
East Horrington Som 44 D5
East Horsley Sur. 50 C5
East Horton Northumb. . . 264 C2
Easthouse Shetland 313 J5
Easthouses Midloth 270 B6
East Howdon T&W. 243 D8
East Howe BCP 19 B7
East Huntspill Som 43 E10
East Hyde C Beds. 85 B10
East Ilkerton Devon 41 D8
East Ilsley W Berks 64 C3
Easting Orkney 314 A7
Eastington Devon. 26 F2
Glos 80 D3
Glos 81 C10
East Keal Lincs. 174 C5
East Kennett Wilts. 62 F6
East Keswick W Yorks . . . 206 E3
East Kilbride S Lanark 268 E2
East Kimber Devon. 12 B5
East Kingston W Sus 35 G9
East Kirkby Lincs 174 C4
East Knapton N Yorks 217 D7
East Knighton Dorset 18 D2
East Knowstone Devon. . . . 26 C4
East Knoyle Wilts 45 G11
East Kyloe Northumb 264 B3
East Kyo Durham 242 G5
East Lambrook Som 28 D6
East Lamington Highld . . . 301 B7
Eastland Gate Hants 33 E11
East Langdon Kent. 55 D10
East Langton Leics. 136 E4
East Langwell Highld. . . . 309 J7
East Lavant W Sus. 22 B5
East Lavington W Sus 34 D6
East Law Northumb. 242 G3
East Layton N Yorks 224 D3
Eastleach Martin Glos 82 D2
Eastleach Turville Glos . 81 D11
East Leake Notts. 153 D11
East Learmouth
Northumb 263 B9
Eastleigh Devon 25 B7
Hants 32 D6
East Leigh Devon 8 E3
Devon. 25 F11
East Lexham Norf. 159 F7
East Lilburn Northumb. . . . 264 E2
Eastling Kent 54 B3
East Linton E Loth 281 F11
East Liss Hants 34 B3
East Lockinge Oxon. 64 B2
East Loftus Redcar. 226 B4
East Looe Corn 6 E5
East Lound N Lincs 188 B3
East Lulworth Dorset 18 E3
East Lutton N Yorks 217 F8
East Lydeard Som. 27 B11
East Lydford Som. 44 G5
East Lyng Som 28 B4
East Mains Aberds 293 D8
Borders 271 F11
S Lanark 268 E2
East Malling Kent. 53 B8
East Malling Heath Kent . . 53 B7
East March Angus. 287 D8
East Marden W Sus 34 E4
East Markham Notts 188 G2
East Marsh NE Lincs 201 E9
East Martin Hants 31 D9
East Marton N Yorks. 204 C4
East Melbury Dorset 30 C5
East Meon Hants. 33 C11
East Mere Devon. 27 D7
East Mersea Essex. 89 C9
East Mey Highld. 310 B7
East Molesey Sur 67 F7
Eastmoor Derbys 186 G4
Norf 140 C4
East Moor W Yorks 197 C10
East Moors Cardiff 59 D8
East Morden Dorset. 18 B4
East Morton W Yorks 205 E7
East Moulsecoomb
Brighton 36 F4
East Ness N Yorks 216 D3
East Newton E Yorks 209 F11
N Yorks 216 D2
Eastney Ptsmth 21 B9
Eastnor Hereford. 98 D4
East Norton Leics. 136 C5
East Nynehead Som 27 C11
East Oakley Hants 48 C5
Eastoft N Lincs 199 D10
East Ogwell Devon 14 G2
Eastoke Hants 21 B10
Easton Bristol 60 E6
Cambs 122 C2
Cumb 239 C10
Cumb 239 F7
Devon. 8 F3
Devon. 13 D10
Dorset 17 G9
Hants 48 G4
IoW 20 D2
Lincs. 155 D8
Norf 160 G2
Som 44 D4
Suff. 126 F5
W Berks 64 E2
Wilts. 61 E11
Easton Grey Wilts. 61 B11
Easton in Gordano
N Som 60 D4
Easton Maudit N Nhants . 121 F7
Easton on the Hill
N Nhants. 137 C10
Easton Royal Wilts. 63 G8
Easton Town Som. 44 G5
Wilts. 61 B11
East Orchard Dorset 30 D4
East Ord Northumb 273 E9
Eastover Som. 43 F10
East Panson Devon. 12 C3
Eastpark Dumfries 238 D2
East Parley BCP 19 B8
East Peckham Kent 53 D7
East Pennard Som 44 F5
East Perry Cambs 122 D3
East Portholland Corn 5 G9
East Portlemouth Devon . . .9 G9
East Prawle Devon 9 G10
East Preston W Sus 35 G9
East Pulham Dorset. 30 F2
East Putford Devon 24 D5
East Quantoxhead Som . . 42 E6
East Rainton T&W 234 B2
East Ravendale NE Lincs . 190 B2
East Raynham Norf 159 D7
Eastrea Cambs. 138 D5
East Rhidorroch Lodge
Highld 307 K7
Eastriggs Dumfries 238 D6
East Rigton W Yorks. 206 E3
Eastrington E Yorks 199 B9
Eastrip Wilts 61 E10
East Rolstone N Som 59 G11
Eastrop Hants 48 C6
East Rounton N Yorks 225 E8
East Row N Yorks 227 C7
East Rudham Norf 158 D6
East Runton Norf 177 E11
East Ruston Norf 160 D6
Eastry Kent 55 C10
East Saltoun E Loth 271 B9
East Sheen London. 67 D8
East Sherford Devon. 7 E11
East Skelston Dumfries . . 247 F8
East Sleekburn
Northumb 253 G7
East Somerton Norf 161 F9
East Stanley Durham. 242 G6
East Stockwith Lincs. 188 C3
East Stoke Dorset. 18 D3
Notts. 172 F3
Som 29 D7
East Stour Dorset 30 C4
East Stour Common
Dorset. 30 C4
East Stourmouth Kent 71 G9
East Stowford Devon. 25 B10
East Stratton Hants. 48 F4
East Street Kent 55 B10
Som 44 F4
East Studdal Kent. 55 D10
East Suisnish Highld 295 B7
East Taphouse Corn 6 C3
East-the-Water Devon 25 B7
East Third Borders 262 B4
East Thirston Northumb . 252 D5
East Tilbury Thurrock 69 D7
East Tisted Hants 49 G8
East Torrington Lincs . . . 189 E10
East Town Som 42 G6
Som 44 E6
Wilts. 45 B11
East Trewent Pembs 73 F8
East Tuddenham Norf . . 159 G11
East Tuelmenna Corn 6 B4
East Tytherley Hants. 32 B3
East Tytherton Wilts. 62 E3
East Village Devon. 26 F4
V Glam 58 E3
Eastville Bristol. 60 E6
Lincs 174 D6
East Wall Shrops 131 E10
East Walton Norf 158 F4
East Water Som. 44 C4
East Week Devon 13 C9
Eastwell Leics 154 D5
East Wellow Hants 32 C4
Eastwell Park Kent 54 D4
East Wemyss Fife 280 B6
East Whitburn W Loth 269 B9
Eastwick Herts 86 C6
Shetland 312 F5
East Wickham London. 68 D3
East Williamston Pembs . . . 73 E9
East Winch Norf 158 F3
East Winterslow Wilts 47 G8
East Wittering W Sus 21 B11
East Witton N Yorks 214 B2
Eastwood Hereford 98 C2
Notts. 171 F7
Southend 69 B10
S Yorks 186 C6
W Yorks. 196 B3
East Woodburn
Northumb. 251 F10
Eastwood End Cambs 139 E8
Eastwood Hall Notts. 171 F7
East Woodhay Hants 64 G2
East Woodlands Som 45 E9
East Worldham Hants. 49 F8
East Worlington Devon. 26 E3
East Worthing W Sus. 35 G11
East Wretham Norf 141 E8
East Youlstone Devon. 24 D3
Eathorpe Warks 119 D7
Eaton Ches E. 168 B5
Ches W 167 C9
Hereford. 115 F10
Leics 154 D5
Norf 142 B4
Notts. 188 F2
Oxon. 82 E6
Shrops 131 F7
Shrops 131 F10
Eaton Bishop Hereford 97 D8
Eaton Bray C Beds. 103 G9
Eaton Constantine
Shrops 131 B11
Eaton Ford Cambs 122 E3
Eaton Green C Beds 103 G9
Eaton Hastings Oxon. 82 F3
Eaton Mascott Shrops . . 131 B10
Eaton on Tern Shrops . . . 150 E3
Eaton Socon Cambs. 122 F3
Eaton upon Tern Shrops . 150 E3
Eau Brink Norf. 157 F11
Eau Withington
Hereford. 97 C10
Eaves Green W Mid. 134 G5
Eavestone N Yorks 214 F4
Ebberly Hill Devon 25 D9
Ebberston N Yorks 217 C7
Ebbesbourne Wake Wilts . 31 C7
Ebblake Hants 31 F10
Ebbw Vale Bl Gwent 77 D11
Ebchester Durham 242 F4
Ebdon N Som. 59 G11
Ebernoe W Sus 35 B7
Ebford Devon 14 D5
Ebley Glos 80 D4
Ebnal Ches W 167 F7
Ebnall Hereford 115 F9
Ebreywood Shrops 149 F10
Ebrington Glos 100 C3
Ecchinswell Hants 48 B4
Ecclaw Borders 272 B5
Ecclefechan Dumfries . . . 238 C5
Eccle Riggs Cumb. 210 B4
Eccles Borders. 272 G5
Gtr Man 184 B3
Kent 69 G8
Ecclesall S Yorks 186 E4
Ecclesfield S Yorks 186 C5
Ecclesgreig Aberds 293 G9
Eccleshall Staffs. 150 D6
Eccleshill W Yorks. 205 F9
Ecclesmachan W Loth . . 279 G11
Eccles on Sea Norf. 161 D8
Eccles Road Norf 141 E10
Eccleston Ches W 166 C6
Lancs 194 D4
Mers 183 B7
Eccleston Park Mers. 183 C7
Eccliffe Dorset. 30 B3
Eccup W Yorks 205 E11
Echt Aberds. 293 C9
Eckford Borders 262 D6
Eckfordmoss Borders 262 D6
Eckington Derbys. 186 F6
Worcs 99 C8
Eckington Corner E Sus . . 23 D8
Ecklands S Yorks 197 G8
Eckworthy Devon. 24 D6
Ecton N Nhants. 120 E6
Staffs 169 D9
Ecton Brook W Nhants. . . . 120 E6
Edale Derbys. 185 D10
Edale End Derbys 185 D11
Edbrook Som. 43 E8
Edburton W Sus. 36 E2
Edderside Cumb 229 B7
Edderton Highld 309 L7
Eddington Kent. 71 F7
W Berks 63 F10
Eddistone Devon. 24 C3
Eddleston Borders 270 F4
Eddlewood S Lanark 268 E4
Edenbridge Kent 52 D2
Edenfield Lancs 195 D9
Edenhall Cumb 231 E7
Edenham Lincs 155 E11
Eden Mount Cumb 211 D8
Eden Park London. 67 F11
Edensor Derbys. 170 B2
Edentaggart Argyll 276 C6
Edenthorpe S Yorks 198 F6
Edentown Cumb 239 F9
Eden Vale Durham 234 D4
Wilts. 45 C11
Ederline Argyll. 275 C9
Edern Gwyn 144 B5
Edford Som. 45 D7
Edgarley Som. 44 F4
Edgbaston W Mid 133 G11
Edgcote W Nhants. 101 B10
Edgcott Bucks 102 G3
Som 41 F10
Edgcumbe Corn 2 C6
Edge Glos 80 D4
Shrops 131 B7
Edgebolton Shrops 149 E11
Edge End Glos 79 C9
Lancs 203 G10
Edgefield Norf. 159 C11
Edgefield Street Norf. . 159 C11
Edge Fold Blackburn. 195 D8
Gtr Man. 195 F8
Edge Green Ches W 167 E7
Gtr Man. 183 B9
Norf 141 F10
Edgehill Warks 101 B7
Edge Hill Mers. 182 C5
Warks 134 D4
Edgeley Gtr Man. 184 D5
Edge Mount S Yorks 186 C3
Edgerley Shrops 148 F6
Edgerston Borders. 262 G5
Edgerton W Yorks. 196 D6
Edgeside Lancs. 195 C10
Edgeworth Glos 80 D6
Edginswell Devon. 9 B7
Edgiock Worcs. 117 E10
Edgmond Telford. 150 F4
Edgmond Marsh Telford. 150 E4
Edgton Shrops 131 F7
Edgware London 85 G11
Edgwick W Mid 134 G6
Edgworth Blackburn. 195 D8
Edham Borders 262 B6
Edial Staffs 133 B11
Edinample Stirling 285 E9
Edinbane Highld 298 D3
Edinburgh Edin. 280 G5
Edinchip Stirling 285 E9
Edingale Staffs 152 G4
Edingight Ho Moray. 302 D5
Edinglassie Ho Aberds . . . 292 B5
Edingley Notts. 171 D11
Edingthorpe Norf. 160 C6
Edingthorpe Green Norf 160 C6
Edington Som 43 E11
Wilts. 46 C2
Edingworth Som. 43 C11
Edintore Moray 302 E4
Edistone Devon 24 C2
Edithmead Som 43 D10
Edith Weston Rutland 137 B8
Edlaston Derbys 169 G11
Edlesborough Bucks. 85 B7
Edlingham Northumb. 252 B4
Edlington Lincs. 190 G2
Edmondsham Dorset 31 E9
Edmondsley Durham. 233 B10
Edmondstown Rhondda . . . 77 G8
Edmondthorpe Leics. 155 F7
Edmonston S Lanark 269 G11
Edmonstone Orkney 314 D5
Edmonton Corn. 10 G5
London 86 G4
Edmundbyers Durham . . . 242 G2
Ednam Borders 262 B6
Ednaston Derbys. 170 G2
Edney Common Essex . . . 87 E11
Edradynate Perth. 286 B2
Edrom Borders. 272 D6
Edstaston Shrops 149 C10
Edstone Warks 118 E3
Edvin Loach Hereford 116 F3
Edwalton Notts. 153 B11
Edwardstone Suff 107 C8
Edwardsville M Tydf. 77 F9
Edwinsford Carms 94 E2
Edwinstowe Notts 171 B10
Edworth C Beds 104 C4
Edwyn Ralph Hereford . . . 116 F2
Edzell Angus. 293 G7
Efail-fôch Neath. 57 B9
Efail Isaf Rhondda 58 C5
Efailnewydd Gwyn 145 B7
Efailwen Carms. 92 F2
Efenechtyd Denb 165 D10
Effingham Sur. 50 C6
Effirth Shetland 313 H5
Efflinch Staffs 152 F3
Efford Devon 26 G5
Plym 7 D10
Egbury Hants 48 C2
Egdon Worcs 117 G8
Egerton Gtr Man 195 E8
Kent 54 D2
Egerton Forstal Kent . . . 53 D11
Egerton Green Ches E 167 E8
Egford Som. 45 D9
Eggbeare Corn 12 D2
Eggborough N Yorks 198 C5
Eggbuckland Plym. 7 D10
Eggesford Station
Devon 25 E11
Eggington C Beds 103 F9
Egginton Derbys. 152 D5
Egginton Common
Derbys 152 D5
Egglesburn Durham. 232 G5
Egglescliffe Stockton . . . 225 C8
Eggleston Durham 232 G5
Egham Sur 66 E4
Egham Hythe Sur. 66 E5
Egham Wick Sur. 66 E3
Egleton Rutland. 137 B7
Eglingham Northumb. 264 F4
Egloshayle Corn 10 G5
Egloskerry Corn 11 D11
Eglwysbach Conwy 180 G4
Eglwys-Brewis V Glam 58 F4
Eglwys Cross Wrex 167 G7
Eglwys Fach Ceredig 128 D3
Eglwyswen Pembs 92 D3
Eglwyswrw Pembs 92 D2
Egmanton Notts 172 B2
Egmere Norf 159 B8
Egremont Cumb 219 C10
Mers. 182 C4
Egton N Yorks 226 D6
Egton Bridge N Yorks. 226 D6
Egypt Bucks 66 B3
Hants 48 E3
W Berks 64 D2
W Yorks. 205 G7
Eiden Highld 309 J7
Eight Ash Green Essex . . . 107 F8
Eighton Banks T&W 243 F7
Eignaig Highld 289 E9
Eign Hill Hereford 97 D10
Eil Highld 291 B10
Eilanreach Highld 295 D10
Eildon Borders 262 C3
Eileanach Lodge Highld . 300 C5
Eilean Anabaich
W Isles 305 H4
Eilean Darach Highld. 307 L6
Eilean Shona Ho Highld . . 289 B8
Einacleite W Isles. 304 F3
Einsiob = *Evenjobb*
Powys 114 E5
Eisgean W Isles. 305 G5
Eisingrug Gwyn. 146 C2
Eland Green Northumb . . . 242 C5
Elan Village Powys. 113 D8
Elberton S Glos 60 B6
Elborough N Som 43 B11
Elbridge Shrops. 149 E7
W Sus 22 C6
Elburton Plym 7 E10
Elcho Perth. 286 E5
Elcock's Brook Worcs. . 117 E10
Elcombe Glos 80 F3
Swindon 62 C6
Elcot W Berks 63 F11
Eldene Swindon 63 C7
Eldernell Cambs 138 D6
Eldersfield Worcs. 98 E6
Elderslie Renfs 267 C8
Elder Street Essex. 105 E11
Eldon Durham. 233 F10
Eldon Lane Durham 233 F10
Eldrick S Ayrs 245 G7
Eldroth N Yorks 212 F5
Eldwick W Yorks 205 E8
Elemore Vale T&W. 234 B3
Elerch = *Bont-goch*
Ceredig. 128 F3
Elfhowe Cumb 221 F9
Elford Northumb 264 C5
Staffs 152 G3
Elford Closes Cambs 123 C10
Elgin Moray. 302 C2
Elgol Highld 295 D7
Elham Kent. 55 E7
Eliburn W Loth 269 B10
Elie Fife 287 G8
Elim Anglesey 178 D5
Eling Hants 32 E5
W Berks 64 D4
Elishader Highld 298 C5
Elishaw Northumb 251 D9
Elizafield Dumfries 238 C2
Elkesley Notts 187 F11
Elkington W Nhants 120 B2
Elkins Green Essex 87 E10
Elkstone Glos. 81 C7
Ellacombe Torbay. 9 C8
Ellan Highld. 301 G8
Elland W Yorks 196 C6
Elland Lower Edge
W Yorks. 196 C6
Elland Upper Edge
W Yorks. 196 C6
Ellary Argyll 275 F8
Ellastone Staffs. 169 G10
Ellel Lancs. 202 B5
Ellemford Borders 272 C4
Ellenborough Cumb 228 D6
Ellenbrook Herts 86 D2
IoM. 192 E4
Ellenglaze Corn. 4 D5
Ellenhall Staffs 150 D6
Ellen's Green Sur. 50 F5
Ellerbeck N Yorks 225 F8
Ellerburn N Yorks 216 C6
Ellerby N Yorks. 226 C5
Ellerdine Telford 150 E2
Ellerdine Heath Telford . 150 E2
Ellerhayes Devon 27 G7
Elleric Argyll. 284 C4
Ellerker E Yorks 200 B2
Ellerton E Yorks 207 F10
N Yorks 224 F5
Shrops 150 D4
Ellesborough Bucks 84 D4
Ellesmere Shrops 149 C8
Ellesmere Park Gtr Man . 184 B3
Ellesmere Port Ches W . . 182 F6
Ellicombe Som 42 E3
Ellingham Hants. 31 F10
Norf 143 E7
Northumb 264 D5
Ellingstring N Yorks 214 C3
Ellington Cambs 122 C3
Northumb 253 E7
Ellington Thorpe Cambs 122 C3
Elliot Angus. 287 D10
Elliots Green Som 45 D9
Elliot's Town Caerph 77 E10
Ellisfield Hants 48 D6
Elliston Borders. 262 D3
Ellistown Leics 153 G8
Ellon Aberds 303 F9
Ellonby Cumb 230 D4
Ellough Suff 143 F8
Elloughton E Yorks 200 B2
Ellwood Glos 79 D9
Elm Cambs. 139 B9
Elmbridge Glos. 80 B5
Worcs 117 D8
Elm Corner Sur. 50 B5
Elm Cross Wilts. 62 D6
Elmdon Essex 105 D9
W Mid 134 G3
Elmdon Heath W Mid. 134 G3
Elmer W Sus 35 G7
Elmers End London. 67 F11
Elmers Green Lancs 194 F3
Elmers Marsh W Sus 34 B5
Elmesthorpe Leics. 135 D9
Elmfield IoW 21 C8
Elm Hill Dorset. 30 B4
Elmhurst Bucks. 84 B4
Staffs 152 G2
Elmley Castle Worcs 99 C9
Elmley Lovett Worcs 117 D7
Elmore Glos. 80 B3
Elmore Back Glos. 80 B3
Elm Park London 68 B4
Elmscott Devon. 24 C2
Elmsett Suff 107 B11
Elms Green Hereford 115 F10
Worcs 116 D4
Elmslack Lancs 211 D9
Elmstead Essex. 107 F11
London 68 E2
Elmstead Heath Essex . 107 G11
Elmstead Market
Essex 107 G11
Elmsted Kent 54 E6
Elmsthorpe Leics 135 D9
Elmstone Kent. 71 G9
Elmstone Hardwicke
Glos. 99 F8
Elmswell E Yorks 208 B5
Suff. 125 E9
Elmton Derbys. 187 G8
Elness Orkney. 314 C6
Elphin Highld 307 H7
Elphinstone E Loth 281 G7
Elrick Aberds 293 C10
Elrig Dumfries. 236 E5
Elrigbeag Argyll 284 F5
Elrington Northumb 241 E9
Elscar S Yorks 197 G11
Elsdon Hereford. 114 G6
Northumb 251 E10
Elsecar S Yorks 186 B5
S Yorks 197 G11
Elsenham Essex 105 F10
Elsenham Sta Essex 105 F10
Elsfield Oxon 83 C8
Elsham N Lincs. 200 E4
Elsing Norf 159 F11
Elslack N Yorks. 204 D4
Elson Hants 33 G10
Shrops 149 B7
Elsrickle S Lanark 269 G11
Elstead Sur. 50 E2
Elsted W Sus. 34 D4
Elsthorpe Lincs 155 E11
Elstob Durham 234 G2
Elston Devon 26 G3
Notts. 172 F3
Wilts. 46 E5
Elstone Devon 25 D11
Elstow Bedford. 103 B11
Elstree Herts 85 F11
Elstronwick E Yorks 209 G10
Elswick Lancs 202 F4
T&W 242 E6
Elswick Leys Lancs. 202 F4
Elsworth Cambs 122 E6
Elterwater Cumb. 220 E6
Eltham London. 68 E2
Eltisley Cambs 122 F5
Elton Cambs 137 E11
Ches W 183 F7
Derbys 170 C2
Glos 80 C2
Gtr Man. 195 E9
Hereford. 115 C9
Notts. 154 B5
Stockton 225 B8
Elton Green Ches W 183 G7
Elton's Marsh Hereford. . . . 97 C9
Eltringham Northumb 242 E3
Elvanfoot S Lanark 259 F11
Elvaston Derbys 153 C8
Elveden Suff. 124 B6
Elvet Hill Durham 233 C11
Elvingston E Loth 281 G9
Elvington Kent. 55 C9
York 207 D9
Elwell Devon. 41 G7
Dorset 17 E9
Elwick Hrtlpl. 234 E5
Northumb 264 B4
Elworth Ches E. 168 C2
Elworthy Som 42 G5
Ely Cambs 139 G10
Cardiff 58 D6
Emberton M Keynes 103 B7
Embleton Cumb 229 E9
Durham. 234 F4
Northumb 264 E6
Embo Highld 311 K2
Emborough Som. 44 C6
Embo Street Highld 311 K2
Embsay N Yorks 204 C6
Emerson Park London 68 B4
Emerson's Green S Glos. . . 61 D7
Emerson Valley
M Keynes. 102 E6
Emery Down Hants 32 F3
Emley W Yorks 197 E8
Emmbrook Wokingham 65 F9
Emmer Green Reading 65 D8
Emmett Carr Derbys 187 F7
Emmington Oxon 84 E2
Emneth Norf. 139 B9
Emneth Hungate Norf . 139 B10
Emorsgate Norf 157 E10
Empingham Rutland 137 B8
Empshott Hants 49 G9
Empshott Green Hants. . . 49 G8
Emscote Warks 118 D5
Emstrey Shrops 149 G10
Emsworth Hants. 22 B2
Enborne W Berks 64 F2
Enborne Row W Berks 64 G2
Enchmarsh Shrops. 131 D10
Enderby Leics 135 D10
Endmoor Cumb 211 C10
Endon Staffs 168 E6
Endon Bank Staffs 168 E6
Energlyn Caerph 58 B6
Enfield London. 86 F4
Worcs 117 D10
Enfield Highway London. . .86 F5
Enfield Lock London 86 F5
Enfield Town London. 86 F4
Enfield Wash London. 86 F5
Enford Wilts 46 C6
Engamoor Shetland 313 H4
Engedi Anglesey 178 F5
Engine Common S Glos . . . 61 C7
Englefield W Berks 64 E6
Englefield Green Sur 66 E3
Englesea-brook Ches E . . 168 E3
English Bicknor Glos 79 B9
Englishcombe Bath. 61 G8
English Frankton
Shrops 149 D9
Engollan Corn 10 G3
Enham Alamein Hants . . 47 D11
Enis Devon. 25 B9
Enisfirth Shetland. 312 F5
Enmore Som. 43 G8
Enmore Field Hereford . . 115 E9
Enmore Green Dorset. 30 C5
Ennerdale Bridge
Cumb. 219 B11
Enniscaven Corn. 5 D9
Enoch Dumfries 247 C9
Enochdhu Perth 292 G2
Ensay Argyll 288 E5
Ensbury BCP 19 B7
Ensbury Park BCP 19 C7
Ensdon Shrops. 149 F8
Ensis Devon. 25 B9
Enslow Oxon. 83 B7
Enstone Oxon. 101 G7
Enterkinfoot Dumfries . . 247 C9
Enterpen N Yorks 225 D9
Enton Green Sur. 50 E3
Enville Staffs 132 F6
Eolaigearraidh W Isles. . 297 L3
Eorabus Argyll 288 G5
Eòropaidh W Isles 304 B7
Epney Glos 80 C3
Epperstone Notts. 171 F11
Epping Essex 87 E7
Epping Green Essex 86 D6
Herts 86 D3
Epping Upland Essex 86 E6
Eppleby N Yorks. 224 C3
Eppleworth E Yorks 208 G6
Epsom Sur 67 G8
Epwell Oxon 101 C7
Epworth N Lincs. 199 G9
Epworth Turbary
N Lincs. 199 G9
Erbistock Wrex 166 G5
Erbusaig Highld. 295 C9
Erchless Castle Highld . . 300 E4
Erdington W Mid. 134 E2
Eredine Argyll 275 C10
Eriboll Highld 308 D4
Ericstane Dumfries. 260 G3
Eridge Green E Sus 52 F5
Erines Argyll. 275 F9
Eriswell Suff. 124 B4
Erith London 68 D4
Erlestoke Wilts. 46 C3
Ermine Lincs. 189 G7
Ermington Devon 8 E2
Ernesettle Plym 7 D8
Erpingham Norf 160 C3
Erriottwood Kent. 54 B2
Errogie Highld 300 G5
Errol Perth 286 E6
Errol Station Perth 286 E6
Erskine Renfs. 277 G9
Erskine Bridge Renfs 277 G9
Ervie Dumfries 236 C2
Erwarton Suff 108 E4
Erwood Powys. 95 C11
Eryholme N Yorks 224 D6
Eryrys Denb 166 D2
Escomb Durham 233 E9
Escott Som. 42 F5
Escrick N Yorks 207 E8
Esgairdawe Carms. 94 C2
Esgairgeiliog Powys 128 B5
Esgyryn Conwy 180 F4
Esh Durham. 233 C9
Esher Sur 66 G6
Eshiels Borders 261 B7
Esholt W Yorks 205 E9
Eshott Northumb 252 D6
Eshton N Yorks 204 B4
Esh Winning Durham. 233 C9
Eskadale Highld. 300 F4
Eskbank Midloth 270 B6
Eskdale Green Cumb. 220 E2
Eskdalemuir Dumfries. . . . 249 D7
Eske E Yorks 209 E7
Eskham Lincs. 190 B5
Eskholme S Yorks 198 D6
Esknish Argyll 274 G4
Esk Valley N Yorks. 226 E6
Eslington Park
Northumb 264 G2
Esperley Lane Ends
Durham. 233 G8
Esprick Lancs. 202 F4
Essendine Rutland 155 G10
Essendon Herts. 86 D3
Essich Highld 300 F6
Essington Staffs 133 C9
Esslemont Aberds 303 G9
Eston Redcar 225 B11
Estover Plym 7 D10
Eswick Shetland. 313 H6
Etal Northumb 263 B10
Etchilhampton Wilts. 62 G4
Etchingham E Sus. 38 B2
Etchinghill Kent 55 F7
Staffs 151 F10
Etchingwood E Sus 37 C8
Etherley Dene Durham . . . 233 F9
Ethie Castle Angus. 287 C10
Ethie Mains Angus 287 C10
Etling Green Norf. 159 G10
Etloe Glos 79 D11
Eton Windsor 66 D3
Eton Wick Windsor. 66 D2
Etruria Stoke 168 F5
Etsell Shrops. 131 C7
Etterby Cumb 239 F9
Etteridge Highld 291 D8
Ettersgill Durham 232 F3
Ettiley Heath Ches E. 168 C2
Ettingshall W Mid 133 D8
Ettingshall Park W Mid. . 133 D8
Ettington Warks 100 B5
Etton E Yorks. 208 E5
Pboro 138 B2
Ettrick Borders 261 G7
Ettrickbridge Borders. 261 E9
Ettrickdale Argyll 275 G11
Ettrickhill Borders 261 G7
Etwall Derbys 152 C5
Etwall Common Derbys . 152 C5
Eudon Burnell Shrops 132 F3
Eudon George Shrops 132 F3
Euston Suff 125 B7
Euximoor Drove Cambs . 139 D9
Euxton Lancs 194 D5
Evanstown Bridgend 58 B3
Evanton Highld. 300 C6
Evedon Lincs 173 F9
Eve Hill W Mid. 133 E8
Evelix Highld 309 K7
Evendine Hereford 98 C5
Evenjobb = *Einsiob*
Powys 114 E5
Evenley W Nhants 101 E11
Evenlode Glos 100 F4
Even Pits Hereford 97 D11
Even Swindon Swindon. . . . 62 B6
Evenwood Durham 233 G9
Evenwood Gate Durham. 233 G9
Everbay Orkney 314 D6
Evercreech Som. 44 F6
Everdon W Nhants 119 F11
Everingham E Yorks 208 E2
Everland Shetland. 312 D8
Everleigh Wilts 47 C8
Everley N Yorks 217 B9
Eversholt C Beds 103 E9
Evershot Dorset 29 G9
Eversley Essex. 69 B8
Hants 65 G9
Eversley Centre Hants 65 G9
Eversley Cross Hants 65 G9
Everthorpe E Yorks. 208 G4
Everton C Beds. 122 G4
Hants 19 C11
Mers. 182 C5
Notts. .187 C11
Evertown Dumfries 239 B9
Evesbatch Hereford 98 B3
Evesham Worcs. 99 C10
Evington Kent 54 D6
Leicester 136 C2
Ewanrigg Cumb. 228 D6
Ewden Village S Yorks 186 B3
Ewell Sur. 67 G8
Ewell Minnis Kent 55 E9
Ewelme Oxon 83 G10
Ewen Glos 81 F8
Ewenny V Glam. 58 D2
Ewerby Lincs 173 F10
Ewerby Thorpe Lincs. . . . 173 F10
Ewes Dumfries 249 E9
Ewesley Northumb 252 E3
Ewhurst Sur. 50 E5
Ewhurst Green E Sus. 38 C3
Sur 50 F5
Ewloe Flint 166 B4
Ewloe Green Flint. 166 B3
Ewood Blackburn. 195 B7
Ewood Bridge Lancs 195 C9
Eworthy Devon. 12 C5
Ewshot Hants. 49 D10
Ewyas Harold Hereford. 97 F7
Exbourne Devon 25 G10
Exbury Hants 20 B4
Exceat E Sus 23 F8
Exebridge Devon. 26 C6
Exelby N Yorks 214 B5
Exeter Devon 14 C4
Exford Som. 41 F11
Exfords Green Shrops. 131 B9
Exhall Warks 118 F2
Warks. 135 F7
Exlade Street Oxon 65 C7
Exley W Yorks 196 C5
Exley Head W Yorks 204 F6
Exminster Devon. 14 D4
Exmouth Devon 14 E6
Exnaboe Shetland 313 M5
Exning Suff. 124 D2
Exted Kent. 55 E7
Exton Devon 14 D5
Hants 33 C10
Rutland. 155 G8
Som 42 G2
Exwick Devon. 14 C4
Eyam Derbys. 186 F2
Eydon W Nhants 119 G10
Eye Hereford. 115 E9
Pboro 138 C4
Suff. 126 C2
Eye Green Pboro. 138 C4
Eyemouth Borders 273 C8
Eyeworth C Beds 104 B4
Eyhorne Street Kent 53 C10
Eyke Suff 126 G6
Eynesbury Cambs. 122 F3
Eynort Highld 294 C5
Eynsford Kent 68 F4
Eynsham Oxon. 82 D6
Eype Dorset. 16 C5
Eyre Highld 295 B7
Highld 298 D4
Eyres Monsell
Leicester. 135 D11
Eythorne Kent. 55 D9
Eyton Hereford. 115 E9
Shrops 131 F7
Shrops 149 G7
Wrex. 166 G4
Eyton on Severn
Shrops 131 B11
Eyton upon the Weald
Moors Telford. 150 G3

F

Faberstown Wilts. 47 C9
Faccombe Hants. 47 B11
Faceby N Yorks. 225 E9
Fachell Gwyn 163 B8
Fachwen Gwyn 163 C9
Facit Lancs 195 D11
Fackley Notts. 171 C7
Faddiley Ches E 167 E9
Faddonch Highld. 295 C11
Fadmoor N Yorks. 216 B3
Faerdre Swansea 75 E11
Fagley W Yorks 205 G9
Fagwyr Swansea 75 E11
Faichem Highld 290 C4
Faifley W Dunb 277 G10
Failand N Som 60 E4
Failford S Ayrs 257 D11
Failsworth Gtr Man. 195 G11
Fain Highld 299 B11
Faindouran Lodge
Moray 292 C2
Fairbourne Gwyn 146 G2
Fairbourne Heath Kent . 53 C11
Fairburn N Yorks 198 B3
Fairburn House Highld . . 300 D4
Fair Cross London 68 B3
Fairfield Clack. 279 C7
Derbys 185 G9
Gtr Man 184 B6
Gtr Man. 195 E10
Kent 39 B7
Mers 182 C5
Stockton 225 B8
Worcs 99 C10
Worcs 117 B8
Fairfield Park Bath 61 F9
Fairfields Glos. 98 E4
Fairford Glos 81 E11
Fair Green Norf. 158 F3
Fairhaven Lancs 193 B10
N Ayrs .255 C10
Fairhill S Lanark. 268 E4
Fair Hill Cumb 230 E6
Fairlands Sur. 50 C3
Fairlee IoW 20 C6
Fairlie N Ayrs 266 D4
Fairlight E Sus 38 E5
Fairlight Cove E Sus. 38 E5
Fairlop London. 87 G7
Fairmile BCP 19 C9
Devon 15 B7
Sur 66 G6
Fairmilehead Edin 270 B4
Fair Moor Northumb 252 F5
Fairoak Caerph 77 F11
Staffs 150 C5
Fair Oak Hants. 33 D7
Hants 64 G5
Lancs 203 D8
Fair Oak Green Hants 65 G7
Fairseat Kent 68 G6
Fairstead Essex 88 B3
Norf 158 F2
Fairview Glos. 99 G9
Fairwarp E Sus. 37 B7
Fairwater Cardiff 58 D6
Torf. 78 G3
Fairwood Wilts 45 C10
Fairy Cottage IoM 192 D5
Fairy Cross Devon. 24 C6
Fakenham Norf. 159 D8
Fakenham Magna Suff. . 125 B8
Fala Midloth. 271 C8
Fala Dam Midloth 271 C8
Falahill Borders. 271 D7
Falcon Hereford. 98 E2
Falcon Lodge W Mid 134 D2
Falconwood London. 68 D3
Falcutt W Nhants 101 C11
Faldingworth Lincs 189 E9
Faldonside Borders 262 C2
Falfield Fife 287 G8
S Glos 79 G11
Falkenham Suff 108 D5
Falkenham Sink Suff. 108 D5
Falkirk Falk. 279 F7
Falkland Fife 286 G6
Falla Borders 262 G6
Fallgate Derbys. 170 C5
Fallin Stirling 278 C6
Fallinge Derbys 170 B3
Fallings Heath W Mid 133 D9
Fallowfield Gtr Man 184 C5
Fallside N Lanark 268 C4
Falmer E Sus. 36 F5
Falmouth Corn 3 C8
Falnash Borders 249 B9
Falsgrave N Yorks 217 B10
Falside W Loth 269 B9
Falsidehill Borders. 272 G3
Falstone Northumb 250 F6
Fanagmore Highld 306 E6
Fancott C Beds. 103 F10
Fangdale Beck
N Yorks 225 G11
Fangfoss E Yorks 207 C11
Fanich Highld 311 J2
Fankerton Falk 278 E5
Fanmore Argyll 288 E6
Fanner's Green Essex. 87 C11
Fannich Lodge Highld. 300 C2
Fans Borders. 272 G2
Fanshowe Ches E 184 G5
Fant Kent 53 B8
Faoilean Highld 295 C7
Far Arnside Cumb. 211 D8
Far Bank S Yorks 198 E6
Far Banks Lancs 194 C2
Far Bletchley M Keynes. . . 103 E7
Farcet Cambs 138 E4
Far Cotton W Nhants 120 F4
Farden Shrops 115 B11
Fareham Hants 33 F9
Far End Cumb 220 F6
Farewell Staffs 151 G11
Far Forest Worcs 116 C4
Farforth Lincs 190 F4
Far Green Glos 80 E3
Farhill Derbys. 170 C5
Far Hoarcross Staffs. 152 E2
Faringdon Oxon 82 F3
Farington Lancs 194 B4
Farington Moss Lancs 194 C4
Farlam Cumb 240 F3
Farlands Booth Derbys. . . . 185 D9
Farlary Highld 309 J7
Far Laund Derbys 170 F5
Farleigh N Som 60 F3
Sur 67 G11
Farleigh Court Sur. 67 G11
Farleigh Green Kent 53 C8
Farleigh Hungerford
Som. 45 B10
Farleigh Wallop Hants 48 D6
Farleigh Wick Wilts. 61 G10
Farlesthorpe Lincs. 191 G7
Farleton Cumb. 211 C10
Lancs 211 F11
Farley Bristol 60 E2
Derbys 170 C3
Shrops 131 B7
Shrops 132 C2
Staffs 169 G9
Wilts. 32 B2
Far Ley Staffs 132 D5
Farley Green Suff. 124 G4
Sur 50 D5
Farley Hill Luton 103 G11
Wokingham. 65 G8
Farleys End Glos. 80 B3
Farlington N Yorks 216 F2
Ptsmth 33 F11
Farlow Shrops 132 G2
Farmborough Bath 61 G7
Farmbridge End Essex. 87 C10
Farmcote Glos. 99 F11

Farmcote *continued*
Shrops 132 E5
Farmington Glos 81 B10
Farmoor Oxon 82 D6
Far Moor Gtr Man 194 G4
Farms Common Corn 2 C5
Farmtown Moray 302 D5
Farm Town Leics 153 F7
Farnah Green Derbys 170 F4
Farnborough Hants 49 C11
London 68 G2
Warks 101 B8
W Berks 64 C2
Farnborough Green
Hants 49 B11
Farnborough Park
Hants 49 B11
Farnborough Street
Hants 49 B11
Farncombe Sur 50 E3
Farndish Bedford 121 E8
Farndon Ches W 166 E6
Notts 172 E3
Farnell Angus 287 B10
Farnham Dorset 31 D7
Essex 105 G9
N Yorks 215 G7
Suff 127 E7
Sur 49 D10
Farnham Common Bucks 66 C3
Farnham Green Essex 105 F9
Farnham Park Bucks 66 C3
Farnham Royal Bucks 66 C3
Farnhill N Yorks 204 D6
Farningham Kent 68 F4
Farnley N Yorks 205 D10
W Yorks 205 G11
Farnley Bank W Yorks 197 E7
Farnley Tyas W Yorks 197 E7
Farnsfield Notts 171 D10
Farnworth Gtr Man 195 F8
Halton 183 D8
Far Oakridge Glos 80 E6
Farr Highld 291 C10
Highld 300 F6
Highld 308 C7
Farraline Highld 300 G5
Farr House Highld 300 F6
Farringdon Devon 14 C6
T&W 243 G9
Farrington Dorset 30 D4
Farrington Gurney Bath 44 B6
Far Royds W Yorks 205 G11
Far Sawrey Cumb 221 F7
Farsley W Yorks 205 F10
Farsley Beck Bottom
W Yorks 205 F10
Farther Howegreen
Essex 88 E4
Farthing Corner
Medway 69 G10
Farthing Green Kent 53 D10
Farthinghoe W Nhants 101 D10
Farthingloe Kent 55 E9
Farthingstone W Nhants 120 F2
Far Thrupp Glos 80 E5
Fartown W Yorks 196 D6
Farway Devon 15 B9
Farway Marsh Devon 28 G4
Fasach Highld 297 G7
Fasag Highld 299 D8
Fascadale Highld 289 B7
Faslane Port Argyll 276 D4
Fasnacloich Argyll 284 C4
Fasnakyle Ho Highld 300 G3
Fassfern Highld 290 F2
Fatfield T&W 243 G8
Fattahead Aberds 302 D6
Faucheldean W Loth 279 G11
Faugh Cumb 240 G2
Faughill Borders 262 C2
Fauld Staffs 152 D3
Fauldhouse W Loth 269 C8
Fauldiehill Angus 287 D9
Fauldshope Borders 261 D10
Faulkbourne Essex 88 B3
Faulkland Som 45 C8
Fauls Shrops 149 C11
Faverdale Darl 224 B5
Faversham Kent 70 G4
Favillar Moray 302 F2
Fawdington N Yorks 215 E8
Fawdon Northumb 264 F2
T&W 242 D6
Fawfieldhead Staffs 169 C9
Fawkham Green Kent 68 F5
Fawler Oxon 63 B10
Oxon 82 B5
Fawley Bucks 65 B9
Hants 33 G7
W Berks 63 C11
Fawley Bottom Bucks 65 B8
Fawley Chapel Hereford 97 F11
Faxfleet E Yorks 199 C11
Faygate W Sus 51 G8
Fazakerley Mers 182 B5
Fazeley Staffs 134 C4
Feagour Highld 291 D7
Fearby N Yorks 214 C3
Fearn Highld 301 B8
Fearnan Perth 285 C11
Fearnbeg Highld 299 D7
Fearnhead Warr 183 C10
Fearn Lodge Highld 309 L6
Fearnmore Highld 299 C7
Fearn Station Highld 301 B8
Fearnville W Yorks 206 F2
Featherstone Staffs 133 B8
W Yorks 198 C2
Featherwood Northumb 251 C8
Feckenham Worcs 117 E10
Fedw Fawr Anglesey 179 E10
Feering Essex 107 G7
Feetham N Yorks 223 F9
Fegg Hayes Stoke 168 E5
Fèith Mhor Highld 301 G8
Feizor N Yorks 212 F5
Felbridge Sur 51 F11
Felbrigg Norf 160 B4
Felcourt Sur 51 E11
Felden Herts 85 E8
Felderland Kent 55 B10
Feldy Ches E 183 F11
Felhampton Shrops 131 F8
Felin-Crai Powys 95 G7
Felindre Carms 75 C7
Carms 93 D7
Carms 93 G11
Carms 94 E3
Carms 94 F4
Ceredig 111 F10
Powys 96 D3
Powys 96 G3
Powys 130 C3
Powys 130 G3
Rhondda 58 C3
Swansea 75 E10
Felindre Farchog Pembs 92 D2
Felinfach Ceredig 111 F10
Felinfach *continued*
Powys 95 E11
Felinfoel Carms 75 E8
Felingwmisaf Carms 93 G10
Felingwmuchaf Carms 93 G10
Felin Newydd Carms 94 D3
Felin-newydd Powys 96 D2
Felin Newydd *= New Mills*
Powys 129 C11
Felin Puleston Wrex 166 F4
Felin-Wnda Ceredig 92 B6
Felinwynt Ceredig 110 G4
Felixkirk N Yorks 215 C9
Felixstowe Suff 108 E5
Felixstowe Ferry Suff 108 D6
Felkington Northumb 273 G8
Felkirk W Yorks 197 E11
Felldyke Cumb 219 B11
Fell End Cumb 222 F4
Fellgate T&W 243 E8
Felling T&W 243 E7
Felling Shore T&W 243 E7
Fell Lane W Yorks 204 E6
Fellside T&W 242 E5
Fell Side Cumb 230 D2
Felmersham Bedford 121 F9
Felmingham Norf 160 D5
Felmore Essex 69 B8
Felpham W Sus 35 H7
Felsham Suff 125 F8
Felsted Essex 106 G3
Feltham London 66 E6
Som 28 D2
Felthamhill London 66 E5
Felthorpe Norf 160 F3
Felton Hereford 97 B11
Northumb 252 C5
N Som 60 F4
Felton Butler Shrops 149 F7
Feltwell Norf 140 E4
Fenay Bridge W Yorks 197 D7
Fence Lancs 204 F2
Fence Houses T&W 243 G8
Fencott Oxon 83 B9
Fen Ditton Cambs 123 E9
Fen Drayton Cambs 122 D6
Fen End Lincs 156 E4
W Mid 118 B4
Fengate Norf 160 E3
Pboro 138 D4
Fenham Northumb 273 G11
T&W 242 D6
Fenhouses Lincs 174 G3
Feniscliffe Blackburn 195 B7
Feniscowles Blackburn 194 B6
Feniton Devon 15 B8
Fenlake Bedford 103 B11
Fenn Green Shrops 132 G5
Fennington Som 27 B11
Fenn's Bank Wrex 149 B10
Fenn Street Medway 69 D9
Fenny Bentley Derbys 169 E11
Fenny Bridges Devon 15 B8
Fenny Castle Som 44 E4
Fenny Compton Warks 119 G8
Fenny Drayton Leics 134 D6
Fenny Stratford
M Keynes 103 E7
Fenrother Northumb 252 E5
Fen Side Lincs 174 D4
Fenstanton Cambs 122 D6
Fenstead End Suff 124 G6
Fen Street Norf 141 G11
Suff 125 B9
Suff 125 B11
Fenton Cambs 122 B6
Cumb 240 F2
Lincs 172 E5
Lincs 188 F4
Northumb 263 C11
Stoke 168 G5
Fentonadle Corn 11 F7
Fenton Barns E Loth 281 E10
Fenton Low Stoke 168 F5
Fenton Pits Corn 5 C11
Fenton Town Northumb 263 C11
Fenwick E Ayrs 267 G9
Northumb 242 C3
Northumb 273 G11
S Yorks 198 D5
Feochaig Argyll 255 F8
Feock Corn 3 B8
Feolin Ferry Argyll 274 G5
Ferguslie Park Renfs 267 C9
Ferindonald Highld 295 E8
Feriniquarrie Highld 296 F7
Ferlochan Argyll 289 E11
Fern Angus 292 G6
Bucks 65 B11
Fern Bank Gtr Man 185 B7
Ferndale Kent 52 E5
Rhondda 77 F7
Ferndown Dorset 31 G9
Ferne Wilts 30 C6
Ferness Highld 301 E9
Ferney Green Cumb 221 F8
Fernham Oxon 82 G3
Fernhill Gtr Man 195 E10
Rhondda 77 F8
W Sus 51 E10
Fern Hill Suff 106 B6
Fernhill Gate Gtr Man 195 F7
Fernhill Heath Worcs 117 F7
Fernhurst W Sus 34 B5
Fernie Fife 287 F7
Ferniebrae Aberds 303 D9
Ferniegair S Lanark 268 E4
Ferniehirst Borders 271 G8
Fernilea Highld 294 B5
Fernilee Derbys 185 F8
Fernsplatt Corn 4 G5
Ferrensby N Yorks 215 G7
Ferring W Sus 35 G9
Ferrybridge W Yorks 198 C3
Ferryden Angus 287 B11
Ferryhill Aberdeen 293 C11
Durham 233 E11
Ferry Hill Cambs 139 G7
Ferryhill Station
Durham 234 E2
Ferry Point Highld 309 L7
Ferryside *= Glan-y-Fferi*
Carms 74 C5
Ferryton Highld 300 C6
Fersfield Norf 141 G11
Fersit Highld 290 F5
Feshiebridge Highld 291 C10
Fetcham Sur 50 B6
Fetterangus Aberds 303 D9
Fettercairn Aberds 293 F8
Fetterdale Fife 287 E8
Fettes Highld 300 D5
Fewcott Oxon 101 F10
Fewston N Yorks 205 C9
Fewston Bents N Yorks 205 C9
Ffairfach Carms 94 G2
Ffair-Rhos Ceredig 112 D4
Ffaldybrenin Carms 94 C2
Ffarmers Carms 94 C3
Ffawyddog Powys 78 B2
Ffodun *= Forden* Powys 130 C4
Ffont y gari *= Font y gary*
V Glam 58 F5
Fforddlas Powys 96 D4
Ffordd-las Denb 165 C10
Ffordd-y-Gyfraith
Bridgend 57 E11
Fforest Carms 75 E9
Fforest-fach Swansea 56 B6
Fforest Gôch Neath 76 E2
Ffostrasol Ceredig 93 B7
Ffos-y-ffin Ceredig 111 E8
Ffos-y-go Wrex 166 E4
Ffridd Powys 130 D3
Ffrith Wrex 166 D3
Ffrwd Gwyn 163 D7
Ffwl y mwn *= Fonmon*
V Glam 58 F4
Ffynnon Carms 74 B5
Ffynnon ddrain Carms 93 G8
Ffynnongroes *= Crosswell*
Pembs 92 D2
Ffynnon Gron Pembs 91 F8
Ffynnongroyw Flint 181 E10
Ffynnon Gynydd Powys 96 C3
Ffynnon-oer Ceredig 111 G10
Fickleshole Sur 67 G11
Fidden Argyll 288 G5
Fiddes Aberds 293 E10
Fiddington Glos 99 E8
Som 43 E8
Fiddington Sands Wilts 46 C4
Fiddleford Dorset 30 E4
Fiddler' Green Norf 141 D10
Fiddler's Ferry Mers 193 C11
Warr 183 D9
Fiddler's Green Glos 99 G8
Hereford 97 D11
Fiddlers Hamlet Essex 87 E7
Field Hereford 114 G6
Som 44 E6
Staffs 151 C10
Field Assarts Oxon 82 C4
Field Broughton Cumb 211 C7
Field Common Sur 66 F6
Field Dalling Norf 159 B10
Field Green Kent 38 B3
Field Head Leics 135 B9
Fields End Herts 85 D8
Field's Place Hereford 115 G8
Fifehead Magdalen
Dorset 30 C3
Fifehead Neville Dorset 30 E3
Fifehead St Quintin
Dorset 30 E3
Fife Keith Moray 302 D4
Fifield Oxon 82 B2
Wilts 46 C6
Windsor 66 D2
Fifield Bavant Wilts 31 B8
Figheldean Wilts 47 D7
Filands Wilts 62 B2
Filby Norf 161 G9
Filby Heath Norf 161 G9
Filchampstead Oxon 83 D7
Filey N Yorks 218 C2
Filgrave M Keynes 103 B7
Filham Devon 8 D2
Filkins Oxon 82 E2
Filleigh Devon 25 B11
Devon 26 E2
Fillingham Lincs 188 D6
Fillongley Warks 134 F5
Filmore Hill Hants 33 B11
Filton S Glos 60 D6
Filwood Park Bristol 60 F5
Fimber E Yorks 217 G7
Finavon Angus 287 B8
Finberry Kent 54 F4
Fincastle Ho Perth 291 G10
Finchairn Argyll 275 C10
Fincham Mers 182 C6
Norf 140 B3
Finchampstead
Wokingham 65 G9
Finchdean Hants 34 E2
Finchingfield Essex 106 E3
Finchley London 86 G3
Findern Derbys 152 C6
Findhorn Moray 301 C10
Findhorn Bridge Highld 301 G8
Findochty Moray 302 C4
Findo Gask Perth 286 E4
Findon Aberds 293 D11
W Sus 35 F10
Findon Mains Highld 300 C6
Findon Valley W Sus 35 F10
Findrack Ho Aberds 293 C8
Finedon N Nhants 121 C8
Fineglen Argyll 275 B10
Fine Street Hereford 96 D6
Fingal Street Suff 126 D4
Fingask Aberds 303 G7
Fingerpost Worcs 116 C4
Fingest Bucks 84 G3
Finghall N Yorks 214 B3
Fingland Cumb 239 F7
Dumfries 259 F7
Finglesham Kent 55 C10
Fingringhoe Essex 107 G10
Finham W Mid 118 B6
Finkle Street S Yorks 186 B4
Finlarig Stirling 285 D9
Finmere Oxon 102 E2
Finnart Perth 285 B9
Finney Green Ches E 184 E5
Staffs 168 F3
Finningham Suff 125 D11
Finningley S Yorks 187 B11
Finnygaud Aberds 302 D5
Finsbury London 67 C10
Finsbury Park London 67 B10
Finstall Worcs 117 D9
Finsthwaite Cumb 211 B7
Finstock Oxon 82 B5
Finstown Orkney 314 E3
Fintry Aberds 303 D7
Dundee 287 D8
Stirling 278 D2
Finwood Warks 118 D3
Finzean Aberds 293 D8
Finzean Ho Aberds 293 D7
Fionnphort Argyll 288 G5
Fionnsbhagh W Isles 296 C6
Firbank Cumb 222 G2
Firbeck S Yorks 187 D9
Firby N Yorks 214 B5
N Yorks 216 F4
Firemore Highld 307 L3
Firgrove Gtr Man 196 E2
Firkin Argyll 285 G7
Firle E Sus 23 D7
Firsby Lincs 175 C7
Firsdown Wilts 47 G8
Firs Lane Gtr Man 194 G6
First Coast Highld 307 K4
Firswood Gtr Man 184 B4
Firth Borders 262 E2
Firth Moor Darl 224 C6
Firth Park S Yorks 186 C5
Fir Toll Kent 54 E2
Fir Tree Durham 233 E8
Fir Vale S Yorks 186 C5
Firwood Fold Gtr Man 195 E8
Fishbourne IoW 21 C7
W Sus 22 C4
Fishburn Durham 234 E3
Fishcross Clack 279 B7
Fisherford Aberds 302 F6
Fishermead M Keynes 103 D7
Fisher Place Cumb 220 B6
Fisherrow E Loth 280 G6
Fishersgate Brighton 36 F3
Fishers Green Herts 104 F4
Fisher's Pond Hants 33 C7
Fisherstreet W Sus 50 G3
Fisherton Highld 301 D7
S Ayrs 257 F7
Fisherton de la Mere
Wilts 46 F4
Fisherwick Staffs 134 B3
Fishery Windsor 65 C11
Fishguard *= Abergwaun*
Pembs 91 D9
Fishlake S Yorks 199 E7
Fishleigh Devon 25 F8
Fishleigh Barton Devon 25 C9
Fishleigh Castle Devon 25 F8
Fishley Norf 161 G8
W Mid 133 C10
Fishmere End Lincs 156 B5
Fishponds Bristol 60 D6
Fishpool Glos 98 F3
Gtr Man 195 F10
N Yorks 205 D10
Fishpools Powys 114 D3
Fishtoft Lincs 174 G5
Fishtoft Drove Lincs 174 F4
Fishtown of Usan
Angus 287 B11
Fishwick Borders 273 E8
Lancs 194 B5
Fiskavaig Highld 294 B5
Fiskerton Lincs 189 G8
Notts 172 E2
Fitling E Yorks 209 G11
Fittleton Wilts 46 D6
Fittleworth W Sus 35 D8
Fitton End Cambs 157 G8
Fitton Hill Gtr Man 196 G2
Fitz Shrops 149 F8
Fitzhead Som 27 B10
Fitzwilliam W Yorks 198 D2
Fiunary Highld 289 E8
Five Acres Glos 79 C9
Five Ash Down E Sus 37 C7
Five Ashes E Sus 37 C9
Five Bells Som 42 E5
Five Bridges Hereford 98 B3
Fivecrosses Ches W 183 F8
Fivehead Som 28 C5
Five Houses IoW 20 D4
Five Lane Ends Lancs 202 C6
Fivelanes Corn 11 E10
Five Lanes Mon 78 G6
Five Oak Green Kent 52 D6
Five Oaks W Sus 35 B9
Five Roads Carms 75 D7
Five Ways Warks 118 D4
Five Wents Kent 53 C10
Fixby W Yorks 196 C6
Flackley Ash E Sus 38 C5
Flack's Green Essex 88 B3
Flackwell Heath Bucks 65 B11
Fladbury Worcs 99 B9
Fladbury Cross Worcs 99 B9
Fladda Shetland 312 E5
Fladdabister Shetland 313 K6
Flagg Derbys 169 B10
Flaggoners Green
Hereford 116 G2
Flamborough E Yorks 218 E4
Flamstead Herts 85 C9
Flamstead End Herts 86 E4
Flansham W Sus 35 G7
Flanshaw W Yorks 197 C10
Flappit Spring W Yorks 205 F7
Flasby N Yorks 204 B4
Flash Staffs 169 B8
Flashader Highld 298 D3
Flask Inn N Yorks 227 E8
Flathurst W Sus 35 C7
Flaunden Herts 85 E8
Flawborough Notts 172 G3
Flawith N Yorks 215 F9
Flax Bourton N Som 60 F4
Flaxby N Yorks 206 B3
Flaxholme Derbys 170 G4
Flaxlands Norf 142 E2
Flaxley Glos 79 B11
Flax Moss Lancs 195 C9
Flaxpool Som 42 F6
Flaxton N Yorks 216 G3
Fleckney Leics 136 E2
Flecknoe Warks 119 E10
Fledborough Notts 188 G4
Fleet Dorset 17 E8
Hants 22 C2
Hants 49 C10
Lincs 157 E7
Fleet Downs Kent 68 E5
Fleetend Hants 33 F8
Fleet Hargate Lincs 157 E7
Fleetlands Hants 33 G9
Fleets N Yorks 213 G9
Fleetville Herts 85 D11
Fleetwood Lancs 202 D2
Fleggburgh =
Burgh St Margaret Norf 161 G8
Fleming Field Durham 234 C3
Flemings Kent 55 B9
Flemingston V Glam 58 E4
Flemington S Lanark 268 D3
S Lanark 268 G4
Flempton Suff 124 D6
Fleoideabhagh W Isles 296 C6
Fletchersbridge Corn 6 B2
Fletcher's Green Kent 52 C4
Fletchertown Cumb 229 C10
Fletching E Sus 36 C6
Fletching Common
E Sus 36 C6
Fleuchary Highld 309 K7
Fleuchlang Dumfries 237 D8
Fleur-de-lis Caerph 77 F11
Flexbury Corn 24 F2
Flexford Hants 32 C6
Sur 50 D2
Flimby Cumb 228 E6
Flimwell E Sus 53 G8
Flint Flint 182 G2
Flint Cross Cambs 105 C8
Flintham Notts 172 F2
Flint Hill Durham 242 G5
Flint Mountain *= Mynydd Fflint* Flint 182 G2
Flinton E Yorks 209 F10
Flint's Green W Mid 134 G5
Flintsham Hereford 114 F6
Flishinghurst Kent 53 F9
Flitcham Norf 158 D4
Flitholme Cumb 222 B5
Flitton C Beds 103 D11
Flitwick C Beds 103 D10
Flixborough N Lincs 199 D11
Flixborough Stather
N Lincs 199 E11
Flixton Gtr Man 184 C2
N Yorks 217 D10
Suff 142 F6
Flockton W Yorks 197 E8
Flockton Green
W Yorks 197 D8
Flockton Moor W Yorks 197 E8
Flodaigh W Isles 296 F4
Flodden Northumb 263 B10
Flodigarry Highld 298 B4
Floodgates Hereford 114 F5
Flood's Ferry Cambs 139 E7
Flood Street Hants 31 D10
Flookburgh Cumb 211 D7
Flordon Norf 142 D3
Flore W Nhants 120 E2
Florence Stoke 168 G6
Flotterton Northumb 251 C11
Flowers Bottom Bucks 84 F4
Flowers Green E Sus 23 C10
Flowery Field Gtr Man 184 B6
Flowton Suff 107 B11
Fluchter E Dunb 277 G11
Flugarth Shetland 313 G6
Flushdyke W Yorks 197 C9
Flush House W Yorks 196 F6
Flushing Aberds 303 E10
Corn 3 C8
Corn 3 D7
Flyford Flavell Worcs 117 G9
Foals Green Suff 126 C5
Fobbing Thurrock 69 C8
Fochabers Moray 302 D3
Fochriw Caerph 77 D10
Fockerby N Lincs 199 D10
Fodderletter Moray 301 G11
Fodderstone Gap Norf 140 B3
Fodderty Highld 300 D5
Foddington Som 29 B9
Foel Powys 147 G9
Foel-gastell Carms 75 C8
Foffarty Angus 287 C8
Foggathorpe E Yorks 207 F11
Foggbrook Gtr Man 184 D6
Fogo Borders 272 F5
Fogorig Borders 272 F5
Fograrth Shetland 313 H4
Fogwatt Moray 302 D2
Foindle Highld 306 E6
Folda Angus 292 G3
Fold Head Lancs 195 D11
Fold Hill Lincs 175 E7
Foldrings S Yorks 186 C3
Fole Staffs 151 B10
Foleshill W Mid 135 G7
Foley Park Worcs 116 B6
Folke Dorset 29 E11
Folkestone Kent 55 F8
Folkingham Lincs 155 C11
Folkington E Sus 23 E9
Folksworth Cambs 138 F2
Folkton N Yorks 217 D11
Folla Rule Aberds 303 F7
Folley Shrops 132 D5
Follifoot N Yorks 206 C2
Follingsby T&W 243 E8
Folly Dorset 30 G2
Pembs 91 G8
Folly Cross Devon 25 F7
Folly Gate Devon 13 B7
Folly Green Essex 106 F6
Fonmon *= Ffwl-y-mwn*
V Glam 58 F4
Fonston Corn 11 C10
Fonthill Bishop Wilts 46 G2
Fonthill Gifford Wilts 46 G2
Fontmell Magna Dorset 30 D5
Fontmell Parva Dorset 30 E4
Fontwell W Sus 35 F7
Font-y-gary *= Ffont-y-gari*
V Glam 58 F5
Foodieash Fife 287 F7
Foolow Derbys 185 F11
Footbridge Glos 99 F10
Footherley Staffs 134 C2
Footrid Worcs 116 C3
Foots Cray London 68 E3
Forbestown Aberds 292 B5
Force Forge Cumb 220 G6
Force Green Kent 52 B2
Force Mills Cumb 220 G6
Forcett N Yorks 224 C3
Ford Argyll 275 C9
Bucks 84 D3
Derbys 186 E6
Devon 8 E2
Devon 8 G5
Devon 24 C6
Devon 28 G2
Glos 99 F11
Hereford 115 F10
Kent 71 F8
Mers 182 B4
Northumb 263 B10
Pembs 91 F9
Plym 7 D9
Shrops 149 G8
Som 27 B9
Som 44 C5
Staffs 169 E9
Wilts 47 G7
Wilts 61 E10
W Sus 35 G7
Forda Devon 12 C6
Devon 40 F3
Fordbridge W Mid 134 F3
Fordcombe Kent 52 E4
Fordell Fife 280 D3
Forden *= Ffodun* Powys 130 C4
Ford End Essex 87 B11
Essex 105 E9
Forder Corn 7 D8
Forder Green Devon 8 B5
Ford Forge Northumb 263 B10
Fordgate Som 43 G10
Ford Green Lancs 202 D5
Stoke 168 E5
Fordham Cambs 124 C2
Essex 107 F8
Norf 140 D2
Fordham Heath Essex 107 F8
Ford Heath Shrops 149 G8
Ford Hill Northumb 263 B11
Fordhouses W Mid 133 C8
Fordingbridge Hants 31 E10
Fordington Lincs 190 G6
Fordley T&W 243 C7
Fordon E Yorks 217 D10
Fordoun Aberds 293 F9
Ford's Green E Sus 36 B6
Suff 125 D11
Fordstreet Essex 107 F8
Ford Street Som 27 D11
Fordton Devon 14 B2
Fordwater Devon 28 G4
Fordwells Oxon 82 C4
Fordwich Kent 55 B7
Fordyce Aberds 302 C5
Forebridge Staffs 151 E8
Foredale N Yorks 212 F6
Forehill S Ayrs 257 E8
Foreland Fields IoW 21 D9
Foreland Ho Argyll 274 G3
Foremark Derbys 152 D6
Forest Becks Lancs 203 C11
Forestburn Gate
Northumb 252 D3
Forest Coal Pit Mon 96 G5
Forestdale London 67 G11
Foresterseat Moray 301 D11
Forest Gate Hants 33 E10
London 68 C2
Forest Green Glos 80 E4
Sur 50 E6
Forest Hall Cumb 221 E10
T&W 243 D7
Forest Head Cumb 240 F3
Forest Hill London 67 E11
Oxon 83 D9
Wilts 63 F8
Forest Holme Lancs 195 B10
Forest-in-Teesdale
Durham 232 F3
Forest Lane Head
N Yorks 206 B2
Forest Lodge Argyll 284 C6
Highld 292 B2
Perth 291 F11
Forest Mill Clack 279 C9
Forest Moor N Yorks 206 B2
Forestreet Devon 24 E5
Forest Row E Sus 52 G2
Forestside W Sus 34 E3
Forest Side IoW 20 D5
Forest Town Notts 171 C9
Forewoods Common
Wilts 61 G10
Forfar Angus 287 B8
Forgandenny Perth 286 F4
Forge Corn 4 F3
Powys 128 D5
Forge Hammer Torf 78 F3
Forge Side Torf 78 D2
Forgewood N Lanark 268 D4
Forgie Moray 302 D3
Forglen Ho Aberds 302 D6
Forgue Aberds 302 E6
Forhill Worcs 117 B11
Formby Mers 193 F10
Forncett End Norf 142 E2
Forncett St Mary Norf 142 E3
Forncett St Peter Norf 142 E3
Forneth Perth 286 C4
Fornham All Saints Suff 124 D6
Fornham St Genevieve
Suff 124 D6
Fornham St Martin Suff 125 D7
Fornighty Highld 301 D9
Forrabury Corn 11 C7
Forres Moray 301 D10
Forrestfield N Lanark 269 B7
Forrest Lodge Dumfries 246 F3
Forry's Green Essex 106 E5
Forsbrook Staffs 169 G7
Forse Highld 310 F6
Forse Ho Highld 310 F6
Forshaw Heath Warks 117 C11
Forsinain Highld 310 E3
Forsinard Highld 310 E2
Forsinard Station Highld 310 E2
Forstal Kent 53 B8
Forston Dorset 17 B9
Fort Augustus Highld 290 C5
Forteviot Perth 286 F4
Fort George Highld 301 D7
Forth S Lanark 269 E8
Forthampton Glos 99 E7
Forthay Glos 80 F2
Forth Road Bridge Edin 280 F2
Fortingall Perth 285 C11
Fortis Green London 67 B9
Fort Matilda Invclyd 276 F5
Forton Hants 33 G10
Hants 48 E2
Lancs 202 C5
Shrops 149 F8
Som 28 F4
Staffs 150 E5
Forton Heath Shrops 149 F8
Fortrie Aberds 302 E6
Aberds 303 D7
Fortrose Highld 301 D7
Fortuneswell Dorset 17 G9
Fort William Highld 290 F3
Forty Green Bucks 84 E3
Bucks 84 G6
Forty Hill London 86 F4
Forward Green Suff 125 F11
Forwood Glos 80 E5
Fosbury Wilts 47 B10
Foscot Oxon 100 G4
Foscote Bucks 102 D4
Wilts 61 D11
W Nhants 102 B3
Fosdyke Lincs 156 C6
Fosdyke Bridge Lincs 156 C6
Foss Perth 285 B11
Foss Cross Glos 81 D9
Fossebridge Glos 81 C9
Fostall Kent 70 G5
Fosten Green Kent 53 F10
Fosterhouses S Yorks 199 E7
Foster's Booth
W Nhants 120 G3
Foster's Green Worcs 117 D9
Foster Street Essex 87 D7
Foston Derbys 152 C3
Leics 136 D2
Lincs 172 G5
N Yorks 216 F3
Foston on the Wolds
E Yorks 209 B8
Fotherby Lincs 190 C4
Fothergill Cumb 228 E6
Fotheringhay N Nhants 137 E11
Foubister Orkney 314 F5
Foul Anchor Cambs 157 F9
Foulbridge Cumb 230 B4
Foulby W Yorks 197 D11
Foulden Borders 273 D8
Norf 140 D5
Foul End Warks 134 E4
Foulford Hants 31 F11
Foulis Castle Highld 300 C5
Foul Mile E Sus 23 B10
Foulride Green E Sus 23 E9
Foulridge Lancs 204 E3
Foulsham Norf 159 E10
Foundry Corn 2 B3
Foundry Hill Norf 159 D11
Fountain Bridgend 57 E11
Fountainhall Borders 271 F8
Four Ashes Bucks 84 F5
Staffs 132 F6
Staffs 133 B8
Suff 125 C10
W Mid 118 B3
Four Crosses Powys 129 B11
Four Crosses *continued*
Powys 148 F5
Staffs 133 B9
Wrex 166 E3
Four Elms Devon 28 F3
Kent 52 D3
Four Foot Som 44 G5
Four Forks Som 43 F8
Four Gates Gtr Man 194 F6
Four Gotes Cambs 157 F9
Four Houses Corner
W Berks 64 F6
Four Lane End S Yorks 197 G9
Four Lane Ends Derbys 170 D5
Four Lane Ends
Blackburn 195 B7
Ches W 167 C9
Gtr Man 195 E9
W Yorks 205 G8
Four Lanes Corn 2 B5
Fourlanes End Ches E 168 D4
Four Marks Hants 49 G7
Four Mile Bridge
Anglesey 178 F3
Four Mile Elm Glos 80 C4
Four Oaks E Sus 38 C5
Glos 98 F3
Kent 70 G3
W Mid 134 D2
W Mid 134 G4
Four Oaks Park W Mid 134 D2
Fourpenny Highld 311 K2
Four Points W Berks 64 D5
Four Pools Worcs 99 C10
Four Roads Carms 74 D6
IoM 192 F3
Fourstones Northumb 241 D9
Four Throws Kent 38 B3
Four Wantz Essex 87 C10
Four Wents Kent 53 F9
Fovant Wilts 31 B8
Foveran Aberds 303 G9
Fowey Corn 6 E2
Fowler's Plot Som 43 F10
Fowley Common Warr 183 B11
Fowlis Angus 287 D7
Fowlis Wester Perth 286 E3
Fowlmere Cambs 105 B8
Fownhope Hereford 97 E11
Foxash Estate Essex 107 E11
Foxbar Renfs 267 C9
Foxbury London 68 E2
Foxcombe Hill Oxon 83 E7
Fox Corner C Beds 103 F8
Sur 50 C3
Foxcote Glos 81 B8
Som 45 B8
Foxcotte Hants 47 D10
Foxdale IoM 192 E3
Foxdown Hants 48 C4
Foxearth Essex 106 C6
Foxendown Kent 69 F7
Foxfield Cumb 210 B4
Foxford W Mid 135 G7
Foxham Wilts 62 D3
Fox Hatch Essex 87 F9
Fox Hill Bath 61 G9
Hereford 98 B3
Foxhills Hants 32 E4
Foxhole Corn 5 E9
Norf 142 D4
Swansea 57 C7
Fox Hole Swansea 56 D5
Foxholes N Yorks 217 E10
Fox Holes Wilts 45 E11
Foxhunt Green E Sus 23 B8
Fox Lane Hants 49 B11
Foxley Hereford 97 B8
Norf 159 E10
Staffs 168 E3
Wilts 61 B11
Foxlydiate Worcs 117 D10
Fox Royd W Yorks 197 D8
Fox Street Essex 107 F10
Foxt Staffs 169 F8
Foxton Cambs 105 B8
Durham 234 F3
Leics 136 E4
N Yorks 225 F8
Foxup N Yorks 213 D7
Foxwist Green Ches W 167 B10
Foxwood Shrops 116 B2
Foy Hereford 97 F11
Foyers Highld 300 G4
Foynesfield Highld 301 D8
Fraddam Corn 2 C3
Fraddon Corn 5 D8
Fradley Staffs 152 G3
Fradley Junction Staffs 152 G2
Fradswell Staffs 151 C9
Fraisthorpe E Yorks 218 G3
Framfield E Sus 37 C7
Framingham Earl Norf 142 C5
Framingham Pigot Norf 142 C5
Framlingham Suff 126 E5
Frampton Dorset 17 B8
Lincs 156 B6
Frampton Cotterell
S Glos 61 C7
Frampton Court Glos 99 E10
Frampton End S Glos 61 C7
Frampton Mansell Glos 80 E6
Frampton on Severn
Glos 80 D2
Frampton West End
Lincs 174 G3
Framsden Suff 126 F3
Framwellgate Moor
Durham 233 C11
France Lynch Glos 80 E6
Franche Worcs 116 B6
Frandley Ches W 183 F10
Frankby Mers 182 D2
Frankfort Norf 160 E6
Franklands Gate
Hereford 97 B10
Frankley Worcs 133 G9
Frankley Green Worcs 133 G9
Frankley Hill Worcs 117 B9
Frank's Bridge Powys 114 F2
Frankton Warks 119 C8
Frankwell Shrops 149 G9
Frans Green Norf 160 G2
Frant E Sus 52 F5
Fraserburgh Aberds 303 C9
Frating Essex 107 G11
Frating Green Essex 107 G11
Fratton Ptsmth 21 B9
Freasley Warks 134 D4
Freathy Corn 7 E8
Frecheville S Yorks 186 E5
Freckenham Suff 124 C3
Freckleton Lancs 194 B2
Fredley Sur 51 C7
Freebirch Derbys 186 G4
Freeby Leics 154 E6
Freefolk Hants 48 D3
Freehay Staffs 169 G8
Freeland Oxon 82 C6
Renfs 267 B9
Freeland Corner Norf 160 F3
Freemantle Soton 32 E6
Freester Shetland 313 H6
Freethorpe Norf 143 B8
Free Town Gtr Man 195 E10
Freezy Water London 86 F5
Freiston Lincs 174 G5
Freiston Shore Lincs 174 G5
Fremington Devon 40 G4
N Yorks 223 F10
Frenchay S Glos 60 D6
Frenchbeer Devon 13 D9
Frenches Green Essex 106 G4
Frenchmoor Hants 32 B3
French Street Kent 52 C3
Frenchwood Lancs 194 B4
Frenich Stirling 285 G8
Frensham Sur 49 E10
Frenze Norf 142 G2
Fresgoe Highld 310 C3
Freshbrook Swindon 62 C6
Freshfield Mers 193 F9
Freshford Bath 61 G9
Freshwater IoW 20 D2
Freshwater Bay IoW 20 D2
Freshwater East Pembs 73 F8
Fressingfield Suff 126 B5
Freston Suff 108 D3
Freswick Highld 310 C7
Fretherne Glos 80 D2
Frettenham Norf 160 F4
Freuchie Fife 286 G6
Freuchies Angus 292 G4
Freystrop Pembs 73 C7
Friarn Som 43 F7
Friar Park W Mid 133 E10
Friars Cliff BCP 19 C9
Friar's Gate E Sus 52 G3
Friar's Hill E Sus 38 E5
Friarton Perth 286 E5
Friday Bridge Cambs 139 C9
Friday Hill London 86 G5
Friday Street E Sus 23 E10
Suff 126 G6
Suff 127 E7
Sur 50 D6
Fridaythorpe E Yorks 208 B3
Friendly W Yorks 196 C5
Friern Barnet London 86 G3
Friesland Argyll 288 D3
Friesthorpe Lincs 189 E9
Frieston Lincs 172 F6
Frieth Bucks 84 G3
Frieze Hill Som 28 B2
Friezeland Notts 171 E7
Frilford Oxon 82 F6
Frilford Heath Oxon 82 F6
Frilsham W Berks 64 E4
Frimley Sur 49 B11
Frimley Green Sur 49 B11
Frimley Ridge Sur 49 B11
Frindsbury Medway 69 E8
Fring Norf 158 C4
Fringford Oxon 102 F2
Friningham Kent 53 B10
Frinkle Green Essex 106 C4
Frinsted Kent 53 B11
Frinton-on-Sea Essex 108 G4
Friockheim Angus 287 C9
Friog Gwyn 146 G2
Frisby Leics 136 C4
Frisby on the Wreake
Leics 154 F3
Friskney Lincs 175 D7
Friskney Eaudyke Lincs 175 D7
Friskney Tofts Lincs 175 E7
Friston E Sus 23 F8
Suff 127 E8
Fritchley Derbys 170 E5
Frith Kent 54 B2
Fritham Hants 32 E2
Frith Bank Lincs 174 F4
Frith Common Worcs 116 D3
Frithelstock Devon 25 D7
Frithelstock Stone Devon 25 D7
Frithend Hants 49 F10
Frith-hill Bucks 84 E6
Frith Hill Sur 50 E3
Frithsden Herts 85 D8
Frithville Lincs 174 E4
Frittenden Kent 53 E10
Frittiscombe Devon 8 G6
Fritton Norf 142 E4
Norf 143 C9
Norf 161 F8
Fritwell Oxon 101 F10
Frizinghall W Yorks 205 F8
Frizington Cumb 219 B10
Frizzeler's Green Suff 124 E5
Frobost W Isles 297 J3
Frocester Glos 80 E3
Frochas Powys 148 G5
Frodesley Shrops 131 C10
Frodingham N Lincs 199 E11
Frodsham Ches W 183 F8
Frogden Borders 263 D7
Frog End Cambs 123 F10
Cambs 123 G8
Froggatt Derbys 186 F2
Froghall Staffs 169 F8
Frogham Hants 31 E11
Kent 55 C9
Froghole Kent 52 C2
Frogholt Kent 55 F7
Frogland Cross S Glos 60 C6
Frog Moor Swansea 56 C3
Frogmore Devon 8 G5
Hants 33 C11
Hants 49 B10
Herts 85 E11
Frognal S Ayrs 257 D8
Frognall Lincs 156 G3
Frogpool Corn 4 G5
Frog Pool Worcs 116 D5
Frogs' Green Essex 105 D11
Frogshail Norf 160 B5
Frogwell Corn 6 B6
Frolesworth Leics 135 E10
Frome Som 45 D9
Fromebridge Glos 80 D3
Fromefield Som 45 D9
Frome St Quintin Dorset 29 G9
Fromes Hill Hereford 98 B3
Fromington Hereford 97 B10
Fron Denb 165 B9
Gwyn 145 B7
Gwyn 163 D8
Powys 113 D11
Powys 129 C8
Powys 130 C4
Powys 130 D3
Shrops 148 B5
Fron-Bache Denb 166 G2
Froncysyllte Wrex 166 G3
Fron-dêg Wrex 166 F3
Frongoch Gwyn 147 B8
Fron Isaf Wrex 166 G3
Frost Devon 26 F3
Frostenden Suff 143 G9
Frostenden Corner Suff 143 G9
Frosterley Durham 232 D6
Frost Hill N Som 60 G2

Frostlane Hants 32 F6
Frost Row Norf 141 C10
Frotoft Orkney 314 D4
Froxfield C Beds 103 E9
Wilts 63 F9
Froxfield Green Hants 34 B2
Froyle Hants 49 E9
Fryern Hill Hants 32 C6
Fryerning Essex 87 E10
Fryerns Essex 69 B8
Fryton N Yorks 216 E3
Fugglestone St Peter
Wilts 46 G6
Fulbeck Lincs 172 E6
Northumb 252 F5
Fulbourn Cambs 123 F10
Fulbrook Oxon 82 C3
Fulflood Hants 33 B7
Fulford Som 28 B2
Staffs 151 B9
York 207 D8
Fulham London 67 D8
Fulking W Sus 36 E2
Fullabrook Devon 40 E4
Fullarton Glasgow 268 C2
N Ayrs 257 B8
Fuller's End Essex 105 F10
Fuller's Moor Ches W 167 E7
Fuller Street Essex 88 B2
Fullerton Hants 47 F11
Fulletby Lincs 190 G3
Fullshaw S Yorks 197 G8
Full Sutton E Yorks 207 B10
Fullwell Cross London 86 G6
Fullwood E Ayrs 267 E8
Gtr Man 196 F2
Fulmer Bucks 66 B3
Fulmodestone Norf 159 C9
Fulneck W Yorks 205 G10
Fulnetby Lincs 189 F9
Fulney Lincs 156 E5
Fulready Warks 100 B5
Fulshaw Park Ches E 184 E4
Fulstone W Yorks 197 F7
Fulstow Lincs 190 B4
Fulthorpe Stockton 234 G4
Fulwell Oxon 101 G7
T&W 243 F9
Fulwood Lancs 202 G6
Som 28 C2
S Yorks 186 D4
Fundenhall Norf 142 D3
Fundenhall Street Norf 142 D2
Funtington W Sus 22 B3
Funtley Hants 33 F9
Funtullich Perth 285 E11
Funzie Shetland 312 D8
Furley Devon 28 G3
Furnace Argyll 284 G4
Carms 74 E6
Carms 75 E8
Ceredig 128 D3
Highld 299 B9
Furnace End Warks 134 E4
Furnace Green W Sus 51 F9
Furnace Wood W Sus 51 F11
Furneaux Pelham Herts 105 F8
Furner's Green E Sus 36 B6
Furness Vale Derbys 185 E8
Furneux Pelham Herts 105 F8
Furnham Som 28 F4
Further Ford End Essex 105 E9
Further Quarter Kent 53 F11
Furtho W Nhants 102 C5
Furze Devon 25 B10
Furzebrook Dorset 18 E4
Furzedown Hants 32 B5
London 67 E9
Furzehill Devon 41 D8
Dorset 31 G8
Furze Hill Hants 31 E11
Furzeley Corner Hants 33 E11
Furze Platt Windsor 65 C11
Furzey Lodge Hants 32 G5
Furzley Hants 32 D3
Furzton M Keynes 102 D6
Fyfett Som 28 E2
Fyfield Essex 87 D9
Glos 82 E2
Hants 47 D9
Oxon 82 F6
Wilts 63 F7
Wilts 63 G7
Fylingthorpe N Yorks 227 D8
Fyning W Sus 34 C4
Fyvie Aberds 303 F7

G

Gabalfa Cardiff 59 D7
Gabhsann bho Dheas
W Isles 304 C6
Gabhsann bho Thuath
W Isles 304 C6
Gable Head Hants 21 B10
Gablon Highld 309 K7
Gabroc Hill E Ayrs 267 E9
Gadbrook Sur 51 D8
Gaddesby Leics 154 G3
Gadebridge Herts 85 D8
Gadfa Anglesey 179 D7
Gadfield Elm Worcs 98 E5
Gadlas Shrops 149 B7
Gadlys Rhondda 77 E7
Gadshill Kent 69 E8
Gaer Newport 59 B9
Powys 96 G3
Gaer-fawr Mon 78 F6
Gaerllwyd Mon 78 F6
Gaerwen Anglesey 179 G7
Gagingwell Oxon 101 F8
Gaick Lodge Highld 291 E9
Gailey Staffs 151 G8
Gailey Wharf Staffs 151 G8
Gainfield Oxon 82 F4
Gainford Durham 224 B3
Gain Hill Kent 53 D8
Gainsborough Lincs 188 C4
Suff 108 C3
Gainsford End Essex 106 D4
Gairletter Argyll 276 E3
Gairloch Highld 299 B8
Gairlochy Highld 290 E3
Gairney Bank Perth 280 B2
Gairnshiel Lodge
Aberds 292 C4
Gaisgill Cumb 222 D2
Gaitsgill Cumb 230 B3
Galadean Borders 271 G11
Galashiels Borders 261 B11
Galdlys Flint 182 G2
Gale Gtr Man 196 D2
Galgate Lancs 202 B5
Galhampton Som 29 B10
Gallaberry Dumfries 247 G11
Gallachoille Argyll 275 E8
Gallanach Argyll 288 C4
Argyll 289 G10
Highld 294 G6
Gallantry Bank Ches E 167 E8
Gallatown Fife 280 C5
Galley Common Warks 134 E6
Galleyend Essex 88 E2
Galley Hill Cambs 122 D6
Lincs 190 F6
Galleywood Essex 88 E2
Galligill Cumb 231 B11
Gallin Perth 285 C9
Gallovie Highld 291 E7
Gallowfauld Angus 287 C8
Gallowhill Glasgow 267 D11
Renfs 267 B9
Gallowhills Aberds 303 D10
Gallows Corner London 87 G8
Gallowsgreen Torf 78 D3
Gallows Green Essex 106 F2
Essex 107 F8
Staffs 169 G9
Worcs 117 E8
Gallows Inn Derbys 171 G7
Gallowstree Common
Oxon 65 C7
Galltair Highld 295 C10
Galltegfa Denb 165 D10
Gallt Melyd *=Meliden*
Denb 181 E9
Gallt-y-foel Gwyn 163 C9
Gallypot Street E Sus 52 F3
Galmington Som 28 C2
Galmisdale Highld 294 G6
Galmpton Devon 8 G3
Torbay 9 D7
Galon Uchaf M Tydf 77 D9
Galphay N Yorks 214 E5
Galston E Ayrs 258 B2
Galtrigill Highld 296 F7
Gam Corn 11 F7
Gamble Hill W Yorks 205 G11
Gamblesby Cumb 231 D8
Gamble's Green Essex 88 C3
Gamelsby Cumb 239 G7
Gamesley Derbys 185 C8
Gamlingay Cambs 122 G4
Gamlingay Cinques
Cambs 122 G4
Gamlingay Great Heath
Cambs 122 G4
Gammaton Devon 25 B7
Gammaton Moor Devon 25 C7
Gammersgill N Yorks 213 C11
Gamston Notts 154 B2
Notts 188 F2
Ganarew Hereford 79 B8
Ganavan Argyll 289 F10
Ganders Green Glos 98 G4
Gang Corn 6 B6
Ganllwyd Gwyn 146 E4
Gannetts Dorset 30 D3
Gannochy Angus 293 F7
Perth 286 E5
Ganstead Highld 310 E7
Ganstead E Yorks 209 G9
Ganthorpe N Yorks 216 E3
Ganton N Yorks 217 D9
Gants Hill London 68 B2
Ganwick Corner Herts 86 F3
Gaodhail Argyll 289 F8
Gappah Devon 14 F3
Garafad Highld 298 C4
Garamor Highld 295 F8
Garbat Highld 300 C4
Garbhallt Argyll 275 D11
Garboldisham Norf 141 G10
Garbole Highld 301 G7
Garden City Bl Gwent 77 D11
Flint 166 B4
Gardeners Green
Wokingham 65 F10
Gardenstown Aberds 303 C7
Garden Village Swansea 56 B5
S Yorks 186 B3
Wrex 166 E4
W Yorks 206 G4
Garderhouse Shetland 313 J5
Gardham E Yorks 208 E5
Gardie Shetland 312 D7
Gardin Shetland 312 G6
Gare Hill Som 45 E9
Garelochhead Argyll 276 C4
Garford Oxon 82 F6
Garforth W Yorks 206 G4
Gargrave N Yorks 204 C4
Gargunnock Stirling 278 C4
Garizim Conwy 179 F11
Garker Corn 5 E10
Garlandhayes Devon 27 D11
Garlands Cumb 239 G10
Garleffin S Ayrs 244 G3
Garlic Street Norf 142 G4
Garlieston Dumfries 236 E6
Garliford Devon 26 B3
Garlinge Kent 71 F10
Garlinge Green Kent 54 C6
Garlogie Aberds 293 C9
Garmelow Staffs 150 D5
Garmond Aberds 303 D8
Garmondsway Durham 234 E2
Garmony Argyll 289 E8
Garmouth Moray 302 C3
Garmston Shrops 132 B2
Garn Powys 130 G2
Garnant Carms 75 C11
Garndiffaith Torf 78 E3
Garndolbenmaen Gwyn 163 G7
Garnedd Conwy 164 E2
Garnett Bridge Cumb 221 F10
Garnetts Essex 87 B10
Garnfadryn Gwyn 144 C5
Garnkirk N Lanark 268 B3
Garnlydan Bl Gwent 77 C11
Garnsgate Lincs 157 E8
Garnswllt Swansea 75 D10
Garn-swllt Swansea 75 D10
Garn-yr-erw Torf 78 C2
Garrabost W Isles 304 E7
Garrachra Argyll 275 E11
Garra Eallabus Argyll 274 F3
Garralburn Moray 302 D4
Garraron Argyll 275 C9
Garras Corn 2 E6
Garreg Flint 181 F10
Gwyn 163 G10
Garrets Green W Mid 134 F2
Garrick Perth 286 F2
Garrigill Cumb 231 C10
Garriston Stirling 285 G7
Garriston N Yorks 224 G3
Garroch Dumfries 246 G3
Garrogie Lodge Highld 291 B7
Garros Highld 298 C4
Garrow Perth 286 C2
Garrowhill Glasgow 268 C3
Garrygualach Highld 290 C3
Garryhorn Dumfries 246 E2
Garsdale Cumb 212 B4
Garsdale Head Cumb 222 G5
Garsdon Wilts 62 B3
Garshall Green Staffs 151 C9
Garsington Oxon 83 E9
Garstang Lancs 202 D5
Garston Herts 85 F10
Garston *continued*
Mers 182 E6
Garswood Mers 183 B9
Gartachoil Stirling 277 C10
Gartbreck Argyll 254 B3
Gartcosh N Lanark 268 B3
Garth Bridgend 57 C11
Ceredig 128 G2
Flint 181 E10
Gwyn 179 G9
Newport 59 B9
Newport 78 G4
Perth 285 B11
Powys 95 B9
Powys 114 C5
Shetland 313 H4
Shetland 313 H6
Wrex 166 G3
Garthamlock Glasgow 268 B3
Garthbeg Highld 291 B7
Garthbrengy Powys 95 E10
Garthdee Aberdeen 293 C11
Gartheli Ceredig 111 F11
Garthmyl Powys 130 D3
Garthorpe Leics 154 E6
N Lincs 199 D11
Garth Owen Powys 130 E2
Garth Row Cumb 221 F10
Garth Trevor Wrex 166 G3
Gartlea N Lanark 268 C5
Gartloch Glasgow 268 B3
Gartly Aberds 302 F5
Gartmore Stirling 277 B10
Gartmore Ho Stirling 277 B10
Gartnagrenach Argyll 255 B8
Gartness N Lanark 268 C5
Stirling 277 D10
Gartocharn W Dunb 277 D8
Garton E Yorks 209 F11
Garton-on-the-Wolds
E Yorks 208 B5
Gartsherrie N Lanark 268 B4
Gartur Stirling 277 B11
Gartymore Highld 311 H4
Garvald E Loth 281 G11
Garvamore Highld 291 D7
Garvard Argyll 274 D4
Garvault Hotel Highld 308 F7
Garve Highld 300 C3
Garvestone Norf 141 B10
Garvock Aberds 293 F9
Invclyd 276 G5
Garvock Hill Fife 280 D2
Garway Hereford 97 G9
Garway Hill Hereford 97 F8
Gaskan Highld 289 B9
Gasper Wilts 45 G9
Gastard Wilts 61 F11
Gasthorpe Norf 141 G9
Gaston Green Essex 87 B7
Gatacre Park Shrops 132 F5
Gatcombe IoW 20 D5
Gateacre Mers 182 D6
Gatebeck Cumb 211 B10
Gate Burton Lincs 188 E4
Gateford Notts 187 E9
Gateford Common
Notts 187 E9
Gateforth N Yorks 198 B5
Gatehead E Ayrs 257 B9
Gate Helmsley N Yorks 207 B9
Gatehouse Northumb 251 F7
Gatehouse of Fleet
Dumfries 237 D8
Gatelawbridge
Dumfries 247 D10
Gateley Norf 159 E9
Gatenby N Yorks 214 B6
Gatesgarth Cumb 220 B3
Gateshead T&W 243 E7
Gatesheath Ches W 167 C7
Gateside Aberds 293 B8
Angus 287 C8
Dumfries 248 E4
E Renf 267 D9
Fife 286 G5
N Ayrs 267 E7
Shetland 312 F4
Gatewen Wrex 166 E4
Gatherley Devon 12 E3
Gathurst Gtr Man 194 F4
Gatlas Newport 78 G4
Gatley Gtr Man 184 D4
Gatley End Cambs 104 C5
Gatton Sur 51 C9
Gattonside Borders 262 B2
Gatwick Glos 80 C2
Gatwick Airport W Sus 51 E9
Gaufron Powys 113 D9
Gaulby Leics 136 C3
Gauldry Fife 287 E7
Gauntons Bank Ches E 167 F9
Gaunt's Common Dorset 31 F8
Gaunt's Earthcott S Glos 60 C6
Gaunt's End Essex 105 E10
Gautby Lincs 189 G11
Gavinton Borders 272 E5
Gawber S Yorks 197 F10
Gawcott Bucks 102 E3
Gawsworth Ches E 168 B5
Gawthorpe W Yorks 197 C9
W Yorks 197 D7
Gawthrop Cumb 212 B3
Gawthwaite Cumb 210 C5
Gay Bowers Essex 88 E3
Gaydon Warks 119 G7
Gayfield Orkney 314 A4
Gayhurst M Keynes 103 B7
Gayle N Yorks 213 B7
Gayles N Yorks 224 D2
Gay Street W Sus 35 C9
Gayton Mers 182 E3
Norf 158 F4
Staffs 151 D9
W Nhants 120 G4
Gayton Engine Lincs 191 D7
Gayton le Marsh Lincs 190 E6
Gayton le Wold Lincs 190 D2
Gayton Thorpe Norf 158 F4
Gaywood Norf 158 E2
Gaza Shetland 312 F5
Gazeley Suff 124 E4
Geanies House Highld 301 B8
Gearraidh Bhailteas
W Isles 297 J3
Gearraidh Bhaird
W Isles 304 F5
Gearraidh Dubh W Isles 296 F4
Gearraidh na h-Aibhne
W Isles 304 E4
Gearraidh na Monadh
W Isles 297 K3
Gearraidh Sheilidh
W Isles 297 J3
Geary Highld 298 C2
Geat Wolford Warks 100 E4
Geddes House Highld 301 D8
Gedding Suff 125 F9
Geddington N Nhants 137 G7
Gedgrave Hall Suff 109 B8
Gedintailor Highld 295 B7
Gedling Notts 171 G10
Gedney Lincs 157 E8
Gedney Broadgate Lincs 157 E8
Gedney Drove End
Lincs 157 D9
Gedney Dyke Lincs 157 D8
Gedney Hill Lincs 156 G6
Gee Cross Gtr Man 185 C7
Geeston Rutland 137 C9
Gegin Wrex 166 E3
Geilston Argyll 276 F6
Geinas Denb 165 B9
Geirinis W Isles 297 G3
Geise Highld 310 C5
Geisiadar W Isles 304 E3
Geldeston Norf 143 E7
Gell Conwy 164 B5
Gelli Pembs 73 B9
Rhondda 77 G7
Gellideg M Tydf 77 D8
Gellifor Denb 165 C10
Gelli-gaer Neath 57 C9
Gelli-hôf Caerph 77 F11
Gelligroes Caerph 77 G11
Gellilydan Gwyn 146 B3
Gellinud Neath 76 E2
Gellinudd Neath 76 E2
Gellyburn Perth 286 D4
Gellygron Neath 76 E2
Gellywen Carms 92 G5
Gelsmoor Leics 153 F8
Gelston Dumfries 237 D9
Lincs 172 G6
Gembling E Yorks 209 B8
Gemini Warr 183 C9
Gendros Swansea 56 B6
Genesis Green Suff 124 F4
Gentleshaw Staffs 151 G11
Geocrab W Isles 305 J3
Georgefield Dumfries 249 E7
George Green Bucks 66 C4
Georgeham Devon 40 F3
George Nympton Devon 26 C2
Georgetown Bl Gwent 77 D10
Georgia Corn 1 B5
Gergask Highld 291 D8
Gerlan Gwyn 163 B10
Germansweek Devon 12 C4
Germiston Glasgow 268 B2
Germoe Corn 2 D3
Gernon Bushes Essex 87 E7
Gerrans Corn 3 B9
Gerrard's Bromley
Staffs 150 C5
Gerrards Cross Bucks 66 B4
Gerrick Redcar 226 C4
Geseilfa Powys 129 E8
Gestingthorpe Essex 106 D6
Gesto Ho Highld 294 B5
Geuffordd Powys 148 G4
Geufron Denb 166 G2
Gibbet Hill Warks 135 G10
W Mid 118 C6
Gibb Hill Ches W 183 F10
Gibbshill Dumfries 237 B9
Gib Heath W Mid 133 F11
Gibraltar Bedford 103 B10
Bucks 84 C3
Kent 55 F8
Gibralter Oxon 83 B7
Gibshill Invclyd 276 G6
Gibsmere Notts 172 F2
Giddeahall Wilts 61 E11
Giddy Green Dorset 18 D2
Gidea Park London 68 B4
Gidleigh Devon 13 D9
Giffard Park M Keynes 103 C7
Giffnock E Renf 267 D11
Gifford E Loth 271 B10
Giffordland N Ayrs 266 F5
Giffordtown Fife 286 F6
Gigg Gtr Man 195 F10
Giggetty Staffs 133 E7
Giggleswick N Yorks 212 G6
Giggshill Sur 67 F7
Gignog Pembs 91 G7
Gilberdyke E Yorks 199 B10
Gilbert's Coombe Corn 4 G3
Gilbert's End Worcs 98 C6
Gilbert's Green Warks 118 C2
Gilbertstone W Mid 134 G2
Gilbert Street Hants 49 G7
Gilchriston E Loth 271 B9
Gilcrux Cumb 229 D8
Gildersome W Yorks 197 B8
Gildersome Street
W Yorks 197 B8
Gildingwells S Yorks 187 D9
Gilesgate Durham 233 C11
Gilesgate Moor
Durham 233 C11
Gileston V Glam 58 F4
Gilfach Caerph 77 F11
Hereford 96 E6
Gilfach Goch Rhondda 58 B3
Gilfachrheda Ceredig 111 F8
Gilgarran Cumb 228 G6
Gill N Yorks 204 E5
Gillamoor N Yorks 216 B3
Gillan Corn 3 E7
Gillar's Green Mers 183 B7
Gillbank Cumb 221 F7
Gillbent Gtr Man 184 E5
Gillen Highld 298 D2
Gillesbie Dumfries 248 E5
Gilling East N Yorks 216 D2
Gillingham Dorset 30 B4
Medway 69 F9
Norf 143 E8
Gilling West N Yorks 224 D3
Gillmoss Mers 182 B6
Gillock Highld 310 D6
Gillow Heath Staffs 168 D5
Gills Highld 310 B7
Gill's Green Kent 53 G9
Gillway Staffs 134 C4
Gilmanscleuch Borders 261 E8
Gilmerton Edin 270 B5
Perth 286 E2
Gilmonby Durham 223 C9
Gilmorton Leics 135 F11
Gilmourton S Lanark 268 G3
Gilnow Gtr Man 195 F8
Gilroyd S Yorks 197 G10
Gilsland Northumb 240 D4
Gilsland Spa Cumb 240 D4
Gilson Warks 134 E3
Gilstead W Yorks 205 F8
Gilston Borders 271 D8
Herts 86 C6
Gilston Park Herts 86 C6
Giltbrook Notts 171 F7
Gilver's Lane Worcs 98 C6
Gilwell Park Essex 86 F5
Gilwern Mon 78 C2
Gimingham Norf 160 B5
Ginclough Ches E 185 F7
Ginger's Green E Sus 23 C10
Giosla W Isles 304 F3
Gipping Suff 125 E11
Gipsey Bridge Lincs 174 F3
Gipsy Row Suff 107 D11
Gipsyville Hull 200 B5
Gipton W Yorks 206 F2
Gipton Wood W Yorks 206 F2
Girdle Toll N Ayrs 266 G6
Girlington W Yorks 205 G8
Girlsta Shetland 313 H6
Girsby Lincs 190 D2
N Yorks 225 D7
Girt Som 29 C10
Girtford C Beds 104 B3
C Beds 122 G3
Girthon Dumfries 237 D8
Girton Cambs 123 E8
Notts 172 B4
Girvan S Ayrs 244 D5
Gisburn Lancs 204 D2
Gisleham Suff 143 F10
Gislingham Suff 125 C11
Gissing Norf 142 F2
Gittisham Devon 15 B8
Givons Grove Sur 51 C7
Glachavoil Argyll 275 F11
Glackmore Highld 300 D6
Glack of Midthird Moray 302 E3
Gladestry Powys 114 F4
Gladsmuir E Loth 281 G9
Glaichbea Highld 300 F5
Glais Swansea 76 E2
Glaisdale N Yorks 226 D5
Glame Highld 298 E5
Glamis Angus 287 C7
Glan Adda Gwyn 179 G9
Glanafon Pembs 73 B7
Glanaman Carms 75 C11
Glan-Conwy Conwy 164 E4
Glandford Norf 177 E8
Glan-Duar Carms 93 C10
Glandwr Caerph 78 E2
Pembs 92 F3
Glan-Dwyfach Gwyn 163 G7
Glandy Cross Carms 92 F2
Glandyfi Ceredig 128 D3
Glan Gors Anglesey 179 F7
Glangrwyney Powys 78 B2
Glanhanog Powys 129 D8
Glanmule Powys 130 E3
Glanrafon Ceredig 128 G2
Glanrhyd Gwyn 144 B5
Pembs 92 C2
Glan-rhyd Gwyn 163 D7
Powys 76 D3
Glantlees Northumb 252 B4
Glanton Northumb 264 G3
Glanton Pike Northumb 264 G3
Glan-traeth Anglesey 178 F3
Glantwymyn *=Cemmaes Road* Powys 128 C6
Glanvilles Wootton
Dorset 29 F11
Glanwern Ceredig 128 F2
Glanwydden Conwy 180 E4
Glan-y-don Flint 181 F11
Glan y Ffer *=Ferryside*
Carms 74 C5
Glan-y-llyn Rhondda 58 C6
Glan-y-môr Carms 74 C4
Glan-y-nant Caerph 77 F10
Powys 129 G8
Glan-yr-afon Anglesey 179 E10
Flint 181 E10
Gwyn 164 G6
Gwyn 165 G8
Shrops 148 E4
Glan-y-wern Gwyn 146 C2
Glapthorn N Nhants 137 E10
Glapwell Derbys 171 B7
Glas-allt Shiel Aberds 292 E4
Glasbury Powys 96 D3
Glaschoil Highld 301 F10
Glascoed Denb 181 G7
Mon 78 E4
Powys 129 F11
Powys 148 G2
Wrex 166 E3
Glascorrie Aberds 292 D5
Perth 286 E2
Glascote Staffs 134 C4
Glascwm Powys 114 G3
Glasdir Flint 181 E10
Glasdrum Argyll 284 C4
Glasfryn Conwy 164 E6
Glasgoed Ceredig 92 B6
Glasgoforest Aberds 293 B10
Glasgow Glasgow 267 B11
Glashvin Highld 298 C4
Glasinfryn Gwyn 163 B9
Glaslwch Newport 59 B9
Glasnacardoch Highld 295 F8
Glasnakille Highld 295 D7
Glasphein Highld 297 G7
Glaspwll Powys 128 D4
Glassburn Highld 300 F3
Glassenbury Kent 53 F8
Glasserton Dumfries 236 F6
Glassford S Lanark 268 F4
Glassgreen Moray 302 C2
Glasshoughton W Yorks 198 C2
Glasshouse Glos 98 G4
Glasshouse Hill Glos 98 G4
Glasshouses N Yorks 214 G3
Glasslie Fife 286 G6
Glasson Cumb 228 D6
Cumb 239 E7
Lancs 202 B4
Glassonby Cumb 231 D7
Glasterlaw Angus 287 B9
Glaston Rutland 137 C7
Glastonbury Som 44 F4
Glatton Cambs 138 F3
Glazebrook Warr 183 C11
Glazebury Warr 183 B11
Glazeley Shrops 132 F4
Gleadless S Yorks 186 E5
Gleadless Valley
S Yorks 186 E5
Gleadmoss Ches E 168 B4
Gleadsmoss Ches E 168 B4
Gleanhead Dumfries 245 G10
Gleann Tholàstaidh
W Isles 304 D7
Gleaston Cumb 210 E5
Glebe Hants 33 D9
Shetland 313 J6
T&W 243 F8
Glecknabae Argyll 275 G11
Gledhow W Yorks 206 F2
Gledrid Shrops 148 B5
Gleiniant Powys 129 E9
Glemsford Suff 106 B6
Glen Dumfries 237 B10
Dumfries 237 D7
Glenallachie Moray 302 E2
Glenalmond College
Perth 286 E3
Glenalmond Ho Perth 286 E3
Glenamachrie Argyll 289 G11
Glenample Stirling 285 E9
Glenancross Highld 295 F8
Glenapp Castle S Ayrs 244 G3
Glenaros Ho Argyll 289 E7
Glen Auldyn IoM 192 C5
Glenbarr Argyll 255 D7
Glenbeg Highld 289 C7
Highld 301 G10
Glen Bernisdale Highld 298 E4
Glenbervie Aberds 293 E9
Glenboig N Lanark 268 B4
Glenborrodale Highld 289 C8
Glenbranter Argyll 276 B2
Glenbreck Borders 260 E3
Glenbrein Lodge Highld 290 B6
Glenbrittle House
Highld 294 C6
Glenbrook Edin 270 B2
Glenbuchat Castle
Aberds 292 B5
Glenbuchat Lodge
Aberds 292 B5
Glenbuck E Ayrs 259 D7
Glenburn Renfs 267 C9
Glenbyre Argyll 289 G7
Glencalvie Lodge Highld 309 L4
Glencanisp Lodge
Highld 307 G6
Glencaple Dumfries 237 C11
Glencarron Lodge
Highld 299 D10
Glencarse Perth 286 E5
Glencassley Castle
Highld 309 J4
Glencat Aberds 293 D7
Glenceitlein Highld 284 C5
Glencoe Highld 284 B4
Glencraig Fife 280 B3
Glencripesdale Highld 289 D8
Glencrosh Dumfries 247 F7
Glendavan Ho Aberds 292 C6
Glendearg Borders 262 B2
Glendevon Perth 286 G3
Glendoebeg Highld 290 C6
Glendoe Lodge Highld 290 C6
Glendoick Perth 286 E6
Glendoll Lodge Angus 292 F4
Glendoune S Ayrs 244 D5
Glenduckie Fife 286 F6
Glendye Lodge Aberds 293 E8
Gleneagles Hotel Perth 286 F3
Gleneagles House Perth 286 G3
Glenearn Perth 286 F5
Glenegedale Argyll 254 B4
Glenelg Highld 295 D10
Glenernie Moray 301 E10
Glenfarg Perth 286 F5
Glenfarquhar Lodge
Aberds 293 E9
Glenferness House
Highld 301 E9
Glenfeshie Lodge
Highld 291 D10
Glenfiddich Lodge
Moray 302 F3
Glenfield Leics 135 B10
Glenfinnan Highld 295 G10
Glenfinnan Lodge
Highld 295 G11
Glenfintaig Ho Highld 290 E4
Glenfoot Perth 286 F5
Glenfyne Lodge Argyll 284 F6
Glengap Dumfries 237 D8
Glengarnock N Ayrs 266 E6
Glengolly Highld 310 C5
Glengorm Castle Argyll 288 D6
Glengoulandie Perth 285 B11
Glengrasco Highld 298 E4
Glenhead Farm Angus 292 G4
Glen Ho Borders 261 C7
Glenholt Plym 7 C10
Glenhoul Dumfries 246 F4
Glenhurich Highld 289 C10
Glenkerry Borders 261 G7
Glenkiln Dumfries 237 B10
Glenkindie Aberds 292 B6
Glenlair Dumfries 237 B9
Glenlatterach Moray 301 D11
Glenlee Dumfries 246 G4
Glenleigh Park E Sus 38 F2
Glenleraig Highld 306 F6
Glenlichorn Perth 285 F11
Glenlicht Ho Highld 290 B2
Glenlivet Moray 301 G11
Glenlochar Dumfries 237 C9
Glenlochsie Perth 292 F2
Glenlocksie Lodge
Perth 292 F2
Glenloig N Ayrs 255 D10
Glenlomond Perth 286 G5
Glenluce Dumfries 236 D4
Glenlussa Ho Argyll 255 E8
Glenmallan Argyll 276 B5
Glenmarkie Lodge
Angus 292 G4
Glenmarksie Highld 300 D3
Glenmavis N Lanark 268 B4
W Loth 269 B9
Glenmaye IoM 192 E3
Glenmayne Borders 261 C11
Glenmeanie Highld 300 D2
Glenmidge Dumfries 247 F9
Glenmoidart Ho Highld 289 B9
Glen Mona IoM 192 D5
Glen Mor Highld 295 B10
Glenmore Argyll 275 B9
Argyll 275 G11
Highld 298 E4
Glenmore Lodge
Highld 291 C11
Glenmoy Angus 292 G6
Glen Nevis House Highld 290 F3
Glennoe Argyll 284 D4
Glen of Newmill Moray 302 D4
Glenogil Angus 292 G6
Glenowen Pembs 73 D7
Glen Parva Leics 135 D11
Glenprosen Lodge
Angus 292 G4
Glenprosen Village
Angus 292 G5
Glenquaich Lodge
Perth 286 D2
Glenquiech Angus 292 G6
Glenquithlie Aberds 303 C8
Glenrath Borders 260 C6
Glenrazie Dumfries 236 C5
Glenreasdell Mains
Argyll 255 B9
Glenree N Ayrs 255 E10
Glenridding Cumb 221 B7
Glenrosa N Ayrs 256 B2
Glenrossal Highld 309 J4
Glenrothes Fife 286 G6
Glensanda Highld 289 E10
Glensaugh Aberds 293 F8
Glensburgh Falk 279 E8
Glenshero Lodge Highld 291 D7
Glenshoe Lodge Perth 292 G3
Glen Sluain Argyll 275 D11
Glenstockadale
Dumfries 236 C2
Glenstriven Argyll 275 F11
Glentaggart S Lanark 259 D8
Glen Tanar House
Aberds 292 D6
Glentarkie Perth 286 F5
Glenternie Borders 260 B6
Glentham Lincs 189 C8
Glentirranmuir Stirling 278 C3
Glenton Aberds 302 G6
Glentress Borders 261 B7
Glentromie Lodge
Highld 291 D9
Glen Trool Lodge
Dumfries 245 G10
Glentrool Village
Dumfries 236 B5
Glentruan IoM 192 B5
Glentruim House Highld 291 D8
Glentworth Lincs 188 D6
Glenuaig Lodge Highld 299 E11
Glenuig Highld 289 B8
Glenure Argyll 284 C4
Glenurquhart Highld 301 C7
Glen Village Falk 279 F7
Glen Vic Askil Highld 298 E3
Glenview Argyll 284 E5
Glen Village Falk 279 F7
Glen Vine IoM 192 E4
Glespin S Lanark 259 D8
Gletness Shetland 313 H6
Glewstone Hereford 97 G11
Glinton Pboro 138 B3
Globe Town London 67 C11
Glodwick Gtr Man 196 G2
Glogue Pembs 92 E4
Glooston Leics 136 D4
Glororum Northumb 264 C5
Glossop Derbys 185 C8
Gloster Hill Northumb 253 C7
Gloucester Glos 80 B4
Gloup Shetland 312 C7
Glutton Green Shetland 310 E7
Gloweth Corn 4 G5
Glusburn N Yorks 204 E6
Glutt Lodge Highld 310 F3
Glutton Bridge Staffs 169 B9
Gluvian Corn 5 C8
Glympton Oxon 101 G8
Glyn Mon 79 F7
Powys 129 F8
Glynarthen Ceredig 92 B6
Glynbrochan Powys 129 G8
Glyn Castle Neath 76 E4
Glyn-Ceiriog Wrex 148 B4
Glyncoch Rhondda 77 G9
Glyncorrwg Neath 57 B11
Glyn-Cywarch Gwyn 146 C2
Glynde E Sus 23 D7
Glyndebourne E Sus 23 C7
Glyndyfrdwy Denb 165 G10
Glynedd *=Glyn neath*
Neath 76 D5
Glyne Gap E Sus 38 F3
Glyn Etwy Bl Gwent 77 D11
Glynhafren Powys 129 G7
Glynllan Bridgend 58 B2
Glynmorlas Shrops 148 B6
Glyn-neath *=Glynedd*
Neath 76 D5
Glynogwr Bridgend 58 B3
Glyntaff Rhondda 58 B5
Glyntawe Powys 76 B4
Gnosall Staffs 150 E6
Gnosall Heath Staffs 150 E6
Goadby Leics 136 D4
Goadby Marwood Leics 154 D5
Goatacre Wilts 62 D4
Goatham Green E Sus 38 C4
Goathill Dorset 29 D11
Goathland N Yorks 226 E6
Goathurst Som 43 G9
Goathurst Common Kent 52 C3
Goat Lees Kent 54 D4
Gobernuisgach Lodge
Highld 308 E4
Gobernuisgeach Highld 310 F3
Gobhaig W Isles 305 H2
Gobley Hole Hants 48 D6
Gobowen Shrops 148 C6
Godalming Sur 50 E3
Goddards Bucks 84 G3
Goddard's Corner Suff 126 D5
Goddard's Green Kent 53 G10
W Berks 65 F7
Goddards' Green W Sus 36 C3
Godden Green Kent 52 B5
Goddington London 68 F3
Godley Gtr Man 185 B7
Godleybrook Staffs 169 G7
Godley Hill Gtr Man 185 C7
Godleys Green E Sus 36 D5
Godmanchester Cambs 122 C4
Godmanstone Dorset 17 B9
Godmersham Kent 54 C5
Godney Som 44 E3
Godolphin Cross Corn 2 C4
Godre'r-graig Neath 76 D3
God's Blessing Green
Dorset 31 G8
Godshill Hants 31 E11
IoW 20 E6
Godstone Sur 51 C10
Godswinscroft Hants 19 B9
Godwell Devon 8 D2
Godwick Norf 159 E8
Godwinscroft Hants 19 B9
Goetre Mon 78 D4
Goferydd Anglesey 178 E2
Goff's Oak Herts 86 E4
Gogar Edin 280 G3
Goginan Ceredig 128 G3
Goirtean a'Chladaich
Highld 290 F2
Golan Gwyn 163 G8
Golant Corn 6 E2
Golberdon Corn 12 G2
Golborne Gtr Man 183 B10
Golcar W Yorks 196 D6
Golch Flint 181 F11
Goldcliff Newport 59 C11
Golden Balls Oxon 83 F9
Golden Cross E Sus 23 C8
E Sus 23 C10
Golden Green Kent 52 D6
Golden Grove Carms 75 B9
Goldenhill Stoke 168 E5
Golden Hill Bristol 60 D5
Hants 19 B11
Pembs 73 E7
Pembs 91 G9
Golden Park Devon 24 C2
Golden Pot Hants 49 E8
Golden Valley Derbys 170 E6
Glos 99 G8
Hereford 98 B3
Golder Field Hereford 115 E11
Golders Green London 67 B9
Goldfinch Bottom
W Berks 64 G4
Goldhanger Essex 88 D6
Gold Hill Dorset 30 E4
Norf 139 E10
Golding Shrops 131 C10
Goldington Bedford 121 G11
Goldsborough N Yorks 206 B3
N Yorks 226 C6
Gold's Cross Bath 60 G5
Golds Green W Mid 133 E9
Goldsithney Corn 2 C2
Goldstone Shrops 150 D4
Goldthorn Park W Mid 133 D8
Goldthorpe S Yorks 198 G3
Goldworthy Devon 24 C5
Golford Kent 53 F9
Golftyn Flint 182 G3
Golgotha Kent 55 D9
Gollanfield Highld 301 D8
Gollawater Corn 4 E5
Gollinglith Foot
N Yorks 214 C3
Golly Wrex 166 D4
Golsoncott Som 42 F4
Golspie Highld 311 J2
Golval Highld 310 C2
Golynos Torf 78 E3
Gomeldon Wilts 47 F7
Gomersal W Yorks 197 B8
Gometra Ho Argyll 288 E5
Gomshall Sur 50 D5
Gonalston Notts 171 F11
Gonamena Corn 11 G11
Gonerby Hill Foot Lincs 155 B8
Gonfirth Shetland 313 G5
Good Easter Essex 87 C10
Gooderstone Norf 140 C5
Goodleigh Devon 40 G6
Goodley Stock Kent 52 C2
Goodmanham E Yorks 208 E3
Goodmayes London 68 B3
Goodnestone Kent 55 C9
Kent 70 G4
Goodrich Hereford 79 B9
Goodrington Torbay 9 D7
Good's Green Worcs 132 G5
Goodshaw Lancs 195 B10
Goodshaw Chapel
Lancs 195 B10
Goodshaw Fold Lancs 195 B10
Goodstone Devon 13 G11
Goodwick *=Wdig* Pembs 91 D8
Goodworth Clatford
Hants 47 E11
Goodyers End Warks 134 F6
Goodyhills Cumb 229 B8
Goole E Yorks 199 C8
Goom's Hill Worcs 117 G10
Goonabarn Corn 5 E9
Goonbell Corn 4 F4
Goon Gumpas Corn 4 G4
Goonhavern Corn 4 E5
Goonhusband Corn 2 D5
Goonlaze Corn 2 B6
Goonown Corn 4 E4
Goonpiper Corn 3 B8
Goonvrea Corn 4 F4
Gooseberry Green Essex 87 F11
Goose Eye W Yorks 204 E6
Gooseford Devon 13 C9
Goose Green Cumb 211 C10
Essex 108 F2
Gtr Man 194 G5
Hants 32 F4
Herts 86 D5
Kent 52 C6
Kent 53 F10
Lancs 194 C3
Norf 142 F2
S Glos 61 C8
W Sus 34 C3
W Sus 35 D10
Gooseham Mill Devon 24 D2
Goosehill W Yorks 197 C11
Goose Hill Hants 64 G4
Goosehill Green Worcs 117 E8
Goosemoor Staffs 150 F6
Goosemoor Green
Staffs 151 G11
Goosenford Som 28 B2
Goose Pool Hereford 97 D9
Goosewell Devon 40 D5
Goosey Oxon 82 G5
Goosnargh Lancs 203 F7
Goostrey Ches E 184 G3
Gorbals Glasgow 267 C11
Gorcott Hill Warks 117 D11
Gord Shetland 313 L6
Gorddinog Conwy 179 G11
Gordon Borders 272 G2
Gordonbush Highld 311 J2
Gordonsburgh Moray 302 C4
Gordonstoun Moray 301 C11
Gordonstown Aberds 302 D5
Aberds 303 F7
Gore Dorset 29 D9
Kent 55 B10
Gorebridge Midloth 270 C6
Gore Cross Wilts 46 C4
Gore End Hants 64 G2
Gorefield Cambs 157 G8
Gorehill W Sus 35 C7
Gore Pit Essex 88 B5
Gore Street Kent 71 F9
Gorgie Edin 280 G4
Gorhambury Herts 85 D10
Goring Oxon 64 C6
Goring-by-Sea W Sus 35 G10
Goring Heath Oxon 65 D7
Gorleston-on-Sea
Norf 143 C10
Gornalwood W Mid 133 E8
Gorrachie Aberds 303 D7
Gorran Churchtown Corn 5 G9
Gorran Haven Corn 5 G10
Gorran High Lanes Corn 5 G9
Gorrenberry Borders 249 D11
Gorrig Ceredig 93 C8
Gorse Covert Warr 183 C11
Gorsedd Flint 181 F11
Gorse Hill Gtr Man 184 B4
Swindon 63 B7
Gorseinon Swansea 56 B5
Gorseness Orkney 314 E4
Gorsethorpe Notts 171 B9
Gorseybank Derbys 170 E3
Gorsgoch Ceredig 111 G9
Gorslas Carms 75 C9
Gorsley Glos 98 F3
Gorsley Common
Hereford 98 F3
Gorsley Ley Staffs 133 B11
Gorstage Ches W 183 G10
Gorstan Highld 300 C3
Gorstanvorran Highld 289 B10
Gorstella Ches W 166 C5
Gorsteyhill Ches E 168 E2
Gorst Hill Worcs 116 C4
Gorstyhill Staffs 168 E2
Gorsty Hill Staffs 151 D11
Gortan Argyll 274 G3
Gortantaoid Argyll 274 F4
Gortenacullish Highld 295 G8
Gorteneorn Highld 289 C8

Gortenfern Highld 289 C8
Gortinanane Argyll 255 C8
Gorton Gtr Man 184 B5
Gortonallister N Ayrs 256 D2
Gosbeck Suff 126 F3
Gosberton Lincs 156 C4
Gosberton Cheal Lincs 156 D4
Gosberton Clough Lincs 156 D3
Goscote W Mid 133 C10
Goseley Dale Derbys 152 E6
Gosfield Essex 106 F5
Gosford Hereford 115 D10
Oxon 83 C7
Gosford Green W Mid 118 B6
Gosforth Cumb 219 E11
T&W 242 D6
Gosforth Valley Derbys 186 F4
Gosland Green Suff 124 G5
Gosling Green Suff 107 C9
Gosmere Kent 54 B4
Gosmore Herts 104 F3
Gospel Ash Staffs 132 E6
Gospel End Village
Staffs 133 E7
Gospel Green W Sus 50 G2
Gospel Oak London 67 B9
Gosport Hants 21 B8
Hants 32 C5
Gossabrough Shetland 312 E7
Gossard's Green C Beds 103 C9
Gossington Glos 80 E2
Gossops Green W Sus 51 F9
Goswick Northumb 273 F11
Gotham Dorset 31 E9
E Sus 38 F2
Notts 153 C10
Gothelney Green Som 43 F9
Gotherington Glos 99 F9
Gothers Corn 5 D9
Gott Argyll 288 E2
Shetland 313 J6
Gotton Som 28 B2
Goudhurst Kent 53 F8
Goukstone Moray 302 D4
Goulceby Lincs 190 F3
Goulton N Yorks 225 E9
Gourdas Aberds 303 E7
Gourdon Aberds 293 F10
Gourock Invclyd 276 F4
Govan Glasgow 267 B11
Govanhill Glasgow 267 C11
Gover Hill Kent 52 C6
Goverton Notts 172 E2
Goveton Devon 8 F5
Govilon Mon 78 C3
Gowanhill Aberds 303 C10
Gowanwell Aberds 303 E8
Gowdall E Yorks 198 C6
Gowerton = Tre-Gwyr
Swansea 56 B5
Gowhole Derbys 185 E8
Gowkhall Fife 279 D11
Gowkthrapple N Lanark 268 E5
Gowthorpe E Yorks 207 C11
Goxhill E Yorks 209 E9
N Lincs 200 C6
Goxhill Haven N Lincs 200 B6
Goybre Neath 57 D9
Goytre Neath 57 D9
Gozzard's Ford Oxon 83 F7
Grabhair W Isles 305 G5
Graby Lincs 155 D11
Gracca Corn 5 D10
Gracemount Edin 270 B5
Grade Corn 2 G6
Graffham W Sus 34 D6
Grafham Cambs 122 D3
Sur 50 E4
Grafton Hereford 97 D9
N Yorks 215 G8
Oxon 82 E3
Shrops 149 F8
Worcs 99 D9
Worcs 115 E11
Grafton Flyford Worcs 117 F9
Grafton Regis W Nhants 102 B5
Grafton Underwood
N Nhants 137 G8
Grafty Green Kent 53 D11
Grahamston Falk 279 E7
Graianrhyd Denb 166 D2
Graig Carms 74 E6
Conwy 180 G4
Denb 181 G9
Rhondda 58 B5
Wrex 148 B4
Graig-Fawr Swansea 75 E10
Graig-fechan Denb 165 E10
Graig Felen Swansea 75 E11
Graig Penllyn V Glam 58 D3
Graig Trewyddfa Swansea 57 B7
Grain Medway 69 D11
Grains Bar Gtr Man 196 F3
Grainsby Lincs 190 B3
Grainthorpe Lincs 190 B5
Grainthorpe Fen Lincs 190 B5
Graiselound N Lincs 188 B3
Grampound Corn 5 F8
Grampound Road Corn 5 E8
Gramsdal W Isles 296 F4
Granborough Bucks 102 F5
Granby Notts 154 B5
Grandborough Warks 119 D9
Grandpont Oxon 83 D8
Grandtully Perth 286 B3
Grange Cumb 220 B5
Dorset 31 G8
E Ayrs 257 B10
Fife 287 G8
Halton 183 E8
Lancs 203 G7
Medway 69 F9
Mers 182 D2
NE Lincs 201 F9
N Yorks 223 G8
Perth 286 E6
Warr 183 C10
Grange Crossroads
Moray 302 D4
Grange Estate Dorset 31 G10
Grange Hall Moray 301 C10
Grange Hill Durham 233 F10
Essex 86 G6
Grangemill Derbys 170 D2
Grange Moor W Yorks 197 D8
Grangemouth Falk 279 E8
Grangemuir Fife 287 G9
Grange of Cree
Dumfries 236 D6
Grange of Lindores Fife 286 F6
Grange-over-Sands
Cumb 211 D8
Grangepans Falk 279 E10
Grange Park London 86 F4
Mers 183 C7
Swindon 62 C6
W Nhants 120 F5
Grangetown Cardiff 59 E7
Redcar 235 G7
Grangetown continued
T&W 243 G10
Grange Villa Durham 242 G6
Grange Village Glos 79 C11
Granish Highld 291 B11
Gransmoor E Yorks 209 B8
Gransmore Green
Essex 106 G3
Granston = Treopert
Pembs 91 E7
Grantchester Cambs 123 F8
Grantham Lincs 155 B8
Grantley N Yorks 214 F4
Grantley Hall N Yorks 214 F4
Grantlodge Aberds 293 B9
Granton Dumfries 248 B3
Edin 280 F4
Grantown Aberds 302 D5
Grantown-on-Spey
Highld 301 G10
Grantsfield Hereford 115 E10
Grantshouse Borders 272 B6
Grant Thorold NE Lincs 201 F9
Graplin Dumfries 237 E8
Grappenhall Warr 183 D10
Grasby Lincs 200 G5
Grasmere Cumb 220 D6
Grasscroft Gtr Man 196 G3
Grassendale Mers 182 D5
Grassgarth Cumb 221 F8
Cumb 230 C2
Grass Green Essex 106 D4
Grassholme Durham 232 G4
Grassington N Yorks 213 G10
Grassmoor Derbys 170 B6
Grassthorpe Notts 172 B3
Grasswell T&W 243 G8
Grateley Hants 47 E9
Gratton Devon 24 E5
Gratwich Staffs 151 C10
Gravel Ches W 167 B11
Gravel Castle Kent 55 D8
Graveley Cambs 122 E4
Herts 104 F4
Gravelhill Shrops 149 G9
Gravel Hill Bucks 85 G8
Gravel Hole Gtr Man 196 F2
Shrops 149 B7
Gravelly Hill W Mid 134 E2
Gravels Shrops 130 D6
Gravelsbank Shrops 130 C6
Graven Shetland 312 F6
Graveney Kent 70 G5
Gravenhill Oxon 101 G11
Gravenhunger Moss
Shrops 168 G2
Gravesend Herts 105 F8
Kent 68 E6
Grayingham Lincs 188 B6
Grayrigg Cumb 221 F11
Grays Thurrock 68 D6
Grayshott Hants 49 F11
Grayson Green Cumb 228 F5
Grayswood Sur 50 G2
Graythorp Hrtlpl 234 F6
Grazeley Wokingham 65 F7
Grazeley Green W Berks 65 F7
Greagdhubh Lodge
Highld 291 D8
Greamchary Highld 310 F2
Greasbrough S Yorks 186 B6
Greasby Mers 182 D3
Greasley Notts 171 F7
Great Abington Cambs 105 B10
Great Addington
N Nhants 121 B9
Great Alne Warks 118 F2
Great Altcar Lancs 193 F10
Great Amwell Herts 86 C5
Great Asby Cumb 222 C3
Great Ashfield Suff 125 D9
Great Ashley Wilts 61 G10
Great Ayton N Yorks 225 C11
Great Baddow Essex 88 E2
Great Bardfield Essex 106 E3
Great Barford Bedford 122 G2
Great Barrington Glos 82 C2
Great Barrow Ches W 167 B7
Great Barton Suff 125 D7
Great Barugh N Yorks 216 D4
Great Bavington
Northumb 251 G11
Great Bealings Suff 108 B4
Great Bedwyn Wilts 63 G9
Great Bentley Essex 108 G2
Great Berry Essex 69 B7
Great Billing W Nhants 120 E6
Great Bircham Norf 158 C5
Great Blakenham Suff 126 G2
Great Blencow Cumb 230 E5
Great Bolas Telford 150 E2
Great Bookham Sur 50 C6
Great Bosullow Corn 1 C4
Great Bourton Oxon 101 B9
Great Bowden Leics 136 F4
Great Bower Kent 54 C4
Great Bradley Suff 124 G3
Great Braxted Essex 88 C5
Great Bricett Suff 125 G10
Great Brickhill Bucks 103 E8
Great Bridge W Mid 133 E9
Great Bridgeford Staffs 151 D7
Great Brington
W Nhants 120 D3
Great Bromley Essex 107 F11
Great Broughton Cumb 228 E6
N Yorks 225 D10
Great Buckland Kent 69 G7
Great Budworth
Ches W 183 F11
Great Burdon Darl 224 B6
Great Burgh Sur 51 B8
Great Burstead Essex 87 G11
Great Busby N Yorks 225 D10
Great Canfield Essex 87 B9
Great Carlton Lincs 190 D6
Great Casterton Rutland 137 B9
Rutland 137 B10
Great Cellws Powys 113 E11
Great Chalfield Wilts 61 G11
Great Chart Kent 54 E3
Great Chatwell Staffs 150 G5
Great Chell Stoke 168 E5
Great Chesterford
Essex 105 C10
Great Cheveney Kent 53 E8
Great Cheverell Wilts 46 C3
Great Chilton Durham 233 E11
Great Chishill Cambs 105 D8
Great Clacton Essex 89 B11
Great Claydons Essex 88 E3
Great Cliff W Yorks 197 D10
Great Clifton Cumb 228 F6
Great Coates NE Lincs 201 F8
Great Comberton Worcs 99 C9
Great Common Suff 143 F7
W Sus 35 B8
Great Corby Cumb 239 G11
Great Cornard Suff 107 C7
Great Cowden E Yorks 209 E10
Great Coxwell Oxon 82 G3
Great Crakehall
N Yorks 224 G4
Great Cransley
N Nhants 120 B6
Great Cressingham
Norf 141 C7
Great Crosby Mers 182 B4
Great Crosthwaite
Cumb 229 G11
Great Cubley Derbys 152 B3
Great Dalby Leics 154 G4
Great Denham Bedford 103 B10
Great Doddington
N Nhants 121 E7
Great Doward Hereford 79 B9
Great Dunham Norf 159 G7
Great Dunmow Essex 106 G2
Great Durnford Wilts 46 F6
Great Easton Essex 106 F2
Leics 136 E6
Great Eccleston Lancs 202 E4
Great Edstone N Yorks 216 C4
Great Ellingham Norf 141 D10
Great Elm Som 45 D8
Great Eppleton T&W 234 B3
Greater Doward Hereford 79 B9
Great Eversden Cambs 123 G7
Great Fencote N Yorks 224 G5
Greatfield Wilts 62 B5
Great Finborough Suff 125 F10
Greatford Lincs 155 G11
Great Fransham Norf 159 G7
Great Gaddesden Herts 85 C8
Greatgap Bucks 84 B6
Greatgate Staffs 169 G9
Great Gate Staffs 169 G9
Great Gidding Cambs 138 G2
Great Givendale
E Yorks 208 C2
Great Glemham Suff 126 E6
Great Glen Leics 136 D3
Great Gonerby Lincs 155 B7
Great Gransden Cambs 122 F5
Great Green Cambs 104 C5
Norf 142 F5
Suff 125 B11
Suff 125 F8
Suff 126 B2
Great Habton N Yorks 216 D5
Great Hale Lincs 173 G10
Great Hallingbury Essex 87 B8
Greatham Hants 49 G9
Hrtlpl 234 F5
W Sus 35 D8
Great Hampden Bucks 84 E4
Great Harrowden
N Nhants 121 C7
Great Harwood Lancs 203 G10
Great Haseley Oxon 83 E10
Great Hatfield E Yorks 209 E9
Great Haywood Staffs 151 E9
Staffs 151 E10
Great Heath W Mid 134 G6
Great Heck N Yorks 198 C5
Great Henny Essex 107 D7
Great Hinton Wilts 46 B2
Great Hivings Bucks 85 E7
Great Hockham Norf 141 E9
Great Holcombe Oxon 83 F10
Great Holland Essex 89 B12
Great Hollands Brack 65 F11
Great Holm M Keynes 102 D6
Great Honeyborough
Pembs 73 D7
Great Horkesley Essex 107 E9
Great Hormead Herts 105 F7
Great Horton W Yorks 205 G8
Great Horwood Bucks 102 E5
Great Houghton
S Yorks 198 F2
W Nhants 120 F5
Great Howarth Gtr Man 196 D2
Great Hucklow Derbys 185 F11
Great Job's Cross Kent 38 B4
Great Kelk E Yorks 209 B8
Great Kendale E Yorks 217 G10
Great Kimble Bucks 84 D4
Great Kingshill Bucks 84 F5
Great Langton N Yorks 224 F5
Great Lea Common
Reading 65 F8
Great Leighs Essex 88 B2
Great Lever Gtr Man 195 F8
Great Limber Lincs 200 F6
Great Linford M Keynes 103 C7
Great Livermere Suff 125 C7
Great Longstone Derbys 186 G2
Great Lumley Durham 233 B11
Great Lyth Shrops 131 B9
Great Malgraves Thurrock 69 C7
Great Malvern Worcs 98 B5
Great Maplestead Essex 106 E6
Great Marton Blackpool 202 F2
Great Marton Moss
Blackpool 202 G2
Great Massingham Norf 158 E5
Great Melton Norf 142 B2
Great Milton Oxon 83 E10
Great Missenden Bucks 84 E5
Great Mitton Lancs 203 F10
Great Mongeham Kent 55 C10
Greatmoor Bucks 102 G4
Great Moor Gtr Man 184 D6
Staffs 132 D6
Great Moulton Norf 142 E3
Great Munden Herts 105 G7
Great Musgrave Cumb 222 C5
Greatness Kent 52 B4
Great Ness Shrops 149 F7
Great Notley Essex 106 G4
Great Oak Mon 78 D5
Great Oakley Essex 108 F3
N Nhants 137 F7
Great Offley Herts 104 F2
Great Ormside Cumb 222 B4
Great Orton Cumb 239 G8
Great Ouseburn
N Yorks 215 G8
Great Oxendon
W Nhants 136 G4
Great Oxney Green
Essex 87 D11
Great Palgrave Norf 158 G6
Great Parndon Essex 86 D6
Great Pattenden Kent 53 E8
Great Paxton Cambs 122 E4
Great Plumpton Lancs 202 G3
Great Plumstead Norf 160 G6
Great Ponton Lincs 155 C8
Great Preston W Yorks 198 B2
Great Purston
W Nhants 101 D10
Great Raveley Cambs 138 G5
Great Rissington Glos 81 B11
Great Rollright Oxon 100 E6
Great Ryburgh Norf 159 D9
Great Ryle Northumb 264 G2
Great Ryton Shrops 131 C9
Great Saling Essex 106 F4
Great Salkeld Cumb 231 D7
Great Sampford Essex 106 D2
Great Sankey Warr 183 D9
Great Saredon Staffs 133 B9
Great Saxham Suff 124 E5
Great Shefford W Berks 63 E11
Great Shelford Cambs 123 G9
Great Shoddesden Hants 47 D9
Great Smeaton N Yorks 224 E6
Great Snoring Norf 159 C8
Great Somerford Wilts 62 C3
Great Stainton Darl 234 G2
Great Stambridge Essex 88 G5
Great Staughton Cambs 122 E2
Great Steeping Lincs 174 C6
Great Stoke S Glos 60 C6
Great Stonar Kent 55 B10
Greatstone-on-Sea Kent 39 C9
Great Stretton Leics 136 C3
Great Strickland Cumb 231 G7
Great Stukeley Cambs 122 C4
Great Sturton Lincs 190 F2
Great Sutton Ches W 182 F5
Shrops 131 G10
Great Swinburne
Northumb 241 B10
Great Tew Oxon 101 F7
Great Tey Essex 107 F7
Great Thirkleby N Yorks 215 D9
Great Thurlow Suff 124 G3
Great Torrington Devon 25 D7
Great Tosson Northumb 252 C2
Great Totham Essex 88 C5
Great Tows Lincs 190 C2
Great Tree Corn 6 D5
Great Urswick Cumb 210 E5
Great Wakering Essex 70 B2
Great Waldingfield Suff 107 C8
Great Walsingham Norf 159 B8
Great Waltham Essex 87 C11
Great Warley Essex 87 G9
Great Washbourne Glos 99 E9
Great Weeke Devon 13 D10
Great Weldon N Nhants 137 F8
Great Welnetham Suff 125 F7
Great Wenham Suff 107 D11
Great Whittington
Northumb 242 C2
Great Wigborough Essex 89 C7
Great Wilbraham
Cambs 123 F10
Great Wilne Derbys 153 C8
Great Wishford Wilts 46 F5
Great Witchingham
Norf 160 E2
Great Witcombe Glos 80 C6
Great Witley Worcs 116 D5
Great Wolford Warks 100 E4
Greatworth W Nhants 101 C11
Great Wratting Suff 106 B3
Great Wymondley Herts 104 F4
Great Wyrley Staffs 133 B9
Great Wytheford
Shrops 149 F11
Great Yarmouth Norf 143 B10
Great Yeldham Essex 106 D5
Greave Gtr Man 184 C6
Lancs 195 C11
Grebby Lincs 174 B6
Greeba IoM 192 D4
Green Denb 165 B9
Pembs 73 E7
Powys 130 E5
Greenacres Gtr Man 196 F2
Greenan Argyll 275 G11
Greenbank Ches W 183 G10
Falk 279 F7
Shetland 312 C7
Green Bank Cumb 211 C7
Green Bottom Corn 4 F5
Glos 79 B11
Greenburn W Loth 269 C8
Green Close N Yorks 212 F4
Green Clough W Yorks 205 G7
Green Crize Hereford 97 D10
Greencroft Durham 242 G5
Green Cross Sur 49 F11
Greendale Ches E 184 F5
Greendikes Northumb 264 D3
Greendown Som 44 C5
Green Down Devon 28 G3
Greendykes Northumb 264 D3
Greenend N Lanark 268 C4
Oxon 100 G6
Green End Bedford 103 B10
Bedford 121 E11
Bedford 122 E2
Bedford 122 G2
Bucks 84 F4
Bucks 103 E8
Cambs 122 C4
Cambs 123 F7
C Beds 103 D11
Herts 85 D8
Herts 104 E5
Herts 104 E6
Herts 104 G6
Herts 105 F7
Lancs 204 D4
N Yorks 226 E6
Warks 134 F5
Greenfaulds N Lanark 278 G5
Greenfield C Beds 103 E11
Glasgow 268 C2
Gtr Man 196 G3
Highld 289 D11
Highld 290 C4
Oxon 84 G2
Greenfield = Maes-Glas
Flint 181 F11
Greenfoot N Lanark 268 B4
Greenford London 66 C6
Greengairs N Lanark 278 G5
Greengarth Hall Cumb 219 E11
Greengate Gtr Man 196 D2
Norf 159 F10
Green Gate Devon 27 D8
Greengates W Yorks 205 F9
Greengill Cumb 229 D8
Green Hailey Bucks 84 E4
Greenhalgh Lancs 202 F4
Greenhall S Lanark 268 D3
Greenham Dorset 28 G6
Som 27 C9
W Berks 64 F3
Green Hammerton
N Yorks 206 B5
Greenhaugh Northumb 251 F7
Green Haworth Lancs 195 B9
Greenhead Borders 261 D11
Dumfries 247 D9
N Lanark 268 E6
Northumb 240 D5
Staffs 169 F7
Green Head Cumb 230 B3
Green Heath Staffs 151 G9
Greenheys Gtr Man 195 G8
Greenhill Dumfries 238 B4
Durham 234 B3
Falk 278 F6
Hereford 98 B4
Kent 71 F7
Leics 153 G8
Greenhill continued
London 67 B7
S Yorks 186 E4
Worcs 99 B10
Worcs 116 B6
Green Hill Kent 53 C9
Lincs 155 B8
Wilts 62 B5
W Yorks 206 F4
Greenhill Bank Shrops 149 B7
Greenhillocks Derbys 170 F6
Greenhills N Ayrs 267 E7
S Lanark 268 E2
Greenhithe Kent 68 E5
Greenholm E Ayrs 258 B2
Greenholme Cumb 221 D11
Greenhouse Borders 262 E3
Greenhow N Yorks 214 G2
Greenhow Hill N Yorks 214 G2
Greenigoe Orkney 314 F4
Greenland Highld 310 C6
S Yorks 186 D5
Greenland Mains Highld 310 C6
Greenlands Bucks 65 B9
Worcs 117 D11
Green Lane Devon 13 F11
Hereford 98 B2
Powys 130 D3
Warks 117 E11
Worcs 118 B6
Greenlaw Aberds 302 D6
Borders 272 F4
Greenlaw Mains Midloth 270 C4
Greenlea Dumfries 238 B2
Greenleys M Keynes 102 C6
Greenloaning Perth 286 G2
Greenlooms Ches W 167 C7
Greenman's Lane Wilts 62 C3
Greenmeadow Swindon 62 B6
Torf 78 F3
Green Moor S Yorks 186 B3
Greenmount Gtr Man 195 E9
Greenmow Shetland 313 L6
Greenoak E Yorks 199 B10
Greenock Invclyd 276 F5
Greenock West Invclyd 276 F5
Greenodd Cumb 210 C6
Green Ore Som 44 C5
Green Parlour Bath 45 C8
Green Quarter Cumb 221 E9
Greenrigg W Loth 269 C8
Greenrow Cumb 238 G4
Greens Borders 249 F11
Green St Green London 68 G3
Greensforge Staffs 133 F7
Greensgate Norf 160 F2
Greenside Cumb 222 E4
Derbys 186 F5
Gtr Man 184 B6
T&W 242 E4
W Yorks 197 D7
Green Side W Yorks 197 E7
W Yorks 205 G11
Greensidehill Northumb 263 F11
Greens Norton
W Nhants 102 B3
Greensplat Corn 5 D9
Greenstead Essex 107 F10
Greenstead Green Essex 106 F6
Greensted Essex 87 E8
Greensted Green Essex 87 E8
Green Street Essex 87 F10
E Sus 38 E3
Glos 80 B5
Glos 80 E3
Herts 85 F11
Herts 105 G9
Worcs 99 B7
Worcs 99 C7
W Sus 35 C10
Greenstreet Green
Suff 107 B10
Green Street Green Kent 68 E5
London 68 G3
Green Tye Herts 86 B6
Greenway Hereford 98 E4
Pembs 91 E11
Som 27 B11
V Glam 58 E5
Worcs 116 C4
Greenwell Cumb 240 F2
Greenwells Borders 262 C3
Greenwich London 67 D11
Suff 108 C3
Wilts 46 G2
Greenwith Common Corn 4 G5
Greenwoods Essex 87 F11
Greeny Orkney 314 D2
Greep Highld 298 E2
Greet Glos 99 E10
Kent 54 B2
Greete Shrops 115 C11
Greetham Lincs 190 G4
Rutland 155 G8
Greetland W Yorks 196 C5
Greetland Wall Nook
W Yorks 196 C5
Greetwell N Lincs 200 G2
Gregg Hall Cumb 221 G9
Gregson Lane Lancs 194 B5
Gregynog Powys 129 D11
Grèin W Isles 297 L2
Greinetobht W Isles 296 D4
Greinton Som 44 F2
Gremista Shetland 313 J6
Grenaby IoM 192 E3
Grendon N Nhants 121 E7
Warks 134 C5
Grendon Bishop
Hereford 115 F11
Grendon Common
Warks 134 D5
Grendon Green
Hereford 115 F11
Grendon Underwood
Bucks 102 G3
Grenofen Devon 12 G5
Grenoside S Yorks 186 C4
Greosabhagh W Isles 305 J3
Gresford Wrex 166 E5
Gresham Norf 160 B3
Greshornish Highld 298 D3
Gressenhall Norf 159 F9
Gressingham Lancs 211 F11
Gresty Green Ches E 168 E2
Greta Bridge Durham 223 C11
Gretna Dumfries 239 D8
Gretna Green Dumfries 239 D8
Gretton Glos 99 E10
N Nhants 137 E7
Shrops 131 D10
Gretton Fields Glos 99 E10
Grewelthorpe N Yorks 214 D4
Greyfield Bath 44 B6
Greygarth N Yorks 214 E3
Grey Green N Lincs 199 F9
Greylake Som 43 G11
Greylake Fosse Som 44 F2
Greynor Carms 75 D9
Greynor-isaf Carms 75 D9
Greyrigg Dumfries 248 F3
Greys Green Oxon 65 C8
Greysouthen Cumb 229 F7
Greystead Northumb 251 F7
Greystoke Cumb 230 E4
Greystoke Gill Cumb 230 F4
Greystone Aberds 292 D6
Aberds 302 F6
Angus 287 C9
Cumb 211 D10
Dumfries 237 B11
Greystonegill N Yorks 212 F3
Greystones S Yorks 186 D4
Warks 99 B11
Greytree Hereford 97 F11
Greywell Hants 49 C8
Griais W Isles 304 D6
Grianan W Isles 304 E6
Gribb Dorset 28 G5
Gribthorpe E Yorks 207 F11
Gridley Corner Devon 12 C3
Griff Warks 135 F7
Griffins Hill W Mid 133 G10
Griffithstown Torf 78 F3
Griffydam Leics 153 F8
Grigg Kent 53 E11
Griggs Green Hants 49 G10
Grillis Corn 2 B5
Grilstone Devon 26 C2
Grimbister Orkney 314 E3
Grimblethorpe Lincs 190 D2
Grimeford Village Lancs 194 E6
Grimes Hill Worcs 117 B11
Grimesthorpe S Yorks 186 C5
Grimethorpe S Yorks 198 F2
Griminis W Isles 296 D3
W Isles 296 F3
Grimister Shetland 312 D6
Grimley Worcs 116 E6
Grimness Orkney 314 G4
Grimoldby Lincs 190 D5
Grimpo Shrops 149 D7
Grimsargh Lancs 203 G7
Grimsbury Oxon 101 C9
Grimsby NE Lincs 201 E9
Grimscote W Nhants 120 G3
Grimscott Corn 24 F3
Grimshaw Blackburn 195 C8
Grimshaw Green Lancs 194 E3
Grimsthorpe Lincs 155 E10
Grimston E Yorks 209 F11
Leics 154 E3
Norf 158 E4
York 207 C8
Grimstone Dorset 17 C8
Grimstone End Suff 125 D8
Grinacombe Moor Devon 12 C4
Grindale E Yorks 218 E2
Grindigar Orkney 314 F5
Grindiscol Shetland 313 K6
Grindle Shrops 132 C5
Grindleford Derbys 186 F2
Grindleton Lancs 203 D11
Grindley Staffs 151 D10
Grindley Brook Shrops 167 G8
Grindlow Derbys 185 F11
Grindon Northumb 273 G8
Staffs 169 E9
Stockton 234 F3
T&W 243 G9
Grindonmoor Gate
Staffs 169 E9
Grindsbrook Booth
Derbys 185 D10
Gringley on the Hill
Notts 188 C2
Grinsdale Cumb 239 F9
Grinshill Shrops 149 E10
Grinstead Hill Suff 125 G11
Grinton N Yorks 223 F10
Griomasaigh W Isles 297 G4
Griomsidar W Isles 304 F5
Grishipoll Argyll 288 D3
Grisling Common E Sus 36 C6
Gristhorpe N Yorks 217 C11
Griston Norf 141 D8
Gritley Orkney 314 F5
Grittenham Wilts 62 C4
Grittlesend Hereford 98 B4
Grittleton Wilts 61 C11
Grizebeck Cumb 210 C4
Grizedale Cumb 220 G6
Groam Highld 300 E5
Grobister Orkney 314 D6
Grobsness Shetland 313 G5
Groby Leics 135 B10
Groes Conwy 165 C8
Neath 57 D9
Groes Efa Denb 165 B10
Groes-faen Rhondda 58 C5
Groes-fawr Denb 165 B10
Groesffordd Gwyn 144 B5
Powys 95 F11
Groesffordd Marli Denb 181 G8
Groeslon Gwyn 163 C8
Gwyn 163 D7
Groes-lwyd Mon 96 G6
Powys 148 G4
Groespluan Powys 130 B4
Groes-wen Caerph 58 B6
Grogport Argyll 255 C9
Gromford Suff 127 F7
Gronant Flint 181 E9
Gronwen Shrops 148 D5
Groombridge E Sus 52 F4
Grosmont Mon 97 G8
N Yorks 226 D6
Gross Green Warks 119 F7
Grotaig Highld 300 G4
Groton Suff 107 C9
Grotton Gtr Man 196 G3
Grougfoot Falk 279 F10
Grove Bucks 103 G8
Dorset 17 G10
Hereford 98 C2
Kent 71 G8
Notts 188 F2
Oxon 82 G6
Pembs 73 E7
Grove End Kent 69 G11
Warks 100 D6
Warks 134 D3
Grove Green Kent 53 B9
Grovehill E Yorks 208 F6
Herts 85 D9
Grove Hill E Sus 23 C10
Kent 71 G8
Grove Park London 67 D8
London 68 E2
Groves Kent 55 B9
Grovesend Swansea 75 E9
Grove Town W Yorks 198 C3
Grove Vale W Mid 133 E10
Grubb Street Kent 68 F5
Grub Street Staffs 150 D5
Grudie Highld 300 C3
Gruids Highld 309 J5
Gruinard House Highld 307 K4
Gruinards Highld 309 K5
Grula Highld 294 C5
Gruline Argyll 289 E7
Gruline Ho Argyll 289 F7
Grumbeg Highld 308 F6
Grumbla Corn 1 D4
Grunasound Shetland 313 K5
Grundisburgh Suff 126 G4
Grunsagill Lancs 203 C11
Gruting Shetland 313 J4
Grutness Shetland 313 N6
Gryn Goch Gwyn 162 F6
Gualachulain Highld 284 C5
Gualin Ho Highld 308 D3
Guardbridge Fife 287 F8
Guard House W Yorks 204 E6
Guarlford Worcs 98 B6
Guay Perth 286 C4
Gubbion's Green Essex 88 B2
Gubblecote Herts 84 C6
Guesachan Highld 289 B10
Guestling Green E Sus 38 E5
Guestling Thorn E Sus 38 D4
Guestwick Norf 159 D11
Guestwick Green Norf 159 D11
Guide Blackburn 195 B8
Guide Bridge Gtr Man 184 B6
Guide Post Northumb 253 F7
Guilden Morden Cambs 104 C5
Guilden Sutton Ches W 166 B6
Guildford Sur 50 D3
Guildford Park Sur 50 D3
Guildiehaugh W Loth 269 B9
Guildtown Perth 286 D5
Guilford Pembs 73 D7
Guilsborough W Nhants 120 C3
Guilsfield = Cegidfa
Powys 148 G4
Guilthwaite S Yorks 187 D7
Guilton Kent 55 B9
Guineaford Devon 40 F5
Guisachan Highld 300 G3
Guisborough Redcar 226 B2
Guiseley W Yorks 205 E9
Guist Norf 159 D9
Guith Orkney 314 C5
Guiting Power Glos 99 G11
Gulberwick Shetland 313 K6
Gullane E Loth 281 E9
Guller's End Worcs 99 D7
Gulling Green Suff 124 F6
Gullom Holme Cumb 231 F9
Gulval Corn 1 C5
Gulworthy Devon 12 G4
Gumfreston Pembs 73 E10
Gumley Leics 136 E3
Gummow's Shop Corn 5 D7
Gunby E Yorks 207 F10
Lincs 155 E8
Lincs 175 B7
Gundenham Som 27 C10
Gundleton Hants 48 G6
Gun Green Kent 53 G9
Gun Hill E Sus 23 C9
Gunn Devon 40 G6
Gunnersbury London 67 D7
Gunnerside N Yorks 223 F9
Gunnerton Northumb 241 C10
Gunness N Lincs 199 E10
Gunnislake Corn 12 G4
Gunnista Shetland 313 J7
Gunstone Staffs 133 C7
Guns Village W Mid 133 E9
Gunter's Bridge W Sus 35 C7
Gunthorpe Lincs 188 B4
Norf 159 C10
Notts 171 G11
Pboro 138 C3
Rutland 137 B7
Gunton Suff 143 D10
Gunville IoW 20 D5
Gunwalloe Corn 2 E5
Gunwalloe Fishing Cove
Corn 2 E5
Gupworthy Som 42 F3
Gurnard IoW 20 B5
Gurnett Ches E 184 G6
Gurney Slade Som 44 D6
Gurnos M Tydf 77 D8
Powys 76 D3
Gushmere Kent 54 B4
Gussage All Saints Dorset 31 E8
Gussage St Andrew
Dorset 31 E7
Gussage St Michael
Dorset 31 E7
Gustard Wood Herts 85 B11
Guston Kent 55 E10
Gutcher Shetland 312 D7
Guthram Gowt Lincs 156 E3
Guthrie Angus 287 B9
Guyhirn Cambs 139 C7
Guyhirn Gull Cambs 139 C7
Guy's Cliffe Warks 118 D5
Guy's Head Lincs 157 D9
Guy's Marsh Dorset 30 C4
Guyzance Northumb 252 C6
Gwaelod-y-garth Cardiff 58 C6
Gwaenysgor Flint 181 E9
Gwalchmai Anglesey 178 F5
Gwalchmai Uchaf
Anglesey 178 F5
Gwallon Corn 2 C2
Gwastad Pembs 91 G10
Gwastadgoed Gwyn 145 G11
Gwastadnant Gwyn 163 D10
Gwaun-Cae-Gurwen
Neath 76 C2
Gwaun-Leision Neath 76 C2
Gwavas Corn 2 D5
Corn 2 G6
Gwbert Ceredig 92 B3
Gwedna Corn 2 C4
Gweek Corn 2 D6
Gwehelog Mon 78 E5
Gwenddwr Powys 95 C11
Gwennap Corn 2 B6
Gwenter Corn 2 F6
Gwernaffield-y-Waun
Flint 166 C2
Gwernafon Powys 129 E8
Gwerneirin Powys 129 F10
Powys 130 G3
Gwernesney Mon 78 E6
Gwernogle Carms 93 E10
Gwernol Denb 166 E2
Gwern y brenin Shrops 148 D6
Gwernydd Powys 129 C11
Gwernymynydd Flint 166 C2
Gwern-y-Steeple V Glam 58 D5
Gwersyllt Wrex 166 E4
Gwespyr Flint 181 E10
Gwills Corn 4 D6
Gwinear Corn 2 B3
Gwinear Downs Corn 2 C4
Gwithian Corn 2 A3
Gwredog Anglesey 178 D6
Gwrhay Caerph 77 F11
Gwyddelwern Denb 165 F9
Gwyddgrug Carms 93 D9
Gwynfryn Wrex 166 E3
Gwystre Powys 113 D11
Gwytherin Conwy 164 C5
Gyfelia Wrex 166 F4
Gyffin Conwy 180 F3
Gylen Park Argyll 289 G10
Gyre Orkney 314 F3
Gyrn Denb 165 D11
Gyrn-goch Gwyn 162 F6

H

Habberley Shrops 131 C7
Worcs 116 B6
Habergham Lancs 204 G2
Habertoft Lincs 175 B8
Habin W Sus 34 C4
Habrough NE Lincs 200 E6
Haccombe Devon 14 G3
Haceby Lincs 155 B10
Hacheston Suff 126 F6
Hackbridge London 67 F9
Hackenthorpe S Yorks 186 E6
Hackford Norf 141 C11
Hackforth N Yorks 224 G4
Hack Green Ches E 167 F10
Hackland Orkney 314 D3
Hackleton W Nhants 120 F6
Hacklinge Kent 55 C10
Hackman's Gate Worcs 117 B7
Hackness N Yorks 227 G9
Orkney 314 G3
Som 43 D10
Hackney London 67 C10
Hackney Wick London 67 C11
Hackthorn Lincs 189 E7
Wilts 47 D7
Hackthorpe Cumb 230 G6
Haclait W Isles 297 G4
Haconby Lincs 156 D2
Hacton London 68 B4
Haddacott Devon 25 C8
Hadden Borders 263 B7
Haddenham Bucks 84 D2
Cambs 123 B9
Haddenham End Field
Cambs 123 B9
Haddington E Loth 281 G10
Lincs 172 C6
Haddiscoe Norf 143 D8
Haddoch Aberds 302 E5
Haddon Cambs 138 E2
Ches E 169 B7
Hade Edge W Yorks 196 F6
Hademore Staffs 134 B3
Haden Cross W Mid 133 F9
Hadfield Derbys 185 B8
Hadham Cross Herts 86 B6
Hadham Ford Herts 105 G8
Hadleigh Essex 69 B10
Suff 107 C10
Hadleigh Heath Suff 107 C9
Hadley London 86 F2
Telford 150 G3
Worcs 117 E7
Hadley Castle Telford 150 G3
Hadley End Staffs 152 E3
Hadley Wood London 86 F3
Hadlow Kent 52 D6
Hadlow Down E Sus 37 C8
Hadlow Stair Kent 52 D6
Hadnall Shrops 149 F10
Hadspen Som 45 G7
Hadstock Essex 105 C11
Hadston Northumb 253 D7
Hady Derbys 186 G5
Hadzor Worcs 117 E8
Haffenden Quarter Kent 53 E11
Hafod Swansea 57 C7
Hafod-Dinbych Conwy 164 E5
Hafod Grove Pembs 92 C2
Hafodiwan Ceredig 111 G7
Hafod-lom Conwy 180 G5
Hafod-y-Green Denb 181 G8
Hafodyrynys Bl Gwent 78 F2
Hag Fold Gtr Man 195 G7
Haggate Gtr Man 196 F2
Lancs 204 F3
Haggbeck Cumb 239 C11
Haggersta Shetland 313 J5
Haggerston London 67 C10
Northumb 273 G10
Hagginton Hill Devon 40 D5
Haggrister Shetland 312 F5
Haggs Falk 278 F5
Haghill Glasgow 268 B2
Hagley Hereford 97 C11
Worcs 133 G8
Hagloe Glos 79 D11
Hagmore Green Suff 107 D9
Hagnaby Lincs 174 C4
Lincs 191 F7
Hagnaby Lock Lincs 174 D4
Hague Bar Derbys 185 D7
Hagworthingham Lincs 174 B4
Haigh Gtr Man 194 F6
S Yorks 197 E9
Haigh Moor W Yorks 197 C9
Haighton Green Lancs 203 G7
Haighton Top Lancs 203 G7
Haile Cumb 219 D10
Hailes Glos 99 E10
Hailey Herts 86 C5
Oxon 64 B6
Oxon 82 C5
Hailsham E Sus 23 D9
Hailstone Hill Wilts 81 G9
Hail Weston Cambs 122 E3
Haimer Highld 310 C5
Haimwood Powys 148 F6
Hainault London 87 G7
Haine Kent 71 F11
Hainford Norf 160 F4
Hains Dorset 30 D3
Hainton Lincs 189 E11
Hainworth W Yorks 205 F7
Hainworth Shaw
W Yorks 205 F7
Hairmyres S Lanark 268 E2
Haisthorpe E Yorks 218 G2
Hakeford Devon 40 F6
Hakin Pembs 72 D5
Halabezack Corn 2 C6
Halam Notts 171 E11
Halamanning Corn 2 C3
Halbeath Fife 280 D2
Halberton Devon 27 E8
Halcon Som 28 B2
Halcro Highld 310 C6
Haldens Herts 86 C2
Hale Cumb 211 D10
Gtr Man 184 D3
Halton 183 E7
Hants 31 D11
Kent 71 F9
Medway 69 F9
Som 30 B3
Sur 49 D10
Hale Bank Halton 183 E7
Hale Barns Gtr Man 184 D3
Halecommon W Sus 34 C4
Hale Coombe N Som 44 B2
Hale End London 86 G5
Hale Green E Sus 23 C9

Hale Mills Corn 4 G5
Hale Nook Lancs 202 E3
Hales Norf 143 D7
Staffs 150 C4
Hales Bank Hereford 116 G2
Halesfield Telford 132 C4
Halesgate Lincs 156 D6
Hales Green Derbys 169 G11
Norf 143 D7
Halesowen W Mid 133 G9
Hales Park Worcs 116 B5
Hales Place Kent 54 B6
Hales Street Norf 142 F3
Hale Street Kent 53 D7
Hales Wood Hereford 98 E2
Halesworth Suff 127 B7
Halewood Mers 183 D7
Half Moon Village Devon 14 B3
Halford Shrops 131 G8
Warks 100 B5
Halfpenny Cumb 211 B10
Halfpenny Furze Carms 74 C3
Halfpenny Green Staffs 132 E6
Halfway Carms 75 E8
Carms 94 E2
Carms 94 E6
S Yorks 186 E6
W Berks 64 F2
Wilts 45 D11
Halfway Bridge W Sus 34 C6
Halfway House Shrops 148 G6
Halfway Houses
Gtr Man 195 F9
Kent 70 E2
Halfway Street Kent 55 D9
Halgabron Corn 11 D7
Halifax W Yorks 196 B5
Halkburn Borders 271 G9
Halket E Ayrs 267 E8
Halkirk Highld 310 D5
Halkyn = *Helygain* Flint 182 G2
Halkyn Mountain Flint 182 G2
Hallam Fields Derbys 153 B9
Halland E Sus 23 B8
Hallaton Leics 136 D5
Hallatrow Bath 44 B6
Hallbankgate Cumb 240 F3
Hall Bower W Yorks 196 E6
Hall Broom S Yorks 186 D3
Hall Cross Lancs 202 G4
Hall Dunnerdale Cumb 220 F4
Halleaths Dumfries 248 G3
Hallen S Glos 60 C5
Hallend Warks 118 D2
Hall End Bedford 103 B10
C Beds 103 D11
Lincs 174 E6
S Glos 61 B8
Warks 134 C5
Hallew Corn 5 D10
Hallfield Gate Derbys 170 D5
Hall Flat Worcs 117 C9
Hallgarth Durham 234 C2
Hall Garth York 207 C9
Hallglen Falk 279 F7
Hall Green Ches E 168 D4
Essex 106 D5
Lancs 194 C3
Lancs 194 F4
W Mid 133 E10
W Mid 134 G2
W Mid 135 G7
Wrex 167 G7
W Yorks 197 D10
Hall Grove Herts 89 C8
Halliburton Borders 261 B11
Borders 272 F3
Hallin Highld 298 D2
Halling Medway 69 G8
Hallingbury Street
Essex 87 B8
Hallington Lincs 190 D4
Northumb 241 B11
Hall i' th' Wood Gtr Man 195 E8
Halliwell Gtr Man 195 E8
Hall of Clestrain Orkney 314 F2
Hall of Tankerness
Orkney 314 F5
Hall of the Forest
Shrops 130 G4
Hallon Shrops 132 D5
Hallonsford Shrops 132 D5
Halloughton Notts 171 E11
Hallow Worcs 116 F6
Hallowes Derbys 186 F5
Hallow Heath Worcs 116 F6
Hallowsgate Ches W 167 B8
Hallrule Borders 262 G3
Halls E Loth 282 G3
Hallsands Devon 9 G11
Hall Santon Cumb 220 E2
Hall's Cross E Sus 23 D11
Hallsford Bridge Essex 87 E9
Halls Green Essex 86 D6
Hall's Green Herts 104 F5
Kent 52 D4
Hallspill Devon 25 C7
Hallthwaites Cumb 210 B3
Hall Waberthwaite
Cumb 220 F2
Hallwood Green Glos 98 E3
Hallworthy Corn 11 D9
Hallyards Borders 260 B6
Hallyburton House
Perth 286 D6
Hallyne Borders 270 G3
Halmer End Staffs 168 F3
Halmond's Frome
Hereford 98 B3
Halmore Glos 79 E11
Halmyre Mains Borders 270 F3
Halnaker W Sus 22 B6
Halsall Lancs 193 E11
Halse Som 27 B10
W Nhants 101 C11
Halsetown Corn 2 B2
Halsfordwood Devon 14 C3
Halsham E Yorks 201 B9
Halsinger Devon 40 F4
Halstead Essex 106 E6
Kent 68 G3
Leics 136 B4
Halstock Dorset 29 F8
Halsway Som 42 F6
Haltcliff Bridge Cumb 230 D3
Halterworth Hants 32 C5
Haltham Lincs 174 C2
Haltoft End Lincs 174 F5
Halton Bucks 84 C5
Halton 183 E8
Lancs 211 G10
Northumb 241 D11
Wrex 148 B6
W Yorks 206 G2
Halton Barton Corn 7 B8
Halton Brook Halton 183 E8
Halton East N Yorks 204 C6
Halton Fenside Lincs 174 C6
Halton Gill N Yorks 213 D7
Halton Green Lancs 211 F10
Halton Holegate Lincs 174 B6
Halton Lea Gate
Northumb 240 F5
Halton Moor W Yorks 206 G2
Halton Shields
Northumb 242 D2
Halton View Halton 183 D8
Halton West N Yorks 204 C2
Haltwhistle Northumb 240 E6
Halvergate Norf 143 B8
Halvosso Corn 2 C6
Halwell Devon 8 E5
Halwill Devon 12 B4
Halwill Junction Devon 24 G6
Halwin Corn 2 C5
Ham Devon 28 G2
Glos 79 F11
Glos 99 G9
Highld 310 B6
Kent 55 C10
London 67 E7
Plym 7 D9
Shetland 313 K1
Som 27 C11
Som 28 B3
Som 28 E3
Som 45 D7
Wilts 63 G10
Hamar Shetland 312 F5
Hamarhill Orkney 314 C5
Hamars Shetland 313 G6
Hambleden Bucks 65 B9
Hambledon Hants 33 E10
Sur 50 F3
Hamble-le-Rice Hants 33 F7
Hambleton Lancs 202 E3
N Yorks 205 C7
N Yorks 207 G7
Hambleton Moss Side
Lancs 202 E3
Hambridge Som 28 C5
Hambrook S Glos 60 D6
W Sus 22 B3
Ham Common Dorset 30 B4
Hameringham Lincs 174 B4
Hamerton Cambs 122 B2
Hametoun Shetland 313 K1
Ham Green Bucks 83 B11
Hants 48 G2
Hereford 98 C4
Kent 38 B5
Kent 69 F10
N Som 60 D4
Wilts 61 G11
Worcs 117 E10
Ham Hill Kent 69 G8
Hamilton S Lanark 268 D3
Hamister Shetland 313 G7
Hamlet Dorset 29 F9
Hammer W Sus 49 G11
Hammer Bottom Hants 49 G11
Hammerfield Herts 85 D8
Hammerpot W Sus 35 F9
Hammersmith Derbys 170 E5
London 67 D8
Hammerwich Staffs 133 B11
Hammerwood E Sus 52 F2
Hammill Kent 55 B9
Hammond Street Herts 86 E4
Hammoon Dorset 30 E4
Ham Moor Sur 66 G5
Hamnavoe Shetland 312 E4
Shetland 312 E6
Shetland 312 F6
Shetland 313 K5
Hamnish Clifford
Hereford 115 F10
Hamp Som 43 F10
Hampden Park E Sus 23 E10
Hampen Glos 81 B9
Hamperden End Essex 105 E11
Hamperley Shrops 131 F8
Hampers Green W Sus 35 C7
Hampeth Northumb 252 B5
Hampnett Glos 81 B10
Hampole S Yorks 198 E4
Hampreston Dorset 19 B7
Hampsfield Cumb 211 C8
Hampson Green Lancs 202 C5
Hampstead London 67 B9
Hampstead Garden Suburb
London 67 B9
Hampstead Norreys
W Berks 64 D4
Hampsthwaite N Yorks 205 B11
Hampton Kent 71 F7
London 66 F6
Shrops 132 F4
Swindon 81 G11
Worcs 99 C10
Hampton Bank Shrops 149 C9
Hampton Beech Shrops 130 B6
Hampton Bishop
Hereford 97 D11
Hampton Fields Glos 80 F5
Hampton Gay Oxon 83 B7
Hampton Green Ches W 167 F8
Glos 80 E5
Hampton Hargate Pboro 138 E3
Hampton Heath Ches W 167 F7
Hampton Hill London 66 E6
Hampton in Arden
W Mid 134 G4
Hampton Loade Shrops 132 F5
Hampton Lovett Worcs 117 D7
Hampton Lucy Warks 118 F5
Hampton Magna Warks 118 D5
Hampton on the Hill
Warks 118 E5
Hampton Park Hereford 97 D10
Soton 32 D6
Hampton Poyle Oxon 83 B8
Hamptons Kent 52 C6
Hampton Vale Pboro 138 E3
Hampton Wick London 67 F7
Hamptworth Wilts 32 D2
Hamrow Norf 159 E8
Hamsey E Sus 36 E6
Hamsey Green London 51 B10
Hamshill Glos 80 E3
Hamstall Ridware Staffs 152 F2
Hamstead IoW 20 C4
W Mid 133 E10
Hamstead Marshall
W Berks 64 F2
Hamsterley Durham 233 E8
Durham 242 F4
Hamstreet Kent 54 G4
Ham Street Som 44 G5
Hamworthy BCP 18 C5
Hanbury Staffs 152 D3
Worcs 117 E9
Hanbury Woodend
Staffs 152 D3
Hanby Lincs 155 C10
Hanchett Village Suff 106 B3
Hanchurch Staffs 168 G4
Handbridge Ches W 166 B6
Handcross W Sus 36 B3
Handforth Ches E 184 E5
Hand Green Ches W 167 C8
Handless Shrops 131 E7
Handley Ches W 167 D7
Derbys 170 C5
Handley Green Essex 87 E11
Handsacre Staffs 151 F11
Handside Herts 86 C2
Handsworth S Yorks 186 D6
W Mid 133 E10
Handsworth Wood
W Mid 133 E11
Handy Cross Bucks 84 G5
Devon 24 B6
Som 42 G6
Hanford Dorset 30 E4
Stoke 168 G5
Hangersley Hants 31 F11
Hanging Bank Kent 52 C3
Hanging Heaton
W Yorks 197 C9
Hanging Houghton
W Nhants 120 C5
Hanging Langford Wilts 46 F4
Hangingshaw Borders 261 C9
Dumfries 248 F4
Hangleton Brighton 36 F3
W Sus 35 G9
Hangsman Hill S Yorks 199 E7
Hanham S Glos 60 E6
Hanham Green S Glos 60 E6
Hankelow Ches E 167 F11
Hankerton Wilts 81 G7
Hankham E Sus 23 D10
Hanley Stoke 168 F5
Hanley Castle Worcs 98 C6
Hanley Child Worcs 116 E3
Hanley Swan Worcs 98 C6
Hanley William Worcs 116 D3
Hanlith N Yorks 213 G8
Hanmer Wrex 149 B9
Hannaford Devon 25 B10
Hannafore Corn 6 E5
Hannah Lincs 191 F8
Hanningfields Green
Suff 125 G7
Hannington Hants 48 B4
Swindon 81 G11
W Nhants 120 C6
Hannington Wick
Swindon 81 F11
Hanscombe End C Beds 104 E2
Hansel Devon 8 F6
Hansel Village S Ayrs 257 C9
Hansley Cross Staffs 169 G9
Hanslope M Keynes 102 B6
Hanthorpe Lincs 155 E11
Hanwell London 67 C7
Oxon 101 C8
Hanwood Shrops 131 B8
Hanwood Bank Shrops 149 G8
Hanworth Brack 65 F11
London 66 E6
Norf 160 B3
Happendon S Lanark 259 C9
Happisburgh Norf 161 C7
Happisburgh Common
Norf 161 D7
Hapsford Ches W 183 G7
Som 45 D9
Hapton Lancs 203 G11
Norf 142 D3
Hararden =*Penarlëg*
Flint 166 B4
Harberton Devon 8 D5
Harbertonford Devon 8 D5
Harbledown Kent 54 B6
Harborne W Mid 133 G10
Harborough Magna
Warks 119 B9
Harborough Parva
Warks 119 B9
Harbottle Northumb 251 C10
Harbour Heights E Sus 36 G6
Harbourland Kent 53 B9
Harbourneford Devon 8 C4
Harbours Hill Worcs 117 D9
Harbour Village Pembs 91 D8
Harbridge Hants 31 E10
Harbridge Green Hants 31 E10
Harburn W Loth 269 C10
Harbury Warks 119 F7
Harby Leics 154 C4
Notts 188 G5
Harcombe Devon 14 E3
Devon 15 C9
Harcourt Corn 3 B8
Harcourt Hill Oxon 83 E7
Hardbreck Orkney 314 F4
Hardeicke Glos 80 C4
Harden S Yorks 197 G7
W Mid 133 C10
W Yorks 205 F7
Hardendale Cumb 221 C11
Hardenhuish Wilts 62 E2
Harden Park Ches E 184 F4
Hardgate Aberds 293 C9
Dumfries 237 C10
N Yorks 214 G5
W Dunb 277 G10
Hardham W Sus 35 D8
Hardhorn Lancs 202 F3
Hardingham Norf 141 C10
Hardings Booth Staffs 169 C9
Hardingstone W Nhants 120 F5
Hardings Wood Staffs 168 E4
Hardington Som 45 C8
Hardington Mandeville
Som 29 E8
Hardington Marsh Som 29 F8
Hardington Moor Som 29 E8
Hardiston Perth 279 B11
Hardisworthy Devon 24 C2
Hardley Hants 32 G6
Hardley Street Norf 143 C7
Hardmead M Keynes 103 B8
Hardrow N Yorks 223 G7
Hardstoft Derbys 170 C6
Hardstoft Common
Derbys 170 C6
Hardway Hants 33 G10
Som 45 G8
Hardwick Bucks 84 B4
Cambs 122 D3
Cambs 123 F7
N Nhants 121 D7
Norf 142 F4
Norf 158 F2
Oxon 82 D5
Oxon 101 C8
Oxon 101 F11
Shrops 131 E7
Stockton 234 G4
S Yorks 187 D7
W Mid 133 D11
Hardwicke Glos 80 C3
Glos 99 F8
Hereford 96 C5
Hardwick Green Worcs 98 E6
Hardwick Village Notts 187 F10
Hardy's Green Essex 107 G8
Hare Som 28 D3
Hare Appletree Lancs 202 B6
Hareby Lincs 174 B4
Harecroft W Yorks 205 F7
Hareden Lancs 203 C8
Hare Edge Derbys 186 G4
Harefield London 85 G9
Soton 33 E7
Harefield Grove London 85 G9
Haregate Staffs 169 D7
Hare Green Essex 107 G11
Hare Hatch Wokingham 65 D10
Harehill Derbys 152 B3
Harehills W Yorks 206 G2
Harehope Borders 270 G4
Northumb 264 E3
Harelaw Durham 242 G5
Hareleeshill S Lanark 268 E5
Hareplain Kent 53 F10
Haresceugh Cumb 231 C8
Harescombe Glos 80 C4
Haresfield Glos 80 C4
Swindon 82 G2
Haresfinch Mers 183 B8
Hareshaw N Lanark 268 C6
Hareshaw Head
Northumb 251 F9
Harestanes E Dunb 278 G3
Harestock Hants 48 G3
Hare Street Essex 86 D6
Herts 104 F6
Herts 105 F7
Harewood W Yorks 206 D2
Harewood End Hereford 97 F10
Harewood Hill W Yorks 204 F6
Harford Carms 94 C2
Devon 8 D2
Devon 40 G6
Hargate Norf 142 E2
Hargate Hill Derbys 185 C8
Hargatewall Derbys 185 F10
Hargrave Ches W 167 C7
N Nhants 121 C10
Suff 124 F5
Harker Cumb 239 E9
Harker Marsh Cumb 229 E7
Harkland Shetland 312 E6
Harknett's Gate Essex 86 D6
Harkstead Suff 108 E3
Harlaston Staffs 152 G4
Harlaw Ho Aberds 303 G7
Harlaxton Lincs 155 C7
Harlech Gwyn 145 C11
Harlequin Notts 154 B3
Harlescott Shrops 149 F10
Harlesden London 67 C8
Harlesthorpe Derbys 187 F7
Harleston Devon 8 F5
Norf 142 G4
Suff 125 E10
Harlestone W Nhants 120 E4
Harle Syke Lancs 204 F3
Harley Shrops 131 C11
S Yorks 186 B5
Harleyholm S Lanark 259 B10
Harley Shute E Sus 38 F3
Harleywood Glos 80 F4
Harling Road Norf 141 F9
Harlington C Beds 103 E10
London 66 D5
S Yorks 198 G3
Harlosh Highld 298 E2
Harlow Essex 86 C6
Harlow Carr N Yorks 205 C11
Harlow Green T&W 243 F7
Harlow Hill Northumb 242 D3
N Yorks 205 C11
Harlthorpe E Yorks 207 F10
Harlton Cambs 123 G7
Harlyn Corn 10 F3
Harman's Corner Kent 69 G11
Harman's Cross Dorset 18 E5
Harmans Water Brack 65 F11
Harmby N Yorks 214 B2
Harmer Green Herts 86 B3
Harmer Hill Shrops 149 E9
Harmondsworth London 66 D5
Harmston Lincs 173 C7
Harnage Shrops 131 C11
Harnham Northumb 242 B3
Wilts 31 B10
Wilts 31 B11
Harnhill Glos 81 E9
Harold Hill London 87 G8
Harold Park London 87 G9
Haroldston West Pembs 72 B5
Haroldswick Shetland 312 B8
Harold Wood London 87 G8
Harome N Yorks 216 C2
Harpenden Herts 85 C10
Harpenden Common
Herts 85 C10
Harper Green Gtr Man 195 F8
Harperley Durham 242 G5
Harper's Gate Staffs 169 D7
Harper's Green Norf 159 E8
Harpford Devon 15 C7
Harpham E Yorks 217 G11
Harpley Norf 158 D5
Worcs 116 E3
Harpole W Nhants 120 E3
Harpsdale Highld 310 D5
Harpsden Oxon 65 C9
Harpsden Bottom Oxon 65 C9
Harpswell Lincs 188 D6
Harpton Powys 114 F4
Harpurhey Gtr Man 195 G11
Harpur Hill Derbys 185 G9
Harraby Cumb 239 G10
Harracott Devon 25 B9
Harrapool Highld 295 C8
Harras Cumb 219 B9
Harraton T&W 243 G7
Harrier Shetland 313 J1
Harrietfield Perth 286 E3
Harrietsham Kent 53 C11
Harringay London 67 B10
Harrington Cumb 228 F5
Lincs 190 G5
N Nhants 136 G5
Harringworth N Nhants 137 D8
Harris Highld 294 F5
Harriseahead Staffs 168 D5
Harriston Cumb 229 C9
Harrogate N Yorks 206 C2
Harrold Bedford 121 F8
Harrop Dale Gtr Man 196 F4
Harrow Highld 310 B6
London 67 B7
Harrowbarrow Corn 7 B7
Harrowbeer Devon 7 B10
Harrowby Lincs 155 B8
Harrowden Bedford 103 B11
Harrowgate Hill Darl 224 B5
Harrowgate Village
Darl 224 B5
Harrow Green Suff 125 G7
Harrow Hill Glos 79 B10
Harrow on the Hill
London 67 B7
Harrow Street Suff 107 D9
Harrow Weald London 85 G11
Harry Stoke S Glos 60 D6
Harston Cambs 123 G8
Harston *continued*
Leics 154 C6
Harswell E Yorks 208 E2
Hart Hrtlpl 234 E5
Hartbarrow Cumb 221 G8
Hartburn Northumb 252 F3
Stockton 225 B8
Hartcliffe Bristol 60 F5
Hart Common Gtr Man 194 F6
Hartest Suff 124 G6
Hartest Hill Suff 124 G6
Hartfield E Sus 52 F3
Highld 299 E7
Hartford Cambs 122 C5
Ches W 183 G10
Som 27 B7
Hartfordbeach
Ches W 183 G10
Hartfordbridge Hants 49 B9
Hartford End Essex 87 B11
Hartforth N Yorks 224 D3
Hartgrove Dorset 30 D4
Hartham Herts 86 C4
Harthill Ches W 167 D8
N Lanark 269 C8
S Yorks 187 E7
Hart Hill Luton 104 G2
Hartington Derbys 169 C10
Hartland Devon 24 C3
Hartle Worcs 117 B8
Hartlebury Shrops 132 D4
Worcs 116 C6
Hartlebury Common
Worcs 116 C6
Hartlepool Hrtlpl 234 E6
Hartley Cumb 222 D5
Kent 53 G9
Kent 68 F6
Northumb 243 B8
Plym 7 D9
Hartley Green Kent 68 F6
Staffs 151 D9
Hartley Mauditt Hants 49 F8
Hartley Westpall Hants 49 B7
Hartley Wintney Hants 49 B9
Hartlington N Yorks 213 G10
Hartlip Kent 69 G10
Hartmoor Dorset 30 C3
Hartmount Highld 301 B7
Hartoft End N Yorks 226 G5
Harton N Yorks 216 G4
Shrops 131 F9
T&W 243 E9
Hartpury Glos 98 F5
Hartsgreen Shrops 132 G5
Hart's Green Suff 125 F7
Hartshead W Yorks 197 C7
Hartshead Green
Gtr Man 196 G3
Hartshead Moor Side
W Yorks 197 C7
Hartshead Moor Top
W Yorks 197 B7
Hartshead Pike
Gtr Man 196 G3
Hartshill Stoke 168 F5
Warks 134 E6
Hart's Hill W Mid 133 F8
Hartshill Green Warks 134 E6
Hartshorne Derbys 152 E6
Hartsop Cumb 221 C8
Hart Station Hrtlpl 234 D5
Hartswell Som 27 B9
Hartwell Staffs 151 B8
W Nhants 120 G5
Hartwith N Yorks 214 G4
Hartwood Lancs 194 D5
N Lanark 268 D6
Hartwoodburn Borders 261 D11
Harvel Kent 68 G6
Harvest Hill W Mid 134 G5
Harvieston Stirling 277 D11
Harvills Hawthorn
W Mid 133 E9
Harvington Worcs 99 B11
Worcs 117 C7
Harvington Cross Worcs 99 B11
Harvington Hill Worcs 99 B10
Harwell Notts 187 C11
Oxon 64 B3
Harwich Essex 108 E5
Harwood Durham 232 E2
Gtr Man 195 E8
Harwood Dale N Yorks 227 F9
Harwood Lee Gtr Man 195 E8
Harwood on Teviot
Borders 249 B10
Harworth Notts 187 C10
Hasbury W Mid 133 G9
Hascombe Sur 50 E3
Haselbech W Nhants 120 B4
Haselbury Plucknett Som 29 E7
Haseley Warks 118 D4
Haseley Green Warks 118 D4
Haseley Knob Warks 118 C4
Haselor Warks 118 F2
Hasfield Glos 98 F6
Hasguard Pembs 72 D5
Haskayne Lancs 193 F11
Hasketon Suff 126 G4
Hasland Derbys 170 B5
Haslemere Sur 50 G2
Haslingbourne W Sus 35 C7
Haslingden Lancs 195 C9
Haslingfield Cambs 123 G8
Haslington Ches E 168 D2
Hasluck's Green W Mid 118 B2
Hassall Ches E 168 D3
Hassall Green Ches E 168 D3
Hassell Street Kent 54 D5
Hassendean Borders 262 E2
Hassingham Norf 143 B7
Hassocks W Sus 36 D3
Hassop Derbys 186 G2
Haster Highld 310 D7
Hasthorpe Lincs 175 B7
Hastigrow Highld 310 C6
Hasting Hill T&W 243 G9
Hastingleigh Kent 54 E5
Hastings E Sus 38 F4
Som 28 D4
Hastingwood Essex 87 D7
Hastoe Herts 84 D6
Haston Shrops 149 E10
Haswell Durham 234 C3
Haswell Moor Durham 234 C3
Haswell Plough Durham 234 C3
Haswellsykes Borders 260 B6
Hatch C Beds 104 B3
Devon 8 F4
Hants 49 C7
Wilts 30 B6
Hatch Beauchamp Som 28 C4
Hatch Bottom Hants 33 E7
Hatch End Bedford 121 E11
London 85 G10
Hatchet Gate Hants 32 G5
Hatchet Green Hants 31 D11
Hatch Farm Hill W Sus 34 B6
Hatch Green Som 28 D4
Hatching Green Herts 85 C10
Hatchmere Ches W 183 G9
Hatch Warren Hants 48 D6
Hatcliffe NE Lincs 201 G8
Hateley Heath W Mid 133 E10
Hatfield Hereford 115 F11
Herts 86 D2
S Yorks 199 F7
Worcs 117 G7
Hatfield Broad Oak Essex 87 B8
Hatfield Chase S Yorks 199 E8
Hatfield Garden Village
Herts 86 D2
Hatfield Heath Essex 87 B8
Hatfield Hyde Herts 86 C2
Hatfield Peverel Essex 88 C3
Hatfield Woodhouse
S Yorks 199 F7
Hatford Oxon 82 G4
Hatherden Hants 47 C10
Hatherleigh Devon 25 G8
Hatherley Glos 99 G8
Hathern Leics 153 E9
Hatherop Glos 81 D11
Hathersage Derbys 186 E2
Hathersage Booths
Derbys 186 E2
Hathershaw Gtr Man 196 G2
Hatherton Ches E 167 F11
Staffs 151 G9
Hatley St George Cambs 122 G5
Hatston Orkney 314 E4
Hatt Corn 7 C7
Hatterseat Aberds 303 G9
Hattersley Gtr Man 185 C7
Hatt Hill Hants 32 B4
Hattingley Hants 48 F6
Hatton Aberds 303 F10
Angus 287 D9
Derbys 152 D4
Lincs 189 F11
London 66 D5
Moray 301 D11
Shrops 131 E9
Warks 118 D4
Warr 183 E9
Hattonburn Aberds 293 C9
Hatton Castle Aberds 303 E7
Hattoncrook Aberds 303 G8
Hatton Grange Shrops 132 C5
Hatton Heath Ches W 167 C7
Hatton Hill Sur 66 G2
Hattonknowe Borders 270 F4
Hatton of Fintray
Aberds 293 B10
Hatton Park N Nhants 121 D7
Haugh E Ayrs 257 D11
Gtr Man 196 E2
Lincs 190 F6
Haugham Lincs 190 E4
Haugh-head Borders 261 B8
Haugh Head Northumb 264 D2
Haughland Orkney 314 E5
Haughley Suff 125 E10
Haughley Green Suff 125 E10
Haughley New Street
Suff 125 E10
Haugh of Glass Moray 302 F4
Haugh of Kilnmaichlie
Moray 301 F11
Haugh of Urr Dumfries 237 C10
Haughs of Clinterty
Aberdeen 293 B10
Haughton Ches E 167 D9
Notts 187 G11
Powys 148 F6
Shrops 132 B4
Shrops 132 D3
Shrops 149 D7
Shrops 149 F11
Staffs 151 E7
Haughton Castle
Northumb 241 C10
Haughton Green
Gtr Man 184 C6
Haughton Le Skerne
Darl 224 B6
Haughurst Hill W Berks 64 G5
Haulkerton Aberds 293 F9
Haultwick Herts 104 G6
Haunn Argyll 288 E5
W Isles 297 K3
Haunton Staffs 152 G4
Hauxton Cambs 123 G8
Havannah Ches E 168 C5
Havant Hants 22 B2
Haven Hereford 97 B11
Hereford 115 G8
Haven Bank Lincs 174 E2
Haven Side E Yorks 201 B7
Havenstreet IoW 21 C7
Havercroft W Yorks 197 E11
Haverfordwest = *Hwlffordd*
Pembs 73 B7
Haverhill Suff 106 B3
Haverigg Cumb 210 D3
Havering-atte-Bower
London 87 G8
Haveringland Norf 160 E3
Haversham M Keynes 102 C6
Haverthwaite Cumb 210 C6
Haverton Hill Stockton 234 G5
Haviker Street Kent 53 D8
Havyatt Som 44 F4
Havyatt Green N Som 60 G3
Hawarden = *Penarläg*
Flint 166 B4
Hawbridge Worcs 99 B8
Hawbush Green Essex 106 G5
Hawcoat Cumb 210 E4
Hawcross Glos 98 E5
Hawddamor Gwyn 146 F3
Hawen Ceredig 92 B6
Hawes N Yorks 213 B7
Hawes' Green Norf 142 D4
Hawes Side Blackpool 202 G2
Hawford Worcs 116 E6
Hawgreen Shrops 150 D2
Hawick Borders 262 F2
Hawkchurch Devon 28 G4
Hawkcombe Som 41 D11
Hawkedon Suff 124 G5
Hawkenbury Kent 52 F5
Kent 53 E10
Hawkeridge Wilts 45 C11
Hawkerland Devon 15 D7
Hawkersland Cross
Hereford 97 B10
Hawkesbury S Glos 61 B9
Warks 135 G7
Hawkesbury Upton
S Glos 61 B9
Hawkes End W Mid 134 G6
Hawkesley W Mid 117 B10
Hawk Green Gtr Man 185 D7
Hawkhill Northumb 264 G6
Hawk Hill Cumb 228 F6
Hawkhope Northumb 250 F6
Hawkhurst Kent 53 G9
Hawkhurst Common
E Sus 23 B8
Hawkinge Kent 55 F8
Hawkin's Hill Essex 106 E3
Hawkley Gtr Man 194 G5
Hants 34 B2
Hawkridge Som 41 G11
Hawksdale Cumb 230 B3
Hawks Green Staffs 151 G9
Hawkshaw Blackburn 195 D9
Hawkshead Cumb 221 F7
Hawkshead Hill Cumb 220 F6
Hawks Hill Bucks 66 B2
Hawk's Hill Sur 51 B7
Hawksland S Lanark 259 B8
Hawkspur Green
Essex 106 E3
Hawks Stones W Yorks 196 B2
Hawkswick N Yorks 213 E9
Hawksworth Notts 172 G3
W Yorks 205 E9
W Yorks 205 F11
Hawkwell Essex 88 G4
Hawley Hants 49 B11
Kent 68 E4
Hawley Bottom Devon 28 G2
Hawley Lane Hants 49 B11
Hawling Glos 99 G11
Hawn Orkney 314 D4
Hawnby N Yorks 215 B10
Hawne W Mid 133 G9
Haworth W Yorks 204 F6
Haws Bank Cumb 220 F6
Hawstead Suff 125 F7
Hawstead Green Suff 125 F7
Hawthorn Durham 234 B4
Hants 49 G7
Rhondda 58 B6
Wilts 61 F11
Hawthorn Corner Kent 71 F8
Hawthorn Hill Brack 65 E11
Lincs 174 D2
Hawthorns Staffs 168 F4
Hawthorpe Lincs 155 D10
Hawton Notts 172 E3
Haxby York 207 B8
Haxey N Lincs 188 B3
N Lincs 199 G9
Haxey Carr N Lincs 199 G9
Haxted Sur 52 D2
Haxton Wilts 46 D6
Hay Corn 10 G5
Haybridge Shrops 116 C2
Som 44 D4
Telford 150 G3
Hayden Glos 99 G8
Haydock Mers 183 B9
Haydon Bath 45 C7
Dorset 29 D11
Som 28 C3
Som 44 D5
Swindon 62 B6
Haydon Bridge
Northumb 241 E8
Haydon Wick Swindon 62 B6
Haye Corn 7 B7
Haye Fm Corn 6 B6
Hayes London 66 C6
London 68 F2
Staffs 169 C9
Hayes End London 66 C5
Hayes Knoll Wilts 81 G10
Hayes Town London 66 C6
Hayfield Derbys 185 D8
Fife 280 C5
Hay Field S Yorks 187 B10
Hayfield Green
S Yorks 187 B11
Haygate Telford 150 G2
Haygrass Som 28 C2
Hay Green Essex 87 E10
Herts 104 D6
Norf 157 F10
Hayhill E Ayrs 257 F11
Hayhillock Angus 287 C9
Haylands IoW 21 C7
Hayle Corn 2 B3
Hayley Green W Mid 133 G8
Hay Mills W Mid 134 G2
Haymoor End Som 28 B4
Haymoor Green
Ches E 167 E11
Hayne Devon 26 F5
Haynes C Beds 103 C11
Haynes Church End
C Beds 103 C11
Haynes West End
C Beds 103 C11
Hay-on-Wye Powys 96 C4
Hayscastle Pembs 91 F7
Hayscastle Cross Pembs 91 G8
Haysford Pembs 91 G8
Hayshead Angus 287 C10
Hayston E Dunb 278 G2
Haystoun Borders 261 B7
Hay Street Herts 105 F7
Haythorne Dorset 31 F8
Hayton Aberdeen 293 C11
Cumb 229 C8
Cumb 240 F2
E Yorks 208 D2
Notts 188 E2
Hayton's Bent Shrops 131 G10
Haytor Vale Devon 13 F11
Haytown Devon 24 E5
Haywards Heath W Sus 36 C4
Haywood S Lanark 269 E9
S Yorks 198 E5
Haywood Oaks Notts 171 D10
Hazard's Green E Sus 23 C11
Hazelbank S Lanark 268 F6
Hazelbeach Pembs 72 E6
Hazelbury Bryan Dorset 30 F2
Hazeleigh Essex 88 E4
Hazel End Essex 105 G9
Hazeley Hants 49 B8
Hazeley Bottom Hants 49 B9
Hazeley Heath Hants 49 B9
Hazeley Lea Hants 49 B8
Hazelgrove Notts 171 F8
Hazel Grove Gtr Man 184 D6
Hazelhurst Gtr Man 195 D9
Gtr Man 195 G9
Gtr Man 196 G3
Hazelslack Cumb 211 D9
Hazelslade Staffs 151 G10
Hazel Street Kent 53 B11
Kent 53 F7
Hazel Stub Suff 106 C3
Hazelton Glos 81 B9
Hazelton Walls Fife 287 E7
Hazelwood Derbys 170 F4
Devon 8 E4
London 68 G2
Hazlehead S Yorks 197 G7
Hazlemere Bucks 84 F5
Hazler Shrops 131 E9
Hazlerigg T&W 242 C6
Hazles Staffs 169 F8
Hazlescross Staffs 169 F8
Hazleton Glos 81 B9
Hazlewood N Yorks 205 C7
Hazon Northumb 252 C5
Heacham Norf 158 B3
Headbourne Worthy
Hants 48 G3
Headbrook Hereford 114 F6
Headcorn Kent 53 E10
Headingley W Yorks 205 F11
Headington Oxon 83 D8
Headington Hill Oxon 83 D8
Headlam Durham 224 B3
Headless Cross Cumb 211 D7
Worcs 117 D10
Headley Hants 49 F10
Hants 64 G4
Sur 51 C8
Headley Down Hants 49 F10
Headley Heath Worcs 117 B11
Headley Park Bristol 60 F5
Head of Muir Falk 278 E6
Headon Devon 24 G5
Notts 188 F2
Heads S Lanark 268 F4
Headshaw Borders 261 E11
Heads Nook Cumb 239 F11
Headstone London 66 B6
Headwell Fife 279 D11
Heady Hill Gtr Man 195 E10
Heage Derbys 170 E5
Healaugh N Yorks 206 D5
N Yorks 223 F10
Heald Green Gtr Man 184 D4
Healds Green Gtr Man 195 F11
Heale Devon 40 D6
Som 28 B5
Som 28 D2
Som 45 E7
Healey Gtr Man 195 D11
Northumb 242 F2
N Yorks 214 C3
W Yorks 197 C8
W Yorks 197 D9
Healey Cote Northumb 252 C4
Healeyfield Durham 233 B7
Healey Hall Northumb 242 F2
Healing NE Lincs 201 E8
Heamoor Corn 1 C5
Heaning Cumb 221 F8
Heanish Argyll 288 E2
Heanor Derbys 170 F6
Heanor Gate Derbys 170 F6
Heanton Punchardon
Devon 40 F4
Heap Bridge Gtr Man 195 E10
Heapham Lincs 188 D5
Hearn Hants 49 F10
Hearnden Green Kent 53 D10
Hearthstane Borders 260 D4
Hearthstone Derbys 170 D4
Hearts Delight Kent 69 G11
Heasley Mill Devon 41 G8
Heast Highld 295 D8
Heath Cardiff 59 D7
Derbys 170 B6
Halton 183 E8
Heath and Reach
C Beds 103 F8
Heath Charnock Lancs 194 E5
Heath Common W Sus 35 E10
W Yorks 197 D11
Heathcot Aberds 293 C10
Heathcote Derbys 169 C10
Shrops 150 D3
Warks 118 E6
Heath Cross Devon 13 B10
Devon 14 C2
Heath End Bucks 84 F5
Bucks 85 D7
Derbys 153 E7
Hants 64 G2
Hants 64 G5
S Glos 61 B7
Sur 49 D10
Warks 118 E4
W Mid 133 C10
W Sus 35 D7
Heather Leics 153 G7
Heathercombe Devon 13 E10
Heatherfield Highld 298 E4
Heather Row Hants 49 C8
Heatherside Sur 50 B2
Heatherwood Park
Highld 311 K2
Heatherybanks Aberds 303 E7
Heathfield Cambs 105 B9
Devon 14 F2
E Sus 37 C9
Glos 80 F2
Hants 33 F9
Lincs 189 C10
N Yorks 214 F2
S Ayrs 257 E9
Som 27 B11
Som 43 G7
Heathfield Village Oxon 83 B8
Heath Green Hants 48 F6
Worcs 117 C11
Heathhall Dumfries 237 B11
Heath Hayes Staffs 151 G10
Heath Hill Shrops 150 G5
Heath House Som 44 D2
Heathlands Wokingham 65 F10
Heath Lanes Telford 150 E2
Heath Park London 68 B4
Heathrow Airport London 66 D5
Heath Side Kent 68 E4
Heathstock Devon 28 G2
Heathton Shrops 132 E6
Heathtop Derbys 152 C4
Heath Town W Mid 133 D8
Heathwaite Cumb 221 F8
N Yorks 225 E9
Heatley Staffs 151 D11
Warr 184 D2
Heaton Gtr Man 195 F7
Lancs 211 G8
Staffs 169 C7
T&W 243 D7
W Yorks 205 G8
Heaton Chapel Gtr Man 184 C5
Heaton Mersey Gtr Man 184 C5
Heaton Moor Gtr Man 184 C5
Heaton Norris Gtr Man 184 C5
Heaton Royds W Yorks 205 F8
Heaton's Bridge Lancs 194 E2
Heaton Shay W Yorks 205 F8
Heaven's Door Som 29 C10
Heaverham Kent 52 B5
Heaviley Gtr Man 184 D6
Heavitree Devon 14 C4
Hebburn T&W 243 E8
Hebburn Colliery T&W 243 D8
Hebburn New Town
T&W 243 E8
Hebden N Yorks 213 G10
Hebden Bridge W Yorks 196 B3
Hebden Green Ches W 167 B10
Hebing End Herts 104 G6
Hebron Anglesey 179 E7
Carms 92 F3
Northumb 252 F5
Heck Dumfries 248 G3

Heckdyke N Lincs 188 B3
Heckfield Hants 65 G8
Heckfield Green Suff 126 B3
Heckfordbridge Essex 107 G8
Heckingham Norf 143 D7
Heckington Lincs 173 G10
Heckmondwike
W Yorks 197 C8
Heddington Wilts 62 F3
Heddington Wick Wilts 62 F3
Heddle Orkney 314 E3
Heddon Devon 25 B11
Heddon-on-the-Wall
Northumb 242 D4
Hedenham Norf 142 E6
Hedge End Dorset 30 F4
Hants 33 E7
Hedgehog Bridge Lincs 174 F3
Hedgerley Bucks 66 B3
Hedgerley Green Bucks 66 B3
Hedgerley Hill Bucks 66 B3
Hedging Som 28 B4
Hedley Hill Durham 233 C9
Hedley on the Hill
Northumb 242 F3
Hednesford Staffs 151 G9
Hedon E Yorks 201 B7
Hedsor Bucks 66 B2
Hedworth T&W 243 E8
Heelands M Keynes 102 D6
Heeley S Yorks 186 E5
Hegdon Hill Hereford 115 G11
Heggerscales Cumb 222 C6
Heggle Lane Cumb 230 D3
Heglibister Shetland 313 H5
Heighington Darl 233 G11
Lincs 173 B8
Heighley Staffs 168 F3
Height End Lancs 195 C9
Heightington Worcs 116 C5
Heights Gtr Man 196 F3
Heights of Brae Highld 300 C5
Heights of Kinlochewe
Highld 299 C10
Heilam Highld 308 C4
Heiton Borders 262 C6
Helbeck Cumb 222 B5
Hele Devon 12 C2
Devon 13 G10
Devon 27 G7
Devon 40 D4
Som 27 C11
Torbay 9 B8
Helebridge Corn 24 G2
Helensburgh Argyll 276 E5
Helford Corn 3 D7
Helford Passage Corn 3 D7
Helham Green Herts 86 B5
Helhoughton Norf 159 D7
Helions Bumpstead
Essex 106 C3
Hellaby S Yorks 187 C8
Helland Corn 11 G7
Som 28 C4
Hellandbridge Corn 11 G7
Hell Corner W Berks 63 G11
Hellesdon Norf 160 G4
Hellesveor Corn 2 A2
Hellidon W Nhants 119 F10
Hellifield N Yorks 204 B3
Hellifield Green
N Yorks 204 B3
Hellingly E Sus 23 C9
Hellington Norf 142 C6
Hellister Shetland 313 J5
Hellman's Cross Essex 87 B9
Helm Northumb 252 D5
N Yorks 223 G8
Helmburn Borders 261 E9
Helmdon W Nhants 101 C11
Helme W Yorks 196 E5
Helmingham Suff 126 F3
Helmington Row
Durham 233 D9
Helmsdale Highld 311 H4
Helmshore Lancs 195 C9
Helmside Cumb 212 B3
Helmsley N Yorks 216 C2
Helperby N Yorks 215 F8
Helperthorpe N Yorks 217 E9
Helpringham Lincs 173 G10
Helpston Pboro 138 B2
Helsby Ches W 183 F7
Helscott Corn 24 G2
Helsey Lincs 191 G8
Helston Corn 2 D5
Helstone Corn 11 E7
Helston Water Corn 4 G5
Helton Cumb 230 G6
Helwith Bridge N Yorks 212 F6
Helygain = *Halkyn* Flint 182 G2
Hemblington Norf 160 G6
Hemblington Corner
Norf 160 G6
Hembridge Som 44 F5
Hemel Hempstead Herts 85 D9
Hemerdon Devon 7 D11
Hemford Shrops 130 C6
Hem Heath Stoke 168 G5
Hemingbrough N Yorks 207 G9
Hemingby Lincs 190 G2
Hemingfield S Yorks 197 G11
Hemingford Abbots
Cambs 122 C5
Hemingford Grey
Cambs 122 C5
Hemingstone Suff 126 G3
Hemington Leics 153 D9
N Nhants 137 F11
Som 45 C8
Hemley Suff 108 C5
Hemlington Mbro 225 C10
Hemp Green Suff 127 D7
Hempholme E Yorks 209 C7
Hempnall Norf 142 E4
Hempnall Green Norf 142 E4
Hempriggs House
Highld 310 E7
Hemp's Green Essex 107 F8
Hempshill Vale Notts 171 G8
Hempstead Essex 106 D2
Medway 69 G9
Norf 160 B2
Norf 161 D8
Hempsted Glos 80 B4
Hempton Norf 159 D8
Oxon 101 E8
Hempton Wainhill Oxon 84 E3
Hemsby Norf 161 F9
Hemsted Kent 54 E6
Hemswell Lincs 188 C6
Hemswell Cliff Lincs 188 D6
Hemsworth Dorset 31 F7
S Yorks 186 E5
W Yorks 198 E2
Hemyock Devon 27 E10
Henaford Devon 24 D2
Hen Bentref Llandegfan
Anglesey 179 G9
Henbrook Worcs 117 D8
Henbury Bristol 60 D5
Ches E 184 G5
Dorset 18 B5
Hendomen Powys 130 D4
Hendon London 67 B8
T&W 243 F10
Hendra Corn 2 B6
Corn 2 C5
Corn 2 D3
Corn 2 F6
Corn 5 C9
Corn 5 D9
Corn 11 E7
Hendrabridge Corn 6 B5
Hendraburnick Corn 11 D8
Hendra Croft Corn 4 D5
Hendre Flint 165 B11
Gwyn 110 B2
Powys 129 D9
Hendre-ddu Conwy 164 B5
Hendredenny Park
Caerph 58 B6
Hendreforgan Rhondda 58 B3
Hendrerwydd Denb 165 C10
Hendrewen Swansea 75 D10
Hendy Carms 75 E9
Hendy-Gwyn Carms 74 B2
Hendy Gwyn = *Whitland*
Carms 73 B11
Hên-efail Denb 165 C9
Heneglwys Anglesey 178 F6
Hen-feddau fawr Pembs 92 E4
Henfield S Glos 61 D7
W Sus 36 D2
Henford Devon 12 C3
Henfords Marsh Wilts 45 E11
Henghurst Kent 54 F3
Hengoed Caerph 77 F10
Denb 165 D9
Powys 114 G4
Shrops 148 C5
Hengrave Norf 160 F2
Suff 124 D6
Hengrove Bristol 60 F6
Hengrove Park Bristol 60 F5
Henham Essex 105 F10
Heniarth Powys 130 B2
Henlade Som 28 C3
Henleaze Bristol 60 D5
Henley Dorset 29 G11
Glos 80 B6
Shrops 115 B10
Shrops 131 F9
Som 44 G2
Suff 126 G3
Wilts 47 B10
Wilts 61 F10
W Sus 34 B5
Henley Common W Sus 34 B5
Henley Green W Mid 135 G7
Henley-in-Arden Warks 118 D3
Henley-on-Thames Oxon 65 C9
Henley's Down E Sus 38 E2
Henley Street Kent 69 F7
Henllan Ceredig 93 C7
Denb 165 B8
Henllan Amgoed Carms 92 G3
Henlle Shrops 148 C6
Henllys Torf 78 G3
Henllys Vale Torf 78 G3
Henlow C Beds 104 D3
Hennock Devon 14 E2
Henny Street Essex 107 D7
Henryd Conwy 180 G3
Henry's Moat Pembs 91 F10
Hensall N Yorks 198 C5
Henshaw Northumb 241 E7
W Yorks 205 E10
Hensingham Cumb 219 B9
Hensington Oxon 83 B7
Henstead Suff 143 F9
Hensting Hants 33 C7
Henstridge Devon 40 E5
Som 30 D2
Henstridge Ash Som 30 C2
Henstridge Bowden
Som 29 C11
Henstridge Marsh Som 30 C2
Henton Oxon 84 E3
Som 44 D3
Henwood Corn 11 G11
Oxon 83 E7
Henwood Green Kent 52 E6
Heogan Shetland 313 J6
Heol-ddu Carms 75 E7
Swansea 56 B6
Heolgerrig M Tydf 77 D8
Heol-laethog Bridgend 58 C2
Heol-las Bridgend 58 C2
Swansea 57 B7
Heol Senni Powys 95 G8
Heol-y-gaer Powys 96 D3
Heol-y-mynydd V Glam 57 G11
Hepburn Northumb 264 E3
Hepple Northumb 251 C11
Hepscott Northumb 252 G6
Hepthorne Lane Derbys 170 C6
Heptonstall W Yorks 196 B3
Hepworth Suff 125 C9
W Yorks 197 F7
Herbrandston Pembs 72 D5
Hereford Hereford 97 C10
Heribusta Highld 298 B4
Heriot Borders 271 E7
Hermiston Edin 280 G3
Hermitage Borders 250 D2
Dorset 29 F10
W Berks 64 E4
W Sus 22 B3
Hermitage Green Mers 183 C10
Hermit Hill S Yorks 197 G10
Hermit Hole W Yorks 205 F7
Hermon Anglesey 162 B5
Carms 93 E7
Carms 94 F3
Pembs 92 E4
Herne Kent 71 F7
Herne Bay Kent 71 F7
Herne Common Kent 71 F7
Herne Hill London 67 E10
Herne Pound Kent 53 C7
Herner Devon 25 B9
Hernhill Kent 70 G5
Herniss Corn 2 C6
Herodsfoot Corn 6 C4
Heron Cross Stoke 168 G5
Heronden Kent 55 C9
Herongate Essex 87 G10
Heronsford S Ayrs 244 G4
Heronsgate Herts 85 G8
Heron's Ghyll E Sus 37 B7
Herons Green Bath 44 B5
Heronston Bridgend 58 D2
Herra Shetland 312 D8
Herriard Hants 49 D7
Herringfleet Suff 143 D9
Herring's Green
Bedford 103 C11
Herringswell Suff 124 C4
Herringthorpe S Yorks 186 C6
Hersden Kent 71 G8
Hersham Corn 24 F3
Sur 66 G6
Herstmonceux E Sus 23 C10
Herston Dorset 18 F6
Orkney 314 G4
Hertford Herts 86 C4
Hertford Heath Herts 86 C4
Hertingfordbury Herts 86 C4
Hesketh Bank Lancs 194 C2
Hesketh Lane Lancs 203 E8
Hesketh Moss Lancs 194 C2
Hesket Newmarket
Cumb 230 D2
Heskin Green Lancs 194 D4
Hesleden Durham 234 D4
Hesleyside Northumb 251 G8
Heslington York 207 C8
Hessay York 206 C6
Hessenford Corn 6 D6
Hessett Suff 125 E8
Hessle E Yorks 200 B4
W Yorks 198 D2
Hest Bank Lancs 211 F9
Hester's Way Glos 99 G8
Hestinsetter Shetland 313 J4
Heston London 66 D6
Hestwall Orkney 314 E2
Heswall Mers 182 E3
Hethe Oxon 101 F11
Hethel Norf 142 C3
Hethelpit Cross Glos 98 F5
Hethersett Norf 142 C3
Hethersgill Cumb 239 D11
Hetherside Cumb 239 D10
Hetherson Green
Ches W 167 F8
Hethpool Northumb 263 D9
Hett Durham 233 D11
Hetton N Yorks 204 B5
Hetton Downs T&W 234 B3
Hetton-le-Hill T&W 234 B3
Hetton-le-Hole T&W 234 B3
Hetton Steads Northumb 264 B2
Heugh Northumb 242 C3
Heugh-head Aberds 292 B5
Heveningham Suff 126 C6
Hever Kent 52 E3
Heversham Cumb 211 C9
Hevingham Norf 160 E3
Hewas Water Corn 5 F9
Hewelsfield Glos 79 E9
Hewelsfield Common
Glos 79 E8
Hewer Hill Cumb 230 D3
Hew Green N Yorks 205 B10
Hewish N Som 60 G2
Som 28 F6
Hewood Dorset 28 G5
Heworth T&W 243 E7
York 207 C8
Hexham Northumb 241 E10
Hextable Kent 68 E4
Hexthorpe S Yorks 198 G5
Hexton Herts 104 E2
Hexworthy Devon 13 G9
Hey Lancs 204 E3
Heybridge Essex 87 F10
Essex 88 D5
Heybridge Basin Essex 88 D5
Heybrook Bay Devon 7 F10
Heydon Cambs 105 C8
Norf 160 D2
Heydour Lincs 155 B10
Heyford Park Oxon 101 F10
Hey Green W Yorks 196 E4
Heyheads Gtr Man 196 G3
Hey Houses Lancs 193 B10
Heylipol Argyll 288 E1
Heylor Shetland 312 E4
Heyope Powys 114 C4
Heyrod Gtr Man 185 B7
Heysham Lancs 211 G8
Heyshaw N Yorks 214 G3
Heyshott W Sus 34 D5
Heyshott Green W Sus 34 D5
Heyside Gtr Man 196 F2
Heytesbury Wilts 46 E2
Heythrop Oxon 101 F7
Heywood Gtr Man 195 E11
Wilts 45 C11
Hibaldstow N Lincs 200 G3
Hibb's Green Suff 125 G7
Hickford Hill Essex 106 C5
Hickleton S Yorks 198 F3
Hickling Norf 161 E8
Notts 154 D3
Hickling Green Norf 161 E8
Hickling Heath Norf 161 E8
Hickling Pastures Notts 154 D3
Hickmans Green Kent 54 B5
Hicks Forstal Kent 71 G7
Hicks Gate Bath 60 F6
Hick's Mill Corn 4 G5
Hickstead W Sus 36 C3
Hidcote Bartrim Glos 100 C3
Hidcote Boyce Glos 100 C3
Hifnal Shrops 132 D4
Higginshaw Gtr Man 196 F2
High Ackworth W Yorks 198 D2
Higham Derbys 170 D5
Fife 286 F6
Kent 69 E8
Lancs 204 F2
Suff 107 D10
Suff 124 E4
S Yorks 197 F10
Higham Common
S Yorks 197 F10
Higham Dykes
Northumb 242 B4
Higham Ferrers
N Nhants 121 D9
Higham Gobion C Beds 104 E2
Higham Hill London 86 G5
Higham on the Hill
Leics 135 D7
Highampton Devon 25 G7
Highams Park London 86 G5
Higham Wood Kent 52 D5
High Angerton Northumb 252 F3
High Bankhill Cumb 231 C7
High Banton N Lanark 278 E4
High Barn Lincs 174 C5
High Barnes T&W 243 F9
High Barnet London 86 F2
High Beach Essex 86 F6
High Bentham N Yorks 212 F3
High Bickington Devon 25 C10
High Biggins Cumb 212 D2
High Birkwith N Yorks 212 D5
High Birstwith N Yorks 205 B10
High Blantyre S Lanark 268 D3
High Bonnybridge Falk 278 F6
High Bradfield S Yorks 186 C3
High Bradley N Yorks 204 D6
High Bray Devon 41 G7
Highbridge Cumb 230 C3
Hants 33 C7
Highld 290 E3
Som 43 D10
Highbridge *continued*
W Mid 133 C10
Highbrook W Sus 51 G11
High Brooms Kent 52 E5
High Brotheridge Glos 80 C5
High Bullen Devon 25 C8
Highburton W Yorks 197 E7
Highbury London 67 B10
Ptsmth 33 G11
Som 45 D7
Highbury Vale
Nottingham 171 G8
High Buston Northumb 252 B6
High Callerton
Northumb 242 C5
High Cark Cumb 211 C7
High Casterton Cumb 212 D2
High Catton E Yorks 207 C10
High Church Northumb 252 F5
Highclere Hants 64 G2
Highcliffe BCP 19 C10
Derbys 186 F2
High Cogges Oxon 82 D5
High Common Norf 141 B9
High Coniscliffe Darl 224 B4
High Crompton Gtr Man 196 F2
High Cross Cambs 123 F8
Corn 2 D6
E Sus 37 B9
Hants 34 B2
Herts 85 F10
Herts 86 B5
Newport 59 B9
Warks 118 D3
W Sus 36 D2
High Crosshill S Lanark 268 C2
High Cunsey Cumb 221 G7
High Dubmire T&W 234 B2
High Dyke Durham 232 F5
High Easter Essex 87 C10
High Eggborough
N Yorks 198 C5
High Eldrig Dumfries 236 C4
High Ellington N Yorks 214 C3
Higher Alham Som 45 E7
Higher Ansty Dorset 30 G3
Higher Ashton Devon 14 E3
Higher Audley Blackburn 195 B7
Higher Bal Corn 4 E4
Higher Ballam Lancs 202 G3
Higher Bartle Lancs 202 G6
Higher Bebington Mers 182 D4
Higher Berry End
C Beds 103 E9
Higher Blackley
Gtr Man 195 G10
Higher Boarshaw
Gtr Man 195 F11
Higher Bockhampton
Dorset 17 C10
Higher Bojewyan Corn 1 C3
Higher Boscaswell Corn 1 C3
Higher Brixham Torbay 9 D8
Higher Broughton
Gtr Man 195 G10
Higher Burrow Som 28 C6
Higher Burwardsley
Ches W 167 D8
High Ercall Telford 149 F11
Higher Chalmington
Dorset 29 G9
Higher Cheriton Devon 27 G10
Higher Chillington Som 28 E5
Higher Chisworth
Derbys 185 C7
Highercliff Corn 6 D4
Higher Clovelly Devon 24 C4
Higher Condurrow Corn 2 B5
Higher Crackington Corn 11 B9
Higher Cransworth Corn 5 B9
Higher Croft Blackburn 195 B7
Higher Denham Bucks 66 B4
Higher Dinting Derbys 185 C8
Higher Disley Ches E 185 E7
Higher Downs Corn 2 C3
Higher Durston Som 28 B3
Higher End Gtr Man 194 G4
Higher Folds Gtr Man 195 G7
Higherford Lancs 204 E3
Higher Gabwell Torbay 9 B8
Higher Green Gtr Man 195 G8
Higher Halstock Leigh
Dorset 29 F8
Higher Heysham Lancs 211 G8
Higher Hogshead
Lancs 195 C11
Higher Holton Som 29 B11
Higher Hurdsfield
Ches E 184 G6
Higher Kingcombe
Dorset 16 B6
Higher Kinnerton Flint 166 C4
Higher Land Corn 12 G3
Higher Marsh Som 30 C2
Higher Melcombe Dorset 30 G2
Higher Menadew Corn 5 D10
Higher Molland Devon 41 G8
Higher Muddiford Devon 40 F5
Higher Nyland Dorset 30 C2
Higher Penwortham
Lancs 194 B4
Higher Pertwood Wilts 45 F11
Higher Porthpean Corn 5 E10
Higher Poynton Ches E 184 E6
Higher Prestacott Devon 12 B3
Higher Rads End
C Beds 103 E9
Higher Ridge Shrops 149 C7
Higher Rocombe Barton
Devon 9 B8
Higher Row Dorset 31 G8
Higher Runcorn Halton 183 E8
Higher Sandford
Dorset 29 C10
Higher Shotton Flint 166 B4
Higher Shurlach
Ches W 183 G11
Higher Slade Devon 40 D4
Higher Street Som 42 E6
Higher Tale Devon 27 G9
Higher Tolcarne Corn 5 B7
Higher Totnell Dorset 29 F10
Highertown Corn 4 G6
Corn 11 E8
Higher Town Corn 5 C10
Scilly 1 F4
Som 42 D3
Higher Tremarcoombe
Corn 6 B5
Higher Vexford Som 42 F6
Higher Walreddon Devon 12 G5
Higher Walton Lancs 194 B5
Warr 183 D9
Higher Wambrook Som 28 F3
Higher Warcombe Devon 40 D3
Higher Weaver Devon 27 G9
Higher Whatcombe
Dorset 30 G4
Higher Wheelton Lancs 194 C6
Higher Whitley
Ches W 183 E10
Higher Wincham
Ches W 183 F11
Higher Woodsford
Dorset 17 D11
Higher Wraxall Dorset 29 G9
Higher Wych Ches W 167 G7
High Etherley Durham 233 F9
High Ferry Lincs 174 F5
Highfield E Yorks 207 F10
Glos 79 E10
Gtr Man 194 G5
Gtr Man 195 F8
Herts 85 D9
N Ayrs 266 E6
Oxon 101 G11
Soton 32 E6
S Yorks 186 D5
T&W 242 F4
High Field Lancs 203 C10
Highfields Cambs 123 F7
Derbys 170 B6
Essex 88 B5
Glos 80 F3
Leicester 136 C2
Northumb 273 E9
Staffs 151 E8
S Yorks 198 F4
High Flatts W Yorks 197 F8
High Forge Durham 242 G6
High Friarside Durham 242 F5
High Gallowhill E Dunb 278 G2
High Garrett Essex 106 F5
Highgate E Sus 52 G2
Kent 53 G9
London 67 B9
Powys 130 D2
S Yorks 198 G3
W Mid 133 F11
High Grange Durham 233 E9
High Grantley N Yorks 214 F4
High Green Cumb 221 E8
Norf 141 B8
Norf 142 B2
Norf 159 G8
Shrops 132 G4
Suff 125 E7
S Yorks 186 B4
Worcs 99 B7
W Yorks 197 E7
High Halden Kent 53 F11
High Halstow Medway 69 D9
High Ham Som 44 G2
High Handenhold
Durham 242 G6
High Harrington Cumb 228 F6
High Harrogate N Yorks 206 B2
High Haswell Durham 234 C3
High Hatton Shrops 150 E2
High Hauxley Northumb 253 C7
High Hawsker N Yorks 227 D8
High Heath Shrops 150 D3
W Mid 133 C10
High Hesket Cumb 230 C5
High Hesleden Durham 234 D5
High Hill Cumb 229 G11
High Houses Essex 87 C11
High Hoyland S Yorks 197 E9
High Hunsley E Yorks 208 F4
High Hurstwood E Sus 37 B7
High Hutton N Yorks 216 F5
High Ireby Cumb 229 D10
High Kelling Norf 177 E10
High Kilburn N Yorks 215 D10
High Lands Durham 233 F8
Highlane Ches E 168 B5
Derbys 186 E6
High Lane Gtr Man 185 D7
Worcs 116 E3
Highlanes Corn 10 G4
Staffs 150 C5
High Lanes Corn 2 B3
High Laver Essex 87 D8
Highlaws Cumb 229 B8
Highleadon Glos 98 G5
High Legh Ches E 184 E2
Highleigh W Sus 22 D4
High Leven Stockton 225 C8
Highley Shrops 132 G4
High Littleton Bath 44 B6
High Longthwaite
Cumb 229 B11
High Lorton Cumb 229 F9
High Marishes N Yorks 216 D6
High Marnham Notts 188 G4
High Melton S Yorks 198 G4
High Mickley Northumb 242 E3
High Mindork Dumfries 236 D5
Highmoor Cumb 229 B11
Oxon 65 B8
High Moor Derbys 187 E7
Lancs 194 E4
Highmoor Cross Oxon 65 C8
Highmoor Hill Mon 60 B3
High Moorsley T&W 234 B2
Highnam Glos 80 B3
Highnam Green Glos 98 G5
High Nash Glos 79 C9
High Newton Cumb 211 C8
High Newton-by-the-Sea
Northumb 264 D6
High Nibthwaite Cumb 210 B5
Highoak Norf 141 C11
High Oaks Cumb 222 G2
High Offley Staffs 150 D5
High Ongar Essex 87 E9
High Onn Staffs 150 F6
High Onn Wharf Staffs 150 F6
High Park Cumb 221 G10
Mers 193 D11
Highridge Bristol 60 F5
High Risby N Lincs 200 E2
Highroad Well Moor
W Yorks 196 B5
High Roding Essex 87 B10
High Rougham Suff 125 E8
High Row Cumb 230 D3
Cumb 230 G3
High Salvington W Sus 35 F10
High Scales Cumb 229 B9
High Sellafield Cumb 219 E10
High Shaw N Yorks 223 G7
High Shields T&W 243 D9
High Shincliffe Durham 233 C11
High Side Cumb 229 E10
High Southwick T&W 243 F9
High Spen T&W 242 F4
High Stakesby N Yorks 227 C7
Highstead Kent 71 F8
Highsted Kent 70 G2
High Stoop Durham 233 C8
Highstreet Kent 70 G5
High Street Corn 5 E9
Kent 53 G8
Pembs 73 B11
Suff 107 B7
Suff 127 C8
Suff 127 F8
Suff 143 G7
Highstreet Green Essex 106 E5
Sur 50 F3
High Street Green Suff 125 F10
High Sunderland
Borders 261 C11
Hightae Dumfries 238 B3
Highter's Heath W Mid 117 B11
High Throston Hrtlpl 234 E5
High Tirfergus Argyll 255 F7
Hightown Ches E 168 C5
Hants 31 G11
Mers 193 G10
Soton 33 E7
Wrex 166 F4
W Yorks 197 C7
High Town Luton 103 G11
Shrops 132 E4
Staffs 151 G9
Hightown Green Suff 125 F9
Hightown Heights
W Yorks 197 C7
High Toynton Lincs 174 B3
High Trewhitt Northumb 252 B2
High Urpeth Durham 242 G6
High Valleyfield Fife 279 D10
High Walton Cumb 219 C9
High Warden Northumb 241 D10
High Water Head Cumb 220 F6
Highway Corn 4 G4
Hereford 97 B9
Som 29 C7
Wilts 62 E4
Windsor 65 C11
Highweek Devon 14 G2
High Westwood Durham 242 F4
High Whinnow Cumb 239 G8
Highwood Devon 27 F10
Dorset 18 D3
Essex 87 E10
Hants 31 F11
Worcs 116 D3
Highwood Hill London 86 G2
High Woolaston Glos 79 F9
High Worsall N Yorks 225 D7
Highworth Swindon 82 G2
Highworthy Devon 24 F6
High Wray Cumb 221 F7
High Wych Herts 87 C7
High Wycombe Bucks 84 G5
Hilborough Norf 140 C6
Hilborough Ho Norf 140 C6
Hilcot Glos 81 B7
Hilcote Derbys 171 D7
Hilcot End Glos 81 E9
Hilcott Wilts 46 B6
Hildenborough Kent 52 D5
Hilden Park Kent 52 D5
Hildersham Cambs 105 B10
Hildersley Hereford 98 G2
Hilderstone Staffs 151 C8
Hilderthorpe E Yorks 218 F3
Hilfield Dorset 29 F10
Hilgay Norf 140 D2
Hill S Glos 79 G10
Warks 119 D9
W Mid 134 D2
Hillam N Yorks 198 B4
Hillbeck Cumb 222 B5
Hillblock Pembs 73 B8
Hillborough Kent 71 F8
Hill Bottom Oxon 64 D6
Hillbourne BCP 18 C6
Hillbrae Aberds 302 E6
Aberds 303 G7
Hill Brow W Sus 34 B3
Hillbutts Dorset 31 G7
Hill Chorlton Staffs 150 B5
Hillcliffe Warr 183 D10
Hillcliffane Derbys 170 F3
Hillcommon Som 27 B11
Hill Common Norf 161 E8
Hill Corner Som 45 D10
Hill Croome Worcs 99 C7
Hillcross Derbys 152 C6
Hill Dale Lancs 194 E3
Hill Deverill Wilts 45 E11
Hilldyke Lincs 174 F4
Hill Dyke Lincs 174 F4
Hillend Fife 280 E2
N Lanark 268 B6
N Som 43 B11
Shrops 132 E6
Swansea 56 C2
Hill End Durham 232 D6
Fife 279 B10
Glos 99 D8
London 85 G8
N Yorks 205 C7
Som 29 E8
Worcs 117 E8
Hillend Green Glos 98 F4
Hillersland Glos 79 C9
Hillerton Devon 13 B10
Hillesden Bucks 102 F3
Hillesden Hamlet Bucks 102 E3
Hillesley Glos 61 B9
Hillfarance Som 27 C11
Hillfarrance Som 27 C11
Hillfield Devon 8 E6
W Mid 118 B2
Hillfields S Glos 60 D6
W Mid 118 B6
Hillfoot Aberds 303 D9
W Yorks 205 G10
Hillfoot End C Beds 104 E2
Hill Furze Worcs 99 B9
Hill Gate Hereford 97 F9
Hillgreen W Berks 64 D3
Hill Green Essex 105 E9
Kent 69 G10
Hillgrove W Sus 34 B6
Hillhampton Hereford 97 B11
Hillhead Aberds 302 F5
Aberds 303 G8
Corn 5 C11
Devon 9 E8
E Ayrs 257 B10
S Ayrs 257 F10
Hill Head Hants 33 G8
Northumb 241 D10
Hillhead of Auchentumb
Aberds 303 D9
Hillhead of Blairy
Aberds 302 D6
Hillhead of Cocklaw
Aberds 303 E10
Hill Hoath Kent 52 E3
Hill Hook W Mid 134 C2
Hillhouse Borders 271 D10
Hill Houses Shrops 116 B2
Hilliard's Cross Staffs 152 G3
Hilliclay Highld 310 C5
Hillingdon London 66 C5
Hillingdon Heath London 66 C5
Hillington Glasgow 267 C10
Norf 158 D4
Hillis Corner IoW 20 C5
Hillmoor Devon 27 E10
Hillmorton Warks 119 C10
Hill Mountain Pembs 73 D7
Hillockhead Aberds 292 B6
Aberds 292 C5
Hillock Vale Lancs 195 B9
Hill of Beath Fife 280 C3
Hill of Drip Stirling 278 B5
Hill of Fearn Highld 301 B8
Hill of Keillor Angus 286 C6
Hill of Mountblairy
Aberds 302 D6
Hill of Overbrae Aberds 303 C8
Hill Park Hants 33 F9
Kent 52 B2
Hillpool Worcs 117 B7
Hillpound Hants 33 D9
Hill Ridware Staffs 151 F11
Hillsborough S Yorks 186 C4
Hillside Aberds 293 D11
Angus 293 G9
Devon 8 C4
Devon 27 F11
Hants 49 C9
Mers 193 E10
Orkney 314 D3
Orkney 314 G4
Shetland 313 G6
Shrops 131 F11
Wilts 81 G9
Hill Side Hants 34 B3
S Yorks 197 G8
Worcs 116 E5
W Yorks 197 D7
Hill Somersal Derbys 152 C2
Hills Town Derbys 171 B7
Hillstreet Hants 32 D4
Hill Street Kent 54 D6
Hillswick Shetland 312 F4
Hilltop Bl Gwent 77 D11
Bucks 85 E7
Derbys 170 C4
Hill Top Derbys 186 F5
Durham 232 G5
Durham 233 C10
Durham 242 G5
Gtr Man 195 G8
Hants 32 G6
Notts 171 F7
N Yorks 214 G3
N Yorks 214 G5
Staffs 133 B7
S Yorks 186 C5
S Yorks 186 D3
S Yorks 187 B7
S Yorks 197 F9
Warks 134 E5
Warks 135 E7
W Mid 133 E9
W Sus 34 C5
W Yorks 196 E5
W Yorks 197 D10
W Yorks 205 G7
W Yorks 205 G11
Hillview T&W 243 G9
Hill View Dorset 18 B5
Hillway IoW 21 D8
Hillwell Shetland 313 M5
Hill Wood W Mid 134 C2
Hill Wootton Warks 118 D6
Hillyfields Hants 32 D5
Hilmarton Wilts 62 D4
Hilperton Wilts 45 B11
Hilperton Marsh Wilts 45 B11
Hilsea Ptsmth 33 G11
Hilston E Yorks 209 G11
Hiltingbury Hants 32 C6
Hilton Aberds 303 F9
Borders 273 E7
Cambs 122 D5
Cumb 231 G10
Derbys 152 C4
Dorset 30 G3
Durham 233 G9
Highld 309 L7
Highld 311 L3
Shrops 132 D5
Staffs 133 B11
Stockton 225 C9
Hilton House Gtr Man 194 F6
Hilton Lodge Highld 300 G2
Hilton of Cadboll Highld 301 B8
Hilton Park Gtr Man 195 G10
Himbleton Worcs 117 F8
Himley Staffs 133 E7
Hincaster Cumb 211 C10
Hinchley Wood Sur 67 F7
Hinchliffe Mill W Yorks 196 F6
Hinchwick Glos 100 E2
Hinckley Leics 135 E8
Hinderclay Suff 125 B10
Hinderton Ches W 182 F4
Hinderwell N Yorks 226 B5
Hindford Shrops 148 C6
Hindhead Sur 49 F11
Hindle Fold Lancs 203 G10
Hindley Gtr Man 194 G6
Northumb 242 F2
Hindley Green Gtr Man 194 G6
Hindlip Worcs 117 F7
Hindolveston Norf 159 D10
Hindon Wilts 46 G2
Hindpool Cumb 210 F3
Hindringham Norf 159 B9
Hindsford Gtr Man 195 G7
Hingham Norf 141 C10
Hinstock Shrops 150 D3
Hintlesham Suff 107 C11
Hinton Glos 79 E11
Hants 19 B10
Hereford 96 D6
S Glos 61 D8
Shrops 131 B8
Som 29 C9
W Nhants 119 G10
Hinton Ampner Hants 33 B9
Hinton Blewett Bath 44 B5
Hinton Charterhouse
Bath 45 B9
Hinton Cross Worcs 99 C10
Hinton-in-the-Hedges
W Nhants 101 D11
Hinton Martell Dorset 31 F8
Hinton on the Green
Worcs 99 C10
Hinton Parva Dorset 31 G7
Swindon 63 C8
Hinton St George Som 28 E6
Hinton St Mary Dorset 30 D3
Hinton Waldrist Oxon 82 F5
Hints Shrops 116 C2
Staffs 134 C3
Hinwick Bedford 121 E8
Hinwood Shrops 131 B7
Hinxhill Kent 54 E5
Hinxton Cambs 105 B9
Hinxworth Herts 104 C4
Hipperholme W Yorks 196 B6
Hipplecote Worcs 116 F4
Hipsburn Northumb 264 G6
Hipswell N Yorks 224 F3
Hirael Gwyn 179 G9
Hiraeth Carms 92 G3
Hirn Aberds 293 C9
Hirnant Powys 147 E11
Hirst N Lanark 269 C7
Northumb 253 F7
Hirst Courtney N Yorks 198 C6
Hirwaen Denb 165 C10
Hirwaun Rhondda 77 D7
Hirwaun Common
Bridgend 58 C2
Hiscott Devon 25 B8
Hislop Borders 249 C9
Hisomley Wilts 45 D11
Histon Cambs 123 E8
Hitcham Suff 125 G9
Hitchill Dumfries 238 D4
Hitchin Herts 104 F3
Hitchin Hill Herts 104 F3
Hitcombe Bottom Wilts 45 E10
Hither Green London 67 E11
Hittisleigh Devon 13 C10
Hittisleigh Barton Devon 13 B10
Hive E Yorks 208 G2
Hixon Staffs 151 D10
Hoaden Kent 55 B9
Hoar Cross Staffs 152 E2
Hoarwithy Hereford 97 F10
Hoath Kent 71 G8
Hoath Corner Kent 52 E3
Hobarris Shrops 114 B6
Hobbister Orkney 314 F3
Hobble End Staffs 133 B10
Hobbles Green Suff 124 G4
Hobbs Cross Essex 87 C7
Essex 87 F7
Hobbs Wall Bath 61 G7
Hob Hill Ches W 167 E7
Hobkirk Borders 262 G3
Hobroyd Derbys 185 C8
Hobson Durham 242 F5
Hoby Leics 154 F3
Hoccombe Som 27 B10
Hockenden London 68 F3
Hockerill Herts 105 G9
Hockering Norf 159 G11
Hockering Heath Norf 159 G11
Hockerton Notts 172 D2
Hockholler Som 27 C11
Hockholler Green Som 27 C11
Hockley Ches E 184 E6
Essex 88 G4
Kent 54 B3
Staffs 134 C4
W Mid 118 B5
Hockley Heath W Mid 118 C3
Hockliffe C Beds 103 F9
Hockwold cum Wilton
Norf 140 F4
Hockworthy Devon 27 D8
Hocombe Hants 32 C6
Hoddesdon Herts 86 D5
Hoddlesden Blackburn 195 C8
Hoddomcross Dumfries 238 C5
Hoddom Mains Dumfries 238 C5
Hoden Worcs 99 B11
Hodgefield Staffs 168 E6
Hodgehill Ches E 168 B4
W Mid 134 F2
Hodgeston Pembs 73 F8
Hodley Powys 130 E3
Hodnet Shrops 150 D2
Hodnetheath Shrops 150 D2
Hodsock Notts 187 D10
Hodsoll Street Kent 68 G6
Hodson Swindon 63 C7
Hodthorpe Derbys 187 F8
Hoe Hants 33 D9
Norf 159 F9
Sur 50 D5
Hoe Benham W Berks 64 F2
Hoe Gate Hants 33 E10
Hoff Cumb 222 B3
Hoffleet Stow Lincs 156 B4
Hogaland Shetland 312 F5
Hogben's Hill Kent 54 B4
Hogganfield Glasgow 268 B2
Hoggard's Green Suff 125 F7
Hoggeston Bucks 102 G6
Hoggington Wilts 45 B10
Hoggrill's End Warks 134 E4
Hogha Gearraidh
W Isles 296 D3
Hog Hatch Sur 49 D10
Hoghton Lancs 194 B6
Hoghton Bottoms Lancs 194 B6
Hogley Green W Yorks 196 F6
Hognaston Derbys 170 E2
Hogpits Bottom Herts 85 E8
Hogsthorpe Lincs 191 G8
Hogstock Dorset 31 F7
Holbeach Lincs 157 E7
Holbeach Bank Lincs 157 D7
Holbeach Clough Lincs 156 D6
Holbeach Drove Lincs 156 G6
Holbeache Worcs 116 B5
Holbeach Hurn Lincs 157 D7
Holbeach St Johns
Lincs 156 F6
Holbeach St Marks
Lincs 157 C7
Holbeach St Matthew
Lincs 157 C8
Holbeck Notts 187 G8
W Yorks 205 G11
Holbeck Woodhouse
Notts 187 G8
Holberrow Green
Worcs 117 F10
Holbeton Devon 8 E2
Holborn London 67 C10
Holborough Kent 69 G8
Holbrook Derbys 170 G5
Suff 108 D3
S Yorks 186 E6
Holbrook Common
S Glos 61 E7
Holbrook Moor Derbys 170 F5
Holbrooks W Mid 134 G6
Holburn Northumb 264 B2
Holbury Hants 32 G6
Holcombe Devon 14 G5
Gtr Man 195 D9
Som 45 D7
Holcombe Brook
Gtr Man 195 E9
Holcombe Rogus Devon 27 D9
Holcot W Nhants 120 D5
Holdbrook London 86 F5
Holden Lancs 203 D11
Holdenby W Nhants 120 D3
Holden Fold Gtr Man 196 F2
Holdenhurst BCP 19 B8
Holder's Green Essex 106 F2
Holders Hill London 86 G2
Holdfast Worcs 99 D7
Holdgate Shrops 131 F11
Holdingham Lincs 173 F9
Holditch Dorset 28 G4
Holdsworth W Yorks 196 B5
Holdworth S Yorks 186 C3
Hole Devon 24 D4
W Yorks 204 F6
Hole Bottom W Yorks 196 C2
Holefield Borders 263 C8
Holehills N Lanark 268 B5
Holehouse Derbys 185 C8
Holehouses Ches E 184 F2

Hole-in-the-Wall
Hereford 98 F2
Holemill Aberdeen 293 C10
Holemoor Devon 24 F6
Hole's Hole Devon 7 B8
Holestane Dumfries 247 D9
Holestone Derbys 170 C4
Hole Street W Sus 35 E10
Holewater Devon 41 F8
Holford Som 43 E7
Holgate York 207 C7
Holker Cumb 211 D7
Holkham Norf 176 E5
Hollacombe Devon 24 G5
Devon 26 G4
Hollacombe Hill Devon 7 E10
Holland Orkney 314 A4
Orkney 314 D6
Sur 52 C2
Holland Fen Lincs 174 F2
Holland Lees Lancs 194 F4
Holland-on-Sea Essex 89 B12
Hollands Som 29 D9
Hollandstoun Orkney 314 A7
Hollee Dumfries 239 D7
Hollesley Suff 109 C7
Hollicombe Torbay 9 C7
Hollies Common Staffs 150 E6
Hollinfare Warr 183 C11
Hollingbourne Kent 53 B10
Hollingbury Brighton 36 F4
Hollingdean Brighton 36 F4
Hollingdon Bucks 103 F7
Hollingrove E Sus 37 C11
Hollingthorpe W Yorks 197 D10
Hollington Derbys 152 B4
E Sus 38 E3
Hants 48 B2
Staffs 151 B11
Hollington Cross Hants 48 B2
Hollington Grove
Derbys 152 B4
Hollingwood Derbys 186 G6
Hollingworth Gtr Man 185 B8
Hollin Hall Lancs 204 F4
Hollin Park W Yorks 206 F2
Hollins Cumb 222 G3
Derbys 186 G4
Gtr Man 195 F8
Gtr Man 195 F10
Gtr Man 195 F11
Staffs 168 D6
Staffs 168 E4
Staffs 169 F7
Hollinsclough Staffs 169 B9
Hollins End S Yorks 186 E5
Hollinsgreen Ches E 168 C2
Hollins Green Warr 183 C11
Hollins Lane Lancs 202 C5
Shrops 149 B10
Hollinswood Telford 132 B4
Hollinthorpe W Yorks 206 G3
Hollinwood Gtr Man 196 G2
Shrops 149 B10
Hollis Green Devon 27 F9
Hollis Head Devon 27 G7
Hollocombe Devon 25 E10
Hollocombe Town
Devon 25 E10
Holloway Derbys 170 D4
Wilts 45 G11
Windsor 65 C10
Holloway Hill Sur 50 E3
Hollow Brook Bath 60 G5
Hollowell W Nhants 120 C3
Hollow Meadows
S Yorks 186 D2
Hollowmoor Heath
Ches W 167 B7
Hollow Oak Dorset 18 C2
Hollows Dumfries 239 B9
Hollow Street Kent 71 G8
Holly Bank W Mid 133 C11
Hollyberry End W Mid 134 G5
Holly Brook Som 44 D4
Hollybush Caerph 77 E11
E Ayrs 257 G9
Stoke 168 G5
Torf 78 G3
Worcs 98 D5
Holly Bush Wrex 166 G6
Hollybush Corner Bucks 66 B3
Suff 125 F8
Hollybushes Kent 54 B2
Hollybush Hill Bucks 66 C3
Essex 89 B10
Hollycroft Leics 135 E8
Holly Cross Windsor 65 C10
Holly End Norf 139 B9
Holly Green Bucks 84 E3
Worcs 99 C7
Holly Hill N Yorks 224 E3
Hollyhurst Shrops 131 D9
Warks 135 F7
Hollym E Yorks 201 B10
Hollywaste Shrops 116 B2
Hollywater Hants 49 G10
Hollywood Worcs 117 B11
Holmacott Devon 25 B8
Holman Clavel Som 28 D2
Holmbridge W Yorks 196 F6
Holmbury St Mary Sur 50 E6
Holmbush Corn 5 E10
Dorset 28 G5
Holmcroft Staffs 151 D8
Holme Cambs 138 F3
C Beds 104 C3
Cumb 211 D10
N Lincs 200 F2
Notts 172 D4
N Yorks 215 C7
W Yorks 196 F6
W Yorks 205 G9
Holmebridge Dorset 18 D3
Holme Chapel Lancs 195 B11
Holme Green C Beds 104 C3
N Yorks 207 E7
Wokingham 65 F10
Holme Hale Norf 141 B7
Holme Hill NE Lincs 201 F9
Holme Lacy Hereford 97 D11
Holme Lane Notts 154 B2
Holme Marsh Hereford 114 G6
Holme Mills Cumb 211 D10
Holme next the Sea
Norf 176 E2
Holme-on-Spalding-Moor
E Yorks 208 F2
Holme on the Wolds
E Yorks 208 D5
Holme Pierrepont Notts 154 B2
Holmer Hereford 97 C10
Holmer Green Bucks 84 F6
Holmes Lancs 194 D2
Holme St Cuthbert
Cumb 229 B8
Holmes Chapel Ches E 168 B3
Holmesdale Derbys 186 F5
Holmesfield Derbys 186 F4
Holme Slack Lancs 203 G7
Holmes's Hill E Sus 23 C8
Holmeswood Lancs 194 D2
Holmethorpe Sur 51 C9
Holmewood Derbys 170 B6
Holme Wood W Yorks 205 G9
Holmfield W Yorks 196 B5
Holmfirth W Yorks 196 F6
Holmhead Angus 293 F7
Dumfries 246 F6
E Ayrs 258 E3
Holmhill Dumfries 247 D9
Holmisdale Highld 297 G7
Holmley Common
Derbys 186 F5
Holmpton E Yorks 201 C11
Holmrook Cumb 219 F11
Holmsgarth Shetland 313 J6
Holmside Durham 233 B10
Holmsleigh Green Devon 28 G2
Holmston S Ayrs 257 E9
Holmwood Corner Sur 51 E7
Holmwrangle Cumb 230 B6
Holne Devon 8 B4
Holnest Dorset 29 E11
Holnicote Som 42 D2
Holsworthy Devon 24 G4
Holsworthy Beacon
Devon 24 F5
Holt Dorset 31 G8
Hants 49 C8
Mers 183 C7
Norf 159 B11
Wilts 61 G11
Worcs 116 E6
Wrex 166 E6
Holtby York 207 C9
Holt End Hants 49 F7
Worcs 117 D11
Holt Fleet Worcs 116 E6
Holt Green Lancs 193 G11
Holt Head W Yorks 196 E5
Holt Heath Dorset 31 G9
Worcs 116 E6
Holt Hill Kent 53 B8
Staffs 152 D2
Holton Oxon 83 D10
Som 29 B11
Suff 127 B7
Holton cum Beckering
Lincs 189 E10
Holton Heath Dorset 18 C4
Holton le Clay Lincs 201 G9
Holton le Moor Lincs 189 B9
Holton St Mary Suff 107 D11
Holt Park W Yorks 205 E11
Holt Pound Hants 49 E10
Holts Gtr Man 196 G3
Holtspur Bucks 84 G6
Holt Wood Dorset 31 F8
Holtye E Sus 52 F3
Holway Dorset 28 G5
Dorset 29 C10
Flint 181 F11
Som 28 C2
Holwell Dorset 30 E2
Herts 104 E3
Leics 154 E4
Oxon 82 D2
Som 45 D8
Holwellbury C Beds 104 E3
Holwick Durham 232 F4
Holworth Dorset 17 E11
Holybourne Hants 49 E8
Holy City Devon 28 G3
Holy Cross T&W 243 D8
Worcs 117 B8
Holyfield Essex 86 E5
Holyhead = Caergybi
Anglesey 178 E2
Holy Island Northumb 273 B11
Holylee Borders 261 B9
Holymoorside Derbys 170 B4
Holyport Windsor 65 D11
Holystone Northumb 251 C11
Holytown N Lanark 268 C5
Holy Vale Scilly 1 G4
Holywell Cambs 122 C6
C Beds 85 B8
Corn 4 D5
Dorset 29 G9
E Sus 23 F9
Glos 80 G3
Hereford 97 C7
Herts 85 F9
Northumb 243 C8
Som 29 E8
Warks 118 D3
Holywell = Treffynnon
Flint 181 F11
Holywell Green
W Yorks 196 D5
Holywell Lake Som 27 C10
Holywell Row Suff 124 B4
Holywood Dumfries 247 G10
Homedowns Glos 99 E8
Homer Shrops 132 C2
Homer Green Mers 193 G10
Homersfield Suff 142 F5
Homerton London 67 B11
Hom Green Hereford 97 G11
Homington Wilts 31 B10
Honeybourne Worcs 100 C2
Honeychurch Devon 25 G10
Honeydon Bedford 122 F2
Honey Hall N Som 60 G2
Honeyhill Wokingham 65 F10
Honey Hill Kent 70 G6
Honeystreet Wilts 62 G6
Honey Street Wilts 62 G6
Honey Tye Suff 107 D9
Honeywick C Beds 103 G9
Honicknowle Plym 7 D9
Honiley Warks 118 C4
Honing Norf 160 D6
Honingham Norf 160 G2
Honington Lincs 172 G6
Suff 125 C8
Warks 100 C5
Honiton Devon 27 G11
Honkley Wrex 166 D4
Honley W Yorks 196 E6
Honley Moor W Yorks 196 E6
Honnington Telford 150 F4
Honor Oak London 67 E11
Honor Oak Park London 67 E11
Honresfeld Gtr Man 196 D2
Hoo Kent 71 G9
Hoober S Yorks 186 B6
Hoobrook Worcs 116 C6
Hood Green S Yorks 197 G10
Hood Hill S Yorks 186 B5
Hood Manor Warr 183 D9
Hooe E Sus 23 D11
Plym 7 E10
Hooe Common E Sus 23 C11
Hoo End Herts 85 B11
Hoofield Ches W 167 C8
Hoo Green Ches E 184 E2
Hoohill Blackpool 202 F2
Hoo Hole W Yorks 196 B4
Hook Cambs 139 E8
Devon 28 F4
Hook *continued*
E Yorks 199 B9
Hants 33 F8
Hants 49 C8
London 67 G7
Pembs 73 C7
Wilts 62 C5
Hook-a-gate Shrops 131 B9
Hook Bank Worcs 98 C6
Hooke Dorset 16 B6
Hook End Essex 87 F9
Oxon 65 C7
W Mid 134 G4
Hooker Gate T&W 242 F4
Hookgate Staffs 150 B4
Hook Green Kent 53 F7
Kent 68 F6
Hook Heath Sur 50 B3
Hook Norton Oxon 101 E7
Hook Park Hants 33 G7
Hook's Cross Herts 104 G5
Hook Street Glos 79 F11
Wilts 62 C5
Hooksway W Sus 34 D4
Hookway Devon 14 B3
Hookwood Sur 51 E9
Hoole Ches W 166 B6
Hoole Bank Ches W 166 B6
Hooley Sur 51 B9
Hooley Bridge Gtr Man 195 E11
Hooley Brow Gtr Man 195 E11
Hooley Hill Gtr Man 184 B6
Hoo Meavy Devon 7 B10
Hoop Mon 79 D8
Hoopers Pool Wilts 45 C10
Hoops Devon 24 C5
Hoo St Werburgh
Medway 69 E9
Hooton Ches W 182 F5
Hooton Levitt S Yorks 187 C8
Hooton Pagnell S Yorks 198 F3
Hooton Roberts S Yorks 187 B7
Hopcroft's Holt Oxon 101 F9
Hope Derbys 185 E11
Devon 9 G8
Highld 308 D4
Powys 130 B5
Shrops 130 C6
Staffs 169 D10
Hope = Yr Hôb Flint 166 D4
Hope Bagot Shrops 115 C11
Hopebeck Cumb 229 G9
Hope Bowdler Shrops 131 E9
Hopedale Staffs 169 D10
Hope End Green Essex 105 G11
Hope Green Ches E 184 E6
Hopeman Moray 301 C11
Hope Mansell Hereford 79 B10
Hope Park Shrops 130 C6
Hopesay Shrops 131 G7
Hopesgate Shrops 130 C6
Hope's Green Essex 69 B9
Hope's Rough Hereford 98 B2
Hopetown W Yorks 197 C11
Hope under Dinmore
Hereford 115 G10
Hopgoods Green
W Berks 64 F4
Hopkinstown Rhondda 77 G9
Hopley's Green Hereford 114 G6
Hopperton N Yorks 206 B4
Hop Pole Lincs 156 G3
Hopsford Warks 135 G8
Hopstone Shrops 132 E5
Hopton Derbys 170 E3
Shrops 149 D11
Shrops 149 E7
Staffs 151 D8
Suff 125 B9
Hoptonbank Shrops 116 B2
Hopton Cangeford
Shrops 131 G10
Hopton Castle Shrops 115 B7
Hoptongate Shrops 131 G10
Hoptonheath Shrops 115 B7
Hopton Heath Staffs 151 D9
Hopton on Sea Norf 143 D10
Hopton Wafers Shrops 116 B2
Hopwas Staffs 134 B3
Hopwood Gtr Man 195 F11
Worcs 117 B10
Hopworthy Devon 24 G4
Horam E Sus 23 B9
Horbling Lincs 156 B2
Horbury W Yorks 197 D9
Horbury Bridge
W Yorks 197 D9
Horbury Junction
W Yorks 197 D10
Horcott Glos 81 E11
Horden Durham 234 C4
Horderley Shrops 131 F8
Hordle Hants 19 B11
Hordley Shrops 149 C7
Horeb Carms 75 D7
Carms 93 F10
Ceredig 93 C7
Flint 166 D3
Horfield Bristol 60 D6
Horgabost W Isles 305 J2
Horham Suff 126 C4
Horkesley Heath Essex 107 F9
Horkstow N Lincs 200 D3
Horkstow Wolds
N Lincs 200 D3
Horley Oxon 101 C8
Sur 51 E9
Horn Ash Dorset 28 G5
Hornblotton Som 44 G5
Hornblotton Green Som 44 G5
Hornby Lancs 211 F11
N Yorks 224 G4
N Yorks 225 D7
Horncastle Lincs 174 B3
Reading 65 E7
Hornchurch London 68 B4
Horncliffe Northumb 273 F8
Horndean Borders 273 F7
Hants 34 E2
Horndon Devon 12 F6
Horndon on the Hill
Thurrock 69 C7
Horne Sur 51 E10
Horner Som 41 D11
Horne Row Essex 88 E3
Horner's Green Suff 107 C9
Hornestreet Essex 107 E10
Horney Common E Sus 37 B7
Horn Hill Som 43 E8
Hornick Corn 5 E9
Horniehaugh Angus 292 G6
Horning Norf 160 F6
Horninghold Leics 136 D6
Horninglow Staffs 152 D4
Horningsea Cambs 123 E9
Horningsham Wilts 45 E10
Horningtoft Norf 159 E8
Horningtops Corn 6 C5
Hornsbury Som 28 E4
Hornsby Cumb 240 G2
Horns Corner Kent 38 B2
Horns Cross Devon 24 C5
E Sus 38 C4
Hornsea E Yorks 209 D10
Hornsea Bridge
E Yorks 209 D10
Hornsea Burton
E Yorks 209 D10
Hornsey London 67 B10
Hornsey Vale London 67 B10
Horns Green Kent 52 B3
Horn Street Kent 55 F7
Kent 69 G7
Hornton Oxon 101 B7
Horpit Swindon 63 C8
Horrabridge Devon 7 B10
Horringer Suff 124 E6
Horringford IoW 20 D6
Horrocks Fold Gtr Man 195 E8
Horrocksford Lancs 203 E10
Horsalls Kent 53 C11
Horsebridge Devon 12 G4
Hants 47 G10
Shrops 131 B7
Horse Bridge Staffs 169 E7
Horsebrook Devon 8 D4
Staffs 151 G7
Horsecastle N Som 60 F2
Horsedown Wilts 61 D10
Horsedowns Corn 2 C4
Horsehay Telford 132 B3
Horseheath Cambs 106 B2
Horseholm Dumfries 238 C2
Horsehouse N Yorks 213 C10
Horseley Heath W Mid 133 E9
Horsell Sur 50 B3
Horsell Birch Sur 50 B3
Horseman's Green
Wrex 166 G6
Horseman Side Essex 87 F8
Horsemere Green W Sus 35 G7
Horsenden Bucks 84 E3
Horsepools Glos 80 C4
Horseway Cambs 139 F8
Horseway Head
Hereford 114 E6
Horsey Norf 161 E9
Som 43 F10
Horsey Corner Norf 161 E9
Horsey Down Wilts 81 G9
Horsford Norf 160 F3
Horsforth W Yorks 205 F10
Horsforth Woodside
W Yorks 205 F10
Horsham Worcs 116 F4
W Sus 51 G7
Horsham St Faith Norf 160 F4
Horshoe Green Kent 52 E3
Horsington Lincs 173 B11
Som 30 C2
Horsley Derbys 170 G5
Glos 80 F4
Northumb 242 D3
Northumb 251 D8
Horsley Cross Essex 108 F2
Horsleycross Street
Essex 108 F2
Horsleyhill Borders 262 F2
Horsley Hill T&W 243 D9
Horsleyhope Durham 233 B7
Horsleys Green Bucks 84 F3
Horsley Woodhouse
Derbys 170 G5
Horsmonden Kent 53 E7
Horspath Oxon 83 E9
Horstead Norf 160 F5
Horsted Green E Sus 23 B7
Horsted Keynes W Sus 36 B5
Horton Bucks 84 B6
Dorset 31 F8
Kent 54 B6
Lancs 204 C3
S Glos 61 C9
Shrops 149 D9
Som 28 E4
Staffs 168 D6
Swansea 56 D3
Telford 150 G3
Wilts 62 G5
Windsor 66 D4
W Nhants 120 G6
Horton Common Dorset 31 F9
Horton Cross Som 28 D4
Horton-cum-Studley
Oxon 83 C9
Horton Green Ches W 167 F7
Horton Heath Dorset 31 F9
Hants 33 D7
Horton in Ribblesdale
N Yorks 212 E6
Horton Kirby Kent 68 F5
Hortonlane Shrops 149 G8
Horton Wharf Bucks 84 B6
Hortonwood Telford 150 G3
Horwich Gtr Man 194 E6
Horwich End Derbys 185 E8
Horwood Devon 25 B8
Horwood Riding S Glos 61 B8
Hoscar Lancs 194 E3
Hose Leics 154 D4
Hoselaw Borders 263 C8
Hoses Cumb 220 G4
Hosey Hill Kent 52 C3
Hosh Perth 286 E2
Hosta W Isles 296 D3
Hoswick Shetland 313 L6
Hotham E Yorks 208 G3
Hothfield Kent 54 D3
Hotley Bottom Bucks 84 E5
Hoton Leics 153 E11
Hotwells Bristol 60 E5
Houbans Shetland 312 F5
Houbie Shetland 312 D8
Houdston S Ayrs 244 D5
Hough Argyll 288 E1
Ches E 168 E2
Ches E 184 F5
Hougham Lincs 172 G5
Hough Green Halton 183 D7
Hough-on-the-Hill
Lincs 172 F6
Hough Side W Yorks 205 G10
Houghton Cambs 122 C5
Cumb 239 F10
Hants 47 G10
Northumb 242 D4
Pembs 73 D7
W Sus 35 E8
Houghton Bank Darl 233 G10
Houghton Conquest
C Beds 103 C10
Houghton Green E Sus 38 C6
Warr 183 C10
Houghton-le-Side
Darl 233 G10
Houghton-le-Spring
T&W 234 B2
Houghton on the Hill
Leics 136 C3
Houghton Regis
C Beds 103 G10
Houghton St Giles Norf 159 B8
Houghwood Mers 194 G4
Houlland Shetland 312 B7
Shetland 312 F7
Shetland 313 H5
Shetland 313 J6
Houlsyke N Yorks 226 D4
Houlton Warwicks 119 C11
Hound Hants 33 F7
Hound Green Hants 49 B8
Hound Hill Dorset 31 G7
Houndmills Hants 48 C6
Houndscroft Glos 80 E5
Houndslow Borders 272 F2
Houndsmoor Som 27 B10
Houndstone Som 29 D8
Houndwood Borders 272 C6
Hounsdown Hants 32 E5
Hounsley Batch N Som 60 G4
Hounslow London 66 D6
Hounslow Green Essex 87 B11
Hounslow West London 66 D6
Hourston Orkney 314 E2
Housabister Shetland 313 H6
Housay Shetland 312 F8
Househill Highld 301 D8
House of Daviot Highld 301 E7
House of Glenmuick
Aberds 292 D5
Houses Hill W Yorks 197 D7
Housetter Shetland 312 E5
Housham Tye Essex 87 C8
Houss Shetland 313 K5
Houston Renfs 267 B8
Houstry Highld 310 F5
Houton Orkney 314 F3
Hove Brighton 36 G3
Hove Edge W Yorks 196 C6
Hoveringham Notts 171 F11
Hoveton Norf 160 F6
Hovingham N Yorks 216 D3
How Cumb 240 F2
Howbeck Bank Ches E 167 F11
Howbrook S Yorks 186 B4
How Caple Hereford 98 E2
Howden Borders 262 E5
E Yorks 199 B8
W Loth 269 B11
Howden Clough
W Yorks 197 B8
Howden-le-Wear
Durham 233 E9
Howdon T&W 243 D8
Howdon Pans T&W 243 D8
Howe Highld 310 C7
Norf 142 C5
N Yorks 214 C6
Howe Bridge Gtr Man 195 G7
Howegreen Essex 88 E4
Howe Green Essex 87 B8
Essex 88 E2
Warks 134 F6
Howell Lincs 173 F10
How End C Beds 103 C10
Howe of Teuchar
Aberds 303 E7
Howe Street Essex 87 C11
Essex 106 E3
Howey Powys 113 F11
Howford Borders 261 B8
Borders 261 E9
Howgate Cumb 228 G5
Midloth 270 D4
Howgill Cumb 222 F2
Lancs 204 D2
N Yorks 205 B7
How Green Kent 52 D3
How Hill Norf 161 F7
Howick Mon 79 F8
Northumb 265 F7
Howick Cross Lancs 194 B4
Howle Durham 233 F7
Telford 150 E3
Howleigh Som 28 D2
Howlett End Essex 105 E11
Howley Glos 80 G2
Som 28 F3
Warr 183 D10
Hownam Borders 263 F7
Hownam Mains Borders 263 E7
Howpasley Borders 249 B8
Howsen Worcs 116 G5
Howsham N Lincs 200 G4
N Yorks 216 G4
Howslack Dumfries 248 B3
Howtel Northumb 263 C9
Howt Green Kent 69 F11
Howton Hereford 97 F8
Howtown Cumb 221 B8
Howwood Renfs 267 C7
How Wood Herts 85 E10
Hoxne Suff 126 B3
Hoxton London 67 C10
Hoy Orkney 314 F2
Hoylake Mers 182 D2
Hoyland S Yorks 197 G11
Hoyland Common
S Yorks 197 G11
Hoylandswaine S Yorks 197 G9
Hoyle W Sus 34 D6
Hoyle Mill S Yorks 197 F11
Hubbard's Hill Kent 52 C4
Hubberholme N Yorks 213 D8
Hubberston Pembs 72 D5
Hubbersty Head Cumb 221 G8
Hubberton Green
W Yorks 196 C4
Hubbert's Bridge Lincs 174 G3
Huby N Yorks 205 D11
N Yorks 215 F11
Hucclecote Glos 80 B5
Hucking Kent 53 B10
Hucknall Notts 171 F8
Huddersfield W Yorks 196 D6
Huddington Worcs 117 F8
Huddisford Devon 24 D4
Huddlesford Staffs 134 B3
Hud Hey Lancs 195 C9
Hudnall Herts 85 C8
Hudnalls Glos 79 E8
Hudswell N Yorks 224 E3
Wilts 61 F11
Huggate E Yorks 208 B3
Hugglepit Devon 24 C4
Hugglescote Leics 153 G8
Hughenden Valley Bucks 84 F5
Hughley Shrops 131 D11
Hugh Mill Lancs 195 C10
Hugh Town Scilly 1 G4
Hugus Corn 4 G5
Huish Devon 25 B7
Devon 25 E8
Wilts 62 G6
Huish Champflower Som 27 B9
Huish Episcopi Som 28 B6
Huisinis W Isles 305 G1
Hulcote C Beds 103 D8
W Nhants 102 B4
Hulcott Bucks 84 B5
Hulland Derbys 170 F2
Hulland Moss Derbys 170 F3
Hulland Ward Derbys 170 F3
Hullavington Wilts 61 C11
Hullbridge Essex 88 G4
Hull End Derbys 185 E9
Hulme Gtr Man 184 B4
Staffs 168 F6
Warr 183 C10
Hulme End Staffs 169 D10
Hulme Walfield Ches E 168 B4
Hulseheath Ches E 184 E2
Hulverstone IoW 20 E3
Hulver Street Suff 143 F9
Humber Devon 14 G3
Hereford 115 F10
Humber Bridge N Lincs 200 C4
Humberston NE Lincs 201 F10
Humberstone Leicester 136 B2
Humberston Fitties
NE Lincs 201 F10
Humbie E Loth 271 C9
Humbledon T&W 243 F9
Humble Green Suff 107 B8
Humbleton E Yorks 209 G10
Northumb 263 D11
Humby Lincs 155 C10
Hume Borders 272 G4
Hummersknott Darl 224 C5
Humshaugh Northumb 241 C10
Huna Highld 310 B7
Huncoat Lancs 203 G11
Huncote Leics 135 D10
Hundalee Borders 262 F4
Hundall Derbys 186 F5
Hunderthwaite Durham 232 G5
Hunderton Hereford 97 D9
Hundleby Lincs 174 B5
Hundle Houses Lincs 174 E3
Hundleshope Borders 260 B6
Hundleton Pembs 73 E7
Hundon Suff 106 B4
Hundred Acres Hants 33 E9
Hundred End Lancs 194 C2
Hundred House Powys 114 G2
Hungarton Leics 136 B3
Hungate W Yorks 197 B11
Hungerford Hants 31 E11
Shrops 131 F10
Som 42 E4
W Berks 63 F10
Windsor 65 E10
Hungerford Green
W Berks 64 D5
Hungerford Newtown
W Berks 63 E11
Hunger Hill Gtr Man 195 F7
Lancs 194 E4
Hungershall Park Kent 52 F5
Hungerstone Hereford 97 D8
Hungerton Lincs 155 D7
Hungladder Highld 298 B3
Hungreyhatton Shrops 150 D3
Hunmanby N Yorks 217 D11
Hunmanby Moor
N Yorks 218 D2
Hunningham Warks 119 D7
Hunningham Hill Warks 119 D7
Hunnington Worcs 133 G9
Hunny Hill IoW 20 D5
Hunsdon Herts 86 C6
Hunsdonbury Herts 86 C6
Hunsingore N Yorks 206 C4
Hunslet W Yorks 206 G2
Hunslet Carr W Yorks 206 G2
Hunsonby Cumb 231 D7
Hunspow Highld 310 B6
Hunstanton Norf 175 G11
Hunstanworth Durham 232 B5
Hunsterson Ches E 167 F11
Hunston Suff 125 D9
W Sus 22 C5
Hunston Green Suff 125 D9
Hunstrete Bath 60 G6
Hunsworth W Yorks 197 B7
Hunt End Worcs 117 E10
Huntenhull Green Wilts 45 D10
Huntercombe End Oxon 65 B7
Hunters Forstal Kent 71 F7
Hunter's Quay Argyll 276 F3
Huntham Som 28 B4
Hunthill Lodge Angus 292 F6
Huntingdon Cambs 122 C4
Huntingfield Suff 126 C6
Huntingford Dorset 45 G10
S Glos 80 G2
Huntington Ches W 166 C6
E Loth 281 F9
Hereford 97 C9
Hereford 114 G5
Staffs 151 G9
Telford 132 B3
York 207 B8
Hunting-tower Perth 286 E4
Huntley Glos 80 B2
Staffs 169 G8
Huntly Aberds 302 F5
Huntlywood Borders 272 G2
Hunton Hants 48 F3
Kent 53 D8
N Yorks 224 G3
Hunton Bridge Herts 85 E9
Hunt's Corner Norf 141 F11
Huntscott Som 42 E2
Hunt's Cross Mers 182 D6
Hunts Green Warks 134 D3
Hunt's Green Bucks 84 E5
W Berks 64 E2
Huntsham Devon 27 C8
Huntshaw Devon 25 C8
Huntshaw Water Devon 25 C8
Hunt's Hill Bucks 84 F4
Hunt's Lane Leics 135 C9
Huntspill Som 43 D10
Huntstile Som 43 G9
Huntworth Som 43 G10
Hunwick Durham 233 E9
Hunworth Norf 159 B11
Hurcott Som 28 D5
Som 29 B8
Worcs 117 B7
Hurdcott Wilts 47 G7
Hurdley Powys 130 E5
Hurdsfield Ches E 184 G6
Hurgill N Yorks 224 E3
Hurlet Glasgow 267 C10
Hurley Warks 134 D4
Windsor 65 C10
Hurley Bottom Windsor 65 C10
Hurley Common Warks 134 D4
Hurlford E Ayrs 257 B11
Hurliness Orkney 314 H2
Hurlston Lancs 194 E2
Hurlston Green Lancs 193 E11
Hurn BCP 19 B8
E Yorks 208 E6
Hurn's End Lincs 174 F6
Hursey Dorset 28 G6
Hursley Hants 32 B6
Hurst Cumb 230 C4
Dorset 17 C11
Gtr Man 196 G2
N Yorks 223 E10
Som 29 D7
Hurst *continued*
Wokingham 65 E9
Hurstbourne Priors
Hants 48 D2
Hurstbourne Tarrant
Hants 47 C11
Hurstead Gtr Man 196 D2
Hurst Green Essex 89 B9
E Sus 38 B2
Lancs 203 F9
Sur 51 C11
W Mid 133 F9
Hurst Hill W Mid 133 E8
Hurstley Hereford 97 B7
Hurst Park Sur 66 F6
Hurstpierpoint W Sus 36 D3
Hurst Wickham W Sus 36 D3
Hurstwood Lancs 204 G3
Hurtmore Sur 50 D3
Hurworth-on-Tees Darl 224 C6
Hurworth Place Darl 224 D5
Hury Durham 223 B9
Husabost Highld 298 D2
Husbands Bosworth
Leics 136 G2
Husbandtown Angus 287 D8
Husborne Crawley
C Beds 103 D9
Husthwaite N Yorks 215 D10
Hutcherleigh Devon 8 E5
Hutchesontown
Glasgow 267 C11
Hutchwns Bridgend 57 F10
Hut Green N Yorks 198 C5
Huthwaite Notts 171 D7
Hutlerburn Borders 261 E10
Huttock Top Lancs 195 C11
Huttoft Lincs 191 F8
Hutton Borders 273 E9
Cumb 230 F4
Essex 87 F10
E Yorks 208 C6
Lancs 194 B3
N Som 43 B11
Hutton Bonville N Yorks 224 E6
Hutton Buscel N Yorks 217 C9
Hutton Conyers N Yorks 214 E6
Hutton Cranswick
E Yorks 208 C6
Hutton End Cumb 230 D4
Hutton Gate Redcar 225 B11
Hutton Hang N Yorks 214 B3
Hutton Henry Durham 234 D4
Hutton-le-Hole
N Yorks 226 G4
Hutton Magna Durham 224 C2
Hutton Mount Essex 87 G10
Hutton Roof Cumb 211 D11
Cumb 230 E3
Hutton Rudby N Yorks 225 D9
Huttons Ambo N Yorks 216 F5
Hutton Sessay N Yorks 215 D9
Hutton Village Redcar 225 C11
Hutton Wandesley
N Yorks 206 C6
Huxham Devon 14 B4
Huxham Green Som 44 F5
Huxley Ches W 167 C8
Huxter Shetland 313 G7
Shetland 313 H3
Shetland 313 H5
Huxton Borders 273 B7
Huyton Mers 182 C6
Huyton Park Mers 182 C6
Huyton Quarry Mers 183 C7
Hwlffordd = Haverfordwest
Pembs 73 B7
Hycemoor Cumb 210 B1
Hyde Glos 80 E5
Glos 99 F11
Gtr Man 184 B6
Hants 31 E11
Hants 48 G3
Hereford 115 F9
Hyde Chase Essex 88 E4
Hyde End W Berks 64 G5
Hyde Heath Bucks 84 E6
Hyde Lea Staffs 151 E8
Hyde Park S Yorks 198 G5
Hydestile Sur 50 E3
Hylton Castle T&W 243 F9
Hylton Red House T&W 243 F9
Hyltons Crossways Norf 160 D4
Hyndburn Bridge
Lancs 203 G10
Hyndford Bridge
S Lanark 269 G8
Hyndhope Borders 261 E9
Hynish Argyll 288 F1
Hyssington Powys 130 E6
Hystfield Glos 79 F11
Hythe Hants 32 F6
Kent 55 G7
Som 44 C2
Sur 66 E4
Hythe End Windsor 66 E4
Hythie Aberds 303 D10
Hyton Cumb 210 B1

I

Iarsiadar W Isles 304 E3
Ibberton Dorset 30 F3
Ible Derbys 170 D2
Ibsley Hants 31 F11
Ibstock Leics 153 G8
Ibstone Bucks 84 G3
Ibthorpe Hants 47 C11
Iburndale N Yorks 227 D7
Ibworth Hants 48 C5
Icelton N Som 59 F11
Ichrachan Argyll 284 D4
Ickburgh Norf 140 E6
Ickenham London 66 B5
Ickenthwaite Cumb 210 B6
Ickford Bucks 83 D11
Ickham Kent 55 B8
Ickleford Herts 104 E3
Icklesham E Sus 38 D5
Ickleton Cambs 105 C9
Icklingham Suff 124 C5
Ickornshaw N Yorks 204 E5
Ickwell C Beds 104 B3
Ickwell Green C Beds 104 B3
Icomb Glos 100 G4
Icy Park Devon 8 F3
Idbury Oxon 82 B2
Iddesleigh Devon 25 F9
Ide Devon 14 C3
Ideford Devon 14 F3
Ide Hill Kent 52 C3
Iden E Sus 38 C6
Iden Green Kent 53 F8
Kent 53 G10
Idle W Yorks 205 F9
Idle Moor W Yorks 205 F9
Idless Corn 4 F6
Idlicote Warks 100 C5
Idmiston Wilts 47 F7
Idole Carms 74 B6
Idridgehay Derbys 170 F3
Idridgehay Green
Derbys 170 F3
Idrigill Highld 298 C3
Idstone Oxon 63 C9
Idvies Angus 287 C9
Iet-y-bwlch Carms 92 F3
Iffley Oxon 83 E8
Ifield W Sus 51 F8
Ifield Green W Sus 51 F9
Ifieldwood W Sus 51 F8
Ifold W Sus 50 G4
Iford BCP 19 C8
E Sus 36 F6
Ifton Heath Shrops 148 B6
Ightfield Shrops 149 B11
Ightfield Heath Shrops 149 B11
Ightham Kent 52 B5
Igtham Common Kent 52 B5
Iken Suff 127 F8
Ilam Staffs 169 E10
Ilchester Som 29 C8
Ilchester Mead Som 29 C8
Ilderton Northumb 264 E2
Ileden Kent 55 C8
Ilford London 68 B2
Som 28 D5
Ilfracombe Devon 40 D4
Ilkeston Derbys 171 G7
Ilketshall St Andrew
Suff 143 F7
Ilketshall St Lawrence
Suff 143 G7
Ilketshall St Margaret
Suff 142 F6
Ilkley W Yorks 205 D8
Illand Corn 11 F11
Illey W Mid 133 G9
Illidge Green Ches E 168 C3
Illington Norf 141 F8
Illingworth W Yorks 196 B5
Illogan Corn 4 G3
Illogan Highway Corn 4 G3
Illshaw Heath W Mid 118 C2
Illston on the Hill Leics 136 D4
Ilmer Bucks 84 D3
Ilmington Warks 100 C4
Ilminster Som 28 E5
Ilsington Devon 13 F11
Ilston Swansea 56 C5
Ilton N Yorks 214 D3
Som 28 D5
Imachar N Ayrs 255 C9
Imber Wilts 46 D3
Imeraval Argyll 254 C4
Immervoulin Stirling 285 F9
Immingham NE Lincs 201 E7
Impington Cambs 123 E8
Ince Ches W 183 F7
Ince Blundell Mers 193 G10
Ince in Makerfield
Gtr Man 194 G5
Inchbae Lodge Highld 300 C4
Inchbare Angus 293 G8
Inchberry Moray 302 D3
Inchbraoch Angus 287 B11
Inchbrook Glos 80 E4
Inchcape Highld 309 J6
Incheril Highld 299 C10
Inchgrundle Angus 292 F6
Inchina Highld 307 K4
Inchinnan Renfs 267 B9
Inchkinloch Highld 308 E5
Inchlaggan Highld 290 C3
Inchlumpie Highld 300 B5
Inchmore Highld 300 E3
Highld 300 E5
Inchnacardoch Hotel
Highld 290 B5
Inchnadamph Highld 307 G7
Inchock Angus 287 C10
Inch of Arnhall Aberds 293 F8
Inchree Highld 290 G2
Inchrory Moray 292 C3
Inchs Corn 5 C9
Inchture Perth 286 E6
Inchyra Perth 286 E5
Indian Queens Corn 5 D8
Inerval Argyll 254 C4
Ingatestone Essex 87 F11
Ingbirchworth S Yorks 197 F8
Ingerthorpe N Yorks 214 F5
Ingestre Staffs 151 E9
Ingham Lincs 188 E6
Norf 161 D7
Suff 125 C7
Ingham Corner Norf 161 D7
Ingleborough Norf 157 F9
Ingleby Derbys 152 D6
Lincs 188 F5
Ingleby Arncliffe
N Yorks 225 E8
Ingleby Barwick
Stockton 225 C9
Ingleby Cross N Yorks 225 E9
Ingleby Greenhow
N Yorks 225 D11
Ingleigh Green Devon 25 F10
Inglemire Hull 209 G7
Inglesbatch Bath 61 G8
Inglesham Swindon 82 F2
Ingleton Durham 233 G9
N Yorks 212 E3
Inglewhite Lancs 202 E6
Ingmanthorpe N Yorks 206 C4
Ingoe Northumb 242 C2
Ingol Lancs 202 G6
Ingoldisthorpe Norf 158 C3
Ingoldmells Lincs 175 B9
Ingoldsby Lincs 155 C10
Ingon Warks 118 F4
Ingram Northumb 264 F2
Ingrams Green W Sus 34 C4
Ingrave Essex 87 G10
Ingrow W Yorks 205 F7
Ings Cumb 221 F8
Ingst S Glos 60 B5
Ingthorpe Rutland 137 B9
Ingworth Norf 160 D3
Inham's End Cambs 138 D5
Inhurst Hants 64 G5
Inkberrow Worcs 117 F10
Inkerman Durham 233 D8
Inkersall Derbys 186 G6
Inkersall Green Derbys 186 G6
Inkford Worcs 117 C11
Inkpen W Berks 63 G11
Inkpen Common
W Berks 63 G11
Inkstack Highld 310 B6
Inlands W Sus 22 B3
Inmarsh Wilts 62 G2
Inn Cumb 221 D8
Innellan Argyll 276 G3
Inner Hope Devon 9 G8
Innerleithen Borders 261 B8
Innerleven Fife 287 G7
Innermessan Dumfries 236 C2
Innerwick E Loth 282 G4
Perth 285 C9

Innie Argyll 275 B9
Inninbeg Highld 289 E8
Innis Chonain Argyll 284 E5
Innistrynich Argyll 284 E5
Innox Hill Som 45 D9
Innsworth Glos 99 G7
Insch Aberds 302 G6
Insh Highld 291 C10
Inshegra Highld 306 D7
Inshore Highld 308 C3
Inskip Lancs 202 F5
Inskip Moss Side Lancs 202 F5
Instoneville S Yorks 198 E5
Instow Devon 40 G3
Insworke Corn 7 E8
Intack Blackburn 195 B8
Intake S Yorks 186 E5
S Yorks 198 G5
W Yorks 205 F10
Interfield Worcs 98 B5
Intwood Norf 142 C3
Inver Aberds 292 D4
Highld 311 L2
Perth 286 C4
Inverailort Highld 295 G9
Inveraldie Angus 287 D8
Inveralivaig Highld 298 E4
Inveralligin Highld 299 D8
Inverallochy Aberds 303 C10
Inveran Highld 299 B8
Highld 309 K5
Inveraray Argyll 284 G4
Inverarish Highld 295 B7
Inverarity Angus 287 C8
Inverarnan Stirling 285 F7
Inverasdale Highld 307 L3
Inverawe Ho Argyll 284 D4
Inverbeg Argyll 276 B6
Inverbervie Aberds 293 F10
Inverboyndie Aberds 302 C6
Inverbroom Highld 307 L6
Invercarron Mains
Highld 309 K5
Invercassley Highld 309 J4
Invercauld House
Aberds 292 D3
Inverchaolain Argyll 275 F11
Invercharnan Highld 284 C5
Inverchoran Highld 300 D2
Invercreran Argyll 284 C4
Inverdruie Highld 291 B11
Inverebrie Aberds 303 F9
Invereck Argyll 276 E2
Inverernan Ho Aberds 292 B5
Invereshie House
Highld 291 C10
Inveresk E Loth 280 G6
Inverey Aberds 292 E2
Inverfarigaig Highld 300 G5
Invergarry Highld 290 C5
Invergelder Aberds 292 D4
Invergeldie Perth 285 E11
Invergordon Highld 301 C7
Invergowrie Perth 287 D7
Inverguseran Highld 295 E9
Inverhadden Perth 285 B10
Inverhaggernie Stirling 285 E7
Inverharroch Moray 302 F3
Inverherive Stirling 285 E7
Inverie Highld 295 F9
Inverinan Argyll 275 B10
Inverinate Highld 295 C11
Inverkeilor Angus 287 C10
Inverkeithing Fife 280 E2
Inverkeithny Aberds 302 E6
Inverkip Invclyd 276 G4
Inverkirkaig Highld 307 H5
Inverlael Highld 307 L6
Inverleith Edin 280 F4
Inverliever Lodge Argyll 275 C9
Inverliver Argyll 284 D4
Inverlochlarig Stirling 285 F8
Inverlochy Argyll 284 E5
Highld 290 F3
Moray 301 G11
Inverlounin Argyll 276 B4
Inverlussa Argyll 275 E7
Inver Mallie Highld 290 E3
Invermark Lodge Angus 292 E6
Invermoidart Highld 289 B8
Invermoriston Highld 290 B6
Invernaver Highld 308 C7
Inverneill Argyll 275 E9
Inverness Highld 300 E6
Invernettie Aberds 303 E11
Invernoaden Argyll 276 B2
Inveronich Argyll 284 G6
Inveroran Hotel Argyll 284 C6
Inverpolly Lodge Highld 307 H5
Inverquharity Angus 287 B8
Inverquhomery Aberds 303 E10
Inverroy Highld 290 E4
Inversanda Highld 289 D11
Invershiel Highld 290 B2
Invershin Highld 309 K5
Invershore Highld 310 F6
Inversnaid Hotel Stirling 285 G7
Invertrossachs Stirling 285 G9
Inverugie Aberds 303 E11
Inveruglas Argyll 285 G7
Inveruglass Highld 291 C10
Inverurie Aberds 303 G7
Invervar Perth 285 C10
Inverythan Aberds 303 E7
Inwardleigh Devon 13 B7
Inwood Shrops 131 D9
Inworth Essex 88 B5
Iochdar W Isles 297 G3
Iping W Sus 34 C5
Ipplepen Devon 8 B6
Ipsden Oxon 64 B6
Ipsley Worcs 117 D11
Ipstones Staffs 169 F8
Ipswich Suff 108 C3
Irby Mers 182 E3
Irby in the Marsh Lincs 175 C7
Irby upon Humber
NE Lincs 201 G7
Irchester N Nhants 121 D8
Ireby Cumb 229 D10
Lancs 212 D3
Ireland C Beds 104 C2
Orkney 314 F3
Shetland 313 L5
Wilts 45 C10
Ireland's Cross Shrops 168 G2
Ireland Wood W Yorks 205 F11
Ireleth Cumb 210 D4
Ireshopeburn Durham 232 D3
Ireton Wood Derbys 170 F3
Irlam Gtr Man 184 C2
Irlams o' th' Height
Gtr Man 195 G9
Irnham Lincs 155 D10
Iron Acton S Glos 61 C7
Ironbridge Telford 132 C3
Iron Bridge Cambs 139 D9
Iron Cross Warks 117 G11
Irongray Dumfries 237 B11
Iron Lo Highld 299 G10
Ironmacannie Dumfries 237 B8
Irons Bottom Sur 51 D9
Ironside Aberds 303 D8
Ironville Derbys 170 E6
Irstead Norf 161 E7
Irstead Street Norf 161 F7
Irthington Cumb 239 E11
Irthlingborough
N Nhants 121 C8
Irton N Yorks 217 C10
Irvine N Ayrs 257 B8
Irwell Vale Lancs 195 C9
Isabella Pit Northumb 253 G8
Isallt Bach Anglesey 178 F3
Isauld Highld 310 C3
Isbister Orkney 314 D2
Orkney 314 E3
Shetland 312 D5
Shetland 313 G7
Isel Cumb 229 E9
Isfield E Sus 36 D6
Isham N Nhants 121 C7
Ishriff Argyll 289 F8
Isington Hants 49 E9
Island Carr N Lincs 200 F3
Islands Common Cambs 122 E3
Islay Ho Argyll 274 G4
Isle Abbotts Som 28 C5
Isle Brewers Som 28 C5
Isleham Cambs 124 C2
Isle of Axholme N Lincs 199 F9
Isle of Dogs London 67 D11
Isle of Man Dumfries 238 B2
Isle of Whithorn
Dumfries 236 F6
Isleornsay Highld 295 D9
Islesburgh Shetland 312 G5
Islesteps Dumfries 237 B11
Isleworth London 67 D7
Isley Walton Leics 153 D8
Islibhig W Isles 304 F1
Islington London 67 C10
Telford 150 E4
Islip N Nhants 121 B9
Oxon 83 C8
Isombridge Telford 150 G2
Istead Rise Kent 68 F6
Isycoed Wrex 166 E6
Itchen Soton 32 E6
Itchen Abbas Hants 48 G4
Itchen Stoke Hants 48 G5
Itchingfield W Sus 35 B10
Itchington S Glos 61 B7
Itteringham Norf 160 C2
Itteringham Common
Norf 160 D3
Itton Devon 13 B9
Mon 79 F7
Itton Common Mon 79 F7
Ivegill Cumb 230 C4
Ivelet N Yorks 223 F8
Iver Bucks 66 C4
Iver Heath Bucks 66 C4
Iverley Staffs 133 G7
Iveston Durham 242 G4
Ivinghoe Bucks 84 B6
Ivinghoe Aston Bucks 85 B7
Ivington Hereford 115 F9
Ivington Green Hereford 115 F9
Ivybridge Devon 8 D2
Ivy Chimneys Essex 86 E6
Ivychurch Kent 39 B8
Ivy Cross Dorset 30 C5
Ivy Hatch Kent 52 C5
Ivy Todd Norf 141 B7
Iwade Kent 69 F11
Iwerne Courtney or Shroton
Dorset 30 E5
Iwerne Minster Dorset 30 E5
Iwood N Som 60 G3
Ixworth Suff 125 C8
Ixworth Thorpe Suff 125 C8

J

Jackfield Telford 132 C3
Jack Green Lancs 194 B5
Jack Hayes Staffs 168 F6
Jack Hill N Yorks 205 C10
Jack-in-the-Green Devon 14 B6
Jacksdale Notts 170 E6
Jack's Green Essex 105 G11
Glos 80 D5
Jack's Hatch Essex 86 D6
Jackson Bridge
W Yorks 197 F7
Jackstown Aberds 303 F7
Jacobstow Corn 11 B9
Jacobstowe Devon 25 G9
Jacobs Well Sur 50 C3
Jagger Green W Yorks 196 D5
Jameston Pembs 73 F9
Jamestown Dumfries 249 D8
Highld 300 D4
W Dunb 277 E7
Jamphlars Fife 280 B4
Janetstown Highld 310 C4
Janke's Green Essex 107 F8
Jarrow T&W 243 D8
Jarvis Brook E Sus 37 B8
Jasper's Green Essex 106 F4
Java Argyll 289 F9
Jawcraig Falk 278 F6
Jaw Hill W Yorks 197 C9
Jaywick Essex 89 C11
Jealott's Hill Brack 65 E11
Jeaniefield Borders 271 G10
Jedburgh Borders 262 E5
Jedurgh Borders 262 F5
Jeffreyston Pembs 73 D9
Jellyhill E Dunb 278 G2
Jemimaville Highld 301 C7
Jennetts Hill W Berks 64 E5
Jennyfield N Yorks 205 B11
Jericho Gtr Man 195 E10
Jersey Farm Herts 85 D11
Jersey Marine Neath 57 C8
Jerviswood S Lanark 269 F7
Jesmond T&W 243 D7
Jevington E Sus 23 E9
Jewell's Cross Corn 24 G3
Jingle Street Mon 79 C7
Jockey End Herts 85 C8
Jodrell Bank Ches E 184 G3
Johnby Cumb 230 E4
John O'Gaunt Leics 136 B4
John O'Gaunts
W Yorks 197 B11
John o'Groats Highld 310 B7
John's Cross E Sus 38 C2
Johnshaven Aberds 293 G9
Johnson Fold Gtr Man 195 E7
Johnson's Hillock
Lancs 194 C5
Johnson Street Norf 161 F7
Johnston Pembs 72 C6
Johnstone Renfs 267 C8
Johnstonebridge
Dumfries 248 E3
Johnstone Mains
Aberds 293 F9
Johnstown Carms 74 B6
Wrex 166 F4
Jolly's Bottom Corn 4 F5
Joppa Corn 2 B3
Edin 280 G6
S Ayrs 257 F10
Jordan Green Norf 159 E11
Jordanhill Glasgow 267 B10
Jordans Bucks 85 G7
Jordanston Pembs 91 E8
Jordanthorpe S Yorks 186 E5
Jordon S Yorks 186 C6
Joyford Glos 79 C9
Joy's Green Glos 79 B10
Jubilee Gtr Man 196 E2
Notts 170 E6
Jugbank Staffs 150 B5
Jump S Yorks 197 G11
Jumpers Common BCP 19 C8
Jumpers Green BCP 19 C8
Jumper's Town E Sus 52 G3
Junction N Yorks 204 D6
Juniper Northumb 241 F10
Juniper Green Edin 270 B3
Jurby East IoM 192 C4
Jurby West IoM 192 C4
Jurston Devon 13 E9
Jury's Gap E Sus 39 D7

K

Kaber Cumb 222 C5
Kaimend S Lanark 269 F9
Kaimes Edin 270 B5
Kaimrig End Borders 269 G11
Kalemouth Borders 262 D6
Kame Fife 287 G7
Kames Argyll 275 B9
Argyll 275 F10
E Ayrs 258 D5
Kates Hill W Mid 133 E9
Kea Corn 4 G6
Keadby N Lincs 199 E10
Keal Cotes Lincs 174 C5
Kearby Town End
N Yorks 206 D2
Kearnsey Kent 55 E9
Kearsley Gtr Man 195 F9
Kearstwick Cumb 212 C2
Kearton N Yorks 223 F9
Kearvaig Highld 306 B7
Keasden N Yorks 212 F4
Kebroyd W Yorks 196 C4
Keckwick Halton 183 E9
Keddington Lincs 190 D4
Keddington Corner
Lincs 190 D5
Kedington Suff 106 B4
Kedleston Derbys 170 G4
Kedslie Borders 271 G11
Keekle Cumb 219 B10
Keelars Tye Essex 107 G11
Keelby Lincs 201 E7
Keele Staffs 168 F4
Keeley Green Bedford 103 B10
Keelham W Yorks 205 G7
Keenley Northumb 241 F7
Keenthorne Som 43 F8
Keeres Green Essex 87 C9
Keeston Pembs 72 B6
Keevil Wilts 46 B2
Kegworth Leics 153 D9
Kehelland Corn 4 G2
Keig Aberds 293 B8
Keighley W Yorks 205 E7
Keil Highld 289 D11
Keilarsbrae Clack 279 C7
Keilhill Aberds 303 D7
Keillmore Argyll 275 E7
Keillor Perth 286 C6
Keillour Perth 286 E3
Keills Argyll 274 G5
Keils Argyll 274 G6
Keinton Mandeville Som 44 G4
Keir Mill Dumfries 247 E9
Keisby Lincs 155 D10
Keiss Highld 310 C7
Keistle Highld 298 D4
Keith Moray 302 D4
Keith Hall Aberds 303 G7
Keith Inch Aberds 303 E11
Keithock Angus 293 G8
Kelbrook Lancs 204 E4
Kelby Lincs 173 G8
Kelcliffe W Yorks 205 E9
Keld Cumb 221 C11
N Yorks 223 E7
Keldholme N Yorks 216 B4
Keld Houses N Yorks 214 G2
Kelfield N Lincs 199 G10
N Yorks 207 F7
Kelham Notts 172 D3
Kelhurn Argyll 276 F6
Kellacott Devon 12 D4
Kellamergh Lancs 194 B2
Kellan Argyll 289 E7
Kellas Angus 287 D8
Moray 301 D11
Kellaton Devon 9 G11
Kellaways Wilts 62 D3
Kelleth Cumb 222 D3
Kelleythorpe E Yorks 208 B5
E Yorks 208 B6
Kelling Norf 177 E9
Kellingley N Yorks 198 C4
Kellington N Yorks 198 C5
Kelloe Durham 234 D2
Kelloholm Dumfries 258 G6
Kells Cumb 219 B9
Kelly Corn 10 G6
Devon 12 E3
Kelly Bray Corn 12 G3
Kelmarsh W Nhants 120 B4
Kelmscott Oxon 82 F3
Kelsale Suff 127 D7
Kelsall Ches W 167 B8
Kelsall Hill Ches W 167 B8
Kelsay Argyll 254 B2
Kelshall Herts 104 D6
Kelsick Cumb 238 G5
Kelso Borders 262 C6
Kelstedge Derbys 170 C4
Kelstern Lincs 190 C3
Kelsterton Flint 182 G3
Kelston Bath 61 F8
Keltneyburn Perth 285 C11
Kelton Dumfries 237 B11
Durham 232 G4
Kelty Fife 280 C2
Keltybridge Fife 280 B2
Kelvedon Essex 88 B5
Kelvedon Hatch Essex 87 F9
Kelvin S Lanark 268 E2
Kelvindale Glasgow 267 B11
Kelvinside Glasgow 267 B11
Kelynack Corn 1 D3
Kemacott Devon 41 D7
Kemback Fife 287 F8
Kemberton Shrops 132 C4
Kemble Glos 81 F7
Kemble Wick Glos 81 F7
Kemerton Worcs 99 D8
Kemeys Commander
Mon 78 E4
Kemincham Ches E 168 B4
Kemnay Aberds 293 B9
Kempe's Corner Kent 54 D4
Kempie Highld 308 D4
Kempley Glos 98 F3
Kempley Green Glos 98 F3
Kempsey Worcs 99 B7
Kempsford Glos 81 F11
Kemps Green Warks 118 C2
Kempshott Hants 48 C6
Kempston Bedford 103 B10
Kempston Church End
Bedford 103 B10
Kempston Hardwick
Bedford 103 B10
Kempston West End
Bedford 103 B9
Kempton Shrops 131 G7
Kemp Town Brighton 36 G4
Kemsing Kent 52 B4
Kemsley Kent 70 F2
Kemsley Street Kent 69 G10
Kenardington Kent 54 G3
Kenchester Hereford 97 C8
Kencot Oxon 82 E3
Kendal Cumb 221 G10
Kendal End Worcs 117 C10
Kendleshire S Glos 61 D7
Kendon Caerph 77 F11
Kendoon Dumfries 246 F4
Kendray S Yorks 197 F11
Kenfig Bridgend 57 E10
Kenfig Hill Bridgend 57 E10
Kengharair Argyll 288 E6
Kenilworth Warks 118 C5
Kenknock Stirling 285 D8
Kenley London 51 B10
Shrops 131 C11
Kenmore Argyll 284 G4
Highld 299 D7
Perth 285 C11
Kenmure Dumfries 237 B8
Kenn Devon 14 D4
N Som 60 F2
Kennacley W Isles 305 J3
Kennacraig Argyll 275 G9
Kennards House Corn 11 E11
Kenneggy Corn 2 D3
Kenneggy Downs Corn 2 D3
Kennerleigh Devon 26 F4
Kennet Clack 279 C8
Kennet End Suff 124 D4
Kennethmont Aberds 302 G5
Kennett Cambs 124 D3
Kennford Devon 14 D4
Kenninghall Norf 141 F10
Kenninghall Heath
Norf 141 G10
Kennington Kent 54 E4
London 67 D10
Oxon 83 E8
Kenn Moor Gate N Som 60 F2
Kennoway Fife 287 G7
Kenny Som 28 D4
Kenny Hill Suff 124 B3
Kennythorpe N Yorks 216 F5
Kenovay Argyll 288 E1
Kensaleyre Highld 298 D4
Kensal Green London 67 C8
Kensal Rise London 67 C8
Kensal Town London 67 C8
Kensary Highld 310 E6
Kensington London 67 D9
Mers 182 C5
Kensworth C Beds 85 B8
Kentallen Highld 284 B4
Kentchurch Hereford 97 F8
Kentford Suff 124 D4
Kentisbeare Devon 27 F9
Kentisbury Devon 40 E6
Kentisbury Ford Devon 40 E6
Kentish Town London 67 C9
Kentmere Cumb 221 E9
Kenton Devon 14 E5
London 67 B7
Suff 126 D3
T&W 242 D6
Kenton Bankfoot T&W 242 D6
Kenton Bar T&W 242 D6
Kenton Corner Suff 126 D4
Kenton Green Glos 80 C3
Kentra Highld 289 C8
Kentrigg Cumb 221 G10
Kents Corn 11 B9
Kents Bank Cumb 211 D7
Kent's Green Glos 98 G4
Kents Hill M Keynes 103 D7
Kent's Oak Hants 32 C4
Kent Street E Sus 38 D3
Kent 53 C7
W Sus 36 C2
Kenwick Shrops 149 C8
Kenwick Park Shrops 149 D8
Kenwyn Corn 4 F6
Kenyon Warr 183 B10
Keoldale Highld 308 C3
Keonchulish Ho Highld 307 K6
Kepdowrie Stirling 277 C11
Kepnal Wilts 63 G7
Keppanach Highld 290 G2
Keppoch Highld 295 C11
Keprigan Argyll 255 F7
Kepwick N Yorks 225 G9
Kerchesters Borders 263 B7
Kerdiston Norf 159 E11
Keresforth Hill S Yorks 197 F10
Keresley W Mid 134 G6
Keresley Newlands
Warks 134 G6
Kerfield Borders 270 G5
Kerley Downs Corn 4 G5
Kernborough Devon 8 G5
Kerne Bridge Hereford 79 B9
Kernsary Highld 299 B8
Kerridge Ches E 184 F6
Kerridge-end Ches E 184 F6
Kerris Corn 1 D4
Kerry = Ceri Powys 130 F2
Kerrycroy Argyll 266 C2
Kerry Hill Staffs 168 F6
Kerrysdale Highld 299 B8
Kerry's Gate Hereford 97 E7
Kersal Gtr Man 195 G10
Kersall Notts 172 C2
Kersbrook Cross Corn 12 F2
Kerscott Devon 25 B10
Kersey Suff 107 C10
Kersey Tye Suff 107 C9
Kersey Upland Suff 107 C9
Kershopefoot Cumb 249 G11
Kersoe Worcs 99 D9
Kerswell Devon 27 F9
Kerswell Green Worcs 99 B7
Kerthen Wood Corn 2 C3
Kesgrave Suff 108 B4
Kessingland Suff 143 F10
Kessingland Beach
Suff 143 F10
Kessington E Dunb 277 G11
Kestle Corn 5 F9
Kestle Mill Corn 5 D7
Keston London 68 G2
Keston Mark London 68 F2
Keswick Cumb 229 G11
Norf 142 C4
Norf 161 C7
Kete Pembs 72 E4
Ketford Glos 98 E4
Ketley Telford 150 G3
Ketley Bank Telford 150 G3
Ketsby Lincs 190 F5
Kettering N Nhants 121 B7
Ketteringham Norf 142 C3
Kettins Perth 286 D6
Kettlebaston Suff 125 G9
Kettlebridge Fife 287 G7
Kettlebrook Staffs 134 C4
Kettleburgh Suff 126 E5
Kettle Corner Kent 53 C8
Kettle Green Herts 86 B6
Kettlehill Fife 287 G7
Kettleholm Dumfries 238 B4
Kettleness N Yorks 226 B6
Kettleshume Ches E 185 F7
Kettleshulme Ches E 185 F7
Kettlesing N Yorks 205 B10
Kettlesing Bottom
N Yorks 205 B10
Kettlesing Head
N Yorks 205 B10
Kettlestone Norf 159 C9
Kettlethorpe Lincs 188 F4
W Yorks 197 D10
Kettletoft Orkney 314 C6
Kettlewell N Yorks 213 E9
Ketton Rutland 137 C9
Kevingtown London 68 F3
Kew London 67 D7
Keward Som 44 E4
Kew Bridge London 67 D7
Kewstoke N Som 59 G10
Kexbrough S Yorks 197 F9
Kexby Lincs 188 D5
York 207 C10
Keybridge Corn 11 G7
Keycol Kent 69 G11
Keyford Som 45 D9
Key Green Ches E 168 C5
N Yorks 226 E6
Keyham Leics 136 B3
Keyhaven Hants 20 C2
Keyingham E Yorks 201 B8
Keymer W Sus 36 D4
Keynsham Bath 61 F7
Keysers Estate Essex 86 D5
Key's Green Kent 53 F7
Keysoe Bedford 121 E11
Keysoe Row Bedford 121 E11
Keyston Cambs 121 B10
Key Street Kent 69 G11
Keyworth Notts 154 C2
Khantore Aberds 292 D4
Kibbear Som 28 C2
Kibblesworth T&W 242 F6
Kibworth Beauchamp
Leics 136 E3
Kibworth Harcourt
Leics 136 E3
Kidbrooke London 68 D2
Kidburngill Cumb 229 G7
Kiddal Lane End
W Yorks 206 F4
Kiddemore Green Staffs 133 B7
Kidderminster Worcs 116 B6
Kiddington Oxon 101 G8
Kidd's Moor Norf 142 C2
Kidlington Oxon 83 C7
Kidmore End Oxon 65 D7
Kidnal Ches W 167 F7
Kidsdale Dumfries 236 F6
Kidsgrove Staffs 168 E4
Kidstones N Yorks 213 C9
Kidwelly = Cydweli
Carms 74 D6
Kiel Crofts Argyll 289 F11
Kielder Northumb 250 E4
Kierfiold Ho Orkney 314 E2
Kiff Green W Berks 64 F5
Kilbagie Fife 279 D8
Kilbarchan Renfs 267 C8
Kilbeg Highld 295 E8
Kilberry Argyll 275 G8
Kilbirnie N Ayrs 266 E6
Kilbowie W Dunb 277 G10
Kilbraur Highld 311 H2
Kilbride Argyll 254 C4
Argyll 275 D9
Argyll 289 G10
Argyll 289 G11
Highld 295 C7
Kilbridemore Argyll 275 D11
Kilbryde Castle Stirling 285 G11
Kilburn Angus 292 G5
Derbys 170 F5
London 67 C9
N Yorks 215 D10
Kilby Leics 136 D2
Kilby Bridge Leics 136 D2
Kilchamaig Argyll 275 G9
Kilchattan Argyll 274 D4
Kilchattan Bay Argyll 266 E2
Kilchenzie Argyll 255 E7
Kilcheran Argyll 289 F10
Kilchiaran Argyll 274 G3
Kilchoan Argyll 275 B8
Highld 288 C6
Kilchoman Argyll 274 G3
Kilchrenan Argyll 284 E4
Kilconquhar Fife 287 G8
Kilcot Glos 98 F3
Kilcoy Highld 300 D5
Kilcreggan Argyll 276 E4
Kildale N Yorks 226 D2
Kildalloig Argyll 255 F8
Kildary Highld 301 B7
Kildaton Ho Argyll 254 C5
Kildavanan Argyll 275 G11
Kildermorie Lodge
Highld 300 B5
Kildonan Dumfries 236 D2
Highld 298 D3
N Ayrs 256 E2
Kildonan Lodge Highld 311 G3
Kildonnan Highld 294 G6
Kildrum N Lanark 278 F5
Kildrummy Aberds 292 B6
Kildwick N Yorks 204 D6
Kilfinan Argyll 275 F10
Kilfinnan Highld 290 D4
Kilgetty Pembs 73 D10
Kilgour Fife 286 G6
Kilgrammie S Ayrs 245 C7
Kilgwrrwg Common Mon 79 F7
Kilhallon Corn 5 E11
Kilham E Yorks 217 G11
Northumb 263 C9
Kilkeddan Argyll 255 E8
Kilkenneth Argyll 288 E1
Kilkenny Glos 81 B8
Kilkerran Argyll 255 F8
Kilkhampton Corn 24 E3
Killamarsh Derbys 187 E7
Killaworgey Corn 5 C8
Killay Swansea 56 C6
Killbeg Argyll 289 E8
Killean Argyll 255 C7
Killearn Stirling 277 D10
Killegruer Argyll 255 D7
Killen Highld 300 D6
Killerby Darl 224 B3
Killichonan Perth 285 B9
Killiechoinich Argyll 289 G10
Killiechonate Highld 290 E4
Killiechronan Argyll 289 E7
Killiecrankie Perth 291 G11
Killiemor Argyll 288 F6
Killiemore House Argyll 288 G6
Killilan Highld 295 B11
Killimster Highld 310 D7
Killin Stirling 285 D9
Killinallan Argyll 274 F4
Killingbeck W Yorks 206 G2
Killinghall N Yorks 205 B11
Killington Cumb 212 B2
Devon 41 D7
Killingworth T&W 243 C7
Killingworth Moor T&W 243 C7
Killingworth Village
T&W 243 C7
Killin Lodge Highld 291 C7
Killivose Corn 2 B4
Killmahumaig Argyll 275 D8
Killochyett Borders 271 F9
Killocraw Argyll 255 D7
Killundine Highld 289 E7
Killylung Dumfries 247 G11
Kilmacolm Invclyd 267 B7
Kilmaha Argyll 275 C10
Kilmahog Stirling 285 G10
Kilmalieu Highld 289 D10
Kilmaluag Highld 298 B4
Kilmany Fife 287 E7
Kilmarie Highld 295 D7
Kilmarnock E Ayrs 257 B10
Kilmaron Castle Fife 287 F7
Kilmartin Argyll 275 D9
Kilmaurs E Ayrs 267 G8
Kilmelford Argyll 275 B9
Kilmeny Argyll 274 G4
Kilmersdon Som 45 C7
Kilmeston Hants 33 B9
Kilmichael Argyll 255 E7
Argyll 275 F10
Kilmichael Glassary
Argyll 275 D9
Kilmichael of Inverlussa
Argyll 275 E8
Kilmington Devon 15 B11
Wilts 45 F9
Kilmington Common
Wilts 45 F9
Kilmoluaig Argyll 288 E1
Kilmonivaig Highld 290 E3
Kilmorack Highld 300 E4
Kilmore Argyll 289 G10
Highld 295 E8
Kilmory Argyll 275 F8
Highld 289 B7
Highld 294 E5
N Ayrs 255 E10
Kilmory Lodge Argyll 275 C8
Kilmote Highld 311 H3
Kilmuir Highld 298 B3
Highld 298 E2
Highld 300 E6
Highld 301 B7
Kilmun Argyll 275 B10
Argyll 276 E3
Kilnave Argyll 274 F3
Kilncadzow S Lanark 269 F7
Kilndown Kent 53 G8
Kiln Green Hereford 79 B10
Wokingham 65 D10
Kilnhill Cumb 229 E10
Kilnhurst S Yorks 187 B7
Kilninian Argyll 288 E5
Kilninver Argyll 289 G10
Kiln Pit Hill Northumb 242 G2
Kilnsea E Yorks 201 D12
Kilnsey N Yorks 213 F9
Kilnwick E Yorks 208 D5
Kilnwick Percy E Yorks 208 C2
Kilnwood Vale W Sus 51 G8
Kiloran Argyll 274 D4
Kilpatrick N Ayrs 255 E10
Kilpeck Hereford 97 E8
Kilphedir Highld 311 H3
Kilpin E Yorks 199 B9
Kilpin Pike E Yorks 199 B9
Kilrenny Fife 287 G9
Kilsby W Nhants 119 C11
Kilspindie Perth 286 E6
Kilsyth N Lanark 278 F4
Kiltarlity Highld 300 E5
Kilton Notts 187 F9
Redcar 226 B4
Som 43 E7
Kilton Thorpe Redcar 226 B3
Kiltyrie Perth 285 D10
Kilvaxter Highld 298 C3
Kilve Som 43 E7
Kilvington Notts 172 G3
Kilwinning N Ayrs 266 G6
Kimberley Norf 141 C11
Notts 171 G8
Kimberworth S Yorks 186 C6
Kimberworth Park
S Yorks 186 C6
Kimblesworth Durham 233 B11
Kimble Wick Bucks 84 D4
Kimbolton Cambs 121 D11
Hereford 115 E10
Kimbridge Hants 32 B4
Kimcote Leics 135 F11
Kimmeridge Dorset 18 F4
Kimmerston Northumb 263 B11
Kimpton Hants 47 D9
Herts 85 B11
Kimworthy Devon 24 E4
Kinabus Argyll 254 C3
Kinbeachie Highld 300 C6
Kinbrace Highld 310 F2
Kinbuck Stirling 285 G11
Kincaidston S Ayrs 257 F9
Kincaple Fife 287 F8
Kincardine Fife 279 D8
Highld 309 L6
Kincardine Bridge Falk 279 D8
Kincardine O'Neil
Aberds 293 D7
Kinclaven Perth 286 D5
Kincorth Aberdeen 293 C11
Kincorth Ho Moray 301 C10
Kincraig Highld 291 C10
Kincraigie Perth 286 C3
Kindallachan Perth 286 C3
Kine Moor S Yorks 197 G9
Kineton Glos 99 F11
Warks 118 G6
Kineton Green W Mid 134 G2
Kinfauns Perth 286 E5
Kingairloch Highld 289 D10
Kingarth Argyll 255 B11
Kingates IoW 20 F6
Kingbeare Corn 11 G11
Kingcoed Mon 78 D6
Kingdown N Som 60 G4
King Edward Aberds 303 D7
Kingerby Lincs 189 C9
Kingfield Sur 50 B4
Kingford Devon 24 F3
Devon 25 D10
Kingham Oxon 100 G5
Kinghay Wilts 30 B5
Kingholm Quay
Dumfries 237 B11
Kinghorn Fife 280 D5
Kingie Highld 290 C3
Kinglassie Fife 280 B4
Kingledores Borders 260 D4
Kingoodie Perth 287 E7
King's Acre Hereford 97 C9
Kingsand Corn 7 E8
Kingsash Bucks 84 D5
Kingsbarns Fife 287 F9
Kingsbridge Devon 8 G4
Som 42 F3
King's Bromley Staffs 152 F2
Kingsbrook Oxfordshire 84 C4
Kingsburgh Highld 298 D3
Kingsbury London 67 B8
Warks 134 D4
Kingsbury Episcopi Som 28 C6
Kingsbury Regis Som 29 D11
King's Caple Hereford 97 F11
Kingscauseway Highld 301 B7
Kingscavil W Loth 279 F10
Kingsclere Hants 48 B4
Kingsclere Woodlands
Hants 64 G4
King's Cliffe N Nhants 137 D10
Kings Clipstone Notts 171 C10
Kingscote Glos 80 F4
Kingscott Devon 25 D8
King's Coughton Warks 117 F11
Kingscourt Glos 80 E4
Kingscross N Ayrs 256 D2
Kingsditch Glos 99 G8
Kingsdon Som 29 B8
Kingsdown Kent 54 B2
Kent 55 D11
Swindon 63 B7
Wilts 61 F10
King's Dyke Cambs 138 D4
Kingseat Fife 280 C2
Kingseathill Fife 280 D2
King's End Worcs 116 G6
Kingsett Devon 12 E6
Kingsey Bucks 84 D2
Kingsfield Hereford 97 B10
Kingsfold Lancs 194 B4
W Sus 51 F7
Kingsford Aberds 293 B7
E Ayrs 267 F8
Worcs 132 G6
Kingsforth N Lincs 200 D4
King's Furlong Hants 48 C6
Kingsgate Kent 71 E11
King's Green Glos 98 E5
Worcs 116 E5
Kingshall Green Suff 125 E8
Kingshall Street Suff 125 E8
Kingsheanton Devon 40 F5
King's Heath W Mid 133 G11
W Nhants 120 E4
Kings Hedges Cambs 123 E9
Kingshill Glos 80 F3
Swindon 62 C6
Kings Hill Glos 81 E8
King's Hill Kent 53 C7
W Mid 133 D9
Kingsholm Glos 80 B4
Kingshouse Hotel
Highld 284 B6
Kingshurst W Mid 134 F3
Kingside Hill Cumb 238 G5
Kingskerswell Devon 9 B7
Kingskettle Fife 287 G7
Kingsknowe Edin 280 G4
Kingsland Anglesey 178 E2
Hereford 115 E8
London 67 C10
Shrops 149 G9
Kings Langley Herts 85 E9
Kingsley Ches W 183 G9
Hants 49 F9
Staffs 169 F8
Kingsley Green W Sus 49 G11
Kingsley Holt Staffs 169 F8
Kingsley Moor Staffs 169 F7
Kingsley Park W Nhants 120 E5
Kingslow Shrops 132 D5
King's Lynn Norf 158 E2
King's Meaburn Cumb 231 G8
Kingsmead Hants 33 E9
Kingsmere Oxon 101 G11
King's Mills Derbys 153 D8
Wrex 166 F4
Kingsmoor Essex 86 D6
Kings Moss Mers 194 G4
Kingsmuir Angus 287 C8
Fife 287 G9
Kings Muir Borders 261 B7
King's Newnham Warks 119 B9
King's Newton Derbys 153 D7
Kingsnordley Shrops 132 F5
Kingsnorth Kent 54 F4
King's Norton Leics 136 C3
W Mid 117 B11
King's Nympton Devon 25 D11
King's Pyon Hereford 115 G8
Kings Ripton Cambs 122 B5
King's Somborne Hants 47 G11
King's Stag Dorset 30 E2
King's Stanley Glos 80 E4
King's Sutton W Nhants 101 D9
King's Tamerton Plym 7 D9
Kingstanding W Mid 133 E11
Kingsteignton Devon 14 G3
Kingsteps Highld 301 D9
King Sterndale Derbys 185 G9
King's Thorn Hereford 97 E10
Kingsthorpe W Nhants 120 E5
Kingsthorpe Hollow
W Nhants 120 E5
Kingston Cambs 122 F6
Devon 8 F2
Devon 9 E8
Dorset 18 F5
Dorset 30 F3
E Loth 281 E10
Gtr Man 184 B6
Hants 31 G11
IoW 20 E5
Kent 55 C7
M Keynes 103 D8
Moray 302 C3
Ptsmth 33 G11
Kingston continued
Suff 108 B5
Kingston Bagpuize Oxon 82 F6
Kingston Blount Oxon 84 F2
Kingston by Sea W Sus 36 G2
Kingston Deverill Wilts 45 F10
Kingstone Hereford 97 D8
Hereford 98 G2
Som 28 E5
Staffs 151 D11
S Yorks 197 F10
Kingstone Winslow Oxon 63 B9
Kingston Gorse W Sus 35 G9
Kingston Lisle Oxon 63 B10
Kingston Maurward
Dorset 17 C10
Kingston near Lewes
E Sus 36 F5
Kingston on Soar
Notts 153 D10
Kingston Park T&W 242 D6
Kingston Russell Dorset 17 C7
Kingston St Mary Som 28 B2
Kingston Seymour
N Som 60 F2
Kingston Stert Oxon 84 E2
Kingston upon Hull Hull 200 B5
Kingston upon Thames
London 67 F7
Kingston Vale London 67 E8
Kingstown Cumb 239 F9
King Street Essex 87 E9
King's Walden Herts 104 G3
Kingsway Bath 61 G8
Halton 183 D8
Kingswear Devon 9 E7
Kingswells Aberdeen 293 C10
Kingswinford W Mid 133 F7
Kingswood Bucks 83 B11
Essex 69 B8
Glos 80 G2
Hereford 114 G5
Herts 85 E10
Kent 53 C10
Powys 130 C4
S Glos 60 E6
Som 42 F6
Sur 51 B8
Warks 118 C3
Warr 183 C9
Kingswood Brook
Warks 118 C3
Kingswood Common
Staffs 132 C6
Worcs 116 D4
Kings Worthy Hants 48 G3
Kingthorpe Lincs 189 F10
Kington Hereford 114 F5
S Glos 79 G10
Worcs 117 F9
Kington Langley Wilts 62 D2
Kington Magna Dorset 30 C3
Kington St Michael Wilts 62 D2
Kingussie Highld 291 C9
Kingweston Som 44 G4
Kinhrive Highld 301 B7
Kininvie Ho Moray 302 E3
Kinkell Bridge Perth 286 F3
Kinknockie Aberds 303 E10
Aberds 303 G9
Kinkry Hill Cumb 240 B2
Kinlet Shrops 132 G4
Kinloch Fife 286 F6
Highld 289 D8
Highld 294 F5
Highld 295 D8
Highld 308 F3
Perth 286 C5
Perth 286 C6
Kinlochan Highld 289 C10
Kinlochard Stirling 285 G8
Kinlochbeoraid Highld 295 G10
Kinlochbervie Highld 306 D7
Kinloch Damph Highld 299 E8
Kinlocheil Highld 289 B11
Kinlochewe Highld 299 C10
Kinloch Hourn Highld 295 E11
Kinloch Laggan Highld 291 E7
Kinlochleven Highld 290 G3
Kinloch Lodge Highld 308 D5
Kinlochmoidart Highld 289 B9
Kinlochmorar Highld 295 F10
Kinlochmore Highld 290 G3
Kinloch Rannoch Perth 285 B10
Kinlochspelve Argyll 289 G8
Kinloid Highld 295 G8
Kinloss Moray 301 C10
Kinmel Bay = Bae Cinmel
Conwy 181 E7
Kinmuck Aberds 293 B10
Kinmundy Aberds 293 B10
Kinnadie Aberds 303 E9
Kinnaird Perth 286 B3
Perth 286 E6
Kinnaird Castle Angus 287 B10
Kinnauld Highld 309 J7
Kinneff Aberds 293 F10
Kinneil Falk 279 E9
Kinnelhead Dumfries 248 C2
Kinnell Angus 287 B10
Kinnerley Shrops 148 E6
Kinnersley Hereford 96 B6
Worcs 99 C7
Kinnerton Powys 114 E4
Kinnerton Green Flint 166 C4
Kinnesswood Perth 286 G5
Kinninvie Durham 233 G7
Kinnordy Angus 287 B7
Kinoulton Notts 154 C3
Kinross Perth 286 G5
Kinrossie Perth 286 D5
Kinsbourne Green Herts 85 B10
Kinsey Heath Ches E 167 G11
Kinsham Hereford 115 E7
Worcs 99 D8
Kinsley W Yorks 198 E2
Kinson BCP 19 B7
Kintallan Argyll 275 E8
Kintbury W Berks 63 F11
Kintessack Moray 301 C9
Kintillo Perth 286 F5
Kintocher Aberds 293 C7
Kinton Hereford 115 C8
Shrops 149 F7
Kintore Aberds 293 B9
Kintour Argyll 254 B5
Kintra Argyll 254 C4
Argyll 288 G5
Kintradwell Highld 311 J3
Kintraw Argyll 275 C9
Kinuachdrachd Argyll 275 D8
Kinveachy Highld 291 B11
Kinver Staffs 132 G6
Kinwalsey Warks 134 F5
Kip Hill Durham 242 G6
Kiplin N Yorks 224 F5
Kippax W Yorks 206 G4
Kippen Stirling 278 C3
Kippford or Scaur
Dumfries 237 D10
Kippilaw Borders 262 D2

Kippilaw Mains Borders 262 D2
Kipping's Cross Kent 52 F6
Kippington Kent 52 C4
Kirbister Orkney 314 D6
Orkney 314 E2
Orkney 314 F3
Kirbuster Orkney 314 D2
Kirby Bedon Norf 142 B5
Kirby Bellars Leics 154 F4
Kirby Cane Norf 143 E7
Kirby Corner W Mid 118 B5
Kirby Cross Essex 108 G4
Kirby Fields Leics 135 C10
Kirby Green Norf 143 E7
Kirby Grindalythe
N Yorks 217 F8
Kirby Hill N Yorks 215 F7
N Yorks 224 D2
Kirby Knowle N Yorks 215 B9
Kirby-le-Soken Essex 108 G4
Kirby Misperton
N Yorks 216 D5
Kirby Moor Cumb 240 E2
Kirby Muxloe Leics 135 C10
Kirby Row Norf 143 E7
Kirby Sigston N Yorks 225 G8
Kirby Underdale
E Yorks 208 B2
Kirby Wiske N Yorks 215 C7
Kirdford W Sus 35 B8
Kirk Highld 310 D6
Kirkabister Shetland 315 K6
Shetland 313 K6
Kirkandrews Dumfries 237 E8
Kirkandrews-on-Eden
Cumb 239 F9
Kirkapol Argyll 288 E2
Kirkbampton Cumb 239 F8
Kirkbean Dumfries 237 D11
Kirkborough Cumb 229 D7
Kirkbrae Orkney 314 B4
Kirk Bramwith S Yorks 198 E6
Kirkbride Cumb 238 F6
Kirkbridge N Yorks 224 G5
Kirkbuddo Angus 287 C9
Kirkburn Borders 261 B7
E Yorks 208 B5
Kirkburton W Yorks 197 E7
Kirkby Lincs 189 C9
Mers 182 B6
N Yorks 225 D10
Kirkby Fenside Lincs 174 C4
Kirkby Fleetham
N Yorks 224 G5
Kirkby Green Lincs 173 D9
Kirkby Hill N Yorks 215 F7
Kirkby in Ashfield
Notts 171 D8
Kirkby-in-Furness
Cumb 210 C4
Kirkby la Thorpe Lincs 173 F10
Kirkby Lonsdale Cumb 212 D2
Kirkby Malham N Yorks 213 G7
Kirkby Mallory Leics 135 C9
Kirkby Malzeard
N Yorks 214 E4
Kirkby Mills N Yorks 216 B4
Kirkbymoorside
N Yorks 216 B3
Kirkby on Bain Lincs 174 C2
Kirkby Overblow
N Yorks 206 D2
Kirkby Stephen Cumb 222 D5
Kirkby Thore Cumb 231 F8
Kirkby Underwood
Lincs 155 D11
Kirkby Wharfe N Yorks 206 E6
Kirkby Woodhouse
Notts 171 E7
Kirkcaldy Fife 280 C5
Kirkcambeck Cumb 240 D2
Kirkcarswell Dumfries 237 E9
Kirkcolm Dumfries 236 C2
Kirkconnel Dumfries 258 G6
Kirkconnell Dumfries 237 C11
Kirkcowan Dumfries 236 C5
Kirkcudbright Dumfries 237 D8
Kirkdale Mers 182 C4
Kirk Deighton N Yorks 206 C3
Kirk Ella E Yorks 200 B4
Kirkfieldbank S Lanark 269 G7
Kirkforthar Feus Fife 286 G6
Kirkgunzeon Dumfries 237 C10
Kirk Hallam Derbys 171 G7
Kirkham Lancs 202 G4
N Yorks 216 F4
Kirkhamgate W Yorks 197 C9
Kirk Hammerton
N Yorks 206 B5
Kirkhams Gtr Man 195 F10
Kirkharle Northumb 252 G2
Kirkheaton Northumb 242 B2
W Yorks 197 D7
Kirkhill Angus 293 G8
E Renf 267 D11
Highld 300 E5
Midloth 270 C4
Moray 302 F2
W Loth 279 G11
Kirkholt Gtr Man 195 E11
Kirkhope Borders 261 E9
Kirkhouse Borders 261 C8
Cumb 240 F3
Kirkiboll Highld 308 D5
Kirkibost Highld 295 D7
Kirkinch Angus 287 C7
Kirkinner Dumfries 236 D6
Kirkintilloch E Dunb 278 G3
Kirk Ireton Derbys 170 E3
Kirkland Cumb 219 B11
Cumb 229 B11
Cumb 231 E8
Dumfries 247 E8
Dumfries 258 G6
S Ayrs 244 E6
Kirkland Guards Cumb 229 C9
Kirk Langley Derbys 152 B5
Kirkleatham Redcar 235 G7
Kirklees Gtr Man 195 E9
Kirklevington Stockton 225 D8
Kirkley Suff 143 E10
Kirklington Notts 171 D11
N Yorks 214 C6
Kirklinton Cumb 239 D10
Kirkliston Edin 280 G2
Kirkmaiden Dumfries 236 F3
Kirk Merrington
Durham 233 E11
Kirkmichael Perth 286 B4
S Ayrs 245 B8
Kirk Michael IoM 192 C4
Kirkmichael Mains
Dumfries 248 F2
Kirkmuirhill S Lanark 268 G5
Kirknewton Northumb 263 C10
W Loth 270 B2
Kirkney Aberds 302 F5
Kirk of Shotts N Lanark 268 C6
Kirkoswald Cumb 231 C7
S Ayrs 244 B6
Kirkpatrick Dumfries 247 E10
Kirkpatrick Durham
Dumfries 237 B9
Kirkpatrick-Fleming
Dumfries 239 C7
Kirk Sandall S Yorks 198 F6
Kirksanton Cumb 210 C2
Kirkshaw N Lanark 268 C4
Kirk Smeaton N Yorks 198 D4
Kirkstall W Yorks 205 F11
Kirkstead Borders 261 E7
Lincs 173 C11
Kirkstile Aberds 302 F5
Kirkstyle Highld 310 B7
Kirkthorpe W Yorks 197 C11
Kirkton Aberds 302 E6
Aberds 302 G6
Angus 286 C6
Angus 287 C8
Angus 287 D8
Argyll 275 C8
Borders 262 G2
Dumfries 247 G11
Fife 280 D4
Fife 287 E7
Highld 295 C10
Highld 299 E9
Highld 301 D7
Highld 309 K7
Perth 286 F3
S Lanark 259 E10
Stirling 285 G9
W Loth 269 B10
Kirktonhill Borders 271 E9
W Dunb 277 G7
Kirkton Manor Borders 260 B6
Kirkton of Airlie Angus 287 B7
Kirkton of Auchterhouse
Angus 287 D7
Kirkton of Auchterless
Aberds 303 E7
Kirkton of Barevan
Highld 301 E8
Kirkton of Bourtie
Aberds 303 G8
Kirkton of Collace
Perth 286 D5
Kirkton of Craig Angus 287 B11
Kirkton of Culsalmond
Aberds 302 F6
Kirkton of Durris
Aberds 293 D9
Kirkton of Glenbuchat
Aberds 292 B5
Kirkton of Glenisla
Angus 292 G4
Kirkton of Kingoldrum
Angus 287 B7
Kirkton of Largo Fife 287 G8
Kirkton of Lethendy
Perth 286 C5
Kirkton of Logie Buchan
Aberds 303 G9
Kirkton of Maryculter
Aberds 293 D10
Kirkton of Menmuir
Angus 293 G7
Kirkton of Monikie
Angus 287 D9
Kirkton of Oyne Aberds 302 G6
Kirkton of Rayne
Aberds 302 G6
Kirkton of Skene
Aberds 293 C10
Kirkton of Tough
Aberds 293 B8
Kirktoun E Ayrs 267 G8
Kirktown Aberds 303 D10
Kirktown of Alvah
Aberds 302 C6
Kirktown of Deskford
Moray 302 C5
Kirktown of Fetteresso
Aberds 293 E10
Kirktown of Mortlach
Moray 302 F3
Kirktown of Slains
Aberds 303 G10
Kirkurd Borders 270 G2
Kirkwall Orkney 314 E4
Kirkwhelpington
Northumb 251 G11
Kirkwood Dumfries 238 B4
N Lanark 268 C4
Kirk Yetholm Borders 263 D8
Kirmington N Lincs 200 E6
Kirmond le Mire Lincs 189 C11
Kirn Argyll 276 F3
Kirriemuir Angus 287 B7
Kirstead Green Norf 142 D5
Kirtlebridge Dumfries 238 C6
Kirtleton Dumfries 249 G7
Kirtling Cambs 124 F3
Kirtling Green Cambs 124 F3
Kirtlington Oxon 83 B7
Kirtomy Highld 308 C7
Kirton Lincs 156 B6
Notts 171 B11
Suff 108 D5
Kirton Campus W Loth 269 B10
Kirton End Lincs 174 G3
Kirton Holme Lincs 174 G3
Kirton in Lindsey
N Lincs 188 B6
Kiskin Cumb 210 B1
Kislingbury W Nhants 120 F3
Kitbridge Devon 28 G4
Kitchenroyd W Yorks 197 F8
Kitebrook Warks 100 E4
Kite Green Warks 118 D3
Kite Hill IoW 21 C7
Kites Hardwick Warks 119 D9
Kit Hill Dorset 30 D4
Kitlye Glos 80 E5
Kit's Coty Kent 69 G8
Kit Green Gtr Man 194 F5
Kittisford Som 27 C9
Kittle Swansea 56 D5
Kitt's End Herts 86 F2
Kitt's Green W Mid 134 F3
Kitt's Moss Gtr Man 184 E5
Kittwhistle Dorset 28 G5
Kittybrewster Aberdeen 293 C11
Kitwell W Mid 133 G9
Kitwood Hants 49 G7
Kivernoll Hereford 97 E9
Kiveton Park S Yorks 187 E7
Knaith Lincs 188 E4
Knaith Park Lincs 188 D4
Knaphill Sur 50 B3
Knapp Hants 32 C6
Perth 286 D6
Som 28 B4
Wilts 31 B8
Knapp Hill Wilts 30 B5
Knapthorpe Notts 172 D2
Knaptoft Leics 136 F2
Knapton Norf 160 C6
York 207 C7
Knapton Green Hereford 115 G8
Knapwell Cambs 122 E6
Knaresborough N Yorks 206 B3
Knarsdale Northumb 240 G5
Knatts Valley Kent 68 G5
Knauchland Moray 302 D5
Knaven Aberds 303 E8
Knave's Ash Kent 71 G7
Knaves Green Suff 126 D2
Knavesmire York 207 D7
Knayton N Yorks 215 B8
Knebworth Herts 104 G5
Knedlington E Yorks 199 B8
Kneesall Notts 172 C2
Kneesworth Cambs 104 C6
Kneeton Notts 172 F2
Knelston Swansea 56 D3
Knenhall Staffs 151 B8
Knettishall Suff 141 G9
Knightacott Devon 41 F7
Knightcote Warks 119 G7
Knightcott N Som 43 B11
Knightley Staffs 150 D6
Knightley Dale Staffs 150 E6
Knighton BCP 18 B6
Devon 7 F10
Dorset 29 E10
Leicester 135 C11
Oxon 63 B9
Som 43 E7
Staffs 150 D4
Staffs 168 G2
Wilts 63 E9
Worcs 117 F10
Knighton = Tref-y-Clawdd
Powys 114 C5
Knighton Fields
Leicester 135 C11
Knighton on Teme
Worcs 116 C2
Knightor Corn 5 D10
Knightsbridge Glos 99 F7
London 67 D9
Knight's End Cambs 139 E8
Knights Enham Hants 47 D11
Knight's Hill London 67 E10
Knightsmill Corn 11 E7
Knightsridge W Loth 269 B10
Knightswood Glasgow 267 B10
Knightwick Worcs 116 F4
Knill Hereford 114 E5
Knipe Fold Cumb 220 F6
Knipoch Argyll 289 G10
Knipton Leics 154 C6
Knitsley Durham 233 B8
Kniveton Derbys 170 E2
Knocharthur Highld 309 J7
Knock Argyll 289 F7
Cumb 231 F9
Moray 302 D5
Knockally Highld 311 G5
Knockan Highld 307 H7
Knockandhu Moray 302 G2
Knockando Moray 301 E11
Knockando Ho Moray 302 E2
Knockandoo Highld 301 G7
Knockbain Highld 300 D6
Knockbreck Highld 298 C2
Knockbrex Dumfries 237 E7
Knockcarrach Highld 290 B6
Knockdee Highld 310 C5
Knockdolian S Ayrs 244 F4
Knockdow Argyll 276 G2
Knockdown Glos 61 B10
Knockenbaird Aberds 302 G6
Knockenkelly N Ayrs 256 D2
Knockentiber E Ayrs 257 B9
Knockerdown Derbys 170 E2
Knockespock Ho Aberds 302 G5
Knockfarrel Highld 300 D5
Knockglass Dumfries 236 D2
Knockhall Kent 68 E5
Knockhall Castle
Aberds 303 G9
Knockholt Kent 52 B3
Knockholt Pound Kent 52 B3
Knockie Lodge Highld 290 B6
Knockin Shrops 148 E6
Knockin Heath Shrops 149 E7
Knockinlaw E Ayrs 257 B10
Knockinnon Highld 310 F5
Knocklaw Northumb 252 C3
Knocklearn Dumfries 237 B9
Knocklearoch Argyll 274 G4
Knockmill Kent 68 G5
Knocknaha Argyll 255 F7
Knocknain Dumfries 236 C1
Knockothie Aberds 303 F9
Knockrome Argyll 274 F6
Knocksharry IoM 192 D3
Knockstapplemore
Argyll 255 F7
Knockvologan Argyll 274 B4
Knodishall Suff 127 E8
Knokan Argyll 288 G6
Knole Som 29 B7
Knollbury Mon 60 B2
Knoll Green Som 43 F8
Knolls Green Ches E 184 F4
Knoll Top N Yorks 214 F3
Knolton Wrex 149 B7
Knolton Bryn Wrex 149 B7
Knook Wilts 46 E2
Knossington Leics 136 B6
Knotbury Staffs 169 B8
Knott End-on-Sea
Lancs 202 D3
Knotting Bedford 121 E10
Knotting Green
Bedford 121 E10
Knottingley W Yorks 198 C4
Knott Lanes Gtr Man 196 G2
Knott Oak Som 28 E5
Knotts Cumb 230 G4
Lancs 203 C11
Knotty Ash Mers 182 C6
Knotty Corner Devon 24 B6
Knotty Green Bucks 84 G6
Knowbury Shrops 115 C11
Knowe Dumfries 236 B5
Shetland 313 G5
Knowefield Cumb 239 F10
Knowehead Aberds 293 C7
Aberds 302 D5
Dumfries 246 E4
Knowes E Loth 282 F2
Knowesgate Northumb 251 F11
Knowes of Elrick
Aberds 302 D6
Knoweton N Lanark 268 D5
Knowetop N Lanark 268 D5
Knowhead Aberds 303 D9
Knowl Bank Staffs 168 F3
Knowle Bristol 60 E6
Devon 15 E7
Devon 26 G3
Devon 27 B8
Devon 40 F3
Hants 33 F9
Shrops 115 C11
Som 43 F10
Wilts 63 G7
W Mid 118 B3
Knowle Fields Worcs 117 F10
Knowlegate Shrops 115 C11
Knowle Green Lancs 203 F8
Sur 66 E4
Knowle Grove W Mid 118 B3
Knowle Hill Sur 66 F3
Knowle Park W Yorks 205 E7
Knowle St Giles Som 28 E4
Knowlesands Shrops 132 E4
Knowles Hill Devon 14 G3
Knowl Green Essex 106 C5
Knowl Hill Windsor 65 D10
Knowlton Dorset 31 E8
Kent 55 C9
Knowl Wall Staffs 151 B7
Knowl Wood W Yorks 196 C2
Knowsley Mers 182 B6
Knowsthorpe W Yorks 206 G2
Knowstone Devon 26 C4
Knox Bridge Kent 53 E9
Knucklas Powys 114 C5
Knuston N Nhants 121 D8
Knutsford Ches E 184 F3
Knutton Staffs 168 F4
Knuzden Brook Lancs 195 B8
Knypersley Staffs 168 D5
Kraiknish Highld 294 C5
Krumlin W Yorks 196 D5
Kuggar Corn 2 F6
Kyleakin Highld 295 C9
Kyle of Lochalsh Highld 295 C9
Kylepark N Lanark 268 C3
Kylerhea Highld 295 C9
Kylesknoydart Highld 295 F10
Kylesku Highld 306 F7
Kylesmorar Highld 295 F10
Kylestrome Highld 306 F7
Kyllachy House Highld 301 G7
Kymin Hereford 97 B11
Mon 79 C8
Kynaston Hereford 97 F10
Shrops 149 E7
Kynnersley Telford 150 F3
Kyre Worcs 116 E2
Kyre Green Worcs 116 E2
Kyre Magna Worcs 116 E2
Kyre Park Worcs 116 E2
Kyrewood Worcs 116 D2

L

Labost W Isles 304 D4
Lacasaidh W Isles 304 F5
Lacasdal W Isles 304 E6
Laceby NE Lincs 201 F8
Laceby Acres NE Lincs 201 F8
Lacey Green Bucks 84 F4
Ches E 184 E4
Lach Dennis Ches W 184 G2
Lache Ches W 166 C5
Lackenby Redcar 225 B11
Lackford Suff 124 C5
Lacock Wilts 62 F2
Ladbroke Warks 119 F8
Laddenvean Corn 3 E7
Laddingford Kent 53 D7
Lade Kent 39 C9
Lade Bank Lincs 174 E5
Ladies Riggs N Yorks 214 F2
Ladmanlow Derbys 185 G8
Ladock Corn 5 E7
Ladwell Hants 32 C6
Lady Orkney 314 B6
Ladybank Fife 287 F7
Ladybrook Notts 171 C8
Ladyburn Invclyd 276 F6
Ladycross Corn 12 D2
Ladyes Hill Warks 118 C5
Lady Green Mers 193 G10
Lady Hall Cumb 210 B3
Lady Halton Shrops 115 B9
Lady House Gtr Man 196 E2
Ladykirk Borders 273 F7
Ladyoak Shrops 131 C7
Lady Park T&W 242 F6
Ladyridge Hereford 97 E11
Ladysford Aberds 303 C9
Lady's Green Suff 124 F5
Ladywell London 67 E11
Shrops 149 C9
W Loth 269 B10
Ladywood Telford 132 C3
W Mid 133 F11
Worcs 117 E7
Lady Wood W Yorks 206 F2
Laffak Mers 183 B8
Laga Highld 289 C8
Lagafater Lodge
Dumfries 236 B3
Lagalochan Argyll 275 B9
Lagavulin Argyll 254 C5
Lagg Argyll 274 F6
N Ayrs 255 E10
Laggan Argyll 254 B3
Highld 289 B9
Highld 290 D4
Highld 291 D8
S Ayrs 245 G7
Lagganlia Highld 291 C10
Laggan Lodge Argyll 289 G8
Lagganmullan Dumfries 237 D7
Lagganulva Argyll 288 E6
Lagness W Sus 22 C5
Laide Highld 307 K3
Laig Highld 294 G6
Laigh Carnduff S Lanark 268 F3
Laigh Fenwick E Ayrs 267 G9
Laigh Glengall S Ayrs 257 F8
Laighmuir E Ayrs 267 F9
Laighstonehall S Lanark 268 E4
Laindon Essex 69 B7
Lair Highld 299 E10
Perth 292 G3
Laira Plym 7 D10
Lairg Highld 309 J5
Lairg Lodge Highld 309 J5
Lairgmore Highld 300 F5
Lairg Muir Highld 309 J5
Laisterdyke W Yorks 205 G9
Laithes Cumb 230 E5
Laithkirk Durham 232 G5
Laity Moor Corn 4 F3
Lake BCP 18 C5
Devon 12 D6
Devon 24 F6
Devon 40 G5
IoW 21 E7
Wilts 46 F6
Lake End Bucks 66 D2
Lakenham Norf 142 B4
Lakenheath Suff 140 G4
Laker's Green Sur 50 F4
Lakesend Norf 139 D10
Lakeside Cumb 211 B7
Thurrock 68 D5
Worcs 117 D11
Laleham Sur 66 F5
Laleston = Trelales
Bridgend 57 F11
Lamanva Corn 3 C7
Lamarsh Essex 107 D7
Lamas Norf 160 E4
Lamb Corner Essex 107 E10
Lambden Borders 272 G4
Lamberden Kent 38 B4
Lamberhead Green
Gtr Man 194 G4
Lamberhurst Kent 53 F7
Lamberhurst Quarter
Kent 53 F7
Lamberton Borders 273 D9
Lambert's End W Mid 133 E9
Lambeth London 67 D10
Lambfair Green Suff 124 G4
Lambfoot Cumb 229 E9
Lambhill Glasgow 267 B11
Lambley Northumb 240 F5
Notts 171 F10
Lambourn W Berks 63 D10
Lambourne Corn 4 E5
Essex 87 F7
Lambourne End Essex 87 G7
Lambourn Woodlands
W Berks 63 D10
Lambridge Bath 61 F9
Lamb's Cross Kent 53 D9
Lambs Green W Sus 51 F8
Lambs' Green Dorset 18 B5
Lambston Pembs 72 B6
Lambton T&W 243 G7
Lamellion Corn 6 C4
Lamerton Devon 12 F5
Lamesley T&W 243 F7
Laminess Orkney 314 C6
Lamington Highld 301 B7
S Lanark 259 C11
Lamlash N Ayrs 256 C2
Lamledra Corn 5 G10
Lamloch Dumfries 246 D2
Lammack Blackburn 195 B7
Lamonby Cumb 230 D4
Lamorick Corn 5 C10
Lamorna Corn 1 E4
Lamorran Corn 5 G7
Lampardbrook Suff 126 E5
Lampeter = Llanbedr Pont
Steffan Ceredig 93 B11
Lampeter Velfrey Pembs 73 C11
Lamphey Pembs 73 E8
Lamplugh Cumb 229 G7
Lamport W Nhants 120 C5
Lampton London 66 D6
Lamyatt Som 45 F7
Lana Devon 12 B2
Devon 24 F4
Lanark S Lanark 269 G7
Lancaster Lancs 211 G9
Lanchester Durham 233 B9
Lancing W Sus 35 G11
Landbeach Cambs 123 D9
Landcross Devon 25 C7
Landerberry Aberds 293 C9
Landewednack Corn 2 G6
Landford Wilts 32 D3
Landford Manor Wilts 32 C3
Landfordwood Wilts 32 C3
Land Gate Gtr Man 194 G5
Landguard Manor IoW 21 E7
Landhill Devon 12 B4
Landican Mers 182 D3
Landimore Swansea 56 C3
Landkey Devon 40 G5
Landkey Newland Devon 40 G5
Landore Swansea 57 B7
Landport E Sus 36 E6
Ptsmth 33 G10
Landrake Corn 7 C7
Landscove Devon 8 B5
Landshipping Pembs 73 C8
Landshipping Quay
Pembs 73 C8
Landslow Green
Gtr Man 185 B7
Landulph Corn 7 C8
Landwade Suff 124 D2
Landywood Staffs 133 B9
Lane Corn 4 C6
Laneast Corn 11 E10
Lane Bottom Lancs 204 F3
W Yorks 205 F7
Lane End Bucks 84 G4
Lane-end Corn 5 B10
Lane End Cumb 220 G2
Derbys 170 C6
Devon 24 G6
Dorset 18 C3
Flint 166 C3
Glos 79 B10
Hants 33 B9
Hants 33 B11
IoW 21 D9
Kent 68 E5
Lancs 204 D3
Sur 49 E10
S Yorks 186 B5
Wilts 45 D10
W Yorks 204 F6
Lane Ends Ches E 168 D2
Ches E 185 E7
Cumb 210 C6
Derbys 152 C4
Gtr Man 185 C7
Lancs 194 D6
Lancs 203 C11
Lancs 203 G11
N Yorks 204 E5
Stoke 168 E5
W Yorks 205 F10
Lane Green Staffs 133 C7
Laneham Notts 188 F4
Lanehead Durham 232 C2
Northumb 251 F7
Lane Head Derbys 185 F11
Durham 224 C2
Gtr Man 183 B10
Pembs 73 E8
W Mid 133 C9
W Yorks 197 F7
Lane Heads Lancs 202 F4
Lanehouse Dorset 17 F9
Lanercost Cumb 240 E3
Lanescot Corn 5 D11
Lanesend Pembs 73 D9
Lanes End Bucks 84 D6
Lane's End Shrops 132 G2
Lanesfield W Mid 133 D8
Laneshaw Bridge Lancs 204 E4
Lane Side Lancs 195 C9
Laney Green Staffs 133 B9
Lanfach Caerph 78 F2
Langaford Devon 12 B4
Langage Devon 7 E11
Langal Highld 289 C9
Langaller Som 28 B3
Langar Notts 154 C4
Langbank Renfs 277 G7
Langbar N Yorks 205 C7
Langbaurgh N Yorks 225 C11
Langburnshiels Borders 250 C2
Langcliffe N Yorks 212 G6
Langdale Highld 308 E6
Langdale End N Yorks 227 G8
Langdon Corn 12 D2
Langdon Beck Durham 232 E3
Langdon Hills Essex 69 B7
Langdown Hants 32 F6
Langdyke Dumfries 238 C3
Fife 287 G7
Langenhoe Essex 89 B8
Langford C Beds 104 C3
Devon 14 B4
Devon 27 G8
Essex 88 D4
Notts 172 D4
Oxon 82 E2
Som 28 B2
Langford Budville Som 27 C10
Langford Green Devon 27 G8
N Som 44 B3
Langham Dorset 30 B3
Essex 107 E10
Norf 177 E8
Rutland 154 G6
Som 28 E4
Suff 125 C9
Langhaugh Borders 260 C6
Langho Lancs 203 G10
Langholm Dumfries 249 G9
Langholme N Lincs 188 B3
Langhope Borders 261 E10
Langland Swansea 56 D6
Langlee Borders 262 B2
Langleeford Northumb 263 E10
Langlee Mains Borders 262 B2
Langlees Falk 279 E7
Langley Ches E 184 G6
Derbys 170 F6
Essex 105 D8
Glos 99 F10
Gtr Man 195 F11
Hants 32 G6
Herts 104 G4
Kent 53 C10
Northumb 241 E8
Oxon 82 B4
Slough 66 D4
Som 27 B9
Warks 118 E3
W Mid 133 F9
W Sus 34 B4
Langley Burrell Wilts 62 D2
Langleybury Herts 85 E9
Langley Common
Derbys 152 B5
Wokingham 65 F9
Langley Corner Bucks 66 C4
Langley Green Derbys 152 B5
Essex 107 G7
Warks 118 E3
W Mid 133 F9
W Sus 51 F9
Langley Heath Kent 53 C10
Langley Marsh Som 27 B9
Langley Mill Derbys 170 F6
Langley Moor Durham 233 C11
Langley Park Durham 233 C10
Langley Street Norf 143 C7
Langley Vale Sur 51 B8
Langloan N Lanark 268 C4
Langney E Sus 23 E10
Langold Notts 187 D9
Langore Corn 12 D2
Langport Som 28 B6
Langrick Lincs 174 F3
Langrick Bridge Lincs 174 F3
Langridge Bath 61 F8
Langridge Ford Devon 25 C9
Langrigg Cumb 222 C5
Cumb 229 B9
Langrish Hants 34 C2
Langsett S Yorks 197 G8
Langshaw Borders 262 B2
Langside Glasgow 267 C11
Perth 285 F11
Langskaill Orkney 314 B4
Langstone Devon 13 E10
Hants 22 C2
Newport 78 G5
Langthorne N Yorks 224 G5
Langthorpe N Yorks 215 F7
Langthwaite N Yorks 223 E10
Langtoft E Yorks 217 F10
Lincs 156 G2
Langton Durham 224 B3
Lincs 174 B2
Lincs 190 G5
N Yorks 216 F5
Langton by Wragby
Lincs 189 F11
Langton Green Kent 52 F4
Suff 126 C2
Langton Herring Dorset 17 E8
Langton Long Blandford
Dorset 30 F5
Langton Matravers
Dorset 18 F6
Langtree Devon 25 D7
Langtree Week Devon 25 D7
Langwathby Cumb 231 E7
Langwell Ho Highld 311 G5
Langwell Lodge Highld 307 J6
Langwith Derbys 171 B8
Langwith Junction
Derbys 171 B8
Langworth Lincs 189 F9
Lanham Green Essex 106 G5
Lanivet Corn 5 C10
Lanjeth Corn 5 E9
Lanjew Corn 5 C9
Lank Corn 11 F7
Lanlivery Corn 5 D11
Lanner Corn 2 B6
Lanreath Corn 6 D3
Lanrick Stirling 285 G10
Lansallos Corn 6 E3
Lansbury Park Caerph 59 B7
Lansdown Bath 61 F8
Glos 99 G8
Lanstephan Corn 12 D2
Lanteglos Corn 11 E7
Lanteglos Highway Corn 6 E3
Lanton Borders 262 E4
Northumb 263 C10
Lantuel Corn 5 B9
Lantyan Corn 6 D2
Lapal W Mid 133 G9
Lapford Devon 26 F2
Lapford Cross Devon 26 F2
Laphroaig Argyll 254 C4
Lapley Staffs 151 G7
Lapworth Warks 118 C3
Larachbeg Highld 289 E8
Larbert Falk 279 E7
Larbreck Lancs 202 E4
Larches Lancs 202 G6
Larden Green Ches E 167 E9
Larg Highld 292 B2
Largie Aberds 302 F6
Largiebaan Argyll 255 F7
Largiemore Argyll 275 E10
Largoward Fife 287 G8
Largs N Ayrs 266 D4
Largue Aberds 302 E6
Largybeg N Ayrs 256 E3
Largymeanoch N Ayrs 256 E2
Largymore N Ayrs 256 E2
Larkfield Invclyd 276 F4
Kent 53 B8
W Yorks 205 F10
Larkhall Bath 61 F9
S Lanark 268 E5
Larkhill Wilts 46 E6
Lark Hill Gtr Man 195 G7
Larklands Derbys 171 G7
Larks' Hill Suff 108 B3
Larling Norf 141 F9
Larport Hereford 97 D11
Larrick Corn 12 F2
Larriston Borders 250 E2
Lartington Durham 223 B10
Lary Aberds 292 C5
Lasborough Glos 80 G4
Lasham Hants 49 E7
Lashenden Kent 53 E10
Lask Edge Staffs 168 D6
Lassington Glos 98 G5
Lassodie Fife 280 C2
Lastingham N Yorks 226 G4
Latcham Som 44 D2
Latchbrook Corn 7 D8
Latchford Herts 105 G7
Oxon 83 E11
Warr 183 D10
Latchingdon Essex 88 E5
Latchley Corn 12 G4
Latchmere Green Hants 64 G6
Latchmore Bank Essex 87 B7
Lately Common Warr 183 B11
Lathallan Mill Fife 287 G8
Lathbury M Keynes 103 B7
Latheron Highld 310 F5
Latheronwheel Highld 310 F5
Latheronwheel Ho
Highld 310 F5
Lathom Lancs 194 E3
Lathones Fife 287 G8
Latimer Bucks 85 F8
Latteridge S Glos 61 C7
Lattiford Som 29 B11
Lattinford Hill Suff 107 D11
Latton Wilts 81 F9
Latton Bush Essex 87 D7
Lauchintilly Aberds 293 B9
Laudale Ho Highld 289 D9
Lauder Borders 271 F10
Lauder Barns Borders 271 F10
Laugharne = Talacharn
Carms 74 C4
Laughern Hill Worcs 116 F5
Laughterton Lincs 188 F4
Laughton E Sus 23 C8
Leics 136 F3
Lincs 155 C11
Lincs 188 B4
Laughton Common
S Yorks 187 D8
E Sus 23 C7
Laughton en le Morthen
S Yorks 187 D8
Launcells Corn 24 F2
Launcells Cross Corn 24 F3
Launceston Corn 12 D2
Launcherley Som 44 E4
Laund Lancs 195 C10
Launton Oxon 102 G2
Laurencekirk Aberds 293 F9
Laurieston Dumfries 237 C8
Falk 279 F8
Lavendon M Keynes 121 G8
Lavenham Suff 107 B8
Laverackloch Moray 301 C11
Laverhay Dumfries 248 D4
Laverlaw Borders 261 B7
Laverley Som 44 F5
Lavernock V Glam 59 F7
Laversdale Cumb 239 E11
Laverstock Wilts 47 G7
Laverstoke Hants 48 D3
Laverton Glos 99 D11
N Yorks 214 E4
Som 45 C9
Lavington Sands Wilts 46 B4
Lavister Wrex 166 D5
Lavrean Corn 5 D10
Lawers Perth 285 D10
Perth 285 E11
Lawford Essex 107 E11
Som 42 F6
Lawford Heath Warks 119 C9
Lawhill Perth 286 F3
Law Hill S Lanark 268 E6
Lawhitton Corn 12 E3
Lawkland N Yorks 212 F5
Lawkland Green
N Yorks 212 F5
Lawley Telford 132 B3
Lawn Swindon 63 C7
Lawnhead Staffs 150 E6
Lawns W Yorks 197 C10
Lawnswood W Yorks 205 F11
Lawnt Denb 165 B8
Lawrence Hill Newport 59 B10
Lawrence Weston
Bristol 60 D4
Lawrenny Pembs 73 D8
Lawrenny Quay Pembs 73 D8
Lawshall Suff 125 G7
Lawshall Green Suff 125 G7
Lawton Hereford 115 F8
Shrops 131 G10
Lawton-gate Ches E 168 D4
Lawton Heath End
Ches E 168 D3
Laxey IoM 192 D5
Laxfield Suff 126 C5
Laxfirth Shetland 313 H6
Shetland 313 J6
Laxford Bridge Highld 306 E7
Laxo Shetland 313 G6
Laxobigging Shetland 312 F6
Laxton E Yorks 199 B9
N Nhants 137 D8
Notts 172 B2
Laycock W Yorks 204 E6
Layer Breton Essex 88 B6
Layer de la Haye Essex 89 B7
Layer Marney Essex 88 B6
Layerthorpe York 207 C8
Layham Suff 107 C10
Laymore Dorset 28 G5
Layters Green Bucks 85 G7
Laytham E Yorks 207 F10
Layton Blackpool 202 F2
Lazenby Redcar 225 B11
Lazonby Cumb 230 D6
Lea Derbys 170 D4
Hereford 98 G3
Lancs 202 G5
Lincs 188 D4
Shrops 131 B8
Shrops 131 F7
Wilts 62 B3
Lea Bridge London 67 B11
Leabrooks Derbys 170 E6
Lea by Backford
Ches W 182 G5
Leacainn W Isles 305 H3
Leac a Li W Isles 305 J3
Leachkin Highld 300 E6
Leacnasaide Highld 299 B7
Leadburn Midloth 270 D4
Leadendale Staffs 151 B8
Leadenham Lincs 173 E7
Leaden Roding Essex 87 C9
Leadgate Cumb 231 C10
Durham 242 G4
T&W 242 F4
Leadhills S Lanark 259 G9
Leadingcross Green
Kent 53 C11
Leadmill Derbys 186 E2
Flint 166 C2
Lea End Worcs 117 B10
Leafield Oxon 82 B4
Wilts 61 F11
Lea Forge Ches E 168 F2
Leagrave Luton 103 G10
Leagreen Hants 19 C11
Lea Green Mers 183 C8
Lea Hall W Mid 134 F2
Lea Heath Staffs 151 D10
Leake Lincs 174 F6
N Yorks 225 G8
Leake Commonside
Lincs 174 E5
Leake Fold Hill Lincs 174 E6
Lealholm N Yorks 226 D5
Lealholm Side N Yorks 226 D5
Lea Line Hereford 98 G3
Lealt Argyll 275 D7
Highld 298 C5
Leam Derbys 186 F2
Lea Marston Warks 134 E4
Leamington Hastings
Warks 119 D8
Leamoor Common
Shrops 131 F8
Leamore W Mid 133 C9
Leamside Durham 234 B2
Leanach Argyll 275 D11
Leanachan Highld 290 F4
Leanaig Highld 300 D5
Leapgate Worcs 116 C6
Leargybreck Argyll 274 F6
Lease Rigg N Yorks 226 E6
Leasey Bridge Herts 85 C11
Leasgill Cumb 211 C9
Leasingham Lincs 173 F9
Leasingthorne Durham 233 F11
Leason Swansea 56 C3
Leasowe Mers 182 C3
Leatherhead Sur 51 B7
Leatherhead Common
Sur 51 B7
Leathern Bottle Glos 80 E2
Leathley N Yorks 205 D10
Leaths Dumfries 237 C9
Leaton Shrops 149 F9
Telford 150 G2
Leaton Heath Shrops 149 F9
Lea Town Lancs 202 G5
Lea Valley Herts 85 B11
Leaveland Kent 54 C4
Leavenheath Suff 107 D9
Leavening N Yorks 216 G5
Leavesden Green Herts 85 E9
Leaves Green London 68 G2
Lea Yeat Cumb 212 B5
Leazes Durham 242 F5
Lebberston N Yorks 217 C11
Leburnick Corn 12 E3
Lechlade-on-Thames
Glos 82 F2
Leck Lancs 212 D2
Leckford Hants 47 F11
Leckfurin Highld 308 D7
Leckgruinart Argyll 274 G3
Leckhampstead Bucks 102 D4
W Berks 64 D2
Leckhampstead Thicket
W Berks 64 D2
Leckhampton Glos 80 B6
Leckie Highld 299 C10
Leckmelm Highld 307 K6
Leckuary Argyll 275 D9
Leckwith V Glam 59 E7
Leconfield E Yorks 208 E6
Ledaig Argyll 289 F11
Ledburn Bucks 103 G8
Ledbury Hereford 98 D4
Ledcharrie Stirling 285 E9
Leddington Glos 98 E3
Ledgemoor Hereford 115 G8
Ledgowan Highld 299 D11
Ledicot Hereford 115 E8
Ledmore Angus 293 G7
Highld 307 H7
Lednagullin Highld 308 C7
Ledsham Ches W 182 G5
W Yorks 198 B3
Ledston W Yorks 198 B2
Ledstone Devon 8 F4
Ledston Luck W Yorks 206 G4
Ledwell Oxon 101 F8
Lee Argyll 288 G6
Devon 40 D3
Devon 40 D5
Hants 32 D5
Lancs 203 B7
London 67 E11
Northumb 241 F10
Shrops 149 C8
Leeans Shetland 313 J5
Lee Bank W Mid 133 F11
Leebotten Shetland 313 L6
Leebotwood Shrops 131 D9
Lee Brockhurst Shrops 149 D10
Leece Cumb 210 F4
Lee Chapel Essex 69 B7
Leechpool Mon 60 B4
Lee Clump Bucks 84 E6
Lee Common Bucks 84 E6
Leeds Kent 53 C10
W Yorks 205 G11
Leedstown Corn 2 C4
Leeford Devon 41 D9
Lee Gate Bucks 84 D5
Lee Ground Hants 33 F8
Lee Head Derbys 185 C8
Leeholme Durham 233 E10
Leek Staffs 169 D7
Leekbrook Staffs 169 E7
Leek Wootton Warks 118 D5
Lee Mill Devon 8 D2
Leeming N Yorks 214 B5
W Yorks 204 G6
Leeming Bar N Yorks 224 G5
Leemings Lancs 203 D10
Lee Moor Devon 7 C11
W Yorks 197 B10
Lee-on-the-Solent
Hants 33 G9

Lee-over-Sands Essex.. 89 C10
Lees Derbys 152 B5
Gtr Man............... 196 G3
W Yorks............... 204 F6
Leesthorpe Leics 154 G5
Leeswood = Coed-Llai
Flint.................. 166 D3
Leetown Perth......... 286 E6
Leftwich Ches W 183 G11
Legar Powys............ 78 B2
Legbourne Lincs 190 E5
Legburthwaite Cumb ... 220 B6
Legerwood Borders 271 G11
Leggatt Hill W Sus 34 C6
Legsby Lincs 189 D10
Leicester Leicester 135 C11
Leicester Forest East
Leics 135 C10
Leicester Grange Warks 135 E8
Leigh Devon 26 E2
Dorset 18 B6
Dorset 29 F10
Dorset 30 F3
Glos 99 F7
Gtr Man............... 195 G7
Kent 52 D4
Shrops 130 C6
Sur 51 D8
Wilts 81 G9
Worcs 116 G5
Leigham Plym 7 D10
Leigh Beck Essex 69 C10
Leigh Common Som 30 B2
Leigh Delamere Wilts... 61 D11
Leigh Green Kent 54 G2
Leighland Chapel Som... 42 F4
Leigh-on-Sea Southend. 69 B10
Leigh Park Hants 22 B2
Leigh Sinton Worcs 116 G5
Leighswood W Mid...... 133 C11
Leighterton Glos 80 G4
Leighton N Yorks 214 D3
Shrops 132 B2
Som 45 E8
Leighton = Tre'r llai
Powys 130 B4
Leighton Bromswold
Cambs................. 122 B2
Leighton Buzzard
C Beds................. 103 F8
Leigh upon Mendip Som . 45 D7
Leigh Woods N Som 60 E5
Leinthall Earls Hereford . 115 D8
Leinthall Starkes
Hereford.............. 115 D8
Leintwardine Hereford . 115 C8
Leire Leics............ 135 E10
Leirinmore Highld 308 C4
Leiston Suff 127 E8
Leitfie Perth............ 286 C6
Leith Edin 280 F5
Leithenhall Dumfries.... 248 D4
Leitholm Borders 272 G5
Lelant Corn 2 B2
Lelant Downs Corn 2 B2
Lelley E Yorks 209 G10
Lem Hill Worcs 116 C4
Lemington T&W 242 E5
Lemmington Hall
Northumb 264 G4
Lempitlaw Borders...... 263 C7
Lemsford Herts.......... 86 C2
Lenacre Cumb 212 B3
Lenborough Bucks....... 102 E3
Lenchwick Worcs........ 99 B10
Lendalfoot S Ayrs 244 F4
Lendrick Lodge Stirling . 285 G9
Lenham Kent 53 C11
Lenham Forstal Kent 54 C2
Lenham Heath Kent...... 54 D2
Lennel Borders 273 G7
Lennoxtown E Dunb 278 F2
Lent Bucks............... 66 C2
Lenten Pool Denb....... 165 B8
Lenton Lincs............ 155 C10
Nottingham............ 153 B11
Lenton Abbey
Nottingham 153 B10
Lentran Highld 300 E5
Lent Rise Bucks.......... 66 C2
Lenwade Norf 159 F11
Leny Ho Stirling 285 G10
Lenzie E Dunb 278 G3
Lenziemill N Lanark 278 G5
Leoch Angus............ 287 D7
Leochel-Cushnie
Aberds 293 B7
Leominster Hereford.... 115 F9
Leomonsley Staffs...... 134 B2
Leonard Stanley Glos.... 80 E4
Leonardston Pembs 72 D6
Leorin Argyll............ 254 C4
Lepe Hants 20 B5
Lephin Highld........... 297 G7
Lephinchapel Argyll 275 D10
Lephinmore Argyll 275 D10
Leppington N Yorks 216 G5
Lepton W Yorks 197 D8
Lepton Edge W Yorks.... 197 D8
Lerigoligan Argyll....... 275 C9
Lerrocks Stirling 285 G11
Lerryn Corn 6 D2
Lerwick Shetland........ 313 J6
Lesbury Northumb 264 G6
Leschangie Aberds 293 B9
Le Skerne Haughton
Darl 224 B6
Leslie Aberds 302 G5
Fife.................... 286 G6
Lesmahagow S Lanark.. 259 B8
Lesnewth Corn 11 C8
Lessendrum Aberds..... 302 E5
Lessingham Norf 161 D7
Lessness Heath London .. 68 D3
Lessonhall Cumb 238 G6
Leswalt Dumfries........ 236 C2
Letchmore Heath Herts. 85 F11
Letchworth Garden City
Herts.................. 104 E4
Letcombe Bassett Oxon. 63 B11
Letcombe Regis Oxon... 63 B11
Letham Angus 287 C9
Falk................... 279 D7
Fife.................... 287 F7
Perth.................. 286 E4
Letham Grange Angus . 287 C10
Lethem Borders......... 250 B5
Lethen Ho Highld 301 D9
Lethenty Aberds 303 E8
Aberds 303 G7
Letheringham Suff 126 F5
Letheringsett Norf 159 B11
Lettaford Devon 13 E10
Lettan Orkney........... 314 B7
Letter Aberds 293 B9
Letterewe Highld 299 B9
Letterfearn Highld 295 C10
Letterfinlay Highld...... 290 D4
Lettermay Argyll........ 284 G5
Lettermorar Highld 295 G9
Lettermore Argyll....... 288 E6
Letters Highld 307 L6
Letterston = Treletert
Pembs.................. 91 F8
Lettoch Highld.......... 292 B2
Highld 301 F10
Moray.................. 302 F3
Perth.................. 291 G11
Letton Hereford.......... 96 B6
Hereford.............. 115 C7
Letton Green Norf 141 B9
Lett's Green Kent........ 52 B3
Letty Brongu Bridgend .. 57 D11
Letty Green Herts 86 C3
Letwell S Yorks.......... 187 D9
Leuchars Fife........... 287 E8
Leuchars Ho Moray 302 C2
Leumrabhagh W Isles... 305 G5
Levalsa Meor Corn........ 5 F10
Levan Invclyd 276 F4
Levaneap Shetland...... 313 G6
Levedale Staffs 151 F7
Level of Mendalgief
Newport................ 59 B10
Level's Green Essex 105 G9
Leven E Yorks 209 D8
Fife.................... 287 G7
Levencorroch N Ayrs.... 256 E2
Levenhall E Loth 281 G7
Levens Cumb 211 B9
Leven Seat W Loth 269 D8
Levens Green Herts..... 105 G7
Levenshulme Gtr Man ... 184 C5
Leventhorpe W Yorks .. 205 G8
Levenwick Shetland..... 313 L6
Lever-Edge Gtr Man..... 195 F8
Leverington Cambs 157 G8
Leverington Common
Cambs................. 157 G8
Leverstock Green Herts . 85 D9
Leverton Lincs.......... 174 F6
W Berks 63 E10
Leverton Highgate Lincs 174 F6
Leverton Lucasgate
Lincs 174 F6
Leverton Outgate Lincs . 174 F6
Levington Suff.......... 108 D4
Levisham N Yorks 226 G6
Levishie Highld 290 B6
Lew Oxon................. 82 D4
Lewannick Corn 11 E11
Lewcombe Dorset 29 F9
Lewdown Devon 12 D4
Lewes E Sus 36 E6
Leweston Pembs.......... 91 G8
Lewisham London........ 67 D11
Lewiston Highld......... 300 G5
Lewistown Bridgend...... 58 B2
Lewknor Oxon............ 84 F2
Leworthy Devon 24 G4
Devon 41 F7
Lewson Street Kent....... 70 G3
Lewth Lancs 202 F5
Lewthorn Cross Devon... 13 F11
Lewtrenchard Devon 12 D5
Lexden Essex........... 107 G9
Ley Aberds.............. 293 B7
Corn 6 B3
Som 41 F10
Leybourne Kent 53 B7
Leyburn N Yorks........ 224 G2
Leycett Staffs........... 168 F3
Leyfields Staffs......... 134 B4
Ley Green Herts 104 G3
Ley Hey Park Gtr Man.... 185 D7
Leyhill Bucks 85 E7
S Glos 79 G11
Ley Hill W Mid.......... 134 D2
Leyland Lancs 194 C4
Leylodge Aberds 293 B9
Leymoor W Yorks 196 D6
Leys Aberds............. 292 C6
Aberds 303 D10
Cumb 219 B11
Perth.................. 286 D6
Staffs 169 F8
Leys Castle Highld 300 E6
Leysdown-on-Sea Kent.. 70 E4
Leys Hill Hereford 79 B9
Leysmill Angus.......... 287 C10
Leys of Cossans Angus . 287 C7
Leysters Hereford...... 115 E11
Leysters Pole Hereford. 115 E11
Leyton London 67 B11
Leytonstone London 67 B11
Lezant Corn 12 F2
Lezerea Corn 2 C5
Leziate Norf 158 F3
Lhanbryde Moray 302 C2
Liatrie Highld 300 F2
Libanus Powys........... 95 F9
Libberton S Lanark..... 269 G9
Libbery Worcs 117 F9
Liberton Edin 270 B5
Liceasto W Isles 305 J3
Lichfield Staffs 134 B2
Lick Perth 286 B2
Lickey Worcs 117 B9
Lickey End Worcs 117 C9
Lickfold W Sus........... 34 B6
Lickhill Worcs 116 C6
Lickleyhead Castle
Aberds 302 G6
Liddaton Devon.......... 12 E5
Liddel Orkney........... 314 H4
Liddesdale Highld....... 289 D9
Liddeston Pembs 72 D5
Liddington Swindon...... 63 C8
Liden Swindon 63 C7
Lidgate Suff 124 F4
Lidget S Yorks.......... 199 G7
Lidget Green W Yorks .. 205 G8
Lidgett Notts 171 B10
Lidgett Park W Yorks ... 206 F2
Lidham Hill E Sus 38 D4
Lidlington C Beds 103 D9
Lidsey W Sus............. 22 C6
Lidsing Kent............. 69 G9
Lidstone Oxon 101 G7
Lieurary Highld 310 C4
Liff Angus 287 D7
Lifford W Mid........... 117 B11
Lifton Devon............. 12 D3
Liftondown Devon 12 D3
Lightcliffe W Yorks...... 196 B6
Lighteach Shrops 149 C10
Lightfoot Green Lancs.. 202 G6
Lighthorne Warks 118 F6
Lighthorne Heath Warks 119 F7
Lighthorne Rough
Warks 118 F6
Lightmoor Telford....... 132 B3
Light Oaks Staffs 168 E6
Lightpill Glos............ 80 E4
Lightwater Sur 66 G2
Lightwood Shrops 132 E2
Shrops 150 D3
Staffs 169 G8
Stoke 168 G6
S Yorks 186 E5
Lightwood Green
Ches E................ 167 G10
Wrex.................. 166 G5
Liglartrie S Ayrs 244 F6
Lilbourne W Nhants 119 B11
Lilburn Tower Northumb. 264 E2
Lilford Gtr Man......... 195 G7
Lillesdon Som 28 C4
Lilleshall Telford........ 150 F4
Lilley Herts 104 F2
W Berks 64 D2
Lilliesleaf Borders 262 E2
Lillingstone Dayrell
Bucks 102 D4
Lillingstone Lovell
Bucks 102 C4
Lillington Dorset......... 29 E10
Warks.................. 118 D6
Lilliput BCP.............. 18 C6
Lilstock Som 43 E7
Lilybank Invclyd 276 G6
Lilyhurst Shrops 150 G4
Lilyvale Kent............. 54 F5
Limbrick Lancs 194 D6
Limbury Luton 103 G11
Limebrook Hereford 115 D7
Limefield Gtr Man...... 195 E10
Limehouse London....... 67 C11
Limehurst Gtr Man 196 G2
Limekilnburn S Lanark . 268 E4
Limekiln Field Derbys... 187 G7
Limekilns Fife 279 E11
Limerigg Falk........... 279 G7
Limerstone IoW 20 E4
Lime Side Gtr Man...... 196 G2
Limestone Brae
Northumb 231 B11
Lime Street Worcs 98 E6
Lime Tree Park W Mid... 118 B5
Limington Som 29 C8
Limpenhoe Norf........ 143 C7
Limpenhoe Hill Norf.... 143 C8
Limpers Hill Wilts 45 G10
Limpley Stoke Wilts 61 G9
Limpsfield Sur 52 C2
Limpsfield Chart Sur 52 C2
Limpsfield Common Sur . 52 C2
Linbriggs Northumb 251 B9
Linburn W Loth.......... 270 B2
Linby Notts 171 E8
Linchmere W Sus 49 G11
Lincluden Dumfries 237 B11
Lincoln Lincs 189 G7
Lincomb Worcs 116 D6
Lincombe Devon........... 8 D4
Devon 40 D3
Lindale Cumb 211 C8
Lindal in Furness Cumb . 210 D5
Lindean Borders 261 C11
Linden Glos 80 B4
Lindfield W Sus 36 B4
Lindford Hants 49 F10
Lindifferon Fife 287 F7
Lindley N Yorks 205 D10
W Yorks................ 196 D6
Lindley Green N Yorks . 205 D10
Lindores Fife 286 F6
Lindow End Ches E...... 184 F4
Lindridge Worcs 116 D3
Lindsell Essex 106 F2
Lindsey Suff 107 C9
Lindsey Tye Suff 107 B9
Lindwell W Yorks 196 C5
Lineholt Worcs 116 D6
Lineholt Common
Worcs 116 D6
Liney Som................ 43 F11
Linfitts Gtr Man 196 F3
Linford Hants............ 31 F11
Thurrock 69 D7
Lingague IoM 192 E3
Lingards Wood W Yorks . 196 E5
Lingbob W Yorks 205 F7
Lingdale Redcar 226 B3
Lingen Hereford......... 115 D7
Lingfield Darl 224 C6
Sur 51 E11
Lingfield Common Sur .. 51 E11
Lingley Green Warr..... 183 D9
Lingley Mere Warr..... 183 D10
Lingreabhagh W Isles... 296 C6
Lingwood Norf.......... 143 B7
Linhope Borders 249 C10
Northumb 263 F11
Linicro Highld........... 298 C3
Link N Som............... 44 B3
Linkend Worcs........... 98 E6
Linkenholt Hants 47 B11
Linkhill Kent............. 38 B4
Linkinhorne Corn........ 12 G2
Linklater Orkney 314 H4
Linklet Orkney 314 A7
Linksness Orkney 314 E5
Orkney 314 F2
Linktown Fife 280 C5
Linley Shrops 131 E7
Shrops 132 D3
Linley Brook Shrops.... 132 D3
Linleygreen Shrops 132 D3
Linley Green Hereford... 116 G3
Linlithgow W Loth...... 279 F10
Linlithgow Bridge
W Loth 279 F9
Linndhu Ho Argyll...... 289 D7
Linneraineach Highld ... 307 J6
Linns Angus 292 F3
Linnyshaw Gtr Man..... 195 G8
Linshiels Northumb..... 251 B9
Linsiadar W Isles 304 E4
Linsidemore Highld 309 K5
Linslade C Beds 103 F8
Linstead Parva Suff.... 126 B6
Linstock Cumb......... 239 F10
Linthorpe Mbro......... 225 B9
Linthurst Worcs 117 C9
Linthwaite W Yorks..... 196 E6
Lintlaw Borders 272 D6
Lintmill Moray 302 C5
Linton Borders.......... 263 D7
Cambs 105 B11
Derbys 152 F5
Hereford................ 98 F3
Kent 53 D9
Northumb 253 E7
N Yorks 213 G9
W Yorks................ 206 D3
Linton Heath Derbys 152 F5
Linton Hill Hereford 98 G3
Linton-on-Ouse
N Yorks 215 G9
Lintridge Glos........... 98 E4
Lintz Durham 242 F5
Lintzford T&W.......... 242 F4
Lintzgarth Durham...... 232 C4
Linwood Hants 31 F11
Lincs.................. 189 D10
Renfs 267 C8
Lionacleit W Isles...... 297 G3
Lional W Isles.......... 304 B7
Lions Green E Sus....... 23 B9
Liphook Hants 49 G10
Lipley Shrops 150 C4
Lippitts Hill Essex 86 F5
Liquo or Bowhousebog
N Lanark 269 D7
Liscard Mers 182 C4
Liscombe Som........... 41 G11
Liskeard Corn 6 C5
Liss Hants 34 B3
Lissett E Yorks 209 B8
Liss Forest Hants 34 B3
Lissington Lincs 189 E10
Lisson Grove London..... 67 C9
Listerdale S Yorks 187 C7
Listock Som 28 C4
Listoft Lincs 191 G8
Liston Essex 107 C7
Liston Garden Essex.... 106 B6
Lisvane Cardiff........... 59 C7
Liswerry Newport........ 59 B10
Litcham Norf 159 F7
Litchard Bridgend........ 58 C2
Litchborough W Nhants . 120 G2
Litchfield Hants 48 C3
Litchurch Derbys 153 B7
Litherland Mers 182 B4
Litlington Cambs 104 C6
E Sus 23 E8
Litmarsh Hereford 97 B10
Little Abington Cambs . 105 B10
Little Addington
N Nhants 121 C9
Little Airmyn E Yorks .. 199 B8
Little Almshoe Herts.... 104 F3
Little Alne Warks 118 E2
Little Altcar Mers...... 193 F10
Little Ann Hants 47 E10
Little Arowry Wrex 167 G7
Little Asby Cumb....... 222 D3
Little Ashley Wilts 61 G10
Little Assynt Highld ... 307 G6
Little Aston Staffs 133 C11
Little Atherfield IoW 20 E5
Little Ayre Orkney..... 314 G3
Little-ayre Shetland.... 313 G5
Little Ayton N Yorks 225 C11
Little Baddow Essex 88 D3
Little Badminton S Glos . 61 C10
Little Ballinluig Perth... 286 B3
Little Bampton Cumb ... 239 F7
Little Bardfield Essex... 106 E3
Little Barford Bedford... 122 F3
Little Barningham Norf . 160 C2
Little Barrington Glos ... 82 C2
Little Barrow Ches W.... 183 G7
Little Barugh N Yorks... 216 D5
Little Bavington
Northumb 241 B11
Little Bayham E Sus 52 F6
Little Bealings Suff..... 108 B4
Littlebeck N Yorks...... 227 D7
Little Beckford Glos 99 E9
Little Bedwyn Wilts...... 63 F9
Little Bentley Essex..... 108 F2
Little Berkhamsted Herts 86 D3
Little Billing W Nhants.. 120 E6
Little Billington C Beds.. 103 G8
Little Birch Hereford 97 E10
Little Bispham Blackpool 202 E2
Little Blakenham Suff .. 108 B2
Little Blencow Cumb.... 230 E5
Little Bloxwich W Mid.. 133 C10
Little Bognor W Sus...... 35 C8
Little Bolehill Derbys ... 170 E3
Little Bollington Ches E . 184 D2
Little Bolton Gtr Man.... 184 B3
Little Bookham Sur 50 C6
Littleborough Devon...... 26 E4
Gtr Man................ 196 D2
Notts................... 188 E4
Little Bosullow Corn 1 C4
Littlebourne Kent 55 B8
Little Bourton Oxon..... 101 C9
Little Bowden Leics..... 136 F4
Little Boys Heath Bucks.. 84 F6
Little Bradley Suff 124 G3
Little Braithwaite
Cumb................. 229 G10
Little Brampton Shrops . 131 G7
Little Braxted Essex 88 C4
Little Bray Devon 41 F7
Little Brechin Angus 293 G7
Littlebredy Dorset 17 D7
Little Brickhill
M Keynes............... 103 E8
Little Bridgeford Staffs . 151 D7
Little Brington
W Nhants 120 E3
Little Bristol S Glos 80 G2
Little Britain Warks..... 118 G2
Little Bromley Essex.... 107 F11
Little Bromwich W Mid . 134 F2
Little Broughton Cumb.. 229 E7
Little Budworth Ches W . 167 B9
Little Burstead Essex ... 87 G11
Littlebury Essex 105 D10
Littlebury Green Essex . 105 D9
Little Bytham Lincs 155 F10
Little Cambridge Essex . 106 F2
Little Canfield Essex.... 105 G11
Little Canford BCP....... 18 B6
Little Carleton Lancs.... 202 F2
Little Carlton Lincs 190 D5
Notts................... 172 D3
Little Casterton
Rutland 137 B10
Little Catwick E Yorks .. 209 E8
Little Catworth Cambs . 122 C2
Little Cawthorpe Lincs.. 190 E5
Little Chalfield Wilts.... 61 G11
Little Chalfont Bucks..... 85 F7
Little Chart Kent......... 54 D2
Little Chart Forstal Kent. 54 D3
Little Chell Stoke 168 E5
Little Chester Derby 153 B7
Little Chesterford
Essex 105 C10
Little Chesterton Oxon. 101 G11
Little Cheverell Wilts ... 46 C3
Little Chishill Cambs ... 105 D8
Little Clacton Essex 89 B11
Little Clanfield Oxon..... 82 E3
Little Clegg Gtr Man.... 196 E2
Little Clifton Cumb...... 229 F7
Little Coates NE Lincs .. 201 F8
Little Colp Aberds 303 E7
Little Comberton Worcs . 99 C9
Little Comfort Corn...... 12 E2
Little Common E Sus..... 38 F2
Lincs 156 D6
Shrops 115 B7
W Sus 34 C6
Little Compton Warks .. 100 E5
Little Corby Cumb...... 239 F11
Little Cornard Suff 107 D7
Littlecote Bucks 102 G6
Littlecott Wilts 46 C6
Little Cowarne Hereford. 116 G2
Little Coxwell Oxon...... 82 G3
Little Crakehall N Yorks . 224 G4
Little Cransley N Nhants. 120 B6
Little Crawley M Keynes . 103 B8
Little Creaton W Nhants . 120 C4
Little Creich Highld 309 L6
Little Cressingham Norf 141 D7
Little Crosby Mers 193 G10
Little Cubley Derbys 152 B3
Little Dalby Leics 154 G5
Little Dawley Telford 132 B3
Littledean Glos.......... 79 C11
Littledean Hill Glos 79 C11
Little Dens Aberds 303 E10
Little Dewchurch
Hereford................ 97 E10
Little Ditton Cambs 124 F3
Little Doward Hereford... 79 B8
Littledown BCP........... 19 C8
Hants 47 B10
Little Downham Cambs 139 G10
Little Drayton Shrops ... 150 C3
Little Driffield E Yorks.. 208 B6
Little Drybrook Glos..... 79 D9
Little Dunham Norf..... 159 G7
Little Dunkeld Perth.... 286 C4
Little Dunmow Essex ... 106 G3
Little Durnford Wilts 46 G6
Little Eastbury Worcs... 116 F6
Little Easton Essex 106 G2
Little Eaton Derbys 170 G5
Little Eccleston Lancs .. 202 E4
Little Ellingham Norf .. 141 D10
Little End Cambs........ 122 F3
Essex 87 E8
E Yorks 208 F2
Little Everdon
W Nhants 119 F11
Little Eversden Cambs .. 123 G7
Little Faringdon Oxon.... 82 E2
Little Fencote N Yorks... 224 G5
Little Fenton N Yorks... 206 F6
Littleferry Highld 311 K2
Littlefield NE Lincs 201 F9
Littlefield Common Sur.. 50 C3
Littlefield Green
Windsor 65 D11
Little Finborough Suff. 125 G10
Little Fransham Norf ... 159 G8
Little Frith Kent.......... 54 B2
Little Gaddesden Herts.. 85 C7
Littlegain Shrops 132 D5
Little Gidding Cambs.... 138 G2
Little Gight Aberds...... 303 F8
Little Glemham Suff 126 F6
Little Glenshee Perth ... 286 D3
Little Gorsley Glos....... 98 F3
Little Gransden Cambs.. 122 F5
Little Green Cambs 104 B5
Notts................... 172 G2
Som 45 D8
Suff.................... 125 C11
Wrex................... 167 G7
Little Grimsby Lincs.... 190 C4
Little Gringley Notts.... 188 E2
Little Gruinard Highld.. 307 L4
Little Habton N Yorks... 216 D4
Little Hadham Herts 105 G8
Little Hale Lincs 173 G10
Norf 141 B8
Little Hallam Derbys ... 171 G7
Little Hallingbury Essex . 87 B7
Littleham Devon.......... 14 E6
Devon 24 C6
Little Hampden Bucks ... 84 E5
Littlehampton W Sus 35 G8
Little Harrowden Glos 80 D4
Little Harrowden
N Nhants 121 C7
Little Harwood
Blackburn 195 B7
Little Haseley Oxon 83 E10
Little Hatfield E Yorks .. 209 E9
Little Hautbois Norf 160 E5
Little Haven Pembs 72 C5
W Sus 51 G7
Little Hay Staffs 134 C2
Little Hayfield Derbys... 185 D8
Little Haywood Staffs.. 151 E10
Little Heath Ches E..... 167 G11
Ches W 166 B6
Herts 85 D8
Herts 86 E3
London 68 B3
Staffs 151 F8
Sur 66 G6
W Berks 65 E7
W Mid 134 G6
Little Heck N Yorks..... 198 C5
Littlehempston Devon..... 8 C6
Little Henham Essex.. 105 E10
Little Henny Essex...... 107 D7
Little Herbert's Glos..... 81 B7
Little Hereford
Hereford............. 115 D11
Little Hill Hereford 97 F9
Som 28 E3
Little Holbury Hants 32 G6
Little Honeyborough
Pembs................... 73 D7
Little Hoole Moss Houses
Lancs.................. 194 C3
Little Horkesley Essex .. 107 E9
Little Hormead Herts ... 105 F8
Little Horsted E Sus...... 23 B7
Little Horton Wilts...... 62 G4
W Yorks............... 205 G9
Little Horwood Bucks... 102 E5
Littlehoughton
Northumb 264 F6
Little Houghton
S Yorks 198 G2
W Nhants 120 F6
Little Hucklow Derbys . 185 F11
Little Hulton Gtr Man... 195 G8
Little Humber E Yorks... 201 C8
Little Hungerford
W Berks 64 E4
Little Ilford London....... 68 B2
Little Ingestre Staffs.... 151 E9
Little Inkberrow Worcs 117 F10
Little Irchester
N Nhants 121 D8
Little Keyford Som....... 45 D9
Little Kimble Bucks 84 D4
Little Kineton Warks..... 118 G6
Little Kingshill Bucks ... 84 F5
Little Knowles Green
Suff 124 F5
Little Langdale Cumb ... 220 E6
Little Langford Wilts..... 46 F4
Little Laver Essex........ 87 D8
Little Layton Blackpool . 202 F2
Little Leigh Ches W ... 183 F10
Little Leighs Essex........ 88 B2
Little Lepton W Yorks ... 197 E8
Little Leven E Yorks 209 D8
Little Lever Gtr Man 195 F9
Little Limber Lincs...... 200 E6
Little Linford M Keynes . 102 C6
Little Load Som........... 29 C7
Little London Bucks 83 C10
Bucks 84 D5
Little London continued
Cambs 139 D8
Essex 105 F9
Essex 106 D3
E Sus 23 B9
Glos 80 B2
Hants 47 D11
Hants 48 B6
Lincs 156 E4
Lincs 157 E8
Lincs 189 D10
Lincs 190 F4
Norf 140 D5
Norf 160 C2
Norf 160 C5
Norf 160 E3
Oxon.................... 83 E8
Powys.................. 129 F10
Shrops 131 F10
Som 44 D6
Suff.................... 125 F10
Worcs 116 C2
W Yorks 205 F10
Little Longstone
Derbys 185 G11
Little Lyntuck Aberds.... 293 B7
Little Lyth Shrops 131 B9
Little Madeley Staffs.... 168 F3
Little Malvern Worcs..... 98 C5
Little Mancot Flint...... 166 B4
Little Maplestead Essex 106 E6
Little Marcle Hereford.... 98 D3
Little Marlow Bucks..... 65 B11
Little Marsden Lancs ... 204 F3
Little Marsh Bucks...... 102 G3
Norf 159 B10
Wilts.................... 45 B11
Little Marton Blackpool.. 202 G2
Little Mascalls Essex 88 E2
Little Massingham Norf. 158 E5
Little Melton Norf 142 B3
Little Merthyr Hereford .. 96 B5
Little Milford Pembs 73 C7
Littlemill Aberds........ 292 D5
E Ayrs 257 F11
Highld 301 D9
Northumb 264 F6
Little Mill Kent........... 53 D7
Mon 78 E4
Little Milton Newport ... 59 B11
Oxon.................... 83 E10
Little Minster Oxon 82 C4
Little Missenden Bucks .. 84 F6
Little Mongeham Kent.. 55 C10
Littlemoor Derbys 170 C5
Dorset 17 E9
Little Moor Gtr Man 184 D6
Lancs.................. 203 E10
Little Moor End Lancs... 195 B8
Littlemore Oxon 83 E8
Little Morrell Warks 118 F6
Littlemoss Gtr Man..... 184 B6
Little Mountain Flint.... 166 C3
Little Musgrave Cumb.. 222 C5
Little Ness Shrops....... 149 F8
Little Neston Ches W ... 182 F3
Little Newcastle Pembs .. 91 F9
Little Newsham Durham. 224 B2
Little Norlington E Sus.... 23 C7
Little Norton Som 29 D7
Little Oakley Essex 108 F4
N Nhants 137 F7
Little Odell Bedford 121 F9
Little Offley Herts 104 F2
Little Onn Staffs 150 F6
Little Ormside Cumb.... 222 B4
Little Orton Cumb....... 239 F9
Leics 134 B6
Little Ouse Norf 140 F2
Little Ouseburn N Yorks . 215 G8
Littleover Derby 152 C6
Little Overton Wrex.... 166 G5
Little Oxney Green
Essex 87 D11
Little Packington Warks 134 G4
Little Parndon Essex..... 86 C6
Little Paxton Cambs 122 E3
Little Petherick Corn 10 G4
Little Pitlurg Moray..... 302 E4
Little Plumpton Lancs... 202 G3
Little Plumstead Norf.. 160 G6
Little Ponton Lincs..... 155 C8
Littleport Cambs....... 139 F11
Little Posbrook Hants ... 33 G8
Little Poulton Lancs 202 F3
Little Preston Kent 53 B8
W Yorks............... 206 G3
Littler Ches W.......... 167 B10
Little Raveley Cambs.... 122 B5
Little Reedness
E Yorks 199 C10
Little Reynoldston
Swansea................. 56 D3
Little Ribston N Yorks .. 206 C3
Little Rissington Glos.. 81 B11
Little Rogart Highld 309 J7
Little Rollright Oxon 100 E5
Little Ryburgh Norf..... 159 D9
Little Ryle Northumb 264 G2
Little Ryton Shrops 131 C9
Little Salisbury Wilts.... 63 G7
Little Salkeld Cumb.... 231 D7
Little Sampford Essex .. 106 E3
Little Sandhurst Brack.. 65 G10
Little Saredon Staffs.... 133 B8
Little Saxham Suff 124 E5
Little Scatwell Highld .. 300 D3
Little Scotland Gtr Man.. 194 E6
Little Sessay N Yorks 215 E9
Little Shelford Cambs... 123 G9
Little Shoddesden Hants. 47 D9
Little Shrewley Warks .. 118 D4
Little Shurdington Glos.. 80 B6
Little Silver Devon 26 F6
Devon 40 E4
Little Singleton Lancs... 202 F3
Little Skillymarno
Aberds 303 D9
Little Skipwith N Yorks .. 207 F9
Little Smeaton N Yorks . 198 D4
N Yorks 224 E6
Little Snoring Norf 159 C9
Little Sodbury S Glos.... 61 C9
Little Sodbury End
S Glos 61 C8
Little Somborne Hants.. 47 G11
Little Somerford Wilts... 62 C3
Little Soudley Shrops ... 150 D4
Little Stainforth
N Yorks 212 F6
Little Stainton Darl 234 G2
Little Stanmore London . 85 G11
Little Stanney Ches W... 182 G6
Little Staughton Bedford 122 E2
Littlestead Green Oxon.. 65 D8
Little Steeping Lincs.... 174 C6
Little Stoke S Glos 60 C6
Staffs 151 C8
Littlestone-on-Sea Kent. 39 C9
Little Stonham Suff..... 126 E2
Little Stretton Leics 136 C3
Little Stretton continued
Shrops 131 E8
Little Strickland Cumb . 221 B11
Little Studley N Yorks .. 214 E6
Little Stukeley Cambs... 122 B4
Little Sugnall Staffs.... 150 C6
Little Sutton Ches W 182 F5
Lincs 157 E9
Shrops 131 G10
Little Swinburne
Northumb 241 B10
Little Tarrington Hereford 98 C2
Little Tew Oxon 101 F7
Little Tey Essex 107 G7
Little Thetford Cambs.. 123 B10
Little Thirkleby N Yorks . 215 D9
Little Thornage Norf... 159 B11
Little Thornton Lancs... 202 E3
Littlethorpe Leics 135 D10
N Yorks 214 F6
Little Thorpe Durham .. 234 C4
W Yorks................ 197 C7
Little Thurlow Suff 124 G3
Little Thurlow Green
Suff 124 G3
Little Thurrock Thurrock . 68 D6
Littleton Bath 60 G5
Ches W 166 B6
Dorset 30 G5
Hants 48 G3
Perth.................. 286 D6
Som 44 G3
Sur 50 D3
Sur 66 F5
Wilts.................... 62 G2
Littleton Common Sur... 66 E5
Littleton Drew Wilts 61 C10
Littleton-on-Severn
S Glos 60 B5
Littleton Panell Wilts.... 46 C4
Littleton-upon-Severn
S Glos 79 G9
Little Torboll Highld.... 309 K7
Little Torrington Devon .. 25 D7
Little Totham Essex..... 88 C5
Little Toux Aberds 302 D5
Littletown Durham...... 234 C2
IoW 20 C6
W Yorks................ 197 C8
Little Town Cumb 220 B4
Lancs.................. 203 F9
Warr.................. 183 C10
Little Tring Herts 84 C6
Little Twycross Leics ... 134 B6
Little Urswick Cumb 210 E5
Little Vantage W Loth ... 270 C2
Little Wakering Essex ... 70 B2
Little Walden Essex.... 105 C10
Little Waldingfield Suff. 107 B8
Little Walsingham Norf. 159 B8
Little Waltham Essex ... 88 C2
Little Walton Warks.... 135 G9
Little Warley Essex 87 G10
Little Warton Warks 134 C5
Little Washbourne Glos.. 99 E9
Little Weighton E Yorks . 208 G5
Little Weldon N Nhants.. 137 F8
Little Welland Worcs..... 98 D6
Little Welnetham Suff... 125 E7
Little Welton Lincs..... 190 D4
Little Wenham Suff 107 D11
Little Wenlock Telford .. 132 B2
Little Weston Som 29 B10
Little Whitehouse IoW .. 20 C5
Little Whittingham Green
Suff 126 B5
Littlewick Green
Windsor 65 D10
Little Wigborough Essex. 89 B7
Little Wilbraham
Cambs................. 123 F10
Littlewindsor Dorset...... 28 G6
Little Wisbeach Lincs... 156 C2
Little Wishford Wilts 46 F5
Little Witcombe Glos 80 B6
Little Witley Worcs 116 E5
Little Wittenham Oxon... 83 G9
Little Wolford Warks... 100 D5
Littlewood Staffs 133 B9
Little Wood Corner Bucks 84 E6
Little Woodcote London.. 67 G9
Littlewood Green
Warks.................. 117 E11
Little Woolgarston
Dorset................... 18 E5
Littleworth Bedford.... 103 C11
Glos 80 E4
Glos 100 D2
Oxon.................... 82 F4
Oxon.................... 83 D9
Oxon.................... 83 G10
Staffs 151 E8
Staffs 151 G10
Staffs 187 B10
Warks.................. 118 E4
Wilts.................... 63 G7
Worcs 117 E9
Worcs 117 G7
W Sus 35 C11
Littleworth Common
Bucks 66 B2
Little Worthen Shrops .. 130 B6
Littleworth End Warks.. 134 D3
Little Wratting Suff..... 106 B3
Little Wymington
Bedford................. 121 D9
Little Wymondley Herts. 104 F4
Little Wyrley Staffs 133 B10
Little Wytheford
Shrops 149 F11
Little Yeldham Essex ... 106 D5
Littley Green Essex 87 B11
Litton Derbys 185 F11
N Yorks 213 E8
Som 44 C5
Litton Cheney Dorset 17 C7
Litton Mill Derbys..... 185 G11
Liurbost W Isles 304 F5
Livermead Torbay......... 9 C8
Liverpool Mers 182 C4
Liverpool Airport Mers . 182 E6
Liversedge W Yorks 197 C8
Liverton Devon 14 F2
Redcar 226 B4
Liverton Mines Redcar.. 226 B4
Liverton Street Kent..... 53 C11
Livesey Street Kent 53 C8
Livingshayes Devon...... 27 G7
Livingston W Loth 269 B11
Livingston Village
W Loth 269 B10
Lix Toll Stirling 285 D9
Lixwm Flint 181 G11
Lizard Corn 2 G6
Llaingoch Anglesey 178 E2
Llaithddu Powys 129 G11
Llampha V Glam.......... 58 D2
Llan Powys 129 C7
Llanaber Gwyn 146 F2
Llanaelhaearn Gwyn.... 162 G5
Llanafan Ceredig 112 C3
Llanafan-fawr Powys... 113 F9
Llanallgo Anglesey...... 179 D7
Llananno Powys 113 C11
Llanarmon Gwyn 145 B8
Llanarmon Dyffryn Ceiriog
Wrex.................. 148 C3
Llanarmon Mynydd-mawr
Powys 148 D2
Llanarmon-yn-Ial
Denb 165 D11
Llanarth Ceredig........ 111 F8
Mon 78 C5
Llanarthne Carms 93 G10
Llanasa Flint........... 181 E10
Llanbabo Anglesey 178 D5
Llanbad Rhondda......... 58 C3
Llanbadarn Fawr
Ceredig................ 128 G2
Llanbadarn Fynydd
Powys 114 B2
Llanbadarn-y-Garreg
Powys 96 B2
Llanbadoc Mon........... 78 E5
Llanbadrig Anglesey ... 178 C5
Llanbeder Newport 78 G5
Llanbedr Gwyn 145 D11
Powys 96 B2
Powys 96 G4
Llanbedr-Dyffryn-Clwyd
Denb 165 D10
Llanbedrgoch Anglesey . 179 E8
Llanbedrog Gwyn....... 144 C6
Llanbedr Pont Steffan
= Lampeter Ceredig...... 93 B11
Llanbedr-y-cennin
Conwy................. 164 B3
Llanberis Gwyn 163 C9
Llanbethery V Glam....... 58 F4
Llanbister Powys 114 C2
Llanblethian = Llanfleiddan
V Glam................... 58 E3
Llanboidy Carms......... 92 G4
Llanbradach Caerph 77 G10
Llanbrynmair Powys.... 129 C7
Llancadle = Llancatal
V Glam................... 58 F4
Llancaiach Caerph 77 F10
Llancarfan V Glam 58 E5
Llancatal = Llancadle
V Glam................... 58 F4
Llancayo Mon 78 E5
Llancloudy Hereford 97 G9
Llancowrid Powys 130 E3
Llancynfelyn Ceredig ... 128 E2
Llan-dafal Bl Gwent 77 E11
Llandaff Cardiff.......... 59 D7
Llandaff North Cardiff ... 59 D7
Llandanwg Gwyn 145 D11
Llandarcy Neath.......... 57 B8
Llandawke Carms........ 74 C3
Llanddaniel Fab
Anglesey............... 179 G7
Llanddarog Carms........ 75 B8
Llanddeiniol Ceredig... 111 C11
Llanddeiniolen Gwyn ... 163 B8
Llandderfel Gwyn....... 147 B9
Llanddeusant Anglesey . 178 D4
Carms 94 G5
Llanddew Powys......... 95 E11
Llanddewi Swansea 56 D3
Llanddewi-Brefi Ceredig 112 F3
Llanddewi Fach Mon.... 78 F4
Llanddewi'r Cwm Powys 95 B10
Llanddewi Rhydderch
Mon..................... 78 C5
Llanddewi Skirrid Mon .. 78 B4
Llanddewi Velfrey
Pembs................... 73 B10
Llanddewi Ystradenni
Powys 114 D2
Llanddoged Conwy 164 C4
Llanddona Anglesey..... 179 F9
Llanddowror Carms....... 74 C3
Llanddulas Conwy 180 F6
Llanddwywe Gwyn...... 145 E11
Llanddyfynan Anglesey.. 179 F8
Llandecwyn Gwyn 146 B2
Llandefaelog Powys 95 E10
Llandefaelog Fach
Powys 95 E10
Llandefaelog-tre'r-graig
Powys 96 F2
Llandefalle Powys 96 D2
Llandegai Gwyn 179 G9
Llandegfan Anglesey ... 179 G9
Llandegla Denb......... 165 E11
Llandegley Powys 114 E2
Llandegveth Mon......... 78 F4
Llandegwning Gwyn.... 144 C5
Llandeilo Carms 94 G2
Llandeilo Graban Powys 95 C11
Llandeilo'r Fan Powys ... 95 E7
Llandeloy Pembs......... 91 F7
Llandenny Mon........... 78 E6
Llandenny Walks Mon 78 E5
Llandevaud Newport...... 78 G6
Llandevenny Mon......... 60 B2
Llandewi Ystradenny
Powys 114 D2
Llandilo Pembs 92 F2
Llandilo-yr-ynys Carms. 93 G9
Llandinabo Hereford 97 F10
Llandinam Powys....... 129 F10
Llandissilio Pembs....... 92 G2
Llandogo Mon............ 79 E8
Llandough V Glam........ 58 E3
V Glam 59 E7
Llandovery = Llanymddyfri
Carms 94 E5
Llandow = Llandw
V Glam................... 58 E2
Llandre Carms 94 C3
Ceredig................ 128 F2
Llandrillo Denb 147 B10
Llandrillo-yn-Rhôs
Conwy................. 180 E4
Llandrindod Wells
Powys 113 E11
Llandrinio Powys 148 F5
Llandruidion Pembs 90 G5
Llandudno Conwy...... 180 E3
Llandudno Junction
= Cyffordd Llandudno
Conwy.................. 180 F3
Llandudoch = St Dogmaels
Pembs................... 92 B3
Llandw = Llandow
V Glam................... 58 E2
Llandwrog Gwyn 163 D7
Llandybie Carms......... 75 B10
Llandyfaelog Carms 74 C6
Llandyfan Carms......... 75 B10
Llandyfriog Ceredig...... 92 C6
Llandyfrydog Anglesey . 178 D6
Llandygwydd Ceredig 92 C4
Llandynan Denb 165 F11
Llandyrnog Denb 165 B10
Llandysilio Powys....... 148 F5
Llandyssil Powys 130 D3
Llandysul Ceredig........ 93 C8
Llanedeyrn Cardiff....... 59 C8

Llanedi Carms 75 D9
Llanedwen Anglesey 163 B8
Llaneglwys Powys 95 D11
Llanegryn Gwyn 110 B2
Llanegwad Carms 93 G10
Llaneilian Anglesey 179 C7
Llanelian yn-Rhôs Conwy 180 F5
Llanelidan Denb 165 E10
Llanelieu Powys 96 E3
Llanellen Mon 78 C4
Llanelli Carms 56 B4
Llanelltyd Gwyn 146 F4
Llanelly Mon 78 C2
Llanelly Hill Mon 78 C2
Llanelwedd Powys 113 G10
Llanelwy = St Asaph Denb 181 G8
Llanenddwyn Gwyn 145 E11
Llanengan Gwyn 144 D5
Llanerch Powys 130 E6
Llanerch Emrys Powys 148 E4
Llanerchymedd Anglesey 178 E6
Llanerfyl Powys 129 B10
Llaneuddog Anglesey 179 D7
Llan eurgain = Northop Flint 166 B2
Llanfabon Caerph 77 G10
Llanfachraeth Anglesey 178 E4
Llanfachreth Gwyn 146 E5
Llanfaelog Anglesey 178 G4
Llanfaelrhys Gwyn 144 D4
Llanfaenor Mon 78 B6
Llanfaes Anglesey 179 F10
Powys 95 F10
Llanfaethlu Anglesey 178 D4
Llanfaglan Gwyn 163 C7
Llanfair Gwyn 145 D11
Llanfair Caereinion Powys 130 B2
Llanfair Clydogau Ceredig 112 G2
Llanfair-Dyffryn-Clwyd Denb 165 D10
Llanfairfechan Conwy 179 F11
Llanfair Kilgeddin Mon 78 D4
Llanfair Kilgheddin Mon 78 D4
Llanfair-Nant-Gwyn Pembs 92 D3
Llanfairpwll-gwyngyll Anglesey 179 G8
Llanfair Talhaiarn Conwy 180 G6
Llanfair Waterdine Shrops 114 B4
Llanfairyneubwll Anglesey 178 F3
Llanfairynghornwy Anglesey 178 C4
Llanfallteg Carms 73 B11
Llanfallteg West Carms 73 B10
Llanfaredd Powys 113 G11
Llanfarian Ceredig 111 B11
Llanfechain Powys 148 E3
Llanfechan Powys 113 G9
Llanfechell Anglesey 178 C5
Llanferres Denb 165 C11
Llan Ffestiniog Gwyn 164 G2
Llanfflewyn Anglesey 178 D5
Llanfigael Anglesey 178 E4
Llanfihangel-ar-arth Carms 93 D9
Llanfihangel-Crucorney Mon 96 G6
Llanfihangel Glyn Myfyr Conwy 165 F7
Llanfihangel-helygen Powys 113 E10
Llanfihangel Nant Bran Powys 95 E8
Llanfihangel-nant-Melan Powys 114 F3
Llanfihangel Rhydithon Powys 114 D3
Llanfihangel Rogiet Mon 60 B2
Llanfihangel Tal-y-llyn Powys 96 F2
Llanfihangel Tor y Mynydd Mon 79 E7
Llanfihangel-uwch-Gwili Carms 93 G9
Llanfihangel-y-Creuddyn Ceredig 112 B3
Llanfihangel-yng-Ngwynfa Powys 147 F11
Llanfihangel yn Nhowyn Anglesey 178 F4
Llanfihangel-y-pennant Gwyn 128 B3
Gwyn 163 F8
Llanfilo Powys 96 E2
Llanfleiddan = Llanblethian V Glam 58 E3
Llanfoist Mon 78 C3
Llanfor Gwyn 147 B8
Llanfrechfa Torf 78 G4
Llanfrothen Gwyn 163 G10
Llanfrynach Powys 95 F11
Llanfwrog Anglesey 178 E4
Denb 165 D10
Llanfyllin Powys 148 F2
Llanfynydd Carms 93 F11
Flint 166 D3
Llanfyrnach Pembs 92 E4
Llangadfan Powys 147 G10
Llangadog Carms 74 D6
Carms 94 F4
Llangadwaladr Anglesey 162 B5
Powys 148 C3
Llangaffo Anglesey 162 B6
Llangain Carms 74 B5
Llangammarch Wells Powys 95 B8
Llangan V Glam 58 D3
Llangarron Hereford 97 G10
Llangasty Talyllyn Powys 96 F2
Llangathen Carms 93 G11
Llangattock Powys 78 B2
Llangattock Lingoed Mon 97 G7
Llangattock nigh Usk Mon 78 D4
Llangattock-Vibon-Avel Mon 79 B7
Llangedwyn Powys 148 E3
Llangefni Anglesey 179 F7
Llangeinor Bridgend 58 B2
Llangeitho Ceredig 112 F2
Llangeler Carms 93 D7
Llangendeirne Carms 75 C7
Llangennech Carms 75 E9
Llangennith Swansea 56 C2
Llangenny Powys 78 B2
Llangernyw Conwy 164 B5
Llangeview Mon 78 E5
Llangewydd Court Bridgend 57 E11
Llangian Gwyn 144 D5
Llangloffan Pembs 91 E8
Llanglydwen Carms 92 F3
Llangoed Anglesey 179 F10
Llangoedmor Ceredig 92 B3
Llangollen Denb 166 G2
Llangolman Pembs 92 F2
Llangors Powys 96 F2
Llangorwen Ceredig 128 G2
Llangovan Mon 79 D7
Llangower Gwyn 147 C8
Llangrannog Ceredig 110 G6
Llangristiolus Anglesey 178 G6
Llangrove Hereford 79 B8
Llangua Mon 97 F7
Llangunllo Powys 114 C4
Llangunnor Carms 74 B6
Llangurig Powys 113 B8
Llangwm Conwy 165 G7
Mon 78 E6
Pembs 73 D7
Llangwnnadl Gwyn 144 C4
Llangwyfan Denb 165 B10
Llangwyfan-isaf Anglesey 162 B4
Llangwyllog Anglesey 178 F6
Llangwyryfon Ceredig 111 C11
Llangybi Ceredig 112 G2
Gwyn 162 G6
Mon 78 F5
Llangyfelach Swansea 56 B6
Llangyndeyrn Carms 75 C7
Llangynhafal Denb 165 C10
Llangynidr Powys 77 B11
Llangyniew Powys 130 B2
Llangynin Carms 74 B2
Llangynog Carms 74 B4
Powys 147 D11
Llangynwyd Bridgend 57 D11
Llanhamlach Powys 95 F11
Llanharan Rhondda 58 C4
Llanharry Rhondda 58 C4
Llanhennock Mon 78 G5
Llanhilleth Bl Gwent 78 E2
Llanhowel Pembs 90 F6
Llanidloes Powys 129 G9
Llaniestyn Gwyn 144 C5
Llanifyny Powys 129 G7
Llanigon Powys 96 D4
Llanilar Ceredig 112 C2
Llanilid Rhondda 58 C3
Llanilltud Fawr = Llantwit Major V Glam 58 F3
Llanio Ceredig 112 F2
Llanion Pembs 73 E7
Llanishen Cardiff 59 C7
Mon 79 E7
Llanllawddog Carms 93 F9
Llanllechid Gwyn 163 B10
Llanllowell Mon 78 F5
Llanllugan Powys 129 C11
Llanllwch Carms 74 B5
Llanllwchaiarn Powys 130 E2
Llanllwni Carms 93 D9
Llanllwyd Shrops 130 G3
Llanllyfni Gwyn 163 E7
Llanmadoc Swansea 56 C2
Llanmaes Cardiff 58 D6
V Glam 58 F3
Llanmartin Newport 59 B11
Llanmerwig Powys 130 E3
Llanmihangel V Glam 58 E3
Llan-mill Pembs 73 C10
Llanmiloe Carms 74 D3
Llanmorlais Swansea 56 C4
Llannefydd Conwy 181 G7
Llannerch-y-môr Flint 181 F11
Llannon Carms 75 D8
Llan-non = Llanon Ceredig 111 D10
Llannor Gwyn 145 B7
Llanon Pembs 90 E6
Llanon = Llan-non Ceredig 111 D10
Llanover Mon 78 D4
Llanpumsaint Carms 93 F8
Llanreath Pembs 73 E7
Llanreithan Pembs 91 F7
Llanrhaeadr Denb 165 C9
Llanrhaeadr-ym-Mochnant Powys 148 D2
Llanrhian Pembs 90 E6
Llanrhidian Swansea 56 C3
Llanrhos Conwy 180 E3
Llanrhyddlad Anglesey 178 D4
Llanrhystud Ceredig 111 D10
Llanrosser Hereford 96 D5
Llanrothal Hereford 79 B7
Llanrug Gwyn 163 C8
Llanrumney Cardiff 59 C8
Llanrwst Conwy 164 C4
Llansadurnen Carms 74 C3
Llansadwrn Anglesey 179 F9
Carms 94 E3
Llansaint Carms 74 D5
Llansamlet Swansea 57 B7
Llansanffraid Glan Conwy Conwy 180 F4
Llansannan Conwy 164 B6
Llansannor V Glam 58 D3
Llansantffraed Ceredig 111 D10
Powys 96 G2
Llansantffraed Cwmdeuddwr Powys 113 D9
Llansantffraed-in-Elwel Powys 113 G11
Llansantffraid-ym-Mechain Powys 148 E4
Llansawel Carms 94 D2
Llansawel = Briton Ferry Neath 57 C8
Llansilin Powys 148 D4
Llansoy Mon 78 E6
Llanspyddid Powys 95 F10
Llanstadwell Pembs 72 D6
Llansteffan Carms 74 C5
Llanstephan Powys 96 C2
Llantarnam Torf 78 G4
Llanteems Mon 96 G6
Llanteg Pembs 73 C11
Llanthony Mon 96 F5
Llantilio Crossenny Mon 78 C5
Llantilio Pertholey Mon 78 B4
Llantood Pembs 92 C3
Llantrisant Anglesey 178 E5
Mon 78 F5
Rhondda 58 C4
Llantrithyd V Glam 58 E4
Llantwit Neath 57 B9
Llantwit Fardre Rhondda 58 B5
Llantwit Major = Llanilltud Fawr V Glam 58 F3
Llanuwchllyn Gwyn 147 C7
Llanvaches Newport 78 G6
Llanvair Discoed Mon 78 G6
Llanvapley Mon 78 C5
Llanvetherine Mon 78 B5
Llanveynoe Hereford 96 E6
Llanvihangel Crucorney Mon 96 G6
Llanvihangel Gobion Mon 78 D4
Llanvihangel-Ystern-Llewern Mon 78 C6
Llanwarne Hereford 97 F10
Llanwddyn Powys 147 F10
Llanwenarth Mon 78 C3
Llanwenog Ceredig 93 B9
Llanwern Newport 59 B11
Llanwinio Carms 92 F5
Llanwnda Gwyn 163 D7
Pembs 91 D8
Llanwnnen Ceredig 93 B10
Llanwnog Powys 129 E10
Llanwrda Carms 94 E4
Llanwrin Powys 128 C5
Llanwrthwl Powys 113 E9
Llanwrtud = Llanwrtyd Wells Powys 95 B7
Llanwrtyd Powys 95 B7
Llanwrtyd Wells = Llanwrtud Powys 95 B7
Llanwyddelan Powys 129 C11
Llanyblodwel Shrops 148 E4
Llanybri Carms 74 C4
Llanybydder Carms 93 C10
Llanycefn Pembs 91 G11
Llanychaer Pembs 91 D9
Llanycil Gwyn 147 C8
Llanycrwys Carms 94 B2
Llanymawddwy Gwyn 147 F8
Llanymddyfri = Llandovery Carms 94 E5
Llanymynech Powys 148 E5
Llanynghenedl Anglesey 178 E4
Llanynys Denb 165 C10
Llan-y-pwll Wrex 166 E5
Llanyrafon Torf 78 G4
Llanyre Powys 113 E10
Llanystumdwy Gwyn 145 B9
Llanywern Powys 96 F2
Llawhaden Pembs 73 B9
Llawnt Shrops 148 C5
Llawrdref Bellaf Gwyn 144 D5
Llawr-y-glyn Powys 129 E8
Llay Wrex 166 D4
Llechcynfarwy Anglesey 178 E5
Llecheiddior Gwyn 163 G7
Llechfaen Powys 95 F11
Llechfraith Gwyn 146 F3
Llechryd Caerph 77 D10
Ceredig 92 C4
Llechrydau Powys 148 C4
Llechwedd Conwy 180 F3
Lledrod Ceredig 112 C2
Llenmerewig Powys 130 E3
Llethrid Swansea 56 C4
Llettyrychen Carms 75 E7
Llidiad Nenog Carms 93 D10
Llidiardau Gwyn 147 B7
Llidiart-y-parc Denb 165 G10
Llithfaen Gwyn 162 G5
Lloc Flint 181 F10
Llong Flint 166 C3
Llowes Powys 96 C3
Lloyney Powys 114 B4
Llugwy Powys 128 D4
Llundain-fach Ceredig 111 F11
Llwydarth Bridgend 57 C11
Llwydcoed Rhondda 77 E7
Llwyn Denb 165 C9
Shrops 130 G5
Llwyncelyn Ceredig 111 F8
Llwyndafydd Ceredig 111 F7
Llwynderw Powys 130 C4
Llwyn-derw Powys 129 G8
Llwyndrain Pembs 92 E5
Llwyn-du Mon 78 B3
Llwynduris Ceredig 92 C4
Llwyndyrys Gwyn 162 G5
Llwyneinion Wrex 166 F3
Llwyngwril Gwyn 110 B2
Llwynhendy Carms 56 B4
Llwyn-hendy Carms 56 B4
Llwynmawr Wrex 148 B4
Llwyn-on Village M Tydf 77 C8
Llwyn-Têg Carms 75 D9
Llwyn-y-brain Carms 73 C11
Llwyn-y-go Shrops 148 E6
Llwynygog Powys 129 E7
Llwyn-y-groes Ceredig 111 F11
Llwynypia Rhondda 77 G7
Llwyn-yr-hwrdd Pembs 92 E4
Llynclys Shrops 148 E5
Llynfaes Anglesey 178 F6
Llysfaen Conwy 180 F5
Llyswen Powys 96 D2
Llysworney V Glam 58 E3
Llys-y-frôn Pembs 91 G10
Llywel Powys 95 E7
Llywernog Ceredig 128 G4
Load Brook S Yorks 186 D3
Loan Falk 279 F9
Loandhu Highld 301 B8
Loanend Northumb 273 E8
Loanhead Aberds 302 D6
Midloth 270 B5
Perth 286 D5
Loanreoch Highld 300 B6
Loans S Ayrs 257 C8
Loansdean Northumb 252 G5
Loans of Tullich Highld 301 B8
Lobb Devon 40 F3
Lobhillcross Devon 12 D5
Lobley Hill T&W 242 E6
Lobthorpe Lincs 155 E9
Loch a Charnain W Isles 297 G4
Loch a' Ghainmhich W Isles 304 F4
Lochailort Highld 295 G9
Lochaline Highld 289 E8
Lochanhully Highld 301 G9
Lochans Dumfries 236 D2
Locharbriggs Dumfries 247 G11
Lochassynt Lodge Highld 307 G6
Lochavich Ho Argyll 275 B10
Lochawe Argyll 284 E5
Loch Baghasdail W Isles 297 K3
Lochbuie Argyll 289 G8
Lochbuie Ho Argyll 289 G8
Lochcallater Lodge Aberds 292 E3
Lochcarron Highld 295 B10
Loch Choire Lodge Highld 308 F6
Lochdhu Highld 310 E4
Lochdochart House Stirling 285 E8
Lochdon Argyll 289 F9
Lochdrum Highld 300 B2
Lochead Argyll 275 E11
Argyll 275 F8
Lochearnhead Stirling 285 E9
Lochee Dundee 287 D7
Loch Eil Highld 290 F2
Lochend Edin 280 G5
Highld 300 F5
Highld 310 C6
Lochend Ho Stirling 277 B11
Locherben Dumfries 247 D11
Lochetive Ho Highld 284 C5
Loch Euphoirt W Isles 296 E4
Lochfoot Dumfries 237 B10
Lochgair Argyll 275 D10
Lochgarthside Highld 291 B7
Lochgelly Fife 280 C3
Lochgilphead Argyll 275 E9
Lochgoilhead Argyll 284 G6
Loch Head Dumfries 236 E5
Dumfries 245 E11
Lochhill Moray 302 C2
Lochhussie Highld 300 D4
Lochinch Castle Dumfries 236 C3
Lochindorb Lodge Highld 301 F9
Lochinver Highld 307 G5
Lochlane Perth 286 E2
Lochletter Highld 300 G4
Loch Loyal Lodge Highld 308 E6
Lochluichart Highld 300 C3
Lochmaben Dumfries 248 G3
Lochmore Cottage Highld 310 E4
Lochmore Lodge Highld 306 F7
Loch nam Madadh W Isles 296 E5
Lochnell Ho Argyll 289 F10
Lochore Fife 280 B3
Lochorodale Argyll 255 F7
Lochportain W Isles 296 D5
Lochran Perth 280 B2
Lochranza N Ayrs 255 B10
Lochs Crofts Moray 302 C3
Loch Sgioport W Isles 297 H4
Lochside Aberds 293 G9
Highld 301 D8
Highld 308 D4
Highld 310 F2
S Ayrs 257 E8
Lochslin Highld 311 L2
Lochstack Lodge Highld 306 E7
Lochton Aberds 293 D9
Lochty Angus 293 G7
Fife 287 G9
Perth 286 E4
Lochuisge Highld 289 D9
Lochurr Dumfries 247 F7
Lochwinnoch Renfs 267 D7
Lochwood Dumfries 248 D3
Glasgow 268 B3
Lockyside Highld 290 F3
Lockengate Corn 5 C10
Lockerbie Dumfries 248 G4
Lockeridge Wilts 62 F6
Lockeridge Dene Wilts 62 F6
Lockerley Hants 32 B3
Lockhills Cumb 230 B6
Locking N Som 43 B11
Lockinge Oxon 64 B2
Locking Stumps Warr 183 C10
Lockington E Yorks 208 D5
Leics 153 D9
Lockleaze Bristol 60 D6
Lockleywood Shrops 150 D3
Locksbottom London 68 F2
Locksbrook Bath 61 G8
Locksgreen IoW 20 C4
Locks Heath Hants 33 F8
Lockton N Yorks 226 G6
Lockwood W Yorks 196 D6
Loddington Leics 136 C5
N Nhants 120 B6
Loddiswell Devon 8 F4
Loddon Norf 143 D7
Loddon Ingloss Norf 142 D6
Lode Cambs 123 E10
Lode Heath W Mid 134 G3
Loders Dorset 16 C5
Lodgebank Shrops 149 D11
Lodge Green N Yorks 223 F9
W Mid 134 G5
Lodge Hill Corn 6 C4
W Mid 133 G10
W Yorks 197 C9
Lodge Lees Kent 55 D8
Lodge Moor S Yorks 186 D3
Lodge Park Worcs 117 D10
Lodsworth W Sus 34 C6
Lodsworth Common W Sus 34 C6
Lodway Bristol 60 D4
Lofthouse N Yorks 214 E2
W Yorks 197 B10
Lofthouse Gate W Yorks 197 C10
Loftus Redcar 226 B4
Logan E Ayrs 258 E3
Loganlea W Loth 269 C9
Logan Mains Dumfries 236 E2
Loggerheads Denb 165 C11
Staffs 150 B4
Logie Angus 293 G8
Fife 287 E8
Moray 301 D10
Logiealmond Lodge Perth 286 D3
Logie Coldstone Aberds 292 C6
Logie Hill Highld 301 B7
Logie Newton Aberds 302 F6
Logie Pert Angus 293 G8
Logierait Perth 286 B3
Login Carms 92 G3
Logmore Green Sur 50 D6
Loidse Mhorsgail W Isles 304 F3
Lolworth Cambs 123 E7
Lomeshaye Lancs 204 F2
Lôn Gwyn 147 C7
Lonbain Highld 298 D6
Londesborough E Yorks 208 D3
London Apprentice Corn 5 E10
London Beach Kent 53 F11
London Colney Herts 85 E11
Londonderry N Yorks 214 B6
W Mid 133 F10
London End Cambs 121 D11
London Fields W Mid 133 E8
London Minstead Hants 32 E3
Londonthorpe Lincs 155 B9
Londubh Highld 307 L3
Lonemore Highld 299 B7
Highld 309 L7
Long Ashton N Som 60 E5
Long Bank Worcs 116 C5
Longbar N Ayrs 266 E6
Longbarn Warr 183 C10
Long Bennington Lincs 172 G4
Longbenton T&W 243 D7
Longborough Glos 100 F3
Long Bredy Dorset 17 C7
Longbridge Plym 7 D10
Warks 118 E5
W Mid 117 B10
Longbridge Deverill Wilts 45 E11
Longbridge Hayes Stoke 168 E5
Longbridgemuir Dumfries 238 D3
Long Buckby W Nhants 120 D2
Long Buckby Wharf W Nhants 120 D2
Longburgh Cumb 239 F8
Longburton Dorset 29 E11
Longcause Devon 8 C5
Long Clawson Leics 154 D4
Longcliffe Derbys 170 D2
Long Common Hants 33 E8
Long Compton Staffs 151 E7
Warks 100 E5
Longcot Oxon 82 G3
Long Crendon Bucks 83 D11
Long Crichel Dorset 31 E7
Longcroft Cumb 238 F6
Falk 278 F5
Longcross Devon 12 F4
Sur 66 F3
Long Cross Wilts 45 G9
Longdale Cumb 222 D2
Longdales Cumb 230 C6
Long Dean Wilts 61 D11
Longden Shrops 131 B8
Longden Common Shrops 131 C8
Long Ditton Sur 67 F7
Longdon Staffs 151 G11
Worcs 98 D6
Longdon Green Staffs 151 G11
Longdon Heath Worcs 98 D6
Longdon Hill End Worcs 98 D6
Longdon on Tern Telford 150 F2
Longdown Devon 14 C3
Longdowns Corn 2 C6
Long Drax N Yorks 199 B7
Longdrum Angus 292 G4
Long Duckmanton Derbys 186 G6
Long Eaton Derbys 153 C9
Longfield Kent 68 F6
Shetland 313 M5
Wilts 45 B11
Longfield Hill Kent 68 F6
Longfleet BCP 18 C6
Longford Derbys 152 B4
Glos 98 G6
Kent 52 B4
London 66 D4
Shrops 150 C2
Telford 150 F4
Warr 183 C10
W Mid 135 G7
Longfordlane Derbys 152 B4
Longforgan Perth 287 E7
Longformacus Borders 272 D3
Longframlington Northumb 252 C4
Long Gardens Essex 106 D6
Long Green Ches W 183 G7
Suff 125 B11
Worcs 98 E6
Longham Dorset 19 B7
Norf 159 F8
Long Hanborough Oxon 82 C6
Longhaven Aberds 303 F11
Longhedge Wilts 45 E10
Longhill Aberds 303 D9
Longhirst Northumb 252 F6
Longhope Glos 79 B11
Orkney 314 G3
Longhorsley Northumb 252 E4
Longhoughton Northumb 264 G6
Longhouse Bath 61 G8
Long Itchington Warks 119 D8
Long John's Hill Norf 142 B4
Longlands Cumb 229 D11
London 68 E2
Longlane Derbys 152 B5
W Berks 64 E3
Long Lane Telford 150 F2
Long Lawford Warks 119 B9
Long Lee W Yorks 205 E7
Longlevens Glos 99 G7
Longley W Yorks 196 C5
W Yorks 196 F6
Longley Estate S Yorks 186 C5
Longley Green Worcs 116 G4
Longleys Perth 286 C6
Long Load Som 29 C7
Longmanhill Aberds 303 C7
Long Marston Herts 84 B5
N Yorks 206 C6
Warks 100 B3
Long Marton Cumb 231 G9
Long Meadow Cambs 123 E10
Long Meadowend Shrops 131 G8
Long Melford Suff 107 B7
Longmoor Camp Hants 49 G9
Longmorn Moray 302 D2
Longmoss Ches E 184 G5
Long Newnton Glos 80 G6
Longnewton Borders 262 D3
Stockton 225 B7
Long Newton E Loth 271 C10
Longney Glos 80 C3
Longniddry E Loth 281 F8
Longnor Shrops 131 C9
Staffs 151 G7
Staffs 169 C9
Longnor Park Shrops 131 C9
Long Oak Shrops 149 E7
Longparish Hants 48 E2
Longpark Cumb 239 E10
E Ayrs 257 B10
Long Park Hants 48 G2
Longport Stoke 168 F5
Long Preston N Yorks 204 B2
Longridge Glos 80 D5
Lancs 203 F8
Staffs 151 F8
W Loth 269 C9
Longridge End Glos 98 G6
Longrigg N Lanark 278 G6
Longriggend N Lanark 278 G6
Long Riston E Yorks 209 E8
Longrock Corn 1 C5
Long Sandall S Yorks 198 F6
Longscales N Yorks 205 B10
Longsdon Staffs 169 E7
Longshaw Gtr Man 194 G4
Staffs 169 F9
Longside Aberds 303 E10
Longsight Gtr Man 184 B5
Long Sight Gtr Man 196 F2
Longslow Shrops 150 B3
Longsowerby Cumb 239 G9
Longstanton Cambs 123 D7
Longstock Hants 47 F11
Longstone Corn 2 B2
Corn 11 G7
Edin 280 G4
Pembs 73 D10
Som 28 B5
Longstowe Cambs 122 G6
Long Stratton Norf 142 E3
Longstreet Wilts 46 C6
Long Street M Keynes 102 B5
Long Sutton Hants 49 D8
Lincs 157 E8
Som 29 B7
Longthorpe Pboro 138 D3
Long Thurlow Suff 125 D10
Longthwaite Cumb 230 G4
Longton Lancs 194 B3
Stoke 168 G6
Longtown Cumb 239 D9
Hereford 96 F6
Longtownmail Orkney 314 F4
Longview Mers 182 C6
Longville in the Dale Shrops 131 E10
Longway Bank Derbys 170 E4
Longwell Green S Glos 61 E7
Long Whatton Leics 153 E9
Longwick Bucks 84 D3
Long Wittenham Oxon 83 G8
Longwitton Northumb 252 F3
Longwood Shrops 132 B2
W Yorks 196 D6
Longwood Edge W Yorks 196 D6
Longworth Oxon 82 F5
Longyester E Loth 271 B10
Lon-las Swansea 57 B8
Lonmay Aberds 303 D10
Lonmore Highld 298 E2
Looe Corn 6 E5
Looe Mills Corn 6 C4
Loose Kent 53 C9
Loosegate Lincs 156 D6
Loose Hill Kent 53 C9
Loosley Row Bucks 84 E4
Lopcombe Corner Wilts 47 F9
Lopen Som 28 E6
Lopen Head Som 28 E6
Loppergarth Cumb 210 D5
Loppington Shrops 149 D9
Lopwell Devon 7 C9
Lorbottle Northumb 252 B2
Lorbottle Hall Northumb 252 B2
Lordsbridge Norf 157 G11
Lord's Hill Soton 32 D5
Lordshill Common Sur 50 E4
Lordswood Soton 32 D6
Lords Wood Medway 69 G9
Lornty Perth 286 C5
Loscoe Derbys 170 F6
W Yorks 198 C2
Loscombe Dorset 16 B6
Losgaintir W Isles 305 J2
Lossiemouth Moray 302 B2
Lossit Argyll 254 B2
Lossit Lodge Argyll 274 G5
Lostford Shrops 150 C2
Lostock Gtr Man 195 F7
Lostock Gralam Ches W 183 F11
Lostock Green Ches W 183 G11
Lostock Hall Lancs 194 B4
Lostock Junction Gtr Man 195 F7
Lostwithiel Corn 6 D2
Loth Orkney 314 C6
Lothbeg Highld 311 H3
Lothersdale N Yorks 204 D5
Lothianbridge Midloth 270 C6
Lothmore Highld 311 H3
Lottisham Som 44 G5
Loudwater Bucks 84 G6
Herts 85 F9
Loughborough Leics 153 F10
Loughor Swansea 56 B5
Loughton Essex 86 F6
M Keynes 102 D6
Shrops 132 G2
Lound Lincs 155 F11
Notts 187 D11
Suff 143 D10
Loundsley Green Derbys 186 G5
Lount Leics 153 F7
Lour Angus 287 C8
Louth Lincs 190 D4
Lovat Highld 300 E5
Lovaton Devon 7 B10
Love Clough Lancs 195 B10
Lovedean Hants 33 E11
Love Green Bucks 66 C4
Lover Wilts 32 C2
Loversall S Yorks 187 B9
Loves Green Essex 87 E10
Lovesome Hill N Yorks 225 F7
Loveston Pembs 73 D9
Lovington Som 44 G5
Low Ackworth W Yorks 198 D3
Low Alwinton Northumb 251 B10
Low Angerton Northumb 252 G3
Lowbands Glos 98 E5
Low Barlings Lincs 189 G9
Low Barugh S Yorks 197 F10
Low Bentham N Yorks 212 F2
Low Biggins Cumb 212 D2
Low Blantyre S Lanark 268 D3
Low Borrowbridge Cumb 222 E2
Low Bradfield S Yorks 186 C3
Low Bradley N Yorks 204 D6
Low Braithwaite Cumb 230 C4
Low Bridge Wilts 62 E3
Lowbridge House Cumb 221 E10
Low Brunton Northumb 241 C10
Low Burnham N Lincs 199 G9
Low Burton N Yorks 214 C4
Low Buston Northumb 252 B6
Lowca Cumb 228 G5
Low Catton E Yorks 207 C10
Low Clanyard Dumfries 236 F3
Low Common Norf 142 E2
Low Compton Gtr Man 196 F2
Low Coniscliffe Darl 224 C5
Low Cotehill Cumb 239 G11
Low Coylton S Ayrs 257 F10
Low Crosby Cumb 239 F10
Lowcross Hill Ches W 167 E7
Low Dalby N Yorks 217 B7
Lowdham Notts 171 F11
Low Dinsdale Darl 224 C6
Lowe Shrops 149 C10
Lowedges S Yorks 186 E4
Lowe Hill Staffs 169 D7
Low Eighton T&W 243 F7
Low Ellington N Yorks 214 C4
Lower Achachenna Argyll 284 E4
Lower Aisholt Som 43 F8
Lower Allscot Shrops 132 D4
Lower Altofts W Yorks 197 C11
Lower Amble Corn 10 G5
Lower Ansty Dorset 30 G3
Lower Ardtun Argyll 288 G5
Lower Arncott Oxon 83 B10
Lower Ashtead Sur 51 B7
Lower Ashton Devon 14 E2
Lower Assendon Oxon 65 C8
Lower Badcall Highld 306 E6
Lower Ballam Lancs 202 G3
Lower Bartle Lancs 202 G5
Lower Basildon W Berks 64 D6
Lower Bassingthorpe Lincs 155 D9
Lower Bearwood Hereford 115 F7
Lower Bebington Mers 182 E4
Lower Beeding W Sus 36 B2
Lower Benefield N Nhants 137 F9
Lower Bentley Worcs 117 D9
Lower Beobridge Shrops 132 E5
Lower Berry Hill Glos 79 C9
Lower Binton Warks 118 G2
Lower Birchwood Derbys 170 E6
Lower Bitchet Kent 52 C5
Lower Blandford St Mary Dorset 30 F5
Lower Blunsdon Swindon 81 G10
Lower Bobbingworth Green Essex 87 D8
Lower Bockhampton Dorset 17 C10
Lower Boddington W Nhants 119 G9
Lower Bodham Norf 160 B2
Lower Bodinnar Corn 1 C4
Lower Bois Bucks 85 E7
Lower Bordean Hants 33 C11
Lower Boscaswell Corn 1 C3
Lower Bourne Sur 49 E10
Lower Bradley W Mid 133 D9
Lower Brailes Warks 100 D6
Lower Breakish Highld 295 C8
Lower Bredbury Gtr Man 184 C6
Lower Breinton Hereford 97 D9
Lower Broadheath Worcs 116 F6
Lower Brook Hants 32 B4
Lower Broughton Gtr Man 184 B4
Lower Brynamman Neath 76 C2
Lower Brynn Corn 5 C9
Lower Buckenhill Hereford 98 E2
Lower Buckland Hants 20 B2
Lower Bullingham Hereford 97 D10
Lower Bullington Hants 48 E3
Lower Bunbury Ches E 167 D9
Lower Burgate Hants 31 D11
Lower Burrow Som 28 C6
Lower Burton Hereford 115 F8
Lower Bush Medway 69 F7
Lower Cadsden Bucks 84 E4
Lower Caldecote C Beds 104 B3
Lower Cam Glos 80 E2
Lower Canada N Som 43 B11
Lower Carden Ches W 167 E7
Lower Catesby W Nhants 119 F10
Lower Cator Devon 13 F9
Lower Caversham Reading 65 E8
Lower Chapel Powys 95 D10
Lower Chedworth Glos 81 C9
Lower Cheriton Devon 27 G10
Lower Chicksgrove Wilts 46 G3
Lower Chute Wilts 47 C10
Lower Clapton London 67 B11
Lower Clent Worcs 117 B8
Lower Clicker Corn 6 C5
Lower Clopton Warks 118 F3
Lower Common Hants 48 E6
Hants 65 G9
Mon 78 B2
Mon 78 E4
Shrops 131 B9
Lower Copthurst Lancs 194 C5
Lower Cotburn Aberds 303 D7
Lower Cousley Wood E Sus 53 G7
Lower Cox Street Kent 69 G10
Lower Cragabus Argyll 254 C4
Lower Creedy Devon 26 G4
Lower Croan Corn 10 G6
Lower Crossings Derbys 185 E8
Lower Cumberworth W Yorks 197 F8
Lower Daggons Hants 31 E9
Lower Darwen Blackburn 195 B7
Lower Dean Bedford 121 D11
Devon 8 C4
Lower Dell Highld 292 B2
Lower Denby W Yorks 197 F8
Lower Denzell Corn 5 B7
Lower Deuchries Aberds 302 D6
Lower Diabaig Highld 299 C7
Lower Dicker E Sus 23 C9
Lower Dinchope Shrops 131 G9
Lower Dowdeswell Glos 81 B8
Lower Down Shrops 130 G6
Lower Drift Corn 1 D4
Lower Dunsforth N Yorks 215 G8
Lower Durston Som 28 B3
Lower Earley Wokingham 65 E9
Lower East Carleton Norf 142 C3
Lower Eastern Green W Mid 118 B5
Lower Edmonton London 86 G4
Lower Egleton Hereford 98 B2
Lower Elkstone Staffs 169 D9
Lower Ellastone Staffs 169 G10
Lower End Bucks 83 D11
Bucks 102 E4
C Beds 103 D8
C Beds 103 G9
Glos 81 E7
N Nhants 121 E7
Oxon 82 B4
W Nhants 120 F6
W Nhants 120 G5
Lower Everleigh Wilts 47 C7
Lower Eythorne Kent 55 D9
Lower Failand N Som 60 E4
Lower Faintree Shrops 132 F3
Lower Falkenham Suff 108 D5
Lower Farringdon Hants 49 F8
Lower Feltham London 66 E5
Lower Fittleworth W Sus 35 D8
Lowerford Lancs 204 F3
Lower Forge Shrops 132 F4
Lower Foxdale IoM 192 E3
Lower Frankton Shrops 149 C7
Lower Freystrop Pembs 73 C7
Lower Froyle Hants 49 E9
Lower Gabwell Devon 9 B8
Lower Gledfield Highld 309 K5
Lower Godney Som 44 E3
Lower Goldstone Kent 71 G9
Lower Gornal W Mid 133 E8
Lower Grange W Yorks 205 G8
Lower Gravenhurst C Beds 104 D2
Lower Green Essex 88 E2
Essex 105 E8
Essex 106 E4
Lower Green *continued*
Gtr Man 184 B2
Herts 104 E3
Kent 52 E5
Kent 52 E6
Norf 159 B9
Staffs 133 B8
Suff 124 D4
Sur 66 F6
Warks 119 D10
W Berks 63 G11
Lower Grove Common Hereford 97 F11
Lower Hacheston Suff 126 F6
Lower Halistra Highld 298 D2
Lower Halliford Sur 66 F5
Lower Halstock Leigh Dorset 29 F8
Lower Halstow Kent 69 F11
Lower Hamswell S Glos 61 E8
Lower Hamworthy BCP 18 C6
Lower Hardres Kent 55 C7
Lower Hardwick Hereford 115 F8
Lower Harpton Powys 114 E5
Lower Hartlip Kent 69 G10
Lower Hartshay Derbys 170 E5
Lower Hartwell Bucks 84 C3
Lower Hatton Staffs 150 B6
Lower Hawthwaite Cumb 210 B4
Lower Haysden Kent 52 D5
Lower Hayton Shrops 131 G10
Lower Hazel S Glos 60 B6
Lower Heath Ches E 168 C5
Lower Hempriggs Moray 301 C11
Lower Heppington Kent 54 C6
Lower Hergest Hereford 114 F5
Lower Herne Kent 71 F7
Lower Heyford Oxon 101 G9
Lower Heysham Lancs 211 G8
Lower Higham Kent 69 E8
Lower Highmoor Oxon 65 B8
Lower Holbrook Suff 108 E3
Lower Holditch Dorset 28 G4
Lower Holloway London 67 B10
Lower Holwell Dorset 31 E9
Lower Hook Worcs 98 C6
Lower Hookner Devon 13 E10
Lower Hopton Shrops 149 E7
W Yorks 197 D7
Lower Hordley Shrops 149 D7
Lower Horncroft W Sus 35 D8
Lower Horsebridge E Sus 23 C9
Lowerhouse Ches E 184 F6
Lancs 204 G2
Lower House Halton 183 D8
Lower Houses W Yorks 197 D7
Lower Howsell Worcs 98 B5
Lower Illey Worcs 133 G9
Lower Island Kent 70 F6
Lower Kersal Gtr Man 195 G10
Lower Kilburn Derbys 170 F5
Lower Kilcott Glos 61 B9
Lower Killeyan Argyll 254 C3
Lower Kingcombe Dorset 17 B7
Lower Kingswood Sur 51 C8
Lower Kinnerton Ches W 166 C4
Lower Kinsham Hereford 115 E7
Lower Knapp Som 28 B4
Lower Knightley Staffs 150 E6
Lower Knowle Bristol 60 E5
Lower Langford N Som 60 G3
Lower Largo Fife 287 G8
Lower Layham Suff 107 C10
Lower Ledwyche Shrops 115 C10
Lower Leigh Staffs 151 B10
Lower Lemington Glos 100 E4
Lower Lenie Highld 300 G5
Lower Lode Glos 99 E7
Lower Lovacott Devon 25 B8
Lower Loxhore Devon 40 F6
Lower Lydbrook Glos 79 B9
Lower Lye Hereford 115 D8
Lower Machen Newport 59 B8
Lower Maes-coed Hereford 96 E6
Lower Mains Clack 279 B9
Lower Mannington Dorset 31 F9
Lower Marsh Som 30 C2
Lower Marston Som 45 E9
Lower Meend Glos 79 E9
Lower Menadue Corn 5 D10
Lower Merridge Som 43 G8
Lower Mickletown W Yorks 198 B2
Lower Middleton Cheney W Nhants 101 C10
Lower Midway Derbys 152 E6
Lower Mill Corn 3 B10
Lower Milovaig Highld 296 F7
Lower Milton Som 44 D4
Lower Moor Wilts 81 G8
Worcs 99 B9
Lower Morton S Glos 79 G10
Lower Mountain Flint 166 D4
Lower Nazeing Essex 86 D5
Lower Netchwood Shrops 132 E2
Lower Netherton Devon 14 G3
Lower New Inn Torf 78 F4
Lower Ninnes Corn 1 C5
Lower Nobut Staffs 151 C10
Lower North Dean Bucks 84 F5
Lower Norton Warks 118 E4
Lower Nyland Dorset 30 C2
Lower Ochrwyth Caerph 59 B8
Lower Odcombe Som 29 D8
Lower Oddington Glos 100 F4
Lower Ollach Highld 295 B7
Lower Padworth W Berks 64 F6
Lower Penarth V Glam 59 F7
Lower Penn Staffs 133 D7
Lower Pennington Hants 20 C2
Lower Penwortham Lancs 194 B4
Lower Peover Ches W 184 G2
Lower Pexhill Ches E 184 G5
Lower Pilsley Derbys 170 C6
Lower Pitkerrie Highld 311 L2
Lower Place Gtr Man 196 E2
London 67 C8
Lower Pollicot Bucks 84 C2
Lower Porthkerry V Glam 58 F5
Lower Porthpean Corn 5 E10
Lower Quinton Warks 100 B3
Lower Rabber Hereford 114 G5
Lower Race Torf 78 E3
Lower Radley Oxon 83 F8
Lower Rainham Medway 69 F10
Lower Ratley Hants 32 C4
Lower Raydon Suff 107 D10
Lower Rea Glos 80 B4

Lower Ridge Devon 28 G2
Shrops 148 C6
Lower Roadwater Som 42 F4
Lower Rochford Worcs 116 D2
Lower Rose Corn 4 E5
Lower Row Dorset 31 G8
Lower Sapey Worcs 116 E3
Lower Seagry Wilts 62 C3
Lower Sheering Essex 87 C7
Lower Shelton C Beds 103 C9
Lower Shiplake Oxon 65 D9
Lower Shuckburgh
Warks 119 E9
Lower Skelty Swansea 56 C6
Lower Slackstead Hants 32 B5
Lower Slade Devon 40 D4
Lower Slaughter Glos 100 G3
Lower Solva Pembs 87 G11
Lower Soothill W Yorks 197 C9
Lower Soudley Glos 79 D11
Lower Southfield
Hereford 98 C3
Lower Stanton St Quintin
Wilts 62 C2
Lower Stoke Medway 69 D10
W Mid 119 B7
Lower Stondon C Beds 104 D3
Lower Stone Glos 79 G11
Lower Stonnall Staffs 133 C11
Lower Stow Bedon Norf 141 E9
Lower Stratton Som 28 D6
Swindon 63 B7
Lower Street E Sus 38 E2
Norf 160 B5
Norf 160 C3
Norf 160 F6
Suff 108 E3
Suff 124 G5
Lower Strensham Worcs 99 C8
Lower Stretton Warr 183 E10
Lower Studley Wilts 45 B11
Lower Sundon C Beds 103 F10
Lower Swainswick Bath 61 F9
Lower Swanwick Hants 33 F7
Lower Swell Glos 100 F3
Lower Sydenham
London 67 E11
Lower Tadmarton Oxon 101 D8
Lower Tale Devon 27 G9
Lower Tasburgh Norf 142 D3
Lower Tean Staffs 151 B10
Lower Thorpe
W Nhants 101 B10
Lower Threapwood
Wrex 166 G6
Lower Thurlton Norf 143 D8
Lower Thurnham Lancs 202 C5
Lower Thurvaston
Derbys 152 B4
Lower Todding Hereford 115 B8
Lower Tote Highld 298 C5
Lowertown Corn 2 D5
Corn 5 C11
Devon 12 E5
Lower Town Devon 27 E8
Hereford 98 C2
Pembs 91 D9
Worcs 117 F7
W Yorks 204 G6
Lower Trebullett Corn 12 F2
Lower Tregunnon Corn 11 E10
Lower Treworrick Corn 6 B4
Lower Tuffley Glos 80 C4
Lower Turmer Hants 31 F10
Lower Twitchen Devon 24 D5
Lower Twydall Medway 69 F10
Lower Tysoe Warks 100 B6
Lower Upham Hants 33 D8
Lower Upnor Medway 69 E9
Lower Vexford Som 42 F6
Lower Wainhill Oxon 84 E3
Lower Walton Warr 183 D10
Lower Wanborough
Swindon 63 C8
Lower Weacombe Som 42 E6
Lower Weald M Keynes 102 D5
Lower Wear Devon 14 D4
Lower Weare Som 44 C2
Lower Weedon
W Nhants 120 F2
Lower Welson Hereford 114 G5
Lower Westholme Som 44 E5
Lower Westhouse
N Yorks 212 E3
Lower Westmancote
Worcs 99 D8
Lower Weston Bath 61 F8
Lower Whatcombe
Dorset 30 G4
Lower Whatley Som 45 D8
Lower Whitley Ches W 183 F10
Lower Wick Glos 80 F2
Worcs 116 G6
Lower Wield Hants 48 E6
Lower Willingdon E Sus 23 E9
Lower Winchendon or
Nether Winchendon
Bucks 84 C2
Lower Withington
Ches E 168 B4
Lower Wolverton Worcs 117 G8
Lower Woodend Aberds 293 B8
Bucks 65 B10
Lower Woodford Wilts 46 G6
Lower Woodley Corn 5 B10
Lower Woodside Herts 86 D2
Lower Woolston Som 29 B11
Lower Woon Corn 5 C10
Lower Wraxall Dorset 29 G9
Som 44 F6
Wilts 61 G10
Lower Wych Ches W 167 G7
Lower Wyche Worcs 98 C5
Lower Wyke W Yorks 197 B7
Lower Yelland Devon 40 G3
Lower Zeals Wilts 45 G9
Lowes Barn Durham 233 C11
Lowesby Leics 136 B4
Lowestoft Suff 143 E10
Loweswater Cumb 229 G8
Low Etherley Durham 233 F9
Low Fell T&W 243 F7
Lowfield S Yorks 186 D5
Lowfield Heath W Sus 51 E9
Low Fold W Yorks 205 F10
Lowford Hants 33 E7
Low Fulney Lincs 156 E5
Low Garth N Yorks 226 D4
Low Gate Northumb 241 E10
N Yorks 214 F5
Low Geltbridge Cumb 240 F2
Lowgill Cumb 222 F2
Lancs 212 G3
Low Grantley N Yorks 214 E4
Low Green N Yorks 205 B10
Suff 125 E7
W Yorks 205 F10
Low Greenside T&W 242 E4
Low Habberley Worcs 116 B6
Low Ham Som 28 B6
Low Hauxley Northumb 253 C7
Low Hawsker N Yorks 227 D8
Low Hesket Cumb 230 B5
Low Hesleyhurst
Northumb 252 D3
Low Hill W Mid 133 C8
Low Hutton N Yorks 216 F5
Lowick Cumb 210 B5
N Nhants 137 G9
Northumb 264 B2
Lowick Bridge Cumb 210 B5
Lowick Green Cumb 210 B5
Low Knipe Cumb 230 G6
Low Laithe N Yorks 214 G3
Low Laithes S Yorks 197 G11
Lowlands Torf 78 F3
Low Leighton Derbys 185 D8
Low Lorton Cumb 229 F9
Low Marishes N Yorks 216 D6
Low Marnham Notts 172 B4
Low Mill N Yorks 226 F3
Low Moor Lancs 203 E10
W Yorks 197 B7
Lowmoor Row Cumb 231 F8
Low Moorsley T&W 234 B2
Low Moresby Cumb 228 G5
Lowna N Yorks 226 G3
Low Newton Cumb 211 C8
Low Newton-by-the-Sea
Northumb 264 E6
Lownie Moor Angus 287 C8
Lowood Borders 262 B2
Low Prudhoe Northumb 242 E4
Low Risby N Lincs 200 E2
Low Row Cumb 229 C9
Cumb 240 E3
N Yorks 223 F9
Low Salchrie Dumfries 236 C2
Low Smerby Argyll 255 E8
Low Snaygill N Yorks 204 D5
Lowsonford Warks 118 D3
Low Street Norf 141 B10
Thurrock 69 D7
Low Tharston Norf 142 D3
Lowther Cumb 230 G6
Lowthertown Dumfries 238 D6
Lowtherville IoW 21 F7
Low Thornley T&W 242 E5
Lowthorpe E Yorks 217 G11
Lowton Gtr Man 183 B10
Som 27 D11
Lowton Common
Gtr Man 183 B10
Lowton Heath Gtr Man 183 B10
Lowton St Mary's
Gtr Man 183 B10
Low Torry Fife 279 D10
Low Town Shrops 132 E4
Low Toynton Lincs 190 G3
Low Valley S Yorks 198 G2
Low Valleyfield Fife 279 D10
Low Walton Cumb 219 C9
Low Waters S Lanark 268 E4
Low Westwood Durham 242 F4
Low Whinnow Cumb 239 G8
Low Whita N Yorks 223 F10
Low Wood Cumb 210 C6
Low Worsall N Yorks 225 C7
Low Wray Cumb 221 E7
Loxbeare Devon 26 D6
Loxford London 68 B2
Loxhill Sur 50 F4
Loxhore Devon 40 F6
Loxhore Cott Devon 40 F6
Loxley S Yorks 186 D4
Warks 118 G5
Loxley Green Staffs 151 C11
Loxter Hereford 98 C4
Loxton N Som 43 B11
Loxwood W Sus 50 G4
Loyter's Green Essex 87 C8
Loyterton Kent 70 G3
Lozells W Mid 133 F11
Lubachlaggan Highld 300 B3
Lubachoinnich Highld 309 K4
Lubberland Shrops 116 B2
Lubcroy Highld 309 J3
Lubenham Leics 136 F4
Lubinvullin Highld 308 C5
Lucas End Herts 86 E4
Lucas Green Lancs 194 C5
Sur 50 B2
Luccombe Som 42 E2
Luccombe Village IoW 21 F7
Lucker Northumb 264 C5
Luckett Corn 12 G3
Lucking Street Essex 106 E6
Luckington Wilts 61 C10
Lucklawhill Fife 287 E8
Luckwell Bridge Som 42 F2
Lucton Hereford 115 E8
Ludag W Isles 297 K3
Ludborough Lincs 190 B3
Ludbrook Devon 8 E3
Ludchurch Pembs 73 C10
Luddenden W Yorks 196 B4
Luddenden Foot
W Yorks 196 C4
Ludderburn Cumb 221 G8
Luddesdown Kent 69 F7
Luddington N Lincs 199 D10
Warks 118 G3
Luddington in the Brook
N Nhants 138 G2
Lude House Perth 291 G10
Ludford Lincs 190 D2
Shrops 115 C10
Ludgershall Bucks 83 B11
Wilts 47 C9
Ludgvan Corn 2 C2
Ludham Norf 161 F7
Ludlow Shrops 115 C10
Ludney Lincs 190 B5
Som 28 E5
Ludstock Hereford 98 D3
Ludstone Shrops 132 E6
Ludwell Wilts 30 C6
Ludworth Durham 234 C3
Luffenhall Herts 104 F5
Luffincott Devon 12 C2
Lufton Som 29 D8
Lugar E Ayrs 258 E3
Lugate Borders 271 G8
Luggate Burn E Loth 282 G2
Lugg Green Hereford 115 E9
Luggiebank N Lanark 278 G5
Lugsdale Halton 183 D8
Lugton E Ayrs 267 E8
Lugwardine Hereford 97 C11
Luib Highld 295 C7
Luibeilt Highld 290 G4
Lulham Hereford 97 C8
Lullenden Sur 52 E2
Lullington Derbys 152 G5
Som 45 C9
Lulsgate Bottom N Som 60 F4
Lulsley Worcs 116 F4
Lulworth Camp Dorset 18 E2
Lumb Lancs 195 C10
Lancs 195 D9
Lumb *continued*
W Yorks 196 C4
W Yorks 197 E7
Lumb Foot W Yorks 204 F6
Lumburn Devon 12 G5
Lumbutts W Yorks 196 C3
Lumby N Yorks 206 G5
Lumley W Sus 22 B3
Lumley Thicks Durham 243 G8
Lumloch E Dunb 268 B2
Lumphanan Aberds 293 C7
Lumphinnans Fife 280 C3
Lumsdaine Borders 273 B7
Lumsden Aberds 302 G4
Lunan Angus 287 B10
Lunanhead Angus 287 B8
Luncarty Perth 286 E4
Lund E Yorks 208 D5
N Yorks 207 G9
Shetland 312 C7
Lundal W Isles 304 E3
Lundavra Highld 290 G2
Lunderton Aberds 303 E11
Lundie Angus 286 D6
Highld 290 B3
Lundin Links Fife 287 G8
Lundwood S Yorks 197 F11
Lundy Green Norf 142 E4
Lunga Argyll 275 C8
Lunna Shetland 312 G6
Lunning Shetland 312 G7
Lunnister Shetland 312 F5
Lunnon Swansea 56 D4
Lunsford Kent 53 B7
Lunsford's Cross E Sus 38 E2
Lunt Mers 193 G10
Luntley Hereford 115 F7
Lunts Heath Halton 183 D8
Lupin Staffs 152 F2
Luppitt Devon 27 F11
Lupridge Devon 8 E4
Lupset W Yorks 197 D10
Lupton Cumb 211 C11
Lurg Aberds 293 C8
Lurgashall W Sus 34 B6
Lurignich Argyll 289 D11
Lurley Devon 26 E6
Lusby Lincs 174 B4
Lushcott Shrops 131 D11
Luson Devon 8 F2
Luss Argyll 277 C7
Lussagiven Argyll 275 E7
Lusta Highld 298 D2
Lustleigh Devon 13 E11
Lustleigh Cleave Devon 13 E11
Luston Hereford 115 E9
Lusty Som 45 G7
Luthermuir Aberds 293 G8
Luthrie Fife 287 F7
Lutley W Mid 133 G8
Luton Devon 14 F4
Devon 27 G9
Luton 103 G11
Medway 69 F9
Lutsford Devon 24 D3
Lutterworth Leics 135 G10
Lutton Devon 7 D11
Devon 8 C3
Lincs 157 D8
N Nhants 138 F2
Lutton Gowts Lincs 157 E8
Lutworthy Devon 26 D3
Luxborough Som 42 F3
Luxley Glos 98 G3
Luxted London 68 G2
Luxton Devon 28 E2
Luxulyan Corn 5 D11
Luzley Gtr Man 196 G3
Luzley Brook Gtr Man 196 F2
Lyatts Som 29 E8
Lybster Highld 310 F6
Lydbury North Shrops 131 F7
Lydcott Devon 41 F7
Lydd Kent 39 C8
Lydden Kent 55 D9
Kent 71 F11
Lyddington Rutland 137 D7
Lydd on Sea Kent 39 C9
Lyde Orkney 314 E3
Shrops 130 C6
Lydeard St Lawrence
Som 42 G6
Lyde Cross Hereford 97 C10
Lyde Green Hants 49 B8
S Glos 61 D7
Lydford Devon 12 E6
Lydford Fair Place Som 44 G5
Lydford-on-Fosse Som 44 G5
Lydgate Derbys 186 F4
Gtr Man 196 G3
W Yorks 196 B2
Lydham Shrops 130 E6
Lydiard Green Wilts 62 B5
Lydiard Millicent Wilts 62 B5
Lydiard Plain Wilts 62 B5
Lydiard Tregoze Swindon 62 C6
Lydiate Mers 193 G11
Lydiate Ash Worcs 117 B9
Lydlinch Dorset 30 E2
Lydmarsh Som 28 F5
Lydney Glos 79 E10
Lydstep Pembs 73 F9
Lye W Mid 133 G8
Lye Cross N Som 60 G3
Lye Green Bucks 85 E7
E Sus 52 G4
Warks 118 D3
Wilts 45 B10
Lye Head Worcs 116 C5
Lye Hole N Som 60 G4
Lyewood Common E Sus 52 F4
Lyford Oxon 82 G5
Lymbridge Green Kent 54 E6
Lyme Green Ches E 184 G6
Lyme Regis Dorset 16 C2
Lymiecleuch Borders 249 C9
Lyminge Kent 55 E7
Lymington Hants 20 B2
Lyminster W Sus 35 G8
Lymm Warr 183 D11
Lymore Hants 19 C11
Lympne Kent 54 F6
Lympsham Som 43 C10
Lympstone Devon 14 E5
Lynbridge Devon 41 D8
Lynch Hants 48 D4
Som 42 D2
Lynchat Highld 291 C9
Lynchgate Shrops 131 F7
Lynch Hill Hants 48 D3
Slough 66 C2
Lyndale Ho Highld 298 D3
Lyndhurst Hants 32 F4
Lyndon Rutland 137 C8
Lyndon Green W Mid 134 F2
Lyne Borders 270 G4
Sur 66 F4
Lyneal Shrops 149 C8
Lyneal Mill Shrops 149 C9
Lyneal Wood Shrops 149 C9
Lyne Down Hereford 98 E2
Lyneham Oxon 100 G5
Wilts 62 D4
Lynemore Highld 301 G10
Lynemouth Northumb 253 E7
Lyne of Gorthleck
Highld 300 G5
Lyne of Skene Aberds 293 B9
Lyness Orkney 314 G3
Lyne Station Borders 260 B6
Lynford Norf 140 E6
Lyng Norf 159 F11
Som 28 B4
Lyngate Norf 160 C5
Lyngford Som 28 B2
Lynmore Highld 301 F10
Lynmouth Devon 41 D8
Lynn Staffs 133 C11
Telford 150 F5
Lynnwood Borders 261 G11
Lynsore Bottom Kent 55 D7
Lynsted Kent 70 G2
Lynstone Corn 24 F2
Lynton Devon 41 D8
Lynwilg Highld 291 B10
Lynworth Glos 99 G9
Lyons T&W 234 B3
Lyon's Gate Dorset 29 F11
Lyon's Green Norf 159 G8
Lyonshall Hereford 114 F6
Lyons Hall Essex 88 B2
Lypiatt Glos 80 D6
Lyrabus Argyll 274 G3
Lytchett Matravers
Dorset 18 B4
Lytchett Minster Dorset 18 C5
Lyth Highld 310 C6
Lytham Lancs 193 B11
Lytham St Anne's
Lancs 193 B10
Lythbank Shrops 131 B9
Lythe N Yorks 226 C6
Lythes Orkney 314 H4
Lythmore Highld 310 C4

M

Maam Argyll 284 F5
Mabe Burnthouse Corn 3 C7
Mabie Dumfries 237 B11
Mabledon Kent 52 E5
Mablethorpe Lincs 191 D8
Macclesfield Ches E 184 G6
Macclesfield Forest
Ches E 185 G7
Macduff Aberds 303 C7
Mace Green Suff 108 C2
Machan S Lanark 268 E5
Macharioch Argyll 255 G8
Machen Caerph 59 B8
Machrie N Ayrs 255 D9
Machrie Hotel Argyll 254 C4
Machrihanish Argyll 255 E7
Machroes Gwyn 144 D6
Machynlleth Powys 128 C4
Machynys Carms 56 B4
Mackerel's Common
W Sus 35 B8
Mackerye End Herts 85 B11
Mackham Devon 27 F11
Mackney Oxon 64 B5
Mackside Borders 262 G4
Mackworth Derbys 152 B6
Macmerry E Loth 281 G8
Madderty Perth 286 E3
Maddington Wilts 46 E5
Maddiston Falk 279 F8
Maddox Moor Pembs 73 C7
Madehurst W Sus 35 E7
Madeley Staffs 168 G3
Telford 132 C3
Madeley Heath Staffs 168 F3
Worcs 117 B9
Madeley Park Staffs 168 G3
Madeleywood Telford 132 C3
Maders Corn 12 G2
Madford Devon 27 E10
Madingley Cambs 123 E7
Madjeston Dorset 30 B4
Madley Hereford 97 D8
Madresfield Worcs 98 B6
Madron Corn 1 C5
Maenaddwyn Anglesey 179 E7
Maenclochog Pembs 91 F11
Maendy V Glam 58 D4
Maenporth Corn 3 D7
Maentwrog Gwyn 163 G11
Maen-y-groes Ceredig 111 F7
Maer Corn 24 F2
Staffs 150 B5
Maerdy Carms 94 G2
Conwy 165 G8
Rhondda 77 F7
Maes-bangor Ceredig 128 G3
Maesbrook Shrops 148 E5
Maesbury Shrops 148 D6
Maesbury Marsh Shrops 148 D6
Maesgeirchen Gwyn 179 G9
Maes-glas Newport 59 B9
Maes Glas *= Greenfield*
Flint 181 F11
Maesgwyn-Isaf Powys 148 G3
Maeshafn Denb 166 C2
Maesllyn Ceredig 93 C7
Maes llyn Ceredig 93 C7
Maesmynis Powys 95 B10
Maes Pennant Flint 181 F11
Maesteg Bridgend 57 C10
Maes-Treylow Powys 114 D5
Maesybont Carms 75 B9
Maesycoed Rhondda 58 B5
Maesycrugiau Carms 93 C9
Maesycwmmer Caerph 77 G11
Maes-y-dre Flint 166 C2
Maesygwartha Mon 78 C2
Maesymeillion Ceredig 93 B8
Maesypandy Powys 129 D9
Maesyrhandir Powys 129 E11
Magdalen Laver Essex 87 D8
Maggieknockater Moray 302 E3
Maggots End Essex 105 F9
Magham Down E Sus 23 C10
Maghull Mers 193 G11
Magor Mon 60 B2
Magpie Green Suff 125 B11
Mahaar Dumfries 236 B2
Maida Vale London 67 C9
Maidenbower W Sus 51 F9
Maiden Bradley Wilts 45 F10
Maidencombe Torbay 9 B8
Maidenhall Suff 108 C3
Maidenhead Windsor 65 C11
Maiden Head N Som 60 F5
Maidenhead Court
Windsor 66 C2
Maiden Law Durham 233 B9
Maiden Newton Dorset 17 B7
Maidenpark Falk 279 E9
Maidens S Ayrs 244 B6
Maidensgrave Suff 108 B5
Maiden's Green Brack 65 E11
Maidensgrove Oxon 65 B8
Maiden's Hall Northumb 252 D6
Maidenwell Corn 11 G8
Lincs 190 F4
Maiden Wells Pembs 73 F7
Maidford W Nhants 120 G2
Maids Moreton Bucks 102 D4
Maidstone Kent 53 B9
Maidwell W Nhants 120 B4
Mail Shetland 313 L6
Mailand Shetland 312 C8
Mailingsland Borders 270 G4
Main Powys 148 F3
Maindee Newport 59 B10
Maindy Cardiff 59 D7
Mainholm S Ayrs 257 E9
Mains Cumb 229 G7
Mainsforth Durham 234 E2
Mains of Airies Dumfries 236 C1
Mains of Allardice
Aberds 293 F10
Mains of Annochie
Aberds 303 E9
Mains of Ardestie
Angus 287 D9
Mains of Arnage Aberds 303 F9
Mains of Auchoynanie
Moray 302 E4
Mains of Baldoon
Dumfries 236 D6
Mains of Balhall Angus 293 G7
Mains of Ballindarg
Angus 287 B8
Mains of Balnakettle
Aberds 293 F8
Mains of Birness Aberds 303 F9
Mains of Blackhall
Aberds 303 G7
Mains of Burgie Moray 301 D10
Mains of Cairnbrogie
Aberds 303 G8
Mains of Cairnty Moray 302 D3
Mains of Clunas Highld 301 E8
Mains of Crichie Aberds 303 E9
Mains of Daltulich
Highld 301 E7
Mains of Dalvey Highld 301 F11
Mains of Dellavaird
Aberds 293 E9
Mains of Drum Aberds 293 D10
Mains of Edingight
Moray 302 D5
Mains of Fedderate
Aberds 303 E8
Mains of Flichity Highld 300 G6
Mains of Hatton Aberds 303 D9
Aberds 303 E7
Mains of Inkhorn Aberds 303 F9
Mains of Innerpeffray
Perth 286 F3
Mains of Kirktonhill
Aberds 293 G8
Mains of Laithers
Aberds 302 E6
Mains of Mayen Moray 302 E5
Mains of Melgund
Angus 287 B9
Mains of Taymouth
Perth 285 C11
Mains of Thornton
Aberds 293 F8
Mains of Towie Aberds 303 E7
Mains of Ulbster Highld 310 E7
Mains of Watten Highld 310 D6
Mainsriddle Dumfries 237 D11
Mainstone Shrops 130 F5
Maisemore Glos 98 G6
Maitland Park London 67 C9
Major's Green W Mid 118 B2
Makeney Derbys 170 G5
Malacleit W Isles 296 D3
Malborough Devon 9 G9
Malcoff Derbys 185 E9
Malden Rushett London 67 G7
Maldon Essex 88 D4
Malehurst Shrops 131 B7
Malham N Yorks 213 G8
Maligar Highld 298 C4
Malinbridge S Yorks 186 D4
Malinslee Telford 132 B3
Malkin's Bank Ches E 168 D3
Mallaig Highld 295 F8
Mallaig Bheag Highld 295 F8
Malleny Mills Edin 270 B3
Malling Stirling 285 G9
Mallows Green Essex 105 F9
Malltraeth Anglesey 162 B6
Mallwyd Gwyn 147 G7
Malmesbury Wilts 62 B2
Malmsmead Devon 41 D9
Malpas Ches W 167 F7
Corn 4 G6
Newport 78 G4
W Berks 64 E6
Malswick Glos 98 F4
Maltby Lincs 190 E4
Stockton 225 C9
S Yorks 187 C8
Maltby le Marsh Lincs 191 E7
Malting End Suff 124 G4
Malting Green Essex 107 G9
Maltings Angus 293 G9
Maltman's Hill Kent 54 E2
Malton N Yorks 216 E5
Malvern Common Worcs 98 C5
Malvern Link Worcs 98 B5
Malvern Wells Worcs 98 C5
Mambeg Argyll 276 D4
Mamble Worcs 116 C3
Mamhilad Mon 78 E4
Manaccan Corn 3 E7
Manadon Plym 7 D9
Manafon Powys 130 C2
Manais W Isles 296 C7
Manar Ho Aberds 303 G7
Manaton Devon 13 E11
Manby Lincs 190 D5
Mancetter Warks 134 D6
Manchester Gtr Man 184 B4
Manchester Airport
Gtr Man 184 D4
Mancot Flint 166 B4
Mancot Royal Flint 166 B4
Mandally Highld 290 C4
Manea Cambs 139 F9
Maney W Mid 134 D2
Manfield N Yorks 224 C4
Mangaster Shetland 312 F5
Mangotsfield S Glos 61 D7
Mangrove Green Herts 104 G2
Mangurstadh W Isles 304 E2
Manhay Corn 2 C5
Manian-fawr Pembs 92 B3
Mankinholes W Yorks 196 C3
Manley Ches W 183 G8
Devon 27 E7
Manley Common
Ches W 183 G8
Manmoel Caerph 77 E11
Man-moel Caerph 77 E11
Mannal Argyll 288 E1
Mannamead Plym 7 D9
Mannerston W Loth 279 F10
Manningford Abbots
Wilts 46 B6
Manningford Bohune
Wilts 46 B6
Manningford Bruce Wilts 46 B6
Manningham W Yorks 205 G9
Mannings Heath W Sus 36 B2
Mannington Dorset 31 F9
Manningtree Essex 107 E11
Mannofield Aberdeen 293 C11
Manor London 68 B2
Manorbier Pembs 73 F9
Manorbier Newton
Pembs 73 F8
Manor Bourne Devon 7 F9
Manordeilo Carms 94 F3
Manor Estate S Yorks 186 D5
Manorhill Borders 262 C5
Manor Hill Corner Lincs 157 F8
Manor House W Mid 135 G7
Manorowen Pembs 91 D8
Manor Park Bucks 84 C4
Ches W 167 B11
E Sus 37 C7
London 68 B2
Notts 153 C11
Slough 66 C3
S Yorks 186 D5
W Yorks 205 D9
Manor Parsley Corn 4 F4
Manor Royal W Sus 51 F9
Man's Cross Essex 106 D5
Mansegate Dumfries 247 G9
Manselfield Swansea 56 D5
Mansel Lacy Hereford 97 B8
Mansell Gamage
Hereford 97 C7
Manselton Swansea 57 B7
Mansergh Cumb 212 C2
Mansewood Glasgow 267 C11
Mansfield E Ayrs 258 G4
Notts 171 C8
Mansfield Woodhouse
Notts 171 C8
Manson Green Norf 141 C10
Mansriggs Cumb 210 C5
Manston Dorset 30 D4
Kent 71 F10
W Yorks 206 F3
Manswood Dorset 31 F7
Manthorpe Lincs 155 B8
Lincs 155 F11
Mantles Green Bucks 85 F7
Manton N Lincs 200 G2
Notts 187 F9
Rutland 137 C7
Wilts 63 F7
Manton Warren N Lincs 200 F2
Manuden Essex 105 F9
Manwood Green Essex 87 C8
Manywells Height
W Yorks 205 F7
Maperton Som 29 B11
Maplebeck Notts 172 C2
Maple Cross Herts 85 G8
Mapledurham Oxon 65 D7
Mapledurwell Hants 49 C7
Maple End Essex 105 D11
Maplehurst W Sus 35 C11
Maplescombe Kent 68 G5
Mapleton Derbys 169 F11
Mapperley Derbys 170 G6
Nottingham 171 G9
Mapperley Park
Nottingham 171 G9
Mapperton Dorset 16 B6
Dorset 18 B4
Mappleborough Green
Warks 117 D11
Mappleton E Yorks 209 E10
Mapplewell S Yorks 197 F10
Mappowder Dorset 30 F2
Maraig W Isles 305 H3
Marazanvose Corn 4 E6
Marazion Corn 2 C2
Marbhig W Isles 305 G6
Marbrack Dumfries 246 E3
Marbury Ches E 167 F9
March Cambs 139 D8
S Lanark 259 G11
Marcham Oxon 83 F7
Marchamley Shrops 149 D11
Marchamley Wood
Shrops 149 C11
Marchington Staffs 152 C2
Marchington Woodlands
Staffs 152 D2
Marchroes Gwyn 144 D6
Marchwiel Wrex 166 F5
Marchwood Hants 32 E5
Marcross V Glam 58 F2
Marden Hereford 97 B10
Kent 53 E8
T&W 243 C9
Wilts 46 B5
Marden Ash Essex 87 E9
Marden Beech Kent 53 E8
Marden's Hill E Sus 52 G3
Marden Thorn Kent 53 E9
Mardleybury Herts 86 B3
Mardu Shrops 130 G5
Mardy Mon 78 B4
Shrops 148 C5
Marefield Leics 136 B4
Mareham le Fen Lincs 174 C3
Mareham on the Hill
Lincs 174 B3
Marehay Derbys 170 F5
Marehill W Sus 35 D9
Maresfield E Sus 37 C7
Maresfield Park E Sus 37 C7
Marfleet Hull 200 B6
Marford Wrex 166 D5
Margam Neath 57 D9
Margaret Marsh Dorset 30 D4
Margaret Roding Essex 87 C9
Margaretting Essex 87 E11
Margaretting Tye Essex 87 E11
Margate Kent 71 E11
Margery Sur 51 C9
Margnaheglish N Ayrs 256 C2
Margreig Dumfries 237 B10
Margrove Park Redcar 226 B3
Marham Norf 158 G4
Marhamchurch Corn 24 G2
Marholm Pboro 138 C2
Marian Flint 181 F9
Marian Cwm Denb 181 F9
Mariandyrys Anglesey 179 E10
Marianglas Anglesey 179 E8
Marian-glas Anglesey 179 E8
Mariansleigh Devon 26 C2
Marian y de *= South Beach*
Gwyn 145 C7
Marian y mor *= West End*
Gwyn 145 C7
Marine Town Kent 70 E2
Marionburgh Aberds 293 C9
Marishader Highld 298 C4
Marjoriebanks Dumfries 248 G3
Mark Dumfries 236 D3
Dumfries 237 C7
S Ayrs 236 B2
Som 43 D11
Markbeech Kent 52 E3
Markby Lincs 191 F7
Mark Causeway Som 43 D11
Mark Cross E Sus 23 C7
E Sus 52 G5
Markeaton Derbys 152 B6
Market Bosworth Leics 135 C8
Market Deeping Lincs 138 B2
Market Drayton Shrops 150 C3
Market Harborough
Leics 136 F4
Markethill Perth 286 D6
Market Lavington Wilts 46 C4
Market Overton Rutland 155 F7
Market Rasen Lincs 189 D10
Market Stainton Lincs 190 F2
Market Warsop Notts 171 B9
Market Weighton
E Yorks 208 E3
Market Weston Suff 125 B9
Markfield Leics 153 G9
Mark Hall North Essex 87 C7
Mark Hall South Essex 87 C7
Markham Caerph 77 E11
Markham Moor Notts 188 G2
Markinch Fife 286 G6
Markington N Yorks 214 F5
Markland Hill Gtr Man 195 F7
Markle E Loth 281 F11
Marksbury Bath 61 G7
Mark's Corner IoW 20 C5
Marks Gate London 87 G7
Marks Tey Essex 107 G8
Markyate Herts 85 B9
Marland Gtr Man 195 E11
Marlas Hereford 97 F8
Marl Bank Worcs 98 C5
Marlborough Wilts 63 F7
Marlbrook Hereford 115 G10
Worcs 117 C9
Marlcliff Warks 117 G11
Marldon Devon 9 C7
Marle Green E Sus 23 B9
Marle Hill Glos 99 G9
Marlesford Suff 126 F6
Marley Kent 55 C7
Kent 55 C10
Marley Green Ches E 167 F9
Marley Heights W Sus 49 G11
Marley Hill T&W 242 F6
Marley Pots T&W 243 F9
Marlingford Norf 142 B2
Mar Lodge Aberds 292 D2
Marloes Pembs 72 D3
Marlow Bucks 65 B10
Hereford 115 B8
Marlow Bottom Bucks 65 B11
Marlow Common Bucks 65 B10
Marlpit Hill Kent 52 D2
Marlpits E Sus 38 E2
Marlpool Derbys 170 F6
Marnhull Dorset 30 D3
Marnoch Aberds 302 D5
Marnock N Lanark 268 B4
Marple Gtr Man 185 D7
Marple Bridge Gtr Man 185 D7
Marpleridge Gtr Man 185 D7
Marr S Yorks 198 F4
Marrel Highld 311 H4
Marr Green Wilts 63 G8
Marrick N Yorks 223 F11
Marrister Shetland 313 G7
Marros Carms 74 D2
Marsden T&W 243 E9
W Yorks 196 E4
Marsden Height Lancs 204 F3
Marsett N Yorks 213 B8
Marsh Bucks 84 D4
Devon 28 E3
W Yorks 196 D6
W Yorks 204 F6
Marshall Meadows
Northumb 273 D9
Marshall's Cross Mers 183 C8
Marshall's Elm Som 44 G3
Marshall's Heath Herts 85 B11
Marshalsea Dorset 28 G5
Marshalswick Herts 85 D11
Marsham Norf 160 E3
Marshaw Lancs 203 C7
Marsh Baldon Oxon 83 F9
Marsh Benham W Berks 64 F2
Marshborough Kent 55 B10
Marshbrook Shrops 131 F8
Marshchapel Lincs 190 B5
Marsh Common S Glos 60 C5
Marsh End Worcs 98 D6
Marshfield Newport 59 C9
S Glos 61 E9
Marshfield Bank
Ches E 167 D11
Marshgate Corn 11 C9
Marsh Gate W Berks 63 F10
Marsh Gibbon Bucks 102 G2
Marsh Green Ches W 183 F8
Devon 14 C6
Gtr Man 194 F5
Kent 52 E2
Staffs 168 D5
Telford 150 G2
Marsh Houses Lancs 202 C5
Marshland St James
Norf 139 B10
Marsh Lane Derbys 186 F6
Glos 79 D9
Marsh Mills Som 43 F7
Marshmoor Herts 86 D2
Marshside Kent 71 F8
Mers 193 D11
Marsh Side Norf 176 E3
Marsh Street Som 42 E3
Marshwood Dorset 16 B3
Marske N Yorks 224 E2
Marske-by-the-Sea
Redcar 235 G8
Marston Ches W 183 F11
Hereford 115 F7
Lincs 172 G5
Oxon 83 D8
Staffs 150 G6
Staffs 151 D8
Warks 119 B8
Warks 134 E4
Wilts 46 B3
Marston Bigot Som 45 E9
Marston Doles Warks 119 F9
Marston Gate Som 45 D9
Marston Green W Mid 134 F3
Marston Hill Glos 81 F10
Marston Jabbett Warks 135 F7
Marston Magna Som 29 C9
Marston Meysey Wilts 81 F10
Marston Montgomery
Derbys 152 B2
Marston Moretaine
C Beds 103 C9
Marston on Dove
Derbys 152 D4
Marston St Lawrence
W Nhants 101 C10
Marston Stannett
Hereford 115 F11
Marston Trussell
W Nhants 136 F3
Marstow Hereford 79 B9
Marsworth Bucks 84 C6
Marten Wilts 47 B9
Marthall Ches E 184 F4
Martham Norf 161 F9
Marthwaite Cumb 222 G2
Martin Hants 31 D9
Kent 55 D10
Lincs 173 D10
Lincs 174 B2
Martindale Cumb 221 B8
Martin Dales Lincs 173 C11
Martin Drove End Hants 31 C9
Martinhoe Devon 41 D7
Martinhoe Cross Devon 41 D7
Martin Hussingtree
Worcs 117 E7
Martin Mill Kent 55 D10
Martin Moor Lincs 174 C2
Martinscroft Warr 183 D11
Martin's Moss Ches E 168 C4
Martinstown Dorset 17 D8
Martinstown or
Winterbourne St Martin
Dorset 17 D8
Martlesham Suff 108 B4
Martlesham Heath Suff 108 B4
Martletwy Pembs 73 C8
Martley Worcs 116 E5
Martock Som 29 D7
Marton Ches E 168 B5
Ches W 167 B10
Cumb 210 D4
E Yorks 209 F9
Lincs 188 E4
Mbro 225 B10
N Yorks 215 G8
N Yorks 216 C4
Shrops 130 C5
Shrops 149 E8
Warks 119 D8
Marton Green Ches W 167 B10
Marton Grove Mbro 225 B9
Marton-in-the-Forest
N Yorks 215 F11
Marton-le-Moor
N Yorks 215 E7
Marton Moor Warks 119 D8
Marton Moss Side
Blackpool 202 G2
Martyr's Green Sur 50 B5
Martyr Worthy Hants 48 G4
Marwick Orkney 314 D2
Marwood Devon 40 F4
Marybank Highld 300 D4
Highld 301 B7
Maryburgh Highld 300 D5
Maryfield Aberds 293 D7
Corn 7 D8
Maryhill Glasgow 267 B11
Marykirk Aberds 293 G8
Maryland Mon 79 D8
Marylebone Gtr Man 194 F5
Marypark Moray 301 F11
Maryport Cumb 228 D6
Dumfries 236 F3
Mary Tavy Devon 12 F6
Maryton Angus 287 B7
Angus 287 B10
Marywell Aberds 293 D7
Aberds 293 D11
Angus 287 C10
Masbrough S Yorks 186 C6
Mascle Bridge Pembs 73 D7
Masham N Yorks 214 C4
Mashbury Essex 87 C11
Masongill N Yorks 212 D3
Masonhill S Ayrs 257 E9
Mastin Moor Derbys 187 F7
Mastrick Aberdeen 293 C10
Matchborough Worcs 117 D11
Matching Essex 87 C8
Matching Green Essex 87 C8
Matching Tye Essex 87 C8
Matfen Northumb 242 C2
Matfield Kent 53 E7
Mathern Mon 79 G8
Mathon Hereford 98 B4
Mathry Pembs 91 E7
Matlaske Norf 160 C3
Matley Gtr Man 185 B7
Matlock Derbys 170 C3
Matlock Bank Derbys 170 C3
Matlock Bath Derbys 170 D3
Matlock Bridge Derbys 170 D3
Matlock Cliff Derbys 170 D4
Matlock Dale Derbys 170 D3
Matshead Lancs 202 E6
Matson Glos 80 B4
Matterdale End Cumb 230 G3
Mattersey Notts 187 D11
Mattersey Thorpe
Notts 187 D11
Matthewsgreen
Wokingham 65 F10
Mattingley Hants 49 B8
Mattishall Norf 159 G11
Mattishall Burgh Norf 159 G11
Mauchline E Ayrs 257 D11
Maud Aberds 303 E9
Maudlin Corn 5 C11
Dorset 28 F5
W Sus 22 B5
Maudlin Cross Dorset 28 F5
Maugersbury Glos 100 F4
Maughold IoM 192 C5
Mauld Highld 300 F4
Maulden C Beds 103 D11
Maulds Meaburn Cumb 222 B2
Maunby N Yorks 215 B7
Maund Bryan Hereford 115 G11
Maundown Som 27 B9
Mauricewood Midloth 270 C4
Mautby Norf 161 G9
Mavesyn Ridware
Staffs 151 F11
Mavis Enderby Lincs 174 B5
Maviston Highld 301 D9
Mawbray Cumb 229 B7
Mawdesley Lancs 194 E3
Mawdlam Bridgend 57 E10
Mawgan Corn 2 D6
Mawgan Porth Corn 5 B7
Maw Green Ches E 168 D2
Mawla Corn 4 F4
Mawnan Corn 3 D7
Mawnan Smith Corn 3 D7
Mawsley N Nhants 120 B6
Mawson Green S Yorks 198 D6
Mawthorpe Lincs 191 G7
Maxey Pboro 138 B2
Maxstoke Warks 134 F4
Maxted Street Kent 54 E6

Maxton Borders 262 C4
Kent 55 E10
Maxwellheugh Borders 262 C6
Maxwelltown Dumfries 237 B11
Maxworthy Corn 11 C11
Mayals Swansea 56 C6
May Bank Staffs 168 F5
Maybole S Ayrs 257 G8
Maybury Sur 50 B4
Maybush Soton 32 E5
Mayer's Green W Mid 133 E10
Mayes Green Sur 50 F6
Mayeston Pembs 73 E8
Mayfair London 67 C9
Mayfield E Sus 37 B9
Midloth 271 C7
Northumb 243 B7
Staffs 169 F11
W Loth 269 B8
Mayford Sur 50 B3
Mayhill Swansea 56 C6
May Hill Mon 79 C8
May Hill Village Glos 98 G4
Mayland Essex 88 E6
Maylandsea Essex 88 E6
Maynard's Green E Sus 23 B9
Mayne Ho Moray 302 C2
Mayon Corn 1 D3
Maypole Kent 68 E4
Kent 71 G7
London 68 G3
Mon 79 B7
Scilly 1 G4
Maypole Green Essex 107 G9
Norf 143 D8
Suff 125 F8
Suff 126 D5
Mays Green Oxon 65 C8
May's Green N Som 59 G11
Sur 50 B5
Mayshill S Glos 61 C7
Maythorn S Yorks 197 F7
Maythorne Notts 171 D11
Maywick Shetland 313 L5
Mead Devon 13 G11
Devon 24 D2
Mead End Hants 19 B11
Hants 33 E11
Wilts 31 C8
Meadgate Bath 45 B7
Meadle Bucks 84 D4
Meadowbank Ches W 167 B11
Edin 280 G5
Meadowend Essex 106 C4
Meadowfield Durham 233 D10
Meadowfoot N Ayrs 266 F4
Meadow Green Hereford 116 F4
Meadow Hall S Yorks 186 C5
Meadow Head S Yorks 186 E4
Meadowley Shrops 132 E3
Meadowmill E Loth 281 G8
Meadows Nottingham 153 B11
Meadowtown Shrops 130 C6
Meads E Sus 23 F10
Meadside Oxon 83 G9
Mead Vale Sur 51 D9
Meadwell Devon 12 E4
Meaford Staffs 151 B7
Meagill N Yorks 205 B9
Mealabost W Isles 304 E6
Mealabost Bhuirgh
W Isles 304 C6
Mealasta W Isles 304 F1
Meal Bank Cumb 221 F10
Meal Hill W Yorks 197 F7
Mealrigg Cumb 229 B8
Mealsgate Cumb 229 C10
Meanwood W Yorks 205 F11
Mearbeck N Yorks 212 G6
Meare Som 44 E3
Meare Green Som 28 B4
Som 28 C3
Mearns Bath 45 B7
E Renf 267 D10
Mears Ashby N Nhants 120 D6
Measborough Dike
S Yorks 197 F11
Measham Leics 152 G6
Meath Green Sur 51 E9
Meathop Cumb 211 C8
Meaux E Yorks 209 F7
Meaver Corn 2 F5
Meavy Devon 7 B10
Medbourne Leics 136 E5
M Keynes 102 D6
Medburn Northumb 242 C4
Meddon Devon 24 D3
Meden Vale Notts 171 B9
Medhurst Row Kent 52 D3
Medlam Lincs 174 D4
Medlar Lancs 202 F4
Medlicott Shrops 131 E8
Medlyn Corn 2 C6
Medmenham Bucks 65 C10
Medomsley Durham 242 G4
Medstead Hants 49 F7
Meerbrook Staffs 169 C7
Meer Common Hereford 115 G7
Meer End W Mid 118 C4
Meerhay Dorset 29 G7
Meers Bridge Lincs 191 D7
Meersbrook S Yorks 186 E5
Meesden Herts 105 E8
Meeson Telford 150 E3
Meeson Heath Telford 150 E3
Meeth Devon 25 F8
Meethe Devon 25 C11
Meeting Green Suff 124 F4
Meeting House Hill
Norf 160 D6
Meggernie Castle Perth 285 C9
Meggethead Borders 260 E5
Meidrim Carms 92 G5
Meifod Denb 165 D8
Powys 148 G3
Meigle N Ayrs 266 B3
Perth 286 C6
Meikle Earnock
S Lanark 268 E4
Meikle Ferry Highld 309 L7
Meikle Forter Angus 292 G3
Meikle Gluich Highld 309 L6
Meikle Obney Perth 286 D4
Meikleour Perth 286 D5
Meikle Pinkerton
E Loth 282 F4
Meikle Strath Aberds 293 F8
Meikle Tarty Aberds 303 G9
Meikle Wartle Aberds 303 F7
Meinciau Carms 75 C7
Meir Stoke 168 G6
Meir Heath Staffs 168 G6
Melbourn Cambs 105 C7
Melbourne Derbys 153 D7
E Yorks 207 E11
S Lanark 269 G11
Melbury Abbas Dorset 30 D5
Melbury Bubb Dorset 29 F9
Melbury Osmond Dorset 29 F9
Melbury Sampford
Dorset 29 F9
Melby Shetland 313 H3
Melchbourne Bedford 121 D10
Melcombe Som 43 G9
Melcombe Bingham
Dorset 30 G3
Melcombe Regis Dorset 17 E9
Meldon Devon 13 C7
Northumb 252 G4
Meldreth Cambs 105 B7
Meldrum Ho Aberds 303 G8
Melfort Argyll 275 B9
Melgarve Highld 290 D6
Meliden = *Gallt Melyd*
Denb 181 E9
Melinbyrhedyn Powys 128 D6
Melin Caiach Caerph 77 F10
Melincourt Neath 76 E4
Melincryddan Neath 57 B8
Melinsey Corn 3 B10
Melin-y-coed Conwy 164 C4
Melin-y-ddôl Powys 129 B11
Melin-y-grug Powys 129 B11
Melin-y-Wig Denb 165 F8
Melkington Northumb 273 G7
Melkinthorpe Cumb 231 F7
Melkridge Northumb 240 E6
Melksham Wilts 62 G2
Melksham Forest Wilts 62 G2
Mellangaun Highld 307 L3
Mellangoose Corn 2 D5
Melldalloch Argyll 275 F10
Mell Green W Berks 64 D3
Mellguards Cumb 230 B4
Melling Lancs 211 E11
Mers 193 G11
Mellingey Corn 10 G4
Melling Mount Mers 194 G2
Mellis Suff 126 C2
Mellis Green Suff 125 C11
Mellon Charles Highld 307 K3
Mellon Udrigle Highld 307 K3
Mellor Gtr Man 185 D7
Lancs 203 G9
Mellor Brook Lancs 203 G8
Mells Som 45 D8
Suff 127 B8
Mells Green Som 45 D8
Melmerby Cumb 231 D8
N Yorks 213 B11
N Yorks 214 D6
Melon Green Suff 124 F6
Melplash Dorset 16 B5
Melrose Borders 262 C2
Melsetter Orkney 314 H2
Melsonby N Yorks 224 D3
Meltham W Yorks 196 E6
Meltham Mills W Yorks 196 E6
Melton E Yorks 200 B3
Suff 126 G5
Meltonby E Yorks 207 C11
Melton Constable Norf 159 C10
Melton Mowbray Leics 154 F5
Melton Ross N Lincs 200 E5
Melvaig Highld 307 L2
Melverley Shrops 148 F6
Melverley Green Shrops 148 F6
Melvich Highld 310 C2
Membland Devon 7 F11
Membury Devon 28 G3
Memsie Aberds 303 C9
Memus Angus 287 B8
Mena Corn 5 C10
Menabilly Corn 5 E11
Menadarva Corn 4 G2
Menagissey Corn 4 F4
Menai Bridge = *Porthaethwy*
Anglesey 179 G9
Mendham Suff 142 G5
Mendlesham Suff 126 D2
Mendlesham Green
Suff 125 E11
Menethorpe N Yorks 216 F5
Mengham Hants 21 B10
Menheniot Corn 6 C5
Menherion Corn 2 B6
Menithwood Worcs 116 D4
Menna Corn 5 E8
Mennock Dumfries 247 B8
Menston W Yorks 205 E9
Menstrie Clack 278 B6
Mentmore Bucks 84 B6
Menzion Borders 260 E3
Meoble Highld 295 G9
Meole Brace Shrops 149 G9
Meols Mers 182 C2
Meon Hants 33 G8
Meonstoke Hants 33 D10
Meopham Kent 68 F6
Meopham Green Kent 68 F6
Meopham Station Kent 68 F6
Mepal Cambs 139 G8
Meppershall C Beds 104 D2
Merbach Hereford 96 B6
Mercaton Derbys 170 G3
Merchant Fields
W Yorks 197 B7
Merchiston Edin 280 G4
Mere Ches E 184 E2
Wilts 45 G10
Mere Brow Lancs 194 D2
Mereclough Lancs 204 G3
Mere Green W Mid 134 D2
Worcs 117 E9
Merehead Wrex 149 B9
Mere Heath Ches W 183 G11
Meresborough Medway 69 G10
Mereside Blackpool 202 G2
Meretown Staffs 150 E5
Mereworth Kent 53 C7
Mergie Aberds 293 E9
Meriden Herts 85 F10
W Mid 134 G4
Merkadale Highld 294 B5
Merkland Dumfries 237 B9
N Ayrs 256 B2
S Ayrs 244 E6
Merkland Lodge Highld 309 G4
Merle Common Sur 52 D2
Merley BCP 18 B6
Merlin's Bridge Pembs 72 C6
Merlin's Cross Pembs 73 E7
Merridale W Mid 133 D7
Merridge Som 43 G8
Merrie Gardens IoW 21 E7
Merrifield Devon 8 F6
Devon 24 G3
Merrington Shrops 149 E9
Merrion Pembs 72 F6
Merriott Dorset 16 B6
Som 28 E6
Merriottsford Som 28 E6
Merritown BCP 19 B8
Merrivale Devon 12 F6
Hereford 98 G2
Merrow Sur 50 C4
Merrybent Darl 224 C4
Merry Field Hill Dorset 31 G8
Merry Hill Herts 85 G10
W Mid 133 D7
Merryhill Green
Wokingham 65 E9
Merrylee E Renf 267 D11
Merry Lees Leics 135 B9
Merrymeet Corn 6 B5
Merry Meeting Corn 11 G7
Merry Oak Soton 32 E6
Mersham Kent 54 F5
Merstham Sur 51 C9
Merston W Sus 22 C5
Merstone IoW 20 E6
Merther Corn 5 G7
Merther Lane Corn 5 G7
Merthyr Carms 93 G7
Merthyr Cynog Powys 95 D9
Merthyr-Dyfan V Glam 58 F6
Merthyr Mawr Bridgend 57 F11
Merthyr Tydfil M Tydf 77 D8
Merthyr Vale M Tydf 77 F9
Merton Devon 25 E8
London 67 E9
Norf 141 D8
Oxon 83 B9
Merton Park London 67 F9
Mervinslaw Borders 262 G5
Meshaw Devon 26 D3
Messing Essex 88 B5
Messingham N Lincs 199 G11
Mesty Croft W Mid 133 E9
Mesur-y-dorth Pembs 87 E11
Metal Bridge Durham 233 E11
Metfield Suff 142 G5
Metherell Corn 7 B8
Metheringham Lincs 173 C9
Methersgate Suff 108 B5
Methil Fife 281 B7
Methilhill Fife 281 B7
Methlem Gwyn 144 C3
Methley W Yorks 197 B11
Methley Junction
W Yorks 197 B11
Methley Lanes
W Yorks 197 B11
Methlick Aberds 303 F8
Methven Perth 286 E4
Methwold Norf 140 E4
Methwold Hythe Norf 140 E4
Mettingham Suff 143 F7
Metton Norf 160 B3
Mevagissey Corn 5 G10
Mewith Head N Yorks 212 F4
Mexborough S Yorks 187 B7
Mey Highld 310 B6
Meyrick Park BCP 19 C7
Meysey Hampton Glos 81 F10
Miabhag W Isles 305 H2
W Isles 305 J3
Miabhig W Isles 304 E2
Mial Highld 299 B7
Michaelchurch Hereford 97 F10
Michaelchurch Escley
Hereford 96 E6
Michaelchurch on Arrow
Powys 114 G4
Michaelston-le-Pit
V Glam 59 E7
Michaelston-y-Fedw
Newport 59 C8
Michaelstow Corn 11 F7
Michealston-super-Ely
Cardiff 58 D6
Michelcombe Devon 8 B3
Micheldever Hants 48 F4
Michelmersh Hants 32 B4
Mickfield Suff 126 E2
Micklebring S Yorks 187 C8
Mickleby N Yorks 226 C6
Micklefield Bucks 84 G5
W Yorks 206 G4
Micklefield Green Herts 85 F8
Mickleham Sur 51 C7
Micklehurst Gtr Man 196 G3
Mickleover Derby 152 C6
Micklethwaite Cumb 239 G7
W Yorks 205 E8
Mickleton Durham 232 G5
Glos 100 C3
Mickletown W Yorks 197 B11
Mickle Trafford Ches W 166 B6
Mickley Derbys 186 F4
N Yorks 214 D5
Shrops 150 C2
Mickley Green Suff 124 F6
Mickley Square
Northumb 242 E3
Midanbury Hants 33 E7
Mid Ardlaw Aberds 303 C9
Mid Auchinleck Invclyd 276 G6
Midbea Orkney 314 B4
Mid Beltie Aberds 293 C8
Mid Calder W Loth 269 B11
Mid Cloch Forbie
Aberds 303 D7
Mid Clyth Highld 310 F6
Middle Assendon Oxon 65 B8
Middle Aston Oxon 101 F9
Middle Balnald Perth 286 B4
Middle Barton Oxon 101 F8
Middle Bickenhill
W Mid 134 G4
Middlebie Dumfries 238 B6
Middle Bockhampton
BCP 19 B9
Middle Bourne Sur 49 E10
Middle Bridge N Som 60 D3
Middle Burnham Som 43 D10
Middle Cairncake
Aberds 303 E8
Middlecave N Yorks 216 E5
Middle Chinnock Som 29 E7
Middle Claydon Bucks 102 F4
Middle Cliff Staffs 169 E8
Middlecliffe S Yorks 198 F2
Middlecott Devon 13 D10
Devon 24 F6
Devon 26 F3
Middle Crackington Corn 11 B9
Middlecroft Derbys 186 G6
Middle Drums Angus 287 B9
Middle Duntisbourne
Glos 81 D7
Middlefield Falk 279 E7
Middleforth Green
Lancs 194 B4
Middle Green Bucks 66 C4
Som 27 D10
Suff 124 D4
Middleham N Yorks 214 B2
Middle Handley Derbys 186 F6
Middle Harling Norf 141 F9
Middle Herrington T&W 243 G9
Middlehill Corn 6 B5
Wilts 61 F10
Middle Hill Pembs 73 C7
Staffs 133 B9
Middlehope Shrops 131 F9
Middle Kames Argyll 275 E10
Middle Littleton Worcs 99 B11
Middle Luxton Devon 28 E2
Middle Madeley Staffs 168 F3
Middle Maes-coed
Hereford 96 E6
Middlemarsh Dorset 29 F11
Middle Marwood Devon 40 F4
Middle Mayfield Staffs 169 G10
Middle Mill Pembs 87 F11
Middlemoor Devon 12 G5
Middlemuir Aberds 303 D9
Aberds 303 E8
Aberds 303 G9
Middleport Stoke 168 F5
Middle Quarter Kent 53 F11
Middle Rainton T&W 234 B2
Middle Rasen Lincs 189 D9
Middlerig Falk 279 F8
Middle Rigg Perth 286 G4
Middle Rocombe Devon 9 B8
Middlesbrough Mbro 234 G5
Middlesceugh Cumb 230 C4
Middleshaw Cumb 211 B11
Middle Side Durham 232 F4
Middlesmoor N Yorks 213 E11
Middle Stoford Som 27 C11
Middle Stoke Devon 13 G9
Medway 69 D10
W Mid 119 B7
Middlestone Durham 233 E11
Middlestone Moor
Durham 233 E10
Middle Stoughton Som 44 D2
Middlestown W Yorks 197 D9
Middle Strath W Loth 279 G8
Middle Street Glos 80 E3
Middle Taphouse Corn 6 C3
Middlethird Borders 272 G3
Middlethorpe York 207 D7
Middleton Aberds 293 B10
Argyll 288 E1
Cumb 212 B2
Derbys 169 C11
Derbys 170 D3
Essex 107 D7
Gtr Man 195 F11
Hants 48 E2
Hereford 115 D10
Hrtlpl 234 E6
IoW 20 D2
Lancs 202 B4
Midloth 271 D7
N Nhants 136 F6
Norf 158 F3
Northumb 252 F3
Northumb 264 B4
N Yorks 204 E5
N Yorks 205 D8
N Yorks 216 B5
Perth 286 C5
Perth 286 F2
Perth 286 G5
Shrops 115 B10
Shrops 130 D5
Shrops 148 D6
Suff 127 D8
Swansea 56 D2
Warks 134 D3
W Yorks 197 B10
Middleton Baggot
Shrops 132 E2
Middleton Cheney
W Nhants 101 C9
Middleton Green Staffs 151 B9
Middleton Hall
Northumb 263 D11
Middleton-in-Teesdale
Durham 232 F4
Middleton Junction
Gtr Man 195 G11
Middleton Moor Suff 127 D8
Middleton of Rora
Aberds 303 E10
Middleton One Row
Darl 225 C7
Middleton-on-Leven
N Yorks 225 D9
Middleton-on-Sea
W Sus 35 G7
Middleton on the Hill
Hereford 115 E10
Middleton-on-the-Wolds
E Yorks 208 D4
Middleton Place Cumb 219 G11
Middleton Priors
Shrops 132 E2
Middleton Quernhow
N Yorks 214 D6
Middleton St George
Darl 224 C6
Middleton Scriven
Shrops 132 F3
Middleton Stoney
Oxon 101 G10
Middleton Tyas N Yorks 224 D4
Middletown Cumb 219 D9
N Som 60 E3
Powys 148 G6
Warks 117 E11
Middle Town Scilly 1 F4
Middle Tysoe Warks 100 C6
Middle Wallop Hants 47 F9
Middle Weald M Keynes 102 D5
Middlewich Ches E 167 B11
Middlewick Wilts 61 E11
Middle Wick Glos 80 F2
Middle Winterslow Wilts 47 G8
Middlewood Ches E 184 E6
Corn 11 F11
S Yorks 186 C4
Middle Woodford Wilts 46 F6
Middlewood Green
Suff 125 E11
Middleyard Glos 80 E4
Middlezoy Som 43 G11
Middridge Durham 233 F11
Midelney Som 28 C6
Midfield Highld 308 C5
Midford Bath 61 G9
Midgard Borders 262 F3
Mid Garrary Dumfries 237 B7
Midge Hall Lancs 194 C4
Midgehole W Yorks 196 B3
Midgeholme Cumb 240 F4
Midgham W Berks 64 F5
Midgham Green W Berks 64 F5
Midgley W Yorks 196 B4
W Yorks 197 E9
Mid Holmwood Sur 51 D7
Midhopestones S Yorks 186 B2
Midhurst W Sus 34 C5
Mid Lambrook Som 28 D6
Midland Orkney 314 F3
Mid Lavant W Sus 22 B5
Midlem Borders 262 D2
Mid Letter Argyll 284 G4
Midlock S Lanark 259 E11
Mid Main Highld 300 F4
Midmar Aberds 293 C8
Midmuir Argyll 289 G11
Mid Murthat Dumfries 248 D3
Midpark Argyll 255 B11
Midplaugh Aberds 302 E5
Midsomer Norton Bath 45 C7
Midton Invclyd 276 F4
Midtown Highld 307 L3
Highld 308 C5
Midtown of Buchromb
Moray 302 E3
Midtown of Glass
Aberds 302 E4
Mid Urchany Highld 301 E8
Midville Lincs 174 D5
Mid Walls Shetland 313 H4
Midway Ches E 184 E6
Som 45 D7
Mid Yell Shetland 312 D7
Miekle Toux Aberds 302 D5
Migdale Highld 309 K6
Migvie Aberds 292 C6
Milarrochy Stirling 277 C8
Milber Devon 14 G3
Milborne Port Som 29 D11
Milborne St Andrew
Dorset 18 B2
Milborne Wick Som 29 C11
Milbourne Northumb 242 B4
Wilts 62 B2
Milburn Aberds 302 E5
Aberds 302 F6
Cumb 231 F9
Milbury Heath S Glos 79 G11
Milby N Yorks 215 F8
Milch Hill Essex 106 G4
Milcombe Corn 6 D4
Oxon 101 E8
Milden Suff 107 B9
Mildenhall Suff 124 C4
Wilts 63 F8
Milebrook Powys 114 C6
Milebush Kent 53 D9
Mile Cross Norf 160 G4
Mile Elm Wilts 62 F3
Mile End Cambs 140 G2
Devon 14 G2
Essex 107 F9
Glos 79 C9
London 67 C11
Suff 124 G6
Mileham Norf 159 F8
Mile Oak Brighton 36 F2
Kent 53 E7
Shrops 148 D6
Staffs 134 C3
Miles Green Staffs 168 F4
Sur 50 B3
Miles Hill W Yorks 205 F11
Milesmark Fife 279 D11
Miles Platting Gtr Man 184 B5
Miles's Green W Berks 64 F4
Mile Town Kent 70 E2
Milfield Northumb 263 C10
Milford Derbys 170 F5
Devon 24 C2
Powys 129 E11
Shrops 149 E8
Staffs 151 E9
Sur 50 E2
Wilts 31 B11
Milford Haven Pembs 72 D6
Milford on Sea Hants 19 C11
Milkhouse Water Wilts 63 G7
Milkieston Borders 270 F4
Milkwall Glos 79 D9
Milkwell Wilts 30 C6
Milland W Sus 34 B4
Millarston Renfs 267 C9
Millbank Aberds 303 E11
Highld 310 C5
Kent 71 F8
Mill Bank W Yorks 196 C4
Millbeck Cumb 229 F11
Millbounds Orkney 314 C5
Millbreck Aberds 303 E10
Millbridge Sur 49 E10
Millbrook C Beds 103 D10
Corn 7 E8
Devon 41 G9
Gtr Man 185 B7
Soton 32 E5
Mill Brow Gtr Man 185 D7
Millburn S Ayrs 257 D10
Millcombe Devon 8 F6
Mill Common Norf 142 C6
Suff 143 G8
Mill Corner E Sus 38 C4
Milldale Staffs 169 E10
Mill Dam N Yorks 212 F3
Millden Lodge Angus 293 F7
Milldens Angus 287 B9
Millend Glos 80 D3
Glos 80 F3
Mill End Bucks 65 C9
Cambs 124 F3
Glos 81 C10
Herts 85 G8
Herts 104 E6
Mill End Green Essex 106 F2
Millendreath Corn 6 E5
Millerhill Midloth 270 B6
Miller's Dale Derbys 185 G10
Miller's Green Derbys 170 E3
Essex 87 D9
Millersneuk E Dunb 278 G3
Millerston Glasgow 268 B2
Mill Farm Aberds 303 C8
Millfield Pboro 138 C3
T&W 243 F9
Millgate Lancs 195 D11
Norf 160 D3
Millgillhead Cumb 229 G7
Mill Green Cambs 106 B2
Essex 87 E10
Hants 64 G4
Herts 86 D2
Norf 142 G2
Shrops 150 D3
Suff 107 C9
Suff 125 F9
Suff 126 E2
W Mid 133 C11
Millhalf Hereford 96 B5
Millhall Kent 53 B8
Mill Hall Dumfries 237 E8
Millhayes Devon 27 E10
Devon 28 G2
Millhead Lancs 211 E9
Millheugh S Lanark 268 E5
Millhill Devon 12 G5
Mill Hill Blackburn 195 B7
Essex 88 G4
E Sus 23 D10
Glos 79 D10
Gtr Man 195 F8
Kent 55 C11
Lincs 175 B8
London 86 G2
Suff 125 G7
Mill Hills Suff 108 B5
Mill Hirst N Yorks 214 G3
Millhouse Argyll 275 F10
Cumb 230 D3
Millhousebridge
Dumfries 248 F4
Millhouse Green
S Yorks 197 G8
Millhouses S Yorks 186 E4
Millhouses *continued*
S Yorks 198 G2
Millikenpark Renfs 267 C8
Millin Cross Pembs 73 C7
Millington E Yorks 208 C2
Millington Green
Derbys 170 F3
Mill Lane Hants 49 C9
Mill Meads London 67 C11
Millmeece Staffs 150 C6
Millmoor Devon 27 E10
Millness Cumb 211 C10
Mill of Brydock Aberds 302 D6
Mill of Chon Stirling 285 G8
Mill of Haldane W Dunb 277 E8
Mill of Kingoodie
Aberds 303 G8
Mill of Lynebain Aberds 302 F4
Mill of Muiresk Aberds 302 E6
Mill of Rango Orkney 314 E2
Mill of Sterin Aberds 292 D5
Mill of Uras Aberds 293 E10
Millom Cumb 210 C3
Millook Corn 11 B9
Millow C Beds 104 C4
Mill Park Argyll 255 G8
Mill Place N Lincs 200 F3
Millpool Corn 2 C3
Corn 11 G8
Millport N Ayrs 266 E3
Millquarter Dumfries 246 G4
Mill Shaw W Yorks 205 G11
Mill Side Cumb 211 C8
Mill Street Kent 53 B7
Norf 159 F11
Suff 107 D9
Milltack Aberds 303 D7
Millthorpe Derbys 186 F4
Lincs 156 C2
Mill Throop BCP 19 B8
Millthrop Cumb 222 G3
Milltimber Aberdeen 293 C10
Milltown Aberds 292 C4
Corn 6 B2
Corn 6 D2
Derbys 170 C5
Devon 40 F5
Highld 301 E9
Milltown of Aberdalgie
Perth 286 E4
Milltown of Auchindoun
Moray 302 E3
Milltown of Craigston
Aberds 303 D7
Milltown of Edinvillie
Moray 302 E2
Milltown of Kildrummy
Aberds 292 B6
Milltown of Rothiemay
Moray 302 E5
Milltown of Towie
Aberds 292 B6
Millwall London 67 D11
Milnathort Perth 286 G5
Milner's Heath Ches W 167 C7
Milngavie E Dunb 277 G11
Milnquarter Falk 278 F6
Milnrow Gtr Man 196 E2
Milnsbridge W Yorks 196 D6
Milnshaw Lancs 195 B9
Milnthorpe Cumb 211 C9
W Yorks 197 D10
Milnwood N Lanark 268 D4
Milo Carms 75 B9
Milson Shrops 116 C2
Milstead Kent 54 B2
Milston Wilts 47 D7
Milthorpe W Nhants 101 B11
Milton Angus 287 C7
Angus 292 E6
Cambs 123 E9
Cumb 211 C10
Cumb 240 E3
Derbys 152 D6
Dumfries 236 D4
Dumfries 237 B10
Dumfries 247 G8
Fife 287 E8
Glasgow 267 B11
Highld 299 E7
Highld 300 D3
Highld 300 E5
Highld 300 F4
Highld 301 B7
Highld 301 E7
Highld 310 D7
Kent 69 E7
Moray 292 B3
Moray 302 C5
Notts 188 G2
N Som 59 G10
Oxon 83 G7
Oxon 101 E8
Pembs 73 E8
Perth 286 F3
Powys 114 G4
Ptsmth 21 B9
Som 29 C7
Stirling 285 G9
Stoke 168 E6
S Yorks 197 G11
W Dunb 277 G8
Wilts 45 G11
Milton Abbas Dorset 30 G4
Milton Bridge Midloth 270 C4
Milton Bryan C Beds 103 E9
Milton Clevedon Som 45 F7
Milton Coldwells Aberds 303 F9
Milton Combe Devon 7 B9
Milton Common Oxon 83 E11
Milton Coombe Devon 7 B9
Milton Damerel Devon 24 E5
Miltonduff Moray 301 C11
Milton End Glos 80 C2
Glos 81 E10
Milton Ernest Bedford 121 F10
Milton Green Ches W 167 D7
Devon 12 F4
Milton Heights Oxon 83 G7
Miltonhill Moray 301 C10
Milton Hill Devon 14 F4
Oxon 83 G7
Miltonise Dumfries 236 B3
Milton Keynes
M Keynes 103 D7
Milton Keynes Village
M Keynes 103 D7
Milton Lilbourne Wilts 63 G7
Milton Malsor W Nhants 120 F4
Milton Morenish Perth 285 D10
Milton of Auchinhove
Aberds 293 C7
Milton of Balgonie Fife 287 G7
Milton of Buchanan
Stirling 277 C8
Milton of Campfield
Aberds 293 C8
Milton of Campsie
E Dunb 278 F3
Milton of Corsindae
Aberds 293 C8
Milton of Cullerlie
Aberds 293 C9
Milton of Cultoquhey
Perth 286 E2
Milton of Cushnie
Aberds 293 B7
Milton of Dalcapon
Perth 286 B3
Milton of Drimmie
Perth 286 B5
Milton of Edradour
Perth 286 B3
Milton of Gollanfield
Highld 301 D7
Milton of Lesmore
Aberds 302 G4
Milton of Logie Aberds 292 C6
Milton of Machany
Perth 286 F3
Milton of Mathers
Aberds 293 G9
Milton of Murtle
Aberdeen 293 C10
Milton of Noth Aberds 302 G5
Milton of Tullich Aberds 292 D5
Milton on Stour Dorset 30 B3
Milton Regis Kent 70 F2
Milton Street E Sus 23 E8
Milton under Wychwood
Oxon 82 B3
Milverton Som 27 B10
Warks 118 D6
Milwich Staffs 151 C9
Milwr Flint 181 G11
Mimbridge Sur 66 G3
Minard Argyll 275 D10
Minard Castle Argyll 275 D10
Minchington Dorset 31 E7
Minchinhampton Glos 80 E5
Mindrum Northumb 263 C8
Minehead Som 42 D3
Minera Wrex 166 E3
Mineshope Corn 11 B9
Minety Wilts 81 G8
Minffordd Gwyn 145 B11
Gwyn 146 G4
Gwyn 179 G9
Mingarrypark Highld 289 C8
Mingoose Corn 4 F4
Miningsby Lincs 174 C4
Minions Corn 11 G11
Minishant S Ayrs 257 G8
Minllyn Gwyn 147 G7
Minnes Aberds 303 G9
Minngearraidh W Isles 297 J3
Minnigaff Dumfries 236 C6
Minnonie Aberds 303 C7
Minnow End Essex 88 C2
Minnygap Dumfries 248 D2
Minshull Vernon
Ches E 167 C11
Minskip N Yorks 215 G7
Minstead Hants 32 E3
Minsted W Sus 34 C5
Minster Kent 70 E3
Kent 71 G10
Minsterley Shrops 131 C7
Minster Lovell Oxon 82 C4
Minsterworth Glos 80 B3
Minterne Magna Dorset 29 G11
Minterne Parva Dorset 29 G11
Minting Lincs 189 G11
Mintlaw Aberds 303 E10
Minto Borders 262 E3
Minto Kames Borders 262 E3
Minton Shrops 131 E8
Minwear Pembs 73 C8
Minworth W Mid 134 E3
Mirbister Orkney 314 E2
Mirehouse Cumb 219 B9
Mireland Highld 310 C7
Mirfield W Yorks 197 D8
Miserden Glos 80 D6
Misery Corner Norf 142 F5
Miskin Rhondda 58 C4
Rhondda 77 F8
Misselfore Wilts 31 C8
Misson Notts 187 C11
Misterton Leics 135 G11
Notts 188 C3
Som 29 F7
Misterton Soss Notts 188 B3
Mistley Essex 108 E2
Mistley Heath Essex 108 E2
Mitcham London 67 F9
Mitcheldean Glos 79 B11
Mitchell Corn 5 E7
Mitchell Hill Borders 260 C3
Mitchellslacks
Dumfries 247 D11
Mitchelston Borders 271 F9
Mitchel Troy Mon 79 C7
Mitcheltroy Common
Mon 79 D7
Mite Houses Cumb 219 F11
Mitford Northumb 252 F5
Mithian Corn 4 E4
Mithian Downs Corn 4 F4
Mitton Staffs 151 F7
Worcs 99 E8
Mixbury Oxon 102 E2
Mixenden W Yorks 196 B5
Mixtow Corn 6 E2
Moat Cumb 239 C10
Moats Tye Suff 125 F10
Mobberley Ches E 184 F3
Staffs 169 G8
Moblake Ches E 167 G11
Mobwell Bucks 84 E5
Moccas Hereford 97 C7
Mochdre Conwy 180 F4
Powys 129 F11
Mochrum Dumfries 236 E5
Mockbeggar Hants 31 F11
Kent 54 E6
Medway 69 E8
Mockerkin Cumb 229 G7
Moclett Orkney 314 B4
Modbury Devon 8 E3
Moddershall Staffs 151 B8
Model Village Derbys 187 G8
Warks 119 E8
Modest Corner Kent 52 E5
Moelfre Anglesey 179 D8
Conwy 181 G7
Powys 148 D3
Moel Tryfan Gwyn 163 D8
Moel-y-crio Flint 165 B11
Moffat Dumfries 248 B3
Moffat Mills N Lanark 268 C5
Mogador Sur 51 C8
Mogworthy Devon 26 D5
Moira Leics 152 F6
Moity Powys 96 C3
Molash Kent 54 C4
Mol-chlach Highld 294 D6
Mold Flint 166 C2
Moldgreen W Yorks 197 D7
Molehill Green Essex 105 G11
Molehill Green *continued*
Essex 106 G4
Molescroft E Yorks 208 E6
Molesden Northumb 252 G4
Molesworth Cambs 121 B11
Molinnis Corn 5 D10
Moll Highld 295 B7
Molland Devon 26 B4
Mollington Ches W 182 G5
Oxon 101 B8
Mollinsburn N Lanark 278 G4
Monachty Ceredig 111 E10
Monachylemore Stirling 285 F8
Monar Lodge Highld 300 E2
Monaughty Powys 114 D4
Monboddo House
Aberds 293 F9
Mondaytown Shrops 130 B6
Mondynes Aberds 293 F9
Monemore Stirling 285 D9
Monevechadan Argyll 284 G5
Monewden Suff 126 F4
Moneyacres E Ayrs 267 E8
Moneydie Perth 286 E4
Moneyhill Herts 85 G8
Money Hill Leics 153 F7
Moneyrow Green
Windsor 65 D11
Moneystone Staffs 169 F9
Mongleath Corn 3 C7
Moniaive Dumfries 247 E7
Monifieth Angus 287 D8
Monikie Angus 287 D8
Monimail Fife 286 F6
Monington Pembs 92 C2
Monk Bretton S Yorks 197 F11
Monk End N Yorks 224 D5
Monken Hadley London 86 F3
Monkerton Devon 14 C5
Monk Fryston N Yorks 198 B4
Monk Hesleden Durham 234 D5
Monkhide Hereford 98 C2
Monkhill Cumb 239 F8
W Yorks 198 C3
Monkhopton Shrops 132 E2
Monkland Hereford 115 F9
Monkleigh Devon 25 C7
Monkmoor Shrops 149 G10
Monknash V Glam 58 E2
Monkokehampton Devon 25 F9
Monkscross Corn 12 G3
Monkseaton T&W 243 C8
Monks Eleigh Suff 107 B9
Monk's Gate W Sus 36 B2
Monks Heath Ches E 184 G4
Monk Sherborne Hants 48 B6
Monkshill Aberds 303 E7
Monks Hill Kent 53 E11
Monksilver Som 42 F5
Monks Kirby Warks 135 G9
Monk Soham Suff 126 D4
Monks Orchard London 67 F11
Monk's Park Wilts 61 F11
Monkspath W Mid 118 B2
Monks Risborough Bucks 84 E4
Monksthorpe Lincs 174 B6
Monkston Park
M Keynes 103 D7
Monk Street Essex 106 F2
Monkswood Midloth 270 C6
Mon 78 E4
W Yorks 206 F2
Monkton Devon 27 G11
Kent 71 G9
Pembs 73 E7
S Ayrs 257 D9
T&W 243 E8
V Glam 58 E2
Monkton Combe Bath 61 G9
Monkton Deverill Wilts 45 F11
Monkton Farleigh Wilts 61 F10
Monktonhall E Loth 280 G6
Monkton Heathfield Som 28 B3
Monkton Up Wimborne
Dorset 31 E8
Monkwearmouth T&W 243 F9
Monkwood Hants 49 G7
Monkwood Green
Worcs 116 E6
Monmarsh Hereford 97 B10
Monmore Green W Mid 133 D8
Monmouth = *Trefynwy*
Mon 79 C8
Monmouth Cap Mon 97 F7
Monnington on Wye
Hereford 97 C7
Monreith Dumfries 236 E5
Monreith Mains
Dumfries 236 E5
Montacute Som 29 D7
Montcliffe Gtr Man 195 E7
Montcoffer Ho Aberds 302 C6
Montford Argyll 266 C2
Shrops 149 G8
Montford Bridge Shrops 149 F8
Montgarrie Aberds 293 B7
Montgomery Powys 130 D4
Montgomery Lines
Hants 49 C11
Monton Gtr Man 184 B3
Montpelier Bristol 60 E5
Montrave Fife 287 G7
Montrose Angus 287 B11
Montsale Essex 89 F8
Monwode Lea Warks 134 E5
Monxton Hants 47 E10
Monyash Derbys 169 B11
Monymusk Aberds 293 B8
Monzie Perth 286 E2
Monzie Castle Perth 286 E2
Moodiesburn N Lanark 278 G3
Moolham Som 28 E5
Moon's Green Kent 38 B5
Moon's Moat Worcs 117 D11
Moonzie Fife 287 F7
Moor Som 28 D6
Mooradale Shetland 312 F6
Moor Allerton W Yorks 205 F11
Mooray Wilts 46 G3
Moorby Lincs 174 C3
Moorclose Cumb 228 F5
Gtr Man 195 F11
Moor Common Bucks 84 G4
Moorcot Hereford 115 F7
Moor Crichel Dorset 31 F7
Moor Cross Devon 8 D2
Moordown BCP 19 C7
Moore Halton 183 E9
Moor Edge W Yorks 205 F7
Moorend Cumb 239 G8
Derbys 170 F2
Dumfries 239 C7
Glos 80 C5
Glos 80 E2
Gtr Man 185 D7
S Glos 61 D7
Moor End Bucks 84 G4
Cambs 105 B7
C Beds 103 G9

Moor End *continued*
Durham 234 C2
EYorks 208 F2
Glos 99 G9
Lancs 202 E3
NYorks 207 F7
NYorks 215 G7
SYorks 197 G9
Worcs 117 F8
WYorks 196 B5
WYorks 206 D4
York 207 B9
Moorend Cross Hereford 98 B4
Moor End Field NYorks 215 F8
Moorends SYorks 199 D7
Moorfield Derbys 185 C8
Moorgate Norf 160 C3
SYorks 186 C6
Moorgreen Hants 33 D7
Notts 171 F7
Moor Green Herts 104 F6
Staffs 169 G7
Wilts 61 F11
WMid 133 G11
Moorhaigh Notts 171 C8
Moorhall Derbys 186 G4
Moor Hall WMid 134 D2
Moorhampton Hereford 97 B7
Moorhaven Village Devon 8 D3
Moorhayne Devon 28 F2
Moorhead WYorks 205 F8
Moor Head WYorks 197 B8
WYorks 197 E8
Moorhey GtrMan 196 G2
Moorhole SYorks 186 E6
Moorhouse Cumb 239 F8
Cumb 239 G7
Notts 172 B3
SYorks 198 E3
Moorhouse Bank Sur 52 C2
Moorhouses Lincs 174 D3
Moorland or Northmoor Green Som 43 G10
Moorledge Bath 60 G5
Moorlinch Som 43 F11
Moor Monkton NYorks 206 B6
Moor Monkton Moor
NYorks 206 B6
Moor of Balvack Aberds 293 B8
Moor of Granary
Moray 301 D10
Moor of Ravenstone
Dumfries 236 E5
Moor Park Cumb 229 D7
Hereford 97 C9
Herts 85 G9
Sur 49 D11
Moor Row Cumb 219 C10
Cumb 229 B10
Moorsholm Redcar 226 C3
Moorside ChesW 182 F3
Dorset 30 D3
Durham 233 B7
GtrMan 195 G9
GtrMan 196 F3
WYorks 197 B8
WYorks 205 F10
Moor Side Lancs 202 F5
Lancs 202 G4
Lincs 174 D2
WYorks 197 B7
WYorks 204 F6
Moorstock Kent 54 F6
Moor Street Kent 69 F10
Moorswater Corn 6 C4
Moorthorpe WYorks 198 E3
Moor Top WYorks 197 C7
Moortown Devon 12 B2
Devon 12 G6
Devon 25 C8
Hants 31 G11
IoW 20 E4
Lincs 189 B9
Telford 150 F2
WYorks 206 F2
Morangie Highld 309 L7
Morar Highld 295 F8
Moravian Settlement
Derbys 153 B8
Môrawelon Anglesey 178 E3
Morayhill Highld 301 E7
Morborne Cambs 138 E2
Morchard Bishop Devon 26 F3
Morchard Road Devon 26 G3
Morcombelake Dorset 16 C4
Morcott Rutland 137 C8
Morda Shrops 148 D5
Morden Dorset 18 B4
London 67 F9
Morden Green Cambs 104 C5
Morden Park London 67 F8
Mordiford Hereford 97 D11
Mordington Holdings
Borders 273 D8
Mordon Durham 234 F2
More Shrops 130 E6
Morebath Devon 27 C7
Morebattle Borders 263 E7
Morecambe Lancs 211 G8
More Crichel Dorset 31 F7
Moredon Swindon 62 B6
Moredun Edin 270 B5
Morefield Highld 307 K6
Morehall Kent 55 F8
Morelaggan Argyll 284 G6
Moreleigh Devon 8 E5
Morenish Perth 285 D9
Moresby Cumb 228 G5
Moresby Parks Cumb 219 B9
Morestead Hants 33 B8
Moreton Dorset 18 D2
Essex 87 D8
Hereford 115 E10
Mers 182 C3
Oxon 82 E6
Oxon 83 E11
Staffs 150 F5
Staffs 152 D2
Moreton Corbet
Shrops 149 E11
Moretonhampstead
Devon 13 D11
Moreton-in-Marsh Glos 100 E4
Moreton Jeffries
Hereford 98 B2
Moreton Morrell Warks 118 F6
Moreton on Lugg
Hereford 97 B10
Moreton Paddox Warks 118 G6
Moreton Pinkney
WNhants 101 B11
Moreton Say Shrops 150 C2
Moreton Valence Glos 80 D3
Moretonwood Shrops 150 C2
Morfa Carms 56 B4
Carms 75 C9
Ceredig 110 G6
Gwyn 144 C3
Morfa Bach Carms 74 C5
Morfa Bychan Gwyn 145 B10
Morfa Dinlle Gwyn 162 D6
Morfa Glas Neath 76 D5
Morfa Nefyn Gwyn 162 G3
Morfydd Denb 165 F10
Morganstown Cardiff 58 C6
Morgan's Vale Wilts 31 C11
Moriah Ceredig 112 B2
Mork Glos 79 D9
Morland Cumb 231 G7
Morley ChesE 184 E4
Derbys 170 G5
Durham 233 F8
WYorks 197 B9
Morley Green ChesE 184 E4
Morleymoor Derbys 170 G5
Morley Park Derbys 170 F5
Morley St Botolph
Norf 141 D11
Morley Smithy Derbys 170 G5
Mornick Corn 12 G2
Morningside Edin 280 G3
NLanark 268 D6
Morningthorpe Norf 142 E4
Morpeth Northumb 252 F6
Morphie Aberds 293 G9
Morrey Staffs 152 F2
Morridge Side Staffs 169 E8
Morrilow Heath Staffs 151 B9
Morris Green Essex 106 E4
Morriston = *Treforys*
Swansea 57 B7
Morristown VGlam 59 E7
Morston Norf 177 E8
Mortehoe Devon 40 D3
Morthen SYorks 187 D7
Mortimer WBerks 65 G7
Mortimer's Cross
Hereford 115 E8
Mortimer West End
Hants 64 G6
Mortlake London 67 D8
Mortomley SYorks 186 B4
Morton Cumb 230 D4
Cumb 239 G9
Derbys 170 C6
IoW 21 D8
Lincs 155 E11
Lincs 172 C5
Lincs 188 C4
Norf 160 F2
Notts 172 E2
SGlos 79 G10
Shrops 148 E5
Morton Bagot Warks 118 E2
Morton Common
Shrops 148 E5
Morton Mains Dumfries 247 D9
Morton Mill Shrops 149 E11
Morton-on-Swale
NYorks 224 G6
Morton Spirt Warks 117 G10
Morton Tinmouth
Durham 233 G9
Morton Underhill
Worcs 117 F10
Morvah Corn 1 B4
Morval Corn 6 D5
Morven Lodge Aberds 292 C5
Morvich Highld 295 C11
Highld 309 J7
Morville Shrops 132 E3
Morville Heath Shrops 132 E3
Morwellham Quay Devon 7 B8
Morwenstow Corn 24 E2
Mosborough SYorks 186 E6
Moscow EAyrs 267 G9
Mose Shrops 132 E5
Mosedale Cumb 230 E3
Moseley WMid 133 D8
WMid 133 G11
Worcs 116 F6
Moses Gate GtrMan 195 F8
Mosley Common
GtrMan 195 G8
Moss Argyll 288 E1
Highld 289 C8
SYorks 198 E5
Wrex 166 E4
Mossat Aberds 292 B6
Mossbank Shetland 312 F6
Moss Bank Halton 183 D8
Mers 183 B8
Mossbay Cumb 228 F5
Mossblown SAyrs 257 E10
Mossbrow GtrMan 184 D2
Mossburnford Borders 262 F5
Mossdale Dumfries 237 B8
Mossedge Cumb 239 D11
Moss Edge Lancs 202 D4
Lancs 202 E4
Mossend NLanark 268 C4
Moss End Brack 65 E11
ChesE 183 F11
Mosser Mains Cumb 229 F8
Mossfield Highld 300 B6
Mossgate Staffs 151 B8
Mossgiel EAyrs 257 D11
Mosshouses Borders 262 B2
Moss Houses ChesE 184 G5
Mosside Angus 287 B8
Moss Lane ChesE 184 G6
Mossley ChesE 168 C5
GtrMan 196 G3
Mossley Brow GtrMan 196 G3
Mossley Hill Mers 182 D5
Moss Nook GtrMan 184 D4
Mers 183 C8
Moss of Barmuckity
Moray 302 C2
Moss of Meft Moray 302 C2
Mosspark Glasgow 267 C10
Moss Pit Staffs 151 E8
Moss Side Cumb 238 G5
GtrMan 184 B4
Moss-side Highld 301 D8
Moss Side Lancs 193 G11
Lancs 194 C4
Lancs 202 G3
Mers 182 B6
Moss-side Moray 302 D5
Mosstodloch Moray 302 D3
Mosston Angus 287 C9
Mosstown Aberds 303 C10
Mossy Lea Lancs 194 E4
Mosterton Dorset 29 F7
Moston ChesE 168 C2
ChesW 182 G6
GtrMan 195 G11
Shrops 149 D11
Moston Green ChesE 168 C2
Mostyn Flint 181 E11
Mostyn Quay Flint 181 E11
Motcombe Dorset 30 B5
Mothecombe Devon 8 F2
Motherby Cumb 230 F4
Motherwell NLanark 268 D5
Motspur Park London 67 F8
Mottingham London 68 E2
Mottisfont Hants 32 B4
Mottistone IoW 20 E4
Mottram in Longdendale
GtrMan 185 B7
Mottram Rise GtrMan 185 B7
Mottram St Andrew
ChesE 184 F5
Mott's Green Essex 87 B8
Mott's Mill ESus 52 F4
Mouldsworth ChesW 183 G8
Moulin Perth 286 B3
Moulsecoomb Brighton 36 F4
Moulsford Oxon 64 C5
Moulsham Essex 88 D2
Moulsoe MKeynes 103 C8
Moultavie Highld 300 B6
Moulton ChesW 167 B11
Lincs 156 E6
NYorks 224 E4
Suff 124 E3
VGlam 58 E5
WNhants 120 D5
Moulton Chapel Lincs 156 F5
Moulton Eaugate Lincs 156 F6
Moulton Park WNhants 120 E5
Moulton St Mary Norf 143 B7
Moulton Seas End Lincs 156 D6
Moulzie Angus 292 F4
Mounie Castle Aberds 303 G7
Mount Corn 4 D5
Corn 6 B2
Highld 301 E9
WYorks 196 D5
Mountain Anglesey 178 E2
WYorks 205 G7
Mountain Air BlGwent 77 D11
Mountain Ash = *Aberpennar*
Rhondda 77 F8
Mountain Bower Wilts 61 D10
Mountain Cross Borders 270 F2
Mountain Street Kent 54 C5
Mountain Water Pembs 91 G8
Mount Ambrose Corn 4 G4
Mount Ballan Mon 60 B3
Mount Batten Plym 7 E9
Mountbenger Borders 261 D8
Mountbengerburn
Borders 261 D8
Mountblow WDunb 277 G9
Mount Bovers Essex 88 G4
Mount Bures Essex 107 E8
Mount Canisp Highld 301 B7
Mount Charles Corn 5 B10
Corn 5 E10
Mount Cowdown Wilts 47 C9
Mount End Essex 87 E7
Mount Ephraim ESus 23 B7
Mounters Dorset 30 D3
Mountfield ESus 38 C2
Mountgerald Highld 300 C5
Mount Gould Plym 7 D9
Mount Hawke Corn 4 F4
Mount Hermon Corn 2 F6
Sur 50 B4
Mount Hill SGlos 61 E7
Mountjoy Corn 5 C7
Mount Lane Devon 12 B3
Mountnessing Essex 87 F10
Mounton Mon 79 G8
Mount Pleasant Bucks 102 E3
ChesE 168 D4
Corn 5 C10
Derbys 152 D6
Derbys 152 F5
Derbys 170 F4
Devon 27 G11
Durham 233 E11
ESus 23 E7
ESus 36 D6
Flint 182 G2
Hants 19 B11
Kent 71 F10
London 85 G8
MTydf 77 F9
Neath 57 B9
Norf 141 E9
Pembs 73 D8
Shrops 149 G9
Stockton 234 G4
Stoke 168 G5
Suff 106 B4
T&W 243 E7
Warks 135 F7
Worcs 99 D10
Worcs 117 E10
WYorks 197 C8
Mount Sion Wrex 166 E3
Mount Skippett Oxon 82 B5
Mountsolie Aberds 303 D9
Mountsorrel Leics 153 F11
Mount Sorrel Wilts 31 C8
Mount Tabor WYorks 196 B5
Mount Vernon Glasgow 268 C3
Mount Wise Corn 7 E9
Mousehill Sur 50 E2
Mousehole Corn 1 D5
Mousen Northumb 264 C4
Mousley End Warks 118 D4
Mouswald Dumfries 238 C3
Mouth Mill Devon 24 B3
Mowbreck Lancs 202 G4
Mow Cop ChesE 168 D5
Mowden Darl 224 B5
Essex 88 C3
Mowhaugh Borders 263 E8
Mowmacre Hill
Leicester 135 B11
Mowshurst Kent 52 D3
Mowsley Leics 136 F2
Moxby NYorks 215 F11
Moxley WMid 133 D9
Moy Argyll 255 E8
Highld 290 E6
Highld 301 F7
Moy Hall Highld 301 F7
Moy Ho Moray 301 C10
Moyles Court Hants 31 F11
Moylgrove = *Trewyddel*
Pembs 92 C2
Moy Lodge Highld 290 E6
Muasdale Argyll 255 C7
Muchalls Aberds 293 D11
Much Birch Hereford 97 E10
Much Cowardne Hereford 98 B2
Much Cowarne Hereford 98 B2
Much Dewchurch
Hereford 97 E9
Muchelney Som 28 C6
Muchelney Ham Som 28 C6
Much Hadham Herts 86 B5
Much Hoole Lancs 194 C3
Much Hoole Moss Houses
Lancs 194 C3
Much Hoole Town
Lancs 194 C3
Muchlarnick Corn 6 D4
Much Marcle Hereford 98 E3
Muchrachd Highld 300 F2
Much Wenlock Shrops 132 C2
Muckairn Argyll 289 F11
Muckernich Highld 300 D5
Mucking Thurrock 69 C7
Muckle Breck Shetland 312 G7
Muckleford Dorset 17 C8
Mucklestone Staffs 150 B4
Muckleton Norf 158 B6
Shrops 149 E11
Muckletown Aberds 302 G5
Muckley Shrops 132 D2
Muckley Corner Staffs 133 B11
Muckley Cross Shrops 132 D2
Muckton Lincs 190 E5
Muckton Bottom Lincs 190 E5
Mudale Highld 308 F5
Mudd GtrMan 185 C7
Muddiford Devon 40 F5
Muddlebridge Devon 40 G4
Muddles Green ESus 23 C8
Mudeford BCP 19 C9
Mudford Som 29 D9
Mudford Sock Som 29 D9
Mudgley Som 44 D2
Mudgock Stirling 277 F11
Mugeary Highld 294 B6
Mugginton Derbys 170 G3
Muggintonlane End
Derbys 170 G3
Muggleswick Durham 232 B6
Mugswell Sur 51 C9
Muie Highld 309 J6
Muir Aberds 292 E2
Muircleugh Borders 271 F10
Muirden Aberds 303 D7
Muirdrum Angus 287 D9
Muiredge Fife 281 B7
Muirend Glasgow 267 C11
Muirhead Angus 287 D7
Fife 286 G6
Fife 287 F8
NLanark 268 B3
SAyrs 257 C8
Muirhouse Edin 280 F4
NLanark 268 D5
Muirhouselaw Borders 262 D4
Muirhouses Falk 279 E10
Muirkirk EAyrs 258 D5
Muirmill Stirling 278 E4
Muir of Alford Aberds 293 B7
Muir of Fairburn Highld 300 D4
Muir of Fowlis Aberds 293 B7
Muir of Kinellar
Aberds 293 B10
Muir of Miltonduff
Moray 301 D11
Muir of Ord Highld 300 D5
Muir of Pert Angus 287 D8
Muirshearlich Highld 290 E3
Muirskie Aberds 293 D10
Muirtack Aberds 303 F9
Muirton Aberds 303 D7
Highld 301 C7
Perth 286 E5
Perth 286 F3
Muirton Mains Highld 300 D4
Muirton of Ardblair
Perth 286 C5
Muirton of Ballochy
Angus 293 G8
Muiryfold Aberds 303 D7
Muker NYorks 223 F8
Mulbarton Norf 142 C3
Mulben Moray 302 D3
Mulberry Corn 5 B10
Mulfra Corn 1 C5
Mulindry Argyll 254 B4
Mulla Shetland 313 G6
Mullardoch House
Highld 300 F2
Mullenspond Hants 47 D9
Mullion Corn 2 F5
Mullion Cove Corn 2 F5
Mumbles Hill Swansea 56 D6
Mumby Lincs 191 G8
Mumps GtrMan 196 F2
Mundale Moray 301 D10
Munderfield Row
Hereford 116 G2
Munderfield Stocks
Hereford 116 G2
Mundesley Norf 160 B6
Mundford Norf 140 E6
Mundham Norf 142 D6
Mundon Essex 88 E5
Mundurno Aberdeen 293 B11
Mundy Bois Kent 54 D2
Munerigie Highld 290 C4
Muness Shetland 312 C8
Mungasdale Highld 307 K4
Mungrisdale Cumb 230 E3
Munlochy Highld 300 D6
Munsary Cottage Highld 310 E6
Munsley Hereford 98 C3
Munslow Shrops 131 F10
Munstone Hereford 97 C10
Murch VGlam 59 E7
Murchington Devon 13 D9
Murcot Worcs 99 C11
Murcott Oxon 83 B9
Wilts 81 G7
Murdieston Stirling 278 B3
Murdishaw Halton 183 E9
Murieston WLoth 269 C11
Murkle Highld 310 C5
Murlaggan Highld 290 D2
Highld 290 E5
Murra Orkney 314 F2
Murrayfield Edin 280 G4
Murrayshall Perth 286 E5
Murraythwaite Dumfries 238 C4
Murrell Green Hants 49 B8
Murrell's End Glos 98 E4
Glos 98 G5
Murrion Shetland 312 F4
Murrow Cambs 139 B7
Mursley Bucks 102 F6
Murston Kent 70 G2
Murthill Angus 287 B8
Murthly Perth 286 D4
Murton Cumb 231 G10
Durham 234 B3
Northumb 273 F9
Swansea 56 D5
T&W 243 C8
York 207 C8
Murton Grange
NYorks 215 B10
Murtwell Devon 8 D5
Musbury Devon 15 C11
Muscliff BCP 19 B7
Muscoates NYorks 216 C3
Muscott WNhants 120 E2
Musdale Argyll 289 G11
Mushroom Green
WMid 133 F8
Musselburgh ELoth 280 G6
Musselwick Pembs 72 D4
Mustard Hyrn Norf 161 F8
Muston Leics 154 B6
NYorks 217 D11
Mustow Green Worcs 117 C7
Muswell Hill London 86 G3
Mutehill Dumfries 237 E8
Mutford Suff 143 F9
Muthill Perth 286 F2
Mutley Plym 7 D9
Mutterton Devon 27 G8
Mutton Hall ESus 37 C9
Muxton Telford 150 G4
Mwdwl-eithin Flint 181 F11
Mwynbwll Flint 165 B11
Mybster Highld 310 D5
Myddfai Carms 94 F5
Myddle Shrops 149 E9
Myddlewood Shrops 149 E9
Myddyn-fych Carms 75 C10
Mydroilyn Ceredig 111 F9
Myerscough Lancs 202 F5
Myerscough Smithy
Lancs 203 G8
Mylor Bridge Corn 3 B8
Mylor Churchtown Corn 3 B8
Mynachdy Cardiff 59 D7
Rhondda 77 F8
Mynachlog-ddu Pembs 92 E2
Mynd Shrops 115 C7
Myndd Llandegai Gwyn 163 B10
Myndtown Shrops 131 F7
Mynydd Bach Ceredig 112 B4
Mynydd-bach Mon 79 G7
Swansea 57 B7
Mynydd-bach-y-glo
Swansea 56 B6
Mynydd Bodafon
Anglesey 179 D7
Mynydd Fflint = *Flint Mountain* Flint 182 G2
Mynydd Gilan Gwyn 144 E5
Mynydd-isa Flint 166 C3
Mynyddislwyn Caerph 77 G11
Mynydd-llan Flint 181 G11
Mynydd Marian Conwy 180 F5
Mynydd Mechell
Anglesey 178 D5
Mynyddygarreg Carms 74 D6
Mynytho Gwyn 144 C6
Myrebird Aberds 293 D9
Myrelandhorn Highld 310 D6
Myreside Perth 286 E6
Myrtle Hill Carms 94 E5
Mytchett Sur 49 B11
Mytchett Place Sur 49 C11
Mytholm WYorks 196 B3
Mytholmes WYorks 204 F6
Mytholmroyd WYorks 196 B4
Mythop Lancs 202 G3
Mytice Aberds 302 F4
Myton Warks 118 E6
Myton Hall NYorks 215 F8
Myton-on-Swale
NYorks 215 F8
Mytton Shrops 149 F8

N

Naast Highld 307 L3
Nab Hill WYorks 197 D7
Nab's Head Lancs 194 B6
Naburn York 207 D7
Nab Wood WYorks 205 F8
Naccolt Kent 54 E4
Nackington Kent 55 C7
Nacton Suff 108 C4
Nadderwater Devon 14 C3
Nafferton EYorks 209 B7
Na Gearrannan WIsles 304 D3
Nag's Head Glos 80 F5
Naid-y-march Flint 181 F11
Nailbridge Glos 79 B10
Nailsbourne Som 28 B2
Nailsea NSom 60 D3
Nailstone Leics 135 B8
Nailsworth Glos 80 F5
Nailwell Bath 61 G8
Nairn Highld 301 D8
Nalderswood Sur 51 D8
Nance Corn 4 G3
Nanceddan Corn 2 C2
Nancegollan Corn 2 C4
Nancemellin Corn 4 G2
Nancenoy Corn 2 D6
Nancledra Corn 1 B5
Nangreaves Lancs 195 D10
Nanhoron Gwyn 144 C5
Nanhyfer = *Nevern*
Pembs 91 D11
Nannau Gwyn 146 E4
Nannerch Flint 165 B11
Nanpantan Leics 153 F10
Nanpean Corn 5 D9
Nanquidno Corn 1 D3
Nanstallon Corn 5 B10
Nant Carms 74 B6
Denb 165 D11
Nant Alyn Flint 165 B11
Nant-ddu Powys 77 B8
Nanternis Ceredig 111 F7
Nantgaredig Carms 93 G9
Nantgarw Rhondda 58 B6
Nant-glas Powys 113 E9
Nantglyn Denb 165 C8
Nantgwyn Powys 113 B9
Nantithet Corn 2 E5
Nantlle Gwyn 163 E8
Nantmawr Shrops 148 E5
Nant Mawr Flint 166 C3
Nantmel Powys 113 D10
Nantmor Gwyn 163 F10
Nant Peris = *Old Llanberis*
Gwyn 163 D10
Nantserth Powys 113 C9
Nant Uchaf Denb 165 D8
Nantwich ChesE 167 E11
Nant-y-Bai Carms 94 C5
Nant-y-Bwch BlGwent 77 C10
Nant-y-cafn Neath 76 D4
Nantycaws Carms 75 B7
Nant y Caws Shrops 148 D5
Nant-y-ceisiad Caerph 59 B8
Nant-y-derry Mon 78 D4
Nant-y-felin Conwy 179 G11
Nant-y-ffin Carms 93 E11
Nantyffyllon Bridgend 57 C11
Nantyglo BlGwent 77 C11
Nant-y-gollen Shrops 148 D4
Nant-y-moel Bridgend 76 G6
Nant-y-pandy Conwy 179 G11
Nant-y-Rhiw Conwy 164 D4
Nantyronen Station
Ceredig 112 B3
Napchester Kent 55 D10
Naphill Bucks 84 F4
Napleton Worcs 99 B7
Napley Staffs 150 B4
Napley Heath Staffs 150 B4
Nappa NYorks 204 C3
Nappa Scar NYorks 223 G9
Napton on the Hill
Warks 119 E9
Narberth = *Arberth*
Pembs 73 C10
Narberth Bridge Pembs 73 C10
Narborough Leics 135 D10
Norf 158 G4
Narfords Som 28 F3
Narkurs Corn 6 D6
Narracott Devon 24 D5
Narrowgate Corner
Norf 161 F8
Nasareth Gwyn 163 E7
Naseby WNhants 120 B3
Nash Bucks 102 E5
Hereford 114 E6
Kent 55 B9
London 68 G2
Newport 59 C10
Shrops 116 C2
Som 29 E8
Nashend Glos 80 D5
Nash End Worcs 132 G5
Nashes Green Hants 49 D7
Nash Lee Bucks 84 D4
Nash Mills Herts 85 E9
Nash Street ESus 23 C8
Kent 68 F6
Nassington NNhants 137 D11
Nastend Glos 80 D3
Nast Hyde Herts 86 D2
Nasty Herts 105 G7
Natcott Devon 24 C3
Nateby Cumb 222 D5
Lancs 202 E5
Nately Scures Hants 49 C8
Natland Cumb 211 B10
Natton Glos 99 E8
Naughton Suff 107 B10
Naunton Glos 100 G2
Worcs 99 D7
Naunton Beauchamp
Worcs 117 G9
Navant Hill WSus 34 B6
Navenby Lincs 173 D7
Navestock Heath Essex 87 F8
Navestock Side Essex 87 F9
Navidale Highld 311 H4
Navity Highld 301 C7
Nawton NYorks 216 C3
Nayland Suff 107 E9
Nazeing Essex 86 D6
Nazeing Gate Essex 86 D6
Nazeing Long Green
Essex 86 E6
Nazeing Mead Essex 86 D5
Neacroft Hants 19 B9
Nealhouse Cumb 239 G8
Neal's Green Warks 134 G6
Neames Forstal Kent 54 B5
Neap Shetland 313 H7
Near Hardcastle
NYorks 214 F2
Near Sawrey Cumb 221 F7
Nearton End Bucks 102 F6
Neasden London 67 B8
Neasham Darl 224 C6
Neat Enstone Oxon 101 G7
Neath = *Castell-nedd*
Neath 57 B8
Neath Abbey Neath 57 B8
Neatham Hants 49 E8
Neath Hill MKeynes 103 C7
Neatishead Norf 160 E6
Neat Marsh EYorks 209 G9
Neaton Norf 141 C8
Nebo Anglesey 179 C7
Ceredig 111 D10
Conwy 164 D4
Gwyn 163 E7
Nebsworth Warks 100 C3
Nechells WMid 133 F11
Necton Norf 141 B7
Nedd Highld 306 F6
Nedderton Northumb 252 G6
Nedge Hill Som 44 C5
Telford 132 B4
Nedging Suff 107 B9
Nedging Tye Suff 107 B10
Needham Norf 142 G4
Needham Green Essex 87 B9
Needham Market Suff 125 G11
Needham Street Suff 124 D4
Needingworth Cambs 122 C6
Needwood Staffs 152 E3
Neen Savage Shrops 116 B3
Neen Sollars Shrops 116 C3
Neenton Shrops 132 F2
Nefod Shrops 148 B6
Nefyn Gwyn 162 G4
Neighbourne Som 44 D6
Neight Hill Worcs 117 F8
Neilston ERenf 267 D9
Neinthirion Powys 129 B9
Neithrop Oxon 101 C8
Nelly Andrews Green
Powys 130 B5
Nelson Caerph 77 F10
Lancs 204 F3
Nelson Village Northumb 243 B7
Nemphlar SLanark 269 G7
Nempnett Thrubwell
NSom 60 G4
Nene Terrace Lincs 138 B5
Nenthall Cumb 231 B11
Nenthead Cumb 231 C11
Nenthorn Borders 262 B5
Neopardy Devon 13 B11
Nepcote WSus 35 F10
Nepgill Cumb 229 F7
Nep Town WSus 36 D2
Nerabus Argyll 254 B3
Nercwys Flint 166 C2
Nerston SLanark 268 D2
Nesbit Northumb 263 C11
Ness ChesW 182 F4
Orkney 314 C4
Nesscliffe Shrops 149 F7
Nessholt ChesW 182 F4
Nesstoun Orkney 314 A7
Neston ChesW 182 F3
Wilts 61 F11
Netchells Green
WMid 133 F11
Netham Bristol 60 E6
Nethanfoot SLanark 268 F6
Nether Alderley ChesE 184 F4
Netheravon Wilts 46 D6
Nether Blainslie
Borders 271 G10
Nether Booth Derbys 185 D10
Netherbrae Aberds 303 D7
Netherbrough Orkney 314 E3
Nether Broughton Leics 154 D3
Netherburn SLanark 268 F6
Nether Burrow Lancs 212 D2
Nether Burrows Derbys 152 B5
Netherbury Dorset 16 B5
Netherby Cumb 239 C9
NYorks 206 D2
Nether Cassock
Dumfries 248 C6
Nether Cerne Dorset 17 B9
Nether Chanderhill
Derbys 186 G4
Netherclay Som 28 C3
Nether Compton Dorset 29 D9
Nethercote Oxon 101 C9
Warks 119 E10
Nethercott Devon 12 B3
Devon 40 F3
Oxon 101 G9
Som 42 G6
Nether Crimond Aberds 303 G8
Netherdale Shetland 313 H3
Nether Dalgliesh
Borders 249 B7
Nether Dallachy Moray 302 C3
Nether Edge SYorks 186 E4
Netherend Glos 79 E9
Nether End Derbys 186 G3
Leics 154 G4
WYorks 197 F8
Nether Exe Devon 26 G6
Netherfield ESus 38 D2
MKeynes 103 D7
Notts 171 G10
Nethergate Norf 159 D11
Nether Glasslaw Aberds 303 D8
Nether Hall Leicester 136 B2
Netherhampton Wilts 31 B10
Nether Handley Derbys 186 F6
Nether Handwick Angus 287 C7
Nether Haugh SYorks 186 B6
Nether Headon Notts 188 F2
Nether Heage Derbys 170 E5
Nether Heyford
WNhants 120 F3
Nether Hindhope
Borders 263 G7
Nether Horsburgh
Borders 261 B8
Nether Howecleuch
SLanark 260 G2
Nether Kellet Lancs 211 F10
Nether Kidston Borders 270 G4
Nether Kinmundy
Aberds 303 E10
Nether Kirton ERenf 267 D9
Netherland Green
Staffs 152 C2
Nether Langwith Notts 187 G8
Netherlaw Dumfries 237 E9
Netherlay Dorset 28 F6
Nether Leask Aberds 303 F10
Netherlee ERenf 267 D11
Nether Lenshie Aberds 302 E6
Netherley Aberds 293 D10
Mers 182 D6
WYorks 196 E4
Nether Loads Derbys 170 B4
Nethermill Dumfries 248 F2
Nethermills Moray 302 D5
Nether Monynut
Borders 272 C4
Nether Moor Derbys 170 B5
Nethermuir Aberds 303 E9
Netherne on-the-Hill
Sur 51 B9
Netheroyd Hill WYorks 196 D6
Nether Padley Derbys 186 F3
Nether Park Aberds 303 D10
Netherplace ERenf 267 D10
Nether Poppleton York 207 B7
Netherraw Borders 262 E3
Nether Row Cumb 230 D2
Nether Savock Aberds 303 E10
Netherseal Derbys 152 G5
Nether Shiels Borders 271 F8
Nether Silton NYorks 225 G9
Nether Skyborry Shrops 114 C5
Nether Street Suff 125 E8
Netherstoke Dorset 29 F8
Nether Stowe Staffs 152 G2
Nether Stowey Som 43 F7
Nether Street Essex 87 C9
Herts 86 B6
Netherthird EAyrs 258 F3
Netherthong WYorks 196 F6
Netherthorpe Derbys 186 G6
SYorks 187 E8
Netherton Aberds 303 E8
Angus 287 B9
ChesW 183 F8
Corn 11 G11
Cumb 228 D6
Devon 14 G3
Glos 81 E11
Hants 47 B11
Hereford 97 F10
Mers 193 G11
NLanark 268 E5
Northumb 251 B11
Oxon 82 F6
Perth 286 B5
Shrops 132 G4
Stirling 277 F11
WMid 133 F8
Worcs 99 C9
WYorks 196 E6
WYorks 197 D9
Netherton of Lonmay
Aberds 303 C10
Nethertown Cumb 219 D9
Highld 310 B7
Lancs 203 F10
Staffs 152 F2
Nether Urquhart Fife 286 G5
Nether Wallop Hants 47 F10
Nether Warden
Northumb 241 D10
Nether Wasdale Cumb 220 E2
Nether Welton Cumb 230 B3
Nether Westcote Glos 100 G4
Nether Whitacre Warks 134 E4
Nether Winchendon or Lower Winchendon
Bucks 84 C2
Netherwitton Northumb 252 E4
Netherwood EAyrs 258 D5
Nether Worton Oxon 101 E8
Nether Yeadon
WYorks 205 E10
Nethy Bridge Highld 301 G10
Netley Hants 33 F7
Netley Hill Soton 33 E7
Netley Marsh Hants 32 E4
Nettacott Devon 14 B4
Netteswell Essex 87 C7
Nettlebed Oxon 65 B8
Nettlebridge Som 44 D6
Nettlecombe Dorset 16 B6
IoW 20 F6
Nettleden Herts 85 C8
Nettleham Lincs 189 F8
Nettlestead Kent 53 C7
Suff 107 B11
Nettlestead Green Kent 53 C7
Nettlestone IoW 21 C8
Nettlesworth Durham 233 B11
Nettleton Glos 80 C6
Lincs 200 G6
Wilts 61 D10
Nettleton Green Wilts 61 D10
Nettleton Hill WYorks 196 D5
Nettleton Shrub Wilts 61 D10
Nettleton Top Lincs 189 B10
Netton Wilts 46 F6
Neuadd Carms 94 G3
Nevendon Essex 88 G2
Nevern = *Nanhyfer*
Pembs 91 D11
Nevilles Cross Durham 233 C11
New Abbey Dumfries 237 C11
New Aberdour Aberds 303 C8
New Addington London 67 G11
Newall WYorks 205 D10
Newall Green GtrMan 184 D4
New Alresford Hants 48 G5
New Alyth Perth 286 C6
Newark Orkney 314 B7
Pboro 138 C4
Newark-on-Trent Notts 172 E3
New Arley Warks 134 F5
New Arram EYorks 208 E6
Newarthill NLanark 268 D5
New Ash Green Kent 68 F6
New Balderton Notts 172 E4
Newball Lincs 189 F9
Newbarn Kent 55 F7
New Barn Kent 68 F6
New Barnet London 86 F3
New Barnetby NLincs 200 E5
Newbarns Cumb 210 E4
New Barton NNhants 121 E7
New Basford Nottingham 171 G9
Newbattle Midloth 270 B6
New Beaupre VGlam 58 E4
New Beckenham London 67 E11
New Bewick Northumb 264 E3
Newbie Dumfries 238 D5
Newbiggin Cumb 210 F5
Cumb 211 D11
Cumb 219 G11
Cumb 230 F5
Cumb 231 B7
Cumb 231 F8
Durham 232 B5
Durham 232 F4
Durham 233 B8
NYorks 213 B9
NYorks 223 G9
Newbiggin-by-the-Sea
Northumb 253 F8
Newbigging Aberds 303 G7
Angus 287 D8
Borders 262 F6
Edin 280 F2
SLanark 269 F10
New-bigging Angus 286 C6
Newbiggings Orkney 314 B6
Newbiggin Hall Estate
T&W 242 D6
Newbiggin-on-Lune
Cumb 222 D4
New Bilton Warks 119 B9
Newbold Derbys 186 G5
GtrMan 196 E2
Leics 136 B5
Leics 153 F8
Newbold Heath Leics 135 B8
Newbold on Avon
Warks 119 B9
Newbold on Stour
Warks 100 B4
Newbold Pacey Warks 118 F5
Newbolds WMid 133 C8
Newbold Verdon Leics 135 C8
New Bolingbroke Lincs 174 D4
New Bolsover Derbys 187 G7
Newborough Pboro 138 B4
Staffs 152 D2
New Boston Mers 183 B9
New Botley Oxon 83 D7
Newbottle T&W 243 G8
WNhants 101 D10
New Boultham Lincs 189 G7
Newbourne Suff 108 C5
New Bradwell MKeynes 102 C6
New Brancepeth
Durham 233 C10
Newbridge Bath 61 F8
Caerph 78 F2
Ceredig 111 F10
Corn 1 C4
Corn 4 G5
Corn 7 B7
Dumfries 237 B11
Edin 280 G2
ESus 52 G3
Hants 32 D3
IoW 20 D4
Lancs 204 F3
NYorks 216 B6
Oxon 82 E6
Pembs 91 E8
Shrops 148 D6
WMid 133 D7
Wrex 166 G3
New Bridge Wrex 166 G3
Newbridge Green Worcs 98 D6
Newbridge-on-Usk Mon 78 G5
Newbridge-on-Wye
Powys 113 F10
New Brighton Flint 166 B3
Mers 182 C4
Wrex 166 E3
WSus 22 B3
WYorks 197 B9
WYorks 205 F8
New Brimington Derbys 186 G6
New Brinsley Notts 171 E7
New Brotton Redcar 235 G9
Newbrough Northumb 241 D9
New Broughton Wrex 166 E4
New Buckenham Norf 141 E11
Newbuildings Devon 26 G3
New Buildings Bath 45 B7
Dorset 18 E5
Newburgh Aberds 303 D9
Aberds 303 G9
Borders 261 F8
Fife 286 F6
Lancs 194 E3
Newburn T&W 242 D5
Newbury Kent 54 B2
WBerks 64 F3
Wilts 45 E10
New Bury GtrMan 195 F8
Newbury Park London 68 B2
Newby Cumb 231 G7
Lancs 204 D2
NYorks 205 D11
NYorks 212 E4
NYorks 215 F7
NYorks 225 C10
NYorks 227 G10
Newby Bridge Cumb 211 B7
Newby Cote NYorks 212 E4
Newby East Cumb 239 F11
Newby Head Cumb 231 G7
New Byth Aberds 303 D8
Newby West Cumb 239 G9
Newby Wiske NYorks 215 B7
Newcastle Bridgend 58 D2
Mon 78 B6
Shrops 130 G4
Newcastle Emlyn = *Castell Newydd Emlyn* Carms 92 C6
Newcastleton or Copshaw Holm Borders 249 F11

Newcastle-under-Lyme
Staffs 168 F4
Newcastle upon Tyne
T&W 242 E6
New Catton Norf 160 G4
Newchapel Powys 129 G9
Staffs 168 E5
Sur 51 E11
Newchapel =Capel Newydd
Pembs 92 D4
New Charlton London 68 D2
New Cheltenham S Glos 61 E7
New Cheriton Hants 33 B9
Newchurch Bl Gwent 77 C11
Carms 93 G7
Hereford 115 G7
IoW 21 D7
Kent 54 G5
Lancs 195 C10
Mon 79 F7
Powys 114 G4
Staffs 152 E2
Newchurch in Pendle
Lancs 204 F2
New Clipstone Notts 171 C9
New Costessey Norf 160 G3
Newcott Devon 28 F2
New Coundon Durham 233 E10
New Cowper Cumb 229 B8
Newcraighall Edin 280 G6
New Crofton W Yorks 197 D11
New Cross Ceredig 112 B2
London 67 D11
Oxon 65 D9
Som 28 D6
New Cross Gate London 67 D11
New Cumnock E Ayrs 258 G4
New Deer Aberds 303 E8
New Delaval Northumb 243 B7
New Delph Gtr Man 196 F3
New Denham Bucks 66 C4
Newdigate Sur 51 E7
New Downs Corn 1 C3
Corn 4 E4
New Duston W Nhants 120 E4
New Earswick York 207 B8
New Eastwood Notts 171 F7
New Edlington S Yorks 187 B8
New Elgin Moray 302 C2
New Ellerby E Yorks 209 F9
Newell Green Brack 65 E11
New Eltham London 68 E2
New End Lincs 190 G2
Warks 118 E2
Worcs 117 F11
Newenden Kent 38 B4
New England Essex 106 C4
Lincs 175 D8
Pboro 138 C3
Som 28 E4
Newent Glos 98 F4
Newerne Glos 79 E10
New Farnley W Yorks 205 G10
New Ferry Mers 182 D4
Newfield Durham 233 E10
Durham 242 G6
Highld 301 B7
Stoke 168 E6
New Fletton Pboro 138 D3
Newford Scilly 1 G4
Newfound Hants 48 C5
New Fryston W Yorks 198 B3
Newgale Pembs 90 G6
New Galloway Dumfries 237 B8
Newgarth Orkney 314 E2
Newgate Lancs 194 F4
Norf 177 E9
Newgate Corner Norf 161 G8
Newgate Street Herts 86 D4
New Gilston Fife 287 G8
New Greens Herts 85 D10
New Grimsby Scilly 1 F3
New Ground Herts 85 C7
Newgrounds Hants 31 E11
Newhailes Edin 280 G6
New Hainford Norf 160 F4
Newhall Ches E 167 F10
Derbys 152 E5
Newhall Green Warks 134 F5
New Hall Hey Lancs 195 C10
Newhall House Highld 300 C6
Newhall Point Highld 301 C7
Newham Lincs 174 E3
Northumb 264 D5
New Hartley Northumb 243 B8
Newhaven Derbys 169 C11
Devon 24 C5
Edin 280 F5
E Sus 36 G6
New Haw Sur 66 G5
Newhay N Yorks 207 G9
New Headington Oxon 83 D9
New Heaton Northumb 273 G7
New Hedges Pembs 73 E10
New Herrington T&W 243 G8
Newhey Gtr Man 196 E2
Newhill Fife 286 F6
Perth 286 G5
S Yorks 186 B6
Newhills Aberdeen 293 C10
New Hinksey Oxon 83 E8
New Ho Durham 232 D3
New Holkham Norf 159 B7
New Holland N Lincs 200 C5
W Yorks 205 F7
Newholm N Yorks 227 C7
New Horwich Derbys 185 E8
New Houghton Derbys 171 B7
Norf 158 D5
Newhouse Borders 262 E2
N Lanark 268 C5
Shetland 313 G6
New House Kent 68 E6
Newhouses Borders 271 G10
New Houses Gtr Man 194 G5
N Yorks 212 E6
New Humberstone
Leicester 136 B2
New Hunwick Durham 233 E9
New Hutton Cumb 221 G11
New Hythe Kent 53 B8
Newick E Sus 36 C6
Newingreen Kent 54 F6
Newington Edin 280 G5
Kent 55 F7
Kent 69 G11
Kent 71 F11
London 67 D10
Notts 187 C11
Oxon 83 F10
Shrops 131 G8
Newington Bagpath Glos 80 G4
New Inn Carms 93 D9
Devon 24 F6
Mon 79 E7
Pembs 91 E11
Torf 78 F4
New Invention Shrops 114 B5
W Mid 133 C9
New Kelso Highld 299 E9
New Kingston Notts 153 D10
New Kyo Durham 242 G5
New Ladykirk Borders 273 F7
New Lanark S Lanark 269 G7
Newland Cumb 210 D6
E Yorks 199 B10
Glos 79 D9
Hull 209 G7
N Yorks 199 C7
Oxon 82 C5
Worcs 98 B5
Newland Bottom Cumb 210 C5
Newland Common
Worcs 117 E8
Newland Green Kent 54 D2
Newlandrig Midloth 271 C7
Newlands Borders 250 E2
Borders 262 E2
Cumb 229 G10
Cumb 230 D2
Derbys 170 F6
Dumfries 247 F11
Glasgow 267 C11
Highld 301 E7
Moray 302 D3
Northumb 242 F3
Notts 171 C9
Staffs 151 E11
Newlands Corner Sur 50 D4
Newlandsmuir S Lanark 268 E2
Newlands of Geise
Highld 310 C4
Newlands of Tynet
Moray 302 C3
Newlands Park Anglesey 178 E3
New Lane Lancs 194 E2
New Lane End Warr 183 B10
New Langholm Dumfries 249 G9
New Leake Lincs 174 D6
New Leeds Aberds 303 D9
Newliston Edin 280 G2
Fife 280 C5
New Lodge S Yorks 197 F10
New Longton Lancs 194 B4
Newlot Orkney 314 E5
New Lubbesthorpe
Leics 135 C10
New Luce Dumfries 236 C3
Newlyn Corn 1 D5
Newmachar Aberds 293 B10
Newmains N Lanark 268 D6
New Malden London 67 F8
Newman's End Essex 87 C8
Newman's Green Suff 107 C7
Newman's Place Hereford 96 B5
Newmarket Glos 80 F4
Suff 124 E2
W Isles 304 E6
New Marske Redcar 235 G8
New Marston Oxon 83 D8
New Marton Shrops 148 C6
New Micklefield
W Yorks 206 G4
Newmill Borders 261 G11
Corn 1 C5
Moray 302 D4
New Mill Aberds 293 E9
Borders 262 G2
Corn 1 C5
Corn 4 F6
Cumb 219 E11
Herts 84 C6
Wilts 63 G7
W Yorks 197 F7
Newmillerdam
W Yorks 197 D10
Newmill of Inshewan
Angus 292 G6
Newmills Corn 11 D11
Fife 279 D10
Highld 300 C6
New Mills Borders 271 F10
Ches E 184 E3
Corn 5 E7
Derbys 185 D7
Glos 79 E10
Hereford 98 D4
New Mills =Felin Newydd
Powys 129 C11
Newmills of Boyne
Aberds 302 D5
Newmiln Perth 286 D5
Newmilns E Ayrs 258 B2
New Milton Hants 19 B10
New Mistley Essex 108 E2
New Moat Pembs 91 F11
Newmore Highld 300 B6
Highld 300 D5
New Moston Gtr Man 195 G11
Newnes Shrops 149 C7
Newney Green Essex 87 D11
Newnham Cambs 123 F8
Glos 79 C11
Hants 49 C8
Herts 104 D4
Kent 54 B3
Warks 118 E3
W Nhants 119 F11
Newnham Bridge Worcs 116 D2
New Ollerton Notts 171 B11
New Oscott W Mid 133 E11
New Pale Ches W 183 G8
Newpark Fife 287 F8
New Park N Yorks 205 B11
New Parks Leicester 135 B11
New Passage S Glos 60 B4
New Pitsligo Aberds 303 D8
New Polzeath Corn 10 F4
Newpool Staffs 168 D5
Newport Corn 12 D2
Devon 40 G5
Dorset 18 C3
Essex 105 E10
E Yorks 208 G3
Glos 79 F11
Highld 311 G5
IoW 20 D6
Newport 59 B10
Norf 161 F10
Som 28 C4
Telford 150 F4
Newport =Trefdraeth
Pembs 91 D11
Newport-on-Tay Fife 287 E8
Newport Pagnell
M Keynes 103 C7
Newpound Common
W Sus 35 B9
Newquay Corn 4 C6
New Quay =Ceinewydd
Ceredig 111 F7
New Rackheath Norf 160 G5
New Radnor Powys 114 E4
New Rent Cumb 230 D5
New Ridley Northumb 242 F3
New Road Side N Yorks 204 E5
W Yorks 197 B7
New Romney Kent 39 C9
New Rossington
S Yorks 187 B10
New Row Ceredig 112 C4
Lancs 203 F8
New Row *continued*
N Yorks 226 C2
Newsam Green
W Yorks 206 G3
New Sarum Wilts 46 G6
New Sawley Derbys 153 C9
Newsbank Ches E 168 B4
New Scarbro W Yorks 205 G10
Newseat Aberds 303 E10
Aberds 303 F7
Newsells Herts 105 D7
Newsham Lancs 202 F6
Northumb 243 B8
N Yorks 215 C7
N Yorks 224 C2
New Sharlston
W Yorks 197 C11
Newsholme E Yorks 199 B8
Lancs 204 C2
W Yorks 204 F6
New Silksworth T&W 243 G9
New Skelton Redcar 226 B3
New Smithy Derbys 185 E9
Newsome W Yorks 196 E6
New Southgate London 86 G3
New Springs Gtr Man 194 F6
New Sprowston Norf 160 G4
New Stanton Derbys 153 B9
Newstead Borders 262 C3
Northumb 264 D5
Notts 171 E8
Staffs 168 G5
W Yorks 197 E11
New Stevenston
N Lanark 268 D5
New Street Kent 68 G6
Staffs 169 E9
Newstreet Lane Shrops 150 B2
New Swanage Dorset 18 E6
New Swannington Leics 153 F8
Newtake Devon 14 G3
New Thirsk N Yorks 215 C8
Newthorpe Notts 171 F7
N Yorks 206 G5
Newthorpe Common
Notts 171 F7
New Thundersley Essex 69 B9
Newtoft Lincs 189 D8
Newton Argyll 275 D11
Borders 262 E3
Borders 262 F2
Bridgend 57 F10
Cambs 105 B8
Cambs 157 G8
Cardiff 59 D8
C Beds 104 C4
Ches W 166 B6
Ches W 167 D8
Ches W 183 F8
Corn 5 C11
Cumb 210 E4
Derbys 170 D6
Dorset 30 E3
Dumfries 239 C7
Dumfries 248 E4
Gtr Man 185 B7
Hereford 96 C5
Hereford 96 E6
Hereford 115 D7
Hereford 115 G10
Highld 301 C7
Highld 301 E7
Highld 306 F7
Highld 310 E7
Lancs 202 F2
Lancs 202 G4
Lancs 203 C9
Lancs 211 E11
Lincs 155 B10
Mers 182 D2
Moray 301 C11
N Nhants 137 G7
Norf 158 F6
Northumb 242 E2
Notts 171 G11
Perth 286 D2
S Glos 79 G10
Shetland 312 E5
Shetland 313 K5
Shrops 132 D4
Shrops 149 C8
S Lanark 259 C10
S Lanark 268 C3
Som 42 F6
Staffs 151 D10
Suff 107 C8
Swansea 56 D6
S Yorks 198 G5
Warks 119 B10
Wilts 32 C2
W Loth 279 F11
W Mid 133 E10
Newton Abbot Devon 14 G3
Newtonairds Dumfries 247 G9
Newton Arlosh Cumb 238 F5
Newton Aycliffe
Durham 233 G11
Newton Bewley Hrtlpl 234 F5
Newton Blossomville
M Keynes 121 G8
Newton Bromswold
N Nhants 121 D9
Newton Burgoland
Leics 135 B7
Newton by Toft Lincs 189 D9
Newton Cross Pembs 91 F7
Newton Ferrers Devon 7 F10
Newton Flotman Norf 142 D4
Newtongrange Midloth 270 C6
Newton Green Mon 79 G8
Newton Hall Durham 233 B11
Northumb 242 D2
Newton Harcourt Leics 136 D2
Newton Heath
Gtr Man 195 G11
Newtonhill Aberds 293 D11
Highld 300 E5
Newton Hill W Yorks 197 C10
Newton Ho Aberds 302 G6
Newton Hurst Staffs 151 D11
Newtonia Ches E 167 B11
Newton Ketton Darl 234 G2
Newton Kyme N Yorks 206 E5
Newton-le-Willows
Mers 183 B9
N Yorks 214 B4
Newton Leys Milton
Keynes 103 E7
Newton Longville
Bucks 102 E6
Newton Mearns
E Renf 267 D10
Newtonmill Angus 293 G8
Newtonmore Highld 291 D9
Newton Morrell
N Yorks 224 D4
Oxon 102 F2
Newton Mulgrave
N Yorks 226 B5
Newton of Ardtoe
Highld 289 B8
Newton of Balcanquhal
Perth 286 F5
Newton of Balcormo
Fife 287 G9
Newton of Falkland
Fife 286 G6
Newton of Mountblairy
Aberds 302 D6
Newton of Pitcairns
Perth 286 F4
Newton on Ayr S Ayrs 257 E8
Newton on Ouse
N Yorks 206 B6
Newton-on-Rawcliffe
N Yorks 226 G6
Newton on the Hill
Shrops 149 E9
Newton on the Moor
Northumb 252 B5
Newton on Trent Lincs 188 G4
Newton Park Argyll 266 B2
Mers 183 C9
Newton Peveril Dorset 18 B4
Newton Poppleford
Devon 15 D7
Newton Purcell Oxon 102 E2
Newton Regis Warks 134 B5
Newton Reigny Cumb 230 E5
Newton Rigg Cumb 230 E5
Newton St Boswells
Borders 262 C3
Newton St Cyres Devon 14 B3
Newton St Faith Norf 160 F4
Newton St Loe Bath 61 G8
Newton St Petrock Devon 24 E6
Newton Solney Derbys 152 D5
Newton Stacey Hants 48 E2
Newton Stewart
Dumfries 236 C6
Newton Tony Wilts 47 E8
Newton Tracey Devon 25 B8
Newton under Roseberry
Redcar 225 C11
Newton Underwood
Northumb 252 F4
Newton upon Derwent
E Yorks 207 D10
Newton Valence Hants 49 G8
Newton with Scales
Lancs 202 G4
Newton Wood Gtr Man 184 B6
New Totley S Yorks 186 F4
Newtown Argyll 284 G4
BCP 18 C6
Bl Gwent 77 C11
Bucks 85 E7
Caerph 78 G2
Cambs 121 D11
Ches E 184 E6
Ches W 183 F8
Corn 2 D3
Corn 11 F11
Cumb 229 B7
Cumb 239 F9
Cumb 240 E2
Derbys 185 E7
Devon 26 B3
Dorset 29 G7
Falk 279 E9
Glos 79 E11
Glos 80 D3
Glos 99 E8
Gtr Man 194 F5
Gtr Man 195 G9
Hants 21 B8
Hants 32 C4
Hants 32 E3
Hants 33 D8
Hants 33 E10
Hants 33 F7
Hants 49 F8
Hants 49 G10
Hants 64 G3
Hereford 97 E10
Hereford 98 C2
Highld 290 C5
IoM 192 E4
IoW 20 C4
Mers 183 B7
Norf 143 B10
Northumb 252 C2
Northumb 263 C11
Northumb 264 D2
Oxon 65 C9
Powys 130 E2
Rhondda 77 F9
Shrops 132 C2
Shrops 149 C9
Shrops 149 E8
Som 28 E3
Som 43 F9
Staffs 133 C9
Staffs 168 C6
Staffs 169 C9
Wilts 30 B6
Wilts 63 G10
W Mid 133 F11
Worcs 116 F5
Worcs 117 E7
New Town Bath 45 B9
Bath 60 G5
Dorset 30 C3
Dorset 30 D6
Dorset 31 D7
Dorset 31 F7
Edin 280 G4
Edin 280 G5
E Loth 281 G8
E Sus 37 C7
Glos 99 E10
Kent 53 B7
Kent 68 E4
Lancs 203 F8
Luton 103 G11
Medway 69 G8
Oxon 100 F5
Reading 65 E8
Shetland 312 E6
Som 29 D9
Som 29 D11
Som 44 D3
Soton 33 E7
Swindon 63 C7
T&W 234 B2
T&W 243 E8
W Berks 64 D6
Wilts 46 C6
Wilts 63 E9
W Mid 133 B11
W Mid 133 E9
W Sus 35 B11
W Yorks 198 C3
Newtown-in-St Martin
Corn 2 E6
Newtown Linford Leics 135 B10
Newtown St Boswells
Borders 262 C3
Newtown Unthank Leics 135 C9
New Tredegar Caerph 77 E10
New Trows S Lanark 259 B8
Newtyle Angus 286 C6
New Ulva Argyll 275 E8
New Village E Yorks 209 G7
S Yorks 198 F5
New Walsoken Cambs 139 B9
New Waltham NE Lincs 201 G9
New Well Powys 113 B11
New Wells Powys 130 D3
New Whittington Derbys 186 F5
New Wimpole Cambs 104 B6
New Winton E Loth 281 G8
New Woodhouses
Shrops 167 G9
New Works Telford 132 B3
New Wortley W Yorks 205 G11
New Yatt Oxon 82 C5
Newyears Green London 66 B5
New York Lincs 174 D2
N Yorks 214 G3
T&W 243 C8
New Zealand Wilts 62 D4
Nextend Hereford 114 F6
Neyland Pembs 73 D7
Niarbyl IoM 192 E3
Nib Heath Shrops 149 F8
Nibley Glos 79 D11
S Glos 61 C7
Nibley Green Glos 80 F2
Nibon Shetland 312 F5
Nicholashayne Devon 27 D10
Nicholaston Swansea 56 D4
Nidd N Yorks 214 G6
Niddrie Edin 280 G5
Nigg Aberdeen 293 C11
Highld 301 B8
Nigg Ferry Highld 301 C7
Nightcott Som 26 B5
Nilig Denb 165 D8
Nimble Nook Gtr Man 196 G2
Nimlet S Glos 61 E8
Nimmer Som 28 E4
Nine Ashes Essex 87 E9
Ninebanks Northumb 241 G7
Nine Elms London 67 D9
Swindon 62 B6
Nine Maidens Downs Corn 2 B5
Nine Mile Burn Midloth 270 D3
Nineveh Worcs 116 C3
Worcs 116 E2
Ninewells Glos 79 C9
Nine Wells Pembs 90 G5
Ninfield E Sus 38 E2
Ningwood IoW 20 D3
Ningwood Common IoW 20 D3
Ninnes Bridge Corn 2 B2
Nisbet Borders 262 D5
Nisthouse Orkney 314 E3
Shetland 313 G7
Nithbank Dumfries 247 D9
Niton IoW 20 F6
Nitshill Glasgow 267 C10
Noah's Arks Kent 52 B5
Noah's Green Worcs 117 E10
Noak Bridge Essex 87 G11
Noak Hill Essex 87 G11
London 87 G8
Nob End Gtr Man 195 F9
Nobland Green Herts 86 B5
Noblethorpe S Yorks 197 F9
Nobold Shrops 149 G9
Nobottle W Nhants 120 E3
Nob's Crook Hants 33 C7
Nocton Lincs 173 C9
Noctorum Mers 182 D3
Nodmore W Berks 64 D2
Noel Park London 86 G4
Nogdam End Norf 143 C7
Nog Tow Lancs 202 G6
Noke Oxon 83 C8
Noke Street Medway 69 E8
Nolton Pembs 72 B5
Nolton Haven Pembs 72 B5
No Man's Heath Ches W 167 F8
Warks 134 B5
Nomansland Devon 26 E4
Herts 85 C11
Wilts 32 D3
No Man's Land Corn 6 D5
Hants 33 B8
Noneley Shrops 149 D9
Noness Shetland 313 L6
Nonikiln Highld 300 B6
Nonington Kent 55 C9
Nook Cumb 211 C10
Noon Nick W Yorks 205 F8
Nonsbrough Shetland 313 H4
Noonsun Ches E 184 F4
Noonvares Corn 2 C3
Noranside Angus 292 G6
Norbiton London 67 F7
Norbreck Blackpool 202 E2
Norbridge Hereford 98 C4
Norbury Ches E 167 F9
Derbys 169 G10
London 67 F10
Shrops 131 E7
Staffs 150 E5
Norbury Common
Ches E 167 F9
Norbury Junction Staffs 150 E5
Norbury Moor Gtr Man 184 D6
Norby N Yorks 215 C8
Shetland 313 H3
Norchard Worcs 116 D6
Norcote Glos 81 E8
Norcott Brook Ches W 183 E10
Norcross Blackpool 202 E2
Nordelph Norf 139 C11
Nordelph Corner Norf 141 C10
Norden Dorset 18 E4
Gtr Man 195 E11
Norden Heath Dorset 18 E4
Nordley Shrops 132 D3
Norham Northumb 273 F8
Norham West Mains
Northumb 273 F8
Nork Sur 51 B8
Norland Town W Yorks 196 C5
Norleaze Wilts 45 C11
Norley Ches W 183 G9
Devon 25 G8
Norley Common Sur 50 E4
Norleywood Hants 20 B3
Norlington E Sus 36 E6
Normacot Stoke 168 G6
Normanby N Lincs 199 D11
N Yorks 216 C4
Redcar 225 B10
Normanby-by-Spital
Lincs 189 D7
Normanby by Stow
Lincs 188 E5
Normanby le Wold
Lincs 189 B10
Norman Cross Cambs 138 E3
Normandy Sur 50 C2
Norman Hill Glos 80 F3
Norman's Bay E Sus 23 D11
Norman's Green Devon 27 G9
Normanston Suff 143 E10
Normanton Derby 152 C6
Leics 172 G4
Normanton *continued*
Lincs 172 F6
Notts 172 E2
Rutland 137 B8
Wilts 46 E6
W Yorks 197 C11
Normanton le Heath
Leics 153 G7
Normanton on Soar
Notts 153 E10
Normanton-on-the-Wolds
Notts 154 C2
Normanton on Trent
Notts 172 B3
Normanton Spring
S Yorks 186 E6
Normanton Turville
Leics 135 D9
Normoss Lancs 202 F2
Norney Sur 50 E2
Norr W Yorks 205 F7
Norrington Common
Wilts 61 G11
Norris Green Corn 7 B8
Mers 182 C5
Norris Hill Leics 152 F6
Norristhorpe W Yorks 197 C8
Norseman Orkney 314 E3
Northacre Norf 141 D9
North Acton London 67 C8
Northall Bucks 103 G9
Northallerton N Yorks 225 G7
Northall Green Norf 159 G9
Northam Devon 24 B6
Soton 32 E6
Northampton W Nhants 120 E5
North Anston S Yorks 187 E8
North Ascot Brack 66 F2
North Aston Oxon 101 F9
Northaw Herts 86 E3
Northay Devon 28 G5
Som 28 E3
North Ayre Shetland 312 F6
North Baddesley Hants 32 D5
North Ballachulish
Highld 290 G2
North Barrow Som 29 B10
North Barsham Norf 159 C8
North Batsom Som 41 G10
Northbeck Lincs 173 G9
North Beer Corn 12 C2
North Benfleet Essex 69 B9
North Bersted W Sus 22 C6
North Berwick E Loth 281 D11
North Bitchburn Durham 233 E9
North Blyth Northumb 253 G8
North Boarhunt Hants 33 E10
North Bockhampton BCP 19 B9
Northborough Pboro 138 B3
Northbourne BCP 19 B7
Kent 55 C10
North Bovey Devon 13 E10
North Bradley Wilts 45 C11
North Brentor Devon 12 E5
North Brewham Som 45 F8
Northbridge Street
E Sus 38 C2
Northbrook Dorset 17 C11
Hants 33 D9
Hants 48 F4
Oxon 101 G9
Wilts 46 C4
North Brook End Cambs 104 C5
North Broomage Falk 279 E7
North Buckland Devon 40 E3
North Burlingham Norf 161 G7
North Cadbury Som 29 B10
North Cairn Dumfries 236 B1
North Camp Hants 49 C11
North Carlton Lincs 188 F6
Notts 187 E9
North Carrine Argyll 255 G7
North Cave E Yorks 208 G3
North Cerney Glos 81 D8
North Chailey E Sus 36 C5
Northchapel W Sus 35 B7
North Charford Wilts 31 D11
North Charlton
Northumb 264 E5
North Cheam London 67 F8
North Cheriton Som 29 B11
Northchurch Herts 85 D7
North Cliff E Yorks 209 D10
North Cliffe E Yorks 208 F3
North Clifton Notts 188 G4
North Close Durham 233 E11
North Cockerington
Lincs 190 C5
North Coker Som 29 E8
North Collafirth
Shetland 312 E5
North Common S Glos 61 E7
Suff 125 B9
North Connel Argyll 289 F11
North Cornelly Bridgend 57 E10
North Corner Corn 3 F7
S Glos 61 C7
North Corriegills
N Ayrs 256 C2
North Corry Highld 289 D10
Northcote Devon 27 G11
North Cotes Lincs 201 G11
Northcott Corn 24 F2
Devon 12 C2
Devon 27 E9
Devon 27 F10
North Country Corn 4 G3
Northcourt Oxon 83 F8
North Court Som 41 F11
North Cove Suff 143 F9
North Cowton N Yorks 224 E5
North Craigo Angus 293 G8
North Crawley
M Keynes 103 C8
North Cray London 68 E3
North Creake Norf 159 B7
North Curry Som 28 B4
North Dalton E Yorks 208 C4
North Darley Corn 11 G11
North Dawn Orkney 314 F4
North Deighton N Yorks 206 C3
North Denes Norf 161 G10
Northdown Kent 71 E11
North Dronley Angus 287 D7
North Drumachter Lodge
Highld 291 F8
North Duffield N Yorks 207 F9
Northdyke Orkney 314 D2
North Dykes Cumb 230 D6
North Eastling Kent 54 B3
Northedge Derbys 170 B5
North Elham Kent 55 E7
North Elkington Lincs 190 C3
North Elmham Norf 159 E9
North Elmsall W Yorks 198 E3
North Elmshall W Yorks 198 E3
North Elphinestone
E Loth 281 G7
Northend Bath 61 F9
Bucks 84 G2
Essex 89 E7
Northend *continued*
Essex 105 D10
Warks 119 G7
North End Bath 60 G6
Bedford 103 B9
Bedford 121 F10
Bucks 102 F4
Bucks 102 F6
Cumb 239 F8
Devon 27 D10
Dorset 30 B4
Durham 233 C11
Essex 87 B11
Essex 106 D5
E Yorks 209 C9
E Yorks 209 E9
E Yorks 209 G11
Hants 31 D10
Hants 33 B9
Hants 64 G2
Leics 153 F11
Lincs 174 G2
Lincs 189 B8
Lincs 190 C5
Lincs 190 D6
Lincs 191 D7
Lincs 201 G10
London 67 B9
London 68 D4
N Lincs 200 C6
Norf 141 E10
Northumb 252 C4
N Som 60 F2
Ptsmth 33 G11
Som 28 B3
Wilts 81 G8
W Sus 35 F10
W Sus 35 G7
W Sus 51 F11
Northenden Gtr Man 184 C4
Northern Moor Gtr Man 184 C4
North Erradale Highld 307 L2
North Evington
Leicester 136 C2
North Ewster N Lincs 199 G10
North Fambridge Essex 88 F5
North Fearns Highld 295 B7
North Featherstone
W Yorks 198 C2
North Feltham London 66 E6
North Feorline N Ayrs 255 E10
North Ferriby E Yorks 200 B3
Northfield Aberdeen 293 C11
Borders 262 D3
Borders 273 B8
Edin 280 G5
E Yorks 200 B4
Highld 301 B7
M Keynes 103 C7
N Nhants 137 E7
Som 43 F9
W Mid 117 B10
Northfields Hants 33 B7
Lincs 137 B10
North Finchley London 86 G3
Northfleet Kent 68 E6
Northfleet Green Kent 68 E6
North Flobbets Aberds 303 F7
North Frodingham
E Yorks 209 C8
Northgate Lincs 156 D3
Som 27 B9
W Sus 51 F9
North Gluss Shetland 312 F5
North Gorley Hants 31 E11
North Green Norf 141 B10
Norf 142 F4
Suff 126 B6
Suff 126 E6
Suff 127 D7
North Greetwell Lincs 189 G8
North Grimston N Yorks 216 F6
North Halley Orkney 314 F5
North Halling Medway 69 F8
North Harrow London 66 B6
North Hayling Hants 22 C2
North Hazelrigg
Northumb 264 C3
North Heasley Devon 41 G8
North Heath W Berks 64 E3
W Sus 35 C9
North Hill Corn 11 F11
North Hillingdon London 66 C5
North Hinksey Oxon 83 D7
North Hinksey Village
Oxon 83 D7
North Ho Shetland 313 J5
North Holmwood Sur 51 D7
North Houghton Hants 47 G10
Northhouse Borders 249 B10
North Howden E Yorks 207 G11
North Huish Devon 8 D4
North Hyde London 66 D6
North Hykeham Lincs 172 B6
North Hylton T&W 243 F8
Northiam E Sus 38 B4
Northill C Beds 104 B2
Northington Glos 80 D2
Hants 48 F5
North Kelsey Lincs 200 G4
North Kelsey Moor
Lincs 200 G5
North Kensington London 67 C8
North Kessock Highld 300 E6
North Killingholme
N Lincs 200 D6
North Kilvington
N Yorks 215 B8
North Kilworth Leics 136 G2
North Kingston Hants 31 G11
North Kirkton Aberds 303 D11
North Kiscadale N Ayrs 256 D2
North Kyme Lincs 173 E11
North Laggan Highld 290 D4
North Lancing W Sus 35 F11
North Landing E Yorks 218 E4
Northlands Lincs 174 E4
Northlea Durham 243 G10
Northleach Glos 81 C10
North Lee Bucks 84 D4
North Lees N Yorks 214 E6
Northleigh Devon 15 B9
Devon 40 G6
North Leigh Kent 54 D6
Oxon 82 C5
North Leverton with
Habblesthorpe Notts 188 E3
Northlew Devon 12 B6
North Littleton Worcs 99 B11
North Looe Sur 67 G8
North Lopham Norf 141 G10
North Luffenham
Rutland 137 C8
North Marden W Sus 34 D4
North Marston Bucks 102 G5
North Middleton
Midloth 271 D7
Northumb 264 E2
North Millbrex Aberds 303 E8
North Molton Devon 26 B2
Northmoor Devon 24 D4
Northmoor *continued*
Oxon 82 E6
Northmoor Corner Som 43 G10
Northmoor Green or
Moorland Som 43 G10
North Moreton Oxon 64 B5
North Mosstown
Aberds 303 D10
North Motherwell
N Lanark 268 D4
North Moulsecoomb
Brighton 36 F4
Northmuir Angus 287 B7
North Mundham W Sus 22 C5
North Muskham Notts 172 D3
North Newbald E Yorks 208 F4
North Newington Oxon 101 D8
North Newnton Wilts 46 B6
North Newton Som 43 G9
Northney Hants 22 C2
North Nibley Glos 80 F2
North Oakley Hants 48 C4
North Ockendon London 68 C5
Northolt London 66 C6
Northop =Llan-eurgain
Flint 166 B2
Northop Hall Flint 166 B3
North Ormesby Mbro 234 G6
North Ormsby Lincs 190 C3
Northorpe Lincs 155 F11
Lincs 156 B4
Lincs 188 B5
W Yorks 197 C8
North Otterington
N Yorks 215 B7
Northover Som 29 C8
Som 44 F3
North Owersby Lincs 189 C9
Northowram W Yorks 196 B6
Northpark Argyll 275 G11
North Perrott Som 29 F7
North Petherton Som 43 G9
North Petherwin Corn 11 D11
North Pickenham Norf 141 B7
North Piddle Worcs 117 G9
North Poorton Dorset 16 B6
Northport Dorset 18 D4
North Port Argyll 284 E4
North Poulner Hants 31 F11
Northpunds Shetland 313 L6
North Queensferry Fife 280 E2
North Radworthy Devon 41 G9
North Rauceby Lincs 173 F8
North Reddish Gtr Man 184 C5
Northrepps Norf 160 B4
North Reston Lincs 190 E5
North Rigton N Yorks 205 D11
North Ripley Hants 19 B9
North Rode Ches E 168 B5
North Roe Shetland 312 E5
North Row Cumb 229 E10
North Runcton Norf 158 F2
North Sandwick
Shetland 312 D7
North Scale Cumb 210 F3
North Scarle Lincs 172 B5
North Seaton Northumb 253 F7
North Seaton Colliery
Northumb 253 F7
North Sheen London 67 D7
North Shian Argyll 289 E11
North Shields T&W 243 D9
North Shoebury Southend 70 B2
North Shore Blackpool 202 F2
Northside Aberds 303 D8
Orkney 314 D2
North Side Cumb 228 F6
Pboro 138 D5
North Skelmanae
Aberds 303 D9
North Skelton Redcar 226 B3
North Somercotes Lincs 190 B6
North Stainley N Yorks 214 D5
North Stainmore Cumb 222 B6
North Stifford Thurrock 68 C6
North Stoke Bath 61 F8
Oxon 64 B6
W Sus 35 E8
North Stoneham Hants 32 D6
Northstowe Cambs 123 D8
North Street Hants 31 D11
Hants 48 G6
Kent 54 B4
Medway 69 E10
W Berks 64 E6
North Sunderland
Northumb 264 C6
North Synton Borders 261 E11
North Tamerton Corn 12 B2
North Tawton Devon 25 G11
North Thoresby Lincs 190 B3
North Tidworth Wilts 47 D8
North Togston Northumb 252 C6
Northton Aberds 293 C9
Northtown Orkney 314 G4
Shetland 313 M5
North Town Devon 25 F8
Hants 49 C11
Som 29 B10
Som 44 E5
Windsor 65 C11
North Tuddenham
Norf 159 G10
Northumberland Heath
London 68 D4
Northville Torf 78 F3
North Walbottle T&W 242 D5
North Walney Cumb 210 F3
North Walsham Norf 160 C5
North Waltham Hants 48 D5
North Warnborough
Hants 49 C8
North Water Bridge
Angus 293 G8
North Waterhayne Devon 28 F3
North Watford Herts 85 F10
North Watten Highld 310 D6
Northway Devon 24 C5
Glos 99 E8
Som 27 B10
Swansea 56 D5
North Weald Bassett
Essex 87 E7
North Weirs Hants 32 G3
North Wembley London 67 B7
North Weston N Som 60 D3
Oxon 83 D11
North Wheatley Notts 188 D3
North Whilborough Devon 9 B7
North Whiteley Moray 302 E4
Northwich Ches W 183 G11
Northwick S Glos 60 B5
Som 43 D11
Worcs 116 F6
North Wick Bath 60 F5
North Widcombe Bath 44 B5
North Willingham
Lincs 189 D11
North Wingfield Derbys 170 B6

North Witham Lincs 155 E8
Northwold Norf 140 D5
Northwood Derbys 170 C3
IoW 20 C5
Kent 71 F11
London 85 G9
Mers 182 B6
Shrops 149 C9
Staffs 168 G5
Stoke 168 F5
Northwood Green Glos 80 B2
Northwood Hills London 85 G9
North Woolwich London 68 D2
North Wootton Dorset 29 E11
Norf 158 E2
Som 44 E5
North Wraxall Wilts 61 D10
North Wroughton
Swindon 63 C7
Norton Devon 9 E7
Devon 24 B3
E Sus 23 E7
Glos 99 G7
Halton 183 E9
Herts 104 E4
IoW 20 D2
Mon 78 B6
Notts 187 G9
N Som 59 G10
Powys 114 D6
Shrops 131 B11
Shrops 131 G9
Shrops 132 C4
Stockton 234 G4
Suff 125 D9
Swansea 56 D3
Swansea 56 D6
S Yorks 186 E5
S Yorks 198 D4
Wilts 61 C11
W Mid 133 G7
W Nhants 120 E2
Worcs 99 B10
Worcs 117 G7
W Sus 22 B6
W Sus 22 D5
Norton Ash Kent 70 G3
Norton Bavant Wilts 46 E2
Norton Bridge Staffs 151 C7
Norton Canes Staffs 133 B10
Norton Canon Hereford 97 B7
Norton Corner Norf 159 D11
Norton Disney Lincs 172 D5
Norton East Staffs 133 B10
Norton Ferris Wilts 45 F9
Norton Fitzwarren Som 27 B11
Norton Green Herts 104 G4
IoW 20 D2
Staffs 168 E6
W Mid 118 C3
Norton Hawkfield Bath 60 G5
Norton Heath Essex 87 E10
Norton in Hales Shrops 150 B4
Norton-in-the-Moors
Stoke 168 E5
Norton-Juxta-Twycross
Leics 134 B6
Norton-le-Clay N Yorks 215 E8
Norton Lindsey Warks 118 E4
Norton Little Green
Suff 125 D9
Norton Malreward Bath 60 F6
Norton Mandeville Essex 87 E9
Norton-on-Derwent
N Yorks 216 E5
Norton St Philip Som 45 B9
Norton Subcourse Norf 143 D8
Norton sub Hamdon Som 29 D7
Norton's Wood N Som 60 E2
Norton Woodseats
S Yorks 186 E5
Norwell Notts 172 C3
Norwell Woodhouse
Notts 172 C2
Norwich Norf 142 B4
Norwick Shetland 312 B8
Norwood Derbys 187 E7
Dorset 29 F8
Norwood End Essex 87 D9
Norwood Green London 66 D6
W Yorks 196 B6
Norwood Hill Sur 51 E8
Norwood New Town
London 67 E10
Norwoodside Cambs 139 D8
Noseley Leics 136 D4
Noss Highld 310 D7
Shetland 313 M5
Noss Mayo Devon 7 F11
Nosterfield N Yorks 214 C5
Nosterfield End Cambs 106 C2
Nostie Highld 295 C10
Notgrove Glos 100 G2
Nottage Bridgend 57 F10
Notter Corn 7 C7
Nottingham Nottingham 153 B11
Notting Hill London 67 C8
Nottington Dorset 17 E9
Notton Wilts 62 F2
W Yorks 197 E10
Nounsley Essex 88 C3
Noutard's Green Worcs 116 D5
Novar House Highld 300 C6
Nova Scotia Ches W 167 B10
Novers Park Bristol 60 F5
Noverton Glos 99 G9
Nowton Suff 125 E7
Nox Shrops 149 G8
Noyadd Trefawr Ceredig 92 B5
Noyadd Wilym Ceredig 92 C4
Nuffield Oxon 65 B7
Nun Appleton N Yorks 207 F7
Nunburnholme E Yorks 208 D2
Nuncargate Notts 171 E8
Nunclose Cumb 230 B5
Nuneaton Warks 135 E7
Nuneham Courtenay
Oxon 83 F9
Nuney Green Oxon 65 D7
Nunhead London 67 D11
Nun Hills Lancs 195 C11
Nun Monkton N Yorks 206 B6
Nunney Som 45 D8
Nunney Catch Som 45 E8
Nunnington N Yorks 216 D3
Nunnykirk Northumb 252 E3
Nunsthorpe NE Lincs 201 F9
Nunthorpe Mbro 225 C10
York 207 C8
Nunton Wilts 31 B11
Nunwick N Yorks 214 E6
Nupdown S Glos 79 F10
Nupend Glos 80 D3
Glos 80 F4
Nup End Bucks 84 B5
Herts 86 B2
Nuper's Hatch Essex 87 G8
Nuppend Glos 79 E10
Nuptown Brack 65 E11
Nursling Hants 32 D5
Nursted Hants 34 C3
Nursteed Wilts 62 G4
Nurston V Glam 58 F5
Nurton Staffs 132 D6
Nurton Hill Staffs 132 D6
Nutbourne W Sus 22 B3
W Sus 35 D9
Nutbourne Common
W Sus 35 D9
Nutburn Hants 32 C5
Nutcombe Sur 49 G11
Nutfield Sur 51 C10
Nut Grove Mers 183 C7
Nuthall Notts 171 G8
Nuthampstead Herts 105 E8
Nuthurst Warks 118 C3
W Sus 35 B11
Nutley E Sus 36 B6
Hants 48 E6
Nuttall Gtr Man 195 D9
Nutwell S Yorks 198 G6
Nybster Highld 310 C7
Nye N Som 60 G2
Nyetimber W Sus 22 D5
Nyewood W Sus 34 C4
Nyland Som 44 C3
Nymet Rowland Devon 26 F2
Nymet Tracey Devon 26 G2
Nympsfield Glos 80 E4
Nynehead Som 27 C10
Nythe Som 44 G2
Swindon 63 B7
Nyton W Sus 22 B6

O

Oadby Leics 136 C2
Oad Street Kent 69 G11
Oakall Green Worcs 116 E6
Oakamoor Staffs 169 G9
Oakbank W Loth 269 B11
Oak Bank Gtr Man 195 F10
Oak Cross Devon 12 B6
Oakdale BCP 18 C6
Caerph 77 F11
N Yorks 205 B11
Oake Som 27 B11
Oake Green Som 27 B11
Oaken Staffs 133 C7
Oakenclough Lancs 202 D6
Oakengates Telford 150 G4
Oakenholt Flint 182 G3
Oakenshaw Durham 233 D10
Lancs 203 G10
W Yorks 197 B7
Oakerthorpe Derbys 170 E5
Oakes W Yorks 196 D6
Oakfield Herts 104 F3
IoW 21 C7
Torf 78 G4
Oakford Ceredig 111 F9
Devon 26 C6
Oakfordbridge Devon 26 C6
Oakgrove Ches E 168 B6
M Keynes 103 D7
Oakham Rutland 137 B7
W Mid 133 F9
Oakhanger Ches E 168 E3
Hants 49 F9
Oakhill Som 44 D6
W Sus 51 G7
Oak Hill Stoke 168 G5
Suff 109 B7
Oakhurst Kent 52 C4
Oakington Cambs 123 E8
Oaklands Carms 74 B6
Herts 86 B2
Powys 113 G10
Oakleigh Park London 86 G3
Oakle Street Glos 80 B3
Oakley BCP 18 B6
Bedford 121 G10
Bucks 83 C10
Fife 279 D10
Glos 99 G9
Hants 48 C5
Oxon 84 E3
Staffs 150 B4
Suff 126 B3
Oakley Court Oxon 64 B6
Oakley Green Windsor 66 D2
Oakley Park Powys 129 F9
Suff 126 B3
Oakley Wood Oxon 64 B6
Oakmere Ches W 167 B9
Oakridge Glos 80 E6
Hants 48 C6
Oakridge Lynch Glos 80 E6
Oaks Shrops 131 C8
Oaksey Wilts 81 G7
Oaks Green Derbys 152 C3
Oakshaw Ford Cumb 240 B2
Oakshott Hants 34 B2
Oaks in Charnwood
Leics 153 F9
Oakthorpe Leics 152 G6
Oak Tree Darl 225 C7
Oakwell W Yorks 197 B8
Oakwood Derby 153 B7
London 86 F3
Northumb 241 D10
Warr 183 C11
W Yorks 206 F2
Oakwoodhill Sur 50 F6
Oakworth W Yorks 204 F6
Oape Highld 309 J4
Oare Kent 70 G4
Som 41 D10
W Berks 64 E4
Wilts 63 G7
Oareford Som 41 D10
Oasby Lincs 155 B10
Oath Som 28 B5
Oathill Dorset 28 F6
Oathlaw Angus 287 B8
Oatlands Glasgow 267 C11
N Yorks 205 C11
Oatlands Park Sur 66 G5
Oban Argyll 289 G10
Highld 295 G10
W Isles 305 H3
Obley Shrops 114 B6
Oborne Dorset 29 D11
Obthorpe Lincs 155 F11
Obthorpe Lodge Lincs 156 F2
Occlestone Green
Ches W 167 C11
Occold Suff 126 C3
Ocean Village Soton 32 E6
Ochiltree E Ayrs 258 E2
Ochr-y-foel Denb 181 F9
Ochtermuthill Perth 286 F2
Ochtertyre Perth 286 E2
Ochtow Highld 309 J4
Ockbrook Derbys 153 B8
Ocker Hill W Mid 133 E9
Ockeridge Worcs 116 E5
Ockford Ridge Sur 50 E3
Ockham Sur 50 B5
Ockle Highld 289 B7
Ockley Sur 50 F6
Ocle Pychard Hereford 97 B11
Octon E Yorks 217 F10
Octon Cross Roads
E Yorks 217 F10
Odam Barton Devon 26 D2
Odcombe Som 29 D8
Odd Down Bath 61 G8
Oddendale Cumb 221 C11
Odder Lincs 188 G6
Oddingley Worcs 117 F8
Oddington Glos 100 F4
Oxon 83 C9
Odell Bedford 121 F9
Odham Devon 25 G7
Odie Orkney 314 D6
Odiham Hants 49 C8
Odsal W Yorks 197 B7
Odsey Cambs 104 D5
Odstock Wilts 31 B10
Odstone Leics 135 B7
Offchurch Warks 119 D7
Offenham Worcs 99 B11
Offenham Cross Worcs 99 B11
Offerton Gtr Man 184 D6
T&W 243 F8
Offerton Green Gtr Man 184 D6
Offham E Sus 36 E5
Kent 53 B7
W Sus 35 F8
Offleyhay Staffs 150 D5
Offleymarsh Staffs 150 D5
Offleyrock Staffs 150 D5
Offord Cluny Cambs 122 D4
Offord D'Arcy Cambs 122 D4
Offton Suff 107 B11
Offwell Devon 15 B9
Ogbourne Maizey Wilts 63 E7
Ogbourne St Andrew
Wilts 63 E7
Ogbourne St George
Wilts 63 E8
Ogden W Yorks 205 G7
Ogdens Hants 31 E11
Ogil Angus 292 G6
Ogle Northumb 242 B4
Ogmore V Glam 57 F11
Ogmore-by-Sea = *Aberogwr*
V Glam 57 F11
Ogmore Vale Bridgend 76 G6
Okeford Fitzpaine Dorset 30 E4
Okehampton Devon 13 B7
Okehampton Camp
Devon 13 C7
Oker Derbys 170 C3
Okewood Hill Sur 50 F6
Okle Green Glos 98 F5
Okraquoy Shetland 313 K6
Okus Swindon 62 C6
Olchard Devon 14 F3
Old W Nhants 120 C5
Old Aberdeen
Aberdeen 293 C11
Old Alresford Hants 48 G5
Oldany Highld 306 F6
Old Arley Warks 134 E5
Old Balornock Glasgow 268 B2
Old Basford Nottingham 171 G8
Old Basing Hants 49 C7
Old Belses Borders 262 E3
Oldberrow Warks 118 D2
Old Bewick Northumb 264 E3
Old Bexley London 68 E3
Old Blair Perth 291 G10
Old Bolingbroke Lincs 174 B4
Oldborough Devon 26 F3
Old Boston Mers 183 B9
Old Bramhope
W Yorks 205 E10
Old Brampton Derbys 186 G4
Old Bridge of Tilt
Perth 291 G10
Old Bridge of Urr
Dumfries 237 C9
Oldbrook M Keynes 103 D7
Old Buckenham Norf 141 E11
Old Burdon T&W 243 G9
Old Burghclere Hants 48 B3
Oldbury Kent 52 B5
Shrops 132 E4
Warks 134 E6
W Mid 133 F9
Oldbury Naite S Glos 79 G10
Oldbury-on-Severn
S Glos 79 G10
Oldbury on the Hill Glos 61 B10
Old Byland N Yorks 215 B11
Old Cambus Borders 272 B6
Old Cardinham Castle
Corn 6 B2
Old Carlisle Cumb 229 B11
Old Cassop Durham 234 D2
Oldcastle Mon 96 G6
Oldcastle Heath Ches W 167 F7
Old Castleton Borders 250 E2
Old Catton Norf 160 G4
Old Chalford Oxon 100 F6
Old Church Stoke
Powys 130 E5
Old Clee NE Lincs 201 F9
Old Cleeve Som 42 E4
Old Colwyn Conwy 180 F5
Old Coppice Shrops 131 B9
Old Corry Highld 295 C8
Oldcotes Notts 187 D9
Old Coulsdon London 51 B10
Old Country Hereford 98 C4
Old Craig Aberds 303 G9
Angus 292 G4
Oldcroft Glos 79 D10
Old Crombie Aberds 302 D5
Old Cryals Kent 53 E7
Old Cullen Moray 302 C5
Old Dailly S Ayrs 244 D6
Old Dalby Leics 154 E3
Old Dam Derbys 185 F10
Old Deer Aberds 303 E9
Old Denaby S Yorks 187 B7
Old Ditch Som 44 D4
Old Dolphin W Yorks 205 G8
Old Down S Glos 60 B6
Old Duffus Moray 301 C11
Old Edlington S Yorks 187 B8
Old Eldon Durham 233 F10
Old Ellerby E Yorks 209 F9
Oldend Glos 80 D3
Old Fallings W Mid 133 C8
Oldfallow Staffs 151 G9
Old Farm Park
M Keynes 103 D8
Old Felixstowe Suff 108 D6
Oldfield Cumb 229 F7
Shrops 132 F3
Worcs 116 E6
W Yorks 196 E6
W Yorks 204 F6
Old Field Shrops 115 B9
Oldfield Brow Gtr Man 184 D3
Oldfield Park Bath 61 G8
Old Fletton Pboro 138 D3
Old Fold T&W 243 E7
Oldford Som 45 C9
Old Ford London 67 C11
Old Forge Hereford 79 B9
Oldfurnace Staffs 169 G8
Old Furnace Torf 78 E3
Old Gate Lincs 157 E8
Old Glossop Derbys 185 C8
Old Goginan Ceredig 128 G3
Old Goole E Yorks 199 C8
Old Gore Hereford 98 F2
Old Graitney Dumfries 239 D8
Old Grimsby Scilly 1 F3
Oldhall Renfs 267 C10
Old Hall Powys 129 G8
Oldhall Green Suff 125 F7
Old Hall Green Herts 105 G7
Oldhall Ho Highld 310 D6
Old Hall Street Norf 160 C6
Oldham Gtr Man 196 F2
Oldham Edge Gtr Man 196 F2
Oldhamstocks E Loth 282 G4
Old Harlow Essex 87 C7
Old Hatfield Herts 86 D2
Old Heath Essex 107 G10
Old Heathfield E Sus 37 C9
Old Hill W Mid 133 F9
Old Hills Worcs 98 B6
Old Hunstanton Norf 175 G11
Oldhurst Cambs 122 B6
Old Hurst Cambs 122 B5
Old Hutton Cumb 211 B11
Oldington Shrops 132 D4
Old Johnstone Dumfries 248 D6
Old Kea Corn 4 G6
Old Kilpatrick W Dunb 277 G9
Old Kinnernie Aberds 293 C9
Old Knebworth Herts 104 G4
Oldland S Glos 61 E7
Oldland Common S Glos 61 E7
Old Langho Lancs 203 F10
Old Laxey IoM 192 D5
Old Leake Lincs 174 E6
Old Leckie Stirling 278 C3
Old Lindley W Yorks 196 D5
Old Linslade C Beds 103 F8
Old Llanberis = *Nant Peris*
Gwyn 163 D10
Old Malden London 67 F8
Old Malton N Yorks 216 E5
Old Marton Shrops 148 C6
Old Mead Essex 105 F10
Oldmeldrum Aberds 303 G8
Old Micklefield
W Yorks 206 G4
Old Mill Corn 12 G3
Old Milton Hants 19 C10
Old Milverton Warks 118 D5
Oldmixon N Som 43 B10
Old Monkland N Lanark 268 C4
Old Nenthorn Borders 262 B5
Old Netley Hants 33 F7
Old Neuadd Powys 129 F11
Old Newton Suff 125 E11
Old Oak Common London 67 C8
Old Park Corn 6 B4
Telford 132 B3
Old Passage S Glos 60 B5
Old Perton Staffs 133 D7
Old Philpstoun W Loth 279 F11
Old Polmont Falk 279 F8
Old Portsmouth Ptsmth 21 B8
Old Quarrington
Durham 234 D2
Old Radnor Powys 114 F5
Old Rattray Aberds 303 D10
Old Rayne Aberds 302 G6
Old Romney Kent 39 B8
Old Shirley Soton 32 E5
Oldshore Beg Highld 306 D6
Old Shoreham W Sus 36 F2
Oldshoremore Highld 306 D7
Old Snydale W Yorks 198 C2
Old Sodbury S Glos 61 C9
Old Somerby Lincs 155 C9
Oldstead N Yorks 215 C10
Old Stillington Stockton 234 G3
Old Storridge Common
Worcs 116 G4
Old Stratford W Nhants 102 C5
Old Struan Perth 291 G10
Old Swan Mers 182 C5
Old Swarland Northumb 252 C5
Old Swinford W Mid 133 G8
Old Tame Gtr Man 196 F3
Old Tebay Cumb 222 D2
Old Thirsk N Yorks 215 C8
Old Tinnis Borders 261 D9
Old Toll S Ayrs 257 E9
Oldtown Aberds 293 C7
Aberds 302 G5
Highld 309 L5
Old Town Cumb 211 C11
Cumb 230 C5
Edin 280 G5
E Sus 23 F9
E Sus 38 F2
E Sus 38 F4
E Yorks 218 F3
Herts 104 F4
Scilly 1 G4
Swindon 63 C7
W Yorks 196 B3
Oldtown of Ord Aberds 302 D6
Old Trafford Gtr Man 184 B4
Old Tree Kent 71 G8
Old Tupton Derbys 170 B5
Oldwalls Swansea 56 C3
Old Warden C Beds 104 C2
Old Warren Flint 166 C4
Oldway Swansea 56 D5
Torbay 9 C7
Old Way Som 28 D5
Oldways End Devon 26 B5
Old Weston Cambs 121 B11
Old Wharf Hereford 98 D4
Oldwhat Aberds 303 D8
Old Whittington Derbys 186 G5
Oldwich Lane W Mid 118 C4
Old Wick Highld 310 D7
Old Wimpole Cambs 122 G6
Old Windsor Windsor 66 E3
Old Wingate Durham 234 D3
Old Wives Lees Kent 54 C5
Old Woking Sur 50 B4
Old Wolverton
M Keynes 102 C6
Oldwood Worcs 115 D11
Old Woodhall Lincs 174 B2
Old Woodhouses
Shrops 167 G9
Old Woodstock Oxon 82 B6
Olgrinmore Highld 310 D4
Olive Green Staffs 152 F2
Oliver's Battery Hants 33 B7
Ollaberry Shetland 312 E5
Ollag W Isles 297 G3
Ollerbrook Booth
Derbys 185 D10
Ollerton Ches E 184 F3
Notts 171 B11
Ollerton *continued*
Shrops 150 D2
Ollerton Fold Lancs 194 C6
Ollerton Lane Shrops 150 D3
Olmarch Ceredig 112 F2
Olmstead Green Essex 106 C2
Olney M Keynes 121 G7
Olrig Ho Highld 310 C5
Olton W Mid 134 G2
Olveston S Glos 60 B6
Olwen Ceredig 93 B11
Ombersley Worcs 116 E6
Ompton Notts 171 B11
Omunsgarth Shetland 313 J5
Onchan IoM 192 E4
Onecote Staffs 169 D9
Onehouse Suff 125 F10
Onen Mon 78 C6
Onesacre S Yorks 186 C3
Ongar Hill Norf 157 E11
Ongar Street Hereford 115 D7
Onibury Shrops 115 B9
Onich Highld 290 G2
Onllwyn Neath 76 C4
Onneley Staffs 168 G3
Onslow Village Sur 50 D3
Onthank E Ayrs 267 G8
Onziebust Orkney 314 D4
Openshaw Gtr Man 184 B5
Openwoodgate Derbys 170 F5
Opinan Highld 299 B7
Highld 307 K3
Orange Lane Borders 272 G5
Orange Row Norf 157 E10
Orasaigh W Isles 305 G5
Orbiston N Lanark 268 D4
Orbliston Moray 302 D3
Orbost Highld 298 E2
Orby Lincs 175 B7
Orchard Hill Devon 24 B6
Orchard Leigh Bucks 85 E7
Orchard Portman Som 28 C2
Orcheston Wilts 46 D5
Orcop Hereford 97 F9
Orcop Hill Hereford 97 F9
Ord Highld 295 D8
Ordale Shetland 312 C8
Ordhead Aberds 293 B8
Ordie Aberds 292 C6
Ordiequish Moray 302 D3
Ordiqhill Aberds 302 D5
Ordley Northumb 241 F10
Ordsall Gtr Man 184 B4
Notts 187 E11
Ore E Sus 38 E4
Oreston Plym 7 E10
Oreton Shrops 132 G3
Orford Suff 109 B8
Warr 183 C10
Organford Dorset 18 C4
Orgreave Staffs 152 F3
S Yorks 186 D6
Oridge Street Glos 98 F5
Orlandon Pembs 72 D4
Orlestone Kent 54 G3
Orleton Hereford 115 D9
Worcs 116 D3
Orleton Common
Hereford 115 D9
Orlingbury N Nhants 121 C7
Ormacleit W Isles 297 H3
Ormathwaite Cumb 229 F11
Ormesby Redcar 225 B10
Ormesby St Margaret
Norf 161 G9
Ormesby St Michael
Norf 161 G9
Ormiclate Castle
W Isles 297 H3
Ormidale Lodge Argyll 275 F11
Ormiscaig Highld 307 K3
Ormiston Borders 262 G2
E Loth 271 B8
Ormsaigbeg Highld 288 C6
Ormsaigmore Highld 288 C6
Ormsary Argyll 275 F8
Ormsgill Cumb 210 E3
Ormskirk Lancs 194 F2
Ornsby Hill Durham 233 B9
Orpington London 68 F3
Orrell Gtr Man 194 F4
Mers 182 B4
Orrell Post Gtr Man 194 G4
Orrisdale IoM 192 C4
Orrock Fife 280 D4
Orroland Dumfries 237 E9
Orsett Thurrock 68 C6
Orsett Heath Thurrock 68 D6
Orslow Staffs 150 F6
Orston Notts 172 G3
Orthwaite Cumb 229 E11
Ortner Lancs 202 C6
Orton Cumb 222 D2
N Nhants 120 B6
Staffs 133 D7
Orton Brimbles Pboro 138 D3
Orton Goldhay Pboro 138 D3
Orton Longueville
Pboro 138 D3
Orton Malborne Pboro 138 D3
Orton-on-the-Hill Leics 134 C6
Orton Rigg Cumb 239 G8
Orton Southgate Pboro 138 E2
Orton Waterville Pboro 138 D3
Orton Wistow Pboro 138 D2
Orwell Cambs 123 G7
Osbaldeston Lancs 203 G8
Osbaldeston Green
Lancs 203 G8
Osbaldwick York 207 C8
Osbaston Leics 135 C8
Shrops 148 E6
Telford 149 F11
Osbaston Hollow Leics 135 B8
Osbournby Lincs 155 B11
Oscroft Ches W 167 B8
Ose Highld 298 E3
Osea Island Essex 88 D6
Osehill Green Dorset 29 F11
Osgathorpe Leics 153 F8
Osgodby Lincs 189 C9
N Yorks 207 G8
N Yorks 217 C11
Osgodby Common
N Yorks 207 F8
Osidge London 86 G3
Oskaig Highld 295 B7
Oskamull Argyll 288 E6
Osleston Derbys 152 B4
Osmaston Derby 153 C7
Derbys 170 G2
Osmington Dorset 17 E10
Osmington Mills Dorset 17 E10
Osmondthorpe W Yorks 206 G2
Osmotherley N Yorks 225 F9
Osney Oxon 83 D8
Ospisdale Highld 309 L7
Ospringe Kent 70 G4
Ossaborough Devon 40 E3
Ossemsley Hants 19 B10
Osset Spa W Yorks 197 D9
Ossett W Yorks 197 C9
Ossett Street Side
W Yorks 197 C9
Ossington Notts 172 C3
Ostend Essex 88 F6
Norf 161 C7
Osterley London 66 D6
Oswaldkirk N Yorks 216 D2
Oswaldtwistle Lancs 195 B8
Oswestry Shrops 148 D5
Otby Lincs 189 C10
Oteley Shrops 149 C8
Otford Kent 52 B4
Otham Kent 53 C9
Otham Hole Kent 53 C10
Otherton Staffs 151 G8
Othery Som 43 G11
Otley Suff 126 F4
W Yorks 205 D10
Otterbourne Hants 33 C7
Otterburn Northumb 251 E9
N Yorks 204 B3
Otterburn Camp
Northumb 251 D9
Otterden Place Kent 54 C2
Otter Ferry Argyll 275 E10
Otterford Som 28 E2
Otterham Corn 11 C9
Otterhampton Som 43 E8
Otterham Quay Kent 69 F10
Otterham Station Corn 11 D9
Otter Ho Argyll 275 F10
Ottershaw Sur 66 G4
Otterspool Mers 182 D5
Otterswick Shetland 312 E7
Otterton Devon 15 D7
Otterwood Hants 32 G6
Ottery St Mary Devon 15 B8
Ottinge Kent 55 E7
Ottringham E Yorks 201 C9
Oughterby Cumb 239 F7
Oughtershaw N Yorks 213 C7
Oughterside Cumb 229 C8
Oughtibridge S Yorks 186 C4
Oughtrington Warr 183 D11
Oulston N Yorks 215 E10
Oulton Cumb 238 G6
Norf 160 D2
Staffs 150 E5
Staffs 151 B8
Suff 143 D10
W Yorks 197 B11
Oulton Broad Suff 143 E10
Oultoncross Staffs 151 C8
Oulton Grange Staffs 151 B8
Oulton Heath Staffs 151 B8
Oulton Street Norf 160 D3
Oundle N Nhants 137 F10
Ounsdale Staffs 133 E7
Ousby Cumb 231 E8
Ousdale Highld 311 G4
Ousden Suff 124 F4
Ousefleet E Yorks 199 C10
Ousel Hole W Yorks 205 E8
Ouston Durham 243 G7
Northumb 241 G7
Northumb 242 C3
Outcast Cumb 210 D6
Out Elmstead Kent 55 C8
Outer Hope Devon 8 G3
Outertown Orkney 314 E2
Outgate Cumb 221 F7
Outhgill Cumb 222 E5
Outhill Warks 118 D2
Outhills Aberds 303 D10
Outlands Staffs 150 C5
Outlane W Yorks 196 D5
Outlane Moor W Yorks 196 D5
Outlet Village Ches W 182 G6
Outmarsh Wilts 61 G11
Out Newton E Yorks 201 C11
Out Rawcliffe Lancs 202 E4
Outwell Norf 139 C10
Outwick Hants 31 D10
Outwood Gtr Man 195 F9
Som 28 B4
Sur 51 D10
W Yorks 197 C10
Outwoods Leics 153 F8
Staffs 150 F5
Staffs 152 E4
Warks 134 G4
Ouzlewell Green
W Yorks 197 B10
Ovenden W Yorks 196 B5
Ovenscloss Borders 261 C11
Over Cambs 123 C7
Ches W 167 B10
Glos 80 B4
S Glos 60 C5
Overa Farm Stud Norf 141 F9
Overbister Orkney 314 B6
Over Burrow Lancs 212 D2
Over Burrows Derbys 152 B5
Overbury Worcs 99 D9
Overcombe Dorset 17 E9
Over Compton Dorset 29 D9
Overend W Mid 133 G9
Over End Cambs 137 E11
Derbys 186 G3
Overgreen Derbys 186 G4
Over Green W Mid 134 E3
Over Haddon Derbys 170 B2
Over Hulton Gtr Man 195 F7
Over Kellet Lancs 211 E10
Over Kiddington Oxon 101 G8
Over Knutsford Ches E 184 F3
Over Langshaw
Borders 271 G10
Overleigh Som 44 F3
Overley Staffs 152 F3
Overley Green Warks 117 F11
Over Monnow Mon 79 C8
Overmoor Staffs 169 F7
Over Norton Oxon 100 F6
Over Peover Ches E 184 G3
Overpool Ches W 182 F5
Overs Shrops 131 D7
Overscaig Hotel Highld 309 G4
Overseal Derbys 152 F5
Over Silton N Yorks 225 G9
Overslade Warks 119 C9
Oversland Kent 54 B5
Oversley Green Warks 117 F11
Overstone W Nhants 120 D6
Over Stowey Som 43 F7
Overstrand Norf 160 A4
Over Stratton Som 28 D6
Over Tabley Ches E 184 E2
Overthorpe W Nhants 101 C9
W Yorks 197 D8
Overton Aberdeen 293 B10
Aberds 293 B9
Ches W 183 F8
Dumfries 237 C11
Glos 80 C2
Hants 48 D4
Invclyd 276 G5
Lancs 202 B4
N Yorks 207 B7
Shrops 115 C10
Overton *continued*
Staffs 151 B10
Swansea 56 D3
W Yorks 197 D9
Overton = *Owrtyn* Wrex 166 G5
Overton Bridge Wrex 166 G5
Overtown Lancs 212 D2
N Lanark 268 E6
Swindon 63 D7
W Yorks 197 D11
Over Town Lancs 195 B11
Over Wallop Hants 47 F9
Over Whitacre Warks 134 E5
Over Worton Oxon 101 F8
Oving Bucks 102 G5
W Sus 22 C6
Ovingdean Brighton 36 G5
Ovingham Northumb 242 E3
Ovington Durham 224 C2
Essex 106 C5
Hants 48 G5
Norf 141 C8
Northumb 242 E3
Owen's Bank Staffs 152 D4
Ower Hants 32 D4
Owermoigne Dorset 17 D11
Owlbury Shrops 130 E6
Owlcotes Derbys 170 B6
Owl End Cambs 122 B4
Owler Bar Derbys 186 F3
Owlerton S Yorks 186 D4
Owlet W Yorks 205 F9
Owlpen Glos 80 F4
Owl's Green Suff 126 D5
Owlsmoor Brack 65 G11
Owlswick Bucks 84 D3
Owlthorpe S Yorks 186 E6
Owmby Lincs 200 G5
Owmby-by-Spital Lincs 189 D8
Ownham W Berks 64 E2
Owrtyn = *Overton* Wrex 166 G5
Owslebury Hants 33 C8
Owston Leics 136 B5
S Yorks 198 E5
Owston Ferry N Lincs 199 G10
Owstwick E Yorks 209 G11
Owthorne E Yorks 201 B10
Owthorpe Notts 154 C3
Owton Manor Hrtlpl 234 F5
Oxborough Norf 140 C4
Oxclose S Yorks 186 E6
T&W 243 F7
Oxcombe Lincs 190 F4
Oxcroft Derbys 187 G7
Oxcroft Estate Derbys 187 G7
Oxen End Essex 106 F3
Oxenhall Glos 98 F4
Oxenholme Cumb 211 B10
Oxenhope W Yorks 204 F6
Oxen Park Cumb 210 B6
Oxenpill Som 44 E2
Oxenton Glos 99 E9
Oxenwood Wilts 47 B10
Oxford Oxon 83 D8
Stoke 168 E5
Oxgang E Dunb 278 G3
Oxgangs Edin 270 B4
Oxhey Herts 85 F10
Oxhill Durham 242 G5
Warks 100 B6
Oxlease Herts 86 D2
Oxley W Mid 133 C8
Oxley Green Essex 88 C6
Oxley's Green E Sus 37 C11
Oxlode Cambs 139 F9
Oxnam Borders 262 F5
Oxnead Norf 160 E4
Oxshott Sur 66 G6
Oxspring S Yorks 197 G9
Oxted Sur 51 C11
Oxton Borders 271 E9
Mers 182 D3
Notts 171 E10
N Yorks 206 E6
Oxton Rakes Derbys 186 G4
Oxwich Swansea 56 D3
Oxwich Green Swansea 56 D3
Oxwick Norf 159 D8
Oykel Bridge Highld 309 J3
Oyne Aberds 302 G6
Oystermouth Swansea 56 D6
Ozleworth Glos 80 G3

P

Pabail Iarach W Isles 304 E7
Pabail Uarach W Isles 304 E7
Pabo Conwy 180 F4
Pace Gate N Yorks 205 C8
Pachesham Park Sur 51 B7
Packers Hill Dorset 30 E2
Packington Leics 153 G7
Packmoor Staffs 168 E5
Packmores Warks 118 D5
Packwood W Mid 118 C3
Packwood Gullet
W Mid 118 C3
Padanaram Angus 287 B8
Padbury Bucks 102 E4
Paddington London 67 C9
Warr 183 D10
Paddlesworth Kent 55 F7
Kent 69 G7
Paddock Kent 54 C3
W Yorks 196 D6
Paddockhaugh Moray 302 D2
Paddockhill Ches E 184 F4
Paddockhole Dumfries 248 G6
Paddock Wood Kent 53 E7
Paddolgreen Shrops 149 C10
Padfield Derbys 185 B8
Padgate Warr 183 D10
Padham's Green Essex 87 F10
Padiham Lancs 203 G11
Padney Cambs 123 C10
Padog Conwy 164 E4
Padside N Yorks 205 B9
Padside Green N Yorks 205 B9
Padson Devon 13 B7
Padstow Corn 10 F4
Padworth W Berks 64 F6
Padworth Common
Hants 64 G6
Paganhill Glos 80 D4
Page Bank Durham 233 D10
Page Moss Mers 182 C6
Page's Green Suff 126 D2
Pagham W Sus 22 D5
Paglesham Churchend
Essex 88 G6
Paglesham Eastend
Essex 88 G6
Paibeil W Isles 296 E3
Paible W Isles 305 J2
Paignton Torbay 9 C7
Pailton Warks 135 G9
Painleyhill Staffs 151 C10
Painscastle Powys 96 B3
Painshawfield Northumb 242 E3
Pains Hill Sur 52 C2
Painsthorpe E Yorks 208 B2
Painswick Glos 80 D5
Painter's Forstal Kent 54 B3
Painters Green Wrex 167 G8
Painter's Green Herts 86 B3
Painthorpe W Yorks 197 D10
Paintmoor Som 28 F4
Pairc Shiaboist W Isles 304 D4
Paisley Renfs 267 C9
Pakefield Suff 143 E10
Pakenham Suff 125 D8
Pale Gwyn 147 B9
Pale Green Essex 106 C3
Palehouse Common
E Sus 23 B7
Palestine Hants 47 E9
Paley Street Windsor 65 D11
Palfrey W Mid 133 D10
Palgowan Dumfries 245 G9
Palgrave Suff 126 B2
Pallaflat Cumb 219 C9
Pallington Dorset 17 C11
Pallion T&W 243 F9
Pallister Mbro 225 B10
Palmarsh Kent 54 G6
Palmer Moor Derbys 152 C2
Palmersbridge Corn 11 F9
Palmers Cross Staffs 133 C7
Sur 50 E4
Palmer's Flat Glos 79 D9
Palmers Green London 86 G4
Palmer's Green Kent 53 E7
Palmerstown V Glam 58 F6
Palmersville T&W 243 C7
Palmstead Kent 55 D7
Palnackie Dumfries 237 D10
Palnure Dumfries 236 C6
Palterton Derbys 171 B7
Pamber End Hants 48 B6
Pamber Green Hants 48 B6
Pamber Heath Hants 64 G6
Pamington Glos 99 E8
Pamphill Dorset 31 G7
Pampisford Cambs 105 B9
Pan IoW 20 D6
Orkney 314 G3
Panborough Som 44 D3
Panbride Angus 287 D9
Pancakehill Glos 81 C9
Pancrasweek Devon 24 F3
Pancross V Glam 58 F4
Pandy Gwyn 128 C2
Gwyn 146 F4
Gwyn 147 D7
Mon 96 G6
Powys 129 C8
Wrex 148 B3
Wrex 166 G6
Pandy'r Capel Denb 165 E9
Pandy Tudur Conwy 164 C5
Panfield Essex 106 F4
Pangbourne W Berks 64 D6
Panhall Fife 280 C6
Panks Bridge Hereford 98 B2
Pannal N Yorks 206 C2
Pannal Ash N Yorks 205 C11
Pannel's Ash Essex 106 C5
Panpunton Powys 114 C5
Panshanger Herts 86 C3
Pant Denb 166 E2
Flint 181 G10
Gwyn 144 C4
M Tydf 77 D9
Powys 129 C11
Shrops 148 E5
Wrex 166 D5
Wrex 166 F3
Pantasaph Flint 181 F11
Pantdu Neath 57 C9
Panteg Ceredig 111 E9
Torf 78 F4
Pantersbridge Corn 6 B3
Pant-glas Gwyn 163 F7
Pant-glâs Powys 128 D5
Pant-glas Shrops 148 C5
Pantgwyn Carms 93 F11
Ceredig 92 B4
Pant-lasau Swansea 57 B7
Pantmawr Cardiff 58 C6
Pant Mawr Powys 129 G7
Panton Lincs 189 F11
Pant-pastynog Denb 165 C8
Pantperthog Gwyn 128 C4
Pantside Caerph 78 F2
Pant-teg Carms 93 F9
Pant-y-Caws Carms 92 F3
Pant-y-crûg Ceredig 112 B3
Pant-y-dwr Powys 113 B9
Powys 113 C9
Pant-y-ffridd Powys 130 C3
Pantyffynnon Carms 75 C10
Pantygasseg Torf 78 F3
Pantymwyn Flint 165 C11
Pant-y-pyllau Bridgend 58 C2
Pant-yr-awel Bridgend 58 B2
Pant-y-Wacco Flint 181 F10
Panxworth Norf 161 G7
Papcastle Cumb 229 E8
Papermill Bank Shrops 149 D11
Papigoe Highld 310 D7
Papil Shetland 313 K5
Papley N Nhants 138 F2
Orkney 314 G4
Papple E Loth 281 G11
Papplewick Notts 171 E8
Papworth Everard
Cambs 122 E5
Papworth St Agnes
Cambs 122 E5
Papworth Village Settlement
Cambs 122 E5
Par Corn 5 E11
Paradise Glos 80 C5
Paradise Green Hereford 97 B10
Paramoor Corn 5 F9
Paramour Street Kent 71 G9
Parbold Lancs 194 E3
Parbrook Som 44 F5
W Sus 35 B9
Parc Gwyn 147 C7
Parc Erissey Corn 4 G3
Parc-hendy Swansea 56 B4
Parchey Som 43 F10
Parciau Anglesey 179 E7
Parcllyn Ceredig 110 G4
Parc Mawr Caerph 77 G10
Parc-Seymour Newport 78 G6
Parc-y-rhôs Carms 93 B11
Pardown Hants 48 D5
Pardshaw Cumb 229 G7
Pardshaw Hall Cumb 229 F8
Parham Suff 126 E6
Park Corn 10 G6
Devon 14 B2
Dumfries 247 E10
Som 44 G3
Swindon 63 C7
Park Barn Sur 50 C3
Park Bottom Corn 4 G3
Park Bridge Gtr Man 196 G2
Park Broom Cumb 239 F10

Park Close Lancs 204 E3
Park Corner Bath 45 B9
E Sus 23 C8
E Sus 52 F4
Oxon 65 B7
Windsor 65 C11
Parkend Glos 79 D10
Glos 80 C3
Park End Bedford 121 G9
Cambs 123 E11
Mbro 225 B10
Northumb 241 B9
Som 43 G7
Staffs 168 E3
Worcs 116 C5
Parkengear Corn 5 F8
Parker's Corner W Berks 64 E6
Parker's Green Herts 104 F6
Kent 52 D6
Parkeston Essex 108 E4
Parkfield Corn 6 B6
S Glos 61 D7
W Mid 133 D8
Parkfoot Falk 278 F6
Parkgate Ches E 184 G3
Ches W 182 F3
Cumb 229 B10
Dumfries 248 F2
Essex 87 B11
Kent 53 G11
Sur 51 E8
S Yorks 186 B6
Park Gate Dorset 30 F2
Hants 33 F8
Kent 55 D7
Suff 124 F4
Worcs 117 C8
W Yorks 197 E8
Park Green Essex 105 F9
Parkhall W Dunb 277 G9
Park Hall Shrops 148 C6
Parkham Devon 24 C5
Parkham Ash Devon 24 C5
Parkhead Cumb 230 C2
Glasgow 268 C2
S Yorks 186 E4
Park Head Cumb 231 C7
Derbys 170 E5
W Yorks 197 F7
Parkhill Aberds 303 E10
Invclyd 277 G7
Park Hill Glos 79 F9
Kent 54 G3
Mers 194 G3
Notts 171 E11
N Yorks 214 F6
S Yorks 186 D5
Parkhill Ho Aberds 293 B10
Parkhouse Mon 79 E7
Parkhouse Green
Derbys 170 C6
Parkhurst IoW 20 C5
Parklands W Yorks 206 F3
Park Lane Staffs 133 B7
Wrex 149 B8
Park Langley London 67 F11
Park Mains Renfs 277 G9
Parkmill Swansea 56 D4
Park Mill W Yorks 197 E9
Parkneuk Aberds 293 F9
Fife 279 D11
Park Royal London 67 C7
Parkside C Beds 103 G10
Cumb 219 B10
Durham 234 B4
N Lanark 268 D6
Staffs 151 D8
Wrex 166 D5
Parkstone BCP 18 C6
Park Street Herts 85 E10
W Sus 50 G6
Park Town Luton 103 G11
Oxon 83 D8
Park Village Northumb 240 E5
W Mid 133 C8
Park Villas W Yorks 206 F2
Parkway Hereford 98 D4
Som 29 C9
Park Wood Kent 53 C9
Medway 69 G10
Parkwood Springs
S Yorks 186 D4
Parley Cross Dorset 19 B7
Parley Green BCP 19 B7
Parliament Heath Suff 107 C9
Parlington W Yorks 206 F4
Parmoor Bucks 65 B9
Parnacott Devon 24 F4
Parney Heath Essex 107 E10
Parr Mers 183 C8
Parracombe Devon 41 E7
Parr Brow Gtr Man 195 G8
Parrog Pembs 91 D10
Parsley Hay Derbys 169 C10
Parslow's Hillock Bucks 84 E4
Parsonage Green Essex 88 D2
Parsonby Cumb 229 D8
Parson Cross S Yorks 186 C5
Parson Drove Cambs 139 B7
Parsons Green London 67 D9
Parson's Heath Essex 107 F10
Partick Glasgow 267 B11
Partington Gtr Man 184 C2
Partney Lincs 174 B6
Parton Cumb 228 G5
Cumb 239 G7
Dumfries 237 B8
Glos 99 G7
Hereford 96 B6
Partridge Green W Sus 35 D11
Partrishow Powys 96 G5
Parwich Derbys 169 E11
Pasford Staffs 132 D6
Passenham W Nhants 102 D5
Passfield Hants 49 G10
Passingford Bridge Essex 87 F8
Passmores Essex 86 D6
Paston Norf 160 C6
Pboro 138 C3
Paston Green Norf 160 C6
Pasturefields Staffs 151 D9
Patchacott Devon 12 B5
Patcham Brighton 36 F4
Patchetts Green Herts 85 F10
Patching W Sus 35 F9
Patchole Devon 40 E6
Patchway S Glos 60 C6
Pategill Cumb 230 F6
Pateley Bridge N Yorks 214 F3
Paternoster Heath Essex 88 C6
Pathe Som 43 G11
Pather N Lanark 268 E5
Pathfinder Village Devon 14 C2
Pathhead Aberds 293 G9
E Ayrs 258 G4
Fife 280 C5
Midloth 271 C7
Path Head T&W 242 E5
Pathlow Warks 118 F3
Path of Condie Perth 286 F4
Pathstruie Perth 286 F4
Patient End Herts 105 F8
Patmore Heath Herts 105 F8
Patna E Ayrs 257 G10
Patney Wilts 46 B5
Patrick IoM 192 D3
Patrick Brompton
N Yorks 224 G4
Patricroft Gtr Man 184 B3
Patrington E Yorks 201 C10
Patrington Haven
E Yorks 201 C10
Patrixbourne Kent 55 B7
Patsford Devon 40 F4
Patterdale Cumb 221 B7
Pattiesmuir Fife 279 E11
Pattingham Staffs 132 D6
Pattishall W Nhants 120 G3
Pattiswick Essex 106 G6
Patton Shrops 131 E11
Patton Bridge Cumb 221 F11
Paul Corn 1 D5
Paulerspury W Nhants 102 B4
Paull E Yorks 201 B7
Paul's Green Corn 2 C4
Paulsgrove Ptsmth 33 F10
Paulton Bath 45 B7
Paulville W Loth 269 B9
Pave Lane Telford 150 F5
Pavenham Bedford 121 F9
Pawlett Som 43 E10
Pawlett Hill Som 43 E9
Pawston Northumb 263 C9
Paxford Glos 100 D3
Paxton Borders 273 E8
Payden Street Kent 54 C2
Payhembury Devon 27 G9
Paynes Green Sur 50 F6
Paynter's Cross Corn 7 C7
Paynter's Lane End Corn 4 G3
Paythorne Lancs 204 C2
Payton Som 27 C10
Peacehaven E Sus 36 G6
Peacehaven Heights
E Sus 36 G6
Peacemarsh Dorset 30 B4
Peak Dale Derbys 185 F9
Peak Forest Derbys 185 F10
Peak Hill Lincs 156 F5
Peakirk Pboro 138 B3
Pean Hill Kent 70 G6
Pear Ash Som 45 G9
Pearsie Angus 287 B7
Pearson's Green Kent 53 E7
Peartree Herts 86 C2
Pear Tree Derby 153 C7
Peartree Green Essex 87 F9
Hereford 97 E11
Soton 32 E6
Sur 50 F3
Peas Acre W Yorks 205 E8
Peasedown St John Bath 45 B8
Peasehill Derbys 170 F6
Peaseland Green Norf 159 F11
Peasemore W Berks 64 D3
Peasenhall Suff 127 D7
Pease Pottage W Sus 51 G9
Peas Hill Cambs 139 D8
Peaslake Sur 50 E5
Peasley Cross Mers 183 C8
Peasmarsh E Sus 38 C5
Som 28 E4
Sur 50 D3
Peaston E Loth 271 B8
Peastonbank E Loth 271 B8
Peathill Aberds 303 C9
Peat Inn Fife 287 G8
Peatling Magna Leics 135 E11
Peatling Parva Leics 135 F11
Peaton Shrops 131 G10
Peatonstrand Shrops 131 G10
Peats Corner Suff 126 E3
Pebmarsh Essex 107 E7
Pebsham E Sus 38 F3
Pebworth Worcs 100 B2
Pecket Well W Yorks 196 B3
Peckforton Ches E 167 D8
Peckham London 67 D10
Peckham Bush Kent 53 D7
Peckingell Wilts 62 E2
Pecking Mill Som 44 F6
Peckleton Leics 135 C9
Pedair-ffordd Powys 148 E2
Pedham Norf 160 G6
Pedlars End Essex 87 D8
Pedlar's Rest Shrops 131 G9
Pedlinge Kent 54 F6
Pedmore W Mid 133 G8
Pednor Bottom Bucks 84 E6
Pednormead End Bucks 85 E7
Pedwell Som 44 F2
Peebles Borders 270 G5
Peel Borders 261 B10
IoM 192 D3
Lancs 202 G3
Peel Common Hants 33 G9
Peel Green Gtr Man 184 B2
Peel Hall Gtr Man 184 D4
Peel Hill Lancs 202 G3
Peel Park S Lanark 268 E2
Peene Kent 55 F7
Peening Quarter Kent 38 B5
Peggs Green Leics 153 F8
Pegsdon C Beds 104 E2
Pegswood Northumb 252 F6
Pegwell Kent 71 G11
Peinaha Highld 298 D4
Peinchorran Highld 295 B7
Peingown Highld 298 B4
Peinlich Highld 298 D4
Peinmore Highld 298 E4
Pelaw T&W 243 E7
Pelcomb Pembs 72 B6
Pelcomb Bridge Pembs 72 B6
Pelcomb Cross Pembs 72 B6
Peldon Essex 89 B7
Pelhamfield IoW 21 C7
Pell Green E Sus 52 G6
Pellon W Yorks 196 B5
Pelsall W Mid 133 C10
Pelsall Wood W Mid 133 C10
Pelton Durham 243 G7
Pelton Fell Durham 243 G7
Pelutho Cumb 229 B8
Pelynt Corn 6 D4
Pemberton Carms 75 E8
Gtr Man 194 G5
Pembles Cross Kent 53 D11
Pembre = *Pembrey*
Carms 74 E6
Pembrey = *Pembre*
Carms 74 E6
Pembridge Hereford 115 F7
Pembroke = *Penfro*
Pembs 73 E7
Pembroke Dock = *Doc*
Penfro Pembs 73 E7
Pembroke Ferry Pembs 73 E7
Pembury Kent 52 E6
Pempwell Corn 12 F3
Penallt Mon 79 C8
Pen-allt Hereford 97 F11
Penally = *Penalun*
Pembs 73 F10
Penalt Hereford 97 F11
Penalun = *Penally*
Pembs 73 F10
Penare Corn 5 G9
Penarlâg = *Hawarden*
Flint 166 B4
Penarron Powys 130 F2
Penarth V Glam 59 E7
Penarth Moors Cardiff 59 E7
Penbeagle Corn 2 B2
Penbedw Flint 165 B11
Pen-bedw Pembs 92 D4
Penberth Corn 1 E4
Penbidwal Mon 96 G6
Penbodlas Gwyn 144 C5
Pen-bont Rhydybeddau
Ceredig 128 G3
Penboyr Carms 93 D7
Penbryn Ceredig 110 G5
Pencader Carms 93 D8
Pencaenewydd Gwyn 162 G6
Pencaerau Neath 57 B8
Pen-caer-fenny Swansea 56 B4
Pencaitland E Loth 271 B8
Pencarnisiog Anglesey 178 G5
Pencarreg Carms 93 B10
Pencarrow Corn 11 E8
Penceiliogi Carms 75 E8
Pencelli Powys 95 F11
Pen-clawdd Swansea 56 B4
Pencoed Bridgend 58 C3
Pencombe Hereford 115 G11
Pen-common Powys 76 D6
Pencoyd Hereford 97 F10
Pencoys Corn 2 B5
Pencraig Anglesey 179 F7
Hereford 97 G11
Powys 147 D10
Pencroesoped Mon 78 D4
Pencuke Corn 11 C9
Pendas Fields W Yorks 206 F3
Pendeen Corn 1 C3
Pendeford W Mid 133 C7
Penderyn Rhondda 77 D7
Pendine = *Pentwyn*
Carms 74 D2
Pendlebury Gtr Man 195 G9
Pendleton Gtr Man 184 B4
Lancs 203 F11
Pendock Worcs 98 E5
Pendoggett Corn 10 F6
Pendomer Som 29 E8
Pendoylan V Glam 58 D5
Pendre Bridgend 58 C2
Gwyn 110 C2
Powys 95 F10
Pendrift Corn 11 G8
Penegoes Powys 128 C5
Penelewey Corn 4 G6
Penenden Heath Kent 53 B9
Penffordd Pembs 91 G11
Penffordd Lâs = *Staylittle*
Powys 129 E7
Penfro = *Pembroke*
Pembs 73 E7
Pengam Caerph 77 F11
Penge London 67 E11
Pengegon Corn 2 B5
Pengelly Corn 11 E7
Pengenffordd Powys 96 E3
Pengersick Corn 2 D3
Pen-gilfach Gwyn 163 C9
Pengold Corn 11 C8
Pengorffwysfa Anglesey 179 C7
Pengover Green Corn 6 B5
Pen-groes-oped Mon 78 D4
Penguithal Hereford 97 G10
Pengwern Denb 181 F8
Penhale Corn 2 F5
Corn 5 D8
Penhale Jakes Corn 2 D4
Penhallick Corn 3 F7
Corn 4 G3
Penhallow Corn 4 E5
Penhalurick Corn 2 B6
Penhalvean Corn 2 B6
Penhelig Gwyn 128 D2
Penhill Devon 40 G4
Swindon 63 B7
Penhow Newport 78 G6
Penhurst E Sus 23 B11
Peniarth Gwyn 128 B2
Penicuik Midloth 270 C4
Peniel Carms 93 G8
Denb 165 C8
Penifiler Highld 298 E4
Peninver Argyll 255 E8
Penisa'r Waun Gwyn 163 C9
Penistone S Yorks 197 G8
Penjerrick Corn 3 C7
Penketh Warr 183 D9
Penkhull Stoke 168 G5
Penkill S Ayrs 244 D6
Penknap Wilts 45 D11
Penkridge Staffs 151 G8
Pen-lan Swansea 56 B6
Pen-Lan-mabws Pembs 91 F7
Penleigh Wilts 45 C11
Penley Wrex 149 B8
Penllech Gwyn 144 C4
Penllergaer Swansea 56 B6
Penllwyn Caerph 77 F11
Ceredig 128 G3
Penllyn V Glam 58 D3
Pen-llyn Anglesey 178 E4
Pen-lon Anglesey 162 B6
Penmachno Conwy 164 E3
Penmaen Caerph 77 F11
Swansea 56 D4
Penmaenan Conwy 180 F2
Penmaenmawr Conwy 180 F2
Penmaenpool Gwyn 146 F3
Penmaen Rhôs Conwy 180 F5
Penmark V Glam 58 F5
Penmarth Corn 2 B6
Penmayne Corn 10 F4
Pen Mill Som 29 D9
Penmon Anglesey 179 E10
Penmore Mill Argyll 288 D6
Penmorfa Ceredig 110 G6
Gwyn 163 G8
Penmynydd Anglesey 179 G8
Penn Bucks 84 G6
W Mid 133 D7
Pennal Gwyn 128 C4
Pennan Aberds 303 C8
Pennance Corn 4 G4
Pennant Ceredig 111 E10
Conwy 164 D5
Denb 147 C10
Denb 165 E8
Powys 129 D7
Pennant Melangell
Powys 147 D10
Pennar Pembs 73 E7
Pennard Swansea 56 D5
Pennar Park Pembs 72 E6
Penn Bottom Bucks 84 G6
Pennerley Shrops 131 D7
Pennington Cumb 210 D5
Gtr Man 183 B11
Hants 20 C2
Pennington Green
Gtr Man 194 F6
Pennorth Powys 96 F2
Penn Street Bucks 84 F6
Pennsylvania Devon 14 C4
S Glos 61 E8
Penny Bridge Cumb 210 C6
Pennycross Argyll 289 G7
Plym 7 D9
Pennygate Norf 160 E6
Pennygown Argyll 289 E7
Penny Green Derbys 187 F8
Penny Hill Lincs 157 D7
W Yorks 196 D5
Pennylands Lancs 194 F3
Pennymoor Devon 26 E5
Pennypot Kent 54 G6
Penny's Green Norf 142 D3
Pennytinney Corn 10 F6
Pennywell T&W 243 F9
Pen-onn V Glam 58 F5
Penparc Ceredig 92 B4
Pembs 91 E7
Penparcau Ceredig 111 B11
Penpedairheol Caerph 77 F10
Mon 78 E4
Penpergym Mon 78 C4
Penperlleni Mon 78 E4
Penpethy Corn 11 D7
Penpillick Corn 5 D11
Penplas Carms 74 B5
Penpol Corn 3 B8
Penpoll Corn 6 E2
Penponds Corn 2 B4
Penpont Corn 11 G7
Dumfries 247 E8
Powys 95 F9
Penprysg Bridgend 58 C3
Penquit Devon 8 E2
Penrallt Gwyn 145 B7
Powys 129 F9
Penrherber Carms 92 D5
Penrhiw Caerph 78 G2
Penrhiwceiber Rhondda 77 F8
Pen-Rhiw-fawr Neath 76 C2
Penrhiwgarreg Bl Gwent 78 E2
Penrhiw-llan Ceredig 93 C7
Penrhiw-pal Ceredig 92 B6
Penrhiwtyn Neath 57 B8
Penrhos Anglesey 178 E3
Gwyn 144 C6
Hereford 114 F6
Penrhôs Mon 78 C6
Penrhos Mon 78 C6
Powys 76 C3
Pen-rhos Wrex 166 E3
Penrhosfeilw Anglesey 178 E2
Penrhos Garnedd Gwyn 179 G9
Penrhyd Lastra Anglesey 178 C6
Penrhyn Bay = *Bae-Penrhyn*
Conwy 180 E4
Penrhyn Castle Pembs 92 B2
Penrhyn-coch Ceredig 128 G2
Penrhyndeudraeth
Gwyn 146 B2
Penrhynside Conwy 180 E4
Penrhyn side Conwy 180 E4
Penrhys Rhondda 77 F8
Penrice Swansea 56 D3
Penrith Cumb 230 E6
Penrose Corn 10 G3
Corn 11 F7
Penrose Hill Corn 2 D4
Penruddock Cumb 230 F4
Penryn Corn 3 C7
Pensarn Carms 74 B6
Conwy 181 F7
Pen-sarn Gwyn 145 D11
Gwyn 162 G6
Pensax Worcs 116 D4
Pensby Mers 182 E3
Penselwood Som 45 G9
Pensford Bath 60 G6
Pensham Worcs 99 C8
Penshaw T&W 243 G8
Penshurst Kent 52 E4
Pensilva Corn 6 B5
Pensnett W Mid 133 F8
Penston E Loth 281 G8
Penstone Devon 26 G3
Penstraze Corn 4 F5
Pentewan Corn 5 F10
Pentiken Shrops 130 G4
Pentir Gwyn 163 B9
Pentire Corn 4 C5
Pentirvin Shrops 130 C6
Pentlepoir Pembs 73 D10
Pentlow Essex 106 B6
Pentlow Street Essex 106 B6
Pentney Norf 158 G4
Penton Corner Hants 47 D10
Penton Grafton Hants 47 D10
Penton Mewsey Hants 47 D10
Pentonville London 67 C10
Pentowin Carms 74 B3
Pentraeth Anglesey 179 F8
Pentrapeod Caerph 77 E11
Pentre Carms 75 C8
Denb 165 D10
Flint 165 C11
Flint 166 B4
Flint 166 C2
Flint 166 D2
Flint 182 G2
Powys 129 F11
Powys 130 B4
Powys 130 E5
Powys 147 D11
Powys 148 G3
Rhondda 77 F7
Shrops 148 D4
Shrops 149 F7
Wrex 148 B2
Wrex 166 G3
Pentrebach Carms 94 E6
M Tydf 77 E9
Rhondda 58 B5
Swansea 75 D10
Pentre-bâch Ceredig 93 B11
Pentre-bach Powys 95 E8
Pentrebane Cardiff 58 D6
Pentrebeirdd Powys 148 G3
Pentre Berw Anglesey 179 G7
Pentre-bont Conwy 164 E2
Pentre Broughton Wrex 166 E4
Pentre Bychan Wrex 166 F4
Pentrecagal Carms 92 C6
Pentre-cefn Shrops 148 D4
Pentre-celyn Denb 165 E11
Powys 129 B7
Pentre-chwyth Swansea 57 B7
Pentre Cilgwyn Wrex 148 B4
Pentre-clawdd Shrops 148 C5
Pentre-coed Shrops 149 B7
Pentre-cwrt Carms 93 D7
Pentre Dolau-Honddu
Powys 95 C9
Pentredwr Denb 165 F11
Pentre-dwr Swansea 57 B7
Pentrefelin Anglesey 178 C6
Carms 93 G11
Ceredig 94 B2
Conwy 180 G4
Denb 166 G2
Gwyn 145 B10
Pentre-Ffwrndan Flint 182 G3
Pentrefoelas Conwy 164 E5
Pentref-y-groes Caerph 77 F11
Pentre-galar Pembs 92 E3
Pentregat Ceredig 111 G7
Pentre-Gwenlais Carms 75 B10
Pentre Gwynfryn Gwyn 145 D11
Pentre Halkyn Flint 182 G2
Pentreheyling Shrops 130 E4
Pentre Hodre Shrops 114 B6
Pentre Isaf Conwy 164 B5
Pentre Llanrhaeadr
Denb 165 C9
Pentre Llifior Powys 130 D2
Pentrellwyn Ceredig 93 C8
Pentre-llwyn-llwyd
Powys 113 G9
Pentre-llyn Ceredig 112 C2
Pentre-llyn cymmer
Conwy 165 E7
Pentre Maelor Wrex 166 F5
Pentre Meyrick V Glam 58 D3
Pentre-newydd Shrops 148 B5
Pentre-Piod Torf 78 E3
Pentre-Poeth Carms 75 E8
Newport 59 B9
Pentre'r beirdd Powys 148 G3
Pentre'r Felin Conwy 164 B4
Pentre'r-felin Denb 165 B10
Powys 95 E8
Pentre-rhew Ceredig 112 G3
Pentre-tafarn-y-fedw
Conwy 164 C4
Pentre-ty-gwyn Carms 94 D6
Pentreuchaf Gwyn 145 B7
Pentre-uchaf Conwy 180 F5
Pentrich Derbys 170 E5
Pentridge Dorset 31 D8
Pentrisil Pembs 91 E11
Pentwyn Caerph 77 E10
Cardiff 59 C8
Pen-twyn Caerph 78 E2
Pentwyn = *Pendine*
Carms 74 D2
Pen-twyn Carms 75 C9
Mon 79 D8
Torf 78 E3
Pentwyn Berthlwyd
Caerph 77 F10
Pentwyn-mawr Caerph 77 F11
Pentyrch Cardiff 58 C6
Penuchadre V Glam 57 G11
Penuwch Ceredig 111 E11
Penwartha Corn 4 E5
Penwartha Coombe Corn 4 E5
Penweathers Corn 4 G6
Penwithick Corn 5 D10
Penwood Hants 64 G2
Penwortham Lane
Lancs 194 B4
Penwyllt Powys 76 B5
Pen-y-Ball Top Flint 181 F11
Penybanc Carms 75 C10
Pen-y-banc Carms 93 G8
Carms 94 G2
Pen-y-bank Caerph 77 E10
Penybedd Carms 74 E6
Penybont Ceredig 128 F2
Powys 114 E2
Pen-y-Bont Bl Gwent 78 D2
Carms 92 F6
Gwyn 128 C4
Gwyn 146 D2
Powys 148 E4
Pen y Bont ar ogwr
= *Bridgend* Bridgend 58 C2
Penybontfawr Powys 147 E11
Penybryn Caerph 77 F10
Pen-y-Bryn Gwyn 145 B9
Gwyn 146 F3
Pembs 92 C3
Powys 130 C3
Shrops 148 B6
Wrex 166 G3
Penycae Wrex 166 F3
Pen-y-cae Bridgend 58 C2
Neath 57 D9
Powys 76 C4
Pen-y-cae-mawr Mon 78 F6
Penycaerau Gwyn 144 D3
Pen-y-cefn Flint 181 F10
Pen-y-clawdd Mon 79 D7
Pen-y-coed Shrops 148 E5
Pen-y-coedcae Rhondda 58 B5
Penycwm Pembs 90 G6
Pen-y-Darren M Tydf 77 D9
Penydre Swansea 75 E11
Pen-y-fai Bridgend 57 E11
Carms 75 E7
Pen-y-fan Carms 56 B4
Mon 79 D8
Penyfeidr Pembs 91 F7
Pen-y-felin Flint 165 B11
Penyffordd Flint 166 C4
Pen-y-ffordd Denb 181 E8
Flint 181 E10
Penyffridd Gwyn 163 D8
Pen y Foel Shrops 148 E5
Penygarn Torf 78 E3
Pen-y-garn Carms 93 E11
Ceredig 128 F2
Penygarnedd Powys 148 E2
Pen-y-garnedd
Anglesey 179 F8
Penygelli Powys 130 E2
Pen-y-gop Conwy 164 G6
Penygraig Rhondda 77 G7
Pen-y-graig Gwyn 144 C3
Penygraigwen Anglesey 178 D6
Penygroes Gwyn 163 E7
Pembs 92 D3
Pen-y-groes Carms 75 C9
Pen-y-groeslon Gwyn 144 C4
Pen-y-Gwryd Hotel
Gwyn 163 D11
Pen-y-lan Cardiff 59 D7
Newport 59 B9
V Glam 58 D3
Pen-y-maes Flint 181 F11
Pen-y-Myndd Carms 75 E7
Penymynydd Flint 166 C4
Pen-y-Park Hereford 96 C5
Penyraber Pembs 91 D9
Pen-yr-englyn Rhondda 76 F6
Penyrheol Caerph 58 B6
Swansea 56 B5
Torf 78 F3
Pen-yr-heol Bridgend 58 C2
Mon 78 C6
Pen-yr-Heolgerrig
M Tydf 77 D8
Pen-y-rhiw Rhondda 58 B5
Penysarn Anglesey 179 C7
Pen-y-stryt Denb 165 E11
Penywaun Rhondda 77 E7
Pen-y-wern Shrops 114 B6
Penzance Corn 1 C5
Peopleton Worcs 117 G8
Peover Heath Ches E 184 G3
Peper Harow Sur 50 E2
Peppercombe Devon 24 C5
Pepper Hill Som 43 F7
W Yorks 196 B6
Peppermoor Northumb 264 F6
Pepper's Green Essex 87 C10
Pepperstock C Beds 85 B9
Perceton N Ayrs 267 G7
Percie Aberds 293 D7
Percuil Corn 3 C9
Percyhorner Aberds 303 C9
Percy Main T&W 243 D8
Per-ffordd-llan Flint 181 F10
Perham Down Wilts 47 D9
Periton Som 42 D3
Perivale London 67 C7
Perkhill Aberds 293 C7
Perkinsville Durham 243 G7
Perlethorpe Notts 187 G11
Perranarworthal Corn 3 B7
Perrancoombe Corn 4 E5
Perran Downs Corn 2 C3
Perranporth Corn 4 E5
Perranuthnoe Corn 2 D2
Perranwell Corn 3 B7
Corn 4 E5
Perranwell Station Corn 3 B7
Perran Wharf Corn 3 B7
Perranzabuloe Corn 4 E5
Perrott's Brook Glos 81 D8
Perry Devon 26 F5
Kent 55 B9
W Mid 133 E11
Perry Barr W Mid 133 E11
Perry Beeches W Mid 133 E11
Perry Common W Mid 133 E11
Perry Crofts Staffs 134 C4
Perryfields Worcs 117 C8
Perryfoot Derbys 185 E10
Perry Green Essex 106 G6
Herts 86 B6
Som 43 F9
Wilts 62 B3
Perrymead Bath 61 G9
Perrystone Hill Hereford 98 F2
Perry Street Kent 68 E6
Som 28 F4
Perrywood Kent 54 B4
Pershall Staffs 150 C6
Pershore Worcs 99 B8
Pert Angus 293 G8
Pertenhall Bedford 121 D11
Perth Perth 286 E5
Perthcelyn Rhondda 77 F9
Perthy Shrops 149 C7
Perton Hereford 97 C11
Staffs 133 D7
Pertwood Wilts 45 F11
Pested Kent 54 C4
Peterborough Pboro 138 D3
Peterburn Highld 307 L2
Peterchurch Hereford 96 D6
Peterculter Aberdeen 293 C10
Peterhead Aberds 303 E11
Peterlee Durham 234 C4
Petersburn N Lanark 268 C5
Petersfield Hants 34 C2
Peter's Finger Devon 12 D3
Peter's Green Herts 85 B10
Petersham London 67 E7
Peters Marland Devon 25 E7
Peterstone Wentlooge
Newport 59 C9
Peterston-super-Ely
V Glam 58 D5
Peterstow Hereford 97 G11
Peter Tavy Devon 12 F6
Petertown Orkney 314 F3
Peterville Corn 4 E4
Petham Kent 54 C6
Petherwin Gate Corn 11 D11
Petrockstow Devon 25 F8
Petsoe End M Keynes 103 B7
Pett E Sus 38 E5
Pettaugh Suff 126 F3
Pett Bottom Kent 54 E6
Kent 55 C7
Petteridge Kent 53 E7
Pettinain S Lanark 269 G9
Pettings Kent 68 G6
Pettistree Suff 126 G5
Pett Level E Sus 38 E5
Petton Devon 27 C8
Shrops 149 D8
Petts Wood London 68 F2
Petty Aberds 303 F7
Pettycur Fife 280 D5
Petty France S Glos 61 B9
Pettymuick Aberds 303 G9
Pettywell Norf 159 E11
Petworth W Sus 35 C7
Pevensey E Sus 23 E10
Pevensey Bay E Sus 23 E11
Peverell Plym 7 D9
Pewsey Wilts 63 G7
Pewsey Wharf Wilts 63 G7
Pewterspear Warr 183 E10
Phantassie E Loth 281 F11
Pharisee Green Essex 106 G2
Pheasants Bucks 65 B9
Pheasant's Hill Bucks 65 B9
Pheasey W Mid 133 D11
Pheonix Green Hants 49 B9
Phepson Worcs 117 F8
Philadelphia T&W 243 G8
Philham Devon 24 C3
Philiphaugh Borders 261 D10
Phillack Corn 2 B3
Philleigh Corn 3 B9
Phillip's Town Caerph 77 E10
Philpot End Essex 87 B10
Philpstoun W Loth 279 F10
Phocle Green Hereford 98 F2
Phoenix Green Hants 49 B9
Phoenix Row Durham 233 F9
Phorp Moray 301 D10
Pibsbury Som 28 B6
Pibwrlwyd Carms 74 B6
Pica Cumb 228 G6
Piccadilly S Yorks 187 B7
Warks 134 D4
Piccadilly Corner Norf 142 F5
Piccotts End Herts 85 D9
Pickburn S Yorks 198 F4
Picken End Worcs 98 C6
Pickering N Yorks 216 C5
Pickering Nook Durham 242 F5
Picket Hill Hants 31 F11
Picket Piece Hants 47 D11
Picket Post Hants 31 F11
Pickford W Mid 134 G5
Pickford Green W Mid 134 G5
Pickhill N Yorks 214 C6
Picklenash Glos 98 F4
Picklescott Shrops 131 D8
Pickles Hill W Yorks 204 F6
Pickletillem Fife 287 E8
Pickley Green Gtr Man 195 G7
Pickmere Ches E 183 F11
Pickney Som 27 B11
Pickstock Telford 150 E4
Pickup Bank Blackburn 195 C8
Pickwell Devon 40 E3
Leics 154 G5
Pickwick Wilts 61 E11
Pickwood Scar W Yorks 196 C5
Pickworth Lincs 155 C10
Rutland 155 G9
Picton Ches W 182 G6
Flint 181 E10
N Yorks 225 D8
Pict's Hill Som 28 B6
Piddinghoe E Sus 36 G6
Piddington Bucks 84 G4
Oxon 83 B10
W Nhants 120 G6
Piddlehinton Dorset 17 B10
Piddletrenthide Dorset 17 B10
Pidley Cambs 122 B6
Pidney Dorset 30 F2
Piece Corn 2 B5
Piercebridge Darl 224 B4
Piercing Hill Essex 86 F6
Pierowall Orkney 314 B4
Piff's Elm Glos 99 F8
Pigdon Northumb 252 F5
Pightley Som 43 F8
Pig Oak Dorset 31 G8
Pigstye Green Essex 87 D10
Pike End W Yorks 196 D4
Pikehall Derbys 169 D11
Pike Hill Lancs 204 G3
Pike Law W Yorks 196 D4
Pikeshill Hants 32 F3
Pikestye Hereford 97 B10
Pilford Dorset 31 G8
Pilgrims Hatch Essex 87 F9
Pilham Lincs 188 C5
Pilhough Derbys 170 C3
Pill N Som 60 D4
Pembs 72 D6
Pillaton Corn 7 C7
Staffs 151 G8
Pillerton Hersey Warks 100 B6
Pillerton Priors Warks 100 B5
Pilleth Powys 114 D5
Pilley Glos 81 B7
Hants 20 B2
S Yorks 197 G10
Pilley Bailey Hants 20 B2
Pillgwenlly Newport 59 B10
Pilling Lancs 202 D4
Pilling Lane Lancs 202 D3
Pillmouth Devon 25 C7
Pillowell Glos 79 D10
Pillows Green Glos 98 F5
Pillwell Dorset 30 D3
Pilmuir Borders 261 G11
Pilning S Glos 60 B5
Pilrig Edin 280 F5
Pilsbury Derbys 169 C10
Pilsdon Dorset 16 B4
Pilsgate Pboro 137 B11
Pilsley Derbys 170 C6
Derbys 186 G2
Pilsley Green Derbys 170 C6
Pilson Green Norf 161 G7
Piltdown E Sus 36 C6
Pilton Devon 40 G5
Edin 280 F4
N Nhants 137 G10
Rutland 137 C8
Som 44 E5
Pilton Green Swansea 56 D2
Piltown Som 44 F5
Pimhole Gtr Man 195 E10
Pimlico Herts 85 D9
Lancs 203 E10
London 67 D9
W Nhants 102 C2
Pimperne Dorset 29 F9
Dorset 30 F6
Pinchbeck Lincs 156 D4
Pinchbeck Bars Lincs 156 D3
Pinchbeck West Lincs 156 E4
Pincheon Green
S Yorks 199 D7
Pinckney Green Wilts 61 G10
Pincock Lancs 194 D5
Pineham Kent 55 D10
M Keynes 103 C7
Pinehurst Swindon 63 B7
Pinfarthings Glos 80 E5
Pinfold Lancs 193 E11
Pinfold Hill S Yorks 197 G9
Pinfoldpond C Beds 103 E8
Pinford End Suff 124 F6
Pinged Carms 74 E6
Pingewood W Berks 65 F7
Pin Green Herts 104 F4
Pinhoe Devon 14 C5
Pinkett's Booth W Mid 134 G5
Pink Green Worcs 117 D11
Pinkie Braes E Loth 281 G7
Pinkney Wilts 61 B11
Pinkneys Green Windsor 65 C11
Pinksmoor Som 27 D10
Pinley W Mid 119 B7
Pinley Green Warks 118 D4
Pin Mill Suff 108 D4
Pinminnoch Dumfries 236 D2
S Ayrs 244 E5
Pinmore S Ayrs 244 E6
Pinmore Mains S Ayrs 244 E6
Pinnacles Essex 86 D6
Pinner London 66 B6
Pinner Green London 85 G10
Pinnerwood Park
London 85 G10
Pin's Green Worcs 98 B6
Pinsley Green Ches E 167 F9
Pinstones Shrops 131 F9
Pinvin Worcs 99 B9
Pinwall Leics 134 C6
Pinwherry S Ayrs 244 F5
Pinxton Derbys 171 E7
Pipe and Lyde Hereford 97 C10
Pipe Aston Hereford 115 C9
Pipe Gate Shrops 168 G2
Pipehill Staffs 133 B11
Pipehouse Bath 45 B9
Piperhall Argyll 266 D2
Piperhill Highld 301 D8
Pipe Ridware Staffs 151 F11
Piper's Ash Ches W 166 B6
Piper's End Worcs 98 E6
Piper's Hill Worcs 117 D9
Piper's Pool Corn 11 E11
Pipewell N Nhants 136 F6
Pippacott Devon 40 F4
Pippin Street Lancs 194 C5
Pipps Hill Essex 69 B7
Pipsden Kent 53 G9
Pipton Powys 96 D3
Pirbright Sur 50 B2
Pirbright Camp Sur 50 B2
Pirnmill N Ayrs 255 C9
Pirton Herts 104 E2
Worcs 99 B7
Pisgah Ceredig 112 B3
Stirling 285 G11
Pishill Oxon 65 B8
Pishill Bank Oxon 84 G2
Pismire Hill S Yorks 186 C5
Pistyll Gwyn 162 G4
Pit Mon 78 D5
Pitagowan Perth 291 G10
Pitblae Aberds 303 C9
Pitcairngreen Perth 286 E4
Pitcalnie Highld 301 B8
Pitcaple Aberds 303 G7
Pitchcombe Glos 80 D5
Pitchcott Bucks 102 G5
Pitcher's Green Suff 125 F8
Pitchford Shrops 131 C10
Pitch Green Bucks 84 E3
Pitch Place Sur 49 F11
Sur 50 C3
Pitcombe Som 45 G7
Pitcorthie Fife 280 D2
Fife 287 G9
Pitcot Som 45 D7
V Glam 57 G11
Pitcox E Loth 282 F2
Pitcur Perth 286 D6
Pitfancy Aberds 302 E5
Pitfichie Aberds 293 B8
Pitforthie Aberds 293 F10
Pitgair Aberds 303 D7
Pitgrudy Highld 309 K7
Pithmaduthy Highld 301 B7
Pitkennedy Angus 287 B9
Pitkevy Fife 286 G6
Pitkierie Fife 287 G9
Pitlessie Fife 287 G7
Pitlochry Perth 286 B3
Pitmachie Aberds 302 G6
Pitmain Highld 291 C9
Pitmedden Aberds 303 G8
Pitminster Som 28 D2
Pitmuies Angus 287 C9
Pitmunie Aberds 293 B8
Pitney Som 29 B7
Pitrocknie Perth 286 C6
Pitscottie Fife 287 F8
Pitsea Essex 69 B8
Pitses Gtr Man 196 G2
Pitsford W Nhants 120 D5
Pitsford Hill Som 42 G6
Pitsmoor S Yorks 186 D5
Pitstone Bucks 84 B6
Pitstone Green Bucks 84 B6
Pitstone Hill Bucks 85 C7
Pitt Hants 33 B7
Pittachar Perth 286 E2
Pitt Court Glos 80 F3
Pittendreich Moray 301 C11
Pittentrail Highld 309 J7
Pittenweem Fife 287 G9
Pitteuchar Fife 280 B5
Pittington Durham 234 C2
Pittodrie Aberds 302 G6
Pitton Swansea 56 D2
Wilts 47 G8
Pitts Hill Stoke 168 E5
Pittswood Kent 52 D6
Pittulie Aberds 303 C9
Pittville Glos 99 G9
Pityme Corn 10 F5
Pity Me Durham 233 B11
Pityoulish Highld 291 B11
Pixey Green Suff 126 B4
Pixham Sur 51 C7
Worcs 98 B6
Pixley Hereford 98 D3
Shrops 150 D3
Pizien Well Kent 53 C7
Place Newton N Yorks 217 E7
Plaidy Aberds 303 D7
Corn 6 E5
Plain-an-Gwarry Corn 4 G3
Plain Dealings Pembs 73 B9
Plains N Lanark 268 B5
Plainsfield Som 43 F7
Plain Spot Notts 171 E7
Plain Street Corn 10 F5
Plaish Shrops 131 D10
Plaistow London 68 C2
London 68 E2
W Sus 50 G4
Plaistow Green Essex 106 F6
Plaitford Wilts 32 D3
Plaitford Green Hants 32 C3
Plank Lane Gtr Man 194 G6
Plans Dumfries 238 D3
Plantation Bridge Cumb 221 F9
Plantationfoot Dumfries 248 E4
Plardiwick Staffs 150 E6
Plasau Shrops 149 E7
Plâs Berwyn Denb 165 G11
Plas-canol Gwyn 145 F11
Plas Coch Wrex 166 E4
Plas Dinam Powys 129 F10
Plas Gogerddan Ceredig 128 G2
Plashet London 68 C2
Plashett Carms 74 D3
Plasiolyn Powys 129 C11
Plas Llwyngwern Powys 128 C5
Plas Meredydd Powys 130 D3
Plas Nantyr Wrex 148 B3
Plasnewydd Powys 129 D9
Plaster's Green Bath 60 G4
Plastow Green Hants 64 G4
Plas-yn-Cefn Denb 181 G8
Platt Kent 52 B6
Platt Bridge Gtr Man 194 G6
Platt Lane Shrops 149 B10
Platts Common
S Yorks 197 G11
Platt's Heath Kent 53 C11
Plawsworth Durham 233 B11
Plaxtol Kent 52 C6
Playden E Sus 38 C6
Playford Suff 108 B4
Play Hatch Oxon 65 D8
Playing Place Corn 4 G6
Playley Green Glos 98 E5
Plealey Shrops 131 B8
Pleamore Cross Som 27 D10
Plean Stirling 278 D6
Pleasant Valley Pembs 73 D10
Pleasington Blackburn 194 B6
Pleasley Derbys 171 C8
Pleasleyhill Notts 171 C8
Pleck Dorset 30 E3
Dorset 30 E2
W Mid 133 D9
Pleckgate Blackburn 203 G9
Pleck or Little Ansty
Dorset 30 G3
Pledgdon Green Essex 105 F11
Pledwick W Yorks 197 D10
Plemstall Ches W 183 G7
Plenmeller Northumb 240 E6
Pleshey Essex 87 C11
Plockton Highld 295 B10

Plocrapol W Isles 305 J3
Plot Gate Som 44 G4
Plot Street Som 44 F5
Ploughfield Hereford 97 C7
Plough Hill Warks 134 E6
Plowden Shrops 131 F7
Ploxgreen Shrops 131 C7
Pluckley Kent 54 D2
Pluckley Thorne Kent 54 E2
Plucks Gutter Kent 71 G9
Plumbland Cumb 229 D9
Plumbley S Yorks 186 E6
Plumford Kent 54 B4
Plumley Ches E 184 F2
Plump Hill Glos 79 B11
Plumpton Cumb 230 D5
E Sus 36 E5
W Nhants 101 B11
Plumpton End
W Nhants 102 B4
Plumpton Foot Cumb 230 D5
Plumpton Green E Sus 36 D5
Plumpton Head Cumb 230 E6
Plumstead London 68 D3
Norf 160 C2
Plumstead Common
London 68 D3
Plumstead Green Norf 160 C2
Plumtree Notts 154 C2
Plumtree Green Kent 53 D10
Plumtree Park Notts 154 C2
Plungar Leics 154 C5
Plush Dorset 30 G2
Plusha Corn 11 E11
Plushabridge Corn 12 G2
Plusterwine Glos 79 F9
Plwmp Ceredig 111 G7
Plymouth Plym 7 E9
Plympton Plym 7 D10
Plymstock Plym 7 E10
Plymtree Devon 27 G9
Pobgreen Gtr Man 196 F4
Pochin Houses Caerph 77 E11
Pocket Nook Gtr Man 183 B10
Pockley N Yorks 216 B2
Pocklington E Yorks 208 D2
Pockthorpe
Norf 141 D8
Norf 158 D6
Norf 159 E10
Norf 159 F11
Pode Hole Lincs 156 E4
Podimore Som 29 C8
Podington Bedford 121 E8
Podmoor Worcs 117 C7
Podmore Norf 159 G9
Staffs 150 B5
Podsmead Glos 80 B4
Poffley End Oxon 82 C5
Pogmoor S Yorks 197 F10
Point Corn 3 B8
Point Clear Essex 89 C9
Pointon Lincs 156 C2
Pokesdown BCP 19 C8
Pol a Charra W Isles 297 K3
Polbae Dumfries 236 B4
Polbain Highld 307 H4
Polbathic Corn 7 D7
Polbeth W Loth 269 C10
Polborder Corn 7 C7
Polbrock Corn 5 B10
Polchar Highld 291 C10
Polebrook N Nhants 137 F11
Pole Elm Worcs 98 B6
Polegate E Sus 23 D9
Pole Moor W Yorks 196 D5
Poles Highld 309 K7
Polesden Lacey Sur 50 C6
Poleshill Som 27 C9
Pole's Hole Wilts 45 C10
Polesworth Warks 134 C5
Polgear Corn 2 B5
Polgigga Corn 1 E3
Polglass Highld 307 J5
Polgooth Corn 5 E9
Poling W Sus 35 G8
Poling Corner W Sus 35 F8
Polkerris Corn 5 E11
Polla Highld 308 D3
Polladras Corn 2 C4
Pollard Street Norf 160 C6
Pollhill Kent 53 C11
Poll Hill Mers 182 E3
Pollie Highld 309 H7
Pollington E Yorks 198 D6
Polliwilline Argyll 255 G8
Polloch Highld 289 C9
Pollok Glasgow 267 C10
Pollokshields Glasgow 267 C11
Polmadie Glasgow 267 C11
Polmarth Corn 2 B6
Polmassick Corn 5 F9
Polmear Corn 5 E11
Polmont Falk 279 F8
Polmorla Corn 10 G5
Polnessan E Ayrs 257 G10
Polnish Highld 295 G9
Polopit N Nhants 121 B10
Polpenwith Corn 2 D6
Polpeor Corn 2 B2
Polperro Corn 6 E4
Polruan Corn 6 E2
Polsham Som 44 E4
Polsloe Devon 14 C4
Polstead Suff 107 D9
Polstead Heath Suff 107 C9
Poltalloch Argyll 275 D9
Poltesco Corn 2 F6
Poltimore Devon 14 B5
Polton Midloth 270 C5
Polwarth Borders 272 E4
Polwheveral Corn 2 D6
Polyphant Corn 11 E11
Polzeath Corn 10 F4
Pomeroy Derbys 169 B10
Pomphlett Plym 7 E10
Ponciau Wrex 166 F3
Pond Close Som 27 B10
Ponde Powys 96 D2
Pondersbridge Cambs 138 E5
Ponders End London 86 F5
Pond Park Bucks 85 E7
Pond Street Essex 105 D9
Pondtail Hants 49 C10
Pondwell IoW 21 C8
Poniou Corn 1 B4
Ponjeravah Corn 2 D6
Ponsanooth Corn 3 B7
Ponsford Devon 27 F8
Ponsonby Cumb 219 D11
Ponsongath Corn 3 F7
Ponsworthy Devon 13 G10
Pont Corn 6 E2
Pont Aber Carms 94 G4
Pont Aber-Geirw Gwyn 146 D5
Pontamman Carms 75 C10
Pontantwn Carms 74 C6
Pontardawe Neath 76 E2
Pontarddulais Swansea 75 E9
Pontarfynach = Devils Bridge Ceredig 112 B4
Pont-ar-gothi Carms 93 G10
Pont ar Hydfer Powys 95 F7
Pont-ar-llechau Carms 94 G4
Pontarsais Carms 93 F8
Pontblyddyn Flint 166 C3
Pontbren Araeth Carms 94 G3
Pontbren Llwyd Rhondda 76 D6
Pontcanna Cardiff 59 D7
Pont Cyfyng Conwy 164 D2
Pont Cysyllte Wrex 166 G3
Pontdolgoch Powys 129 E10
Pont Dolydd Prysor
Gwyn 146 B4
Pontefract W Yorks 198 C3
Ponteland Northumb 242 C5
Ponterwyd Ceredig 128 G4
Pontesbury Shrops 131 B7
Pontesbury Hill Shrops 131 B7
Pontesford Shrops 131 B8
Pontfadog Wrex 148 B4
Pontfaen Pembs 91 E10
Pont-faen Powys 95 E9
Shrops 148 B5
Pont Fronwydd Gwyn 146 E6
Pont-gareg Pembs 92 C2
Pontgarreg Ceredig 110 G6
Ponthen Shrops 148 F6
Pont-Henri Carms 75 D7
Ponthir Torf 78 G4
Ponthirwaun Ceredig 92 B5
Pont Hwfa Anglesey 178 E2
Pontiago Pembs 91 D8
Pont iets = Pontyates
Carms 75 D7
Pontithel Powys 96 D3
Pontllanfraith Caerph 77 F11
Pontlliw Swansea 75 E10
Pont-Llogel Powys 147 F10
Pontllyfni Gwyn 162 E6
Pontlottyn Caerph 77 D10
Pontneddfechan Powys 76 D6
Pontnewydd Torf 78 F3
Pont-newydd Carms 74 D6
Flint 165 B11
Pontnewynydd Torf 78 E3
Pont Pen-y-benglog
Gwyn 163 C10
Pontrhydfendigaid
Ceredig 112 D4
Pont Rhydgaled Powys 128 G6
Pont Rhyd-goch
Conwy 163 C11
Pont-Rhyd-sarn Gwyn 147 D7
Pont Rhyd-y-berry
Powys 95 D9
Pont Rhyd-y-cyff
Bridgend 57 D11
Pontrhydyfen Neath 57 C9
Pont-rhyd-y-groes
Ceredig 112 C4
Pontrhydyrun Torf 78 F3
Pont-Rhythallt Gwyn 163 C8
Pontrilas Hereford 97 F7
Pontrobert Powys 148 G2
Pont-rug Gwyn 163 C8
Pont Senni = Sennybridge
Powys 95 F8
Ponts Green E Sus 23 B11
Pontshill Hereford 98 G2
Pont-siôn Ceredig 93 B8
Pont Siôn Norton
Rhondda 77 G9
Pontsticill M Tydf 77 C9
Pont-Walby Neath 76 D5
Pontwgan Conwy 180 G3
Pontyates = Pont-iets
Carms 75 D7
Pontyberem Carms 75 C8
Pont-y-blew Shrops 148 B6
Pontyclun Rhondda 58 C4
Pontycymer Bridgend 76 G6
Pontyglasier Pembs 92 D2
Pont-y-gwaith Rhondda 77 G8
Pontymister Caerph 78 G2
Pontymoel Torf 78 E3
Pont-y-pant Conwy 164 E3
Pont y Pennant Gwyn 147 E8
Pontypool Torf 78 E3
Pontypridd Rhondda 58 B5
Pont yr Afon-Gam
Gwyn 164 G2
Pont-yr-hafod Pembs 91 F8
Pont-y-rhyl Bridgend 58 B2
Pont-Ystrad Denb 165 C9
Pont-y-wal Powys 96 D2
Pontywaun Caerph 78 G2
Pooksgreen Hants 32 E5
Pool Corn 4 G3
W Yorks 205 D10
Poolbrook Worcs 98 C5
Poole BCP 18 C6
N Yorks 198 B3
Som 27 C10
Poole Keynes Glos 81 F8
Poolend Staffs 169 D7
Poolestown Dorset 30 D2
Poolewe Highld 307 L3
Pooley Bridge Cumb 230 G5
Pooley Street Norf 141 G11
Poolfold Staffs 168 D5
Poolhead Shrops 149 C9
Pool Head Hereford 115 G11
Pool Hey Lancs 193 D11
Poolhill Glos 98 F4
Poolmill Hereford 97 G11
Pool o' Muckhart Clack 286 G4
Pool Quay Powys 148 G5
Poolsbrook Derbys 186 G6
Poolside Moray 302 E4
Poolstock Gtr Man 194 G5
Pooltown Som 42 F3
Pootings Kent 52 D3
Pope Hill Pembs 72 C6
Pope's Hill Glos 79 C11
Popeswood Brack 65 F10
Popham Devon 41 G8
Hants 48 E5
Poplar London 67 C11
Poplar Grove Lincs 190 B6
Poplars Herts 104 G5
Popley Hants 48 C6
Porchester Nottingham 171 G9
Porchfield IoW 20 C4
Porin Highld 300 D3
Poringland Norf 142 C5
Porkellis Corn 2 C5
Porlock Som 41 D11
Porlockford Som 41 D11
Porlock Weir Som 41 D11
Portachoillan Argyll 255 B8
Port Allen Perth 286 E6
Port Ann Argyll 275 E10
Port Appin Argyll 289 E11
Port Arthur Shetland 313 K5
Portash Wilts 46 G3
Port Askaig Argyll 274 G5
Portavadie Argyll 275 G10
Port Bannatyne Argyll 275 G11
Port Brae Fife 280 C5
Port Bridge Devon 9 D7
Portbury N Som 60 D4
Port Carlisle Cumb 238 E6
Port Charlotte Argyll 254 B3
Portchester Hants 33 F10
Portclair Highld 290 B6
Port Clarence Stockton 234 G5
Port Dinorwic = Y Felinheli
Gwyn 163 B8
Port Driseach Argyll 275 F10
Port Dundas Glasgow 267 B11
Porteath Corn 10 F5
Port Edgar Edin 280 F2
Port Ellen Argyll 254 C4
Port Elphinstone Aberds 293 B9
Portencalzie Dumfries 236 B2
Portencross N Ayrs 266 F3
Porterfield Renfs 267 B9
Port Erin IoM 192 F2
Port Erroll Aberds 303 F10
Porter's End Herts 85 B11
Portesham Dorset 17 D8
Portessie Moray 302 C4
Port e Vullen IoM 192 C5
Port-Eynon Swansea 56 D3
Portfield Argyll 289 G9
Som 28 B6
W Sus 22 B5
Portfield Gate Pembs 72 B6
Portgate Devon 12 D4
Port Gaverne Corn 10 E6
Port Glasgow Invclyd 276 G6
Portgordon Moray 302 C3
Portgower Highld 311 H4
Porth Corn 4 C6
Rhondda 77 G8
Porthallow Corn 3 E7
Corn 6 E4
Porthcawl Bridgend 57 F10
Porth Colmon Gwyn 144 C3
Porthcothan Corn 10 G3
Porthcurno Corn 1 E3
Portheiddy Pembs 90 E6
Port Henderson Highld 299 B7
Porthgain Pembs 90 E6
Porthgwarra Corn 1 E3
Porthhallow Corn 3 E7
Porthill Shrops 149 G9
Staffs 168 F5
Port Hill Oxon 65 B7
Porthilly Corn 10 F4
Porth Kea Corn 4 G6
Porthkerry V Glam 58 F5
Porthleven Corn 2 D4
Porthllechog = Bull Bay
Anglesey 178 C6
Porthloo Scilly 1 G4
Porthmadog Gwyn 145 B11
Porthmeor Corn 1 B4
Porth Navas Corn 3 D7
Porthoustock Corn 3 E8
Porthpean Corn 5 E10
Porthtowan Corn 4 F3
Porth Tywyn = Burry Port
Carms 74 E6
Porth-y-felin Anglesey 178 E2
Porthyrhyd Carms 75 B8
Carms 94 D4
Porth-y-waen Shrops 148 E5
Portico Mers 183 C7
Portincaple Argyll 276 C4
Portington Devon 12 F4
E Yorks 207 G11
Portinnisherrich Argyll 275 B10
Portinscale Cumb 229 G11
Port Isaac Corn 10 E5
Portishead N Som 60 D3
Portkil Argyll 276 E5
Portknockie Moray 302 C4
Port Lamont Argyll 275 F11
Portland Som 44 F3
Portlethen Aberds 293 D11
Portlethen Village
Aberds 293 D11
Portlevorchy Highld 306 D7
Portling Dumfries 237 D10
Port Lion Pembs 73 D7
Portloe Corn 3 B10
Port Logan Dumfries 236 E2
Portlooe Corn 6 E4
Portmahomack Highld 311 L3
Port Mead Swansea 56 B6
Portmeirion Gwyn 145 B11
Portmellon Corn 5 G10
Port Mholair W Isles 304 E7
Port Mor Highld 288 B6
Portmore Hants 20 B2
Port Mulgrave N Yorks 226 B5
Portnacroish Argyll 289 E11
Portnahaven Argyll 254 B2
Portnalong Highld 294 B5
Portnaluchaig Highld 295 G8
Portnancon Highld 308 C4
Port Nan Giùran
W Isles 304 E7
Port nan Long W Isles 296 D4
Portnellan Stirling 285 E8
Stirling 285 F8
Port Nis W Isles 304 B7
Portobello Edin 280 G6
T&W 243 F7
W Mid 133 D9
W Yorks 197 D10
Port of Menteith Stirling 285 G9
Porton Wilts 47 F7
Portpatrick Dumfries 236 D2
Port Quin Corn 10 E5
Portrack Stockton 225 B9
Port Ramsay Argyll 289 E10
Portreath Corn 4 F3
Portree Highld 298 E4
Port St Mary IoM 192 F3
Portscatho Corn 3 B9
Portsea Ptsmth 33 G10
Portsea Island Ptsmth 33 G11
Portskerra Highld 310 C2
Portskewett Mon 60 B4
Portslade Brighton 36 F3
Portslade-by-Sea
Brighton 36 G3
Portslade Village
Brighton 36 F3
Portsmouth Ptsmth 21 B9
W Yorks 196 B2
Port Solent Ptsmth 33 F10
Portsonachan Argyll 284 E4
Portsoy Aberds 302 C5
Port Sunlight Mers 182 E4
Port Sutton Bridge
Lincs 157 E9
Portswood Soton 32 E6
Port Talbot Neath 57 D9
Porttanachy Moray 302 C3
Port Tennant Swansea 57 C7
Portuairk Highld 288 C6
Portvasgo Highld 308 C5
Portway Dorset 18 D2
Glos 98 E5
Hereford 97 B9
Hereford 97 D9
Som 28 B6
Portway continued
Som 44 F3
W Mid 133 F9
Worcs 117 C11
Port Wemyss Argyll 254 B2
Port William Dumfries 236 E5
Portwood Gtr Man 184 C6
Portwrinkle Corn 7 E7
Posenhall Shrops 132 C3
Poslingford Suff 106 B5
Posso Borders 260 C6
Postbridge Devon 13 F9
Postcombe Oxon 84 F2
Post Green Dorset 18 C5
Postling Kent 54 F6
Postlip Glos 99 F10
Post Mawr = Synod Inn
Ceredig 111 G8
Postwick Norf 142 B5
Potarch Aberds 293 D8
Potash Suff 108 D2
Potbridge Hants 49 C8
Pot Common Sur 50 E2
Potholm Dumfries 249 F9
Potmaily Highld 300 F4
Potman's Heath Kent 38 B5
Potsgrove C Beds 103 F9
Potten End Herts 85 D8
Potten Street Kent 71 F9
Potter Brompton
N Yorks 217 D9
Pottergate Street Norf 142 E3
Potterhanworth Lincs 173 B9
Potterhanworth Booths
Lincs 173 B9
Potter Heigham Norf 161 F8
Potter Hill Leics 154 E4
S Yorks 186 B4
Potterne Wilts 46 B3
Potterne Wick Wilts 46 B4
Potternewton W Yorks 206 F2
Potters Bar Herts 86 E3
Potters Brook Lancs 202 C5
Potters Corner Kent 54 E3
Potter's Cross Staffs 132 G6
Potters Crouch Herts 85 D10
Potter's Forstal Kent 53 D11
Potter's Green E Sus 37 C8
W Mid 135 G7
Pottersheath Herts 86 B2
Potters Hill N Som 60 F4
Potters Marston Leics 135 D9
Potter Somersal Derbys 152 B2
Potterspury W Nhants 102 C5
Potter Street Essex 87 D7
Potterton Aberds 293 B11
W Yorks 206 F4
Pottery Field W Yorks 206 G2
Potthorpe Norf 159 E8
Pottington Devon 40 G5
Potto N Yorks 225 E9
Potton C Beds 104 B4
Pott Row Norf 158 E4
Pott Shrigley Ches E 184 F6
Pouchen End Herts 85 D8
Poughill Corn 24 F2
Devon 26 F5
Poulner Hants 31 F11
Poulshot Wilts 46 B3
Poulton Ches W 166 D5
Glos 81 E10
Mers 182 C4
Mers 182 E4
Poulton-le-Fylde Lancs 202 F2
Pound Som 28 D6
Pound Bank Worcs 98 B5
Worcs 116 C4
Poundbury Dorset 17 C9
Poundffald Swansea 56 C5
Poundfield E Sus 52 G4
Poundford E Sus 37 C9
Poundgate E Sus 37 B7
Poundgreen Wokingham 65 F7
Pound Green E Sus 37 C8
Hants 48 B5
IoW 20 D2
Suff 124 G4
Worcs 116 B5
Pound Hill W Sus 51 F9
Poundland S Ayrs 244 F5
Poundon Bucks 102 F2
Poundsbridge Kent 52 E4
Poundsgate Devon 13 G10
Poundstock Corn 11 B10
Pound Street Hants 64 G3
Pounsley E Sus 37 C8
Poverest London 68 F3
Povey Cross Sur 51 E9
Powburn Northumb 264 F3
Powderham Devon 14 E5
Powder Mills Kent 52 D5
Powers Hall End Essex 88 B4
Powerstock Dorset 16 B6
Powfoot Dumfries 238 D4
Pow Green Hereford 98 C4
Powhill Cumb 238 F6
Powick Worcs 116 G6
Powler's Piece Devon 24 D5
Powmill Perth 279 B10
Pownall Park Ches E 184 E4
Powntley Copse Hants 49 E8
Poxwell Dorset 17 E10
Poyle Slough 66 D4
Poynings W Sus 36 E3
Poyntington Dorset 29 D11
Poynton Ches E 184 E6
Telford 149 F11
Poynton Green Telford 149 F11
Poyntzfield Highld 301 C7
Poyston Pembs 73 B7
Poyston Cross Pembs 73 B7
Poystreet Green Suff 125 F9
Praa Sands Corn 2 D3
Pratling Street Kent 53 B8
Pratt's Bottom London 68 G3
Praze Corn 2 B3
Praze-an-Beeble Corn 2 B4
Predannack Wollas Corn 2 F5
Prees Shrops 149 C11
Preesall Lancs 202 D3
Preesall Park Lancs 202 D3
Prees Green Shrops 149 C11
Preesgweene Shrops 148 B5
Prees Heath Shrops 149 B11
Preeshenlle Shrops 148 C6
Prees Higher Heath
Shrops 149 B11
Prees Lower Heath
Shrops 149 C11
Prees Wood Shrops 149 C11
Prenbrigog Flint 166 C3
Prendergast Pembs 73 B7
Pembs 90 G6
Prenderguest Borders 273 D8
Prendwick Northumb 264 G2
Pren-gwyn Ceredig 93 C8
Prenteg Gwyn 163 G9
Prenton Mers 182 D4
Prescot Mers 183 C7
Prescott Devon 27 E9
Glos 99 F9
Prescott continued
Shrops 132 G3
Shrops 149 E8
Presdales Herts 86 C5
Preshome Moray 302 C4
Press Derbys 170 B5
Pressen Northumb 263 B8
Prestatyn Denb 181 E9
Prestbury Ches E 184 F6
Glos 99 G9
Presteigne Powys 114 E6
Presthope Shrops 131 D11
Prestleigh Som 44 E6
Prestolee Gtr Man 195 F9
Preston Borders 272 D5
Brighton 36 F4
Devon 14 G3
Dorset 17 E10
E Loth 281 F11
E Loth 281 G7
E Yorks 209 G9
Glos 81 E8
Glos 98 E3
Herts 104 G3
Kent 70 G4
Kent 71 G8
Lancs 194 B4
London 67 B7
Northumb 264 D5
Rutland 137 C7
Shrops 149 G10
Torbay 9 C7
T&W 243 D8
Wilts 62 D4
Wilts 63 E9
Preston Bagot Warks 118 D3
Preston Bissett Bucks 102 F3
Preston Bowyer Som 27 B10
Preston Brockhurst
Shrops 149 E10
Preston Brook Halton 183 E9
Preston Candover Hants 48 E6
Preston Capes
W Nhants 119 G11
Preston Crowmarsh
Oxon 83 G10
Preston Deanery
W Nhants 120 F5
Prestonfield Edin 280 G5
Preston Fields Warks 118 D3
Preston Grange T&W 243 C8
Preston Green Warks 118 D3
Preston Gubbals Shrops 149 F9
Preston-le-Skerne
Durham 234 G2
Preston Marsh Hereford 97 B11
Prestonmill Dumfries 237 D11
Preston Montford
Shrops 149 G8
Preston on Stour Warks 118 G4
Preston-on-Tees
Stockton 225 B8
Preston on the Hill
Halton 183 E9
Preston on Wye Hereford 97 C7
Prestonpans E Loth 281 G7
Preston Pastures Worcs 100 B3
Preston Plucknett Som 29 D8
Preston St Mary Suff 125 G8
Preston-under-Scar
N Yorks 223 G11
Preston upon the Weald
Moors Telford 150 F3
Preston Wynne Hereford 97 B11
Prestwich Gtr Man 195 G10
Prestwick Northumb 242 C5
S Ayrs 257 D9
Prestwold Leics 153 E11
Prestwood Bucks 84 E5
Staffs 133 F7
Staffs 169 G10
Prey Heath Sur 50 B3
Price Town Bridgend 76 G6
Prickwillow Cambs 139 G11
Priddy Som 44 C4
Pride Park Derbys 153 B7
Priestacott Devon 24 F6
Priestcliffe Derbys 185 G10
Priestcliffe Ditch
Derbys 185 G10
Priest Down Bath 60 G6
Priestfield W Mid 133 D8
Worcs 98 C6
Priesthaugh Borders 249 C11
Priesthill Glasgow 267 C10
Priesthorpe W Yorks 205 F10
Priest Hutton Lancs 211 E10
Priestley Green
W Yorks 196 B6
Prieston Borders 262 D2
Priestside Dumfries 238 D4
Priestthorpe W Yorks 205 F8
Priest Weston Shrops 130 D5
Priestwood Brack 65 F11
Kent 69 G7
Priestwood Green Kent 69 G7
Primethorpe Leics 135 E10
Primrose T&W 243 E8
Primrose Corner Norf 160 G6
Primrose Green Norf 159 F11
Primrosehill Herts 85 E9
Primrose Hill Bath 61 F8
Lancs 193 F11
London 67 C9
W Mid 133 F8
Primrose Valley
N Yorks 218 D2
Primsland Worcs 117 E8
Prince Hill Ches E 168 G2
Prince Royd W Yorks 196 D6
Princes End W Mid 133 E9
Princes Gate Pembs 73 C10
Prince's Marsh Hants 34 B3
Princes Park Mers 182 D5
Princes Risborough
Bucks 84 E4
Princethorpe Warks 119 C8
Princetown Caerph 77 C10
Devon 13 G7
Prinsted W Sus 22 B3
Printstile Kent 52 E5
Prion Denb 165 C9
Prior Muir Fife 287 F9
Prior Park Northumb 273 E9
Prior Rigg Cumb 239 D11
Priors Frome Hereford 97 D11
Priors Halton Shrops 115 B9
Priors Hardwick Warks 119 F9
Priorslee Telford 150 G4
Priors Marston Warks 119 F9
Prior's Norton Glos 99 G7
Priors Park Glos 99 E7
Priorswood Som 28 B2
Priory Pembs 72 D6
Priory Green Suff 107 C8
Priory Heath Suff 108 C3
Priory Wood Hereford 96 B5
Prisk V Glam 58 D4
Pristacott Devon 25 B8
Priston Bath 61 G7
Pristow Green Norf 142 F2
Prittlewell Southend 69 B11
Privett Hants 21 B7
Hants 33 B11
Prixford Devon 40 F4
Probus Corn 5 F7
Proncy Highld 309 K7
Prospect Cumb 229 C8
Prospect Village Staffs 151 G10
Prospidnick Corn 2 C4
Provanmill Glasgow 268 B2
Prowse Devon 26 F4
Prudhoe Northumb 242 E3
Prussia Cove Corn 2 D3
Ptarmigan Lodge
Stirling 285 G7
Pubil Perth 285 C8
Publow Bath 60 G6
Puckeridge Herts 105 G7
Puckington Som 28 D5
Pucklechurch S Glos 61 D7
Pucknall Hants 32 B5
Puckrup Glos 99 D7
Puckshole Glos 80 D4
Puddaven Devon 8 C5
Puddinglake Ches W 168 B2
Pudding Pie Nook Lancs 202 F6
Puddington Ches W 182 G4
Devon 26 E4
Puddle Corn 5 D11
Puddlebridge Som 28 E4
Puddledock Kent 52 C3
Kent 68 E4
Norf 141 E11
Puddletown Dorset 17 C11
Pudleigh Som 28 E4
Pudleston Hereford 115 F11
Pudsey W Yorks 196 B2
W Yorks 205 G10
Pulborough W Sus 35 D8
Pulcree Dumfries 237 D7
Pule Hill W Yorks 196 B5
Puleston Telford 150 E4
Pulford Ches W 166 D5
Pulham Dorset 30 F2
Pulham Market Norf 142 F3
Pulham St Mary Norf 142 F4
Pullens Green S Glos 79 G10
Pulley Shrops 131 B9
Pullington Kent 53 G10
Pulloxhill C Beds 103 E11
Pulverbatch Shrops 131 C8
Pumpherston W Loth 269 B11
Pumsaint Carms 94 C3
Puncheston = Cas-Mael
Pembs 91 F10
Puncknowle Dorset 16 D6
Punnett's Town E Sus 37 C10
Purbrook Hants 33 F11
Purewell BCP 19 C9
Purfleet Thurrock 68 D5
Puriton Som 43 E10
Purleigh Essex 88 E4
Purley London 67 G10
Purley on Thames
W Berks 65 D7
Purlogue Shrops 114 B5
Purlpit Wilts 61 F11
Purls Bridge Cambs 139 F9
Purn N Som 43 B10
Purse Caundle Dorset 29 D11
Purslow Shrops 131 G7
Purston Jaglin W Yorks 198 D2
Purtington Som 28 F5
Purton Glos 79 E11
W Berks 64 D3
Wilts 62 B5
Purton Common Wilts 62 B5
Purton Stoke Wilts 81 G9
Purwell Herts 104 F4
Pury End W Nhants 102 B4
Pusey Oxon 82 F5
Putley Hereford 98 D2
Putley Common Hereford 98 D2
Putley Green Hereford 98 D3
Putloe Glos 80 D3
Putney London 67 D8
Putney Heath London 67 E8
Putney Vale London 67 E8
Putnoe Bedford 121 G11
Putsborough Devon 40 E3
Putson Hereford 97 D10
Puttenham Herts 84 C5
Sur 50 D2
Puttock End Essex 106 C6
Puttock's End Essex 87 B9
Putton Dorset 17 E9
Puxey Dorset 30 E3
Puxley W Nhants 102 C5
Puxton N Som 60 G2
Pwll Carms 75 E7
Powys 130 C3
Pwll-clai Flint 181 G11
Pwllcrochan Pembs 72 E6
Pwll-glas Denb 165 E10
Pwllgloyw Powys 95 E10
Pwllheli Gwyn 145 B7
Pwll-Mawr Cardiff 59 D8
Pwll-melyn Flint 181 G11
Pwllmeyric Mon 79 G8
Pwll-trap Carms 74 B3
Pwll-y-glaw Neath 57 C9
Pwllypant Caerph 59 B7
Pye Bridge Derbys 170 E6
Pyecombe W Sus 36 E3
Pye Corner Devon 14 B4
Kent 53 D11
Newport 59 B9
S Glos 60 D6
Pye Green Staffs 151 G9
Pye Hill Notts 170 E6
Pyewipe NE Lincs 201 E9
Pyle IoW 20 F5
Swansea 56 D5
Pyle = Y Pîl Bridgend 57 E10
Pylehill Hants 33 D7
Pyle Hill Sur 50 B3
Pyleigh Som 42 G6
Pylle Som 44 F6
Pymore or Pymoor
Cambs 139 F9
Pype Hayes W Mid 134 E2
Pyrford Sur 50 B4
Pyrford Green Sur 50 B4
Pyrford Village Sur 50 B4
Pyrland Som 28 B2
Pyrton Oxon 83 F11
Pytchley N Nhants 121 C7
Pyworthy Devon 24 G4

Q

Quabbs Shrops 130 G4
Quabrook E Sus 52 G2
Quadring Lincs 156 C4
Quadring Eaudike Lincs 156 C4
Quags Corner W Sus 34 C5
Quainton Bucks 84 B2
Quaker's Yard M Tydf 77 F9
Quaking Houses
Durham 242 G5
Quality Corner Cumb 219 B9
Quarhouse Glos 80 E5
Quarley Hants 47 E9
Quarmby W Yorks 196 D6
Quarndon Derbys 170 G4
Quarndon Common
Derbys 170 G4
Quarrelton Renfs 267 C8
Quarrendon Bucks 84 B4
Quarr Hill IoW 21 C7
Quarriers Village
Invclyd 267 B7
Quarrington Lincs 173 G9
Quarrington Hill
Durham 234 D2
Quarrybank Ches W 167 B8
Quarry Bank W Mid 133 F8
Quarryford E Loth 271 B11
Quarryhead Aberds 303 C9
Quarry Heath Staffs 151 G8
Quarryhill Highld 309 L7
Quarry Hill Staffs 134 C4
Quarrywood Moray 301 C11
Quarter S Lanark 268 E4
Quartley Devon 27 B7
Quatford Shrops 132 E4
Quatquoy Orkney 314 E3
Quatt Shrops 132 F5
Quebec Durham 233 C9
W Sus 34 C3
Quedgeley Glos 80 C4
Queen Adelaide Cambs 139 G11
Queenborough Kent 70 E2
Queen Camel Som 29 C9
Queen Charlton Bath 60 F6
Queen Dart Devon 26 D4
Queenhill Worcs 99 D7
Queen Oak Dorset 45 G9
Queen's Bower IoW 21 E7
Queensbury London 67 B7
W Yorks 205 G8
Queen's Corner W Sus 34 B5
Queensferry Edin 280 F2
Flint 166 B4
Queen's Head Shrops 148 D6
Queenslie Glasgow 268 B3
Queen's Park Bedford 103 B10
Blackburn 195 B7
Ches W 166 B6
Essex 87 F11
W Nhants 120 E5
Queenstown Blackpool 202 F2
Queen Street Kent 53 D7
Wilts 62 B4
Queensville Staffs 151 E8
Queenzieburn N Lanark 278 F3
Quemerford Wilts 62 F4
Quendale Shetland 313 M5
Quendon Essex 105 E10
Queniborough Leics 154 G2
Quenington Glos 81 E10
Quernmore Lancs 202 B6
Queslett W Mid 133 E11
Quethiock Corn 6 C6
Quhamm Shetland 312 G6
Quholm Orkney 314 E2
Quick Gtr Man 196 G3
Quick Edge Gtr Man 196 G3
Quicks Green W Berks 64 D5
Quidenham Norf 141 F10
Quidhampton Hants 48 C4
Wilts 46 G6
Quilquox Aberds 303 F9
Quina Brook Shrops 149 C10
Quinbury End W Nhants 120 G2
Quindry Orkney 314 G4
Quinton W Mid 133 G9
W Nhants 120 G5
Quintrell Downs Corn 5 C7
Quixhill Staffs 169 G10
Quoditch Devon 12 B4
Quoig Perth 286 E2
Quoisley Ches E 167 F8
Quoit Corn 5 C8
Quorndon or Quorn
Leics 153 F11
Quothquan S Lanark 259 B11
Quoyloo Orkney 314 D2
Quoynee Highld 310 D6
Quoyness Orkney 314 F2
Quoys Shetland 312 B8
Shetland 313 G6

R

Raasay Ho Highld 295 B7
Rabbit's Cross Kent 53 D9
Rableyheath Herts 86 B2
Raby Cumb 238 G5
Mers 182 F4
Racecourse Suff 108 C3
Racedown Hants 47 E9
Rachan Mill Borders 260 C4
Rachub Gwyn 163 B10
Rack End Oxon 82 E6
Rackenford Devon 26 D5
Rackham W Sus 35 E9
Rackheath Norf 160 G5
Rackley Som 43 C11
Racks Dumfries 238 C2
Rackwick Orkney 314 B4
Orkney 314 G2
Radbourne Derbys 152 B5
Radcliffe Gtr Man 195 F9
Northumb 253 C7
Radcliffe on Trent Notts 154 B2
Radclive Bucks 102 E3
Radcot Oxon 82 F3
Raddery Highld 301 D7
Raddington Som 27 B8
Raddon Devon 26 G6
Radernie Fife 287 G8
Radfall Kent 70 G6
Radfield Kent 70 G2
Radford Bath 45 B7
Nottingham 171 G9
Oxon 101 G8
W Mid 134 G6
Worcs 117 F10
Radfordbridge Oxon 101 G8
Radford Semele Warks 118 E6
Radipole Dorset 17 E9
Radlet Som 43 F8
Radlett Herts 85 F11
Radley Oxon 83 F8
Radley Green Essex 87 D10
Radley Park Oxon 83 F8
Radlith Shrops 131 B8
Radmanthwaite Notts 171 C8
Radmoor Shrops 150 E2
Radmore Green Ches E 167 D9
Radmore Wood Staffs 151 D11
Radnage Bucks 84 F3
Radnor Corn 4 G4
Radnor Park W Dunb 277 G9
Radstock Bath 45 C7
Radstone W Nhants 101 C11
Radway Warks 101 B7
Radway Green Ches E 168 E3
Radwell Bedford 121 F10
Radwell continued
Herts 104 D4
Radwinter Essex 106 D2
Radwinter End Essex 106 D2
Radyr Cardiff 58 C6
Raehills Dumfries 248 E3
Raera Argyll 289 G10
Rafborough Hants 49 B11
Rafford Moray 301 D10
Raga Shetland 312 D6
Ragdale Leics 154 F3
Ragdon Shrops 131 E9
Raggalds W Yorks 205 G7
Ragged Appleshaw
Hants 47 D10
Raginnis Corn 1 D5
Raglan Mon 78 D6
Ragmere Norf 141 E11
Ragnal Wilts 63 E10
Ragnall Notts 188 G4
Rahane Argyll 276 D4
Rahoy Highld 289 D8
Raigbeg Highld 301 G8
Rails S Yorks 186 D3
Rainbow Hill Worcs 117 F7
Rainford Mers 194 G3
Rainford Junction Mers 194 G3
Rainham London 68 C4
Medway 69 F10
Rainhill Mers 183 C7
Rainhill Stoops Mers 183 C8
Rainow Ches E 185 F7
Rainowlow Ches E 185 F7
Rain Shore Gtr Man 195 D11
Rainsough Gtr Man 195 G10
Rainton Dumfries 237 D8
N Yorks 215 D7
Rainton Bridge T&W 234 B2
Rainton Gate Durham 234 B2
Rainworth Notts 171 D9
Raisbeck Cumb 222 D2
Raise Cumb 231 B10
Rait Perth 286 E6
Raithby Lincs 190 E4
Raithby by Spilsby Lincs 174 B5
Rake W Sus 34 B4
Rake Common Hants 34 B3
Rake End Staffs 151 F11
Rake Head Lancs 195 C10
Rakes Dale Staffs 169 G9
Rakeway Staffs 169 G8
Rakewood Gtr Man 196 E2
Raleigh Devon 40 G5
Ralia Lodge Highld 291 D9
Rallt Swansea 56 C4
Ram Carms 93 B11
Ram Alley Wilts 63 G8
Ramasaig Highld 297 G7
Rame Corn 2 C6
Corn 7 F8
Rameldry Mill Bank
Fife 287 G7
Ram Hill S Glos 61 D7
Ram Lane Kent 54 D3
Ramnageo Shetland 312 C8
Rampisham Dorset 29 G9
Rampside Cumb 210 F4
Rampton Cambs 123 D8
Notts 188 F3
Ramsbottom Gtr Man 195 D9
Ramsburn Moray 302 D5
Ramsbury Wilts 63 E9
Ramscraigs Highld 311 G5
Ramsdean Hants 34 C2
Ramsdell Hants 48 B5
Ramsden London 68 F3
Oxon 82 B5
Worcs 99 B8
Ramsden Bellhouse
Essex 88 G2
Ramsden Heath Essex 88 F2
Ramsden Wood
W Yorks 196 C2
Ramsey Cambs 138 F5
Essex 108 E4
IoM 192 C5
Ramseycleuch Borders 261 G7
Ramsey Forty Foot
Cambs 138 F6
Ramsey Heights Cambs 138 F5
Ramsey Island Essex 89 D7
Ramsey Mereside
Cambs 138 F5
Ramsey St Mary's
Cambs 138 F5
Ramsgate Kent 71 G11
Ramsgill N Yorks 214 E2
Ramshaw Durham 232 B5
Durham 233 F8
Ramsholt Suff 108 C6
Ramshorn Staffs 169 F9
Ramsley Devon 13 C8
Ramslye Kent 52 F5
Ramsnest Common Sur 50 G2
Ranais W Isles 304 F6
Ranby Lincs 190 F2
Notts 187 E11
Rand Lincs 189 F10
Randwick Glos 80 D4
Ranfurly Renfs 267 C7
Rangag Highld 310 E5
Rangemore Staffs 152 E3
Rangeworthy S Glos 61 B7
Rankinston E Ayrs 257 G11
Rank's Green Essex 88 B3
Ranmoor S Yorks 186 D4
Ranmore Common Sur 50 C6
Rannerdale Cumb 220 B3
Rannoch Lodge Perth 285 B9
Rannoch Station Perth 285 B8
Ranochan Highld 295 G10
Ranskill Notts 187 D11
Ranton Staffs 151 E7
Ranton Green Staffs 150 E6
Ranworth Norf 161 G7
Rapkyns W Sus 50 G6
Raploch Stirling 278 C5
Rapness Orkney 314 B5
Rapps Som 28 D4
Rascal Moor E Yorks 208 F2
Rascarrel Dumfries 237 E9
Rashielee Renfs 277 G9
Rashiereive Aberds 303 G9
Rashwood Worcs 117 D8
Raskelf N Yorks 215 E9
Rassal Highld 299 E8
Rassau Bl Gwent 77 C11
Rastrick W Yorks 196 C6
Ratagan Highld 295 D11
Ratby Leics 135 B10
Ratcliff London 67 C11
Ratcliffe Culey Leics 134 D6
Ratcliffe on Soar Leics 153 D9
Ratcliffe on the Wreake
Leics 154 G2
Ratford Wilts 62 E3
Ratfyn Wilts 47 E7
Rathen Aberds 303 C10
Rathillet Fife 287 E7
Rathmell N Yorks 204 B2
Ratho Edin 280 G2

Ratho Station Edin. 280 G2
Rathven Moray 302 C4
Ratlake Hants 32 C6
Ratley Warks 101 B7
Ratling Kent 55 C8
Ratlinghope Shrops 131 D8
Ratsloe Devon 14 B5
Rattar Highld 310 B6
Ratten Row Cumb 230 B3
Cumb 230 C2
Lancs 202 E4
Norf 157 G10
Rattery Devon 8 C4
Rattlesden Suff 125 F9
Rattray Perth 286 C5
Raughton Cumb 230 B3
Raughton Head Cumb 230 B3
Raunds N Nhants 121 C9
Ravelston Edin 280 G4
Ravenfield S Yorks 187 B7
Ravenglass Cumb 219 F11
Ravenhead Mers 183 C8
Ravenhills Green Worcs 116 G4
Raveningham Norf 143 D7
Ravenscar N Yorks 227 E9
Ravenscliffe Stoke 168 E4
W Yorks 205 F9
Ravenscraig Invclyd 276 F5
Ravensdale IoM 192 C4
Ravensden Bedford 121 G11
Ravenseat N Yorks 223 E7
Raven's Green Essex 108 G2
Ravenshall Staffs 168 F3
Ravenshead Notts 171 E9
Ravensmoor Ches E 167 E10
Ravensthorpe Pboro 138 C3
W Nhants 120 C3
W Yorks 197 C8
Ravenstone Leics 153 G8
M Keynes 120 G6
Ravenstonedale Cumb 222 E4
Ravenstown Cumb 211 D7
Ravenstruther S Lanark 269 F8
Ravenswood Village
Settlement Wokingham 65 G10
Ravensworth N Yorks 224 D2
Raw N Yorks 227 D8
Rawcliffe E Yorks 199 C7
York 207 C7
Rawcliffe Bridge
E Yorks 199 C7
Rawdon W Yorks 205 F10
Rawdon Carrs W Yorks 205 F10
Rawfolds W Yorks 197 C7
Rawgreen Northumb 241 F10
Raw Green S Yorks 197 F9
Rawmarsh S Yorks 186 B6
Rawnsley Staffs 151 G10
Rawreth Essex 88 G3
Rawreth Shot Essex 88 G3
Rawridge Devon 28 F2
Rawson Green Derbys 170 F5
Rawtenstall Lancs 195 C10
Rawthorpe W Yorks 197 D7
Rawyards N Lanark 268 B5
Raxton Aberds 303 F8
Raydon Suff 107 D11
Raygill N Yorks 204 D4
Raylees Northumb 251 E10
Rayleigh Essex 88 G4
Rayne Essex 106 G4
Rayners Lane London 66 B6
Raynes Park London 67 F8
Reabrook Shrops 131 C7
Reach Cambs 123 D11
Read Lancs 203 G11
Reader's Corner Essex 88 E2
Reading Reading 65 E8
Readings Glos 79 B10
Reading Street Kent 54 G2
Kent 71 F11
Readymoney Corn 6 E2
Ready Token Glos 81 E10
Reagill Cumb 222 B2
Rearquhar Highld 309 K7
Rearsby Leics 154 G3
Reasby Lincs 189 F9
Rease Heath Ches E 167 E10
Reaster Highld 310 C6
Reaulay Highld 299 D7
Reawick Shetland 313 J5
Reawla Corn 2 B4
Reay Highld 310 C3
Rechullin Highld 299 D8
Reculver Kent 71 F8
Red Ball Devon 27 D9
Redberth Pembs 73 E9
Redbourn Herts 85 C10
Redbournbury Herts 85 C10
Redbourne N Lincs 189 B7
N Lincs 200 G3
Redbridge Dorset 17 D11
London 68 B2
Soton 32 E5
Red Bridge Lancs 211 D9
Redbrook Mon 79 C8
Wrex 167 G8
Red Bull Ches E 168 D4
Staffs 150 B4
Redburn Highld 300 C5
Highld 301 E9
Northumb 241 E7
Redcar Redcar 235 G8
Redcastle Angus 287 B10
Highld 300 E5
Redcliff Bay N Som 60 D2
Redcroft Dumfries 237 B9
Redcross Worcs 117 C7
Red Dial Cumb 229 B11
Reddicap Heath W Mid 134 D2
Redding Falk 279 F8
Reddingmuirhead Falk 279 F8
Reddish Gtr Man 184 C5
Warr 183 D11
Redditch Worcs 117 D10
Rede Suff 124 F6
Redenhall Norf 142 G5
Redenham Hants 47 D10
Redesdale Camp
Northumb 251 D8
Redesmouth Northumb 251 G9
Redford Aberds 293 F9
Angus 287 C9
Dorset 29 F10
Durham 233 E7
W Sus 34 B5
Redfordgreen Borders 261 F9
Redgorton Perth 286 E4
Redgrave Suff 125 B10
Redheugh Angus 292 G6
Redhill Aberds 293 C9
Aberds 302 F6
Herts 104 E6
Notts 171 F9
N Som 60 G4
Shrops 131 B9
Shrops 150 G4
Staffs 150 D6
Sur 51 C9
Telford 150 G4
Red Hill BCP 19 B7
Red Hill *continued*
Hants 34 E2
Hereford 97 D10
Kent 53 C7
Leics 135 D10
Pembs 72 B6
Warks 118 F2
Worcs 117 G7
W Yorks 198 B2
Redhills Cumb 230 F6
Devon 14 C4
Redhouse Argyll 275 G9
Red House Common
E Sus 36 C5
Redhouses Argyll 274 G4
Redisham Suff 143 G8
Red Lake Telford 150 G3
Redland Bristol 60 D5
Orkney 314 D3
Redland End Bucks 84 E4
Redlands Dorset 17 E9
Som 44 G3
Swindon 81 G11
Redlane Som 28 E2
Redlingfield Suff 126 C3
Red Lodge Suff 124 C3
Red Lumb Gtr Man 195 D10
Redlynch Som 45 G8
Wilts 32 C2
Redmain Cumb 229 E8
Redmarley D'Abitot Glos 98 E5
Redmarshall Stockton 234 G3
Redmile Leics 154 B5
Redmire N Yorks 223 G10
Redmonsford Devon 24 D4
Redmoor Corn 5 C11
Redmoss Aberds 303 F8
Rednal Shrops 149 D7
W Mid 117 B10
Redpath Borders 262 B3
Red Pits Norf 159 D11
Redpoint Highld 299 C7
Red Post Corn 24 F3
Red Rail Hereford 97 F10
Red Rice Hants 47 E10
Red Rock Gtr Man 194 F5
Red Roses Carms 74 C2
Red Row Northumb 253 D7
Redruth Corn 4 G3
Red Scar Lancs 203 G7
Redscarhead Borders 270 G4
Redstocks Wilts 62 G2
Red Street Staffs 168 E4
Redtye Corn 5 C10
Redvales Gtr Man 195 F10
Red Wharf Bay Anglesey 179 E8
Redwick Newport 60 C2
S Glos 60 B4
Redwith Shrops 148 E6
Redworth Darl 233 G10
Reed Herts 105 D7
Reed End Herts 104 D6
Reedham Lincs 174 D2
Norf 143 C8
Reedley Lancs 204 F2
Reedness E Yorks 199 C9
Reed Point Lincs 174 E2
Reeds Beck Lincs 174 B2
Reedsford Northumb 263 C9
Reeds Holme Lancs 195 C10
Reedy Devon 14 D2
Reen Manor Corn 4 E5
Reepham Lincs 189 G8
Norf 159 E11
Reeth N Yorks 223 F10
Reeves Green W Mid 118 B5
Refail Powys 130 C3
Regaby IoM 192 C5
Regil Bath 60 G4
Regoul Highld 301 D8
Reiff Highld 307 H4
Reigate Sur 51 C9
Reigate Heath Sur 51 C8
Reighton N Yorks 218 D2
Reighton Gap N Yorks 218 D2
Reinigeadal W Isles 305 H4
Reisque Aberds 293 B10
Reiss Highld 310 D7
Rejerrah Corn 4 D5
Releath Corn 2 C5
Relubbus Corn 2 C3
Relugas Moray 301 E9
Remenham Wokingham 65 C9
Remenham Hill
Wokingham 65 C9
Remony Perth 285 C11
Rempstone Notts 153 E11
Remusaig Highld 309 J7
Rendcomb Glos 81 D8
Rendham Suff 126 E6
Rendlesham Suff 126 G6
Renfrew Renfs 267 B10
Renhold Bedford 121 G11
Renishaw Derbys 186 F6
Renmure Angus 287 B10
Rennington Northumb 264 F6
Renshaw Wood Shrops 132 B6
Renton W Dunb 277 F7
Renwick Cumb 231 C7
Repps Norf 161 F8
Repton Derbys 152 D6
Reraig Highld 295 C10
Reraig Cot Highld 295 B10
Rerwick Shetland 313 M5
Rescassa Corn 5 G9
Rescobie Angus 287 B9
Rescorla Corn 5 D10
Resipole Highld 289 C9
Reskadinnick Corn 4 G2
Resolfen = *Resolven*
Neath 76 E4
Resolis Highld 300 C6
Resolven = *Resolfen*
Neath 76 E4
Restalrig Edin 280 G5
Reston Borders 273 C7
Cumb 221 F9
Restronguet Passage Corn 3 B8
Restrop Wilts 62 B5
Resugga Green Corn 5 D10
Reswallie Angus 287 B9
Retallack Corn 5 B8
Retew Corn 5 D8
Retford Notts 188 E2
Retire Corn 5 C10
Rettendon Essex 88 F3
Rettendon Place Essex 88 F3
Revesby Lincs 174 C3
Revesby Bridge Lincs 174 C4
Revidge Blackburn 195 B7
Rew Devon 9 G9
Devon 13 G11
Dorset 29 F11
Rewe Devon 14 B4
Rew Street IoW 20 C5
Rexon Devon 12 D4
Rexon Cross Devon 12 D4
Reybridge Wilts 62 F2
Reydon Suff 127 B9
Reydon Smear Suff 127 B9
Reymerston Norf 141 B10
Reynalton Pembs 73 D9
Reynoldston Swansea 56 C3
Rezare Corn 12 F3
Rhadyr Mon 78 E5
Rhaeadr Gwy = *Rhayader*
Powys 113 D9
Rhandir Conwy 180 G4
Rhandirmwyn Carms 94 C5
Rhayader = *Rhaeadr Gwy*
Powys 113 D9
Rhedyn Gwyn 144 C5
Rhegreanoch Highld 307 H5
Rhemore Highld 289 D7
Rhencullen IoM 192 C4
Rhenetra Highld 298 D4
Rhes-y-cae Flint 181 G11
Rhewl Denb 165 C10
Denb 165 F11
Shrops 148 C6
Wrex 149 B7
Rhewl-fawr Flint 181 E10
Rhewl-Mostyn Flint 181 E11
Rhian Highld 309 H5
Rhicarn Highld 307 G5
Rhiconich Highld 306 D7
Rhicullen Highld 300 B6
Rhidorroch Ho Highld 307 K6
Rhiews Shrops 150 B2
Rhifail Highld 308 E7
Rhigolter Highld 308 D3
Rhigos Rhondda 76 D6
Rhilochan Highld 309 J7
Rhippinllwyd Ceredig 92 C5
Ceredig 110 G6
Rhiroy Highld 307 L6
Rhitongue Highld 308 D6
Rhivichie Highld 306 D7
Rhiw Gwyn 144 D4
Rhiwabon = *Ruabon*
Wrex 166 G4
Rhiwbebyll Denb 165 B10
Rhiwbina Cardiff 59 C7
Rhiwbryfdir Gwyn 163 F11
Rhiwceiliog Bridgend 58 C3
Rhiwderin Newport 59 B9
Rhiwen Gwyn 163 C9
Rhiwfawr Neath 76 C2
Rhiwinder Rhondda 58 B4
Rhiwlas Gwyn 147 B8
Gwyn 163 B9
Powys 148 C3
Rhode Som 43 G9
Rhode Common Kent 54 B5
Rhodes Gtr Man 195 F11
Rhodesia Notts 187 F9
Rhodes Minnis Kent 55 E7
Rhodiad Pembs 90 F5
Rhonadale Argyll 255 D8
Rhondda Rhondda 77 F7
Rhonehouse or Kelton Hill
Dumfries 237 D9
Rhoose V Glam 58 F5
Rhos Carms 93 D7
Rhôs Denb 165 C10
Neath 76 E2
Rhos Powys 148 F5
Rhosaman Carms 76 C2
Rhosbeirio Anglesey 178 C5
Rhoscefnhir Anglesey 179 F8
Rhoscolyn Anglesey 178 F3
Rhôs Common Powys 148 F5
Rhoscrowther Pembs 72 E6
Rhosddu Wrex 166 E4
Rhos-ddû Gwyn 144 B5
Rhosdylluan Gwyn 147 D7
Rhosesmor Flint 166 B2
Rhosfach Pembs 92 F2
Rhos-fawr Gwyn 145 B7
Rhosgadfan Gwyn 163 D8
Rhosgoch Anglesey 178 D6
Powys 96 B3
Rhos-goch Powys 96 B3
Rhosgyll Gwyn 163 G7
Rhos Haminiog Ceredig 111 E10
Rhos-hill Pembs 92 C3
Rhoshirwaun Gwyn 144 D3
Rhos Isaf Gwyn 163 D7
Rhoslan Gwyn 163 G7
Rhoslefain Gwyn 110 B2
Rhosllanerchrugog
Wrex 166 F3
Rhôs Lligwy Anglesey 179 D7
Rhosmaen Carms 94 G2
Rhosmeirch Anglesey 179 F7
Rhosneigr Anglesey 178 G4
Rhosnesni Wrex 166 E5
Rhôs-on-Sea Conwy 180 E4
Rhosrobin Wrex 166 E4
Rhossili Swansea 56 D2
Rhosson Pembs 90 F4
Rhostrehwfa Anglesey 178 G6
Rhostryfan Gwyn 163 D7
Rhostyllen Wrex 166 F4
Rhoswiel Shrops 148 B5
Rhosybol Anglesey 178 D6
Rhos-y-brithdir Powys 148 E2
Rhosycaerau Pembs 91 D8
Rhosygadair Newydd
Ceredig 92 B4
Rhosygadfa Shrops 148 C6
Rhos-y-garth Ceredig 112 C2
Rhosygilwen Pembs 92 C4
Rhos-y-gwaliau Gwyn 147 C8
Rhos-y-llan Gwyn 144 B4
Rhos-y-Madoc Wrex 166 G4
Rhosymedre Wrex 166 G3
Rhos-y-meirch Powys 114 D5
Rhosyn-coch Carms 92 G5
Rhu Argyll 275 G9
Argyll 276 E5
Rhuallt Denb 181 F9
Rhubodach Argyll 275 F11
Rhuddall Heath Ches W 167 C9
Rhuddlan Ceredig 93 C9
Denb 181 F8
Rhue Highld 307 K5
Rhulen Powys 96 B2
Rhunahaorine Argyll 255 C8
Rhyd Ceredig 92 C5
Gwyn 163 G10
Powys 129 C9
Rhydaman = *Ammanford*
Carms 75 C10
Rhydargaeau Carms 93 F8
Rhydcymerau Carms 93 D11
Rhydd Worcs 98 B6
Rhyd-Ddu Gwyn 163 E9
Rhydd Green Worcs 98 B6
Rhydding Neath 57 B8
Rhydfudr Ceredig 111 D11
Rhydgaled Conwy 165 C7
Rhydgaled = *Chancery*
Ceredig 111 B11
Rhydlewis Ceredig 92 B6
Rhydlios Gwyn 144 C3
Rhydlydan Conwy 164 E5
Powys 129 E11
Rhydmoelddu Powys 113 B11
Rhydness Powys 96 C2
Rhydowen Carms 92 F3
Ceredig 93 B8
Rhyd-Rosser Ceredig 111 D11
Rhydspence Hereford 96 B4
Rhydtalog Flint 166 D2
Rhyd-uchaf Gwyn 147 B8
Rhydwen Gwyn 146 F4
Rhydwyn Anglesey 178 D4
Rhyd-y-Brown Pembs 91 G11
Rhyd-y-clafdy Gwyn 144 B6
Rhydycroesau Powys 148 C4
Rhyd-y-cwm Shrops 130 G3
Rhydyfelin Carms 92 D5
Ceredig 111 B11
Powys 129 E11
Rhondda 58 B5
Rhyd-y-foel Conwy 180 F6
Rhyd-y-fro Neath 76 D2
Rhydygele Pembs 91 G7
Rhyd-y-gwin Swansea 75 E11
Rhyd-y-gwystl Gwyn 145 B8
Rhydymain Gwyn 146 E6
Rhyd-y-meirch Mon 78 D4
Rhyd-y-meudwy Denb 165 E10
Rhydymwyn Flint 166 B2
Rhyd-y-pandy Swansea 75 E11
Rhyd-yr-onen Gwyn 128 C2
Rhyd-y-sarn Gwyn 163 G11
Rhydywrach Carms 73 B11
Rhyl Denb 181 E8
Rhymney Caerph 77 D10
Rhyn Wrex 148 B6
Rhynd Fife 287 E8
Perth 286 E5
Rhynie Aberds 302 G4
Highld 301 B8
Ribbesford Worcs 116 C5
Ribblehead N Yorks 212 D5
Ribble Head N Yorks 212 D5
Ribbleton Lancs 203 G7
Ribby Lancs 202 G4
Ribchester Lancs 203 F8
Riber Derbys 170 D4
Ribigill Highld 308 D5
Riby Lincs 201 F7
Riby Cross Roads Lincs 201 F7
Riccall N Yorks 207 F8
Riccarton E Ayrs 257 B10
Richards Castle
Hereford 115 D9
Richborough Port Kent 71 G10
Richings Park Bucks 66 D4
Richmond London 67 E7
N Yorks 224 E3
S Yorks 186 D6
Richmond Hill W Yorks 206 G2
Richmond's Green
Essex 106 F2
Rich's Holford Som 42 G6
Rickard's Down Devon 24 B6
Rickarton Aberds 293 E10
Rickerby Cumb 239 F10
Rickerscote Staffs 151 E8
Rickford N Som 44 B3
Rickinghall Suff 125 B10
Rickleton T&W 243 G7
Rickling Essex 105 E9
Rickling Green Essex 105 F10
Rickmansworth Herts 85 G9
Rickney E Sus 23 D10
Riddell Borders 262 E2
Riddings Derbys 170 E6
Riddlecombe Devon 25 E10
Riddlesden W Yorks 205 E7
Riddrie Glasgow 268 B2
Ridgacre W Mid 133 G10
Ridge Bath 44 B5
Dorset 18 D4
Hants 32 D4
Herts 86 E2
Lancs 211 G9
Som 28 F3
Wilts 46 G3
Ridgebourne Powys 113 E11
Ridge Common Hants 34 C2
Ridge Green Sur 51 D10
Ridgehill N Som 60 G4
Ridge Hill Gtr Man 185 B7
Ridge Lane Warks 134 E5
Ridgemarsh Herts 85 G8
Ridge Row Kent 55 E8
Ridgeway Bristol 60 D6
Derbys 170 E5
Derbys 186 E6
Kent 54 E5
Newport 59 B9
Pembs 73 D10
Som 45 D8
Staffs 168 E5
Ridgeway Cross Hereford 98 B4
Ridgeway Moor Derbys 186 E6
Ridgewell Essex 106 C4
Ridgewood E Sus 23 B7
Ridgmont C Beds 103 D9
Ridgway Shrops 131 F7
Sur 50 B4
Riding Gate Som 30 B2
Riding Mill Northumb 242 E2
Ridley Kent 68 G6
Northumb 241 E7
Ridley Stokoe Northumb 250 F6
Ridleywood Wrex 166 E6
Ridlington Norf 160 C6
Rutland 136 C6
Ridlington Street Norf 160 C6
Ridsdale Northumb 251 G10
Riechip Perth 286 C4
Riemore Perth 286 C4
Rienachait Highld 306 F5
Rievaulx N Yorks 215 B11
Riff Orkney 314 E4
Riffin Aberds 303 E7
Rifle Green Torf 78 D3
Rift House Hrtlpl 234 E5
Rigg Dumfries 239 D7
Riggend N Lanark 278 G5
Rigsby Lincs 190 F6
Rigside S Lanark 259 B9
Riley Green Lancs 194 B6
Rileyhill Staffs 152 F2
Rilla Mill Corn 11 G11
Rillaton Corn 11 G11
Rillington N Yorks 217 E7
Rimac Lincs 191 C7
Rimington Lancs 204 D2
Rimpton Som 29 C10
Rimswell E Yorks 201 B10
Rimswell Valley
E Yorks 201 B10
Rinaston Pembs 91 F9
Rindleford Shrops 132 D4
Ringasta Shetland 313 M5
Ringford Dumfries 237 D8
Ringing Hill Leics 153 F9
Ringinglow S Yorks 186 E3
Ringland Newport 59 B11
Norf 160 G2
Ringles Cross E Sus 37 C7
Ringlestone Kent 53 B9
Kent 53 B11
Ringley Gtr Man 195 F9
Ringmer E Sus 36 E6
Ringmore Devon 8 F3
Ring o' Bells Lancs 194 E3
Ringorm Moray 302 E2
Ring's End Cambs 139 C7
Ringsfield Suff 143 F8
Ringsfield Corner Suff 143 F8
Ringshall Herts 85 C7
Suff 125 G10
Ringshall Stocks Suff 125 G10
Ringstead N Nhants 121 B9
Norf 176 E2
Ringtail Green Essex 87 B11
Ringwood Hants 31 F11
Ringwould Kent 55 D11
Rinmore Aberds 292 B6
Rinnigill Orkney 314 G3
Rinsey Corn 2 D3
Rinsey Croft Corn 2 D4
Riof W Isles 304 E3
Ripe E Sus 23 C8
Ripley Derbys 170 E5
Hants 19 B9
N Yorks 214 G5
Sur 50 B5
Riplingham E Yorks 208 G5
Ripon N Yorks 214 E6
Ripper's Cross Kent 54 E3
Rippingale Lincs 155 D11
Ripple Kent 55 D10
Worcs 99 D7
Ripponden W Yorks 196 D4
Rireavach Highld 307 K5
Risabus Argyll 254 C4
Risbury Hereford 115 G10
Risby E Yorks 208 G6
Lincs 189 C10
Suff 124 D5
Risca Caerph 78 G2
Rise E Yorks 209 E9
Rise Carr Darl 224 B5
Riseden E Sus 52 G6
Kent 53 F8
Rise End Derbys 170 D3
Risegate Lincs 156 D4
Riseholme Lincs 189 F7
Risehow Cumb 228 E6
Riseley Bedford 121 E10
Wokingham 65 G8
Rise Park London 87 G8
Nottingham 171 F9
Rishangles Suff 126 D3
Rishton Lancs 203 G10
Rishworth W Yorks 196 D4
Rising Bridge Lancs 195 B9
Risingbrook Staffs 151 E8
Risinghurst Oxon 83 D9
Rising Sun Corn 12 G3
Risley Derbys 153 B9
Warr 183 C10
Risplith N Yorks 214 F4
Rispond Highld 308 C4
Rivar Wilts 63 G10
Rivenhall Essex 88 B4
Rivenhall End Essex 88 B4
River Kent 55 E9
W Sus 34 C6
River Bank Cambs 123 D10
Riverhead Kent 52 B4
Rivers' Corner Dorset 30 E3
Riverside Cardiff 59 D7
Plym 7 D8
Stirling 278 C6
Worcs 117 D10
Riverside Docklands
Lancs 194 B4
Riverton Devon 40 G6
Riverview Park Kent 69 E7
Rivington Lancs 194 E6
Rixon Dorset 30 E3
Rixton Warr 183 C11
Roach Bridge Lancs 194 B5
Roaches Gtr Man 196 G3
Roachill Devon 26 C4
Roade W Nhants 120 G5
Road Green Norf 142 E5
Roadhead Cumb 240 C2
Roadmeetings S Lanark 269 F7
Roadside Highld 310 C5
Roadside of Catterline
Aberds 293 F10
Roadside of Kinneff
Aberds 293 F10
Roadwater Som 42 F4
Road Weedon W Nhants 120 F2
Roag Highld 298 E2
Roa Island Cumb 210 G4
Roast Green Essex 105 E9
Roath Cardiff 59 D7
Roath Park Cardiff 59 D7
Roberton Borders 261 G10
S Lanark 259 D10
Robertsbridge E Sus 38 C2
Robertstown Moray 302 E2
Rhondda 77 E8
Roberttown W Yorks 197 C7
Robeston Back Pembs 73 B9
Robeston Cross Pembs 72 D5
Robeston Wathen Pembs 73 B9
Robeston West Pembs 72 D5
Robhurst Kent 54 G2
Robin Hill Staffs 168 D6
Robin Hood Derbys 186 G3
Lancs 194 E4
W Yorks 197 B10
Robinhood End Essex 106 D4
Robin Hood's Bay
N Yorks 227 D9
Robins W Sus 34 B4
Robinson's End Warks 134 E6
Roborough Devon 7 C10
Devon 25 D9
Rob Roy's House Argyll 284 F5
Robroyston Glasgow 268 B2
Roby Mers 182 C6
Roby Mill Lancs 194 F4
Rocester Staffs 152 B2
Roch Pembs 91 G7
Rochdale Gtr Man 195 E11
Roche Corn 5 C9
Roche Grange Staffs 169 C7
Rochester Medway 69 F8
Northumb 251 D8
Rochford Essex 88 G5
Worcs 116 D2
Roch Gate Pembs 91 G7
Rock Caerph 77 F11
Corn 10 F4
Devon 28 G3
Neath 57 C9
Northumb 264 E6
Som 28 C4
Worcs 116 C4
W Sus 35 E10
Rockbeare Devon 14 C6
Rockbourne Hants 31 D10
Rockcliffe Cumb 239 E9
Dumfries 237 D10
Flint 182 G3
Lancs 195 C11
Rockcliffe Cross Cumb 239 E8
Rock End Staffs 168 D5
Rock Ferry Mers 182 D4
Rockfield Highld 311 L3
Mon 79 C7
Rockford Devon 41 D9
Hants 31 F11
Rockgreen Shrops 115 B10
Rockhampton S Glos 79 G11
Rockhead Corn 11 E7
Rockhill Shrops 114 B5
Rockingham N Nhants 137 E7
Rockland All Saints
Norf 141 D9
Rockland St Mary Norf 142 C6
Rockland St Peter Norf 141 D9
Rockley Notts 188 G2
Wilts 63 E7
Rockley Ford Som 45 C8
Rockness Glos 80 F4
Rockrobin E Sus 52 G6
Rocksavage Halton 183 E8
Rocks Park E Sus 37 C7
Rockstowes Glos 80 F3
Rockville Argyll 276 C4
Rockwell End Bucks 65 B9
Rockwell Green Som 27 C10
Rocky Hill Scilly 1 G4
Rodbaston Staffs 151 G8
Rodborough Glos 80 E4
Rodbourne Swindon 62 C6
Wilts 62 C2
Rodbourne Bottom Wilts 62 C2
Rodbourne Cheney
Swindon 62 B6
Rodbridge Corner
Essex 107 C7
Rodd Hereford 114 E6
Roddam Northumb 264 E2
Rodden Dorset 17 E8
Rodd Hurst Hereford 114 E6
Roddymoor Durham 233 D9
Rode Som 45 C10
Rodeheath Ches E 168 B5
Rode Heath Ches E 168 D3
Rode Hill Som 45 C10
Roden Telford 149 F11
Rodford S Glos 61 C7
Rodgrove Som 30 C2
Rodhuish Som 42 F4
Rodington Telford 149 G11
Rodington Heath
Telford 149 G11
Rodley Glos 80 C2
W Yorks 205 F10
Rodmarton Glos 80 F6
Rodmell E Sus 36 F6
Rodmer Clough
W Yorks 196 B3
Rodmersham Kent 70 G2
Rodmersham Green Kent 70 G2
Rodney Stoke Som 44 C3
Rodsley Derbys 170 G2
Rodway Som 43 F9
Telford 150 F3
Rodwell Dorset 17 F9
Roebuck Low Gtr Man 196 F3
Roecliffe N Yorks 215 F7
Roe Cross Gtr Man 185 B7
Roedean Brighton 36 G4
Roe End Herts 85 B8
Roe Green Gtr Man 195 G9
Herts 86 D2
Herts 104 E6
Roehampton London 67 E8
Roe Lee Blackburn 203 G9
Roesound Shetland 312 G5
Roestock Herts 86 D2
Roffey W Sus 51 G7
Rogart Highld 309 J7
Rogart Station Highld 309 J7
Rogate W Sus 34 C4
Roger Ground Cumb 221 F7
Rogerstone Newport 59 B9
Rogerton S Lanark 268 D2
Roghadal W Isles 296 C6
Rogiet Mon 60 B3
Rogue's Alley Cambs 139 B7
Roke Oxon 83 G10
Rokemarsh Oxon 83 G10
Roker T&W 243 F10
Rollesby Norf 161 F8
Rolleston Leics 136 C4
Notts 172 E2
Rollestone S Yorks 186 E5
Wilts 46 E5
Rollestone Camp Wilts 46 E5
Rolleston-on-Dove
Staffs 152 D4
Rolls Mill Dorset 30 E3
Rolston E Yorks 209 D10
Rolstone N Som 59 G11
Rolvenden Kent 53 G10
Rolvenden Layne Kent 53 G11
Romaldkirk Durham 232 G5
Romanby N Yorks 225 G7
Roman Hill Suff 143 E10
Romannobridge Borders 270 F3
Romansleigh Devon 26 C2
Rome Angus 293 G7
Romesdal Highld 298 D4
Romford Dorset 31 F9
Kent 52 E6
London 68 B4
Romiley Gtr Man 184 C6
Romney Street Kent 68 G4
Rompa Shetland 313 L6
Romsey Hants 32 C5
Romsey Town Cambs 123 F9
Romsley Shrops 132 G5
Worcs 117 B9
Romsley Hill Worcs 117 B9
Ronachan Ho Argyll 255 B8
Ronague IoM 192 E3
Rondlay Telford 132 B4
Ronkswood Worcs 117 G7
Rood End W Mid 133 F10
Rookby Cumb 222 C6
Rook End Essex 105 E11
Rookhope Durham 232 C4
Rooking Cumb 221 B8
Rookley IoW 20 E6
Rookley Green IoW 20 E6
Rooks Bridge Som 43 C11
Rooksey Green Suff 125 G8
Rooks Hill Kent 52 C5
Rooksmoor Glos 80 E4
Rook's Nest Som 42 G5
Rook Street Wilts 45 G10
Rookwith N Yorks 214 B4
Rookwood W Sus 21 B11
Roos E Yorks 209 G11
Roose Cumb 210 F4
Roosebeck Cumb 210 F5
Roosecote Cumb 210 F4
Roost End Essex 106 C4
Rootham's Green
Bedford 122 F2
Rooting Street Kent 54 D3
Rootpark S Lanark 269 E9
Ropley Hants 48 G6
Ropley Dean Hants 48 G6
Ropley Soke Hants 49 G7
Ropsley Lincs 155 C9
Rora Aberds 303 D10
Rorandle Aberds 293 B8
Rorrington Shrops 130 C5
Rosarie Moray 302 E3
Roscroggan Corn 4 G3
Rose Corn 4 E5
Roseacre Kent 53 B9
Lancs 202 F4
Rose-an-Grouse Corn 2 B2
Rose Ash Devon 26 C3
Rosebank E Dunb 278 G3
S Lanark 268 F6
Rosebery Midloth 270 D6
Rosebrae Moray 301 C11
Rosebrough Northumb 264 D4
Rosebush Pembs 91 F11
Rosecare Corn 11 B9
Rosedale Herts 86 E4
Rosedale Abbey
N Yorks 226 F4
Roseden Northumb 264 E2
Rosedinnick Corn 5 B8
Rosedown Devon 24 C3
Rosefield Highld 301 D8
Rose Green Essex 107 F8
Suff 107 C9
Suff 107 D8
W Sus 22 D6
Rose Grove Lancs 204 G2
Rosehall Highld 309 J4
N Lanark 268 C4
Rosehaugh Mains
Highld 300 D6
Rosehearty Aberds 303 C9
Rosehill Blackburn 195 C8
Corn 4 E5
Corn 5 C10
Gtr Man 184 D3
London 67 F9
Pembs 72 B5
Shrops 150 C3
T&W 243 D8
Rose Hill Bucks 66 C2
Derbys 153 B7
E Sus 23 B7
Gtr Man 195 F8
Lancs 204 G2
Oxon 83 E8
Suff 108 C3
Sur 51 D7
Roseisle Moray 301 C11
Roseland Corn 6 C5
Roselands E Sus 23 E10
Rosemarket Pembs 73 D7
Rosemarkie Highld 301 D7
Rosemary Lane Devon 27 E11
Rosemelling Corn 5 D10
Rosemergy Corn 1 B4
Rosemount Perth 286 C5
Rosenannon Corn 5 B9
Rosenithon Corn 3 E8
Roser's Cross E Sus 37 C9
Rose Valley Pembs 73 E8
Rosevean Corn 5 D10
Rosevear Corn 2 E5
Roseville W Mid 133 E8
Rosevine Corn 3 B9
Rosewarne Corn 2 B4
Corn 4 G2
Rosewell Midloth 270 C5
Roseworth Stockton 234 G4
Roseworthy Corn 2 B4
Corn 4 F5
Roseworthy Barton Corn 2 B4
Rosgill Cumb 221 B10
Rosherville Kent 68 E6
Roshven Highld 289 B9
Roskear Croft Corn 4 G3
Roskhill Highld 298 E2
Roskill House Highld 300 D6
Roskorwell Corn 3 E7
Rosley Cumb 230 B2
Roslin Midloth 270 C5
Rosliston Derbys 152 F4
Rosneath Argyll 276 E5
Ross Borders 273 C9
Dumfries 237 E8
Northumb 264 B4
Perth 285 E11
Rossett Wrex 166 D5
Rossett Green N Yorks 206 C2
Ross Green Worcs 116 E5
Rossie Ochill Perth 286 F4
Rossie Priory Perth 286 D6
Rossington S Yorks 187 B10
Rosskeen Highld 300 C6
Rossland Renfs 277 G8
Rossmore BCP 19 C7
Ross-on-Wye Hereford 98 G2
Roster Highld 310 F6
Rostherne Ches E 184 E2
Rostholme S Yorks 198 F5
Rosthwaite Cumb 220 C5
Cumb 220 G4
Roston Derbys 169 G10
Rosudgeon Corn 2 D3
Rosyth Fife 280 E2
Rotchfords Essex 107 E8
Rotcombe Bath 44 B6
Rothbury Northumb 252 C3
Rotherbridge W Sus 35 C7
Rotherby Leics 154 F3
Rotherfield E Sus 37 B9
Rotherfield Greys Oxon 65 C8
Rotherfield Peppard
Oxon 65 C8
Rotherham S Yorks 186 C6
Rotherhithe London 67 D11
Rothersthorpe
W Nhants 120 F4
Rotherwas Hereford 97 D10
Rotherwick Hants 49 B8
Rothes Moray 302 E2
Rothesay Argyll 275 G11
Rothiebrisbane Aberds 303 F7
Rothiemay Crossroads
Moray 302 E5
Rothiemurchus Lodge
Highld 291 C11
Rothienorman Aberds 303 F7
Rothiesholm Orkney 314 D6
Rothley Leics 153 G11
Northumb 252 F2
Rothley Plain Leics 153 G11
Rothley Shield East
Northumb 252 E2
Rothmaise Aberds 302 F6
Rothwell Lincs 189 B11
N Nhants 136 G6
W Yorks 197 B10
Rothwell Haigh
W Yorks 197 B10
Rotsea E Yorks 209 C7
Rottal Angus 292 G5
Rotten End Essex 106 F4
Suff 127 D7
Rotten Green Hants 49 B9
Rotten Row W Berks 64 E5
W Mid 118 B3
Rottingdean Brighton 36 G5
Rottington Cumb 219 C9
Rotton Park W Mid 133 F10
Roud IoW 20 E6
Rougham Norf 158 E6
Suff 125 E8
Rougham Green Suff 125 E8
Rough Bank Gtr Man 196 E2
Roughbirchworth
S Yorks 197 G9
Roughburn Highld 290 E5
Rough Close Staffs 151 B8
Rough Common Kent 54 B6
Roughcote Staffs 168 G6
Rough Haugh Highld 308 E7
Rough Hay Staffs 152 E4
Roughlee Lancs 204 E2
Roughley W Mid 134 D2
Roughmoor Som 28 B2
Swindon 62 B6
Roughrigg N Lanark 278 G6
Roughsike Cumb 240 B2
Roughton Lincs 174 C2
Norf 160 B4
Shrops 132 E5
Roughton Moor Lincs 174 C2
Roughway Kent 52 C6
Roundbush Essex 88 E5
Round Bush Herts 85 F10
Roundbush Green Essex 87 C9
Round Green Luton 103 G11
Roundham Som 28 F6
Roundhay W Yorks 206 F2
Round Maple Suff 107 C9
Round Oak Shrops 131 G7
W Mid 133 F8
Round's Green W Mid 133 F9
Roundshaw London 67 G10
Round Spinney
W Nhants 120 D5
Roundstonefoot
Dumfries 248 B4
Round Street Kent 69 F7
Roundstreet Common
W Sus 35 B9
Roundswell Devon 40 G4
Roundthorn Gtr Man 184 D4
Roundthwaite Cumb 222 E2
Roundway Wilts 62 G4
Roundyhill Angus 287 B7
Rousdon Devon 15 C11
Rousham Oxon 101 G9
Rous Lench Worcs 117 G10
Routenburn N Ayrs 266 C3
Routh E Yorks 209 E7
Rout's Green Bucks 84 F3
Row Corn 11 F7
Cumb 211 B8
Cumb 231 E8
Rowanburn Dumfries 239 B10
Rowanfield Glos 99 G8
Rowardennan Stirling 277 B7
Rowarth Derbys 185 D8
Row Ash Hants 33 E8
Rowbarton Som 28 B2
Rowberrow Som 44 B3
Row Brow Cumb 229 D7
Rowde Wilts 62 G3
Rowden Devon 13 B8
N Yorks 205 B11
Rowe Head Cumb 210 D5
Rowen Conwy 180 G3
Rowfoot Northumb 240 E5
Rowford Som 28 B2
Row Green Essex 106 G4
Row Heath Essex 89 B10
Rowhedge Essex 107 G10
Rowhill Sur 66 G4
Rowhook W Sus 50 G6
Rowington Warks 118 D4
Rowington Green
Warks 118 D4
Rowland Derbys 186 G2
Rowlands Castle Hants 34 E2
Rowlands Gill T&W 242 F5
Rowland's Green
Hereford 98 D3
Rowledge Sur 49 E10
Rowlestone Hereford 97 F7
Rowley E Yorks 208 G5
Shrops 130 B6
Rowley Green London 86 F2
Rowley Hill W Yorks 197 E7
Rowley Park Staffs 151 E8
Rowley Regis W Mid 133 F9
Rowley's Green W Mid 134 G6
Rowling Kent 55 C9
Rowly Sur 50 E4
Rownall Staffs 169 F7
Rowner Hants 33 G9
Rowney Green Worcs 117 C10
Rownhams Hants 32 D5
Row-of-trees Ches E 184 F4
Rowrah Cumb 219 B11
Rowsham Bucks 84 B4
Rowsley Derbys 170 B3
Rowstock Oxon 64 B3
Rowston Lincs 173 D9
Rowthorne Derbys 171 C7
Rowton Ches W 166 C6
Shrops 149 G7
Telford 150 F2
Rowton Moor Ches W 166 C6
Row Town Sur 66 G4
Roxburgh Borders 262 C5
Roxburgh Mains
Borders 262 D5
Roxby N Lincs 200 D2
N Yorks 226 B5
Roxeth London 66 B6
Roxton Bedford 122 G3
Roxwell Essex 87 D10
Royal British Legion Village
Kent 53 B8
Royal Leamington Spa
Warks 118 D6
Royal Oak Darl 233 G10
Lancs 194 G2
N Yorks 218 D2
Royal's Green Ches E 167 G10
Royal Tunbridge Wells
= *Tunbridge Wells* Kent 52 F5
Royal Wootton Bassett
Wilts 62 C5
Roybridge Highld 290 E4
Royd S Yorks 197 G8
Roydhouse W Yorks 197 E8
Royd Moor S Yorks 197 G8
W Yorks 198 E2
Roydon Essex 86 D6
Norf 141 G11
Norf 158 E4
Roydon Hamlet Essex 86 D6
Royds Green W Yorks 197 B11
Royston Glasgow 268 B2
Herts 105 C7
S Yorks 197 E11
Royston Water Som 28 E2
Royton Gtr Man 196 F2
Ruabon = *Rhiwabon*
Wrex 166 G4

Ruaig Argyll 288 E2
Ruan High Lanes Corn 3 B10
Ruan Lanihorne Corn 5 G7
Ruan Major Corn 2 F6
Ruan Minor Corn 2 F6
Ruarach Highld 295 C11
Ruardean Glos 79 B10
Ruardean Hill Glos 79 B10
Ruardean Woodside Glos 79 B10
Rubery Worcs 117 B9
Rubha Ghaisinis W Isles 297 G4
Rubha Stoer Highld 306 F5
Ruchazie Glasgow 268 B3
Ruchill Glasgow 267 B11
Ruckcroft Cumb 230 C6
Ruckhall Hereford 97 D9
Ruckinge Kent 54 G4
Ruckland Lincs 190 F4
Rucklers Lane Herts 85 E9
Ruckley Shrops 131 C10
Rudbaxton Pembs 91 G9
Rudby N Yorks 225 D9
Ruddington Notts 153 C11
Ruddle Glos 79 C11
Rudford Glos 98 G5
Rudge Shrops 132 D6
Som 45 C10
Rudge Heath Shrops 132 D5
Rudgeway S Glos 60 B6
Rudgwick W Sus 50 G5
Rudhall Hereford 98 F2
Rudheath Ches W 183 G11
Rudheath Woods Ches W 184 G2
Rudhja Garbh Argyll 289 E11
Rudley Green Essex 88 E4
Rudloe Wilts 61 E10
Rudry Caerph 59 B7
Rudston E Yorks 217 F11
Rudyard Staffs 169 D7
Ruewood Shrops 149 D9
Rufford Lancs 194 D3
Rufforth York 206 C6
Ruffs Notts 171 F8
Rugby Warks 119 B10
Rugeley Staffs 151 F10
Ruggin Som 27 D11
Ruglen S Ayrs 245 C7
Rugley Northumb 264 G5
Ruilick Highld 300 E5
Ruishton Som 28 C3
Ruisigearraidh W Isles 296 C5
Ruislip London 66 B5
Ruislip Common London 66 B5
Ruislip Gardens London 66 B5
Ruislip Manor London 66 B6
Ruiton W Mid 133 E8
Ruloe Ches W 183 G9
Rumach Highld 295 G8
Rumbling Bridge Perth 279 B10
Rumbow Cottages Worcs 117 B8
Rumburgh Suff 142 G6
Rumbush W Mid 118 B2
Rumer Hill Staffs 133 B9
Rumford Corn 10 G3
Falk 279 F8
Rumney Cardiff 59 D8
Rumsam Devon 40 G5
Rumwell Som 27 C11
Runcorn Halton 183 E8
Runcton W Sus 22 C5
Runcton Holme Norf 140 B2
Rundlestone Devon 13 G7
Runfold Sur 49 D11
Runhall Norf 141 B11
Runham Norf 143 B10
Norf 161 G9
Runham Vauxhall Norf 143 B10
Running Hill Head Gtr Man 196 F4
Runnington Som 27 C10
Running Waters Durham 234 C2
Runsell Green Essex 88 D3
Runshaw Moor Lancs 194 D4
Runswick Bay N Yorks 226 B6
Runwell Essex 88 G2
Ruscombe Glos 80 D4
Wokingham 65 D9
Ruscote Oxon 101 C8
Rushall Hereford 98 E2
Norf 142 G3
Wilts 46 B6
W Mid 133 C10
Rushbrooke Suff 125 E7
Rushbury Shrops 131 E10
Rushcombe Bottom BCP 18 B5
Rushden Herts 104 E6
N Nhants 121 D9
Rushenden Kent 70 E2
Rusher's Cross E Sus 37 B10
Rushey Mead Leicester 136 B2
Rushford Devon 12 F4
Norf 141 G8
Rushgreen Warr 183 D11
Rush Green Essex 89 B11
Herts 86 C5
Herts 104 G4
London 68 B4
Norf 141 B11
Rush-head Aberds 303 E8
Rush Hill Bath 61 G8
Rushington Hants 32 E5
Rushlake Green E Sus 23 B10
Rushland Cross Cumb 210 B6
Rushley Green Essex 106 D5
Rushmere C Beds 103 F8
Suff 143 F9
Rushmere St Andrew Suff 108 B4
Rushmere Street Suff 108 B4
Rushmoor Sur 49 E11
Telford 150 G2
Rushmore Hants 33 E11
Rushmore Hill London 68 G3
Rushock Hereford 114 F6
Worcs 117 C7
Rusholme Gtr Man 184 B5
Rushton Ches W 167 C9
Dorset 18 D3
N Nhants 136 G6
N Yorks 217 C9
Shrops 132 B2
Rushton Spencer Staffs 168 C6
Rushwick Worcs 116 G6
Rushyford Durham 233 F11
Rushy Green E Sus 23 C7
Ruskie Stirling 285 G10
Ruskington Lincs 173 E9
Rusland Cumb 210 B6
Rusling End Herts 104 G4
Rusper W Sus 51 F8
Ruspidge Glos 79 C11
Russel Highld 299 E8
Russell Hill London 67 G10
Russell's Green E Sus 38 E2
Russell's Hall W Mid 133 F8
Russell's Water Oxon 65 B8
Russel's Green Suff 126 C5
Russ Hill Sur 51 E8
Rusthall Kent 52 F5
Rustington W Sus 35 G9
Ruston N Yorks 217 C9
Ruston Parva E Yorks 217 G11
Ruswarp N Yorks 227 D7
Ruthall Shrops 131 F11
Rutherford Borders 262 C4
Rutherglen S Lanark 268 C2
Ruthernbridge Corn 5 B10
Ruthin V Glam 58 D3
Ruthin = Ruthun Denb 165 D10
Ruthrieston Aberdeen 293 C11
Ruthun = Ruthin Denb 165 D10
Ruthven Aberds 302 E5
Angus 286 C6
Highld 291 D9
Highld 301 F8
Ruthven House Angus 287 C7
Ruthvoes Corn 5 C8
Ruthwaite Cumb 229 D10
Ruthwell Dumfries 238 D3
Ruxley London 68 E3
Ruxton Hereford 97 F11
Ruxton Green Hereford 79 B8
Ruyton-XI-Towns Shrops 149 E7
Ryal Northumb 242 C2
Ryal Fold Blackburn 195 C7
Ryall Dorset 16 C4
Worcs 99 C7
Ryarsh Kent 53 B7
Rychraggan Highld 300 F4
Rydal Cumb 221 D7
Ryde IoW 21 C7
Rydens Sur 66 F6
Rydeshill Sur 50 C3
Rydon Devon 14 G3
Rye E Sus 38 C6
Ryebank Shrops 149 C10
Rye Common Hants 49 C9
Ryecroft S Yorks 186 B6
W Yorks 205 F7
Ryecroft Gate Staffs 168 C6
Ryeford Glos 80 E4
Rye Foreign E Sus 38 C5
Rye Harbour E Sus 38 D6
Ryehill E Yorks 201 B8
Ryeish Green Wokingham 65 F8
Ryelands Hereford 115 F9
Rye Park Herts 86 C5
Rye Street Worcs 98 D5
Ryeworth Glos 99 G9
Ryhall Rutland 155 G10
Ryhill W Yorks 197 E11
Ryhope T&W 243 G10
Rylah Derbys 171 B7
Rylands Notts 153 B10
Rylstone N Yorks 204 B5
Ryme Intrinseca Dorset 29 E9
Ryther N Yorks 207 F7
Ryton Glos 98 E4
N Yorks 216 D5
Shrops 132 C5
T&W 242 E5
Warks 135 F7
Ryton-on-Dunsmore Warks 119 C7
Ryton Woodside T&W 242 E4

S

Sabden Lancs 203 F11
Sabine's Green Essex 87 F8
Sackers Green Suff 107 D8
Sacombe Herts 86 B4
Sacombe Green Herts 86 B4
Sacriston Durham 233 B10
Sadberge Darl 224 B6
Saddell Argyll 255 D8
Saddell Ho Argyll 255 D8
Saddington Leics 136 E3
Saddle Bow Norf 158 F2
Saddlescombe W Sus 36 E3
Saddle Street Dorset 28 G5
Sadgill Cumb 221 D9
Saffron's Cross Hereford 115 G10
Saffron Walden Essex 105 D10
Sageston Pembs 73 E9
Saham Hills Norf 141 C8
Saham Toney Norf 141 C8
Saighdinis W Isles 296 E4
Saighton Ches W 166 C6
Sain Dunwyd = St Donats V Glam 58 F2
St Abbs Borders 273 B8
St Abb's Haven Borders 273 B8
St Agnes Corn 4 E4
Scilly 1 H3
St Albans Herts 85 D10
St Allen Corn 4 E6
St Andrews Fife 287 F9
St Andrew's Major V Glam 58 E6
St Andrew's Wood Devon 27 F9
St Annes Lancs 193 B10
St Anne's Park Bristol 60 E6
St Ann's Dumfries 248 E3
Nottingham 171 G9
St Ann's Chapel Corn 12 G4
Devon 8 F3
St Anthony Corn 3 C9
St Anthony-in-Meneage Corn 3 D7
St Anthony's T&W 243 E7
St Anthony's Hill E Sus 23 E10
St Arvans Mon 79 F8
St Asaph = Llanelwy Denb 181 G8
St Athan = Sain Tathon V Glam 58 F4
Sain Tathon = St Athan V Glam 58 F4
St Augustine's Kent 54 C6
St Austell Corn 5 E10
St Austins Hants 20 B2
St Bees Cumb 219 C9
St Blazey Corn 5 E11
St Blazey Gate Corn 5 E11
St Boswells Borders 262 C3
St Breock Corn 10 G5
St Breward Corn 11 F7
St Briavels Glos 79 E9
St Briavels Common Glos 79 E8
St Bride's Pembs 72 C4
St Brides Major = Saint-y-Brid V Glam 57 G11
St Bride's Netherwent Mon 60 B2
St Brides-super-Ely V Glam 58 D5
St Brides Wentlooge Newport 59 C9
Saintbridge Glos 80 B5
St Budeaux Plym 7 D8
Saintbury Glos 100 D2
St Buryan Corn 1 D4
St Catherine Bath 61 E9
St Catherine's Argyll 284 G5
St Catherine's Hill BCP 19 B8
St Chloe Glos 80 E4
St Clears = Sanclêr Carms 74 B3
St Cleer Corn 6 B5
St Clement Corn 4 G6
St Clether Corn 11 E10
St Colmac Argyll 275 G11
St Columb Major Corn 5 C8
St Columb Minor Corn 4 C6
St Columb Road Corn 5 D8
St Combs Aberds 303 C10
St Cross Hants 33 B7
St Cross South Elmham Suff 142 G5
St Cyrus Aberds 293 G9
St David's Perth 286 E3
St David's = Tyddewi Pembs 90 F5
St Day Corn 4 G4
St Decumans Som 42 E5
St Dennis Corn 5 D9
St Denys Soton 32 E6
St Devereux Hereford 97 E8
St Dials Torf 78 G3
St Dogmaels = Llandudoch Pembs 92 B3
St Dominick Corn 7 B8
St Donat's = Sain Dunwyd V Glam 58 F2
St Edith's Wilts 62 G3
St Endellion Corn 10 F5
St Enoder Corn 5 D7
St Erme Corn 4 E6
St Erney Corn 7 D7
St Erth Corn 2 B3
St Erth Praze Corn 2 B3
St Ervan Corn 10 G3
St Eval Corn 5 B7
St Ewe Corn 5 F9
St Fagans Cardiff 58 D6
St Fergus Aberds 303 D10
St Fillans Perth 285 E10
St Florence Pembs 73 E9
St Gennys Corn 11 B8
St George Bristol 60 E6
Conwy 181 F7
St George in the East London 67 C10
St Georges N Som 59 G11
St George's Gtr Man 184 B4
Telford 150 G4
V Glam 58 D5
St George's Hill Sur 66 G5
St George's Well Devon 27 F8
St Germans Corn 7 D7
St Giles Lincs 189 G7
London 67 C10
St Giles in the Wood Devon 25 D8
St Giles on the Heath Devon 12 C3
St Giles's Hill Hants 33 B7
St Gluvias Corn 3 C7
St Godwalds Worcs 117 D9
St Harmon Powys 113 C9
St Helena Warks 134 C5
St Helen Auckland Durham 233 F9
St Helens Cumb 228 E6
IoW 21 D8
Mers 183 B8
St Helen's E Sus 38 E4
S Yorks 197 F11
St Helen's Wood E Sus 38 E4
St Helier London 67 F9
St Hilary Corn 2 C3
V Glam 58 E4
Saint Hill Devon 27 F9
W Sus 51 F11
St Ibbs Herts 104 F3
St Illtyd Bl Gwent 78 E2
St Ippollytts Herts 104 F3
St Ishmael's Pembs 72 D4
St Issey Corn 10 G4
St Ive Corn 6 B6
St Ive Cross Corn 6 B6
St Ives Cambs 122 C6
Corn 2 A2
Dorset 31 G10
St James Dorset 30 C5
London 67 C9
Norf 160 E5
St James's End W Nhants 120 E4
St James South Elmham Suff 142 G6
St Jidgey Corn 5 B8
St John Corn 7 E8
St Johns London 67 D11
Warks 118 C5
St John's E Sus 52 G4
IoM 192 D3
Kent 52 B4
Kent 52 E5
Sur 50 B3
Worcs 116 G6
W Yorks 206 F4
St John's Chapel Devon 25 B8
Durham 232 D3
St John's Fen End Norf 157 G10
St John's Highway Norf 157 G10
St John's Park IoW 21 C8
St John's Town of Dalry Dumfries 246 G4
St John's Wells Aberds 303 F7
St John's Wood London 67 C9
St Judes IoM 192 C4
St Julians Herts 85 D10
Newport 59 B10
St Just Corn 1 C3
St Justinian Pembs 90 F4
St Just in Roseland Corn 3 B9
St Katharines Wilts 63 G9
St Katherine's Aberds 303 F7
St Keverne Corn 3 E7
St Kew Corn 10 F6
St Kew Highway Corn 10 F6
St Keyne Corn 6 C4
St Lawrence Corn 5 B10
Essex 89 E7
IoW 20 F6
Kent 71 F11
St Leonards Dorset 31 G10
E Sus 38 F3
S Lanark 268 E2
St Leonard's Bucks 84 D6
St Leonard's Street Kent 53 B7
St Levan Corn 1 E3
St Luke's Derby 152 B6
London 67 C10
St Lythans V Glam 58 E6
St Mabyn Corn 10 G6
St Madoes Perth 286 E5
St Margarets Herts 86 C5
London 67 E7
St Margaret's Hereford 97 E7
St Margaret's at Cliffe Kent 55 E11
St Margaret's Hope Orkney 314 G4
St Margaret South Elmham Suff 142 G6
St Mark's Glos 99 G8
IoM 192 E3
St Martin Corn 2 E6
Corn 6 E5
St Martins Perth 286 D5
St Martin's Shrops 148 B6
St Martin's Moor Shrops 148 B6
St Mary Bourne Hants 48 C2
St Marychurch Torbay 9 B8
St Mary Church V Glam 58 E4
St Mary Cray London 68 F3
St Mary Hill V Glam 58 D3
St Mary Hoo Medway 69 D10
St Mary in the Marsh Kent 39 B9
St Mary's Orkney 314 F4
St Mary's Bay Kent 39 B9
St Maughans Mon 79 B7
St Maughans Green Mon 79 B7
St Mawes Corn 3 C8
St Mawgan Corn 5 B7
St Mellion Corn 7 B7
St Mellons Cardiff 59 C8
St Merryn Corn 10 G3
St Mewan Corn 5 E9
St Michael Caerhays Corn 5 G9
St Michael Church Som 43 G10
St Michael Penkevil Corn 5 G7
St Michaels Kent 53 F11
Torbay 9 C7
Worcs 115 D11
St Michael's Hamlet Mers 182 D5
St Michael's on Wyre Lancs 202 E5
St Michael South Elmham Suff 142 G6
St Minver Corn 10 F5
St Monans Fife 287 G9
St Neot Corn 6 B3
St Neots Cambs 122 E3
St Newlyn East Corn 4 D6
St Nicholas Herts 104 F5
Pembs 91 D7
V Glam 58 E5
St Nicholas at Wade Kent 71 F9
St Nicholas South Elmham Suff 142 G6
St Nicolas Park Warks 135 E7
St Ninians Stirling 278 C5
St Olaves Norf 143 D9
St Osyth Essex 89 B10
St Osyth Heath Essex 89 B10
St Owens Cross Hereford 97 G10
St Pancras London 67 C10
St Paul's Glos 80 B4
St Paul's Cray London 68 F3
St Paul's Walden Herts 104 G3
St Peters Kent 71 F11
St Peter's Glos 99 G8
T&W 243 E7
St Peter South Elmham Suff 142 G6
St Peter The Great Worcs 117 G7
St Petrox Pembs 73 F7
St Pinnock Corn 6 C4
St Quivox S Ayrs 257 E9
St Ruan Corn 2 F6
Saint's Hill Kent 52 E4
St Stephen Corn 5 E8
St Stephens Corn 7 D8
Herts 85 D10
St Stephen's Corn 12 D2
St Teath Corn 11 E7
St Thomas Devon 14 C4
Swansea 57 C7
St Tudy Corn 11 F7
St Twynnells Pembs 73 F7
St Veep Corn 6 E2
St Vigeans Angus 287 C10
St Vincent's Hamlet Essex 87 G9
St Wenn Corn 5 C9
St Weonards Hereford 97 G9
St Winnow Corn 6 D2
Saint y Brid = St Brides Major V Glam 57 G11
St y-Nyll V Glam 58 D5
Saith ffynnon Flint 181 F11
Salcombe Devon 9 G9
Salcombe Regis Devon 15 D9
Salcott-cum-Virley Essex 88 C6
Salden Bucks 102 F6
Sale Gtr Man 184 C3
Saleby Lincs 191 F7
Sale Green Worcs 117 F8
Salehurst E Sus 38 C2
Salem Carms 94 F2
Ceredig 128 G3
Corn 4 G4
Salen Argyll 289 E7
Highld 289 C8
Salendine Nook W Yorks 196 D6
Salenside Borders 261 E11
Salesbury Lancs 203 G9
Saleway Worcs 117 F8
Salford C Beds 103 D8
Gtr Man 184 B4
Oxon 100 F5
Salford Ford C Beds 103 D8
Salford Priors Warks 117 G11
Salfords Sur 51 D9
Salhouse Norf 160 G6
Saligo Argyll 274 G3
Salisbury Wilts 31 B10
Salkeld Dykes Cumb 230 D6
Sallachan Highld 289 C11
Sallachy Highld 295 B11
Highld 309 J5
Salle Norf 160 E2
Salmans Kent 52 E4
Salmonby Lincs 190 G4
Salmond's Muir Angus 287 D9
Salmonhutch Devon 14 B2
Salperton Glos 99 G11
Salperton Park Glos 81 B9
Salph End Bedford 121 G11
Salsburgh N Lanark 268 C6
Salt Staffs 151 D9
Salta Cumb 229 B7
Saltaire W Yorks 205 F8
Saltash Corn 7 D8
Saltburn Highld 301 C7
Saltburn-by-the-Sea Redcar 235 G9
Saltby Leics 155 D7
Salt Coates Cumb 238 G5
Saltcoats Cumb 219 F11
E Loth 281 E9
N Ayrs 266 G4
Saltcotes Lancs 193 B11
Saltdean Brighton 36 G5
Salt End E Yorks 201 B7
Salter Lancs 212 G2
Salterbeck Cumb 228 F5
Salterforth Lancs 204 D3
Salters Heath Hants 48 B6
Saltershill Shrops 150 D2
Salters Lode Norf 139 C11
Salter Street W Mid 118 C2
Salterswall Ches W 167 B10
Salterton Wilts 46 F6
Saltfleet Lincs 191 C7
Saltfleetby All Saints Lincs 191 C7
Saltfleetby St Clement Lincs 191 C7
Saltfleetby St Peter Lincs 190 D6
Saltford Bath 61 F7
Salt Hill Slough 66 C3
Salthouse Cumb 210 F4
Norf 177 E9
Saltley W Mid 133 F11
Saltmarsh Newport 59 C11
Saltmarshe E Yorks 199 C9
Saltness Orkney 314 G2
Shetland 313 J4
Saltney Flint 166 B5
Salton N Yorks 216 D4
Saltrens Devon 25 C7
Saltwell T&W 243 E7
Saltwick Northumb 242 B5
Saltwood Kent 55 F7
Salum Argyll 288 E2
Salvington W Sus 35 F10
Salwarpe Worcs 117 E7
Salwayash Dorset 16 B5
Sambourne Warks 117 E11
Wilts 45 E11
Sambrook Telford 150 E4
Samhla W Isles 296 E3
Samlesbury Lancs 203 G7
Samlesbury Bottoms Lancs 194 B6
Sampford Arundel Som 27 D10
Sampford Brett Som 42 E5
Sampford Chapple Devon 25 G10
Sampford Courtenay Devon 25 G10
Sampford Moor Som 27 D10
Sampford Peverell Devon 27 E8
Sampford Spiney Devon 12 G6
Sampool Bridge Cumb 211 B9
Samuel's Corner Essex 70 B3
Samuelston E Loth 281 G9
Sanachan Highld 299 E8
Sanaigmore Argyll 274 F3
Sanclêr = St Clears Carms 74 B3
Sancreed Corn 1 D4
Sancton E Yorks 208 F4
Sand Highld 307 K4
Shetland 313 J5
Som 44 D2
Sandaig Highld 295 E9
Sandal W Yorks 197 D10
Sandale Cumb 229 C10
Sandal Magna W Yorks 197 D10
Sandavore Highld 294 G6
Sandbach Ches E 168 C3
Sandbach Heath Ches E 168 C3
Sandbank Argyll 276 E3
Sandbanks BCP 18 D6
Kent 70 G4
Sandborough Staffs 152 F2
Sandbraes Lincs 200 G6
Sandend Aberds 302 C5
Sanderstead London 67 G10
Sandfields Glos 99 G8
Neath 57 C8
Staffs 134 B2
Sandford Cumb 222 B4
Devon 26 G4
Dorset 18 D4
Hants 31 G11
IoW 20 E6
N Som 44 B2
Shrops 148 E6
Shrops 149 C11
S Lanark 268 G4
Worcs 99 B7
W Yorks 205 F11
Sandford Batch N Som 44 B2
Sandfordhill Aberds 303 E11
Sandford Hill Stoke 168 G6
Sandford on Thames Oxon 83 E8
Sandford Orcas Dorset 29 C10
Sandford St Martin Oxon 101 F8
Sandgate Kent 55 G7
Sand Gate Cumb 211 D7
Sandgreen Dumfries 237 D7
Sandhaven Aberds 303 C9
Argyll 276 E3
Sandhead Dumfries 236 E2
Sandhill Bucks 102 F4
Cambs 139 F11
S Yorks 198 F2
Sandhills Dorset 29 E11
Dorset 29 G9
Mers 182 C4
Oxon 83 D9
Sur 50 F2
W Yorks 206 F3
Sandhoe Northumb 241 D11
Sandhole Argyll 275 D11
Sand Hole E Yorks 208 F2
Sandholme E Yorks 208 G2
Lincs 156 B6
Sandhurst Brack 65 G10
Glos 98 G6
Kent 38 B3
Sandhurst Cross Kent 38 B3
Sandhutton N Yorks 215 C7
Sand Hutton N Yorks 207 B9
Sandiacre Derbys 153 B9
Sandilands Lincs 191 E8
S Lanark 259 B9
Sandiway Ches W 183 G10
Sandleheath Hants 31 E10
Sandling Kent 53 B9
Sandlow Green Ches E 168 B3
Sandness Shetland 313 H3
Sandon Essex 88 E2
Herts 104 E6
Staffs 151 C8
Sandonbank Staffs 151 D8
Sandown IoW 21 E7
Sandown Park Kent 52 E6
Sandpit Dorset 28 G6
Sandpits Glos 98 F6
Sandplace Corn 6 D5
Sandridge Herts 85 C11
Wilts 62 F2
Sandringham Norf 158 D3
Sands Bucks 84 G4
Sandsend N Yorks 227 C7
Sands End London 67 D9
Sandside Cumb 210 D6
Cumb 211 C9
Orkney 314 F2
Sand Side Cumb 210 C4
Lancs 202 C4
Sandside Ho Highld 310 C3
Sandsound Shetland 313 J5
Sandtoft N Lincs 199 F8
Sandvoe Shetland 312 D5
Sandway Kent 53 C11
Sandwell W Mid 133 F10
Sandwich Kent 55 B10
Sandwich Bay Estate Kent 55 B11
Sandwick Cumb 221 B8
Orkney 314 H4
Shetland 313 L6
Sandwith Cumb 219 C9
Sandwith Newtown Cumb 219 C9
Sandy Carms 75 E7
C Beds 104 B3
Sandybank Orkney 314 C5
Sandy Bank Lincs 174 E3
Sandy Carrs Durham 234 C3
Sandycroft Flint 166 B4
Sandy Cross E Sus 37 C9
Sur 49 D11
Sandy Down Hants 20 B2
Sandyford Dumfries 248 E6
Stoke 168 E5
Sandygate Devon 14 G3
IoM 192 C4
S Yorks 186 D4
Sandy Gate Devon 14 C5
Sandy Haven Pembs 72 D5
Sandyhills Dumfries 237 D10
Sandylake Corn 6 C2
Sandylands Lancs 211 G8
Som 27 C10
Sandylane Swansea 56 D5
Sandy Lane Wilts 62 F3
Wrex 166 G5
W Yorks 205 F8
Sandypark Devon 13 D10
Sandysike Cumb 239 D9
Sandy Way IoW 20 E5
Sangobeg Highld 308 C4
Sangomore Highld 308 C4
Sanham Green W Berks 63 F10
Sankey Bridges Warr 183 D9
Sankyns Green Worcs 116 E5
Sanna Highld 288 C6
Sanndabhaig W Isles 297 G4
W Isles 304 E6
Sannox N Ayrs 255 C11
Sanquhar Dumfries 247 B7
Sansaw Heath Shrops 149 E10
Santon Cumb 220 E2
N Lincs 200 E2
Santon Bridge Cumb 220 E2
Santon Downham Suff 140 F6
Sapcote Leics 135 E9
Sapey Bridge Worcs 116 F4
Sapey Common Hereford 116 E4
Sapiston Suff 125 B8
Sapley Cambs 122 C4
Sapperton Derbys 152 C3
Glos 80 E6
Lincs 155 C10
Saracen's Head Lincs 156 D6
Sarclet Highld 310 E7
Sardis Carms 75 D9
Pembs 73 D10
Sarisbury Hants 33 F8
Sarn Bridgend 58 C2
Flint 181 F10
Powys 130 E4
Sarnau Carms 74 B4
Ceredig 110 G6
Gwyn 147 B9
Powys 95 E10
Powys 148 F4
Sarn Bach Gwyn 144 D6
Sarnesfield Hereford 115 G7
Sarn Meyllteyrn Gwyn 144 C4
Saron Carms 75 C10
Carms 93 D7
Denb 165 C8
Gwyn 163 B8
Gwyn 163 D7
Sarratt Herts 85 F8
Sarratt Bottom Herts 85 F8
Sarre Kent 71 G9
Sarsden Oxon 100 G5
Sarsden Halt Oxon 100 G5
Sarsgrum Highld 308 C3
Sasaig Highld 295 E8
Sascott Shrops 149 G8
Satley Durham 233 C8
Satmar Kent 55 F9
Satran Highld 294 B6
Satron N Yorks 223 F8
Satterleigh Devon 25 C11
Satterthwaite Cumb 220 G6
Satwell Oxon 65 C8
Sauchen Aberds 293 B8
Saucher Perth 286 D5
Sauchie Clack 279 C7
Sauchieburn Aberds 293 G8
Saughall Ches W 182 G5
Saughall Massie Mers 182 D3
Saughton Edin 280 G4
Saughtree Borders 250 D3
Saul Glos 80 D2
Saundby Notts 188 D3
Saundersfoot = Llanusyllt Pembs 73 E10
Saunderton Bucks 84 E3
Saunderton Lee Bucks 84 F4
Saunton Devon 40 F3
Sausthorpe Lincs 174 B5
Saval Highld 309 J5
Savary Highld 289 E8
Saveock Corn 4 F5
Saverley Green Staffs 151 B9
Savile Park W Yorks 196 C5
Savile Town W Yorks 197 C8
Sawbridge Warks 119 D10
Sawbridgeworth Herts 87 B7
Sawdon N Yorks 217 B8
Sawley Derbys 153 C9
Lancs 203 D11
N Yorks 214 F4
Sawood W Yorks 204 G6
Sawston Cambs 105 B9
Sawtry Cambs 138 G3
Sawyers Hill Wilts 81 G8
Sawyer's Hill Som 27 C11
Saxby Leics 154 F6
Lincs 189 D8
W Sus 35 G7
Saxby All Saints N Lincs 200 D3
Saxelbye Leics 154 E4
Saxham Street Suff 125 E11
Saxilby Lincs 188 F5
Saxlingham Norf 159 B10
Saxlingham Green Norf 142 D4
Saxlingham Nethergate Norf 142 D4
Saxlingham Thorpe Norf 142 D4
Saxmundham Suff 127 E7
Saxondale Notts 154 B3
Saxon Street Cambs 124 F3
Saxtead Suff 126 D5
Saxtead Green Suff 126 E5
Saxtead Little Green Suff 126 D5
Saxthorpe Norf 160 C2
Saxton N Yorks 206 F5
Sayers Common W Sus 36 D3
Scackleton N Yorks 216 E2
Scadabhagh W Isles 305 J3
Scaftworth Notts 187 C11
Scagglethorpe N Yorks 216 E6
Scaitcliffe Lancs 195 B9
Scaladal W Isles 305 G3
Scalan Moray 292 B4
Scalasaig Argyll 274 D4
Scalby E Yorks 199 B10
N Yorks 227 G10
Scald End Bedford 121 F10
Scaldwell W Nhants 120 C5
Scaleby Cumb 239 E11
Scalebyhill Cumb 239 E10
Scale Hall Lancs 211 G9
Scale Houses Cumb 231 B7
Scales Cumb 210 E5
Cumb 230 F2
Cumb 231 C7
Lancs 202 G5
Scalford Leics 154 E5
Scaling Redcar 226 C4
Scaliscro W Isles 304 F3
Scallasaig Highld 295 D10
Scallastle Argyll 289 F8
Scalloway Shetland 313 K6
Scalpay W Isles 305 J4
Scalpay Ho Highld 295 C8
Scalpsie Argyll 255 B11
Scamadale Highld 295 F9
Scamblesby Lincs 190 F3
Scamland E Yorks 207 E11
Scammadale Argyll 289 G10
Scamodale Highld 289 B10
Scampston N Yorks 217 D7
Scampton Lincs 189 F7
Scaniport Highld 300 F6
Scapa Orkney 314 F4
Scapegoat Hill W Yorks 196 D5
Scar Orkney 314 B6
Scarborough N Yorks 217 B10
Scarcewater Corn 5 E8
Scarcliffe Derbys 171 B7
Scarcroft W Yorks 206 E3
Scarcroft Hill W Yorks 206 E3
Scardroy Highld 300 D2
Scarff Shetland 312 E4
Scarfskerry Highld 310 B6
Scargill Durham 223 C11
Scar Head Cumb 220 G5
Scarinish Argyll 288 E2
Scarisbrick Lancs 193 E11
Scarness Cumb 229 E10
Scarning Norf 159 G9
Scarrington Notts 172 G2
Scarth Hill Lancs 194 F2
Scarthingwell N Yorks 206 F5
Scartho NE Lincs 201 F9
Scarvister Shetland 313 J5
Scarwell Orkney 314 D2
Scatness Shetland 313 M5
Scatraig Highld 301 F7
Scatwell Ho Highld 300 D3
Scawby N Lincs 200 F3
Scawsby S Yorks 198 G5
Scawthorpe S Yorks 198 F5
Scawton N Yorks 215 C10
Scayne's Hill W Sus 36 C5
Scethrog Powys 96 F2
Scholar Green Ches E 168 D4
Scholemoor W Yorks 205 G8
Scholes Gtr Man 194 F5
S Yorks 186 B5
W Yorks 197 B7
W Yorks 197 F7
W Yorks 204 F6
W Yorks 206 F3
Scholey Hill W Yorks 197 B11
School Aycliffe Durham 233 G11
Schoolgreen Wokingham 65 F8
School Green Ches W 167 C10
Essex 106 E4
IoW 20 D2
W Yorks 205 G8
Schoolhill Aberds 293 D11
School House Dorset 28 G5
Sciberscross Highld 309 H7
Scilly Bank Cumb 219 B9
Scissett W Yorks 197 E8
Scleddau Pembs 91 E8
Scofton Notts 187 E10
Scole Norf 126 B2
Scole Common Norf 142 G2
Scolpaig W Isles 296 D3
Scone Perth 286 E5
Sconser Highld 295 B7
Scoonie Fife 287 G7
Scoor Argyll 274 B5
Scopwick Lincs 173 D9
Scoraig Highld 307 K5
Scorborough E Yorks 208 D6
Scorrier Corn 4 G4
Scorriton Devon 8 B4
Scorton Lancs 202 D6
N Yorks 224 E5
Sco Ruston Norf 160 E5
Scotbheinn W Isles 296 F4
Scotby Cumb 239 G10
Scotch Corner N Yorks 224 E4
Scotches Derbys 170 F4
Scotforth Lancs 202 B5
Scotgate W Yorks 196 E6
Scot Hay Staffs 168 F4
Scothern Lincs 189 F8
Scotland Leics 136 D3
Leics 153 E7
Lincs 155 C10
W Berks 64 F5
Scotland End Oxon 100 E6
Scotland Gate Northumb 253 G7
Scotlands W Mid 133 C8
Scotland Street Suff 107 D9
Scotlandwell Perth 286 G5
Scot Lane End Gtr Man 194 F6
Scotsburn Highld 301 B7
Scotscalder Station Highld 310 D4
Scotscraig Fife 287 E8
Scots' Gap Northumb 252 F2
Scotston Aberds 293 F9
Perth 286 C3
Scotstoun Glasgow 267 B10
Scotstown Highld 289 C10
Scotswood T&W 242 E5
Windsor 66 F2
Scottas Highld 295 E9
Scotter Lincs 199 G11
Scotterthorpe Lincs 199 G11
Scottlethorpe Lincs 155 E11
Scotton Lincs 188 B5
N Yorks 206 B2
N Yorks 224 F3
Scottow Norf 160 E5
Scott Willoughby Lincs 155 B11
Scoughall E Loth 282 E2
Scoulag Argyll 266 D2
Scoulton Norf 141 C9
Scounslow Green Staffs 151 D11
Scourie Highld 306 E6
Scourie More Highld 306 E6
Scousburgh Shetland 313 M5
Scout Dike S Yorks 197 G8
Scout Green Cumb 221 D11
Scouthead Gtr Man 196 F3
Scowles Glos 79 C9
Scrabster Highld 310 B4
Scraesburgh Borders 262 F5
Scrafield Lincs 174 B4
Scragged Oak Kent 69 G10
Scrainwood Northumb 251 B11
Scrane End Lincs 174 G5
Scrapsgate Kent 70 E2
Scraptoft Leics 136 B2
Scrapton Som 28 E3
Scratby Norf 161 F10
Scrayingham N Yorks 216 G4
Scredda Corn 5 E10
Scredington Lincs 173 G9
Screedy Som 27 B9
Scremby Lincs 174 B6
Scremerston Northumb 273 F10
Screveton Notts 172 G2
Scrivelsby Lincs 174 B3
Scriven N Yorks 206 B2
Scronkey Lancs 202 D4
Scrooby Notts 187 C11
Scropton Derbys 152 C3
Scrub Hill Lincs 174 D2
Scruton N Yorks 224 G5
Scrwgan Powys 148 E3
Scuddaborg Highld 298 C3
Scuggate Cumb 239 C10
Sculcoates Hull 209 G7
Sculthorpe Norf 159 C7
Scunthorpe N Lincs 199 E11
Scurlage Swansea 56 D3
Sea Som 28 E4
Seaborough Dorset 28 F6
Seabridge Staffs 168 G4
Seabrook Kent 55 G7
Seaburn T&W 243 F10
Seacombe Mers 182 C4
Seacox Heath Kent 53 G8
Seacroft Lincs 175 C9
W Yorks 206 F3
Seadyke Lincs 156 B6
Seafar N Lanark 278 G5
Seafield Highld 311 L3
Midloth 270 C5
S Ayrs 257 E8
W Loth 269 B10
Seaford E Sus 23 F7
Seaforth Mers 182 B4
Seagrave Leics 154 F2
Seagry Heath Wilts 62 C3
Seaham Durham 234 B4
Seahouses Northumb 264 C6
Seal Kent 52 B4
Sealand Flint 166 B5
Seale Sur 49 D11
Seamer N Yorks 217 C10
N Yorks 225 C9
Seamill N Ayrs 266 F4
Sea Mill Cumb 210 F5
Sea Mills Bristol 60 D5
Corn 10 G4
Sea Palling Norf 161 D8
Searby Lincs 200 F5
Seasalter Kent 70 F5
Seascale Cumb 219 E10
Seathorne Lincs 175 B9
Seathwaite Cumb 220 C4
Cumb 220 F4
Seatle Cumb 211 C7
Seatoller Cumb 220 C4
Seaton Corn 6 E6
Cumb 228 E6
Devon 15 C10
Durham 243 G9
E Yorks 209 D9
Kent 55 B8
Northumb 243 B8
Rutland 137 D8
Seaton Burn T&W 242 C6
Seaton Carew Hrtlpl 234 F6
Seaton Delaval Northumb 243 B8
Seaton Ross E Yorks 207 E11
Seaton Sluice Northumb 243 B8
Seatown Aberds 302 C5
Aberds 303 D11
Dorset 16 C4
Seaureaugh Moor Corn 2 B6
Seave Green N Yorks 225 E11
Seaview IoW 21 C8
Seaville Cumb 238 G5
Seavington St Mary Som 28 E6
Seavington St Michael Som 28 D6
Seawick Essex 89 C10
Sebastopol Torf 78 F3
Sebay Orkney 314 F5
Sebergham Cumb 230 C3
Sebiston Velzian Orkney 314 D2
Seckington Warks 134 B5
Second Coast Highld 307 K4
Second Drove Cambs 139 F10
Sedbergh Cumb 222 G3
Sedbury Glos 79 G8
Sedbusk N Yorks 223 G7
Seddington C Beds 104 B3
Sedgeberrow Worcs 99 D10
Sedgebrook Lincs 155 B7
Sedgefield Durham 234 F3
Sedgeford Norf 158 B4
Sedgehill Wilts 30 B5
Sedgemere W Mid 118 B4
Sedgley W Mid 133 E8
Sedgley Park Gtr Man 195 G10
Sedgwick Cumb 211 B10
Sedlescombe E Sus 38 D3
Sedlescombe Street E Sus 38 D3
Sedrup Bucks 84 C3
Seed Kent 54 B2
Seed Lee Lancs 194 C5
Seedley Gtr Man 184 B4
Seend Wilts 62 G2
Seend Cleeve Wilts 62 G2
Seend Head Wilts 62 G2
Seer Green Bucks 85 G7
Seething Norf 142 D6
Seething Wells London 67 F7
Sefton Mers 193 G11
Segensworth Hants 33 F8
Seggat Aberds 303 E7
Seghill Northumb 243 C7
Seifton Shrops 131 G9

Seighford Staffs 151 D7
Seilebost W Isles 305 J2
Seion Gwyn 163 B8
Seisdon Staffs 132 E6
Seisiadar W Isles 304 E7
Selattyn Shrops 148 C5
Selborne Hants 49 G8
Selby N Yorks 207 G8
Selgrove Kent 54 B4
Selham W Sus 34 C6
Selhurst London 67 F10
Selkirk Borders 261 D11
Sellack Hereford 97 F11
Sellack Boat Hereford 97 F11
Sellafirth Shetland 312 D7
Sellan Corn 1 C4
Sellibister Orkney 314 B7
Sellick's Green Som 28 D2
Sellindge Kent 54 F6
Selling Kent 54 B4
Sells Green Wilts 62 G3
Selly Hill N Yorks 227 D7
Selly Oak W Mid 133 G10
Selly Park W Mid 133 G11
Selmeston E Sus 23 D8
Selsdon London 67 G10
Selsey W Sus 22 E5
Selsfield Common
W Sus 51 G10
Selside Cumb 221 F10
N Yorks 212 D5
Selsley Glos 80 E4
Selsmore Hants 21 B10
Selson Kent 55 B10
Selsted Kent 55 E8
Selston Notts 171 E7
Selston Common Notts 171 E7
Selston Green Notts 171 E7
Selwick Orkney 314 F2
Selworthy Som 42 D2
Semblister Shetland 313 H5
Semer Suff 107 B9
Sem Hill Wilts 30 B5
Semington Wilts 61 G11
Semley Wilts 30 B5
Sempringham Lincs 156 C2
Send Sur 50 B4
Send Grove Sur 50 C4
Send Marsh Sur 50 B4
Senghenydd Caerph 77 G10
Sennen Corn 1 D3
Sennen Cove Corn 1 D3
Sennybridge = *Pont Senni*
Powys 95 F8
Serlby Notts 187 D10
Serrington Wilts 46 F5
Sessay N Yorks 215 D9
Setchey Norf 158 G2
Setley Hants 32 G4
Seton E Loth 281 G8
Seton Mains E Loth 281 F8
Setter Shetland 312 E6
Shetland 313 H5
Shetland 313 J7
Shetland 313 L6
Settiscarth Orkney 314 E3
Settle N Yorks 212 G6
Settrington N Yorks 216 E6
Seven Ash Som 43 G7
Sevenhampton Glos 99 G10
Swindon 82 G2
Seven Kings London 68 B3
Sevenoaks Kent 52 C4
Sevenoaks Common
Kent 52 C4
Sevenoaks Weald Kent 52 C4
Seven Sisters = *Blaendulais*
Neath 76 D4
Seven Springs Glos 81 B7
Seven Star Green Essex 107 F8
Severn Beach S Glos 60 B4
Severnhampton Swindon 82 G2
Severn Stoke Worcs 99 C7
Sevick End Bedford 121 G11
Sevington Kent 54 E4
Sewards End Essex 105 D11
Sewardstone Essex 86 F5
Sewardstonebury Essex 86 F5
Sewell C Beds 103 G9
Sewerby E Yorks 218 F3
Seworgan Corn 2 C6
Sewstern Leics 155 E7
Sexhow N Yorks 225 D9
Sezincote Glos 100 E3
Sgarasta Mhor W Isles 305 J2
Sgiogarstaigh W Isles 304 B7
Sgiwen = *Skewen* Neath 57 B8
Shabbington Bucks 83 D11
Shab Hill Glos 80 B6
Shackerley Shrops 132 B6
Shackerstone Leics 135 B7
Shacklecross Derbys 153 C8
Shackleford Sur 50 D2
Shackleton W Yorks 196 B3
Shacklewell London 67 B10
Shacklford Sur 50 D2
Shade W Yorks 196 C2
Shadforth Durham 234 C2
Shadingfield Suff 143 G8
Shadoxhurst Kent 54 F3
Shadsworth Blackburn 195 B8
Shadwell Glos 80 F3
London 67 C11
Norf 141 G8
W Yorks 206 F2
Shaffalong Staffs 169 E7
Shaftenhoe End Herts 105 D8
Shaftesbury Dorset 30 C5
Shafton S Yorks 197 E11
Shafton Two Gates
S Yorks 197 E11
Shaggs Dorset 18 E3
Shakeford Shrops 150 D3
Shakerley Gtr Man 195 G7
Shakesfield Glos 98 E3
Shalbourne Wilts 63 G10
Shalcombe IoW 20 D3
Shalden Hants 49 E7
Shalden Green Hants 49 E7
Shaldon Devon 14 G4
Shalfleet IoW 20 D4
Shalford Essex 106 F4
Som 45 G8
Sur 50 D4
Shalford Green Essex 106 F4
Shalloch Moray 302 D3
Shallowford Devon 25 B11
Devon 41 E8
Staffs 151 D7
Shalmsford Street Kent 54 C5
Shalstone Bucks 102 D2
Shamley Green Sur 50 E4
Shandon Argyll 276 D5
Shandwick Highld 301 B8
Shangton Leics 136 D4
Shankhouse Northumb 243 B7
Shanklin IoW 21 E7
Shannochie N Ayrs 255 E10
Shannochill Stirling 277 B10
Shanquhar Aberds 302 F5
Shanwell Fife 287 E8
Shanzie Perth 286 B6
Shap Cumb 221 B11
Shapridge Glos 79 B11
Shapwick Dorset 30 G6
Som 44 F2
Sharcott Wilts 46 B6
Shard End W Mid 134 F3
Shardlow Derbys 153 C8
Shareshill Staffs 133 B8
Sharlston W Yorks 197 D11
Sharlston Common
W Yorks 197 D11
Sharmans Cross W Mid 118 B2
Sharnal Street Medway 69 E9
Sharnbrook Bedford 121 F9
Sharneyford Lancs 195 C11
Sharnford Leics 135 E9
Sharnhill Green Dorset 30 F2
Sharoe Green Lancs 202 G6
Sharow N Yorks 214 E6
Sharpenhoe C Beds 103 E11
Sharperton Northumb 251 C11
Sharples Gtr Man 195 E8
Sharpley Heath Staffs 151 B9
Sharpness Glos 79 E11
Sharpsbridge E Sus 36 C6
Sharp's Corner E Sus 23 B9
Sharpstone Bath 45 B9
Sharp Street Norf 161 E7
Sharpthorne W Sus 51 G11
Sharptor Corn 11 G11
Sharpway Gate Worcs 117 D9
Sharrington Norf 159 B10
Sharrow S Yorks 186 D4
Sharston Gtr Man 184 D4
Shatterford Worcs 132 G5
Shatterling Kent 55 B9
Shatton Derbys 185 E11
Shaugh Prior Devon 7 C10
Shavington Ches E 168 E2
Shaw Gtr Man 196 F2
Swindon 62 B6
W Berks 64 F3
Wilts 61 F11
W Yorks 204 F6
Shawbank Shrops 131 G9
Shawbirch Telford 150 G2
Shawbury Shrops 149 E11
Shawclough Gtr Man 195 E11
Shaw Common Glos 98 F3
Shawdon Hall Northumb 264 G3
Shawell Leics 135 G10
Shawfield Gtr Man 195 E11
Staffs 169 C9
Shawfield Head
N Yorks 205 C11
Shawford Hants 33 C7
Som 45 C9
Shawforth Lancs 195 C11
Shaw Green Herts 104 E5
Lancs 194 D4
N Yorks 205 C11
Shawhead Dumfries 237 B10
N Lanark 268 C4
Shaw Heath Ches E 184 F3
Gtr Man 184 D5
Shawhill Dumfries 238 D6
Shawlands Glasgow 267 C11
Shaw Lands S Yorks 197 F10
Shaw Mills N Yorks 214 G5
Shawsburn S Lanark 268 E5
Shaw Side Gtr Man 196 F2
Shawton S Lanark 268 F3
Shawtonhill S Lanark 268 F3
Shay Gate W Yorks 205 F8
Sheandow Moray 302 F2
Shear Cross Wilts 45 E11
Shearington Dumfries 238 D2
Shearsby Leics 136 E2
Shearston Som 43 G9
Shebbear Devon 24 F6
Shebdon Staffs 150 D5
Shebster Highld 310 C4
Sheddens E Renf 267 D11
Shedfield Hants 33 E9
Sheen Staffs 169 C10
Sheepbridge Derbys 186 G5
Sheepdrove W Berks 63 D10
Sheep Hill Durham 242 F5
Sheeplane C Beds 103 E8
Sheepridge Bucks 65 B11
W Yorks 197 D7
Sheepscar W Yorks 206 G2
Sheepscombe Glos 80 C5
Sheepstor Devon 7 B11
Sheepwash Devon 25 F7
Northumb 253 F7
Sheepway N Som 60 D3
Sheepy Magna Leics 134 C6
Sheepy Parva Leics 134 C6
Sheering Essex 87 C8
Sheerness Kent 70 E2
Sheerwater Sur 66 G4
Sheet Hants 34 C3
Shrops 115 C10
Sheets Heath Sur 50 B2
Sheffield Corn 1 D5
S Yorks 186 D5
Sheffield Bottom
W Berks 65 F7
Sheffield Green E Sus 36 C6
Sheffield Park S Yorks 186 D5
Shefford C Beds 104 D2
Shefford Woodlands
W Berks 63 E11
Sheigra Highld 306 C6
Sheildmuir N Lanark 268 D5
Sheinton Shrops 132 C2
Shelderton Shrops 115 B8
Sheldon Derbys 169 B11
Devon 27 F10
W Mid 134 G3
Sheldwich Kent 54 B4
Sheldwich Lees Kent 54 B4
Shelf Bridgend 58 C2
W Yorks 196 B6
Shelfanger Norf 142 G2
Shelfield Warks 118 E2
W Mid 133 C10
Shelfield Green Warks 118 E2
Shelfleys W Nhants 120 F4
Shelford Notts 171 G11
Warks 135 F8
Shell Worcs 117 F9
Shelland Suff 125 E10
Shellbrook Leics 152 F6
Shelley Essex 87 E9
Suff 107 D10
W Yorks 197 E8
Shelley Woodhouse
W Yorks 197 E8
Shell Green Halton 183 D8
Shellingford Oxon 82 G4
Shellow Bowells Essex 87 D10
Shellwood Cross Sur 51 D8
Shelsley Beauchamp
Worcs 116 E4
Shelsley Walsh Worcs 116 E4
Shelthorpe Leics 153 F10
Shelton Bedford 121 D10
Norf 142 E4
Shelton *continued*
Notts 172 G3
Shrops 149 G9
Stoke 168 F5
Shelton Green Norf 142 E4
Shelton Lock Derby 153 C7
Shelton under Harley
Staffs 150 B6
Shelve Shrops 130 D6
Shelvin Devon 27 G11
Shelvingford Kent 71 F8
Shelwick Hereford 97 C10
Shelwick Green
Hereford 97 C10
Shenfield Essex 87 G10
Shenington Oxon 101 C7
Shenley Herts 85 E11
Shenley Brook End
M Keynes 102 D6
Shenleybury Herts 85 E11
Shenley Church End
M Keynes 102 D6
Shenley Fields W Mid 133 G10
Shenley Lodge
M Keynes 102 D6
Shenley Wood
M Keynes 102 D6
Shenmore Hereford 97 D7
Shennanton Dumfries 236 C5
Shennanton Ho
Dumfries 236 C5
Shenstone Staffs 134 C2
Worcs 117 C7
Shenstone Woodend
Staffs 134 C2
Shenton Leics 135 C7
Shenval Highld 300 G4
Moray 302 G2
Shenvault Moray 301 E10
Shepeau Stow Lincs 156 G6
Shephall Herts 104 G5
Shepherd Hill W Yorks 197 C9
Shepherd's Bush London 67 C8
Shepherd's Gate Norf 157 F11
Shepherd's Green Oxon 65 C8
Shepherd's Hill Sur 50 G2
Shepherd's Patch Glos 80 E2
Shepherd's Port Norf 158 C3
Shepherdswell or
Sibertswold Kent 55 D9
Shepley W Yorks 197 F7
Shepperdine S Glos 79 F10
Shepperton Sur 66 F5
Shepperton Green Sur 66 F5
Shepreth Cambs 105 B7
Shepshed Leics 153 F9
Shepton Beauchamp
Som 28 D6
Shepton Mallet Som 44 E6
Shepton Montague Som 45 G7
Shepway Kent 53 C9
Sheraton Durham 234 D4
Sherberton Devon 13 G8
Sherborne Bath 44 B5
Dorset 29 D10
Glos 81 C11
Sherborne St John Hants 48 B6
Sherbourne Warks 118 E5
Sherbourne Street Suff 107 C9
Sherburn Durham 234 C2
N Yorks 217 D9
Sherburn Grange
Durham 234 C2
Sherburn Hill Durham 234 C2
Sherburn in Elmet
N Yorks 206 G5
Shere Sur 50 D5
Shereford Norf 159 D7
Sherfield English Hants 32 C3
Sherfield on Loddon
Hants 49 B7
Sherfin Lancs 195 B9
Sherford Devon 8 G5
Dorset 18 C4
Som 28 C2
Sheriffhales Shrops 150 G5
Sheriff Hill T&W 243 E7
Sheriff Hutton N Yorks 216 F3
Sheriff's Lench Worcs 99 B10
Sheringham Norf 177 E11
Sherington M Keynes 103 B7
Sheringwood Norf 177 E11
Shermanbury W Sus 36 D2
Shernal Green Worcs 117 E8
Shernborne Norf 158 C4
Sherrard's Green Worcs 98 B5
Sherrardspark Herts 86 C2
Sherriffhales Shrops 150 G5
Sherrington Wilts 46 F3
Sherston Wilts 61 B11
Sherwood Nottingham 171 G9
Sherwood Green Devon 25 C9
Sherwood Park Kent 52 E6
Shettleston Glasgow 268 C2
Shevington Gtr Man 194 F4
Shevington Moor
Gtr Man 194 E4
Shevington Vale
Gtr Man 194 F4
Sheviock Corn 7 D7
Shewalton N Ayrs 257 B8
Shibden Head W Yorks 196 B5
Shide IoW 20 D5
Shiel Aberds 292 B4
Shiel Bridge Highld 295 D11
Shieldaig Highld 299 B8
Highld 299 D8
Shieldhall Glasgow 267 B10
Shieldhill Dumfries 248 F2
Falk 279 F7
S Lanark 269 G10
Shield Row Durham 242 G6
Shielfoot Highld 289 C8
Shielhill Angus 287 B8
Invclyd 276 G4
Shifford Oxon 82 E5
Shifnal Shrops 132 B4
Shilbottle Northumb 252 B5
Shilbottle Grange
Northumb 252 B6
Shildon Durham 233 F10
Shillford E Renf 267 D8
Shillingford Devon 27 C7
Oxon 83 G9
Shillingford Abbot Devon 14 D4
Shillingford St George
Devon 14 D4
Shillingstone Dorset 30 E4
Shillington C Beds 104 E2
Shillmoor Northumb 251 B9
Shilton Oxon 82 D3
Warks 135 G8
Shilvington Northumb 252 G5
Shimpling Norf 142 G3
Suff 125 G7
Shimpling Street Suff 125 G7
Shincliffe Durham 233 C11
Shiney Row T&W 243 G8
Shinfield Wokingham 65 F8
Shingay Cambs 104 B6
Shingham Norf 140 C5
Shingle Street Suff 109 C7
Shinner's Bridge Devon 8 C5
Shinness Highld 309 H5
Shipbourne Kent 52 C5
Shipdham Norf 141 B9
Shipdham Airfield Norf 141 B9
Shipham Som 44 B2
Shiphay Torbay 9 B7
Shiplake Oxon 65 D9
Shiplake Bottom Oxon 65 C8
Shiplake Row Oxon 65 D9
Shiplate N Som 43 B11
Shiplaw Borders 270 F4
Shipley Derbys 170 G6
Northumb 264 F4
Shrops 132 D6
W Sus 35 C10
W Yorks 205 F8
Shipley Bridge Sur 51 E10
Shipley Common
Derbys 171 G7
Shipley Shiels Northumb 251 E7
Shipmeadow Suff 143 F7
Shipping Pembs 73 D10
Shippon Oxon 83 F7
Shipston-on-Stour
Warks 100 C5
Shipton Bucks 102 F5
Glos 81 B8
N Yorks 207 B7
Shrops 131 E11
Shipton Bellinger Hants 47 D8
Shipton Gorge Dorset 16 C5
Shipton Green W Sus 22 C4
Shipton Lee Bucks 102 G4
Shipton Moyne Glos 61 B11
Shipton Oliffe Glos 81 B8
Shipton on Cherwell
Oxon 83 B7
Shipton Solers Glos 81 B8
Shiptonthorpe E Yorks 208 E3
Shipton-under-Wychwood
Oxon 82 B3
Shirburn Oxon 83 F11
Shirdley Hill Lancs 193 E11
Shirebrook Derbys 171 B8
Shirecliffe S Yorks 186 C4
Shiregreen S Yorks 186 C5
Shirehampton Bristol 60 D4
Shiremoor T&W 243 C8
Shirenewton Mon 79 G7
Shire Oak W Mid 133 C11
Shireoaks Derbys 185 E9
Notts 187 E9
Shires Mill Fife 279 D10
Shirkoak Kent 54 F2
Shirland Derbys 170 D6
Shirlett Shrops 132 D3
Shirley Derbys 170 G2
Hants 19 B9
London 67 F11
Soton 32 E6
W Mid 118 B2
Shirley Heath W Mid 118 B2
Shirley holms Hants 19 B11
Shirley Warren Soton 32 E5
Shirl Heath Hereford 115 F8
Shirrell Heath Hants 33 E9
Shirwell Devon 40 F5
Shirwell Cross Devon 40 F5
Shiskine N Ayrs 255 E10
Shitterton Dorset 18 C2
Shobdon Hereford 115 E8
Shobley Hants 31 F11
Shobnall Staffs 152 E4
Shobrooke Devon 26 G5
Shoby Leics 154 F3
Shocklach Ches W 166 F6
Shocklach Green
Ches W 166 F6
Shoeburyness Southend 70 C2
Sholden Kent 55 C11
Sholing Soton 32 E6
Sholing Common Soton 33 E7
Sholver Gtr Man 196 F3
Shootash Hants 32 C4
Shooters Hill London 68 D2
Shootersway Herts 85 D7
Shoot Hill Shrops 149 G8
Shop Corn 10 G3
Corn 24 E2
Devon 24 E5
Shop Corner Suff 108 E4
Shopford Cumb 240 C3
Shopnoller Som 43 G7
Shopp Hill W Sus 34 B6
Shopwyke W Sus 22 B5
Shore Gtr Man 196 D2
W Yorks 196 B2
Shore Bottom Devon 28 G2
Shoreditch London 67 C10
Som 28 C2
Shoregill Cumb 222 E5
Shoreham Kent 68 G4
Shoreham Beach W Sus 36 G2
Shoreham-by-Sea
W Sus 36 F2
Shore Mill Highld 301 C7
Shoresdean Northumb 273 F9
Shores Green Oxon 82 D5
Shoreside Shetland 313 J4
Shoreswood Northumb 273 F8
Shoreton Highld 300 C6
Shorley Hants 33 B9
Shorncliffe Camp Kent 55 F7
Shorncote Glos 81 F8
Shorne Kent 69 E7
Shorne Ridgeway Kent 69 E7
Shorne West Kent 69 E7
Shortacombe Devon 12 D6
Shortacross Corn 6 D5
Shortbridge E Sus 37 C7
Short Cross W Mid 133 G9
Shortfield Common Sur 49 E10
Shortgate E Sus 23 B7
Short Green Norf 141 F11
Shorthampton Oxon 100 G6
Shortheath Hants 49 F9
Sur 49 E10
Short Heath Derbys 152 G6
W Mid 133 C9
W Mid 133 E11
Shorthill Shrops 131 B8
Shortlands London 67 F11
Shortlanesend Corn 4 F6
Shortlees E Ayrs 257 B10
Shortmoor Devon 28 G2
Dorset 29 G7
Shorton Torbay 9 C7
Shortroods Renfs 267 B9
Shortstanding Glos 79 C9
Shortstown Bedford 103 B11
Short Street Wilts 45 D10
Shortwood Glos 80 F4
S Glos 61 D7
Shorwell IoW 20 E5
Shoscombe Bath 45 B8
Shoscombe Vale Bath 45 B8
Shotatton Shrops 149 E7
Shotesham Norf 142 D5
Shotgate Essex 88 G3
Shotley N Nhants 137 D8
Suff 108 D4
Shotley Bridge Durham 242 G3
Shotleyfield Northumb 242 G3
Shotley Gate Suff 108 E4
Shottenden Kent 54 C4
Shottermill Sur 49 G11
Shottery Warks 118 G3
Shotteswell Warks 101 B8
Shottisham Suff 108 C6
Shottle Derbys 170 F4
Shottlegate Derbys 170 F4
Shotton Durham 234 D4
Durham 234 F3
Flint 166 B4
Northumb 242 B6
Northumb 263 C8
Shotton Colliery
Durham 234 C3
Shotts N Lanark 269 C7
Shotwick Ches W 182 G4
Shouldham Norf 140 B3
Shouldham Thorpe Norf 140 B3
Shoulton Worcs 116 F6
Shover's Green E Sus 53 G7
Shraleybrook Staffs 168 F3
Shrawardine Shrops 149 F8
Shrawley Worcs 116 E6
Shreding Green Bucks 66 C4
Shrewley Warks 118 D4
Shrewley Common
Warks 118 D4
Shrewsbury Shrops 149 G9
Shrewton Wilts 46 E5
Shripney W Sus 22 C6
Shrivenham Oxon 63 B8
Shropham Norf 141 E9
Shroton or Iwerne Courtney
Dorset 30 E5
Shrub End Essex 107 G9
Shrubs Hill Sur 66 F3
Shrutherhill S Lanark 268 F5
Shucknall Hereford 97 C11
Shudy Camps Cambs 106 C2
Shulishadermor Highld 298 E4
Shulista Highld 298 B4
Shuna Ho Argyll 275 C8
Shurdington Glos 80 B6
Shurlock Row Windsor 65 E10
Shurnock Worcs 117 E10
Shurrery Highld 310 D4
Shurrery Lodge Highld 310 D4
Shurton Som 43 E8
Shustoke Warks 134 E4
Shute Devon 15 B11
Devon 26 G5
Shute End Wilts 31 B11
Shutford Oxon 101 C7
Shut Heath Staffs 151 E7
Shuthonger Glos 99 D7
Shutlanger W Nhants 120 G4
Shutta Corn 6 E5
Shutt Green Staffs 133 B7
Shuttington Warks 134 B5
Shuttlesfield Kent 55 E7
Shuttlewood Derbys 187 G7
Shuttleworth Gtr Man 195 D10
Shutton Hereford 98 F3
Shwt Bridgend 57 D11
Siabost bho Dheas
W Isles 304 D4
Siabost bho Thuath
W Isles 304 D4
Siadar W Isles 304 C5
Siadar Iarach W Isles 304 C5
Siadar Uarach W Isles 304 C5
Sibbaldbie Dumfries 248 F4
Sibbertoft W Nhants 136 G3
Sibdon Carwood Shrops 131 G8
Sibford Ferris Oxon 101 D7
Sibford Gower Oxon 101 D7
Sible Hedingham Essex 106 E5
Sibley's Green Essex 106 F2
Sibsey Lincs 174 E5
Sibsey Fen Side Lincs 174 E4
Sibson Cambs 137 D11
Leics 135 C7
Sibster Highld 310 D7
Sibthorpe Notts 172 F3
Notts 188 G2
Sibton Suff 127 D7
Sibton Green Suff 127 C7
Sicklesmere Suff 125 E7
Sicklinghall N Yorks 206 D3
Sid Devon 15 D8
Sidbrook Som 28 B3
Sidbury Devon 15 C8
Shrops 132 F3
Sidcot N Som 44 B2
Sidcup London 68 E3
Siddal W Yorks 196 C6
Siddick Cumb 228 E6
Siddington Ches E 184 G4
Glos 81 F8
Siddington Heath
Ches E 184 G4
Sidemoor Worcs 117 C9
Side of the Moor
Gtr Man 195 E8
Sidestrand Norf 160 B5
Sidford Devon 15 C8
Sidlesham W Sus 22 D5
Sidlesham Common
W Sus 22 C5
Sidley E Sus 38 F2
Sidlow Sur 51 D9
Sidmouth Devon 15 D8
Sidway Staffs 150 B5
Sigford Devon 13 G11
Sigglesthorne E Yorks 209 D9
Sighthill Edin 280 G3
Glasgow 268 B2
Sigingstone = *Tresigin*
V Glam 58 E3
Signet Oxon 82 C2
Sigwells Som 29 C10
Silchester Hants 64 G6
Sildinis W Isles 305 G4
Sileby Leics 153 F11
Silecroft Cumb 210 C2
Silfield Norf 142 D2
Silford Devon 24 B6
Silian Ceredig 111 G11
Silkstead Hants 32 C6
Silkstone S Yorks 197 F9
Silkstone Common
S Yorks 197 G9
Silk Willoughby Lincs 173 G9
Silloth Cumb 238 G4
Sills Northumb 251 C8
Sillyearn Moray 302 D5
Siloh Carms 94 D4
Silpho N Yorks 227 G9
Silsden W Yorks 204 D6
Silsoe C Beds 103 D11
Silton Dorset 30 B3
Silverburn Midloth 270 C4
Silverdale Lancs 211 E9
Staffs 168 F4
Silverdale Green Lancs 211 E9
Silver End Essex 88 B4
W Mid 133 F8
Silvergate Norf 160 D3
Silver Green Norf 142 E5
Silverhill E Sus 38 E3
Silver Hill E Sus 38 B2
Silverhill Park E Sus 38 E4
Silver Knap Som 29 C11
Silverknowes Edin 280 F4
Silverley's Green Suff 126 B5
Silvermuir S Lanark 269 F8
Silverstone W Nhants 102 C3
Silver Street Glos 80 E3
Kent 69 G11
Som 27 C11
Som 44 G4
Worcs 117 B11
Silverton Devon 27 G7
W Dunb 277 F8
Silvertonhill S Lanark 268 E4
Silvertown London 68 D2
Silverwell Corn 4 F4
Silvington Shrops 116 B2
Silwick Shetland 313 J4
Sim Hill S Yorks 197 G9
Simister Gtr Man 195 F10
Simmondley Derbys 185 C8
Simm's Cross Halton 183 D8
Simm's Lane End Mers 194 G4
Simonburn Northumb 241 C9
Simonsbath Som 41 F9
Simonsburrow Devon 27 D10
Simonside T&W 243 E8
Simonstone Lancs 203 G11
N Yorks 223 G7
Simprim Borders 272 F6
Simpson M Keynes 103 D7
Pembs 72 B5
Simpson Cross Pembs 72 B5
Simpson Green W Yorks 205 F9
Sinclair's Hill Borders 272 E6
Sinclairston E Ayrs 257 F11
Sinclairtown Fife 280 C5
Sinderby N Yorks 214 C6
Sinderhope Northumb 241 G8
Sinderland Green
Gtr Man 184 C2
Sindlesham Wokingham 65 F9
Sinfin Derby 152 C6
Sinfin Moor Derby 153 C7
Singdean Borders 250 C3
Singleborough Bucks 102 E5
Single Hill Bath 45 B8
Singleton Lancs 202 F3
W Sus 34 E5
Singlewell Kent 69 E7
Singret Wrex 166 D4
Sinkhurst Green Kent 53 E10
Sinnahard Aberds 292 B6
Sinnington N Yorks 216 B4
Sinton Worcs 116 E6
Sinton Green Worcs 116 E6
Sion Hill Bath 61 F8
Sipson London 66 D5
Sirhowy Bl Gwent 77 C11
Sisland Norf 142 D6
Sissinghurst Kent 53 F9
Sisterpath Borders 272 F5
Siston S Glos 61 D7
Sithney Corn 2 D4
Sithney Common Corn 2 D4
Sithney Green Corn 2 D4
Sittingbourne Kent 70 G2
Six Ashes Staffs 132 F5
Six Bells Bl Gwent 78 E2
Sixhills Lincs 189 D11
Six Hills Leics 154 E2
Sixmile Kent 54 E6
Six Mile Bottom Cambs 123 F11
Sixpenny Handley Dorset 31 D7
Sizewell Suff 127 E9
Skaigh Devon 13 C8
Skail Highld 308 E7
Skaill Orkney 314 C4
Orkney 314 E2
Orkney 314 F5
Skares E Ayrs 258 F2
Skateraw E Loth 282 F4
Skaw Shetland 312 B8
Shetland 312 G7
Skeabost Highld 298 E4
Skeabrae Orkney 314 D2
Skeeby N Yorks 224 E4
Skeete Kent 54 E6
Skeffington Leics 136 C4
Skeffling E Yorks 201 D11
Skegby Notts 171 C7
Notts 188 G3
Skegness Lincs 175 C9
Skelberry Shetland 313 G6
Shetland 313 M5
Skelbo Highld 309 K7
Skelbo Street Highld 309 K7
Skelbrooke S Yorks 198 E4
Skeldyke Lincs 156 B6
Skelfhill Borders 249 C11
Skellingthorpe Lincs 188 G6
Skellister Shetland 313 H6
Skellorn Green Ches E 184 E6
Skellow S Yorks 198 E4
Skelmanthorpe W Yorks 197 E8
Skelmersdale Lancs 194 F3
Skelmonae Aberds 303 F8
Skelmorlie N Ayrs 266 B3
Skelmuir Aberds 303 E9
Skelpick Highld 308 D7
Skelton Cumb 230 D4
E Yorks 199 B9
N Yorks 223 E11
Redcar 226 B3
York 207 B7
Skelton-on-Ure
N Yorks 215 F7
Skelwick Orkney 314 B4
Skelwith Bridge Cumb 220 E6
Skendleby Lincs 174 B6
Skendleby Psalter Lincs 190 G6
Skene Ho Aberds 293 C9
Skenfrith Mon 97 G9
Skerne E Yorks 208 B6
Skerne Park Darl 224 C5
Skeroblingarry Argyll 255 E8
Skerray Highld 308 C6
Skerricha Highld 306 D7
Skerryford Pembs 72 C6
Skerton Lancs 211 G9
Sketchley Leics 135 E8
Sketty Swansea 56 C6
Skewen = *Sgiwen* Neath 57 B8
Skewes Corn 5 B9
Skewsby N Yorks 216 E2
Skeyton Norf 160 D4
Skeyton Corner Norf 160 D5
Skiag Bridge Highld 307 G7
Skibo Castle Highld 309 L7
Skidbrooke Lincs 190 C6
Skidbrooke North End
Lincs 190 B6
Skidby E Yorks 208 G6
Skilgate Som 27 B7
Skillington Lincs 155 D7
Skinburness Cumb 238 F4
Skinflats Falk 279 E8
Skinidin Highld 298 E2
Skinner's Bottom Corn 4 F4
Skinners Green W Berks 64 F2
Skinnet Highld 308 C5
Skinningrove Redcar 226 B4
Skipness Argyll 255 B9
Skippool Lancs 202 E3
Skiprigg Cumb 230 B3
Skipsea E Yorks 209 B9
Skipsea Brough E Yorks 209 C9
Skipton N Yorks 204 C5
Skipton-on-Swale
N Yorks 215 D7
Skipwith N Yorks 207 F9
Skirbeck Lincs 174 G4
Skirbeck Quarter Lincs 174 G4
Skirethorns N Yorks 213 G9
Skirlaugh E Yorks 209 F8
Skirling Borders 260 B3
Skirmett Bucks 65 B9
Skirpenbeck E Yorks 207 B10
Skirwith Cumb 231 E8
Skirza Highld 310 C7
Skitby Cumb 239 D10
Skitham Lancs 202 E4
Skittle Green Bucks 84 E3
Skulamus Highld 295 C8
Skullomie Highld 308 C6
Skyborry Green Shrops 114 C5
Skye Green Essex 107 G7
Skye of Curr Highld 301 G9
Skyfog Pembs 90 F6
Skyreholme N Yorks 213 G11
Slack Derbys 170 C4
W Yorks 196 B3
W Yorks 196 D5
Slackcote Gtr Man 196 F3
Slackhall Derbys 185 E9
Slackhead Moray 302 C4
Slack Head Cumb 211 D9
Slackholme End Lincs 191 G8
Slacks of Cairnbanno
Aberds 303 E8
Slad Glos 80 D5
Sladbrook Glos 98 F5
Slade Devon 27 F10
Devon 40 D4
Kent 54 C2
Pembs 72 B6
Slade End Oxon 83 G9
Slade Green London 68 D4
Slade Heath Staffs 133 B8
Slade Hooton S Yorks 187 D8
Sladen Green Hants 48 C2
Sladesbridge Corn 10 G6
Slades Green Worcs 99 E7
Slaggyford Northumb 240 G5
Slaidburn Lancs 203 C10
Slaithwaite W Yorks 196 E5
Slaley Derbys 170 D3
Northumb 241 F11
Slamannan Falk 279 G7
Slape Cross Som 43 F10
Slapewath Redcar 226 B2
Slapton Bucks 103 G8
Devon 8 G6
W Nhants 102 B2
Slateford Edin 280 G4
Slate Haugh Moray 302 C4
Slatepit Dale Derbys 170 B4
Slattocks Gtr Man 195 F11
Slaugham W Sus 36 B3
Slaughterbridge Corn 11 D8
Slaughterford Wilts 61 E10
Slaughter Hill Ches E 168 D2
Slawston Leics 136 E5
Slay Pits S Yorks 199 F7
Sleaford Hants 49 F10
Lincs 173 F9
Sleagill Cumb 221 B11
Sleap Shrops 149 D9
Sleapford Telford 150 F2
Sleapshyde Herts 86 D2
Sleastary Highld 309 K6
Slebech Pembs 73 B8
Sledge Green Worcs 98 E6
Sledmere E Yorks 217 G8
Sleetbeck Cumb 240 B2
Sleet Moor Derbys 170 E6
Sleight Dorset 18 B5
Sleights N Yorks 227 D7
Slepe Dorset 18 C4
Sliabhna h-Airde
W Isles 296 F3
Slickly Highld 310 C6
Sliddery N Ayrs 255 E10
Slideslow Worcs 117 C9
Sligachan Hotel Highld 294 C6
Sligneach Argyll 288 G4
Sligrachan Argyll 276 C3
Slimbridge Glos 80 E2
Slindon Staffs 150 C6
W Sus 35 F7
Slinfold W Sus 50 G5
Sling Glos 79 D9
Gwyn 163 B10
Slingsby N Yorks 216 E3
Slioch Aberds 302 F5
Slip End C Beds 85 B9
Herts 104 D5
Slippery Ford W Yorks 204 E6
Slipton N Nhants 121 B9
Slitting Mill Staffs 151 F10
Slochd Highld 301 G8
Slockavullin Argyll 275 D9
Slogan Moray 302 E3
Sloley Norf 160 E5
Sloncombe Devon 13 D10
Sloothby Lincs 191 G7
Slough Slough 66 D3
Slough Green Som 28 C3
W Sus 36 B3
Slough Hill Suff 125 G7
Sluggan Highld 301 G8
Sluggans Highld 298 E4
Slumbay Highld 295 B10
Sly Corner Kent 54 G3
Slyfield Sur 50 C3
Slyne Lancs 211 F9
Smailholm Borders 262 B4
Smallbridge Gtr Man 196 D2
Smallbrook Devon 14 B3
Glos 79 E9
Smallburgh Norf 160 E6
Smallburn Aberds 303 E10
E Ayrs 258 D5
Smalldale Derbys 185 E11
Derbys 185 F9
Small Dole W Sus 36 E2
Small End Lincs 174 D6
Smalley Derbys 170 G6
Smalley Common
Derbys 170 G6
Smalley Green Derbys 170 G6
Smallfield Sur 51 E10
Smallford Herts 85 D11
Small Heath W Mid 134 F2
Smallholm Dumfries 238 B4
Small Hythe Kent 53 G11
Smallmarsh Devon 25 C10
Smallrice Staffs 151 C9
Smallridge Devon 28 G4
Smallshaw Gtr Man 196 G2
Smallthorne Stoke 168 E5
Small Way Som 44 G6
Smallwood Ches E 168 C4
Worcs 117 D10
Smallwood Green Suff 125 F8
Smallwood Hey Lancs 202 D3
Smallworth Norf 141 G10
Smannell Hants 47 D11
Smardale Cumb 222 D4
Smarden Kent 53 E11
Smarden Bell Kent 53 E11
Smart's Hill Kent 52 E4
Smaull Argyll 274 G3
Smeatharpe Devon 27 E11
Smeaton Fife 280 C5
Smeeth Kent 54 F5
Smeeton Westerby
Leics 136 E3
Smelthouses N Yorks 214 G3
Smercleit W Isles 297 K3
Smerral Highld 310 F5
Smestow Staffs 133 E7
Smethcott Shrops 131 D9
Smethwick W Mid 133 F10
Smethwick Green
Ches E 168 C4
Smirisary Highld 289 B8
Smisby Derbys 152 F6
Smite Hill Worcs 117 F7
Smithaleigh Devon 7 D11
Smithbrook W Sus 34 C6
Smith End Green Worcs 116 G5
Smithfield Cumb 239 D10
Smith Green Lancs 202 C5
Smithies S Yorks 197 F11
Smithincott Devon 27 E9
Smithley S Yorks 197 G11
Smith's End Herts 105 D8
Smiths Green Ches E 184 G4
Smith's Green Ches E 168 E3
Essex 105 G11
Essex 106 C3
Smithston Aberds 302 G5
Smithstown Highld 299 B7
Smithton Highld 301 E7
Smithwood Green Suff 125 G8
Smithy Bridge Gtr Man 196 D2
Smithy Gate Flint 181 F11
Smithy Green Ches E 184 G2
Gtr Man 184 D5
Smithy Houses Derbys 170 F5
Smithy Lane Ends Lancs 194 E2
Smockington Leics 135 F9
Smock Alley W Sus 35 D9
Smoky Row Bucks 84 D4
Smoogro Orkney 314 F3
Smug Oak Herts 85 E10
Smyrton S Ayrs 244 G4
Smythe's Green Essex 88 B6
Snagshall E Sus 38 C3
Snaigow House Perth 286 C4
Snailbeach Shrops 131 C7
Snails Hill Som 29 E7
Snailswell Herts 104 E3
Snailwell Cambs 124 D2
Snainton N Yorks 217 C8
Snaisgill Durham 232 F5
Snaith E Yorks 198 C6
Snape N Yorks 214 C5
Suff 127 F7
Snape Green Lancs 193 E11
Snape Hill Derbys 186 F5
S Yorks 198 G2
Snapper Devon 40 G5
Snaresbrook London 67 B11
Snarestone Leics 134 B6
Snarford Lincs 189 E9
Snargate Kent 39 B7
Snarraness Shetland 313 H4
Snatchwood Torf 78 E3
Snave Kent 39 B8
Sneachill Worcs 117 G8
Snead Powys 130 E6
Snead Common Worcs 116 D4
Sneads Green Worcs 117 D7
Sneath Common Norf 142 F3
Sneaton N Yorks 227 D7
Sneatonthorpe N Yorks 227 D8
Snedshill Telford 132 B4
Sneinton Nottingham 153 B11
Snelland Lincs 189 E9
Snelston Derbys 169 G11
Snetterton Norf 141 E9
Snettisham Norf 158 C3
Sneyd Green Stoke 168 F5
Sneyd Park Bristol 60 D5
Snibston Leics 153 G8
Snig's End Glos 98 F5
Snipeshill Kent 70 G2
Sniseabhal W Isles 297 H3
Snitter Northumb 252 C2
Snitterby Lincs 189 C7
Snitterfield Warks 118 F4
Snitterton Derbys 170 C3
Snitton Shrops 115 B11
Snittongate Shrops 115 B11
Snodhill Hereford 96 C6
Snodland Kent 69 G7
Snods Edge Northumb 242 G3
Snowden Hill S Yorks 197 G9
Snowdown Kent 55 C8
Snow End Herts 105 E8
Snow Hill Ches E 167 E10
W Yorks 197 C10
Snow Lea W Yorks 196 D5
Snowshill Glos 99 E11
Snow Street Norf 141 G11
Snydale W Yorks 198 D2
Soake Hants 33 E11
Soar Anglesey 178 G5
Carms 94 F2
Devon 9 G9
Gwyn 146 B2
Powys 95 E9
Soar-y-Mynydd Ceredig 112 G5
Soberton Hants 33 D10
Soberton Heath Hants 33 E10
Sockbridge Cumb 230 F6
Sockburn Darl 224 D6
Sockety Dorset 29 F7
Sodom Denb 181 G9
Shetland 313 G7
Wilts 62 C4
Sodylt Bank Shrops 148 B6
Soham Cambs 123 C11
Soham Cotes Cambs 123 B11
Soho London 67 C9
Som 45 D7
W Mid 133 F10
Solas W Isles 296 D4
Soldon Cross Devon 24 E4
Soldridge Hants 49 G7
Sole Street Kent 54 D5

Sole Street *continued*
Kent 69 F7
Solfach =*Solva* Pembs 90 G5
Solihull W Mid 118 B2
Solihull Lodge W Mid 117 B11
Sollers Dilwyn Hereford 115 F8
Sollers Hope Hereford 98 E2
Sollom Lancs 194 D3
Solva =*Solfach* Pembs 90 G5
Somerby Leics 154 G5
Lincs 200 F5
Somercotes Derbys 170 E6
Somerdale Bath 61 F7
Somerford BCP 19 C9
Ches E 168 B4
Staffs 133 B7
Somerford Keynes Glos 81 G8
Somerley W Sus 22 D4
Somerleyton Suff 143 D9
Somersal Herbert
Derbys 152 B2
Somersby Lincs 190 G4
Somersham Cambs 123 B7
Suff 107 B11
Somers Town London 67 C9
Ptsmth 21 B8
Somerton Newport 59 B10
Oxon 101 F9
Som 29 B7
Suff 124 G6
Somerton Hill Som 29 B7
Somerwood Shrops 149 G11
Sompting W Sus 35 G11
Sompting Abbotts
W Sus 35 F11
Sonning Wokingham 65 D9
Sonning Common Oxon 65 C8
Sonning Eye Oxon 65 D9
Sontley Wrex 166 F4
Sookholme Notts 171 B8
Sopley Hants 19 B9
Sopwell Herts 85 D11
Sopworth Wilts 61 B10
Sorbie Dumfries 236 E6
Sordale Highld 310 C5
Sorisdale Argyll 288 C4
Sorley Devon 8 F4
Sorn E Ayrs 258 D3
Sornhill E Ayrs 258 C2
Sortat Highld 310 C6
Sotby Lincs 190 F2
Sothall S Yorks 186 E6
Sots Hole Lincs 173 C10
Sotterley Suff 143 G9
Soudley Shrops 131 E9
Shrops 150 D4
Soughley S Yorks 197 G7
Soughton =*Sychdyn*
Flint 166 B2
Soulbury Bucks 103 F7
Soulby Cumb 222 C4
Cumb 230 F5
Souldern Oxon 101 E10
Souldrop Bedford 121 E9
Sound Ches E 167 F10
Shetland 313 H5
Shetland 313 J6
Sound Heath Ches E 167 F10
Soundwell S Glos 60 D6
Sourhope Borders 263 E8
Sourin Orkney 314 C4
Sourlie N Ayrs 266 G6
Sour Nook Cumb 230 C3
Sourton Devon 12 C6
Soutergate Cumb 210 C4
South Acre Norf 158 G6
South Acton London 67 D7
South Alkham Kent 55 E8
Southall London 66 C6
South Allington Devon 9 G10
South Alloa Falk 279 C7
Southam Cumb 219 C9
Glos 99 F9
Warks 119 E8
South Ambersham
W Sus 34 C6
Southampton Soton 32 E6
South Anston S Yorks 187 E8
South Ascot Windsor 66 F2
South Ashford Kent 54 E4
South Auchmachar
Aberds 303 E9
Southay Som 28 D6
South Baddesley Hants 20 B3
South Ballachulish
Highld 284 B4
South Balloch S Ayrs 245 D8
South Bank Redcar 234 G6
York 207 C7
South Barrow Som 29 B10
South Beach Northumb 243 B8
South Beach =*Marian-y-de*
Gwyn 145 C7
South Beddington
London 67 G9
South Benfleet Essex 69 B9
South Bents T&W 243 E10
South Bersted W Sus 22 C6
South Blainslie
Borders 271 G10
South Bockhampton BCP 19 B9
Southborough Kent 52 E5
London 67 F7
London 68 F2
Southbourne BCP 19 C8
W Sus 22 B3
South Bramwith
S Yorks 198 E6
South Brent Devon 8 D3
South Brewham Som 45 F8
South Bromley London 67 C11
Southbrook Wilts 45 G10
South Broomage Falk 279 E7
South Broomhill
Northumb 252 D6
Southburgh Norf 141 C9
South Burlingham Norf 143 B7
Southburn E Yorks 208 C5
South Cadbury Som 29 B10
South Cairn Dumfries 236 C1
South Carlton Lincs 189 F7
Notts 187 E9
South Carne Corn 11 E10
South Cave E Yorks 208 G4
South Cerney Glos 81 F8
South Chailey E Sus 36 D5
South Chard Som 28 F4
South Charlton
Northumb 264 E5
South Cheriton Som 29 C11
Southchurch Southend 70 B2
South Church Durham 233 F10
South Cliffe E Yorks 208 F3
South Clifton Notts 188 G4
South Clunes Highld 300 E5
South Cockerington
Lincs 190 D5
South Common Devon 28 G4
Southcoombe Oxon 100 F6
South Cornelly Bridgend 57 E10
South Corriegills
N Ayrs 256 C2
South Corrielaw
Dumfries 248 G5
Southcote Reading 65 E7
Southcott Corn 11 B9
Devon 24 D6
Wilts 47 B7
Southcourt Bucks 84 C4
South Cove Suff 143 G9
South Creagan Argyll 289 E11
South Creake Norf 159 B7
Southcrest Worcs 117 D10
South Crosland
W Yorks 196 E6
South Croxton Leics 154 G3
South Croydon London 67 G10
South Cuil Highld 298 C3
South Dalton E Yorks 208 D5
South Darenth Kent 68 F5
Southdean Borders 250 B4
Southdene Mers 182 B6
South Denes Norf 143 C10
Southdown Bath 61 G8
Corn 7 E8
South Down Hants 33 C7
Som 28 E2
South Duffield N Yorks 207 G9
South Dunn Highld 310 D5
South Earlswood Sur 51 D9
Southease E Sus 36 F6
South Elkington Lincs 190 D3
South Elmsall W Yorks 198 E3
South Elphinstone
E Loth 281 G7
Southend Argyll 255 G7
Bucks 65 B9
Glos 80 F2
London 67 E11
Oxon 83 E9
W Berks 64 D2
W Berks 64 E5
Wilts 63 E7
South End Bedford 103 B10
Bucks 103 F7
Cumb 210 G4
E Yorks 209 E9
Hants 31 D10
South-end Herts 86 B6
South End N Lincs 200 C6
Norf 141 E9
Southend-on-Sea
Southend 69 B11
Southerhouse Shetland 313 K5
Southerly Devon 12 D6
Southernby Cumb 230 D3
Southern Cross Brighton 36 F3
Southernden Kent 53 D11
Southerndown V Glam 57 G11
Southerness Dumfries 237 D11
Southern Green Herts 104 E6
South Erradale Highld 299 B7
Southery Norf 140 E2
Southey Green Essex 106 E5
South Fambridge Essex 88 F5
South Farnborough
Hants 49 C11
South Fawley W Berks 63 C11
South Ferriby N Lincs 200 C3
Southfield Northumb 243 B7
South Field E Yorks 200 B4
Windsor 66 D3
Southfields London 67 E9
Thurrock 69 C7
Southfleet Kent 68 E6
South Flobbets Aberds 303 F7
Southford IoW 20 F6
South Garth Shetland 312 D7
South Garvan Highld 289 B11
Southgate Ceredig 111 A11
London 86 G3
Norf 159 C7
Norf 160 E2
Swansea 56 D5
W Sus 51 F9
South Glendale W Isles 297 K3
South Gluss Shetland 312 F5
South Godstone Sur 51 D11
South Gorley Hants 31 E11
South Gosforth T&W 242 D6
South Green Essex 87 G11
Essex 89 B8
Kent 69 G11
Norf 157 F10
Norf 159 G11
Suff 126 B3
South Gyle Edin 280 G3
South-haa Shetland 312 E5
South Hackney London 67 C11
South Ham Hants 48 C6
South Hampstead London 67 C9
South Hanningfield Essex 88 F2
South Harefield London 66 B5
South Harrow London 66 B6
South Harting W Sus 34 D3
South Hatfield Herts 86 D2
South Hayling Hants 21 B10
South Hazelrigg
Northumb 264 C3
South Heath Bucks 84 E6
Essex 89 B10
South Heighton E Sus 23 E7
South-heog Shetland 312 E5
South Hetton Durham 234 B3
South Hiendley
W Yorks 197 E11
South Hill Corn 12 G2
N Som 43 B10
Pembs 72 C4
South Hinksey Oxon 83 E8
South Hole Devon 24 C2
South Holme N Yorks 216 D3
South Holmwood Sur 51 D7
South Hornchurch
London 68 C4
South Huish Devon 8 G3
South Hykeham Lincs 172 C6
South Hylton T&W 243 F9
Southill C Beds 104 C3
Dorset 17 E9
Southington Hants 48 D4
South Kelsey Lincs 189 B8
South Kensington London 67 D9
South Kessock Highld 300 E6
South Killingholme
N Lincs 201 D7
South Kilvington
N Yorks 215 C8
South Kilworth Leics 136 G2
South Kirkby W Yorks 198 E2
South Kirkton Aberds 293 C9
South Kiscadale N Ayrs 256 D2
South Knighton Devon 14 G2
Leicester 136 C2
South Kyme Lincs 173 F11
South Lambeth London 67 D10
South Lancing W Sus 35 G11
Southlands Dorset 17 F9
South Lane S Yorks 197 F9
Southleigh Devon 15 C10
South Leigh Oxon 82 D5
South Leverton Notts 188 E3
South Littleton Worcs 99 B11
South Lopham Norf 141 G10
South Luffenham
Rutland 137 C8
South Malling E Sus 36 E6
Southmarsh Som 45 G8
South Marston Swindon 63 B7
Southmead Bristol 60 D5
South Merstham Sur 51 C9
South Middleton
Northumb 263 E11
South Milford N Yorks 206 G5
South Millbrex Aberds 303 E8
South Milton Devon 8 G4
South Mimms Herts 86 E2
Southminster Essex 89 F7
South Molton Devon 26 B2
Southmoor Oxon 82 F5
South Moor Durham 242 G5
South Moreton Oxon 64 B5
South Mundham W Sus 22 C5
South Muskham Notts 172 D3
South Newbald E Yorks 208 F4
South Newbarns Cumb 210 F4
South Newington Oxon 101 E8
South Newsham
Northumb 243 B8
South Newton Wilts 46 G5
South Normanton
Derbys 170 D6
South Norwood London 67 F10
South Nutfield Sur 51 D10
South Ockendon Thurrock 68 C5
Southoe Cambs 122 E3
Southolt Suff 126 D3
South Ormsby Lincs 190 F5
Southorpe Pboro 137 C11
South Ossett W Yorks 197 D9
South Otterington
N Yorks 215 B7
Southover Dorset 17 C8
E Sus 36 F6
E Sus 37 B11
South Owersby Lincs 189 C9
Southowram W Yorks 196 C6
South Oxhey Herts 85 G10
South Park Sur 51 D8
South Pelaw Durham 243 G7
South Perrott Dorset 29 F7
South Petherton Som 28 D6
South Petherwin Corn 12 E2
South Pickenham Norf 141 C7
South Pill Corn 7 D8
South Pool Devon 8 G5
South Poorton Dorset 16 B6
Southport Mers 193 D10
South Port Argyll 284 E4
Southpunds Shetland 313 L6
South Quilquox Aberds 303 F8
South Radworthy Devon 41 G9
South Rauceby Lincs 173 F8
South Raynham Norf 159 E7
South Reddish Gtr Man 184 C5
Southrepps Norf 160 B5
South Reston Lincs 190 E6
Southrey Lincs 173 B10
Southrop Glos 81 E11
Oxon 101 E7
Southrope Hants 49 E7
South Ruislip London 66 B6
South Runcton Norf 140 B2
South Scarle Notts 172 C4
Southsea Ptsmth 21 B8
Wrex 166 E4
South Shian Argyll 289 E11
South Shields T&W 243 D9
South Shore Blackpool 202 G2
South Side Durham 233 F8
Orkney 314 D5
South Somercotes Lincs 190 C6
South Stainley N Yorks 214 G6
South Stainmore Cumb 222 C6
South Stanley Durham 242 G5
South Stifford Thurrock 68 D6
Southstoke Bath 61 G8
South Stoke Oxon 64 C6
W Sus 35 F8
South Stour Kent 54 F4
South Street E Sus 36 D5
Kent 54 B5
Kent 68 G6
Kent 69 G10
Kent 70 F6
London 52 B2
South Tawton Devon 13 C9
South Tehidy Corn 4 G3
South Thoresby Lincs 190 F6
South Tidworth Wilts 47 D8
South Tottenham
London 67 B10
Southtown Norf 143 B10
Orkney 314 G4
Som 28 D4
Som 44 F5
South Town Devon 14 E5
Hants 49 F7
South Twerton Bath 61 G8
South Ulverston Cumb 210 D6
South View Hants 48 C6
Southville Devon 8 G4
Torf 78 F3
South Voxter Shetland 313 G5
Southwaite Cumb 230 C4
South Walsham Norf 161 G7
Southwark London 67 D10
South Warnborough
Hants 49 D8
Southwater W Sus 35 B11
Southwater Street
W Sus 35 B11
Southway Plym 7 C9
Som 44 E4
South Weald Essex 87 G9
South Weirs Hants 32 G3
Southwell Dorset 17 G9
Notts 172 E2
South Weston Oxon 84 F2
South Wheatley Corn 11 C10
Notts 188 D3
South Whiteness
Shetland 313 J5
Southwick Hants 33 F10
N Nhants 137 E10
Som 43 D11
T&W 243 F9
Wilts 45 B10
W Sus 36 F2
South Widcombe Bath 44 B5
South Wigston Leics 135 D11
South Willesborough
Kent 54 E4
South Willingham
Lincs 189 E11
South Wimbledon London 67 E9
South Wingate Durham 234 E4
South Wingfield Derbys 170 D5
South Witham Lincs 155 F8
Southwold Suff 127 B10
South Wonford Devon 24 F5
South Wonston Hants 48 F3
Southwood Derbys 153 E7
Hants 49 B10
Norf 143 B7
Som 44 G5
Worcs 116 E4
South Woodford London 86 G6
South Woodham Ferrers
Essex 88 F4
South Wootton Norf 158 E2
South Wraxall Wilts 61 G10
South Yardley W Mid 134 G2
South Yarrows Highld 310 E7
South Yeo Devon 25 G8
South Zeal Devon 13 C9
Soval Lodge W Isles 304 F5
Sowber Gate N Yorks 215 B7
Sowerby N Yorks 215 C8
W Yorks 196 C4
Sowerby Bridge
W Yorks 196 C5
Sowerby Row Cumb 230 D3
Sower Carr Lancs 202 E3
Sowley Green Suff 124 G4
Sowood W Yorks 196 D5
Sowood Green W Yorks 196 D5
Sowton Devon 14 C5
Sowton Barton Devon 14 D2
Soyal Highld 309 K5
Soyland Town W Yorks 196 C4
Spacey Houses N Yorks 206 C2
Spa Common Norf 160 C5
Spalding Lincs 156 E4
Spaldington E Yorks 207 G11
Spaldwick Cambs 122 C2
Spalford Notts 172 B4
Spanby Lincs 155 B11
Spango Invclyd 276 G4
Spanish Green Hants 49 B7
Sparham Norf 159 F11
Sparhamhill Norf 159 F11
Spark Bridge Cumb 210 C6
Sparkbrook W Mid 133 G11
Sparkford Som 29 B10
Sparkhill W Mid 133 G11
Sparkwell Devon 7 D11
Sparl Shetland 312 G5
Sparnon Corn 1 E3
Sparnon Gate Corn 4 G3
Sparrow Green Norf 159 G9
Sparrow Hill Som 44 C2
Sparrowpit Derbys 185 E9
Sparrow's Green E Sus 52 G6
Sparsholt Hants 48 G2
Oxon 63 B10
Spartylea Northumb 232 B3
Spath Staffs 151 B11
Spaunton N Yorks 226 G4
Spaxton Som 43 F8
Spean Bridge Highld 290 E4
Spear Hill W Sus 35 D10
Spearywell Hants 32 B4
Speckington Som 29 C9
Speed Gate Kent 68 F5
Speedwell Bristol 60 E6
Speen Bucks 84 F4
W Berks 64 F3
Speeton N Yorks 218 E2
Speke Mers 182 E6
Speldhurst Kent 52 E5
Spellbrook Herts 87 B7
Spelsbury Oxon 101 G7
Spelter Bridgend 57 C11
Spen W Yorks 197 B7
Spencers Wood
Wokingham 65 F8
Spen Green Ches E 168 C4
Spennells Worcs 116 C6
Spennithorne N Yorks 214 B2
Spennymoor Durham 233 E11
Spernall Warks 117 E11
Spetchley Worcs 117 G7
Spetisbury Dorset 30 G6
Spexhall Suff 143 G7
Speybank Highld 291 C10
Spey Bay Moray 302 C3
Speybridge Highld 301 G10
Speyview Moray 302 E2
Spillardsford Aberds 303 D10
Spilsby Lincs 174 B6
Spindlestone Northumb 264 C5
Spinkhill Derbys 187 F7
Spinney Hill W Nhants 120 E5
Spinney Hills Leicester 136 C2
Spinningdale Highld 309 L6
Spion Kop Notts 171 B9
Spirthill Wilts 62 D3
Spital Mers 182 E4
Windsor 66 D3
Spitalbrook Herts 86 D5
Spitalfields London 67 C10
Spitalhill Derbys 169 F11
Spital Hill S Yorks 187 C10
Spital in the Street
Lincs 189 D7
Spital Tongues T&W 242 D6
Spithurst E Sus 36 D6
Spittal Dumfries 236 D5
E Loth 281 F9
E Yorks 207 C11
Highld 310 D5
Northumb 273 E10
Pembs 91 G9
Stirling 277 D10
Spittalfield Perth 286 C5
Spittal Houses S Yorks 186 B5
Spittal of Glenmuick
Aberds 292 E5
Spittal of Glenshee
Perth 292 F3
Spittlegate Lincs 155 C8
Spixworth Norf 160 F4
Splatt Corn 10 F4
Corn 11 D10
Devon 25 F10
Som 43 F8
Splayne's Green E Sus 36 C6
Splott Cardiff 59 D7
Spofforth N Yorks 206 C3
Spondon Derby 153 B8
Spon End W Mid 118 B6
Spon Green Flint 166 C3
Spooner Row Norf 141 D11
Spoonleygate Shrops 132 D6
Sporle Norf 158 G6
Spotland Bridge
Gtr Man 195 E11
Spott E Loth 282 F3
Spratton W Nhants 120 C4
Spreakley Sur 49 E10
Spreyton Devon 13 B9
Spriddlestone Devon 7 E10
Spridlington Lincs 189 E8
Sprig's Alley Oxon 84 F3
Springbank Glos 99 G8
Spring Bank Cumb 229 G10
Springboig Glasgow 268 C3
Springbourne BCP 19 C8
Springburn Glasgow 268 B2
Spring Cottage Leics 152 F6
Spring End N Yorks 223 F9
Springfield Argyll 275 F11
Caerph 77 F11
Dumfries 239 D8
Essex 88 D2
Fife 287 F7
Gtr Man 194 F5
Highld 300 C6
M Keynes 103 D7
Moray 301 D10
W Mid 133 D8
W Mid 133 F9
W Mid 133 G11
Springfields Stoke 168 G5
Spring Gardens Som 45 D9
Spring Green Lancs 204 E4
Spring Grove London 67 D7
Springhead Gtr Man 196 G3
Springhill E Renf 267 D10
IoW 20 B6
N Lanark 269 D7
Staffs 133 B11
Staffs 133 C9
Spring Hill Gtr Man 196 F2
Lancs 195 B8
W Mid 133 D7
Springholm Dumfries 237 C10
Springkell Dumfries 239 B7
Spring Park London 67 F11
Springside N Ayrs 257 B9
Springthorpe Lincs 188 D5
Spring Vale S Yorks 197 G9
Spring Valley IoM 192 E4
Springwell Essex 105 C10
T&W 243 F7
T&W 243 F9
Springwells Dumfries 248 E3
Sproatley E Yorks 209 G9
Sproston Green Ches W 168 B2
Sprotbrough S Yorks 198 G4
Sproughton Suff 108 C2
Sprouston Borders 263 B7
Sprowston Norf 160 G4
Sproxton Leics 155 E7
N Yorks 216 C2
Sprunston Cumb 230 B3
Spunhill Shrops 149 C8
Spurlands End Bucks 84 F5
Spurstow Ches E 167 D9
Spurtree Shrops 116 D2
Spynie Moray 302 C2
Spyway Dorset 16 C6
Square and Compass
Pembs 91 E7
Squires Gate Blackpool 202 G2
Sraid Ruadh Argyll 288 E1
Srannda W Isles 296 C6
Sronphadruig Lodge
Perth 291 F9
Stableford Shrops 132 D5
Staffs 150 B6
Stacey Bank S Yorks 186 C3
Stackhouse N Yorks 212 F6
Stackpole Pembs 73 F7
Stackpole Quay Pembs 73 F7
Stacksford Norf 141 E11
Stacksteads Lancs 195 C10
Stackyard Green Suff 107 B9
Staddiscombe Plym 7 E10
Staddlethorpe E Yorks 199 B10
Staddon Devon 24 C3
Devon 24 G5
Staden Derbys 185 G9
Stadhampton Oxon 83 F10
Stadhlaigearraidh
W Isles 297 H3
Stadmorslow Staffs 168 D5
Staffield Cumb 230 C6
Staffin Highld 298 C4
Stafford Staffs 151 E8
Stafford Park Telford 132 B4
Stafford's Corner Essex 89 B7
Stafford's Green Dorset 29 C10
Stagbatch Hereford 115 F9
Stagden Cross Essex 87 C10
Stagehall Borders 271 G9
Stagsden Bedford 103 B9
Stagsden West End
Bedford 103 B9
Stag's Head Devon 25 B11
Stain Highld 310 C7
Stainburn Cumb 228 F6
N Yorks 205 D10
Stainby Lincs 155 E8
Staincliffe W Yorks 197 C8
Staincross S Yorks 197 E10
Staindrop Durham 233 G8
Staines Green Herts 86 C3
Staines-upon-Thames
Sur 66 E4
Stainfield Lincs 155 D11
Lincs 189 G10
Stainforth N Yorks 212 F6
S Yorks 198 E6
Staining Lancs 202 F3
Stainland W Yorks 196 D5
Stainsacre N Yorks 227 D8
Stainsby Derbys 170 B6
Lincs 190 G4
Stainton Cumb 211 B10
Cumb 230 F5
Cumb 239 F9
Durham 223 B11
Mbro 225 C9
N Yorks 224 F2
S Yorks 187 C9
Stainton by Langworth
Lincs 189 F9
Staintondale N Yorks 227 F9
Stainton le Vale Lincs 189 C11
Stainton with Adgarley
Cumb 210 E5
Stair Cumb 229 G10
E Ayrs 257 E10
Stairfoot S Yorks 197 F11
Stairhaven Dumfries 236 D4
Staithes N Yorks 226 B5
Stakeford Northumb 253 F7
Stake Hill Gtr Man 195 F11
Stakenbridge Worcs 117 B7
Stake Pool Lancs 202 D4
Stalbridge Dorset 30 D2
Stalbridge Weston
Dorset 30 D2
Stalham Norf 161 D7
Stalham Green Norf 161 E7
Stalisfield Green Kent 54 C3
Stallen Dorset 29 D10
Stallingborough
NE Lincs 201 E7
Stalling Busk N Yorks 213 B8
Stallington Staffs 151 B8
Stalmine Lancs 202 D3
Stalmine Moss Side
Lancs 202 D3
Stalybridge Gtr Man 185 B7
Stambermill W Mid 133 G8
Stamborough Som 42 F4
Stambourne Essex 106 D4
Stambourne Green
Essex 106 D4
Stamford Lincs 137 B10
Stamford Bridge
Ches W 167 B7
E Yorks 207 B10
Stamfordham Northumb 242 C3
Stamford Hill London 67 B10
Stamperland E Renf 267 D11
Stamshaw Ptsmth 33 G10
Stanah Cumb 220 B6
Lancs 202 E3
Stanborough Herts 86 C2
Stanbridge C Beds 103 G9
Dorset 31 G8
Stanbridgeford C Beds 103 G9
Stanbrook Essex 106 F2
Worcs 98 B6
Stanbury W Yorks 204 F6
Stand Gtr Man 195 F9
N Lanark 268 B5
Standburn Falk 279 G8
Standeford Staffs 133 B8
Standen Kent 53 E11
Standen Hall Lancs 203 E10
Standen Street Kent 53 G10
Standerwick Som 45 C10
Standford Hants 49 G10
Standford Bridge
Telford 150 E4
Standingstone Cumb 229 B11
Cumb 229 E7
Standish Glos 80 D4
Gtr Man 194 E5
Standish Lower Ground
Gtr Man 194 F5
Standlake Oxon 82 E5
Standon Hants 32 B6
Herts 105 G7
Staffs 150 B6
Standon Green End
Herts 86 B5
Stane N Lanark 269 D7
Stanecastle N Ayrs 257 B8
Stanfield Norf 159 E8
Stoke 168 E5
Stanford C Beds 104 C3
Kent 54 F6
Norf 141 E7
Shrops 148 G6
Stanford Bishop
Hereford 116 G3
Stanford Bridge Worcs 116 D4
Stanford Dingley
W Berks 64 E5
Stanford End Wokingham 65 G8
Stanford Hills Notts 153 E10
Stanford in the Vale
Oxon 82 G4
Stanford-le-Hope
Thurrock 69 C7
Stanford on Avon
W Nhants 119 B11
Stanford on Soar Notts 153 E10
Stanford on Teme
Worcs 116 D4
Stanford Rivers Essex 87 E8
Stanfree Derbys 187 G7
Stanground Pboro 138 D4
Stanhill Lancs 195 B8
Stanhoe Norf 158 B6
Stanhope Borders 260 D4
Durham 232 D5
Kent 54 E3
Stanion N Nhants 137 F8
Stank Cumb 210 E4
Stanklyn Worcs 117 C7
Stanks W Yorks 206 F3
Stanley Derbys 170 G6
Durham 242 G5
Lancs 194 F3
Notts 171 C7
Perth 286 D5
Shrops 132 G3
Shrops 132 G5
Staffs 168 E6
Wilts 62 E3
W Yorks 197 C10
Stanley Common
Derbys 170 G6
Stanley Crook Durham 233 D9
Stanley Downton Glos 80 E4
Stanley Ferry W Yorks 197 C11
Stanley Gate Lancs 194 G2
Stanley Green BCP 18 C6
Ches E 184 E5
Shrops 149 B10
Stanley Hill Hereford 98 C3
Stanley Moor Staffs 168 E6
Stanley Pontlarge Glos 99 E9
Stanleytown Rhondda 77 G8
Stanlow Ches W 182 F6
Staffs 132 D5
Stanmer Brighton 36 F4
Stanmore Hants 33 B7
London 85 G11
Shrops 132 E4
W Berks 64 D3
Stanner Powys 114 F5
Stannergate Dundee 287 D8
Stannersburn Northumb 250 F6
Stanners Hill Sur 66 G3
Stanningfield Suff 125 F7
Stanningley W Yorks 205 G10
Stannington Northumb 242 B6
S Yorks 186 D4
Stanpit BCP 19 C9
Stansbatch Hereford 114 E6
Stansfield Suff 124 G5
Stanshope Staffs 169 E10
Stanstead Suff 106 B6
Stanstead Abbotts Herts 86 C5
Stansted Kent 68 G6
Stansted Airport Essex 105 G11
Stansted Mountfitchet
Essex 105 G10
Stanthorne Ches W 167 B11
Stanton Glos 99 E11
Mon 96 G6
Northumb 252 F4
Staffs 169 F10
Suff 125 C9
Stantonbury M Keynes 102 C6
Stanton by Bridge
Derbys 153 D7
Stanton-by-Dale Derbys 153 B9
Stanton Chare Suff 125 C9
Stanton Drew Bath 60 G5
Stanton Fitzwarren
Swindon 81 G11
Stanton Gate Notts 153 B9
Stanton Harcourt Oxon 82 D6
Stanton Hill Notts 171 C7
Stanton in Peak Derbys 170 C2
Stanton Lacy Shrops 115 B9
Stanton Lees Derbys 170 C3
Stanton Long Shrops 131 E11
Stanton-on-the-Wolds
Notts 154 C2
Stanton Prior Bath 61 G7
Stanton St Bernard Wilts 62 G5
Stanton St John Oxon 83 D9
Stanton St Quintin Wilts 62 D2
Stanton Street Suff 125 D9
Stanton under Bardon
Leics 153 G9
Stanton upon Hine Heath
Shrops 149 E11
Stanton Wick Bath 60 G6
Stantway Glos 80 C2
Stanwardine in the Fields
Shrops 149 E8
Stanwardine in the Wood
Shrops 149 D8
Stanway Essex 107 G8
Glos 99 E11
Stanway Green Essex 107 G9
Suff 126 C4
Stanwell Sur 66 E5
Stanwell Moor Sur 66 E4
Stanwick N Nhants 121 C9
Stanwick-St-John
N Yorks 224 C3
Stanwix Cumb 239 F10
Stanycliffe Gtr Man 195 F11
Stanydale Shetland 313 H4
Staoinebrig W Isles 297 H3
Stape N Yorks 226 G5
Stapehill Dorset 31 G9
Stapeley Ches E 167 F11
Stapenhill Staffs 152 E5
Staple Kent 55 B9
Som 42 E6
Staplecross E Sus 38 C3
Staple Cross Devon 27 C8
Staplefield W Sus 36 B3
Staple Fitzpaine Som 28 D3
Stapleford Cambs 123 G9
Herts 86 B4
Leics 154 F6
Lincs 172 D5
Notts 153 B9
Wilts 46 F5
Stapleford Abbotts Essex 87 G8
Stapleford Tawney Essex 87 F8
Staplegrove Som 28 B2
Staplehay Som 28 C2
Staple Hill S Glos 61 D7
Worcs 117 C9
Staplehurst Kent 53 E9
Staple Lawns Som 28 D3
Staplers IoW 20 D6
Staples Hill W Sus 35 B8
Staplestreet Kent 70 G5
Stapleton Bristol 60 D6
Cumb 240 C2
Hereford 114 D6
Leics 135 D8
N Yorks 198 D4
N Yorks 224 C5
Shrops 131 C9
Som 29 C7
Stapley Som 27 E11
Staploe Bedford 122 E2
Staplow Hereford 98 C3
Stapness Shetland 313 J4
Star Anglesey 179 G8
Fife 287 G7
Pembs 92 E4
Som 44 B2
Stara Orkney 314 D2
Starbeck N Yorks 206 B2
Starbotton N Yorks 213 E9
Starcross Devon 14 E5
Stareton Warks 118 C6
Stargate T&W 242 E5
Star Hill Mon 79 E7
Starkholmes Derbys 170 D4
Starling Gtr Man 195 E9
Starlings Green Essex 105 E9
Starr's Green E Sus 38 D3
Starston Norf 142 G4
Start Devon 8 G6
Startforth Durham 223 B10
Start Hill Essex 105 G10
Startley Wilts 62 C2
Startop's End Bucks 84 C6
Starveall S Glos 61 B9
Starvecrow Kent 52 D5
Statenborough Kent 55 B10
Statford St Andrew Suff 127 E7
Statham Warr 183 D11
Stathe Som 28 B5
Stathern Leics 154 C5
Station Hill Cumb 229 B11
Station Town Durham 234 D4
Statland Common
Norf 141 D10
Staughton Green Cambs 122 D2
Staughton Highway
Cambs 122 E2
Staughton Moor Cambs 122 E2
Staunton Glos 79 C8
Glos 98 F5
Staunton in the Vale
Notts 172 G4
Staunton on Arrow
Hereford 115 E7
Staunton on Wye
Hereford 97 B7
Staupes N Yorks 205 B10
Staveley Cumb 211 B7
Cumb 221 F9
Derbys 186 G6
N Yorks 215 G7
Staveley-in-Cartmel
Cumb 211 B7
Staverton Devon 8 C5
Glos 99 G7
Wilts 61 G11
W Nhants 119 E10
Staverton Bridge Glos 99 G7
Stawell Som 43 F11
Stawley Som 27 C9
Staxigoe Highld 310 D7
Staxton N Yorks 217 D10
Staylittle Ceredig 128 F2
Staylittle =*Penffordd-Lâs*
Powys 129 E7
Staynall Lancs 202 E3
Staythorpe Notts 172 E3
Stead W Yorks 205 D8
Steam Mills Glos 79 B10
Stean N Yorks 213 E11
Steanbow Som 44 F5
Stearsby N Yorks 216 E2
Steart Som 29 B9
Som 43 D9
Stebbing Essex 106 G3
Stebbing Green Essex 106 G3
Stechford W Mid 134 F2
Stede Quarter Kent 53 F11
Stedham W Sus 34 C5
Steel Northumb 241 F10
Northumb 251 G9
Steel Bank S Yorks 186 D4
Steel Cross E Sus 52 G4
Steelend Fife 279 C10
Steele Road Borders 250 E2
Steeleroad-end Borders 250 E2
Steel Green Cumb 210 D3
Steel Heath Shrops 149 B10
Steen's Bridge
Hereford 115 F10
Steep Hants 34 B2
Steephill IoW 21 F7
Steep Lane W Yorks 196 C4
Steeple Dorset 18 E4
Essex 88 E6
Steeple Ashton Wilts 46 B2
Steeple Aston Oxon 101 F9
Steeple Barton Oxon 101 G8
Steeple Bumpstead
Essex 106 C3
Steeple Claydon Bucks 102 F3
Steeple Gidding Cambs 138 G2
Steeple Langford Wilts 46 F4
Steeple Morden Cambs 104 C5
Steep Marsh Hants 34 B3
Steeraway Telford 132 B3
Steeton W Yorks 204 E6
Stein Highld 298 D2
Steinmanhill Aberds 303 E7
Stella T&W 242 E5
Stelling Minnis Kent 54 D6
Stelvio Newport 59 B9
Stembridge Som 28 C6
Swansea 56 C3
Stemster Highld 310 C5
Stemster Ho Highld 310 C5
Stenalees Corn 5 D10
Stenaquoy Orkney 314 C5
Stencoose Corn 4 F4
Stenhill Devon 27 E9
Stenhouse Dumfries 247 E8
Edin 280 G4
Stenhousemuir Falk 279 E7
Stenigot Lincs 190 E3
Stennack Corn 2 B5
Stenness Shetland 312 F4
Stenscholl Highld 298 C4
Stenso Orkney 314 D3
Stenson Derbys 152 D6
Stenton E Loth 282 G2
Fife 280 B5
Stentwood Devon 27 F10
Stenwith Lincs 154 B6
Stepaside Corn 5 F9
Pembs 73 D10
Powys 129 F11
Stepping Hill Gtr Man 184 D6
Steppingley C Beds 103 D10
Stepps N Lanark 268 B3
Sterndale Moor Derbys 169 B10
Sternfield Suff 127 E7
Sterridge Devon 40 D5
Stert Wilts 46 B4
Sterte BCP 18 C6
Stetchworth Cambs 124 F2
Stevenage Herts 104 G4
Steven's Crouch E Sus 38 D2
Stevenston N Ayrs 266 G5
Stevenstone Devon 25 D8
Steventon Hants 48 D4
Oxon 83 G7
Shrops 115 C10
Steventon End Essex 105 C11
Stevington Bedford 121 G9
Stewards Essex 87 D7
Steward's Green Essex 87 E7
Stewartby Bedford 103 C10
Stewarton Argyll 255 F7
E Ayrs 267 F8
Stewkley Bucks 103 F7
Stewkley Dean Bucks 102 F6
Stewley Som 28 D4
Stewton Lincs 190 D5
Steyne Cross IoW 21 D8
Steyning W Sus 35 E11
Steynton Pembs 72 D6
Stibb Corn 24 E2
Stibbard Norf 159 D9
Stibb Cross Devon 24 E6
Stibb Green Wilts 63 G8
Stibbington Cambs 137 D11
Stichill Borders 262 B6
Sticker Corn 5 E9
Stickford Lincs 174 D5
Stick Hill Kent 52 E3
Sticklepath Devon 13 C8
Devon 40 G5
Som 28 E4
Som 42 F4
Sticklinch Som 44 F5
Stickling Green Essex 105 E9
Stickney Lincs 174 D4
Stiffkey Norf 177 E7
Stifford's Bridge Hereford 98 B4
Stiff Street Kent 69 G11
Stileway Som 44 E3
Stillingfleet N Yorks 207 E7
Stillington N Yorks 215 F11
Stockton 234 G3
Stilton Cambs 138 F3
Stinchcombe Glos 80 F2
Stinsford Dorset 17 C10
Stiperstones Shrops 131 C7
Stirchley Telford 132 B4
W Mid 133 G11
Stirkoke Ho Highld 310 D7
Stirling Aberds 303 E11
Stirling 278 C5
Stirtloe Cambs 122 D3
Stirton N Yorks 204 C5
Stisted Essex 106 G5
Stitchcombe Wilts 63 F8
Stitchin's Hill Worcs 116 G5
Stithians Corn 2 B6
Stittenham Highld 300 B6
Stivichall W Mid 118 B6
Stixwould Lincs 173 B11
Stoak Ches W 182 G6
Stobhill Northumb 252 G6
Stobhillgate Northumb 252 F6
Stobieside S Lanark 258 B4
Stobo Borders 260 B5
Stoborough Dorset 18 D4
Stoborough Green
Dorset 18 D4
Stobs Castle Borders 250 B2
Stobshiel E Loth 271 C9
Stobswood Northumb 252 E6
Stock Essex 87 F11
Lancs 204 D3
N Som 60 G3
Stockbridge Hants 47 G11
S Yorks 198 F5
W Sus 22 C5
W Yorks 205 E7
Stockbridge Village
Mers 182 C6
Stockbury Kent 69 G10
Stockcross W Berks 64 F2
Stockend Glos 80 D4
Stocker's Head Kent 54 C3
Stockerston Leics 136 D6
Stockfield W Mid 134 G2
Stock Green Worcs 117 F9
Stockheath Hants 22 B2
Stock Hill Suff 125 D9
Stockholes Turbary
N Lincs 199 F9
Stockiemuir Stirling 277 E10
Stocking Hereford 98 E2
Stockingford Warks 134 E6
Stocking Green Essex 105 D11

Stocking Pelham Herts 105 F9
Stockland Devon 28 G2
Stockland Bristol Som 43 E8
Stockland Green Kent 52 E5
W Mid 133 E11
Stockleigh English Devon 26 F5
Stockleigh Pomeroy
Devon 26 G5
Stockley Wilts 62 F4
Stocklinch Som 28 D5
Stockport Gtr Man 184 C5
Stocksbridge S Yorks 186 B3
Stocksfield Northumb 242 E3
Stocks Green Kent 52 D5
Stockstreet Essex 106 G6
Stockton Hereford 115 E10
Norf 143 E7
Shrops 130 C5
Shrops 132 D4
Telford 150 F5
Warks 119 E8
Wilts 46 F3
Stockton Brook Staffs 168 E6
Stockton Heath Warr 183 D10
Stockton-on-Tees
Stockton 225 B8
Stockton on Teme
Worcs 116 D4
Stockton on the Forest
York 207 B9
Stocktonwood Shrops 130 C5
Stockwell Devon 27 G7
Glos 80 C6
London 67 D10
Stockwell End W Mid 133 C7
Stockwell Heath Staffs 151 E11
Stockwitch Cross Som 29 C9
Stockwood Bristol 60 F6
Dorset 29 F9
Stock Wood Worcs 117 F10
Stockwood Vale Bath 60 F6
Stodday Lancs 202 B5
Stodmarsh Kent 71 G8
Stody Norf 159 C11
Stoer Highld 307 G5
Stoford Som 29 E9
Wilts 46 F5
Stoford Water Devon 27 F9
Stogumber Som 42 F5
Stogursey Som 43 E8
Stoke Devon 24 C2
Hants 22 C2
Hants 48 C2
Medway 69 D10
Plym 7 D9
Suff 108 C3
W Mid 119 B7
Stoke Abbott Dorset 29 G7
Stoke Albany N Nhants 136 F6
Stoke Aldermoor
W Mid 119 B7
Stoke Ash Suff 126 C2
Stoke Bardolph Notts 171 G10
Stoke Bishop Bristol 60 D5
Stoke Bliss Worcs 116 E3
Stoke Bruerne
W Nhants 102 B4
Stoke by Clare Suff 106 C4
Stoke-by-Nayland Suff 107 D9
Stoke Canon Devon 14 B4
Stoke Charity Hants 48 F3
Stoke Climsland Corn 12 G3
Stoke Common Hants 33 C7
Stoke Cross Hereford 116 G2
Stoke D'Abernon Sur 50 B6
Stoke Doyle N Nhants 137 F10
Stoke Dry Rutland 137 D7
Stoke Edith Hereford 98 C2
Stoke End Warks 134 D3
Stoke Farthing Wilts 31 B9
Stoke Ferry Norf 140 D4
Stoke Fleming Devon 9 F7
Stokeford Dorset 18 D3
Stoke Gabriel Devon 8 D6
Stoke Gifford S Glos 60 D6
Stoke Golding Leics 135 D7
Stoke Goldington
M Keynes 102 B6
Stokegorse Shrops 131 G11
Stoke Green Bucks 66 C3
Stokeham Notts 188 F3
Stoke Hammond Bucks 103 F7
Stoke Heath Shrops 150 D3
W Mid 135 G7
Worcs 117 D8
Stoke Hill Devon 14 C4
Hereford 98 B2
Stoke Holy Cross Norf 142 C4
Stokeinteignhead Devon 14 G4
Stoke Lacy Hereford 98 B2
Stoke Lane Hereford 116 G2
Stoke Lyne Oxon 101 F11
Stoke Mandeville Bucks 84 C4
Stokenchurch Bucks 84 F3
Stoke Newington
London 67 B10
Stokenham Devon 8 G6
Stoke on Tern Shrops 150 D2
Stoke-on-Trent Stoke 168 F5
Stoke Orchard Glos 99 F8
Stoke Park Suff 108 C3
Stoke Poges Bucks 66 C3
Stoke Pound Worcs 117 D9
Stoke Prior Hereford 115 F10
Worcs 117 D8
Stoke Rivers Devon 40 F6
Stoke Rochford Lincs 155 D8
Stoke Row Oxon 65 C7
Stoke St Gregory Som 28 B4
Stoke St Mary Som 28 C3
Stoke St Michael Som 45 D7
Stoke St Milborough
Shrops 131 G11
Stokesay Shrops 131 G8
Stokesby Norf 161 G8
Stokesley N Yorks 225 D10
Stoke sub Hamdon Som 29 D7
Stoke Talmage Oxon 83 F11
Stoke Trister Som 30 B2
Stoke Wake Dorset 30 F3
Stoke Water Dorset 29 G7
Stoke Wharf Worcs 117 D9
Stokoe Northumb 250 F6
Stolford Som 43 D8
Stondon Massey Essex 87 E9
Stone Bucks 84 C3
Glos 79 F11
Kent 38 B6
Kent 68 E5
Som 44 G5
Staffs 151 C8
S Yorks 187 D9
Worcs 117 B7
Stonea Cambs 139 E9
Stoneacton Shrops 131 E10
Stone Allerton Som 44 C2
Ston Easton Som 44 C6
Stonebow Worcs 99 B8
Stonebridge Essex 70 B2
London 67 C8
Norf 141 E8
Stonebridge continued
N Som 43 B11
Sur 51 D7
W Mid 134 G4
Stone Bridge Corner
Pboro 138 C5
Stonebridge Green Kent 54 D2
Stonebroom Derbys 170 D6
Stonebyres Holdings
S Lanark 268 G6
Stone Chair W Yorks 196 B6
Stoneclough Gtr Man 195 F9
Stonecombe Devon 40 E6
Stone Cross E Sus 23 E10
E Sus 37 B8
E Sus 52 G6
Kent 52 F4
Kent 54 F4
Kent 55 B10
W Mid 133 E10
Stonecrouch Kent 53 G7
Stonedge Borders 250 B3
Stone-edge Batch
N Som 60 E3
Stoneferry Hull 209 G8
Stonefield Argyll 289 F11
S Lanark 268 D3
Staffs 151 C7
Stonefield Castle Hotel
Argyll 275 F9
Stonegate E Sus 37 B11
N Yorks 226 D5
Stonegrave N Yorks 216 D3
Stonegravels Derbys 186 G5
Stonehall Kent 55 D9
Worcs 99 B7
Stonehaugh Northumb 241 B7
Stonehaven Aberds 293 E10
Stone Head N Yorks 204 E4
Stone Heath Staffs 151 B9
Stonehill Sur 66 G4
Stone Hill Kent 54 D2
Kent 54 F5
S Glos 60 E6
S Yorks 199 F7
Stonehills Hants 33 G7
Stonehouse Aberds 303 F8
Glos 80 D4
Northumb 240 F5
Plym 7 E9
S Lanark 268 F5
Stone House Cumb 212 B5
Stonehouses Staffs 169 G7
Stone in Oxney Kent 38 B6
Stoneleigh London 67 G8
Warks 118 C6
Stoneley Green Ches E 167 E10
Stonely Cambs 122 D2
Stonepits Worcs 117 F10
Stonequarry W Sus 52 F2
Stoner Raise Cumb 230 B4
Stoner Hill Hants 34 B2
Stonesby Leics 154 E6
Stonesfield Oxon 82 B5
Stones Green Essex 108 F3
Stone Street Kent 52 C5
Suff 107 D9
Suff 143 G7
Stonestreet Green Kent 54 F5
Stonethwaite Cumb 220 C5
Stoneton Warks 119 G9
Stonewells Moray 302 C2
Stonewood Kent 68 E5
Stoneyard Green
Hereford 98 C4
Stoneybank E Loth 280 G6
Stoneybreck Shetland 313 N2
Stoneyburn W Loth 269 C9
Stoneycombe Devon 9 B7
Stoneycroft Mers 182 C5
Stoney Cross Hants 32 E3
Stoneyfield Gtr Man 195 E11
Moray 301 D11
Stoneyford Derbys 170 F6
Devon 27 F8
Stoneygate Aberds 303 F10
Leicester 136 C2
Stoney Hill Worcs 117 C9
Stoneyhills Essex 88 F6
Stoneykirk Dumfries 236 D2
Stoneylane Shrops 115 B11
Stoney Middleton
Derbys 186 F2
Stoney Royd W Yorks 196 C5
Stoney Stanton Leics 135 E9
Stoney Stoke Som 45 G8
Stoney Stratton Som 45 F7
Stoney Stretton Shrops 131 B7
Stoneywood Aberdeen 293 B10
Falk 278 E5
Stonganess Shetland 312 C7
Stonham Aspal Suff 126 F2
Stonnall Staffs 133 C11
Stonor Oxon 65 B8
Stonton Wyville Leics 136 D4
Stony Batter Hants 32 B3
Stony Cross Devon 25 B8
Hereford 98 B4
Hereford 116 D2
Stony Dale Notts 172 G2
Stonyfield Highld 300 B6
Stonyford Hants 32 D4
Stony Gate T&W 243 G9
Stony Green Bucks 84 F5
Stony Heap Durham 242 G4
Stony Heath Hants 48 B5
Stony Houghton Derbys 171 B7
Stony Knaps Dorset 28 G5
Stonyland Devon 25 B8
Stony Littleton Bath 45 B8
Stonymarsh Hants 32 B4
Stony Stratford
M Keynes 102 C5
Stoodleigh Devon 26 D6
Stop-and-Call Pembs 91 D8
Stopes S Yorks 186 D3
Stopgate Devon 28 F2
Stopham W Sus 35 D8
Stopper Lane Lancs 204 D2
Stopsley Luton 104 G2
Stoptide Corn 10 F4
Stores Corner Suff 109 B7
Storeton Mers 182 E4
Storiths N Yorks 205 C7
Stormontfield Perth 286 E5
Stormore Wilts 45 D10
Stornoway W Isles 304 E6
Storridge Hereford 98 B4
Storrington W Sus 35 E9
Storrs Cumb 221 G7
S Yorks 186 D3
Storth Cumb 211 C9
Storwood E Yorks 207 E10
Stotfield Moray 302 B2
Stotfold C Beds 104 D4
Stottesdon Shrops 132 G3
Stoughton Leics 136 C2
Sur 50 C3
W Sus 34 E4
Stoughton Cross Som 44 D2
Stoul Highld 295 F9
Stoulton Worcs 99 B8
Stourbridge W Mid 133 G8
Stourpaine Dorset 30 F5
Stourport on Severn
Worcs 116 C6
Stour Provost Dorset 30 C3
Stour Row Dorset 30 C4
Stourton Staffs 133 F7
Warks 100 D5
Wilts 45 G9
W Yorks 206 G2
Stourton Caundle Dorset 30 D2
Stourton Hill Warks 100 D6
Stout Som 44 G2
Stove Orkney 314 C6
Shetland 313 L6
Stoven Suff 143 G8
Stow Borders 271 G9
Lincs 155 B11
Lincs 188 E5
Stow Bardolph Norf 140 B2
Stow Bedon Norf 141 D9
Stowbridge Norf 140 B2
Stow cum Quy Cambs 123 E10
Stowe Glos 79 D9
Hereford 96 B5
Lincs 156 G2
Shrops 114 C6
Staffs 152 G2
Stowe-by-Chartley
Staffs 151 D10
Stowe Green Glos 79 D9
Stowell Glos 81 C9
Som 29 C11
Stowey Bath 44 B5
Stowfield Hereford 79 B9
Stowford Devon 12 B4
Devon 12 D4
Devon 24 E3
Devon 25 B10
Devon 41 E7
Stowgate Lincs 156 G3
Stowlangtoft Suff 125 D9
Stow Lawn W Mid 133 D8
Stow Longa Cambs 122 C2
Stow Maries Essex 88 F4
Stowmarket Suff 125 F10
Stow-on-the-Wold
Glos 100 F3
Stow Park Newport 59 B10
Stowting Kent 54 E6
Stowting Common Kent 54 E6
Stowting Court Kent 54 E6
Stowupland Suff 125 F11
Straad Argyll 275 G11
Strachan Aberds 293 D8
Strachurmore Argyll 284 G5
Stradbroke Suff 126 C4
Stradishall Suff 124 G4
Stradsett Norf 140 C3
Stragglethorpe Lincs 172 E6
Straid S Ayrs 244 E4
Straight Soley Wilts 63 E10
Straith Dumfries 247 F8
Straiton Edin 270 B5
S Ayrs 245 C9
Straloch Aberds 303 G8
Perth 292 G2
Stramshall Staffs 151 B11
Strand Glos 80 C2
London 67 C10
Strands Cumb 210 C3
Strang IoM 192 E4
Strangeways Gtr Man 184 B4
Strangford Hereford 97 F11
Stranghow Redcar 226 B3
Strangways Wilts 46 E6
Stranog Aberds 293 D10
Stranraer Dumfries 236 C2
Strata Florida Ceredig 112 D4
Stratfield Mortimer
W Berks 65 G7
Stratfield Saye Hants 65 G7
Stratfield Turgis Hants 49 B7
Stratford C Beds 104 B3
Glos 99 D7
London 67 C11
Stratford Marsh London 67 C11
Stratford New Town
London 67 C11
Stratford St Andrew
Suff 127 E7
Stratford St Mary Suff 107 E10
Stratford Sub Castle
Wilts 46 G6
Stratford Tony Wilts 31 B9
Stratford-upon-Avon
Warks 118 F3
Strath Highld 299 B7
Highld 310 D6
Strathallan Castle Perth 286 F3
Strathan Highld 295 F11
Highld 307 G5
Highld 308 C5
Strathan Skerray Highld 308 C6
Strathaven S Lanark 268 G4
Strathavon Lo Moray 301 G11
Strathblane Stirling 277 F11
Strathcanaird Highld 307 J6
Strathcarron Highld 299 E9
Strathcoil Argyll 289 F8
Strathcoul Highld 310 D5
Strathdon Aberds 292 B5
Strathellie Aberds 303 C10
Strathgarve Lodge
Highld 300 C4
Strathkinness Fife 287 F8
Strathmashie House
Highld 291 D7
Strathmiglo Fife 286 F6
Strathmore Lodge
Highld 310 E5
Strathpeffer Highld 300 D4
Strathrannoch Highld 300 B3
Strathtay Perth 286 B3
Strathvaich Lodge
Highld 300 B3
Strathwhillan N Ayrs 256 B2
Strathy Highld 300 B6
Highld 310 C2
Strathyre Stirling 285 F9
Stratton Corn 24 F2
Dorset 17 C9
Glos 81 E8
Stratton Audley Oxon 102 F2
Stratton Chase Bucks 85 G7
Stratton-on-the-Fosse
Som 45 C7
Stratton St Margaret
Swindon 63 B7
Stratton St Michael
Norf 142 E4
Stratton Strawless Norf 160 E4
Stravithie Fife 287 F9
Strawberry Bank Cumb 211 B8
Strawberry Hill E Sus 52 F5
London 67 E7
W Yorks 198 C2
Streat E Sus 36 D5
Streatham London 67 E10
Streatham Hill London 67 E10
Streatham Park London 67 E9
Streatham Vale London 67 E9
Streatley C Beds 103 F11
W Berks 64 C5
Street Cumb 222 D2
Lancs 202 C6
N Yorks 226 E4
Som 28 F5
Som 44 F3
Street Ash Som 28 E3
Street Ashton Warks 135 G9
Street Dinas Shrops 148 B6
Street End Hants 33 D9
Kent 54 C6
W Sus 22 D5
Street Gate T&W 242 F6
Streethay Staffs 152 G2
Streethouse W Yorks 197 C11
Street Houses N Yorks 206 D6
Streetlam N Yorks 224 F6
Street Lane Derbys 170 F5
Streetly W Mid 133 D11
Street Lydan Wrex 149 B8
Streetly End Cambs 106 B2
Street of Kincardine
Highld 291 B11
Street on the Fosse Som 44 F6
Strefford Shrops 131 F8
Strelley Notts 171 G8
Strensall York 216 G2
Strensham Worcs 99 C8
Stretch Down Devon 26 E4
Stretcholt Som 43 E9
Strete Devon 8 F6
Stretford Gtr Man 184 C4
Hereford 115 F10
Stretford Court Hereford 115 F8
Strethall Essex 105 D9
Stretham Cambs 123 C10
Strettington W Sus 22 B5
Stretton Ches W 166 E6
Derbys 170 C5
Rutland 155 F8
Staffs 151 G7
Staffs 152 D5
Warr 183 E10
Stretton en le Field
Leics 152 G6
Stretton Grandison
Hereford 98 C2
Stretton-on-Dunsmore
Warks 119 C8
Stretton-on-Fosse
Warks 100 D4
Stretton Sugwas
Hereford 97 C9
Stretton under Fosse
Warks 135 G8
Stretton Westwood
Shrops 131 D11
Strichen Aberds 303 D9
Strines Gtr Man 185 D7
Stringston Som 43 E7
Strixton N Nhants 121 E8
Stroat Glos 79 F9
Strode N Som 60 G4
Strom Shetland 313 J5
Stromeferry Highld 295 B10
Stromemore Highld 295 B10
Stromness Orkney 314 F2
Stronaba Highld 290 E4
Stronachlachar Stirling 285 F8
Stronachullin Lodge
Argyll 275 F9
Stronchreggan Highld 290 F2
Stronchrubie Highld 307 H7
Strone Argyll 255 F7
Argyll 274 G6
Argyll 276 E3
Highld 290 E3
Highld 291 D9
Highld 300 G5
Invclyd 276 G5
Stronelairg Lodge
Highld 291 C7
Stroneskar Argyll 275 C9
Stronmachair Stirling 285 G8
Stronmilchan Argyll 284 E5
Stronord Dumfries 236 C6
Stronsaul Argyll 276 F2
Strontian Highld 289 C10
Stronvar Stirling 285 E9
Strood Kent 53 G11
Medway 69 F8
Strood Green Sur 51 D8
W Sus 35 C8
W Sus 50 G6
Strothers Dale
Northumb 241 F11
Stroud Glos 80 D4
Hants 34 C2
Sur 50 F2
Stroude Sur 66 F4
Strouden BCP 19 C8
Stroud Green Essex 88 G5
Glos 80 D4
London 67 B10
Stroul Argyll 276 E4
Stroupster Highld 310 C7
Stroxton Lincs 155 C8
Stroxworthy Devon 24 D4
Struan Highld 294 B5
Perth 291 G10
Strubby Lincs 191 E7
Structon's Heath Worcs 116 D5
Strugg's Hill Lincs 156 B5
Strumpshaw Norf 142 B6
Strutherhill S Lanark 268 F5
Struthers Fife 287 G7
Struy Highld 300 F3
Stryd Anglesey 178 E2
Stryd y Facsen Anglesey 178 E4
Stryt-issa Wrex 166 F3
Stuartfield Aberds 303 E9
Stubb Norf 161 E8
Stubbermere W Sus 22 B3
Stubber's Green
W Mid 133 C10
Stubbings Windsor 65 C10
Stubbing's Green Suff 125 C11
Stubbington Hants 33 G9
Stubbins Lancs 195 D9
Lancs 202 E6
Stubble Green Cumb 219 F11
Stubbles W Berks 64 D5
Stubbs Cross Kent 54 F3
Stubbs Green Norf 143 D7
Stubb's Green Norf 142 D5
Stubhampton Dorset 30 E6
Stub Place Cumb 219 G11
Stubshaw Cross
Gtr Man 194 G5
Stubton Lincs 172 F5
Stubwood Staffs 151 B11
Stuckgowan Argyll 285 G7
Stuckton Hants 31 E11
Studdal Kent 55 D10
Studd Hill Kent 71 F7
Studfold N Yorks 212 E6
Stud Green Ches E 168 C2
Windsor 65 D11
Studham C Beds 85 B8
Studland Dorset 18 E6
Studley Warks 117 E11
Wilts 62 E3
Studley Green Bucks 84 F3
Wilts 45 B10
Studley Roger N Yorks 214 E5
Studley Royal N Yorks 214 E5
Stump Cross Essex 105 C10
Stumps Cross Glos 99 E11
Stuntney Cambs 123 B11
Stunts Green E Sus 23 C10
Sturbridge Staffs 150 C6
Sturford Wilts 45 E10
Sturgate Lincs 188 D5
Sturmer Essex 106 C3
Sturminster Common
Dorset 30 E3
Sturminster Marshall
Dorset 31 G7
Sturminster Newton
Dorset 30 E3
Sturry Kent 71 G7
Stursdon Corn 24 E2
Sturton N Lincs 200 G3
Sturton by Stow Lincs 188 E5
Sturton le Steeple Notts 188 E3
Stuston Suff 126 B2
Stutton N Yorks 206 E5
Suff 108 E3
Styal Ches E 184 E4
Styants Bottom Kent 52 B5
Stydd Lancs 203 F9
Styrrup Notts 187 C10
Suainebost W Isles 304 B7
Suardail W Isles 304 E6
Succoth Aberds 302 F4
Argyll 284 G6
Suckley Worcs 116 G4
Suckley Green Worcs 116 G4
Suckley Knowl Worcs 116 G4
Suckquoy Orkney 314 H4
Sucksted Green Essex 105 F11
Sudborough N Nhants 137 G9
Sudbourne Suff 127 G8
Sudbrook Lincs 173 G7
Mon 60 B4
Sudbrooke Lincs 189 F8
Sudbury Derbys 152 C3
London 67 C7
Suff 107 C7
Sudden Gtr Man 195 E11
Suddie Highld 300 D6
Sudgrove Glos 80 D6
Suffield Norf 160 C4
N Yorks 227 G9
Sugnall Staffs 150 C5
Sugwas Pool Hereford 97 C9
Suisnish Highld 295 D7
Suladale Highld 298 D3
Sulaisiadar W Isles 304 E7
Sulby IoM 192 C4
Sulgrave T&W 243 F8
W Nhants 101 B11
Sulham W Berks 64 E6
Sulhampstead W Berks 64 F6
Sulhampstead Abbots
W Berks 64 F6
Sulhampstead Bannister
Upper End W Berks 64 F6
Sulhamstead W Berks 64 F6
Sulland Orkney 314 B5
Sullington W Sus 35 E9
Sullington Warren
W Sus 35 E9
Sullom Shetland 312 F5
Sullom Voe Oil Terminal
Shetland 312 F5
Sully V Glam 59 F7
Sumburgh Shetland 313 N6
Summerbridge N Yorks 214 G4
Summer Bridge
N Yorks 214 G4
Summercourt Corn 5 D7
Summerfield Kent 55 B9
Norf 158 B5
Worcs 116 C6
Summerfield Park
W Mid 133 F10
Summergangs Hull 209 G8
Summer Heath Bucks 84 G2
Summerhill Newport 59 B10
Pembs 73 D11
Staffs 133 B11
Telford 150 F4
Worcs 116 B6
Wrex 166 E4
Summer Hill E Sus 23 D9
W Mid 133 E9
Summerhouse Darl 224 B4
Summerlands Cumb 211 B10
Som 29 D8
Summerleaze Mon 60 B2
Summerley Derbys 186 F5
Summerscales N Yorks 205 C8
Summersdale W Sus 22 B5
Summerseat Gtr Man 195 E9
Summerston Glasgow 277 G11
Summerstown Bucks 102 G3
London 67 E9
Summertown Oxon 83 D8
Summit Gtr Man 195 E10
Gtr Man 196 D2
Gtr Man 196 F2
Sunbrick Cumb 210 E5
Sunbury Common Sur 66 E5
Sunbury-on-Thames Sur 66 F6
Sundayshill S Glos 79 G11
Sundaywell Dumfries 247 G8
Sunderland Argyll 274 G3
Cumb 229 D9
Lancs 202 B4
T&W 243 F9
Sunderland Bridge
Durham 233 D11
Sundhope Borders 261 D8
Sundon Park Luton 103 F11
Sundridge Kent 52 B3
London 68 E2
Sun Green Gtr Man 185 B7
Sunhill Glos 81 E10
Sunipol Argyll 288 D5
Sunken Marsh Essex 69 C10
Sunk Island E Yorks 201 D9
Sunningdale Windsor 66 F3
Sunninghill Windsor 66 F2
Sunningwell Oxon 83 E7
Sunniside Durham 233 D8
T&W 242 F6
T&W 243 G8
Sunny Bank Gtr Man 195 F10
Sunny Bower Lancs 203 G10
Sunnybrow Durham 233 E9
Sunnyfields S Yorks 198 F4
Sunny Hill Derby 152 C6
Sunnyhurst Blackburn 195 C7
Sunnylaw Stirling 278 B5
Sunnymead Oxon 83 D8
Sunnymeads Windsor 66 D4
Sunnymede Essex 87 G11
Sunnyside S Yorks 187 C7
Sunnyside continued
W Sus 51 F11
Sunset Hereford 114 F6
Sunton Wilts 47 C8
Surbiton London 67 F7
Surby IoM 192 E3
Surfleet Lincs 156 D5
Surfleet Seas End Lincs 156 D5
Surlingham Norf 142 B6
Surrex Essex 107 G7
Suspension Bridge
Norf 139 E10
Sustead Norf 160 B3
Susworth Lincs 199 G10
Sutcombe Devon 24 E4
Sutcombemill Devon 24 E4
Sutherland Grove
Argyll 289 E11
Suton Norf 141 D11
Sutors of Cromarty
Highld 301 C8
Sutterby Lincs 190 G5
Sutterton Lincs 156 B5
Sutterton Dowdyke
Lincs 156 C5
Sutton Bucks 66 D4
Cambs 123 B8
C Beds 104 B4
Devon 8 G4
E Sus 23 F7
Kent 55 D10
Lincs 172 E5
London 67 G9
Mers 183 C8
Norf 161 E7
Notts 154 B5
Notts 187 E11
N Yorks 198 B3
Oxon 82 D6
Pboro 137 D11
Pembs 72 B6
Shrops 132 F4
Shrops 149 D7
Shrops 149 G10
Shrops 150 C3
Som 44 G6
Staffs 150 E5
Suff 108 B6
S Yorks 198 E5
W Sus 35 D7
Sutton Abinger Sur 50 D6
Sutton at Hone Kent 68 E5
Sutton Bassett
N Nhants 136 E5
Sutton Benger Wilts 62 D2
Sutton Bingham Som 29 E8
Sutton Bonington
Notts 153 E10
Sutton Bridge Lincs 157 E9
Sutton Cheney Leics 135 C8
Sutton Coldfield W Mid 134 D2
Sutton Corner Lincs 157 D8
Sutton Courtenay Oxon 83 G8
Sutton Crosses Lincs 157 E8
Sutton Cum Lound
Notts 187 E11
Sutton End W Sus 35 D7
Sutton Forest Side
Notts 171 D8
Sutton Gault Cambs 123 B8
Sutton Green Ches W 182 F5
Sur 50 C4
Wrex 166 F6
Sutton Hall Shrops 132 C4
Sutton Heath Mers 183 C8
Sutton Hill Telford 132 C4
Sutton Holms Dorset 31 F9
Sutton Howgrave
N Yorks 214 D6
Sutton in Ashfield Notts 171 D7
Sutton-in-Craven
N Yorks 204 E6
Sutton Ings Hull 209 G8
Sutton in the Elms
Leics 135 E10
Sutton Lakes Hereford 97 B10
Sutton Lane Ends
Ches E 184 G6
Sutton Leach Mers 183 C8
Sutton Maddock Shrops 132 C4
Sutton Mallet Som 43 F11
Sutton Mandeville Wilts 31 B7
Sutton Manor Mers 183 C8
Sutton Marsh Hereford 97 C10
Sutton Mill N Yorks 204 E6
Sutton Montis Som 29 C10
Sutton on Hull Hull 209 G8
Sutton on Sea Lincs 191 E8
Sutton-on-the-Forest
N Yorks 215 G11
Sutton on the Hill
Derbys 152 C4
Sutton on Trent Notts 172 B3
Sutton Poyntz Dorset 17 E10
Sutton Row Wilts 31 B7
Sutton St Edmund Lincs 157 G7
Sutton St James Lincs 157 F7
Sutton St Michael
Hereford 97 B10
Sutton St Nicholas
Hereford 97 B10
Sutton Scarsdale
Derbys 170 B6
Sutton Scotney Hants 48 F3
Sutton Street Suff 108 C6
Sutton under Brailes
Warks 100 D6
Sutton-under-
Whitestonecliffe
N Yorks 215 C9
Sutton upon Derwent
E Yorks 207 D10
Sutton Valence Kent 53 D10
Sutton Veny Wilts 45 E11
Sutton Waldron Dorset 30 D5
Sutton Weaver Ches W 183 F8
Sutton Wick Bath 44 B5
Oxon 83 G7
Swaby Lincs 190 F5
Swadlincote Derbys 152 F6
Swaffham Norf 140 B6
Swaffham Bulbeck
Cambs 123 E11
Swaffham Prior Cambs 123 E11
Swafield Norf 160 C5
Swaile's Green E Sus 38 C3
Swainby N Yorks 225 E9
Swain House W Yorks 205 F9
Swainshill Hereford 97 C9
Swainsthorpe Norf 142 C4
Swainswick Bath 61 F9
Swaithe S Yorks 197 G11
Swalcliffe Oxon 101 D7
Swalecliffe Kent 70 F6
Swallow Lincs 201 G7
Swallow Beck Lincs 173 B7
Swallowcliffe Wilts 31 B7
Swallowfield Wokingham 65 G8
Swallowfields Devon 8 C5
Swallowhurst Cumb 220 G2
Swallownest S Yorks 187 E7
Swallows Cross Essex 87 F10
Swalwell T&W 242 E6
Swampton Hants 48 C2
Swanage Dorset 18 F6
Swanbach Ches E 167 G11
Swanbister Orkney 314 F3
Swanborough Swindon 81 G11
Swan Bottom Bucks 84 D6
Swanbourne Bucks 102 F6
Swanbridge V Glam 59 F7
Swan Green Ches W 184 G2
Suff 126 C5
Swanland E Yorks 200 B3
Swanley Glos 80 F2
Kent 68 F4
Swanley Bar Herts 86 E3
Swanley Village Kent 68 F4
Swanmore Hants 33 D9
IoW 21 C7
Swannay Orkney 314 D2
Swannington Leics 153 F8
Norf 160 F2
Swanpool Lincs 189 G7
Swanscombe Kent 68 E6
Swansea = Abertawe
Swansea 56 C6
Swanside Mers 182 C6
Swanston Edin 270 B4
Swan Street Essex 107 F7
Swanton Abbott Norf 160 D5
Swanton Hill Norf 160 D5
Swanton Morley Norf 159 F10
Swanton Novers Norf 159 C10
Swanton Street Kent 53 B11
Swan Village W Mid 133 E9
Swanwick Derbys 170 E6
Hants 33 F8
Swanwick Green Ches E 167 F9
Swarby Lincs 173 G8
Swarcliffe W Yorks 206 F3
Swardeston Norf 142 C4
Swarister Shetland 312 E7
Swarkestone Derbys 153 D7
Swarland Northumb 252 C5
Swarraton Hants 48 F5
Swartha W Yorks 205 D7
Swarthmoor Cumb 210 D5
Swartland Orkney 314 D2
Swathwick Derbys 170 B5
Swaton Lincs 156 B2
Swavesey Cambs 123 D7
Sway Hants 19 B11
Swayfield Lincs 155 E9
Swaythling Soton 32 D6
Sweet Green Worcs 116 E2
Sweetham Devon 14 B3
Sweethaws E Sus 37 B8
Sweethay Som 28 C2
Sweetholme Cumb 221 B11
Sweethouse Corn 5 C11
Sweets Corn 11 B9
Sweetshouse Corn 5 C11
Sweffling Suff 126 E6
Swell Som 28 C5
Swelling Hill Hants 49 G7
Swepstone Leics 153 G7
Swerford Oxon 101 E7
Swettenham Ches E 168 B4
Swetton N Yorks 214 E3
Swffryd Caerph 78 F2
Swiftsden E Sus 38 B2
Swift's Green Kent 53 E11
Swilland Suff 126 G3
Swillbrook Lancs 202 G5
Swillington W Yorks 206 G3
Swillington Common
W Yorks 206 G3
Swimbridge Devon 25 B10
Swimbridge Newland
Devon 40 G6
Swinbrook Oxon 82 C3
Swincliffe N Yorks 205 B10
W Yorks 197 B8
Swincombe Devon 41 E7
Swinden N Yorks 204 C3
Swinderby Lincs 172 C5
Swindon Glos 99 G8
Staffs 133 E7
Swindon 63 C7
Swine E Yorks 209 F8
Swinefleet E Yorks 199 C9
Swineford S Glos 61 F7
Swineshead Bedford 121 D11
Lincs 174 G2
Swineshead Bridge
Lincs 174 G2
Swinethorpe Lincs 172 B5
Swiney Highld 310 F6
Swinford Leics 119 B11
Oxon 82 D6
Swingate Notts 171 G8
Swingbrow Cambs 139 F7
Swingfield Minnis Kent 55 E8
Swingfield Street Kent 55 E8
Swingleton Green Suff 107 B9
Swinhoe Northumb 264 D6
Swinhope Lincs 190 B2
Swining Shetland 312 G6
Swinister Shetland 312 E5
Shetland 313 L6
Swinithwaite N Yorks 213 B10
Swinmore Common
Hereford 98 C3
Swinnie Borders 262 F4
Swinnow Moor
W Yorks 205 G10
Swinscoe Staffs 169 F10
Swinside Cumb 229 G10
Swinside Townfoot
Borders 262 F6
Swinstead Lincs 155 E10
Swinton Borders 272 F6
Glasgow 268 C3
Gtr Man 195 G9
N Yorks 214 D4
N Yorks 216 E5
S Yorks 186 B6
Swinton Bridge S Yorks 187 B7
Swinton Hill Borders 272 F6
Swintonmill Borders 272 F6
Swinton Park Gtr Man 195 G9
Swiss Valley Carms 75 E8
Swithland Leics 153 G10
Swordale Highld 300 C5
Highld 309 K6
Swordland Highld 295 F9
Swordly Highld 308 C7
Sworton Heath Ches E 183 E11
Swyddffynnon Ceredig 112 D3
Swynnerton Staffs 151 B7
Swyre Dorset 16 D6
Sycamore Devon 28 F3
Sychdyn = Soughton
Flint 166 B2
Sychtyn Powys 129 B9
Sydallt Wrex 166 D4
Syde Glos 81 C7
Sydenham London 67 E11
Oxon 84 E2
Som 43 F10
Sydenham Damerel
Devon 12 F4
Syderstone Norf 158 C6
Sydling St Nicholas
Dorset 17 B8
Sydmonton Hants 48 B3
Sydney Ches E 168 D2
Syerston Notts 172 F2
Syke Gtr Man 195 D11
Sykehouse S Yorks 198 D6
Sykes Lancs 203 C8
Syleham Suff 126 B4
Sylen Carms 75 D8
Symbister Shetland 313 G7
Symington Borders 271 F8
S Ayrs 257 C9
S Lanark 259 B11
Symondsbury Dorset 16 C4
Symonds Green Herts 104 F4
Symonds Yat Hereford 79 B9
Synderford Dorset 28 G5
Synod Inn = Post Mawr
Ceredig 111 G8
Synton Borders 261 E11
Synton Mains Borders 261 E11
Synwell Glos 80 G3
Syre Highld 308 E6
Syreford Glos 99 G10
Syresham W Nhants 102 C2
Syster Highld 310 C6
Syston Leics 154 G2
Lincs 172 G6
Sytchampton Worcs 116 D6
Sytch Ho Green Shrops 132 E5
Sytch Lane Telford 150 E2
Sywell N Nhants 120 D6

T

Taagan Highld 299 C10
Tabley Hill Ches E 184 F2
Tabor Gwyn 146 F5
Tàbost W Isles 304 B7
Tabost W Isles 305 G5
Tachbrook Mallory
Warks 118 E6
Tacker Street Som 42 F4
Tackley Oxon 101 G9
Tacleit W Isles 304 E3
Tacolneston Norf 142 D2
Tadcaster N Yorks 206 E5
Tadden Dorset 31 G7
Taddington Derbys 185 G10
Glos 99 E11
Taddiport Devon 25 D7
Tadhill Som 45 D7
Tadley Hants 64 G6
Oxon 64 B4
Tadlow Cambs 104 B5
C Beds 104 B5
Tadmarton Oxon 101 D7
Tadnoll Dorset 17 D11
Tadwick Bath 61 E8
Tadworth Sur 51 B8
Tafarnau-bach
Bl Gwent 77 C10
Tafarn-y-bwlch Pembs 91 E11
Tafarn-y-gelyn Denb 165 C11
Taff Merthyr Garden Village
M Tydf 77 F10
Taff's Well Rhondda 58 C6
Tafolwern Powys 129 C7
Tai Conwy 164 C3
Taibach Neath 57 D9
Tai-bach Powys 148 D3
Taigh a Ghearraidh
W Isles 296 D3
Taigh Bhalaigh W Isles 296 D3
Tai-mawr Conwy 165 G7
Tai-morfa Gwyn 144 D5
Tain Highld 309 L7
Highld 310 C6
Tai'-nant Wrex 166 F3
Tainlon Gwyn 162 E6
Tairbeart W Isles 305 H3
Tai'r-Bull Powys 95 F9
Tairgwaith Neath 76 C2
Tai'r-heol Caerph 77 G10
Tai'r-ysgol Swansea 57 B7
Tai-Ucha Denb 165 D8
Takeley Essex 105 G11
Takeley Street Essex 105 G10
Talacharn = Laugharne
Carms 74 C4
Talachddu Powys 95 E11
Talacre Flint 181 E10
Talardd Gwyn 147 D7
Talaton Devon 15 B7
Talbenny Pembs 72 C4
Talbot Green Rhondda 58 C4
Talbot Heath BCP 19 C7
Talbot's End S Glos 80 G2
Talbot Village BCP 19 C7
Talbot Woods BCP 19 C7
Tale Devon 27 G9
Talerddig Powys 129 C8
Talgarreg Ceredig 111 G8
Talgarth Powys 96 E3
Talgarth's Well Swansea 56 D2
Talisker Highld 294 B5
Talke Staffs 168 E4
Talke Pits Staffs 168 E4
Talkin Cumb 240 F3
Talladale Highld 299 B9
Talla Linnfoots Borders 260 E4
Tallaminnoch S Ayrs 245 D10
Talland Corn 6 E4
Tallarn Green Wrex 166 G6
Tallentire Cumb 229 D8
Talley Carms 94 E2
Tallington Lincs 137 B11
Talmine Highld 308 C5
Talog Carms 92 F6
Talsarn Carms 94 F5
Tal-sarn Ceredig 111 F10
Talsarnau Gwyn 146 B2
Talskiddy Corn 5 B8
Talwrn Anglesey 179 F7
Wrex 166 F3
Tal-y-bont Ceredig 128 F3
Conwy 164 B3
Gwyn 145 E11
Gwyn 179 G10
Talybont-on-Usk Powys 96 G2
Tal-y-cafn Conwy 180 G3
Tal-y-coed Mon 78 B6
Talygarn Rhondda 58 C4
Talyllyn Powys 96 F2
Tal-y-llyn Gwyn 128 B4
Talysarn Gwyn 163 E7
Tal-y-waenydd Gwyn 163 F11
Talywain Torf 78 E3
Tal-y-wern Powys 128 C6
Tamanabhagh W Isles 304 F2
Tame Bridge N Yorks 225 D10
Tamer Lane End
Gtr Man 194 G6
Tamerton Foliot Plym 7 C9

Tame Water Gtr Man 196 F3
Tamfourhill Falk 279 E7
Tamworth Staffs 134 C4
Tamworth Green Lincs 174 G5
Tancred N Yorks 206 B5
Tandem W Yorks 197 D7
Tanden Kent 54 F2
Tandlehill Renfs 267 C8
Tandridge Sur 51 C11
Tanerdy Carms 93 G8
Tanfield Durham 242 F5
Tanfield Lea Durham 242 G5
Tang N Yorks 205 B10
Tangasdal W Isles 297 M2
Tang Hall York 207 C8
Tangiers Pembs 73 B7
Tangley Hants 47 C10
Tanglwst Carms 92 E6
Tangmere W Sus 22 B6
Tangwick Shetland 312 F4
Tangy Argyll 255 E7
Tan Hills Durham 233 B11
Tan Hinon Powys 129 F7
Tanhouse Lancs 194 F3
Tanis Wilts 62 G3
Tankersley S Yorks 197 G10
Tankerton Kent 70 F6
Tanlan Flint 181 E10
Tan-lan Conwy 164 C3
Gwyn 163 G10
Tanlan Banks Flint 181 E10
Tannach Highld 310 E7
Tannachie Aberds 293 E9
Tannadice Angus 287 B8
Tanner's Green Worcs 117 C11
Tannington Suff 126 D4
Tannington Place Suff 126 D4
Tannochside N Lanark 268 C4
Tan Office Suff 126 E2
Tan Office Green Suff 124 F5
Tansley Derbys 170 D4
Tansley Hill W Mid 133 F9
Tansley Knoll Derbys 170 C4
Tansor N Nhants 137 E11
Tanterton Lancs 202 G6
Tantobie Durham 242 G5
Tanton N Yorks 225 C10
Tanwood Worcs 117 C8
Tanworth-in-Arden
Warks 118 C2
Tan-y-bwlch Gwyn 163 G11
Tanyfron Wrex 166 E3
Tan-y-fron Conwy 165 C7
Tan-y-graig Anglesey 179 F8
Gwyn 144 B6
Tanygrisiau Gwyn 163 F11
Tan-y-groes Ceredig 92 B5
Tan-y-mynydd Gwyn 144 C6
Tan-y-pistyll Powys 147 D11
Tan-yr-allt Denb 181 E9
Gwyn 163 E7
Tanyrhydiau Ceredig 112 D4
Tanysgafell Gwyn 163 B10
Taobh a Chaolais
W Isles 297 K3
Taobh a' Ghlinne
W Isles 305 G5
Taobh a Thuath Loch
Aineort W Isles 297 J3
Taobh a Tuath Loch
Baghasdail W Isles 297 J3
Taobh Siar W Isles 305 H3
Taobh Tuath W Isles 296 C5
Taplow Bucks 66 C2
Tapnage Hants 33 E9
Tapton Derbys 186 G5
Tapton Hill S Yorks 186 D4
Tarbat Ho Highld 301 B7
Tarbert Argyll 255 B7
Argyll 275 E7
Argyll 275 G9
Tarbet Argyll 285 G7
Highld 295 F9
Highld 306 E6
Tarbock Green Mers 183 D7
Tarbolton S Ayrs 257 D10
Tarbrax S Lanark 269 D10
Tardebigge Worcs 117 D10
Tardy Gate Lancs 194 B4
Tarfside Angus 292 F6
Tarland Aberds 292 C6
Tarleton Lancs 194 C3
Tarleton Moss Lancs 194 C2
Tarlogie Highld 309 L7
Tarlscough Lancs 194 E2
Tarlton Glos 81 F7
Tarn W Yorks 205 F9
Tarnbrook Lancs 203 B7
Tarnock Som 43 C11
Tarns Cumb 229 B8
Tarnside Cumb 221 G8
Tarporley Ches W 167 C9
Tarpots Essex 69 B9
Tarr Som 42 G6
Tarraby Cumb 239 F10
Tarrant Crawford
Dorset 30 G6
Tarrant Gunville Dorset 30 E6
Tarrant Hinton Dorset 30 E6
Tarrant Keyneston
Dorset 30 G6
Tarrant Launceston
Dorset 30 F6
Tarrant Monkton Dorset 30 F6
Tarrant Rawston Dorset 30 F6
Tarrant Rushton Dorset 30 F6
Tarrel Highld 311 L2
Tarring Neville E Sus 36 G6
Tarrington Hereford 98 C2
Tarrington Common
Hereford 98 D2
Tarryblake Ho Moray 302 E5
Tarsappie Perth 286 E5
Tarskavaig Highld 295 E7
Tarts Hill Shrops 149 B8
Tarves Aberds 303 F8
Tarvie Highld 300 D4
Perth 292 G2
Tarvin Ches W 167 B7
Tarvin Sands Ches W 167 B7
Tasburgh Norf 142 D4
Tasley Shrops 132 E3
Taston Oxon 101 G7
Tat Bank W Mid 133 F9
Tatenhill Staffs 152 E4
Tatenhill Common
Staffs 152 E3
Tathall End M Keynes 102 B6
Tatham Lancs 212 F2
Tathwell Lincs 190 E4
Tatling End Bucks 66 B4
Tatsfield Sur 52 B2
Tattenhall Ches W 167 D7
Tattenhoe M Keynes 102 E6
Tatterford Norf 159 D7
Tattersett Norf 158 C6
Tattershall Lincs 174 D2
Tattershall Bridge
Lincs 173 D11
Tattershall Thorpe
Lincs 174 D2
Tattingstone Suff 108 D2
Tattingstone White Horse
Suff 108 D2
Tattle Bank Warks 118 E3
Tatton Dale Ches E 184 E2
Tatworth Som 28 F4
Taunton Gtr Man 196 G2
Som 28 C2
Taverham Norf 160 G3
Taverners Green Essex 87 B9
Tavernspite Pembs 73 C11
Tavistock Devon 12 G5
Taw Green Devon 13 B9
Tawstock Devon 25 B9
Taxal Derbys 185 F8
Tay Bridge Dundee 287 E8
Tayinloan Argyll 255 C7
Taymouth Castle Perth 285 C11
Taynish Argyll 275 E8
Taynton Glos 98 G4
Oxon 82 C2
Taynuilt Argyll 284 D4
Tayport Fife 287 E8
Tayvallich Argyll 275 E8
Tea Green Herts 104 G2
Tealby Lincs 189 C11
Tealing Angus 287 D8
Teams T&W 242 E6
Team Valley T&W 242 E6
Teanford Staffs 169 G8
Teangue Highld 295 E8
Teanna Mhachair
W Isles 296 E3
Teasley Mead E Sus 52 F4
Tebay Cumb 222 E2
Tebworth C Beds 103 F9
Tedburn St Mary Devon 14 C2
Teddington Glos 99 E9
London 67 E7
Teddington Hands Worcs 99 E9
Tedsmore Shrops 149 D7
Tedstone Delamere
Hereford 116 F3
Tedstone Wafer
Hereford 116 F3
Teesville Redcar 225 B10
Teeton W Nhants 120 C3
Teffont Evias Wilts 46 G3
Teffont Magna Wilts 46 G3
Tegryn Pembs 92 E4
Teigh Rutland 155 F7
Teigncombe Devon 13 D9
Teigngrace Devon 14 G2
Teignmouth Devon 14 G4
Teign Village Devon 14 E2
Telford Telford 132 B3
Telham E Sus 38 E3
Tellisford Som 45 B10
Telscombe E Sus 36 G6
Telscombe Cliffs E Sus 36 G5
Templand Dumfries 248 F3
Temple Corn 11 G8
Glasgow 267 B10
Midloth 270 D6
Wilts 45 E10
Windsor 65 C10
Temple Balsall W Mid 118 B4
Temple Bar Carms 75 B9
Ceredig 111 G10
W Sus 22 B5
Templeborough
S Yorks 186 C6
Temple Cloud Bath 44 B6
Templecombe Som 30 C2
Temple Cowley Oxon 83 E8
Temple End Essex 106 C6
Suff 124 G3
Temple Ewell Kent 55 E9
Temple Fields Essex 87 C7
Temple Grafton Warks 118 G2
Temple Guiting Glos 99 F11
Templehall Fife 280 C5
Temple Herdewyke
Warks 119 G7
Temple Hill Kent 68 D5
Temple Hirst N Yorks 198 C6
Templeman's Ash Dorset 28 G6
Temple Normanton
Derbys 170 B6
Temple Sowerby Cumb 231 F8
Templeton Devon 26 E5
Pembs 73 C10
W Berks 63 F11
Templeton Bridge Devon 26 E5
Templetown Durham 242 G4
Tempsford C Beds 122 G3
Ten Acres W Mid 133 G11
Tenandry Perth 291 G11
Tenbury Wells Worcs 115 D11
Tenby = Dinbych-y-Pysgod
Pembs 73 E10
Tencreek Corn 6 E4
Tendring Essex 108 G2
Tendring Green Essex 108 F2
Tendring Heath Essex 108 F2
Ten Mile Bank Norf 140 D2
Tenston Orkney 314 E2
Tenterden Kent 53 G11
Terfyn Conwy 180 F6
Gwyn 163 C9
Terhill Som 43 G7
Terling Essex 88 B3
Ternhill Shrops 150 C2
Terpersie Castle Aberds 302 G5
Terras Corn 5 E8
Terregles Banks
Dumfries 237 B11
Terrible Down E Sus 23 B7
Terrick Bucks 84 D4
Terriers Bucks 84 G5
Terrington N Yorks 216 E3
Terrington St Clement
Norf 157 E10
Terrington St John
Norf 157 G10
Terryhorn Aberds 302 F4
Terry's Green Warks 118 C2
Terwick Common W Sus 34 C4
Teston Kent 53 C8
Testwood Hants 32 E5
Tetbury Glos 80 G5
Tetbury Upton Glos 80 F5
Tetchill Shrops 149 C7
Tetchwick Bucks 83 B11
Tetcott Devon 12 B2
Tetford Lincs 190 G4
Tetley N Lincs 199 E9
Tetney Lincs 201 G10
Tetney Lock Lincs 201 G10
Tetsworth Oxon 83 E11
Tettenhall W Mid 133 D7
Tettenhall Wood W Mid 133 D7
Tetworth Cambs 122 G4
Teuchan Aberds 303 F10
Teversal Notts 171 C7
Teversham Cambs 123 F9
Teviothead Borders 249 B10
Tewel Aberds 293 E10
Tewin Herts 86 C3
Tewin Wood Herts 86 B3
Tewitfield Lancs 211 E10
Tewkesbury Glos 99 E7
Teynham Kent 70 G3
Teynham Street Kent 70 G3
Thackley W Yorks 205 F9
Thackley End W Yorks 205 F9
Thackthwaite Cumb 229 G8
Thainston Aberds 293 F8
Thakeham W Sus 35 D10
Thame Oxon 84 D2
Thames Ditton Sur 67 F7
Thames Haven Thurrock 69 C8
Thames Head Glos 81 F7
Thamesmead London 68 C3
Thanington Kent 54 B6
Thankerton S Lanark 259 B11
Tharston Norf 142 E3
Thatcham W Berks 64 F4
Thatto Heath Mers 183 C8
Thaxted Essex 106 E2
The Aird Highld 298 D4
Theakston N Yorks 214 B6
Thealby N Lincs 199 D11
The Alders Staffs 134 C3
Theale Som 44 D3
W Berks 64 E6
The Arms Norf 141 D7
Thearne E Yorks 209 F7
The Bage Hereford 96 C5
The Balloch Perth 286 F2
The Bank Ches E 168 D4
The Banks Gtr Man 185 D7
Wilts 62 D4
The Barony Ches E 167 E11
Orkney 314 D2
The Barton Wilts 62 D5
The Batch S Glos 61 E7
The Beeches Glos 81 E8
The Bell Gtr Man 194 F4
The Bents Staffs 151 C10
Theberton Suff 127 D8
The Blythe Staffs 151 D10
The Bog Shrops 131 D7
The Borough Dorset 30 E2
London 67 D10
The Bourne Sur 49 E10
Worcs 117 F9
The Bows Stirling 285 G11
The Braes Highld 295 B7
The Brampton Staffs 168 F4
The Brand Leics 153 G10
The Bratch Staffs 133 E7
The Breck Orkney 314 F3
The Brents Kent 70 G4
The Bridge Dorset 30 E3
The Broad Hereford 115 E9
The Brook Suff 125 B11
The Brushes Derbys 186 F5
The Bryn Mon 78 D4
The Burf Worcs 116 D6
The Butts Hants 49 F8
Som 45 D9
The Camp Glos 80 D6
Herts 85 D11
The Cape Warks 118 D5
The Chart Kent 52 C3
The Chequer Wrex 167 G7
The Chuckery W Mid 133 D10
The City Bucks 84 F3
The Cleaver Hereford 97 F10
The Close W Sus 22 C5
The Colony Oxon 100 D6
The Common Bath 60 G6
Bucks 102 E5
Dorset 30 E3
Shrops 150 D3
Suff 108 B2
Swansea 56 C4
Wilts 47 G8
Wilts 61 G11
Wilts 62 C4
W Sus 51 G7
The Corner Kent 53 E8
Shrops 131 F8
The Cot Mon 79 F8
The Craigs Highld 309 K4
The Crofts E Yorks 218 E4
The Cronk IoM 192 C4
The Cross Hands Leics 134 C6
The Cwm Mon 79 G7
Theddingworth Leics 136 F3
Theddlethorpe All Saints
Lincs 191 D7
Theddlethorpe St Helen
Lincs 191 D7
The Dell Suff 143 D9
The Delves W Mid 133 D10
The Den N Ayrs 266 E6
The Dene Durham 242 G4
Hants 47 C11
The Down Kent 53 F7
Shrops 132 E3
The Downs Sur 50 F3
The Dunks Wrex 166 E4
The Eals Northumb 251 F7
The Eaves Glos 79 D10
The Fall W Yorks 197 B10
The Fence Glos 79 D8
The Flat Glos 80 B3
The Flatt Cumb 240 B3
The Flourish Derbys 153 B8
The Folly Herts 85 C11
S Glos 61 E8
The Fording Hereford 98 F3
The Forge Hereford 114 F6
The Forstal Kent 54 F4
The Forties Derbys 152 F6
The Four Alls Shrops 150 C3
The Fox Wilts 62 B6
The Foxholes Shrops 132 G2
The Frenches Hants 32 C4
The Frythe Herts 86 C2
The Garths Shetland 312 B8
The Gibb Wilts 61 D10
The Glack Borders 260 B6
The Gore Shrops 131 G11
The Grange Norf 160 E2
N Yorks 225 F11
The Green Cambs 122 D5
C Beds 85 B8
Cumb 210 C3
Cumb 211 D7
Essex 88 B3
Hants 32 B3
M Keynes 103 C7
Norf 141 C11
Norf 159 B11
Oxon 101 F9
Shrops 130 G6
S Yorks 197 G8
Warks 118 F4
Wilts 45 G11
W Nhants 102 C5
The Grove Dumfries 237 B11
Durham 242 G3
Herts 85 F9
Shrops 131 B7
Shrops 131 G8
Worcs 99 C7
The Gutter Derbys 170 F5
The Gutter *continued*
Worcs 117 B9
The Hacket S Glos 61 B7
The Hague Derbys 185 C8
The Hall Shetland 312 D8
The Hallands N Lincs 200 C5
The Ham Wilts 45 C11
The Handfords Staffs 151 E7
The Harbour Kent 53 D10
The Haven W Sus 50 G5
The Headland Hrtlpl 234 E6
The Heath Norf 159 D8
Norf 160 E3
Norf 160 E4
Staffs 151 C11
Suff 108 D2
The Hem Shrops 132 B4
The Hendre Mon 79 C7
The Herberts V Glam 58 E3
The Hermitage Cambs 123 C7
The High Essex 86 C6
The Highlands E Sus 38 F2
The Hill Cumb 210 C3
The Hobbins Shrops 132 E4
The Hollands Staffs 168 D6
The Hollies Notts 172 E4
The Holmes Derbys 153 B7
The Holt Wokingham 65 D10
The Hook Worcs 98 C6
The Hope Shrops 115 B10
The Howe Cumb 211 B9
IoM 192 F2
The Humbers Telford 150 G3
The Hundred Hereford 115 E10
The Hyde London 67 B8
Worcs 98 C6
The Hythe Essex 107 G10
The Inch Edin 280 G5
The Knab Swansea 56 D6
The Knap V Glam 58 F5
The Knapp Hereford 116 G3
S Glos 79 G11
The Knowle W Mid 133 F9
The Laches Staffs 133 B8
The Lake Dumfries 237 E8
The Lakes Worcs 116 B5
The Lawe T&W 243 D9
The Lawns E Yorks 208 G6
Thelbridge Barton Devon 26 E3
The Leacon Kent 54 G3
The Leath Shrops 131 F11
The Lee Bucks 84 E6
The Lees Kent 54 C4
The Leigh Glos 99 F7
The Leys Staffs 134 C4
The Lhen IoM 192 B4
The Ling Norf 142 D6
The Lings Norf 141 B10
S Yorks 199 F7
The Linleys Wilts 61 F11
Thelnetham Suff 125 B10
The Lunt W Mid 133 D9
Thelveton Norf 142 G3
Thelwall Warr 183 D10
The Manor W Sus 22 C4
The Marsh Ches E 168 C4
Hereford 115 F9
Powys 130 D6
Shrops 150 D3
Staffs 150 D6
Suff 125 B11
Suff 126 B2
Wilts 62 C5
Themelthorpe Norf 159 E11
The Middles Durham 242 G6
The Mint Hants 34 B3
The Moor Flint 166 B4
Kent 38 B3
The Moors Hereford 97 E10
The Mount Hants 64 G2
Reading 65 E8
The Mumbles = Y Mwmbwls
Swansea 56 D6
The Murray S Lanark 268 E2
The Mythe Glos 99 E7
The Nant Wrex 166 E3
The Narth Mon 79 D8
The Neuk Aberds 293 D9
Thenford W Nhants 101 C10
The Node Herts 104 G4
The Nook Shrops 149 C11
Shrops 150 E3
The North Mon 79 D8
The Oval Bath 61 G8
The Park Glos 99 G8
The Parks S Yorks 198 F6
The Pitts Wilts 31 B9
The Platt Oxon 83 E9
The Pludds Glos 79 B10
The Point Devon 14 E5
The Pole of Itlaw
Aberds 302 D6
The Port of Felixstowe
Suff 108 E5
The Potteries Stoke 168 F5
The Pound Glos 98 E4
The Quarry Glos 80 F2
Shrops 149 G9
The Quarter Kent 53 E11
Kent 53 G11
The Rampings Worcs 99 E7
The Rectory Lincs 156 G2
The Reddings Glos 99 G8
Therfield Herts 104 D6
The Rhos Pembs 73 C8
The Rhydd Hereford 97 E9
The Riddle Hereford 115 E9
The Ridge Wilts 61 F11
The Ridges Wokingham 65 G10
The Ridgeway Herts 86 E3
The Riding Northumb 241 D10
The Riggs Borders 261 C8
The Rink Borders 261 C11
The Rise Windsor 66 F2
The Rock Telford 132 B3
The Rocks Kent 53 B8
S Glos 61 C8
The Roe Denb 181 G8
The Rookery Herts 85 G10
Staffs 168 D5
The Row Lancs 211 D9
The Rowe Staffs 150 B6
The Ryde Herts 86 D2
The Sands Sur 49 D11
The Scarr Glos 98 F4
The Shoe Wilts 61 E10
The Shruggs Staffs 151 C8
The Slack Durham 233 F8
The Slade W Berks 64 F4
The Smeeth Norf 157 G10
The Smithies Shrops 132 D3
The Spa Wilts 62 G2
The Spring Warks 118 C5
The Square Torf 78 F3
The Stocks Kent 38 B6
Wilts 62 G2
The Straits Hants 49 F9
W Mid 133 E8
The Strand Wilts 46 B2
The Swillett Herts 85 F8
The Sydnall Shrops 150 C3
Thetford Lincs 156 F2
Norf 141 G7
The Thrift Cambs 104 D6
The Throat Wokingham 65 F10
The Toft Staffs 151 F8
The Towans Corn 2 B3
The Town Scilly 1 F3
The Twittocks Glos 99 D7
The Tynings Glos 80 B6
The Vale W Mid 133 G11
The Valley Ches E 167 D11
Kent 54 C3
Leics 154 F4
Pembs 73 D10
The Vauld Hereford 97 B10
The Village Newport 78 G4
Windsor 66 E3
W Mid 133 F7
The Walshes Worcs 116 C6
The Warren Kent 54 E3
Wilts 63 F8
The Waterwheel Shrops 131 C7
The Weaven Hereford 97 E10
The Wells Sur 67 G7
The Wern Wrex 166 E3
The Willows NE Lincs 201 F8
The Wood Shrops 148 E6
Shrops 149 D9
The Woodlands Leics 136 D3
Suff 107 C11
Suff 108 D3
The Woods W Mid 133 D10
The Wrangle Bath 44 B4
The Wrythe London 67 F9
The Wyke Shrops 132 B4
The Wymm Hereford 97 B10
Theydon Bois Essex 86 F6
Theydon Garnon Essex 87 F7
Theydon Mount Essex 87 F7
The Yeld Shrops 131 G11
Thicket Mead Bath 45 B7
Thick Hollins W Yorks 196 E6
Thickthorn Hall Norf 142 B3
Thickwood Wilts 61 E10
Thimbleby Lincs 190 G2
N Yorks 225 F9
Thimble End W Mid 134 E2
Thinford Durham 233 E11
Thingley Wilts 61 E11
Thingwall Mers 182 E3
Thirdpart N Ayrs 266 F3
Thirlby N Yorks 215 C9
Thirlestane Borders 271 F11
Thirn N Yorks 214 B4
Thirsk N Yorks 215 C8
Thirtleby E Yorks 209 G9
Thistleton Lancs 202 F4
Rutland 155 F8
Thistley Green Essex 88 B2
Suff 124 B3
Thixendale N Yorks 216 G6
Thockrington Northumb 241 B11
Tholomas Drove Cambs 139 B7
Tholthorpe N Yorks 215 F9
Thomas Chapel Pembs 73 D10
Thomas Close Cumb 230 C4
Thomastown Aberds 302 F5
Rhondda 58 B4
Thompson Norf 141 D8
Thomshill Moray 302 D2
Thong Kent 69 E7
Thongsbridge W Yorks 196 F6
Thoralby N Yorks 213 B10
Thoresby Notts 187 G10
Thoresthorpe Lincs 191 F7
Thoresway Lincs 189 B11
Thorganby Lincs 190 B2
N Yorks 207 E9
Thorgill N Yorks 226 F4
Thorington Suff 127 C8
Thorington Street Suff 107 D10
Thorlby N Yorks 204 C5
Thorley Herts 87 B7
IoW 20 D3
Thorley Houses Herts 105 G9
Thorley Street Herts 87 B7
IoW 20 D3
Thormanby N Yorks 215 E9
Thorn Devon 13 D9
Powys 114 E5
Thornaby on Tees
Stockton 225 B9
Thornage Norf 159 B11
Thornborough Bucks 102 E4
N Yorks 214 D5
Thornbury Devon 24 F6
Hereford 116 F2
S Glos 79 G10
W Yorks 205 G9
Thornby Cumb 239 G7
W Nhants 120 B3
Thorncliff W Yorks 197 E8
Thorncliffe Staffs 169 D8
Thorncombe Dorset 28 G5
Dorset 30 G5
Thorncombe Street Sur 50 E4
Thorncote Green
C Beds 104 B3
Thorncross IoW 20 E4
Thorndon Suff 126 D2
Thorndon Cross Devon 12 C6
Thorne Corn 24 G2
S Yorks 199 E7
Thorne Coffin Som 29 D8
Thornehillhead Devon 24 D6
Thorne Moor Devon 12 D3
Thornend Wilts 62 D3
Thorner W Yorks 206 E3
Thornes Staffs 133 C11
W Yorks 197 D10
Thorne St Margaret Som 27 C9
Thorney Bucks 66 D4
Notts 188 G5
Pboro 138 C5
Som 28 C6
Thorney Close T&W 243 G9
Thorney Crofts E Yorks 201 C8
Thorney Green Suff 125 E11
Thorney Hill Hants 19 B9
Thorney Island W Sus 22 C3
Thorney Toll Pboro 138 C6
Thorneywood Notts 171 G9
Thornfalcon Som 28 C3
Thornford Dorset 29 E10
Thorngrafton Northumb 241 D7
Thorngrove Som 43 G11
Thorngumbald E Yorks 201 B8
Thornham Norf 176 E2
Thornham Fold
Gtr Man 195 F11
Thornham Magna Suff 126 C2
Thornham Parva Suff 126 C2
Thornhaugh Pboro 137 C11
Thornhill Cardiff 59 C7
Cumb 219 D10
Derbys 185 E11
Dumfries 247 D9
Soton 33 E7
Stirling 278 B3
Torf 78 F3
Thornhill *continued*
Wilts 62 D5
W Yorks 197 D9
Thorn Hill S Yorks 186 C6
Thornhill Edge W Yorks 197 D8
Thornhill Lees W Yorks 197 D8
Thornhill Park Hants 33 E7
Thornhills W Yorks 197 C7
Thornholme E Yorks 218 G2
Thornicombe Dorset 30 G5
Thornielee Borders 261 B10
Thornley Durham 233 D8
Durham 234 D3
Thornliebank E Renf 267 D10
Thornly Park Renfs 267 C9
Thornroan Aberds 303 F8
Thorns N Yorks 223 E7
Suff 124 F4
Thornseat S Yorks 186 C2
Thornsett Derbys 185 D8
Thorns Green Ches E 184 E3
Thornthwaite Cumb 229 F10
N Yorks 205 B9
Thornton Angus 287 C7
Bucks 102 D5
E Yorks 207 D11
Fife 280 B5
Lancs 202 E2
Leics 135 B9
Lincs 174 B2
Mbro 225 C9
Mers 193 G10
Northumb 273 F9
Pembs 72 D6
W Yorks 205 G8
Thornton Curtis N Lincs 200 D5
Thorntonhall S Lanark 267 D11
Thornton Heath London 67 F10
Thornton Hough Mers 182 E4
Thornton in Craven
N Yorks 204 D4
Thornton in Lonsdale
N Yorks 212 E3
Thornton-le-Beans
N Yorks 225 G7
Thornton-le-Clay
N Yorks 216 F3
Thornton-le-Dale
N Yorks 216 C6
Thornton le Moor Lincs 189 B9
Thornton-le-Moor
N Yorks 215 B7
Thornton-le-Moors
Ches W 182 G6
Thornton-le-Street
N Yorks 215 B8
Thorntonloch E Loth 282 G4
Thornton Park Northumb 273 F8
Thornton Rust N Yorks 213 B9
Thornton Steward
N Yorks 214 B3
Thornton Watlass
N Yorks 214 B4
Thornwood Common
Essex 87 D7
Thornydykes Borders 272 F2
Thoroton Notts 172 G3
Thorp Gtr Man 196 F2
Thorp Arch W Yorks 206 D4
Thorpe Cumb 230 F5
Derbys 169 E11
E Yorks 208 D5
Lincs 191 E7
Norf 143 D8
Notts 172 F3
N Yorks 213 G10
Sur 66 F4
Thorpe Abbotts Norf 126 B3
Thorpe Acre Leics 153 E10
Thorpe Arnold Leics 154 E5
Thorpe Audlin W Yorks 198 D3
Thorpe Bassett N Yorks 217 E7
Thorpe Bay Southend 70 B2
Thorpe by Water
Rutland 137 D7
Thorpe Common Suff 108 D5
Thorpe Constantine
Staffs 134 B5
Thorpe Culvert Lincs 175 C7
Thorpe Edge W Yorks 205 F9
Thorpe End Norf 160 G5
Thorpe Fendykes Lincs 175 C7
Thorpe Green Essex 108 G3
Lancs 194 C5
Suff 125 G8
Sur 66 F4
Thorpe Hamlet Norf 142 B4
Thorpe Hesley S Yorks 186 B5
Thorpe in Balne
S Yorks 198 E5
Thorpe in the Fallows
Lincs 188 E6
Thorpe Langton Leics 136 E4
Thorpe Larches Durham 234 F3
Thorpe Latimer Lincs 156 B2
Thorpe Lea Sur 66 E4
Thorpe-le-Soken Essex 108 G3
Thorpe le Street
E Yorks 208 E2
Thorpe le Vale Lincs 190 C2
Thorpe Malsor
N Nhants 120 B6
Thorpe Mandeville
W Nhants 101 B10
Thorpe Market Norf 160 B4
Thorpe Marriot Norf 160 F3
Thorpe Morieux Suff 125 G8
Thorpeness Suff 127 F9
Thorpe on the Hill Lincs 172 B6
W Yorks 197 B10
Thorpe Row Norf 141 B9
Thorpe St Andrew Norf 142 B5
Thorpe St Peter Lincs 175 C7
Thorpe Salvin S Yorks 187 E8
Thorpe Satchville Leics 154 G4
Thorpe Street Suff 125 B10
Thorpe Thewles
Stockton 234 G4
Thorpe Tilney Lincs 173 D10
Thorpe Underwood
N Nhants 136 G5
N Yorks 206 B5
Thorpe Waterville
N Nhants 137 G10
Thorpe Willoughby
N Yorks 207 G7
Thorpe Wood N Yorks 207 G7
Thorpland Norf 140 B2
Thorrington Essex 89 B9
Thorverton Devon 26 G6
Thoulstone Wilts 45 D10
Thrandeston Suff 126 B2
Thrapston N Nhants 121 B9
Thrashbush N Lanark 268 B5
Threapland Cumb 229 D9
N Yorks 213 G9
Threapwood Ches W 166 F6
Staffs 169 G8
Three Ashes Hants 64 G6
Hereford 97 G10
Shrops 115 B7
Three Ashes *continued*
Som 45 D7
Three Bridges Argyll 284 F4
Lincs 190 D6
W Sus 51 F9
Three Burrows Corn 4 F4
Three Chimneys Kent 53 F10
Three Cocked Hat Norf 143 D8
Three Cocks = Aberllynfi
Powys 96 D3
Three Crosses Swansea 56 C5
Three Cups Corner
E Sus 37 C10
Three Fingers Wrex 167 G7
Three Gates Dorset 29 F10
Threehammer Common
Norf 160 E6
Three Hammers Corn 11 D10
Three Holes Norf 139 C10
Three Holes Cross Corn 10 G6
Threekingham Lincs 155 B11
Three Leg Cross E Sus 53 G7
Three Legged Cross
Dorset 31 F9
Threelows Staffs 169 F9
Three Maypoles W Mid 118 B2
Three Mile Cross
Wokingham 65 F8
Threemilestone Corn 4 G5
Threemiletown W Loth 279 F11
Three Oaks E Sus 38 E4
Threepwood Borders 271 G10
Three Sisters Denb 165 C9
Threewaters Corn 5 B10
Threlkeld Cumb 230 F2
Threshers Bush Essex 87 D7
Threshfield N Yorks 213 G9
Thrigby Norf 161 G9
Thringarth Durham 232 G4
Thringstone Leics 153 F8
Thrintoft N Yorks 224 G6
Thriplow Cambs 105 B8
Throapham S Yorks 187 D8
Throckenholt Lincs 139 B7
Throcking Herts 104 E6
Throckley T&W 242 D5
Throckmorton Worcs 99 B9
Throop Dorset 18 C2
Throphill Northumb 252 F4
Thropton Northumb 252 C2
Throsk Stirling 279 C7
Througham Glos 80 D6
Throughgate Dumfries 247 G9
Throwleigh Devon 13 C9
Throwley Kent 54 B3
Throwley Forstal Kent 54 C3
Throxenby N Yorks 217 B10
Thrumpton Notts 153 C10
Notts 188 E2
Thrumster Highld 310 E7
Thrunton Northumb 264 G3
Thrupe Som 44 D6
Thrupp Glos 80 E5
Oxon 82 F3
Oxon 83 B7
Thruscross N Yorks 205 B9
Thrushelton Devon 12 D4
Thrussington Leics 154 F2
Thruxton Hants 47 D9
Hereford 97 E8
Thrybergh S Yorks 187 B7
Thulston Derbys 153 C8
Thunder Bridge
W Yorks 197 E7
Thundergay N Ayrs 255 C9
Thunder Hill Norf 161 F8
Thunder's Hill E Sus 23 C9
Thundersley Essex 69 B9
Thundridge Herts 86 B5
Thurcaston Leics 153 G11
Thurcroft S Yorks 187 D7
Thurdon Corn 24 E3
Thurgarton Norf 160 C3
Notts 171 F11
Thurgoland S Yorks 197 G9
Thurlaston Leics 135 D10
Warks 119 C9
Thurlbear Som 28 C3
Thurlby Lincs 156 F2
Lincs 172 C6
Lincs 191 F7
Thurleigh Bedford 121 F11
Thurlestone Devon 8 G3
Thurloxton Som 43 G9
Thurlstone S Yorks 197 G8
Thurlton Norf 143 D8
Thurlton Links Norf 143 D8
Thurlwood Ches E 168 D4
Thurmaston Leics 136 B2
Thurnby Leics 136 C2
Thurne Norf 161 F8
Thurnham Kent 53 B10
Lancs 202 C5
Thurning N Nhants 137 G11
Norf 159 D11
Thurnscoe S Yorks 198 F3
Thurnscoe East S Yorks 198 F3
Thursby Cumb 239 G8
Thursford Norf 159 C9
Thursford Green Norf 159 C9
Thursley Sur 50 F2
Thurso Highld 310 C5
Thurso East Highld 310 C5
Thurstaston Mers 182 E2
Thurston Suff 125 D8
Thurston Clough
Gtr Man 196 F3
Thurston End Suff 124 G5
Thurstonfield Cumb 239 F8
Thurstonland W Yorks 197 E7
Thurton Norf 142 C6
Thurvaston Derbys 152 B2
Derbys 152 B4
Thuxton Norf 141 B10
Thwaite N Yorks 223 F7
Suff 126 D2
Thwaite Flat Cumb 210 E4
Thwaite Head Cumb 220 G6
Thwaites W Yorks 205 E7
Thwaite St Mary Norf 142 E6
Thwaites Brow W Yorks 205 E7
Thwing E Yorks 217 E11
Tibbermore Perth 286 E4
Tibberton Glos 98 G5
Telford 150 E3
Worcs 117 F8
Tibenham Norf 142 F2
Tibshelf Derbys 170 C6
Tibshelf Wharf Notts 171 C7
Tibthorpe E Yorks 208 B5
Ticehurst E Sus 53 G7
Tichborne Hants 48 G5
Tickencote Rutland 137 B9
Tickenham N Som 60 E3
Ticket Wood Devon 8 G4
Tickford End M Keynes 103 C7
Tickhill S Yorks 187 C9
Tickleback Row Brack 65 E11
Ticklerton Shrops 131 E9
Tickmorend Glos 80 F4
Ticknall Derbys 153 E7
Tickton E Yorks 209 E7
Tidbury Green W Mid 117 B11
Tidcombe Wilts 47 B9
Tiddington Oxon 83 E11
Warks 118 F4
Tidebrook E Sus 37 B10
Tideford Corn 6 D6
Tideford Cross Corn 6 C6
Tidenham Glos 79 F9
Tidenham Chase Glos 79 F9
Tideswell Derbys 185 F11
Tidmarsh W Berks 64 E6
Tidmington Warks 100 D5
Tidnor Hereford 97 D11
Tidpit Hants 31 D9
Tidworth Wilts 47 D8
Tiers Cross Pembs 72 C6
Tiffield W Nhants 120 G3
Tifty Aberds 303 E7
Tigerton Angus 293 G7
Tigh-na-Blair Perth 285 F11
Tighnabruaich Argyll 275 F10
Tighnacachla Argyll 274 G3
Tighnafiline Highld 307 L3
Tighness Argyll 284 G6
Tigley Devon 8 C5
Tilbrook Cambs 121 D11
Tilbury Thurrock 68 D6
Tilbury Green Essex 106 C4
Tilbury Juxta Clare
Essex 106 C5
Tile Cross W Mid 134 F3
Tilegate Green Essex 87 D8
Tile Hill W Mid 118 B5
Tilehouse Green W Mid 118 B3
Tilehurst Reading 65 E7
Tilekiln Green Essex 105 G10
Tiley Dorset 29 F11
Tilford Sur 49 E11
Tilford Common Sur 49 E11
Tilford Reeds Sur 49 E11
Tilgate W Sus 51 G9
Tilgate Forest Row
W Sus 51 G9
Tilkey Essex 106 G6
Tilland Corn 6 C6
Tillathrowie Aberds 302 F4
Tillers' Green Glos 98 E3
Tilley Shrops 149 D10
Tilley Green Shrops 149 D10
Tillicoultry Clack 279 B8
Tillietudlem S Lanark 268 F6
Tillingham Essex 89 E7
Tillington Hereford 97 B9
Staffs 151 E8
W Sus 35 C7
Tillington Common
Hereford 97 B9
Tillislow Devon 12 C3
Tillworth Devon 28 G4
Tillyarblet Angus 293 G7
Tillybirloch Aberds 293 C8
Tillycorthie Aberds 303 G9
Tilly Down Hants 47 D10
Tillydrine Aberds 293 D8
Tillyfour Aberds 293 B7
Tillyfourie Aberds 293 B8
Tillygarmond Aberds 293 D8
Tillygreig Aberds 303 G8
Tillykerrie Aberds 303 G8
Tilly Lo Aberds 293 C7
Tillynaught Aberds 302 C5
Tilmanstone Kent 55 C10
Tilney All Saints Norf 157 F11
Tilney cum Islington
Norf 157 G11
Tilney Fen End Norf 157 G10
Tilney High End Norf 157 F11
Tilney St Lawrence
Norf 157 G10
Tilsdown Glos 80 F2
Tilshead Wilts 46 D4
Tilsmore E Sus 37 C9
Tilsop Shrops 116 C2
Tilstock Shrops 149 B10
Tilston Ches W 167 E7
Tilstone Bank Ches W 167 D9
Tilstone Fearnall
Ches W 167 C9
Tilsworth C Beds 103 G9
Tilton on the Hill Leics 136 B4
Tilts S Yorks 198 F5
Tiltups End Glos 80 F4
Tilty Essex 105 F11
Timberden Bottom Kent 68 G4
Timberhonger Worcs 117 C8
Timberland Lincs 173 D10
Timbersbrook Ches E 168 C5
Timberscombe Som 42 E3
Timble N Yorks 205 C9
Timbold Hill Kent 54 B2
Timbrelham Corn 12 E3
Timperley Gtr Man 184 D3
Timsbury Bath 45 B7
Hants 32 C4
Timsgearraidh W Isles 304 E2
Timworth Suff 125 D7
Timworth Green Suff 125 D7
Tincleton Dorset 17 C11
Tindale Cumb 240 F4
Tindale Crescent
Durham 233 F9
Tindon End Essex 106 E2
Tingewick Bucks 102 E3
Tingley W Yorks 197 B9
Tingon Shetland 312 E4
Tingrith C Beds 103 E10
Tingwall Orkney 314 D3
Tinhay Devon 12 E3
Tinkers End Bucks 102 F5
Tinshill W Yorks 205 F11
Tinsley S Yorks 186 C6
Tinsley Green W Sus 51 F9
Tintagel Corn 11 D7
Tintern Parva Mon 79 E8
Tintinhull Som 29 D8
Tintwistle Derbys 185 B8
Tinwald Dumfries 248 G2
Tinwell Rutland 137 B10
Tipner Ptsmth 33 G10
Tippacott Devon 41 D9
Tipper's Hill Warks 134 F5
Tipperty Aberds 302 C6
Aberds 303 G9
Tipple Cross Devon 12 D3
Tipps End Norf 139 D10
Tip's Cross Essex 87 E9
Tiptoe Hants 19 B11
Tipton W Mid 133 E8
Tipton Green W Mid 133 E9
Tipton St John Devon 15 C7
Tiptree Essex 88 B5
Tiptree Heath Essex 88 B5
Tirabad Powys 95 C7
Tiraghoil Argyll 288 G5
Tircanol Swansea 57 B7
Tirdeunaw Swansea 57 B7
Tirinie Perth 291 G10
Tirley Glos 98 F6
Tirley Knowle Glos 98 F6
Tiroran Argyll 288 G6

Tirphil Caerph 77 E10
Tirril Cumb 230 F6
Tirryside Highld 309 H5
Tir-y-berth Caerph 77 F11
Tir-y-dail Carms 75 C10
Tisbury Wilts 30 B6
Tisman's Common
W Sus 50 G5
Tissington Derbys 169 E11
Titchberry Devon 24 B2
Titchfield Hants 33 F8
Titchfield Common Hants 33 F8
Titchfield Park Hants 33 F8
Titchmarsh N Nhants 121 B10
Titchwell Norf 176 E3
Titcomb W Berks 63 F11
Tithby Notts 154 B3
Tithebarn Staffs 169 G9
Tithe Barn Hillock Mers 183 B9
Titley Hereford 114 E6
Titlington Northumb 264 F4
Titmore Green Herts 104 F4
Titsey Sur 52 C2
Titson Corn 24 G2
Tittenhurst Windsor 66 F3
Tittensor Staffs 151 B7
Titterhill Shrops 131 G10
Tittle Row Windsor 65 C11
Tittleshall Norf 159 E7
Titton Worcs 116 D6
Titty Hill W Sus 34 B5
Tiverton Ches W 167 C9
Devon 27 E7
Tivetshall St Margaret
Norf 142 F3
Tivetshall St Mary Norf 142 F3
Tividale W Mid 133 E9
Tivington Som 42 D2
Tivington Knowle Som 42 E2
Tivoli Cumb 228 G5
Tivy Dale S Yorks 197 F9
Tixall Staffs 151 E9
Tixover Rutland 137 C9
Toab Orkney 314 F5
Shetland 313 M5
Toadmoor Derbys 170 E4
Toad Row Suff 143 F10
Tobermory Argyll 289 D7
Toberonochy Argyll 275 C8
Tobha Beag W Isles 296 D5
Tobha Mor W Isles 297 H3
Tobhtarol W Isles 304 E3
Tobson W Isles 304 E3
Toby's Hill Lincs 191 C7
Tocher Aberds 302 F6
Tockenham Wilts 62 D4
Tockenham Wick Wilts 62 C4
Tockholes Blackburn 195 C7
Tockington S Glos 60 B6
Tockwith N Yorks 206 C5
Todber Dorset 30 C4
Todding Hereford 115 B8
Toddington C Beds 103 F10
Glos 99 E10
W Sus 35 G8
Toddlehills Aberds 303 E10
Todd's Green Herts 104 F4
Todenham Glos 100 D4
Todhill Angus 287 D8
Todhills Cumb 239 E9
Durham 233 E10
Todlachie Aberds 293 B8
Todmorden W Yorks 196 C2
Todpool Corn 4 G4
Todrig Borders 261 F10
Todwick S Yorks 187 E7
Toft Cambs 123 F7
Lincs 155 F11
Shetland 312 F6
Warks 119 C9
Toft Hill Durham 233 F9
Lincs 174 C2
Toft Monks Norf 143 E8
Toft next Newton Lincs 189 D8
Toftrees Norf 159 D7
Tofts Highld 310 C7
Toftshaw W Yorks 197 B7
Toftwood Norf 159 G9
Togston Northumb 252 C6
Tokavaig Highld 295 D8
Tokers Green Oxon 65 D8
Tokyngton London 67 C7
Tolastadh a Chaolais
W Isles 304 E3
Tolastadh bho Thuath
W Isles 304 D7
Tolborough Corn 11 F9
Tolcarne Corn 2 B5
Corn 2 C5
Tolcarne Wartha Corn 2 B5
Toldish Corn 5 D8
Tolgus Mount Corn 4 G3
Tolhurst E Sus 53 G7
Tolladine Worcs 117 F7
Tolland Som 42 G6
Tollard Farnham Dorset 30 D6
Tollard Royal Wilts 30 D6
Toll Bar Mers 183 C7
Rutland 137 B10
S Yorks 198 F5
Tollbar End W Mid 119 B7
Toll End W Mid 133 E9
Tollerford Dorset 17 B7
Toller Fratrum Dorset 17 B7
Toller Porcorum Dorset 17 B7
Tollerton Notts 154 C2
N Yorks 215 G10
Toller Whelme Dorset 29 G8
Tollesbury Essex 89 C7
Tollesby Mbro 225 B10
Tolleshunt D'Arcy Essex 88 C6
Tolleshunt Knights Essex 88 C6
Tolleshunt Major Essex 88 C5
Tollie Highld 300 D5
Toll of Birness Aberds 303 F10
Tolm W Isles 304 E6
Tolmers Herts 86 E4
Tolpuddle Dorset 17 C11
Tolskithy Corn 4 G3
Tolvaddon Downs Corn 4 G3
Tolvah Highld 291 D10
Tolworth London 67 F7
Tomaknock Perth 286 E2
Tom an Fhuadain
W Isles 305 G5
Tomatin Highld 301 G8
Tombreck Highld 300 F6
Tombui Perth 286 B2
Tomchrasky Highld 290 B4
Tomdoun Highld 290 C3
Tomich Highld 300 B6
Highld 300 G3
Tomich House Highld 300 E5
Tomintoul Aberds 292 D3
Moray 292 B3
Tomlow Warks 119 E9
Tomnaven Moray 302 F4
Tomnavoulin Moray 302 G2
Tomperrow Corn 4 G5
Tompkin Staffs 168 E6
Tompset's Bank E Sus 52 G2
Tomsleibhe Argyll 289 F8
Tomthorn Derbys 185 F9
Ton Mon 78 F5
Ton Breigam V Glam 58 D3
Tonbridge Kent 52 D5
Tonderghie Dumfries 236 F6
Tondu Bridgend 57 E11
Tone Som 27 C10
Tonedale Som 27 C10
Tone Green Som 27 C11
Tong Kent 53 D10
Shrops 132 B5
W Yorks 205 G10
Tonge Leics 153 E8
Tonge Corner Kent 70 F2
Tonge Fold Gtr Man 195 F8
Tonge Moor Gtr Man 195 E8
Tong Forge Shrops 132 B5
Tong Green Kent 54 C3
Tongham Sur 49 D11
Tongland Dumfries 237 D8
Tong Norton Shrops 132 B5
Tong Park W Yorks 205 F9
Tong Street W Yorks 205 G9
Tongue Highld 308 D5
Tongue End Lincs 156 F3
Tongwell M Keynes 103 C7
Tongwynlais Cardiff 58 C6
Tonmawr Neath 57 B10
Tonna =Tonnau Neath 57 B9
Tonnau =Tonna Neath 57 B9
Ton-Pentre Rhondda 77 F7
Ton-teg Rhondda 58 B5
Tontine Lancs 194 G4
Tonwell Herts 86 B4
Tonypandy Rhondda 77 G7
Ton-y-pistyll Caerph 77 F11
Tonyrefail Rhondda 58 B4
Toot Baldon Oxon 83 E9
Toothill Hants 32 D5
Swindon 62 C6
W Yorks 196 C6
Toot Hill Essex 87 E8
Staffs 169 G9
Tooting Graveney London 67 E9
Topcliffe N Yorks 215 D8
W Yorks 197 B9
Topcroft Norf 142 E5
Topcroft Street Norf 142 E5
Top End Bedford 121 E10
Top Green Notts 172 F3
Topham S Yorks 198 D6
Topleigh W Sus 34 D6
Top Lock Gtr Man 194 F6
Top of Hebers Gtr Man 195 F11
Top o' th' Lane Lancs 194 C5
Top o' th' Meadows
Gtr Man 196 F3
Toppesfield Essex 106 D4
Toppings Gtr Man 195 E8
Toprow Norf 142 D3
Topsham Devon 14 D5
Top Valley Nottingham 171 F9
Torbeg N Ayrs 255 E10
Torboll Farm Highld 309 K7
Torbothie N Lanark 269 D7
Torbreck Highld 309 J7
Torbrex Stirling 278 C5
Torbryan Devon 8 B6
Torbush N Lanark 268 D6
Torcross Devon 8 G6
Torcroy Highld 291 D9
Tore Highld 300 D6
Torfrey Corn 6 E2
Torgyle Highld 290 B5
Torinturk Argyll 275 G9
Torkington Gtr Man 184 D6
Torksey Lincs 188 F4
Torlum W Isles 296 F3
Torlundy Highld 290 F3
Tormarton S Glos 61 D9
Tormisdale Argyll 254 B2
Tormitchell S Ayrs 244 E6
Tormore Highld 295 E8
N Ayrs 255 D9
Tornagrain Highld 301 E7
Tornahaish Aberds 292 C4
Tornapress Highld 299 E8
Tornaveen Aberds 293 C8
Torness Highld 300 G5
Toronto Durham 233 E9
Torpenhow Cumb 229 D10
Torphichen W Loth 279 G9
Torphin Edin 270 B4
Torphins Aberds 293 C8
Torpoint Corn 7 E8
Torquay Torbay 9 C8
Torquhan Borders 271 F8
Torr Devon 7 E11
Devon 8 C2
Torra Argyll 254 B4
Torran Argyll 275 C9
Highld 298 E5
Highld 301 B7
Torrance E Dunb 278 G2
Torrans Argyll 288 G6
Torranyard N Ayrs 267 G7
Torre Som 42 E4
Torbay 9 C8
Torridon Highld 299 D9
Torridon Ho Highld 299 D8
Torries Aberds 293 B8
Torrin Highld 295 C7
Torrisdale Highld 308 C6
Torrisdale Castle Argyll 255 D8
Torrisdale-Square
Argyll 255 D8
Torrish Highld 311 H3
Torrisholme Lancs 211 G9
Torroble Highld 309 J5
Torroy Highld 309 K5
Torrpark Corn 11 D10
Torry Aberdeen 293 C11
Aberds 302 F4
Torryburn Fife 279 D10
Torsonce Borders 271 G9
Torsonce Mains Borders 271 G9
Torterston Aberds 303 E10
Torthorwald Dumfries 238 B2
Tortington W Sus 35 F8
Torton Worcs 116 C6
Tortworth S Glos 80 G2
Torvaig Highld 298 E4
Torver Cumb 220 G5
Torwood Falk 278 E6
Torwoodlee Mains
Borders 261 B11
Torworth Notts 187 D11
Tosberry Devon 24 C3
Toscaig Highld 295 B9
Toseland Cambs 122 E4
Tosside N Yorks 203 B11
Tostock Suff 125 E9
Totaig Highld 295 C10
Highld 298 D2
Totardor Highld 294 B5
Tote Highld 298 E4
Totegan Highld 310 C2
Tote Hill Hants 32 C4
W Sus 34 C5
Totford Hants 48 F5
Totham Hill Essex 88 C5
Totham Plains Essex 88 C5
Tothill Lincs 190 E6
Tot Hill Hants 64 G3
Totland IoW 20 D2
Totley S Yorks 186 F4
Totley Brook S Yorks 186 E4
Totley Rise S Yorks 186 E4
Totmonslow Staffs 151 B9
Totnell Dorset 29 F10
Totnes Devon 8 C6
Totnor Hereford 97 E11
Toton Notts 153 C10
Totronald Argyll 288 D3
Totscore Highld 298 C3
Tottenham London 86 G4
Tottenham Hale London 67 B10
Tottenhill Norf 158 G2
Tottenhill Row Norf 158 G2
Totteridge Bucks 84 G5
London 86 G2
Totternhoe C Beds 103 G9
Totteroak S Glos 61 C8
Totterton Shrops 131 F7
Totties W Yorks 197 F7
Tottington Gtr Man 195 E9
Norf 141 D7
Tottlebank Cumb 210 C6
Tottleworth Lancs 203 G10
Totton Hants 32 E5
Touchen End Windsor 65 D11
Toulston N Yorks 206 E5
Toulton Som 43 G7
Toulvaddie Highld 311 L2
Tournaig Highld 307 L3
Toux Aberds 303 D9
Tovil Kent 53 C9
Towan Corn 10 G3
Towan Cross Corn 4 F4
Toward Argyll 266 B2
Towcester W Nhants 102 B3
Towednack Corn 1 B5
Towerage Bucks 84 G4
Tower End Norf 158 F3
Tower Hamlets Kent 55 E10
Towerhead N Som 44 B2
Tower Hill Ches E 184 F6
Devon 12 C3
Essex 108 E4
Herts 85 E8
Mers 194 G2
Sur 51 D7
W Mid 133 E11
W Sus 35 B11
Towersey Oxon 84 D2
Tow House Northumb 241 E7
Towie Aberds 292 B6
Aberds 302 G5
Aberds 303 C8
Towiemore Moray 302 E3
Tow Law Durham 233 D8
Town Barton Devon 14 C2
Townend Derbys 185 E9
Staffs 151 B9
W Dunb 277 F8
Town End Bucks 84 F3
Cambs 139 D8
Cumb 211 B7
Cumb 211 C8
Cumb 212 C2
Cumb 220 D6
Cumb 221 E8
Cumb 221 F7
Cumb 231 F8
Derbys 185 F11
E Yorks 207 C10
Mers 183 D7
W Yorks 196 D5
Townfield Durham 232 B5
Town Fields Ches W 167 B10
Towngate Cumb 230 B6
Lincs 156 G2
Town Green Gtr Man 183 B9
Lancs 194 F2
Norf 161 G7
Townhead Argyll 275 G11
Cumb 229 D7
Cumb 230 D6
Cumb 231 E8
Dumfries 237 E8
N Lanark 268 B4
Northumb 251 E9
S Ayrs 244 C6
S Yorks 186 E4
S Yorks 197 G7
Town Head Cumb 220 D6
Cumb 221 E8
Cumb 222 C2
Cumb 222 C3
Cumb 231 F7
Cumb 231 F8
Cumb 231 G8
Cumb 231 G9
Derbys 185 F11
N Yorks 204 B2
N Yorks 212 F5
Staffs 169 F8
W Yorks 204 D6
Townhead of Greenlaw
Dumfries 237 C9
Townhill Fife 280 D2
Swansea 56 C6
Townhill Park Hants 33 E7
Town Kelloe Durham 234 D3
Townlake Devon 12 G4
Townland Green Kent 54 G2
Town Lane Gtr Man 183 B11
Town Littleworth E Sus 36 D6
Town of Lowton Mers 183 B10
Town Park Telford 132 B3
Town Row E Sus 52 G5
Townsend Bath 44 B5
Bucks 84 D2
Devon 25 B10
Herts 85 D10
Oxon 63 B11
Pembs 72 D4
Som 44 C4
Stoke 168 F6
Wilts 46 B3
Wilts 46 B4
Towns End Hants 48 B5
Som 30 D2
Town's End Bucks 102 G2
Dorset 18 B3
Dorset 18 E5
Dorset 29 F9
Som 45 D7
Townsend Fold Lancs 195 C10
Townshend Corn 2 C3
Town Street Glos 98 F6
Townwell S Glos 79 G11
Town Yetholm Borders 263 D8
Towthorpe E Yorks 217 G8
York 207 B8
Towton N Yorks 206 F5
Towyn Conwy 181 F7
Toxteth Mers 182 D5
Toynton All Saints Lincs 174 C5
Toynton Fen Side Lincs 174 C5
Toynton St Peter Lincs 174 C6
Toy's Hill Kent 52 C3
Trabboch E Ayrs 257 E10
Traboe Corn 2 E6
Trabrown Borders 271 F10
Tracebridge Som 27 C9
Tradespark Highld 301 D8
Orkney 314 F4
Trafford Park Gtr Man 184 B3
Traigh Ho Highld 295 F8
Trailong Powys 95 F9
Trallwn Rhondda 77 G9
Swansea 57 B7
Tramagenna Corn 11 E7
Tram Inn Hereford 97 E9
Tranch Torf 78 E3
Tranent E Loth 281 G8
Tranmere Mers 182 D4
Trantlebeg Highld 310 D2
Trantlemore Highld 310 D2
Tranwell Northumb 252 G5
Trapp Carms 75 B11
Traprain E Loth 281 F11
Trap's Green Warks 118 D2
Trapshill W Berks 63 G11
Traquair Borders 261 C8
Trash Green W Berks 65 F7
Travellers' Rest Carms 74 B5
Trawden Lancs 204 F4
Trawscoed Powys 95 E11
Trawsfynydd Gwyn 146 B4
Trawsnant Ceredig 111 D11
Treadam Mon 78 B5
Treaddow Hereford 97 G10
Treal Corn 2 F6
Trealaw Rhondda 77 G8
Treales Lancs 202 G4
Trearddur Anglesey 178 F3
Treaslane Highld 298 D3
Treath Corn 3 D7
Treator Corn 10 F4
Tre-Aubrey V Glam 58 E4
Trebanog Rhondda 77 G8
Trebanos Neath 76 E2
Trebarber Corn 5 C7
Trebartha Corn 11 F11
Trebarwith Corn 11 D7
Trebarwith Strand Corn 10 D6
Trebeath Corn 11 D11
Tre-Beferad V Glam 58 F3
Trebell Green Corn 5 C11
Treberfydd Powys 96 F2
Trebetherick Corn 10 F4
Trebilcock Corn 5 C9
Treble's Holford Som 43 G7
Tre-boeth Swansea 57 B7
Treborough Som 42 F4
Trebudannon Corn 5 C7
Trebullett Corn 12 F2
Treburgett Corn 11 F7
Treburgie Corn 6 C4
Treburley Corn 12 F3
Treburrick Corn 10 G3
Trebyan Corn 5 C11
Trecastle Powys 95 F7
Trecenydd Caerph 58 B6
Trecott Devon 25 G10
Trecwn Pembs 91 E9
Trecynon Rhondda 77 E7
Tredannick Corn 10 G6
Tredaule Corn 11 E10
Tredavoe Corn 1 D5
Treddiog Pembs 91 F7
Tredegar Bl Gwent 77 D10
Trederwen Powys 148 F5
Tre-derwen Powys 148 F4
Tredethy Corn 11 G7
Tredington Glos 99 F8
Warks 100 C5
Tredinnick Corn 1 C4
Corn 5 D10
Corn 6 B3
Corn 6 D4
Corn 10 G4
Tredogan V Glam 58 F5
Tredomen Caerph 77 G10
Powys 96 E2
Tredown Devon 24 D2
Tredrizzick Corn 10 F5
Tredunnock Mon 78 G5
Tredustan Powys 96 E2
Tredworth Glos 80 B4
Treen Corn 1 B4
Corn 1 E3
Treesmill Corn 5 D11
Treeton S Yorks 186 D6
Trefaes Gwyn 144 C5
Trefanny Hill Corn 6 D4
Trefasser Pembs 91 D7
Trefdraeth Anglesey 178 G6
Trefdraeth =Newport
Pembs 91 D11
Trefecca Powys 96 E2
Trefechan Ceredig 111 A11
M Tydf 77 D8
Wrex 166 F3
Trefeglwys Powys 129 E9
Trefeitha Powys 96 E2
Trefenter Ceredig 112 D2
Treffgarne Pembs 91 G9
Treffynnon Pembs 90 F6
Treffynnon =Holywell
Flint 181 F11
Trefgarn Owen Pembs 91 F7
Trefil Bl Gwent 77 C10
Trefilan Ceredig 111 F11
Trefin =Trevine Pembs 90 E6
Treflach Shrops 148 D5
Trefnanney Powys 148 F4
Trefnant Denb 181 G9
Trefonen Shrops 148 D5
Trefor Anglesey 178 E5
Gwyn 162 F5
Treforda Corn 11 E7
Treforest Rhondda 58 B5
Treforgan Ceredig 92 B4
Tre-Forgan Neath 76 D3
Treforys =Morriston
Swansea 57 B7
Trefriw Conwy 164 C3
Trefrize Corn 12 F2
Tref y Clawdd =Knighton
Powys 114 C5
Trefynwy =Monmouth
Mon 79 C8
Tregada Corn 12 E2
Tregadgwith Corn 1 D4
Tregadillett Corn 12 E2
Tre-gagle Mon 79 D8
Tregaian Anglesey 178 F6
Tregajorran Corn 4 G3
Tregamere Corn 5 C8
Tregardock Corn 10 E6
Tregare Mon 78 C6
Tregarland Corn 6 D5
Tregarlandbridge Corn 6 D4
Tregarne Corn 3 E7
Tregaron Ceredig 112 F3
Tregarrick Mill Corn 6 D4
Tregarth Gwyn 163 B10
Tregath Gwyn 163 B10
Tregatillian Corn 5 C8
Tregatta Corn 11 D7
Tregavarah Corn 1 D4
Tregear Corn 2 E5
Tregeare Corn 11 D10
Tregeiriog Wrex 148 C3
Tregele Anglesey 178 C5
Tregellist Corn 10 F6
Tregeseal Corn 1 C3
Tregew Corn 3 C8
Tre-Gibbon Rhondda 77 E7
Tregidden Corn 3 E7
Treginnis Pembs 90 G4
Treglemais Pembs 90 F6
Tregole Corn 11 B9
Tregolls Corn 2 B6
Tregolwyn =Colwinston
V Glam 58 D2
Tregona Corn 5 B7
Tregonce Corn 10 G4
Tregonetha Corn 5 C9
Tregonna Corn 10 G4
Tregonning Corn 5 D7
Tregony Corn 5 G8
Tregoodwell Corn 11 E8
Tregorden Corn 10 G6
Tregorrick Corn 5 E10
Tregoss Corn 5 C9
Tregoyd Powys 96 D4
Tregoyd Mill Powys 96 D3
Tregreenwell Corn 11 E7
Tregrehan Mills Corn 5 E10
Tregroes Ceredig 93 C8
Tregullon Corn 5 C11
Tregunna Corn 10 G5
Tregurrian Corn 5 B7
Tregurtha Downs Corn 2 C2
Tre Gwyr =Gowerton
Swansea 56 B5
Tregyddulan Pembs 91 D7
Tregynon Powys 129 D11
Tre-gynwr Carms 74 B6
Trehafod Rhondda 77 G8
Trehafren Powys 129 E11
Trehan Corn 7 D8
Treharris M Tydf 77 F9
Trehemborne Corn 10 G3
Treherbert Rhondda 76 F6
Tre-hill V Glam 58 E5
Trehunist Corn 6 C6
Tre-Ifor Rhondda 77 D7
Trekeivesteps Corn 11 G10
Trekenner Corn 12 F2
Trekenning Corn 5 C8
Treknow Corn 11 D7
Trelales =Laleston
Bridgend 57 F11
Trelan Corn 2 F6
Tre-lan Flint 165 B11
Trelash Corn 11 C9
Trelassick Corn 5 E7
Trelawnyd Flint 181 F9
Trelech Carms 92 E5
Treleddyd-fawr Pembs 90 F5
Treleigh Corn 4 G4
Treletert =Letterston
Pembs 91 F8
Trelew Corn 3 B8
Trelewis M Tydf 77 F10
Treligga Corn 11 E7
Trelights Corn 10 F5
Trelill Corn 10 F6
Trelion Corn 5 E8
Treliske Corn 4 F6
Trelissick Corn 3 B8
Treliver Corn 5 B9
Trellech Mon 79 D8
Trelleck Grange Mon 79 E7
Trelogan Flint 181 E10
Treloquithack Corn 2 D5
Trelowia Corn 6 D5
Trelowth Corn 5 E9
Trelystan Powys 130 C5
Tremadog Gwyn 163 G9
Tremail Corn 11 D9
Tremain Ceredig 92 B4
Tremaine Corn 11 D10
Tremains Bridgend 58 D2
Tremar Corn 6 B5
Trematon Corn 7 D7
Trematon Castle Corn 7 D8
Tremayne Corn 2 B4
Trembraze Corn 6 B5
Tremedda Corn 1 B5
Tremeirchion Denb 181 G9
Tremethick Cross Corn 1 C4
Tremore Corn 5 C10
Tremorebridge Corn 5 C10
Tremorfa Cardiff 59 D8
Tre-Mostyn Flint 181 F10
Trenance Corn 4 C6
Corn 5 B7
Corn 5 C9
Corn 10 G4
Trenant Corn 6 B4
Corn 10 G5
Trenarren Corn 5 F10
Trenay Corn 6 B3
Trench Telford 150 G3
Trench Green Oxon 65 D7
Trench Wood Kent 52 D5
Trencreek Corn 4 C6
Trencrom Corn 2 B2
Trendeal Corn 5 E7
Trenear Corn 2 C5
Treneglos Corn 11 D10
Trenerth Corn 2 B4
Trenewan Corn 6 E3
Trengune Corn 11 C9
Trenhorne Corn 11 F11
Treningle Corn 5 B10
Treninnick Corn 4 C6
Trenoon Corn 2 F6
Trenoweth Corn 3 C7
Trent Dorset 29 D9
Trentham Stoke 168 G5
Trentishoe Devon 40 D6
Trentlock Derbys 153 C9
Trent Vale Stoke 168 G5
Trenwheal Corn 2 C4
Treoes V Glam 58 D2
Treopert =Granston
Pembs 91 E7
Treorchy =Treorci
Rhondda 77 F7
Treorci =Treorchy
Rhondda 77 F7
Treowen Caerph 78 F2
Powys 130 E2
Tre-pit V Glam 58 E2
Trequite Corn 10 F6
Tre'r-ddôl Ceredig 128 E3
Trerhyngyll V Glam 58 D4
Trerise Corn 2 F6
Trer llai =Leighton
Powys 130 B4
Trerose Corn 3 D7
Trerulefoot Corn 6 D6
Tresaith Ceredig 110 G5
Tresamble Corn 3 B7
Tresarrett Corn 11 G7
Tresavean Corn 2 B6
Tresawle Corn 5 F7
Tresawsen Corn 4 F5
Trescoll Corn 5 C10
Trescott Staffs 132 D6
Trescowe Corn 2 C3
Tresean Corn 4 D5
Tresevern Croft Corn 2 B6
Tresham Glos 80 G3
Tresigin =Sigingstone
V Glam 58 E3
Tresillian Corn 5 F7
Tresimwn =Bonvilston
V Glam 58 E5
Tresinney Corn 11 E8
Tresinwen Pembs 91 C7
Treskerby Corn 4 G4
Treskillard Corn 2 B5
Treskilling Corn 5 D10
Treskinnick Cross Corn 11 B10
Treslothan Corn 2 B5
Tresmeer Corn 11 D10
Tresowes Green Corn 2 D3
Tresoweshill Corn 2 D4
Tresparrett Corn 11 C8
Tresparrett Posts Corn 11 C8
Tressady Highld 309 J7
Tressait Perth 291 G10
Tresta Shetland 312 D8
Shetland 313 H5
Treswell Notts 188 F3
Treswithian Corn 4 G2
Treswithian Downs
Corn 4 G2
Tre-Taliesin Ceredig 128 E3
Trethellan Water Corn 2 B6
Trethevy Corn 11 D7
Trethewey Corn 1 E3
Trethillick Corn 10 F4
Trethomas Caerph 59 B7
Trethosa Corn 5 E8
Trethowel Corn 5 E10
Trethurgy Corn 5 D10
Tretio Pembs 90 F5
Tretire Hereford 97 G10
Tretower Powys 96 G3
Treuddyn Flint 166 D3
Trevadlock Corn 11 F11
Trevail Corn 4 D5
Trevalga Corn 11 D7
Trevalgan Corn 1 A5
Trevalyn Wrex 166 D5
Trevance Corn 10 G4
Trevanger Corn 10 F5
Trevanson Corn 10 G5
Trevarrack Corn 1 C5
Trevarren Corn 5 C8
Trevarrian Corn 4 B6
Trevarrick Corn 5 G9
Trevarth Corn 4 G4
Trevaughan Carms 73 B11
Carms 93 G7
Tre-vaughan Carms 93 G8
Treveal Corn 1 A5
Trevegean Corn 1 D3
Treveighan Corn 11 F7
Trevellas Corn 4 E4
Trevelmond Corn 6 C4
Trevelver Corn 10 G5
Trevemper Corn 4 D6
Treven Corn 11 D7
Trevena Corn 2 D4
Trevenen Corn 2 D5
Trevenen Bal Corn 2 D5
Trevenning Corn 11 F7
Treveor Corn 5 G9
Treverbyn Corn 5 D10
Corn 6 B4
Treverva Corn 3 C7
Trevescan Corn 1 E3
Trevethin Torf 78 E3
Trevia Corn 11 E7
Trevigro Corn 6 B6
Trevilder Corn 10 G6
Trevilla Corn 3 B8
Trevilson Corn 4 D6
Trevine Corn 10 F5
Trevine =Trefin Pembs 90 E6
Treviscoe Corn 5 D8
Treviskey Corn 2 B6
Trevithal Corn 1 D5
Trevoll Corn 4 D6
Trevone Corn 10 F3
Trevor Wrex 166 G3
Trevorrick Corn 10 G4
Trevor Uchaf Denb 166 G2
Trevowah Corn 4 D5
Trevowhan Corn 1 B4
Trew Corn 2 D4
Trewalder Corn 11 E7
Trewarmett Corn 11 D7
Trewartha Corn 2 B2
Corn 3 B10
Trewassa Corn 11 D8
Treween Corn 11 E10
Trewellard Corn 1 C3
Trewen Corn 11 E7
Corn 11 E11
Mon 79 G7
Trewennack Corn 2 D5
Trewennan Corn 11 E7
Trewern Powys 148 G5
Trewetha Corn 10 E6
Trewethen Corn 10 F6
Trewethern Corn 10 F6
Trewey Corn 1 B5
Trewidland Corn 6 D5
Trewindle Corn 6 C2
Trewint Corn 6 C5
Corn 11 B9
Corn 11 E10
Trewithian Corn 3 B9
Trewithick Corn 11 D11
Trewollock Corn 5 G10
Trewoodloe Corn 12 G2
Trewoofe Corn 1 D4
Trewoon Corn 2 F5
Corn 5 E9
Treworga Corn 5 G7
Treworgan Common
Mon 78 D6
Treworlas Corn 3 B9
Treworld Corn 11 C8
Trewornan Corn 10 G5
Treworrick Corn 6 B4
Treworthal Corn 3 B9
Trewyddel =Moylgrove
Pembs 92 C2
Trewyn Devon 24 G4
Tre-wyn Mon 96 G6
Treyarnon Corn 10 G3
Treyford W Sus 34 D4
Trezaise Corn 5 D9
Trezelah Corn 1 C5
Triangle Glos 79 E8
Staffs 133 B11
W Yorks 196 C4
Trickett's Cross Dorset 31 G9
Triffleton Pembs 91 G9
Trillacott Corn 11 D11
Trimdon Durham 234 E3
Trimdon Colliery
Durham 234 D3
Trimdon Grange
Durham 234 D3
Trimingham Norf 160 B5
Trimley Lower Street
Suff 108 D5
Trimley St Martin Suff 108 D5
Trimley St Mary Suff 108 D5
Trimpley Worcs 116 B5
Trimsaran Carms 75 E7
Trims Green Herts 87 B7
Trimstone Devon 40 E3
Trinafour Perth 291 G9
Trinant Caerph 78 E2
Tring Herts 84 C6
Tringford Herts 84 C6
Tring Wharf Herts 84 C6
Trinity Angus 293 G8
Devon 27 F7
Edin 280 F4
Trinity Fields Staffs 151 D8
Trisant Ceredig 112 B4
Triscombe Som 43 F7
Trislaig Highld 290 F2
Trispen Corn 4 E6
Tritlington Northumb 252 E6
Troan Corn 5 D7
Trochry Perth 286 C3
Trodigal Argyll 255 E7
Troearhiwgwair
Bl Gwent 77 D11
Troedrhiwdalar Powys 113 G9
Troedrhiwffenyd Ceredig 93 C8
Troedrhiwfuwch Caerph 77 E10
Troedyraur Ceredig 92 B6
Troedyrhiw M Tydf 77 E9
Trofarth Conwy 180 G5
Trolliloes E Sus 23 C10
Tromode IoM 192 E4
Trondavoe Shetland 312 F5
Troon Corn 2 B5
S Ayrs 257 C8
Trooper's Inn Pembs 73 C7
Trosaraidh W Isles 297 K3
Trossachs Hotel Stirling 285 G9
Troston Suff 125 C7
Trostre Carms 56 B4
Trostrey Common Mon 78 E5
Troswell Corn 11 C11
Trotshill Worcs 117 F7
Trotten Marsh W Sus 34 B4
Trottiscliffe Kent 68 G6
Trotton W Sus 34 C4
Trough Gate Lancs 195 C11
Troutbeck Cumb 221 E8
Cumb 230 F3
Troutbeck Bridge Cumb 221 F8
Troway Derbys 186 F5
Trowbridge Cardiff 59 C8
Wilts 45 B11
Trowell Notts 153 B9
Trow Green Glos 79 D9
Trowle Common Wilts 45 B10
Trowley Bottom Herts 85 C9
Trows Borders 262 C5
Trowse Newton Norf 142 B4
Troydale W Yorks 205 G10
Troy Town Kent 52 D2
Kent 54 E5
Medway 69 F8
Truas Corn 11 D7
Trub Gtr Man 195 F11
Trudoxhill Som 45 E8
Trueman's Heath
Worcs 117 B11
True Street Devon 8 C6
Trull Som 28 C2
Trumaisgearraidh
W Isles 296 D4
Trumfleet S Yorks 198 E6
Trumpan Highld 298 C2
Trumpet Hereford 98 D3
Trumpington Cambs 123 F8
Trumpsgreen Sur 66 F3
Trunch Norf 160 C5
Trunnah Lancs 202 E2
Truro Corn 4 G6
Truscott Corn 12 D2
Trusham Devon 14 E3
Trusley Derbys 152 B5
Trussall Corn 2 D5
Trussell Corn 11 D10
Trusthorpe Lincs 191 E8
Truthan Corn 4 E6
Truthwall Corn 2 C2
Trwstllewelyn Powys 130 D3
Tryfil Anglesey 178 E6
Trysull Staffs 133 E7
Trythogga Corn 1 C5
Tubbs Mill Corn 5 G9
Tubney Oxon 82 F6
Tubslake Kent 53 G9
Tuckenhay Devon 8 D6
Tuckermarsh Devon 7 B8
Tuckerton Som 28 B3
Tuckhill Shrops 132 F5
Tuckingmill Corn 4 G3
Corn 11 F7
Wilts 30 B6
Tucking Mill Bath 61 G9
Tuckton BCP 19 C8
Tuddenham Suff 108 B3
Suff 124 C4
Tuddenham St Martin
Suff 108 B3
Tudeley Kent 52 D6
Tudeley Hale Kent 52 D6
Tudhay Devon 28 G4
Tudhoe Durham 233 D11
Tudhoe Grange
Durham 233 E11
Tudorville Hereford 97 G11
Tudweiliog Gwyn 144 B4
Tuebrook Mers 182 C5
Tuesley Sur 50 E3
Tuesnoad Kent 54 E2
Tuffley Glos 80 C4
Tufnell Park London 67 B9
Tufton Hants 48 D3
Pembs 91 F10
Tugby Leics 136 C5
Tugford Shrops 131 F11
Tughall Northumb 264 D6
Tulchan Lodge Angus 292 F3
Tullecombe W Sus 34 B4
Tullibardine Perth 286 F3
Tullibody Clack 279 B7
Tullich Argyll 284 F4
Highld 299 E9
Highld 300 G6
Tullich Muir Highld 301 B7
Tulliemet Perth 286 B3
Tulloch Aberds 293 F9
Aberds 303 F8
Highld 290 E5
Perth 286 E4
Tulloch Castle Highld 300 C5
Tullochgorm Argyll 275 D10
Tulloch-gribban Highld 301 G9
Tullochroisk Perth 285 B11
Tullochvenus Aberds 293 C7
Tulloes Angus 287 C9
Tullybannocher Perth 285 E11
Tullybelton Perth 286 D4
Tullycross Stirling 277 D9
Tullyfergus Perth 286 C6
Tullymurdoch Perth 286 B5
Tullynessle Aberds 293 B7
Tulse Hill London 67 E10
Tumble =Y Tymbl Carms 75 C8
Tumbler's Green Essex 106 F6
Tumby Lincs 174 D2
Tumby Woodside Lincs 174 D3
Tummel Bridge Perth 285 B11
Tumpy Green Glos 80 E2
Tumpy Lakes Hereford 97 B10
Tunbridge Hill Medway 69 E10
Tunbridge Wells =Royal
Tunbridge Wells Kent 52 F5
Tunga W Isles 304 E6
Tungate Norf 160 D5
Tunley Bath 45 B7
Glos 80 E6
Tunnel Hill Worcs 98 C6
Tunnel Pits N Lincs 199 G8
Tunshill Gtr Man 196 E2
Tunstall E Yorks 209 G12
Kent 69 G11
Lancs 212 E2
Norf 143 B8
N Yorks 224 F4
Staffs 150 D5
Stoke 168 E5
Suff 127 G7
T&W 243 G9
Tunstead Derbys 185 G10
Gtr Man 196 G4
Norf 160 E5
Tunworth Hants 49 D7
Tupsley Hereford 97 C10
Tupton Derbys 170 B5
Turbary Common BCP 19 C7
Turfdown Corn 5 B11
Turf Hill Gtr Man 196 E2
Turfholm S Lanark 259 B8
Turfmoor Devon 28 G3
Shrops 149 F7
Turgis Green Hants 49 B7
Turin Angus 287 B9
Turkdean Glos 81 B10
Turkey Island Hants 33 E9
W Sus 34 D3
Turkey Tump Hereford 97 F10
Tur Langton Leics 136 E4
Turleigh Wilts 61 G10
Turleygreen Shrops 132 F5
Turlin Moor BCP 18 C5
Turmer Hants 31 F10
Turn Lancs 195 D10
Turnalt Argyll 275 C9
Turnastone Hereford 97 D7
Turnberry S Ayrs 244 B6
Turnchapel Plym 7 E9
Turnditch Derbys 170 F3
Turner Green Lancs 203 G8
Turner's Green E Sus 23 B10
E Sus 52 G6
Warks 118 D3
W Berks 64 F4
Turners Hill W Sus 51 F10
Turners Puddle Dorset 18 C2
Turnerwood S Yorks 187 E8
Turnford Herts 86 E5
Turnhouse Edin 280 G3
Turnhurst Stoke 168 E5
Turnstead Milton
Derbys 185 E8
Turnworth Dorset 30 F4
Turrerich Perth 286 D2
Turriff Aberds 303 D7
Tursdale Durham 234 D2
Turton Bottoms
Blackburn 195 D8
Turves Cambs 138 D6
Turves Green W Mid 117 B10
Turvey Bedford 121 G8
Turville Bucks 84 G3
Turville Heath Bucks 84 G2
Turweston Bucks 102 D2
Tushielaw Borders 261 F8
Tutbury Staffs 152 D4
Tutnall Worcs 117 C9
Tutnalls Glos 79 E10
Tutshill Glos 79 G8
Tutt Hill Kent 54 D3
Tuttington Norf 160 D4
Tutts Clump W Berks 64 E5
Tutwell Corn 12 F3
Tuxford Notts 188 G2
Twatt Orkney 314 D2
Shetland 313 H5
Twechar E Dunb 278 F4
Tweedale Telford 132 C4
Tweeddaleburn Borders 270 E5
Tweedmouth Northumb 273 E9
Tweedsmuir Borders 260 E3
Twelve Heads Corn 4 G5
Twelve Oaks E Sus 37 C11
Twelvewoods Corn 6 B4
Twemlow Green Ches E 168 B3
Twenties Kent 71 F10
Twenty Lincs 156 E3
Twerton Bath 61 G8
Twickenham London 67 E7
Twigworth Glos 98 G6
Twineham W Sus 36 D3
Twineham Green W Sus 36 C3
Twinhoe Bath 45 B8
Twinstead Essex 107 D7
Twinstead Green Essex 106 D6
Twiss Green Warr 183 B11
Twist Devon 28 G3
Twiston Lancs 204 E2
Twitchen Devon 41 G9
Shrops 115 B7
Twitchen Mill Devon 41 G9
Twitham Kent 55 B9
Twitton Kent 52 B4
Two Bridges Devon 13 G8
Glos 79 D11
Two Burrows Corn 4 F4
Two Dales Derbys 170 C3
Two Gates Staffs 134 C4
Two Mile Ash M Keynes 102 D6
W Sus 35 B10
Two Mile Hill Bristol 60 E6
Two Mile Oak Cross Devon 8 B6
Two Mills Ches W 182 G5
Two Pots Devon 40 E4
Two Waters Herts 85 D9
Twr Anglesey 178 E2
Twycross Leics 134 C6
Twydall Medway 69 F9
Twyford Bucks 102 F3
Derbys 152 D6
Dorset 30 D5
Hants 33 C7
Leics 154 G4

Twyford continued
Lincs 155 E8
Norf 159 E10
Oxon 101 D9
Shrops 148 D6
Wokingham 65 D9
Worcs 99 B10
Twyford Common
Hereford 97 D10
Twyn-Allws Mon 78 C3
Twynholm Dumfries 237 D8
Twyning Glos 99 D7
Twyning Green Glos 99 D8
Twynllanan Carms 94 G5
Twynmynydd Carms 75 C11
Twyn Shôn-Ifan Caerph 77 G11
Twynyrodyn M Tydf 77 D9
Twyn-yr-odyn V Glam 58 E6
Twyn-y-Sheriff Mon 78 D6
Twywell N Nhants 121 B9
Tyberton Hereford 97 D7
Tyburn W Mid 134 E2
Tyby Norf 159 D11
Ty-coch Swansea 56 C6
Tycroes Carms 75 C10
Tycrwyn Powys 148 F2
Tyddewi = St Davids
Pembs 90 F5
Tydd Gote Lincs 157 F9
Tydd St Giles Cambs 157 F8
Tydd St Mary Lincs 157 F8
Tyddyn Powys 129 F9
Tyddyn Angharad Denb 165 F9
Tyddyn Dai Anglesey 178 C6
Tyddyn-mawr Gwyn 163 G9
Ty-draw Conwy 164 D5
Swansea 57 C7
Tye Hants 22 C2
Tye Common Essex 87 G11
Tyegate Green Norf 161 G7
Tye Green Essex 87 C10
Essex 87 D7
Essex 87 F11
Essex 105 D11
Essex 105 G10
Essex 106 G5
Tyersal W Yorks 205 G9
Ty-fry Mon 78 F6
Tyganol V Glam 58 E4
Ty-hen Carms 92 G6
Gwyn 144 C3
Ty-isaf Carms 56 B4
Tyla Mon 78 C2
Tylagwyn Bridgend 58 B2
Tyldesley Gtr Man 195 G7
Tyle Carms 94 F3
Tyle-garw Rhondda 58 C4
Tyler Hill Kent 70 G6
Tylers Causeway Herts 86 D3
Tylers Green Bucks 84 G6
Tyler's Green Essex 87 D8
Sur 51 C11
Tyler's Hill Bucks 85 E7
Ty Llwyn Bl Gwent 77 D11
Tylorstown Rhondda 77 F8
Tylwch Powys 129 G9
Ty-mawr Anglesey 179 D7
Ty Mawr Carms 93 C10
Ty-mawr Conwy 181 F7
Ty Mawr Cwm Conwy 164 F6
Tynant Rhondda 58 B5
Ty-nant Conwy 165 G7
Gwyn 147 D8
Tyncelyn Ceredig 112 E2
Tyndrum Stirling 285 D7
Tyne Dock T&W 243 D9
Tyneham Dorset 18 E3
Tynehead Midloth 271 D7
Tynemouth T&W 243 D9
Tyne Tunnel T&W 243 D8
Tynewydd Ceredig 92 B4
Neath 76 D4
Rhondda 76 F6
Ty-Newydd Ceredig 111 D10
Tyning Bath 45 B7
Tyninghame E Loth 282 F2
Tyn-lon Gwyn 163 D7
Tynron Dumfries 247 E8
Tyntesfield N Som 60 E4
Tyntetown Rhondda 77 F9
Ty'n-y-bryn Rhondda 58 B4
Tyn-y-celyn Wrex 148 B3
Tyn-y-coed Shrops 148 D4
Ty'n-y-coedcae Caerph 59 B7
Tyn-y-cwm Swansea 75 E10
Tynyfedw Conwy 165 B7
Ty'n-y-fedwen Powys 148 C2
Ty'n-y-ffordd Denb 181 G8
Tyn-y-ffridd Powys 148 C2
Ty'n-y-garn Bridgend 57 E11
Tynygongl Anglesey 179 E8
Tynygraig Ceredig 112 D3
Tyn-y-graig Powys 113 G10
Ty'n-y-groes Conwy 180 G3
Ty'n-y-maes Gwyn 163 C10
Tyn-y-pwll Anglesey 178 D6
Ty'n-yr-eithin Ceredig 112 E3
Tynyrwtra Powys 129 F7
Tyrells End C Beds 103 E9
Tyrell's Wood Sur 51 B7
Ty'r-felin-isaf Conwy 164 C5
Ty Rhiw Rhondda 58 C6
Tyrie Aberds 303 C9
Tyringham M Keynes 103 B7
Tyseley W Mid 134 G2
Ty-Sign Caerph 78 G2
Tythecott Devon 24 D6
Tythegston Bridgend 57 F11
Tytherington Ches E 184 F6
S Glos 61 B7
Som 45 D9
Wilts 46 E2
Tytherleigh Devon 28 G4
Tytherton Lucas Wilts 62 E2
Tyttenhanger Herts 85 D11
Ty-uchaf Powys 147 E10
Tywardreath Corn 5 E11
Tywardreath Highway
Corn 5 D11
Tywyn Conwy 180 F3
Gwyn 110 C2

U

Uachdar W Isles 296 F3
Uags Highld 295 B9
Ubbeston Green Suff 126 C6
Ubley Bath 44 B4
Uckerby N Yorks 224 E4
Uckfield E Sus 37 C7
Uckinghall Worcs 99 D7
Uckington Glos 99 G8
Shrops 131 B11
Uddingston S Lanark 268 C3
Uddington S Lanark 259 C9
Udimore E Sus 38 D5
Udley N Som 60 G3
Udny Green Aberds 303 G8
Udny Station Aberds 303 G9
Udston S Lanark 268 D3
Udstonhead S Lanark 268 F4
Uffcott Wilts 62 D6
Uffculme Devon 27 E9
Uffington Lincs 137 B11
Oxon 63 B10
Shrops 149 G10
Ufford Pboro 137 C11
Suff 126 G5
Ufton Warks 119 E7
Ufton Green W Berks 64 F6
Ufton Nervet W Berks 64 F6
Ugadale Argyll 255 E8
Ugborough Devon 8 D3
Ugford Wilts 46 G5
Uggeshall Suff 143 G8
Ugglebarnby N Yorks 227 D7
Ughill S Yorks 186 C3
Ugley Essex 105 F10
Ugley Green Essex 105 F10
Ugthorpe N Yorks 226 C5
Uidh W Isles 297 M2
Uig Argyll 276 E2
Argyll 288 D3
Highld 296 F7
Highld 298 C3
Uigen W Isles 304 E2
Uigshader Highld 298 E4
Uisken Argyll 274 B4
Ulaw Aberds 303 G9
Ulbster Highld 310 E7
Ulcat Row Cumb 230 G4
Ulceby Lincs 190 G6
N Lincs 200 E6
Ulceby Skitter N Lincs 200 E6
Ulcombe Kent 53 D10
Uldale Cumb 229 D10
Uley Glos 80 F3
Ulgham Northumb 252 E6
Ullapool Highld 307 K6
Ullcombe Devon 28 F2
Ullenhall Warks 118 D2
Ullenwood Glos 80 B6
Ulleskelf N Yorks 206 E6
Ullesthorpe Leics 135 F10
Ulley S Yorks 187 D7
Ullingswick Hereford 97 B11
Ullington Worcs 100 B2
Ullinish Highld 294 B5
Ullock Cumb 229 G7
Cumb 229 G10
Ulnes Walton Lancs 194 D4
Ulpha Cumb 220 G3
Ulrome E Yorks 209 B9
Ulshaw N Yorks 214 B2
Ulsta Shetland 312 E6
Ulva House Argyll 288 F6
Ulverley Green W Mid 134 G2
Ulverston Cumb 210 D5
Ulwell Dorset 18 E6
Umberleigh Devon 25 C10
Unapool Highld 306 F7
Unasary W Isles 297 J3
Under Bank W Yorks 196 F6
Underbarrow Cumb 221 G9
Undercliffe W Yorks 205 G9
Underdale Shrops 149 G10
Underdown Devon 14 D3
Underhill London 86 F3
Wilts 45 G11
Underhoull Shetland 312 C7
Underling Green Kent 53 D9
Underriver Kent 52 C5
Underriver Ho Kent 52 C5
Under the Wood Kent 71 F8
Under Tofts S Yorks 186 D4
Underton Shrops 132 E3
Underwood Newport 59 B11
Notts 171 E7
Pembs 73 C7
Plym 7 D10
Undley Suff 140 G3
Undy Mon 60 B2
Ungisiadar W Isles 304 F3
Unifirth Shetland 313 H4
Union Cottage Aberds 293 D10
Union Mills IoM 192 E4
Union Street E Sus 53 G8
United Downs Corn 4 G4
Unstone Derbys 186 F5
Unstone Green Derbys 186 F5
Unsworth Gtr Man 195 F10
Unthank Cumb 230 B3
Cumb 230 D5
Cumb 231 C8
Derbys 186 F4
Unthank End Cumb 230 D5
Upavon Wilts 46 C6
Up Cerne Dorset 29 G11
Upchurch Kent 69 F10
Upcott Devon 24 D2
Devon 25 F9
Devon 25 F11
Devon 40 F3
Hereford 114 G6
Som 27 C11
Upend Cambs 124 F3
Up End M Keynes 103 B8
Up Exe Devon 26 G6
Upgate Norf 160 F2
Upgate Street Norf 141 E11
Norf 142 E5
Up Green Hants 65 G9
Uphall Dorset 29 G9
W Loth 279 G11
Uphall Station W Loth 279 G11
Upham Devon 26 F5
Hants 33 C8
Uphampton Hereford 115 E7
Worcs 116 E6
Up Hatherley Glos 99 G8
Uphempston Devon 8 C6
Uphill N Som 43 B10
Uphill Manor N Som 43 B10
Up Holland Lancs 194 F4
Uplands Glos 80 D5
Swansea 56 C6
Uplawmoor E Renf 267 D8
Upleadon Glos 98 F5
Upleadon Court Glos 98 F5
Upleatham Redcar 226 B2
Uplees Kent 70 G3
Uploders Dorset 16 C6
Uplowman Devon 27 D8
Uplyme Devon 16 C2
Up Marden W Sus 34 E3
Upminster London 68 B5
Up Mudford Som 29 D9
Up Nately Hants 49 C7
Upnor Medway 69 E9
Upottery Devon 28 F2
Uppacott Devon 25 B9
Uppat Highld 311 J2
Uppend Essex 105 F9
Upper Affcot Shrops 131 F8
Upper Ardchronie
Highld 309 L6
Upper Ardgrain
Aberds 303 F9
Upper Ardroscadale
Argyll 275 G11
Upper Arley Worcs 132 G5
Upper Armley W Yorks 205 G11
Upper Arncott Oxon 83 B10
Upper Astley Shrops 149 F10
Upper Aston Shrops 132 E6
Upper Astrop
W Nhants 101 D10
Upper Badcall Highld 306 E6
Upper Bangor Gwyn 179 G9
Upper Basildon W Berks 64 D5
Upper Batley W Yorks 197 B8
Upper Battlefield
Shrops 149 F10
Upper Beeding W Sus 35 E11
Upper Benefield
N Nhants 137 F9
Upper Bentley Worcs 117 D9
Upper Bighouse Highld 310 D2
Upper Birchwood
Derbys 170 E6
Upper Blainslie
Borders 271 G10
Upper Boat Rhondda 58 B6
Upper Boddam Aberds 302 F6
Upper Boddington
W Nhants 119 G9
Upper Bogrow Highld 309 L7
Upper Bogside Moray 302 D2
Upper Bonchurch IoW 21 F7
Upper Booth Derbys 185 D10
Upper Borth Ceredig 128 F2
Upper Boyndlie Aberds 303 C9
Upper Brailes Warks 100 D6
Upper Brandon Parva
Norf 141 B10
Upper Breakish Highld 295 C8
Upper Breinton Hereford 97 C9
Upper Broadheath
Worcs 116 F6
Upper Brockholes
W Yorks 196 B5
Upper Broughton Notts 154 D3
Upper Broxwood
Hereford 115 G7
Upper Bruntingthorpe
Leics 136 F2
Upper Brynamman
Carms 76 C2
Upper Buckenhill
Hereford 97 E11
Upper Bucklebury
W Berks 64 F4
Upper Bullington Hants 48 E3
Upper Burgate Hants 31 D11
Upper Burnhaugh
Aberds 293 D10
Upper Bush Medway 69 F7
Upperby Cumb 239 G10
Upper Caldecote
C Beds 104 B3
Upper Cam Glos 80 F3
Upper Canada N Som 43 B11
Upper Canterton Hants 32 E3
Upper Catesby
W Nhants 119 F10
Upper Catshill Worcs 117 C9
Upper Chapel Powys 95 C10
Upper Cheddon Som 28 B2
Upper Chicksgrove Wilts 31 B7
Upper Church Village
Rhondda 58 B5
Upper Chute Wilts 47 C9
Upper Clapton London 67 B10
Upper Clatford Hants 47 E11
Upper Coberley Glos 81 B7
Upper College Shrops 149 C11
Upper Colwall Hereford 98 C5
Upper Common Hants 48 D6
Upper Cotburn Aberds 303 D7
Upper Cotton Staffs 169 F9
Upper Coullie Aberds 293 B9
Upper Cound Shrops 131 C11
Upper Coxley Som 44 E4
Upper Cudworth
S Yorks 197 F11
Upper Culphin Aberds 302 D6
Upper Cumberworth
W Yorks 197 F8
Upper Cwmbran Torf 78 F3
Upperdale Derbys 185 G11
Upper Dallachy Moray 302 C3
Upper Deal Kent 55 C11
Upper Dean Bedford 121 D10
Devon 8 C4
Upper Denby W Yorks 197 D8
W Yorks 197 F8
Upper Denton Cumb 240 D4
Upper Derraid Highld 301 F10
Upper Diabaig Highld 299 C8
Upper Dicker E Sus 23 D9
Upper Dinchope Shrops 131 G9
Upper Dormington
Hereford 97 D11
Upper Dounreay Highld 310 C4
Upper Dovercourt Essex 108 E4
Upper Dowdeswell Glos 81 B8
Upper Druimfin Argyll 289 D7
Upper Dunsforth
N Yorks 215 G8
Upper Dunsley Herts 84 C6
Upper Eashing Sur 50 E3
Upper Eastern Green
W Mid 134 G5
Upper Eathie Highld 301 C7
Upper Edmonton London 86 G4
Upper Egleton Hereford 98 C2
Upper Elkstone Staffs 169 D9
Upper Ellastone Staffs 169 G10
Upper Elmers End
London 67 F11
Upper End Derbys 185 F9
Glos 81 C10
Glos 81 D8
Leics 154 G4
Upper Enham Hants 47 D11
Upper Farmcote Shrops 132 E5
Upper Farringdon Hants 49 F8
Upper Feorlig Highld 298 E2
Upper Fivehead Som 28 C4
Upper Forge Shrops 132 F4
Upper Framilode Glos 80 C3
Upper Froyle Hants 49 E9
Upper Gambolds Worcs 117 D9
Upper Gills Highld 310 B7
Upper Glenfintaig
Highld 290 E4
Upper Godney Som 44 E3
Upper Goldstone Kent 71 G9
Upper Gornal W Mid 133 E8
Upper Gravenhurst
C Beds 104 D2
Upper Green Essex 105 E8
Mon 78 B5
Suff 124 E4
W Berks 63 G11
W Yorks 197 B9
Upper Grove Common
Hereford 97 F11
Upper Guist Norf 159 D10
Upper Hackney Derbys 170 C3
Upper Hale Sur 49 D10
Upper Halistra Highld 298 D2
Upper Halliford Sur 66 F5
Upper Halling Medway 69 G7
Upper Ham Worcs 99 D7
Upper Hambleton
Rutland 137 B8
Upper Hamnish
Hereford 115 F10
Upper Harbledown Kent 54 B6
Upper Hardres Court
Kent 55 C7
Upper Hardwick
Hereford 115 F8
Upper Hartfield E Sus 52 G3
Upper Hartshay Derbys 170 E5
Upper Haselor Worcs 99 C10
Upper Hatton Staffs 150 B6
Upper Haugh S Yorks 186 B6
Upper Hawkhillock
Aberds 303 F10
Upper Hayesden Kent 52 E5
Upper Hayton Shrops 131 G10
Upper Heath Shrops 131 F11
Upper Heaton W Yorks 197 D7
Upper Hellesdon Norf 160 G4
Upper Helmsley
N Yorks 207 B9
Upper Hengoed Shrops 148 C5
Upper Hergest Hereford 114 G5
Upper Heyford Oxon 101 F9
W Nhants 120 F3
Upper Hill Glos 79 F11
Hereford 115 G9
Upper Hindhope
Borders 251 B7
Upper Holloway London 67 B9
Upper Holton Suff 127 B8
Upper Hopton W Yorks 197 D7
Upper Horsebridge
E Sus 23 C9
Upper Howsell Worcs 98 B5
Upper Hoyland
S Yorks 197 G11
Upper Hulme Staffs 169 C8
Upper Hyde IoW 21 E7
Upper Ifold Sur 50 G4
Upper Inglesham Swindon 82 F2
Upper Inverbrough
Highld 301 F8
Upper Kergord Shetland 313 H6
Upper Kidston Borders 270 G4
Upper Kilcott Glos 61 B9
Upper Killay Swansea 56 C5
Upper Killeyan Argyll 254 C3
Upper Kinsham
Hereford 115 D7
Upper Knockando
Moray 301 E11
Upper Lambourn
W Berks 63 C10
Upper Landywood
Staffs 133 B9
Upper Langford N Som 44 B3
Upper Langwith Derbys 171 B8
Upper Layham Suff 107 C10
Upper Leigh Staffs 151 B10
Upper Lenie Highld 300 G5
Upper Littleton N Som 60 G5
Upper Loads Derbys 170 B4
Upper Lochton Aberds 293 D8
Upper Lode Worcs 99 E7
Upper Longdon Staffs 151 G11
Upper Longwood
Shrops 132 B2
Upper Ludstone Shrops 132 D6
Upper Lybster Highld 310 F6
Upper Lydbrook Glos 79 B10
Upper Lyde Hereford 97 C9
Upper Lye Hereford 115 D7
Upper Maes-coed
Hereford 96 D6
Upper Marsh W Yorks 204 F6
Upper Midhope S Yorks 186 B2
Upper Midway Derbys 152 E5
Uppermill Gtr Man 196 F3
Upper Milovaig Highld 297 G7
Upper Milton Oxon 82 B3
Som 44 D4
Upper Minety Wilts 81 G8
Upper Mitton Worcs 116 C6
Upper Moor Worcs 99 B9
Upper Moor Side
W Yorks 205 G10
Upper Morton S Glos 79 G11
Upper Nash Pembs 73 E8
Upper Netchwood
Shrops 132 E2
Upper Newbold Derbys 186 G5
Upper Nobut Staffs 151 B10
Upper North Dean Bucks 84 F4
Upper Norwood London 67 F10
W Sus 34 D6
Upper Obney Perth 286 D4
Upper Ochrwyth Caerph 59 B8
Upper Oddington Glos 100 F4
Upper Ollach Highld 295 B7
Upper Padley Derbys 186 F2
Upper Pickwick Wilts 61 E11
Upper Pollicott Bucks 84 C2
Upper Poppleton York 207 C7
Upper Port Highld 301 G10
Upper Postern Kent 52 D6
Upper Quinton Warks 100 B3
Upper Race Torf 78 F3
Upper Ratley Hants 32 C4
Upper Ridinghill
Aberds 303 D10
Upper Rissington Glos 82 B2
Upper Rochford Worcs 116 D2
Upper Rodmersham Kent 70 G2
Upper Sandaig Highld 295 D9
Upper Sanday Orkney 314 F5
Upper Sapey Hereford 116 E3
Upper Saxondale Notts 154 B3
Upper Seagry Wilts 62 C2
Upper Shelton C Beds 103 C9
Upper Sheringham
Norf 177 E10
Upper Shirley London 67 G11
Soton 32 E6
Upper Siddington Glos 81 F8
Upper Skelmorlie
N Ayrs 266 B4
Upper Slackstead Hants 32 B5
Upper Slaughter Glos 100 G3
Upper Solva Pembs 90 G5
Upper Soudley Glos 79 C11
Uppersound Shetland 313 J6
Upper Stanton Drew
Bath 60 G6
Upper Staploe Bedford 122 F2
Upper Stoke Norf 142 C5
W Mid 135 G7
Upper Stondon C Beds 104 D2
Upper Stowe W Nhants 120 F2
Upper Stratton Swindon 63 B7
Upper Street Hants 31 D11
Norf 142 G3
Norf 160 B5
Upper Street continued
Norf 160 E6
Norf 160 F6
Norf 161 F7
Suff 108 E2
Suff 124 G5
Suff 126 G2
Upper Strensham
Worcs 99 D8
Upper Studley Wilts 45 B10
Upper Sundon C Beds 103 F10
Upper Swainswick Bath 61 F9
Upper Swanmore Hants 33 D9
Upper Swell Glos 100 F3
Upper Sydenham
London 67 E10
Upper Tankersley
S Yorks 186 B4
Upper Tean Staffs 151 B10
Upperthong W Yorks 196 F6
Upperthorpe Derbys 187 E7
N Lincs 199 G9
Upper Threapwood
Ches W 166 F6
Upper Thurnham Lancs 202 C5
Upper Tillyrie Perth 286 G5
Upperton E Sus 23 E10
Oxon 83 G11
W Sus 35 C7
Upper Tooting London 67 E9
Upper Tote Highld 298 D5
Uppertown Derbys 170 C4
Highld 300 F4
Highld 310 B7
Northumb 241 C9
Orkney 314 G4
Upper Town Derbys 170 D3
Derbys 170 E2
Durham 233 D7
Hereford 97 B11
N Som 60 F4
Suff 125 D8
Wilts 62 D3
W Yorks 204 G6
Upper Treverward
Shrops 114 B5
Upper Tysoe Warks 100 C6
Upper Up Glos 81 F8
Upper Upham Wilts 63 D8
Upper Upnor Medway 69 E9
Upper Vobster Som 45 D8
Upper Walthamstow
London 67 B11
Upper Wardington
Oxon 101 B9
Upper Wardley W Sus 34 B4
Upper Weald M Keynes 102 D5
Upper Weedon
W Nhants 120 F2
Upper Welland Worcs 98 C5
Upper Wellingham
E Sus 36 E6
Upper Welson Hereford 114 G5
Upper Westholme Som 44 E5
Upper Weston Bath 61 F8
Upper Weybread Suff 126 B4
Upper Whiston S Yorks 187 D7
Upper Wick Glos 80 F2
Worcs 116 G6
Upper Wield Hants 48 F6
Upper Wigginton
Shrops 148 B6
Upper Winchendon
Bucks 84 C2
Upper Witton W Mid 133 E11
Upper Wolvercote Oxon 83 D7
Upper Wolverton
Worcs 117 G8
Upperwood Derbys 170 D3
Upper Woodend
Aberds 293 B8
Upper Woodford Wilts 46 F6
Upper Woolhampton
W Berks 64 F5
Upper Wootton Hants 48 C5
Upper Wraxall Wilts 61 E10
Upper Wyche Hereford 98 C5
Uppincott Devon 26 G5
Uppingham Rutland 137 D7
Uppington Dorset 31 F8
Shrops 132 B2
Upsall N Yorks 215 B9
Upsher Green Suff 107 C8
Upshire Essex 86 E6
Up Somborne Hants 47 G11
Upstreet Kent 71 G8
Up Sydling Dorset 29 G10
Upthorpe Glos 80 E3
Suff 125 C9
Upton Bucks 84 C3
Cambs 122 B3
Ches W 166 B6
Corn 11 G11
Corn 24 G2
Cumb 230 D2
Devon 8 G4
Devon 27 G9
Dorset 17 E10
Dorset 18 C5
E Yorks 209 C8
Hants 32 D5
Hants 47 B11
IoW 21 C7
Kent 71 F11
Lincs 188 D5
London 68 C2
Mers 182 D3
Mers 183 D7
Norf 161 G7
Notts 172 E2
Notts 188 F2
Oxon 64 B4
Oxon 82 C2
Pboro 138 C2
Slough 66 D3
Som 27 B7
Som 29 B7
Warks 118 F2
Wilts 45 G11
W Nhants 120 E4
W Yorks 198 E3
Upton Bishop Hereford 98 F2
Upton Cheyney S Glos 61 F7
Upton Cressett Shrops 132 E3
Upton Crews Hereford 98 F2
Upton Cross Corn 11 G11
Upton End C Beds 104 E2
Upton Field Notts 172 E2
Upton Green Norf 161 G7
Upton Grey Hants 49 D7
Upton Heath Ches W 166 B6
Upton Hellions Devon 26 G4
Upton Lea Bucks 66 C3
Upton Lovell Wilts 46 E2
Upton Magna Shrops 149 G11
Upton Noble Som 45 F8
Upton Park London 68 C2
Upton Pyne Devon 14 B4
Upton Rocks Halton 183 D8
Upton St Leonards Glos 80 C5
Upton Scudamore Wilts 45 D11
Upton Snodsbury Worcs 117 G8
Upton upon Severn
Worcs 99 C7
Upton Warren Worcs 117 D8
Upwaltham W Sus 34 E6
Upware Cambs 123 C10
Upwell Norf 139 C9
Upwey Dorset 17 E9
Upwick Green Herts 105 G9
Upwood Cambs 138 G5
Uradale Shetland 313 K6
Urafirth Shetland 312 F5
Uragaig Argyll 274 D4
Urchfont Wilts 46 B4
Urdimarsh Hereford 97 B10
Ure Shetland 312 F4
Ure Bank N Yorks 214 E6
Urgashay Som 29 C9
Urgha W Isles 305 J3
Urgha Beag W Isles 305 H3
Urishay Common
Hereford 96 D6
Urlar Perth 286 C2
Urlay Nook Stockton 225 C7
Urmston Gtr Man 184 C3
Urpeth Durham 242 G6
Urquhart Highld 300 D5
Moray 302 C2
Urra N Yorks 225 E11
Urray Highld 300 D5
Ushaw Moor Durham 233 C10
Usk Mon 78 E5
Usselby Lincs 189 C9
Usworth T&W 243 F8
Utkinton Ches W 167 B8
Utley W Yorks 204 E6
Uton Devon 14 B2
Utterby Lincs 190 C4
Uttoxeter Staffs 151 C11
Uwchmynydd Gwyn 144 D3
Uxbridge London 66 C5
Uxbridge Moor London 66 C5
Uyea Shetland 312 D5
Uyeasound Shetland 312 C7
Uzmaston Pembs 73 C7

V

Vachelich Pembs 90 F5
Vadlure Shetland 313 J4
Vagg Som 29 D8
Vaila Hall Shetland 313 J4
Vaivoe Shetland 312 G7
Vale W Yorks 196 B2
Vale Down Devon 12 D6
Vale of Health London 67 B9
Valeswood Shrops 149 E7
Valley = Y Fali Anglesey 178 F3
Valleyfield Dumfries 237 D8
Valley Park Hants 32 C6
Valley Truckle Corn 11 E7
Valsgarth Shetland 312 B8
Valtos Highld 298 C5
Van Caerph 59 B7
Powys 129 F9
Vange Essex 69 B8
Vanlop Shetland 313 M5
Varchoel Powys 148 G4
Varfell Corn 2 C2
Varteg Torf 78 D3
Vassa Shetland 313 H6
Vastern Wilts 62 C5
Vatsetter Shetland 312 E7
Shetland 313 L5
Vatten Highld 298 E2
Vaul Argyll 288 E2
Vauxhall London 67 D10
Mers 182 C4
W Mid 133 F11
Vaynol Hall Gwyn 163 B8
Vaynor M Tydf 77 C8
Veensgarth Shetland 313 J6
Velator Devon 40 F3
Veldo Hereford 97 C11
Velindre Powys 96 D3
Vellanoweth Corn 2 C2
Vellow Som 42 F5
Velly Devon 24 C3
Veness Orkney 314 D5
Venn Devon 8 F4
Venngreen Devon 24 E5
Venn Green Devon 24 E5
Vennington Shrops 130 B6
Venn Ottery Devon 15 C7
Venn's Green Hereford 97 B10
Venny Tedburn Devon 14 B2
Venterdon Corn 12 G3
Ventnor IoW 21 F7
Vention Devon 40 E3
Venton Devon 7 D11
Ventongimps Corn 4 E5
Ventonleague Corn 2 B3
Venus Hill Herts 85 E8
Veraby Devon 26 B3
Vermentry Shetland 313 H5
Vernham Bank Hants 47 B10
Vernham Dean Hants 47 B10
Vernham Row Hants 47 B10
Vernham Street Hants 47 B11
Vernolds Common
Shrops 131 G9
Verwood Dorset 31 F9
Veryan Corn 3 B10
Veryan Green Corn 5 G8
Vicarage Devon 15 D10
Vicarscross Ches W 166 B6
Vickerstown Cumb 210 F3
Victoria Corn 5 C9
S Yorks 197 F7
Victoria Dock Village
Hull 200 B6
Victoria Park Bucks 84 C4
Victory Gardens
Renfs 267 B10
Vidlin Shetland 312 G6
Viewpark N Lanark 268 C4
Vigo W Mid 133 C10
Vigo Village Kent 68 G6
Vinegar Hill Mon 60 B2
Vinehall Street E Sus 38 C3
Vines Cross E Sus 23 B9
Viney Hill Glos 79 D11
Vinney Green S Glos 61 D7
Virginia Water Sur 66 F3
Virginstow Devon 12 C3
Viscar Corn 2 C6
Vobster Som 45 D8
Voe Shetland 312 E5
Shetland 313 G6
Vogue Corn 4 G4
Vole Som 43 D11
Vowchurch Hereford 97 D7
Vowchurch Common
Hereford 97 D7
Voxmoor Som 27 D10
Voxter Shetland 312 F5
Voy Orkney 314 E2
Vron Gate Shrops 130 B6
Vulcan Village Mers 183 C9

W

Waberthwaite Cumb 220 G2
Wackerfield Durham 233 G9
Wacton Hereford 116 F2
Norf 142 E3
Wacton Common Norf 142 F3
Wadbister Shetland 313 J6
Wadborough Worcs 99 B8
Wadbrook Devon 28 G4
Waddesdon Bucks 84 B2
Waddeton Devon 9 D7
Waddicar Mers 182 B5
Waddingham Lincs 189 B7
Waddington Lancs 203 E10
Lincs 173 C7
Waddingworth Lincs 189 G11
Waddon Devon 14 F3
London 67 G10
Wadebridge Corn 10 G5
Wadeford Som 28 E4
Wade Hall Lancs 194 C4
Wadenhoe N Nhants 137 G10
Wades Green Ches E 167 C11
Wadesmill Herts 86 B5
Wadhurst E Sus 52 G6
Wadshelf Derbys 186 G4
Wadsley S Yorks 186 C4
Wadsley Bridge S Yorks 186 C4
Wadswick Wilts 61 F10
Wadwick Hants 48 C2
Wadworth S Yorks 187 B9
Waen Denb 165 B10
Denb 165 C7
Flint 181 G11
Powys 129 E9
Waen Aberwheeler
Denb 165 B9
Waen-fâch Powys 148 F4
Waen Goleugoed Denb 181 G9
Waen-pentir Gwyn 163 B9
Waen-wen Gwyn 163 B9
Wag Highld 311 G4
Wagbeach Shrops 131 C7
Wagg Som 28 B6
Waggersley Staffs 151 B7
Waggs Plot Devon 28 G4
Wainfelin Torf 78 E3
Wainfleet All Saints
Lincs 175 D7
Wainfleet Bank Lincs 175 D7
Wainfleet St Mary Lincs 175 D8
Wainfleet Tofts Lincs 175 D7
Wainford Norf 142 E6
Waingroves Derbys 170 F6
Wainhouse Corner Corn 11 B9
Wain Lee Staffs 168 D5
Wainscott Medway 69 E8
Wainstalls W Yorks 196 B4
Waitby Cumb 222 D5
Waithe Lincs 201 G9
Wakefield W Yorks 197 C10
Wake Green W Mid 133 G11
Wake Hill N Yorks 214 E3
Wake Lady Green
N Yorks 226 F3
Wakeley Herts 104 F6
Wakerley N Nhants 137 D9
Wakes Colne Essex 107 F7
Wakes Colne Green
Essex 107 E7
Walberswick Suff 127 C9
Walberton W Sus 35 F7
Walbottle T&W 242 D5
Walby Cumb 239 E10
Walcombe Som 44 D5
Walcot Bath 61 F9
Lincs 155 B11
N Lincs 199 C11
Oxon 82 B4
Shrops 130 F6
Swindon 63 C7
Telford 149 G11
Worcs 99 B8
Walcote Leics 135 G11
Warks 118 F2
Walcot Green Norf 142 G2
Walcott Lincs 173 D10
Norf 161 C7
Walden N Yorks 213 C10
Walden Head N Yorks 213 C9
Walden Stubbs N Yorks 198 D5
Waldersey Cambs 139 C8
Waldershaigh S Yorks 186 B3
Walderslade Medway 69 G9
Walderton W Sus 34 E3
Walditch Dorset 16 C5
Waldley Derbys 152 B2
Waldridge Durham 243 G7
Waldringfield Suff 108 C5
Waldringfield Heath
Suff 108 B5
Waldron E Sus 23 B8
Waldron Down E Sus 37 C8
Wales Som 29 C9
S Yorks 187 E7
Wales Bar S Yorks 187 E7
Walesby Lincs 189 C10
Notts 187 G11
Walesby Grange Lincs 189 C10
Wales End Suff 106 B5
Waleswood S Yorks 187 E7
Walford Hereford 97 G11
Hereford 115 C7
Shrops 149 E8
Som 28 B3
Staffs 150 C6
Walford Heath Shrops 149 F8
Walgherton Ches E 167 F11
Walgrave W Nhants 120 C6
Walham Glos 98 G6
Walham Green London 67 D9
Walhampton Hants 20 B2
Walkden Gtr Man 195 G8
Walker T&W 243 E7
Walkerburn Borders 261 B9
Walker Fold Lancs 203 E9
Walkeringham Notts 188 C3
Walkerith Lincs 188 C3
Walkern Herts 104 F5
Walker's Green Hereford 97 B10
Walker's Heath W Mid 117 B11
Walkerville N Yorks 224 F4
Walkford BCP 19 C10
Walkhampton Devon 7 B10
Walkington E Yorks 208 F5
Walkley S Yorks 186 D4
Walkmill Shrops 131 E7
Walk Mill Lancs 204 G3
Walkmills Shrops 131 D9
Wall Corn 2 B4
Northumb 241 D10
Staffs 134 B2
Wallacestone Falk 279 F8
Wallaceton Dumfries 247 F8
Wallacetown S Ayrs 245 C7
S Ayrs 257 E8
Shetland 313 H5
Wallands Park E Sus 36 E6
Wallasey Mers 182 C4
Wallbank Lancs 195 D11
Wall Bank Shrops 131 E10
Wallbrook W Mid 133 E8
Wallcrouch E Sus 53 G7
Wallend London 68 C2
Wall End Cumb 210 C4
Kent 71 G8
Waller's Green Hereford 98 D3
Walley's Green Ches E 167 C11
Wall Heath W Mid 133 F7
Wall Hill Gtr Man 196 F3
Wallingford Oxon 64 B6
Wallington Hants 33 F9
Herts 104 E5
London 67 G9
Wallington Heath
W Mid 133 C9
Wallingwells Notts 187 E9
Wallis Pembs 91 F10
Wallisdown BCP 19 C7
Walliswood Sur 50 F6
Wall Mead Bath 45 B7
Wall Nook Durham 233 B10
Wallow Green Glos 80 F4
Wallridge Northumb 242 B3
Walls Shetland 313 J4
Wallsend T&W 243 D7
Wallston V Glam 58 E6
Wallsuches Gtr Man 195 E7
Wallsworth Glos 98 G6
Wall under Heywood
Shrops 131 E10
Wallyford E Loth 281 G7
Walmer Kent 55 C11
Walmer Bridge Lancs 194 C3
Walmersley Gtr Man 195 E10
Walmgate Stray York 207 C8
Walmley W Mid 134 E2
Walmsgate Lincs 190 F5
Walnut Grove Perth 286 E5
Walnut Tree M Keynes 103 D7
Walnuttree Green Herts 105 G9
Walpole Som 43 E10
Suff 127 C7
Walpole Cross Keys
Norf 157 F10
Walpole Highway Norf 157 G10
Walpole Marsh Norf 157 F9
Walpole St Andrew
Norf 157 F10
Walpole St Peter Norf 157 F9
Walrow Som 43 D10
Walsal End W Mid 118 B4
Walsall W Mid 133 D10
Walsall Wood W Mid 133 C10
Walsden W Yorks 196 C2
Walsgrave on Sowe
W Mid 135 G7
Walsham le Willows
Suff 125 C9
Walshaw Gtr Man 195 E9
Walshford N Yorks 206 C4
Walsoken Cambs 157 G9
Walson Mon 97 G8
Walston S Lanark 269 F11
Walsworth Herts 104 E4
Walters Ash Bucks 84 F4
Walter's Green Kent 52 E4
Walterston V Glam 58 E5
Walterstone Hereford 96 F6
Waltham Kent 54 D6
NE Lincs 201 G9
Waltham Abbey Essex 86 E5
Waltham Chase Hants 33 D9
Waltham Cross Herts 86 E5
Waltham on the Wolds
Leics 154 D6
Waltham St Lawrence
Windsor 65 D10
Waltham's Cross Essex 106 E3
Walthamstow London 67 B11
Walton Bucks 84 C4
Cumb 240 E2
Derbys 170 B5
Leics 135 F11
Mers 182 C5
M Keynes 103 D7
Pboro 138 C3
Powys 114 F5
Shrops 115 B9
Som 44 F3
Staffs 151 C7
Staffs 151 D7
Suff 108 D5
Telford 149 F11
Warks 118 G5
W Yorks 197 D11
W Yorks 206 D4
Walton Cardiff Glos 99 E8
Walton Court Bucks 84 C4
Walton East Pembs 91 G10
Walton Elm Dorset 30 D3
Walton Grounds
W Nhants 101 E10
Walton Heath Hants 33 F10
Walton Highway Norf 157 G9
Walton in Gordano
N Som 60 E2
Walton-le-Dale Lancs 194 B5
Walton Manor Oxon 83 D8
Walton-on-Thames Sur 66 F6
Walton on the Hill
Staffs 151 E9
Sur 51 B8
Walton-on-the-Naze
Essex 108 G5
Walton on the Wolds
Leics 153 F11
Walton-on-Trent
Derbys 152 F4
Walton Pool Worcs 117 B8
Walton St Mary N Som 60 E2
Walton Summit Lancs 194 B5
Walton Warren Norf 158 F4
Walton West Pembs 72 C5
Walwen Flint 181 F10
Flint 181 G11
Flint 182 F2
Walwick Northumb 241 C10
Walworth Darl 224 B4
London 67 D10
Walworth Gate Darl 233 G10
Walwyn's Castle Pembs 72 C5
Wambrook Som 28 F3
Wampool Cumb 238 G6
Wanborough Sur 50 D2
Swindon 63 C8
Wandel Dyke S Lanark 259 D11
Wandle Park London 67 F10
Wandon End Herts 104 G2
Wandsworth London 67 E9
Wangford Suff 127 B9
Wanlip Leics 154 G2
Wanlockhead Dumfries 259 G9
Wannock E Sus 23 E9
Wansford E Yorks 209 B7
Pboro 137 D11
Wanshurst Green Kent 53 D9
Wanson Corn 24 G1

Wanstead London 68 B2
Wanstrow Som 45 E8
Wanswell Glos 79 E11
Wantage Oxon 63 B11
Wants Green Worcs 116 F5
Wapley S Glos 61 D8
Wappenbury Warks 119 D7
Wappenham W Nhants 102 B2
Wapping London 67 C10
Warbleton E Sus 23 B10
Warblington Hants 22 B2
Warborough Oxon 83 G9
Warboys Cambs 138 G6
Warbreck Blackpool 202 F2
Warbstow Corn 11 C10
Warbstow Cross Corn 11 C10
Warburton Gtr Man 184 D2
Warburton Green
Gtr Man 184 E3
Warcop Cumb 222 B4
Warden Kent 70 E4
Northumb 241 D10
Powys 114 E6
Ward End W Mid 134 F2
Warden Hill Glos 99 G8
Warden Point IoW 20 D2
Warden Street C Beds 104 C2
Ward Green Suff 125 E10
S Yorks 197 G10
Ward Green Cross
Lancs 203 F8
Wardhedges C Beds 103 D11
Wardhill Orkney 314 D6
Wardington Oxon 101 B9
Wardlaw Borders 261 F7
Wardle Ches E 167 D10
Gtr Man 196 D2
Wardle Bank Ches E 167 D10
Wardley Gtr Man 195 G9
Rutland 136 C6
T&W 243 E7
W Sus 34 B4
Wardlow Derbys 185 G11
Wardour Wilts 30 B6
Wardpark N Lanark 278 F5
Wardrobes Bucks 84 E4
Wardsend Ches E 184 E6
Wardy Hill Cambs 139 G9
Ware Herts 86 C5
Kent 71 G9
Wareham Dorset 18 D4
Warehorne Kent 54 G3
Warenford Northumb 264 D4
Waren Mill Northumb 264 C4
Warenton Northumb 264 C4
Wareside Herts 86 B5
Waresley Cambs 122 G4
Worcs 116 C6
Ware Street Kent 53 B9
Warfield Brack 65 E11
Warfleet Devon 9 E7
Wargate Lincs 156 C4
Wargrave Mers 183 C9
Wokingham 65 D9
Warham Hereford 97 D9
Norf 176 E6
Warhill Gtr Man 185 B7
Waring's Green W Mid 118 C2
Wark Northumb 241 B9
Northumb 263 B8
Wark Common
Northumb 263 B8
Warkleigh Devon 25 C10
Warkton N Nhants 121 B7
Warkworth Northumb 252 B6
W Nhants 101 C9
Warlaby N Yorks 224 G6
Warland W Yorks 196 C2
Warleggan Corn 6 B3
Warleigh Bath 61 G9
Warley Essex 87 G9
Warley Town W Yorks 196 B5
Warley Woods W Mid 133 F10
Warlingham Sur 51 B11
Warmbrook Derbys 170 E3
Warmfield W Yorks 197 C11
Warmingham Ches E 168 C2
Warminghurst W Sus 35 D10
Warmington N Nhants 137 E11
Warks 101 B8
Warminster Wilts 45 D11
Warminster Common
Wilts 45 E11
Warmlake Kent 53 C10
Warmley S Glos 61 E7
Warmley Hill S Glos 61 E7
Warmley Tower S Glos 61 E7
Warmonds Hill
N Nhants 121 D9
Warmsworth S Yorks 198 G4
Warmwell Dorset 17 D11
Warnborough Green
Hants 49 C8
Warndon Worcs 117 F7
Warners End Herts 85 D8
Warnford Hants 33 C10
Warnham W Sus 51 G7
Warningcamp W Sus 35 F8
Warninglid W Sus 36 B2
Warpsgrove Oxon 83 F10
Warren Ches E 184 G5
Dorset 18 C3
Pembs 72 F6
S Yorks 186 B5
Warrenby Redcar 235 F7
Warren Corner Hants 34 B2
Hants 49 D10
Warren Heath Suff 108 C4
Warren Row Windsor 65 C10
Warren's Green Herts 104 F5
Warren Street Kent 54 C2
Warrington M Keynes 121 G7
Warr 183 D10
Warriston Edin 280 F5
Warsash Hants 33 F7
Warsill N Yorks 214 F4
Warslow Staffs 169 D9
Warsop Vale Notts 171 B8
Warstock W Mid 117 B11
Warstone Staffs 133 B9
Warter E Yorks 208 C3
Warthermarske N Yorks 214 D4
Warthill N Yorks 207 B9
Wartle Aberds 293 C7
Wartling E Sus 23 D11
Wartnaby Leics 154 E4
Warton Lancs 194 B2
Lancs 211 E9
Northumb 252 C2
Warks 134 C5
Warton Bank Lancs 194 B2
Warwick Warks 118 E5
Warwick Bridge Cumb 239 F11
Warwick on Eden
Cumb 239 F11
Warwicksland Cumb 239 B10
Warwick Wold Sur 51 C10
Wasbister Orkney 314 C3
Wasdale Head Cumb 220 D3
Wash Derbys 185 E9
Washall Green Herts 105 E8
Washaway Corn 5 B10
Washbourne Devon 8 E5
Washbrook Som 44 C2
Suff 108 C2
Washbrook Street Suff 108 C2
Wash Common W Berks 64 G3
Wash Dyke Norf 157 F10
Washerwall Staffs 168 F6
Washfield Devon 26 D6
Washfold N Yorks 223 E11
Washford Som 42 E5
Worcs 117 D11
Washford Pyne Devon 26 E4
Washingborough Lincs 189 G8
Washingley Cambs 138 F2
Washington T&W 243 F8
W Sus 35 E10
Washington Village
T&W 243 F8
Washmere Green Suff 107 B8
Washpit W Yorks 196 F6
Wash Water W Berks 64 G3
Washwood Heath
W Mid 134 F2
Wasing W Berks 64 G5
Waskerley Durham 233 B7
Wasperton Warks 118 F5
Wasp Green Sur 51 D10
Wasps Nest Lincs 173 C9
Wass N Yorks 215 D11
Waste Green Warks 118 D4
Wastor Devon 8 F2
Watchet Som 42 E5
Watchfield Oxon 63 B8
Som 43 D10
Watchgate Cumb 221 F10
Watchhill Cumb 229 C9
Watch House Green
Essex 106 G3
Watchill Dumfries 238 D6
Dumfries 248 G3
Watcombe Torbay 9 B8
Watendlath Cumb 220 B5
Water Devon 13 E11
Lancs 195 B10
Waterbeach Cambs 123 D9
W Sus 22 B5
Waterbeck Dumfries 238 B6
Waterdale Herts 85 E10
Waterden Norf 159 B7
Waterditch Hants 19 B9
Water Eaton M Keynes 103 E7
Oxon 83 C8
Waterend Bucks 84 F3
Cumb 229 G8
Glos 80 C3
Herts 86 C2
Water End Bedford 104 B2
C Beds 103 D11
C Beds 104 B5
Essex 105 C11
E Yorks 207 F11
Hants 49 C7
Herts 85 C8
Herts 86 E2
Waterfall Staffs 169 E9
Waterfoot Argyll 255 D9
Cumb 230 G5
E Renf 267 D11
Lancs 195 C10
Waterford Hants 20 B2
Herts 86 C4
Water Fryston W Yorks 198 B3
Water Garth Nook Cumb 210 F3
Watergate Corn 6 E4
Corn 11 E8
Watergore Som 28 D6
Waterhales Essex 87 F8
Waterham Kent 70 G5
Waterhay Wilts 81 G9
Waterhead Angus 292 F6
Cumb 221 E7
Devon 8 F3
Dumfries 248 E5
Waterhead on Minnoch
S Ayrs 245 E9
Waterheads Borders 270 E4
Waterheath Norf 143 E8
Waterhouses Durham 233 C9
Staffs 169 E9
Water Houses N Yorks 213 F7
Wateringbury Kent 53 C7
Waterlane Glos 80 E6
Waterlip Som 45 E7
Waterloo BCP 18 C6
Blackburn 195 B7
Corn 11 G8
Derbys 170 C6
Gtr Man 196 G2
Highld 295 C8
Mers 182 B4
N Lanark 268 E6
Norf 126 B2
Norf 143 E8
Norf 160 F4
Pembs 73 E7
Perth 286 D4
Shrops 149 C9
Waterloo Park Mers 182 B4
Waterloo Port Gwyn 163 C7
Waterlooville Hants 33 F11
Waterman Quarter Kent 53 E10
Watermead Glos 80 B5
Watermeetings
S Lanark 259 G11
Watermill E Sus 38 E2
Watermillock Cumb 230 G4
Watermoor Glos 81 E8
Water Newton Cambs 138 D2
Water Orton Warks 134 E3
Waterperry Oxon 83 D10
Waterrow Som 27 B9
Watersfield W Sus 35 D8
Watersheddings
Gtr Man 196 F2
Waterside Aberds 292 B5
Aberds 303 G10
Blackburn 195 C8
Bucks 85 E7
Cumb 229 B10
Derbys 185 E8
E Ayrs 245 B10
E Ayrs 267 G9
E Dunb 278 G3
E Renf 267 D10
Sur 51 D11
S Yorks 199 E7
Telford 150 F2
Waterslack Lancs 211 D9
Water's Nook Gtr Man 195 F7
Waterstein Highld 297 G7
Waterstock Oxon 83 D10
Waterston Pembs 72 D6
Water Stratford Bucks 102 E3
Waters Upton Telford 150 F2
Waterthorpe S Yorks 186 E6
Waterton Aberds 303 F9
Bridgend 58 D2
Water Yeat Cumb 210 B5
Watford Herts 85 F10
W Nhants 120 D2
Watford Gap Staffs 134 C2
Watford Heath Herts 85 G10
Watford Park Caerph 58 B6
Wath Cumb 222 D3
N Yorks 214 D6
N Yorks 214 F2
N Yorks 216 D3
Wath Brow Cumb 219 C10
Watherston Borders 271 F8
Wath upon Dearne
S Yorks 198 G2
Watledge Glos 80 E4
Watley's End S Glos 61 C7
Watlington Norf 158 G2
Oxon 83 G11
Watnall Notts 171 F8
Watsness Shetland 313 H3
Watten Highld 310 D6
Wattisfield Suff 125 C10
Wattisham Suff 125 G10
Wattisham Stone Suff 125 G10
Wattlefield Norf 142 D2
Wattlesborough Heath
Shrops 149 G7
Watton E Yorks 208 C6
Norf 141 C8
Watton at Stone Herts 86 B4
Watton Green Norf 141 C8
Watton's Green Essex 87 F8
Wattston N Lanark 268 B5
Wattstown Rhondda 77 G8
Wattsville Caerph 78 G2
Wauchan Highld 295 G11
Waulkmill Lodge Orkney 314 F3
Waun Gwyn 163 C9
Powys 148 F4
Waunarlwydd Swansea 56 B6
Waun Beddau Pembs 90 F5
Waunclunda Carms 94 E3
Waunfawr Gwyn 163 D8
Waun Fawr Ceredig 128 G2
Waungilwen Carms 92 D6
Waungron Swansea 75 E9
Waunlwyd Bl Gwent 77 D11
Waun-Lwyd Bl Gwent 77 D11
Waun-y-clyn Carms 75 E7
Waun y Gilfach Bridgend 57 D10
Wavendon M Keynes 103 D8
Wavendon Gate
M Keynes 103 D8
Waverbridge Cumb 229 B10
Waverley S Yorks 186 D6
Waverton Ches W 167 C7
Cumb 229 B10
Wavertree Mers 182 D5
Wawcott W Berks 63 F11
Wawne E Yorks 209 F7
Waxham Norf 161 D8
Waxholme E Yorks 201 B10
Way Kent 71 F10
Waye Devon 13 G11
Wayend Street Hereford 98 D4
Wayfield Medway 69 F9
Wayford Som 28 F6
Waymills Shrops 167 G9
Wayne Green Mon 78 B6
Way's Green Ches W 167 B10
Waytown Devon 24 C5
Devon 40 G5
Way Village Devon 26 E5
Way Wick N Som 59 G11
Wdig = Goodwick Pembs 91 D8
Weachyburn Aberds 302 D6
Weacombe Som 42 E6
Weald Oxon 82 E4
Wealdstone London 67 B7
Wearde Corn 7 D8
Weardley W Yorks 205 E11
Weare Som 44 C2
Weare Giffard Devon 25 C7
Wearhead Durham 232 D3
Wearne Som 28 B6
Weasdale Cumb 222 E3
Weasenham All Saints
Norf 158 E6
Weasenham St Peter
Norf 159 E7
Weaste Gtr Man 184 B4
Weatherhill Sur 51 E10
Weatheroak Hill Worcs 117 C11
Weaverham Ches W 183 G10
Weavering Street Kent 53 B9
Weaverslake Staffs 152 F2
Weaverthorpe N Yorks 217 E9
Webbington Som 43 B11
Webheath Worcs 117 D10
Webscott Shrops 149 E9
Wecock Hants 33 E11
Wedderlairs Aberds 303 F8
Wedderlie Borders 272 E2
Weddington Kent 55 B9
Warks 135 E7
Wedhampton Wilts 46 B5
Wedmore Som 44 D2
Wednesbury W Mid 133 D9
Wednesbury Oak
W Mid 133 E9
Wednesfield W Mid 133 C8
Weecar Notts 172 B4
Weedon Bucks 84 B4
Weedon Bec W Nhants 120 F2
Weedon Lois W Nhants 102 B2
Weeford Staffs 134 C2
Week Devon 8 C5
Devon 12 E5
Devon 25 B9
Devon 26 D2
Weeke Devon 26 F3
Hants 48 G3
Week Green Corn 11 B10
Weekley N Nhants 137 G7
Weekmoor Som 27 B10
Weeks IoW 21 C7
Week St Mary Corn 11 B10
Weel E Yorks 209 F7
Weeley Essex 108 G2
Weeley Heath Essex 108 G3
Weem Perth 286 C2
Weeping Cross Staffs 151 E8
Weethley Warks 117 F11
Weethley Bank Warks 117 G11
Weethley Gate Warks 117 G11
Weeting Norf 140 F5
Weeton E Yorks 201 C11
Lancs 202 G3
N Yorks 205 D11
Weetwood W Yorks 205 F11
Weetwood Common
Ches W 167 B8
Weetwood Hall
Northumb 264 D2
Weir Essex 69 B10
Lancs 195 B11
Weirbrook Shrops 148 E6
Weir Quay Devon 7 C8
Welborne Norf 159 G11
Welborne Common
Norf 141 B11
Welbourn Lincs 173 E7
Welburn N Yorks 216 C3
Welburn *continued*
N Yorks 216 F4
Welbury N Yorks 225 E7
Welby Lincs 155 B9
Welches Dam Cambs 139 F9
Welcombe Devon 24 D2
Weld Bank Lancs 194 D5
Weldon N Nhants 137 F8
Northumb 252 D4
Welford W Berks 64 E2
W Nhants 136 G2
Welford-on-Avon
Warks 118 G3
Welham Leics 136 E5
Notts 188 E2
Som 45 G7
Welham Green Herts 86 D2
Well Hants 49 D9
Lincs 190 G6
N Yorks 214 C5
Welland Worcs 98 C5
Welland Stone Worcs 98 D6
Wellbank Angus 287 D8
Well Bottom Dorset 30 D6
Wellbrook E Sus 37 B9
Welldale Dumfries 238 D5
Well End Bucks 65 B11
Herts 86 F2
Weller's Town Kent 52 E4
Wellesbourne Warks 118 F5
Well Green Gtr Man 184 D3
Wellheads Aberds 302 F4
Well Heads W Yorks 205 G7
Well Hill Kent 68 G3
Wellhouse W Berks 64 E4
W Yorks 196 E5
Welling London 68 D3
Wellingborough
N Nhants 121 D7
Wellingham Norf 159 E7
Wellingore Lincs 173 D7
Wellington Cumb 219 E11
Hereford 97 B9
Som 27 C10
Telford 150 G3
Wellington Heath
Hereford 98 C4
Wellington Hill W Yorks 206 F2
Wellisford Som 27 C9
Wellow Bath 45 B8
IoW 20 D3
NE Lincs 201 F9
Notts 171 B11
Wellow Wood Hants 32 C3
Well Place Oxon 65 B7
Wellpond Green Herts 105 G8
Wellroyd W Yorks 205 F10
Wells Som 44 D5
Wellsborough Leics 135 C7
Wells Green Ches E 167 E11
Wells-next-the-Sea
Norf 176 E6
Wellsprings Som 28 B2
Well Street Kent 53 B7
Wellstye Green Essex 87 B10
Wellswood Torbay 9 C8
Welltown Corn 6 B2
Well Town Devon 26 F6
Wellwood Fife 279 D11
Welney Norf 139 E10
Welsford Devon 24 C3
Welshampton Shrops 149 B8
Welsh Bicknor Hereford 79 B9
Welsh End Shrops 149 B10
Welsh Frankton Shrops 149 C7
Welsh Harp London 67 B8
Welsh Hook Pembs 91 F8
Welsh Newton Hereford 79 B7
Welsh Newton Common
Hereford 79 B8
Welshpool Powys 130 B4
Welsh St Donats V Glam 58 D4
Welshwood Park Essex 107 F10
Welstor Devon 13 G10
Welton Bath 45 C7
Cumb 230 C3
E Ayrs 258 D2
E Yorks 200 B3
Lincs 189 F8
W Nhants 119 D11
Welton Hill Lincs 189 E8
Welton le Marsh Lincs 175 B7
Welton le Wold Lincs 190 D3
Welwick E Yorks 201 C10
Welwyn Herts 86 B2
Welwyn Garden City
Herts 86 C2
Wem Shrops 149 D10
Wembdon Som 43 F9
Wembley London 67 B7
Wembley Park London 67 B7
Wembury Devon 7 F10
Wembworthy Devon 25 F11
Wemyss Bay Invclyd 266 B3
Wenallt Ceredig 112 C3
Gwyn 146 F4
Gwyn 165 G7
Wendens Ambo Essex 105 D10
Wendlebury Oxon 83 B9
Wendling Norf 159 G8
Wendover Bucks 84 D5
Wendover Dean Bucks 84 E5
Wendron Corn 2 C5
Wendy Cambs 104 B6
Wenfordbridge Corn 11 F7
Wenhaston Suff 127 B8
Wenhaston Black Heath
Suff 127 C8
Wennington Cambs 122 B4
Lancs 212 E2
London 68 C4
Wensley Derbys 170 C3
N Yorks 213 B11
Wentbridge W Yorks 198 D3
Wentnor Shrops 131 E7
Wentworth Cambs 123 B9
S Yorks 186 B5
Wenvoe V Glam 58 E6
Weobley Hereford 115 G8
Weobley Marsh
Hereford 115 G8
Weoley Castle W Mid 133 G10
Wepham W Sus 35 F8
Wepre Flint 166 B3
Wereham Norf 140 C3
Wereham Row Norf 140 C3
Wereton Staffs 168 E3
Wergs W Mid 133 C7
Wern Gwyn 145 B10
Powys 77 B10
Powys 147 G9
Powys 148 E5
Powys 148 G5
Shrops 148 C5
Swansea 56 C4
Wern ddu Shrops 148 D4
Werneth Gtr Man 196 G2
Werneth Low Gtr Man 185 C7
Wernffrwd Swansea 56 C4
Wern-Gifford Mon 96 G6
Wernlas Shrops 148 E6
Wern-olau Swansea 56 B5
Wernrheolydd Mon 78 C5
Wern Tarw Bridgend 58 C3
Wern-y-cwrt Mon 78 D5
Wern-y-gaer Flint 166 B2
Wernyrheolydd Mon 78 C5
Werrington Corn 12 D2
Pboro 138 C3
Staffs 168 F6
Wervin Ches W 182 G6
Wescoe Hill N Yorks 205 D11
Wesham Lancs 202 G4
Wessington Derbys 170 D5
West Aberthaw V Glam 58 F4
Westacott Devon 40 G5
West Acre Norf 158 F5
West Acton London 67 C7
West Adderbury Oxon 101 D9
West Allerdean
Northumb 273 F9
West Allotment T&W 243 C8
West Alvington Devon 8 G4
West Amesbury Wilts 46 E6
West Anstey Devon 26 B5
West Appleton N Yorks 224 G4
West Ardhu Argyll 288 D6
West Ardsley W Yorks 197 B9
West Ardwell Dumfries 236 E2
West Arthurlie E Renf 267 D9
West Ashby Lincs 190 G3
West Ashford Devon 40 F4
West Ashling W Sus 22 B4
West Ashton Wilts 45 B11
West Auckland Durham 233 F9
West Ayton N Yorks 217 C9
West Bagborough Som 43 G7
West Bank Bl Gwent 78 D2
Halton 183 E8
West Barkwith Lincs 189 E11
West Barnby N Yorks 226 C6
West Barnes London 67 F8
West Barns E Loth 282 F3
West Barsham Norf 159 C8
West Bay Dorset 16 C5
West Beckham Norf 160 B2
West Bedfont Sur 66 E5
West Benhar N Lanark 269 C7
Westbere Kent 71 G7
West Bergholt Essex 107 F9
West Bexington Dorset 16 D6
West Bilney Norf 158 F4
West Blackdene Durham 232 D3
West Blackdown Devon 12 E5
West Blatchington
Brighton 36 F3
West Bold Borders 261 B9
West Boldon T&W 243 E9
Westborough Lincs 172 G5
Westbourne BCP 19 C7
Suff 108 B2
W Sus 22 B3
Westbourne Green
London 67 C9
West Bourton Dorset 30 B3
West Bowling W Yorks 205 G9
West Bradford Lancs 203 E10
West Bradley Som 44 F5
West Bretton W Yorks 197 E9
West Bridgford Notts 153 B11
West Brompton London 67 D9
West Bromwich
W Mid 133 E10
Westbrook Hereford 96 C5
Kent 71 E10
Sur 50 E3
Warr 183 C9
W Berks 64 E2
Wilts 62 F3
Westbrook Green Norf 142 G2
Westbrook Hay Herts 85 D8
West Broughton Derbys 152 C2
West Buckland Devon 41 G7
Som 27 C11
Westburn S Lanark 268 C3
West Burnside Aberds 293 F8
West Burrafirth
Shetland 313 H4
West Burton N Yorks 213 B10
W Sus 35 E7
Westbury Bucks 102 D2
Shrops 131 B7
Wilts 45 C11
Westbury Leigh Wilts 45 C11
Westbury-on-Severn
Glos 80 C2
Westbury on Trym Bristol 60 D5
Westbury Park Bristol 60 D5
Westbury-sub-Mendip
Som 44 D4
West Butsfield Durham 233 C8
West Butterwick
N Lincs 199 F10
Westby Lancs 202 G3
Lincs 155 D9
West Byfleet Sur 66 G4
West Caister Norf 161 G10
West Calder W Loth 269 C10
West Camel Som 29 C9
West Carlton W Yorks 205 E10
West Carr Hull 209 G7
N Lincs 199 F8
West Chadsmoor Staffs 151 G9
West Challow Oxon 63 B11
West Charleton Devon 8 G5
West Chelborough Dorset 29 F8
West Chevington
Northumb 252 D6
West Chiltington W Sus 35 D9
West Chiltington Common
W Sus 35 D9
West Chinnock Som 29 E7
West Chirton T&W 243 D8
West Chisenbury Wilts 46 C6
West Clandon Sur 50 C4
West Cliff BCP 19 C7
N Yorks 227 C7
West Cliffe Kent 55 E10
Westcliff-on-Sea
Southend 69 B11
West Clyne Highld 311 J2
West Clyth Highld 310 F6
Highld 310 F6
West Coker Som 29 E8
Westcombe Som 29 B7
Som 45 F7
West Common Hants 32 G6
West Compton Dorset 17 C7
Som 44 E5
West Cornforth Durham 234 E2
Westcot Oxon 63 B10
Westcote Glos 100 G4
Westcotes Leicester 135 C11
Westcott Bucks 84 B2
Devon 27 G8
Shrops 131 C8
Sur 50 D6
Westcott Barton Oxon 101 F8
Westcourt Wilts 63 G8
West Cowick E Yorks 199 C7
West Cranmore Som 45 E7
Westcroft M Keynes 102 E6
W Mid 133 C8
West Cross Kent 53 G10
Swansea 56 D6
West Crudwell Wilts 80 G6
West Cullery Aberds 293 C9
West Curry Corn 11 C11
West Curthwaite Cumb 230 B2
West Darlochan Argyll 255 E7
Westdean E Sus 23 F8
West Dean Wilts 32 B3
W Sus 34 E5
West Deeping Lincs 138 B2
West Denant Pembs 72 C6
Westdene Brighton 36 F3
West Denton T&W 242 D5
West Derby Mers 182 C5
West Dereham Norf 140 C3
West Didsbury Gtr Man 184 C4
West Down Devon 40 E4
Hants 47 F11
Westdown Camp Wilts 46 D4
Westdowns Corn 11 E7
West Downs Corn 5 C10
West Drayton London 66 D5
Notts 188 G2
West Dulwich London 67 E10
West Ealing London 67 C7
West Edge Derbys 170 C4
West Ella E Yorks 200 B4
Westend Oxon 100 G6
S Glos 79 G10
West End Bedford 121 E11
Bedford 121 G9
Brack 65 E11
Brack 66 G2
Caerph 78 F2
Cumb 239 F8
Dorset 30 G6
E Yorks 201 B9
E Yorks 208 G4
E Yorks 209 B9
E Yorks 209 G9
E Yorks 217 G11
Glos 80 F5
Hants 33 E7
Hants 33 F9
Hants 48 F6
Herts 86 D3
Kent 54 B2
Kent 71 F7
Lancs 195 B8
Lancs 211 G8
Leics 153 F8
Lincs 174 F5
Lincs 190 B5
Mon 78 F6
Norf 141 B8
Norf 161 G10
N Som 60 F3
N Yorks 205 B8
N Yorks 206 E6
N Yorks 207 F7
Oxon 64 B5
Oxon 82 E6
S Glos 61 B8
S Lanark 269 F9
Som 44 C5
Som 45 G7
Suff 143 G9
Sur 49 E10
Sur 66 G6
S Yorks 199 F7
Wilts 30 C6
Wilts 31 C7
Wilts 62 D3
Windsor 65 D10
Worcs 99 D11
W Sus 36 D2
W Yorks 197 B7
W Yorks 205 F10
West End = Marian-y-mor
Gwyn 145 C7
West End Green Hants 65 G7
Westend Town
Northumb 241 D7
West-end Town V Glam 58 F3
Westenhanger Kent 54 F6
Wester Aberchalder
Highld 300 G5
Wester Arboll Highld 311 L2
Wester Auchinloch
N Lanark 278 G3
Wester Auchnagallin
Highld 301 F10
Wester Balgedie Perth 286 G5
Wester Brae Highld 300 C6
Wester Broomhouse
E Loth 282 F3
Wester Craiglands
Highld 301 D7
Wester Culbeuchly
Aberds 302 C6
Westerdale Highld 310 D5
N Yorks 226 D3
Wester Dalvoult Highld 291 B11
Wester Dechmont
W Loth 269 B10
Wester Deloraine
Borders 261 E8
Wester Denoon Angus 287 C7
Wester Ellister Argyll 254 B2
Wester Essendy Perth 286 C5
Wester Essenside
Borders 261 E10
Wester Feddal Perth 286 G2
Westerfield Shetland 313 H5
Suff 108 B3
Wester Fintray Aberds 293 B10
Westerfolds Moray 301 C11
Wester Galgantray
Highld 301 E8
Westergate W Sus 22 C6
Wester Gospetry Fife 286 G5
Wester Gruinards
Highld 309 K5
Wester Hailes Edin 270 B4
Westerham Kent 52 C2
Westerhope T&W 242 D5
Wester Housebyres
Borders 262 B2
Wester Kershope
Borders 261 D9
Wester Lealty Highld 300 B6
Westerleigh S Glos 61 D8
Westerleigh Hill S Glos 61 D8
Wester Lix Stirling 285 E9
Wester Milton Highld 301 D9
Wester Mosshead
Aberds 302 F5
Western Bank Cumb 229 B10
Western Downs Staffs 151 E8
Wester Newburn Fife 287 G8
Western Heights Kent 55 E10
Western Hill Durham 233 C11
Western Park Leicester 135 C11
Wester Ord Aberds 293 C10
Wester Parkgate
Dumfries 248 F2
Wester Quarff Shetland 313 K6
Wester Skeld Shetland 313 J4
Wester Strath Highld 300 D6
Westerton Aberds 293 B9
Aberds 302 E5
Angus 287 B10
Durham 233 E10
Moray 302 D3
W Sus 22 B5
Westertown Aberds 303 F7
Wester Watten Highld 310 D6
Westerwick Shetland 313 J4
West Ewell Sur 67 G8
West Farleigh Kent 53 C8
West Farndon
W Nhants 119 G10
West Felton Shrops 148 D6
West Fenton E Loth 281 E9
West Ferry Dundee 287 D8
Westfield Bath 45 C7
Cumb 228 F5
E Sus 38 D4
Hants 21 B10
Hereford 98 B4
Highld 310 C4
N Lanark 278 G4
Norf 141 B9
Redcar 235 G7
Sur 50 B4
S Yorks 186 E6
W Loth 279 G8
W Yorks 197 C8
W Yorks 205 E9
West Field N Lincs 200 D6
York 207 C7
Westfields Dorset 30 F2
Hereford 97 C9
West Fields W Berks 64 F3
Westfields of Rattray
Perth 286 C5
Westfield Sole Kent 69 G9
West Firle E Sus 23 D7
West Fleetham
Northumb 264 D5
West Flodden
Northumb 263 C10
Westford Som 27 C10
West Garforth W Yorks 206 G3
Westgate Durham 232 D4
N Lincs 199 F9
Norf 176 E4
Norf 177 E7
Westgate Hill W Yorks 197 B8
Westgate on Sea Kent 71 E10
Westgate Street Norf 160 E3
West Ginge Oxon 64 B2
West Gorton Gtr Man 184 B5
West Grafton Wilts 63 G8
West Green Hants 49 B8
London 67 B10
S Yorks 197 F11
W Sus 51 F9
West Greenskares
Aberds 303 C7
West Grimstead Wilts 32 B2
West Grinstead W Sus 35 C11
West Haddlesey
N Yorks 198 B5
West Haddon W Nhants 120 C2
West Hagbourne Oxon 64 B4
West Hagley Worcs 133 G8
Westhall Aberds 302 G6
Suff 143 G8
West Hall Cumb 240 D3
West Hallam Derbys 170 G6
Westhall Hill Oxon 82 C3
West Halton N Lincs 200 C2
Westham Dorset 17 F9
E Sus 23 E10
Som 44 D2
West Ham Hants 48 C6
London 68 C2
Westhampnett W Sus 22 B5
West Hampstead London 67 B9
West Handley Derbys 186 F5
West Hanney Oxon 82 G6
West Hanningfield Essex 88 F2
West Hardwick
W Yorks 198 D2
West Harling Norf 141 G9
West Harlsey N Yorks 225 F8
West Harnham Wilts 31 B10
West Harptree Bath 44 B5
West Harrow London 66 B6
West Harting W Sus 34 C3
West Harton T&W 243 E9
West Hatch Som 28 C3
Wilts 30 B6
Westhay Som 44 E2
Westhead Lancs 194 F2
West Head Norf 139 B11
West Heath Ches E 168 C4
Hants 48 B5
Hants 49 B11
London 68 D3
W Mid 117 B10
West Helmsdale Highld 311 H4
West Hendon London 67 B8
West Hendred Oxon 64 B2
West Herrington T&W 243 G8
West Heslerton N Yorks 217 D8
West Hewish N Som 59 G11
Westhide Hereford 97 C11
Westhill Aberds 293 C10
E Yorks 209 F10
Highld 301 E7
West Hill Devon 15 C7
E Sus 38 E4
E Yorks 218 F3
London 67 E8
N Som 60 D3
Som 30 B2
Staffs 151 G9
Wilts 61 F11
W Sus 51 G10
West Hoathly W Sus 51 G11
West Holme Dorset 18 D3
West Holywell T&W 243 C8
Westhope Hereford 115 G9
Shrops 131 F9
West Horndon Essex 68 B6
Westhorp W Nhants 119 G10
Westhorpe Lincs 156 C4
Notts 171 E11
Suff 125 D10
West Horrington Som 44 D5
West Horsley Sur 50 C5
West Horton Northumb 264 C2
West Hougham Kent 55 E9
Westhoughton Gtr Man 195 F7
West Houlland Shetland 313 H4
Westhouse N Yorks 212 E3
Westhouses Derbys 170 D6
West Houses Lincs 174 E4
West Howe BCP 19 B7
West Howetown Som 42 G2
Westhumble Sur 51 C7
West Huntington York 207 B8
West Huntspill Som 43 E10
West Hurn BCP 19 B8
West Hyde Herts 85 G8
West Hynish Argyll 288 F1
West Hythe Kent 54 G6
West Ilkerton Devon 41 D8
West Ilsley W Berks 64 C3
Westing Shetland 312 C7
Westington Glos 100 D2
West Itchenor W Sus 22 C3
West Jesmond T&W 243 D7
West Keal Lincs 174 C5
West Kennett Wilts 62 F6
West Kensington London 67 D8
West Kilbride N Ayrs 266 F4
West Kilburn London 67 C8
West Kingsdown Kent 68 G5
West Kingston W Sus 35 G9
West Kington Wilts 61 D10
West Kington Wick
Wilts 61 D10
West Kinharrachie
Aberds 303 F9
West Kirby Mers 182 D2
West Kirkby Mers 182 D2
West Knapton N Yorks 217 D7
West Knighton Dorset 17 D10
West Knoyle Wilts 45 G11
West Kyloe Northumb 273 G11
West Kyo Durham 242 G5
Westlake Devon 8 E2
West Lambrook Som 28 D6
Westland Argyll 275 G11
Westland Green Herts 105 G8
Westlands Staffs 168 G4
Worcs 117 E7
West Langdon Kent 55 D10
West Langwell Highld 309 J6
West Lavington Wilts 46 C4
W Sus 34 C5
West Layton N Yorks 224 D2
Westlea Northumb 252 G6
Swindon 62 C6
West Lea Durham 234 B4
West Leake Notts 153 D10
West Learmouth
Northumb 263 B9
Westleigh Devon 25 B7
Devon 27 D9
Gtr Man 194 G6
West Leigh Devon 25 F11
Hants 22 B2
Som 42 G6
Westleton Suff 127 D8
West Lexham Norf 158 F6
Westley Shrops 131 B7
Suff 124 E6
Westley Heights Essex 69 B7
Westley Waterless
Cambs 124 F2
West Lilling N Yorks 216 F2
Westlington Bucks 84 C3
Westlinton Cumb 239 E9
West Linton Borders 270 E2
West Liss Hants 34 B3
West Littleton S Glos 61 D9
West Lockinge Oxon 64 B2
West Looe Corn 6 E5
West Luccombe Som 41 D11
West Lulworth Dorset 18 E2
West Lutton N Yorks 217 F8
West Lydford Som 44 G5
West Lydiatt Hereford 97 C11
West Lyn Devon 41 D8
West Lyng Som 28 B4
West Lynn Norf 158 E2
West Mains Borders 271 F11
S Lanark 268 E2
West Malling Kent 53 B7
West Malvern Worcs 98 B5
Westmancote Worcs 99 D8
West Marden W Sus 34 E3
West Marina E Sus 38 F3
West Markham Notts 188 G2
Westmarsh Kent 71 G9
West Marsh NE Lincs 201 E9
West Marton N Yorks 204 C3
West Mathers Aberds 293 G9
West Melbury Dorset 30 C5
West Melton S Yorks 198 G2
West Meon Hants 33 C10
West Meon Woodlands
Hants 33 B10
West Merkland Highld 308 F3
West Mersea Essex 89 C8
Westmeston E Sus 36 E4
Westmill Herts 104 E3
Herts 105 F7
West Milton Dorset 16 B6
Westminster London 67 D10
West Minster Kent 70 E2
West Molesey Sur 66 F6
West Monkseaton T&W 243 C8
West Monkton Som 28 B3
West Moor T&W 243 C7
Westmoor End Cumb 229 D8
West Moors Dorset 31 G9
West Morden Dorset 18 B4
West Morriston Borders 272 G2
West Morton W Yorks 205 E7
West Mudford Som 29 C9
Westmuir Angus 287 B7
West Muir Angus 293 G7
West Myreriggs Perth 286 C6
Westness Orkney 314 D3
West Ness N Yorks 216 D3
West Newham Northumb 242 B3
Westnewton Cumb 229 C8
Northumb 263 C10
West Newton E Yorks 209 F9
Norf 158 D3
Som 28 B3
West Norwood London 67 E10
Westoe T&W 243 D9
West Ogwell Devon 14 G2
Weston Bath 61 F8
Ches E 168 E2
Ches E 184 G5
Devon 15 D9
Devon 27 G10
Dorset 17 G9
Dorset 29 F8
Halton 183 E8
Hants 34 C2
Hereford 115 F7
Herts 104 E5
Lincs 156 D5
Notts 172 B3
N Yorks 205 D9
Pembs 73 C8
Shrops 114 C6
Shrops 131 E11
Shrops 148 D5
Shrops 149 D11
S Lanark 269 F10
Soton 32 E6
Staffs 151 D9
Suff 143 F8
W Berks 63 E11
W Nhants 101 B11
Weston Bampfylde
Som 29 C10

Weston Beggard
Hereford 97 C11
Westonbirt Glos 61 B11
Weston by Welland
N Nhants 136 E5
Weston Colley Hants 48 F4
Weston Colville Cambs 124 G2
Westoncommon Shrops 149 D8
Weston Common Soton 33 E7
Weston Corbett Hants 49 D7
Weston Coyney Stoke 168 G6
Weston Ditch Suff 124 B3
Weston Favell
W Nhants 120 E5
Weston Green Cambs 124 G2
Norf 160 G2
Sur 67 F7
Weston Heath Shrops 150 G5
Weston Hills Lincs 156 E5
Weston in Arden Warks 135 F7
Westoning C Beds 103 E10
Weston-in-Gordano
N Som 60 E2
Weston Jones Staffs 150 E5
Weston Longville Norf 160 F2
Weston Lullingfields
Shrops 149 E8
Weston Manor IoW 20 D2
Weston Mill Plym 7 D9
Weston-on-Avon
Warks 118 G3
Weston-on-the-Green
Oxon 83 B8
Weston-on-Trent
Derbys 153 D8
Weston Park Bath 61 F8
Weston Patrick Hants 49 D7
Weston Point Halton 183 E7
Weston Rhyn Shrops 148 B5
Weston-sub-Edge Glos 100 C2
Weston-super-Mare
N Som 59 G10
Weston Town Som 45 E8
Weston Turville Bucks 84 C5
Weston under Lizard
Staffs 150 G6
Weston under Penyard
Hereford 98 G2
Weston under Wetherley
Warks 119 D7
Weston Underwood
Derbys 170 G3
M Keynes 121 G7
Westonwharf Shrops 149 D8
Westonzoyland Som 43 G11
West Orchard Dorset 30 D4
West Overton Wilts 62 F6
Westow N Yorks 216 F5
Westowe Som 42 G6
Westown Devon 27 E10
Perth 286 E6
West Panson Devon 12 C2
West Park Hrtlpl 234 E5
Hull 200 B5
Mers 183 B7
T&W 243 D9
W Yorks 205 F11
West Parley Dorset 19 B7
West Pasture Durham 232 G4
West Peckham Kent 52 C6
West Pelton Durham 242 G6
West Pennard Som 44 F4
West Pentire Corn 4 C5
West Perry Cambs 122 D2
West Pontnewydd Torf 78 F3
West Poringland Norf 142 C5
West Porlock Som 41 D11
Westport Argyll 255 E7
Som 28 D5
West Portholland Corn 5 G9
West Porton Renfs 277 G8
West Pulham Dorset 30 F2
West Putford Devon 24 D5
West Quantoxhead Som 42 E6
Westquarter Falk 279 F8
Westra V Glam 58 E6
West Rainton Durham 234 B2
West Rasen Lincs 189 D9
West Ravendale
NE Lincs 190 B2
West Raynham Norf 159 D7
West Retford Notts 187 E11
Westridge Green
W Berks 64 D5
Westrigg W Loth 269 B8
Westrip Glos 80 D4
Westrop Wilts 61 E11
Westrop Green W Berks 64 E4
West Rounton N Yorks 225 E8
West Row Suff 124 B3
West Royd W Yorks 205 F9
West Rudham Norf 158 D6
West Ruislip London 66 B5
Westrum N Lincs 200 F4
West Runton Norf 177 E11
Westruther Borders 272 F2
Westry Cambs 139 D7
West Saltoun E Loth 271 B9
West Sandford Devon 26 G4
West Sandwick Shetland 312 E6
West Scholes W Yorks 205 G7
West Scrafton N Yorks 213 C11
West Shepton Som 44 E6
West Sherford Devon 7 E10
West Side Bl Gwent 77 D11
Orkney 314 C5
West Skelston Dumfries 247 F8
West Sleekburn
Northumb 253 G7
West Somerton Norf 161 F9
West Southbourne BCP 19 C8
West Stafford Dorset 17 D10
West Stockwith Notts 188 C3
West Stoke Devon 13 G9
Som 29 D7
W Sus 22 B4
West Stonesdale
N Yorks 223 E7
West Stoughton Som 44 D2
West Stour Dorset 30 C3
West Stourmouth Kent 71 G9
West Stow Suff 124 C6
West Stowell Wilts 62 G6
West Strathan Highld 308 C5
West Stratton Hants 48 E4
West Street Kent 54 C2
Kent 55 C10
Medway 69 D8
Suff 125 C9
West Tanfield N Yorks 214 D5
West Taphouse Corn 6 C3
West Tarbert Argyll 275 G9
West Tarring W Sus 35 G10
West Third Borders 262 B4
West Thirston Northumb 252 D5
West Thorney W Sus 22 C3
Westthorpe Derbys 187 F7
West Thurrock Thurrock 68 D5
West Tilbury Thurrock 69 D7
West Tisted Hants 33 B11
West Tofts Norf 140 E6
Perth 286 D5
West Tolgus Corn 4 G3
West Torrington Lincs 189 E10
West Town Bath 60 G4
Devon 14 B3
Devon 24 C4
Hants 21 B10
Hereford 115 E8
N Som 60 F3
Som 44 F4
W Sus 36 D3
West Tytherley Hants 32 B3
West Tytherton Wilts 62 E2
Westvale Mers 182 B6
West Vale W Yorks 196 C5
West View Hrtlpl 234 D5
West Village V Glam 58 E3
Westville Devon 8 G4
Notts 171 F8
West Walton Norf 157 G9
West Walton Highway
Norf 157 G9
Westward Cumb 229 C11
Westward Ho! Devon 24 B6
West Watergate Corn 6 E4
West Watford Herts 85 F10
Westweekmoor Devon 12 C4
Westwell Kent 54 D3
Oxon 82 D2
Westwell Leacon Kent 54 D3
West Wellow Hants 32 D3
Westwells Wilts 61 F11
West Wemyss Fife 280 C6
Westwick Cambs 123 D8
Durham 223 B11
Norf 160 D5
West Wick N Som 59 G11
West Wickham Cambs 106 B2
London 67 F11
Westwick Row Herts 85 D9
West Williamston Pembs 73 D8
West Willoughby Lincs 173 G7
West Winch Norf 158 F2
West Winterslow Wilts 47 G8
West Wittering W Sus 21 B11
West Witton N Yorks 213 B11
Westwood Devon 14 B6
Devon 14 E5
Kent 55 D7
Kent 71 F11
Notts 171 E7
Pboro 138 D3
S Lanark 268 E2
Wilts 45 B10
Wilts 46 G6
West Woodburn
Northumb 251 F9
West Woodhay W Berks 63 G11
Westwood Heath
W Mid 118 B5
West Woodlands Som 45 E9
Westwood Park Essex 107 E9
Gtr Man 184 B3
Westwoodside N Lincs 188 B3
West Worldham Hants 49 F8
West Worlington Devon 26 E3
West Worthing W Sus 35 G10
West Wratting Cambs 124 G2
West Wycombe Bucks 84 G4
West Wylam Northumb 242 E4
Westy Warr 183 D10
West Yatton Wilts 61 E11
West Yell Shetland 312 E6
West Yeo Som 43 G10
West Yoke Kent 68 F5
West Youlstone Corn 24 D3
Wetham Green Kent 69 F10
Wetheral Cumb 239 G11
Wetheral Plain Cumb 239 F11
Wetherby W Yorks 206 D4
Wetherden Suff 125 E10
Wetherden Upper Town
Suff 125 D10
Wetheringsett Suff 126 D2
Wethersfield Essex 106 E4
Wethersta Shetland 312 G5
Wetherup Street Suff 126 E2
Wetley Rocks Staffs 169 F7
Wetmore Staffs 152 E5
Wettenhall Ches E 167 C10
Wettenhall Green
Ches E 167 C10
Wettles Shrops 131 F8
Wetton Staffs 169 D10
Wetwang E Yorks 208 B4
Wetwood Staffs 150 C5
Wexcombe Wilts 47 B9
Wexham Street Bucks 66 C3
Weybourne Norf 177 E10
Sur 49 D11
Weybread Suff 142 G4
Weybridge Sur 66 G5
Weycroft Devon 16 B2
Weydale Highld 310 C5
Weyhill Hants 47 D10
Weymouth Dorset 17 F9
Weythel Powys 114 F4
Whaddon Bucks 102 E6
Cambs 104 B6
Glos 80 C4
Glos 99 G9
Wilts 31 B11
Wilts 61 G11
Whaddon Gap Cambs 104 B6
Whale Cumb 230 G6
Whaley Derbys 187 G8
Whaley Bridge Derbys 185 E8
Whaley Thorns Derbys 187 G8
Whaligoe Highld 310 E7
Whalley Lancs 203 F10
Whalley Banks Lancs 203 F10
Whalley Range Gtr Man 184 C4
Whalleys Lancs 194 F3
Whalton Northumb 252 G4
Wham N Yorks 212 G5
Whaplode Lincs 156 E6
Whaplode Drove Lincs 156 G6
Whaplode St Catherine
Lincs 156 E6
Wharf Warks 119 G8
Wharfe N Yorks 212 F5
Wharles Lancs 202 F4
Wharley End C Beds 103 C8
Wharmley Northumb 241 D9
Wharncliffe Side
S Yorks 186 C3
Wharram le Street
N Yorks 217 F8
Wharram Percy
N Yorks 217 G7
Wharton Ches W 167 B11
Hereford 115 F10
Lincs 188 C4
Wharton Green
Ches W 167 B11
Whashton N Yorks 224 D3
Whasset Cumb 211 C10
Whatcombe Dorset 30 G4
Whatcote Warks 100 C6
Whatcroft Ches W 167 B11
Whateley Staffs 134 D4
Whatfield Suff 107 B10
Whatley Som 28 F5
Som 45 D8
Whatlington E Sus 38 D3
Whatmore Shrops 116 C2
Whatsole Street Kent 54 E6
Whatstandwell Derbys 170 E4
Whatton Notts 154 B4
Whauphill Dumfries 236 E6
Whaw N Yorks 223 E9
Wheal Alfred Corn 2 B3
Wheal Baddon Corn 4 G5
Wheal Busy Corn 4 G4
Wheal Frances Corn 4 E5
Wheal Kitty Corn 4 E4
Wheal Rose Corn 4 G4
Wheatacre Norf 143 E9
Wheatcroft Derbys 170 D5
Wheatenhurst Glos 80 D3
Wheathall Shrops 131 C9
Wheathampstead Herts 85 C11
Wheathill Shrops 132 G2
Som 44 G5
Wheat Hold Hants 64 G5
Wheatley Devon 14 C4
Hants 49 E9
Oxon 83 D9
S Yorks 198 G5
W Yorks 196 B5
Wheatley Hill Durham 234 D3
Wheatley Hills S Yorks 198 G6
Wheatley Lane Lancs 204 F2
Wheatley Park S Yorks 198 F5
Wheaton Aston Staffs 151 G7
Wheddon Cross Som 42 F2
Wheedlemont Aberds 302 G4
Wheelbarrow Town Kent 55 D7
Wheeler End Bucks 84 G4
Wheelerstreet Sur 50 E2
Wheelock Ches E 168 D3
Wheelock Heath
Ches E 168 D2
Wheelton Lancs 194 C5
Lancs 194 C6
Lancs 194 D5
Lancs 194 D6
Wheen Angus 292 F5
Wheldale W Yorks 198 B3
Wheldrake York 207 D9
Whelford Glos 81 F11
Whelley Gtr Man 194 F5
Whelpley Hill Herts 85 E7
Whelpo Cumb 230 D2
Whelp Street Suff 107 B8
Whelston Flint 182 F2
Whempstead Herts 104 G6
Whenby N Yorks 216 F2
Whepstead Suff 124 F6
Wherry Town Corn 1 D5
Wherstead Suff 108 C3
Wherwell Hants 47 E11
Wheston Derbys 185 F10
Whetley Cross Dorset 29 G7
Whetsted Kent 53 D7
Whetstone Leics 135 D11
London 86 G3
Whettleton Shrops 131 G8
Whicham Cumb 210 C2
Whichford Warks 100 E6
Whickham T&W 242 E6
Whickham Fell T&W 242 F6
Whiddon Devon 40 F5
Whiddon Down Devon 13 C9
Whifflet N Lanark 268 C4
Whigstreet Angus 287 C8
Whilton W Nhants 120 E2
Whilton Locks
W Nhants 120 E2
Whimble Devon 24 G5
Whim Farm Borders 270 E4
Whimple Devon 14 B6
Whimpwell Green Norf 161 D7
Whinburgh Norf 141 B10
Whinfield Darl 224 B6
Whinhall N Lanark 268 B5
Whin Lane End Lancs 202 E3
Whinmoor W Yorks 206 F3
Whinney Hill Stockton 225 B7
S Yorks 187 C7
Whinnieliggate
Dumfries 237 D9
Whinnyfold Aberds 303 F10
Whinny Heights
Blackburn 195 B7
Whins of Milton Stirling 278 C5
Whins Wood W Yorks 205 F7
Whipcott Devon 27 D9
Whippendell Botton
Herts 85 E9
Whippingham IoW 20 C6
Whipsiderry Corn 4 C6
Whipsnade C Beds 85 B8
Whipton Devon 14 C5
Whirley Grove Ches E 184 F5
Whirlow S Yorks 186 E4
Whisby Lincs 172 B6
Whissendine Rutland 154 G6
Whissonsett Norf 159 E8
Whisterfield Ches E 184 G4
Whistlefield Argyll 276 C2
Argyll 276 C4
Whistley Green
Wokingham 65 E9
Whistlow Oxon 101 F9
Whiston Mers 183 C7
Staffs 151 G7
Staffs 169 F8
S Yorks 186 D6
W Nhants 120 E6
Whiston Cross Mers 183 C7
Shrops 132 C5
Whitacre Heath Warks 134 E4
Whitbarrow Village
Cumb 230 F4
Whitbeck Cumb 210 C2
Whitbourne Hereford 116 F4
Whitbourne Moor Wilts 45 D10
Whitburn T&W 243 E10
W Loth 269 C8
Whitburn Colliery
T&W 243 E10
Whitby Ches W 182 F5
N Yorks 227 C7
Whitbyheath Ches W 182 F5
Whitchurch Bath 60 F6
Bucks 102 G5
Cardiff 59 C7
Devon 12 G5
Hants 48 D3
Hereford 79 B9
Pembs 90 F5
Shrops 167 G8
Som 30 C2
Whitchurch Canonicorum
Dorset 16 B3
Whitchurch Hill Oxon 64 D6
Whitchurch-on-Thames
Oxon 64 D6
Whitcombe Dorset 17 D10
Whitcombe *continued*
Som 29 C10
Whitcot Shrops 131 E7
Whitcott Keysett Shrops 130 G5
Whiteacen Moray 302 E2
Whiteacre Kent 54 D6
Whiteacre Heath Warks 134 E4
Whiteash Green Essex 106 E5
White Ball Som 27 D9
Whitebirk Blackburn 195 B8
Whitebog Highld 301 C7
Whitebridge Highld 290 B6
Whitebrook Mon 79 D8
Whiteburn Borders 271 F11
Whitebushes Sur 51 D9
Whitecairn Dumfries 236 D4
Whitecairns Aberds 293 B11
Whitecastle S Lanark 269 G10
Whitechapel Lancs 203 E7
London 67 C10
Whitechurch Maund
Hereford 97 B11
Whitecleat Orkney 314 F5
Whitecliff Glos 79 C9
Whiteclosegate Cumb 239 F10
White Colne Essex 107 F7
White Coppice Lancs 194 D6
Whitecote W Yorks 205 F10
Whitecraig E Loth 281 G7
Whitecraigs E Renf 267 D11
Whitecroft Glos 79 D10
Whitecrook W Dunb 267 B10
Whitecross Corn 2 C2
Corn 6 E2
Corn 10 G5
Falk 279 F9
Som 28 C6
Staffs 151 E7
White Cross Bath 44 B5
Bath 44 B6
Corn 2 E5
Corn 5 D7
Hereford 97 C9
Som 43 D10
Wilts 45 G9
White Cross Hill Cambs 123 B9
White End Worcs 98 E5
Whiteface Highld 309 L7
Whitefarland N Ayrs 255 C9
Whitefaulds S Ayrs 245 B7
Whitefield Aberds 303 G7
Dorset 18 C4
Gtr Man 195 F10
Perth 286 D5
Som 27 B9
Whitefield Lane End
Mers 183 D7
Whiteflat E Ayrs 258 D2
Whiteford Aberds 303 G7
Whitegate Ches W 167 B10
White Gate Gtr Man 195 G11
Som 28 F4
White Grit Shrops 130 D6
Whitehall Blackburn 195 C7
Bristol 60 E6
Devon 27 E10
Devon 40 F4
Hants 49 C8
Herts 104 E6
W Sus 35 C10
White Hall Herts 104 G5
Whitehall Village
Orkney 314 D6
Whitehaven Cumb 219 B9
Shrops 148 E5
Whitehawk Brighton 36 G4
Whitehawk Gate W Mid 133 F9
Whitehill E Sus 37 B8
Hants 49 G9
Kent 54 B4
Midloth 271 B7
Moray 302 D5
S Lanark 268 D4
Staffs 168 E3
White Hill Bath 45 B8
Wilts 45 G10
W Yorks 204 E6
Whitehills Aberds 302 C6
S Lanark 268 E2
T&W 243 E7
White Hills W Nhants 120 E4
Whiteholme Blackpool 202 E2
Whitehough Derbys 185 E8
Whitehouse Aberds 293 B8
Argyll 275 G9
White House Suff 108 B2
Whitehouse Common
W Mid 134 D2
Whitehouse Green
W Berks 65 F7
White Houses Notts 188 F2
Whiteinch Glasgow 267 B10
Whitekirk E Loth 281 E10
Whiteknights Reading 65 E8
Whiteknowes Aberds 293 C7
Whitelackington Som 28 D5
White Lackington
Dorset 17 B10
White Ladies Aston
Worcs 117 G8
Whitelaw S Lanark 268 G2
Whiteleaf Bucks 84 E4
Whiteleas T&W 243 E9
Whiteleaved Oak Glos 98 D5
Whitelee Borders 262 C3
Northumb 250 B6
White Lee W Yorks 197 B8
Whitelees S Ayrs 257 C9
White-le-Head Durham 242 G5
Whiteley Bank IoW 21 E7
Whiteley Green Ches E 184 F6
Whiteley Village Sur 66 G5
White Lund Lancs 211 G8
Whitelye Mon 79 E8
Whitemans Green W Sus 36 B4
White Mill Carms 93 G9
Whitemire Moray 301 D9
Whitemoor Corn 5 D9
Nottingham 171 G8
Warks 118 C5
Wilts 118 C5
White Moor Derbys 170 F5
Whitemore Staffs 168 C5
Whitenap Hants 32 C5
White Ness Shetland 313 J5
White Notley Essex 88 B3
White Oak Kent 68 F4
Whiteoak Green Oxon 82 C4
White Ox Mead Bath 45 B8
Whiteparish Wilts 32 C2
White Pit Lincs 190 F5
Whitepits Wilts 45 F10
White Post Kent 52 E4
Notts 171 D10
Whiterashes Aberds 303 G8
Whiterigg Borders 262 C3
Whiterock Bridgend 58 D2
White Rocks Hereford 97 G8
White Roding or White Roothing Essex 87 C9
Whiterow Highld 310 E7
White's Green W Sus 34 B6
Whiteshill Glos 80 D4
S Glos 60 D6
Whiteside Northumb 240 D6
W Loth 269 B9
Whitesmith E Sus 23 C8
Whitespots Dumfries 247 F10
White Stake Lancs 194 B4
Whitestaunton Som 28 E3
Whitestone Aberds 293 D8
Devon 14 C3
Devon 40 D3
Warks 135 F7
White Stone Hereford 97 C11
Whitestones Aberds 303 D8
Whitestreet Green Suff 107 D9
Whitewall Common Mon 60 B2
Whitewall Corner
N Yorks 216 E5
White Waltham Windsor 65 D10
Whiteway Bath 61 G8
Dorset 18 E3
Glos 80 C6
Glos 80 F4
Whitewell Aberds 303 C9
Corn 11 E7
Highld 291 C11
Lancs 203 D9
Wrex 167 G7
Whitewell Bottom
Lancs 195 C10
Whiteworks Devon 13 G8
Whitfield Kent 55 D10
Northumb 241 F7
S Glos 79 G11
W Nhants 102 D2
Whitfield Court Sur 50 B3
Whitfield Hall Northumb 241 F7
Whitford Devon 15 B11
Whitford = *Chwitffordd*
Flint 181 F10
Whitgift E Yorks 199 C10
Whitgreave Staffs 151 D7
Whithaugh Borders 249 F11
Whithebeir Orkney 314 C5
Whithorn Dumfries 236 E6
Whiting Bay N Ayrs 256 D2
Whitington Norf 140 D4
Whitkirk W Yorks 206 G3
Whitland = *Hendy-Gwyn*
Carms 73 B11
Whitlaw Borders 271 F9
Whitleigh Plym 7 C9
Whitletts S Ayrs 257 E9
Whitley Gtr Man 194 F5
N Yorks 198 C5
Reading 65 E8
S Yorks 186 C4
Wilts 61 F11
W Mid 119 B7
Whitley Bay T&W 243 C9
Whitley Bridge N Yorks 198 C5
Whitley Chapel
Northumb 241 F10
Whitley Head W Yorks 204 E6
Whitley Heath Staffs 150 D6
Whitley Lower W Yorks 197 D8
Whitley Reed Ches W 183 E10
Whitley Row Kent 52 C3
Whitley Sands T&W 243 C9
Whitley Thorpe N Yorks 198 C5
Whitley Wood Reading 65 F8
Whitlock's End W Mid 118 B2
Whitminster Glos 80 D3
Whitmoor Devon 27 E9
Whitmore Dorset 31 F9
Staffs 168 G4
Whitmore Park W Mid 134 G6
Whitnage Devon 27 D8
Whitnash Warks 118 E6
Whitnell Som 43 F8
Whitney Bottom Som 28 E4
Whitney-on-Wye
Hereford 96 B5
Whitrigg Cumb 229 D10
Cumb 238 F6
Whitriggs Borders 262 F3
Whitsbury Hants 31 D10
Whitslaid Borders 271 G11
Whitsome Borders 273 E7
Whitsomehill Borders 273 F7
Whitson Newport 59 C11
Whitstable Kent 70 F6
Whitstone Corn 11 B11
Whittingham Northumb 264 G3
Whittingslow Shrops 131 F8
Whittington Glos 99 G10
Lancs 212 D2
Norf 140 D4
Shrops 148 C6
Staffs 133 G7
Staffs 134 B3
Staffs 150 C5
Warks 134 D5
Worcs 117 G7
Whittington Moor
Derbys 186 G5
Whittlebury W Nhants 102 C3
Whittleford Warks 134 E6
Whittle-le-Woods
Lancs 194 C5
Whittlesey Cambs 138 D5
Whittlesford Cambs 105 B9
Whittlestone Head
Blackburn 195 D8
Whitton Borders 263 E7
Hereford 115 C8
London 66 E6
N Lincs 200 C2
Northumb 252 C3
Powys 114 D5
Shrops 115 C11
Stockton 234 G3
Suff 108 B2
Whittonditch Wilts 63 E9
Whittonstall Northumb 242 F3
Whittytree Shrops 115 B8
Whitway Hants 48 B3
Whitwell Derbys 187 F8
Herts 104 G3
IoW 20 F6
N Yorks 224 F5
Rutland 137 B8
Whitwell-on-the-Hill
N Yorks 216 F4
Whitwell Street Norf 160 E2
Whitwick Leics 153 F8
Whitwood W Yorks 198 C2
Whitworth Lancs 195 D11
Whixall Shrops 149 C10
Whixley N Yorks 206 B4
Whoberley W Mid 118 B6
Wholeflats Falk 279 E8
Whome Orkney 314 G3
Whorlton Durham 224 C2
N Yorks 225 E9
Whydown E Sus 38 F2
Whygate Northumb 241 B7
Whyke W Sus 22 C5
Whyle Hereford 115 E11
Whyteleafe Sur 51 B10
Wibdon Glos 79 F9
Wibsey W Yorks 205 G8
Wibtoft Leics 135 F9
Wichenford Worcs 116 E5
Wichling Kent 54 B2
Wick BCP 19 C8
Devon 27 G11
Highld 310 D7
S Glos 61 E8
Shetland 313 K6
Som 28 B6
Som 43 C10
Som 43 E8
V Glam 58 E2
Wilts 31 C11
Worcs 99 B9
W Sus 35 G8
Wicken Cambs 123 C11
W Nhants 102 D4
Wicken Bonhunt Essex 105 E9
Wickenby Lincs 189 E9
Wicken Green Village
Norf 158 C6
Wick Episcopi Worcs 116 G6
Wickersley S Yorks 187 C7
Wicker Street Green
Suff 107 C9
Wickford Essex 88 G3
Wickham Hants 33 E9
W Berks 63 E11
Wickham Bishops Essex 88 C4
Wickhambreaux Kent 55 B8
Wickhambrook Suff 124 G4
Wickhamford Worcs 99 C11
Wickham Green Suff 125 D11
W Berks 63 E11
Wickham Heath W Berks 64 F2
Wickham Market Suff 126 F6
Wickhampton Norf 143 B8
Wickham St Paul Essex 106 D6
Wickham's Cross Som 44 G4
Wickham Skeith Suff 125 D11
Wickham Street Suff 124 G5
Suff 125 D11
Wick Hill Brack 65 E11
Kent 53 E10
Wokingham 65 G9
Wickhurst Kent 52 D4
Wicklane Bath 45 B7
Wicklewood Norf 141 C11
Wickmere Norf 160 C3
Wickridge Street Glos 98 F6
Wick Rocks S Glos 61 E8
Wick St Lawrence
N Som 59 F11
Wickstreet E Sus 23 D8
Wick Street Glos 80 D5
Wickwar S Glos 61 B8
Widbrook Wilts 45 B10
Widcombe Bath 61 G9
Widdington Essex 105 E10
Widdrington Northumb 253 D7
Widdrington Station
Northumb 252 E6
Widecombe in the Moor
Devon 13 F10
Widegates Corn 6 D5
Widemarsh Hereford 97 C10
Widemouth Bay Corn 24 G2
Wideopen T&W 242 C6
Widewall Orkney 314 G4
Widewell Plym 7 C9
Widford Essex 87 D11
Herts 86 B6
Widgham Green Cambs 124 F3
Widham Wilts 62 B5
Widley Hants 33 F11
Widmer End Bucks 84 F5
Widmerpool Notts 154 D2
Widmoor Bucks 66 B2
Widmore London 68 F2
Widnes Halton 183 D8
Wierton Kent 53 D9
Wig Powys 130 F2
Wigan Gtr Man 194 F5
Wiganthorpe N Yorks 216 E3
Wigbeth Dorset 31 F8
Wigborough Som 28 D6
Wig Fach Bridgend 57 F10
Wiggaton Devon 15 C8
Wiggenhall St Germans
Norf 157 G11
Wiggenhall St Mary Magdalen Norf 157 G11
Wiggenhall St Mary the Virgin Norf 157 G11
Wiggenhall St Peter
Norf 158 G2
Wiggens Green Essex 106 C3
Wiggington Staffs 134 B4
Wigginstall Staffs 169 C9
Wigginton Herts 84 C6
Oxon 101 E7
Shrops 148 B6
Staffs 134 B4
York 207 B7
Wigginton Bottom Herts 84 D6
Wigginton Heath Oxon 101 D7
Wigglesworth N Yorks 204 B2
Wiggonby Cumb 239 G7
Wiggonholt W Sus 35 D9
Wighill N Yorks 206 D5
Wighton Norf 159 B8
Wightwick Manor Staffs 133 D7
Wigley Derbys 186 G4
Hants 32 D4
Wigmarsh Shrops 149 D7
Wigmore Hereford 115 D8
Medway 69 G10
Wigsley Notts 188 G5
Wigsthorpe N Nhants 137 G10
Wigston Leics 136 D2
Wigston Magna Leics 136 D2
Wigston Parva Leics 135 F9
Wigthorpe Notts 187 E9
Wigtoft Lincs 156 B5
Wigton Cumb 229 B11
Wigtown Dumfries 236 D6
Wigtwizzle S Yorks 186 B2
Wike W Yorks 206 E2
Wike Well End S Yorks 199 E7
Wilbarston N Nhants 136 F6
Wilberfoss E Yorks 207 C10
Wilberlee W Yorks 196 E5
Wilburton Cambs 123 C9
Wilby N Nhants 121 D7
Norf 141 F10
Suff 126 C4
Wilcot Wilts 62 G6
Wilcott Shrops 149 F7
Wilcott Marsh Shrops 149 F7
Wilcove Corn 7 D8
Wilcrick Newport 60 B2
Wilday Green Derbys 186 G4
Wildboarclough Ches E 169 B7
Wilden Bedford 121 F11
Worcs 116 C6
Wildern Hants 33 E7
Wildernesse Kent 52 B4
Wilderspool Warr 183 D10
Wilderswood Gtr Man 194 E6
Wilde Street Suff 124 B4
Wildhern Hants 47 C11
Wildhill Herts 86 D3
Wildmanbridge
S Lanark 268 E6
Wild Mill Bridgend 58 C2
Wildmoor Hants 49 B7
Oxon 83 F7
Worcs 117 B9
Wildridings Brack 65 F11
Wildsworth Lincs 188 B4
Wildwood Staffs 151 E8
Wilford Nottingham 153 B11
Wilgate Green Kent 54 B3
Wilkesley Ches E 167 G10
Wilkhaven Highld 311 L3
Wilkieston W Loth 270 B2
Wilkinthroop Som 29 C11
Wilkin Throop Som 29 C11
Wilksby Lincs 174 C3
Willacy Lane End Lancs 202 F5
Willand Devon 27 E8
Som 27 E11
Willand Moor Devon 27 E8
Willard's Hill E Sus 38 C2
Willaston Ches E 167 E11
Ches W 182 F4
Shrops 149 B11
Willen M Keynes 103 C7
Willenhall W Mid 119 B7
W Mid 133 D9
Willerby E Yorks 208 G6
N Yorks 217 D10
Willersey Glos 100 D2
Willersley Hereford 96 B6
Willesborough Kent 54 E4
Willesborough Lees
Kent 54 E4
Willesden London 67 C8
Willesden Green London 67 C8
Willesley Leics 152 G6
Wilts 61 B11
Willett Som 42 G6
Willey Shrops 132 D3
Warks 135 G9
Willey Green Sur 50 C2
Willhayne Som 28 E4
Williamhope Borders 261 C10
Williamscott Oxon 101 B9
William's Green Suff 107 C9
Williamslee Borders 270 G6
Williamstown Rhondda 77 G8
Williamthorpe Derbys 170 B6
Willian Herts 104 E4
Willicote Pastures
Worcs 100 B3
Willingale Essex 87 D9
Willingcott Devon 40 E3
Willingdon E Sus 23 E9
Willingham Cambs 123 C8
Suff 143 G8
Willingham by Stow
Lincs 188 E5
Willingham Green
Cambs 124 G2
Willington Bedford 104 B2
Derbys 152 D5
Durham 233 D9
Kent 53 C9
T&W 243 D8
Warks 100 D5
Willington Corner
Ches W 167 B8
Willington Quay T&W 243 D8
Willisham Suff 125 G11
Willisham Tye Suff 125 G11
Willitoft E Yorks 207 F10
Williton Som 42 E5
Willoughbridge Staffs 168 G3
Willoughby Lincs 191 G7
Warks 119 D10
Willoughby Hills Lincs 174 F4
Willoughby-on-the-Wolds
Notts 154 D2
Willoughby Waterleys
Leics 135 E11
Willoughton Lincs 188 C6
Willowbank Bucks 66 B5
Willow Green Ches W 183 F10
Worcs 116 F5
Willow Holme Cumb 239 F9
Willows Gtr Man 195 F8
Willows Green Essex 88 B2
Willowtown Bl Gwent 77 C11
Will Row Lincs 191 D7
Willsbridge S Glos 61 E7
Willslock Staffs 151 C11
Willstone Shrops 131 D9
Willsworthy Devon 12 E6
Wilmcote Warks 118 F3
Wilmington Bath 61 G7
Devon 15 B10
E Sus 23 E8
Kent 68 E4
Wilmington Green E Sus 23 D8
Wilminstone Devon 12 F5
Wilmslow Ches E 184 E4
Wilmslow Park Ches E 184 E5
Wilnecote Staffs 134 C4
Wilney Green Norf 141 G11
Wilpshire Lancs 203 G9
Wilsden W Yorks 205 F7
Wilsden Hill W Yorks 205 F7
Wilsford Lincs 173 G8
Wilts 46 B6
Wilts 46 F6
Wilsham Devon 41 D9
Wilshaw W Yorks 196 F6
Wilsic S Yorks 187 B9
Wilsill N Yorks 214 G3
Wilsley Green Kent 53 F9
Wilsley Pound Kent 53 F9
Wilsom Hants 49 F8
Wilson Hereford 97 G11
Leics 153 E8
Wilsontown S Lanark 269 D9
Wilstead Bedford 103 C11
Wilsthorpe Derbys 153 C9
Lincs 155 G11
Wilstone Herts 84 C6
Wilstone Green Herts 84 C6
Wilthorpe S Yorks 197 F10
Wilton Borders 261 G11
Cumb 219 C10
Hereford 97 G11
N Yorks 217 C7
Redcar 225 B11
Som 28 C2
Wilts 46 G5
Wilts 63 G9
Wilton Park Bucks 85 G7
Wiltown Devon 27 D11
Som 28 C5
Wimbish Essex 105 D11
Wimbish Green Essex 106 D2
Wimblebury Staffs 151 G10
Wimbledon London 67 E8
Wimble Hill Hants 49 D10
Wimblington Cambs 139 E8
Wimboldsley Ches W 167 C11
Wimbolds Trafford
Ches W 182 G6
Wimborne Minster
Dorset 18 B6
Wimborne St Giles
Dorset 31 E8
Wimbotsham Norf 140 B2
Wimpole Cambs 104 B6
Wimpson Soton 32 E5
Wimpstone Warks 100 B4
Wincanton Som 30 B2
Winceby Lincs 174 B4
Wincham Ches W 183 F11
Winchburgh W Loth 279 G11
Winchcombe Glos 99 F10
Winchelsea E Sus 38 D6
Winchelsea Beach E Sus 38 D6
Winchester Hants 33 B7
Winchestown Bl Gwent 77 C11
Winchet Hill Kent 53 E8
Winchfield Hants 49 C9
Winchfield Hurst Hants 49 C9
Winchmore Hill Bucks 84 G6
London 86 G4
Wincle Ches E 169 B7
Wincobank S Yorks 186 C5
Winder Cumb 219 B10
Windermere Cumb 221 F8
Winderton Warks 100 C6
Windhill Highld 300 E5
S Yorks 198 G3
W Yorks 205 F9
Wind Hill Cumb 210 E5
Pembs 73 F9
Windhouse Shetland 312 D6
Winding Wood W Berks 63 E11
Windle Hill Ches W 182 F4
Windlehurst Gtr Man 185 D7
Windlesham Sur 66 G2
Windley Derbys 170 F4
Windmill Corn 10 G3
Flint 181 G11
Flint 182 G2
Windmill Hill Bristol 60 E5
E Sus 23 C10
Halton 183 E9
Kent 69 F10
Som 28 D4
Worcs 99 B8
W Yorks 197 D11
Windrush Glos 81 C11
Windsor N Lincs 199 E9
Windsor 66 D3
Windsoredge Glos 80 E4
Windsor Green Suff 125 G7
Windwhistle Som 28 F5
Windy Arbor Mers 183 D7
Windy Arbour Warks 118 C5
Windydoors Borders 261 B10
Windygates Fife 287 G7
Windyharbour Ches E 184 G4
Windy Hill Wrex 166 E4
Windyknowe W Loth 269 B9
Windy Nook T&W 243 E7
Windywalls Borders 263 C7
Windy-Yett E Ayrs 267 E9
Wineham W Sus 36 C2
Winestead E Yorks 201 C9
Winewall Lancs 204 E4
Winfarthing Norf 142 F2
Winford IoW 21 E7
N Som 60 F4
Winforton Hereford 96 B5
Winfrith Newburgh
Dorset 18 E2
Wing Bucks 103 G7
Rutland 137 C7
Wingate Durham 234 D4
Wingates Gtr Man 195 F7
Northumb 252 D4
Wingerworth Derbys 170 B5
Wingfield C Beds 103 F10
Suff 126 B4
S Yorks 186 B6
Wilts 45 B10
Wingfield Green Suff 126 B4
Wingfield Park Derbys 170 E5
Wingham Kent 55 B8
Wingham Green Kent 55 B8
Wingham Well Kent 55 B8
Wingmore Kent 55 D7
Wingrave Bucks 84 B5
Winkburn Notts 172 D2
Winkfield Brack 66 E2
Winkfield Place Brack 66 E2
Winkfield Row Brack 65 E11
Winkhill Staffs 169 E9
Winkhurst Green Kent 52 D3
Winklebury Hants 48 C6
Winkleigh Devon 25 F10
Winksley N Yorks 214 E5
Winkton BCP 19 B9
Winlaton T&W 242 E5
Winlaton Mill T&W 242 E5
Winless Highld 310 D7
Winllan Powys 148 E4
Winmarleigh Lancs 202 D5
Winmarleigh Moss
Lancs 202 D4
Winnal Hereford 97 E9
Winnal Common Hereford 97 E9
Winnall Hants 33 B7
Worcs 116 D6
Winnard's Perch Corn 5 B8
Winnersh Wokingham 65 E9
Winnington Ches W 183 G10
Staffs 150 B4
Winnington Green
Shrops 148 G6
Winnothdale Staffs 169 G8
Winscales Cumb 228 F6
Winscombe N Som 44 B2
Winsdon Hill Luton 103 G11
Winsford Ches W 167 B10
Som 42 G2
Winsham Devon 40 F3
Som 28 F5
Winshill Staffs 152 E5
Winsh-wen Swansea 57 B7
Winsick Derbys 170 B6
Winskill Cumb 231 D7
Winslade Devon 24 D5
Hants 49 D7
Winsley N Yorks 214 G4
Wilts 61 G10
Winslow Bucks 102 F5
Winslow Mill Hereford 98 D2
Winson Glos 81 D9
Winson Green W Mid 133 F10
Winsor Hants 32 E4
Winstanley Gtr Man 194 G5
Winstanleys Gtr Man 194 F5
Winster Cumb 221 G8
Derbys 170 C2
Winston Durham 224 B2
Suff 126 E3
Winstone Glos 81 D7
Winston Green Suff 126 E3
Winswell Devon 25 E7
Winterborne Bassett
Wilts 62 E6
Winterborne Came
Dorset 17 D10

Winterborne Clenston
Dorset 30 G4
Winterborne Herringston
Dorset 17 D9
Winterborne Houghton
Dorset 30 G4
Winterborne Kingston
Dorset 18 B3
Winterborne Monkton
Wilts 62 E6
Winterborne Muston
Dorset 18 B3
Winterborne Stickland
Dorset 30 G4
Winterborne Tomson
Dorset 18 B3
Winterborne Whitechurch
Dorset 30 G4
Winterborne Zelston
Dorset 18 B3
Winterbourne Kent 54 B5
S Glos 60 C6
W Berks 64 E3
Winterbourne Abbas
Dorset 17 C8
Winterbourne Bassett
Wilts 62 E6
Winterbourne Dauntsey
Wilts 47 G7
Winterbourne Down
S Glos 61 D7
Winterbourne Earls Wilts 47 G7
Winterbourne Gunner
Wilts 47 F7
Winterbourne Monkton
Dorset 17 D9
Winterbourne Steepleton
Dorset 17 D8
Winterbourne Stoke
Wilts 46 E5
Winterbrook Oxon 64 B6
Winterburn N Yorks 204 B4
Winterfield Bath 45 B7
Winter Gardens Essex 69 C9
Winterhay Green Som 28 D5
Winterhead N Som 44 B2
Winteringham N Lincs 200 C2
Winterley Ches E 168 D2
Wintersett W Yorks 197 D11
Wintershill Hants 33 D8
Winterton N Lincs 200 D2
Winterton-on-Sea Norf 161 F9
Winter Well Som 28 C3
Winthorpe Lincs 175 B9
Notts 172 D4
Winton BCP 19 C7
Cumb 222 C5
E Sus 23 E8
Gtr Man 184 B3
N Yorks 225 F8
Wintringham N Yorks 217 E7
Winwick Cambs 138 G2
Warr 183 C10
W Nhants 120 C2
Winwick Quay Warr 183 C10
Winyard's Gap Dorset 29 F7
Winyates Worcs 117 D11
Winyates Green Worcs 117 D11
Wirksworth Derbys 170 E3
Wirksworth Moor
Derbys 170 E4
Wirswall Ches E 167 G8
Wisbech Cambs 139 B9
Wisbech St Mary Cambs 139 B8
Wisborough Green
W Sus 35 B8
Wiseton Notts 188 D2
Wishanger Glos 80 D6
Wishaw N Lanark 268 D5
Warks 134 E3
Wisley Sur 50 B5
Wispington Lincs 190 G2
Wissenden Kent 54 E2
Wissett Suff 127 B7
Wistanstow Shrops 131 F8
Wistanswick Shrops 150 D3
Wistaston Ches E 167 E11
Wistaston Green
Ches E 167 E11
Wiston Pembs 73 B8
S Lanark 259 C11
W Sus 35 E10
Wiston Mains S Lanark 259 C11
Wistow Cambs 138 G5
Leics 136 D2
N Yorks 207 F7
Wiswell Lancs 203 F10
Witcham Cambs 139 G9
Witchampton Dorset 31 F7
Witchford Cambs 123 B10
Witcombe Som 29 C7
Withacott Devon 24 D6
Witham Essex 88 C4
Witham Friary Som 45 E8
Witham on the Hill
Lincs 155 F11
Witham St Hughs Lincs 172 C5
Withcall Lincs 190 E3
Withdean Brighton 36 F4
Witherenden Hill E Sus 37 B10
Withergate Norf 160 D5
Witheridge Devon 26 E4
Witheridge Hill Oxon 65 C7
Witherley Leics 134 D6
Withermarsh Green
Suff 107 D10
Withern Lincs 190 E6
Withernsea E Yorks 201 B10
Withernwick E Yorks 209 E9
Withersdale Street Suff 142 G5
Withersdane Kent 54 D5
Withersfield Suff 106 B3
Witherslack Cumb 211 C8
Witherwack T&W 243 F9
Withial Som 44 F5
Withiel Corn 5 B9
Withiel Florey Som 42 G3
Withielgoose Corn 5 B10
Withielgoose Mills Corn 5 B10
Withington Glos 81 B8
Gtr Man 184 C5
Hereford 97 C11
Shrops 149 G11
Staffs 151 B10
Withington Green
Ches E 184 G4
Withington Marsh
Hereford 97 C11
Withleigh Devon 26 E6
Withnell Lancs 194 C6
Withnell Fold Lancs 194 C6
Withybed Green Worcs 117 C10
Withybrook Som 45 D7
Warks 135 G8
Withybush Pembs 73 B7
Withycombe Som 41 F11
Som 42 E4
Withycombe Raleigh
Devon 14 E6
Withyditch Bath 45 B8
Withyham E Sus 52 F3
Withy Mills Bath 45 B7
Withymoor Village
W Mid 133 F8
Withypool Som 41 F10
Withystakes Staffs 169 F7
Withywood Bristol 60 F5
Witley Sur 50 F2
Witnells End Worcs 132 G5
Witnesham Suff 126 G3
Witney Oxon 82 C5
Wittensford Hants 32 E3
Wittering Pboro 137 C11
Wittersham Kent 38 B5
Witton Angus 293 F7
Norf 142 B6
W Mid 133 E11
Worcs 117 E7
Witton Bridge Norf 160 C6
Witton Gilbert Durham 233 B10
Witton Hill Worcs 116 E5
Witton-le-Wear Durham 233 E8
Witton Park Durham 233 E9
Wiveliscombe Som 27 B9
Wivelrod Hants 49 F7
Wivelsfield E Sus 36 C4
Wivelsfield Green E Sus 36 C5
Wivenhoe Essex 107 G10
Wivenhoe Cross Essex 107 G10
Wiveton Norf 177 E8
Wix Essex 108 F3
Wixams Bedford 103 C10
Wixford Warks 117 G11
Wixhill Shrops 149 D11
Wixoe Suff 106 C4
Woburn C Beds 103 E8
Woburn Sands
M Keynes 103 D8
Wofferwood Common
Hereford 116 G3
Wokefield Park W Berks 65 F7
Woking Sur 50 B4
Wokingham Wokingham 65 F10
Wolborough Devon 14 G3
Woldhurst W Sus 22 C5
Woldingham Sur 51 B11
Woldingham Garden Village
Sur 51 B11
Wold Newton E Yorks 217 E10
NE Lincs 190 B2
Wolfclyde S Lanark 260 B2
Wolferd Green Norf 142 D5
Wolferlow Hereford 116 E3
Wolferton Norf 158 D3
Wolfhampcote Warks 119 D10
Wolfhill Perth 286 D5
Wolf's Castle Pembs 91 F9
Wolfsdale Pembs 91 G8
Wolfsdale Hill Pembs 91 G8
Woll Borders 261 E11
Wollaston N Nhants 121 E8
Shrops 148 G6
W Mid 133 G7
Wollaton Nottingham 153 B10
Wollerton Shrops 150 C2
Wollerton Wood Shrops 150 C2
Wollescote W Mid 133 G8
Wollrig Borders 261 E11
Wolsingham Durham 233 D7
Wolstanton Staffs 168 F5
Wolstenholme
Gtr Man 195 D11
Wolston Warks 119 B8
Wolsty Cumb 238 G4
Wolterton Norf 160 C3
Wolvercote Oxon 83 D7
Wolverham Ches W 182 F6
Wolverhampton W Mid 133 D8
Wolverley Shrops 149 C9
Worcs 116 B6
Wolverstone Devon 27 G10
Wolverton Hants 48 B5
Kent 55 E9
M Keynes 102 C6
Shrops 131 F9
Warks 118 E4
Wilts 45 G9
Wolverton Common
Hants 48 B5
Wolvesnewton Mon 79 F7
Wolvey Warks 135 F8
Wolvey Heath Warks 135 F8
Wolviston Stockton 234 F5
Womaston Powys 114 E5
Wombleton N Yorks 216 C3
Wombourne Staffs 133 E7
Wombridge Telford 150 G3
Wombwell S Yorks 197 G11
Womenswold Kent 55 C8
Womersley N Yorks 198 D4
Wonastow Mon 79 C7
Wonderstone N Som 43 B10
Wonersh Sur 50 D4
Wonford Devon 14 C4
Wonson Devon 13 D9
Wonston Dorset 30 F2
Hants 48 F3
Wooburn Bucks 66 B2
Wooburn Green Bucks 66 B2
Wood Pembs 91 G7
Som 28 D4
Woodacott Devon 24 F5
Woodacott Cross Devon 24 F5
Woodale N Yorks 213 D10
Woodbank Argyll 255 F7
Ches W 182 G5
Shrops 131 F11
Woodbastwick Norf 160 F6
Woodbeck Notts 188 F3
Wood Bevington
Warks 117 G11
Woodborough Notts 171 F10
Wilts 46 B6
Woodbridge Dorset 30 D5
Dorset 30 E2
Glos 81 C8
Northumb 253 F7
Suff 108 B5
Woodbridge Hill Sur 50 C3
Woodbridge Walk Suff 109 B7
Wood Burcote
W Nhants 102 B3
Woodburn Common
Bucks 66 B2
Woodburn Moor Bucks 84 G6
Woodbury Devon 14 D6
Woodbury Salterton
Devon 14 D6
Woodchester Glos 80 E4
Woodchurch Kent 54 G2
Mers 182 D3
Woodcock Wilts 45 E11
Woodcock Heath
Staffs 151 D11
Woodcock Hill Herts 85 G9
W Mid 133 G10
Woodcombe Som 42 D3
Woodcot Hants 33 G9
Woodcote London 67 G10
Oxon 64 C6
Sur 51 B8
Telford 150 F5
Woodcote Green London 67 G9
Worcs 117 C8
Woodcott Hants 48 C2
Woodcroft Glos 79 F8
Woodcutts Dorset 31 D7
Wood Dalling Norf 159 D11
Woodditton Cambs 124 F3
Woodeaton Oxon 83 C8
Wood Eaton Staffs 150 F6
Wooden Pembs 73 D10
Woodend Ches E 185 D7
Cumb 219 C10
Cumb 220 F3
Cumb 229 F10
Cumb 229 G7
Essex 87 C9
Fife 280 B4
Notts 171 C7
Staffs 152 D3
W Loth 279 F11
W Nhants 102 B2
W Sus 22 B4
Wood End Bedford 103 B10
Bedford 121 D11
Bedford 121 F11
Bucks 102 E5
C Beds 103 C9
Gtr Man 196 F2
Hereford 98 C2
Herts 104 F6
Warks 118 C2
Warks 134 D4
Warks 134 F5
Windsor 66 E2
W Mid 133 C8
W Mid 135 G7
Wood Enderby Lincs 174 C3
Woodend Green Essex 105 F11
W Nhants 102 B2
Wood End Green London 66 C5
Woodend Ho Argyll 275 G11
Woodfalls Wilts 31 C11
Woodfield Glos 80 F2
Oxon 101 G11
S Ayrs 257 E8
Wood Field Sur 51 B7
Woodford Corn 24 E2
Devon 8 E5
Glos 79 F11
Gtr Man 184 E5
London 86 G6
N Nhants 121 B9
Plym 7 D10
Som 42 F5
Som 44 E4
Woodford Bridge London 86 G6
Woodford Green London 86 G6
Woodford Halse
W Nhants 119 G10
Woodford Wells London 86 G6
Woodgate Devon 27 D10
Norf 159 F10
W Mid 133 G9
Worcs 117 D9
W Sus 22 C6
Wood Gate Staffs 152 D3
Woodgate Hill Gtr Man 195 E10
Woodgates End Essex 105 F11
Woodgates Green
Worcs 116 C2
Woodgate Valley
W Mid 133 G10
Woodgreen Hants 31 D11
Oxon 82 C5
Wood Green Essex 86 E6
London 86 G4
Norf 142 E4
W Mid 133 D9
Worcs 116 D6
Woodhall Herts 86 C2
Invclyd 276 G6
N Yorks 207 G9
N Yorks 223 G9
Wood Hall Essex 105 E9
Woodhall Hills
W Yorks 205 F10
Woodhall Spa Lincs 173 C11
Woodham Bucks 84 B2
Durham 233 F11
Sur 66 G4
Woodham Ferrers Essex 88 F3
Woodham Mortimer
Essex 88 E4
Woodham Walter Essex 88 D4
Woodhatch Sur 51 D9
Woodhaven Fife 287 E8
Wood Hayes W Mid 133 C8
Woodhead Aberds 303 F7
Woodheads Borders 271 F10
Woodhey Gtr Man 195 D9
Mers 182 D4
Woodhey Green Ches E 167 E9
Woodhill Essex 88 E3
N Som 60 D3
Shrops 132 G4
Som 28 B5
Woodhorn Northumb 253 F7
Woodhouse Cumb 211 C10
Cumb 219 B9
Hants 47 D11
Leics 153 F10
N Lincs 199 F9
S Yorks 186 D6
W Yorks 196 C6
W Yorks 197 C11
W Yorks 205 E7
W Yorks 205 F11
Wood House Lancs 203 C10
Woodhouse Down S Glos 60 B6
Woodhouse Eaves
Leics 153 G10
Woodhouse Green
Staffs 168 C6
Woodhouselee Midloth 270 C4
Woodhouselees
Dumfries 239 C9
Woodhouse Mill
S Yorks 186 D6
Woodhouse Park
Gtr Man 184 D4
Woodhouses Ches W 183 F8
Cumb 239 G8
Gtr Man 184 C3
Gtr Man 196 G2
Staffs 133 B11
Staffs 152 F3
Woodhurst Cambs 122 B6
Woodingdean Brighton 36 F5
Woodington Hants 32 C4
Woodkirk W Yorks 197 C9
Woodlake Dorset 18 C3
Woodland Cumb 210 B4
Devon 8 B5
Devon 8 D2
Durham 233 F7
Kent 54 E6
Woodland Head Devon 13 B11
Woodlands Aberdeen 293 B10
Aberds 293 D9
Aberds 303 G8
Dorset 31 F9
Dumfries 238 B3
Gtr Man 185 B7
Hants 32 E4
Highld 300 C5
Kent 68 G5
London 67 D7
N Yorks 206 C2
Som 43 E7
Som 44 F4
S Yorks 198 F4
Wokingham 65 C9
W Yorks 196 B5
Woodlands Common
Dorset 31 F9
Woodlands Park
Windsor 65 D11
Woodlands St Mary
W Berks 63 E10
Woodlane Shrops 150 D3
Staffs 152 E2
Wood Lane Shrops 149 C8
Staffs 168 E4
Wood Lanes Ches E 184 E6
Woodleigh Devon 8 F4
Woodlesford W Yorks 197 B11
Woodley Gtr Man 184 C6
Hants 32 C5
Wokingham 65 E9
Woodley Green
Wokingham 65 E9
Woodleys Oxon 82 B6
Woodlinkin Derbys 170 F6
Woodloes Park Warks 118 D5
Woodmancote Glos 80 F3
Glos 81 D8
Glos 99 F9
Worcs 99 C8
W Sus 22 B3
W Sus 36 E2
Woodmancott Hants 48 E5
Woodmansey E Yorks 209 F7
Woodmansgreen W Sus 34 B5
Woodmans Green E Sus 38 D3
Woodmansterne Sur 51 B9
Woodmill Staffs 152 E2
Woodminton Wilts 31 C8
Woodnesborough Kent 55 B10
Woodnewton N Nhants 137 E10
Woodnook Lancs 195 B9
Lincs 155 C8
Wood Norton Norf 159 D10
Worcs 99 B10
Woodplumpton Lancs 202 G6
Woodram Som 28 D2
Woodrising Norf 141 C9
Wood Road Gtr Man 195 E9
Woodrow Bucks 84 F6
Cumb 229 B10
Dorset 30 E3
Dorset 30 F2
Worcs 117 B7
Worcs 117 D11
Wood Row W Yorks 197 B11
Woods Hereford 96 B5
Woods Bank W Mid 133 D9
Wood's Corner E Sus 23 B11
Woodsden Kent 53 G9
Woodseats Derbys 185 C7
Wood Seats S Yorks 186 B4
Woodseaves Shrops 150 C3
Staffs 150 D5
Woodsend Pembs 72 C5
Wilts 63 D8
Woods End Gtr Man 184 B2
Woodsetton W Mid 133 E8
Woodsetts S Yorks 187 E9
Woodsfield Worcs 98 B6
Woodsfold Lancs 202 F5
Woodsford Dorset 17 C11
Wood's Green E Sus 52 G6
Woodside Aberdeen 293 C11
Aberds 303 E10
Bedford 121 G11
Brack 66 E2
C Beds 85 B9
Ches E 167 C10
Ches W 183 G8
Derbys 170 G5
Derbys 187 G7
Dumfries 238 B2
Durham 233 F9
Essex 87 E7
Fife 287 G8
Hants 20 C2
Herts 85 E10
Herts 86 D3
IoW 20 C6
London 67 F10
N Lincs 199 G8
Perth 286 D6
Shrops 130 G6
Telford 132 C3
W Mid 133 F8
W Yorks 196 B6
Woodside Green Essex 87 B8
Kent 54 C2
Woodside of Arbeadie
Aberds 293 D9
Woodside Park London 86 G3
Woods Moor Gtr Man 184 D6
Woodspeen W Berks 64 F2
Woodspring Priory
N Som 59 F10
Wood Stanway Glos 99 E11
Woodstock Kent 70 G2
Oxon 82 B6
Pembs 91 F10
Woodston Pboro 138 D3
Wood Street Norf 161 E7
Sur 50 C3
Wood Street Village Sur 50 C3
Woodthorpe Derbys 187 G7
Leics 153 F10
Lincs 190 E6
Notts 171 G9
York 207 D7
Woodton Norf 142 E5
Woodtown Devon 24 C6
Devon 25 B7
Woodvale Mers 193 E10
Woodville Derbys 152 F6
Dorset 30 C4
Woodville Feus Angus 287 C10
Woodwall Green Staffs 150 C5
Wood Walton Cambs 138 G4
Woodway Oxon 64 C4
Woodway Park W Mid 135 G7
Woodwell N Nhants 121 B9
Woodwick Orkney 314 D3
Woodworth Green
Ches E 167 D9
Woodyates Dorset 31 D8
Woody Bay Devon 41 D7
Woofferton Shrops 115 D10
Wookey Som 44 D4
Wookey Hole Som 44 D4
Wool Dorset 18 D2
Woolacombe Devon 40 E3
Woolage Green Kent 55 D8
Woolage Village Kent 55 C8
Woolaston Glos 79 F9
Woolaston Common Glos 79 E9
Woolaston Slade Glos 79 E9
Woolaston Woodside
Glos 79 E9
Woolavington Som 43 E10
Woolbeding W Sus 34 C5
Wooldale W Yorks 197 F7
Wooler Northumb 263 D11
Woolfall Heath Mers 182 C6
Woolfardisworthy Devon 26 F4
Woolfardisworthy or
Woolsery Devon 24 C4
Woolfold Gtr Man 195 E9
Woolfords Cottages
S Lanark 269 D10
Woolford's Water Dorset 29 F11
Woolgarston Dorset 18 E5
Woolgreaves W Yorks 197 D10
Woolhampton W Berks 64 F5
Woolhope Hereford 98 D2
Woolhope Cockshoot
Hereford 98 D2
Woolland Dorset 30 F3
Woollard Bath 60 G6
Woollaston Staffs 151 F7
Woollaton Devon 25 E7
Woollensbrook Herts 86 C5
Woolley Bath 61 F8
Cambs 122 C3
Corn 24 D3
Derbys 170 C5
Wilts 61 G10
W Yorks 197 E10
Woolley Bridge Gtr Man 185 B8
Woolley Green Wilts 61 G10
Windsor 65 C11
Woolmere Green Worcs 117 E9
Woolmer Green Herts 86 B3
Woolmer Hill Sur 49 G11
Woolmersdon Som 43 G9
Woolminstone Som 28 F6
Woolpack Corner Kent 53 F11
Woolpit Suff 125 E9
Woolpit Green Suff 125 E9
Woolpit Heath Suff 125 E9
Woolridge Glos 98 G6
Woolsbridge Dorset 31 F9
Woolscott Warks 119 D9
Woolsery or
Woolfardisworthy
Devon 24 C4
Woolsgrove Devon 26 G3
Woolsington T&W 242 D5
Woolstanwood Ches E 167 D11
Woolstaston Shrops 131 D9
Woolsthorpe Lincs 155 E8
Woolsthorpe by Belvoir
Lincs 154 C6
Woolsthorpe-by-
Colsterworth Lincs 155 E8
Woolston Corn 6 B5
Devon 8 G4
Shrops 131 F8
Shrops 148 E6
Som 29 B10
Som 42 F5
Soton 32 E6
Warr 183 D10
Woolstone Glos 99 E9
M Keynes 103 D7
Oxon 63 B9
Woolston Green Devon 8 B5
Woolton Mers 182 D6
Woolton Hill Hants 64 G2
Woolvers Hill N Som 59 G11
Woolverstone Suff 108 D3
Woolverton Som 45 C9
Woolwell Devon 7 C10
Woolwich London 68 D2
Woolwich Ferry London 68 D2
Woon Corn 5 D10
Woonton Hereford 115 E10
Hereford 115 G7
Wooperton Northumb 264 E2
Woophlaw Borders 271 G9
Woore Shrops 168 G2
Wooton Shrops 115 C11
Shrops 132 F5
Wootten Green Suff 126 C4
Wootton Bedford 103 B10
Hants 19 B10
Hereford 97 D11
Hereford 114 G6
IoW 20 C6
Kent 55 D8
N Lincs 200 D5
Oxon 82 B6
Oxon 83 E7
Shrops 115 B9
Shrops 148 D6
Staffs 150 D6
Staffs 169 F10
W Nhants 120 F5
Wootton Bourne End
Bedford 103 B9
Wootton Bridge IoW 20 C6
Wootton Broadmead
Bedford 103 C10
Wootton Common IoW 20 C6
Wootton Courtenay Som 42 E2
Wootton Fitzpaine Dorset 16 B3
Wootton Green C Beds 103 C9
W Mid 118 B4
Wootton Rivers Wilts 63 G7
Woottons Staffs 151 B11
Wootton St Lawrence
Hants 48 C5
Wootton Wawen Warks 118 E3
Worbarrow Dorset 18 F3
Worcester Worcs 117 F7
Worcester Park London 67 F8
Wordsley W Mid 133 F7
Wordwell Suff 124 C6
Worfield Shrops 132 D5
Worgret Dorset 18 D4
Work Orkney 314 E4
Workhouse Common
Norf 161 E7
Workhouse End Bedford 122 G2
Workhouse Green Suff 107 D8
Workhouse Hill Essex 107 E9
Workington Cumb 228 F5
Worksop Notts 187 F9
Worlaby Lincs 190 F4
N Lincs 200 E4
Worlds End Hants 33 E10
W Mid 134 G2
World's End Bucks 84 D5
London 86 F4
Suff 125 F9
W Berks 64 D3
W Sus 36 D4
Worle N Som 59 G11
Worlebury N Som 59 G10
Worleston Ches E 167 D11
Worley Glos 80 F4
Worlingham Suff 143 F8
Worlington Devon 40 G3
Suff 124 C3
Worlingworth Suff 126 D4
Wormadale Shetland 313 J5
Wormald Green
N Yorks 214 G6
Wormbridge Hereford 97 E8
Wormbridge Common
Hereford 97 E8
Wormegay Norf 158 G3
Wormelow Tump
Hereford 97 E9
Wormhill Derbys 185 G10
Wormingford Essex 107 E8
Worminghall Bucks 83 D10
Wormington Glos 99 D10
Worminster Som 44 E5
Wormiston Ho Fife 287 G10
Wormit Fife 287 E7
Wormleighton Warks 119 G8
Wormley Herts 86 D5
Sur 50 F2
Wormleybury Herts 86 D5
Wormley West End Herts 86 D4
Worms Ash Worcs 117 C8
Wormshill Kent 53 B11
Worms Hill Kent 53 F8
Wormsley Hereford 97 B8
Wornish Nook Ches E 168 B4
Worplesdon Sur 50 C3
Worrall S Yorks 186 C4
Worrall Hill Glos 79 C10
Worsbrough S Yorks 197 G11
Worsbrough Bridge
S Yorks 197 G11
Worsbrough Common
S Yorks 197 F10
Worsbrough Dale
S Yorks 197 G11
Worsham Oxon 82 C3
Worsley Gtr Man 195 G8
Worsley Hall Gtr Man 194 F5
Worsley Mesnes
Gtr Man 194 G5
Worstead Norf 160 D6
Worsthorne Lancs 204 G3
Worston Devon 7 E11
Lancs 203 E11
Worswell Devon 7 F10
Worten Kent 54 E3
Worth Kent 55 B10
Som 44 D4
W Sus 51 F9
Worth Abbey W Sus 51 G10
Wortham Suff 125 B11
Worthen Shrops 130 C6
Worthenbury Wrex 166 F6
Worthing Norf 159 F9
W Sus 35 G10
Worthington Leics 153 E8
Worth Matravers Dorset 18 F5
Worthy Som 41 D11
Worthybrook Mon 79 C7
Worting Hants 48 C6
Wortley Glos 80 G3
S Yorks 186 B4
W Yorks 205 G11
Worton N Yorks 223 G9
Oxon 83 C7
Wilts 46 B3
Wortwell Norf 142 G5
Wotherton Shrops 130 C5
Wothorpe Pboro 137 B10
Wotter Devon 7 C11
Wotton Glos 80 B4
Sur 50 D6
Wotton-under-Edge
Glos 80 G3
Wotton Underwood
Bucks 83 B11
Woughton on the Green
M Keynes 103 D7
Woughton Park
M Keynes 103 D7
Wouldham Kent 69 G8
Woundale Shrops 132 E5
Wrabness Essex 108 E3
Wraes Aberds 302 F5
Wrafton Devon 40 F3
Wragby Lincs 189 F10
W Yorks 198 D2
Wragholme Lincs 190 B5
Wramplingham Norf 142 B2
Wrangaton Devon 8 D3
Wrangbrook W Yorks 198 E3
Wrangham Aberds 302 F6
Wrangle Lincs 174 E6
Wrangle Bank Lincs 174 E6
Wrangle Lowgate Lincs 174 E6
Wrangle Low Ground
Lincs 174 E6
Wrangway Som 27 D10
Wrantage Som 28 C4
Wrawby N Lincs 200 F4
Wraxall Dorset 29 G9
N Som 60 E3
Som 44 F6
Wray Lancs 212 F2
Wray Common Sur 51 C9
Wraysbury Windsor 66 E4
Wrayton Lancs 212 E2
Wrea Green Lancs 202 G3
Wreaks End Cumb 210 B4
Wreath Som 28 F4
Wreay Cumb 230 B4
Cumb 230 G4
Wrecclesham Sur 49 D10
Wrekenton T&W 243 F7
Wrelton N Yorks 216 B5
Wrenbury Ches E 167 F9
Wrenbury cum Frith
Ches E 167 F9
Wrench Green N Yorks 217 B9
Wreningham Norf 142 D3
Wrentham Suff 143 G9
Wrenthorpe W Yorks 197 C10
Wrentnall Shrops 131 C8
Wressle E Yorks 207 G10
N Lincs 200 F3
Wrestlingworth C Beds 104 B5
Wretham Norf 141 F8
Wretton Norf 140 D3
Wrexham Wrex 166 E4
Wreyland Devon 13 E11
Wribbenhall Worcs 116 B5
Wrickton Shrops 132 F2
Wrightington Bar Lancs 194 E4
Wright's Green Warr 183 E10
Wright's Green Essex 87 B8
Wrinehill Staffs 168 F3
Wringsdown Corn 12 D2
Wrington N Som 60 G3
Wrinkleberry Devon 24 C4
Writhlington Bath 45 C8
Writtle Essex 87 D11
Wrockwardine Telford 150 G2
Wrockwardine Wood
Telford 150 G4
Wroot N Lincs 199 G8
Wrose W Yorks 205 F9
Wrotham Kent 52 B6
Wrotham Heath Kent 52 B6
Wroughton Swindon 62 C6
Wroxall IoW 21 F7
Warks 118 C4
Wroxeter Shrops 131 B11
Wroxhall Warks 118 C4
Wroxham Norf 160 F6
Wroxton Oxon 101 C8
Wyaston Derbys 169 G11
Wyatt's Green Essex 87 F9
Wybers Wood NE Lincs 201 F8
Wyberton Lincs 174 G4
Wyboston Bedford 122 F3
Wybunbury Ches E 168 F2
Wychbold Worcs 117 D8
Wych Cross E Sus 52 G2
Wychnor Staffs 152 F3
Wychnor Bridges Staffs 152 F3
Wyck Hants 49 F9
Wyck Rissington Glos 100 G3
Wycliffe Durham 224 C2
Wycoller Lancs 204 F4
Wycomb Leics 154 E5
Wycombe Marsh Bucks 84 G5
Wyddial Herts 105 E7
Wydra N Yorks 205 C10
Wye Kent 54 D5
Wyebanks Kent 54 C2
Wyegate Green Glos 79 D9
Wyesham Mon 79 C8
Wyfordby Leics 154 F5
Wyke Dorset 30 B3
Shrops 132 C2
Sur 50 C2
W Yorks 197 B7
Wyke Champflower Som 45 G7
Wykeham Lincs 156 D5
N Yorks 216 D6
N Yorks 217 C9
Wyken Shrops 132 E5
W Mid 135 G7
Wyke Regis Dorset 17 F9
Wykey Shrops 149 E7
Wykin Leics 135 D8
Wylam Northumb 242 E4
Wylde Hereford 115 D9
Wylde Green W Mid 134 E2
Wyllie Caerph 77 G11
Wylye Wilts 46 F4
Wymans Brook Glos 99 G8
Wymbush M Keynes 102 D6
Wymering Ptsmth 33 F10
Wymeswold Leics 154 E2
Wymington Bedford 121 E9
Wymondham Leics 155 F7
Norf 142 C2
Wymondley Bury Herts 104 F4
Wymott Lancs 194 C4
Wyndham Bridgend 76 G6
Wyndham Park V Glam 58 D5
Wynds Point Hereford 98 C5
Wynford Eagle Dorset 17 B7
Wyng Orkney 314 G3
Wynn's Green Hereford 98 B2
Wynyard Village
Stockton 234 F4
Wyre Piddle Worcs 99 B9
Wysall Notts 154 D2
Wyson Hereford 115 D10
Wythall Worcs 117 B11
Wytham Oxon 83 D7
Wythburn Cumb 220 C6
Wythenshawe Gtr Man 184 D4
Wythop Mill Cumb 229 F9
Wyton Cambs 122 C5
E Yorks 209 G9
Wyverstone Suff 125 D10
Wyverstone Green
Suff 125 D10
Wyverstone Street
Suff 125 D10
Wyville Lincs 155 D7
Wyvis Lodge Highld 300 B4

Y

Yaddlethorpe N Lincs 199 F11
Yafford IoW 20 E4
Yafforth N Yorks 224 G6
Yair Borders 261 C11
Yalberton Torbay 9 D7
Yalding Kent 53 C7
Yanley N Som 60 F5
Yanworth Glos 81 C9
Yapham E Yorks 207 C11
Yapton W Sus 35 G7
Yarberry N Som 43 B11
Yarborough NE Lincs 201 F9
Yarbridge IoW 21 D8
Yarburgh Lincs 190 C5
Yarcombe Devon 28 F2
Yard Som 42 F5
Yarde Som 42 F5
Yardhurst Kent 54 E3
Yardley W Mid 134 F2
Yardley Gobion
W Nhants 102 C5
Yardley Hastings
W Nhants 121 F7
Yardley Wood W Mid 118 B2
Yardro Powys 114 F4
Yarford Som 28 B2
Yarhampton Worcs 116 D5
Yarhampton Cross
Worcs 116 D5
Yarkhill Hereford 98 C2
Yarlet Staffs 151 D8
Yarley Som 44 D4
Yarlington Som 29 B11
Yarlside Cumb 210 F4
Yarm Stockton 225 C8
Yarmouth IoW 20 D3
Yarnacott Devon 40 G6
Yarnbrook Wilts 45 C11
Yarnfield Staffs 151 C7
Yarningale Common
Warks 118 D3
Yarnscombe Devon 25 C9
Yarnton Oxon 83 C7
Yarpole Hereford 115 E9
Yarrow Borders 261 D9
Northumb 250 F6
Som 43 D11
Yarrow Feus Borders 261 D8
Yarrowford Borders 261 C10
Yarsop Hereford 97 B8
Yarwell N Nhants 137 D11
Yate S Glos 61 C8
Yateley Hants 65 G10
Yate Rocks S Glos 61 C8
Yatesbury Wilts 62 E5
Yattendon W Berks 64 E5
Yatton Hereford 115 D8
N Som 60 F2
Yatton Keynell Wilts 61 D11
Yaverland IoW 21 D8
Yawthorpe Lincs 188 C5
Yaxham Norf 159 G10
Yaxley Cambs 138 E3
Suff 126 C2
Yazor Hereford 97 B8
Y Bala = *Bala* Gwyn 147 B8
Y Bont Faen = *Cowbridge*
V Glam 58 E3
Y Borth = *Borth* Ceredig 128 E2
Yeabridge Som 28 D6
Yeading London 66 C6
Yeadon W Yorks 205 E10
Yealand Conyers Lancs 211 E10
Yealand Redmayne
Lancs 211 D10
Yealand Storrs Lancs 211 D9
Yealmbridge Devon 7 E11
Yealmpton Devon 7 E11
Yearby Redcar 235 G8
Yearngill Cumb 229 C8
Yearsley N Yorks 215 E11
Yeaton Shrops 149 F8
Yeaveley Derbys 169 G11
Yedingham N Yorks 217 D7
Yelden Bedford 121 D10
Yeldersley Hollies
Derbys 170 G2
Yeldon Bedford 121 D10
Yelford Oxon 82 E5
Yelland Devon 40 G3
Yelling Cambs 122 E5
Yelsted Kent 69 G10
Yelvertoft W Nhants 119 B11
Yelverton Devon 7 B10
Norf 142 C5
Yenston Som 30 C2
Yeoford Devon 13 B11
Yeolmbridge Corn 12 D2
Yeo Mill Devon 26 B4
Yeo Vale Devon 24 C6
Yeovil Som 29 D9
Yeovil Marsh Som 29 D8
Yeovilton Som 29 C8
Yerbeston Pembs 73 D9
Yesnaby Orkney 314 E2
Yetlington Northumb 252 B2
Yetminster Dorset 29 E9
Yett N Lanark 268 D5
Yettington Devon 15 D7
Yetts o' Muckhart Clack 286 G4
Yew Green Warks 118 D4
Yewhedges Kent 54 B3
Yew Tree Gtr Man 185 B7
W Mid 133 D10
Yewtree Cross Kent 55 E7
Y Fali = *Valley* Anglesey 178 F3
Y Felinheli = *Port Dinorwic*
Gwyn 163 B8
Y Ferwig Ceredig 92 B3
Y Ffôr Gwyn 145 B7
Y-Ffrith Denb 181 E8
Y Gors Ceredig 112 B2
Y Gribyn Powys 129 E8
Yieldshields S Lanark 269 E7
Yiewsley London 66 C5
Yinstay Orkney 314 E5
Y Mwmbwls = *The Mumbles*
Swansea 56 D6
Ynus-tawelog Swansea 75 D10
Ynys Gwyn 145 B11
Ynysboeth Rhondda 77 F9
Ynysddu Caerph 77 G11
Ynysforgan Swansea 57 B7
Ynysgyfflog Gwyn 146 G2
Ynyshir Rhondda 77 G8
Ynys-isaf Powys 76 C3
Ynyslas Ceredig 128 E2
Ynysmaerdy Neath 57 B8
Rhondda 58 C4
Ynysmeudwy Neath 76 D2
Neath 76 D2
Ynys Tachwedd Ceredig 128 E2
Ynystawe Swansea 75 E11
Ynyswen Powys 76 C4
Rhondda 77 F7
Ynysybwl Rhondda 77 G9
Ynysygwas Neath 57 C9
Yockenthwaite N Yorks 213 D8
Yockleton Shrops 149 G7
Yodercott Devon 27 E9
Yokefleet E Yorks 199 C10
Yoker W Dunb 267 B10
Yonder Bognie Aberds 302 E5
Yondertown Devon 7 D11
Yopps Green Kent 52 C6
York Lancs 203 G10
York 207 C7
Yorkletts Kent 70 G5
Yorkley Glos 79 D10
Yorkley Slade Glos 79 D10
York Town Sur 65 G11
Yorton Shrops 149 E10
Yorton Heath Shrops 149 E10
Yottenfews Cumb 219 D10
Youlgrave Derbys 170 C2
Youlstone Devon 24 D3
Youlthorpe E Yorks 207 B11
Youlton N Yorks 215 G9
Youngsbury Herts 86 B5
Young's End Essex 88 B2
Young Wood Lincs 189 G10
Yoxall Staffs 152 F2
Yoxford Suff 127 D7
Y Pîl = *Pyle* Bridgend 57 E10
Yr Hôb = *Hope* Flint 166 D4
Ysbyty Cynfyn Ceredig 112 B5
Ysbyty Ifan Conwy 164 F4
Ysbyty Ystwyth Ceredig 112 C4
Ysceifiog Flint 181 G11
Ysgeibion Denb 165 D9
Yspitty Carms 56 B5
Ystalyfera Neath 76 D3
Ystrad Rhondda 77 F7
Ystrad Aeron Ceredig 111 F10
Ystradfellte Powys 76 C6
Ystradffin Carms 94 B5
Ystradgynlais Powys 76 C3
Ystradmeurig Ceredig 112 D4
Ystrad-mynach Caerph 77 G10
Ystradowen Carms 76 C2
V Glam 58 D4
Ystrad Uchaf Powys 129 C11
Ystumtuen Ceredig 112 B4
Ythanbank Aberds 303 F9
Ythanwells Aberds 302 F6
Ythsie Aberds 303 F8
Y Tymbl = *Tumble* Carms 75 C8
Y Waun = *Chirk* Wrex 148 B5

Z

Zeal Monachorum Devon 26 G2
Zeals Wilts 45 G9
Zelah Corn 4 E6
Zennor Corn 1 B5
Zoar Corn 3 F7
Zouch Notts 153 E10

County and unitary authority boundaries

Ordnance Survey National Grid

The blue lines which divide the Navigator map pages into squares for indexing match the Ordnance Survey National Grid and correspond to the small squares on the boundary map below. Each side of a grid square measures 10km on the ground.

The National Grid 100-km square letters and kilometre values are indicated for the grid intersection at the outer corners of each page. For example, the intersection SE6090 at the upper right corner of page 215 is 60km East and 90km North of the south-west corner of National Grid square SE.

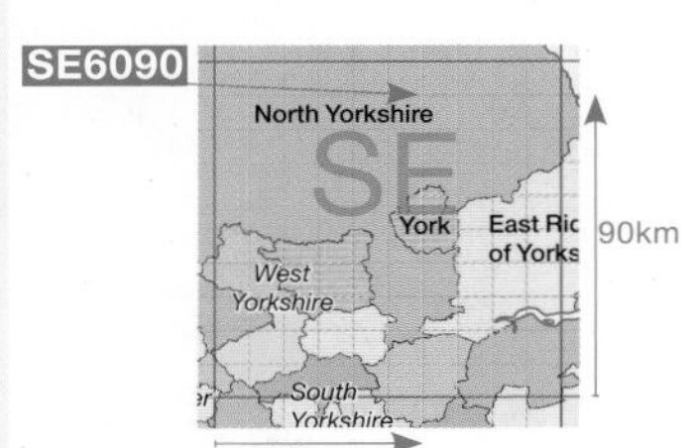

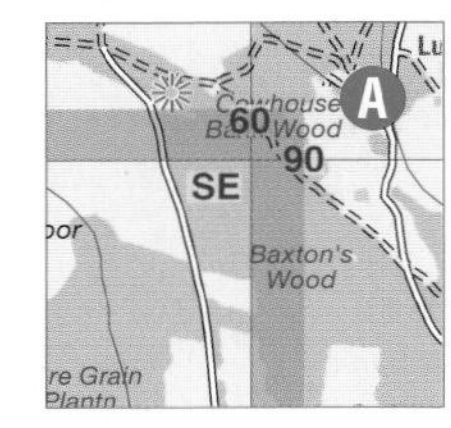

Using GPS with Navigator mapping

Since Navigator Britain is based on Ordnance Survey mapping, and rectified to the National Grid, it can be used with in-car or handheld GPS for locating identifiable waypoints such as road junctions, bridges, railways and farms, or assessing your position in relation to any of the features shown on the map.

On your receiver, choose British Grid as the location format and for map datum select Ordnance Survey (this may be described as Ord Srvy GB or similar, or more specifically as OSGB36). Your receiver will automatically convert the latitude/longitude co-ordinates transmitted by GPS into compatible National Grid data.

Positional accuracy of any particular feature is limited to 50–100m, due to the limitations of the original survey and the scale of Navigator mapping.

For further information see www.gps.gov.uk

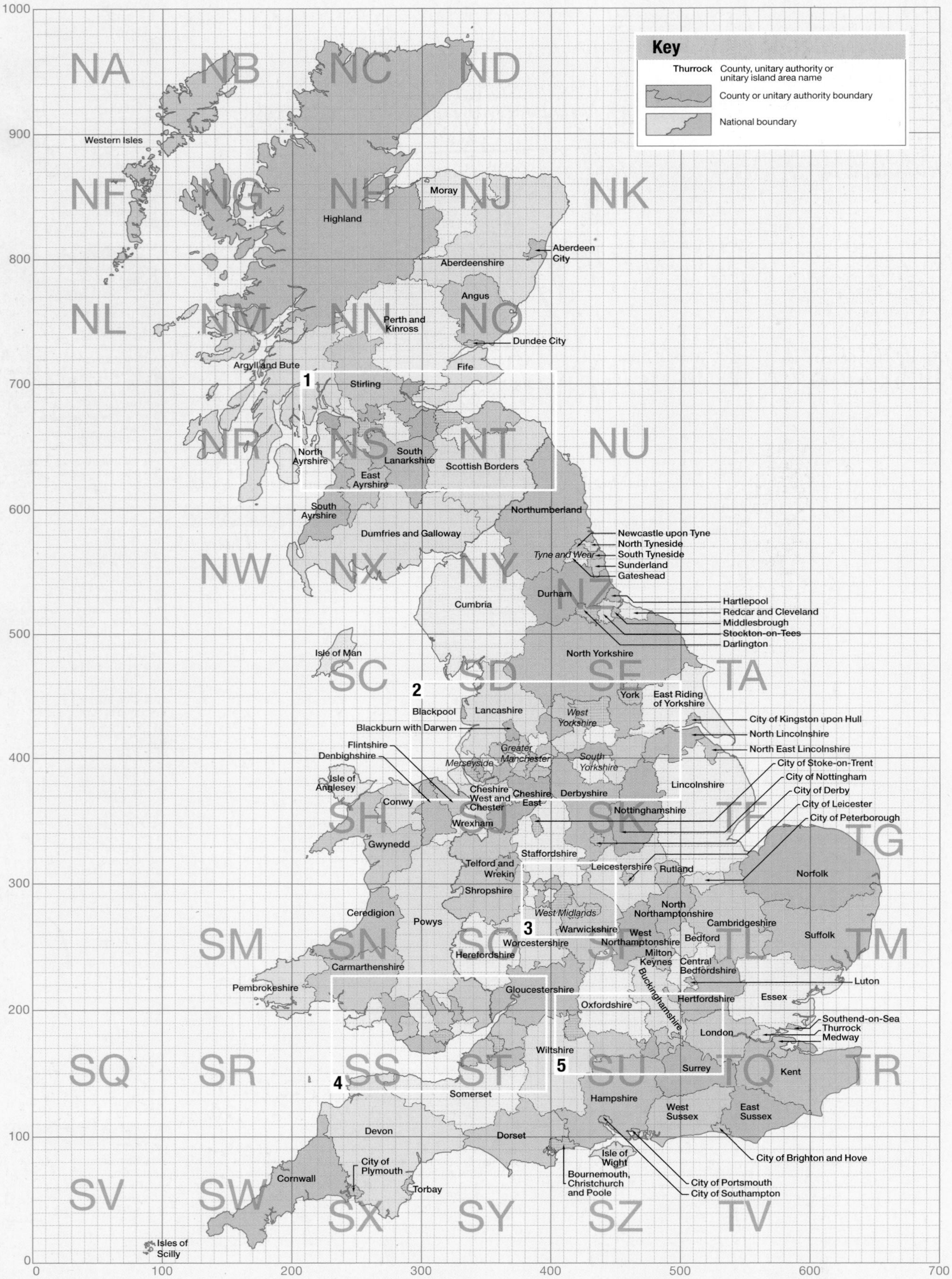

Greater London

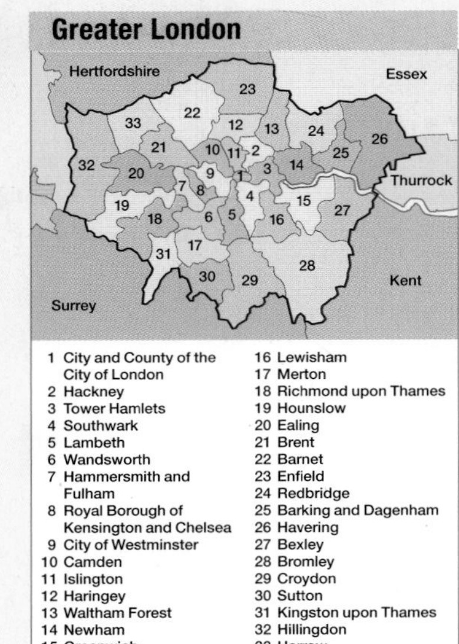

Key

Thurrock — County, unitary authority or unitary island area name

County or unitary authority boundary

National boundary

NA NB NC ND NF NG NH NJ NK NL NM NN NO NR NS NT NU NW NX NY NZ SC SD SE TA SH SJ SK TF TG SM SN SO SP TL TM SQ SR SS ST SU TQ TR SV SW SX SY SZ TV

Western Isles, Highland, Moray, Aberdeenshire, Aberdeen City, Angus, Perth and Kinross, Dundee City, Argyll and Bute, Fife, Stirling, North Ayrshire, South Lanarkshire, East Ayrshire, Scottish Borders, South Ayrshire, Dumfries and Galloway, Northumberland, Newcastle upon Tyne, North Tyneside, Tyne and Wear, South Tyneside, Sunderland, Gateshead, Cumbria, Durham, Hartlepool, Redcar and Cleveland, Middlesbrough, Stockton-on-Tees, Darlington, Isle of Man, North Yorkshire, York, East Riding of Yorkshire, Blackpool, Lancashire, West Yorkshire, Blackburn with Darwen, City of Kingston upon Hull, North Lincolnshire, North East Lincolnshire, Flintshire, Denbighshire, Greater Manchester, Merseyside, South Yorkshire, City of Stoke-on-Trent, City of Nottingham, Isle of Anglesey, Cheshire West and Chester, Cheshire East, Derbyshire, Lincolnshire, City of Derby, Conwy, City of Leicester, Nottinghamshire, City of Peterborough, Wrexham, Gwynedd, Staffordshire, Telford and Wrekin, Leicestershire, Rutland, Norfolk, Shropshire, West Midlands, North Northamptonshire, Ceredigion, Powys, Warwickshire, Cambridgeshire, West Northamptonshire, Bedford, Suffolk, Worcestershire, Herefordshire, Milton Keynes, Central Bedfordshire, Carmarthenshire, Luton, Pembrokeshire, Gloucestershire, Buckinghamshire, Hertfordshire, Essex, Oxfordshire, Southend-on-Sea, Thurrock, London, Medway, Wiltshire, Surrey, Kent, Somerset, Hampshire, West Sussex, East Sussex, Devon, Dorset, City of Brighton and Hove, Isle of Wight, City of Plymouth, Cornwall, Torbay, Bournemouth, Christchurch and Poole, City of Portsmouth, City of Southampton, Isles of Scilly

1 2 3 4 5

0 100 200 300 400 500 600 700

1000 900 800 700 600 500 400 300 200 100 0

1 Central Scotland

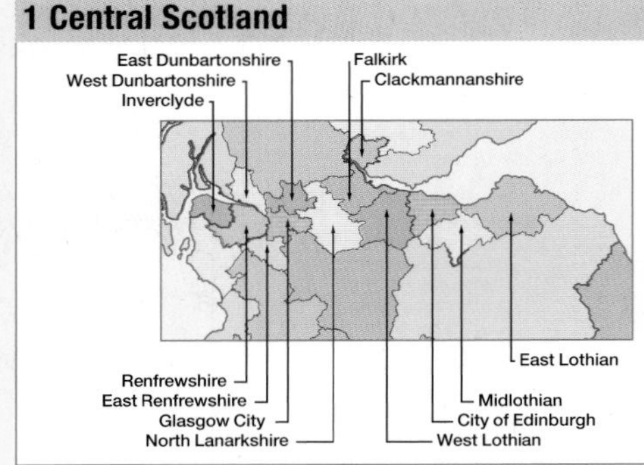

2 Northern England

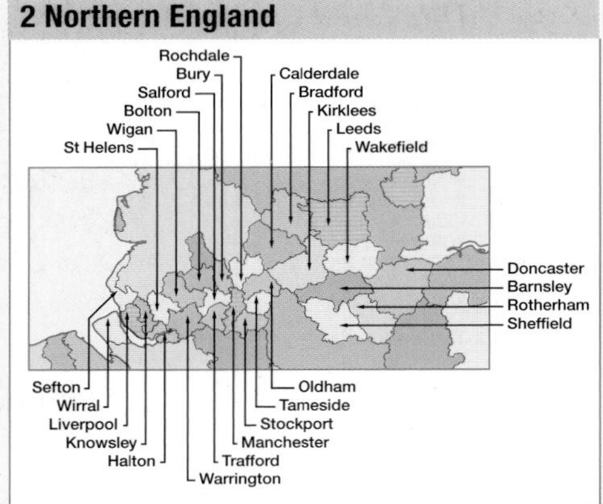

3 West Midlands

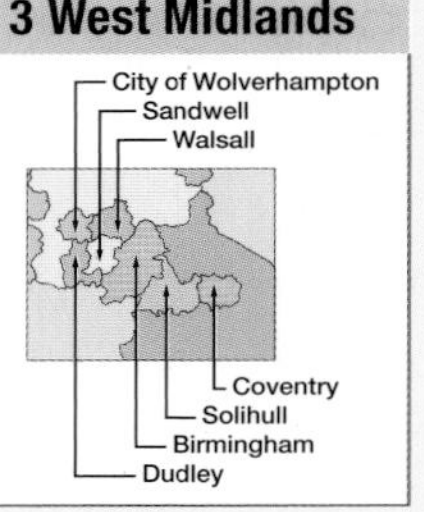

4 South Wales and Bristol area

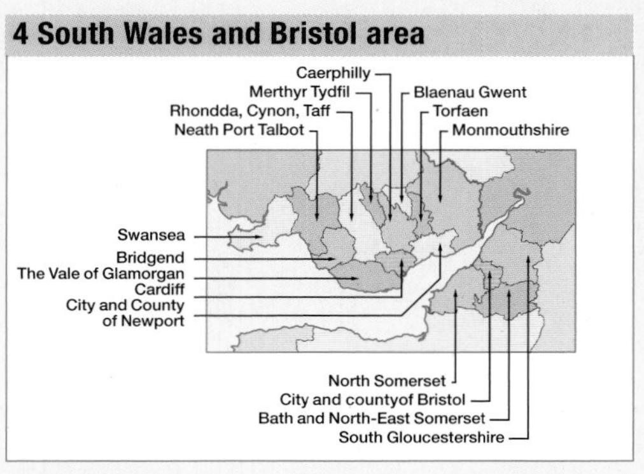

5 Thames Valley

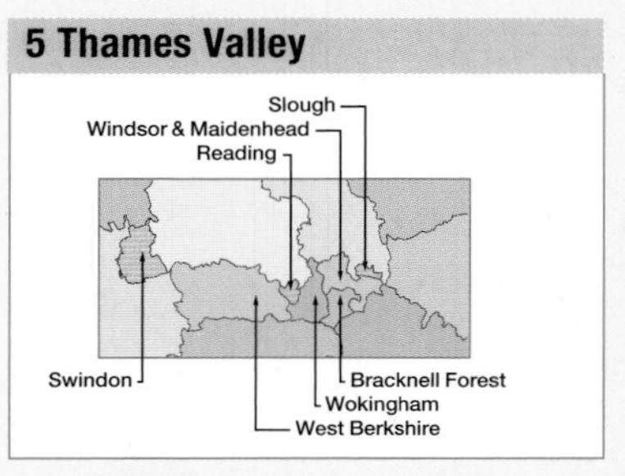

ROAD ATLAS

SUPER CLEAR SCALE
1.5 miles to 1 inch
1:100 000*

NO.1 BEST SELLER

NAVIGATOR® BRITAIN

CONTENTS

II **Key to map symbols**
III **Restricted motorway junctions**
IV **Route planning maps**
X **Distances** and journey times
1 **Road maps of Britain**
315 **Urban approach maps**

315 **Bristol** *approaches*
316 **Birmingham** *approaches*
318 **Cardiff** *approaches*
319 **Edinburgh** *approaches*
320 **Glasgow** *approaches*
321 **Leeds** *approaches*
322 **London** *approaches*
326 **Liverpool** *approaches*
327 **Manchester** *approaches*
328 **Newcastle** *approaches*
329 **Nottingham** *approaches*
330 **Sheffield** *approaches*

331 **Town plans**

331 Aberdeen, Aberystwyth, Ashford, Ayr, Bangor, Barrow-in-Furness, Bath, Berwick-upon-Tweed
332 Birmingham, Blackpool, Bournemouth, Bradford, Brighton, Bristol, Bury St Edmunds
333 Cambridge, Canterbury, Cardiff, Carlisle, Chelmsford, Cheltenham, Chester, Chichester, Colchester
334 Coventry, Derby, Dorchester, Dumfries, Dundee, Durham, Edinburgh, Exeter
335 Fort William, Glasgow, Gloucester, Grimsby, Hanley, Harrogate, Holyhead, Hull
336 Inverness, Ipswich, Kendal, King's Lynn, Leeds, Lancaster, Leicester, Lewes
337 Lincoln, Liverpool, Llandudno, Llanelli, Luton, Macclesfield, Manchester
338 London
340 Maidstone, Merthyr Tydfil, Middlesbrough, Milton Keynes, Newcastle, Newport, Newquay, Newtown, Northampton
341 Norwich, Nottingham, Oban, Oxford, Perth, Peterborough, Plymouth, Poole, Portsmouth
342 Preston, Reading, St Andrews, Salisbury, Scarborough, Shrewsbury, Sheffield, Southampton
343 Southend-on-Sea, Stirling, Stoke, Stratford-upon-Avon, Sunderland, Swansea, Swindon, Taunton, Telford
344 Torquay, Truro, Wick, Winchester, Windsor, Wolverhampton, Worcester, Wrexham, York

345 **Index to town plans**
361 **Index to road maps of Britain**
402 **County and unitary authority boundaries**

www.philips-maps.co.uk

First published in 1994 by Philip's,
a division of Octopus Publishing Group Ltd
www.octopusbooks.co.uk
Carmelite House
50 Victoria Embankment
London EC4Y 0DZ
An Hachette UK Company
www.hachette.co.uk

Fifteenth edition 2022
First impression 2022

ISBN 978-1-84907-614-2 (flexi-bound)
ISBN 978-1-84907-613-5 (spiral-bound)

Cartography by Philip's

Data for the caravan sites provided by The Camping and Caravanning Club.

Information for the selection of Wildlife Trust nature reserves provided by The Wildlife Trusts.

Information for National Parks, Areas of Outstanding Natural Beauty, National Trails and Country Parks in Wales supplied by the Countryside Council for Wales.

Information for National Parks, Areas of Outstanding Natural Beauty, National Trails and Country Parks in England supplied by Natural England. Data for Regional Parks, Long Distance Footpaths and Country Parks in Scotland provided by Scottish Natural Heritage.

Information for Forest Parks supplied by the Forestry Commission

Information for the RSPB reserves provided by the RSPB

Gaelic name forms used in the Western Isles provided by Comhairle nan Eilean.

Data for the National Nature Reserves in England provided by Natural England. Data for the National Nature Reserves in Wales provided by Countryside Council for Wales. Darparwyd data'n ymwneud â Gwarchodfeydd Natur Cenedlaethol Cymru gan Gyngor Cefn Gwlad Cymru.

Information on the location of National Nature Reserves in Scotland was provided by Scottish Natural Heritage.

Data for National Scenic Areas in Scotland provided by the Scottish Executive Office. Crown copyright material is reproduced with the permission of the Controller of HMSO and the Queen's Printer for Scotland. Licence number C02W0003960.

*Parts of Scotland at smaller scale

Printed in China

Road map symbols

M25	**Motorway**
16, 17	**Motorway junctions** – full access, restricted access
	Toll motorway
Pease Pottage Services	**Motorway service area**
	Motorway under construction
S	**Primary route** – dual, single carriageway, services – under construction, narrow
Cardiff	**Primary destination**
25, 26	**Numbered junctions** – full, restricted access
	A road – dual, single carriageway – under construction, narrow
	B road – dual, single carriageway – under construction, narrow
	Minor road – dual, single carriageway
	Drive or track
	Urban side roads
	Roundabout, multi-level junction
2	**Distance in miles**
	Tunnel
Toll	**Toll, steep gradient** – points downhill
CLEVELAND WAY	**National trail** – England and Wales
GREAT GLEN WAY	**Long distance footpath** – Scotland
YATTON	**Railway with station, level crossing, tunnel**
ROPLEY	**Preserved railway with level crossing, station, tunnel**
	Tramway
	National boundary
	County or unitary authority boundary
	Car ferry, catamaran
	Passenger ferry, catamaran
	Hovercraft
V, P	**Internal ferry** – car, passenger
	Principal airport, other airport or airfield
MENDIP HILLS	**Area of outstanding natural beauty, National Forest** – England and Wales, **Forest park**, **National park**, **National scenic area** – Scotland, **Regional park**
	Woodland
	Beach – sand, shingle
KENNET AND AVON CANAL	**Navigable river or canal**
6	**Lock, flight of locks, canal bridge number**
C, CF, CS, LS	**Caravan or camping sites** – CCC* Club Site, Ready Camp Site, Camping in the Forest Site – CCC Certificated Site, Listed Site
P&R, ▲965	**Viewpoint, park and ride, spot height** – in metres
	Linear antiquity
29	**Adjoining page number**
SY 70 80	**Ordnance Survey National Grid reference** – see page 402

*Categories defined by the Camping and Caravanning Club of Great Britain

Road map scale 1: 100 000 or 1.58 miles to 1 inch

0 1 2 3 4 5 km
0 1 2 3 miles

Road map scale (Isle of Man and parts of Scotland)
1: 200 000 or 3.15 miles to 1 inch

0 1 2 3 4 5 6 7 8 9 10 km
0 1 2 3 4 5 6 miles

Tourist information

Example	Symbol
BYLAND ABBEY	**Abbey or priory**
WOODHENGE	**Ancient monument**
SEALIFE CENTRE	**Aquarium or dolphinarium**
CITY MUSEUM AND ART GALLERY	**Art collection or museum**
TATE ST IVES	**Art gallery**
1644	**Battle site and date**
ABBOTSBURY SWANNERY	**Bird sanctuary or aviary**
BAMBURGH CASTLE	**Castle**
YORK MINSTER	**Cathedral**
SANDHAM MEMORIAL CHAPEL	**Church of interest**
	Country park
SEVEN SISTERS	– England and Wales
LOCHORE MEADOWS	– Scotland
ROYAL BATH & WEST SHOWGROUND	**County show ground**
MONK PARK FARM	**Farm park**
HILLIER GARDENS AND ARBORETUM	**Garden, arboretum**
ST ANDREWS	**Golf course** – 18-hole
TYNTESFIELD	**Historic house**
SS GREAT BRITAIN	**Historic ship**
HATFIELD HOUSE	**House and garden**
CUMBERLAND PENCIL MUSEUM	**Museum**
MUSEUM OF DARTMOOR LIFE	– Local
NAT MARITIME MUSEUM	– Maritime or military
	Marina
SILVERSTONE	**Motor racing circuit**
	Nature reserves
HOLTON HEATH	– National nature reserve
BOYTON MARSHES	– RSPB reserve
DRAYCOTT SLEIGHTS	– Wildlife Trust reserve
	Picnic area
WEST SOMERSET RAILWAY	**Preserved railway**
THIRSK	**Racecourse**
LEAHILL TURRET	**Roman antiquity**
THRIGBY HALL	**Safari park**
FREEPORT BRAINTREE	**Shopping village**
MILLENNIUM STADIUM	**Sports venue**
ALTON TOWERS	**Theme park**
	Tourist information
NATIONAL RAILWAY MUSEUM	**Transport collection**
LEVANT MINE	**World heritage site**
HELMSLEY	**Youth hostel**
MARWELL	**Zoo**
SUTTON BANK VISITOR CENTRE, GLENFIDDICH DISTILLERY	**Other place of interest**

Approach map symbols

M6	**Motorway**
	Toll motorway
6, 5	**Motorway junction** – full, restricted access
S	**Service area**
	Under construction
A6	**Primary route** – dual, single carriageway
S	**Service area**
	Multi-level junction
	roundabout
	Under construction
A195	**A road** – dual, single carriageway
B1288	**B road** – dual, single carriageway
	Minor road – dual, single carriageway
	Ring road
3	**Distance in miles**
COSELEY	**Railway with station**
LOXDALE	**Tramway with station**
M	**Underground or metro station**
	Congestion charge area

Restricted motorway junctions

M1	Northbound	Southbound
2	No exit	No access
4	No exit	No access
6A	No exit. Access from M25 only	No access. Exit to M25 only
7	No exit. Access from A414 only	No access. Exit to A414 only
17	No access. Exit to M45 only	No exit. Access from M45 only
19	No exit to A14	No access from A14
21A	No access	No exit
23A		Exit to A42 only
24A	No exit	No access
35A	No access	No exit
43	No access. Exit to M621 only	No exit. Access from M621 only
48	No exit to A1(M) southbound	

M3	Eastbound	Westbound
8	No exit	No access
10	No access	No exit
13	No access to M27 eastbound	
14	No exit	No access

M4	Eastbound	Westbound
1	Exit to A4 eastbound only	Access from A4 westbound only
2	Access from A4 eastbound only	Access to A4 westbound only
21	No exit	No access
23	No access	No exit
25	No exit	No access
25A	No exit	No access
29	No exit	No access
38		No access
39	No exit or access	No exit
42	Access from A483 only	Exit to A483 only

M5	Northbound	Southbound
10	No exit	No access
11A	No access from A417 eastbound	No exit to A417 westbound

M6	Northbound	Southbound
3A	No access.	No exit. Access from M6 eastbound only
4A	No exit. Access from M42 southbound only	No access. Exit to M42 only
5	No access	No exit
10A	No access. Exit to M54 only	No exit. Access from M54 only
11A	No exit. Access from M6 Toll only	No access. Exit to M6 Toll only
20	No exit to M56 eastbound	No access from M56 westbound
20A	No exit	No access
24	No exit	No access
25	No access	No exit
30	No exit. Access from M61 northbound only	No access. Exit to M61 southbound only
31A	No access	No exit
45	No access	No exit

M6 Toll	Northbound	Southbound
T1		No exit
T2	No exit, no access	No access
T5	No exit	No access
T7	No access	No exit
T8	No access	No exit

M8	Eastbound	Westbound
6	No exit	No access
6A	No access	No exit
7	No Access	No exit
7A	No exit. Access from A725 northbound only	No access. Exit to A725 southbound only
8	No exit to M73 northbound	No access from M73 southbound
9	No access	No exit
13	No exit southbound	Access from M73 southbound only
14	No access	No exit
16	No exit	No access
17	No exit	
18		No exit
19	No exit to A814 eastbound	No access from A814 westbound
20	No exit	No access
21	No access from M74	No exit
22	No exit. Access from M77 only	No access. Exit to M77 only
23	No exit	No access
25	Exit to A739 northbound only. Access from A739 southbound only	
25A	No exit	No access
28	No exit	No access
28A	No exit	No access
29A	No exit	No access

M9	Eastbound	Westbound
2	No access	No exit
3	No exit	No access
6	No access	No exit
8	No exit	No access

M11	Northbound	Southbound
4	No exit	No access
5	No access	No exit
8A	No access	No exit
9	No access	No exit
13	No access	No exit
14	No exit to A428 westbound	No exit. Access from A14 westbound only

M20	Eastbound	Westbound
2	No access	No exit
3	No exit Access from M26 eastbound only	No access Exit to M26 westbound only
10	No access	No exit
11A	No access	No exit

M23	Northbound	Southbound
7	No exit to A23 southbound	No access from A23 northbound
10A	No exit	No access

M25	Clockwise	Anticlockwise
5	No exit to M26 eastbound	No access from M26 westbound
19	No access	No exit
21	No exit to M1 southbound. Access from M1 southbound only	No exit to M1 southbound. Access from M1 southbound only
31	No exit	No access

M27	Eastbound	Westbound
10	No exit	No access
12	No access	No exit

M40	Eastbound	Westbound
3	No exit	No access
7	No exit	No access
8	No exit	No access
13	No exit	No access
14	No access	No exit
16	No access	No exit

M42	Northbound	Southbound
1	No exit	No access
7	No access Exit to M6 northbound only	No exit. Access from M6 northbound only
7A	No access. Exit to M6 southbound only	No exit
8	No exit. Access from M6 southbound only	Exit to M6 northbound only. Access from M6 southbound only

M45	Eastbound	Westbound
M1 J17	Access to M1 southbound only	No access from M1 southbound
With A45	No access	No exit

M48	Eastbound	Westbound
M4 J21	No exit to M4 westbound	No access from M4 eastbound
M4 J23	No access from M4 westbound	No exit to M4 eastbound

M49	Southbound	Northbound
18A	No exit to M5 northbound	No access from M5 southbound

M53	Northbound	Southbound
11	Exit to M56 eastbound only. Access from M56 westbound only	Exit to M56 eastbnd only. Access from M56 westbound only

M56	Eastbound	Westbound
2	No exit	No access
3	No access	No exit
4	No exit	No access
7		No access
8	No exit or access	No exit
9	No access from M6 northbound	No access to M6 southbound
15	No exit to M53	No access from M53 northbound

M57	Northbound	Southbound
3	No exit	No access
5	No exit	No access

M60	Clockwise	Anticlockwise
2	No exit	No access
3	No exit to A34 northbound	No exit to A34 northbound
4	No access from M56	No exit to M56
5	No exit to A5103 southbound	No exit to A5103 northbound
14	No exit	No access
16	No exit	No access
20	No access	No exit
22		No access
25	No access	
26		No exit or access
27	No exit	No access

M61	Northbound	Southbound
2	No access from A580 eastbound	No exit to A580 westbound
3	No access from A580 eastbound. No access from A666 southbound	No exit to A580 westbound
M6 J30	No exit to M6 southbound	No access from M6 northbound

M62	Eastbound	Westbound
23	No access	No exit

M65	Eastbound	Westbound
9	No access	No exit
11	No exit	No access

M66	Northbound	Southbound
1	No access	No exit

M67	Eastbound	Westbound
1A	No access	No exit
2	No exit	No access

M69	Northbound	Southbound
2	No exit	No access

M73	Northbound	Southbound
2	No access from M8 eastbound	No exit to M8 westbound

M74	Northbound	Southbound
3	No access	No exit
3A	No exit	No access
7	No exit	No access
9	No exit or access	No access
10		No exit
11	No exit	No access
12	No access	No exit

M77	Northbound	Southbound
4	No exit	No access
6	No exit	No access
7	No exit	
8	No access	No access

M80	Northbound	Southbound
4A	No access	No exit
6A	No exit	No access
8	Exit to M876 northbound only. No access	Access from M876 southbound only. No exit

M90	Northbound	Southbound
1	Access from A90 north-bound only	No access. Exit to A90 south-bound only
2A	No access	No exit
7	No exit	No access
8	No access	No exit
10	No access from A912	No exit to A912

M180	Eastbound	Westbound
1	No access	No exit

M621	Eastbound	Westbound
2A	No exit	No access
4	No exit	
5	No exit	No access
6	No access	No exit

M876	Northbound	Southbound
2	No access	No exit

A1(M)	Northbound	Southbound
2	No access	No exit
3		No access
5	No exit	No exit, no access
14	No exit	No access
40	No access	No exit
43	No exit. Access from M1 only	No access. Exit to M1 only
57	No access	No exit
65	No access	No exit

A3(M)	Northbound	Southbound
1	No exit	No access
4	No access	No exit

A38(M) with Victoria Rd, (Park Circus) Birmingham	
Northbound	No exit
Southbound	No access

M4 Junctions 25, 25A, 26

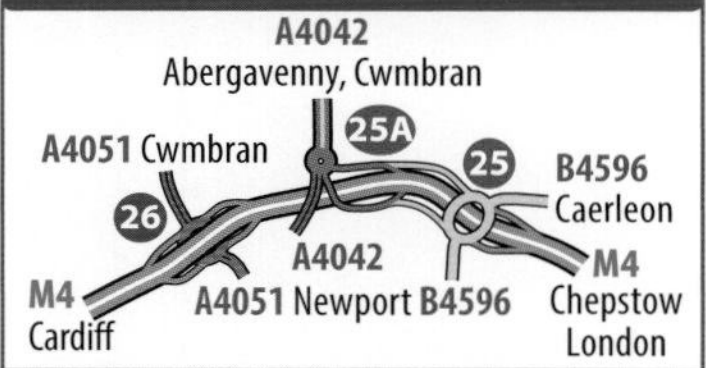

A4042
Abergavenny, Cwmbran
A4051 Cwmbran
25A
25
B4596
Caerleon
26
A4042
M4
Chepstow
London
M4
Cardiff
A4051 Newport B4596

A48(M)	Northbound	Southbound
M4 Junc 29	Exit to M4 eastbound only	Access from M4 westbound only
29A	Access from A48 eastbound only	Exit to A48 westbound only

A57(M)	Eastbound	Westbound
With A5103	No access	No exit
With A34	No access	No exit

A58(M)	Southbound
With Park Lane and Westgate, Leeds	No access

A64(M)	Eastbound	Westbound
With A58 Clay Pit Lane, Leeds	No access from A58	No exit to A58

A74(M)	Northbound	Southbound
18	No access	No exit
22		No exit to A75

A194(M)	Northbound	Southbound
A1(M) J65 Gateshead Western Bypass	Access from A1(M) northbound only	Exit to A1(M) southbound only

M6 Junc 20 · M56 Junc 9

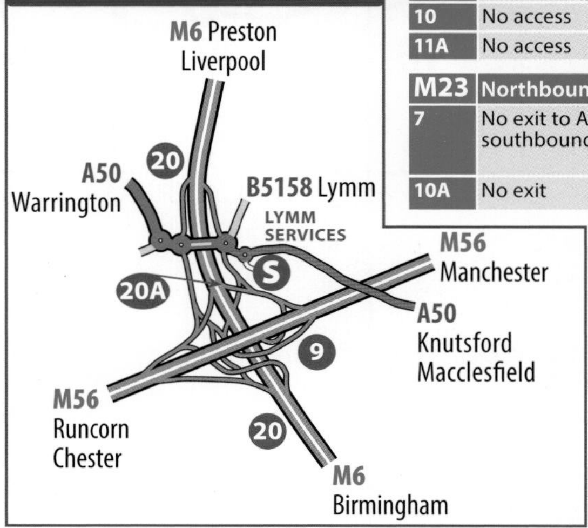

M6 Preston
Liverpool
A50
Warrington
20
B5158 Lymm
LYMM SERVICES
S
M56
Manchester
20A
A50
Knutsford
Macclesfield
9
M56
Runcorn
Chester
20
M6
Birmingham

M3 Junctions 13, 14 · M27 Junction 4

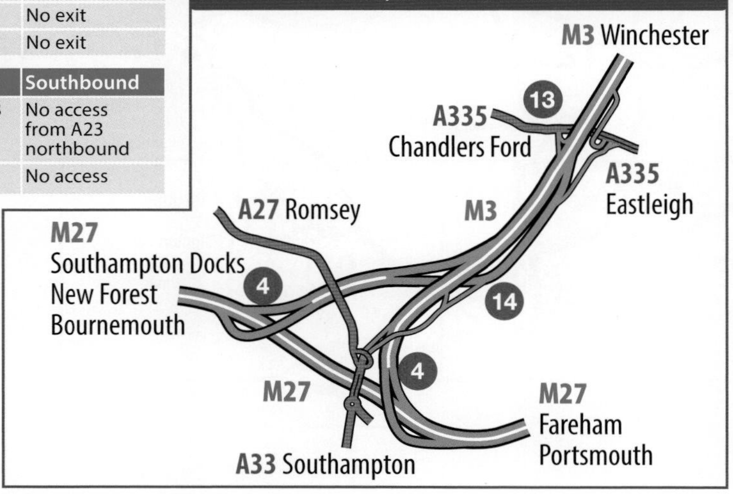

M3 Winchester
13
A335
Chandlers Ford
A335
Eastleigh
A27 Romsey
M3
M27
Southampton Docks
New Forest
Bournemouth
4
14
4
M27
M27
Fareham
Portsmouth
A33 Southampton

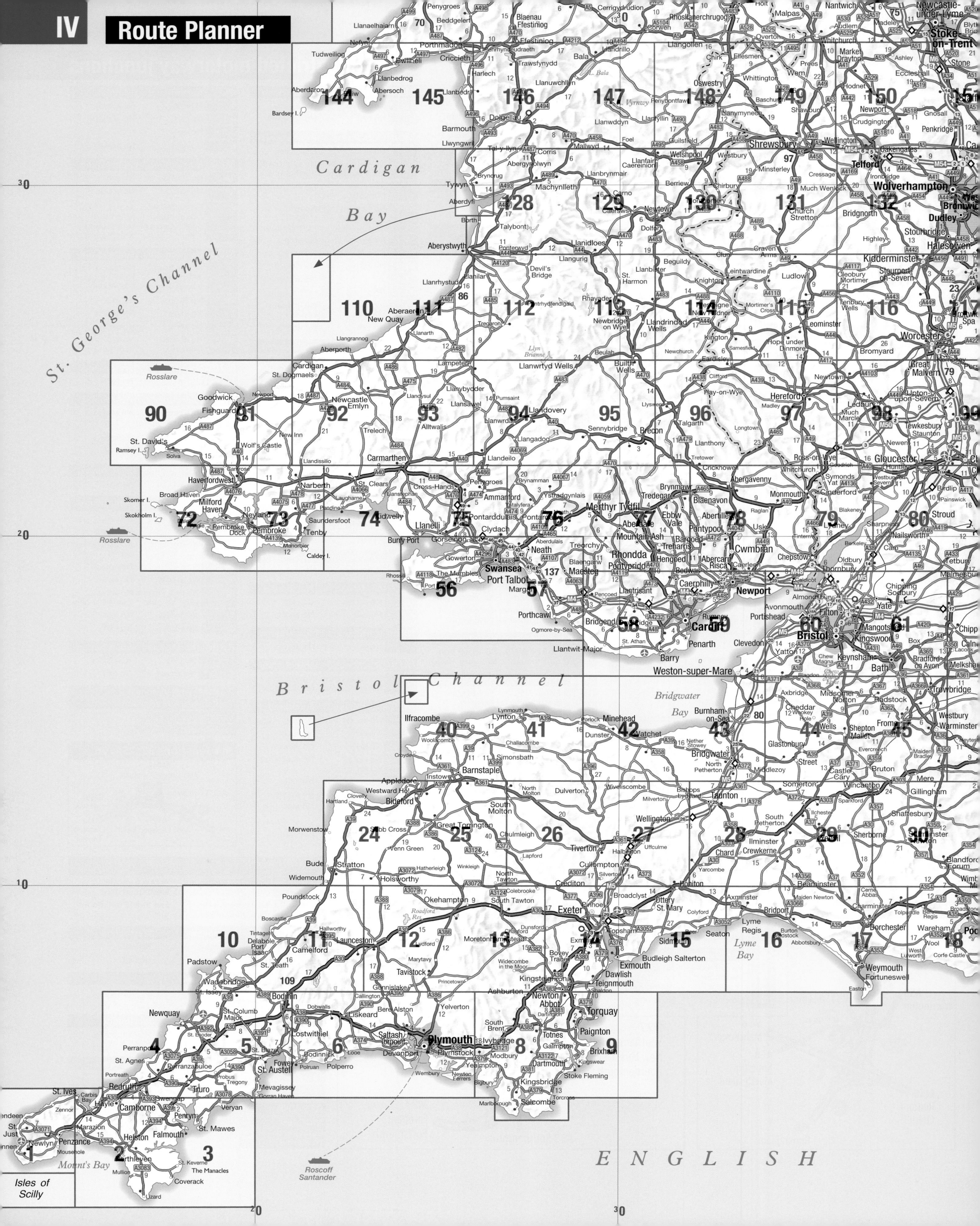
Cardigan Bay
St. George's Channel
Bristol Channel
Bridgwater Bay
Lyme Bay
Mount's Bay
ENGLISH
Rosslare
Roscoff Santander
Isles of Scilly
144
145
146
147
148
149
150
128
129
130
131
132
110
111
112
113
114
115
116
90
91
92
93
94
95
96
97
98
72
73
74
75
76
77
78
79
80
56
57
58
59
60
61
40
41
42
43
44
45
24
25
26
27
28
29
30
10
11
12
13
14
15
16
17
18
1
2
3
4
5
6
8
9
109
137
Aberystwyth
Machynlleth
Dolgellau
Barmouth
Pwllheli
Criccieth
Porthmadog
Bala
Oswestry
Shrewsbury
Welshpool
Newtown
Telford
Wolverhampton
Dudley
Stoke-on-Trent
Kidderminster
Worcester
Hereford
Leominster
Ludlow
Llandrindod Wells
Builth Wells
Brecon
Abergavenny
Monmouth
Gloucester
Cardigan
Fishguard
St. David's
Haverfordwest
Milford Haven
Pembroke
Tenby
Carmarthen
Llanelli
Swansea
Neath
Port Talbot
Bridgend
Merthyr Tydfil
Pontypridd
Caerphilly
Newport
Cardiff
Barry
Penarth
Chepstow
Bristol
Bath
Weston-super-Mare
Clevedon
Wells
Glastonbury
Bridgwater
Taunton
Minehead
Lynton
Ilfracombe
Barnstaple
Bideford
Tiverton
Exeter
Exmouth
Teignmouth
Newton Abbot
Torquay
Paignton
Brixham
Dartmouth
Kingsbridge
Salcombe
Plymouth
Tavistock
Okehampton
Launceston
Bude
Bodmin
Newquay
St. Austell
Truro
Falmouth
Redruth
Camborne
Penzance
Helston
St. Ives
Dorchester
Weymouth
Bridport
Honiton
Yeovil
Sherborne
Shaftesbury
Trowbridge
Frome
Stroud
Chippenham

V
Motorway
junctions - full,restricted
Toll motorway
Services
Primary route
single/dual carriageway
A Road
B Road
Distances - in miles
major
minor
Railway
National boundary
Ferry route
Airport
Scale 1:1129000 1cm = 11.29km 1 inch = 17.82 miles
0 5 10 15 20 25 30 35 40 45 50 miles
0 10 20 30 40 50 60 70 80 km
CHANNEL
Strait of Dover
LONDON
BIRMINGHAM
Nottingham
Derby
Leicester
Coventry
Northampton
Peterborough
Cambridge
Norwich
Ipswich
Colchester
Oxford
Reading
Luton
Southend-on-Sea
Brighton
Southampton
Portsmouth
Bournemouth
Calais
Hoek van Holland
Dunkerque
Dieppe
Caen Le Harve
Bilbao Santander
Guernsey Jersey Cherbourg St. Malo

Edinburgh
Glasgow
Paisley
Kilmarnock
Ayr
Irvine
Troon
Arran
Brodick
Campbeltown
Firth of Clyde
North Channel
Belfast
Bangor
Newtownards
Larne
Lisburn
Downpatrick
Newcastle
Stranraer
Luce Bay
Newton Stewart
Dumfries
Solway Firth
Carlisle
Workington
Whitehaven
Keswick
Penrith
Kendal
Windermere
Barrow-in-Furness
Morecambe Bay
Lancaster
Isle of Man
Douglas
Ramsey
Peel
Castletown
Port Erin
IRISH SEA
Blackpool
Preston
Blackburn
Southport
Liverpool
Liverpool Bay
Birkenhead
St. Helens
Manchester
Wigan
Bolton
Chester
Wrexham
Crewe
Stoke-on-Trent
Anglesey
Holyhead
Bangor
Caernarfon
Rhyl
Colwyn Bay
Conwy
Dublin
Belfast
Liverpool
Douglas
254
255
256
257
258
259
260
261
262
263
266
267
268
269
270
271
272
273
244
245
246
247
248
249
250
251
236
237
238
239
240
241
228
229
230
231
232
219
220
221
222
223
192
210
211
212
213
202
203
204
193
194
195
178
179
180
181
182
183
184
162
163
164
165
166
167
168

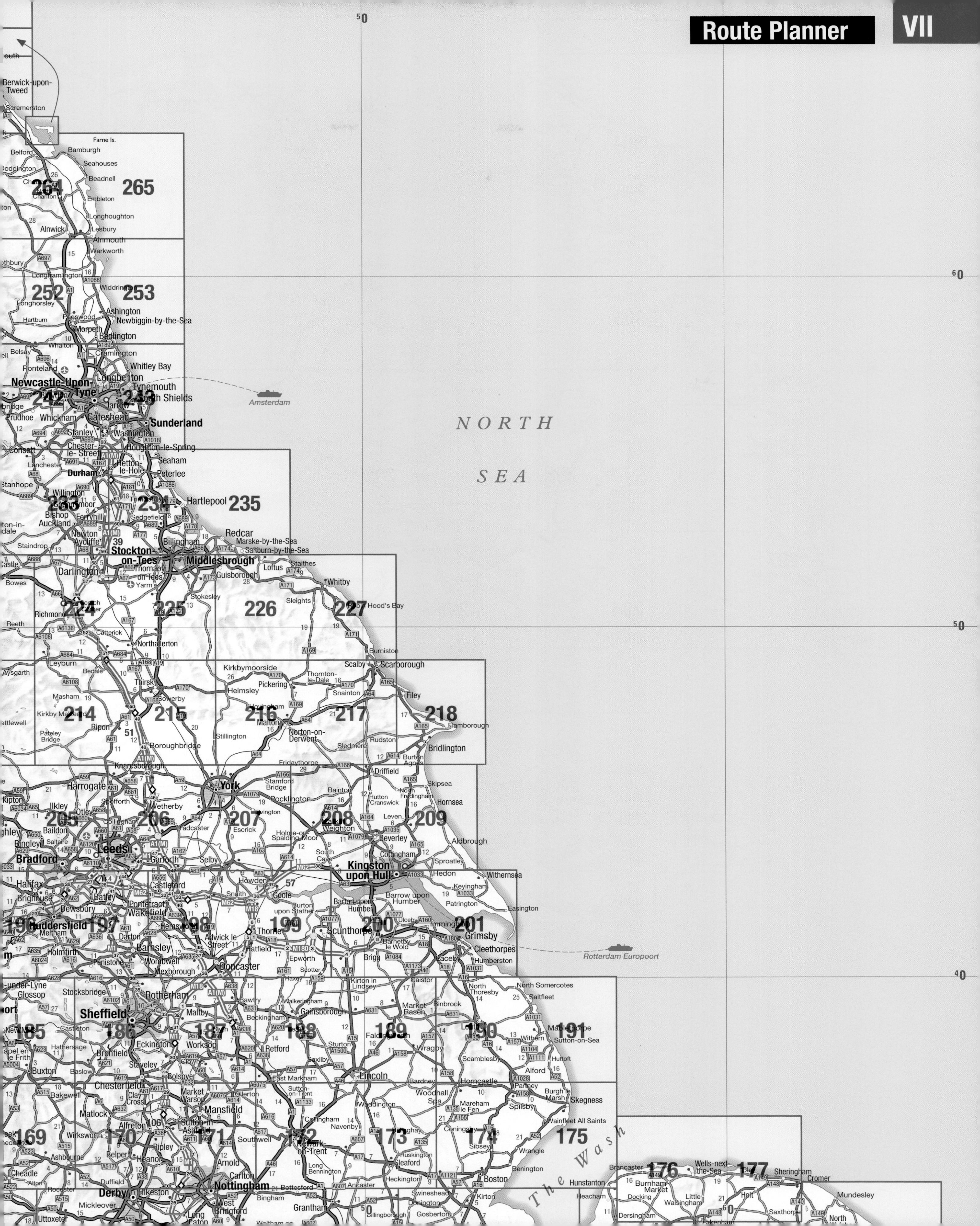
NORTH
SEA
Amsterdam
Rotterdam Europoort
The Wash
Berwick-upon-Tweed
Scremerston
Farne Is.
Belford
Bamburgh
Seahouses
Beadnell
Embleton
Longhoughton
Lesbury
Alnwick
Alnmouth
Warkworth
Longframlington
Widdrington
Longhorsley
Hartburn
Pegswood
Morpeth
Ashington
Newbiggin-by-the-Sea
Bedlington
Whalton
Belsay
Cramlington
Ponteland
Whitley Bay
Longbenton
Newcastle-Upon-Tyne
Tynemouth
South Shields
Jarrow
Gateshead
Whickham
Prudhoe
Sunderland
Stanley
Washington
Houghton-le-Spring
Consett
Chester-le-Street
Seaham
Lanchester
Durham
Hetton-le-Hole
Peterlee
Stanhope
Willington
Hartlepool
Bishop Auckland
Ferryhill
Sedgefield
Newton Aycliffe
Redcar
Marske-by-the-Sea
Saltburn-by-the-Sea
Staindrop
Stockton-on-Tees
Billingham
Middlesbrough
Darlington
Thornaby on Tees
Yarm
Guisborough
Loftus
Staithes
Whitby
Bowes
Stokesley
Richmond
Sleights
Hood's Bay
Reeth
Catterick
Northallerton
Burniston
Leyburn
Bedale
Scalby
Scarborough
Aysgarth
Kirkbymoorside
Pickering
Thornton-le-Dale
Snainton
Filey
Thirsk
Helmsley
Sowerby
Masham
Malton
Norton-on-Derwent
Flamborough
Ripon
Stillington
Rudston
Bridlington
Pateley Bridge
Boroughbridge
Sledmere
Burton Agnes
Knaresborough
Fridaythorpe
Driffield
Skipsea
Harrogate
York
Stamford Bridge
Bainton
Hutton Cranswick
North Frodingham
Hornsea
Ilkley
Otley
Spofforth
Wetherby
Pocklington
Leven
Bingley
Baildon
Tadcaster
Escrick
Market Weighton
Beverley
Aldbrough
Bradford
Leeds
Garforth
Holme-on-Spalding-Moor
Cottingham
Selby
South Cave
Sproatley
Kingston upon Hull
Hedon
Withernsea
Halifax
Castleford
Howden
Goole
Keyingham
Brighouse
Batley
Pontefract
Barrow upon Humber
Patrington
Dewsbury
Wakefield
Burton upon Stather
Barton-upon-Humber
Easington
Huddersfield
Meltham
Hemsworth
Thorne
Scunthorpe
Immingham
Grimsby
Darton
Adwick le Street
Cleethorpes
Holmfirth
Barnsley
Hatfield
Barnetby le Wold
Humberston
Penistone
Wombwell
Epworth
Brigg
Laceby
Mexborough
Doncaster
Glossop
Stocksbridge
Rotherham
Bawtry
Kirton in Lindsey
Caistor
North Thoresby
North Somercotes
Saltfleet
Sheffield
Maltby
Beckingham
Gainsborough
Market Rasen
Binbrook
Louth
Mablethorpe
Castleton
Hathersage
Eckington
Worksop
Retford
Faldingworth
Wragby
Withern
Sutton-on-Sea
Chapel en le Frith
Dronfield
Sturton
Saxilby
Scamblesby
Huttoft
Buxton
Staveley
Clowne
Alford
Bolsover
Lincoln
East Markham
Horncastle
Chesterfield
Bakewell
Clay Cross
Market Warsop
Ollerton
Sutton-on-Trent
Bardney
Partney
Burgh le Marsh
Skegness
Matlock
Mansfield
Woodhall Spa
Waddington
Mareham le Fen
Spilsby
Alfreton
Sutton in Ashfield
Coleby
Navenby
Coningsby
Wainfleet All Saints
Wirksworth
Southwell
Newark-on-Trent
Sibsey
Ashbourne
Belper
Ripley
Heanor
Arnold
Long Bennington
Ruskington
Sleaford
Wrangle
Cheadle
Carlton
Heckington
Boston
Benington
Brancaster
Wells-next-the-Sea
Sheringham
Cromer
Hunstanton
Burnham Market
Derby
Ilkeston
Nottingham
Bottesford
Ancaster
Swineshead
Donington
Kirton
Heacham
Docking
Little Walsingham
Holt
Mundesley
Mickleover
West Bridgford
Bingham
Grantham
Billingborough
Gosberton
Dersingham
Fakenham
Saxthorpe
Uttoxeter
Long Eaton
North Walsham

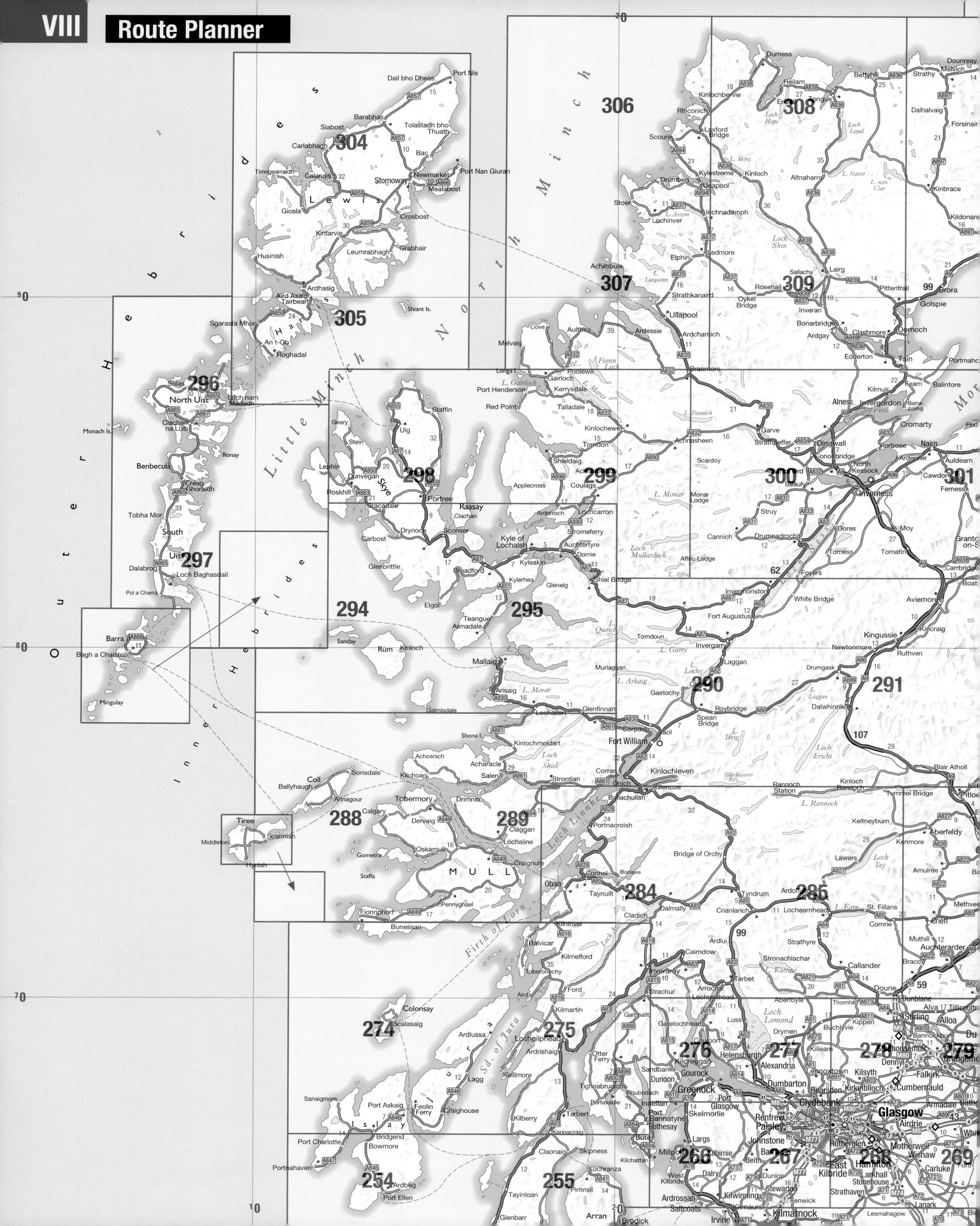

Outer Hebrides
Inner Hebrides
North Minch
Little Minch
Lewis
Harris
North Uist
Benbecula
South Uist
Barra
Skye
Raasay
Rum
Coll
Tiree
Mull
Colonsay
Islay
Jura
Arran
Firth of Lorn
Sd. of Jura
Loch Linnhe
Moray Firth
Cromarty Firth
Port Nis
Dail bho Dheas
Barabhas
Siabost
Carlabhagh
Tolastadh bho Thuath
Bac
Stornoway
Newmarket
Port Nan Giuran
Mealabost
Timsgearraidh
Calanais
Giosla
Crosbost
Kintarvie
Leumrabhagh
Grabhair
Husinish
Ardhasig
Aird Asaig
Tairbeart
Shiant Is.
Sgarasta Mhor
An t-Ob
Roghadal
Solas
Loch nam Madadh
Monach Is.
Clachan na Luib
Ronay
Creag Ghoraidh
Tobha Mor
Dalabrog
Loch Baghasdail
Pol a Charra
Bagh a Chaisteil
Mingulay
Durness
Kinlochbervie
Rhiconich
Laxford Bridge
Scourie
Kylestrome
Kinloch
Drumbeg
Ullapool
Stoer
Lochinver
Inchnadamph
Elphin
Ledmore
Achiltibuie
Strathkanaird
Ardcharnich
Braemore
Cove
Aultbea
Ardessie
Melvaig
Poolewe
Gairloch
Kerrysdale
Port Henderson
Red Point
Talladale
Kinlochewe
Torridon
Shieldaig
Achnasheen
Garve
Strathpeffer
Dingwall
Conon Bridge
Beauly
Inverness
North Kessock
Nairn
Cawdor
Fortrose
Cromarty
Invergordon
Alness
Tain
Dornoch
Golspie
Brora
Helmsdale
Bettyhill
Tongue
Strathy
Melvich
Dounreay
Altnaharra
Kinbrace
Lairg
Bonar Bridge
Ardgay
Edderton
Inverness
Staffin
Uig
Portree
Dunvegan
Roskhill
Bracadale
Drynoch
Sconser
Carbost
Glenbrittle
Broadford
Elgol
Kyle of Lochalsh
Kyleakin
Dornie
Shiel Bridge
Glenelg
Armadale
Mallaig
Arisaig
Lochailort
Glenfinnan
Fort William
Corpach
Spean Bridge
Roybridge
Fort Augustus
Invergarry
Drumnadrochit
Foyers
Aviemore
Kingussie
Newtonmore
Dalwhinnie
Blair Atholl
Kinlochleven
Glencoe
Ballachulish
Strontian
Salen
Acharacle
Kilchoan
Tobermory
Dervaig
Craignure
Oban
Connel
Taynuilt
Dalmally
Tyndrum
Crianlarich
Killin
Lochearnhead
Callander
Aberfeldy
Crieff
Comrie
Inveraray
Tarbet
Arrochar
Lochgilphead
Tarbert
Campbeltown
Port Askaig
Bowmore
Port Ellen
Port Charlotte
Dunoon
Rothesay
Greenock
Gourock
Helensburgh
Dumbarton
Alexandria
Clydebank
Paisley
Glasgow
Stirling
Falkirk
Cumbernauld
Airdrie
Motherwell
Hamilton
East Kilbride
Largs
Ardrossan
Saltcoats
Irvine
Kilmarnock
Brodick
Lochranza

Shetland Islands
Norwick
Haroldswick
Baltasound
Unst
Cullivoe
Gutcher
Belmont
Fetlar
Funzie
Isbister
Mid Yell
Yell
Burravoe
Ulsta
312
Hillswick
St Magnus Bay
Out Skerries
Brae
Voe
Vidlin
Whalsay
Symbister
Sandness
Neap
Dale
Aith
Walls
Foula
Easter Skeld
Lerwick
I. of Noss
Scalloway
313
Hamnavoe
West Burra
Northpunds
Scousburgh
Boddam
Aberdeen Kirkwall
Sumburgh
Fair Isle
Orkney Islands
Westray
Hollandstoun
N. Ronaldsay
The North Sound
Pierowall
Midbea
Burness
Rapness
Overbister
Eday
Sanday
Wasbister
Stronsay
The Barony
Twatt
Redland
Dounby
314
Balfour
Stronsay Firth
Finstown
Kirkwall
Stromness
Mainland
Aberdeen Lerwick
Orphir
Gritley
Copinsay
Hoy
Scapa Flow
Flotta
Lyness
St. Margaret's Hope
South Ronaldsay
South Walls
Burwick
Pentland Firth
Scrabster
Thurso
Mey
Dunnet
Castletown
John o' Groats
Nybster
Keiss
Sordale
Halkirk
Hastigrow
Reiss
Watten
Mybster
Wick
310
Thrumster
Achavanich
Ulbster
Lybster
Latheron
Dunbeath
Berriedale
Ousdale
Helmsdale
311
Firth
Burghead
Lossiemouth
Findochty
Portknockie
Kinloss
Kingston
Buckie
Portsoy
Elgin
Banff
Macduff
Rosehearty
Fraserburgh
Inverallochy
Forres
Fochabers
Craibstone
New Aberdour
Crimond
Kellas
Mulben
Aberchirder
New Pitsligo
Strichen
Rothes
Keith
302
Turriff
Maud
303
Mintlaw
Peterhead
Archiestown
Charlestown of Aberlour
Fortrie
Old Deer
Huntly
Boddam
Lettoch
Marypark
Dufftown
Methlick
Cruden Bay
Colpy
Tarves
Ellon
Insch
Tomnavoulin
Cabrach
Oldmeldrum
Rhynie
Lumsden
Newburgh
Kirkwall Lerwick
Tomintoul
Inverurie
Kemnay
Newmachar
Alford
Kintore
Dyce
Balmedie
Strathdon
Ordhead
Bridge of Don
Aberdeen
Westhill
Cults
Tarland
Torphins
Peterculter
Crathie
Aboyne
Portlethen
Braemar
Ballater
Banchory
Newtonhill
292
293
Stonehaven
Spittle of Glenshee
Clova
Fettercairn
Inverbervie
Laurencekirk
Marykirk
Johnshaven
Kirkton of Glenisla
Dykehead
Tannadice
Brechin
Montrose
Kirriemuir
Bridge of Cally
Forfar
Friockheim
Inverkeilor
Alyth
Rattray
Blairgowrie
Glamis
Carmyllie
Meigle
Dunkeld
Coupar Angus
Monikie
Arbroath
Carnoustie
Invergowrie
Dundee
Monifieth
287
286
Balbeggie
Tayport
Newport-on-Tay
Leuchars
Perth
Scone
Wormit
Firth of Tay
Newburgh
St. Andrews
Bridge of Earn
Cupar
Auchtermuchty
Ceres
Crail
Ladybank
Falkland
Leslie
Anstruther
Kinross
Markinch
St. Monance
Glenrothes
Leven
Elie
I. of May
Lochgelly
Buckhaven
Firth of Forth
Cowdenbeath
Kirkcaldy
North Berwick
Burntisland
281
282
283
280
Dunbar
Queensferry
Prestonpans
East Linton
Edinburgh
Tranent
Haddington
Livingston
Musselburgh
Dalkeith
Gifford
Cockburnspath
St. Abb's
Coldingham
Eyemouth
Loanhead
Bonnyrigg
Grantshouse
Penicuik
Gorebridge
Ayton
Chirnside
270
271
272
273
Berwick-upon-Tweed
Preston
Duns
West Linton
Westruther
Fountainhall
Lauder
Greenlaw
Swinton
Scremerston
Blyth Bridge
Leitholm
Peebles
Stow
Gordon
Coldstream
Innerleithen
Earlston
Galashiels
Broughton
Farne Is.

Distances and journey times

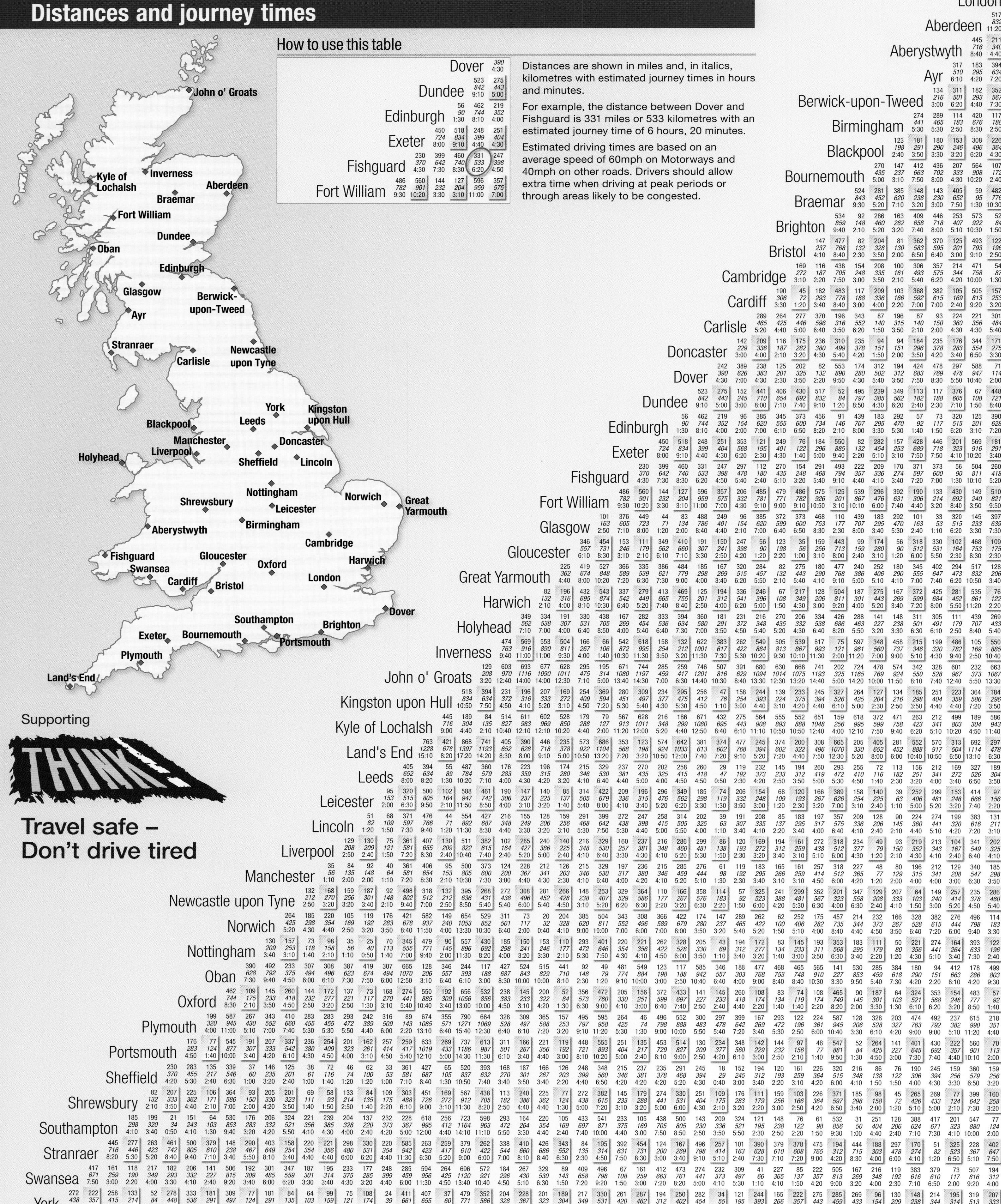

How to use this table

Dover						*390* 4:30
Dundee					523 *842* 9:10	275 *443* 5:00
Edinburgh				56 *90* 1:30	462 *744* 8:10	219 *352* 4:00
Exeter			450 *724* 8:00	518 *834* 9:10	248 *399* 4:40	251 *404* 4:30
Fishguard		230 *370* 4:30	399 *642* 7:30	460 *740* 8:30	331 *533* 6:20	247 *398* 4:50
Fort William	486 *782* 9:30	560 *901* 10:20	144 *232* 3:30	127 *204* 3:10	596 *959* 11:00	357 *575* 7:00

Distances are shown in miles and, in italics, kilometres with estimated journey times in hours and minutes.

For example, the distance between Dover and Fishguard is 331 miles or 533 kilometres with an estimated journey time of 6 hours, 20 minutes.

Estimated driving times are based on an average speed of 60mph on Motorways and 40mph on other roads. Drivers should allow extra time when driving at peak periods or through areas likely to be congested.

	Swansea	Stranraer	Southampton	Shrewsbury	Sheffield	Portsmouth	Plymouth	Oxford	Oban	Nottingham	Norwich	Newcastle upon Tyne	Manchester	Liverpool	Lincoln	Leicester	Leeds	Land's End	Kyle of Lochalsh	Kingston upon Hull	John o' Groats	Inverness	Holyhead	Harwich	Great Yarmouth	Gloucester	Glasgow	Fort William	Fishguard	Exeter	Edinburgh	Dundee	Dover	Doncaster	Carlisle	Cardiff	Cambridge	Bristol	Brighton	Braemar	Bournemouth	Blackpool	Birmingham	Berwick-upon-Tweed	Ayr	Aberystwyth	Aberdeen	London
Aberdeen																																																517 *832* 11:20
Aberystwyth																																															445 *716* 8:40	211 *340* 4:40
Ayr																																														317 *510* 6:10	183 *295* 4:20	394 *634* 7:20
Berwick-upon-Tweed																																													134 *216* 3:00	311 *501* 6:20	182 *293* 4:40	352 *567* 7:30
Birmingham																																												274 *441* 5:30	289 *465* 5:30	114 *183* 2:50	420 *676* 8:30	117 *188* 2:50
Blackpool																																											123 *198* 2:40	181 *291* 3:50	180 *290* 3:30	153 *246* 3:20	308 *496* 6:20	226 *364* 4:30
Bournemouth																																										270 *435* 5:00	147 *237* 3:10	412 *663* 7:50	436 *702* 8:00	207 *333* 4:30	564 *908* 10:20	107 *172* 2:40
Braemar																																									524 *843* 9:30	281 *452* 5:20	385 *620* 7:10	148 *238* 3:20	143 *230* 3:00	405 *652* 7:50	59 *95* 1:30	482 *776* 10:30
Brighton																																								534 *859* 9:40	92 *148* 2:10	286 *460* 5:20	163 *262* 3:20	409 *658* 7:40	446 *718* 8:00	253 *407* 5:10	573 *922* 10:30	52 *84* 1:50
Bristol																																							147 *237* 4:10	477 *768* 8:40	82 *132* 2:30	204 *328* 3:50	81 *130* 2:00	362 *583* 6:50	370 *595* 6:40	125 *201* 3:00	493 *793* 9:10	122 *196* 2:50
Cambridge																																						169 *272* 3:10	116 *187* 2:20	438 *705* 7:50	154 *248* 3:00	208 *335* 3:50	100 *161* 2:10	306 *493* 5:40	357 *575* 6:20	214 *344* 4:20	471 *758* 10:00	54 *87* 1:30
Cardiff																																					190 *306* 3:30	45 *72* 1:20	182 *293* 3:40	483 *778* 8:40	117 *188* 3:00	209 *336* 4:00	103 *166* 2:20	368 *592* 7:00	382 *615* 7:00	105 *169* 2:40	505 *813* 9:20	157 *253* 3:20
Carlisle																																				289 *465* 5:20	264 *425* 4:40	277 *446* 5:00	370 *596* 6:40	196 *316* 3:50	343 *552* 6:20	87 *140* 1:50	196 *315* 3:50	87 *140* 2:10	93 *150* 2:00	224 *360* 4:30	221 *356* 4:30	301 *484* 5:40
Doncaster																																			142 *229* 3:00	209 *336* 4:00	116 *187* 2:10	175 *282* 3:20	236 *380* 4:30	310 *499* 5:40	235 *378* 4:20	94 *151* 1:50	94 *151* 2:00	184 *296* 3:50	235 *378* 4:20	176 *283* 3:40	344 *554* 6:50	171 *275* 3:30
Dover																																		242 *390* 4:30	389 *626* 7:00	238 *383* 4:30	125 *201* 2:30	202 *325* 3:50	82 *132* 2:20	553 *890* 9:50	174 *280* 4:30	312 *502* 5:40	194 *312* 3:50	424 *683* 7:50	478 *769* 8:30	297 *478* 5:50	588 *947* 10:40	71 *114* 2:00
Dundee																																	523 *842* 9:10	275 *443* 5:00	152 *245* 3:00	441 *710* 8:00	406 *654* 7:10	430 *692* 7:40	517 *832* 9:10	52 *84* 1:20	495 *797* 8:50	239 *385* 4:30	349 *562* 6:20	113 *182* 2:40	117 *188* 2:30	376 *605* 7:10	67 *108* 1:50	448 *721* 8:40
Edinburgh																																56 *90* 1:30	462 *744* 8:10	219 *352* 4:00	96 *154* 2:00	385 *620* 7:00	345 *555* 6:10	373 *600* 6:50	456 *734* 8:20	91 *146* 2:10	439 *707* 8:00	183 *295* 3:30	292 *470* 5:30	57 *92* 1:40	73 *117* 1:50	320 *515* 6:20	125 *201* 3:10	390 *628* 7:20
Exeter																															450 *724* 8:00	518 *834* 9:10	248 *399* 4:40	251 *404* 4:30	353 *568* 6:20	121 *195* 2:30	249 *401* 4:30	76 *122* 1:40	184 *296* 5:00	550 *885* 9:40	82 *132* 2:20	282 *454* 5:10	157 *253* 3:10	428 *689* 7:50	446 *718* 7:50	201 *323* 4:10	569 *916* 10:20	181 *291* 3:40
Fishguard																														230 *370* 4:30	399 *642* 7:30	460 *740* 8:30	331 *533* 6:20	247 *398* 4:50	297 *478* 5:40	112 *180* 2:40	270 *435* 5:10	154 *248* 3:20	291 *468* 5:40	493 *794* 9:10	222 *357* 4:40	209 *336* 4:10	170 *274* 3:40	371 *597* 7:20	373 *600* 7:00	56 *90* 1:30	504 *811* 10:10	260 *418* 5:20
Fort William																													486 *782* 9:30	560 *901* 10:20	144 *232* 3:30	127 *204* 3:10	596 *959* 11:00	357 *575* 7:00	206 *332* 4:30	485 *781* 9:10	479 *771* 9:00	486 *782* 9:10	575 *926* 10:50	125 *201* 3:10	539 *867* 10:10	296 *476* 6:00	392 *631* 7:40	190 *306* 4:40	133 *214* 3:20	430 *692* 8:40	149 *240* 3:50	510 *821* 9:50
Glasgow																												101 *163* 2:50	376 *605* 7:10	449 *723* 8:00	44 *71* 1:20	83 *134* 2:00	488 *786* 8:40	249 *401* 4:40	96 *154* 2:10	385 *620* 7:00	372 *599* 6:40	373 *600* 6:50	468 *753* 8:30	110 *177* 2:30	439 *707* 8:00	183 *295* 3:40	292 *470* 5:30	101 *163* 2:40	33 *53* 1:10	320 *515* 6:20	145 *233* 3:30	397 *639* 7:30
Gloucester																											346 *557* 6:10	454 *731* 8:30	153 *246* 3:10	111 *179* 2:10	349 *562* 6:10	410 *660* 7:10	191 *307* 3:30	150 *241* 2:50	247 *398* 4:20	56 *90* 1:20	123 *198* 2:20	35 *56* 1:00	159 *256* 3:10	443 *713* 8:00	99 *159* 2:40	174 *280* 3:10	56 *90* 1:20	318 *512* 6:00	330 *531* 5:50	102 *164* 2:30	468 *753* 8:30	109 *175* 2:30
Great Yarmouth																										225 *362* 4:40	419 *674* 8:00	527 *848* 10:20	366 *589* 7:20	335 *539* 6:30	386 *621* 7:30	484 *779* 9:00	185 *298* 4:00	167 *269* 3:40	320 *515* 6:20	284 *457* 5:50	82 *132* 2:10	275 *443* 5:40	180 *290* 4:10	477 *768* 9:10	240 *386* 5:00	252 *406* 5:10	180 *290* 4:10	345 *555* 7:00	402 *647* 7:40	294 *473* 6:20	517 *832* 10:50	128 *206* 3:40
Harwich																									82 *132* 2:10	196 *316* 4:00	432 *695* 8:10	543 *874* 10:30	337 *542* 6:40	279 *449* 5:20	413 *665* 7:40	469 *755* 8:40	125 *201* 2:50	194 *312* 4:00	336 *541* 6:20	246 *396* 5:00	67 *108* 1:50	217 *349* 4:30	128 *206* 3:00	504 *811* 9:20	187 *301* 4:00	275 *443* 5:20	167 *269* 3:40	372 *599* 7:20	425 *684* 8:00	281 *452* 5:50	535 *861* 11:20	76 *122* 2:20
Holyhead																								349 *562* 7:10	334 *538* 7:00	191 *307* 4:00	330 *531* 6:40	438 *705* 8:50	167 *269* 4:00	282 *454* 5:40	333 *536* 6:40	394 *634* 7:30	360 *580* 7:00	181 *291* 3:50	231 *372* 4:50	216 *348* 5:40	270 *435* 5:20	206 *332* 4:30	334 *538* 6:40	426 *686* 8:20	288 *463* 5:50	141 *227* 3:20	148 *238* 3:30	311 *501* 6:30	305 *491* 6:10	111 *179* 2:50	439 *707* 8:40	269 *433* 5:40
Inverness																							474 *763* 9:40	569 *916* 11:00	553 *890* 11:00	504 *811* 9:30	166 *267* 4:00	66 *106* 1:40	542 *872* 10:30	618 *995* 11:30	158 *254* 3:50	132 *212* 3:20	622 *1001* 11:30	383 *617* 7:30	262 *422* 5:30	549 *884* 10:20	505 *813* 9:30	539 *867* 10:10	617 *993* 11:30	75 *121* 2:00	597 *961* 11:20	348 *560* 7:00	458 *737* 9:00	215 *346* 5:10	199 *320* 4:30	486 *782* 9:40	105 *169* 2:50	550 *885* 10:40
John o' Groats																						129 *208* 3:20	603 *970* 12:40	693 *1116* 14:00	677 *1090* 14:00	628 *1011* 12:30	295 *475* 7:10	195 *314* 5:00	671 *1080* 13:40	744 *1197* 14:30	285 *459* 7:00	259 *417* 6:30	746 *1201* 14:40	507 *816* 10:30	391 *629* 8:40	680 *1094* 13:30	630 *1014* 12:30	668 *1075* 13:20	741 *1193* 14:40	202 *325* 5:00	724 *1165* 14:20	478 *769* 10:00	574 *924* 11:50	342 *550* 8:10	328 *528* 7:40	601 *967* 12:40	232 *373* 5:50	663 *1067* 13:30
Kingston upon Hull																					518 *834* 10:50	394 *634* 7:50	231 *372* 4:50	196 *316* 4:10	207 *333* 5:20	169 *272* 3:10	254 *409* 4:50	369 *594* 7:20	280 *451* 5:30	309 *497* 5:40	234 *377* 4:30	295 *475* 5:30	256 *412* 4:50	47 *76* 1:10	158 *254* 3:00	244 *393* 4:40	139 *224* 3:10	233 *375* 4:20	245 *394* 4:40	327 *526* 6:10	264 *425* 5:00	127 *204* 2:30	134 *216* 2:50	185 *298* 3:50	251 *404* 4:40	223 *359* 4:40	364 *586* 7:20	184 *296* 3:50
Kyle of Lochalsh																				445 *716* 9:00	189 *304* 4:40	84 *135* 2:10	514 *827* 10:40	611 *983* 12:10	602 *969* 12:10	528 *850* 10:20	179 *288* 4:40	79 *127* 2:00	567 *913* 11:20	628 *1011* 12:00	216 *348* 5:20	186 *299* 4:40	671 *1080* 12:50	432 *695* 8:40	275 *443* 6:10	564 *908* 11:10	555 *893* 10:50	552 *888* 10:50	651 *1048* 12:40	159 *256* 4:00	618 *995* 12:10	372 *599* 7:50	471 *758* 9:40	263 *423* 6:20	212 *341* 5:10	499 *803* 10:20	189 *304* 4:50	586 *943* 11:40
Land's End																			763 *1228* 15:10	421 *678* 8:20	868 *1397* 17:20	741 *1193* 14:20	405 *652* 8:30	390 *628* 8:00	446 *718* 9:10	235 *378* 5:00	573 *922* 10:50	686 *1104* 13:20	353 *568* 7:20	123 *198* 3:20	574 *924* 10:50	642 *1033* 12:00	381 *613* 7:40	374 *602* 7:20	477 *768* 9:10	245 *394* 5:20	374 *602* 7:20	200 *322* 4:40	308 *496* 7:50	665 *1070* 12:30	205 *330* 5:20	405 *652* 8:00	281 *452* 6:00	552 *888* 10:40	570 *917* 10:50	313 *504* 6:50	692 *1114* 13:10	297 *478* 6:30
Leeds																		405 *652* 8:00	394 *634* 8:20	55 *89* 1:30	487 *784* 10:20	360 *579* 7:10	176 *283* 4:00	223 *359* 4:30	196 *315* 4:20	174 *280* 3:20	215 *346* 4:10	329 *530* 6:40	237 *381* 4:40	270 *435* 5:00	202 *325* 4:00	258 *415* 4:50	260 *418* 4:50	29 *47* 0:50	119 *192* 2:30	232 *373* 4:20	145 *233* 2:50	194 *312* 3:50	260 *419* 5:00	293 *472* 5:30	255 *410* 4:50	72 *116* 1:40	113 *182* 2:30	156 *251* 3:20	212 *341* 4:00	169 *272* 3:40	327 *526* 6:50	189 *304* 3:50
Leicester																	95 *153* 2:00	320 *515* 6:30	500 *805* 9:50	102 *164* 2:10	588 *947* 11:50	461 *742* 8:50	190 *306* 4:00	147 *237* 3:10	140 *225* 3:20	85 *137* 1:40	314 *505* 5:40	422 *679* 8:00	209 *336* 4:10	196 *315* 3:40	296 *476* 5:20	349 *562* 6:20	185 *298* 3:30	74 *119* 1:30	206 *332* 3:50	154 *248* 3:00	68 *109* 1:20	120 *193* 2:30	166 *267* 3:20	389 *626* 7:00	158 *254* 3:10	140 *225* 2:40	39 *63* 1:10	252 *406* 5:00	299 *481* 5:20	153 *246* 3:20	414 *666* 7:40	97 *156* 2:20
Lincoln																51 *82* 1:20	68 *109* 1:50	371 *597* 7:30	476 *766* 9:40	44 *71* 1:20	554 *892* 11:30	427 *687* 8:30	216 *348* 4:40	155 *249* 3:30	128 *206* 3:20	159 *256* 3:10	291 *468* 5:30	399 *642* 7:50	272 *438* 5:30	247 *398* 4:40	258 *415* 5:00	314 *505* 5:50	202 *325* 4:00	39 *63* 1:10	191 *307* 3:40	208 *335* 4:10	85 *137* 2:20	183 *295* 3:40	197 *317* 4:00	357 *575* 6:40	209 *336* 4:10	128 *206* 2:40	90 *145* 2:10	224 *360* 4:40	274 *441* 5:10	199 *320* 4:20	383 *616* 7:20	131 *211* 3:10
Liverpool															129 *208* 2:50	130 *209* 2:40	75 *121* 1:50	361 *581* 7:20	407 *655* 8:30	130 *209* 2:40	511 *822* 10:40	382 *615* 7:40	102 *164* 2:40	265 *427* 5:20	240 *386* 5:00	140 *225* 2:40	216 *348* 4:10	329 *530* 6:40	160 *257* 3:30	237 *381* 4:30	216 *348* 4:10	286 *460* 5:20	299 *481* 5:30	86 *138* 1:50	120 *193* 2:30	169 *272* 3:20	194 *312* 3:40	161 *259* 3:10	272 *438* 5:10	318 *512* 6:00	234 *377* 4:30	49 *79* 1:20	93 *150* 2:10	219 *352* 4:30	213 *343* 4:10	104 *167* 2:40	341 *549* 6:40	202 *325* 4:10
Manchester														35 *56* 1:10	84 *135* 2:00	92 *148* 2:00	40 *64* 1:10	361 *581* 7:20	406 *654* 8:30	95 *153* 2:10	500 *805* 10:30	373 *600* 7:30	124 *200* 3:00	228 *367* 4:40	212 *341* 4:30	126 *203* 2:30	215 *346* 4:10	329 *530* 6:40	197 *317* 4:00	236 *380* 4:20	215 *346* 4:10	285 *459* 5:20	276 *444* 5:10	61 *98* 1:30	119 *192* 2:30	183 *295* 3:40	165 *266* 3:10	161 *259* 3:10	257 *414* 4:50	318 *512* 6:00	227 *365* 4:20	48 *77* 1:20	80 *129* 2:00	196 *315* 4:00	212 *341* 4:00	129 *208* 3:00	340 *547* 6:30	185 *298* 3:50
Newcastle upon Tyne													132 *212* 2:50	168 *270* 3:20	159 *256* 3:20	187 *301* 3:40	92 *148* 2:10	498 *802* 9:40	318 *512* 7:00	132 *212* 2:50	395 *636* 8:50	268 *431* 5:40	272 *438* 5:40	308 *496* 6:00	281 *452* 5:40	266 *428* 4:50	148 *238* 3:10	253 *407* 5:20	329 *529* 6:20	364 *586* 6:30	110 *177* 2:20	166 *267* 3:20	358 *576* 6:30	114 *183* 2:20	57 *92* 1:50	325 *523* 6:00	241 *388* 4:20	299 *481* 5:30	352 *567* 6:30	201 *323* 4:00	347 *558* 6:30	129 *208* 2:40	207 *333* 4:10	64 *103* 1:50	149 *240* 3:00	257 *414* 5:20	235 *378* 4:50	286 *460* 5:40
Norwich												264 *425* 5:20	185 *298* 4:30	220 *354* 4:40	105 *169* 2:50	119 *192* 3:20	176 *283* 3:50	421 *678* 8:40	582 *937* 11:50	149 *240* 4:00	654 *1053* 13:30	529 *852* 10:30	311 *501* 6:40	73 *117* 2:00	20 *32* 0:40	204 *328* 4:10	385 *620* 9:00	504 *811* 10:00	343 *552* 7:00	308 *496* 6:00	366 *589* 7:00	422 *679* 8:00	174 *280* 3:50	147 *237* 3:20	289 *465* 5:40	262 *422* 5:20	62 *100* 1:50	252 *406* 5:10	175 *282* 4:00	457 *735* 8:40	214 *344* 4:40	232 *373* 4:50	166 *267* 3:50	328 *528* 6:40	382 *615* 7:20	276 *444* 6:00	496 *798* 9:40	114 *183* 3:30
Nottingham											130 *209* 3:40	157 *253* 3:10	73 *118* 1:40	98 *158* 2:10	35 *56* 1:10	25 *40* 0:50	70 *113* 1:40	345 *555* 7:00	479 *771* 9:40	90 *145* 2:00	557 *896* 11:30	430 *692* 8:20	185 *298* 4:00	150 *241* 3:20	153 *246* 3:30	110 *177* 2:10	293 *472* 5:30	401 *646* 7:50	220 *354* 4:30	221 *356* 4:10	262 *422* 4:50	328 *528* 6:00	205 *330* 3:50	43 *69* 1:10	194 *312* 3:40	172 *277* 3:20	83 *134* 1:40	145 *233* 3:00	193 *311* 3:50	353 *568* 6:30	183 *295* 3:40	111 *179* 2:20	50 *80* 1:20	221 *356* 4:30	274 *441* 5:10	164 *264* 3:40	393 *633* 7:30	122 *196* 2:40
Oban										390 *628* 7:30	492 *792* 9:40	233 *375* 4:50	307 *494* 6:00	308 *496* 6:10	387 *623* 7:30	419 *674* 7:50	307 *494* 6:00	665 *1070* 12:50	128 *206* 3:10	346 *557* 6:40	244 *393* 6:10	117 *188* 3:00	427 *687* 8:30	524 *843* 10:00	515 *829* 10:00	441 *710* 8:10	92 *148* 2:30	49 *79* 1:20	481 *774* 9:10	549 *884* 10:00	123 *198* 3:00	117 *188* 2:50	585 *942* 10:40	346 *557* 6:40	188 *303* 4:00	477 *768* 9:00	468 *753* 8:40	465 *748* 8:40	565 *910* 10:30	141 *227* 3:30	530 *853* 9:50	285 *459* 5:40	384 *618* 7:30	180 *290* 4:20	94 *151* 2:20	412 *663* 8:10	178 *286* 4:20	499 *803* 9:30
Oxford									462 *744* 8:30	109 *175* 2:10	145 *233* 3:50	260 *418* 4:50	144 *232* 2:50	172 *277* 3:20	137 *221* 2:50	73 *117* 1:30	168 *270* 3:10	274 *441* 5:40	550 *885* 10:40	192 *309* 3:40	656 *1056* 13:00	532 *856* 10:00	238 *383* 4:50	145 *233* 3:10	200 *322* 4:20	52 *84* 1:30	356 *573* 6:30	472 *760* 9:00	205 *330* 4:10	156 *251* 3:00	372 *599* 6:40	433 *697* 7:40	141 *227* 2:50	145 *233* 2:40	260 *418* 4:40	108 *174* 2:20	83 *134* 1:40	74 *119* 1:40	108 *174* 2:20	465 *749* 8:20	90 *145* 2:00	187 *301* 3:30	64 *103* 1:30	324 *521* 6:10	353 *568* 6:20	154 *248* 3:20	483 *777* 8:50	57 *92* 1:40
Plymouth								199 *320* 4:00	587 *945* 11:00	267 *430* 5:10	343 *552* 7:00	410 *660* 7:40	283 *455* 5:30	283 *455* 5:30	293 *472* 5:50	242 *389* 4:40	316 *509* 6:00	89 *143* 2:20	674 *1085* 13:10	355 *571* 6:40	790 *1271* 15:40	664 *1069* 12:30	328 *528* 6:40	309 *497* 6:10	365 *588* 7:20	157 *253* 3:20	495 *797* 9:10	595 *958* 11:20	264 *425* 5:30	46 *74* 1:30	496 *798* 9:00	552 *888* 10:00	300 *483* 5:50	297 *478* 5:40	399 *642* 7:20	167 *269* 3:40	293 *472* 5:30	122 *196* 2:50	224 *361* 6:00	587 *945* 10:40	128 *206* 3:30	328 *528* 6:10	203 *327* 4:20	474 *763* 9:00	492 *792* 9:00	237 *382* 5:10	615 *990* 11:20	218 *351* 4:40
Portsmouth							176 *283* 4:50	77 *124* 1:40	545 *877* 10:00	191 *307* 3:40	207 *333* 4:20	337 *542* 6:10	236 *380* 4:30	254 *409* 4:50	201 *323* 4:00	162 *261* 3:10	257 *414* 4:50	259 *417* 5:40	633 *1019* 12:10	269 *433* 5:00	737 *1186* 14:30	613 *987* 11:30	311 *501* 6:10	166 *267* 3:40	221 *356* 4:40	119 *192* 3:00	448 *721* 8:10	555 *893* 10:20	251 *404* 5:00	135 *217* 2:40	453 *729* 8:10	514 *827* 9:00	130 *209* 2:50	234 *377* 4:20	348 *560* 6:10	142 *229* 3:00	144 *232* 2:50	97 *156* 2:10	48 *77* 1:40	547 *881* 9:50	52 *84* 1:30	264 *425* 4:50	141 *227* 3:00	401 *645* 7:30	430 *692* 7:40	222 *357* 4:40	560 *901* 10:10	70 *113* 2:00
Sheffield						230 *370* 4:20	283 *455* 5:30	135 *217* 2:40	339 *546* 6:30	37 *60* 1:00	146 *235* 3:20	125 *201* 2:40	38 *61* 1:00	72 *116* 1:40	46 *74* 1:20	62 *100* 1:20	33 *53* 1:00	361 *581* 7:10	427 *687* 8:40	65 *105* 1:30	520 *837* 10:50	393 *632* 7:40	168 *270* 3:40	187 *301* 3:50	166 *267* 3:40	126 *203* 2:20	248 *399* 4:40	348 *560* 6:50	215 *346* 4:20	237 *381* 4:20	235 *378* 4:20	291 *468* 5:20	245 *394* 4:30	18 *29* 0:40	152 *245* 3:00	194 *312* 3:40	120 *193* 2:20	161 *259* 3:10	226 *364* 4:20	320 *515* 6:00	216 *348* 4:10	86 *138* 1:50	76 *122* 1:50	190 *306* 4:00	245 *394* 4:30	159 *256* 3:30	360 *579* 6:50	159 *256* 3:20
Shrewsbury					82 *132* 2:10	207 *333* 3:50	225 *362* 4:40	106 *171* 2:10	364 *586* 7:00	93 *150* 2:00	205 *330* 4:20	201 *323* 3:50	69 *111* 1:40	58 *93* 1:50	133 *214* 2:50	84 *135* 1:40	109 *175* 2:20	303 *488* 6:10	451 *726* 9:00	169 *272* 3:10	567 *912* 11:30	438 *705* 8:20	113 *182* 2:50	240 *386* 4:40	225 *362* 4:40	77 *124* 1:30	272 *438* 5:00	382 *615* 7:20	145 *233* 3:10	179 *288* 3:20	274 *441* 5:00	330 *531* 6:00	251 *404* 4:30	109 *175* 2:10	176 *283* 3:20	111 *179* 2:20	159 *256* 3:00	103 *166* 2:50	226 *364* 4:20	371 *597* 6:50	185 *298* 3:40	98 *158* 2:00	45 *72* 1:20	265 *426* 5:10	269 *433* 5:00	77 *124* 2:10	399 *642* 7:30	160 *258* 3:20
Southampton				185 *298* 4:10	199 *320* 3:40	21 *34* 0:50	151 *243* 4:10	64 *103* 1:30	530 *853* 9:40	176 *283* 3:20	206 *332* 4:20	324 *521* 5:50	221 *356* 4:10	239 *385* 4:30	204 *328* 4:00	137 *220* 2:40	232 *373* 4:20	228 *367* 5:00	618 *995* 12:00	256 *412* 4:40	723 *1164* 14:10	598 *963* 11:10	293 *472* 5:50	164 *264* 3:30	220 *354* 4:40	105 *169* 2:40	433 *697* 7:40	541 *871* 10:00	233 *375* 4:40	105 *169* 3:00	438 *705* 7:50	500 *805* 8:50	143 *230* 2:50	209 *336* 3:50	324 *521* 5:50	121 *195* 2:30	148 *238* 2:50	76 *122* 2:20	61 *98* 1:50	532 *856* 9:30	31 *50* 1:00	251 *404* 4:40	128 *206* 2:40	388 *624* 7:10	417 *671* 7:30	201 *323* 4:10	547 *880* 10:00	77 *124* 2:00
Stranraer			445 *716* 8:20	277 *446* 5:30	263 *423* 5:20	461 *742* 8:40	500 *805* 9:40	379 *610* 7:10	148 *238* 3:40	290 *467* 5:50	403 *649* 8:10	158 *254* 3:40	220 *354* 4:40	221 *356* 4:40	298 *480* 6:00	330 *531* 6:20	220 *354* 4:40	585 *942* 11:30	263 *423* 6:30	259 *417* 5:20	379 *610* 9:00	262 *422* 6:00	338 *544* 7:00	410 *660* 8:10	426 *686* 8:40	343 *552* 6:30	84 *135* 2:30	195 *314* 4:50	392 *631* 7:50	454 *731* 8:30	124 *200* 3:00	167 *269* 3:40	496 *798* 9:10	257 *414* 5:10	101 *163* 2:40	390 *628* 7:30	379 *610* 7:10	378 *608* 7:20	475 *765* 9:00	194 *312* 4:20	444 *715* 8:30	188 *303* 4:00	297 *478* 6:00	170 *274* 4:10	51 *82* 1:20	325 *523* 6:50	228 *367* 5:10	402 *647* 7:50
Swansea		417 *671* 7:50	161 *259* 3:00	118 *190* 2:20	217 *349* 4:00	182 *293* 3:30	206 *332* 4:10	141 *227* 2:40	506 *815* 9:20	192 *309* 3:40	301 *485* 6:00	347 *559* 6:20	187 *301* 3:30	195 *314* 3:40	233 *375* 4:30	177 *285* 3:20	248 *399* 4:40	285 *459* 6:00	594 *956* 11:30	264 *425* 4:50	696 *1120* 13:40	572 *921* 10:40	184 *296* 4:50	267 *430* 5:10	329 *530* 6:30	89 *143* 1:50	409 *658* 7:20	496 *798* 9:20	67 *108* 1:50	161 *259* 3:00	412 *663* 7:20	473 *761* 8:20	274 *441* 5:00	232 *373* 4:10	309 *497* 5:30	41 *66* 1:10	227 *365* 4:10	85 *137* 1:50	222 *357* 4:20	505 *813* 9:00	167 *269* 3:20	216 *348* 4:00	119 *192* 2:30	383 *616* 7:10	379 *610* 6:50	73 *117* 2:00	507 *816* 9:20	194 *312* 4:00
York	272 *438* 5:10	222 *357* 4:40	258 *415* 5:10	133 *214* 2:40	52 *84* 1:20	278 *448* 5:10	333 *536* 6:20	181 *291* 3:20	309 *497* 6:00	77 *124* 1:40	181 *291* 4:20	84 *135* 2:20	64 *103* 1:30	99 *159* 2:10	75 *121* 1:50	108 *174* 2:10	24 *39* 0:50	411 *661* 8:00	407 *655* 8:20	37 *60* 1:10	479 *771* 10:10	352 *566* 7:00	204 *328* 4:20	228 *367* 4:40	201 *323* 4:20	189 *304* 3:30	217 *349* 4:10	330 *531* 6:30	261 *420* 5:10	287 *462* 5:10	194 *312* 3:40	250 *402* 4:40	282 *454* 5:10	34 *55* 1:00	121 *195* 2:30	244 *393* 4:40	165 *266* 3:10	222 *357* 4:10	275 *443* 5:10	285 *459* 5:20	269 *433* 5:00	96 *154* 2:00	130 *209* 2:40	148 *238* 3:10	214 *344* 4:00	195 *314* 4:10	319 *513* 6:10	207 *333* 4:10

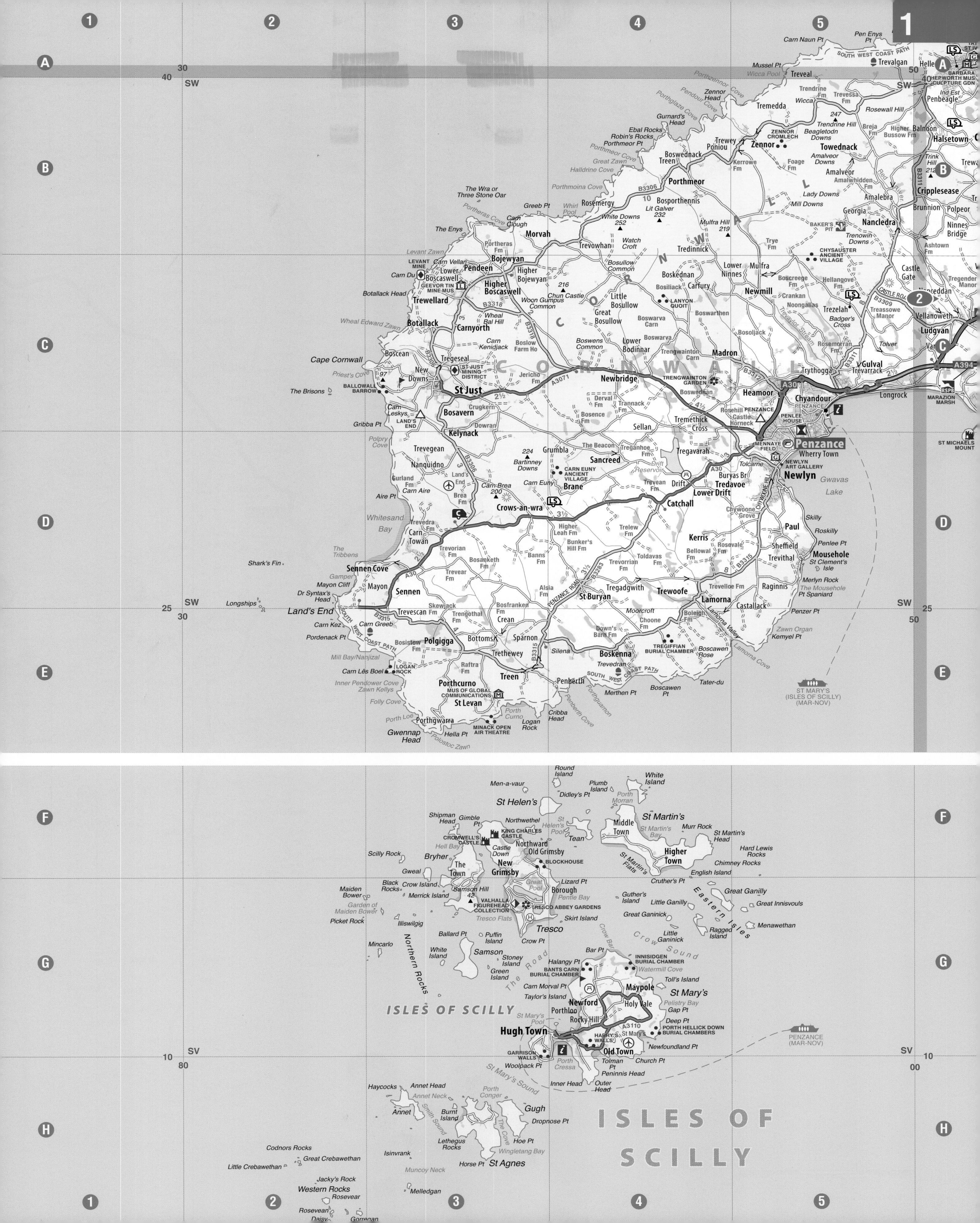

1
1
2
3
4
5
A
B
C
D
E
F
G
H
30
40
SW
50
SW
25
Carn Naun Pt
Pen Enys Pt
SOUTH WEST COAST PATH
Trevalgan
Mussel Pt
Wicca Pool
Treveal
Helle
BARBARA HEPWORTH MUS & SCULPTURE GDN
Ind Est
Penbeagle
Porthzennor Cove
Zennor Head
Pendour Cove
Porthglaze Cove
Trendrine Fm
Wicca Fm
Trevessa Fm
Tremedda
247
Trendrine Hill
Rosewall Hill
Gurnard's Head
Beagletodn Downs
Breja Fm
Higher Bussow Fm
Balnoon
Halsetown
Ebal Rocks
Robin's Rocks
Porthmeor Pt
Trewey
Poniou
Zennor
ZENNOR CROMLECH
Towednack
Porthmeor Cove
Great Zawn
Halldrine Cove
Boswednack
Treen
Kerrowe Fm
Foage Fm
Amalveor Downs
Amalveor
Trink Hill
212
B3311
Porthmoina Cove
B3306
Porthmeor
Amalwhidden Fm
Amalebra
Cripplesease
The Wra or Three Stone Oar
Rosemergy
10
Bosporthennis
Lit Galver
232
Lady Downs
Mill Downs
Brunnion
Polpeor
Greeb Pt
Whirl Pool
Porthcras Cove
White Downs
252
Mulfra Hill
219
Georgia
Nancledra
Ninnes Bridge
Carn Clough
BAKER'S PIT
The Enys
Morvah
Watch Croft
Trevowhan
Tredinnick
Trye Fm
Trenowin Downs
Ashtown Fm
Levant Zawn
Portheras Fm
Bojewyan
CHYSAUSTER ANCIENT VILLAGE
LEVANT MINE
Carn Vellan
Pendeen
Bosullow Common
Lower Ninnes
Mulfra
Castle Gate
Carn Du
Lower Boscaswell
GEEVOR TIN MINE MUS
Higher Bojewyan
216
Boskednan
Boscreege Fm
Hellangove Fm
Tregender Manor
Higher Boscaswell
Chun Castle
Bosiliack
Carfury
Newmill
Crankan
Botallack Head
Trewellard
Woon Gumpus Common
Little Bosullow
LANYON QUOIT
Noongallas
Trezelah
B3309
CASTLE ROAD
2
Nanceddan
Treassowe Manor
Vellanoweth
Wheal Bal Hill
B3318
Boswarthen
Badger's Cross
Ludgvan
Wheal Edward Zawn
Botallack
Great Bosullow
Boswarva Carn
Carnyorth
Bosoljack
Trevaylor Stream
Rosemorran Fm
Tolver
Carn Kenidjack
Lower Bodinnar
Boswarva
Bosiow Farm Ho
Bowens Common
Tregwainton Carn
B3311
Gulval
Cape Cornwall
Boscean
Tregeseal
ST JUST MINING DISTRICT
CORNWALL
Madron
Trythogga
Trevarrack
A394
Priest's Cove
New Downs
Jericho Fm
A3071
Newbridge
TRENGWAINTON GARDEN
B3312
Longrock
97
BALLOWALL BARROW
St Just
A30
Heamoor
Chyandour
The Brisons
Bosavern
Crugkern
Derval Fm
Boswednan
RSPB MARAZION MARSH
Carn Leskys
LAND'S END
Trannack Fm
Rosehill
PENZANCE
Castle Horneck
PENZANCE
PENLEE HOUSE
Gribba Pt
Kelynack
Dowran
Bosence Fm
Sellan
Tremethick Cross
Polpry Cove
MENNAYE FIELD
Penzance
ST MICHAELS MOUNT
Trevegean
The Beacon
Treganhoe Fm
Wherry Town
224
Bartinney Downs
Grumbla
Sancreed
Tregavarah
NEWLYN ART GALLERY
Nanquidno
Land's End
CARN EUNY ANCIENT VILLAGE
Drift Reservoir
Tolcarne
Newlyn
Gurland Fm
Carn Aire
Carn Euny
Brane
Trevean Fm
Drift
A30
Buryas Br
Tredavoe
Gwavas Lake
Carn Brea
200
Lower Drift
Aire Pt
Brea Fm
Crows-an-wra
Catchall
CHYWOONE HILL
Chywoone Grove
Whitesand Bay
Trevedra Fm
Higher Leah Fm
Trelew Fm
Skilly
Roskilly
Carn Towan
Kerris
Paul
Penlee Pt
The Tribbens
Trevorian Fm
Bunker's Hill Fm
Rosevale Fm
Sheffield
Mousehole
Bellowal Fm
St Clement's Isle
Shark's Fin
Sennen Cove
Bosanketh Fm
Banns Fm
Trevorrian Fm
Toldavas Fm
B3315
Trevithal
Gamper
Mayon Cliff
Mayon
Trevear Fm
Merlyn Rock
Dr Syntax's Head
A30
PENZANCE ROAD
B3283
Tregadgwith
Trewoofe
Trevelloe Fm
Raginnis
The Mousehole
Sennen
Alsia Fm
St Buryan
Lamorna
Pt Spaniard
Longships
Land's End
Skewjack
Bosfranken Fm
Castallack
Trevescan Fm
Trengothal Fm
Crean
Moorcroft
Penzer Pt
Carn Kez
Carn Greeb
Choone Fm
Boleigh Fm
Zawn Organ
Pordenack Pt
Bottoms
Sparnon
Down's Barn Fm
Lamorna Valley
Kemyel Pt
Polgigga
Bosistow Fm
Trethewey
Silena
Boskenna
Lamorna Cove
Mill Bay/Nanjizal
TREGIFFIAN BURIAL CHAMBER
Boscawen Rose
Raftra Fm
Carn Lês Boel
LOGAN ROCK
Treen
Trevedran
Penberth
Tater-du
Inner Pendower Cove
Zawn Kellys
Porthcurno
MUS OF GLOBAL COMMUNICATIONS
SOUTH WEST COAST PATH
ST MARY'S (ISLES OF SCILLY) (MAR-NOV)
St Levan
Merthen Pt
Boscawen Pt
Folly Cove
Porth Curno
Logan Rock
Cribba Head
Penberth Cove
Porthguarnon
Porth Loe
Porthgwarra
MINACK OPEN AIR THEATRE
Gwennap Head
Hella Pt
Folostoc Zawn
Round Island
White Island
Men-a-vaur
Plumb Island
Didley's Pt
Porth Morran
St Helen's
St Martin's
Shipman Head
Gimble Pt
Northwethel
St Helen's Pool
Middle Town
Murr Rock
St Martin's Head
CROMWELL'S CASTLE
KING CHARLES CASTLE
Tean
St Martin's Bay
Hell Bay
Castle Down
Northward
Higher Town
Hard Lewis Rocks
Scilly Rock
Bryher
Old Grimsby
Chimney Rocks
The Town
New Grimsby
BLOCKHOUSE
St Martin's Flats
English Island
Gweal
Black Rocks
Crow Island
Great Pool
Lizard Pt
Cruther's Pt
Maiden Bower
Samson Hill
42
Borough
Pentle Bay
Great Ganilly
Merrick Island
Guther's Island
Little Ganilly
Great Innisvouls
Garden of Maiden Bower
VALHALLA FIGUREHEAD COLLECTION
TRESCO ABBEY GARDENS
Eastern Isles
Picket Rock
Tresco Flats
Skirt Island
Great Ganinick
Illiswilgig
Menawethan
Tresco
Ragged Island
Ballard Pt
Puffin Island
Little Ganinick
Crow Bar
Crow Sound
Mincarlo
Samson
Crow Pt
White Island
Stoney Island
Bar Pt
Northern Rocks
INNISIDGEN BURIAL CHAMBER
Halangy Pt
Green Island
BANTS CARN BURIAL CHAMBER
Watermill Cove
Toll's Island
The Road
Carn Morval Pt
Maypole
St Mary's
Taylor's Island
Newford
ISLES OF SCILLY
Porthloo
Holy Vale
Pelistry Bay
Gap Pt
St Mary's Pool
Rocky Hill
Deep Pt
Hugh Town
A3110
PORTH HELLICK DOWN BURIAL CHAMBERS
PENZANCE (MAR-NOV)
HARRY'S WALLS
St Mary's
GARRISON WALLS
Old Town
Newfoundland Pt
SV
10
80
Woolpack Pt
Porth Cressa
Tolman Pt
Church Pt
SV
10
00
Peninnis Head
St Mary's Sound
Inner Head
Outer Head
Haycocks
Annet Head
Porth Conger
Annet Neck
Gugh
Annet
Burnt Island
Smith Sound
The Cove
Dropnose Pt
ISLES OF SCILLY
Lethegus Rocks
Hoe Pt
Wingletang Bay
Codnors Rocks
Isinvrank
Great Crebawethan
Little Crebawethan
Horse Pt
St Agnes
Muncoy Neck
Jacky's Rock
Western Rocks
Melledgan
Rosevear
Rosevean
Daisy
Gorregan

2
St Ives
ST IVES BAY
St Ives Head or The Island
Clodgy Pt
Porthminster Pt
Carbis Bay
Halsetown
Lelant
Hayle
Phillack
Copperhouse
Gwithian
Connor Downs
Angarrack
Camborne
Tuckingmill
Pool
Carn Brea
Carnkie
Lanner
Gwennap
Carharrack
Roseworthy
Barripper
Troon
Four Lanes
Stithians
Penhalvaen
Praze-an-Beeble
St Erth
St Erth Praze
Canon's Town
Crowlas
Ludgvan
Nancledra
Gulval
Longrock
Marazion
St Michaels Mount
Perranuthnoe
St Hilary
Goldsithney
Relubbus
Townshend
Leedstown
Fraddam
Godolphin Cross
Crowntown
Nancegollan
Releath
Porkellis
Wendron
Helston
Breage
Ashton
Germoe
Praa Sands
Rinsey
Porthleven
Sithney
Gweek
Constantine
Mawgan
Garras
St Martin
Trewennack
Culdrose
Gunwalloe
Cury
Cross Lanes
Mullion
Mullion Cove
Penhale
Goonhilly Downs
Kuggar
Ruan Minor
Cadgwith
St Ruan
Grade
Lizard
Lizard Point
Landewednack
Church Cove
MOUNT'S BAY
CORNWALL
Cudden Pt
Hoe Pt
Trewavas Head
Rinsey Head
Tye Rocks
Porthleven Sands
Loe Bar
Halzephron Cliff
Poldhu Pt
Predannack Head
Vellan Head
Kynance Cove
Enoch Rock
A30
A394
A3083
A393
B3301
B3302
B3280
B3303
B3304
B3297
B3293
B3296
SOUTH WEST COAST PATH
0 1 2 3 miles
0 1 2 3 4 5 km
A B C D E F G H
1 2 3 4 5 6

3
Playing Place
Old Kea
St Michael Penkevil
Lamorran
Ruan River
Caerhays
West Portholland
East Portholland
Treveor
Fernsplatt
Coombe
Helston Water
Quenchwell
Chygwyne
Cowlands
Coombe
Higher Trelease Fm
Tretheake Manor
Sunny Corner
Hick's Mill
Cusgarne
Greenwith Common
Carnon Downs
Killiganoon
Veryan Green
May's Rock
Porthluney Cove
BOSWINGER
Frogpool
Tregye
Penelewey
Pelgerran Wood
Treworga
Treburthes
Greeb Pt
Penare
Penveor Pt
Perranwell
Perranwell Station
Perranarworthal
Devoran
Goonpiper
Penpol
Trevilla
Trelissick
TRELISSICK GARDEN
Borlase Wood
Philleigh
Ruan High Lanes
Trewartha
Melinsey
Veryan
Portloe
Hartriza Pt
Shag Rock
VERYAN BAY
High Pt
Lizard Pool
Dodman Pt
DEVORAN & PERRAN
Chycoose
Point
Feock
Treworthal
Treworlas
Crugsillick Manor
Lower Mill
Tregamenna Manor Fm
Manare Pt
Tregairewoon Fm
Carne
Pennare Fm
Perran Wharf
Devichoys Wood
Carclew
Restronguet Creek
Restronguet Passage
Harcourt
Commerrans Fm
Curgurrell
Pibyah Rock
Gerrans Bay
Shannick Pt
Rosen Cliff 101
Kiberick Cove
Lemoria Rock
Gull Rock
Nare Head
Trewithian
Burnthouse
Angarrick
Treluswell
Roskrow
Weir Pt
CARRICK ROADS
Messack Fm
Rosevine
Mylor Bridge
Mylor Creek
Messack Pt
Trethewell
St Just in Roseland
St Just Pool
Gerrans
Portscatho
Treliever
A394
A39
RAZE THE ROOF
PENRYN
Carveth
Penryn
Bissom
Trelew
Penarrow Pt
Mylor Churchtown
Mabe Burnthouse
St Gluvias
Ind Est
Tregew
Flushing
Percuil
Antron Fm
College Res
Trefusis Pt
St Mawes
ST MAWES CASTLE
Greeb Pt
Argal Manor
Mongleath
Falmouth
NAT MARITIME MUS CORNWALL
FALMOUTH DOCKS
Castle Pt
St Mawes Harbour
Porthmellin Head
Porth Fm
Towan Beach
Argal Res
Budock Water
PENMERE
Bus Pk
PENDENNIS CASTLE
St Anthony
Bohortha
Killigerran Head
Porthbear Beach
Lamanva
Trewen Fm
Boslowick
FALMOUTH TOWN
Gyllyngvase Beach
Pendennis Pt
St Anthony Head
Place Barton
Treverva
Swan Pool
Zone Pt
Penjerrick
Penrose Fm
Pennance Pt
Treworval Fm
Carlidnack
Bareppa
Maenporth
High Cliff
Drift Fm
Boskensoe Fm
Mawnan Smith
FALMOUTH BAY
Bream Cove
Porth Navas
GLENDURGAN GARDEN
Trerose
Rosemullion Head
Helford Passage
TREBAH GDNS
Mawnan
SOUTH WEST COAST PATH
Durgan
Toll Pt
River
Treath
St Anthony-in-Meneage
Helford
Flushing
Gillan Harbour
Manaccan
Nare Pt
Polnare Cove
Nare Head
Gillan
Carne
Nare Cove
Beacon 112
Roskorwell
Porthallow
Porthkerris Pt
Tregidden
Tregarne
Polpidnick Fm
Trelease Mill
Trelease Fm
Laddenvean
Porthoustock
Rosenithon
St Keverne
Ind Est
Godrevy Cove
Carn-du Rocks
Grugwith
Roskilly
Crousa Common
Roskilly's Open Fm
B3293
Zoar
B3294
Lowland Pt
North Corner
Polcoverack Fm
Penhallick
Coverack
COVERACK
Ponsongath
Perprean Cove
Ebber Rocks
Treleaver Cliff
Black Head
SW
10
00
40
A
B
C
D
E
F
G
H
7
8
9
10
11

Trescore Islands
Porth Mear
Park Head
Diggory's Island
10
Queen Bess Rock
BEDRUTHEN STEPS
Pendarves Island
Carnewas Island
Trerathick Pt
Trenance Pt
Berryl's Pt
Beacon Cove
Griffin's Pt
Stem Pt
Watergate Bay
Watergate or Tregurrian Beach
Horse Rock
Zacry's Islands
Trevelgue Head
Flory Island
Whipsiderry
Towan Head
Gazzle
Newquay
Fistral Beach
BLUE REEF AQUARIUM
Porth
St Columb Minor
Pentire Point East
NEWQUAY ZOO
Trenance
Gusti Veor
Trencreek
Chapel
Pentire Point West
Porth Joke
Crantock Beach
Pentire
Kelsey Head
Treninnick
Lane
A392
The Gannel
West Pentire
Crantock
Trevemper
Holywell Bay
Holywell Beach
The Kelseys
Cubert Common
Trevithick Manor
Trevilley Court Fm
Gwills
Kestle Mill
Carter's or Gull Rocks
HOLYWELL BAY FUN PARK
Trevowah
Carines
Penhale Pt
Holywell
Carevick
Hoblyn's Cove
Tresean
Trevail
Trenissick
Trerew Fm
Trewerry Mill
TRERICE
Ligger Pt
Ellenglaze
Cubert
Trescowthick
Trewolla
Trevoll
Treoffal
Benny Mill
BENNY HALT
LAPPA VALLEY STEAM RAILWAY
Ligger or Perran Bay
Neeham
Perran Beach
ST PIRAN'S CHURCH (REMS)
Mount
PERRAN CROSS
Treworthen
Rejerrah
Cargoll
St Newlyn East
Cotty's Pt
Hendra Croft
Treludderow Manor
Penhallow Moor
Trevilson
Reen Sands
Rose
PERRAN ROUND
Lower Rose
Scotland Fm
Shepherds Fm
Fiddlers Green
Droskyn Pt
Reen Manor
Rosehill
Newlyn Downs
PERRANPORTH
Perranporth
Cligga Head
Carnebo Fm
Goonhavern
Bawden Rocks or Man & His Man
Hanover Cove
Reen Cross
Sixty Acres Fm
Bolingey
B3285
Perrancoombe
Green Island
Trevellas Porth
Anchor
Cocks
Penwartha Coombe
Carnkief
Perranwell
Killigrew
Newdowns Head
Cross Coombe
Trevellas
Perranzabuloe
Penwartha
Lambourne
Wheal Frances
Zelah Hill
Deer Park Wood
Zelah
Blowinghouse
A30
Trefronick Fm
Crams
St Agnes Head
Carn Gowla
New Downs
Wheal Kitty
Ventongimps
Chyverton Ho
Tolgroggan Fm
CORNWALL
St Agnes
Peterville
Barkla Shop
Truthan
Tubby's Head
Higher Bal
ST AGNES BEACON
192
Penhallow
Gollawater
HEALEYS CORNISH CYDER FARM
Boswellick
St Allen
Goonown
Mithian
Callestick
Marazanvose
Higher Callestick Fm
Chapel Porth
Goonvrea
ST AGNES MINING DISTRICT
Goonbell
Mithian Downs
Nanteague Fm
Pennare
Treworgan
Tresawsen
Penwartha Ho
Allet
B3284
Towan Cross
Mingoose
Coldharbour
Pendale
Porth Towan
Banns
Silverwell
St Clement Woods
Shortlanesend
Mount Hawke
Gover Fm
Roscarnick Fm
Tregavethan Manor
Roseworthy
Higher Carvinack
Idless
Calerick
Polwhele
Porthtowan
Penhallow Fm
Truro Fm
Trevaskis
Treheveras
Killagorden
Gullyn Rock
Sheep Rock
Factory Fm
Two Burrows
Little Croft West
Treworder
Manor Parsley
Blackwater
Three Burrows
Boscolla
Featherbeds
Buckshead
PORTREATH HARBOUR
Menagissey
Skinner's Bottom
Penstraze
Croft West
Nancemere
Tregurra
Kenwyn
Gull Rock
Horse Rock
Portreath
Laity Moor
Mawla
Carnhot
Green Bottom
P&R
New Mill
Cambrose
Forge
Stencoose
Boscawen Fm
Jolly's Bottom
Ind Est
Treliske
ROYAL CORNWALL MUSEUM
Samphire Island
Basset's Cove
B3300
Bridge
Nance
PORTREATH
CORNWALL GOLD TOLGUS MILL
Parc Erissey
Wheal Rose
Wheal Busy
Saveock
Bus Pk
Gloweth
Threemilestone
Highertown
Truro
Chacewater
GWENNAP MINING DISTRICT
Tomperrow
Kerley Downs
Newbridge
Radnor
WHEAL PEEVOR MINE
Sparnon Gate
Scorrier
Salem
Illogan
Gilbert's Coombe
Killifreth
Creegbrawse
Cusveorth Coombe
Carrine Common
Penweathers
St Clement
North Cliffs
TEHIDY
Paynter's Lane End
North Country
Treleigh
Highway
Treskerby
Todpool
Baldhu
Hugus
Hugus Fm
Goodern Manor Fm
Kea
Malpas
Fishing Cove
Navax Pt
Hell's Mouth
Deadman's Cove
Oak Wood
Old Merrose Fm
Park Bottom
West Tolgus
Tolgus Mount
Redruth
Mount Ambrose
Plain-an-Gwarry
Vogue
St Day
Cox Hill
Goon Gumpas
Hale Mills
Calenick
Porth Kea
B3301
Coombe
CORNWALL
Red River
CORNISH MINES & ENGINES
REDRUTH MINING DISTRICT
Grofthandy
Twelve Heads
Wheal Baddon
Carlyon
Old Kea
Gwithian
Roscroggan
Tolvaddon Downs
Tolskithy
Menadarva
Reskadinnick
Roskear Croft
Illogan Highway
Church Town
Busveal
Trevethan
Carharrack
United Downs
Fernsplatt Coombe
Bissoe
Helston Water
Quenchwell
Chygwyne
Playing Place
Nancemellin
Pool
Carnbrea
Carn Marth 235
Cowlands
Kehelland
Treswithian Downs
Rosewarne
Tuckingmill
CARN BREA 225
Sunny Corner
Hick's Mill
Carnon Downs
Cornhill Fm
Brea
Penhallick
Bosleake
Church Coombe
Pennance
Cusgarne
Greenwith Common
Killiganoon
TREVARNON ROUND
Treswithian
CAMBORNE MINING DISTRICT
Trevarth
Frogpool
Tregye
Come-to-Good
Penelewey
Camborne
Piece
Carnkie
Lanner
Gwennap
PERRANWELL
Perran Station
Trelissick
TRELISSICK GARDEN
Treskillard
Buller Downs
Treviskey
Tresavean
Comford
Trevarth Fm
Tresamble
Perranwell
Devoran
Goonpiper
Penpol
Trevilla
Filtrick Fm
Four Lanes
Grillis
Perranarworthal
Point
Trethellan Water
Penhalurick
Crosspost Fm
KENNALL VALE
DEVORAN & PERRAN
Chycoose
Feock
SHIRE HORSE TRUST & CARRIAGE
Troon
Pencoys
Perran Wharf
Carclew
Seareaugh
Killivose
Treslothan
Trenowin
Angarrack
Manor Downs
0 1 2 3 miles
0 1 2 3 4 5 km
SW
60
70
40
A
B
C
D
E
F
G
H
2
3
4
5
6
1

6
Cardinham Moor
Hard Head
Redhill Downs
Colliford Downs
Bunning's Park
Lord's Park Fm
Westerlake Fm
Sparretts Fm
THE HURLERS STONE CIRCLES
Craddock Moor
Minions
Upton Cross
Dunslea
CARADON MINING DISTRICT
Caradon Hill 369
Gonamena
Caradon Town
Downgate
Browda
Trewoodle
Golberdon
Higher Carblake
Praze
Millpool
St Bellarmin's Tor
Maidenwell
Carburrow Tor
Letter Moor
Redhill Downs
Draynes Common
Sibleyback Lake
Crylla Fm
Tokenbury Manor
Pensilva
Trevigro
Haye Fm
Racecourse Downs
Cardinham Downs
Fore Downs
Warleggan Down
Hobb's Hill
Mutton's Downs
Wortha
Northwood
Carpuan
Draynes
GOLITHA FALLS
Trekeivesteps
Commonmoor
Darite
Higher Tremarcoombe
TRETHEVY QUOIT
Crow's Nest
Tokenbury Corner
Middlehill
Ind Est
Charaton Cross
Bicton Manor
Bicton Wood
Redland Fm
Appledore
Lidcutt Wood
Milltown
Cardinham
Treslea Downs
Pantersbridge
Carne Wood
Warleggan
Tremaddock Fm
Berry Down
282
Trenant
KING DONIERT'S INSCRIBED STONE
Treworrick
St Cleer
Trecarne
Tremar
Newton Fm
Rosecraddoc Manor
Woolston
Frogwell
Callywith Wood
Deviock Wood
Hurtstocks Wood
Old Cardinham Castle
Mount
Lestow Fm
Goonzion Downs
St Neot
Wayland
Gang
St Ive
A390
Merryhue
Cooksland
Ind Est
Callabarrett Wood
Long Downs
Higher Hill Fm
Welltown
Lower Hill
CARNGLAZE SLATE CAVERNS
Treverbyn Mill
Treverbyn
Lampretten Ho
Trethinnick Fm
Treleathick
Thornton
Parkfield
St Ive Cross
Dunnerdake Fm
Durnaford Fm
Margate Wood
Kingswood Downs
Pinsla Park
Tawna Downs
Well Wood
Trenay
Carnglaze Caverns
Woodland Fm
Bokenna Wood
Ashford Br
Treworgey Manor
Venton Veor
East Tuelmenna
Woodhill Manor
Tengrove Fm
Penhawger Fm
Trebeigh Wood
Cutkive Wood
Venton Ho
Ludcott Fm
COLESLOGGETT HALT
Laneskin Wood
Redrice Wood
Holtroad Downs
Tredinnick
Ley
Twelvewoods
Doublebois
High Wood
Hendrabridge
Trembraze
Merrymeet
Westdown Wood
Vicarage Wood
Hammett
Crendle Down
Turfdown
Fletchersbridge
Bear Wood
Cabilla Wood
Lebail Wood
Drawbridge
A38
Dobwalls
Old Park
LISKEARD MUS
Bus Pk
Liskeard
Addington
Pengover Green
Trehunsey Br
Quethiock
Goodmerry Fm
Bazley's Plantn
Haft Wood
Penkestle Downs
Hall Downs
Draw Wood
Largin Wood
Bodithiel Fm
Middle Taphouse
B3360
Treburgie
Moorswater
Looe Mills
Ind Est
Stony Br
Tregondale Fm
Hepwell Br
Trehunist
Leigh Fm
Pounda
Trebrown
Newbridge Wood
BODMIN PARKWAY
LANHYDROCK HOUSE
Cutmadoc
Newton
Great Wood
West Taphouse
Tithe Hall Fm
Gelly Fm
East Taphouse
Trevelmond
Boduel
COOMBE
Camellion
LISKEARD
Tencreek Fm
Roseland
Tregrill
Trewint
Lambest
Blunts
Bofarnel Downs
Bofarnel
Bedwindle Fm
A390
Cripstone Fm
B3359
St Pinnock
Lodge Hill
Pennyglaze
Menheniot
Doddycross
Pathada Wood
Maudlin
Sweethouse
Fairy Cross
Trewindle
Babbington
Connon
Braddock
Cliver Wood
Scawns Fm
Trussel Br
East Looe River
B3252
Bodway
RESTORMEL CASTLE
Druid's Hill
Crickapit Mill
Penfrane Manor
Trevillis Wood
West Trevillies
Trethawle Fm
Lower Clicker
MENHENIOT
Coldrenick
Trehurst
Tilland
Molenick
Tideford Cross
Wilton Fm
Roselyon
Deerpark Wood
Trenchwa Wood
Lametton Mill
B3269
B3268
Hillhead
Sandylake
West Drive
Brooks
Beara Fm
Woodlay Fm
Herodsfoot
St Keyne
B3254
KEYNE
Great Trethew
Hornington
Lean Park Fm
Berry Fm
Cutmere
Lostwithiel
LOSTWITHIEL
Millham Fm
Trebarrel
Polmartin Fm
Hollowpark
208
Bury Down
Trewidland
Fursdon
Bylane End
B3251
Trebrownbridge Wood
Bethany
Budge's Shop
Kernock Mill
Tideford
Bridgend
Beacon Hill
Coombe Fm
Polpiece
Black Down
Windsor Wood
CAUSELAND
Landlooe Br
Pensipple
Catchfrench Manor
A38
Bawdoe Fm
Couch's Mill
Netherton
Penhuffle Wood
Polvean Cross
Tawell Fm
Botallick
Abovetown
B3359
Landare Fm
Tremadart Wood
Churchbridge
Polvean Wood
Lower Trenode
Wilton Fm
Trerulefoot
Bake Manor
Castle
Newham Fm
Duloe
Westnorth
Wringworthy
A387
Lydcott Wood
Bake Wood
Milltown
Lantyan
St Winnow
Ribby Fm
Winnick
Bocaddon
Pengute Fm
Trefanny Hill
Gillhill Wood
Tredinnick
Tregarlandbridge
Tregarland
Higherdiff
Bin Down
Widegates
Shortacross
Hessenford
A374
Great Wood
Lerryn
Lanreath
Tregarrick Mill
Tregarrick Wood
SANDPLACE
Sandplace
Morval
Cleese Fm
Polbath
Carruggatt Wood
Lantyan Wood
Wooda Fm
Trevollard
East Court Wood
Muchlarnick
Puffiland Fm
No Man's Land
Bokenver Wood
Trelowia
Minard Fm
GOLANT
Penquite Cliff
Treesmill
Treire Fm
Court Wood
Hall Wood
Snowden's Bridge
Keveral Wood
Carcoe Fm
Narkurs
Lawhibbet Fm
Torfrey
St Veep
Haye Fm
Tregarrick Fm
Pelynt
Milcombe
Great Tree
B3253
Kilgogue Fm
Golant
Trefrawl
Lancare Fm
Catherinepark Wood
Kiln Wood
Ten Acre Wood
Watergate
Trenant Wood
St Martin
MONKEY SANCTUARY
Penhale Fm
Seaton
B3247
Tywardreath
Trenython Manor
B3269
Penpoll
Peakswater
Bake Fm
B3359
Trelay Fm
Trelawne Manor
Ind Est
Millendreath
Plaidy
Bodigga Cliff
Colmer Rocks
Downderry
SOUTH WEST COAST PATH
Trezare Fm
Penpoll Creek
Polveithan Fm
Lanteglos Highway
Penkelly
Polean Fm
Barcelona
LOOE
Trad Est
Shutta
East Looe
Polmear
Mixtow
Colvithick Wood
Trevedda Fm
Whitecross
Trethake Fm
Trenewan
West Watergate
POLPERRO ROAD
West Looe
Looe
LOOE MUSEUM
Looe Bay
Hannafore
Hannafore Pt
PASSAGE LANE
Bodinnick
Pont
Tremeer Fm
Great Tratford
Great Kellow Fm
A387
Tencreek
Portlooe
Polkerris
B3415
Fowey
Carneggan Fm
Frogmore Fm
Lansallos
Carey Park
Porthallow
Talland
Talland Bay
Portnadler Bay
ST GEORGE'S ISLAND MARINE NATURE RESERVE
St George's or Looe Island
WHITSAND
Readymoney
Menabilly
ST CATHERINE'S CASTLE
Pont Pill
Churchtown Fm
CORNWALL
Crumplehorn
Brent
HERITAGE MUS OF SMUGGLING & FISHING
Polruan
West Coombe
Lantic Bay
Hard Hd 132
Polperro
Downend Pt
Coombe Hawne
Washing Rocks
Blackbottle Rock
Lantivet Bay
Pencarrow Head
Shag Rock
Chapel Cliff
Southground Pt
Sandy Cove
SX
70
40
10
A
B
C
D
E
F
G
H
1
2
3
4
5
6
11
12
0
1
2
3 miles
0
1
2
3
4
5 km

Kelly Bray
Monkscross
Chilsworthy
St Ann's Chapel
Gunnislake
Tamar Valley Mining District
Hurdlich Horn
Morwelldown Plantn
Hartshole Fm
Birch Wood
River Tavy
Higher Walreddon
West Down
Grenofen
Fullamoor
Eggworthy Fm
Leeden Tor 389
Cramber Tor
445
Kit Hill
333
Earth Work
Bowling Green
Silver Valley
Rising Sun
Donkey Pk
Albaston
Drakewalls
Morwell Wood
Bedford Br
Dunridge
Holewell Fm
Higher Pittisham
Horseyeatt Welltown
Leather Tor
Whiteworks
Peek Hill 400
Nun's Cross Fm
Callington
Harrowbarrow
Metherell
Norris Green
Mount Lodge
Dupath Well Chapel
Cleave Fm
Corneal
Morwellham Quay
Maddacleave Wood
Hocklake Fm
Berra Tor
Uppaton
Horrabridge
Walkhampton
Gnatham Barton
Down Tor 366
Lower Lowery
Burrator Reservoir
Combshead Tor
454
Coombe Fm
Rill Fm
Ashton
Cotehele
Calstock
Buckland Monachorum
The Garden House
Harrowbeer
Dousland
Yennadon Down
Sheeps Tor
Newbridge
Viverdon Down
Trehill Fm
Morden Fm
St Dominick
Hatch Wood
Denham Br
Didham Fm
Crapstone Ho
Crapstone
Axtown
Yelverton
Sheepstor
Ditsworthy Warren
Hartor Tors
Tuckermarsh
Bohetherick
Helston Fm
Bere Alston
Tamar
Buckland Abbey
Meavy
Yeo Fm
Ringmoor Cott
Callisham Down
Gutter Tor 350
Upper Plym Valley
Amy Down
Bealbury
Heathfield Fm
Lockridge Fm
Woolacombe Fm
Fishacre Wood
Chub Tor
Olderwood Plantn
Dartmoor
Giant's Hill
Halton Barton
Crocadon Wood
Well Fm
Norton Fm
Milton Combe
Coombe Fm
Hoo Meavy
Lovaton
Ringmoor Down
St Mellion Park
St Mellion
Halton Quay
Hole's Hole
Cotts
Down Fm
Valley
Bickham
Clearbrook
Catstor Down
Legis Tor
Willings Walls Warren
Hentor Warren
National Park
Langcombe Hill
Trewashford Fm
Polborder
Weir Quay
Hole Fm
Lopwell
North Wood
Trowlesworthy Tors 348
Lee Moor
Herod Wood
Paynter's Cross
Pillaton
Kernock
Crosspark Wood
Ley Fm
Cadover Br
492
Shell Top 475
Penn Moor
A388
South Sillaton
Pillatonmill
Howton
New Park Fm
Bere Ferrers
River Tamar
Blaxton Wood
Bame Wood
Lower Upperton
Shaden Moor
Shaugh Moor
Penn Beacon 427
Leigh Fm
Cargreen
Thorn Pt
New Barn Fm
A386
Leigh
Devon
Nethershaugh Fm
Shaugh Prior
Hatt Ho
Hatt
Cross Fm
Rumbulllion Fm
Weir Pt
River Tavy
Roborough
Bickleigh
Bickleigh Vale
Beatland Corner
Collard Tor
Wotter
Lee Moor
Dendles Waste
Trewandra
Wotton Fm
Botusfleming
Landulph
Kingsmill Lake
Neal Pt
Warleigh Pt
Warleigh Point
North Coombe Fm
Widewell
Bus Pk
Woolwell
Hartstone Fm
Faunstone Fm
Tolchmoor Gate
Rook Tor
Landrake
Lantallack Cross
Liskeard Road
A38
Notter
Carkeel
Ind Est
Skinham Pt
Warren Pt
Tamerton Foliot
P&R
Glenholt
Whitleigh
Southway
Great Shaugh Wood
Little Pethill Fm
Crownhill Down
Headon Down
Quick Br
Newpark Waste
Saltash Services
Trematon
South Pill
Latchbrook
Burraton
Ernesettle
Crownhill Fort
Bus Pk
Estover
Cann Wood
Delamore Ho
Drakeland Corner
Dartmoor Zoological Park
Smallhanger
Yondertown
Cornwood
Berry Hill
Saltash
Forder
Mary Newman's Cottage
Toll
St Budeaux
King's Tamerton
Honicknowle
Manadon
Crownhill
Derriford
Long Down
Bude Fm
Hemerdon Ball 212
Lutton
Moor Cross
St Erney
Burraton Coombe
Wearde
Riverside
Trehan
Trematon Castle
St Stephens
Bull Pt
Ham
Pennycross
The Park Way
Leigham
Plym Valley Railway
Longbridge
Woodford
Newnham Park
Hemerdon
Sparkwell
St Germans
Antony Passage
Churchtown Farm Community
Weston Mill Lake
Barne Barton
Weston Mill
Ind Est
Eggbuckland
P&R
Hemerdon Ho
Lower Venton Fm
Mark's Br
Cadleigh Lodge
Jupiter Pt
Antony House
Wilcove
Hamoaze
Keyham
Ford
Peverell
Home Park
Compton
Efford
Crabtree
Plymouth
Mannamead
Chaddlewood
Plympton
Underwood
Venton
Lee Mill
Sheviock Wood
Berry Down
Sheviock
Erth Hill
Lynher River or St Germans
Maryfield
Bus Pk
Dockyard
Stoke
Devonport
Mutley
Mount Gould
Laira
Saltram House
River Plym
Smithaleigh
Hunsdon Fm
Torpoint
Bus Cen
Brickfields Rec Gnd
Stonehouse
The Box
Langage
Blackpool
Crafthole
Antony
Deadman's Pt
St John's Lake
Merchant's House
National Marine Aquarium
Royal Citadel
Billacombe
West Sherford
East Sherford
Southwood Wood
Poppie's Br
Portwrinkle
Trethill Cliffs
St John
Sango Island
Cremyll
Devils Pt
Western King Pt
Cattedown
Oreston
Pomphlett
Elburton Road
Plymstock
Elburton
Efford Fm
Lotherton Br
Worston
Long Sands
Hounster Hill
Bus Pk
Inswork
Southdown
Mount Edgcumbe
Mount Batten Pt
Turnchapel
Hooe
Combe
Yeo Fm
Stonycross Fm
Tregantle Cliff
Sharrow Pt
Freathy
Millbrook
Millbrook Lake
Drake's Island
Dunstone Pt
Jennycliff Bay
South West Coast Path
Barn Fm
Coombe Fm
Brixton
Yealmpton
Yealmbridge
Bulland Wood
Dunstone
Bay
Anderton
The Sound
Spriddlestone
Torr
Picklecombe Pt
Staddiscombe
Spriddlestone Ho
Coffleet Creek
River Yealm
Ashcombe Fm
Holbeton
Kingsand
Cawsand
Staddon Pt
Bovisand Bay
Bovisand Lodge
Down Thomas
Raneleigh Fm
Hollacombe Hill
Wembury Wood
South Devon
Captain Blake's Pt
Pier Cellars
Manor Bourne
Steer Pt
Luson
Polhawn Cove
Rame
Roscoff Santander (Mar-Nov)
Knighton
B3186
Collaton Fm
Creacombe Fm
South West Coast Path
Lillery's Cove
Penlee Pt
Heybrook Bay
Wembury
Newton Ferrers
Pool Mill Fm
Preston Fm
Alston Hall
Battisborough Cross
Rame Head
Renney Rocks
Wembury Pt
Blackstone Rocks
Season Pt
Warren Pt
Bridgend
Membland
Poole Fm
Haye Fm
Mothecombe
Mouthstone Pt
Noss Mayo
St Anchorite's Rock
Gara Pt
Worswell
South West Coast Path
Wadham Rocks
Erme Mouth
Blackstone Pt
Netton Fm
Stoke Ho
Blackaterry Pt
Mary's Rocks
Hilsea Pt
Stoke Pt
Beacon Pt
SX 60 70
SX 40 60
A B C D E F G H
7 8 9 10 11 12 13

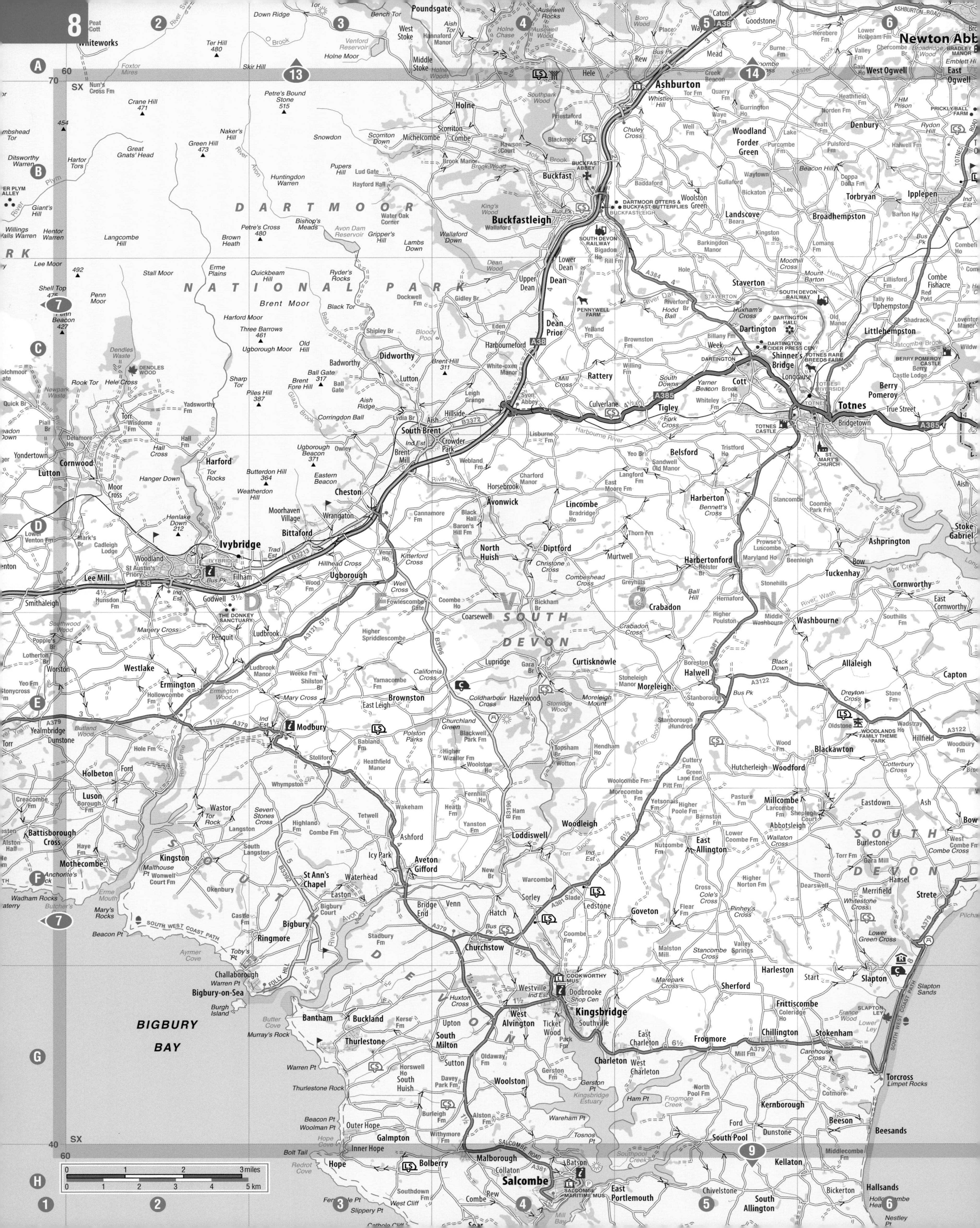

8
Peat Cott
Whiteworks
Down Ridge
Bench Tor
Poundsgate
West Stoke
Aish Tor
Hannaford Manor
Holne Chase
Ausewell Rocks
Ausewell Wood
Boro Wood
Place
Caton
Goodstone
Ashburton Road
Lower Holbeam Fm
Herebere Fm
Newton Abb
Ter Hill 480
Venford Reservoir
Holne Moor
Middle Stoke
Mead
Rew
Bus Pk
A38
Valley Fm
Chercombe Br
Broadridge Wood
Bradley Manor
Emblett Hi
Foxtor Mires
Skir Hill
13
Hele
Ashburton
Creek Beacon
14
West Ogwell
East Ogwell
SX
Nun's Cross Fm
Petre's Bound Stone 515
Crane Hill 471
Holne
Southpark Wood
Whistley Hill
Tor Fm
Quarry Fm
Gurrington Ho
Heathfield Fm
HM Prison
Norden Fm
Prickly Ball Farm
454
Lambshead Tor
Naker's Hill
Green Hill 473
Great Gnats' Head
Snowdon
Scorriton Down
Michelcombe
Scorriton
Combe
Priestaford Ho
Blackmoor
Rawson Court
Chuley Cross
Well Fm
Waye Fm
Woodland
Lake
Yeatt Fm
Denbury
Rydon Hill
Ditsworthy Warren
Harton Tors
Pupers Hill
Lud Gate
Hayford Hall
Huntingdon Warren
Brook Manor
Brook Wood
Holy Brook
Buckfast Abbey
Buckfast
Forder Green
Purcombe Fm
Pulsford Fm
Halwell Fm
Totnes Road
Beacon Hill
Baddaford
Gullaford
Waytown
Coppa Dolla Fm
Plym
Giant's Hill
River Plym
DARTMOOR
Water Oak Corner
Bishop's Meads
King's Wood
Buckfastleigh
Wallaford
Dartmoor Otters & Buckfast Butterflies
Woolston Green
Bickaton
Torbryan
Ipplepen
Willings Walls Warren
Hentor Warren
Petre's Cross 480
Avon Dam Reservoir
Gripper's Hill
Langcombe Hill
Brown Heath
Lambs Down
Wallaford Down
South Devon Railway
Bigadon Ho
Landscove
Beara
Broadhempston
Barton Ho
Kingston Ho
Barkingdon Manor
Lomans Fm
Bus Pk
Combefi Ho
Lee Moor
492
Stall Moor
Erme Plains
Quickbeam Hill
Ryder's Rocks
Dean Wood
Lower Dean
Dean
Upper Dean
Moothill Cross
Mount Barton
Hole
A384
Rill Fm
Combe Fishacre
Lillisford Fm
Shell Top 476
Penn Beacon 427
Penn Moor
NATIONAL PARK
Brent Moor
Black Tor
Dockwell Fm
Gidley Br
Staverton
South Devon Railway
Red Post
Tally Ho
Uphempston
Riverford Br
Hood Ball
Pennywell Farm
Staverton
Huxham's Cross
Dartington Hall
Harford Moor
Three Barrows 461
Ugborough Moor
Old Hill
Shipley Br
Bloody Pool
Eden Fm
Dean Prior
Yelland Fm
Dartington
Old Manor
Shadrack
Loventor Manor
Littlehempston
Dendles Waste
Dendles Wood
Badworthy
Didworthy
Brent Hill 311
Harbourneford
A38
Brownston Fm
Billany Fm
Week
Dartington Cider Press Cen
Shinner's Bridge
Totnes Rare Breeds Farm
Gatcombe Brook
Berry Pomeroy Castle
Berry Castle Lodge
Wildw
Colchmoor Gate
Rook Tor
Hele Cross
Sharp Tor
Ball Gate 317
Brent Fore Hill
Ball Gate
Lutton
White-oxen Manor
Willing Fm
Rattery
Yarner Beacon
Cott
Longcause
Totnes Riverside
Berry Pomeroy
Newpark Waste
Quick Br
Piall Br
Torr Wisdome Fm
Yadsworthy Fm
Piles Hill 387
Aish Ridge
Corringdon Ball
Leigh Grange
Syon Abbey
Mill Cross
South Downs
A385
Culverlane
Brook Ho
Whiteley Fm
Tigley
Fork Cross
Totnes
True Street
Bridgetown
A385
Delamore Ho
Yondertown
Cornwood
Lutton
Hall Cross
Hall Fm
Harford
Tor Rocks
Ugborough Beacon 371
Owley
Hillside
Aish
Lydia Br
South Brent
Ind Est
Brent Mill
Crowder Park
B3372
Lisburne Fm
Harbourne River
Totnes Castle
St Mary's Church
Webland Fm
Yeo Br
Sandwell Old Manor
Belsford
Tristford Ho
Hanger Down
Butterdon Hill 364
Eastern Beacon
River Avon
Charford Manor
Langford Fm
East Moore Fm
Aish
Moor Cross
Weatherdon Hill
Cheston
Horsebrook
Avonwick
Lincombe
Harberton
Bennett's Cross
Stancombe
Coombe Park Fm
Henlake Down 212
Moorhaven Village
Wrangaton
Cannamore Fm
Black Hall
Baron's Hill Fm
Bradridge Ho
Lower Venton Fm
Mark's Br
Cadleigh Lodge
Woodland
Ivybridge
Bittaford
Trad Est
B3213
Venn Ho
Kitterford Cross
North Huish
Diptford
Thorn Fm
Prowse's Luscombe
Maryland Ho
Harbertonford
Ashprington
Stoke Gabriel
St Austin's Priory
Lee Mill
Filham
Hillhead Cross
Ugborough
Christone Cross
Murtwell
Rolster Br
Beenleigh
Bow
Tuckenhay
Bow Creek
A38
Hunsdon Fm
Ind Est
Bus Pk
Wood Fm
Well Cross
Combeshead Cross
Greyhills Fm
Ball Hill
Hernaford
Stonehills
Cornworthy
Smithaleigh
Godwell
The Donkey Sanctuary
Fowlescombe Gate
Coombe Ho
Bickham Br
Crabadon
Higher Poulston
Middle Washbourne
River Wash
East Cornworthy
Southwood Wood
Marjery Cross
Penquit
Ludbrook
Coarsewell
SOUTH
DEVON
Crabadon Cross
Washbourne
Southhills Fm
Popple's Br
Lotherton
Worston
A3121
Higher Spriddlescombe
B3196
Lupridge
Gara Br
Curtisknowle
Black Down
Boreston
Halwell
Allaleigh
Capton
Yeo Fm
Stonycross
Westlake
Ermington
Ludbrook Manor
Weeke Fm
Shilston Br
Yarnacombe Fm
California Cross
Coldharbour Cross
Hazelwood
Stoneleigh Manor
Moreleigh
Moreleigh Mount
A3122
Bus Pk
Dreyton Cross
Stone Fm
Hollowcombe Fm
Ermington Wood
Mary Cross
Brownston
East Leigh
Storridge Wood
Stanborough Ho
Oldstone
Woodlands Family Theme Park
Wadstray Ho
Hillfield
A3122
Yealmbridge
Dunstone
A379
Butland Wood
Ind Est
Modbury
Babland Fm
Polston Parks
Churchland Green
Blackwell Park Fm
Stanborough Hundred
Woodbury Fm
Torr
Hole Fm
Stoliford
Higher Wizaller Fm
Woolston Ho
Topsham Br
Wotton
Hendham Ho
Torr Brook
Wood Fm
Blackawton
Cotterbury Cross
Holbeton
Ford
Heathfield Manor
Whympston
Cuttery Fm
Green Lane End
Woolcombe Fm
Hutcherleigh
Woodford
Creacombe
Luson
Borough Fm
Wastor
Tor Rock
Seven Stones Cross
Highland Fm
Tetwell
Wakeham
Fernhill Ho
Heath Fm
Ham Fm
B3196
Morecombe Fm
Pitt Fm
Yetsonais Fm
Higher Poole Fm
Pasture Fm
Millcombe
Larcombe Fm
Shepleigh Court
Eastdown
Ash
Bow
Battisborough Cross
Langston
Combe Fm
Yanston Fm
Barnston Fm
Abbotsleigh
Alston Hall
Haye Fm
Kingston
South Langston
Ashford
Loddiswell
Woodleigh
East Allington
Lower Coombe Fm
Wallaton Cross
Nutcombe Fm
SOUTH
Burlestone
West Combe Fm
Combe Cross
Mothecombe
Malthouse Pt
Wonwell Court Fm
B3392
Icy Park
Aveton Gifford
New Br
Torr
Ind Est
Torr Fm
Gara Mill
Anchorite's Rock
Okenbury
St Ann's Chapel
Waterhead
Warcombe
Higher Norton Fm
Thorn
Dearswell
DEVON
Hansel
Merrifield
Whitestone Cross
Strete
Wadham Rocks
Erme Mouth
Butcher's Rock
Mary's Rocks
Castle Fm
Easton
Bigbury Court
Bridge End
Venn
Sorley
Slade
Ledstone
A381
Cross
Cole's Cross
Flear Fm
Pinhey's Cross
Goveton
Pilcha
7
South West Coast Path
Beacon Pt
Bigbury
Ringmore
River Avon
Stadbury Fm
Hatch
Bus Pk
A379
Coombe Fm
Lower Green Cross
Aymer Cove
Toby's Pt
Churchstow
Malston Mill
Stancombe Cross
Valley Springs
Challaborough
Warren Pt
Folly Hill
Cookworthy Mus
Westville
Ind Est
Dodbrooke Shop Cen
Marepark Cross
Harleston
Start
Slapton
Slapton Sands
Bigbury-on-Sea
Burgh Island
Huxton Cross
West Alvington
Kingsbridge
Sherford
Frittiscombe
Coleridge Ho
France Wood
Slapton Ley
BIGBURY BAY
Butter Cove
Murray's Rock
Bantham
Buckland
Kerse Fm
Upton
South Milton
Ticket Wood
Southville
East Charleton
Frogmore
Chillington
Stokenham
Lower Ley
South West Coast Path
Thurlestone
Pack Fm
Charleton
West Charleton
Mill Fm
A379
Carehouse Cross
Torcross
Limpet Rocks
Warren Pt
Horswell Ho
Sutton
Oldaway Fm
Woolston
Gerston Fm
Gerston Pt
Kingsbridge Estuary
Thurlestone Rock
South Huish
Davey Park Fm
Ham Pt
Frogmore Creek
North Pool Fm
Kernborough
Cotmore
Burleigh Fm
Alston Fm
Wareham Pt
Beacon Pt
Woolman Pt
Outer Hope
Hope Cove
Galmpton
Withymore Fm
Tosnos Pt
Ford
Dunstone
South Pool
Beeson
Beesands
SX
Bolt Tail
Inner Hope
Salcombe Road
Southpool Creek
9
Middlecombe Fm
Redrot Cove
Hope
Bolberry
Malborough
Batson
Kellaton
Collaton
Salcombe
Salcombe Maritime Mus
East Portlemouth
Chivelstone
Bickerton
Hallsands
Southdown Fm
West Cliff
Slippery Pt
Combe
Rew
South Allington
Hollowcombe Head
Nestley Pt
0 1 2 3 miles
0 1 2 3 4 5 km
A B C D E F G H
1 2 3 4 5 6

Netherton
Combeinteignhead
Shaldon Wildlife Trust
The Ness Ho
The Beacon
Buckland
Newtake
Haccombe
Wolborough
Milber
Labrador Bay
Aller Park
Lower Gabwell
Higher Gabwell
Abbotskerswell
Coffinswell
Blackaller's Cove
Aller
Daccombe
Kingskerswell
Maidencombe
Rock Ho
Bell Rock
Watcombe Head
Stoneycombe
Barton
Watcombe
Dainton
St Marychurch
North Whilborough
Edginswell
Bygones
BABBACOMBE BAY
Hele
Babbacombe
Shiphay
Compton
Torre
Torquay
Ellacombe
Black Head
Kent's Cavern
Chelston
Cockington
Wellswood
Anstey's Cove
Marldon
Lead Stone or Flat Rock
Living Coasts
Thatcher Rock
Daddyhole Cove
Peaked Tor Cove
Churscombe
Shorton
Preston
Livermead
Hollicombe
Paignton
Blagdon
Oldway
TOR BAY
Collaton St Mary
St Michaels
Roundham Head
Paignton Zoo
Goodrington Sands
Splashdown Quaywest
Goodrington
Saltern Cove
Yalberton
Broadsands
Elberry Cove
Fishcombe Pt
Port Bridge
Berry Head
Waddeton
Galmpton
Brixham Heritage Museum
The Golden Hind
Churston Ferrers
Cod Rock
Durl Head
Brixham
Higher Brixham
St Mary's Bay
Dittisham
Greenway
Sharkham Pt
Dartmouth Steam Railway
Southdown Cliff
Hillhead
SOUTH DEVON
Man Sands
Crabrock Pt
Cod Rocks
Long Sands
Woodhuish Fm
Dartmouth
Scabbacombe Sands
Scabbacombe Head
Kingston
Coleton Fishacre Gdn
Kingswear
Norton
Warfleet
Ivy Cove
Dartmouth Castle
Pudcombe Cove
Kelly's Cove
Eastern Black Rock
Outer Froward Pt
Blackstone Pt
Stoke Fleming
Combe Pt
Meg Rocks
Blackpool
START BAY
Woolston
Charleton
Torcross
Limpet Rocks
South Huish
Kingsbridge Estuary
Ham Pt
Frogmore Creek
Kernborough
Wareham Pt
Beeson
Galmpton
Ford
Dunstone
Beesands
Tosnos Pt
South Pool
Bolberry
Malborough
Batson
Kellaton
Collaton
Salcombe
East Portlemouth
Chivelstone
Bickerton
Hallsands
Hollowcombe Head
South Allington
Nestley Pt
Combe
Rew
West Cliff
Soar
Mill Bay
South Sands
Catholic Cliff
Overbecks Museum & Garden
Start Pt
Lantern Rock
Black Stone
Shag Rock
Deckler's Cliff
Gorah Rocks
Sleadon Rocks
East Prawle
Ballsaddle Rock
Bolt Head
Little Mew Stone
Ball Rock
Gammon Head
Langerstone Pt
Prawle Pt
Sharpers Head

10
2
3
4
5
6
A
B
C
D
E
F
G
H
1
80
00
SW
70
The Island
Tintagel Head
Dunderhole Pt
TINTAGEL
Penhallic Pt
Gull Rock
Port William
Dennis Pt
Backways Cove
Start Pt
Trerubies Cove
Tregardock Cliff
Jacket's Pt
Crookmoyle Rock
Delabole Pt
Dannonchapel
Port Isaac Bay
Barrett's Zawn
Ranie Pt
SOUTH WEST COAST PATH
Varley Head
Kellan Head
Scamor Pt
Lobber Pt
Tresungers Pt
Port Gaverne
Trewetha
Treore Fm
B3267
Pine Haven
Reedy Cliff
Port Isaac
Port Quin
Doyden Pt
Port Quin Bay
Trevan Pt
Carnweather Pt
The Mouls
Rumps Pt
Com Head
Newland
Pentire Pt
83
Pentire Fm
Scarrabine Fm
Porteath
Plain Street
Trelights
Pendoggett
Poltreworgey
Pentireglaze Haven
Padstow Bay
New Polzeath
Hayle Bay
Trenant
Polzeath
Carruan
Shilla Mill
St Endellion
Gunvenna
Gulland Rock
Pepper Hole
Stepper Pt
The Narrows
Butter Hole
Gunver Head
Trebetherick
Harbour Cove
Daymer Bay
Trewiston Fm
Trevanger
Treglyn Down
Pennytinney
Lanow Fm
Tregellist
Trelill
Pityme
St Minver
Trevine
Trewethern
Trequite
Tredrizzick
St Kew
Greater Brighter Fm
Trevose Head
Stinking Cove
Merope Rocks
Round Hole
Mother Ivey's or Polventon Bay
Porthmissen Bridge
Crugmeer
Tregirls Fm
Trebetherick Pt
Gun Pt
Splatt
Penmayne
Treglyn Fm
Rooke Fm
Chapel Amble
Carclaze Fm
Quies
Dinas Head
Trevone Bay
Round Hole
Trethillick
PRIDEAUX PLACE
Rock
Trefresa Fm
Blakes Keiro
B3314
Harlyn Bay
Trevone
Harlyn
Treator
Stoptide
Porthilly Cove
Porthilly
Penpont Fm
Hendra
St Kew Highway
Booby's Bay
Constantine Bay
Constantine Bay
B3276
Padstow
PADSTOW MUSEUM
Town Bar
Gutt Bridge
Lower Amble
Treworman
Trevelver
Trethevan Fm
Treyarnon Pt
Ind Est
Windmill
Dinas
NATIONAL LOBSTER HATCHERY
Trethias Island
Warren Cove
Pepper Cove
Fox Cove
TREYARNON BAY
Treyarnon
Towan
Trewithen Fm
Treravel Fm
St Merryn
A389
Dennis Hill
Oldtown
Oldtown Cove
Cant Cove
River Camel
River Amble
Tregorden
Kelly
A39
Rocksea Fm
Dinham's Br
Trehemborne
Carnevas
Trevorrick
Shop
Sea Mills
Tregonce
Trevorrick
Trevilgus Fm
Bodellick
Tregunna
Perlees Fm
Trevanson
Burniere
Bodieve
Ball
Three Holes Cross
Minnows Islands
Will's Rock
Porthcothan Bay
Highlanes
CORNWALL
Burgois
Edmonton
Dunveth
Ind Est
Trenant
St Mabyn
Trescore Islands
Trevean
Tregonna
Whitecross
Penhale
Wadebridge
Hingham Mill
Trevilder
Trethick Fm
Porthcothan
Trevethan
Porth Mear
Trevio
Treburick Fm
Little Petherick
Mellingey
Trevance
St Issey
ROYAL CORNWALL SHOWGROUND
St Breock
Egloshayle
Clapper
Sladesbridge
Lower Croan
Croanford
PENCARROW HOUSE
High Cove
Trevemedar
Treburrick
Lewidden
St Merryn Airfield (disused)
Treglinnick
Treleigh Fm
Tregingey Fm
B3274
Trenance
Trevear Fm
Tredruston Fm
Trelyll Fm
Polmorla
Treraven
Tredannick
Park
Trescowe Brake
Park Head
Effins
Penrose
Pentruse Fm
Blable Ho
Hay
Pengelly Fm
River Camel
Costislost
Bozion Fm
Diggory's Island
Tregona
St Ervan
Rumford
Tredinnick
Pawton Manor Fm
Bishop's Wood
Polgeel Wood
Queen Bess Rock
BEDRUTHEN STEPS
Trerair Fm
Bogee Fm
St Jidgey
Cannalidgey
Hustyn Wood
Burlorne
Tregoose
Polbrock
Washaway
Lane-end
Downhill
Trevisker Fm
CAMEL CREEK ADVENTURE PARK
Mount Charles
St Eval Airfield (disused)
St Eval
Bear's Downs
Long Stone
Trelow Downs
Scotland Corner
208
Higher
Brocton
Penaligon Downs
High Cove
Trenance Pt
Bogee
0
1
2
3 miles
0
1
2
3
4
5 km

7
8
9
10
11
12
24
5
6
A
B
C
D
E
F
G
H
Black Rock
Wanson Mouth
Wanson
Widemouth Fm
Box's
Budd's Titson
Titson
Langford Barton
Marhayes Manor
Merrifield
Bradford Manor
Coppathorne
Burracott
Bakesdown
Tankins Fm
Strawberry Bank
Foxhole Pt
Millook Haven
Millook
Penhalt Fm
Causewell
Penfound Manor
Furze Fm
Poundstock
Bangors
Odd Mill
Thorne
Westcott Plantn
Dizzard Pt
Trevoulter Fm
Thinwood Fm
Plymswood Fm
Steele Hill
Whitstone Head
Whitstone
West Balsdon
Affaland Wood
Elgar Wood
River Tamar
Dizzard
Treskinnick Cross
Tregole
Barton Hele
Swannacott Wood
Wadfast
Blagdon Manor Fm
Tamar
Tarragon
Trengayor
Meads Fm
Penhallym
Week Green
Week St Mary
Newpark
Haydon Moor Plantns
Pencannow Pt
St Genny's
Crackington Haven
Trewint
PENHALLAM
Reeve Ho
Greena Moor
Street
Way Fm
North Tamerton
Bray's Pt
Tremoutha Haven
Chilpark
Trewergie Barton
Coxford
Trencreek
Treforda
Sudcott
GREENA MOOR
Semersdon Fm
Trelay
Ash
Willsworthy Cross
Dipper Fm
Suttondown Plantn
Ogbeare Hall
Samphire Rock
Middle Crackington
Mineshope
Higher Crackington
Rosecare
Jacobstow
Kents
Southcott
Sweets
Creddacott Fm
Greenamoor Br
Alvacott
Wainhouse Corner
A39
Tobarn
High Cliff
Pengold
Hill
Pencuke
Rosecare Villa Fm
Higher Whiteleigh
Brendon Barton
Villaton Fm
Beardon Plantn
Roundhayes Fm
Headon
Middle Wheatley
Exe
Newton Fm
Copper Fm
Cansford Fm
West Curry
Curry Lane
Beardon
Gull Rock
Collamoor Head
Trengune
Exemoor Fm
Maxworthy Cross
Underhill
SOUTH WEST COAST PATH
Tresparrett Posts
South Wheatley
Cauldworthy Water
Maxworthy
Clubworthy
Fire Beacon Pt
Langdon
Darracott Park
Beeny Cliff
Seals Hole
Ringford Fm
Tresparrett Down
Witheven
Canworthy
Cauldworthy Bridge
Tascott Fm
North Beer
Beeny
Cockport
Trevillian
Trenannick
Copthorne
Bennacott
Boscastle
B3263
Tremorle
Tresparrett
Marshgate
Caroe
Kernick Fm
Hendra
Canworthy Water
Winsdon
Penally Pt
Hennett
Tredown
Fonston
Troswell
Langdon Fm
Museum of Witchcraft & Magic
Forrabury
Grower Rock
Short Island
Long Island
Welltown Manor
Treworld
Trebiffin
Lesnewth
River Valency
Otterham
Otterham Mill
Fentrigan
Warbstow Cross
Warbstow
Gorracott
Brazacott
Godcott
Lye Rock
Bossiney Haven
Trevalga
Trehane Fm
Polrunny Fm
Otterham Down
Hallgarden
Trelash
Tredarrup
Downinney
Elmfield
Braywood Fm
Billacott
Forda
Langdon
Tredorn Fm
Otterham Station
Youlstone
Trillacott
Bittens Fm
Ind Est
North Petherwin
Tamar Otter & Wildlife Centre
Langdon Cross
Tintagel Castle
Trethevy
St Nectan's Glen
Tredole Fm
Tregatherall Fm
Coppiestone Fm
Trewonnard
Trussell
Westcott
Tremaine
Petherwin Gate
Treforda
Reddivallen
Halwill Barton
Sedan Fm
Cornwall at War Museum
Treglith
Splatt
Treburtle
River Ottery
Halgabron
Bossiney
Tintagel
Old Post Office
Cardew
Tregeen
Lane End
Three Hammers
Trehummer
Treludick
Penheale Manor
Weston
Hellescott Bridge
Treneglos
Grovetoe
Hendraburnick
Hendraburnick Down
Davidstow
Hallworthy
Wilsey Down
Lanzion
Trebeath
Tregeardown Beacon
Beepark Copse
Underwood
Treven
Tregatta
Truas
Waterpit Down
Tresoke
Trelay
Kensey
Tresmeer
219
Egloskerry
Trewarmett
Condolden Fm
Trewassa
Tremail
Kittow's Moor
Badgall
Badharlick
Langore
B3263
Trevilla Park
Starapark
Treglasta Fm
Cold Northcott
Badgall Downs
Torrpark
Tregeare
Trebarwith
Penpethy
Higher Trether Fm
The Vale of Avalon
Higher Tremail Fm
Tredwen Barton
River Inny
A395
Napp's Moor
High Hall
Tregeare Down
Athill Fm
Trewithick
Truscott
Gall Hill
Trenouth Fm
B3314
Collan's Cross
Davidstow Moor Airfield (disused)
Red Down
Newmills
Slaughterbridge
Trevivian
Launceston Steam Railway
Treligga
Rockhead
Trenuth Fm
Ta Mill
River Kensey
Newmills
The Hidden Valley Discovery Park
Higher Trevallett Fm
Delabole
Trethern Fm
Davidstow Woods
Basil Fm
St Clether
Treven
Laneast
Laneast Downs
Old Tree Ho
Pengelly
Camelford
A39
Tregoodwell
Davidstow Moor
Trevillian's Gate
Piper's Pool
Tregadillett
Westdown Road
Trevia
Hendra
Crowdy Reservoir
New Park Fm
Trecollas Fm
Lower Tregunnon
Gimblett's Mill
Trethorne Leisure Park
Trebursye Manor
Trewen
Bowithick
Penpont
Higher Tregunnon
Trewen
Kennards House
Daw's House
Newhall Manor
Lanteglos
Valley Truckle
Pencarrow
Aldermoor Fm
Roughtor Fm
Lower Moor
Lanlavery Rock
324
Oldpark
Pennydevern
Bray Down
346
Trebray
Water
Treween
Trenarrett
Trethinna
Hicks Mill
Holyway Cross
Penfoot
Tramagenna
Trewalder
Buttern Hill
346
Oldhay
Trerithick
Trecongdon
West Petherwin
Trewennan
Treforda
Watergate
Tresinney
Little Rough Tor
Rough Tor
400
High Moor
Trekennick Tor
Newhay
Polyphant
Two Bridges
Botathan
South Petherwin
B3267
Treveilley
Highertown
Poldue Downs
South Carne
St Nonna's Church
Tredaule
Tregillis
Helstone
Maiden Tor
Leskernick Hill
329
Wesley's Cottage
Fivelanes
Altarnun
Lewannick
Knightsmill
Tregreenwell
Widewalls Fm
New Hall
Louden Hill
Roughtor Moors
Brown Willy
420
Trewint Downs
Trewint
Trebant
Tinney Hall
Trewanta Hall Fm
Treliaske Ho
St Teath
Tor
Wesley Cottage
A30
Plusha
Treveighan
Helsbury Fm
Trenilk
Trenanick
Treburgett
Harpur's Downs
Candra Hill
Brownwilly Downs
Codda Tor
The Beacon
369
Tregenna
Trevague
Treburland
Trevadlock
Example Cross
Drinnick Fm
Trewinnow Cross
Alex Tor
294
Casehill Downs
Garrow Downs
331
Butters Tor
316
Bodmin
Poldhu
Tregune
Fox Tor
323
Upton Barton
River Lynher
Larrick
Tregawn
Corgelly Fm
Catshole Tor
345
Codda
Illand
Michaelstow
Fentonadle
Wood Park
Treswallock Downs
King Arthur's Downs
Garrow Tor
Moor
Halvana Plantn
Tolcarne Tor
Trenhorne
Congdon's Shop
Newtown
Trenewth
Pengelly
Trevenning
Tuckingmill
Churchtown
King Arthur's Hall
Emblance Downs
Scribble Downs
Priddacombe Downs
Tolborough
East Moor
Ridge
Trebartha
Coad's Green
Langstone
Lanoy
Gam
Lamphill Woods
Penwood Ho
Butterstor Downs
Palmersbridge
Carey Tor
Bastreet Downs
Glubhole Fm
Trewithey
Treween
St Breward
Penrose
Lady Down
Row
Carkees Tor
Shallow Water Common
Roughlands Fm
Jamaica Inn (Hotel)
Museum of Smuggling
Bolventor
Rushyford Gate
Withey Brook
Hawk's Tor
329
Castick Fm
North Hill
Penhole
Trefrize
St Tudy
Loskeyle Fm
Delford Br
Carbilly Tor
266
Hawk's Tor
307
Toddy Park
River Fowey
Treworth Tor
Twelve Men's Moor
Berriowbridge
Lank
De Lank River
Stripple Stones
Hawkstor Downs
Brockabarrow Common
Stanning Hill
Minzies Downs
Dozmary Hill
Trezibbett
Smallacoombe Downs
Kilmar Tor
396
Middlewood
Kingbeare
Bathpool
North Coombe Fm
Clampit
B3257
Tresquare
Wenfordbridge
13½
Bradford
Hawk's Tor Fm
Bearah Tor
Kerrow
Menacrin Downs
Bois Ho
Dozmary Pool
Newel Tor
344
Botternell
Pengelly
Penpont
Pendrift
Metherin
Temple New Br
Gillhouse Downs
Harrowbridge Hill Fm
Ninestones Fm
Patrieda Barton
Poley's Br
Keybridge
Merry Meeting
Carwen
Temple Tor
Sharptor
North Darley
Rillaton
B3266
Longstone
Bodrigan
Spittal
Tresarrett
Blisland
Temple
Blacktor Downs
Simon's Stone
Brown Gelly
342
Hill Tor
Henwood
Rilla Mill
Trequites
Helligan Barton
Helligan Wood
Waterloo
Merrifield
Browngelly Downs
Stowe's Hill
381
Darleyford
Netherton
Upton
Withey Brook
Withybrook Marsh
Sterts Arts Centre
Upton Cross
Plushabridge
Browda
Shell Woods
Coldrinnick Woods
Trehudreth Downs
Bunning's Park
Collford Lake
Westerlake Fm
Sparretts Fm
The Hurlers Stone Circles
Dunslea
Ley Mill
Caradon Town
Tredethy
Cardinham Moor
Hard Head
Redhill Downs
Lord's Park Fm
Caradon Mining District
Downgate
Hellandbridge
Colvannick Tor
Colliford Downs
Craddock Moor
Minions
Caradon Hill
369
Colquite Woods
Broads Fm
Helland
Carburrow Tor
Redhill Downs
Draynes Common
Siblyback Lake
Tokenbury Manor
Scrawsdon Fm
Higher Carblake
Bodmin
Praze
Millpool
St Bellarmin's Tor
Maidenwell
Letter Moor
Crylla Fm
Gonamena
Pensilva
SX
70
30
Racecourse Downs
Trago
Whitebarrow Fm
Mutton's Downs
Tokenbury Corner
Helland Wood
Cardinham Downs
Fore Downs
Warleggan Down
Hobb's Hill
282
Northwood
Worthy
Darite
Middlehill
Ind Est
Charaton Cross
Outlands Wood
Racecourse Fm
Lidcutt Wood
Milltown
Cardinham
Pantersbridge
Warleggan
Carpuan
Berry Down
Draynes
Golitha Falls
King Doniert's Inscribed Stone
Higher Tremarcoombe
Trethevy Quoit
Crow's Nest
Clerkenw
East Wood
Deviock Wood
Treslea Downs
Carne Wood
Tremaddock Fm
Trenant
Treworrick
Trecarne
St Cleer
Tremar
Woolston
St Petroc's Church
Callywith Wood
Old Cardinham
Mount
St Neot
Rosecraddoc Manor
Wayland
Gang
SX
00
30
B3254
Tamar
Langdon
Langore
Tregillis
B3254
Notter

Launceston
Tavistock
Lifton
Lydford
Tinhay
Milton Abbot
Gunnislake
Calstock
Horrabridge
Mary Tavy
Peter Tavy
Bridestowe
Sourton
Halwill
Beaworthy
Ashwater
Clawton
Tamar Valley
Cornwall
Roadford Lake
A30
A386
A388
A390
A3079
B3254
B3257
B3362
Kelly Bray
Callington
St Dominick
Bere Alston
Lewdown
Chillaton
Lamerton
Sydenham Damerel
Stoke Climsland
Coryton
Broadwoodwidger
Germansweek
Whitchurch
Grenofen
Walkhampton
Dousland
Buckland Monachorum
Cotehele
Morwellham Quay
Tamar Valley Mining District
Launceston Steam Railway
Tavistock Museum
Lydford Castle
Lydford Gorge
Dingle's Fairground Heritage Centre
Tamar Otter & Wildlife Centre
Sourton Cross Services
0 1 2 3 miles
0 1 2 3 4 5 km

Exbourne
Sampford Courtenay
North Tawton
Sampford Chapple
Okehampton
Museum of Dartmoor Life
Okehampton Castle
Okehampton Bracken Tor
Belstone
Sticklepath
Finch Foundry
South Tawton
South Zeal
Whiddon Down
Spreyton
Hittisleigh
Cheriton Bishop
Crockernwell
Drewsteignton
Castle Drogo
Sandypark
Easton
Chagford
Gidleigh
Murchington
Wonson
Throwleigh
Teigncombe
Kestor Rock 436
Frenchbeer
Moretonhampstead
Doccombe
Dunsford
Colebrooke
Coleford
Yeoford
Hillerton
Itton
Taw Green
Okehampton Camp 436
Meldon
Meldon Reservoir
Yes Tor 619
High Willhays 621
Black-a-Tor Copse
Cosdon Hill
Hangingstone Hill 604
Cut Hill 604
D E V O N
D A R T M O O R
N A T I O N A L
P A R K
Fernworthy Reservoir
Fernworthy Forest
Sittaford Tor 537
Quintin's Man 552
Whitehorse Hill 601
Chagford Common
Water Hill 489
Warren House Inn
Grimspound (Earthwork)
Hameldown Tor 529
North Bovey
Lettaford
Manaton
Lustleigh
Becky Falls Woodland Park
Hound Tor
Haytor Vale
Haytor Information Centre
Widecombe in the Moor
Postbridge
Postbridge Information Centre
Clapper Bridge
Bellever
Wistman's Wood
Merrivale Prehistoric Settlement
Rundlestone
Two Bridges
Princetown
National Park Visitor Centre
HM Prison
Dartmeet
Hexworthy
Ponsworthy
Poundsgate
Buckland in the Moor
Ilsington
Liverton
Sigford
Bickington
Ashburton
Holne
Woodland
Whiteworks
Sheepstor
Burrator Reservoir
Bovey Tracey Heritage Centre
House of Marbles
East Dartmoor Woods & Heaths
Dartmoor Expedition Centre
Brimley
A30
A382
A386
B3212
A38
SX
80
00
70

Crediton
Thorverton
Shobrooke
Efford
Raddon
Berrysbridge
Ellerhayes
Killerton House
Nether Exe
Rewe
Columbjohn
Budlake
Clyst Hydon
Clyst St Lawrence
Westwood
Hollacombe
Neopardy
Salmonhutch
Fordton
Uton
Hookway
Sweetham
Newton St Cyres
Brampford Speke
Nettacott
Stoke Canon
Brookleigh
Venny Tedburn
Upton Pyne
Half Moon Village
West Town
Langford
Pye Corner
Huxham
Ratsloe
Poltimore
Broadclyst
Dog Village
Jack in the Green
Hand and Pen
Cowley
Cranbrook
Rockbeare
Tedburn St Mary
Town Barton
Heath Cross
Whitestone
Pathfinder Village
Halsfordwood
Nadderwater
Exwick
Duryard
Pennsylvania
Stoke Hill
Pinhoe
Blackhorse
Clyst Honiton
Exeter International
Marsh Green
Exeter
Polsloe
Whipton
Monkerton
Heavitree
Sowton
Aylesbeare
Brook
Bilsdon
Longdown
Wheatley
St Thomas
Redhills
Wonford
Sandy Gate
Clyst St Mary
Farringdon
Ide
Alphington
Countess Wear
Nine Oaks
Dunsford
Reedy
Butts
Shillingford Abbot
Clyst St George
Woodbury Salterton
Shillingford St George
Topsham
Ebford
Exminster
Sowton Barton
Dunchideock
Clapham
Bridfordmills
Bridford
Doddiscombsleigh
Kennford
Exton
Woodbury
Kenn
Christow
Court Barton
Bennah
Underdown
Lympstone
Powderham
Kenton
Higher Ashton
Lower Ashton
Trusham
Harcombe
Starcross
Exmouth
Withycombe Raleigh
Littleham
The Point
Hennock
Chudleigh
Ashcombe
Cockwood
Dawlish Warren
Bovey Tracey
Chudleigh Knighton
Ideford
Luton
Dawlish
Brimley
Ilsington
Heathfield
Liverton
Coldeast
Blackpool
Preston
Sandygate
Bishopsteignton
Holcombe
Teigngrace
Kingsteignton
Teignmouth
Shaldon
Highweek
Newton Abbot
Lower Netherton
Combeinteignhead
Netherton
Stokeinteignhead
Buckland
Milber
Wolborough
West Ogwell
East Ogwell
Aller Park
Abbotskerswell
Coffinswell
Kingskerswell
Maidencombe
River Exe
River Teign
3 miles
5 km

Payhembury
Awliscombe
Raleigh
ALLHALLOWS MUSEUM
Northcote
Mount Pleasant
Lower Ridge
Ham
Hawley Bottom
Smallridge
Higher Cheriton
Colestocks
Buckerell
Honiton
Littletown
Cleave
Wilmington
Dalwood
Weycroft
Newtown
Talaton
Talewater
Feniton
Hamlet
Offwell
Widworthy
Axminster
Fenny Bridges
Gittisham
Alfington
Millbrook
Larkbeare
Gosford
Blannicombe
Shute
Kilmington
Fairmile
Coombelake
Taleford
Woodford
Watchcombe
Umborne
Tricombe
Northleigh
Hampton
Wyke Green
Ottery St Mary
Church Green
Farway
Seaton Junction
Whitford
Maidenhayne
Trill
Raleigh
Woodbridge
Musbury
West Hill
Broad Oak
Wiggaton
Fluxton
Colyton
Kingsdon
Road Green
Southleigh
Holcombe
Higher Metcombe
Metcombe
Venn Ottery
Tipton St John
Cotford
Sidbury
Holyford
Colyford
Combpyne
Rousdon
St Dympna's
Seaton
Axmouth
Southerton
Harpford
Bowd
Sidford
Harcombe
Burrow
Bridge End
Trow
Street
Hawkerland
Goosemoor
Newton Poppleford
Northmostown
Stowford
Salcombe Regis
Weston
Beer
SEATON BAY
Vicarage
Branscombe
Bulverton
Sid
Kingston
Colaton Raleigh
Cotmaton
Sidmouth
Beer Head
DORSET & EAST DEVON COAST
Chit Rocks
High Peak
Tortoiseshell Rocks
Big Picket Rock
Hern Point Rock
Ladram Bay
Smallstones Pt
Chiselbury Bay
North Star
Otterton
East Budleigh
Brandy Head
Black Head
Danger Pt
Kersbrook
Knowle
Little Knowle
Budleigh Salterton
FAIRLYNCH ARTS CENTRE & MUSEUM
Dunscombe Cliff
Weston Cliff
Littlecombe Shoot
Haven Cliff
Culverhole Pt
Dowlands Cliffs and Landslips
AXMOUTH TO LYME REGIS UNDERCLIFFS
Humble Pt
E A S T   D E V O N
A30
A35
A3052
A375
B3174
B3176
B3178
B3172
SY
7
8
9
10
11
A
B
C
D
E
F
G
H
16
27
28

All Saints
Holditch
Smallridge
Waggs Plot
Wadbrook
Castle
Tudhay
Hawkchurch
Brimley
Tillworth
Weycroft
Millway Rise
Axminster
Millbrook
Sector
Blackpool Corner
Marshwood
Lambert's Castle Hill
Birdsmoorgate
Marshalsea
Bettiscombe
Pilsdon
Pilsdon Pen
Cockpit Hill 277
Lewesdon Hill 272
Redlands Yard
Waddon Hill
Beaminster
Beaminster Museum
Shortmoor
Toller Whelme
Stoke Abbott
Stoke Water
Whitecross
Netherbury
Mapperton
Hooke
North Bowood
Lower Strode
South Bowood
Monkwood
Furleigh Cross
Melplash
North Poorton
South Poorton
Loscombe
Kingsland
Waytown
Oxbridge
Hincknowle
Salwayash
Camesworth
Lambrook
The Mount
Powerstock
West Milton
Nettlecombe
Mangerton
Wooth
Dottery
Pymore
Bradpole
Loders
Uploders
Eggardon Hill 252
D O R S E T
Broad Oak
Bluntshay
Abbey Gate
Wyke Green
Raymond's Hill
Monkton Wyld
Champernhayes Marsh
Wootton Fitzpaine
Whitchurch Canonicorum
Ryall
Morcombelake
North Chideock
Symondsbury
Allington
Court Orchard
Coneygar
St Andrew's Well
Bridport
Bridport Museum
Yondover
Askerswell
Spyway
Walditch
Bothenhampton
Shipton Gorge
Chilcombe
Skilling
Watton
Eype
Higher Eype
Lower Eype
Eype's Mouth
West Bay
West Cliff
East Cliff
Burton Bradstock
Southover
Burton Cliff
Burton Mere
Puncknowle
Swyre
The Knoll 181
West Bexington
Dorset & East Devon Coast
South West Coast Path
Chideock
Seatown
Golden Cap 191
Langdon Hill
St Gabriel's Mouth
Wear Cliffs
Ridge Cliff
East Ebb Cove
Charmouth
Charmouth Heritage Coast Centre
Catherston Leweston
Penn
Harcombe Bottom
Fern Hill
Dragon's Hill
Uplyme
Yawl
Holcombe
Combpyne
Rousdon
Ware
Lyme Regis
Dinosaurland
Aquarium
Cobb
Seven Rock Pt
Pinhay Bay
Humble Pt
Axmouth to Lyme Regis Undercliffs
Dowlands Cliffs and Landslips
Trill
A35
A3052
B3165
B3157
B3162
B3163
A3066
DORCHESTER ROAD
WEST ROAD
L Y M E
B A Y
SY
70
30
0 1 2 3 miles
0 1 2 3 4 5 km
A B C D E F G H
1 2 3 4 5 6
15
28
29

Higher Wraxall
Wraxall
Lower Wraxall
Higher Chalmington
Chalmington
Up Sydling
Peak End Hill 207
Cerne Abbas Giant
Abbey
Cerne Abbas
Weam Common Hill
Cerne Park
Plush
Nettlecombe Fm
Lyscombe Fm
Higher Down
Tenant's Hill
Higher Southcombe Fm
Bramblecombe
Newton Fm
Gallows Corner
Long Close Fm
Sandhills
Castle Hill 183
Cattistock
Higher Kingcombe
Lower Kingcombe
Kingcombe Meadows Reserve
Lancombe Fm
Grove Stall Fm
Chilfrome
Whitesheet Hill
Dorchester Road
Folly Hill
Peak End Hill
Cowdown Hill
Higher City Fm
Sydling St Nicholas
Huish Fm
Hill Barn
Dickley Down
Smacam Down
Lower Barton Fm
Buck Hill 211
Green Hill
Pound Fm
Bow's Hill
Manor Ho
Piddletrenthide
Kingrove Bottom
Dole's Ash Fm
Thorncombe
Whitcombe Hill
Cheselbourne
Whitelands Downs
Dole's Hill Plantn
Cheselbourne West Down
Chebbard Fm
Dewlish
Parsonage Fm
Lawn Barn Fm
Bagber Fm
Deverel Fm
Toller Porcorum
Frogmore Fm
Tollerford
Maiden Newton
Fore Hill
Norden Hill
Combe Bottom
Combe Hill
South Field Hill
Ridge Hill
Nether Cerne
East Hill
College Down
White Lackington
Coombe Bottom
Toller Fratrum
Hog Cliff
Crete Hill
Magiston Hill
Bushes Barn
Godmanstone
Heave Coppice
Holcombe Bottom
Piddlehinton
Bourne Fm
Druce Higher Barn
Puddletown Down
Park Hill
Milborne Wood
Milborne St Andrew
Weatherby Castle
Colesmoor Fm
Ferndown Fm
Wynford Wood
Manor Fm
Wynford Eagle
Chammen's Hill
Hog Cliff Hill
Cruxton
South Field Hill
Magiston Fm
Forston Barn
Fairmile Fm
New Buildings
Little Puddle Bottom
Muston Fm
Little Puddle Hill
Hill's Copse
Basan Hill
Lower Fm
Milborne Wood Fm
Fryer's Br
Bardolf Manor
Devil's Brook
Hill Barn
Ashley Barn
Roger's Hill Fm
Shatcombe Fm
Crockway Fm
Frampton
Grimstone Down
Stratton Down
Forston
Charlton Higher Down
Wolfeton Clump
Peak Coppice
Laycock Fm
Waterston Manor
Druce Fm
Northbrook
West Compton
Wynford Ho
Round Hill Plants
Notton Hill Barn
Southover
Longlands Fm
Frampton Ho
Hog Hill
Haydon Hill
North Street
Charlton Down
Athelhampton
Burleston
Martyrs Museum
Tolpuddle
Grimstone
Stratton
Ash Hill
Leap Gate
Hill Barn
Home Fm
Troy Town Fm
Yellowham Wood
Puddletown
Green Hill
Athelhampton
Admiston Fm
Park Fm
South Ho
Affpuddle
Compton Valence
Littlewood Fm
Muckleford
Bradford Peverell
River Frome
Charminster
Grey's Wood
Higher Kingston Fm
Puddletown Forest
Puddletown Heath
Ilsington Wood
Southover Heath
Sares Wood
Affpuddle Heath
Dorset
Hogleaze Fm
Town Hill Fm
Penn Hill
Wolfeton House
Higher Burton Fm
Silver's Lane
Higher Bockhampton
Hardy's Cottage & Garden
Castle Hill
Tincleton
Clyffe Ho
Marl Pits Wood
Bryants Puddle Heath
Oakers Wood
Tout Hill
North Barn Fm
Kingston Russell
Lower Skippet Fm
Combe Bottom
Burton
Military Mus
Old Crown Court
County Mus
Stinsford
Kingston Maurward
Pine Lodge Fm
Norris Mill Fm
Snipe Moor
Pallington
Waddock Drove
Tutankhamun Mus
Poundbury
Dinosaur Museum
Kingston Maurward Animal Park & Gdns
Lower Bockhampton
Frome Mead
White Mead
Woodsford
Waddock Fm
Winterbourne Poor Lot Barrows
Martin's Down
Black Down
Winterbourne Abbas
Nine Stones
Lambert's Hill
Bradford Down
Dorchester
Litton Cheney
Long Bredy
North Hill
Winterbourne Steepleton
Dorchester West
Dorchester South
Maumbury Rings
Lower Lewell Fm
Hurst Heath
Hurst
Whatcombe Down
Lower Fm
River Bride
Littlebredy
White Hill
Loscombe Fm
Rew Manor
Max Gate
Frome Hill
West Stafford
Higher Woodsford
Moreton
Park's Dairy Fm
Tenants Hill
Littlebredy Fm
Old Warren
Sheep Down
Martinstown or Winterbourne St Martin
Hog Hill
Maiden Castle
Maiden Castle Fm
Conygar Hill
P&R
South Winterborne
Stafford Fm
Knighton Heath Wood
Crossways
Warmwell Road
Redbridge
West Lodge
Kingston Russell Stone Circle
Valley of Stones
Black Down
Goldcombe Fm
Hardy Monument
Crow Hill
Ashley Chase Ho
Gorwell Fm
Shorn Hill
Great Hill
Winterborne Monkton
Ashton Fm
Monkton Hill
Herrington Fm
Winterborne Herrington
Winterborne Came
Whitcombe Manor
Whitcombe
Lewell Lodge
Empool Heath
West Knighton
Holiday Pk
Outer Heath
Bus Pk
Mill House Cider Museum
Whitcombe Vale
Abbotsbury Castle
Wears Fm
White Hill
South West Coast Path
Portesham Hill
Corton Down
Bayard Barn
Bayard Hill
Came Down
Higher Came Fm
Cole Hill Wood
Cripton Cottage
Whitcombe Barn
Broadmayne
Warmwell Heath
Knap Fm
Tadnoll
Blacknoll
Abbey (Rems)
Abbotsbury
Abbotsbury Plains
Portesham
Ridgeway Hill Tunnel
Warren Barn
Came Wood
Beech Fm
Brick Hill
Warmwell
Goose Hill
Coryates
Friar Waddon Hill
Ridgeway Hill
Holcombe Bottom
Glebe Fm
Warmwell Down Barn
Owermoigne
Galton
West Fossil Fm
Portway
Abbotsbury Sub-Tropical Gardens
St Catherine's Chapel
Chapel Hill
Abbotsbury Children's Farm
Abbotsbury Swannery
Rodden Barn Fm
Upwey
Elwell
Bincombe Hill
Bincombe
White Horse Hill
White Horse
Wareham Road
Winfrith Newburgh
Rodden
Merry Hill
Bramdon Lane
Hewish Fm
Upwey Manor
Broadwey
Green Hill
Water Supply
Poxwell Manor
Poxwell
Chesters Hill
Rodden Ridge
Wyke Wood
Hewish Hill
Holwell Fm
Lorton Ho
Littlemoor
Sutton Poyntz
River Jordan
White Horse Fm
Preston
Osmington Ho
Moigns Down
Holworth
Grange Dairy
Chaldon Herring or East Chaldon
New Barn Fm
Manor Ho
Tatton Ho
Tatton Fm
Nottington
Lorton Meadows Nature Reserve
Jordan Hill Roman Temple
Osmington
Osmington Mills
Upton
Spring Bottom Hill
South Down Fm
Burning Cliff
Chaldon Down
Langton Herring
West Fleet
Buckland Ripers
Redlands
Corfe Hill
Old Manor
Overcombe
Lodmoor
Sea Life Centre
Bowleaze Cove
Redcliff Pt
Black Head
England Coast Path
Chideock Fm
Bagwell Fm
Moor Fm
Coldharbour
Radipole
Furzy Cliff
Dorset & East Devon Coast
Ringstead Bay
Newlands Fm
Chesil Beach
Weymouth Gateway Sculptures
Chickerell
Southill
Radipole Lake
Melcombe Regis
RSPB Lodmoor
Weymouth Bay
Fleet
Putton
Gore Cove
Sea Barn Fm
East Fleet
Retail Pk
Greenhill
Swyre Head
St Oswald's Bay
Bat's Head
Bennetts Water Gardens
Charlestown
Westham
Weymouth
Deep Sea Adventure
Chickerell Road
Danger area
Nothe Fort
Lanehouse
Rodwell
Dorset & East Devon Coast
Southlands
Wyke Regis
North Ship Channel
East Ship Channel
Small Mouth
Portland Harbour
Portland Castle
Nat. Sailing Academy
Castletown
Portland
Balaclava Bay
South Ship Channel
Fortuneswell
HM Prison
Bus Cen
Chiswell
Portland
Clay Ope
Ind Est
HM YOI
Grove
Easton
Grove Cliff
Shop Cen
Weston
Portland Museum
Church Ope Cove
Freshwater Bay
Southwell
Bill of Portland
A35
A37
A352
A353
A354
A356
B3143
B3147
B3150
B3153
B3154
B3155
B3156
B3157
B3159
B3390
SY
80
00
70
A
B
C
D
E
F
G
H
7
8
9
10
11
18
29
30

Milton Abbas
Higher Whatcombe
Whatcombe
Lower Whatcombe
Charlton Down
North Fm
South Fm
Field Dairy Fm
Shapwick
Kingston Lacy
Hillbutts
Tadden
Hound Hill
Chilbridge
Merry Field Hill
Pilford
Canford Bottom
Colehill
Winterborne Whitechurch
Chescombe Fm
Hewish Fm
Long Close Fm
30
31
Great Coll Wood
Field Dairy
Moorcourt Fm
Stag Gate
Sturminster Marshall
Barford Fm
Wynne Copse
Cowgrove
Minster
Deans Court
Wimborne Minster
Leigh
Little Canford
Deverel Down
North Down
East Fm
West Fm
Bagber Fm
Deverel Fm
Lawn Barn Fm
Winterborne Kingston
Anderson Manor
Winterborne Zelston
Mapperton
Almer
East Almer Fm
Lion Lodge
Charborough Park
Newton Peveril
Henbury
Combe Almer
Lambs Green
Sleight
East End
Ashington
Oakley
Merley
Canford Magna
Canford School
Milborne St Andrew
Weatherby Castle
Bere Down
Anderson
Dairy Ho
Botany Bay Barn
Huish
Marsh Br
High Wood
Brock Hill
Dullar Fm
Green Fields Fm
Henbury Plantn
Knoll Fm
Rushcombe Bottom
Corfe Mullen
Rose Lawn Coppice
Bearwood
Muddox Barrow Fm
East Field Fm
Bloxworth Down
West Morden
West Park Fm
Lytchett Ho
Barrow Hill
Stony Down Plantn
Hill View
Corfe Hills
Broadstone
Canford Heath
West Howe
Hill Barn
Roke Fm
Ashley Barn
Roger's Hill Fm
Town's End
Bere Wood
Morden
Dolman's Hill
Bartom's Hill
Lytchett Matravers
Poor Common
Upton Heath
Lodge Hill
Tolpuddle
Tolpuddle Ball
Martyrs Museum
Bere Regis
Shitterton
Black Hill
Woodbury Hill
Bloxworth Ho
Bloxworth
Newport
East Bloxworth
Whitefield
Morden Mill
East Morden
Whitmore Bottom
Lytchett Heath
Beacon Hill
Upton Heath
Hillbourne
Waterloo
Canford Heath
Bus Pk
Tower Park Leisure Compl
17
Affpuddle
Turners Puddle
Hollow Oak
Throop
Doddings Fm
Lower Woodbury Fm
Woodlake
Oak Hill
Black Heath
Sherford
Park Corner
Slepe
Post Green
Bere Fm
Lytchett Minster
Creekmoor
Upton
Newtown
Oakdale
Affpuddle Heath
Briants Puddle
Chamberlayne's Fm
Lane End
Bere Heath
Sugar Hill
Wareham Forest
Morden Park
Sherford Br
Farmer Palmer's
Organford
Pike's Fm
Sherford River
Ind Est
Stanley Green
Branksome
Sares Wood
Mart Pits Wood
Bryants Puddle Heath
Oakers Wood
Throop Heath
Moreton Plantn
Chamberlayne's Heath
Warren
Philliols Fm
Stroud Br
Gore Heath
Holton Heath
Lytchett Bay
Hamworthy
Turlin Moor
Holes Bay
Sterte
Longfleet
Parkstone
Pallington
Tonerspuddle Heath
Warren Heath
Gallows Hill
Decoy Heath
Morden Bog
East Holton
Rockley Sands
Lake
Poole
Scaplen's Court Mus
Lilliput
Waddock Cross
Clouds Hill
Bere Heath
Trent Vale Fm
Great Ovens Hill
Holton Heath
Wood Bar Looe
Lower Hamworthy
Hurst
DORSET
Bovington Heath
Wool Heath
Trigon Hill
Cold Harbour
Northport Heath
Sandford
Gold Pt
Keysworth Pt
Patchins Pt
Poole Harbour
Moreton
Snelling Fm
Longthorns
Monkey World
South Heath
Budden's Fm
Carey Heath
Keysworth Fm
Arne Bay
Shipstal Pt
Maryland
The Villa
Brownsea Island
West Lodge
Cranes Moor
Bovington Camp
The Tank Museum
Woolbridge Heath
Great Plantn
Stokeford Heath
Trigon Fm
Northport
Wareham
Swineham Pt
Arne
RSPB
Furzey Island
North Haven Pt
Sandbanks
Broomhill Br
Tout Hill
Whitcombe Vale
East Burton
Wool
Bindon Abbey (Rems)
Stokeford
Binnegar Hall
Binnegar
Worgret Heath
Museum
Priory of Lady St Mary
Arne Reedbeds
Fitzworth Pt
Green Island
South Deep
Jerry's Pt
South Haven Pt
Shell Bay
Tadnoll
Blacknoll
Knighton Heath
Giddy Green
Braytown
Quarr Hill
Rushton
River Frome
Worgret
Holmebridge
Holme Priory
Ridge
Middlebere Fm
Ower Bay
Cleavel Pt
Brand's Bay
West Burton Fm
East Stoke
New Buildings
Woodstreet Fm
Cole Wood
Highwood Heath
East Holme
Stoborough
Stoborough Green
Hartland Moor
Slepe Fm
Purbeck Heaths
Wytch Fm
Newton Bay
Newton
Goathorn Plantn
Drove Island
Studland Beach & Nature Reserve
West Fossil Fm
Portway
East Knighton
Highwood
West Holme
Doreys Fm
Hartland Stud
Middlebere Heath
Oil Terminal
Rempstone Heath
Wytch Heath
Newton Heath
Greenlands Fm
Little Sea
Winfrith Newburgh
Coombe Wood
Coombe Keynes
Coombe Heath
West Holme Heath
Holme Heath
Creech Bottom
Grange Barn
Creech Heath
Furzebrook
Norden Heath
Purbeck Heaths
Studland Bay
Chaldon Herring or East Chaldon
Vine's Down Bldgs
Marley Wood
Marley Wood House
Shaggs
Park Lodge
Hurst Mill
Povington Heath
Grange Heath
Creech
Blue Pool
Norden
Bushey
Lower Bushey Fm
Higher Bushey Fm
The Agglestone
Black Down
Redend Pt
Winfrith Hill
Belhuish Ho
Park Wood
Home Fm
Whiteway
East Creech
Stonehill Down
Knowle Hill
Corfe Castle
Rollington Fm
Rempstone Hall
Godlington Heath
Studland
Chideock Fm
Daggers Gate
Burngate Fm
Lulworth Castle
East Lulworth
Great Wood
Barneston Manor
Cocknowle
Model Village & Garden
Corfe Castle
Little Woolgarston
Woolgarston
Ailwood Fm
Knitson Fm
Ulwell
Newlands Fm
Lulworth Camp
Danger Area
Povington Hill
West Creech Hill
Grange Arch
Animal Sanctuary
Church Knowle
West Bucknowle
Town's End
Swanage Railway
New Buildings
Godlington Manor
Swyre Head
Dungy Head
Lulworth Cove
West Lulworth
Heritage Centre
Whiteway Hill
Purbeck Hills
Steeple
Blackmanston Fm
Bradle Fm
West Orchard Fm
Blashenwell Fm
Lynch Fm
Harman's Cross
New Swanage
Swanage Bay
St Oswald's Bay
Bat's Head
Bindon Hill
Worbarrow Bay
Tyneham
Gad Cliff
Worbarrow
The Etches Collection
Kimmeridge
Smedmore Hill
Orchard Hill Fm
Kingston
West Street
Dunshay Manor
New Barn
Herston Halt
Ind Est
Swanage
Lulworth Cove
Mupe Bay
Brandy Bay
Kimmeridge Bay
Hobarrow Bay
Swyre Head
Coombe Bottom
Compact Fm
Langton Matravers
Herston
Peveril Pt
Swalland Fm
South West Coast Path
Kimmeridge Ledges
Rope Lake Head
Westhill Fm
Acton
Eastington Fm
Durlston Bay
Hounstout Cliff
Renscombe Fm
Worth Matravers
California Fm
Durlston
Durlston Head
Tilly Whim Caves
Egmont Pt
Chapman's Pool
Anvil Pt
Blackers Hole
Seacombe Cliff
Dorset & East Devon Coast
St Aldhelm's or St Alban's Head
A31
A35
A350
A351
A352
A354
A3049
B3075
B3070
B3071
B3067
B3068
B3069
B3351
B3369
Poole Road
Blandford Road North
Sandford Road
Holton Heath
Corfe Road
Morden Road
Gravel Hill
Newtown Hill
Waddock Drove
Ferry Road
Valley Road
New Road
SY
00
70
80
0 1 2 3 miles
0 1 2 3 4 5 km
A B C D E F G H
1 2 3 4 5 6

19
Ferndown
Christchurch
Bournemouth
Boscombe
Southbourne
Highcliffe
New Milton
Barton on Sea
Milford on Sea
Lymington
Keyhaven
POOLE BAY
CHRISTCHURCH BAY
Hengistbury Head
The Needles
Alum Bay
Totland Bay
Hurst Beach
CHERBOURG
JERSEY
GUERNSEY
ST MALO
Handfast Point or The Foreland
The Pinnacles
DORSET & EAST DEVON COAST
Canford Cliffs
Poole Head
Branksome Chine
Westbourne
Sway
Hordle
Downton
Everton
Pennington
Bransgore
Hurn
Kinson
Winton
Moordown
Talbot Village
Mudeford
Stanpit
Purewell
Somerford
Walkford
Ashley
Bashley
Wootton
Beckley
Hinton
Burton
Winkton
Sopley
Ripley
Avon
Kingston
Bisterne
Holdenhurst
West Parley
Parley Cross
Longham
Dudsbury
Bear Cross
Ensbury
Springbourne
Pokesdown
Iford
Tuckton
Wick
Jumpers Green
RUSSELL-COTES MUSEUM
SAMMY MILLER MOTORCYCLE MUSEUM
HIGHCLIFFE CASTLE
THE NEEDLES OLD BATTERY
THE NEEDLES PARK
7
8
9
10
11
A
B
C
D
E
F
G
H
20
31
32
SZ

THE
HANTS
ISLE OF WIGHT
Lymington
Newport
Cowes
East Cowes
Blackfield
Langley
Calshot
Hill Head
Hatchet Gate
Otterwood
Setley
Battramsley
Boldre
Pilley
Bull Hill
Norleywood
South Baddesley
East End
Portmore
Walhampton
Buckland
Lower Buckland
Mount Pleasant
St Austins
Pennington
Woodside
Waterford
Everton
Lower Pennington
Lymore
Milford on Sea
Keyhaven
Exbury
Bucklers Hard
Lepe
West Common
East Boldre
Needs Ore Pt
Hurst Beach
Hurst Castle
Sconce Pt
Yarmouth
Norton
Norton Green
Freshwater
Totland
Totland Bay
Colwell Bay
Warden Point
Colwell
Weston Manor
Pound Green
Freshwater Bay
Afton
The Needles
Compton Bay
Brook
Mottistone
Hulverstone
Brighstone
Brighstone Bay
Limerstone
Shorwell
Yafford
Thorncross
Kingston
Little Atherfield
Atherfield Green
Chale Green
Pyle
Chale
Chale Bay
Blackgang
Niton
St Lawrence
Whitwell
Shalcombe
Calbourne
Newbridge
Wellow
Thorley
Thorley Street
Bouldnor
Cranmore
Ningwood
Shalfleet
Hamstead
Newtown
Newtown Bay
Porchfield
Locksgreen
Parkhurst
Parkhurst Forest
Northwood
Gurnard
Gurnard Bay
Rew Street
Thorness Bay
Hunny Hill
Forest Side
Gunville
Carisbrooke
Clatterford
Shide
Bowcombe
Blackwater
Gatcombe
Chillerton
Rookley
Godshill
Roud
Wroxall
Whippingham
Wootton Bridge
Wootton Common
Fairlee
Staplers
Downend
Arreton
Merstone
Horringford
Barton
Dallimores
Woodside
Littletown
Sandford
St Catherine's Down
St Catherine's Pt
Knoles
Kingates
Bierley
Southford
Nettlecombe
Atherfield Pt
Shepherd's Chine
Chilton Chine
Grange Chine
The Undercliff
Cowes Roads
Osborne Bay
Old Castle Pt
A3054
A3055
A3020
B3401
B3399
B3323
A3021
A3056
32
33
19
SZ
30
70
0 1 2 3 miles
0 1 2 3 4 5 km
A B C D E F G H
1 2 3 4 5 6

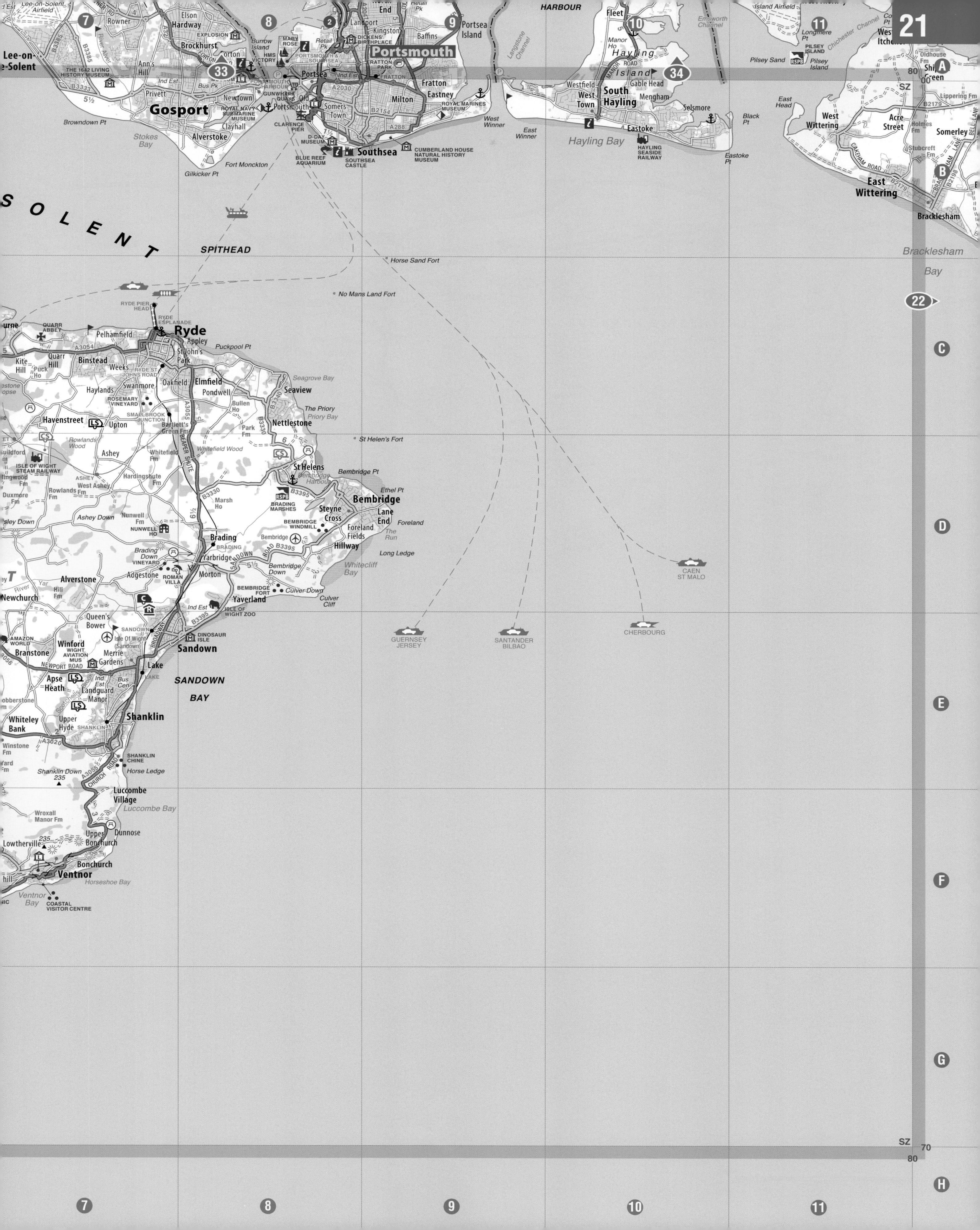
Lee-on-the-Solent
Rowner
Elson
Hardway
Brockhurst
Ann's Hill
Privett
Gosport
Alverstoke
Browndown Pt
Stokes Bay
Gilkicker Pt
Fort Monckton
Burrow Island
Portsmouth
Landport
Kingston
Baffins
Portsea Island
Portsea
Fratton
Eastney
Milton
Old Portsmouth
Somers Town
Southsea
SOUTHSEA CASTLE
BLUE REEF AQUARIUM
D-DAY MUSEUM
CUMBERLAND HOUSE NATURAL HISTORY MUSEUM
ROYAL MARINES MUSEUM
ROYAL NAVY SUBMARINE MUSEUM
THE 1642 LIVING HISTORY MUSEUM
MARY ROSE
HMS VICTORY
GUNWHARF QUAYS
CLARENCE PIER
DICKENS' BIRTHPLACE
HARBOUR
West Winner
East Winner
Fleet
Manor Ho
Hayling Island
Westfield
West Town
South Hayling
Gable Head
Mengham
Eastoke
Selsmore
Hayling Bay
HAYLING SEASIDE RAILWAY
Black Pt
Eastoke Pt
Emsworth Channel
Langstone Channel
Chichester Channel
Longmere Pt
PILSEY ISLAND
Pilsey Island
Pilsey Sand
East Head
West Wittering
Acre Street
Somerley
East Wittering
Bracklesham
Bracklesham Bay
Oldhouse Fm
Lippering Fm
Holmes Fm
Stubcroft Fm
SOLENT
SPITHEAD
Horse Sand Fort
No Mans Land Fort
St Helen's Fort
RYDE PIER HEAD
RYDE ESPLANADE
Ryde
Appley
St John's Park
Puckpool Pt
QUARR ABBEY
Pelhamfield
Quarr Hill
Binstead
Kite Hill
Weeks
Swanmore
Haylands
Oakfield
Elmfield
Pondwell
ROSEMARY VINEYARD
SMALLBROOK JUNCTION
Bullen Ho
Seagrove Bay
Seaview
The Priory
Priory Bay
Nettlestone
Havenstreet
Upton
Rowlands Wood
Ashey
Whitefield Fm
Whitefield Wood
Hardingshute Fm
Park Fm
ISLE OF WIGHT STEAM RAILWAY
West Ashey
Rowlands Fm
Duxmore Fm
Ashey Down
Nunwell Fm
NUNWELL HO
St Helens
Bembridge Harbour
Bembridge Pt
Ethel Pt
BRADING MARSHES
Marsh Ho
Steyne Cross
Bembridge
Lane End
Foreland
Foreland Fields
BEMBRIDGE WINDMILL
The Run
Hillway
Long Ledge
Brading
Brading Down
VINEYARD
Yarbridge
Adgestone
ROMAN VILLA
Morton
Bembridge Down
Whitecliff Bay
BEMBRIDGE FORT
Culver Down
Culver Cliff
Yaverland
ISLE OF WIGHT ZOO
Alverstone
Newchurch
Queen's Bower
AMAZON WORLD
Branstone
Winford
WIGHT AVIATION MUS
Merrie Gardens
DINOSAUR ISLE
Sandown
Lake
SANDOWN BAY
Apse Heath
Landguard Manor
Whiteley Bank
Upper Hyde
Shanklin
Winstone Fm
SHANKLIN CHINE
Horse Ledge
Shanklin Down
Luccombe Village
Luccombe Bay
Wroxall Manor Fm
Dunnose
Upper Bonchurch
Lowtherville
Bonchurch
Ventnor
Horseshoe Bay
Ventnor Bay
COASTAL VISITOR CENTRE
CAEN ST MALO
GUERNSEY JERSEY
SANTANDER BILBAO
CHERBOURG
SZ

Havant
Leigh Park
Stockheath
Bedhampton
Rowlands Castle
Stansted Forest
Warblington
Emsworth
Langstone
Southbourne
Prinsted
Nutbourne
Hermitage
Westbourne
Woodmancote
Funtington
West Ashling
East Ashling
Walderton
Stoughton
Woodend
West Stoke
Mid Lavant
East Lavant
Summersdale
Westerton
Strettington
Westhampnett
Halnaker
Boxgrove
Tangmere
Oving
Aldingbourne
Westergate
Eartham
Chichester
Fishbourne
Broadbridge
Bosham
Chidham
Apuldram
Stockbridge
Whyke
Portfield
Donnington
Merston
Runcton
Colworth
North Mundham
South Mundham
Hunston
Sidlesham
Pagham
Nyetimber
Rose Green
Aldwick
North Bersted
South Bersted
Bognor Regis
CHICHESTER HARBOUR
Thorney Island
West Thorney
LANGSTONE HARBOUR
Northney
North Hayling
Stoke
Fleet
Hayling Island
South Hayling
West Town
Eastoke
Mengham
Hayling Bay
West Itchenor
Birdham
Shipton Green
West Wittering
East Wittering
Bracklesham
Bracklesham Bay
Earnley
Somerley
Highleigh
WEST SUSSEX
Church Norton
Selsey
Selsey Bill
Pagham Harbour
CAEN ST MALO
CHERBOURG
SANTANDER BILBAO
0 1 2 3 miles
0 1 2 3 4 5 km

Uckfield
Rocks Park
Blackboys
Pounsley
Waldron Down
in Hand
Heathfield
Cade Street
Old Heathfield
Punnett's Town
Three Cups Corner
Brightling
Oxley's Green
Hollingrove
Twelve Oaks
Cackle Street
Framfield
Ridgewood
New Town
Little London
Waldron
Tilsmore
Sandy Cross
Maynard's Green
Rushlake Green
Warbleton
Dallington
Darwell Hole
Netherfield
Little Horsted
Horsted Green
Mount Ephraim
Palehouse Common
Hawkhurst Common
Foxhunt Green
Sharp's Corner
Horam
Vines Cross
Chapman's Town
Churches Green
Penhurst
Ponts Green
Brownbread Street
Steven's Crouch
Halland
East Hoathly
Shortgate
Laughton Common
Laughton
Burlow
Marle Green
Foul Mile
Trolliloes
Cowbeech
Bodle Street Green
Chiddingly
Whitesmith
Gun Hill
Grove Hill
Cowbeech Hill
Chilsham
Herstmonceux
Windmill Hill
Marlpits
Ninfield
Lower Street
Golden Cross
Nash Street
Muddles Green
Holmes's Hill
Broomham
Lower Horsebridge
Hellingly
Upper Horsebridge
Magham Down
Golden Cross
Boreham Street
Hooe Common
Russell's Green
Glyndebourne
Mark Cross
Ripe
Chalvington
Lower Dicker
Upper Dicker
Hailsham
Wartling
Hooe
Little Common
Cooden
West Firle
Selmeston
Arlington
Caneheath
Summer Hill
Pevensey Levels
Rickney
Alciston
Berwick
Wilmington Green
Polegate
Hankham
Mill Hill
Pevensey
Norman's Bay
Westham
Stone Cross
Friday Street
Pevensey Bay
Wilmington
Milton Street
Folkington
Willingdon
Alfriston
Litlington
Hampden Park
Langney
St Anthony's Hill
Jevington
Norton
Bishopstone
East Blatchington
Sutton
Seaford
Exceat
Westdean
Friston
Upperton
Roselands
Old Town
Eastbourne
Meads
East Dean
Holywell
Birling Gap
Beachy Head
Seven Sisters
Cuckmere Haven
Seaford Head
EAST SUSSEX
TQ
TV
36
37
38
A B C D E F G H
7 8 9 10 11

BARNSTAPLE
OR
BIDEFORD BAY
Westward Ho!
Northam Burrows
Sandymere
Mermaid's Pool
Buckleigh
Silford
Rickard's Down
Orchard Hill
Bideford
Abbotsham
The Big Sheep
Greencliff
Cockington Fm
Knotty Corner
Affinity Devon
Babbacombe Mouth
Babbacombe Cliff
South West Coast Path
Ford
High Park
Fairy Cross
Woodtown
Yeo Vale
Peppercombe
Northway
Alwington
Littleham
Gauter Pt
Buck's Cross
Buck's Mills
Hoops
Horns Cross
Goldworthy
Waytown
Foxdown Manor
Broad Parkham
Newhaven
Tuckingmill
Bulland
Sedborough
Bocombe
Cabbacott
Parkham
Buckland Brewer
Parkham Ash
Dyers Moor Fm
Babeleigh Barton
Venton Fm
Gorwood Fm
Melbury Hill 216
Melbury Fm
Park Fm
Bearah Fm
Thorne Fm
Bilsford
Buda
Craneham
Ash Fm
Winslade
Lower Twitchen
Powler's Piece
Common Moor
Lydeland Water
Wrangworthy Cross
Narracott
Eckworthy
Tythecott
Ashbury
Hartland Pt
Barley Bay
Shipload Bay
Eldern Pt
Chapman Rock
Exmansworthy Cliff
Gawlish Cliff
Beckland Bay
Windbury Pt
Blackchurch Rock
Blagdon Fm
Titchberry
Gawlish Fm
Damehole Pt
Upright Cliff
Blegbury
Beckland Fm
Mouth Mill
Norton
Cheristow
Yapham Fm
Wood Rock
Gallant Rock
Clovelly Court
Hartland Abbey
Highdown Cotts
Abbey River
Hartland Quay Mus
Ballhill
Rosedown
Ind Pk
Mettaford Fm
Velly
Wrinkleberry
Hugglepit
Clovelly
Bight a Doubleyou
Burscott
Stoke
Hartland
Hescott Fm
Holloford Fm
Kernstone Fm
North
Leigh Fm
Natcott
Highford Fm
Warmleigh Fm
Speke's Mill Mouth
Burnstone
Docton Mill & Gardens
Galsham Fm
Philham
Higher Clovelly
Milky Way Adventure Park
Slade Fm
Staddon
Baxworthy Cross
Burford
Milford
Elmscott
Devon
Eddistone
Welsford
Stitworthy Fm
Seckington Fm
Seckington Water
Clifford Water
Clifford
West Town
Cranford
Cranford Water
Woolfardisworthy
Mansley Cliff
Tosberry
Docton
Nabor Pt
Gull Rock
Sandhole Cliff
Hardisworthy
Firebeacon
Golden Park
Welsford Moor
Bursdon Moor
Maid's Moor
Alminstone Cross
South Hole
Embury Beacon 157
Putshole Fm
Lutsford
Bursdon
Summerwell Fm
Gorvin Fm
Huddisford
West Moor
Stroxworthy
Duerdon
Gorrell Fm
Ramtor Rock
Hendon Moor 233
Runland Fm
Claw Cross
Welcombe Mouth
Welcombe
Tredown
Henaford
Meddon
Horton Br
Marshall Fm
Fordmill Fm
Ashmansworthy
Nutton Fm
Marsland Mouth
Mead
Darracott
Upcott
Shorston Fm
Brimford Br
Horton Fm
Dipple
Hole
Marsland Cliff
Marsland Water
Gooseham Mill
Marsland Manor
Woolley
Holyrood Ho
Kismeldon Bridge
Yeol Mouth
Cornakey Cliff
Gooseham
Hackmarsh
Northmoor
Cory
Kismeldon Fm
East Putford
Cholash Fm
Bibbear Fm
Southcott
Thornehillhead
Henna Cliff 143
Eastcott
Newlands Fm
Volehouse Fm
West Putford
Waffapool
Galsworthy
Holwell Fm
Wonders Corner
Vicarage Cliff
Lucky Hole
Morwenstow
Rule Cross
Crimp
Youlstone
Dinworthy
Heath Fm
Gnome Reserve & Wild Flower Garden
Bountis Thorne
Stowford
Withacott
Crosstown
West Youlstone
East Youlstone
Trentworthy Fm
Redmonsford
Silworthy Cross
Hankford Barton
Eastacott
Higher Sharpnose Pt
St John the Baptist Church
Woodford Cross
Shop
Ryall Fm
West Down
Wheelers Cross
Colscott
Bower
Haytown
Doves Moor
Stibb Cross
Hill
Ash Fm
Darzle Fm
Middlefields Fm
Wrasford Moor
Bradworthy Common
Hippa Rock
Eastaway Manor
Woodford
Ham Fm
Stursdon
Uppacott Fm
Bradworthy
Bulkworthy
Stowford
Worden
Cleverdon
Roseland Cross
Abbots Bickington
Venn Fm
Stibb Hollow
Stanbury Mouth
Lower Sharpnose Pt
Elmsworthy Fm
Lympscott Fm
Upper Tamar Lake
Lamberal Water
River Tamar
Kimworthy
Northcott
North Lane
Brendon
Fives Lanes Cross
Woodford Br
Downmoor Cross
Badworthy Fm
Taylor's Cross
Woodlands Fm
Bradworthy Cross
South Lane
Youldon Fm
Coombe Fm
Newton St Petrock
Rowd Fm
Steeple Pt
Duckpool
Burridge Fm
Darracott
Instaple Fm
Matcott
Venn Green
Shop
Walland
Coombe
Lee Wood
Penstowe Park
Stowe Wood
Kilkhampton
Thurdon
Alfardisworthy
Crosslands Fm
Sutcombe
Upcott
Hawkwell
Sutcombemill
Forestreet
Sudden
Ladford
St James's Church
Forda
Lower Tamar Lake
Waldon Fm
River Waldon
Buttermoor
Caute
Houndapit Fm
Stowe Cliffs
Stibb
Lymsworthy Fm
Lutsford Fm
Shilland Fm
Soldon Cross
Hole Fm
Gratton
Grawley
Penninknold
Long Rock
Cornwall
Killock Fm
Halls
Hessaford Fm
Lopthorne Fm
Higher Pigsdon Fm
Bude Aqueduct
Wooda Fm
Youldonmoor Cross
Langadon Fm
Milton Damerel
Berry Fm
Waite Fm
Gidcott Mill
Sandy Mouth
Menachurch Pt
Dunsmouth Fm
Ivyleaf Fm
Moreton Pound Fm
Mboreton Mill
Cross Fm
Pitt Cross
Shebbear
Northcott Mouth
Crockwood Fm
Northcott
Hunthill Wood
Venn Fm
Dunsdon
Woodsdown Hill
Holsworthy Beacon
South Wonford
Old Wood
Thornbury
Highworthy
Maer
Poughill
Bush
Hersham
Headon Fm
Gearns Fm
Vognacott
Woodacott
Woodacott Cross
Windy Cross
Wrangle Pt
Stamford Hill
Colebrook Fm
Great Moreton
Lana
Ugworthy Barton
Babbington
Yellowland Fm
Brendon
Bason
Bradford
Alfacott
North Worden
Bude Haven
Flexbury
Grimscott
Leigh Wood
Burmsdon Fm
Kingsford
Vaglefield Fm
Portlane Br
Priestacott
Compass Pt
The Castle Bude
Bude
Stratton
Launcells Cross
Chilsworthy
Hoggs Park
Cookbury
Cookbury Moor Plantn
Ebbingford Manor
Ind Est
Launcells
Prustacott Fm
Scorsham Fm
Red Post
Pancrasweek
Thorne Fm
Parnacott
Blagdonmoor Wharf
Arliemoor Fm
Middlecott
Holemoor
Grove Park
Marsh
Barton Gate
Youldon Fm
Pitworthy
Hammworthy Fm
River Deer
Forda Fm
Lynstone
Rodd's Bridge
Shernick
Bramble Wood
Stadson Fm
Phillips's Pt
Upton
Thorne
Phillips Fm
West Grove
Brayshill
Buttsbear Cross
Small Brook
Burnard's Ho
Trewyn
Ind Est
Stanbury Cross
Lakes
Cookbury Wick
Anvil Corner
Higher Kennelands
Flares
Marhamchurch
Hobbacott
Treyeo
Jewell's Cross
Grove
Holladon Fm
Derril Water
Holsworthy
Waterloo Fm
Staddon
Southcombe Fm
Garlands Fm
Brandis Corner
Whiteleigh Water
Helebridge
Hilton
Churchtown
Derril
Derriton
Little Knowle Fm
Whimble
Eastacombe Fm
Fernlea Fm
Dunsland Cross
Lashbrook Moor Plantn
Kingslake Fm
Widemouth Sand
Helscott
Widemouth Bay
Woodknowle
Rattenbury
Great Beer Fm
Bridgerule
Pyworthy
Broadshell Cross
Chasty
Hollacombe
Claw Moor Plantn
Weekpark Plantn
Whiteleigh Meadow
Shepard Island
Chilla
Trelay
Hackthorne
Furze Cross
Hopworthy
Headon Southcott Fm
Little Claw Moor
Morcombe Plantn
Black Rock
Titson
Tackbeare Fm
Holsworthy Woods
Common Moor
Clawmoor Fm
Wanson Mouth
Widemouth
Box's Shop
Budd's Titson
Marhayes Manor
Langford Barton
Bradford Manor
Crinacott Fm
Paronage Wood
Brooks House
Leworthy
Sillick Moor
Winscott Cross
Claw Bridge
Cookworthy Moor Plantn
Halwill Moor Plantn
Wanson
Merrifield
Affalon Moor
North Down
Langaford Moor
Lane End
Coppathorne
Burracott Fm
Bakesdown
Tankins Fm
Strawberry Bank
Millook
Poundstock
Causewell
Penfound Fm
Furze Fm
Westcott Plantn
Forda Mill
Corfcott Green
Town Fm
Clawton
Buckhorn
Haye Fm
Hunscott Fm
East Down
Langaford
Halwill
Thorne
Affaland Wood
Elger Wood
North Beer
Sandymoor Cross
Quodditch Cross
Rectory Fm
Halwill
Whitstone
Whitstone Head
Treskinnick Cross
Steele Hill
Swannacott Wood
West Balsdon
Stowford Wood
River Claw
Quodditchmoor Plantns
Stowford
Raggot
East Youlstone
Barton
Wadfast
Blagdon
New
Landhill
Trego
Station Road
2 3 4 5 6
A B C D E F G H
1 2 3 4 5 6
40
11
12
20
30
SS
00
0 1 2 3 miles
0 1 2 3 4 5 km

25
Crow Rock
Instow Sands
Instow
Appledore
N DEVON MARITIME MUSEUM
The Quay
Worlington
Bickleton
Fremington
Combrew
Bickington
Newport
Portmor
Landkey
Harford
Sandick
West Buckland School
Elwell
East Buckland
Charles Bottom
Roundswell
Rumsam
Bishops Tawton
Landkey Newland
Swimbridge Newland
Sandick Cross
Hurscott
Yarnacott
Yeoland
West Buckland
Huxtable Fm
Gubbs Fm
Brayley Hill
Fullingcott Fm
Hollamoor Clump
Eastacombe
Upcott Fm
Tawstock
Swimbridge
Kerscott
High Down
Leary Moors
Heddon
Park
Huish
TAPELEY PARK GARDENS
Westleigh
Coombe Fm
Trayhill
Huish Moor
St John's Chapel
Stonyland
Rushcott Fm
Prospect Corner
Uppacott
Downrew Ho
Horswell Fm
Hannaford
Hangman's Hill
Bydown Ho
Lane End Fm
Tower Fm
Oxford Down
Shallowford
Bremridge Wood
Holmacott
Horwood
Eastleigh
Eastleigh Manor
Ball Hill
Halmpstone Manor
Summer Moor
Frogmor
Tower Moor
Barton Cross
Filleigh
Stag's Head
Whitehills Plantn
QUINCE HONEY FARM
Harepie Cross
Lower Lovacott
Newton Tracey
Harracott
Week
Bickell Cross
Upcott Fm
Wellesley Fm
Cobbaton
Stowford
Pristacott
Bartridge Common
Weach Barton Fm
East-the-Water
Ind Est
Woodville Fm
Woodtown
Gammaton
Bulworthy
Webbery
Stony Cross
Chapelton
Herner
COBBATON COMBAT VEHICLE MUS
East Stowford
Lerwill Fm
Furze
Coombe Fm
Hiscott
Ensis
Langham Lake
CHAPELTON
Horestone Cotts
ST HIERITHA'S CHURCH
Chittlehampton
Townsend
Riding Cross
Ford Br
Bray Br
Nadrid Water
South Molton
Stone
Common Moors
Alverdiscott
South Moor
Hollick Fm
Gammaton Moor
Borough Fm
Ham Fm
Shortridge Fm
Rooks Fm
Cleave Fm
Buck's Mill
Langley Cross
Fishleigh Barton
Higher Ho
Umberleigh Ho
Whey Fm
Halswell Fm
Pillmouth
Landcross
Hallspill
Oldiscleave Fm
Haddacott
Garnacott Fm
Hill Fm
Bremridge Fm
Chantry
Greendown Fm
Cleave Fm
Thorne Fm
Lashingcott Moor
Yarnscombe
Brown's Hill Head
UMBERLEIGH
Umberleigh
Eastacott
Pugsley
Broden Hill
Clapworthy
Parsonage Fm
Broomhouse Fm
George Nympton
Huntshaw Water
Huntshaw
Boode Fm
Horse Moor
Atherington
Warkleigh
Meethe
Warkleigh Ho
Culverhill Fm
Trayne
The Hill
Weare Giffard
Park
Huntshaw Mill Bridge
Eastacombe
Orchard Fm
Cloggshill Cross
Langridge Ford
Smallmarsh
Shortridge
Claytown
Satterleigh
Great Oakwell Fm
Annery
Saltrens
Haycroft Fm
Footlands
Weirmarsh Fm
Park Fm
Haynetow
Littlewood Fm
Jose's Cross
Downes Ho
Beam Ho
Furze Fm
Furzebeam Hill
Darracott Res
BELLE VUE CROSS
Ward Fm
Churchcombe Fm
Cranford Cross
Heale Town
Wooton
Little Silver
Chittlehamholt
Bias Wood
Monkleigh
TORRINGTON MUS
Moortown
Peagham Barton
Way Barton
Hill Fm
Sherwood Green
Welcombe
High Bickington
Southwood
Arshaton Wood
Manor Ho
Hele Wood
Colley Lake
Down Fm
Collacott Fm
Broomham Moor
Huxford Fm
Culleigh
Great Torrington
Ind Est
High Bullen
Stevenstone
Dodscott
Barn Down
Beara Moor
Ebberly Hill
Beechwood Ho
Snape
Kinnings
Collins
Smitha
Frithelstock
DARTINGTON CRYSTAL
Servis Fm
St Giles in the Wood
Weel Fm
Beara
Libbaton
Bale's Ash
Kingford
River Taw
Abbot's Marsh
PORTSMOUTH ARMS
Snydies Fm
Park Wood
Kingsnympton Park
Hummacott
King's Nympton
Cleave
Castle Hill
Frithelstock Stone
Frizenham
Taddiport
Ley Fm
Kingscott
Stoney Ford
Winscott Barton
Natty Cross
Week
Upcott
Bouchland Fm
Head Wood
Head Mill
Hill Head
Great Lightleigh
Garland Cross
RHS GARDEN ROSEMOOR
South Hill
Watergate
Whitsley Barton
Week Down
Handford
Bedport
Hill Fm
Spittle Fm
Waddington
Cutland Ho
West Garland Fm
Little Torrington
North Healand
South Healand
Woodlands
Castle Hill
Wansley Barton
Roborough
Burrington Moor Cross
Eaglescott
Pavington
Burrington
KINGS NYMPTON
King's Hill
Newnham Barton Fm
Cadbury Barton
Five Lane End
Birchill Fm
Smytham Manor
Hall Ho
Ramscliffe Fm
Great Barlington
SHEPPATON LANE
Balls Corner
Elstone
Dobb's Moor
Hollam
Gribble Inn
Brealeys
Long Wood
River Torridge
Golland
Colleton Mills
Beacon
Parsonage Horridge Moor
Langtree Week
Langtree
West Arson
Austins
Beaford
Down Fm
Firsdon Fm
Cowflop Cross
Beaford Moor
Potheridge Gate
Pinkhill Fm
Beaford Br
Frost's Corner
Molly
Cottwood
Ash Wood
Bithefin Moor
Colleton Manor
Ind Est
Chulmleigh
Huntacott
Suddon Fm
Berry Cross
Peters Marland
Colehouse Fm
Riddlecombe
Hook Fm
Leigh Ho
Dart Br
Sydham
Winswell Moor
Winswell
Hillies Wood
Buckland Fm
Cudworthy Moor
Dolton Beacon
Ashreigney
Copy Lake
Kersham
Bridge Reeve
Chawleigh Week
Savourys
Moortown
Woollaton
Eastwood
Merton Mill
Greatwood Fm
Halsdon Ho
Venton
Iddlecott
B3217
Wood Fm
Hollocombe Moor
Lodgey Cross
Eagle Down
Horridge
Gosse's Fm
Kennydown Fm
Heywood Wood
Merton Moors
Grange Fm
Merton
Rosehill
HALSDON
Dolton
Cross Fm
Aller Fm
Hollocombe Town
Stable Green
Ashley
Labdon
Saul's Fm
Heywood Ho
EGGESFORD
Eggesford Station
Southcott
Alscott Fm
Marland Moor
Huish
New Bridge
Ham Fm
Venton Fm
Hollocombe
Lane End
Zeal Fm
Galmington
Grascott
Haddiport
Berry Fm
Broadmead
Chapple Fm
Dowland
Dowland Moor
Heath Hill
Heath Fm
Flashdown Wood
Battledown Cross
Netherton Fm
Hook Fm
North Town
Petrockstow
Park Fm
Upcott
Coombe Fm
Loosedon Cross
Berner's Cross
Wheatland Fm
Wembworthy
Upcott
Spekes Cross
Hayne Fm
Eggesford
Buckland Filleigh
Hallwood Fm
Little Mere River
Brimblecombe Brake
Whitemoor
Bryony Hill
Gerrydown Fm
Winkleigh Wood
Partridge Walls
Higher Park
Upcott Wood
Buckland Mill
Waydown Plantn
Swardicott
Meeth
Eastpark
Iddesleigh
Seckington Cross
Winkleigh
West Brushford Fm
Reeve
River Taw
Nymet Rowland
South Hill Fm
Devon Lodge
Oakley Ho
B3220
Down Fm
South Hill
Newcourt Barton
Crockers Hele
Bondstones
STATION ROAD
Barwick
Bullhead Fm
Ingleigh Green
Fourways Cross
Bullow Brook
Stony Br
Graysbridge Fm
Luxton Moor
Taw Green
Brushford
Coldridge
Sheepwash
Bridge Town
Nethercott Ho
Bude Fm
Hill Fm
Lake
Barntown
Taw Bridge
Southmoor Fm
Ditsham
Totleigh Barton
River Torridge
Hele Bridge
Middlecott
Oak Fm
West Leigh
Birch Fm
Black Torrington
Smithsland
Barton
Fishleigh Lake
Mill Fm
Monkokehampton
Broadwood Kelly
Riddlestone Fm
Bankland Fm
Keyethern Fm
Fishleigh Castle
Vellaford Fm
Stafford Beer
Splatt
Thorn Corner
East Leigh
Upcott Fm
Beara Court
Glebe Fm
Stockleigh Fm
Pangkor Ho
Deckport Cross
Seldon Fm
Holme Down
Hole Brook
Corstone Moor
Moorend Fm
Lewersland Fm
Bondleigh
Cholhouse
Leigh Cross
Highampton
Heane Fm
Hatherleigh
Hill Barton
Pulworthy Brook
Burdon Grange
Warren Fm
Venton Cross
Ind Est
Woodhall Br
Tor Down Fm
Lake
Honeychurch Moor
Ashridge Court
Hole Fm
Ashridge Moor Cross
Kerswell
Stewdon Fm
Woodhall
Cadham
Honeychurch
Redpost Cross
Great Beere Moor
Reeve Castle
Chilla Moor
Odham
Locks Park
BASSET'S CROSS
Dunsland Court
Bouchers Hill
Staddon Fm
Nichols Nymet Ho
Cleave Fm
Broomford Manor
Exbourne
Bridge Fm
Waddaford
Stonequarry Fm
Leasefield Fm
Water
Stewdon Moor
Rutleigh Ball Fm
Landsend Fm
Marshford Fm
Medland Brook
Jacobstowe
Stockbeare Fm
Sampford Courtenay
North Tawton
Stone Fm
Nichols Nymett Cross
Hampson
Whiddon Moor
River Lew
Gribbleford Fm
Langabeare Barton
Northview Manor
Norley
South Yeo
Narracott Fm
Langabeer Moor
Sampford Chapple
Trecott
Newland Mill
Broadnymett Moor
Hole Stock Bridge
Teachmore Fm
South Dornaford
Swanstone Moor
Chapple Moor
Culm Cross
de Bathe Fm
Halse Fm
Beaworthy
Inwardleigh
Preston Moor
Dornaford Park
Comm Moor
Falcadon Fm
Cocktree Moor
Trew Fm
Crowden
Northlew
Heath Fm
Oak Cross
Lamerton Cross
Beacon Cross
North Wood Moor
Itton
Ham Fm
West Beghear
East Kimber
Homing Down
Westlake Fm
Eastacombe Fm
Rowden
Itton Moor
Heath Moor
Berrydown Plantn
Black Moor
South Hill Fm
Patchacott
Loveland Fm
Ashbury
Folly
Hill Barto
Wood Fm
Appledore
Belstone Corner
Halford Manor
Bowbeer
Sixty Acre Moor
Waytown
A39
A361
A36
A377
A386
A388
A3124
A3072
B3227
B3226
B3232
B3233
B3096
B3042
B3216
B3220
B3217
A399
P&R
SS
70
00
7
8
9
10
11
12
13
26
40
41
A
B
C
D
E
F
G
H

Heasley Mill
Twitchen
Twitchen Mill
Hawkridge
Mounsey Hill 374
South Hill
West Anstey Common
North Molton
Molland
Bickingcott
Champson
West Anstey
East Anstey
Dulverton
Battleton
Brushford
Nightcott
Exebridge
Oldways End
Yeo Mill
Bottreaux Mill
Veraby
South Molton
Garliford
Newtown
Bish Mill
Bishops Nympton
Ash Mill
George Nympton
Alswear
Mariansleigh
Knowstone
East Knowstone
Roachill
Oakfordbridge
Oakford
Rose Ash
Romansleigh
Meshaw
Creacombe
Rackenford
Stoodleigh
Stoodleigh Beacon 301
King's Nympton
Cadbury Barton
Week
Lutworthy
Queen Dart
Mogworthy
Loxbeare
Washfield
Chulmleigh
Witheridge
Nomansland
Templeton Bridge
Templeton
Calverleigh
Cheldon
Chawleigh
West Worlington
East Worlington
Drayford
Thelbridge Barton
Cruwys Morchard
Withleigh
Cotteylands
Eggesford Station
D E V O N
Washford Pyne
Puddington
Pennymoor
Way Village
Filleigh
Black Dog
Little Silver
Well Town
Eastington
Lapford
Nymet Rowland
Coldridge
Morchard Bishop
Woolfardisworthy
Poughill
Upham
Cadeleigh
Kennerleigh
Stockleigh English
Cheriton Fitzpaine
Bickleigh
Bickleigh Castle
Oldborough
West Leigh
East Leigh
Zeal Monachorum
Down St Mary
Morchard Road
Ash Bullayne
Newbuildings
East Village
Upton Hellions
Cadbury
Chitterley
Stockleigh Pomeroy
Copplestone
Bow
Knowle
West Sandford
Sandford
Up Exe
Thorverton
Shobrooke
Efford
Coleford
Crediton
Nymet Tracey
Nether Exe
Rewe
Colebrooke
Shute
Sweetham
Brampford Speke
Hookway
Newton St Cyres
Hillerton
Yeoford
Venny
Stoke Canon
A361
A377
A396
A3072
B3227
B3137
B3096
B3042
B3226
B3222
0 1 2 3 miles
0 1 2 3 4 5 km

Brompton Regis
Clatworthy
Brompton Ralph
Tolland
Lawrence
Cothelstone
East Combe
Combe Florey
Pyleigh
Handy Cross
Tarr
West Leigh
Cushuish
Hartford
Upton
Huish Champflower
Maundown
Langley Marsh
Langley
Ford
Hoccombe
Chapel Leigh
Northway
Ash Priors
Bishops Lydeard
East Lydeard
Yarford
Fulford
Pickney
Nailsbourne
Haddon Hill
Skilgate
Chipstable
Wiveliscombe
Northgate
Castle
Fitzhead
Pond Close
Halse
Cotford St Lukes
Preston Bowyer
Heathfield
Norton Fitzwarren
Langford
Staplegrove
Milverton
Hillcommon
Oake
Oake Green
Waterrow
Raddington
Blackwell
Quartley
Morebath
Petton
Shillingford
Bathealton
Hillfarance
Bishop's Hull
S O M E R S E T
Bampton
Clayhanger
Poleshill
Langford Budville
Chipley
Sandylands
Gundenham
East Nynehead
Nynehead
Bradford-on-Tone
Comeytrowe
Kittisford
Appley
Ashbrittle
Stawley
Wellisford
Runnington
Tonedale
Wellington
Rockwell Green
Thorne St Margaret
Holywell Lake
Chelston
Hockholler
West Buckland
Huntsham
Hockworthy
Greenham
Payton
Westford
Sampford Arundel
Middle Green
Ford Street
Angersleigh
Cove
Holcombe Rogus
Whipcott
White Ball
Wrangway
Red Ball
Westleigh
Burlescombe
North End
Nicholashayne
Wellington Monument
Simonsburrow
Clayhidon
East Mere
Chevithorne
Uplowman
Whitnage
Appledore
Culm Davy
Brownheath
Bolham
Chettiscombe
Cowleymoor
Sampford Peverell
Halberton
Culmstock
Hemyock
Rosemary Lane
Churchstanton
Stapley
Tiverton
Uffculme
Craddock
Ashill
Bolham Water
Churchinford
Ash Thomas
Willand
Smithincott
Abbey
Smeatharpe
Butterleigh
Cullompton
Kentisbeare
Blackborough
D E V O N
B L A C K D O W N
H I L L S
Sheldon
Dunkeswell
Upottery
Dulford
Kerswell
Luppitt
Colebrook
Bradninch
Mutterton
Westcott
Broadhembury
Wolverstone
Beacon
Wick
Monkton
Silverton
Langford
Hele
Norman's Green
Plymtree
Payhembury
Awliscombe
Combe Raleigh
Cotleigh
Ellerhayes
Clyst Hydon
Tale
Honiton
Budlake
Clyst St Lawrence
Colestocks
Buckerell
Talaton
Feniton
Gittisham
Offwell
Wilmington
Westwood
Fenny Bridges
Alfington

Taunton
Chard
Ilminster
Axminster
Langport
South Petherton
SOMERSET
DEVON
DORSET
BLACKDOWN HILLS
Broomfield
Kingston St Mary
Cheddon Fitzpaine
Monkton Heathfield
North Newton
Thurloxton
Burrow-bridge
Othery
Athelney
Lyng
Stoke St Gregory
Creech St Michael
North Curry
Ruishton
Henlade
Thornfalcon
Curry Rivel
Huish Episcopi
Muchelney
Drayton
Fivehead
Curry Mallet
Beercrocombe
Isle Abbotts
Isle Brewers
Hatch Beauchamp
West Hatch
Bishop's Hull
Norton Fitzwarren
Staplegrove
Trull
Staplehay
Pitminster
Blagdon Hill
Churchstanton
Churchinford
Stoke St Mary
Orchard Portman
Staple Fitzpaine
Bickenhall
Curland
Ashill
Broadway
Horton
Donyatt
Ilton
Puckington
Barrington
Shepton Beauchamp
Kingsbury Episcopi
Stocklinch
Seavington St Michael
Seavington St Mary
Lopen
Dinnington
Hinton St George
Dowlish Wake
Kingstone
Whitestaunton
Buckland St Mary
Combe St Nicholas
Wadeford
Cricket Malherbie
Chillington
Cudworth
Chaffcombe
Crewkerne
Winsham
Wayford
Clapton
Seaborough
Cricket St Thomas
Whatley
Forton
Tatworth
South Chard
Chardstock
Thorncombe
Holditch
Hawkchurch
Membury
Stockland
Yarcombe
Upottery
Rawridge
Monkton
Cotleigh
Dalwood
Wilmington
Offwell
Weycroft
Smallridge
Churchill
Tytherleigh
Burstock
Broadwindsor
Bettiscombe
Pilsdon
Marshwood
Blackney
Drimpton
Marsh
Howley
Newcott
Millhayes
Heathstock
Kilmington
Taunton Deane Services
A303
A358
A30
A35
A378
A361
A372
M5
0 1 2 3 miles
0 1 2 3 4 5 km

Somerton
Littleton
Kingweston
Keinton Mandeville
Lydford-on-Fosse
Castle Cary
Alford
Shepton Montague
Bratton Seymour
Wincanton
Charlton Mackerell
Charlton Adam
Babcary
Foddington
North Barrow
South Barrow
Galhampton
Yarlington
Lovington
North Cadbury
Holton
Cary Fitzpaine
Kingsdon
Long Sutton
Podimore
Sparkford
Blackford
Maperton
Lattiford
North Cheriton
South Cheriton
Compton Pauncefoot
South Cadbury
West Camel
Queen Camel
Sutton Montis
Bridgehampton
Yeovilton
Ilchester
Limington
Chilton Cantelo
Marston Magna
Rimpton
Corton Denham
Charlton Horethorne
Stowell
Templecombe
Abbas Combe
Long Load
Stapleton
Ash
Martock
Tintinhull
Chilthorne Domer
Ashington
Mudford
Adber
Sandford Orcas
Milborne Wick
Poyntington
Milborne Port
Yenston
Hurst
Stoke sub Hamdon
Montacute
Norton sub Hamdon
Preston Plucknett
Yeovil
Sherborne
Over Compton
Nether Compton
Trent
Oborne
Goathill
Purse Caundle
Haydon
Chiselborough
Odcombe
Brympton
East Chinnock
West Chinnock
West Coker
North Coker
East Coker
Barwick
Stoford
Bradford Abbas
Thornford
North Wootton
Alweston
Folke
Bishop's Caundle
Stourton Caundle
Longburton
Lillington
Beer Hackett
Knighton
Yetminster
Ryme Intrinseca
Closworth
Hardington Mandeville
Hardington Marsh
Pendomer
Haselbury Plucknett
North Perrott
Crewkerne
Misterton
South Perrott
Halstock
Melbury Osmond
Leigh
Chetnole
Holnest
Glanvilles Wootton
Hermitage
Middlemarsh
Duntish
Pulham
Melbury Bubb
Melbury Sampford
Corscombe
Chedington
West Chelborough
Evershot
Holywell
Batcombe
Hilfield
Minterne Magna
Buckland Newton
Rampisham
Frome St Quintin
Up Cerne
Alton Pancras
Cerne Abbas
Beaminster
Wraxall
Chalmington
Up Sydling
Hooke
Cattistock
Sydling St Nicholas
Piddletrenthide
Netherbury
Melplash
Chilfrome
North Poorton
Toller
Maiden Newton
White Lackington
DORSET
A37
A303
A30
A359
A3088
A356
A352
A357
A371
A372
B3151
B3153
B3148
B3145

Stavordale
Pen Ridge Fm
Zeals
Lower Zeals
Mere
Charnage
Upton
Roundhill Grange
Brickhouse Fm
Pear Ash
Penselwood
Wolverton
Castle Ground Fm
Rook Street
Woodlands Manor
Southbrook
Limpers Hill
Bush Fm
Broadmead Fm
The Green
Milton
Sheephouse Fm
Fonthill Gifford
Rectory Fm
Shalford
Greenlands Fm
Leigh Common
Queen Oak
Bourton
White Hill
Barrow Street
Park Corner Fm
Underhill
Holloway
East Knoyle
Ruddlemoor Fm
Moorhayes Fm
Cuttlesham Fm
Charlton Musgrove
Southmarsh
Redmoor Fm
West Swainsford
Lugmarsh Fm
Kinghay
Tisbury
Tuckingmill
Wincanton
Riding Gate
Huntingford
Westleaze Fm
Higher Holbrook Fm
Windmill Hill
Bayford
Slodbrook Fm
Silton
West Bourton
Snaggs Fm
Friars Hayes Fm
New Leaze Fm
Upper Leigh Fm
Sycamore Fm
Clapton Fm
Lower Park Fm
Westmarsh Fm
Pitts Fm
Newtown
Pythouse
East Hatch
Hatch
Suddon Grange
West Hill
Wincanton Museum
Stoke Trister
Tinker's Hill
Milton on Stour
Bloomer's Fm
Sweetwell Fm
Lower Leigh Fm
Billhay Fm
Mitchell's Fm
Whistley Fm
Lawn Fm
Gutchpool Fm
Sedgehill
Hook Valley Fm
Stileway Fm
Milton Fm
North End
Park Ho
West Hatch
Cucklington
Colesbrook
Wolfridge Fm
Whitebridge Fm
Childscourt School
Frith Fm
Hale
Bainley Hill Fm
Peacemarsh
Bowridge Hill
Woodwater Fm
Knapp Hill
Sedgehill Manor
Peaked Fm
Wardour
Brains Fm
Horwood Fm
Baskets Fm
Wyke
Gillingham
Semley
Sutor Fm
Plaishbridge Fm
King's Court Wood
North Hayes Fm
Sem Hill
Broad Oak Fm
Ark Fm
Old Wardour Castle
Lattiford
Grove Fm
Meadow Vale Fm
Clinger Fm
Gillingham Museum
Bay
Elm Hill
Gutch Common
Hook Copse
Malkin Hill Fm
Marsh Court
Higher Marsh Fm
Westbrook Fm
Ham Common
Shorts Green Fm
Westwood Fm
Title Path Hill
Leggatts Fm
Park Gate Fm
Horwood Fm
North Cheriton
Gould's Fm
Langham
Eccliffe
Forest Lodge Fm
Avenue Fm
Hart Hill Fm
Hatts Fm
Barkers Hill
Beauchamp Fm
Nower's Copse
Motcombe
Bittles Green
Buckhorn Weston
Madjeston
Thanes Fm
Donhead St Mary
Donhead St Andrew
South Cheriton
Rodgrove
Hartmoor
Bugley
Shearstock Fm
Hunger Hill Fm
Whitehouse Fm
Wincombe Park
Wincombe
White Sheet Hill
Bow Brook
Pitt House Fm
Caggypole Fm
Bye Fm
Bleet Fm
Hunger Hill
Sherborne Causeway
Bus Pk
Eastleaze Fm
Sans Fm
West End
Horsington
Abbas Combe
Combe Throop
Abbey Ford Br
Pelsham Fm
Kington Magna
Bowden
Clay Hill Ho
Enmore Green
Ivy Cross
Dockham Bottom
Donhead Hall
Milkwell
Birdbush
Brook Waters
Rowberry Ho
Wilkinthroop
Templecombe
Higher Nyland
Lower Fm
New Town
Stour Hill
High Br
East Stour
Terrace Fm
Fry's Fm
East Stour Common
Duncliffe Hill
Green's Fm
Cherry Orchard Fm
Alcester
Gold Hill Museum
Shaftesbury
Abbey
St James
Coombe
Ludwell
Charlton
Ferne
Chapel Fm
West Wood
Common Lane Fm
Gartell Lt Rly
Lower Nyland
West Stour
Hawker's Fm
Duncliffe Wood
Jolliffe's Fm
Coles Lane Fm
Cannfield Fm
Spring Fm
Cann Common
Cann
Manor Fm
Windmill Hill
Yenston
Mohuns Park
Coking Fm
Fifehead Magdalen
Stour Provost
Woodville
Yeatman's Fm
Payhouse Fm
Holm and Ivy Fm
Gear's Mill
Win Green
Lower Bowden Fm
Whitchurch
Lower Marsh
Henstridge
Henstridge Marsh
Factory Fm
Manor Fm
Trill Br
Pigeon House Fm
Stour Row
Great House Fm
HM Prison
West Melbury
East Melbury
Charlton Down
Monk's Down
Henstridge Bowden
Henstridge Ash
Good's Fm
Gore Fm
Guy's Marsh
Allan's Fm
Melbury Abbas
Ashcombe Ho
Inwood
Doncliffe Hall Fm
Kit Hill
Blackven Common
Quarry Fm
Toomer Hill
Trad Est
Hains
Gannetts
Todber
Hayes Fm
Wadmill Fm
Breeze Hill
Melbury Wood
Melbury Hill
Quarry Bottom
Ashcombe Bottom
Ashcombe Farm Cott
Berwick Down
Towns End
Pillwell
Moorside
Lymburghs Fm
Budden's Fm
Ashmore Down
Compton Abbas
Ashgrove Fm
Woodley Down
Triangle Fm
Prior's Down
Marnhull
Twyford
East Compton
Fore Top
Hatts Barn
Gray's Fm
Mounters
Toogoods Fm
Margaret Marsh
Hartgrove
Compton Abbas
West Wood
Ashmore
Tollard Royal
Stalbridge Park
Copse Ho
Stalbridge
Bus Pk
Woodbridge
Elbury Hill
Fontmell Wood
Shepherd's Bottom
Cranborne Chase
Pleck
Walton Elm
Crib-house Fm
Lushes Fm
East Orchard
Bedchester
Fontmell Down
Longcombe Bottom
Tollard Park
Purse Caundle
Frith Ho
Stalbridge Weston
Bibberne Fm
Bungays Fm
Hewletts Fm
Chivrick's Brook
Ramshill Fm
Pen Hill
Fontmell Magna
Fontmell Hill Ho
Larmer Tree Gardens
Manor Fm
Sturt Fm
Stalbridge Common
Marsh Fm
King's Mill Br
Cutt Mill
Northwood Fm
West Orchard
Winchells Fm
Vale Fm
Balfour's Wood
Well Bottom
Tollard Green
Rookery Fm
Trip's Fm
Haddon Lodge
Poolestown
Ryalls Fm
Hinton St Mary
Manor Fm
Manston
Stubhampton Bottom
Farnham Woods
Bagber Br
Sutton Waldron
Caesar's Camp
Tollard Farnham
Plumley Wood
Holtham Plantn
Hargrove Fm
Twinwood Coppice
Farrington
Peggs Fm
Combe Bottom
Sutton Hill
West Lodge
Ashmore Wood
Ashmore Bottom
Manor Fm
Hookswood Ho
Stourton Caundle
Cook's Fm
Blackmoor Vale
Cook's Lane
Colber Fm
Manston Road
Manston Ho
Clayesmore School
Iwerne Minster
Busseys Stool Fm
Chettle Down
Tut Hill Fm
Warr Br
Thornhill Park
Mullins' Fm
Pleak House Fm
Ind Est
Rixon
Hammoon
Fontmell Parva
Gallows Corner
Brookman's Valley
Hill Fm
Earl's Hill
Dungrove Hill
Main Down
Bishop's Caundle
Brunsell Knap Fm
Caundle Brook
Stroud Fm
Lydlinch
Sturminster Newton Museum
Sturminster Newton
Fiddleford Manor
Preston Ho
Rolls Mill
Road Lane Fm
Twofords Br
Lydlinch Common
Hawkins Fm
Stock Gaylard Ho
Bagber
The Bridge
Newton
Fiddleford
Gold Hill
Child Okeford
Iwerne Courtney or Shroton
Preston Hill
Stubhampton
Tarrant Gunville
Chettle
Cox's Water
Brickles Wood
Puxey
Piddles Wood
Sturminster Common
New Cross Gate
Fort
Hambledon Hill
Ranston Hill Bldgs
Ranston Hill
Preston Wood
Grammars Hill
Handcock's Bottom
Gunville Down
Westbury Fm
White Kennels
Higher Wood Br
Holwell
Hydes Fm
New House Fm
Salkeld Br
Rivers Corner
Broad Oak
Angiers Fm
Manor Ho
Hambledon Hill
Home Fm
Woodbridge
Blackrow Fm
Holebrook Fm
Plumber Manor
Darknoll Fm
Conygar Coppice
Hayward Br
Buckshaw Fm
Borough
The
Little Rodmore Fm
Berry Fm
Deadmoor Common
Haydon Fm
Banbury Hill
Etheridge Fm
Hanford
Coombe Bottom
Everley Fm
Free Down
Pimperne Wood
Newfield Fm
Hinton Bushes
Barton Hill
Tarrant Hinton
Barnes Cross
Crouch Hill
Pleck
Packers Hill
King's Stag
Rooksmoor Copse
Fifehead Neville
Roome Fm
Okeford Fitzpaine
Shillingstone
Roman Fort
Hod Hill
Ash
Stourpaine Down
Pimperne Down
Hyde Hill Plantn
New Gorse
Woodrow
Fifehead St Quintin
Whitmore Coppice
The Common
Stroud Fm
Hartcliff Fm
Alders Coppice
Smethered Fm
Kingston
Lydden Ho
Lowbrook Fm
Belchalwell
Belchalwell Street
Eastcombe Wood
Blandford Forest
River Iwerne
Stourpaine
Downend Fm
France Firs
Pimperne
Tarrant Launceston
Warry's Plantns
Harbin's Fm
Pulham Gorse
Hartmoor Fm
East Pulham
Woodrow
Turnworth Ho
Stud Ho
Tarrant Monkton
Pulham
Glebe Fm
Hazelbury Bryan
Pidney
Leigh
Turnworth Clump
Turnworth Down
Hillcombe Coppice
Norton Wood
Durweston
Hammett's Fm
Bus Pk
Blandford Camp
Pitt's Fm
Newlands Fm
West Pulham
Wonston
Droop
Mount Pleasant Fm
Bell Hill
Nutford Fm
Royal Signals Museum
Blackland Plantn
Duntish Elms Fm
Towns End Fm
Cannings Court
Long Wood
Ibberton
Manor France Fm
Ind Est
Letton Park
Luton Fm
Luton Down
Hill
Beaulieu Wood
Park Gate
Fir Tree Fm
Crate Wood
Manor Ho
Ibberton Long Down
Turnworth
Shepherd's Corner Fm
The Hanging
Websley Fm
Bryanston School
Bryanston
Tarrant Rawston
Duntish
Hammond Street Fm
Westfields
Hill Fm
Woolland
South Down
Hedge End
Field Grove
Broadley Wood
Bryanston Park
The Down Wood
Woolford's Water
Skinners Fm
Stoke Wake
Rawlsbury Camp (Earthwork)
Woolland Hill
Normandy Fm
Blandford Forum
Museum
Walnut Avenue
Mappowder
Chaston Fm
Bulbarrow Hill (Earthwork)
Houghton North Down
Knife Hill Fm
Old Warren Plantn
Blandford St Mary
Langton Long Blandford
Ashley Wood
Tarrant Rushton
Rew
Sharnhill Green
Saunders Fm
Hatherly Fm
Delcombe Wood
Delcombe Down
North Barn Fm
Stickland Hill Fm
Lower Blandford St Mary
Buckland Newton
Henley
Bookham
Noake Fm
Thurnwood Fm
Humber Wood
Crockers Fm
Pleck or Little Ansty
Moots Copse
Higher Houghton Fm
Winterborne Houghton
Winterborne Stickland
The Plantation
Littleton
Manor Dairy Fm
Preston Fm
Melcombe Park
Breach Wood
Higher Ansty
Manor Fm
Park Wood
The Old Rectory
Fox Ground Down
Charlton Marshall
Tarrant Keyneston
Church Hill
Ball Hill
Folly
Spring Wood Fm
Hill Wood
Ansty Cross
Delcombe Fm
Quarleston Fm
Skelder Ho
Winterborne Clenston
Little Down
Thorncombe Fm
Thorncombe
Keynston Mill
Barcombe Fm
Alton Pancras
Watcombe Bottom
Lower Ansty
Hilton
Crincombe Bottom
Charity Wood
Field Barn
Charlton on the Hill
Glebe Fm
Tarrant Crawford
Bishops Court Dairy
Holcombe Dairy
Higher Hill
Higher Melcombe
Melcombe Bingham
Cross Lanes
Aller
Coombe Hill
Park Fm
Whatcombe Wood
Milton Park Wood
Oatclose Wood
Higher Whatcombe
Whatcombe
Spetisbury
Melmoth's Hill
Milton Abbey
Henning Hill
Plush
Nettlecombe Fm
Luccombe Fm
Gorcombe Fm
West End
North Fm
Shapwick
Tenant's Hill
Plush Hill
Lyscombe Fm
Newton Fm
Milton Abbas
Luccombe Down
Whatcombe Ho
Lower Whatcombe
South Fm
Higher Southcombe Fm
Bramblecombe
Long Close Fm
Field Dairy Fm
Manor Ho
New Barn Fm
East Hill
Thorncombe Fm
Manor Ho
Gallows Corner
Hewish Fm
Chescombe Fm
Winterborne Whitechurch
Charlton Down
East Down
Field Dairy
Moorcourt Fm
Westley Wood
Dole's Ash Fm
Piddletrenthide
Whitcombe
Selbourne
Whitelands Downs
Bagber Fm
Deverel Down
West Fm
East Fm
North Down
Stag Gate
Newton Peveril
Kingrove Bottom
College Down
Hill Plantn
Cheselbourne West Down
Lawn Barn Fm
Deverel Fm
Almer
East Almer Fm
Lion Lodge
White Lackington
Chebbard Fm
Dewlish
Parsonage Fm
Deverel Fm
Winterborne Kingston
Bushes Fm
Mapperton
Winterborne
Charborough
Marsh Fm
Dullar Fm
D O R S E T
A303
A357
A350
A30
A3030
A354
B3081
B3092
B3091
B3143
B3082
B3075
A B C D E F G H
1 2 3 4 5 6
29 45 46 17 18
0 1 2 3 miles
0 1 2 3 4 5 km

31
Salisbury
Ringwood
Wilton
Ditchampton
Dinton
Baverstock
Barford St Martin
Burcombe
Quidhampton
Bemerton
Netherhampton
Stratford Sub Castle
New Sarum
Bishopdown
Laverstock
Milford
West Harnham
East Harnham
Harnham
Britford
Alderbury
Whaddon
West Grimstead
Chicksgrove
Lower Chicksgrove
Upper Chicksgrove
Teffont Evias
Teffont Magna
Compton Chamberlayne
Fovant
Sutton Mandeville
Sutton Row
Swallowcliffe
Ansty
Stratford Tony
Coombe Bissett
Homington
Odstock
Nunton
Bodenham
Longford Castle
Broad Chalke
Bishopstone
Knapp
Fifield Bavant
Mount Sorrel
Stoke Farthing
Croucheston
Ebbesbourne Wake
West End
Alvediston
Bowerchalke
Misselfore
Woodminton
W I L T S H I R E
C R A N B O U R N E   C H A S E   A N D
W E S T   W I L T S H I R E   D O W N S
H A M P S H I R E
D O R S E T
Charlton-All-Saints
Downton
Wick
Morgan's Vale
Redlynch
Lover
Woodfalls
North Charford
Hale
Martin Drove End
Martin
East Martin
Tidpit
Cobley
Woodyates
New Town
Deanland
Pentridge
Whitsbury
Rockbourne
Upper Street
Outwick
Breamore
Woodgreen
North Street
Flood Street
Upper Burgate
Burgate
Lower Burgate
Damerham
North End
South End
Fordingbridge
Ashford
Sandleheath
Godshill
Stuckton
Frogham
Blissford
Hyde
Hungerford
North Gorley
South Gorley
Ibsley
Mockbeggar
Linwood
Moyles Court
Rockford
Highwood
Blashford
Bickton
Alderholt
Camel Green
Charing Cross
Daggons
Cripplestyle
Crendell
Lower Daggons
Cranborne
Boveridge
Lower Holwell
Edmondsham
Gotham
Verwood
Romford
Woodlands
Woodlands Common
Dewlands Common
Three Legged Cross
Ashley Heath
Ashley
St Ives
St Leonards
West Moors
Ferndown
Trickett's Cross
Stapehill
Colehill
Canford Bottom
Wimborne Minster
Oakley
Canford Magna
Hampreston
Longham
Dudsbury
West Parley
Woodcutts
Sixpenny Handley
Dean
Farnham
Minchington
Gussage St Andrew
Cashmoor
Monkton Up Wimborne
Wimborne St Giles
Gussage St Michael
Gussage All Saints
Knowlton
Long Crichel
Moor Crichel
Manswood
Witchampton
Chalbury
Chalbury Common
Horton
Hinton Martell
Gaunt's Common
Holt Wood
Mannington
Holt
Stanbridge
Hinton Parva
Clapgate
Furzehill
Broom Hill
Pilford
Hillbutts
Pamphill
Tadden
Kingston
Bisterne
Moortown
Burley Street
Burley
Picket Post
Linford
North Poulner
Poulner
Thorney Hill
North Ripley
Ripley
Avon
Bransgore
Shirley
Sopley
Merley
Henbury
Sturminster Marshall
A30
A36
A338
A354
A31
A348
B3078
B3081
B3089
B3080
B3072
B3073
B3347

Pitton
West Winterslow
Horsebridge
King's Somborne
Ashley
Sparsholt
Ham Green
West Tytherley
East Tytherley
Farley
East Grimstead
West Dean
Alderbury
Whaddon
West Grimstead
Lockerley
East Dean
Butt's Green
Mottisfont
Dunbridge
Braishfield
Michelmersh
Timsbury
Pucknall
Hursley
Standon
Compton
Brook
Lower Brook
Kimbridge
Carter's Clay
Whiteparish
Newton
Kent's Oak
Upper Ratley
Awbridge
Newtown
Abbotswood
Ampfield
Knapp
Ladwell
Cupernham
Romsey
Sherfield English
Wellow Wood
Plaitford Green
Landford Manor
Plaitford
Landford
West Wellow
East Wellow
Whitenap
Halterworth
Chandler's Ford
North Baddesley
Eastleigh
Chilworth
Morgan's Vale
Redlynch
Lover
Woodfalls
North Charford
Hale
Hamptworth
Nomansland
Canada
Ridge
Lee
Rownhams
Nursling
Bassett
Swaythling
Wigley
Ower
Bramshaw
Furzley
Hillstreet
Stonyford
Calmore
Testwood
Totton
Brook
Fritham
Cadnam
Copythorne
Winsor
Bartley
Netley Marsh
Rushington
Millbrook
Eling
Southampton
SOUTHAMPTON
Shirley
Portswood
Northam
Woolston
Itchen
Upper Canterton
Stoney Cross
Minstead
Newtown
Broomy Lodge
Woodlands
Ashurst
Foxhills
Hounsdown
Pooksgreen
Marchwood
Linwood
Emery Down
Lyndhurst
Bank
Clayhill
Pikeshill
Hythe
Dibden
Applemore
Dibden Purlieu
Picket Post
Burley Lodge
Denny Lodge
Hardley
Holbury
Burley Street
Burley
Bisterne Close
Brockenhurst
Balmerlawn
Beaulieu
Hatchet Gate
Hill Top
Setley
East Boldre
Bucklers Hard
Exbury
Sway
Battramsley
Pilley
Bull Hill
Wootton
Bransgore
THE NEW FOREST NATIONAL PARK
HAM
M27
M271
A36
A27
A31
A35
A337
A326
A3090
B3054
B3056
0 1 2 3 miles
0 1 2 3 4 5 km

Winchester
Weeke
Harestock
Easton
Avington
Ovington
New Alresford
Bishop's Sutton
Ropley
Ropley Dean
Charlwood
Monkwood
Colemore
Tichborne
Winnall
St Giles's Hill
Fulflood
Sleepers Hill
Stanmore
Chilcomb
Cheriton
New Cheriton
North End
Bramdean
West Tisted
Lane End
Hinton Ampner
HINTON AMPNER
Filmore Hill
Bailey Green
Privett
High Cross
Oliver's Battery
Compton
Compton End
Morestead
Beauworth
Kilmeston
Brockwood
West Meon Woodlands
Froxfield Green
Lower Bordean
Northfields
Shawford
Otterbourne
Twyford
Owslebury
Baybridge
Longwood Dean Fm
West Meon
East End
Warnford
Langrish
Colden Common
Hensting
Blackdown
Beacon Hill 201
Exton
East Meon
Ramsdean
Frogmore
Fisher's Pond
Crowdhill
MARWELL ZOOLOGICAL PARK
Upham
Lower Upham
Dean
Ashton
Corhampton
Meonstoke
Coombe
Bishopstoke
Fair Oak
Durley Street
Wintershill
Newtown
Bishop's Waltham
Hoe
Upper Swanmore
Droxford
Brockbridge
Chidden
Clanfield
Horton Heath
Durley
Brown Heath
Swanmore
Soberton
Hillpound
Glebe
Waltham Chase
Shirrell Heath
Soberton Heath
Hambledon
Catherington
Long Common
Boorley Green
Curdridge
Shedfield
Kingsmead
Hoe Gate
Newtown
Horndean
West End
Botley
Hedge End
Curbridge
Wickham
Hundred Acres
North Boarhunt
Forest Gate
Anthill Common
Denmead
Lovedean
Cowplain
Netley Hill
Hightown
Lowford
Old Netley
Burridge
Bursledon
Swanwick
Lower Swanwick
Tapnage
Knowle
Funtley
Crockerhill
Walton Heath
Southwick
Waterlooville
Havant
Leigh Park
Hound
Netley
Park Gate
Sarisbury
Segensworth
Titchfield Park
Wallington
Boarhunt
Purbrook
Bedhampton
Hamble-le-Rice
Locks Heath
Titchfield Common
Warsash
Fleetend
Abshot
Titchfield
Fareham
West End
Portchester
Paulsgrove
Wymering
Cosham
Drayton
Farlington
Langstone
Newtown
Hook
Fleetlands
PORTSMOUTH
PORTSMOUTH HARBOUR
Hilsea
Tipner
Fawley
Ashlett
Calshot
Stubbington
Peel Common
Bridgemary
Meon
Hill Head
Hardway
Elson
Rowner
Brockhurst
North End
Portsea Island
LANGSTONE HARBOUR
Lee-on-the-Solent
Gosport
Portsmouth
Portsea
Fratton
Eastney
Milton
Southsea
Alverstoke
Clayhall
Privett
Somers Town
Stanswood Bay
Stokes Bay
SOUTH DOWNS NATIONAL PARK
SOUTHAMPTON WATER
M27
M3
M275
A3(M)
A31
A32
A272
A27
Hayling I

Valence
Empshott
Greatham
Longmoor Camp
Liphook
Linchmere
Kingsley Green
Fernhurst
Fisherstreet
Colemore
Hawkley
Liss Forest
Langley
West Liss
East Liss
Liss
Rake
Hill Brow
Rogate Common
Milland
Upper Wardley
Woodmansgreen
Chorley Common
Redford
Henley Common
Henley
Lickfold
Lurgashall
Bexleyhill
High Cross
Froxfield Green
Steep Marsh
Steep
Petersfield
Sheet
Langrish
Stroud
Durleighmarsh
Rogate
Fyning
Terwick Common
Borden
Titty Hill
Trotton
Chithurst
Iping
Stedham
Woolbeding
Easebourne
Lodsworth
Ramsdean
Weston
Nursted
Buriton
Dumpford
Nyewood
Minsted
Midhurst
Selham
Halfway Bridge
West Lavington
South Ambersham
South Harting
East Harting
Elsted
Treyford
Didling
Bepton
Cocking
Heyshott
Graffham
Clanfield
Chalton
North Marden
Hooksway
East Lavington
WEST SUSSEX
SOUTH DOWNS NATIONAL PARK
Catherington
Horndean
Compton
Up Marden
West Marden
East Marden
Chilgrove
West Dean
Singleton
Charlton
East Dean
Upwaltham
Blendworth
Finchdean
Forestside
Deanlane End
Cowplain
Rowlands Castle
Stoughton
Walderton
Havant
Leigh Park
Stockheath
Bedhampton
Warblington
Emsworth
Westbourne
Woodmancote
Funtington
West Ashling
East Ashling
Woodend
West Stoke
Mid Lavant
East Lavant
Westerton
Halnaker
Boxgrove
Strettington
Summersdale
Westhampnett
Tangmere
Nyton
Hambrook
Southbourne
Nutbourne
Hermitage
Langstone
Broadbridge
Bosham
Chichester
Fishbourne
Apuldram
Stockbridge
Oving
Aldingbourne
Westergate
Woodgate
Chidham
Northney
North Hayling
Stoke
West Thorney
CHICHESTER HARBOUR
Thorney Island
LANGSTONE HARBOUR
Fleet
Donnington
Merston
Colworth
Lidsey
Runcton
Shripney
North Mundham
Hunston
West Itchenor
Bosham Hoe
Shipton Green
Birdham
South Mundham
North Bersted
South Bersted
Rose Green
Bognor Regis
Aldwick
Nyetimber
Pagham
West Wittering
Somerley
Highleigh
Street End
Hayling Island
Hayling Bay
0 1 2 3 miles
0 1 2 3 4 5 km

Loxwood
Plaistow
Ifold
Broadbridge Heath
Horsham
Slinfold
The Haven
Northchapel
Mackerel's Common
Roundstreet Common
Five Oaks
Itchingfield
Southwater Street
Mannings Heath
Ebernoe
Kirdford
Wisborough Green
Newpound Common
Billingshurst
Barns Green
Southwater
Monk's Gate
Balls Cross
Strood Green
Parbrook
Copsale
Nuthurst
Brooks Green
Coneyhurst
Maplehurst
Upperton
Gunter's Bridge
Adversane
Dragons Green
Tillington
Petworth
Bedham
Coolham
Cowfold
Shipley
West Grinstead
Broadford Bridge
Byworth
Codmore Hill
North Heath
Gay Street
Broomer's Corner
Littleworth
Dial Post
Fittleworth
Stopham
Nutbourne
West Chiltington
Partridge Green
Pulborough
Marehill
Goose Green
Duncton
Hardham
Coldwaltham
Thakeham
Spear Hill
Barlavington
Wiggonholt
West Chiltington Common
Ashington
Ashurst
Henfield
Sutton
Watersfield
Greatham
Abingworth
Bignor
Storrington
Sullington
Rock
Hole Street
Wiston
West Burton
Bury
Amberley
Cootham
Rackham
Washington
Steyning
Houghton
Bramber
Madehurst
North Stoke
North End
Upper Beeding
South Stoke
Offham
Findon
Burpham
Wepham
Botolphs
Slindon
Warningcamp
Patching
Clapham
Coombes
Arundel
Crossbush
High Salvington
Walberton
Binsted
Hammerpot
Findon Valley
North Lancing
Tortington
Poling
Salvington
Lancing
Barnham
Lyminster
Angmering
Durrington
Sompting
Ford
Wick
Hangleton
West Tarring
Broadwater
Yapton
Toddington
East Worthing
South Lancing
Climping
East Preston
Ferring
Worthing
Littlehampton
Rustington
Goring-by-Sea
West Worthing
Bilsham
Flansham
Middleton-on-Sea
Atherington
Elmer
Felpham
A272
A24
A29
A283
A27
A259
A280
A264
A281
A2032
B2133
B2139
B2138
B2135
50
51
36
TQ
A
B
C
D
E
F
G
H
7
8
9
10
11

36
Horsham
Tilgate Forest Row
Handcross
Balcombe
West Hill
Ardingly
Highbrook
Wych Cross
Chelwood Gate
Chelwood Common
Danehill
Horsted Keynes
Nutley
Mannings Heath
Ashfold Crossways
Slaugham
Staplefield
Lower Beeding
Monk's Gate
Nuthurst
Warninglid
Crabtree
Slough Green
Brook Street
Whitemans Green
Cuckfield
Lindfield
Haywards Heath
Scayne's Hill
Sheffield Green
Splayne's Green
Fletching
Maplehurst
Cowfold
Bolney
Ansty
Chownes Mead
Bolnore
Lyoth Common
Fletching Common
Grisling Common
Crosspost
Kent Street
Twineham Green
Twineham
Wineham
Hickstead
Goddards Green
Abbotsford
Burgess Hill
Wivelsfield
Wivelsfield Green
North Chailey
Newick
Chailey
South Street
Littleworth
Partridge Green
Shermanbury
Sayers Common
World's End
Ditchling Common
Spithurst
West End
Henfield
High Cross
Blackstone
Albourne Green
Albourne
Hurstpierpoint
Hurst Wickham
Keymer
Ditchling
Plumpton Green
Chiltington
Barcombe Cross
Barcombe
Hassocks
Bedlam Street
Nep Town
Woodmancote
Streat
East Chiltington
Clayton
Westmeston
Plumpton
Cooksbridge
Hamsey
Small Dole
Poynings
Fulking
Edburton
Pyecombe
Saddlescombe
Offham
Upper Beeding
Bramber
Castle Town
Botolphs
South Malling
Wallands Park
Lewes
Southover
Patcham
Coldean
Stanmer
Falmer
Kingston near Lewes
Beddingham
BRIGHTON AND HOVE
Mile Oak
Hangleton
West Blatchington
Westdene
Withdean
Hollingbury
Moulsecoomb
Preston
Hollingdean
Bevendean
Woodingdean
Iford
Rodmell
Southease
Old Shoreham
Portslade
Southwick
Kingston by Sea
Fishersgate
Hove
Aldrington
Shoreham-by-Sea
Portslade-by-Sea
Brighton
Kemp Town
Whitehawk
Roedean
Ovingdean
Telscombe
Piddinghoe
Rottingdean
Saltdean
Telscombe Cliffs
Peacehaven
Newhaven
Peacehaven Heights
Harbour Heights
South Lancing
SOUTH DOWNS WAY
A23
A27
A272
A275
A26
A259
A283
A281
A22
0 1 2 3 miles
0 1 2 3 4 5 km

Crowborough
St John's
Steel Cross
Poundfield
Rotherfield
Town Row
Mark Cross
Wadhurst
Best Beech Hill
Stone Cross
Shover's Green
Three Leg Cross
Ticehurst
Wallcrouch
Riseden
Tidebrook
Bardown
Stonegate
Coggins Mill
Mayfield
Witherenden Hill
Etchingham
Whitehill
Alderbrook
Jarvis Brook
Poundgate
Duddleswell
Fairwarp
High Hurstwood
Cackle Street
Maresfield
Five Ash Down
Pound Green
Hadlow Down
Five Ashes
Butcher's Cross
Burwash
Burwash Common
Burwash Weald
Buxted
Ringles Cross
Uckfield
Cross in Hand
Mutton Hall
Broad Oak
Cade Street
Heathfield
Old Heathfield
Three Cups Corner
Punnett's Town
Brightling
Oxley's Green
Blackboys
Framfield
Ridgewood
Little London
Waldron
Maynard's Green
Rushlake Green
Dallington
Darwell Hole
Netherfield
Little Horsted
Horam
Warbleton
Foxhunt Green
Penhurst
Halland
East Hoathly
Burlow
Foul Mile
Ponts Green
Shortgate
Chiddingly
Whitesmith
Gun Hill
Cowbeech
Bodle Street Green
Laughton
Golden Cross
Herstmonceux
Windmill Hill
Ninfield
Glyndebourne
Ripe
Lower Dicker
Upper Dicker
Hellingly
Lower Horsebridge
Upper Horsebridge
Magham Down
Boreham Street
Hooe Common
Chalvington
Hailsham
Wartling
Hooe
Little Common
Selmeston
Arlington
Caneheath
Summer Hill
Pevensey Levels
Rickney
Hooe Level
Alciston
Berwick
Polegate
Hankham
Pevensey
Norman's Bay
Wilmington
Folkington
Westham
Pevensey Bay
Alfriston
Willingdon
Hampden Park
Langney
Litlington
Jevington
St Anthony's Hill
Roselands
Norton
Bishopstone
East Blatchington
Seaford
Westdean
Friston
Eastbourne
EAST SUSSEX
A22
A26
A27
A259
A265
A267
A271
A272
A2290
B2100
B2102
B2192
B2124
TQ
A
B
C
D
E
F
G
H

Flimwell
Leg Cross
Berner's Hill
Seacox Heath
Dale Hill
Ringden Fm
High Street
Hawkhurst
Highgate
Four Throws
Woodsden
Pipsden
Gun Green
Iden Green
Beacon Hill
West Cross
Dingleden
C M BOOTH COLLECTION OF HISTORIC VEHICLES
Rolvenden
Rolvenden Layne
Small Hythe
SMALLHYTHE PLACE
Reading Street
Appledore Heath
Bulleign
Pashley Manor
PASHLEY MANOR GDNS
Wardsbrook Fm
Horns Corner
The Moor
Field Green
Sandhurst
Standen Street
Great Job's Cross
Peening Quarter
Swiftsden
Three Gates Fm
Burgh Wood
Cooper's Corner
Stone House Fm
Conghurst Fm
Linkhill
Lamberden
Kensham Fm
KENT & EAST SUSSEX RAILWAY
Potman's Heath
Maytham Wharf
Isle of Oxney
Moon's Green
Wittersham
Stone
Stone in Oxney
The Stocks
Burgh Hill
Hurst Green
Etchingham
ETCHINGHAM
Haremere Hall
Silver Hill
Sandhurst Cross
Newenden
Frogs Hill
Rother Levels
Ham Green
Blackbrook Fm
Tophill Fm
Newbridge Fm
Bodiam
BODIAM CASTLE
Bodiam Br
South Park
Lower Northlands Fm
Northiam
GREAT DIXTER
Dixter Wood
FARM WORLD
Knelle Wood
River Rother
Underwood's Fm
Bugsell Mill Fm
Bush Barn
Northbridge Street
Willard's Hill
Salehurst
ROTHER VALLEY RLY CENTRE
ROBERTSBRIDGE
Robertsbridge
Squibs Fm
Snagshall
Ewhurst Green
Sempstead Wood
Mill Corner
Beckley
Four Oaks
Flackley Ash
Clayhill
Peasmarsh
Iden
Houghton Green
Playden
Rye Foreign
Bowler's Town
East Guldeford
Oxley's Green
Brightling Hall
Glottenham Manor
Collier's Green
Horns Cross
Staplecross
Lordship Wood
Swaile's Green
Cripp's Corner
The Grange
The Beacon
EAST SUSSEX
Great Stent Fm
Beckley Furnace
Beckley Woods
Groves
Partridge Fm
Clayton Fm
Rye
YPRES TOWER
LAMB HOUSE
HERITAGE CENTRE & TOWN MODEL
Hollingrove
Cackle Street
Darwell Reservoir
Darwell Wood
Mountfield
John's Cross
Vinehall Street
Footland Wood
Brede High Wood
Chitcombe
Broad Oak
Broadland Row
Conster Manor
Powdermill Res
Tillingham Fm
Udimore
Camber Castle
Rye Harbour
RYE HARBOUR
Darwell Hill
Darwell Hole
Netherfield
Crowhurst Wood
Woodmans Green
Sedlescombe
Goatham Green
Cackle Street
Brede
Pickdick Fm
Great Sowdens Wood
Cock Marling
Brede Level
Winchelsea
WINCHELSEA COURT HALL MUSEUM
Rye Marsh Fm
Nook Beach
Canadia
Whatlington
Sedlescombe Street
BREDE STEAM GIANTS
Pestalozzi Children's Village
Penhurst
Battle
BATTLE ABBEY
1066
Ashburnham Forge
Steven's Crouch
Kent Street
Westfield
Doleham
Lidham Hill
Guestling Thorn
Broad Street
Icklesham
Winchelsea Beach
Pett Level
Starr's Green
Telham
Beauport Park
Catsfield
Catsfield Stream
Crowhurst
Marlpits
Ninfield
Lower Street
Henley's Down
Three Oaks
Pett
Guestling Green
Cliff End
Baldslow
Friar's Hill
Hollington
Silverhill Park
St Helen's
Ore
Fairlight
Fairlight Cove
Hooe Common
Lunsford's Cross
Silverhill
Bohemia
Blacklands
St Helen's Wood
Broomsgrove
Clive Vale
Belmont
Fairlight Glen
Covehurst Bay
Ecclesbourne Glen
Hooe
Gotham
The Highlands
Sidley
COMBE VALLEY COUNTRYSIDE PARK
Harley Shute
Bulverhythe
West Hill
ST CLEMENTS CAVE
SHIPWRECK HERITAGE CENTRE
BLUE REEF AQUARIUM
Hastings
Old Town
Little Common
Glenleigh Park
Pebsham
Glyne Gap
West Marina
St Leonards
Galley Hill
Cooden
Bexhill
DE LA WARR PAVILION
My Lord's Rock
Hooe Level
COODEN BEACH
Norman's Bay
TQ
0 1 2 3 miles
0 1 2 3 4 5 km

Great Heron Wood
Park Hill
Corner
Smith's Fm
Thrift Cott
Higham Fm
Bridge Fm
Johnson's Corner
Wey Street Fm
Will's Fm
Brooker Fm
Manor Ho
Newchurch
Gammon's Fm
Forty Acre Cott
Burmarsh
Donkey Street
HORNE'S PLACE CHAPEL
The Dowels
Stockbridge Ho
Poplar Ho
Norwood Fm
New Barn Fm
Orgarswick Fm
Chapel Cottage Fm
Sutton Fm
HYTHE ROAD
Dymchurch Wall
A259
B2080
APPLEDORE
Bridge Fm
Ham Fm
Whitehall Fm
Snave
Romney
Willow Fm
Lodgeland Fm
Pickney Bush Fm
Blackmanstone Br
DYMCHURCH
DYMCHURCH MARTELLO TOWER
Dymchurch
Sellinge Fm
Brenzett Green
Hope Fm
New House Fm
Moat Ho
Poplar Fm
Marsh
North Fording Bungalow
St Mary in the Marsh
ROMNEY, HYTHE & DYMCHURCH RAILWAY
Snargate
Priory Fm
Spring Fm
Melon Fm
Ivychurch
A2070
ST MARY'S BAY
St Mary's Bay
Highknock Channel
Fairfield Court
Brodnyx
ROMNEY WARREN
Honeychild Manor
Becket Barn Fm
Brenzett
Brenzett Place
AERONAUTICAL MUSEUM
Blue House Fm
Yoakes Court Fm
Beechcroft Fm
DYMCHURCH ROAD
Fairfield
Brattle Ho
Old Hall Fm
Rhewall Fm
Sewer
ROMNEY WARREN HALT
ROMNEY MARSH
ROMNEY MARSH VISITOR CENTRE
Poplar Hall
New
Hope Fm
Bush Fm
A259
Warren Fm
Dean Court
Brookland
Sycamore Fm
Old Romney
New Romney
NEW ROMNEY
Phoenix Caisson
Hook Ho
Coldharbour Fm
LYDD ROAD
B2071
New Buildings Fm
Whitehouse Fm
Court Lodge
Hammonds Corner
Littlestone-on-Sea
White Kemp Sewer
Blue House Fm
Kemp's Hill
Romney Sands
GULDEFORD LANE
Old Cheyne Court
Midley Cotts
Hawthorn Corner
ROMNEY ROAD
Walland
Coldicott Fm
Belgar Fm
Greatstone-on-Sea
Guldeford Lane Corner
Baynham Fm
Westbrook Fm
B2075
Footway Fm
Court
Newland Fm
Marsh
ROMNEY SANDS
Little Cheyne Court
Little Scotney
Westbroke Ho
Jack's Court
Kent Ditch
Lydd (London Ashford)
Barn Fm
Lydd
Lade
Pigwell
Rod Ho
Scotney Court
Denge Marsh
Lydd-on-Sea
LYDD INTERNATIONAL RACEWAY
DUNGENESS
RSPB
Halfway Bush
Point Fm
Danger area
Boulderwall Fm
Camber
Jury's Gap
Holmstone
Lydd Ranges
West Ripe
Manor Fm
DUNGENESS
Open Pits
Broomhill Level
Camber Sands
South Brooks
Brickwall Fm
RYE BAY
Broomhill Sands
Dungeness Power Sta
DUNGENESS
Dungeness
THE OLD LIGHTHOUSE
54
55
7
8
9
10
11
A
B
C
D
E
F
G
H
TR
20
30
00

56
56
SS
Hen & Chickens
Seals' Rock
North West Pt
North East Pt
Gannets' Rock
Gannets' Bay
St James's Stone
Tibbetts Hill 138
LUNDY MARINE NATURE RESERVE
Tibbett's Pt
Jenny's Cove
Lundy
Dead Cow Pt
Ackland's Moor 142
Lundy Roads
BIDEFORD (APRIL-OCT) ILFRACOMBE (APRIL-OCT)
Halftide Rock
Beacon Hill
Rat Island
Castle Hill
Surf Pt
South West Pt
LUNDY (APRIL-OCT)
Capstone Pt
Samson's Bay
Water Mouth
WATERMOUTH CASTLE
Rawn's Rocks
Blackstone Pt
Elwill Bay
Trentishoe
Hele Bay
Little Hangman 218
Gt Hangman 318
Hangman Pt
SOUTH WEST COAST PATH
Ilfracombe
Hele
HELE CORN MILL
Hole Fm
Holdstone Down 349
South Dean Fm
Trentishoe Down
Shag Pt
Flat Pt
MUSEUM
Chambercombe
Goosewell
Lester Cliff
Girt Down
Bull Pt
Pensport Rock
Lee Bay
CHAMBERCOMBE MANOR
Berrynarbor
Lee
Combe Martin
Lee
Lincombe
Higher Slade
Kitstone Hill
NORTH DEVON
Rockham Bay
North Morte Fm
Higher Warcombe
Whitestone
Lower Slade
Warmscombe Fm
Sterridge
Morte Pt
Mortehoe
Shaftsboro Fm
Campscott Fm
Slade Resrs
Oakridge Fm
Two Pots
Stoneditch Hill
Henstridge
WILDLIFE & DINOSAUR PARK
Borough Cross
Little Shelfin Fm
Grunta Pool
Manor Fm
Trimstone
Ind Est
Hore Down Fm
Ettiford Fm
Berry Down Cross
South Ley
Kentisbury
Woolacombe
Mill Rock
Cheglinch
Morte Bay
Ossaborough
Willingcott
Outer Narracott
Bugford
Stonecombe
Ivycott
Bradwell
Dean
Dean Cross
Patchole
Roadway
Bittadon
Kentisbury Ford
Black Rock
Putsborough Sand
Pickwell Down
Spreacombe Manor
North Downs
West Down
Fullabrook
Burland Fm
Baggy Pt
Pickwell
Castle Street Fm
Buckland Down
Little Silver
Churchill
Arlington
Putsborough
Vention
Fullabrook Down
East Down
Croyde Bay
North Buckland
Georgeham
Metcombe Down
Hewish Down
ARLINGTON COURT
Ora Hill
Forda
Croyde
Nethercott
Winsham Down Ho
Halsinger Down
Patsford
Milltown
Cross
Darracott
Upcott
Halsinger
Winsham
Swindon Down
Loxhore
South Hole Fm
Incledon Fm
Knowle
Middle Marwood
Whiddon
Crockers
Muddiford
CROYDE ROAD SAUNTON ROAD
Buckland Manor
Boode
Higher Muddiford
Lobb
Marwood
Guineaford
Saunton
Whitehall
MARWOOD HILL
Kingsheanton
Shirwell Cross
Shirwell
Sandy Lane Fm
Braunton
Pippacott
Prixford
BROOMHILL SCULPTURE GARDENS
Shop Cen
Luscott Barton
Waterlake
Saunton Sands
Braunton Down
Mainstone
Springfield Cross
Heanton Punchardon
West Ashford
Velator
Wrafton
Ashford
Upcott Ho
Burridge
Stoke Rivers
Braunton Burrows
Braunton Marsh
Chivenor
Penhill Pt
Bradiford
Raleigh
Snapper
Goodleigh
Horsey Island
Allen's Rock
Pilton
Waytown
Airy Pt
Danger area
Saltpill Duck Pond
Penhill
Pottington
Derby
Barnstaple
MUSEUM OF BARNSTAPLE & NORTH DEVON
Gunn
LUNDY (APRIL-OCT)
River Taw
ST ANNE'S CHAPEL & MUSEUM
Broad Sands
Lower Yelland
Muddlebridge
Sticklepath
Westacott
Yelland
Fremington
Bickington
Newport
Crow Pt
Combrew
Brynsworthy
Landkey
Crow Rock
Instow Sands
The Quay
Worlington
Bickleton
Myrtle Cott
Roundswell
Rumsam
Landkey Newland
Swimbridge Newland
Appledore
N DEVON MARITIME MUSEUM
Sandymere
NORTHAM BURROWS
Instow
Fullingcott Fm
Upcott Fm
Hollamoor Clump
Bishops Tawton
Yarnacott
Riverton
Diddywell
Huish
Eastacombe
Swimbridge
24
25
St John's Chapel
Tawstock
Hannaford
TAPELEY PARK GARDENS
Huish Moor
Stonyland
Downrew Ho
Westleigh
Rushcott Fm
Prospect Corner
Uppacott
Horswell Fm
Hangman's Hill
Northam
Holmacott
Eastleigh Manor
Halmpstone Manor
Rickard's
Silford
Horwood
Summer
3 miles
5 km

Foreland Pt
Countisbury Cove
Woody Bay
Wringcliff Bay
Crock Pt
Lee Bay
Lynton
CLIFF RLY
Countisbury
Kipscombe Hill 343
Old Burrow Hill 345
Sugarloaf Hill
Embelle Wood
Culbone Wood
Gore Pt
Porlock Bay
Hurlstone Pt
Selworthy Sand
Martinhoe
LYN & EXMOOR MUSEUM
Lynmouth
Lynbridge
Wind Hill
LYNTON
WATERSMEET HOUSE
Coombe Fm
Ashton Fm
Southern Wood
Yenworthy Fm
Broomstreet Fm
CULBONE CHURCH
Worthy
Toll
Yarner Fm
Dean
Caffyns Fm
Barton Wood
Leeford
Wilsham
Brendon
Malmsmead
Fellingscott
West Lyn
Kemacott
Martinhoe Common
A39
East Ilkerton
Barbrook
Combe Park Ho
Bridge Ball
Hillsford Br
Tippacott
Rockford
Slocombeslade
North Common
Lillycombe Ho
Porlock Weir
Worthy Wood
Porlockford
West Porlock
Bossington
EXMOOR OWL & HAWK CENTRE
Lynch
Allerford
LYNTON & BARNSTAPLE RAILWAY
WOODY BAY
WILDNER TOP
Killington
Stock Castle
Scob Hill
Oare
Oareford
Cloud Fm
Malmsmead Hill 389
Robber's Br
Smalla Combe
Westcott Brake
Pitt Fm
Court Place
The Park
Porlock
Doverhay
West Ilkerton
Martinhoe Cross
Stock Common
Roborough Castle
Cheriton
Shilstone Hill 405
Tippacott Ridge
Great Black Hill
Weirwood Common
Porlock Common
Shillett Wood
Homebush Wood
Hawk Combe
Glen Lodge
Horner
West Luccombe
Brandish Street
KILLINGTON LANE
Beacon Castle
Bodley
Parracombe
Churchtown
Ilkerton Ridge
Furzehill
Shallowford
Dry Br
Withycombe Ridge
Stowey Ridge
Mill Hill
Chalk Water
HAWKCOMBE WOODS
Parracombe Common
South Common
Cannon Hill
Furzehill Common
Cheriton Ridge
Pig Hill
Brendon Common 412
B3223
Doone Country
Black Hill
Weir Water
Tarr Ball Hill
317 Ley Hill
Horner Wood
Nutscale Water
Rowley Down
Butter Hill
Saddle Gate
Exmoor
Forest
Hoaroak
West Lyn River
Hoaroak Water
Farley Water
Badgworthy Hill
Hoccombe Water
Manor Allotment
Kittuck Meads
Madacombe
Babe Hill
Luccombe Hill
Blackmoor Gate
Thorn Hill
Brendon Two Gates
Larkbarrow
Alderman's Barrow 447
Lucott Cross 465
The Mound 373
THE DUNKERY & HORNER WOOD
Wilmersham Common
Robin How
Challacombe Common
Winaway
475 Hoaroak Hill
Hoar Tor
Exe Plain
Trout Hill
East Pinford
Swap Hill
East Water
Higher Down
Challacombe Res
Pinkery Pond
The Chains 487
Blackpitts Gate
Swap Hill 444
Almsworthy Common
Dunkery Beacon 519
Barton Gate
Swincombe
North Regis 417
Pinkery Fm
PINKERY CENTRE FOR OUTDOOR LEARNING
EXMOOR NATIONAL PARK
Friendship Fm
Yelland Cross
B3358
Stowford
Challacombe
NORTH LANE
Barton Town
Old Close Bottom
Prayway Head
River Exe
Warren Fm
Ashcombe Bottom
Allcombe Water
Exford Common
Hoar Moor
Codsend Moors
Dunkery Gate 387
A399
Challacombe Mill
Leeham Ford Br
Shoulsbarrow Fm
Weirs Combe
Sloley Stone
Duredon Fm
Clovenrocks Br
Gallon Ho
Higher Riscombe Fm
Hill Fm
Pitsworthy Fm
River Quarme
Kitnor Heath
Higher Ho
Codsend
Knightacott
Northland Corner
Wallover Down
Cornham Fm
Barle Water
Simonsbath
Honeymead Fm
Pennycombe Water
Ashott Barton
Edgcott
Coombe Fm
B3224
Larcombe Fm
Horsecombe Fm
Luckwell Bridge
Fullaford Down
Squallacombe
Winstitchen Fm
White Water
Thornemead
White Cross
Ley
Exford
CHURCH HILL
EXFORD
Leworthy
Rockley Fm
Bray Common
Little Bray Cross
Horcombe
Blue Gate
SOMERSET
Chibbet Post
North Court
ROOM HILL ROAD
Staddon Hill
Torre Fm
Hoe Fm
Silkwood Top
Berry Hill
River Bray
Buckworthy
Pickedstones
Staddon Fm
Haxton Down
Down Fm
Wort Wood
Lydcott Hall
East Down Wood
Whitefield Down
Five Barrows Cross
Kinsford Gate
Emmett's Grange
Kinsford Water
Wintershead Fm
Horsen Fm
Great Ferny Ball
Blackland Fm
Hillway Fm
Road Hill
Nethercote
Kemps
Benton
Mockham Down Gate
Lydcott
Little Bray
Cross Gate
Holewater
Beara Hill Head
Poltimore Arms (PH)
Lyddicombe Bottom
Gravel Pit Cross
Long Holcombe
Horsen Hill 443
Landacre Br
Withypool
Withycombe
Barnacott Fm
Mockham Down
Fyldon Common
River Barle
Waterhouse Fm
Comer's Gate
Winn Brook
Kimbland Fm
Brayfordhill
Brayford
High Bray
Hall
Yarde Gate Fm
North Radworthy
Sherdon Fm
Woolcombe Allot
Woolcombe Fm
Withypool Common
Withypool Hill 398
North Batsom
West Batsom
Winsford Hill 426
Burrow Wood
Winsford
Copple
Edbrooke Ho
West Howet
Slade Fm
Fyldon
Shortacombe
Sherdon Water
Porchester's Post 388
West Water
Great Bradley
The Allotment
Yellowcombe
Goodwells Head
The Old Rectory
Molland Cross
Higher Molland
Bentwichen
North Heasley
Long Wood
Longstone Wells
Darlick Moors
Withypool Cross
Halscombe Allot
Willingford Fm
Westwater Allot
Westwater Fm
Spire Cross
Summerway
Charles
Popham
Sportsman's Inn (PH)
Litton Water
Danes Brook
Draydon Knap
Elwell
Upcott Fm
Hudley Mill
Newtown Br
Hunnawins Fm
Radworthy Down
South Radworthy
North Molton Ridge
Twitchen Ridge
Hawkridge Plain
Hill Fm
TARR STEPS WOODLAND
Parsonage Fm
Tarr Fm
Liscombe
Little River
Spire
Old Ashway
West Buckland School
East Buckland
Charles Bottom
Tabor Hill
Heasley Mill
Balls Cross
TARR STEPS
Ashway Side
Mounsey Hill 374
326
South Hill
Macmillan Way West
South Wood
Bampfylde Hill
Barcombe Down
Wheatclose Cross
Moorhouse Ridge
Hawkridge Common
West Buckland
Huxtable Fm
Holywell Cross
Holywell Res
Twitchen Mill
Cloggs Fm
Lyshwell Fm
Shircombe Fm
Hawkridge
Hawkridge Ridge
Brayley Hill
Steep Head
Brinsworthy
Twitchen
Hollowcombe
Litchadon Fm
High Bullen Fm
Millbrook
Cussacombe Gate
Molland Common
Nadrid
North Molton
Pitt Fm
Pulham Fm
Pulsworthy Fm
Kerswell Fm
West Anstey Common
Whiterocks Down
Draydon Fm
Mounsey Castle
Marsh Hall Ho
A361
Leary Moors
Heddon
Oxford Down
Hallowford
Bremridge Wood
Wheatlands Fm
Coombe
Snurridge
South Cockerham
West Park
Burcombe
River Mole
Sannacott Fm
Limeslake Fm
Waterbrooks Fm
Bickingcott
Luckworthy
Champson
Molland
Smallacombe
Stone
Woodland Fm
West
Two Moor Way
Five Cross Ways
Old Berry Fm
SS
60
30
90

BRISTOL CHANNEL
58
41
26
27
SS
Hurlstone Pt
Selworthy Sand
Selworthy Beacon 308
SOUTH WEST COAST PATH
Greenaleigh Pt
Bossington
EXMOOR OWL & HAWK CENTRE
Lynch
Memorial Hut
Porlock
Allerford
Selworthy
Woodcombe
Minehead
Madbrain Sands
Warren Pt
BUTLINS
Higher Town
Doverhay
Brandish Street
Holnicote
Bratton
Hindon Fm
Wydon Fm
Moor Wood
West Luccombe
Horner
Glen Lodge
A39
Blackford
Tivington
Troytes Fm
Great Headon Plantn
Periton
HOPCOTT ROAD
Alcombe
Dunster Beach
Luccombe
Knowle Top
Tivington Knowle
Periton Hill 295
Staunton Plantn
Penny Hill
Ellicombe
Marsh Street
Blue Anchor Bay
Quantock's Head
Ley Hill 317
Horner Wood
Huntscott
Wootton Courtenay
MINEHEAD
DOLL MUSEUM
Knowle Hill
Dunster
HOME FARM
Watchet
Warren Bay
St Audrie's Bay
Blue Ben
Black Rock
East Quantoxhead
Parkhouse Fm
East Wood
Luccombe Hill
Brockwell
DUNKERY VINEYARD
Aville Fm
DUNSTER WATERMILL
DUNSTER CASTLE GARDENS
Blue Anchor
BLUE ANCHOR
EASTBURY ROAD
WATCHET
DONIFORD BEACH HALT
Perry Fm
Higher Street
Robin How 428
River Avill
A396
Whits Wood
Marshwood Fm
Chapel Cleeve
Binham Fm
Old Cleeve
Bye Fm
Kentsford Fm
St Decumans
Five Bells
Doniford
Rydon Fm
Egrove Fm
The Home Fm
Amitabha Buddhist Centre
Townsend Fm
Kilve Court
Pardlestone Fm
Fairgarden Fm
Well Fm
Cowbridge
Hur Wood
Broadwood Fm
Carhampton
Briddicott Fm
STATION ROAD
WEST SOMERSET RAILWAY
FIVE BELLS
WILLITON
West Wood
West Quantoxhead
Dunkery Beacon 519
Burrow
Timberscombe
Elsworthy
Bickham
Aller Hill
Withycombe
RAILWAY MUS
TROPIQUARIA ANIMAL & ADVENTURE PARK
Williton
High Bridge
Wibble Fm
Staple
Staple Plantn
West Hill Beacon Hill 310
Pardlestone Hill
Pitt Br
Croydon Ho
Gupworthy Fm
Combe Fm
Bilbrook
Hungerford
WASHFORD
Washford
CLEEVE ABBEY
Washford Cross
Sampford Brett
Torweston Fm
Lower Weacombe
Weacombe
Longstone Hill
Dunkery Gate 387
West Harwood Fm
Croydon Hill
Black Hill 353
Torre
CIDER FARM
Orchard Wyndham
Bicknoller Post
Ford Fm
Oaktrow Wood
EXMOOR
365
Lodge Fm
Escott Fm
Fair Cross
Woolston
Bicknoller
CUTCOMBE HILL
Cutcombe
Stowey Fm
Well
381
Rodhuish Common
Rodhuish
Clitsome Fm
Beggearn Huish
Black Down Wood
Capton
Quantock Moor Fm
Thorncombe Hill
NATIONAL PARK
Golsoncott
Lower Roadwater
Yarde
Chilcombe
Thorncombe Ho
Newton
Luckwell Bridge
Wheddon Cross
Couple Cross
Nurcott Fm
Churchtown
Monkham Hill
Croydon Hall
Woodford
Yellow Wood Fm
Vellow
A358
Halsway Manor
Kersham Hill 361
Slowley Wood
Slowley Fm
Roadwater
Nettlecombe Court
Rowdon Fm
Escott
Wayshill
Black Hill 358
Hoe Fm
Triscombe
White Moor
Luxborough
Tacker Street
Kingswood
Hurley Fm
Torre Fm
Honeywell Ho
SOMERSET
Lype Hill 423
Colly Hill
Kingsbridge
Washford River
Monksilver
Coombe Cross
Catford Cott
Halsway
Crowcombe Park
Newcombe Fm
Pooltown
Langridge Wood
Woodadvent Fm
Birchanger Fm
Stogumber
STOGUMBER
Crowcombe Court
Crowcombe
B3224
390
Quarme Hill
Chargot Ho
Langham Fm
Kennisham Hill
Court Fm
Chapman's Fm
Stamborough
Leighland Chapel
Chidgley
Sticklepath
Wood Fm
Water Fm
THE CHURCH HOUSE
Kemps
Great Cott
South Quarme Fm
South Quarme Allotment
Chargot Wood
Hook Hill Fm
Bird's Hill
WEST SOMERSET RAILWAY
Leigh Cott
Lawford
Withycombe
Luckyard Fm
Stone Lodge
Goosemoor
Langham Hill
Brendon Hills
Treborough Common
Treborough
Colton Fm
Pond Wood
Ashbeer
Lower Vexford
Higher Vexford
Flaxpo
Winsford
Exton Hill 348
Witheridge Fm
Weekfield Fm
Gupworthy
WITHIEL HILL
Sminhays Corner
Eastern Wood
B3190
Elworthy
Heathfield Fm
Burrow Wood
Coppleham
Edbrooke Ho
West Howetown
Kendle Fm
Ford Fm
Eastcott Fm
Burrow Fm
Brendon Hill
Raleigh's Cross Inn
Holcombe Water Fm
Colwell Fm
Hartrow Manor
Willett Ho
Rexton Fm
Coleford Water
CROWCOMBE HEATHFIELD
Crowcombe Heathfield
Rich's Holford
Yellowcombe
The Allotment
Exton
Leigh Fm
Withiel Fm
Brendon Hill Fm
Tone Fm
Tripp Bottom
Willett
New Marsh
Rook's Nest
Willett Hill
Coleford Fm
Courtsley
Summerway
Bridgetown
Combeshead Fm
King's Brompton Fm
Blagdon Hill
Withiel Florey
Swansea Fm
Fryan Fm
Emble Fm
Westowe
Draydon Knap
Holtam Fm
Howetown Fm
Kings Brompton Forest
Middleton Bottom
Tripp Fm
Broadway Head Fm
Whitmoor Fm
Nethercott
Cophole Fm
Middleton Court
Battin's Fm
Lydeard St Lawrence
East Town
Tolland
Combe Wood
326
South Hill
Higher Foxhanger Fm
Brompton Regis
Rugg's Fm
East Withy Fm
Brown Fm
Week Fm
Brompton Ralph
Hele Fm
Bowden Fm
Manor Fm
Courtland Fm
Clatworthy Reservoir
Broford Fm
Kents
Ditch Fm
Rowes Fm
Clatworthy
Middle Stone Fm
Pitsford Hill
Handy Cross
Pyleigh
Chilly Bridge
Daws Fm
Redcross Fm
Venne Cott
Hill Fm
White's Fm
Harwood Fm
Tarr
Pitpear Fm
Halscombe Fm
Harewood Fm
Wimbleball Lake/Res
West Withy Fm
Perry Fm
Parsonage Fm
Cording's Fm
Combe Bottom
Moor Mill Fm
West Leigh
Homeleaze Fm
Ash Wood
Lyncombe Fm
316 Court
Hartford Bottom
West Hill Wood
Upton Fm
Hayne Fm
Bittescombe Manor
Coombe Fm
Huish Champflower
Whitefield
Hoccombe
Chapel Leigh
Draydon Fm
Mounsey Castle
Shute Fm
Huish Moor
Langley Marsh
Langley
Burrow Hill Fm
Northway
Brewers Fm
Sholford Fm
Maundown
Ford
Halse Water
Pond Close
355
Haddon Fm
Upton
Godhams Fm
Lotley Fm
Washbattle Br
Maundown Hill
Greenway Fm
Northgate
Croford Ho
Fitzhead
Halse
Old Berry Fm
B3222 Hele Br
Chapple Fm
Blindwell
Oxenleaze
Heydon Hill
Bulland
Castle
B3227
B3188
B3191
A358
0 1 2 3 miles
0 1 2 3 4 5 km

7
8
9
10
11
Weston-super-Mare
Tower Rock
Rudder Rock
Calf Rock
Steep Holm
59
Weston Bay
TROPICANA
Clarence Park
Worlebury Camp
Locking
Banwell
Hutton
Uphill
Oldmixon
Elborough
Hillend
Knightcott
Lower Canada
Upper Canada
Yarberry
Bleadon
Wonderstone
Shiplate
Christon
Loxton
South Hill
Webbington
Crook Peak
Compton Bishop
Hay Wood
Hellenge Hill
Bleadon Hill
Hamwood
Loxton Hill
Purn
Coombe Fm
WALBOROUGH
The Grange
Fiddler's Pt
Brean Down
Black Pt
Berrow Flats
Brean
Brean Fm
Warren Fm
Diamond Fm
Ham Fm
ANIMAL FARM ADVENTURE PARK
BREAN THEME PARK
Northam Fm
Ford Common
Pitland Rhyne
Wick Fm
Wick
Bridge Fm
Berrow Manor
Batch
Holm Fm
Lympsham
Poplar Fm
Eastertown
North Yeo Fm
Rackley
Crab Hole
Biddisham
Lower Fm
Edingworth
Sedgemoor Services
M5
44
A38
Badgworth
Tarnock
Rooks Bridge
Weare
BRIDGWATER
BAY
Brent Road
Ham
Burton Row
East Brent
Brent Knoll
Berrow
Lake Ho
Stone Allerton
Allerton Moor
Chapel Allerton
New Homestead Fm
Ashton
Binham Moor
White Cross
Edithmead
Burnham-on-Sea
Middle Burnham
B3140
Burnham Level
Worston Ho
Somerset Court
22
Northwick
Dutch Court Fm
Wellfield Ho
Vole
Plaish Fm
Perry Fm
Blackford Moor
West Stoughton
Mark
Mark Causeway
Yarrow
B3139
Stert Island
Stert Flats
Stert Pt
Fenning Island
Highbridge
Alstone
Walrow
Magnolia Ho
Southwick
Watchfield
Mark Moor
Stook Ho
Little Moor
Totney Fm
Westham
Lands End Fm
Hinkley Point Power Station
ENGLAND COAST PATH
Hinkley Point C under construction
BRIDGWATER BAY
Steart
Stockland Reach
The Island
Huntspill
Malthouse Fm
Bason Bridge
Hackness
SECRET WORLD WILDLIFE RESCUE
East Huntspill
Cote
Cripp's Fm
Liberty Fm
River Bridge
River Brue
Tealham Moor
Stolford
Catsford Common
Little Dowden's Fm
Wick Moor
Whitewick
Chalcott Fm
Woolstone Fm
Idson Fm
WWT STEART MARSHES NATURE RESERVE
Wall Common
Marsh Fm
Park Fm
Lilstock
Knighton
Shurton
Burton
Wick
Gunter's Grove
Kilton
Stogursey
Farringdon Hill Fm
Cock Fm
Cole Pool
Stockland Bristol
Stockland Manor
Otterhampton
Hill Ho
Higher Hill Fm
Stringston
Great Plantn
Water Fm
Steyning Manor
Cockwood
Kilve
West Huntspill
Bleak Br
Dodds Fm
Stretcholt
Black Ditch
Withy Grove Fm
HUNTSPILL RIVER
Withy Fm
Huntspill River
Gold Corner
Chilton Moor
Burtle Hill
Burtle
Hurst Fm
Pawlett
North Fm
Pawlett Hams
Gaunt's Fm
Pawlett Hill
Puriton Level
Woolavington Level
Causeway
Combwich
Combwich Reach
River Parrett
Hill Fm
Moor House Fm
Plud Fm
Fairfield Wood
Monkton
Stockland Lovell Manor
Wrenmore Fm
Dyche
Barnsworthy Fm
Holford
Woodlands
Dodington
Durborough Fm
Stogursey Brook
Beere Manor Fm
Coultings
Peadon Fm
Putnell Fm
Walpole
23
Puriton
Woolavington
Catcott
CATCOTT
Catcott Heath
Edington Heath
Hallicks Fm
Down End
Dumball
Kings Sedgemoor
Knowle Hill
Cossington
Nidons
Bonson
Horn Hill
Rodway Fm
Roobies Fm
Perry Mill Fm
Pinnacle Hill
Woodlands Hill
Nether Stowey
Fiddington
Edbrook
Cannington Park
CANNINGTON COLL
Rodway
Cannington
Dairy House Fm
Horsey Pill
Crandon Br
A39
Bawdrip
Chilton Polden
Edington
Catcott
Grange
Shervage Wood
Duke's Plantn
COLERIDGE COTTAGE
Dowsborough
Inwood Fm
Whitnell
Keenthorne
Knoll Green
Padnoller Ho
Withiel Fm
Brymore School
Ashford
Groom House Fm
Manor Fm
Perry Court Fm
Perry Green
Chilton Trinity
A38 Bristol Road
Manor Fm
Knowle
Horsey
King's Fm
Bawdrip Level
Ford Fm
Bath Road
Kent Fm
Bincombe
Cross Fm
Friarn
Over Stowey
Adscombe
Aley
Seven Wells Wood
Marsh Mills
Radlet
Currypool Fm
The Grange
Bradley Green
Wembdon Fm
Bridgwater
Bath Road
Slape Cross
Bradney
Peasy Fm
Pendon Hill
Stawell
Cock Hill
Manor Fm
Robin Upright's Hill
Quantock Combe
Pepper Hill
Rowdens Fm
Charlinch
Charlynch
Splatt
Gothelney Hall
Gothelney Green
Crossmoor Fm
Clayhill Fm
Wembdon
Newtown
Quantock Road
East Bower
Sydenham
Eastover
Westfield Fm
Parchey
Chedzoy
West Moor
Ball Hill
Sutton Fm
Fursland Fm
Moorlinch
Great Hill
Tuxwell Fm
Plainsfield
Hawkridge Reservoir
Spaxton
Four Forks
Holmes Fm
Postridge Fm
Durleigh Reservoir
Northfield
BLAKE MUS
Ind Est
Fowler's Plot
Mount Close Batch
Sutton Mallet
Pit Hill
Sharpen Hill
Greylake Fosse
Great Wood
Floorey Down
Round Hill
Pightley
Durleigh Brook
Rexworthy Fm
Bare Ash
Durleigh
Hamp Brook
Hamp
Westonzoyland Road
Aisholt Wood
Hawkridge Common
Durborough Fm
Wills Neck
Bagborough Hill
Triscombe
Aisholt
Lower Aisholt
Enmore Castle
Enmore
Troakes Fm
Willstock Fm
Bridgwater Services
Dunwear
Penzoy Fm
Bussex
Westonzoyland
Liney
Burdenham Fm
GREYLAKE RSPB
Briarwood Fm
Smokeham
Lydeard Hill
Lower Merridge
Good's Fm
Merridge
Broomfield Hall
Andersfield
Goathurst
TEMPLE OF HARMONY
Rhode
Double Br
A372
South Moor
Westonzoyland
Greylake
Rock Fm
Bagborough Ho
West Bagborough
Bishpool Fm
Gib Hill
Courtway
Wind Down
Rockhouse Fm
Higher Heathcombe Fm
Oakenford Fm
Balls Fm
Compass
Huntworth
S O M E R S E T
Andersea
Langmead
Owery Fm
Greylake
River Cary
Seven Ash
Ind Est
Heathfield
Park End
Twenty Acre Plantn
Huntstile
Gooding's Fm
Woolmersdon
North Petherton
24
Copse Fm
Linden Fm
Raymond's Fm
Weston Level
WESTONZOYLAND PUMPING STATION
SOMERSET LEVELS
Shopnoller
Terhill
Buncombe Wood
Westleigh Fm
Lydeard Fm
Lydeard Cross
The Thickets
Rooks Castle Fm
Melcombe
Boomer
Shovel Ho
Fordgate
Petherton Park Fm
Hoopers Elm Fm
Thorngrove
Middlezoy
Nether Moor
Shride Fm
Langacre Rhyne
Charity Fm
Turn Hill
Cothelstone Fm
Cothelstone
Cothelstone Hill
Badger Copse
Ducks Pool
Ball Covert
FYNE COURT
Broomfield
Stream Fm
Wort Wood
King's Cliff Wood
Staffland Fm
Northmoor Green or Moorland
Moorland House Fm
Othery
Beer
Aller Wood
Breach Wood
East Combe
Toulton
Ivyton Fm
Raswell Fm
Owl Hill Fm
Haddon Fm
Clavelshay
Taunton Road
Churchill Fm
Godfrey's Corner
North Newton
Northmoor Main Drain
New House Fm
Middlemoor Br
West Yeo
Saltmoor Fm
Lower Salt Moor
A372
Hunter's Lodge
Pathe
Beer Road
Cushuish
Pixford Fm
Beech Copse
Kingston Beacon
Oggshole Fm
Volis Cross
Cheddon Down
Manor Ho
Shearston
Thurloxton
St Michael Church
Maunsel Ho
Northmoor Corner
MAUNSEL LOCKS BRIDGWATER & TAUNTON CANAL
Stanmoor Bridge
East Lydeard
Portman Fm
Bishops Lydeard
Sandhill Park
Fennington
Yarf
27
Kingston St Mary
Hill Fm
Quantock Fm
Burlinch
Coombe
West Newton
Tuckerton
Bankland
Banklan
28
East Lyng
Burrow-bridge
Longstone
Aller Hill
Ash Priors
BISHOPS LYDEARD
Greenway
Back Stream
Fennington Weir
Lower Portman Fm
Pickney
Fulford
Nailsbourne
Gadd's Bottom
Mill Cross
Volis Fm
Upper Cheddon
Hestercombe
Gotton
HESTERCOMBE GARDENS
Adsborough
Primmore Corner
Hedging
Outwood
Outwood Ho
Lyng
Athelney Hill
Athelney
Stan Moor
Stathe
Aller
Aller Court Fm
Middle Moor
Edgeborough Fm
Stonehouse Fm
Conquest Fm
Noah's Hill
West Monkton
Walford
Higher Durston
Durston
Lower Buckland Fm
A361
Main Road
Parsonage Fm
Curload
Hook Bridge
Stathe Court
Combe
Goosenford
Yarde
Durston
West Lyng
A
B
C
D
E
F
G
H

Brinsea
Cowslip Green
Butcombe
Chew Stoke
Stanton Wick
Chelwood
BATH
NORTH EAST
Banwell
Churchill
Lower Langford
Langford Green
Rickford
Burrington
Blagdon
Nempnett Thrubwell
West Town
Chew Valley Lake
Bishop Sutton
Sutton Wick
Clutton
Temple Cloud
Hallatrow
Sandford
Dinghurst
Upper Langford
Rowberrow
Star
Shipham
Winscombe
Sidcot
Ubley
Compton Martin
West Harptree
East Harptree
Hinton Blewett
South Widcombe
Farrington Gurney
Litton
Webbington
Compton Bishop
Cross
Lower Weare
Axbridge
KING JOHN'S HUNTING LODGE
Cheddar Reservoir
CHEDDAR
CHEDDAR SHOWCAVES & GORGE
Cheddar
Bradley Cross
MENDIP HILLS
Charterhouse
Mendip Forest
Priddy
Chewton Mendip
Ston Easton
Chilcompton
Emborough
Weare
Hythe
Clewer
Stone Allerton
Chapel Allerton
Draycott
Rodney Stoke
Westbury-sub-Mendip
EBBOR ROCKS
EBBOR GORGE
WOOKEY HOLE CAVES & PAPERMILL
Wookey Hole
Green Ore
Binegar
Gurney Slade
Ashwick
Oakhill
West Horrington
East Horrington
Cocklake
West Stoughton
Wedmore
Blackford
Westham
Heath House
Mudgley
Theale
Latcham
Panborough
Wookey
Wells
Dulcote
Dinder
Croscombe
Shepton Mallet
Doulting
Burtle
Westhay
Godney
Polsham
Coxley
Southway
Worminster
North Wootton
West Compton
Pilton
East Compton
Cannard's Grave
Edington
Catcott
Shapwick
Ashcott
Meare
Glastonbury
GLASTONBURY TOR
Edgarley
West Pennard
East Pennard
Pylle
Evercreech
Moorlinch
Pedwell
Greinton
Street
Walton
Overleigh
Butleigh Wootton
Baltonsborough
Butleigh
Southwood
SOMERSET
Ansford
Castle Cary
Greylake
Henley
High Ham
Dundon
Compton Dundon
Kingweston
West Lydford
East Lydford
Lydford-on-Fosse
Alford
Keinton Mandeville
Lovington
Wheathill
Othery
Littleton
Hurcott
Charlton Mackerell
Charlton Adam
Babcary
North Barrow
South Barrow
Galhampton
Somerton
Pitney
Langport
A38
A368
A37
A39
A371
A361
A372
B3151
B3139
B3135
B3153
0 1 2 3 miles
0 1 2 3 4 5 km

45
SOMERSET
CRANBOURNE CHASE AND
WEST WILTSHIRE DOWNS
WILTSHIRE
Bradford on-Avon
Holt
Trowbridge
Westbury
Warminster
Frome
Radstock
Midsomer Norton
Peasedown St John
Paulton
Farmborough
Priston
Inglesbatch
Southstoke
Monkton Combe
Limpley Stoke
Freshford
Winsley
Turleigh
Westwood
Avoncliff
Staverton
Hilperton
Semington
Great Hinton
Steeple Ashton
West Ashton
Yarnbrook
North Bradley
Southwick
Heywood
Dilton Marsh
Chapmanslade
Upton Scudamore
Bishopstrow
Boreham
Norton Bavant
Sutton Veny
Longbridge Deverill
Brixton Deverill
Monkton Deverill
Kingston Deverill
Pertwood
Chicklade
Hindon
West Knoyle
East Knoyle
Mere
Zeals
Stourton
Kilmington
Maiden Bradley
Horningsham
Longleat Park
Gare Hill
Witham Friary
Wanstrow
Nunney
Trudoxhill
Leighton
East Cranmore
West Cranmore
Dean
Heale
Chesterblade
Batcombe
Upton Noble
Bruton
Milton Clevedon
North Brewham
South Brewham
Hardway
Redlynch
Cole
Pitcombe
Shepton Montague
Bratton Seymour
Yarlington
Wincanton
Charlton Musgrove
Stoney Stoke
Penselwood
Bourton
Queen Oak
Silton
Huntingford
Milton on Stour
Sedgehill
Stoke Trister
Bayford
West Bourton
Holwell
Tytherington
Mells
Great Elm
Vobster
Coleford
Holcombe
Highbury
Stratton-on-the-Fosse
Kilmersdon
Charlton
Hemington
Faulkland
Buckland Dinham
Hardington
Laverton
Lullington
Beckington
Rode
Woolverton
Norton St Philip
Tellisford
Farleigh Hungerford
Hinton Charterhouse
Wellow
Shoscombe
Camerton
Timsbury
Dunkerton
Combe Hay
Twinhoe
Berkley
Oldford
Standerwick
Corsley
Corsley Heath
Sturford
Crockerton
Shear Cross
Whatley
Chantry
Leigh upon Mendip
Stoke St Michael
Downhead
Nettlebridge
A36
A361
A350
A303
A362
A366
A359
A3098
B3092
B3095
B3081
61
8
9
10
11
7
29
30
46

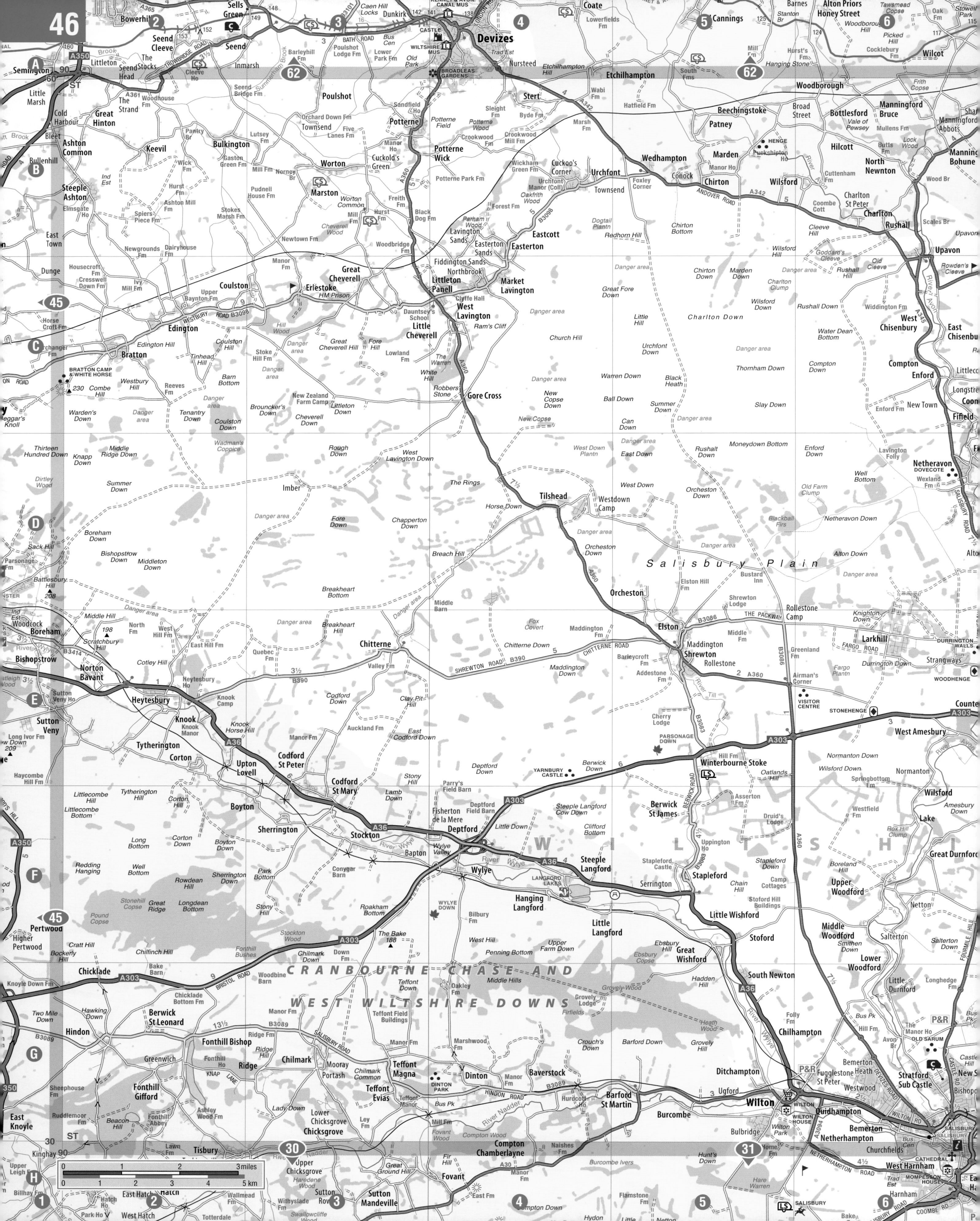
Bowerhill
Sells Green
Seend Cleeve
Seend
The Stocks
Seend Head
Semington
Littleton
Inmarsh
Barleyhill Fm
Caen Hill Locks
Dunkirk
Kennet & Avon Canal Mus
Castle
Wiltshire Mus
Devizes
Poulshot Lodge Fm
Lower Park Fm
Old Park
Broadleas Gardens
Coate
Lowerfields Fm
Cannings
Barnes
Stanton Br
Alton Priors
Honey Street
Woodborough Hill
Tawsmead Copse
Oak Fm
Stowell Park
Picked Hill
Cocklebury Fm
Wilcot
Mill Fm
Hurst's Fm
Hanging Stone
South Fms
Nursteed
Trad Est
Etchilhampton Hill
Etchilhampton
Woodborough
Frith Copse
Little Marsh
The Strand
Woodhouse Fm
Seend Bridge Fm
Poulshot
Sandfield Ho
Stert
Sleight Fm
Byde Fm
Wabi Fm
Hatfield Fm
Beechingstoke
Broad Street
Bottlesford
Vale of Pewsey
Manningford Bruce
Manningford Abbots
Cold Harbour
Great Hinton
Orchard Down Fm
Townsend
Potterne
Potterne Field
Potterne Wood
Crookwood Fm
Crookwood Mill Fm
Marsh Fm
Patney
Mullens Fm
Bleet
Ashton Common
Keevil
Pantry Br
Bulkington
Lutsey Fm
Five Lanes Fm
Manor Ho
Potterne Wick
Wickham Green Fm
Cuckoo's Corner
Urchfont
Wedhampton
Henge
Puckshipton Ho
Marden
Hilcott
Butts Fm
Lock Wood
Manningford Bohune
Bullenhill
Gaston Green Fm
Wick Fm
Worton
Cuckold's Green
Urchfont Manor (Coll)
Foxley Corner
Manor Ho
Conock
Chirton
Wilsford
Cuttenham Fm
North Newnton
Wood Br
Steeple Ashton
Ind Est
Hurst Fm
Mill Fm
Norney Br
Marston
Potterne Park Fm
Oakfrith Wood
Townsend
Andover Road
Coombe Cott
Charlton St Peter
Elmsgate Ho
Ashton Mill Fm
Pudnell House Fm
Worton Common
Freith Fm
Forest Fm
Charlton
Rushall
Scales Br
Spiers Piece Fm
Stokes Marsh Fm
Mill Fm
Hurst Fm
Black Dog Fm
Parham Wood
Eastcott
Dogtail Plantn
Redhorn Hill
Chirton Bottom
Cleeve Hill
Upavon
East Town
Newgrounds Fm
Dairyhouse Fm
Newtown Fm
Cheverell Wood
Woodbridge Fm
Lavington Sands
Easterton Sands
Easterton
Wilsford Hill
Goddard's Cleeve
Dunge
Housecroft Fm
Cresswell Down Fm
Ivy Mill Fm
Manor Fm
Great Cheverell
Fiddington Sands
Northbrook
Littleton Panell
Market Lavington
Chirton Down
Marden Down
Danger area
Rushall Hill
Old Cleeve
Rowden's Cleeve
Upper Baynton Fm
Coulston
Erlestoke
HM Prison
Clyffe Hall
West Lavington
Great Fore Down
Charlton Clump
Horse Croft Fm
Westbury Road
Edington
Hill Wood
Dauntsey's School
Little Cheverell
Ram's Cliff
Little Hill
Charlton Down
Wilsford Down
Rushall Down
Widdington Fm
West Chisenbury
East Chisenbury
Edington Hill
Coulston Hill
Stoke Hill Fm
Great Cheverell Hill
Fore Hill
Lowland Fm
Church Hill
Urchfont Down
Water Dean Bottom
Bratton
Tinhead Hill
The Warren
White Hill
Thornham Down
Compton Down
Compton
Enford
Littlecott
Bratton Camp & White Horse
Combe Hill
Westbury Hill
Reeves Fm
Barn Bottom
New Zealand Farm Camp
Littleton Down
Robbers' Stone
Gore Cross
New Copse Down
Warren Down
Ball Down
Black Heath
Summer Down
Slay Down
Enford Fm
New Town
Longstreet
Warden's Down
Tenantry Down
Coulston Down
Brouncker's Down
Cheverell Down
New Copse
Can Down
Fifield
Beggar's Knoll
Wadman's Coppice
Thirteen Hundred Down
Middle Ridge Down
Knapp Down
Rough Down
West Lavington Down
West Down Plantn
East Down
Rushall Down
Moneydown Bottom
Enford Down
Lavington Folly
Netheravon
Dovecote
Dirtley Wood
Summer Down
Imber
The Rings
Tilshead
Westdown Camp
West Down
Orcheston Down
Well Bottom
Wexland Fm
Old Farm Clump
Fore Down
Chapperton Down
Horse Down
Blackball Firs
Netheravon Down
Boreham Down
Sack Hill
Bishopstrow Down
Middleton Down
Breach Hill
Orcheston Down
Alton Down
Salisbury Plain
Parsonage Down
Battlesbury Hill
Breakheart Bottom
Elston Hill Fm
Bustard Inn
Orcheston
Middle Barn
Shrewton Lodge
Rollestone Camp
Knighton Down
Woodcock
Boreham
Middle Hill
North Fm
West Hill Fm
Breakheart Hill
Fox Covert
Maddington Fm
Elston
The Packway
Middle Fm
Larkhill
Scratchbury Hill
East Hill Fm
Quebec Fm
Chitterne
Chitterne Down
Chitterne Road
Maddington
Shrewton
Rollestone
Barleycroft Fm
Greenland Fm
Fargo Road
Fargo Plantn
Durrington Down
Durrington Walls
Strangways
Bishopstrow
Norton Bavant
Cotley Hill
Valley Fm
Shrewton Road
Maddington Down
Addestone Fm
Airman's Corner
Woodhenge
Heytesbury Ho
Heytesbury
Sutton Veny Ho
Sutton Veny
Knook Camp
Codford Down
Clay Pit Hill
River Till
Visitor Centre
Stonehenge
West Amesbury
Knook
Knook Manor
Knook Horse Hill
Auckland Fm
East Codford Down
Cherry Lodge
Long Ivor Fm
Tytherington
Corton
Manor Fm
Codford St Peter
Upton Lovell
Yarnbury Castle
Berwick Down
Hill Fm
Winterbourne Stoke
Oatlands Hill
Normanton Down
Wilsford Down
Normanton
Springbottom Fm
Haycombe Hill Fm
Littlecombe Hill
Littlecombe Bottom
Tytherington Hill
Corton Hill
Deptford Down
Stony Hill
Codford St Mary
Parry's Field Barn
Lamb Down
Boyton
Sherrington
Fisherton de la Mere
Deptford Field Barn
Deptford
Little Down
Steeple Langford Cow Down
Asserton Fm
Berwick St James
Druid's Lodge
Westfield Fm
Wilsford
Amesbury Down
Lake
Long Bottom
Corton Down
Boyton Down
Stockton
Wylye Valley
Bapton
Clifford Bottom
Uppington Ho
Rox Hill Clump
Great Durnford
Redding Hanging
Well Bottom
Rowdean Hill
Sherrington Down
Park Bottom
Conygar Barn
Wylye
Steeple Langford
Stapleford Castle
Stapleford Down
Boreland Hill
Upper Woodford
Stonehill Copse
Great Ridge
Longdean Bottom
Langford Lakes
Hanging Langford
Serrington
Stapleford
Chain Hill
Camp Cottages
Stoford Hill Buildings
Pound Copse
Stony Hill
Roakham Bottom
Wylye Down
Bilbury Fm
Little Langford
Little Wishford
Netton
Pertwood
Higher Pertwood
Stockton Wood
The Bake
West Hill
Penning Bottom
Upper Farm Down
Ebsbury Hill
Great Wishford
Stoford
Middle Woodford
Salterton
Salterton Down
Smithen Down
Lower Woodford
Cratt Hill
Bockerly Hill
Chilfinch Hill
Fonthill Bushes
Chilmark Down
Down Fm
Ebsbury Copse
Chicklade
Bake Barn
Woodbine Barn
Cranbourne Chase and West Wiltshire Downs
Teffont Down
Oakley Fm
Middle Hills
Grovely Wood
Hadden Hill
South Newton
Little Durnford
Longhedge Fm
Knoyle Down Fm
Chicklade Bottom Fm
Hawking Down
Berwick St Leonard
Grovely Lodge
Firfields
Two Mile Down
Hindon
Manor Fm
Teffont Field Buildings
Heath Wood
Folly Fm
Chilhampton
Bus Pk
Hill Fm
Fonthill Bishop
Ridge Fm
Ridge Hill
Manor Fm
Marshwood Fm
Crouch's Down
Barford Down
Grovely Hill
The Manor Ho
Avon Br
Old Sarum
Greenwich
Fonthill Ho
Ridge
Chilmark
Mooray
Portash
Chilmark Common
Teffont Magna
Dinton Park
Dinton
Manor Fm
Baverstock
Ditchampton
Bemerton Heath
Fugglestone St Peter
Stratford Sub Castle
Westwood
Sheephouse Fm
Fonthill Gifford
Teffont Evias
Teffont Manor
Hindon Road
Hurdcott Ho
Barford St Martin
Ugford
Wilton
Wilton House
Quidhampton
Lady Down
Bus Pk
Mill Fm
Burcombe
Bemerton
Netherhampton
Rudd lemoor Fm
Beacon Hill
Fonthill Abbey
Ashley Wood Fm
Lower Chicksgrove
Chicksgrove
Ley Fm
Fovant Wood
Compton Wood
River Nadder
Bulbridge
Wilton Park
Churchfields
East Knoyle
Kinghay
Lawn Fm
Tisbury
Upper Chicksgrove
Fir Hill
Compton Chamberlayne
Naishes Fm
Hunt's Down
Netherhampton Road
West Harnham
Upper Leigh Fm
Harnham Wood
Great Ground Hill
Fovant
Manor Fm
Burcombe Ivers
Hare Warren
Trad Est
Mompesson House
Cathedral
Billhay Fm
East Hatch
Hatch
Park Ho
West Hatch
Wallmead Fm
Totterdale
Withyslade Fm
Swallowcliffe Wood
Sutton Row
Sutton Mandeville
East Fm
Compton Down
Hydon
Flamstone Fm
Little
Netton
Salisbury
Harnham
Coombe Rd
Bake
0 1 2 3 miles
0 1 2 3 4 5 km

47
Pewsey
Milton Lilbourne
Burbage
Eastcourt
Wilton
Marten
Buttermere
Rivar
Combe
West Grafton
East Grafton
Southcott
Oxenwood
Tidcombe
Fosbury
Henley
Wexcombe
Linkenholt
Faccombe
Netherton
Vernham Row
Vernham Street
Vernham Dean
Ashmansworth
Littledown
Upton
Aughton
Brunton
Collingbourne Kingston
Lower Everleigh
Everleigh
East Everleigh
Sunton
Cadley
Collingbourne Ducis
Chute Standen
Upper Chute
Lower Chute
Chute Cadley
Tangley
Ibthorpe
Hurstbourne Tarrant
The Dene
Stoke
Wildhern
Hatherden
Ludgershall
Faberstown
Redenham
Tidworth
North Tidworth
South Tidworth
Perham Down
Great Shoddesden
Little Shoddesden
Ragged Appleshaw
Appleshaw
Clanville
Penton Mewsey
Penton Grafton
Penton Corner
Foxcotte
Charlton
Little London
Upper Enham
Enham Alamein
Knights Enham
Smannell
Woodhouse
East Anton
Picket Piece
Andover Down
Figheldean
Ablington
Brigmerston
Milston
Durrington
Bulford
Bulford Camp
Ratfyn
Amesbury
Kimpton
Fyfield
Thruxton
Weyhill
Mullenspond
East Cholderton
Shipton Bellinger
Andover
Anna Valley
Amport
Monxton
Abbotts Ann
Little Ann
Upper Clatford
Goodworth Clatford
Quarley
Grateley
Cholderton
Palestine
Red Rice
Newton Tony
Allington
Boscombe
Wherwell
Newton Stacey
Chilbolton
Cottonworth
Fullerton
Leckford
Idmiston
Over Wallop
Middle Wallop
Nether Wallop
Longstock
Porton
Gomeldon
Stockbridge
Winterbourne Dauntsey
Winterbourne Gunner
Winterbourne Earls
Lopcombe Corner
East Winterslow
Middle Winterslow
West Winterslow
The Common
Firsdown
Ford
Broughton
North Houghton
Houghton
Little Somborne
Up Somborne
Pitton
Laverstock
Salisbury
Milford
Bossington
King's Somborne
Ashley
Horsebridge
West Tytherley
Stony Batter
The Green
East Tytherley
Farley
Britford
East Grimstead
Frenchmoor
Compton
Brook
Furzedown
N O R T H
W E S S E X   D O W N S
H A M P S H I R E
A338
A342
A303
A343
A30
A3057
A345
B3084
63
31
32
48

Woolton Hill
East End
Broad Laying
Penwood
Pound Street
Earlstone Common
Burghclere
Plastow Green
Fair Oak
Axmansford
Inhurst
Baughurst
Tadley
Silchester
Heath
Highclere
Whitway
Ecchinswell
Kingsclere
Wolverton
Wolverton Common
Pamber Green
Little London
Faccombe
Ashmansworth
Old Burghclere
Sydmonton
Ramsdell
Monk Sherborne
Sherborne St John
Crux Easton
Hannington
Upper Wootton
Ibworth
Woodcott
Litchfield
Dunley
North Oakley
Popley
Hurstbourne Tarrant
Binley
Wootton St Lawrence
Oakridge
South View
Winklebury
Stoke
NORTH WESSEX DOWNS
Worting
Basingstoke
Eastrop
Cole Henley
Quidhampton
Newfound
Buckskin
South Ham
Swampton
Deane
Clarken Green
Church Oakley
Oakley
Kempshott
St Mary Bourne
Foxdown
Overton
Ashe
East Oakley
Brighton Hill
Lynch Hill
Whitchurch
Laverstoke
Freefolk
Southington
Hatch Warren
Cliddesden
Steventon
Broadmere
Tufton
Picket Piece
Andover Down
Hurstbourne Priors
North Waltham
Farleigh Wallop
Dummer
Ellisfield
Longparish
Middleton
East Aston
Popham
Nutley
Forton
Bransbury
HAMPSHIRE
Axford
Woodmancott
Preston Candover
Bradley
Wherwell
Barton Stacey
Bullington
Upper Bullington
West Stratton
Newton Stacey
Chilbolton
Egypt
Hunton
East Stratton
Chilton Candover
Lower Wield
Sutton Scotney
Wonston
Stoke Charity
Micheldever
Brown Candover
Upper Wield
Northington
Hattingley
Chilbolton Down
South Wonston
Abbotstone
Crawley
Old Alresford
Bighton
Long Park
Kings Worthy
Martyr Worthy
Itchen Abbas
Itchen Stoke
Gundleton
Up Somborne
Littleton
Headbourne Worthy
Easton
Avington
Ovington
New Alresford
Bishop's Sutton
Sparsholt
Weeke
Hyde
Winchester
Tichborne
Ropley Dean
Winnall
No Man's Land
Cheriton
Stanmore
Chilcomb
Bramdean
New Cheriton
0 1 2 3 miles
0 1 2 3 4 5 km

Stratfield Saye
West End Green
Fair Oak Green
Heckfield
Eversley
Sandhurst
Yateley
Blackwater
Camberley
Bramshill
Stratfield Turgis
Turgis Green
Bramley
Hound Green
Hazeley
Hawley
Frimley
Sherfield on Loddon
Hartley Westpall
Mattingley
Hartfordbridge
Lyde Green
Hartley Wintney
Frimley Green
Farnborough Green
Church End
Rotherwick
West Green
Phoenix Green
Cove
West Heath
Chineham
Mytchett
Hook
Winchfield
Pondtail
Farnborough
Daneshill
Newnham
Fleet
Old Basing
Hatch
Nately Scures
Andwell
Up Nately
Dogmersfield
Crookham Village
Church Crookham
North Camp
Ash Vale
North Warnborough
Odiham
Mapledurwell
Greywell
Colt Hill
Mill Lane
Ash
Aldershot
Ewshot
Bowling Alley
Tongham
Badshot Lea
Upton Grey
Tunworth
Winslade
Crondall
Long Sutton
South Warnborough
Weston Patrick
Herriard
Farnham
Dippenhall
Compton
Runfold
Seale
The Sands
Well
Wrecclesham
Bentley
Southrope
Bagmore
Lower Froyle
Upper Froyle
Froyle
The Bourne
Rowledge
Golden Pot
Shalden
Lasham
Bentworth
Holybourne
Binsted
Blacknest
Alton
Wilson
Beech
Wyck
Wheatley
Frensham
Millbridge
Tilford
Elstead
East Worldham
Kingsley
Sleaford
Chawton
West Worldham
Hartley Mauditt
Medstead
Four Marks
Lower Farringdon
Upper Farringdon
Oakhanger
Bordon Camp
Bordon
Lindford
Headley
Arford
Grayshott
Hindhead
Selborne
Blackmoor
Whitehill
Conford
Bramshott
Haslemere
Kitwood
East Tisted
Newton Valence
Empshott
Liphook
Greatham
Longmoor Camp
Camelsdale
Linchmere
Colemore
Monkwood
West Tisted
Hawkley
Liss Forest
Liss
Fernhurst
Kingsley Green
Farnham
SURREY
50
65
33
34

Chobham
Bagshot Heath
Lightwater
West End
Castle Green
Byfleet
West Byfleet
Cobham
Oxshott
Whiteley Village
Frimley
Frimley Green
Farnborough Green
Deepcut
Mytchett
Bisley
Knaphill
Woking
Horsell
Sheerwater
Pyrford
Wisley
Ripley
Ockham
Old Woking
Send
Send Marsh
Brookwood
Pirbright
Worplesdon
Fox Corner
Burpham
East Horsley
West Horsley
Effingham
Fetcham
Little Bookham
Great Bookham
West Clandon
East Clandon
Merrow
Ash Vale
Ash
Normandy
Wyke
Flexford
Wood Street
Onslow Village
Guildford
Tongham
Wanborough
Puttenham
Compton
Shalford
Chilworth
Albury
Shere
Gomshall
Abinger Hammer
Wotton
Westcott
Ranmore Common
Peaslake
Holmbury St Mary
Coldharbour
Farncombe
Godalming
Bramley
Wonersh
Shamley Green
Elstead
Milford
Witley
Thursley
Hambledon
Hascombe
Cranleigh
Ewhurst
Forest Green
Walliswood
Oakwoodhill
Dunsfold
Alfold
Rudgwick
Slinfold
Chiddingfold
Grayswood
Haslemere
Ramsnest Common
Loxwood
Plaistow
Ifold
Kingsley Green
Fernhurst
Roundstreet Common
Five Oaks
Itchingfield
SURREY HILLS
SURREY
0 1 2 3 miles
0 1 2 3 4 5 km

Epsom
Banstead
Purley
Sanderstead
Coulsdon
Kenley
Whyteleafe
Warlingham
Chipstead
Ashtead
Leatherhead
Burgh Heath
Tadworth
Kingswood
Woldingham
Caterham
Walton on the Hill
Headley
Mickleham
Merstham
Limpsfield
Oxted
SURREY HILLS
Reigate
Redhill
Nutfield
Bletchingley
Godstone
Tandridge
Dorking
Brockham
Betchworth
Buckland
Earlswood
South Nutfield
South Godstone
Crowhurst
Leigh
Sidlow
Salfords
Outwood
North Holmwood
South Holmwood
Horley
Smallfield
Lingfield
Newdigate
Charlwood
Gatwick Airport
Burstow
Newchapel
Dormansland
Felbridge
Copthorne
East Grinstead
Capel
Ifield
Three Bridges
Crawley
Pound Hill
Worth
Turners Hill
Rusper
Colgate
Faygate
Broadfield
Tilgate
Pease Pottage
Handcross
Balcombe
Ardingly
Horsham
Roffey
West Hoathly
Sharpthorne
Highbrook
Sunnyside
Kingsfold
WEST SUSSEX
Staplefield
Slaugham
M25
M23
A22
A23
A24
A25
A264
A217
67
52
35
36

Leaves Green
Downe
Biggin Hill
Tatsfield
Titsey
Limpsfield
Oxted
Hurst Green
Holland
Lingfield
Dormansland
East Grinstead
Sunnyside
Ashurst Wood
Forest Row
Wych Cross
Chelwood Gate
Cudham
Knockholt
Knockholt Pound
Halstead
Shoreham
Otford
Chevening
Dunton Green
Chipstead
Riverhead
Sevenoaks
Westerham
Brasted
Sundridge
Crockham Hill
Edenbridge
Marlpit Hill
Four Elms
Hever
Chiddingstone
Markbeech
Cowden
Hartfield
Withyham
Crowborough
Penshurst
Leigh
Hildenborough
Tonbridge
Southborough
Royal Tunbridge Wells
Rusthall
Langton Green
Groombridge
Frant
Pembury
Hadlow
Ightham
Borough Green
Platt
Seal
Kemsing
Heaverham
Wrotham
Plaxtol
Shipbourne
Fordcombe
Ashurst
Rotherfield
Mark Cross
Tidebrook
KENT DOWNS
KENT
HIGH WEALD
EAST SUSSEX
Ashdown Forest
0 1 2 3 miles
0 1 2 3 4 5 km

Snodland
Burham
Eccles
Birling
Ryarsh
Addington
Leybourne
Larkfield
New Hythe
Ditton
Aylesford
Boxley
Detling
Thurnham
Bredhurst
Stockbury
South Green
Bredgar
Bicknor
Wormshill
Frinsted
Milstead
Hucking
Sandling
Allington
Royal British Legion Village
East Malling
West Malling
Offham
King's Hill
Maidstone
Penenden Heath
Bearsted
Roseacre
Weavering Street
Grove Green
Barming Heath
East Barming
Fant
Tovil
Wateringbury
Teston
West Farleigh
East Farleigh
Loose
Shepway
Willington
Otham
Leeds
Broomfield
Hollingbourne
Eyhorne Street
Harrietsham
Lenham
KENT
DOWNS
Nettlestead
Nettlestead Green
Coxheath
Boughton Monchelsea
Langley
Langley Heath
Kingswood
Chart Sutton
Sutton Valence
Ulcombe
Boughton Malherbe
Grafty Green
Yalding
Hunton
Benover
Laddingford
Linton
Chainhurst
East Peckham
Hale Street
Branbridges
Beltring
Paddock Wood
Collier Street
Marden
Staplehurst
Headcorn
Hawkenbury
Egerton
Smarden
Brenchley
Horsmonden
Matfield
Lamberhurst
Goudhurst
Kilndown
Cranbrook
Sissinghurst
Frittenden
Biddenden
High Halden
Bethersden
Tenterden
Rolvenden
Benenden
Hawkhurst
Flimwell
Ticehurst
Wadhurst
Stonegate
Sandhurst
Newenden
Hartley
Iden Green
HIGH WEALD
Bedgebury Forest
Bewl Water
Maidstone Services
Knox Bridge
Cross-at-Hand
Wilsley Pound
Four Throws
The Moor
Small Hythe
Woodchurch
London Beach
St Michaels
M20
M2
A20
A21
A229
A262
A274
A28
A228
A26
A249
A268
B2163
B2162
B2079
B2085
B2086
B2082
B2087
B2099
69
54
38
37

54
Rodmersham
Rodmersham Green
Upper Rodmersham
Lynsted
Cellarhill
Lewson Street
Norton Ash
Oaks
Davington
Ospringe
The Brents
Faversham
Goodnestone
Preston
Culmers
Fostall
Dargate
Dargate Common
Hernhill
Staplestreet
Boughton Street
Dunkirk
Denstroude
Honey Hill
Blean
Rough Common
Upper Harbledown
Harbledown
Woodstock
Newbury
Kingsdown
Bexon
Milstead
Dungate
Erriottwood
Bluetown
Hollybushes
Newnham
Doddington
West End
Eastling
North Eastling
Painter's Forstal
Whitehill
Plumford
Selgrove
North Street
Gosmere
Sheldwich
Sheldwich Lees
Copton
Crouch
South Street
Hickmans Green
Winterbourne
Oversland
Hogben's Hill
Neames Forstal
Selling
Rhode Common
Chartham Hatch
Thanington
Timbold Hill
Wichling
Seed
Tong
Yewhedges
Hockley
Throwley
Little Frith
Frith
Perrywood
Wyebanks
Otterden Place
Slade
Throwley Forstal
Badlesmere
Old Wives Lees
Shottenden
Chilham
Bagham
Shalmsford Street
Chartham
Horton
West Street
Payden Street
Warren Street
Tong Green
The Valley
Leaveland
Dane Street
Great Bower
Mountain Street
Garlinge Green
Street End
Lenham
Stalisfield Green
North Downs
KENT
DOWNS
Molash
Pested
Challock
Paddock
Stocker's Head
Charing Hill
Godmersham
King's Wood
Petham
Sandway
Leadingcross Green
Lenham Heath
Charing Heath
Charing
Bilting
Crundale
Sole Street
Waltham
Eastwell Park
Boughton Aluph
Boughton Corner
Boughton Lees
Westwell Leacon
Westwell
Dunn Street
Egerton
Egerton Forstal
Pluckley
Pluckley Thorne
Little Chart
Little Chart Forstal
Ram Lane
Wye
Hassell Street
Bodsham
North Leigh
Whiteacre
Goat Lees
Kennington
Bockhanger
Bybrook
Hothfield
Potters Corner
Hastingleigh
Brook
Troy Town
Elmsted
Lymbridge Green
Mockbeggar
Fir Toll
Chambers Green
Maltman's Hill
Ripper's Cross
Great Chart
Ashford
South Ashford
Willesborough
Willesborough Lees
Hinxhill
Sevington
Stowting
Brabourne
Brabourne Lees
Woodland
Haffenden Quarter
Wissenden
Bethersden
Stanhope
Kingsnorth
Mersham
Smeeth
Postling
Brissenden Green
Tanden
Shadoxhurst
Stubbs Cross
Cheeseman's Green
Finberry
Sellindge
Stanford
High Halden
Bliby
Clap Hill
Aldington
Westenhanger
Henghurst
Bromley Green
Aldington Frith
Newingreen
Pedlinge
Shirkoak
Bonnington
Lympne
Robhurst
Orlestone
Bilsington
Court-at-Street
West Hythe
Woodchurch
Hamstreet
Ruckinge
Tenterden
Brook Street
Kenardington
Warehorne
Palmarsh
Leigh Green
Burmarsh
Newchurch
Appledore Heath
Reading Street
Small Hythe
Appledore
Snave
Romney Marsh
Dymchurch
Brenzett Green
Snargate
St Mary in the Marsh
Stone
Isle of Oxney
The Dowels
M2
M20
A2
A28
A20
A251
A252
A2070
A259
70
53
38
39
0 1 2 3 miles
0 1 2 3 4 5 km

SANDWICH BAY
Shell Ness
Sandwich Flats
Richborough Port
Westmarsh
Westbere
Stodmarsh
Sturry
Fordwich
Canterbury
Littlebourne
Bekesbourne
Patrixbourne
Bridge
Nackington
Lower Hardres
Bishopsbourne
Kingston
Barham
Bossingham
Derringstone
Denton
Wingmore
Elham
Ottinge
Lyminge
Etchinghill
Beachborough
Newington
Cheriton
Saltwood
Hythe
Sandgate
Seabrook
Folkestone
Channel Tunnel
Hawkinge
Capel-le-Ferne
West Hougham
Drellingore
Densole
Swingfield Minnis
Swingfield Street
Selsted
Wootton
Lydden
Coldred
Shepherdswell or Sibertswold
Coxhill
Eythorne
Elvington
Barfrestone
Womenswold
Woolage Green
Snowdown
Aylesham
Adisham
Nonington
Easole Street
Chillenden
Goodnestone
Knowlton
Wingham
Ickham
Wickhambreaux
Preston
Elmstone
Hoaden
Ash
Staple
Durlock
Guilton
Marshborough
Woodnesborough
Eastry
Betteshanger
Tilmanstone
Northbourne
Sandwich
Stone Cross
Worth
Ham
Finglesham
Sholden
Deal
Walmer
Great Mongeham
Little Mongeham
Ripple
Sutton
East Studdal
Kingsdown
Ringwould
Martin
Martin Mill
East Langdon
West Langdon
Whitfield
Guston
West Cliffe
St Margaret's at Cliffe
SOUTH FORELAND
Temple Ewell
River
Ewell Minnis
Alkham
Buckland
Maxton
Aycliff
Farthingloe
Dover
Western Docks
Eastern Docks
Shakespeare Cliff
Channel Tunnel
CALAIS DUNKERQUE
K E N T
STRAIT OF DOVER
A B C D E F G H
7 8 9 10 11
TR 60
TR 30
40

Pembrey
(Pembre)
Burry Port
(Porth Tywyn)
Achddu
Craig
Lettyrychen
Pwll
Cwmbach
Furnace
Felinfoel
Llangennech
Waungron
Dafen
Sandy
Llanelli
Pen-y-fan
Ty-isaf
Morfa
Machynys
Bryn
Llwyn-hendy
Pemberton
Penceiliogi
Bynea
Yspitty
Loughor
Gorseinon
Penllergaer
Penyrheol
Pontlliw
Garden Village
Grovesend
Swansea West Services
Cadle
Fforest-fach
Port Mead
Pen-lan
Mynydd-bach-y-glo
Gendros
Cwmdu
Cockett
Townhill
Waunarlwydd
Gowerton
(Tre-Gwyr)
Penclawdd
Pen-clawdd
Crofty
Llanmorlais
Wernffrwd
Three Crosses
Blue Anchor
Dunvant
(Dynfant)
Killay
Upper Killay
Sketty
Brynmill
Uplands
Swansea
Abertawe
Blackhills
Black Pill
Mayals
West Cross
The Mumbles
(Y Mwmbwls)
Mumbles Head
Oystermouth
Newton
Langland
Norton
Mumbles Hill
Murton
Manselfield
Bishopston
Kittle
Oldway
Pennard
Southgate
Parkmill
Nicholaston
Penmaen
Ilston
Lunnon
Llethrid
River Loughor
Afon Llwchwr
Whiteford Pt
Trwyn Whiteford
Berges Island
Whiteford Sands
Llanrhidian Sands
Llanrhidian
Landimore
Cheriton
Llanmadoc
Burry Holms
Hills Tor
Broughton Bay
Llangennith
Hillend
Burry Green
Stembridge
Oldwalls
THE GOWER
GWYR
Gower Peninsula
Arthur's Stone
Burial Chamber
Reynoldston
Little Reynoldston
Knelston
Llanddewi
RHOSSILI BAY
Rhossili
Rhossili Down
Middleton
Pitton
Pilton Green
Scurlage
Penrice
Oxwich
Oxwich Castle
Oxwich Green
Horton
Overton
Port-Eynon
Port-Eynon Pt
Trwyn Port Eynon
PORT EYNON BAY
OXWICH BAY
BAE OXWICH
Oxwich Pt
Worm's Head
BRISTOL CHANNEL
MÔR HAFREN
A4118
B4295
B4271
B4247
A484
A4240
74
75
47
46
0 1 2 3 miles
0 1 2 3 4 5 km

Clydach
Faerdre
Ynystawe
Pant-lasau
Cwmrhydyceirw
Morriston
(Treforys)
Clase
Graig Trewyddfa
Treboeth
Landore
Llansamlet
Trallwn
Heol-las
Birchgrove
Tai'r-ysgol
Lon-las
Skewen
Winsh-wen
Cwm
Bon-y-maen
Cefn-hengoed
Pentre-dwr
Coed Darcy
Llandarcy
Jersey Marine
Pentre-chwyth
Kilvey Hill
Foxhole
Port Tennant
St Thomas
P&R
Crymlyn Burrows
Swansea Works
West Pier
THE NATIONAL WATERFRONT MUS
PLANTASIA
Crymlyn Bog & Pant-y-Sais
Tennant Canal
Fabian Way
Cefn-y-Garth
Mynydd Drumau
Glanbran Ho
Stanley Wood
Darran Wood
Neath Abbey
Melincryddan
Bryn-coch
Rhyddin
Cadoxton-Juxta-Neath
Cilfrew
Aberdulais
Aberdulais Falls
Fforest Gôch
Tonna (Tonnau)
Neath
Castell-Nedd
The Gnoll
Mosshouse Wood
Mount Pleasant
Cimla
Afan Valley Road
Neath Canal
Briton Ferry
(Llansawel)
Pant-Howel-Ddu
Gelli-gaer
Mynydd-y-Gaer
314
Bwlch
Baglan
Baglan Bay
Bae Baglan
River Neath
Wales Coast Path
Brynbryddan
Mynydd Dinas
258
Pantdu
Cwmafan
Ynysygwas
Caerhendy
Cwmavon Road
Corlannau
Aberavon
Sandfields
Aberavon Sands
Witford Pt
Port Talbot
Harbourside Park under dev
Taibach
Pen-y-cae
Goytre
Cwm Dyffryn
Ergyd Isaf
Margam
Margam Sands
Steel Works
Brombil
Groes
Margam Park
Stones
Eglwys Nunydd Reservoir
Kenfig House Fm
Water Street
Ind Est
Caegarw
Llanmihangel
Kenfig Sands
Kenfig Pool & Dunes
Kenfig Pool
Kenfig
Visitor Centre
Penymynydd
Mawdlam
North Cornelly
South Cornelly
Pyle (Y Pil)
Shop Cen
Kenfig Hill
Bedford
Cefn Cross
Cefn Cribbwr
Pen-y-castell
Ty-Tanglwyst Fm
Ballas Fm
Sker Pt
Sker Court
Parc Newydd Fm
The Grove
Flynnon-wen Rocks
Rest Bay
Nottage
Lock's Common
Hutchwns Pt
Hutchwns
Porthcawl
Porthcawl Museum
Porthcawl Pt
Sandy Bay
Coney Beach
Rhych Pt
Trecco Bay
Clevis
Newton
Black Rocks
Newton Pt
Newton Down
The Beacons
Manor Fm
Bridgend Road
Clement Fm
Court
Wig Fach
Tythegston
Whitney Fm
Laleston
Stormy Down
Upper Park
Candleston Castle
Merthyr Mawr Warren
Merthyr Mawr
Ogmore Castle
Ogmore
Ogmore Road
Ogmore-by-Sea
(Aberogwr)
Black Rocks
Tusker Rock
Groes Fm
Heol-y-mynydd
St Brides Major
(Saint-y-Brid)
Pitcot
Penuchadre
Southerndown
Glamorgan Heritage Coast Centre
Dunraven Bay
Durval Fm
Castle-upon-Alun
Old Castle Down
Wallas Fm
Tre-p
Nash Pt
Melincourt
Melin Cwrt Waterfalls
Clyne
Wenallt Wood
Coed Gawdir
Banwen Torybetel
Carn Caca
Moel yr Hyrddod
Carn Caglau
493
Mynydd Corrwg Fechan
Coetgae'r Derlwyn
Mynydd Blaen-Nant-du
Glyncorrwg
Aton Corrwg
Mynydd Ynyscorrwg
502
Mynydd Abergwynfi
Glyn Corrwg
Mynydd Blaengwynfi
Blaen-gwynfi
Coetgae Isaf
Mynydd Blaenafan
Abercregan
Aber-gwynfi
Nant y Fedw
Cymer
Foel Fawr
347
Croeserw
Mynydd Fforch-Dwm
Tyle'r waun
Mynydd Nant-y-bar
Mynydd Rhiwgregen
Mynydd Blaenafon
Cwm Gwenffrwd
Cwm Blaenpelenna
Tonmawr
Cefn Morfudd
307
Cefn-Saeson
Baradychwallt
AFAN ARGOED
Cwm Afan
Duffryn
Efail-fâch
280
Mynydd Pen-Rhys
Cerrig Llwydion
Pontrhydyfen
370
Foel Fynyddau
Pwll-y-glaw
Rock
Cwm
Moel y Fen
Afan Argoed
Mynydd Penhydd
South Wales Miners Museum
Cwm yr Argoed
Pen Disgwylfa
FOREST PARK
Brynheulog
Foely Dyffryn
366
Caerau
Blaencaerau
Llynfi River
Dyffryn
Rhiw Tor Cymry
Spelter
Mynydd Bach
433
Blaen Cwmdû
Nantyffyllon
Mynydd Caerau
555
Craig Walter
Werfa
568
Blaengarw
Pwll-y-garn
Mynydd Llangeinwr
Bryn
Cil-y-Gofid
Mynydd Bychan
Moel Gallt-y-cwm
272
Cwm Farteg
319
Mynydd Bach
Cwm Wernderi
Maesteg
Neath Road
Llwydarth
Bryn-Rhug Fm
Garth Hill
257
Garth
Cwm Garw Fechan
Moel Cynhordy
Pontycymer
Cwm Gelli-wern
Cwm Sychbant
Cwm Nant-y-glo
Cwmfelin
Cwm y Garn
Margam Forest
Mynydd Margam
344
Cwm Cerdin
Moel Troed-y-rhiw
Pont Rhyd-y-cyff
Cynhordy Fm
Mynydd Moelgeila
Pont-y-rhyl
Craig-yr-Hudol
Llangynwyd
Waun y Gilfach
Gilfach
Gadlys
Bryn-Cynan
BRIDGEND
PEN-Y-BONT AR OGWR
Nant y Gadlys
Craig Cwm Maelwg
Mynydd y Castell
319
Moel Ton-mawr
Cwm Cynffig
Craig yr Aber
Mynydd Baedan
251
Coytrahen
Tylacoch Fm
Shwt
Llangeinor
Bettws
Ton Mawr Fm
Twyn-yr-hydd
Pentre Fm
Pen-y-bryn
Aberbaiden Fm
Ffordd-y-Gyfraith
Cwm-ffos
Park Fm
Parc Slip Nature Reserve
Fountain
Tondu
Brynmenyn
Bryncethin
Aberkenfig
(Abercynffig)
Sarn
Cymdda
Sarn Park Services
Ty'n-y-garn
McArthur Glen Bridgend
Derwen
Pen-y-cae
Pen-y-fai
Pant Fm
Court Colman
Pendre
Llangewydd Court
Cefn Glas
Bryntirion
Newcastle
Bridgend
Tremains
Whiterock
Tyla Fm
Ton Fm
Ewenny
Beech Fm
Tair Cross Down
SWANSEA BAY
BAE ABERTAWE
M4
A48
A483
A465
A4230
A4107
A4063
A4061
A4106
A4229
A473
B4282
B4281
B4283
B4524
B4265
SS
90
00
70
7
8
9
10
11
A
B
C
D
E
F
G
H

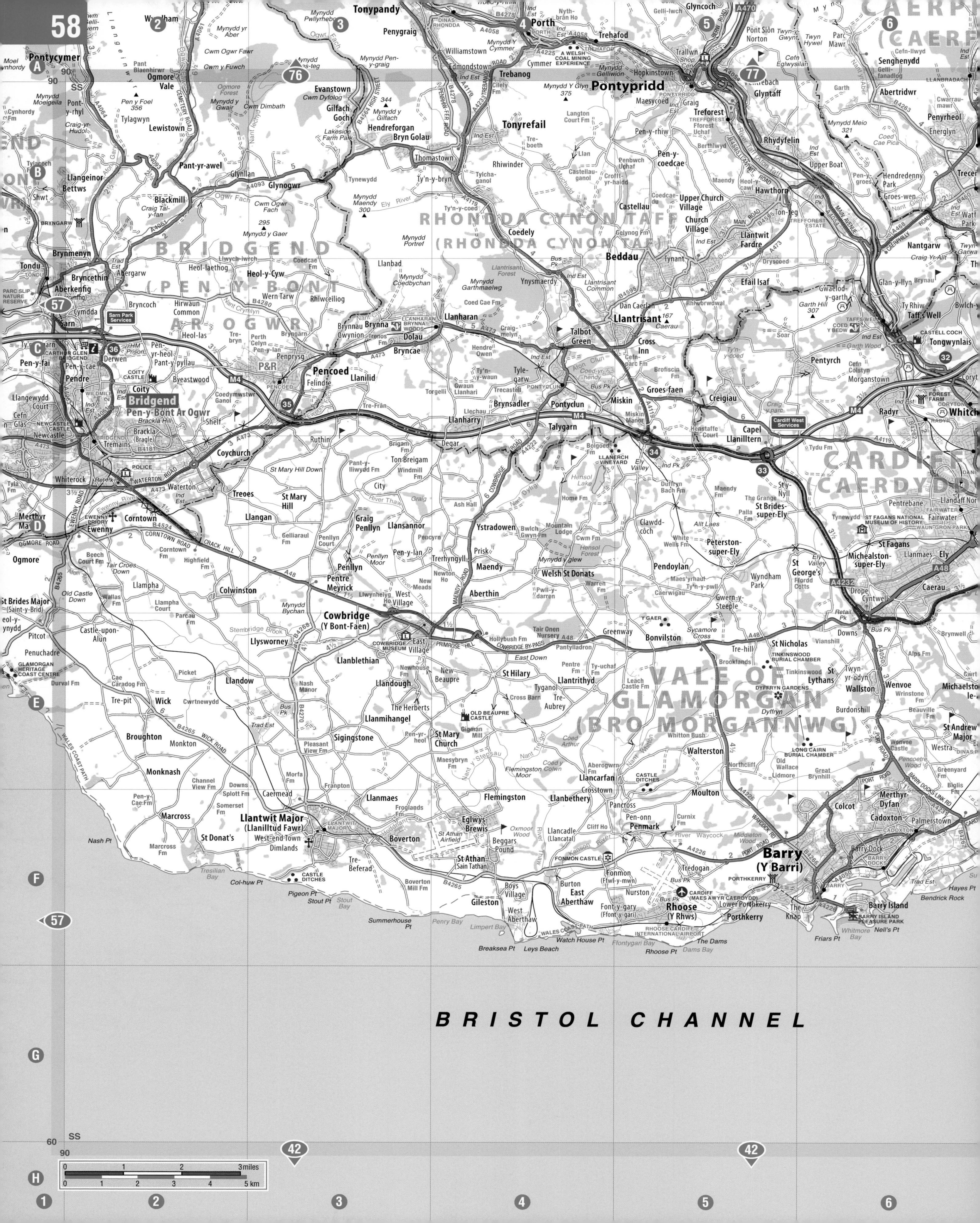
BRISTOL CHANNEL
VALE OF GLAMORGAN (BRO MORGANNWG)
BRIDGEND (PEN-Y-BONT AR OGWR)
RHONDDA CYNON TAFF (RHONDDA CYNON TAF)
CARDIFF (CAERDYDD)
Bridgend
Pontypridd
Barry (Y Barri)
Cowbridge (Y Bont-Faen)
Llantwit Major (Llanilltud Fawr)
Llantrisant
Pencoed
Rhoose (Y Rhws)
Barry Island
St Athan (Sain Tathan)
Tonypandy
Porth
Penarth

Cwm felin fach
Crosskeys
Wattsville
Newtown
Black Vein
Brynawel
Risca
Penrhiw
Danygraig
Pontymister
Ty-Sign
Sirhowy Valley
Mynydd Dimlaith
Mynydd Y Grug
Twyn Yr Oerfel
Mynydd Machen
Bedwas
Trethomas
Machen
Chatham
Upper Ochrwyth
Nant-y-ceisiad
Craig-y-Rhacca
Ty-canol
Pwllypant
Caerphilly
(Caerffili)
Ty'n-y-coedcae
Lower Machen
Draethen
Mynydd Bwlch
Rudry
Lansbury Park
Mynydd Rudry
Van
The Warren
Caerphilly Common
Caerphilly Tunnel
Pant Glas Fm
Parc Ceen Onn
Coed Craig Ruperra
Ruppera Home Fm
Coed Coesau-whips
Cefn Mably Woods
Fair Oak Fm
Lisvane
Llanishen
Cardiff Gate Services
Began
Church Fm
Shop Cen
Pantmawr
Rhiwbina
Birchgrove
Cyncoed
Pentwyn
Llanedeyrn
Llanrumney
St Mellons
Trowbridge
Rumney
Heath
Roath Park
Mynachdy
Gabalfa
Llandaff
Pontcanna
Maindy
Cathays
Blackweir
Roath
Pen-y-lan
Tremorfa
Canton
Cathays Park
Splott
Cardiff
Caerdydd
Cardiff Flats
Riverside
Butetown
East Moors
Grangetown
Millennium Centre
Welsh Assembly
Orchard Ledges
Leckwith
Penarth Moors
Cardiff Bay
Llandough
International Sports Village
Cardiff Bay Barrage
Dinas Powys
Cogan
Penarth Head
Turner House
Murch
Penarth
Old Cogan Hall Fm
Morristown
Lower Penarth
The Stairs
Cosmeston
Cosmeston Lakes
Roundbush Rocks
Medieval Village
De Sully Grange
Cog
Ranny Bay
Lavernock
Lavernock Pt
Lavernock Point
Sully
Swanbridge
St Mary's Well Bay
Sully Island
Ynys Sili
Rogerstone
Fourteen Locks
Cefn
High Cross
Rhiwderin
Garth
Bassaleg
Pentre-poeth
Park Ho
Pye Corner
Dyffryn Court
Holly Ho
Clearwell
Michaelston-y-Fedw
Pen-y-lan
Penylan Fm
Fairwater Fm
Druidstone Ho
Coedkernew
Castleton
Marshfield
Blacktown
Tymawr Fm
Hawse Fm
St Brides Wentlooge
Rhubina Fm
Orchard Fm
New Ho
Peterstone Gout
Peterstone Wentlooge
Pilldu
Sluice Fm
Pwll-Mawr
Ty-to-maen Fm
Rumney Great Wharf
Peterstone Great Wharf
Newton
Maerdy Fm
Lamby
Bettws
Malpas
Newport
Casnewydd
Park Fm
Brynglas
Caerleon
National Legion Museum
Roman Bath & Amphitheatre
The Village
St Julians
Christchurch
Chepstow Hill
Priory Wood
Cat's Ash
Llanbeder
Coed-y-caerau
Penrhos Fm
New Wood
Barrack Hill
Crindau
Barnardtown
Summerhill
Beechwood
Maindee
Allt-yr-yn
Ridgeway
Caerau Park
St Woolos
Stow Park
Glasllwch
Gaer
Stelvio
Pillgwenlly
Level of Mendalgief
Lawrence Hill
Bishpool
Ringland
Alway
Somerton
Lisweery
Coldra
Langstone
Little Milton
Llanwern
Underwood
Bishton
Wilcrick
Llanmartin
Glan Llyn under dev
Transporter Bridge
Geraint Thomas National Velodrome of Wales
Tredegar House
Duffryn
Maes-glas
Cleppa Park
Lower Lake
Pye Corner
Broadstreet Common
Moor Barn
Tatton Fm
Bowleaze Common
Green Moor
Greenmoor
Whitson Court
North Row Fm
Nash Works
Nash
Uskmouth
Nash Power Sta
Henton Fm
Whitson
Goldcliff
Saltmarsh
Newport Wetlands
River Usk (Afon Wysg)
New Gout
Sea Reach
West Usk Lighthouse
Goldcliff Pill
Porton Ho
Gold Cliff
Broad Mead
Wales Coast Path
Llandevenny
Severn Estuary
Aber Hafren
Monkstone
Flat Holm
North West Pt
Lighthouse Pt
Tower Rock
Rudder Rock
Calf Rock
Steep Holm
Pigeon Ho
Margaret's Bay
Ladye Bay
Walton St Mary
Clevedon Bay
Salthouse Bay
Church Hill
Clevedon
East Clevedon
Blackstone Rocks
Dowlais Fm
Treble House Fm
Seawall Fm
Riverside Fm
Channel View
Middle Lane Fm
Bullocks Fm
Kingston Seymour
Langford Grounds
St Thomas's Head
Woodspring Bay
Wharf Fm
Ham Fm
Wick Warth
Swallow Cliff
Middle Hope
Sand Pt
Woodspring Priory
Sandbay Fm
Iceton
Yeo Bank Fm
Tutshill Ear
Wemberham Cott
North Somerset
Sand Fm
Wick St Lawrence
Ebdon
Bourton
East Hewish
West Hewish
Hewish
Sand Bay
Norton
Kewstoke
Worlebury
Worle
St Georges
May's Green
Puxton
Birnbeck Island
Ashcombe Park
Milton
West Wick
Way Wick
Puxton Park
Rolstone
East Rolstone
Box Bush Fm
Weston-super-Mare
Marine Lake
Tropicana
Weston Milton
Wolvershill Manor
Lower Gout Fm
Rookery Fm
Clarence Park
Weston Bay
Helicopter Mus
Drove Fm
Woolvers Hill
Court Fm
Banwell
Stonebridge
West End Fm
Locking
Elborough
Hutton
Fiddler's Pt
Brean Down
Black Pt
Uphill
Uphill Manor
Oldmixon
Lower Canada
Upper Canada
Hillend
Knightcott
The Caves
Banwell Hill
Banwell Castle
Yarberry
Walborough
The Grange
Hay Wood
Christon Plantn
Towerhead
A
B
C
D
E
F
G
H
7
8
9
10
11
43
60
77
78

Llanvaches
Penhow
Llanmartin
Bishton
Llandevenny
Wilcrick
Magor
Magor Services
Undy
Rogiet
Caldicot
Portskewett
Sudbrook
Crick
Mathern
Beachley
Caldicot Level
Redwick
Summerleaze
Welsh Grounds
Bedwin Sands
Severn Road Bridge
Prince of Wales Bridge
Severn Tunnel
Aust
Severn View Services
Littleton-on-Severn
Elberton
Olveston
Alveston
Thornbury
Rudgeway
Tockington
Almondsbury
Pilning
Severn Beach
New Passage
Redwick
Northwick
Easter Compton
Patchway
Bradley Stoke
Stoke Gifford
Filton
Winterbourne
Frenchay
Hambrook
Catbrain
Hallen
Henbury
Avonmouth
Shirehampton
Pill
Portishead
Redcliff Bay
Portbury
Easton-in-Gordano
Clapton-in-Gordano
Weston-in-Gordano
Walton-in-Gordano
Clevedon
Gordano Services
King Road
Westbury on Trym
Horfield
Stapleton
Fishponds
Redland
Clifton
Bristol
Bedminster
Knowle
Brislington
Hanham
Keynsham
Long Ashton
Failand
Wraxall
Tickenham
Nailsea
Flax Bourton
Backwell
Yatton
Congresbury
Wrington
Felton
Winford
Dundry
Chew Magna
Chew Stoke
Pensford
Whitchurch
Blagdon
Ubley
Burrington
Langford
Churchill
Kingston Seymour
Puxton
Hewish
Brinsea
Redhill
Butcombe
Nempnett Thrubwell
Stanton Drew
Bishopsworth
Hartcliffe
Withywood
Chew Valley Lake
CITY AND COUNTY OF BRISTOL
NORTH SOMERSET
BATH NORTH EAST
Bristol International
M4
M5
M48
M49
M32
A38
A37
A369
A370
A4
A403
A4174
0 1 2 3 miles
0 1 2 3 4 5 km

Upper Morton
Whitfield
Charfield
Kingswood
Abbey Gatehouse
Wortley
Alderley
Tresham
Leighterton
Doughton
Cromhall
Cromhall Common
Talbot's End
Churchend
Hillesley
Lower Kilcott
Upper Kilcott
Westonbirt
Westonbirt Arboretum
Shipton Moyne
Milbury Heath
Tytherington
Wickwar
Chase Hill
Oldbury on the Hill
Knockdown
Willesley
Easton Grey
Itchington
Bagstone
Hawkesbury
Hawkesbury Upton
Didmarton
Sopworth
Sherston
Pinkney
Foxley
Rangeworthy
Latteridge
Iron Acton
Engine Common
Yate Rocks
Horton
Dunkirk
Petty France
Little Badminton
Luckington
Norton
Totteroak
Little Sodbury End
Little Sodbury
Badminton
Badminton Park
Alderton
Hullavington
Frampton Cotterell
Nibley
Yate
Chipping Sodbury
Old Sodbury
Goose Green
Westerleigh Common
Mayshill
Rodford
Frampton End
Coalpit Heath
Acton Turville
Littleton Drew
Grittleton
Stanton St Quintin
Winterbourne Down
Westerleigh
Wapley
Dodington
Codrington
Tormarton
Burton
Nettleton
Leigh Delamere
Leigh Delamere Services
Kington St Michael
SOUTH
GLOUCESTERSHIRE
COTSWOLDS
WILTSHIRE
Mangotsfield
Pucklechurch
Hinton
Dyrham
Dyrham Park
West Kington
Castle Combe
Yatton Keynell
Shortwood
Siston
Abson
West Littleton
North Wraxall
Ford
West Yatton
Allington
Hardenhuish
Kingswood
Warmley
Bridge Yate
Doynton
Marshfield
The Shoe
Slaughterford
Biddestone
Frogwell
Sheldon Manor
Wick
Pennsylvania
Cold Ashton
Thickwood
Colerne
Eastrip
Upper Pickwick
Middlewick
Pickwick
Cross Keys
Oldland
Willsbridge
Avon Valley Railway
Bitton
Upton Cheyney
Lansdown
Langridge
Tadwick
St Catherine
Three Shire Stones
Corsham
Corsham Court
Easton
Westrop
Thingley
Notton
Avon Valley Adventure & Wildlife Park
North Stoke
Woolley
Upper Swainswick
Swainswick
Northend
Box
Box Hill
Alcombe
Hawthorn
Neston
Gastard
Chapel Knapp
Saltford
Kelston
Upper Weston
Beckford's Tower
Charlcombe
Batheaston
Bathford
Kingsdown
Henley
Atworth
Beanacre
Whitley
Shaw
Weston
Newbridge
Lower Weston
Bath
Walcot
Bathampton
Bathwick
Roman Baths
The Recreation Ground
Claverton
Monkton Farleigh
Corston
Newton St Loe
Twerton
Odd Down
Combe Down
Monkton Combe
Warleigh
South Wraxall
Broughton Common
Broughton Gifford
Melksham
Holt
Stanton Prior
Englishcombe
Marksbury
Inglesbatch
Hunstrete
Priston
Southstoke
Midford
Tucking Mill
Limpley Stoke
Freshford
Bradford-on-Avon
Bradford Leigh
Winsley
Turleigh
Avoncliff
Staverton
Hilperton
Semington
Farmborough
Wellow
Peasedown
Dunkerton
Carlingcott
Combe Hay
Twinhoe
Westwood
Trowle Common
Trowbridge
SOMERSET
M4
A4
A46
A36
A350
A420
A433

62
The Priory
Newnton Ho
Murcott
Eastcourt Ho
Braydon Brook Fm
Oaksey Nursery
Flisteridge Wood
Lyngrove Fm
Lower Moor
Grove Fm
Hillside
Leigh
Chelworth Lower Green
Farfield Fm
Newlands Fm
Lower Blunsdon
Marsh Fm
Merchants Fm
Bishoper Fm
Hankerton Field Fm
Hankerton
Cloatley Manor
Cloatley
Upper Minety
Sawyers Hill
Minety
Flower's Fm
Field Fm
Gryphon Lodge Fm
Leighfield Lodge Fm
B4040
Leighfield Fm
Cox Hill
Stoke Common Fm
Purton Stoke
CRICKLADE ROAD
Dudgemore Fm
Chapel Fm
Upper Widhill Fm
Eagle Lodge
Manor Fm
Shipton Moyne
Fosse Tilery Fm
Gilboa Fm
Bell Fm
Bullock's Horn
Cloatley End
Woodward Fm
Braydon Hall
Old Copse
Buryhill Fm
White Lodge
Hayes Knoll
SWINDON & CRICKLADE RAILWAY
Blunsdon St Andrew
Quobwell Fm
Griffins Barn Fm
Brokenborough
Andover's Gorse
Stonehill Fm
Park Copse
Stonehill Wood
Watts Wood
Bentham Ho
New Fm
BLUNSDON
Haydon
Haydon Wick
Filands
Perry Green
Charlton
B4040
Lype Fm
Swatnage Wood
Stone Hill
Summer House Fm
Ravensbrook Fm
Gospel Oak Fm
Pry Fm
WILTSHIRE
Fosse Fm
Boakley Fm
Cranmore Fm
Back Br
Bus Pk
ABBEY HOUSE
CHARLTON ROAD
Garsdon
Turk's Fm
Pond Fm
Nineteen Acre Wood
Great Withy Wood
Ravensroost Wood
RAVENSROOST WOOD AND MEADOWS
Red Lodge
Battlelake Fm
Purton Common
Paven Hill
Widham
The Fox
Greenmeadow
Moredon
Malmesbury
ABBEY
Milbourne
Twatley Manor Fm
Hyam Fm
Hyam Wood
Manor Fm
Garsdon Wood
Great Elm Fm
Braydon Pond
Pond Lodge
Worthy Hill Fm
Grove Fm
Moonsleaze Fm
Braydon Manor
Braydon Green Fm
MUSEUM
Purton
Dogridge
Purton Ho
Common Platt
ATHELSTAN
Arches Fm
Foxley Grove
Thornhill Fm
Coombe Green
Lea
Winkworth Fm
Somerford Common
Queen Street
Park View Fm
The Firs
Brockhurst Wood
Green Hill
Restrop
Roughmoor
Pinehurst
Burton Hill
Cow Br
Sundey Hill Fm
Somerford Fm
Wood Hill
Penn's Lodge Fm
Webb's Wood
Lydiard Plain
Manor Ho
Lydiard Millicent
Rodbourne Cheney
Foxley
Foxley Green
Cowage Grove
Kings Heath
Lawn Fm
Burnt Heath Fm
Cleverton
Lea Wood
Clitchbury Manor
Ramps Hill
Braydon Side
Woodbridge
Koffs Fm
Frith Copse
Lydiard Green
Greatfield
Nine Elms
Trad Est
Shaw
Maunditts Park Fm
Little Somerford
B4042
Malthouse Fm
Lodge Fm
The Common
Callow Hill
Purley Fm
Flaxlands Wood
Highgate Fm
Midgehall Copse
Flaxlands Manor Fm
Park Copse
LYDIARD HOUSE
Lydiard Tregoze
Westlea
Rodbourne
Even Swindon
Norton
Bradfield Wood
West Park Wood
Corston
Rodbourne Rail Fm
Angrove Fm
East End Fm
Causeway End
Brinkworth
Hook
Hook Street
Letterage Copse
LYDIARD PARK
Grange Park
Toothill
Freshbrook
Ballard's Ash
Royal Wootton Bassett
Coped Hall
The Marsh
Midge Hall
SWINDON RD
Spittleborough Fm
M4
Windmill Hill
GREAT WESTERN WAY
Area under dev
Okus
STEAM
Rodbourne
Somerford Br
Idover Demesne Fm
Crew's Fm
Manor Fm
White's Fm
Dovey's Fm
Hooker's Gate Fm
Great Somerford
Dauntsey
Little Smithcot Fm
Great Smithcot Fm
Grittenham
Olivemead Fm
Goddards Fm
Grove Fm
Old Park Fm
A3102
Wickfield Fm
Upper Studley Fm
B4005
Common Fm
Kingway Barn
Cleeve Ho
Rodbourne Bottom
Binscombe Wood
Idover Ho
Hullavington
Hullavington Airfield (Disused)
Startley
Seagry Heath
Seagry Wood
River Avon
Greenman's Lane
Great Wood
Chessley Hill Fm
Brynard's Hill
Ind Est
Bus Pk
Costow Fm
Wharf Fm
Glebe Fm
North Wroughton
Lower Stanton St Quintin
Avil's Fm
Upper Seagry
Lower Seagry
Sodom
Snell's Fm
Great Wood Fm
Hart Fm
Tockenham Wick
HUNTS MILL ROAD
Vastern
Greenhill Common Fm
Brinkworth Brook
Can Court Fm
Wootton Meadows
Elcombe House Fm
Swallett Gate
Corner Fm
Bowd's Fm
Vale Fm
Vowley Fm
Great Chaddington Fm
Lower Basset Down Fm
Elcombe
Nables Fm
Stanton St Quintin
Stanton Park
Clanville
Dauntsey Lock
Park Fm
Waite Hill Fm
THE HILLOCKS
Shaw Fm
Little Park Fm
Wootton Fields Fm
Salthrop Ho
Chilton Fm
Upper Town
Bittlesea Fm
The Banks
Greenhill Fms
Queens Court Fm
The Barton
Cotmarsh
Bincknoll Fm
Clouts Wood
Red Barn
A4122
Draycot Cerne
Summerlands Fm
MAIN ROAD
Bright's Fm
Bradenstoke
Lyneham
Tockenham
Clyffe Pypard Wood
Greenway Fm
Upper Ham Fm
BINCKNOLL CASTLE
Quidhampton Wood
Salthrop Fm
Leigh Delamere Services
Whitelands Fm
Sutton Benger
Draycot Ho
Christian Malford
Bradenstoke Abbey
Church End
Tockenham Court Fm
Thornhill
WHITE HORSE
Bincknoll Wood
Moorshall Fm
Priory Fm
Kington St Michael
The Old Rectory
Thornend
Melsome Wood
Middlehill Fm
Parsonage Fm
Littletown Farmhouse
Preston
Broad Town
Uffcott
Bowldown
Lake Fm
Catcomb Wood
New Zealand
Bushton
Thickthorn Fm
Wood Street Fm
Cockroost Fm
Hackpen Fm
Kington Langley
Langley Gate Fm
Sutton Lane Fm
Foxham
Freegrove Fm
Springfield Ho
Broadtown Hill
Manor Fm
The Weir
Elm Cross
Down Fm
Tor Hill
Heywood Fm
Lodge Fm
Grove Fm
Avon
West End
Cadenham Manor
Stockham Marsh Fm
Catcomb
Goatacre
Clyffe Pypard
CLYFFE PYPARD
Uffcott Down
Barbury Hill
BARBURY CASTLE
Fowlswick Fm
Bolehyde Manor
Allington
CEPEN PARK
Manor Fm
Thornhill Fm
Langley Fm
Teal Fm
Hare Street Fm
Beacon Hill
Marsh Fm
Windmill Hill
Woodhill Park
Nebo Fm
Highden
Broad Hinton
Langley Burrell
Bird's Marsh
Barrow Fm
Kellaways
Charlcutt
Spirthill
Leekshedge Fm
Witcomb Fm
Corton Manor Fm
Bupton Hill Fm
Fiddlers Hill
Hardenhuish
Allington Bar
Peckingell
Tytherton Lucas
Catbrook Ho
East Tytherton
Cowage Brook
Hilmarton
SWINDON ROAD
Clevancy
Stanmore Copse
Winterbourne Bassett
Rabson Manor
Hackpen Hill
Preshute Down
SHELDON MANOR
Westfield Ho
West Tytherton
Bremhill Wick
Bremhill Grove
Honeybed Wood
Hanger Park Fm
Bremhill Ho
Cowick Fm
Hilmarton Manor
Lower Penn Fm
Rodwell Fm
Lower End Fm
Highway
Highway Hill
Whyr Fm
Gorse Copse
Berwick Bassett
Man's Head
Frogwell
Retail Pk
CHIPPENHAM MUSEUM
New Leaze Fm
Scotts Mill
Bencroft Hill
Wick Hill
Turnham Wood
Whitley Fm
Beversbrook Fm
Breach Fm
Dugdales Fm
Manor Fm
Roach Wood
Berwick Bassett Clump
Wick Down Fm
Chiverlins Fm
A350
Chippenham
Harden's Fm
Low Bridge
Fisher's Brook
High Penn Fm
Freeth Fm
Monkton Field
Monkton Down
Temple Fm
Temple Bottom
Rowden Hill
Hither Fm
Stanley
Bremhill
Compton Bassett
Compton Hill
Nolands Fm
Grey Wethers or Sarsen Stones
Patterdown Fm
Englands
LONDON ROAD
Pound Fm
Stanley Abbey Fm
Ratford
Swerves Fm
Abberd Brook
Compton Bassett Ho
Yatesbury
Winterbourne Monkton
WINDMILL HILL
River Kennet
Showell Fm
Forest Gate Fm
Conigre Fm
Calne Marsh
Sands Fm
NORTH
Lower Lodge Fm
Studley
Calne
Cherhill Field
Yatesbury Field
East Fm
FYFIELD DOWN
Easton
Westrop
Cocklemore Brook
Pewsham Ho
Derry Hill
Buck Hill
Bassett's Moor
LACKHAM
Wiltshire College (Lackham)
Horse Copse
Lower Sands Fm
Cherhill
Upper Fm
Manor Fm
Overton Down
Clatford Down
Thingley
Golden Gates
Pigsty Copse
BOWOOD HOUSE
Pinhills Fm
Pillars Lodge
Quemerford
WHITE HORSE
Cherhill Down
AVEBURY MANOR
Avebury
AVEBURY STONE CIRCLE & MUSEUM
Courtlands Fm
Notton
Naish Hill Fm
Great Wood
Bowood Lake
Blackland Park
Theobald's Green
Knoll Down
Avebury Trusloe
Down Barn
Fyfield Hill
Chapel Knapp
Ray Mill
Reybridge
Bewley Common
Nethermore Fm
The Warren
Cuff's Corner
Holly Ditch Fm
Mile Elm
Ranscombe Bottom
Calstone Down
West Down
SILBURY HILL
West Kennett
STONE AVENUE
Gastard
Lacock
LACOCK ABBEY
FOX TALBOT MUSEUM
Tossels Fm
Rough Leaze Fm
Blackland
Calstone Wellington
Beckhampton
THE SANCTUARY (OVERTON HILL)
North Fm
A4
Lockeridge Ho
Scott's Fm
Sandy Lane
Stockley
Danger area
WEST KENNETT LONG BARROW
Beckhampton Penning
West Overton
Lockeridge
Bowden Hill
Bowden Hill Ho
Spye Park Ho
Broad's Green
Wans Ho
Bell Fm
Heddington Wick
Splatts Ho
Harley Fm
Morgan's Hill
MORGAN'S HILL
Furze Knoll
North Down
East Kennett
LONG BARROW
White Hill
Locke Dene
Beanacre
Silverstreet Wood
Chittoe
DEVIZES ROAD
Hampsley Hollow
Baltic Fm
Bishop's Canning Down
Hemp Knoll
Allington Down
Lurkeley Hill
Halfway Fm
Manor Fm
Turnpike Fm
Heddington
King's Play Hill
Easton Down
Hursley Bottom
Whitley
Shaw
Rhotteridge Fm
Bromham House Fm
Netherstreet Fm
Boreham Wood
Beechfield Ho
Forest Fm
Prickmoor Wood
A3102 WESTBROOK ROAD
Sloperton Fm
Westbrook
Beacon Hill
Hill Cott
ROUNDWAY DOWN 1643
Roughridge Hill
All Cannings Down
Furze Hill
Shaw Ho
Oakley Fm
Sandridge
Bromham
Oliver's Castle
Roundway Hill
Tan Hill
Melksham Forest
New Road Fm
SANDRIDGE COMMON
Sandridge Park
Sandridge Fm
The Fruit Fm
Moorhouse Fm
St Edith's
WHITE HORSE
Bourton
Easton Fm
Bishops Cannings
Harepath Fm
New Town
Draycot Hill
Gopher Wood
Golden Ball Hill
Melksham
Snarlton Fm
Durlett Fm
Rowdeford School
Roundway
Horton Mill Fm
Townsend Fm
Clifford's Hill
PEWSEY DOWNS
Milk Hill
Walker's Hill
Huish
Draycot Payne
The Spa
Tanhouse Fm
Redstocks
Broad Lane Fm
Berhills Fm
Wick Fm
Rowde Hill Fm
Rowde
Iron Pear Tree Fm
Roundway Hill Fm
Trad Est
Ind Est
Horton Br
Horton
Allington
The Knoll
Lower Mill Fm
Cannings Cross Fm
Stanton St Bernard
East Field
West Stowell
Berryfield
BATH ROAD
A365
Sells Green
Tanis
Caen Hill Locks
Dunkirk
KENNET & AVON CANAL MUS
LONDON ROAD
Little Horton
Calcote Fm
KENNET AND AVON CANAL
All Cannings Br
Alton Barnes
Alton Priors
Honey Street
Tawsmead Copse
Oak Fm
Stowell Park
Whaddon Grove Fm
Outmarsh
Bowerhill
Seend Cleeve
CASTLE
Devizes
WILTSHIRE MUS
Coate
Lowerfields Fm
All Cannings
Stanton Br
Woodborough Hill
Picked Hill
Cocklebury Fm
Wilcot
Semington
Littleton
The Stocks
Seend Head
TROWBRIDGE ROAD
Seend
Inmarsh
Cleeve Ho
Barleyhill Fm
Poulshot Lodge Fm
Bus Cen
Lower Park Fm
Old Park
BROADLEAS GARDENS
Trad Est
Nursteed
Etchilhampton Hill
Etchilhampton
South Fms
Mill Fm
Hurst's Fm
Hanging Stone
Seend Bridge Fm
Summerham Brook
Poulshot
Stert
Wabi Fm
Woodborough
Frith Copse
Little Marsh
Orchard Down Fm
Townsend
Five Lanes
Sandfield Ho
Potterne
Potterne Field
Sleight Fm
Potterne Wood
Byde Fm
Crookwood Fm
Marsh Fm
Hatfield Fm
Beechingstoke
Broad Street
Patney
Bottlesford
Vale of Pewsey
Manningford Bruce
Mullens Fm
Manningford Abbots
Ashton Common
Keevil
Pantry Fm
Bulkington
Lutsey Fm
Manor Ho
Potterne Wick
Marden
HENGE
Puckshipton
Hilcott
Lock Wood
Semington Brook
miles
km

Burytown Fms
Castle Hill
Broad Blunsdon
Stanton Fitzwarren
Swanborough
Redlands
Severnhampton
Broadbush
Stanton Park
Park Fm
Watchfield
Longcot
Fernham
Baulking
Goosey
Denchworth
Shrivenham
Defence Coll of Management & Tech
Cleveland Fm
Uffington
St Mary's Church
Woolstone
Kingston Lisle
Fawler
Westcot
Sparsholt
Childrey
West Challow
East Challow
Wantage
Charlton
Belmont
Vale & Downland Museum
Letcombe Regis
Letcombe Bassett
Upper Stratton
Kingsdown
Stratton St Margaret
Lower Stratton
Gorse Hill
Nythe
Covingham
Swindon
Walcot
Eldene
Dorcan
New Town
Museum & Art Gallery
Lawn
Park
Liden
Coate
Coate Water
South Marston
Bourton
Compton Beauchamp
Knighton
Kingstone Winslow
Uffington White Horse & Castle
White Horse Hill
The Ridgeway Path
Ashbury
Wayland's Smithy
Idstone
Bishopstone
Hinton Parva
Wanborough
Liddington
Badbury Wick
Badbury
Chiseldon
Wroughton
Hodson
Ashdown House
Lambourne Downs
Upper Lambourn
Lambourn
Eastbury
East Garston
Fawley
South Fawley
North Wessex Downs
West Berkshire
Oxon
Swindon
Baydon
Membury Services
Aldbourne
Lambourn Woodlands
Woodlands St Mary
Great Shefford
Shefford Woodlands
Weston
Welford
Chaddleworth
Upper Upham
Draycot Foliat
Barbury Castle
Burderop Down
Woodsend
Ogbourne St George
Southend
Ogbourne St Andrew
Ogbourne Maizey
Rockley
Ramsbury
Whittonditch
Preston
Crooked Soley
Straight Soley
Chilton Foliat
Hungerford Newtown
Wickham
Leverton
Axford
Mildenhall
Marlborough
Manton
Clatford
Forest Hill
Froxfield
Hungerford
Eddington
Avington
Kintbury
Halfway
Savernake Forest
Cadley
Chisbury
Chisbury Chapel
Little Bedwyn
Bagshot
Sanham Green
Anvilles
Titcomb
Clench Common
The Warren
Great Bedwyn
Durley
Inkpen
Upper Green
Lower Green
West Woodhay
Wootton Rivers
Oare
New Mill
Crofton
Crofton Beam Engines
Wilton
Wilton Windmill
Shalbourne
Ham
Rivar
Stibb Green
Burbage
Eastcourt
Pewsey
Pewsey Wharf
Milton Lilbourne
Easton Royal
Little Salisbury
Fyfield
Kepnal
West Grafton
East Grafton
Marten
Buttermere
Walbury Hill
Combe
East Woodhay
Southcott
Oxenwood
Wexcombe
Tidcombe
Henley
Linkenholt
Faccombe
M4
A4
A338
A346
A419
A420
B4000
B4001
B4192
B4507
Bath Road
London Road
Ermin Street
River Kennet
Kennet & Avon Canal
81
82
47
15
14
64

Steventon
Didcot
Wantage
Wallingford
Harwell
Rowstock
East Hendred
Ardington
Lockinge
Blewbury
Upton
West Hagbourne
East Hagbourne
South Moreton
North Moreton
Cholsey
Moulsford
South Stoke
Goring
Streatley
Woodcote
Crowmarsh Gifford
Brightwell cum Sotwell
Aston Tirrold
Aston Upthorpe
Chilton
West Ilsley
East Ilsley
Compton
Farnborough
Catmore
Brightwalton
Lilley
Chaddleworth
Leckhampstead
Peasemore
Beedon
Chieveley
Hampstead Norreys
Aldworth
Ashampstead
Yattendon
Hermitage
Frilsham
Bradfield
Pangbourne
Tidmarsh
Sulham
Theale
Englefield
Bucklebury
Curridge
Boxford
Winterbourne
Welford
Wickham
Speen
Donnington
Shaw
Newbury
Thatcham
Midgham
Woolhampton
Aldermaston
Brimpton
Crookham
Greenham
Enborne
Hamstead Marshall
Kintbury
Stockcross
Headley
Burghclere
Highclere
Kingsclere
Tadley
Baughurst
Ashford Hill
Ecchinswell
Woolton Hill
East Woodhay
Ball Hill
Silchester
Padworth
Ufton Nervet
Mortimer West End
Bramley
Pamber Heath
NORTH WESSEX DOWNS
OXFORDSHIRE
WEST BERKSHIRE
THE RIDGEWAY PATH
M4
A34
A339
A4
A417
A329
A340
63
82
83
48
A
B
C
D
E
F
G
H
1
2
3
4
5
6
0 1 2 3 miles
0 1 2 3 4 5 km

Greenfield
Turville Heath
Turville
Fingest
Bolter End
Lane End
Booker
Cressex
Loudwater
Pishill
Skirmett
Frieth
Moor Common
Flackwell Heath
Cookley Green
Russell's Water
Southend
Stonor
Parmoor
Pheasants
Rockwell End
Marlow Bottom
Wooburn Green
Park Corner
Maidensgrove
Well End
Little Marlow
Nuffield
Nettlebed
Fawley
Hambleden
Lower Woodend
Marlow
Bovingdon Green
Bourne End
Port Hill
Fawley Bottom
Greenlands
Mill End
Medmenham
Bisham
Cookham
Cookham Dean
Cookham Rise
Bix
Middle Assendon
Lower Assendon
Aston
Remenham
Hurley
Highmoor Cross
Stoke Row
Checkendon
Shepherd's Green
Satwell
Rotherfield Greys
Rotherfield Peppard
Henley-on-Thames
Remenham Hill
Furze Platt
Maidenhead
Taplow
Sonning Common
Harpsden
Crazies Hill
Holly Cross
Warren Row
Burchett's Green
Littlewick Green
Cox Green
Bray Wick
Bray
Kidmore End
Lower Shiplake
Shiplake
Binfield Heath
Wargrave
Knowl Hill
White Waltham
Woodlands Park
Holyport
Goring Heath
Cane End
Tokers Green
Emmer Green
Caversham
Dunsden Green
Play Hatch
Sonning
Charvil
Twyford
Hare Hatch
Ruscombe
Waltham St Lawrence
Paley Street
Touchen End
Stud Green
Fifield
Mapledurham
Purley on Thames
Tilehurst
Reading
Woodley
Hurst
Whistley Green
Shurlock Row
Hawthorn Hill
Jealott's Hill
Moss End
Warfield
Maiden's Green
Winkfield
Calcot
Calcot Row
Southcote
Whitley
Earley
Winnersh
Sindlesham
Binfield
Popeswood
Bullbrook
Winkfield Row
Bracknell
Wokingham
Emmbrook
Shinfield
Arborfield
Arborfield Cross
Eastheath
Easthampstead
Amen Corner
Harmans Water
Crown Wood
Three Mile Cross
Grazeley
Burghfield
Burghfield Hill
Spencers Wood
Swallowfield
Barkham
The Throat
Holme Green
Hanworth
Birch Hill
Arborfield Garrison
Wick Hill
Crowthorne
Stratfield Mortimer
Beech Hill
Riseley
Farley Hill
Finchampstead
Eversley
Eversley Cross
Little Sandhurst
Sandhurst
Bagshot
Stratfield Saye
Heckfield
Bramshill
Yateley
Camberley
Frimley
Hawley
Blackwater
York Town
Stratfield Turgis
Turgis Green
Hound Green
Hazeley
Hartley Wespall
WOKINGHAM
READING
WINDSOR & MAIDENHEAD
BRACKNELL FOREST
BUCKS

Beaconsfield
Loudwater
Flackwell Heath
Seer Green
Jordans
Chalfont St Peter
Gerrards Cross
Northwood
Harefield
Ruislip
Harrow
Pinner
Eastcote
Ruislip Common
Denham
Ickenham
Uxbridge
Hillingdon
Northolt
Greenford
Southall
Hayes
Yiewsley
West Drayton
Heston
Hounslow
Cranford
Harmondsworth
Heathrow Airport
Burnham
Slough
Taplow
Farnham Common
Stoke Poges
Iver Heath
Iver
Langley
Cippenham
Eton
Eton Wick
Windsor
Datchet
Colnbrook
Poyle
Stanwell
Feltham
Twickenham
Hanworth
Holyport
Bray
Dorney
Old Windsor
Wraysbury
WINDSOR & MAIDENHEAD
BUCKS
Winkfield
Cranbourne
Englefield Green
Egham
Staines-upon-Thames
Ashford
Sunbury-on-Thames
Hampton
Ascot
Sunninghill
Sunningdale
Virginia Water
Thorpe
Chertsey
Shepperton
Walton-on-Thames
Addlestone
Weybridge
Esher
Bagshot
Windlesham
Lightwater
Chobham
Woodham
Byfleet
West Byfleet
Cobham
Woking
Knaph
Pyrford
Wisley
Heathrow
M4
M25
M40
M3
A4
A30
A40
A312
A316
A308
A322
65
84
85
50
0 1 2 3 miles
0 1 2 3 4 5 km

Stanmore
Finchley
Woodford
Wealdstone
Hendon
Wood Green
Hornsey
Tottenham
Walthamstow
Wanstead
Leytonstone
Leyton
Wembley
Hampstead
Highgate
Stoke Newington
Islington
Hackney
Willesden
Camden
Shoreditch
Bethnal Green
Harlesden
Paddington
Finsbury
Holborn
City
Poplar
Ealing
Acton
Blackwall Tunnel
Hammersmith
Kensington
Westminster
Southwark
Bermondsey
Chiswick
Chelsea
Lambeth
Greenwich
Brentford
Kew Br
Battersea
Fulham
Camberwell
Deptford
Peckham
Lewisham
Isleworth
Richmond
Mortlake
Clapham
Brixton
Putney
Wandsworth
Balham
Catford
Richmond Park
LONDON
Teddington
Wimbledon
Streatham
Sydenham
Penge
Beckenham
Bromley
Kingston upon Thames
New Malden
Merton
Mitcham
South Norwood
Surbiton
Morden
Croydon
Sutton
Carshalton
Chessington
Cheam
Wallington
Ewell
Epsom
Purley
Banstead
Coulsdon
Chipstead
Ashtead
Whyteleafe
Warlingham

Woodford
Woodford Bridge
Grange Hill
Hainault
Harold Hill
Collier Row
Gidea Park
Romford
Harold Wood
Great Warley
Little Warley
Barkingside
Redbridge
Wanstead
Leytonstone
Newbury Park
Seven Kings
Goodmayes
Chadwell Heath
Rush Green
Hornchurch
Upminster
Cranham
West Horndon
East Horndon
Bulphan
Ilford
Barking
Becontree
Dagenham
Elm Park
Hacton
Corbets Tey
North Ockendon
South Hornchurch
Rainham
Wennington
Aveley
South Ockendon
THURROCK
North Stifford
Little Thurrock
Grays
Purfleet
West Thurrock
South Stifford
Stratford
West Ham
East Ham
LONDON
Canning Town
Beckton
Creekmouth
Thamesmead
Blackwall Tunnel
Silvertown
North Woolwich
Woolwich Ferry
Woolwich
Plumstead
Abbey Wood
Belvedere
Erith
Greenwich
Charlton
Blackheath
Kidbrooke
Shooters Hill
Welling
Bexleyheath
Crayford
Barnehurst
Slade Green
Dartford
Dartford Crossing
Greenhithe
Stone
Northfleet
Swanscombe
Gravesend
Eltham
Lee
Hither Green
Falconwood
Blackfen
Bexley
Old Bexley
Coldblow
Sidcup
Mottingham
Grove Park
Chislehurst
North Cray
Foots Cray
Ruxley
Hextable
Swanley
Wilmington
Hawley
Sutton at Hone
Darenth
South Darenth
Bean
Betsham
Southfleet
Longfield
Hartley
New Barn
Istead Rise
Bromley
Bickley
Widmore
Shortlands
Petts Wood
St Paul's Cray
St Mary Cray
Orpington
Hayes
Bromley Common
Farnborough
Locksbottom
Keston
Green St Green
Chelsfield
Well Hill
Crockenhill
Farningham
Eynsford
Horton Kirby
Fawkham Green
New Ash Green
West Kingsdown
Maplescombe
KENT DOWNS
Shoreham
Halstead
Badger's Mount
Knockholt Pound
Cudham
Downe
Biggin Hill
Otford
Kemsing
Heaverham
Wrotham
Stansted
Fairseat
Vigo Village
Culverstone Green
Trottiscliffe
KENT
M25
M20
M26
A2
A20
A13
A12
A127
0 1 2 3 miles
0 1 2 3 4 5 km

ESSEX
Rayleigh
Rochford
Hockley
Hawkwell
Laindon
Basildon
Pitsea
Vange
North Benfleet
Thundersley
South Benfleet
Hadleigh
Eastwood
Leigh-on-Sea
Southend-on-Sea
Westcliff-on-Sea
Prittlewell
Southchurch
Chalkwell
London Southend Airport
Canvey Island
Winter Gardens
Stanford-le-Hope
Corringham
Fobbing
Coryton
Thames Haven
DP World London Gateway
Mucking
Linford
East Tilbury
West Tilbury
River Thames
Cliffe
Cooling
High Halstow
St Mary Hoo
Allhallows
Allhallows-on-Sea
Isle of Grain
Grain
Lower Stoke
Stoke
Middle Stoke
Hoo St Werburgh
Chattenden
Higham
Shorne
Wainscott
Upnor
MEDWAY
River Medway
Strood
Rochester
Chatham
Gillingham
Rainham
Walderslade
Wayfield
Hempstead
Wigmore
Medway Services
Upchurch
Lower Halstow
Newington
Sittingbourne
Queenborough
Rushenden
Iwade
Kemsley
Milton Regis
Bobbing
Borden
Stockbury
Bredhurst
Boxley
Aylesford
Snodland
Halling
Cuxton
Wouldham
Burham
Eccles
Cobham
Luddesdown
Birling
Leybourne
Ditton
Larkfield
KENT
DOWNS
North Downs Way
Gravesend Reach
Long Reach
Southend Pier
Thurrock Thameside Nature Reserve
Cliffe Pools
Hadleigh Castle
Upnor Castle
Chatham Historic Dockyard
Rochester Castle
Cathedral
Dickens World
Kit's Coty House
87
88
70
53
TQ
A
B
C
D
E
F
G
H
1
2
3
4
5
6
7
8
9
10
11

Paglesham Eastend
Horseshoe Corner
Rugwood Fm
Eastwick Head
Island
Great Burwood Fm
Rugwood Head
Barling Marsh
Potton Island
88
89
Aspins Head
Roper's Fm
Barling Hall Fm
Fleet Head
New England Island
The Broomway
Butler's Fm
Bolts Fm
Barling
New England Creek
Shelford Head
High Ho
Stonebridge
Little Wakering Wick
Rushley Island
Havengore Island
Maplin Sands
Smither's Fm
Shopland Hall
Little Wakering
Oxenham Fm
Sharpness Head
Clay Street Fm
Oldbury Fm
Havengore Head
Haven Pt
HIGH STREET
B1017
Ind Est
Great Wakering
Samuel's Corner
Wakering Stairs
Bournes Green
A1159
North Shoebury
Southchurch
A13
Black Grounds
THORPE BAY
Thorpe Bay
Pig's Bay
KURSAAL
B1016
Cambridge Town
SHOEBURYNESS
SEA LIFE ADVENTURE
EASTERN ESPLANADE
THORPE ESPLANADE
Shoeburyness
PIER RLY
69
Southend Pier
Shoebury Ness
West Knock
East Knock
THAMES ESTUARY
Roas Bank
Grain Spit
Grain
Garrison Pt
Jacob's Bank
Blue Town
Cheyney Rock
SHEERNESS-ON-SEA
Sheerness
A249
Marine Town
Minster Marshes
Scrapsgate
Mile Town
The Lappel
A250
Queenborough Spit
West Minster
Halfway Houses
ABBEY
East End
West Swale
Deadmans Island
B2008
QUEENBOROUGH ROAD
MINSTER ROAD
Minster
Trouts
Warden Pt
QUEENBOROUGH
Queenborough
Neats Court
LOWER ROAD
Scocles Fm
Norwood Manor
Barnland Fm
Warden
A2500
Eastchurch
Rushenden
Long Reach
Neatscourt Marshes
Parsonage Fm
New Hook Fm
Old Hook Fm
Groves Fm
HM Prison
LEYSDOWN ROAD
Bay View
B2231
Old Rides Fm
Leysdown-on-Sea
Minster Marshes
Southlees Marshes
FERRY ROAD
SHEPPEY WAY
Stray Marshes
Isle of Sheppey
Capel Hill Fm
COASTAL PARK
Muswell Manor
Ferry Marshes
The Dray
Windmill Creek
Leysdown Marshes
Ind Est
SWALE
Ridham Dock
ELMLEY
Eastchurch Marshes
Capel Fleet
Harty
Marshes
Elmley Island
ELMLEY MARSHES
Kings Hill Fm
Elmley Marshes
Spitend Marshes
Isle of Harty
THE SWALE
Shell Ness
TANKERTON BAY
Long Rock
Iwade
Coldharbour Marshes
Dutchman's Island
Elliots Fm
Whitstable
Swalecliffe
Tankerton
Lower Island
Pheasant Fm
Shrubsole Fm
The Lillies
The Swale
Peg Fleet
Spitend Pt
Mocketts
Sayes Court
WHITSTABLE BAY
KEMSLEY DOWN
Kemsley
Fowley Island
SITTINGBOURNE & KEMSLEY LIGHT RLY
South Deep
Conyer Creek
The Ferry Inn
Horse Sands
The Oaze
Seasalter
Duncan Down
South Street
Chestfield
Milton Regis
Tonge Corner
Blacketts
South Oaze
COURT HALL MUS
Binny Cotts
Teynham Level
Conyer
Cleve Marshes
Graveney Marshes
Seasalter Level
Bogshole Fm
A299
Clapham Hill
Radfall
Chalkwell
Murston
Teynham Street
Nagden Marshes
Fox's Cross
SITTINGBOURNE
Uplees
Court Lodge
Graveney Marshes
Teynham Court
Poplar Hall
Graveney Hill
Monkshill Fm
Yorkletts
Burgess Fm
Clowes Wood
Snipeshill
Bax
Barrow Green
Luddenham Court
Oare
Ham Marshes
Nagden
Broom Street
Pean Hill
Sittingbourne
HERITAGE MUS
Bapchild
Radfield
Haywood
Teynham
Deerton Street
Nash's Fm
B2045
Ham Fm
Highstreet
Waterham
Graveney
Culmers
Heart's Delight
Little Dully
Dully Ho
Rodmersham
Cellarhill
The Old Farm Ho
Four Oaks
Davington
SHEPHERD NEAME BREWERY
CHART GUNPOWDER MILLS
Sandbanks
Dargate Common
Denstroude
Red Lion Ho
Well Court
Tunstall
Nouds Fm
Batteries Fm
Lewson Street
Beacon Hill
The Brents
Faversham
Goodnestone
Langdon Court
Fostall
Honey Hill
Amery Court
Highsted
Rodmersham Green
Upper Rodmersham
Lynsted
Norton Ash
LONDON ROAD
Ospringe
FLEUR DE LIS HERITAGE CENTRE
Ind Est
Ewell Fm
Hernhill
Dargate
Acorn Cott
Blean Wood
Hothe Court Fm
Tyler Hill
Grove End
Oakwood Fm
Pitstock Fm
Loyterton
Judd's Hill
MAISON DIEU
Perry Court
B2040
Fairbrook Fm
Holly Hill
North Bishopden Wood
BLEAN WOODS
Blean
Woodstock
Newbury
Kingsdown
Lynsted Park
Monk Fm
54
Preston
Staplestreet
MOUNT EPHRAIM
Courte Fm
Nash Ct
Brenley Corner
Dunkirk
Church Wood
Hassenden
BLEAN WOODS
Rough Common
Penfield
Whitehill
Hansletts Ho
Copton
M2
A2
Boughton Street
Bexon
Churchman's Fm
Painter's Forstal
Plumford
Brenley Ho
BOUGHTON BYPASS
Upper Harbledown
Homestall Wood
Hall Place
CANTERBURY WEST
Bluetown
Sharsted Court
Champion Court
College Wood
Scooks Farm Ho
Selgrove
Sole Street Ho
Crouch
South Street
Hickmans Green
Forester's Lodge Fm
Fishpond Wood
Harbledown
Newnham
North
Owens Court
A251
BIGBURY CAMP
0 1 2 3 miles
0 1 2 3 4 5 km

7
8
9
10
11
A
B
C
D
E
F
G
H
89
40
90
TR
NORTH
SEA
Margate
Westgate on Sea
Birchington
Reculver
RECULVER TOWER & ROMAN FORT
Herne Bay
Hampton
Beltinge
Hillborough
Bishopstone
Eddington
Greenhill
Herne
Broomfield
Hoath
Chislet
Upstreet
Sarre
St Nicholas at Wade
Monkton
Minster
Acol
Manston
Isle of Thanet
Garlinge
Westbrook
Cliftonville
Kingsgate
Northdown
St Peters
Broadstairs
Ramsgate
Pegwell
Cliffs End
Sandwich Bay
Pegwell Bay
Shell Ness
Richborough Port
Sandwich
Ash
Grove
Preston
Elmstone
Wingham Wildlife Park
Sturry
Fordwich
Canterbury
Westbere
Hersden
Stodmarsh
Wickhambreaux
Littlebourne
Wade Marsh
Plumpudding Island
River Wantsum
Minnis Bay
Grenham Bay
St Mildred's Bay
Nayland Rock
North Foreland
Long Nose Spit
Botany Bay
Dumpton Gap
West Stourmouth
East Stourmouth
Westmarsh
Upper Goldstone
Lower Goldstone
Richborough Castle
A28
A299
A253
A256
A255
A254
55
TR
60
40

ST BRIDES BAY
BAIE SAIN FFRAID
90
91
Newgale Sands
Maidenhall Pt
Rickets Head
Black Cliff
Madoc's Haven
Druidston Haven
Settling Nose
Black Pt
Sleek Stone
Broad Haven
(Aberllydan)
The Settlands
Little Haven
Goultrop Roads
Borough Head
Ticklas Pt
Stack Rocks
Howney Stone
Mill Haven
Halfway Rock
Wavey Haven
St Brides Haven
The Nab Head
Tower Pt
Wooltack Pt
Trwyn Wooltack
Haven Pt
High Pt
Musselwick Sands
Martin's Haven
Garland Stone
Skomer Head
Pigstone Bay
SKOMER ISLAND
Skomer Island
Ynys Skomer
The Wick
North Haven
Little Sound
The Neck
Midland Island
Summer Only
Deadman's Bay
SKOMER MARINE NATURE RESERVE VISITOR CENTRE
Rainy Rock
MARLOES SANDS
Albion Sands
Gateholm Stack
Gateholm Island
Ynys Gateholm
Marloes Sands
Broad Sound
Skokholm Island
Ynys Skokholm
Little Bay Pt
SKOKHOLM ISLAND
The Stack
East Bay
Mad Bay
Long Pt
Hog Bay
Long Nose
Quarry Pt
The Head
Frank's Pt
Crab Rocks
Hooper's Pt
Westdale Bay
Great Castle Head
Iron Pt
Long Pt
Welshman's Bay
Little Castle Pt
Frenchman's Bay
Mill Bay
St Ann's Head
Pentir St Ann
Kete
West Blockhouse Pt
Watwick Bay
Watwick Pt
Castlebeach Bay
Dale Pt
Dale Roads
Dale
Townsend
Red Cliff
Little Marloes Fm
Crabhall Fm
Marloes
Marloes Court
Musselwick Fm
St Bride's
Windmill Park
Pearson Fm
Ripperston Fm
WALES COAST PATH
LLWYBR ARFORDIR PENFRO
PEMBROKESHIRE COAST PATH
South Hill
Talbenny
Orlandon
Slatemill Bridge
Butterhill Fm
Slatehill Fm
Marles Fm
B4327
PEMBROKESHIRE COAST
NATIONAL PARK
Musselwick
St Ishmael's
Lindsway Bay
Watch House Pt
Bicton
Sandy Haven
Hasguard
Hasguard Hall
Hasguard Cross
Little Castle Head
Great Castle Head
South Hook Pt
Herbrandston
Sandyhaven Pill
Capeston
Stack Rock
Milford Haven
Aberdaugleddyf
Thorn Island
Chapel Bay
West Angle Bay
Angle
Angle Pt
Rat Island
The Hall
B4320
Angle Bay
Bae Angle
Castles Bay
Sheep Island
Ynys y Defaid
Parsonsquarry Bay
Carters Green
East Pickard Bay
Gravel Bay
Freshwater West
Kilpaison Burrows
B4319
Gupton Fm
Great Furzenip
Frainslake Sands
Brownslade Burrows
Blucks Pool
Berry Slade
Danger area
Wind Bay
Linney Head
Pen-y-holt Bay
Bulliber Down
Mount Sion Down
ELEGUG STACKS
Flimston Bay
The Wash
Mewsford Pt
PEMBROKESHIRE
COAST NATIONAL PARK
Artillery Range
Brownslade
Castlemartin
Axton Hill
Cold Comfort
Warren
Merrion
MERRION CROSS
Corston
Newton Corseside
Wallaston Green
B4320
Rhoscrowther
Popton Pt
Bullwell Bay
Sawdern Pt
Oil Refinery
Pwllcrochan
Pennar Mouth
Pembroke Power Sta
Lambeath Fm
ROSSLARE
Wear Pt
Milford Haven
Aberdaugleddau
Hakin
Pill
Hubberston
MILFORD HAVEN
Bus Pk
Liddeston
Priory
Trad Est
Thornton
Steynton
STEINTON ROAD
Lodge Fm
Oil Refinery
Robeston Cross
Robeston West
Woodsend
Moor Fm
Walwyn's Castle
Hooks
Fenton
Walton West
Broadway
Nattshook Fm
B4341
Timber Hill
Haroldston West
Castle High
Rosehill
Corner Fm
HANGSTONE DAVEY
Hill Fm
Druidston
Rogeston
West Lambeston
Lambston
Nolton
Nolton Haven
Trapps Fm
Simpson
Folkeston Hill
Keeston Moor
Keeston Br
Knock Brook
Simpson Cross
Keeston
Pelcomb Cross
Pelcomb
Pelcomb Bridge
Dunston Grove
Sutton
Sutton Lodge
Cuckoo Grove
HAVEN ROAD
HAVERFORDWEST TOWN MUS
Albert Town
Trad Est
Portfield Gate
Skerryford
DALE ROAD
B4327
Dreenhill
Merlin's Bridge
West Denant
Denant
Ratford Bridge
Barn Fm
North Johnston Fm
Bus Pk
Pope Hill
JOHNSTON
Johnston
Annikel
Tiers Cross
Rose Cottage Fm
Deemshill
A4076
MILFORD ROAD
Rose Hill
Hayston Mill
Hayston Hall
Upper Scoveston
Scoveston
Scoveston Fort
A477
Black Bridge
Honeyborough
B4325
Venn Fm
Waterston
Leonardston
Oil Refinery
Llanstadwell
Wood
Church Hill
Roch
Roch Gate
Ferny Glen
Cuffern
Dudwells
Robleston Hall
Haysford
Wolfsdale
Chapel Hill
Folly
Camrose
Camrose Brook
Cleddau Lodge
Cuttybridge
Knock Fm
Red Hill
Slade
A487
Pelcomb Fm
Western
Newgale
A
B
C
D
E
F
G
H
1
2
3
4
5
6
70
20
SM
SR
90
0
1
2
3 miles
0
1
2
3
4
5 km

Rudbaxton
Scolton Manor
Lower Haythog Fm
Mountjoy Fm
Clarbeston Road
Clarbeston
Rhyd-y-Brown
New Mill
Bletherston
Brechfa
Llandissilio
Wauntfrwd
Cilhengroes
Hiraeth
Gwarmacwydd
Henllan Amgoed
Gellydogin
91
92
Lamborough
Clarbeston Grange
Gwernant Fm
Llandre Br
Crug-y-deri
Dyffryn-Conin
Castell-gwyn
Lan
Wernlygoes
Bowling Fm
Poyston
Poyston Cross
Earthworks
Gelli
Gellyolau
Clunderwen
Llanfallteg West
Llanfallteg
Rhydywrach
Parciau
Blaenwernddu
Cwmfelin Boeth
Haverfordwest
Pembrokeshire County Show Ground
Clover Hill
Lower Hill
Hooks Hill
Cotland Mill
Longlands Fm
Llwyndyrys
Pen-parc
Great Vaynor
Bryn Fm
Sarnlas
Cilpost Fm
Whitland Abbey
Trad Est
Crundale
Cartlett Brook
Tanyard Fm
Wiston
Conkland Hill
Manor Fm
Corner Fm
Cotland Fm
Plain Dealings
Trefwynt Fm
Bethesda
Trewern
Lanlliwe
Withybush
Fenton Brook
Holgan
Llawhaden
Llawhaden Castle
Penllwyn Ho
Pen-troydin
Caermaenau Fawr
Ffynnon
Gwyndy Fm
Whitland (Hendy-Gwyn)
Prendergast
Arnolds Down
Merryborough
Wood Barn
Wiston Wood
Hobbin's Hill
Park Ho
Colby Fm
Abystree
Middle Hook Fm
Redstone Cross
Blackmoor Hill
Redstone Bank
Henllan
Llanddewi Velfrey
Caerau Gaer
Lampeter Vale
High Street
Trevaughan
Llwyn-y-brain
Haverfordwest Hwlffordd
Cotts Park
Deep Lake
Arnolds Hill
Millin Brook
Slebech
West End
Colby Mill
Kenox
Canaston Bridge
Robeston Wathen
Rushacre Fm
Afon Marlais
Whitley Fm
Lan-mill
Hillblock
The Rhos
Slebech Park
Pickle Wood
Robeston Back
Narberth (Arberth)
Narberth Bridge
Narberth Mus
Crinow
Lampeter Velfrey
Lowmead Fm
Uzmaston
Church Hill
Millin Cross
Picton Home Fm
Blackpool
Canaston Wood
Dyffryn Fm
Gilfach Fm
Golden Grove
Rosen Green
Picton Park
Minwear Wood
Blue Lagoon Water Park
Camp Hill
Cloyne Fm
Fern Hill
Black Hill
Boulston
Picton Castle
Minwear
Nash Fm
Oakwood
Narberth Mountain
Cold Blow
Cilrhiw Ho
Lower Llantydwell
Tavernspite
Lower Freystop
Hook Reach
Western Cleddau
Eastern Cleddau
Cott Fm
The Grove
Princes Gate
South Treffgarne
Upper Llantydwell
West Rose
Red Roses
Little Milford
Underwood
Picton Pt
Folly Fm
Mounton Fm
Cross Hands
Martin Hill
Merry Vale
Chapel Hill
Templeton
Middleton Fm
New House
Three Wells
Hazel Grove
Hook
Maddox Moor
Trooper's Inn
Landshipping
Landshipping Quay
Whitlow
New Park
Martletwy
Dynaston
A4115
Rose Down
Ludchurch
Trenewydd
Llanteg
West Pool
Syke
Clareston
Deerland
North Wood
Woodhouse Grange
Weston
Cwm Deri Vineyard
Ramshorn Fm
Pengelli Forest
Blaencilgoed Fm
The Longstone
Amroth Road
Marros Mountain
East Moor
Tally-Ho
Llangwm
Guilford
Black Tar
Burnett's Hill
Baglan Fm
Yerbeston Mountain
Cloverhill Fm
Longstone
Black Moor
Garness Mill
Pendeilo
Hill Mountain
Blacktar Pt
Moithan Moor
Tedion Mountain
Campshill Fm
Yerbeston
Reynalton
Thomas Chapel
Kilgetty Fm
Marros
Rosemarket
Great Westfield
Coedcanlas Fm
Vallen
Loveston
Folly Farm
Pembrokeshire Coast National Park
Port Lion
Beggars Reach
Garron Pill
Mountain Park Fm
Moor Fm
Broom
Stepaside
Colby Woodland Garden
Summerhill
Marros Beacon
Houghton
Benton Wood
Oak Hill
Bishop's Br
Shipping
Kilgetty
Telpyn Fm
Newton Fm
Penceed
Lawrenny
Cresswell Castle
Langdon
Begelly
Amroth
Telpyn Pt
Marros Sands
Milton Fm
Pembrokeshire
Lawrenny Quay
Cresswell River
New Park
Cresswell Quay
Cresselly
Lanesend
Jeffreyston
Dawes Fm
Sardis
Churchton
Pleasant Valley
Mead Lodge
Ferry Hill
Williamston
West Williamston
Carew Mountain
Cresselly Big Wood
Wooden
Pentlepoir
Saundersfoot
Wiseman's Bridge
Coppet Hall Pt
Great Honeyborough
Glenowen
Burton Ferry
Burton Mountain
Daugleddau
Coast National Park
Freestone Hall
Broadmoor
Cold Inn
Ridgeway
The Valley
Saundersfoot (Llanussyllt)
Saundersfoot Bay
Bae Saundersfoot
Neyland
Burton
Mount Pleasant
Bateman's Hill
Upton Castle Gardens
Carew River
Carew Newton
New Shipping Pt
Whitehill
Norchard Fm
East Williamston
Hobbs Pt
Pembroke Ferry
Llanion
Waterloo
Cosheston Pt
Cosheston
Lane Head
Mayeston
Hakin Pt
Carew Castle & Cross
Crickchurch Fm
Redberth
Islands Fm
Broadfield
Monkstone Pt
Pembroke Dock
Ford Pt
Carew
Sageston
Pembroke Road
Bangeston Hall
Golden Hill
Brotherhill
Milton
Carew Cheriton
Upper Nash
New Inn Fm
Trevayne
Llanreath
Pennar
Pembroke Dock Doc Penfro
Windsor Hill Fm
Penny Bridge
North Down
Winter Hall
Furze Hill
Summerton
Manor Wildlife Park
Elm Grove
Tenby Dinosaur Park
Cornish Down
New Hedges
Waterwynch
Pembrokeshire Coast Path
Llwybr Arfordir Penfro
Wales Coast Path
Bentlass
Pembroke Castle
Pembroke (Penfro)
Monkton
Grove
Windsor Fm
South Hills
Lamphey Bishop's Palace
Hazel Hill
St Florence
Gumfreston
Tarr Fm
The Ritec
Tenby Roads
Tenby
Dinbych-y-Pysgod
St Catherine's Island
Tenby Museum
Tudor Merchant's House
Hundleton
Windmill Hill
Merlin's Cross
Rose Valley
Lamphey
Hodgeston Hill
Beaver's Hill
Manorbier Newton
Maiden Wells
Hill Fm
Lammaston Fm
Hodgeston
Manorbier
Norchard Fm
Penally (Penalun)
Freshwater East
Herbertsmoor
Jameston
Wales Coast Path
Danger area
Caldey Roads
(Summer Only)
Giltar Pt
Yerbeston
West Moor Cliff
Moor Fm
Park Fm
Lydstep
Lydstep Haven
Caldey Sound
St Petrox
Cheriton or Stackpole Elidor
The Downs
East Trewent
Trewent Pt
Swanlake Bay
East Moor Cliff
Manorbier Bay
Priest's Nose
King's Quoit
Wind Hill
Skrinkle Haven
Lydstep Pt
St Margaret's Island
Sandy Bay
Eel Pt
Priory Bay
Star Cliff
Den Pt
Caldey Pt
Caldey Island Ynys Bŷr
Sandtop Bay
Small Ord Pt
Drinkim
West Beacon Pt
Chapel Pt
Old Castle Head
Greenala Pt
Stackpole
Stackpole Quay
Lily Ponds
Fish Ponds
Barafundle Bay
Bosherston
Danger area
Saddle Pt
Stackpole Head
Star Rock
St Govans Chapel
Trevallen Downs
Long Matthew Pt
St Govan's Head
Pen St Gofan
A40
A477
A478
A4075
B4314
B4313
B4315
B4316
B4318
B4319
B4322
B4328
B4584
B4585
B4586
A4139
A4076
Carew Lane
Ford Lane
SN
SS
20
90
A
B
C
D
E
F
G
H
7
8
9
10
11
74

CARMARTHEN BAY
BAE CAERFYRDDIN
CARMARTHENSHIRE
SIR GAERFYRDDIN
Carmarthen
Caerfyrddin
Tanerdy
Abergwili
Pen-y-banc
Bryn Myrddin
Ffynnon ddrain
Trevaughan
Merthyr
Cwmduhen
Cefnmystrych
Nantybwla
ROMAN AMPHITHEATRE
CARMARTHEN COUNTY MUSEUM
Llangunnor
Tre-gynwr
Nant
Pensarn
Johnstown
Llanllwch
UNITED COUNTIES SHOWGROUND
CORS GOCH LLANLLWCH
P&R
Travellers Rest
Maes-y-Prior
Llethrach
Derllys Court
Trebersed
Cwmau Bach
Pentre'r-hydd
Sarnau
Pen-pontbren
Nantyrhebog
Cwmcoch
Penplas
Wernolau
Wern Ddu
Pibwrlwyd
Bolahaul Fm
A48
A40
Cwmffrwd
Bwlchymynydd
Oaklands
Croesyceiliog
Llwynfilltir
Pistyll
Idole
Lan Ho
Gelliddu
Rhydw
Bancycapel
Parry's Castle
Cloigyn
Pen-y-maes
Towy Castle Fm
Llwyngwcw
Llwyncelyn
Pencelli Fm
Pontan
Crugan-fawr
Ystradferthyr
Ystrad-fawr
Llandyfaelog
Cilgadan Hall
Iscoed Home Fm
Llancwm Fm
Pentre
Wer
Cilfeithy Fm
Wenallt
Allt-Cunedda
Mynydd y Garreg
Mynyddygarreg
Goitre
Glyn Abbey
Penlan Uchaf
Allt Fm
Rogerlay
Llangadog
Garreg Fm
Pont-newydd
KIDWELLY CASTLE
Kidwelly
(Cydweli)
B4308
Meat
Ty Cornel Fm
Waun y-clyn
Pinged
Bryndias Fm
Ty Mawr
FFWRD FARM MIRE
Penllwyn Uchaf
Penybedd
Penllwyn Isaf
Draenog
Cenrhos
Graig
Achddu
Pembrey
(Pembre)
Furnace
PEMBREY & BURRY PORT
Pembrey Forest
WALES COAST PATH
Danger area
Cefn Sidan Sands
Gwendraeth
Tywyn Pt
Salmon Point Scar
Penallt Fm
Llansaint
Tanylan Fm
St Ishmael
Broadway
Pengay Fm
Broadlay
Ferryside
(Glan-y-Fferi)
FERRYSIDE
River Towy Afon Tywi
Morfa Bach
Gilfach
Llwyn-du
Penhen
Llangain
Glogue
Dolaumeinion
Llaethdy
Ystradwalter
Cwrt Malle
LLANSTEFFAN ROAD
B4312
Llangynog
Ffynnon
Moelfre
Glasfryn
Waundas
Nantego
Coomb
(Cheshire Home)
Penycoed
Cwmllyfri
Tre-huddion
Lanmartin
Hendre
Llanybri
Lan Fm
Ferry Fm
Cwm-celyn
Down Fm
Llansteffan
The Green
LLANSTEFFAN CASTLE
Lord's Park
St Anthony's Well
Wharley Pt
Black Scar
Pentowyn
River Taf Afon Taf
Ginst Pt
Laugharne Sands
Laugharne Burrows
East Ho
Longridge
East Marsh
Hurst Ho
West Marsh
Pendine Sands
Dolwen Pt
Gilman Pt
Ragwen Pt
Marros Sands
Telpyn Pt
Telpyn Fm
Marros Beacon
Marros
Garness Fm
Pendine
(Pentywyn)
Llanmiloe
Tremoilet Fm
Castle Lloyd Fm
Westmead Fm
A4066
Plashett
Brook
Llansadurnen
Colston Fm
East Pool
West Pool
Syke
Marros Mountain
Garness Mill
Hazel Grove
Red Roses
West Rose
Windleway
Manor Court
B4314
Llandawke
Laugharne
(Talacharn)
LAUGHARNE CASTLE
DYLAN THOMAS BOATHOUSE
Broadway
Glan-y-môr
Milton Fm
Cross Inn
Whitehill Down
Hall Down
Halfpenny Furze
New Mill
Woodhouse Fm
Cildywyll
Vaynor Fm
Cnwce
Brunant
Brynamlwg
Brandy Hill
Lowmead Fm
B4328
Llanddowror
Moor Fm
Four Wheels
A477
Old Pale
Little Pale
River Taf Afon Taf
Great Pale
Dolenwydd
Clog-y-fran
Backe
Pwll-trap
Zabulon
Moor
Fforest Fm
Ind Est
Whitland
(Hendy-Gwyn)
WHITLAND
Trevaughan
Llwyn-y-brain
High Street
St Clears
Sanclêr
Ty'r Gate
THE GATE CRAFT CENTRE
Lower Court
Croes-y-ceiliog
Ardderfin
Gelli
Maenllwyd
Asgood Fm
Pwllygrafel
Cowin Grove
College Fm
Bancyfelin
Wern Fm
Derry Hall
Bron-y-gaer
Pentowin
Penlan
Penuwch
Blaenycoed
Pen-y-coed
Llwynbychan
The Grove
Llwyndewi
Pont-y-Fenni
Whitland Abbey
Cilpost Fm
Aber
Pengwern
Troedyrhiw
Llangynin
Berthlwyd
Plascerdin
Pantyrhas
Fynnonfoida
Llwyngwydd
Blaencediw
Baily Mawr
Bank y llain
Penback Fm
Nantyreglwys
Dyffryn Marlais
Pantygroes
Gellydogin
Caerlleon
Garllegan Fawr
Penlan
Llangarthginning
Meidrim
MEIDRIM ROAD
B4299
Esgair
Pantyderi
Drefach
Rhosyn-coch
Sarnau Fm
Bwlch Fm
Hafod Fm
B4298
Cwm
Pen-y-Isaf
Nant Cynnen
Afon Cynin
Wales Coast Path
Berges Island
Whiteford Sands
Hills Tor
Broughton Bay
Twlc Pt
Minor Pt
Burry Holms
Spaniard Rocks
Llanmadoc
Llanmadoc Hill
Tankeylake Moor
Llangennith Moors
Kennexstone
Diles Lake
Hillend
Coety Green
Llangennith
Hardings Down
Druids Lodge
White Moor
Rhossili Down
RHOSSILI
BAY
The Beacon
Kingshall
RHOSSILI VISITOR CENTRE
Rhossili
Talgarth's Well
Blow Hole
Devil's Bridge
SN
SS
0 1 2 3 miles
0 1 2 3 4 5 km

Gwynfe
Maesadda
Hirlwyn-isaf
Truman
Carreg Yr Ogof
585
Pen-Rhiw-goch
Cwm Sawdde Fechan
Twyn-Swnd
Waun Lefrith
Bannau Sir Gaer
Llyn y Fan Fach
Brest Twrch
Carnau Nant-Menyn
Llyn y Fan Fawr
Waun Leuci
Y Gelli
Fan Bwlch Chwyth
Craig Cwm-du
Garnwen
Tyleglas
Tyle-garw
Fan Hir
Ffforest Fawr
94
95
Gellybevan Fm
Pont Clydach
Cefn y Cylchau
Esgair Hir
Banwen Gwyn
Waun Haffes
Yr Allt
Bryn Melyn
Fan Dringarth
Rhiw-ddu
Clogau Mawr
Cefn y Truman
Y Mynydd Du
NATIONAL PARK
Fan Gihirych
725
Fan Llia
632
Fan Nedd
Ystradfellte Reservoir
Wernwgan
Carn Pen-y-clogau
Carn Cennen
Foel Fraith
602
Blaen y Cylchau
Foel Fawr
616
Garreg-lwyd
Garreg Fraith
Bylchau Rhos-fain
Fan Frith
BANNAU BRYCHEINIOG
471
Bwlch y Ddau-wynt
Cefn Carn-Fadog
512
Disgwlfa
Cwm Haffes
Tafarn-y-Garreg (PH)
Tair Carn Uchaf
CARMARTHENSHIRE
(SIR GAERFYRDDIN)
558
Carreg-Goch
Castell y Geifr
Glyntawe
Carn yr Onnen
Cwm Pedol
507
Pen yr Helyg
Tyle Garw
NATIONAL SHOWCAVES CENTRE FOR WALES
DAN-YR-OGOF
ALLT RHONGYR
Penwyllt
OGOF FFYNNON DDU
Carreg Cadno
POWYS
Drysgol
Foel Deg-arbedd
Craig Derlwyn
Cefn Mawr
Dorwen ar Giedd
Craig-y-nos
Carreg Lwyd
Sand Hill
Cynghordy
Dorwen
Nant Fydd
Llwyn-y-moch
Cribarth
423
Pant-y-wal
Rhongyr-isaf
Saith Maen
Pant Mawr
Heolyrhedyn Fm
Upper Brynamman
THE BLACK MOUNTAIN CENTRE
Brynamman
Rhosaman
Pen-y-wern
Bryn Bugeiliaid
382
Twyn Brynffaldau
BRECON BEACONS
Pen-y-cae
Ynyswen
Garw-leisiau
Ystradfellte
Gwaun Cefnygarreg
75
Lower Brynamman
Cefn-bryn-brain
Giedd Forest
Abercraf
Berthlwyd Fm
Plas-y-darren
MELLTE GORGE
Garnant
Ind Est
Cwmllynfell
Cae'r-Lan
Caehopkin
WALES APE & MONKEY SANCTUARY
HENRHYD FALLS
NATIONAL PARK
Gwaun-Leision
Tairgwaith
Ystradowen
Blaen nant
Tyhwnt
Cwmgiedd
Ynys-isaf
Cae'r-bont
Coelbren
Coed y Rhaiadr
Gwaun Bryn-bwch
Porth yr Ogof
Hepste fawr
Tir-dyweunydd
Cwmhelen
Bryncethin Fm
Gwaun-Cae-Gurwen
Penlle'rfedwen
Pen-Rhiw-fawr
Cwm-twrch Uchaf
Penrhos
Hendre-ladis
Mynydd Drum
Onllwyn
Tonyfildre
BANNAU BRYCHEINIOG
Pont Rhyd-y-cnau
Hendre-bolon
Gelli-fawr
Mynydd Uchaf
Rhiwfawr
Mynydd Bach
Cwm-twrch Isaf
YSTRADFAWR
Ystradgynlais
Gors Llwyn
Dysgwylfa
Bronwydd
Pont Melin-fach
Bryn-cûl
Cwmgors
Bryn-melyn
Sgwd-yr-Eira
Nantricket
Cwm-nant Hopkin
Gelliwarog
Tynewydd
Dyffryn Cellwen
INTER VALLEY ROAD
Fforch Egel Fm
Betting-uchaf
Gilfach-yr-haidd
Gurnos
Bus Pk
Glan-rhyd
Bryndulais
Seven Sisters (Blaendulais)
FALLS
Tresgyrch-Fawr
351
Ystalyfera
Foel Penderyn
371
Pen-common
Craig y Ddinas
Pontbren Llwyd
Mynydd Y Garth
321
Mynydd Allt-y-grug
339
Y Darren Widdon
352
Varteg
Nant Hir
Pwllwatkin Fm
Pendyrran Fm
Nant-y-cafn
Pontneddfechan
Mynydd Carn-y-Cnart
Garth
Gelliwlca Fawr
Godre'r-graig
Varteg Hill
Rhos Common
Cefn-Isaf Fm
Glyn-neath (Glynedd)
Penderyn Reservoir
Gelli-luog
Craig Clwyd Fechan
Craig Clwyd
Aber-pergwm Wood
Morfa Glas
Cefn Rhigos
Ind Est
Ty-melin Uchaf
Cilmaengwyn
Cwm Du
Tre-Forgan
Pont-Walby
NEATH PORT TALBOT
Ynysmeudwy
Bus Pk
Coed-du
Gelli-benuchel
Rhigos
Bryn
Cwm Gwrelych
Cwm-hwnt
Rhyd-y-fro
Craig Llangiwg
Gellygron
Mynydd Marchywel
Cwm Rhyd-y-gau
Blaengwrach
Llechart-fach Fm
Mynydd Gellionnen
Wigfa
Hendrecaradog
Crynant (Creunant)
Cwmgwrach
Cwm yr Argoed
Rheola Forest
Vale of Neath
GLANTAWE RIVERSIDE
Cilybebyll
Gellinudd
Crugau Wood
Allt Rheola
Craig y pant
Hirwaun Common
Pontardawe
Craig Trebanos
418
Craig Nedd
(CASTELL-NEDD PORT TALBOT)
Garn-Fach
600
Lyn Fawr
Rhos
Tyrau Wood
383
Mynydd Resolfen
Mynydd Pen-y-cae
Trebanos
Alltwen
Resolven (Resolfen)
Glyn Castle
Mynydd Beili-glas
Craig-y-Duke
Cilhendre
Tirlan
Abergarwed
Carn Brynllydan
485
Lluest-wen Res
Penydre
Pentrehaearn Fm
Bryn-caws Fm
Llwyngriffith Fm
Pont-dwfnant
Llwyn-coedwr
MELIN CWRT WATERFALLS
Melincourt
Nant y Felin
Garn Goch
Mynydd Ystradffernol
Twyn Rh
Faerdre
Fforest Gôch
Banwen Fm
Erwsaethau Fm
Tir-isaf Fm
Coetgae'r Derlwyn
Cefntyle-brych
Clydach
Ind Est
Mynydd Drumau
Mynydd Blaenrhondda
Y Garn Bica
516
Cefn-y-Garth
272
Mountain Wood
Cilfrew
Clyne
Carn Caca
Moel yr Hyrddod
Carn Caglau
493
Mynydd Corrwg Fechan
Glais
Bryn-coch
Aberdulais
ABERDULAIS FALLS
Banwen Torybetel
Blaenrhondda
Glanbran Ho
Stanley Wood
Cadoxton-Juxta-Neath
Wenallt Wood
Mynydd Blaen-Nant-du
Glyncorrwg
Cwm Lluest
Tynewydd
Heol-las
Darran Wood
Rhydding
Tonna (Tonnau)
Blaencwm
Birchgrove
Neath Abbey
Mynydd Ynyscorrwg
502
Treherbert
44
Tai'r-ysgol
Lon-las
SKEWEN
THE GNOLL
Mosshouse Wood
Mynydd Fforch-Dwm
Tyle'r waun
Mynydd Abergwynfi
TREHERBERT
Cwm Saerbren
Craig Selsig
Pen-yr-englyn
Llansamlet
Skewen
NEATH ABBEY
Neath
Castell-Nedd
Cefn Morfudd
307
Mynydd Blaenafon
Mynydd Nant-y-bar
Mynydd Rhiwgregen
Glyn Corrwg
Mynydd Blaengwynfi
Mynydd Tyle-coch
Trallwn
43
Melincryddan
Mount Pleasant
Cimla
Bus Pk
Tonmawr
AFAN ARGOED
Abercregan
Blaen-gwynfi
75
Bus Cen
Cefn-Saeson
Baradychwallt
Coetgae Isaf
Mynydd Blaenafan
Cwm-parc
Cefn-hengoed
Pentre-dwr
Coed Darcy
Llandarcy
Cwm Afan
Cymer
Foel Fawr
347
Croeserw
Aber-gwynfi
Efail-fach
Duffryn
Brynheulog
Blaencaerau
Mynydd Caerau
555
Craig Ogwr
BWLCH
Craig y Geifr
Werfa
568
CRYMLYN BOG & PANT-Y-SAIS
Briton Ferry (Llansawel)
Pant-Howel-Ddu
Jersey Marine
Ind Est
Cerrig Llwydion
280
Mynydd Pen-Rhys
SOUTH WALES MINERS MUSEUM
AFAN ARGOED
Foely Dyffryn
366
Cwm yr Argoed
Caerau
Craig Walter
Ty-draw
42
Gelli-gaer
Pontrhydyfen
Mynydd-y-Gaer
314
370
Foel Fynyddau
Cwm
Mynydd Penhydd
Pen Disgwylfa
Dyffryn
Cwm Nant-y-moel
Swansea Works
Crymlyn Burrows
Baglan
Bwlch
Pwll-y-glaw
Rock
Moel y Fen
FOREST PARK
Rhiw Tor Cymry
Spelter
Mynydd Bach
433
Blaen Cwmdû
Blaengarw
Nant-y-moel
Baglan Bay
Bae Baglan
Brynbryddan
Nantyffyllon
Price Town
Witford Pt
Mynydd Dinas
258
Pantdu
Cwmafan
Mynydd Bychan
Coll-y-Gelli
Bryn
Ynysygwas
Caerhendy
Cwm Farteg
Moel Gallt-y-cwm
272
319
Mynydd Bach
Maesteg
Bryn-Rhug Fm
Cwm Garw Fechan
Cwm Gelli-wern
Wyndham
Mynydd y Aber
Sandfields
Aberavon
Aberavon Sands
Corlannau
Cwm Wernderi
Cwm Sychbant
Llwydarth
Garth Hill
257
Garth
Moel Cynhordy
Pontycymer
Pant Blaenhirwr
Ogmore Vale
Cwm Ogwr Fa
Cwm y Fuwch
Port Talbot
57
40
41
Pen-y-cae
Cwm Dyffryn
Cwm Nant-y-glo
Cwmfelin
58
Mynydd Moelgeila
Pen y Foel
356
Ogmore Forest
Mynydd y Gwair
Goytre
Cwm y Garn
Margam Forest
Mynydd Margam
344
Moel Troed-y-rhiw
Pont Rhyd-y-cyff
Cynhordy Fm
Pont-y-rhyl
Tylagwyn
Cwm Cerdin
Llangynwyd
Craig-yr-Hudol
Lewistown
Taibach
Ergyd Isaf
Waun y Gilfach
BRIDGEND
Gadlys
0 1 2 3 miles
0 1 2 3 4 5 km

Brecon Beacons
95
96
Aber-Village
Danywenallt
Llangynidr
Coed-yr-ynys
Cwmcrawnon
Tretower Castle & Court
Ffawyddog
Llangattock
Abercynafon
Torpantau
Pontsticill Reservoir
Brecon Mountain Railway
Pontsticill
Vaynor
Nant-ddu
Garwnant Visitor Centre
Llwyn-on Village
Llwyn-on Reservoir
Penderyn
Hirwaun
Penywaun
Trefil
Rassau
Garnlydan
Brynmawr
Beaufort
Nantyglo
Blaina
Dukestown
Tafarnau-bach
Princetown
Tredegar
Ebbw Vale
(Glyn Ebwy)
Rhymney
(Rhymni)
Georgetown
Pontlottyn
Abertysswg
Fochriw
Cefn-coed-y-cymmer
Gurnos
Dowlais
Pen-y-Darren
Cyfarthfa Castle & Museum
Heads of the Valleys Road
Merthyr Tydfil
Merthyr Tudful
MERTHYR TYDFIL
(MERTHYR TUDFUL)
Gellideg
Pen-yr-Heolgerrig
Twynyrodyn
Pentrebach
Abercanaid
Troedyrhiw
Aberdare
(Aberdâr)
Aber-nant
Robertstown
Llwydcoed
Trecynon
Cwmdare
Gadlys
RHONDDA CYNON TAFF
Cwmbach
Aberaman
Cwmaman
Mountain Ash
(Aberpennar)
Penrhiwceiber
Aberfan
Merthyr Vale
Treharris
Bedlinog
Cwmfelin
Deri
New Tredegar
(Tredegar Newydd)
Tirphil
Bargoed
(Bargod)
Aberbargoed
Gilfach
Pengam
Blackwood
(Coed Duon)
Oakdale
Markham
Argoed
Hollybush
BLAENAU GWENT
Gelligaer
Hengoed
Nelson
Llancaiach
Ystrad Mynach
Maesycwmmer
Abercynon
Ynysybwl
Ynyshir
Porth
Trehafod
Pontypridd
Treforest
Cilfynydd
Glyncoch
Maerdy
Ferndale
Treorchy
(Treorci)
Pentre
Rhondda
Ystrad
Ton-Pentre
Gelli
Tylorstown
Llwynypia
Clydach Vale
Tonypandy
Trealaw
Penygraig
Williamstown
Trebanog
Tonyrefail
Cymmer
Llanbradach
Senghenydd
Abertridwr
Penyrheol
Bedwas
Caerphilly
CAERPHILLY
(CAERFFILI)
Abercarn
Crosskeys
Wattsville
Ynysddu
Cwm
Trinant
Pontllanfraith
Newbridge
Rhondda Heritage Park
A470
A465
A4059
A4233
A469
A472
A4048
A4046

BRECON BEACONS NATIONAL PARK
BANNAU BRYCHEINIOG
MONMOUTHSHIRE (SIR FYNWY)
BLAENAU GWENT
TORFAEN (TOR-FAEN)
NEWPORT CASNEWYDD
Abergavenny Y Fenni
Pontypool (Pont-y-pŵl)
Cwmbran
Usk (Brynbuga)
Caerleon
Crickhowell
Blaenavon
Abertillery
Raglan
Risca
Crosskeys
Abersychan
Griffithstown
Pontnewydd
Llanfoist
Gilwern
Govilon
Blaina
Nantyglo
Abercarn
Crumlin
Newbridge
Llanhilleth
Trinant
Oakdale
Croesyceiliog
Llantarnam
Malpas
Bettws
Rogerstone
Christchurch
Penhow
Llanvaches
Parc-Seymour
Newbridge-on-Usk
Llantrisant
Llangybi
Little Mill
Monkswood
Goetre
Penperlleni
Llanover
Llanellen
Llanvetherine
Llantilio Crossenny
Llanvihangel Crucorney
Llantilio Pertholey
Mardy
Llangattock
Llanelly
Clydach
Blackrock
Cwmbran
Caerleon
0 1 2 3 miles
0 1 2 3 4 5 km

Broad Oak
Llangarron
Llancloudy
Pencraig
Coughton
Pontshill
Lea
Walford
Goodrich
Marstow
Kerne Bridge
Hope Mansell
Mitcheldean
Longhope
Llanrothal
Llangrove
Welsh Newton
Whitchurch
Welsh Bicknor
Ruardean
Drybrook
St Maughans
Maypole
Buckholt
Ganarew
Symonds Yat
English Bicknor
Lower Lydbrook
Upper Lydbrook
Brierley
Ruardean Woodside
Nailbridge
Blaisdon
Flaxley
Rockfield
Dixton
Christchurch
Staunton
Berry Hill
Five Acres
Edge End
Cinderford
Littledean
Elton
Monmouth
Trefynwy
Over Monnow
Wyesham
Coleford
Broadwell
Coalway
FOREST OF DEAN
FOREST PARK
GLOUCESTERSHIRE
Ruspidge
Newnham
Ruddle
Arlingham
Upper Soudley
Wonastow
Penallt
Redbrook
Newland
Milkwall
Ellwood
Parkend
Yorkley
Blakeney
Awre
Mitchel Troy
Pen-twyn
Clearwell
Hoop
Whitebrook
Stowe Green
Trow Green
Whitecroft
Pillowell
Viney Hill
Bream
Llangovan
Trellech
Llandogo
St Briavels
Coldharbour
New Mills
Lydney
Newerne
Purton
Parkhouse
Llanishen
Catbrook
Trelleck Grange
Tintern Parva
Brockweir
Hewelsfield
Aylburton
Sharpness
Halmore
Newtown
Wanswell
Chapel Hill
Devauden
Netherend
Brookend
Woolaston
Alvington
Berkeley
River Severn
Sheperdine Sands
Wibdon
Stroat
Tidenham
Woodcroft
Bevington
St Arvans
Itton Common
Shepperdine
Woodford
Stone
Tutshill
Sedbury
Chepstow
Cas-gwent
Shirenewton
Mynydd-bach
SOUTH GLOUCESTERSHIRE
Rockhampton
Oldbury-on-Severn
Thornbury
Morton
Mathern
Beachley
Crick
Caerwent
Littleton-on-Severn
Aust
Elberton
Alveston
Tytherington
Caldicot
Portskewett

Cheltenham
Charlton Kings
Whittington
Syreford
Salperton
Notgrove
Cold Aston
Bourton-on-the-Water
Wyck Rissington
Upper Rissington
Little Rissington
Andoversford
Dowdeswell
Shipton Solers
Shipton
Shipton Oliffe
Hazleton
Turkdean
Clapton-on-the-Hill
Seven Springs
Coberley
Kilkenny
Foxcote
Compton Abdale
Withington
Hampnett
Farmington
Great Rissington
Cowley
Cassey Compton
Northleach
Sherborne
Great Barrington
Cockleford
Colesbourne
Yanworth
Stowell
Eastington
Windrush
Elkstone
Chedworth
Fossebridge
Little Barrington
C O T S W O L D S
Coln St Dennis
Aldsworth
Syde
Winstone
Rendcomb
Foss Cross
Coln Rogers
G L O U C E S T E R S H I R E
Woodmancote
Calmsden
Winson
Duntisbourne Abbots
Duntisbourne Leer
North Cerney
Ablington
Upper End
Bagendon
Arlington
Bibury
Duntisbourne Rouse
Middle Duntisbourne
Daglingworth
Barnsley
Eastleach Turville
Hatherop
Coln St Aldwyns
Eastleach Martin
Ready Token
Baunton
Quenington
Netherton
Fyfield
Stratton
Southrop
Cirencester
Ampney Crucis
Sunhill
Ampney St Mary
Coates
Preston
Ampney St Peter
Fairford
Milton End
Chesterton
Poulton
Horcott
Siddington
Harnhill
Meysey Hampton
Tarlton
Driffield
Whelford
Lechlade-on-Thames
Inglesham
Ewen
Dunfield
Marston Meysey
Kempsford
Kemble
Shorncote
South Cerney
Down Ampney
Poole Keynes
Somerford Keynes
Cerney Wick
Latton
Castle Eaton
Hannington Wick
Upper Inglesham
Chelworth
Ashton Keynes
Oaksey
Cricklade
Chelworth Upper Green
Hannington
Highworth
Crudwell
Eastcourt
Leigh
Murcott
Upper Minety
Hankerton
Cloatley
Minety
Purton Stoke
Broad Blunsdon
Stanton Fitzwarren
Sevenhampton
Perry Green
Charlton
Garsdon
W I L T S H I R E
S W I N D O N
Haydon Wick
Upper Stratton
Penhill
Purton Common
Widham
South Marston
82
62
63
99
100
7
8
9
10
11

Westcote
Church Westcote
Foscot
Bould
Idbury
Nether Westcote
Upper Rissington
Little Rissington
Great Rissington
Fifield
Lyneham
Chadlington
Spelsbury
Taston
Charlbury
Glympton
Kiddington
Wootton
Woodleys
Chilson
Shorthampton
Walcot
Ascott-under-Wychwood
Ascott d'Oyley
Milton under Wychwood
Shipton-under-Wychwood
Upper Milton
Fawler
Finstock
Stonesfield
Combe
Blenheim Palace
Long Hanborough
Church Hanborough
Freeland
East End
North Leigh
New Yatt
Hailey
Ramsden
Leafield
Whiteoak Green
Langley
Fordwells
Asthall Leigh
Field Assarts
COTSWOLDS
Great Barrington
Little Barrington
Taynton
Windrush
Westhall Hill
Fulbrook
Burford
Upton
Swinbrook
Asthall
Little Minster
Minster Lovell
Crawley
Witney
Cogges
Newland
Woodgreen
Shores Green
High Cogges
Eynsham
Barnard Gate
South Leigh
Church End
Westwell
Signet
Holwell
Bradwell Grove
Shilton
Carterton
Brize Norton
Curbridge
Ducklington
Lew
Hardwick
Sutton
Stanton Harcourt
Eastleach Turville
Eastleach Martin
Filkins
Broughton Poggs
Kencot
Alvescot
Black Bourton
Bampton
Aston
Yelford
Brighthampton
Standlake
West End
OXFORDSHIRE
Fyfield
Southrop
Broadwell
Langford
Cote
Cowleaze Corner
Weald
Clanfield
Little Clanfield
Little Faringdon
Grafton
Shifford
Chimney
Newbridge
Northmoor
Moreton
Appleton
Radcot
Duxford
Kelmscott
Lechlade-on-Thames
Buckland Marsh
Carswell Marsh
Longworth
Hinton Waldrist
Kingston Bagpuize
Fyfield
Netherton
Tubney
Frilford Heath
Inglesham
Eaton Hastings
Thrupp
Buckland
Southmoor
Frilford
Buscot
Littleworth
Pusey
Garford
Upper Inglesham
Faringdon
Gainfield
Charney Bassett
Highworth
Coleshill
Great Coxwell
Shellingford
Hatford
Bow
Lyford
Little Coxwell
Stanford in the Vale
West Hanney
East Hanney
Goosey
Fernham
Baulking
Denchworth
Watchfield
Longcot
Severnhampton
Grove
Uffington
West Challow
Wantage
Charlton
Ardington Wick
West Hendred
Woolstone
Kingston
Childrey
Compton
South Marston
Belmont
Challow
3 miles
5 km

Bicester Village
Kingsmere
Chesterton
Little Chesterton
Wendlebury
Ambrosden
Blackthorn
Grendon Underwood
Tackley
Nethercott
Kirtlington
Weston-on-the-Green
Bletchingdon
Merton
Lower Arncott
Upper Arncott
Piddington
Ludgershall
Kingswood
Woodham
Wotton Underwood
Bunkers Hill
Shipton on Cherwell
Hampton Poyle
Fencott
Murcott
Charlton on Otmoor
Kidlington
Oddington
Islip
Boarstall
Brill
Ashendon
Dorton
Upper Pollicott
Begbroke
Gosford
Noke
Horton-cum-Studley
Oakley
Little London
Chilton
Yarnton
Water Eaton
Woodeaton
Beckley
BUCKINGHAMSHIRE
Easington
Cutteslowe
Elsfield
Stanton St John
Wolvercote
Upper Wolvercote
Wytham
Summertown
Marston
Worminghall
Long Crendon
Lower End
Forest Hill
Headington
Barton
Ickford
Shabbington
Binsey
Oxford
Holton
Waterperry
Waterstock
Wheatley
Botley
Osney
North Hinksey
New Hinksey
Temple Cowley
Horspath
Tiddington
Thame
Moreton
North Weston
Cumnor
Chawley
South Hinksey
Cowley
Iffley
Rose Hill
Littlemore
Kennington
Cuddesdon
Great Milton
Denton
Garsington
Little Milton
Great Haseley
Little Haseley
Tetsworth
Sandford on Thames
Toot Baldon
Marsh Baldon
OXFORDSHIRE
Chislehampton
Stadhampton
Abingdon-on-Thames
Radley
Nuneham Courtenay
Drayton St Leonard
Berinsfield
Newington
Chalgrove
Easington
Pyrton
Shirburn
Culham
Clifton Hampden
Dorchester
Warborough
Cuxham
Watlington
Long Wittenham
Little Wittenham
Berrick Salome
Britwell Salome
Drayton
Sutton Courtenay
Appleford
Shillingford
Benson
Ewelme
Milton
Steventon
Didcot
Wallingford
Harwell
East Hendred
East Hagbourne
Crowmarsh Gifford
Oxford Services
M40
A40
A34
A418
A329
A4074
A415
A420
A41
101
102
84
64
65

Creslow
Oving
Whitchurch
Ledburn
Slapton
Quainton
Pitchcott
Aston Abbotts
Mentmore
Horton
Kingswood
Hardwick
Wingrave
Crafton
Cheddington
Westcott
Waddesdon
Weedon
Rowsham
Hulcott
Pitstone
Wotton Underwood
Bierton
Long Marston
Marsworth
Ashendon
Upper Winchendon
Puttenham
Wilstone
Aylesbury
Upper Pollicott
Lower Hartwell
Southcourt
Buckland
Aston Clinton
Tring
Stone
Dinton
Chilton
Cuddington
Westlington
Weston Turville
Halton
Easington
Chearsley
Stoke Mandeville
Bishopstone
Ford
Wendover
Long Crendon
Haddenham
Terrick
Aston Sandford
Kimble Wick
Ellesborough
Little Kimble
Great Kimble
Kingsey
Owlswick
Meadle
Thame
Towersey
Ilmer
Longwick
Askett
Dunsmore
Moreton
Monks Risborough
Little Hampden
The Lee
Princes Risborough
Emmington
Henton
Saunderton
Tetsworth
Sydenham
Chinnor
Oakley
Prestwood
Great Missenden
Adwell
Postcombe
Kingston Blount
Crowell
Aston Rowant
Bledlow Ridge
Lewknor
Radnage
Stokenchurch
Naphill
Hughenden Valley
Pyrton
Shirburn
West Wycombe
Downley
Hazlemere
Ibstone
Northend
High Wycombe
Penn
Christmas Common
Turville
Fingest
Lane End
Booker
Wycombe Marsh
Loudwater
Beaconsfield
Frieth
Skirmett
Flackwell Heath
OXON
BUCKINGHAMSHIRE
CHILTERNS
M40
A41
A413
A418
A4010
A4129
A40
Aylesbury Vale Parkway
Haddenham & Thame Parkway
Princes Risborough
Grand Union Canal
Waddesdon Manor
Wycombe Museum
Hughenden Manor
West Wycombe Park
Wycombe Air Park (Booker)
Beaconsfield Services
0 1 2 3 miles
0 1 2 3 4 5 km

Dunstable
Luton
London Luton
Harpenden
Wheathampstead
Kimpton
Redbourn
St Albans
Hemel Hempstead
Berkhamsted
Tring
Aldbury
Ivinghoe Aston
Edlesborough
Eaton Bray
Totternhoe
Whipsnade
Kensworth
Caddington
Markyate
Flamstead
Studham
Dagnall
Ringshall
Little Gaddesden
Great Gaddesden
Nettleden
Potten End
Northchurch
Dudswell
Bourne End
Boxmoor
Apsley
Felden
Bovingdon
Chesham
Chipperfield
Kings Langley
Abbots Langley
Leavesden Green
Garston
Watford
North Watford
Bushey
Oxhey
South Oxhey
Radlett
Shenley
London Colney
Bricket Wood
Colney Street
Aldenham
Borehamwood
Elstree
Edgware
Stanmore
Harrow Weald
Wealdstone
Harrow
Pinner
Northwood
Rickmansworth
Chorleywood
Croxley Green
Sarratt
Chenies
Latimer
Little Chalfont
Amersham
Chalfont St Giles
Chalfont St Peter
Chalfont Common
Jordans
Seer Green
Gerrards Cross
Denham
Harefield
Ruislip Common
Eastcote
Maple Cross
Mill End
Batchworth Heath
Moor Park
Sandridge
Jersey Farm
Marshalswick
Fleetville
Colney Heath
Tyttenhanger
Hatching Green
Batford
Kinsbourne Green
Blackmore End
Ayot St Lawrence
Ayot St Peter
Whitwell
Breachwood Green
Peter's Green
East Hyde
Slip End
Pepperstock
Markyate
Piccotts End
Gadebridge
Leverstock Green
Bedmond
Primrosehill
Chiswell Green
Park Street
Potters Crouch
Childwick Green
Flowers
C H I L T E R N S
H E R T F O R D S H I R E
M1
M25
A41
A405
A414
A5183
TL
TQ
Shenleybury
Letchmore Heath
Ridge
Green Street
London Gateway Services

H E R T F O R D S H I R E
L O N D O N
ESS
Knebworth
Bragbury End
Watton at Stone
Whempstead
Dane End
Hook's Cross
Codicote
Datchworth
Woolmer Green
Sacombe
High Cross
Much Hadham
Hadham Cross
Welwyn
Oaklands
Digswell
Tewin
Stapleford
Chapmore End
Tonwell
Wadesmill
Thundridge
Ware
Wareside
Widford
Hunsdon
Welwyn Garden City
Panshanger
Hertingfordbury
Hertford
Hertford Heath
Bengeo
Hatfield
Hatfield Garden Village
Hatfield Hyde
Cole Green
Letty Green
Essendon
Bayford
Brickendon
Hoddesdon
Broxbourne
Great Amwell
Stanstead Abbotts
St Margarets
Rye Park
Roydon
Eastwick
Lee Valley Regional Park
Welham Green
Brookmans Park
Cuffley
Northaw
Wormley
Turnford
Cheshunt
Waltham Cross
Waltham Abbey
Nazeing
Potters Bar
South Mimms
South Mimms Services
Shenley
Borehamwood
Barnet
East Barnet
Enfield
Southgate
Edmonton
Chingford
Loughton
Buckhurst Hill
Woodford
Finchley
Friern Barnet
Tottenham
Wood Green
Walthamstow
Hornsey
Mill Hill
Edgware
Kingsbury
London Gateway Services
Enfield Chase
Epping Forest
104
105
85
67
68
0 1 2 3 miles
0 1 2 3 4 5 km

Great Notley
Tye Green
Cressing
Coggeshall Hamlet
Feering
Kelvedon
Messing
Tiptree
Layer Marney
Silver End
White Notley
Faulkbourne
Rivenhall
Rivenhall End
Great Leighs
Little Leighs
Fairstead
Terling
Witham
Chipping Hill
Great Braxted
Little Braxted
Tolleshunt Knights
Tolleshunt Major
Tolleshunt D'Arcy
Goldhanger
Great Totham
Little Totham
Wickham Bishops
Hatfield Peverel
Nounsley
Boreham
Broomfield
Springfield
Chelmsford
Great Baddow
Danbury
Little Baddow
Woodham Walter
Langford
Heybridge
Heybridge Basin
Maldon
Osea Island
Northey Island
ESSEX
Woodham Mortimer
Purleigh
Cock Clarks
Mundon
Maylandsea
Mayland
Steeple
Latchingdon
Cold Norton
Stow Maries
Woodham Ferrers
Bicknacre
East Hanningfield
West Hanningfield
South Hanningfield
Hanningfield Reservoir
Galleywood
Stock
Ramsden Heath
Runwell
Wickford
Battlesbridge
Hullbridge
South Woodham Ferrers
North Fambridge
South Fambridge
Althorne
Creeksea
Canewdon
Ashingdon
Hockley
Hawkwell
Rochford
Rayleigh
Thundersley
North Benfleet
Pitsea
Eastwood
Paglesham Churchend
Paglesham Eastend
Great Stambridge
Barling
Little Wakering
0 1 2 3 miles
0 1 2 3 4 5 km

Rowhedge
Alresford
Great Bentley
Weeley
Weeley Heath
Thorpe-le-Soken
Thorpe Park
Kirby Cross
Layer de la Haye
Malting Green
Abberton
Abberton Reservoir
Fingringhoe
Fingringhoe Wick Nature Reserve
South Green
Langenhoe
Thorrington
Aingers Green
South Heath
Hollybush Hill
St Osyth Heath
Row Heath
Little Clacton
Great Holland
Cook's Green
Burrsville Park
Brightlingsea
Hurst Green
Peldon
Great Wigborough
Little Wigborough
Copt Hall Marshes Nature Reserve
Mersea Island
East Mersea
West Mersea
Mersea Island Mus
Cudmore Grove
Colne Estuary
Blue Row
Point Clear
St Osyth
St Osyth Priory
Great Clacton
Clacton-on-Sea
Holland-on-Sea
Jaywick
Seawick
Lee-over-Sands
Colne Bar
Colne Pt
St Osyth Beach
Blackwater Estuary
Tollesbury
Tollesbury Wick Marshes
The Nass
River Blackwater
Bradwell Waterside
St Peter's on the Wall
East End
Bradwell on Sea
Ramsey Island
St Lawrence
Tillingham
Dengie
Asheldham
Southminster
Montsale
Deal Hall
Burnham-on-Crouch
River Crouch
Foulness Sands
Foulness Pt
Wallasea Wetlands
Wallasea Island
Churchend
Courtsend
Foulness Island
River Roach
Potton Island
New England Island
Rushley Island
Havengore Island
Maplin Sands
TM
TR
A
B
C
D
E
F
G
H
7
8
9
10
11
107
108
70
71

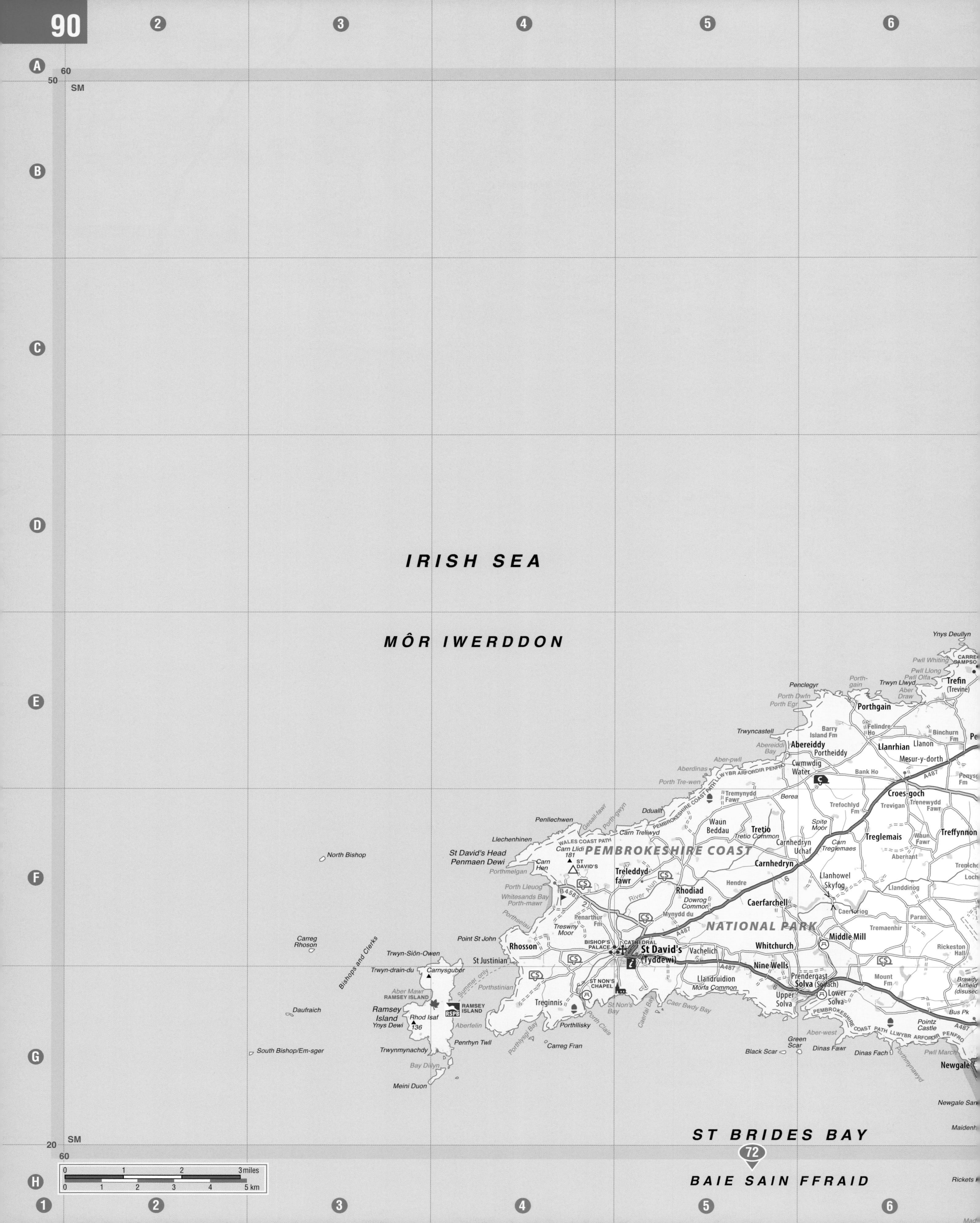
IRISH SEA
MÔR IWERDDON
ST BRIDES BAY
BAIE SAIN FFRAID
PEMBROKESHIRE COAST
NATIONAL PARK
St David's
(Tyddewi)
Ramsey Island
Ynys Dewi
North Bishop
South Bishop/Em-sger
Bishops and Clerks
Carreg Rhoson
Daufraich
Meini Duon
St David's Head
Penmaen Dewi
Porthgain
Abereiddy
Trefin
(Trevine)
Llanrhian
Croes-goch
Treglemais
Treffynnon
Carnhedryn
Caerfarchell
Middle Mill
Whitchurch
Solva
Newgale
Rhodiad
Treleddyd-fawr
Rhosson
Treginnis
Porthllisky
St Justinian
Point St John
Penllechwen
Llechenhinen
Dinas Fawr
Dinas Fach
Black Scar
Green Scar
Nine Wells
Prendergast
Lower Solva
Upper Solva
Llanhowel
Skyfog
Trevigan
Ynys Deullyn
Penclegyr
Trwyncastell
A487
B4583
72

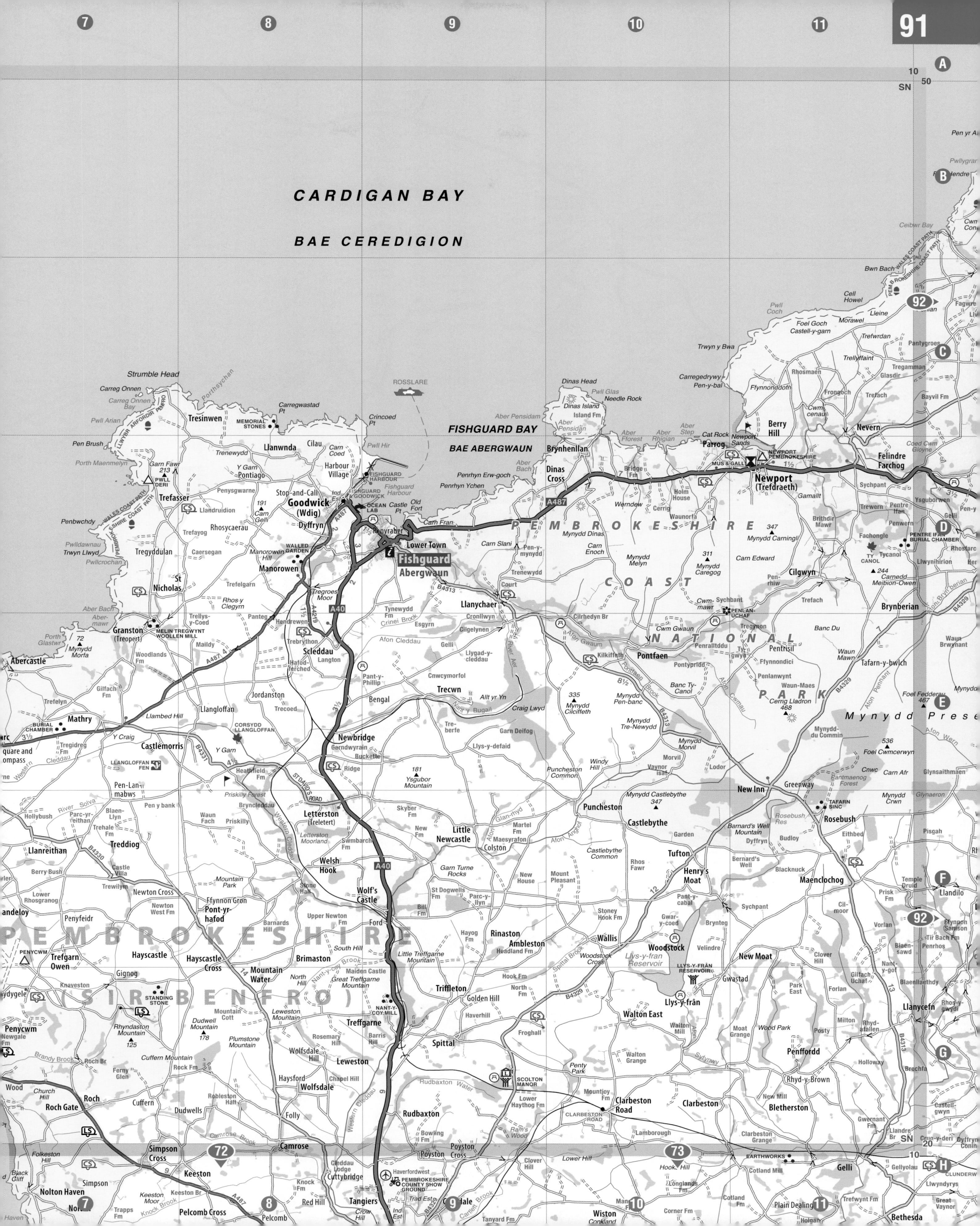
7
8
9
10
11
CARDIGAN BAY
BAE CEREDIGION
FISHGUARD BAY
BAE ABERGWAUN
ROSSLARE
Strumble Head
Carreg Onnen
Carreg Onnen Bay
Porthsychan
Pwll Arian
Pen Brush
Porth Maenmelyn
Garn Fawr 213
PWLL DERI
Tresinwen
MEMORIAL STONES
Carregwastad Pt
Crincoed Pt
Llanwnda
Cilau
Carn Coed
Harbour Village
Pwll Hir
FISHGUARD HARBOUR
Trenewydd
Y Garn Pontiago
Penysgwarne
Trefasser
Llanduridion
Stop-and-Call
Goodwick (Wdig)
Dyffryn
OCEAN LAB
Castle Pt
Old Fort
Fishguard Harbour
Penbwchdy
Pwlldawnau
Trwyn Llwyd
Pwllcrochan
Trefayog
Rhosycaerau
Carn Gelli
Tregyddulan
Caersegan
Manorowen Hill
WALLED GARDEN
Manorowen
Renyraber
Lower Town
Fishguard
Abergwaun
Carn Fran
St Nicholas
Trefelgarn
Rhos-y Clegyrn
Tregroes Moor
Aber Bach
Aber-mawr
Granston (Treopert)
MELIN TREGWYNT WOOLLEN MILL
Trellys-y-Coed
Panteg
Hendrewen
Porth Glastwr
Mynydd Morfa 72
Maildy
Trebrython
Scleddau
Langton
Abercastle
Woodlands Fm
Hafod-Iferched
Pant-y-Phillip
Bengal
Jordanston
Trecoed
Trefelyn
Gilfach Fm
Mathry
BURIAL CHAMBER
Llambed Hill
Llangloffan
CORSYDD LLANGLOFFAN
Y Craig
Castlemorris
Tregidreg Fm
Y Garn
LLANGLOFFAN FEN
Heathfield Fm
Pen-Lan-mabws
Pen y bank
Priskilly Forest
Bryncleddau
River Solva
Blaen-Llyn
Parc-yr-eithan
Hollybush
Waun Fach
Priskilly
Trehale Fm
Treddiog
Llanreithan
Berry Bush
Castle Villa
Trewilym
Newton Cross
Lower Rhosgranog
Mountain Park
Newton West Fm
Ffynnon Grøn
Pont-yr-hafod
Penyfeidr
PEMBROKESHIRE
(SIR BENFRO)
PENYCWM
Trefgarn Owen
Hayscastle
Hayscastle Cross
Gignog
Knaveston
STANDING STONE
Rhyndaston Mountain 125
Penycwm
Newgale Fm
Brandy Brook
Roch Br
Ferny Glen
Cuffern Mountain
Rock Fm
Dudwell Mountain 178
Plumstone Mountain
Mountain Water
Mountain Cott
Wood
Church Hill
Roch
Roch Gate
Cuffern
Robleston Hall
Dudwells
Simpson Cross
Camrose Brook
Camrose
Folkeston Hill
Black Cliff
Simpson
Keeston
Keeston Moor
Keeston Br
Nolton Haven
Trapps Fm
Knock Brook
Pelcomb Cross
Pelcomb
Newbridge
Garndwyrain
Buckette
Ridge
Letterston (Treletert)
Letterston Moorland
Swmbarch Fm
Welsh Hook
Wolf's Castle
Stone Hall
Upper Newton Fm
Ford
Barnards Hill
Brimaston
South Hill
North Hill
Maiden Castle
Great Treffgarne Mountain
NANT-Y-COY MILL
Leweston Mountain
Treffgarne
Rosemary Hill
Barris Hill
Wolfsdale Hill
Leweston
Haysford
Wolfsdale
Chapel Hill
Folly
Western Cleddau
Rudbaxton
Bowling Fm
Poyston
Poyston Cross
Cleddau Lodge
Cuttybridge
Haverfordwest
PEMBROKESHIRE COUNTY SHOW GROUND
Knock Fm
Red Hill
Tangiers
Crow Hill
Trad Est
Ind Est
Clover Hill
Tanyard Fm
ST DAVID'S ROAD
Tynewydd Fm
Crinei Brook
Esgyrn
Afon Cleddau
Gelli
Cnwcymorfol
Trecwn
Allt yr Yn
Nant y Bugail
Craig Lwyd
Tre-berfe
Garn Deifog
Llys-y-defaid
Ysgubor Mountain 181
Skyber Fm
New Fm
Little Newcastle
Glan-rhyd
Martel Fm
Maesyrafon
Colston
Garn Turne Rocks
St Dogwells Fm
Parc-y-llyn
Bill Fm
Hayog Fm
Rinaston
Ambleston
Headland Fm
Little Treffgarne Mountain
Triffleton
Golden Hill
Haverhill
Hook Fm
North Fm
Spittal
Spittal Brook
SCOLTON MANOR
Rudbaxton Water
Lower Haythog Fm
Ram's Wood
CLARBESTON ROAD
Lower Hill
Dinas Head
Pwll Glas
Needle Rock
Dinas Island
Island Fm
Aber Pensidan
Aber Ffwrd
Aber Rhigian
Aber Step
Brynhenllan
Dinas Cross
Penrhyn Erw-goch
Penrhyn Ychen
Bridge Fm
Werndew
Gerrig
Holm House
Waunorfa
PEMBROKESHIRE COAST NATIONAL PARK
Mynydd Dinas
Carn Slani
Pen-y-mynydd
Carn Enoch
Trenewydd
Court
Llanychaer
Cronllwyn
Cilgelynen
Llygad-y-cleddau
River Ael
Cilrhedyn Br
Afon Gwaun
Kilkiffeth
Pontfaen
Pontyprìdd
Banc Ty-Canol
Mynydd Melyn
Mynydd Carningli 347
Mynydd Caregog 311
Carn Edward
Cwm-mawr
Sychbant
PENLAN-UCHAF
Cwm Gwaun
Penrallt-ddu
Ty-gwyn
Mynydd Cilciffeth 335
Mynydd Pen-banc
Mynydd Tre-Newydd
Pontfaen Brook
Windy Hill
Puncheston Common
Mynydd Morvil
Morvil
Vaynor isaf
Lodor
Puncheston
Mynydd Castlebythe 347
Castlebythe
Afon Angof
Castlebythe Common
Rhos Fawr
Mount Pleasant
New House
Stoney Hook Fm
Wallis
Woodstock Cross
Llys-y-fran Reservoir
Woodstock
LLYS-Y-FRAN RESERVOIR
Llys-y-frân
Walton East
Walton Mill
Walton Grange
Froghall
Penty Park
Mountjoy Fm
Clarbeston Road
Clarbeston
Lamborough
Hook
Hook Hill
Longlands Fm
Wiston
Conkland
Corner Fm
Man Fm
Pwll Coch
Trwyn y Bwa
Carregedrywy
Pen-y-bal
Cat Rock
Parrog
Newport Sands
Berry Hill
NEWPORT PEMBROKESHIRE
MUS & GALL
Newport (Trefdraeth)
Gamallt
Cell Howel
Morawel
Lleine
Foel Goch
Castell-y-garn
Trefwrdan
Trellyffaint
Tregamman
Glasdir
Rhosmaen
Ffynnondofn
Frongoch
Trefach
Cwm-cenau
Nevern
Coed Cwm Glowne
Felindre Farchog
Sychpant
Trewern
Pentre Ifan
Penwern
Brithdir Mawr
Fachongle
PENTRE IFAN BURIAL CHAMBER
TY CANOL
Tycanol
Carnedd Meibion-Owen 244
Cilgwyn
Pen-rhiw
Trefach
Brynberian
Afon Brynberian
Banc Du
Tregynon
Pentrisil
Ffynnondici
Penlanwynt
Waun-Maes
Cerrig Lladron 468
Afon Cwmau
Waun Mawn
Tafarn-y-bwlch
Afon Pennant
Foel Feddau 467
Mynydd Preseli
Mynydd-du Commin
Foel Cwmcerwyn 536
Cnwc
Carn Afr
Pantmaenog Forest
Glynsaithmaen
Glynaeron
New Inn
Greenway
Mynydd Crwn
TAFARN SINC
Rosebush
Rosebush Res
Barnard's Well Mountain
Dyffryn
Budloy
Garden
Tufton
Henry's Moat
Bernard's Well
Blacknuck
Maenclochog
Eithbed
Pisgah
Temple Druid
Prisk Fm
Llandilo
Pant-y-cabal
Sychpant
Gwar-y-coed
Brynteg
Velindre
Cil-moor
Vorlan
Ffynnon Samson
Tir Bach Fm
Penrhos
Blaen-sawd
New Moat
Clover Hill
Gwastad
Nant-y-goi
Blaenllaethdy
Park East
Forlan
Gilfach Uchaf
Llanycefn
Rhos-y-gwydl
Moat Grange
Wood Park
Posty
Milton
Rhyd-afallen
Penffordd
Holloway
Brechfa
Rhyd-y-Brown
New Mill
Bletherston
Gwernant Fm
Llandre Br
Crug-y-deri
Dyffryn Conin
Clarbeston Grange
EARTHWORKS
Cotland Mill
Gelli
Gellyolau
CLUNDERW
Llwyndyrys
Cotland Fm
Plain Dealing
Trefwynt Fm
Great Vaynor
Holgan
Bethesda
Sylvnwy
Bwn Bach
Ceibwr Bay
PEMBROKESHIRE COAST PATH
WALES COAST PATH
LLWYBR ARFORDIR CYMRU
Pantygroes
Bayvil Fm
Ysguborwen
Pen-y-bryn
Gelli
Rhosfarc
Llwynihirion
Waun Brwynant
Mynydd Prescelly
A487
A40
A4219
B4313
B4329
B4330
B4331
92
72
73
A
B
C
D
E
F
G
H
SN
10
20
50

Cardigan Island
Carreg Lydan
Pen yr Hwbyn
Clos-y-graig
Pen Tew
Nantycroy
Ty Gwyn
Nantmawr
Blaenplwyf
Ceredigion Coast Path
Aberporth
Parcllyn
Dyffryn
Tresaith
Penbryn
Penmorfa
Ffynnon Berw
Maes-y-Ffynnon
Pwllglas
Sarnau
Brynhoffnant
Perthygopa
Allt-goch
North Fawr
Pant yr Holiad
Dyffryn-bern
Cemaes Head
Gwbert
Towyn Warren
Y Ferwig
Felinwynt
Rhosygadair Fawr
Rhosygadair Newydd
West Wales Airport, Aberporth
Cwmporthman
Login
Tre-cefn
Pen-rhiw
Troedyrhiw
Trefere
Ffynnonwen
Rocklands
Cwm
Tyhen
Internal Fire Mus of Power
Rhippinllwyd
Allt-y-goed
Penrhyn Castle
Poppit Sands
Pen yr Afr
Pengarn
Cippyn
Pwllygranant
Foel Hendre
Pantirion
Clawddcam
Cwm Connell
Ceibwr Bay
St Dogmaels (Llandudoch)
St Dogmael's Abbey
Manian-fawr
Albro Castle
Tregibby Fm
Caemorgan
New Mill
Banc-y-Warren
Penparc
Cardigan
Aberteifi
Castle
Bus Pk
Bridgend
Ind Est
Teifi Marshes Nature Reserve
Llangoedmor
Treforgan
Cwrt Fm
Bronydd
Noyadd Wilym
Tremain
Blaenannerch
Glanrhyd
Tan-y-groes
Blaenporth
Maengwyn
Glynarthen
Glasgoed
Cwmcoednerth
College Mawr
Gilfach
Hendraws
Glandulas
Brithdir
Penlon Betws
Pantdaniel
Coedperthi
Bettws Ifan
Ffynnongog
Pen-y-banc
Esgergraig
Felin-Wnda
Hawen
Capel Gwnda
Beulah
Plas Troedyraur
Troedyraur
Brongest
Wern Gadno
Bryngwyn
Penbwllaid
Beulah Road
Cwrt Hen
Bronwion
Ponthirwaun
Rhosfawr
Fronlas
Parcybwla
Trefaes-Fach
Allt-y-cadno
Noyadd Trefawr
Ffynnoncipil
Lan
Rhos-wen
Ffynnon Tynewydd
Cryngae Mawr
Blaenwenen
Parc-y-Gors
Wernynad
Pantgwyn
Dyffryn
Pantinker
Waunwhiod
Moylgrove
Bwn Bach
Pembrokeshire Coast Path
Glandwr Fm
Hafod Grove
Monington
Penwaun
Welsh Wildlife Centre
Forest
Coedmor
Glanhelyg
Glanolmarch
Scotland Hill Fm
Blaen-pant
Penrallt-y-Bie Fm
Pengwernfach
Llandygwydd
Bryngwrog
Capel Tygwydd
Blaensyllty
Pant-y-bwla
Blaengwenllan Cross
Blaen-Cil-Llech
Llechryd
Castle Malgwyn Fm
Llwynduris
Rhyd
Penwernfawr
Brongwyn
Cilfallen
Rhippinllwyd
Lleine
Fagwreinon
Trefigin
Llwyngwydd
Rhydgaled
Pantygrwndy
Tredefaid
Cwm Plysgog
Cilgerran Castle
Pen-lan
Cilgerran
Trefwrdan
Pantygroes
Pantgwyn Mawr
Parke
Penbanc
Croft
Felinganol
Pen-y-bryn
Bridell
Penparceithin
Penfai
Stradmore Mansion
Alltybwla
Cenarth
National Coracle Centre
Cwm-cou
Adpar
Cilgwyn
Llandyfriog
Berthyfedwen
Tregamman
Glasdir
Trefach
Bayvil Fm
Crugiau
Trewenfron
Llantood
Maes-y-felin
Penwenallt Fm
Carreg-wen
Penlan-Cenarth
Gelliorlas
Gilfo Fm
Newcastle Emlyn (Castell Newydd Emlyn)
Bus Cen
Aber-Arad
Glwen Fm
Pentrecagal
Blaenhalen
Nevern
Pontgarreg
Pencelly
Palle Fm
Pen-cwm
Ty-hen Fm
Rhos-hill
Cilast-isaf
Rhosygilwen
Pentre
Cilrhue Fach
Abercych
Allt Boeth
Felindre Farchog
Coed Cwm Gloyne
Pengelli Forest
Castell Henllys Iron Age Fort
Court
Baengafren
Penycoed
Bwlchgarreg-lwyd
Mynydd Crogwy
Cilast-uchaf
Pen-bedw
Newchapel
Clynfyw
Tyhir
Pengwern
Penrherber
Sychpant
Ysguborwen
Henllan
Eglwyswrw
Penderi
Penlanfeigan
Cilwendeg
Cilgwyn
Penlangarreg
Nantyrhawl
Clifforest Fm
Trewern
Pentre Ifan
Gelli
Pen-y-benglog
Pantygarn
Dyfed Shire Horse Farm
Eglwyswrw Common
Brynbwa
Pistyll Meigan
Dyffryn-Meigan
Boncath
Penrallty
Afon Dulas
Lancych
Glyneithinog
Caws Cenarth Cheese
Letty-clyd
Hendy
Rhydyfelin
Pontgarreg
Cwmhiraeth
Fachongle
Pentre Ifan Burial Chamber
Ty Canol
Tycanol
Rhostarced
Llanfair-Nant-Gwyn
Neuadd
Arleth
Werndddofn
Dolalau-isaf
Blaenffos
Blaenachddu
Pen y Garn
Capel Iwan
Cwmpengraig
Llwynihirion
Hendre
Temple Gate
Crosswell
Pontyglasier
Fountain Hill
Clover Hill
Eglwyswen
Moelfre
Cwmcych
Afon Mamog
Cil-waunydd Fawr
Cwmgelli Fm
Blaen Bran
Carnedd Meibion-Owen
Brynberian
Pensarn
Pantyrodyn
Wern Ddu
Glynmaen
Annedd Wen
Dyffryn Mawr
Gorsfraith
Cidigill
Dolpwll
Bwlchygroes
Dyffryn Cefn Faes
Cwm Cneifa
Crynga
Hafod
Pengribyn
Cwmorgan
Black-oak
Penygroes
Tygwyn
Ty-canol
Rhydwen
Fronlas
Lleinau
Frenni Fawr
Penlan-uchaf
Frenni Fach
Dolau-llannerch
Star
Nant Neel
Nant-llan-fach
Drysgol-goch
Ty-mawr
Llwyndrain
Dyffryn
Clyn felin-fach
Crugygorllwyn
Maudland Ho
Tanglwst
Waun Brwynant
Pembrokeshire
(Sir Benfro)
Tafarn-y-bwlch
Foel Drygarn
Fort
Crymych
Llainbanal
Crug-yr-hwch
Troedyrhiw
Nentydd
Glogue Fm
Llwyn-yr-hwrdd
Penbanc
Tegryn
Pantyrheddwch
Coed-llwyd
Tyddyn
Penwaun Fm
Ddolwen
Carn Goedog
Carn Bresab
Carn Bica
Mynydd-bach
Foel Fedderau
Carn Sian
Carnmenyn
Carn Gyfrwy
Mynydd Preseli
Nant-y-geifr-fawr
Glogue
Hermon
Nantyweirglodd
Pantgwyn-mawr
Blaengilfach
Cadifor Hall
Highgate
Maes-pwll
Plasyrhafod
Triol
Afon Wern
Craig Talfynydd
Caermeini
Foel Cwmcerwyn
Pentre-galar
Llanfyrnach
Rhyd-y-gath
Bryn-eithin
Trehenry
Tre fawr
Llwyncelyn-lan
Hen-feddau fawr
Greenhall
Rhoscrugebolion
Nantycyw
Carregwen
Crugiwan
Bryn-Iwan
Waun-ceiliogau
Nantycerrig
Carn Afr
Cnwc
Glynsaithmaen
Mynachlog-ddu
Rhos fach
Graig
Pantygwyddel
Clynblewog Fm
Dinas
Trelech
Rhospwllygawnen
Clungarthen
Maniwan
Parcymynydd
Trafel-y-pwll
Nantcwmrhys
Mynydd Crwn
Glynaeron
Llain
Waun Isaf
Gors Fawr
Trefach
Pen-yr-allt
Foel-Drych
Pentre Glas
Bribwll
Pant-y-gelli
Ffynnonau Dyfnant
Llanwinio Common
Gilfachwen Fm
Llain-lwyd
Glyn Dewi
Fronlas
Gilfachygestin
Wern
Blaendyffryn
Fferm-y-Capel
Pisgah
Allt-y-gog
Pont yr Haiarn
Gwarllwyn
Glandwr
Penlan
Blaenpant
Rhyd-goch
Pengraig
Crees-llan
Berthlwyd
Cilevan
Gilfach-y-Bettws
Trenoeth
Blaenparsel
Pengraigfawr
Rhosfach
Llandre
Ynysfawr
Carn Besi
Iet-y-bwlch
Rhydowen
Ffynonwen
Elwyn
Castell-mawr
Plasparcau
Cwm
Castell Mawr
Woodlands
Clunpurfaith
Blaendyfod
Nantyrolchfa
Penalltfangor
Hebron
Glyngarw
Temple Druid
Prisk Fm
Llandilo
Llangolman Common
Dandderwen
Gilfach-ddofn
Llangolman
Glandy Cross
Castell Garw
Maes-y-felin
Llanglydwen
Pilmawr
Trefach
Blaenwaun
Felindre
Treparcau
Pantmelyn
Glasfryn
Pencaerau Mawr
Blaenbryn
Brynmeini
Vorlan
Ffynon Samson
Tir Bach Fm
Penrhos
Llwynyrebol
Pant-y-Caws
Dolwilym
Llwynhugh
Fron Fm
Afon Tigen
Dyffryn Brodyn
Cwmbach
Llanwinio
Pwll-y-march
Pen-y-bont
Llwyn-crwn
Cwmgest
Sychpant
Blaengofer
Pantyllyn
Blaen-sawd
Clyngwyn
Cilau-fawr
Maen-hir
Coynant
Gwal y Filiast
Trehir Uchaf
Glyntaf
Cefn-y-pant
Pencraig
Pant-y-maen
Panthowell
Castell Gorwyn
Talog
Nant-y-gof
Efailwen
Blaenafon
Pantyrodyn
March-gwyn
Cilhernin
Fronhaul
Penrallt
Canerw
Frowen
Lan
Cwmfelin Mynach
Wernberni
Wernolau Fawr
Maesgwynne
Pensarn
Lleinau
Blaengelli
Blaenpant
Clifforch
Crugydeirne
Ty-hen
Fachddu
Penrallt Trawscoed
Pant-y-Grwn
Cilhir-Uchaf
Ffynnonwen
Gilfach Uchaf
Blaenllaethdy
Llanycefn
Rhos-y-gwyd
Marble Hall
Plas-y-bedw
Penlan
Cilgynydd
Llechclawdd
Penhenrhiw
Cilsant
Pengraig
Gellywen
Eithin-doun-isaf
Felin-pandy
Abernant
Rhyd-afallen
Login
Ffynnonwen
Cross-hands
Llanboidy
Blaencwmmau
Goetre-uchaf
Maen-côch
Plas-paun
Eithin-duon-uchaf
Dyffryn
Plas-y-parciau
Tal-y-fan-uchaf
Posty-Uchaf
Pantyg-Cendy
Holloway
Brechfa
Bush Fm
Cilowen
Cwm-miles
Waunffrwd
Ffoswinau
Hafod
Cilanw
Pencnwc
Goetre Fawr
Caerlleon
Nantyreglwys
Corngafr
Garllegan Fawr
Bwlchgwynt
Brynwl
Glandwr
Talfan Isaf
Cwm
Posty-isaf
Nant-y-bair
Afon Cynnen
Llandissilio
Cilhengroes
Castell Draenog
Gellydogin
Pantygroes
Blaencediw
Dyffryn Marlais
Baily Mawr
Penback Fm
Bank y llain
Penlan
Llangarthginning
Rhosyn-coch
Drefach
Sarnau Fm
Bwlch Fm
Cwmduhen
Castell-gwyn
Hiraeth
Gwarmacwydd
Henllan Amgoed
Lan
Wernlygoes
Fynnonfoida
Llwyngwydd
Pantyrhas
Playcerdin
Cethin Fm
Meidrim
Hafod Fm
Gwernant Fm
Llandre Br
Dyffryn-Conin
Rhydywrach
Parciau
Blaenwernddu
Llanfallteg
Llangynin
Berthlwyd
Troedyrhiw
Esgair
Pentowin
Pantyderi
Pen-pontbren
Sarnau
Gellyc
Pengwern
Penuwch
Blaenycoed
Penlan
Bron-y-gaer
Cwmfelin Boeth
Sarnlas
Great Vaynor
Bryn Fm
Cilpost Fm
Whitland Abbey
Aber
Llwynbychan
Pen-y-coed
Meidrim Road
Derry Hall
Wern Fm
Bancyfelin
Nantyrhos
Bethesda
Trewern
A487
A478
A484
A486
B4548
B4333
B4334
B4570
B4582
B4332
B4329
B4313
B4299
B4298
B4571
A
B
C
D
E
F
G
H
1
2
3
4
5
6
91
110
73
74
SN
0 1 2 3 miles
0 1 2 3 4 5 km

Pentregat
Blaenbedw Fawr
Talgarreg
Gorsgoch
Cribyn
Silian
Lampeter
(Llanbedr Pont Steffan)
Olwen
Cellan
Pentrefelin
Cwmann
Ram
Capel Cynon
Bwlch-y-fadfa
Castell-Howell
Aber
Cwrt-newydd
Llanwnnen
Pentre-bach
Ffostrasol
Pont-siân
Maesymeillion
Cwmsychpant
Rhydowen
Llanwenog
Dre-fach
Alltyblaca
Pencarreg
Parc-y-rhôs
Croes-lan
Tregroes
Pren-gwyn
Llanybydder
Maesllyn
Brynteg
Rhuddlan
Glan-Dûar
Ty Mawr
Horeb
Capel Dewi
Aber-banc
Penrhiw-llan
Llandysul
Maesycrugiau
Aber-Giâr
Llangeler
Drefach
Llanfihangel-ar-arth
Llanllwni
Pentre-cwrt
Saron
Drefelin
Bancyffordd
Rhydcymerau
Llidiad Nenog
New Inn
Pencader
Gwyddgrug
Rhos
Forest of Brechfa
Allt Brechfa
Dolgran
Gwernogle
Abergorlech
Cwmduad
Alltwalis
Nant-y-ffin
Hermon
Brechfa
Llanpumsaint
Llanllawddog
Pontarsais
Horeb
Cynwyl Elfed
Llanfynydd
Capel Isaac
Rhydargaeau
Pant-teg
Pantgwyn
Bwlchnewydd
Felingwmuchaf
Newchurch
Bronwydd Arms
Peniel
Felingwmisaf
Pentrefelin
Capel Gwyn
Llanfihangel-uwch-Gwili
Court Henry
Broad Oak
Llangathen
Ffynnon ddrain
Trevaughan
Nantgaredig
Pont-ar-gothi
Cilsan
Merthyr
Carmarthen
Caerfyrddin
Tanerdy
Abergwili
White Mill
Capel Dewi
Llanegwad
Felindre
Dryslwyn
Llangunnor
Llanarthne
Golden Grove
Johnstown
Llanllwch
Pensarn
Nantycaws
Penrhiwgoch
CARMARTHENSHIRE
SIR GAERFYRDDIN
CEREDIGION
A40
A485
A486
A475
A484
B4459
B4338
B4336
B4310
B4300
111
74
75
94

Llanfair Clydogau
Penlan
Pont Glanrhyd
Graigddu
Groes
Bryn Glas
Bryn Du
Egair Maen
Llethr Gwyn
Pen Rhiw-Clochdy
Esgair Gwair
Pen Rhiwclochdy
Foel Fraith
Llyn Brianne Reservoir
Tywi Forest
Allt Tywi
Nant-y-Neuadd
Nant-y-medd
Penlanmedd
Pentre
Dyffryn
Cwm Twrch
Llethr Du
Bryn Mwysau
Llethr Erwast
Lan Fawr 429
Hafod Las
Penbanc
Bryn Mawr
Blaen-Twrch
Carn Nant-yr-ast 440
Craig Pysgotwr
Craig Cnwch-glas
Allt y Fedw
Pen y Foel
Cefn Uchaf
Cellan
Pentrefelin
Craig Twrch
Bryn Ceiliogau
Bryn Glas
Esgair Hendre
Craig Siarls
Bryn Arau Duon
Craig Ddu
Llyn Brianne Reservoir
Pen Rhiwbie
Mynydd Trawsnant
Henog
Coed Llwynifan
Coed Tangaer
Cwmann
Ram
Sychnant
Cerrig Cyffion
Esgair Tan-Lan
393 Banc y Garth
Allt Rhyd y Groes
Craig Clangwyn
Rhuddallt
Gwenffrwd-Dinas
Cefn Ystrad-ffin
Bryn-hirfaen
Esgaircorn
Tynant
Blaen Rhisglog Plantn
Cefn Branddu
Dinas
Ystradffin
Carn Twrch 487
Craig Galltyberau
409
Kings Park
Waunbant
Cae Caradog
Esgair-crwys
Parc-mawr
Tyllwyd
Crugiau Merched 459
Craig Llys-fedw
Esgair Dafydd
A482
Llanycrwys
Troed-y-bryn
Foel
Aber Branddu
Craig Troed-y-rhiw-fer
Pen Deriwyn
Pyllau-crynion
Ffarmers
Banc y Graig
Banc y Ddau Fryn
Mynydd Mallaen
Craig Beinon
Nant-y-Bai
Cnwch 320
Rhandirmwyn
Bryn Nicol
Fwng
Bryn Gareg
Ffaldybrenin
Bryn-Brân
Allt yr Hebog
Cwrt-y-cadno
Cefn y Bryn
Esgair Ferchon 433
429
Craig Ddu
Craig Rhosan
93
Cwmcanol
Pantycelyn Fm
Harford
Pen banc
Banc Maes-yr-Haidd
Aber-Mangoed
Glan-meddyg
Craig Llech-gwynt
Penrhyn
Gwernpwll
Llanerchindda
Dryslwyn
Mount Fm
Pen Lan-dalau
Llandre
Rhyd-lydan
Blaen-Ceiment
Banc Bronffin
Cefn Bach
Afon Merchon
Rhiw Cilgwyn 412
Home Fm
Dolfallt
Esgairdawe
Maes-troyddyn-fawr
Dolaucothi Gold Mines
Caeo Forest
Banc Blaendyffryn
Rhiw-mallaen
Ty'n-y-waun
Cefnhirfryn
Cynghordy
Cynghordy Hall
Lletherhir
Gwarcoed
Wern
Pumsaint
Caio
Cwm-Fran-fawr
365 Pen Lifau
Cilycwm
Pantybryn
341
Bryniau
Tan-y-coed
Coed-y-gof
Cwm-Einon-fawr
Derwen Fawr Fm
Felin Newydd
Maescadog
Nantwrch
Llwyn-Owen
Ochr-y-fforest
Pen y Gaer
Divlyn
A483
Banc Cefngarreg
Brechfa Forest
Froodvale Fm
Maesglas Fm
Benlan
Pen-y-banc
Gilwen
Cefn-trenfa
Cefn-y-gefail
Pantglas
Cwmcoedifor
Esgair
Pengelli
Pistyllgwyn
Pantyderwen
Crugybar
Borthyn
Bwlchcefnsarth
Porthyrhyd
Cae-glâs
Ysgrafell
Siloh
Troed-y-rhiw
Tyn-y-coed
Little Hall
Noethgrug
Ty'n-y-coed
Cwmhowel
The Croft
CARMARTHENSHIRE
Talog
Bwlch-tre-banau
Llwyncynhyrys
Cefnrickett
Dolauhirion
Mwmffri 302
Cefncoed
B4302
Rhos
Cwmgogerddan
Hafod Br
Garregfechan
Abercrychan
Gellyrhydd
Penywaun
Llansawel
Ynys Fm
Castell
Bancyglyn
Pen y Ddinas
Dolaugleision
Talley Lakes
Pigyn Shon-Nicholas
Mynydd Llansadwrn
Blaen-y-cwm
Troed-y-rhiw
Plas-newydd
Poor Man's Wood
Cefn Crug
Gellyfelen
Babel
Rhydyglyn
Tre-glog
Acheth
Banc Beili-Tew 278
Edwinsford
Pantiauau
Tyrheol
Cors Farlais
Cwmargenau
Wern
Penrhiw
Talrhyn
Maesllydan Hall
Garddfady Fm
Pentre-ty-gwyn
Gwarllwyn
B4310
Blaencwm
Moelfre
Bryngwyn
Blaenmarlais
Cwm-marchon
Gilfach
Llandovery
Llanymddyfri
Glangwydderig
Cefnpwllhen
Cwm-cwta
Abergorlech
Parcmawr
Parcydilfa
Cilyllynfawr
Cwm-gwlaw-fawr
SIR GAERFYRDDIN
Cwm-Mynys
Mount Pleasant
Pentwyn
Allt y Ferdre
Cefn Arthen 309
Pentrebach
Halfway
Mynydd Cynros 329
Talley Abbey
Talley
Cwm-byr
Cefn Fm
Cwmdwr
Llwyncelyn
Cefnucheldre
Lwyd Jack
Cwm-Rhuddan
Fron Fm
Cwm Dwr
Cilwr Fm
Beili Bedw
Coedhirion
Wauncluda
Llanwrda
Penrock
Cefn-cerrig
Dagfa
A40
Llanerch-goch
Hafod Fawr
Pistyll-gwyn
Pant-yr-esgair
Fan
Llansadwrn
Dolgarreg
Cwm-gwyn
Cae-gwyn
Llwynywormwood
Y Pigwn
Pistyll Uchaf
Mynydd Figyn
Cwmcerrig
Aberdaunant
Felindre
Cwmcowddu
Myrtle Hill
Pen-twyn
Mynydd Bach Trecastell
Cwmdu
Halfway
Bryn
Brownhill Fm
Glan-Towy
Pentir Bach 198
Glasallt-fawr
Cilgwyn
Myddfai
Cwm Nant-y-Beudy
Pistyll-south
Tirpant
Goetre Fm
Cefn Parc
Cefn Maes
A4069
Cilgwyn Wood
Esgair-llaethdy
Pant-y-ffynnon
Newfoundland Fm
Parc-glâs
Green Grove
Gelli-felen
Sarnau
429
Mynydd Myddfai
Soar
Taliaris
Llwynpiod
Ashfield
Llangadog
Afon Brân
Lletyrhyddod
Cefn-gwrych
Usk Reservoir
Ffrwdwen
Cwm-cragen
Onen-fawr
Cefn-glasfryn
Carreg-Sawdde Common
Cwm-Brân
Mandinam
Tirpaun
Hermon
Glandulais
Felindre
Coed Caer Bedw
Gilfach
Cefngeudrum
Gwydre
Penrhiw Uchaf
429 Fedw Fawr
Ffrwd
Mount
Pistyllgwyn
Cefncilwg
Capel Isaac
Salem
Glanbrydan Park
Manordeilo
Tyle
Dolau Fm
Bryngwyn Fm
Cefn-y-coed Common
Tirmawr
Rhiwiau 354
Pantmeinog
Stangau
Gelli
Talsarn
Blaenllechach
Arhosfa'r Garreg-Lwyd
River Usk
Foel Darw 424
Blaenau Uchaf
Blaenau Isaf
Cwmifor
Cae-mawr
Caeaubychain Bach
Rhiwiau-uchaf
Tir-Howel
Dyffryn Ceidrych
Bont Fawr
Pant-Hywel
Cilmaen
Mynydd Y Llan 423
Bryn Mawr 457
426
Pantgwyn
Caegroes
Llwydcoed-uchaf
New Inn
Closglas
Capel-isaf
Bethlehem
Coed-mawr
Twynllanan
Llanddeusant
Waun Lwyd
Hafod
Hafodneddyn
Bryn-hyfryd
Capel-y Tydist
Carn Goch
Y Gaer Hillfort
Pont-ar-llechau
Nant-gwynne
Tredomen
Blaenau
Pentrefelin
Cilwern
Llwyncelyn Fm
Pen-y-banc
Pen-y-banc
Rhosmaen
Pontbren Araeth
Crug Glas
Tan-y-lan
Pen crug
Acheth
Blaensawdde
Birdshill
Dinefwr Park
Ind Est
Crymlym Manor
Gurnos
Trichrug 415
Banc Carreg-feol-gam
Bailey Home Fm
Llwynfron
Penmaen
BRECON BEACONS NATIONAL PARK
Fan Foel
Moel Feri 591
Castle Woods
Newton House
Llandeilo
Dyffryn Tywi
Cilsan
Brynteg
Dafadfa-isaf
Capel Gwynfe
Pont Aber
Maes-y-ffynnon
Tyle Du
Carreg Yr Ogof 585
Llyn y Fan Fach
Bannau Brycheiniog 802
Llyn y Fan Fawr
Ffairfach
Treyeb Wood
Hafod Fm
Neuadd
Pontbren
Maesadda
Pen-Rhiw-goch
Waun Lefrith
Bannau Sir Gaer
College Fm
B4300
Treiorwg
Cefn-fedw
Hirlwyn-isaf
Truman
Cwm Sawdde Fechan
Twyn-Swnd
Brest Twrch
Fan Hir
Maerdy
Maes-Evan
Gelli-groes
Tynywaun
Gellybevan Fm
Carnau Cont-Menyn
Golden Grove
Parklane
Onen-fawr
Penhill Fm
Blaencennen Fm
Pont Clydach
556 Cefn y Cylchau
Egair Hir
Waun Haffes
Carreg Cennen Castle & Farm Centre
Clogau Mawr
Cefn y Truman
Mynydd Du
Banwen Gwyn
Wern Dolau
Rhyd-y-ffynnon Fm
Meusydd Hall
Cwmcennen
Cwrtbrynbeirdd
Beddau'r Derwydd
Banc Wernwgan
521 Carn Pen-y-clogau
Carn Cennen
Foel Fraith 602
Blaen y Cylchau
Foel Fawr
616
Tirygoitre
0 1 2 3 miles
0 1 2 3 4 5 km

Cefn Crug
Crugwydd
Cefn Cynllaith
Cefn Blaeneinon
Irfon Forest
Pen-Y-Garn
Carcwm
Beulah
Trefan
Cefn-poeth
Ty-mawr
Tysegur
Llwyngwyn
Cilmery
Cilmeri
Rhosferig
Park Wells
Cilmery Fm
ROYAL WELSH SHOWGROUND
Llanelwedd
Noyadd
Tynllwyn
Aderedw Hill
Oaklands
Builth Wells
Llanfair-ym-Muallt
Llanfaredd
Wernfawr
Tyn-y-graig
Llwyn-cus
Llanfechan Ho
Garth Bank
Ty'h-y-ffos
Hendre
Llanfechan
Coed Cowyn
Garth
Pistyllgwyn
Penfedw
Llwyncadwgan
Caerau
Cwm Irfon
Cefn Alltwinau
Ffosyrhyddod
Coed Clunmelyn
Garth Ho
Dolmenyn
Gwaralit
Erwhelm
Maes-y-cwm
Llanwrtyd
Llawes-heli
Llwynbrain
Ty-gwyn
Y Foel
Gilfach
Dal-y-gaer
Gwarafog Ho
Cwmrhybin
Moelfre
Llanddewi'r Cwm
Pwllgwyn
Ysgiog
Middle Hall
Blaenmilo Fm
Cefnhingog Fm
Tynycoed Fm
Pennau
Banc y Cwm
Maesmynis
Pantypyllau
Gwar-henallt
Henallt
Court Fm
Aberedw
Bronffynnon
Glancamddwr
Llangammarch Wells
Cae'r-mynach
The Warren
Trawstir
Pant-y-llyn Hill
Alltmawr
Llanwrtyd Wells
(Llanwrtud)
Ind Est
Aber-Dulas uchaf
Park
Troed-y-rhiw
Pen-y-garreg
Banc y Celyn
Hendy
Aberedw Rocks
Penmaenllwyd
Llwyneuadd
Egsair Moel
Cwm-mwyn
Llawr-dre-fawr
Berthddu
Glancledan Fawr
Caedn
Cefn-gorwydd
Ty-uchaf
Drovers' Arms
Danger area
Blaen Bwch Fm
Waun Hirwaun
Blaenfirnant
Blaen-Gwenddwr
Blaen Henllan
Llandeilo Graban
Cefn-esgair
Gelli crugiau
Bryn-beili
Cefn
Cynala
Drum-ddu
Llethr-ddu
Yr Allt
Fosgoy
Penlanlwyd
Tynllwyni
Cwm Dwfnant
Pentre Dolau-Honddu
Fron Fm
Cwm Owen
Nant yr Offeiriad
Groes-wen
Gwenddwr
Erwood
Twyn y Garth
Abergefail
Mynydd Eppynt
Danger area
Cefn Gledwen
Bryn-du
Artillery Range
Login
Pool Hall
Cwm Crickadarn
Crickadarn
Ty-isaf Fm
Cefn Llwydlo
Penlanwen
Twyn Rhyd-car
Llwyn-rhidyll
Llwyn-gwyn
Spite Inn Fm
Nant Crysan
Tirabad
Caerau
Crug-du
Pantycelyn
Tynrhos
Pen-y-lan
Penrhiw
Ty-mawr
Twyn-y-Post
Waun Gynllwch
Cefn Llwydallt
Tyleheulog
Dyrysgol
Brynffo Fm
Cefn Coch
Gwrhyd
Sennybridge Training Area
Cefn Trum-Yr-Hwch
Upper Chapel
Fforest
Cefn Clawdd
Cefn Gaer Commons
Stockley Wood
Cornelau
Baily Bach
Baily Brith
Tynwaun
Cefn Merthyr Cynog
Pantgwyn
Cefn Bach
Llaneglwys Wood
Esgair
Penrheol
Mynydd Fforest
Nantymynach
Nant-yr-arian
Tir Bach
Cwm Egnant
Alltarnog
Gaer-fawr
Ysgwydd Hwch
Llaneglwys
Merthyr Cynog
Garreg Fawr
Cwmache
Blaendyryn
Pont Rhyd-y-berry
Clpebyll
Bwlchserth Fm
Llandefalle Hill
Pentrenewbury
Cilfodig Fm
Ponde
Bryn-y-Garn
Cwm Ffrydyll
Cwm-pistyll
Tynewydd Fm
Rhiw
Cwm Nant-y-moch
Cwm Mawan
Cwm-Llythin
Fanolau Fm
Lower Chapel
Wernddyfwg
Cwm-Gwilym
Cefnmachllys
Caebetran
Twyn-y-Gaer
Llandefalle
Pwll-y-cwrw
Felin-newydd
Mynydd Bwlch-y-groes
Nant Eithrim
Llandeilo'r Fan
Gwar-y-felin
Cwm Erchan
Maen Richard
Blaengwy
Mynydd Bach
Lloegr
Funglas
Trawscoed
Trehenry
Pontybat Fm
Llanfihangel Nant Bran
Pentregwyn
Battle Hill
Pont-faen
Cilmanharen
Garthbrengy
Garth-isaf
Cwm Llech
Twyn Brynhicet
Pen-y-lan
Pentre-lloegr
Ynys-gyfarch
Cefn Sarnau
Pwllgloyw
Cilgwyn
Coedgenau
Cefncoed Bach
Talachddu
Felinfach
Tylecrwn
Glyn Celyn
Penishawain
Danger area
Pwllacca
Tir-y-felin
Trawscoed
Cefn Uchaf
Twyn Disgwylfa
Mynydd Aberyscir
Battle Fawr
Llwyncelyn
Sarnau
Llandefaelog Fach
Llandefaelog
Pant-y-cored
Trefeitha
Nantgwared
Llwyngronw
Fedw
Blaenclydach
Pentre-bach
Cefn Twrch
Pen-y-bryn
Soar
Ffinnant-isaf
Cwm-Gwengad
Pytinglas
Gelli-geiloges
Oaklands
Lower Penwaen
Pentwyn
Yr Allt
Gwenffrwd
Battle
Penoyre
Pytindu
Llanddew
Bailea
Rhiwbergoch
Llywel
Bronydd-mawr
POWYS
Gilfach-uchaf
Ynys-y-bont
Cusop
Cradoc
Pen-y-Crug
Pontgwilym
Bishop's Meadow
Wern
Alexanderstone
Drostre
Pentre'r-felin
Park Fm
Trallong
Cwmlliw
Tirmawr
Aberbran
Aberyscir
BRECON GAER ROMAN FORT
Brecon
Aberhonddu
Pennant
Gludy
Pendre
Ffynnonau
CATHEDRAL
BRECON CASTLE
REGIMENTAL MUS. OF THE ROYAL WELSH
BRECKNOCK MUSEUM (Y GAER)
BRECON (TY'N-Y-CAEAU)
Groesffordd
Llechfaen
Llanywern
Waun-y-mynach Common
Gwndwnw
Graiggoch Fm
Yr Allt
Trecastle
Pantysgallog
Sennybridge
(Pontsenni)
River Usk
Abersefin
Penwern
Penpont
Llanfaes
Llanspyddid
Garngaled
Ind Est
Cwmwysg
Penrhiw
Pont Newydd
Bwysfa
Llwyn-cor
Penywingon
Defynnog
Cwm Camlais
Twyny Gaer
Cefn Llechid
Blaenrheon
Closcedi
Tyisha
Bolgoed
Glanafon Fm
Cwm Clydach
Tir-y-graig
Cwm Camlais-fawr
Mynydd Illtud
Cilwhybert
Cwrt Gilbert
Cefn Cantref
Upper Cantref Fm
Abercynrig Mill
Slade Fm
Talyllyn
Llanfrynach
Tynewydd
Manest Court
Scethrog
Tai'r-Bull
Libanus
NATIONAL PARK VISITOR CENTRE
Brynbolgoed
Twyn
Abersenny
Abersenni Uchaf
Tylebychan
Heolfanog
Modrydd
Nant Cwm Llwch
Fforest Fach
Marchogdir
Cwm Crai
Crai
Llwyneuadd
Beiligwern
Cwmbrynich Fm
Cwmclyn
Forest Lodge
Glo Garnhyd
Wenallt
Twyn-cil-rhew
Allt Ddu
Plas-y-gaer
Neuadd
Pontbrengarreg
Rhiwiau
Bailea
Blaen-nant Fm
Pencelli
Monmouthshire & Brecon Canal
Gelli-wlyb
Felin-Crai
Cwm Newynydd
Bailea Fm
Maeswalter
Blaenbrynich
Coed Ty-mawr
Pen Milan
Cwm-llwch
Cefn Cyll
Tyle-llwyd
Cwm Oergwm
Cross Oak
Talybont-on-Usk
Waungoch
Penwaundwr
Nantcoch
Heol Senni
Gelliau isaf
Cnewr
CRAIG CERRIG GLEISIAD A FAN FRYNYCH
Fan Frynych
BRECON BEACONS
Blaenglyn
Bryn
Cwm Cwy
Aber-Village
DANYWENALLT
Waun Leuci
Cwm Pedest
Cray Reservoir
Y Gelli
Fan Bwlch Chwyth
Neuadd
Garnlwyd
Garnwen
Wern-fawr
Craig Cwm-du
Nant Cwm-du
Craig Cerrig-gleisiad
Y Gyrn
Pen y Fan
Corn Du
Cribin
Bryn Teg
Cwm Cynwyn
Cwm Oergwm
Cwm Cwareli
Blaen Cwm Banw
Tyle-Clydach
Wenallt
Forest Fawr
Tyleglas
Tyle-garw
Craig y Fro
Brecon Beacons
Craig Gwaun-taf
Craig Cwm Cynwyn
Craig Pwllfa
Twyn-Du
Danywenal
PARK
Yr Allt
Bryn Melyn
Fan Dringarth
Bryn Du
Fan Fawr
Tyle Brith
Pont ar Daf
Rhiw yr Ysgyfarnog
Cefn Cul
Tor Glas
Craig Fan Las
Gwalciau'r Cwm
Craig y Fan
Fan Gihirych
Fan Llia
Pant Gilfach-wen
Cefn yr Henriw
Beacons Reservoir
Cwm Crew
Neuadd Reservoirs
Craig-y-fan-ddu
Allt Lwyd
Talybont Forest
Fan Nedd
Fan Fraith
Nant Tywynni
Gwaun
Brynmelyn
A483
A470
A40
A4215
A4067
B4519
B4520
B4567
B4602
B4601
B4558
7
8
9
10
11
76
77
96
113

Newchurch
Michaelchurch on Arrow
Brilley Mountain
Upper Welson
Lower Welson
Almeley
Upcott
Rhulen
Bryngwyn
Dol-y-cannau
Crowther's Pool
Brilley
Little Merthyr
Millhalf
Eardisley
Llanbadarn-y-Garreg
Cradle Rocks
Rhos-goch
Rhos Goch Common
Whitney-on-Wye
Winforton
Willersley
Rhydspence
Letton
Llanbedr
Painscastle
Clifford
Clifford Castle
Priory Wood
Merbach
Llandeilo Graban
Bronydd
Pen-y-Park
Hardwicke
Bredwardine
Erwood
Crickadarn
Llanstephan
Clyro
Hay-on-Wye
(Y Gelli Gandryll)
Hay on Wye Castle
The Bage
Arthur's Stone
Moccas Park
River Wye
Llowes
Cusop
Dorstone
Rhydness
Boughrood
Cwmbach
Llanigon
Glasbury
Heol-y-gaer
Snodhill
Cefn Hill
Llyswen
Pipton
Three Cocks
Tregoyd
Llanrosser
Hinton
Brechfa Pool
Velindre
Craswall Priory (Rems)
Urishay Common
Hay Bluff
677
Craswall
Llandefalle
Bronllys
Bronllys Castle
Felinnewydd
Pont-y-wal
Lord Hereford's Knob or Twmpa
690
Upper Maes-coed
Michaelchurch Escley
Talgarth
Llanelieu
Llanfilo
Felinfach
Middle Maes-coed
Newton
Capel-y-ffin
Tredustan
Trefecca
Pwll-y-Wrach
Tredomen
Llanveynoe
P O W Y S
Grwyne Fawr Reservoir
Llandefaelog-tre'r-graig
Pengenffordd
Castell Dinas
450
BRECON BEACONS
NATIONAL PARK
Lower Maes-coed
Llanywern
Llanfihangel Tal-y-llyn
Llangors
Waun Fach
811
Longtown
Longtown Castle
Talyllyn
Llanthony
Llanthony Priory
Clodock
BANNAU BRYCHEINIOG
Llanhamlach
Llangasty Talyllyn
Llangorse Lake
The Black Mountains
Y Mynyddoedd Duon
Scethrog
Cathedine
Pencelli
Walterstone
Cwmrhos
Oldcastle
Cross Oak
Llansantffraed
Cwmdu
Cwmyoy
Talybont-on-Usk
Bwlch
Tre-wyn
Pandy
Aber-Village
Danywenallt
Gaer
Tretower
Tretower Castle & Court
Stanton
Llanfihangel Crucorney
Llanvihangel Court
Coed-yr-ynys
Llanbedr
Forest Coal Pit
Crossways
Bettws
Crickhowell
(Crug Hywel)
Sugar Loaf
596
Ffawyddog
Llangattock
Llangenny
A40
A438
A470
A479
A4078
A4350
A4348
A4351
A4352
A465
A4111
A4112
A4594
A4558
A4560
B4350
95
114
77
78
0 1 2 3 miles
0 1 2 3 4 5 km

Weobley
Weobley Marsh
Sarnesfield
Bush Bank
King's Pyon
Westhope
Dinmore
Bodenham
Saffron's Cross
Bodenham Moor
Maund Bryan
Ledgemoor
Logaston
Newchurch
Canon Pyon
Wellington
Highway
Wormsley
Norton Canon
Calver Hill
Hurstley
Moorhampton
Yarsop
Yazor
Mansel Lacy
Foxley
Tillington Common
Tillington
Burghill
Staunton on Wye
Mansell Gamage
Monnington on Wye
Brinsop
Credenhill
Kenchester
Bishopstone
Byford
Moccas
Bridge Sollers
Stretton Sugwas
Swainshill
Preston on Wye
Ploughfield
Lulham
Canon Bridge
Blakemere
Tyberton
Madley
Cublington
Shenmore
Clehonger
Allensmore
Kingstone
Vowchurch
Turnastone
Thruxton
Winnal
Cockyard
Kerry's Gate
Didley
St Devereux
Wormbridge
Kilpeck
Bacton
Abbey Dore
Ewyas Harold
Howton
Pontrilas
Rowlestone
Monmouth Cap
Llangua
Kentchurch
Grosmont
Garway Hill
White Rocks
Garway
Skenfrith
Norton
Crossway
Llanrothal
Welsh Newton
St Weonards
Tretire
Broad Oak
Llancloudy
Llangarron
Llangrove
Marstow
Goodrich
Kerne Bridge
Walford
Pencraig
Ross-on-Wye
Peterstow
Wilton
Bridstow
Glewstone
Hereford
Holmer
Moreton on Lugg
Marden
Sutton St Nicholas
Sutton St Michael
Withington
Shucknall
Lugwardine
Bartestree
Weston Beggard
Tupsley
Hampton Bishop
Mordiford
Dinedor
Holme Lacy
Fownhope
Grafton
Callow
Much Dewchurch
Much Birch
Kivernoll
Wormelow Tump
Little Birch
Little Dewchurch
Bolstone
Ballingham
Carey
Hoarwithy
King's Caple
Sellack
Harewood End
Pencoyd
Michaelchurch
Orcop Hill
Orcop
Bagwy Llydiart
Hereford
Wye
Valley
Ledgemoor
Ullingswick
Felton
Burley Gate
Preston Wynne
Ocle Pychard
Westhide
Yarkhill
Newtown
Tarrington
Stoke Edith
Dormington
Priors Frome
Checkley
Woolhope
Sollers Hope
Falcon
Brockhampton
How Caple
Fawley Chapel
Foy
Hole-in-the-Wall
Brampton Abbotts
Coughton
Tudorville
Kingsthorne
Dewsall Court
Portway
Twyford Common
Dinedor Cross
Mordiford
Lower Bullingham
Bullinghope
A49
A438
A465
A4103
A4110
A480
A466
A40
A4137
B4349
B4348
B4352
B4399
B4224
B4521
B4347
SO
115
7
8
9
10
11
78
79
98
A
B
C
D
E
F
G
H

98
MALVERN HILLS
HEREFORDSHIRE
GLOUCES
Malvern Link
Great Malvern
West Malvern
Malvern Wells
Little Malvern
Ledbury
Newent
Bromyard
Much Cowarne
Stoke Lacy
Bishops Frome
Castle Frome
Cradley
Colwall
Colwall Stone
Eastnor
Eastnor Castle
Bosbury
Coddington
Wellington Heath
Tarrington
Stoke Edith
Trumpet
Pixley
Woolhope
Putley
Much Marcle
Little Marcle
Preston
Dymock
Kempley
Upton Bishop
Brampton Abbotts
Ross Spur Services
Weston under Penyard
Linton
Gorsley
Aston Crews
Clifford's Mesne
Glasshouse Hill
Huntley
Mitcheldean
Longhope
Birdwood
Tibberton
Rudford
Highleadon
Hartpury
Maisemore
Ashleworth
Sandhurst
Twigworth
Longford
Gloucester
Staunton
Corse
Eldersfield
Pendock
Redmarley D'Abitot
Bromsberrow Heath
Welland
Hanley Swan
Hanley Castle
Castlemorton
Longdon
Birtsmorton
Upleadon
Malswick
Kent's Green
Taynton
Bulley
Powick
Madresfield
Newland
Guarlford
Three Counties Showground
Hellens Manor
St Mary's Church Kempley
Clutter's Cave
Eden's Hill
Dick Whittington Farm Park
National Waterways Museum
Highnam Woods
Candlemakers
M50
A449
A417
A438
A4103
A40
116
97
79
80
0 1 2 3 miles
0 1 2 3 4 5 km

WORCESTERSHIRE
COTSWOLDS
Pershore
Evesham
Tewkesbury
Cheltenham
Broadway
Winchcombe
Bishop's Cleeve
Charlton Kings
Upton upon Severn
Bredon
Eckington
Fladbury
Cropthorne
Wyre Piddle
Throckmorton
Bishampton
Norton
Harvington
Offenham
Bengeworth
Hampton
Badsey
Aldington
Bretforton
Wickhamford
Childswickham
Sedgeberrow
Hinton on the Green
Ashton under Hill
Aston Somerville
Dumbleton
Wormington
Toddington
Stanton
Stanway
Laverton
Buckland
Snowshill
Didbrook
Hailes
Greet
Gretton
Alderton
Teddington
Beckford
Kemerton
Overbury
Conderton
Elmley Castle
Bricklehampton
Little Comberton
Great Comberton
Birlingham
Defford
Besford
Strensham
Upper Strensham
Lower Strensham
Ripple
Twyning
Kinsham
Northway
Ashchurch
Aston Cross
Walton Cardiff
Deerhurst
Apperley
Tredington
Stoke Orchard
Gotherington
Woolstone
Oxenton
Alstone
Dixton
Prescott
Langley
Postlip
Cleeve Hill
Woodmancote
Southam
Prestbury
Swindon
Uckington
Elmstone Hardwicke
Boddington
Coombe Hill
Leigh
Staverton
Golden Valley
Down Hatherley
Parton
Churchdown
Badgeworth
Shurdington
Leckhampton
Up Hatherley
Sandfields
Pittville
Battledown
Oakley
Whittington
Sevenhampton
Brockhampton
Charlton Abbots
Hawling
Guiting Power
Kineton
Temple Guiting
Farmcote
Ford
Cutsdean
Taddington
Salperton
Notgrove
Aylworth
Barton
Shipton
Syreford
Dowdeswell
Upper Dowdeswell
Lower Dowdeswell
Andoversford
Shipton Solers
Shipton Oliffe
Foxcote
Kilkenny
Kingsditch
Arle
Staverton Bridge
Hatfield
Kempsey
Stoulton
Drake's Broughton
Pinvin
Peopleton
Egdon
Upper Wolverton
Ab Lench
Atch Lench
Church Lench
Abbots Salford
Salford Priors
Cleeve Prior
North Littleton
Middle Littleton
South Littleton
Marlcliff
Bickmarsh
Willersey
Kersoe
Netherton
Wadborough
Pirton
Kinnersley
Naunton
Bushley
Forthampton
Chaceley
Hardwicke
Fiddington
Newtown
A46
A44
A435
A436
A40
M5
M50
B4084
B4035
B4632

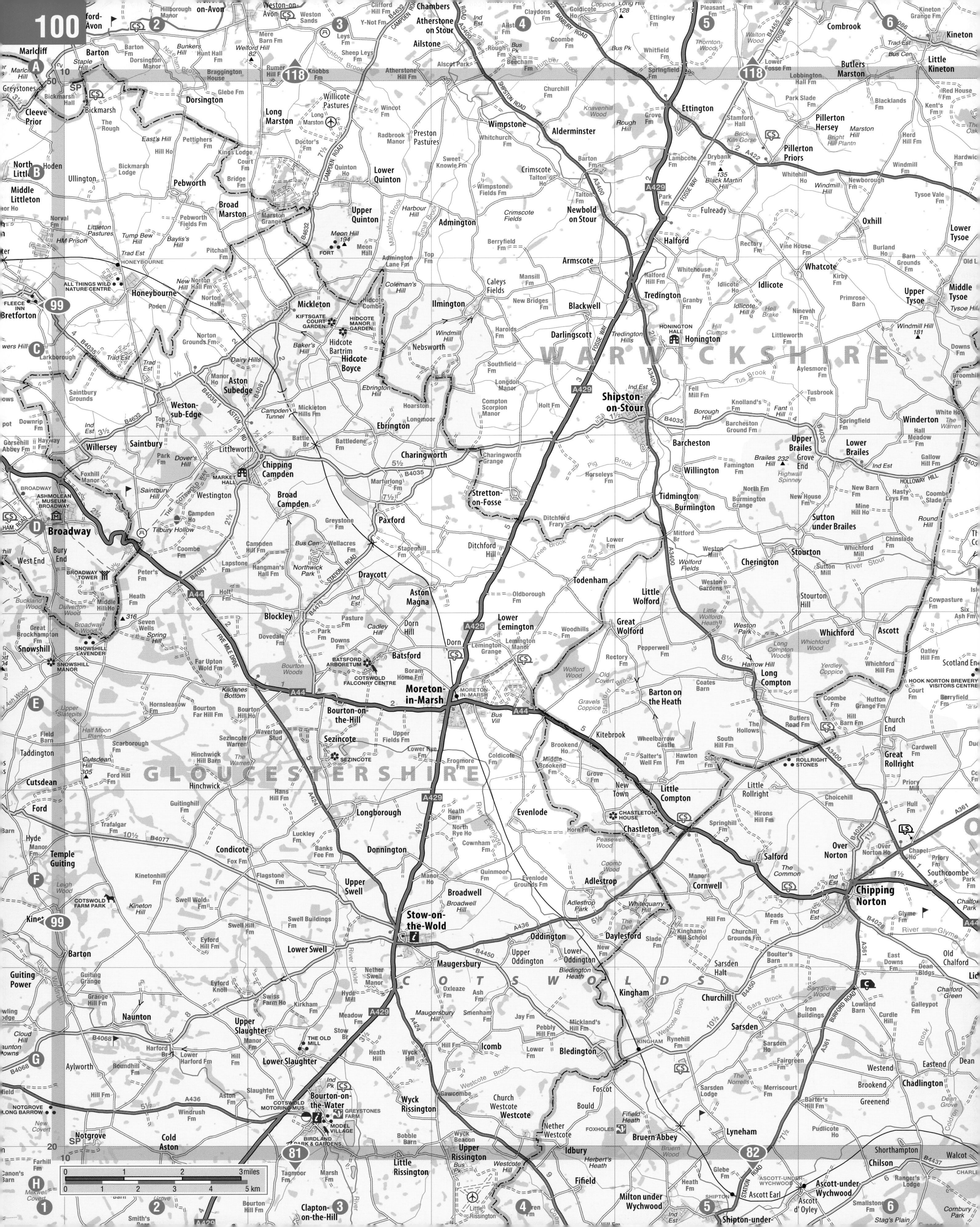

WARWICKSHIRE
GLOUCESTERSHIRE
COTSWOLDS
Marlcliff
Barton
Bidford-on-Avon
Weston-on-Avon
Welford-on-Avon
Chambers
Atherstone on Stour
Ailstone
Alscot Park
Clifford Chambers
Long Marston
Dorsington
Bickmarsh
Cleeve Prior
Greystones
Pebworth
Broad Marston
Lower Quinton
Upper Quinton
Admington
Ilmington
Mickleton
Hidcote Bartrim
Hidcote Boyce
Hidcote Manor Garden
Kiftsgate Court Garden
Nebsworth
Wimpstone
Whitchurch Fm
Preston Pastures
Alderminster
Ettington
Pillerton Hersey
Pillerton Priors
Butlers Marston
Combrook
Kineton
Little Kineton
Newbold on Stour
Crimscote
Armscote
Halford
Fulready
Tredington
Blackwell
Darlingscott
Shipston-on-Stour
Honington
Honington Hall
Idlicote
Whatcote
Oxhill
Upper Tysoe
Middle Tysoe
Lower Tysoe
North Littleton
Middle Littleton
Ullington
Honeybourne
Bretforton
All Things Wild Nature Centre
Fleece Inn
Aston Subedge
Weston-sub-Edge
Saintbury
Willersey
Chipping Campden
Broad Campden
Westington
Ebrington
Charingworth
Paxford
Barcheston
Willington
Tidmington
Burmington
Upper Brailes
Lower Brailes
Winderton
Sutton under Brailes
Stretton-on-Fosse
Broadway
Broadway Tower
Ashmolean Museum Broadway
Blockley
Draycott
Aston Magna
Batsford
Batsford Arboretum
Cotswold Falconry Centre
Ditchford Hill
Todenham
Little Wolford
Great Wolford
Cherington
Stourton
Whichford
Ascott
Long Compton
Barton on the Heath
Hook Norton Brewery Visitors Centre
Snowshill
Snowshill Manor
Snowshill Lavender
Moreton-in-Marsh
Dorn
Lower Lemington
Bourton-on-the-Hill
Sezincote
Kitebrook
Little Compton
Little Rollright
Great Rollright
Rollright Stones
Cutsdean
Taddington
Ford
Hinchwick
Longborough
Evenlode
Chastleton
Chastleton House
Salford
Over Norton
Chipping Norton
Temple Guiting
Condicote
Donnington
Upper Swell
Broadwell
Adlestrop
Cornwell
Cotswold Farm Park
Stow-on-the-Wold
Lower Swell
Oddington
Upper Oddington
Lower Oddington
Daylesford
Maugersbury
Kingham
Churchill
Sarsden
Guiting Power
Naunton
Upper Slaughter
Lower Slaughter
Icomb
Bledington
Aylworth
Bourton-on-the-Water
Cotswold Motoring Mus
Model Village
Birdland Park & Gardens
Wyck Rissington
Church Westcote
Westcote
Foscot
Bould
Lyneham
Chadlington
Notgrove
Cold Aston
Little Rissington
Upper Rissington
Idbury
Bruern Abbey
Fifield
Milton under Wychwood
Ascott-under-Wychwood
Ascott Earl
Ascott d'Oyley
Chilson
Shorthampton
Walcot
Clapton-on-the-Hill
Shipton-under-
A429
A44
A424
A436
A3400
A422
A361
B4035
B4632
B4081
B4479
B4450
B4077
B4068
B4026
B4437
99
118
81
82
0 1 2 3 miles
0 1 2 3 4 5 km

Banbury
Bicester
Brackley
Middleton Cheney
Deddington
Adderbury
Bloxham
Charlbury
Kidlington
Enstone
Steeple Aston
Upper Heyford
Lower Heyford
Kirtlington
Aynho
King's Sutton
Souldern
Croughton
Fritwell
Ardley
Chesterton
Wendlebury
Weston-on-the-Green
Middleton Stoney
Tackley
Wootton
Woodstock
Cropredy
Warmington
Farnborough
Avon Dassett
Shenington
Alkerton
Hornton
Horley
Hanwell
Wroxton
Drayton
Epwell
Shutford
Swalcliffe
Sibford Ferris
Sibford Gower
Tadmarton
Broughton
Milcombe
Wigginton
Hook Norton
South Newington
Barford St John
Barford St Michael
Swerford
Great Tew
Little Tew
Over Worton
Nether Worton
Duns Tew
North Aston
Middle Aston
Somerton
Sandford St Martin
Westcott Barton
Middle Barton
Steeple Barton
Glympton
Thenford
Marston St Lawrence
Greatworth
Sulgrave
Culworth
Thorpe Mandeville
Chacombe
Evenley
Mixbury
Cottisford
Hardwick
Hethe
Fringford
Stoke Lyne
Caversfield
Bucknell
Fewcott
Baynard's Green
Charlton
Newbottle
Hinton-in-the-Hedges
Halse
Radstone
Whitfield
Helmdon
Weedon Lois
Moreton Pinkney
Canons Ashby
Eydon
Chipping Warden
Aston le Walls
Wardington
Mollington
Claydon
Great Bourton
Little Bourton
Williamscott
WEST NORTHANTS
OXFORDSHIRE
Cherwell Valley Services
M40
A422
A423
A361
A4260
A43
A41
A44
B4100
B4031
B4030

WEST NORTHANTS
BUCKINGHAMSHIRE
Towcester
Buckingham
Stony Stratford
Wolverton
Winslow
Bicester
Brackley
Silverstone
Whittlebury
Potterspury
Deanshanger
Steeple Claydon
Middle Claydon
Padbury
Tingewick
Finmere
Maids Moreton
Akeley
Leckhampstead
Thornborough
Great Horwood
Little Horwood
Marsh Gibbon
Quainton
Whitchurch
Hanslope
Castlethorpe
Stoke Bruerne
Paulerspury
Yardley Gobion
Grafton Regis
Lillingstone Lovell
Lillingstone Dayrell
Chackmore
Dadford
Twyford
Charndon
Calvert
Edgcott
Grendon Underwood
Kingswood
North Marston
Granborough
Oving
Pitchcott
Hardwick
Creslow
Cublington
Dunton
Hoggeston
Swanbourne
Mursley
Drayton Parslow
Stewkley
Launton
Stratton Audley
Poundon
Newton Purcell
Barton Hartshorn
Chetwode
Preston Bissett
Hillesden
Gawcott
Radclive
Water Stratford
Westbury
Shalstone
Turweston
Whitfield
Biddlesden
Evenley
Mixbury
Fringford
Hethe
Wappenham
Slapton
Abthorpe
Blakesley
Duncote
Caldecote
Tiffield
Roade
Ashton
Alderton
Shutlanger
Greens Norton
Bradden
Weedon Lois
Syresham
Crowfield
Radstone
Beachampton
Calverton
Loughton
Shenley Church End
Bradwell
Tattenhoe
Whaddon
Nash
Singleborough
Adstock
Addington
East Claydon
Botolph Claydon
Denham
Tetchwick
Woodham
Weedon
Rowsham
Lower Arncott
Blackthorn
Ambrosden
0 1 2 3 miles
0 1 2 3 4 5 km

Olney
Weston Underwood
Brayfield
Newton Blossomville
Clifton Reynes
COWPER & NEWTON MUSEUM
Bromham
Biddenham
Bedford
Goldington
Putnoe
Brickhill
Woodside
Great Denham
Queen's Park
Fenlake
Kempston
Elstow
Harrowden
Cardington
Cople
Shortstown
Emberton
Petsoe End
Filgrave
Tyringham
Hardmead
Astwood
Stagsden
Stagsden West End
Kempston West End
Box End
Wood End
Keeley Green
Wootton
Kempston Hardwick
Wixams
Cotton End
Herring's Green
Littleworth
Wilstead
Haynes
Sherington
Chicheley
Lathbury
North Crawley
Little Crawley
Newport Pagnell
Tickford End
Brook End
East End
Bourne End
Upper Shelton
Wootton Broadmead
Stewartby
Broad Green
Cranfield
Lower Shelton
Caulcott
Marston Moretaine
Houghton Conquest
Chapel End
Haynes West End
Haynes Church End
Moulsoe
Great Linford
Blakelands
Giffard Park
Pineham
Tongwell
Willen
Downhead Park
Northfield
Milton Keynes Village
Atterbury
Broughton
Woolstone
Springfield
Oakgrove
Fishermead
Milton Keynes
Kingston
Monkston Park
Distribution Park
Salford
Salford Ford
Hulcote
Lidlington
Millbrook
How End
Ampthill
Maulden
Clophill
Beadlow
Green End
Duck End
Water End
Woughton on the Green
Eaglestone
Oldbrook
Coffee Hall
Brinklow
Kents Hill
Wavendon
Wavendon Gate
Cross End
Lower End
Woburn Sands
Aspley Guise
Brogborough
Bougton End
Denel End
Flitton
Wardhedges
Silsoe
Walnut Tree
Old Farm Park
Browns Wood
Walton
Woughton Park
Netherfield
Beanhill
Simpson
Bleak Hall
Caldecotte
Bletchley
Aspley Heath
Husborne Crawley
Ridgmont
Steppingley
Flitwick
Greenfield
Pulloxhill
Bow Brickhill
Higher Berry End
Fenny Stratford
Far Bletchley
Water Eaton
Newton Leyes
Birchmoor Green
Woburn
Froxfield
Tyrells End
Eversholt
Church End
Higher Rads End
Tingrith
Westoning
Little Brickhill
Pinfoldpond
Great Brickhill
Sheeplane
Harlington
Sharpenhoe
Barton-le-Clay
Higham Gobion
Hexton
Stoke Hammond
Potsgrove
Milton Bryan
Battlesden
Bragenham
Fox Corner
Heath and Reach
Toddington
Streatley
Upper Sundon
Fancott
Chalgrave
Lower Sundon
Soulbury
Hollingdon
Rushmere
Old Linslade
Hockliffe
Tebworth
Wingfield
Chalton
Sundon Park
Clipstone
Leighton Buzzard
Eggington
Linslade
Stanbridge
Tilsworth
Houghton Regis
Bidwell
Parkside
Limbury
Stopsley
Biscot
Burcott
Billington
Little Billington
Stanbridgeford
Leagrave
Luton
Wing
Ledburn
Lower End
Totternhoe
Sewell
Beecroft
Dunstable
High Town
Round Green
Hart Hill
Eaton Green
Eaton Bray
Honeywick
Slapton
Moor End
Downside
Chaul End
Farley Hill
Caddington
Northall
Edlesborough
Horton
Horton Wharf
Wingrave
Crafton
Mentmore
Nup End
Ivinghoe Aston
Whipsnade
Kensworth
Church End
Slip End
Woodside
Pepperstock
Cheddington
CENTRAL BEDFORDSHIRE
CHILTERNS
LUTON
M1
A5
A6
A421
A428
A4146
A505
A507

CENTRAL
BEDFORDSHIRE
CHILTERNS
LUTON
Blunham
Willington
Moggerhanger
Sandy
Girtford
Everton
Potton
Cockayne Hatley
Hatley St George
Arrington
New Wimpole
Croydon
Wendy
Tadlow
Whaddon
Cople
Cardington
Hatch
Beeston
Thorncote Green
Northill
Ickwell Green
Upper Caldecote
Biggleswade
Sutton
Wrestlingworth
Eyeworth
Dunton
Guilden Morden
Steeple Morden
Abington Pigotts
Bassingbourn
Litlington
Old Warden
Southill
Broom
Stanford
Langford
Edworth
Hinxworth
Ashwell
Haynes
Shefford
Clifton
Henlow
Arlesey
Stotfold
Newnham
Radwell
Bygrave
Baldock
Letchworth Garden City
Norton
Clophill
Campton
Meppershall
Upper Stondon
Lower Stondon
Shillington
Pirton
Ickleford
Hitchin
Walsworth
Willian
Great Wymondley
Little Wymondley
Graveley
Weston
Clothall
Wallington
Sandon
Therfield
Kelshall
Rushden
Cottered
Cromer
Ardeley
Walkern
Benington
Stevenage
Aston
Knebworth
Codicote
Kimpton
Whitwell
St Paul's Walden
Langley
Preston
Lilley
Great Offley
Barton-le-Clay
Hexton
Pegsdon
Stopsley
Hart Hill
Watton at Stone
Sacombe
Datchworth
Woolmer Green
Whempstead
Dane End
Haultwick
Old Knebworth
A1
A1(M)
A505
A507
A600
A602
B658
B1042
B1040
B1037
B197
A1198
A10
A6
122
103
85
86
0 1 2 3 miles
0 1 2 3 4 5 km

CAMBRIDGESHIRE
ESSEX
123
106
86
87
Orwell
Barrington
Harston
Hauxton
Little Shelford
Stapleford
Babraham
Sawston
Newton
Whittlesford
Pampisford
Little Abington
Great Abington
Hildersham
Linton
Balsham
West Wickham
Shepreth
Foxton
Meldreth
Melbourn
Fowlmere
Thriplow
Heathfield
Duxford
Hinxton
Ickleton
Stump Cross
Great Chesterford
Little Chesterford
Hadstock
Bartlow
Ashdon
Royston
Heydon
Chrishall
Elmdon
Strethall
Littlebury
Saffron Walden
Great Chishill
Little Chishill
Barley
Littlebury Green
Duddenhoe End
Bridge Green
Wendens Ambo
Audley End
Newport
Reed
Barkway
Nuthampstead
Langley
Arkesden
Debden
Wimbish
Radwinter
Buckland
Anstey
Meesden
Wicken Bonhunt
Clavering
Rickling
Widdington
Wyddial
Brent Pelham
Buntingford
Great Hormead
Hare Street
Berden
Quendon
Stocking Pelham
Furneaux Pelham
Ugley
Henham
Broxted
Westmill
Braughing
Manuden
Elsenham
Stansted Mountfitchet
Farnham
Albury
Puckeridge
Standon
Little Hadham
Much Hadham
Bishop's Stortford
Birchanger
Stansted Airport
Takeley
Great Hallingbury
Thorley
Sawbridgeworth
Great Easton
Little Easton
Great Munden
Barwick
Hatfield Forest
Great Canfield

Balsham
Weston Green
Little Bradley
Little Thurlow
Great Thurlow
Assington Green
Thurston End
Boxted
Stanstead
West Wickham
Streetly End
Withersfield
Great Wratting
Barnardiston
Hundon
Poslingford
Glemsford
Horseheath
Little Wratting
Brockley Green
Chilton Street
Cavendish
Haverhill
Kedington
Clare
Pentlow
Bartlow
Shudy Camps
Castle Camps
Sturmer
Boyton End
Stoke by Clare
Foxearth
Wixoe
Baythorne End
Steeple Bumpstead
Helions Bumpstead
Birdbrook
Ridgewell
Ashen
Ovington
Belchamp St Paul
Belchamp Otten
Belchamp Walter
Tilbury Juxta Clare
Little Yeldham
Bulmer
Hempstead
Radwinter
Stambourne
Great Yeldham
Gestingthorpe
Toppesfield
Cornish Hall End
Wimbish
Great Sampford
Wickham St Paul
ESSEX
Gainsford End
Castle Hedingham
Sible Hedingham
Great Maplestead
Little Maplestead
Little Sampford
Finchingfield
Thaxted
Halstead
Wethersfield
Great Bardfield
Little Bardfield
Gosfield
Shalford
Monk Street
Lindsell
High Garrett
Great Saling
Bardfield Saling
Great Easton
Panfield
Stisted
Bocking
Braintree
Bradwell
Great Dunmow
Rayne
Little Dunmow
Great Notley
Felsted
Black Notley
Tye Green
Cressing
Silver End
Barnston
White Notley
Hatfield Peverel
ESSEX
0 1 2 3 miles
0 1 2 3 4 5 km

SUFFOLK
DEDHAM VALE
Sudbury
Colchester
Hadleigh
Long Melford
Lavenham
Shimpling
Alpheton
Preston St Mary
Kettlebaston
Hitcham
Wattisham
Wattisham Stone
Ringshall Stocks
Barking Tye
Willisham Tye
Willisham
Great Bricett
Nedging Tye
Naughton
Offton
Somersham
Little Blakenham
Great Blakenham
Bildeston
Whelp Street
Bridge Street
Brent Eleigh
Monks Eleigh
Chelsworth
Nedging
Swingleton Green
Milden
Semer
Ash Street
Whatfield
Elmsett
Flowton
Burstallhill
Burstall
Aldham
Lindsey
Lindsey Tye
Stackyard Green
Drakestone Green
Humble Green
Little Waldingfield
Acton
Cuckoo Tye
Great Waldingfield
Upsher Green
Newman's Green
Priory Green
Rose Green
Parliament Heath
Round Maple
Mill Green
Broad Street
Castling's Heath
Kersey Tye
Kersey Upland
Edwardstone
Groton
Gosling Green
William's Green
Wicker Street Green
Horner's Green
Sherbourne Street
Bower House Tye
Hadleigh Heath
Polstead Heath
Boxford
Newton
Great Cornard
Cornard Tye
Chilton
Ballingdon
Middleton
Sackers Green
Little Cornard
Stone Street
Calais Street
Whitestreet Green
Hagmore Green
Henny Street
Great Henny
Assington
Workhouse Green
Polstead
Shelley
Raydon
Lower Raydon
Layham
Upper Layham
Lower Layham
Hintlesham
Washbrook Street
Chattisham
Washbrook
Coles Green
Copdock
Mace Green
The Woodlands
Little Wenham
Gipsy Row
Great Wenham
Capel St Mary
Holton St Mary
Bentley
Harrow Street
Leavenheath
Stoke-by-Nayland
Mill Street
Bell's Corner
Withermarsh Green
Thorington Street
Higham
Lattinford Hill
East Bergholt
Brantham
Cattawade
Twinstead Green
Twinstead
Lamarsh
Dorking Tye
Honey Tye
Alphamstone
Bures Green
Nayland
Bures
Boxted
Stratford St Mary
Dedham
Pebmarsh
Cross End
Mount Bures
Little Horkesley
Wormingford
Boxted Cross
Boxted Heath
Langham
Dedham Heath
Lamb Corner
Birchall Corner
Lawford
Manningtree
Colne Engaine
Countess Cross
Wakes Colne Green
Wakes Colne
White Colne
Chappel
Great Horkesley
Westwood Park
Horkesley Heath
Fordham
West Bergholt
Mile End
Ardleigh
Little Bromley
Fox Street
Parson's Heath
Great Bromley
Fordstreet
Great Tey
Aldham
Gallows Green
Eight Ash Green
Seven Star Green
Braiswick
Welshwood Park
Crockleford Heath
Crockleford Hill
Elmstead Market
Elmstead Heath
Marks Tey
Little Tey
Stanway
Lexden
Beacon End
Abbey Field
The Hythe
Old Heath
Copford
Copford Green
Shrub End
Maypole Green
Wivenhoe Cross
Wivenhoe
Frating Green
Frating
Alresford
Hare Green
Balls Green
Coggeshall
Broad Green
Surrex
Skye Green
Easthorpe
Heckfordbridge
Blackheath
Berechurch
Rowhedge
Feering
Kelvedon
Gore Pit
Messing
Hardy's Green
Birch
Layer de la Haye
Malting Green
Birch Green
Layer Breton
Layer Marney
Abberton
Langenhoe
Fingringhoe
South Green
Thorrington
Abberton Reservoir
River Colne
River Stour
Colne Valley
FLATFORD MILL VISITOR CENTRE
THE MUNNINGS ART MUSEUM
EAST ANGLIAN RAILWAY MUSEUM
COLCHESTER ZOO
BETH CHATTO GARDENS
BOURNE MILL
FINGRINGHOE WICK NATURE RESERVE
WOLVES WOOD
KENTWELL HALL
MELFORD HALL
GAINSBOROUGH'S HOUSE
GUILDHALL
ST JAMES'S CHAPEL
WATTISHAM STATION HERITAGE
A134
A131
A1071
A1141
A12
A120
A137
A133
B1115
B1070
B1068
B1508
B1029
B1027
B1022
B1026
B1025
B1024
B1023
B1352
125
108
88
89

Barham
Henley
Witnesham
Grundisburgh
Burgh
Hasketon
Melton
Bromeswell
Friday Street
Upper Street
Great Blakenham
Claydon
Little Blakenham
Nettlestead
Somersham
Akenham
Culpho
Boot Street
Great Bealings
Little Bealings
Woodbridge
Tuddenham St Martin
Tuddenham
Westerfield
Playford
Whitton
Castle Hill
Bramford
White House
Westbourne
Rushmere St Andrew
Rushmere Street
Kesgrave
Martlesham
Martlesham Heath
Waldringfield Heath
Waldringfield
Sutton
Sutton Common
Shottisham
Sutton Street
Sproughton
Burstall
Ipswich
California
Rose Hill
Hintlesham
Washbrook Street
Chantry
Maidenhall
Stoke
Broke Hall
Warren Heath
Brightwell
Newbourne
Hemley
Ramsholt
Gainsborough
Priory Heath
Nacton Heath
Bucklesham
Copdock
Coles Green
Mace Green
Belstead
Wherstead
Nacton
Amberfield
Kirton
Falkenham
Bawdsey
Levington
Freston
Woolverstone
Pin Mill
Chelmondiston
Trimley St Martin
Felixstowe Ferry
Capel St Mary
SUFFOLK
Tattingstone
Tattingstone White Horse
The Woodlands
Thorpe Common
Trimley Lower Street
Trimley St Mary
Bentley
Holbrook
Lower Holbrook
Walton
Old Felixstowe
Felixstowe
Church End
Shotley
Erwarton
Harkstead
Stutton
Upper Street
Brantham
SUFFOLK COAST AND HEATHS
Shop Corner
Shotley Gate
The Port of Felixstowe
Cattawade
River Stour
River Orwell
Mistley
Manningtree
Lawford
Wrabness
Parkeston
Harwich
Dovercourt
Upper Dovercourt
Ramsey
Little Oakley
Bradfield
Bradfield Heath
Mistley Heath
New Mistley
Little Bromley
Horsleycross Street
Wix
Great Oakley
Horsley Cross
Tendring Heath
Goose Green
Stones Green
Tendring Green
Tendring
Little Bentley
Beaumont
Hare Green
Balls Green
Frating Green
Thorpe Green
Weeley
Thorpe-le-Soken
Kirby-le-Soken
Kirby Cross
Walton-on-the-Naze
Great Bentley
Weeley Heath
Aingers Green
Row Heath
Frinton-on-Sea
Great Holland
Thorrington
Little Clacton
Hamford Water
Pennyhole Bay
Crabknowe Spit
Pye Sand
The Naze
Skipper's Island
Horsey Island
HOEK VAN HOLLAND
Landguard Pt
Shotley Pt
0 1 2 3 miles
0 1 2 3 4 5 km

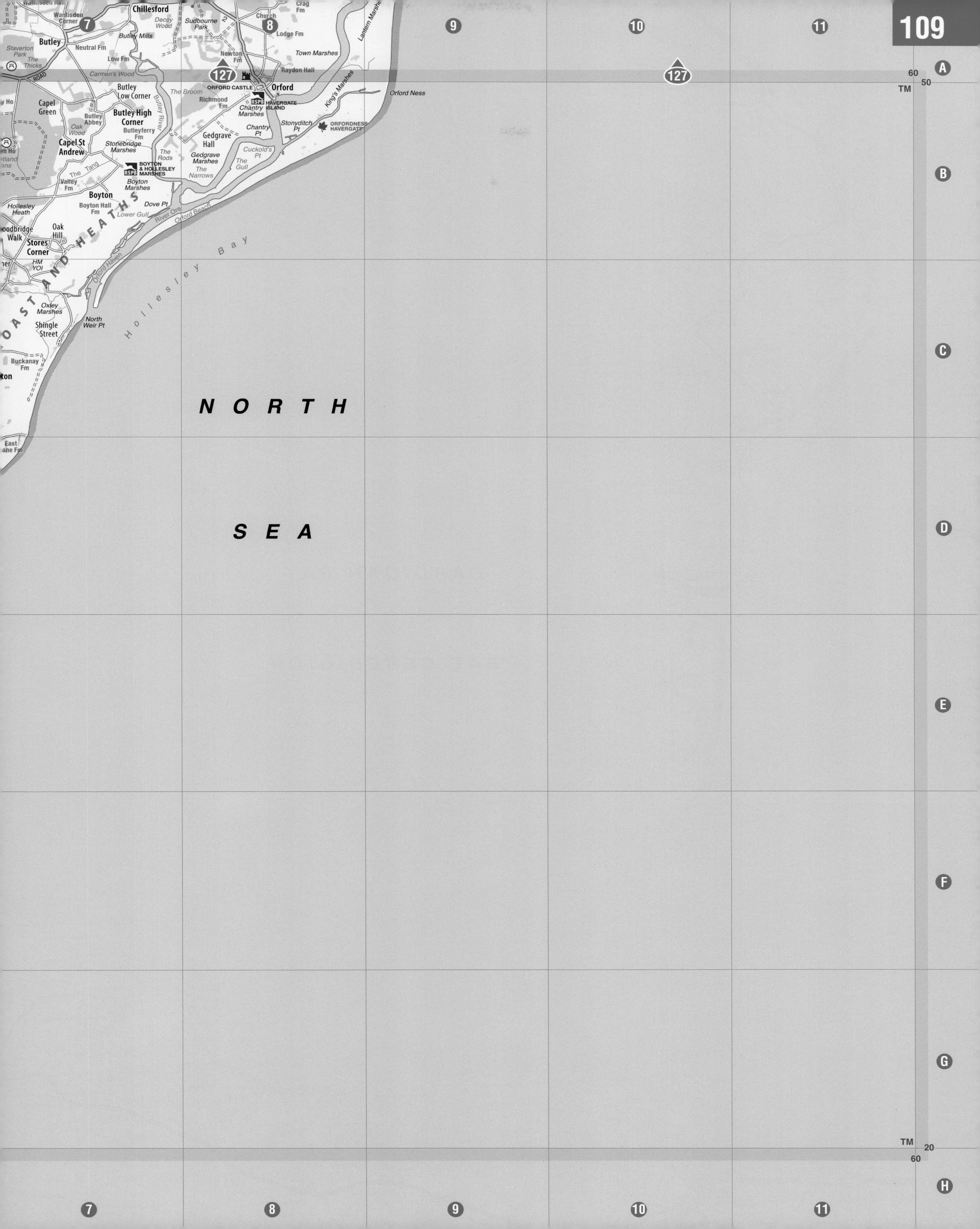

Chillesford
Wantisden Corner
Butley
Decoy Wood
Sudbourne Park
Church
Crag Fm
Lodge Fm
Butley Mills
Neutral Fm
Staverton Park
The Thicks
Low Fm
Newton Fm
Town Marshes
Lantern Marshes
Carmen's Wood
127
ORFORD CASTLE
Orford
Raydon Hall
Orford Ness
Butley Low Corner
The Broom
Richmond Fm
HAVERGATE ISLAND
King's Marshes
Capel Green
Butley Abbey
Butley High Corner
Butleyferry Fm
Butley River
Chantry Marshes
Chantry Pt
Stonyditch Pt
ORFORDNESS-HAVERGATE
Oak Wood
Capel St Andrew
Stonebridge Marshes
Gedgrave Hall
Cuckold's Pt
The Rods
Gedgrave Marshes
The Gull
The Narrows
The Tang
BOYTON & HOLLESLEY MARSHES
Valley Fm
Boyton Marshes
Boyton
Hollesley Heath
Boyton Hall Fm
Dove Pt
Lower Gull
River Ore
Orford Beach
Woodbridge Walk
Oak Hill
Stores Corner
HM YOI
COAST AND HEATHS
Orford Haven
Hollesley Bay
Oxley Marshes
Shingle Street
North Weir Pt
Buckanay Fm
East Lane Fm
NORTH
SEA
TM
60
50
20
A
B
C
D
E
F
G
H
7
8
9
10
11

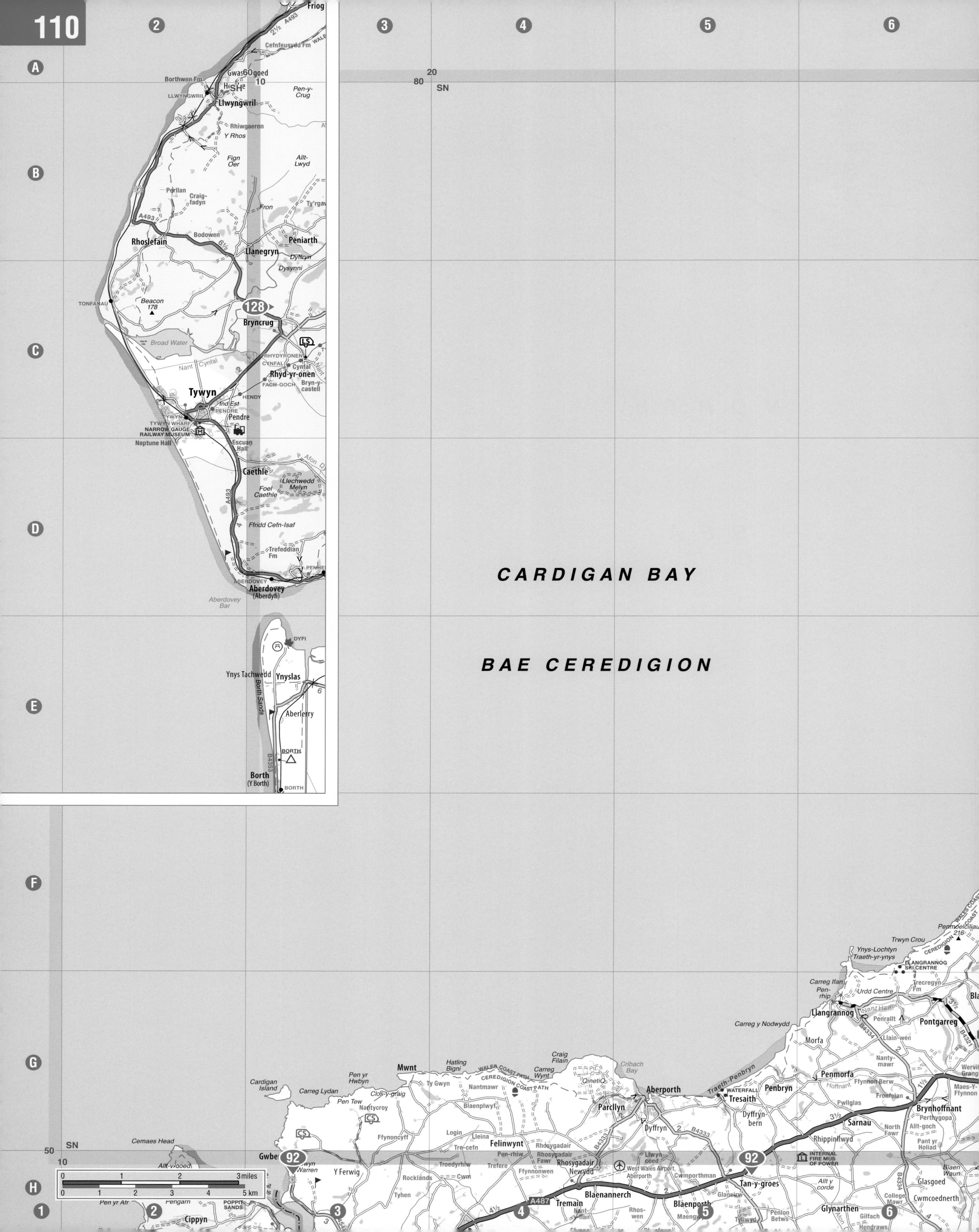

CARDIGAN BAY
BAE CEREDIGION
Friog
Llwyngwril
Rhoslefain
Llanegryn
Peniarth
Bryncrug
Tywyn
Rhyd-yr-onen
Pendre
Caethle
Aberdovey
(Aberdyfi)
Aberdovey Bar
Ynys Tachwedd
Ynyslas
Aberleffry
Borth
(Y Borth)
Broad Water
NARROW GAUGE RAILWAY MUSEUM
Neptune Hall
Llangrannog
Pontgarreg
Penmorfa
Penbryn
Tresaith
Aberporth
Parcllyn
Mwnt
Felinwynt
Rhosygadair
Blaenannerch
Tan-y-groes
Brynhoffnant
Sarnau
Glynarthen
Cwmcoednerth
Glasgoed
Tremain
Blaenporth
Y Ferwig
Cippyn
Cardigan Island
Cemaes Head
Carreg y Nodwydd
Ynys-Lochtyn
Traeth-yr-ynys
LLANGRANNOG SKI CENTRE
INTERNAL FIRE MUS OF POWER
West Wales Airport, Aberporth

Aberystwyth
Trefechan
Penparcau
Southgate
Rhydyfelin
Llanfarian
Chancery (Rhydgaled)
Blaenplwyf
Penderi Cliffs
Wales Coast Path
Ceredigion Coast Path
Llanddeiniol
Llangwyryfon
Llanrhystud
Ty-Newydd
Trefenter
Rhyd-Rosser
Llansantffraed
Llanon (Llan-non)
Rhydfudr
Trawsnant
Fantasy Farm Park
Nebo
Rhos Haminiog
Cross Inn
Aberarth
Aberaeron
Bethania
Penuwch
Pennant
Monachty
Crynfryn
New Quay (Ceinewydd)
New Quay Head
Birds Rock
Traethy Coubal
Cei-bach
Gilfachrheda
Maen-y-groes
Llanerchaeron
Cilcennin
Newbridge
Ciliau Aeron
Bwlch-Llan
Capel Betws Lleucu
Llwyncelyn
Henfynyw
Ffos-y-ffin
Oernant
Cross Inn
Nanternis
Llanarth
Oakford
Trefilan
Tal-sarn
Gartheli
Llwyn-y-groes
Llundain-fach
Abermeurig
Caerwedros
Dihewyd
Ystrad Aeron
Felinfach
Temple Bar
Llwyndafydd
Synod Inn
Mydroilyn
CEREDIGION (SIR CEREDIGION)
Caledrhydiau
Ffynnon-oer
Llangybi
Plwmp
Pentregat
Talgarreg
Gorsgoch
Cribyn
Silian
Betws Bledrws
Capel Cynon
Bwlch-y-fadfa
Castell-Howell
Cwrt-newydd
Olwen
Lampeter (Llanbedr Pont Steffan)
A487
A482
A485
A486
B4577
B4337
B4342
B4338
B4459
B4576
B4343
112
128
93

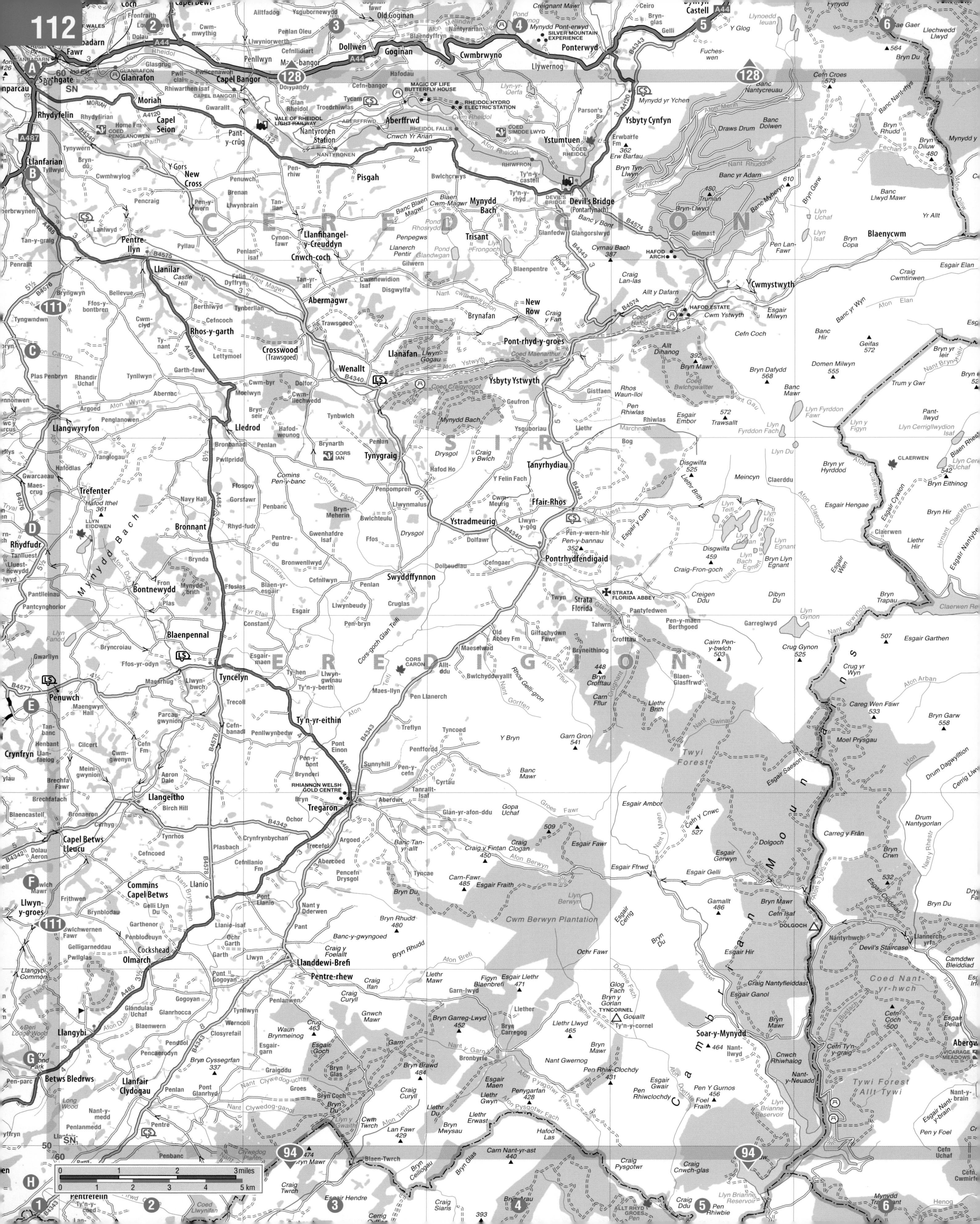

Old Goginan
Dollwen
Goginan
Cwmbrwyno
Ponterwyd
Castell
SILVER MOUNTAIN EXPERIENCE
Mynydd Pont-erwyd
Glanrafon
Capel Bangor
Penllwyn
Moriah
Rhydyfelin
Capel Seion
Aberffrwd
VALE OF RHEIDOL LIGHT RAILWAY
MAGIC OF LIFE BUTTERFLY HOUSE
RHEIDOL HYDRO ELECTRIC STATION
Ystumtuen
Ysbyty Cynfyn
Llanfarian
New Cross
Pisgah
Devil's Bridge (Pontarfynach)
Mynydd Bach
Trisant
Llanfihangel-y-Creuddyn
Cnwch-coch
Pentre-llyn
Llanilar
Abermagwr
Cwmystwyth
HAFOD ESTATE
Rhos-y-garth
Crosswood (Trawsgoed)
Wenallt
Llanafan
Pont-rhyd-y-groes
Ysbyty Ystwyth
Llangwyryfon
Lledrod
Tynygraig
Tanyrhydiau
Trefenter
Bronnant
Ystradmeurig
Ffair-Rhos
Pontrhydfendigaid
Rhydfudr
Swyddffynnon
Bontnewydd
Strata Florida
STRATA FLORIDA ABBEY
Blaenpennal
Tyncelyn
Penuwch
Ty'n-yr-eithin
Crynfryn
Llangeitho
Tregaron
RHIANNON WELSH GOLD CENTRE
Capel Betws Lleucu
Commins Capel Betws
Llanio
Llwyn-y-groes
Cockshead
Olmarch
Llanddewi-Brefi
Pentre-rhew
Cwm Berwyn Plantation
Soar-y-Mynydd
Llangybi
Betws Bledrws
Llanfair Clydogau
Devil's Staircase
Coed Nant-yr-hwch
Twyi Forest
Tywi Forest Allt Tywi
CEREDIGION
SIR CEREDIGION
Cambrian Mountains
Claerwen
Blaenycwm
Llyn Brianne Reservoir
0 1 2 3 miles
0 1 2 3 4 5 km

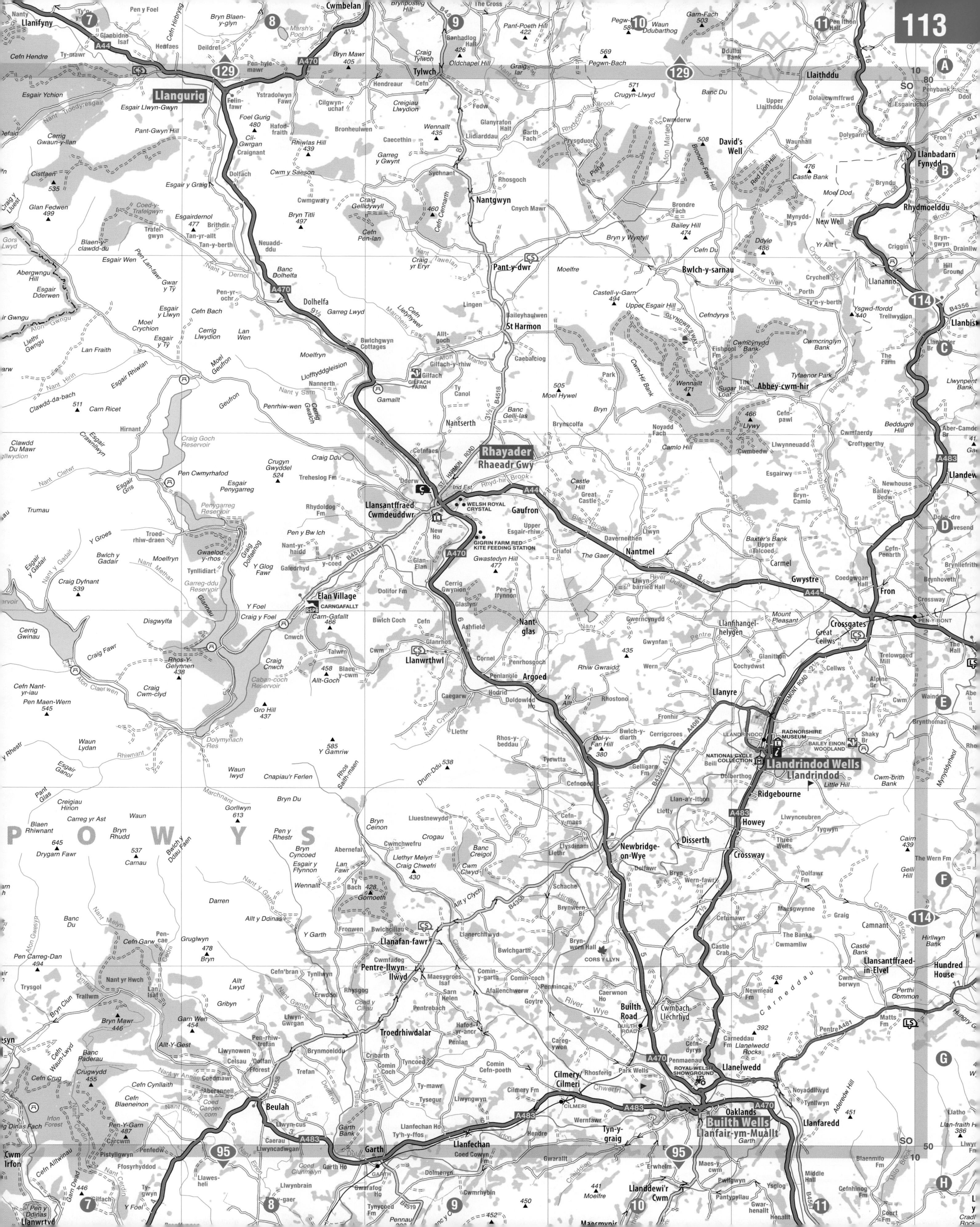
Llanifyny
Cwmbelan
Pen y Foel
Bryn Blaen-y-glyn
Marsh's Pool
Cefn Hirbrysg
Glanbidw isaf
Cefn Hendre
Ty-mawr
A44
Henfaes
Deildref
Bryn Mawr 405
Pen-hyle-mawr
A470
129
Llangurig
Esgair Ychion
Felin-fawr
Ystradolwyn Fawr
Cilgwyn-uchaf
Creigiau Llwydion
Hendreaur
Cefn
Tylwch
Craig Tylwch
Banhadlog Hall 426
Oldchapel Hill
The Cross
Pant-Poeth Hill 422
Craig-lar
Pegw-584
Waun Ddubarthog
569 Pegwn-Bach
Garn-Fach 503
Pen Ithon Hall
Ddultu Bank
Llaithddu
571 Crugyn-Llwyd
Banc Du
Upper Llaithddu
Dolauewmffrwd
Penybank
Esgairuchaf
Ddol
Esgair Llwyn-Gwyn
Foel Gurig 480
Hafod-fraith
Cil-Gwrgan
Craignant
Pant-Gwyn Hill
Cerrig Gwaun-y-llan
Bronheulwen
Wennallt 435
Caecethin
Rhiwlas Hill 439
Fedw
Glanyrafon Hall
Llidiarddau
Garth Fach
Cwmderw
508
David's Well
Waunhall
Dolygarn
Llanbadarn Fynydd
Cistfaen 535
Dolfach
Esgair y Graig
Cwm y Saeson
Garreg y Gwynt
Sychnant
Rhosgoch
Nantgwyn
Cnych Mawr
Prysgduon
Pistyll
Brondre-Fawr Hill
Red Lion Hill
476 Castle Bank
Moel Dod
Bryndu
Rhydmoelddu
Glan Fedwen 499
Coed-y-Trafelgwyn
Esgairdernol 477
Brithdir
Tan-yr-allt
Trafel-gwyn
Cwmgwary
Craig Gellidywyll
Bryn Titli 497
460 Cefn Cennarth
Brondre Fach
Bailey Hill 474
Mynydd-llys
New Well
Bryn y Wyntyll
Ddyle 486
Yr Allt
Criggin
Bryn-gwyn
Drainllwyn
Gors Lwyd
Blaen-y-clawdd-du
Tan-y-berth
Neuadd-ddu
Cefn Pen-lan
Nant Tawelan
Craig yr Eryr
Pant-y-dwr
Moelfre
Cefn Du
Bwlch-y-sarnau
Crychell
Llananno
Hill Ground
Abergwngu Hill
Esgair Dderwen
Esgair Wen
Pen Lan-fawr
Gwar y Tŷ
Banc Dolhelfa
Nant y Dernol
Pen-yr-ochr
Dolhelfa
Garreg Lwyd
Cefn Llechywel
Castell-y-Garn 494
Upper Esgair Hill
Porth
Ty'n-y-berth
Ysgwd-ffordd 440
Trellwydion
114
Llanbister
Esgair y Llwyn
Cefn Bach
Moel Crychion
Cerrig Llwydion
Esgair y Tŷ
Lan Wen
Lingen
Baileyhaulwen
St Harmon
Glyndŵr's Way
Cefndyrys
Fishpool Fm
Cwmcynydd Bank
Cwmcringlyn Bank
The Farm
Llethr Gwngu
Afon Gwngu
Lan Fraith
Moel Geufron
Moelfryn
Bwlchgwyn Cottages
Allt-goch
Gilfach-y-rhiw
Caebalciog
Park
Cwm-Hir Bank
Wennallt 471
The Hall
Sugar Loaf
Abbey-cwm-hir
Tyfaenor Park
Llwynpent Bank
Clawdd-da-bach
511
Carn Ricet
Esgair Rhiwlan
Nant Hirin
Nant y Sarn
Llofftyddgleision
Nannerth
Gilfach Farm
Gamallt
Ty Canol
505 Moel Hywel
Geufron
Penrhiw-wen
Cerrig Gwalch
B4518
Banc Gelli-las
Bryn
466 Llywy
Cefn-pawl
Beddugre Hill
Aber-Camddwr Br
Hirnant
Nantserth
Brynscolfa
Noyadd Fach
Camlo Hill
Cwmfaerdy
Croftyperthy
Clawdd Du Mawr
Craig Goch Reservoir
Esgair Crawnllwyn
Crugyn Gwyddel 524
Craig Ddu
Cefnfaes
Rhayader
Rhaeadr Gwy
Llwynneuadd
Cwmbedw
A483
Llandewi
Nant Cletwr
Pen Cwmyrhafod
Esgair Penygarreg
Treheslog Fm
Dderw
Ind Est
Rhyd-hir Brook
Castle Hill
Great Castle
Esgairwy
Newhouse
Bailey-bedw
Esgair Gris
Trumau
Penygarreg Reservoir
Rhydoldog Fm
Llansantffraed Cwmdeuddwr
Welsh Royal Crystal
Gaufron
Black Brook
Bryn-Camlo
Dol-y-dre
Y Groes
Troed-rhiw-draen
Pen y Bw Ich
New Ho
Gigrin Farm Red Kite Feeding Station
Upper Esgair-rhiw
Daverneithen
Clwyn
Baxter's Bank
Upper Talcoed
Cefn-Penarth
Esgair y Gadair
Bwlch y Gadair
Gwaelod-y-rhos
Craig Dolfaenog
Nant-yr-haidd
Ty'n-y-coed
Glan-Elan
Criafol
The Gaer
Nantmel
Carmel
Brynllefrith
Nant Methan
Moelfryn
Tynlldiart
Y Glog Fawr
Galedrhyd
Gwastedyn Hill 477
Llwyn-barried Hall
River Dulas
Gwystre
Coedgwgan Hall
Fron
Brynhoveth
Craig Dyfnant 539
Garreg-ddu Reservoir
Elan Village
Carngafallt
Dolifor Fm
Cerrig Gwynion
Glaslyn
Pen-y-ffynnon
Crossway
Pen-y-Bont
Disgwylfa
Y Foel
Craig y Foel
Carn-Gafallt 466
Bwlch Coch
Cefn
Ashfield
Nant-glas
Gwerncynydd
Llanfihangel-helygen
Mount Pleasant
Crossgates
Great Cellws
Cerrig Gwinau
Cnwch
Glanrhos
Llanwrthwl
435
Gwynfan
Pentre Brook
Glanithon
Cellws
Trelowgoed Mill
The Hall
Craig Fawr
Rhos-Y-Gelynnen 438
Craig Cnwch
458 Blaen-y-cwm
Cwm
Allt-Goch
Talwrn
Cornel
Penrhosgoch
Argoed
Rhiw Gwraidd
Wern
Cochydwst
Alpine Br
Afon Claerwen
Craig Cwm-clyd
Caban-coch Reservoir
Gro Hill 437
Penlanole
Hodrid
Caegarw
Doldowlod Ho
Yr Allt
Rhostono
Llanyre
Cwm
Cefn Nant-yr-iau
Pen Maen-Wern 545
Nant Cymrun
Llethr
Fronhir
Bwlch-y-diarth
Cerrigcroes
A4081
Llandrindod
Radnorshire Museum
Bailey Einon Woodland
Shaky Br
Brynthomas
Waun Lydan
Dolymynach Res
Rhiwnant
585 Y Gamriw
Rhos-y-beddau
Dol-y-Fan Hill 380
Gelligarn Fm
National Cycle Collection
Beili
Llandrindod Wells
Llandrindod
Dolberthog
Little Hill
Cwm-brith Bank
Mynyddyrhoel
Esgair Ganol
Waun lwyd
Cnapiau'r Ferlen
Rhos Saith-maen
Drum-Ddu 538
Tycwtta
Cefncoed
B4358
Ridgebourne
Pant Glas
Creigiau Hinon
Waun
Carreg yr Ast
Bryn Du
Marchnant
Gorllwyn 613
Bryn Ceinon
Lluestnewydd
Cefn-y-maes
Lletty
Llan-a'r-Ithon
Howey
Llwynceubren
Tygwyn
Blaen Rhiwnant
Bryn Rhudd
Bwlch y Ddau Faen
Pen y Rhestr
Crogau
Llysdinam
Newbridge-on-Wye
Disserth
Three Wells
Cairn 439
POWYS
645 Drygarn Fawr
537 Carnau
Bryn Cyncoed
Abernefal
Cwmchwefru
Llethyr Melyn
Banc Creigol
Craig Chwefri 430
Cwm Clwyd
Llethr
Dolfawr
Bryn
Crossway
The Wern Fm
Gelli Hill
Esgair y Ffynnon
Lan Fawr
Wennallt
Ty Bach
428 Gomoeth
Allt y Clych
Schache
Wern-fawr
Dolfawr Fm
Darren
Nant y Gath
Allt y Ddinas
Brynwern Br
Maesgwynne
Graig
Camnant
Banc Du
Nant Melyn
Cefn Garw
Pen-cae
Fronwen
Bwlchcilau
Llanafan-fawr
Llanerchllwyd
Cefnmawr
The Banks
Cwmamliw
Hirllwyn Bank
Gruglwyn
478 Bryn
Y Garth
Bwlchgarth
Bryn-wern Hall
Cors y Llyn
Castle Crab
Castle Bank
Llansantffraed-in-Elvel
Hundred House
Pen Carreg-Dan 494
Nant yr Hwch
Cwmfadog
Pentre-llwyn-llwyd
Comin-y-garth
Comin-coch
436
Newmead Fm
Cwm-berwyn
Perthi Common
Trysgol
Lan Isaf
Allt Lwyd
Cefn'bran
Tynllwyn
Maesygroes Isaf
Afallenchwerw
Penmincae
Caerwnon Ho
Builth Road
Cwmbach Llechrhyd
Carneddau
Bryn Clun
Trallwm
Gribyn
Erwddol
Rhysgog
Coed y Cilau
Sarn Helen
Gwytre
River Wye
Matts Fm
Pentrebach
Bryn Mawr 446
Garn Wen 454
Nant Gwnfel
Llwyn-Gwrgan
Troedrhiwdalar
Hafod-yr-ancr
Penlan
Careg-ywen
Carneddau Fm
Llanelwedd Rocks
392
A481
Allt-Y-Gest
Pen-rhiw-trefan
Llwynowen
Brynmoelddu
Celsau
Dolfan
Cribarth
Comin Coch
Tyncoed
Comin Cefn-poeth
Cefn-dyrys
Penmaenau
Llanelwedd
Royal Welsh Showground
Cefn Waun Lwyd
Banc Paderau
Crugwydd 455
Cefn Crug
Cefn Cynllaith
Coedmawr
Aberannell
Forest
Trefan
Ty-mawr
Cilmery/Cilmeri
Rhosferig
Park Wells
Chwefri
Noyaddllwyd
Tynllwyn
Aderedw Hill
Cefn Blaeneinon
Coed Caeper-com
Nant Elwon
Tysegur
Llwyngwynn
Cilmery Fm
Cilmeri
Oaklands
A483
A470
451
Llanfaredd
Llatho
Lan-fraith Ho 386
Dinas Fach
Irfon Forest
Pen-Y-Garn 487
Cwm Irfon
Penfedw
Beulah
Llwyn-cus
Caerau
Llwyncadwgan
Garth Bank
Llanfechan Ho
Ty'h-y-ffos
Llanfechan
Hendre
Wernfawr
Tyn-y-graig
Builth Wells
Llanfair-ym-Muallt
Garth
Pistyllgwyn
Cefn Alltwinau
Ffosyrhyddod
Llawes-heli
Coed Clunmelyn
Garth Ho
Coed Cowyn Fm
Dolmenyn
Gwaralit
Erwhelm
Maes-y-cwm
Blaenmilo Fm
Middle Hall
95
Garn Dwad
Ty-gwyn
Y Foel
Gilfach
Llwynbrain
Gwarafog Ho
Cwmrhybin
441 Moelfre
Llanddewi'r Cwm
Pwllgwyn
Pantypyllau
Ysgiog
Gwar-henallt
Cefnhirog Fm
Court Fm
Pen y Ddinas
Llanwrtyd
Tynycoed Fm
Pennau
450
452
Maesmynis
B4567
B4519

Felindre
Bettws-y-crwyn
Clun
Clunton
Beguildy
Gwerneirin
Quabbs
Churchbank
Llanbadarn Fynydd
Dutlas
Upper Treverward
Hobarris
Rhydmoelddu
Purlogue
New Invention
Chapel Lawn
Llanfair Waterdine
Knucklas
Skyborry Green
Stowe
Llanbister
Crug
Milebrook
Knighton (Tref-y-Clawdd)
Llangunllo
Rhos-y-meirch
Llandewi Ystradenny
Bleddfa
Monaughty
Pilleth
Dolau
Whitton
Norton
Llanfihangel Rhydithon
Cascob
Dolley Green
Radnor Forest
Fforest Faesyfed
Fron
Maes-Treylow
Stapleton
Penybont
Discoed
Beggar's Bush
Presteigne (Llanandras)
Llandegley
P O W Y S
Kinnerton
Evenjobb
Rodd
Nash
Knill
New Radnor (Maesyfed)
Walton
Titley
Old Radnor
Yardro
Burlingjobb
Flintsham
Stanner
Llanfihangel-nant-Melan
Dolyhir
Kington
Lyonshall
Frank's Bridge
Upper Hergest
Lower Hergest
Llansantffraed-in-Elvel
Hundred House
Gladestry
Kingswood
Huntington
Hengoed
Colva
Glascwm
Cregrina
Newchurch
Michaelchurch on Arrow
Lower Welson
Eardisley
Rhulen
Bryngwyn
Brilley
Millhalf
Llanbadarn-y-Garreg
A483
A488
A44
A481
A4113
A4112
A4111
B4356
B4355
B4372
B4362
B4357
B4594
B4368
Glyndwr's Way
0 1 2 3 miles
0 1 2 3 4 5 km

SHROPSHIRE HILLS
HEREFORDSHIRE
Aston on Clun
Little Brampton
Purslow
Clunbury
Twitchen
Hopton Castle
Hoptonheath
Bedstone
Bucknell
Buckton
Walford
Brampton Bryan
Letton
Birtley
Lingen
Limebrook
Kinsham
Byton
Combe Moor
Stokesay
Broome
Norton
Culmington
Vernolds Common
Onibury
Aldon
Brandhill
Clungunford
Abcott
Shelderton
Marlow
Lower Todding
Todding
Leintwardine
Kinton
Whitton
Downton on the Rock
Burrington
Bromfield
Old Field
Bringewood Forge
Lady Halton
Priors Halton
Ludlow
Ludford
Stanton Lacy
Middleton
Henley
Rockgreen
Snitton
Farden
Cleedownton
Hayton's Bent
Hopton Cangeford
Bitterley
Cleeton St Mary
Knowbury
Cleehill
Hints
Hope Bagot
Knowle
Caynham
Whitton
Steventon
Overton
Ashford Bowdler
Ashford Carbonell
Middleton
Greete
Burford
Tenbury Wells
Boraston
Nash
Little Hereford
Gosford
Woofferton
Brimfield
Richards Castle
Orleton
Comberton
Aston
Elton
Adforton
Wigmore
Leinthall Starkes
Leinthall Earls
Yatton
Ongar Street
Lower Lye
Aymestrey
Mortimer's Cross
Lucton
Yarpole
Bircher
Croft
Eye
Moreton
Ashton
Middleton on the Hill
St Michaels
Berrington
Leysters Pole
Kimbolton
Stockton
Grafton
Pudleston
Hatfield
Luston
Eyton
Lugg Green
Shobdon
Ledicot
Kingsland
Cobnash
Staunton on Arrow
Shirl Heath
Cholstrey
Lawton
Leominster
Barons Cross
Eaton
Eardisland
Pembridge
Monkland
Ivington
Ivington Green
Stoke Prior
Humber
Docklow
Steen's Bridge
Grendon Green
Bredenbury
Marston
Bearwood
Luntley
Sollers Dilwyn
Dilwyn
Broxwood
Haven
Brierley
Wharton
Risbury
Marston Stannett
Aulden
Birley
Knapton Green
Upper Hill
Marlbrook
Newton
Hegdon Hill
Pencombe
Bowley
Hope under Dinmore
Bodenham
Bodenham Moor
Maund Bryan
Little Cowarne
Weobley
Weobley Marsh
Sarnesfield
Ledgemoor
King's Pyon
Westhope
Bush Bank
Canon Pyon
Wellington
Ullingswick
Felton
Moreton Jeffries
Norton
A49
A44
A456
A4110
A4112
A417
A4113
A4117
A4361

SHROPSHIRE
Cleedownton
Bromdon
Farlow
Oreton
Prescott
Bagginswood
Knowle Hill
Kinlet
SEVERN VALLEY RAILWAY
Shatterford
Kingsford
Blakeshall
BODENHAM ARBORETUM & EARTH CENTRE
ARLEY ARBORETUM & GARDENS
Upper Arley
Silvington
Catherton
Clee Hill
Cleeton St Mary
Titterstone Clee
Hoptonbank
Neen Savage
Buttonoak
Pound Green
Trimpley
Habberley
Low Habberley
Fairfield
Wolverley
Franche
Kidderminster
Foxwood
Doddington
Hopton Wafers
Cleobury Mortimer
Hollywaste
Wyre Forest
WYRE FOREST
Wribbenhall
Bewdley
Blakebrook
Foley Park
WEST MIDLAND SAFARI PARK
Lem Hill
Far Forest
Fingerpost
Cleehill
Hints
Knowle
Coreley
Milson
Bayton
Pound Bank
Callow Hill
Ribbesford
Blackstone
Summerfield
Bliss Gate
Bayton Common
Wilden
Neen Sollars
Nash
Mamble
Clows Top
Rock
Stourport-on-Severn
Heightington
Hartlebury
Areley Kings
Boraston
Knighton on Teme
Newnham Bridge
Frith Common
Pensax
Astley Cross
Dunley
Waresley
Burford
Tenbury Wells
Rochford
Lower Rochford
Upper Rochford
Lindridge
Eardiston
Stockton on Teme
Abberley
Astley
Lincomb
Crossway Green
Orleton
Hanley William
Stanford on Teme
Great Witley
Highwood
Broad Heath
Stanford Bridge
Kingswood Common
Noutard's Green
Frog Pool
Dunhampton
Sytchampton
Hanley Child
Witley Court
Shrawley
Uphampton
Ombersley
Kyre Park
Stoke Bliss
Sweet Green
Upper Sapey
Sapey Common
Shelsley Walsh
Shelsley Beauchamp
Little Witley
Holt Heath
Holt Fleet
Holt
Bank Street
Clifton upon Teme
Harpley
High Lane
Wolferlow
Collington
Thornbury
Hatfield
Grimley
Sinton Green
Wichenford
Martley
Tedstone Wafer
Tedstone Delamere
Edvin Loach
Edwyn Ralph
Berrow Green
Horsham
Moseley
Hallow
Shoulton
Grendon Green
Whitbourne
Ankerdine Hill
Doddenham
Broad Green
Lower Broadheath
Upper Broadheath
ELGAR'S BIRTHPLACE MUSEUM
BROCKHAMPTON ESTATE
Bromyard
Bromyard Downs
Sapey Bridge
Knightwick
Lulsley
Broadwas
Worcester
Bringsty Common
Hegdon Hill
Linley Green
Suckley Knowl
Alfrick
Leigh
Brockamin
Bransford
St John's
Rushwick
Pencombe
Alfrick Pound
MALVERN HILLS
Suckley
Stanford Bishop
Little Cowarne
Munderfield Row
Munderfield Stocks
Acton Beauchamp
Longley Green
Old Storridge Common
Leigh Sinton
Powick
Bowling Green
Ullingswick
Stoke Lacy
Acton Green
Pole Elm
Callow End
Storridge
Malvern
Newland
Stanbrook
Bishops Frome
Evesbatch
Ridgeway
0 1 2 3 miles
0 1 2 3 4 5 km

WORCESTERSHIRE
Hagley
West Hagley
Hagley Park
Churchill
Stakenbridge
Blakedown
Broome
Holy Cross
Clent
Clent Hills
Romsley
Rumbow Cottages
Walton Pool
Dayhouse Bank
Hunnington
Lower Illey
Illey
Frankley Services
Woodgate
Kitwell
Frankley
Frankley Green
Weoley Castle
Griffins Hill
Shenley Fields
Bournville
Selly Manor
Cadbury World
Stirchley
Ten Acres
King's Heath
Alcester Lane's End
Yardley Wood
Billesley
Northfield
King's Norton
Lifford
Brandwood End
Highter's Heath
Warstock
Solihull Lodge
Walker's Heath
Turves Green
Longbridge
West Heath
Rednal
Cofton Hackett
Cofton Common
Rubery
Eachway
Beacon Hill
Lickey
Lickey Hills
Lydiate Ash
Hawkesley
Wast Hills
Wast Hill Tunnel
Hollywood
Major's Green
Shirley Heath
Whitlock's End
Trueman's Heath
Drakes Cross
Bateman's Green
Silver Street
Grimes Hill
Tidbury Green
Wythall
The Transport Museum Wythall
Headley Heath
Forhill
Lea End
Hopwood
Hopwood Park Services
Arrowfield Top
Weatheroak Hill
Inkford
Birch Acre
Tanner's Green
Forshaw Heath
Terry's Green
Portway
Hob Hill
Ladbrook Hall
Wood End
Gilbert's Green
Aspley Heath
Branson's Cross
Carpenter's Hill
Heath Green
Rowney Green
Alvechurch
Withybed Green
Cobley Hill
Apes Dale
Blackwell
Linthurst
Burcot
Lickey End
Hall Flat
Catshill
Marlbrook
Staple Hill
Bellevue
Upper Catshill
Barnt Green
Fairfield
Wildmoor
Madeley Heath
Bell End
Bell Heath
The Gutter
Chapman's Hill
Waseley Hills
Belbroughton
Hackman's Gate
Drayton
Hartle
Broom Hill
Woodrow
Harvington
Harvington Hall
Stone
Stone House Cottage Garden
Stanklyn
Mustow Green
Shenstone
Bluntington
Tanwood
Chaddesley Corbett
Chaddesley Woods
Woodcote Green
Dodford
Alfred's Well
Worms Ash
Bournheath
Dordale
Brockencote
Cakebole
Rushock
Park Gate
Timberhonger
Perryfields
Sidemoor
Slideslow
Tutnall
Broad Green
Short Wood Tunnel
Stoney Hill
Aston Fields
Charford
Finstall
Bromsgrove
St Godwalds
Upper Gambolds
Stoke Heath
Stoke Prior
Stoke Pound
Avoncroft Museum of Historic Buildings
Upton Warren
Elmley Lovett
Cutnall Green
Broad Common
Broad Alley
Bryan's Green
Cooksey Green
Cooksey Corner
Elmbridge
Doverdale
Hampton Lovett
Crutch Hill
Wychbold
Rashwood
Henbrook
Astwood
Sharpway Gate
Piper's Hill
Harbours Hill
Stoke Wharf
Woodgate
Bentley
Upper Bentley
Lower Bentley
Foster's Green
Fosters Green Meadows
Forest Hill
Hanbury
Hanbury Hall
Tardebigge
Webheath
Foxlydiate
Batchley
Redditch
Smallwood
Riverside
Enfield
Forge Mill Needle Museum
Church Hill
Moon's Moat
Holt End
Beoley
Pink Green
Trap's Green
Gorcott Hill
Winyates Green
Arrow Valley
Southcrest
Lodge Park
Ipsley
Matchborough
Washford
Mappleborough Green
Headless Cross
Woodrow
Greenlands
Crabbs Cross
Hunt End
Elcock's Brook
Mount Pleasant
Ham Green
Cruise Hill
Green Lane
Studley
Morton Bagot
Dagtail End
Astwood Bank
Littlewood Green
Middletown
Sambourne
Feckenham
Shurnock
Bradley Green
Noah's Green
Berrow Hill
Droitwich Spa
Witton
Westlands
Berry Hill
Hill End
Salwarpe
Chawson
Copcut
Primsland
Newland Common
Hadzor
Shernal Green
Goosehill Green
Mere Green
Woolmere Green
Gallows Green
Broughton Green
Dunhampstead
Saleway
Phepson
Shell
Himbleton
Earl's Common
White Cottage
Stock Green
Stock Wood
Morton Underhill
Holberrow Green
Edgiock
New End
Coughton
Coughton Court
Cladswell
Cookhill
Knowle Fields
Dormston
Little Inkberrow
Inkberrow
Stonepits
Knighton
Alcester
Oversley Green
Arrow
Ragley Hall
Weethley
Ladywood
Martin Hussingtree
Brownheath Common
Oddingley
Tibberton
Sale Green
Neight Hill
Huddington
Grafton Flyford
The Bourne
Kington
Crowle
Crowle Green
Moor End
Fernhill Heath
Hindlip
Lower Town
Sixways Stadium
Astwood
Blackpole
Brickfields
Warndon
Trotshill
Tolladine
Rainbow Hill
Ronkswood
The Commandery
Red Hill
Cherry Orchard
Whittington
St Peter the Great
Spetchley
Spetchley Park & Gardens
Sneachill
Broughton Hackett
Bredicot
Upton Snodsbury
Churchill
North Piddle
Flyford Flavell
Abberton
Radford
Abbots Morton
Rous Lench
Goom's Hill
Weethley Gate
Wood Bevington
Dunnington
Cock Bevington
Iron Cross
Wixford
Broom
Exhall
Little Britain
White Ladies Aston
Naunton Beauchamp
Bishampton
Ab Lench
Church Lench
Atch Lench
Salford Priors
Abbots Salford
Marlcliff
Bidford-on-Avon
Barton
Cleeve Prior
Greystones
Bickmarsh
Harvington
Harvington Cross
Norton
Wood Hall
Worcestershire Parkway
Egdon
Upper Wolverton
Lower Wolverton
Peopleton
Littleworth
Hatfield
Kempsey
Brook End
Green Street
Napleton
Stonehall
Hawbridge
Wadborough
Drake's Broughton
Walcot
Pinvin
Throckmorton
Pershore Airfield (disused)
Sheriff's Lench
Badger's Hill
Hill Furze
Stonebow

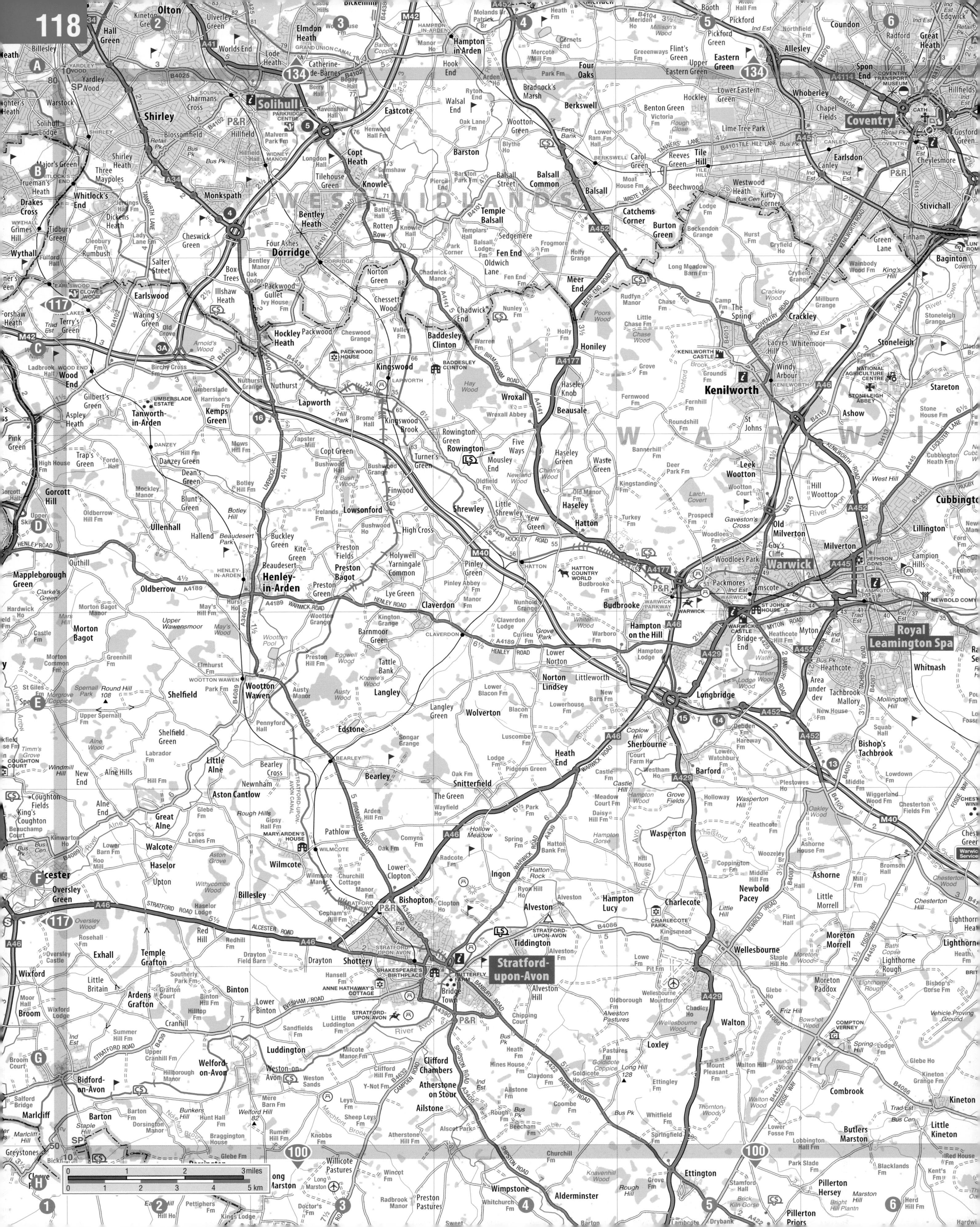

Olton
Hall Green
Elmdon Heath
Hampton in Arden
Meriden
Booth
Pickford
Coundon
Radford
Great Heath
Edgwick
Billesley
Worlds End
Lode Heath
Catherine-de-Barnes
Hook End
Four Oaks
Flint's Green
Eastern Green
Allesley
Spon End
Yardley Wood
Warstock
Solihull
Shirley
Sharmans Cross
Blossomfield
Eastcote
Walsal End
Bradnock's Marsh
Berkswell
Benton Green
Lower Eastern Green
Whoberley
Chapel Fields
Coventry
Hillfields
Solihull Lodge
Copt Heath
Barston
Wootton Green
Carol Green
Reeves Green
Tile Hill
Lime Tree Park
Earlsdon
Canley
Cheylesmore
Gosford Green
Major's Green
Shirley Heath
Three Maypoles
Trueman's Heath
Drakes Cross
Whitlock's End
Monkspath
Tilehouse Green
Knowle
Balsall Street
Balsall Common
Balsall
Westwood Heath
Kirby Corner
Stivichall
Bentley Heath
WEST MIDLANDS
Temple Balsall
Catchems Corner
Burton Green
Grimes Hill
Tidbury Green
Dickens Heath
Cheswick Green
Four Ashes
Dorridge
Rotten Row
Sedgemere
Fen End
Oldwich Lane
Finham
Green Lane
Baginton
Wythall
Salter Street
Box Trees
Norton Green
Meer End
Earlswood
Illshaw Heath
Packwood Gullet
Chessetts Wood
Chadwick End
Nunley Fm
Rudfyn Manor
Camp Fm
The Spring
Crackley
Terry's Green
Waring's Green
Hockley Heath
Packwood
Baddesley Clinton
Honiley
Kenilworth Castle
Ladyes Hill
Whitemoor
Stoneleigh
Wood End
Kingswood
Lapworth
Nuthurst
Umberslade
Kemps Green
Tanworth-in-Arden
Wroxall
Haseley Knob
Beausale
Windy Arbour
Kenilworth
Stareton
National Agriculture Centre
Stoneleigh Abbey
Ashow
Aspley Heath
Gilbert's Green
Rowington Green
Rowington
Five Ways
Mousley End
Haseley Green
Waste Green
St Johns
Leek Wootton
Pink Green
Danzey Green
Copt Green
Turner's Green
WARWI
Gorcott Hill
Dean's Green
Blunt's Green
Finwood
Shrewley
Haseley
Hatton
Hill Wootton
Ullenhall
Lowsonford
Little Shrewley
Yew Green
Old Milverton
Lillington
Cubbington
Hallend
Buckley Green
High Cross
Guy's Cliffe
Milverton
Mappleborough Green
Oldberrow
Beaudesert
Henley-in-Arden
Preston Fields
Kite Green
Preston Bagot
Holywell
Yarningale Common
Pinley Green
Woodloes Park
Warwick
Packmores
Emscote
Campion Hills
Morton Bagot
Lye Green
Claverdon
Budbrooke
Hampton on the Hill
Myton
Royal Leamington Spa
Whitnash
Barnmoor Green
Lower Norton
Bridge End
Heathcote
Tattle Bank
Norton Lindsey
Littleworth
Longbridge
Tachbrook Mallory
Shelfield
Wootton Wawen
Langley
Wolverton
Sherbourne
Bishop's Tachbrook
Edstone
Heath End
Barford
Little Alne
New End
Bearley Cross
Bearley
Snitterfield
The Green
Aston Cantlow
Newnham
Great Alne
Walcote
Pathlow
Wasperton
Ashorne
Haselor
Wilmcote
Lower Clopton
Ingon
Newbold Pacey
Upton
Alcester
Oversley Green
Billesley
Bishopton
Alveston
Hampton Lucy
Charlecote
Little Morrell
Red Hill
Exhall
Temple Grafton
Drayton
Shottery
Stratford-upon-Avon
Tiddington
Wellesbourne
Moreton Morrell
Lighthorne
Lighthorne Heath
Wixford
Little Britain
Ardens Grafton
Binton
Lower Binton
Bridge Town
Alveston Hill
Walton
Moreton Paddox
Broom
Cranhill
Luddington
Loxley
Compton Verney
Welford-on-Avon
Weston-on-Avon
Clifford Chambers
Atherstone on Stour
Combrook
Kineton
Bidford-on-Avon
Marlcliff
Barton
Ailstone
Little Kineton
Butlers Marston
Greystones
Ettington
Pillerton Hersey
Wimpstone
Alderminster
Preston Pastures
Pillerton Priors
Long Marston
0 1 2 3 miles
0 1 2 3 4 5 km

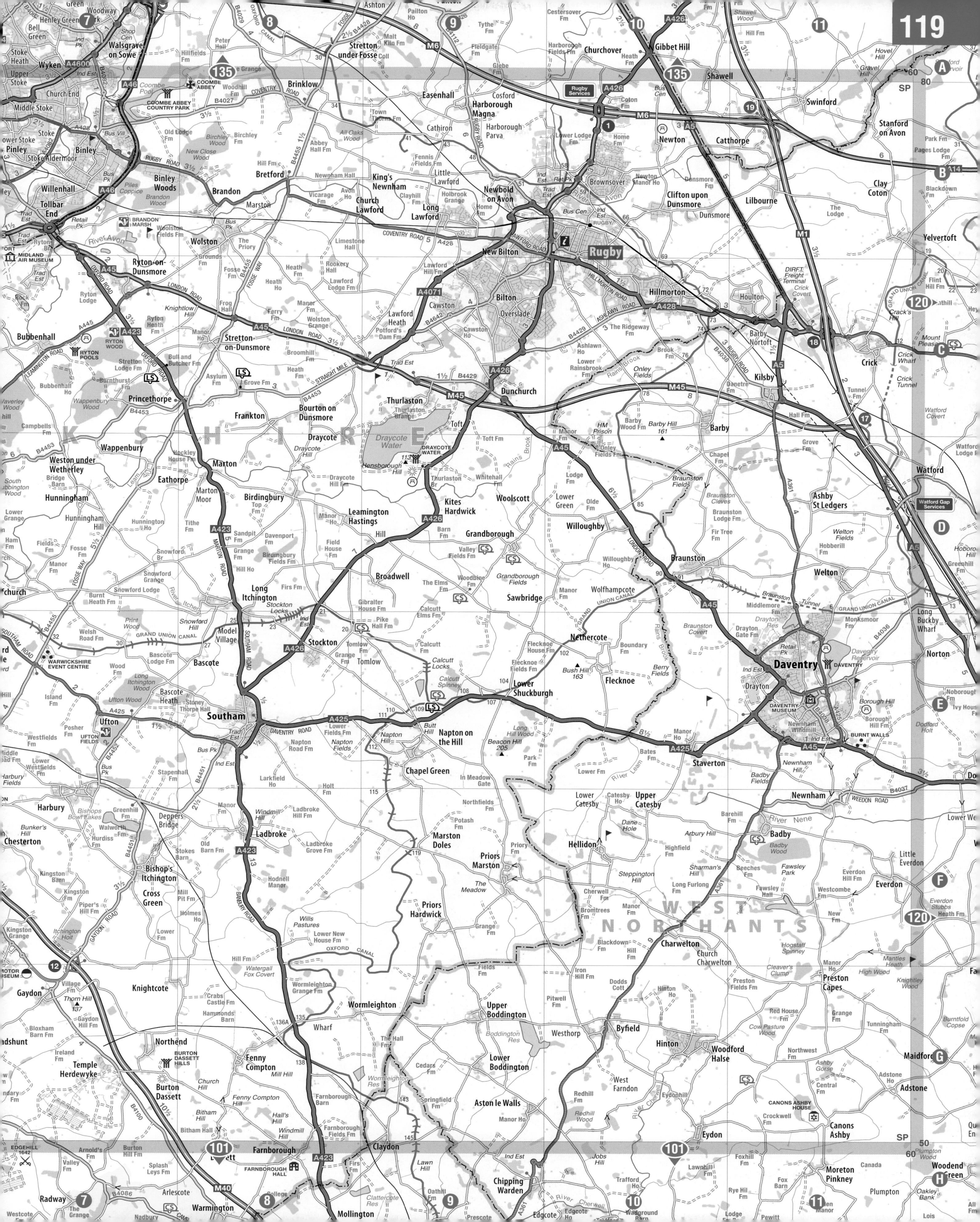

Henley Green
Woodway
Bell Green
Stoke Heath
Walsgrave on Sowe
Wyken
Upper Stoke
Church End
Middle Stoke
Stoke
Pinley
Binley
Stoke Aldermoor
Willenhall
Tollbar End
Binley Woods
Brandon
Brinklow
Stretton under Fosse
Easenhall
Harborough Magna
Harborough Parva
Cathiron
Churchover
Gibbet Hill
Shawell
Swinford
Stanford on Avon
Newton
Catthorpe
Coombe Abbey Country Park
Bretford
King's Newnham
Church Lawford
Little Lawford
Long Lawford
Newbold on Avon
Brownsover
Clifton upon Dunsmore
Lilbourne
Clay Coton
Dunsmore
Wolston
Ryton-on-Dunsmore
Rugby
New Bilton
Bilton
Overslade
Hillmorton
Houlton
Yelvertoft
Midland Air Museum
Cawston
Lawford Heath
Bubbenhall
Stretton-on-Dunsmore
Barby Nortoft
Kilsby
Crick
Princethorpe
Frankton
Bourton on Dunsmore
Thurlaston
Dunchurch
Toft
Barby
Draycote
Draycote Water
Wappenbury
Weston under Wetherley
Eathorpe
Marton
Hunningham
Birdingbury
Leamington Hastings
Kites Hardwick
Woolscott
Willoughby
Watford
Ashby St Ledgers
Grandborough
Broadwell
Braunston
Welton
Sawbridge
Long Itchington
Stockton
Nethercote
Flecknoe
Model Village
Bascote
Daventry
Norton
Drayton
Southam
Ufton
Lower Shuckburgh
Napton on the Hill
Chapel Green
Staverton
Newnham
Harbury
Deppers Bridge
Ladbroke
Marston Doles
Priors Marston
Hellidon
Upper Catesby
Lower Catesby
Badby
Little Everdon
Everdon
Chesterton
Bishop's Itchington
Cross Green
Priors Hardwick
WEST NORTHANTS
Charwelton
Church Charwelton
Preston Capes
Gaydon
Knightcote
Wormleighton
Upper Boddington
Byfield
Hinton
Woodford Halse
Maidford
Northend
Fenny Compton
Temple Herdewyke
Lower Boddington
West Farndon
Adstone
Burton Dassett
Aston le Walls
Canons Ashby
Eydon
Farnborough
Claydon
Chipping Warden
Moreton Pinkney
Woodend Green
Radway
Arlescote
Warmington
Mollington
Edgcote
Plumpton
M6
M1
M45
M40
A45
A423
A426
A425
A428
A5
A361
Grand Union Canal
Oxford Canal
River Avon
River Nene

WEST NORTHANTS
Northampton
Welford
Naseby
Clipston
Arthingworth
Rothwell
Kelmarsh
Harrington
Orton
Thorpe Malsor
Loddington
Stanford on Avon
Clay Coton
Elkington
Cold Ashby
Haselbech
Maidwell
Draughton
Great Cransley
Little Cransley
Mawsley
Broughton
Yelvertoft
Thornby
Winwick
Lamport
Hanging Houghton
Cottesbrooke
Old
Scaldwell
Walgrave
Crick
West Haddon
Guilsborough
Coton
Hollowell
Creaton
Little Creaton
Brixworth
Hannington
Ravensthorpe
Teeton
Spratton
Holcot
Watford
Watford Gap Services
Holdenby
East Haddon
Pitsford
Long Buckby
Sywell
Mears Ashby
Chapel Brampton
Church Brampton
Boughton
Moulton
Overstone
Great Brington
Little Brington
Whilton
Whilton Locks
Long Buckby Wharf
Harlestone
Norton
Muscott
Brockhall
Nobottle
New Duston
Dallington
Kingsthorpe
Queen's Park
Kingsley Park
Moulton Park
Boothville
Spinney Hill
Great Billing
Little Billing
Ecton
Ecton Brook
Weston Favell
Abington
Abington Vale
Duston
Harpole
Dodford
Flore
Upton
Kislingbury
Lower Weedon
Upper Weedon
Weedon Bec
Road Weedon
Upper Heyford
Nether Heyford
Briar Hill
Far Cotton
Delapre Abbey
Hardingstone
Great Houghton
Little Houghton
Brafield-on-the-Green
Cogenhoe
Denton
Little Everdon
Church Stowe
Upper Stowe
Bugbrooke
Rothersthorpe
Milton Malsor
Collingtree
Wootton
Shelfleys
Northampton Services
Farthingstone
Litchborough
Pattishall
Grimscote
Cold Higham
Astcote
Eastcote
Gayton
Blisworth
Courteenhall
Grange Park
Quinton
Preston Deanery
Hackleton
Piddington
Horton
Maidford
Adstone
Tiffield
Roade
Caldecote
Duncote
Blakesley
Quinbury End
Shutlanger
Hulcote
Ashton
Hartwell
Stoke Bruerne
Towcester
Greens Norton
Eakley Lanes
Ravenstone
Salcey Forest
Stoke Goldington
Long Street
Plumpton
Canada
Cinch Stadium at Franklins Gdns
Sixfields Stadium
Hunsbury Hill
Billing Aquadrome
Northamptonshire Ironstone Railway Trust
Northampton & Lamport Railway
Holdenby House and Icarus Falconry
Coton Manor Gardens
Cottesbrooke Hall & Gardens
Lamport Hall
Althorp
Old Dairy Farm Country Shopping & Craft Centre
Canal Museum
Stoke Park Pavilions
Pitsford Water
Naseby Reservoir
Hollowell Reservoir
Ravensthorpe Reservoir
Stanford Reservoir
Sywell Reservoir
Grand Union Canal
River Nene
Blisworth Tunnel
0 1 2 3 miles
0 1 2 3 4 5 km

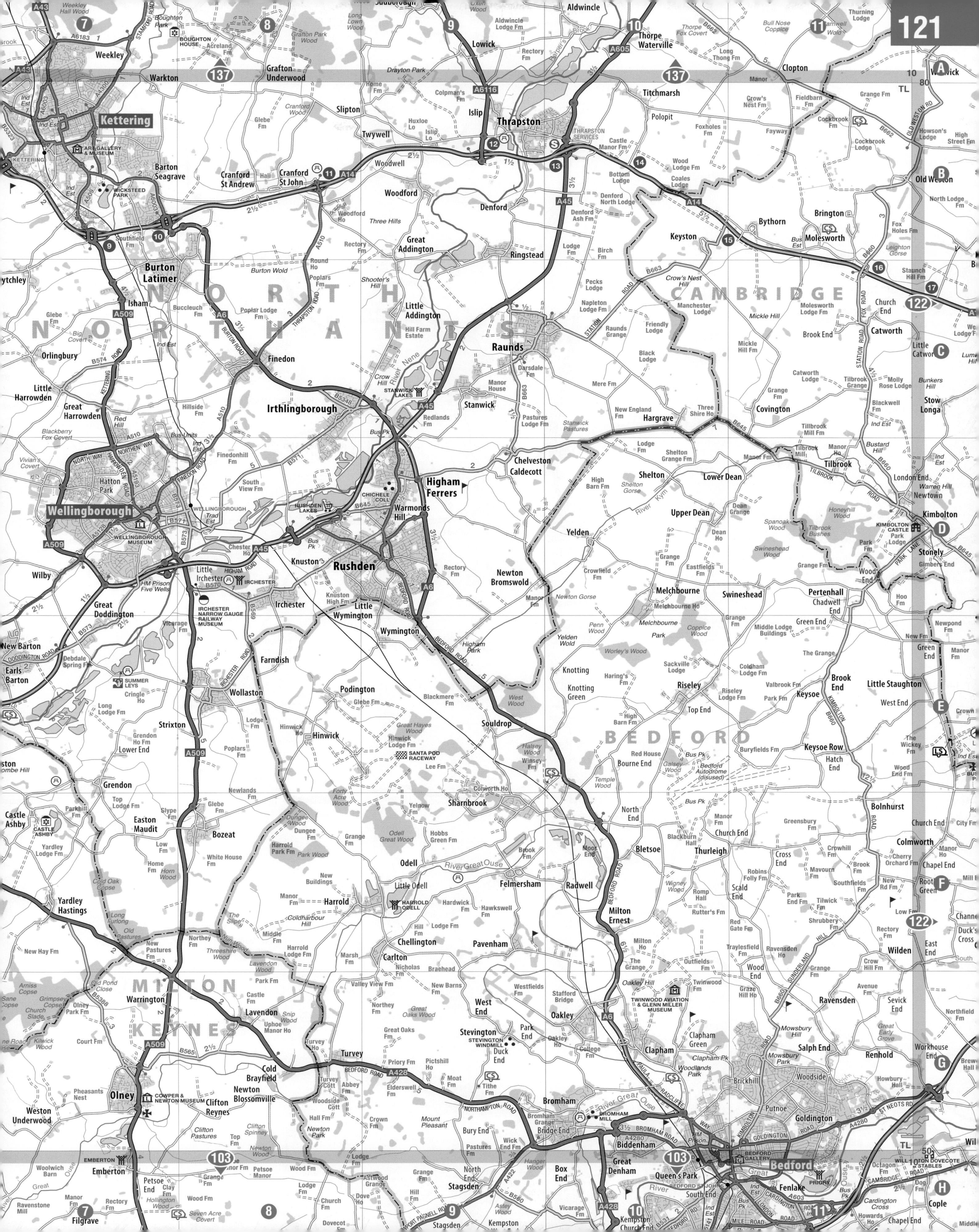
Weekley Hall Wood
Boughton Park
BOUGHTON HOUSE
Acreland Fm
Grafton Park Wood
Long Lown Wood
Oxen Wood
Aldwincle
Aldwincle Lodge Fm
Lowick
Rectory Fm
Thorpe Waterville
Thorpe Fox Covert
Long Thong Fm
Bull Nose Coppice
Thurning Lodge
Weekley
Warkton
Grafton Underwood
Drayton Park
Clopton
Kettering
Home Fm
Colpman's Fm
Islip
Titchmarsh
Crow's Nest Fm
Fieldbarn Fm
Grange Fm
Cranford Wood
Slipton
Thrapston
Polopit
Glebe Fm
Twywell
Huxloe Lo
Slip Lo
THRAPSTON SERVICES
Foxholes Fm
Fayway
Cockbrook Fm
Cockbrook Lodge
Howson's Lodge
High Street Fm
ART GALLERY & MUSEUM
Castle Manor Fm
Woodwell
Wood Lodge Fm
Barton Seagrave
Cranford St Andrew
Hall
Cranford St John
Bottom Lodge
Coales Lodge
Old Weston
WICKSTEED PARK
Woodford
Denford
Denford North Lodge
North Lodge Fm
Woodford Ho
Three Hills
Denford Ash Fm
Bythorn
Brington
Southfield Fm
Great Addington
Rectory Fm
Ringstead
Lodge Fm
Birch Fm
Keyston
Bus Est
Molesworth
Fox Holes Fm
Leighton Gorse
Burton Latimer
Round Ho
Burton Wold
Poplars Fm
Shooter's Hill
Pecks Lodge
Crow's Nest Hill
Staunch Hill Fm
ytchley
Isham
Buccleuch Fm
Poplar Lodge Fm
Little Addington
Napleton Lodge Fm
Manchester Lodge
Mickle Hill
Molesworth Lodge Fm
Church End
CAMBRIDGE
NORTH
NORTHANTS
Glebe Fm
Big Covert
Hill Farm Estate
Raunds
Raunds Grange
Friendly Lodge
Brook End
Catworth
Orlingbury
Finedon
Black Lodge
Mickle Hill Fm
Little Catworth
Darsdale Fm
Bunkers Hill
Little Harrowden
Crow Hill
River Nene
STANWICK LAKES
Manor House
Mere Fm
Catworth Lodge
Tilbrook Grange
Molly Rose Lodge
Stow Longa
Great Harrowden
Hillside Fm
Irthlingborough
Stanwick
Grange Fm
Blackwell Fm
Redlands Fm
Pastures Lodge Fm
Stanwick Pastures
New England Fm
Hargrave
Three Shire Ho
Covington
Ind Est
Red Hill
Blackberry Fox Covert
Bus Pk
Tillbrook Mill Fm
Bustard Hill
Vivian's Covert
Finedonhill Fm
Chelveston
Caldecott
Lodge Fm
Shelton Grange Fm
Manor Fm
Tilbrook Mill
Tilbrook
London End
Hatton Park
South View Fm
Higham Ferrers
High Barn Fm
Shelton
Shelton Gorse
Lower Dean
Warren Hill
Newtown
CHICHELE COLL
River Kym
Dean Grange
Honeyhill Wood
Kimbolton
Wellingborough
WELLINGBOROUGH
RUSHDEN LAKES
Warmonds Hill
Upper Dean
Spanoak Wood
KIMBOLTON CASTLE
Park Lodge
WELLINGBOROUGH MUSEUM
Trad Est
Yelden
Dean Ho
Tilbrook Bushes
Swineshead Wood
Park Fm
Stonely
Gimbers End
Chester Ho
Bus Pk
Grange Fm
Eastfields Fm
Grange Fm
Wilby
Little Irchester
Knuston
Rushden
Rectory Fm
Newton Bromswold
Crowfield Fm
Wood End
HM Prison Five Wells
IRCHESTER
Melchbourne
Swineshead
Pertenhall
Chadwell End
Hoo Fm
Great Doddington
IRCHESTER NARROW GAUGE RAILWAY MUSEUM
Irchester
Knuston High Fm
Little Wymington
Manor Fm
Newton Gorse
Melchbourne Ho
Green End
Newpond Fm
Vicarage Fm
Wymington
Penn Wood
Melchbourne Park
Grange Fm
Middle Lodge Buildings
Coppice Wood
New Barton
Yelden Wold
New Fm
Green End
Manor Fm
Earls Barton
Debdale Spring Fm
Farndish
Higham Park
Worley's Wood
The Grange
Knotting
Haring's Fm
Sackville Lodge
Coldham Lodge Fm
SUMMER LEYS
Cringle Ho
Wollaston
Podington
Glebe Fm
Blackmere Fm
Knotting Green
Riseley
Riseley Lodge Fm
Valbrook Fm
Park Fm
Brook End
Keysoe
Little Staughton
West End
Long Lodge Fm
Strixton
Lodge Fm
Hinwick Ho
Great Hayes Wood
West Wood
Souldrop
High Barn Fm
Top End
Hinwick
Hinwick Lodge Fm
SANTA POD RACEWAY
BEDFORD
Buryfields Fm
Keysoe Row
Hatch End
Grendon Ho Fm
Lower End
Poplars Fm
Lee Fm
Halsey Wood
Winsey Fm
Red House
Bourne End
Galsey Wood
Bedford Autodrome (disused)
Wood End Fm
Grendon
Newlands Fm
Forty Acre Wood
Colworth Ho
Temple Wood
Castle Ashby
CASTLE ASHBY
Top Lodge Fm
Parkhill Fm
Easton Maudit
Slype Fm
Glebe Fm
Yelnow Wood
Sharnbrook
North End
Bolnhurst
Yardley Lodge Fm
Bozeat
Dungee Wood
Dungee Fm
Grange Fm
Odell Great Wood
Hobbs Green Fm
Manor Fm
Church End
Blackburn Hall
Greensbury Fm
Church End
Low Fm
Harrold Park Fm
Park Wood
Brook Fm
Moor End
Bletsoe
Thurleigh
Cross End
Crowhill Fm
Colmworth
Home Fm
White House Fm
Horn Wood
Odell
River Great Ouse
Cherry Orchard Fm
Chapel End
Cold Oak Copse
New Buildings
Felmersham
Radwell
Robins Folly Fm
Mavourn Fm
Brook Fm
Southfields Fm
Roots Green
Yardley Hastings
Little Odell
Wigney Wood
Scald End
Manor Fm
Harrold
HARROLD ODELL
Hardwick Fm
Hawkswell Fm
Milton Ernest
Romp Hall
Park End Fm
Tilwick Fm
New Rd Fm
Long Furlong
The Slipe
Coldharbour Hill
Rutter's Fm
Shrubbery Fm
Low Fm
Old Pastures
Middle Fm
Hill Fm
Lodge Fm
Red Gate Fm
Rectory Fm
New Hay Fm
New Pastures Fm
Northey Fm
Threeshire Wood
Chellington
Pavenham
Milton Ho
Traylesfield Fm
Ravensden Ho
Wilden
East End
Harrold Lodge Fm
Marsh Fm
Carlton
The Grange
Outfields Fm
Wood End
Grange Fm
Crow Hill Fm
MILTON
Lavendon Wood
Nicholas Fm
Braehead
Oakley Hill
Twinwood Fm
Grange Fm
Arniss Copse
Old Pond Close
Park Fm
Valley View Fm
New Barns Fm
Westfields Fm
TWINWOOD AVIATION & GLENN MILLER MUSEUM
Graze Hill Ho
Avenue Fm
Grimpsey Copse
Church Slade
Olney Park Fm
Warrington
Castle Fm
Northey Fm
Great Oaks Wood
West End
Stafford Bridge
Oakley
Ravensden
Sevick End
Northfield Fm
Lavendon
Snip Wood
KEYNES
Uphoe Manor Ho
Great Oaks Fm
Stevington
STEVINGTON WINDMILL
Park End
Oakley Ho
Clapham
Clapham Green
Mowsbury Hill
Salph End
Great Early Grove
Renhold
Kilwick Wood
Court Fm
Turvey Ho
Priory Fm
Pictshill Fm
Duck End
College Fm
Clapham Pk
Mowsbury Park
Workhouse End
Turvey
Woodlands Park
Brickhill
Woodside
Cold Brayfield
Turvey Cott
Abbey Fm
Moat Fm
Tithe Fm
Howbury Hall
Newton Blossomville
Elderswell Fm
Pheasants Nest
Olney
COWPER & NEWTON MUSEUM
Clifton Reynes
Woodside Cott
Bromham
Putnoe
Goldington
Weston Underwood
Hall Fm
Crown Fm
Mount Pleasant
Bromham Grange
BROMHAM MILL
Bridge End
Newton Park
Clifton Pastures
Clifton Spinney
Top Fm
Bury End
Pastures Fm
Wick End Fm
Biddenham
HM Prison
BEDFORD GALLERY
Bedford
Newton Wood
Lodge Fm
Hanger Wood
Great Denham
Queen's Park
WILL 1O DOVECOTE & STABLES
Woolwich Barn
EMBERTON
Emberton
Manor Fm
Petsoe Manor
Wood Fm
Grange Fm
North End
Box End
Octagon Fm
Petsoe End
Clay Fm
Hollington Wood
Astwood Grange
Stagsden
Ind Est
Fenlake
PRIORY
Oog Fm
Ravenstone Mill
Manor Fm
Rectory Fields
Wood Fm
Lodge Fm
Church Fm
Dove Ho
Hill Fm
Astey Wood
South End
Cardington Cross
Cople
Filgrave
Seven Acre Covert
Dovecot
Stagsden
Vicarage Fm
Kempston
Kempston Church End
Howards Fm
Chapel End
Green End
Manor Fm
Mill Fm
Ind Est
Hatch
Little Staughton
Stonely
Channel End
Duck's Cross
Wilden

Little Gidding
Steeple Gidding
Winwick
Hamerton Zoo Park
Hamerton
Monks Wood
Wood Walton
Great Raveley
Little Raveley
Wistow
Warboys
Fenton
Pidley
138
Wennington
Abbots Ripton
Broughton
Kings Ripton
Old Hurst
Woodhurst
Raptor Foundation
Upton
Alconbury Weald
Alconbury Airfield (disused)
Alconbury Weston
Alconbury
Buckworth
Old Weston
Barham
Leighton Bromswold
Woolley
Little Stukeley
Great Stukeley
Owl End
Sapley
Huntingdon
Hartford
Wyton
Houghton
St Ives
Hemingford Abbots
Hemingford Grey
Norris Museum
The Manor
Needingworth
Holywell
Cromwell Mus
Hinchingbrooke House
Brampton
Brampton Park
Brampton Hut Services
Godmanchester
Wood Green Animal Shelter
Fen Drayton Lakes
Fenstanton
Galley Hill
Fen Drayton
Catworth
Little Catworth
Spaldwick
Easton
Ellington
Ellington Thorpe
Stow Longa
Grafham
Grafham Water
Brampton Wood
Kimbolton
Kimbolton Castle
Buckden
Buckden Towers
Offord Cluny
Offord D'Arcy
West Perry
East Perry
Stirtloe
Hilton
Conington
Stonely
Staughton Green
Great Staughton
Staughton Highway
Dillington
Diddington
Southoe
Great Paxton
Papworth St Agnes
Graveley
Boxworth
Elsworth
Knapwell
Little Staughton
Little Paxton
Paxton Pits Nature Reserve
Hail Weston
Toseland
Yelling
Papworth Village Settlement
Papworth Everard
CAMBRIDGESHI
Bushmead Priory
Bushmead
Duloe
Staploe
Eaton Ford
St Neots
Eynesbury
Eaton Socon
Croxton
Eltisley
Cambourne
Childerley
Caxton
Bolnhurst
Colmworth
Upper Staploe
Honeydon
BEDFORD
Little Barford
Abbotsley
Great Gransden
Great Gransden Windmill
Bourn Windmill
Bourn
Caldecote
Kingston
Wyboston
Chawston
Colesden
Wilden
Little Gransden
Longstowe
Roxton
Tempsford
Waresley
Waresley & Gransden Wood
Renhold
Green End
Great Barford
Blunham
Tetworth
Gamlingay Cinques
Gamlingay
Everton
Hatley St George
East Hatley
Arrington
Wimpole Hall Home Farm
Wimpole
Willington
Willington Dovecote & Stables
Moggerhanger
Sandy
Potton
Cockayne Hatley
Croydon
New Wimpole
Deepdale
Girtford
Cople
Chapel End
Hatch
Beeston
The Lodge
Wendy
104
121
A1(M)
A1
A14
A141
A1307
A428
A421
A603
A1198
B1040
B1043
B1046
B1042
1
2
3miles
1
2
3
4
5 km

Mepal
Witcham
Wardy Hill
Coveney
Queen Adelaide
Ely
Oliver Cromwell's House
Cathedral & Mus
Somersham
Chatteris Road
Sutton
Wentworth
Witchford
Stuntney
South Fen
Haddenham
Haddenham End Field
Colne
Bluntisham
Earth
Earith
The Hermitage
Wilburton
Stretham
Little Thetford
Barway
Soham Cotes
Soham
Aldreth
Old Bedford River
River Great Ouse
Ouse Fen
Willingham
Over
Swavesey
Church End
Chittering
Upware
Wicken
Wicken Fen
Burwell
Reach
Cottenham
Rampton
Northstowe
Longstanton
Boxworth End
Oakington
Westwick
Landbeach
Waterbeach
Denny End
Farmland Mus & Denny Abbey
Swaffham Prior
Lolworth
Bar Hill
Histon
Impington
Girton
Milton
Horningsea
Clayhithe
Lode
Anglesey Abbey
Swaffham Bulbeck
Commercial End
Bottisham
Dry Drayton
Kings Hedges
Madingley
Arbury
Chesterton
Fen Ditton
Stow cum Quy
Little Wilbraham
Great Wilbraham
Hardwick
Coton
American Forces Cemetery
Cambridge
Kettle's Yard
King's College Chapel
Museum of Technology
Fitzwilliam Museum
University Botanic Garden
Newnham
Coldham's Common
Romsey Town
Teversham
Cherry Hinton
Fulbourn
Six Mile Bottom
Highfields
Toft
Comberton
Green End
Barton
Grantchester
Trumpington
Great Eversden
Little Eversden
Haslingfield
Harlton
Great Shelford
Stapleford
Hauxton
Little Shelford
Harston
Gog Magog Hills
Wandlebury
West Wratting
Weston Colville
Balsham
Orwell
Barrington
Newton
Sawston
Babraham
Pampisford
Great Abington
Abington
Hildersham
Shepreth
Foxton
Whittlesford
Shepreth Wildlife Park
Newmarket
National Stud
A10
A14
A142
A1123
A1303
A11
M11
A428
A603
A1134
A1307
B1049
B1050
B1102

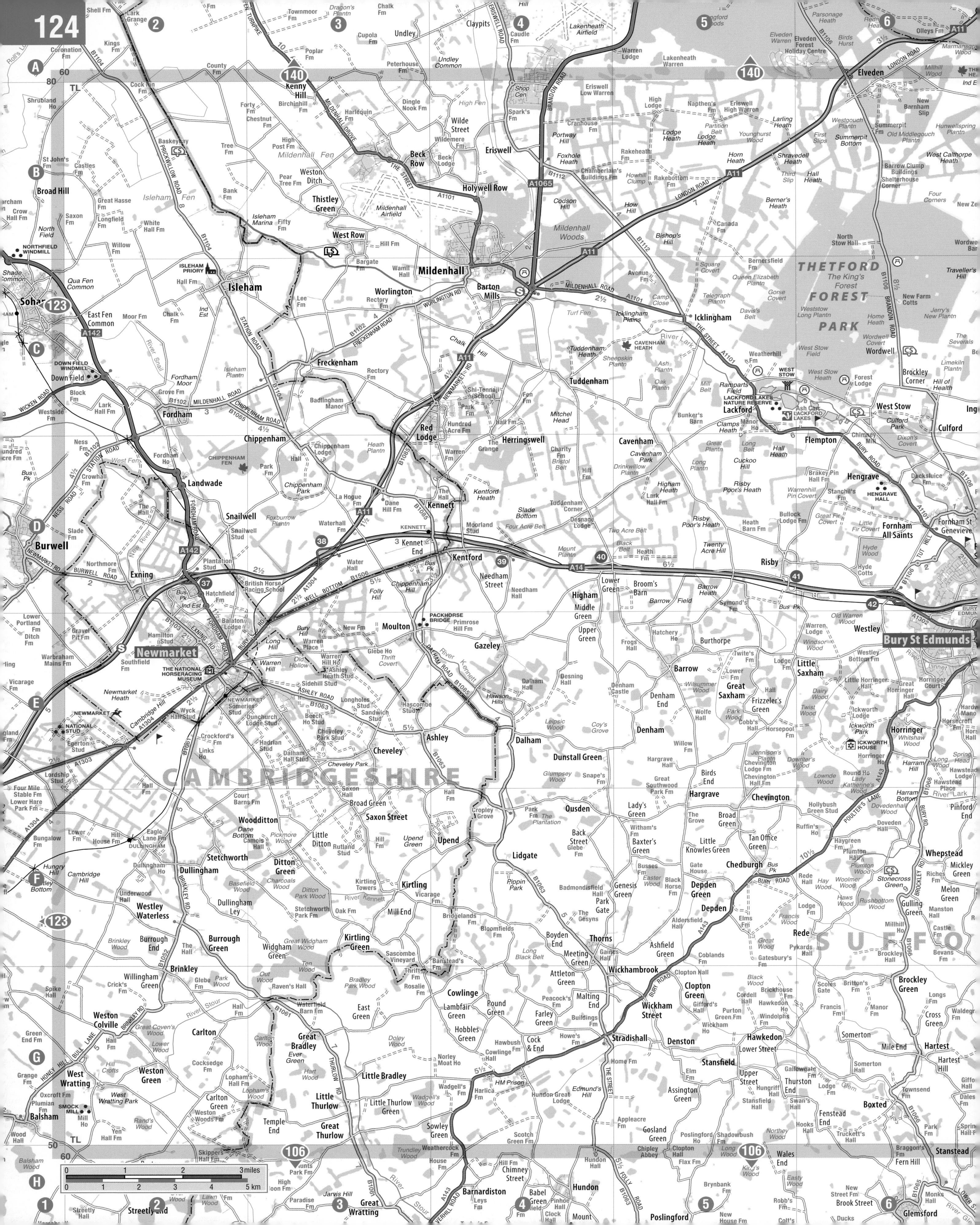

Mildenhall
Isleham
Soham
Burwell
Newmarket
Fordham
Chippenham
Freckenham
Worlington
Barton Mills
Eriswell
Holywell Row
Beck Row
West Row
Thistley Green
Icklingham
Elveden
THETFORD FOREST PARK
Tuddenham
Herringswell
Red Lodge
Kennett
Kentford
Cavenham
Lackford
Flempton
Hengrave
Culford
West Stow
Fornham All Saints
Risby
Higham
Barrow
Bury St Edmunds
Westley
Little Saxham
Great Saxham
Horringer
Moulton
Gazeley
Dalham
Ashley
Cheveley
Exning
Landwade
Snailwell
Woodditton
Saxon Street
Upend
Kirtling
Kirtling Green
Dullingham
Stetchworth
Ditton Green
Westley Waterless
Burrough Green
Brinkley
Weston Colville
Carlton
West Wratting
Balsham
Great Bradley
Little Bradley
Little Thurlow
Great Thurlow
Cowlinge
Lidgate
Ousden
Denham
Hargrave
Chevington
Chedburgh
Depden
Thorns
Wickhambrook
Stradishall
Denston
Hawkedon
Stansfield
Hartest
Boxted
Stanstead
Glemsford
Hundon
Barnardiston
Great Wratting
Poslingford
CAMBRIDGESHIRE
SUFFO
Mildenhall Airfield
Lakenheath Airfield
Mildenhall Woods
Isleham Fen
Mildenhall Fen
THE NATIONAL HORSERACING MUSEUM
ICKWORTH HOUSE
HENGRAVE HALL
LACKFORD LAKES NATURE RESERVE
A11
A14
A142
A1304
A143
A1065
A1101
B1085
B1063
B1061
B1106
140
106
123
TL
1 2 3 4 5 6
A B C D E F G H
0 1 2 3 miles
0 1 2 3 4 5 km

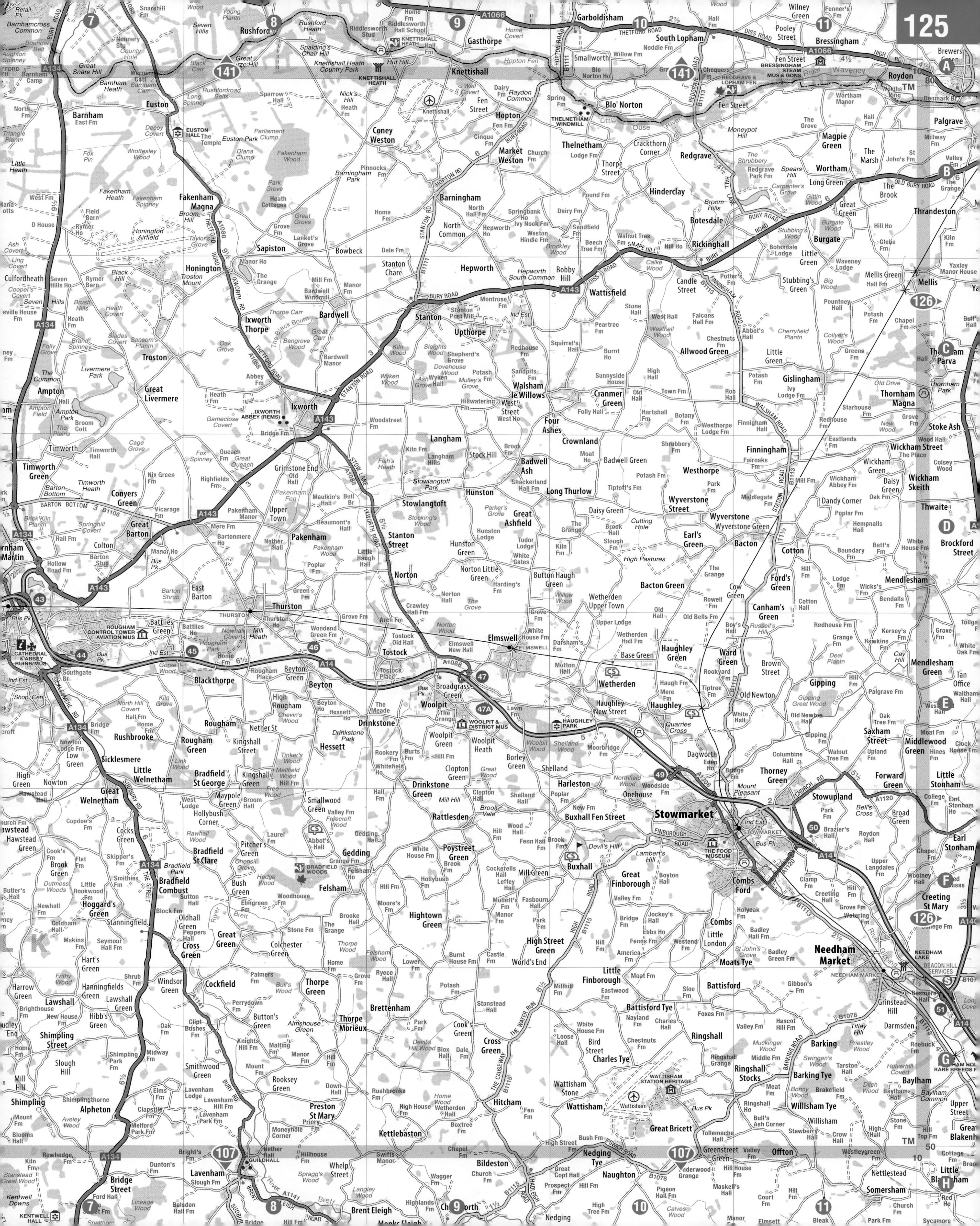

141
126
107
A
B
C
D
E
F
G
H
7
8
9
10
11
43
44
45
46
47
47A
49
50
51
A1066
A134
A143
A1088
A14
A1120
A1141
A1308
B1111
B1113
B1115
B1078
B1106
Rushford
Garboldisham
South Lopham
Bressingham
Roydon
Gasthorpe
Knettishall
Knettishall Heath Country Park
Euston
Barnham
Hopton
Blo' Norton
Fen Street
Palgrave
Coney Weston
Market Weston
Thelnetham
Redgrave
Magpie Green
Wortham
Thorpe Street
Hinderclay
Barningham
Botesdale
Rickinghall
Thrandeston
Fakenham Magna
Sapiston
Honington
Hepworth
Wattisfield
Burgate
Mellis
Bardwell
Stanton
Upthorpe
Ixworth Thorpe
Troston
Allwood Green
Gislingham
Thornham Magna
Walsham le Willows
Ampton
Great Livermere
Ixworth
Four Ashes
Cranmer Green
Langham
Crownland
Finningham
Stoke Ash
Timworth
Timworth Green
Stock Hill
Badwell Ash
Westhorpe
Wickham Skeith
Conyers Green
Pakenham
Stowlangtoft
Hunston
Long Thurlow
Wyverstone Street
Wyverstone
Great Ashfield
Thwaite
Great Barton
Stanton Street
Bacton
Cotton
Brockford Street
Norton
Earl's Green
Mendlesham
Thurston
Bacton Green
Ford's Green
Canham's Green
Elmswell
Tostock
Ward Green
Haughley Green
Wetherden
Mendlesham Green
Blackthorpe
Beyton
Woolpit
Haughley
Old Newton
Gipping
Rougham
Rushbrooke
Drinkstone
Hessett
Saxham Street
Middlewood Green
Sicklesmere
Little Welnetham
Great Welnetham
Bradfield St George
Stowmarket
Stowupland
Harleston
Buxhall Fen Street
Rattlesden
Drinkstone Green
Forward Green
Little Stonham
Earl Stonham
Bradfield St Clare
Gedding
Buxhall
Great Finborough
Combs Ford
Felsham
Bradfield Combust
Hoggard's Green
Hightown Green
Creeting St Mary
Needham Market
Combs
High Street Green
Great Green
Cross Green
Cockfield
Thorpe Green
Little Finborough
Battisford
Lawshall
Shimpling Street
Brettenham
Thorpe Morieux
Battisford Tye
Ringshall
Cross Green
Barking
Charles Tye
Ringshall Stocks
Barking Tye
Baylham
Hitcham
Wattisham
Great Bricett
Willisham Tye
Shimpling
Alpheton
Preston St Mary
Kettlebaston
Offton
Nedging Tye
Naughton
Bildeston
Lavenham
Bridge Street
Whelp Street
Brent Eleigh
Somersham
Little Blakenham
Stowmarket
The Food Museum
Wattisham Station Heritage
Woolpit & District Mus
Haughley Park
Rougham Control Tower Aviation Mus
Cathedral & Abbey Ruins/Mus
Euston Hall
Thelnetham Windmill
Bressingham Steam Mus & Gdns
Redgrave & Lopham Fen
Ixworth Abbey (Rems)
Bradfield Woods
Guildhall
Kentwell Hall
Needham Lake
Beacon Hill Services
River Waveney
Little Ouse River
River Gipping

Covehithe
Frostenden
Brampton
Stoven
Mill Common
Westhall
Uggeshall
Clay Common
South Cove
Cove Bottom
Spexhall
Rumburgh
Wissett
Broadway
Halesworth
Holton
Wangford
Reydon
Reydon Smear
Southwold
SOUTHWOLD MUSEUM
Blyford
Wenhaston
Blythburgh
Blackheath
Walberswick
Walpole
Bramfield
Thorington
Sibton Green
High Street
Darsham
Sibton
Hemp Green
Yoxford
Westleton
Dunwich
DUNWICH MUSEUM
Dunwich Forest
SUFFOLK COAST
Middleton
Middleton Moor
Rotten End
North Green
Theberton
Eastbridge
Minsmere Level
MINSMERE
Curlew Green
Kelsale
Carlton
Saxmundham
LEISTON ABBEY
Leiston
LONG SHOP MUSEUM
Sizewell
Knodishall
Benhall Green
Benhall Street
Sternfield
Coldfair Green
Aldringham
Friston
Farnham
Thorpe Ness
Thorpeness
Gromford
Snape
SNAPE MALTINGS
Blaxhall
Aldeburgh
ALDEBURGH MUS
Fort Green
Iken
Tunstall
Tunstall Forest
High Street
Sudbourne
Chillesford
Butley
Orford
Orford Ness
ORFORDNESS HAVERGATE
Butley High Corner
Capel Green
Capel St Andrew
Gedgrave Hall
SUFFOLK COAST AND HEATHS
Aldeburgh Bay
TM

SNOWDONIA NATIONAL PARK
PARC CENEDLAETHOL ERYRI
CEREDIGION
(SIR CEREDIGION)
Machynlleth
Tywyn
Aberdovey (Aberdyfi)
Llwyngwril
Abergynolwyn
Llanegryn
Bryncrug
Pandy
Rhyd-yr-onen
Tal-y-llyn
Minffordd
Corris
Corris Uchaf
Aberllefenni
Aberangell
Esgairgeiliog
Pantperthog
Pen-y-bont
Pennal
Derwenlas
Glaspwll
Glandyfi
Eglwys Fach
Furnace
Ynyslas
Borth (Y Borth)
Upper Borth
Llancynfelyn
Tre'r-ddôl
Tre-Taliesin
Tal-y-bont
Dôl-y-Bont
Llandre
Pen-y-garn
Bow Street
Penrhyn-coch
Clarach
Plas Gogerddan
Comins Coch
Capel Dewi
Llanbadarn Fawr
Waun Fawr
Capel Bangor
Goginan
Cwmbrwyno
Ponterwyd
Dyffryn Castell
Ysbyty Cynfyn
Ystumtuen
Aberffrwd
Bont-goch (Elerch)
Salem
Pen-bont Rhydybeddau
Forge
Penegoes
Tal-y-wern
Melinbyrhedyn
Pant-glas
Aberhosan
Darowen
Abercegir
Cemmaes
Cemmaes Road (Glantwymyn)
Commins Coch
Llanwrin
Dol-fôr
Pant Mawr
Nant-y-moch Reservoir
Plynlimon / Pumlumon Fawr
River Dovey / Afon Dyfi
Dyfi Forest
A487
A493
A489
A44
B4405
B4353
B4572
B4343
B4404
146
110
112
0 1 2 3 miles
0 1 2 3 4 5 km

7
Mallwyd
8
Mynydd Talyglannau
Bryn Ysguthan
Gesail-ddu
9
Maes-llymystyn
Esgair y Maes
Foel
Pont Twrch
Cefn-du
Cefniau
Blowty
10
Dolpebyll
Llangadfan
Ffridd Maesceleynog
Neuadd-wen
Pen-y-criben
11
Tyn-y-rhyd
Esgair Ddu
Cwm Tafolog
147
Carnedd Wen 523
Ffridd Goch
Lletty-Mawr
A458
Stone Ho
Parc
Hafan
Afon Banwy
Gro
Berth-Fawr
Tynrhos
A
SJ
Llechwedd Mawr
Cwm Gast
Tafolog
Carnedd y Cylch
Gwrachen
Bryn-derwen
Goetre
Goetre Fach
Llanerfyl
Moel Bentyrch 338
Four Crosses
Cefndre
Caen-y-mynydd
Bryn-glas Hall
Glascoed
Heniarth
Mynydd y Cemais
Blaen-Tafolog
Mynydd Lluest Fach
Waun Lwyd
Ffridd Ganol
Nant Craigyfran
Pen Coed
Plasynghraen
Diosg
Pentyrch
Hen-efail
NEW ROAD
Afon Einion
Dolgead Hall
Clegyrnant
Y Rhos
Caerbwla
Disgwylfa 386
Hirros Hall
Hirrhos Uchaf
Maes-y-glydfa
Craig Fawr
Waun-gau
Dôl Fawr
Mynydd Rhiw-Saeson
Cwm Pen Llydan
Penylau Gwynion 450
Llyn Gwyddior
Cannon
Afon Cannon
Dolwen
Moel Ddolwen
Sychtyn
Hafod
Glyn
Melin-y-grug
Llanoddian Hall
B
Ind Est
Fron 412
Glaslyn
Gelli Gethin
Cwmllwynog
Rhosaflo
Melin-y-ddôl
Parc-y-rhiw
Rhiw-hiriaeth Isaf
Llanfair Caereinion
Neinthirion
Dolau
Belan Hall
Mynydd Waun Fawr
Llyn Hir
Belan
Rhiw hiriaeth
Mount Pleasant
Pentre-Celyn
Moel Eiddew 453
Plas-rhiw-Saeson
Llechwedd Du
GLYNDWR'S WAY
Cors Fforchog
Cwmderwen
Bryn y Castell 368
Cross Fm
Plasiolyn
Tynllwyn
Eron-goch
Waun Fawr
Bryn-moel
Waun
Pandy
Dol-y-garreg wen-isaf
Bryn y Lloi
Mynydd Lluest-y-graig
Pant-y-milwyr
Bryn-penarth
Ystrad Uchaf
Gwern-y-bwlch
Brynaere
Cerrig y Tân
Esgair Priciau
Ffridd Fawr
Ffridd-Rhyd-Ddu 424
Foel Fawr
Lletty Gwilym Isaf
Tan-y-graig
Penarth
130
Coed Ffridd-fawr
Esgair
Pentremawr
Berth-las
Banc y Gorlan
Afon Gam
Pentre-lludw
Carreg-y-big
Tyn-y-coed
Lawnt
B4389
Maesprydd
A470
Ty Pella
Llanbrynmair
Bryn Gwyn
Twmpath Melyn 439
Nant Wythan
Gwaenydd
Frongoch Hall
Cefn Coch
Belan-deg
Tafolwern
Tyn-y-coed
Cwm Bustach
Corun-y-Ffridd 371
Dolfach
Mynydd y Gribin
Llanllugan
Dwyrhiw
Gwernydd
Manafon
C
Cwmbychan-mawr
B4518
Braich-Odnant
Moel Caetwpa
Afon Iaen
Mynydd yr Hendre
414 Y Foel
Gwaun-y-maglau
Ty Bach
Sychnant
Glan-yr-afon
Llanwyddelan
Old Hall
Plas Esgair
Llan
Gelli
Newydd Fynyddog 412
Fron
Talerddig
Rhyd
Mynydd Pistyll-du
Mynydd Dwyriw
Pant
Adfa
Bryn Fm
Dolgair
New Mills
Cefn-twlch
Pen Rhiw-Mwyn 388
Tawelfan
Bont-Dolgadfan
Cwm Llwyd
Cwm Ednant
Cwmcalch Isaf
Glanhanog
Hendre
Dol-friog
Carneddau (ruin)
Mynydd Clogau 402
Castell-y-Isaf
Trawsgelli
Argoed
Lower Fachwen
Dolymelinau
Cae Madog
Brynbach
Ffridd yr Ystrad
Brynderwen
Aberclawdd
Tregynon
Pwllan
404 Banc Bronderwgoed
Cwmcalch Uchaf
419
Derlwyn
Yr Allt
Y Glonc 461
Mynydd Cerrigllwydion
Cochsidan
Bechan Brook
Skew Br
The Heath
Craigfryn
Lleustuchaf
Bryn Du
Sarnbigog
Rallt
Pikins
Gwgia
Brynheulog
Ty'n y Bryn
D
Llannerch-yr-aur
Esgair Geulan
Pennant
Wig
Mynydd Penypistyll
Bryn Amlwg 488
Pen y Pigyns
Allt Fawr
Garreg-Hir 485
Llyn Mawr
Llyn y Tarw
GREGYNOG
Brithdir
Henfaes
Mynydd Cil-Cwm 527
Bryn Du
Wylfa
Sarn
Plas Llysyn
Mynydd Llwytgoed
Cilcwm
Creigiau Pennant
Hendre
Pantle
Afon Cledan
Bryn-côch
Tynyreithin
Carno
Parc-y-rhiw
Llyn Du
Cefn-llydan
Finger Post
Ty'n-y-banadl
Cwm-mawr
Pont Crugnant
449
Blaen-y-cwm
Bryn yr Aran
Pentre
Plasnewydd
Llwydcoed
Bwlch-y-ffridd
Bryncoch
Ddifed
New Ho
Cwm
Highgate Hill
Trannon
Allt-Du
Trawscoed
Wgi-fawr
Maesypandy
Gwern-y-pwll
Bettws Hall
Hafod
Nant Rhyd-Essian
Penbedw
Garth Hill
Red Ho
Bryn Moel
Dylife
P
O
W
Y
S
Waun Garno
396 Bryn y Gadair
Clatter
Mynydd Garth-Pwt
Sylwfa Wood
Bryn-yr-Oerfa 460
Bryn Mawr 450
Esgair Hir
Dolbachog
Blaencerniog
Gors Goch
Afon Carnog
Pontdolgoch
Alltwnnog
Llanwnog
Llwyn-y-gog
Fachwen Pool
Hirnant
Llechwedd Du
Rhiw Dyfeity Fawr
Fuches
Staylittle (Penffordd-Lâs)
Gamallt
Mawnog Bryn-glas
Bryn Crugog 447
Colwyn Brook
Hafod
Foel y Belan
Tyn sarn
B4568
Rhydlydan
Bryn-y-pentre Wood
Point Fm
Tynyreithin Hall
Rhydyfelin
Newtown
Y Drenewydd
E
Clywedog
Llwynygog
Yfridd Nantyrhafod 433
Waen-y-gittin
Cwm-gwernog
Long Hill
Oerle
Ystradfaelog
Cefncoch
Cefn Gwyn
Wig Br
B4569
Gwynfynydd
Caersws
7½
Aberhafesp
A489
Red Ho
MILFORD ROAD
Red Ho
Fedw-Ddu
Nant-yr-hafod
Braichyfedw
Y Gribyn
Foel Dyrnol
Llawr-y-glyn
Geseilfa
Waen
Rhiwen
Gleiniant
Frydd
Argoed
Ddraenen Ddu
CAERSWS
Carnedd
LONG LENGTH
Bronfelin Hall
ORIEL DAVIES GALLERY
Milford
Trehafren
Garth Owen
Maesyrhandir
NEWTOWN
Dduallt
Cadwgan
Gwernafon
The Hill 385
Fforest
Cilhaul
Bodaioch Hall
Trefeglwys
Cefn Carnedd 279
Allt y Gaer
Glanhafren Hall
Lan 421
Esgairieth
Derwllwydion
Afon Cerist
Trewythen
Llandinam Hall
Cwmllwydion
Bryn-helyg
Pen-y-bryn
Stepaside
Cwmbiga
Llyn Clywedog
B4518
Maesyblawd
Dolgwden
Pen y Coed
Hornby
Gwerneirin
Plas Dinam
Cefn-hir
Little London
DOLFOR ROAD
Nant-y-Gwrdu
Banc-y-Groes 419
Dinas 445
Waun y Gadair
Lluest-wen
482 Bryn y Fan
Cwmdylluan
Llyn Ebyr
Coedmawr
Gelli Hir
Broneirion
Llandinam
Moel Lart 438
Cobblers Gate
Mochdre
Glascoed
Penhempen
Graig
GLYNDWR'S WAY
Forest Hafren
Rhosfawr
Trawscoed
Hafod
Carreg
F
Dolfor Court
470 Mynydd y Groes
Gendrum
Bryn-y-Tail 403
Llyn y Fan
Y Fan
Van
Croesllwyn
Tyddyn
Coed Mawr
Afon Severn
River Severn
Bryntail
Garth
Cefngoleugoed
Gellilefrith
Cefn
Giant's Grave 516
Yr Allt
Mochdre Brook
Old Neuadd
Bryn Mawr
B4569
Penrallt
Oakley Park
Lower Penrhuddlan
Pentre
Cwm
Gias
Yr Esgair
Cwm Deildre
Glyn
Afon Clywedog
Morfodion
Bont-newydd
Dolwen
Tynyrwrtha
Maenhinon 344
Tan Hinon
Cefnpenarth
Allt Goch
Berth-lwyd Coppice
Allt y Moch
Pencraig Rocks
480 Glôg Fm Glog
Black Gate
Panty-yr-esgair
Old Hall
Glan-y-nant
OLD MARKET HALL
Llanidloes
Clydfannau
Coed y Gaer
Y Foel Glyn-Feinion 435
519 Waunlluestowain
Seven Wells
Banc Cefnperfedd
Cider Ho
Foel-goch
Glynhafren
Bronheulwen
Llwyn-derw
Caenfedw
Gorn Hill
Pen-y-banc
Glyn-Feinion
Craig Dugwin
Bryn Dadlau
Camnant
Bryn Cwmrhiwdre
Neuadd-goch Bank
Fuches
Mount Severn
BRYN-DU ROAD
Newchapel
Bryn-côch
Tach
Dethenydd
River Ithon
Beili
Banc Du
Afon Bidno
Castell-greidd
Glynbrochan
Afon Brochan
Ind Est
Bryndu
Moelfre 428
Blaenbythigion
Pen Bwlch-y-Groes
Blaen Pathog
368 Brynposteg Hill
Blue Lins Brook
A483
Allt Pant-mawr
Ffos y Ffwdan
Cwmbelan
Waun
Graig
Cwm
Carn Bryn
G
Nanty
Pen y Foel
Cefn Hirbrysg
Bryn Blaen-y-glyn
Marsh's Pool
4½
B4518
The Cross
Pant-Poeth Hill 422
Pegw-Mawr 584
Waun Ddubarthog
Garn-Fach 503
Pen Ithon Hall
Garn
Llanifyny
Ty'n-y-rhos
Glanbidno Isaf
A44
Henfaes
Deildref
Banhadlog Hall
426 Oldchapel Hill
569 Pegwn-Bach
Ddulfai Bank
Cefn Hendre
Ty-mawr
Pen-hyle-mawr
Bryn Mawr 405
Craig Tylwch
Graig Ias
Nant Gwyddos
16
Llaithddu
A470
Tylwch
SO
80
10
CS
113
Llangurig
Ystradolwyn Fawr
Hendreaur
Cefn
571 Crugyn-Llwyd
Banc Du
Penybank
Esgair Ychion
Nant Troedyresgair
Esgair Llwyn-Gwyn
Cefn-fawr
Cilgwyn-uchaf
Creigiau Llwydion
Fedw
Brook
Cwmderw
Upper Llaithddu
Dolauewmffrwd
Esgairuchaf
Ddol
H
Foel Gurig 480
Hafod-fraith
Bronheulwen
Wennallt 435
Glanyrafon Halt
Rhydwdyau Brook
Nant Marteg
Dolgarn
Cerrig Gwaun-y-llan
Pant-Gwyn Hill
Cil-Gwrgan
Craignant
Rhiwlas Hill 439
Caecethin
Garreg
Llidiarddau
Garth Fach
Prysgduon
508
David's Well
Waunhall
Llanbadarn

148
129
114
Welshpool
Y Trallwng
Newtown
Y Drenewydd
Montgomery
(Trefaldwyn)
Llanfair
Caereinion
Bishop's
Castle
Clun
Newcastle
Kerry
Sarn
Abermule
Berriew
Churchstoke
Chirbury
Forden
Kingswood
Buttington
Trewern
Guilsfield
Castle Caereinion
Manafon
New Mills
Tregynon
Bettws
Cedewain
Llanmerewig
Glanmule
Llandyssil
Garthmyl
Pentreheyling
Priest
Weston
Hyssington
Lydham
Colebatch
Brockton
Mainstone
Cefn Einion
Bettws-y-crwyn
Anchor
Felindre
Beguildy
Dolfor
Hodley
Hendomen
Leighton
Marton
Worthen
Binweston
Trelystan
Middleton
The Marsh
Wotherton
Rorrington
Meadowtown
Stockton
Pentre
Aston
Owlbury
Snead
Churchbank
Whitcott
Keysett
Bicton
Duffryn
Quabbs
Clun
Forest
POWYS
A458
A483
A490
A489
A488
B4385
B4386
B4388
B4390
B4368
Offa's Dyke Path
Glyndŵr's Way
Kerry Hill
Long Mountain
River Severn
River Clun
River Teme
POWIS CASTLE
POWYSLAND MUS
WELSHPOOL & LLANFAIR LIGHT RAILWAY
ANDREW LOGAS MUSEUM OF SCULPTURE
DOLFORWYN CASTLE
MONTGOMERY CASTLE
MITCHELL'S FOLD STONE CIRCLE
HOUSE ON CRUTCHES MUS
CLUN CASTLE
ORIEL DAVIES GALLERY
Mid-Wales
0 1 2 3 miles
0 1 2 3 4 5 km

Rowton
Preston
Charlton
Westbury
Yockleton
Cruckmeole
Cruckton
Hanwood
Meole Brace
Emstrey
Attingham Park
Atcham
Norton
Uppington
Aston
Stoney Stretton
Edge
Lea
Hinton
Farley
Bayston Hill
Annscroft
Wroxeter Roman City (Viroconium)
Wroxeter
Cross Houses
Donnington
Rushton
Westley
Asterley
Pontesbury
Pontesford
Plealey
Longden
Great Lyth
Lyth Hill
Condover
Cantlop Bridge
Berrington
Longwood
Eaton Constantine
Dryton
Minsterley
Radlith
Oaks
Stapleton
Cantlop
Cound
Leighton
Ploxgreen
Habberley
Wrentnall
Church Pulverbatch
Pulverbatch
Dorrington
Great Ryton
Wheathall
Pitchford
Golding
Acton Pigott
Cressage
Snailbeach
Crowsnest
Westcott
Acton Burnell
Acton Burnell Castle
Frodesley
Harley
Stiperstones
Longnor
Ruckley
Kenley
Picklescott
Woolstaston
Leebotwood
Langley Chapel & Gatehouse
Causewaywood
Church Preen
Hughley
Stretton Westwood
Shropshire
The Bog
Ratlinghope
Bridges
All Stretton
Plaish
Enchmarsh
Presthope
Cardington
Gretton
Caer Caradog Hill
Easthope
Bourton
Carding Mill Valley
Church Stretton
Longville in the Dale
Brockton
East Wall
Norbury
Wentnor
The Long Mynd
Wall Bank
Hope Bowdler
Wall under Heywood
Wilderhope Manor
Weston
Little Stretton
Rushbury
Shipton
Asterton
Minton
Ticklerton
Stanton Long
Marshbrook
Acton Scott
Hatton
Eaton
Wenlock Edge
Broadstone
Holdgate
Ditton Priors
Myndtown
Whittingslow
Harton
Middlehope
Corve Dale
Plowden
Horderley
Woolston
Alcaston
Westhope
Aston Munslow
Munslow
Tugford
Abdon
Edgton
Wistanstow
Upper Affcot
Strefford
Diddlebury
Upper Heath
Cheny Longville
Lower Dinchope
Corfton
Peaton
Clee St Margaret
Hopesay
Newington
Sibdon Carwood
Halford
Seifton
Great Sutton
Kempton
Craven Arms
Culmington
Stoke St Milborough
Aston on Clun
Stokesay
Norton
Shropshire Hills
Little Brampton
Broome
Clunbury
Vernolds Common
Hayton's Bent
Cleedownton
Hopton Cangeford
Twitchen
Onibury
Stanton Lacy
Clungunford
Cleeton St Mary
Shelderton
Wootton
Hopton Castle
A5
A49
A458
A488
A489
B4368
B4371
B4370
B4365
B4364
B4378
B4386
B4380
A4169
SJ
SO
149
115
132

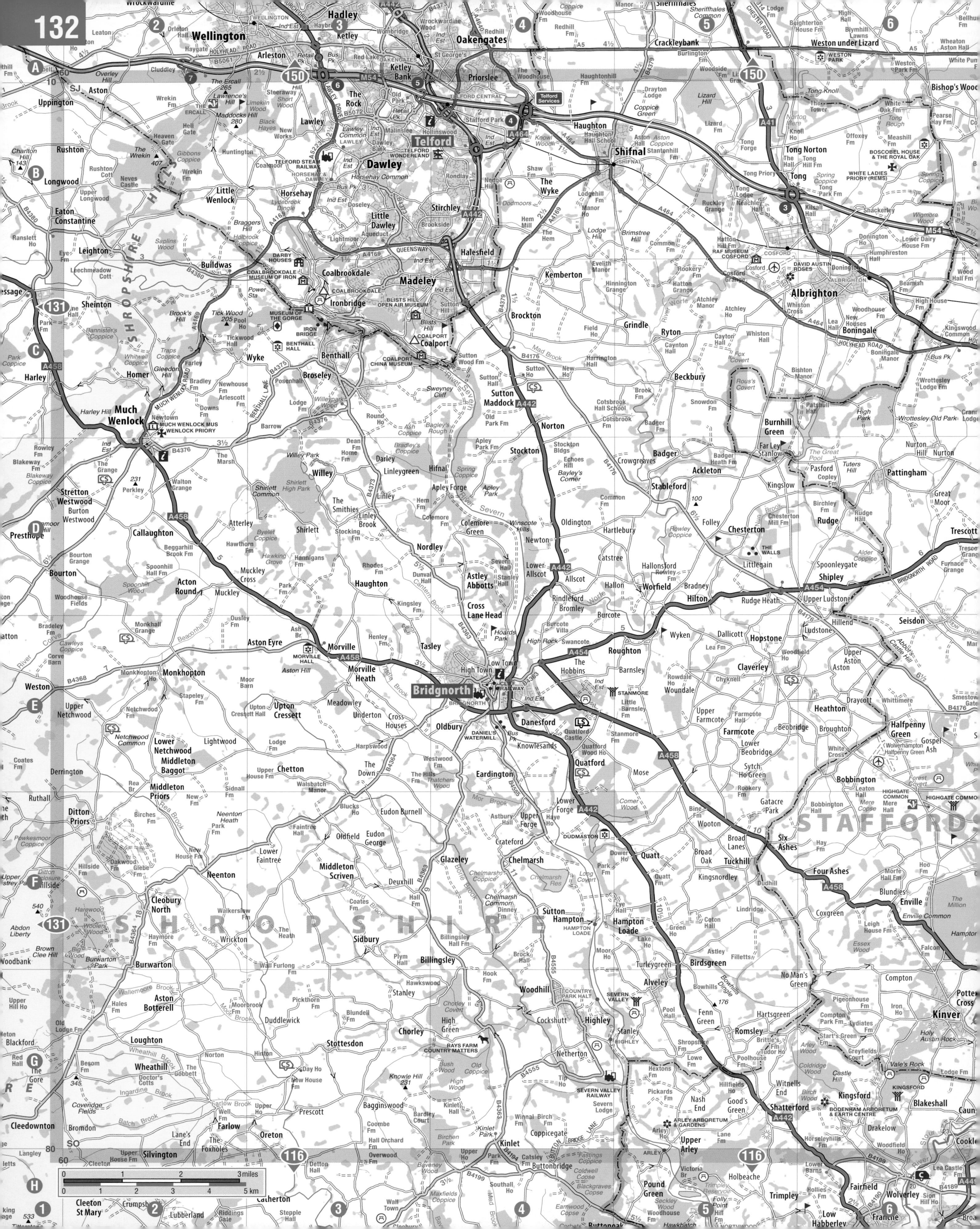
Wellington
Hadley
Ketley
Oakengates
Crackleybank
Weston under Lizard
Arleston
Ketley Bank
Priorslee
Telford
Dawley
Shifnal
Haughton
Tong
Tong Norton
Lawley
Horsehay
Little Dawley
Stirchley
Halesfield
Little Wenlock
Coalbrookdale
Madeley
Ironbridge
Coalport
Benthall
Broseley
Buildwas
Leighton
Eaton Constantine
Longwood
Rushton
Uppington
Aston
Sheinton
Harley
Much Wenlock
Homer
Wyke
Barrow
Kemberton
Brockton
Grindle
Ryton
Beckbury
Albrighton
Boningale
Sutton Maddock
Norton
Stockton
Badger
Ackleton
Stableford
Burnhill Green
Pattingham
Chesterton
Rudge
Shipley
Hilton
Worfield
Allscot
Oldington
Hartlebury
Catstree
Willey
Linleygreen
Darley
Apley Forge
Shirlett
Atterley
Callaughton
Stretton Westwood
Presthope
Bourton
Muckley Cross
Acton Round
Muckley
Nordley
Astley Abbotts
Cross Lane Head
Haughton
Tasley
Morville
Aston Eyre
Monkhopton
Weston
Upper Netchwood
Upton Cressett
Bridgnorth
Oldbury
Danesford
Quatford
Roughton
Wyken
Hopstone
Claverley
Heathton
Farmcote
Seisdon
Halfpenny Green
Bobbington
STAFFORDSHIRE
SHROPSHIRE
Eardington
Chetton
Middleton Priors
Derrington
Ditton Priors
Neenton
Middleton Scriven
Glazeley
Chelmarsh
Quatt
Tuckhill
Six Ashes
Four Ashes
Enville
Cleobury North
Burwarton
Sidbury
Billingsley
Sutton
Hampton
Hampton Loade
Alveley
Birdsgreen
Kinver
Aston Botterell
Stottesdon
Chorley
Highley
Romsley
Loughton
Wheathill
Kingsford
Blakeshall
Cleedowntown
Farlow
Oreton
Prescott
Kinlet
Silvington
Upper Arley
Shatterford
Pound Green
Trimpley
Wolverley
Fairfield
Cleeton St Mary
Catherton
M54
A458
A442
A454
A464
A41
A5
B4176
B4363
B4364
B4555
B4373
B4376
B4368
B4379
0 1 2 3 miles
0 1 2 3 4 5 km

Stretton
Oldfallow
Wimblebury
Cannock Wood
Gentleshaw
Farewell
Chorley
Horsebrook
Gailey
Hatherton
Heath Hayes
Cannock
Bridgtown
Norton East
Norton Canes
Chase Terrace
Chasetown
Burntwood
Leomansley
Kiddemore Green
Brewood
Hammerwich
Standeford
Great Saredon
Churchbridge
Cheslyn Hay
Great Wyrley
Norton Canes Services
Shareshill
Coven
Featherstone
Little Wyrley
Hobble End
Brownhills
Muckley Corner
Wall
Hilton Park Services
Springhill
Clayhanger
Shire Oak
Stonnall
Shenstone
Codsall
Fordhouses
Bushbury
Essington
Bloxwich
Pelsall
Walsall Wood
Shelfield
Vigo
Holly Bank
Thornes
Lower Stonnall
Oxley
Wood Hayes
Ashmore Park
New Invention
Short Heath
Harden
Rushall
Leighswood
Aldridge
Footherley
Watford Gap
Little Aston
Wergs
Perton
Tettenhall Wood
Heath Town
Wednesfield
Willenhall
Bentley
Coal Pool
Birchills
Walsall
Caldmore
Palfrey
Streetly
Four Oaks
Wolverhampton
Compton
Castlecroft
Merridale
Blakenhall
Moseley
Bilston
Darlaston
Bradmore
Penn
Lower Penn
Goldthorn Park
Spring Hill
Ettingshall
Pleck
The Delves
Great Barr
Yew Tree
Kingstanding
Banners Gate
New Oscott
Boldmere
Orton
Sedgley
Coseley
Moxley
Bradley
Wednesbury
Friar Park
Grove Vale
Wombourne
Trysull
Gospel End Village
Upper Gornal
Tipton
Ocker Hill
Hill Top
Charlemont
Hamstead
Perry Barr
Perry Common
Blakeley
Himley
The Black Country
Lower Gornal
Gornalwood
Dudley
Dudley Port
Great Bridge
Tividale
West Bromwich
Handsworth
Aston
Erdington
Gravelly Hill
Swindon
Wall Heath
Kingswinford
Russell's Hall
Netherton
Oldbury
Smethwick
Sandwell
Winson Green
Nechells
Brierley Hill
Pensnett
Rowley Regis
Langley Green
Bearwood
Saltley
Wordsley
Amblecote
Quarry Bank
Old Hill
Blackheath
Edgbaston
Birmingham
Stourton
Stourbridge
Wollaston
Lye
Cradley
Halesowen
Harborne
Chad Valley
Sparkbrook
Balsall Heath
Sparkhill
Whittington
Pedmore
Norton
Wollescote
Hasbury
Hayley Green
California
Selly Oak
Moseley
Woodgate
Bartley Green
Weoley Castle
Bournville
Stirchley
Kings Heath
Hall Green
Hagley
Frankley Services
Illey
Frankley
Cotteridge
Churchill
Clent
Romsley
Northfield
King's Norton
Blakedown
Broome
Holy Cross
Warstock
Solihull Lodge
West Midlands
Midlands

Lichfield
Leomansley
Streethay
Huddlesford
Elford
Harlaston
Edingale
Haunton
Clifton Campville
Chilcote
Measham
Appleby Magna
Appleby Parva
Whittington
Hademore
Wigginton
Thorpe Constantine
No Man's Heath
Newton Regis
Seckington
Austrey
Norton-Juxta-Twycross
Wall
Hopwas
Leyfields
Tamworth
Shuttington
Alvecote
Amington
Shenstone
Weeford
Hints
Little Hay
Bonehill
Fazeley
Glascote
Polesworth
Warton
Orton-on-the-Hill
Watford Gap
Drayton Bassett
Dosthill
Wilnecote
Birchmoor
Dordon
St Helena
Grendon
Sheepy Magna
Sheepy Parva
Little Aston
Hill
Roughley
Streetly
Four Oaks
Middleton
Kingsbury
Whittington
Grendon Common
Baddesley Ensor
Baxterley
Atherstone
Mancetter
Witherley
Ratcliffe Culey
Sutton Coldfield
Hurley
Bentley
Wishaw
Bodymoor Heath
Marston
Lea Marston
Ridge Lane
Oldbury
Hartshill
New Oscott
Wylde Green
Walmley
Over Green
Pype Hayes
Erdington
Curdworth
Minworth
Whiteacre Heath
Nether Whitacre
Furnace End
Church End
Shustoke
Over Whitacre
Ansley
Stockingford
Castle Bromwich
Water Orton
Coleshill
Tyburn
Gravelly Hill
Castle Vale
Old Arley
New Arley
Astley
Kitt's Green
Tile Cross
Maxstoke
Fillongley
Corley Ash
Corley
Bedworth Heath
Birmingham
Yardley
Sheldon
Marston Green
Little Packington
Keresley
Acock's Green
Elmdon
Meriden
Olton
Bickenhill
Hampton in Arden
Coundon
Allesley
Berkswell
Coventry
WARWICKSHIRE
WEST MIDLANDS
STAFFS
M6 TOLL
M42
M6
A5
A38
A452
A45
0 1 2 3 miles
0 1 2 3 4 5 km

THE NATIONAL FOREST
LEICESTERSHIRE
Ibstock
153
Ellistown
Stanton under Bardon
Markfield
Newtown Linford
Anstey
Thurcaston
Cropston
Birstall
Wanlip
Heather
Swepstone
Newton Burgoland
Battram
Bagworth
Thornton
Field Head
Groby
Ratby
Glenfield
Leicester
Belgrave
Odstone
Nailstone
Barton in the Beans
Shackerstone
Congerstone
Bilstone
Carlton
Barlestone
Osbaston
Newbold Verdon
Botcheston
Newtown Unthank
Kirby Muxloe
Leicester Forest East
Leicester Forest East Services
Market Bosworth
Cadeby
Wellsborough
Desford
Peckleton
Braunstone
Braunstone Town
New Lubbesthorpe
Western Park
Westcotes
Clarendon Park
Stoneygate
Knighton
Aylestone
North Evington
Shenton
Sutton Cheney
Kirkby Mallory
Upton
Stapleton
Dadlington
Earl Shilton
Thurlaston
Enderby
Glen Parva
Eyres Monsell
South Wigston
Narborough
Huncote
Whetstone
Blaby
Littlethorpe
Stoke Golding
Barwell
Elmesthorpe
Potters Marston
Normanton Turville
Higham on the Hill
Croft
Cosby
Countesthorpe
Kilby Bridge
Foston
Hinckley
Stoney Stanton
Sapcote
Sutton in the Elms
Weddington
Nuneaton
Burbage
Sketchley
Aston Flamville
Sharnford
Primethorpe
Broughton Astley
Willoughby Waterleys
Peatling Magna
Attleborough
Whitestone
Burton Hastings
Smockington
Frolesworth
Leire
Dunton Bassett
Ashby Magna
Bruntingthorpe
Peatling Parva
Wolvey Heath
Copston Magna
Claybrooke Magna
Claybrooke Parva
Ashby Parva
Griff
Marston Jabbett
Bramcote
Shelford
Wolvey
Wibtoft
Ullesthorpe
Gilmorton
Upper Bruntingthorpe
Bedworth
Weston in Arden
Bramcote Mains
Ryton
Bulkington
Cloudesley Bush
Bitteswell
Kimcote
Walton
Lutterworth
Exhall
Hawkesbury
Barnacle
Shilton
Willey
Hopsford
Withybrook
Cross in Hand
Misterton
Walcote
Ansty
Monks Kirby
Brockhurst
Little Walton
Pailton
Street Ashton
Cotesbach
South Kilworth
Foleshill
Walsgrave on Sowe
Wyken
Stretton under Fosse
Churchover
Gibbet Hill
Shawell
Brinklow
Easenhall
Harborough Magna
Harborough Parva
Swinford
Stanford on Avon
Cathiron
Newton
Catthorpe
Binley
Pinley
M1
M69
M6
A5
A47
A46
A50
A426
A4303
Rugby Services
119
136

Syston
Barsby
Thorpe Satchville
Burrough on the Hill
Somerby
Cold Overton
Barleythorpe
Oakham
Wanlip
Barkby
Twyford
South Croxton
Birstall
Thurmaston
Barkby Thorpe
Beeby
John O'Gaunt
Newbold
Marefield
Owston
Knossington
Braunston-in-Rutland
Rushey Mead
Hungarton
Lowesby
Nether Hall
New Humberstone
Humberstone
Keyham
Scraptoft
Cold Newton
Tilton on the Hill
Halstead
Belgrave
Crown Hills
North Evington
Evington
Bushby
Thurnby
Houghton on the Hill
Billesdon
Skeffington
Loddington
Ridlington
Highfields
LEICESTER CITY
Clarendon Park
Stoneygate
Stoughton
Frisby
Gaulby
Tugby
Belton in Rutland
Knighton Fields
South Knighton
Aylestone Park
Knighton
Oadby
Little Stretton
King's Norton
Rolleston
East Norton
Allexton
Wardley
Illston on the Hill
Wigston
Wigston Magna
Noseley
Goadby
South Wigston
Great Glen
Scotland
Burton Overy
Carlton Curlieu
Newton Harcourt
Stockerston
The Woodlands
Shangton
Horninghold
Kilby Bridge
Care Village
Glooston
Hallaton
LEICESTERSHIRE
Wistow
Stonton Wyville
Cranoe
Blaston
Kilby
Bulwick
Kibworth Harcourt
Tur Langton
Slawston
Fleckney
Smeeton Westerby
Kibworth Beauchamp
Church Langton
Medbourne
Peatling Magna
Arnesby
Saddington
East Langton
Thorpe Langton
Welham
Weston by Welland
Drayton
Shearsby
Bruntingthorpe
Gumley
Foxton
Ashley
Sutton Bassett
Middleton
East Carlton
Peatling Parva
Knaptoft
Mowsley
Upper Bruntingthorpe
Laughton
Great Bowden
Wilbarston
Stoke Albany
Dingley
Brampton Ash
Carlton Purlieus
Walton
Lubenham
Little Bowden
Market Harborough
Theddingworth
Marston Trussell
East Farndon
Braybrooke
Husbands Bosworth
Great Oxendon
North Kilworth
Rushton
Desborough
Sibbertoft
WEST NORTHANTS
South Kilworth
Clipston
Arthingworth
Rothwell
Welford
Harrington
Kelmarsh
Thorpe Underwood
Naseby
Orton
Loddington
Thorpe Malsor
0 1 2 3 miles
0 1 2 3 4 5 km

Oakham
Rutland Water
Egleton
Upper Hambleton
Burley
Exton
Whitwell
Empingham
Tickencote
Great Casterton
Little Casterton
Ryhall
Belmesthorpe
Greatford
Barholm
Stowe
Uffington
Tallington
West Deeping
Northfields
Stamford
Tinwell
Wothorpe
Burghley House
Pilsgate
Barnack
Bainton
Ashton
Ufford
Southorpe
Wittering
Thornhaugh
Sacrewell Farm & Country Centre
Wansford
Stibbington
Sutton
Upton
Sibson
Water Newton
Yarwell
Nassington
Apethorpe
Woodnewton
King's Cliffe
Easton on the Hill
Collyweston
Duddington
Tixover
Ketton
Aldgate
Geeston
Normanton
Edith Weston
North Luffenham
South Luffenham
Lyndon
Manton
Wing
Pilton
Preston
Ayston
Glaston
Morcott
Barrowden
Uppingham
Bisbrooke
Seaton
Wakerley
Lyddington
Thorpe by Water
Harringworth
Shotley
Laxton
Blatherwycke
Bulwick
Gretton
Caldecott
Rockingham
Deene
Deenethorpe
Southwick
Fotheringhay
Elton
Over End
Eaglethorpe
Tansor
Cotterstock
Glapthorn
Warmington
Corby
Great Weldon
Little Weldon
Upper Benefield
Lower Benefield
Oundle
Ashton
Polebrook
Lutton
Stanion
Great Oakley
Little Oakley
Brigstock
Stoke Doyle
Barnwell St Andrew
Barnwell
Barnwell All Saints
Armston
Hemington
Luddington in the Brook
Pilton
Wadenhoe
Achurch
Aldwincle
Thurning
Wigsthorpe
Thorpe Waterville
Lowick
Clopton
Winwick
Geddington
Newton
Sudborough
Weekley
Warkton
Grafton Underwood
Slipton
Twywell
Islip
Thrapston
Titchmarsh
Kettering
NORTH NORTHANTS
A1
A6003
A606
A47
A43
A427
A6116
A605
A6121
A1175
A4300
A6183
B1443
B1081
B672
B662
B671
121
138
155
7
8
9
10
11
12

Market Deeping
Deeping St James
Towngate
Deeping Gate
West Deeping
Tallington
Maxey
Northborough
Etton
Glinton
Peakirk
Helpston
Bainton
Ashton
Ufford
Crowland
Nene Terrace
Newborough
Eye
Eye Green
Thorney
Thorney Toll
PETERBOROUGH
Werrington
Gunthorpe
Paston
Walton
Marholm
Dogsthorpe
New England
Ravensthorpe
Millfield
Eastfield
Newark
Westwood
Longthorpe
Fengate
Castor
Ailsworth
Sutton
Stibbington
Upton
Peterborough
Woodston
New Fletton
Old Fletton
Stanground
Orton Wistow
Orton Waterville
Orton Longueville
Orton Brimbles
Orton Malborne
Orton Goldhay
Orton Southgate
Alwalton
Chesterton
Water Newton
Hampton Hargate
Hampton Vale
Farcet
Yaxley
Haddon
Elton
Morborne
Norman Cross
Folksworth
Stilton
Washingley
Caldecote
Denton
Lutton
Papley
Chapel End
Holme
Conington
Glatton
Sawtry
Great Gidding
Little Gidding
Steeple Gidding
Winwick
Hamerton
Coppingford
Luddington in the Brook
Hemington
Whittlesey
Inham's End
Eastrea
Coates
Turves
Pondersbridge
Ramsey Mereside
Ramsey St Mary's
Ramsey Heights
Ramsey
Ramsey Forty Foot
Benwick
Bury
Upwood
Great Raveley
Little Raveley
Wistow
Church End
Wood Walton
Wennington
Warboys
Fenton
Abbots Ripton
Chapel Head
Bedford Level
North Level
CAMBRIDGESHIRE
Stone Bridge Corner
North Side
Peterborough Services
NENE VALLEY RAILWAY
FERRY MEADOWS
FLAG FEN ARCHAEOLOGY PARK
PETERBOROUGH MUSEUM
THE WESTON HOMES STADIUM
EAST OF ENGLAND SHOWGROUND
SACREWELL FARM & COUNTRY CENTRE
CASTOR HANGLANDS
HOLME FEN
WOODWALTON FEN
MONKS WOOD
UPWOOD MEADOWS
HAMERTON ZOO PARK
RURAL MUSEUM
RAMSEY ABBEY GATEHOUSE
Peterborough (Conington)
Peterborough (Sibson)
Upwood Airfield (disused)
0 1 2 3 miles
0 1 2 3 4 5 km

Gorefield
Leverington
Leverington Common
Wisbech
Walsoken
New Walsoken
Peckover House
Wisbech & Fenland Museum
Fenland & West Norfolk Aviation Mus
St John's Fen End
Tilney Fen End
Wiggenhall St Mary Magdalen
Marshland St James
Marshland Fen
Parson Drove
Church End
Wisbech St Mary
Murrow
Bunker's Hill
Tholomas Drove
Rogue's Alley
Elm
Emneth
Emneth Hungate
Collett's Bridge
Holly End
Begdale
Friday Bridge
N O R F O L K
Stowbridge
West Head
Guyhirn
Guyhirn Gull
Waldersey
Coldham
Outwell
Downham Market
Barroway Drove
Bardolph Fen
Upwell
Nordelph
Salters Lode
Denver
Denver Sluice
Three Holes
Fordham
Ring's End
Chainbridge
Westry
Norwoodside
Peas Hill
Badgeney
Euximoor Drove
Iron Bridge
Little London
March
Town End
Christchurch
Tipps End
Lakesend
Ten Mile Bank
Bedford Level
Middle Level
Hilgay Fen
WWT Welney Wetland Centre
Welney
Flood's Ferry
Knight's End
Stonea
Wimblington
Eastwood End
Suspension Bridge
Gold Hill
Apes Hall
Brandon Creek
Doddington
Manea
Purls Bridge
Horseway
Chatteris
Welches Dam
Ouse Washes
Pymoor
Oxlode
Dunkirk
Littleport
Sandhill
Black Bank
California
Little Downham
Langwood Fen
Block Fen
Ferry Hill
Chettisham
Queen Adelaide
Prickwillow
Mile End
Coveney
Wardy Hill
Mepal
Witcham
Ely
Oliver Cromwell's House
Sutton Gault
Sutton
Witchford
Somersham
Stuntney
Old Bedford River
The New Bedford River or Hundred Foot Drain
River Great Ouse
Sixteen Foot Drain
Forty Foot or Vermuden's Drain
A47
A141
A142
A10
A1101
A1122
B1098
B1099
B1100
B1093
B1411
B1382
B1104
157
140
123
7
8
9
10
11
A
B
C
D
E
F
G
H

Mary Magdalen
Watlington
Tottenhill
Wormegay
Shouldham Warren
Marham
Narborough Field
Great Palgrave
Sporle
Swaffham
Runcton Holme
South Runcton
Fodderstone Gap
Shouldham
Shouldham Thorpe
Marham Airfield
Thorpland
Stowbridge
Wimbotsham
Stow Bardolph
Stradsett
Fincham
Barton Bendish
Beachamwell
Shingham
Cockley Cley
THETFORD
FOREST
PARK
Downham Market
Broomhill
Bexwell
Crimplesham
Eastmoor
Gooderstone
N O R F O L K
Denver
Wereham
Boughton
Oxborough
Oxburgh Hall Garden & Estate
Gooderstone Water Gardens
West Dereham
Wereham Row
Wretton
Stoke Ferry
Whittington
Foulden
Hilborough
Fordham
Bodney
Hilgay
Ten Mile Bank
Northwold
Didlington
Brookville
Little London
Ickburgh
Methwold
Methwold Hythe
Cranwich
Mundford
Lynford Arboretum & Lakes
Southery
West Tofts
Breckland
Lynford
Brandon Creek
Feltwell
Weeting
Weeting Castle
Weeting Heath
Grime's Graves
Brandon Bank
Little Ouse
Hockwold cum Wilton
Santon Downham
Lakenheath Fen
Brandon
Heritage Centre
High Lodge Forest Centre
Thetford Warren Lodge
Level
Shippea Hill
Prickwillow
Mile End
SUFFOLK
Lakenheath
Lakenheath Airfield
Undley
Claypits
Elveden
Eriswell
Wilde Street
Beck
Mildenhall Fen
A10
A134
A1122
A1065
A47
A1101
A11
158
139
124

NORFOLK
Little Fransham
Lyon's Green
Scarning
Toftwood
Mattishall Burgh
Clint Green
Mattishall
East Tuddenham
Yaxham
Daffy Green
Necton
West End
Westfield
Winburgh
Brakefield Green
Welborne
Welborne Common
Colton
Bradenham
Holme Hale
Thorpe Row
High Green
Upper Brandon Parva
Brandon Parva
Barford
Shipdham
Garvestone
Thuxton
Runhall
Barnham Broom
North Pickenham
Little Hale
Crowshill
Letton Green
High Common
North Green
Reymerston
The Lings
The Grove
Low Street
Danemoor Green
Wramplingham
Carleton Forehoe
Ashill
Cranworth
Southburgh
Woodrising
Hardingham
Kimberley
Nordelph Corner
Saham Hills
Saham Toney
Ovington
Carbrooke
Caudlesprings
Drurylane
Great Cressingham
Chalkhill
Neaton
Watton Green
Frost Row
Hingham
Hackford
Crownthorpe
Wicklewood
Wymondham
Watton
Scoulton
Deopham
Highoak
Little Cressingham
Little Ellingham
Deopham Stalland
Statland Common
Deopham Green
Morley St Botolph
Suton
Merton
Griston
Northacre
Caston
Bush Green
Anchor Corner
The Arms
Rockland St Peter
Bow Street
Spooner Row
Thompson
Stow Bedon
Great Ellingham
Fiddlers Green
Besthorpe
Pockthorpe
Rockland All Saints
Tottington
Attleborough
Burgh Common
Bunwell Bottom
Stanford
Breckles
Lower Stow Bedon
Mount Pleasant
Shropham
Great Hockham
North End
Puddledock
Church Green
Old Buckenham
Carleton Rode
Snetterton
Stacksford
Eccles Road
South End
Ragmere
New Buckenham
East Wretham
Wretham
Stonebridge
Illington
Wilby
Larling
Harling Road
Hunt's Corner
Banham
Croxton
Quidenham
Kenninghall
Bridgham
East Harling
Middle Harling
Dam Green
Edge Green
Winfarthing
Kenninghall Heath
Thetford
Brettenham
Shadwell
West Harling
North Lopham
Fersfield
Shelfanger
Rushford
Gasthorpe
Garboldisham
South Lopham
Pooley Street
Bressingham
Knettishall
Smallworth
Euston
Blo' Norton
Fen Street
Hopton
Coney Weston
Thelnetham
Barnham
Redgrave
A11
A1066
A134
A1075
A47
159
125
142

Hellesdon
Old Catton
Sprowston
Thorpe End
Blofield Heath
Hemblington Corner
Costessey
Costessey Park
Longdell Hills
New Costessey
Upper Hellesdon
Mile Cross
New Sprowston
New Catton
Great Plumstead
Easton
ROYAL NORFOLK SHOWGROUND
Colton
Marlingford
Bowthorpe
Bunker's Hill
Thorpe St Andrew
Norwich
Thorpe Hamlet
Witton
Blofield
Brundall
Bawburgh
Earlham
Colney
SAINSBURY CENTRE FOR VISUAL ARTS
CASTLE & MUS
WHITLINGHAM COUNTRY PARK
Barford
Postwick
Great Melton
Little Melton
Cringleford
Eaton
Lakenham
Trowse Newton
Whitlingham Marsh
SURLINGHAM CHURCH MARSH
Surlingham
Wramplingham
High Green
Carleton Forehoe
Thickthorn Hall
Hethersett
Keswick
Kirby Bedon
BUCKENHAM MARSHES
ROCKLAND MARSHES
Kimberley Park
Intwood
Arminghall
Caistor St Edmund
Framingham Pigot
Bramerton
Rockland St Mary
Claxton
Lower East Carleton
Kidd's Moor
Ketteringham
Swardeston
Dunston
Framingham Earl
Hellington
Ashby St Mary
Wymondham
WYMONDHAM ABBEY
East Carleton
Stoke Holy Cross
Upper Stoke
Poringland
Yelverton
Alpington
Bergh Apton
Thurton
Mill Common
Hethel
Mulbarton
Swainsthorpe
West Poringland
Bracon Ash
Silfield
Penny's Green
Wreningham
Howe
Wolferd Green
Hawes' Green
Shotesham
Brooke
Sisland
Mundham
Suton
Ashwellthorpe
Toprow
Newton Flotman
Saxlingham Thorpe
Stubb's Green
Spooner Row
Flordon
Foxhole
Saxlingham Nethergate
Kirstead Green
Seething
Fundenhall
Hapton
Lower Tasburgh
Saxlingham Green
Loddon Ingloss
Church Wattlefield
Fundenhall Street
Low Tharston
Tasburgh
Black Carr
Bunwell Bottom
Tacolneston
INDUSTRIAL STEAM MUS
Hempnall
Thwaite St Mary
Bunwell
Forncett End
Tharston
Forncett St Mary
Stratton St Michael
Road Green
Woodton
Cordwell
Flaxlands
Forncett St Peter
NORFOLK
Hempnall Green
Silver Green
Topcroft
Hedenham
Upgate Street
Carleton Rode
Bustard's Green
Long Stratton
Morningthorpe
Fritton
Lundy Green
Bedingham Green
Bunwell Hill
Low Common
Hargate
Wacton
Wood Green
Topcroft Street
Upgate Street
Cobbler's Green
Ditchingham
Pottergate Street
Aslacton
Shelton
Shelton Green
Shelton Common
Misery Corner
Wainford
New Buckenham
Cargate Common
Great Moulton
Wacton Common
Outney Common
Bungay
Tibenham
Hardwick
Harris Green
Darrow Green
Great Green
Pristow Green
Sneath Common
Tibenham Airfield
Colegate End
Cole's Common
North Green
Denton
Earsham
Goose Green
Hales Street
Bush Green
Tivetshall St Margaret
Alburgh
Flixton
Short Green
Winfarthing
Tivetshall St Mary
Pulham Market
Piccadilly Corner
Homersfield
Gissing
Pulham St Mary
Wortwell
Boyland Common
Mill Green
Semere Green
Starston
Redenhall
St Cross South Elmham
St Peter South Elmham
Shelfanger
Bridge Green
Shimpling
Garlic Street
Harleston
St Margaret South Elmham
Burston
Dickleburgh Moor
Rushall
Mendham
SOUTH ELMHAM HALL
Audley End
Dickleburgh
Needham
St Nicholas South Elmham
Bressingham Common
Westbrook Green
High Common
100TH BOMB GROUP MEMORIAL MUSEUM
Shotford Heath
Snow Street
Walcot Green
Thelveton
Mendham Marshes
Brewers Green
Diss
Frenze
Scole Common
Upper Street
Withersdale Street
St James South Elmham
Roydon
Thorpe Abbotts
Brockdish
Weybread
Metfield
Billingford
BILLINGFORD WINDMILL
Upper Weybread
Oakley
Earsham Street
Syleham
Stuston
Needham
Mendham
0 1 2 3 miles
0 1 2 3 4 5 km

Caister-on-Sea
West Caister
West End
Runham
Stokesby
Fishley
Acle
North Burlingham
Burlingham Green
Damgate
Lingwood
Beighton
South Burlingham
Moulton St Mary
Tunstall
Halvergate
THE
BROADS
Breydon Water
Great Yarmouth
Newtown
Runham Vauxhall
Cobholm Island
Southtown
Fisher's Marshes
ELIZABETHAN HOUSE, LADY EVA & TOLHOUSE MUSEUMS
SEA LIFE CENTRE
PLEASURE BEACH
North Beach
The Beach
South Denes
Buckenham
Hassingham
Freethorpe
Southwood
Wickhampton
BERNEY ARMS WINDMILL
BERNEY MARSHES & BREYDON WATER
BURGH CASTLE
Burgh Castle
Bradwell
Gorleston-on-Sea
Gorleston Cliffs
Cantley
Limpenhoe
Limpenhoe Hill
PETTITS ANIMAL ADVENTURE PARK
Reedham
Chedgrave Marshes
River Yare
River Waveney
Belton
Howard's Common
Belton Common
Browston Green
REDWINGS HORSE SANCTUARY (CALDECOTT)
Hopton on Sea
Langley Street
Hardley Street
Nogdam End
Chedgrave
Loddon
Heckingham
Lower Thurlton
Thurlton
Thurlton Marshes
Fritton
ST OLAVE'S PRIORY
St Olaves
Bunker's Hill
Bloodman's Corner
The Dell
Cuckoo Green
Lound
Blundeston
Corton
Corton Cliffs
Herringfleet
SOMERLEYTON HALL
Somerleyton
Haddiscoe
Thorpe
Hales
Raveningham
RAVENINGHAM GARDENS
HALES HALL BARN & GARDENS
PLEASUREWOOD HILLS LEISURE PARK
Gunton
Oulton
Normanston
LOWESTOFT MARITIME MUS
North Beach
Lowestoft Denes
Lowestoft Ness
Maypole Green
Brundish
Toft Monks
Kirby Cane
Stockton
Wheatacre
Waterheath
Aldeby
Burgh St Peter
Waterloo
Oulton Broad
Lowestoft
Roman Hill
CARLTON MARSHES NATURE RESERVE
Ellingham
Kirby Row
Geldeston
Gillingham
Dockeney
Dunburgh
Beccles
BECCLES DISTRICT MUSEUM
River Waveney
Barsham Marshes
Beccles Marshes
Castle Marsh
Kirkley
Claremont Pier
Pakefield
Pakefield Cliffs
Carlton Colville
EAST ANGLIA TRANSPORT MUS
Mettingham
Shipmeadow
Barsham
Worlingham
North Cove
Barnby
Gisleham
Ringsfield
Ringsfield Corner
Ilketshall St Andrew
Weston
Ellough
Hulver Street
Mutford
Rushmere
Kessingland
AFRICA ALIVE!
Kessingland Beach
Henstead
SUFFOLK
Redisham
Shadingfield
Sotterley
West End
Benacre
Benacre Ness
The Denes
Ilketshall St Lawrence
Stone Street
Cox Common
Brampton
Wrentham
Mill Common
Stoven
Frostenden
Covehithe
Westhall
Clay Common
South Cove
Spexhall
Uggeshall
Cove Bottom
Wissett
Broadway
HALESWORTH AIRFIELD MEM MUS
Upper Holton
Wangford
Reydon Smear
Halesworth
161
127

2
3
4
5
6
A
B
C
D
E
F
G
H
1
SH
10
40
Trwyn Porth Dinllaen
Carreg Ddu
Porth Dinllaen
Borth Wen
Penrhyn Nefyn
Porth Nefyn
Bodeilias
Pistyll
Moel Ty-Gwyn
Wern
Tir Bach
Tyddyn Uchaf
Morfa Nefyn
Aber Geirch
LLŶN MARITIME MUSEUM
Mynydd Nefyn
Bodeilian
162
Nefyn
Garn Boduan
280
Hendre Penprys
Penrhyn Cwmistir
Cwmistir
Groesffordd
Edern
Plasyngheidio
Tan-y-graig
B4417
B4412
A497
B4354
Glanrhyd
Moelypenmaen
Porth Towyn
Rhos-y-llan
Porth Ysglaig
Towyn
Tref-erwyn
Maesoglan
Glan-y-gors
Hendre
Boduan
Coed Bodfel
Cefn Leisiog
CORS GEIRCH
Porth Ysgaden
Nyffryn
Y Ddôl
Meillionen
Tudweiliog
Mochras
Traian
Penrallt
Porth Gwylan
Tan-llan
Brynodol
Madryn Castle
Mathan Isaf
Cefn Mine
Gwyndy
Pwllgoed
Moel Caerau
Pennllech Bach
Ty-mawr
Rhos-ddû
Dinas
Galltr y Beren
Penrhyn Melyn
Cefntreuddyn
Cefnamwlch
371
Carn Fadryn
CARN FADRUN (FORT)
B4415
Tan-y-bryn
Porth Colmon
Ffridd-goch
Ffridd-wen
Penybryn
Tyn Llidiart
Myfyr
Tyn Simdda
Garn Bach
Garnfadryn
Rhyd-y-clafdy
Penrhos
Traeth Penllech
Porth Wen Bâch
Berthaur
Porth Colmon Morfa
Bryn Geinach
Penllech
Mynydd Cefnamwlch
182
Tregwm
Bryn-mawr
Llaniestyn
Penbodlas
Bryn Celyn Hall
Cefn Llanfair
Polish Home
Porth Ty-mawr
Pen-y-graig
Wern Fawr
Tyddyncaled
Afon
Tynewydd
Carneddol
Porth Widlin
WALES COAST PATH
Llangwnnadl
Cellar Fm
Sarn Meyllteyrn
Trefaes
Inkermann Br
Rhedyn
Foel Bach
Penarwel
Henllys
Carreg y
Porth Ferin
Penrhyn Mawr
Maen Mellt
Dinas
Porth Iago
Ty-mawr
Ty-hen
Lleiniau
Pen-y-bryn
Pant
B4413
Tyn-y-coed
Bryncroes
Trygarn
Bronphilip Fm
Nanhoron
Foel Fawr
Mynytho Common
Llanbedrog
Plas Glyn-y-weddw
A499
Brynhunog Fawr
Llety'r Wym
Pen-y-groeslon
Coch-y-moel
Botwnnog
Capel Newydd
Mynytho
Mynydd Tirycwmwd
132
Trwyn Llanbedrog
Trwyn Glas
Porth Oer
Porth y Wrâch
Methlem
Tocia
Hirwaun
Faerdre
Gelliwig
Bryn Llewelyn
Coed-y-fron
Tan-y-mynydd
Rhydlios
NEOLITHIC AXE FACTORY
Tyddyn Corn Fm
Llandegwning
Talsarn
Saithbont
Barach
Nant
Rhandir
Bodwi
Dinas Bâch
Mynydd Carreg
Rhoshirwaun
Cruga Bach
304
Mynydd Rhiw
Tyn-y-parc
Tyddyn Gwyn
Fach Fm
The Warren
Dinas Fawr
Felin Uchaf
Meillionydd
Neigwl Ganol
Capel Carmel
Porthorion
WALES COAST PATH
Llawrdref Bellaf
Llangian
St Tudwal's Road
Penbennar
Glangors
PLAS-YN-RHIW
Ty Mawr
Glan Soch
Carreg
Bryn-mawr
Mynydd Ystum
Ty Cerrig
Abersoch
Angorfa St Tudwal
Morfa Gors
Hendre
Afon Daron
Penycaerau
Rhiw
Trefollwyn
Braich Anelog
Anelog
Ty Croes Mawr
Mynydd Graig
PORTH NEIGWL OR HELL'S MOUTH
Punt Gwynedd
Towyn
Llanengan
Porth Tocyn
Llanllawen
Porth Llanllawen
MYNYDD-Y-CRAIG HEADLAND
Maen Du
Aberdaron
Llanfaelrhys
Tai-morfa
Sarn Bach
Penrhyn Du
Porth Bach
St Tudwal's Island East
Braich y Noddfa
Mynydd Mawr
Uwchmynydd
Bryn Fm
Porth Cadlan
Porth Ysgo
Newydd Fm
Bwlchtocyn
Marchroes
Braich y Pwll
160
Porth Simdde
Aberdaron Bay
Trwyn y Penrhyn
Ogof Lwyd
Trwyn Talfarach
Cim
Gwyddel
Porth Cloch
Ebolion
Nant Fm
Corn Fm
Trwyn Maen Melyn
Bodermid
Trwyn y Fulfran
Nant-y-big
St Tudwal's Island West
Trwyn y Gwyddel
MYNUDD CILAN
Porth Ceiriad
Pistyll Cim
Porth Felen
Ynys Gwylan-fawr
Trwyn Carreg-y-tir
Mynydd Gilan
Pared-mawr
Trwyn yr Wylfa
Porth y Pistyll
Ynys Gwylan-bâch
Trwyn y Ffosle
Parwyd
Hen Borth
Cilan Uchaf
Trwyn Llech-y-doll
Pen y Cil
Trwyn Cilan
Maen Bugail
Bardsey Sound
Swnt Enlli
Bae y Rhigol
Trwyn y Gorlech
Bae'r Nant
ST MARY'S ABBEY (RUINS) OLD CROSSES
Maen Iau
Plas-bach
Bardsey Island
Ynys Enlli
Carreg yr Honwy
YNYS ENLLI
Porth Solfach
Cafn Enlli
Ystwffwl Glas
Henllwyn
Ogof Lladron
Ogof Diban
G W Y N E D D
L L E Y N
0
1
2
3 miles
0
1
2
3
4
5 km

Penrhyn Llyn
Ysgubor Plas
Cefn Isaf
Tyddyn Cestyll
Llwyndyrys
Trallwyn Hall
Maen-llwyd
Pencaenewydd
Pentyrch isaf
Talafon
Castell Gwgan
Lôn-las
Llangybi
Maes Gwyn Uchaf
Fron-oleu
Bettws Bach
Rhoslan
Bryniau Ystumcegid
Bryn Hywel
Garnedd-hir
Garth Fm
Y Fedw 267
Prenteg
Pont Croesor
Bryn
Mynydd-mawr
Plas
Geufron
Pencraig
Penbryn
Rhosgyll
Tyddyn cethin
Tyddyn-Iolyn
Braich-y-saint
Penmorfa
Glan-y-morfa
Allt-wen
Coed Tremadog
Tremadog
Welsh Highland Heritage Railway
Welsh Highland Railway
Fron
Tyn Coed
Ynysieci
Bryn llefrith
Felin Bencoed
Tyddyn-y-felin
Glyncoed
Llwyn-dwyfog
Tyddyn
Dynana
Pentreuchaf
Rhos-fawr
Rhyd-y-gwystl
Bryngwdyn
Llanarmon
Pen-y-Mount
Y Garth
Penrhyndeudraeth
Ty Du Isaf
Coed Rhos-fawr
Tyn-rhos-fawr
Y Ffôr
Cromlech
Pen-carth
Cabin Wood
Trefan
Pentrefelin
Wern
Moel-y-Gest 262
Bus Pk
Porthmadog
Railway Museum
Porthmadog Harbour
Minffordd
Bryn Rodyn
Llannerch
Brynaerau
Chwilog
Llanystumdwy
Pen-y-Bryn
Criccieth
Coed-y-llyn
Rhosydd
Bryngoleu
Brynllaeth
Clogwyn
Penarth Bach
Penarth Fawr
Lloyd George Museum
Criccieth Castle
Morfa Bychan
Maritime Mus
Borth-y-Gest
Britannia Terr
Boston Lodge Halt
Llandecwyn
Llannor
Tan-y-graig
Abererch
Broom Hall
Afon Wen
Bont Fechan
Muriau
Portmeirion
Brynhynog
Gorphwysfa
Hafan y Mor
Penychain
Black Rock Sand
Wales Coast Path
Traeth Bach
Talsarnau
Efailnewydd
Pensarn Fm
Denio
Penrallt
Pwllheli
Bryn-ynys
Allt Fawr
Ind Est
Penrhyn
Cerrig y Barcdy
Pen-ychain
Harlech Pt
Ynys
Tygwyn
Glan-y-wern
Glyn-y-warch
Carreg yr Imbill
West End
Marian-y-mor
South Beach
Traeth Crugan
Morfa Harlech
Tyn-yr-acrau
Coed Penmaen
Moel Goch 369
Glyn Morfa
Merthyr Fm
Foel Senigl
Tremadog Bay
Bae Tremadog
Harlech
Harlech Castle
Ffridd Fm
Maesyraelfor
Tyddyn Felin
Llanfair
Hafod-y-llyn
Llandanwg
Slate Caverns
Pen-y-bont
Pen-sarn
Coed Lletywalter
Pentre Gwynfryn
Llanbedr
Coed Aberartro
Shell Island
Hendy
Uwchlaw'r-coed
Taltreuddyn
Pen-y-bryn
Morfa Dyffryn
Llwynion-fechan
Ynys-Gwrtheyrn
Coed Ystumgwern
Tal y ffnonau
Llanenddwyn
Waun Hir
Dyffryn Burial Chamber
Meifod-uchaf
Cors-y-Gedol
Dyffryn Ardudwy
Llanddwywe
Tal-y-bont
Llecheiddior
Eithin-fynydd
Mynydd Egryn
Plas-canol
Llwyndu Fm
Llanaber
Barmouth (Abermaw)
RNLI Lifeboat Museum
Fairbourne Railway
Barmouth Bay
Bae Bermo
Golf Halt
Fairbourne
Cefnfeusydd Fm
Borthwen Fm
Gwastadgoed
Hendre
Llwyngwril
Rhiwgaeron
Y Rhos
Fign
162
163
146
A B C D E F G H
7 8 9 10 11

Llan Ffestiniog
Maentwrog
Tan-y-bwlch
Penrhyndeudraeth
Minffordd
Portmeirion
Talsarnau
Trawsfynydd
Llyn Trawsfynydd
Pont Dolydd Prysor
Bronaber
Harlech Castle
Cors-y-Gedol
Tal-y-bont
Barmouth (Abermaw)
Barmouth Bay
Bae Bermo
Fairbourne
Friog
Arthog
Ynysgyfflog
Llanelltyd
Penmaenpool
Bontddu
Caerdeon
Dolgellau
Brithdir
Bont Newydd
Rhydymain
Ganllwyd
Llanfachreth
Coed y Brenin Forest Park
Snowdonia National Park
Parc Cenedlaethol Eryri
Cadair Idris
Minffordd
Tal-y-llyn
Corris Uchaf
Aberllefenni
Aberangell
Llanfihangel-y-pennant
Buarthmeini
Pont Fronwydd
Arenig Fawr
Rhinog Fawr
Rhinog Fach
Diffwys
Llyn Cwm Bychan
Afon Mawddach
Dyfi Forest
Mynydd Moel
Rhobell Fawr
Dduallt
Maentwrog
Gellilydan
Cilfor
Eisingrug
Glyn-Cywarch
Pen-y-bont
Llanaber
Plas-canol
Abergwynant
Rhydwen
Tabor
Capel Hermon
Bed-y-coedwr
Pont Aber-Geirw
Cwm-hesgen
Nannau
Blaen-y-cwm
Dolgellau
A470
A487
A493
A494
A496
B4391
B4416
B4405
0 1 2 3 miles
0 1 2 3 4 5 km

DENBIGHSHIRE
(SIR DDYNBYCH)
POWYS
Bala
Y Bala
Llanfor
Bethel
Sarnau
Cefn-ddwysarn
Llandderfel
Frongoch
Llidiardau
Rhyd-uchaf
Rhiwlas
Cynwyd
Llandrillo
Pennant
Llanycil
Parc
Llangower
Llanuwchllyn
Pandy
Rhosdylluan
Talardd
Ty-nant
Aber-Hirnant
Penllyn Forest
Rhos-y-gwaliau
Alltforgan
Pennant Melangell
Llangynog
Pencraig
Tan-y-pistyll
Pistyll Rhaeadr
Tyn-y-fedwen
Penybontfawr
Penygarnedd
Hirnant
Ty-uchaf
Lake Vyrnwy
Llanwddyn
Abertridwr
Blaen-y-cwm
Tycrwyn
Llanfihangel-yng-Ngwynfa
Pont-Llogel
Dolanog
Pontrobert
Ddôl-Cownwy
Dyfnant Forest
Aber-Rhiwlech
Pont y Pennant
Llanymawddwy
Cywarch
Bryn Sion
Aber Cowarch
Cwm-Cewydd
Mallwyd
Wern
Foel
Llangadfan
Llanerfyl
Four Crosses
Heniarth
Cadair Berwyn 827
Cadair Bronwen 784
Moel Sych 827
Aran Benllyn 885
Aran Fawddwy 907
Llyn Tegid or Bala Lake
Bala Lake Railway
River Dee
Afon Eiddew
A494
A4212
A458
B4391
B4401
B4402
B4403
B4393
B4395
B4396
B4382
B4501
Y Berwyn
Lake Vyrnwy RSPB
Glyndŵr's Way
164
165
148
129
7
8
9
10
11
A
B
C
D
E
F
G
H
SJ

Llangollen
Cefn-mawr
Froncysyllte
Pentre
Halton
Chirk (Y Waun)
CHIRK CASTLE
Glyn-Ceiriog
Pontfadog
Llwynmawr
Bronygarth
Chirk Bank
Preesgweene
Weston Rhyn
St Martin's
Ifton Heath
Street Dinas
WREXHAM (WRECSAM)
Pandy
Craignant
Tregeiriog
Llechrydau
Selattyn
Gobowen
Llanarmon Dyffryn Ceiriog
Hengoed
Hindford
Rhiwlas
Pant-glas
Whittington
WHITTINGTON CASTLE
Tyn-y-fedwen
Tyn-y-ffridd
Cefn Canol
Llawnt
Rhydycroesau
Babbinswood
Llangadwaladr
POWYS
Oswestry
CAMBRIAN RAILWAY MUS
Middleton
Tai-bach
Moelfre
Llansilin
Felin Newydd
Tyn-y-coed
Morda
Wootton
Llanrhaeadr-ym-Mochnant
Cefn Coch
Trefonen
Ball
Maesbury
Maesbury Marsh
West Felton
SHROPSHIRE
Treflach
Nantmawr
Morton
Woolston
Penybontfawr
Penygarnedd
Llangedwyn
Pen-y-bont
Porth-y-waen
Llynclys
Rhos-y-brithdir
Llanyblodwel
Crickheath
Osbaston
Knockin
Bwlchyddar
Pant
Maesbrook
Abernaint
Llansantffraid-ym-Mechain
Llanymynech
Kinnerley
Llanfechain
Llanfyllin
Llandysilio
Four Crosses
Crosslanes
Tycrwyn
Bwlch-y-cibau
Waen Fach
Deuddwr
Llandrinio
Melverley Green
Melverley
Sarnau
Arddleen
Main
Trefnanney
Crewgreen
Criggion
Coedway
Pentrebeirdd
Geuffordd
Wern
Meifod
Pontrobert
Glascoed
Maesgwyn-Isaf
Varchoel
Pool Quay
Middletown
Wollaston
Guilsfield (Cegidfa)
Groes-lwyd
Trewern
Halfway House
Cloddiau
Nelly Andrews Green
Buttington
Vennington
Heniarth
0 1 2 3 miles
0 1 2 3 4 5 km

Erbistock
Overton (Owrtyn)
Horseman's Green
Three Fingers
Eglwys Cross
Whitewell
Whitchurch
Chemistry
Waymills
Broughall
Lightwood Green
Sandy Lane
Redbrook
Street Lydan
Penley
Hanmer
Little Green
The Chequer
Tilstock Road
Ash Magna
Knolton Bryn
Knolton
Rhewl
Tarts Hill
Arowry
Bronington
Alkington
Brown Moss Nature Reserve
Ightfield
Dudleston
Pentre-coed
Gadlas
Dudleston Heath
Tilstock
Prees Heath
Coptiviney
Breaden Heath
Fenn's Whixall & Bettisfield Mosses
Fenn's Moss
Hollinwood
Prees Higher Heath
Elson
Ellesmere
The Mere
Welshampton
Balmer Heath
Bettisfield
Welsh End
Shropshire Union Canal
Whixall
Sandford
Perthy
Welsh Frankton
Colemere
Lyneal
Northwood
Waterloo
Quina Brook
Prees
Darliston
Prees Lower Heath
Fauls
Tetchill
Lee
Wood Lane
Edstaston
Lower Frankton
Hordley
Wolverley
Newtown
Lowe
Prees Green
Kenwick
Horton
Wem
English Frankton
Loppington
Lower Hordley
Cockshutt
Marchamley
Weston
Wixhill
Hawkstone Historic Park & Follies
Hodnet Hall Gardens
Rednal
Stanwardine in the Wood
The Wood
Noneley
Commonwood
Tilley
Aston
Lee Brockhurst
Haughton
Grimpo
Bagley
Petton
Burlton
Sleap
Hopton
Moston
Weston Lullingfields
Westoncommon
Shropshire
Eardiston
Wykey
Stanwardine in the Fields
Marton
Alderton
Clive
Yorton
Preston Brockhurst
Stanton upon Hine Heath
High Hatton
Shotatton
Myddle
Grinshill
Moreton Corbet
Ruyton-XI-Towns
Brownhill
Baschurch
Harmer Hill
Shawbury
Edgebolton
Muckleton
Kynaston
Prescott
Walford
Merrington
Preston Gubbals
Hadnall
Rowton
Kinton
Nesscliffe
Great Ness
Little Ness
Yeaton
Walford Heath
Bomere Heath
Astley
Poynton Green
Great Wytheford
Walton
Wilcott
Grafton
Leaton
Bings Heath
High Ercall
Felton Butler
Fitz
Albrighton
Pentre
Ensdon
Forton Heath
Mytton
Battlefield
Haughton
Roden
Shrawardine
Montford Bridge
Harlescott
Rodington
Alberbury
Montford
Bicton
Ditherington
Uffington
Ford
Shrewsbury
Shelton
Coton Hill
Withington
Shoot Hill
Copthorne
Upton Magna
Rowton
Cardeston
Porthill
Preston
Walcot
Charlton
Hortonlane
Meole Brace
Emstrey
Attingham Park
Westbury
Yockleton
Nox
Cruckton
Cruckmeole
Hanwood
Bayston Hill
Norton
Uppington
Aston
Stoney Stretton
Edge
Lea
Atcham
Wroxeter Roman City (Viroconium)
Farley
Hinton
Wroxeter
Donnington
Rushton
A5
A49
A41
A53
A528
A458
B5476
B5063
Shrewsbury Road
Holyhead Road

Coxbank
Heath
Wilkesley
Ireland's Cross
Pipe Gate
Aston
Madeley Park
Hanchurch
Whitmore
Knighton
Adderley
Willoughbridge
Dorothy Clive Garden
Baldwin's Gate
Bearstone
Blackbrook
Ightfield
Norton in Hales
Maer
Stableford
Newstreet Lane
Chapel Chorlton
Calverhall
Mucklestone
Betton
Loggerheads
Ashley
Ashley Heath
Hookgate
Podmore
Cranberry
Standon
Cotes
Almington
Moreton Say
Market Drayton
Hales
Chatcull
Longford
Sandford
Bletchley
Wetwood
Millmeece
Fauls
Fairoak
Croxtonbank
Slindon
Croxton
Ternhill
Sutton
The Four Alls
Chipnall
Lostford
Sugnall
Sturbridge
Woodseaves
Rosehill
Wollerton
Cheswardine
Pershall
Stoke Heath
Bishop's Offley
Marchamley
Hodnet
Wistanswick
Soudley
Eccleshall
Hodnet Hall Gardens
Stoke on Tern
Mill Green
Lockleywood
Adbaston
Knighton
Hopton
Hinstock
High Offley
Wootton
Ellerton
Shebdon
Woodseaves
Lawnhead
Ollerton
Sambrook
Radmoor
High Hatton
Child's Ercall
Weston Jones
Knightley Dale
Knightley
Norbury
Howle
Pickstock
Eaton on Tern
Ellerdine Heath
Puleston
Sutton
Forton
Muckleton
Great Bolas
Cold Hatton
Edgmond Marsh
Gnosall
Tibberton
Cherrington
Rowton
Waters Upton
Edgmond
Coton
Gnosall Heath
Newport
Walton
Adeney
Longford
Outwoods
High Ercall
Crudgington
Church Aston
Chetwynd Aston
Church Eaton
Kynnersley
Brockton
Moreton
Longdon on Tern
High Onn
Sleapford
Orslow
Lilleshall
Eyton upon the Weald Moors
Preston upon the Weald Moors
Hoo Zoo Dinosaur World
Great Chatwell
Rodington
Muxton
Heath Hill
Weston Heath
Marston
Bratton
Donnington
Admaston
Lilyhurst
Brineton
Trench
Donnington Wood
Wrockwardine
Hadley
Sheriffhales
Blymhill
Walcot
Ketley
Wellington
Oakengates
Charlton
Arleston
Crackleybank
Weston under Lizard
Ketley Bank
Priorslee
Aston
Uppington
The Rock
Haughton
Bishop's Wood
Lawley
Telford
Shifnal
Tong Norton
Rushton
Boscobel House & The Royal Oak
SHROPSHIRE
TELFORD AND WREKIN
0 1 2 3 miles
0 1 2 3 4 5 km

Trentham
Meir
Lightwood
Meir Heath
Blythe Bridge
Forsbrook
Draycott in the Moors
Mobberley
Freehay
Alton
Gallows Green
Bradley in the Moors
Denstone
Rough Close
Greatgate
Rocester
Barlaston
World of Wedgwood
Tittensor
Cresswell
Upper Tean
Croxden
Hollington
Lower Tean
Checkley
Knenhall
Fulford
Combridge
Moddershall
Upper Leigh
Lower Leigh
Fole
Crakemarsh
Beamhurst
Creighton
Oulton
Meaford
Church Leigh
Middleton Green
Cotwalton
Withington
Stramshall
Stone
Hilderstone
Garshall Green
Dods Leigh
Lower Nobut
Dagdale
Bramshall
The Heath
Walton
Little Stoke
Dayhills
Field
Yarnfield
Milwich
Coton Hill
Coton
Blount's Green
Uttoxeter
Gratwich
Aston-by-Stone
Fradswell
Norton Bridge
Burston
Sandon
Willslock
Kingstone
Izaak Walton Cottage Museum
Chebsey
Yarlet
Whitgreave
Grindley
Gorsty Hill
Marston
Gayton
Great Bridgeford
Salt
Weston
Stowe-by-Chartley
Chartley Moss
Amerton Farm & Craft Centre
Drointon
Hopton
Hixon
Holmcroft
Seighford
Newton
Stafford
Ingestre
Abbots Bromley
Ranton
Doxey
Coton Clanford
Long Compton
Derrington
Tixall
Great Haywood
Admaston
Whitecross
Forebridge
Little Haywood
Shugborough Estate
Weeping Cross
Colwich
Staffordshire
Haughton
Moss Pit
Milford
Walton on the Hill
Colton
Blithbury
Brocton
Coppenhall
Allimore Green
Etchinghill
Rugeley
Hamstall Ridware
Bradley
Acton Trussell
Bednall
Apeton
Dunston
Cannock Chase
Hill Ridware
Nethertown
Slitting Mill
Levedale
Longridge
Brereton
Armitage
Handsacre
Mitton
Upper Longdon
Longdon
Whiston
Pye Green
Penkridge
Congreve
Huntington
Longdon Green
Lapley
Hednesford
Hazelslade
Littleworth
Farewell
Stretton
Cannock Wood
Gentleshaw
Wimblebury
Oldfallow
Chorley
Horsebrook
Gailey
Hatherton
Heath Hayes
Cannock
Norton East
Chase Terrace
Burntwood
Lichfield
Kiddemore Green
Brewood
Bridgtown
Chasetown
Norton Canes
Standeford
Churchbridge
M6
A34
A50
A51
A518
A513
A5
A449
A460
A515

DERBYSHIRE
STAFFS
THE NATIONAL FOREST
Derby
Burton upon Trent
Uttoxeter
Lichfield
Tutbury
Swadlincote
Mickleover
Allestree
Normanton
Littleover
Willington
Repton
Horninglow
Stretton
Branston
Stapenhill
Winshill
Newhall
Woodville
Hilton
Etwall
Findern
Egginton
Rolleston-on-Dove
Hatton
Scropton
Sudbury
Doveridge
Rocester
Marchington
Hanbury
Barton-under-Needwood
Alrewas
Yoxall
King's Bromley
Elford
Edingale
Croxall
Harlaston
Clifton Campville
Measham
Appleby Magna
Overseal
Linton
Rosliston
Walton-on-Trent
Coton in the Elms
Lullington
Netherseal
Kedleston
Quarndon
Brailsford
Ednaston
Mackworth
Longford
Cubley Common
Great Cubley
Alkmonton
Yeaveley
Rodsley
Hollington
Longlane
Thurvaston
Radbourne
Dalbury
Burnaston
Marston Montgomery
Somersal Herbert
Oaks Green
Church Broughton
Sutton on the Hill
Foston
Tatenhill
Needwood
Newchurch
Anslow
Fradley
Elmhurst
Streethay
Whittington
Hademore
Thorpe Constantine
No Man's Heath
Newton Solney
Bretby
Hartshorne
Milton
Twyford
Stenson
Castle Gresley
Church Gresley
Moira
Donisthorpe
Oakthorpe
Chilcote
Hamstall Ridware
Blithbury
Handsacre
Newborough
Draycott in the Clay
Marston on Dove
Lichfield Trent Valley
National Memorial Arboretum
Conkers National Forest Discovery Centre
A50
A38
A515
A511
A444
A52
A513
A5121
A51
A5192
A5127
A516
A514
A42
A5206
A5132
River Dove
River Trent
River Mease
Trent Valley
Trent & Mersey Canal
0 1 2 3 miles
0 1 2 3 4 5 km
151
169
170
134

NOTTINGHAM
Nottingham
West Bridgford
Beeston
Stapleford
Long Eaton
Sandiacre
Risley
Chaddesden
Spondon
Borrowash
Breaston
Draycott
Alvaston
Chellaston
Melbourne
Castle Donington
Kegworth
Shepshed
Loughborough
Coalville
Whitwick
Ashby-de-la-Zouch
Ibstock
Markfield
Newtown Linford
Anstey
Birstall
Mountsorrel
Sileby
Rothley
Cossington
Barrow upon Soar
Quorn or Quorndon
Woodhouse Eaves
Ruddington
Clifton
Keyworth
East Leake
Gotham
Sutton Bonington
Wymeswold
Rempstone
NOTTINGHAMSHIRE
DERBY CITY
LEICESTERSHIRE
THE NATIONAL FOREST
Charnwood Forest
EAST MIDLANDS
Donington Park Services
Trowell Services
170
171
154
135

Carlton
Stoke Bardolph
Newton
Burrowsmoor Holt
Scarrington
Alverton
Radcliffe on Trent
Colwick
Netherfield
Saxondale
Bingham
Aslockton
Orston
Normanton
Whatton
Bottesford
Holme Pierrepont
Upper Saxondale
Harlequin
Elton
Easthorpe
Muston
Adbolton
Holme Lane
Gamston
Bassingfield
West Bridgford
Cropwell Butler
Tithby
Cropwell Bishop
Barnstone
Granby
Sutton
Redmile
Stenwith
Edwalton
NOTTINGHAMSHIRE
Vale of Belvoir
Cotgrave
Langar
Barkestone-le-Vale
Plungar
Belvoir
Belvoir Castle
Woolsthorpe by Belvoir
Tollerton
Clipston
Owthorpe
Colston Bassett
Plumtree
Normanton-on-the-Wolds
Plumtree Park
Keyworth
Stanton-on-the-Wolds
Kinoulton
Harby
Stathern
Harston
Knipton
Hose
Hickling
Widmerpool
Long Clawson
Eaton
Eastwell
Branston
Croxton Kerrial
Wysall
Goadby Marwood
Nether Broughton
Upper Broughton
Willoughby-on-the-Wolds
Waltham on the Wolds
Wycomb
Scalford
Chadwell
Stonesby
Wymeswold
Old Dalby
Holwell
Ab Kettleby
Wartnaby
Potter Hill
Grimston
Saxelbye
Burton on the Wolds
Six Hills
LEICESTERSHIRE
Shoby
Ragdale
Asfordby
Asfordby Hill
Thorpe Arnold
Brentingby
Wyfordby
Freeby
Saxby
Garthorpe
Walton on the Wolds
Melton Mowbray
Melton Carnegie Museum
Stapleford
Seagrave
Hoby
Frisby on the Wreake
Kirby Bellars
Rotherby
Brooksby
Burton Lazars
Thrussington
Sileby
Ratcliffe on the Wreake
Rearsby
Little Dalby
Great Dalby
Nether End
Upper End
Whissendine
Leesthorpe
Cossington
East Goscote
Gaddesby
Queniborough
Ashby Folville
Pickwell
Syston
Thorpe Satchville
Barsby
Burrough on the Hill
Somerby
Cold Overton
Barkby
South Croxton
Twyford
Barleythorpe
John O'Gaunt
Newbold
Marefield
Owston
Knossington
Beeby
Oakham
A46
A52
A606
A607
A6006
A6
B676
B6047
171
172
153
136
0 1 2 3 miles
0 1 2 3 4 5 km

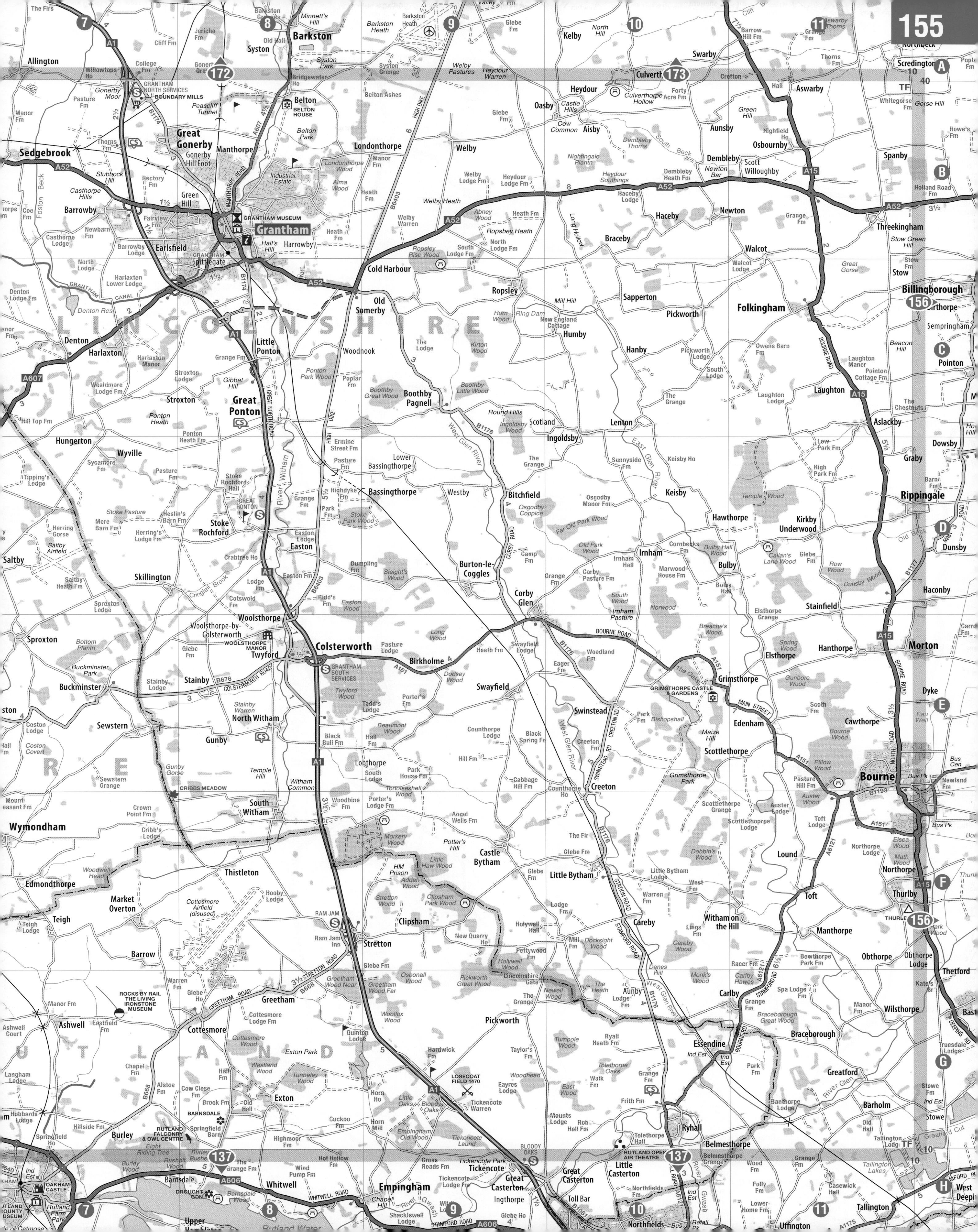

Barkston
Syston
Allington
Kelby
Swarby
Culverth 173
Heydour
Oasby
Aisby
Aswarby
Aunsby
Osbournby
Dembleby
Scott Willoughby
Spanby
172
Belton
BELTON HOUSE
Great Gonerby
Manthorpe
Londonthorpe
Welby
Sedgebrook
Barrowby
GRANTHAM MUSEUM
Grantham
Harrowby
Earlsfield
Spittlegate
Cold Harbour
Haceby
Newton
Braceby
Walcot
Threekingham
Ropsley
Sapperton
Pickworth
Folkingham
Billingborough 156
Old Somerby
LINCOLNSHIRE
Humby
Hanby
Denton
Harlaxton
Little Ponton
Woodnook
Boothby Pagnell
Laughton
Pointon
Stroxton
Great Ponton
Scotland
Lenton
Ingoldsby
Aslackby
Hungerton
Wyville
Dowsby
Graby
Bassingthorpe
Westby
Bitchfield
Keisby
Rippingale
Hawthorpe
Kirkby Underwood
Stoke Rochford
Easton
Irnham
Bulby
Dunsby
Saltby
Skillington
Burton-le-Coggles
Corby Glen
Haconby
Stainfield
Woolsthorpe
Woolsthorpe-by-Colsterworth
WOOLSTHORPE MANOR
Sproxton
Colsterworth
Twyford
Birkholme
Elsthorpe
Hanthorpe
Morton
Buckminster
Stainby
GRANTHAM SOUTH SERVICES
Swayfield
Grimsthorpe
GRIMSTHORPE CASTLE & GARDENS
Dyke
North Witham
Swinstead
Edenham
Cawthorpe
Sewstern
Gunby
Scottlethorpe
Bourne
CRIBBS MEADOW
South Witham
Creeton
Wymondham
Castle Bytham
Lound
Thistleton
Little Bytham
Northorpe
Edmondthorpe
Market Overton
Toft
Thurlby
Teigh
Clipsham
Careby
Witham on the Hill
Manthorpe
156
RAM JAM
Stretton
Barrow
Obthorpe
Thetford
ROCKS BY RAIL THE LIVING IRONSTONE MUSEUM
Greetham
Carlby
Ashwell
Pickworth
Wilsthorpe
Cottesmore
Essendine
Braceborough
LOSECOAT FIELD 1470
Greatford
Exton
Burley
RUTLAND FALCONRY & OWL CENTRE
BARNSDALE
Ryhall
Barholm
Belmesthorpe
Stowe
137
Tickencote
Great Casterton
Little Casterton
RUTLAND OPEN AIR THEATRE
Whitwell
Empingham
OAKHAM CASTLE
RUTLAND COUNTY MUSEUM
Upper Hambleton
Rutland Water
Toll Bar
Northfields
Uffington
Tallington
West Deeping
RUTLAND
A1
A52
A15
A151
A607
A606
A6121
B1176
B6403
B676
B668
B1174
STAMFORD ROAD
BOURNE ROAD

Helpringham
Swineshead
Kirton Holme
Wyberton
Frampton
Kirton
Sandholme
Skeldyke
Seadyke
Bucklegate
Spanby
Swaton
Bicker
Drayton
Asperton
Wigtoft
Sutterton
Algarkirk
Donington
Northorpe
Threekingham
Horbling
Billingborough
Birthorpe
Sempringham
Pointon
Millthorpe
Aslackby
Dowsby
Graby
Rippingale
Dunsby
Haconby
Morton
Dyke
Bourne
Thurlby
Obthorpe
Thetford
Wilsthorpe
Baston
Langtoft
Barholm
Stowe
Towngate
Market Deeping
Deeping St James
Frognall
Tallington
Maxey
Northborough
Quadring
Gosberton
Westhorpe
Gosberton Clough
Risegate
Surfleet
Surfleet Seas End
Fosdyke
Crossgate
Pinchbeck
Pinchbeck West
Pinchbeck Bars
Northgate
Spalding
Little London
Pode Hole
Clay Lake
Fulney
Low Fulney
Weston
Weston Hills
Moulton
Whaplode
Moulton Seas End
Austendike
Whaplode St Catherine
Cowbit
Moulton Chapel
Moulton Eaugate
Peak Hill
Deeping St Nicholas
Tongue End
Twenty
Hop Pole
Crowland
Shepeau Stow
Whaplode Drove
Holbeach Drove
Gedney Hill
Dowsdale
LINCOLNSHIRE

THE WASH
Scrane End
Freiston Low
Marsh Fm
HM Prison
The Scalp
River Witham
The Haven
Wyberton Marsh
FRAMPTON MARSH
The Cots
Fosdyke Wash
Fleet Haven Outfall
Lundy's Fm
Hospital Cotts
Leadenhall Fm
Willow Tree Ho
Reckerby Fm
Bingham Lodge
Thimbleby Ho
Lawyers' Fm
Trevethoe Fm
Leaden Hall
Holbeach St Matthew
Wards Fm
Sot's Hole
Christie Ho
Hartley Fm
Acre Ho
Browns Fm
Dawsmere Ho
Red House Fm
Wiles Fm
Dawsmere
Holbeach St Marks
Holbeach Marsh
Woodstoke Ho
Oldershaw Fm
Bleak House Fm
Dawsmere Creek
Keightley House Fm
Home Fm
Cardwell Ho
Gedney Marsh
Gedney Drove End
Middle Marsh Ho
Poplars Fm
Norfolk House Fm
Marsh Fm
Bertie Lodge
Crowmarsh Fm
Manor Fm
Onslow Fm
Black Barn
Red House Fm
The Grove
Fleet Haven
Red House Fm
Boat Mere Fm
Welby Ho
Clays Fm
Coney Garth Ho
Old White Ho
Brook House Fm
Lodge Fm
Crab's Hole
Holbeach Bank
Holbeach Hurn
Sutton Corner
Lutton Leam
Osbourne Ho
Woodhouse Fm
Hurn Hall
Lutton Marsh
Bull Dog Sand
Penny Hill
Cackle Hill
Hovenden Ho
Gedney Dyke
Lutton Grange
Leamlands
THE WASH
Laurel Lodge Fm
Welby Fm
Lutton
Guy's Head
Lynn Channel
Holbeach
Old Leam Fm
Terrington Marsh
Admiral's Fm
Fleet Hargate
Lutton Gowts
Chapelgate
Monmouth Ho
Lighthouse Fm
Kamarad Fm
Walkers Marsh
Horseshoe Hole Fm
Ongar Hill
Harrington Hall Fm
Gedney
King John Fm
Maze Fm
Nene Lodge Fm
Pierrepont Fm
Fleet Lodge
Oak Lodge
Manor Ho
Stonegate Ho
Avenue Fm
Little London
Common Fm
Westmere House Fm
Balaclava Fm
Fleet
Broadgate Ho
Manor Ho
New Ho
The Laurels Fm
River Great Ouse
Millbank Fm
Long Sutton
Bridge Fm
Weatherall Fm
Fern Fm
Myrobella Fm
Garnsgate
Westmere Fm
Port Sutton Bridge
East Anglian Fm
Red House Fm
Hurdletree Ho
Gedney Broadgate
Little Sutton
Wingland Marsh
Wingland Grange
Bentinck Fm
Greenmarsh Fm
Primrose Fm
Pulvertoft Hall Fm
White He Fm
Grove Fm
Sutton Bridge
Rhoon Fm
Marsh Fm
Elder Lodge
Bleak House Fm
Bellmount
Fen House Fm
Fen Fm
Onslow Fm
Fields Fm
Orange Row
West Lynn
Saturday Br
Moorswood Fm
Old Gate
Sutton Crosses
Home Fm
Nene Outfall Cut
Alma Lodge
Clenchwarton
TRUE'S YARD FISHERFOLK MUS
ST GEORGE'S GUILDHALL
Clark's Hill
Poplar Ho
Red Foreman's Br
Willow Tree Fm
South Holland Lodge
Petersponit Fm
Poplar Tree Fm
Emorsgate
South Green
Terrington St Clement
Hoe Fm
Margaretta Ho
CUSTOM HOUSE
Fleet Fen
Red House Fm
Holland Ho
South Holland Ho
Strawberry Hall
Tydd St Mary's Marsh
Walpole Cross Keys
Lovell's Hall
Kenwick Hall
KING'S LYNN
Sycamore Lodge
Clifton's Br
Wood Fm
Gibbons Fm
Balsamfield Ho
Kenwick Fm
Sutton St James
Tydd St Mary
The Grange
Old Hall
The Elms
Bell's Br
DRAW DIKE
White Cross Fm
Gunthorpe Fm
Old Inclosed Marsh
Highenden Ho
Cherry Fm
Hay Green
Shepherd's Gate
Tilney All Saints
Manor Fm
Lowgate Ho
Tydd Gote
Corner Fm
Walpole Marsh
Walpole St Andrew
Bustards Fm
Jankinsfield Fm
Merries Fm
Leedsgate Fm
Manor Hill Fm
Manor Hill Corner
Tretton Manor Fm
Hannath Hall
Foul Anchor
River Nene
Flower Fm
Tilney High End
Trafford Ho
Four Gotes
White House Fm
Wash Dyke
Broken Cross
Islington Lodge
Dunton Hall
Broadgate Ho
Cole Ho
Kirkgate Br
Silverwood Fm
White Ho Fm
Islington Hall Fm
Coy Br
Sandygate Fm
Tydd St Giles
Rose Hall
Walpole St Peter
St Peter's Lodge
Duncan's Fm
Hornfield Ho
Park Ho
Church End
Bank Fm
Eau Brink
Saddle Bow
Hallgate Fm
Ingleborough Fm
NORFOLK
Salgate Fm
Lodge Fm
Marsh Fm
Oaktree Fm
Ingleborough
White Hall Fm
Grangehill Fm
Ewings Fm
Aylmer Hall
Wiggenhall St Germans
Abbey Fm
Poplartree Fm
Honington House Fm
Terrington St John
Wiggenhall St Mary the Virgin
Guanock Ho
North Level Main Drain
Newton
Ferry Fm
Walpole Highway
St John's Highway
Hirdling Ho
Tilney St Lawrence
Thornton's Br
Mole Grove Fm
Chestnut Ho
Grange Fm
Elm Tree Ho
Sutton St Edmund
CAMBRIDGE
Priory Fm
Faulkner Ho
West Walton
Ratten Row
Tilney cum Islington
Wiggenhall St Peter
Fenwick Ho
Poplartree Fm
Guanock Ho
West Walton Highway
Black Ditch Level
Lordsbridge
Peter's Drove Br
Ivy Fm
Fitton End
Barrycott Lodge
Magdalen Br
Holly Tree Fm
Barbers Fm
Oxfield Fm
West Drove Fm
Green Lane Fm
White House Fm
Marshland
Decoy Fm
Park Ho
Walton Highway
Smeeth Lode
Gorefield
St John's Fen End
Eye Fm
Richmond Hall
Floral Fm
Grassgate Ho
FENLAND & WEST NORFOLK AVIATION MUS
Harp's Hall
Rosary Fm
Blacklane Fm
Harold's Br
Trinity Hall
Tilney Fen End
Gravel Bank Fm
Leverington
Leverington Common
Walpole Gate
Subscription Br
Wiggenhall St Mary Magdalen
Hawthorn Fm
Tydd St Mary's Fen
Hundred Acre Fm
The Smeeth
WATLINGTON
Holland's Fm
Manor Fm
Carlton Fm
Walsoken
Trafford Ho
Wisbech
Barrett's Br
Rosedale
Parsonage Fm
Main Drain
Chancellor's
PECKOVER HOUSE
New Walsoken
Paradise Fm
Marshland St James
Highfield Fm
Cheyney Br
Chequers Corner
Popenhoe Ho
Clough's Cross
Wood Mills Fm
Manor Ho
Smeeth House Fm
Forty Foot Br
Rungay's Br
Parson Drove
Church End
Bellamy's Br
WISBECH & FENLAND MUSEUM
Banyer Hall
Dike
Inham Hall
Wisbech
Oxburgh
Marshland Fen
River Great Ouse
A17
A47
A1101
B1359
B1515
B1390
B1165
B1166
B1169
B198
B1187
GEDNEY RD
WASHWAY ROAD
MARSH ROAD
FEN ROAD
ST JAMES ROAD
WISBECH RD
FISHERGATE
CHURCH LANE
SUTTON RD
HIGH ROAD
LEVERINGTON COMMON
LYNN ROAD
MAIN ROAD
TF
60
40
10
174
175
158
139
7
8
9
10
11
A
B
C
D
E
F
G
H

THE WASH
NORFOLK COAST
NORFOLK
Hunstanton
Ringstead
Heacham
Sedgeford
Docking
Stanhoe
Snettisham
Shepherd's Port
Ingoldisthorpe
Shernborne
Fring
Bircham Newton
Great Bircham
Bircham Tofts
Bagthorpe
Barmer
Syderstone
Dersingham
Anmer
Tattersett
Wolferton
Sandringham
West Newton
Flitcham
East Rudham
West Rudham
New Houghton
Harpley
Babingley
Castle Rising
Hillington
North Wootton
Congham
Roydon
Little Massingham
Great Massingham
South Wootton
Grimston
Pott Row
Gaywood
West Lynn
Clenchwarton
King's Lynn
Fairstead
Gayton
Leziate
Ashwicken
Hardwick
Gayton Thorpe
Rougham
Weasenham All Saints
Fair Green
Tower End
West Winch
Middleton
East Winch
East Walton
West Bilney
Saddle Bow
North Runcton
Wiggenhall St Germans
Blackborough End
Setchey
Pentney
West Acre
Castle Acre
Newton
South Acre
Wiggenhall St Peter
Narborough
Tottenhill Row
Great Palgrave
Wormegay
Wiggenhall St Mary Magdalen
Watlington
Tottenhill
Marham
Shouldham
Shouldham Thorpe
Runcton
Swaffham
Summerfield
Muckleton
Blenheim Park
Wicken Green Village
Stubborn Sand
Ferrier Sand
Peter Black Sand
Bull Dog Sand
Lynn Channel
River Great Ouse
River Nar
PEDDARS WAY & NORFOLK COAST PATH
A148
A149
A47
A10
A1065
A1122
A1078
A1076
B1454
B1153
B1155
B1440
B1439
B1145
175
176
157
140
0 1 2 3 miles
0 1 2 3 4 5 km

NORFOLK COAST
NORFOLK
176
177
160
141
Fakenham
Dereham
Holt
Reepham
Briston
Wells & Walsingham Light Railway
Great Walsingham
Little Walsingham
Binham
Wighton
Warham
Langham
Glandford
Saxlingham
Letheringsett
Field Dalling
Hindringham
Thursford
Little Snoring
Great Snoring
Houghton St Giles
North Barsham
West Barsham
East Barsham
Sculthorpe
Kettlestone
Fulmodestone
Barney
Melton Constable
Hindolveston
Stibbard
Great Ryburgh
Little Ryburgh
Guist
Foulsham
Twyford
Bintree
Foxley
Bawdeswell
Billingford
North Elmham
Worthing
Swanton Morley
Beetley
Gressenhall
Longham
Mileham
Litcham
Beeston
Wendling
Scarning
Toftwood
Mattishall
North Tuddenham
Hockering
Honingham
Yaxham
Necton
Little Fransham
Great Fransham
Little Dunham
Great Dunham
East Lexham
Tittleshall
Wellingham
Whissonsett
Horningtoft
Colkirk
Oxwick
Hempton
Shereford
Tatterford
Toftrees
Helhoughton
West Raynham
East Raynham
South Raynham
Dunton
North Creake
New Holkham
Waterden
Egmere
Southgate
Edgefield
Hempstead
Corpusty
Heydon
Salle
Lenwade
Weston Longville
Elsing
Lyng
Sparham
Mill Street
Woodgate
Hoe
Westfield
Welborne
Colton
Barford
Brandon Parva
A148
A1067
A1065
A47
B1145
B1110
B1146
B1105
B1354

Sheringham
Cromer
Overstrand
Sidestrand
Northrepps
Trimingham
NORFOLK COAST
Mundesley
High Kelling
Bodham
West Beckham
East Beckham
Aylmerton
Felbrigg
Crossdale Street
Gresham
Baconsthorpe
Hempstead
Bessingham
Sustead
Metton
Roughton
Thorpe Market
Southrepps
Gimingham
Trunch
Lower Street
Knapton
Paston
Bacton
Edgefield
Plumstead
Matlaske
Thurgarton
Hanworth
Alby Hill
Aldborough
Wickmere
Little Barningham
Erpingham
Calthorpe
Colby
Suffield
Antingham
Bradfield
Swafield
Edingthorpe
North Walsham
Itteringham
Saxthorpe
Corpusty
Wolterton
Ingworth
Blickling
Banningham
Felmingham
Tungate
Crostwight
Honing
Heydon
Oulton
Silvergate
Aylsham
Tuttington
Skeyton
Westwick
Worstead
Dilham
Smallburgh
Salle
Cawston
Southgate
Marsham
Brampton
Oxnead
Sloley
Scottow
Reepham
Booton
Eastgate
Brandiston
Hevingham
Buxton
Lamas
Little Hautbois
Sco Ruston
Tunstead
Ashmanhaugh
Neatishead
Alderford
Swannington
Waterloo
Hainford
Horstead
Coltishall
Hoveton
Wroxham
Belaugh
Attlebridge
Morton
Felthorpe
Horsford
Newton St Faith
Frettenham
Crostwick
Horsham St Faith
Spixworth
Weston Longville
Thorpe Marriot
Taverham
Drayton
Ringland
Rackheath
Salhouse
Woodbastwick
Hellesdon
Old Catton
Sprowston
Costessey
Easton
Honingham
Thorpe End
Great Plumstead
Blofield
Brundall
Norwich
Thorpe St Andrew
Earlham
Bowthorpe
Colton
Barford
A148
A140
A149
A1067
A1270
A47
A1151
A1074
177
159
142

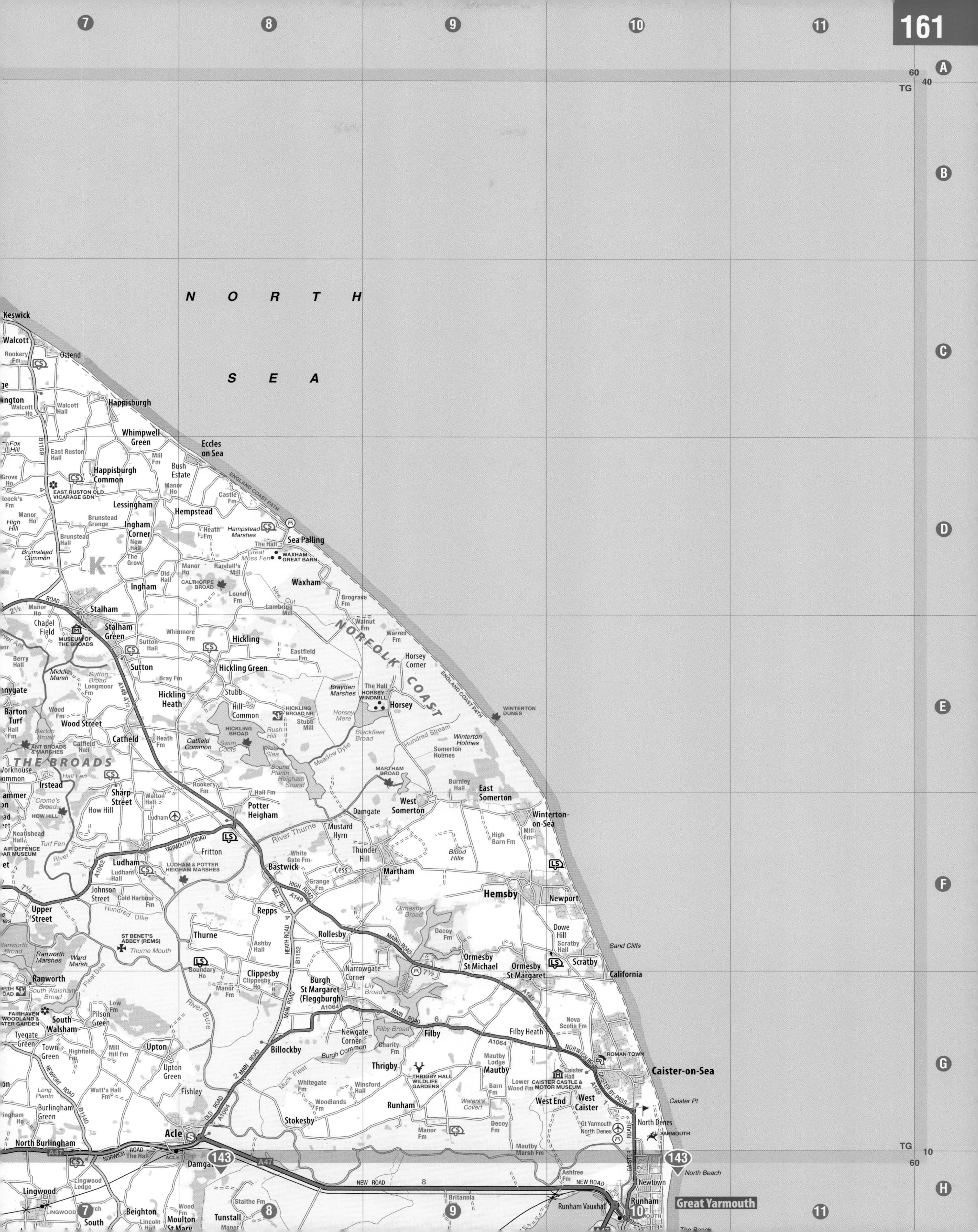

NORTH SEA
Keswick
Walcott
Ostend
Happisburgh
Whimpwell Green
Eccles on Sea
Happisburgh Common
Lessingham
Hempstead
Sea Palling
Ingham Corner
Waxham
Ingham
Stalham
Stalham Green
Hickling
Sutton
Hickling Green
Hickling Heath
Horsey
NORFOLK COAST
ENGLAND COAST PATH
WINTERTON DUNES
Catfield
THE BROADS
Wood Street
Irstead
Sharp Street
Potter Heigham
West Somerton
East Somerton
Winterton-on-Sea
Damgate
Martham
Ludham
Bastwick
Fritton
Hemsby
Newport
Repps
Rollesby
Thurne
Scratby
California
Ormesby St Michael
Ormesby St Margaret
Clippesby
Burgh St Margaret (Fleggburgh)
Ranworth
South Walsham
Upton
Billockby
Filby
Filby Heath
Caister-on-Sea
Thrigby
Mautby
West Caister
West End
Runham
Stokesby
Acle
North Burlingham
Lingwood
Beighton
Moulton St Mary
Tunstall
Runham Vauxhall
Great Yarmouth
North Denes
Newtown
Upper Street
Ludham & Potter Heigham Marshes
St Benet's Abbey (rems)
Thrigby Hall Wildlife Gardens
Caister Castle & Motor Museum
Museum of the Broads
East Ruston Old Vicarage Gdn
Waxham Great Barn
Horsey Windmill
Hickling Broad NR
Martham Broad
A149
A1064
A47
A1062
B1152
B1159
B1140
143

CAERNARFON
BAY
BAE CAERNARFON
178
144
145
SH
70
20
40
BARCLODIAD Y GAWRES BURIAL CHAMBER
Nobla
Porth Trecastell
Llangwyfan-isaf
Gate Ho
Merddyn-y-Bit
Penhenllys
Bodgedwydd
Glanrafon
Ty-mawr
Treiddon
Tyn-rhos-uchaf
Tre-Ddafydd-uchaf
Bodwrdin
Trefeilir
Bethel
Tan Lan
Capel Mawr
Paradwys
Trefdraeth
Glanrafon Fm
Afon Cefni
Clafdy
Aberffraw
A4080
Afon Ffraw
Llyn Coron
Llangadwaladr
Hermon
Mynydd Esgair-Ebrill
Coed Llywelyn
Bodorgan
Malltraeth
Pen-y-Bont Fm
Llangaffo
Glanmorfa
Tyddyn-y-fawd
Frondeg-Uchaf
Cefn Mawr
Maesoglan
Caethle
Danger area
Porth China
Porth Cwyfan
Penrhyn
Braich-lwyd
Traeth Mawr
Aber Ffraw Bay
Trefi
Bodowen
Porth-cadwaladr
Porth Twyn-mawr
Malltraeth Sands
TACLA TAID TRANSPORT MUSEUM
Ind Est
ISLE OF A
Newborough (Niwbwrch)
Dwyran
Newborough Forest
ANGLESEY MODEL VILLAGE
Pen-lon
(SIR YN
NEWBOROUGH WARREN & YNYS LLANDDWYN
Allt Niwbwrch
ISLE OF ANGLESEY
YNYS MÔN
Malltraeth Bay
Bae Malltraeth
WALES COAST PATH
Gwddn Llandwyn
Ynys Llanddwyn
Newborough Warren
Traeth Melynog
Abermenai Pt
Foryd B
South Sands
Warren Fm
Caernarfon
AIRWORLD AVIATION MUSEUM
Morfa Dinlle
Blythe
Dinas Dinlle
Llandwr
A499
Pontllyfni
CRAIG-DINAS
Aberdesach
Afon Desach
Tainlon
Clynnog-fawr
Penrhiwiau
Capel Uchaf
ST BEUNO'S WELL
Cwmgwared
Bryn Ifan
Bryn-yr-eryr
Gyrn-goch
Gyrn Goch 492
509 Bwlch Mawr
Corsy-wlad
Afon Dwyfach
Morfa
Trwyn y Tâl
Gwydir
Hengwm
522 Gyrn Ddu
Trefor
297 Moel Penllechog
Moel Bronmoid 416
Pen-Y-Gaer 389
Cwm
Hedre-fawr
Cwm-coryn Fm
Trwyn y Gorlech
LLEYN PENINSULA
Porth y Nant
Yr Eifl 564
TRE'R-CEIRI (FORT)
Llanaelhaearn
Moelfre
Bronmiod Fm
Cwm Cilio
Brychyni
Pen-sarn
Penrhyn Glas
Mount Pleasant
Gelliau
Hafod
B4417
Bryn Mawr
Cae'r-ferch
Mynachdy Bach
Llithfaen
Mynydd Carnguwch 359
Brynbychan
Tyddyn-Cethin
Ynys-wen
Moel Gwynus
Carnguwch Fawr
Pont y Gydros
Cefn-caer-ferch
Cefnydd
Carnguwch Bach
Penrhyn Bodeilas
Pistyll
Lleyn Pen
Murcyplau
Tyn Lon
Moel Ty-Gwyn
Gwyniasa
Maen-llwyd
Pentyrch-isaf
Penrh
Carreg Ddu
Trwyn Porth Dinllaen
Borth Wen
Porth Dinllaen
Penrhyn Nefyn
Porth Nefyn
Wern
Tir Bach
Ysgubor Plas
Cefn Isaf
Tyddyn Cestyll
Trallwyn Hall
Pencaenewydd
Lôn-fas
Llangybi
Talafon
Morfa Nefyn
LLŶN MARITIME MUSEUM
Tyddyn Uchaf
Llwyndyrys
Castell Gwgan
Penbryn
Aber Geirch
LON ISAF
Mynydd Nefyn
Bodeilian
Bryn
Mynydd-mawr
Geufron
Ynysleci
Brynllefrith
Plas Du
Nefyn
Tyn Coed
Glyncoed
Llwyn-dwyfog
Hendre Penprys
Fron
Garn Boduan 280
B4412
A497
Penrhyn Cwmistir
Edern
Pentreuchaf
Rhos-fawr
Rhyd-y-gwystl
Pencraig
Bryngwdyn
Llanarmon
Coed Rhos-fawr
Plasyngheidio
Tan-y-graig
B4354
Ty Du Isaf
Tyn-rhos-fawr
Y Ffôr
Cromlech
Chwilog
Glanrhyd
Moelypenmaen
Bryn Rodyn
Llannerch
Penarth Bach
Rhos-y-llan
Porth Towyn
Tref-erwyn
Maesoglan
Rhosydd
Bryngoleu
Clogwyn
Pont
0 1 2 3 miles
0 1 2 3 4 5 km
A
B
C
D
E
F
G
H
1
2
3
4
5
6

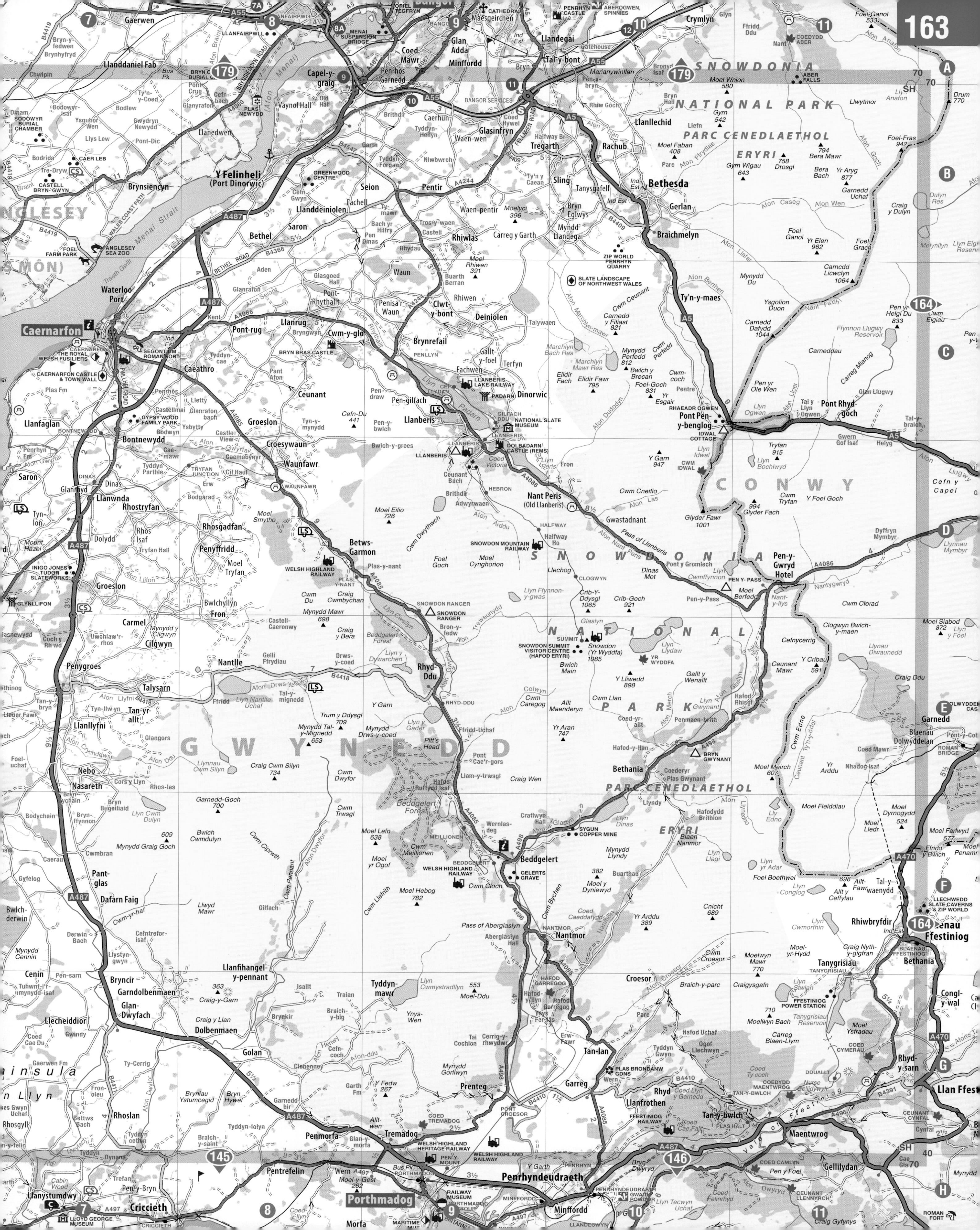

SNOWDONIA
NATIONAL PARK
PARC CENEDLAETHOL
ERYRI
CONWY
GWYNEDD
ANGLESEY
Bangor
Caernarfon
Porthmadog
Gaerwen
Llanddaniel Fab
Llanfairpwll
Menai Suspension Bridge
Coed Mawr
Glan Adda
Maesgeirchen
Minffordd
Llandegai
Tal-y-bont
Crymlyn
Capel-y-graig
Penrhos Garnedd
Vaynol Hall
Caerhun
Glasinfryn
Waen-wen
Tregarth
Rachub
Llanllechid
Bethesda
Gerlan
Braichmelyn
Y Felinheli (Port Dinorwic)
Brynsiencyn
Llanedwen
Seion
Pentir
Llanddeiniolen
Sling
Tanysgafell
Saron
Bethel
Rhiwlas
Carreg y Garth
Moelyci 396
Waun
Moel Rhiwen 391
Rhiwen
Clwt-y-bont
Deiniolen
Waterloo Port
Pont-rug
Llanrug
Cwm-y-glo
Brynrefail
Caeathro
Ceunant
Pen-gilfach
Llanberis
Dinorwic
Fachwen
Llyn Padarn
Llanfaglan
Bontnewydd
Groeslon
Croesywaun
Waunfawr
Saron
Llanwnda
Rhostryfan
Dinas
Rhosgadfan
Penyffridd
Moel Tryfan
Betws-Garmon
Welsh Highland Railway
Snowdon Mountain Railway
Groeslon
Fron
Carmel
Cilgwyn
Penygroes
Nantlle
Talysarn
Tan-yr-allt
Llanllyfni
Nebo
Nasareth
Rhyd-Ddu
Llyn Cwellyn
Snowdon Ranger
Snowdon (Yr Wyddfa) 1085
Snowdon Summit Visitor Centre (Hafod Eryri)
Nant Peris (Old Llanberis)
Pass of Llanberis
Gwastadnant
Glyder Fawr 1001
Glyder Fach 994
Tryfan 915
Y Garn 947
Elidir Fawr 795
Carnedd y Filiast 821
Mynydd Perfedd 812
Foel-Goch 831
Pont Pen-y-benglog
Ogwen
Pont Rhyd-goch
Ty'n-y-maes
Carnedd Dafydd 1044
Carnedd Llewelyn 1064
Yr Elen 962
Foel Grach
Foel-Fras 942
Drum 770
Moel Wnion 580
Gyrn 542
Pen-y-Gwryd Hotel
Pen-y-Pass
Pen y Gromlech
Crib-Goch 921
Crib-Y-Ddysgl 1065
Y Lliwedd 898
Dyffryn Mymbyr
Moel Siabod 872
Cwm Clorad
Ceunant Mawr
Y Cribau 591
Bethania
Llyn Gwynant
Yr Aran 747
Mynydd Drws-y-coed
Trum y Ddysgl 709
Mynydd Tal-y-Mignedd 653
Craig Cwm Silyn 734
Garnedd-Goch 700
Mynydd Graig Goch 609
Moel Hebog 782
Moel Lefn 638
Beddgelert
Beddgelert Forest
Gelerts Grave
Sygun Copper Mine
Nantmor
Pass of Aberglaslyn
Cnicht 689
Yr Arddu 389
Moel y Dyniewyd 382
Moel Meirch 607
Moel Dyrnogydd 524
Moel Farlwyd 577
Garnedd
Blaenau Dolwyddelan
Rhiwbryfdir
Blaenau Ffestiniog
Tanygrisiau
Ffestiniog Power Station
Moelwyn Mawr 770
Moelwyn Bach 710
Croesor
Llanfihangel-y-pennant
Tyddyn-mawr
Moel-Ddu 553
Dolbenmaen
Garndolbenmaen
Bryncir
Glan-Dwyfach
Golan
Tan-lan
Plas Brondanw Gdns
Garreg
Llanfrothen
Rhyd
Tan-y-bwlch
Maentwrog
Gellilydan
Rhyd-y-sarn
Llan Ffestiniog
Prenteg
Tremadog
Penmorfa
Pentrefelin
Criccieth
Llanystumdwy
Lloyd George Museum
Penrhyndeudraeth
Minffordd
Morfa
Rhoslan
Llecheiddior
Dafarn Faig
Pant-glas
A55
A5
A487
A4085
A4086
A498
A470
A496
A497
B4366
B4409
B4410
B4418
B4547

Pontwgan
Tal-y-cafn
Eglwysbach
Graig
Rhandir
Trofarth
Llanfair Talhaiarn
Gell
Cefn-coch
Pentre Isaf
Pentre'r Felin
Llanbedr-y-cennin
Tal-y-Bont
Castell
Dolgarrog
Llangernyw
Hendre-ddu
Llansannan
Bryn-nantllech
Bryn-glas
Pandy Tudur
Tan-lan
Llanddoged
Trefriw
Pentre-tafarn-y-fedw
Llanrwst
Tŷ'r-felin-isaf
Gwytherin
Tai
Cornel
Melin-y-coed
Capel Curig
Pont Cyfyng
GWYDYR
FOREST PARK
Betws-y-Coed
Nebo
CONWY
Capel Garmon
Pont-y-pant
Dolwyddelan
Garnedd
Pentre-bont
Dinas Mawr
Glan Conwy
Padog
Pentrefoelas
Rhydlydan
Glasfryn
Cefn-brith
Hafod-Dinbych
SNOWDONIA
NATIONAL
PARK
Penmachno
Carrog
Cwm Penmachno
Ysbyty Ifan
Cerrigydrudion
Ty Mawr Cwm
PARC CENEDLAETHOL
ERYRI
Blaenau Ffestiniog
Bethania
Congl-y-wal
Rhyd-y-sarn
Llan Ffestiniog
Pont yr Afon-Gam
Bont Newydd
Migneint
Llyn Celyn
Ciltalgarth
Glan-yr-afon
Frongoch
Pen-y-gop
Llidiardau
Rhyd-uchaf
A470
A5
A548
A543
B5113
B5106
B4407
B4391
A4212
180
163
146
147
0 1 2 3 miles
0 1 2 3 4 5 km

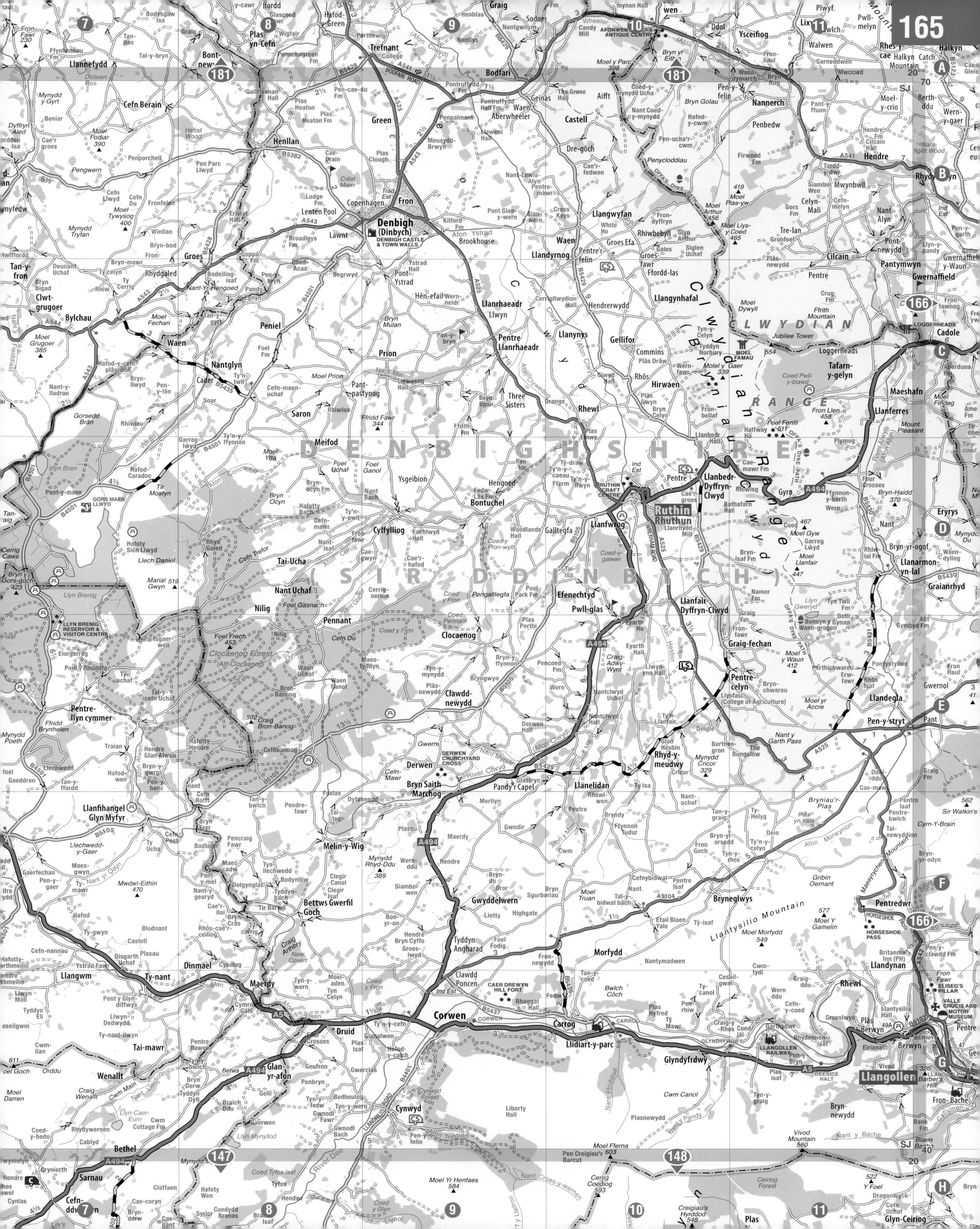

165
Denbigh (Dinbych)
Denbigh Castle & Town Walls
Ruthin Rhuthun
Ruthin Craft Centre
Corwen
Llangollen
DENBIGHSHIRE (SIR DDINBYCH)
Clwydian Range (Bryniau Clwyd)
Vale of Clwyd
Clocaenog Forest (Allt Clocaenog)
Llantysilio Mountain
Llyn Brenig
Llyn Brenig Reservoir & Visitor Centre
Gors Maen Llwyd
Trefnant
Bodfari
Henllan
Llannefydd
Cefn Berain
Bylchau
Nantglyn
Groes
Peniel
Prion
Saron
Meifod
Cyffylliog
Bontuchel
Llanrhaeadr
Pentre Llanrhaeadr
Llandyrnog
Llangwyfan
Llangynhafal
Llanynys
Gellifor
Hirwaen
Rhewl
Llanbedr-Dyffryn-Clwyd
Llanfwrog
Efenechtyd
Pwll-glas
Llanfair-Dyffryn-Clwyd
Graig-fechan
Pentrecelyn
Clawdd-newydd
Derwen
Derwen Churchyard Cross
Bryn Saith Marchog
Clocaenog
Nant Uchaf
Nilig
Pennant
Tai-Ucha
Llanelidan
Rhyd-y-meudwy
Melin-y-Wig
Bettws Gwerfil Goch
Gwyddelwern
Tyddyn Angharad
Morfydd
Bryneglwys
Llandegla
Pen-y-stryt
Llanarmon-yn-Ial
Graianrhyd
Eryrys
Llanferres
Maeshafn
Tafarn-y-gelyn
Loggerheads
Cadole
Cilcain
Pantymwyn
Gwernaffield
Nannerch
Halkyn
Ysceifiog
Afonwen Craft & Antique Centre
Moel Famau
Jubilee Tower
Offa's Dyke Path
Horseshoe Pass
Llandynan
Rhewl
Elisegs Pillar
Valle Crucis Abbey
Motor Museum
Berwyn
Llangollen Railway
Glyndyfrdwy
Carrog
Llidiart-y-parc
Druid
Cynwyd
Caer Drewyn Hill Fort
Maerdy
Dinmael
Ty-nant
Llangwm
Tai-mawr
Glan-yr-afon
Wenallt
Bethel
Sarnau
Llanfihangel Glyn Myfyr
Pentre-llyn cymmer
Cerrig-y-drudion
Waen
Copenhagen
Fron
Lawnt
Brookhouse
Green
River Clwyd
River Dee
Moel Fferna
181
166
147
148

Halkyn
Oakenholt
Flint Mountain (Mynydd Fflint)
182
Kelsterton
Golftyn
Connah's Quay
Shotton
Garden City
Queensferry
Sealand
Saughall
Mollington
Backford
Wervin
Picton
Chester
Upton
Newton
Hoole
Mickle Trafford
Upton Heath
Hoole Bank
Blacon
Abbot's Meads
Saltney
Lache
Handbridge
Vicarscross
Littleton
Rowton
Huntington
Northop (Llan-eurgain)
Northop Hall
Rhosesmor
Cefn-eurgain
Hendre
Rhydymwyn
Soughton (Sychdyn)
Sandycroft
Mancot
Mancot Royal
Hawarden (Penarlâg)
Ewloe
Ewloe Green
Aston
New Brighton
Alltami
Buckley (Bwcle)
Mold
Yr Wyddgrug
Mynydd-isa
Prenbrigog
Pantymwyn
Gwernaffield
Nant Alyn
Pont-newydd
Drury
Lane End
Spon Green
Nant Mawr
Little Mountain
Bretton
Broughton
Old Warren
Cadole
Gwernymynydd
Llong
Penymynydd
Lower Kinnerton
Balderton
Gorstella
Dodleston
Eccleston
Higher Kinnerton
Kinnerton Green
Penyffordd
Belgrave
Bruera
FLINTSHIRE
(SIR Y FFLINT)
Maeshafn
Nercwys
Llanferres
Pontblyddyn
Leeswood (Coed-Llai)
Pulford
Aldford
Treuddyn
Coed-Talon
Hope (Yr Hôb)
Burton Green
Golly
Lavister
Eryrys
Caergwrle
Bridge End
Burton
Rossett
Trevalyn
Llanarmon-yn-Ial
Graianrhyd
Llanfynydd
Bryn Common
Cefn-y-bedd
Ffrith
Llay
Marford
Churton
Farndon
Rhydtalog
Sydallt
Gresford
Holt
Glascoed
Four Crosses
Bwlchgwyn
Brymbo
Gwersyllt
Rhosrobin
Borras Head
Crewe-by-Farndon
Crewe
Llandegla
Pen-y-stryt
Gwynfryn
Minera
Coedpoeth
Gatewen
Garden Village
Acton
Llan-y-pwll
New Broughton
New Brighton
Rhosnesni
Wrexham
Wrecsam
Ridleywood
Castletown
Isycoed
Shocklach Green
Bersham
Rhostyllen
Bowling Bank
Marchwiel
Talwrn
Pentredwr
Rhosllanerchrugog
Johnstown
Sontley
Cross Lanes
Worthenbury
Llandynan
Cock Bank
Gyfelia
Eyton
Bangor-is-y-coed
Threapwood
Ruabon (Rhiwabon)
Acrefair
Overton Bridge
Cloy
Pandy
Berwyn
Garth
Trevor
Pont Cysyllte
Cefn-mawr
Llangollen
Rhos-y-Madoc
Erbistock
Overton (Owrtyn)
Horseman's Green
Froncysyllte
Halton
Penley
Street Lydan
Chirk (Y Waun)
Knolton
Dudleston
Pentre-coed
WREXHAM
(WRECSAM)
148
149
165
0 1 2 3 miles
0 1 2 3 4 5 km

CHESHIRE EAST
Hartford
Davenham
Moulton
Winsford
Over
Wharton
Sandiway
Cuddington
Delamere Forest Park
Kelsall
Tarvin
Tarporley
Cotebrook
Little Budworth
Oulton Park
Church Minshull
Wettenhall
Alpraham
Calveley
Beeston
Beeston Castle
Bunbury
Spurstow
Peckforton
Burwardsley
Higher Burwardsley
Bulkeley
Barbridge
Wardle
Aston juxta Mondrum
Worleston
Crewe
Wistaston
Willaston
Nantwich
Acton
Burland
Faddiley
Stoneley Green
Ravensmoor
Wrenbury
Aston
Sound
Broomhall
Audlem
Buerton
Hankelow
Hatherton
Walgherton
Wybunbury
Shavington
Stapeley
Broxton
Barnhill
Bickerton
Malpas
Hampton Heath
Edge Green
Duckington
No Man's Heath
Bickley Moss
Norbury
Marbury
Wirswall
Whitchurch
Chemistry
Waymills
Broughall
Ash Magna
Tilstock
Alkington
Bronington
Redbrook
Hanmer
Grindley Brook
Brooklands
Burleydam
Wilkesley
Coxbank
Adderley
Norton in Hales
Ightfield
Cholmondeley Castle Gardens & Chapel
Shropshire Union Canal
River Weaver
River Gowy
SJ
70
A
B
C
D
E
F
G
H
7
8
9
10
11
168
183
149
150

CHESHIRE EAST
STOKE-ON-TRENT
Middlewich
Holmes Chapel
Sandbach
Elworth
Congleton
Crewe
Alsager
Kidsgrove
Biddulph
Tunstall
Burslem
Hanley
Newcastle-under-Lyme
Stoke-on-Trent
Fenton
Longton
Madeley
Audley
Haslington
Wheelock
Goostrey
Twemlow Green
Blackden Heath
Withington Green
Siddington
Lower Withington
Marton
Gawsworth
Warren
Bosley
Rodeheath
North Rode
Buglawton
Astbury
Mossley
Timbersbrook
Brereton Heath
Somerford
Swettenham
Byley
Cranage
Warmingham
Moston Green
Winterley
Wybunbury
Walgherton
Hatherton
Shavington
Weston
Betley
Balterley
Wrinehill
Checkley
Woore
Onneley
Keele
Silverdale
Knutton
Chesterton
Bradwell
Talke
Red Street
Mow Cop
Knypersley
Endon
Baddeley Green
Milton
Bucknall
Meir
Trentham
Hanford
Barlaston
Clayton
Whitmore
Madeley Park
Baldwin's Gate
Maer
Stableford
Knighton
Pipe Gate
Ireland's Cross
Keele Services
Sandbach Services
M6
A34
A50
A500
A53
A51
A52
A54
A534
A525
A520
A523
A536
A527
184
150
151
167
0 1 2 3 miles
0 1 2 3 4 5 km

Forest
Clough
Derbyshire Br
Canholes
Harpur Hill
Cowdale
King Sterndale
Blackwell
Priestcliffe
Taddington
Ashford in the Water
Trentabank
Cuckoo Rocks
High Ash Fm
Axe Edge Moor
Cheeks Hill
Ladmanlow
Chelmorton
Sterndale Moor
Flagg
Sheldon
Wildboarclough
Allgreave
Knotbury
Axe Edge
Colshaw
Flash
Earl Sterndale
Monyash
Over Haddon
Wincle
Danebridge
Gradbach Mill
Hollinsclough
Glutton Bridge
Crowdicote
Longnor
Fawfieldhead
Newtown
Pilsbury
Parsley Hay
Youlgrave
Middleton
Heaton
Roche Grange
Meerbrook
Upper Hulme
Sheen
Brund
Hartington
Heathcote
Newhaven
Biggin
Pikehall
Blackshaw Moor
Thorncliffe
Upper Elkstone
Lower Elkstone
Warslow
Hulme End
Ecton
Poolend
Ball Haye Green
Leek
Lowe Hill
Bradnop
Onecote
Butterton
Wetton
Alstonefield
Hope
Milldale
Alsop en le Dale
Parwich
Ballidon
Longsdon
Horse Bridge
Leekbrook
Cheddleton
Basford Green
Grindonmoor Gate
Grindon
Ford
Bottom House
New Street
Winkhill
Waterfall
Waterhouses
Calton
Ilam
Thorpe
Tissington
Bradbourne
Fenny Bentley
Kniveton
Wetley Rocks
Ipstones
Cauldon
Blore
Cellarhead
Consall
Blakeley Lane
Foxt
Froghall
Whiston
Swinscoe
Mapleton
Kingsley
Kingsley Holt
Cotton
Oakamoor
Ramshorn
Wootton
Stanton
Mayfield
Ashbourne
Clifton
Spitalhill
Church Mayfield
Farley
Dilhorne
Cheadle
Threapwood
Alton
Ellastone
Snelston
Osmaston
Wyaston
Caverswall
Forsbrook
Blythe Bridge
Freehay
Mobberley
Lightwood
Norbury
Roston
Yeaveley
Rodsley
Draycott in the Moors
Greatgate
Denstone
Quixhill
Croxden
Hollington
Rocester
Stubwood
Cubley Common
Cresswell
Lower Tean
Checkley
Fulford
Great Cubley
Alkmonton
Marston Montgomery
Upper Tean
STAFFORDSHIRE
PEAK DISTRICT NATIONAL PARK
DERBYSHIRE
A515
A53
A523
A52
A50
A6
A54
A520
A522
185
151
152
170

Hassop
Baslow
Chesterfield
Old Brampton
Wadshelf
Brampton
Calow
Duckmanton
Hady
Ashford in the Water
Pilsley
Eastmoor
Chatsworth Park
Edensor
Bakewell
Holymoorside
Walton
Birdholme
Hasland
Sutton Scarsdale
Over Haddon
Beeley
Slatepit Dale
Swathwick
Wingerworth
Grassmoor
Temple Normanton
Heath
Rowsley
Holmewood
Northwood
Tupton
Old Tupton
North Wingfield
Youlgrave
Alport
Stanton in Peak
Uppertown
Brockhurst
Kelstedge
Alton
Middleton
Bradford
Darley Dale
Two Dales
Ashover
Clay Cross
Churchtown
Birchover
Upper Hackney
Milltown
Stretton
Tibshelf
Darley Bridge
Wensley
Elton
Winster
Matlock
Tansley Knoll
Woolley
Brightgate
Tansley
Pikehall
Matlock Bath
Starkholmes
Higham
Stonebroom
Shirland
Newton
Blackwell
Grangemill
Bonsall
Ible
Aldwark
Lea
Wessington
Westhouses
Cromford
Wheatcroft
South Normanton
Middleton
Holloway
South Wingfield
Longcliffe
Bolehill
Alfreton
Ballidon
Parwich
Brassington
Crich
Whatstandwell
Oakerthorpe
Wirksworth
Somercotes
Carsington
Hopton
Fritchley
Bradbourne
Miller's Green
Alderwasley
Swanwick
Callow
Bullbridge
Pentrich
Riddings
Ironville
Knockerdown
Ripley
Ambergate
Toadmoor
Hognaston
Kirk Ireton
Heage
Codnor
Kniveton
Beighton Hill
Shottle
Belper Lane End
Broadholme
Atlow
Idridgehay
Marehay
Biggin
Far Laund
Ashbourne
Hulland Ward
Hulland
Belper
Turnditch
Cowers Lane
Bradley
Hazelwood
Denby
Heanor
Kilburn
Milford
Holbrook
Smalley
Marlpool
DERBYSHIRE
Windley
Osmaston
Mugginton
Duffield
Coxbench
Shipley
Weston Underwood
Mapperley
Shirley
Ednaston
Brailsford
Flaxholme
Little Eaton
Stanley Common
West Hallam
Kedleston
Morley
Yeaveley
Rodsley
Quarndon
Stanley
Hollington
Breadsall
Allestree
Dale Abbey
Kirk Langley
Longlane
PEAK DISTRICT NATIONAL PARK
0 1 2 3 miles
0 1 2 3 4 5 km

171
NOTTINGHAMSHIRE
SHERWOOD FOREST
SHERWOOD PINES FOREST PARK
CITY OF NOTTINGHAM
Bolsover
New Bolsover
Carr Vale
Hills Town
Scarcliffe
Palterton
Rylah
Whaley
Whaley Thorns
Nether Langwith
Langwith
Upper Langwith
Cuckney
Norton
Meden Vale
Church Warsop
Market Warsop
Langwith Junction
Shirebrook
Sookholme
Spion Kop
Budby
Thoresby
Perlethorpe
Walesby
Edwinstowe
New Ollerton
Ollerton
Boughton
Wellow
Ompton
Kirton
Kneesall
Glapwell
Stony Houghton
New Houghton
Rowthorne
Pleasley
Pleasleyhill
Moorhaigh
Radmanthwaite
Mansfield Woodhouse
Clipstone
Kings Clipstone
Lidgett
Gorsethorpe
Newlands
Forest Town
Mansfield
Ladybrook
Teversal
Skegby
Stanton Hill
Dalestorth
Fackley
Dunsill
Stanley
Huthwaite
Sutton in Ashfield
Sutton Forest Side
Hilcote
Commonside
Kirkby in Ashfield
Cox Moor
Rainworth
Bilsthorpe
Bilsthorpe Moor
Eakring
Maplebeck
Winkburn
Kirklington
White Post
Farnsfield
Edingley
Blidworth
Brick-Kiln End
Haywood Oaks
Blidworth Bottoms
Ravenshead
Annesley Woodhouse
Nuncargate
Annesley
Newstead
Selston
Bagthorpe
Underwood
New Brinsley
Brinsley
Jacksdale
Papplewick
Linby
Hucknall
Calverton
Oxton
Halam
Southwell
Easthorpe
Westhorpe
Halloughton
Normanton
Maythorne
Epperstone
Woodborough
Gonalston
Thurgarton
Hoveringham
Lowdham
Caythorpe
Kneeton
Lambley
Burton Joyce
Bulcote
Gunthorpe
East Bridgford
Newton
Shelford
Stoke Bardolph
Radcliffe on Trent
Bingham
Saxondale
Upper Saxondale
Harlequin
Holme Pierrepont
Adbolton
Moorgreen
Westville
Beauvale
Eastwood
Watnall
Kimberley
Nuthall
Giltbrook
Awsworth
Cotmanhay
Swingate
Cossall
Strelley
Trowell
Kirk Hallam
Ilkeston
Stanton-by-Dale
Bestwood Village
Bestwood
Bulwell
Top Valley
Rise Park
Arnold
Redhill
Daybrook
Woodthorpe
Mapperley
Mapperley Park
Sherwood
Porchester
Gedling
Carlton
Netherfield
Colwick
Basford
Old Basford
New Basford
Cinderhill
Aspley
Broxtowe
Bilborough
Whitemoor
Wollaton
Lenton
Lenton Abbey
Dunkirk
Radford
St Ann's
Sneinton
Bramcote Hills
Nottingham
A60
A617
A614
A6097
A616
A38
A611
A610
A52
A46
A6514
M1
187
172
153
154

NOTTINGHAMSHIRE
West Markham
Tuxford
Fledborough
South Clifton
Wigsley
Harby
Doddington
Birchwood
Skegby
High Marnham
Low Marnham
Spalford
Egmanton
Normanton on Trent
Grassthorpe
Weston
Kirton
Laxton
Eagle Moor
Eagle
Whisby
North Scarle
Girton
Sutton on Trent
Moorhouse
Ompton
Eagle Barnsdale
Thorpe on the Hill
South Hykeham
Besthorpe
Ossington
Kneesall
Carlton on Trent
South Scarle
Morton
Swinderby
Haddington
Norwell Woodhouse
Norwell
Kersall
Collingham
Cromwell
Witham St Hughs
Thurlby
Aubourn
Maplebeck
Caunton
Bathley
Holme
North Muskham
Brough
Bassingham
Winkburn
Knapthorpe
Little Carlton
Langford
Norton Disney
Stapleford
Carlton le Moorland
South Muskham
Winthorpe
Hockerton
Kelham
Averham
Upton
Southwell
Easthorpe
Normanton
Staythorpe
Rolleston
Farndon
Newark-on-Trent
Coddington
Barnby in the Willows
Beckingham
Brant Broughton
Leadenham
Stragglethorpe
Balderton
New Balderton
Hawton
Fiskerton
Morton
Fenton
Claypole
Stubton
Bleasby
East Stoke
Thorpe
Thurgarton
Caythorpe
Brandon
Frieston
Elston
Syerston
Cotham
Hoveringham
Hough-on-the-Hill
Dry Doddington
Kneeton
Flintham
Sibthorpe
Long Bennington
Westborough
Gelston
Hougham
Marston
Shelton
Staunton in the Vale
Screveton
East Bridgford
Car Colston
Hawksworth
Flawborough
Kilvington
Foston
Thoroton
Alverton
Newton
Scarrington
Orston
Normanton
Allington
Barkston
Syston
Aslockton
Whatton
Bingham
Bottesford
Easthorpe
Elton
Sedgebrook
Great Gonerby
Manthorpe
Belton
A1
A46
A17
A616
A617
A6097
A52
0 1 2 3 miles
0 1 2 3 4 5 km

Lincoln
LINCOLNSHIRE LIFE
LINCOLN CASTLE
CATHEDRAL
LINCOLN ARBORETUM
BISHOP'S PALACE
Willingham Fen
FOSSDYKE NAVIGATION CANAL
River Witham
Boundary Fm
Old River Witham
Tile House Beck
Young Wood
Moat Ho
Austacre Wood
Great Fm
Waddingworth
Red Ho
New Boultham
Trad Est
Retail Pk
LNER STADIUM
GUILDHALL
Shop Cen
Washingborough
Heighington Fen
Branston Island
Abbey Hills
Scotgrove Wood
Lawfield Fm
New Park Wood
Moor Fm
Spotted Lodge
Hill Fm
Manor Fm
Glebe Fm
Highfield Ho
Canwick
INTERNATIONAL BOMBER COMMAND CTR
Boultham
Swallow Beck
Boultham Moor
Bracebridge
Whitehall
Canwick Manor Fm
Ashfield Ho
Bracebridge Heath
Cliff Fm
Washingborough Top Fm
Heighington
Bracken Hill Fm
Third Hill Fm
Branston Booths
Delph Fm
Branstone Fen
Red House Fm
Poplars Fm
BRANSTON CAUSEWAY
Bardney Lock
Bardney
Bardney Common
Tupholme Hall Fm
High Cell Ho
Birt Hill
Catchwater Drain
Grange Fm
Sand Nook Fm
Bucknall
HORNCASTLE STREET
Edlington Scrubbs
Horsington
Firgrove Fm
BARDNEY LIMEWOODS
Southrey Wood
Birch Wood
Poplar Grove
Campney Grange Fm
Poplar Fm
BUCKNALL ROAD
Mapleton Fm
Poolham Hall
Darwood Fm
High Dar Wood
Branston
Whitehouse Fm
Branston Moor
Branston Lodge
Potterhanworth Booths
Longhills Hall
Ind Est
Potterhanworth Wood
Abbey Warren Fm
Horsington Wood
Stixwould Wood
Southrey
Duckpool Br
Halstead Hall
Bracebridge Low Fields
Grange Fm
Fox Covert
Potterhanworth
Barff Fm
Neville Wood
Cherrystone Cott
River Witham
Holmes Fm
Stixwould
Newstead Fm
Halstead Wood
Reeds Beck Fm
Moorside Fm
Reeds Beck
Mere Hall
Potterhanworth Heath
Wasps Nest
Nocton
Dunston Fen
Ash House Fm
Delph
Red Br
Waterloo Fm
Bracken Wood
East Mere Ho
Nocton Grange
Abbey Hill
Nocton
Fen Fm
Sots Hole
Tanvats
Waddington
Lowfields Fm
Beaufoe Manor
Highfield Fm
Nocton Heath
Nocton Wood
Engine Fm
Metheringham Delph
Willow Fm
Blankney Dales
Stixwould Grange
Roughton Moor
Lincoln Lane Fm
Barn Fm
Glebe Fm
Dunston
Metheringham Low Fields
Black Horse Fm
Woodhall Spa
Harmston Heath
Ram Fm
Glebe Fm
Fenside Fm
Dales Head Dike
Glebe Fm
Kirkstead Br
Kirkstead Hall
Kirkstead
Landsdale Ho
Harmston
WHITE LANE
TOWER LANE
Coleby Lodge Fm
Dunston Heath
Hall Fm
Metheringham
Metheringham Barff Fm
CAR DYKE (ROMAN CANAL)
Martin Fen
Martin Dales
Harmston Field
Low Fields Fm
Hall Fm
Heath Grange Fm
Heath Ho
METHERINGHAM HEATH LANE
MOOR LANE
Barff Fm
Carr Dyke Fm
Linwood Hall Fm
MARTIN SOUTH DROVE
Timberland Dales
Coleby
Coleby Low Fields
Coleby Heath
Boothby Heath Fm
Metheringham Lodge
Blankney Park
Blankney
North Moor Ho
Timberland Delph
Dales Br
Tonge Fm
Park Fm
HEATH LANE
Boothby Graffoe
Green Man Wood
Blankney Grange
Blankney Heath
Westmoor Fm
METHERINGHAM AIRFIELD VISITOR CENTRE
Martin
THORPE CAMP VISITOR CENTRE
Green Man Fm
Scopwick Low Field Fm
Thorpe Tilney Fen
Thorpe Tilney Dales
Lodge Fm
LINCOLNSHIRE
Boothby Graffoe Low Fields
Scopwick Ho
Timberland
Bank Fm
Navenby Low Fields
Navenby
Navenby Heath
Scopwick Lodge Fm
Scopwick Heath
MAIN STREET
Scopwick
Kirkby Green
Evans' Fm
Thorpe Tilney
Tattershall
TATTERSHALL CASTLE
Peacocks Fm
Vine Ho
Heath Fm
Temple High Grange Fm
HEATH ROAD
Sheffield Ho
Walcott Hurn
Walcott Dales
Wellingore
Highfield House Fm
Gorse Hill Covert
RAF DIGBY OPS ROOM MUSEUM
Rowston
Crown Fm
Walcott
HIGH STREET
Billinghay Hurn
Witham House Fm
Wellingore Low Fields
Rowston Field Fm
Field Fm
WALCOTT ROAD
Skirth
Glebe Fm
Ashby Hall
Rowston Grange
Billinghay
SLEAFORD
Tattershall Bridge
Stennett's Fm
Dogdyke
Wood Fm
Fox Covert
CLIFF ROAD
Thompson's Bottom
Heath Fm
Ashby Lodge
Ashby de la Launde
Allens Fm
Home Fm
TATTERSHALL RD
Billinghay Dales
Griffin's Fm
Digby
Digby Gorse
Grange Fm
North Kyme Common
Chapel Hill
Welbourn
Warren Houses
Slate House Fm
Brook
Digby Fen
Dorrington
Temple Fm
Springwell
Bloxholm
Dorrington Grange
Fen Ho
Drove Fm
North Kyme Fen
South Barn Fm
Temple Bruer
Peacock Lodge
Pitts Fm
Home Fm
Cocked Hat Fm
Cocked Hat Plantn
Manor Fm
Hill Fm
LINCOLN ROAD
The Dales
North Kyme
Fendale Fm
Moor Wood
Dorrington
NORTH INGS FARM MUSEUM
North Hills
Wong Fm
Vacherie Ho
High Dyke Fm
Cottage Fm
Moor Fm
Crossways Fm
Praie Grounds
Decoy Ho
House Fm
Clayfields Fm
Leadenham Heath
Stocks Heath Fm
Hill Top Fms
Homestead Fm
New Fm
Dale Fm
Dunsby House
Ind Est
Poplar Fm
Grange Fm
MAIN STREET
FERRY LANE
Terry Booth Fm
Reed Point
Roxholm Grange
Roxholm Hall
Ruskington
RUSKINGTON
Anwick
SLEAFORD ROAD
The Grange
Park Ho
Lawn Hill Fm
Shepherds Fm
Culbeck
Bus Pk
Reeves Plantn
Hall Fm
WOOD LANE
Kyme Eau
Heath Fm
RAF College Cranwell
CRANWELL AVENUE
Cranwell
Old Hall Fm
Haverholme Priory
Cobbler's Lock
River Slea
Mill Fm
Moor Fm
Ewerby Waithe Common
South Kyme
Sycamore Ho
Maryland
Bleak House
Cranwell
Westfield Wood
MOOR LANE
White Ho
Fox Covert
Pattingden Ho
Chestnut House Fm
Hill Fm
Caythorpe Heath
Leasingham Moor
Old River Slea
Barns Fm
Westfield Fm
Leasingham
Ewerby Thorpe
Fenmore Fm
CLAY BANK
Elms Fm
Frieston Heath Fm
Ermine Street Fm
Rauceby Grange
Heath Fm
CRANWELL AVIATION HERITAGE CENTRE
Moor Fm
Evedon Mill
Ewerby
Whitehouse Fm
Mill Green Fm
Five Willow Wath Fm
North Rauceby Heath
Bus Pk
Holdingham
Evedon
Sparrow Gorse
Woodside Fm
High Wood
North Rauceby
Galley Hill
Bargate Hill
Walks Fm
Howell Fen
Sadland Fm
Normanton
HIGH DIKE
Sudbrook Ho
South Rauceby
Hall
Field Fm
Sleaford
Bouncing Hill
The Grange
Kirkby la Thorpe
Howell
Heckington Eau
Glebe Fm
Carlton Scroop
Sudbrook Hill Fm
Lodge Fm
Crowland Fm
Boiling Wells Fm
COGGLESFORD WATERMILL
SLEAFORD MUSEUM
NAT CENTRE FOR CRAFT & DESIGN
Mount Lane Fm
Boughton
Wash Dike
Star Fen
Holme Ho
Six Hundreds Fm
GRANTHAM RD
SLEAFORD
Asgarby
The Beck
Winkhill
SIDEBAR LANE
Sudbrook
ANCASTER
South Rauceby Lodge
Quarrington
Mareham Lane Fm
Bone's Fm
Sardesons Fm
Heckington
Hall Fm
East Heckington
West Willoughby
Waterloo Fm
River Slea
RAUCEBY
Westfield Fm
SLEAFORD RD
HECKINGTON
Mile Ho
The Rake
Ancaster
TOWN END
Lodge Fm
Lodge Fm
HECKINGTON WINDMILL
Poplar Fm
High Field House
WILLOUGHBY ROAD
Grange Fm
Wilsford Warren
Beacon Hill
Grange Fm
Great Hale
Hall Fm
Slate House Fm
Wilsford
Silk Willoughby
Willoughby Gorse
Saltbox Fm
Bellhouse Fm
Burton Fm
Willoughby Heath
The Valley
Valley Fm
Kelby Fm
Cliff Beck
Hercocks Fm
Highfields Ho
Crow Lane Fm
White Ho
Barkston Heath
Barkston Heath
Glebe Fm
Burton Pedwardine
Little Hale
Broadhurst Fm
Bra End
Kelby
North Hill
Barrow Hill Fm
Grange Fm
Aswarby Thorns
Burton Cliff
Burton Br
Willoughby Ho
Northbeck
MAIN ROAD
Glebe Fm
Syston Grange
Welby Pastures
Heydour Warren
Swarby
Thorns Fm
Scredington
Poplar Fm
Helpringham
Park Ho
North Beck
South Forty Foot Drain
Lowgrounds Fm
Crow Hall
Culverthorpe
Crofton
Hall
Aswarby
Thorpe Latimer
Belton Ashes
Oasby
Castle Hills
Culverthorpe Hollow
Forty Acre Fm
Whitegorse Fm
Gorse Hill
Poplartree Fm
Glebe Fm
Cow Common
Aisby
Green Hill
Aunsby
Highfield Ho
Rowe's Fm
Swaton Common
Eau End
Cow Bridge
Welby
Osbournby
Manor Fm
Nightingale
Dembleby
Spanby
Londonthorpe
Manor

LINCOLNSHIRE
Horncastle
Woodhall Spa
Coningsby
Tattershall
Spilsby
Boston
Sibsey
Stickney
Wrangle
Swineshead
Kirton
Edlington
Thimbleby
Langton
Horsington
Old Woodhall
Thornton
Martin
Reeds Beck
Roughton
Roughton Moor
Kirkby on Bain
Kirkstead
Haltham
Wood Enderby
Toft Hill
Mareham le Fen
Revesby
Revesby Bridge
Moorby
Miningsby
East Kirkby
Hagnaby
Scrivelsby
Dalderby
Hameringham
Asgarby
Lusby
Winceby
Mareham on the Hill
High Toynton
Low Toynton
Scrafield
Greetham
Ashby Puerorum
Hagworthingham
Bag Enderby
Harrington
Sutterby
Fordington
Aswardby
Sausthorpe
Langton
Partney
Skendleby
Grebby
Dalby
Raithby by Spilsby
Hundleby
Mavis Enderby
Hareby
Old Bolingbroke
West Keal
East Keal
Keal Cotes
Toynton All Saints
Toynton St Peter
Toynton Fen Side
Halton Holegate
Ashby by Partney
Monksthorpe
Great Steeping
Little Steeping
Halton Fenside
Stickford
Midville
Eastville
New Leake
New Bolingbroke
Hagnaby Lock
West Fen
East Fen
Fen Side
Medlam
Carrington
Frithville
West Houses
Northlands
Sibsey Fen Side
Lade Bank
Leake Commonside
Wrangle Bank
Wrangle Lowgate
Old Leake
Leverton
Leverton Highgate
Leverton Outgate
Leverton Lucasgate
Benington
Benington Sea End
Butterwick
Freiston
Freiston Shore
Skirbeck
Skirbeck Quarter
Fishtoft
Tamworth Green
Scrane End
Hill Dyke
Boston Long Hedges
Halltoft End
Cowbridge
Frith Bank
Fishtoft Drove
Anton's Gowt
Langrick
Langrick Bridge
Gipsey Bridge
Newham
Bunker's Hill
Sandy Bank
New York
Scrub Hill
Hundle Houses
Haven Bank
Reed Point
Holland Fen
Amber Hill
Brothertoft
Boston West
Hedgehog Bridge
Chapel Hill
Dogdyke
Tattershall Bridge
Tattershall Thorpe
Tumby
Tumby Woodside
Moor Side
Reedham
Hawthorn Hill
Chain Bridge
Hubbert's Bridge
Swineshead Bridge
East Heckington
North End
Baythorpe
Fenhouses
Kirton Holme
Frampton West End
Kirton End
Wyberton
Frampton
Sandholme
Holland Fen
River Witham
The Haven
Butterwick Low
Freiston Low
Wyberton Marsh
Frampton Marsh
TATTERSHALL CASTLE
TATTERSHALL COLLEGE
BATTLE OF BRITAIN MEMORIAL FLIGHT
THORPE CAMP VISITOR CENTRE
LINCOLNSHIRE AVIATION HERITAGE CENTRE
BOLINGBROKE CASTLE
SNIPE DALES
NORTHCOTE HEAVY HORSE CENTRE
LINCOLNSHIRE WILDLIFE PARK
SIBSEY TRADER MILL
ST BOTOLPH'S CHURCH
MAUD FOSTER MILL
GUILDHALL
JAKEMANS COMMUNITY STADIUM
FRAMPTON MARSH
FREISTON SHORE
WINCEBY 1643
A16
A52
A17
A153
A155
A158
A1121
B1183
B1184
B1192
190
173
156
157
A
B
C
D
E
F
G
H
1
2
3
4
5
6
TF
70
40
20
miles
km

Willoughby
Hogsthorpe
Sloothby
Slackholme End
Hasthorpe
Habertoft
Addlethorpe
Ingoldmells
FANTASY ISLAND
Ingoldmells Pt
HARDY'S ANIMAL FARM
Welton le Marsh
Candlesby
Orby
Gunby
GUNBY HALL
BUTLIN'S SKEGNESS
Ashington End
Seathorne
Winthorpe
Mill Hill
Burgh le Marsh
BURGH LE MARSH WINDMILL
Bratoft
South View
Firsby
Irby in the Marsh
NATURELAND SEAL SANCTUARY
Skegness
THE LIFEBOAT STATION MUSEUM
THE VILLAGE CHURCH FARM
AQUARIUM
Croft
Thorpe Culvert
Thorpe St Peter
Seacroft
Wainfleet Common
New England
Wainfleet Bank
Wainfleet All Saints
MAGDALEN COLLEGE MUS
BATEMANS BREWERY
Wainfleet Tofts
Wainfleet St Mary
GIBRALTAR POINT
GIBRALTAR POINT NNR
Gibraltar Point
Wainfleet Harbour
Inner Knock
Wainfleet Sand
Friskney Eaudyke
Friskney
Friskney Tofts
Friskney Flats
The Horseshoe
Wrangle Flats
THE WASH
Gore Pt
HOLME DUNES
HOLME BIRD OBSERVATORY
Holme next the Sea
Old Hunstanton
St Edmund's Pt
Hunstanton
SEA LIFE SANCTUARY
Ringstead
A52
A158
191
157
158

HOLKHAM BAY
BRANCASTER BAY
SCOLT HEAD ISLAND
Harbour Channel
Brancaster Harbour
Brancaster Marsh
Norton Creek
Trowland Creek
Burnham Harbour
West Sands
High Cape
The Run
Bob Hall's Sand
Big Gap
Holkham Gap
Holkham Meals
Lodge Marsh
Warham Salt Marshes
East Fleet
Gore Pt
HOLME DUNES
HOLME BIRD OBSERVATORY
NORFOLK COAST PATH
PEDDARS WAY
Holme next the Sea
Thornham
TITCHWELL MARSH
Titchwell
Brancaster
Marsh Side
BRANCASTER ACTIVITY CENTRE
Brancaster Staithe
Burnham Deepdale
Deepdale Marsh
Norton Marsh
Burnham Norton
Burnham Overy Staithe
Overy Marsh
Burnham Overy Town
Marsh House Fm
Gun Hill
Burrow Gap
Dale Hole
Howe Hill
Holkham
HOLKHAM
Wells-next-the-Sea
WELLS-NEXT-THE-SEA
STIFFKEY ROAD
COAST ROAD
THE MIDDEN
Peterstone Fm
WELLS ROAD
Leath Ho
Bone's Belt
HOLKHAM HALL
Holkham Park
The Temple
NORFOLK
COAST
HIGH STREET
Manor Ho
Barrow Common
The Downs
Hawker's Hill Fm
Westgate
Burnham Market
Westgate Fm
Sussex Fm
Beacon Hill
Gallow Hill
Burnham Thorpe
Gravelpit Hill
Manor Ho
Lucas Hill Wood
Old Common Plantn
Golden Gates
Gallow Hill
Northgate Hall Fm
Warham
WARHAM ST MARY HALT
WELLS & WALSINGHAM LIGHT RAILWAY
Branthill Fm
Branthill Cotts
Scarboro Wood
Longlands Fm
The Belt
Hall
Hunstanton Park
Beacon Hill
Lyng Fm
Bluestone Fm
Choseley Fm
Field Ho
Crow Hall Fm
Ringstead
Downs Fm
Ringstead Downs
Courtyard Fm
Lugden Hill Fm
Sunderland Fm
Friar's Thorne Fm
Cradle Hall Fm
Muckleton
Field Barn
CREAKE ABBEY (REMS)
Abbey Fm
New Holkham
Blunt's Corner
Field Barn
Wighton
WIGHTON HALT
Crabbe Castle Fm
Setons Halt
River Stiffkey
Neat's Ling
Thornham Corner
Summerfield
Church Fm
NORFOLK LAVENDER
St Catherine's Cross
BRANCASTER ROAD
BURNHAM ROAD
BURNHAM ROAD
High Barn
High House Fm
Shammer Ho
Wringate Fm
North Creake
High Hills
Shepherd's Hill
Chantry Hills
Quarles Fm
East Common
Haggard's Lodge
Bunker's Hill
Edgar Fm
Egmere Fm
Egmere
WALSINGHAM
Berry Hall
Great Walsi
Little Walsingham
WALSINGHAM GROUNDS & SHIREHALL MUS
East Hall
SEDGEFORD ROAD
DOCKING RD
Docking
The Park
Sedgeford
Eaton
158
FAKENHAM ROAD
Docking Common
Docking Lodge
Stanhoe
Sly's Barn
Manor Ho
South Creake
Waterden Fm
Waterden
Compton Hall
North Barsham Fm
Barwick Ho
Barwick Hall Fm
Bloodgate Hill
Glover's Fm
Church Fm
Fring
Snettisham
Inmere Fm
Honey Hills
HONEY HILLS
Bircham Newton
Hyde Park
Hubbards Fm
Southgate
The Gorse
North Barsham
Canister Hall Fm
Houghton St Giles
Great Snoring
West Barsham
Buildings Fm
SNETTISHAM PARK
Snettisham Ho
Ingoldisthorpe
Red Barn Fm
Moor Fm
Great Bircham
Barmer
Leicester Square Fm
East Barsham
White Hall
Syderstone
Cranmer Hall
Waterhouse Fm
Thorpland Hall
Little
Shernborne Hall
Shernborne
BIRCHAM MILL
Bircham Tofts
Bagthorpe
Syderstone Common
Blenheim Park
RAF SCULTHORPE HERITAGE CENTRE
Sculthorpe Airfield (disused)
Manor Fm
Sculthorpe
Lodge Fm
Thorpland Lodge Fm
Bircham Common
Tofts Hill
Frizzleton Fm
Coxford Wood
Wicken Green Village
The Grange
Grove Fm
Alet
LYNN RD
Mill Ho
Dersingham
Ling Ho
Manor Fm
Doddshill Fm
Tofts Dale
Coxford Heath
Tattersett
Dunton Patch
Dunton
A148
Fakenham
A1067
Heath Fm
Sculthorpe Moor
Heath House Fm
Anmer
Gatesend Hill
Manor Fm
159
Shereford
The Heath
Fakenham Common
Penstthorpe Hall
Dersingham Wood
The Carr
Big Wood
HOUGHTON HALL
New Buildings
North Pole Fm
Coxford
Doughton
Hempton
FAKENHAM
Park Ho
SANDRINGHAM HOUSE
Commodore Wood
Cross Belt
Bunker's Hill
Houghton Park
The Mayflower
New Houghton
East Rudham
LYNN ROAD
Broomsthorpe
Pynkney Hall
Tatterford
Southmill Fm
Manor Ho
A1065
DEREHAM ROAD
Norton Hall
Starmoor Wood
West
Harpley Common
Sandringham
A149
B1153
B1454
B1155
B1355
B1105
TF
60
70
30
0 1 2 3 miles
0 1 2 3 4 5 km

7
8
9
10
11
A
B
C
D
E
F
G
H
TG
20
60
30
Blakeney Pit
Warham Hole
West Sand
Cabbage Creek
South Side
Pits Pt
The Marrams
BLAKENEY
Stiffkey Freshes
Stiffkey Salt Marshes
Stiffkey Greens
Morston Salt Marshes
Great Barnett
Agar Creek
New Cut
CLEY MILL
BLAKENEY GUILDHALL
CLEY MARSHES
COAST ROAD
PEDDARS WAY AND NORFOLK COAST PATH
Warborough Hill
MORSTON RD
Morston
Stiffkey
Cockthorpe Common
Cockthorpe
Battledore Hill
Blakeney
Joe's Hill
LANGHAM ROAD
B1156
Sparrow Hill
Wiveton
Wiveton Downs
Cley next the Sea
Newgate
Gravelpit Hill
Salthouse
A149
Gallow Hill
MUCKLEBURGH COLLECTION
Weybourne
SHERINGHAM ROAD
WEYBOURNE RD
Sheringham
SHERINGHAM
HILLSIDE SHIRE HORSE SANCTUARY
West Runton
Beeston Regis
East Runton
CROMER
NORFOLK COAST
Langham Lodge
Oulton Hill
Glandford
Summer House Hill
Swan Lodge
The Wing
Lowes Fm
The Hangs
Kelling
NORTH NORFOLK RAILWAY (THE POPPY LINE)
KELLING HEATH HALT
Kelling Heath
Sheringham Hall
Oak Wood
WEYBOURNE
SHERINGHAM PARK
Weybourne Heath
The Dales
Upper Sheringham
LODGE HILL
HOLWAY ROAD
A1082
Sheringwood
Pretty Corner
Stone Hill
The Roman Camp
The Valley
Stone Hill
HOLT ROAD
A148
Langham
Long Lane Fm
Short Lane Fm
Old Barn
Westgate
BINHAM PRIORY & WAYSIDE CROSS
Binham
Ellis Fm
Saxlingham
Manor House Fm
Smoker's Hole
Bayfield Hall
Cley Park
Lawn Fm
Hundred Acre Wood
Highborough Fm
High Kelling
Bodham
East Beckham
West Beckham
Aylmerton
Barn Plantn
Great Wood
Felbrigg
FELBRIGG HALL
Roundwood Hill
Green
Abbot Fm
Field Ho
Foxburrow Fm
County Fm
Field Dalling
Little Marsh
Eastmoor Fm
Horse Hill
Letheringsett
Pereer's Hills
Holt Hall (Coll)
Gresham's School
THE GALLERY
HOLT RD
Breck Fm
LETHERINGSETT WATERMILL
Little Thornage
Common Hill
Holt
CROMER ROAD
Heath Fm
Hill Ho
Manor Ho
Rookery Fm
Lower Bodham
Bodham Hill
Stonepit Hill
Rounce's Coverts
Gresham
Common Plantn
Red Ho
BACONSTHORPE CASTLE (REMS)
Beckett's Fm
Baconsthorpe
Hell Hole
Up Wood
Clipstreet Fm
Bale Hall
Lower Green
Bale
Sharrington
Stowe Ollands
Ingmote Hill
THORNAGE ROAD
Heath Ho
Dam Hill
River Glaven
Hempstead
Manor Ho
Thurgarton Old Hall
Bessingham
Sustead
Metton
Hall Fm
Hindringham
Grange Fm
Bullfer Grove
Brinton
Thornage
Hill Ho
B1110
King's Hills
Edgefield Woods
Edgefield Hall
Lowes Fm
Bunker's Hill
The Dales
Pond Hills
Hole Fm
Hall Fm
Barningham Hall
Manor Ho
Hanworth
160
Vinepark Fm
Thursford Green
THURSFORD COLLECTION
Frog Hall Fm
Gunthorpe Park
Gunthorpe
Lobb's Valley
Burgh Stubbs
Stody
The Green
Hunworth
Starlings' Hill
Plumstead Green
Plumstead
Matlaske
Hall Fm
Aldborough Hall
Thurgarton
Hanworth Hall
Manor Fm
Little Snoring
Thursford
Old Coach House
Pigg's Grave
Briningham
Burgh Hall
Breck Fm
Little Wood
Range Fm
Barningham Green
Lower Street
Aldborough
Alby Hill
The Lings
B1354
Wood Fm
FAKENHAM ROAD
Fuel Fm
White Ollands Fm
Thwaite Hill Fm
Wickmere
Abbey
A148
Forty Acre Plantn
River Stiffkey
Barney
Neat's Close
Park Fm
Melton Constable
Briston
Fir Patch
Edgefield Street
B1149
Old Covert
Mere Fm
Little Barningham
Park Fm
Thwaite Hall
Thwaite Common
Erpingham Ho
Little Wood
Swanton Novers
Swanton Great Wood
Melton Hall
Bunker's Hill
Dairy Fm
New Covert
Shrub Fm
Mannington Hall
MANNINGTON GARDENS
Wolterton Park
Wolterton
Calthorpe
Erpingham
ALBY CRAFTS & GARDENS
Kettlestone
Croxton
Fulmodestone
SWANTON NOVERS
Brown's Covert
Briston Common
Roper Fm
Craymere Beck
Moor Hall
Holly Fm
Mossymere Wood
White House Fm
Scarrow Beck
Itteringham
Clipstone Ho
Common End
Raw Hall
Tipples' Fm
The Lake
Holmes's Wood
Wood Severals
Washpit Plantn
Rookery Fm
Blackwater Br
Little London
Saxthorpe
Moorgate
A140
Common Fm
159
Manor Fm
PENSTHORPE NATURAL PARK
Park Fm
Fulmodeston Severals
Hindolveston
Burnthouse Fm
Roundabout Fm
Nethergate
Holly Heath Fm
Corpusty
Irmingland Hall
Itteringham Common
Great Wood
Park Fm
Ingworth
Thurning
Hall Fm
Foundry Hill
Red Pits
Oulton Lodge
The Tower
Blickling
BLICKLING HALL
Abbotts Hall
Field Barn
Hindolveston Wood
Black Water
Oak Grove
Cropton Hall
Oulton
Hercules Wood
Flash Pit Fm
Drabblegate
Little Ryburgh
Stibbard
Holly Hill
Wood Norton
Ashcroft Fm
Norton
Coldham Hall
Church Fm

178
The Skerries
Harry Furlough's Rocks
Wylfa Head
Wylfa Power Sta
Porth Llanlleiana
Hell's Mouth/Porth Cynfor
Porthllechog (Bull Bay)
Llanbadrig
Cemaes
Carmel Head
Pen Carmel
Hen Borth
Porth y Dyfn
WALES COAST PATH
Tregele
Burwen
Amlwch
Llanfairynghornwy
Llanfechell
Rhosbeirio
Bodewryd
Porth y Bribys
Mynydd y Garn
Llanrhyddlad
Mynydd Mechell
Llanfflewyn
Carreglefn
Rhosgoch
Rhosybol
Parys Mountain
Rhydwyn
Church Bay
Porth Swtan
Porth Trwyn
ISLE OF ANGLESEY
YNYS MÔN
HOLYHEAD BAY
BAE CAERGYBI
Llanfaethlu
Llanbabo
Llyn Alaw
Gwredog
Tyn-y-pwll
DUBLIN
Porth Tywyn-mawr
LLYNNON WINDMILL
Llanddeusant
Llandyfrydog
Llanfwrog
Elim
Llanerchymedd
Llantrisant
Stryd y Facsen
Bachau
Gogarth Bay
BREAKWATER
Soldiers' Pt
HOLYHEAD MARITIME MUSEUM
Salt Island
Holyhead
Caergybi
CAER Y TWR (FORT)
Holyhead Mountain
Mountain
Llaingoch
Porth-y-felin
Morawelon
Nimrod Rocks
Goferydd
HOLYHEAD MTN HUT CIRCLES
Pont Hwfa
HOLYHEAD ROMAN FORT
Stryd
Twr
Pen-las Rock
SOUTH STACK CLIFFS
Kingsland
Penrhos
PENRHOS FEILW STANDING STONES
TY-MAWR STANDING STONE
Penrhosfeilw
TREFIGNATH BURIAL CHAMBER
Beddmanarch Bay
Llanfachraeth
TREGWEHELYDD STANDING STONE
Pen-llyn
Llanfigael
Carmel
Llanynghenedl
Rallt Fm
Shop Fm
PRESADDFED BURIAL CHAMBER
Llechcynfarwy
Newlands Park
Valley (Y Fali)
Bodedern
Trefor
Llangwyllog
Porth Ruffydd
Porth Dafarch
Trearddur
Trearddur Bay
Isallt Bach
Holy Island
Ynys Gybi
Porth Diana
Raven's Pt
Caergeiliog
Llanfihangel yn Nhowyn
Four Mile Bridge
Bryngwran
Llynfaes
Bodffordd
Llanfairyneubwll
VALLEY WETLANDS
Capel-gwyn
Gwalchmai
Engedi
Heneglwys
Rhoscolyn
Rhoscolyn Head
Silver Bay
Borthwen
Ddrydwy
Dothan
TY-NEWYDD BURIAL CHAMBER
Cerrigceinwen
Llangristiolus
Ynys Feirig
Rhosneigr
Llanfaelog
Pencarnisiog
Bryn Du
DIN DRYFOL BURIAL CHAMBER
Soar
Capel Mawr
Porth Nobla
BARCLODIAD Y GAWRES BURIAL CHAMBER
Bethel
Trefdraeth
Porth Trecastell
Llangwyfan-isaf
Llangadwaladr
Aberffraw
Hermon
Malltraeth
Llangaffo
162

7
8
9
10
11
A
B
C
D
E
F
G
H
180
Amlwch Port
Porthyrychen
Porth Eilian
Llaneilian
Fresh Water Bay
Pengorffwysfa
Cerrig-mân
Porthygwichiaid
Porth Helygen
Porth yr Aber
Ynys Dulas
Garreg Allan
Nebo
Dulas
Gwlybycoed
Traeth yr Ora
Llaneuddog
City Dulas
Tyddyn Isaf
Lligwy Bay
ISLE OF ANGLESEY
YNYS MÔN
Brynrefail
Moelfre
MOELFRE SEAWATCH CENTRE
Y Swnt
DIN LLIGWY
LLIGWY BURIAL CHAMBER
Rhôs Lligwy
Ty-mawr
Mynydd Bodafon
Plas Bodafon
Llanallgo
Caerhoslligwy
Maenaddwyn
Parciau
Marianglas
Penciau
Frigan
Tynygongl
Borth-wen
Brynteg
Benllech
Benllech Sand
Dinas
Capel Coch
Cefn-du Mawr
Nant Isaf
Nant-uchaf
CORS ERDDREINIOG
Nant Newydd
CORS GOCH
Ynys Isaf
Bettws
Red Wharf Bay
Red Wharf Bay Traeth-coch
Llanbedrgoch
Erddreiniog
Maen Eryr
Prysan
Hendre
Glan Gors
Gwenfro Isaf
STANDING STONE
Llanddyfnan
Gwenfro Uchaf
Pencefn
Tan-y-graig
Pentraeth Forest
Pentraeth
STONE SCIENCE
Rhosmeirch
Tyn Beudy
CORS BODEILIO
Hendre Fm
Talwrn
Clegyrdy-bach
OREL YNYS MÔN
Clegyrdy-mawr
Gylched
Pencraig
Plas Penmynydd
Ceint
Ty-coch
Dyffryn
Taihirion
Rhoscefnhir
Trefor
Pen-y-garnedd
Hendrefor
Hafotty Covert
Llansadwrn
Bodgylched
Penmynydd
Hirdre-faig
Cefn-poeth
Tyddyn
Y Dolydd
Twll-y-clawdd
Castell
Tyddyn Mawr
Rhyd-y-arian
Bwlch-gwyn
Cefn Du Isaf
Ty'n Buarth
PILI PALAS
Menai Bridge (Porthaethwy)
Pentre Berw
Tyn Cae
Llanfairpwll-gwyngyll
Star
Gaerwen
LLANFAIRPWLL
Ind Est
Bryn-y-fedwen
Brynhyfryd
Llanddaniel Fab
Chwipin
BRYN CELLI DDU BURIAL CHAMBER
Pont Crug
Glanyrafon
PLAS NEWYDD
Afon Menai
Capel-y-graig
Vaynol Hall
Old Hall
Bodowyr-isaf
BODOWYR BURIAL CHAMBER
Ysgubor Wen
Bodlew
Gwydryn Newydd
Pont-Dic
Llanedwen
Lew
MENAI SUSPENSION BRIDGE
ORIEL TEGFRYN
Bangor
Garth
Upper Bangor
STORIEL
Hirael
CATHEDRAL
Maesgeirchen
Coed Mawr
Glan Adda
Minffordd
Penrhos Garnedd
Caerhun
Tyddyn-Hellyn
Brithdir
Pen-y-wen
Glasinfryn
Coed Hywel
Tregarth
Halfway Br
Rachub
Llanllechid
Bryn
Tal-y-bont
Llandegai
PENRHYN CASTLE
ABEROGWEN SPINNIES
Marianywinllan
Pen-y-bryn
Rhiw Goch
Afon Ogwen
BANGOR SERVICES
WALES COAST PATH
Crymlyn
Glyn
Ffridd Ddu
Bronydd Isaf
Abergwyngregyn
COEDYDD ABER
ABER FALLS
SNOWDONIA
NATIONAL PARK
PARC CENEDLAETHOL ERYRI
Moel Wnion 580
Gyrn 542
Llefn
Moel Faban 408
Bera Mawr
Llwytmor
Foel-Ganol 533
Drosgl 621
Pen Bryn-du
Bwlch y Ddeufaen
Drum 770
Foel-Fras 942
Nant
Gorddinog
Cammarnaint
Garreg Fawr 356
Nant-y-felin
Nant-y-pandy
Llanfairfechan
LLANFAIRFECHAN
Garizim
Penmaenan
Moelf 435
Afon Anafon
CONWY BAY
BAE CONWY
Puffin Island or Priestholm Ynys Seiriol
Outer Road
Fedw Fawr
Mariandyrys
Glan-yr-afon
Caim
PENMON PRIORY
Penmon
Lavan Sands
Penhwnllys
Bryn Ddol
Cefn
Wern Fm
Llanddona
Llangoed
Bryn Celyn
Carwad
Pen-y-bryn
Ffordd Deg
Rhos Newydd
Rhôs
Bryn Cogail
Llanfaes
Fryars Road
BEAUMARIS CASTLE
GAOL & COURTHOUSE
ALLT GOCH FAWR
Coed Cefn
Cefn
Beaumaris
Gallows Point
Trwyn y Penrhyn
Hen Bentref Llandegfan
Llandegfan
BEAUMARIS ROAD
SH
70
00
163

IRISH SEA
MÔR IWERDDON
Great Ormes Head
Pen-y-Gogarth
Hornby Cave
GREAT ORME
GREAT ORME RAILWAY
GREAT ORME COPPER MINE
CABIN LIFT
Toll
Llandudno Bay or Ormes Bay
Llandudno
THE PARADE
Cregiau Rhiwledyn
Little Ormes Head
Penrhyn Bay (Bae Penrhyn)
Penrhynside
Craig-y-don
Rhôs Pt
Rhôs-on-Sea
Llandrillo-yn-Rhos
Colwyn Bay (Bae Colwyn)
Conwy Sands
Llanrhos
Deganwy
Glanwydden
Bryn Pydew
Llandudno Junction (Cyffordd Llandudno)
Tywyn
Penmaen Rhôs
WELSH MOUNTAIN ZOO
Mochdre
Old Colwyn
Llanddulas
Abergele
Penmaenmawr
Penmaenan
Dwygyfylchi
Capelulo
Llechwedd
Gyffin
Conwy
CONWY CASTLE
Dolwyd
Bryn-rhys
Llansanffraid Glan Conwy
Pentrefelin
Bryn-y-maen
Llanelian-yn-Rhos
Llysfaen
Rhyd-y-foel
Dolwen
Betws-yn-Rhos
Llanfairfechan
Nant-y-pandy
SNOWDONIA NATIONAL PARK
PARC CENEDLAETHOL ERYRI
Henryd
Rowen
Ty'n-y-groes
Pontwgan
Tal-y-cafn
BODNANT GARDEN
Graig
Eglwysbach
Dawn
Hafod-lom
Trofarth
Chwefforda
Pentre'r Felin
Gell
Cefn-coch
Pentre Isaf
Llanfair Talhaiarn
Tal-y-Bont
GWRYCH CASTLE & GARDENS
CONWY
0 1 2 3 miles
0 1 2 3 4 5 km

7
8
9
10
11
A
B
C
D
E
F
G
H
182
165
Rhyl
(Y Rhyl)
Prestatyn
Kinmel Bay
(Bae Cinmel)
Towyn
Rhuddlan
Dyserth
Meliden
(Gallt Melyd)
Gronant
Talacre
Point of Ayr
(Yr Parlwr Du)
Gwespyr
Llanasa
Ffynnongroyw
Mostyn Quay
Mostyn
Trelogan
Whitford
(Chwitffordd)
Holywell
(Treffynon)
Greenfield
Carmel
Gorsedd
Pant-y-Wacco
Caerwys
St Asaph
(Llanelwy)
Trefnant
Bodfari
Tremeirchion
Bodelwyddan
St George
Glascoed
Cefn Berain
Llannefydd
Nannerch
Halkyn
West Kirby
Hilbre Island
Little Hilbre Island
Salisbury Middle
DENBIGHSHIRE
(SIR DDINBYCH)
FLINTSHIRE
(SIR Y FFLINT)
CLWYDIAN RANGE
Halkyn Mountain

LIVERPOOL
BAY
Crosby Channel
Crosby
ANTONY GORMLEY SCULPTURES
BELFAST
DOUGLAS (NOV-MARCH) DUBLIN
DOUGLAS (MARCH-NOV)
Little Crosby
Sefton
Thornton
Netherton
Blundellsands
Brighton le Sands
Great Crosby
Buckley Hill
Aintree
Melling
Melling Mount
Waddicar
Northwood
Kirkby
Westvale
Southdene
Waterloo Park
Waterloo
Ford
Litherland
Orrell
Seaforth
Fazakerley
Gillmoss
Croxteth
Knowsle
Bootle
Walton
Norris Green
Sandhills
Kirkdale
Clubmoor
West Derby
Stockbridge Village
MERSEYSIDE
Tuebrook
Anfield
Everton
Fincham
Woolfall Heath
Longview
Vauxhall
Liverpool
Dovecot
Knotty Ash
Swanside
Page Moss
Roby
Huyton
Kensington
Old Swan
Broad Green
Edge Hill
Bowing Park
Wavertree
Childwall
Belle Vale
Netherley
Princes Park
Toxteth
Dingle
Mossley Hill
Calderstones
Gateacre
Woolton
Allerton
Aigburth
Grassendale
Otterspool
St Michael's Hamlet
Hunt's Cross
Garston
Speke Hall
LIVERPOOL (JOHN LENNON)
Liverpool Airport
River Mersey
Garston Channel
Eastham Sands
Eastham Locks
Stanlow Banks
New Brighton
Wallasey
Egremont
Liscard
Leasowe
Moreton
Poulton
Bidston
Bidston Hill
Seacombe
Claughton
Birkenhead
Tranmere
Rock Ferry
New Ferry
Bebington
Bromborough Pool
Port Sunlight
Dove Point
East Hoyle Bank
Meols
Hoylake
Hilbre Island
West Kirby
Saughall Massie
Upton
Greasby
Newton
Frankby
Grange
Noctorum
Oxton
Woodchurch
Arrowe Hill
Prenton
Caldy
Landican
Irby
Thurstaston
Thingwall
Storeton
Woodhey
Higher Bebington
Lower Bebington
Pensby
Barnston
Brimstage
Spital
Poulton
Bromborough
Eastham Ferry
Heswall
Dawpool Bank
The Dales
Thornton Hough
Brookhurst
Eastham
Gayton
Raby
Parkgate
Hinderton
Gayton Sands
Neston
Little Neston
Willaston
Hooton
Childer Thornton
Little Sutton
Overpool
Ellesmere Port
Stanlow
Ness
CHESHIRE WEST & CHESTER
NESS BOTANIC GARDENS
Great Sutton
Whitby
Wolverham
Greenfield (Maes-Glas)
Walwen
Whelston
Holywell (Treffynon)
Bagillt
Dolphin
Flint (Y Fflint)
Mount Pleasant
Pentre-Ffwrndan
Halkyn
Oakenholt
Rockcliffe
Flint Mountain (Mynydd Fflint)
Halkyn Mountain
Burton
Puddington
Ledsham
Capenhurst
Two Mills
Woodbank
Shotwick
Whitbyheath
Little Stanney
Backford Cross
Stoak
Dunkirk
Backford
Wervin
Picton
Mollington
Saughall
Moston
Mickle Trafford
Upton Heath
Upton
Hoole Bank
Newton
Chester
Sealand
Garden City
Shotton
Connah's Quay
Golftyn
Kelsterton
Wimbolds Trafford
Thornton-le-Moors
0 1 2 3 miles
0 1 2 3 4 5 km

Rainford
Billinge
Longshaw
Bryn
Bryn Gates
Abram
Westleigh
Tyldesley
Leigh
Ashton-in Makerfield
Golborne
Lowton
Lowton Common
Pennington
Astley
Haydock
Newton-le-Willows
St Helens
Eccleston
Prescot
Huyton
Whiston
Rainhill
Culcheth
Croft
Winwick
Burtonwood
Glazebury
Cadishead
Warrington
Hollins Green
Rixton
Woolston
Martinscroft
Padgate
Orford
Dallam
Great Sankey
Penketh
Widnes
Runcorn
Halton
Latchford
Thelwall
Lymm
Grappenhall
Stockton Heath
Appleton
Moore
Daresbury
Stretton
Hale
Frodsham
Helsby
Kingsley
Weaverham
Northwich
Hartford
Davenham
Moulton
Cuddington
Sandiway
Kelsall
Delamere
Oakmere
Manley
Mouldsworth
Alvanley
Dunham-on-the-Hill
Plumley
Lostock Gralam
Great Budworth
Comberbach
Barnton
Anderton
Marston
Pickmere
High Legh
Arley
Whitley Reed
Higher Whitley
Lower Whitley
Preston Brook
Dutton
Aston
Sutton Weaver
CHESHIRE WEST & CHESTER
HALTON
WARRINGTON
DELAMERE FOREST PARK

Worsley
Swinton
Pendlebury
Broughton Park
Moston
Failsworth
Hollinwood
Kersal
Harpurhey
Newton Heath
Boothstown
Higher Green
Astley Green
Lancashire Mining Museum
RHS Garden Bridgewater
Westwood Park
Monton
Ellesmere Park
Charlestown
Strangeways
Cheetham Hill
Salford
Droylsden
Ashton
Eccles
Patricroft
Winton
Barton upon Irwell
Peel Green
Dumplington
Ordsall
Hulme
Manchester
Ardwick
Openshaw
Gorton
Denton
Audenshaw
Dukinfield
Irlam
Flixton
Urmston
Davyhulme
Trafford Park
Stretford
Old Trafford
Moss Side
Rusholme
Levenshulme
Reddish
Fallowfield
Chorlton-cum-Hardy
Withington
Cadishead
Glazebrook
Carrington
Partington
Ashton upon Mersey
Sale
Brooklands
Northern Moor
West Didsbury
Didsbury
Heaton Mersey
Heaton Moor
Heaton Chapel
Heaton Norris
South Reddish
Bredbury
Stockport
Northenden
Timperley
Broadheath
Altrincham
Wythenshawe
Gatley
Cheadle
Cheadle Heath
Cheadle Hulme
Edgeley
Heaviley
Offerton
Hazel Grove
Warburton
Heatley
Lymm
Dunham Town
Bowdon
Hale
Hale Barns
Woodhouse Park
Heald Green
Bramhall
Manchester Airport
Ashley
Styal
Handforth
Poynton
Woodford
Mobberley
Morley Green
Wilmslow
Rostherne
Tatton Park
Knutsford
Over Tabley
Holehouses
Alderley Edge
Prestbury
Bollington
Nether Alderley
Chelford
Ollerton
Marthall
Over Peover
Lower Peover
Peover Heath
Plumley
Lostock Gralam
Pickmere
Monks Heath
Macclesfield
Hurdsfield
Tytherington
Broken Cross
Henbury
Siddington
Withington Green
Lower Withington
Goostrey
Jodrell Bank Visitor Centre
Blackden Heath
Lach Dennis
Allostock
Warren
Gawsworth
Sutton Lane Ends
Langley
Gurnett
Oakgrove
Twemlow Green
Cranage
Holmes Chapel
Marton
Highlane
Lower Pexhill
0 1 2 3 miles
0 1 2 3 4 5 km

Mossley
Stalybridge
Mottram in Longdendale
Hyde
Godley
Hattersley
Broadbottom
Tintwistle
Hadfield
Hollingworth
Padfield
Gamesley
Old Glossop
Glossop
Simmondley
Charlesworth
Chisworth
Compstall
Marple
Marple Bridge
Mellor
Charlestown
Chunal
Little Hayfield
Hayfield
Thornsett
Birch Vale
New Mills
Newtown
Low Leighton
Disley
Strines
Furness Vale
Bridgemont
Buxworth
Chinley
Chinley Head
Whaley Bridge
Horwich End
Taxal
Kettleshulme
Chapel-en-le-Frith
Chapel Milton
Sparrowpit
Dove Holes
Peak Dale
Fernilee
Combs
Burbage
Buxton
Fairfield
Harpur Hill
King Sterndale
Cowdale
Chelmorton
Taddington
Sterndale Moor
Flagg
Wildboarclough
Macclesfield Forest
Walker Barn
Rainow
Crowden
Longdendale
Edale
Nether Booth
Barber Booth
Castleton
Hope
Bradwell
Aston
Bamford
Thornhill
Brough
Shatton
Peak Forest
Tideswell
Litton
Wardlow
Great Hucklow
Little Hucklow
Foolow
Eyam
Wheston
Hargatewall
Tunstead
Wormhill
Miller's Dale
Blackwell
Priestcliffe
Cressbrook
Little Longstone
Great Longstone
Ashford in the Water
Sheldon
Ashopton
Ladybower Res
Derwent Reservoir
Howden Moors
Bleaklow
Kinder Scout
Edale Moor
Vale of Edale
Mam Tor
Snake Road
PEAK DISTRICT NATIONAL PARK
High Peak
Hope Forest
Derwent Moors
DERBYSHIRE
A628
A57
A6
A623
A624
A515
A53
A54
A537
A6013
M67
196
197
186
169

Langsett
Cubley
Oxspring
Crane Moor
Birdwell
Upper Hoyland
Platts Common
Jump
Hemingfield
Brampton
Wath upon Dearne
Hoyland
Elsecar
Roughbirchworth
Snowden Hill
Thurgoland
Pilley
Tankersley
Chapeltown
Midhopestones
Upper Midhope
Wortley
West Melton
Stocksbridge
Deepcar
Finkle Street
Howbrook
Westwood
Mortomley
Harley
Wentworth
Barrow
Bolsterstone
Ewden Village
High Green
Upper Tankersley
Thorpe Hesley
Nether Haugh
Upper Haugh
Wigtwizzle
Broomhead Moor
Upper Commons
PEAK DISTRICT NATIONAL PARK
Wharncliffe Side
Oughtibridge
Grenoside
Ecclesfield
Kimberworth
Rotherham
High Bradfield
Low Bradfield
Worrall
Parson Cross
Shiregreen
Wincobank
Middlewood
Wadsley
Wadsley Bridge
Ughill
Stacey Bank
Dungworth
Stannington
Hillsborough
Malinbridge
Owlerton
Pitsmoor
Carbrook
Attercliffe
Brinsworth
Tinsley
Moorgate
SOUTH YORKSHIRE
Hollow Meadows
Walkley
Sheffield
Crookes
Darnall
Treeton
Catcliffe
Handsworth
Ladybower
Ashopton
Fulwood
Ranmoor
Highfield
Arbourthorne
Manor Estate
Woodhouse
Bamford
Thornhill
Aston
Hathersage
Ecclesall
Millhouses
Whirlow
Ringinglow
Norton Woodseats
Gleadless
Hackenthorpe
Beighton
Abbeydale
Beauchief
Dore
Totley
Bradway
Jordanthorpe
Highlane
Mosborough
Eckington
Upper Padley
Nether Padley
Grindleford
Dronfield
Dronfield Woodhouse
Holmesfield
Owler Bar
Coal Aston
Apperknowle
Marsh Lane
Middle Handley
West Handley
Unstone
Unstone Green
Abney
Bretton
Foolow
Eyam
Stoney Middleton
Froggatt
Curbar
Calver
Baslow
Hassop
Rowland
Great Longstone
Little Longstone
Ashford in the Water
Pilsley
Edensor
Bakewell
DERBYSHIRE
New Whittington
Old Whittington
Common Side
Barlow
Staveley
Brimington
Newbold
Chesterfield
Old Brampton
Brampton
Tapton
Duckmanton
Calow
Arkwright Town
Hady
Birdholme
Walton
Holymoorside
Eastmoor
Wadshelf
Overgreen
Moorhall
Wildays Green
Sutton Scarsdale
Hasland

Mexborough
Conisbrough
Warmsworth
Bessacarr
New Edlington
Old Edlington
Loversall
Wadworth
New Rossington
Rossington
Finningley
Blaxton
Auckley
Branton
Thrybergh
Ravenfield
Micklebring
Braithwell
Maltby
Hellaby
Wickersley
Bramley
Tickhill
Bawtry
Harworth
Bircotes
Austerfield
Misson
Newington
Scaftworth
Everton
Harwell
Stainton
Stone
Firbeck
Oldcotes
Styrrup
Serlby
Scrooby
Ranskill
Mattersey
Mattersey Thorpe
Blyth
Torworth
Langold
Carlton in Lindrick
Letwell
Gildingwells
Dinnington
Laughton en le Morthen
Thurcroft
Ulley
Aughton
Aston
Swallownest
Todwick
North Anston
South Anston
Kiveton Park
Wales
Woodsetts
Wallingwells
Hodsock
Bilby
Barnby Moor
Sutton
Lound
Wigthorpe
Gateford
Shireoaks
Worksop
Rhodesia
Manton
Kilton
Ranby
Babworth
Retford
Ordsall
Eaton
Scofton
Harthill
Thorpe Salvin
Killamarsh
Norwood
Spinkhill
Barlborough
Whitwell
Clowne
Creswell
Elmton
Holbeck
Norton
Cuckney
Whaley Thorns
Nether Langwith
Langwith
Bolsover
Carburton
Budby
Perlethorpe
Walesby
Bothamsall
Haughton
Elkesley
Gamston
West Drayton
Milton
Market Warsop
Church Warsop
Meden Vale
New Ollerton
Kirton
Palterton
Scarcliffe
Shuttlewood
SOUTH YORKSHIRE
NOTTINGHAMSHIRE
SHERWOOD FOREST
M18
M1
A1(M)
A1
A57
A60
A631
A614
A619
A638
198
199
188
171
A
B
C
D
E
F
G
H

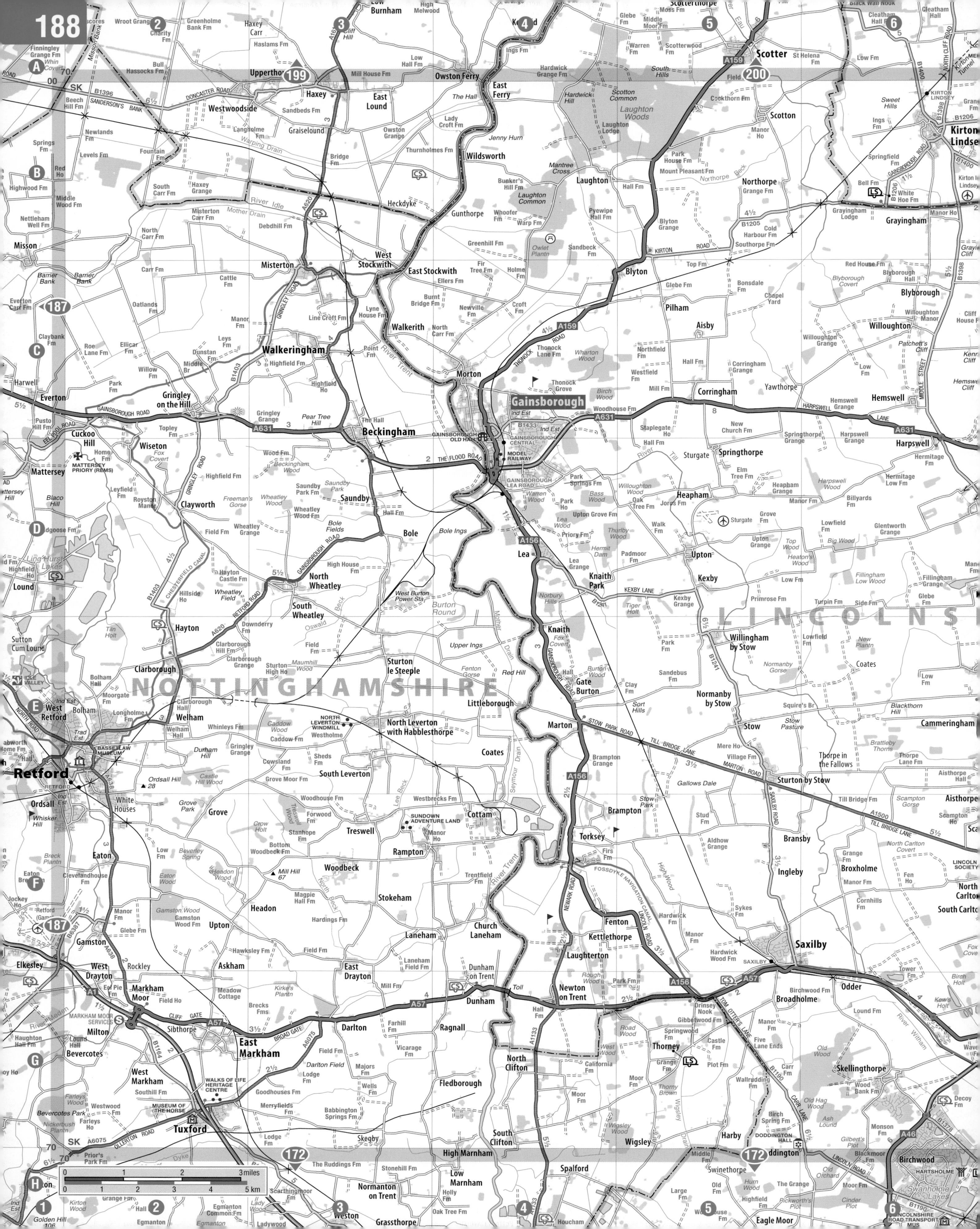
Wroot Grange
Greenholme Bank Fm
Haxey Carr
Low Burnham
High Melwood
Kelfield
Scotterthorpe
Moss Fm
Cleatham Hall Fm
Cleatham Hall
Finningley Grange Fm
Charity Fm
Haslams Fm
Cliff Hill
Glebe Fm
Middle Moor Fm
Warren Fm
Scotterwood Fm
Low Hall Fm
Ings Fm
Scotter
St Helena Fm
Low Fm
Bull Fm
Hassocks Fm
Upperthorpe
Mill House Fm
Owston Ferry
Hardwick Grange Fm
South Hills
Field
Kirton Tunnel
SK
B1396
DONCASTER ROAD
Haxey
East Ferry
Hardwick Hill
Scotton Common
Cockthorn Fm
Kirton Lindsey
Beech Hill Fm
SANDERSON'S BANK
Westwoodside
East Lound
The Hall
Laughton Woods
Scotton
Sweet Hills
Sandbeds Fm
Lady Croft Fm
Laughton Lodge
Ings Fm
Newlands Fm
Langholme Fm
Graiselound
Owston Grange
Jenny Hurn
Manor Ho
Springs Fm
Warping Drain
Thurnholmes Fm
Wildsworth
Levels Fm
Fountain Fm
Bridge Fm
Mantree Cross
Park House Fm
Springfield Fm
Mount Pleasant Fm
GAINSBOROUGH ROAD
Red Ho
Haxey Grange
Bunker's Hill Fm
Laughton
Northorpe Beck
Northorpe
Highwood Fm
South Carr Fm
Laughton Common
Hall Fm
Northorpe Grange Fm
Bell Fm
White Hoe Fm
Middle Wood Fm
River Idle
Heckdyke
Pyewipe Hall Fm
Grayingham Lodge
Grayingham
Manor Ho
Nettleham Well Fm
Misterton Carr Fm
Mother Drain
Gunthorpe
Whoofer Fm
Warp Fm
Blyton Grange
B1205
Cold Harbour Fm
Southorpe Fm
Debdhill Fm
North Carr Fm
Misson
Greenhill Fm
Owlet Plantn
Sandbeck Fm
KIRTON ROAD
Grayingham Cliff
West Stockwith
Misterton
East Stockwith
Fir Tree Fm
Holme Fm
Top Fm
Red House Fm
Blyborough Covert
Blyborough Hall
Barrier Bank
Carr Fm
Cattle Fm
Ellers Fm
Blyton
Glebe Fm
Bonsdale Fm
Chapel Yard
Blyborough
Everton Carr Fm
Oatlands Fm
GRINGLEY ROAD
Burnt Bridge Fm
Newville Fm
Croft Fm
Pilham
Willoughton Manor
Cliff House Fm
Manor Fm
Line Croft Fm
Lyne House Fm
Walkerith
North Carr Fm
A159
Aisby
Willoughton
Claybank Fm
Leys Fm
Roe Lane Fm
Ellicar Fm
Dunstan Fm
Walkeringham
Point Fm
River Trent
Thonock Lane Fm
Wharton Wood
Northfield Fm
Willoughton Grange
Patchett's Cliff
Kenn Cliff
Highfield Fm
Corringham Grange
Low Fm
Middle Br
B1403
Willow Fm
Highfield Ho
THONOCK ROAD
Westfield Fm
Hall Fm
Harwell
Park Fm
Morton
Thonock Grove
Yawthorpe
Hemswell Cliff
Everton
Gringley on the Hill
Gainsborough
Birch Wood
Mill Fm
Corringham
MIDDLE STREET
Hemswell
GAINSBOROUGH ROAD
Gringley Grange
Pear Tree Hill
The Hall
Ind Est
Woodhouse Fm
Hemswell Grange
Pusto Hill Fm
A631
B1433
HARPSWELL LANE
Cuckoo Hill
Topley Fm
Beckingham
GAINSBOROUGH OLD HALL
GAINSBOROUGH CENTRAL
New Church Fm
Stapiegate Ho
Springthorpe Grange
Harpswell Grange
A631
Harpswell
Wiseton
Home Fm
Fox Covert
Wood Fm
THE FLOOD ROAD
MODEL RAILWAY
Hall Fm
Sturgate
Springthorpe
Hermitage Fm
Mattersey
MATTERSEY PRIORY (REMS)
Highfield Fm
Beckingham Wood
River Till
Elm Tree Fm
Hermitage Low Fm
Leyfield Fm
Saundby Park Fm
Saundby Park
GAINSBOROUGH LEA ROAD
Park Springs Fm
Willoughton Wood
Heapham Grange
Harpswell Wood
Blaco Hill
Royston Manor
Clayworth
Freeman's Gorse
Wheatley Wood
Saundby
Warren Wood
Park Ho
Bass Wood
Oak Tree Fm
Jores Fm
Heapham
Manor Fm
Billyards Fm
Wheatley Wood Fm
Hall Fm
Upton Grove Fm
Sturgate
Grove Fm
Lowfield Fm
Glentworth Grange
Field Fm
Wheatley Grange
Bole Fields
Bole
Bole Ings
Lea Wood
Walk Fm
Priory Fm
Thurlby Wood
Big Wood
Upton Grange
Top Wood
A156
Lea
Hermit Dam
Padmoor Fm
Upton
Heaton's Wood
Fillingham Low Wood
Fillingham Grange
Lound
Hayton Castle Fm
High House Fm
North Wheatley
Lea Grange
Knaith Park
KEXBY LANE
Kexby
Low Fm
Glebe Fm
CHESTERFIELD CANAL
Hillside Ho
Wheatley Field
RETFORD ROAD
West Burton Power Sta
Norbury Hills
Tiger Holt
Kexby Grange
Primrose Fm
Turpin Fm
Side Fm
South Wheatley
Burton Round
Sutton Cum Lound
Hayton
A620
Downderry Fm
Oswald Beck
Knaith
Fox Covert
LINCOLNSHIRE
Willingham by Stow
Lowfield Fm
New Plantn
Tin Holt
Clarborough Hill Fm
Field Fm
Upper Ings
Park Fm
Normanby Gorse
Coates
Clarborough Grange
Maumhill Wood
Sturton High Ho
Sturton le Steeple
Fenton Grange
Red Hill
Burton Wood
Hall
Sandebus Fm
Low Fm
Clarborough
IDLE VALLEY
Bolham Hall
Moorgate Fm
NOTTINGHAMSHIRE
Gate Burton
Clay Fm
Normanby by Stow
Clarborough Hall
Littleborough
Sort Hills
Squire's Br
Blackthorn Hill
West Retford
Bolham
Longholme Fm
Welham
Caddow Wood
NORTH LEVERTON WINDMILL
North Leverton with Habblesthorpe
Marton
STOW PARK ROAD
Stow
Stow Pasture
Cammeringham
Trad Est
Welham Hall
Whinleys Fm
Caddow Fm
Westholme
TILL BRIDGE LANE
Mere Ho
Brattleby Thorns
BASSETLAW MUSEUM
Durham Hill
Gringley Grange
Sheds Fm
Coates
Brampton Grange
Village Fm
Thorpe in the Fallows
Thorpe Lane Fm
Retford
Cowsland Fm
Ordsall Hill
Castle Hill Wood
South Leverton
Seymour Drain
MARTON ROAD
Sturton by Stow
Aisthorpe Hall
Grove Moor Fm
Gallows Dale
Ordsall
White Houses
Grove Park
Woodhouse Fm
Westbrecks Fm
Stow Park
SAXILBY ROAD
Till Bridge Fm
Scampton Gorse
Aisthorpe
Whisker Hill
Grove
Treswell Wood
Forwood Fm
SUNDOWN ADVENTURE LAND
Cottam
Brampton
A1500
Scampton Ho
Crow Holt
Stanhope Fm
Treswell
Lee Beck
Manor Ho
Torksey
Stud Fm
Bransby
North Carlton Covert
Low Fm
Beverley Spring
Bottom Woodbeck Fm
Rampton
Firs Fm
Aldhow Grange
Grange Fm
Broxholme
LINCOLN SOCIETY
Eaton
Breck Plantn
Headon Wood
Mill Hill
Woodbeck
Trentfield Fm
FOSSDYKE NAVIGATION CANAL
High Wood
Ingleby
Fen Ho
Manor Fm
Eaton
Clevelandhouse Fm
Eaton Wood
North Beck
Magpie Hall Fm
Stokeham
NEWARK ROAD
Sykes Fm
Cornhills Fm
North Carlton
South Carlton
Jockey
Retford
Manor Fm
Headon
Gamston Wood
Gamston Wood Fm
Hardings Fm
Church Laneham
Fenton
LINCOLN ROAD
Hardwick Fm
Upton
Laneham
Kettlethorpe
Manor Fm
Gamston
Glebe Fm
Hawksley Fm
Field Fm
Laughterton
Hardwick Wood Fm
Saxilby
Elkesley
Rockley
Askham
Laneham Field Fm
Dunham on Trent
Rough Wood
Park Fm
Saxilby
Tower Fm
Birch Holt
Cove Fm
West Drayton
East Drayton
Mill Fm
Toll
Newton on Trent
A156
A57
Odder
Eel Pie Fm
Markham Moor
Meadow Cottage
Kirke's Plantn
Dunham
Drinsey Nook
Birchwood Fm
Broadholme
Field Ho
Brecks Fms
A57
Hall Fm
TOM OTTER'S LANE
Gibbetwood Fm
Lound Fm
Kew's Holt
MARKHAM MOOR SERVICES
CLIFF GATE
Sibthorpe
Darlton
Farhill Fm
Ragnall
Road Wood
Springwood Fm
Manor Fm
River Witham
Milton
A57
BROAD GATE
A6075
Thorney
Castle Fm
Five Lane Ends
Haughton Hall Fm
Lound Hall
East Markham
Vicarage Fm
West Wood
California Fm
Grange Fm
Plot Fm
Old Wood
Wave
Bevercotes
Field Fm
Darlton Field
Majors Fm
North Clifton
Carr Fm
Skellingthorpe
West Markham
WALKS OF LIFE HERITAGE CENTRE
Lodge Fm
Wells Fm
Fledborough
Moor Fm
Thorny Brown
Wallrudding Fm
B1190
Wood Bank Fm
Southill Fm
Goodhouses Fm
Moor Fm
Old Hag Wood
Decoy Fm
Farleys Wood
Westwood Fm
MUSEUM OF THE HORSE
Merryfields Fm
Babbington Springs Fm
Wigsley Wood
Wigsley Drain
CARR LANE
Ash Lound
Bevercotes Park
Nickerbush Plantn
Farleys Ho
Tuxford
Lodge Fm
Skegby
South Clifton
Wigsley
Birch Spring Fm
Gilbert's Plot
Monson Fm
A46
B1378
SK
A6075
OLLERTON ROAD
Harby
DODDINGTON HALL
Doddington
Blackmoor Fm
Birchwood
Prior's Park Fm
Dyke
High Marnham
Middle Fm
LINCOLN ROAD
HARTSHOLME
The Ruddings Fm
Stonehill Fm
Low Marnham
Spalford
Swinethorpe
Old Orchard
Hurn Wood
The Grange
Moor Fm
Swanholme Lakes
Scarthingmoor Fm
Normanton on Trent
Holly Fm
Large Fm
Old Fm
Highfield Fm
Pickworth's Plot
Cinder Plot
B1190
Kirton Wood
Grange Fm
Hall
Egmanton Common Fm
Lady Wood
Oak Tree Fm
Woodhouse Fm
LINCOLNSHIRE ROAD TRANSPORT MUS
Golden Hill
Egmanton
Egmanton
Ladywood
Weston
Grassthorpe
Houcham
Eagle Moor
0 1 2 3 miles
0 1 2 3 4 5 km
199
200
187
172
A
B
C
D
E
F
G
H
1
2
3
4
5
6

Hibaldstow
North Kelsey
North Kelsey Moor
Cabourne
Caistor
Sandbraes
Canada
Redbourne
Cuxwold
Rothwell
Nettleton
Moortown
South Kelsey
Holton le Moor
Croxby
Thorganby
Brandy Wharf
Waddingham
Thornton le Moor
Thoresway
Swinhope
LINCOLNSHIRE
WOLDS
Normanby le Wold
Brookenby
Snitterby
North Owersby
South Owersby
Usselby
Claxby
Binbrook
Stainton le Vale
Atterby
Otby
Bishop Norton
Kingerby
Kirkby
Osgodby
Walesby
Kirmond le Mire
Bishopbridge
Glentham
Tealby
Spital in the Street
Middle Rasen
Market Rasen
Caenby
Caenby Corner
West Rasen
Ludford
Toft next Newton
North Willingham
Normanby-by-Spital
Newton by Toft
Sixhills
Owmby-by-Spital
Newtoft
Little London
Saxby
Linwood
Legsby
Buslingthorpe
Faldingworth
Spridlington
Bleasby
Hainton
Lissington
South Willingham
Cold Hanworth
Friesthorpe
East Torrington
Hackthorn
Snarford
West Torrington
Wickenby
Benniworth
Holton cum Beckering
East Barkwith
Welton Hill
Welton
Snelland
West Barkwith
Fulnetby
Dunholme
Reasby
Rand
Panton
Sotby
Stainton by Langworth
Scothern
Bullington
Wragby
Great Sturton
Langworth
Sudbrooke
Newball
Langton by Wragby
Hatton
Riseholme
Nettleham
Apley
Kingthorpe
Barlings
Reepham
North Greetwell
Low Barlings
Minting
Ermine
Bunker's Hill
St Giles
Cherry Willingham
Stainfield
Gautby
Lincoln
Fiskerton
Wispington
Washingborough
Young Wood
Waddingworth
New Boultham
Canwick
Boultham
Heighington
Branston Booths
Bardney
Bucknall
Horsington
Bracebridge
Potterhanworth
A15
A46
A631
A1103
A158
B1205
B1225
B1203
B1202
B1399
B1190
River Witham
Fossdyke Navigation
7
8
9
10
11
200
201
173
190
A
B
C
D
E
F
G
H
TF

Beelsby
Brigsley
North End
Tetney Lock
North Coates Airfield
Tetney
Ashby Hill
Ashby cum Fenby
Hatcliffe
Waithe
North Cotes
201
Grainsby
West Ravendale
East Ravendale
North Thoresby
Marshchapel
Donna Nook
Croxby
Thorganby
Wold Newton
Fulstow
Eskham
Wragholme
Grainthorpe
Poplar Grove
North Somercotes
RAF BINBROOK HERITAGE CENTRE
Brookenby
Ludborough
Covenham Reservoir
Grainthorpe Fen
Conisholme
Church End
Binbrook
189
Covenham St Bartholomew
Covenham St Mary
South Somercotes
North Ormsby
Utterby
Yarburgh
Kirmond le Mire
Fotherby
North End
Skidbrooke
Little Grimsby
Alvingham
Thorpe le Vale
North Elkington
North Cockerington
Great Tows
Kelstern
Ludford
Keddington
South Cockerington
Saltfleetby St Peter
South Elkington
Louth
Grimoldby
Welton le Wold
Little Welton
Burgh on Bain
Girsby
Stewton
Manby
ST JAMES CHURCH
Hubbards Hills
Hallington
Little Carlton
Gayton le Wold
Biscathorpe
Great Carlton
Raithby
Legbourne
Gayton le Marsh
South Willingham
Withcall
Maltby
Little Cawthorpe
North Reston
South Reston
Donington on Bain
Tathwell
Dovendale
Tothill
Withern
Benniworth
Haugham
Stenigot
Muckton
CADWELL PARK
Authorpe
Woodthorpe
LINCOLNSHIRE
LINCOLNSHIRE WOLDS
Market Stainton
Cawkwell
Maidenwell
Claythorpe
Sotby
Goulceby
Scamblesby
Burwell
CLAYTHORPE WATERMILL & WILDFOWL GARDENS
Belleau
Ranby
Farforth
Ruckland
Aby
White Pit
Swaby
Great Sturton
Oxcombe
South Thoresby
Ketsby
Haugh
Rigsby
ALFORD MANOR HOUSE & FOLK MUSEUM
Belchford
South Ormsby
Calceby
Hemingby
Tetford
Driby
Baumber
Minting
Fulletby
Salmonby
Brinkhill
Ulceby Cross
Ulceby
Somersby
Wispington
West Ashby
Bag Enderby
Harrington
Sutterby
Fordington
Skendleby Psalter
Edlington
Ashby Puerorum
Claxby St Andrew
WOLDS WILDLIFE PARK
Low Toynton
Greetham
Aswardby
Langton
Dalby
Thimbleby
Hagworthingham
Skendleby
174
Horncastle
High Toynton
Sausthorpe
Scrafield
Winceby
SNIPE DALES
Grebby
Partney
Old
Thornton
Mareham on the Hill
Lusby
0 1 2 3 miles
0 1 2 3 4 5 km

NORTH SEA
Saltfleet
Saltfleet Haven
Sea View Fm
Rimac
SALTFLEETBY THEDDLETHORPE DUNES
Saltfleetby All Saints
Theddlethorpe St Helen
Theddlethorpe All Saints
Gas Terminal
North End
THE SEAL SANCTUARY & WILDLIFE CENTRE
Will Row
Meers Bridge
Westfield Fm
Stain Hill
Meers Bank
Mablethorpe Hall
FUN FAIR
Mablethorpe
Trusthorpe
Strubby Grange
Earl's Br
Poplar Fm
Grange Fm
Bamber's Br
Willow Fm
Strubby
Thorpe
Trusthorpe Hall
Maltby le Marsh
Manor Ho
Sutton on Sea
Sandilands
Poplar Lodge Fm
Mill Hill
Beesby
Abbey Fm
Beesby Grange
Hagnaby
Hannah
Sea Bank Fm
America Fm
Saleby
Markby
Priory Fm
Cob Hill
Saleby Manor
Glebe Fm
The Grange
College Fm
Asserby Turn
Asserby
Willow Fm
Black House Fm
Thoresthorpe
Bilsby
Dryby Fm
Wold Sea Fm
Manor Fm
Anderby Creek
Alford
The Grange
Moat Ho
Huttoft
The Manor
Anderby
Bilsby Field
Thurlby
Farlesthorpe Fen
ON YOUR MARQUES
Wolla Bank
Mumby
Manor Ho
Langham Fm
Manor Fm
Chapel Six Marshes
Farlesthorpe
School Fm
Mill Hill
Mickleberry Hill
Authorpe Row
Chapman's Fm
Chapel Pt
Mawthorpe
Elsom Fm
Cumberworth
Cherry Fm
Helsey
Croft Fm
Bonthorpe
Manor Fm
Chapel St Leonards
Willoughby
Listoft
Hogsthorpe
Poplar Fm
Burlands Beck
Willoughby High Drain
Willoughby Wood
Hogsbeck Ho
Sloothby
Howlet Ho
Slackholme End
Hope Fm
Beeches Fm
Welton Low Wood
Welton High Wood
Thwaite Hall
Hasthorpe
Welbourne Fm
HARDY'S ANIMAL FARM
Highfield Fm
Habertoft
Ingoldmells
Candlesby Hill
Rookery Fm
Welton le Marsh
Boothby Hall
Addlethorpe
FANTASY ISLAND
Ingoldmells Pt
Manor Fm
Boothby Grange
Whitehouse
Corner
A1031
A1104
A157
A1111
A52
B1449
B1196
SALTFLEET ROAD
MABLETHORPE RD
THEDDLETHORPE RD
ALFORD ROAD
SUTTON ROAD
BEESBY ROAD
HUTTOFT ROAD
EAST ST
SUTTON ROAD
THURLBY ROAD
LONG LANE
MUMBY ROAD
MAWTHORPE HILL ROAD
HANBY LANE
SKEGNESS ROAD
BAKER'S LANE
175
TF
70
00
A
B
C
D
E
F
G
H
7
8
9
10
11

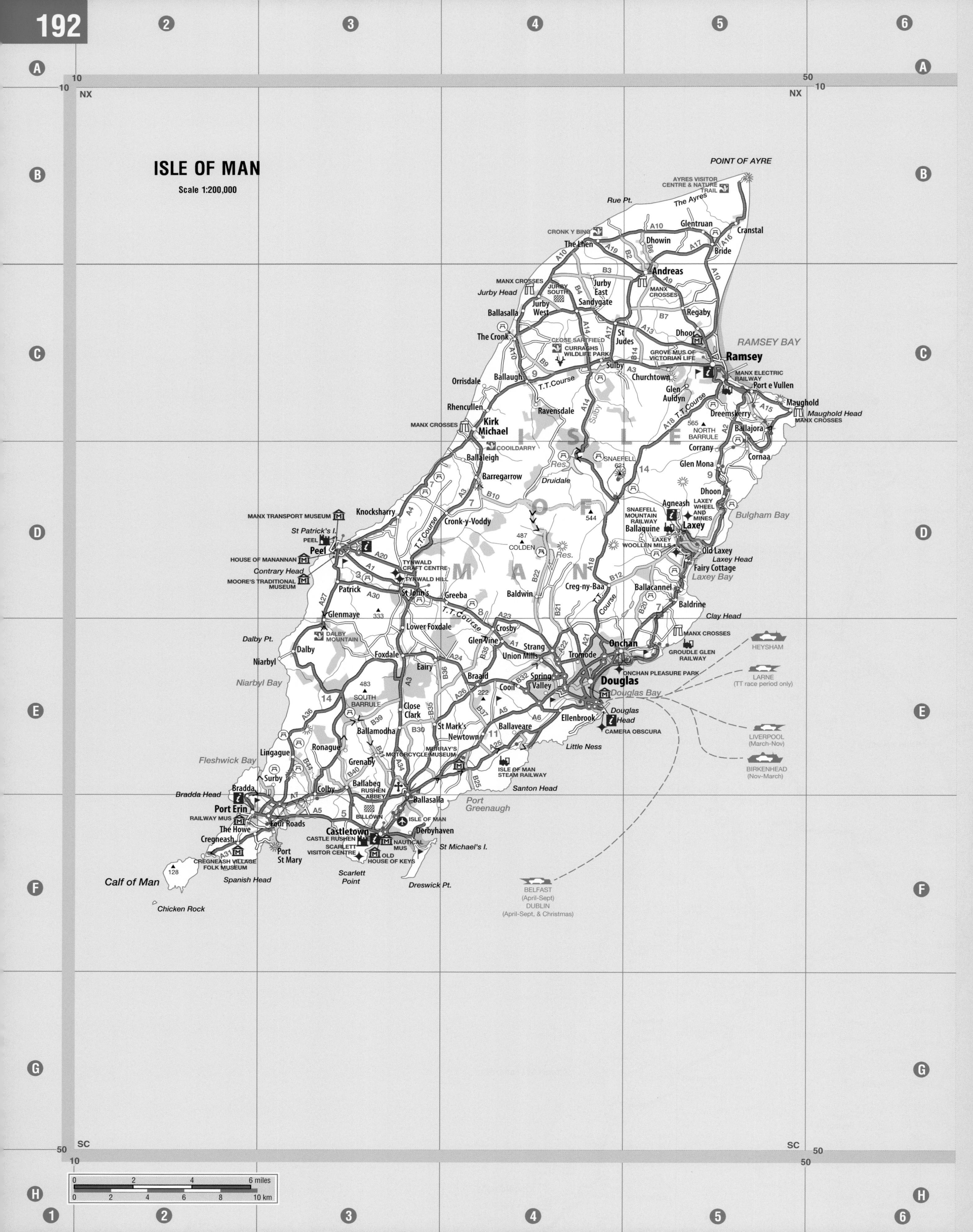
ISLE OF MAN
Scale 1:200,000
POINT OF AYRE
AYRES VISITOR CENTRE & NATURE TRAIL
Rue Pt.
The Ayres
CRONK Y BING
Glentruan
Cranstal
Dhowin
The Lhen
Bride
Andreas
MANX CROSSES
Jurby Head
JURBY SOUTH
Jurby East
Jurby West
Sandygate
Ballasalla
Regaby
The Cronk
Dhoor
St Judes
CLOSE SARTFIELD
CURRAGHS WILDLIFE PARK
GROVE MUS OF VICTORIAN LIFE
RAMSEY BAY
Ramsey
Sulby
Churchtown
MANX ELECTRIC RAILWAY
Orrisdale
Ballaugh
T.T.Course
Glen Auldyn
Port e Vullen
Rhencullen
Ravensdale
Dreemskerry
Maughold
Maughold Head
Kirk Michael
NORTH BARRULE
Ballajora
COOILDARRY
ISLE
Corrany
Ballaleigh
SNAEFELL
Cornaa
Glen Mona
Barregarrow
Druidale
Dhoon
MANX TRANSPORT MUSEUM
Knocksharry
SNAEFELL MOUNTAIN RAILWAY
Agneash
LAXEY WHEEL AND MINES
Bulgham Bay
St Patrick's I.
PEEL
Cronk-y-Voddy
OF
Ballaquine
Laxey
Peel
COLDEN
LAXEY WOOLLEN MILLS
Old Laxey
HOUSE OF MANANNAN
Laxey Head
Contrary Head
TYNWALD CRAFT CENTRE
Fairy Cottage
MOORE'S TRADITIONAL MUSEUM
TYNWALD HILL
MAN
Laxey Bay
Patrick
St John's
Greeba
Baldwin
Creg-ny-Baa
Ballacannel
Glenmaye
Baldrine
Clay Head
Lower Foxdale
Crosby
Dalby Pt.
DALBY MOUNTAIN
Glen Vine
MANX CROSSES
Dalby
Strang
Onchan
HEYSHAM
Niarbyl
Foxdale
Union Mills
Tromode
GROUDLE GLEN RAILWAY
Eairy
ONCHAN PLEASURE PARK
LARNE
(TT race period only)
Niarbyl Bay
Braaid
Spring Valley
Douglas
SOUTH BARRULE
Cooil
Douglas Bay
Close Clark
Douglas Head
Ellenbrook
CAMERA OBSCURA
Ballamodha
St Mark's
Newtown
Ballaveare
LIVERPOOL
(March-Nov)
Fleshwick Bay
Lingague
Ronague
MURRAY'S MOTORCYCLE MUSEUM
Little Ness
Grenaby
Surby
ISLE OF MAN STEAM RAILWAY
BIRKENHEAD
(Nov-March)
Bradda Head
Bradda
Ballabeg
RUSHEN ABBEY
Santon Head
Colby
Ballasalla
Port Erin
Port Greenaugh
RAILWAY MUS
BILLOWN
The Howe
Four Roads
ISLE OF MAN
Castletown
Derbyhaven
Cregneash
CASTLE RUSHEN
NAUTICAL MUS
St Michael's I.
SCARLETT VISITOR CENTRE
Port St Mary
OLD HOUSE OF KEYS
CREGNEASH VILLAGE FOLK MUSEUM
Calf of Man
Spanish Head
Scarlett Point
Dreswick Pt.
BELFAST
(April-Sept)
DUBLIN
(April-Sept, & Christmas)
Chicken Rock
0 2 4 6 miles
0 2 4 6 8 10 km

193
Lytham St Anne's
St Annes
Salter's Bank
Fairhaven
Ansdell
Lytham
Lytham Hall
Lytham Windmill Museum
Church Scar
Fairhaven Lake
Crusader Bank
North Hollow
Blackpool
Great Marton Moss
Peel
Higher Ballam
Lower Ballam
Moss Side
Westby
Warton
Warton Bank
Saltcotes
Hey Houses
River Ribble
Hesketh Sands
Ribble Estuary
Banks Sands
George's Brow
Banks Marsh
Long Bank
Great Bank
Foulnaze
Marshside Sands
Crossens Marsh
Horse Bank
Angry Brow
Southport Sands
Fiddler's Ferry
Banks
Crossens
Marshside
Botanic Garden
Eco Visitor Centre
Marine Lake
Southport Model Railway Village
The Atkinson
Churchtown
High Park
Southport
Blowick
Birkdale Sands
Birkdale
Brown Edge
Hillside
Birkdale Hills
Pool Hey
Snape Green
Carr Cross
Scarisbrick
Shirdley Hill
Bescar
Drummersdale
Smithy Lane Ends
Ainsdale
Ainsdale-on-Sea
Ainsdale Sands
Ainsdale Hills
Woodvale
Ainsdale Sand Dunes
LANCS
Halsall Moss
Halsall
Pinfold
Hurlston Green
Hurlston
Primrose Hill
Barton
Haskayne
Downholland Moss
Downholland Cross
Ormskirk
Aughton Park
Aughton
Town Green
Mad Wharf
Formby Hills
Freshfield
Formby
Formby Pt
Little Altcar
Great Altcar
Alt Bridge
Cabin Hill
Taylor's Bank
Formby Bank
North End
Hightown
Lady Green
Carr Houses
Ince Blundell
Homer Green
Lunt
Maghull
Lydiate
Sefton
Little Crosby
Thornton
Netherton
Melling
Melling Mount
Moss Side
Crosby Channel
Blundellsands
Brighton le Sands
Great Crosby
Buckley Hill
Aintree
Waddicar
Westvale
Antony Gormley Sculptures
Crosby
Waterloo

Preston
Fulwood
Ribbleton
Ingol
Cadley
Dowbridge
Newton
Scales
Lea Town
Clifton
Freckleton
Warton
Kellamergh
Hutton
Longton
Middleforth Green
Penwortham Lane
Walton-le-Dale
Bamber Bridge
Lostock Hall
Farington
Higher Walton
Samlesbury
Much Hoole
Becconsall
Hesketh Bank
Tarleton
Bretherton
Leyland
Clayton-le-Woods
Clayton Green
Whittle-le-Woods
Wheelton
Brinscall
Euxton
Croston
Mere Brow
Sollom
Holmeswood
Eccleston
Chorley
Heskin Green
Mawdesley
Bispham Green
Rufford
Tarlscough
Coppull
Adlington
Rivington
Horwich
Burscough
Burscough Bridge
Parbold
Newburgh
Standish
Shevington
Blackrod
Ormskirk
Skelmersdale
Dalton
Orrell
Wigan
Aspull
Hindley
Westhoughton
Ince in Makerfield
Pemberton
Up Holland
Rainford
Billinge
Ashton-in-Makerfield
Garswood
Abram
Platt Bridge
Bickershaw
LANCASHIRE
River Ribble
River Douglas
Leeds & Liverpool Canal
M6
M61
M58
M65
A59
A6
A49
A5209
A570
A577
A58
202
203
193
182
183
0 1 2 3 miles
0 1 2 3 4 5 km

Great Harwood
Clayton-le-Moors
Hapton
Rishton
Accrington
Church
Oswaldtwistle
Blackburn
Darwen
Haslingden
Rawtenstall
Bacup
Whitworth
Ramsbottom
Edgworth
Bolton
Bury
Heywood
Rochdale
Middleton
Royton
Radcliffe
Farnworth
Whitefield
Prestwich
Walkden
Atherton
Tyldesley
Worsley
Swinton
Pendlebury
Salford
Eccles
Leigh
Failsworth
Droylsden
LANCASHIRE
BLACKBURN WITH DARWEN
GREATER MANCHESTER
Forest of Rossendale

Heptonstall Moor
High Greenwood
Hardcastle Crags
Shackleton
Pecket Well
Old Town
Chiserley
Wainstalls
Illingworth
Queensbury
Ogden
Causeway Foot
Clayton
Great Horton
Buttershaw
Stiperden Moor
Colden
Heptonstall
Hebden Bridge
Blackshaw Head
Mytholm
Charlestown
Mytholmroyd
Midgley
Luddenden
Booth
Mount Tabor
Ovenden
Wheatley
Pellon
Halifax
Northowram
Hipperholme
Shelf
Stone Chair
Portsmouth
Cornholme
Pudsey
Lydgate
Todmorden
Mankinholes
Lumbutts
Eastwood
Luddenden Foot
Sowerby Bridge
Sowerby
Savile Park
Copley
Southowram
Brighouse
Rastrick
Clough Foot
Walsden
Shade
Langfield Common
Cragg Vale
Triangle
Lumb
Mill Bank
Greetland
Elland
Warland
Soyland Moor
Ripponden
Barkisland
Stainland
Holywell Green
Birchencliffe
Lindley
Whitworth
Facit
Shawforth
Calderbrook
Summit
Rishworth
Rishworth Moor
Booth Wood
Outlane
Oakes
Wardle
Littleborough
Smallbridge
Healey
Rochdale
Milnrow
Newhey
Rakewood
Hollingworth Lake
Scapegoat Hill
Golcar
Leymoor
Paddock
Lockwood
Slaithwaite
Linthwaite
Marsden
Meltham
Netherton
Honley
Brockholes
Denshaw
Bleak Hey Nook
Castleton
Royton
Shaw
Chadderton
Oldham
Delph
Diggle
Dobcross
Uppermill
Greenfield
Lees
Wessenden Moor
Netherthong
Upperthong
Holmfirth
Holmbridge
Holme
Saddleworth Moor
PEAK DISTRICT NATIONAL PARK
GREATER MANCHESTER
Failsworth
Hollinwood
Mossley
Hazelhurst
Stalybridge
Droylsden
Crowden
Ashton-under-Lyne
M62
A58
A646
A629
A62
A640
A672
A635
A6024
184
185
195
204
205
0 1 2 3 miles
0 1 2 3 4 5 km

YORKSHIRE
SOUTH YORKSHIRE
Bradford
Dewsbury
Wakefield
Barnsley
Batley
Morley
Ossett
Horbury
Middleton
Rothwell
Cleckheaton
Heckmondwike
Liversedge
Birstall
Mirfield
Normanton
Crigglestone
Darton
Royston
Cudworth
Worsbrough
Wombwell
Hoyland
Penistone
Stocksbridge
Denby Dale
Skelmanthorpe
Clayton West
Dodworth
Hartshead Moor Services
Woolley Edge Services
Leeds Skelton Lake Services
Thurlstone Moors

Micklefield
Kippax
Prestor
Great Preston
Ledston Luck
Ledston
Ledsham
Lumby
South Milford
Steeton Hall
Monk Fryston
Hillam
Hambleton
Thorpe Willoughby
Brayton
East Common
Fairburn
Burton Salmon
Gateforth
Burn
Allerton Bywater
Lower Mickletown
Mickletown
Methley
Methley Junction
New Fryston
Wheldale
Water Fryston
Poole
Birkin
West Haddlesey
Chapel Haddlesey
Camblesforth
Castleford
Airedale
Brotherton
Byram
Beal
NORTH
Kellington
Temple Hirst
Hirst Courtney
Carlton
Whitwood
Cutsyke
Glasshoughton
Ferrybridge
Sutton
Kellingley
Knottingley
Eggborough
Hut Green
Hensall
Normanton
Hopetown
Loscoe
New Town
North Featherstone
Pontefract
Woodhouse
Old Snydale
Ackton
Strawberry Hill
Grove Town
Chequerfield
Carleton
Darrington
Cridling Stubbs
High Eggborough
Whitley
Great Heck
Little Heck
Gowdall
West Cowick
Pollington
Streethouse
Snydale
Featherstone
Purston Jaglin
West Hardwick
Sharlston
YORKSHIRE
Stapleton
Womersley
Balne
Foulby
High Ackworth
East Hardwick
Wentbridge
Little Smeaton
Walden Stubbs
Eskholme
Topham
Sykehouse
Wragby
Brakenhill
Low Ackworth
Thorpe Audlin
Kirk Smeaton
Fenwick
Fitzwilliam
Ackworth Moor Top
Badsworth
Norton
Ryhill
Kinsley
Hemsworth
Upton
Campsall
Askern
Moss
Fosterhouses
Havercroft
South Hiendley
North Elmsall
Wrangbrook
Instoneville
Far Bank
Haywood
SOUTH
Braithwaite
Shafton
Brierley
Moorthorpe
Skelbrooke
Sutton
Burghwallis
Owston
Kirk Bramwith
South Bramwith
YORKSHIRE
South Kirkby
South Elmsall
Hampole
Skellow
Carcroft
Thorpe in Balne
Upper Cudworth
Cudworth
Grimethorpe
Barnby Dun
Adwick le Street
Woodlands
Toll Bar
Almholme
Dunsville
Clayton
Hooton Pagnell
Kirk Sandall
Great Houghton
Brodsworth
Highfields
Arksey
New Village
Edenthorpe
Thurnscoe
Little Houghton
Bentley
Armthorpe
Darfield
Billingley
Hickleton
Marr
Goldthorpe
Scawsby
Cusworth
Wheatley
Wheatley Hills
Intake
Nutwell
Wombwell
Bolton upon Dearne
Barnburgh
Harlington
Doncaster
Hyde Park
Newton
Hexthorpe
Doncaster Common
Cantley
Brampton
Adwick upon Dearne
High Melton
Sprotbrough
Bessacarr
Elsecar
Wath upon Dearne
Mexborough
Cadeby
Warmsworth
Balby
Old Denaby
Denaby Main
Conisbrough
Swinton
Loversall
New Edlington
Rossington

EAST RIDING OF YORKSHIRE
NORTH LINCOLNSHIRE
Wressle
Woodhall
Newhay
Hemingbrough
Brind
North Howden
Portington
Hive
Sandholme
Newport
Walling Fen
Newsholme
Cavil
Eastrington
Newland
Scalby
Gilberdyke
Staddlethorpe
Bennetland
Barmby on the Marsh
Long Drax
Asselby
Knedlington
Howden
Balkholme
Greenoak
Bellasize
Kilpin Pike
Kilpin
Boothferry
Drax
Little Airmyn
Airmyn
Hook
Skelton
Laxton
Broomfleet
Newland
Goole
Blacktoft
Faxfleet
Yokefleet
Saltmarshe
Whitton
Rawcliffe
East Cowick
Rawcliffe Bridge
Old Goole
Swinefleet
Reedness
Little Reedness
Whitgift
Ousefleet
Adlingfleet
Alkborough
Walcot
West Halton
Coleby
Garthorpe
Fockerby
Burton Stather
Burton upon Stather
Thealby
Pincheon Green
Luddington
Eastoft
Normanby
Flixborough
Moorends
Thorne Waste or Moors
Crowle Waste or Moors
Flixborough Stather
Amcotts
Dragonby
Fishlake
Thorne
Canal Side
Wike Well End
Crowle
Windsor
Ealand
Keadby
Gunness
Crosby
Frodingham
Scunthorpe
Brumby
Hatfield
Althorpe
Burringham
Derrythorpe
Sandtoft
Woodhouse
Westgate
Grey Green
Belton
Church Town
Isle of Axholme
Hatfield Woodhouse
West End
Hatfield Moors
Beltoft
West Butterwick
East Butterwick
Ashby
Yaddlethorpe
Bottesford
Messingham
Epworth
Epworth Turbary
Wroot
Low Burnham
Kelfield
Susworth
Scotterthorpe
Scotter
Blaxton
Finningley
Upperthorpe
Haxey
Westwoodside
East Lound
Owston Ferry
East Ferry
Scotton
Wildsworth
M62
M18
M180
M181
A63
A614
A161
A18
A159
207
208
187
188
200

West End
South Cave
Riplingham
Eppleworth
Inglemire
Newland
Stoneferry
Sutton Ings
Summergangs
KINGSTON UPON HULL
Sculcoates
208
209
Brantingham
Ellerker
Kirk Ella
West Ella
Willerby
Anlaby
East Ella
Anlaby Park
West Park
MKM STADIUM
Victoria Dock Village
THE DEEP
WILBERFORCE HOUSE
Alexandra Dock
King George Dock
Marfleet
Swanland
Welton
Elloughton
Brough
Melton
North Ferriby
Hessle
Northfield
Gipsyville
Pickering Park
Humber Dale
HUMBER BRIDGE
St Andrews Quay
Kingston upon Hull
CLIVE SULLIVAN WAY
YORKSHIRE WOLDS WAY
Whitton Ness
Whitton Channel
Redcliff Channel
Humber Bridge
Hessle Haven
Skitter Ness
Goxhill Haven
River Humber
Chowder Ness
Read's Island
South Channel
Whitton
199
Bishopthorpe
Winteringham
Barton Cliff
FAR INGS
WATER'S EDGE
Barton Waterside
BARTON-ON-HUMBER
ST PETER'S CHURCH
Barton-upon Humber
BAYSGARTH HOUSE MUSEUM
NEW HOLLAND
New Holland
Barrow Haven
Barrow upon Humber
Goxhill
South End
East Halton
The Elms
West Halton
SLUICE LANE
South Ferriby
Coleby
Northlands
Horkstow Wolds
Barton Grange
Kingsforth
Thealby
Winterton
Horkstow
Sedgeworth Fm
THORNTON ABBEY
Thornton Curtis
NORTH LINCOLNSHIRE
FARM MUS
NORMANBY HALL
Roxby
Saxby Wolds
Saxby All Saints
Burnham
Wootton
North Killingholme
Sheffield's Hill
Ulceby Skitter
Ulceby
Bonby
Dragonby
Appleby
High Risby
Low Risby
Risby Warren
Worlaby
Habrough
Crosby Warren
Elsham
Croxton
ELSHAM HALL
Frodingham
NORTH LINCOLNSHIRE MUSEUM
Santon
Kirmington
Melton Ross
New Barnetby
HUMBERSIDE AIRPORT
Scunthorpe
Brumby
Barnetby le Wold
Little Limber
Wressle
Broughton
WRAWBY POSTMILL
Wrawby
Ashby
Great Limber
Bottesford
Holme
Brigg
Castlethorpe
Mill Place
Bigby
Somerby
LINCOLNSHIRE
Scawby
Searby
Messingham
Greetwell
Sturton
Howsham
Owmby
Grasby
Clixby
Manton
Cadney
North Kelsey
North Kelsey Moor
Cabourne
Hibaldstow
Caistor
Scotter
GAINSTHORPE DESERTED MEDIEVAL VILLAGE
Redbourne
188
189
Nettleton
North End
Moortown
Kirton in Lindsey
South Kelsey
Holton
Nettleton Top
3 miles
5 km

EAST RIDING OF YORKSHIRE
NORTH EAST LINCOLNSHIRE
River Humber
Mouth of the Humber
Grimsby Roads
Hedon
Salt End
Haven Side
Preston
West End
Burstwick
Thorngumbald
Paull
Ryehill
Camerton
Keyingham
Ottringham
Roos
Tunstall
North End
Elstronwick
Burton Pidsea
Waxholme
Rimswell
Owthorne
Withernsea
Halsham
East End
Hollym
Winestead
Patrington
Patrington Haven
Holmpton
Out Newton
Welwick
Weeton
Skeffling
Easington
Kilnsea
Sunk Island
Little Humber
Thorney Crofts
Stone Creek
Sunk Island Sands
Hawkin's Pt
The Plumbs
Skeffling Clays
Easington Clays
Trinity Sands
Kilnsea Clays
SPURN DISCOVERY CENTRE
SPURN
SPURN POINT NATURE RESERVE
Humber Pilot Station
Spurn Head
Stony Binks
Bull Sand Fort
ROTTERDAM
Foulholme Sands
North Killingholme Haven
South Killingholme Haven
Immingham Dock
Immingham
Stallingborough
Healing
Keelby
Riby
Riby Cross Roads
Aylesby
Laceby
Irby upon Humber
Swallow
Cuxwold
Beelsby
Hatcliffe
Croxby
Grimsby
Pyewipe
Great Coates
West Marsh
Little Coates
Littlefield
Wellow
Nunsthorpe
Bradley
Scartho
New Waltham
Weelsby
Old Clee
Grant Thorold
East Marsh
Cleethorpes
CLEETHORPES LIGHT RAILWAY
THE JUNGLE ZOO
Humberston
Humberston Fitties
Waltham
Holton le Clay
Barnoldby le Beck
Brigsley
Ashby cum Fenby
Waithe
Tetney
Tetney Lock
North Coates
Marshchapel
Grainsby
North Thoresby
East Ravendale
West Ravendale
Tetney High Sands
Northcoates Pt
Horse Shoe Pt
A1033
A180
A160
A18
A46
A16
A1173
A1031
B1362
B1445
209
189
190

Heysham
Lower Heysham
Higher Heysham
Half Moon Bay
Heysham Nuclear Power Sta
Lancaster
Castle Lancaster
Ashton Memorial
Williamson Park & Butterfly House
Abraham Heights
Aldcliffe
Heaton
Scotforth
Douglas
Heysham Lake
Middleton Sands
Middleton
Overton
Colloway Marsh
River Lune
Stodday
Bailrigg
Burrow Heights
Quernmore
Hare Appletree
Sunderland Bank
Sunderland
Bazil Pt
Fishnet Pt
Glasson
Conder Green
Galgate
Ellel
Shoulder of Lune
Sunderland Point
Plover Scar
Lower Thurnham
Thurnham
Upper Thurnham
River Conder
Smith Green
Hampson Green
Ortner
Cockersand Abbey Fm
Bank Houses
Cockerham Sands
Cockerham
Pattys Fm
Marsh Houses
Marsh Lane
Potters Brook
Forton
Clifton Hill
Bay Horse
Lancaster (Forton) Services
Street
Dolphinholme
Five Lane Ends
Cockerham Marsh
Braides
Sand Side
River Cocker
Hollins Lane
Pilling Sands
Preesall Sands
North Wharf
Fleetwood
Rossall Pt
Cocker's Dyke Houses
Knott End-on-Sea
Pilling Lane
Pilling Marsh
Fluke Hall
Ladies Hill
Dam Side
Pilling
Stake Pool
Moss Edge
Cockerham Moss
Winmarleigh
Winmarleigh Moss
Cabus
Scorton
Oakenclough
Preesall
Hackensall Hall
Head Dyke Lane
Scronkey
Pilling Moss
Ford Green
Nateby
Garstang
Calder Vale
Affinity Lancashire
Preesall Park
Stalmine
Stalmine Moss Side
Barnaby's Sands
Eagland Hill
Bowgreave
Bonds
Rossall School
Cleveleys
River Wyre
Burn Naze
Trunnah
Staynall
Cold Row
Hambleton
Skitham
Moss Edge
Rawcliffe Moss
Churchtown
Catterall
Stubbins
Claughton
Thornton
Stanah
Anchorsholme
Little Bispham
Norbreck
Whiteholme
Norcross
Little Thornton
Out Rawcliffe
Ratten Row
St Michael's on Wyre
Breedy Butts
Little Eccleston
Great Eccleston
Brock
Bispham
Blackpool
Skippool
Little Poulton
Carleton
Warbreck
Poulton-Le-Fylde
Hardhorn
Little Singleton
Singleton
Copp
Elswick
Thistleton
Crossmoor
Inskip
Myerscough
Bilsborrow
Duncombe
Matshead
North Shore
Queenstown
Layton
Normoss
Newton
Staining
Esprick
Roseacre
Woodsfold
Cuddy Hill
Barton
Blackpool Tower & Circus
Sea Life Centre
Central Pier
Blackpool Zoo
Marton Mere
Stanley Park
Great Marton
Greenhalgh
Medlar
Wharles
Catforth
Corner Row
Broughton
Woodplumpton
Hawes Side
Marton Moss Side
Mereside
Little Marton
Mythop
Weeton
Swillbrook
Lightfoot Green
Blackpool Pleasure Beach
Common Edge
Peel Hill
Little Plumpton
Great Plumpton
Wesham
Mowbreck
Bolton Houses
Treales
Lower Bartle
Higher Bartle
Sharoe Green
South Shore
Squires Gate
Great Marton Moss
Peel
Westby
Kirkham
Dowbridge
Cottam
Ingol
Cadley
Fulwood
Wrea Green
Ribby
Lea Town
Crusader Bank
Higher Ballam
Lower Ballam
Moss Side
Hall Cross
Newton
Scales
Newton with Scales
Clifton
Lea
Larches
Preston
Bryning
Kellamergh
Freckleton
Riverside Docklands
Higher Penwortham
Frenchwood
Saltcotes
Lytham St Anne's
Ansdell
Fairhaven
Warton
M6
M55
A6
A585
A583
A584
A586
A588
A589
A683
A5085
B5269
B5290
B5270
B5377
B5272
B5266
B5260
B5259
B6241
B6242
210
211
193
194
0 1 2 3 miles
0 1 2 3 4 5 km
SD

211
212
194
195
204
FOREST OF BOWLAND
FOREST OF BOWLAND
LANCASHIRE
FOREST OF BOWLAND
Gisburn Forest
Tarnbrook
Lee
Abbeystead
Marshaw
Calder Fell
Bleasdale Moors
Bleasdale
Sykes
Hareden
Dunsop Bridge
Newton
Slaidburn
Easington
Whitewell
Cow Ark
Browsholme Hall
Chipping
Hesketh Lane
Whitechapel
Walker Fold
Longridge
Ribchester
Little Town
Hurst Green
Great Mitton
Waddington
West Bradford
Chatburn
Clitheroe
Low Moor
Downham
Worston
Pendle Hill
Pendleton
Barrow
Wiswell
Sabden
Whalley
Billington
Old Langho
Langho
Copster Green
Salesbury
Wilpshire
Balderstone
Osbaldeston
Mellor
Mellor Brook
Samlesbury
Ribbleton
Grimsargh
Goosnargh
Haighton Green
Great Harwood
Clayton-le-Moors
Rishton
Church
Accrington
Blackburn
Padiham
Read
Simonstone
Higham
Hapton
Huncoat
Altham
Tosside
Wigglesworth
Rathmell
Grunsagill
Knotts
Holden
Bolton-by-Bowland
Sawley
Grindleton
Forest Becks
Lane Ends
Wood House
Sawley Abbey
Stonyhurst
Slaidburn Road
Clitheroe Road
Whalley Road
Preston Road
Longsight Road
Preston New Road
A59
A671
A666
A677
A678
A680
A6119
B6243
B6245
B6246
B6478
M6
M65

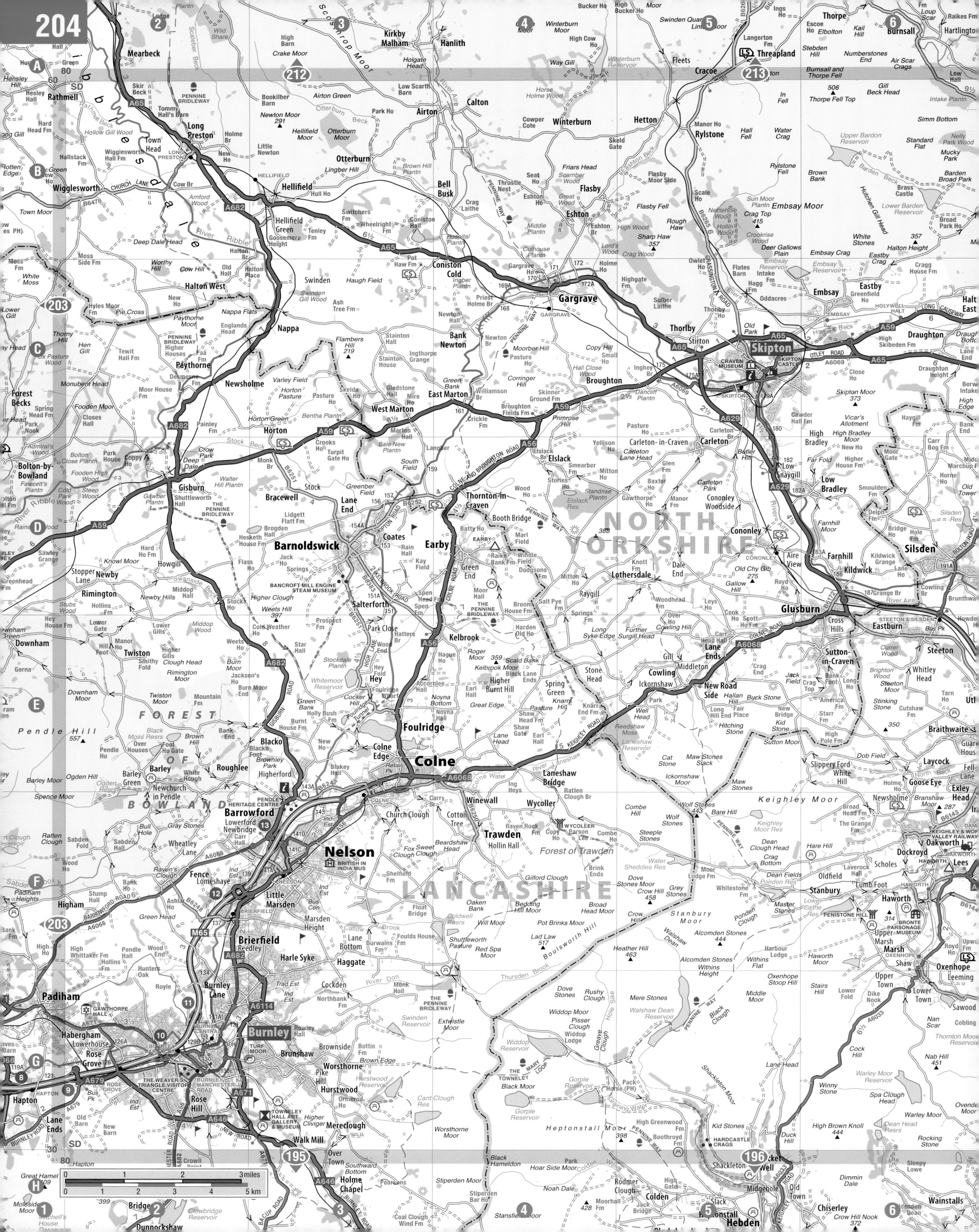

Mearbeck
Rathmell
Long Preston
Wigglesworth
Hellifield
Otterburn
Airton
Calton
Kirkby Malham
Hanlith
Winterburn
Hetton
Cracoe
Threapland
Rylstone
Burnsall
Thorpe
Hartlington
Flasby
Eshton
Bell Busk
Coniston Cold
Gargrave
Embsay Moor
Embsay
Eastby
Halton West
Swinden
Nappa
Paythorne
Newsholme
Thorlby
Stirton
Skipton
Draughton
Broughton
East Marton
West Marton
Horton
Gisburn
Bolton-by-Bowland
Bracewell
Barnoldswick
Coates
Earby
Thornton-in-Craven
Elslack
Carleton
Carleton-in-Craven
Cononley
Farnhill
Kildwick
Silsden
Glusburn
Lothersdale
Cross Hills
Eastburn
Steeton
Sutton-in-Craven
Cowling
Salterforth
Kelbrook
Foulridge
Colne
Laneshaw Bridge
Wycoller
Trawden
Nelson
Barrowford
Brierfield
Burnley
Padiham
Hapton
Rose Grove
Worsthorne
Hurstwood
Cliviger
Mereclough
Walk Mill
Holme Chapel
Colden
Hebden
Haworth
Oxenhope
Oakworth
Stanbury
Laycock
Braithwaite
NORTH YORKSHIRE
LANCASHIRE
FOREST OF BOWLAND
Pendle Hill
Forest of Trawden
Keighley Moor
Boulsworth Hill
PENNINE WAY
PENNINE BRIDLEWAY
River Ribble
River Aire
A65
A59
A682
A56
A6068
A629
A6069
A646
A671
A679
M65
212
213
203
195
196
0 1 2 3 miles
0 1 2 3 4 5 km

NORTH YORKSHIRE
NIDDERDALE
WEST YORKSHIRE
Pock Stones Moor
Barden Fell
Rocking Moor
Denton Moor
Skyreholme
Howgill
Barden Scale
Bolton Abbey
Hazlewood
Bolton Bridge
Beamsley
Langbar
Addingham
Ilkley
Middleton
Denton
Askwith
Burley in Wharfedale
Otley
Newall
Weston
Timble
Fewston
Blubberhouses
Pace Gate
Hill End
West End
Thruscross
Padside
Thornthwaite
Dacre
Dacre Banks
Darley
Darley Head
Birstwith
Hampsthwaite
Killinghall
Ripley
Burnt Yates
Bedlam
Clint
Kettlesing
Kettlesing Head
Kettlesing Bottom
Felliscliffe
Harrogate
Harlow Hill
Oatlands
Pannal
Beckwithshaw
Brackenthwaite
Spacey Houses
North Rigton
Stainburn
Braythorn
Lindley Green
Farnley
Clifton
Leathley
Huby
Dunkeswick
Weeton
Castley
Pool
Arthington
Weardley
Bramhope
Eccup
Menston
Burley Woodhead
Guiseley
Yeadon
Rawdon
Horsforth
Cookridge
Tinshill
Holt Park
Adel
Alwoodley
Moor Allerton
Chapel Allerton
Meanwood
Headingley
Leeds
Armley
Holbeck
Hunslet
Beeston
Keighley
Riddlesden
East Morton
Micklethwaite
Crossflatts
Bingley
Eldwick
Baildon
Shipley
Saltaire
Idle
Apperley Bridge
Calverley
Rodley
Farsley
Stanningley
Bramley
Pudsey
Kirkstall
Bradford
Heaton
Manningham
Allerton
Thornton
Clayton
Queensbury
Wibsey
Bierley
Tong
Drighlington
Gildersome
Churwell
Morley
Cottingley
Cullingworth
Wilsden
Denholme
Harden
Illingworth
Shelf
Low Moor
Odsal
Wortley
Farnley
New Farnley
LEEDS BRADFORD INTERNATIONAL AIRPORT
213
214
196
197
206

Brearton
Brearton Moor
Farnham
Ferrensby
Arkendale
Arkendale Moor
214
Great Ouseburn
Little Ouseburn
Marton Cottage Fm
Great Ouseburn Moor
Linton-on-Ouse
Newton on Ouse
Ember Hill
Beningbrough
Beningbrough Park
BENINGBROUGH HALL
215
Killinghall
Nidd Viaduct
Scotton
Scriven
Coneythorpe
Flaxby
Knaresborough
KNARESBOROUGH
MOTHER SHIPTON'S CAVE
CASTLE & MUS
Allerton Mauleverer
ALLERTON CASTLE
Whixley
Tancred
Thorpe Underwood
Nun Monkton
Moor Monkton
Green Hammerton
Kirk Hammerton
Hopperton
Bilton
New Park
Starbeck
Forest Lane Head
Calcutt
Forest Moor
Goldsborough
Goldsborough Moor
High Harrogate
Harrogate
ENVIROVENT STADIUM
Woodlands
Harlow Hill
GT YORKSHIRE SHOWGROUND
HORNBEAM PARK
205
Oatlands
Rossett Green
Pannal
Spacey Houses
Follifoot
PLUMPTON ROCKS
Little Ribston
Walshford
Hunsingore
Cattal
Marston Moor
Hessay
Tockwith
1644
Cowthorpe
North Deighton
Spofforth
SPOFFORTH CASTLE
Ingmanthorpe
Wetherby Services
Bickerton
Long Marston
Rufforth
Hutton Wandesley
Kirk Deighton
Bilton in Ainsty
Kirkby Overblow
Sicklinghall
Wetherby
WETHERBY
Walton
Angram
Askham Richard
Healaugh
Dunkeswick
Weeton
Netherby
Chapel Hill
Linton
Wighill
Bilbrough
Collingham
Boston Spa
Thorp Arch
Catterton
Newton Kyme
Toulston
Harewood
HAREWOOD HOUSE
East Keswick
Compton
Clifford
Bramham
Weardley
Bardsey
East Rigton
Tadcaster
Oxton
Colton
Stutton
Wike
Bracken Park
Scarcroft
Scarcroft Hill
Thorner
BRAMHAM PARK
1408
Bolton Percy
Kirkby Wharfe
Ulleskelf
Alwoodley
Moor Allerton
Shadwell
WEST YORKSHIRE
Kiddal Lane End
Towton
Potterton
Chapel Allerton
Roundhay
Wellington Hill
Monkswood
Green Hill
St John's
1461
Scarthingwell
Barwick in Elmet
Scholes
Aberford
Saxton
Church Fenton
Potternewton
Seacroft
Leeds
Woodhouse
Barkston
Barkston Ash
Gipton
Harehills
Sheepscar
Manston
Parlington
LOTHERTON HALL
Little Fenton
Biggin
Whitkirk
Halton
Austhorpe
Colton
Garforth
East Garforth
West Garforth
Old Micklefield
Garden Village
New Micklefield
Sherburn in Elmet
Osmondthorpe
Halton Moor
Cross Green
TEMPLE NEWSAM
HOME FARM RARE BREEDS
Swillington Common
Newthorpe
South Milford
Hunslet
Beeston
THWAITE MILLS WATERMILL MUSEUM
Stourton
Leeds Skelton Lake Services
Swillington
Kippax
Ledston Luck
Lumby
Little Preston
Ledsham
Monk Fryston
Great Preston
197
198
Rothwell
Oulton
Ledston
Fairburn
Hillam
Burton
0 1 2 3 miles
0 1 2 3 4 5 km

Flaxton
Harton
Leppington
Acklam
Strensall
Claxton
Scrayingham
Bossall
Kirk Gates
Wigginton
Haxby
Earswick
Towthorpe
Sand Hutton
Buttercrambe
Kirby Underdale
Painsthorpe
Bugthorpe
Shipton
Skelton
Overton
West Huntington
New Earswick
Upper Helmsley
Gate Helmsley
Stockton on the Forest
Warthill
Skirpenbeck
Full Sutton
Youlthorpe
Bishop Wilton
Nether Poppleton
Rawcliffe
Huntington
Holtby
Stamford Bridge
Gowthorpe
Great Givendale
Clifton
Heworth
York
Knapton
Murton
Dunnington
Low Catton
High Catton
Town End
Fangfoss
Spittal
Meltonby
Acomb
Holgate
Osbaldwick
Grimston
Kexby
Wilberfoss
Bolton
Yapham
South Bank
Nunthorpe
Heslington
Walmgate Stray
Woodthorpe
Fulford
Newton upon Derwent
Barmby Moor
Pocklington
Askham Bryan
Middlethorpe
Bishopthorpe
Elvington
Allerthorpe
Copmanthorpe
CITY OF YORK
Crockey Hill
Sutton upon Derwent
EAST RIDING
OF YORKSHIRE
Naburn
Acaster Malbis
Wheldrake
Thornton
Storwood
Melbourne
Deighton
Bielby
Scamland
Escrick
Everingham
Appleton Roebuck
Acaster Selby
East Cottingwith
Thorganby
Seaton Ross
Stillingfleet
Ellerton
Laytham
Kelfield
Aughton
Holme-on-Spalding-Moor
Riccall
Skipwith
Cawood
North Duffield
Harlthorpe
Foggathorpe
Water End
Highfield
Bubwith
Dawker Hill
NORTH YORKSHIRE
Wistow
Gunby
Gribthorpe
Willitoft
Barlby
Osgodby
Breighton
Bursea
Selby
Lund
South Duffield
Spaldington
Cliffe
Wressle
Thorpe Willoughby
East Common
Brayton
Brind
North Howden
Portington
Newhay
Hemingbrough
Newsholme
Cavil
Eastrington
Gateforth
Burn
Barlow
Barmby on the Marsh
Howden
Asselby
Knedlington

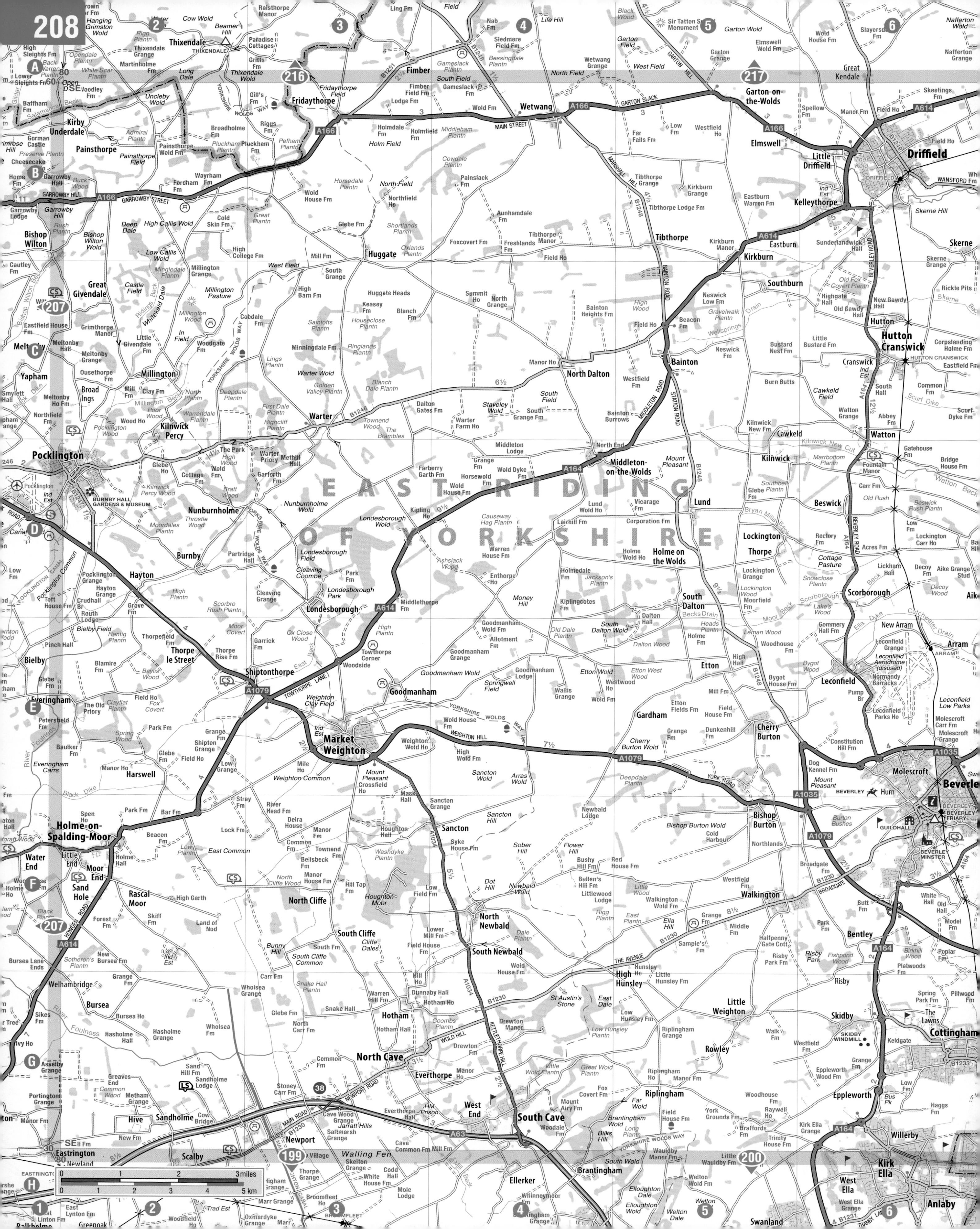
EAST RIDING OF YORKSHIRE
216
217
207
199
200
Thixendale
Fimber
Fridaythorpe
Wetwang
Garton-on-the-Wolds
Driffield
Little Driffield
Elmswell
Kelleythorpe
Kirby Underdale
Painsthorpe
Garrowby Hill
Bishop Wilton
Great Givendale
Huggate
Tibthorpe
Kirkburn
Eastburn
Southburn
Skerne
Hutton
Hutton Cranswick
Bainton
North Dalton
Millington
Yapham
Meltonby
Warter
Kilnwick Percy
Pocklington
Middleton-on-the-Wolds
Watton
Kilnwick
Beswick
Lund
Nunburnholme
Burnby
Hayton
Londesborough
Lockington
Thorpe
Holme on the Wolds
South Dalton
Scorborough
Arram
Leconfield
Bielby
Thorpe le Street
Shiptonthorpe
Goodmanham
Etton
Everingham
Market Weighton
Gardham
Cherry Burton
Harswell
Molescroft
Beverley
Holme-on-Spalding-Moor
Sancton
Bishop Burton
Water End
Moor End
Sand Hole
Rascal Moor
North Cliffe
North Newbald
Walkington
South Cliffe
South Newbald
Bentley
High Hunsley
Little Weighton
Bursea
Hotham
Skidby
Cottingham
North Cave
Rowley
Everthorpe
Riplingham
Eppleworth
West End
South Cave
Willerby
Hive
Sandholme
Newport
Scalby
Eastrington
Brantingham
Ellerker
Kirk Ella
West Ella
Anlaby
Swanland
Welton
A166
A614
A1079
A164
A1034
A63
A1035
B1248
B1246
B1230
YORKSHIRE WOLDS WAY
0 1 2 3 miles
0 1 2 3 4 5 km

Ruston Parva
Harpham
Lowthorpe
Nafferton
Fraisthorpe
Fraisthorpe Sands
Barmston Sands
Barmston
Gransmoor
Great Kelk
Lissett
Gembling
Ulrome
Ulrome Sands
Wansford
Foston on the Wolds
Beeford
Upton
Skipsea Brough
Skipsea
Skipsea Sands
Brigham
Church End
North Frodingham
Rotsea
Dunnington
Atwick
Atwick Sands
Hempholme
Bewholme
Double Gates
North Cliff
Burshill
Baswick Steer
Brandesburton
Hornsea
Seaton
Hornsea Mere
Hornsea Bridge
Hornsea Burton
South Cliff
Rolston Sands
Leven
Catwick
Little Leven
Sigglesthorne
Rolston
Goxhill
Mappleton
Mappleton Sands
Eske
Routh
Little Hatfield
Great Hatfield
Great Cowden
Cowden Sands
Tickton
Long Riston
Rise
Arnold
Withernwick
Skirlaugh
New Ellerby
Marton
Meaux
Weel
Aldbrough
East Newton
Woodmansey
Old Ellerby
West Newton
Thearne
Wawne
Flinton
Dunswell
Swine
Coniston
Garton
Grimston
Humbleton
Fitling
Sproatley
Thirtleby
Ganstead
Hilston
Bransholme
Wyton
Bilton
Owstwick
Sutton on Hull
Lelley
Elstronwick
Tunstall
Sutton Ings
Burton Pidsea
Stoneferry
North End
Summergangs
Preston
Roos
Sculcoates
Kingston upon Hull
Marfleet
West End
Salt End
Hedon
Haven Side
Burstwick
Newland
Inglemire
West Carr
Victoria Dock Village
A165
A1035
A1033
A1079
B1242
B1244
B1249
B1238
B1240
B1243
217
218
200
201
7
8
9
10
11
A
B
C
D
E
F
G
H
TA
30
60

Foldgate Fm
Corney Fell
Sele Bottom
Dunnerdale Fells
Scrithwaite Fm
Dry Hall
Troughton Hall
F U R N E S S
Stable Harvey Moss
Sunny Bank
Thrang Crag Wood
Top o Selside
335
Bowkerstead Fm
Corney
Swallowhurst
Littlecell Bottom
Buck Barrow
549
Plough Fell
Frith Hall
Ulpha Park
Lind End
Hesketh Hall
Bracelet Hall
Woodland Grove
Pool Scar
Yew Bank
Brown Howe
Grass Paddocks
Long Crags
Force Mills
The Hooks
Flatts
Corney Hall
Prior Park
Penn
Green Bank
Broughton Mills
Bridge End
Birk Knott
Bethecar Moor
Force Forge
Thwaites Fell
220
10
Ford
90
SD
Seaton Hall
Low Kinmont
Stoneside Hill
422
Lane End
Rosthwaite
Tarn Riggs
Beacon Tarn
High Nibthwaite
Whitestock Hall
Thwaite Moss
Hycemoor
Bootle
Cross House
Mere Crags
Moss Side Fm
Green Moor
Woodland Fell
Wool Knott
Greenholme Fm
Ickenthwaite
Bootle Fell
Woodland
Arklid Intake
Arklid Fm
Stock Wood
Rusland
Fellgreen
Swinside Fell
Windy Slack
Lower Hawthwaite
Woodland Hall
Water Yeat
Bank End
Blawith Knott
Houkler Hall
Blawith
Rusland Moss
Furness Fells
Fellside
Broomhill
Duddon Bridge
A595
A593
Manor Fm
Black Moss
Longlife Wood
Nibthwaite Grange
Park Wood
Side Ho
Stoupdale Crags
472
Gray Stones
Graystone Ho
Ash House
Broughton in Furness
Fell End
Birch Bank
Lin Crag Fm
Bandrake Head
Kirkthwaite Cottage
Low Hay Bridge
Kiskin
Knott Hill
Buckman Brow
Hill Park
Oxen Park
Annaside
River Annas
Little Fell
Fell Gate
High Hay Bridge
Barfield Tarn
Black Combe
Hazel Mount
Eccle Riggs
Wreaks End
Far Houses
Heathwaite Fm
Lowick Bridge
Sayles Fm
Burn Knott
Baystone Bank Res
Coal Gate
Well Wood
Subberthwaite Common
Colton
Monk Foss Fm
Lady Hall
Duddon Mosses
White Moss
Kirkby Park Wood
Lowick
Bank Wood
Beckside Fm
298
Great Burney
Ashlack Hall
Beck Stones
Stone Dykes
Lowick Hall
Esps Fm
Bouth
Old Hall Fm
Ridding Side Fm
Fore Slack
Whicham Mill
600
Foxfield
Hallthwaites
Grizebeck
Wood Gate
Lowick Green
Abbots Reading Fm
Brockwood Hall
Bankend
A5092
Millergill Beck
Hallbeck Ho
Mire Ho
The Green
Arnaby
Beanthwaite
Lowick Common
Beck Bottom
Spark Bridge
Tottlebank
Ireland Moss
Strands
Gawthwaite
Whitbeck
Dunningwell
Dove Bank
B5281
Hollow Oak
Haverthwaite
Gutterby Spa
Green Road
Chapels
Lowick High Common
Black Crags
Hill End
Whicham Valley
Angerton Marsh
Kirkby Hall
Groffa Crag
England Coast Path
Woods
Wall End
Brunt Riggs
Legbarrow Pt
Whicham Hall
Millom Park
Park Ho
The Hill
Kirkby-in-Furness
Broughton Beck
Penny Bridge
Whicham
Millom Marsh
Gill House Beck
Moor Ho
Blade Moss
Greenodd
Silecroft
Sand Side
Beck Side
Gunson Height
Well Ho
Mearness Fm
Roudsea Wood
Low Ho
Low Hall
Out Park
Shooting House Hill
Hollowmire
Mansriggs Hall
Bowstead Gates
Duddon Sands
Soutergate
Mearness Point
Stribers Moss
Duddon Channel
Osmotherley Moor
Mansriggs
Arrad Foot
Nab Point
Beck Wood
Borwick Rails Harbour
Kirksanton
Hestham Hall Fm
Millom
Millom Heritage & Arts Centre
Bank House Moor
Higher Lath Fm
Newland Bottom
Plumpton Cottage Fm
Roudsea Wood & Mosses
Haverigg Pool
Ind Est
Borwick Rails
Dunnerholme
Harlock Res
Harlock Hill
Newland
Great Oath Hill
65
Ashes Pt
Hazelhurst Pt
Old Hall Fm
Barrow Monument
Cumbria Crystal
Steel Green
HM Prison
RSPB
Hodbarrow
Marsh Grange
Copse Hill
Pennington Res
Ewe Dale
Ulverston
Laurel & Hardy Mus
Leven Viaduct
Stewner Park Fm
Poaka Beck Res
Haverigg
Hodbarrow Point
Ireleth
Ghyll Fm
High Greaves
Stone Cross
Plumpton Bight
South Ulverston
Canal Foot
Old Park Wood
Haverigg Point
Wortbrig Scar
Askam
Askam in Furness
Tippins Lane
Far Old Park Fm
Pennington Ho
Pennington
Outcast
Hammerside Pt
Martin
Loppergarth
Rowe Head
Swarthmoor Hall
Swarthmoor
Dragley Beck
Sandside
Croftlands
Cartmel Sands
Greenscoe Fm
High Haume Fm
Lindal Moor
Trinkeld Fm
Priory Road
A5087
A590
Roanhead Fm
Mouzel Fm
Tytup Hall
Lindal in Furness
Chapel Island
Sandscale Haws
Safari Zoo Cumbria
Flat Woods
Edge Hill
Conishead Priory & Manjushri Kadampa Meditation Centre
Duddon Sands
Lenibrick Point
Thwaite Flat
Great Urswick
Bardsea
Wellhouse Fm
Urswick Tarn
Lowsy Point
Dalton Castle
Dalton-in-Furness
Cowpren Point
Scarth Channel
Scarth Bight
Park Road
Sinkfall
Dalton
Skells Lodge
Bolton Heads
Holme Bank
Sea Wood
Ulverston Sands
Little Urswick
Sunbrick
Ind Est
Billincoat Fm
Baycliff
Shope Tree Scar
North End Marsh
Stainton with Adgarley
Scales
Hawcoat
Newton
North Walney
Walney Meetings
North Stank Fm
Mere Tarn
Wind Hill
Ulverston Channel
Bow Bridge
Maskel Point
Ormsgill
Furness Abbey
Gleaston Watermill
Barrow (Walney Island)
Walney Road
Croslands Park
New Close Fm
Gleaston
Colt Park
Aldingham
The Dunes Hotel Stadium
Newbarns
Beacon Hill
Dendron
Stank
Barrow-in-Furness
Holbeck
Bus Pk
The Dock Mus
Hindpool
Yarlside
Scarbarrow Hill
Newbiggin
Earnse Pt
North Walney
South Newbarns
Roose
Sea Mill
North Scale
Salthouse
Leece
Roosecote
Vickerstown
Barrow Island
Ind Est
Moor Head Cottages
Page Bank Fm
Waterfront under dev
Walney Channel
Roosebeck
Peasholmes Fm
Water Garth Nook
Roosecote Sands
Rampside Road
Coast Road
Roosebeck Sands
Tummer Hill Marsh
Biggar Sands
Westfield Point
Lancaster Sound
Biggar
Rampside
Isle of Walney
Rampside Sands
South Channel
Long Rein Point
Roa Island
Snab Sands
Wylock Marsh
Piel Channel
Foulney Island
Snab Pt
Sheep Island
Piel Castle
Piel Island
Piel Harbour
South End
Scar End Point
Haws Point
South Walney
South East Point
Piel Bar
SD
60
10
202
Douglas
0 1 2 3 miles
0 1 2 3 4 5 km
A B C D E F G H
1 2 3 4 5 6

Killington Lake Services (Southbound Only)
Burton-in-Kendal Services (Northbound Only)
LAKE DISTRICT NATIONAL PARK
ARNSIDE AND SILVERDALE
MORECAMBE BAY
LANCS
Kendal
Natland
Oxenholme
Sedgwick
Stainton
Endmoor
Gatebeck
Crooklands
Milton
Hincaster
Levens
Sampool Bridge
Brigsteer
Crosthwaite
Underbarrow
Gregg Hall
Bowland Bridge
Cartmel Fell
Finsthwaite
Lakeside
Newby Bridge
Staveley-in-Cartmel
Backbarrow
Ayside
High Newton
Low Newton
Witherslack
Town End
Meathop
Lindale
Field Broughton
Cartmel
Grange-over-Sands
Allithwaite
Kents Bank
Flookburgh
Holker
Cark
Milnthorpe
Heversham
Leasgill
Storth
Beetham
Arnside
Silverdale
Yealand Redmayne
Yealand Conyers
Warton
Carnforth
Burton-in-Kendal
Holme
Clawthorpe
Farleton
Lupton
Hutton Roof
Kearstwick
Low Biggins
Whittington
Nether Burrow
Tunstall
Newton
Arkholme
Capernwray
Borwick
Priest Hutton
Melling
Wrayton
Over Kellet
Nether Kellet
Bolton-le-Sands
Hest Bank
Slyne
Bare
Torrisholme
Morecambe
Heysham
Lancaster
Halton
Caton
Brookhouse
Hornby
Wray
Farleton
Aughton
Claughton
Caton Green
Gressingham
Tatham
Crossgill
Quernmore
Scotforth
Aldcliffe
Heaton
Middleton
Salter
Caton Moor
Littledale
Killington
Mansergh
Old Town
Old Hutton
Middleshaw
New Hutton
Millholme
Kent Channel
Keer Channel
Salt Marsh
Kent Viaduct
A6
A65
A590
A591
A683
A589
A601(M)
M6
221
212
202
203

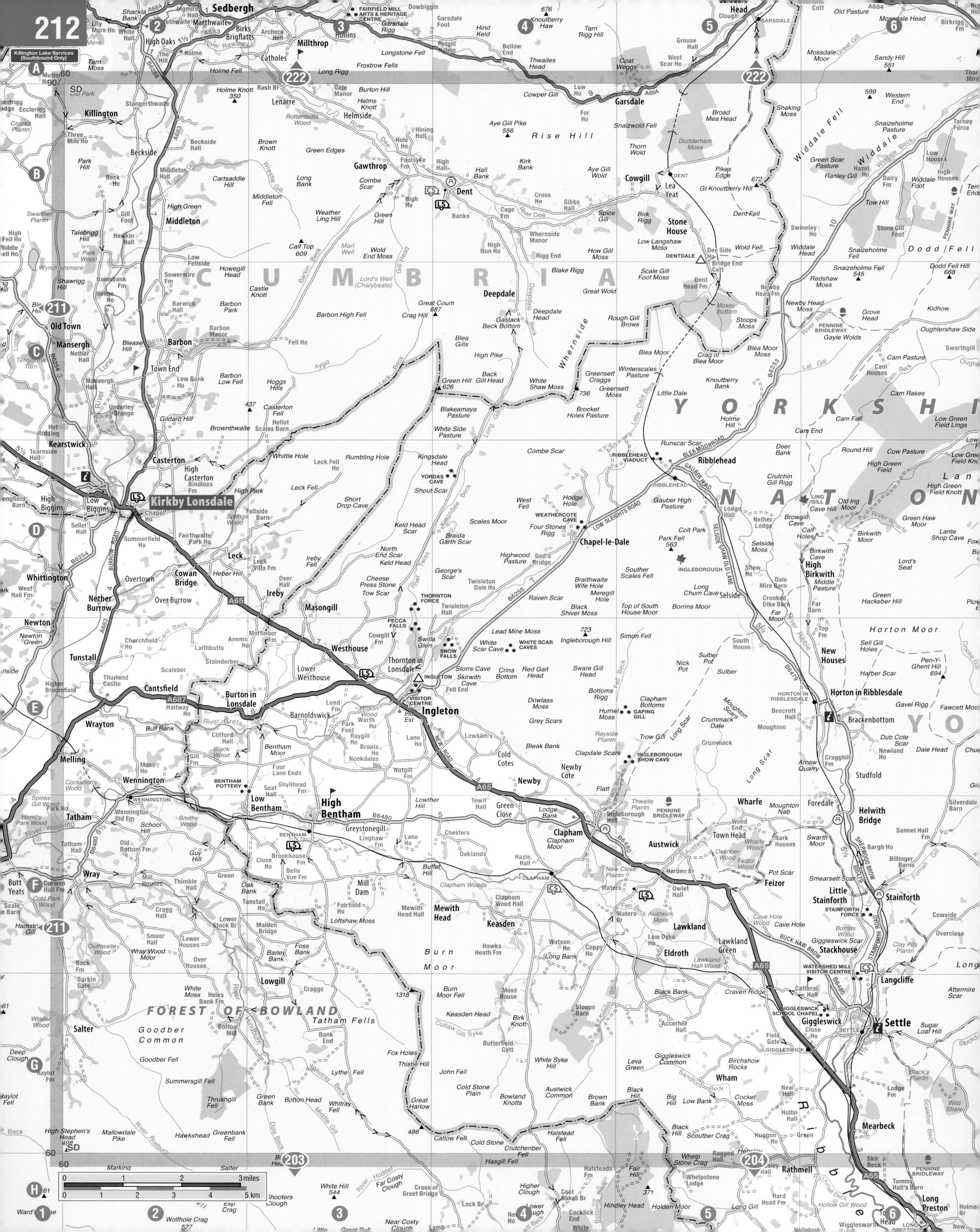

212
Killington Lake Services (Southbound Only)
Sedbergh
Millthrop
Killington
Gawthrop
Dent
Cowgill
Garsdale
Lea Yeat
Stone House
Middleton
Deepdale
Rise Hill
C U M B R I A
Y O R K S H I
N A T I O N
Whernside
Ribblehead
Old Town
Mansergh
Barbon
Kearstwick
Casterton
Kirkby Lonsdale
Leck
Cowan Bridge
Whittington
Nether Burrow
Ireby
Masongill
Chapel-le-Dale
Ingleborough Hill
Newton
Tunstall
Westhouse
Thornton in Lonsdale
Ingleton
Cantsfield
Burton in Lonsdale
Wrayton
Melling
Wennington
Low Bentham
High Bentham
Newby
Clapham
Austwick
Horton in Ribblesdale
Helwith Bridge
Tatham
Wray
Mewith Head
Keasden
Lawkland
Eldroth
Little Stainforth
Stainforth
Stackhouse
Langcliffe
Giggleswick
Settle
Lowgill
Salter
FOREST OF BOWLAND
Tatham Fells
Burn Moor
Wham
Mearbeck
Rathmell
Long Preston
Feizor
Wharfe
Foredale
Selside
Studfold
Horton Moor
Dodd Fell
Widdale Fell
A65
A683
A687
A684
B6255
B6479
B6480
B6254
222
211
203
204
0 1 2 3 miles
0 1 2 3 4 5 km

Hardraw Force Waterfall
Hardrow
Sedbusk
Sedbusk High Pasture
Cote Pasture
Helm
Low Mill Outdoor Centre
Newbiggin
Nappa Scar
Swinehaw Bottom
Blue Scar
Bolton
Bolton Castle
Preston-under-Scar
Redmire
Leyburn
Wensleydale
Hawes
Dales Countryside Museum
Wensleydale Creamery
Gayle
Burtersett
Bainbridge
Askrigg
Worton
Woodhall
Carperby
Cubeck
Thornton Rust
Aysgarth
Aysgarth Falls
Swinithwaite
West Witton
Wensley
Countersett
Semer Water
Addlebrough 476
Thornton Rust Moor
Aysgarth Moor
Castle Dykes
Thoralby
West Burton
Newbiggin
Bishopdale Valley
Carlton
Melmerby
Coverham
Caldbergh
Agglethorpe
Middleham High Moor
Melmerby Moor
Penhill 546
Stalling Busk
Marsett
Raydale
Carpley Green
Stake Fell 495
Black Pasture
Heck Brow
Fairy Haw
Drumaldrace 614
Sleddale Pasture
Wether Fell
Bishopdale
Burton Pasture
Harland Hill 535
Carlton Moor
Gammersgill
West Scrafton
Coverdale
Walden
Walden Head
Horsehouse
Braidley
Woodale
Kidstones
Kidstones Bank
Kidstones Fell
Naughtberry Hill 573
Denman's Hill 482
Little Haw 486
Great Haw 544
Masham Moor
North Moor
Oughtershaw
Beckermonds
Yorkshire Dales
Yockenthwaite
Deepdale
Hubberholme
Cray
Buckden
Buckden Pike 702
Langstrothdale Chase
National Park
Foxup
Halton Gill
Tor Mere Top 617
Starbotton
Nidderdale
Angram Reservoir
Scar House Reservoir
Great Whernside 704
Little Whernside 604
Middlesmoor
Lofthouse
Stean
Litton
Littondale
Arncliffe
Kettlewell
Hawkswick
Wharfedale
North Yorkshire
Darnbrook Fell
Pennine Way
Stean Moor
Meugher 575
Conistone Moor
Kilnsey
Kilnsey Crag
Kilnsey Park
Conistone
Grass Wood Nature Reserve
Grassington
Grassington Folk Mus
Threshfield
Linton
Hebden
Thorpe
Burnsall
Hartlington
Appletreewick
Skyreholme
Parcevall Hall Gdns
Stump Cross Caverns
Grimwith Reservoir
Appletreewick Moor
Hebden Moor
Heathfield Moor
Malham Tarn
Malham
Malham Cove
Gordale Scar
Kirkby Malham
Hanlith
Airton
Calton
Winterburn
Hetton
Cracoe
Rylstone
Threapland
Bordley
Water Houses
Fountains Fell
Scosthrop Moor
Barden Fell
Pock Stones Moor
Drebley
Howgill
Simon's Seat 485
Appletreewick
The Settle Loop
Upper Barden Reservoir
Winterburn Reservoir

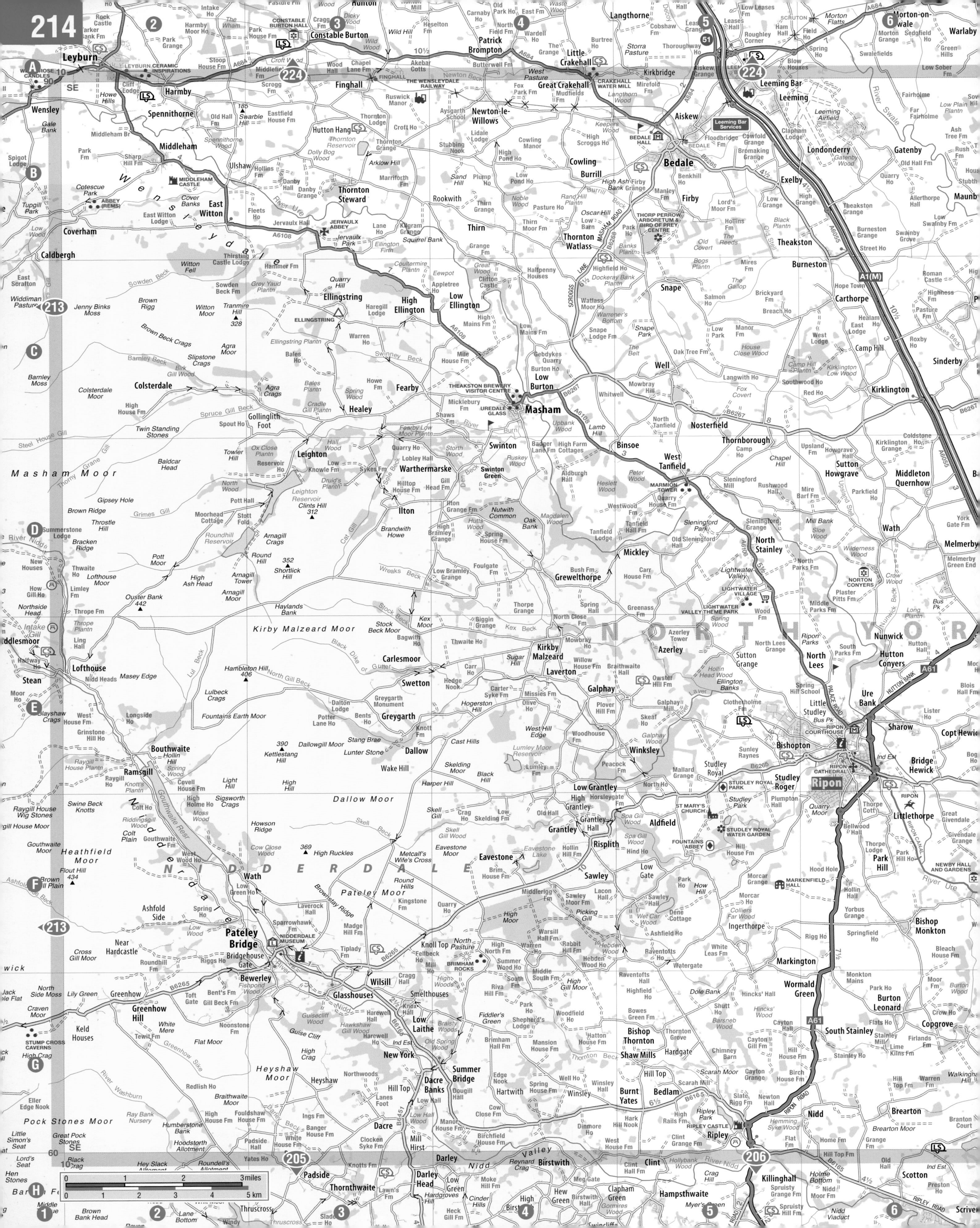
Leyburn
Wensley
Harmby
Spennithorne
Middleham
Constable Burton
Finghall
Patrick Brompton
Little Crakehall
Great Crakehall
Langthorne
Kirkbridge
Leeming Bar
Leeming
Aiskew
Bedale
Newton-le-Willows
Hutton Hang
Thornton Steward
East Witton
Coverham
Caldbergh
Ulshaw
Jervaulx Abbey
Rookwith
Thirn
Cowling
Burrill
Firby
Exelby
Londonderry
Gatenby
Thornton Watlass
Snape
Theakston
Burneston
Carthorpe
Camp Hill
Sinderby
Ellingstring
High Ellington
Low Ellington
Wensleydale
Masham
Low Burton
Well
Fearby
Healey
Colsterdale
Leighton
Warthermarske
Swinton
Ilton
Binsoe
West Tanfield
Nosterfield
Thornborough
Kirklington
Sutton Howgrave
Middleton Quernhow
Wath
Melmerby
North Stainley
Mickley
Grewelthorpe
Masham Moor
Kirby Malzeard Moor
Kirkby Malzeard
Laverton
Carlesmoor
Swetton
Greygarth
Dallow
Galphay
Azerley
North Lees
Nunwick
Hutton Conyers
Ure Bank
Sharow
Copt Hewick
Bishopton
Ripon
Studley Royal
Studley Roger
Bridge Hewick
Littlethorpe
Winksley
Low Grantley
High Grantley
Grantley
Aldfield
Risplith
Sawley
Eavestone
Lofthouse
Stean
Middlesmoor
Ramsgill
Bouthwaite
Wath
Nidderdale
Dallow Moor
Pateley Moor
Pateley Bridge
Bridgehouse Gate
Bewerley
Wilsill
Glasshouses
Smelthouses
Low Laithe
Greenhow
Greenhow Hill
Heathfield Moor
Heyshaw Moor
New York
Summer Bridge
Dacre Banks
Dacre
Hartwith
Bishop Thornton
Shaw Mills
Hardgate
Ingerthorpe
Markington
Wormald Green
Burton Leonard
South Stainley
Bishop Monkton
Copgrove
Bedlam
Burnt Yates
Winsley
Brearton
Nidd
Ripley
Darley
Birstwith
Clint
Killinghall
Scotton
Hampsthwaite
Padside
Thornthwaite
Darley Head
Pock Stones Moor
Keld Houses
North Yorkshire
A1(M)
A61
A6108
A684
B6265
B6267
B6165
0 1 2 3 miles
0 1 2 3 4 5 km

NORTH YORK MOORS
NATIONAL PARK
HOWARDIAN
HILLS
The Hambleton Hills
Thirsk
Sowerby
Thornton-le-Beans
Thornton-le-Moor
Thornton-le-Street
North Kilvington
South Kilvington
South Otterington
Newby Wiske
Kirby Wiske
Newsham
Sowber Gate
Borrowby
Knayton
Leake
Cowesby
Kepwick
Nether Silton
Silton Grange
Upsall
Kirby Knowle
Boltby
Felixkirk
Thirlby
Sutton-under-Whitestonecliffe
Old Thirsk
Norby
New Thirsk
Carlton Miniott
Sandhutton
Holme
Skipton-on-Swale
Catton
Baldersby St James
Topcliffe
Asenby
Rainton
Dishforth
Cundall
Crakehill
Dalton
Sessay
Little Sessay
Hutton Sessay
Little Hutton
Birdforth
Thormanby
Carlton Husthwaite
Husthwaite
Bagby
Balk
Great Thirkleby
Little Thirkleby
Kilburn
High Kilburn
Oldstead
Wass
Byland Abbey
Coxwold
Ampleforth
Yearsley
Oulston
Brandsby
Stearsby
Crayke
Easingwold
Raskelf
Fawdington
Brafferton
Helperby
Moor End Field
Norton-le-Clay
Marton-le-Moor
Kirby Hill
Langthorpe
Milby
Boroughbridge
Aldborough
Roecliffe
Minskip
Staveley
Ferrensby
Arkendale
Grafton
Marton
Lower Dunsforth
Upper Dunsforth
Great Ouseburn
Little Ouseburn
Branton Green
Aldwark
Flawith
Alne
Tholthorpe
Tollerton
Youlton
Linton-on-Ouse
Cross Lanes
Huby
Sutton-on-the-Forest
Stillington
Marton-in-the-Forest
Moxby
Newton on Ouse
Thorpe Underwood
Whixley
Coneythorpe
Flaxby
Knaresborough
Shipton
Wigginton
Skelton-on-Ure
Helmsley
Rievaulx
Old Byland
Cold Kirby
Scawton
Hawnby
Murton Grange
Carlton
Mount Pleasant
High Bannisuce 319
Sutton Bank
Hambleton Inn
Gormire Lake
Hood Hill
Scawton Moor
Yearsley Moor
Gilling Park
River Swale
River Ouse
River Kyle
A19
A168
A167
A61
A170
A1(M)
B1448
B1257
B1363
SUTTON ROAD
STATION ROAD
YORK ROAD
HIGH STREET
COTE LANE
MAIN STREET
SE 90
SE 60
225
216
206
207
A
B
C
D
E
F
G
H
7
8
9
10
11
49
48
50
WORLD OF JAMES HERRIOT
SION HILL HALL
BOB HUNTER HOME OF THE WREN
SUTTON BANK NATIONAL PARK CENTRE
WHITE HORSE
KILBURN MOUSEMAN VISITOR CENTRE
BYLAND ABBEY
SHANDY HALL
NEWBURGH PRIORY
RIEVAULX ABBEY
RIEVAULX TERRACE & TEMPLE
HELMSLEY CASTLE
DUNCOMBE PARK
SUTTON PARK
ALDBOROUGH ROMAN TOWN
STAVELEY NATURE RESERVE
ALLERTON CASTLE
MONK PARK FARM

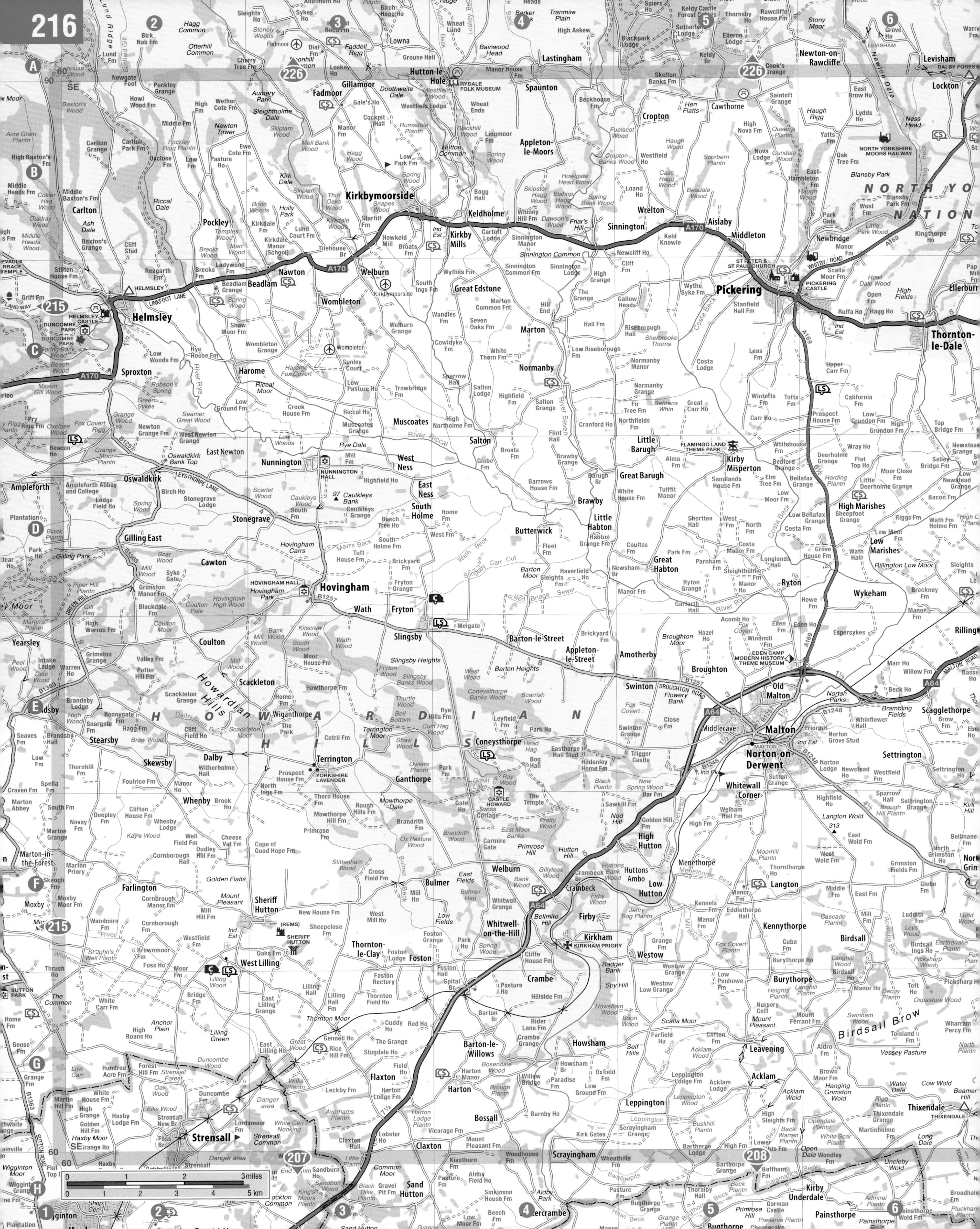
Helmsley
Kirkbymoorside
Pickering
Malton
Norton-on-Derwent
Old Malton
Hovingham
Strensall
Thornton-le-Dale
Lastingham
Spaunton
Appleton-le-Moors
Cropton
Sinnington
Wrelton
Aislaby
Middleton
Keldholme
Kirkby Mills
Nawton
Beadlam
Wombleton
Welburn
Great Edstone
Marton
Normanby
Salton
Muscoates
Harome
Sproxton
Pockley
Carlton
Oswaldkirk
Ampleforth
Nunnington
West Ness
East Ness
South Holme
Stonegrave
Gilling East
Cawton
Coulton
Yearsley
Scackleton
Wath
Fryton
Slingsby
Butterwick
Brawby
Little Habton
Great Habton
Little Barugh
Great Barugh
Kirby Misperton
High Marishes
Low Marishes
Ryton
Wykeham
Barton-le-Street
Appleton-le-Street
Amotherby
Swinton
Broughton
Terrington
Ganthorpe
Coneysthorpe
Dalby
Skewsby
Whenby
Stearsby
Sheriff Hutton
Farlington
Marton-in-the-Forest
Moxby
West Lilling
Thornton-le-Clay
Foston
Bulmer
Welburn
Whitwell-on-the-Hill
Crambe
Kirkham
Westow
Firby
High Hutton
Low Hutton
Huttons Ambo
Menethorpe
Langton
Kennythorpe
Birdsall
Burythorpe
Leavening
Acklam
Leppington
Howsham
Barton-le-Willows
Flaxton
Harton
Bossall
Claxton
Scrayingham
Sand Hutton
Thixendale
Settrington
Scagglethorpe
Whitewall Corner
Middlecave
Levisham
Lockton
Newton-on-Rawcliffe
Howardian Hills
HOWARDIAN HILLS
NORTH YORK MOORS NATIONAL PARK
Birdsall Brow
A170
A169
A64
B1257
B1363
B1248
226
215
207
208
CASTLE HOWARD
NUNNINGTON HALL
HOVINGHAM HALL
KIRKHAM PRIORY
FLAMINGO LAND THEME PARK
EDEN CAMP MODERN HISTORY THEME MUSEUM
RYDALE FOLK MUSEUM
NORTH YORKSHIRE MOORS RAILWAY
PICKERING CASTLE
HELMSLEY CASTLE
DUNCOMBE PARK
0 1 2 3 miles
0 1 2 3 4 5 km

NORTH YORK MOORS FOREST PARK
NORTH YORKSHIRE
EAST RIDING OF YORKSHIRE
The Wolds
Scarborough
Scalby
Newby
Barrowcliff
Falsgrave
Seamer
Eastfield
Osgodby
Cayton
Filey
Gristhorpe
Lebberston
Hunmanby
Muston
Staxton
Flixton
Folkton
Willerby
Ganton
Sherburn
East Heslerton
West Heslerton
Potter Brompton
Yedingham
Scampston
West Knapton
East Knapton
Wintringham
Thorpe Bassett
Place Newton
Foxholes
Fordon
Wold Newton
Burton Fleming
Thwing
Octon
Octon Cross Roads
Langtoft
Butterwick
Weaverthorpe
Helperthorpe
East Lutton
West Lutton
Kirby Grindalythe
Duggleby
Wharram le Street
Sledmere
Cottam
Kilham
Rudston
Thornholme
Burton Agnes
Harpham
Ruston Parva
Lowthorpe
Nafferton
Driffield
Garton-on-the-Wolds
Wetwang
Fimber
Fridaythorpe
Great Kendale
Great Kelk
Elmswell
Ebberston
Allerston
Wilton
Snainton
Brompton
Wykeham
Ruston
Hutton Buscel
West Ayton
East Ayton
Irton
Sawdon
Wrench Green
Everley
Hackness
Suffield
Langdale End
Broxa
Silpho
Throxenby
Wharram Percy
Towthorpe
Scarborough Castle
Sea Life Scarborough
Rotunda Museum
Scarborough Sports Village
Sledmere House
Burton Agnes Hall
Wolds Way Lavender
Scampston Hall
A170
A171
A165
A64
A1039
B1261
B1249
B1253
B1248
B1251
B1252
A166
A614
227
218
208
209

NORTH SEA
FILEY BAY
BRIDLINGTON BAY
EAST RIDING OF YORKSHIRE
Yons Nab
Lebberston Cliff
Gristhorpe Cliff
217
Cunstone Nab
The Wyke
Cliff Fm
Club Pt
WOLDS WAY
Newbiggin
North Cliff
Filey Brigg
Brigg End
Filey Sands
Gristhorpe
Filey Field
A1039
Filey
Carr Ho
Beacon Hill
MUSTON ROAD
A165
Muston
Muston Grange
Muston Sands
Lowfield Fm
Hunmanby Sands
Royal Oak
Pilmoor Fm
Foxhill Fm
Primrose Valley
MOOR ROAD
Hunmanby Gap
Hunmanby
Airy Hill Fm
Hunmanby Moor
Ind Est
Moor Fm
Reighton Sands
Hill Fm
HUNMANBY
Rosedale Fm
Moor Ho
Reighton Gap
Graffitoe Fm
Speeton Sands
Howe Fm
Barf Fm
Vicarage Fm
Moor Fm
Reighton
Speeton Hills
Speeton Cliffs
HUNMANBY ROAD
Dale Fm
Speeton
Speeton Moor
Buckton Cliffs
Speeton Grange
Reighton Field
SPEETON GATE
Buckton Hall
BEMPTON CLIFFS
RSPB
Bempton Cliffs
Scale Nab
Standard Hill
Cat Nab
Bempton Grange
Wandale Fm
Gull Nook
Speeton
Field Greenlands Fm
Hill Fm
Bartindale Fm
Wasters Plantn
High Huntow Fm
Buckton
Dykes Plantn
Thornwick Bay
Bempton
DANE'S DYKE
North Cliff
FLAMBOROUGH CLIFFS NATURE RESERVE
Burton Fleming
Grindale Field
North Dale
B1229
FLAMBOROUGH ROAD
North Landing
Cradle Head
BEMPTON
North Moor
Stottle Bank Nook
Maidensgrave Fm
Newsham Field
Butterwicks Fm
BEMPTON
Flatmere Plantn
Selwicks Bay
Grindale
SCARBOROUGH ROAD
High Barn
B1255
NORTH MARINE ROAD
Flamborough Head
Finley Hill
East Leys Fm
North Mount
Lynhams
LIGHTHOUSE ROAD
FLAMBOROUGH HEAD LIGHTHOUSE
Fox Covert Plantn
Charlestone Fm
Field Ho
The Crofts
B1259
High Stacks
FLAMBOROUGH ROAD
Old Fall Plantn
Flamborough
Danes Dyke Fm
Beacon Fm
Highcliffe Manor
Beacon Hill
North Wood
High Easton Fm
Ind Est
MARTON GATE
SEWERBY HALL & GARDEN
South Landing
East Crags Wood
Sewerby
Springdale Fm
Binsdale Fm
Sewerby Rocks
Boynton
Eastfield Fm
MARTON ROAD
BONDVILLE MODEL VILLAGE
B1253
PRIORY
North Sands
West Lawn Wood
Fish Ponds Wood
Wandale Fm
BAYLE MUS
Old Town
Ruds
Carr Plantn
Thorpe Hall
BRIDLINGTON
Bridlington
Sands Wood
South Side Mount
Temple Fm
Carnaby Temple
High Wood
West Hill
The Spa
Wold Gate
Hallowkiln Wood
Ind Est
Hilderthorpe
Tufthill Fm
Bessingby
Haisthorpe Field
Carnaby
KINGSGATE
P&R
Thornholme Field
Haisthorpe
A614
A165
A1038
Burton Agnes Field
Thornholme
BRIDLINGTON ANIMAL PARK
Wilsthorpe
South Sands
BURTON AGNES HALL
Ind Est
Carnaby Moor
BURTON AGNES MANOR HOUSE
Brackendale Fm
Harpham Grange
Burton Agnes
Oak Wood Fm
Auburn Fm
Hords Covert
Burton Agnes Stud Fm
A165
Fraisthorpe Sands
Demming Fm
Harpham
Burtoncarr Ho
Fraisthorpe
Thornholme Moor
Little Kelk Fm
Gransmoor Wood
Low Stonehills
Turtle Hill Fm
Woodside Fm
Hamiltonhill Fm
High Stonehills
BRIDLINGTON
Gransmoor Low Ho
Gransmoor Lodge
209
Barmston Sands
Barmston
Barmston Main Drain
Great Kelk
Park Ho
Lissett
Allison Lane End
Ulrome
TA
10
30
90
60
0 1 2 3 miles
0 1 2 3 4 5 km

7
8
9
10
11
A
B
C
D
E
F
G
H
228
229
210
220
NX
NY
SC
SD
90
20
10
Lowca
Moresby
Parton
Parton Bay
Tanyard Bay
Redness Pt
Bransty
Whitehaven
WHITEHAVEN
THE BEACON
THE RUM STORY
CORKICKLE
Bleach Green
Low Moresby
Tivoli
Quality Corner
Harras
Scilly Bank
Moresby Parks
Moresby Moss
WALK MILL
Boon Wood
Wilson Park
Keekle Head Fm
247
High Park
Moorside Parks
Dub Hall
Tutehill Fm
Kidburngill
Woodend
Havercroft
Crossgates
Millgillhead
Lamplugh
Owsen Fell
Dockray Nook
Felldyke
Blake Fell
Lamplugh Fell
Knock Murton
Middle Fell
Asby
Arlecdon
Arlecdon Hill
Rowrah
Leys
Sandsclose
Acrewalls
Keltonfell Top
Kirkland
Kelton Fell
Banna Fell
Croasdale
Ghyll Fm
HIGH LEYS
Winder
Bleak Ho
MAIN STREET
Frizington
Salter Hall
Stockhow Hall
Ennerdale Bridge
Routen Fm
How Hall Fm
Ennerdale Water
Kells
Saltom Bay
Woodhouse
LOW ROAD
Mirehouse
Hensingham
Summergrove Hall
Ind Est
High Low Hall
Weddicar Hall
Frizington Hall
Troughton Ho
Low Ho
Keekle
Frizington Parks
Parkside
Cleator Moor
Wath Brow
High Waterside
Longmoor
Swinside End
Low Waterside
Birk Moss
Crag Farm House
Angler's Crag
Crag Fell
Grike
North Head
Sandwith
Demesne
Low Hall
Moor Row
Cleator
River Ehen
Cathow
Flat Fell
Blakeley Moss
389
Blakeley Raise
Boathow Crag
St Bees Head
Rottington
ENGLAND COAST PATH
Parkhouse Fm
Low Walton
Bigrigg
Woodend
Dent
Dent Cott
LONGLANDS LAKE
Cow Field
Uldale Fm
Lankrigg Moss
541
Lank Rigg
High Walton
Southam
Pallaflat
Row Foot
Cobra Castle
Lowther Park
South Head
ST BEES HEAD
RSPB
ST BEES
St Bees
High Ho
Sike Ho
Gillfoot
Briscoe
Wilton
Ghyll Fm
Latter Barrow
354
Kinniside Common
Latterbarrow Beck
Bleaberry
Fairladies Fm
Marlborough Hall
Ashley Grove
EGREMONT CASTLE
Egremont
Grange
High House Fm
408
Boat How
Town Bank
Catgill Hall
Great Wood
How Hills
Carleton
Haile Hall
Head of Haile
Cold Fell
Side End
Worm Gill
Scalderskew Wood
Couldertone
Thornhill
Haile
Ind Est
Middletown
C U M B R I A
Town End
Strudda Bank
Stockdale Moor
Stone Pike
345
Beckcote Fm
Wheel Fell
Ponsonby Fell
NETHERTOWN
Nethertown
COP LANE
Yeorton Hall Fm
Blackbeck
Moor House
Laverock How
Blengdale Forest
Beckermet
Stephney
Calder Bridge
Hollow Moor
Braystones
BRAYSTONES
Petersburgh
Middlebank
Sella Park Ho
Ponsonby
Bleng Fell
Greenmoor Side
Yottenfews
Church House Fm
Ponsonby Old Hall
High Sellafield
New Mill
Bolton Wood
Sellafield Works
Wind Hall
Wellington
Calder Hall
Newton Manor
Hawkbarrow Fm
Rainors
Julian Holme
Gateriggs
SELLAFIELD
Calder
Fleming Hall
Gosforth
Row Fm
Harecroft Hall (School)
Hollins
Seascale Hall
How Fm
Moorside Fm
Field End
Santon
Seascale
SEASCALE
High House Fm
Hewrigg Fm
Hall Santon
Santon Bridge
HALLSENNA MOOR
Hall Senna
Addy Ho
Greengarth Hall
Alkbank Fm
Irton Hall
Irton Park
Holmrook
Cragg Fm
Stubble Green
DRIGG
Drigg
River Irt
Carleton Hall
Wood End
Barn Scar
Danger area
MURT
MITESIDE HALT
MUNCASTER MILL
WATERMILL
Mite Houses
Saltcoats
RAVENGLASS FOR ESKDALE
RLY MUS
Ravenglass
CASTLE & HAWK & OWL CENTRE
Hall
Waberthwaite
Drigg Point
River Esk
Newbiggin
Wabert
Lane End
Middleton Place
Swallowhurst
The Nooks
Flatts
Tarn Bay
Stub Place
Seaton Hall
Hycemoor
Hill Fm
BOOTLE
Selker Bay
Cross Ho
Bootle
Broomhill
A595
A5094
A5086
B5306
B5295
B5294
B5345
B5344
LOOP ROAD SOUTH
Pow Beck
Kirk Beck
River Keekle
Dub Beck
Collergate Beck
Croasdale Beck
Calder
Newmill Beck
River Bleng
River Mite

Lamplugh
Loweswater
Loweswater Fell
Felldyke
Knock Murton
Blake Fell
Lamplugh Fell
Little Dodd
Mellbreak
Middle Fell
Gavel Fell 526
Hen Comb 509
Kelton Fell
Banna Fell
Croasdale
Crummock Water
Rannerdale
Hause Point
Low Bank
Ling Crags
Lanthwaite
Grasmoor
Whiteside
Hopegill Head
Sand Hill
Eel Crag
Force Crag
Crag Hill
Scar Crag
Wandope
Ard Crags
High Moss
Causey Pike
Rowling End
Stair
Swinside
Newlands
Little Town
Cat Bells
Derwent Isle
Derwent Water
Stable Hills
Falcon Crag
Low Moss
Castlerigg Fell
Ashness Br
Bleaberry Fell
Goat Crag
Castle Rock
Legburthwaite
Stanah
Fisher Place
Watson's Dodd
Great Dodd
Stybarrow Dodd
Sticks Pass
Calfhow Pike
Dale Bottom
High Rigg
Yew Crag
Low Bridge End Fm
Derwent Fells
High Snab Bank
Scope End
Knott Rigg
Newlands Pass
Keskadale Beck
Robinson Crags
Robinson 737
High Crags
Hindscarth 727
Littledale Edge
Buttermere
Buttermere Moss
Buttermere Fell
High Spy 653
Castle Nook
Dalehead Crags
Dale Head 753
High Scawdel
Gatesgarth
Black Crag
Narrow Moor
Grange
Borrowdale
King's How
Bowder Stone
Castle Crag
Brown Dodd
Watendlath
Watendlath Tarn
Brund Fell
Hazel Bank
Rosthwaite
Ashness Fell
High Seat 608
Castle Crag
Reecastle Crag
Middle Crag
Armboth Fell
Raven Crag
Thirlmere
Brown Crag
Raise 883
Keppel Cove
Cockrigg Crags
Fisher Crag
Hause Point
Helvellyn 950
Nethermost Pike
High Crags
Comb Crags
Wythburn
Dollywaggon Pike 858
Willie Wife Moor
Steel End
Steel Fell 553
Seat Sandal
Wythburn Fells
Grisedale Tarn
Routen Fm
Great Borne 616
Gale Fell
Scaw Well
Starling Dodd 633
Little Dodd
Bowness Knott
Red Pike 755
Dodd
Burtness Wood
Ennerdale Water
Ennerdale Forest
Ennerdale
Ennerdale Fell
Angler's Crag
Crag Fell
Boathow Crag
High Stile 806
Grey Crags
High Crag 744
Honister Pass
Warnscale Bottom
Fleetwith Pike 648
Yew Crag
Honister Hause
Borrowdale (Longthwaite)
Seatoller
Stonethwaite
Borrowdale Fells
Bull Crag
Coldbarrow Fell
High Saddle
Ullscarf 726
Standing Crag
Tarn Crags
Sail Hills
Iron Crag
Steeple 841
Pillar 892
Robinson's Cairn
Black Sail
Scarth Gap Pass
Black Sail Pass
River Liza
Grey Knotts 697
Brandreth 715
Seathwaite
Base Brown 646
Thornythwaite Fell
Capell Crag
Hind Crag
Stockley Bridge
Combe Head
White Crag
Blea Rock
Sergeant's Crag
Greenup Edge
Silver Cove
Little Gowder Crag
Caw Fell 667
Haycock 797
Gowder Crag
Scoat Fell
Scoat Tarn
Red Pike
Mosedale Beck
Kirkfell Crags
Gillercomb Head
Green Gable 801
Great Gable 899
Kirk Fell
Glaramara 783
South Crag
Cam Crag
Brown Crag
Calf Crag
Gibson Knott
Cumbria
Mountains
Lake District National Park
Bleaberry Gill
Boat How 408
Stockdale Head
Hause 420
Blackbeck Knotts
Gosforth Crag
Dore Head
Wasdale Fell
Sty Head
Lingmell Beck
Allen Crags 785
Ash Crags
High Raise 762
Fergill Crag
High White Stones
Tarn Crag
Easedale Tarn
Helm Crag
Slapestone Edge
Grasmere
Stone Arthur
Town Head
Stockdale Moor
River Bleng
Seatallan 692
High Fell
Yewbarrow
Wasdale Head
Lingmell Crag
Great End 910
Esk Hause
Tongue Head
Black Crags
Martcrag Moor
Thunacar Knott
Pavey Ark
Blea Crag
Yew Crag
Nether Wasdale Common
Copeland Forest
Knott Ends
Dropping Crag
Middle Fell 582
Long Crag
Glade How
Buckbarrow
Hollow Moor
Windsor Fm
Lingmell Gill
Hollow Stones
Scafell Pike 977
Broad Crag
Esk Pike
Rakehead Crag
Wasdale Head Hall Fm
Scafell 964
Dow Crag
Pike de Bield Moss
Bow Fell 902
Green Tongue
Langdale Pikes 736
Stickle Tarn
Langdale Fell
Middle Fell Fm
Pye Howe
Tarn Crag
Allan Bank
Town End
Langdale
Chapel Stile
Dow Bank
Elterwater
Wast Water
Maiden Castle
Broad Tongue
Cam Spout Crag
Gait Crags
Green Hole
Bowfell Links
Crinkle Crags
Stool End
Side Pike
Wall End
Great Langdale Beck
Nether Wasdale
Wasdale Hall
Illgill Head 604
Burnmoor Tarn
Quagrigg Moss
Silverybield Crag
Adam-a-Cove 859
Gladstone Knott
Pike of Blisco 705
Blake Rigg
Bleatarn Ho
Lingmoor Fell
Little Langdale
Wilson Place
Bolton Wood
Hawkbarrow Fm
Julian Holme
Gaterigghow
Stangends
Tongue Moor
Whin Rigg
Eskdale Fell
Great How
High Scarth Crag
Black Crag
Little Stand 727
Cold Pike
Black Crag
Horse Crags
Hollin Crag
Raiñors
Hollins
Crag Ho
Gill Ho
Boat How
Heron Crag
Brock Crag
Ulpha Fell
Wrynose Pass
River Brathay
Fell Foot
Little Langdale Tarn
Stang End
Park Fell
Black Fell
Santon
Irton Fell
Bakerstead
River Mite
Yew Crags
Border End
Hardknott Pass
Hardknott Roman Fort
Wet Side Edge
Rough Crags
River Duddon
Great Intake
Moss Rigg Wood
Field End
Great Bank
Miterdale Forest
Low Place
Eskdale Mill
Boot
Great Barrow
Eskdale
Taw Ho
Cockley Beck Fell
Cockley Beck
Black Hall
Hinning House Fell 773
Tilberthwaite High Fells
Wetherlam 763
Furness Fells
Hewrigg Fm
Hall Santon
Santon Bridge
Irton Pike
Ain Ho
Beckfoot
Armont Ho
Crowhow End
Castle How
Dale Head
Grey Friar
Swirl How 802
Black Sails
Lad Stones
Ivy Crag
Harry Guards Wood
Arnside Intake
Aikbank Fm
Irton Hall
Irton Park
Keyhow
Eskdale Green
Fisherground Halt
Dalegarth for Boot
Wha House Fm
Birker Fell
Demming Crag
Mill House Fm
Irton Road
The Green
Forge Ho
Muncaster Head
Harter Fell 649
Kepple Crag
Dow Crag
Brandy Crag
Hinning Ho
Troutal Fell
Great How Crags
High Fell
Above Beck Fells
Yewdale Fells
Tarn Hows
Rose Castle
Carleton Hall
Wood End
Cragg Fm
Ravenglass & Eskdale Railway
Murthwaite Halt
Mitesite Halt
Garner Bank
Hare Gill
Kepple Crag
Crook Crag
Green Crag 489
Long Crag
Levers Water
Coniston Coppermines
Far End
High Water Head
Hawkshead Hill
High Cross
Seathwaite Tarn
Little Cove
Dow Crag
Brim Fell
Coniston Holly How
Coniston
Ruskin Museum
Muncaster Mill
Watermill
River Esk
Linbeck Gill
Water Crag
Rough Crag
Birker Fell
Wormshell How
Wallowbarrow Heald
High Tongue
Tongue Ho
Seathwaite Fells
Goat's Water
The Old Man of Coniston 803
The Bell
Hollin Bank Fm
Hawkshead
Cragg Fm
Hinning Ho
Raven Crag
Great Worm Crag
Low Crag 292
Long Ho
Long House Gill
Bowmanstead
Cat Bank
Steam Yacht Gondola
Tent Lodge
Ravenglass
Muncaster Castle & Hawk & Owl Centre
Birkby Fell
Devoke Water
Woodend
Brown Rigg
Hollin House Tongue
Turner Hall Fm
Walna Scar
Little Arrow Moor
Spoon Hall
Haws Bank
Lands Point
Barnscar
Seathwaite
Newfield Wood
Ash Gill Beck
Bleathwaite Pasture
Park Coppice
Brantwood
Lawson Park
Hall Waberthwaite
The Knott
Woodend Height 494
Ulpha Fell
Nook Moor Ho
Hall Dunnerdale
Low Hall
White Pike
Torver High Common
Hare Crags
Scar Head
Torver
Grizedale Forest Park Visitor Centre
Grizedale
Broad Oak
Stainton Beck
Stainton Fell
Stainton Pike 498
Hesk Fell
Hazel Head
High Kiln Bank Fm
Caw 529
Caw Moss
Dunnerdale Fells
Lag Bank
Broughton Moor
The Knott
Torver Common Wood
Hoathwaite Fm
Torver Back Common
Newbiggin
Grange
Samgarth
Rowantree Force
Withe Bottom
Fox Crags
Whitrow Beck
Waberthwaite
Welcome Nook
Waberthwaite Fell
Whitfell 572
Hole Ho
Ulpha
Church Ho
Far Kiln Bank
Moor Fm
Under Crag
Coniston Water
Lane End
High Corney
Rainsborrow Wood
Birks Wood
Hoses
Lord's Wood
Green Rigg
Bank End
Torver Low Common
The Park
Satterthwaite
Far Bank
Burn Moor
Bigert Mire
Whistling Green
Hare Hall
Ball Hall
Dry Hall
The Hawk
Troughton Hall
Oxen House Bay
Rigg Wood
Great Hill
Foldgate Fm
Corney Fell
Sele Bottom
Frith Hall
Dunnerdale Fells
Scrithwaite Fm
Lind End
Bracelet Hall
Sunny Bank
Stable Harvey Moss
Thrang Crag Wood
Top o Selside 335
Long Crags
Grass Paddocks
Bowkerstead
Corney
Littlecell Bottom
Buck Barrow 549
Plough Fell
Ulpha Park
Hesketh Hall
Pool Scar
Woodland Grove
Yew Bank
Brown Howe
Force Mills
Swallowhurst
The Nooks
Flatts
Corney Hall
Prior Park
Thwaites Fell
Penn
Green Bank
Broughton Mills
Bridge End
Rosthwaite
Tarn Riggs
Birk Knott
Allan Tarn
Bethecar Moor
Force Forge
Low Kinmont
Seaton Hall
Stoneside Hill
Lane End
Beacon Tarn
High Nibthwaite
Whitestock Hall
Crosslands
Ickenthwaite
Woodland
Green Moor
Woodland Fell
Wool Knott
Greenholme Fm
Lower Hawthwaite
Moss Side Fm
Woodland Hall
Water Yeat
High Wood
Arklid Fm
Arklid Intake
Stock Wood
Rusland Moss
Rusland
Rushland Cross
Bootle
Fellside
Swinside Fell
Windy
Duddon Bridge
Bank End
Manor Fm
Black Moss
Longlie Wood
Blawith Knott
Blawith
Nibthwaite
Colton Beck
Furness Fells
A591
A593
A595
B5289
B5322
B5343
B5285
0 1 2 3 miles
0 1 2 3 4 5 km
NY
SD
219
229
230
210

Dowthwaitehead
Dockray
Gowbarrow Fell
Gowbarrow Park
AIRA FORCE WATERFALL
Knotts
Ullswater
Glencoyne Park
Aira Point
Howtown
Sandwick
Martindale
Martindale Common
Helton Fell
Whale
Little Strickland
Butterwick
Bampton
Bampton Grange
Bomby
Rosgill
Reagill
Sleagill
Newby Head
HELVELLYN
Glenridding
Patterdale
Grasmere
Grasthwaite Howe
Dale Head
The Nab
Red Crag
Haweswater Reservoir
SHAP ABBEY
Shap
Keld
KELD CHAPEL
Hardendale
Oddendale
Bridgend
Hartsop
Grisedale
Deepdale
Dovedale
Fairfield
LAKE DISTRICT NATIONAL PARK
High Street
Kidsty Pike
HAWESWATER
Mardale Common
Shap Fells
Wet Sleddale Reservoir
KIRKSTONE PASS
Kentmere Reservoir
Kentmere
Sadgill
Long Sleddale
Sleddale Forest
CUMBRIA
RYDAL MOUNT
Rydal
Ambleside
Clappersgate
Waterhead
AMBLESIDE ROMAN FORT
STAGSHAW GARDEN
Troutbeck
Town End
Borrowdale
Greenholme
Tebay Services North
Bretherdale Head
Roundthwaite
Forest Hall
Lowbridge House
LONG SLEDDALE
WINDERMERE
BROCKHOLE NATIONAL PARK VISITOR CENTRE
HOLEHIRD
Low Wray
BLELHAM BOG
Outgate
High Wray
Troutbeck Bridge
Windermere
Staveley
Ings
Elfhowe
Garnett Bridge
Selside
Watchgate
WINDERMERE STEAMBOATS & MUSEUM
THE WORLD OF BEATRIX POTTER
Bowness-on-Windermere
Ferney Green
Cowen Head
Bowston
Garth Row
Patton Bridge
Grayrigg
Far Sawrey
Near Sawrey
HILL TOP
Crook
Plantation Bridge
Burneside
Meal Bank
Storrs
Winster
Crosthwaite
Underbarrow
Kendal
KENDAL CASTLE
ABBOT HALL ART GALLERY & MUSEUM
Killington Reservoir
Killington Lake Services (Southbound Only)
Gregg Hall
Lowther Park
New Hutton
Millholme
Ludderburn
Hartbarrow
Tarnside
Strawberry Bank
Bowland Bridge
Brigsteer
Natland
Oxenholme
OXENHOLME LAKE DISTRICT
Middleshaw
Killington
YMCA LAKESIDE
STOTT PARK BOBBIN MILL
Cartmel Fell
Row
The Howe
SIZERGH CASTLE
Barrows Green
Old Hutton
Windermere
A591
A592
A5284
A684
A685
A6
M6

Crackenthorpe
Appleby-in-Westmorland
231
232
Murton
Hilton
Colby
Kings Meaburn
Morland Moor
Newby End Fm
Sleagill
Reagill
Maulds Meaburn
Crosby Ravensworth
Hardendale
221
Oddendale
Shap Summit
Coalpit Hill
Crosby Ravensworth Fell
Burrells
Hoff
Drybeck
Great Ormside
Little Ormside
Sandford
Warcop
Brackenber
Coupland
Great Asby
Little Asby
Town Head
Asby Winderwath Common
High Pike 372
Great Asby Scar
Orton
Raisbeck
Tebay Services South
Tebay Services North
Greenholme
Gaisgill
Old Tebay
Tebay
J38 Truckstop Services
Kelleth
Newbiggin-on-Lune
Ravenstonedale
Coldbeck
Bowderdale
Weasdale
Crosby Garrett
Smardale
Soulby
Bleatarn
Great Musgrave
Little Musgrave
Brough
North Stainmore
Church Brough
Brough Sowerby
Kaber
Barras
Winton
Kirkby Stephen
Hartley
Nateby
Waitby
Heggerscales
Rookby
CUMBRIA
Nine Standards Rigg
Birkdale Common
Angram Common
Mallerstang
Mallerstang Common
Outhgill
Shoregill
Abbotside Common
Howgill Fells
Langdale Fell
Ravenstonedale Common
Brant Fell
Baugh Fell
Wild Boar Fell 708
The Calf 676
Roundthwaite
Low Borrowbridge
Lowgill
Beck Foot
Howgill
Firbank
Cautley
Sedbergh
Millthrop
Brigflatts
Garsdale
Garsdale Head
Grisdale
Cotterdale
Killington Reservoir
Killington Lake Services (Southbound Only)
212
Rise Hill
Widdale Fell
A66
A685
A683
A684
M6
B6259
B6260
B6270
B6276
0 1 2 3 miles
0 1 2 3 4 5 km

Romaldkirk
Kinninvie
Grassholme
Hunderthwaite
Hury
Cotherstone
Barnard Castle
Startforth
Lartington
Stainton
Westwick
Boldron
Bowes
Gilmonby
Greta Bridge
Brignall
Scargill
Barningham
Newsham
Dalton
Whaw
Langthwaite
Arkle Town
Reeth
Fremington
Healaugh
Kearton
Feetham
Gunnerside
Ivelet
Satron
Crackpot
Low Row
Muker
Thwaite
Keld
Angram
Ravenseat
West Stonesdale
Grinton
Marrick
Hurst
Washfold
Skelton
Marske
Stainton
Bellerby
Leyburn
Wensley
Preston-under-Scar
Redmire
Castle Bolton
Carperby
Woodhall
Askrigg
Newbiggin
Bainbridge
Worton
Cubeck
Hawes
Gayle
Burtersett
Hardrow
Simonstone
Sedbusk
High Shaw
Swinithwaite
West Witton
Aysgarth
Thornton Rust
Countersett
D U R H A M
N O R T H
Y O R K S H I R E
YORKSHIRE DALES
NATIONAL PARK
Bowes Moor
Stainmore Forest
Deep Dale
Arkengarthdale Moor
Kexwith Moor
Hurst Moor
Gayles Moor
Melbecks Moor
Whitaside Moor
Askrigg Common
Abbotside Common
Wensleydale
River Swale
River Tees
River Greta
River Ure
Balderhead Reservoir
Blackton Reservoir
Hury Reservoir
Selset Reservoir
Pennine Way
A66
A67
A688
A684
B6270
B6277
B6278
Tan Hill
Mirk Fell 571
Great Pinseat 583
Calver Hill 487
Whit Fell 411
Great Knipe 515
Moudy Mea 522
Collinson's Hill 434
Citron Seat 446
Cleasby Hill 511
How Tallon 447
Arndale Hill 515
Blea Barf 540
Lovely Seat 675
Rogan's Seat 672
Buttertubs Pass
The Bowes Museum
Egglestone Abbey
Bowes Castle
Bolton Castle
Maiden Castle
Swaledale Museum
Aysgarth Falls
Hardraw Force Waterfall
Dales Countryside Museum
Wensleydale Creamery
232
233
224
213
A B C D E F G H
7 8 9 10 11

Raby Park
Raby Castle
Wackerfield
Hilton
Houghton-le-Side
Heighington
Brafferton
Great Stainton
Staindrop
Ingleton
Killerby
Summerhouse
Walworth Gate
Coatham Mundeville
Cleatlam
Langton
Headlam
Denton
Walworth
Beaumont Hill
Barmpton
Little Newsham
Winston
Gainford
Archdeacon Newton
Harrowgate Village
Harrowgate Hill
Great Burdon
Sadberge
Faverdale
Haughton Le Skerne
DURHAM
Piercebridge
Carlbury
Branksome
Cockerton
Head of Steam Darlington Railway Museum
Piercebridge Roman Bridge & Fort
High Coniscliffe
Whorlton
Ovington
Wycliffe
Merrybent
Mowden
Darlington
Hummersknott
Lingfield
Caldwell
Eppleby
Manfield
Low Coniscliffe
Cleasby
Blackwell
Skerne Park
Eastbourne
The Northern Echo Arena
Greta Bridge
Hutton Magna
Lane Head
Forcett
Carlton
Stanwick-St-John
Aldbrough St John
Stapleton
Iron Age Fortifications
Newsham
East Layton
West Layton
Hurworth Place
Hurworth-on-Tees
Neasham
Croft-on-Tees
Newton Morrell
Barton
Melsonby
Eryholme
Dalton
Ravensworth
Gayles
Dalton-on-Tees
Croft Circuit
Kirby Hill
Whashton
Hartforth
Gayles Moor
NORTH YORKSHIRE
Scotch Corner
Scotch Corner Services
Middleton Tyas
Gilling West
Moulton
North Cowton
Great Smeaton
Moulton Hall
East Cowton
Uckerby
Skeeby
Atley Hill
Birkby
Richmond
Georgian Theatre
Richmond Castle
Green Howards Museum
Hurgill
Easby Abbey
Easby
Marske
Skelton
Hudswell
Scorton
Catterick Bridge
Bolton-on-Swale
Whitwell
Streetlam
Danby Wiske
Colburn
Brompton-on-Swale
Hipswell
Walkerville
Catterick Garrison
Downholme
Catterick
Kiplin Hall
Kiplin
Great Langton
Stainton
Scotton
Tunstall
East Appleton
West Appleton
Kirkby Fleetham
Yafforth
Barden
East Hauxwell
Hornby
Hackforth
Great Fencote
Little Fencote
Bellerby
Garriston
Arrathorne
Thrintoft
Ainderby Steeple
Scruton
Hunton
Langthorne
Morton-on-Swale
Warlaby
Constable Burton Hall
Constable Burton
Patrick Brompton
Leyburn
Leyburn Ceramic Inspirations
Harmby
Little Crakehall
Great Crakehall
Crakehall Water Mill
Finghall
The Wensleydale Railway
Leeming Bar
Leeming
Newton-le-Willows
Aiskew
Bedale Hall
Leeming Bar Services
Middleham
Hutton Hang
Wensley
Scotch Corner
0 1 2 3 miles
0 1 2 3 4 5 km

Middlesbrough
Stockton-on-Tees
STOCKTON ON TEES
Billingham Beck
Transporter Bridge (Toll)
Riverside Stadium
Clarence
South Bank
Grangetown
Eston
Lazenby
Wilton
Teesville
Lackenby
Dunsdale
Normanby
Ormesby
REDCAR AND CLEVELAND
Guisborough
Hutton Gate
North Ormesby
Pallister
Berwick Hills
Linthorpe
Marton Grove
Acklam
Park End
Marton
Easterside
Captain Cook Birthplace Museum
Tollesby
Coulby Newham
Mount Pleasant
Nunthorpe
Brookfield
Hemlington
Stainton
Thornton
Maltby
MIDDLESBROUGH
Thornaby on Tees
Preston Park Museum & Gdns
Preston-on-Tees
Ingleby Barwick
Bishopton
Carlton
Redmarshall
Hardwick
Bishopsgarth
Whinney Hill
Fairfield
Hartburn
Elton
Longnewton
Urlay Nook
Eaglescliffe
Egglescliffe
Teesside Airport
Teesside International Airport
Middleton One Row
Aislaby
Yarm
High Leven
Hilton
Newby
Seamer
Tanton
Great Ayton
Captain Cook Schoolroom Mus
Captain Cook's Monument
Little Ayton
Newton under Roseberry
Roseberry Topping
Hutton Village
Langbaurgh
Kildale
Easby
Battersby
Stokesley
Tame Bridge
Middleton-on-Leven
Kirklevington
Low Worsall
High Worsall
Girsby
Picton
Crathorne
Rudby
Hutton Rudby
Enterpen
Sexhow
Great Busby
Kirkby
Great Broughton
Ingleby Greenhow
Hornby
Appleton Wiske
West Rounton
East Rounton
Potto
Goulton
Carlton in Cleveland
Faceby
Whorlton
Swainby
Welbury
Deighton
Ingleby Arncliffe
Ingleby Cross
Exelby South
Exelby North
Cleveland Hills
Cringle Moor
Urra
Urra Moor
Chop Gate
Seave Green
Lovesome Hill
East Harlsey
West Harlsey
Mount Grace Priory
Osmotherley
Osmotherley Moor
NORTH YORK MOORS NATIONAL PARK
Ellerbeck
Winton
Brompton
Northallerton
Foxton
Kirby Sigston
Thimbleby
Over Silton
Nether Silton
Bullamoor
Hawnby
Fangdale Beck
Cross Holme
The Grange
Kepwick
Leake
Cowesby
Thornton-le-Beans
Thornton-le-Moor
Borrowby
North Otterington
Sowber Gate
Newby
Knayton
Murton Grange
Dale Town Common
Daleside
Cleveland Way
Black Hambleton
Rievaulx Moor
A19
A66
A172
A174
A171
A173
A167
A684
234
235
226
215
NZ
SE
A
B
C
D
E
F
G
H
7
8
9
10
11

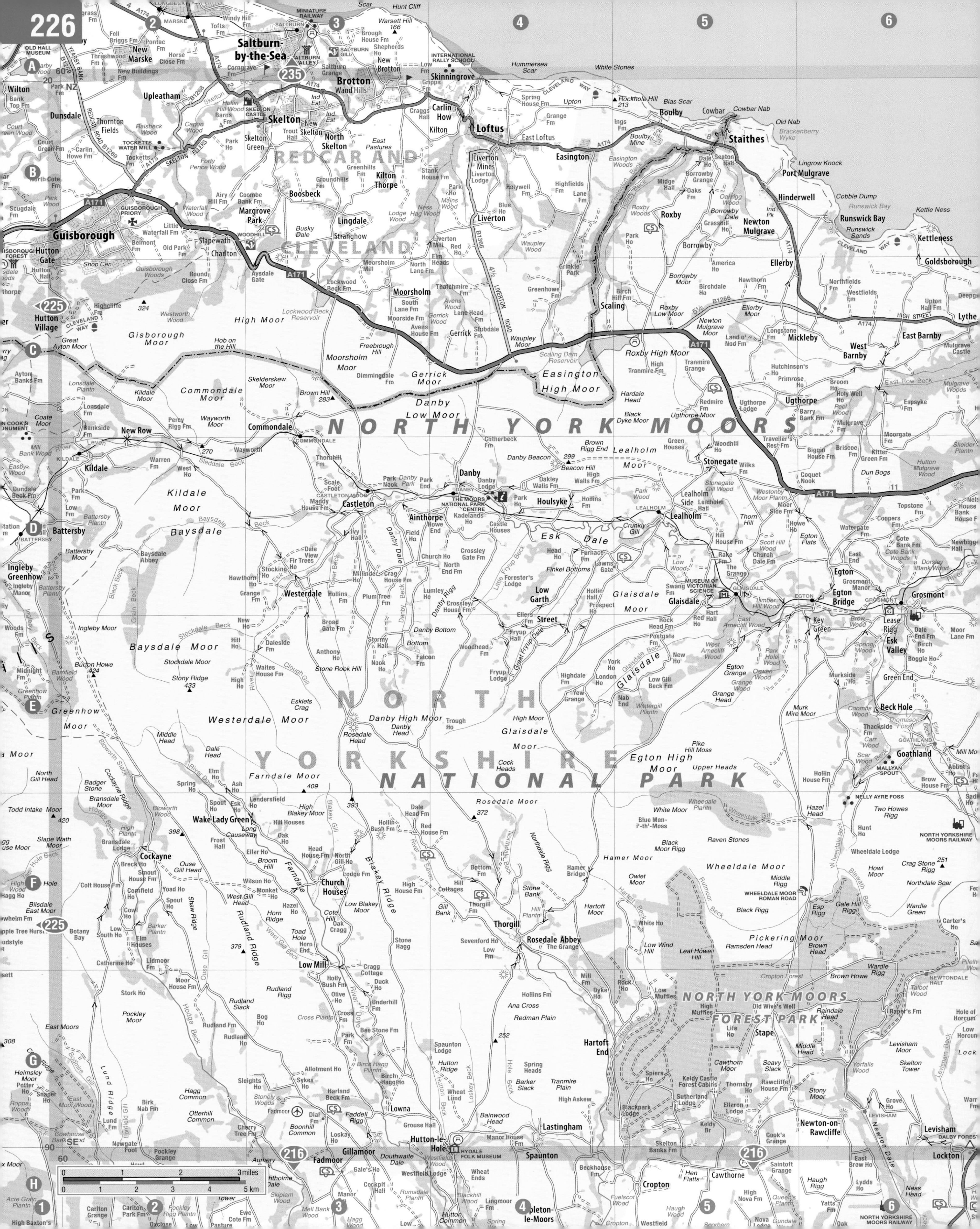

Saltburn-by-the-Sea
Guisborough
Skelton
Brotton
Loftus
Staithes
Danby
Castleton
Westerdale
Lealholm
Glaisdale
Egton
Grosmont
Goathland
Rosedale Abbey
Hutton-le-Hole
Lastingham
Gillamoor
Fadmoor
Levisham
NORTH YORK MOORS
NORTH YORKSHIRE NATIONAL PARK
REDCAR AND CLEVELAND
NORTH YORK MOORS FOREST PARK

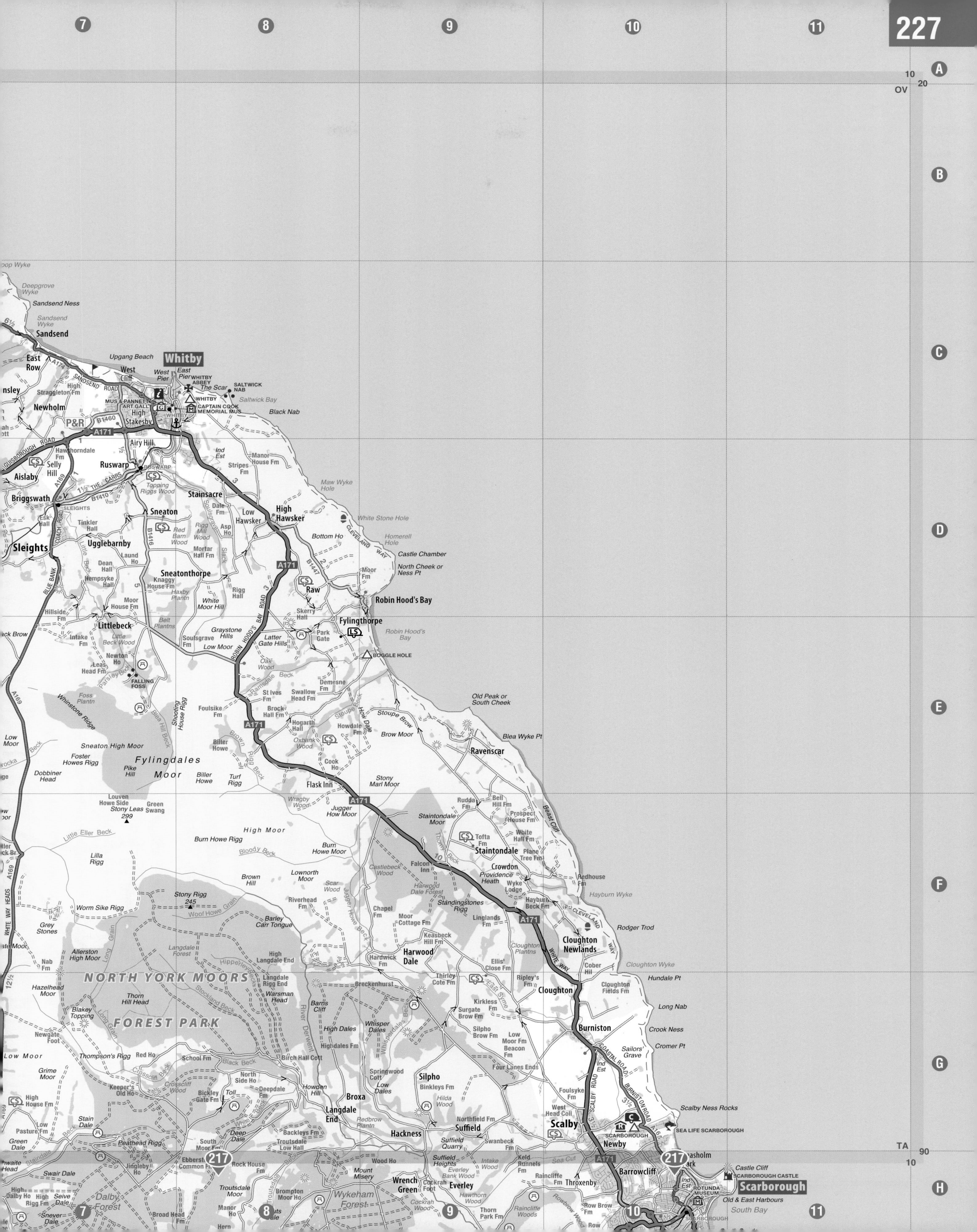

Whitby
Sandsend
Sandsend Ness
East Row
Newholm
Upgang Beach
West Cliff
Whitby Abbey
Saltwick Nab
Saltwick Bay
Black Nab
Captain Cook Memorial Mus
High Stakesby
Airy Hill
Ruswarp
Aislaby
Briggswath
Sleights
Stainsacre
Sneaton
Ugglebarnby
High Hawsker
Low Hawsker
Sneatonthorpe
Raw
Robin Hood's Bay
Fylingthorpe
Boggle Hole
Littlebeck
Falling Foss
Fylingdales Moor
Flask Inn
Ravenscar
Old Peak or South Cheek
Blea Wyke Pt
Staintondale
Cloughton Newlands
Cloughton
Burniston
Harwood Dale
Hayburn Wyke
Rodger Trod
Hundale Pt
Long Nab
Crook Ness
Cromer Pt
NORTH YORK MOORS
FOREST PARK
Langdale End
Broxa
Hackness
Silpho
Suffield
Scalby
Scalby Ness Rocks
Sea Life Scarborough
Newby
Barrowcliff
Throxenby
Everley
Wrench Green
Scarborough
Scarborough Castle
Castle Cliff
Rotunda Museum
Old & East Harbours
South Bay
Dalby Forest
Wykeham Forest
A171
A169
217

EAST
STEWARTRY
COAST
Auchencairn
Auchencairn Bay
Drungans
Auchencairn Ho
Hestan Island
Almorness Pt
White Port
Moyl
Balcary Bay
Balcary Pt
Airds Cott
Airds
Airds Pt
Cairn Hill
Nether Hazelfield
Rascarrel
Rascarrel Bay
Castle Muir Pt
Barlocco Bay
NX
237
238
219
Bank End
SENHOUSE ROMAN MUSEUM
LAKE DISTRICT COAST AQUARIUM
MARITIME MUS
Maryport
THE WAVE CENTRE
Netherton
Ewanrigg
Risehow Fm
Risehow
Fothergill
Woodside
Flimby
Standing
St Helens
Camerton Grange
A596
Stud Fm
Siddick
Seaton
Camerton
Camerton Hall
Ribton Hall
North Side
Hawk Hill
Salmon Hall
Barepot
Stainburn Hall Fm
Great Clifton
Clifton Hall
WORKINGTON HALL
Stainburn
Workington
A66
HELENA THOMPSON MUSEUM
Close End
Moorclose
Schoose
Quarry Hill
Mossbay
A596
Westfield
East Town End Fm
Moss Bay
Salterbeck
Winscales
A595
Harrington
High Harrington
Gale Ho
Lucy Close Fm
Wythemoor Ho
Lillyhall Industrial Estate
Distington Works
Grayson Green
West Ghyll End Fm
Harrington Parks
Wythemoor Head
Branthwaite Row Fm
Kelmore Hill Fm
Park Ho
Distington
Gilgarran
Cunning Pt
Barngill Ho
Common End
High House Fm
Lowca
Pica
Wilson Park
Keekle Head Fm
Providence Bay
Moresby
Boon Wood
High Park
Parton Bay
Parton
Low Moresby
Tutehill Fm
Moresby Moss
Tivoli
Tanyard Bay
A595
Redness Pt
Bransty
Moresby Parks
Sandsclose
Harras
Scilly Bank
Ind Est
WALK MILL
Acrewalls
Arlecdon Hill
Whitehaven
THE BEACON
THE RUM
River Keekle
Dub Beck
ENGLAND COAST PATH
MAIN ROAD
0 1 2 3 miles
0 1 2 3 4 5 km

Blitterlees
Abbey Town
Kingside Hill
Kelsick
Lessonhall
Oulton
Moorhouse
Parton
Crofton
Micklethwaite
Wolsty
Beckfoot
Highlaws
Pelutho
Aldoth
Dundraw
Moor Row
Waverbridge
Wigton
Western Bank
Kirkland
Newtown
Tarns
Blencogo
Holme St Cuthbert
Mawbray
Goodyhills
Common Moss
Bromfield
Langrigg
Parkgate
Waverton
Old Carlisle
Highmoor
Dubmill Pt
Salta
Edderside
New Cowper
Mealrigg
High Scales
Waterside
Red Dial
Brackenthwaite
Westnewton
Bolton Low Houses
Westward
Allonby
Allonby Bay
Aspatria
Watchhill
Fletchertown
Mealsgate
Hayton
Prospect
Oughterside
Baggrow
Blennerhasset
Harriston
Boltongate
Sandale
Allerby
Crosby Villa
Crosscanonby
Threapland
Plumbland
Parsonby
Bothel
Torpenhow
Ireby
Whitrigg
Moor Park
Crosby
Bullgill
Gilcrux
High Ireby
Uldale
Branthwaite
Fell Side
Birkby
Greengill
Dearham
Row Brow
Tallentire
Sunderland
Blindcrake
Bewaldeth
Orthwaite
Broughton Moor
Dovenby
Bridekirk
Redmain
Isel
Little Broughton
Great Broughton
Bassenthwaite
Papcastle
Brigham
Cockermouth
Embleton
Lambfoot
Wythop Mill
Skiddaw Forest
Nepgill
Bridgefoot
Greysouthen
Little Clifton
Eaglesfield
LAKE DISTRICT NATIONAL PARK
Oldfield
Deanscales
Brandlingill
High Lorton
Low Lorton
Lorton Vale
Thornthwaite
WHINLATTER FOREST PARK
Millbeck
Applethwaite
Ormathwaite
Dean
Pardshaw
Mosser
Ullock
Thackthwaite
Braithwaite
Portinscale
Keswick
Brigham
Chestnut Hill
Mockerkin
Castlerigg
Woodend
Crossgates
Lamplugh
Loweswater
Stair
Swinside
Newlands
Derwent Water
Asby
Loweswater Fell
Castlerigg Fell
Rannerdale
Derwent Fells
Skiddaw 931
Bassenthwaite Lake
Cumbria
Solway Coast

Baldwinholme
Brisco
Durdar
Dalston
Thursby
Moorend
Crofton
Micklethwaite
West End
Low Whinnow
West Curthwaite
East Curthwaite
Cardew
Cardewlees
Cumdivock
Chalkfoot
Broomfield
Buckabank
Bridge End
Unthank
Sprunston
Foulbridge
Wreay
Burthwaite
Cotehill
Hornsby
Holmwrangle
Lockhills
Aiketgate
Armathwaite
Towngate
Ainstable
Hawksdale
Raughton
Gaitsgill
Raughton Head
Stockdalewath
Highbridge
Ivegill
Brackenthwaite
Rosley
Welton
Nether Welton
Grassgarth
Brothybeck
Sebergham
Churchtown
Middlesceugh
Low Braithwaite
Mellguards
Southwaite Services
Southwaite
Low Hesket
High Hesket
Old Town
Nunclose
Longdales
Ruckcroft
Dale
Inglewood
Forest
Hurst
Thomas Close
Calthwaite
Morton
Hutton End
Plumpton Foot
Townhead
Lazonby Fell
Plumpton
Brockleymoor
New Rent
Hutton-in-the-Forest
Unthank
Skelton
Unthank End
Ellonby
Lamonby
Plumpton Head
Catterlen
Laithes
Little Blencow
Great Blencow
Johnby
Newton Reigny
Newton Rigg
Fair Hill
Penrith
Castletown
Pategill
Carleton
Eamont Bridge
Clifton
Greystoke
Berrier
Motherby
Penruddock
Hutton
Stainton
Redhills
Sockbridge
Tirril
Dacre
Soulby
Pooley Bridge
Waterfoot
Askham
Lowther
Hackthorpe
Helton
Whale
Caldbeck
Hesket Newmarket
Whelpo
Upton
Ratten Row
Parkhead
Newlands
Southernby
Sowerby Row
Millhouse
Fell Side
Caldbeck Fells
High Row
Heggle Lane
Hutton Roof
Mosedale
Mungrisdale
CUMBRIA
LAKE DISTRICT NATIONAL PARK
Skiddaw Forest
Scales
Troutbeck
Beckces
Threlkeld
Matterdale End
Dockray
Watermillock
Knotts
Longthwaite
Wreay
Ullswater
Howtown
Martindale
Sandwick
Bampton
Butterwick
Low Knipe
Matterdale Common
Dowthwaitehead
Great Dodd
Dale Bottom
Fisher Place
Greystoke Forest
A595
A596
A66
A6
A591
A592
A5091
M6
B5305
B5299
B5288
B5320
0 1 2 3 miles
0 1 2 3 4 5 km

240
241
232
221
222
7
8
9
10
11
A
B
C
D
E
F
G
H
NY
80
50
20
Cumrew Fell
Geltsdale Middle
Three Pikes 585
Hartchyside
Bertram Hill
Shawhead
Dewley Fell
Dewley Field
Willyshaw Rigg
497
Ouston Fell
NINEBANKS
Hawkuplee
Spartywell
Farneyside
Knarsdale Common
Butt Hill
Far Town
LINTLEY
Ayle Common
Long Cross
White Hill
Mohope Head
Park Ho
Broadlee
Kevenn Moor
Newbiggin
Newbiggin Fell
Blotting Raise 591
Croglin Fell
The Combs
Green Hill
Thornhope Fell
Ayle
KIRKHAUGH
Kirkside Wood
Clarghyll Hall
White Ho
Mohope Moor
Halley Moor
The Nook
Limestone Brae
Broad Mea
High Shield
Lawyer's Cross
Farlam Currick
Grey Nag 656
Black Hill
Castle Nook
Whitley Castle
SOUTH TYNEDALE RAILWAY
Newshield Moss
Hard Rigg
Broad Meadows
New Ho
The Meres
Black Cleugh
Sumburgh Ho
Fieldhead
Scarrowmanwick Fell
Wanwood Hill
Blagill
Hesleywell Moor
Middle Rigg
Croglin
Scarrowmanwick
Thack Moor 609
637
Tom Smith's Stone
Raise
ALSTON
Alston
Foreshield
East Cocklake
Carrshield
Smallburns Moor
Carrshield Moor
Caber Fm
Davygill
Croglin High Hall
Watch Hill
Whitewell Fm
Browngill
The Dodd
614
Middle Moor
Scale Houses
Renwick Fell
Woldgill Moss
Park Fell
Black Ho
Bayle Hill Fm
Middle Fell
Nenthall
Galligill
Whimsey Hill
Coalcleugh
Lowhall Building
Long Moor
Dyrah
The Dod
Watcher's Hill
Horse Edge
Hill Ho
Bayles
Greenends
Whin Fell
Crindledyke Fm
Lincowell
Green Rigg
Long Tongue
664 Black Fell
Gilderdale Forest
Brownside Moss
Ghyll Ho
Rise
Middle Fell
Nettle Hall
Welgill
Black Hill
Coalcleugh Moor
Scales Moor
Skelling Moor
Harescugh Fell
Leadgate
575
Nenthead
Slate Hill
Renwick
Hartside Cotts
Rotherhope Tower
Meadow Flatt
Rice Head
Alston Moor
Old Mill
NENTHEAD MINES
Harescugh
How Moor
Ravenbridge Mill
HARTSIDE HEIGHT
Benty Hill
Meathaw Hill 486
Cropshall
Nunnery Hill
Shaw Side
Scales
Huddlesceugh Hall
Busk
Blackburn Bank
Dryburn
High Skydes
KILLHOPE MINING
Cowhorn Hill
High Whill
Low Mill
Viol Moor
Gamblesby Fell
Cawood Hill
Flinty Fell 614
Loaning Head
Knoutberry Hill
Kirkoswald
Park Head
Twotop Hill
Fiend's Fell 634
Rotherhope Fell
Garrigill
Nag's Head
Unthank
Hazel Rigg
Viol Moor
Long Crags
Staneshaw Rigg
Crossgill
Pasture Houses
Ash Gill
Mount Pleasant
Old Parks
Black Burn
Long Grain
Lamb's Head 648
The Mains
Gamblesby
Glassonbybeck
Little Knapside Hill 657
Smittergill Head
Hound Hill 596
Alston Moor
Lee Hos
High Ashgill
709
Dead Stones
White Edge
Glassonby
Eden Lacy
Lacy's Caves
Maughanby Fm
Todhills
Hause in the Scar
685 Knapside Hill
Melmerby Fell
Rigg End
Ousby Fell
Pikeman Hill
West Ashgill
Paper Hill
Pasture Ho
Hole Ho
Windy Brow
Burnhope Moor
Melmerby Mire
Tarn Ho
Melmerby High Scar
Hill Ho
Tynehead
Yad Moss
Burnhope Seat 746
LONG MEG & HER DAUGHTERS
Marian Lodge
Melmerby
Stony Rigg
Bullman Hills
PENNINE WAY
Long Man Hill
Little Salkeld
Robberby Fm
Colstons Fm
Gale Hall
Cuns Fell
Green Fell 740
Raehow End
NORTH
Lambgreen Hills
Round Hill 686
Slack's Rigg
Scaud Hill
Hunsonby
Ousby Moor
Jardine's Fm
Muska Hill
Brown Hill
Skirwith Fell
Fallow Hill
Crossgill Head
Calvert End
Tyne Head
Tynehead Fell
Bellbeaver Rigg 620
Yad Moss
Harwood Common
Ashgill Head
Winskill
Crewgarth
Ousby
Row
Rayson Hall
Thack Moor
Frog Hall
Langwathby
LANGWATHBY
Beck Mill
Townhead
High Cap
Kirkdale
Cross Fell 893
Tees Head
River Tees
Viewing Hill
Greencomb Sike
Kirkland Fell
Little Dun Fell
Hard Hill 678
Metalband Hill
Hardship Fell
Edenhall
Langwathby Moor
Skirwith High Moor
Bank Hall
Kirkland
Wildboar Scar
Middle Tongue
Great Dun Fell 848
Milburn Forest
Moor Ho
Dodgen Pot
Home Fm
High Barn
Appleside Hill
Skirwith
Skirwith Abbey
Whamthorn Plantn
Hanging Walls of Mark Anthony
MOOR HOUSE UPPER TEESDALE
West Common
Moorlands Plantn
Primrose Bank
Grumply Hill
Iron Howe
Green Castle
Backside Fell
Touting Hill
Dolphenby
Blencarn
High Slack
PENNINES
Knock Fell
Udford
Moorside
Red Carle
Cow Green Reservoir
Highbarn Cott
Cross How
Lounthwaite
Hornby Hall
Underwood
Burney Hill
Culgaith
Loscars
Green Fell
Woodside
Meldon Hill 767
Milburn
Howgill Castle
Dufton Fell
CAULDRON SNOUT WATERFALL
Whinfell Ho
Newbiggin
Mill Rigg Fm
Moorlands Head
Kirk Ho
High Scald Fell
Haversheaf Hall
Gullom Holme
Milburn Grange
Knock Pike
Sawmill Cotts
Whinfell Forest
Ash Hill
ACORN BANK GARDEN
Slakes Fm
Close Ho
Brownber Hill
Oglebird Plantn
Temple Sowerby
Housay Park
Halefield Fm
Low Abbey
Knock
Rasp Hill
Knock Moor
Leacet Hill
WHINFELL FOREST VILLAGE
Salter Wood
Skygarth Fm
Lowmoor Row
Hale Grange
Stamp Hill Fm
Knock Cross
Dufton Pike
Bluethwaite Hill
Backstone Edge
Narrowgate Beacon
HIGH CUP NICK
Maize Beck
CLIBURN MOSS
Town Head
Kirkby Thore
Town End
Town Head
Marton Moor
Coatsike Fm
Pusgill Ho
Brown Howe
Melkinthorpe
Shaw Ho
Ousen Stand
Bridge End
Sleastonhow
Birks Head
Marton Ho
DUFTON
Dufton
Bow Hall
503 Peeping Hill
High Cup Gill
Danger area
Mickle Fell
Wood Ho
Cliburn
Long Marton
Park Ho
Murton Fell
Melkinthorpe Wood
Leith Bank
Crossrigg Hall
Winter Ho
Edenbank Fm
Trout Beck
Town Head
Middle Tongue
Street Ho
Glenton Vale
Town Wood
Eden Grove
Redlands Bank
Broom
Dufton Wood
Town End
Stanley Bank Plantn
Bolton
Brampton
Sealehowe Wood
Harbour Flatt
594 Murton Pike
Keekham Beck Head
Hilton Fell
Great Strickland
Morland
Croft Ends
Brampton Tower
Brackenthwaite
Greystone Ho
Dallan Bank
Syke Ho
Town Head
Roger Head
Crackenthorpe
Murton
Mell Fell
Amber Hill
Little Fell 745
Burton Fell
Philip Reed Moor
Keld
Edenfields
Bolton Lodge
Hangingshaw
Sheriff Park
Newby Head
Sandriggs Fm
Strickland Lodge Fm
High Field
King's Meaburn
New Bewley Castle
Colby Laithes
Low Barn
Shepherd's Cott
Newby
Newby End Fm
Morland Moor
Burwain Hall
Penny Hill
Colby
Battlebarrow Ho
APPLEBY
Gale Ho
Langton Field
Roman Fell
Christy Bank
Warcop Fell
Thrimby Hall
White Stone
Hilton
Stoneriggs
Appleby-in-Westmorland
Little Strickland
White Stone
Dedra Banks
Littlebeck
Brackenber Moor
Brackenber
Bankwood
Thrimby Grange
Bedlands Gate
Jerusalem
Bandley Wood
Long Fell
Tinside Rigg
Helbeck Fell
Brown Howe
Sleagill Head
Sleagill
Lowfield
Sideway Bank
Burrells
Low Bank End
Coupland
Middle Fell
Musgrave Fell
Seavy Rigg
Seat Hill
Barwise Hall
Greyber
Meaburn
Pattinson's
A66
A686
A689
B6413
B6412
B6277
B6294
B6260
B6542
A689
Gelt Burn
New Water
Croglin Water
Raven Beck
Sally Grain
Eden
River Eden
River South Tyne
River Nent
Knar Burn
Ayle Burn
Woldgill Burn
Thornhope Burn
Crook Burn
Force Burn
Lodgegill Sike
Swindale Beck
Great Rundale Beck
Milburn Beck
Crowdundle Beck
Blencarn Beck
Hole Sike
Sunnygill Beck
Dale Beck
Robberby Water
Hazelrigg Beck
Loo Gill
Trout Beck
Moss Burn
Rough Sike
Green Burn
Grain Beck
Maize Beck
Swarth Beck
Hilton Beck
Swindale Edge
Great Millstone Sike
Goal Sike
Connypot Beck
Scraith Burn
Wellhope Burn
Wellhope Burn
Sandyford Sike
Whitewalls Burn
Aglionby Beck
Smittergill Burn
Rowling Burn
Cash Burn
Dry Burn
Dufton Ghyll Burn
Cross Gill
Little Gill
Black Burn
Gilderdale Burn
Briggle Beck
Leith
River Eamont
Tarn Gill
Pike
Bove Wood
Helbeck Fell
Kentmere Fell
10½
7½
5½
4½
3½
11½
6
4
5
22

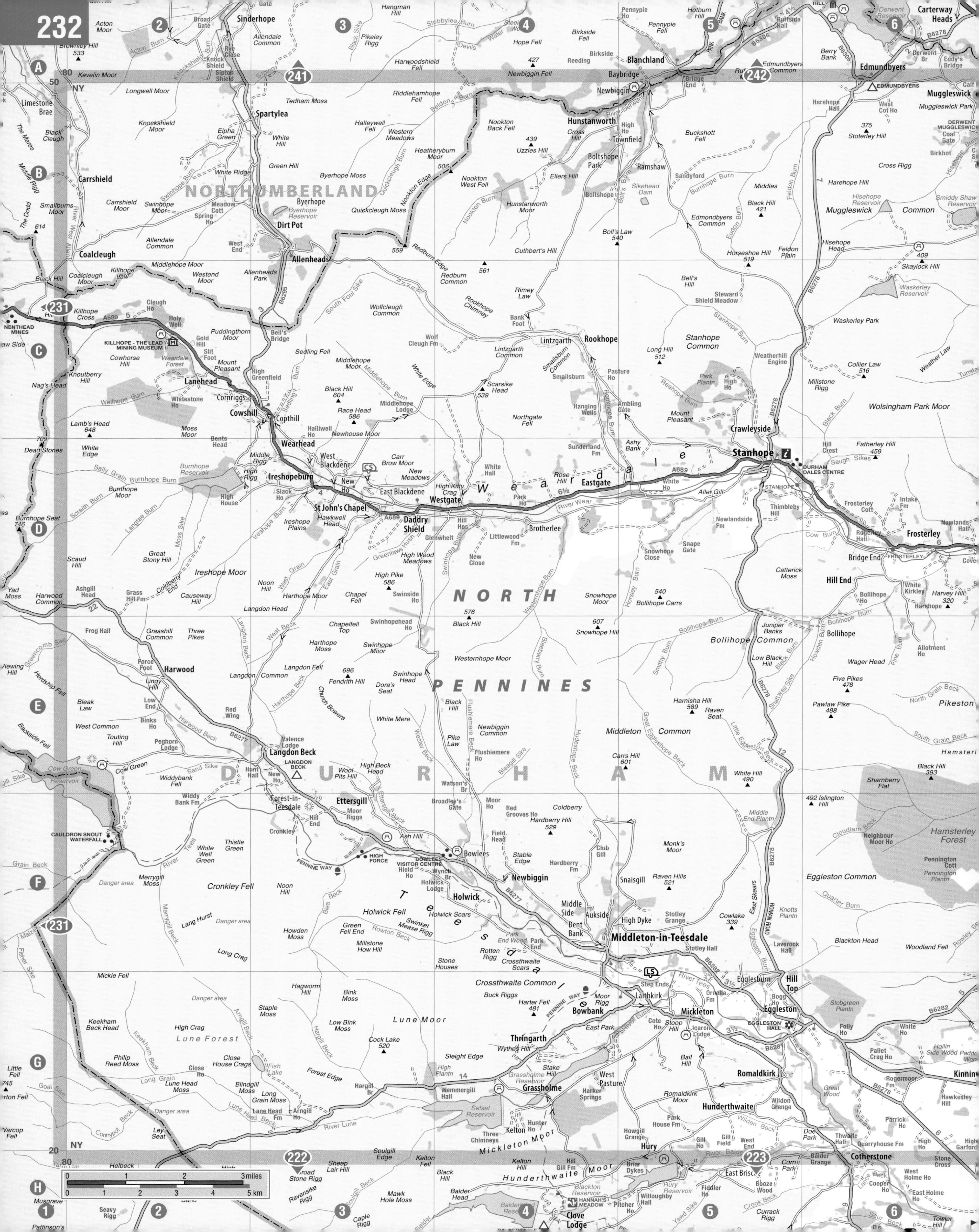
NORTHUMBERLAND
NORTH PENNINES
DURHAM
Weardale
Teesdale
Acton Moor
Sinderhope
Hangman Hill
Pennypie Ho
Hotburn Hill
Carterway Heads
Broad Gate
Allendale Common
Pikeley Rigg
Stobbylee Burn
Pennypie Fell
Ruffside Hall
Brownley Hill 533
Rye Close
Hope Fell
Birkside Fell
Berry Bank
Derwent Br
Eddy's Bridge
Knock Shield
Sipton Shield
Harwoodshield Fell
427
Reading
Birkside
Blanchland
Edmundbyers Common
Edmundbyers
Kevelin Moor
Newbiggin Fell
Baybridge
Bridge End
EDMUNDBYERS
Muggleswick
Longwell Moor
Riddlehamhope Fell
Newbiggin
Harehope Hall
Muggleswick Park
Limestone Brae
Tedham Moss
West Cot Ho
Spartylea
Nookton Back Fell
Hunstanworth
High Ho
DERWENT MUGGLESWICK
The Meres
Knockshield Moor
Halleywell Fell
Western Meadows
Townfield
Buckshott Fell
375 Stoterley Hill
Coal Gate
Black Cleugh
Elpha Green
White Hill
Heatheryburn Moor
439 Uzzles Hill
Cross Hill
Birkhot
Middle Rigg
Green Hill
506
Boltshope Park
Ramshaw
Cross Rigg
Carrshield
White Ridge
Byerhope Moss
Nookton Edge
Nookton West Fell
Ellers Hill
Sandyford
Middles
Harehope Hill
Byerhope
Sikehead Dam
Hisehope Reservoir
Smiddy Shaw Reservoir
Smallburns Moor
Carrshield Moor
Swinhope Moor
Meadow Cott
Byerhope Reservoir
Quickcleugh Moss
Hunstanworth Moor
Boltshope
Black Hill 421
Muggleswick
Common
The Dodd
Spring Ho
Dirt Pot
Edmondbyers Common
614
Allendale Common
West End
Boll's Law 540
Horseshoe Hill 519
Feldon Plain
Hisehope Head
409
Coalcleugh
559
Redburn Edge
Cuthbert's Hill
Skayiock Hill
Killhope Law
Middlehope Moor
Allenheads
561
Black Hill
Coalcleugh Moor
Westend Moor
Allenheads Park
Redburn Common
Bell's Hill
Waskerley Reservoir
Rimey Law
Steward Shield Meadow
Killhope Cross
Cleugh Ho
South Fou Sike
Wolfcleugh Common
Rookhope Chimney
NENTHEAD MINES
A689
Holy Well
Bank Foot
Waskerley Park
Law Side
Gold Hill
Puddingthorn Moor
Bell's Bridge
Wolf Cleugh Fm
Lintzgarth
Rookhope
Stanhope Common
KILLHOPE - THE LEAD MINING MUSEUM
Slit Foot
Sedling Fell
Lintzgarth Common
Long Hill 512
Weatherhill Engine
Collier Law 516
Weather Law
Cowhorse Hill
Weardale Forest
Mount Pleasant
Middlehope Moor
Smallsburn Common
Knoutberry Hill
Lanehead
High Greenfield
White Edge
Scarsike Head
539
Smallsburn
Pasture Ho
Park Plantn
High Ho
Millstone Rigg
Nag's Head
Corniggs
Black Hill 604
Middlehope Lodge
Hanging Wells
Ambling Gate
Mount Pleasant
Wolsingham Park Moor
Wellhope Burn
Whitestone Ho
Cowshill
Copthill
Race Head 586
Northgate Fell
Lamb's Head 648
Halliwell Ho
Newhouse Moor
Crawleyside
Moss Moor
Wearhead
Sunderland Fm
709
Dead Stones
Bents Head
Ashy Bank
Fatherley Hill 459
White Edge
West Blackdene
Carr Brow Moor
Stanhope
Hill Crest
DURHAM DALES CENTRE
Burnhope Reservoir
Middle Rigg
New Meadows
White Hall
Rose Hill
Eastgate
Saugh Sikes
High Rigg
Ireshopeburn
New Ho
East Blackdene
High Kitty Crag
Westgate
White Ho
Allen Gill
STANHOPE
Burnhope Moor
Slack Ho
High House
St John's Chapel
Park Ho
River Wear
Thimbleby Hill
Frosterley Cott
Intake Fm
Burnhope Seat 746
Scraith Burn
Ireshope Plains
Hawkwell Head
Daddry Shield
Hill Hos
Brotherlee
Newlandside Fm
Newlands Hall
Glenwhelt
Littlewood Fm
Rogerley Hall
Frosterley
Scaud Hill
Great Stony Hill
Greenlaws Hush
High Wood Meadows
New Close
Snowhope Close
Snape Gate
Bridge End
FROSTERLEY
Ireshope Moor
Catterick Moss
Yad Moss
Harwood Common
Ashgill Head
Grass Hill Fm
Coldberry End
Causeway Hill
Noon Hill
Harthope Moor
Chapel Fell
High Pike 586
Swinside Ho
NORTH
Snowhope Moor
540 Bollihope Carrs
Hill End
Bollihope Ho
White Kirkley
Harvey Hill 320
Harehope
Langdon Head
576 Black Hill
Frog Hall
Grasshill Common
Three Pikes
Chapelfell Top
Swinhopehead Ho
607 Snowhope Hill
Juniper Banks
Bollihope
Harthope Moss
Swinhope Moor
Bollihope Common
Allotment Ho
Viewing Hill
Force Foot
Harwood
Westernhope Moor
Low Black Hill
Wager Head
Langdon Fell
696 Fendrith Hill
Langdon Common
Lingy Hill
Swinhope Head
Dora's Seat
Herdship Fell
PENNINES
Five Pikes 478
Bleak Law
Low End
Church Bowers
Black Hill
Harnisha Hill 589
Raven Seat
Pawlaw Pike 488
North Grain Beck
Pikeston
West Common
Binks Ho
Red Wing
White Mere
Newbiggin Common
Middleton
Common
Touting Hill
Peghorn Lodge
Harwood Beck
B6277
Valence Lodge
Pike Law
South Grain Beck
Hamsterl
Backside Fell
Langdon Beck
Flushiemere Ho
Carrs Hill 601
Black Hill 393
Cow Green
Cow Green Reservoir
Sand Sike
Hunt Hall
LANGDON BECK
Wool Pits Hill
High Beck Head
White Hill 490
Shamberry Flat
Widdybank Fell
New Ho
Watson's Br
Widdy Bank Fm
Forest-in-Teesdale
Ettersgill
Moor Riggs
Broadley's Gate
Moor Ho
Red Grooves Ho
Coldberry
Hardberry Hill 529
492 Islington Hill
Middle End Plantn
CAULDRON SNOUT WATERFALL
Hill End
Cronkley
Ash Hill
Field Head
Club Gill
Monk's Moor
Neighbour Moor Ho
Hamsterley Forest
Thistle Green
White Well Green
HIGH FORCE
Bowlees
BOWLEES VISITOR CENTRE
Stable Edge
Hardberry Fm
Pennington Cott
Pennington Plantn
Grain Beck
PENNINE WAY
Wynch Br
Newbiggin
Snaisgill
Raven Hills 521
Eggleston Common
Merrygill Moss
Cronkley Fell
Noon Hill
Holwick Lodge
Holwick
Danger area
Middle Side
Aukside
Stotley Grange
Cowlake 339
Knotts Plantn
Quarter Burn
Holwick Fell
Holwick Scars
Dent Bank
High Dyke
East Skears
Lang Hurst
Green Fell End
Swinket Mease Rigg
Middleton-in-Teesdale
Howden Moss
Rowton Beck
Park End Wood
Park End
Blackton Head
Woodland Fell
Laverock Hall
Millstone How Hill
Stotley Hall
Long Crag
Rotten Rigg
Crossthwaite Scars
Stone Houses
Mickle Fell
B6282
Egglesburn
Hill Top
Step Ends
River Tees
Crossthwaite Common
Hagworth Hill
Bink Moss
Buck Riggs
Moor Rigg
Lartington
Lathkirk
Ornella Fm
Bogg Ho
Stobgreen Plantn
Danger area
Staple Moss
Harter Fell 481
Bowbank
Mickleton
Eggleston
Low Bink Moss
Lune Moor
EGGLESTON HALL
Keekham Beck Head
Cote Ho
Stoop Hill
Icaron Lodge
Folly Ho
White Ho
High Crag
Lune Forest
Cock Lake 520
East Park
Thringarth
Philip Reed Moss
Close House Crags
Sleight Edge
Wythes Hill
Hollin Side Wood
Pallet Crag Ho
Little Fell 745
Close Ho
Fish Lake
Forest Edge
High Plantn
Stake Hill
West Pasture
Bail Hill
Romaldkirk
Long Grain
Lune Head Moss
Blindgill Moss
Grassholme Reservoir
Rogermoor Fm
Kinninvie
Hargill Br
Wemmergill Hall
Grassholme
Harker Springs
Romaldkirk Moor
Great Wood
Hawkesley Hill
Long Grain Moss
Danger area
Lane Head Fm
Arngill Ho
Wildon Grange
Hunderthwaite
Selset Reservoir
Hunter Ho
Park House Fm
Parrick Ho
Varcop Fell
Ley Seat
River Lune
Three Chimneys
Kelton Ho
Mickleton Moor
Howgill Grange
Wilden Beck
Doe Park
Thwaite Hall
Quarryhouse Fm
High Ho
High Garford
Gill Ho
Gill Field
West End
Hury
Helbeck
Soulgill Edge
Kelton Fell
Kelton Hill
Gill Fm
River Balder
Balder Grange
Cotherstone
Stone Cross
Broad Stone Rigg
Sheep Lair Hill
Black Hill
Hunderthwaite Moor
Briar Dykes
Hury Reservoir
East Briscoe
Corn Park
Booze Wood
Cooper Ho
West Holme Ho
East Holme Ho
Musgrave
Ravensike Rigg
Mawk Hole Moss
Balder Head
Blackton Reservoir
HANNAH'S MEADOW
Fiddler Ho
Willoughby Hall
Crook Beck
Seavy Rigg
Caple Rigg
Clove Lodge
Pitcher Ho
Yawd Sike
Currack Rigg
Scur Beck
Towler Hill
Pattinson's
0 1 2 3 miles
0 1 2 3 4 5 km
231
241
242
222
223
NY
80
50
20

Consett
Leadgate
Annfield Plain
Bridgehill
South Moor
Stanley
The Middles
Craghead
Villa
Pelaw
Chester-le-Street
Waldridge
Edmondsley
Chester Moor
Great Lumley
Lumley Thicks
Allensford
Moorside
Castleside
Delves
Knitsley
Iveston
Maiden Law
Quaking Houses
Burnhope
Holmside
Plawsworth
Nettlesworth
Sacriston
Kimblesworth
Lanchester
Newbiggin
Ornsby Hill
Healeyfield
Waskerley
East Butsfield
West Butsfield
Satley
Cornsay
Cornsay Colliery
Quebec
Esh
Langley Park
Witton Gilbert
Bearpark
Pity Me
Framwellgate Moor
Aykley Heads
Ushaw Moor
Esh Winning
Durham
Gilesgate
Gilesgate Moor
Sherburn
Belmont
Broompark
Nevilles Cross
Elvet Hill
Shincliffe
High Shincliffe
New Brancepeth
Langley Moor
Meadowfield
Brandon
Waterhouses
Hedley Hill
East Hedleyhope
High Stoop
Inkerman
Wolsingham North Moor
Tow Law
Sunniside
Stanley Crook
Brancepeth
Bowburn
Croxdale
Sunderland Bridge
Hett
Tursdale
Wolsingham
Thornley
Billy Row
Roddymoor
Crook
Oakenshaw
Willington
Page Bank
Tudhoe
Helmington Row
Sunnybrow
Fir Tree
Craigside
Byers Green
Spennymoor
Mount Pleasant
Thinford
Cornforth
Howden-le-Wear
Newfield
Middlestone Moor
Ferryhill
Hunwick
High Grange
Bedburn
Hamsterley
Witton-le-Wear
Redford
Binchester Blocks
Westerton
Kirk Merrington
Ferryhill Station
Chilton Lane
Witton Park
Toronto
Escomb
Woodside
New Coundon
Coundon
Leasingthorne
Middlestone
Leeholme
Low Etherley
High Etherley
Phoenix Row
Toft Hill
Etherley Dene
Tindale Crescent
St Helen Auckland
Bishop Auckland
South Church
Coundon Grange
Eldon
Old Eldon
Chilton
Rushyford
Shildon
Newton Aycliffe
Middridge
Woodham
Morley
South Side
Woodland
Copley
Butterknowle
Lane Head
Howle
High Lands
Ramshaw
West Auckland
Evenwood
Cockfield
Evenwood Gate
Bildershaw
Royal Oak
Redworth
Heighington
Aycliffe
Preston-le-Skerne
Houghton-le-Side
Hilton
Bolam
Wackerfield
Raby Castle
Staindrop
Ingleton
Killerby
Summerhouse
Walworth
Cleatlam
Langton
Headlam
Denton
Staindrop
Coatham Mundeville
Brafferton
Beaumont Hill
A68
A689
A691
A690
A688
A167
A6072
A692
A693
A1(M)
D U R H A M
242
243
234
223
224

Houghton-Le-Spring
Seaham
Hetton-le-Hole
Murton
Seaton
Northlea
Burdon
Philadelphia
Newbottle
Grasswell
Sunniside
Burnside
Fence Houses
Bournmoor
New Lambton
Great Lumley
Colliery Row
East Rainton
Middle Rainton
West Rainton
Leamside
Low Moorsley
High Moorsley
Easington Lane
South Hetton
Elemore Vale
Dalton-le-Dale
Cold Hesledon
Dawdon
Parkside
Deneside
West Lea
Hawthorn
Pittington
Carrville
Belmont
Gilesgate
Durham
Sherburn
Sherburn Hill
Littletown
High Haswell
Haswell
Haswell Plough
Easington
Easington Colliery
Little Thorpe
Horden
Peterlee
Shotton Colliery
Shotton
Ludworth
Thornley
Wheatley Hill
Wingate
Blackhall Colliery
Blackhall Rocks
Castle Eden
Hesleden
High Hesleden
Monk Hesleden
Crimdon Park
Shadforth
Shincliffe
High Shincliffe
Old Cassop
Cassop
Bowburn
Old Quarrington
Quarrington Hill
Kelloe
Coxhoe
Station Town
Hutton Henry
Sheraton
Hart
Hart Station
Deaf Hill
Trimdon Colliery
Trimdon
Trimdon Grange
Cornforth
West Cornforth
Ferryhill
Ferryhill Station
Chilton Lane
Mainsforth
Bishop Middleham
Fishburn
Butterwick
Sedgefield
Chilton
Bradbury
Mordon
Elwick
Dalton Piercy
West Park
High Throston
Hartlepool
Middleton
The Headland
Seaton Carew
Rift House
Owton Manor
Brierton
Greatham
Graythorp
Newton Bewley
Wolviston
Billingham
Cowpen Bewley
Haverton Hill
Port Clarence
Wynyard Village
Thorpe Larches
Grindon
Foxton
Stillington
Old Stillington
Whitton
Thorpe Thewles
Carlton
Redmarshall
Bishopton
Great Stainton
Little Stainton
Aycliffe
Preston-le-Skerne
Brafferton
Newton Ketton
Norton
Roseworth
Hardwick
Bishopsgarth
Fairfield
Stockton-on-Tees
Middlesbrough
South Bank
North Ormesby
Mount Pleasant
Portrack
Hartburn
Linthorpe
Marton Grove
Berwick Hills
Pallister
Tees Mouth
Seal Sands
Hartlepool Bay
Parton Rocks
Featherbed Rocks
Liddle Stack
Nose's Pt
Chourdon Pt
Shippersea Bay
Shot Rock
Fox Holes
Horden Pt
North Sands
Seaton Sands
TYNE AND WEAR
DURHAM
HARTLEPOOL
DARLINGTON
STOCKTON-ON-TEES
A19
A1(M)
A181
A182
A179
A689
A177
A688
A167
A178
A1185
243
233
224
225
0 1 2 3 miles
0 1 2 3 4 5 km

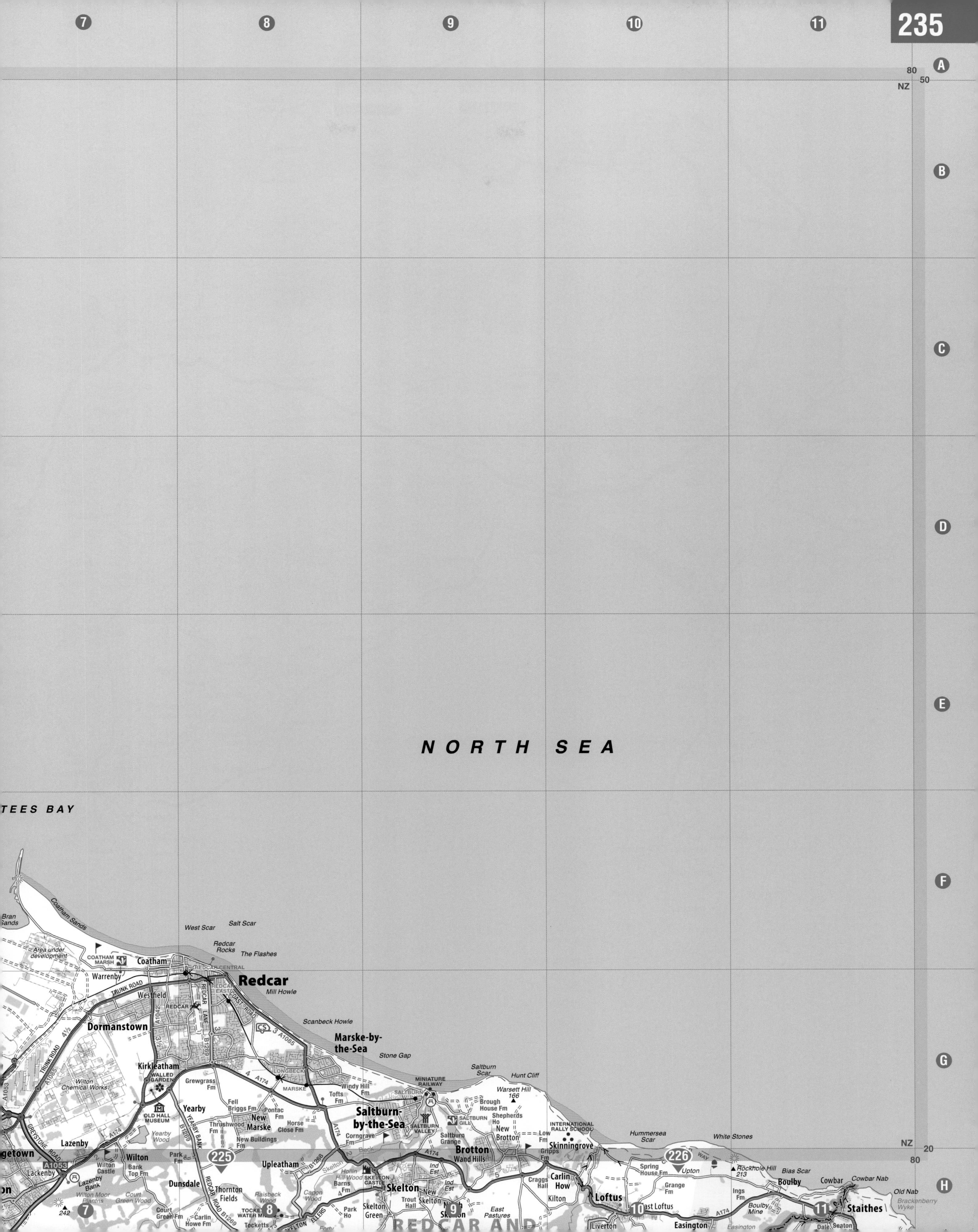
7
8
9
10
11
A
B
C
D
E
F
G
H
NORTH SEA
TEES BAY
Coatham Sands
West Scar
Salt Scar
Redcar Rocks
The Flashes
Coatham
Warrenby
Redcar
Mill Howle
Westfield
Dormanstown
Scanbeck Howle
Marske-by-the-Sea
Stone Gap
Kirkleatham
Wilton Chemical Works
Saltburn Scar
Hunt Cliff
Warsett Hill 166
Yearby
New Marske
Saltburn-by-the-Sea
Lazenby
Wilton
Brotton
Skinningrove
Hummersea Scar
White Stones
Upleatham
Dunsdale
Skelton
Carlin How
Loftus
Boulby
Cowbar
Cowbar Nab
Staithes
Easington
East Loftus
Kilton
225
226
REDCAR AND
NZ
80
50
20

Ballantrae Bay
Ballantrae
Garleffin
Heronsford
Glen Tig
Cosses
Balkissock
Water of Tig
Barrhill
Cairnlea
Laggan
Eldrick
Black Clauchrie
Moan
Palgowan
G A L L O W A Y
Glentrool Forest
Loch Enoch
Loch Neldricken
Loch Valley
Silver Flowe
Bruce's Stone
Glen Trool Lodge
Trool
Gleanhead
Loch Trool
Glentrool Visitor Centre
Glentrool Village
Cairnderry
Downan Pt.
Downan
Glenapp Castle
Smyrton
Auchencrosh
Arecleoch Forest
244
245
Drumlamford Loch
Dornal
Dalnaw
Bargrennan
Loch Dee
F O R E S T
716
Lamachan Hill
D U M F R I
P A R K
G A L L O W
Belfast
Larne
Milleur Pt.
Mark
Glen App
439
Beneraird
Lagafater Lodge
Chirmorrie
Miltonise
Loch Dornal
Loch Ochiltree
Clachaneasy
Loch Maberry
Polbae
Loch Middle
Kirroughtree Forest
Craig Airie Fell
Loch Derry
287
257
Laggangairn Standing Stones
Knowe
Wood of Cree
Wild Goat Park
Auchinleck
353
Corsewall Pt.
Barnhills
North Cairn
Portencalzie
Mahaar
Corsewall
Kirkcolm
Loch Connell
Ervie
Low Salchrie
Leswalt
Craigencross
Cairnryan
Bankhead
The Wig
LOCH RYAN
Penwhirn Res.
Main Water of Luce
Cross Water of Luce
Braid Fell
High Eldrig
Artfield Fell
244
Carseriggan
Penninghame Forest
Glenrazie
Boreland
Cumloden
Penkiln Burn
Palnure Burn
Barfad
Challoch
Minnigaff
Creebridge
Bargaly
Newton Stewart
Kirroughtree Visitor Centre
Stronord
Palnure
Balmurrie
Black Loch
Balminnoch
Loch Heron
Loch Ronald
213
Shennanton Ho.
Shennanton
Blackpark
Benfield
New Luce
Southern Upland Way
Auchmantle
Innermessan
Lochinch Castle
Black Loch
Castle Kennedy Gardens
White Loch
Drumphail
205
Airyligg
Tarf Water
Barraer
123
Carty Port
Baltersan
Glenstockadale
Auchnotteroch
Stranraer
Castle of St John Visitor Centre
Stranraer Museum
Aird
Castle Kennedy
Knockglass
Soulseat Loch
Mark
Glenwhan Gardens
Dunragit
Whitecairn
Balmesh
Glenluce Abbey
Glenluce
Carscreugh
Dergoals
Craighlaw Mains
Kirkcowan
Dernaglar Loch
Knock Moss
High Mindork
Spittal
Causeway End
Carsegowan
Grange of Cree
Creetown
Torhousemuir
Torhouse Stone Circle
Bladnoch
Wigtown
Wigtown Sands
Scotland's Book Town
Carsluith
T H E R H I N S
Black Hd.
Dunskey Ho.
Lochans
182
Colfin
Pinminnoch
Droughduil
Torrs Warren
Castle of Park
Milton
Stairhaven
Whitefield Loch
131
Fell Loch
Castle Loch
T H E M A C H A R S
Portpatrick
Awhirk
Stoneykirk
Luce Sands
Auchenmalg
Drumwalt
Mochrum Loch
Culmazie
Visitor Centre
Mains of Baldoon
Baldoon Sands
Braehead
Kirkinner
Port of Spittal Bay
Kildonan
Auchenmalg Bay
Culshabbin
Airlies
Alticry
197
Loch Head
Barrachan
Whauphill
Culscadden
Cairngarroch
Cairngarroch Bay
Kirkmadrine Stones
Sandhead
Sandhead Bay
Money Hd.
Chapel Finian
Elrig
Mote of Druchtag
75
Mochrum
Sorbie
Garlieston
Clachanmore
Hole Stone Bay
West Ardwell
Ardwell
Ardwell Mains
Chapel Rossan Bay
Ardwell Pt.
Milton Pt.
Airyhassen
Drumtroddan
Drummoddie
Drumtroddan Stones
Galloway Gardens
Logan Mains
Logan Botanic Garden
Balgowan Pt.
L U C E B A Y
Port William
Monreith Mains
Moor of Ravenstone
Castlewigg
Cults
Cruggleton
Mull of Logan
Logan Fish Pond Marine Life Centre
Port Nessock or Port Logan Bay
Port Logan
Barsalloch Pt.
Monreith
Bishopton
Chapel Outon
Priory and Museum
Whithorn
Whithorn Trust Discovery Centre
Cairnywellan Hd.
Monreith Bay
Glasserton
Clanyard Bay
Low Clanyard
Laggantalluch Hd.
Kirkmaiden
Drummore
164
Damnaglaur
Cailliness Pt.
146
Fell of Carleton
St Ninian's Cave
Kidsdale
Tonderghie
Isle of Whithorn
Port Castle Bay
Cutcloy
Burrow Head
Crammag Hd.
Maryport
Cairngaan
Mull of Galloway
Port Kemin
MULL OF GALLOWAY
A77
A751
A75
A718
A714
A712
A747
A716
A746
B7027
B738
B798
B7043
B7077
B7084
B7042
B7065
B7041
B733
B735
B7052
B7005
B7085
B7004
B7021
B7063
NX
80
00
20
0 2 4 6 miles
0 2 4 6 8 10 km
A B C D E F G H
1 2 3 4 5 6

246
247
238
228
219

DUMFRIES AND GALLOWAY
SOLWAY FIRTH
NITH ESTUARY
Blackshaw Bank
Lockerbie
Halleaths
Heck
Hightae
Smallholm
Greenhill
Blackford
Castlemilk
Kettleholm
Middleshaw
Kirkwood
Dalton
Ecclefechan
Hoddomcross
Hoddom Mains
Burnswark
Middlebie
Kirtlebridge
Eaglesfield
Brydekirk
Creca
Charlesfield
Annan
Welldale
Shawhill
Newbie
Watchill
Dornock
Powfoot
Cummertrees
Ruthwell
Clarencefield
Plans
Carrutherstown
Langdyke
Mouswald
Cleughbrae
Collin
Greenlea
Woodside
Elizafield
Racks
Torthorwald
Horseholm
Longbridgemuir
Bankend
Glencaple
Kelton
Shearington
Blackshaw
Eastpark
Bowhouse
Greystone
The Grove
Georgetown
Overton
Carsethorn
Bowness-on-Solway
Cardurnock
Anthorn
Whitrigg
Kirkbride
Newton Arlosh
Skinburness
Silloth
Calvo
Seaville
Causewayhead
Greenrow
Blitterlees
Kingside Hill
Abbey Town
Kelsick
Dundraw
Waverbridge
Beckfoot
Pelutho
Highlaws
Newtown
Blencogo
CAERLAVEROCK CASTLE
WILDFOWL & WETLAND CENTRE
SAVINGS BANKS MUSEUM
THOMAS CARLYLE'S BIRTHPLACE
RUTHWELL CROSS
LOCHMABEN CASTLE
RAMMERSCALES
BURNSWARK HILL FORT
BIRRENS FORT
CAMPFIELD MARSH
BOWNESS ON SOLWAY
SOUTH SOLWAY MOSSES
THORNHILL MOSS & MEADOW
ARBIGLAND GARDENS
JOHN PAUL JONES COTTAGE MUSEUM
DUMFRIES & GALLOWAY AVIATION MUS
A75
A74(M)
A701
A709
A780
B725
B724
B723
B7020
B7076
B722
B6357
B5300
B5301
B5302
B5307
237
248
228
229
0 1 2 3 miles
0 1 2 3 4 5 km

Kirtleton
Crosslands
West Linnbridgeford
Craigs
Hotts
High Muir
Gowd Muir
Collin Hags 255
Bloch Fm
Kerr Height
Leaheads Hill
Viewy Knowe
Kerr
Allfornought Hill
Outer Hill
March Cottage
Allfornought
Solwaybank
Wattaman
Barnglies
Tomshielburn
Tarcoon
Chapelhills
Mossknowe
Newbie
Greenrigg
High Stenries
Kennedy's Corner
Bell's Flow
Bogrie
Bogra
Craigshaws
Outerland
The Forest
Springkell
Branteth
Bellstown
Burnfoot
Cadgillside
Hillhead Fm
Cadgill Wood
Parkhead
Milltown
Scotland Gate
Nethertown
Evertown
Canonbie
Hollows
Loophill
Enthorn
Claygate
Byreburnside
Gilnockie Tower
Hagg Hill
Irvine Ho
Mumbie Cottages
Tarrasfoot Hill
Burian Hill
Greenburn
Outer Woodhead
Orchard
Upper Millsteads
Under Millsteads
Hardenside
The Hill
Albierig
Tinnisburn Forest
Green Knowe
Greena Hill
Harelaw Pike
Harelaw Mill
Barrascrofts
Harelawhill
Archerbeck
Airlee
Rowanburn
Esk Bank
Old Hall
Nook
Kingfield Ho
Liddel Lodge
Bushfield
Stonegarthside Hall
Longcleughside
Crookburn Hill
Baileyhead
Arthur Seat
Lads Lodge
Liddel Park
KIELDER FOREST PARK
Chamot Hill
Bartle's Hill
Sheala Hill
Crossings
Sleetbeck
Catlowdy
Warwicksland
Chapel Hill
Beyond the Moss
Beyond-the-Wood
Dykehead
Riggcroft
Riddings Fm
Hilltop
Barns
Woodhouselees
Riddingshill
High Plains
Scuggate
Scugg Fm
Redgate Head
Shawstown
Hope's Ho
Raeburn
Trough Head
Wakey Hill
Nether Hill
Kinkry Hill
Roadhead
Roan Fm
Haggbeck
Westfield Ho
High Parkfoot
Friar Hill
Selbystown
Lynecrook
Kays Bank
Woodhouselees Plantn
Todhillwood
Craw's Knowe
Cadgillfoot
Cubbyhill
Englishtown
Scots Dyke
Scotsdike
Logan Mains
Chapelknowe
Gillshaw Wood
Gillshaw Flow
Stubby Knowe
Campers' Corner
Frankstown Fm
Corries Mill
Southwoodhead
Dunskellyrig
Merkland Cross
Fauldingcleugh
Nether Woodhouse
Hayfield
Raeburn Flow
Raeburnfoot
Raeburn
Milligansbush
Batenbush
Silverhill Wood
Netherby
Livingstone Ho
Moat
Bruntons Hill
Carwinley
The Green
Netherhirst
Todhillrigg Fm
Easton
Park Ho
Park Rigg
Skyehead
Low Luckens
Gibstown
Jenkinstown
New Pallyards
Shankhill
Lynedale
Harper Hill
Stapleton
Oakshaw Hill
Laws Hall
Cleughfoot Wood
Whiteclosergigg
Patties Hill
Newton
Bruce's Cave
Kirkpatrick-Fleming
Hollee
Broats
Mossknowe
Williamsfield
Valley
Aitchisons Bank
Slackbraes Wood
Low Plains
Stealandsburn
White Close
Calvertsholm
Old Blacksmiths Shop Centre
Gretna Green Services
Solway Moss
Solway Moss 1542
DLO Smalmstown
Smalmstown
Gap Wood
Sandbed
Longtown
Jackson Rigg
Wellknowe Rigg
Brackenhill Rigg
High Dubwath
Barracks
Bolton Fell
Boltonfellend
Prior Rigg
Prior House
Mossedge
Hall Hills
Todholes
Nutberry Moss
Riggheads
Gretna Green
Stonehouse
Springfield
Mill Hill
Fauld Mill
Brisco Hill
Black Snib
Kirklinton Hall
Appleby Ho
Henry's Hill
Cocklet Hill Fm
White Moss
Gretna
Caledonia Park
Rigg
Irvington
Green
Old Graitney
DLO Longtown
River Esk
Francismoor Wood
Kirklinton
Hethersgill
Lonning Park
Leaps
Walton Moss
Prior Rigg
Broomhill Moss
Walton Moss
Bush-on-Lyne Fm
East Cliff
Hetherside
Kirklinton Park
Westhills Moss
Redkirk Pt
Sarkfoot Pt
Mossband Hall
Burnfoot
Hopesike Woods
Hornickhill
Sandysike
Alstonby Hall
Clift Ho
Willow Hill
Willow Bank
Skitby
Smithfield
Hill Ho
Brown Dyke
West Knowe
Breaks Moss
Browhouses
Mossband Hall Marsh
Metal Bridge
Justicetown
Westlinton
Alstonby Grange
Standingstone Rigg
Brown Rigg
Highberries
Blackhouse Plantns
Torduff Pt
Channel of River Esk
Rockliffe Marsh
Far Gulf
Near Gulf
Halltown
Wether Hill
Young's Close
Hespin Wood
Moor Ho
Ross Castle
Todhills
Todhills Rest Area
Rockcliffe Moss
Dyke Nook
Scaleby Moss
The Nooks
Brightenflat
Hall Flatt
Scalebyhill
Scaleby
Fordsyke
Barclose
Woodhead
Moorcock Plantn
Bullerskie
Laversdale
Morrell Hill
Seat Hill Fm
Kylesyke Hill
Heads Wood
The Beck Fm
Newtown
Rockcliffe Cross
Castletown House
Blackford
Wide open Dykes
Longpark
Scaleby Castle
Burghmarsh Pt
CUMBRIA
River Eden
Old Sandsfield
New Sandsfield
Casson Dyke Fm
Rockcliffe
Harker
Ind Est
Houghton Ho
Green Acres
High Knells
Dykeside
Brunstock Beck
Walldub
Knells Ho
Walby
Wall Head
White Moss
Hadrian's Wall Path
Solway Aviation Mus
Irthington
Red Hills
Old Church Fm
Middle Fm
Burgh Marsh
Bankend
Cargohill
Harker Grange
Walby Farm Park
Vallum (course of)
Stanegate (course of)
Carlisle Lake District Airport
Beanlands Park
Rulehome Br
Drumburgh
Watch Hill
North End
Burgh by Sands
Hadrian's Wall (course of)
Beaumont
St Ann's Well
Cargo
Bus Pk
Kingstown
Houghton
Brunstock
Low Crosby
Crosby-on-Eden
Watch Cross
Park Barns
Easton
Boustead Hill
Longburgh
West End
Monkhill Lough
Monkhill
Kirkandrews on Eden
Grinsdale
Kingmoor Ho
Kingstown Road
Tarraby
Park Broom
Warwick Holme
Linstock
Holme Ends
The Hall
Bank Head
Newby East
Edmond Castle
Western Ridge
Drumburgh Moss
Fingland Rigg
Farhill
Hill Fm
Hosket Hill
Etterby
Belah
Edentown
Stanwix
Knowefield
Moor Ho
Whiteclosegate
Holme Gate
Little Corby
Corby Hill
Toppin Castle
Fingland Moss
Fingland
Thurstonfield
Moorhouse
Stainton
Willow Holme
Carlisle Castle
Rickerby
Aglionby
Warwick on Eden
Warwick Bridge
Finglandrigg Woods
Longrigg
Ploughlands
Kirkbampton
Cumberland Bird of Prey Centre
Thurstonfield Lough
Cobble Hall
Moorhouse Road
Ind Est
Tullie House Museum & Art Gallery
Brunton Park
Warwick Road
Moorhouse Hall
Warwick Moor Wood
Corry Ho
Burnrigg
Allenwood
Stockdale Hall
How
Cote
Fenton
Fenton Lane Head
Windmill Ho
Oughterby
Woodlands
Belle Vue
Newtown
Carlisle
Botcherby
Scotby Ho
Wetheral Plain
Low Wood
Broadwath
Heads Nook
Little Bampton
Prior Rigg
Little Orton
Town Walls
Denton Holme
Scotby
Gleneairn Mill
Faugh
Westfield Ho
Lanshaw Ho
Bampton Beck
Quarry Gill
Park Ho
Flat
Bank Ho
Orton Moss
Suttle Ho
Morton
Wigton Road
Dalston Road
Longsowerby
London Road
Currock
Harraby
Garlands
Orchard Ho
Scotby Shield
Wetheral
Great Corby
Corby Castle
Moss Knowe
Park Ho
Aikton Ho
Great Orton
Fisher Gill
Red Ho
Newby West
Upperby
Gladsmuir
Birk Hill
Aikton
Roblaw Hall
Wiggonby
Fallow Field
Orton Park Fm
Newby Cross
Cummersdale
Blackwell
Carleton
Wetheral Pasture
High Wood
Cumwhinton
Cote Ho
Morley Hill
Whitehea
Gamelsby
River Wampool
Down Hall
Thornby
Wiggon Rigg
Woodhouses
Orton Rigg
Baldwinholme
Orton Grange Fm
Lingyclose Head
Sowerby Wood
Carlisle
High Woodbank
River Petteril
Scugger Ho
Brisco
Brisco Hill
Shield Head
Clint Head Fm
Cumwhitton
Wrayside
Hardcake Hall
High Whinnow
Greyrigg Ho
Parton
Moorhouse
Moorhouse Hall
Nealhouse
Wood Fm
Cardewlees
Blackhall Wood
Floshes
Durdar
Springfield Fm
Eden Banks
Low Cotehill
Moorthwaite Moss
Dockray Rigg
Low Whinnow
Bankend
Moorend
Dalston
River Caldew
Oakland Ho
Burthwaite Hill
Newbiggin Hall
Knott Hill
Dockray Hall
Micklethwaite
Crofton
Thursby
Flanders
Hillhouse Nook
Durdar Ho
Carleton Ho
Cotehill
Standingstone
Spittal
West End
Evening Hill
Cardew Hall
Nooklane Foot
Pow Bank
Ratten Row
Stone Raise
Burthwaite
Wragmire Ho
Warathwaite Head
Fishgarth Wood
Bridge Ho
Greenwood Ho
West Woodside
West Curthwaite
Cardew Lodge
Cardew
Green Head
Wragmire Moss
Stoney Wath Fm
Hazel Head
Moorthwaite Lough
Cumdivock
Buckabank
Bridge End
Unthank
Wray
Wreay Hall
High Stand Plantn
Wigton
Kirkland
Ghyll Head Fm
Chalkfoot
East Curthwaite
Nook
Sprunston
Bankdale Fm
Foulbridge
Petteril Crook's Mill
Ivy Cottage
Lowthian Gill
Hawksdale
Broomfield
Jacob's Gill
Speet

Kershope Forest
Bewcastle Fell
Black Knowe 492
Rushy Knowe
Black Cleugh
Allerybank
Sighty Crag 518
Horse Head
Black Knors 248
Whitelyne Common
Long Bar
Smuggy's Pike
Long Crags
Hopehouse
Baileyhead
Crookburn Hill
Black Stantling
The Shanks
Kielder Mires
Clintburn
The Flatt
Slaty Crag
Long Crag 456
Greyfell Common
Lowe Bush
Paddaburn
Muckle Samuel's Crags
Watch Rigg
Tarn Beck
Irthing Head
Little Dodd Hill
High Cap Edge
Arthur Seat
Holmehead
Blackpool Gate
Crew Crag
Gaylock Hill
Whitehill
Green
Crew Moor
Whiteside End
Cammock Rigg
White Brae
Breakshaw Hill
Churnsike Lodge
Felecia Crags
Round Hill 310
Crossings
Oakshaw Ford
Bankhead
Park Head
Grey Hill
Bullcleugh Gate
Blackrigg Foot
Danger area
Shank End
Wreay Hill
Great Tongue Rigg
Round Top 325
Wark
Sleetbeck
Shawhead
Brownhill
Rawney
New Ho
Butterburn Flow
Gowany Knowe
Spy Rigg
Long Rigg
West Cleugh
Heather Ho
Park
Peel o'Hill
Borderrigg
Leafy Rigg
Hen Hill
Great Watch Hill
Haining
Kinkry Hill
Roughsike
Ann's Hill
Bewcastle
Barron's Pike
Roadhead
Kirkbeckstown
Noblestown
Scotstown
Kilnstown
Kirk Beck
Shopford
Gilbert's Hill
Greymare Hill
Whipper Slack
Blackshaws Sike
Lampert
Butterburn
Gowk Bank
Westfield Ho
High Parkfoot
Jock's Hill
Butterburn Hill
Cheeseburn Hill
Bushley Bank
Side Fell
Hen Hill
Rough Sike
Deer Hill
Black Fell
Grindon Green
Lynecrook
Kays Bank
Bellbank
Birk Bush
Cocklett Rigg
Luke's Ho
Collin Bank
Green Knowe
Low King Hill
Jerrycalf Rigg
Berry Hill
Spadeadam Forest
Tip Hill
Great Buckster
The Show
Low Park
The Beacon 310
Gillalees Beacon
White Rigg
Standingstone Rigg
Gavelock Hill
Hopealone
Robinrock Flothers
Harper Hill
Stapleton
Allergarth
Askerton Park
Green Rigg
Middle Shield Rigg
Kingturn Rigg
Rashbush Rigg
Crowrigg Sike
Wileysike
Bell's Braes
Hugh's Hill
Patties Hill
Low Park
Mollen Wood
Parkgate Cotts
Spadeadam Fm
Dumblar Rigg
Forster's Hill
Peat Rigg
White Rigg
Burn Divot
White Close
High Green Hill
Rinnion Hills
Ash Moss
Long Moss
River Irthing
Rushey Hill
Black Rigg
Thirlwall Common (North Side)
Whiteside
Wall Shield
Benkshill
Highstead Ash
Jamie's Hill Sike
Watch Hill
Moss Peteral
Bolton Fell
Kirkcambeck
Gallowberry
Palmer Hill
Waterhead Common
Popping Stone
Wardrew Fm
Seed Rigg
Benks Hill
Ventners Hall
Edges Green
Cowburn Rigg
Swallow Crags
CUMBRIA
Lees Hill
West Hall
Kingbridge Ford Br
Tweedy Hill
Gilsland Spa
War Carr
Cairny Croft
Hangingshields Rigg
Chesters Pike
Cleughfoot
Sook Hill
Well Ho
Leaps Rigg
Barns
Hill Ho
Knorren Beck
B6318
Barron House
Gilsland
Burnt Walls
Low Old Shields
Hadrian's Wall
Hadrian's Wall (Course of)
Cawfields Milecastle
Pennine Way
Vallum (Course of)
Broomhill Moss
Walton Moss
Spout Bank
Swaites
Park Nook
Craigsyke Ford
Miller Hill
Midgeholme Moss
Willowford Bridge Abutment
Harrow's Scar Milecastle
Birdoswald (Camboglanna) Roman Fort
Poltross Burn Milecastle
Gap
Walltown
Cockmount Hill
Haltwhistle Common
Milestone Ho
Stanegate (Course of)
Hainings Ho
White Hill
Walton Woodhead
Allieshaw Rigg
Leahill Turret
Kiln Hill
Birdoswald
Greenhead
Fell End
Breaks Moss
Hill Head
Walton Wood
Craig Hill
High Ho
Denton Mains
Thirlwall Castle
Wardoughan
Edge Hill
Lees Hall
Low Rigg
Blackhouse Plantns
Garthside
Hare Hill
Banks
Bank's East Turret
Upper Denton
Gapshield
The College Fm
Blenkinsopp Hall
Haltwhistle
Hollin Crags
Town Foot
Common Ho
Melkridge
Walton
Howgill
Banks Ho
Nook
Mains Rigg
Low Ho
Low House Fm
Morrell Hill
Low Wall
Lanercost
Lanercost Priory
Trywell Lodge
Thirlwall Common (South Side)
Todholes
Blenkinsopp Common
Hole Ho
Haltwhistle Ind Est
B6322
A69
Kylesyke Hill
Heads Wood
Kellwood
Burtholme
St Mary's Vale
Denton Hall
Low Broom Hill
Lodges
Hill Head
Cross Bank
Bellister Castle
Sandyford Rigg
Plenmeller
East Unthank
Unthank Hall
The Beck Fm
River Irthing
Low Row
Black Rigg
Wain Rigg
Wydon Eals
Newtown
Cotehill Fm
Naworth Park
Denton Foot
Birch Craig
Cleugh Head
Denton Ho
Denton Fell
Featherstone Common
Broomhouse
Warren Ho
Howden Burn
Irthington
Red Hills
Kirby Moor
Quarrybeck Ho
Low Houses
Glencune Burn
Hartleyburn Common (North Side)
Cross Rigg
Bridge End
Broomhouse Common
Bridle Green
Blackcleugh Rigg
Brampton
Old Church Fm
Irthing Ind Est
Miltonrigg Wood
Scarrow Hill
Greentarn Rigg
Whamoss Rigg
Peat Gate
Park Village
Plenmeller Common
Middle Fm
Beanlands Park
Ruleholme
A689
Aaron's Town
Milton Hall
Milton Hill
Milton
Kirkhouse
Moss Ho
Greenside Rigg
Follysyke Cotts
Cocklit Hill
Byers Hall
Rowfoot
Ramshaw Fell
Cairn End
Park Barns
Wood's Hill
Low Geltbridge
Gelt Woods
Talkin Tarn
Farlam
Boon Hill
Hallbankgate
Highfell
Clesketts
Geltsdale
Tarnhouse Rigg
Tindale
Haining Burn
Midgeholme
Halton Lea Gate
Hill Ho
Clover Hill
Burn Ho
Lambley Fm
Wood Houses
Coanwood
Hargill Ho
Todhillwood
Peat Hill
Edmond Castle
Western Ridge
Hayton
Talkin
Turkey Hall
Forest Head
Whinney Fell
Bishop Hill
Bruthwaite Forest
Tindale Fells
Tindale Tarn
Black Burn
Byers Fell
Lambley Common
Lambley
Hag Wood
Quarry Ho
Stonehouse
Burn Ho
Garbutt Hill
Wolf Hills
Laws Fell
Hayton Castle
Street Ho
How
Cote Hill
Greenwell
Chapel Ho
Hill Ho
Talkin Fell 381
Talkin Head Fm
Kelky Fell
Brown Fell
Cold Fell 621
Blackburn Head
Hartleyburn Common (South Side)
Haltonlea Fell
Byers Pike 458
Butt of Blackburn
Tows Bank
Whitwham
Coanwood Common
Ashholme Common
Brown Rigg
Redscar Burn
Fenton
Allenwood
Stockdale Hall
Heads Nook
Fenton Lane Head
Whin Hill
Ring Gate
Castle Carrock
Garth Head
River Gelt
Simmerson Hill
Larchet Hill
Eals
Knowe Head
Wallace's Crags
Eals Fell
Dun Hill
Blaeberry
Faugh
Hayton Moss
Tarn Lodge
Oaktree Hall
Long Dyke
Glencairn Mill
Moss Knowe
Park Ho
Knotts Wood
Tarnmonath Fell
Castle Carrock Fell
Glendue Fell
Faugh Cleugh
Side Ho
Knarsdale Hall
The Bog
Snope Common
Pike Rigg
Mainsrigg Fell
Nixon Head
Geltsdale Ho
Binney Bank
Great Blacklaw Hill 595
Thinhope Burn
Knarsdale
Williamston Common
Low Bradshaw Hill
Whitfield Moor
Whitfield Law
King's Forest of Geltsdale
PENNINE
NORTH
Town Green
Longdyke Fm
Albyfield
Morley Hill
Whitehead Hill
Black Dub
482
Cardunneth Pike
Middle Top
West Dun Hill
Black Hill
Knarsdale Forest
Slaggyford
Aules Hill
Barhaugh Common
Dewley Fell
Cumwhitton
Turnberry Ho
Carlatton Mill
Moorthwaite Moss
Chapel Well
Eden Banks
Cumrew Fell
Geltsdale Middle
New Water
Three Pikes 585
Hartchyside
Bertram Hill
Far Ho
Knar Burn
Shawhead
Dewley Field
Willyshaw Rigg 497
Knarsdale Common
Ayle Common
Long Cross
Cumrew
Hornsby
Butt Hill
Gelt Burn
Lintley
Far Town
Fishgarth Wood
Far Hornsby Gate
Gateshaw Mill
Newbiggin
Newbiggin Fell
Blotting Raise 591
Green Hill
Thornhope Fell
Kirkhaugh
Ayle
Clarghyll Hall
Croglin Fell
The Combs
Broad Mea
High Shield
Castle Nook
Whitlow Castle
Kirkside Wood
South Tynedale Railway
White Ho
Newshield Moss
Lawson Hill
Cairnhead
Sumburgh
Grey Nag
High Stand Plantn
A686
B6413
B6318
0 1 2 3 miles
0 1 2 3 4 5 km
230
231
239
250

Dun's Pike
Watson's Walls
Shillington Common
Ealinghamrigg Common
Ealingham Rigg
Redesmouth
Countesspark Wood
Fell
Green Rigg
Lough Hill
Cowstand Hill
Birney Hill
Sweethope Crags
Cairnglastenhope
Pundershaw
Stone Ho
Shitlington Crags
Anton Hill
Waterfalls
White Ho
Great Bavington
Merry Shiels
Greatlaw
Shitlington Hall
Bridge Ho
Lee Hall Fm
Lee Hall
Tone Hall
Lowshield Green
Carrycoats Hall
Low Fell
Quarry Ho
Newonstead Fm
Bavington Hill Head
White Ho
Pundershaw Burn
Esp Hill
Esp Mill
High Carry Ho
River North Tyne
Pitland Hills
Brier Hill
Low Carry Ho
Rushey Law
Colt Crag Reservoir
Colt Crag
Thockrington
Little Bavington
Bavington Hall
Camstone Rigg
Watergate Moor
Manor Fm
Warksfield Head
South Fm
Rubbingstob Hill
Thockrington Crags
Short Knowes
Moss Barns
Blackaburn
Crossridge
Birtley
Rouchester Fm
Folly Moss
Bavington Mount
Leadgate
Gold Island
Longstrother
Pasture Ho
Blackaburn
Birk Hill
Horneystead
The Ash
Threpwood Hill
Dinley Hill
Gunnerton Fell
Little Swinburne
Kirkheaton Wind Farm
Harelaw
Windy Edge
The Barnes
Woodley Shield
Wark
Comogan Fm
Parkhouse Fm
Hallington Reservoir
Hallington High Fm
White Hill
Whygate
Warks Haugh
Pit Ho
Barrasford Park
Fell Ho
Hallington
Coldcotes
Stonehaugh
Sadbury Hill
High Moralee
Low Moralee
Blackhill Fm
Mallowburn Cottages
Great Swinburne
Whiteside Law
Moatlaw
Willowbog
Broadpool Common
Standard Hill
Bleaklaw
Park End
Steward's Ho
Green's Fell
Swinburne Castle
Colwell
Liddell Hall
Hallington New Ho
Coldcotes Hill
Lyndhurst
Short Moor
Gunnerton
Middleburn
Black Rigg
Coalcleugh
Burnmouth Cotts
N O R T H U M B E R L A N D
Shepherdshield
Allgood Fm
Fell Lane Fm
Wood Hall Fm
Well Ho
High Well Ho
Ryal
Haggle Rigg
Red Burn
Burn Ho
Nunwick Mill
Black Law
Simonburn
Ellwood Ho
Barrasford
Barrasford Green
Bingfield East Quarter
Long Edge
Hopeshield Burn
Hall Barns
Fairshaw Fm
Haughton Castle
Middle Fm
Beaumont Ho
New Bingfield
Bingfield Eastside
Bell Crags
Townshield Bank
Simonburn Common
Stooprigg
Greenhaugh
Uppertown
Wester Hall
Edge Ho
Byreshaw Hill
Bellcrag Flow
Haughton Common
Crook Burn
Banno Crags
Sharpley
Haughton Pasture
Chollerton
Low Errington
Bingfield
Todridge Fell
Long Rigg
Well Rigg
Long Crag
Cockplay
Haughton Mains
Errington Red Ho
Todridge
Shellbraes
Crow Crags
Hemmel Rigg
Teppermoor
Rye Hill
Lincoln Hill
Humshaugh
Keepwick Fm
Halleypike Lough
Black Carts Turret
Carrawburgh Temple of Mithras
Chollerford
Walwick
Cocklaw
Rose's Bower
Sweet Rigg
Queen's Crags
Hadrian's Wall (course of)
Vallum (course of)
Hadrian's Wall Path
Walwick Fell
Beukley
The Whiggs
Great Whittington
Stonefolds
Sewingshields Crags
Wall Turrets & Milecastle
Old Repeater Station
Brown Moor
Torney's Fell
Chesters Museum
Chesters (Cilurnum) Roman Fort
Low Brunton
Grottington Fm
Broomlee Lough
Greenlee Lough
Lane Ho
Brunton Bank
Errington Hill Head
Greenlee Lough
Housesteads (Vercovicium) Roman Fort & Museum
Middle Ho
Howden Hill
Frankham Fell
Brunton Turret
Planetrees Roman Wall
Hill Head
Little Whittington
Bonnyrigg Hall
Hotbank Crags
Cowey Sike
Settlingstones
Wall
Halton Red House
Crag Lough
Hadrian's Wall
Grindon Mill Hills
Grindon Hill
Stonecroft Ho
Newbrough Lodge
Frankham
Written Crag
Codlaw Hill
Wall Fen Fm
Port Gate
Winshields Milecastle
Grindon Lough
Settlingstones
Fourstones
River North Tyne
Front Street
Cross Bank
East Wood
Stagshaw Bank
Carr Houses
Steel Rigg
Bradley Hall
Grandy's Knowe
Newbrough
Stagshaw High Ho
Halton
Hindshield
Fell Cott
Fern Hill Fm
The Sill at Hadrian's Wall
Muckle Moss
Honeycrook Burn
High Warden
Nether Warden
Carr Hill
Black Hill
Holly Hall
Long Stone
Thorngrafton Common
Whinnetley Moss
Haydon Fell
Allerwash Hall
Woodshield Fm
Wharmley
Greenshaw Plain
Warden
Salmonswell Fm
Stagshaw Ho
Chantry Fm
Chesterholm (Vindolanda) Roman Fort & Museum
High Ho
East Mill Hills
Acomb
Beaufront Hill Head
Sandhoe
Aydon Castle
Birkshaw
Westley Bank
Bridge End
Broom Park
The Riding
Shawwell Ho
Aydon
Westend Town
Thorngrafton
Whitechapel Hill
Prior Ho
Chesterwood
Bush Fm
Glendue
Ind Est
Oakwood
Beaufront Castle
Hampstead
Aydon Road
Henshaw
Bardon Mill
Haydon Bridge
Wood Hall
Hackford Fm
Tyne Green
Anick
Anick Grange
Tow House
Lipwood Hall
Hill Ho
High Wood
Bridge End
Tyne Green
Corstopitum Roman Station
Redburn
Crow Hall
South Tyne
Lipwood Well
Haydon Bridge
Lowe's Fell
Low Gate
Hexham
Hexham Abbey
Wide Haugh
Corbridge
Thornbrough
High Barns
River
Ellfoot Ho
Moot Hall
Delegate Hall
Border History Mus
Cock Wood
Dilston Park
Dilston Physic Gdn
Howden Dene
High Barn
Beltingham
Ridley
Elrington
Bagraw Fm
Breckon Hill
Dilston
Haughstrother Wood
Wool Ho
Burn Ho
Allen Banks & Staward Gorge
West Land Ends
Threepwood
Benson's Fell
Oakerland
Swallowship Hill
High Town
West Fell
Prospect Hill
Grey Court
Vauce Wood
Blackhall Plantns
Plover Hill
Black Ho
Sunnyside
Riding Mill
Farrow Shields
Ridley Common
Plankey Mill
Yellow Rigg
Blackhill Fm
Hexham
Peterel Field
Lamb Shield
Linnels
Temperley Grange
Beauclerc
Hag Bank
Harlow Field
Langley
Red Ho
Hole Ho
Birks
West Dipton Burn
Nilston Rigg
Stublick Hill
Stublick Moor
The Paise
Loadman
Greenridge
Dipton Wood
Broomhaugh
Kingswood Common
Kingswood Rigg
Staward Manor
Stublick Sike
Diptonmill
Channel Well
Dotland Park
Red Hemmels
High Plains
Beacon Hill
Fell Ho
Haining Hall
Catton Beacon
Greenrigg Moor
Edge Ho
Todburn Steel
Broomley Pit Ho
Crag Head
Emmerley Hill
Rebel Hill
Anchey Sike
Spitalshield Moor
Lord's Lot
Linnel Wood
Ordley
Lee
Hirst Hill
Marley Cote Walls
Eastwood Ho
Dingbell Hill
Church Burn
Highfield Fm
White Ho
Cook's Ho
Juniper
Black Hall
Finechambers
Whitfield
Old Town
Bulman's Rigg
Low Lane Ho
Barker Ho
Dalton
Whitley Mill
Dye House
Shield Hall
Low Ho
Peel Flatt
Burnt Ho
Bearsbridge
Hindley Hill
Catton
Lea Hall
Gaterley Hill
Moss Well
Reeds Rigg
Hamburn Hall
Steel
Slaley
Healey Mill
Stone Hall
Lough Hill
Raven Currick Rigg
Springwell Ho
Whitley Chapel
Mire Ho
Emley
Chapel Ho
River East Allen
Eshells Moor
Dukesfield
Ridley Halls
Hill Top
Keenley
Pia Troon
Whapweasel Burn
Strothers Dale
Holly Hill
White Ho
Park Head
Whitfield Hall
Quarry Ho
Thornley Gate
Moorhouse Gate
Salmon Field
Rawgreen
Leadpipe Hill
Fell Cotts
Burnt Ridge
Steel Hall
Monk Cott
High Oustley
Broadwood Halls
Allendale Town
Crawberry Hill
Rowley Head
Stotsfold Hall
Fell Plantn
Kellas
Burntridge Moor
Stotsfold Fm
Rennys Barn
Spring Ho
Trygill
Colpitts Grange
Parmentley Hall
Wentworth Place
Finney Hill
Glen Hill
Gate Ho
Wager Ho
Scotch Halls
Herds Law
Slaley Forest
Morley Hill
Round Hill
Park Gill
Rowley Burn
King's Law
White Hall
Espershields Fm
Parmentley Cott
Mount Pleasant
Nettle Hill
Acton Fell
Middle Edge
Studdon Park
Green Hill
Hexhamshire Common
Broadwall Ho
Park Ho
Embley Fell
War Law
Pithouse Fell
Wall Ho
Haggburn Gate
Acton Burn
Ninebanks
Park
Lilswood Grange
Blanchland Moor
Ouston
Drybum Moor
Garrets Hill
Grouse Ho
Burntshield Haugh
Burntshieldhaugh Fell
Loaning Ho
Cowbyers Fell
Derwent Reservoir
Round Hill
Herd's Ho
Green Dike
Newfold Ho
Ladle Well
Linn Burn
Dean Rigg
Black Hill
Sinderhope Gate
Hangman Hill
Whitewalls Burn
Hawkuplee
Spartywell
Sinderhope
Pennypie Ho
Hotburn Hill
Ninebanks
Farneyside
Broad Gate
Stobbylee Burn
Steelcrags Wood
Pennypie Fell
Ruffside Hall
Acton Moor
Allendale Common
Greenleycleugh
Brownley Hill
Black Sike
Pikeley Rigg
Hope Fell
Birkside Fell
Ouston Fell
Devils Water
Park Ho
Acton Burn
Knockshield Burn
Rye Close
Harwoodshield Fell
Birkside
Reeding
Blanchland
Berry Bank
White Hill
Mohope Head
Broadlee
Knock Shield
Kevelin Moor
Newbiggin Fell
Baybridge
Edmundbyers Common
Sipton Shield
Ruffside Moor
Mohope Moor
The Nook
Limestone Brae
Longwell Moor
Riddlehamhope Fell
Newbiggin
Harehope Hall
Halley Moor
Tedham Moss
Spartylea
Beldon Burn
Hunstanworth
River Derwent
Broad Meadows
New Ho
Black Cleugh
Knockshield Moor
Halleywell Fell
Western Meadows
Nookton Back Fell
High Ho
Townfield
Buckshott Fell
The Meres
Hesleywell Moor
Elpha Green
White Hall
Heatheryburn Moor
Ouzles Hill
Cross Hill
Boltshope
A68
A69
A686
A695
A6079
B6318
B6319
B6320
B6342
B6303
B6304
B6305
B6306
B6307
B6295
B6531
B6306
B6530
Dere Street
Corbridge
Bank
251
242
231
232
A
B
C
D
E
F
G
H
7
8
9
10
11
NY
80
50
00

A696
Shaftoe Crags
Mirlaw Ho
Shaftoe Grange
East Shaftoe Hall
Bolam Low Ho
Gallowhill
Whalton
Glebe Ho
Manor Ho
Hill Head
Watch Hill
Shilvington
North Whitehouse Fm
Clifton Fm
Nedderton
Bedlington
Clock Mill
Park Head
Sandyford
Foulmartlaw
Kiplaw
Cock Hill
Dovecote Fm
Netherton Moor Fm
Merry Shiels
Harnham
Middlepart
Howburn Br
East Low Ho
Duddo Hill
Low Hough Ho
Capheaton
Toft Hill
Harnham Buildings
Shortflatt
The Folly
Ogle Dene Ho
West Low Ho
Shilvington Br
Saltwick
Broadlaw
Low Middle Moor
Hartford Bridge
Greatlaw
Bradford
Sir Edward's Lake
Saugh Ho
Hedchester Law
Stannington
Plessey Woods
Plessey Hall Fm
Bavington Hill Head
White Ho
Belsay
Ogle Hill Head
Ogle
Twizell Cott
Bellasis Fm
Bavington Hall
Moss Barns
River Blyth
Toft Hill
Brandy Well Hall
Belsay Barns
Belsay Dene Ho
Belsay Hall, Castle & Gardens
Crawford's Hill
Bonas Hill
Whinney Hill Fm
Ogle South Fm
Bellasis Bridge
Stannington Bridge
Northumberlandia
Shotton
Bavington Mount
Northumberland College Zoo
Carter Moor
Bog Ho
Northumberland Cheese Farm
Down Hill
Moor Plantn
Fisher Lane
Kirkheaton Wind Farm
Kirkheaton
Mount Huly
Slate Hill
Nun Hill
Kirkley West Fm
Kirkley Mill
Berwick Hill Low Ho
Horton Grange Low Ho
Ewe Hill
Blagdon Hall
Blagdon Park
Shotton Grange
Hallington High Fm
Kearsley Fell
Tongues Fm
Wallridge
Black Heddon
West Newham
Cadgers Burn
Benridge Hall
Kirkley Dam Ho
Old Horton Grange
Horton Grange
Waterloo Plantn
Hallington
Moatlaw
Ingoe Moor
Lynup Hill
Milbourne Grange
East Grange
West Grange
Higham Dykes
Berwick Hill
Brenkley
Hoys Wood
Arcot Hill
Hallington New Ho
Robsheugh Burn
The Byerley Stud
Ingoe
South Hall
Blackheddon Br
Milbourne
West Cotes
Park Ho
Seaton Burn
Gardener's Houses Fm
Ryal
Low Hall
Milbourne Hall
Smallburn
Carr Grange Fm
North East Mason Fm
Bingfield East Quarter
White Riggs
New Bingfield
Bingfield Eastside
Robsheugh Fm
South East Fm
Coldcotes Moor
Eland Green
Eland Hall
Prestwick Carr
Big Waters
Westerheugh
Heugh
Dyke Ho
Hillhead Plantn
Red House Fm
Ponteland
Dinnington
Brunswick Village
Corneyside
N O R T H U M B E R L A N D
Whittington White Ho
Fenwick
Chapel Fm
Cairn House Fm
Woodside Fm
Clickemin
Tofts Hill
Hack Hall
Morley Hill Fm
Ind Est
Wideopen
Low Hall
Matfen
Marlpit Plantn
Stamfordham
Dalton
Dissington East Houses
Benacres Plantns
Prestwick
Newcastle International Airport
Hazlerigg
Todridge
Shellbraes
Burnside
Lane Ho
Mill Ho
Broomy Hill
Dissington Hall
Donkins House Fm
Rotary Way
West Brunton Fm
P&R
Thornham Hill
South Lough Ho
North Lough Ho
Bridge End
Cheeseburn Grange
Rose's Bower
Beukley
Dewlaw
Richmond Hill
Grange Ho
Eachwick
Darras Hall
Hold House
Woolsington Hall
The Whiggs
Great Whittington
Ouston
Bog Ho
Ouston Moor
Ouston Airfield (disused)
Street Houses
Kyloe Ho
Dissington Old Hall
Medburn
Callerton Hall
High Callerton
Woolsington
Kenton Bankfoot
Mile Plantn
West Moorehouses
Lowfell Plantns
Plough Inn
Dissington Lane Ho
Birney Hall
Black Callerton
Kingston Park
Little Whittington
Coldside
Nesbitt Hill Head
Callerton Grange
Callerton Lane End
Ouse Burn
Fawdon
Gosforth
Halton Red House
East Moorhouses
Dodley
Breckney Hill
Whorlton Hall
Halton Shields
Wall Houses
Hadrian's Wall Path
Harlow Hill
Turpin's Hill
Lough Ho
Callerton
Coxlodge
Kip Hill
Carr Houses
Heddon Ho
Dewley Fm
Fell House Fm
Newbiggin Hall Estate
Kenton Bar
Halton
Vallum (course of)
Hadrian's Wall (course of)
Heddon Mill
North Walbottle
Kenton
White House
Laker Hall
Welton
Welton Fm
Northside Fm
High Seat
Heddon-on-the-Wall
Kenton Lane
Chantry Fm
Aydon Castle
Newton Fell Ho
Bogle Burn
North Dunslaw Holm
Houghton
Throckley
Westerhope
Blakelaw
Nuns Moor
Shawwell Ho
Aydon
Heathery Edge
Nafferton Fm
Horsley
Bank Top
Heddon Hall
Walbottle
West Denton
East Denton
Fenham
Town Moor
Newton Hall
Thornbrough High Barns
Thornbrough Kiln Ho
Stelling Hall
Whittle Fm
High Barns
Horsley Wood
Holeyn Hall
Rift Fm
Throckley Mill
Tyne Riverside
Newburn
Denton Burn
Spital Tongues
Great North Museum
Thornbrough
Newton
Mount Huly
George Stephenson's Birthplace
Wylam
Clara Vale
Lemington
Bell's Close
Benwell
St James' Park
Brocks Bushes
Overdene
Shaw Ho
Bearl
Tyne Riverside
Castle Hill Fm
Bar Moor
Ryton
Benwell Roman Temple
Howden Dene
Corbridge
Ovingham
Low Prudhoe
Daniel Fm
Crookhill
Blaydon Haughs
Scotswood
Discovery
Stella
Stargate
Elswick
Ovington
Ind Est
West Wylam
Crawcrook
Path Head
Scotswood Road
Utilita Arena
High Barns
Bywell Home Fm
Peepy
Prudhoe
Bradley Hall
Ryton Woodside
Blaydon
Dunston Staithes
Teams
Grey Court
Short Wood
River Tyne
Eltringham
Cherryburn
Priestclose Wood
Bradley Fell
Greenside
Low Greenside
Blaydon Burn
Axwell Park
Dunston
Prospect Hill
Riding Mill
Styford Hall
Stockfield Hall
West Road
Mickley Square
Edgewell House Fm
Metrocentre
Swalwell
Temperley Grange
Beauclerc
Low Shilford
Bywell
Branch End
Kyo Hall
Norman's Riding Fm
Winlaton
Whickham Thorns Centre
Dunston Hill
Lobley Hill
Broomhaugh
Roe Ho
Stocksfield
High Mickley
Buck's Nook
Coalburns
Reeley Mires Fm
Ricklees Fm
Barlow
Whickham
Ridley Mill
Painshawfield
Mickley Grange
Dukeshagg Fm
Winlaton Mill
Fellside
Whickham Highway
Team Valley
Red Hemmels
High Plains
Bromley
Coalburns Fm
Thornley Bank
Derwent Walk
Whickham Hill
Marshall Lands Fm
Broomley Pit Ho
Grange
New Ridley
Broomley-Fell Fm
Hedley on the Hill
Hedley Park Fm
Currock Hill
Horse Gate
High Spen
Low Thornley
Spen Banks
Snipes Dene Wood
Long Hill
Whickham Fell
Trench Hall
Broomleyfell Plantn
Hindley
Leadgate
Hooker Gate
Low Spen Fm
Hollin Hill Fm
Sunniside
Street Gate
Eastwood Ho
Airey Hill Fm
Labourn's Fell
Gibside Chapel & Avenue
Rowlands Gill
Head Wood
Chowdene
Healey
Burnt Ho
Lingey Field
Apperley Dene
Hedley Grange Fm
Chopwell Wood
Gibside Hall
Fellside Fm
High Park Wood
Lady Park
Lamesley
Healey Mill
Low Fotherley
Highfield
Healey Hall
High Fotherley
Bridges Fm
Watch Hill
Kipperlynn
Milkwellburn Wood
Chopwell
Lintzford Wood
Sheep Hill
Leazes Hall
Marley Hill
Hill Top
Fotherley Buildings
Whittonstall
Hollings Hill
Blackhall Mill
Carr Ho
Lintzford
Leazes
Byermoor
Mitcheson's Gate
Kellas Plantn
Scales Cross
Fairley
Whittonstall Hall Fm
Broad Oak Fm
Derwentcote Steel Furnace
Friarside
Crookgate Bank
Andrews House
Tanfield Railway
Ravensworth Grange
Kibblesworth
Fell Cotts
Wood Ho
Park Wood
Low Westwood
Hagg Fm
Hamsterley Mill
Burnopfield
Causey
Hedley Hall Fm
Kibblesworth Grange
Morrowfield Fm
Hamsterley
Lintzford Road
Lintz
Causey Arch
Greymare Hill
St Andrew's Church
Newlands
Ebchester
High Westwood
Hamsterley Hall
Pickering Nook
Hobson
Tanfield
Causey Road
Causey Hall Fm
Cooper Ho
Riding Fm
West Minsteracres
Barleyhill
Newlands Grange
Waskerleyedge Plantn
The Dene
Loft Ho
Straightneck Wood
Clough Dene
East Tanfield
Pockerley Buildings
Espershields Fm
Kiln Pit Hill
East Law
Broom Hill
Southfield Fm
Ewehurst Wood
Hill Top
Tantobie
Tanfield Leith Fm
Beamish Hall
High Forge
Wall Ho
New House Fm
Alty Holm Fm
Medomsley
Bradley Hall
Dipton
Flint Hill
White-le-Head
Tanfield Lea
Beamish Open Air Museum
Kip Hill
Shield Row
High Urpeth
High Handenhold
Pelton
Pithouse Fell
School Ho
Shotleyfield
Shotley Park
Billingside Wood
Pontop Hall
Front Street
Harperley
East Stanley
Beamish
Derwent Reservoir
Cronkley
Fine Ho
Shotleyfell Plantn
Burnmill Bank
Shotley Hall
Shotley Bridge
Pontop Pike
Stob Ho
Kyo
East Kyo
Oxhill
Stanley
West Pelton
Newfield
Pow Hill
Benfieldside
Blackhill
Bunker Hill
Leadgate
East Castle
Catchgate
Harelaw
West Kyo
South Stanley
Eden Hill Fm
Grange Villa
Ruffside Hall
Carterway Heads
Snods Edge
North Snods
Black Hedley
Bridgehill
Durham Road
Annfield
Greencroft
Annfield Plain
South Moor
Shop Cen
Twizell Hall
Greenhead
South Snods
Orchard Field
Consett
Low Brooms Fm
Stony Heap
New Kyo
The Middles
Craghead
Berry Bank
Derwent Br
Eddy's Bridge
Durhamfield
Allensford Bank
The Grove
Retail Pk
Crookhall
Handwell Hill
Durham Hill
Quaking Houses
Broomy Holm
Edmundbyers Common
Edmundbyers
Allensford
Templetown
Iveston
Park Head
Waldridge
West House Fm
Muggleswick
Calf Hall
Moorside
Greencroft Park
Maiden Law
Holmside Hall
Wheatley Green Fm
Congburn
Edmondsley
Combfield
How's Fm
Delves
Stockerley Br
Esp Green
Chapmans Well
Morrow Edge Fm
High Wood
Holmside
Daisy Hill
Stoterley Hill
Dean Howl Fm
Castleside
Middles Fm
Knitsley
East Knitsley
Hurbuck Cotts
Howden Bank
Wheatley Hill
Warland Green
Sacriston Wood
Nettlesworth
Coal Gate
Birkhot
Carp Shield
Healeyfield
Middle Heads
Dyke
Knitsley
Low Meadows
Ornsby Hill
Burnhope
Charlaw Fell
Hill Ho
D U R H A M
Whitehill
NZ
0 1 2 3 miles
0 1 2 3 4 5 km

Blyth
Cowpen
Isabella Pit
253
Newsham
South Beach
New Delaval
South Newsham
East Hartford
Shankhouse
Nelson Village
Cramlington
East Cramlington
New Hartley
Seaton
Seaton Sluice
Hartley
ST MARY'S LIGHTHOUSE
SEATON DELAVAL HALL
Seaton Terrace
Seaton Delaval
Holywell
Seghill
Annitsford
Fordley
Dudley
Burradon
East Holywell
West Holywell
Backworth
Earsdon
Whitley Sands
SPANISH CITY
Whitley Bay
Monkseaton
Camperdown
Killingworth
Killingworth Village
West Moor
Shiremoor
West Monkseaton
Murton
Preston Grange
New York
Cullercoats
Marden
TYNEMOUTH AQUARIUM
Palmersville
Forest Hall
West Allotment
Preston
Tynemouth
CASTLE & PRIORY
Longbenton
STEPHENSON RAILWAY MUS
Billy Mill
Battle Hill
North Shields
AMSTERDAM
Chirton
West Chirton
Percy Main
Holy Cross
Willington
Howdon
Newcastle upon Tyne
Wallsend
ARBEIA ROMAN FORT & MUSEUM
The Lawe
OCEAN BEACH PLEASURE PARK
South Shields
Jesmond
Heaton
Rosehill
Willington Quay
East Howdon
Howdon Pans
ROYAL QUAYS
High Shields
Westoe
Frenchman's Bay
SEGEDUNUM ROMAN FORT
River Tyne
Tyne Tunnel
Jarrow
JARROW HALL
ST PAUL'S MONASTERY
Tyne Dock
West Park
Hebburn Colliery
THE LEAS & MARSDEN ROCK
Horsley Hill
Marsden
Harton
West Harton
Simonside
Byker
Walker
Hebburn New Town
Hebburn
SOUTER LIGHTHOUSE
Cleadon Park
Cleadon Hills Fm
Lizards Fm
East Gateshead
Felling Shore
GATESHEAD INTERNATIONAL STADIUM
St Anthony's
Monkton
Primrose
Biddick Hall
Whiteleas
Cleadon Grange
Old Fold
Bill Quay
Pelaw
Hedworth
Cleadon
Whitburn Colliery
Whitburn
Mount Pleasant
Felling
Heworth
Wardley
Fellgate
Boldon Colliery
Boldon North Br
East Boldon
West Boldon
New Town
Boldon
South Bents
Whitburn Bay
Deckham
Carr Hill
Windy Nook
Sheriff Hill
Leam Lane
Scot's Ho
Beacon Lough
Whitehills
Wrekenton
Low Fell
Follingsby
Downhill
Witherwack
Carley Hill
High Southwick
Hylton Red House
Marley Pots
Southwick
Seaburn
Fulwell
Roker
Harlow Green
Eighton Banks
Springwell
Usworth
Donwell
NORTH EAST LAND, SEA & AIR MUS
Hylton Castle
Castletown
Monkwearmouth
STADIUM OF LIGHT
NATIONAL GLASS CENTRE
Deptford
Ayres Quay
Low Eighton
BOWES RAILWAY
Concord
Sulgrave
Albany
Washington
Pallion
Millfield
Bishopwearmouth
Birtley
Blackfell
Washington Village
Glebe
Barmston
North Hylton
South Hylton
Sunderland
Hendon
Oxclose
Washington Services
Portobello
WASHINGTON OLD HALL
Columbia
WILDFOWL & WETLAND TRUST
Offerton
Pennywell
High Barnes
Humbledon
Biddick
Ayton
Lambton
Grindon
Springwell
Hastings Hill
Hillview
Grangetown
Barley Mow
Ouston
Fatfield
Harraton
Rickleton
PENSHAW MONUMENT
HERRINGTON COUNTRY PARK
Thorney Close
Middle Herrington
Farringdon
New Silksworth
West Herrington
New Herrington
East Herrington
Penshaw
Doxford Park
Tunstall
Ryhope
South Pelaw
Pelton Fell
Shiney Row
Philadelphia
Stony Gate
RYHOPE ENGINES MUSEUM
Thristley House Fm
East Fm
Burdon
Seaham Grange
THE ANKERS
Chester-le-Street
Bournmoor
Newbottle
Grasswell
New Lambton
Sunniside
Burnside
DOWN AT THE FARM
Warden Law
Old Burdon
Burn Hall Fm
EMIRATES RIVERSIDE
Lumley Thicks
Fence Houses
Seaton
Northlea
Chester Moor
Great Lumley
Lumley Grange
Houghton-Le-Spring
Colliery Row
Dubmire
234
Seaham
West Lea
Deneside
Liddle Stack
Plawsworth
Harbour House Fm
Charles Pit Cotts
Cocken White
Lumley Moor Fm
Chilton Moor
RAINTON MEADOWS NAT RES
Rainton Bridge
New Town
Hetton Downs
Great Eppleton
Hetton-le-Hole
Slingley Hill
Dalton Moor
Haverley Ho
Dalton-le-Dale
Dawdon
Nose's Pt
Parkside
A B C D E F G H
7 8 9 10 11
NZ

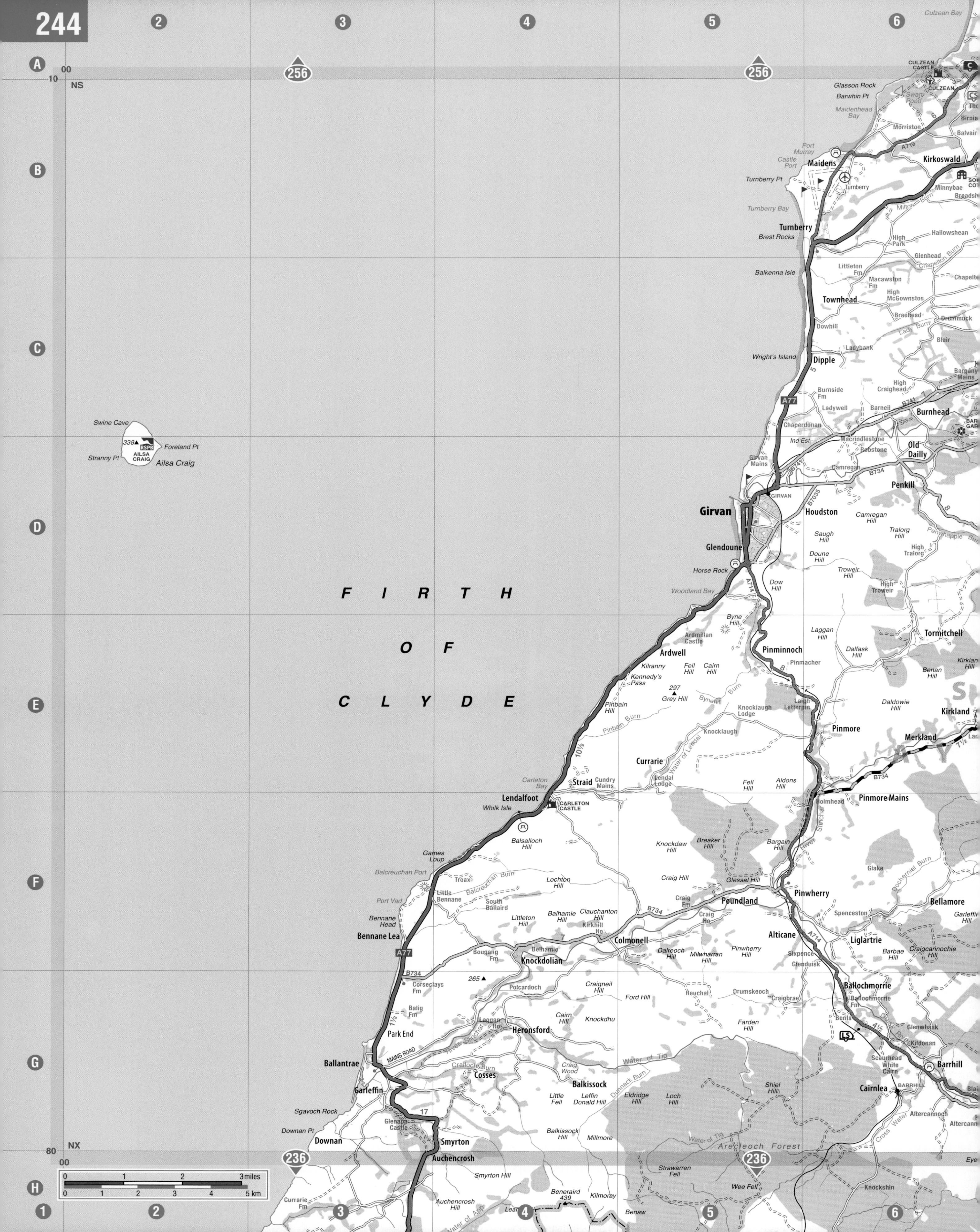
2
3
4
5
6
A
B
C
D
E
F
G
H
1
256
236
NS
NX
Culzean Bay
CULZEAN CASTLE
CULZEAN
Glasson Rock
Barwhin Pt
Swan Pond
Maidenhead Bay
Morriston
Birnie
Balvair
Port Murray
Castle Port
Maidens
A719
Kirkoswald
Turnberry Pt
Turnberry
Minnybae
Broadshaw
Milton Burn
Turnberry Bay
Turnberry
Brest Rocks
Hallowshean
High Park
Glenhead
Chapelton Burn
Balkenna Isle
Littleton Fm
Macawston Fm
Chapelton
Townhead
High McGownston
Braehead
Drummuck
Dowhill
Lady Burn
Blair
Ladybank
Wright's Island
Dipple
Bargany Mains
High Craighead
Burnside Fm
A77
Ladywell
Barneil
B741
Burnhead
Chaperdonan
Ind Est
Macrindlestone
Old Dailly
Robstone
Girvan Mains
Camregan
B734
Penkill
GIRVAN
B7035
Girvan
Houdston
Camregan Hill
Saugh Hill
Tralorg Hill
Penwhapple Burn
Glendoune
High Tralorg
Doune Hill
Horse Rock
Troweir Hill
Dow Hill
High Troweir
Woodland Bay
A714
Byne Hill
Laggan Hill
Tormitchell
Ardmillan Castle
Pinminnoch
Ardwell
Dalfask Hill
Pinmacher
Kilranny
Fell Hill
Cairn Hill
Kennedy's Pass
Benan Hill
297
Grey Hill
Byne Burn
Laigh Letterpin
Daldowie Hill
Kirkland
Pinbain Hill
Knocklaugh Lodge
Pinmore
Pinbain Burn
Knocklaugh
Merkland
Water of Lendal
Currarie
B734
Carleton Bay
Straid
Cundry Mains
Lendal Lodge
Fell Hill
Aldons Hill
Pinmore Mains
Lendalfoot
CARLETON CASTLE
Whilk Isle
Holmhead
Balsalloch Hill
Knockdaw Hill
Breaker Hill
Bargain Hill
River Stinchar
Games Loup
Glake
Balcreuchan Port
Troax
Balcreuchan Burn
Lochton Hill
Craig Hill
Glessal Hill
Pinwherry
Little Bennane
Craig Fm
Poundland
Bellamore
Port Vad
South Ballaird
Spenceston
Bennane Head
Littleton Hill
Balhamie Hill
Clauchanton Hill
Kirkhill Ho
Craig Ho
Garleffin Hill
Bennane Lea
Colmonell
Alticane
Liglartrie
A77
Bougang Fm
Belhamie
Knockdolian
Dalreoch Hill
Milwharran Hill
Pinwherry Hill
Slxpence
Barbae Hill
Craigcannochie Hill
B734
Glenduisk
Corseclays Fm
265
Polcardoch
Craigneil Hill
Ford Hill
Reuchal
Drumskeoch
Craigbrae
Ballochmorrie
Ballochmorrie Fm
Balig Fm
Cairn Hill
Knockdhu
Farden Hill
Bents
Glenwhask
Park End
Laggan Ho
Heronsford
Kildonan
MAINS ROAD
River Stinchar
Water of Tig
Scaurhead
White Cairn
Ballantrae
Craig Wood
Barrhill
Crailloch Burn
Cosses
Balkissock
Shiel Hill
Garleffin
BARRHILL
Cairnlea
Little Fell
Leffin Donald Hill
Dunnack Burn
Eldrigde Hill
Loch Hill
Sgavoch Rock
17
Glenapp Castle
Altercannoch
Cross Water
Downan Pt
Balkissock Hill
Millmore
Water of Tig
Altercannoch
Downan
Smyrton
Arecleoch Forest
Auchencrosh
Strawarren Fell
Eye
Smyrton Hill
Wee Fell
Knockshin
Currarie Fm
Benerard 439
Kilmoray
Auchencrosh Hill
Benaw
Water of App
Swine Cave
338
RSPB
AILSA CRAIG
Foreland Pt
Stranny Pt
Ailsa Craig
FIRTH OF CLYDE
0 1 2 3 miles
0 1 2 3 4 5 km

EAST AYRSHIRE
SOUTH AYRSHIRE
Carrick
GALLOWAY FOREST PARK
DUMFRIES AND GALLOWAY
Maybole
Whitefaulds
COLLEGIATE CHURCH
CROSSRAGUEL ABBEY
Kirkmichael
Aitkenhead
Crosshill
Kirkoswald
Dailly
Wallacetown
Ruglen
Kilkerran
Straiton
Patna
Polnessan
Burnfoot
Waterside
SCOTTISH INDUSTRIAL RAILWAY CENTRE
DALMELLINGTON ROAD
Burnton
Dalmellington
Bellsbank
Town's Common
Craigmalloch
LOCH DOON CASTLE
Loch Doon
Loch Head
Loch Finlas
Loch Bradan Reservoir
Tallaminnoch
Tairlaw Toll
Stinchar Br
South Balloch
Dalwyne
Pinvalley
Barr
Alton Albany Fm
Waterhead on Minnoch
Mount Shellie
Shalloch on Minnoch
Macaterick
Tarfessock
Kirriereoch Hill
Merrick
Benyellary
Bennan
Black Clauchrie
South Ho
Eldrick
Cairnderry
Glen Trool Lodge
BRUCE'S STONE
Glentrool
Glentrool Village
GLENTROOL VISITOR CENTRE
Stroan Br
SOUTHERN UPLAND WAY
Loch Trool
Gleanhead
Palgowan
Mulldonoch
SILVER FLOWE
Rhinns of Kells
Corserine
Meikle Craigtarson
Backhill of Bush (Bothy)
Craiglee
Mid Lump
Kirerroch
BLAIRQUHAN CASTLE
Water of Girvan
River Stinchar
River Cree
Water of Minnoch
B741
B7023
B7045
A77
A713
A714
B734
B7027
257
236
246
A
B
C
D
E
F
G
H
7
8
9
10
11
NS
NX
10
50
80

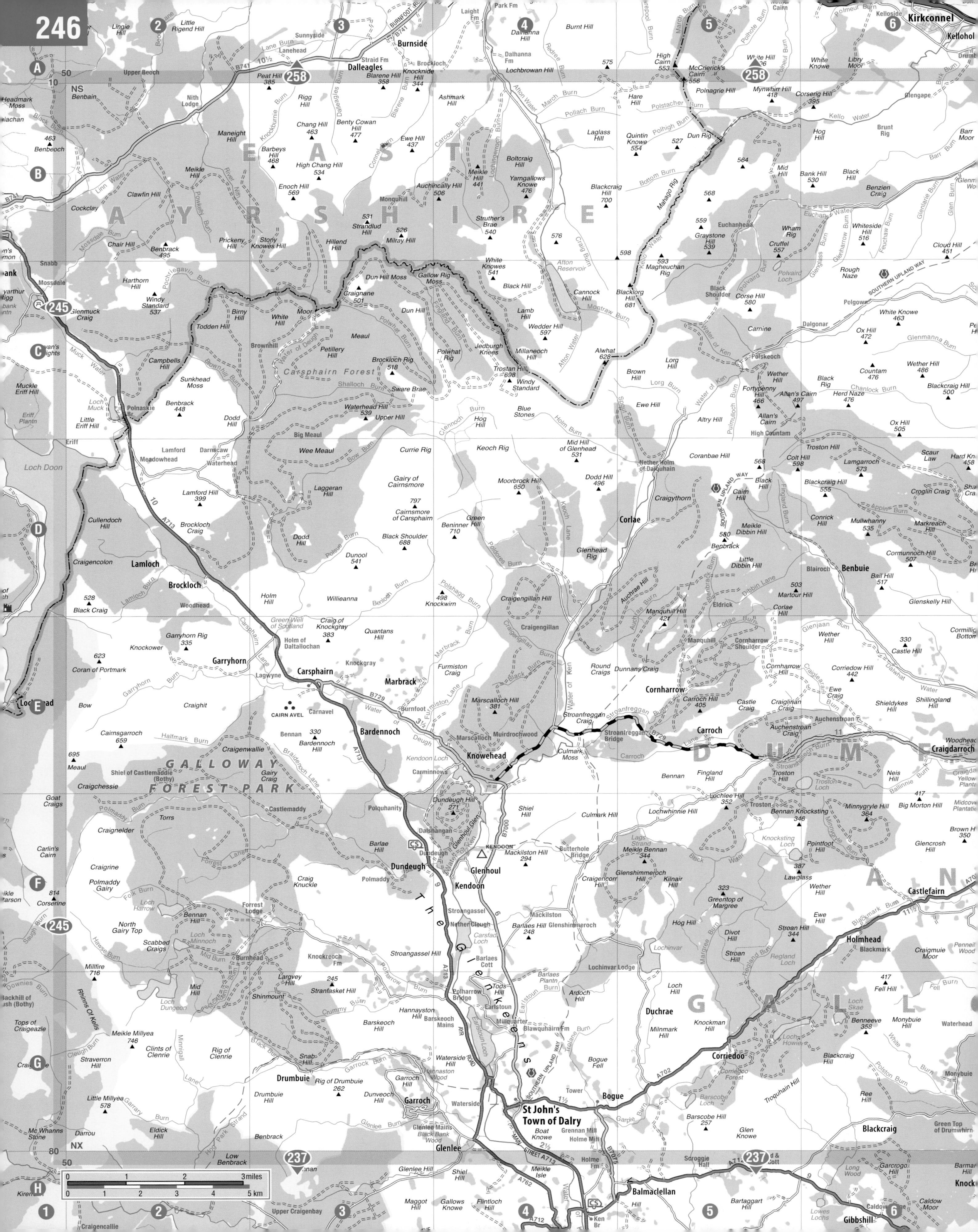

EAST AYRSHIRE
GALLOWAY FOREST PARK
DUMFRIES AND GALLOWAY
Kirkconnel
Kelloholm
Burnside
Dalleagles
Sunnyside
Lanehead
Upper Beoch
Peat Hill 385
Blarene Hill 358
Knocknide Hill 344
Lochbrowan Hill
Burnt Hill
Dalhanna Hill
High Cairn 553
McCrierick's Cairn 556
White Hill 506
Polnagrie Hill
Mynwhirr Hill 418
Corserig Hill 395
Glengape
Benbain
Nith Lodge
Rigg Hill
Chang Hill 463
Benty Cowan Hill 477
Ewe Hill 437
Ashmark Hill
Hare Hill
Quintin Knowe 554
Laglass Hill
Dun Rig
Hog Hill
Brunt Rig
Barr Moor
Benbeoch 463
Maneight Hill
Barbeys Hill 468
High Chang Hill 534
Boltcraig Hill
Meikle Hill 441
Yarngallows Knowe 476
Enoch Hill 569
Auchincally Hill 506
Monguhill
Blackcraig Hill 700
Mid Hill
Bank Hill 530
Black Hill
Benzien Craig
Clawfin Hill
Cockclay
Strandlud Hill 531
Milray Hill 526
Struther's Brae 540
Euchanhead
Wham Rig
Whiteside Hill 516
Chair Hill
Benbrack 495
Prickeny Hill
Stony Knowes Hill
Hillend Hill
Graystone Hill 539
Cruffel 557
Cloud Hill 451
Afton Reservoir
Magheuchan Rig 593
Rough Naze
SOUTHERN UPLAND WAY
Harthorn Hill
Windy Standard 537
Dun Hill Moss
Gallow Rig Moss
Craignane 501
White Knowes 541
Black Hill
Cannock Hill
Blacklorg Hill 681
Black Shoulder
Corse Hill 580
Polgown
Glenmuck Craig
Birny Hill
White Hill
Moor
Dun Hill
Lamb Hill
Wedder Hill 597
White Knowe 463
Todden Hill
Brownhill
Meaul
Carnine
Dalgonar
Ox Hill 472
Campbells Hill
Petillery Hill
Brockloch Rig 518
Polwhat Rig
Jedburgh Knees
Millaneoch Hill
Alwhat 628
Lorg Hill
Polskeoch
Wether Hill 486
Carsphairn Forest
Trostan Hill 698
Windy Standard
Brown Hill
Sunkhead Moss
Muckle Eriff Hill
Sware Brae
Black Rig
Countam 476
Fortypenny Hill 466
Allan's Cairn 497
Herd Naze 476
Blackcraig Hill 500
Polnaskie Br.
Benbrack 448
Waterhead Hill 539
Upper Hill
Dodd Hill
Blue Stones
Hog Hill
Ewe Hill
Altry Hill
Allan's Cairn
Ox Hill 505
Little Eriff Hill
Big Meaul
High Countam
Lamford
Darnscaw
Meadowhead
Waterhead
Wee Meaul
Currie Rig
Keoch Rig
Mid Hill of Glenhead 531
Nether Holm of Dalquhairn
Coranbae Hill
Troston Hill
Colt Hill 598
Lamgarroch 573
Scaur Law
Loch Doon
Lamford Hill 399
Laggeran Hill
Gairy of Cairnsmore
Moorbrock Hill 650
Dodd Hill 496
Black Hill 568
Cairn Hill
Blackcraig Hill 555
Croglin Craig
Craigythorn
Cairnsmore of Carsphairn 797
Green Hill
Beninner 710
Corlae
Cullendoch Hill
Brockloch Craig
Conrick Hill
Mullwhanny 535
Markreach Hill
Meikle Dibbin Hill
Dodd Hill
Black Shoulder 688
Benbrack 580
Glenhead Rig
Craigencolon
Lamloch
Dunool 541
Little Dibbin Hill
Cormunnoch Hill 507
Brockloch
Blairoch
Benbuie
Ball Hill 517
Woodhead
Holm Hill
Willieanna
Knockwirn 498
Craigengillan Hill
Martour Hill 503
Glenskelly Hill
Black Craig 528
Manquhill Hill 421
Eldrick
Corlae Hill
Green Well of Scotland
Craig of Knockgray 383
Holm of Daltallochan
Quantans Hill
Craigengillan
Manquhill
Cornharrow Shoulder
Wether Hill
Castle Hill 330
Garryhorn Rig 335
Knockower
Coran of Portmark 623
Garryhorn
Carsphairn
Knockgray
Marbrack
Furmiston Craig
Round Craigs
Dunnany Craig
Cornharrow Hill
Corriedow Hill 442
Lagwyne
Bow
Craighit
CAIRN AVEL
Carnavel
Burnfoot
Marscalloch Hill 381
Cornharrow
Carroch Hill 405
Castle Craig
Craiglinan Craig
Ewe Craig
Shieldykes Hill
Shillingland Hill
Auchenstroan
Auchenstroan Craig
Cairnsgarroch 659
Bennan
Bardennoch Hill 330
Bardennoch
Muirdrochwood 650
Stroanfreggan Craig
Stroanfreggan Bridge
Carroch
Craigdarroch
Craigenwallie
Marscalloch
Knowehead
Culmark Moss
Meaul 695
Shiel of Castlemaddie (Bothy)
Gairy Craig
Kendoon Loch
Carminnows
Bennan
Fingland Hill
Troston Hill
Neis Hill
Craigchessie
Castlemaddy
Goat Craigs
Dundeugh Hill 271
Polquhanity
Dalshangan
Shiel Hill
Culmark Hill
Lochwhinnie Hill
Lochlee Hill 352
Troston
Bennan Knocksting 346
Minnygryle Hill 364
Big Morton Hill 417
Craignelder
Torrs
Carlin's Cairn
Barlae Hill
Dundeugh
KENDOON
Mackilston Hill 294
Butterhole Bridge
Meikle Bennan 344
Knocksting Loch
Pointfoot Hill
Glencrosh Hill
Brown Hill 350
Craigrine
Polmaddy Gairy
Polmaddy
Craig Knuckle
Glenhoul
Kendoon
Craigencorr Hill
Glenshimmeroch Hill
Kilnair Hill
Lawglass 387
Wether Hill
Castlefairn
Corserine 814
Loch Harrow
Forrest Lodge
Greentop of Margree 323
Stroangassel
Nether Clough
Mackilston
Glenshimmeroch
Hog Hill
Ewe Hill
North Gairy Top
Bennan Hill
Loch Minnoch
Scabbed Craigs
Carsfad Loch
Barlaes Hill 248
Divot Hill
Stroan Hill 344
Holmhead
Blackmark
Craigmuie Moor
Knockreoch
Stroangassel Hill
Barlaes Cott
Lochinvar
Lochinvar Lodge
Stroan Hill
Regland Loch
Millfire 716
Burnhead
Stranfasket Hill 245
Largvey Hill
Mid Hill
Shinmount
Tods Hill
Polharrow Bridge
Earlstoun
Barlaes Plantn
Ardoch Hill
Loch Hill
Fell Hill 417
Loch Dungeon
Rhinns Of Kells
Hannayston Hill
Barskeoch Mains
Barskeoch Hill
Millquarter
Earlstoun Loch
Duchrae
Knockman Hill
Loch Skae
Benneeve 358
Monybuie Hill
Waterhead
Tops of Craigeazle
Meikle Millyea 746
Clints of Clenrie
Rig of Clenrie
Blawquhairn Fm
Milnmark Hill
Loch Howie
Blackcraig Hill
Straverron Hill
Snab Hill
Waterside Hill
Hannaston Wood
Bogue Fell
Corriedoo
Corriedoo Forest
Drumbuie
Rig of Drumbuie 262
Garroch Hill
Garroch
Dunveoch Hill
Tower
Bogue
Troquhain Hill
Ree Hill
Little Millyea 578
Drumbuie Hill
Waterside
St John's Town of Dalry
Barscobe Loch
Barscobe Hill 257
Blackcraig
Green Top of Drumwhirn
Mc Whanns Stone
Darrou
Eldrick Hill
Benbrack
Glenlee Mains
Black Bank Wood
Boat Knowe
Grennan Mill
Holme Mill
Glen Knowe
Glenlee
Low Benbrack
Holme Fm
Scroggie Hall
Long Wood
Garcrogo Hill
Barmark Hill
Glenlee Hill
Shiel Hill
Meikle Isle
Balmaclellan
Maggot Hill
Gallows Knowe
Flintloch Hill
Bartaggart Hill
Lowes Lochs
Caldow Moor
Gibbshill
Upper Craigenbay
Craigencallie
Kirerroch
Ken Br
Water of Ken
Water of Deugh
Afton Water
Kello Water
Euchan Water
Polharrow Burn
Black Water
The Glenkens
MAIN STREET
A713
A702
A712
A762
B729
B7000
B741
B7075
A76
BURNFOOT RD
NS
NX
10
50
80
258
245
237
A B C D E F G H
1 2 3 4 5 6
0 1 2 3 miles
0 1 2 3 4 5 km

Crawick
Sanquhar
Sanquhar Post Office
Tollbooth Museum
Burnfoot
Blackaddie Br
Barrmoor Cotts
Old Barr
Euchan Cott
Ulzieside Plantn
Mains Plantn
Brandleys Cott
Bogg
Lochside
Auchentaggart Moor
Auchengruith
Mennock
Mennock Pass
Mennock Water
Eliock Br
South Mains
Eliock Grange
Wether Hill
Brown Hill 476
White Dod 531
Glenclach Burn
Middle Moor
Meikle Snout
420 Auchensow Hill
Glenimshaw Burn
Cock Hill
Yell Hill
551 Threehope Height
Lang Cleuch
Thirstane Hill 583
East Mount Lowther 631
Whiteside
Wether Hill
Cold Moss
Steygail 573
Enterkin Burn
Lowther Hill 725
Crooked Bank 591
Riccart Cleuch
Riccart Law Rig
Lang Cleuch
Stowgill
Comb Head
Laght Hill 507
Earn Law
Watermeetings Forest
Pin Stane
Mid Height
Threep Moor
Lion Hill
Daerside
Coom Rig
Hitteril
Sweetshaw Brae 448
Southern Upland Way
Mid Hill
Hods Hill
Beld Knowe
Mount Joe
Lowther Hills
Daer Reservoir
Hitteril Hill 491
Meikle Shag 501
Hem Hill
Comb Law 645
Sweetshaw Rig
Earlside 449
Mosshope Fell
Type Knowes 448
Gill Knowe
White Burn
Aylmerbank Wood
340 Cairn Hill
Brown Hill
Whing Burn
Back Burn
Dalpeddar Hill
Cairn Hill 449
Coshogle Rig 372
Dern Craig
Dalveen Pass
Dalveen Toll Cott
Littlemerk Hill
Glengenny Muir 291
Lime Cleuch
Ha Cleuch
Dinabid Linn
Pettylung
Black Hill 531
Well Hill 606
Capel Hill
Watchman's Brae 594
Rodger Law 688
Catlaw Dod
Hirstane Rig 622
Nether Law
Rivox Fell
Whiting Head
Corridow Hill 470
Kirk Hill
Twentyshilling Hill 397
Eliock Burn
Eliock Wood
Kirkbride
Coshogle
Chapel
Muircleuch
Penbane
Durisdeer Hill
Whiteside Hill 554
Hangingshaw Hill
Welltrees Tappin
Peat Hill
Shiel Hill
Glengenny Burn
Minny E'hill
Burnsands Burn
Glenwhargen Craig 482
Fardingmullach Muir
Crairiepark
Enterkinfoot
Eastside
Durisdeermill
Durisdeer
Durisdeer Parish Church
Little Scaw'd Law
Scaw'd Law 663
Ballencleuch Law
Ewe Gair 559
Over Law 483
Annant Hill
Jarney Knowes 505
Wether Hill
Bught Knowe
Breconside Hill 366
Blackbank Plantn
Crairiehill
Thrushlands
Muiryhill
Carronglen
Blackgrain Shoulder
Carsehope Middens
Shiel Dod 668
Little Hill
Lamb Hill 542
Kinnel Water
Peat Craig
Dalzean Snout 407
Dunduff 428
Cairnkinna Hill 552
Birny Rig
Berry Holes
Rig Plantn
Auchensell Wood
Drumcruilton
Glenaggart
Nether Hill 397
Glenleith Fell 612
Wedder Law 672
Whiteside Hill
Five Wells
Earncraig Hill 611
Mid Height 555
Craighoar Hill
Hallscaur Craig
Woodend Craig
Mote Hill
Cleuchhead Hill Plantn
Enoch
East Morton Hill
Kettleton Burn
Blackhill Moss
Gana Hill 668
Daer Hass
Harestanes Height 566
Penbreck 609
Craigbuie Hill
Craigdasher 440
Riddings Bank
Merkland Hill
Goukthorn Plantn
Drumlanrig Park
East Morton
Par Hill
Little Fell
Berry Grain
Garroch Fell 606
Mount Glass
Chanlockfoot Cott
Chanlock Burn
Drumshinnoch
Holestane
Morton Mains
Morton Castle
The Shaw
443
Tod Craig Hill 519
Hard Hill 494
697 Queensberry
Lamb Hill
Keb Hill
Countam 502
Whitecraig Head
Brown Hill
Drumlanrig Castle & Gardens
Drumlanrig Woods
Holm of Drumlanrig
Auchenknight Wood
Auchenleck Hill 447
The Dod 425
Wester Hill
Crichton's Cairn
Grit Hill
New Ho Glengowan Hill
Fiddlers Moss
Arkland Craig 347
Arkland Burn
Townhead Wood
Poets Corner
Newhouse Plantn
Cairnpark
Carronbridge
Morton Wood
Cairns Hill
Rashy Height
Garroch Water
Capel Burn
Blue Cairn 333
Lamb Craigs 417
Appin Lodge
Cairney Knowe
Far Hill
Parfin
Cleuch
Bogrie Wood
Tibbers Wood
Morton Mill
Kirkland
Riddings
Sandrum
Townfoot
Fellend
512 Wee Queensberry
The Law
Glendinning
Torbraehead 400
Muckle Wood
Wet Wood
Doons
Auchenbainzie
Auchenbainzie Hill 302
Ewe Hill
Waterside Mains
Greenhead
Braidshaw Rig
Clog Knowe
Locherben
Killyminshaw Hill 333
Nether Dod
Auchenbrack
Lambgang Plantation
Hillhead Plantation
Nithbank
Langmyre Mains
Kirk Plantn
Highland
Gatelawbridge
Linnburn Hill 254
Knockbrack
Mitchellslacks
Muir Hill
Thistlemark Hill
Brown Knowe
Corfardine
Laight Hill
Glengar Hill
Woodhead
Burnhead
Stepends
Holmhill
Thornhill
Blacknest Ho
Crichope Linn
Benthead
Glass Rig
Branrigg
Mounthoolie Br
Auchengibbert Hill 372
Bennan
Penpont
Floors
Byreholm
Morton Holm
Laught Mains
Knocktimpen 315
Dollard Hill
Sowens Knowe
Morins Hill
Holehouse
Kirkconnel Burn
Craignee Wood
Tynron Doon Fort
Templand Mains
Cample
Townburn Wood
Loch Ettrick
Mc Mount
Gubhill Rig
Whaup Knowe
White Hill
Maqueston Hill
Corriedow Hill
Killiewarren
Tynron Doon
Margmony Hill 326
Stenhouse
Tynron
Shinnel Water
Keir Mill
Trigony Ho
Rosehill
Closeburn
Closeburn Mains
Lamb Hill
Great Hill 353
Shield Knowe
Green Hill
Forest of Ae
Tererran Hill
Bardennoch Hill
Capenoch Moor
Penfillan Moor
Waterside Mains
Beuchen Moor
Beuchan
High Mains
Barnmuir Hill
Shawsholm
Watchman Hill
Bruce's Well
Glencorse Hill
Burnfoot
Larchvie
Brownmoor Hill
Craigdarroch Hill 325
Caitloch
Barbuie
Hillhead
Bardennoch
Ewanston
Peelton Hill
Barr Hill
Wauk Hill 357
Beuchanhill Plantation
Park
Kirkpatrick Hill
Birswick
Nether Rig
Auchencairn Height
Auchengeith Hill
Knockespen
Crawfordton Hill
Shancastle Doon
Maxwelton Hill
Laggan Park
Keir Hills
Barjarg Tower
Barjarg Moor
Kirkpatrick
Nithsdale
Moniaive
Dungalston
Kirkland
Maxwelton House
Maxwelton Mains
Kirkcudbright Fm
Ingleston Mains
The Mull 327
Gracefield
Berscar
Whitespots
Clauchrie Hill
Clauchrie Plantn
Pennyland Moor
Big Craig
Ae Village
Wood Hill
Wood Fm
Relic Hill
Green Craig
Old Crawfordton
Castlehill
Crossford
Straith
Fleuchlarg Hill
Auchenage
Barndennoch
Barburgh Mill
Blackcraig Hill
Fern Hill
Wardlaw
Cocklet Hill
Lakehead Fm
Red Scar
Ell Rig
Girharrow Hill 389
Dalmacallan Forest
Dalmacallan Hill
Slatehouse Hill
Wallaceton
Burnside
Fleughlarg
Braco
Blackwood Ho
Lambrig Wood
Glenmidge
Black Wood
The Forest
Shaw's Hill
Watchman Moor
Gledenholm Moor
Kirkmichael Mains
Craes Hill
Skelston Moor
Boreland
Coatston
Dardarroch Woodhouse
Benan Hill
Barrhill
Auldgirth
Duncow Common
Lanrick Hall
Fulton Moor
Bogrie Hill 432
Shillingland Moor
Knockoure
West Skelston
East Skelston
Goosedubs
Whitedike
Birkshaw
Crawston Hill
Gateside
Cairnhall
Merkland
Lochmailing
Glenbrae Wood
Dalswinton
Newlands
Bog Hall
Ellerslee
North Riddingwood
Guillyburn
Johnfield Moss
Lochurr Hill
Lochurr
Loch Urr
Sundaywell
Sundaywell Moor
Castramon Moor
Gilmerston
Garrieston
Dunscore
Laggan
Springfield
Throughgate
Mc Cheynston
Burnhead
Friars Carse
Ellisland Mus & Farm
Bankhead
Bankfoot
Douganstyle
Dalswinton
Braehead
Longbank
Auchencairn
Black Mark
Craigenputtock Moor
Castramon Hill
Castramon Burn
Glenesslin Burn
Glenesslin
Nethertown Moor
Milton
Poundland
Mansegate
Lagganhill
Mc Murdoston
Kilroy
Isle
Duncow
Riddingwood Ho
Duncow Ho
Hazelrig Fm
Nether Whiteside Moor
Craighead Plantn
Burnside
Milliganton
Farthingwell
Craigdasher Hill
Lettrick Hill
Whiteside Hill
Collieston Hill
Dunesslin Moor
Stroquhan Hill
Greenside Fm
Killyleoch Hill
Townhead Wood
Mc Cubbington
Heathfield
High Farthingwell
Sunnyhill
Portrack Ho
Cowhill Tower
Kemys Hall
Gallaberry
Amisfield
Darngarroch Hill 373
Barr Hill
Upper Stroquhan Hill
Speddoch Hill
Barbuie Fm
Morrington
Berryland
Bellfield Fm
Williamsfield
Killylung
Druids Park
Carzield
Kilblane
Cullivait
Kirkton
Tinwald
Muil Hill 347
Newtonairds Wood
Birkbush
Newtonairds
Captainton
Fourmerkland
Nether Gribton
Gribton
Cormaddie
Holywood
Abbey
Templand Hill
Tinwald Parks
Glaisters
Slongaber Hill
Steilston Ho
Burnside of Balterson
Locharbriggs
Tinwald Ho
Marglolly Br
Bishop Forest Hill
Drumpark
Hall of Drumpark
Routin Br
Irongray
Cluden Lodge
Cludden
Over Broomrigg Fm
Heathfield
Auchenhay Hill
Glenkiln Res
Cornlee Hill
Margreig
Skeoch Hill
Midrig
Lag
See Morris Hill
The Grove
Maryfield
Newbridge
Newbridge Fm
Lincluden College
Ind Est
Dumfries & Galloway Aviation Mus
The Grove
Glenclair Hill
Bank
A76
A702
A701
B729
B797
B740
259
248
237
7
8
9
10
11
A
B
C
D
E
F
G
H
NS
NX
00
10
80

A74(M)
Ericstane
Granton
Howslack
Capplegill
Roundstonefoot
Moffat
MOFFAT MUSEUM
Coatsgate
Beattock
Easter Earshaig
Kinnelhead
Craigieburn
CRAIGIEBURN
Dumcrieff
Mid Murthat
Laverhay
Leithenhall
Minnygap
Lochwood
Newton
Plantationfoot
Waterhead
Sandyford
Raehills
St Ann's
Johnstonebridge
Springwells
Chapelhill
Dinwoodie Mains
Annandale Water Services
Blackacre
Courance
Boreland
Gillesbie
Greyrigg
Parkgate
Nethermill
Sibbaldbie
Templand
Comrie
Millhousebridge
Corrie Common
Shieldhill
Applegarthtown
Paddockhole
Marjoriebanks
Watchill
Lochmaben
Halleaths
LOCHMABEN CASTLE
Tinwald
Lockerbie
LOCKERBIE
Bankshill
Heck
Greenhill
Blackford
Hightae
Burnswark
BURNSWARK HILL FORT
Eskdalemuir Forest
Forest of Ae
Ae Village
Annandale
DUMFRIES & GALLOWAY
Davington
Nether Cassock
SOUTHERN UPLAND WAY
A701
A708
A709
B7076
B7020
B723
B7068
260
247
238
0 1 2 3 miles
0 1 2 3 4 5 km

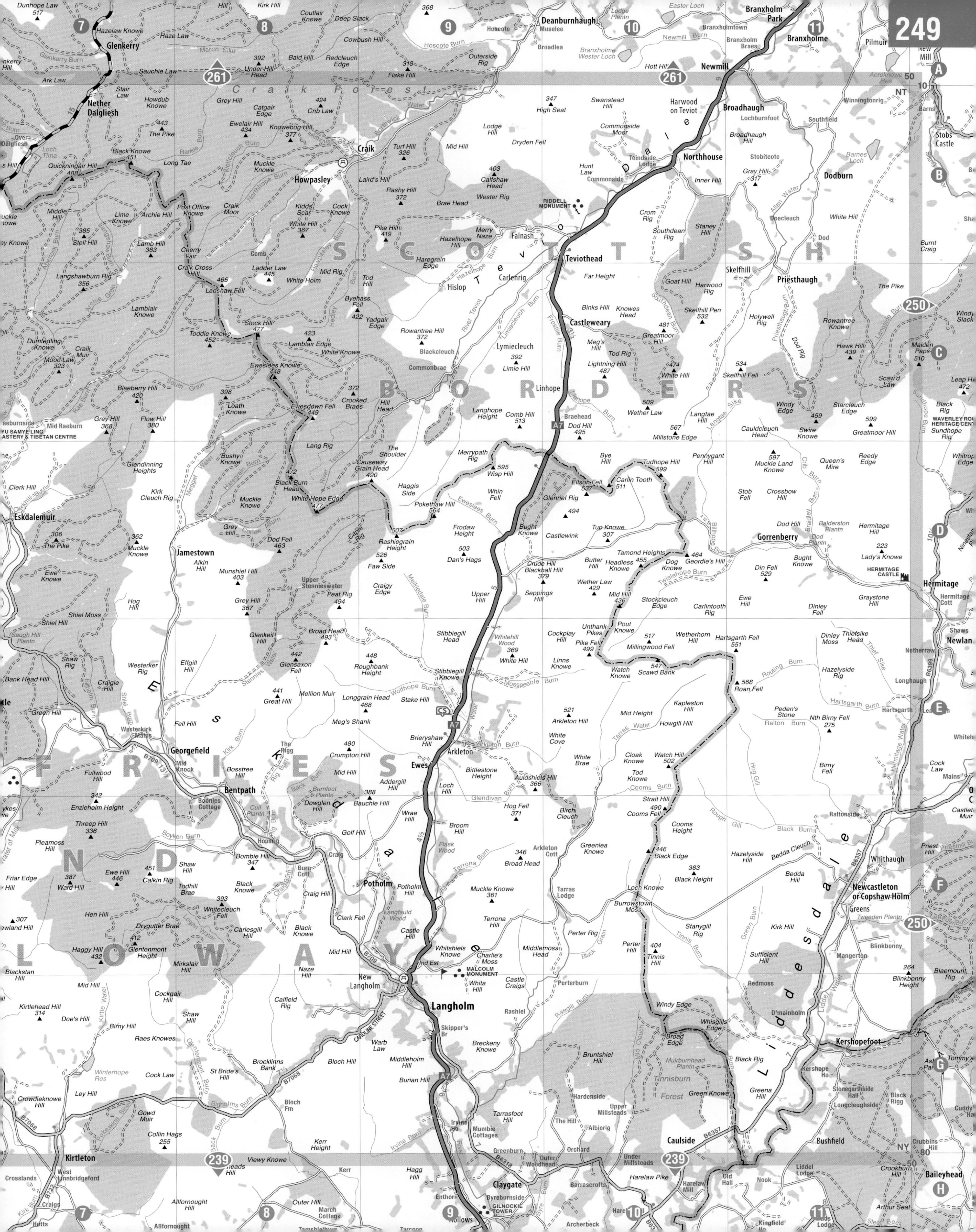

Dunhope Law
517
Hazelaw Knowe
Glenkerry
Haze Law
Kirk Hill
Coutlair Knowe
Deep Slack
Cowbush Hill
Deanburnhaugh
Muselee
Hoscote
Broadlea
Lodge Plantn
Easter Loch
Branxholm Park
Branxholmtown
Newmill Burn
Branxholm Braes
Branxholme
Branxholme Wester Loch
Pilmuir
New Mill
Glenkerry Burn
March Sike
Under Hill Head
Bald Hill
Redcleuch Edge
Flake Hill
Outerside Rig
Hoscote Burn
Hott Hill
Newmill
Sauchie Law
261
Ark Law
Craik Forest
Acreknowe Res
NT
Stair Law
Nether Dalgliesh
Howdub Knowe
Grey Hill
Catgair Edge
Crib Law
High Seat
Swanstead Hill
Harwood on Teviot
Broadhaugh
Lochburnfoot
Winningtonrig
Southfield
Barns
Stobs Castle
Ewelair Hill
The Pike
Knowebog Hill
Craik
Turf Hill
Lodge Hill
Mid Hill
Dryden Fell
Commonside Moor
Broadhaugh Hill
Stobitcote
Barnes Loch
Black Knowe
Quickningair Hill
Long Tae
Muckle Knowe
Howpasley
Laird's Hill
Calfshaw Head
Rashy Hill
Hunt Law
Commonside
Teindside Lodge
Northhouse
Gray Hill
Inner Hill
Dodburn
Middle Hill
Lime Knowe
Archie Hill
Post Office Knowe
Craik Moor
Kidds Scar
Cock Knowe
Brae Head
Wester Rig
RIDDELL MONUMENT
Crom Rig
Doecleuch
White Hill
Stell Hill
Lamb Hill
Pike Hill
Hazelhope Hill
Merry Naze
Falnash
Southdean Rig
Staney Hill
Dod
Burnt Craig
Cherry Lair
Comb
Mid Rig
Haregrain Edge
Teviothead
SCOTTISH
Craik Cross Hill
Ladder Law
Ladshaw Fell
White Holm
Tod Hill
Hislop
Carlenrig
Far Height
Skelfhill
Goat Hill
Harwood Rig
Priesthaugh
The Pike
Langshawburn Rig
Lamblair Knowe
Byehass Fell
Yadgair Edge
Binks Hill
Knowes Head
Skelfhill Pen
Holywell Rig
Rowantree Knowe
250
Windy Slack
Stock Hill
Toddle Knowe
Rowantree Hill
Blackcleuch
Castleweary
Greatmoor Hill
Hawk Hill
Maiden Paps
Dumfedling Knowe
Craik Muir
Mood Law
Lamblair Edge
White Knowe
Lymiecleuch
Meg's Hill
Tod Rig
Dod Rig
Eweslees Knowe
Commonbrae
Limie Hill
Lightning Hill
White Hill
Skelfhill Fell
Scaw'd Law
Leap Hill
BORDERS
Blaeberry Hill
Crooked Braes
Hill Head
Linhope
Windy Edge
Starcleuch Edge
Black Rig
Loath Knowe
Ewesdown Fell
Langhope Height
Comb Hill
Braehead
Wether Law
Langtae Hill
Swire Knowe
SAMYE LING MONASTERY & TIBETAN CENTRE
Mid Raeburn
Grey Hill
Flow Hill
Dod Hill
Millstone Edge
Cauldcleuch Head
Greatmoor Hill
WAVERLEY ROUTE HERITAGE CENTRE
Sundhope Rig
Lang Rig
The Shoulder
Merrypath Rig
Bye Hill
Tudhope Hill
Pennygant Hill
Muckle Land Knowe
Queen's Mire
Reedy Edge
Whitrope Edge
Glendinning Heights
Bushy Knowe
Causeway Grain Head
Wisp Hill
Carlin Tooth
Ellson Fell
Clerk Hill
Kirk Cleuch Rig
Black Burn Head
Haggis Side
Whin Fell
Glenrief Rig
Stob Fell
Crossbow Hill
Eskdalemuir
Muckle Knowe
White Hope Edge
Pokethaw Hill
Frodaw Height
Bught Knowe
Castlewink
Tup Knowe
Dod Hill
Balderston Plantn
Hermitage Hill
The Pike
Grey Hill
Dod Fell
Rashiegrain Height
Dan's Hags
Tamond Heights
Headless Knowe
Geordie's Hill
Gorrenberry
Lady's Knowe
Muckle Knowe
Jamestown
Alkin Hill
Faw Side
Crude Hill
Blackhall Hill
Butter Hill
Dog Knowe
Bught Knowe
Din Fell
HERMITAGE CASTLE
Hermitage
Ewe Knowe
Munshiel Hill
Upper Stennieswater
Craigy Edge
Wether Law
Seppings Hill
Mid Hill
Hog Hill
Grey Hill
Peat Rig
Upper Hill
Stockcleuch Edge
Carlintooth Rig
Ewe Hill
Dinley Fell
Graystone Hill
Hermitage Cott
Shiel Moss
Shiel Hill
Glenkeil Hill
Broad Head
Stibbiegill Head
Whitehill Wood
Cockplay Hill
Unthank Pikes
Pout Knowe
Millingwood Fell
Wetherhorn Hill
Hartsgarth Fell
Dinley Moss
Thiefsike Head
Shaws
Newlan
Netherraw
Saugh Hill Plantn
Shaw Rig
Glensaxon Fell
Roughbank Height
White Hill
Pike Fell
Linns Knowe
Watch Knowe
Scawd Bank
Westerker Rig
Effgill Hill
Stibbiegill Knowe
Mosspeeble Burn
Hazelyside Rig
Bank Head Hill
Craigie Hill
Great Hill
Mellion Muir
Longgrain Head
Wolfhope Burn
Stake Hill
Roan Fell
Longhaugh
Green Hill
Westerkirk Mains
Fell Hill
Meg's Shank
Arkleton Hill
Mid Height
Kapleston Hill
Howgill Hill
Peden's Stone
Nth Birny Fell
Ralton Burn
Hartsgarth
Georgefield
Mid Knock
The Rigg
Crumpton Hill
Brieryshaw Hill
Arkleton
White Cove
Cloak Knowe
Watch Hill
White Brae
Birny Fell
Cock Law
Mains
FRIES
Fullwood Hill
Bosstree Hill
Mid Hill
Ewes
Addergill Hill
Bittlestone Height
Auldshiels Hill
Tod Knowe
Cooms Burn
Bentpath
Boonies Cottage
Burnfoot Plantn
Dowglen Hill
Bauchle Hill
Loch Hill
Glendivan Burn
Hog Fell
Strait Hill
Cooms Fell
Birch Cleuch
Raltonside
Enzieholm Height
Threep Hill
Golf Hill
Wrae Hill
Broom Hill
Cooms Height
Black Burn
Rough Gill
Priest Hill
Hopsrig
Boyken Burn
Pleamoss Hill
Craig
Flask Wood
Arkleton Cott
Greenlea Knowe
Black Edge
Hazelyside Hill
Bedda Cleuch
Whithaugh
Shaw Hill
Bombie Hill
Burn Cott
Broad Head
Black Height
Bedda Hill
Friar Edge
Ward Hill
Ewe Hill
Calkin Rig
Todhill Brae
Black Knowe
Potholm
Potholm Hill
Craig Hill
Muckle Knowe
Tarras Lodge
Loch Knowe
Burrowstown Moss
Newcastleton or Copshaw Holm
Greens
Tweeden Plantn
Hen Hill
Whitecleuch Fell
Langfauld Wood
Clark Fell
Terrona Hill
Stanygill Rig
Kirk Hill
Drygutter Brae
Glentenmont Height
Carlesgill Hill
Black Knowe
Castle Hill
Whitshiels Knowe
Charlie's Moss
Middlemoss Head
Perter Rig
Perter Hill
Tinnis Hill
Sufficient Hill
Blinkbonny
Mangerton
Haggy Hill
Mid Hill
Mirkslair Hill
Naze Hill
Blackstan Hill
New Langholm
MALCOLM MONUMENT
Whita Hill
Castle Craigs
Perterburn
Liddesdale
Blinkbonny Height
Blaemount Rig
Redmoss
Mid Hill
Cockgair Hill
Calfield Rig
Langholm
Rashiel
Windy Edge
D'mainholm
Kirtlehead Hill
Doe's Hill
Shaw Hill
Birny Hill
CARLINE STREET
Skipper's Br
Whisgills Edge
Raes Knowes
Warb Law
Breckeny Knowe
Bruntshiel Hill
Broad Edge
Kershopefoot
Winterhope Res
Cock Law
St Bride's Hill
Brocklinns Bank
Bloch Hill
Middleholm Hill
Muirburnhead Plantn
Black Rig
Kershope Ho
Tommy's
Tinnisburn Forest
Burian Hill
Ley Hill
Green Knowe
Greena Hill
Stonegarthside Hall
Black Rigg
Crowdieknowe Hill
Bloch Fm
Bigholms Burn
Hardenside
Upper Millsteads
Longcleughside
Gowd Muir
Irvine Ho
Tarrasfoot Hill
The Hill
Albierig
Mumbie Cottages
Collin Hags
Heart Height
Irvine Burn
Greenburn
Orchard
Caulside
Bushfield
Crubbins Hill
NY
Kirtleton
239
Viewy Knowe
Outer Woodhead
Under Millsteads
Crosslands
West Linnbridgeford
Kerr
Hagg Hill
Claygate
Barrascrofts
Harelaw Pike
Harelaw Mill
Old Hall
Nook
Liddel Lodge
Crookburn Hill
Baileyhead
Craigs
Allfornought Hill
Outer Hill
March Cottage
Enthorn
Byreburnside
GILNOCKIE TOWER
Hare
Arthur Seat
Hutts
Allfornought
Hollows
Archerbeck
Kingfield

Bonchester Bridge
Bonchester Hill
Hobkirk
Cleuch Head
Mackside
Chesters
Southdean
Southdean Lodge
Highlee Hill
Weasel Hill
Lethem
Huntford
Bught Knowe
REDESWIRE FRAY 1575
Carter Bar
Catcleuch Shin
Whitelee
Lumsdon Law
Ramshope Lodge
Catcleugh
Catcleugh Reservoir
Philip Law 414
Hophills Nob 359
Knock Hills
Deerlee Knowe
Lamblair Edge
Arks Edge
Fairwood Fell
Leap Hill
Edgerston
Edgerston Rig
Falside
Roughlee
White Hill
Hareshaw Knowe
Crink Law
Steele Knowe
Croft Plantn
Doorpool Hill
Birneyknowe
Colliforthill
Colislinn
Adderston Lee
Hoggfield Hill
New Mill
Highend
Stonedge
Winningtonrig
White Hill
Stobs Castle
Cogsmill
Peat Law
Stonedge Forest
Stonedge Hill
Wolflee Hill 393
Cribs Hole
Wauchope Fm
Crag Bank
CRAGBANK WOOD
Hell's Hole
Sim's Knowe
Berryfell Fm
Berryfell Hill
Pike Fell 400
Templehall Hill
Wauchope Common
Black Hill
Peden's Cleuch
Millmoor Rig
Tamshiel Rig
Burns
Scaw'd Law
Green Law
Black Cleuch
Shankend Fm
Burnt Craig
Harwood Moss
Brown's Hill
Brockie Law
Wellcleuch Plantn
Green Law
Meadow Cleuch
Shankend Hill
The Pike
Langburnshiels
Cooper's Cleuch
Wyndburgh Hill 507
Wauchope Forest
Hardlee Flow
Dun Knowe
Windy Slack
Wigg Knowe
Dog Knowe
Fanna Hill 514
Note o' the Gate
Rushy Rig
Needs Law 444
Dun Tae
Knox Knowe 500
Carter Fell 556
WHITELEE MOOR
Cross Cleugh
Scrathy Holes
Maiden Paps 510
Outer Knowe Head 415
Kiln Knowe
Whitegrain Fell
Lamblair Hill 498
Singdean
East Hill
Coomb Edge
Wheelrig Head 448
Hartshorn Pike 545
Haggie Knowe
Limestone Knowe 551
Upper Stony Holes
Grey Mares Knowe 516
White Crags
Kielderhead Moor
KIELDERHEAD
Chattlehope Crag
Redesdale Forest
Girdle Fell
Cairn Cleugh
Leap Hill 472
Sandy Edge
Lime Kiln Edge
Scaw'd Law
Black Rig
Whitrope Cottages
WAVERLEY ROUTE HERITAGE CENTRE
Sundhope Rig
Greatmoor Hill
Mid Hill
Coopercleuch Knowe
Dod Fell
Heather Knowe
Craigy Knowe
Peel Fell 602
The Cheviot Hills
Wool Meath
Woolmeath Edge
Long Crag
Reedy Edge
Whitrope Edge
White Knowe
Stitchel Hill 318
Caddroun Rig
Saughtree Fell
Liddesdale
Rushy Knowe
Mid Fell
West Kielder Moor
Kielder Head
Woody Crags
East Kielder Moor
Blackmar Law
KIELDER
Scaup Pikes
Scaup
Bran's Walls
Blakehope Nick
Street Head
Berrymoor Edge 459
Whitropefoot
Bell Hill
Biccarton Junction
Windy Knowe
Hob Knowe
Deadwater
Wirchet
Deadwater Fell 569
Greyhound Law
Ewe Hill
Hermitage Hill
Lady's Knowe 223
HERMITAGE CASTLE
Hermitage
Blackwood Hill
Shiel Knowe
Saughtree
Thorlieshope
Thorlieshope Pike 360
Thorlieshope Heights
Bells Moor
Ravenshill Moor
FOREST PARK
Three Pikes
Hogswood Moor
Monk Side 513
Wether Lair
Smallhope Rigg
Long Crag
Round Law
Emblehope Moor
Graystone Hill
Hermitage Cott
Arnton Fell
Bught Knowe
Burnmouth Fm
Yarrow Knowe 295
Foulmire Heights
SCOTTISH BORDERS
Shaws
Newlands
Netherraw
Larriston
Larriston Rigg
Hirst Craig
403
Loch Knowe
Crag Head
Kielder
Greys Pike 445
Mount Common
Hawk Knowe
Burn Grange
Harper Crag
Longhaugh
The Steele
Steele Road
Steeleroad-end
Hewisbridge Cott
Rain's Hill
Black Fell
Bewshaugh
Cat Cairn
Butteryhaugh
KIELDER CASTLE VISITOR CENTRE
Devil's Lapful
Wainhope
Millstone Crag
Earl's Seat
The Dodd 353
Leahaugh
Larriston Fells 512
Buckside Knowe
Gowanburn
Whitehaugh
Dinlabyre
Kirndean
Black Knowe
Bakethin Res
Pithouse Crags
Bellingburn
Bellingburn Head
Rabbit Crag
Highfield
Cock Law
Mains
Hobb's Flow
Coal Grain
Buck Fell
Kielder Forest
The Cross
Ewe Knowe
Old Castleton
Flight Moss
Akenshawburn
Ferny Knowe
Wellhaugh
Pope's Hill
Castleton Muir
Harden Moss
Watch Knowe
Wilson's Pike
Hawkhope
Priest Hill
Harden Hill
Scotch Knowe
The Forks
Rushy Knowe
Wind Hill
Hawkhope
Hawkhope Hill
Green Eyes Crags
Whithaugh
Stell Knowe
Dinmontlair Knowe
Caplestone Fell
Eliott's Pike
KIELDER WATER BIRDS OF PREY CENTRE
Kielder Water
Falstone
Yarrow
Newcastleton or Copshaw Holm
Greens
Black Knowe
Newcastleton Forest
Lazy Knowe
Greenside
Scald Pike
Bullcrag Edge
TOWER KNOWE VISITOR CENTRE
Yarrow Moor
Stannersburn
Stokoe
Tweeden Plantn
Long Knowe
Kershopehead
Glendhu Hill 514
Dove Crags
High Long Ho
Kateshaw Hill
Rough Pike
Stower Hill
Low Cranecleugh
White Side
Ridge End
River North Tyne
Blinkbonny
Blinkbonny Height 264
Blaemount Rig
Lishaw Rigg
Muckle Knowe
Geordy's Pike
Long Rigg
Broomy Hill
Drove Rigg
Dings Rigg
Smalesmouth
English Kershope
Robbie's Rigg
Black Hill
Will's Knowe
Broomylinn
Jock's Pike
CUMBRIA
Skelton Pike
Reamy Rigg
Beckhead Crag
Stot Crags
Gill Pike
The Rigg
Kyloe Crags
Archy's Rigg
Roughside Moor
Hopefoot
Ash Park
Tommy's Fell
Kershope Forest
Christianbury Crag 487
Burnt Tom Crags
Byreshield Hill
Long Crags
Black Crags
Blacklyne Common
Story's Gairs
Christy's Crags
Bolts Law 395
Black Rigg
Cuddy's Hall
Blacklyne Ho
Bewcastle Fells
Kettle Hall
Sighty Crag 518
Horse Head
Black Knowe 492
Rushy Knowe
Black Cleugh
Allerybank
Black Knors 248
Crubbins Hill
Bailey Head
Long Bar
Whitelyne Common
Smuggy's Pike
Long Crags
Hopehouse
Chirdon Burn
Black Knors
Black Stantling
The Shanks
KIELDER MIRES
Slaty Crag
Long Crag 456
The Flatt
Watch Rigg
Greyfell Common
Lowe Bush
Paddaburn
Muckle Samuel's Crags
Little Dodd Hill
High Cap Edge
Crew Crag
Irthing Head
Blind Sike
Whitehill
Gaylock Hill
Cammock
Holmehead
Nook
Blackpool Gate
Arthur Seat
0 1 2 3 miles
0 1 2 3 4 5 km
262
249
240

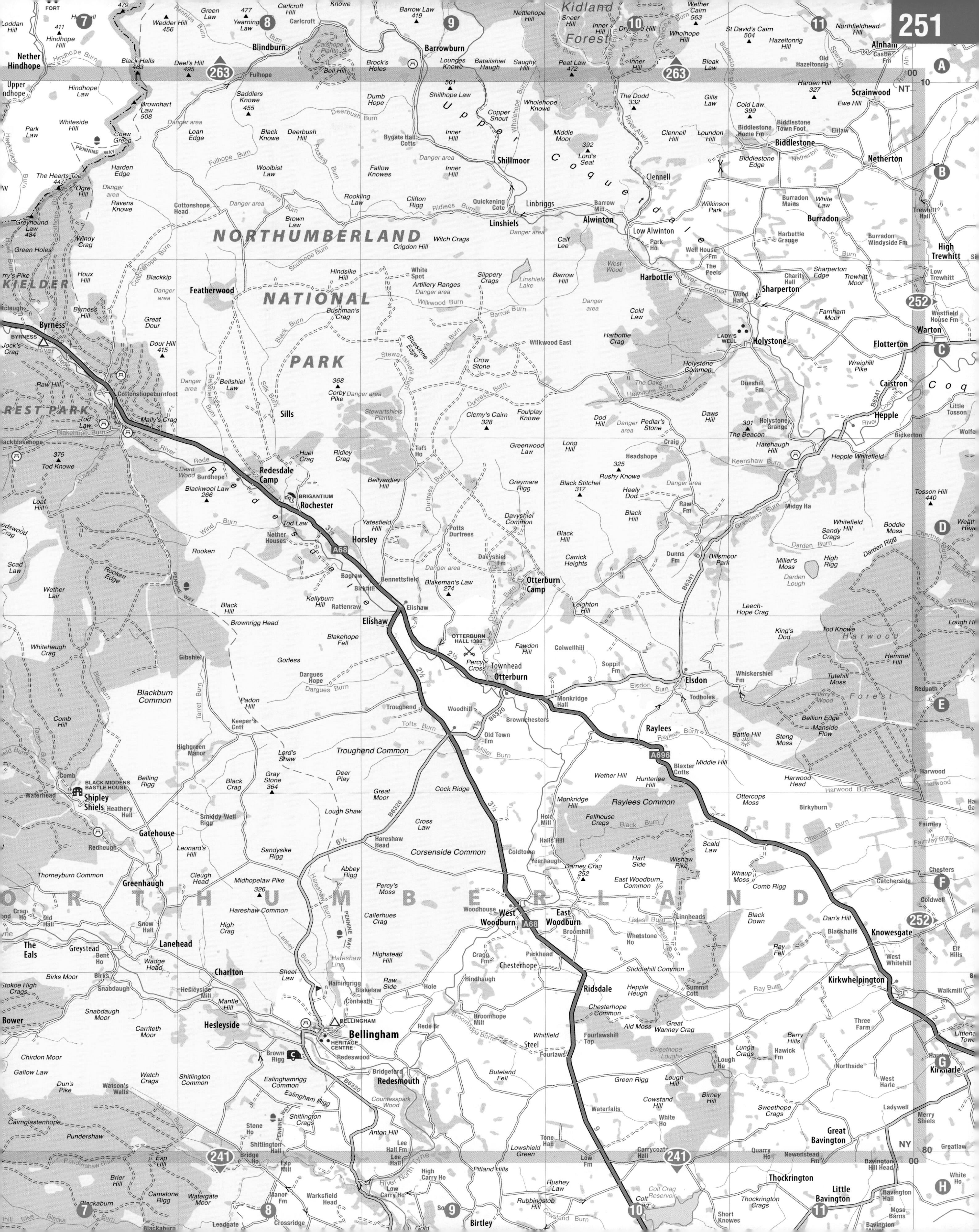

Loddan Hill
Nether Hindhope
Hindhope Hill
Green Law
Yearning Law
Wedder Hill
Carlcroft Hill
Carlcroft
Blindburn
Barrowburn
Barrow Law
Nettlehope Hill
Kidland Forest
Sneer Hill
Inner Hill
Wether Cairn
Wholhope Hill
St David's Cairn
Hazeltonrig Hill
Northfieldhead Hill
Alnham
Castle Fm
Black Halls
Deel's Hill
Fulhope
Brock's Holes
Lounges Knowe
Bataishiel Haugh
Saughy Hill
Peat Law
Bleak Law
Old Hazeltonrig
Harden Hill
Scrainwood
Upper Hindhope
Hindhope Law
Brownhart Law
Saddlers Knowe
Dumb Hope
Shillhope Law
Upper Coquetdale
Copper Snout
Wholehope Knowe
The Dodd
Gills Law
Cold Law
Ewe Hill
Whiteside Hill
Park Law
Chew Green
Pennine Way
Loan Edge
Black Knowe
Deerbush Hill
Bygate Hall Cotts
Inner Hill
Middle Moor
Lord's Seat
Clennell Hill
Loundon Hill
Biddlestone Home Fm
Biddlestone Town Foot
Biddlestone
Elilaw
Netherton
Harden Edge
Woolbist Law
Fallow Knowes
Danger area
Shillmoor
Biddlestone Edge
The Hearts Toe
Ogre Hill
Ravens Knowe
Cottonshope Head
Rookling Law
Clifton Rigg
Quickening Cote
Linbriggs
Barrow Mill
Clennell
Alwinton
Linshiels
Burradon Mains
White Law
Burradon
Trewhitt Hall
Greyhound Law
Windy Crag
Green Holes
Brown Law
Witch Crags
Crigdon Hill
Low Alwinton
Park Ho
Calf Lee
Well House Fm
Harbottle Grange
Burradon Windyside Fm
High Trewhitt
NORTHUMBERLAND NATIONAL PARK
Houx Hill
KIELDER
Blackkip
Featherwood
Hindsike Hill
White Spot
Artillery Ranges
Slippery Crags
Linshiels Lake
Barrow Hill
West Wood
Harbottle
The Peels
Charity Hall
Sharperton Edge
Trewhitt Moor
Low Trewhitt
Sharperton
Wood Hall
Byrness Hill
Byrness
Great Dour
Bushman's Crag
Wilkwood Burn
Barrow Burn
Cold Law
Farnham Moor
Westfield House Fm
Warton
Jock's Crag
Dour Hill
Bluestone Edge
Wilkwood East
Harbottle Crag
Lady's Well
Holystone
Flotterton
Crow Stone
Holystone Common
Wreighill Pike
Raw Hill
Cottonshopeburnfoot
Danger area
Bellshiel Law
Corby Pike
Caistron
REST PARK
Sills
Stewartshiels Plantn
The Oaks
Dueshill Fm
Tod Law
Mally's Crag
Clemy's Cairn
Foulplay Knowe
Dod Hill
Pedlar's Stone
Daws Hill
Holystone Grange
Hepple
Little Tosson
Blakehope Burn
Toft Ho
The Beacon
Bickerton
Tod Knowe
Dead Wood
Burdhope
Huel Crag
Ridley Crag
Greenwood Law
Long Hill
Craig
Harehaugh Hill
Hepple Whitefield
Redesdale Camp
Headshope
Rushy Knowe
Blackwool Law
Rochester
Brigantium
Bellyardley Hill
Greymare Rigg
Black Stitchel
Heely Dod
Tosson Hill
Loaf Hill
Tod Law
Yatesfield Hill
Potts Durtrees
Davyshiel Common
Black Hill
Raw Fm
Midgy Ha
Whitefield Hill
Boddle Moss
Nether Houses
Horsley
Black Hill
Sandy Crags
Darden Rigg
Scad Law
Rooken
Rooken Edge
A68
Davyshiel Fm
Carrick Heights
Dunns Fm
Billsmoor Park
Miller's Moss
High Rigg
Wether Lair
Bagraw
Birkhill
Bennettsfield
Blakeman's Law
Otterburn Camp
Darden Lough
Kellyburn Hill
Rattenraw
Elishaw
Leighton Hill
Leech-Hope Crag
Black Hill
Brownrigg Head
Elishaw
Otterburn Hall 1388
King's Dod
Tod Knowe
Harwood
Lough Hill
Whiteheugh Crag
Blakehope Fell
Fawdon Hill
Colwellhill
Gibshiel
Gorless
Percy's Cross
Townhead
Soppit Fm
Hemmel Hill
Dargues Hope
Otterburn
Elsdon
Whiskershiel Fm
Tutehill Moss
Blackburn Common
Padon Hill
Troughend
Monkridge Hall
Todholes
Forest
Redpath
Woodhill
B6320
Brownchesters
Keeper's Cott
Raylees
Harry's Wood
Bellion Edge
Manside Flow
Comb Hill
Old Town Fm
Battle Hill
Steng Moss
Highgreen Manor
Lord's Shaw
Troughend Common
A696
Middle Hill
Blaxter Cotts
Harwood
Black Middens Bastle House
Belling Rigg
Black Crag
Gray Stone
Deer Play
Wether Hill
Hunterlee Hill
Harwood Head
Shipley Shiels
Waterhead
Heathery Hall
Great Moor
Cock Ridge
Monkridge Hill
Raylees Common
Ottercops Moss
Birkyburn
Smiddy-Well Rigg
Lough Shaw
Fellhouse Crags
Hole Mill
Fairnley
Gatehouse
Redheugh
Cross Law
Hareshaw Head
Halls Hill
Leonard's Hill
Sandysike Rigg
Corsenside Common
Coldtown
Yearhaugh
Scald Law
Hart Side
Wishaw Pike
Thorneyburn Common
Abbey Rigg
Darney Crag
East Woodburn Common
Whaup Moss
Comb Rigg
Chesters
Catcherside
Greenhaugh
Cleugh Head
Midhopelaw Pike
Percy's Moss
NORTHUMBERLAND
Hareshaw Common
Woodhouse
West Woodburn
East Woodburn
Linnheads
Black Down
Dan's Hill
Blackhalls
Coldwell
Knowesgate
Old Hall
The Eals
Greystead
Snow Hall
High Crag
Callerhues Crag
Lisles Burn
Broomhill
Whetstone Ho
Lanehead
Bent Ho
Wadge Head
Highstead Hill
Cragg Fm
Parkhead
Chesterhope
Ray Fell
West Whitehill
Elf Hills
Birks Moor
Birks
Charlton
Sheel Law
Raw Side
Hindhaugh
Stiddlehill Common
Kirkwhelpington
Stokoe High Crags
Snabdaugh
Hesleyside Mill
Mantle Hill
Hainingrigg
Blakelaw
Hole
Conheath
Ridsdale
Hepple Heugh
Summit Cott
Ray Burn
Walkmill
Snabdaugh Moor
Bower
Carriteth Moor
Hesleyside
Bellingham
Heritage Centre
Rede Br
Broomhope Mill
Chesterhope Common
Aid Moss
Great Wanney Crag
Three Farm
Whitfield
Fourlawshill Top
Steel
Fourlaws
Sweethope Loughs
Lunga Crags
Berry Hills
Hawick Fm
Chirdon Moor
Brown Rigg
Redeswood
Gallow Law
Watch Crags
Shitlington Common
Bridgeford
Redesmouth
Buteland Fell
Lough Ho
Northside
Kirkharle
Duns Pike
Watson's Walls
Ealinghamrigg Common
Ealingham Rigg
Green Rigg
Lough Hill
Birney Hill
West Harle
Countesspark Wood
Cowstand Hill
Sweethope Crags
Ladywell
Cairnglastenhope
Shitlington Crags
Waterfalls
White Ho
Merry Shiels
Pundershaw
Stone Ho
Anton Hill
Great Bavington
Tone Hall
Lowshield Green
Carrycoats Hall
Quarry Ho
Newonstead Fm
Greatlaw
Esp Hill
Shitlington Hall
Bridge Ho
Esp Mill
Lee Hall Fm
Lee Hall
Low Fm
Bavington Hill Head
Brier Hill
Camstone Rigg
High Carry Ho
Pitland Hills
Colt Crag Reservoir
Thockrington
White Ho
Watergate Moor
Manor Fm
Warksfield Head
Low Carry Ho
Rushey Law
Rubbingstob Hill
Thockrington Crags
Little Bavington
Bavington Hall
Blackaburn
Leadgate
Crossridge
Birtley
Short Knowes
Moss Barns
Bavington

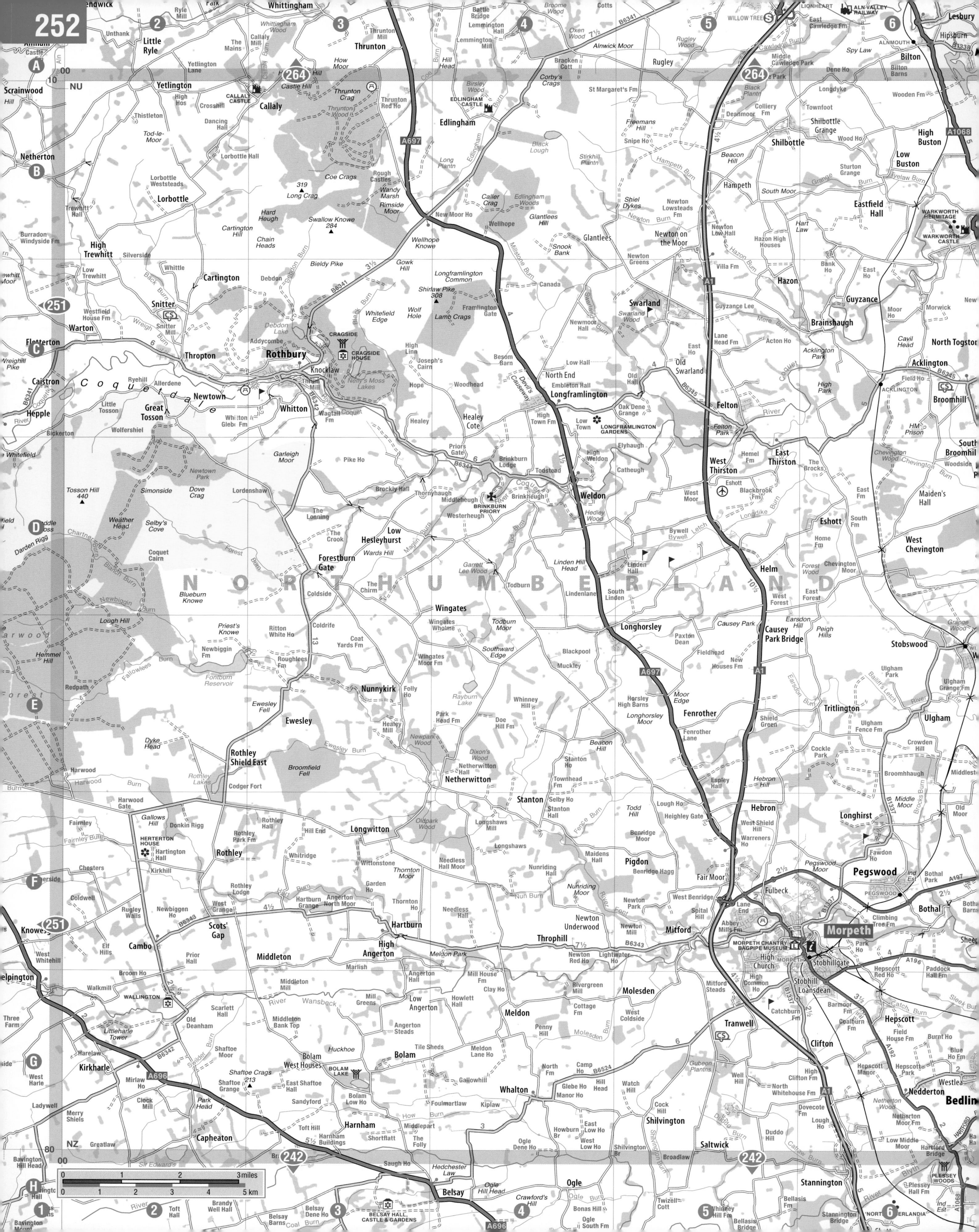
264
251
242
NORTHUMBERLAND
Coquetdale
Alnwick
Whittingham
Thrunton
Little Ryle
Unthank
The Mains
Callaly Mill
Battle Bridge
Lemmington Hall
Lemmington Mill
Broome Wood
Oxen Wood
Cotts
B6341
Alnwick Moor
Rugley Wood
Rugley
Willow Tree
Lionheart
Aln Valley Railway
East Cawledge Fm
Cawledge Park
Middle Cawledge Park
Spy Law
Alnmouth
Lesbury
Hipsburn
B1338
Bilton
Bilton Barns
Dene Ho
Scrainwood
Yetlington
Yetlington Lane
Callaly Castle
Callaly
Castle Hill
Thrunton Crag
Thrunton Wood
Thrunton Red Ho
How Moor
Hill Head
Bracken Cott
Corby's Crags
St Margaret's Fm
Black Plantn
Colliery Fm
Deanmoor
Longdyke
Wooden Fm
Townfoot
Shilbottle Grange
Shilbottle
Wood Ho
High Buston
Low Buston
A1068
Netherton
Thistleton
High Hos
Crosshill
Dancing Hall
Tod-le-Moor
Lorbottle Hall
Edlingham Castle
Edlingham
A697
Long Plantn
Black Lough
Freemans Hill
Snipe Ho
Stirkhill Plantn
Beacon Hill
Hampeth
Hampeth Burn
South Moor
Sturton Grange
Tyelaw Burn
Eastfield Hall
Lorbottle Weststeads
Lorbottle
Coe Crags
319 Long Crag
Rough Castles
Wandy Marsh
Rimside Moor
Caller Crag
Edlingham Woods
Shiel Dykes
Newton Lowsteads Fm
Newton Burn
Trewhitt Hall
Hard Heugh
Swallow Knowe 284
New Moor Ho
Wellhope
Glantlees Hill
Newton Low Hall
Hart Law
Warkworth Hermitage
Warkworth Castle
Burradon Windyside Fm
High Trewhitt
Silverside
Cartington Hill
Chain Heads
Wellhope Knowe
Snook Bank
Glantlees
Newton on the Moor
Hazon High Houses
Low Trewhitt
Whittle
Bieldy Pike
Gowk Hill
Longframlington Common
Millstone Burn
Newton Greens
Villa Fm
Bank Ho
East Ho
Hazon
Cartington
Debdon
Debdon Burn
B6341
Shirlaw Pike 308
Canada
Swarland
Guyzance
Snitter
Westfield House Fm
Warton
Snitter Mill
Whitefield Edge
Wolf Hole
Lamb Crags
Framlington Gate
Swarland Wood
Guyzance Lee
Newmoor Hall
Moor Ho
Morwick
Brainshaugh
Flotterton
Debdon Lake
Addycombe
Cragside
Cragside House
High Linn
Joseph's Cairn
Lane Head Fm
Mere Burn
Acton Ho
Cavil Head
North Togston
Thropton
Rothbury
Besom Barn
East Ho
Low Hall
Old Swarland
Acklington Park
Acklington
Caistron
Ryehill
Allerdene
Knocklaw
Thrum Mill
Nelly's Moss Lakes
Hope
Woodhead
Devil's Causeway
North End
Embleton Hall
Longframlington
Old Hall
B6345
High Park
Field Ho
Acklington
Broomhill
Hepple
Newtown
Little Tosson
Great Tosson
Whitton
Whitton Glebe Fm
Wagtail Fm
B6342
Healey
Healey Cote
High Town Fm
Low Town
Longframlington Gardens
Oak Dene Grange
Felton
Felton Park
HM Prison
Bickerton
Wolfershiel
Garleigh Moor
Priors Gate
Elyhaugh
South Broomhill
Whitefield
Newtown Park
Simonside
Dove Crag
Lordenshaw
Pike Ho
Brinkburn Lodge
B6344
Todstead
High Weldon
Catheugh
West Thirston
Hemel Fm
East Thirston
Chevington Wood
The Brocks
Woodside
Tosson Hill 440
Brockly Hall
Thornyhaugh
Middleheugh
Brinkburn Priory
Brinkheugh
Weldon
Eshott
Blackbrook Fm
West Moor
Hedley Wood
Longdike Burn
East Fm
Maiden's Hall
Weather Head
Selby's Cove
The Lonning
The Crook
Low Hesleyhurst
Westerheugh
Todburn
Bywell
Bywell Letch
South Fm
Darden Rigg
Chartners Burn
Coquet Cairn
Forestburn Gate
Wards Hill
Magin Burn
Garrett Lee Wood
Linden Hill Head
Linden Hall
Home Fm
Helm
West Chevington
Blanch Burn
Forest Burn
The Chirm
Coldside
Todburn
Lindenlane
South Linden
West Forest
Forest Wood
Chevington Moor
East Forest
Newbiggin Burn
Blueburn Knowe
Wingates
Wingates Wholme
Todburn Moor
Longhorsley
Causey Park
Causey Park Bridge
Eardson Hill
Peigh Hills
Stobswood
Lough Hill
Priest's Knowe
Ritton White Ho
Coldrife
Coat Yards Fm
Southward Edge
Blackpool
Paxton Dene
Fieldhead
New Houses Fm
Hemmel Hill
Newbiggin Fm
Roughlees
Wingates Moor Fm
Muckley
Ulgham Park
Ulgham Grange Fm
Fallowlees Burn
Fontburn Reservoir
Redpath
Nunnykirk
Folly Ho
Rayburn Lake
Whinney Hill
Horsley High Barns
Longhorsley Moor
Moor Edge
Fenrother
Shield Green
Tritlington
Ulgham
Ewesley Fell
Ewesley
Healey Mill
Park Head Fm
Doe Hill Fm
Fenrother Lane
Ulgham Fence Fm
Crowden Hill
Dyke Head
Rothley Shield East
Newpark Wood
Ewesley Burn
Dixon's Wood
Netherwitton Hall
Netherwitton
Beacon Hill
Stanton Ho
Cockle Park
Broomfield Fell
Harwood
Rothley Lakes
Codger Fort
Townhead Fm
Espley Hall
Hebron Hill
Broomhaugh
Middlest
Harwood Gate
Stanton
Selby Ho
Stanton Hall
Todd Hill
Lough Ho
Heighley Gate
Hebron
Middle Moor
B1337
Longhirst
Old Moor
Fairnley
Gallows Hill
Donkin Rigg
Rothley Hall
Hill End
Longwitton
Oldpark Wood
Longshaws Mill
Fence Burn
Benridge Moor
West Shield Hill
Warreners Ho
Herterton House
Hartington Hall
Rothley Park Fm
Rothley
Whitridge
Wittonstone
Needless Hall Moor
Longshaws
Maidens Hall
Pigdon
Benridge Hagg
Fawdon Ho
Pegswood Moor
Pegswood
Bothal Park
A197
Chesters
Kirkhill
Thornton Moor
Nunriding Hall
Fair Moor
Fulbeck
Rothley Lodge
Garden Ho
Nunriding Moor
Nun Burn
West Benridge
Newton Park
Spital Hill
Lane End
Bothal
Coldwell
Rugley Walls
Newbiggen Ho
West Grange
Hartburn Grange
Angerton North Moor
Thornton Ho
Needless Hall
Newton Underwood
Newton Hall
Abbey Mills Fm
Climbing Tree Fm
Knowesgate
Elf Hills
Cambo
Scots' Gap
B6343
Hartburn
High Angerton
Meldon Park
Throphill
Mitford
Morpeth Chantry Bagpipe Museum
Morpeth
Park Ho
West Whitehill
Prior Hall
Middleton
Marlish
Newton Red Ho
Lightwater Ho
High Church
Stobhillgate
Hepscott Red Ho
Paddock Hall Fm
A196
Belpington
Broom Ho
Angerton Hall
Mill House Fm
Clay Ho
High Common Ho
Stobhill
Loansdean
Walkmill
Middleton Mill
Rivergreen Mill
Molesden
Mitford Steads
Wallington
River Wansbeck
Mill Greens
Low Angerton
Howlett Hill
Cottage Fm
Barmoor Fm
Coalburn Fm
Catch Burn
Sleek Burn
Three Farm
Littleharle Tower
Scarlett Hall
Old Deanham
Middleton Bank Top
Angerton Steads
Meldon
Penny Hill
West Coldside
Molesden Burn
Catchburn Fm
Tranwell
Hepscott
Field House Fm
Burnt Ho
Harelaw
Kirkharle
B6342
Shaftoe Moor
Huckhoe
Bolam West Houses
Tile Sheds
Bolam
Meldon Lane Ho
Clifton
Blue Ho Fm
West Harle
A696
Mirlaw Ho
Shaftoe Crags 213
Shaftoe Grange
Bolam Lake
East Shaftoe Hall
Gallowhill
North Fm
Camp Ho
B6524
Glebe Ho
Manor Ho
Hill Head
Watch Hill
Gubeon Plantns
Well Hill
High Clifton Fm
North Whitehouse Fm
Hepscott Manor
Hepscott Park
Westlea
Nedderton
Bedlington
Ladywell
Clock Mill
Park Head
Sandyford
Bolam Low Ho
Foulmartlaw
Kiplaw
Whalton
Cock Hill
Shilvington
Dovecote Fm
Netherton Wood
Netherton Moor Fm
Merry Shiels
Capheaton
Toft Hill
Harnham
Harnham Buildings
Middlepart
How Burn
Shortflatt
The Folly
Ogle Dene Ho
Howburn Br
East Low Ho
West Low Ho
Shilvington Br
Shilvington Burn
Saltwick
Duddo Hill
Lough Ho
Low Middle Moor
Hartford Bridge
Greatlaw
Sir Edward's Lake
Saugh Ho
Hedchester Law
Broadlaw
Catraw Burn
Plessey Woods
Bavington Hill Head
Belsay
Ogle Hill Head
Crawford's Hill
Ogle
Ogle Burn
Twizell Cott
Stannington
River Blyth
Plessey Hall Fm
Brandy Well Hall
Toft Hall
River
Belsay Dene Ho
Belsay Hall, Castle & Gardens
Bonas Hill
Ogle South Fm
Whinney Hill Fm
Bellasis Fm
Bellasis Bridge
Stannington Bridge
Northumberlandia
Belsay Barns
Coal Burn
Bavington Mount
A696
A1
A697
B6343
A192
A1068
NU
NZ
0 1 2 3 miles
0 1 2 3 4 5 km

265
265
243
243

Coul Pt.
Machir Bay
Sunderland
Kilchoman
Gortan
Conisby
Lyrabus
Blackrock
Redhouse
Esknish
Daill
Islay Ho
Bridgend
Bruichladdich
Kilchiaran Bay
274
Bowmore
BOWMORE ROUND CHURCH
MUSEUM OF ISLAY LIFE
PORT CHARLOTTE
Port Charlotte
A846
A847
B8016
Tormisdale
RHINNS
OF
ISLAY
232
Lossit
Lossit Pt.
Kelsay
Nerabus
Claddach
Rubha na Faing
Portnahaven
Easter Ellister
Wester Ellister
Port Wemyss
Orsay
Rinns Pt.
LOCH INDAAL
Gartbreck
Laggan
Bridge Ho
Laggan Pt.
Duich
Torra
I S L A Y
LAGGAN BAY
Glenegedale
ISLAY
Castlehill
Arivoichallum
Machrie Hotel
Kintra
Port Alsaig
Rubha Mòr
Leorin
Cornabus
Imeraval
Lower Cragabus
Dùn Mòr Ghil
THE OA
152
Risabus
Lower Killeyan
Upper Killeyan
Kinabus
Inerval
AMERICAN MONUMENT
Mull of Oa
202
Rubha nan Leacan
Port Ellen
Kilbride
Lagavulin
Ardbeg
ARDBEG DISTILLERY
LAGAVULIN DISTILLERY
LAPHROAIG DISTILLERY
Laphroaig
Texa
Mulindry
Cattadale
Kilennan
471 BEINN BHAN
491 BEINN BHEIGEIR
267 BEINN DUBH
347 BEINN SHOLUM
Loch Beinn Uraraidh
Kintour
Claggain Bay
Ardtalla
Carraig Mhór
Ardmore Pt.
KILDALTON CHURCH AND CROSSES
Eilean Craobhach
Eilean a'Chuirn
Eilean Bhride
Kildaton Ho
Eilean Imersay
Camas an Staca
Am Fraoch Eilean
McArthur's Hd.
Cabrach
Strone
Rubha na Tràille
Brosdale I.
PORT ASKAIG
BALLYCASTLE
A R G Y
A N
B U T
Earadale Pt.
Rubh'a'Mharaiche
MULL OF KINTYRE
NORTH CHANNEL
Rathlin Island
Ballycastle Bay
Ballycastle
Bushmills
NR
10
60
00
0 2 4 6 miles
0 2 4 6 8 10 km
A B C D E F G H
1 2 3 4 5 6

Campbeltown
Kintyre
Isle of Arran
North Arran
North Ayrshire
Kilbrannan Sound
Sound of Gigha
Sound of Bute
Island of Bute
Gigha Island
Cara Island
Gigalum Island
Inchmarnock
Holy Island
Island Davaar
Sanda Island
Sheep I.
Pladda
Ailsa Craig
Little Cumbrae Island
Rothesay
Tarbert
Lochranza
Brodick
Lamlash
Whiting Bay
Blackwaterfoot
Carradale
Skipness
Claonaig
Kennacraig
Whitehouse
Clachan
Tayinloan
Glenbarr
Bellochantuy
Machrihanish
Southend
Saddell
Grogport
Pirnmill
Catacol
Sannox
Corrie
Kildonan
Lagg
Sliddery
Kilmory
Machrie
Dougarie
Imachar
Shiskine
Kingarth
Loch Ranza
Goat Fell
Glen Sannox
Glen Rosa
Glen Iorsa
Machrie Bay
Drumadoon Bay
Brodick Bay
Lamlash Bay
Saddell Bay
Carradale Bay
Port Righ
Campbeltown Loch
Machrihanish Bay
Bellochantuy Bay
Brunerican Bay
Polliwilline Bay
West Loch Tarbert
Mull of Kintyre
Kilchattan Bay
Mount Stuart House and Gardens
Lochranza Castle
Isle of Arran Distillery
Isle of Arran Heritage Museum
Brodick Castle
Machrie Moor Standing Stones
King's Cave
Skipness Castle
Saddell Abbey
Campbeltown Heritage Centre
Davaar Island Cave Painting
Achamore Gardens
Clan Macalister Centre
Sculptured Stones
St Blane's Chapel
Glenashdale Falls
Torrylinn Cairn
Kilpatrick Dun
Carn Ban
A83
A841
B842
B8001
B880
B843
B878
B881
A844
ARDROSSAN
BALLYCASTLE
TARBET (Oct-Mar)
CAMPBELTOWN (May-Sept Sat only)
ARDROSSAN (May-Sept) BRODICK (May-Sept, Sat only)
NS
275
266
256
244

FIRTH OF CLYDE
Isle of Arran
NORTH AYRSHIRE
Brodick
Merkland
Glenrosa
Brodick Castle
Cladach
Old Quay
Isle of Arran Heritage Museum
Strathwhillan
North Corriegills
South Corriegills
Corriegills Pt
Clauchlands
Clauchlands Pt
Hamilton Isle
Margnaheglish
Blairbeg
Lamlash
Cordon
Holy Island
Mullach Mor
Pillar Rock Pt
Gortonallister
Auchencairn
Kingscross
Knockenkelly
Sandbraes
North Kiscadale
Whiting Bay
South Kiscadale
Glenashdale Falls
Largymore
Largymeanoch
Largybeg
Largybeg Pt
Dippin Head
Dippin
Levencorroch
Auchenhew
Kildonan
East Bennan
West Bennan
Bennan Head
Pladda
Sound of Pladda
Auchareoch
Ardrossan
Campbeltown (May-Sept Sat only)
Saltcoats
Culzean Castle
Culzean Bay
Broad Craig
Glasson Rock
Barwhin Pt
Maidenhead Bay
Morriston
Balvaird
255
266
244
0 1 2 3 miles
0 1 2 3 4 5 km

Sneddon Law
Cowans Law
Thrashy Knowe
Pley Moss
Long Green
Braidley Moss
Mossmulloch
Caldermill
Laigh Crewburn
Hill Fm
Hall of Kype
Little Kype East
Little Kype West
Newmains
High Dyke
Hookhead
Midlinbank Fm
High Hazliebank
Hazliebank
Muirside
Burnfoot Fm
Wallacegill Muir
Calder Moss
Coldwakning
Hallfield
Gilmourton
267
268
Alton
Muirhouse
High Bowhill
Mount
Stobieside
Westertoun Fm
Lochar Water
Middle Rig
Kypewater
NS
Little Glen
Hareleaa Hill
West Dykehead Fm
Brownhill
West Newton
Cronan
Knevocklaw
Drumclog
A71
Syde Fm
High Dykes
Willochsheuch Moss
Kype Lodge
Crawlaw
Loudoun Mains
West Heads
Foulpapple
Templehill
Loudoun Hill 316
Drumboy Fm
Rench Fm
Torfoot Fm
Martinside
Hungryhill
Howletburn
East Heads
Gamesland
B745
Kype Res
Allanton Newlands
Side Hill
Feeshie Moss
Rough Moss
Dunside Res
Bankhead
Waterside
Newmilns
Darvel
DARVEL ROAD
A71
Bransfield Fm
WINDY
WIZEN
Lochgate
North Halls
Berry Moss
Galston
Strath
Greenholm
Lanfine Home Fm
High Greenbank Fm
Gorsebraehead
High Newton
Cairnsaigh
Peelhill
Overhouse
Harting Rig
Dunside Rig
Auchenbart
Stonyhall
Windyhill
Sparnelbank
Molemount Fm
A719
King's Moss
Auchengilloch 462
Grouse Hill
Logan Fm
Clinchyard
Millands
Changue Hill
Tulloch Hill 300
Laigh Plewland
Dungavel Hill 457
Goodbush Hill 475
Bellisle
Middlefield
Eastfield Fm
High Plewland
Glengavel Reservoir
Brow Hill
Mule Hill
Main Castle
Mill Rig
Spirebush Hill 469
Nutberry Hill 522
Drumdroch
Sornhill
Newfield
Greenfield
Cairnhill
Milrig
West Burnhead
Mean Muir
Logan Moss
Distinkhorn 386
Anderside Hill
Black Loch Moss
Bankend Rig
Regal Hill
257
Whitehill
Langside
Lawdyke
Bogend
Wynds
Tongue
Brown's Muir
Flacket Hill
Avon Head
Laird Knowe
Little Hartmidden
Twopenny Knowe
Bibblon Hill 431
Dippal Rig
Starpet Rig 451
Priesthill Height 493
Bruntwood Mains
Low Holehouse
Meadowhead
Crofthead
Auchmaenoch
Knockdon
Grange Muir
Hart Hill
Burnt Hill
Meanlour Hill
Head of Greenock Water
Hare Craig
Roughdyke Fm
Boghead
South Auchenbrain
Wedder Hill 434
Reppoch Knowe
Craigs Hill
Weitshaw Muir
Blackside
Middlefield Law 466
Priesthill
Sclanor Hill
A76
Barwheys
Barboigh
Auchmillan
Auchmillanhill
Darnhay
Blackbriggs
Oxenshaw
Weitshaw
Pepper Knowe
Auchenlongford Hill
Stony Hill
Dun Rig
Greenock Bridge
Black Hill
Upper Hall
Glenbuck
Brigland
Garfield
Redgate
Wealth of Waters
Heath Cottage
Meath Hill
Aikencleugh
Netherwood
Laigh Hall
Lightshaw
Tardoes
Mauchline Mains
Sorn Mains
Tincorn Hill
Greenock Mains
Limmerhaugh Muir
Marchouse Hill
Burnfoot Moor
Muirkirk
Crossflatt
Earl Hill
Mauchline
Welton
Grassmillees
Blindburn
Sorn
Sorn Castle
Catrine Mains
Nethershield
Daldilling
Dalgain
B743
Smallburn
SMALLBURN ROAD
A70
Kames
Auldhouseburn
Brack Hill
Hawk Hill
Catrine
Whiteflat
Barrshouse
Upper Heilar
Midwellwood Fm
Haugh
Kingencleugh Ho
Logan
Gilmilnscroft
High Wood
Little Cairn Table
The Steel
EAST
AYRSHIRE
Barskimming Mains
Syke
High Clews
Catrineshaw
Kenstey
Brackenhill
B705
Bogend
Roundshaw Fm
Airds Moss
Boghead Lane
Wood Hill
Cairn Table 593
Little Heateth
Meikle Heateth
Drumfork
Glenshaw Rock Fm
Cairn Hill
Fingland Hill 462
Slateholde
Treeshill
Townhead
Darnlaw
Back Rogerton
Common
Cronberry
MUIRKIRK ROAD
Knockbreck
Whiteyards
Wardlaw Hill 497
Panbreck Hill
Mid Hill
Blackfauldhead
Knowe
Knagshill
Commondyke Fm
Dalfad Moss
Auchinleck
B7036
BARONY ROAD
Dykes Fm
Lugar
Wallaceton
Ochiltree
Thirdpart
Boswell Mausoleum
Holmhead
Stony Hill 562
Carston
Lugar Water
Logan
Low Moss
Gass Water
Dornal Moss
Glenmuir Hill
Connor Hill
Drummond's Knowe
White Hill 480
Laigh Tarbeg
Mote Toll
Ochiltree Mains
A70
Dumfries House
Cumnock
Kier Hardie Statue
Barshare
Little Auchengibbert
Crosslar
Garleffan Fm
High Dalblair
East Foredibban Hill
Nether Black Law
Black Law
Grimgrew
Orchardton
Ind Est
Netherthird
Holm Burn
Dalblair
Whiteholm
Benalt 382
Black Hill 431
Fingland Lane
Back o' Hill
Rottenrow
High Carston
Crosshill
Horsecleugh Fm
Craigens
Borland Mains
Avisyard Hill 330
Roughhill Moss
Auchtitench Hill 467
Earl Hill
Knockshinnock
Barmickhill
Bus Pk
Airds Hill
Over Guelt
Shiel Rig
Crook Brae 385
Clocklowie Hill 442
Dennigall Hill
Burnock Mill
Skares
SKARES ROAD
B7046
Garlaff
Mossback
Greenside
High Burnside
Borland
DUMFRIES ROAD
Crawford Hill
Cairnscadden Hill 314
Edge Hill 345
Auchlin
Auchencloigh
The Muir
Glaisnock
Calton Fm
High Polqueys
Millstone Knowe
Halfmerk Hill 453
Black Loch
Kirkland Hill
Craigdullyeart Hill
Niviston Hill 460
Lethans Hill
Todholes Hill 481
Carnivan Hill 324
White Knowe
Benston Fm
Lochhill
Rottenyard
Roughside
Auchlin Rig
Creoch Loch
Polqueys
Corsencon Hill 475
Glenwharrie
Burnockhead
High Mount 365
Carsgailoch Hill
Pathhead
Hall of Mansfield
Hall of Auchincross
Loch o' th' Lowes
New Cumnock
Mansfield
Mansfield Mains
Lagrae
Kirkland
Guffock Hill
Todholes
Greenhill
Fordmouth
North Boig
Corsencon
Black Hill
Stannery Knowe 363
Dalricket Mill
Woodend
Connel Park
East Polquhirter
Meikle Westland
Glen Hall
Laigh Cairn
Over Cairn
Brown Hill
Kirkland Plantn
Tappet Hill
Dalgig
Hungry Hill
Bankglen
West Polquhirter
High Park
West Park Fm
Burntonhill
High Cairn
Nether Cairn
Rigg Fm
Kelloside
Kirkconnel
Kelloholm
Mid Hill
Laight Fm
Kyle Forest
Over Hill
Lingie Hill
Little Rigend Hill
Burnt Hill
Dalhanna Hill
BURNFOOT ROAD
B741
Burnside
Sunnyside
Lanehead
Dalhanna Fm
Lochbrowan Hill
High Cairn 553
McCrierick's Cairn 556
White Hill 406
White Knowe
Libry Moor
Upper Beoch
Peat Hill 385
Dalleagles
Strath Fm
Blarene Hill 358
Knocknide Hill 344
Brockloch
246
Benbain
Ashmark Hill
Hare Hill
Polnagrie Hill
Corserig Hill 395
Glengape
Headmark Moss
Chang Hill 463
Benty Cowan Hill 477
Ewe Hill 437
Laglass Hill
Quintin Knowe 554
Hog Hill
Brunt Rig
Barr Moor
Barbeys Hill
Maneight Hill
Afton Water
Pollach Burn
Polstacher Burn
Kello Water
3 miles
5 km

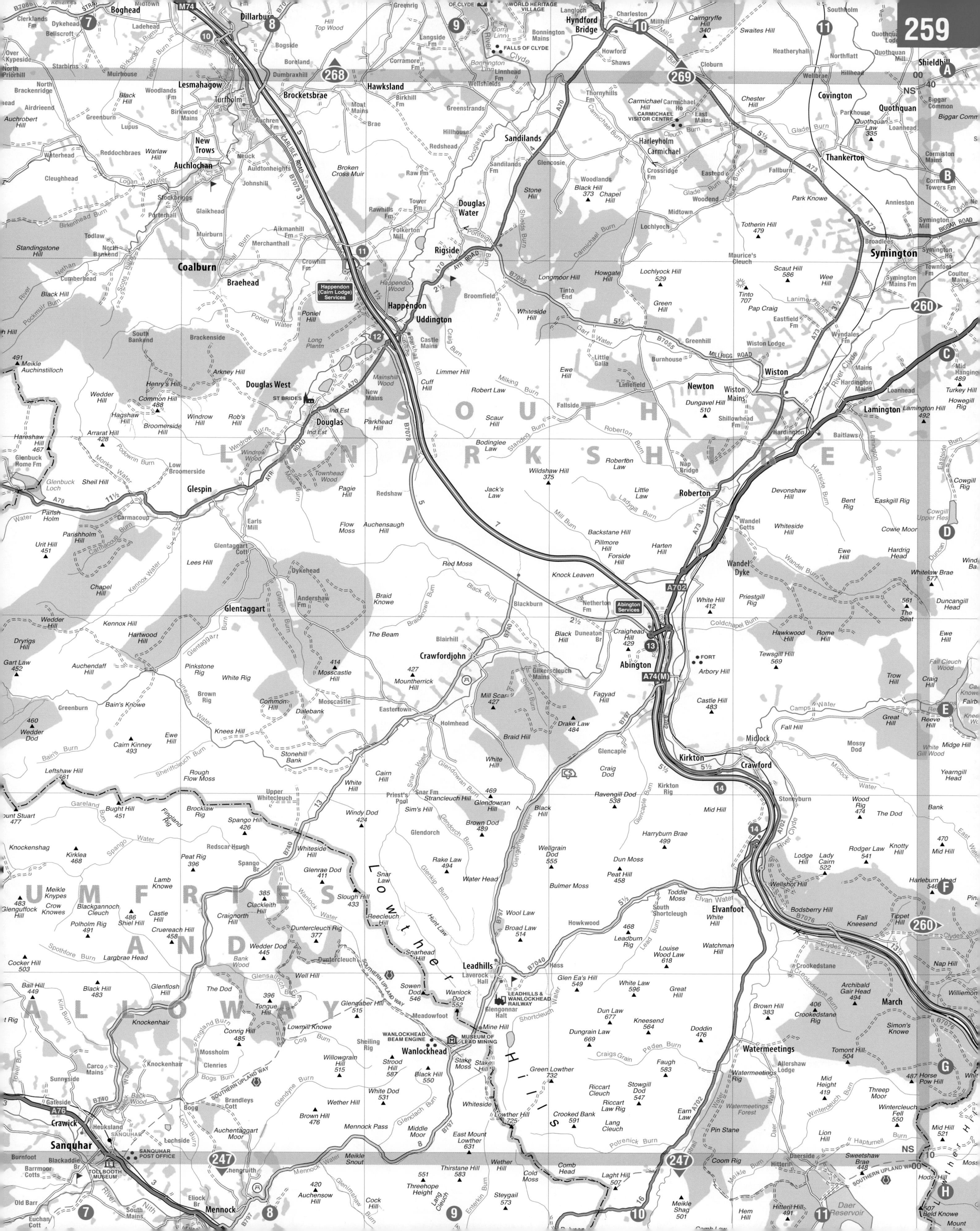

259
Boghead
Dillarburn
Hyndford Bridge
Charleston
Southholm
Clerklands Fm
Dykehead
Bellscroft
Ladehead
Hill Top Wood
FALLS OF CLYDE
Bonnington Mains
Cairngryffe Hill 340
Swaites Hill
Langside Fm
Corramore Fm
Howford
Shaws
Heatheryhall
Northflatt
Quothquan Mill
Shieldhill
Starbirns
Muirhouse
Dumbraxhill
Bogside
Boreland
Linnhead Fm
Cloburn
Wellbrae
Hillhead
North Brackenridge
Lesmahagow
Turfholm
Brocketsbrae
Hawksland
Birkhill Fm
Thornyhills Fm
Carmichael Hill
Carmichael Ho
CARMICHAEL VISITOR CENTRE
East Mains
Chester Hill
Covington
Quothquan
Biggar Common
Airdrieend
Auchrobert Hill
Black Hill
Woodlands Fm
Greenburn
Lupus
Birkwood Mains
Moat Mains
Brae
Greenstrands
Auchren Fm
Quothquan Law 335
Loanhead
Hillhouse
Sandilands
Harleyholm
Carmichael
Glade Burn
New Trows
Warlaw Hill
Redshead
Thankerton
Cormiston Mains
Waterhead
Reddochbraes
Auchlochan
Neuck
Auldtonheights
Broken Cross Muir
Raw Fm
Sandilands Fm
Glencosie
Crossridge Fm
Eastend
Fallburn
Cleughhead
Johnshill
Woodlands Fm
Black Hill 373
Chapel Hill
Stone Hill
Woodend
Park Knowe
Cormiston Towers Fm
Stockbriggs
Porterhall
Glaikhead
Rawhills Fm
Tower Fm
Douglas Water
Midtown
Annieston
Birkenhead Burn
Aikmanhill Fm
Folkerton Mill
Lochlyoch
Totherin Hill 479
Symington Mill
BIGGAR ROAD
Todlaw
Muirburn
Merchanthall
Broadlees
Standingstone Hill
North Bankend
Crowhill Fm
Rigside
Maurice's Cleuch
Symington
Coalburn
Braehead
Happendon (Cairn Lodge) Services
Happendon Wood
Longmoor Hill
Howgate Hill
Lochlyock Hill 529
Scaut Hill 586
Wee Hill
Townfoot Fm
Coulter Mains
Cumberhead
Tinto End
Tinto 707
Symington Mains Fm
Black Hill
Broomfield
Pap Craig
Lanimer Burn
Happendon
Uddington
Whiteside Hill
Green Hill
Eastfield Fm
South Bankend
Brackenside
Poniel Hill
Poniel Water
Long Plantn
Castle Mains
Craig Burn
Garf Water
Greenhill
Wiston Lodge
Wyndales Fm
Meikle Auchinstilloch 491
Arkney Hill
Henry's Hill
Limmer Hill
Little Galla
Burnhouse
MILLRIGG ROAD
Wiston
Mains
Mid Hanging 489
Ewe Hill
Hardington Mains
Wedder Hill
Douglas West
ST BRIDES
Common Hill 488
Cuff Hill
Mainshill Wood
New Mains
Robert Law
Milking Burn
Limefield
Newton
Wiston Mains
Loanhead
Turkey Hill
Howgill Rig
Hagshaw Hill
Windrow Hill
Rob's Hill
Broomerside Hill
Douglas
Ind Est
Parkhead Hill
Fallside
Dungavel Hill 510
Shillowhead Fm
Lamington
Lamington Hill 492
Hardington Ho
Baitlaws
Hareshaw Hill 467
Arrarat Hill 428
Scaur Hill
Bodinglee Law
Standing Burn
Roberton Burn
S O U T H L A N A R K S H I R E
Glenbuck Home Fm
Windrow Wood
Low Broomerside
Townhead Wood
Roberton Law
Nap Bridge
Glenbuck Loch
Sheil Hill
Monks Water
Wildshaw Hill 375
Hartside Burn
Cowgill Rig
Glespin
Pagie Hill
Redshaw
Jack's Law
Little Law
Roberton
Devonshaw Hill
Bent Rig
Easkgill Rig
Parish Holm
Carmacoup
Ladygill Burn
Cowgill Upper Res
Parishholm Hill
Earls Mill
Flow Moss
Auchensaugh Hill
Mill Burn
Backstane Hill
Wandel Cotts
Whiteside Hill
Cowie Moor
Urit Hill 451
Pillmore Hill
Forside Hill
Harten Hill
Glentaggart Cott
Ewe Hill
Hardrig Head
Lees Hill
Red Moss
Knock Leaven
Wandel Dyke
Whitelaw Brae 577
Chapel Hill
Dykehead
Black Burn
Blackburn
A702
Netherton Fm
Abington Services
White Hill 412
Priestgill Rig
561 The Seat
Duncangill Head
Glentaggart
Andershaw Fm
Braid Knowe
Wedder Hill
Kennox Hill
Hartwood Hill
The Beam
Blairhill
Black Hill
Duneaton Br
Craighead Hill 429
Coldchapel Burn
Hawkwood Hill
Rome Hill
Ewe Hill
Dryrigs Hill
Crawfordjohn
Abington
FORT
Arbory Hill
Tewsgill Hill 569
Fall Cleuch Wood
Gart Law 452
Auchendaff Hill
Pinkstone Rig
White Rig
414 Mosscastle Hill
427 Mounterrick Hill
Gilkerscleuch Mains
A74(M)
Trow Hill
Craig Hill
Brown Rig
Common Hill
Mosscastle
Dalebank
Mill Scar 427
Fagyad Hill
Castle Hill 483
Greenburn
Bain's Knowe
Eastertown
Camps Water
Great Hill
Reeve Hill
460 Wedder Dod
Ewe Hill
Knees Hill
Holmhead
Drake Law 484
Fall Hill
Midlock
Mossy Dod
Midge Hill
Cairn Kinney 493
Stonehill Bank
Braid Hill
Glencaple
White Gill Wood
Bain's Burn
Sheriffcleuch Burn
Rough Flow Moss
White Hill
Kirkton
Crawford
Leftshaw Hill 461
Cairn Hill
Craig Dod
Yearngill Head
White Hill
Upper Whitecleuch
Snar Water
Glendowran Burn
Ravengill Dod 538
Kirkton Rig
Gareland Burn
Bught Hill 451
Brocklaw Rig
Priest's Pool
Snar Fm
Strancleuch Hill
469 Glendowran Hill
Stoneyburn
Wood Rig 474
The Dod
Bank
Fingland Rig
Spango Hill 426
Windy Dod 424
Sim's Hill
Black Hill
Mid Hill
Brown Dod 489
Harryburn Brae 499
Mount Stuart 477
Knockenshag
Spango Water
Redscar Heugh
Whiteside Hill
Glendorch
Wellgrain Dod 555
Dun Moss
Lodge Hill
Lady Cairn 522
Rodger Law 541
Knotty Hill
470 Mid Hill
Kirklea 468
Peat Rig 396
Spango Br
Glenrae Dod 411
Rake Law 494
Water Head
Peat Hill 458
Lamb Knowe
Snar Law
Bulmer Moss
Harleburn Head 546
Meikle Knypes
D U M F R I E S A N D G A L L O W A Y
483 Glenguffock Hill
Crow Knowes
Blackgannoch Cleuch
385 Clackleith Hill
Slough Hill 433
Lowther Hills
Toddle Moss
South Shortcleuch
Elvan Water
Elvanfoot
Wellshot Hill
Bodsberry Hill
486 Shiel Hill
Castle Hill
Craignorth Hill
Reecleuch Hill
Hunt Law
Wool Law
White Hill
Fall Kneesend
Tippet Hill
Polholm Rig 491
Cruereach Hill 458
Duntercleuch Rig 377
Broad Law 514
Howkwood
468 Leadburn Rig
Clydes Burn
Spothfore Burn
Largbrae Head
Wedder Dod 445
Snarhead Hill
Louise Wood Law 618
Watchman Hill
Cocker Hill 503
Bank Wood
Duntercleuch
Leadhills
Hass
Crookedstane
Nap Hill
Ball Hill 449
Black Hill 483
Glenflosh Hill
Well Hill
Sowen Dod 546
Laverock Hall
Glen Ea's Hill 549
White Law 596
Great Hill
Archibald Gair Head 494
The Dod
396 Tongue Hill
Glengaber Hill 515
Wanlock Dod 552
LEADHILLS & WANLOCKHEAD RAILWAY
Glengonnar Halt
Dun Law 677
Brown Hill 383
406 Crookedstane Rig
March
Knockenhair
Meadowfoot
Conrig Hill 485
Lowmill Knowe
Mine Hill
Kneesend 564
Doddin 476
Simon's Knowe
WANLOCKHEAD BEAM ENGINE
Sheiling Rig
MUSEUM OF LEAD MINING
Dungrain Law 669
Mossholm
Wanlockhead
Shortcleuch Water
Tomont Hill 504
Clenries
Willowgrain Hill 515
Strood Hill 587
Stake Moss
Stake Hill
Craigs Grain
Peden Burn
Watermeetings
Carco Mains
Knockenhair
Faugh 583
Allershaw Lodge
Sunnyside
Bogs Burn
Green Lowther 732
Black Hill 550
Watermeetings Rig
487 Horse Pow Hill
Mid Height 419
Brandleys Cott
Riccart Cleuch
Stowgill Dod 547
Three Moor
Gateside
White Dod 531
Riccart Law Rig
Watermeetings Forest
Wether Hill
Whiteside
Wintercleuch Fell 550
Crawick
Heuksland
Auchentaggart Moor
Brown Hill 476
Lowther Hill 725
Crooked Bank 591
Lang Cleuch
Earn Law
Pin Stane
Mennock Pass
Middle Moor
Lion Hill
Mid Hill 521
Sanquhar
Lochside
East Mount Lowther 631
Potrenick Burn
Hapturnell
Burnfoot
Blackaddie
SANQUHAR POST OFFICE
Meikle Snout
Wether Hill
Comb Head
Coom Rig
Daerside
Sweetshaw Brae 448
Barrmoor Cotts
TOLLBOOTH MUSEUM
Whengruith
Mennock Water
Thirstane Hill 583
Cold Moss
Laght Hill 507
Hitteril
SOUTHERN UPLAND WAY
Hods Hill
Old Barr
Ellock Br
420 Auchensow Hill
551 Threehope Height
Lang Cleuch
Steygail 573
Meikle Shag 501
Hitteril Hill 491
Daer Reservoir
507 Beld Knowe
Euchan Cott
South Mains
Mennock
Cock Hill
Hem Hill
Mount
River Nith
River Clyde
247
260
268
269

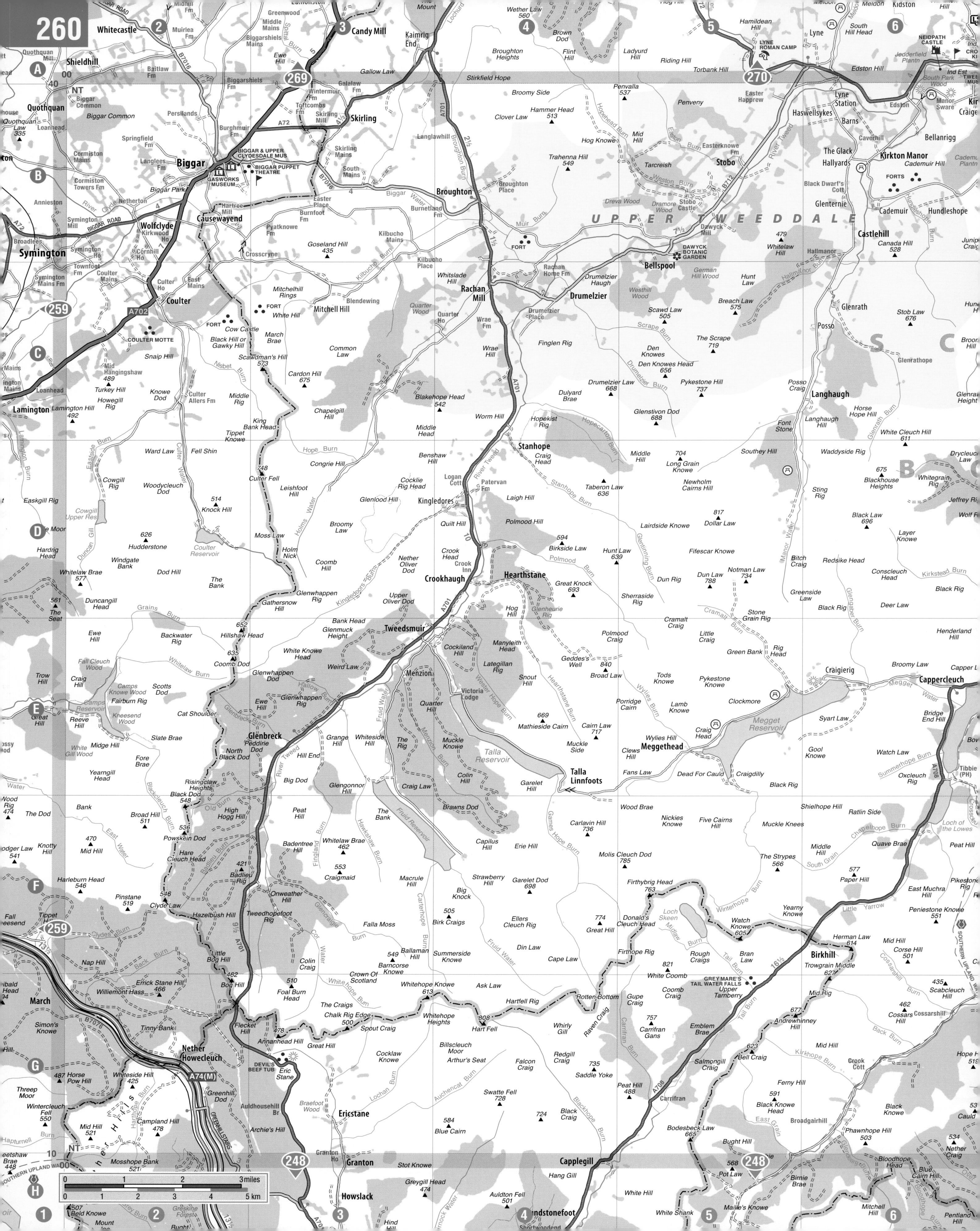
Whitecastle
Candy Mill
Kaimrig End
Wether Law 560
Brown Dod
Hamildean Hill
Lyne
Lyne Roman Camp
Kidston
South Hill Head
Neidpath Castle
Shieldhill
Quothquan
Biggar Common
Muirlea Fm
Middle Mains
Biggarshiels Mains
Ewe Hill
Gallow Law
Broughton Heights
Flint Hill
Ladyurd Hill
Riding Hill
Torbank Hill
Edston Hill
Stirkfield Hope
Baitlaw Fm
Biggarshiels Fm
Wintermuir Fm
Galalaw Fm
Toftcombs
Skirling Mill
Skirling
Broomy Side
Penvalla 537
Penveny
Easter Happrew
Lyne Station
Haswellsykes
Barns
Edston
Manor Sware
Quothquan Law 335
Loanhead
Persilands
Burghmuir Fm
A72
Clover Law
Hammer Head 513
Hog Knowe
Mid Hill
Easterknowe Fm
Caverhill
Bellanrigg
Springfield Fm
Langlawhill
Skirling Mains
Trahenna Hill 549
Tarcreish
Stobo
The Glack
Hallyards
Kirkton Manor
Cademuir Hill
Cormiston Mains
Langlees Fm
Biggar
Biggar & Upper Clydesdale Mus
Biggar Puppet Theatre
Gasworks Museum
South Mains
Cormiston Towers Fm
Biggar Park
Broughton
Broughton Place
Weston Burn
Black Dwarf's Cott
Forts
Anniesston
Netherton
Easter Place
Burnetland Fm
Dreva Wood
Dramore Wood
Stobo Castle
Glenternie
Cademuir
Hundleshope
Symington Mill
Biggar Road
Hartree Mill
Causewayend
Burnfoot Fm
Muir Burn
Upper Tweeddale
Dawyck Mill
Castlehill
Wolfclyde
Kirkwood Ho
Pyatknowe Fm
Kilbucho Mains
Fort
479 Whitelaw Hill
Canada Hill 528
Broadlees
Symington
Cornhill Ho
Crosscryne
Goseland Hill 435
Kilbucho Place
Dawyck Botanic Garden
Bellspool
Hallmanor
Townfoot Fm
Coulter Mains
Whitslade Hill
Rachan Home Fm
Drumelzier Haugh
German Hill Wood
Hunt Law
Symington Mains Fm
Culter Ho
East Mains
Mitchelhill Rings
Rachan Mill
Drumelzier
Westhill Wood
Coulter
A702
Fort
White Hill
Mitchell Hill
Blendewing
Quarter Wood
Quarter Ho
Drumelzier Place
Scawd Law 505
Breach Law 575
Glenrath
Stob Law 676
Cow Castle
Wrae Fm
Scrape Burn
Posso
Coulter Motte
Black Hill or Gawky Hill
March Brae
Common Law
Wrae Hill
Finglen Rig
The Scrape 719
Den Knowes
Den Knowes Head 656
Glenrathope
Snaip Hill
Scawdman's Hill 573
Mid Hangingshaw 489
Cardon Hill 675
Drumelzier Law 668
Pykestone Hill 737
Posso Craig
Turkey Hill
Knowe Dod
Culter Allers Fm
Middle Rig
Howegill Rig
Blakehope Head 542
Dulyard Brae
Langhaugh
Lamington
Lamington Hill 492
Chapelgill Hill
King Bank Head
Worm Hill
Hopekist Rig
Glenstivon Dod 688
Font Stone
Langhaugh Hill
Horse Hope Hill
Middle Head
Tippet Knowe
Stanhope
White Cleuch Hill 611
Ward Law
Fell Shin
Hope Burn
Benshaw Hill
Craig Head
Middle Hill
704 Long Grain Knowe
Southey Hill
Waddyside Rig
675 Blackhouse Heights
Drycleuch Law
Congrie Hill
748 Culter Fell
Cocklie Rig Head
Logan Cott
Paterван Fm
Taberon Law 636
Newholm Cairns Hill
Sting Rig
Whitegrain Rig
Cowgill Rig
Woodycleuch Dod
Leishfoot Hill
Glenlood Hill
Kingledores
Laigh Hill
Jeffrey Rig
Eskgill Rig
514 Knock Hill
817 Dollar Law
Cowgill Upper Res
Quilt Hill
Polmood Hill
Lairdside Knowe
Black Law 696
Wolf Cr
Broomy Law
Layer Knowe
Moss Law
594 Birkside Law
Hunt Law 639
Fifescar Knowe
626 Hudderstone
Coulter Reservoir
Holm Nick
Crook Head
Crook Inn
Nether Oliver Dod
Harding Head
Windgate Bank
Coomb Hill
Dun Law 788
Notman Law 734
Bitch Craig
Redsike Head
Conscleuch Head
Dod Hill
The Bank
Hearthstane
Great Knock 693
Dun Rig
Whitelaw Brae 577
Crookhaugh
Greenside Law
Black Rig
Glenwhappen Rig
Upper Oliver Dod
Sherraside Rig
Stone Grain Rig
Deer Law
561 The Seat
Duncangill Head
Gathersnow Hill
Hog Hill
Glenheurie Rig
Grains Burn
Bank Head
Glenmuck Height
Tweedsmuir
Cramalt Craig
652 Hillshaw Head
Polmood Craig
Little Craig
Henderland Hill
Ewe Hill
Backwater Rig
Manyleith Head
Green Bank
Rig Head
635 Coomb Dod
White Knowe Head
Cockiland Hill
Lategillan Rig
Geddes's Well
840 Broad Law
Broomy Law
Capper Law
Fall Cleuch Wood
Craigierig
Trow Hill
Craig Hill
Weird Law
Menzion
Snout Hill
Tods Knowe
Pykestone Knowe
Cappercleuch
Camps Knowe Wood
Scotts Dod
Glenwhappen Dod
Victoria Lodge
Fairburn Rig
Quarter Hill
Porridge Cairn
Clockmore
Megget Water
Camps Reservoir
Glenwhappen Rig
Lamb Knowe
Syart Law
Bridge End Hill
Great Hill
Cat Shoulder
Kneesend Wood
669 Mathieside Cairn
Cairn Law 717
Craig Head
Megget Reservoir
Reeve Hill
Glenbreck
Grange Hill
Whiteside Hill
Slate Brae
Peddirie Dod
Wylies Hill
Meggethead
Muckle Side
Midge Hill
The Rig
Muckle Knowe
Talla Reservoir
Gool Knowe
Watch Law
White Gill Wood
North Black Dod
Hill End
Clews Hill
Tibbie (PH)
Fore Brae
Talla Linnfoots
Fans Law
Dead For Cauld
Craigdilly
Oxcleuch Rig
Yearngill Head
Big Dod
Glengonnor Hill
Colin Hill
A708
Risingclaw Heights
Craig Law
Garelet Hill
Black Rig
Black Dod 548
Bank
Peat Hill
The Bank
Brawns Dod
Wood Brae
Shielhope Hill
Ratlin Side
The Dod
Broad Hill 511
High Hogg Hill
Nickies Knowe
Five Cairns Hill
Muckle Knees
536
Carlavin Hill 736
Quave Brae
470 Mid Hill
Powskein Dod
Badentree Hill
Whitelaw Brae 462
Capilus Hill
Erie Hill
Middle Hill
Peat Hill
Knotty Hill
Hare Cleuch Head
Molis Cleuch Dod 785
The Strypes 566
421 Badlieu Rig
553 Craigmaid
Macrule Hill
Strawberry Hill
Garelet Dod 698
577 Paper Hill
Harleburn Head 546
Firthybrig Head 763
Onweather Hill
Big Knock
East Muchra Hill
Pinstane 519
546 Clyde Law
Hazelbush Hill
Tweedhopefoot Rig
505 Birk Craigs
Ellers Cleuch Rig
774 Great Hill
Donald's Cleuch Head
Yearny Knowe
Peniestone Knowe 551
Loch Skeen
Watch Knowe 605
Falla Moss
Herman Law 614
Mid Hill
Corse Hill 501
Nap Hill
Colin Craig
549 Barncorse Knowe
Ballaman Hill
Summerside Knowe
Din Law
Firthope Rig
Rough Craigs
Bran Law
Birkhill
Trowgrain Middle 627
Little Bog Hill
Errick Stane Hill 466
Williemont Hass
462 Bog Hill
510 Foal Burn Head
Crown Of Scotland
Whitehope Knowe 613
Ask Law
Cape Law
821 White Coomb
Grey Mare's Tail Water Falls
Upper Tarnberry
Mid Rig
435 Scabcleuch Hill
March
Hartfell Rig
Rotten Bottom
Gupe Craig
Coomb Craig
677 Andrewhinney Hill
462 Cossars Hill
Cossarshill
Simon's Knowe
The Craigs
Chalk Rig Edge 500
Spout Craig
Whitehope Heights
808 Hart Fell
Whirly Gill
Raven Craig
757 Carrifran Gans
Emblem Brae
Tinny Bank
Flecket Hill
478 Annanhead Hill
Great Hill
Billscleuch Moor
Arthur's Seat
Mid Hill
Nether Howecleuch
Devil's Beef Tub
Eric Stane
Cocklaw Knowe
Falcon Craig
Redgill Craig
735 Saddle Yoke
623 Bell Craig
Salmongill Craig
Crook Cott
Hope Hill 519
487 Horse Pow Hill
Whiteside Hill 425
A74(M)
Peat Hill 488
Ferny Hill
Threep Moor
Greenhill Dod
Auldhousehill Br
Swatte Fell 728
Carrifran
591 Black Knowe Head
Black Knowe
Wintercleuch Fell 550
Braefoot Wood
Ericstane
724
Black Craig
Broadgairhill
Phawnhope Hill 503
Mid Hill 521
Campland Hill 478
Archie's Hill
584 Blue Cairn
Bodesbeck Law 665
534 Nether Craig
Granton Ho
Bught Hill
Mosshope Bank 521
Granton
Stot Knowe
Capplegill
568 Pot Law
Bloodhope Head
Southern Upland Way
Greygill Head 474
Hang Gill
Birnie Brae
Blue Cairn Hill
Howslack
Auldton Fell 501
White Hill
Maille's Knowe
Mitchell Hill
Pentland Hill
507 Beld Knowe
Mount
Hind
White Shank
Shortwoodend
0 1 2 3 miles
0 1 2 3 4 5 km
269
270
259
248

Peebles
Eshiels
Kerfield
Glentress
Cardrona
Kirkburn
Haystoun
Kailzie Gardens
Laverlaw
Cardrona Forest
Innerleithen
St Ronan's Wells
Robert Smail's Printing Works
Walkerburn
Holylee
West Bold
Haugh-head
Traquair House
Traquair
The Riggs
Kirkhouse
Glen Ho
Elibank and Traquair Forest
Tweed Valley
Scottish Borders
Forest Park
Southern Upland Way
Minch Moor
Broadmeadows
Yarrowford
Hangingshaw
Yarrow
Yarrow Feus
Catslackburn
Mountbenger
Mountbengerburn
Sundhope
Dryhope
Dryhope Tower
Kirkstead
Craig Douglas
Ettrickbridge
Howford
Brockhill
Helmburn
Hutlerburn
Kirkhope
Hyndhope
Gilmanscleuch
Wester Deloraine
Newburgh
Crosslee
Tushielaw
Wardlaw
Ettrick
Ettrickhill
James Hogg Monument
Ramseycleuch
Buccleuch
Glenkerry
Nether Dalgliesh
Redfordgreen
Roberton
Borthwickshiels
Borthwickbrae
Burnfoot
Deanburnhaugh
Newmill
Branxholm Park
Branxholme
Broadhaugh
Northhouse
Craik
Crak Forest
Ettrick Forest
Todrig
Langhope
Wester Essenside
Salenside
Woll
Ashkirk
Synton Mains
Headshaw
Dryden
North Synton
Bowismiln
Clerklands
Fauldshope
Carterhaugh
Bowhill
Bowhill House & Country Park
Philiphaugh
Halliwell's House Museum
Sir Walter Scott's Courtroom
Selkirk
Selkirk Common
Hartwoodburn
Oakwood Mill
Lindean
Ovenscloss
Sunderland Hall
High Sunderland
Yair
Yair Hill Forest
Boleside
Glenmayne
Abbotsford House
Galashiels
Old Gala House
The Great Tapestry of Scotland
Balmoral
Buckholm
Halliburton
Langlee
Caddonfoot
Caddonlee
Clovenfords
Peel
Ashiestiel
Thornielee
Blackhaugh
Caitha Bowland
Windydoors
Bowshank
Bow
Ferniehirst
Colquhar
Nether Horsburgh
Wilton
Hawick Museum
Hawick
Drumlanrig's Tower
Cauld
Lynnwood
Pilmuir
Newton
Colmslie
Glendearg
270
271
262
249
A7
A72
A707
A708
A699
B709
B7009
B7039
B711
B6400
B710
B7062
B7060
B6360
NT
50
40
10
A
B
C
D
E
F
G
H
7
8
9
10
11

Colmsliehill
Bluecairn
Birkenside
Legerwood Hill
West Morriston
Hume
Falsidehill
Over Langshaw
Kedslie Hill
Kedslie
Chapel on Leader
271
272
Fans
Fans Hill
Hareheugh Craigs
Colmslie
Langshaw
Mosshouses
Cairneymount
Earlston Mains
Darlingfield
Lurgie Craigs
Sweethope Hill
Stichill
Ladhope Moor
Glendearg
Chatto Craigs
Craigsford Mains
Earlston
Cowdenknowes Mains
Mellerstain House
Blinkbonny
Parkend
Stichill Eastfield
Kaimflat
Caldronbrae
Harpertoun
Buckholm Hill
Darling's Hill
Halliburton
Easter Housebyres
Sorrowlessfield Mains
Brotherstone Moor
Rachelfield
Hundy Mundy
Girrick
Nenthorn
Newtonlees
Ednam
Ednam Hill
Langlee Mains
Langlee
Western Housebyres
Ferny Hill
Redpath Hill
Brotherstone Hill
East Third
Smailholm
Old Nenthorn
Spotsmains
Courthill
Edenbank
Hendersyde Fm
Galashiels
Easter Langlee
Gattonside Mains
Redpath
Brotherstone
Craighouse
West Third
Smailholm Mains
Easter Muirdean
Kaimknowe
Berryhill
Kelso
Hendersyde Park
Lowood
Gattonside
Eildon and Leaderfoot
Priorwood Gardens
Melrose Abbey
Leaderfoot
Halidean Mill
Bettyfield
Floors Home Fm
Salmon Fishing Museum
Floors Castle
Abbotsford House
Darnick
Melrose
Whitrighill
Smailholm Tower
Haymount
Gala Hill
Touting Birk's Hill
Boleside
261
Abbotsmoss
Huntlyburn Ho
Dingleton
The Three Hills Roman Heritage Centre
Newstead
Bemersyde
Butchercote
Bemersyde Moss
Fox Covert
Sucklawridge
Kelso Abbey
Maxwellheugh
Border Union Showground
Springwood
Wallacenick
Roxburgh Barns
Faldonside
Cauldshiels Loch
Eildon Hills
Eildon
Monksford
Maidenhall
Clintmains
Dalcove Mains
Manorhill
Trows
Spylaw
Maisondieu
Leadfoot
Newtown St Boswells
Dryburgh
Mertoun Br
Magdalene Hall
Mertoun Gardens
Rutherford Lodge
Cauldshiels Hill
Lindean
Bowden Moor
Greenwells
Whiterigg
Dryburgh Abbey
Lessudden Bank
River Tweed
Roxburgh Mill
Heiton Mill
Heiton
Faughill Moor
Faughill
Bowden
Whitelee
St Boswells
Fens
Benrig
Littledean
Ploughlands
Riddletonhill
Rutherford Mains
Roxburgh Newtown
Roxburgh
Ladyrig
Maxton
Rutherford
Over Whitlaw Fm
Lindean Moor
Mainhill
Camieston
Charlesfield
Big Wood
Roxburgh Moor
Roxburgh Mains
Sunlaws Mill
Greenhead
Whitlaw Mosses
Kippilaw Mains
Northfield
Thornielaw
Forest Lodge
Morridgehall
Muirhouselaw
Steelmoor Plantn
Upper Nisbet Moor
Duke's Strip
Graham's Law
Grahamslaw Plantn
Bowmont Forest
Prieston
Old Prieston
Eastfield
Kippilaw
Elliston
Fox Covert
Midlem
Greenend
Longnewton
Longnewton Forest
Ancrum Moor 1545
Upper Nisbet
Kalemouth
Ormiston Mains
Caverton Hillhead
Old Caverton
Whitmuir Hall
Midlem Mill
Mirighall
Clarilaw
Alerigg
Down Law
Peniel Heugh
Waterloo Monument
Blackrig Plantn
Mosstower
Ploughlands
Eckford
Eckfordmoss
Marlefield
Whitmuir
Shawburn
Toftbarns
Cavers Carre
Chesterknowes
Alewater
Playknowe Plantn
Chapel Fm
Bewlie Mains
Bewlie
Belses Mill Fm
Belses
Pinnacle
Palacehill
Lilliardsedge Park
Woodhead Fm
Howden
Woodside
Nisbet
Nisbetmill
Kirkmains
Wooden Loch
Crailing Tofts
Crailing
Clerklands
Lilliesleaf
Riddell
Craggs
West Middles
Old Belses
Rawflat
Bloomfield
Whitehouse
Ancrum
Harestanes Countryside Visitor Centre
Shortacres
Crailing Ho
Wooden Hill
Rocky Covert
North Synton
Netherraw
Greenhouse
Belses Muir
Ancrum Craig
Broom Covert
Copland
Ancrum West Mains
Bonjedward
Mounthooly
Baittens
Littledeanlees
Blakeman's Crag
Castle Knowe
Cessford
Bowismiln
Newhouse
Firth
Hermiston
Harelaw
Droveroad Plantn
Catshawhill
Troneyhill
Minto Kames
North Lodge
Teviot Dale
Grange Banks
Chesters
Chesters Grange
Lanton Mill
Langdales
Bank Hill
Mount Ulston
Crailinghall
Marchcleuch
Synton
Hunttaw
Black Craig
Barnhills Moor Plantn
Barnhills Fm
Lanton
Lanton Moor
Ulston Moor
Crouchie Wood
Old Hall
Samieston
Newlands
Hassendean Common
Minto Hills
Lambslair Plantn
Cleuchhead
Newton
Mary Queen of Scots House
Wildcat Gate
Overwells Cott
Cappuck Br
Rennieston
Faw Laws
Upper Samieston
Hassendean
Minto
Deanfoot
Menslaws
Spittal-on-Rule
Gospel Hall Fm
Lanton Hill
Jedburgh
Jedburgh Abbey
Howden
Harden Mains
Shibden Hill
Whitton Loch
Hallywell Hill
Horsleyhill
Melgund Glen
Jedburgh Castle Jail Mus
Todlaw
Dunion Hill
Hunthill
Hardenpeel
Crook Knowes
Clarilaw
Knowetownhead
Teviot Bank
Hassendean Bank
Denholm
Bedrule Mill
Bedrule
Black Law
Hundalee
Hag Plantn
Ferniehirst Castle
Scraesburgh
Oxnam
Townfoot Hill
Bloodylaws Hill
Newton
East Boonraw
Appletreehall
Midshiels
Ashybank
Denholm Dean
Spital Tower
Langlee
Glendouglas
Kersheugh
Oxnamrow Hill
Cunzierton Fm
Gala Law
Burnhead
Bucklands
Stirches Mains
Cavers Mains
Mill Court
Midgard
Denholmhill
Gilboa Wood
West Lees
Watch Knowe
Swinnie
Gilliestongues
Mossburnford
Oxnam Sawmill
Swinside Hall
Harker Hill
Burnfoot
Hawick
Heip Hill
Midgard
Effledge
Whitriggs
Fort
Rubers Law
Billerwell
Swinnie Plantn
Bairnkine
Mossburnford Bank
Newbigging
Wilton
Hawick Museum
Cauldmill
Cavers Knowes
Nether Tofts
Old Fodderlee
Easter Fodderlee
Dolphinston
Deanbrae
Hallrule
Wester Fodderlee
Woodhouse
Peg Law
Cauld
Drumlanrig's Tower
Kaimend
Ormiston
Kirkton
Burnt Plantn
Faw Hill
Camptown
Falla
North Riccalton
Lynnwood
Vertish Hill
Hallrule Mill
Weens Ho
Abbotrule
Ruletownhead
Mervinslaw
Lawsuit Law
Dod Hill
White Hill
Kirkton Hill
Weensmoor Fm
Bonchester Bridge
Bonchester Hill
Belling Hill
Mervins Law
Stotfield Hill
Moor Head
Scaw'd Law
Coliforthill
Colislinn
Adderston Lee
Birneyknowe
Hobkirk
Doorpool Hill
Falside
Roughlee
Edgerston
Edgerston Rig
Philip Law
Pilmuir
New Mill
Hoggfield Hill
Highend
Cleuch Head
Crown Plantn
Mackside
Chesters
Southdean Mill
Bught Knowe
Acreknowe Res
Winningtonrig
White
Stonedge
250
Folly Plantn
Spar Plantn
Law Plantn
Southdean
Croft Plantn
White Hill
Hareshaw Knowe
Knock Hills
Hophills Nob
Ephope Law
Southdean Lodge
Lethem
Wolfhee Hill
Cribs Hole
Highlee Hill
Weasel Hill
Steele Knowe
Crink Law
Huntford
Deerlee Knowe
Lamb Edge
Stobs Castle
Cogsmill
Stonedge Hill
Barnes
Charlie's
Bught
Redesmire
A68
A7
A698
A699
A6091
A6088
B6397
B6356
B6404
B6398
B6400
B6358
B6357
B6399
B6405
B6359
B6453
B6401
B6436
B6352
B6350
B6364
B6374
B6360
B6361
A6089
Scottish Borders
NT
0 1 2 3 miles
0 1 2 3 4 5 km

Eccles
Brae Dunstan
Fernyrig Cott
Crown Gorse
Dunglass Wood
Kincham Wood
Lennel
Donaldson's Lodge
Melkington
Castle Heaton
Duddo Hill
Woods Low Wood
Bowsden
Bowsden W
Eccles Ho
Eccles Newton
Bartlehill
Birgham Wood
THE HIRSEL
Hirsel Lake
Western Park
Peter's Plantn
Coldstream
New Heaton
Syning Hill
Heaton Moor
Black Bank
Tindal Ho
Barleymill Bank
Hazely Hill
High Wood
Rhodes Hill
Barmoor Hill
Barmoor Castle
Barmoor Lane End
Moss Hall
Saint Foin
Birgham
Dundock Wood
Cornhill-on-Tweed
Heaton Covert
Pallinsburn Ho
ETAL CASTLE
Etal
Etal Rhodes
Etal Moor
Barmoor Ridge
Lochton
Eden Hall
Springhill
Carham Hall
Gallows Hill
Wark
Bareless
Campfield
Cookstead
HEATHERSLAW LIGHT RAILWAY
HEATHERSLAW CORNMILL
Letham Hill
Ford Forge
Crookham
HEATHERSLAW
Common Cott
Ford Common
Hay Fm
Barmoor South Moor
Redhouse Moor
Moss Wood
LADY WATERFORD HALL
Bar Moor
FORT
Kemping Moss
Kemping Moss Ho
Barmoore Red Ho
Ednam East Mill
River Tweed
Redden
Carham
West Learmouth
Lamb Knowe
Crookham Westfield
Branxton Bldgs
Windy Law
Branxton
Pace Hill
Mount Pleasant
Ford
Ford Hill
Goatscrag Hill
FLODDEN FIELD 1513
East Learmouth
Redden Burn
Hadden
Nottylees
Wark Common
Wark Common Fm
Selby's Hill
Blake Law
Tithe Hill
Branxton Hill
Encampment Fm
Dovehole Crag
Biteabout Fm
Hetton North Fm
Wark Westcommon
Pressen
Howburn
Brown Rigg
Hagg
Moneylaws Covert
Flodden Hill
Floddenford Plantn
White Hill
Kimmerston
Doddington North Moor
Sprouston
Kerchesters
Pressen Burn
Holefield
Flodden
Kersquarter
Moneylaws Hill 246
Barley Hill
Howtel
West Flodden
Whitton Hill
Fenton Hill
Fenton Ho
Polka Cott
Downham
Fenton Mill
Fenton Town
Fenton
Nesbit
Windywalls
Potsclose
Eastfield of Lempitlaw
Horse Rigg
Mindrum Mill
Wester Hill
Redscar Br
Milfield
West Fenton
Hoselaw Mains
Bowmont Water
Housedon Hill 267
THE RINGSES
Mindrum
Pawston
Kilham
Reedsford
Coldside Hill
Thirlings
Galewood
Newtown
Doddington
Doddington Moor
Lempitlaw
Hoselaw
Camp Hill
White Hill
Marleyknowe
DOD LAW
Shepherds Ho
Hoselaw Loch
Wideopen Moor
Pawston Lake
Whaup Moor
Kilham Hill
Canno Mill
Lanton
Ewart Park
Bridge End
Coupland
Black Knowe Covert
Din Moss
Bowmont Hill
River Glen
Blakelaw
Graden Moor
Castle Law
Hare Law
Longknowe Hill 346
Westnewton
Lanton Mill
Kirknewton
Yeavering
East Wood
Doddington Br
Blakelaw Covert
Shotton
HOMILDON HILL 1402
Thirlestane Hill
Venchen Hill
Shotton Hill
Mid Hill
West Hill
Yeavering Bell
YEAVERING BELL (CAMP) 361
Akeld Hill
Akeld
Turvelaws Fm
Way to Wooler
Greenlees
Yetholm Mains
Elsdonburn Shank
White Hill
Wooler
Thirlstane
The Stank
KIRK YETHOLM
Coldsmouth Hill 414
Hethpool
The Bell
Easter Tor 438
Tom Tallon's Crag 353
White Law
Humbleton Buildings
Gains Law 319
Humbleton
Lochside
Lochtower
Town Yetholm
Kirk Yetholm
Elsdon Burn
Humbleton Hill
Frogden
Linton Hill
Yetholm Loch
331 Staerough Hill
Green Humbleton
343 Gt Hetha
Ell's Knowe
Newton Tors
Bell's Valley
Coldberry Hill
Brown's Law
WOOLER
Caverton Mains
Linton Covert
232 Yetholm Law
PENNINE WAY
397 Madam Law
537
Scaldhill
347 Fredden Hill
Commonburn Ho
Hare Law
Earle Mill
Haugh Head
Crookhouse
LINTON CHURCH
Linton
273 High Side
Primside Fm
Shereburgh
White Law
Whitehall
Wooler Common
Earle Whin
Earle
Linton Burnfoot
327 Sunnyside Hill
Watch Hill
NORTHUMBERLAND
Morebattle Tofts
Wildgoose Hill
Loft Hill
Great Moor
Middleton Hall
Morebattle
Latchly Hill 403
Saughieside Hill 487
Steely Crag 365
Morebattle Mains
Crookedshaws Hill
Wood Hill 334
Kaim Rig
Kip Knowe
Steer Rig
Foulburn Gair
NORTHUMBERLAND NATIONAL PARK
Blackhaggs Rigg
Preston Hill 526
Snear Hill
Coronation Wood
Brands Hill 319
Happy Valley
Colgate Mill
North Middleton
Curr Burn
Black Hag 549
Coldburn
Coldburn Hill 485
Broadhope Hill 517
Morebattle Hill 219
Grubbit Law
Cushat End 345
Percy Law
Black Hill
564 The Curr
Lambden Burn
Goldscleugh
Cold Law
South Middleton
Cliftoncote
Fawcett Shank
Blackseat Hill 461
Rackside 337
Harrow Law
Hownam Grange
Blakedean
Mounthooly
MOUNTHOOLY
601 The Schil
Whitton
Hownam Law 449
FORT
Attonburn
Blackdean Curr 501
West Hill 717
Scald Hill 549
Langleeford
Middleton Dean
Ilderton
Deanbrae Law
Braemoor Knowe 312
Elisheugh Hill
White Law 417
Bizzle Crags
Mid Hill
Housey Crags
Middleton Crags
Heddon Wood
Mowhaugh
Langleeford Hope
Langlee Crags
Dod Hill
Chesterhouse Hill
Place Hill
Mow Law
Sourhope
Fasset Hill
Dod Hill 445
Hen Hole
815 The Cheviot
Threestoneburn Ho
Heddon Hill
Hownam Mains
The Kip
Auchope Cairn 726
Cairn Hill 777
714 Hedgehope Hill
Threestoneburn Wood
Harelaw Burn
313 Thowliestane Hill
Hownam Steeple
Wondrum Hill
Hownam
Mallie Side
Hare Law 314
344 Windy Law
Berry Hills
Craik Moor
Mow Law 432
Swindon Hill
Score Head 582
Crookedsike Head
Scotsman's Knowe
652 Comb Fell
534 Gt Standrop
569 Dunmoor Hill
Cunyan Crags
Reaveley Hill
Reaveley Greens
Hare Law
Philogar Hill
Chatto
Tronshaw Hill
Blackbrough Hill
Crock Law
Green Knowe
Kingseat Burn
King's Seat
531 King's Seat
Coldlaw Hope
Linhope Burn
Long Crag
Five Stones
Dod Law
Pudding Law 428
Mid Hill
418 The Bank
Butt Roads 524
Quickening Outer Cleugh
538 Shielcleugh Edge
Chatto Craig
Henshaw Law
399 Green Hill
Belshaw's Knowe
Cock Law
Lint Lands 510
Nagshead Knowe
High Cantle 482
Ritto Hill
Linhope
Greensidehill
Knock Hill
Ingram
Church Hope Hill
Mossy Law
River Breamish
Shill Moor Cairn 528
Meggrim's Knowe
Hartside Hill
Ewe Hill
395 Whitestone Hill
Humblemoor Hill
Windy Gyle 619
High Bleakhope
Wether Hill
Cowie Law
Mozie Law 552
Beefstand Hill 562
Bloodybush Edge 610
Thorny Hill
507 Callaw Cairn
Black Braes
Hazely Law 499
Uswayford
Bush Knowe
Little Dod
Het Hill
Cochrane Pike 335
Little Ward Law
Cushat Law 615
Broad Law
Hangingshaw Hill
Standard Knowe
Lamb Hill 511
Yarnspath Law
Leafield Edge
Ewe Hill
Lumsden Hill
483 Ward Law
Loft Hill 460
543
Green Knowe
Cobden
Woden Law 422
483 Raeshaw Fell
Beef Stand
Mid Hill
Wether Hill
Sting Head
548 Hogdon Law
Hart Law 341
FORT
Broad Flow
Hindside Knowe
Middle Hill
High Knowes
Prendwick
Scraesburgh Fell 479
Hunthall Hill
Green Law
477 Yearning Law
Carlcroft Hill
Carlcroft
Barrow Law 419
Nettlehope Hill
Kidland Forest
Sneer Hill
Wether Cairn 563
Northfieldhead Hill
411 Hindhope Hill
Wedder Hill 456
Inner Hill
Dryhope Hill
Wholhope Hill
St David's Cairn 504
Hazeltonrig Hill
Alnham
Unthank
Loddan Hill
Nether Hindhope
Blindburn
Carshope Plantn
Barrowburn
Brock's Holes
Lounges Knowe
Batailshiel Haugh
Saughy Hill
Inner Hill
Bleak Law
Old Hazeltonrig
Alnham Castle Fm
Black Halls 463
Deel's Hill 495
Fulhope
Bell Hill
Peat Law 472
Upper Hindhope
Hindhope Law
Saddlers Knowe 455
Dumb Hope
501 Shillhope Law
Wholehope Knowe
The Dodd 332
Gills Law
Harden Hill 327
Scrainwood
Brownhart Law 508
Loan Edge
Copper Snout
Cold Law 399
Ewe Hill
Biddlestone Town Foot
Park Law
Whiteside Hill
Chew Green
Deerbush Hill
Bygate Hall Cotts
Inner Hill
Middle Moor
Clennell Hill
Lounden Hill
Biddlestone Home Fm
Biddlestone
Netherton
392 Lord's Seat
Shillmoor
Upper Coquetdale
The Cheviot Hills
Danger area
272
273
264
251
NT 40
NT 10
00
A
B
C
D
E
F
G
H
7
8
9
10
11
A698
A6112
A697
B6350
B6352
B6353
B6354
B6396
B6401
B6351
B6348
B6525
B6461

Wooler
Lowick
Barmoor Castle
Barmoor Lane End
West Kyloe
East Kyloe
Fenham
Buckton
Elwick
Ross
Detchant
Middleton
Holburn
Hetton Steads
North Hazelrigg
South Hazelrigg
Belford
Easington
Waren Mill
Budle
Bamburgh
Glororum
Burton
Spindlestone
Bradford
Mousen
Adderstone
Bellshill
Warenton
Lucker
Seahouses
North Sunderland
Elford
Beadnell
Benthall
Swinhoe
Newham
West Fleetham
Warenford
Newstead
Chathill
Tughall
Preston
Ellingham
Rosebrough
Chatton
Chillingham
Hepburn
Chatton Moor
Greendykes
West Horton
East Horton
Doddington
Haugh Head
Earle
Middleton Hall
North Middleton
South Middleton
Lilburn Tower
East Lilburn
Newtown
Ilderton
Roseden
Roddam
Wooperton
Old Bewick
New Bewick
Harehope
Eglingham
Brownieside
North Charlton
South Charlton
Brunton
Christon Bank
Embleton
High Newton-by-the-Sea
Low Newton-by-the-Sea
Dunstan
Rock
Rennington
Stamford
Littlemill
Broxfield
Littlehoughton
Peppermoor
Denwick
Hawkhill
Lesbury
Bilton
Alnwick
Abberwick
Bolton
Broome Park
Shipley
Titlington
Beanley
Powburn
Brandon
Branton
Ingram
Fawdon
Glanton
Glanton Pike
Shawdon Hall
Whittingham
Great Ryle
Little Ryle
Prendwick
Alnham
Eslington Park
Yetlington
Thrunton
Edlingham
Rugley
Shilbottle
High Buston
Netherton
Farne Islands
Inner Farne
Staple Sound
Budle Bay
Beadnell Bay
Ross Back Sands
NORTHUMBERLAND
0 1 2 3 miles
0 1 2 3 4 5 km

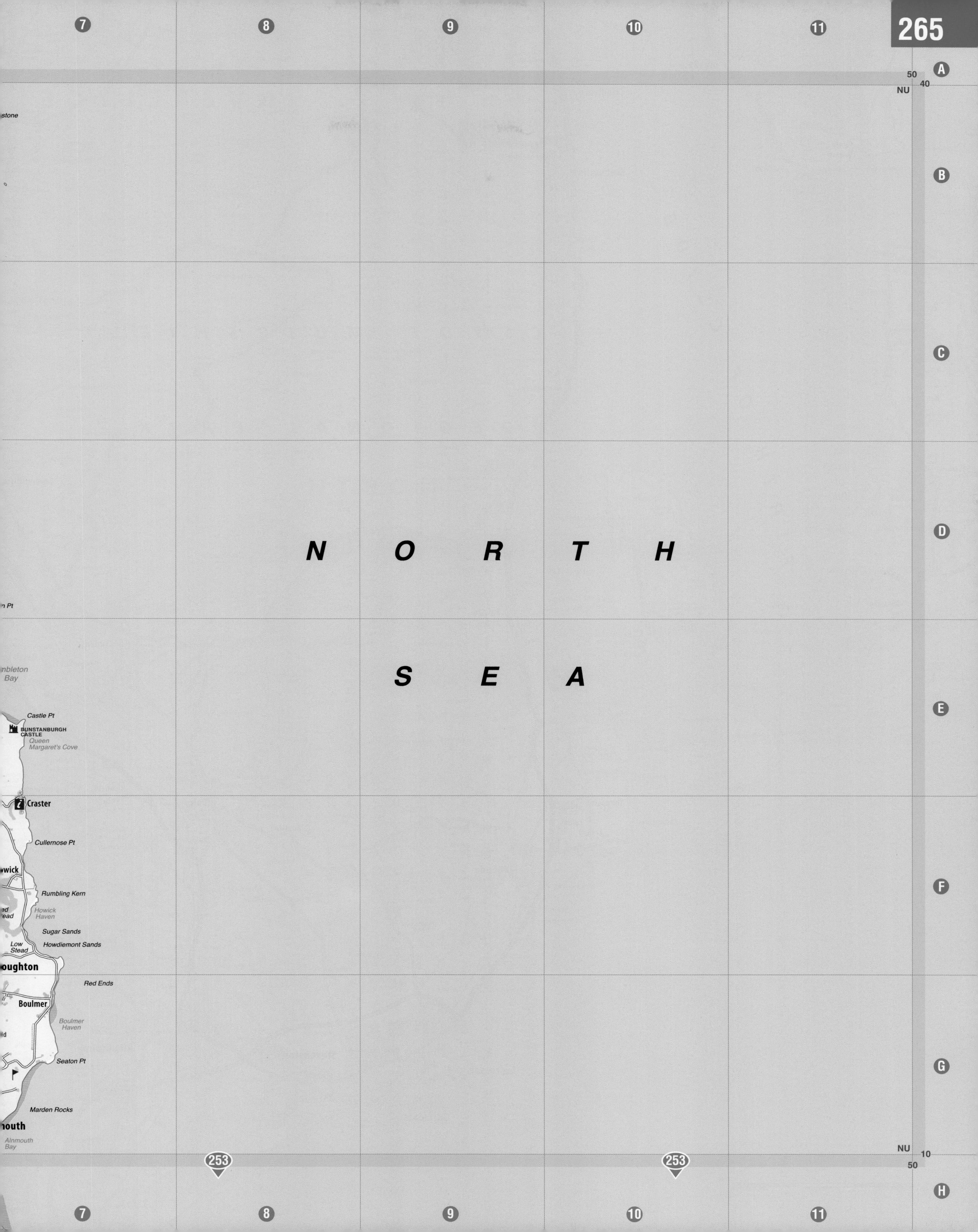
7
8
9
10
11
A
B
C
D
E
F
G
H
50
40
NU
10
50
NU
N O R T H
S E A
Castle Pt
DUNSTANBURGH CASTLE
Queen Margaret's Cove
Craster
Cullernose Pt
Rumbling Kern
Howick Haven
Sugar Sands
Howdiemont Sands
Low Stead
Red Ends
Boulmer
Boulmer Haven
Seaton Pt
Marden Rocks
Alnmouth Bay
253
253

FIRTH OF CLYDE
INVERCLYDE
CLYDE-MUIRSHIEL REGIONAL PARK
NORTH AYRSHIRE
Island of Bute
Great Cumbrae Island
Little Cumbrae Island
Beinn Ruadh 323
Cnoc a' Mhadaih
Buachailean 346
Innellan Hill
Innellan
Port Lamont
Knockdow
Achafour Fm
Newton Park
Castle Toward
Toward Fm
Toward
Toward Quay
Toward Pt
Ardyne Pt
Ardbeg Pt
Ardbeg
Rothesay Bay
Craigmore
Bogany Pt
Ardencraig Gardens
Montford
Ascog Bay
Ascog Pt
Victorian Fernery
Ascog
Loch Ascog
Kerrycroy Bay
Kerrycroy
Cnocnicoill Wood
Scoulag Pt
Scoulag
Mount Stuart
New Fm
Torr Wood
Piperhall
Kerrylamont Bay
Meikle Kilchattan Butts
Bruchag Pt
Kingarth
Kerrytonlia Pt
Kilchattan Bay
Suidhe Chatain
White Port
Covin Hill
St Blane's Chapel
Fort
Glen Callum
Blanes Hill
Glencallum Bay
Barr Hill
Port Leithne
Garroch Head
Inverkip Bay
Inverkip
Everton
Daff Res
Leapmoor Forest
Finnock Bog Fm
High Finnock
Wemyss Pt
Wemyss Bay
Forbes Place
Blood Moss
White Hill
Shielhill
Crawhin Hill
Crawhin Res
Garvock
Gryfe Reservoirs
Dykefoot
Colaouse Hill
Wenchly Top
Garvock Hill
Berry Hill
Rottenburn Br
Creuch Hill 441
Little Creuch Hill
Laverock Stone
Cairncurran Hill
Priestside Fm
Auchenbothie Mains
Jock's Craig
Balrossie School
East Green
Kelly Res
Ferret of Keith Moor
Knockminwood Hill
Lairds Seat
Hardridge Hill 258
Hardridge Fm
Blackwater
Upper Skelmorlie
Skelmorlie
Fardens
Black Fell
North Burnt Hill
Blacketty Water
Duchal Moor
Dunnairbuck Hill
Hyndal Hill
Smeath Hill
High Branchal
Outerwards
Outerwards Res
Coplie Hill
Meigle
Meigle Bay
South Burnt Hill
Comers Hill
Peat Hill
Burnt Hill 486
Queenside Muir
Queenside Loch
Queenside Hill
Craig of Todholes
Craig Minnan
Windy Hill 316
Thornlybank Hill 277
Muirshiel
Blackhouse Moor
Constablewood
Hill Of Stake 522
East Girt Hill
Misty Law 510
Hannah Law 396
Mistlaw Muir
Kaim Dam
Brisbane Mains
Rowantree Hill
Bessel Moor
Waterhead Moor
Girtley Hill
Long Hill
High Corby Knowe
Glenward Hill
Turnave Hill
Routenburn
Kilburn Fm
Box Law
Brown Hill
Wooy Hill
Lairdside Hill 338
Linthills
Largs
Largs Bay
Old Kirk
Haylie Chambered Tomb
Castle Hill
Greeto Br
Feuside Hill
Blacklaw Moss
Blacklaw 466
Wings Law
Ladyland Moor
Auchenbourach 360
Dunconnel Hill
Bridgend
Lochwinnoch
White Bay
Stinking Bay
Skate Pt
Portrye
Gavin's Glen
Horse Hill
Downcraig Ferry
Fairhaven
Bell Bay
Glaid Stone
Tonnel Hill
Fintray Bay
Sheriff's Common
Baliochmartin Bay
Clashfarland Pt
Castle Bay
Knockside Hills
Jock's Knowe
Rough Hill
Greensid Hill
Langdike Moss
Pundeavon Res
Lamb Hill
Burnt Hill
High Blaeberry Craigs
Jeffreystock Fm
Glengarth
Wallace Fm
Gowk Stone
Sheriff's Port
Museum of the Cumbraes
Millport
Millport Bay
Kelburn Country Centre
Brown Hill
Muirhead Reservoir
Camphill Reservoir
Whatside Hills
Blaeloch Hill 407
Cock Law
Lairdside Hill
Gooseton Hill
North Dykes
Lochridge
Fairlie
Fairlie Glen
The Marine Station & David Robertson Mus
Keppel Pier
Farland Pt
Doughend Hole
Aird Hill
Portachur Pt
The Tan
Fairlie Roads
Diamond Hill
Green Hill
Sheep Hill
South Campbill
Auchencloigh
Farm of Place
Kilbirnie
Kilbirnie Loch
Glengarnock
Beith
Southannan Sands
Black Hill
Kaim Hill
Langside Hill
Raven's Craig Glen
Green Hill
Longbar
Sheanawally Pt
Long Bay
Hunterston Sands
Inner Brigurd Pt
Whiteside Hill
Cockrobin Hill
Knockendon Reservoir
Thornyside
Mains
Glengarnock
Biglies Fm
Glenburn Res
Caldron Hill
Crosbie Hills
Brownhill Fm
Coalburn
Barcosh
Meadow Pt
Stoney Port
Broad Islands
Lighthouse Hill
Trail Isle
Castle Island
Waterloo Pt
Gull Pt
Little Brigurd
Hunterston Power Sta
Dykes Plantn
Ward Fm
Brownhill Ho
The Den
Hawking Craig
Goldenberry Hill
Auldmuir Res
Pitcon Mains
Drakemyre
Highfield
Bankhead Moss
Swindridge Muir
Burntongues
Ryefield Ho
Broadlie Ho
Caaf Reservoir
Thirdpart
Carlung Fm
Carlung Ho
Portencross
Glenton Hill
Gill Hill
Ladyside Hill
Laigh Baidland
Greenhirst
Dalry
Giffordland
Lynn Glen
Blairland
Knollhead
Lambridden Fm
Foxcover Plantn
Templandmuir Fm
Ardneil
West Kilbride
Ballees Fm
Faulds Fm
Law Hill
Dykehead
Munnoch Reservoir
Munnoch Res
Farland Head
Mhor
Ardneil Bay
Meadowfoot
Cubrieshaw Hall
Knockewart Hills
Holmbyre
Bankhead
Blair Mill
Dykeneuk Moss
Bell Stane
Seamill
Brither Rocks
Busbie Muir Res
Rowanside Hills
Yonderhouses
Newhouse
Auchenskeith
Jameston
Lissens Moss
Muirlaught Fm
Laigh Gooseloan
Lylestone
South Inch
Kirkland Glen
Craigspark
Dalgarven
Gateside
Ayrshire Museum of Country Life & Costume
Sevenacres Mains
Boydston Fm
Meikle Laught
Stevenston or Ashgrove Loch
Mill Glen Res
Montfode
Scart Rock
Wood Fm
Bannoch
Chapelhill
Sharphill
Middlepart
Castlehill
Kilwinning
Kilwinning Abbey
Bensile
Doura Mains
Horse Isle
North Bay
Broad Rock
Dykesmains
Stevenston
Retail Pk
Ardrossan
Ardrossan Castle
Ardrossan South Beach
Ardrossan Town
Ardrossan Harbour
Glencairn Street
Dubbs
Eglinton Castle
Eglinton
Doura
Brodick
South Bay
North Ayrshire Heritage Centre
Auchenharvie
Stevenston
Saltcoats
Outer Nebbock
Inner Nebbock
Campbeltown (May-Sept only)
Girdle Toll
Stanecastle
Irvine
Bogside Flats
Magnum
Scottish Maritime Museum
Fullarton
Bourtreehill
Broomlands
Dreghorn
0 1 2 3 miles
0 1 2 3 4 5 km

Bearsden
Bishopton
West Porton
Rossland
Dargavel Village
Erskine
Mountblow
Dalmuir
Radnor Park
Drumchapel
Kessington
Bishopbriggs
Kilmacolm
Clydebank
Inchinnan
Knightswood
Summerston
Lambhill
Temple
Yoker
Scotstoun
Jordanhill
Anniesland
Kelvindale
Maryhill
Ruchill
Springburn
Renfrew
Whiteinch
Partick
Kelvinside
Dowanhill
Houston
Quarriers Village
Bridge of Weir
Crosslee
Craigends
Ranfurly
Linwood
Govan
RENFREWSHIRE
Brookfield
Kilbarchan
Johnstone
Paisley
Glasgow
Hillington
Cardonald
Mosspark
Pollokshields
Govanhill
Millarston
Elderslie
Castlehead
Blackhall
Charleston
Thornly Park
Tandlehill
Quarrelton
Millikenpark
Pollok
CITY OF GLASGOW
Rutherglen
Glenburn
Foxbar
Hurlet
Priesthill
Shawlands
Cathcart
Newlands
Howwood
Nitshill
Mansewood
Waterside
Crossmill
Barrhead
Dovecothall
Carnwadric
Thornliebank
Arden
Merrylee
Giffnock
Castlemilk
Gateside
West Arthurlie
Auchenback
Netherlee
Stamperland
Sheddens
Neilston
Springhill
Whitecraigs
Clarkston
Shillford
Crookfur
Newton Mearns
Busby
Netherplace
Broom
Kirkhill
Uplawmoor
Waterfoot
Thorntonhall
Peel Park
EAST
Hairmyres
Newlandsmuir
Lugton
Eaglesham
Halket
RENFREWSHIRE
Barrmill
Greenhills
Burnhouse
Gabroc Hill
Fullwood
Dunlop
Kingsford
Stewarton
Fenwick
Laigh Fenwick
Waterside
Cunninghamhead
Kilmaurs
Onthank
EAST
Moscow
Springside
Knockentiber
Crosshouse
Knockinlaw
Kilmarnock
AYRSHIRE

NORTH LANARKSHIRE
CITY OF GLASGOW
SOUTH LANARKSHIRE
Bishopbriggs
Lumloch
Milton
Colston
Robroyston
Auchinairn
Balornock
Springburn
Barmulloch
Millerston
Provanmill
Hogganfield
Royston
Germiston
Riddrie
Ruchazie
Garthamlock
Craigend
Cranhill
Queenslie
Carntyne
Haghill
Dennistoun
Greenfield
Springboig
Barlanark
Calton
Gorbals
Bridgeton
Shettleston
Barrachnie
Garrowhill
Baillieston
Mount Vernon
Braidfauld
Fullarton
Dalmarnock
Oatlands
Govanhill
Polmadie
Rutherglen
Croftfoot
Burnside
Castlemilk
Cambuslang
Flemington
Carmyle
Newton
Westburn
Eastfield
Carmunnock
Muirend
Linn Park
Jellyhill
Auchinloch
Millersneuk
Wester Auchinloch
Stepps
Garnkirk
Muirhead
Chryston
Moodiesburn
Bridgend
Mollinsburn
Gartcosh
Marnock
Glenboig
Greenfoot
Glenmavis
Townhead
Gartsherrie
Coatbridge
Langloan
Dundyvan
Old Monkland
Kirkshaw
Shawhead
Rosehall
Carnbroe
Bargeddie
Birkenshaw
Tannochside
Viewpark
Broomhouse
Easterhouse
Swinton
Airdrie
Thrashbush
Riggend
Wattston
Stand
Plains
Caldercruix
Hillend
Longriggend
Greengairs
Craigneuk
Gartlea
Calderbank
Chapelhall
Coatdyke
Petersburn
Gartness
Salsburgh
Newhouse
Holytown
New Stevenston
Mossend
Bellshill
Uddingston
Bothwell
Fallside
Orbiston
Milnwood
Newarthill
Carfin
Cleland
Hartwood
Forgewood
North Motherwell
Motherwell
Craigneuk
Wishaw
Newmains
Coltness
Cambusnethan
Morningside
Netherton
Pather
Waterloo
Bogside
Overtown
Law
Dalserf
Rosebank
Netherburn
Crossford
Hazelbank
Carluke
Blantyre
High Blantyre
Stonefield
Low Blantyre
Burnbank
Hamilton
Udston
Earnock
Fairhill
Meikle Earnock
Cadzow
Eddlewood
Silvertonhill
Ferniegair
Allanton
Larkhall
Machan
Hareleeshill
Shawsburn
Strutherhill
Birkenshaw
Knowetop
Knoweton
Muirhouse
Dechmont Hill
Nerston
East Kilbride
Calderwood
College Milton
Peel Park
East Mains
West Mains
Saint Leonards
Thorntonhall
Hairmyres
Westwood
The Murray
Newlandsmuir
Kelvin
Whitehills
Greenhills
Auldhouse
Quarter
Limekilnburn
Millheugh
Shawtonhill
Chapelton
Shawton
Udstonhead
Glassford
Stonehouse
Carnduff
Strathaven
Sandford
Flemington
Kirkmuirhill
Blackwood
Boghead
Dillarburn
Auchenheath
Lesmahagow
Turfholm
Brocketsbrae
Whitelaw
Caldermill
Gilmourton
Stobieside
Auchrobert Hill
Middle Rig
Mossmulloch
Hareshaw
Draffan
Tillietudlem
Craignethan Castle
M8
M73
M74
M80
A725
A71
A726
A723
A73
A721
278
267
258
259
0 1 2 3 miles
0 1 2 3 4 5 km

Uphall
Westfield
Dechmont
Wester Dechmont
Uphall Station
Pumpherston
Livingston
East Calder
Mid Calder
Oakbank
Bathgate
Boghall
Armadale
Bathville
Blackridge
Mayfield
Whiteside
Windyknowe
Westrigg
Blackburn
Seafield
Livingston Village
Kirkton
Deans
Eliburn
Ladywell
Knightsridge
Howden
Dedridge
Adambrae
Bellsquarry
Murieston
Polbeth
West Calder
Harthill
Whitburn
East Whitburn
Croftmalloch
Eastfield
West Benhar
Hirst
Longridge
Stoneyburn
Bents
Loganlea
Addiewell
Fauldhouse
Greenburn
Breich
Shotts
Dykehead
Stane
Torbothie
Springhill
Harburn
Allanton
Woolfords Cottages
Tarbrax
Climpy
Wilsontown
Rootpark
Haywood
Auchengray
Forth
Braehead
Carluke
Yieldshields
Roadmeetings
Kilncadzow
Carnwath
Carstairs
Carstairs Junction
West End
Ravenstruther
Cartland
Lanark
New Lanark
Kirkfieldbank
Hyndford Bridge
Kaimend
Newbigging
Walston
Dunsyre
Dolphinton
Libberton
Pettinain
Whitecastle
Shieldhill
Elsrickle
Candy Mill
Kaimrig End
Melbourne
Covington
Quothquan
Thankerton
Sandilands
Skirling
W E S T   L O T H I A N
M8
A70
A71
A702
A706
A721
279
259
260
270

Ratho Station
Ratho
Sighthill
Hermiston
Wester Hailes
Kingsknowe
Morningside
Craiglockhart
Craigmillar
Newcraighall
Dalkeith
Edinburgh
Bonnington
Wilkieston
Burnwynd
Currie
Juniper Green
Colinton
Swanston
Braid
Liberton
Fairmilehead
Kaimes
Gilmerton
Danderhall
Millerhill
Kirknewton
Balerno
Malleny Mills
Straiton
Loanhead
Bilston
Eskbank
Newbattle
Bonnyrigg and Lasswade
Polton
Roslin
Rosewell
Newtongrange
Woodhouselee
Easter Howgate
Milton Bridge
Pentland Hills
Pentland Hills Regional Park
Auchendinny
Penicuik
Silverburn
Kirkhill
Carrington
Temple
Gorebridge
Midlothian
Nine Mile Burn
Howgate
Carlops
Leadburn
Rosebery
Scottish Borders
Whim Farm
Cowdenburn
West Linton
Waterheads
Halmyre Mains
Damside
Romannobridge
Mountain Cross
Eddleston
Dolphinton
Blyth Bridge
Kirkurd
Melbourne
Castle Craig
Drochil
Tweed Valley Forest Park
Williamslee
Colquhar
Hallyne
Lyne
Peebles
Kerfield
Kings Muir
Cardrona
Kirkburn
Kirkton Manor
Moorfoot
A70
A71
A702
A701
A703
A72
A6094
B6372
A720
M8
280
269
260
261
0 1 2 3 miles
0 1 2 3 4 5 km

Wallyford
Macmerry
Penston
New Winton
Elphinstone
North Elphinstone
South Elphinstone
New Town
Samuelston
Bolton
Garvald
Nunraw Abbey
Crossgatehall
Cousland
Ormiston
Pencaitland
Gifford
Carfrae
White Castle (Fort)
East Saltoun
West Saltoun
Glenkinchie Distillery
Peastonbank
Danskine
Rangely Kip
Whitehill
Fordel Mains
Chesterhill
Oxenfoord Castle
Preston Hall
Gilchriston
Quarryford
Longyester
Green Castle
Peaston
Mayfield
Dewartown
Pathhead
Vogrie
Long Newton
Humbie
Stobshiel
East Lothian
Newlandrig
Crichton
Crichton Castle
Fala Dam
Fala
Blegbie
Widow's Knowe
Priest Law
Lammer Law
Settlement
Borthwick
North Middleton
Tynehead
Blackcastle
Soutra Hill
Crib Law
Seenes Law
Middleton
Dun Law
Tollishill Fort
Hunt Law
Falahill
Gilston
Headshaw Hill
Turf Law
Hillhouse
Addinston
Longcroft Hillfort
Constable Hill
Heriot
Carcant
Kirktonhill
Oxton
Longshaw Law
Borthwick Hall
Southern Upland Way
Fountainhall
Allanshaugh
Lauder
Thirlestane Castle
Thirlestane
Whiteburn
Blythe
Torquhan
Symington
Mitchelston
Stow
Killochyett
Watherston
Boon
Lauderdale
Legerwood
Kirkhill
Upper Blainslie
Nether Blainslie
Threepwood
Wooplaw
Colmslie
Langshaw
Bow
Caitha Bowland
Windydoors
Blackhaugh
Buckholm
West Morriston
Earlston
A68
A7
A697

EAST LOTHIAN
SCOTTISH BORDERS
Lammermuir
Oldhamstocks
Cockburnspath
Cove
Reed Pt
Siccar Pt
Meikle Poo Craig
Hirst Rocks
Old Cambus
Dunbar Common
Clints Dod
WHITE CASTLE (FORT)
Rangely Kip
Lammermuir Hills
Spartleton Edge
Monynut Edge
Ecclaw
Grantshouse
Nether Monynut
Abbey St Bathans
Whiteadder Reservoir
Cranshaws
Ellemford
EDINSHALL BROCH
Longformacus
Southern Upland Way
Preston
Lintlaw
Cumledge
Blanerne
Edrom
EDROM CHURCH
Duns
Duns Law
JIM CLARKE MOTORSPORT MUS
MANDERSTON
Buxley
Clockmill
Cheeklaw
Gavinton
Choicelee
Wedderlie
Twin Law
Dirrington Gt Law
Dirrington Lit Law
Westruther
Polwarth
Sinclair's Hill
Fogo
Sisterpath
Bogend
Swinton
SWINTON KIRK
Merse
Swintonmill
Halliburton
Thornydykes
Whiteburn
Houndslow
Greenlaw
Gordon
GREEN KNOWE TOWER
Legerwood
Huntlywood
Middlethird
Easter Howlaws
Lambden
Leitholm
Orange Lane
Eccles
Hume
HUME
Falsidehill
West Morriston
Fans
Coldstream
THE HIRSEL
Birgham
Stichill
Carham
Wark
A1
A697
A6105
A6112
A1107
A6089
B6456
B6355
B6365
B6460
B6461
B6364
282
271
262
263
0 1 2 3 miles
0 1 2 3 4 5 km

283
263
264
NORTHUMBERLAND
Holy Island (Lindisfarne)
Goswick Sands
Snook Pt
Beal Pt
Causeway
LINDISFARNE
Snipe Pt
Keel Head
Emmanuel Head
Beal Sands
Holy Island Sands
LINDISFARNE HERITAGE CENTRE
Holy Island
LINDISFARNE CASTLE
LINDISFARNE PRIORY
Castle Pt
Hole Mouth
Granary Pt
Fenham
Guile Pt
Burrows Hole
Lowmoor Pt
Tealhole Pt
Ross Pt
Ross Back Sands
Buckton
Fast Castle Head
Wheat Stack
FAST CASTLE
Oatlee Hill
Lumsdaine
Lumsdaine Moor
Cross Law
SETTLEMENT
Coldingham Loch
Mire Loch
St Abb's Head
ST ABB'S HEAD
Horsecastle Bay
Bell Hill
Starney Bay
Northfield
St Abbs
St Abb's Haven
Coldingham Bay
Yellow Craig
Moorside Plantn
Buskinburn Ho
Coldingham Moor
Long Latch
Huxton
SCHOOL ROAD
Temple Hall
PRIORY
Coldingham
Press Castle
Press Mains
Abbey Park
Three Burn Grange
Grange Plantn
Gallows Law
Callercove Pt
Hairy Ness
EYEMOUTH MUSEUM
Eyemouth
Hallydown
Ale Water
North Wood
Ind Est
Blackhill
Cairncross
Scout Pt
Horse Head
Fancove Head
Heugh Head
Littledean Fm
Aytonwood Ho
Fox Covert
Howburn
MAIN STREET
Reston
East Reston Mill
Ayton Mains
Breeches Rock
Loanside
Auchencrow
Berrybank
Ayton
AYTON CASTLE
Burnmouth
Ross
Ross Pt
Peelwalls Ho
Cocklaw
Ayton Hill 199
Chester Hill
Bowie's Plantn
Prenderguest
Peelwalls Fm
Hilton Bay
Causeway Bank
Horn Burn
Millerton Hill
Billiemire Burn
Greenfield Plantns
Lamberton Moor
Lamberton Beach
Meg's Dub
Oldcastles
Edington Covert
Westmains Moor
Foulden Hill
North Crowlea Plantn
Witches' Knowe
Lamberton
Deans Hill
Mordington Holdings
Marshall Meadows Bay
Chirnside
Hag Wood
Lazybeds Plantn
Kilbann
Marshall Meadows
Foulden New Mains
FOULDEN TITHE BARN
Mordington Ho
St John's Haven
Chirnsidebridge
Nether Mains
Foulden
Clappers
West Edge Fm
Stuartslaw
West Foulden
Foulden Bastle
Mains
Edrington Ho
Whiteadder Water
DUNS ROAD
1333
Bus Pk
Allanton
Hutton Hall Barns
Broadmeadows Ho
Clarabad Mill
Edrington Mains
Halidon Hill
Highfields
Sharper's Head
Bucket Rocks
Hutton
Meadow House Mains
Paxton North Mains
Baldersbury Hill
Berwick-upon-Tweed
BERWICK BARRACKS & MAIN GUARD
BERWICK BOROUGH MUS
BERWICK
Broomdykes
Hutton Mains
Spital Mains
Paxton
New Mills
Grangeburn Mill Fm
Mill Fm
Tweedmouth
Blackadder Bank
Sunwick Fm
SHIELFIELD PARK
Sandstell Pt
Spittal
Highcliffe
Doons Law
Winfield
PAXTON HOUSE
River Tweed
Bear's Head
Whitsome
Hilton
Fishwick
UNION SUSPENSION BRIDGE
Loanend
East Ord
Ord Mains
ETAL ROAD
Prior Park
Redshin Cove
Jardinefield
Fishwick Mains
Longridge Towers
Tweedmouthmoor
Borewell Fm
Whitsomehill
Horncliffe
Horncliffe Mains
Saltpan Rocks
East Newton
Horndean
Green Hill
Norham East Mains
Velvet Hall
Ewe Hill
Murton
Scremerston
Fellow Hills
Horndean Burn
Norham West Mains
Thornton Park
Murton White Ho
Unthank Fm
Unthank Blue Ho
Old Town Covert
New Ladykirk
Thornton Cottage
Cheswick Black Rocks
Ladykirk
NORHAM CASTLE
Emerick Fm
Royalty Fm
Thornton Mains
Allerdean Mill
Scremerston Hill
Scremerston Town Fm
Greenside Cotts
Norham
Morris Hall
Thornton
Allerdeanmill Burn
Camphouses
Shoreswood
Shoreswood Hall
Cheswick Sands
Cheswick Ho
Cheswick
Fox Covert
Shoresdean
West Allerdean
Allerdean Grange
Allerdean Greens
Simprim Mains
East Newbiggin
Battle Moor
Grievestead Moor
Coal Burn
Cheswick Buildings
Windmill Hill
Goswick
Ladykirk House
Milne Graden East Mains
Great Haugh
Ancroft Northmoor
Ancroft
Wideopen Plantn
Grindon
Ancroft Mill
Goswick Sands
Holy Island (Lindisfarne)
Milne Graden West Mains
Tillmouth Fm
Felkington
Ancroft Southmoor
Bridge Mill
Haggerston
Snook Pt
Westmoor Plantn
Haydon Dean
Berrington Law
Berrington Ho
Brockmill Fm
Beal Pt
Tweedmill
Shellacres
Toft Hill
Mattilees Hill
Berrington Lough
Berrington
New Haggerston
Beal
Causeway
LINDISFARNE
Twizel Mill
Brick Kiln Plantn
Dean Burn
Bowsden Moor
Duddo
Mattilees Cott
Beal Sands
Holy Island Sands
Fadden Hill
Common Plantn
Castle Heaton
Jacks Law
Lickar Dean
West Mains Inn
Duddo Hill
Bowsden
Lowick Mill
Donaldson's Lodge
Woodside Fm
Low Wood
Bowsden West Fm
Old Dryburn
Mount Hooley
Melkington
Tindal Ho
Black Bank
Hazely Hill
High Wood
Barmoor Hill
Dry Burn
Hunting Hall
Granary Pt
Fenham
Syning Hill
Peter's Plantn
New Heaton
Heaton Moor
Barleymill Bank
Rhodes Hill
Black Heddon
West Kyloe
Fenwick
Cornhill-on-Tweed
Heaton Covert
ETAL CASTLE
Etal Rhodes
Etal Moor
Barmoor Ridge
Barmoor Castle
Barmoor Lane End
Moss Hall
Lowick
East Kyloe
Kyloe Hills
Fenwick Wood
Lowmoor Pt
Pallinsburn Ho
HEATHERSLAW LIGHT RAILWAY
Etal
Letham Hill
Moss Wood
Kyloe Wood
Tealhole Pt
Cookstead
HEATHERSLAW CORNMILL
Ford Forge
Ford Common Cott
Bareless
Campfield
Crookham Westfield
Crookham
HEATHERSLAW
Hay Fm
LADY WATERFORD HALL
Ford Common
FORT
Barmoor South Moor
Redhouse Moor
Moorhouse
Shepherdskirk Hill 202
Buckton Moor
Buckton
Branxton
Windy Law
Bar Moor
Barmoore
NU
15
45
40
10
A1
A6105
A698
A1107
B6438
B6355
B6437
B6461
B6470
B6354
B6525
B6353

Iona
IONA HERITAGE CENTRE
Baile Mor
Stac an Aoineidh
Sligneach
SOUTH WEST MULL MAKERS
Fionnphort
Aridhglas
Fidden
Tiraghoil
A849
Eorabus
Achnahard
Knokan
Lower Ardtun
Bunessan
Lee
Loch Assapol
18
376
CRUACHAN MIN
BROLASS
Beach
376
Leidle
BEINN NA CROISE
Carsaig
Carsaig Bay
Rubha Dubh
288
289
Erraid
Knockvologan
ROSS OF MULL
Uisken
Scoor
Ardalanish
Ardchiavaig
CARSAIG ARCHES
Malcolm's Pt.
Soa I.
Eilean a'Chalmain
125
Rubha nam Braithrean
Rubh Ardalanish
Torran Rocks
NM
OBAN
Dubh Artach
Rubh'a'Geadha
Balnahard
Kiloran Bay
Uragaig
COLONSAY HOUSE GARDENS
Kiloran
Kilchattan
B8086
B8087
136
Scalasaig
COLONSAY
Loch Staosnaig
B8085
Ardskenish
Garvard
Rubha Dubh
Balerominhor
PRIORY
Dubh Eilean
Oronsay
Eilean nan Ron
Corpach Bay
Shian Bay
453
RAINBERG MOR
Shian
Loch Righ Mòr
318
Rubh'an t-Sàilein
Loch Tarbert
Rubha Lang-aoinidh
Rubha a'Mhail
Rubha Bholsa
Lagg
439
Loch an Aircil
Loch Lesgamaill
364
SGARBH BREAC
Nave Island
Ardnave Pt.
J U R A
785
755
PAPS OF JURA
15
A846
Ardmenish
Loch a Chnuic Bhric
Gortantaoid
Bunnahabhain
BUNNAHABHAIN DISTILLERY
316
SOUND OF ISLAY
JURA FOREST
Corran
Carraig Bhan
Ardnave
Kilnave
Cnocbreac
Knockrome
Lowlandman's Bay
Killinallan
Leargybreck
Ardfernal
Garra Eallabus
Loch Gruinart
Glean Astaile
An Clachan
Sanaigmore
B8018
Caol Ila
Loch na Mile
561
CAOL ILA DISTILLERY
Port Askaig
Leckgruinart
Feolin Ferry
FINLAGGAN CENTRE
Braigo
Smaull
LOCH GRUINART RSPB
LOCH GRUINART NATURE RESERVE VISITORS CENTRE
Loch Finlaggan
Keills
Keils
Ballinaby
Carnduncan
Craigens
Loch Cam
Loch Ballygrant
Gleann Ullibh
Craighouse
ISLE OF JURA DISTILLERY
Small Isles
Saligo Bay
Saligo
Aoradh
B8017
Tighnacachla
Ballygrant
Lossit Lodge
342
BRAT BHEINN
Crackaig
Loch Gorm
Balole
Kilmeny
A846
Coul Pt.
Coull
Foreland Ho
I S L A Y
Knocklearoch
Cabrach
Camas an Staca
Strone
Lyrabus
Esknish
Sunderland
Blackrock
Redhouses
A847
Daill
267
BEINN DUBH
Machir Bay
Kilchoman
B8018
Gortan
Islay Ho
Conisby
Bridgend
Am Fraoch Eilean
Rubha na Tràille
Brosdale I.
Bruichladdich
Kilchiaran
Bowmore
NR
Kilchiaran Bay
254
ISLAY LIFE MUSEUM
BOWMORE ROUND CHURCH
A846
Cattadale
Tormisdale
RHINNS
PORT CHARLOTTE
Mulindry
Port Charlotte
Kilennan
0 2 4 6 miles
0 2 4 6 8 10 km
15
Gartbreck
Laggan
Lossit
OF
Lossit Pt.
Kelsay
Nerabus
Bridge Ho
471
BEINN BHAN
491
BEINN BHEIGEIR
Carraig Mhór
A B C D E F G H
1 2 3 4 5 6

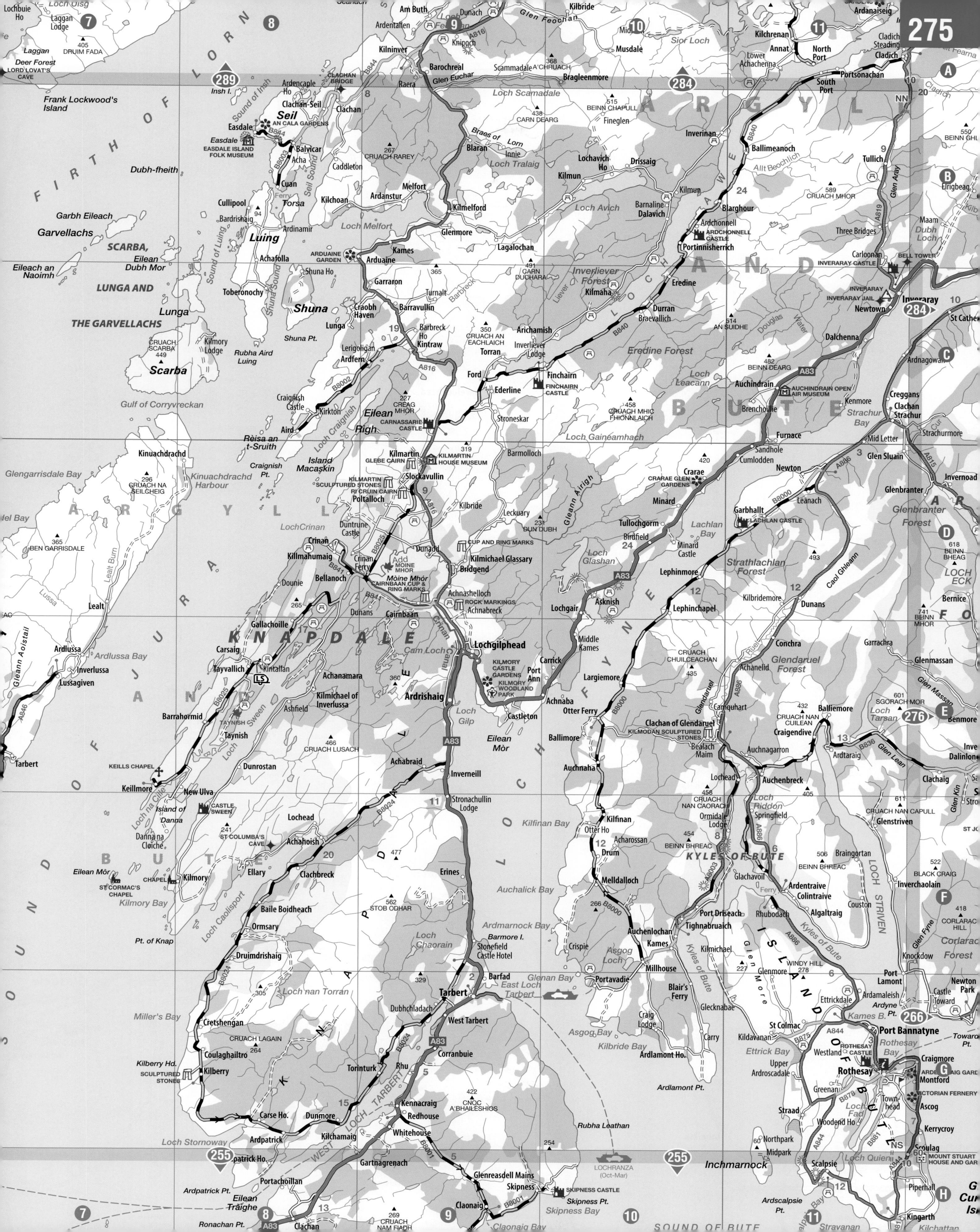

Strachurmore
Beinn Tharsuinn 619
Drimsynie
Inverlochlarig
Lochgoilhead
Coilessan
Morelaggan
Ben Reoch 661
Cruach na Ciobs
Corrow
Coilessan Glen
Cnoc Coinnich 761
Tullich Hill 632
Firkin
Beinn Bhreac 681
Tombuidhe
Creag Dhubh
Beinn Luibhean
Lettermay
The Steeple
Tom Nan Gamhna
Garbh
Creagan
ARGYLL
284
Glen Sluain
465 Beinn Lagan
Curra Lochain
Blairilomond
Carn Glas 502
Dùn Mòr
Inverlounin
FOREST
Carnach Mòr
Tullich Fm
Stob Gobhlach
Doune
Douglas Water
Cruach nam Miseag
Beinn Reithe 653
INVERBEG GALLERY
Glen Douglas
Inverbeg
779 Beinn Bheula
767 Creag Sgoilte
Meall Reamhar
Glenbranter
Invernoaden
Beinn Dubhain
Lochain nan Cnàimh
Beach
PARK
Srón Mallanach
Doune Hill 734
Glenshellish Fm
Glen Branter
Glenbranter Forest
Coire Ealt
Cnoc na Tricriche
Cormonachan Glen
Loch Goil
Tom Molach
The Saddle
Beinn Lochain
Sgurr a' Choinnich
Beannan
Rubha na Beithe
Glenmallan
Tom Buidhe
Cruach an t-Sidhein
Mid Hill
642 Beinn Dubh
Craigbrack
Carrick Castle
CARRICK CASTLE
Beinn Bhreac
Meall Daraich
Beinn Bhreac
Glen Mollochan
703 Beinn Eich
Dornoch Point
Island
Stuck
530
275
ARGYLL
Cruachan Bhuic 635
Carraig na Maraig
Toll nam Muc
Carraig nan Ròn
Portincaple
Whistlefield
Beinn a Mhanaich 709
Gleann na Caorainn
Edentaggart
Luss Water
618 Beinn Bheag
Whistlefield
Cnoc Madaidh
Cnoc Fraorach
Maol an Fheidh
Meall Breac
Rubha Garbh
Cruach an Draghair
Rubha nan Eoin
Beinn Chaorach 713
Coire Coinghil
Coille-eughain Hill
The Strone
Bernice Glen
Larach Hill
Allt Reinain
Creachan Mor 657
Knap Burn
Shelling Burn
656 Beinn Tharsuinn
657 Creag an Leinibh
Beinn Ruisg 595
Tharsuinn 643
Bernice
Loch Eck
FOREST
Toll a' Bhuic
Garelochhead
GARELOCHHEAD
Auchengaich Burn
Auchengavin Burn
Beinn Mhor 741
Meall Dubh
Sligrachan
Loch Long
Cnoc na h-Airighe
ARGYLL
Garrachra Glen
Meall an t-Sith
Sligrachan Hill
Castle Craig
Allt Coille Mheadhanaich
Port an Lochain
Rockville
Strone House
Auchengaich
Auchengaich Hill
Balenock 638
Coire Cuinne
Creachan Hill 536
Coire an
Paper Cave
Drynain
Drynain Glen
Mambeg
Lochan Ghlas Laogh
Faslane Bay
AND BUTE
Capull Cloiche 577
Clach Bheinn 643
Barnacabber
Faslane Port
Garrachra
664 Beinn Ruadh
PARK
Shepherd's Pt
Glen Fruin
Finlas Water
Shemore
Creachan Mor 571
Glenmassan
Stronvochlan
Finart Bay
Carraig Mhaol
Carnban Pt
Fruin Water
Cnap Rheamhar
Ardentinny
Garelochhead Forest
Rahane
Gare Loch
Shantron Hill
Creachan Beag 547
Creag Liath
Coulport
Duchlage
Stronlonag
Stonefield
Glen Massan
Maol Riabhach
ROSNEATH ROAD
West Kilbride
Bailymenoch
Blairglas
Creag Dhonnaiche
Benmore Home Fm
BENMORE BOTANIC GARDENS
Inverchapel Burn
Meall Dubh
Stronchullin Hill
Little Rahane
Shandon
East Kilbride
580 An Creachan
Eckford Ho
Ardpeaton
Airlig
Blairvadach
Inverlauren
601 Sgorach Mor
Corarsik
Benmore
Uig
Creag Mhòr
Gairletter
Gairletter Pt
Hattonburn
Highlandman's Wood
Drumfad
Dumfin
Blairmore Hill
Clynder
Daligan
Glenlean
Glen Lean
432 Meall an Fhamhair
Rashfield
Puck's Glen
Cnoc a'Mhadaidh
Knockderry Fm
Stroul Bay
Stroul
Rhu
GLENARN GARDEN
THE HILL HOUSE
HELENSBURGH UPPER
Bannachra Muir
Clachaig Hill 521
Ballochyle Hill
Invereck
Ardbeg
Kilmun Hill
Bellcairn
SHORE ROAD
Rosneath
Cairndhu Pt
Helensburgh
313 Ben Bowie
Allt Coire Cheathaich
Ballochyle
Dalinlongart
KILMUN ARBORETUM
Blairmore
Garelochhead Forest
Clachan Fm
Rosneath Bay
Castle Pt
THE ROWAN GALLERY
HELENSBURGH CENTRAL
Townhead
B836
Clachaig
Sandhaven
MIDGE LANE
Kilmun
Graham's Pt
Cove
Lindowan Res
Rosneath Home Fm
Robert Ness
Craigendoran
Camis Eskan Fm
Camis Eskan Ho
Killoeter
Little Eachaig River
Dalinlongart Hill
Holy Loch
Strone
Gallow Hill
Culwatty Bay
Perch Rock
CRAIGENDORAN
Meall Criche
Meall Buidhe
Gibb's Pt
Barons Pt
Portkil
Rosneath Pt
Mid Hill
Glen Kin
Sandbank
Lazaretto Pt
Ardnadam
Strone Pt
Kilcreggan
Portkil Bay
Portkil Pt
Colgrain
Cruach nan Capull 611
Finbracken Hill
Stronsaul
Bus Pk
Ind Est
Black Craig 568
Leacann nan Gall
Hunter's Quay
Lyleston Fm
Kilmal
Ardmore
Glenstriven
Kempock Pt
KEMPOCK STONE
Fort Matilda
GOUROCK
Kirn
Gourock
West Bay
Greenock Ocean Terminal
Kelhurn
Giant's Knowe 504
Bishop's Seat
Ashton
FORT MATILDA
MCLEAN MUS & ART GALLERY
River Clyde
ST JOHN'S CHURCH
East Bay
Dunoon
HIGHLAND MARY'S STATUE
McInroy's Pt
CLOCH ROAD
Midton
Greenock West
Greenock
Horse Seat
Cloch Pt
Levan
Ind Est
Coves Res
GREENOCK WEST
GREENOCK CENTRAL
Garvel Pt
Cartsdyke
Pillar Bank
275
522 Black Craig
West Bay
Berry Burn
CLOCH LIGHTHOUSE
Burneven Hill
Larkfield
Central
Inverchaolain
Kilbride Hill
Braeside
Branchton
Ravenscraig
DRUMFROCHAR
CARTSDYKE
Bridgend
CAPPIELOW PARK
Ladyburn
Port Glasgow
472 Blar Buidhe
Corlarach Hill 391
Bullwood
Spango
Overton
WHINHILL
Strone Farm
KILMACOLM ROAD
Strone
BOGSTON
Gibshill
Lilybank
GREENOCK ROAD
Blairbuie
Bull Rock
Lunderston
IBM
New Yetts Res
Whinhill Res
PORT GLASGOW
NEWARK CASTLE
WOODHALL
Brackley Pt
Colarach Hill 419
Garrowchorran Hill
BULLWOOD ROAD
Lunderston Bay
INVERKIP ROAD
Greenock Cut
Whitelees Moor
Burnhead Moor
Harelaw Res
Devol
Mid Auchinlech
Broadfield
395 Kilmarnock Hill
Corlarach Forest
Ardgowan
Bankfoot
Loch Thom
Corlick Hill
Devol Moor
Bardrainney
Ardgowan Pt
Compensation Res
Dunrod Hill
Darndaff Moor
Glen Fyne
Beinn Ruadh 323
Inverkip Bay
Inverkip
Shielhill
Cunston Cott
Cnoc a' Mhadaidh
Berfern Hill
Everton
Crawhin Hill
Gryfe Reservoirs
Dykefoot
Priestside Fm
Auchenbothie Mains
Buachailean 346
Finnock Bog Fm
Leapmoor Forest
Daff Res
Crawhin Res
Garvock
Gryfe Water
Knockdow
Achafour Fm
Innellan Hill
Innellan
High Finnock Fm
Colaouse Hill
Cairncurran Hill
Port Lamont
NS
Newton Park
SHORE ROAD
266
Wemyss Pt
Wemyss Bay
Jock's Craig
Green Water
Forbes Place
Blood Moss
Wenchly Top
Garvock Hill
Rottenburn Fm
INVERCLYDE
266
Berry Hill
Creuch Hill 441
Little Creuch Hill
Laverock Stone
Balrossie School
White Hill
Red Burn
WEMYSS BAY
Ferret of
Burnbank Water
Hardridge Hill
East Green
Castle Toward
Toward Fm
0 1 2 3 miles
0 1 2 3 4 5 km
A B C D E F G H
1 2 3 4 5 6

QUEEN ELIZABETH FOREST PARK
STIRLING
LOCH LOMOND AND THE TROSSACHS NATIONAL PARK
WEST DUNBARTONSHIRE
EAST DUNBARTONSHIRE
Loch Lomond
Loch Ard
Lake of Menteith
Aberfoyle
Milton
Kirkton
Balleich
Cobleland
Gartmore
Barbadoes
Gartur
Dykehead
Port of Menteith
Malling
Arnprior
Buchlyvie
Gartachoil
Dalmary
Rowardennan
Milarrochy
Balmaha
Milton of Buchanan
Drymen
Croftamie
Gartocharn
Balfron
Balfron Station
Killearn
Spittal
Gartness
Boquhan
Ballikinrain
Fintry
Harvieston
Craighat
Dumgoyne
Stockiemuir
Blairquhosh
Netherton
Blanefield
Strathblane
Clachan of Campsie
Mugdock
Milngavie
Bearsden
Blairskaith
Bardowie
Balmore
Cadder
Jellyhill
Bishopbriggs
Kessington
Summerston
Drumchapel
Knightswood
Lambhill
Springburn
Maryhill
Temple
Scotstoun
Yoker
Clydebank
Dalmuir
Duntocher
Hardgate
Old Kilpatrick
Erskine Bridge
Bowling
Milton
Dumbarton
Bonhill
Alexandria
Balloch
Jamestown
Renton
Castlehill
Dennystown
Brucehill
Kirktonhill
Luss
Langbank
Bishopton
Erskine
Kilmacolm
Renfrew
Inchinnan
Kilpatrick Hills
Conic Hill
Inchmurrin
Inchcailloch
Inchtavannach
Inchconnachan
Inchlonaig
A82
A811
A81
A809
A807
A814
A8
M8
M898
B8050

Doune
Dunblane
Deanston
Ruskie
Boquhapple
Thornhill
Flanders Moss
Blair Drummond
Bridge of Allan
Dykehead
Arnprior
Kippen
Cauldhame
Old Leckie
Gargunnock
Glentirranmuir
Blair Drummond Moss
Raploch
Stirling
Cambuskenneth
Cambusbarron
Torbrex
St Ninians
Bannockburn
Gargunnock Hills
Carleatheran 485
Fintry Hills
Fintry
Harvieston
Ballochearn
S T I R L I N G
Touchadam Muir
Earl's Hill
Easter Cringate
Loch Walton
Cairnoch Hill
Carron Valley Reservoir
Carron Bridge
Muirmill
Campsie Fells
Meikle Bin
Kilsyth Hills
Tomtain
Denny
Dunipace
Fankerton
Stoneywood
Plean
Torwood
Bonnybridge
Dennyloanhead
Longcroft
Banknock
Castlecary
Kilsyth
Lennoxtown
Clachan of Campsie
Milton of Campsie
Queenzieburn
Twechar
Croy
Cumbernauld
Kirkintilloch
Lenzie
Bishopbriggs
Cadder
Chryston
Moodiesburn
Muirhead
Glenboig
Stepps
Springburn
Condorrat
Westfield
Balloch
Abronhill
Greengairs
Riggend
Caldercruix
EAST DUNBARTONSHIRE
NORTH LANARKSHIRE
285
286
277
268

CLACKMANNANSHIRE
FIFE
Alva
Tillicoultry
Dollar
Yetts o' Muckhart
Crook of Devon
Pool of Muckhart
Rumbling Bridge
Drum
Coldrain
Powmill
Cleish
Hardiston
Cleish Hills
Blairingone
Devonside
Coalsnaughton
Tullibody
Branshill
Fairfield
Sauchie
Keilarsbrae
Fishcross
Forest Mill
Cambus
Alloa
Clackmannan
Kennet
South Alloa
Dunmore
Kilbagie
Hill End
Saline
Steelend
Balgonar
Knockhill
Cowstrandburn
Blairhall
Comrie
Oakley
Carnock
Gowkhall
Milesmark
Townhill
Wellwood
Kingseathill
Bellyeoman
Dunfermline
Crossford
Cairneyhill
High Valleyfield
Low Valleyfield
Newmills
Low Torry
Torryburn
Culross
Blairburn
Kincardine
Kincardine Bridge
Airth
Letham
Charlestown
Limekilns
Rosyth
Pitcorthie
Queensferry Crossing
Stenhousemuir
Carronshore
Carron
Skinflats
Grangemouth
Bo'ness
Grangepans
Carriden
Muirhouses
Falkirk
Laurieston
Camelon
Grahamston
Bainsford
Redding
Polmont
Brightons
Westquarter
Reddingmuirhead
Glen Village
Callendar Park
Rumford
Maddiston
Whitecross
Linlithgow Bridge
Linlithgow
Grougfoot
Blackness
Philpstoun
Old Philpstoun
Queensferry
Newton
Winchburgh
Threemiletown
Bridgend
Kingscavil
Shieldhill
California
Standburn
Avonbridge
Slamannan
Crossburn
Binniehill
Westfield
Torphichen
Broxburn
Uphall
Dechmont
Wester Dechmont
Uphall Station
Pumpherston
Bathgate
Boghall
Armadale
Livingston
Ecclesmachan
Newbridge
Burnside
Kirkhill
M9
M8
M876
A985
A907
A977
A91
A823
A706
A801
A803
A904

Loch Leven
Loch Leven Castle
Castle Island
St Serf's Island
286
Scotlandwell
Portmoak Moss
Auchmuirbridge
The Knock
Strathenry Ho
Leslie
Croft Outerly
Macedonia
South Parks
Glenrothes
Rimbleton
Auchmuty
Tanshall
Caskieberran
Markinch
Milton of Balgonie
Balcurvie
Windygates
Woodside
Balgonie Castle
Cameron Bridge
Cameron
Pitteuchar
Stenton
East Finglassie
Coaltown of Balgonie
Kinglassie
Thornton
Greenend
Glenrothes with Thornton
Redford
Ore Bridge
Ore Mills
Mackie's Mill
Earlseat Fm
East Wemyss
Coaltown of Wemyss
West Wemyss
Boreland
Blair
Dysart
Blair Pt
Sinclairtown
Gallatown
Dunnikier
Carberry
Smeaton
Templehall
Pathhead
Hayfield
Panhall
Ravenscraig Castle
Kirkcaldy
Kirkcaldy Galleries
Port Brae
Kirkcaldy Sands
Link Sands
Linktown
Stark's Park
Long Craig
Newliston
Chapel
Cardenden
Cluny
Auchterderran
Bowhill
Dogton Stone
Harestanes
Balgreggie Fm
Woodend
Jamphlars
Whinnyhall
Bowhouse Fm
Strathruddie
Capledrae
Kirkland
Ballingry
Lochore
Crosshill
Lochore Meadows
Fife Regional Park
Loch Ore
Inchgill Fm
Hare Law
Glencraig
Clune Plantn
Lochgelly
Lumphinnans
Lochgelly Ind Est
Loch Gelly
Powguild
Lochend
Glenniston
Bankhead of Raith
Camilla Loch
East Balbarton
Clentrie Fm
Dronachy Burn
Boglily
Auchtertool
Auchtertool Ho
Lochhead
Balweary
Lambert's Mill
Kilrie Fm
West Balbairdie
Meadowfield
Balbie Fm
Orrock
Grange
Grange Cottages
Stenhouse
Stenhouse Reservoir
Balmule
Torry Hill
Kinghorn Loch
Linton Court
Kinghorn
Hummel Rocks
Kinghorn Ness
Pettycur
Alexander III Monument
Kirkton
Burntisland
Black Rocks
Ross Pt
Common Rocks
Humbie Wood
Aberdour Castle & Gardens
Aberdour
Silversands Bay
Hawkcraig Pt
Bell Rock
Port Haven
Barnhill Bay
Braefoot Bay
Braefoot Pt
Mortimer's Deep
Car Craig
Swallow Craig
St Colm's Abbey
Inchcolm
Inchkeith
Iron Craig
Long Craig
FIRTH OF FORTH
Cow & Calves
Inchmickery
Cramond Island
Drum Sands
Hound Pt
Peatdraught Bay
St Bridget's Church
Dalgety Bay
Donibristle Bay
Downing Pt
Hillend
The Dales
Dalgety Bay
Inverkeithing
St Davids Harbour
East Ness
West Ness
Jamestown
Inverkeithing Bay
Ferry Hills
Port Laing
Carlingnose Point
North Queensferry
Deep Sea World
Inch Garvie
Whitehouse Pt
Forth Bridge
Forth Road Bridge
Maid of the Forth Cruises
Queensferry Crossing
St Margaret's Hope
Rosyth
Castlandhill
Pattiesmuir
Limekilns
Dunfermline
Bellyeoman
Garvock Hill
Brucefield
Pitcorthie
Annfield Ho
Duloch
Halbeath
Kingseathill
Headwell
Wellwood
Townhill
Kingseat
Crossgates
Fordell
Donibristle
Cullaloe Hills
Cullaloe Cotts
Scotts Walls
Drumcooper
Woodlee
Prathouse
Calais Muir Wood
Monziehall
Broomieside
Bouprie Banks
Otterston Loch
Hill of Beath
Cowdenbeath
Cowdenend
Lassodie
Kirkton Fm
Kelty
Keltybridge
Blairadam
Maryburgh
Lochran
Gairney Bank
Cleish
Templeton Fm
Craigduckie
Bowershall
Roscobie Hills
Gaskie Hill
Valley of Balmule
Loch Fitty
Craigencat Craigs
Hilton Fm
Lower Oakfield
Thornton Wood
Benarty Hill
Benarty Wood
Binn Wood
Hopetoun House
Port Edgar
Queensferry
Newton
Dalmeny
Dalmeny House
Burnshot Wood
Newbigging
Dundas Castle
Dundas Mains
Westfield Fm
Humbie Fm
Craigbrae Fm
Carlowrie Fm
Kirkliston
Turnhouse
Edinburgh Airport
Royal Highland Showground
Newliston
Newbridge
East Mains of Ingliston
Gogar Mains
Gogar
Ratho Station
Burnside
Ratho
Ratho Hall
Union Canal
Hermiston
Baberton Mains
Juniper Green
Wester Hailes
Sighthill
South Gyle
Edinburgh Park
Stenhouse
Saughton
Slateford
Longstone
Kingsknowe
Colinton
Oxgangs
Comiston
Swanston
Fairmilehead
Morningside
Craiglockhart
Royal Observatory
Blackford Hill
Braid
Braid Hills
Liberton
Kaimes
Gracemount
Gilmerton
Danderhall
Millerhill
Craigmillar
Craigmillar Castle
The Inch
Prestonfield
Newington
Duddingston
Bingham
Brunstane
Newhailes
Musselburgh
Fisherrow Sands
Joppa
Portobello
Northfield
Meadowbank
Abbeyhill
Arthur's Seat
Salisbury Crags
Palace of Holyroodhouse
Museum of Childhood
St Giles Cathedral
National Mus of Scotland
Old Town
New Town
Castle
Dean
Haymarket
Dalry
Gorgie
Merchiston
Murrayfield
Corstorphine
Edinburgh Zoo
Clermiston
Blackhall
Ravelston
Craigleith
Inverleith
Royal Botanic Garden
Warriston
Broughton
Pilrig
Lochend
Restalrig
Craigentinny
Easter Road
Edinburgh
Leith
Newhaven
HMY Britannia
Black Rocks
Granton
Granton Harbour
Granton Pt
Trinity
Pilton
Muirhouse
Silverknowes
Lauriston Castle
Cramond
Davidson's Mains
Drylaw
Barnton
Braepark
Cramond Bridge
Craigiehall
Edinburgh Gate
Lennie Mains
Snab Pt
Birnie Rocks
West Craigie Fm
East Craigie
Bughtlin
Ingliston
Norton Mains
Clifton Hall
Clifton Mains
Addiston Mains
Bonnington
Ratho Mains
Craigiehall Temple
Newcraighall
Stoneybank
Whitehill Mains
Edmonstone
Shawfair
Hilltown
Old Craighall
Whitecraig
Drum
Dreghorn
Bonaly
Torphin
Cocklaw
Malcolmstone
Burnwynd
EDINBURGH
CITY OF EDINBURGH
FIFE
270
279
Queensferry
0 1 2 3 miles
0 1 2 3 4 5 km

Leven
Methil
Buckhaven
Scoonie
Innerleven
Largo Bay
Earlsferry
Elie
St Monans
Ardross
Grange
North Berwick
Dirleton
Gullane
Aberlady
Longniddry
Cockenzie and Port Seton
Prestonpans
Tranent
Haddington
East Linton
Drem
East Fortune
Athelstaneford
Ballencrieff
Spittal
Kingston
Whitekirk
Tyninghame
Auldhame
Scoughall
Traprain
Luggate Burn
Garvald
Papple
Samuelston
Bolton
Gifford
Pencaitland
Ormiston
New Winton
Elphinstone
Wallyford
Macmerry
Penston
Gladsmuir
Elvingston
Huntington
Seton
Meadowmill
Crossgatehall
Cousland
Carfrae
EAST LOTHIAN
Bass Rock
Craigleith
Fidra

NORTH SEA
Isle of May
North Ness
South Ness
ISLE OF MAY
287
281
272
Bass Rock
Gin Head
TANTALLON CASTLE
Auldhame
Car Rocks
Scoughall
Scoughall Rocks
New Mains
Whitekirk Covert
Peffer Sands
Ravensheugh Sands
Frances Craig
Whitekirk
Whitekirk Br
Tyninghame Links
Binning Wood
Tyne Sands
Oak Wood
Heckies Hole
JOHN MUIR
Belhaven Bay
Long Craigs
Scart Rock
Meikle Spiker
Belhaven
BELHAVEN ROAD
Dunbar
Tyninghame
Smeaton Ho
Salt Greens Plantn
Firth Plantn
Hedderwick Hill
JOHN MUIR'S BIRTHPLACE
Preston Mains
Preston
PRESTON MILL & PHANTASSIE DOOCOT
Phantassie
Knowes
West Barns
EDINBURGH RD
A199
A1087
A198
A1
Mill Stone Neuk
White Sands
Barns Ness
Ind Est
Broxburn
East Barns
Howmuir
Hedderwick
South Belton
Old Belton
Belhaven
Bielhill
Bielmill
Traprain
Grangemuir
Wester Broomhouse
Spott
Spott Fm
Doon Hill
Little Pinkerton
Meikle Pinkerton
Pinkerton Hill
Dunbar Cement Works
Chapel Pt
Skateraw Harbour
Torness Pt
Long Craig
Thorntonloch Power Sta
Skateraw
Thorntonloch
Crowhill
Pitcox
Meiklerig Wood
Spott West Mains
Spott Mill
Ruchlaw Mains
Stenton
Luggate Burn
Whittinghame Mains
Whittinghame Ho
Ruchlaw West Mains
Bennet's Burn
Pressmennan Wood
THE CHESTERS (FORT)
Highside Hill
Brunt Hill
The Brunt
Thurston Manor
Innerwick
Thurston Mains
Thurston Mains Burn
Old Branxton
Bilsdean Creek
Reed Pt
Cove Harbour
Cove
Cove Fm
Pease Bay
Red Rock
Greenheugh Pt
Siccar Pt
Meikle Poo Craig
Hirst Rocks
Papple
Deuchrie Dod
Deuchrie Wood
Rammer Wood
Halls
Blaik Law
High Wood
Berry Hill
Needle Hill
Blackcastle Hill
Oldhamstocks Mains
DUNGLASS COLLEGIATE CHURCH
Belvidere Wood
Cockburnspath
Dovecot Hall
Oldhamstocks
Garvald Grange
Garvald
Birks Plantn
Stoneypath Tower
Robin Tup's Plantn
Lothian Edge
Sheeppath Glen
Stottencleugh
PEASE DEAN
EAST LOTHIAN
NUNRAW ABBEY
Garvald Mains
Common Plantn
Moorcock Hall
Deuchrie Edge
Watch Law
Bransly Hill
Birny Knowe
Neuk Fm
Old Cambus Townhead
Old Cambus
Old Townhead
Stockbridge
Tower Fm
Dunbar
Friardykes Dod
Saddle Hill
Wightman Hill
Heriot Water
Ecclaw
SETTLEMENT
Penmanshiel Wood
Greenside Hill
Meikle Black Law
A1107
WHITE CASTLE (FORT)
NT
0 1 2 3 miles
0 1 2 3 4 5 km

7
8
9
10
11
A
B
C
D
E
F
G
H
10
00
NT
NT
70
10
Fast Castle Head
Wheat Stack
Telegraph Hill
FAST CASTLE
Oatlee Hill
Dowlaw Burn
Lumsdaine
Lumsdaine Moor
Cross Law
Coldingham Loch
Moorside Plantn
SETTLEMENT
273
St Abb's Head
ST ABB'S HEAD
Mire Loch
Horsecastle Bay
Bell Hill
Starney Bay
273

Strontian
Ardnastang
Camuschoirk
Glen Tarbert
A861
289
Inversanda Bay
Inversanda
Sallachan
Sallachan Pt.
Clovullin
Ardgour
Corran
Inchree
Glenrigh Forest
Bunree
Keppanach
Onich
Cuilcheanna Ho.
A82
North Ballachulish
Callert Ho.
MAM NA GUALAINN
Kinlochmore
Kinlochleven
THE ALUMINIUM STORY
Caolasnacon
290
BLACKWATER R
HIGHLAND WAY
Loch Eilde Mor
LOCH LINNHE
Kentallen
South Ballachulish
Ballachulish
GLENCOE FOLK MUSEUM
Glencoe
GLENCOE VISITOR CENTRE
AONACH
Glen Coe
Altnafeadh
BEINN A' CHRULAISTE
Kingshouse Hotel
GLENCOE SKI CENTRE
BEN NEVIS AND GLEN COE
BIDEAN NAM BIAN
Royal Forest
Dalness
Glen Etive
Alltchaorunn
SGOR NA H-ULAIDH
Glen an Fhiodh
Lochuisge
Loch Uisge
B8043
CREACH BHEINN
FUAR BHEINN
Kilmalieu
Kingairloch
North Corry
Camasnacroise
Loch a'Choire
BEINN MHEADHOIN
KINGAIRLOCH
Ardsheal
Greenfield
Duror
Glenduror Forest
Achad nan Darach
Rubha Mor
Cuil Bay
Beinn a'Bheithir
Eilean Balnagowan
Keil
Glen Duror
Salachan Glen
Bealach
FRAOCHAIDH
Lurignich
Shuna I.
Appin House
A828
Glen Stockdale
Elleric
Glen Creran
Glenure
Glen Ure
BEINN FHIONNLAIDH
Invercharnan
Glenceitlein
STOB DUBH
CLACH LEATHAD
BLACK
BEINN A' CHAISIL
Glensanda
Loch nan Clach
Portnacroish
Ardtur
KINLOCHLAICH HOUSE GARDENS
Appin
Strath of Appin
Port Appin
Port Ramsay
LYNN OF LORN
Eriska
Creagan
Fasnacloich
Invercreran
BEINN CHURALAIN
GLASDRUM WOOD
Glasdrum
Druimavuic
BEINN SGULAIRD
Lochetive Ho.
Gualachulain
STOB GHABHAR
WEST HIGHLAND WAY
STOB COIR'AN ALBANNAICH
Eignaig
Clachan
North Shian
Rudhja Garbh
Loch Creran
South Creagan
South Shian
BEINN TRILLEACHAN
Clashgour
Forest Lodge
Black Mount
Lismore
Balliveolan
Achnacroish
Balure
SHIAN WOOD
Barcaldine
Sutherland Grove
Barcaldine Forest
CREACH BHEINN
Abhainn Dalach
Allt Easach
BEN STARAV
Loch Dochard
Inveroran Hotel
Camas Gorm
Baligrundle
LORN
Baravullin
Dalrannoch
Ferlochan
Bernera I.
Achinduin
Kilcheran
Lochnell Ho
Kiel Crofts
BENDERLOCH
Benderloch
Ledaig
Gleann Salach
B845
BEINN NAN AIGHENAN
Allt Hallater
Bridge of Orchy
Eilean Dubh
Dalnarrow
Eilean Musdile
Ardmucknish Bay
Achnacree
Achnaba
ARDCHATTAN PRIORY GARDENS
ARDCHATTAN PRIORY
BEINN MHEADHONACH
Cadderlie
LOCHETIVE
Inverliver
Glen Liver
Glen Kinglass
Glennoe
Glen Noe
Glen Orchy
BEINN MHIC-MHONAIDH
Arichastlich
BEINN UDLAIDH
Eilean Mor
DUNSTAFFNAGE CASTLE
North Connel
Connel
Black Crofts
FALLS OF LORA
Achnacloich
ACHNACLOICH GARDEN
Muckairn
Bonawe
Dunbeg
Achlaven
Stonefield
A85
CRAIGNURE CASTLEBAY LOCHBOISDALE COLL TIREE
Ganavan
Dunollie
Oban
MCCAIG'S TOWER
OBAN DISTILLERY
Black Lochs
Fearnoch Forest
Brochroy
BONAWE IRON FURNACE
INVERAWE FISHERIES AND SMOKERIES EXHIBITION
Inverawe Ho.
Taynuilt
BEN CRUACHAN
BEINN EUNAICH
Glen Strae
Duiletter
Allt Mhoille
Glen Lochy
Arrivain
B8074
Altnacraig
Kerrera
Balliemore
Barranrioch
Balindore
ANGUS'S GARDEN
BARGUILLEAN
Airdeny
GLEN NANT
Ichrachan
Bridge of Awe
Pass of Brander
Cruachan Reservoir
Falls of Cruachan
KILCHURN CASTLE
Lochawe
B8077
Stronmilchan
Strath of Orchy
Achnafalnich
Inverlochy
Ardmore
Glenamachrie
Glen Lonan
Glen Nant
Dalmally
Corryghoil
Glenview
MCINTYRE MONUMENT
Bach I.
Gylen Park
Gallanach
Killiechoinich
Loch Nell
Cologin
Kilbride
Kilmore
Barran
BEINN GHLAS
Loch Nant
CRUACHAN DAM VISITOR CENTRE
Loch Tromlee
ARDANAISEIG GARDENS
Ardanaiseig
Innis Chonain
INISHAIL CHAPEL
Inishail
Teatle Water
BEN LUI
Eas a'Ghaill
Rubha Seanach
Sound of Kerrera
Am Buth
Dunach
Loch Feochan
Glen Feochan
Kilbride
Midmuir
Musdale
Sior Loch
Kilchrenan
Annat
North Port
Cladich Steading
Cladich
Innistrynich
Allt Fearna
MEALL NAN TIGHEARN
Ardentallen
Knipoch
A816
COLONSAY
Kilninver
Barochreal
Glen Euchar
Scammadale
A'CHRUACH
Bragleenmore
Lower Achachenna
Portsonachan
South Port
Lochan Shira
Loch Stron Mor
CLACHAN BRIDGE
Raera
Loch Scamadale
BEINN CHAPULL
ARGYLL AND BUTE
CARN DEARG
Fineglen
BEINN GHLAS
BEINN BHUIDHE
Clachan
Braes of Lorn
Blaran
Innie
Inverinan
B840
Ballimeanoch
Allt Beochlich
Tullich
Glen Aray
Rob Roy's House
Glen Shira
Brannie Burn
Glen Fyne
Allt na Lairige
Glenfyne Lodge
MAOL BREAC
Balvicar
CRUACH RAREY
Caddleton
Loch Tralaig
Lochavich Ho
Drissaig
Kilmun
Elrigbeag
Seil Sound
Melfort
Ardanstur
Kilchoan
Kilmelford
Loch Avich
Barnaline
Dalavich
Blarghour
CRUACH MHOR
Kilblaan Burn
Clachan
Achadunan
275
Melfort
Glenmore
Ardchonnell
ARDCHONNELL CASTLE
Portinnisherrich
Maam
Dubh Loch
Three Bridges
Loch Sloy
ARDUAINE GARDEN
Arduaine
Kames
Lagalochan
CARN DUCHARA
Inverliever Forest
Eredine
Carloonan
BELL TOWER
INVERARAY CASTLE
Drishaig
A83
Cairndow
ARDKINGLAS WOODLAND GARDEN
Glen Kinglas
Shuna Ho
Garraron
Turnalt
Barbreck
Kilmaha
Liever
LOCH AWE
INVERARAY JAIL
Inveraray
Newtown
Ardno
A815
BEINN AN LOCHAIN
Rest and Be Thankful
BEINN IME
Shuna
Craobh Haven
Barravullin
Durran
Braevallich
AN SUIDHE
Douglas Water
St Catherine's
Hell's Glen
B828
Lunga
Barbreck Ho
Kintraw
CRUACH AN EACHLAICH
Arichamish
Inverliever Lodge
Torran
Eredine Forest
Dalchenna
CRUACH NAN CAPULL
B839
Monevechadan
Glen Croe
Succoth
Shuna Pt.
Lerigoligan
Ardfern
BEINN DEARG
Ardnagowan
BEN DONICH
ARDGARTAN VISITOR CENTRE
Ardgartan
A83
Ford
Finchairn
FINCHAIRN CASTLE
Loch Leacann
Auchindrain
AUCHINDRAIN OPEN AIR MUSEUM
B8002
CREAG MHOR
Ederline
Kenmore
Creggans
Clachan Strachur
Drimsynie
Inveronich
Lochgoilhead
Kirkton
Eilean Righ
Loch Craignish
CARNASSARIE CASTLE
Stroneskar
CRUACH MHIC FHIONNLAICH
Brenchoillie
Strachur Bay
Strachurmore
BEINN LOCHAIN
Corrow
Lettermay
CNOC COINNICH
Coilessan
Creagan Sith
Ardgartan Forest
Island Macaskin
Kilmartin
GLEBE CAIRN
KILMARTIN HOUSE MUSEUM
Barnolloch
Loch Gaineamhach
275
Furnace
Sandhole
Cumlodden
Mid Letter
Glen Sluain
A886
276
Inverlounin
Ardgoil Forest
Crarae
CRARAE GLEN GARDENS
Newton
Invernoaden
BEINN BHEULA
Loch Goil
DOUNE HILL
Poltalloch
Kilbride
Leckuary
Gleann Airigh
Minard
B8000
Garbhallt
Leanach
Glenbranter
Glenbranter Forest
LACHLAN CASTLE
THE SADDLE
Tullochgorm
Duntrune
Lachlan
A814
0 2 4 6 miles
0 2 4 6 8 10 km

285
Rannoch Forest
BEINN MHOLACH
SRON BHEAG
BEINN A' CHUALLAICH
Trinafour
Auchleeks Ho.
GLEN ERROCHTY
Tummel Forest
Tressait
Tummel Bridge
LOCH TUMMEL
Lick
Foss
LEUM UILLEIM
Black Water
Rannoch Station
Bridge of Ericht
Killichonan
Craiganor Lodge
Kinloch Rannoch
Dunalastair
Dunalastair Water
Tullochroisk
Crossmount
Inverhadden
Carie
LOCH RANNOCH
Rannoch Lodge
Loch Eigheach
Finnart
Bridge of Gaur
Camghouran
Black Wood of Rannoch
Rannoch Forest
STOB NA CRUAICHE
Loch Laidon
Loch Gaineamhach
RANNOCH MOOR
Loch Bà
Water of Tulla
LOCH RANNOCH AND GLEN LYON
TAY FOREST
SCHIEHALLION
Loch Kinardochy
Glengoulandie
MEALL A' MHUIC
MEALL BUIDHE
CARN GORM
CARN MAIRG
Garth
Keltneyburn
Camserney
Dull
CASTLE MENZIES
WADE'S BRIDGE
BOLFRACKS GARDEN
Invervar
Carnbahn
Camusvrachan
Innerwick
Balnahanaid
Loch an Daimh
Bridge of Balgie
Meggernie Castle
Gallin
ST FILLAN'S CHURCH & FORTINGALL YEW
Fortingall
Bridge of Lyon
Comrie
Taymouth Castle
Mains of Taymouth
Croftmoraig
Kenmore
SCOTTISH CRANNOG CENTRE
Remony
Fearnan
Acharn
Falls of Acharn
Achallader
BEINN A' CHREACHAIN
MEALL BUIDHE
STUCHD AN LOCHAIN
Pubil
Cashlie
Glen Lyon
Loch Lyon
Stronuich Reservoir
BEINN MHANACH
BIENN AN DOTHAIDH
BEN LAWERS
Lawers
LOCH TAY
Ardradnaig
BEINN BHREAC
Garrow
MEALL NAN TARMACHAN
Loch na Lairige
Ardtalnaig
Claggan
Gleann a' Chilleine
BEINN HEASGARNICH
BEINN DÒRAIN
Kenknock
Glen Lochay
Breadalbane
Duncroisk
Carie
Kiltyrie
Milton Morenish
Morenish
Ardeonaig
Finglen Burn
MEALL NAM CARAN
Almond
Auchnafree
FALLS OF LOCHAY AND FISH LIFT
Boreland
MOIRLANICH LONGHOUSE
Finlarig
Killin
Monemore
Achmore
FALLS OF DOCHART
CREAG MHOR
Batavaime
BEINN ODHAR
BEINN CHEATHAICH
BEN CHALLUM
CREAG UCHDAG
Clifton
Tyndrum
Bovain
Auchlyne
Lix Toll
Wester Lix
Ardchyle
Ledcharrie
GLEN DOCHART
Auchtertyre
Dalrigh
Strath Fillan
Lochdochart House
Auchessan
Loch Iubhair
Inverhaggernie
Loch Dochart
Benmore
Portnellan
Inverherive
Crianlarich
CRIANLARICH
BEN MORE
STOB BINNEIN
WEST HIGHLAND WAY
Glen Ogle
Loch Lednock Reservoir
BEN CHONZIE
Invergeldie
Funtullich
Carroglen
Glen Lednock
Loch Turret Reservoir
SRON MHOR
Dalveich
Ardveich
Lochearnhead
Craggan
Edinchip
LOCH EARN
Derry
St Fillans
EDINAMPLE FALLS
Edinample
Ardvorlich
Ardtrostan
Dundurn
RIVER EARN
Dalchonzie
Dunira
MELVILLE MONUMENT
Comrie
Lawers
COMRIE CROFT
Ochtertyre
Quoig
Tullybannocher
EARTHQUAKE HOUSE
Aberuchill Castle
Ross
Dalginross
Glascorrie
Lochlane
CRIEFF VISITORS' CENTRE
Derrydaroch
Glen Falloch
Falls of Falloch
LOCH LOMOND
Braes of Balquhidder
ROB ROY'S GRAVE
Balquhidder
Auchtubh
Balquhidder Station
Glenample
Monachylemore
Craigruie
Stronvar
Loch Voil
Loch Doine
Inverlochlarig
Ballimore
Strathyre Forest
Strathyre
Ardoch
Immervoulin
BEINN A' CHROIN
BEN VORLICH
Forest of Glenartney
AUCHINGARRICH WILDLIFE CENTRE
Culloch
Torlum Wood
Dalchruin
Glen Artney
Water of Ruchill
Tigh-na-Blair
Auchinner
Auchnashelloch
Ochtermuthill
AND THE
STOB A' CHOIN
BEINN EACH
Ardchullarie More
BEN CLACH
Langside
TROSSACHS
BEINN BHREAC
BENVANE
Loch Lubnaig
STIRLING
Portnellan
Strath Gartney
Drumardoch
UAMH BHEAG
Glenlichorn
Braco Castle
ARDOCH ROMAN CAMP
Stronachlachar
Garrison
ROB ROY'S CAVE
INVERSNAID
Inversnaid Hotel
Brenachoile Lodge
Glen Finglas Res.
LOCH KATRINE
NATIONAL
Loch Arklet
Loch Ard Forest
BEN LEDI
THE GREAT TROSSACHS FOREST
Anie
Pass of Leny
Coilea-chrombe
FALLS OF LENY
Kilmahog
Bochastle
Leny Ho.
CALLANDER
Callander
ROB ROY AND TROSSACHS VISITOR CENTRE
BRACKLINN FALLS
Easter Brackland
Wester Feddal
The Trossachs
TROSSACHS PIER COMPLEX
SS SIR WALTER SCOTT
Trossachs Hotel
Brig o' Turk
Coilantogle
Callandrode
Auchenlaich
Drumloist
Braes of Doune
The Bows
Dalbrack
Lerrocks
Kilbryde Castle
Kinbuck
Ashfield
Frenich
BEN VENUE
Duncraggan
Lendrick Lodge
Loch Achray
THE TROSSACHS
Invertrossachs
Loch Venachar
Loch Drunkie
Achray Forest
LOCH PARK
Cailness
Loch Chon
Tarbet
Craig Rostan
LOMOND
BEN LOMOND
Kinlochard
D. MARSHALL LODGE VISITOR CENTRE
Menteith Hills
Torrie Forest
Loch Rusky
Drumvaich
Burn of Cambus
Lanrick
Deanston
Doune
Dunblane
CATHEDRAL
Sheriff Muir
Stronmachair
Altskeith
Drumlean
Milton
Port of Menteith
Brae of Boquhapple
Mill of Chon
Couligartan
Loch Ard
Aberfoyle
Kirkton
INCHMAHOME PRIORY
Bigram
Ruskie
Goodie Water
Thornhill
Blair Drummond
Easter Row
BLAIR DRUMMOND SAFARI PARK
LEIGHTON LIBRARY
Badgergate
Ptarmigan Lodge
Firkin
QUEEN ELIZABETH
Balleich
Cobleland
Malling
Lake of Menteith
Lochend Ho
Gartur
Dykehead
FLANDERS MOSS
Flanders Moss
Blairdrummond Moss
Sunnylaw
Bridge of Allan
Blairlogie
Rowardennan
BEN LOMOND BUNKHOUSE
BEINN UIRD
Duchray Water
Loch Ard Forest
FOREST PARK
Gartmore
Gartmore Ho
Inverbeg
INVERBEG GALLERY
Rowardennan Forest
BEINN BHREAC
Forth
Drip Moss
Dalmary
Causeway-head
NATIONAL WALLACE MONUMENT
Kelty Water
Douglas

Tummel Forest
LOCH TUMMEL
Tummel Bridge
Tressait
Queen's View
Falls of Tummel
Foss
Lick
TULACH HILL
470
ATHOLL COUNTRY LIFE
Aldclune
Killiecrankie
KILLIECRANKIE VISITOR CENTRE
Bonskeid House
Balavoulin
Loch Bhac
Fincastle Ho.
Tenandry
841
BEN VRACKIE
Moulin
Pitlochry
Kinnaird
EDRADOUR DISTILLERY
Milton of Edradour
BLAIR ATHOL DISTILLERY VISITOR CENTRE
Balmore
Loch Faskally
EXPLORER'S GARDEN
LINN OF TUMMEL
QUEEN'S VIEW CENTRE
Dalnavaid
Tarvie
Straloch
Glen Brerachan
Enochdhu
641
CREAG DHUBH
Kirkmichael
Middle Balnald
Loch Broom
534
MEALL REAMHAR
Ashintully Castle
KNOCK OF BALMYLE
444
Ballintuim
STRATHARDLE
Lair
744
MOUNT BLAIR
Blacklunans
520
CAIRN GIBBS
Forest of Alyth
Black Water
Folda
Glenmarkie Lodge
Glenhead Farm
Backwater Res.
Brewlands Bridge
Longdrum
Freuchies
Kirkton of Glenisla
Bellaty
497
CREIGH HILL
Dykends
Loch of Lintrathen
PEEL FARM TRAIL
BALDUFF HILL
425
REEKIE LINN WATERFALL
Bridge of Craigisla
Auchrannie
Tullymurdoch
Bamff
Shanzie
780
FARRAGON HILL
Loch Derculich
FOREST PARK
Milton of Dalcapon
Strathtay
Ballechin
Grandtully
Little Ballinluig
Balnaguard
Logierait
Ballinluig
Tulliemet
561
CREAG NAM MIAL
Blackcraig Forest
Netherton
Milton of Drimmie
Bridge of Cally
Cochrage Muir
Glengoulandie
Appin of Dull
CLUNY HOUSE GARDENS
Edradynate
Tombuie
ST MARY'S CHURCH
CASTLE MENZIES
Weem
Camserney
Dull
DEWAR'S ABERFELDY DISTILLERY
WADE'S BRIDGE
Aberfeldy
Falls of Moness
Comrie
Taymouth Castle
BOLFRACKS GARDEN
Croftmoraig
Urlar
532
Balnacmeil
Kincraigie
Kindallachan
Guay
Dowally
Loch Ordie
Forest of Clunie
Loch Benachally
Riemore
509
DEUCHARY HILL
Loch Skiach
Dalguise
Craigvinean Forest
Loch Kennard
Dalmarnock
Riechip
Butterstone
Lornty Burn
Middleton
Lornty
Craighall
Courthill
308
Westfields of Rattray
Tullyfergus
CATERAN ECOMUSEUM
Pitrocknie
Alyth
New Alyth
Ruthven
Balhary
Kenmore
SCOTTISH CRANNOG CENTRE
Remony
566
Urlar Burn
Loch Hoil
Glen Cochill
Tombane Burn
Balinloan Burn
RIVER TAY
Forneth
Achalader
Blairgowrie
Kinloch
Rattray
Leitfie
MEIGLE SCULPTURED STONE MUSEUM
Meigle
Loch of Lowes
LOCH OF LOWES NATURE RESERVE
Concraigie
Loch of Clunie
Loch of Drumellie
Clunie
Craigie
Wester Essendy
Muirton of Ardblair
Rosemount
Kinloch
Longleys
Arthurstone
Dunkeld
Little Dunkeld
Birnam
Snaigow House
Kirkton of Lethendy
Scotston
690
MEALL DEARG
THE HERMITAGE
WATERFALL
Ballinlick
Inver
Trochry
Spittalfield
West Myreriggs
Ardler
Newbigging
Keillor
Garrow
Delvine
Caputh
404
Quaich
Turrerich
Glen Quaich
Loch Freuchie
Cablea
Strathbraan
PERTH AND KINROSS
Obney Hills
Meikle Obney
Upper Obney
Gellyburn
Murthly
Muir of Thorn
Ardoch
Meikleour
BEECH HEDGE
Kinclaven
Ballathie
Coupar Angus
Markethill
Kettins
Campmuir
Hallyburton House
Hill of Keillor
Glenquaich Lodge
Amulree
Braan
Balquharn
Waterloo
Cargill
Woodside
Burrelton
Leys
Pitcur
Lundie
805
MEALL NAM FUARAN
Corrymuckloch
Little Glenshee
Bankfoot
Airntully
Whitefield
SIDLAW
Littleton
Almond
Auchnafree
623
MEALL NAN CAORAICH
Milton Burn
Ordie Burn
Tullybelton
West Tofts
Stanley
Wolfhill
Loanhead
Dunsinnan
Saucher
Collace
KING'S SEAT
377
Newton
Logiealmond Lodge
Logiealmond
Shochie Burn
Guildtown
Kinrossie
Kirkton of Collace
St Martins
Bandirran
Abernyte
Knapp
931
BEN CHONZIE
GLEN ALMOND
Sma' Glen
648
MEALL TARSUINN
Chapelhill
Harrietfield
Newmiln
Downhill
Stormontfield
Balbeggie
BRAES OF THE CARSE
Ballindean
Rossie
Loch Turret Reservoir
Shaggie Burn
Glenalmond Ho.
Buchanty
Glenalmond College
Moneydie
Luncarty
Redgorton
PERTH
Kinnaird
Craigdallie
Westown
Inchture
Drummick
Pitcairngreen
SCONE PALACE
Rait
East Bonhard
Kilspindie
288
POLE HILL
Carroglen
Glen Turret
Monzie
Monzie Castle
FALLS OF TURRET
Ochtertyre
Lawers
COMRIE CROFT
Quoig
Hosh
Gilmerton
350
Fowlis Wester
STANDING STONES
Keillour
Craigend
Methven
Almondbank
Huntingtower
Lochty
Tulloch
Muirton
Scone
Murrayshall
MUSEUM & ART GALLERY
FERGUSSON GALLERY
Gannochy
CARSE OF GOWRIE
Grange
Myreside
Errol Station
MELVILLE MONUMENT
Comrie
GLENTURRET DISTILLERY
Crieff
Milton of Cultoquhey
Tomaknock
Keillour Forest
Pow Water
Balgowan
Braegrum
Burnside
Tibbermore
Letham
HUNTINGTOWER CASTLE
BROXDEN SERVICES
Cherrybank
Perth
BRANKLYN GARDEN
Balthayock
Kinfauns Forest
Kinfauns
Glendoick
Errol
Carthagena Bank
Ross
Dalginross
Glascorrie
Lochlane
Pittachar
Madderty
Chapelhill
Clathy
Findo Gask
Milltown of Aberdalgie
Aberdalgie
Craigie
Friarton
Walnut Grove
ELCHO
Elcho
Glencarse
Leetown
Chapelhill
Port Allen
FIRTH
Ballinbreich
CRIEFF VISITOR CENTRE
The Balloch
Concraig
Mains of Innerpeffray
St David's
Dupplin Castle
Tarsappie
Rhynd
Inchyra
St Madoes
Mugdrum I.
LAING MUSEUM
Newburgh
Higham
Culloch
Torlum Wood
DRUMMOND CASTLE GARDENS
OLD CHURCH & TOWER
Muthill
STRATHEARN
INNERPEFFRAY LIBRARY
Kirkton
Kinkell Bridge
Lawhill
Earn
Craigend
Bridge of Earn
Forteviot
Forgandenny
Kintillo
Easter Rhynd
Dunbog
Ochtermuthill
Machany Water
Milton of Machany
Strathallan Castle
Aberuthven
Ardargie House Hotel
Glenearn
Dron
Aberargie
Abernethy
ROUND TOWER
Grange of Lindores
Lindores
Langside
Drumness
Middleton
Tullibardine
TULLIBARDINE CHAPEL
Auchterarder
Dunning
Newton of Pitcairns
Glenfoot
Pitmedden Forest
Colzie
Monimail
Collessie
Newhill
Glenlichorn
Garrick
Milton
Muirton
Rossie Ochill
Pathstruie
Glentarkie
Auchtermuchty
Kinloch
Gifffordtown
Braco Castle
ARDOCH ROMAN CAMP
BLACKHALL ROMAN CAMPS
Gleneagles Hotel
GLENEAGLES
Path of Condie
Glenfarg Res.
Newton of Balcanquhal
Arngask
Glenfarg
Strathmiglo
Dunshalt
Charlottetown
Howe of Fife
Bullie Burn
Wester Feddal
Braco
Blackford
Gleneagles House
Coulshill
Common of Dunning
Water of May
Duncrievie
Newhill
Gateside
Nether Urquhart
Kilgour
FALKLAND PALACE
Newton of Falkland
STRATHALLAN
Greenloaning
Dam of Quoiggs
TULLIBARDINE DISTILLERY
Braes of Ogilvie
485
STEEL'S KNOWE
Glen Eagles
Middle Rigg
497
INNERDOUNY HILL
Athron Hall
Middleton
Burnside
WEST LOMOND
522
Falkland
FIFE
LOMOND HILLS
Freuchie
Allan Water
Kinbuck
Ashfield
Balhaldie
Sheriff Muir
1715
543
Glendevon Resvrs.
Glen Devon
Glendevon
South Queich
Craigow
Upper Tillyrie
Dalqueich
BURLEIGH CASTLE
Milnathort
Wester Gospetry
Glenlomond
Wester Balgedie
Easter Balgedie
MICHAEL BRUCE'S COTTAGE
Kinnesswood
REGIONAL PARK
Glasslie
Pitkevy
Cadham
Burnfoot
Castle Hill Reservoir
611
Carnbo
KINROSS SERVICES
Kinross
LOCH LEVEN
LOCHLEVEN CASTLE
LOCH LEVEN
KINROSS HOUSE
St Serf's Island
CATHEDRAL
Dunblane
631
BLAIRDENON HILL
721
BEN CLEUCH
Pool o' Muckhart
Yetts o' Muckhart
Drum
Coldrain
Gairney Bank
Scotlandwell
Auchmuirbridge
Leslie
GLENROTHES
Pisgah
LEIGHTON LIBRARY
Dunblane
Badgergate
KING'S SEAT HILL
CASTLE CAMPBELL
DOLLAR GLEN
Crook of Devon
Rumbling Bridge
RUMBLING BRIDGE GORGE
LOCH LEVEN
Kinglassie
Stenton
Thornton
Ballingry
Lochore
Woodend
Auchterderran
Cluny
Powmill
Cleish
356
BENARTY HILL
Devonside
Dollar
Blairingone
Hardiston
Cleish Hills
Lochran
HORSE LOWS
Crosshill
Causewayhead
NATIONAL WALLACE MONUMENT
Tullibody
Alva
Fishcross
AFFINITY STERLING MILLS
Coalsnaughton
Hill End
DOGTON STONE
Ore
0 2 4 6 miles
0 2 4 6 8 10 km

Easter Lednathie
Redheugh
Glenogil
Auchnacree
Menmuir
Tigerton
Newtonmill
Craigo
Lochside
St Cyrus
Milton Ness
Morphie
Pathhead
Balnamoon
Mains of Balhall
Lochty
Belliehill
Balrownie
Little Brechin
Keithock
Trinity
Logie
North Craigo
Hillside
Maltings
Glenquiech
Deuchar
Fern
Ogil
Noranside
Careston
Hornieheugh
Dykehead
CAPTAIN SCOTT & DR WILSON CAIRN
668 CAT LAW
Noran Water
BRECHIN CASTLE CENTRE
Brechin
CATHEDRAL & ROUND TOWER
CALEDONIAN RAILWAY
Kirkhill
Dun
Pearsie
Cortachy
Memus
Careston Castle
South Esk
Tannadice
Cadger Path
Aldbar Castle
Bridge of Dun
Kinnaird Castle
Barnhead
Montrose Basin
Montrose
MUSEUM AND ART GALLERY
Scurdie Ness
WILLIAM LAMB MEMORIAL STUDIO
Balloch
Inverquharity
Murthill
Finavon
Netherton
Mains of Melgund
Middle Drums
Inchbraoch
MONTROSE BASIN VISITOR CENTRE
Ferryden
409 MILE HILL
Shielhill
Oathlaw
Crosston
ABERLEMNO SCULPTURED STONES
Aberlemno
Farnell
Bonnyton
Maryton
MONTROSE BASIN
Kirkton of Craig
Kirkton of Kingoldrum
Kinnordy
Northmuir
Montreathmont Forest
Carcary
Dunninald
Long Craig
Fishtown of Usan
LOCH OF KINNORDY NATURE RESERVE
Kirriemuir
BARRIE'S BIRTHPLACE
Carse Gray
Pitkennedy
Rossie Moor
Westerton
Boddin Pt.
Westmuir
Mosside
Blackgate
252
Turin
Montreathmont Moor
Renmure
Braehead of Lunan
Kirkton of Airlie
GATEWAY TO THE GLENS MUS
Maryton
Mains of Ballindarg
Lunanhead
RESTENNETH PRIORY
Rescobie
Dubton
Bolshan
Lunan
Craigton
Padanaram
FORFAR LOCH
Forfar
Reswallie
Balgavies
Glasterlaw
LUNAN BAY
Roundyhill
Drumgley
THE MEFFAN GALL & MUS
Burnside
Milldens
Guthrie
Kinnell
Redcastle
Airlie
Leys of Cossans
ST ORLAND'S STONE
Kingsmuir
Pitmuies
Letham
PITMUIES GARDEN
Friockheim
Boysack
Inverkeilor
Ruthven House
EASSIE SCULPTURED STONE
GLAMIS CASTLE
Dean Water
Dunnichen
Caldhame
Lownie Moor
Bowriefauld
Idvies
Chapelton
Lunan Water
Lang Craig
Ethie Mains
Glamis
Douglastown
Craichie
Leysmill
Cauldcots
Inchock
Red Head
Ethie Castle
Castleton
Charleston
Thornton
Kirkton
Lour
Tulloes
Cononsyth
Drunkendub
Balkeerie
Eassie
Foffarty
Mosston
Colliston
Boysack
Letham Grange
Kirkinch
Milton
Gateside
Inverarity
Whigstreet
Greystone
Redford
St Vigeans
Auchmithie
Wester Denoon
ARK HILL 340
Kirkbuddo
Woodville
Feus
Marywell
Meg's Craig
ST VIGEANS STONES & MUSEUM
Nether Handwick
Gallowfauld
Hayhillock
Carmyllie
Denhead of Arbilot
Hayshead
Cliffburn
The Deil's Heid
ARBROATH ABBEY
Carrot
Arbroath
Arbirlot
SIGNAL TOWER MUSEUM
Coldstream
CROMBIE
Husbandtown
Fauldiehill
Easter Knox
Elliot
Bonnyton
Balkemback
Tealing
Todhill
Kirkton of Monikie
Balmirmer
Kirkton of Auchterhouse
Newbigging
Monikie
Craigton
Salmond's Muir
Auchterhouse
North Dronley
Leoch
Muir of Pert
Inveraldie
East March
Wellbank
CARLUNGIE SOUTERRAIN
Monikie Burn
Muirdrum
Hatton
Bucklerheads
Drumsturdy
Clayholes
BARRY MILL
East Haven
Dronley
Bridgefoot
Burnside of Duntrune
Kellas
Newbigging
Panbride
Muirhead
Birkhill
CLATTO
SOUTERRAIN ARDESTIE
Barry
Carnoustie
Fintry
Baldovie
Mains of Ardestie
Fowlis
CAMPERDOWN AND TEMPLETON WOODS
Downfield
Douglas & Angus
CARNOUSTIE
Barry Links
Liff
DUNDEE
Denhead of Gray
VERDANT WORKS
MUS OF TRANSPORT
Craigie
BROUGHTY CASTLE
West Ferry
Monifieth
Benvie
Lochee
MILLS OBSERVATORY
MUS AND ART GALL
Stannergate
Broughty Ferry
Barnhill
BROUGHTY CASTLE MUSEUM
Longforgan
Invergowrie
Dundee
V&A DUNDEE
Tay Bridge
Buddon Ness
Castle Huntly
Kingoodie
UNIVERSITY BOTANIC GARDENS
DUNDEE
DISCOVERY POINT
Newport-on-Tay
Scotscraig
Tayport
TENTSMUIR
Woodhaven
Tay Rail Bridge
Wormit
Shanwell
Tentsmuir
Fetterdale Forest
Balmerino
BALMERINO ABBEY
Kirkton
Bottomcraig
Pickletillem
Coultra
Gauldry
Rhynd
Carrick
Hazelton Walls
Kilmany
Lucklawhill
Creich
Balmullo
Leuchars
LEUCHARS NORMAN CHURCH
Rathillet
Logie
Milton
Brunton
Eden Mouth
Luthrie
Muirhead
Guardbridge
EDEN ESTUARY CENTRE
ST ANDREWS BAY
Moonzie
Dairsie or Osnaburgh
Kincaple
ST ANDREWS
ST ANDREWS AQUARIUM
Lindifferon
221 MOUNT HILL
Kilmaron Castle
Foodieash
WORLD GOLF MUS
St Andrews
CATH & ST RULE'S TOWER
Strathkinness
Clatto
Newpark
Fernie
Cupar
Kemback
Blebocraigs
ST ANDREWS BOTANIC GARDEN
Brownhills
Buddo Ness
Boarhills
Babbet Ness
Bow of Fife
Cupar Muir
CRAIGTOUN
Balone
Denhead
217
Prior Muir
SCOTTISH DEER CENTRE
HILL OF TARVIT
Pitscottie
Kingsbarns
Cambo Ness
CAMBO GARDENS
Springfield
Bridgend
Ceres
Baldinnie
Cameron Res.
Cameron Burn
Stravithie
Carr Brigs
Eden
SCOTSTARVIT TOWER
Craigrothie
FIFE FOLK MUSEUM
Dunino
Tullybothy Craigs
Ladybank
Pitlessie
Chance Inn
Peat Inn
Beleybridge
Balcomie
Craighead
Cults
Struthers
Falfield
Radernie
Kingsmuir
Wormiston
Fife Ness
CRAIL TOLBOOTH
Balmalcolm
Burnturk
Kettlehill
Woodside
Lathones
Lochty
SCOTLAND'S SECRET BUNKER
New Gilston
Crail
CRAIL MUSEUM AND HERITAGE CENTRE
Kame
Largoward
Carnbee
Pitcorthie
Rameldry Mill Bank
Montrave
Wester Newburn
Lathallan Mill
KELLIE CASTLE AND GARDEN
Pitkierie
West Ness
FIFE COASTAL PATH
Langdyke
Kilrenny
Arncroach
Newton of Balcormo
Grangemuir
Anstruther Easter
Star
Baintown
Kirkton of Largo
Drumeldrie
Colinsburgh
SCOTTISH FISHERIES MUSEUM
Kennoway
Bonnybank
Lundin Links
ROBINSON CRUSOE STATUE
Abercrombie
Pittenweem
Anstruther Wester
Kilconquhar
Scoonie
Lower Largo
Balchrystie
ST FILLAN'S CAVE
ST MONAN'S WINDMILL
BALGONIE CASTLE
Balcurvie
SILVERBURN PARK
Ardross
St Monans
ST MONAN'S CHURCH
LETHAM GLEN
Leven
Milton of Balgonie
Windygates
Innerleven
Largo Bay
Ruddons Pt.
Grange
Elie
ISLE OF MAY
Methil
Earlsferry
Sauchar Pt.
Chapel Ness
Isle of May
Buckhaven
MUSEUM
FIFE COASTAL PATH
Coaltown of Wemyss
292
293
281
282
A
B
C
D
E
F
G
H
7
8
9
10
11
NO
80
60
00

Muck
Port Mor
Gallanach
Eilean nan Each
Sound of Eigg
Sanna Point
Sanna Bay
Sanna
Achnaha
Portuairk
Point of Ardnamurchan
Ardnamurchan Lighthouse
Achosnich
Ormsaigmore
Ormsaigbeg
Kilchoan Bay
An Acairseid
Cairns of Coll
Eilean Mor
Rubha Mor
Sorisdale
Bousd
Cornaigmore
Cliad Bay
Arnabost
Gallanach
Grishipoll
Clabhach
Ballyhaugh
Loch Cliad
Hogh Bay
COLL
Arinagour
Oban
Totronald
Feall Bay
Arileod
Uig
Acha
Breachacha Castle
Friesland
Loch Eatharna
Eilean Ornsay
Calgary Pt.
Gunna
Crossapol Bay
Soa
Loch Breachacha
Castlebay (Apr - Oct, Wed only)
TIREE
Vaul Bay
Balephetrish Bay
Cornaigmore
Vaul
Salum
Caolas
Rubha Dubh
Kirkapol
Ruaig
Gott Bay
Cornaigbeg
Kenovay
Gott
Scarinish
Tiree
Baugh
Heanish
Crossapol
Heylipol
Moss
Hynish Bay
Balinoe
Balemartine
Mannal
West Hynish
Hynish
Rubha Traigh an Duin
Ardmore Bay
Ardmore Pt.
Quinish Pt.
Glengorm Castle
Mull Museum
Tobermory
Rubha an Aird
Caliach Pt.
Caliach
Sunipol
Croig
Mornish
Penmore Mill
Mishnish
Quinish
Cuin
Mull Theatre
Dervaig
Achnadrish
Calgary
Calgary Bay
West Ardhu
The Old Byre Heritage Centre
Druimnacroish
Loch Frisa
Treshnish Pt.
Ensay
Carn Mor
Kengharair
Bellart
Haunn
Achnacraig
Rubh a'Chaoil
Burg
Kilninian
Achleck
Fanmore
Ballygown
Treshnish Isles
Fladda
Lunga
Eilean Dioghlum
Loch Tuath
Eas Fors Waterfall
Beinn na Drise
Gometra
Gometra Ho
Baligortan
Bearnus
Ulva
Ardalum Ho
Ulva House
Laggan Bay
Lagganulva
Oskamull
Sound of Ulva
Loch na Keal
Bac Mor
Eorsa
Isle of
Little Colonsay
Staffa
Fingal's Cave
Inch Kenneth Chapel
Inch Kenneth
Balnahard
Mackinnon's Cave
Balmeanach
Erisgeir
Beinn na Sreine
Glen Seilisdeir
Ardmeanach
Tiroran
The Burg
Burg
Kilfinichen Bay
Loch Scridain
Eilean Annraidh
Maclean's Cross
Iona Abbey and Cathedral
Rubha nan Cearc
Iona Heritage Centre
Iona
Baile Mor
Sound of Iona
South West Mull Makers
Kintra
Aridhglas
Loch na Lathaich
Stac an Aoineidh
Sligneach
Fionnphort
Fidden
Tiraghoil
Eorabus
Achnahard
Knokan
Lower Ardtun
Lee
Bunessan
Loch Assapol
Cruachan Min
Torrans
Erraid
Knockvologan
Ross of Mull
Soa I.
Ardalanish
Ardchiavaig
Uisken
Scoor
Malcolm's Pt.
Eilean a'Chalmain
Rubh Ardalanish
Rubha nam Braithrean
Gunna
TIREE
Vaul Bay
Balephetrish Bay
Sraid Ruadh
Cornaigmore
Balevullin
Hough
Kilmoluaig
Cornaigbeg
Kenovay
Kirkapol
Vaul
Salum
Caolas
Rubha Dubh
Ruaig
Gott Bay
Soa
Gott
Kilkenneth
Moss
Scarinish
Tiree
Baugh
Middleton
Heylipol
Crossapol
Heanish
Loch a'Phuill
Barrapol
Balinoe
Hynish Bay
Rubha Traigh an Duin
Balephuil
Balemartine
Mannal
West Hynish
Hynish
Balephuil Bay
Port Snoig
0 2 4 6 miles
0 2 4 6 8 10 km

Chathastail
ARISAIG (April-Sept)
Druimindarroch
Polnish
Loch Beoraid
Arieniskill
Lochailort
A830
Ranochan
796 SGURR AN UTHA
Glenfinnan Lodge
Glen Dubh Lighe
Loch nan Uamh
Inverailort
Loch Eilt
STATION MUSEUM
GLENFINNAN MONUMENT
Wauchan
SOUND OF ARISAIG
Ardnish
Laggan
Glenfinnan
Eilean nan Gobhar
Loch Ailort
Alisary
Kinlocheil
Fassfern
Samalaman I.
Glenuig Bay
Roshven
869 DRUIM FIACLACH
Callop
Drumsallie
LOCH EIL
Smirisary
Glenuig
882 ROIS-BHEINN
882 BEINN ODHAR BHEAG
Guesachan
South Garvan
Duisky
MORAR, MOIDART AND ARDNAMURCHAN
Baramore
Eilean Shona
666 BEINN GAIRE
755 MEALL NAN CREAG LEAC
Glen Garvan
Rubha Aird Druimnich
Farquhar's Pt.
Invermoidart
Kinlochmoidart
MOIDART
Scamodale
Shona Ho
CASTLE TIORAM
Ardmolich
Glenmoidart Ho
Gaskan
Cona Glen
770 STOB COIRE A'CHEARCAILL
Ockle Pt.
Cùl Doirlinn
Loch Moidart
Newton of Ardtoe
Brunery
SGOR AN TARMACHAIN 756
Fascadale
Kilmory
Ardtoe
Gorstanvorran
Ockle
Shielfoot
Mingarrypark
A861
LOCH SHIEL
Glen Hurich
Branault
Gortenfern
Kentra
Langal
Dalnabreck
Dalelia
Polloch
786 BEINN MHEADHOIN
Conaglen House
357 BEINN BHREAC
Kentra Bay
Blain
Moss
Glenhurich
Loch Doilet
Arivegaig
Acharacle
Ardshealach
888 SGURR DHOMHNUILL
Glen Scaddle
Aryhoulan
ARDNAMURCHAN
Gorteneorn
Kinlochan
Loch Mudle
HIGHLAND
SUNART
Ardgour
SGURR NA H-EANCHAINNE 730
845 BEINN RESIPOL
ARIUNDLE OAKWOOD
Chreagain
Glen Gour
MINGARY CASTLE
490 MEALL NAN EACH
Salen
Resipole
Ariundle
Strontian
701
Ardgour
Clovullin
Corran
Corran Narrows
528 BEN HIANT
Glenbeg
GLENBORRODALE
Scotstown
Anaheilt
Ardery
Sallachan
Inchree
Bunree
Ardslignish
Glenborrodale
512 BEN LAGA
B8007
LOCH SUNART
Ardnastang
Strontian
885 GARBH BHEINN
Archnalea
Sallachan Pt.
Cuilcheanna Ho.
Maclean's Nose
Eilean Mor
Laga
Camas Salach
Camuschoirk
A861
Glen Tarbert
Oronsay
Carna
Glencripesdale
516 MEALL AN DAMHAIN
Laudale Ho
Liddesdale
Tarbert
Inversanda Bay
Inversanda
LOCH LINNHE
169
Auliston Pt.
Doirlinn
582 BEINN NAM BEATHRACH
583 CREACH BHEINN
A828
Kentallen
TOBERMORY
Rahoy
Loch Teacuis
571 BEINN IADAIN
Lochuisge
765 FUAR BHEINN
B8043
Kilmalieu
Ardsheal
Greenfield
Duror
Glendurо
Achadh nan Darach
Calve I.
Drimnin Ho
Barr
Kinloch
Crosben
A884
Loch Uisge
Rubha Mor
Cuil Bay
Beinn a'Bheithir
TOBERMORY DISTILLERY
Drimnin
MORVERN
Gleann Dubh
Beach
Kingairloch
Eilean Balnagowan
Keil
Glen Duror
Upper Druimfin
Bonnavoulin
451 BEINN BHUIDHE
Clounlaid
North Corry
Camasnacroise
Loch a'Choire
Salachan Glen
Bealach
879 FRAOCHAIDH
550 STIOTHEAN NA RAPLAICH
Loch Arienas
739 BEINN MHEADHOIN
KINGAIRLOCH
Lurignich
A848
Rhemore
Acharn
Ardnacross
Killundine
Gleann Geal
Shuna I.
Appin House
Stockdale
Elleric
SOUND OF MULL
B849
Claggan
Larachbeg
KINLOCHALINE CASTLE
ARDTORNISH GARDENS
Achranich
Loch Tearnait
437 BEINN A' CHAISIL
Portnacroish
Ardtur
Glen Stockdale
KINLOCHLAICH HOUSE GARDENS
Appin
Fasnacloich
Invercreran
BEINN CHURALAIN
GLASDRUM WOOD
Glasdrum
Fiunary
Savary
Rannoch
Loch nan Clach
Glensanda
Port Ramsay
Port Appin
Strath of Appin
Creagan
Aros Mains
Lochaline
Loch Aline
GLAIS BHEINN 479
AN SLEAGHACH 513
LYNN OF LORN
Eriska
North Shian
Rudhja Garbh
Rubha Mor
ARDTORNISH CASTLE
Inninbeg
Eignaig
Glenaros Ho
SOUND OF MULL
Fishnish Bay
Ardtornish Pt.
Clachan
South Shian
Loch Creran
South Creagan
Salen
Pennygown
Inninmore Bay
Camas Gorm
Garbh Shlios
Lismore
Balliveolan
Achnacroish
B8045
Balure
SHIAN WOOD
Sutherland Grove
Barcaldine
810 CREACH BHEINN
Kellan
Killiechronan
Killbeg
Corrynachenchy
Balmeanach
A849
Baligrundle
Dalrannoch
Barcaldine Forest
Gruline
B8035
412
Garmony
Scallastle Bay
Rubha an Ridire
Bernera I.
Achinduin
LORN
Baravullin
Ferlochan
708
Gruline Ho
ISLAND OF MULL
Alltrech
Java
Craignure Bay
Kilcheran
Eilean Dubh
Lochnell Ho
Kiel Crofts
BENDERLOCH
Gleann Salach
Knock
Benmore Lodge
Loch Bà
Gaodhail
Scallastle
Craignure
Benderloch
Ledaig
Achnaba
B845
Tomsleibhe
591 BEINN A'GHRAIG
Glen Cannel
766 DUN DA GHAOITHE
Duart Bay
Duart Pt.
DUART CASTLE
Dalnarrow
Eilean Musdile
Ardmucknish Bay
Achnacree
Achnacree Bay
ARDCHATTAN PRIORY GARDENS
ARDCHATTAN PRIORY
715 MEALL MHEADHONACH
761 BEINN TALAIDH
ARGYLL AND BUTE
Druimsornaig
Eilean Mor
North Connel
DUNSTAFFNAGE CASTLE
Black Crofts
FALLS OF LORA
Connel
Achnacloich
ACHNACLOICH GARDEN
Bonawe
966 BEN MORE
704 CORRA-BHEINN
Lochdon
Dunbeg
Achlaven
Muckairn
Stonefield
Ganavan
BONAWE IRON FURNACE
INVERAWE SMOKERIES
Inverawe
Glen More
Ishriff
Lussa
A849
Loch Don
CASTLEBAY COLL TIREE LOCHBOISDALE (Winter only)
Dunollie
A85
Black Lochs
Fearnoch Forest
Taynuilt
MCCAIG'S TOWER
OBAN DISTILLERY
Balindore
Ichrachan
Strathcoil
Grass Pt.
Coladoir
Aird of Kinloch
A849
Loch Airdeglais
Auchnacraig
Kerrera
Altnacraig
Oban
Barranrioch
ANGUS'S GARDEN
BARGUILLEAN
GLEN NANT
Airdeny
Glen Nant
Balliemore
Glenamachrie
383
Glen Lonan
BEN BUIE 717
698 CREACH BEINN
248
Loch Spelve
Ardmore
Killiechoinich
Loch Nell
Loch Fuaron
Kinlochspelve
Croggan
Rubha nan Sailthean
Bach I.
Gylen Park
Gallanach
Cologin
Pennycross
Portfield
Sound of Kerrera
Kilbride
Kilmore
Barran
515 BEINN GHLAS
Loch Nant
Lochbuie
Barachandroman
Rubha Seanach
Dunach
Kilbride
Am Buth
Loch Feochan
Glen Feochan
503 BEINN NA CROISE
Lochbuie Ho
Loch Uisg
Laggan Lodge
Ardentallen
Midmuir
Sior Loch
Kilchrenan
Leidle
Glenbyre
Loch Buie
A816
Knipoch
Annat
Carsaig
405 DRUIM FADA
Laggan
Kilninver
368 A'CHRUACH
Musdale
376
Lower Achachenna
Deer Forest
LORD LOVAT'S CAVE
Carsaig Bay
Rubha Dubh
Insh I.
Barochreal
Scammadale
Bragleenmore
Glen Euchar
Raera
CLACHAN BRIDGE
Ardencaple Ho
B844
Frank Lockwood's Island
Clachan-Seil
Clachan
Scamadale
515 BEINN CHAPULL
438 CARN DEARG
Fineglen
Sound of Insh
Seil
AN CALA GARDENS
FIRTH OF LORN
COLONSAY
Easdale
EASDALE ISLAND FOLK MUSEUM
Braes of Lorn
Inverinan
Balvicar
Blarain
Innie
B840
Ballimeanoch
267 CRUACH RAREY
Lochavich Ho
Loch Tralaig
Acha
Caddleton
Dissaig
Allt Beochlich
295
290
284
274
275

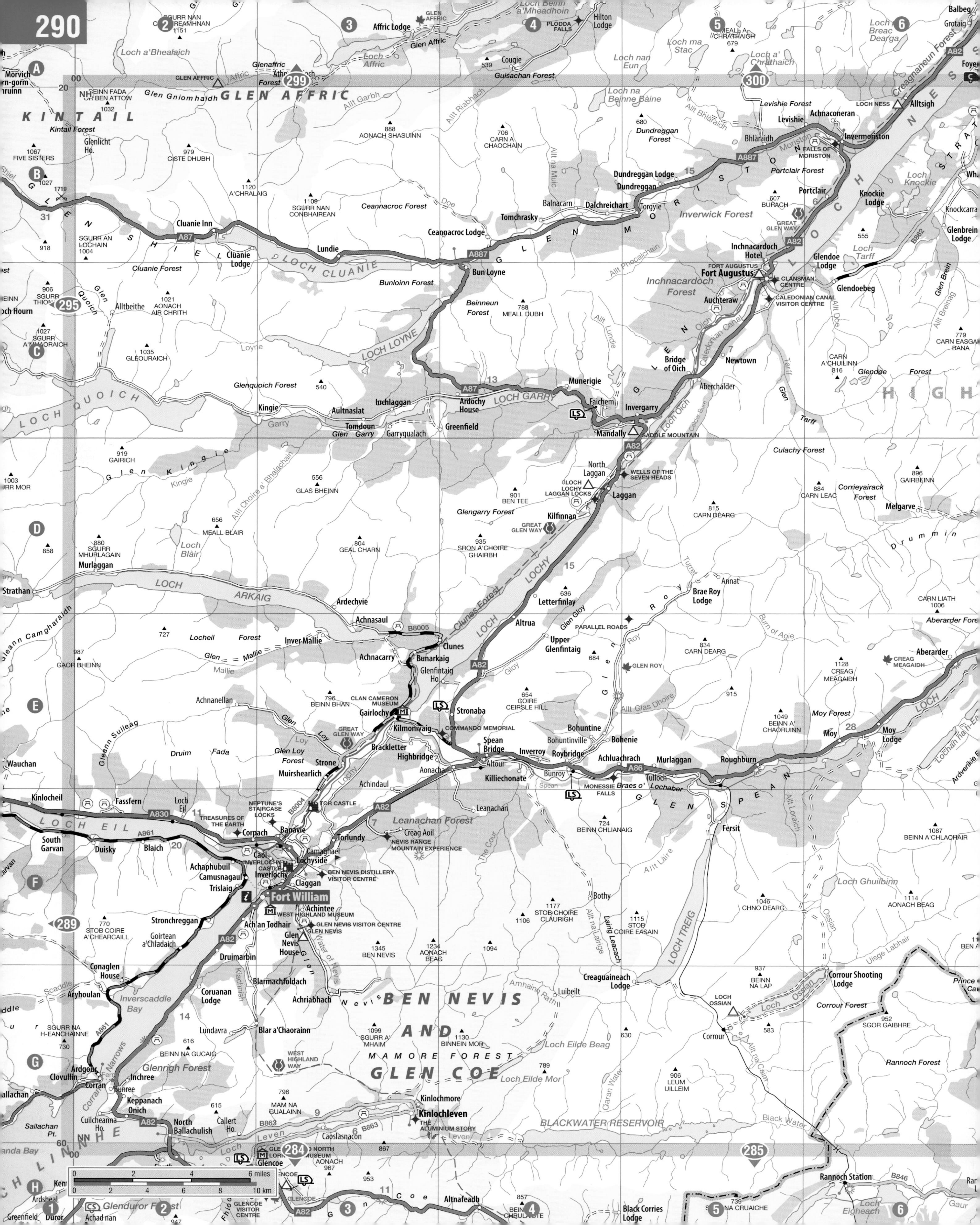
GLEN AFFRIC
KINTAIL
BEN NEVIS AND MAMORE FOREST GLEN COE
Fort William
Fort Augustus
Loch Lochy
Loch Arkaig
Loch Quoich
Loch Garry
Loch Cluanie
Loch Loyne
Loch Eil
Loch Treig
Loch Ness
Blackwater Reservoir
Kinlochleven
Glencoe
Spean Bridge
Invergarry
Invermoriston
Corpach
Banavie
Caol
Inverlochy
Corran
Onich
North Ballachulish
Rannoch Station
Corrour
Roybridge
Tulloch
Laggan
Clunes
Achnacarry
Glen Roy
Glen Nevis
Glen Spean
Glen Moriston
Glen Garry
Glen Loy
Glen Shiel
Cluanie Inn
Tomdoun
Letterfinlay
Fort Augustus
Loch Linnhe
Corran Narrows
0 2 4 6 miles
0 2 4 6 8 10 km
289
295
299
300
284
285

291
MONADHLIATH MOUNTAINS
CAIRNGORM NATIONAL PARK
CAIRNGORM MOUNTAINS
THE CAIRNGORM MOUNTAINS
FOREST OF ATHOLL
PERTH AND KINROSS
GLEN GARRY
LOCH TUMMEL
LOCH RANNOCH
STRATH
Newtonmore
Kingussie
Aviemore
Carrbridge
Boat of Garten
Kincraig
Dalwhinnie
Laggan
Blair Atholl
Pitlochry
Killiecrankie
Calvine
Struan
Kinloch Rannoch
Tummel Bridge
Inverdruie
Coylumbridge
Glenmore
Rothiemurchus
Glenmore Forest Park
Abernethy Forest
Gaick Forest
Gaick Lodge
Glenfeshie Lodge
Glenfeshie Forest
Dalnaspidal Lodge
Dalnacardoch Lodge
Sronphadruig Lodge
Bruar Lodge
Forest Lodge
Ben Alder Lodge
Garrogie Lodge
Coignafearn Lodge
Coignafearn Forest
Killin Lodge
Stronelairg Lodge
Garvamore
Crathie
Cluny Castle
Catlodge
Etteridge
Glentruim House
Ruthven
Insh
Feshiebridge
Loch Insh
Loch Alvie
Loch an Eilein
Loch Morlich
Loch Einich
Loch Cuaich
Loch an t-Seilich
Loch Ericht
HIGHLAND FOLK MUSEUM
CLAN MCPHERSON MUS
HIGHLAND WILDLIFE PARK
DALWHINNIE DISTILLERY
BLAIR CASTLE
CLAN DONNACHAIDH MUSEUM
ATHOLL COUNTRY LIFE
KILLIECRANKIE VISITOR CENTRE
EDRADOUR DISTILLERY
BLAIR ATHOL DISTILLERY VISITOR CENTRE
EXPLORER'S GARDEN
STRATHSPEY RAILWAY
LANDMARK FOREST ADVENTURE PARK
CAIRNGORM CHAIRLIFT, & SKI CENTRE
1309 BEN MACDUI
1296 BRAERIACH
1245 CAIRN GORM
1111 SGORAN DUBH MOR
1120 BEINN A' GHLO
841 BEN VRACKIE
A9
A86
A889
B9152
B970
B8079
B847
B846
B8019
A924
A95
292
285
286
300
301

Lynemore
Inverlochy
Knockandhu
Achdregnie
Auchnarrow
Glenlivet Forest
Strathavon Lo.
Fodderletter
Croughly
Braes of Glenlivet
Clashnoir
Chapeltown
Nethy Bridge
Blairgorm
Dirdhu
Bridge of Brown
Broomhill
Aultmore
Cullachie
Birchfield
Dell Lodge
Lettoch
East Croftmore
Clachaig
Dell
LOCH GARTEN
Abernethy Forest
568 BADDOCH
Dorback Lodge
Larg
Forest Lodge
ABERNETHY CENTRE
ABERNETHY
Aundorach
Braes of Abernethy
Bridge of Avon
Milton
Tomintoul
Delnabo
TOMINTOUL & GLENLIVET DISCOVERY CENTRE
TOMINTOUL
588
588 CARN MEADHONACH
Scalan
Blairnamarrow
Conglass Water
MORAY
LECHT SKI CENTRE
LADDER HILLS
804 CARN MOR
632 HILL OF THREE STONES
Badenyon
Glenbuchat Lodge
658
Water of Buchat
Water of Nochty
Belnacraig
Kirkton of Glenbuchat
Glenbuchat Castle
721 THE BUCK
B9002
ST MARY'S CHURCH
Clova
SCOTTISH SCULPTURE WORKSHOP
Lumsden
Mossat
Kildrummy
Rinmore
KILDRUMMY CASTLE & GARDEN
Milltown of Kildrummy
Glenkindie
Towie
Milltown of Towie
Sinnahard
Balnakeil
718 THE SOCACH
Shiel
Glen Ernan
Ernan Water
Bellabeg
Edinglassie Ho.
Forbestown
Strathdon
Waterside
Inverernan Ho.
Candacraig Ho.
Heugh-head
Boultenstone
Deskryshiel
Tornashean Forest
531 CRAIG OF BUNZEACH
Hillockhead
Deskry Water
673
821 GEAL CHARN
688
MEALL A'BHUACHAILLE 810
GLENMORE VISITOR CENTRE
CAIRNGORM REINDEER CENTRE
Glenmore Lodge
GLENMORE
742
Water of Caiplich
Dalestie
Avon
Water of Ailnack
711
792 CARN EALASAID
Milltown
Colnabaichin
Don
Allt Tuileach
Cock Bridge
Corgarff
Tornahaish
CORGARFF CASTLE
Delnadamph
Burn of Loin
742 BIG GARVOUN
Inchrory
GLEN AVON
CAIRNGORM
CAIRNGORM CHAIRLIFT & SKI CENTRE
1090 BYNACK MORE
Faindouran Lodge
715 THE BRUACH
Forest of Glenavon
Loch Builg
823 BROWN COW HILL
744
749
Morven Lodge
871 MORVEN
Bridgefoot
Easter Davoch
Migvie
Coynach
Balgrennie
Logie Coldstone
Tarland
TOMNAVERIE STONE CIRCLE
Milton of Logie
Glendavan Ho.
Ordie
299 SCAR HILL
CAIRNGORM
CAIRN GORM 1245
1245
Loch Avon
1107
1171 BEN AVON
MOUNTAINS
1082 BEINN A'CHAORRUINN
NATIONAL
Gairnshiel Lodge
Glen Fenzie
Lary
MUIR OF DINNET
604
BURN O VAT
Loch Davan
Loch Kinord
Clarack
Dinnet
BENMACDUI 1309
Loch Etchachan
THE CAIRNGORM MOUNTAINS
1089 CARN EAS
900 CULARDOCH
743 GEALLAIG HILL
M T S.
Glen Gairn
Bridge of Gairn
Milton of Tullich
Cullsh
Coilacriech
Muir of Dinnet
Deecastle
Glascorrie
Ballater
Greystone
Glen Tanar House
1155 DERRY CAIRNGORM
931 BEINN BHREAC
Bush Crathie
CRATHIE CHURCH
Crathie
Littlemill
Dee
BALMORAL CASTLE AND GARDENS
Inver
Invergelder
Easter Balmoral
Khantore
ROYAL LOCHNAGAR DISTILLERY VISITOR CENTRE
Bridge of Muick
House of Glenmuick
Birkhall
Mill of Sterin
529
Glen Tanar
Water of Tanar
GLEN TANAR
CARN NA DROCHAIDE 818
PARK
Derry Lodge
Derry Burn
Lui Water
Glen Lui
BRAEMAR CASTLE
BRAEMAR
Invercauld House
Allanaquoich
Braemar
KINDROCHIT CASTLE
Mar Lodge
Claybokie
MAR LODGE ESTATE
INVEREY
Forest of Mar
LINN OF DEE
Muir
Inverey
Tomintoul
Balintuim
Auchallater
Ballochbuie Forest
DEESIDE AND LOCHNAGAR
Glen Gelder
601
Aucholzie
LINN OF MUICK WATERFALL
Glen Muick
CLACHAN YELL 526
Forest of Glen Tanar
727 COCK CAIRN
742 HILL OF CAT
GRAMPIAN
Geldie Burn
818 CARN LIATH
674
Glen Ey
Allt Connie
BALMORAL FOREST
850 CONACHCRAIG
1150 LOCHNAGAR
Allt-na-giubhsaich
SPITTAL OF GLENMUICK VISITOR CENTRE
Spittal of Glenmuick
721 FASHEILACH
939 MOUNT KEEN
Callater Burn
Lochcallater Lodge
Loch Callater
834
Glen Callater
Baddoch
Dubh Loch
Glas-allt Shiel
Loch Muick
Glen Mark
Water of Mark
Glenmark
Burn of Branny
920 CARN BHAC
1012 CAIRN BANNOCH
998 BROAD CAIRN
Glen Lee
696 MONAWEE
Invermark Lodge
Auchronie
Tarfside
1019 CARN AN TUIRC
958 TOLMOUNT
Water of Unich
Loch Lee
Inchgrundle
Drumgreen
1048 BEINN IUTHARN MHOR
939 AN SOCACH
Loch Vrotachan
GLENSHEE SKI CENTRE
Loch nan Eun
933 THE CAIRNWELL
Devil's Elbow
832 LAIR OF ALDARARIE
Moulzie
Glendoll Lodge
Glen Doll
Braedownie
MUCKLE CAIRN 826
Glen Effock
PERTH
1068 GLAS MAOL
Caenlochan Forest
Glendoll Forest
CORRIE FEE
Loch Brandy
CRUYS 741
Water of Saughs
691 WEST KNOCK
Loch Loch
1051 GLAS TULAICHEAN
905 FINALTY HILL
947 DRIESH
GLEN CLOVA
Clova
Glenlocksie Lodge
BEN GULABIN 806
Tulchan Lodge
758
778 WHITE HILL
Waterhead
Hunthill Lodge
1120 EINN A'GHLO
AND
Glenlochsie
808 MONAMEANACH
Linns
B955
Wheen
ANGUS
903 BEN VUIRICH
Spittal of Glenshee
801 BEN EARB
Glenshoe Lodge
Loch Beanie
Auchavan
Delnamer
Old Craig
Glenprosen Lodge
Kilburn
Rottal
756 FINBRACKS
Dalhenzean
Corrydon
794 MEALL UAINE
740 BADENDUN HILL
Glen Prosen
Balnaboth
PROSEN
Glenprosen Village
512
KINROSS
702 DUCHRAY HILL
Dalnaglar Castle
Meikle Forter
Folda
Glenisla Forest
Glenmarkie Lodge
611
Clachnabrain
545 AULD DARKNEY
Glenmoy
Dalnavaid
Tarvie
Straloch
Glen Brerachan
Enochdhu
Glen Shee
Cray
Lair
B951
744 MOUNT BLAIR
Glenhead Farm
Backwater Res.
Easter Lednathie
South Esk
Redheugh
Auchnacree
Glenogil
Deuchar
Glenquiech
Ogil
Fern
Ashintully Castle
Brewlands Bridge
Freuchies
Longdrum
Horniehaugh
Dykehead
Noranside
641 NO CREAG DHUBH
Kirkmichael
STRATH
Blacklunans
Kirkton of Glenisla
668 CAT LAW
CAPTAIN SCOTT & DR WILSON CAIRN
Newmill of Inshewan
Middle Balnald
520 CAIRN GIBBS
Bellaty
497 CREIGH HILL
Balintore
Pearsie
Memus
Tannadice
Dykends
Balloch
Inverquharity
Murthill
Shielhill
Finavon
Oathlaw
EDRADOUR DISTILLERY
BLAIR ATHOL DISTILLERY VISITOR CENTRE
Milton of Edradour
534 MEALL REAMHAR
TOCK OF BALMYLE
444
Forest of Alyth
Loch of Lintrathen
409 MILE HILL
Kirkton of Kingoldrum
Kinnordy
Northmuir
B957
A95
A939
B9008
A944
A97
B9119
A93
B976
B970
A924
A93
B955
0 2 4 6 miles
0 2 4 6 8 10 km
301
302
291
286
287
1 2 3 4 5 6
A B C D E F G H

Knockespock Ho.
Bogs
Auchleven
Pittodrie
Garioch
Kirkton of Bourtie
Pettymuick
Cultercullen
Foveran
Coldwells Croft
Whitehaugh Forest
Lickleyhead Castle
BENNACHIE 528
Newbigging
BATTLE OF HARLAW MEMORIAL
Mains of Blackhall
Chapel of Garioch
Balhalgardy
BRANDSBUTT STONE
Burgh Muir
Hillbrae
Whiterashes
Affleck
Woodlands
Udny Station
Tillygreig
Tillycorthie
Milltimber
Rashierieve
Hatterseat
Muckletown
GARIOCH
Inverurie
Keith Hall
Hillhead
Nether Crimond
Tillykerrie
Stralochy
Ardo Ho.
Delfrigs
BERRY HILLS
ABERDEENSHIRE
Manar Ho.
Middlemuir
Terpersie Castle
Tullynessle
Keig
Castle Forbes
Upper Woodend
Lower Woodend
Bograxie
Burnhervie
Westerton
Overton
Aquhythie
Port Elphinstone
KINKELL CHURCH
Kinmuck
Balbithan Ho.
Middleton
Newmachar
Reisque
Blackbraes
Kinmundy
Craigie
Causeyend
Whitecairns
Belhelvie
Drumhead
Balmedie
BALMEDIE
LORD ARTHUR'S CAIRN
Bridge of Alford
Montgarrie
HAUGHTON
Rorandle
Pitfichie Forest
Pitfichie
Blairdaff
Dalmadilly
Grantlodge
Upper Coullie
Clovenstone
Burgh Muir
Balbithan
Wester Fintray
Cairnpark
Cothall
Drumligair
Auchintoul
Alford
GRAMPIAN TRANSPORT MUS
HERITAGE MUSEUM
Gateside
Pitmunie
Kemnay
Cottown
Kintore
Hatton of Fintray
OLD CHURCH
Potterton
Muir of Alford
Asloun
Kingsford
Whitehouse
Todlachie
Monymusk
Craigearn
Leylodge
Muir of Kinellar
Woodlands
Parkhill Ho.
Blackdog
Ley
Little Lynturk
Torries
Kirkton of Tough
Tillyfourie
Moor of Balvack
Causeyton
Leschangie
Lauchintilly
CASTLE FRASER
Cluny Castle
Letter
Glasgoforest
Blackburn
Overton
Dyce
Mundurno
Muir of Fowlis
Bridgend
Tillyfour
Corrennie Forest
Corrennie Moor
Ordhead
Sauchen
Achath
Lyne of Skene
Bogentory
Blackchambers
Haughs of Clinterty
ABERDEEN
Stoneywood
Denmore
Milton of Cushnie
Leochel-Cushnie
CRAIGIEVAR CASTLE
Whiteknowes
Kintocher
BENAQUHALLIE
Milton of Corsindae
Bankhead
Corsindae
Old Kinnernie
Dunecht
Skene Ho.
East Auchronie
Chapel of Stoneywood
Newhills
Bankhead
Bucksburn
Hayton
Bridge of Don
BRIG O BALGOWNIE
CRUICKSHANK BOTANIC GARDEN
ST MACHAR'S CATHEDRAL
Old Aberdeen
KIRKWALL LERWICK
Tilly
Lo.
Tullochvenus
Comers
Midmar
STONE CIRCLE
Tillybirloch
Culfosie
Loch of Skene
Kirkton of Skene
Westhill
Woodside
Northfield
Mastrick
Kittybrewster
KING'S COLLEGE VISITOR CENTRE
Aberdeen
ABERDEEN SCIENCE CENTRE
Altdargue
Perkhill
Tornaveen
Marionburgh
Echt
Easter Culfosie
Garlogie
Cairnie
Elrick
Kingswells
Craskins
CULSH SOUTERRAIN
Findrack Ho.
Drumlasie
Lurg
Midmar Forest
South Kirkton
Wester Ord
Easter Ord
GORDON HIGHLANDERS MUSEUM
Mannofield
Ferryhill
Girdle Ness
Knowehead
Wartle
Lumphanan
Torry
DAVID WELCH WINTER GARDENS
Nigg Bay
Greg Ness
Landerberry
Northton
Redhill
Blacktop
Ruthrieston
Kincorth
Milton of Auchinhove
PEEL RING OF LUMPHANAN
HILL OF FARE
Burn of Corrichie
West Cullery
Benthoul
Holemill
Contlaw
Milton of Murtle
Cults
Bieldside
Garthdee
Nigg
DOONIES FARM
Coull
Oldtown
Auchlossan
Torphins
Milton of Cullerlie
Hardgate
Craigton
Banchory-Devenick
Balnagowan
SLUG OF DESS FALLS
Mid Beltie
Milton of Campfield
Hattonburn
Hirn
DRUM CASTLE
Peterculter
Coalford
Milltimber
Heathcot
Charlestown
Cove Bay
Aboyne
Kincardine O'Neil
Maryfield
Tillydrine
Blainacraig Ho
Brathens
Myrebird
Bruckiebog
Drumoak
Mains of Drum
Kirkton of Maryculter
Burnhead
Auchlunies
Hare Ness
Marywell
Birsemore
Backhill of Trustach
Bridge of Canny
East Mains
Upper Lochton
The Neuk
CRATHES CASTLE AND GARDENS
Schoolhill
Hillside
Findon Ness
Findon
Potarch
BANCHORY MUSEUM
Woodside of Arbeadie
Crathes
Stranog
Muirskie
Badentoy Park
Auchlee
Portlethen Village
Portlethen
Birse
Ballogie
Marywell
Blackhall
Arbeadie
Banchory
ROYAL DEESIDE RLY
Kirkton of Durris
Woodlands
Denside
Upper Burnhaugh
Cammachmore
Chapelton of Elsick
Downies
Cammachmore Bay
Burn of Cattie
Blackhall Forest
Deebank
Bridge of Feugh
Crossroads
TOM'S CAIRN
Auchattie
Belts of Collonach
Durris Forest
Borrowfield
Cookney
Newtonhill
CARNFERG
Glencat
Finzean Ho
Tillygarmond
Boghead
Finzean
Strachan
Blackness
Blairdryne
CAIRN MON EARN
Netherley
Muchalls
Percie
Whitestone
Lochton
Backburn
RAEDYKES ROMAN CAMP
Bridge of Muchalls
Forest of Birse
Union Cottage
Water of Feugh
Garrol Hill
MONGOUR
Mergie
Rickarton
Water of Aven
MOUNT SHADE
Water of Dye
Burn of Sheeoch
Cowie Water
KERLOCH
Garron Pt.
Cowie
Glendye Lodge
Bridge of Dye
Kirktown of Fetteresso
Tewel
TOLBOOTH MUSEUM
Stonehaven
Fetteresso Forest
Burn of Tennet
MOUNT BATTOCK
Glen Dye
Tannachie
Carmont
Castle Haven
DUNNOTTAR CASTLE
New Mill
Thornyhive Bay
Drumtochty Forest
Mains of Dellavaird
BURNS FAMILY MEMORIALS
MELUNCART
Glenfarquhar Lodge
Glenbervie
Drumlithie
Fiddes
Barras
Mill of Uras
FOWLSHEUGH
Crawton
Blackcraigs
Drumtochty Castle
Cairn o' Mount
Pitforthie
THE RETREAT GLEN ESK FOLK MUS
Millden Lodge
Dalhastnie
Strath Finella
Monboddo House
Mondynes
Cocketty
Roadside of Catterline
Crawton Bay
Catterline
Clatterin Bridge
Glensaugh
Auchenblae
Brownmuir
Braidon Bay
Todhead Point
Holmhead
East Cairnbeg
Fordoun
Parkneuk
Roadside of Kinneff
Arbuthnott
Mains of Balnakettle
Auchmull
Thainston
Craigmoston
GRASSIC GIBBON CENTRE
ARBUTHNOTT CHURCH
Kinneff
FETTERCAIRN DISTILLERY VISITOR CENTRE
Howe of the Mearns
Davo Mains
Mains of Allardice
HILL OF WIRREN
Fettercairn
Balbegno Castle
Scotston
ARBUTHNOTT HOUSE GARDENS
Little John's Haven
Inverbervie
Bent
West Burnside
Haulkerton
Dalbog
Mains of Thornton
Tulloch
Bervie Bay
Meikle Strath
Witton
Gannochy
Inch of Arnhall
Laurencekirk
Garvock
Gourdon
Craigendowie
EDZELL CASTLE AND GARDENS
Sauchieburn
Johnstone Mains
Garvock Hill
Redford
Benholm
Bridgend
Balfield
Dunlappie
Edzell
Luthermuir
Dykelands
Johnshaven
Rome
North Water Bridge
Mains of Kirktonhill
Luther Water
Kirkton of Menmuir
Ledmore
Tigerton
Inchbare
Pert
North Esk
Marykirk
Bush
Ecclesgreig
Milton of Mathers
West Mathers
Balnamoon
Balrownie
Newtonmill
Craigo
Lochside
St Cyrus
Milton Ness
Mains of Balhall
Lochty
Belliehill
Little Brechin
Keithock
Logie Pert
Muirton of Ballochy
Logie
Morphie
North Craigo
ST CYRUS
Pathhead
West Muir
Trinity
Hillside
Careston
Brechin
HOUSE OF DUN
Kirkhill
Maltings
BRECHIN CASTLE CENTRE
CATHEDRAL ROUND TOWER
CALEDONIAN RAILWAY
Dun
Careston Castle
South Esk
Aldbar Castle
Bridge of Dun
Montrose Basin
Montrose
MUSEUM AND ART GALLERY
Scurdie Ness
Netherton
Mains of Melgund
Middle Drums
Kinnaird Castle
Barnhead
Inchbraoch
MONTROSE BASIN VISITOR CENTRE
WILLIAM LAMB MEMORIAL STUDIO
Crosston
ABERLEMNO SCULPTURED STONES
Aberlemno
Farnell
Balnaboth
Maryton
Ferryden
Kirkton of Craig
ESK
MORAY
STRATHMORE
A
B
C
D
E
F
G
H
7
8
9
10
11
302
303
287
NJ
NO
A90
A92
A93
A94
A96
A944
A956
A957
A980
A935
B974
B9077
B979
B993
B977
B9119
B966
B967
B9120

Ramasaig
Hoe Rape
Hoe Point
Macleod's Tables
488 HEALABHAL BHEAG
Roag
Orbost
Vatten
Harlosh
Balmore
Loch Varkasaig
Feorlig
Balmeanach
Loch Connan
Ose
Loch Caroy
Eabost West
Eabost
Ullinish
Bracadale
Struan
Coillore
Totardor
Loch Duagrich
Tungadal
Snizort
Shulishadermor
Heatherfield
AROS CENTRE
Glenmore
Mugeary
Glen Varragill
Geodha Mor
Harlosh I.
Tarner I.
Loch Bracadale
Wiay
Idrigill Point
MACLEOD'S MAIDENS
Oronsay
Gesto Ho
Portnalong
Ardtreck
Fiskavaig
Rubha nan Clach
Loch Harport
Fernilea
439 ROINEVAL
ARNAVAL 369
TALISKER DISTILLERY
Carbost
Drynoch
Crossal
Gleann Oraid
Merkadale
Satran
Talisker Bay
Talisker
Sligachan Hotel
Eynort
Glen Brittle Forest
Grula
445 BEINN BHREAC
459
SGURR NAN GILLEAN 964
SGURR A'GHREADAIDH 973
MINGINISH
THE CU
Loch Eynort
Kraiknish
Glen Brittle
GLENBRITTLE
CUILLIN HILLS
Glenbrittle House
Bualintur
Culnaneam
992 SGURR ALASDAIR
924 SGURR NAN EAG
Loch Coruisk
Loch Brittle
Rubh an Dunain
Soay Sound
Soay
Mol-chlach
Canna
A'Chill
Garrisdale Pt.
Canna Harbour
Sanday
Rubha Shamhnan Insir
Kilmory
Sound of Canna
Guirdil Bay
388
Kilmory Glen
Kinloch Glen
Rubha na Roinne
MALLAIG (Sun only)
A'Bhrideanach
Kinloch
Loch Scresort
571 ORVAL
RÙM
KINLOCH CASTLE
Rubha Port na Caranean
Schooner Pt.
Oigh-sgeir
Harris
Glen Harris
812 ASKIVAL
781 AINSHVAL
Rubha Sgorr an t-Snidhe
THE SMALL ISLES
SOUND OF RÙM
Rubha nam Meirleach
Bay of Laig
Cleadale
Laig
Rubha an Fhasaidh
Eigg
Sandavore
393 AN SGURR
Galmisdale
SOUND OF EIGG
Eilean nan Each
Gallanach
Port Mor
137
Muck
297
298
288
NG
NM
0 2 4 6 miles
0 2 4 6 8 10 km

ISLAND OF RAASAY
INNER SOUND
Applecross
Kyle of Lochalsh
Kyleakin
Broadford
SKYE
Scalpay
LOCH CARRON
LOCH ALSH
Plockton
Dornie
Shiel Bridge
KINTAIL
HIGHLAND
KNOYDART
SOUND OF SLEAT
Mallaig
Morar
LOCH MORAR
LOCH NEVIS
Arisaig
Lochailort
Glenfinnan
MORAR, MOIDART AND ARDNAMURCHAN
SOUND OF ARISAIG
LOCH QUOICH
Armadale Castle
Inverie
Glenelg
Lochcarron
Strathcarron

SOUTH LEWIS, HARRIS
AND NORTH UIST
NA HEARADH
(HARRIS)
UIBHIST A TUATH
(NORTH UIST)
BEINN NA
FAOGHLA
(BENBECULA)
ST KILDA
St Kilda or Hirta
(Hiort)
Boreray
Soay
CNOC GLAS
CONACHAIR
MULLACH BI
ST KILDA
Loch a' Ghlinne
Bagh a Bhaile
Dun
Tarasaigh
(Taransay)
Paible
Caolas Tharasaigh
Rubha Sgeirigin
Toe Head
Coppay
CHAIPAVAL
Rubha'an Teampuill
Taobh Tuath
SEALLAM
Borve Lodge
Buirgh
SCARISTA STANDING STONE
Sgarasta Mhor
BLEAVAL
Horgabost
Seilebost
LUSKENTYRE BEACH
Losgaintir
LUSKENTYRE
South Harris Forest
Tairbeart
(Tarbert)
Direcleit
Aird Asaig
Taobh Siar
Leacainn
Cul na h-Aird
Isay
OLD WHALING STATION
Lochan Lacasdail
Oban Beag
Urgha
Urgha Beag
Carragraich
Caolas Scalpaigh
Carnach
Scalpay
Sgeotasaigh
Rubha C
a Bhaigh
Loch Ceann Dibig
Loch an Tairbeart
Miabhag
Drinisiadar
Kennacley
Plocropol Pt.
Plocrapol
Scadabhagh
Greosabhagh
Loch Greosabhagh
Rubha Bhocaig
Leac a Li
Collam
Cliuthar
Caolas Stocinis
Stockinish I.
Aird Mhighe
Liceasto
Geocrab
Beacrabhaic
Manais
Loch Langabhat
Fleoideabhagh
Loch Fleoideabhagh
Cuidhtinis
Loch Fionnsbhagh
Fionnsbhagh
Boirseam
Lingreabhagh
Lingarabay I.
Roghadal
ST CLEMENT'S CHURCH
Renish Pt.
Vallay
Langay
Borghasdal
Srannda
Cairminis
Carminish Is.
Killegray
Ensay
An t-Ob (Leverburgh)
Loch Steiseabhat
ROINEABHAL
UIG
Brenish Pt.
Pabaidh
(Pabbay)
Shillay
Little Shillay
Sound of Shillay
Quinish
Sound of Spuir
Spuir
Caolas Phabaidh
Eilean
Bhearnaraigh
(Berneray)
Boreray
Ruisigearraidh
BERNERAY
Borgh
Baile
Caolas Bhearnaraigh
Caolas a'Mhòrain
CAOLAS NA HEARADH
Groay
Gilsay
Lingay
Scaravay
Haskeir I.
Haskeir Eagach
Aird a'Mhòrain
Veilish Pt.
Vallay
Lingay
Oronsay
Torogay
Port nan Long
Baile Mhic Phail
Trumaisgearraidh
Griminish Pt.
Griminis
Taigh Bhalaigh
Ceathramh Meadhanach
Greinetobht
Solas
Malacleit
Vallay Strand
Scolpaig
SCOLPAIG TOWER
Baile Mhartainn
Manish Pt.
Taigh a Ghearraidh
BALRANALD
Hosta
Aird an Runair
Hogha Gearraidh
Baile Raghaill
Glen Drolla
Causamul
Rubha Port Scolpaig
Ceann a Bhaigh
Paibeil
Baile Mor
Claddach-knockline
CLACH MHOR A CHE STANDING STONES
Cladach Chireboist
MARRIVAL
Loch nan Geireann
Loch Fada
Loch Sgealtair
TAIGH CHEARSABHAGH MUSEUM & ARTS CENTRE
Loch Scadabhagh
Loch nam Madadh (Lochmaddy)
Loch nam Madadh
Sursay
Opsay
Tahay
Tobha Beag
Loch Amhlsaraigh
Bagha Chaise
Braigh Chalasaigh
Lochportain
Hermetray
Groatay
Weaver's Pt.
Rubha nam Plèac
Madadh Gruamach
An t-Aigeach
Rubha Mhic Gille-mhicheil
BARPA LANGASS CAIRN
Loch Hunа
SOUTH LEE
Loch Langais
Loch Euphoirt
Loch Euphoirt
Saighdinis
Loch Carabhat
Loch Obasaraigh
EAVAL
AN CAOLAS MHONACH
Na h-eileanan Monach
(Heisker or Monach
Islands)
Shillay
Stockay
Ceann Iar
Ceann Ear
Kirkibost Island
Vorogay
Clachan na Luib
Teanna Mhachair
Samhla
Corunna
Baile Sear
(Baleshare)
Bail Uachdraich
TRINITY TEMPLE
Cairinis
Bail Iochdrach
Cladach Chairinis
Gearraidh Dubh
Oitir Mhór
Beul an Toim
BENBECULA
Baile Glas
Griomasaigh
(Grimsay)
Floddaybeg
Floddaymore
Ronay
Uachdar
Baile a Mhanaich
Scotbheinn
Bagh Mor
Ceallan
Caolas Fhlodaigh
Gramsdal
Flodaigh
Flodday
Cnoc Rolum
Aird
Baile nan Cailleach
Sliabhna h-Airde
Griminis
Torlum
Rubha na Rodagrich
Maragay Mor
Loch Uisgeabhagh
Ard Beag
TRUMPAN CH
Trumpan
Ardmore Pt.
Lower Halistra
Mingay
Isay
Dunvegan Head
LOCH DUNVEGA
Galtrigill
Borreraig
Uig
Husabost
Feriniquarrie
Claigan
An Ceannaich
Loch Pooltiel
NF
NA
NG
305
298
A859
A865
A867
B893
B894
B892
S
E
L
S
I
N
R

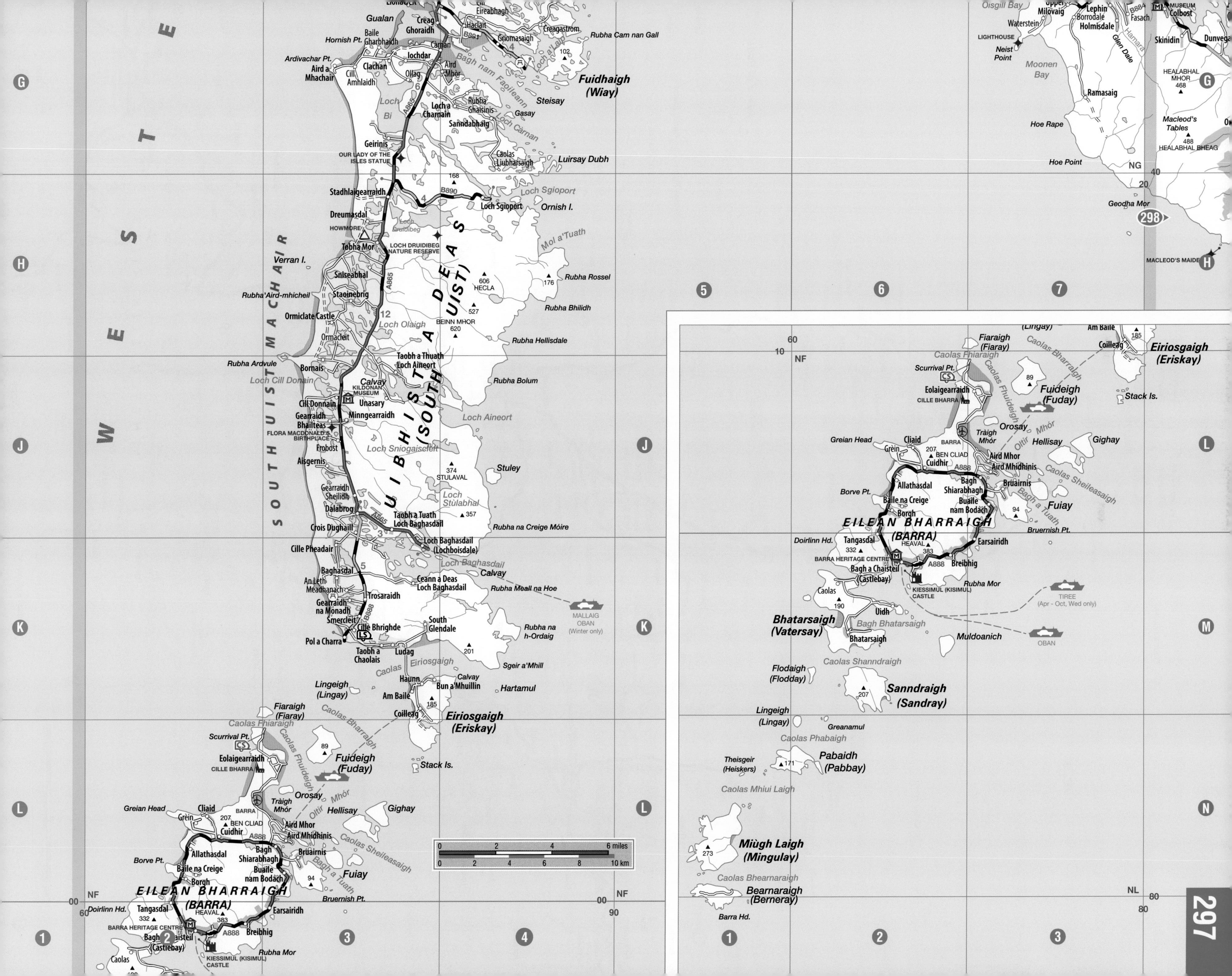
Uibhist a Deas (South Uist)
South Uist Machair
Eilean Bharraigh (Barra)
Eiriosgaigh (Eriskay)
Fuidhaigh (Wiay)
Bhatarsaigh (Vatersay)
Sanndraigh (Sandray)
Pabaidh (Pabbay)
Miùgh Laigh (Mingulay)
Bearnaraigh (Berneray)
Fuideigh (Fuday)
Fiaraigh (Fiaray)
Lingeigh (Lingay)
Flodaigh (Flodday)
Theisgeir (Heiskers)
Gighay
Hellisay
Fuiay
Orosay
Muldoanich
Stack Is.
Calvay
Stuley
Hartamul
Greanamul
Loch Baghasdail (Lochboisdale)
Loch Sgioport
Loch Aineort
Loch Druidibeg Nature Reserve
Howmore
Tobha Mor
Stadhlaigearraidh
Dreumasdal
Geirinis
Our Lady of the Isles Statue
Iochdar
Creag Ghoraidh
Baile Gharbhaidh
Gualan
Cill Amhlaidh
Aird a Mhachair
Ardivachar Pt.
Hornish Pt.
Carnan
Eireabhagh
Griomasaigh
Creagastrom
Loch Carnan
Luirsay Dubh
Ornish I.
Beinn Mhor 620
Hecla 606
Stulaval 374
Rubha Cam nan Gall
Rubha Rossel
Rubha Bhilidh
Rubha Hellisdale
Rubha Bolum
Rubha na Creige Móire
Rubha Meall na Hoe
Rubha na h-Ordaig
Sgeir a'Mhill
Sniseabhal
Staoinebrig
Ormiclate Castle
Ormacleit
Bornais
Rubha Ardvule
Loch Cill Donain
Cill Donnain
Kildonan Museum
Gearraidh Bhailteas
Flora MacDonald's Birthplace
Frobost
Aisgernis
Dalabrog
Crois Dughaill
Cille Pheadair
Baghasdal
Smercleit
Pol a Charra
Gearraidh na Monadh
Trosaraidh
Cille Bhrighde
Taobh a Chaolais
Ludag
Haunn
Am Baile
Coilleag
Bun a'Mhuillin
South Glendale
Ceann a Deas Loch Baghasdail
Taobh a Tuath Loch Baghasdail
Taobh a Thuath Loch Aineort
Unasary
Minngearraidh
Caolas Bharraigh
Caolas Fhuideigh
Caolas Fhiaraigh
Caolas Sheileasaigh
Bagh a Tuath
Bruernish Pt.
Eolaigearraidh
Cille Bharra
Scurrival Pt.
Traigh Mhor
Aird Mhidhinis
Bruairnis
Earsairidh
Breibhig
Rubha Mor
Kiessimul (Kisimul) Castle
Bagh a Chaisteil (Castlebay)
Barra Heritage Centre
Heaval 383
Ben Cliad 207
Cuidhir
Bagh Shiarabhagh
Buaile nam Bodach
Allathasdal
Baile na Creige
Borgh
Borve Pt.
Grein
Greian Head
Cliaid
Tangasdal
Doirlinn Hd.
Caolas
Uidh
Bagh Bhatarsaigh
Caolas Shanndraigh
Caolas Phabaigh
Caolas Mhiui Laigh
Caolas Bhearnaraigh
Barra Hd.
Tiree (Apr - Oct, Wed only)
Oban
Mallaig Oban (Winter only)
Verran I.
Rubha'Aird-mhicheil
Mol a'Tuath
Neist Point
Lighthouse
Waterstein
Milovaig
Moonen Bay
Hoe Rape
Hoe Point
Ramasaig
Glen Dale
Holmisdale
Borrodale
Lephin
Fasach
Hamara
Colbost
Museum
Skinidin
Dunvegan
Healabhal Mhor 468
Healabhal Bheag 488
Macleod's Tables
Macleod's Maidens
Geodha Mor
Oisgill Bay
298
0 2 4 6 miles
0 2 4 6 8 10 km

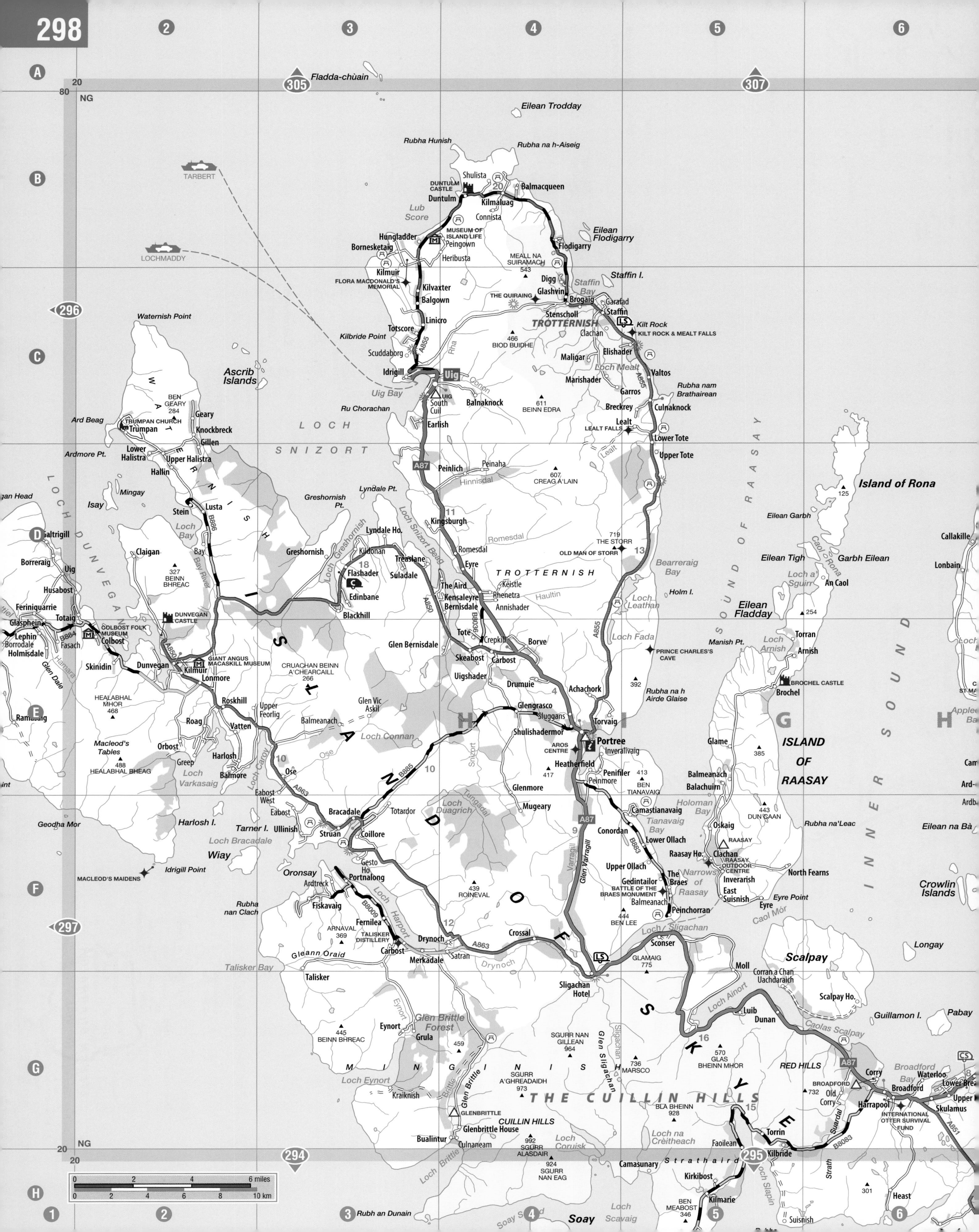

2
3
4
5
6
A
B
C
D
E
F
G
H
1
20
80
NG
305
307
Fladda-chùain
Eilean Trodday
Rubha Hunish
Rubha na h-Aiseig
TARBERT
Shulista
DUNTULM CASTLE
Duntulm
20
Balmacqueen
Kilmaluag
Connista
Lub Score
MUSEUM OF ISLAND LIFE
Hungladder
Peingown
Bornesketaig
Eilean Flodigarry
Flodigarry
LOCHMADDY
Heribusta
MEALL NA SUIRAMACH
543
Kilmuir
FLORA MACDONALD'S MEMORIAL
Kilvaxter
Digg
Staffin I.
Staffin Bay
Glashvin
Balgown
THE QUIRAING
Brogaig
Garafad
Staffin
296
Waternish Point
Stenscholl
TROTTERNISH
Kilt Rock
KILT ROCK & MEALT FALLS
Linicro
Totscore
Kilbride Point
Clachan
466
BIOD BUIDHE
A855
Rha
Elishader
Scuddaborg
Maligar
Loch Mealt
Ascrib Islands
Idrigill
Uig
Conon
Marishader
Valtos
Uig Bay
UIG
South Cuil
Balnaknock
611
BEINN EDRA
Garros
Rubha nam Brathairean
BEN GEARY
284
Geary
Ru Chorachan
Breckrey
Culnaknock
Ard Beag
TRUMPAN CHURCH
Trumpan
Knockbreck
Earlish
LOCH
Lealt
LEALT FALLS
Lower Tote
Gillen
Lower Halistra
Upper Halistra
SNIZORT
Upper Tote
Ardmore Pt.
A87
Peinlich
Peinaha
607
CREAG A'LAIN
Hinnisdal
Leaft
Hallin
Island of Rona
Mingay
Lyndale Pt.
125
Isay
Greshornish Pt.
Stein
Lusta
Loch Bay
B886
11
Kingsburgh
Eilean Garbh
Lyndale Ho.
Loch Snizort Beag
Loch Greshornish
Greshornish
719
THE STORR
OLD MAN OF STORR
13
Callakille
Galtrigill
Claigan
Bay
Kildonan
Treaslane
Romesdal
Eilean Tigh
Garbh Eilean
Borreraig
Uig
Bay River
327
BEINN BHREAC
18
Flashader
Suladale
Eyre
TROTTERNISH
Bearreraig Bay
Loch a' Sguirr
Caol Rona
Lonbain
Husabost
An Caol
Feriniquarrie
Edinbane
The Aird
Kensaleyre
Bernisdale
Keistle
Rhenetra
Haultin
Holm I.
Glasphein
DUNVEGAN CASTLE
Blackhill
Annishader
Loch Leathan
Eilean Fladday
254
Totaig
Lephin
B884
COLBOST FOLK MUSEUM
Colbost
A850
B8036
Borrodale
Fasach
Holmisdale
Tote
Torran
Crepkill
Borve
Loch Fada
Manish Pt.
Loch Arnish
Arnish
Glen Dale
Hamara
Glen Bernisdale
Skeabost
Carbost
PRINCE CHARLES'S CAVE
Skinidin
Dunvegan
GIANT ANGUS MACASKILL MUSEUM
Kilmuir
CRUACHAN BEINN A'CHEARCAILL
266
Uigshader
Lonmore
392
BROCHEL CASTLE
Brochel
Drumuie
Achachork
Rubha na h Airde Glaise
HEALABHAL MHOR
468
Roskhill
Upper Feorlig
Glen Vic Askil
Glengrasco
4
Sluggans
Ramasaig
Balmeanach
Torvaig
Roag
Vatten
Shulishadermor
Glame
ISLAND OF RAASAY
Macleod's Tables
Orbost
Loch Connan
Portree
AROS CENTRE
Inveralivaig
385
488
HEALABHAL BHEAG
Greep
Harlosh
Ose
B885
10
Heatherfield
Penifiler
413
BEN TIANAVAIG
417
Loch Varkasaig
Balmore
Loch Caroy
10
Ose
Peinmore
Balmeanach
Balachuirn
Eabost West
A863
Glenmore
Bracadale
Loch Duagrich
Tungadal
Mugeary
Camastianavaig
Holoman Bay
Geodha Mor
Harlosh I.
Tarner I.
Eabost
Ullinish
Totardor
A87
Tianavaig Bay
443
DUN CAAN
Rubha na'Leac
Eilean na Bà
Loch Bracadale
Struan
Coillore
9
Conordan
B883
Oskaig
Wiay
Lower Ollach
RAASAY
Raasay Ho.
Clachan
RAASAY OUTDOOR CENTRE
MACLEOD'S MAIDENS
Idrigill Point
Gesto Ho
Oronsay
Portnalong
Loch Harport
Varragill
Glen Varragill
Upper Ollach
The Braes
Narrows of Raasay
North Fearns
Ardtreck
Gedintailor
BATTLE OF THE BRAES MONUMENT
Inverarish
East Suisnish
Crowlin Islands
Rubha nan Clach
Fiskavaig
B8009
439
ROINEVAL
Balmeanach
Eyre Point
Eyre
Fernilea
Peinchorran
297
ARNAVAL
369
TALISKER DISTILLERY
12
444
BEN LEE
Caol Mòr
Loch Sligachan
Drynoch
Crossal
Sconser
Longay
Gleann Oraid
Carbost
A863
Satran
GLAMAIG
775
Scalpay
Talisker Bay
Merkadale
Drynoch
Moll
Talisker
Sligachan Hotel
Corran a Chan Uachdaraich
Loch Ainort
Scalpay Ho.
Eynort
Glen Brittle Forest
Luib
Dunan
Guillamon I.
Pabay
445
BEINN BHREAC
Eynort
Grula
SGURR NAN GILLEAN
964
Glen Sligachan
16
Caolas Scalpay
459
570
GLAS BHEINN MHOR
736
MARSCO
RED HILLS
A87
Broadford Bay
Corry
Waterloo
Lower Breakish
MINGINISH
SKYE
Loch Eynort
SGURR A'GHREADAIDH
973
BROADFORD
Broadford
Old Corry
732
Harrapool
Upper Breakish
Kraiknish
Glen Brittle
THE CUILLIN HILLS
BLA BHEINN
928
15
INTERNATIONAL OTTER SURVIVAL FUND
Skulamus
GLENBRITTLE
CUILLIN HILLS
Glenbrittle House
Suardal
A851
Loch na Creitheach
Torrin
Bualintur
Culnaneam
992
SGURR ALASDAIR
Loch Coruisk
Faoilean
Kilbride
B8083
20
NG
294
924
SGURR NAN EAG
Camasunary
Strathaird
295
Strath
Loch Brittle
Kirkibost
Loch Slapin
301
Heast
0
2
4
6 miles
8
10 km
BEN MEABOST
346
Kilmarie
Rubh an Dunain
Soay Sound
Soay
Loch Scavaig
Suisnish
ISLE OF SKYE
SOUND OF RAASAY
INNER SOUND
LOCH DUNVEGAN

Naast
Tournaig
Aird Dubh
Loch na Sealga
Strath More
Clachan
Inverbroom
Auchlunachan
INVEREWE GARDEN
Loch Bad a'Chreamh
Londubh
680
BEINN A'CHAISGEIN BEAG
Port Erradale
North Erradale
Poolewe
Loch Kernsary
Fisherfield Forest
Strath na Sealga
Achneigie
Dundonnell
Forest
Auchindrean
Braemore
CORRIESHALLOCH GORGE
Rubha Bàn
Big Sand
Longa Island
Caolas Beag
CARN DEARG
Lonemore
Mial
Strath
Kernsary
Inveran
Loch Tollaidh
908
BEINN DEARG MHOR
Fain
Smithstown
GAIRLOCH MUSEUM
Gairloch
Dubh Loch
FIONN LOCH
914
BEINN A' CHLAIDHEIMH
MEALL AN DOIREAN
420
LOCH GAIRLOCH
Ardlair
791
BEINN AIRIGH CHARR
Braemore Forest
Bodantionail
Charlestown
Aird
Port Henderson
Badachro
Leacnasaide
Kerrysdale
807
Loch a'Bhraoin
BEINN LAIR
860
Opinan
Shieldaig
Eilean Subhainn
LOCH MAREE ISLANDS
Letterewe Forest
1019
MULLACH COIRE MHIC FHEARCHAIR
934
1110
SGURR MOR
Kerry
Loch Bad an Sgalaig
VICTORIA FALLS
Letterewe
Furnace
Lochan Fada
South Erradale
Loch Clàir
Talladale
Loch Garbhaig
748
GROBAN
999
A'CHAILLEACH
Redpoint
Erradale
Dubh Loch
A832
19
980
SLIOCH
949
MEALL GORM
Abhainn a'Chadh'Bhuidhe
Fannich
Forest
Loch Gaineamhach
WESTER ROSS
300
Fannich Lodge
Flowerdale
Forest
BEINN NAN RAMH
711
875
BAOSBHEINN
Forest
Loch na h-Oidhche
Glen Grudie
692
Kinlochewe Forest
LOCH FANNICH
Heights of Kinlochewe
Leckie
Strath Chrombuill
Craig
Shieldaig
Loch a'Bhealaich
624
BEINN BHREAC
878
Taagan
Lochrosque Forest
Kinlochewe Forest
BEINN EIGHE
Anancaun
Incheril
Abhainn Bruachaig
Rubha na Fearn
Loch
985
BEINN ALLIGIN
1010
BEINN EIGHE
Kinlochewe
933
FIONN BHEINN
Fearnmore
Upper Diabaig
Lower Diabaig
Cromasaig
Glen Docherty
Dosmuckeran
A832
Fearnbeg
Torridon
WESTER ROSS
Arinacrinachd
Alligin Shuas
Torridon Forest
1054
LIATHACH
Badavanich
A832
Achnasheen
Reaulay
Rechullin
Loch a'Chroisg
Cuaig
Kenmore
Loch a'Chracaich
Ardheslaig
Inveralligin
Torridon Ho.
Fasag
TORRIDON
Glen Torridon
Loch Clair
Coulin Lodge
Abhainn Dubh
Ledgowan Forest
Ledgowan
Loch Shieldaig
Upper Loch Torridon
Torridon VISITOR CENTRE
Torridon
782
SGURR DUBH
Loch Coulin
550
CARN-BEAG
Loch Gowan
Abhainn Chuaig
Balgy
Annat
Abhainn Thrail
Coulin
Allt na h-Eirigh
Shieldaig
A896
Coulin Forest
538
CARN MHARTUIN
Loch Gaineamhach
493
CROIC-BHEINN
Abhainn Dubh
Ben-damph Forest
678
CARN BREAC
A890
Glen Carron
Loch Sgamhain
Scardroy
Loch an Eoin
BEN SHIELDAIG
439
Loch Damh
Lair
Glencarron Lodge
Loch Beannacharain
626
BEINN A'CHLACHAIN
Glenshieldaig Forest
902
BEINN DAMH
993
MAOL CHEAN-DEARG
907
Ashnashellach Lodge
Craig
18
928
Loch Lundie
513
Abhainn Dearg
Lair
Glencarron and Glenuig Forest
Glenuaig Lodge
Glen Fhiodhaig
Meig
849
BAC AN EICH
HARTFIELD HOUSE
Hartfield
Applecross Forest
Applecross Ho.
Kinloch Damph
Balnacra
Achnashellach Forest
Loch Dughaill
Loch na Caoidhe
Loch Coultrie
Coulags
Arineckaig
862
1007
MAOILE LUNNDAIDH
814
Applecross
896
BEINN BHAN
Couldoran
1053
Tullich
New Kelso
Strathcarron
West Monar Forest
East Monar Forest
Camusterrach
BEALACH NA BA
Rassal
Tornapress
Kirkton
Achintee
Loch an Laoigh
LURG MHOR
986
Loch Monar
Monar Lodge
Culduie
710
MEALL GORM
Russel
Sanachan
A896
Glen Mor
Ardarroch
Slumbay
Lochcarron
Attadale Ho.
GARDEN
594
Bendronaig Lodge
Loch Calavie
Toscaig
Achintraid
Attadale
An Gead Loch
Loch an Tachdaidh
Uisge Misgeach
Loch Kishorn
STROME CASTLE
Kishorn I.
Reraig
395
Cot
Stromemore
Ardnarff
A890
Attadale
Forest
Loch Cruoshie
Uags
Ardaneaskan
LOCH CARRON
Stromeferry
486
CARN NAN IOMAIREAN
Loch an Iasaich
706
AN CRUACHAN
1150
SGURR NA LAPAICH
1086
AN RIABHACHAN
An Dubh-aird
Plockton
14
Achmore
Killilan Forest
Glencannich
AONACH BUIDHE
899
1069
Port Cam
Braeintra
Duirinish
Drumbuie
Achnandarach
SGUMAN COINNTICH
879
East Benula Forest
Loch House
Erbusaig
Gleann Udalain
Sallachy
Allt-nan-sugh
Killilan
Iron Lo.
Loch Mullardoch
Glen Cannich
Black Is.
Badicaul
Balmacara Square
Loch Long
Faddonch
Allt na Doire Gaibhre
Kyle of Lochalsh
Reraig
Auchertyre
Conchra
Camas-luinie
Carnach
1005
1053
TOLL CREAGACH
CASTLE MOIL
Balmacara
LOCHALSH WOODLAND GARDEN
Kirkton
A87
Nostie
Ardelve
Bundalloch
Carndu
Glen Elchaig
Loch nan Eun
Loch na Leitreach
West Benula Forest
Gleann Sithidh
Gleann A'Choilich
1111
TOM A CHOINICH
Kyleakin
BRIGHT WATER VISITOR CENTRE
LOCH ALSH
Avernish
Glas Eilean
Dornie
EILEAN DONAN CASTLE
634
Elchaig
FALLS OF GLOMACH
1183
CARN EIGE
Gleann nam Fiadh
Ardintoul Pt.
Totaig
Keppoch
Ardintoul
Letterfearn
SGURR AN AIRGID
841
SGURR NAN CEATHREAMHNAN
1151
GLEN AFFRIC
Affric Lodge
SGURR NA COINNICH
739
KYLERHEA OTTER HAVEN
Kyle Rhea
Glen Arroch
Allt Mòr
Ferry
Inverinate
Dorusduain
Loch a'Bhealaich
Glen Affric
Loch Affric
Loch Duich
603
BEINN A'CHUIRN
Ruarach
Morvich
Glenaffric Forest
Athnamulloch
539
Kylerhea
Bernera
Galltair
Glenelg
295
BARRACKS
Scallasaig
RATAGAN
Ratagan
Carn-gorm
Ault a'chruinn
GLEN AFFRIC
Affric
BEINN FADA OR BEN ATTOW
1032
Glen Gniomh
290
GLEN AFFRIC
Allt Garbh
Allt Riabhach
610
BEN ASLAK
Glenelg Bay
Cosag
Eilanreach
Glen More
Cnoc Fhionn
Inverhshiel
Shiel Bridge
KINTAIL
Kintail Forest
Glenlicht Ho.
888
AONACH SHASUINN
706
CARN A' CHAOCHAIN
GLENELG BROCHS
Balvraid
Abhainn a' Ghlinne Bhig
779
1067
FIVE SISTERS
979
CISTE DHUBH
NH
20
80
A B C D E F G H
7 8 9 10 11

Deanich Lodge
Diebidale
Forest
Loch a'Chairn
Gleann Beag
Crom Loch
Glen Diebidale
CARN CHUINNEAG
BEINN THARSUINN
Meikle Gluich
Aultnamain Inn
Auchindrean
Braemore
BEINN DEARG
309
Corriemuick Forest
Abhainn na Glasa
Loch a'Chaorainn
BEINN A'CHAISTEIL
BEINN THARSUINN
CORRIESHALLOCH GORGE
MEALL LEACACHAIN
Loch Vaich
Lubachlaggan
Kildermorie Forest
Kildermorie Lodge
Braeantra
Strath Rusdale
Strath Rory
Abhainn Droma
Dirrie More
Strathvaich Forest
MEALL A' GHRIANAIN
Inchbae Forest
BEINN NAN EUN
Black Water
Loch Morie
Baldoon
Strathy
CNOC CORR GUINIE
Braemore Forest
Lochdrum
Loch Droma
Strathvaich Lodge
Strathrannoch
Inchlumpie
Loanreoch
Ardross
Ardross Forest
Kinhr
Loch Glascarnoch
A835
Strath Vaich
Strath Rannoch
Wyvis Lodge
Boath
Ardross Castle
Easter Ardross
Stittenham
Dalnavie
QUEEN'S CAIRN
Loch Glass
Wester Lealty
Badachonacher
Newmore
Achandunie
BEINN LIATH MHOR A' GHIUBHAIS LI
SGURR MOR
Aultguish Inn
Culzie Lodge
Nonikiln
Moultavie
Mossfield
FYRISH MONUMENT
Alness
Achnagarron
Kinlochluichart Forest
MEALL GORM
MEALL MHIC IOMHAIR
Inchbae Lodge
Garbat Forest
BEN WYVIS
Eileanach Lodge
Glen Glass
Novar House
Dalmore
DALMORE DISTILLERY
Fannich Forest
299
Garbat
Allt nan Caorach
Assynt Ho.
Alness Bay
Fannich Lodge
Loch Fannich
Corriemoillie Forest
Redburn
Evanton
Culcairn
Ferryton
Resolis
Aultdearg
Swordale
Drummond
Cromarty Firth
Alnessferry
Newhall
Foulis Castle
Cullicudden
Newmills
LITTLE WYVIS
Strathgarve Forest
Clach Liath
Ardullie
Strath Sgitheach
STOREHOUSE OF FOULIS
Springfield
Easter Brae
AN CABAR
Lochluichart
Corriemoillie
CIOCH MHOR
Forest
Shoreton
Wester Brae
Millbuie
Achanalt
Grudie
Gorstan
Strathgarve Lodge
Woodlands
Kinbeachie
Black Isle
Dosmuckeran
A832
Loch Luichart
Garve
Heights of Brae
Mountgerald
Findon Mains
Culbo
Strath Bran
Loch Achanalt
Loch Garve
Tulloch Castle
A862
A9
Braefindon
Bottacks
Fodderty
Dingwall
Culbokie
ROGIE FALLS
Auchterneed
A834
MOUNT EAGLE
Killen
Loch Bhad Ghaineamhaich
SGURR MARCASAIDH
Tarvie
HIGHLAND MUS OF CHILDHOOD
Knockfarrel
MACDONALD MONUMENT
Urquhart
Wester Strath
Glenmarksie
Craigdarroch
Strathpeffer
Loch Ussie
Alcaig
Belmaduthy
Little Scatwell
Loch Achilty
Comrie
Lochussie
Tollie
Rosehaugh Mains
Loch Meig
Jamestown
Maryburgh
Corntown
Duncanston
Knockbain
Porin
Dalnacroich
Torrachilty Wood
SGURR A'MHUILINN
Milton
Achlorachan
Curin
Scatwell Ho
Contin
Suddie
Gowan
Bridgend
Strathconon
TORR ACHILTY DAM FISH LIFT
Conon Bridge
Easter Kinkell
Roskill House
Loch Achonachie
Conon House
Leanaig
CARN MHARTUIN
Gleann Meinich
Marybank
Bishop Kinkell
A835
Bennetsfield
Munlochy
Strathconon
Glenmeanie
Muirton Mains
Fairburn House
Urray
Muckernich
Munlochy Bay
Scardroy
Muir of Fairburn
Newmore
Tore
Allangrange Mains
Loch Beannacharain
GLEN ORD DISTILLERY
Kilcoy
Glackmore
Drumderfit
Carnoch
CARN NA COINNICH
Cabaan Forest
Balvaird
Drynie Park
Fettes
Bogallan
Inverchoran
Auchmore
Muir of Ord
Arpafeelie
Drumsmittal
Forest
Orrin Reservoir
Ardnagrask
A832
Redcastle
Kilmuir
BAC AN EICH
Loch nan Eun
Corry of Ardnagrask
Aultvaich
Windhill
Milton
Craigrory
Craigton
Corriehallie Forest
Gleann Goibhre
Tomich House
Charlestown
Glen Orrin
Clashandorran
North Kessock
Loch na Caoidhe
CNOC EILLE MOR
Loch nam Bonnach
Dunmore
Beauly Firth
Longman
Ruilick
BEAULY PRIORY
Lovat
Groam
South Kessock
Highland
Drumindorsair
Beauly
Kirkhill
Bunchrew
Balblair
Inchmore
A862
Lentran
CRAIG PHADRIG FORT
BALNAIN HOUSE
Culcabock
Beauly
Kilmorack
B9164
Leachkin
INVERNESS CASTLE
GARRISON ENCOUNTER
BEINN A'BHA'ACH ARD
Breakachy
AIGAS DAM FISH LADDER
Balchraggan
Drumchardine
FLORAL HALL & VISITOR CENTRE
East Monar Forest
SGURR A'CHOIRE GHLAIS
Erchless Forest
Crask of Aigas
Beaufort Castle
Easter Moniack
Newtonhill
Dunain Ho.
Inverness
Cabrich
Erchless Castle
Aigas Forest
Culburnie
Kiltarlity
The Aird
PRINGLE WEAVERS
Castle Village
Monar Lodge
Neaty Burn
Inchmore
Craigdhu
South Clunes
Caledonian Canal
Leys Castle
Glen
Culligran Falls
AN LEACAINN
Dochgarroch
Braulen Lodge
Struy
Camault Muir
Glaichbea
Ness
Glen Strathfarrar
Farrar
Mid Main
Eskadale
Druimkinnerras
Dochfour Ho.
Scaniport
Loch Beannacharan
Boblainy
Strath Dores
Essich
Glenstrathfarrar Forest
Ardchuilk
Strathfarrar
Struy Forest
Mauld
Ardendrain
Lochend
Loch a'Mhuillidh
Boblainy Forest
Lairgmore
Drumashie Moor
Loch Bruicheach
Carnoch
Glen Convinth
Cragganvallie
GREAT GLEN WAY
Aldourie Castle
Dalveall
SGOR NA DIOLLAID
Strathglass
A82
Glassburn
CAIRN GORM
Abriachan
ABRIACHAN GARDEN NURSERY
Balnafoich
Glencannich Forest
Muchrachd
Balmore
MEALL NAN CAORACH
Balchraggan
Dores
Loch Ashie
Dunlichity Lodge
Liatrie
CARN NAM BAD
Strathnairn
Mullardoch House
Cannich
Glen Urquhart
Balbeg
Balnagrantach
LOCH NESS CENTRE & EXHIBITION
MEALL NA H-EILRIG
Loch Duntelchaig
Farr
Fasnakyle Forest
CAIRN
Buntait
Uppertown
Loch Mullardoch
Glen Cannich
Corrimony
Braefield
Balnain
Potmaily
Milton
Achnabat
Rychraggan
Drumnadrochit
A831
CORRIMONY
Shenval
BCC LOCH NESS
Loch Meiklie
Lochletter
Enrick
STAC NA CATHAIG
Mains of Flichity
DOG FALLS
Lewiston
Urquhart Bay
Tullich
Brinmore
Strone
Fasnakyle Ho
TOLL CREAGACH
Affric
Glenurquhart Forest
Upper Lenie
Lower Lenie
URQUHART CASTLE
COBB MEMORIAL
Divach
Torness
Loch Ruthven
LOCH RUTHVEN
East Croachy
Tomich
Guisachan
Abhainn Deabhag
Enrick
Aberarder House
Balcladaich
Balmacaan Forest
Coiltie
Bunloit
Glen Affric
Loch Beinn a'Mheadhoin
Ancarraig
Balchraggan
GLEN AFFRIC
Hilton Lodge
PLODDA FALLS
Balbeg
Inverfarigaig
CARN NA SAOBHAIDH
Affric Lodge
Loch nam Breac Dearga
Grotaig
Easter Boleskine
FARIGAIG FOREST CENTRE
Aultnagoire
Errogie
Glen Affric
MEALL A' CHRATHAICH
Loch ma Stac
Loch a' Chrathaich
Creagnaneun Forest
Fairaline
Dunmaglass Lodge
Cougie
Loch nan Eun
Foyers
Farigaig Forest
Lyne of Gorthleck
Guisachan Forest
NH
Easter Aberchalder
Loch na Beinne Baine
290
Levishie Forest
LOCH NESS
Alltsigh
Wester Aberchalder
291
BEINN BHREAC MHOR
Levishie
Achnaconeran
Lochgarthside
Loch Mhor
CARN ODHAR
Allt Bhlaraidh
Bailebeag
Dundreggan Forest
Bhlaraidh
Invermoriston
Moriston
FALLS OF MORISTON
Corriegarth Lodge
Garthbeg
CHAOCHAIN
A887
Strath Errick
0 2 4 6 miles
0 2 4 6 8 10 km

8
9
10
11
A
B
C
D
E
F
G
H
309
311
302
291
292
NJ
20
80
Tarbat Discovery Centre
Bindal
Portmahomack
Seafield
Rockfield
Glenmorangie Distillery
Aldie Watermill
St Duthus's Chapel
Tarlo
Morangie
Tain
Tain Through Time Visitor Centre
Tain Tolbooth
Upper Bogrow
Quarryhill
Balcherry
Balnagall
Inver
Arboll
Tarrel
Toulvaddie
Arthurville
Aldie
Hilton
Lochslin
Wester Arboll
Lower Pitkerrie
Geanies House
Morangie Forest
Kingscauseway
Loandhu
Rhynie
Fearn Station
East Lamington
Hartmount
Lamington
Marybank
Newfield
Logie Hill
Hill of Fearn
Fearn
Fearn Abbey
Cadboll
Hilton of Cadboll
Pithmaduthy
Scotsburn
Kildary
Arabella
Loans of Tullich
Broomton
Balintore
Shandwick Stone
Shandwick
Tullich Muir
Milton
Tarbat Ho.
Ankerville
Chapelhill
Nigg Bay
Kilmuir
Pitcalnie
Port an Righ
Barbaraville
Nigg
Sands of Nigg
Mount Canisp
King's Cave
Balintraid
Saltburn
Balnapaling
Balnabruaich
Castlecraig
Invergordon
Ferry
Nigg Ferry
Newhall Point
Cromarty
Cromarty Court House
Cromarty Bay
Udale Bay
Hugh Miller's Birthplace Cottage & Museum
Sutors of Cromarty
Shore Mill
Newton
Jemimaville
Davidston
Navity
Muirton
Glenurquhart
Upper Eathie
Craighead
MORAY FIRTH
Whitebog
Balmungie
Whiteness Head
Groam House Museum and Pictish Centre
Rosemarkie
Rosemarkie Bay
Fort George
Fortrose
Kirkton
Baddock
The Highlanders' Mus
Ardersier
Chanonry Pt.
Heritage Exhibition
Milton of Gollanfield
Gollanfield
Muir of the Clans
Fisherton
Inverness
Lochside
Castle Stuart
Clephanton
Cawdor
Alturlie Pt.
Tornagrain
Croy
Kilravock Castle
Cawdor Castle and Gardens
Morayhill
Newton
Easter Galcantray
Achindown
Cantraywood
Culloden Forest
Balloch
Culloden
Smithton
Newlands
Western Galgantray
Cantraydoune
Cantraybruich
Culloden Battlefield
Clava Cairns
Assich Forest
Westhill
Castletown
Mains of Daltulich
House of Daviot
Beinn Bhuidhe Mhor
Craggie
Daviot
Auchnahillin
Beinn Bhreac
Carn nan Tri-Tighearnan
Moy Burn
Meall a'Bhreacraibh
Meall Mor
Moy Hall
Loch Moy
Moy
Strathdearn Forest
Carn na h-Easgainn
Upper Inverbrough
Balvraid
Tomatin Distillery
Tomatin
Raigbeg
Corrybrough
Findhorn Bridge
Carn a'Choire Mhoir
Carn Glas-Choire
Beinn Bhreac
Glen Kyllachy
Kyllachy House
Clune
Knockandoo
Corrievorrie
Slochd
Garbole
Dalmigavie Lodge
STRATHDEARN
Glen Mazeran
Dalmigavie
Coignascallan
Findhorn
Culbin Sands
Nairn Museum
Nairn Literary Institute Museum
Nairn
Druim
Kingsteps
Tradespark
Boath Dovecote
Auldearn
Moss-side
Househill
Geddes House
Foynesfield
Lalken Forest
Rosefield
Regoul
Piperhill
Culcharry
Littlemill
Mid Urchany
Achavraat
Kirkton of Barevan
Mains of Clunas
Redburn
Newlands of Fleenas Wood
Ardclach Tower
Ardclach
Balmore
Glenferness House
Carn Sgumain
Banchor
Dulsie
Milltown
Drynachan Lodge
Daless
Ballachrochin
Leonach Burn
Tomlachlan Burn
Carn an t-Sean-Liathanaich
The Bar
Culbin Forest
Maviston
Cloddymoss
Kintessack
Brodie Castle
Brodie
Dyke
Earlsmill
Blackhills
Darnaway Castle
Whitemire
Conicavel
Easter Milton
Wester Milton
Lethen Ho
Clune
Achavelgin
Darnaway Forest
Fornighty
Logie Steading Visitor Centre
Logie
Coulmony Ho.
Relugas
Mount
Ferness
Aitnoch
Hill of Aitnoch
Lochindorb
Lochindorb Castle
Lochindorb Lodge
Carn-Ruigh Charrach
Dava
Findhorn
Findhorn Bay
Kincorth Ho.
Kinloss Abbey
Kinloss
Grange Hall
Springfield
Sueno's Stone
Moy Ho.
Forres
Nelson Tower
Blervie Castle
Mundale
Dallas Dhu Distillery
Rafford
Califer
Altyre Ho.
Moor of Granary
Damhead
Altyre Woods
Drumine Forest
Phorp
Newtyle Forest
MORAY
Loch Dallas
Glenernie
Beachans
Divie
Shenvault
Dorback Burn
Carn Kitty
Larig Hill
Burn of Tulchan
Carn na Loine
Upper Derraid
Auchnagallin
Wester Auchnagallin
Glaschoil
Lynmore
Delliefure
Camerory
Cottartown
Upper Port
Dreggie
Glenbeg
Grantown Museum
Grantown-on-Spey
Anagach
Craggan
Achnahannet
Beinn Mhor
Clan Grant Mausoleum & Church
Dulnain Bridge
Speybridge
Revack Estate
Congash
Cromdale
Auchroisk
Haughs of Cromdale
Tulloch-gribban
Skye of Curr
Lochanhully
Duthil
Carrbridge
Landmark Forest Adventure Park
Ellan
Sluggan
Ferth Mhor
Speyside Centre
Broomhill
Balnacruie
Cullachie
Drumuillie
Deishar
Dalnahaitnach
Chapelton
Boat of Garten
Kinveachy
Wester Dalvoult
Avielochan
Birchfield
East Croftmore
Loch Garten
Loch Garten Abernethy
Abernethy Forest
Street of Kincardine
Aundorach
Strathspey Railway
Lower Dell
Dell Lodge
Lettoch
Clachaig
Abernethy Centre
Forest Lodge
Larg
Baddoch
Dorback Lodge
Eil
Caggan
Dulnain
Allt Lorgy
Nethy Bridge
Blairgorm
Aultmore
Dirdhu
CAIRNGORMS NATIONAL PARK
Speyside Way
Lynemore
Creggan a'Chaise
Bridge of Brown
Burghead Visitor Centre
Burghead
Hopeman
Cummingston
Roseisle
College of Roseisle
Roseisle Forest
Burghead Bay
Duffus
Old Duffus
Gordonstoun
Duffus Castle
Palace of Spynie
Spynie
Covesea Skerries
Covesea
Lossiemouth Fisheries & Community Museum
Stotfield
Lower Hempriggs
Quarrywood
Rosebrae
Newton
Laverackloch
Bishopmill
Elgin
Elgin Museum
Elgin Cathedral
Old Mills
Moray Motor Museum
New Elgin
Glassgreen
Coltfield
Alves
Ardgye
Miltonhill
East Grange
Cloves
Pittendreich
Miltonduff
Mains of Burgie
Muir of Miltonduff
Mayne Ho.
Monaughty Forest
Pluscarden Abbey
Auchtertyre
Paddockhaugh
Birnie Church
Barnhill
Foresterseat
Thornhill
Stoneyfield
Upper Bogside
Black Burn
Dallas Forest
Kellas
Glenlatterach
Briach
Hatton
Branchill
Dallas Lodge
Dallas
Craigroy
Cairn Uish
Mill Buie
Ballachraggan
Burn of Roth
Carn na Cailliche
Elchies Forest
Lossie
Archiestown
Cardhu Distillery
Speyside Way
Upper Knockando
Cardow
Knockando Ho.
Knockando
Carron
Daugh of Kinermony
Allt a Ghealaidh
Marypark
Glenfarclas Distillery
Bellehiglash
Cragganmore Distillery
Cragganmore
Advie
Bridge of Avon
Dalchirach
Haugh of Kilnmaichlie
Craggan
Lettoch
Dalriach
Mains of Dalvey
STRATHSPEY
Drumin
Downan
Glenlivet Distillery
Glenlivet
Shenval
Auchbreck
Castleton
HILLS OF CROMDALE
Strath Avon
Ballcorach
Tomnavoulin
Carn Daimh
Knockandhu
Inverlochy
Auchnarrow
Glenlivet Forest
Burn of Lochy
Strathavon Lo.
Croughly
Fodderletter
Clashnoir
Braes of Chapeltown
Bridge of Avon
Milton
Tomintoul & Glenlivet Discovery Centre
Tomintoul
Delnabo
Carn Meadhon
Conglass Water

311
NJ
Halliman Skerries
Covesea Skerries
LOSSIEMOUTH FISHERIES & COMMUNITY MUSEUM
Covesea
Stotfield
Branderburgh
Lossiemouth
Duffus
Gordonstoun
Old Duffus
DUFFUS CASTLE
PALACE OF SPYNIE
Loch Spynie
Lossie Forest
SPEY BAY
Portknockie
Findochty
Cullen Bay
Logie Hd.
Sandend Bay
Redhythe Pt.
Boyne Bay
Knock Hd.
Boyndie Bay
Spynie
Leuchars Ho.
Stonewells
Lochhill
Kingston
SCOTTISH DOLPHIN CENTRE
TUGNET ICE HOUSE
Spey Bay
Gordonsburgh
Buckie
Buckpool
Portessie
Bauds of Cullen
Cullen
Old Cullen
FINDLATER CASTLE
Sandend
Portsoy
Seatown
Whitehills
Inverboyndie
Banff
Quarrywood
Laverackloch
Elgin
Bishopmill
ELGIN MUSEUM
CATHEDRAL
CASHMERE VISITOR CENTRE
OLD MILLS
MORAY MOTOR MUSEUM
Moss of Meft
Urquhart
Burniestrype
Garmouth
Porttanachy
Nether Dallachy
Upper Dallachy
Rathven
Connage
Lintmill
Birkenbog
Bogtown
JOINER'S WORKSHOP
Easter Whyntie
Boyndie
Auds
Pittendreich
New Elgin
Darkland
Lhanbryde
Lochs Crofts
Bogmoor
SPEYSIDE WAY
Portgordon
Slackhead
Cairnfield Ho.
Drybridge
Slate Haugh
Milton
Fordyce
Tillynaught
DUFF HOUSE
Miltonduff
Mayne Ho.
Glassgreen
Moss of Barmuckity
COXTON TOWER
Auchenhalrig
Newlands of Tynet
BAXTERS HIGHLAND VILLAGE
Broadley
Preshome
ST. GREGORY'S CHAPEL
Shiel Muir
Kirktown of Deskford
DESKFORD CHURCH
Ardiecow
Drochedlie
Wester Culbeuchly
Montcoffer
Muir of Miltonduff
Paddockhaugh
Mosstodloch
FOCHABERS FOLK MUSEUM HERITAGE CENTRE
Fochabers
Braes of Enzie
Clochan
Berryhillock
Brodiesord
Newmills of Boyne
Alehousebum
Tipperty
Oldtown of Ord
Mill of Brydock
Kirktown of Alvah
Auchtertyre
Clackmarras
Longmorn
Blackhills
Dipple
Speymouth Forest
Craibstone
Little Toux
Mickle Toux
Upper Culphin
Cornhill
Loanhead
Fattahead
Greenlaw
Foresterseat
BIRNIE CHURCH
Fogwatt
Altonside
Orbliston
Ordiequish
MILLSTONE HILL
Gordonstown
Weachyburn
Drywells
Upper Bogside
Thornshill
MILLBUIES
Westerton
Teindland Forest
Goukstone
Mains of Edingight
Edingight Ho.
KNOCK HILL
Ordiquhill
Grantown
Blacklaw
Finnygaud
Lower Deuchries
Coleburn
Inchberry
Wood of Ordiequish
Forgie
Broadrashes
Garralburn
Deerhill
Grange Crossroads
Whitehill
Sillyearn
Glen of Newmill
Hill of Mountblairy
Glenlatterach
Aultmore
Crannoch
Bracobrae
Davoch of Grange
Knock
Knowes of Elrick
Knowehead
Ramsburn
Crombie Castle
Cranna
Aberchirder
MORAY
Mains of Cairnty
Newmill
Drumnagorrach
Farmtown
Old Crombie
Bogton
Auchinroath
Newlands
Glen of Rothes
Shalloch
Fife Keith
Keith
STRATHISLA DISTILLERY
Nethermills
Knauchland
Moss-side
Marnoch
Clunie
Carnousie
CAIRN UISH
Balnabreich
Mulben
Rosarie
Aikenway
Rothes
GLEN GRANT DISTILLERY
Burn of Rothes
Rosarie Forest
Mains of Auchoynanie
Tarryblake Ho.
Rothiemay Crossroads
Auldtown of Carnoustie
Mains of Laithers
Elchies Forest
CARN NA CAILLICHE
Arndilly Ho.
BEN AIGAN
Belnagarrow
KEITH AND DUFFTOWN RLY
Blackhillock
Poolside
North Whiteley
Balloch Wood
Milltown of Rothiemay
Mains of Mayen
Hillbrae
Inverkeithny
Auchininna
Whiteacen
MACALLAN DISTILLERY
Dandaleith
Maggieknockater
Towiemore
Edintore
Glen of Coachford
Ruthven
Yonder Bognie
Bogniebrae
Midplaugh
FOURMAN HILL
Archiestown
CARDHU DISTILLERY
Cardow
Ringorm
Craigellachie
Kininvie Ho.
Drummuir Castle
Little Pitlurg
Coachford
Cairnie
Haddoch
Milburn
Forgue
Fortrie
Brownhill
Upper Knockando
Robertstown
SPEYSIDE VISITOR CENTRE
SPEYSIDE COOPERAGE VISITOR CENTRE
Midtown of Buchromb
Drummuir
THE BIN
The Bin Forest
Corse of Kinnoir
Cobairdy
Pitfancy
GLENDRONACH DISTILLERY
Drumblair
Carlincraig
Knockando
Knockando Ho.
Carron
Speyview
Glenallachie
Charlestown of Aberlour
Balvenie
Glack of Midthird
Slogan
Midtown of Glass
Drumdelgie
Daugh of Cairnborrow
NORDIC SKI CENTRE
HUNTLY CASTLE
Lessendrum
Corse
Denmoss
Balgaveny
Daugh of Kinermony
Milltown of Edinvillie
BALVENIE CASTLE
GLENFIDDICH DISTILLERY
Milltown of Auchindoun
Cairnborrow
Westerton
Huntly
Drumblade
Largue
Aucharnie
SPEYSIDE WAY
Dufftown
Torry
Terryhorn
Wellheads
Brideswell
Slioch
Logie Newton
Marypark
Sheandow
Kirktown of Mortlach
Haugh of Glass
Deveron
Drumdollo
Denend
Ythanwells
Badenscoth
Bellehiglash
GLENFARCLAS DISTILLERY
MEIKLE CONVAL
Lettoch
AUCHINDOUN CASTLE
STRATHBOGIE
Thomastown
Redhill
Craggenmore
THE SCALP
Bailiesward
Wester Mosshead
Milburn
Bridge of Avon
Glen Rinnes
Dullan Water
Bridgend
Hillhead
Greystone
Bainshole
Fisherford
BEN RINNES
Favillar
Glen Fiddich
Succoth
Tillathrowie
Kirkstile
Shanquhar
Corncatteracht
Dalchirach
Haugh of Glenmaichlie
Kirkhill
Ballochford
Mill of Lynebain
Tomnaven
Coynachie
Culdrain
Blackburn
Glens of Foudland
HILL OF FOUDLAND
Kirkton of Culsalmond
Rothmaise
Craggan
Glenfiddich Lodge
Clashindarroch Forest
Kirkney
Gartly
Colpy
Cairnhill
Drumin
Downan
Bridgend
Clashindarroch
Cults
KNOCKANDY HILL
Largie
Wrangham
Bonnyton
GLENLIVET DISTILLERY
Glenlivet
Badeach
Glenfiddich Forest
Inverharroch
Ardwell
Mytice
Kirkney Water
LEITH HALL
Upper Boddam
Wraes
Knockenbaird
Aulton
Shenval
Black Water
Milton of Lesmore
Smithston
Newton Ho.
Old Rayne
Auchbreck
Castleton
Blackwater Lodge
ROUND HILL
Auchmair
Milton of Noth
Kennethmont
Oldtown
Ardlair
The Shevock
Insch
Pitmachie
Ardoyne
Tomnavoulin
Cabrach
Belhinnie
Cottown
Towie
Blackwater Forest
Aldivalloch
Aldunie
Rhynie
Clatt
Duncanstone
Westhall
CARN AN T-SUIDHE
Wheedlemont
Craig Castle
Auchmenzie
Knockespock Ho.
Leslie
Kirkton
Oyne
Kirkton of Oyne
Glenlivet Forest
Knockandhu
Achdregnie
ST MARY'S CHURCH
Bogs
Auchleven
Lickleyhead Castle
BENNACHIE
Auchnarrow
Livet
THE BUCK
Clova
SCOTTISH SCULPTURE WORKSHOP
Lumsden
Coldwells Croft
Whitehaugh Forest
Clashnoir
Braes of Glenlivet
Chapeltown
HILL OF THREE STONES
CORREEN HILLS
Muckletown
ABERDEEN
GARIO
Croughly
Scalan
Glenton
Milton
TOMIN
Glenbuchat Lodge
Badenyon
Mossat
LORD ARTHUR'S CAIRN
Terpersie Castle
Tully
Keig
Castle Forbes
Upper Woodend
Lower Woodend
Bridge of Alford
Montgarrie
HAUGHTON
Rorandle
Pitfichie Forest
Rinmore
Kildrummy
Milltown of Kildrummy
Water of Buchat
Belnacraig
KILDRUMMY CASTLE & GARDEN
Auchintoul
Muir of
Alford
GRAMPIAN TRANSPORT MUS
Gateside
Pitfichie
Kirkton of
Glenbuchat
Conglass Water
Water of Nochty
0 2 4 6 miles
0 2 4 6 8 10 km
292
293
301

7
8
9
10
11
A
B
C
D
E
F
G
H
20
80
NK
Troup Hd.
Pennan Hd.
Quarry Hd.
SANDHAVEN MEAL MILL
Pittulie
FRASERBURGH HERITAGE CENTRE
Fraserburgh
Rosehearty
PITSLIGO CASTLE
Sandhaven
Broadsea
Kinnaird Head
KINNAIRD CASTLE LIGHTHOUSE & SCOTLAND'S LIGHTHOUSE MUSEUM
MACDUFF MARINE AQUARIUM
Head of Garness
Gamrie Bay
Crovie
TROUP HEAD
Gardenstown
Pennan
Braco Park
Peathill
Fraserburgh Bay
Cairnbulg Pt.
Inverallochy
MAGGIE'S HOOSIE
Easter Silverford
Dubford
Glenquithlie
Mill Farm
Towie
Percyhorner
Coburty
Pitblae
Easter Cardno
Cairnbulg Castle
St Combs
West Greenskares
Longmanhill
Cummerton
Ardlawhill
New Aberdour
Upper Boyndlie
Mid Ardlaw
Memsie
Cairnmuir
Gowanhill
Mosstown
Inzie Head
Park
Cushnie
231 WINDYHEADS HILL
Tyrie
MEMSIE BURIAL CAIRN
Ardglassie
Rathen
Strathellie
Netherton of Lonmay
Minnonie
Hill of Overbrae
Nether Glasslaw
Ladysford
Whitewell
Quarryhead
Cairness
Loch of Strathbeg
Netherbrae
Broadleys
Mountsolie
Spillardsford
Fortrie
Pitgair
Mid Cloch Forbie
Craigmaud
North Skelmanae
Hillhead of Auchentumb
Newburgh
Mains of Hatton
Crimonmogate
Seatown
Rattray Head
Muirton
Gorrachie
Bracklamore
Lonmay
LOCH OF STRATHBEG
King Edward
Milltack
Auchlinn
Crudie
227 HILL OF FISHRIE
Middlemuir
230 MORMOND HILL
Ferniebrae
Crimond
Old Rattray
Milltown of Craigston
Cowbog
New Pitsligo
Knowhead
Hillfoot
Nether Park
Blackhill
Plaidy
Craigston Castle
Cauldwells
Northside
Balnamoon
Strichen
North Mosstown
Fintry
Lower Cotburn
New Byth
Borrohill
New Leeds
Longhill
Upper Ridinghill
Balearn
Gas Terminal
Muirden
Upper Cotburn
Bonnykelly
Adziel
North Ugie Water
Leys
St Fergus Moss
St Fergus
Garmond
Whitestones
Ironside
Little Skillymarno
Denhead
Backfolds
Outhills
Kirktown
Scotstown Hd.
Muiryfold
Cairnhill
Balthangie
Oldwhat
South Auchmachar
Fetterangus
Hythie
Rora Moss
Gallowhills
North Kirkton
Turriff
DELGATIE CASTLE
Cuminestown
Mains of Fedderate
Cuttyhill
Rora
Lunderton
Kirkton Hd.
Middle Cairncake
Aulton of Atherb
Forest of Deer
Toux
Woodside
Middleton of Rora
Little Colp
Delgaty Forest
Culsh
DEER ABBEY
Dunshillock
Newseat
INVERUGIE CASTLE
Inverugie
UGIE SALMON FISH HOUSE
Craighill
Maud
ADEN
Mintlaw
Water
Longside
Buchanhaven
Hatton Castle
Darra
Howe of Teuchar
Slacks of Cairnbanno
New Deer
MAUD RAILWAY MUSEUM
Backhill of Clackriach
Old Deer
ABERDEENSHIRE FARMING MUSEUM
South Ugie
Flushing
Torterston
Peterhead
Rush-head
Stuartfield
Inverquhomery
ARBUTHNOT MUSEUM & ART GALLERY
Birkenhills
Burnside
Drymuir
Bulwark
Parkhill
Hillhead of Cocklaw
Keith Inch
Crofts of Invertherne
Heatherybanks
Bodiechell
Cairnbanno Ho.
Mains of Crichie
Millbreck
Nether Kinmundy
Toddlehills
Invernettie
Peterhead Bay
Mains of Towie
179
North Millbrex
Netherton
Middlemuir
Nethermuir
Crichie
Sandford Bay
Dykeside
Riffin
Steinmanhill
South Millbrex
Balquhindachy
Knaven
Clochan
Kinnadie
Clola
Easterton of Lenabo
Little Dens
Blackhill
Millbank
Boddam
Seggat
Inverythan
Gourdas
Crofts of Meikle Ardo
Gowanwell
Skelmuir
Nether Savock
Buchan Ness
Kirkton of Auchterless
Tifty
Lethenty
Cottown
Cairnorrie
Barrack
Auchnagatt
Mains of Annochie
Kinknockie
Smallburn
Sandfordhill
Stirling
Monkshill
Burnend
Brownhill
Backhill of Fortrie
Moss of Cruden
Croft of Tillymaud
Burreldales
Backhill
FYVIE CASTLE
Little Gight
Mains of Inkhorn
Drakemyre
Backhill
Stoneygate
Coldwells
Longhaven
Stonehouse
Ardo
Skelmonae
Ardallie
Teuchan
Gordonstown
Fyvie
Woodhead
Quilquox
13
Milton Coldwells
Upper Hawkhillock
Auchiries
North Haven
BULLERS OF BUCHAN
Rothiebrisbane
St John's Wells
Crofts of Haddo
Methlick
South Quilquox
Hatton
Twa Havens
Rothienorman
Petty
Collynie
Drumwhindle
Muirtack
Arthrath
Eastertown of Auchleuchries
Cruden Bay
SLAINS CASTLE
Cromblet
North Flobbets
Barthol Chapel
HADDO
Cairnleith Crofts
Mains of Arnage
Berefold
Toll of Birness
Chapel Hill
Port Erroll
Upper Ardgrain
Bogbrae
Bay of Cruden
Folla Rule
St Katherine's
South Flobbets
HADDO HOUSE AND GARDENS
Ythanbank
Hilton
Mains of Birness
Nether Leask
Newseat
Cross of Jackston
Earlsford
Wedderlairs
Inverebrie
Whinnyfold
Byebush
Balgove
Thornroan
Broomfield
Meikle Wartle
Jackstown
Tulloch
Raxton MEDIEVAL TOMB
Knockothie
P&R
Artrochie
Blackhill
Westertown
Redmoss
West Kinharrachie
Auchmacoy
Bethelnie
Craigdam
Tarves
Ythsie
Esslemont
Ellon
Waterton
Alehousehill
Kirkton Rayne
Meldrum Ho.
Auquhorthies
Kirkton of Logie Buchan
VISITOR CENTRE
Kirktown of Slains
LOANHEAD STONE CIRCLE
Mounie Castle
Whitefield
Mains of Cairnbrogie
TOLQUHON CASTLE
F O R M A R T I N E
Ulaw
Cross Stone
Collieston
Durno
Daviot
PITMEDDEN GARDENS
Pitmedden
Waterside
Meikle Tarty
Knockhall Castle
St Catherine's Dub
FORVIE
Sands of Forvie
Fingask
Tipperty
Hackley Hd. or Forvie Ness
Pitcaple
Barra Castle
Oldmeldrum
Cairnbrogie
Udny Green
Mill of Kingoodie
Tarty Burn
Kinknockie
193
Old Craig
Harlaw Ho.
Chapel of Garioch
1411
Lethenty
Kirkton of Bourtie
Hattoncrook
Pettymuick
Culterculien
Foveran
Newburgh
Balhalgardy
Whiterashes
Affleck
Woodlands
Udny Station
Foveran Burn
BATTLE OF HARLAW MEMORIAL
BRANDSBUTT STONE
Mains of Blackhall
Burgh Muir
Hillbrae
Tillygreig
Tillycorthie
Minnes
Drums
Newburgh Bar
237
Inverurie
Hillhead
Nether Crimond
186
Rashiereive
Hatterseat
Tillykerrie
Ardo Ho.
Manar Ho.
Keith Hall
Straloch
Delfrigs
Port Elphinstone
Kinmuck
293
Middlemuir
Burnhervie
Aquhythie
Westerton
Overton
KINKELL CHURCH
Balbithan Ho.
Newmachar
Reisque
Craigie
Causeyend
Drumhead
Dalmadilly
Clovenstone
Burgh Muir
Balbithan
Wester Fintray
Cairnpark
Blackbraes
Kinmundy
Whitecairns
Belhelvie
BALMEDIE
Balmedie
Cothall
Drumligair
Kintore
Cottown
Kemnay
A90
A952
A950
A981
A98
A947
A920
A96
A975
B9031
B9032
B9033
B9107
B9093
B9105
B9027
B9170
B9029
B9106
B9030
B9005
B9000
B9001
B977
B979
B999
B993

RUBHA ROBHANAIS (BUTT OF LEWIS)
CHURCH OF ST MOULAG
HARBOUR VIEW GALLERY
Cunndal
Eòropaidh
Coig Peighinnean
Port Nis
Adabroc
Lional
Tàbost
Suainebost
Cros
Cross Sands
Aird Dhail
Dail bho Dheas
Dail bho Thuath
Sgiogarstaigh
Glen Cross
Cuiashader
Cellar Head
Gabhsann bho Thuath
Gabhsann bho Dheas
Mealabost Bhuirgh
Bail Àrd Bhuirgh
Coig Peighinnean Bhuirgh
Siadar
Siadar Iarach
Siadar Uarach
Baile an Truiseil
TRUSHAL STONE
Rubha Leathann
Aird Barvas
Loch Langabhat
Loch Mór Shanndabhat
Barabhas Iarach
Barabhas Uarach
Barabhas
Brù
Arnol
LOCH NA MUILNE
BLACK HOUSE MUSEUM
Labost
Bragar
Siabost bho Thuath
Siabost bho Dheas
SHAWBOST NORSE MILL
SHAWBOST MUSEUM
Pairc Shiabost
Bàgh Dhail Beag
GEARRANNAN BLACKHOUSE VILLAGE
GARENIN
Dail Beag
Dail Mor
Na Gearrannan
Borghastan
Carlabhagh
Ciribhig
Dun Chàrlabhaigh
DUN CARLOWAY BROCH
Loch Chàrlabhaigh
Little Bernera
Campay
Floday
Harsgeir
Bostadh
IRON AGE HOUSE
Crothair
An Galan Uigeach
AN CAOLAS
Pabay Mor
Tobson
NORSE MILL
Tolastadh a Chaolais
Loch Ròg an Ear
Vacsay
Bhalasaigh
Breacleit
Great Bernera
Circebost
Barraglom
Tacleit
Iarsiadar
Tobhtarol
Crulabhig
Vuia Mór
Vuia Beag
Aird Uig
Bhaltos
Cnip
Cliobh
Miabhig
Uigen
Riof
Loch Ròg
Floday
Bàgh Fhiabhaig
Timsgearraidh
Cradhlastadh
Càrnais
Ard More Mangersta
Mangurstadh
Eadar Dha Fhadhail
SUAINAVAL
Cairisiadar
Geisiadar
Ungisiadar
Einacleite
Aird Fenish
Aird Brenish
Islibhig
MEALISVAL
Breanais
Mealasta
Loch Suaineabhal
Loch Grunabhat
Loch Chaolartan
Giosla
Loch Fuaroil
BEINN MHEADHONACH
Loch Cro Criosdaig
Loidse Mhorsgail
Loch Morsgail
Loch Coirigerod
Tamanabhagh
Caolas an Ei
a Island
Keava
Eilean Kearstay
Calanais
CALANAIS VISITOR CENTRE
CALANAIS STANDING STONES
CALANAIS SMALL STONE CIRCLES
Gearraidh na h-Aibhne
Linsiadar
Lundal
Loch Smuaisabhal
Loch Tungabhat
Loch Ròg
Scaliscro
Breascleit
Loch Lacasabhat Ard
BEINN BRAGAR
Gleann Bhruthadail
Glen Bragar
Loch Urghag
Loch Breibhat
Gleann Mór Barvas
ISLE OF LEWIS (EILEAN LEODHAIS)
Loch Scarabhat Mhòr
Loch Mór an Stàirr
BEINN MHOLACH
Loch nan Stearnag
Lacasdal
Loch Urabhal
Loch a' Ghainmhich
Acha Mor
ACHMORE STONE CIRCLE
Loch Tobhta Bridein
Loch nam Falcag
Loch Airigh na h-Airde
Loch Trealabhal
Laxay
Soval Lodge
Baile Ailein
Lacasaidh
Abhainn Ghearadha
MUIRNEAG
Bail' Ur Tholastaidh
Tolastadh bho Thuath
Tolsta Head
Loch Sgeireach Mor
Griais
Gleann Thollastaidh
Port Bun a'Ghlinne
Creag Fhraoch
Cnoc an t-Solais
Bac
Col
Col Uarach
Vatisker Pt.
Breibhig
Coll Sands
Aird Thunga
Tunga
Sròn Ruadh
BROAD BAY OR LOCH A TUATH
Grianan
Newmarket
Lacasdal
An Gleann Ur
Cnoc Màiri
LEWS CASTLE & MUS NAN EILEAN
LEWIS LOOM CENTRE
AN LANNTAIR GALLERY
STORNOWAY
Stornoway
Sanndabhaig
Mealabost
Tolm
ST COLUMBA'S
Aiginis
Airinis
Holm I.
Arnish Moor
Loch Orasaigh
Griomsidar
Ben Casgro
Liurbost
Ranais
Raerinish Pt.
Crosbost
Barkin Is.
Tabhaidh Mhor
Eilean Chaluim Chille
Ceos
Crobeag
Cromor
Eilean Orasaidh
Eireasort
ULLAPOOL
A' Chearc
Port Nan Giùran
Rubha an t-Siumpain
Cnoc Amhlaigh
Port Mholair
Aird
Sulaisiadar
Garrabost
EYE PENINSULA
Seisiadar
Pabail Uarach
Pabail Iarach
An Cnoc
Suardail
Bàgh Phabail
306
307

SOUTH LEWIS,
HARRIS AND
CEANN A TUATH NA HEARADH
NORTH UIST
LOCH A SIAR
LOCH LANGABHAT
PARK OR PAIRC
NA HEARADH (HARRIS)
CAOLAS NAN EILEAN
CAOLAS NA HEARADH
HIGHLAND
Kearstay
Scarp
Huisinis
Hushinish Pt.
Beitearsaig
Gobhaig
Horsanish
Forest of Harris
Abhainn Suidhe
Arda Mòra
Clasmol
Miabhag
Bun Abhainn Eadarra
OLD WHALING STATION
Soay Beag
Soay Mór
Taransay Glorigs
Camus an t-suithean
Tarasaigh (Taransay)
Paible
Rubha Sgeirigin
Cul na h-Aird
Aird Asaig
Isay
Leacainn
Taobh Siar
Tairbeart (Tarbert)
Direcleit
Oban
Urgha Beag
Urgha
Losgaintir
LUSKENTYRE BEACH
South Harris Forest
BEN LUSKENTYRE
Caolas Tharasaigh
Seilebost
Horgabost
Borve Lodge
Buirgh
SCARISTA STANDING STONE
Sgarasta Mhor
Toe Head
CHAIPAVAL
Rubha'an Teampuill
Taobh Tuath
SEALLAM!
BLEAVAL
Loch Langabhat
Aird Mhighe
Liceasto
Geocrab
Beacrabhaic
Fleoideabhagh
Manais
Loch Steiseabhat
An t-Ob (Leverburgh)
ROINEABHAL
Fionnsbhagh
Boirseam
Lingreabhagh
Cuidhtinis
Loch Fleoideabhagh
Loch Fionnsbhagh
Lingarabay I.
Roghadal
Borghasdal
ST CLEMENT'S CHURCH
Srannda
Cairminis
Carminish Is.
Ensay
Killegray
Langay
Vallay
Renish Pt.
BERNERAY (N. UIST)
Groay
Gilsay
Lingay
Scaravay
Sursay
Opsay
Tahay
Hermetray
Bàgha Chàise
Groatay
Weaver's Pt.
Madadh Gruamach
UIG
Loch Ceann Dibig
Miabhag
Loch an Tairbeart
Drinisiadar
Kennacley
Plocropol Pt.
Plocrapol
Greosabhagh
Leac a Li
Collam
Cliuthar
Caolas Stocinis
Stockinish I.
Scadabhagh
Rubha Bhocaig
Loch Greosabhagh
Sgeotasaigh
Carragraich
Caolas Scalpaigh
Carnach
Rudha Crago
Scalpay
Ceann a Bhaigh
Eilean Scalpaigh (Scalpay)
Lochan Lacasdail
Reinigeadal
RHENIGIDALE
Loch Trollamarig
Maraig
Eilean Anabaich
Loch Shiphoirt
Scaladal
Aird a' Mhulaidh
Aline Lodge
Seaforth I.
STULAVAL
TIRGA MOR
ULLAVAL
UISGNAVAL MORE
CLISHAM
BEINN MHOR
CRIONAIG
Loch a'Ghlinne
Loch Tealasabhagh
Loch Crabhadail
Loch Bodabhat
Loch Reasort
Abhainn Bheararaigh
Ulladail
Bràighe Mór
Caolas an Scarp
Bàgh Huisinis
Beiniseabhal
Morsgail Forest
Strandabhat
Ceann Tarabhaigh
Airidh a Bhruaich
Aird an Troim
Ceann Shiphoirt
Loch Sgibacleit
Tabost
KERSHADER
Loch nan Eilean
Taobh a' Ghlinne
Grabhair
Marbhig
Calbost
Loch Odhairn
Kebock Head
Tom an Fhuadain
Loch Shanndabhat
Orasaigh
Leumrabhagh
Eisgean
Loch Shell or Loch Sealg
Srianach
Eilean Iubhard
Loch Claidh
Loch Bhrollum
Mol Truisg
Gob Rubh'Uisenis
Rubha Bhrollum
Rubha a'Bhaird
Garbh Eilean
Eilean Mhuire
Na h-Eileanan Mòra (Shiant Islands)
Eilean an Tighe
Fladda-chùain
Eilean Trodday
Rubha Hunish
Rubha na h-Aiseig
Shulista
DUNTULM CASTLE
Duntulm
Balmacqueen
Kilmaluag
Connista
Lub Score
MUSEUM OF ISLAND LIFE
Peingown
Hungladder
Borneskitaig
Heribusta
Eilean Flodigarry
Flodigarry
MEALL NA SUIRAMACH
Staffin I.
Staffin Bay
Kilmuir
FLORA MACDONALD'S MEMORIAL
Kilvaxter
Balgown
Linicro
Totscore
THE QUIRAING
Digg
Glashvin
Brogaig
Garafad
Staffin
Stenscholl
TROTTERNISH
Clachan
Kilt Rock
KILT ROCK & MEALT FALLS
Waternish Point
A859
B887
B8060
307
298
296
NG
0 2 4 6 miles
0 2 4 6 8 10 km

CAPE WRATH
Kearvaig
371 SGRIBHIS-BHEINN
Geodha Ruadh na Fola
Bay of Keisgaig
Inshore
Loch Keisgaig
308
Achie
Geodha Ruadh
457 FASHVEN
Am Balg
423 BEINN DEARG
Sandwood Loch
485 CREAG RIABHACH
Rubh'an Fhir Léithe
Loch na Gainimh
Strath Shinary
332 GHLAS BHEINN
Sheigra
Balchrick
Blairmore
Droman
Oldshore Beg
Oldshoremore
Eilean Roin Mor
521 FARRMHEALL
Rhig
Gualin Ho.
19
Loch Clash
Kinlochbervie
Badcall
B801
Inshegra
Achriesgill
Bagh Loch an Roin
Loch Inchard
Rhivichie
9
Achlyness
L. na Claise Carnaich
Loch Dughaill
Ceathramh Garbh
Rhiconich
Ardmore Pt.
Rubha Ruadh
Ardmore
Portlevorchy
Skerricha
A838
GANU MOR 908
Foinaven
Fanagmore
Tarbet
NORTH-WEST SUTHERLAND
Loch Laxford
Loch a'Garbh-bhaid Mòr
Loch Dionard
Handa Island
Foindle
Loch nam Brac
A894
Laxford Bridge
Loch an Easa Uaine
Sound of Handa
Badnabay
787 ARKLE
Scourie Bay
Scourie More
Scourie
Gorm Loch
Laxford
Lochstack Lodge
Rubh'Aird an t-Sionnaich
308
Stack
719 BEN STACK
Upper Badcall
Lower Badcall
Strath Stack
Airdachuilinn
Badcall Bay
18
BEINN AUSKAIRD 386
Achfary
332
Eil. a'Bhreitheimh
Duartbeg
Loch Crocach
REAY FOREST
Rubha a'Mhucard
A894
Lochmore Lodge
Meall Mór
Calbha Mór
Duartmore Bridge
Loch More
Loch na Creige Duibhe
Point of Stoer
Oldany Island
Eddrachillis Bay
Calbha Beag
Duartmore Forest
Loch a'Chairn Bhain
Loch an Leathaid Bhuain
Cirean Geardail
R. nan Còsan
Eilean Chrona
Culkein Drumbeg
Loch Nedd
Kylestrome
547 Forest
161
Ardvar
Glendhu
Rubha Stoer
Culkein
Clashnessie Bay
Oldany
Kylesku
Loch Glendhu
Gleann
Dubh
Cluas Deas
Drumbeg
B869
Unapool
566
Achnacarnin
Nedd
8
530 BEINN AIRD DA LOCH
Clashmore
Loch Poll
Glenleraig
Newton
Loch Glencoul
70
80
NB
30
80
NC
1
2
3
4
5
6
7
8
A
B
C
D
E
F

Stoer
Clachtoll
Rubh'a' Mhill Dheirg
Bay of Stoer
R. Leumair
Achmelvich Bay
Rhicarn
Achmelvich
Rubha Rodha
Baddidarach
Lochinver
Soyea I.
Loch Inver
Kirkaig Pt.
Badnaban
A'Chleit
Strathan
Loch Kirkaig
Inverkirkaig
Rubha na Breige
Eilean Mór
Rubha Coigeach
ENARD BAY
Camas Eilean Ghlais
Rubha Mor
Reiff
Rubh'a' Choin
Inverpolly Lodge
Brae of Achnahaird
Altandhu
SUMMER ISLES SMOKEHOUSE
Eilean Mullagrach
Loch Vatachan
Isle Ristol
Polbain
Glas-leac Mór
Aird of Coigach
Loch Osgaig
Achiltibuie
Tanera Beg
Badentarbat Bay
Polglass
BEN MOR COIGACH
Badenscallie
Summer Isles
Tanera Mór
Horse Sound
ACHININVER
Glas-leac Beag
Horse I.
Achduart
Culnacraig
BEINN MOR COIGACH
Eilean Dubh
Priest I.
Bottle I.
Carn nan Sgeir
Loch an Leothaid
Loch Crócach
Loch Beannach
Lochassynt Lodge
QUINAG
Little Assynt
Brackloch
Glencanisp Lodge
Loch Fe...
ARDVRECK CASTLE
Skiag Bridge
EAS COUL AULIN WATERFALL
BEINN UIDHE
BEINN LEOID
Loch an Eircill
Gorm Loch Mór
Inchnadamph
Inchnadamph Forest
ASSYNT-
COIGACH
Glencanisp
SUILVEN
Forest
Fionn Loch
Loch na Gainimh
CANISP
Stronchrubie
BEN MORE ASSYNT
MEALL AN AONAICH
Falls
Rhegreanoch
Loch Awe
Cam Loch
Loch Veyatie
Loch Sionascaig
Polly
Ledmore
Altnacealgach Hotel
Loch Ailsh
Benmore Lodge
Inverpolly Forest
STAC POLLAIDH
CUL MOR
Drumrunie Forest
Loch an Doire Dhuibh
Elphin
Knockan
Loch Urigill
KNOCKAN CRAG
Loch Bad a'Ghaill
Linneraineach
CUL BEAG
Loch Lurgainn
HIGHLAND
CROMALT HILLS
Drumrunie
Loch Craggie
COIGACH
Langwell Lodge
Strathcanaird
Rappach
Strath nan Lon
MEALL AN FHUARAIN
Blughasary
Strath Kanaird
Keonchulish
Camas Mór
Isle Martin
Loch Kanaird
STORNOWAY
Greenstone Point
Cailleach Hd.
Annat Bay
Rubha Beag
Opinan
Ardmair
Rhue
ISLE MARTIN MICRO MUSEUM
Allt Beinn Donuill
Rappach Water
Duag Bridge
Rhidorroch Forest
Scoraig
Carnach
Stattic Pt.
Rubha Mor
LITTLE LOCH BROOM
Mellon Udrigle
Rireavach
Morefield
Ullapool
Loch Achall
Rhidorroch Ho.
ULLAPOOL MUSEUM
Loch an Daimh
Glen Achall
Gruinard I.
Badluarach
BEINN GHOBHLACH
Mungasdale
Achgarve
Dumamuck
Braes of Ullapool
East Rhidorroch Lodge
Strath Mulzie
Corriemulzie Lodge
Srón a' Gheodha Dhuibh
Eilean Furadh Mór
Rubha Reidh
Camas Mór
Gruinard Bay
Gruinard House
Allt na h-Airbhe
BEINN EILIDEACH
LECKMELM SHRUBBERY AND ARBORETUM
Mellon Charles
Laide
First Coast
Badcaul
Badrallach
Leckmelm
Loch an Draing
Cove
Ormiscaig
Bualnaluib
Sand
Second Coast
Inchina
Badbea
Blarnalearoch
MEALL DUBH
MEALL NAM BRADHAN
Loch a'Choire Mhoir
Tighnafiline
Isle of Ewe
Little Gruinard
Ardessie
Camusnagaul
Rhiroy
Ardcharnich
Dòuchary
AN CUAIDH
Mellangaun
Aultbea
Firemore
Drumchork
Loch a'Bhaid-luachraich
SAIL MHOR
Dundonnell Hotel
Dundonnell
Ardindrean
SEANA BHRAIGH
Loch Sguod
Melvaig
Inverasdale
LOCH EWE
Strath Beag
Eilean Darach
Letters
Aultgrishan
Midtown
Little Gruinard
Loch Fada
Dundonnell House
Inverlael Forest
Seana Chamas
Brae
Rubha 'Ard na Bà
AN TEALLACH
Strathnasheallag Forest
Inverlael
LAEL FOREST GARDEN
Lael Forest
Lael
Clachan Inverbroom
Naast
Tournaig
Aird Dubh
Loch na Sealga
Peterburn
Auchlunachan
Gleann B
Loch Bad a'Chreamh
INVEREWE GARDEN
BEINN A'CHAISGEIN BEAG
Dundonnell
Forest
Port Erradale
Londubh
Fisherfield Forest
Auchindrean
Broom
BEINN DEARG
North Erradale
Poolewe
Loch Kernsary
Achneigie
Strath na Sealga
Strath More
Braemore
Rubha Bàn
Big Sand
BEINN DEARG MHOR
Fain
Tollomuick For.
Longa Island
CARN DEARG
Lonemore
Mial
Strath
Kernsary
Inveran
CORRIESHALLOCH GORGE
Caol Beag
Smithstown
GAIRLOCH MUSEUM
Gairloch
Loch Maree
FIONN LOCH
Dubh Loch
MEALL AN DOIREAN
BEINN A' CHLAIDHEIMH
MEALL LEACAC
Abhainn Cuileig
Dundonnell
Dirri
CARN BAN
Freevater
0 2 4 6 miles
0 2 4 6 8 10 km
NG
NH
304
305
309
299
G
H
J
K
L
1
2
3
4
5
6
7
8
A837
A894
A835
A832
B869
B8021
B8057

CAPE WRATH
Kearvaig
Geodha Ruadh na Fola
Bay of Keisgaig
Geodha Ruadh
Am Balg
Loch Keisgaig
Sandwood Loch
Strath Shinary
Sheigra
Balchrick
Blairmore
Droman
Oldshore Beg
Oldshoremore
Kinlochbervie
Badcall
Inshegra
Achriesgill
Rhivichie
Achlyness
Ceathramh Garbh
Rhiconich
Ardmore
Portlevorchy
Skerricha
Foindle
Laxford Bridge
Badnabay
Scourie
Lower Badcall
Lochstack Lodge
Achfary
Lochmore Lodge
Airdachuilinn
Kylestrome
Kylesku
Unapool
Newton
Ardvar
Duartmore Bridge
Kinloch
Aultanrynie
West Merkland
NORTH-WEST SUTHERLAND
REAY FOREST
Loch Dionard
Strath Dionard
Foinaven
Arkle
Ben Stack
Gualin Ho.
Rhigolter
Inshore
Achiemore
Keoldale
Sangomore
Balnakeil
Durness
Smoo Cave
Leirinmore
Sangobeg
Rispond
Faraid Head
Sarsgrum
Kyle of Durness
Loch Eriboll
Eilean Hoan
Eilean Choraidh
Portnancon
Eriboll
Kempie
Heilam
Polla
Strath Beag
Whiten Head
Hope
Lochside
Loch Hope
Ben Hope
Strathmore
Alltnacaillich
Dun Dornaigil Broch
Gobernuisgach Lodge
Glen Golly
A'Mhoine
Rubha Thormaid
Achuvoldrach
Kyle of Tongue
Tongue
Castle Varrich
Kirkiboll
Rhitongue
Ribigill
Kinloch Lodge
Ben Loyal
Loch Loyal
Loch Loyal Lodge
Inchkinloch
Altnaharra
Mudale
Clebrig
Loch Naver
Strathan
Midfield
Portvasgo
Talmine
Skinnet
Midtown
Rabbit Is.
Eilean nan Ron
Skerray
Coldbackie
Borgie
Borgie Forest
Torrisdale
Invernaver
Bettyhill
Strathnaver Museum
Farr
Swordly
Kirtomy
Armadale
Lednagullin
Strathy Forest
Leckfurin
Skelpick
Achanlochy Clearance Village
Achagary
Carnachy
Rhifail
Strathnaver
Skail
Langdale
Syre
Dalvina Lo.
Rosal Clearance Trail
Grumbeg
Naver Forest
Garvault Hotel
Badanloch Forest
Badanloch Lodge
HIGHLAND

LOCH SHIN
Shin Forest
Oykel Forest
Amat Forest
Strath Oykel
Glen Cassley
Strath Tirry
Strath Fleet
Strathcarron
Strath Brora
BEN ARMINE FOREST
EASTER ROSS
DORNOCH FIRTH
ASSYNT-COIGACH
CROMALT HILLS
Rhidorroch Forest
Inverlael Forest
Freevater Forest
Benmore Forest
Inchnadamph Forest
Morangie Forest
Lairg
Bonar Bridge
Dornoch
Tain
Edderton
Ardgay
Invershin
Rosehall
Oykel Bridge
Ledmore
Inchnadamph
Elphin
Knockan
Drumrunie
Crask Inn
Overscaig Hotel
Altnacealgach Hotel
Skiag Bridge
Lochassynt Lodge
Little Assynt
Rogart
Pittentrail
Kirkton
Embo
Spinningdale
Clashmore
Skibo Castle
Loch Fleet
Loch Migdale
Loch Craggie
Loch Ailsh
Loch Urigill
Cam Loch
Loch Awe
Fionn Loch Mor
Loch a'Ghriama
Loch an Daimh
Loch na Claise Moire
Loch Buidhe
Loch Laro
Strath Mulzie
Glen Einig
Glen Achall
Strath nan Lon
Strath More
Rappach Water
Corriemulzie Lodge
Deanich Lodge
Alladale Lodge
Glencalvie Lodge
Kildermorie Lodge
The Craigs
Croich
Amatnatua
Culrain
Carbisdale Castle
Falls of Shin Visitor Centre
Ferrycroft Visitor Centre
Knockan Crag
Ardvreck Castle
Eas Coul Aulin Waterfall
Corrieshalloch Gorge
Leckmelm Shrubbery and Arboretum
Lael Forest Garden
Croich Church
Hector Macdonald Monument
Glenmorangie Distillery
Tain Through Time Visitor Centre
Dornoch Cathedral
Historylinks
Witches Stone
Skelbo Castle
Whiteness Sands
Dornoch Sands
Cambuscurrie Bay
1084 BEINN DEARG
927 SEANA BHRAIGH
364 AN STUC
838 CARN CHUINNEAG
998 BEN MORE ASSYNT
718 BREABAG
715 MEALL AN AONAICH
704 BEN ARMINE
961 MEALL NAN CON
849 CUL MOR
808 QUINAG
A836
A837
A838
A839
A835
A949
A9
B9168
B9176
A894
311
307
300
301
6 miles
10 km

DUNCANSBY HEAD
Stacks of Duncansby
John o' Groats
Island of Stroma
Nethertown
Uppertown
Langaton Point
Red Head
Mell Head
Men of Mey
St John's Pt.
Boars of Duncansby
Gills Bay
Huna
Canisbay
Kirkstyle
Gills
Freswick
Freswick Bay
Skirza Head
Skirza
Tofts
Ness Head
BUCHOLLY CASTLE
CAITHNESS BROCH CENTRE
Auckengill
Brough Head
Nybster
KEISS CASTLE
Keiss
Stain
SINCLAIR'S BAY
CASTLE SINCLAIR
CASTLE GIRNIGOE
Noss Head
Noss
Sealky Head
Staxigoe
Papigoe
Broadhaven
Wick Bay
Wick
WICK HERITAGE MUS
Ackergill
Old Wick
South Hd.
CASTLE OF OLD WICK
Gote O'Tram
Hempriggs House
Helman Hd.
Newton
Whiterow
Thrumster
Sarclet
Sarclet Hd.
Mains of Ulbster
Ulbster
Whaligoe
Bruan
Lybster
Invershore
Latheronwheel
Latheron
LAIDHAY CROFT
Knockinnon
Dunbeath Water
Braemore
CLAN GUNN HERITAGE CENTRE
Forse
Swiney
Camster
GREY CAIRNS OF CAMSTER
Rumster Forest
Watten
Loch Watten
Mybster
Spittal
Halkirk
Thurso
Thurso Bay
THURSO CASTLE
Scrabster
Holborn Hd.
Spear Hd.
Brims Ness
Brims Castle
Crosskirk
Bridge of Forss
DUNNET HEAD
Briga Hd.
Dunnet
Dunnet Bay
NATURAL HISTORY VISITOR CENTRE
Castletown
Castlehill
Murkle
Clardon
Clardon Hd.
Brough
Hunspow
The Thirl
MARY ANN'S COTTAGE
St John's Loch
CASTLE OF MEY
East Mey
Mey
Scarfskerry Pt.
Scarfskerry
Ham
Rattar
Barrock
Corsback
Inkstack
STROMNESS
Reay
Sandside Bay
Sandside Ho.
Fresgoe
Red Pt.
Dounreay
Isauld
Achvarasdal
Strathy Point
Strathy Bay
Strathy
Melvich
Melvich Bay
Portskerra
Bighouse
Baligill
Golval
STRATH HALLADALE
Achiemore
Craigtown
Dalhalvaig
Forsinain
Forsinard
Forsinard Station
FORSINARD FLOWS
Kinbrace
Achentoul
Lochside
Badanloch Lodge
Badanloch Forest
Garvault Hotel
Achentoul Forest
Armadale
Armadale Bay
Lednagullin
Aultiphurst
Brawl
Totegan
Altnabreac Station
Lochdhu
Dalnawillan Lodge
Strathmore Lodge
Loch Calder
Loch Shurrery
Loch Dubh nan Geodh
Loch Sletill
Loch Strathy
Strathy Forest
BEN GRIAM BEG
BEN GRIAM MORE
BEN ALISKY
Knockfin Heights
Glutt Lodge
HIGHLAND
BURWICK (May-Sept)
ST MARGARETS HOPE

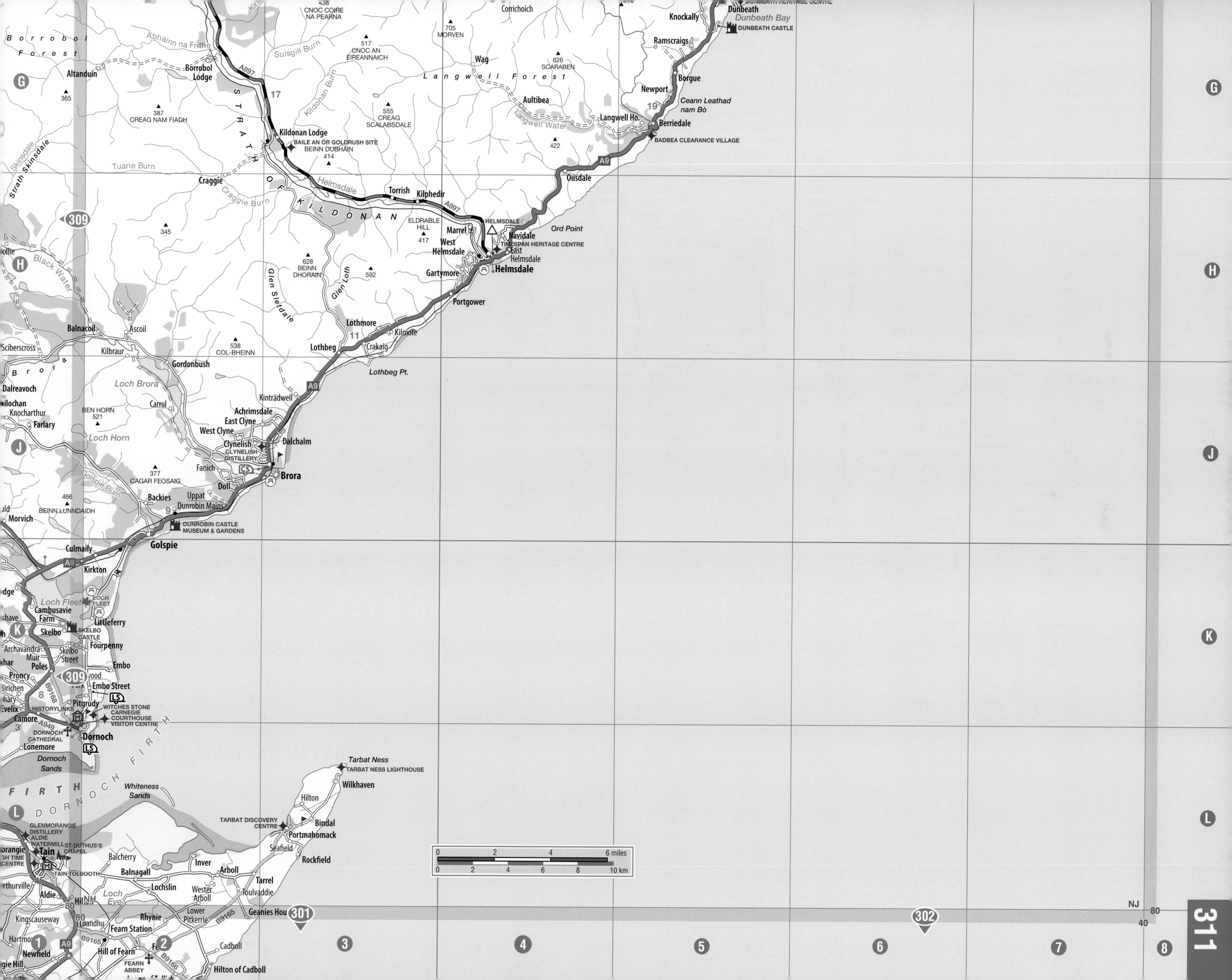
Borrobol Forest
Abhainn na Frithe
Altanduin
Borrobol Lodge
365
387
CREAG NAM FIADH
Strath Skinsdale
Skinsdale
Tuarie Burn
A897
17
STRATH OF KILDONAN
Kildonan Lodge
BAILE AN OR GOLDRUSH SITE
BEINN DUBHAIN
414
Suisgill Burn
Kildonan Burn
CNOC COIRE NA PEARNA
517
CNOC AN EIREANNAICH
555
CREAG SCALABSDALE
705
MORVEN
Wag
Corrichoich
Langwell Forest
626
SCARABEN
Aultibea
Langwell Water
422
Langwell Ho.
Knockally
Dunbeath
Dunbeath Bay
DUNBEATH CASTLE
Ramscraigs
Borgue
Newport
19
Ceann Leathad nam Bò
Berriedale
BADBEA CLEARANCE VILLAGE
A9
Ousdale
Craggie
Craggie Burn
Helmsdale
Torrish
Kilphedir
ELDRABLE HILL
417
Marrel
West Helmsdale
HELMSDALE
Navidale
Ord Point
TIMESPAN HERITAGE CENTRE
East Helmsdale
Helmsdale
Gartymore
Portgower
309
345
Black Water
628
BEINN DHORAIN
Glen Sletdale
Glen Loth
592
Lothmore
Kilmote
11
Lothbeg
Crakaig
Lothbeg Pt.
Balnacoil
Ascoil
Sciberscross
Kilbraur
538
COL-BHEINN
Gordonbush
Brora
Loch Brora
Dalreavoch
Knocharthur
Farlary
BEN HORN
521
Loch Horn
Carrol
Kintradwell
Achrimsdale
East Clyne
West Clyne
Clynelish
CLYNELISH DISTILLERY
Dalchalm
Fanich
377
CAGAR FEOSAIG
Brora
Golspie Burn
466
BEINN LUNNDAIDH
Morvich
Backies
Uppat
Doll
Dunrobin Mains
9
DUNROBIN CASTLE MUSEUM & GARDENS
Culmaily
Golspie
Kirkton
Loch Fleet
LOCH FLEET
Cambusavie Farm
Littleferry
Skelbo
SKELBO CASTLE
Archavandra Muir
Skelbo Street
Fourpenny
Poles
Embo
Pronc y
Embo Street
B9168
8
HISTORYLINKS
Pitgrudy
WITCHES STONE
CARNEGIE COURTHOUSE
VISITOR CENTRE
Camore
A949
DORNOCH CATHEDRAL
Dornoch
Lonemore
Dornoch Sands
DORNOCH FIRTH
Whiteness Sands
Tarbat Ness
TARBAT NESS LIGHTHOUSE
Wilkhaven
Hilton
TARBAT DISCOVERY CENTRE
Bindal
Portmahomack
Seafield
Rockfield
GLENMORANGIE DISTILLERY
ALDIE WATERMILL
ST DUTHUS'S CHAPEL
Tain
TAIN TOLBOOTH
Balcherry
Balnagall
Inver
Arboll
Tarrel
Lochslin
Loch Eye
Wester Arboll
Toulvaddie
Aldie
Hill
NH
80
Kingscauseway
Loandhu
Rhynie
Lower Pitkerrie
B9165
Geanies Hou
301
Fearn Station
Hartmo
Newfield
A9
Hill of Fearn
FEARN ABBEY
B9166
Cadboll
Hilton of Cadboll
0
2
4
6 miles
0
2
4
6
8
10 km
NJ
80
40
302
G
H
J
K
L
1
2
3
4
5
6
7
8

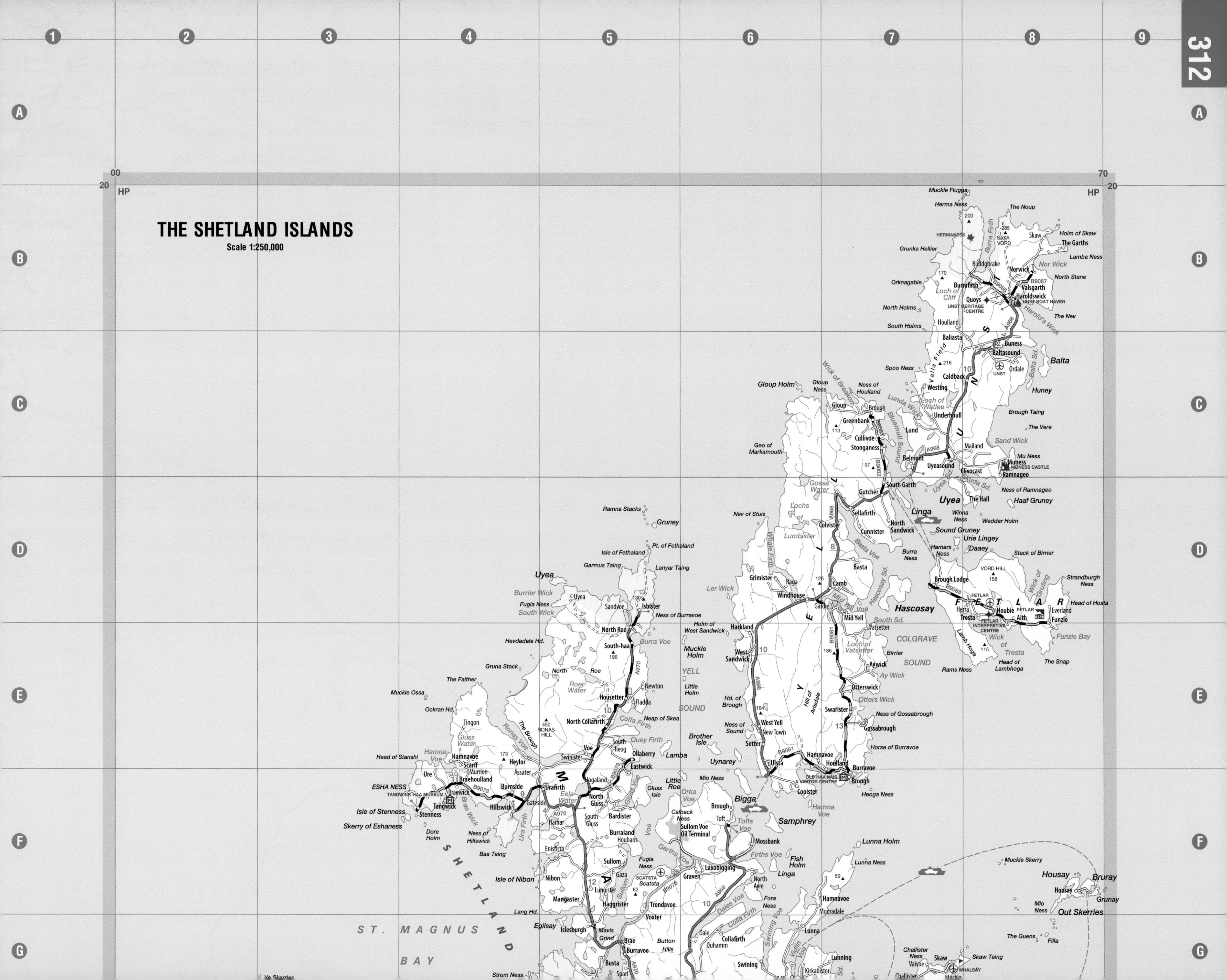
THE SHETLAND ISLANDS
Scale 1:250,000
Muckle Flugga
Herma Ness
The Noup
Holm of Skaw
The Garths
Lamba Ness
North Stane
The Nev
Haroldswick
Baltasound
Balta
Huney
Uyeasound
Belmont
Uyea
Linga
Hascosay
Colgrave Sound
Fetlar
Houbie
Funzie
Gutcher
Cullivoe
Mid Yell
Burravoe
Ulsta
West Yell
Whale Firth
Yell Sound
Bigga
Samphrey
Sullom Voe Oil Terminal
Brae
Voxter
Hillswick
Esha Ness
Stenness
Ronas Hill
North Roe
Isbister
Lunna Holm
Housay
Bruray
Grunay
Out Skerries
St. Magnus Bay
Shetland

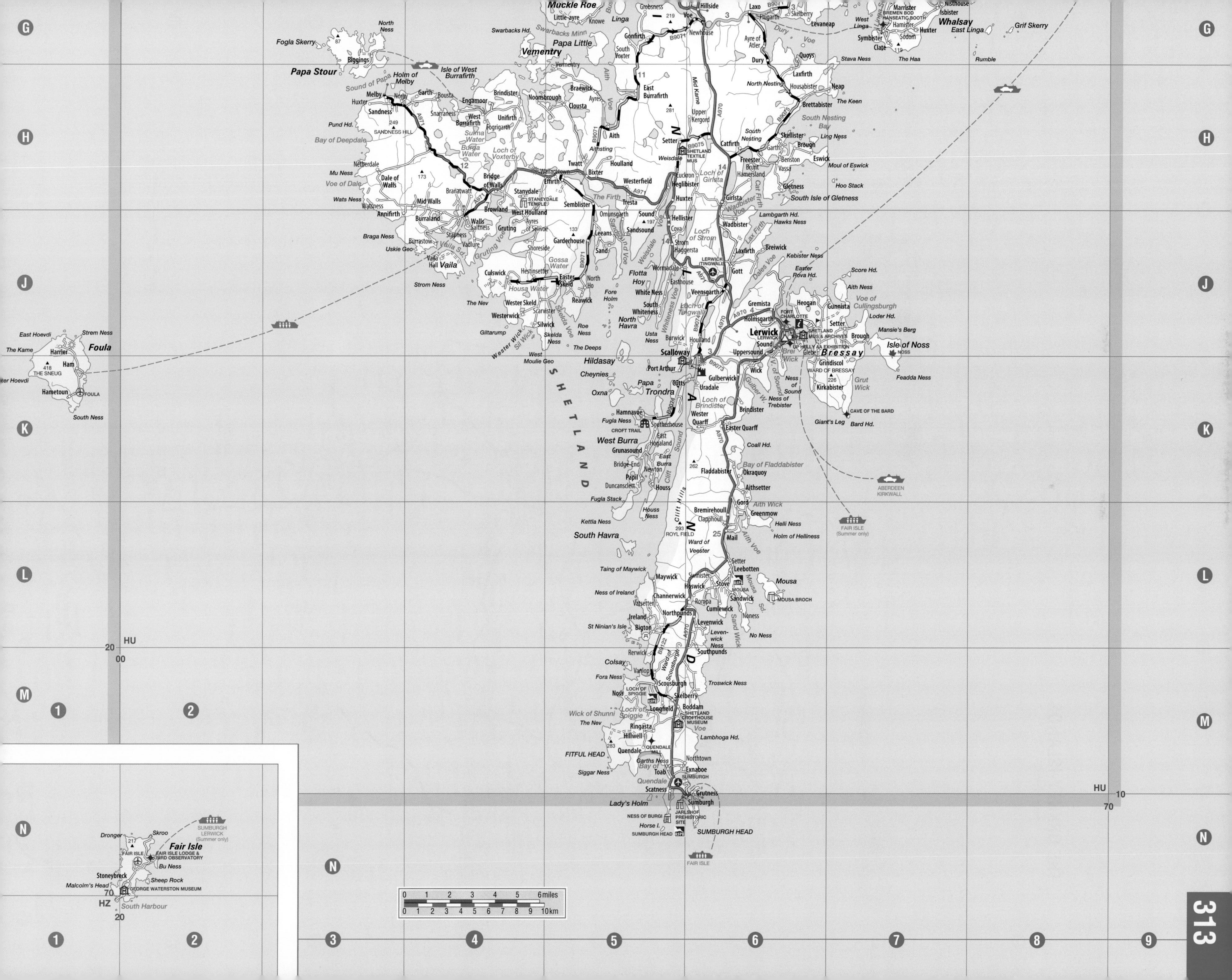
SHETLAND
Muckle Roe
Papa Little
Vementry
Papa Stour
Fogla Skerry
Isle of West Burrafirth
Holm of Melby
Sound of Papa
Melby
Sandness
Huxter
Bay of Deepdale
Voe of Dale
Dale of Walls
Mid Walls
Walls
Bridge of Walls
Vaila
Foula
The Sneug
Hametoun
Harrier
Ham
Strom Ness
East Hoevdi
The Kame
South Ness
Whalsay
East Linga
Grif Skerry
Symbister
Laxo
Skelberry
Voe
Hillside
Aith
Bixter
Twatt
Weisdale
Setter
Mid Kame
Catfirth
South Nesting
Girlista
Wadbister
Laxfirth
Gott
Tingwall
Veensgarth
Gremista
Lerwick
Bressay
Isle of Noss
Voe of Cullingsburgh
Grut Wick
Cave of the Bard
Bard Hd.
Giant's Leg
Hildasay
Scalloway
Port Arthur
Papa
Trondra
Oxna
Cheynies
Hamnavoe
West Burra
East Burra
Papil
Houss
Fugla Stack
Kettla Ness
South Havra
Clift Hills
Royl Field
Fladdabister
Bay of Fladdabister
Brindister
Easter Quarff
Wester Quarff
Gulberwick
Uradale
Aith Wick
Aithsetter
Bremirehoull
Mail
Aith Voe
Cunningsburgh
Mousa
Mousa Broch
Sandwick
Leebotten
Hoswick
Channerwick
Maywick
Bigton
St Ninian's Isle
Levenwick
Southpunds
Colsay
Scousburgh
Loch of Spiggie
Boddam
Shetland Crofthouse Museum
Quendale
Fitful Head
Toab
Bay of Quendale
Sumburgh
Grutness
Jarlshof Prehistoric Site
Sumburgh Head
Lady's Holm
Horse I.
Ness of Burgi
Aberdeen Kirkwall
Fair Isle (Summer only)
Fair Isle
Sumburgh Lerwick (Summer only)
Fair Isle Lodge & Bird Observatory
George Waterston Museum
Skroo
Dronger
Stoneybreck
Malcolm's Head
South Harbour
Sheep Rock
Bu Ness
A970
A971
B9071
0 1 2 3 4 5 6 miles
0 1 2 3 4 5 6 7 8 9 10 km
HU
HZ

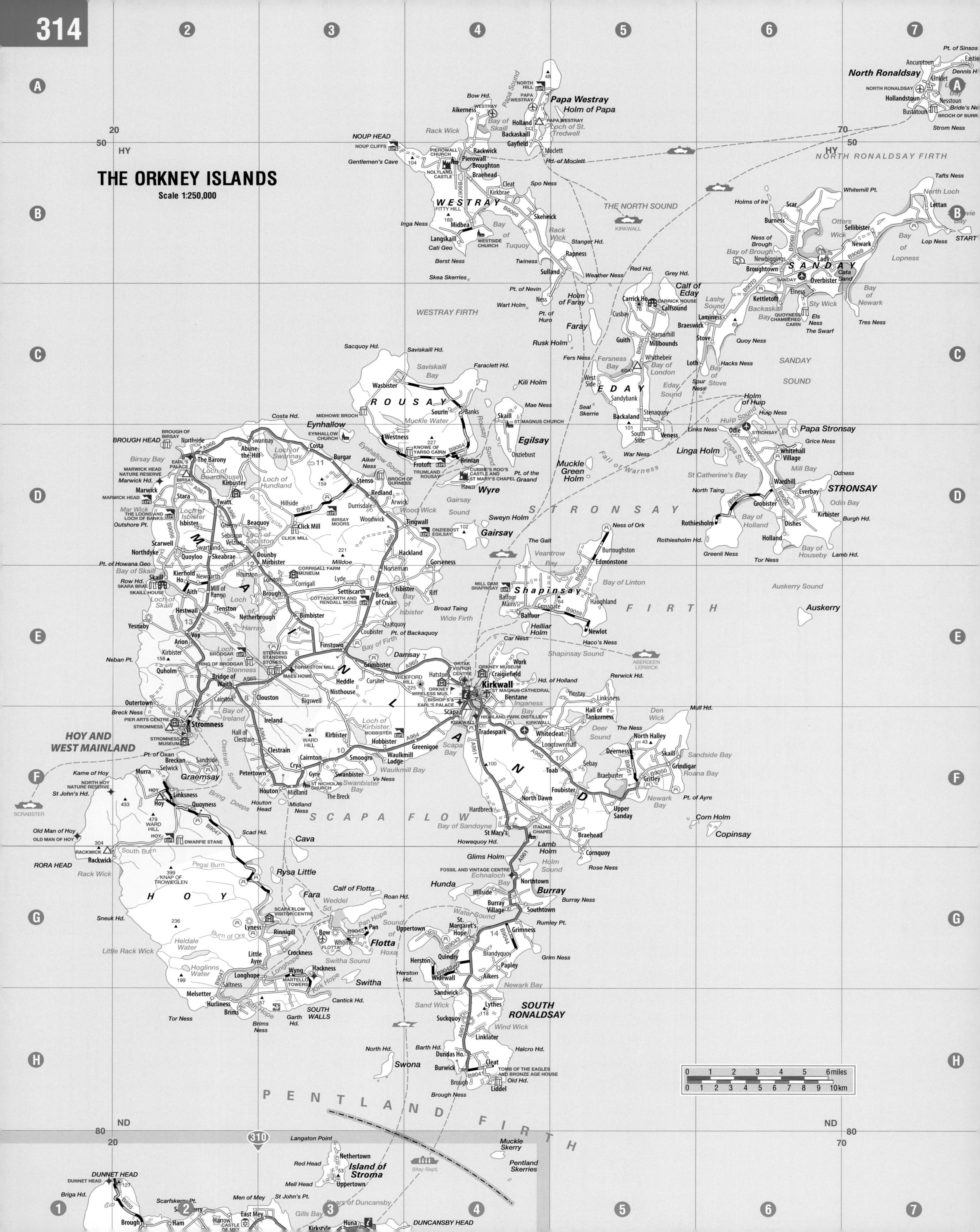
THE ORKNEY ISLANDS
Scale 1:250,000
North Ronaldsay
Hollandstoun
Bustatoun
Dennis Hd.
Strom Ness
NORTH RONALDSAY FIRTH
Papa Westray
Holm of Papa
NOUP HEAD
Noltland Castle
WESTRAY
Pierowall
Rackwick
Broughton
Fitty Hill
Midbea
Inga Ness
Langskaill
Rapness
Tuquoy
WESTRAY FIRTH
THE NORTH SOUND
SANDAY
Kettletoft
Lady
Overbister
Stove
Tres Ness
Calf of Eday
Calfsound
Carrick Ho.
EDAY
Faray
Holm of Faray
SANDAY SOUND
Papa Stronsay
STRONSAY
Whitehall Village
Odness
Rothiesholm
Holland
Auskerry
Auskerry Sound
Linga Holm
ROUSAY
Wasbister
Sourin
Brinian
Frotoft
Trumland
Eynhallow
Egilsay
Wyre
Gairsay
Muckle Green Holm
S T R O N S A Y   F I R T H
Shapinsay
Balfour
Haco's Ness
Helliar Holm
Shapinsay Sound
ABERDEEN LERWICK
BROUGH HEAD
Birsay
Marwick
Twatt
Dounby
Skaill
Skara Brae
Stenness
Evie
Tingwall
Finstown
Stenness
Ring of Brodgar
Maes Howe
Harray
Bridge of Waith
Stromness
Orphir
Kirkwall
St Magnus Cathedral
Bishop's & Earl's Palace
Highland Park Distillery
Scapa
Inganess Bay
Deer Sound
Tankerness
Mull Hd.
Toab
Deerness
Copinsay
Corn Holm
M A I N L A N D
HOY AND WEST MAINLAND
Graemsay
Hoy
Linksness
Old Man of Hoy
Rackwick
Rora Head
Ward Hill
Lyness
Longhope
Flotta
Fara
Cava
Rysa Little
Swona
SOUTH WALLS
Switha
Brims Ness
Tor Ness
SCAPA FLOW
Houton
Hunda
Burray
St Mary's
Lamb Holm
Italian Chapel
Glims Holm
St. Margaret's Hope
SOUTH RONALDSAY
Herston
Widewall
Burwick
Brough Ness
Tomb of the Eagles
PENTLAND FIRTH
Muckle Skerry
Pentland Skerries
Island of Stroma
DUNNET HEAD
DUNCANSBY HEAD
Huna
SCRABSTER
0 1 2 3 4 5 6 miles
0 1 2 3 4 5 6 7 8 9 10km

BRISTOL
AVONMOUTH
PATCHWAY
FILTON
KINGSWOOD
Easter Compton
Over
Compton Greenfield
Wildlife Place Project
Cribbs Causeway
Mall Sh Ctr
Aerospace Bristol Museum
Catbrain
Planet Ice
Berwick
Hallen
Bradley Stoke
Little Stoke
Great Stoke
Broad Mead
Stoke Gifford
Harry Stoke
Bristol Parkway
Winterbourne
Winterbourne Down
North Corner
Frampton Cotterell
Frampton End
Watley's End
Mayshill
Coalpit Heath
Ram Hill
Kendleshire
Henfield
Pye Corner
Whiteshill
Lyde Green
Depot
Avonmouth Docks
The Royal Portbury Dock
Lawrence Weston
Blaise Castle House
Blaise Castle
Henbury
Brentry
Southmead
Filton Abbey Wood
Frenchay
Bromley Heath
Downend
Emersons Green
Mangotsfield
Roman Villa
Shirehampton
Portway Parkway
Westbury on Trym
Eastfield
Henleaze
Horfield
Memorial Stadium (Bristol Rovers FC)
Lockleaze
Broomhill
River Frome
Fishponds
Sea Mills
Golden Hill
Stoke Bishop
Pill
Gordano Services
Easton-in-Gordano
Ham Green
Portbury
Westbury Park
Bishopston
The Bristol County Ground
Ashley Down
Stapleton
Eastville
Hillfields
Shortwood
Soundwell
Siston
Sneyd Park
Redland
Clay Hill
Speedwell
Goose Green
Siston Common
Webb's Heath
Leigh Woods
Abbots Leigh
Clifton Down
Cotham
Montpelier
Stapleton Road
Warmley
Avon Gorge
Clifton Suspension Bridge
Clifton
Cabot Tower
St. George
Crew's Hole
Lower Failand
Bridge Yate
North Common
Hotwells
SS Great Britain
Arnolfini
Bristol Temple Meads
River Avon
St. Anne's Park
Conham
Hanham
Cadbury Heath
Oldland Station
Tyntesfield
Failand
Tyntesfield Plantation
Ashton Court Estate
Bower Ashton
Bedminster
Ashton Gate (Bristol City FC & Bristol Bears Rugby)
Windmill Hill
Arno's Vale
Broom Hill
Oldland
Longwell Green
Hanham Green
Avon Valley Railway
Bitton
Clean Air Zone
Ashton Vale
Knowle
Brislington
Lower Knowle
Cambridge Batch
Long Ashton
Bedminster Down
Filwood Park
Novers Park
Flowers Hill
Flax Bourton
Headley Park
Hengrove
Stockwood
Keynsham
Avon Valley Adventure & Wildlife Park
Barrow Wood
Highridge
Hartcliffe
Withywood
Whitchurch
Barrow Gurney
Barrow Common
AVON RING ROAD
PORTWAY
BRUNEL WAY
HENGROVE WAY
BRIDGWATER ROAD
WELLS ROAD
BATH ROAD
KEYNSHAM BY-PASS
M4
M5
M32
M49
A4
A38
A37
A369
A370
A403
A420
A431
A432
A4018
A4032
A4162
A4174
A4175
A3029
P&R
0 1 2 miles
0 1 2 3 km

WOLVERHAMPTON
WILLENHALL
Bentley
WALSALL
BILSTON
DARLASTON
WEDNESBURY
COSELEY
SEDGLEY
TIPTON
Upper Gornal
Wren's Nest NNR
BLACK COUNTRY LIVING MUSEUM
DUDLEY ZOO & CASTLE
The Black Country
Gornalwood
DUDLEY
Himley Park
HIMLEY HALL
BAGGERIDGE COUNTRY PARK
Nature Centre
WEST BROMWICH
Lyndon
NEWTON
SANDWELL VALLEY COUNTRY PARK
THE HAWTHORNS
Sandwell
Oakham
OLDBURY
Pensnett
Netherton
Merry Hill Centre
ROWLEY REGIS
Langley Green
SMETHWICK
Wordsley
THE RED HOUSE GLASS CONE
BRIERLEY HILL
Old Hill
Blackheath
AMBLECOTE
Hurst Green
Warley Woods
Lye
Cradley
World's End
STOURBRIDGE
HALESOWEN
WOODGATE VALLEY COUNTRY PARK
Pedmore
Wychbury Hill
HALESOWEN ABBEY (REMS)
Woodgate
Weoley Castle
Hagley Wood
Uffmoor Wood
Twiland Wood
FRANKLEY SERVICES
Bartley Resr
Hagley Park
Hagley
Shenley
Fields
HAGLEY
M5
M6
A454
A41
A4123
A461
A459
A456
A458
A491
A4036

Clean Air Zone
Hardwick
Four Oaks
Streetly
Middleton
New Park Wood
Bracebridge Pool
Blackroot Pool
Upper Nut Hurst
Sutton Park National Nature Reserve
Keeper's Pool
Doe Bank Wood
Westwood Coppice
Holly Hurst
Wyndley Pool
Powell's Pool
Pheasey
SUTTON COLDFIELD
Reddicap Heath
Town Hall
Sutton Coldfield Visitor Centre
Ash End House Farm
New Hall Country Park
Kingstanding
Wylde Green
Over Green
Short Heath
Walmley
Hamstead
Nature Centre
Alexander Stadium
Perry Park
Witton Lakes
Erdington
Curdworth
Minworth
Castle Vale
Water Orton
WATER ORTON
Villa Park
Aston Hall
Aston
Castle Bromwich
Castle Bromwich Hall
Bromford
Winson Green
Jewellery Quarter
BIRMINGHAM
Kingshurst
Lea Hall
Edgbaston Resr
Utilita Arena Birmingham
Nat Sea Life
Conv Ctr
Brindley Place
Birmingham New Street
Moor Street
Thinktank
St Andrew's Stadium
Birmingham Eco Park
Blakesley Hall
Bordesley Green
Yardley
Garet's Green
Marston Green
Lyndon Green
Sheldon Country Park
Birmingham Botanical Gardens
Edgbaston
Tyseley Locomotive Works
Birmingham International Airport
Sheldon
Cannon Hill Park
Nature Centre
Moseley
Acock's Green
Selly Park
Selly Oak
Moor Green
Elmdon Park
Sarehole Mill
Ulverley Green
Selly Manor
Cadbury World
Stirchley
Bournville
Hampton Coppice
Lode Heath
River Tame
Birmingham & Fazeley Canal
Grand Union Canal
Worcester and Birmingham Canal
Tame Valley Canal
River Cole
M6
M6 Toll
A38(M)
A34
A38
A45
A452
A4040
0 1 2 miles
0 1 2 3 km

CARDIFF
(CAERDYDD)
CAERPHILLY
(CAERFFILI)
Church Village
Groes-wen
Van
Coed Parc-y-Van
Rudry
Berllangollen
Coed Craig Ruperra
Garth
Park Wood
Coed Coesau-Whips
Llwyncelyn
Watford
Caerphilly Common
The Warren
Nantgarw
Coed y Gedrys
Thornhill
Cefn Mably Woods
Michaelston-y-Fedw
Glan-y-llyn
Gwaelod-y-garth
Grath Hill
Taff's Well
(Ffynnon-Taf)
Coed-y-Wenallt
Castleton
Soar
Garth Wood
Tongwynlais
Lisvane
(Llys Faen)
Began
Marshfield
Blacktown
Pentyrch
Llanishen
Llanedeyrn
Morganstown
Pantmawr
Pentwyn
St. Mellons
(Llaneirwg)
Rhiwbina
Radyr
Cyncoed
Llanrumney
Birchgrove
Peterstone Wentlooge
(Llanbedr Gwynllŵg)
Trowbridge
Whitchurch
Heath
Rumney
(Rhymni)
Llandaff North
Roath Park
Pwll-Mawr
Newton
Gabalfa
Maindy
Fairwater
Llandaff
(Llandaf)
St Fagans
(Sain Ffagan)
Pontacanna
Cathays
Roath
St Brides-super-Ely
(Llansanffraid-ar-Elai)
Canton
Tremorfa
Ely
(Tre-lai)
Splott
St George's
Michaelston-super-Ely
Riverside
Drope
Caerau
Saltmead
Culverhouse Cross
Butetown
Downs
Valegate Retail Park
Leckwith
Grangetown
St Nicholas
(Sain Nicolas)
Twyn-yr-odyn
Tinkinswood Burial Chamber
Wallston
Wenvoe
(Gwenfo)
Michaelston-le-Pit
Llandough
St Lythans
Cardiff Bay Barrage
Taff Vale
River Taff
River Ely
Rhymney River
The Lake
Llanishen Reservoir
Bute E Dock
Roath Dock
Qn Alexandra Dock
Treforest Estate
Parc Cefn Onn
Lisvane & Thornhill
Cardiff Gate Services
Cardiff Gate Retail Park
Cardiff West Services
Forest Farm
Castell Coch
Llandaff Cathedral
Sophia Gardens Stad
St Fagans National Museum of History
Cathays National Museum Cardiff
Cardiff Castle
Cardiff Arms Park
Principality Stadium
Cardiff City
Cardiff International Sports Stad
Cardiff Central
Cardiff Bay
Ninian Park
Wales Millennium Centre
National Assembly
BBC Roath Lock Studios
Techniquest
Ice Arena
Cardiff International Pool
Cardiff International White Water
Cogan
Aber
Castle
Heath High Level
Heath Low Level
Ty Glas
Coryton
Taffs Well
M4
A48(M)
A48
A470
A469
A468
A4232
A4119
A4160
A4161
A4055
A4050
A4054
A4234
A473
B4595
B4600
B4263
B4562
B4487
B4239
B4262
B4488
B4267
B4261
28
29
29A
30
32
33
2 miles
3 km
18
31
32

0 1 2 miles
0 1 2 3 km
Cramond Island
Drum Sands
Dalmeny House
Long Green
Burnshot Wood
Glenpunty Wood
Craigiehall
Cramond Bridge
Cramond
Lauriston Castle
Cammo
Clermiston
Granton Harbour
Granton
Wardie
Newhaven
Port of Leith
HMY Britannia
Ocean Terminal Centre
Scottish Executive
Middle Craigs
Eastern Craigs
Leith
Leith Links
Drylaw
Craigleith
Blackhall
Royal Botanic Garden
Craigentinny
Portobello
Calton Hill
Palace of Holyroodhouse
Scottish Parliament
Holyrood Park
Arthur's Seat
Dunsapie Loch
Northfield
EDINBURGH
West Coates
National Museum of Scotland
Meadow Park
Murrayfield
Corstophine
RZSS Edinburgh Zoo
Scottish National Gallery of Modern Art
Edinburgh Airport
Edinburgh Gateway
Gyle Centre
South Gyle
Merchiston
Churchill
Prestonfield
Commonwealth Pool
Duddingston Loch
Bingham
Joppa
Fisherrow Sands
MUSSELBURGH
Newhailes
Inveresk
Stoneybank
Niddrie
Nether Liberton
Royal Observatory
Craigmillar Castle
The Inch
Old Craighall
Edinburgh Services
Inveresk Lodge Gardens
Longstone
Craiglockhart
Water of Leith Visitor Centre
Hermiston
Baberton
Colinton
Comiston
Braid Hills
Liberton
Alnwickhill
Moredun
Danderhall
Easter Millerhill
Gilmerton
Bonaly
Torphin
Dreghorn Services
Muirhouse
Dalkeith Park
Nature Trail
DALKEITH
Newmills
CURRIE
Torduff Resr
Clubbiedean Resr
Bonaly Country Park
Bonaly Resr
Malleny Garden
Midlothian Snowsports Centre
Hillend Country Park
LOANHEAD
Eskgrove
BONNYRIGG
Easthouses
Harlaw Resr
Pentland Hills
The City of Edinburgh By-Pass

GLASGOW
Drumchapel
Kessington
BISHOPBRIGGS
Auchinloch
Moodiesburn
Chryston
MUIRHEAD
Gartcosh
STEPPS
Robroyston
Balornock
Springburn
Milton
Firhill
Kelvinside
Knightswood
Jordanhill
Partick
Govan
Ibrox
Hillington
Pollokshields
Crossmyloof
Govanhill
Langside
Crookston
Priesthill
Nitshill
Hillpark
Muirend
Cathcart
Orchard Park
Giffnock
Netherlee
Williamwood
CLARKSTON
Crookfur
Carmunnock
Castlemilk
Croftfoot
RUTHERGLEN
CAMBUSLANG
Flemington
Westburn
Newton
UDDINGSTON
Blantyre
Birkenshaw
Broomhouse
Muirhead
Bargeddie
Swinton
Easterhouse
Craigend
Riddrie
Dennistoun
Carntyne
Springboig
Mont Vernon
Braidfauld
Clyde Gateway East
Gallowgate
Dechmont Hill
River Clyde
White Cart Water
Forth and Clyde Canal
Hogganfield Loch
Frankfield Loch
Bishop Loch
Johnston Loch
Gadloch
Possil Loch
Wilderness Plantation
Nature Reserve
Alexandra Park
Tollcross Park
Richmond Park
King's Park
Queen's Park
Bellahouston Park
Victoria Park
Dawsholm Park
Glasgow Green
Pollok Country Park
Rouken Glen Park
Cathkin Braes Country Park
Nature Trail Linn Park
Waulkmill Glen Reservoir
Ryatt Linn Resr
Glasgow Botanic Gardens
Celtic Park
Firhill Stadium
Hampden Park
Scotstoun Stadium
Emirates Arena & Sir Chris Hoy Velodrome
SECC
The SSE Hydro
Science Centre
Riverside Museum
Museum & Art Gallery
Springburn Museum
The People's Palace & Winter Garden
House for an Art Lover
Provan Hall
Glasgow Fort
Hagg's Castle
Burrell Collection
Pollok House
Crookston Castle
Bothwell Castle
David Livingstone Centre
Holmwood House
Braehead Shopping Centre
Silverburn Shopping Centre
Clyde Tunnel
Govt Offices
0 1 2 miles
0 1 2 3 km

2 miles
3 km
LEEDS
Shadwell
Scholes
Arthursdale
Saw Wood
Swarcliffe
Manston
Austhorpe
Colton
Whitekirk
Halton Moor
Monkswood
Brooklands
Parklands
Oakwood
Harehills
Osmondthorpe
Knowsthorpe
Roundhay Park
Tropical World
Lady Wood
Park Villas
Swillington
Swillington Commom
Little Preston
Woodlesford
Rothwell Haigh
ROTHWELL
Oulton
Carlton
Robin Hood
Ouzlewell Green
Newsam Green
Temple Newsam House
Temple Newsam Country Park
Home Farm
Dawson's Wood
Avenue Wood
Rothwell Country Park
Leeds Skelton Lake Services
Thwaite Mills Industrial Museum
River Aire
Aire & Calder Navigation
Hunslet
Holbeck
Bank
Royal Armouries
Thackray Mus of Medicine
Civic Hall
City Art Gall
Town Hall
University of Leeds
Hyde Park
Burley
Burley Park
Headingley
Meanwood
Hollies Botanical Gardens
Beckett Park
Leeds Beckett Univ
West Park
Ireland Wood
Adel
Kirkstall Abbey
Kirkstall Forge
Leeds Industrial Museum
Armley
Upper Wortley
Farnley
New Farnley
Hawksworth
Cragg Hill
HORSFORTH
Hill Top
Bramley
Park Spring
PUDSEY
Farsley
CALVERLEY
Calverley Wood
Lodge Wood
Cragg Wood
West End
Leeds Bradford International Airport
Fulneck
Fulneck Moravian Museum
Tong
Park Wood
Black Carr
Cross Flatts Park
Beeston
Churwell
White Rose Centre
South Leeds Stadium
Middleton Railway
Middleton Park
Middleton
Thorpe on the Hill
The Fall
MORLEY
Topcliffe
Tingley Common
Troy Hill
Bruntcliffe
Gildersome
Drighlington
BIRKENSHAW
Birstall
Copley Hill
Sports Centre
Bagshaw Museum
Oakwell Hall Country Park
Red House
Cockpit Round
Almshouses Wood
Moss Carr Wood
Barrowby Park
The Springs Shopping Centre
RING ROAD
YORK ROAD
SELBY ROAD
PONTEFRACT LANE
WAKEFIELD ROAD
DEWSBURY ROAD
ELLAND ROAD
OTLEY ROAD
HORSFORTH NEW RD
STANNINGLEY BY-PASS
BRADFORD ROAD
MOORTOWN RING ROAD
A64 A6120 A58 A61 A63 A639 A653 A643 A62 A660 A65 A647 A657 A6110 A650 A654 A642 A6029 A652 A58(M) A64(M)
M1 M62 M621
43

BUSHEY
OXHEY
Bushey Heath
Elstree
Arkley
Barnet Gate
Stirling Corner
Underhill
EAST BARNET
BARNET
Totteridge
Whetstone
Osidge
Brockley Hill
Edgware Bury
LONDON GATEWAY SERVICES
Stanmore Common
BENTLEY PRIORY
South Oxhey
Oxhey Woods
Apex Corner
Woodside Park
North Finchley
FRIERN BARNET
Colney Hatch
EDGWARE
Canons Park
STANMORE
Mill Hill
Mill Hill East
Mill Hill Circus
West Finchley
Hatch End
Harrow Weald
Little Stanmore
Grahame Park
Burnt Oak
STONEX STADIUM
Five Ways Corner
Church End
FINCHLEY
Coldfall Wood
Headstone Lane
Headstone
Belmont
HENDON
Muswell Hill
Henlys Corner
Fortis Green
East Finchley
Highgate Wood
Queen's Wood
PINNER
HEADSTONE MANOR & MUS
Civic Centre
Wealdstone
Queensbury
Colindale
HARROW
KENTON
Greenhill
Kingsbury
Temple Fortune
Hampstead Garden Suburb
Eastcote Village
North Harrow
West Harrow
Eastcote
West Hendon
Brent Cross Shopping Centre
Brent Cross
Golders Green
Highgate
Northwick Park
Harrow on the Hill
Preston Road
Barn Hill
Brent Reservoir (Welsh Harp)
Staples Corner
Rayners Lane
Ruislip Manor
Roxeth
North Wembley
Child's Hill
Golders Hill Park
Hampstead Heath
Highgate Ponds
Parliament Hill
Dartmouth Park
Wembley Park
Neasden Circle
Neasden
Dollis Hill
Gladstone Park
Cricklewood
HAMPSTEAD
Gospel Oak
South Ruislip
South Harrow
Sudbury
WEMBLEY
WEMBLEY ARENA
WEMBLEY STADIUM
WILLESDEN
Belsize Park
Swiss Cottage
West Hampstead
Polish War Memorial
NORTHOLT
Target Rbdt
Stonebridge Park
BRENT MUSEUM
Brondesbury
Kilburn
Primrose Hill
LONDON ZOO
Regents Park
Perivale
Alperton
Stonebridge
Harlesden
Kensal Rise
St. John's Wood
Maida Vale
White Hart Rbdt
Greenford Rbdt
GREENFORD
Hanger Lane
Park Royal
Old Oak Common
Wormwood Scrubs Park
LINFORD CHRISTIE OUTDOOR SPORTS CENTRE
Yeading
West Acton
Gipsy Corner
EALING
Westbourne Park
Marylebone Flyover
MARYLEBONE
MADAME TUSSAUD'S
NORTH CIRCULAR ROAD
WESTERN AVENUE
WATFORD WAY
EDGWARE ROAD
EDGWARE WAY
BARNET WAY
GREAT NORTH WAY
Grand Union Canal
0
1
2 miles
0
1
2
3 km

PADDINGTON
Mayfair
Pimlico
CHELSEA
BATTERSEA
Hyde Park
Kensington Gardens
Knightsbridge
Bayswater
Notting Hill
Holland Park
HAMMERSMITH
FULHAM
Parsons Green
WANDSWORTH
Clapham Common
Balham
Wandsworth Common
Upper Tooting
Tooting Bec
Tooting
Collier's Wood
Mitcham Common
Earlsfield
Southfields
Wimbledon Park
WIMBLEDON
MERTON
MORDEN
Morden Park
Lower Morden
Rosehill
West Hill
PUTNEY
Putney Heath
Putney Vale
Wimbledon Common
BARNES
River Thames
Shepherd's Bush
ACTON
South Acton
Bedford Park
CHISWICK
Grove Park
Mortlake
East Sheen
Roehampton
Kingston Vale
Coombe
NEW MALDEN
Motspur Park
Raynes Park
Richmond Park
North Sheen
RICHMOND
Richmond Hill
Kew
Gunnersbury Park
Petersham
Ham
KINGSTON UPON THAMES
Norbiton
Berrylands
SURBITON
West Ealing
Northfields
HANWELL
BRENTFORD
Syon Park
Old Deer Park
St Margarets
TEDDINGTON
Hampton Wick
Hampton Court Park
Thames Ditton
Bushy Park
TWICKENHAM
ISLEWORTH
Woodlands
HOUNSLOW
Whitton
Drayton Green
Osterley Park
Norwood Green
HESTON
Dormer's Wells
SOUTHALL
North Hyde
Hounslow West
Hounslow Heath
HANWORTH
Hanworth Park
Hampton
FELTHAM
SUNBURY
Fieldcommon
WALTON-ON-THAMES
Hayes Town
Cranford
Low Emission Zone
Ultra Low Emission Zone

Low Emission Zone
Ultra Low Emission Zone
2 miles
3 km
LOUGHTON
CHIGWELL
CHINGFORD
WOODFORD
SOUTHGATE
EDMONTON
FRIERN BARNET
WOOD GREEN
TOTTENHAM
WALTHAMSTOW
WANSTEAD
ILFORD
BARKING
HORNSEY
STOKE NEWINGTON
LEYTON
STRATFORD
HACKNEY
WEST HAM
EAST HAM
CAMDEN TOWN
ISLINGTON
SHOREDITCH
BETHNAL GREEN
BOW
FINSBURY
MARYLEBONE
HAMPSTEAD

Hyde Park
Mayfair
Green Park
St James's Palace
Houses of Parliament
Westminster Br
Waterloo Br
Blackfriars Br
Aldgate
Tower Br
POPLAR
Canning Town
Custom House
Blackwall
Blackwall Tunnel
Limehouse
Wapping
Canary Wharf
West India Docks
Royal Albert Dock
London City Airport
King George V Dock
Royal Victoria Dock
River Thames
Silvertown
Thames Barrier
North Woolwich
Woolwich Ferry
North Greenwich
Rotherhithe
ISLE OF DOGS
Millwall
BERMONDSEY
CHELSEA
Pimlico
LAMBETH
Vauxhall Cross
Elephant & Castle
Walworth
Kennington
DEPTFORD
GREENWICH
Greenwich Park
WOOLWICH
Plumstead
Charlton
Woolwich Common
East Wickham
Shooters Hill
Battersea Park
BATTERSEA
Camberwell Green
CAMBERWELL
Peckham
New Cross
Eltham Common
Oxleas Wood
Kidbrooke
BLACKHEATH
Blackheath Park
Falconwood
CLAPHAM
BRIXTON
East Dulwich
Nunhead
Brockley
LEWISHAM
Hither Green
ELTHAM
Clapham Common
Peckham Rye Park
Honor Oak
Ladywell
Yorkshire Grey
Eltham Palace
Avery Hill
Wandsworth Common
Balham
Grange Mills
Brockwell Park
Dulwich Park
Lee
Catford Gyratory
Forest Hill
CATFORD
Upper Tooting
Tooting Bec Common
Tooting Bec
Tulse Hill
STREATHAM
West Dulwich
Dulwich
Mottingham
New Eltham
Bellingham
Bell Green
Grove Park
Longlands
Furzedown
Norwood
Crystal Palace National Sports Centre
PENGE
Downham
Elmstead Wood
Elmstead
CHISLEHURST
Streatham Common
Collier's Wood
Streatham Vale
Beckenham Place Park
Plaistow
Sundridge Park
Chislehurst Common
Scadbury Nature Reserve
Norbury
Anerley
BECKENHAM
BROMLEY
Widmore
Bickley
MITCHAM
Mitcham Common
South Norwood
Elmers End
Eden Park
Shortlands
Petts Wood
Selhurst
Woodside
Southborough
London approaches
325

Great Crosby
CROSBY
ANTONY GORMLEY SCULPTURES - ANOTHER PLACE
Waterloo
Town Hall
Seaforth
RIMROSE VALLEY COUNTRY PARK
LITHERLAND
Melling
Kirkby Park
AINTREE
AINTREE RACE COURSE
Westvale
KIRKBY
Fazakerley
Croxteth
Knowsley
BOOTLE
Docks
Walton
West Derby
CROXTETH COUNTRY PARK
Stockbridge Village
Ferries to Belfast, Douglas & Dublin
New Brighton
Stanley Park
Anfield
WALLASEY
Newsham Park
Huyton with Roby
Roby
Broad Green
Kingsway
Queensway
Birkenhead Park
BIRKENHEAD
LIVERPOOL
MUS OF LIVERPOOL
MARITIME MUSEUM
TATE LIVERPOOL
Royal Albert Dock
BEATLES STORY
M&S BANK ARENA
Edge Hill
Wavertree
WAVERTREE TECHNOLOGY PARK
Childwall
Toxteth
Sefton Park
Dingle
CALDERSTONES PARK
Oxton
Tranmere
Aigburth
SUDLEY HOUSE
Woolton
Otterspool
Allerton
HALEWOOD COUNTRY PARK
River Mersey
Hunt's Cross
GARSTON
LADY LEVER ART GALLERY
PORT SUNLIGHT MUS
Port Sunlight
BEBINGTON
Spital
Brimstage
Bromborough
Eastham Ferry
EASTHAM COUNTRY PARK
SPEKE HALL
LIVERPOOL JOHN LENNON AIRPORT
Terminal Building
LIVERPOOL AIRPORT
SPEKE
0 1 2 miles
0 1 2 3 km
M57
M62
M53
A5036
A580
A59
A562
A561
A41
A5058

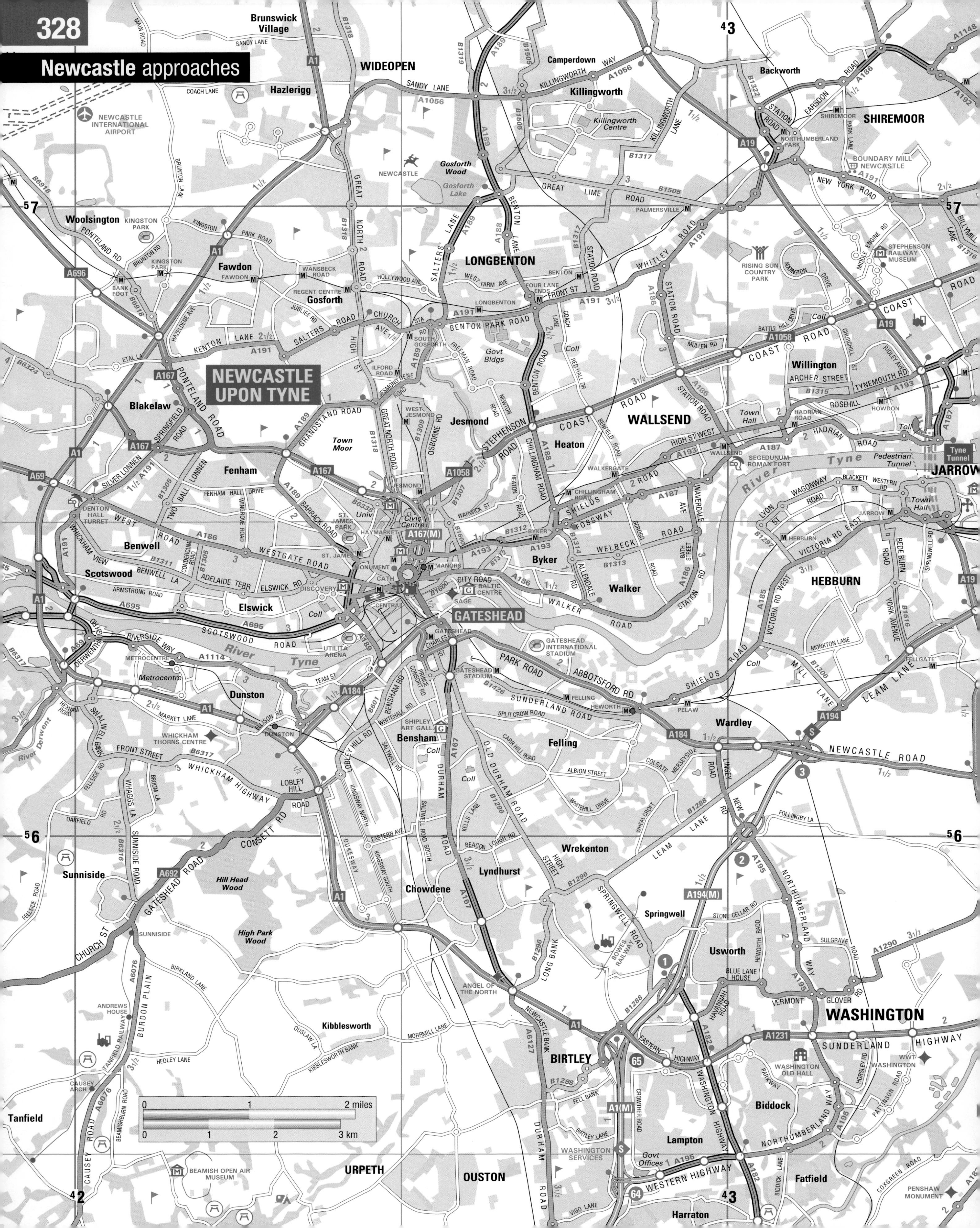
Brunswick Village
Hazlerigg
WIDEOPEN
Camperdown
Killingworth
Killingworth Centre
Backworth
SHIREMOOR
NEWCASTLE INTERNATIONAL AIRPORT
Gosforth Wood
Gosforth Lake
NEWCASTLE
Woolsington
KINGSTON PARK
Fawdon
Gosforth
LONGBENTON
RISING SUN COUNTRY PARK
STEPHENSON RAILWAY MUSEUM
BOUNDARY MILL NEWCASTLE
NEWCASTLE UPON TYNE
Blakelaw
Town Moor
Jesmond
Govt Bldgs
Willington
WALLSEND
Heaton
Town Hall
SEGEDUNUM ROMAN FORT
Tyne Tunnel
Pedestrian Tunnel
JARROW
Fenham
DENTON HALL TURRET
Univ
Civic Centre
Benwell
Scotswood
Byker
Walker
HEBBURN
Elswick
DISCOVERY
GATESHEAD
BALTIC CENTRE
SAGE
UTILITA ARENA
GATESHEAD INTERNATIONAL STADIUM
River Tyne
Metrocentre
Dunston
WHICKHAM THORNS CENTRE
River Derwent
SHIPLEY ART GALL
Bensham
Felling
Wardley
LOBLEY HILL
Wrekenton
Sunniside
Hill Head Wood
Chowdene
Lyndhurst
Springwell
BOWES RAILWAY
Usworth
High Park Wood
ANGEL OF THE NORTH
BLUE LANE HOUSE
WASHINGTON
ANDREWS HOUSE
Kibblesworth
BIRTLEY
WASHINGTON OLD HALL
WWT WASHINGTON
Biddock
CAUSEY ARCH
Tanfield
Lampton
WASHINGTON SERVICES
Govt Offices
BEAMISH OPEN AIR MUSEUM
URPETH
OUSTON
Fatfield
PENSHAW MONUMENT
Harraton
0 1 2 miles
0 1 2 3 km

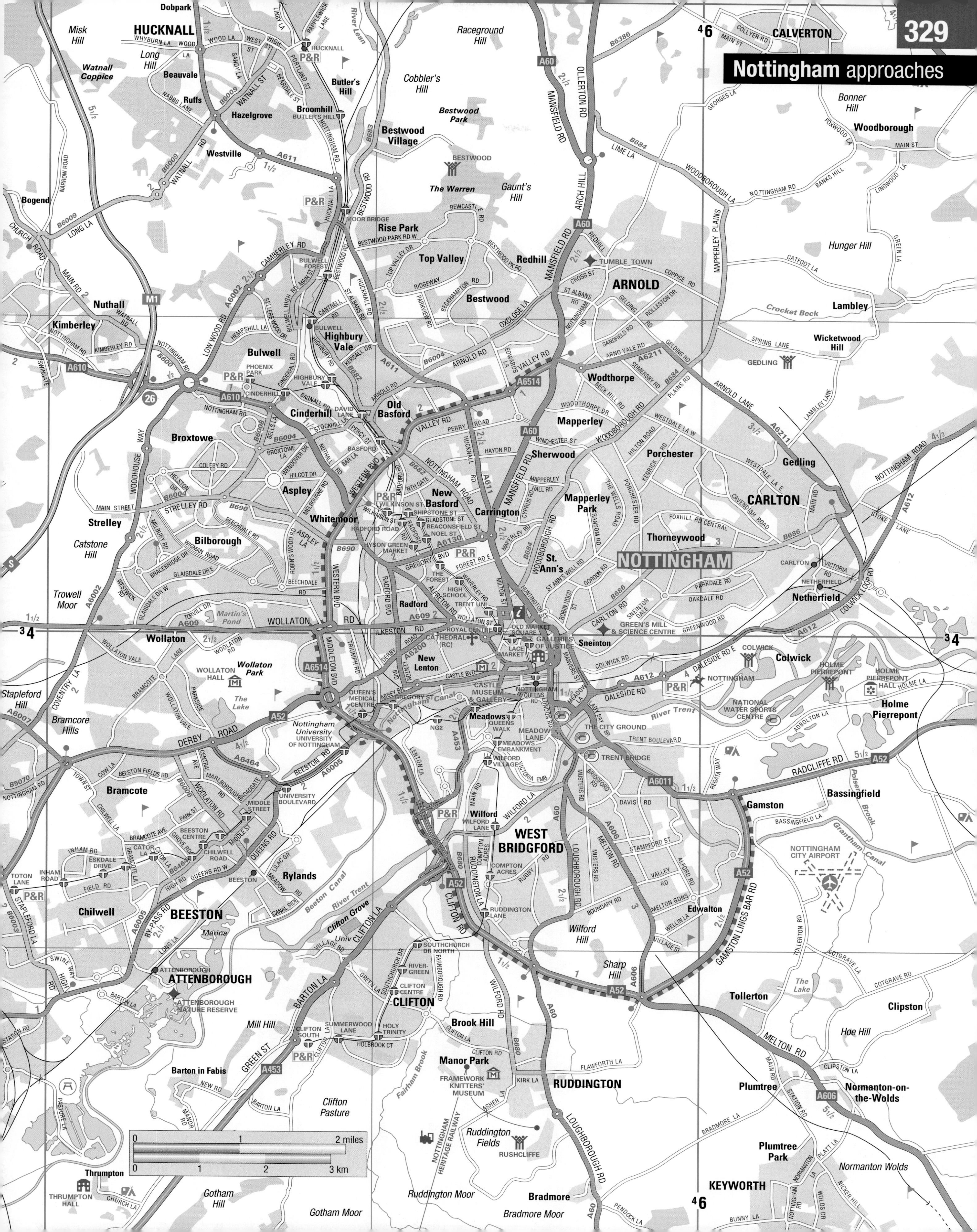
Dobpark
HUCKNALL
Misk Hill
Watnall Coppice
Long Hill
Beauvale
Ruffs
Hazelgrove
Butler's Hill
Broomhill
Raceground Hill
Cobbler's Hill
Bestwood Park
Bestwood Village
CALVERTON
Bonner Hill
Woodborough
Westville
BESTWOOD
The Warren
Gaunt's Hill
Bogend
Rise Park
Top Valley
Redhill
TUMBLE TOWN
ARNOLD
Hunger Hill
Bestwood
Nuthall
Kimberley
Bulwell
Highbury Vale
Lambley
Crocket Beck
Wicketwood Hill
GEDLING
Wodthorpe
Cinderhill
Old Basford
Mapperley
Broxtowe
Sherwood
Porchester
Gedling
Aspley
New Basford
Carrington
Mapperley Park
CARLTON
Strelley
Whitemoor
Bilborough
Thorneywood
Catstone Hill
St. Ann's
NOTTINGHAM
Trowell Moor
Radford
Netherfield
Martin's Pond
WOLLATON
Wollaton
Sneinton
GREEN'S MILL & SCIENCE CENTRE
Colwick
New Lenton
WOLLATON HALL
Wollaton Park
The Lake
HOLME PIERREPONT HALL
Holme Pierrepont
Stapleford Hill
Bramcore Hills
Meadows
River Trent
NATIONAL WATER SPORTS CENTRE
THE CITY GROUND
TRENT BRIDGE
Nottingham University
UNIVERSITY OF NOTTINGHAM
Bramcote
Gamston
Bassingfield
Wilford
WEST BRIDGFORD
NOTTINGHAM CITY AIRPORT
Rylands
Chilwell
BEESTON
Beeston Canal
Clifton Grove
Edwalton
Wilford Hill
Sharp Hill
ATTENBOROUGH
ATTENBOROUGH NATURE RESERVE
CLIFTON
Tollerton
The Lake
Clipston
Mill Hill
Brook Hill
Hoe Hill
Barton in Fabis
Manor Park
FRAMEWORK KNITTERS' MUSEUM
RUDDINGTON
Plumtree
Normanton-on-the-Wolds
Clifton Pasture
Fairham Brook
Ruddington Fields
RUSHCLIFFE
NOTTINGHAM HERITAGE RAILWAY
Plumtree Park
Normanton Wolds
Thrumpton
THRUMPTON HALL
Gotham Hill
Ruddington Moor
Bradmore
KEYWORTH
Gotham Moor
Bradmore Moor
0 1 2 miles
0 1 2 3 km

ROTHERHAM
SHEFFIELD
ECCLESFIELD
GRENOSIDE
HILLSBOROUGH
Wickersley
Sunnyside
Listerdale
Dalton Magna
Dalton Parva
Dalton
Whinney Hill
Brecks
Herringthorpe
Moorgate
Whiston
Morthen
Brampton en le Morthen
Upper Whiston
Ulley
Aston
Aughton
Wales
Woodall
Norwood
Killamarsh
Upperthorpe
Rother Valley Lake
Eastwood
Clifton Park
Broom
Canklow
Masbrough
Greasbrough
Bradgate
Kimberworth Park
Kimberworth
Dropping Well
Blackburn
Tinsley
Jordan
Brinsworth
Catcliffe
Treeton
Guilthwaite
Waverley
Handsworth
Orgreave
Woodhouse Mill
Woodhouse
Fence
Swallownest
Beighton
Sothall
Holbrook
Halfway
Westfield
Waterthorpe
Drakehouse
Hackenthorpe
Moorhole
Owlthorpe
Plumbley
Highlane
Birley
Frecheville
Normanton Spring
Richmond
Hollins End
Intake
Gleadless
Ridgeway
Ridgeway Moor
Ford
Lightwood
Darnall
Greenland
Carbrook
Brightside
Attercliffe
Manor Estate
Manor Park
Sheffield Park
Arbourthorne
Wincobank
Concord Park
Shiregreen
Pismire Hill
Firth Park
Grimesthorpe
Pitsmoor
Fir Vale
Burngreave
Parson Cross
Longley Estate
Shirecliffe
Parkwood Springs
Wadsley Bridge
Owlerton
Birley Carr
Birley Edge
Oughtibridge
Beeley Wood
Wharncliffe Wood
Wadsley
Worrall
Loxley
Knowle Top
Malinbridge
Walkley
Steel Bank
Crookesmoor
Crookes
Tapton Hill
Sandygate
Ranmoor
Fulwood
Greystones
Ecclesall
Sharrow
Nether Edge
Brincliffe
Carter Knowle
Millhouses
Parkhead
Whirlow
Abbeydale
Abbeydale Park
Totley Rise
Totley Bents
Heeley
Lowfield
Meersbrook
Newfield Green
Hemsworth
Backmoor
Gleadless Valley
Norton Woodseats
Norton
Jordanthorpe
Meadow Head
Greenhill
Lowedges
Sheffield Services
Sheffield Station/Sheffield Hallam
Meadowhall Ctr.
Tinsley Park
Dore House Industrial Estate
River Rother
River Sheaf
River Rivelin
R. Don
Limb Brook
Ecclesall Wood
Botanical Gardens
Bishop's House
Heeley City Farm
Magna Science Adventure Centre
Utilita Arena
Valley Centertainment
Ridgeway Cottage Industry Centre
Sheffield to Keadby Canal
M1
M18
A57
A61
A6102
A630
A631
A618
2 miles
3 km

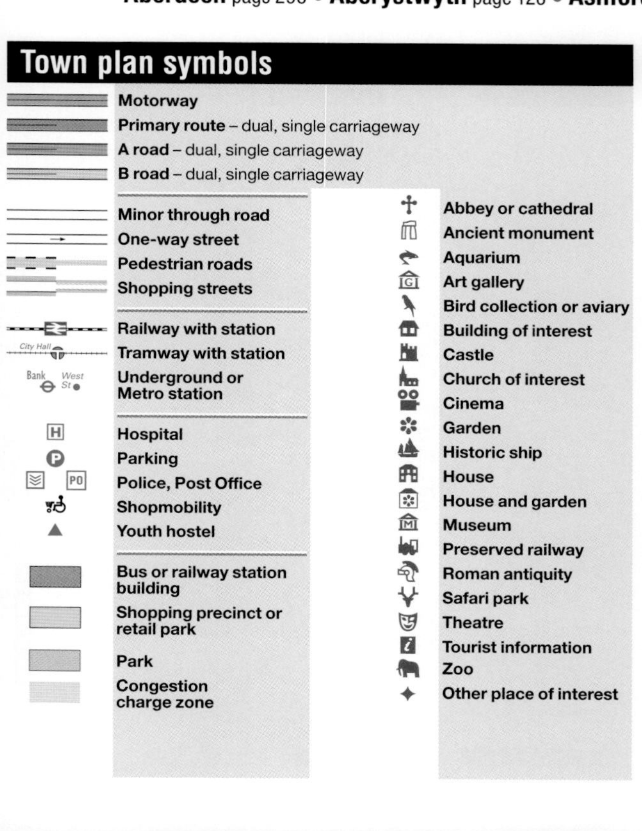
Town plan symbols
Motorway
Primary route – dual, single carriageway
A road – dual, single carriageway
B road – dual, single carriageway
Minor through road
One-way street
Pedestrian roads
Shopping streets
Railway with station
Tramway with station
Underground or Metro station
Hospital
Parking
Police, Post Office
Shopmobility
Youth hostel
Bus or railway station building
Shopping precinct or retail park
Park
Congestion charge zone
Abbey or cathedral
Ancient monument
Aquarium
Art gallery
Bird collection or aviary
Building of interest
Castle
Church of interest
Cinema
Garden
Historic ship
House
House and garden
Museum
Preserved railway
Roman antiquity
Safari park
Theatre
Tourist information
Zoo
Other place of interest

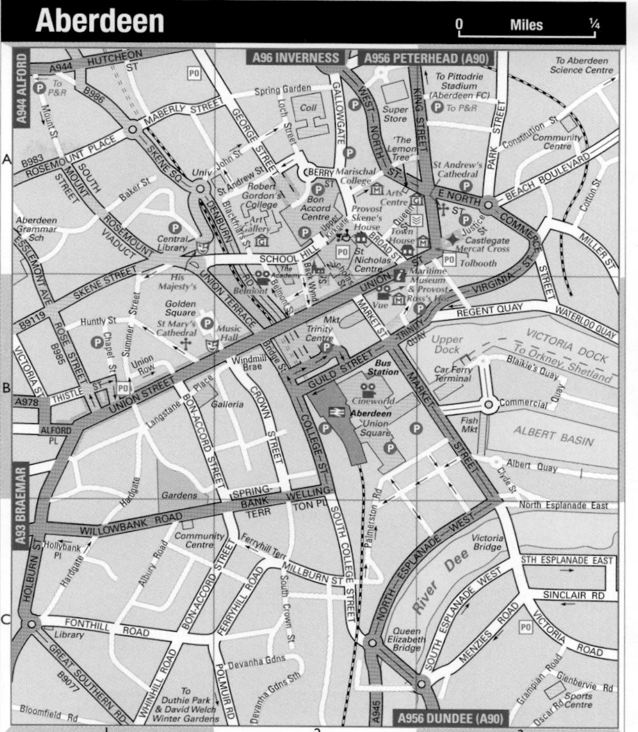
Aberdeen
0 Miles ¼

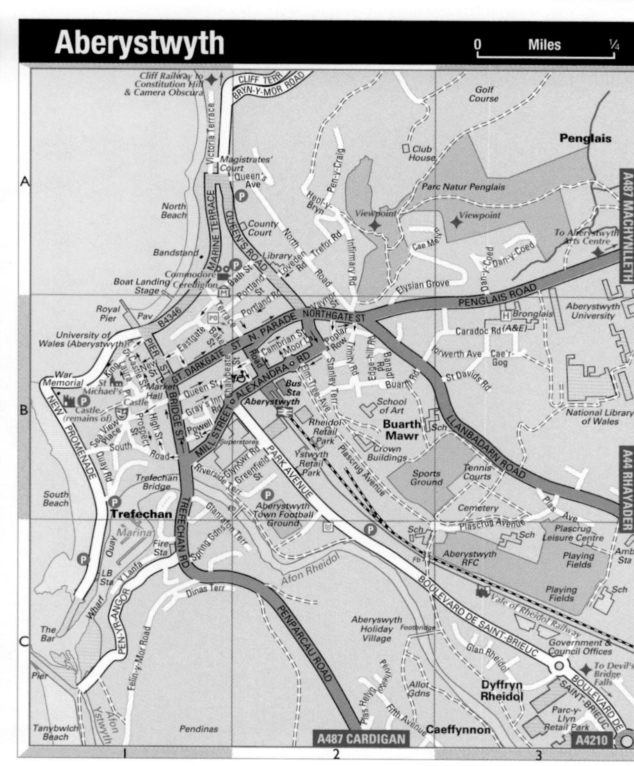
Aberystwyth
0 Miles ¼

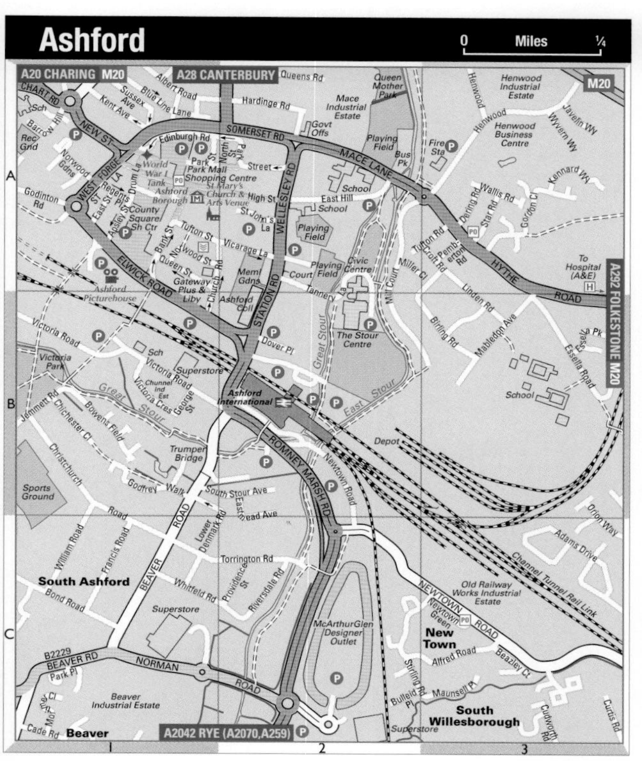
Ashford
0 Miles ¼

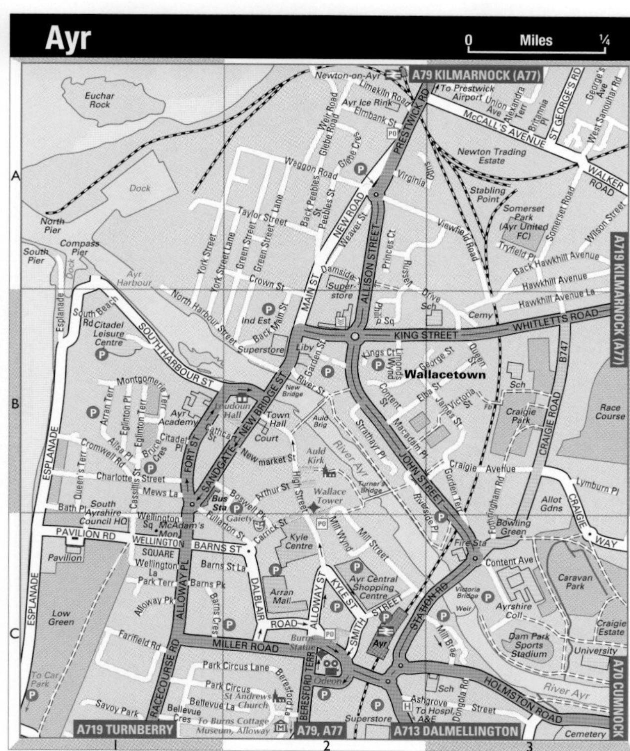
Ayr
0 Miles ¼

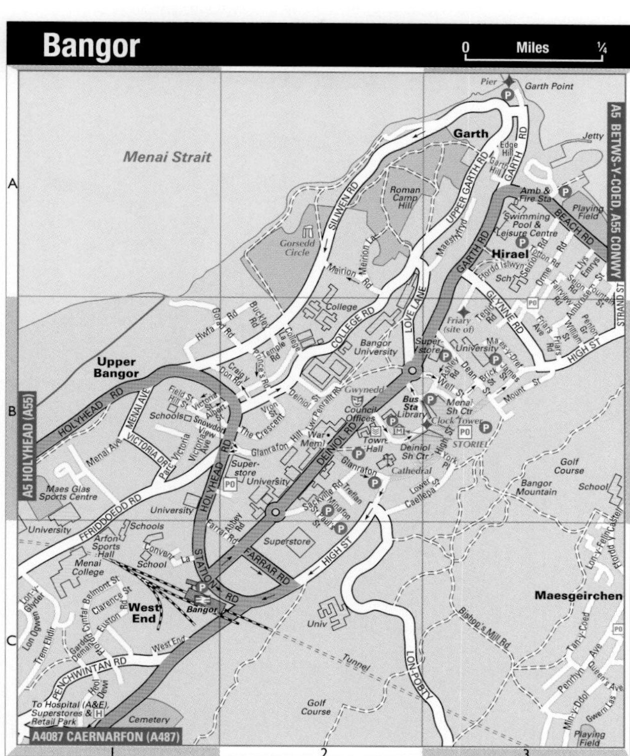
Bangor
0 Miles ¼

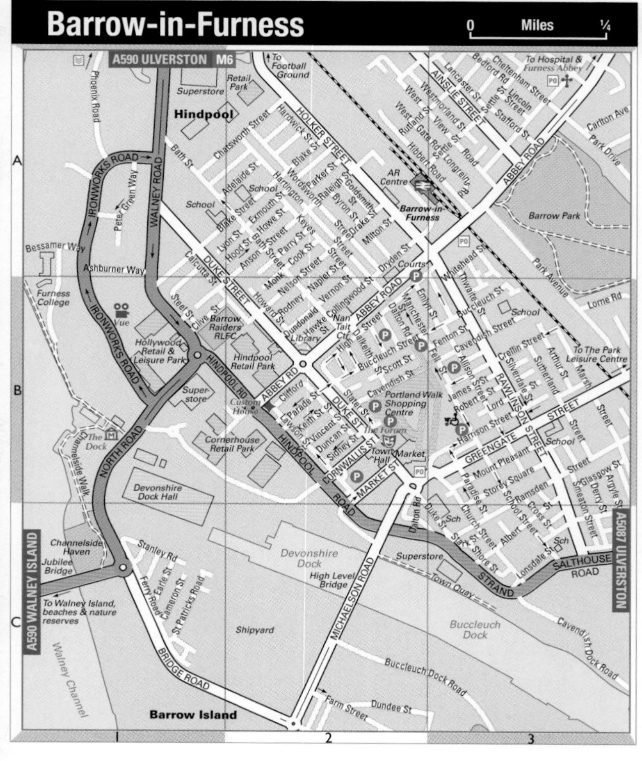
Barrow-in-Furness
0 Miles ¼

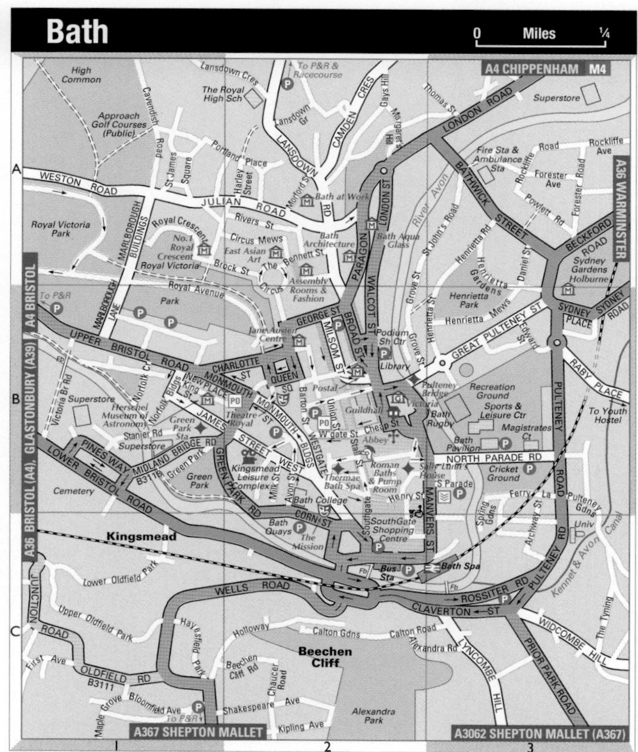
Bath
0 Miles ¼

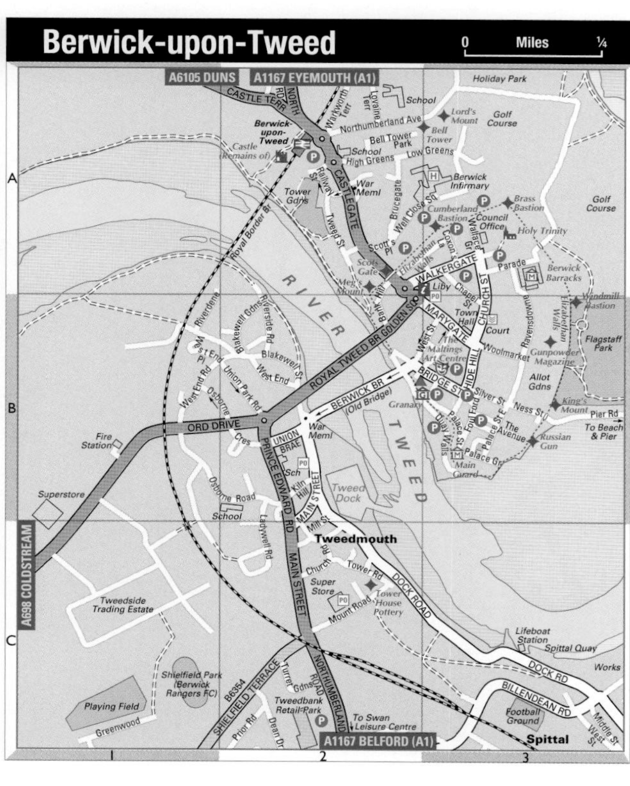
Berwick-upon-Tweed
0 Miles ¼

Birmingham
0 Miles ¼
A4040 OUTER RING ROAD
A41 WOLVERHAMPTON M5
A34 WALSALL M6 A38(M) TO M6
A5127 SUTTON COLDFIELD
A47 CASTLE BROMWICH M6
A457 DUDLEY
A456 KIDDERMINSTER M5
A4540 RING ROAD
A38 BROMSGROVE
A441 REDDITCH
A41 STRATFORD-UPON-AVON (A34, A3400) M42
A45 COVENTRY, AIRPORT & NEC M42
GIB HEATH
WINSON GREEN
NEW TOWN
ASTON
BROOKFIELDS
DUDDESTON
LADYWOOD
BORDESLEY
Edgbaston Reservoir

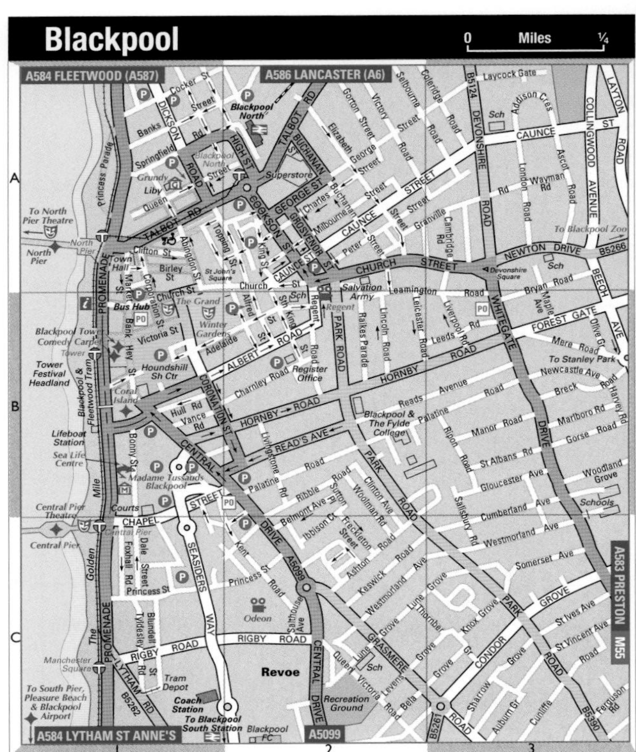
Blackpool
0 Miles ¼
A584 FLEETWOOD (A587)
A586 LANCASTER (A6)
A583 PRESTON M55
A584 LYTHAM ST ANNE'S
A5099
Revoe

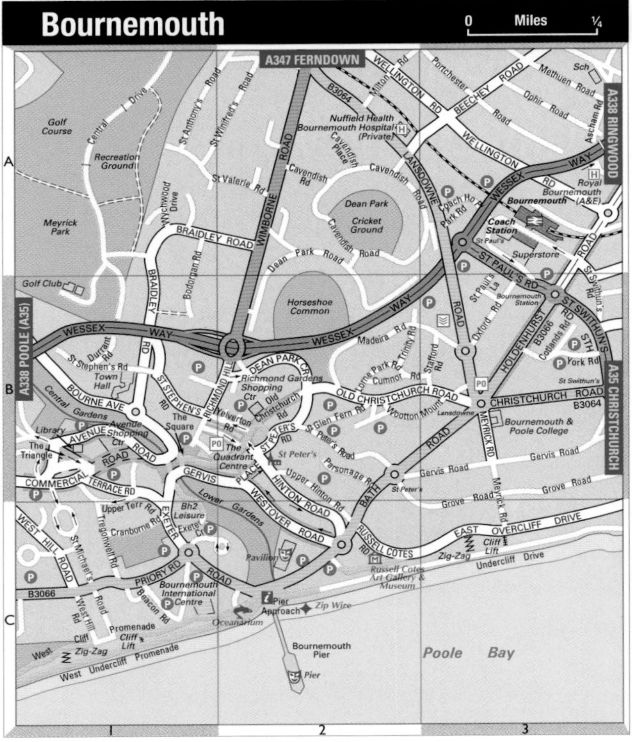
Bournemouth
0 Miles ¼
A347 FERNDOWN
A338 RINGWOOD
A35 POOLE (A35)
A35 CHRISTCHURCH
Poole Bay
Horseshoe Common
Dean Park Cricket Ground
Meyrick Park
Golf Course

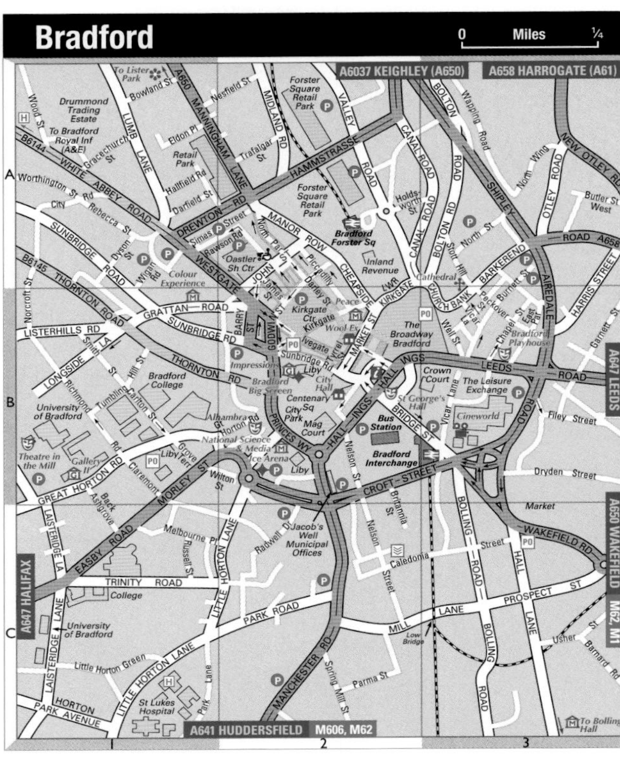
Bradford
0 Miles ¼
A6037 KEIGHLEY (A650)
A658 HARROGATE (A61)
A647 LEEDS
A650 WAKEFIELD M62, M1
A647 HALIFAX
A641 HUDDERSFIELD M606, M62

Brighton
0 Miles ¼
A23 CRAWLEY M23
A270 LEWES (A27)
A270 WORTHING (A27)
A259 WORTHING
A259 NEWHAVEN
West Pier (derelict)
Brighton Pier (Palace Pier)

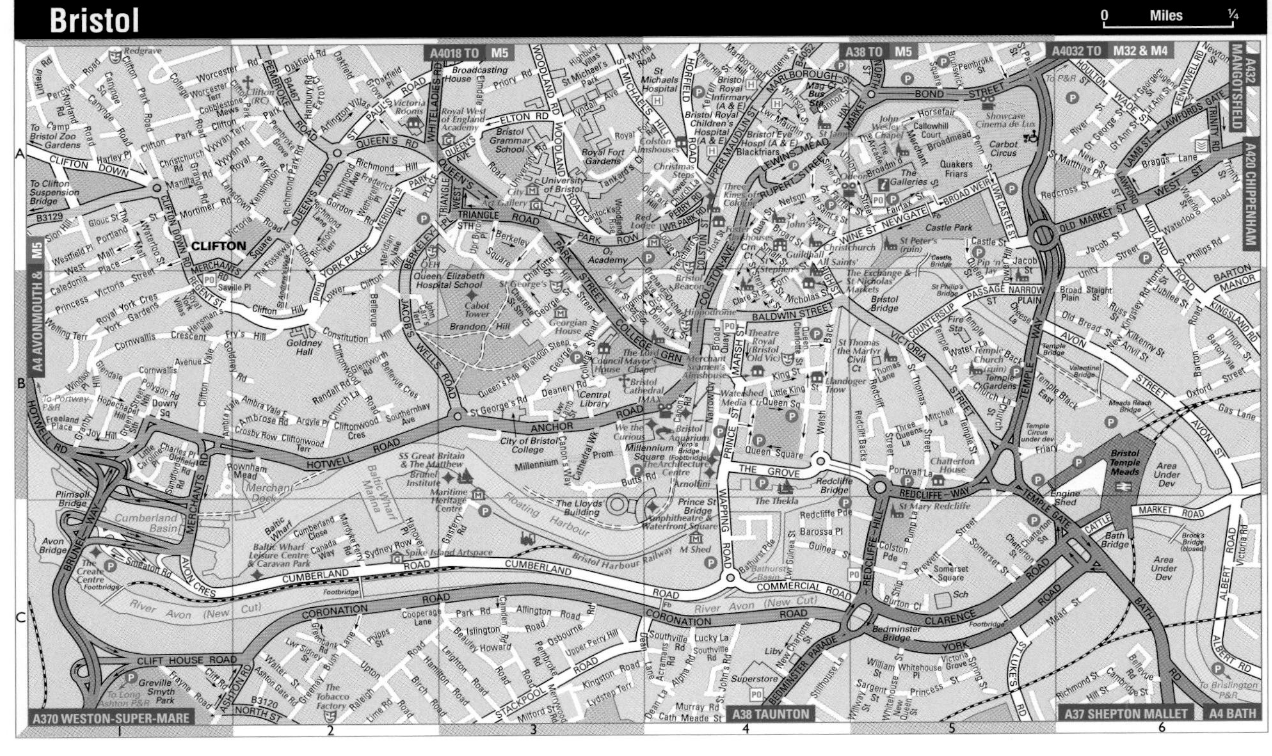
Bristol
0 Miles ¼
A4018 TO M5
A38 TO M5
A4032 TO M32 & M4
A432 MANGOTSFIELD
A420 CHIPPENHAM
A4 AVONMOUTH & M5
A370 WESTON-SUPER-MARE
A38 TAUNTON
A37 SHEPTON MALLET
A4 BATH
CLIFTON
River Avon (New Cut)
Floating Harbour

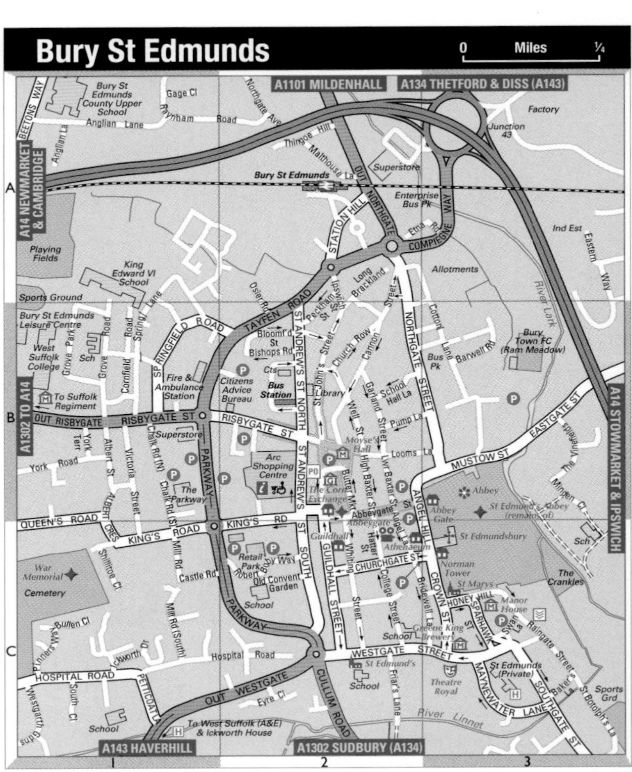
Bury St Edmunds
0 Miles ¼
A1101 MILDENHALL
A134 THETFORD & DISS (A143)
A14 NEWMARKET & CAMBRIDGE
A14 STOWMARKET & IPSWICH
A1302 TO A14
A143 HAVERHILL
A1302 SUDBURY (A134)
River Linnet

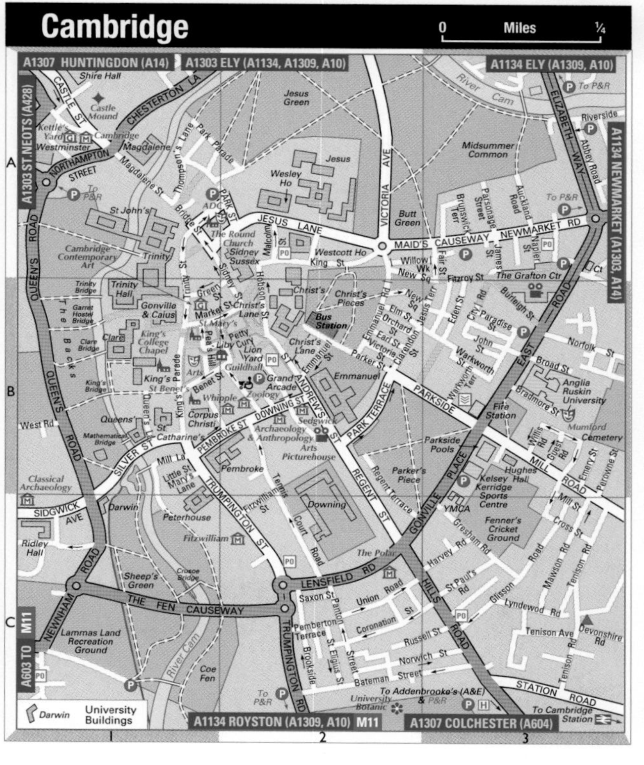
Cambridge
0 Miles ¼
A1307 HUNTINGDON (A14)
A1303 ELY (A1134, A1309, A10)
A1134 ELY (A1309, A10)
A1134 NEWMARKET (A1303, A14)
A1303 ST NEOTS (A428)
A603 TO M11
A1134 ROYSTON (A1309, A10) M11
A1307 COLCHESTER (A604)
Midsummer Common
Jesus Green
Parker's Piece
Bus Station
LENSFIELD RD
THE FEN CAUSEWAY
University Buildings

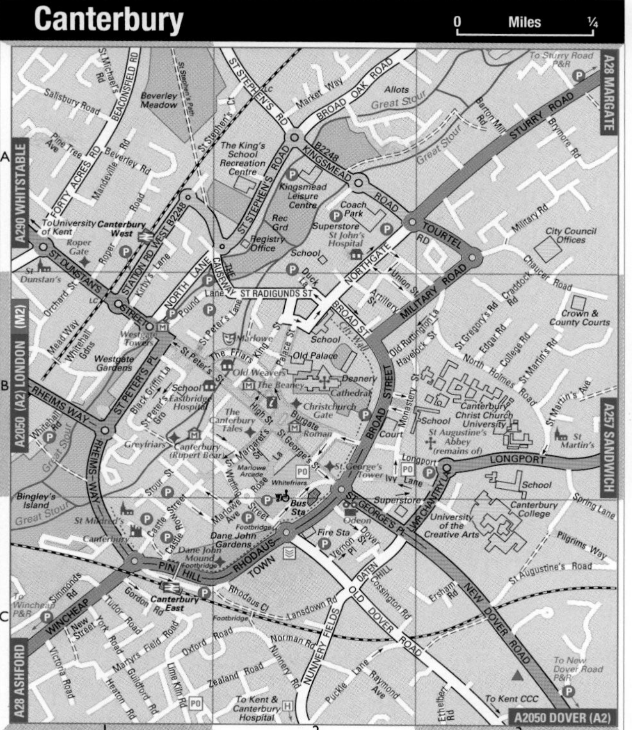
Canterbury
0 Miles ¼
A28 MARGATE
A290 WHITSTABLE
A2050 (A2) LONDON (M2)
A257 SANDWICH
A28 ASHFORD
A2050 DOVER (A2)
Bus Sta
Canterbury East
Canterbury West
Cathedral

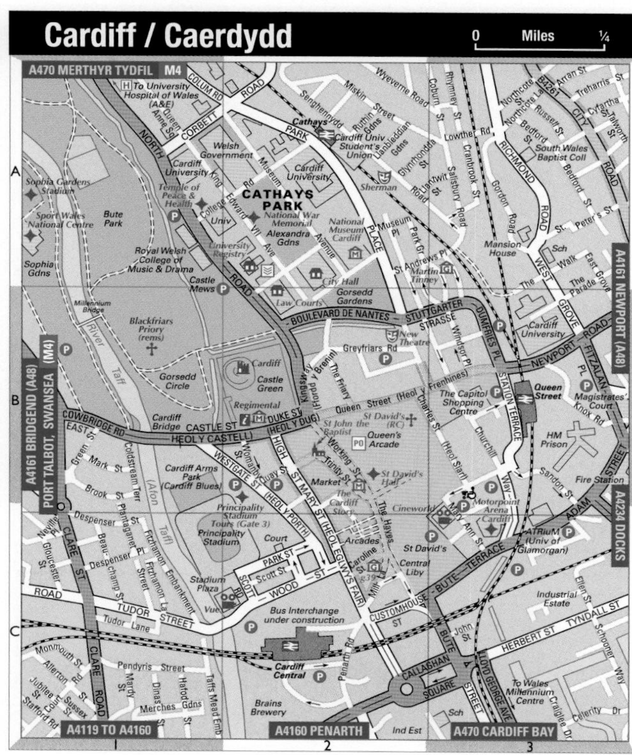
Cardiff / Caerdydd
0 Miles ¼
A470 MERTHYR TYDFIL M4
A4161 NEWPORT (A48)
A4161 BRIDGEND (A48) PORT TALBOT, SWANSEA (M4)
A4234 DOCKS
A4119 TO A4160
A4160 PENARTH
A470 CARDIFF BAY
CATHAYS PARK
BOULEVARD DE NANTES
Cardiff Central
Queen Street

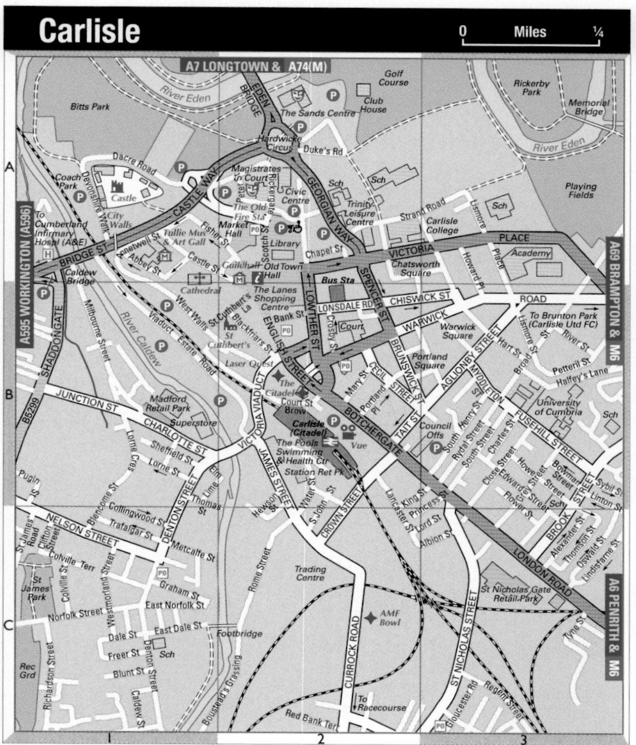
Carlisle
0 Miles ¼
A7 LONGTOWN & A74(M)
A595 WORKINGTON (A596)
A69 BRAMPTON & M6
A6 PENRITH & M6
Bus Sta
Carlisle Citadel

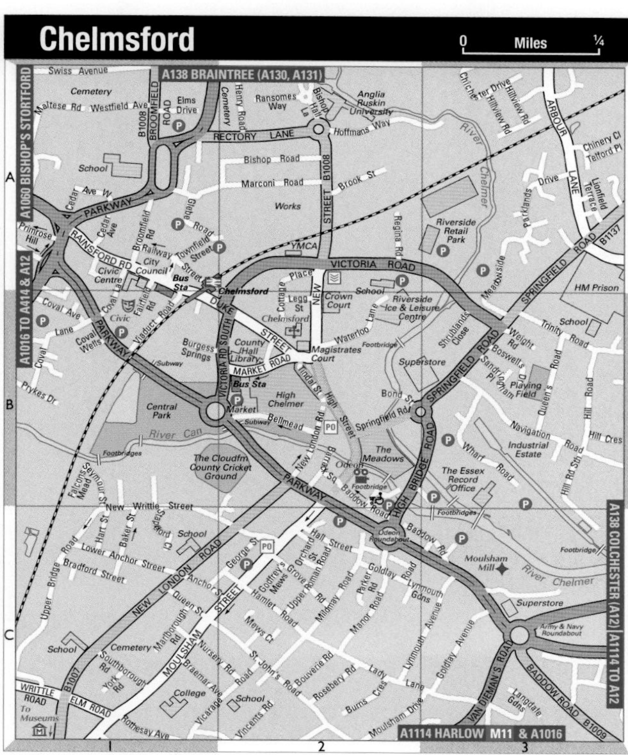
Chelmsford
0 Miles ¼
A138 BRAINTREE (A130, A131)
A1060 BISHOP'S STORTFORD
A1016 TO A414 & A12
A138 COLCHESTER (A12) A1114 TO A12
A1114 HARLOW M11 & A1016
VICTORIA ROAD
PARKWAY
Bus Sta
Chelmsford

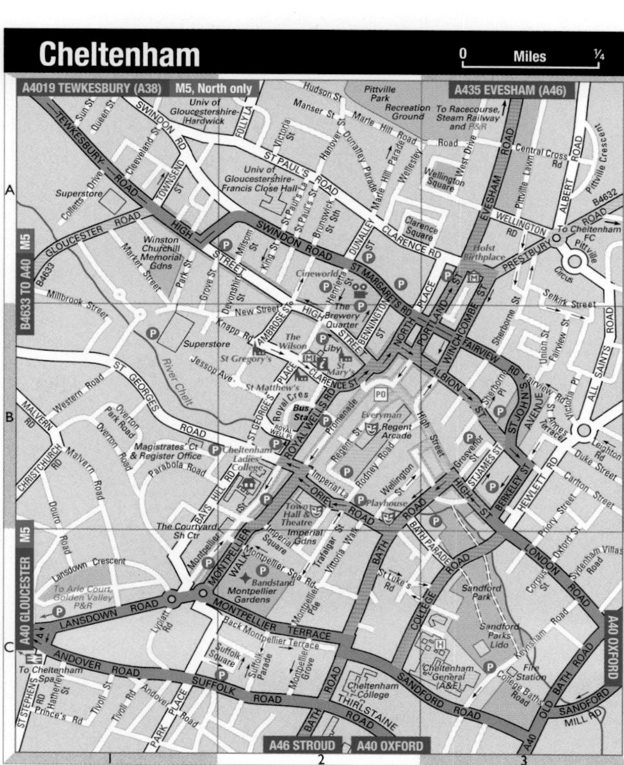
Cheltenham
0 Miles ¼
A4019 TEWKESBURY (A38) M5, North only
A435 EVESHAM (A46)
B4633 TO A40 M5
A40 GLOUCESTER M5
A40 OXFORD
A46 STROUD A40 OXFORD
SWINDON ROAD
MONTPELLIER TERRACE
LANSDOWN ROAD

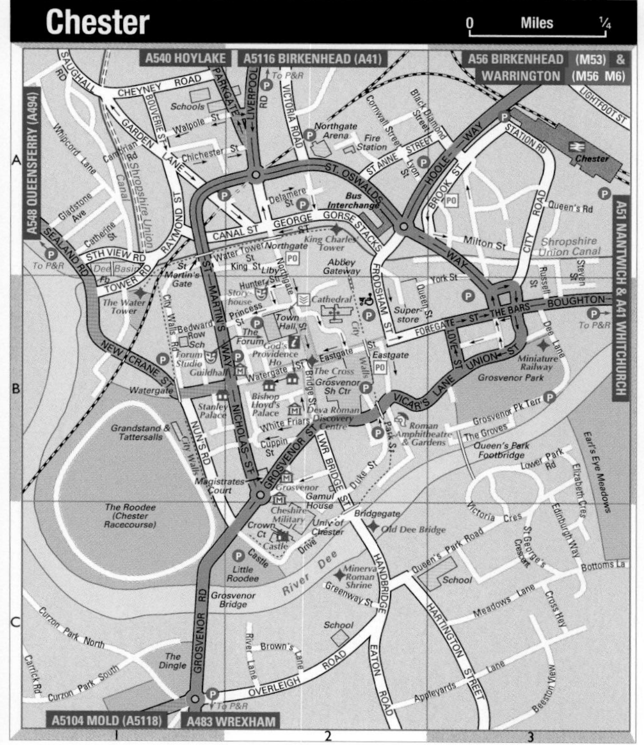
Chester
0 Miles ¼
A540 HOYLAKE
A5116 BIRKENHEAD (A41)
A56 BIRKENHEAD (M53) & WARRINGTON (M56 M6)
A548 QUEENSFERRY (A494)
A51 NANTWICH & A41 WHITCHURCH
A5104 MOLD (A5118)
A483 WREXHAM
The Roodee (Chester Racecourse)
River Dee
Bus Interchange

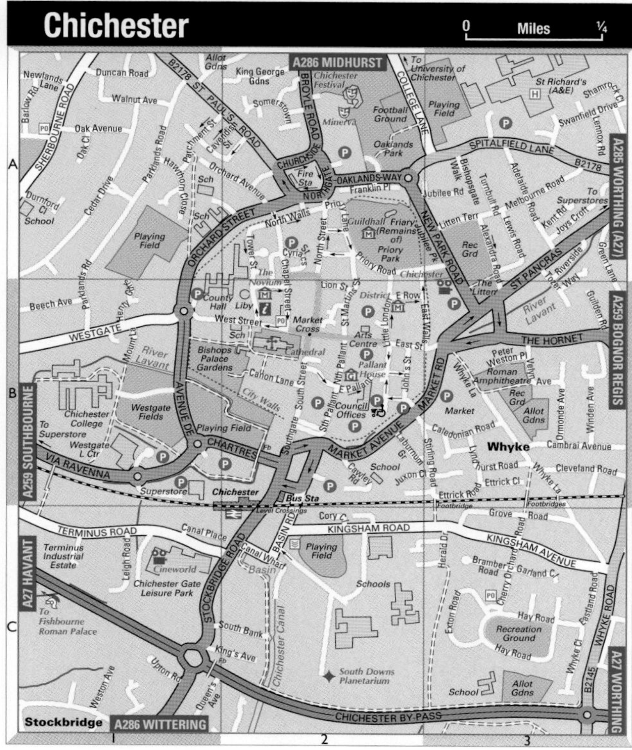
Chichester
0 Miles ¼
A286 MIDHURST
A285 WORTHING (A27)
A259 BOGNOR REGIS
A259 SOUTHBOURNE
A27 HAVANT
A27 WORTHING
Stockbridge
A286 WITTERING
CHICHESTER BY-PASS
Whyke
Bus Sta

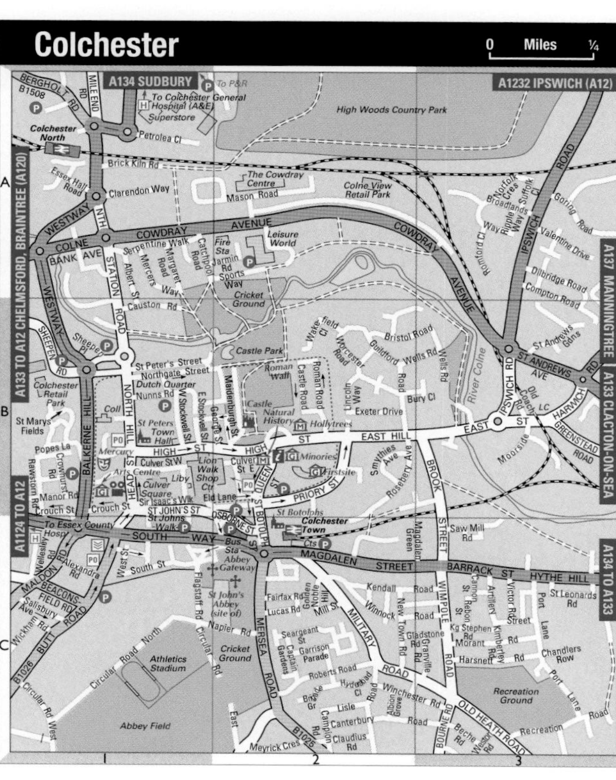
Colchester
0 Miles ¼
A134 SUDBURY
A1232 IPSWICH (A12)
A133 TO A12 CHELMSFORD, BRAINTREE (A120)
A137 MANNINGTREE A133 CLACTON-ON-SEA
A134 TO A133
A12 TO A12
High Woods Country Park
Castle Park
MAGDALEN STREET

Coventry

0 Miles ¼

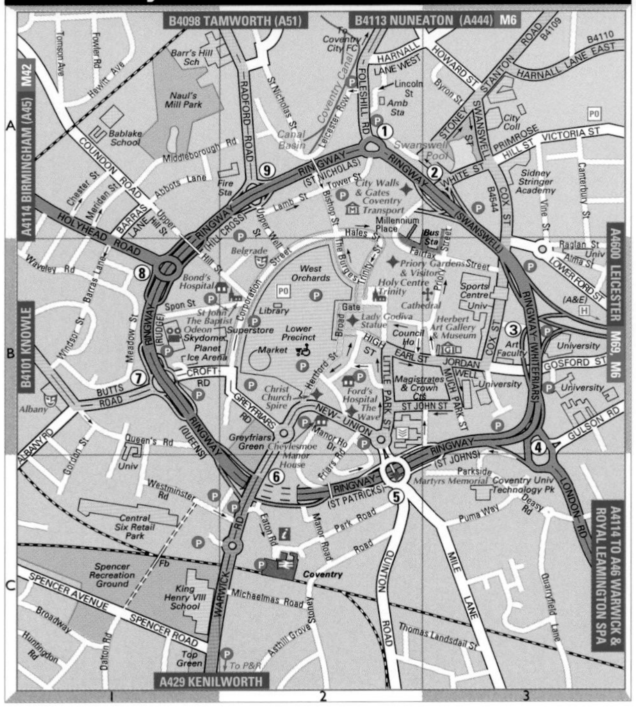

B4098 TAMWORTH (A51) · B4113 NUNEATON (A444) M6 · A4114 BIRMINGHAM (A45) M42 · B4101 KNOWLE · A4600 LEICESTER M69 M6 · A4114 TO A46 WARWICK & ROYAL LEAMINGTON SPA · A429 KENILWORTH

Ringway · Coventry Canal Basin · Coventry Transport Museum · Cathedral · Holy Trinity · Priory Gardens · Herbert Art Gallery & Museum · University · Lady Godiva Statue · Greyfriars Green · Coventry Univ Technology Pk · Central Six Retail Park · Spencer Recreation Ground · King Henry VIII School · Coventry

Derby

0 Miles ¼

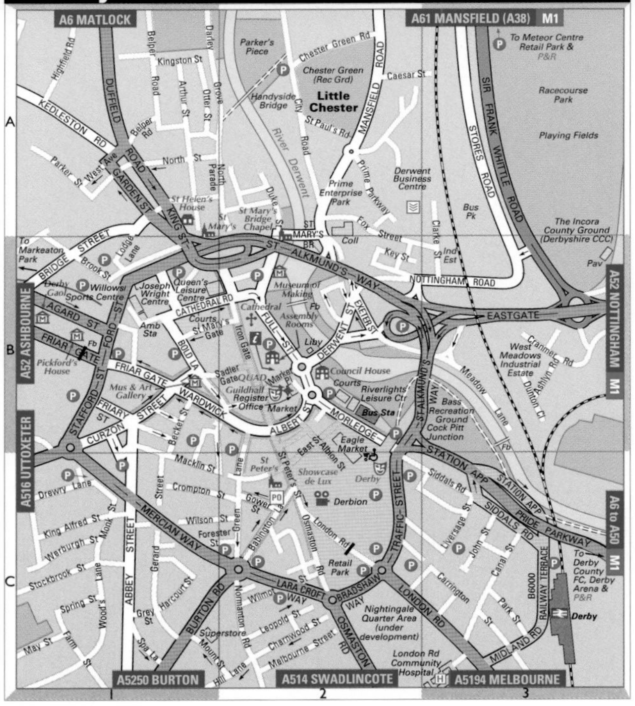

A6 MATLOCK · A61 MANSFIELD (A38) M1 · A52 ASHBOURNE · A516 UTTOXETER · A52 NOTTINGHAM M1 · A6 to A50 M1 · A5250 BURTON · A514 SWADLINCOTE · A5194 MELBOURNE

Little Chester · Parker's Piece · Racecourse Park · Derwent Business Centre · Cathedral · Museum of Making · Assembly Rooms · Council House · Riverlights Leisure Ctr · Bus Sta · Derbion · Derby County FC, Derby Arena & P&R · Derby

Dorchester

0 Miles ¼

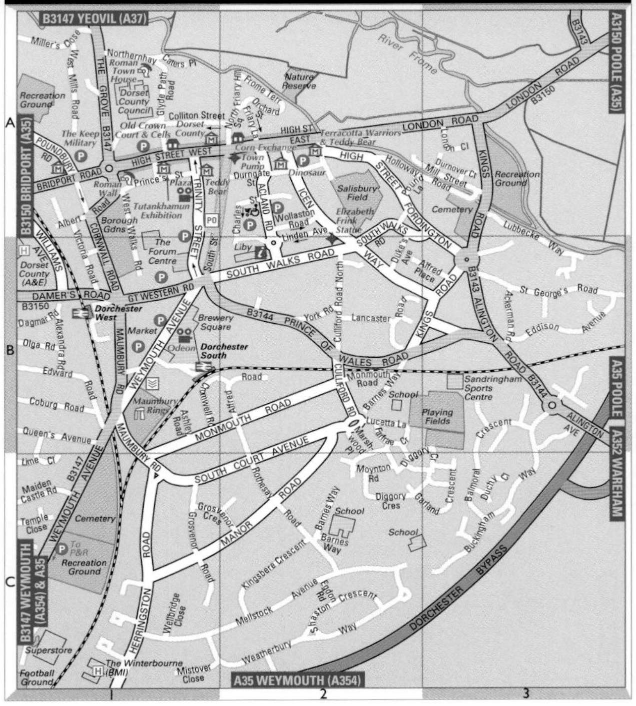

B3147 YEOVIL (A37) · A3150 POOLE (A35) · B3150 BRIDPORT (A35) · A35 POOLE A352 WAREHAM · B3147 WEYMOUTH (A354) A35 · A35 WEYMOUTH (A354)

River Frome · Dorset County Council · High St West · High St East · London Road · Tutankhamun Exhibition · Dorset County Museum · Salisbury Field · Dorchester South · Dorchester West · Brewery Square · South Court Avenue · Dorchester Bypass

Dumfries

0 Miles ¼

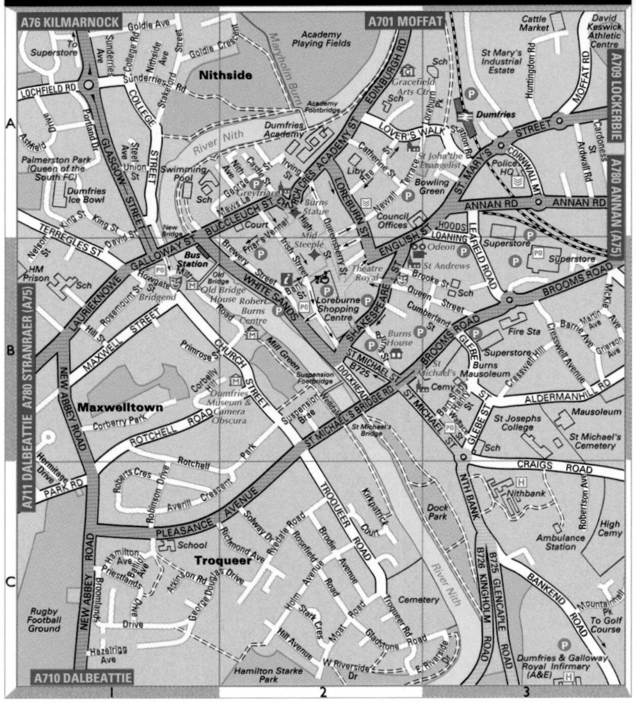

A76 KILMARNOCK · A701 MOFFAT · A709 LOCKERBIE · A780 ANNAN (A75) · A780 STRANRAER (A75) · A711 DALBEATTIE · A710 DALBEATTIE

Nithside · Dumfries Academy · River Nith · Loreburne Shopping Centre · Maxwelltown · Troqueer · Dumfries & Galloway Royal Infirmary (A&E)

Dundee

0 Miles ¼

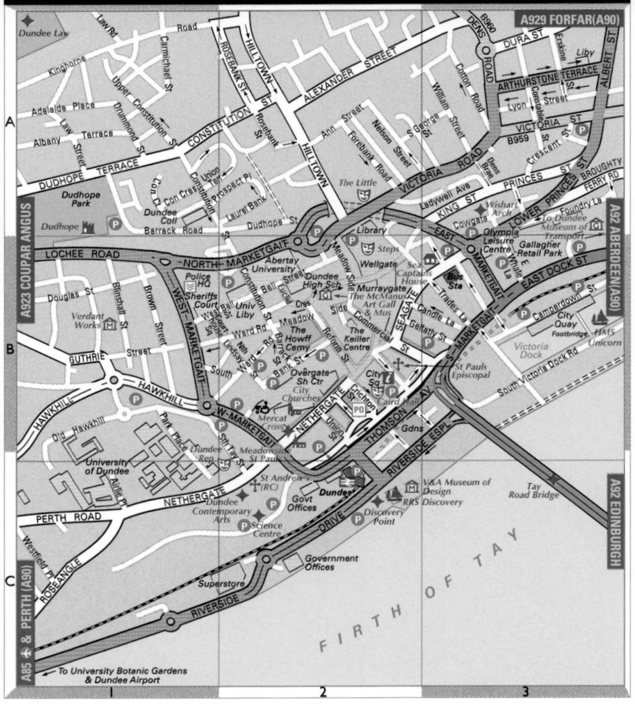

A929 FORFAR (A90) · A923 COUPAR ANGUS · A92 ABERDEEN (A90) · A85 & PERTH (A90) · A92 EDINBURGH

Dudhope Park · Abertay University · Overgate Sh Ctr · University of Dundee · V&A Museum of Design · RRS Discovery · Tay Road Bridge · FIRTH OF TAY

Durham

0 Miles ¼

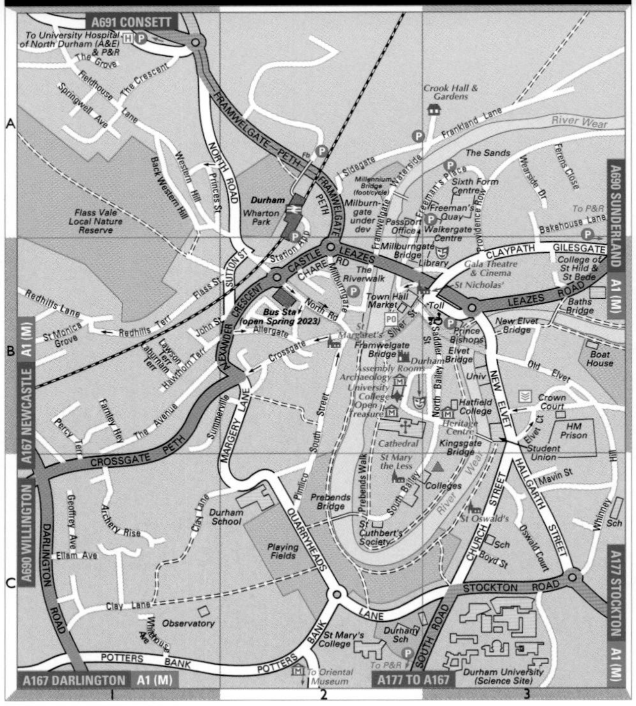

A691 CONSETT · A690 SUNDERLAND A1 (M) · A167 NEWCASTLE A1 (M) · A690 WILLINGTON · A177 STOCKTON A1 (M) · A167 DARLINGTON A1 (M) · A177 TO A167

River Wear · Wharton Park · Flass Vale Local Nature Reserve · Market Place · Castle · Cathedral · Durham School · Durham University (Science Site)

Edinburgh

0 Miles ¼

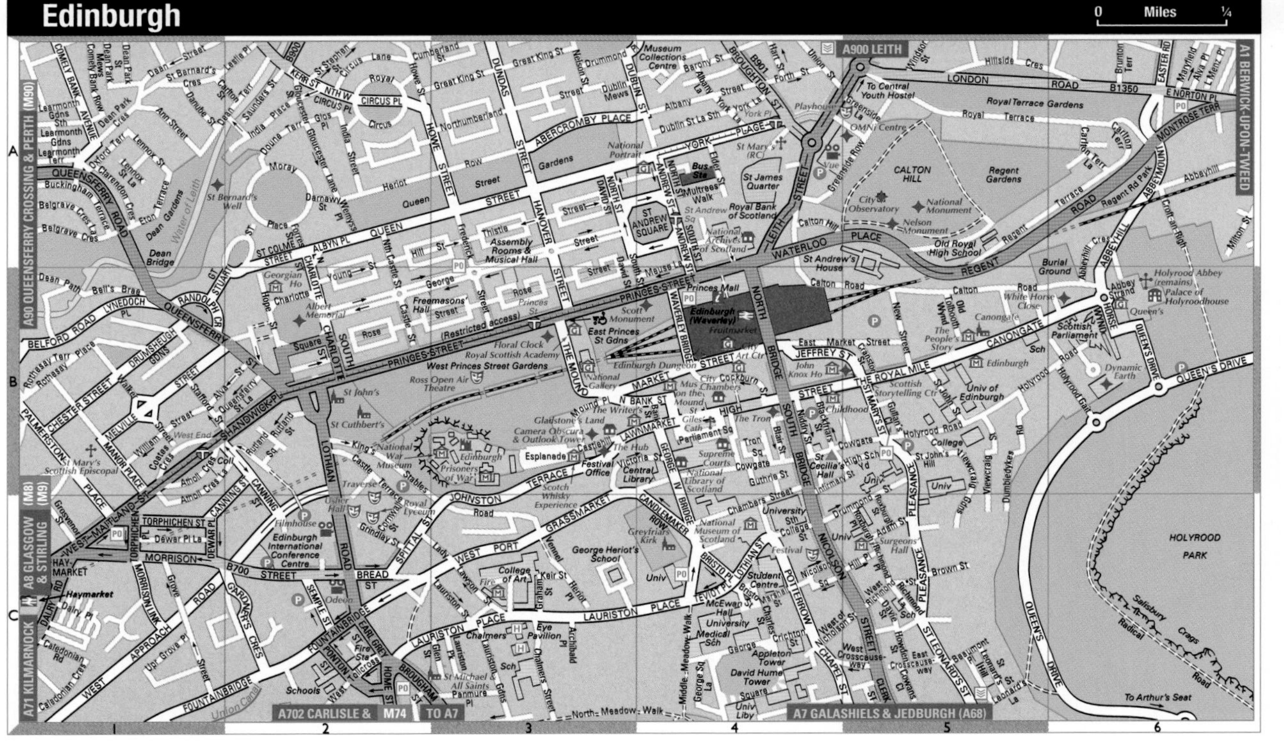

Exeter

0 Miles ¼

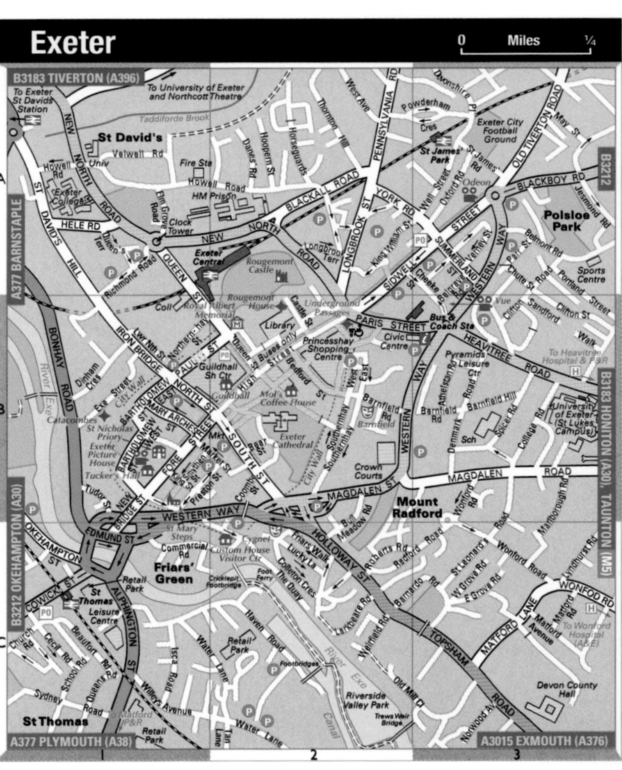

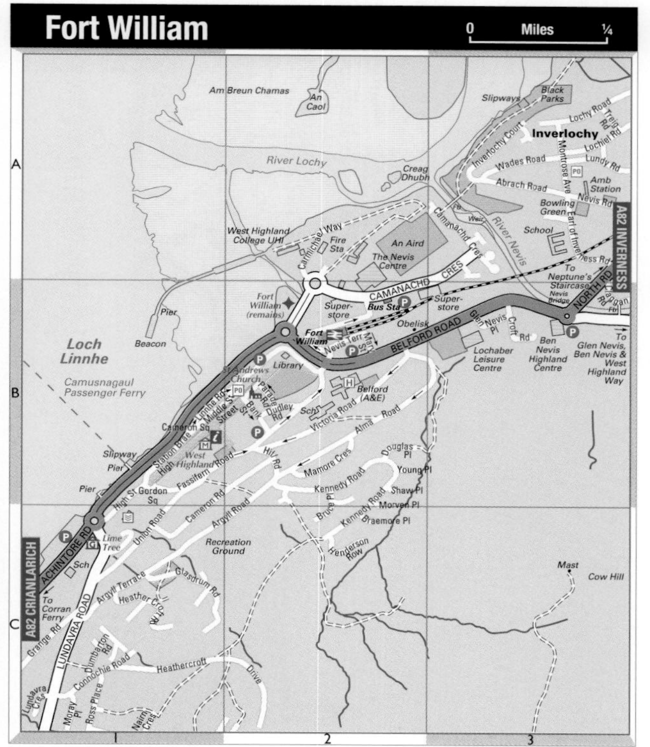
Fort William
0 Miles ¼
Inverlochy
River Lochy
Loch Linnhe
Camusnagaul Passenger Ferry
A82 INVERNESS
A82 CRIANLARICH
BELFORD ROAD
Lochaber Leisure Centre
Belford (A&E)
Recreation Ground
Cow Hill
Inverlochy Castle
Banavie
Corpach

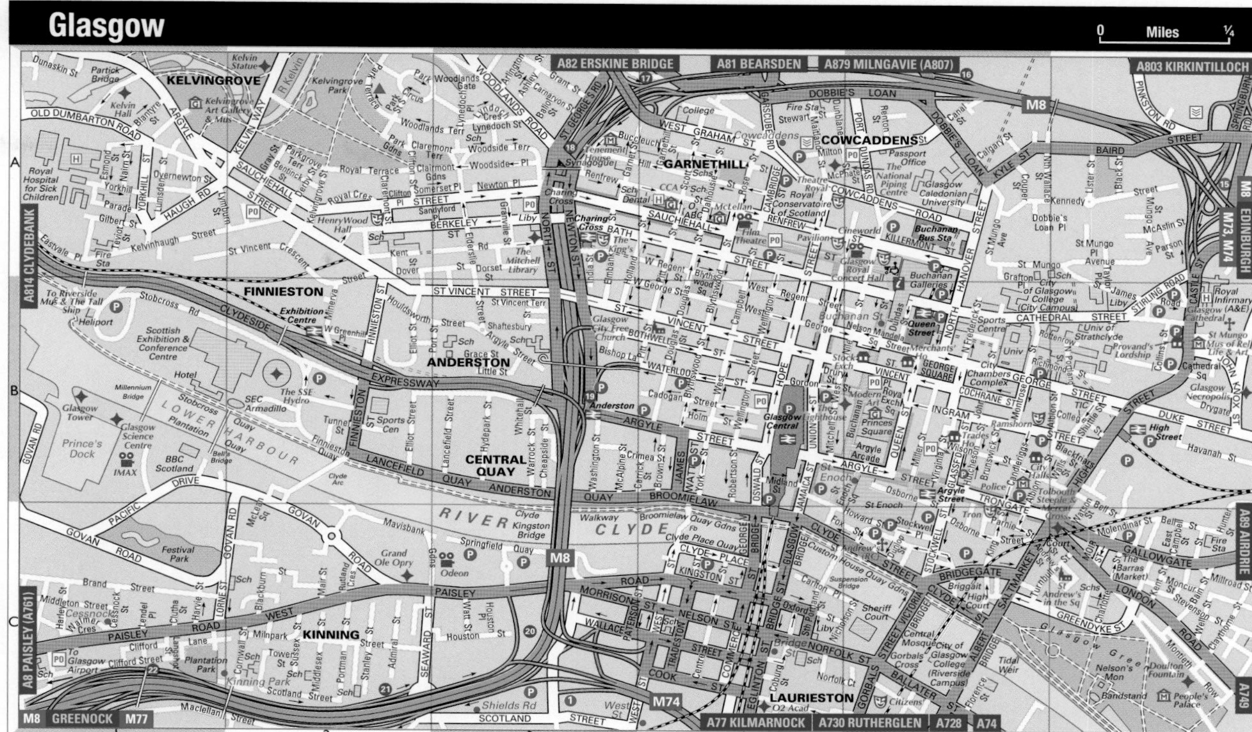
Glasgow
0 Miles ¼
A82 ERSKINE BRIDGE
A81 BEARSDEN
A879 MILNGAVIE (A807)
A803 KIRKINTILLOCH
KELVINGROVE
COWCADDENS
GARNETHILL
FINNIESTON
ANDERSTON
CENTRAL QUAY
KINNING
LAURIESTON
RIVER CLYDE
A814 CLYDEBANK
A8 PAISLEY (A761)
M8 GREENOCK
M77
A77 KILMARNOCK
A730 RUTHERGLEN
A728
A74
A749
A89 AIRDRIE
M8 EDINBURGH M73, M74
M8
M74
Glasgow Central
Queen Street
Buchanan Bus Sta
Glasgow Green
The SSE Hydro
SEC Armadillo

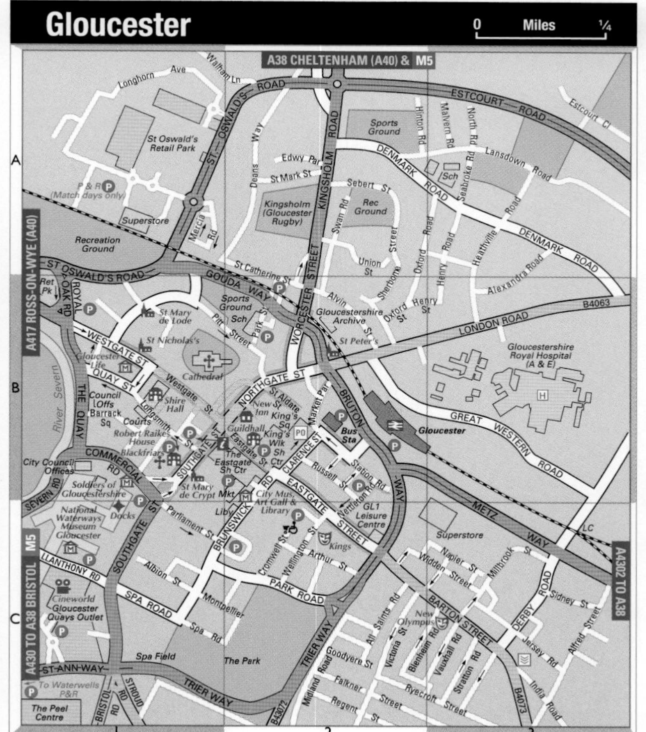
Gloucester
0 Miles ¼
A38 CHELTENHAM (A40) & M5
A417 ROSS-ON-WYE (A40)
A430 TO A38 BRISTOL M5
A4302 TO A38
ESTCOURT ROAD
LONDON ROAD
GREAT WESTERN ROAD
Gloucestershire Royal Hospital (A & E)
Kingsholm (Gloucester Rugby)
Cathedral
The Park
River Severn
Gloucester

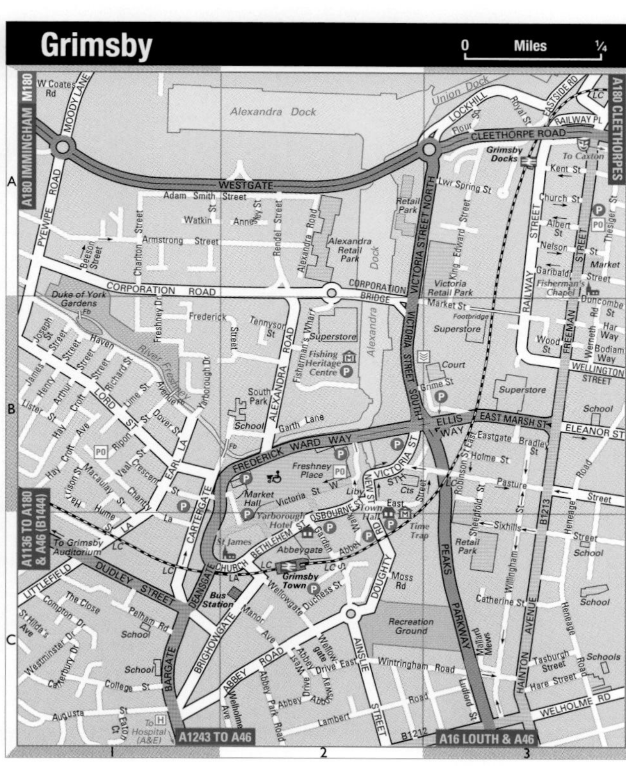
Grimsby
0 Miles ¼
A180 IMMINGHAM M180
A180 CLEETHORPES
A1136 TO A180 & A46 (B1444)
A1243 TO A46
A16 LOUTH & A46
Alexandra Dock
Grimsby Docks
WESTGATE
CORPORATION ROAD
Victoria Retail Park
Grimsby Town
Bus Station
Recreation Ground

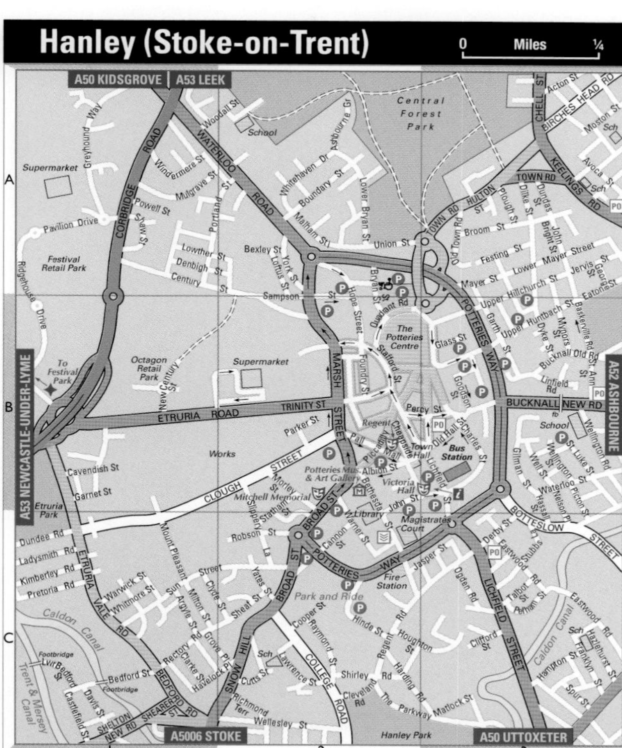
Hanley (Stoke-on-Trent)
0 Miles ¼
A50 KIDSGROVE
A53 LEEK
A53 NEWCASTLE-UNDER-LYME
A52 ASHBOURNE
A5006 STOKE
A50 UTTOXETER
Central Forest Park
Festival Retail Park
ETRURIA ROAD
The Potteries Centre
Bus Station
Caldon Canal
Hanley Park

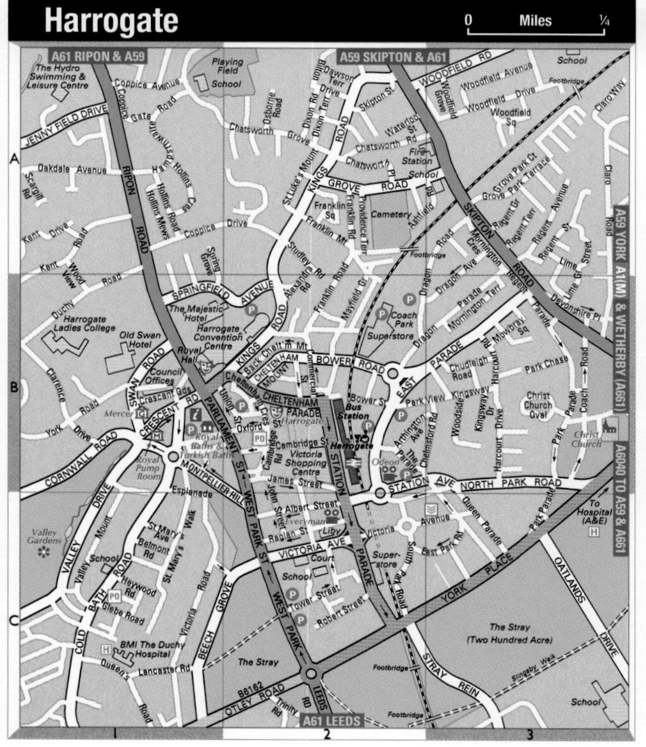
Harrogate
0 Miles ¼
A61 RIPON & A59
A59 SKIPTON & A61
A59 YORK A1(M) & WETHERBY (A661)
A6040 TO A59 & A661
A61 LEEDS
Harrogate Ladies College
Harrogate Convention Centre
The Stray (Two Hundred Acre)
Valley Gardens
Victoria Shopping Centre

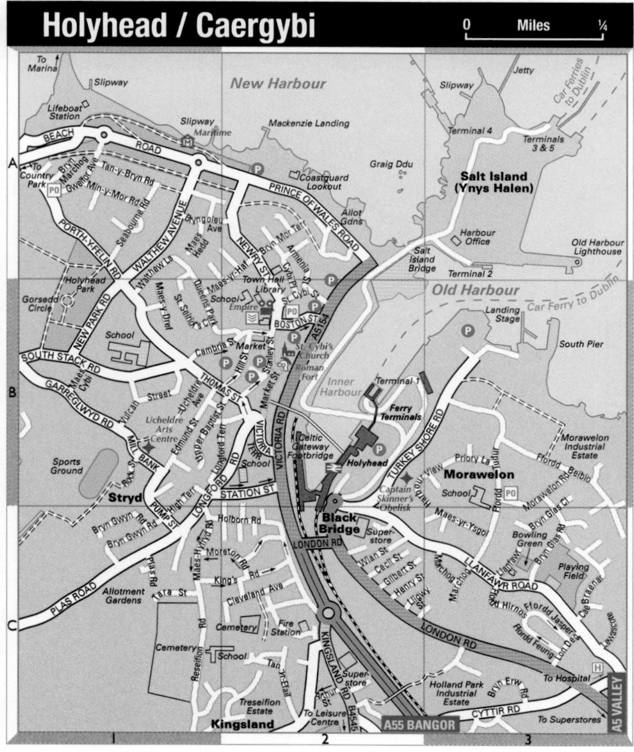
Holyhead / Caergybi
0 Miles ¼
New Harbour
Old Harbour
Salt Island (Ynys Halen)
Inner Harbour
Ferry Terminals
Morawelon
Stryd
Kingsland
A55 BANGOR
A5 VALLEY
Car Ferry to Dublin

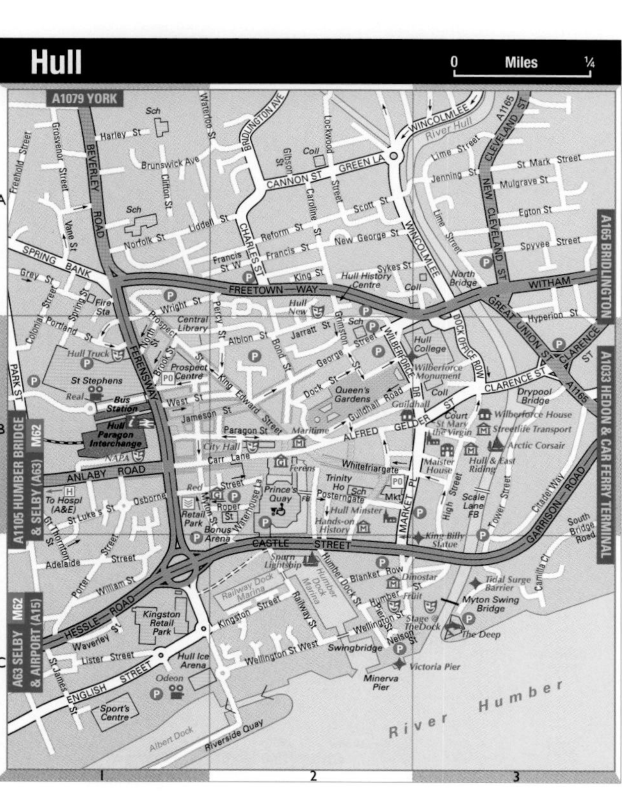
Hull
0 Miles ¼
A1079 YORK
A165 BRIDLINGTON
A1033 HEDON & CAR FERRY TERMINAL
A1105 HUMBER BRIDGE & SELBY (A63)
M62
A63 SELBY & AIRPORT (A15)
FREETOWN WAY
CASTLE STREET
Hull Paragon Interchange
Queen's Gardens
The Deep
River Humber
River Hull

Inverness

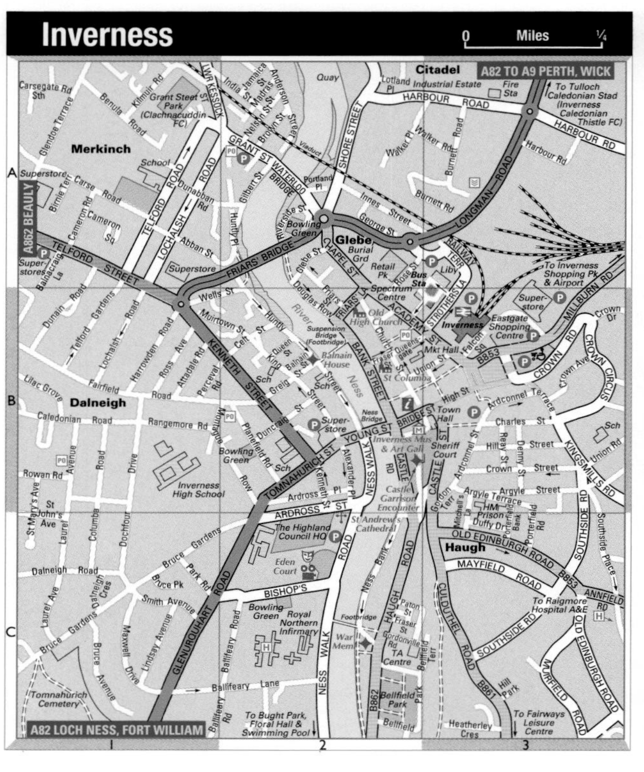

Ipswich

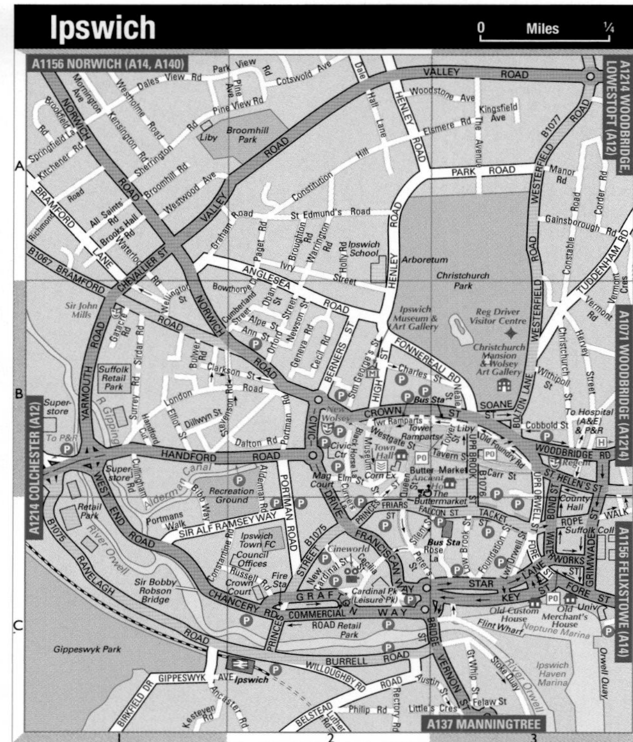

Kendal

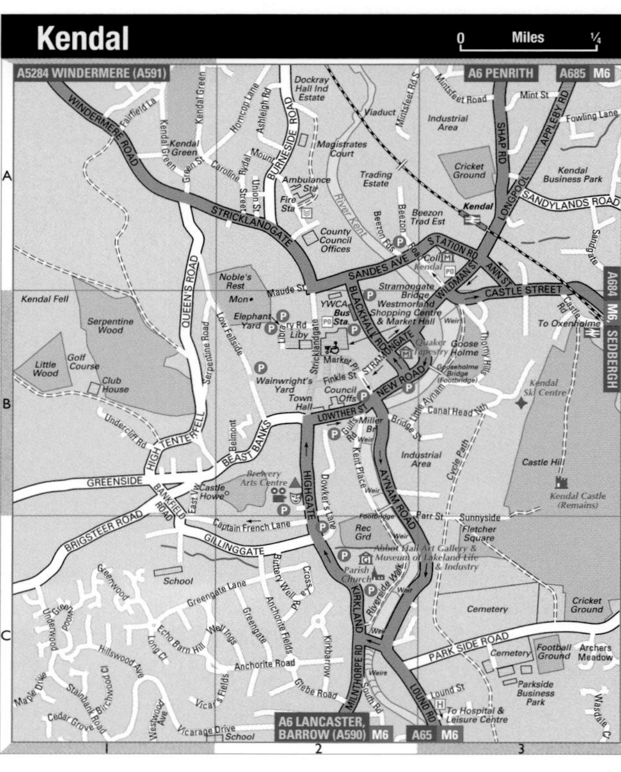

King's Lynn

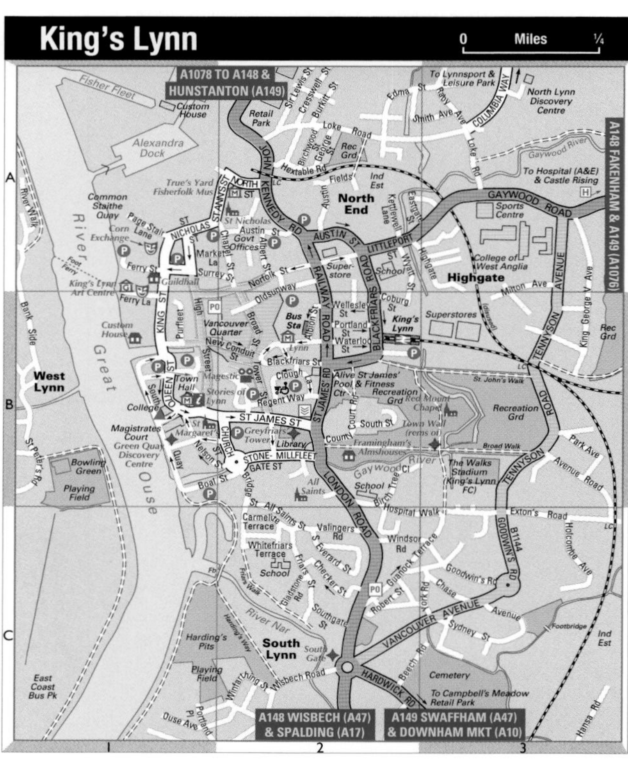

Leeds

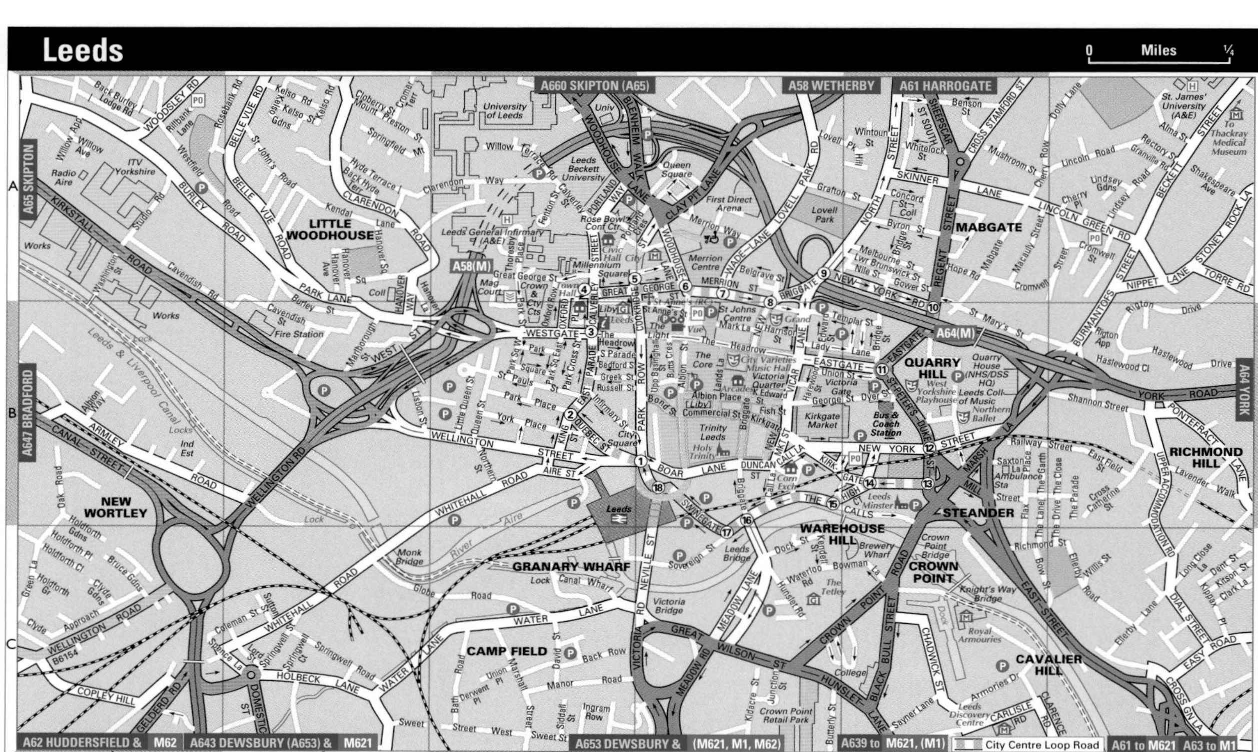

Lancaster

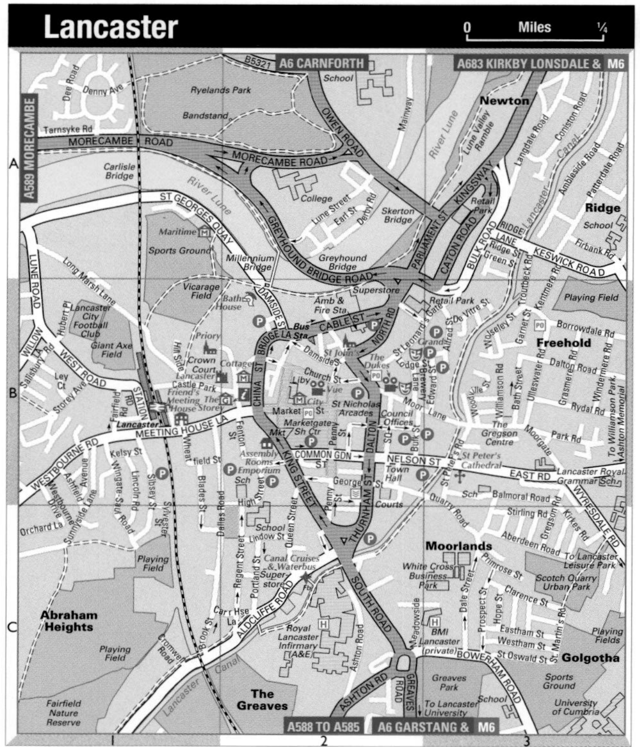

Leicester

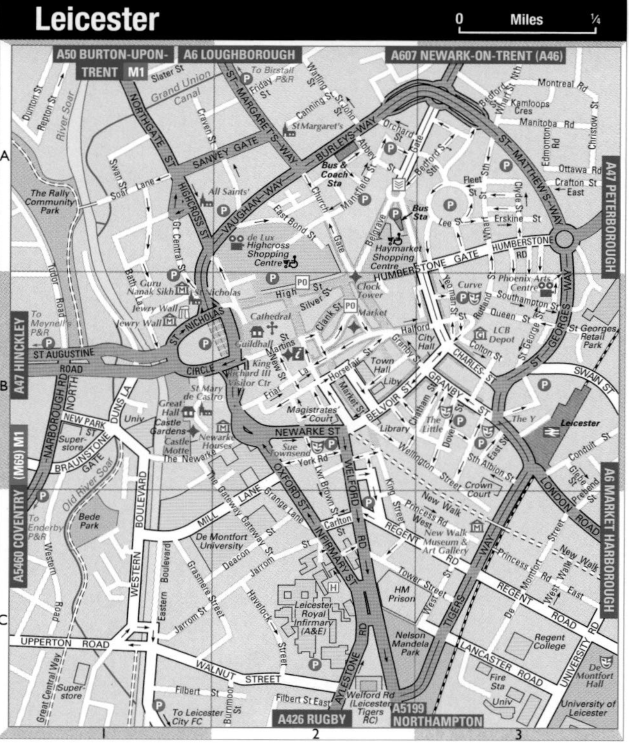

Lewes

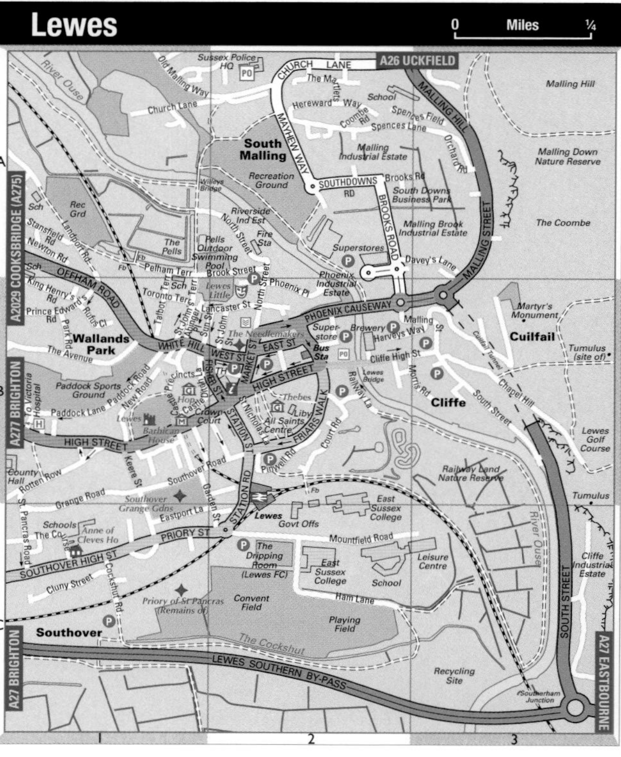

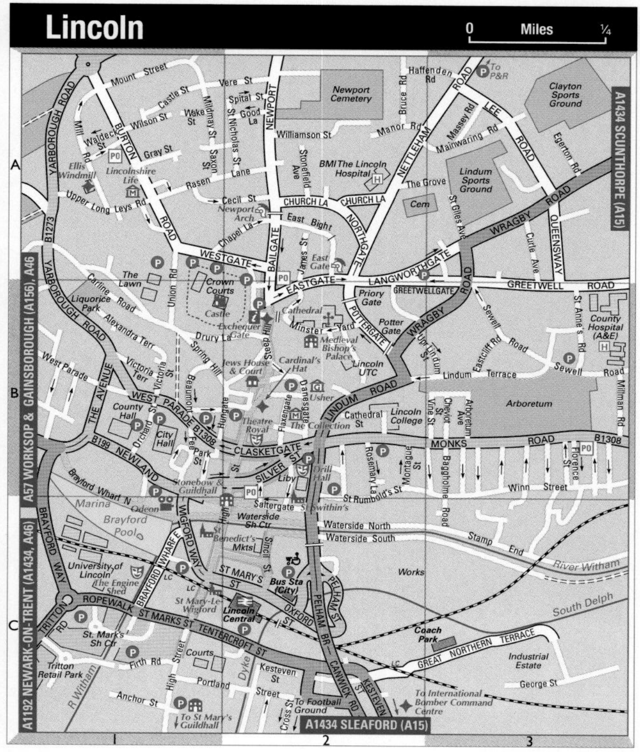
Lincoln
0 Miles ¼
A1434 SCUNTHORPE (A15)
A46
A57 WORKSOP & GAINSBOROUGH (A156)
A1192 NEWARK-ON-TRENT (A1434, A46)
A1434 SLEAFORD (A15)
Newport Cemetery
Clayton Sports Ground
Lindum Sports Ground
Arboretum
Brayford Pool
River Witham
South Delph
Works
Industrial Estate
Coach Park
Tritton Retail Park
Castle
Cathedral
University of Lincoln
County Hospital (A&E)

Liverpool
0 Miles ¼
A5036 TO A565
A565 SOUTHPORT
A5038 KIRKDALE
A59 PRESTON M57 & M58 & KINGSWAY TUNNEL
A580 TO A59
A5049 WEST DERBY
A57 WARRINGTON
A5047 TO M62 & MANCHESTER
A5036 TO A562
A561 GARSTON
A5038 TO A561
A5039 TO A562
A5048 TO A562
RIVER MERSEY
Princes Dock
Princes Jetty
Moorfields
Lime Street
Liverpool Central
Queen Square Bus Stn
Chavasse Park
Canning Dock
Royal Albert Dock
Metropolitan Cathedral (RC)
University of Liverpool
Royal Liverpool University (A&E)
Abercromby Square
Sydney Jones Liby

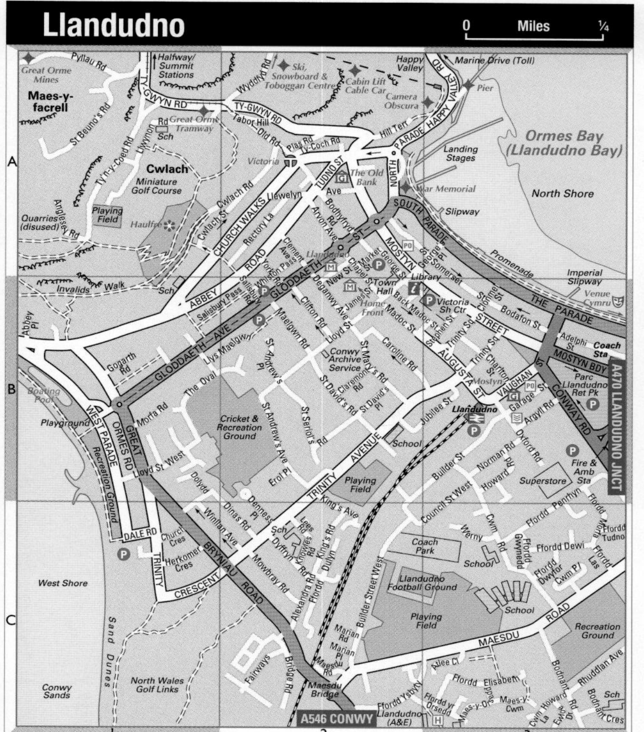
Llandudno
0 Miles ¼
Great Orme Mines
Maes-y-facrell
Cwlach
Ormes Bay (Llandudno Bay)
North Shore
Landing Stages
Slipway
Imperial Slipway
West Shore
Conwy Sands
North Wales Golf Links
Cricket & Recreation Ground
Llandudno Football Ground
Playing Field
A470 LLANDUDNO JNCT
A546 CONWY

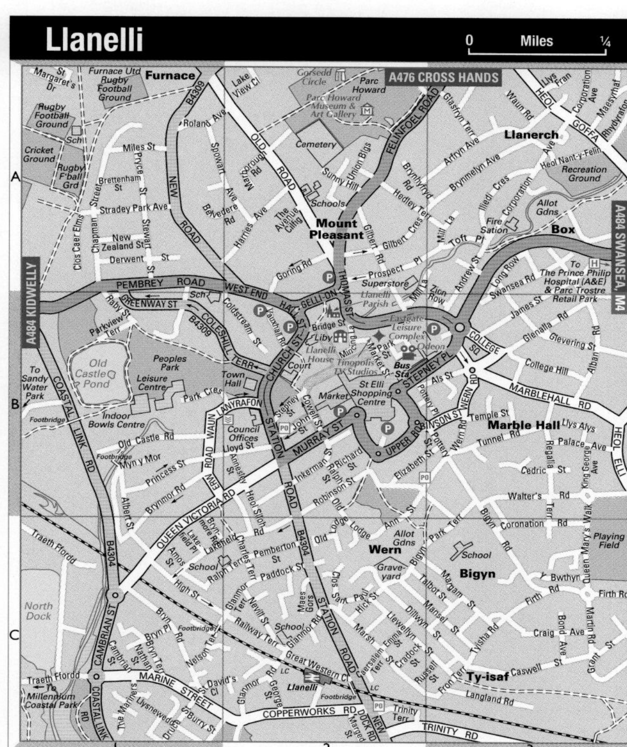
Llanelli
0 Miles ¼
A476 CROSS HANDS
A484 SWANSEA, M4
A484 KIDWELLY
Furnace
Llanerch
Mount Pleasant
Box
Peoples Park
Old Castle Pond
Marble Hall
Wern
Bigyn
Ty-isaf
North Dock
Millennium Coastal Park
Llanelli

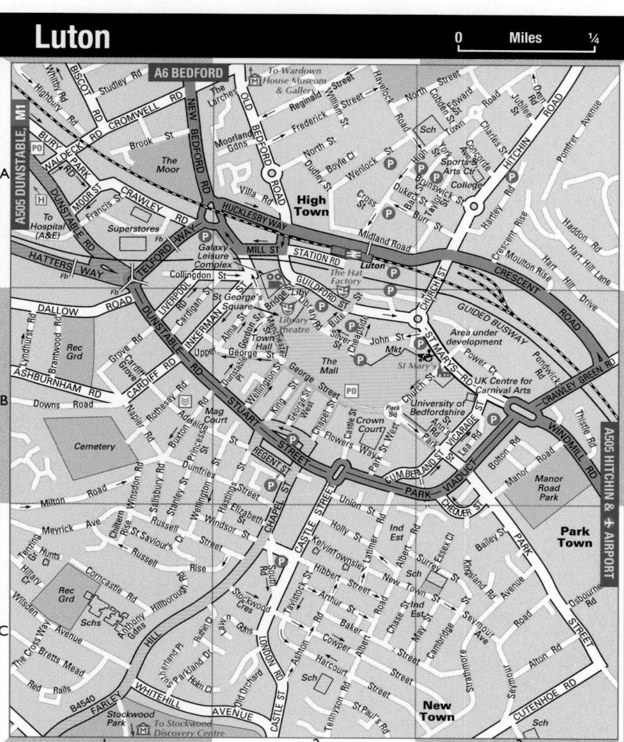
Luton
0 Miles ¼
A6 BEDFORD
A505 DUNSTABLE, M1
A505 HITCHIN & AIRPORT
High Town
The Moor
Luton
Cemetery
Park Town
New Town
Stockwood Park
Manor Road Park
University of Bedfordshire
UK Centre for Carnival Arts

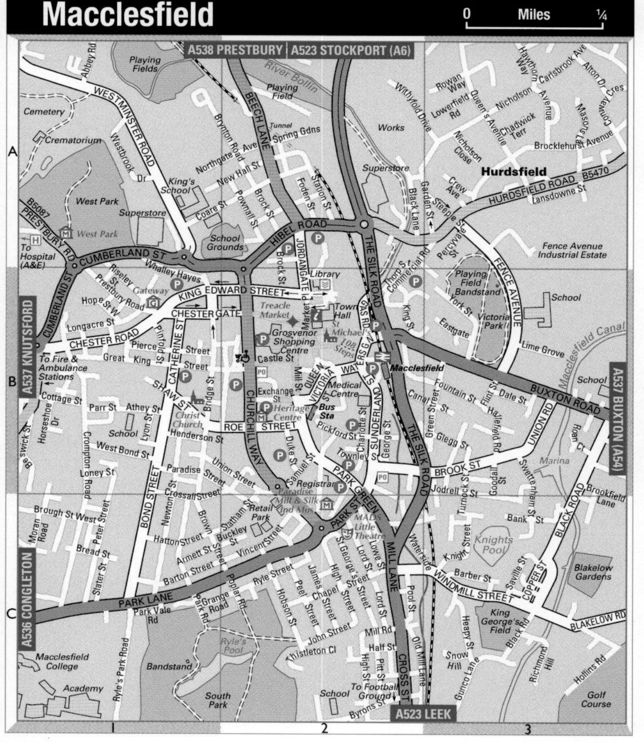
Macclesfield
0 Miles ¼
A538 PRESTBURY
A523 STOCKPORT (A6)
A537 KNUTSFORD
A536 CONGLETON
A523 LEEK
A537 BUXTON (A54)
Hurdsfield
West Park
Crematorium
Cemetery
Fence Avenue Industrial Estate
Macclesfield
Knights Pool
Blakelow Gardens
Macclesfield College
South Park
Golf Course

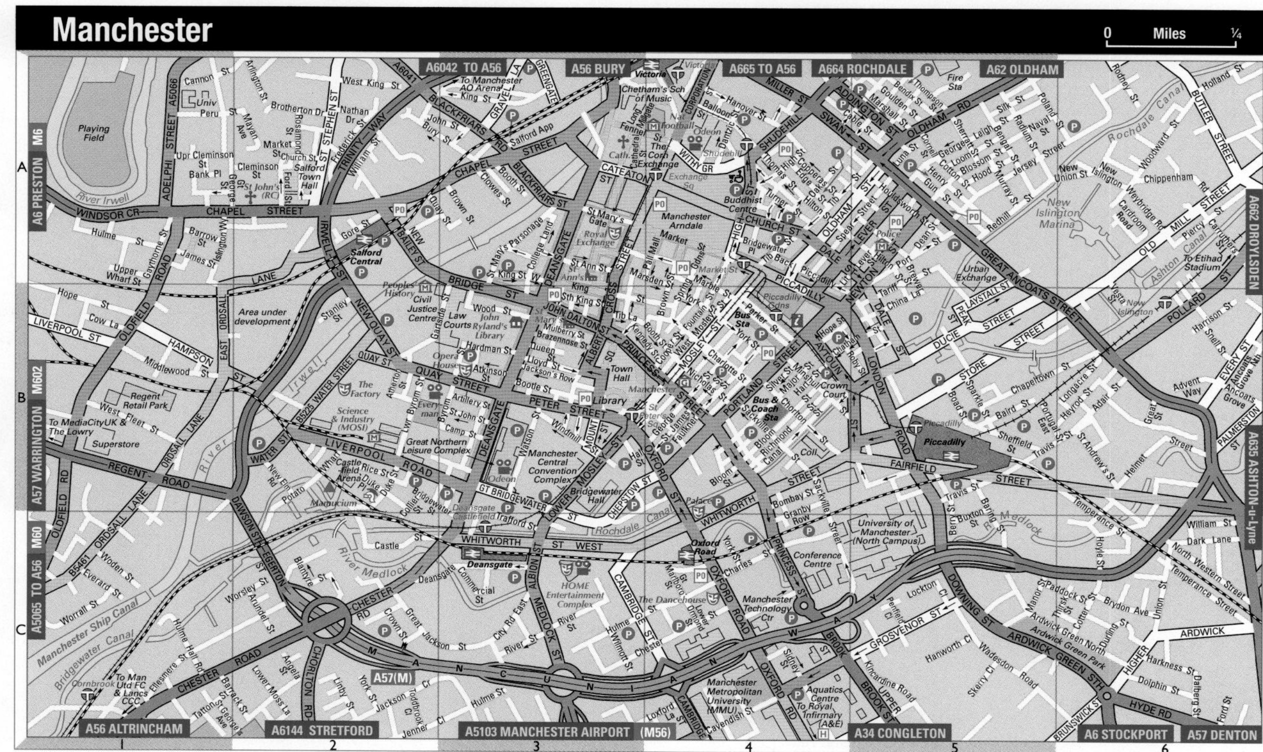
Manchester
0 Miles ¼
A6042 TO A56
A56 BURY
A665 TO A56
A664 ROCHDALE
A62 OLDHAM
A6 PRESTON
A662 DROYLSDEN
A635 ASHTON-u-Lyne
A57 WARRINGTON
M602
A5063 TO A56
M60
A56 ALTRINCHAM
A6144 STRETFORD
A5103 MANCHESTER AIRPORT (M56)
A34 CONGLETON
A6 STOCKPORT
A57 DENTON
Salford Central
Manchester Arndale
Piccadilly
Oxford Road
Deansgate
University of Manchester (North Campus)
Manchester Technology Centre
New Islington Marina
Rochdale Canal
Bridgewater Canal
Manchester Ship Canal
River Irwell
River Medlock
A57(M)
MANCUNIAN WAY

ST. JOHN'S WOOD
REGENT'S PARK
SOMERS TOWN
LISSON GREEN
PADDINGTON
FITZROVIA
BLOOMSBURY
SOHO
MAYFAIR
ST JAMES'S
HYDE PARK
KENSINGTON GARDENS
GREEN PARK
ST JAMES'S PARK
KNIGHTSBRIDGE
BROMPTON
WESTMINSTER
PIMLICO
THE SERPENTINE
Lord's Cricket Ground (MCC & Middlesex CCC)
London Zoo
Regent's Park Boating Lake
Queen Mary's Gardens
Open Air Theatre
London Central Mosque
Regents College
London Business School
Madame Tussaud's
Euston
King's Cross
St Pancras International
British Library
University College London (UCL)
University of London
British Museum
University of Westminster
Wallace Collection
Marble Arch
Speakers Corner
Roosevelt Memorial
Piccadilly Circus
National Gallery
Trafalgar Square
Nelson's Column
Horse Guards' Parade
Buckingham Palace Gardens
Queen Victoria Memorial
Wellington Arch
Apsley House
Hyde Park Corner
Victoria
Westminster Cathedral (RC)
Westminster Abbey
Natural History Museum
Science Museum
Victoria & Albert Museum
Royal Albert Hall
Imperial College London
Albert Memorial
Serpentine Gallery
Saatchi Gallery
Tate Britain
Victoria Coach Station
Marylebone
Paddington Basin
EUSTON ROAD
MARYLEBONE ROAD
OXFORD STREET
PICCADILLY
PARK LANE
KNIGHTSBRIDGE
BAYSWATER ROAD
EDGWARE ROAD
VICTORIA STREET
CROMWELL ROAD

5
6
7
8
B
C
D
E
F
HOXTON
FINSBURY
SHOREDITCH
CLERKENWELL
HOLBORN
THE CITY
SOUTHWARK
SOUTH BANK
NEWINGTON
LAMBETH
BERMONDSEY
RIVER THAMES
Bunhill Fields
The Barbican
Liverpool Street
Lincoln's Inn Fields
St Paul's Cathedral
Tate Modern
Shakespeare's Globe Theatre
The Tower of London
London Bridge
Waterloo
Elephant & Castle
Imperial War Museum
Lambeth Palace
County Hall
London Eye
Royal Festival Hall
Borough Market
Southwark Cathedral
Guy's Hospital
The Shard
Tower Bridge
Blackfriars
Cannon Street
Fenchurch Street
Moorgate
Farringdon
Old Spitalfields Market
Miles
0
½

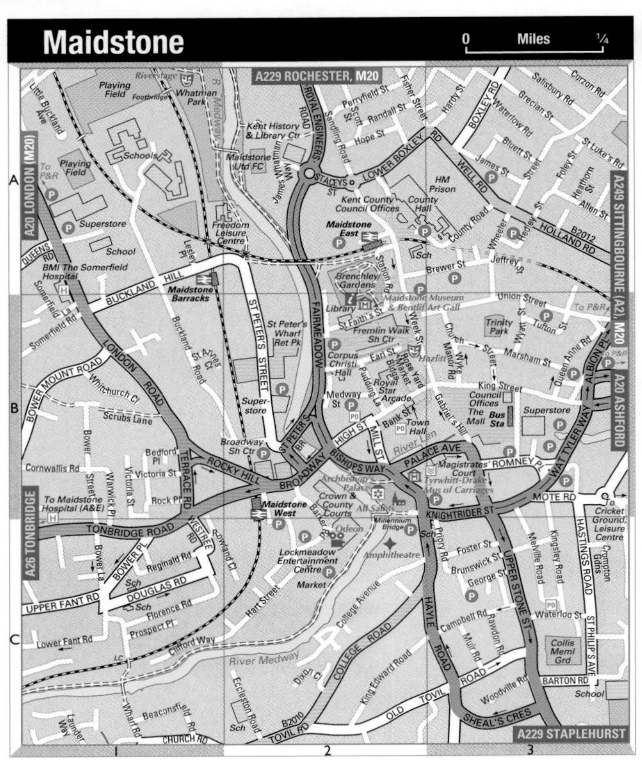
Maidstone
0 Miles ¼
A229 ROCHESTER, M20
A20 LONDON (M20)
A249 SITTINGBOURNE (A2) M20
A20 ASHFORD
A26 TONBRIDGE
A229 STAPLEHURST

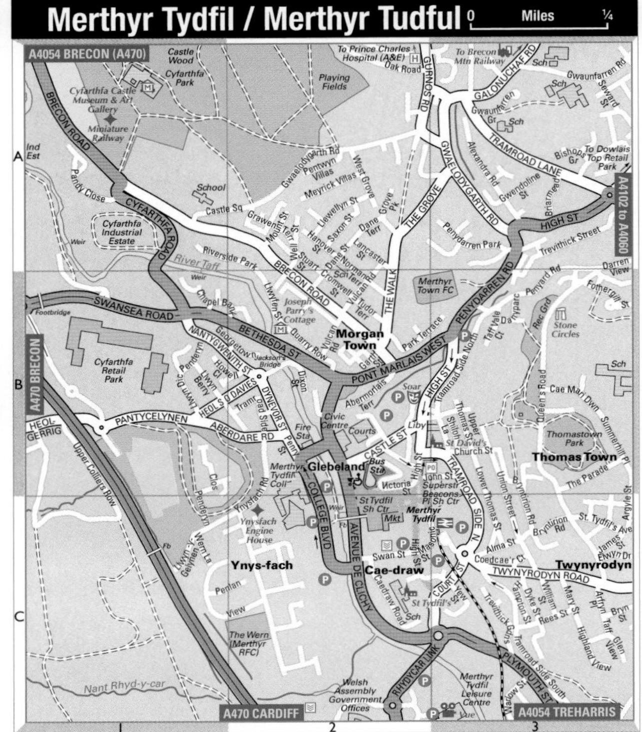
Merthyr Tydfil / Merthyr Tudful
0 Miles ¼
A4054 BRECON (A470)
A470 BRECON
A4102 to A4060
A470 CARDIFF
A4054 TREHARRIS

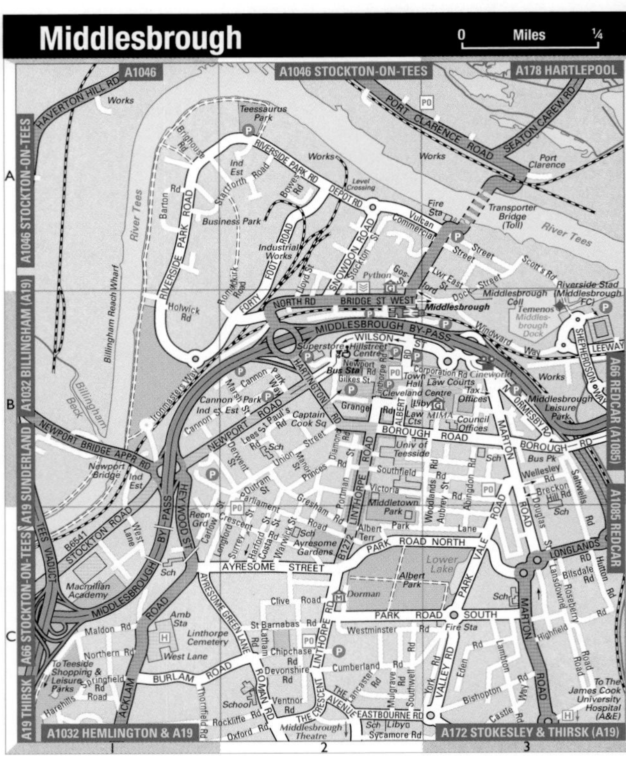
Middlesbrough
0 Miles ¼
A1046
A1046 STOCKTON-ON-TEES
A178 HARTLEPOOL
A66 REDCAR (A1085)
A1085 REDCAR
A1032 HEMLINGTON & A19
A172 STOKESLEY & THIRSK (A19)

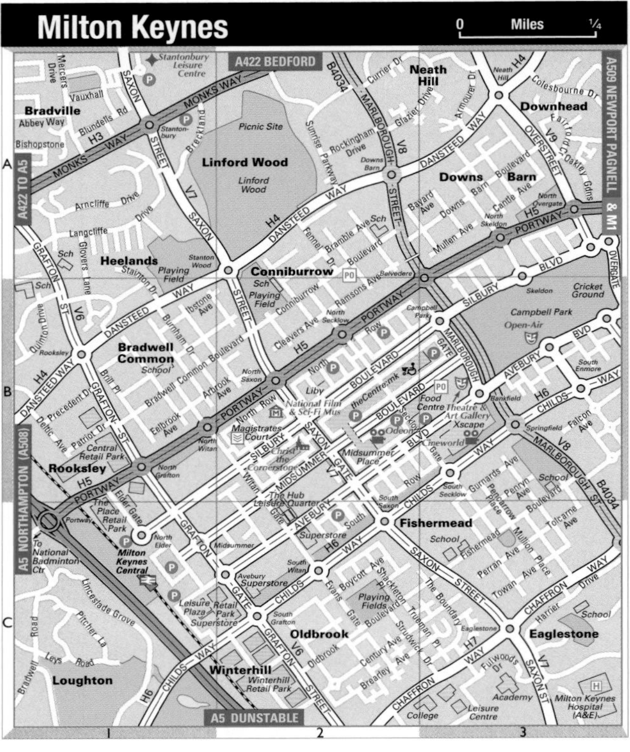
Milton Keynes
0 Miles ¼
A422 BEDFORD
A509 NEWPORT PAGNELL & M1
A422 TO A5
A5 NORTHAMPTON (A508)
A5 DUNSTABLE

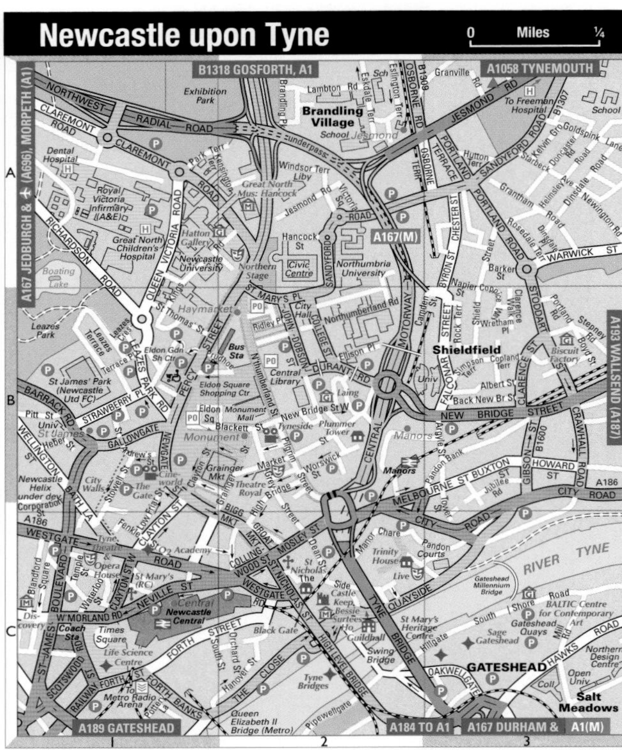
Newcastle upon Tyne
0 Miles ¼
B1318 GOSFORTH, A1
A1058 TYNEMOUTH
A193 WALLSEND (A187)
A189 GATESHEAD
A184 TO A1
A167 DURHAM & A1(M)

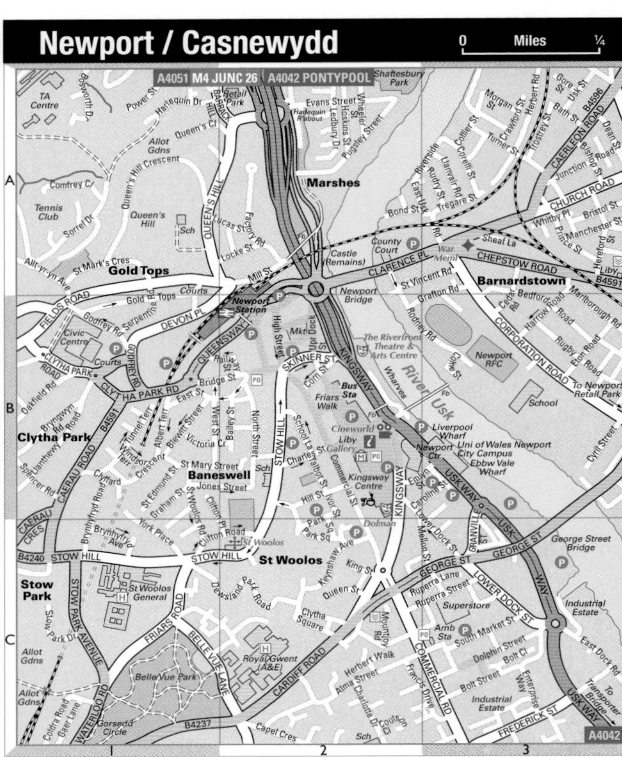
Newport / Casnewydd
0 Miles ¼
A4051 M4 JUNC 26
A4042 PONTYPOOL
A4042

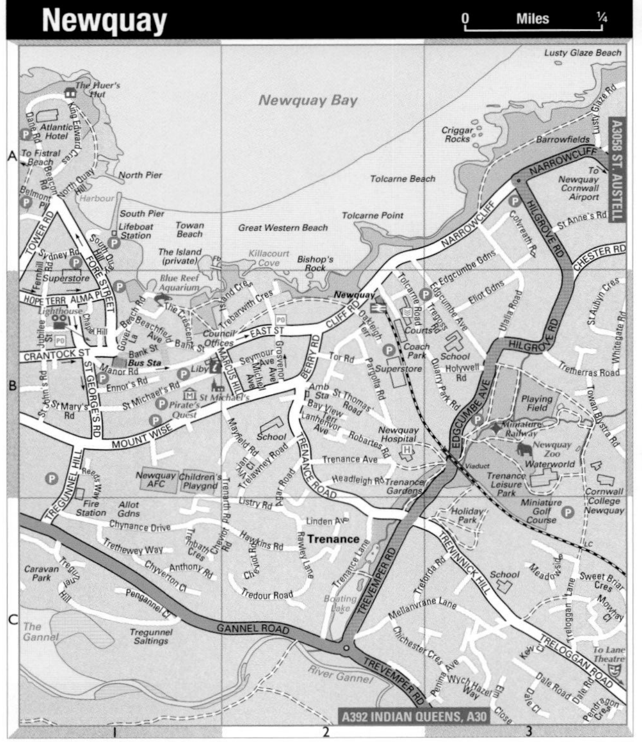
Newquay
0 Miles ¼
Newquay Bay
A3058 ST AUSTELL
A392 INDIAN QUEENS, A30

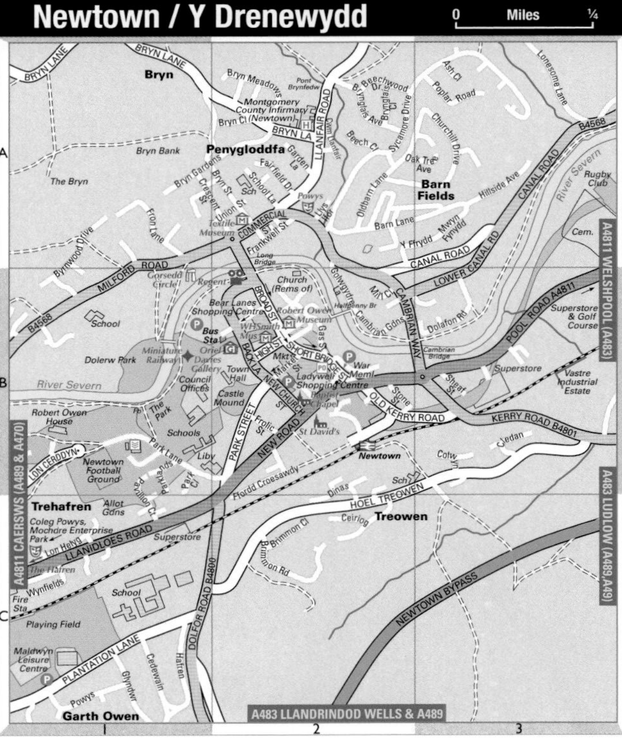
Newtown / Y Drenewydd
0 Miles ¼
A483 WELSHPOOL (A483)
A489 & A470 CAERSWS
A483 LUDLOW (A489)
A483 LLANDRINDOD WELLS & A489

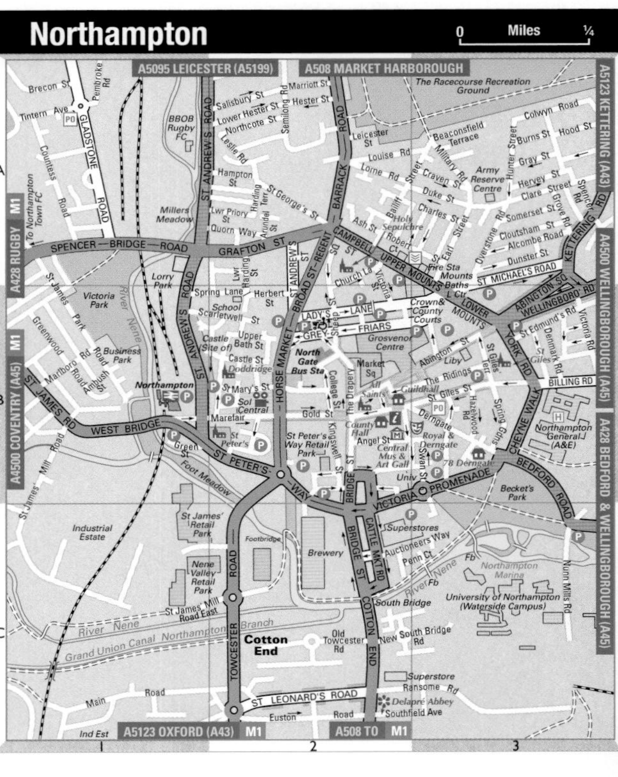
Northampton
0 Miles ¼
A5095 LEICESTER (A5199)
A508 MARKET HARBOROUGH
A5123 KETTERING (A43)
A428 RUGBY M1
A5199 COVENTRY (A45) M1
A5123 OXFORD (A43) M1
A508 TO M1

Norwich

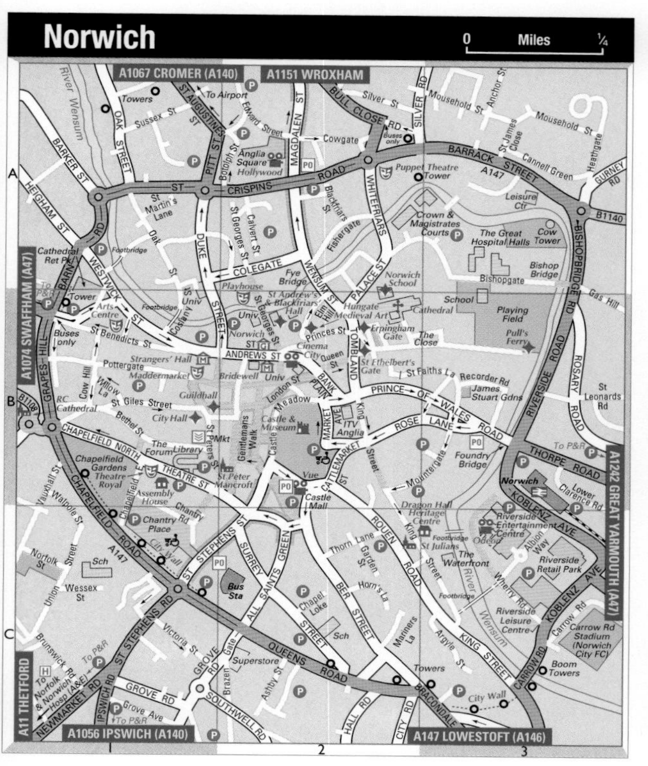

Nottingham

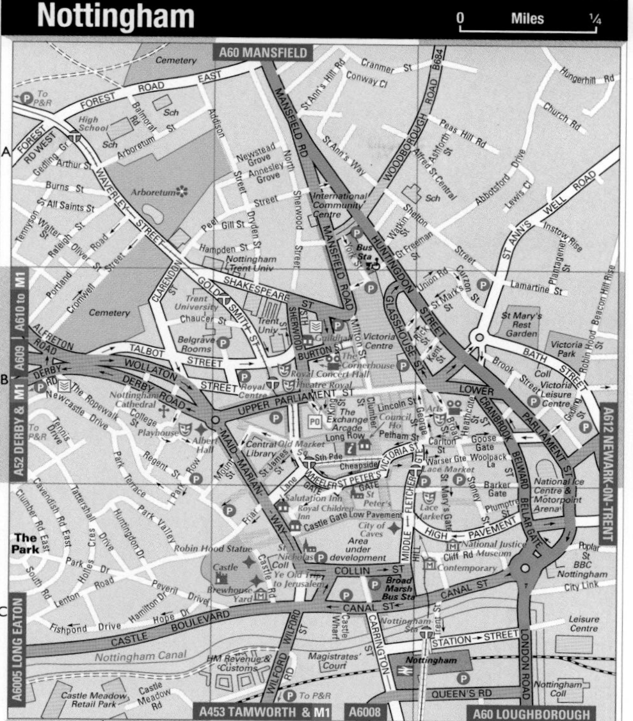

Oban

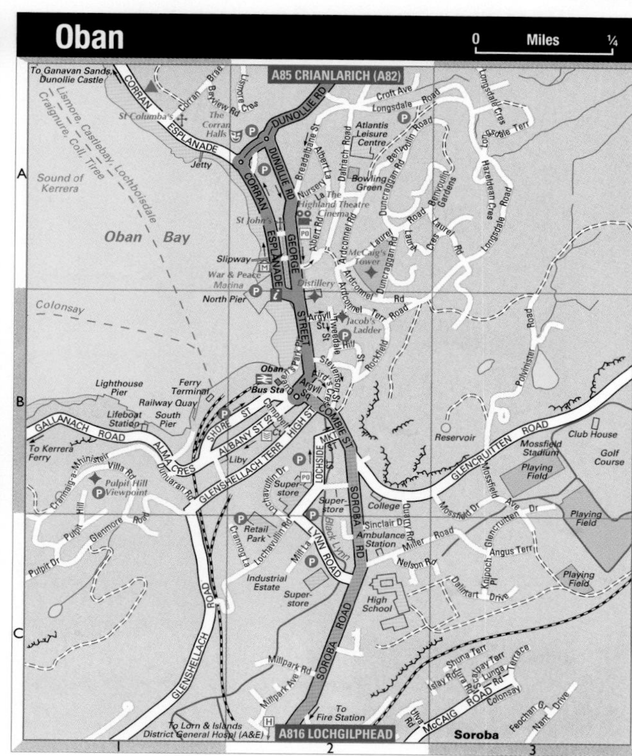

Oxford

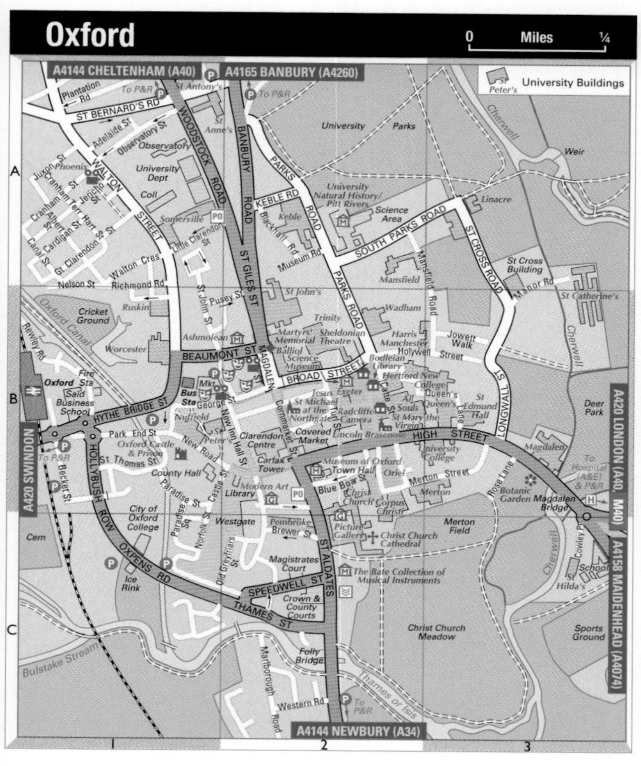

Perth

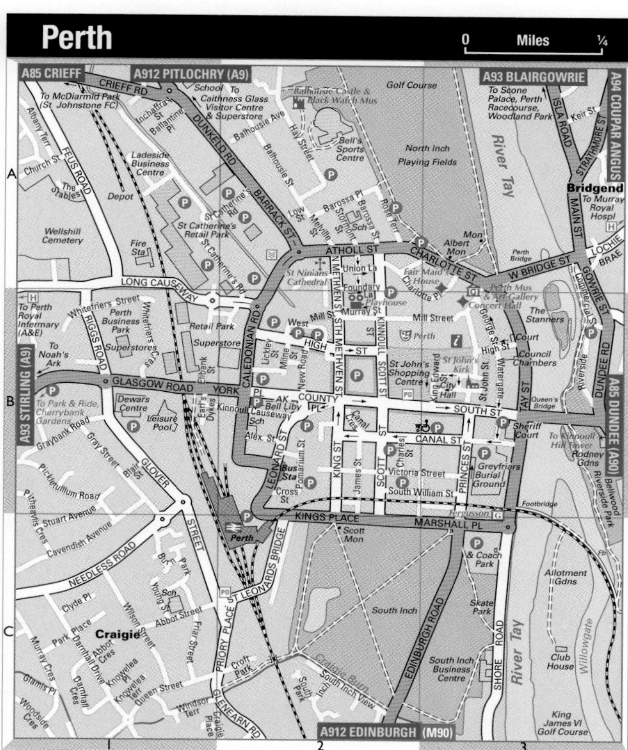

Peterborough

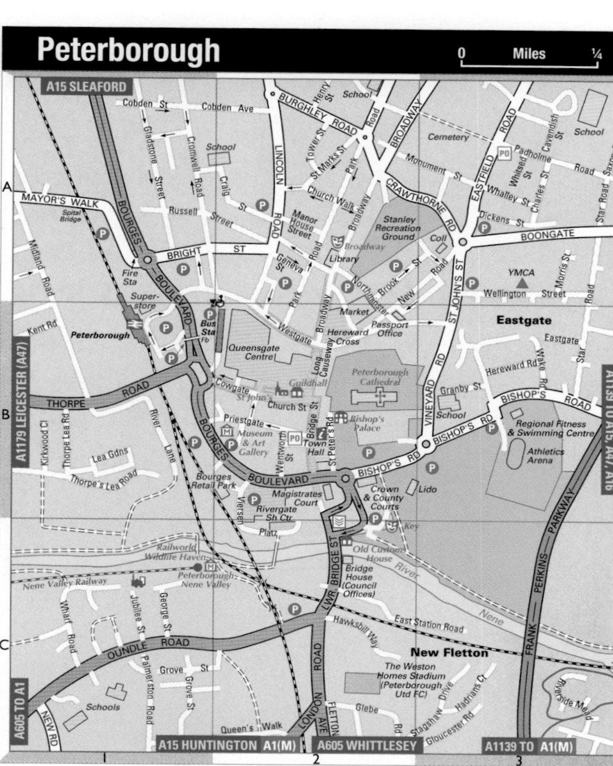

Plymouth

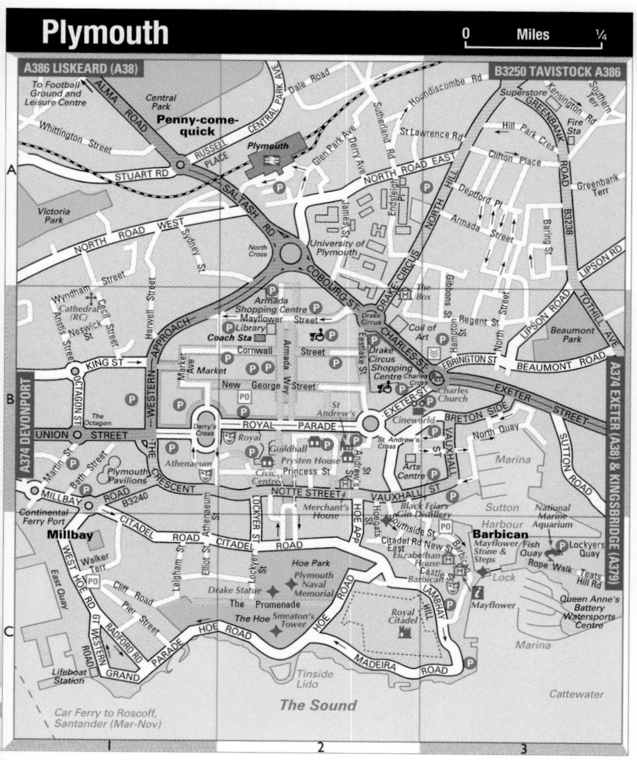

Poole

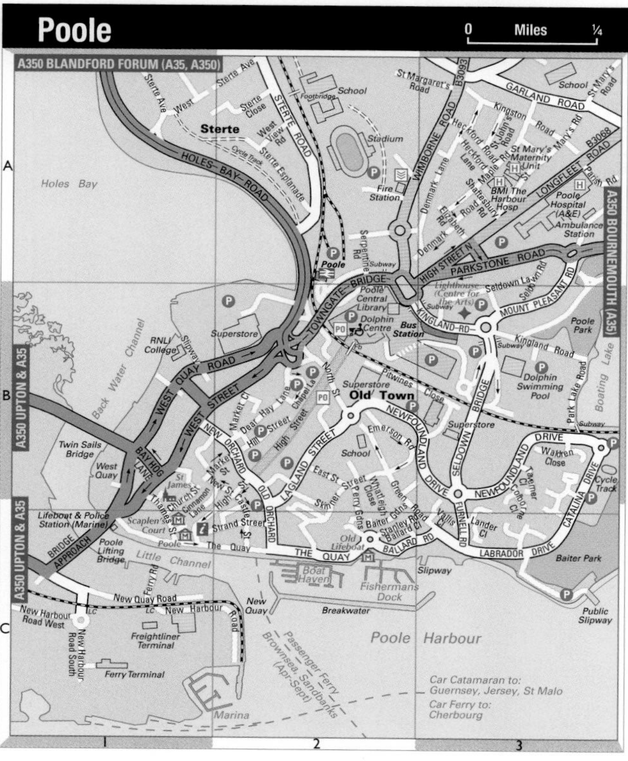

Portsmouth

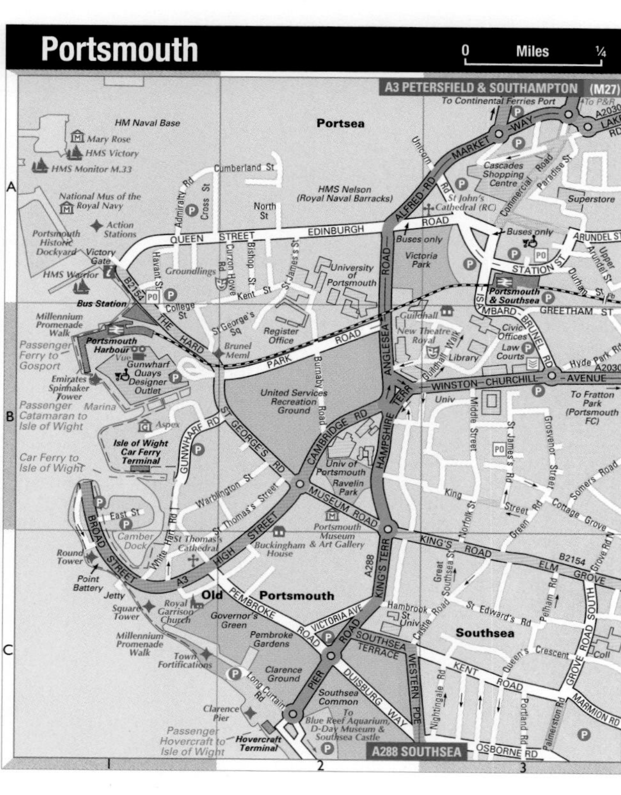

Preston

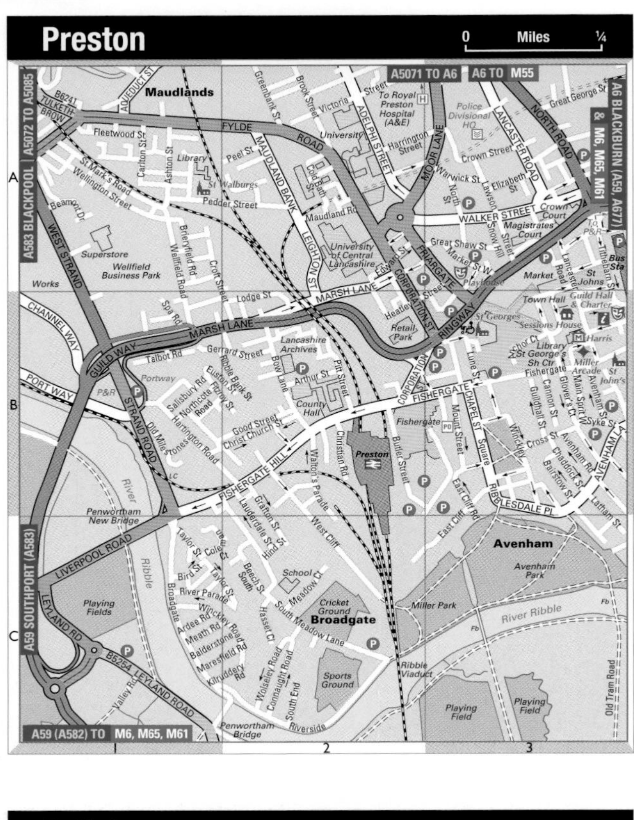

Reading

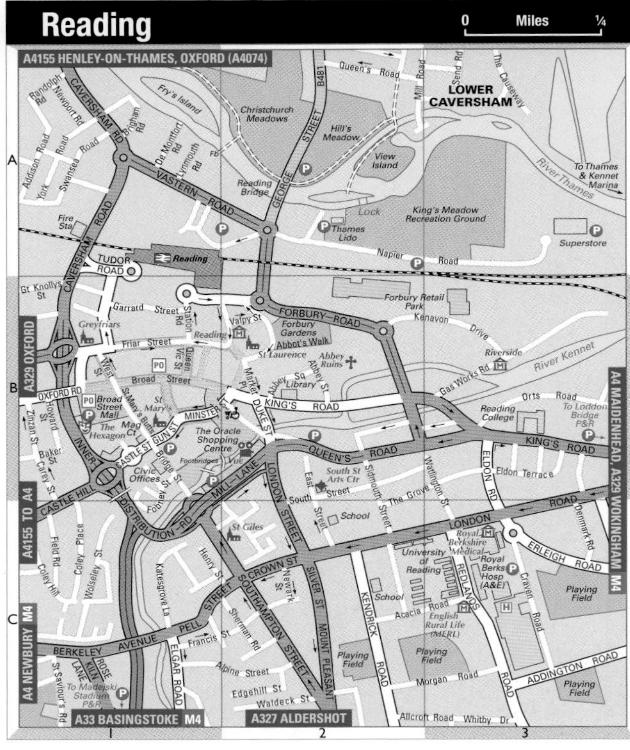

St Andrews

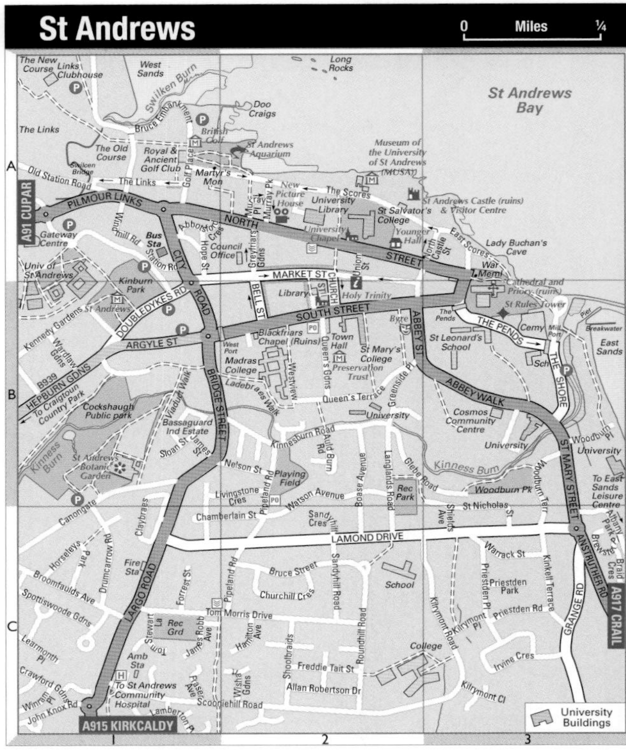

Salisbury

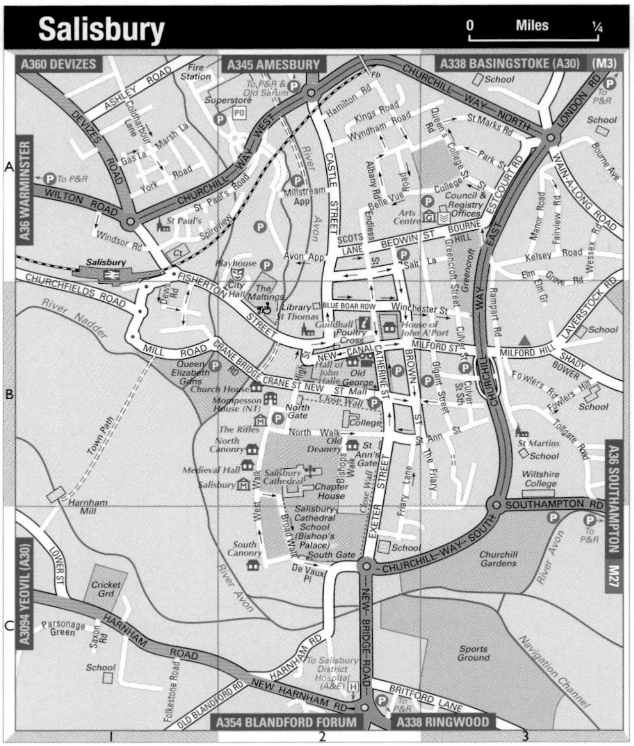

Scarborough

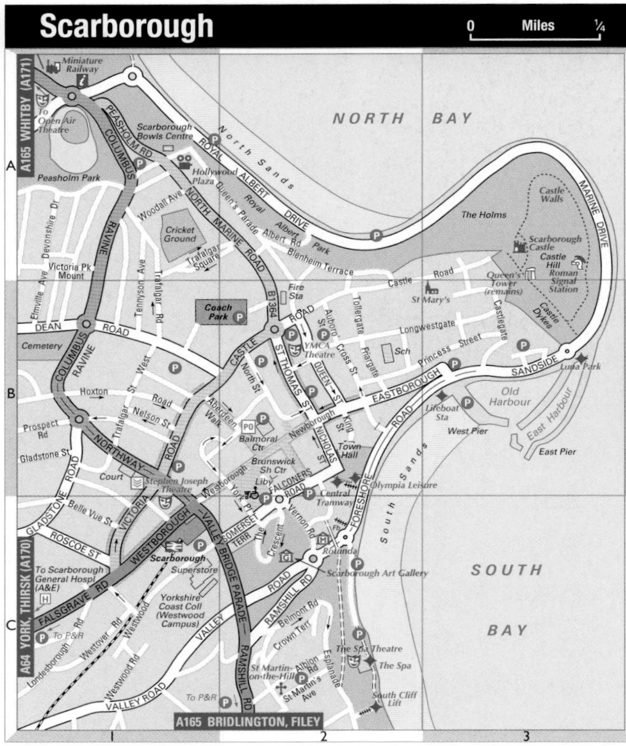

Shrewsbury

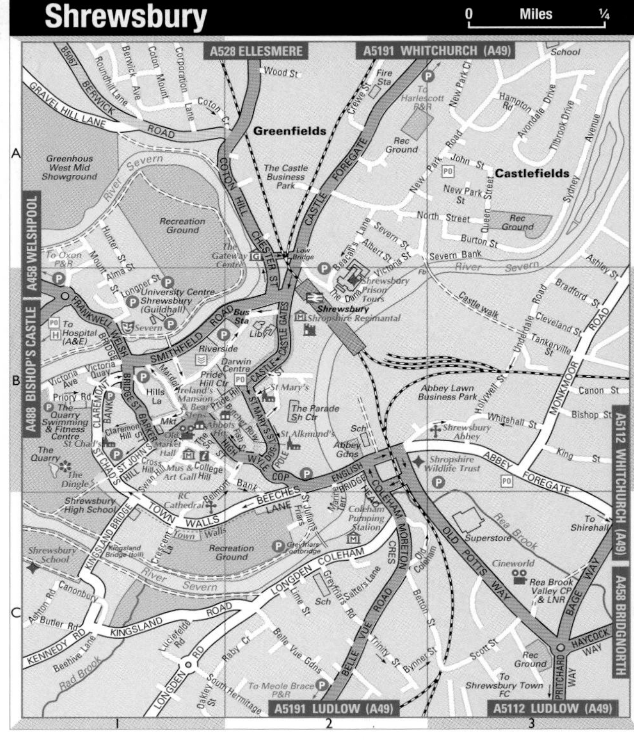

Sheffield

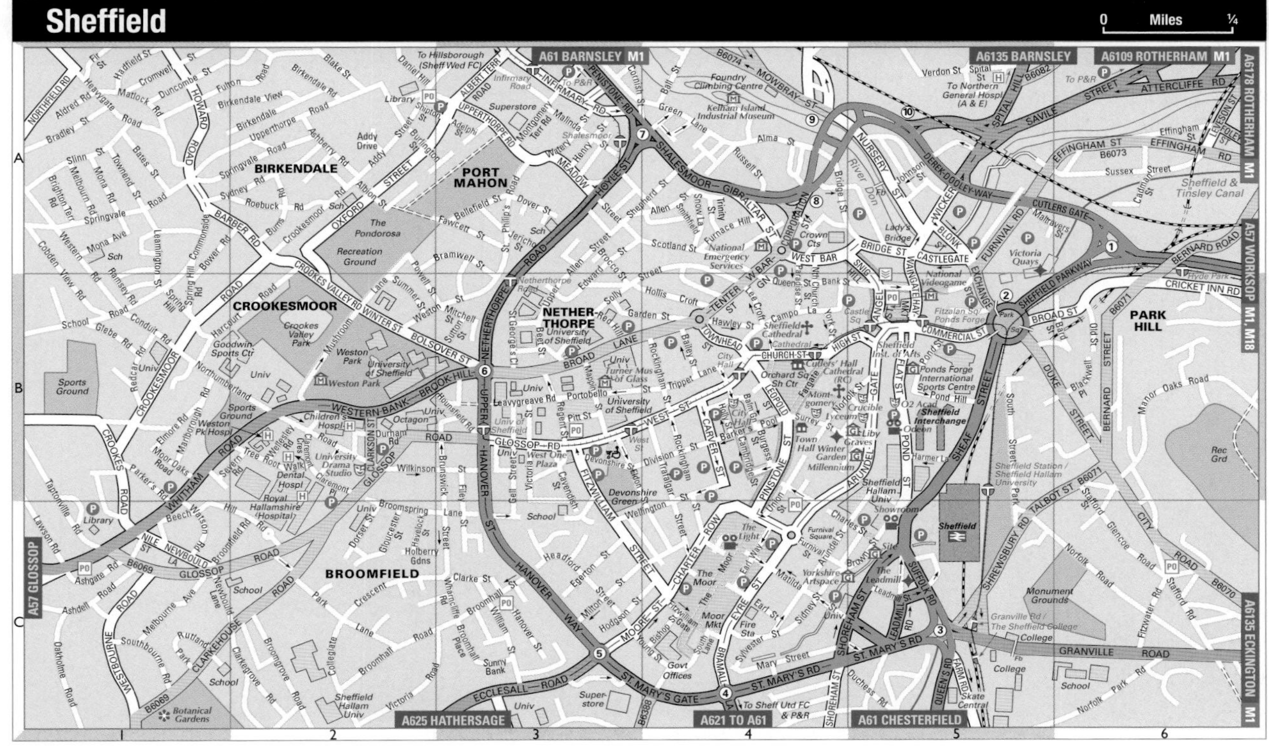

Southampton

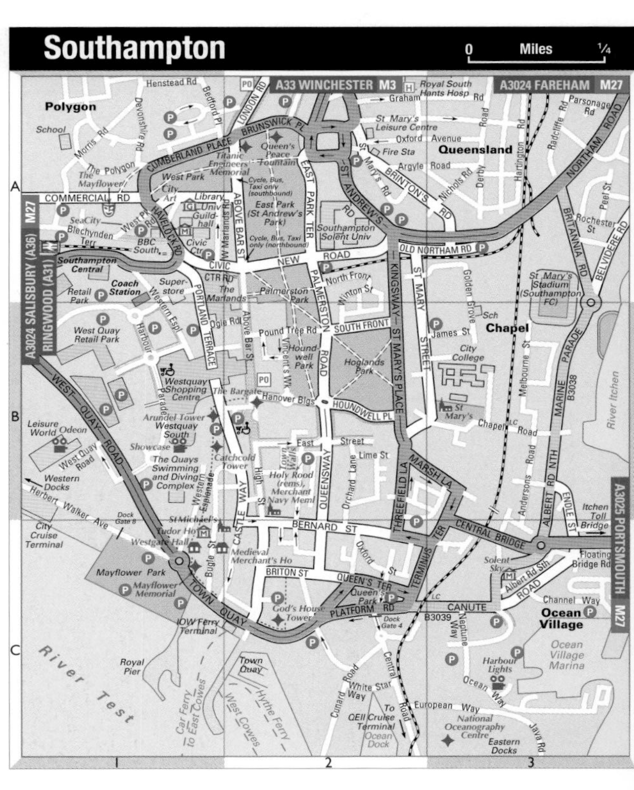

Southend-on-Sea

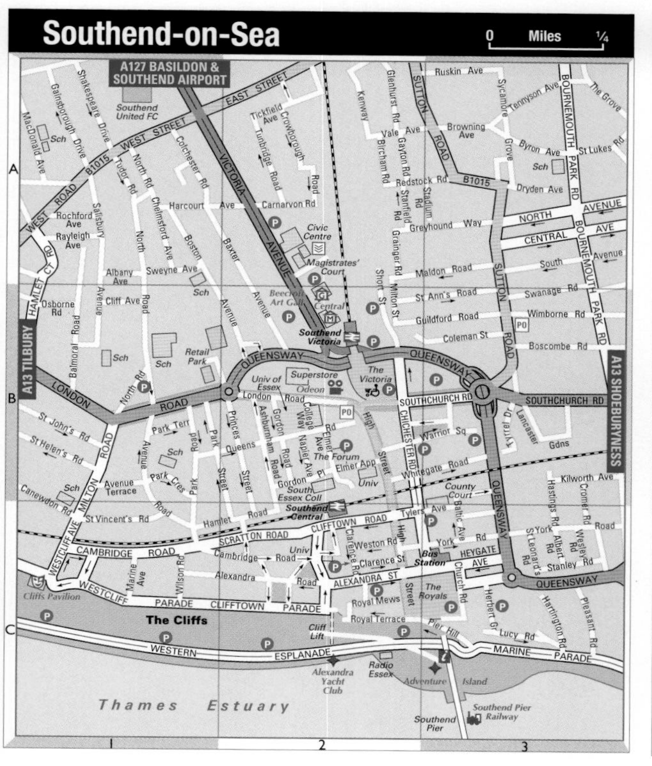

Stirling

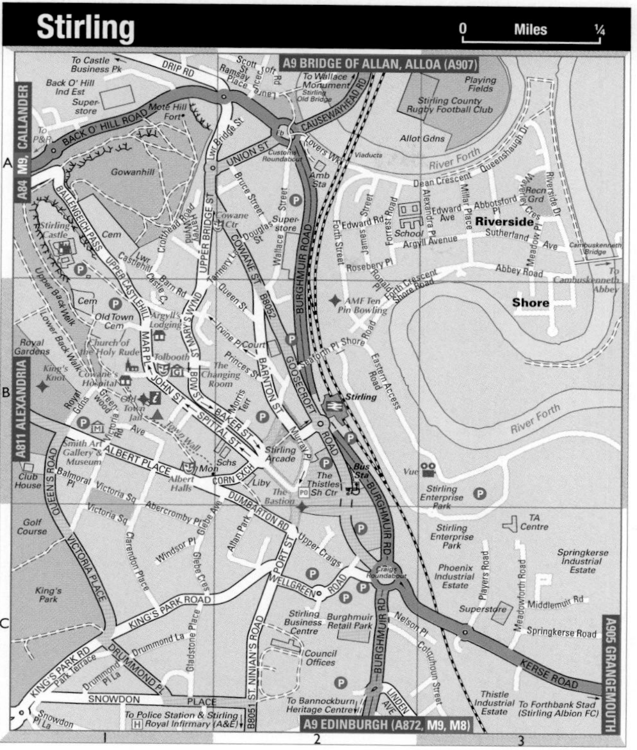

Stoke

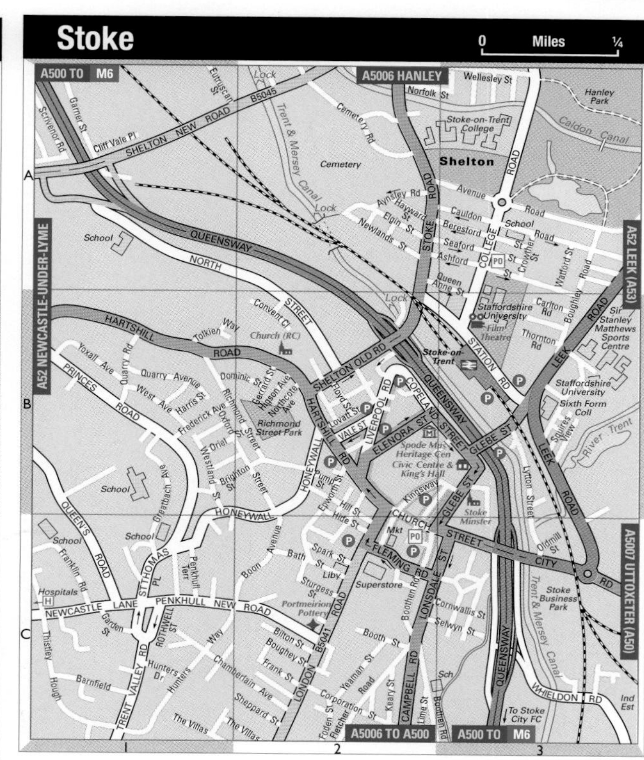

Stratford-upon-Avon

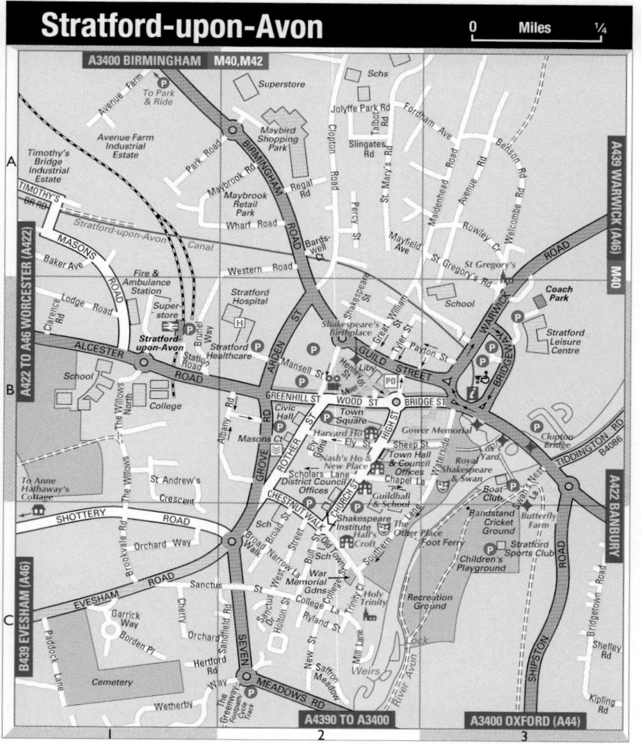

Sunderland

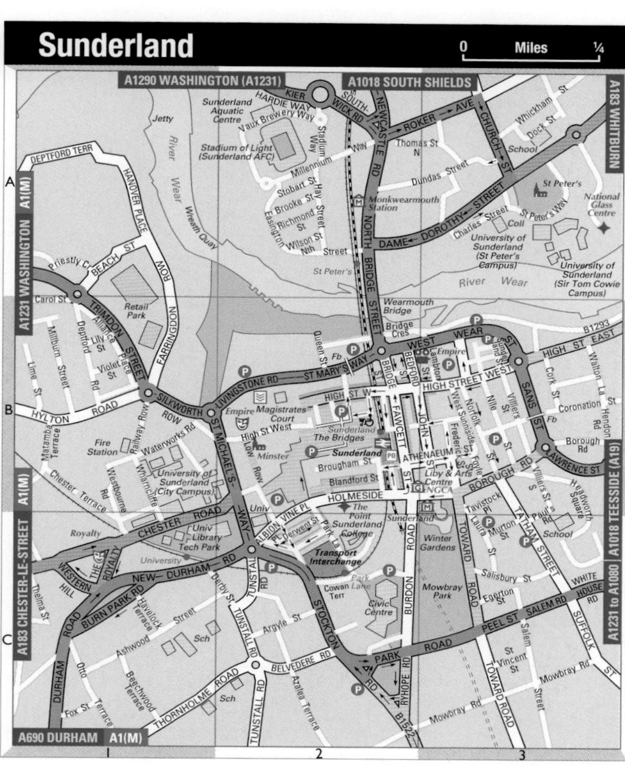

Swansea / Abertawe

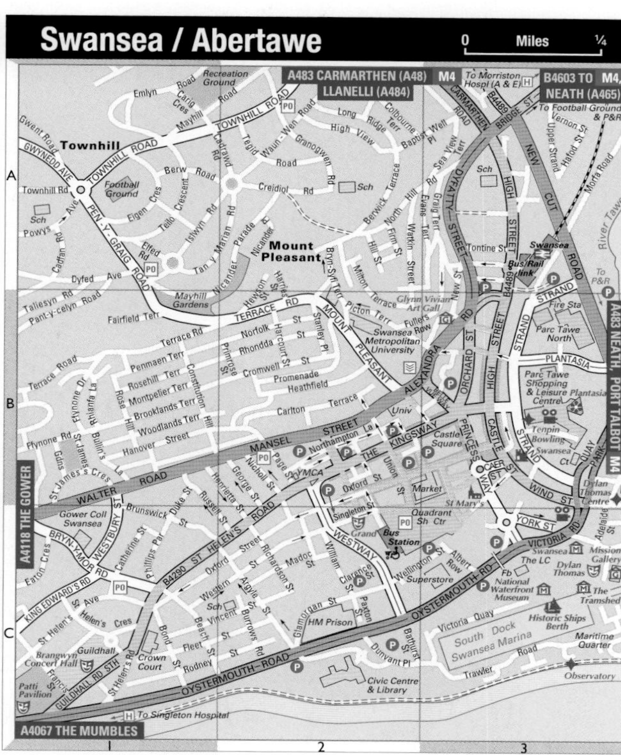

Swindon

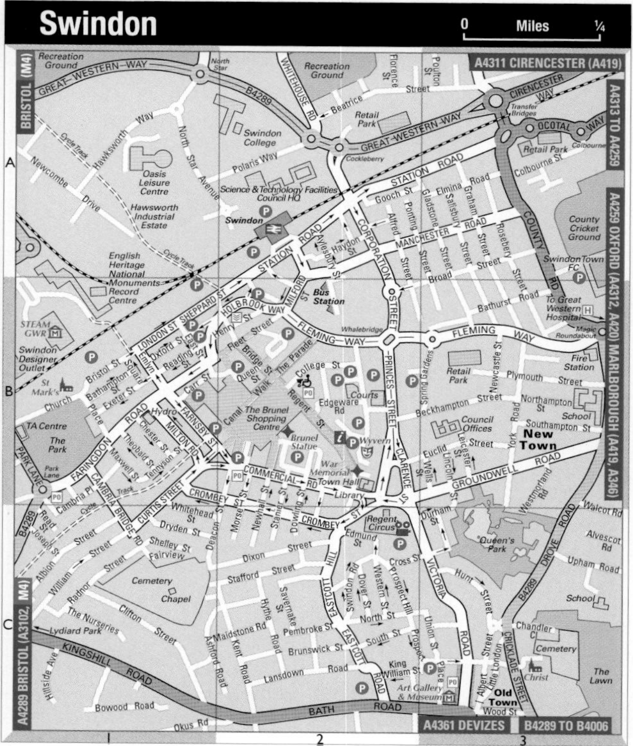

Taunton

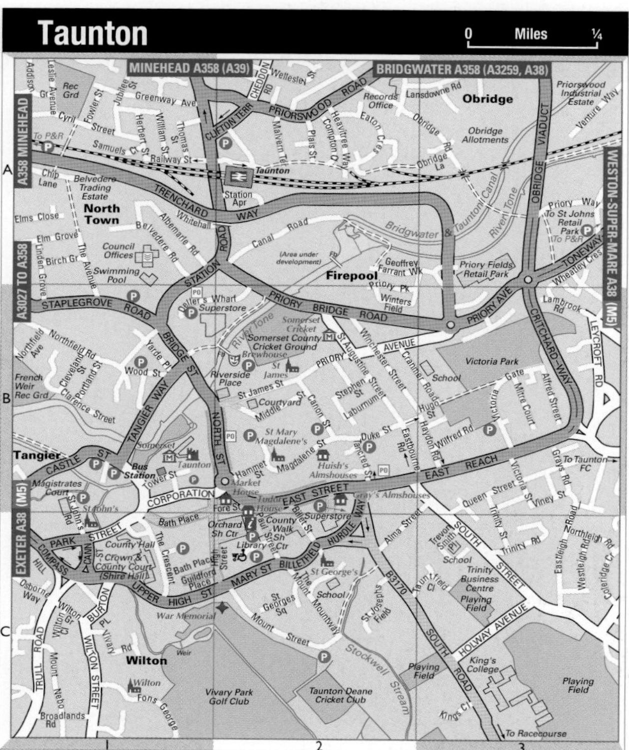

Telford

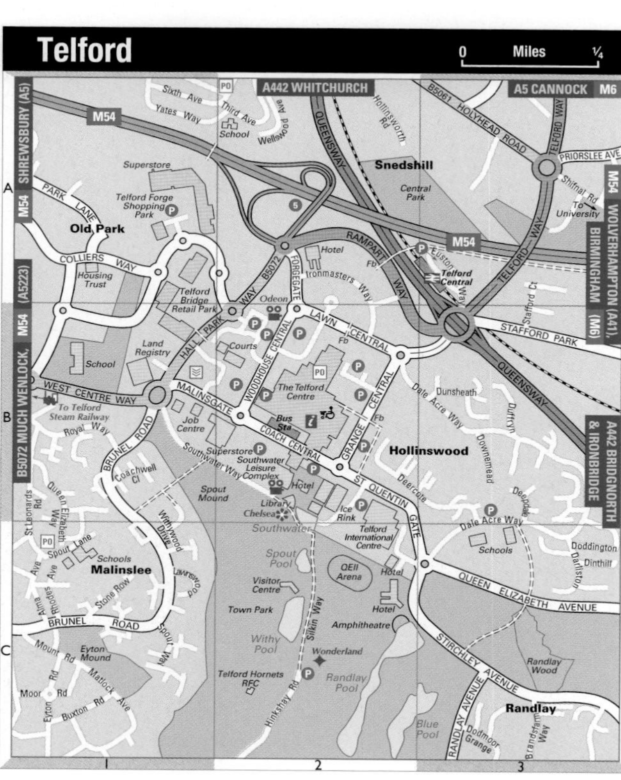

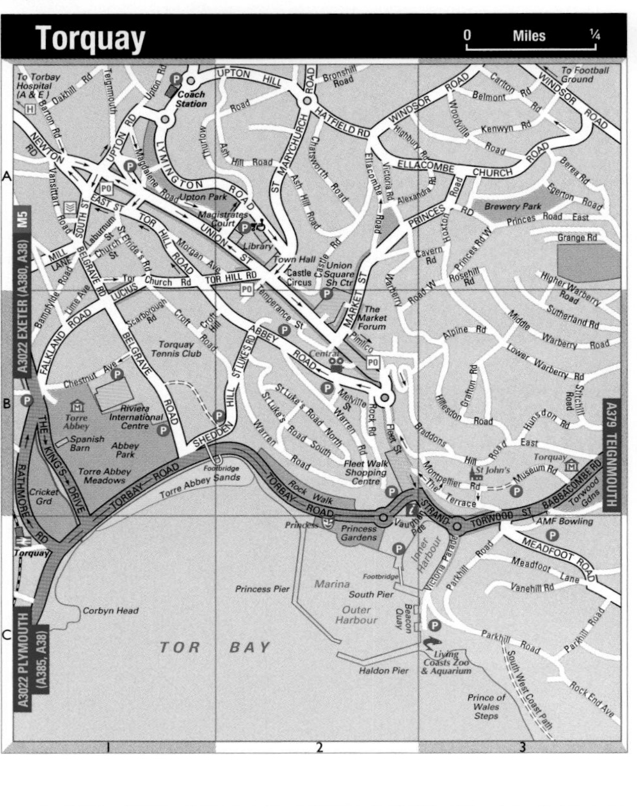
Torquay
0 Miles ¼
A3022 EXETER (A380, A38) M5
A379 TEIGNMOUTH
A3022 PLYMOUTH (A385, A38)
TOR BAY

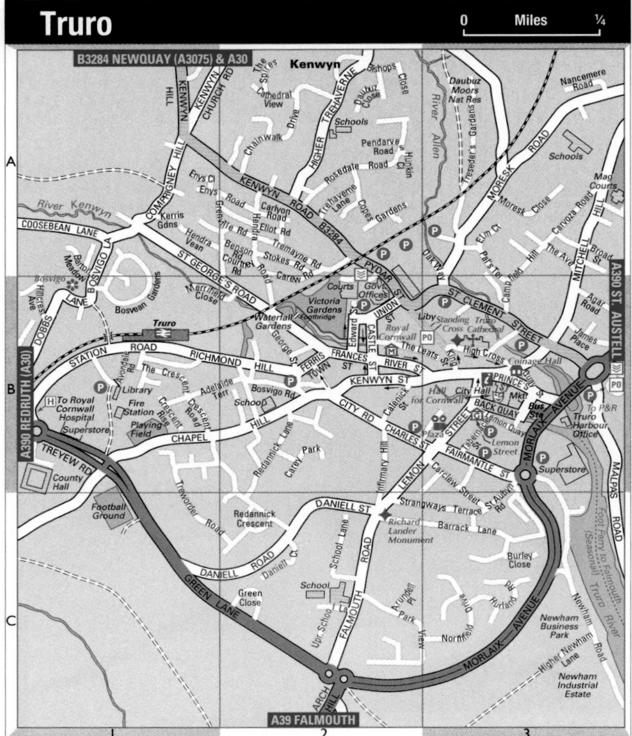
Truro
0 Miles ¼
B3284 NEWQUAY (A3075) & A30
A390 ST AUSTELL
A390 REDRUTH (A30)
A39 FALMOUTH

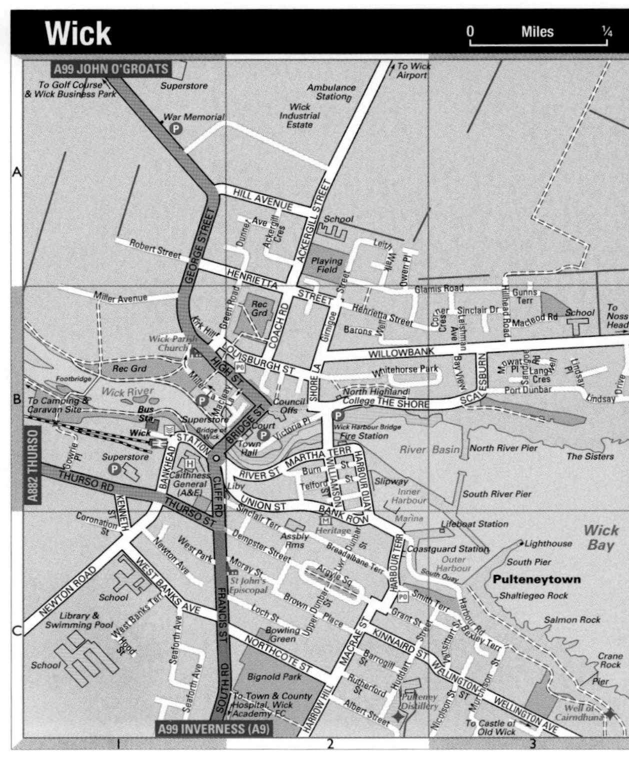
Wick
0 Miles ¼
A99 JOHN O'GROATS
A882 THURSO
A99 INVERNESS (A9)
Wick Bay
Pulteneytown

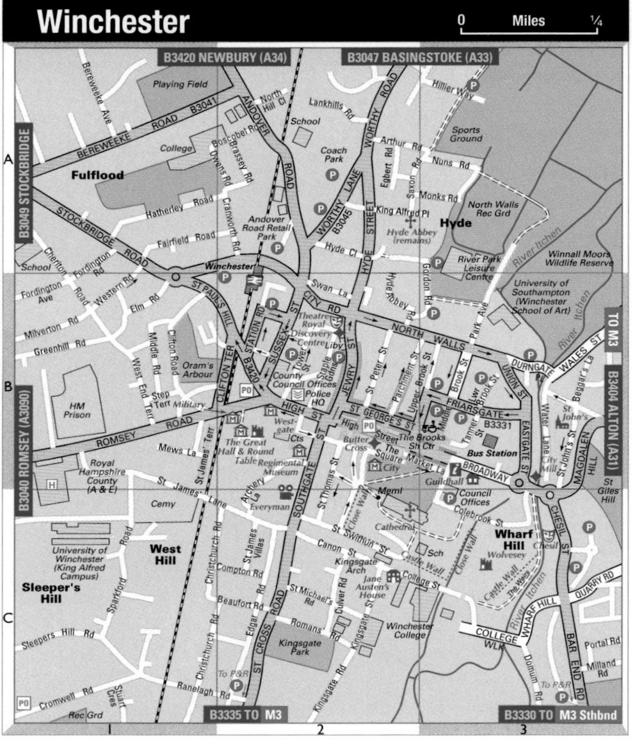
Winchester
0 Miles ¼
B3420 NEWBURY (A34)
B3047 BASINGSTOKE (A33)
B3049 STOCKBRIDGE
B3040 ROMSEY (A3090)
B3404 ALTON (A31)
B3335 TO M3
B3330 TO M3 Sthbnd

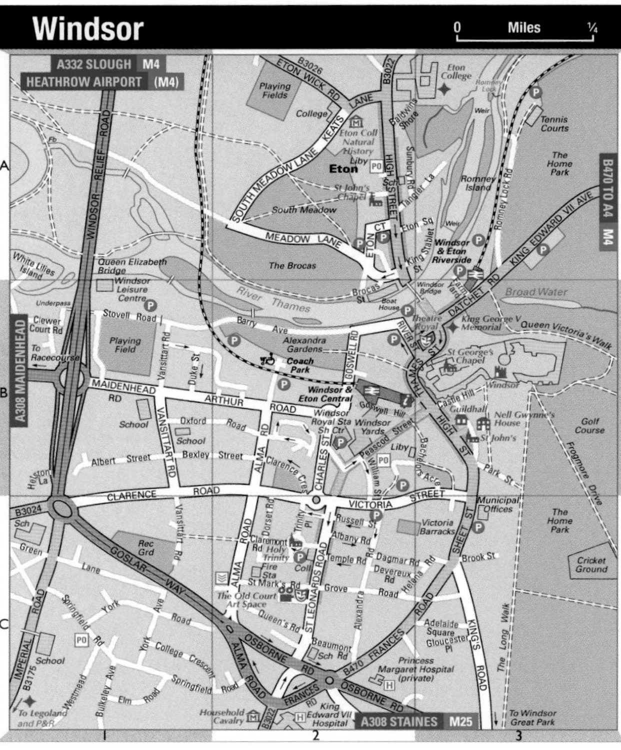
Windsor
0 Miles ¼
A332 SLOUGH M4
HEATHROW AIRPORT (M4)
B470 TO A4 M4
A308 MAIDENHEAD
A308 STAINES M25

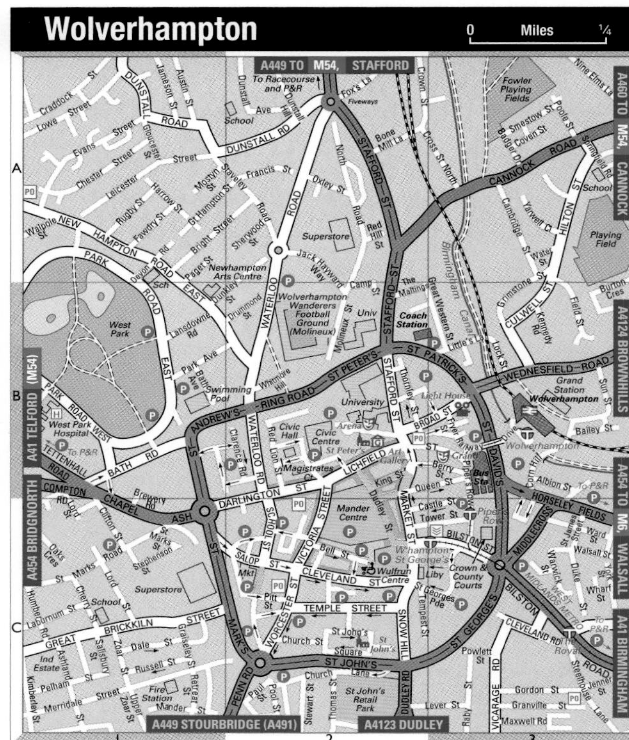
Wolverhampton
0 Miles ¼
A449 TO M54, STAFFORD
A460 TO M54 CANNOCK
A4124 BROWNHILLS
A454 TO M6 WALSALL
A41 BIRMINGHAM
A41 TELFORD (M54)
A454 BRIDGNORTH
A449 STOURBRIDGE (A491)
A4123 DUDLEY

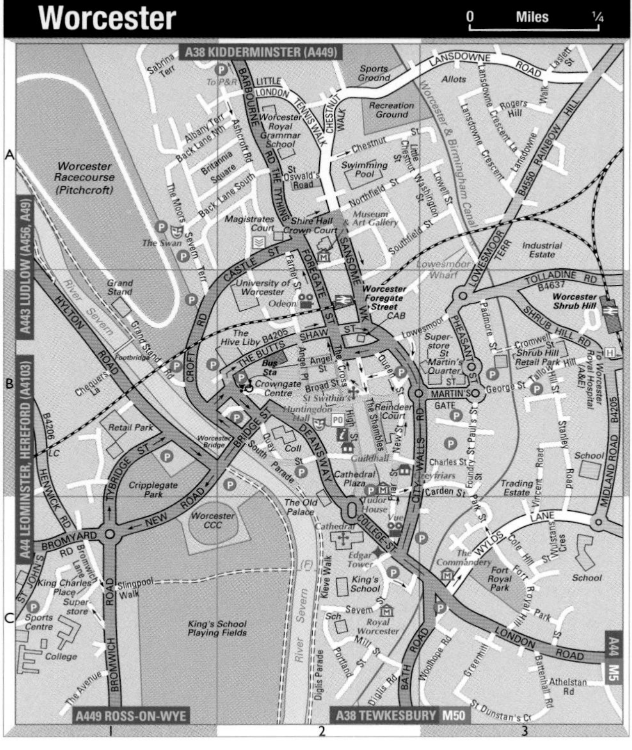
Worcester
0 Miles ¼
A38 KIDDERMINSTER (A449)
A443 LUDLOW (A456, A49)
A44 LEOMINSTER, HEREFORD (A4103)
A449 ROSS-ON-WYE
A38 TEWKESBURY M50
A44 M5

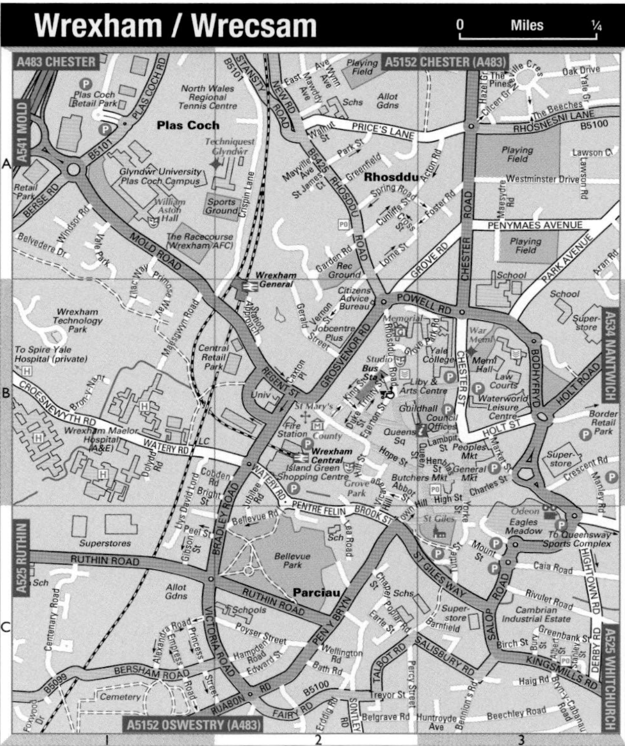
Wrexham / Wrecsam
0 Miles ¼
A483 CHESTER
A5152 CHESTER (A483)
A541 MOLD
A534 NANTWICH
A525 RUTHIN
A525 WHITCHURCH
A5152 OSWESTRY (A483)

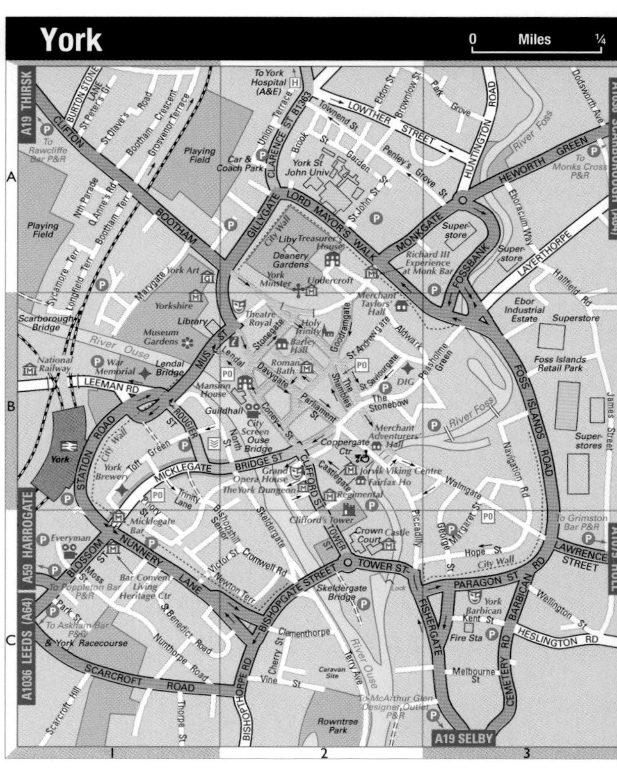
York
0 Miles ¼
A19 THIRSK
A1036 SCARBOROUGH (A64)
A59 HARROGATE
A1036 LEEDS (A64)
A1079 HULL
A19 SELBY

Town plan indexes

Aberdeen 331
Aberdeen B2
Aberdeen Grammar School A1
Academy, The B2
Albert Basin B3
Albert Quay B3
Albury Rd C1
Alford Place B1
Art Gallery A2
Arts Centre A2
Back Wynd A2
Baker St A1
Beach Boulevard A3
Belmont B2
Belmont St B2
Berry St A2
Blackfriars St A2
Blaikie's Quay B3
Bloomfield Rd C1
Bon Accord Centre A2
Bon-Accord St B1/C1
Bridge St B2
Broad St A2
Bus Station B2
Car Ferry Terminal B3
Castlegate A3
Central Library A1
Chapel St B1
Cineworld B2
Clyde St B3
College A2
College St B2
Commerce St A3
Commercial Quay B3
Community Centre A3/C1
Constitution St A3
Cotton St A3
Crown St B2
Denburn Rd A2
Devanha Gardens C2
Devanha Gdns South C2
East North St A3
Esslemont Avenue A1
Ferryhill Rd C2
Ferryhill Terrace C2
Fish Market B3
Fonthill Rd C1
Galleria B1
Gallowgate A2
George St A2
Glenbervie Rd C3
Golden Square B1
Grampian Rd C3
Great Southern Rd C1
Guild St B2
Hardgate B1/C1
His Majesty's Theatre A1
Holburn St C1
Hollybank Place C1
Huntly St B1
Hutcheon St A1
Information Centre B2
John St A2
Justice St A3
King St A2
Langstane Place B1
Lemon Tree, The A2
Library C1
Loch St A2
Maberly St A1
Marischal College A2
Maritime Mus & Provost Ross's House B2
Market B2
Market St B2/B3
Menzies Rd C3
Mercat Cross A3
Millburn St C2
Miller St A3
Mount St A1
Music Hall B1
North Esp East C3
North Esp West C2
Oscar Rd C3
Palmerston Rd C2
Park St A3
Police Station A2
Polmuir Rd C2
Post Office A1/A2/A3/B1/C3
Provost Skene's Ho A2
Queen Elizabeth Br C2
Queen St A2
Regent Quay B3
Regent Road B3
Robert Gordon's Coll A2
Rose St B1
Rosemount Place A1
Rosemount Viaduct A1
St Andrew St A2
St Andrew's Cath A3
St Mary's Cathedral B1
St Nicholas Centre A2
St Nicholas St A2
School Hill A2
Sinclair Rd C3
Skene Square A1
Skene St B1
South College St C2
South Crown St C2
South Esp East C3
South Esp West C3
South Mount St A1
Sports Centre C3
Spring Garden A2
Springbank Terrace C2
Summer St B1
Superstore A2
Thistle St B1
Tolbooth A3
Town House A2
Trinity Centre B2
Union Row B1
Union Square B2
Union St B1/B2
University A2
Upper Dock B3
Upper Kirkgate A2
Victoria Bridge C3
Victoria Dock B3
Victoria Rd C3
Victoria St B2
Virginia St A3
Vue B2
Waterloo Quay B3
Wellington Place B2
West North St A2
Whinhill Rd C1
Willowbank Rd C1
Windmill Brae B2

Aberystwyth 331
Aberystwyth Holiday Village C2
Aberystwyth Library and Ceredigion Archives A2
Aberystwyth RFC C3
Aberystwyth Sta B2
Aberystwyth Town Football Ground B2
Aberystwyth Univ B3
Alexandra Rd B2
Ambulance Station C3
Baker St B1
Banadl Rd B2
Bandstand A1
Bar, The C1
Bath St A2
Boat Landing Stage A1
Bvd de Saint-Brieuc C3
Bridge St B1
Bronglais Hospital B3
Bryn-y-Mor Rd A2
Buarth Rd B2
Bus Station B2
Cae Melyn A2
Cae'r-Gog B3
Cambrian St B2
Caradoc Rd B3
Caravan Site C2
Castle Theatre B1
Castle (remains of) B1
Castle St B1
Cemetery B3
Ceredigion Mus A1
Chalybeate St B1
Cliff Terrace A2
Club House A2
Commodore A1
County Court A2
Crown Buildings B2
Dan-y-Coed A3
Dinas Terrace C1
Eastgate B1
Edge-hill Rd B2
Elm Tree Avenue B2
Elysian Grove A2
Felin-y-Mor Rd C1
Fifth Avenue C2
Fire Station C1
Glanrafon Terrace B1
Glan Rheidol C3
Glyndwr Rd B2
Golf Course A3
Government & Council Offices C3
Gray's Inn Rd B1
Great Darkgate St B1
Greenfield St B2
Heol-y-Bryn A2
High St B1
Infirmary Rd A2
Iorwerth Avenue B3
King St B1
Lauraplace B1
Lifeboat Station C1
Llanbadarn Rd B3
Loveden Rd A2
Magistrates Court A1
Marina C1
Marine Terrace A1
Market Hall B1
Mill St B1
Moor Lane B2
National Lbry of Wales B3
New Promenade B1
New St B1
North Beach A1
North Parade B2
North Rd A2
Northgate St B2
Parc Natur Penglais A3
Parc-y-Llyn Retail Pk C3
Park Avenue B2
Pavillion B1
Pen-y-Craig A2
Pen-yr-angor C1
Pendinas C1
Penglais Rd B3
Penrheidol C2
Pier St B1
Plas Avenue B3
Plas Helyg C2
Plascrug Avenue B2/C3
Plascrug Leisure Ctr C3
Police Station C2
Poplar Row B2
Portland Rd B2
Portland St A2
Post Office B1/B3
Powell St B1
Prospect St B1
Quay Rd B1
Queen St B1
Queen's Avenue A2
Queen's Rd A2
Rheidol Retail Park B2
Riverside Terrace B1
St Davids Rd B3
St Michael's B1
School of Art B2
Seaview Place B1
Shopmobility B2
South Beach B1
South Rd B1
Sports Ground B2
Spring Gardens C1
Stanley Terrace B2
Superstore B1/B2
Superstore B2/C3
Swimming Pool & Leisure Centre C3
Tanybwlch Beach C1
Tennis Courts B3
Terrace Rd B1
Trefechan Bridge B1
Trefechan Rd C2
Trefor Rd A2
Trinity Rd B2
University of Wales (Aberystwyth) B1
Vale of Rheidol Railway C3
Vaynor St B2
Victoria Terrace A1
Viewpoint A2
Viewpoint A3
War Memorial B1
Wharf Quay C1
Y Lanfa C1
Ystwyth Retail Park B2

Ashford 331
Adams Drive C3
Albert Rd A1
Alfred Rd C3
Apsley St A1
Ashford Borough Museum A1
Ashford College B2
Ashford International Station B2
Ashford Picturehouse A1
Bank St A1
Barrowhill Gardens A1
Beaver Industrial Est C1
Beaver Rd C1
Beazley Court C3
Birling Rd B3
Blue Line Lane A1
Bond Rd C1
Bowens Field B1
Bulleid Place C2
Business Park A2
Cade Rd C1
Chart Rd A1
Chichester Close B1
Christchurch Rd B1
Chunnel Industrial Est B1
Church Rd A1
Civic Centre A2
County Square Shopping Centre A1
Croft Rd A3
Cudworth Rd C3
Curtis Rd C3
Dering Rd A3
Dover Place B2
Drum Lane A1
East Hill A2
East St A1
Eastmead Avenue B2
Edinburgh Rd A1
Elwick Rd A1
Essella Park B3
Essella Rd B3
Fire Station A3
Forge Lane A1
Francis Rd C1
Gateway Plus and Liby A1
George St B1
Godfrey Walk B1
Gordon Close A3
Government Offices A2
Hardinge Rd A2
Henwood A3
Henwood Bsns Centre A3
Henwood Ind Est A3
High St A2
Hythe Rd A3
Javelin Way A3
Jemmett Rd B1
Kennard Way A3
Kent Avenue A1
Linden Rd B3
Lower Denmark Rd C1
Mabledon Avenue B3
Mace Industrial Est A2
Mace Lane A2
Maunsell Place C3
McArthurGlen Designer Outlet C2
Memorial Gardens A2
Mill Court A2
Miller Close A2
Mortimer Close C1
New St A1
Newtown Green C3
Newtown Rd B2/C3
Norman Rd C1
North St A2
Norwood Gardens A1
Norwood St A1
Old Railway Works Industrial Estate C3
Orion Way C3
Pk Mall Shopping Ctr A1
Park Place A1
Park St A1/A2
Pemberton Rd A3
Police Station A1
Post Office A1
Providence St C2
Queen St A1
Queens Rd A2
Regents Place A1
Riversdale Rd C2
Romney Marsh Rd B2
St John's Lane A2
St Mary's Church & Arts Venue A1
Somerset Rd A2
South Stour Avenue B2
Star Rd A3
Station Rd B2
Stirling Rd C2
Stour Centre, The B2
Superstore B1
Sussex Avenue A1
Tannery Lane A2
Torrington Rd C2
Trumper Bridge B1
Tufton Rd A3
Tufton St A1
Vicarage Lane A2
Victoria Crescent B1
Victoria Park B1
Victoria Rd B1
Wallis Rd A3
Wellesley Rd A2
West St A1
Whitfeld Rd C1
William Rd C1
World War I Tank A1
Wyvern Way A3

Ayr 331
Ailsa Place B1
Alexandra Terrace A3
Allison St B2
Alloway Park C1
Alloway Place C1
Alloway St C2
Arran Mall C2
Arran Terrace B1
Arthur St B2
Ashgrove St C2
Auld Brig B2
Auld Kirk B2
Ayr C2
Ayr Academy B1
Ayr Central Shopping Centre C2
Ayr Harbour A1
Ayr Ice Rink A2
Ayrshire College C3
Back Hawkhill Avenue A3
Back Main St B2
Back Peebles St A2
Barns Crescent C1
Barns Park C1
Barns St C1
Barns Street Lane C1
Bath Place B1
Bellevue Crescent C1
Bellevue Lane C1
Beresford Lane C2
Beresford Terrace C2
Boswell Park B2
Britannia Place A3
Bruce Crescent B1
Burns Statue C2
Bus Station B1
Carrick St C2
Cassillis St B1
Cathcart St B1
Charlotte St B1
Citadel Leisure Ctr B1
Citadel Place B1
Compass Pier A1
Content Avenue C3
Content St B2
Craigie Avenue B3
Craigie Rd B3
Craigie Way B3
Cromwell Rd B1
Crown St A2
Dalblair Rd C2
Dam Park Sports Stadium C3
Damside A2
Dongola Rd C3
Eglinton Place B1
Eglinton Terrace B1
Elba St B2
Elmbank St A2
Esplanade B1
Euchar Rock A1
Farifield Rd C1
Fort St B1
Fothringham Rd C3
Fullarton St C1
Gaiety C2
Garden St B2
George St B2
George's Avenue A3
Glebe Crescent A2
Glebe Rd A2
Gorden Terrace B3
Green St A2
Green Street Lane A2
Hawkhill Avenue A3
Hawkhill Avenue Lane B3
High St B2
Holmston Rd C3
James St B3
John St B2
King St B2
Kings Court B2
Kyle Centre C2
Kyle St C2
Library B2
Limekiln Rd A2
Limonds Wynd B2
Loudoun Hall B2
Lymburn Place B3
Macadam Place B2
Main St B2
Mcadam's Monument C1
Mccall's Avenue A3
Mews Lane B1
Mill Brae C3
Mill St C2
Mill Wynd C2
Miller Rd C1
Montgomerie Terrace B1
New Bridge B2
New Bridge St B2
New Rd B2
Newmarket St B2
Newton-on-Ayr Sta A2
North Harbour St B1
North Pier A1
Odeon C2
Park Circus C1
Park Circus Lane C1
Park Terrace C1
Pavilion Rd C1
Peebles St A2
Philip Square B2
Police Station B2
Prestwick Rd B1
Princes Court A2
Queen St B3
Queen's Terrace B1
Racecourse Rd C1
River St B2
Riverside Place B2
Russell Drive A2
St Andrews Church C2
St George's Rd A3
Sandgate B1
Savoy Park C1
Smith St C2
Somerset Park (Ayr United FC) A3
Somerset Rd A3
South Beach Rd B1
South Harbour St B1
South Pier A1
Station Rd C2
Strathayr Place B2
Superstore A2/B2
Taylor St A2
Town Hall B2
Tryfield Place A3
Turner's Bridge B2
Union Avenue A3
Victoria Bridge C3
Victoria St B3
Viewfield Rd A3
Virginia Gardens A2
Waggon Rd A2
Walker Rd A3
Wallace Tower B2
Weaver St A2
Weir Rd A2
Wellington Lane C1
Wellington Square C1
West Sanouhar Rd A3
Whitletts Rd B3
Wilson St A3
York St A1
York Street Lane B1

Bangor 331
Abbey Rd C2
Albert St B1
Ambrose St A3
Ambulance Station A3
Arfon Sports Hall C1
Ashley Rd B3
Bangor Mountain B3
Bangor Station C1
Bangor University B2
Beach Rd A3
Belmont St C1
Bishop's Mill Rd C3
Brick St B3
Buckley Rd B2
Bus Station B3
Caellepa B2
Caernarfon Rd C1
Cathedral B2
Cemetery C1
Clarence St C1
Clock Tower B3
College B2/C2
College Lane B2
College Rd B2
Convent Lane C1
Council Offices B2
Craig y Don Rd B2
Crescent, The B2
Dean St B3
Deiniol Rd B2
Deiniol Shopping Ctr B2
Deiniol St B2
Edge Hill A3
Euston Rd C1
Fairview Rd A3
Farrar Rd C2
Ffordd Cynfal C1
Ffordd Islwyn A3
Ffordd y Castell C3
Ffriddoedd Rd B1
Field St B1
Fountain St A3
Friars Avenue B3
Friars Rd B3
Friary (Site of) B3
Gardd Deman C1
Garth Hill A3
Garth Point A3
Garth Rd A3
Glanrafon B2
Glanrafon Hill B2
Glynne Rd B3
Golf Course B3
Golf Course C2
Gorad Rd B1
Gorsedd Circle A2
Gwern Las C3
Heol Dewi C1
High St B3/C2
Hill St B1
Holyhead Rd B1
Hwfa Rd B1
James St B3
Library B2
Llys Emrys A3
Lon Ogwen C1
Lon-Pobty C2
Lon-y-Felin C3
Lon-y-Glyder C1
Love Lane B2
Lower Penrallt Rd B2
Lower St B2
Maes Glas Sports Ctr B1
Maes-y-Dref B3
Maeshyfryd A3
Meirion Lane A2
Meirion Rd A2
Menai Avenue B1
Menai College C1
Menai Shopping Ctr B3
Min-y-Ddol C3
Minafon B2
Mount St B3
Orme Rd A3
Parc Victoria B1
Penchwintan Rd C1
Penlon Grove B3
Penrhyn Avenue C3
Pier A3
Police Station B2
Post Office B2/B3/C3
Prince's Rd B2
Queen's Avenue C3
Sackville Rd B2
St Paul's St B2
Seion Rd A3
Seiriol Rd A3
Siliwen Rd A2
Snowdon View B1
Station Rd C1
STORIEL B2
Strand St B3
Superstore B3/C2
Swimming Pool and Leisure Centre A3
Tan-y-Coed C3
Tegid Rd B3
Temple Rd B2
Theatr Gwynedd B2
Totton Rd A3
Town Hall B2
Treflan B2
Trem Elidir C1
University B2
Upper Garth Rd A3
Victoria Avenue B1
Victoria Drive B1
Victoria St B1
Vron St B2
Well St B3
West End C1
William St B3
York Place B3

Barrow-in-Furness 331
Abbey Rd A3/B2
Adelaide St A2
Ainslie St A3
Albert St C3
Allison St B3
Anson St A2
AR Centre B2
Argyle St B3
Arthur St B3
Ashburner Way A1
Barrow Park A3
Barrow Raiders RLFC B1
Barrow-in-Furness Station A2
Bath St A1/B2
Bedford Rd A3
Bessamer Way A1
Blake St A1/A2
Bridge Rd C1
Buccleuch Dock C3
Buccleuch Dock Rd C2/C3
Buccleuch St B2/B3
Byron St A2
Calcutta St A1
Cameron St C1
Carlton Avenue A3
Cavendish Dock Rd C3
Cavendish St B2/B3
Channelside Haven C1
Channelside Walk B1
Chatsworth St A2
Cheltenham St A3
Church St C3
Clifford St B2
Clive St B1
Collingwood St B2
Cook St A2
Cornerhouse Retail Pk B2
Cornwallis St B2
Courts A2
Crellin St B3
Cross St C3
Custom House B2
Dalkeith St B2
Dalton Rd B2/C2
Derby St B3
Devonshire Dock C2
Devonshire Dock Hall B1
Dock Museum, The B1
Drake St A2
Dryden St A2
Duke St A1/B2/C3
Duncan St B2
Dundee St C2
Dundonald St B2
Earle St C1
Emlyn St B2
Exmouth St A2
Farm St C2
Fell St B3
Fenton St B3
Ferry Rd C1
Forum, The B2
Furness College B1
Glasgow St B3
Goldsmith St A2
Greengate St B3
Hardwick St A2
Harrison St B2
Hartington St A2
Hawke St B2
Hibbert Rd A2
High Level Bridge C2
High St B2
Hindpool Rd B2
Hindpool Retail Park B2
Holker St A2
Hollywood Retail & Leisure Park B1
Hood St A2
Howard St B2
Howe St A2
Ironworks Rd A1/B1
James St B3
Jubilee Bridge C1
Keith St B2
Keyes St A2
Lancaster St A3
Lawson St B2
Library B2
Lincoln St A3
Longreins Rd A3
Lonsdale St C3
Lord St B3
Lorne Rd B3
Lyon St A2
Manchester St B2
Market B2
Market St B2
Marsh St B3
Michaelson Rd C2
Milton St A2
Monk St B2
Mount Pleasant B3
Nan Tait Centre B2
Napier St B2
Nelson St B2
North Rd B1
Open Market B2
Parade St B2
Paradise St B3
Park Avenue A3
Park Drive A3
Parker St A2
Parry St A2
Peter Green Way A1
Phoenix Rd A1
Police Station B2
Portland Walk Shopping Centre B2
Raleigh St A2
Ramsden St B3
Rawlinson St B3
Robert St B3
Rodney St B2
Rutland St A2
St Patricks Rd C1
St Vincent St B2
Salthouse Rd C3
School St B3
Scott St B2
Settle St A3
Shore St C3
Sidney St B2
Silverdale St B3
Slater St B2
Smeaton St B3
Stafford St A3
Stanley Rd C1
Stark St C3
Steel St B1
Storey Square B3
Strand C3
Superstore A1/B1/C3
Sutherland St B3
Thwaite St B3
Town Hall B2
Town Quay C3
Vernon St B2
Vue Cinema B2
Walney Rd A1
West Gate Rd A2
West View Rd A3
Westmorland St A3
Whitehead St A3
Wordsworth St A2

Bath 331
Alexandra Park C2
Alexandra Rd C2
Ambulance Station A3
Approach Golf Courses (Public) A1
Archway St C3
Assembly Rooms & Fashion Museum A2
Avon St B2
Barton St B2
Bath Abbey B2
Bath Aqua Glass A2
Bath at Work Mus A2
Bath College B2
Bath Rugby (The Rec) B3
Bath Spa Station C3
Bathwick St A3
Beckford Road A3
Beechen Cliff Rd C2
Bennett St A2
Bloomfield Avenue C1
Broad Quay C2
Broad St B2
Brock St A1
Bus Station C2
Calton Gardens C2
Calton Rd C2
Camden Crescent A2
Cavendish Rd A1
Cemetery B1
Charlotte St B2
Chaucer Rd C2
Cheap St B2
Circus Mews A2
Claverton St C2
Corn St C2
Cricket Ground B3
Daniel St A3
East Asian Art Mus A2
Edward St B3
Ferry Lane B3
Fire Station A3
First Avenue C1
Forester Avenue A3
Forester Rd A3
Gays Hill A2
George St B2
Great Pulteney St B3
Green Park B1
Green Park Rd B2
Green Park Station B1
Grove St B2
Guildhall B2
Harley St A2
Hayesfield Park C1
Henrietta Gardens A3
Henrietta Mews B3
Henrietta Park B3
Henrietta Rd A3
Henrietta St B3
Henry St B2
Herschel Museum of Astronomy B1
High Common A1
Holburne Museum B3
Holloway C2
James St West B1/B2
Jane Austen Centre B2
Julian Rd A1
Junction Rd C1
Kingsmead Leisure Complex B2
Kipling Avenue C2
Lansdown Crescent A1
Lansdown Grove A2
Lansdown Rd A2
Library B2
London Rd A3
London St A2
Lower Bristol Rd B1
Lower Oldfield Park C1
Lyncombe Hill C3
Magistrates' Court B3
Manvers St B3
Maple Grove C1
Margaret's Hill A2
Marlborough Bldgs A1
Marlborough Lane B1
Midland Bridge Rd B1
Milk St B2
Milsom St B2
Mission The B2
Monmouth St B2
Morford St A2
Museum of Bath Architecture, The A2
New King St B1
No 1 Royal Cres A1
Norfolk Buildings B1
Norfolk Crescent B1
North Parade Rd B3
Oldfield Rd C1
Paragon A2
Pines Way B1
Podium Shopping Ctr B2
Police Station B3
Portland Place A2
Post Office B2/C2
Postal Museum B2
Powlett Rd A3
Prior Park Rd C3
Pulteney Bridge B2
Pulteney Gardens B3
Pulteney Rd B3/C3
Queen Square B2
Raby Place B3
Recreation Ground B3
Rivers St A2
Rockliffe Avenue A3
Rockliffe Rd A3
Roman Baths & Pump Room B2
Rossiter Rd C3
Royal Avenue A1
Royal Crescent A1
Royal High School, The A2
Royal Victoria Park A1
St James Square A1
St John's Rd A3
Sally Lunn's House B2
Shakespeare Avenue C2
Shopmobility B2
South Parade B3
SouthGate Shopping Centre C2
Sports & Leisure Ctr B3
Spring Gardens C3
Stall St B2
Stanier Rd B1
Superstore A3/B1
Sydney Gardens A3
Sydney Place B3
Sydney Rd B3
Theatre Royal B2
Thermae Bath Spa B2
Thomas St A3
Tyning, The C3
Union St B2
University C3
Upper Bristol Rd B1
Upper Oldfield Park C1
Victoria Art Gallery B2
Victoria Bridge Rd B1
Walcot St B2
Wells Rd C1
Westgate Buildings B2
Westgate St B2
Weston Rd A1
Widcombe Hill C3

Berwick-upon-Tweed 331
Avenue, The B3
Bank Hill B2
Bell Tower A3
Bell Tower Park A2
Berwick Barracks A3
Berwick Br B2
Berwick Infirmary A3
Berwick-upon-Tweed A2
Billendean Rd C3
Blakewell Gardens B3
Blakewell St B2
Brass Bastion A3
Bridge St B2
Brucegate St A2
Castle (Remains of) A2
Castle Terrace A2
Castlegate A2
Chapel St A3
Church Rd C2
Church St B3
Council Offices A3
Court B3
Coxon's Lane A3
Cumberland Bastion A3
Dean Drive C2
Dock Rd C2/C3
Elizabethan Walls A2/B3
Fire Station B1
Flagstaff Park B3
Football Ground C3
Foul Ford B3
Golden Square B2
Golf Course A3
Granary B3
Greenwood C1
Gunpowder Magazine B3
Hide Hill B3
High Greens A2
Holy Trinity A3
Information Centre A2
Kiln Hill B2
King's Mount B3
Ladywell Rd C2
Library A3
Lifeboat Station C3
Lord's Mount A3
Lovaine Terrace A2
Low Greens A3
Main Guard B3
Main St B2/C2
Maltings Art Centre, The B3
Marygate B3
Meg's Mount A2
Middle St C3
Mill St C2
Mount Rd C2
Museum B3
Ness St B3
North Rd A2
Northumberland Ave A2
Northumberland Rd C2
Ord Drive B1
Osborne Crescent B2
Osborne Rd B1
Palace Grove B3
Palace St B3
Palace St East B3
Parade A3
Pier Rd B3
Playing Field C1
Police Station B3
Post Office B2/B3/C2
Prince Edward Rd B2
Prior Rd C2
Quay Walls B3
Railway St A2
Ravensdowne B3
Riverdene B1
Riverside Rd B2
Royal Border Br A2
Royal Tweed Br B2
Russian Gun B3
Scots Gate A2
Scott's Place A2
Shielfield Park (Berwick Rangers FC) C1
Shielfield Terrace C2
Silver St B3
Spittal Quay C3
Superstore B1/C1/C2
Tower Gardens A2
Tower Ho Pottery C2
Tower Rd C2
Town Hall B3
Turret Gardens C2
Tweedbank Retail Pk C2
Tweed Dock B2
Tweed St A2
Tweedside Trading Est C1
Union Brae B2
Union Park Rd B2
Walkergate A3
Wallace Grove A3
War Memorial A2
War Memorial B2
Warkworth Terrace A2
Well Close Square A2
West End B2
West End Place B1
West End Rd B1
West St B3
West St C3
Windmill Bastion B3
Woolmarket B3
Works C3

Birmingham 332
Abbey St A2
Aberdeen St A1
Acorn Grove B2
Adams St A5
Adderley St C5
Albert St B4
Albion St B2
Alcester St C5
Aldgate Grove A3
All Saint's St A2
All Saints Rd A2
Allcock St C5
Allesley St A4
Allison St C4
Alma Crescent B6
Alston Rd C1
Arcadian Centre C4
Arthur St C6
Assay Office B3
Ashted Circus B5
Aston Expressway A5
Aston St B4

Aston University ... B4/B5
Avenue Rd ... A5
Bacchus Rd ... A1
Bagot St ... B4
Banbury St ... B5
Barford Rd ... B1
Barford St ... C4
Barn St ... C5
Barnwell Rd ... C6
Barr St ... A3
Barrack St ... B5
Barwick St ... B4
Bath Row ... C3
Beaufort Rd ... C1
Belmont Row ... B5
Benson Rd ... A1
Berkley St ... C3
Bexhill Grove ... C3
Birchall St ... C5
Birmingham City FC ... C6
Birmingham City Hospital (A&E) ... A1
Birmingham City Univ ... B3
Birmingham Wheels Park ✦ ... B6
Bishopsgate St ... C3
Blews St ... A4
Bloomsbury St ... A6
Blucher St ... C3
Bordesley St ... C4
Bowyer St ... C5
Bradburne Way ... A5
Bradford St ... C5
Branston St ... A3
Brearley St ... A4
Brewery St ... A4
Bridge St ... C3
Bridge St West ... A4
Brindley Drive ... B3
Brindley Place ... C3
Broad St ... C3
Broad St Cineworld ... C2
Broadway Plaza ✦ ... C2
Bromley St ... C5
Bromsgrove St ... C4
Brookfield Rd ... A2
Browning St ... C2
Bryant St ... A1
BT Tower ✦ ... B3
Buckingham St ... A3
Bull St ... B4
Bull St ... B4
Bullring ... C4
Cambridge St ... C3
Camden Drive ... B3
Camden St ... B2
Cannon St ... C4
Cardigan St ... B5
Carlisle St ... A1
Carlyle Rd ... C1
Caroline St ... B3
Carver St ... B2
Cato St ... A6
Cattell Rd ... C6
Cattells Grove ... A6
Cawdor Crescent ... C1
Cecil St ... B4
Cemetery ... A2/B2
Cemetery Lane ... A2
Centenary Square ... C3
Ctr Link Industrial Est ... A6
Charlotte St ... B3
Cheapside ... C4
Chester St ... A5
Children's Hospital (A&E) ... B4
Church St ... B4
Claremont Rd ... A2
Clarendon Rd ... C1
Clark St ... C1
Clement St ... B3
Clissold St ... B2
Cleveland St ... B4
Coach Station ... C5
College St ... B2
Colmore Circus ... B4
Colmore Row ... B4
Commercial St ... C3
Constitution Hill ... B3
Convention Ctr, The ... C3
Cope St ... B2
Coplow St ... B1
Corporation St ⇌ ... C4
Council House ... B3
County Court ... B4
Coveley Grove ... A2
Coventry Rd ... C6
Coventry St ... C5
Cox St ... B3
Crabtree Rd ... A2
Cregoe St ... C3
Crescent Avenue ... A2
Crescent Theatre ... C3
Crescent, The ... A2
Cromwell St ... A6
Cromwell St ... B3
Cube, The ... C3
Curzon Circle ... B5
Curzon St ... B5
Custard Factory ✦ ... C5
Cuthbert Rd ... B1
Dale End ... B4
Dart St ... C6
Dartmouth Circus ... A4
Dartmouth Middleway ... A5
Dental Hospital ... B4
Deritend ... C5
Devon St ... A6
Devonshire St ... A1
Digbeth High St ... C4
Dolman St ... B6
Dover St ... A1
Duchess Rd ... C2
Duddeston ⇌ ... B6
Duddeston Manor Rd ... B5
Duddeston Mill Rd ... B6
Duddeston Mill Trading Estate ... B6
Dudley Rd ... B1
Edgbaston Village ... C2
Edmund St ... B3
Edward St ... B3
Elkington St ... A4
Ellen St ... B2
Ellis St ... C3
Erskine St ... B6
Essex St ... C4
Everyman ... C3
Eyre St ... B2
Farm Croft ... A3
Farm St ... A3
Fazeley St ... B4/C5
Felstead Way ... B5
Finstall Close ... B5
Five Ways ... C2
Five Ways ... C2
Fiveway Shopping Ctr ... C2
Fleet St ... B3
Floodgate St ... C5
Ford St ... A2
Fore St ... C4
Forster St ... B5
Francis Rd ... C2
Francis St ... B5
Frankfort St ... A4
Frederick St ... B3
Freeth St ... C1
Freightliner Terminal ... B6
Garrison Circus ... C5
Garrison Lane ... C6
Garrison St ... B6
Gas St ... C3
Geach St ... A4
George St ... B3
George St West ... B2
Gibb St ... C5
Gilby Rd ... C2
Gillott Rd ... B1
Glover St ... C5
Goode Avenue ... A2
Goodrick Way ... A6
Gordon St ... B6
Graham St ... B3
Grand Central Shopping Centre ... C4
Granville St ... C3
Gray St ... C6
Great Barr St ... C5
Great Charles St Queensway ... B3
Great Francis St ... B6
Great Hampton Row ... A3
Great Hampton St ... A3
Great King St ... A3
Great King St North ... A3
Great Lister St ... A5
Great Tindal St ... C2
Green Lane ... C6
Green St ... C5
Greenway St ... C6
Grosvenor St West ... C2
Guest Grove ... A3
Guild Close ... C2
Guildford Drive ... A4
Guthrie Close ... A3
Hagley Rd ... C1
Hall St ... B3
Hampton St ... A3
Handsworth New Rd ... A1
Hanley St ... B4
Harford St ... A3
Harmer Rd ... A2
Harold Rd ... C1
Hatchett St ... A4
Heath Mill Lane ... C5
Heath St ... B1
Heaton St ... A2
Heneage St ... B5
Henrietta St ... B4
Herbert Rd ... C6
High St ... C4
High St ... C5
Hilden Rd ... B5
Hill St ... C3/C4
Hindlow Close ... B6
Hingeston St ... B2
Hippodrome Theatre ... C4
HM Prison ... A1
Hockley Circus ... A2
Hockley Hill ... A3
Hockley St ... A3
Holliday St ... C3
Holloway Circus ... C4
Holloway Head ... C3
Holt St ... B5
Horse Fair ... C4
Hospital St ... A4
Howard St ... B3
Howe St ... B5
Hubert St ... A5
Hunters Rd ... A2
Hunters Vale ... A3
Huntly Rd ... C2
Hurst St ... C4
Icknield Port Rd ... B1
Icknield Square ... B2
Icknield St ... A2/B2
IKON ... C3
Inge St ... C4
Irving St ... C3
James Watt Queensway ... B4
Jennens Rd ... B5
Jewellery Quarter ⇌ ... A3
Jewellery Quarter ... A3
Jewellery Quarter Museum ... B3
John Bright St ... C4
Keeley St ... C6
Kellett Rd ... B5
Kent St ... C4
Kenyon St ... B3
Key Hill ... A3
Key Hill Circus ... A2
Kilby Avenue ... C2
King Edwards Rd ... B2
King Edwards Rd ... C3
Kingston Rd ... C6
Kirby Rd ... A1
Ladywood Arts & Leisure Centre ... B1
Ladywood Circus ... C1
Ladywood Middleway ... C2/C3
Ladywood Rd ... C1
Lancaster St ... B4
Landor St ... B6
Law Courts ... B4
Lawley Middleway ... B5
Ledbury Close ... C2
Ledsam St ... B2
Lees St ... A1
Legge Lane ... B3
Lennox St ... A3
Library ... A6/C3
Library ... C3
Lighthorne Avenue ... B2
Link Rd ... B1
Lionel St ... B3
Lister St ... B5
Little Ann St ... C5
Little Hall Rd ... A6
Liverpool St ... C5
Livery St ... B3/B4
Lodge Rd ... A1
Lord St ... A5
Love Lane ... A5
Loveday St ... B4
Lower Dartmouth St ... C6
Lower Loveday St ... B4
Lower Tower St ... A4
Lower Trinity St ... C5
Lucus Circus ... A3
Ludgate Hill ... B3
Mailbox Centre & BBC ... C3
Margaret St ... B3
Markby Rd ... A1
Marroway St ... B1
Maxstoke St ... C6
Melvina Rd ... A6
Meriden St ... C4
Midland St ... B6
Milk St ... C5
Mill St ... A5
Millennium Point ... B5
Miller St ... A4
Milton St ... A4
Moat Lane ... C4
Montague Rd ... C1
Montague St ... C5
Monument Rd ... C1
Moor St Queensway ... C4
Moor Street ⇌ ... C4
Moorsom St ... A4
Morville St ... C2
Mosborough Cres ... A3
Moseley St ... C4
Mott St ... B3
Mus & Art Gallery ... B3
Musgrave Rd ... A1
National Sea Life Centre ... C3
Navigation St ... C3
Nechell's Park Rd ... A6
Nechells Parkway ... B5
Nechells Place ... A6
New Alexandra ... C3
New Bartholomew St ... C4
New Canal St ... C5
New John St West ... A3
New Spring St ... B2
New St ... C4
New Street ⇌ ... C4
New Summer St ... A4
New Town Row ... A4
Newhall Hill ... B3
Newhall St ... B3
Newton St ... B4
Newtown ... A4
Noel Rd ... C1
Norman St ... A1
Northbrook St ... B1
Northwood St ... B3
Norton St ... A2
Odeon ... C2
Old Crown House ... C5
Old Rep Theatre, The ... C4
Old Snow Hill ... B4
Oliver Rd ... C1
Oliver St ... A5
Osler St ... C1
Oxford St ... C5
Palmer St ... C5
Paradise Circus Queensway ... C3
Paradise St ... C3
Park Rd ... A2
Park St ... C4
Pavilions ... C4
Paxton Rd ... A2
Peel St ... A1
Pershore St ... C4
Phillips St ... A4
Pickford St ... C5
Pinfold St ... C4
Pitsford St ... A2
Plough & Harrow Rd ... C1
Police Station ... A4/B4/C2/C4
Pope St ... B2
Portland Rd ... C1
Post Office ... A5/B1/B3/B5/C3/C5
Preston Rd ... A1
Price St ... B4
Princip St ... B4
Printing House St ... B4
Priory Queensway ... B4
Pritchett St ... A4
Proctor St ... A5
Radnor St ... A2
Rea St ... C4
Regent Place ... B3
Register Office ... C3
Repertory Theatre ... C3
Reservoir Rd ... C1
Richard St ... A5
River St ... C5
Rocky Lane ... A5/A6
Rodney Close ... C2
Roseberry St ... B2
Rotton Park St ... B1
Royal Birmingham Conservatoire ✦ ... B5
Rupert St ... A5
Ruston St ... C2
Ryland St ... C2
St Andrew's Ind Est ... C6
St Andrew's Rd ... C6
St Andrew's St ... C6
St Bolton St ... C6
St Chads ... B4
St Chad's Cath (RC) ✝ ... B4
St Chads Queensway ... B4
St Clements Rd ... A6
St George's St ... A3
St James Place ... B5
St Marks Crescent ... B2
St Martin's ... C4
St Paul's ... B3
St Paul's ... B3
St Paul's Square ... B3
St Philip's ✝ ... B4
St Stephen's St ... A4
St Thomas' Peace Garden ... C3
St Vincent St ... C2
Saltley Rd ... A6
Sand Pits Parade ... B3
Severn St ... C3
Shadwell St ... B4
Sheepcote St ... C2
Shefford Rd ... A4
Sherborne St ... C2
Shylton's Croft ... C2
Skipton Rd ... C2
Smallbrook Queensway ... C4
Smith St ... A3
Snow Hill ⇌ ... B4
Snow Hill Queensway ... B4
Soho, Benson Rd ... A1
South Rd ... A2
Spencer St ... B3
Spring Hill ... B2
Staniforth St ... B4
Station St ... C4
Steelhouse Lane ... B4
Stephenson St ... C4
Steward St ... B2
Stirling Rd ... C1
Stour St ... B2
Suffolk St Queensway ... C3
Summer Hill Rd ... B2
Summer Hill St ... B2
Summer Hill Terrace ... B2
Summer Lane ... A4
Summer Row ... B3
Summerfield Cres ... B1
Summerfield Park ... B1
Superstore ... B2
Sutton St ... C3
Swallow St ... C3
Sydney Rd ... C6
Symphony Hall ... C3
Talbot St ... A1
Temple Row ... C4
Temple St ... C4
Templefield St ... C6
Tenby St ... B3
Tenby St North ... B2
Tennant St ... C2/C3
Thimble Mill Lane ... A6
Thinktank (Science & Discovery) ... B5
Thomas St ... A4
Thorpe St ... C4
Tilton Rd ... C6
Tower St ... A4
Town Hall ... C3
Town Hall ... C3
Trent St ... C5
Turner's Buildings ... A1
Unett St ... A3
Union Terrace ... B5
Upper Trinity St ... C5
Utilita Arena ✦ ... C2
Uxbridge St ... A3
Vauxhall Grove ... B5
Vauxhall Rd ... B5
Vernon Rd ... C1
Vesey St ... B4
Viaduct St ... B5
Victoria Square ... C3
Villa St ... A3
Vittoria St ... B3
Vyse St ... B3
Walter St ... A6
Wardlow Rd ... A5
Warstone Lane ... B2
Washington St ... C3
Water St ... B3
Waterworks Rd ... C1
Watery Lane ... C5
Western Rd ... B1
Wharf St ... A2
Wheeler St ... A3
Whitehouse St ... A5
Whitmore St ... A2
Whittall St ... B4
Wholesale Market ... C4
Wiggin St ... B1
Willes Rd ... A1
Windsor Industrial Est ... A5
Windsor St ... A5
Windsor St ... B5
Winson Green Rd ... A1
Witton St ... C6
Wolseley St ... C6
Woodcock St ... B5

Blackpool 332

Abingdon St ... A1
Addison Crescent ... A3
Adelaide St ... B1
Albert Rd ... B2
Alfred St ... B2
Ascot Rd ... A3
Ashton Rd ... C2
Auburn Grove ... C3
Bank Hey St ... B1
Banks St ... A1
Beech Avenue ... A3
Bela Grove ... C2
Belmont Avenue ... B2
Birley St ... A1
Blackpool & Fleetwood Tram ... B1
Blackpool & the Fylde College ... B2
Blackpool FC ... C2
Blackpool North ⇌ ... A2
Blackpool North ... A2
Blackpool Tower ✦ ... B1
Blundell St ... C1
Bonny St ... B1
Breck Rd ... B3
Bryan Rd ... A3
Buchanan St ... A2
Bus Hub ... B1
Cambridge Rd ... A3
Caunce St ... A2/A3
Central Drive ... B1/C2
Central Pier ✦ ... C1
Central Pier ... C1
Central Pier Theatre ... C1
Chapel St ... C1
Charles St ... A2
Charnley Rd ... B2
Church St ... A1/A2
Clinton Avenue ... B2
Coach Station ... A2/C1
Cocker St ... A1
Coleridge Rd ... A3
Collingwood Avenue ... A3
Comedy Carpet ✦ ... B1
Condor Grove ... C3
Cookson St ... A2
Coronation St ... B1
Corporation St ... A1
Courts ... B1
Cumberland Avenue ... B3
Cunliffe Rd ... C3
Dale St ... C1
Devonshire Rd ... A3
Devonshire Square ... A3
Dickson Rd ... A1
Elizabeth St ... A2
Ferguson Rd ... C3
Forest Gate ... B3
Foxhall Rd ... C1
Freckleton St ... C2
George St ... A2
Gloucester Avenue ... B3
Golden Mile, The ... C1
Gorse Rd ... B3
Gorton St ... A2
Grand Theatre, The ... B1
Granville Rd ... A2
Grasmere Rd ... C2
Grosvenor St ... A2
Grundy Art Gallery ... A1
Harvey Rd ... B3
Hornby Rd ... B2
Houndshill Shopping Centre ... B1
Hull Rd ... B1
Ibbison Court ... C2
Kent Rd ... C2
Keswick Rd ... C2
King St ... A2
Knox Grove ... C3
Laycock Gate ... A3
Layton Rd ... A3
Leamington Rd ... B2
Leeds Rd ... B3
Leicester Rd ... B2
Levens Grove ... C2
Library ... A1
Lifeboat Station ... B1
Lincoln Rd ... B2
Liverpool Rd ... B3
Livingstone Rd ... B2
London Rd ... A3
Lune Grove ... C2
Lytham Rd ... C1
Madame Tussaud's Blackpool ... B1
Manchester Square ... C1
Manor Rd ... B3
Maple Avenue ... B3
Market St ... A1
Marlboro Rd ... B3
Mere Rd ... B3
Milbourne St ... A2
Newcastle Avenue ... B3
Newton Drive ... A3
North Pier ✦ ... A1
North Pier ... A1
North Pier Theatre ... A1
Odeon ... C2
Olive Grove ... B3
Palatine Rd ... B2
Park Rd ... B2/C3
Peter St ... A2
Post Office ... A1/B1/B2/B3
Princess Parade ... A1
Princess St ... C1/C2
Promenade ... A1/C1
Queen St ... A1
Queen Victoria Rd ... C2
Raikes Parade ... B2
Reads Avenue ... B2
Regent Cinema ... B2
Regent Rd ... B2
Register Office ... B2
Ribble Rd ... B2
Rigby Rd ... C1/C2
Ripon Rd ... B3
St Albans Rd ... B3
St Ives Avenue ... C3
St John's Square ... A1
St Vincent Avenue ... C3
Salisbury Rd ... B3
Salthouse Avenue ... C2
Salvation Army Ctr ... A2
Sands Way ... C2
Sea Life Centre ... B1
Seasiders Way ... C1
Selbourne Rd ... A2
Sharrow Grove ... C3
Somerset Avenue ... C3
South King St ... B2
Springfield Rd ... A1
Sutton Place ... B2
Talbot Rd ... A1/A2
Thornber Grove ... C2
Topping St ... A1
Tower ... B1
Town Hall ... A1
Tram Depot ... C1
Tyldesley Rd ... C1
Vance Rd ... B1
Victoria St ... B1
Victory Rd ... A2
Wayman Rd ... A3
Westmorland Ave. ... C2/C3
Whitegate Drive ... B3
Winter Gardens Theatre ... B1
Woodland Grove ... B3
Woolman Rd ... B2

Bournemouth 332

Ascham Rd ... A3
Avenue Rd ... B1
Ave Shopping Centre ... B1
Bath Rd ... C2
Beacon Rd ... C1
Beechey Rd ... A3
Bodorgan Rd ... B1
Bourne Avenue ... B1
Bournemouth ⇌ ... A3
Bh2 Leisure ... C1
Bournemouth & Poole College ... B3
Bournemouth International Centre ... C1
Bournemouth Pier ... C2
Bournemouth Sta ... B3
Braidley Rd ... A1
Cavendish Place ... A2
Cavendish Rd ... A2
Central Drive ... A1
Central Gardens ... B1
Christchurch Rd ... B3
Cliff Lift ... C1/C3
Coach House Place ... A3
Coach Station ... A3
Commercial Rd ... B1
Cotlands Rd ... B3
Cranborne Rd ... C1
Cricket Ground ... A2
Cumnor Rd ... B2
Dean Park ... A2
Dean Park Crescent ... B2
Dean Park Rd ... A2
Durrant Rd ... B1
East Overcliff Drive ... C3
Exeter Crescent ... C1
Exeter Rd ... C1
Gervis Place ... B1
Gervis Rd ... B3
Glen Fern Rd ... B2
Golf Club ... B2
Grove Rd ... B3
Hinton Rd ... C2
Holdenhurst Rd ... B3
Horseshoe Common ... B2
Information Centre ... C2
Lansdowne ... B3
Lansdowne Rd ... A2
Lorne Park Rd ... B2
Lower Gardens ... B1/C2
Madeira Rd ... B2
Methuen Rd ... A3
Meyrick Park ... A1
Meyrick Rd ... B3
Milton Rd ... A2
Nuffield Health Bournemouth Hospital (private) ... A2
Oceanarium ... C2
Old Christchurch Rd ... B2
Ophir Rd ... A3
Oxford Rd ... B3
Park Rd ... A3
Parsonage Rd ... B2
Pavilion ... C2
Pier Approach ... C2
Pier Theatre ... C2
Police Station ... C3
Portchester Rd ... A3
Post Office ... B1/B3
Priory Rd ... C1
Quadrant, The ... B2
Recreation Ground ... A1
Richmond Gardens Shopping Centre ... B2
Richmond Hill Rd ... B1
Russell-Cotes Art Gallery & Museum ... C2
Russell Cotes Rd ... C2
St Anthony's Rd ... A1
St Michael's Rd ... C1
St Paul's ... A3
St Paul's Lane ... B3
St Paul's Rd ... A3
St Peter's ... B2
St Peter's ... B2
St Peter's Rd ... B2
St Stephen's Rd ... B1/B2
St Swithun's ... B3
St Swithun's Rd ... B3
St Swithun's Rd South ... B3
St Valerie Rd ... A2
St Winifred's Rd ... A2
Square, The ... B1
Stafford Rd ... B3
Terrace Rd ... B1
Town Hall ... B1
Tregonwell Rd ... C1
Triangle, The ... B1
Trinity Rd ... B2
Undercliff Drive ... C3
Upper Hinton Rd ... B2
Upper Terrace Rd ... C1
Wellington Rd ... A2/A3
Wessex Way ... A3/B1/B2
West Cliff Promenade ... C1
West Hill Rd ... C1
West Undercliff Prom ... C1
Westover Rd ... B2
Wimborne Rd ... A2
Wootton Mount ... B2
Wychwood Drive ... A1
Yelverton Rd ... B2
York Rd ... B3
Zig-Zag Walks ... C1/C3
Zip Wire ✦ ... C2

Bradford 332

Alhambra ... B2
Back Ashgrove ... B1
Barkerend Rd ... A3
Barnard Rd ... C3
Barry St ... B2
Bolling Rd ... C3
Bolton Rd ... A3
Bowland St ... A1
Bradford Big Screen ✦ ... B2
Bradford College ... B1
Bradford Forster Square ⇌ ... A2
Bradford Interchange ⇌ ... B3
Bradford Playhouse ... B3
Bridge St ... B2
Britannia St ... B2
Broadway Bradford, The ... B2
Burnett St ... B3
Bus Station ... B2
Butler St West ... A3
Caledonia St ... C2
Canal Rd ... A2
Carlton St ... B1
Cathedral ✝ ... A3
Centenary Square ... B2
Chapel St ... B3
Cheapside ... A2
Church Bank ... B3
Cineworld ... B3
City Hall ... B2
City Rd ... A1
Claremont ... B1
Colour Experience ... B1
Croft St ... B2
Crown Court ... B3
Darfield St ... A1
Darley St ... A2
Drewton Rd ... A1
Drummond Trading Estate ... A1
Dryden St ... B3
Dyson St ... A1
Easby Rd ... C1
East Parade ... B3
Eldon Place ... A1
Filey St ... B3
Forster Sq Retail Pk ... A2
Gallery II ... B1
Garnett St ... B3
Godwin St ... B2
Gracechurch St ... A1
Grattan Rd ... B1
Great Horton Rd ... B1/B2
Grove Terrace ... B1
Hall Ings ... B2
Hall Lane ... C3
Hallfield Rd ... A1
Hammstrasse ... A2
Harris St ... B3
Holdsworth St ... A2
Ice Arena ✦ ... B2
Impressions ... B2
Information Centre ... B2
Inland Revenue ... A2
Ivegate ... B2
Jacob's Well Municipal Offices ... B2
James St ... A2
John St ... A2
Kirkgate ... B2
Kirkgate Centre ... B2
Laisteridge Lane ... C1
Leeds Rd ... B3
Leisure Exchange, The ... B3
Library ... B1/B2
Listerhills Rd ... B1
Little Horton Green ... C1
Little Horton Lane ... C1
Longside Lane ... B1
Lower Kirkgate ... B2
Lumb Lane ... A1
Magistrates Court ... B2
Manchester Rd ... C2
Manningham Lane ... A1
Manor Row ... A2
Market ... C3
Market St ... B2
Melbourne Place ... C1
Midland Rd ... A2
Mill Lane ... C2
Morley St ... B1
National Science and Media Museum ... B2
Nelson St ... B2/C2
Nesfield St ... A2
New Otley Rd ... A3
Norcroft St ... B1
North Parade ... A2
North St ... A3
North Wing ... A3
Oastler Shopping Ctr ... A2
Otley Rd ... A3
Park Avenue ... C1
Park Lane ... C1
Park Rd ... C2
Parma St ... C2
Peace Museum ... B2
Peckover St ... B3
Piccadilly ... A2
Police Station ... C2
Post Office ... B1/B2/B3/C3
Princes Way ... B2
Prospect St ... C3
Radwell Drive ... C2
Rawson Rd ... A1
Rebecca St ... A1
Richmond Rd ... B1
Russell St ... C1
St George's Hall ... B2
St Lukes Hospital ... C1
Shipley Airedale Rd ... A3/B3
Shopmobility ... A2
Simes St ... A1
Smith St ... B1
Spring Mill St ... C2
Stott Hill ... A3
Sunbridge Rd ... A1/B1/B2
Theatre in the Mill ... B1
Thornton Rd ... A1/B1
Trafalgar St ... A2
Trinity Rd ... C1
Tumbling Hill St ... B1
Tyrrel St ... B2
Univ of Bradford ... B1/C1
Usher St ... C3
Valley Rd ... A2
Vicar Lane ... B3
Wakefield Rd ... C3
Wapping Rd ... A3
Well St ... B3
Westgate ... A1
White Abbey Rd ... A1
Wigan Rd ... A1
Wilton St ... B1
Wood St ... A1
Wool Exchange ... B2
Worthington St ... A1

Brighton 332

Addison Rd ... A1
Albert Rd ... B2
Albion Hill ... B3
Albion St ... B3
Ann St ... A3
Baker St ... A3
Black Lion St ... C2
Brighton ⇌ ... A2
Brighton Centre ... C2
Brighton Fishing Museum ... C2
Brighton Pier (Palace Pier) ✦ ... C3
Brighton Zip Wire ✦ ... C3
British Airways i360 Tower ✦ ... C1
Broad St ... C3
Buckingham Place ... A2
Buckingham Rd ... B2
Cannon Place ... C1
Carlton Hill ... B3
Chatham Place ... A1
Cheapside ... A3
Church St ... B2
Churchill Square Shopping Centre ... B2
Clifton Hill ... B1
Clifton Place ... B1
Clifton Rd ... B1
Clifton St ... A2
Clifton Terrace ... B1
Clyde Rd ... A3
Coach Station ... C3
Compton Avenue ... A2
Davigdor Rd ... A1
Denmark Terrace ... B1
Ditchling Rd ... A3
Dome ... B2
Duke St ... B2
Duke's Lane ... C2
Dyke Rd ... A1/B2
East St ... C2
Edward St ... B3
Elmore Rd ... B3
Fleet St ... A2
Frederick St ... B2
Gardner St ... B2
Gloucester Place ... B3
Gloucester Rd ... B2
Goldsmid Rd ... A1
Grand Junction Rd ... C2
Grand Parade ... B3
Grove Hill ... B3
Guildford St ... A2
Hampton Place ... B1
Hanover Terrace ... A3
High St ... C3
Highdown Rd ... A1
Information Centre ... C2
John St ... B3
Jubilee Clock Tower ... B2
Kemp St ... B2
Kensington Place ... B2
Kings Rd ... C1
Lanes, The ... C2
Law Courts ... B3
Lewes Rd ... A3
Library ... B2
London Rd ... A3
Madeira Drive ... C3
Marine Parade ... C3
Middle St ... C2
Montpelier Place ... B1
Montpelier Rd ... B1
Montpelier St ... B1
Mus & Art Gallery ... B3
New England Rd ... A2
New England St ... A2
New Rd ... B2
Nizells Avenue ... A1
Norfolk Rd ... B1
Norfolk Terrace ... B1
North Rd ... B2
North St ... B2
Odeon ... C2
Old Shoreham Rd ... A1
Old Steine ... C3
Osmond Rd ... A1
Over St ... B2
Oxford St ... A3
Park Crescent Terrace ... A3
Phoenix Brighton ... B3
Phoenix Rise ... A3
Police Station ... B3
Post Office ... A1/A3/C3
Preston Rd ... A2
Preston St ... B1
Prestonville Rd ... A1
Queen's Rd ... B2
Queen Square ... B2
Regency Square ... C1
Regent St ... B2
Richmond Place ... B3
Richmond St ... B3
Richmond Terrace ... A3
Rose Hill Terrace ... A3
Royal Pavilion ... B2
St Bartholomew's ... A3
St James's St ... C3
St Nicholas Rd ... B2
St Nicholas' ... B2
St Peter's ... A3
Sea Life Brighton ... C3
Shaftesbury Rd ... A3
Ship St ... C2
Sillwood Rd ... B1
Sillwood St ... B1
Southover St ... A3
Spring Gardens ... B2
Stanford Rd ... A1
Stanley Rd ... A3
Surrey St ... B2
Sussex St ... B3
Swimming Pool ... B3
Sydney St ... B3
Temple Gardens ... B1
Terminus Rd ... A2
Theatre Royal ... B2
Tidy St ... B2
Town Hall ... C2
Toy & Model Mus ... A2
Trafalgar St ... B2
Union Rd ... A3
University of Brighton ... B3
Upper Lewes Rd ... A3
Upper North St ... B1
Viaduct Rd ... A3
Victoria Gardens ... B3
Victoria Rd ... B1
Volk's Electric Railway ✦ ... C3
West Pier (derelict) ... C1
West St ... C2
Western Rd ... B1
Whitecross St ... B2
YHA ... C3
York Place ... B3
York Rd ... B1

Bristol 332

Acramans Rd ... C4
Albert Rd ... C6
Alfred Hill ... A4
All Saint's St ... A4
All Saints' ... B4
Allington Rd ... C3
Alpha Rd ... C4
Ambra Vale ... B1
Ambra Vale East ... B2
Ambrose Rd ... B2
Amphitheatre & Waterfront Square ✦ ... C4
Anchor Rd ... B3
Anvil St ... B6
Arcade, The ... A5
Architecture Centre, The ✦ ... B4
Argyle Place ... B2
Arlington Villas ... A2
Arnolfini ✦ ... B4
Art Gallery ... A3
Ashton Gate Rd ... C2
Ashton Rd ... C1
Avon Bridge ... C1
Avon Crescent ... C1
Avon St ... B6
Baldwin St ... B4
Baltic Wharf ... C2
Baltic Wharf Leisure Ctr & Caravan Park ✦ ... C2
Baltic Wharf Marina ... C2
Barossa Place ... C4
Barton Manor ... B6
Barton Rd ... B6
Barton Vale ... B6
Bath Rd ... C6
Bathurst Basin ... C4
Bathurst Parade ... C4
Beauley Rd ... C3
Bedminster Bridge ... C5
Bedminster Parade ... C4
Bellevue ... B2
Bellevue Crescent ... B2
Bellevue Rd ... C6
Berkeley Place ... A2
Berkeley Square ... A3
Birch Rd ... C2
Blackfriars ... A4
Bond St ... A5
Braggs Lane ... A6
Brandon Hill ... B3
Brandon Steep ... B3
Bristol Aquarium ... B4
Bristol Beacon ... B4
Bristol Bridge ... B5
Bristol Cath (CE) ✝ ... B3
Bristol Eye Hospital (A&E) ... A4
Bristol Grammar School ... A3
Bristol Harbour Railway ... C3
Bristol Royal Children's Hospital ... A4
Bristol Royal Infirmary (A&E) ... A4
Bristol Temple Meads Station ⇌ ... B6
Broad Plain ... B6
Broad Quay ... B4
Broad St ... A4
Broad Weir ... A5
Broadcasting House ... A3
Broadmead ... A5

Brunel Institute ✦ B3
Brunel Way C1
Brunswick Square A5
Burton Close C5
Bus Station A4
Butts Rd B3
Cabot Circus A5
Cabot Tower ✦ B3
Caledonia Place B1
Callowhill Court A5
Cambridge St C6
Camden Rd C3
Camp Rd A1
Canada Way C2
Cannon St A4
Canon's Way B3
Cantock's Close A3
Canynge Rd A1
Canynge Square A1
Castle Park A5
Castle St A5
Cathedral Walk B3
Catherine Meade St C4
Cattle Market Rd C6
Central Library B3
Charles Place B1
Charlotte St B3
Charlotte St South B3
Chatterton House B5
Chatterton Square C5
Chatterton St C5
Cheese Lane B5
Christchurch A4
Christchurch Rd A1
Christmas Steps ✦ A4
Church Lane B2/B5
Church St B5
City Museum A3
City of Bristol College B3
Civil and Family Justice Centre B5
Clare St B4
Clarence Rd C5
Cliff Rd C1
Clift House Rd C1
Clifton Cathedral (RC) ✝ A2
Clifton Down A1
Clifton Down Rd A1
Clifton Hill B2
Clifton Park A1/A2
Clifton Park Rd A1
Clifton Rd A2
Clifton Vale B1
Cliftonwood Crescent B2
Cliftonwood Rd B2
Cliftonwood Terrace B2
Cobblestone Mews A1
College Green B3
College Rd A1
College St B3
Colston Almshouses A4
Colston Avenue B4
Colston Parade C5
Colston St A4
Commercial Rd C4
Constitution Hill B2
Cooperage Lane C2
Corn St B4
Cornwallis Avenue B1
Cornwallis Crescent B1
Coronation Rd C2/C4
Council House B3
Counterslip B5
Create Centre, The ✦ C1
Crosby Row B2
Crown Court A4
Culver St B3
Cumberland Basin C1
Cumberland Close C2
Cumberland Rd C2/C3
Dean Lane C4
Deanery Rd B3
Denmark St B4
Dowry Square B1
Eaton Crescent A2
Elmdale Rd A3
Elton Rd A3
Eugene St A4/A6
Exchange and St Nicholas' Markets, The B4
Fairfax St A4
Fire Station B5
Floating Harbour C3
Fosseway, The A2
Foster Almshouses A4
Frayne Rd C1
Frederick Place A2
Freeland Place B1
Friary B5
Frogmore St B3
Fry's Hill B2
Galleries shopping centre, The A5
Gas Lane B6
Gasferry Rd C3
Georgian House B3
Glendale B1
Glentworth Rd B2
Gloucester St A1
Goldney Hall B2
Goldney Rd B1
Gordon Rd A2
Granby Hill B1
Grange Rd A1
Great Ann St A6
Great George Rd B3
Great George St A6/B3
Green St North B1
Green St South B1
Greenay Bush Lane C2
Greenbank Rd C2
Greville Smyth Park C1
Grove, The B4
Guildhall A4
Guinea St C4
Hamilton Rd C3
Hanbury Rd A2
Hanover Place C2
Harley Place A1
Haymarket A5
Hensman's Hill B1
High St B4
Highbury Villas A3
Hill St B3
Hill St C6
Hippodrome B4
Hopechapel Hill B1
Horfield Rd A4
Horsefair, The A5
Horton St B6
Host St A4
Hotwell Rd B1/B2
Houlton St A6
Howard Rd C3
IMAX Cinema B4
Islington Rd C3
Jacob St A5/A6
Jacob's Wells Rd B2
John Carr's Terrace B2
John Wesley's Chapel A5
Joy Hill B1
Jubilee St B6
Kensington Place A2
Kilkenny St B6
King St B4
Kingsland Rd B6
Kingston Rd C3
Lamb St A6
Lansdown Rd A2
Lawford St A6
Lawfords Gate A6
Leighton Rd C3
Lewins Mead A4
Lime Rd C2
Litfield Rd A1
Little Ann St A6
Little Caroline Place B1
Little George St A6
Little King St B4
Llandoger Trow B4
Lloyds' Building, The C3
Lodge St A4
Lord Mayor's Chapel, The B4
Lower Castle St A5
Lower Church Lane A4
Lower Clifton Hill B2
Lower Guinea St C4
Lower Lamb St B3
Lower Maudlin St A4
Lower Park Rd A4
Lower Sidney St C2
Lucky Lane C4
Lydstep Terrace C3
M Shed C4
Magistrates' Court A4
Manilla Rd A1
Mardyke Ferry Rd C2
Maritime Heritage Centre B3
Marlborough Hill A4
Marlborough St A4
Marsh St B4
Mead St C5
Merchant Dock B2
Merchant Seamen's Almshouses B4
Merchant St A5
Merchants Rd A1
Merchants Rd C1
Meridian Place A2
Meridian Vale A2
Merrywood Rd C3
Midland Rd A6
Milford St C3
Millennium Promenade B3
Millennium Square B3
Mitchell Lane B5
Mortimer Rd A1
Murray Rd C4
Myrtle Rd A3
Narrow Plain B5
Narrow Quay B4
Nelson St A4
New Charlotte St C4
New Kingsley Rd B6
New Queen St C5
New St A6
Newgate A5
Newton St A6
Norland Rd A1
North St C2
O2 Academy B3
Oakfield Grove A2
Oakfield Place A2
Oakfield Rd A2
Old Bread St B6
Old Market St A6
Old Park Hill A4
Oldfield Rd B1
Orchard Avenue B4
Orchard Lane B4
Orchard St B4
Osbourne Rd C3
Oxford St B6
Park Place A2
Park Rd C3
Park Row A3
Park St A3
Passage St B5
Pembroke Grove A2
Pembroke Rd A2
Pembroke Rd C3
Pembroke St A5
Penn St A5
Pennywell Rd A6
Percival Rd A1
Pero's Bridge B4
Perry Rd A4
Phipps St C2
Pip 'n' Jay B5
Plimsoll Bridge B1
Police Station A6
Polygon Rd B1
Portland St A1
Portwall Lane B5
Post Office A1/A3/A5/ B1/B4/C4/C5
Prewett St C5
Prince St B4
Prince St Bridge C4
Princess St C5
Princess Victoria St B1
Priory Rd A3
Pump Lane C5
QEH Theatre A2
Quakers Friars A5
Quay St A4
Queen Charlotte St B4
Queen Elizabeth Hospital School B2
Queen Square B4
Queen St A5
Queen's Avenue A3
Queen's Parade B3
Queen's Rd A2/A3
Raleigh Rd C2
Randall Rd B2
Red Lodge A4
Redcliffe Backs B5
Redcliffe Bridge B4
Redcliffe Hill C5
Redcliffe Parade C4
Redcliffe St B5
Redcliffe Way B5
Redcross St A6
Redgrave Theatre A1
Regent St B1
Richmond Hill A2
Richmond Hill Avenue A2
Richmond Lane A2
Richmond Park Rd A2
Richmond St C6
Richmond Terrace A2
River St A6
Rownham Mead B2
Royal Fort Rd A3
Royal Park A2
Royal West of England Academy A3
Royal York Crescent B1
Royal York Villas B1
Rupert St A4
Russ St B6
St Andrew's Walk B2
St George's B3
St George's Rd B3
St James A4
St John's A4
St John's Rd C4
St Luke's Rd C5
St Mary Redcliffe C5
St Matthias Park A6
St Michael's Hill A3
St Michael's Hosp A4
St Michael's Park A3
St Nicholas St B4
St Paul St A5
St Paul's Rd A2
St Peter's (ruin) A5
St Philip's Bridge B5
St Philips Rd A6
St Stephen's B4
St Stephen's St B4
St Thomas St B5
St Thomas the Martyr B5
Sandford Rd B1
Sargent St C5
Saville Place B1
Ship Lane C5
Shopmobility A5
Showcase Cinema de Lux A5
Silver St A4
Sion Hill A1
Small St A4
Smeaton Rd C1
Somerset Square C5
Somerset St C5
Southernhay Avenue B2
Southville Rd C4
Spike Island Artspace C2
Spring St C5
Superstore C4
SS Great Britain and the Matthew B2
Stackpool Rd C3
Staight St B6
Stillhouse Lane C4
Sydney Row C2
Tankard's Close A3
Temple Back B5
Temple Back East B5
Temple Bridge B5
Temple Church B5
Temple Circus B5
Temple Gate C5
Temple St B5
Temple Way B5
Terrell St A4
Theatre Royal (Bristol Old Vic) B4
Thekla B4
Thomas Lane B5
Three Kings of Cologne A4
Three Queens Lane B5
Tobacco Factory, The C2
Tower Hill B5
Tower Lane A4
Trenchard St A4
Triangle South A3
Triangle West A3
Trinity Rd A6
Trinity St A6
Tyndall Avenue A3
Union St A5
Union St B6
Unity St A6
Unity St B3
University of Bristol A3
University Rd A3
Upper Byron Place A3
Upper Maudlin St A4
Upper Perry Hill C3
Upton Rd C2
Valentine Bridge B6
Victoria Grove C5
Victoria Rd C6
Victoria Rooms A2
Victoria Square A2
Victoria St B5
Vyvyan Rd A1
Vyvyan Terrace A1
Wade St A6
Walter St C2
Wapping Rd C4
Water Lane B5
Waterloo Rd A6
Waterloo St A1
Waterloo St A6
Watershed Media Centre ✦ B4
We the Curious ✦ B3
Welling Terrace B1
Welsh Back B4
West Mall A1
West St A6
Westfield Place A1
Wetherell Place A2
Whitehouse Place C5
Whitehouse St C5
Whiteladies Rd A2
Whitson St A4
William St C5
Willway St C5
Windsor Place B1
Wine St A4
Woodland Rd A3
Woodland Rise A3
Worcester Rd A1
Worcester Terrace A1
YHA B4
York Gardens B1
York Place A2
York Rd C5

Bury St Edmunds 332

Abbey Gardens B3
Abbey Gate B3
Abbeygate B2
Abbeygate St B2
Albert Crescent B1
Albert St B1
Angel Hill B2
Angel Lane B2
Anglian Lane A1
Arc Shopping Centre B2
Athenaeum C2
Baker's Lane C3
Barwell Rd B3
Beetons Way A1
Bishops Rd B2
Bloomfield St B2
Bridewell Lane C2
Bullen Close C1
Bury St Edmunds ≥ A2
Bury St Edmunds County Upper Sch A1
Bury St Edmunds Leisure Centre B1
Bury Town FC (Ram Meadow) B3
Bus Station B2
Business Park B3
Butter Market B2
Cannon St B2
Castle Rd C1
Cemetery C1
Chalk Rd (N) B1
Chalk Rd (S) B1
Church Row B2
Churchgate St C2
Citizens Advice Bureau B2
College St C2
Compiegne Way A3
Corn Exchange, The B2
Cornfield Rd B1
Cotton Lane B3
Courts B2
Covent Garden C2
Crown St C3
Cullum Rd C2
Eastern Way A3
Eastgate St B3
Enterprise Bsns Park A2
Etna Rd A2
Eyre Close C2
Fire & Ambulance Sta B1
Friar's Lane C2
Gage Close A1
Garland St B2
Greene King Brewery C3
Grove Park B1
Grove Rd B1
Guildhall C2
Guildhall St C2
Hatter St C2
High Baxter St B2
Honey Hill C3
Hospital Rd C1/C2
Ickworth Drive C1
Industrial Estate A3
Information Centre B2
Ipswich St A2
King Edward VI Sch A1
King's Rd C1/B2
Library B2
Long Brackland A2
Looms Lane B2
Lwr Baxter St B2
Malthouse Lane A2
Manor House C3
Maynewater Lane C3
Mill Rd C1
Mill Rd (South) C1
Minden Close B3
Moyse's Hall B2
Mustow St B3
Norman Tower C3
Northgate Avenue A2
Northgate St B2
Osier Rd A2
Out Northgate A2
Out Risbygate B1
Out Westgate C2
Parkway B1/C2
Parkway, The B1
Peckham St B2
Petticoat Lane C1
Phoenix Day Hosp C1
Pinners Way C1
Police Station C3
Post Office B2
Pump Lane B2
Queen's Rd B1
Raingate St C3
Raynham Rd A1
Retail Park C2
Risbygate St B1/B2
Robert Boby Way C2
St Andrew's St North B2
St Andrew's St South B2
St Botolph's Lane C3
St Edmund's C2
St Edmund's Abbey (Remains) ✦ B3
St Edmunds Hospital (Private) C3
St Edmundsbury ✝ C3
St John's St B2
St Marys C3
School Hall Lane B2
Shillitoe Close C1
South Close C1
Southgate St C3
Sparhawk St C3
Spring Lane B1
Springfield Rd B1
Station Hill A2
Swan Lane C3
Tayfen Rd B2
Theatre Royal C3
Thingoe Hill A2
Victoria St B1
Vinefields, The B3
War Memorial ✦ C1
Well St B2
West Suffolk College B1
Westgarth Gardens C1
Westgate St C2
Whiting St C2
York Rd B1
York Terrace B1

Cambridge 333

Abbey Rd A3
ADC A2
Anglia Ruskin Univ B3
Archaeology & Anthropology B2
Arts Picturehouse B2
Arts Theatre B1
Auckland Rd A3
Backs, The B1
Bateman St C2
Benet St B1
Bradmore St B3
Bridge St A1
Broad St B3
Brookside C2
Brunswick Terrace A3
Burleigh St B3
Bus Station B2
Butt Green A2
Cambridge Contemporary Art Gallery B1
Castle Mound ✦ A1
Castle St A1
Cemetery B3
Chesterton Lane A1
Christ's (College) B2
Christ's Lane B2
Christ's Pieces B2
City Rd B3
Clare Bridge B1
Clare (College) B1
Clarendon St B2
Coe Fen C2
Coronation St C2
Corpus Christi (Coll) B1
Court A3
Cross St C3
Crusoe Bridge C1
Darwin (College) C1
Devonshire Rd C3
Downing (College) C2
Downing St B2
Earl St B2
East Rd B3
Eden St B3
Elizabeth Way A3
Elm St B2
Emery St B3
Emmanuel (College) B2
Emmanuel Rd B2
Emmanuel St B2
Fair St A3
Fen Causeway, The C1
Fenner's Cricket Gd C3
Fire Station B3
Fitzroy St A3
Fitzwilliam Mus C2
Fitzwilliam St C2
Garrett Hostel Bridge B1
Glisson Rd C3
Gonville & Caius (Coll) B1
Gonville Place C2
Grafton Centre, The A3
Grand Arcade B2
Green St B1
Gresham Rd C3
Guest Rd B3
Guildhall B2
Harvey Rd C3
Hills Rd C3
Hobson St B2
Hughes Hall (College) B3
James St A3
Jesus (College) A2
Jesus Green A2
Jesus Lane A2
Jesus Terrace B3
John St B3
Kelsey Kerridge Sports Centre B3
Kettle's Yard A1
King's Bridge B1
King St A2
King's (College) B1
King's Coll Chapel B1
King's Parade B1
Lammas Land Rec Gd C1
Lensfield Rd C2
Library B2
Lion Yard B2
Little St Mary's Lane B1
Lyndewod Rd C3
Magdalene (College) A1
Magdalene St A1
Maid's Causeway A3
Malcolm St A2
Market St B1
Mathematical Bridge B1
Mawson Rd C3
Midsummer Common A3
Mill Lane B1
Mill Rd B3
Mill St C3
Mumford B3
Mus of Cambridge A1
Museum of Classical Archaeology C1
Napier St A3
New Square A2
Newmarket Rd A3
Newnham Rd C1
Norfolk St B3
Northampton St A1
Norwich St C2
Orchard St B2
Panton St C2
Paradise St B3
Park Parade A1
Park St A2
Park Terrace B2
Parker St B2
Parker's Piece B2
Parkside B3
Parkside Pools B3
Parsonage St A3
Pea's Hill B1
Pemberton Terrace C2
Pembroke (College) B2
Pembroke St B1
Perowne St B3
Peterhouse (College) C1
Petty Cury B2
Polar Museum, The C2
Police Station B3
Post Office A3/B2/C1/C2/C3
Queen's Lane B1
Queen's Rd B1
Queens' (College) B1
Regent St B2
Regent Terrace B2
Ridley Hall (College) C1
Riverside A3
Round Church, The A1
Russell St C2
St Andrew's St B2
St Benet's B1
St Catharine's (Coll) B1
St Eligius St C2
St John's (College) A1
St Mary's B1
St Paul's Rd C3
Saxon St C2
Sedgwick Museum B2
Sheep's Green C1
Shire Hall A1
Sidgwick Avenue C1
Sidney St A2
Sidney Sussex (Coll) A2
Silver St B1
Station Rd C3
Tenison Avenue C3
Tenison Rd C3
Tennis Court Rd B2
Thompson's Lane A1
Trinity (College) A1
Trinity Bridge B1
Trinity Hall (College) B1
Trinity St B1
Trumpington Rd C2
Trumpington St B1
Union Rd C2
University Botanic Gardens C2
Victoria Avenue A2
Victoria St B2
Warkworth St B3
Warkworth Terrace B3
Wesley House (Coll) A2
West Rd B1
Westcott House (Coll) A2
Westminster (Coll) A1
Whipple B2
Willis Rd B3
Willow Walk A2
YMCA C3
Zoology B2

Canterbury 333

Artillery St B2
Barton Mill Rd A3
Beaconsfield Rd A1
Beaney, The B2
Beverley Meadow A1
Beverley Rd A1
Bingley's Island B1
Black Griffin Lane B1
Broad Oak Rd A2
Broad St B2
Brymore Rd A3
Burgate B2
Bus Station C2
Canterbury Castle C1
Canterbury Christ Church University B3
Canterbury College C3
Canterbury East ≥ C1
Canterbury Tales, The ✦ B2
Canterbury West ≥ A1
Castle Row C1
Castle St C1
Cathedral ✝ B2
Causeway, The A2
Chaucer Rd A3
Christchurch Gate ✦ B2
City Council Offices A3
City Wall B2
Coach park A2
College Rd B3
Cossington Rd C2
Court B2
Craddock Rd A3
Crown & County Courts B3
Dane John Gardens C2
Dane John Mound ✦ C1
Deanery B2
Dover St C2
Duck Lane B2
Eastbridge Hosp B1
Edgar Rd B3
Ersham Rd C3
Ethelbert Rd C3
Fire Station C2
Forty Acres Rd A1
Friars, The B2
Gordon Rd C1
Greyfriars ✦ B1
Guildford Rd C1
Havelock St B2
Heaton Rd C1
High St B2
Information Ctr A2/B2
Ivy Lane B2
New St C1
King St B2
King's School B2/B3
King's School Recreation Ctr, The A2
Kingsmead Leisure Ctr A2
Kingsmead Rd A2
Kirby's Lane B1
Lansdown Rd C2
Lime Kiln Rd C1
Longport B3
Lower Chantry Lane C3
Mandeville Rd A1
Market Way A2
Marlowe Arcade B2
Marlowe Avenue C2
Marlowe Theatre B2
Martyrs Field Rd C1
Mead Way B1
Military Rd B2
Monastery St B2
Museum of Canterbury (Rupert Bear Mus) B1
New Dover Rd C3
New St C1
Norman Rd C2
North Holmes Rd B3
North Lane B1
Northgate A2
Nunnery Fields C2
Nunnery Rd C2
Oaten Hill C2
Odeon Cinema C2
Old Dover Rd C2
Old Palace B2
Old Ruttington Lane B2
Old Weavers B2
Orchard St B1
Oxford Rd C1
Palace St B2
Pilgrims Way C3
Pin Hill C1
Pine Tree Avenue A1
Police Station C2
Post Office B2, C1
Pound Lane B1
Puckle Lane C2
Raymond Avenue C2
Recreation Ground A2
Registry Office A2
Rheims Way B1
Rhodaus Close C2
Rhodaus Town C2
Roman Museum B2
Roper Gateway A1
Roper Rd A1
Rose Lane B2
Shopmobility B2
St Augustine's Abbey (remains) ✝ B3
St Augustine's Rd C3
St Dunstan's A1
St Dunstan's St A1
St George's Place C2
St George's St B2
St George's Tower ✦ B2
St Gregory's Rd B3
St John's Hospital A2
St Margaret's St B2
St Martin's B3
St Martin's Avenue B3
St Martin's Rd B3
St Michael's Rd A1
St Mildred's C1
St Peter's Grove B1
St Peter's Lane B2
St Peter's Place B1
St Peter's St B1
St Radigunds St B2
St Stephen's Court A1
St Stephen's Path A1
St Stephen's Rd A2
Salisbury Rd A1
Simmonds Rd C1
Spring Lane C3
Station Rd West B1
Stour St B1
Sturry Rd A3
Tourtel Rd A3
Tudor Rd C1
Union St B2
University for the Creative Arts C3
Vernon Place C2
Victoria Rd C1
Watling St B2
Westgate Gardens B1
Westgate Towers B1
Whitefriars B2
Whitehall Gardens B1
Whitehall Rd B1
Wincheap C1
York Rd C1
Zealand Rd C2

Cardiff Caerdydd 333

Adam St B3
Alexandra Gardens A2
Allerton St C1
Arran St A3
ATRiuM (University of Glamorgan) C3
Beauchamp St C1
Bedford St A3
Blackfriars Priory (rems) ✝ B1
Boulevard De Nantes B2
Brains Brewery C2
Brook St B1
Bute Park A1
Bute St C2
Bute Terrace C3
Callaghan Square C2/C3
Capitol Shopping Centre, The B3
Cardiff Arms Park (Cardiff Blues) B1
Cardiff Bridge B1
Cardiff Castle B2
Cardiff Central Sta ≥ C2
Cardiff Story, The B2
Cardiff Univ A1/A2/B3
Cardiff University Student's Union A2
Caroline St C2
Castle Green B2
Castle Mews A1
Castle St (Heol y Castell) B1
Cathays Station ≥ A2
Celerity Drive C3
Central Library C2
Charles St (Heol Siarl) B3
Churchill Way B3
City Hall A2
City Rd A3
Clare Rd C1
Clare St C1
Coburn St A3
Coldstream Terrace B1
College Rd A1
Colum Rd A1
Court C2
Court Rd C1
Craiglee Drive C3
Cranbrook St A3
Customhouse St C2
Cyfartha St A3
Despenser Place C1
Despenser St C1
Dinas St C1
Duke St (Heol y Dug) B2
Dumfries Place B3
East Grove A3
Ellen St C3
Fire Station B3
Fitzalan Place B3
Fitzhamon Emb C1
Fitzhamon Lane C1
Friary, The B2
g39 B2
Gloucester St C1
Glynrhondda St A2
Gordon Rd A3
Gorsedd Gardens B2
Green St B1
Greyfriars Rd B2
Hafod St C1
Hayes, The B2
Herbert St C3
High St B2
HM Prison B3
Industrial Estate C3
Information Centre B2
John St C3
Jubilee St C1
King Edward VII Ave A1
Kingsway (Ffordd y Brenin) B2
Knox Rd B3
Law Courts B2
Llanbleddian Gdns A2
Llantwit St A2
Lloyd George Avenue C3
Lower Cathedral Rd B1
Lowther Rd A3
Magistrates Court B3
Mansion House A3
Mardy St C1
Mark St B1
Market B2
Mary Ann St C3
Merches Gardens C1
Mill Lane C2
Millennium Bridge B1
Miskin St A2
Monmouth St C1
Motorpoint Arena Cardiff ✦ C3
Museum Avenue A2
Museum Place A2
National Museum Cardiff A2
National War Meml ✦ A2
Neville Place C1
New Theatre B2
Newport Rd B3
Northcote Lane A3
Northcote St A3
Parade, The A3
Park Grove A4
Park Place A2
Park St C2
Penarth Rd C2
Pendyris St C1
Plantaganet St C1
Post Office B2
Principality Stadium C1
Principality Stadium Tours (Gate 3) ✦ B2
Quay St B2
Queen's Arcade B2
Queen Anne Square A1
Queen St (Heol y Frenhines) B2
Queen St Station ≥ B3
Regimental Museums B2
Rhymney St A3
Richmond Rd A3
Royal Welsh College of Music and Drama A1
Russell St A3
Ruthin Gardens A2
St Andrews Place A2
St David's B2/C2
St David's ✝ B2
St David's Hall ✦ B2
St John the Baptist B2
St Mary St (Heol Eglwys Fair) B2
St Peter's St A3
Salisbury Rd A3
Sandon St B3
Schooner Way C3
Scott Rd C2
Scott St C2
Senghennydd Rd A2
Sherman Theatre A2
Sophia Gardens A1
Sophia Gardens Stadium ✦ A1
South Wales Baptist College A3
Sport Wales National Centre ✦ A1
Stafford Rd C1
Stadium Plaza C1
Station Terrace B3
Stuttgarter Strasse B2
Sussex St C1
Taffs Mead Embankment C1
Talworth St A3
Temple of Peace & Health ✦ A1
Treharris St A3
Trinity St B2
Tudor Lane C1
Tudor St C1
Tyndall St C3
Vue C1
Walk, The A3
Welsh Government A1
West Grove A3
Westgate St (Heol y Porth) B2
Windsor Place B3
Womanby St B2
Wood St C2
Working St B2
Wyeverne Rd A2

Carlisle 333

Abbey St A1
Aglionby St B3
Albion St C3
Alexander St C3
AMF Bowl ✦ C2
Annetwell St A1
Bank St B2
Bitts Park A1
Blackfriars St B2
Blencome St C1
Blunt St C1
Botchergate B2
Boustead's Grassing C2
Bowman St B3
Bridge St A1
Broad St B3
Brook St C3
Brunswick St B2
Bus Station B2
Caldew Bridge A1
Caldew St C1
Carlisle (Citadel) Station ≥ B2
Carlisle College A2
Castle A1
Castle St A1
Castle Way A1
Cathedral ✝ A1
Cecil St B2
Chapel St A2
Charles St B3
Charlotte St B1
Chatsworth Square A2
Chiswick St B2
Citadel, The ✦ B2
City Walls A1
Civic Centre A2
Clifton St C1
Close St B3
Collingwood St C1
Colville St C1
Colville Terrace C1
Council Offices B3
Court B2
Court St Brow B2
Crosby St B2
Crown St C2
Currock Rd C2
Dacre Rd A1

Dale St C1
Denton St C1
Devonshire Walk A1
Duke's Rd A2
East Dale St C1
East Norfolk St C1
Eden Bridge A2
Edward St B3
Elm St B1
English St B2
Fire Station A2
Fisher St A1
Flower St B3
Freer St C1
Fusehill St B3
Georgian Way A2
Gloucester Rd C3
Golf Course A2
Graham St C1
Grey St B3
Guildhall Museum A2
Halfey's Lane B3
Hardwicke Circus A2
Hart St B3
Hewson St C2
Howard Place A3
Howe St B3
Information Centre A2
James St B2
Junction St B1
King St B2
Lancaster St B2
Lanes Shopping Centre, The B2
Laser Quest ✦ B2
Library A2
Lime St B1
Lindisfarne St C3
Linton St B3
Lismore Place A3
Lismore St B3
London Rd C3
Lonsdale Rd B2
Lord St C3
Lorne Crescent B1
Lorne St B1
Lowther St B2
Madford Retail Park B1
Magistrates' Court A2
Market Hall A2
Mary St B2
Memorial Bridge A3
Metcalfe St C1
Milbourne St B1
Myddleton St B3
Nelson St C1
Norfolk St C1
Old Fire Sta, The A2
Old Town Hall A2
Oswald St C3
Peter St A2
Petteril St B3
Pools B2
Portland Place B2
Portland Square B2
Post Office A2/B2/C1/C3
Princess St C2
Pugin St B1
Red Bank Terrace C2
Regent St C3
Richardson St C1
Rickerby Park A3
Rickergate A2
River St B3
Rome St C2
Rydal St B3
St Cuthbert's B2
St Cuthbert's Lane B2
St James' Park C1
St James' Rd C1
St Nicholas Gate Retail Park C3
St Nicholas St C3
Sands Centre, The A2
Scotch St A2
Shaddongate B1
Sheffield St B1
Shopmobility A2
South Henry St B3
South John St C2
South St B3
Spencer St B2
Station Retail Park B2
Strand Rd A2
Superstore B1
Sybil St B3
Tait St B2
Thomas St B1
Thomson St C3
Trafalgar St C1
Trinity Leisure Centre A2
Tullie Museum & Art Gallery A1
Tyne St C3
University of Cumbria B3
Viaduct Estate Rd B1
Victoria Place A2
Victoria Viaduct B2
Vue B2
Warwick Rd B2
Warwick Square B3
Water St B2
West Walls B1
Westmorland St C1

Chelmsford 333

Anchor St C1
Anglia Ruskin Univ A2
Arbour Lane A3
Baddow Rd B2/C3
Baker St C1
Barrack Square B2
Bellmead B2
Bishop Hall Lane A2
Bishop Rd A2
Bond St B2
Boswells Drive B3
Bouverie Rd C2
Bradford St C1
Braemar Avenue C1
Brook St A2
Broomfield Rd A1
Burgess Springs B3
Burns Crescent C2
Bus Station B1/B2
Cedar Avenue A1
Cedar Avenue West A1
Cemetery A1
Cemetery A2
Cemetery C1
Central Park B1
Chelmsford ✝ B2
Chelmsford ≹ A1
Chichester Drive A3
Chinery Close A3
City Council A1
Civic Centre A1
Civic Theatre B1
Cloudfm County Cricket Ground, The B2
College C1
Cottage Place A2
County Hall B2
Coval Avenue B1
Coval Lane B1
Coval Wells B1
Crown Court B2
Duke St B2
Elm Rd C1
Elms Drive A1
Essex Record Office, The B3
Fairfield Rd B1
Falcons Mead B1
George St C2
Glebe Rd A1
Godfrey's Mews C2
Goldlay Avenue C3
Goldlay Rd C2
Grove Rd C2
Hall St C2
Hamlet Rd C2
Hart St C1
Henry Rd A2
High Bridge Rd B2
High Chelmer Shopping Centre B2
High St B2
Hill Crescent B3
Hill Rd B3
Hill Rd Sth B3
Hillview Rd A3
HM Prison A3
Hoffmans Way A2
Hospital B2
Lady Lane C2
Langdale Gardens C3
Legg St B2
Library B2
Lionfield Terrace A3
Lower Anchor St C1
Lynmouth Avenue C2
Lynmouth Gardens C3
Magistrates Court B2
Maltese Rd A1
Manor Rd C2
Marconi Rd A2
Market B2
Market Rd B2
Marlborough Rd C1
Meadows Shopping Centre, The B2
Meadowside A3
Mews Court C2
Mildmay Rd C2
Moulsham Drive C2
Moulsham Mill ✦ C3
Moulsham St C1/C2
Navigation Rd B3
New London Rd B2/C1
New St A2/B2
New Writtle St C1
Nursery Rd C2
Orchard St C2
Odeon B2
Parker Rd C2
Parklands Drive A3
Parkway A1/B1/B2
Police Station A2
Post Office B2/C2
Primrose Hill A1
Prykes Drive B1
Queen St C1
Queen's Rd B3
Railway St A1
Rainsford Rd A1
Ransomes Way A2
Rectory Lane A2
Regina Rd A2
Riverside Ice & Leisure Centre B2
Riverside Retail Park A3
Rosebery Rd C2
Rothesay Avenue C1
St John's Rd C2
Sandringham Place B3
Seymour St B1
Shopmobility B2
Shrublands Close B3
Southborough Rd C1
Springfield Rd A3/B2/B3
Stapleford Close C1
Superstore B2/C3
Swiss Avenue A1
Telford Place A3
Tindal St B2
Townfield St A1
Trinity Rd B3
University B1
Upper Bridge Rd C1
Upper Roman Rd C2
Van Dieman's Rd C3
Viaduct Rd B1
Vicarage Rd C1
Victoria Rd A2
Victoria Rd South B2
Vincents Rd C2
Waterloo Lane B2
Weight Rd B3
Westfield Avenue A1
Wharf Rd B3
Writtle Rd C1
YMCA A2
York Rd C1

Cheltenham 333

Albert Rd A3
Albion St B3
All Saints Rd B3
Ambrose St B2
Andover Rd C1
Back Montpellier Terr C2
Bandstand ✦ C2
Bath Parade B2
Bath Rd C2
Bays Hill Rd C1
Bennington St B2
Berkeley St B3
Brewery Quarter, The A2
Brunswick St South A2
Bus Station B2
Carlton St B3
Central Cross Road A3
Cheltenham College C2
Cheltenham FC A3
Cheltenham General (A&E) C3
Cheltenham Ladies' College B2
Christchurch Rd B1
Cineworld A2
Clarence Rd A2
Clarence Square A2
Clarence St B2
Cleeveland St A1
College Baths Road C3
College Rd C2
Colletts Drive A1
Corpus St C3
Devonshire St A2
Douro Rd B1
Duke St B3
Dunalley Parade A2
Dunalley St A2
Everyman B2
Evesham Rd A3
Fairview Rd B3
Fairview St B3
Fire Station C3
Folly Lane A2
Gloucester Rd A1
Grosvenor St B3
Grove St A1
Hanover St A2
Hatherley St C1
Henrietta St A2
Hewlett Rd B3
High St B2/B3
Holst Birthplace Museum A3
Hudson St A2
Imperial Gardens C2
Imperial Lane B2
Imperial Square C2
Information Centre B2
Keynsham Rd C3
King St A2
Knapp Rd B2
Lansdown Crescent C1
Lansdown Rd C1
Leighton Rd B3
Library B2
London Rd C3
Lypiatt Rd C1
Magistrates' Court & Register Office B1
Malvern Rd B1
Manser St A2
Market St A1
Marle Hill Parade A2
Marle Hill Rd A2
Millbrook St A1
Milsom St A2
Montpellier Gardens C2
Montpellier Grove C2
Montpellier Parade C2
Montpellier Spa Rd C2
Montpellier St C1
Montpellier Terrace C2
Montpellier Walk C2
New St B2
North Place B2
Old Bath Rd C3
Oriel Rd B2
Overton Park Rd B1
Overton Rd B1
Oxford St C3
Parabola Rd B1
Park Place C1
Park St A1
Pittville Circus A3
Pittville Crescent A3
Pittville Lawn A3
Pittville Park A2
Playhouse B2
Portland St B3
Prestbury Rd A3
Prince's Rd C1
Priory St B3
Promenade B2
Queen St A1
Recreation Ground A2
Regent Arcade B2
Regent St B2
Rodney Rd B2
Royal Crescent B2
Royal Well Place B2
Royal Wells Rd B2
St George's Place B2
St Georges Rd B1
St Gregory's B2
St James St B3
St John's Avenue B3
St Luke's Rd C2
St Margarets Rd A2
St Mary's B2
St Matthew's B2
St Paul's Lane A2
St Paul's Rd A2
St Paul's St A2
St Stephen's Rd C1
Sandford Parks Lido C3
Sandford Mill Road C3
Sandford Park C3
Sandford Rd C2
Selkirk St A3
Sherborne Place B3
Sherborne St B3
Suffolk Parade C2
Suffolk Rd C1
Suffolk Square C1
Sun St A1
Swindon Rd B2
Sydenham Villas Rd C3
Tewkesbury Rd A1
The Courtyard B1
Thirlstaine Rd C2
Tivoli Rd C1
Tivoli St C1
Town Hall & Theatre B2
Townsend St A1
Trafalgar St C2
Union St B3
Univ of Gloucestershire (Francis Close Hall) A2
Univ of Gloucestershire (Hardwick) A1
Victoria Place B3
Victoria St A2
Vittoria Walk C2
Wellesley Rd A2
Wellington Rd A3
Wellington Square A3
Wellington St B2
West Drive A3
Western Rd B1
Wilson, The B2
Winchcombe St B3
Winston Churchill Memorial Gardens A1

Chester 333

Abbey Gateway A2
Appleyards Lane C3
Bars, The B3
Bedward Row B1
Beeston View C3
Bishop Lloyd's Palace B2
Black Diamond St A2
Bottoms Lane C3
Boughton B3
Bouverie St A1
Bus Interchange A2
Bridge St B2
Bridgegate C2
Brook St A3
Brown's Lane C2
Cambrian Rd A1
Canal St A2
Carrick Rd C1
Castle C2
Castle Drive C2
Cathedral ✝ B2
Catherine St A1
Cheshire Military Museum C2
Chester ≹ A3
Cheyney Rd A1
Chichester St A1
City Rd A3
City Walls B1/B2
City Walls Rd B1
Cornwall St A2
Cross Hey C3
Cross, The ✦ B2
Crown Court C2
Cuppin St B2
Curzon Park North C1
Curzon Park South C1
Dee Basin A1
Dee Lane B3
Delamere St A2
Deva Roman Discovery Centre B2
Dingle, The C1
Duke St B2
Eastgate B2
Eastgate St B2
Eaton Rd C2
Edinburgh Way C3
Elizabeth Crescent B3
Fire Station A2
Foregate St B2
Forum Studio B2
Forum, The B2
Frodsham St B2
Gamul House B2
Garden Lane A1
George St A2
Gladstone Avenue A1
God's Providence House B2
Gorse Stacks A2
Greenway St C2
Grosvenor Bridge C1
Grosvenor Museum B2
Grosvenor Park B3
Grosvenor Park Terrace C1
Grosvenor Shopping Centre B2
Grosvenor St B2
Groves Rd B3
Groves, The B3
Guildhall Museum B1
Handbridge C2
Hartington St C3
Hoole Way A2
Hunter St B2
Information Centre B2
King Charles' Tower ✦ A2
King St A2
Library B2
Lightfoot St A3
Little Roodee C2
Liverpool Rd A2
Love St B3
Lower Bridge St B2
Lower Park Rd B3
Lyon St A2
Magistrates Court B2
Meadows Lane C3
Meadows, The B3
Milton St A3
Minerva Roman Shrine ✦ C2
Miniature Railway ✦ B3
New Crane St B1
Nicholas St B2
Northgate A2
Northgate Arena A2
Northgate St A2
Nun's Rd B1
Old Dee Bridge ✦ C2
Overleigh Rd C2
Park St B2
Police Station B2
Post Office A2/A3
Princess St B2
Queen St B2
Queen's Park Rd C3
Queen's Rd A3
Race Course B1
Raymond St A1
River Lane C2
Roman Amphitheatre & Gardens B2
Roodee (Chester Racecourse), The B1
Russell St A3
St Anne St A2
St George's Crescent C3
St Martin's Gate A1
St Martin's Way B1
St Oswalds Way A2
Saughall Rd A1
Sealand Rd A1
South View Rd A1
Stanley Palace B1
Station Rd A3
Steven St A3
Storyhouse B2
Superstore B2
Tower Rd B1
Town Hall B2
Union St B3
University of Chester C2
Vicar's Lane B2
Victoria Crescent C3
Victoria Rd A2
Walpole St A1
Water Tower St A1
Water Tower, The ✦ B1
Watergate B1
Watergate St B2
Whipcord Lane A1
White Friars B2
York St B3

Chichester 333

Adelaide Rd A3
Alexandra Rd A3
Arts Centre B2
Ave de Chartres B1/B2
Barlow Rd A1
Basin Rd C2
Beech Avenue B1
Bishops Palace Gardens B2
Bishopsgate Walk A3
Bramber Rd C3
Broyle Rd A2
Bus Station B2
Caledonian Rd B3
Cambrai Avenue B3
Canal Place C1
Canal Wharf C2
Canon Lane B2
Cathedral ✝ B2
Cavendish St A1
Cawley Rd B2
Cedar Drive A1
Chapel St A2
Cherry Orchard Rd C3
Chichester ≹ B2
Chichester By-Pass C2/C3
Chichester College B1
Chichester Cinema B3
Chichester Festival A2
Chichester Gate Leisure Park C1
Churchside A2
Cineworld C1
City Walls B2
Cleveland Rd B3
College Lane A2
Cory Close C2
Council Offices B2
County Hall B2
District B2
Duncan Rd A1
Durnford Close A1
East Pallant B2
East Row B2
East St B2
East Walls B3
Eastland Rd C3
Ettrick Close B3
Ettrick Rd B3
Exton Rd C3
Fire Station A2
Football Ground A2
Franklin Place A2
Friary (Rems of) A2
Garland Close C3
Green Lane A3
Grove Rd C3
Guilden Rd B3
Guildhall A2
Hawthorn Close A1
Hay Rd C3
Henty Gardens B1
Herald Drive C3
Hornet, The B3
Information Centre B2
John's St B2
Joys Croft A3
Jubilee Park A3
Jubilee Rd A3
Juxon Close B2
Kent Rd A3
King George Gardens A2
King's Avenue C2
Kingsham Avenue C3
Kingsham Rd C2
Laburnum Grove B2
Leigh Rd C1
Lennox Rd A3
Lewis Rd A3
Library B2
Lion St B2
Litten Terrace A3
Litten, The A3
Little London B2
Lyndhurst Rd B3
Market B3
Market Avenue B2
Market Cross B2
Market Rd B3
Melbourne Rd A3
Minerva A2
Mount Lane B1
New Park Rd A3
Newlands Lane A1
North Pallant B2
North St A2
North Walls A2
Northgate A2
Novium, The B2
Oak Avenue A1
Oak Close A1
Oaklands Park A2
Oaklands Way A2
Orchard Avenue A1
Orchard St A1
Ormonde Avenue B3
Pallant House B2
Parchment St A1
Parklands Rd A1/B1
Peter Weston Place B3
Police Station C2
Post Office A1/B2/C3
Priory Lane A2
Priory Park A2
Priory Rd A2
Queen's Avenue C1
Riverside A3
Roman Amphitheatre B3
St Cyriacs A2
St Martins' St B2
St Pancras A3
St Paul's Rd A2
St Richard's Hospital (A&E) A3
Shamrock Close A3
Sherbourne Rd A1
Somerstown A2
South Bank C2
South Downs Planetarium ✦ C2
South Pallant B2
South St B2
Southgate B2
Spitalfield Lane A3
Stirling Rd B3
Stockbridge Rd C1/C2
Swanfield Drive A3
Terminus Ind Est C1
Tower St A2
Tozer Way A3
Turnbull Rd A3
Upton Rd C1
Velyn Avenue B3
Via Ravenna B1
Walnut Avenue A1
West St B2
Westgate B1
Westgate Fields B1
Westgate Leisure Ctr B1
Weston Avenue C1
Whyke Close C3
Whyke Lane B3
Whyke Rd C3
Winden Avenue B3

Colchester 333

Abbey Gateway ✝ C2
Albert St A1
Albion Grove C2
Alexandra Rd C1
Artillery St C3
Arts Centre B1
Balkerne Hill B1
Barrack St C3
Beaconsfield Rd C1
Beche Rd C3
Bergholt Rd A1
Bourne Rd C3
Brick Kiln Rd A1
Brigade Grove C2
Bristol Rd B2
Broadlands Way A3
Brook St B3
Bury Close B2
Bus Station C2
Butt Rd C1
Campion Rd C2
Cannon St C3
Canterbury Rd C2
Captain Gardens C2
Castle B2
Castle Park B2
Castle Rd B2
Catchpool Rd A1
Causton Rd B1
Chandlers Row C3
Circular Rd East C2
Circular Rd North C1
Circular Rd West C1
Clarendon Way A1
Claudius Rd C2
Colchester ≹ A1
Colchester Camp Abbey Field C1
Colchester Retail Park B1
Colchester Town ≹ C2
Colne Bank Avenue A1
Colne View Retail Park A2
Compton Rd A3
Cowdray Avenue A1/A2
Cowdray Centre, The A2
Crouch St B1
Crowhurst Rd B1
Culver Square Shopping Centre B1
Culver St East B2
Culver St West B1
Dilbridge Rd A3
East Hill B2
East St B3
East Stockwell St B1
Eld Lane B1
Essex Hall Rd A1
Exeter Drive B2
Fairfax Rd C2
Fire Station A2
Firstsite B2
Flagstaff Rd C1
Garrison Parade C2
George St B2
Gladstone Rd C2
Golden Noble Hill C2
Goring Rd A3
Granville Rd C3
Greenstead Rd B3
Guildford Rd B2
Harsnett Rd C3
Harwich Rd B3
Head St B1
High St B1/B2
High Woods Country Park A2
Hollytrees B2
Hyderabad Close C2
Hythe Hill C3
Information Centre B2
Jarmin Rd A2
Kendall Rd C2
Kimberley Rd C3
King Stephen Rd C3
Leisure World A2
Library B1
Lincoln Way B2
Lion Walk Shopping Centre B1
Lisle Rd C2
Lucas Rd C2
Magdalen Green C3
Magdalen St C2
Maidenburgh St B2
Maldon Rd C1
Manor Rd B1
Margaret Rd A1
Mason Rd A2
Mercers Way A1
Mercury B1
Mersea Rd C2
Meyrick Crescent C2
Mile End Rd A1
Military Rd C2
Mill St C2
Minories B2
Moorside B3
Morant Rd C3
Napier Rd C2
Natural History B2
New Town Rd C2
Norfolk Crescent A3
North Hill B1
North Station Rd A1
Northgate St B1
Nunns Rd B1
Odeon B1
Old Coach Rd B3
Old Heath Rd C3
Osborne St B2
Petrolea Close A1
Police Station C1
Popes Lane B1
Port Lane C3
Post Office B2/C1
Priory St B2
Queen St B2
Rawstorn Rd B1
Rebon St C3
Recreation Rd C3
Ripple Way A3
Roberts Rd C2
Roman Rd B2
Roman Wall B2
Romford Close A3
Rosebery Avenue B2
St Andrews Avenue B3
St Andrews Gardens B3
St Botolph St B2
St Botolphs B2
St John's Abbey (site of) ✝ C2
St John's St B1
St Johns Walk Shopping Centre B1
St Leonards Rd C3
St Marys Fields B1
St Peter's St B1
St Peters B1
Salisbury Avenue C1
Saw Mill Rd C3
Sergeant St C2
Serpentine Walk A1
Sheepen Place B1
Sheepen Rd B1
Sir Isaac's Walk B1
Smythies Avenue B2
South St C1
South Way C1
Sports Way A2
Suffolk Close A3
Superstore A1
Town Hall B1
Valentine Drive A3
Victor Rd C3
Wakefield Close B2
Wellesley Rd C1
Wells Rd B2/B3
West St C1
West Stockwell St B1
Weston Rd C3
Westway A1
Wickham Rd C1
Wimpole Rd C3
Winchester Rd C2
Winnock Rd C2
Worcester Rd B2

Coventry 334

Abbots Lane A1
Albany B1
Albany Rd B1
Alma St B3
Ambulance Station A2
Art Faculty B3
Asthill Grove C2
Bablake School A1
Barras Lane A1/B1
Barr's Hill School A1
Belgrade B2
Bishop St A2
Bond's Hospital B1
Broad Gate B2
Broadway C1
Burges, The B2
Bus Station A3
Butts Radial B1
Byron St A3
Canterbury St A3
Cathedral ✝ B3
Central Six Retail Park C1
Chester St A1
Cheylesmore Manor House B2
Christ Church Spire ✦ B2
City College A3
City Walls & Gates ✦ A2
Corporation St B2
Council House B2
Coundon Rd A1
Coventry Station ≹ C2
Coventry Transport Museum A2
Coventry University Technology Park C3
Cox St A3
Croft Rd B1
Dalton Rd C1
Deasy Rd C3
Earl St B2
Eaton Rd C2
Fairfax St B3
Foleshill Rd A2
Ford's Hospital B2
Fowler Rd A1
Friars Rd C2
Gordon St C1
Gosford St B3
Greyfriars Green B2
Greyfriars Rd B2
Gulson Rd B3
Hales St A2
Harnall Lane East A3
Harnall Lane West A2
Herbert Art Gallery & Museum B3
Hertford St B2
Hewitt Avenue A1
High St B2
Hill St B1
Holy Trinity B2
Holyhead Rd A1
Howard St A3
Huntingdon Rd C1
Information Centre C2
Jordan Well B3
King Henry VIII Sch C1
Lady Godiva Statue ✦ B2
Lamb St A2
Leicester Row A2
Library B2
Lincoln St A2
Little Park St B2
London Rd C3
Lower Ford St B3
Lower Precinct Shopping Centre B2
Magistrates & Crown Courts B2
Manor House Drive B2
Manor Rd C2
Market B2
Martyrs Memorial ✦ C2
Meadow St B1
Meriden St A1
Michaelmas Rd C2
Middleborough Rd A1
Mile Lane C3
Millennium Place A2
Much Park St B3
Naul's Mill Park A1
New Union B2
Odeon B1
Park Rd C2
Parkside C3
Planet Ice Arena B1
Post Office A3,B2
Primrose Hill St A3
Priory Gardens & Visitor Centre B2
Priory St B3
Puma Way C3
Quarryfield Lane C3
Queen's Rd B1
Quinton Rd C2
Radford Rd A2
Raglan St B3
Ringway (Hill Cross) A1
Ringway (Queens) B1
Ringway (Rudge) B1
Ringway (St Johns) B3
Ringway (St Nicholas) A2
Ringway (St Patricks) C2
Ringway (Swanswell) A2
Ringway (Whitefriars) B3
St John St B3
St John the Baptist B2
St Nicholas St A2
Sidney Stringer Acad A3
Skydome B1
Spencer Avenue C1
Spencer Rec Gnd C1
Spencer Rd C1
Spon St B1
Sports Centre B3
Stoney Rd C2
Stoney Stanton Rd A3
Superstore B2
Swanswell Pool A3
Thomas Landsdail St C2
Tomson Avenue A1
Top Green C1
Tower St A2
Trinity St B2
University B3
University Sports Ctr B3
Upper Hill St A1
Upper Well St A2
Victoria St A3
Vine St A3
Wave, The ✦ B2
Warwick Rd C2
Waveley Rd B1
West Orchards Shopping Centre B2
Westminster Rd C1
White St A3
Windsor St B1

Derby 334

Abbey St C1
Agard St B1
Albert St B2
Albion St B2
Ambulance Station B1
Arthur St A1
Ashlyn Rd B3
Assembly Rooms B2
Babington Lane C2
Bass Recreation Gd B3
Becket St B1
Belper Rd A1
Bold Lane B1
Bradshaw Way C2
Bradshaw Way Retail Park C2
Bridge St B1
Brook St B1
Burton Rd C1
Bus Station B2
Business Park A3
Caesar St A2
Canal St C3
Carrington St C3
Cathedral ✝ B2
Cathedral Rd B1
Charnwood St C2
Chester Green Rd A2
City Rd A2
Clarke St A3
Cock Pitt Junction B3
Council House B2
Courts B1
Cranmer Rd B3
Crompton St C1
Crown & County Courts B2
Curzon St B1
Darley Grove A1
Derbion C2
Derby ≹ C3
Derby C2
Derby Gaol B1
Derwent Bsns Centre A2
Derwent St B2
Drewry Lane C1
Duffield Rd A1
Duke St A2
Dunton Close B3
Eagle Market C2
East St B2
Eastgate B3
Exeter St B2
Farm St C1
Ford St B1
Forester St C1
Fox St A2
Friar Gate B1
Friary St B1
Full St B2
Garden St A1
Gerard St C1
Gower St C2
Green Lane C2
Grey St C1
Guildhall B2
Handyside Bridge A2
Harcourt St C1
Highfield Rd A1
Hill Lane C2
Incora County Ground (Derbyshire CCC), The B3
Information Centre B2
Iron Gate B2
John St C3
Joseph Wright Centre B1
Kedleston Rd A1
Key St B2
King Alfred St C1
King St A1
Kingston St A1
Lara Croft Way C2
Leopold St C2
Liversage St C3
Lodge Lane B1
London Rd C2
London Rd Community Hospital C2
Macklin St C1
Mansfield Rd A2
Market B2
Market Place B2
May St C1
Meadow Lane B3
Melbourne St C2
Mercian Way C1
Midland Rd C3
Monk St C1
Morledge B2
Mount St C1
Mus & Art Gallery B1

Museum of Making .B2
North Parade .A1
North St .A1
Nottingham Rd .B3
Osmaston Rd .C2
Otter St .A1
Park St .C3
Parker St .A1
Pickford's House .B1
Police Station .A2, B2
Post Office .A1/A2/B1/C2/C3
Pride Parkway .C3
Prime Enterprise Park A2
Prime Parkway .A2
QUAD ✦ .B2
Queens Leisure Ctr .B1
Racecourse Park .A3
Railway Terrace .C3
Register Office .B2
Riverlights Leisure Ctr B2
Sadler Gate .B1
St Alkmund's Way .B1/B2
St Helens House ✦ .A1
St Mary's .A1
St Mary's Bridge .A2
St Mary's Bridge Chapel .A2
St Mary's Gate .B1
St Paul's Rd .A2
St Peter's .C2
St Peter's St .C2
Showcase De Lux .C2
Siddals Rd .C3
Sir Frank Whittle Rd .A3
Spa Lane .C1
Spring St .C1
Stafford St .B1
Station Approach .C3
Stockbrook St .C1
Stores Rd .A3
Traffic St .C2
Wardwick .B1
Werburgh St .C1
West Avenue .A1
West Meadows Ind Est B3
Wharf Rd .A2
Wilmot St .C2
Wilson St .C1
Wood's Lane .C1

Dorchester 334

Ackerman Rd .B3
Acland Rd .A2
Albert Rd .A1
Alexandra Rd .B1
Alfred Place .B3
Alfred Rd .B2
Alington Avenue .B3
Alington Rd .B3
Ashley Rd .B1
Balmoral Crescent .C3
Barnes Way .B2/C2
Borough Gardens .A1
Brewery Square .B1
Bridport Rd .A1
Buckingham Way .C3
Caters Place .A1
Cemetery .A3/C1
Charles St .A2
Coburg Rd .B1
Colliton St .A1
Cornwall Rd .A1
Cromwell Rd .B1
Culliford Rd .B2
Culliford Rd North .B2
Dagmar Rd .B1
Damer's Rd .B1
Diggory Crescent .C2
Dinosaur Museum .A2
Dorchester Bypass .C2
Dorchester South Station .B1
Dorchester West Station .B1
Dorset County (A&E) .B1
Dorset County Council Offices .A1
Dorset County Mus .A1
Duchy Close .C3
Duke's Avenue .B2
Durngate St .A2
Durnover Court .A3
Eddison Avenue .B3
Edward Rd .B1
Egdon Rd .C2
Elizabeth Frink Statue ✦ .B2
Farfrae Crescent .B2
Forum Centre, The .B1
Friary Hill .A2
Friary Lane .A2
Frome Terrace .A2
Garland Crescent .C3
Glyde Path Rd .A1
Grosvenor Crescent .C1
Grosvenor Rd .C1
Grove, The .A1
Gt Western Rd .B1
Herringston Rd .C1
High St East .A2
High St Fordington .A2
High Street West .A1
Holloway Rd .A2
Icen Way .A2
Information Centre .B2
Keep Military Museum, The .A1
Kings Rd .A3/B3
Kingsbere Crescent .C2
Lancaster Rd .B2
Library .A1
Lime Close .C1
Linden Avenue .B2
London Close .A3
London Rd .A2/A3
Lubbecke Way .A3
Lucetta Lane .B2
Maiden Castle Rd .C1
Manor Rd .C2
Market .B1
Marshwood Place .B2
Maumbury Rd .B1
Maumbury Rings .B1
Mellstock Avenue .C2
Mill St .A3
Miller's Close .A1
Mistover Close .C1
Monmouth Rd .B1/B2
Moynton Rd .C2
Nature Reserve .A2
North Square .A2
Northernhay .A1
Odeon .B1
Old Crown Court & Cells .A1
Olga Rd .B1
Orchard St .A2
Plaza .A1
Police Station .B1
Post Office .A1
Pound Lane .A2
Poundbury Rd .A1
Prince of Wales Rd .B2
Prince's St .A1
Queen's Avenue .B1
Roman Town House .A1
Roman Wall .A1
Rothesay Rd .C2
St George's Rd .B3
Salisbury Field .A2
Sandringham Sports Centre .B3
Shaston Crescent .C2
Smokey Hole Lane .B3
South Court Avenue .C1
South St .B1
South Walks Rd .B2
Superstore .C3
Teddy Bear Mus .A1
Temple Close .C1
Terracotta Warriors & Teddy Bear Mus .A2
Town Hall .A2
Town Pump ✦ .A2
Trinity St .A1
Tutankhamun Exhibition .A1
Victoria Rd .B1
Weatherbury Way .C2
Wellbridge Close .C1
West Mills Rd .A1
West Walks Rd .A1
Weymouth Avenue .C1
Williams Avenue .B1
Winterbourne (BMI) .C1
Wollaston Rd .A2
York Rd .B2

Dumfries 334

Academy St .A2
Aldermanhill Rd .B3
Ambulance Station .C3
Annan Rd .A3
Ardwall Rd .A3
Ashfield Drive .A1
Atkinson Rd .C1
Averill Crescent .C1
Balliol Avenue .C1
Bank St .B2
Bankend Rd .C3
Barn Slaps .B3
Barrie Avenue .B3
Beech Avenue .A1
Bowling Green .A3
Brewery St .B1
Bridgend Theatre .B1
Brodie Avenue .C2
Brooke St .B2
Broomlands Drive .C1
Brooms Rd .B3
Buccleuch St .A2
Burns House .B2
Burns Mausoleum .B3
Burns St .B2
Burns Statue ✦ .A2
Bus Station .B1
Cardoness St .A3
Castle St .A2
Catherine St .A2
Cattle Market .A3
Cemetery .B3
Cemetery .C2
Church Crescent .A2
Church St .B2
College Rd .A1
College St .A1
Corbelly Hill .B1
Corberry Park .B1
Cornwall Mt .A3
Council Offices .A2
Court .A2
Craigs Rd .C3
Cresswell Avenue .B3
Cresswell Hill .B3
Cumberland St .B3
David Keswick Athletic Centre .A3
David St .B1
Dock Park .C3
Dockhead .B2
Dumfries .A3
Dumfries Academy .A2
Dumfries Ice Bowl .A1
Dumfries Museum & Camera Obscura .B2
Dumfries & Galloway Royal Infirmary (A&E) .C3
East Riverside Drive .C3
Edinburgh Rd .A2
English St .B2
Fire Station .B3
Friar's Vennel .A2
Galloway St .B1
George Douglas Drive .C1
George St .A2
Gladstone Rd .C2
Glasgow St .A1
Glebe St .B3
Glencaple Rd .C3
Goldie Avenue .A1
Goldie Crescent .A1
Golf Course .C3
Gracefield Arts Ctr .A2
Greyfriars .A2
Grierson Avenue .B3
Hamilton Avenue .C1
Hamilton Starke Park .C2
Hazelrigg Avenue .C1
Henry St .B3
Hermitage Drive .C1
High Cemetery .C3
High St .A2
Hill Avenue .C2
Hill St .B1
HM Prison .B1
Holm Avenue .C2
Hoods Loaning .A3
Howgate St .B1
Huntingdon Rd .A3
Information Centre .B2
Irish St .B2
Irving St .A2
King St .A1
Kingholm Rd .C3
Kirkpatrick Court .C2
Laurieknowe .B1
Leafield Rd .B3
Library .A2
Lochfield Rd .A1
Loreburn Park .A3
Loreburn St .A2
Loreburne Shopping Centre .B2
Lover's Walk .A2
Martin Avenue .B3
Mausoleum .B3
Maxwell St .B1
McKie Avenue .B3
Mews Lane .A2
Mid Steeple ✦ .B2
Mill Green .B2
Mill Rd .B1
Moat Rd .C2
Moffat Rd .A3
Mountainhall Park .C3
Nelson St .B1
New Abbey Rd .B1/C1
New Bridge .B1
Newall Terrace .A2
Nith Avenue .A2
Nith Bank .C3
Nithbank Hospital .C3
Nithside Avenue .A1
Odeon .B2
Old Bridge .B1
Old Bridge House .B1
Palmerston Park (Queen of the South FC) .A1
Park Rd .C1
Pleasance Avenue .C1
Police Headquarters .A3
Police Station .A2/A3
Portland Drive .A1
Post Office .B1/B2/B3
Priestlands Drive .C1
Primrose St .B1
Queen St .B3
Queensberry St .A2
Rae St .A2
Richmond Avenue .C2
Robert Burns Ctr .B2
Roberts Crescent .C1
Robertson Avenue .C3
Robinson Drive .C1
Rosefield Rd .C2
Rosemount St .B1
Rotchell Park .C1
Rotchell Rd .B1
Rugby Football Gd .C1
Ryedale Rd .C2
St Andrews .B2
St John the Evangelist .A2
St Josephs College .B3
St Mary's Ind Est .A3
St Mary's St .A3
St Michael St .B2
St Michael's .B2
St Michael's Bridge .B2
St Michael's Bridge Rd B2
St Michael's Cemetery B3
Shakespeare St .B2
Solway Drive .C2
Stakeford St .A1
Stark Crescent .C2
Station Rd .A3
Steel Avenue .A1
Sunderries Avenue .A1
Sunderries Rd .A1
Superstore .B3
Suspension Brae .B2
Swimming Pool .A1
Terregles St .B1
Theatre Royal .B2
Troqueer Rd .C2
Union St .A1
Wallace St .B3
Welldale .B2
West Riverside Drive .C2
White Sands .B2

Dundee 334

Abertay University .B2
Adelaide Place .A1
Airlie Place .C1
Albany Terrace .A1
Albert St .A3
Alexander St .A2
Ann St .A2
Arthurstone Terrace .A3
Bank St .B2
Barrack Rd .A1
Barrack St .B2
Bell St .B2
Blinshall St .B1
Broughty Ferry Rd .A3
Brown St .B1
Bus Station .B3
Caird Hall .B2
Camperdown St .B3
Candle Lane .B3
Carmichael St .A1
City Churches .B2
City Quay .B3
City Square .B2
Commercial St .B2
Constable St .A3
Constitution Crescent .A1
Constitution Court .A1
Constitution St .A1/B2
Cotton Rd .A3
Courthouse Square .B1
Cowgate .A3
Crescent St .A3
Crichton St .B2
Dens Brae .A3
Dens Rd .A3
Discovery Point ✦ .C2
Douglas St .B1
Drummond St .A1
Dudhope Castle .A1
Dudhope St .A2
Dudhope Terrace .A1
Dundee .C2
Dundee Contemporary Arts ✦ .C2
Dundee High School .B2
Dundee Law ✦ .A1
Dundee Rep .C2
Dunhope Park .A1
Dura St .A3
East Dock St .B3
East Marketgait .B3
East Whale Lane .B3
Erskine St .A3
Euclid Crescent .B2
Forebank Rd .A2
Foundry Lane .A3
Gallagher Retail Park .B3
Gellatly St .B3
Government Offices .C2
Guthrie St .B1
Hawkhill .B1
Hilltown .A2
HMS Unicorn ✦ .B3
Howff Cemetery, The .B2
Information Centre .B2
Keiller Shopping Centre .B2
Keiller Centre, The .B2
King St .A3
Kinghorne Rd .A1
Ladywell Avenue .A3
Laurel Bank .A2
Law Rd .A1
Law St .A1
Library .A2/A3
Library and Steps Theatre .A2
Little Theatre, The .A2
Lochee Rd .B1
Lower Princes St .A3
Lyon St .A3
McManus Art Gallery & Museum, The .B2
Meadow Side .B2
Meadowside St Pauls .B2
Mercat Cross ✦ .B2
Murraygate .B2
Nelson St .A2
Nethergate .B2/C1
North Lindsay St .B2
North Marketgait .B2
Old Hawkhill .B1
Olympia Leisure Centre .B3
Overgate Shopping Centre .B2
Park Place .B1
Perth Rd .C1
Police Station .B1
Post Office .B2
Princes St .A3
Prospect Place .A2
Reform St .B2
Riverside Drive .C2
Riverside Esplanade .C2
Roseangle .C1
Rosebank St .A2
RRS Discovery .C2
St Andrew's .C2
St Pauls Episcopal .B3
Science Centre ✦ .C2
Seagate .B2
Sheriffs Court .B1
Shopmobility .B2
South George St .A2
South Marketgait .B3
South Tay St .B2
South Victoria Dock Road .B3
South Ward Rd .B2
Tay Road Bridge ✦ .C3
Thomson Avenue .B2
Trades Lane .B3
Union St .B2
Union Terrace .A1
University Library .B2
University of Dundee .B1
Upper Constitution Street .A1
Verdant Works ✦ .B1
V&A Museum of Design .C2
Victoria Dock .B3
Victoria Rd .A2
Victoria St .A3
Ward Rd .B1
Wellgate .B2
West Bell St .B1
West Marketgait .B1/B2
Westfield Place .C1
William St .A3
Wishart Arch ✦ .A3

Durham 334

Alexander Crescent .B2
Allergate .B2
Archery Rise .C1
Assembly Rooms .B2
Avenue, The .B1
Back Western Hill .A1
Bakehouse Lane .A3
Baths Bridge .B3
Boat House .B3
Boyd St .C3
Bus Station .B2
Castle Chare .B2
Cathedral .B2
Church St .C3
Clay Lane .C1
Claypath .B3
College of St Hild & St Bede .B3
County Hospital .B1
Crescent, The .A1
Crook Hall & Gardens .A3
Crossgate .B2
Crossgate Peth .C1
Crown Court .B3
Darlington Rd .C1
Durham .A2
Durham Castle .B2
Durham School .C2
Durham University (Science Site) .C3
Ellam Avenue .C1
Elvet Bridge .B3
Elvet Court .B3
Farnley Hey .B1
Ferens Close .A3
Fieldhouse Lane .A1
Flass St .B1
Flass Vale Local Nature Reserve .A1
Framwelgate Bridge .B2
Framwelgate .A2
Framwelgate Peth .A2
Framwelgate Waterside .A2
Frankland Lane .A3
Freeman's Place .A3
Freeman's Quay Leisure Centre .A3
Gala Theatre & Cinema .B3
Geoffrey Avenue .C1
Gilesgate .B3
Grey College .C3
Grove, The .A1
Hallgarth St .C3
Hatfield College .B3
Hawthorn Terrace .B1
Heritage Centre .B3
HM Prison .B3
John St .B1
Kingsgate Bridge .B3
Laburnum Terrace .B1
Lawson Terrace .B1
Leazes Rd .B2/B3
Library .B2
Margery Lane .B2
Market .B2
Mavin St .C3
Millburngate .B2
Millburngate Bridge .B2
Millennium Bridge (foot/cycle) .A2
Mountjoy Research Centre .C3
Mus of Archaeology .B2
New Elvet .B3
New Elvet Bridge .B3
North Bailey .B3
North End .A1
Observatory .C1
Old Elvet .B3
Open Treasure .B2
Oriental Museum .C2
Oswald Court .C3
Passport Office .A2
Percy Terrace .B1
Pimlico .C2
Police Station .B3
Post Office .A1/B2
Potters Bank .C1/C2
Prebends Bridge .C2
Prebends Walk .C2
Prince Bishops Shopping Centre .B3
Princes St .A1
Providence Row .A3
Quarryheads Lane .C2
Redhills Lane .B1
Redhills Terrace .B1
Riverwalk, The .B2
Saddler St .B3
St Cuthbert's Society .C2
St Margaret's .B2
St Mary the Less .C2
St Mary's College .C2
St Monica Grove .B1
St Nicholas' .B3
St Oswald's .C3
Sands, The .A3
Shopmobility .B3
Sidegate .A2
Silver St .B2
Sixth Form College .A3
South Bailey .C2
South Rd .C3
South St .B2
Springwell Avenue .A1
Station Approach .B2
Stockton Rd .C3
Student Union .B3
Summerville .B1
Sutton St .B2
Town Hall .B2
University Arts Block .B3
University College ✦ .B2
Walkergate Centre .A3
Wearside Drive .A3
Western Hill .A1
Wharton Park .A2
Whinney Hill .C3
Whitehouse Avenue .C1
YHA .C3

Edinburgh 334

Abbey Strand .B6
Abbeyhill .A6
Abbeyhill Crescent .B6
Abbeymount .A6
Abercromby Place .A3
Adam St .C5
Albany Lane .A4
Albany St .A4
Albert Memorial ✦ .B2
Albyn Place .A2
Alva Place .A6
Alva St .B1
Ann St .A1
Appleton Tower .C4
Archibald Place .C3
Assembly Rooms & Musical Hall .A3
Atholl Crescent .B1
Atholl Crescent Lane .C1
Bank St .B4
Barony St .A4
Beaumont Place .C5
Belford Rd .B1
Belgrave Crescent .A1
Belgrave Cres Lane .A1
Bell's Brae .B1
Blackfriars St .B4
Blair St .B4
Bread St .C2
Bristo Place .C4
Bristo St .C4
Brougham St .C2
Broughton St .A4
Brown St .C5
Brunton Terrace .A6
Buckingham Terrace .A1
Burial Ground .A6
Bus Station .A4
Caledonian Crescent .C1
Caledonian Rd .C1
Calton Hill .A4
Calton Hill .A5
Calton Rd .B4
Camera Obscura & Outlook Tower ✦ .B3
Candlemaker Row .C4
Canning St .B2
Canongate .B5
Canongate .B5
Carlton St .A1
Carlton Terrace .A6
Carlton Terrace Lane .A6
Castle St .B2
Castle Terrace .B2
Castlehill .B3
Central Library .B4
Chalmers Hospital .C3
Chalmers St .C3
Chambers St .C4
Chapel St .C4
Charles St .C4
Charlotte Square .B2
Chester St .B1
Circus Lane .A2
Circus Place .A2
City Art Centre .B4
City Chambers .B4
City Observatory ✦ .A5
Clarendon Crescent .A1
Clerk St .C5
Coates Crescent .B1
Cockburn St .B4
College of Art .C3
Comely Bank Avenue .A1
Comely Bank Row .A1
Cornwall St .C2
Cowans Close .C5
Cowgate .B4
Cranston St .B5
Crichton St .C4
Croft-An-Righ .A6
Cumberland St .A2
Dalry Place .C1
Dalry Rd .C1
Danube St .A1
Darnawy St .A2
David Hume Tower .C4
Davie St .C5
Dean Bridge .A1
Dean Gardens .A1
Dean Park Crescent .A1
Dean Park Mews .A1
Dean Park St .A1
Dean Path .B1
Dean St .A1
Dean Terrace .A1
Dewar Place .C1
Dewar Place Lane .C1
Doune Terrace .A2
Drummond Place .A3
Drummond St .C5
Drumsheugh Gardens .B1
Dublin Mews .A3
Dublin St .A4
Dublin St Lane South .A4
Dumbiedykes Rd .B5
Dundas St .A3
Dynamic Earth ✦ .B6
Earl Grey St .C2
East Crosscauseway .C5
East Market St .B4
East Norton Place .A6
East Princes St Gdns .B3
Easter Rd .A6
Edinburgh (Waverley) .B4
Edinburgh Castle .B3
Edinburgh Dungeon ✦ .B4
Edinburgh International Conference Centre .C2
Elder St .A4
Esplanade .B3
Eton Terrace .A1
Eye Pavilion .C3
Festival Office .B3
Festival Theatre Edinburgh .C4
Filmhouse .C2
Fire Station .C2
Floral Clock ✦ .B3
Forres St .A2
Forth St .A4
Fountainbridge .C2
Frederick St .A3
Freemasons' Hall .B3
Fruitmarket .B4
Gardner's Crescent .C2
George Heriot's School .C3
George IV Bridge .B4
George Square .C4
George Square Lane .C4
George St .B3
Georgian House .B2
Gladstone's Land .B3
Glen St .C3
Gloucester Lane .A2
Gloucester Place .A2
Gloucester St .A2
Graham St .C3
Grassmarket .C3
Great King St .A3
Great Stuart .B1
Greenside Lane .A5
Greenside Row .A5
Greyfriars Kirk .C4
Grindlay St .C2
Grosvenor St .C1
Grove St .C1
Gullan's Close .B5
Guthrie St .B4
Hanover St .A3
Hart St .A4
Haymarket .C1
Haymarket Station .C1
Heriot Place .C3
Heriot Row .A2
High School Yard .B5
High St .B4
Hill Place .C5
Hill St .A2
Hillside Crescent .A5
Holyrood Abbey (Remains) .A6
Holyrood Gait .B6
Holyrood Park .C6
Holyrood Rd .B5
Home St .C2
Hope St .B2
Horse Wynd .B6
Howden St .C5
Howe St .A2
Hub, The ✦ .B3
India Place .A2
India St .A2
Infirmary St .B4
Information Centre .B4
Jeffrey St .B4
John Knox House .B4
Johnston Terrace .C3
Keir St .C3
Kerr St .A2
King's Stables Rd .B2
Lady Lawson St .C3
Lauriston Gardens .C3
Lauriston Park .C3
Lauriston Place .C3
Lauriston St .C3
Lawnmarket .B3
Learmonth Gardens .A1
Learmonth Terrace .A1
Leith St .A4
Lennox St .A1
Lennox St Lane .A1
Leslie Place .A2
London Rd .A5
Lothian Rd .B2
Lothian St .C4
Lower Menz Place .A6
Lynedoch Place .B1
Manor Place .B1
Market St .B4
Marshall St .C4
Maryfield .A6
McEwan Hall .C4
Medical School .C4
Melville St .B1
Meuse Lane .B4
Middle Meadow Walk .C4
Milton St .A6
Montrose Terrace .A6
Moray Place .A2
Morrison Link .C1
Morrison St .C1
Mound Place .B3
Mound, The .B3
Multrees Walk .A4
Mus Collections Ctr .A4
Mus of Childhood .B5
Mus of Edinburgh .B5
Museum of Fire .C3
Mus on the Mound .B4
National Archives of Scotland .A4
National Museum of Scotland .C4
National Gallery .B3
National Library of Scotland .B4
National Monument ✦ A5
National Portrait Gallery .B4
National War Mus .B3
Nelson Monument ✦ .A5
Nelson St .A3
New St .B5
Nicolson Square .C4
Nicolson St .C4
Niddry St .B4
North Bank St .B3
North Bridge .B4
North Castle St .A2
North Charlotte St .A2
North Meadow Walk .C3
North St Andrew St .A4
North St David St .A3
North West Circus Pl .A2
Northumberland St .A3
Odeon .C2
Old Royal High School .A5
Old Tolbooth Wynd .B5
OMNi Centre ✦ .A4
Oxford Terrace .A1
Palace of Holyroodhouse .B6
Palmerston Place .B1
Panmure Place .C3
Parliament Square .B4
People's Story, The B5
Playhouse Theatre .A4
Pleasance .C5
Police Station .A4
Ponton St .C2
Post Office .A3/B4/B5/C1/C2/C4
Potterrow .C4
Princes Mall .B4
Princes St .B3
Princes St .B3
Prisoners of War .B3
Queen's Gallery .B6
Queen St .A2
Queen Street Gardens .A3
Queen's Drive .B6/C6
Queensferry Rd .A1
Queensferry St .B1
Queensferry Street La .B2
Radical Rd .C6
Randolph Crescent .B1
Regent Gardens .A5
Regent Rd .B5
Regent Rd Park .A6
Regent Terrace .A5
Richmond Lane .C5
Richmond Place .C5
Rose St .B2
Ross Open Air Theatre .B3
Rothesay Place .B1
Rothesay Terrace .B1
Roxburgh Place .C5
Roxburgh St .C5
Royal Bank of Scotland .A4
Royal Circus .A2
Royal Lyceum .C2
Royal Mile, The .B5
Royal Scottish Acad B3
Royal Terrace .A5
Royal Terrace Gdns .A5
Rutland Square .B2
Rutland St .B2
St Andrew Square .A4
St Andrew Square .A4
St Andrew's House .A4
St Bernard's Cres .A1
St Bernard's Well ✦ .A1
St Cecilia's Hall .B4
St Colme St .A2
St Cuthbert's .B2
St Giles' .B4
St James Quarter Shopping Centre .A4
St John St .B5
St John's .B2
St John's Hill .B5
St Leonard's Hill .C5
St Leonard's Lane .C5
St Leonard's St .C5
St Mary's .A4
St Mary's Scottish Episcopal .B1
St Mary's St .B5
St Michael & All Saints .C3
St Stephen St .A2
Salisbury Crags .C6
Saunders St .A2
Scotch Whisky Experience ✦ .B3
Scott Monument ✦ .B4
Scottish Parliament .B6
Scottish Storytelling Centre ✦ .B5
Semple St .C2
Shandwick Place .B2
South Bridge .B4
South Charlotte St .B2
South College St .C4
South Learmonth Gardens .A1
South St Andrew St .A4
South St David St .A3
Spittal St .C2
Stafford St .B1
Student Centre .C4
Surgeons' Hall .C5
Supreme Courts .B4
Teviot Place .C4
Thistle St .A3
Torphichen Place .C1
Torphichen St .C1
Traverse Theatre .B2
Tron Square .B4
Tron, The ✦ .B4
Union St .A4
University .C4
University Library .C4
Univ of Edinburgh .B5
Upper Grove Place .C1
Usher Hall .C2
Vennel .C3
Victoria St .B3
Viewcraig Gardens .B5
Viewcraig St .B5
Vue .A4
Walker St .B1
Waterloo Place .A4
Waverley Bridge .B4
Wemyss Place .A2
West Approach Rd .C1
West Crosscauseway .C5
West End .B1
West Maitland St .C1
West of Nicholson St .C4
West Port .C3
West Princes St Gdns .B3
West Richmond St .C5
West Tollcross .C2
White Horse Close ✦ .B6
William St .B1
Windsor St .A5
Writer's Mus, The .B4
York Lane .A4
York Place .A4
York Place .A4
Young St .B2

Exeter 334

Alphington St .C1
Athelstan Rd .B3
Barnardo Rd .C3
Barnfield Hill .B3
Barnfield Rd .B2/B3
Barnfield Theatre .B2
Bartholomew St East .B1
Bartholomew St West .B1
Bear St .B2
Beaufort Rd .C1
Bedford St .B2
Belgrave Rd .A3
Belmont Rd .A3
Blackall Rd .A2
Blackboy Rd .A3
Bonhay Rd .B1
Bull Meadow Rd .C2
Bus & Coach Station .B3
Castle St .B2
Catacombes ✦ .B1
Cecil Rd .C1
Cheeke St .A3
Church Rd .C1
Chute St .A3
City Wall .B1/B2
Civic Centre .B2
Clifton Rd .B3
Clifton St .B3
Clock Tower .A1
College Rd .B3
Colleton Crescent .C2
Commercial Rd .C1
Coombe St .B2
Cowick St .C1
Crown Courts .B2
Custom House Visitor Centre .C2
Cygnet Theatre .C2
Danes' Rd .A2
Denmark Rd .B3
Devon County Hall .C3
Devonshire Place .A3
Dinham Crescent .B1
East Grove Rd .C3
Edmund St .C1
Elm Grove Rd .A1
Exe St .B1
Exeter Cathedral .B2
Exeter Central Sta .A1
Exeter City Football Ground .A3
Exeter College .A1
Exeter Picture Ho .B1
Fire Station .A1
Fore St .B1
Friars Walk .C2
Guildhall .B2
Guildhall Shopping Ctr B2
Haven Rd .C2
Heavitree Rd .B3
Hele Rd .A1
High St .B2
HM Prison .A2
Holloway St .C2
Hoopern St .A2
Horseguards .A2
Howell Rd .A1
Information Centre .B3
Iron Bridge .B1
Isca Rd .C1
Jesmond Rd .A3
King St .B1
King William St .A2
Larkbeare Rd .C2
Leisure Centre .C1
Library .B2
Longbrook St .A2
Longbrook Terrace .A2
Lower North St .B1
Lucky Lane .C2
Lyndhurst Rd .C3
Magdalen Rd .B3
Magdalen St .B2
Market .B2
Market St .B2
Marlborough Rd .C3
Mary Arches St .B1
Matford Avenue .C3
Matford Lane .C3
Matford Rd .C3
May St .A3
Mol's Coffee House B2
New Bridge St .B1
New North Rd .A1/A2
North St .B1
Northernhay St .B1
Norwood Avenue .C3
Odeon .A3
Okehampton St .C1
Old Mill Close .C2
Old Tiverton Rd .A3
Oxford Rd .A3
Paris St .B2
Parr St .A3
Paul St .B1
Pennsylvania Rd .A2
Portland Street .A3
Post Office .A3/B2/C1
Powderham Crescent .A3
Preston St .B1
Princesshay Shopping Centre .B2
Pyramids Leisure Ctr .B3
Quay, The .C2
Queen St .A1
Queen's Terrace .A1
Queens Rd .C1

Radford Rd C2
Richmond Rd A1
Roberts Rd C2
Rougemont Castle A2
Rougemont House B2
Royal Albert Memorial Museum B2
St David's Hill A1
St James' Pk Sta A3
St James' Rd A3
St Leonard's Rd C3
St Mary Steps C1
St Nicholas Priory B1
St Thomas Station C1
Sandford Walk B3
School Rd C1
Sidwell St A2
Smythen St B1
South St B2
Southernhay East B2
Southernhay West B2
Spicer Rd B3
Sports Centre A3
Summerland St A3
Sydney Rd C1
Tan Lane C2
Thornton Hill A2
Topsham Rd C3
Tucker's Hall B1
Tudor St B1
Underground Passages B2
University of Exeter (St Luke's Campus) B3
Velwell Rd A1
Verney St A3
Vue B3
Water Lane C1/C2
Weirfield Rd C2
Well St A3
West Avenue A2
West Grove Rd C3
Western Way A3/B1/B2
Willeys Avenue C1
Wonford Rd B3/C3
York Rd A2

Fort William 335

Abrach Rd A3
Achintore Rd C1
Alma Rd B2
Am Breun Chamas A2
Ambulance Station A3
An Aird A2
Argyll Rd C1
Argyll Terrace C1
Bank St B2
Belford Hospital B2
Ben Nevis Highland Centre B3
Black Parks A3
Braemore Place C2
Bruce Place C2
Bus Station A2
Camanachd Cres A3/B2
Cameron Rd C1
Cameron Square B1
Carmichael Way A2
Claggan Rd B3
Connochie Rd C1
Cow Hill C3
Creag Dhubh A2
Croft Rd B3
Douglas Place B2
Dudley Rd B2
Dumbarton Rd C1
Earl of Inverness Rd A3
Fassifern Rd B1
Fire Station A2
Fort William B2
Fort William (Remains) B2
Glasdrum Rd C1
Glen Nevis Place B3
Gordon Square B1
Grange Rd C1
Heathercroft Drive C1
Heather Croft Rd C1
Henderson Row C2
High St B1
Hill Rd B2
Information Centre A3
Inverlochy Court A3
Kennedy Rd B2/C2
Library B2
Lime Tree Gallery C1
Linnhe Rd B1
Lochaber Leisure Ctr. B3
Lochiel Rd A3
Lochy Rd A3
Lundavra Crescent C1
Lundavra Rd C1
Lundy Rd A3
Mamore Crescent B2
Mary St B2
Middle St B1
Montrose Avenue A3
Moray Place C1
Morven Place C2
Nairn Crescent C1
Nevis Bridge B3
Nevis Centre, The A2
Nevis Rd A3
Nevis Terrace B2
North Rd B3
Obelisk B2
Parade Rd B2
Police Station C1
Post Office A3/B2
Ross Place C1
St Andrews B2
Shaw Place B2
Station Brae B1
Superstore B3
Treig Rd A3
Union Rd C1
Victoria Rd B2
Wades Rd A3
West Highland B1
West Highland College UHI A2
Young Place B2

Glasgow 335

Admiral St C2
Albert Bridge C5
Albion St B5
Anderston B3
Anderston Quay B3
Argyle Arcade B5
Argyle St A1/A2/B3/B4/B5
Argyle Street B5
Arlington St A3
Arts Centre B3
Ashley St A3
Bain St C6
Baird St A6
Baliol St A3
Ballater St C5
Barras (Market), The C6
Bath St A3
BBC Scotland B1
Bell St C6
Bell's Bridge B1
Bentinck St A2
Berkeley St A3
Bishop Lane B3
Black St A6
Blackburn St C2
Blackfriars St B6
Blantyre St A1
Blythswood Square A4
Blythswood St B4
Bothwell St B4
Brand St C1
Breadalbane St A2
Bridge St C4
Bridge St C4
Bridgegate C5
Briggait C5
Broomielaw B4
Broomielaw Quay Gardens B3
Brown St B4
Brunswick St B5
Buccleuch St A3
Buchanan Bus Station A5
Buchanan Galleries A5
Buchanan St B5
Buchanan St B5
Cadogan St B4
Caledonian University A5
Calgary St A5
Cambridge St A4
Canal St A5
Candleriggs B5
Carlton Place C4
Carnarvon St A3
Carrick St B4
Castle St B6
Cathedral Square B6
Cathedral St B5
Central Mosque C5
Ctr for Contemporary Arts A4
Centre St C4
Cessnock C1
Cessnock St C1
Charing Cross A3
Charlotte St C6
Cheapside St B3
Cineworld A5
Citizens' Theatre C5
City Chambers Complex B5
City Halls B5
City of Glasgow College (City Campus) B5
City of Glasgow College (Riverside Campus) C5
Clairmont Gardens A2
Claremont St A2
Claremont Terrace A2
Claythorne St C6
Cleveland St A3
Clifford Lane C1
Clifford St C1
Clifton Place A2
Clifton St A2
Clutha St C1
Clyde Arcade B2
Clyde Place C4
Clyde Place Quay C4
Clyde St C5
Clyde Walkway C3
Clydeside Expressway B2
Coburg St C4
Cochrane St B5
College St B6
Collins St B6
Commerce St C4
Cook St C4
Cornwall St C2
Couper St A5
Cowcaddens A4
Cowcaddens Rd A4
Crimea St B3
Custom Ho Quay Gdns C4
Dalhousie St A4
Dental Hospital A4
Derby St A2
Dobbie's Loan A4/A5
Dobbie's Loan Place A5
Dorset St A3
Douglas St B4
Doulton Fountain C6
Dover St A2
Drury St B4
Drygate B6
Duke St B6
Dunaskin St A1
Dunblane St A4
Dundas St B5
Dunlop St C5
East Campbell St C6
Eastvale Place A1
Eglinton St C4
Elderslie St A3
Elliot St B2
Elmbank St A3
Esmond St A1
Exhibition Centre B2
Festival Park C1
Film Theatre A4
Finnieston Quay B2
Finnieston St B2
Fire Station C6
Florence St C5
Fox St C5
Gallowgate C6
Garnet St A3
Garnethill St A4
Garscube Rd A4
George Square B5
George St B5
George V Bridge C4
Gilbert St A1
Glasgow Bridge C4
Glasgow Cathedral B6
Glasgow Central B4
Glasgow City Free Church B4
Glasgow Green C6
Glasgow Necropolis B6
Glasgow Royal Concert Hall A5
Glasgow Science Centre B1
Glasgow Tower B1
Glassford St B5
Glebe St A6
Gorbals Cross C5
Gorbals St C5
Gordon St B4
Govan Rd B1/C1/C2
Grace St B3
Grafton Place A5
Grand Ole Opry C2
Grant St A3
Granville St A3
Gray St A2
Greendyke St C6
Grey Eagle St B7
Harley St C1
Harvie St C1
Haugh Rd A1
Havanah St B6
Heliport B1
Henry Wood Hall A2
High Court C5
High St B6
High Street B6
Hill St A3
Holland St A3
Holm St B4
Hope St A5
Houldsworth St B2
Houston Place C3
Houston St C3
Howard St C5
Hunter St C6
Hutcheson St B5
Hydepark St B3
Imax Cinema B1
India St A3
Information Centre B5
Ingram St B5
Jamaica St B4
James Watt St B4
John Knox St B6
John St B5
Kelvin Hall A1
Kelvin Statue A2
Kelvin Way A2
Kelvingrove Art Gallery & Museum A1
Kelvingrove Park A2
Kelvingrove St A2
Kelvinhaugh St A1
Kennedy St A6
Kent Rd A2
Killermont St A5
King St B5
King's, The A3
Kingston Bridge C3
Kingston St C4
Kinning Park C2
Kyle St A5
Lancefield Quay B2
Lancefield St B3
Langshot St C1
Lendel Place C1
Lighthouse, The B4
Lister St A6
Little St B3
London Rd C6
Lorne St C1
Lower Harbour B1
Lumsden St A1
Lymburn St A1
Lyndoch Crescent A3
Lynedoch Place A3
Lynedoch St A3
Maclellan St C1
Mair St C2
Maitland St A4
Mansell St C7
Mavisbank Gardens C2
Mcalpine St B3
Mcaslin St A6
McLean Square C2
McLellan Gallery A4
McPhater St A4
Merchants' House B5
Middlesex St C2
Middleton St C1
Midland St B4
Miller St B5
Millennium Bridge B1
Millroad St C6
Milnpark St C2
Milton St A4
Minerva St B2
Mitchell St West B4
Mitchell Lby, The A3
Modern Art Gallery B5
Moir St C6
Molendinar St C6
Moncur St C6
Montieth Row C6
Montrose St B5
Morrison St C3
Nairn St A1
National Piping Centre, The A5
Nelson Mandela Sq B5
Nelson St C4
Nelson's Monument C6
Newton Place A3
Newton St A3
Nicholson St C4
Nile St B5
Norfolk Court C4
Norfolk St C4
North Frederick St B5
North Hanover St B5
North Portland St B6
North St A3
North Wallace St A5
O2 ABC A4
O2 Academy C4
Odeon C3
Old Dumbarton Rd A1
Osborne St B5/C5
Oswald St B4
Overnewton St A1
Oxford St C4
Pacific Drive B1
Paisley Rd C3
Paisley Rd West C1
Park Circus A2
Park Gardens A2
Park St South A2
Park Terrace A2
Parkgrove Terrace A2
Parnie St C5
Parson St A6
Partick Bridge A1
Passport Office A5
Pavilion Theatre A4
Pembroke St A3
People's Palace C6
Pitt St A4/B4
Plantation Park C1
Plantation Quay B1
Police Museum B5
Police Station A4/A6
Port Dundas Rd A5
Port St B2
Portman St C2
Prince's Dock B1
Princes Square B5
Provand's Lordship B6
Queen St B5
Queen Street B5
Ramshorn B5
Renfrew St A3/A4
Renton St A5
Richmond St B5
Robertson St B4
Rose St A4
Rottenrow B5
Royal Concert Hall A5
Royal Conservatoire of Scotland A4
Royal Crescent A2
Royal Exchange Sq B5
Royal Highland Fusiliers Museum A3
West Glasgow Ambulatory Care A1
Royal Infirmary B6
Royal Terrace A2
Rutland Crescent C2
St Andrew's in the Square C6
St Andrew's (RC) C5
St Andrew's St C5
St Enoch B5
St Enoch Shopping Ctr B5
St Enoch Square B4
St George's Rd A3
St James Rd B6
St Kent St C6
St Mungo Avenue A5/A6
St Mungo Museum of Religious Life & Art B6
St Mungo Place A6
St Vincent Crescent A2
St Vincent Place B5
St Vincent St B3/B4
St Vincent Terrace B3
Saltmarket C5
Sandyford Place A3
Sauchiehall St A2/A4
SEC Armadillo B2
School of Art A4
Sclater St B7
Scotland St C2
Scott St A4
Scottish Exhibition & Conference Centre B1
Seaward St C2
Shaftesbury St B3
Sheriff Court C5
Shields Rd C3
Shopmobility A5
Shuttle St B6
Somerset Place A2
South Portland St C4
Springburn Rd A6
Springfield Quay C3
SSE Hydro The B2
Stanley St C2
Stevenson St C6
Stewart St A4
Stirling Rd B6
Stobcross Quay B1
Stobcross Rd B1
Stock Exchange B5
Stockwell Place C5
Stockwell St B5
Stow College A4
Sussex St C2
Synagogue A3
Taylor Place A6
Tenement House A3
Teviot St A1
Theatre Royal A4
Tolbooth Steeple & Mercat Cross C6
Tower St C2
Trades House B5
Tradeston St C4
Transport Museum A1
Tron C5
Trongate B5
Tunnel St B2
Turnbull St C5
Union St B4
Univ of Strathclyde B6
Victoria Bridge C5
Virginia St B5
Wallace St C3
Walls St B6
Walmer Crescent C1
Warrock St B3
Washington St B3
Waterloo St B4
Watson St B6
Watt St C3
Wellington St B4
West Campbell St B4
West George St B4
West Graham St A4
West Greenhill Place B2
West Regent St A4
West Regent St B4
West St C4
West St C4
Whitehall St B3
Wilkes St C7
Wilson St B5
Woodlands Gate A3
Woodlands Rd A3
Woodlands Terrace A2
Woodside Place A3
Woodside Terrace A3
York St B4
Yorkhill Parade A1
Yorkhill St A1

Gloucester 335

Albion St C1
Alexandra Rd B3
Alfred St C3
All Saints Rd C2
Alvin St B2
Arthur St C2
Barrack Square B1
Barton St C2
Blackfriars B1
Blenheim Rd C2
Bristol Rd C1
Brunswick Rd C2
Bruton Way B2
Bus Station B2
Cineworld C1
City Council Offices B1
City Museum, Art Gallery & Library B2
Clarence St B2
Commercial Rd B1
Council Offices B1
Courts B1
Cromwell St C2
Deans Way A2
Denmark Rd A3
Derby Rd C3
Docks C1
Eastgate St B2
Eastgate, The B1
Edwy Parade A2
Estcourt Close A3
Estcourt Rd A3
Falkner St C2
GL1 Leisure Centre C2
Gloucester Cath B1
Gloucester Life B1
Gloucester Quays Outlet C1
Gloucester Station B2
Gloucestershire Archive B2
Gloucestershire Royal Hospital (A&E) B3
Goodyere St C2
Gouda Way A1
Great Western Rd B3
Guildhall B2
Heathville Rd A3
Henry Rd B3
Henry St B2
Hinton Rd A2
India Rd C3
Information Centre B1
Jersey Rd C3
King's C2
King's Walk Shopping Centre B2
Kingsholm (Gloucester Rugby) A2
Kingsholm Rd A2
Lansdown Rd A3
Library C2
Llanthony Rd C1
London Rd B3
Longhorn Avenue A1
Longsmith St B1
Malvern Rd A3
Market B2
Market Parade B2
Mercia Rd A1
Metz Way C3
Midland Rd C2
Millbrook St C3
Montpellier C1
Napier St C3
National Waterways Mus Gloucester C1
Nettleton Rd C2
New Inn B2
New Olympus C3
North Rd A3
Northgate St B2
Oxford Rd A2
Oxford St B2
Park & Ride Gloucester A1
Park Rd C2
Park St B2
Park, The C2
Parliament St C1
Peel Centre, The C1
Pitt St B1
Police Station B1
Post Office B2
Quay St B1
Quay, The B1
Recreation Ground A1/A2
Regent St C2
Robert Raikes Ho B1
Royal Oak Rd B1
Russell St B2
Ryecroft St C2
St Aldate St B2
St Ann Way C1
St Catherine St A2
St Mark St A2
St Mary de Crypt B1
St Mary de Lode B1
St Nicholas's B1
St Oswald's Rd A1
St Oswald's Retail Pk A1
St Peter's B2
Seabroke Rd A3
Sebert St A2
Severn Rd C1
Sherborne St B2
Shire Hall B1
Sidney St C3
Soldiers of Gloucestershire B1
Southgate St B1/C1
Spa Field C1
Spa Rd C1
Sports Ground A2/B2
Station Rd B2
Stratton Rd C3
Stroud Rd C1
Superstore A1
Swan Rd A2
Trier Way C1/C2
Union St A2
Vauxhall Rd C3
Victoria St C2
Walham Lane A1
Wellington St C2
Westgate Retail Park B1
Westgate St B1
Widden St C2
Worcester St B2

Grimsby 335

Abbey Drive East C2
Abbey Drive West C2
Abbey Park Rd C2
Abbey Rd C2
Abbey Walk C2
Abbeygate Shopping Centre C2
Abbotsway C2
Adam Smith St A1/A2
Ainslie St C2
Albert St A3
Alexandra Dock A2/B2
Alexandra Rd A2/B2
Alexandra Retail Park A2
Annesley St A2
Armstrong St A1
Arthur St B1
Augusta St C1
Bargate C1
Beeson St A1
Bethlehem St C2
Bodiam Way B3
Bradley St B3
Brighowgate C1/C2
Bus Station C2
Canterbury Drive C1
Cartergate B1/C1
Catherine St C3
Chantry Lane B1
Charlton St A1
Church Lane C2
Church St A3
Cleethorpe Rd A3
Close, The C1
College St C1
Compton Drive C1
Corporation Bridge A2
Corporation Rd A1
Court B2/B3
Crescent St B1
Deansgate C1
Doughty Rd C2
Dover St B1
Duchess St C2
Dudley St C1
Duke of York Gardens B1
Duncombe St B3
Earl Lane B1
East Marsh St B3
East St B2
Eastgate B3
Eastside Rd A3
Eaton Court C1
Eleanor St B3
Ellis Way B3
Fisherman's Chapel A3
Fisherman's Wharf B2
Fishing Heritage Centre B2
Flour Square A3
Frederick St B1
Frederick Ward Way B2
Freeman St A3/B3
Freshney Drive B1
Freshney Place B2
Garden St C2
Garibaldi St A3
Garth Lane B2
Grime St B3
Grimsby Docks Sta A3
Grimsby Town Sta C2
Hainton Avenue C3
Har Way B3
Hare St C3
Harrison St B1
Haven Avenue B1
Hay Croft Avenue B1
Hay Croft St B1
Heneage Rd B3/C3
Henry St B1
Holme St B3
Hume St C1
James St B1
Joseph St B1
Kent St A3
King Edward St A3
Lambert Rd C2
Library B2
Lime St B1
Lister St B1
Littlefield Lane C1
Lockhill A3
Lord St B1
Lower Spring St A3
Ludford St C3
Macaulay St B1
Mallard Mews C3
Manor Avenue C2
Market A3
Market Hall B2
Market St B3
Moody Lane A3
Moss Rd C2
Nelson St A3
New St B2
Osbourne St B2
Pasture St B3
Peaks Parkway C3
Pelham Rd C1
Police Station A3
Post Office B1/B2
Pyewipe Rd A1
Railway Place A3
Railway St A3
Recreation Ground C2
Rendel St A2
Retail Park A2/B3
Richard St B1
Ripon St B1
Robinson St East B3
Royal St A3
St Hilda's Avenue C1
St James C2
Sheepfold St B3/C3
Shopmobility B2
Sixhills St C3
South Park B2
Superstore B3/B2
Tasburgh St C3
Tennyson St B2
Thesiger St A3
Time Trap C2
Town Hall B2
Veal St B1
Victoria Retail Park A3
Victoria St North A2
Victoria St South B2
Victoria St West B2
Watkin St A1
Welholme Avenue C2
Welholme Rd C3
Wellington St B3
Wellowgate C2
Werneth Rd B3
West Coates Rd A1
Westgate A2
Westminster Drive C1
Willingham St C3
Wintringham Rd C2
Wood St B3
Yarborough Drive B1
Yarborough Hotel C2

Hanley 335

Acton St A3
Albion St B2
Argyle St C1
Ashbourne Grove A2
Avoca St A3
Baskerville Rd B3
Bedford Rd C1
Bedford St C1
Bethesda St B2
Bexley St A2
Birches Head Rd A3
Botteslow St C3
Boundary St A2
Broad St C2
Broom St A3
Bryan St A2
Bucknall New Rd B3
Bucknall Old Rd B3
Bus Station C3
Cannon St C2
Castlefield St C1
Cavendish St B1
Central Forest Park A2
Century Retail Park B1
Charles St B3
Cheapside B2
Chell St A3
Cinema A2
Clarke St C1
Cleveland Rd C2
Clifford St C3
Clough St B2
Clough St East B2
Clyde St C1
College Rd C2
Cooper St C2
Corbridge Rd A1
Cutts St C2
Davis St C1
Denbigh St A1
Derby St C3
Dilke St A3
Dudson Ctr, The A2
Dundas St A3
Dundee Rd C1
Dyke St B3
Eastwood Rd C3
Eaton St A3
Etruria Park B1
Etruria Rd B1
Etruria Vale Rd C1
Festing St A3
Festival Heights Retail Park A1
Festival Retail Park A1
Fire Station C2
Foundry St B2
Franklyn St C3
Garnet St B1
Garth St B3
George St A3
Gilman St B3
Glass St B3
Goodson St B3
Greyhound Way A1
Grove Place C1
Hampton St C3
Hanley Park C2
Hanley Park C2
Harding Rd C2
Hassall St B3
Havelock Place C1
Hazlehurst St C3
Hinde St C2
Hope St B2
Houghton St C2
Hulton St A3
Information Centre B2
Jasper St C2
Jervis St A3
John Bright St A3
John St B2
Keelings Rd A3
Kimberley Rd C1
Ladysmith Rd C1
Lawrence St C2
Leek Rd C3
Library C2
Lichfield St C3
Linfield Rd B3
Loftus St A2
Lower Bedford St C1
Lower Bryan St A2
Lower Mayer St A3
Lowther St A1
Magistrates Court C2
Malham St A2
Marsh St B2
Matlock St C3
Mayer St A3
Milton St C1
Mitchell Arts Centre B2
Moston St A3
Mount Pleasant C1
Mulgrave St A1
Mynors St B3
Nelson Place B3
New Century St B1
Octagon Retail Park B1
Ogden Rd C3
Old Hall St B3
Old Town Rd A3
Pall Mall B2
Palmerston St C3
Park and Ride C2
Parkway, The C2
Pavilion Drive A1
Pelham St C3
Percy St B2
Piccadilly B2
Picton St B3
Plough St A3
Police Station C2
Portland St A1
Post Office A3/B2
Potteries Centre, The B2
Potteries Museum & Art Gallery B2
Potteries Way B1
Powell St A1
Pretoria Rd C1
Quadrant Rd B2
Ranelagh St C2
Raymond St C2
Rectory Rd C1
Regent Rd C2
Regent Theatre B2
Richmond Terrace C2
Ridgehouse Drive A1
Robson St C2
St Ann St B3
St Luke St B3
Sampson St B2
Shaw St A1
Sheaf St C2
Shearer St C1
Shelton New Rd C1
Shirley Rd C2
Slippery Lane C2
Shopmobility B3
Snow Hill C2
Spur St C3
Stafford St B2
Stubbs Lane C3
Sun St C1
Supermarket A1/B2
Superstore B2
Talbot St C3
Town Hall B2
Town Rd A3
Trinity St B2
Union St A2
Upper Hillchurch St A3
Upper Huntbach St B3
Victoria Hall B3
Warner St C2
Warwick St C1
Waterloo Rd A1
Waterloo St B3
Well St B3
Wellesley St C2
Wellington Rd B3
Wellington St B3
Whitehaven Drive A2
Whitmore St C1
Windermere St A1
Woodall St A1
Yates St C2
York St A2

Harrogate 335

Albert St C2
Alexandra Rd B2
Arthington Avenue B2
Ashfield Rd A2
Back Cheltenham Mount B2
Beech Grove C1
Belmont Rd C1
Bilton Drive A2
BMI The Duchy Hospital C1
Bower Rd B2
Bower St B2
Bus Station B2
Cambridge Rd B2
Cambridge St B2
Cemetery A2
Chatsworth Grove A2
Chatsworth Place A2
Chatsworth Rd A2
Chelmsford Rd B3
Cheltenham Cres B2
Cheltenham Mt B2
Cheltenham Parade B2
Christ Church B3
Christ Church Oval B3
Chudleigh Rd B3
Clarence Drive B1
Claro Rd A3
Claro Way A3
Coach Park B2
Coach Rd B3
Cold Bath Rd C1
Commercial St B2
Coppice Avenue A1
Coppice Drive A1
Coppice Gate A1
Cornwall Rd B1
Council Offices B1
Crescent Gardens B1
Crescent Rd B1
Dawson Terrace A2
Devonshire Place B3
Dixon Rd A2
Dixon Terrace A2
Dragon Avenue B3
Dragon Parade B2
Dragon Rd B2
Duchy Rd B1
East Parade B2
East Park Rd C3
Esplanade B1
Everyman C2
Fire Station A2
Franklin Mount A2
Franklin Rd B2
Franklin Square A2
Glebe Rd C1
Grove Park Court A3
Grove Park Terrace A3
Grove Rd A2
Hampsthwaite Rd A1
Harcourt Drive B3
Harcourt Rd B3
Harrogate B2
Harrogate Convention Centre B1
Harrogate Justice Centre (Magistrates' and County Courts) C2
Harrogate Ladies Coll B1
Harrogate Theatre B2
Heywood Rd C1
Hollins Crescent A1
Hollins Mews A1
Hollins Rd A1
Hydro Leisure Ctr, The A1
Information Centre B1
James St B2
Jenny Field Drive A1
John St B2
Kent Drive A1
Kent Rd A1
Kings Rd A2
Kingsway B3
Kingsway Drive B3
Lancaster Rd C1
Leeds Rd C2
Lime Grove B3
Lime St A3
Mayfield Grove B2
Mercer B1
Montpellier Hill B1
Mornington Crescent A3
Mornington Terrace B3
Mowbray Square B3
North Park Rd B3
Oakdale Avenue A1
Oatlands Drive C3
Odeon B2
Osborne Rd A2
Otley Rd C2
Oxford St B2
Parade, The B2
Park Chase B3
Park Parade B3
Park View B2
Parliament St B1
Police Station C3
Post Office B2/C1
Providence Terrace A2
Queen Parade C3
Queen's Rd C1
Raglan St C2
Regent Avenue A3
Regent Grove A3
Regent Parade A3
Regent St A3
Regent Terrace A3
Ripon Rd A1
Robert St C2
Royal Baths & Turkish Baths B1
Royal Pump Room B1
St Luke's Mount A2
St Mary's Avenue C1
St Mary's Walk C1
Scargill Rd A1
Skipton Rd A3

Skipton St A2
Slingsby Walk C3
South Park Rd C2
Spring Grove A1
Springfield Avenue B1
Station Avenue B2
Station Parade B2
Stray Rein C3
Stray, The C2/C3
Studley Rd A2
Superstore B2/C1
Swan Rd B1
Tower St C2
Trinity Rd C2
Union St B2
Valley Drive C1
Valley Gardens C1
Valley Mount C1
Victoria Avenue C2
Victoria Rd C1
Victoria Shopping Ctr B2
Waterloo St A2
West Park C2
West Park St C2
Wood View A1
Woodfield Avenue A3
Woodfield Drive A3
Woodfield Grove A3
Woodfield Rd A3
Woodfield Square A3
Woodside B3
York Place C3
York Rd B1

Holyhead Caergybi 335

Armenia St A2
Arthur St C2
Beach Rd A1
Boston St B2
Bowling Green C3
Bryn Erw Rd C3
Bryn Glas Close C3
Bryn Glas Rd C3
Bryn Gwyn Rd C1
Bryn Marchog A1
Bryn Mor Terrace A2
Bryngoleu Avenue A1
Cae Braenar C3
Cambria St B1
Captain Skinner's Obelisk B2
Cecil St C2
Celtic Gateway Footbridge B2
Cemetery C1/C2
Cleveland Avenue C2
Coastguard Lookout A2
Court B2
Cybi Place A2
Cyttir Rd C3
Edmund St B1
Empire B2
Ferry Terminals B2
Ffordd Beibio B3
Ffordd Feurig C3
Ffordd Hirnos C3
Ffordd Jasper C3
Ffordd Tudur B3
Fire Station C2
Garreglwyd Rd B1
Gilbert St C2
Gorsedd Circle B1
Gwelfor Avenue A1
Harbour Office A3
Harbour View B3
Henry St C2
High Terrace C1
Hill St B2
Holborn Rd C2
Holland Park Ind Est C3
Holyhead Park B1
Holyhead Station B2
King's Rd C2
Kingsland Rd C2
Lewascote C3
Library B2
Lifeboat Station A1
Llanfawr Close C3
Llanfawr Rd C3
Lligwy St C2
Lon Deg C3
London Rd C3
Longford Rd B1
Longford Terrace B1
Maes Cybi B1
Maes Hedd A1
Maes-Hyfryd Rd C1
Maes-y-Dref B1
Maes-yr-Haf A2/B1
Maes-yr-Ysgol C3
Marchog C3
Marina A1
Maritime Museum A1
Market B2
Market St B2
Mill Bank B1
Min-y-Mor Rd A1
Morawelon Ind Est B3
Morawelon Rd B3
Moreton Rd C1
New Park Rd B1
Newry St A2
Old Harbour Lighthouse A3
Plas Rd C1
Police Station B2
Porth-y-Felin Rd A1
Post Office A1/B2/B3
Prince of Wales Rd A2
Priory Lane B3
Pump St C1
Queens Park B1
Reseifion Rd C1
Rock St B1
Roman Fort B2
St Cybi St B2
St Cybi's Church B2
St Seiriol's Close B1
Salt Island Bridge A2
Seabourne Rd A1
South Stack Rd B1
Sports Ground B1
Stanley St B2
Station St B2
Superstore C2
Tan-y-Bryn Rd A1
Tan-yr-Efail C2
Tara St C1
Thomas St B1
Town Hall A2
Treseifion Estate C2
Turkey Shore Rd B2
Ucheldre Arts Ctr B1
Ucheldre Avenue B1
Upper Baptist St B1
Victoria Rd B2
Victoria Terrace B2
Vulcan St B1
Walthew Avenue A1
Walthew Lane A1
Wian St C2

Hull 335

Adelaide St C1
Albert Dock C1
Albion St B2
Alfred Gelder St B2
Anlaby Rd B1
Arctic Corsair B3
Beverley Rd A1
Blanket Row C2
Bond St B2
Bonus Arena B2
Bridlington Avenue A2
Brook St B1
Brunswick Avenue A1
Bus Station B1
Camilla Close C3
Cannon St A2
Caroline St A2
Carr Lane B2
Castle St C2
Central Library B1
Charles St A2
Citadel Way B3
Clarence St B3
Cleveland St A3
Clifton St A1
Colonial St B1
Court B2
Deep, The C3
Dinostar C2
Dock Office Row B3
Dock St B2
Drypool Bridge B3
Egton St A3
English St C1
Ferens Gallery B2
Ferensway B1
Fire Station A1
Francis St A2
Francis St West A2
Freehold St A1
Freetown Way A2
Früit Theatre C2
Garrison Rd B3
George St B2
Gibson St A2
Great Thornton St B1
Great Union St A3
Green Lane A2
Grey St A1
Grimston St B2
Grosvenor St A1
Guildhall B2
Guildhall Rd B2
Hands-on History B2
Harley St A1
Hessle Rd C1
High St B3
Hull Minster B2
Hull Paragon Interchange Sta B1
Hull & East Riding Museum B3
Hull Ice Arena C1
Hull City Hall B2
Hull College B3
Hull History Centre A2
Hull New Theatre A2
Hull Truck Theatre B1
Humber Dock Marina C2
Humber Dock St C2
Humber St C2
Hyperion St A3
Information Centre B1
Jameson St B1
Jarratt St B2
Jenning St A3
King Billy Statue C2
King Edward St B2
King St A2
Kingston Retail Park C1
Kingston St C2
Liddell St A1
Lime St A3
Lister St C1
Lockwood St A2
Maister House B3
Maritime Museum B2
Market B2
Market Place B2
Minerva Pier C2
Mulgrave St A3
Myton Swing Bridge C3
Myton St B1
NAPA (Northern Acad of Performing Arts) B1
Nelson St C2
New Cleveland St A3
New George St A2
Norfolk St A1
North Bridge A3
North St B1
Odeon C1
Old Harbour C3
Osborne St B1
Paragon St B2
Park St B1
Percy St A2
Pier St C2
Police Station B1
Porter St C1
Portland St B1
Post Office B1/B2
Posterngate B2
Prince's Quay B2
Prospect Centre B1
Prospect St B1
Queen's Gardens B2
Railway Dock Marina C2
Railway St C2
Real B1
Red Gallery B1
Reform St A2
Retail Park B1
Riverside Quay C2
Roper St B2
St James St C1
St Luke's St B1
St Mark St A3
St Mary the Virgin B3
St Stephens Shopping Centre B1
Scale Lane Footbridge B3
Scott St A2
South Bridge Rd B3
Sport's Centre C1
Spring Bank A1
Spring St B1
Spurn Lightship C2
Spyvee St A3
Stage @TheDock C3
Sykes St A2
Tidal Surge Barrier C3
Tower St B3
Trinity House B2
Vane St A1
Victoria Pier C2
Waterhouse Lane B2
Waterloo St A1
Waverley St C1
Wellington St C2
Wellington St West C2
West St B1
Whitefriargate B2
Wilberforce Drive B2
Wilberforce House B3
Wilberforce Monument B3
William St C1
Wincolmlee A3
Witham A3
Wright St A1

Inverness 336

Abban St A1
Academy St B2
Alexander Place B2
Anderson St A2
Annfield Rd C3
Ardconnel St B3
Ardconnel Terrace B3
Ardross Place B2
Ardross St B2
Argyle St B3
Argyle Terrace B3
Attadale Rd B1
Ballifeary Lane C2
Ballifeary Rd C1/C2
Balnacraig Lane A1
Balnain House B2
Balnain St B2
Bank St B2
Bellfield Park C2
Bellfield Terrace C3
Benula Rd A1
Birnie Terrace A1
Bishop's Rd C2
Bowling Green B2
Bridge St B2
Brown St A2
Bruce Avenue C1
Bruce Gardens C1
Bruce Park C1
Burial Ground A2
Burnett Rd A3
Bus Station B3
Caledonian Rd B1
Cameron Rd A1
Cameron Square A1
Carse Rd A1
Carsegate Rd Sth A1
Castle Garrison Encounter B2
Castle Rd B2
Castle St B3
Celt St B2
Chapel St A2
Charles St B3
Church St B2
Columba Rd B1/C1
Crown Avenue B3
Crown Circus B3
Crown Drive B3
Crown Rd B3
Crown St B3
Culduthel Rd C3
Dalneigh Crescent C1
Dalneigh Rd C1
Denny St B3
Dochfour Drive B1/C1
Douglas Row B2
Duffy Drive C3
Dunabban Rd A1
Dunain Rd B1
Duncraig St B2
Eastgate Shopping Ctr B3
Eden Court C2
Fairfield Rd B1
Falcon Square B3
Fire Station A3
Fraser St B2
Fraser St C2
Friars' Bridge A2
Friars' Lane B2
Friars' St A2
George St A2
Gilbert St A2
Glebe St A2
Glendoe Terrace A1
Glenurquhart Rd C1
Gordon Terrace B3
Gordonville Rd C2
Grant St A2
Grant Street Park (Clachnacuddin FC) A1
Greig St B2
Harbour Rd A3
Harrowden Rd B1
Haugh Rd C2
Heatherley Crescent C3
High St B3
Highland Council Headquarters, The C2
Hill Park C3
Hill St B3
HM Prison B3
Huntly Place A2
Huntly St B2
India St A2
Industrial Estate A3
Information Centre B2
Innes St A2
Inverness B3
Inverness High Sch B1
Inverness Museum & Art Gallery B2
Jamaica St A2
Kenneth St B2
Kilmuir Rd A1
King St B2
Kingsmills Rd B3
Laurel Avenue B1/C1
Library A3
Lilac Grove B1
Lindsay Avenue C1
Lochalsh Rd A1/B1
Longman Rd A3
Lotland Place A2
Lower Kessock St A1
Madras St A2
Maxwell Drive C1
Mayfield Rd C3
Millburn Rd B3
Mitchell's Lane C3
Montague Row B2
Muirfield Rd C3
Muirtown St B1
Nelson St A2
Ness Bank C2
Ness Bridge B2
Ness Walk B2/C2
Old Edinburgh Rd C3
Old High Church B2
Park Rd C1
Paton St C2
Perceval Rd B1
Planefield Rd B2
Police Station A3
Porterfield Bank C3
Porterfield Rd C3
Portland Place A2
Post Office A2/B1/B2
Queen St B2
Queensgate B2
Railway Terrace A3
Rangemore Rd B1
Reay St B3
Riverside St A2
Rose St A2
Ross Avenue B1
Rowan Rd B1
Royal Northern Infirmary C2
St Andrew's Cath C2
St Columba B2
St John's Avenue C1
St Mary's Avenue C1
Sheriff Court B3
Shore St A2
Smith Avenue C1
Southside Place C3
Southside Rd C3
Spectrum Centre B2
Strothers Lane B3
Superstore A1/B2
TA Centre C2
Telford Gardens B1
Telford Rd A1
Telford St A1
Tomnahurich Cemetery C1
Tomnahurich St B2
Town Hall B3
Union Rd B3
Union St B3
Victorian Market B3
Walker Place A2
Walker Rd A3
War Memorial C2
Waterloo Bridge A2
Wells St B1
Young St B2

Ipswich 336

Alderman Rd B2
All Saints' Rd A1
Alpe St B2
Ancaster Rd C1
Ancient House B3
Anglesea Rd B2
Ann St B2
Arboretum A2
Austin St C2
Avenue, The A3
Belstead Rd C2
Berners St B2
Bibb Way B1
Birkfield Drive C1
Black Horse Lane B2
Bolton Lane B3
Bond St C3
Bowthorpe Close B2
Bramford Lane A1
Bramford Rd A1
Bridge St C2
Brookfield Rd A1
Brooks Hall Rd A1
Broomhill Park A2
Broomhill Rd A1
Broughton Rd A2
Bulwer Rd B1
Burrell Rd C2
Bus Station B3
Butter Market B2
Buttermarket Shopping Centre, The B3
Cardinal Pk Leisure Pk C2
Carr St B3
Cecil Rd B2
Cecilia St C2
Chancery Rd C2
Charles St B2
Chevallier St A1
Christchurch Mansion & Wolsey Art Gallery B3
Christchurch Park A3
Christchurch St B3
Cineworld C2
Civic Centre B2
Civic Drive B2
Clarkson St B1
Cobbold St B3
Commercial Rd C2
Constable Rd A3
Constantine Rd C1
Constitution Hill A2
Corder Rd A3
Corn Exchange B2
Cotswold Avenue A2
Council Offices C2
County Hall B3
Crown Court C2
Crown St B2
Cullingham Rd B1
Cumberland St B2
Curriers Lane B2
Dale Hall Lane A2
Dales View Rd A1
Dalton Rd B2
Dillwyn St B1
Elliot St B1
Elm St B2
Elsmere Rd A3
Falcon St C2
Felaw St C3
Fire Station C2
Flint Wharf C3
Fonnereau Rd B2
Fore St C3
Foundation St C3
Franciscan Way C2
Friars St C2
Gainsborough Rd A3
Gatacre Rd B1
Geneva Rd B2
Gippeswyk Avenue C1
Gippeswyk Park C1
Grafton Way C2
Graham Rd A1
Great Whip St C3
Grimwade St C3
Handford Cut B1
Handford Rd B1
Henley Rd A2
Hervey St B3
High St B2
Holly Rd A2
Ipswich Haven Marina C3
Ipswich Museum & Art Gallery B2
Ipswich School A2
Ipswich Station C2
Ipswich Town FC (Portman Road) C2
Ivry St A2
Kensington Rd A1
Kesteven Rd C1
Key St C3
Kingsfield Avenue A3
Kitchener Rd A1
Library A1
Little's Crescent C2
London Rd B1
Low Brook St C3
Lower Orwell St C3
Luther Rd C2
Magistrates Court B2
Manor Rd A3
Mornington Avenue A1
Museum St B2
Neale St B3
New Cardinal St C2
New Cut East C3
New Cut West C3
New Wolsey B2
Newson St B2
Norwich Rd A1/B1
Oban St B2
Old Custom House C3
Old Foundry Rd B3
Old Merchant's Ho C3
Orford St B2
Paget Rd A2
Park Rd A3
Park View Rd A2
Peter's St C2
Philip Rd C2
Pine Avenue A2
Pine View Rd A2
Police Station B2
Portman Rd B2
Portmans Walk C1
Post Office B2
Princes St C2
Prospect St B1
Queen St B2
Ranelagh Rd C1
Recreation Ground B1
Rectory Rd C2
Regent Theatre B3
Reg Driver Visitor Centre B3
Retail Park C1
Retail Park C2
Richmond Rd A1
Rope Walk C3
Rose Lane C2
Russell Rd C2
St Edmund's Rd A2
St George's St B2
St Helen's St B3
Sherrington Rd A1
Shopmobility B2
Silent St C2
Sir Alf Ramsey Way C1
Sir Bobby Robson Bridge C1
Sirdar Rd B1
Sir John Mills Theatre B1
Soane St B3
Springfield Lane A1
Star Lane C3
Stevenson Rd B1
Stoke Quay C3
Suffolk College C3
Suffolk Retail Park B1
Superstore B1
Surrey Rd B1
Tacket St C3
Tavern St B3
Tower Ramparts B2
Tower Ramparts Shopping Centre B2
Tower St B3
Town Hall B2
Tuddenham Rd A3
University C3
Upper Brook St B3
Upper Orwell St B3
Valley Rd A2
Vermont Crescent B3
Vermont Rd B3
Vernon St C3
Warrington Rd A2
Waterloo Rd A1
Waterworks St C3
Wellington St B1
West End Rd B1
Westerfield Rd A3
Westgate St B2
Westholme Rd A1
Westwood Avenue A1
Willoughby Rd C2
Withipoll St B3
Woodbridge Rd B3
Woodstone Avenue A3
Yarmouth Rd B1

Kendal 336

Abbot Hall Art Gallery & Museum of Lakeland Life & Industry C2
Ambulance Station A2
Anchorite Fields C2
Anchorite Rd C2
Ann St A3
Appleby Rd A3
Archers Meadow C3
Ashleigh Rd A2
Aynam Rd B2
Bankfield Rd B1
Beast Banks B2
Beezon Fields A2
Beezon Rd A2
Beezon Trad Estate A3
Belmont B2
Birchwood Close C1
Blackhall Rd B2
Brewery Arts Ctr B2
Bridge St B2
Brigsteer Rd C1
Burneside Rd A2
Bus Station B2
Buttery Well Rd C2
Canal Head North B3
Captain French Lane C2
Caroline St A2
Castle Hill B3
Castle Howe B2
Castle Rd B3
Castle St A3/B3
Cedar Grove C1
Council Offices B2
County Council Offices A2
Cricket Ground A3
Cricket Ground C3
Cross Lane C2
Dockray Hall Ind Est A2
Dowker's Lane B2
East View B1
Echo Barn Hill C1
Elephant Yard B2
Fairfield Lane A1
Finkle St B2
Fire Station A2
Fletcher Square C3
Football Ground C3
Fowling Lane A3
Gillinggate C2
Glebe Rd C2
Golf Course B1
Goose Holme B3
Gooseholme Bridge B3
Green St A1
Greengate C2
Greengate Lane C1/C2
Greenside B1
Greenwood C1
Gulfs Rd B2
High Tenterfell B1
Highgate B2
Hillswood Avenue C1
Horncop Lane A2
Kendal B2
Kendal Business Park A3
Kendal Castle (Remains) B3
Kendal Fell B1
Kendal Green A1
Kendal Ski Centre B3
Kendal Station A3
Kent Place B2
Kirkbarrow C2
Kirkland C2
Library B2
Library Rd B2
Little Aynam B3
Little Wood B1
Long Close C1
Longpool A3
Lound Rd C3
Lound St C3
Low Fellside B2
Lowther St B2
Magistrates Court A2
Maple Drive C1
Market Place B2
Maude St B2
Miller Bridge B2
Milnthorpe Rd C2
Mint St A3
Mintsfeet Rd A3
Mintsfeet Rd South A2
New Rd B2
Noble's Rest B2
Parish Church C2
Park Side Rd C3
Parkside Bsns Park C3
Parr St B3
Police Station A2
Post Office A3/B2
Quaker Tapestry B2
Queen's Rd B1
Riverside Walk C2
Rydal Mount A2
Sandes Avenue A2
Sandgate A3
Sandylands Rd A3
Serpentine Rd B1
Serpentine Wood B1
Shap Rd A3
South Rd C2
Stainbank Rd C1
Station Rd A3
Stramongate B2
Stramongate Bridge B2
Stricklandgate A2/B2
Sunnyside C3
Thorny Hills B3
Town Hall B2
Undercliff Rd B1
Underwood C1
Union St A2
Vicar's Fields C2
Vicarage Drive C1/C2
Wainwright's Yard B2
Wasdale Close C3
Well Ings C2
Westmorland Shopping Centre & Market Hall B2
Westwood Avenue C1
Wildman St A3
Windermere Rd A1
YHA B2
YWCA B2

King's Lynn 336

Albert St A2
Albion St B2
Alive St James' Swimming Pool B2
All Saints B2
All Saints St B2
Austin Fields A2
Austin St A2
Avenue Rd B3
Bank Side B1
Beech Rd C2
Birch Tree Close B2
Birchwood St A2
Blackfriars Rd B2
Blackfriars St B2
Boal St B1
Bridge St B2
Broad St B2
Broad Walk B3
Burkitt St A2
Bus Station A2
Carmelite Terrace C2
Chapel St A2
Chase Avenue C3
Checker St C2
Church St B2
Clough Lane B2
Coburg St B2
College of West Anglia A3
Columbia Way A3
Common Staithe Quay A1
Corn Exchange A1
County Court Rd B2
Cresswell St A2
Custom House A1
East Coast Business Park C1
Eastgate St A2
Edma St A2
Exton's Rd C3
Ferry Lane B1
Ferry St A1
Framingham's Almshouses B2
Friars St C2
Friars Walk C2
Gaywood Rd A3
George St A2
Gladstone Rd C2
Goodwin's Rd C3
Green Quay Discovery Centre B1
Greyfriars' Tower B2
Guanock Terrace C2
Guildhall A1
Hansa Rd C3
Harding's Way C2
Hardwick Rd C2
Hextable Rd A2
High St B1
Holcombe Avenue C3
Hospital Walk C2
Information Centre B1
John Kennedy Rd A2
Kettlewell Lane A2
King George V Avenue B3
King St B1
King's Lynn Art Centre A1
King's Lynn Station B2
Library B2
Littleport St A2
Loke Rd A2
London Rd B2
Lynn Museum B2
Magistrates Court B1
Majestic B2
Market Lane A1
Millfleet B2
Milton Avenue A3
Nar Valley Walk C2
Nelson St B1
New Conduit St B2
Norfolk St A2
North Lynn Discovery Centre A3
North St A2
Oldsunway B2
Ouse Avenue C1
Page Stair Lane A1
Park Avenue B3
Police Station B2
Portland Place C1
Portland St B2
Purfleet B1
Queen St B1
Raby Avenue A3
Railway Rd A2
Red Mount Chapel B3
Regent Way B2
River Walk A1
Robert St C2
Shopmobility B2
St Ann's St A1
St James St B2
St James' Rd B2
St John's Walk B3
St Margaret's B1
St Nicholas A2
St Nicholas St A1
St Peter's Rd B1
Sir Lewis St A2
Smith Avenue A3
South Everard St C2
South Gate C2
South Quay B1
South St B2
Southgate St C2
Stonegate St B2
Stories of Lynn B1
Surrey St A1
Sydney St C3
Tennyson Avenue B3
Tennyson Rd B3
The Walks Stadium (King's Lynn FC) B3
Tower St B2
Town Hall B1
Town Wall (Remains) B3
True's Yard Fisherfolk Museum A2
Valingers Rd C2
Vancouver Avenue C2
Vancouver Quarter B2
Waterloo St B2
Wellesley St B2
Whitefriars Terrace C2
Windsor Rd C2
Winfarthing St C2
Wisbech Road C2
Wyatt St A2
York Rd C3

Lancaster 336

Aberdeen Rd C3
Aldcliffe Rd C2
Alfred St B3
Ambleside Rd A3
Ambulance & Fire Station B3
Ashfield Avenue B1
Ashton Rd C2
Assembly Rooms Emporium B2
Balmoral Rd B3
Bath House B2
Bath St B3
Blades St B1
BMI Lancaster (private) C3
Borrowdale Rd B3
Bowerham Rd C3
Brewery Lane B2
Bridge Lane B2
Brook St C1
Bulk Rd A3
Bulk St B2
Bus Station B2
Cable St B2
Canal Cruises & Waterbus C2
Carlisle Bridge A1
Carr House Lane C2
Castle B1
Castle Park B1
Caton Rd A3
China St B2
Church St B2
City Museum B2
Clarence St C3
Common Garden St B2
Coniston Rd A3
Cottage Museum B2
Council Offices B2
Courts B2
Cromwell Rd C2
Crown Court B1
Dale St C3
Dallas Rd B1/C1
Dalton Rd B3
Dalton Square B2
Damside St B2
De Vitre St B3
Dee Rd A1
Denny Avenue A1
Derby Rd A2
Dukes, The B2
Earl St A2
East Rd B3
Eastham St C3
Edward St B3
Fairfield Nature Reserve C1
Fairfield Rd B1
Fenton St B2
Firbank Rd A3
Friend's Meeting House B1
Garnet St B3
George St B2
Giant Axe Field B1
Grand B2
Grasmere Rd B3
Greaves Park C3
Greaves Rd C2
Green St B3
Gregson Centre, The B3
Gregson Rd C3
Greyhound Bridge A2
Greyhound Bridge Rd A2
High St B2
Hill Side B1
Hope St C3
Hubert Place B1
Information Centre B2
Kelsy St B1
Kentmere Rd B3
Keswick Road A3
King St B2
Kingsway A3
Kirkes Rd C3
Lancaster City Football Club B1
Lancaster Royal Grammar School B3
Lancaster Station B1
Langdale Rd A3
Ley Court B1
Library B2
Lincoln Rd B1
Lindow St C2
Lodge St B2
Long Marsh Lane B1
Lune Rd A1
Lune St A2
Lune Valley Ramble A3
Mainway A2
Maritime Museum A1
Marketgate Shopping Centre B2
Market St B2
Meadowside C2
Meeting House Lane B1
Millennium Bridge A2
Moor Lane B2
Moorgate B3
Morecambe Rd A1/A2
Nelson St B2
North Rd B2
Orchard Lane C1
Owen Rd A2
Park Rd B3
Parliament St A3
Patterdale Rd A3
Penny St B2
Police Station B2
Portland St C2
Post Office B2/B3
Primrose St C3
Priory B1
Prospect St C3
Quarry Rd B3
Queen St C2
Regent St C2
Ridge Lane A3
Ridge St A3
Royal Lancaster Infirmary (A&E) C2
Rydal Rd B3
Ryelands Park A1
St Georges Quay A1
St John's B2
St Leonard's Gate B2
St Martin's Rd C3
St Nicholas Arcades Shopping Centre B2
St Oswald St C3
St Peter's B3
St Peter's Rd B3
Salisbury Rd B1
Scotch Quarry Urban Park C3
Sibsey St B1
Skerton Bridge A2
South Rd C2
Station Rd B1
Stirling Rd C3
Storey Avenue B1
Storey, The B2
Sunnyside Lane C1
Sylvester St C1
Tarnsyke Rd A1
Thurnham St C2
Town Hall B2
Troutbeck Rd B3
Ulleswater Rd B3
University of Cumbria C3
Vicarage Field B1
Vue B2
West Rd B1
Westbourne Drive C1
Westbourne Rd B1
Westham St C3
Wheatfield St B1
White Cross Business Park C2
Williamson Rd B3
Willow Lane B1
Windermere Rd B3
Wingate-Saul Rd B1
Wolseley St B3
Woodville St B3
Wyresdale Rd C3

Leeds 336

Aire St B3
Albion Place B4
Albion St B4
Albion Way B1
Alma St A6
Ambulance Station B5
Arcades B4
Armley Rd B1
Armories Drive C5
Back Burley Lodge Rd A1
Back Hyde Terrace A2
Back Row C3
Bath Rd C3
Beckett St A6
Bedford St B3
Belgrave St A4
Belle Vue Rd A2
Benson St A5
Black Bull St C5
Blenheim Walk A3
Boar Lane B4
Bond St B4
Bow St C5
Bowman Lane C4
Brewery C4
Brewery Wharf C5
Bridge St A5/B5
Briggate B4
Bruce Gardens C1
Burley Rd A1
Burley St B1
Burmantofts St B6
Bus & Coach Station B5
Butterly St C4
Butts Crescent B4
Byron St A5
Call Lane B4
Calls, The B5
Calverley St A3/B3
Canal St B1
Canal Wharf C3
Carlisle Rd C5
Cavendish Rd A1
Cavendish St A2
Chadwick St C5
Cherry Place A6
Cherry Row A5
City Museum A4
City Varieties Music Hall B4
City Square B3
Civic Hall A3
Clarence Road C5
Clarendon Rd A2
Clarendon Way A3
Clark Lane C6
Clay Pit Lane A4
Cloberry St A2
Close, The B6
Clyde Approach C1
Clyde Gardens C1
Coleman St C2
Commercial St B4
Concord St A5
Cookridge St A4
Copley Hill C1
Core, The B4
Corn Exchange B4
Cromer Terrace A2
Cromwell St A5
Cross Catherine St B6
Cross Green Lane C6
Cross Stamford St A5
Crown & County Courts A3
Crown Point Bridge C5
Crown Point Rd C4
Crown Point Retail Pk C4
David St C3
Dent St C6
Derwent Place C3
Dial St C6
Dock St C4
Dolly Lane A6
Domestic St C2
Drive, The B6
Duke St B5
Duncan St B4
Dyer St B5
East Field St B6
East Parade B3
East St C5
Eastgate B5
Easy Rd C6
Edward St B4
Ellerby Lane C6
Ellerby Rd C6
Fenton St A3
Fire Station B2
First Direct Arena A4
Fish St B4
Flax Place B5
Garth, The B5
Gelderd Rd C1
George St B4
Globe Rd C2
Gower St A5
Grafton St A4
Grand Theatre B4
Granville Rd A6
Great George St A3
Great Wilson St C4
Greek St B3
Green Lane C1
Hanover Avenue A2
Hanover Lane A2
Hanover Square A2
Hanover Way A2
Harewood St B4
Harrison St B4
Haslewood Close B6
Haslewood Drive B6
Headrow, The B3/B4
High Court B5
Holbeck Lane C2
Holdforth Close C1
Holdforth Gardens B1
Holdforth Grove C1
Holdforth Place C1
Holy Trinity B4
Hope Rd A5
Hunslet Lane C4
Hunslet Rd C4
Hyde Terrace A2
Infirmary St B3
Information Centre B3
Ingram Row C3
ITV Yorkshire A1
Junction St C4
Kelso Gardens A2
Kelso Rd A2
Kelso St A2
Kendal Lane A2
Kendell St C4
Kidacre St C4
King Edward St B4
King St B3
Kippax Place C6
Kirkgate B4
Kirkgate Market B4
Kirkstall Rd A1
Kitson St C6
Knight's Way Bridge C5
Lady Lane B4
Lands Lane B4
Lane, The B5
Lavender Walk B6
Leeds Art Gallery B3
Leeds Beckett Univ A3
Leeds Bridge C4
Leeds Coll of Music B5
Leeds Discovery Ctr C5
Leeds General Infirmary (A&E) A3
Leeds Minster B5
Leeds Station B3
Library B3/B4
Light, The B4
Lincoln Green Rd A6
Lincoln Rd A6
Lindsey Gardens A6
Lindsey Rd A6
Lisbon St B3
Little Queen St B3
Long Close Lane C6
Lord St C2
Lovell Park A4
Lovell Park Hill A4
Lovell Park Rd A4
Lower Brunswick St A5
Mabgate A5
Macauly St A5
Magistrates Court A3
Manor Rd C3
Mark Lane B4
Marlborough St B2
Marsh Lane B5
Marshall St C3
Meadow Lane C4
Meadow Rd C4
Melbourne St A5
Merrion Centre A4
Merrion St A4
Merrion Way A4
Mill St B5
Millennium Square A3
Monk Bridge C2
Mount Preston St A2
Mushroom St A5
Neville St C4
New Briggate A4/B4
New Market St B4
New York Rd A5
New York St B5
Nile St A5
Nippet Lane A6
North St A4
Northern Ballet B5
Northern St B3
Oak Rd B1
Oxford Place B3
Oxford Row A3
Parade, The B6
Park Cross St B3
Park Lane A2
Park Place B3
Park Row B4
Park Square B3
Park Square East B3
Park Square West B3
Park St B3
Police Station B5
Pontefract Lane B6
Portland Crescent A3
Portland Way A3
Post Office B4/B5
Quarry House (NHS/DSS Headquarters) B5
Quebec St B3
Queen St B3
Radio Aire A1
Railway St B5
Rectory St A6
Regent St A5
Richmond St C5
Rigton Approach B6
Rigton Drive B6
Rillbank Lane A1
Rosebank Rd A1
Rose Bowl Conference Centre A3
Royal Armouries C5
Russell St B3
St Anne's Cath (RC) A4
St Anne's St B4
St James' Hospital A6
St John's Rd A2
St Johns Centre B4
St Mary's St B5
St Pauls St B3
Saxton Lane B5
Sayner Lane C5
Shakespeare Avenue A6
Shannon St B6
Sheepscar St South A5
Siddall St C3
Skinner Lane A5
South Parade B3
Sovereign St C4
Spence Lane C2
Springfield Mount A2
Springwell Court C2
Springwell Rd C2
Springwell St C2
Stoney Rock Lane A6
Studio Rd A1
Sutton St C2
Sweet St C3
Sweet St West C3
Swinegate B4
Templar St B5
Tetley, The C4
Thoresby Place A3
Torre Rd A6
Town Hall A3
Trinity Leeds B4
Union Place C3
Union St B5
University of Leeds A3
Upper Accommodation Rd B6
Upper Basinghall St B4
Vicar Lane B4
Victoria Bridge C4
Victoria Gate B4
Victoria Quarter B4
Victoria Rd C4
Vue B4
Wade Lane A4
Washington St A1
Water Lane C3
Waterloo Rd C4
Wellington Rd B2/C1
Wellington St B3
West St B2
West Yorkshire Playhouse B5
Westfield Rd A1
Westgate B3
Whitehall Rd B3/C2
Whitelock St A5
Willis St C6
Willow Approach A1
Willow Avenue A1
Willow Terrace Rd A3
Wintoun St A5
Woodhouse Lane A3/A4
Woodsley Rd A1
York Place B3
York Rd B6

Leicester 336

Abbey St A2
All Saints' A1
Aylestone Rd C2
Bath Lane A1
Bede Park C1
Bedford St A3
Bedford St South A3
Belgrave Gate A2
Belvoir St B2
Braunstone Gate B1
Burleys Way A2
Burnmoor St C2
Bus & Coach Station A2
Canning St A2
Carlton St C2
Castle Motte B1
Castle Gardens B1
Cathedral B2
Charles St B3
Chatham St B2
Christow St A3
Church Gate A2
City Hall B3
Clank St B2
Clock Tower B2
Clyde St A3
Colton St B3
Conduit St B3
Crafton St East A3
Craven St A1
Crown Courts B3
Curve B3
De Lux A2
De Montfort Hall C3
De Montfort St C3
De Montfort Univ C1
Deacon St C2
Dover St B3
Duns Lane B1
Dunton St A1
East St B3
East Bond Street A2
Eastern Boulevard C1
Edmonton Rd A3
Erskine St A3
Filbert St C1
Filbert St East C2
Fire Station C3
Fleet St A3
Friar Lane B2
Friday St A2
Gateway St C2
Gateway, The C2
Glebe St B3
Granby St B3
Grange Lane C2
Grasmere St C1
Great Central St A1
Great Hall B1
Guildhall B2
Guru Nanak Sikh Museum B1
Halford St B2
Havelock St C2
Haymarket Shopping Centre A2
High St A2
Highcross Shopping Centre A2
Highcross St A1
HM Prison C2
Horsefair St B2
Humberstone Gate B2
Humberstone Rd A3
Infirmary St C2
Information Centre B2
Jarrom St C2
Jewry Wall B1
Kamloops Crescent A3
King Richard III Visitor Centre B2
King St B2
Lancaster Rd C3
LCB Depot B3
Lee St A3
Leicester Royal Infirmary (A&E) C2
Leicester Station B3
Library B2
London Rd C3
Lower Brown St B2
Magistrates' Court B2
Manitoba Rd A3
Mansfield St A2
Market B2
Market St B2
Mill Lane C2
Montreal Rd A3
Narborough Rd North B1
Nelson Mandela Park C2
New Park St B1
New St B2
New Walk C3
New Walk Museum & Art Gallery C3
Newarke Houses B2
Newarke St B2
Newarke, The B1
Northgate St A1
Orchard St A2
Ottawa Rd A3
Oxford St C2
Phoenix Arts Centre B3
Police Station A3
Post Office B2
Prebend St C3
Princess Rd East C3
Princess Rd West C3
Queen St B3
Rally Community Park, The A2
Regent College C3
Regent Rd C2/C3
Repton St A1
Rutland St B3
St Augustine Rd B1
St Georges Retail Park B3
St George St B3
St Georges Way B3
St John St A2
St Margaret's A2
St Margaret's Way A2
St Martins B2
St Mary de Castro B1
St Matthew's Way A3
St Nicholas B1
St Nicholas Circle B1
Sanvey Gate A2
Silver St B2
Slater St A1
Soar Lane A1
South Albion St B3
Southampton St B3
Sue Townsend Theatre B2
Swain St B3
Swan St A1
Tigers Way C3
Tower St C3
Town Hall B2
Tudor Rd B1
University of Leicester C3
University Rd C3
Upperton Rd C1
Vaughan Way A2
Walnut St C2
Watling St A2
Welford Rd B2
Welford Rd (Leicester Tigers RC) C2
Wellington St B2
West St C3
West Walk C3
Western Boulevard C1
Western Rd C1
Wharf St North A3
Wharf St South A3
Y Theatre, The B3
Yeoman St B3
York Rd B2

Lewes 336

Abinger Place B1
All Saints Centre B2
Anne of Cleves Ho C1
Avenue, The B1
Barbican Ho Mus B1
Brewery B2
Brook St A2
Brooks Rd A2
Bus Station B2
Castle Ditch Lane B1
Castle Precincts B1
Chapel Hill B3
Church Lane A1/A2
Cliffe High St B2
Cliffe Industrial Est C3
Cluny St C1
Cockshut Rd C1
Convent Field C2
Coombe Rd A2
County Hall B1
Course, The C1
Court Rd B2
Crown Court B2
Cuilfail Tunnel B3
Davey's Lane A3
Dripping Room, The (Lewes FC) C2
East St B2
East Sussex College C2
Eastport Lane C1
Fire Station A2
Fisher St B2
Friars Walk B2
Garden St B1
Government Offices C2
Grange Rd B1
Ham Lane C2
Harveys Way B2
Hereward Way A2
High St B1/B2
Hop Gallery B2
Information Centre B2
Keere St B1
King Henry's Rd B1
Lancaster St B2
Landport Rd A1
Leisure Centre C3
Lewes Bridge B2
Lewes Castle B1
Lewes Golf Course B3
Lewes Southern By-Pass C2
Lewes Station B2
Library C2
Malling Brook Ind Est A3
Malling Down Nature Reserve A3
Malling Hill A3
Malling Industrial Est A2
Malling St A3/B3
Market St B2
Martlets, The A2
Martyr's Monument B3
Mayhew Way A2
Morris Rd B3
Mountfield Rd C2
Needlemakers, The B2
New Rd B1
Newton Rd A1
North St A2/B2
Offham Rd B1
Old Malling Way A1
Orchard Rd A3
Paddock Lane B1
Paddock Rd B1
Paddock Sports Gd B1
Park Rd B1
Pelham Terrace A1
Pells Outdoor Swimming Pool A1
Pells, The A1
Phoenix Causeway B2
Phoenix Industrial Est B2
Phoenix Place B2
Pinwell Rd B2
Police Station B2
Post Office B2
Prince Edward's Rd B1
Priory of St Pancras (remains of) C1
Priory St C1
Railway Lane B2
Railway Land Nature Reserve B3
Rotten Row B1
Riverside Ind Est A2
Rufus Close B1
St John St B2
St John's Terrace B1
St Nicholas Lane B2
St Pancras Rd C1
Sewage Works C3
South Downs Bsns Pk A3
South St B3/C3
Southdowns Rd A2
Southerham Junction C3
Southover Grange Gardens B1
Southover High St C1
Southover Rd B1
Spences Field A3
Spences Lane A2
Stansfield Rd A1
Station Rd B2
Station St B2
Sun St B1
Superstore A2/B2
Sussex Police HQ A2
Talbot Terrace B1
Thebes Gallery B2
Toronto Terrace B1
Town Hall B2
West St B2
White Hill B1
Willeys Bridge A1

Lincoln 337

Alexandra Terrace B1
Anchor St C1
Arboretum B3
Arboretum Avenue B3
Avenue, The B1
Baggholme Rd B3
Bailgate A2
Beaumont Fee B1
BMI The Lincoln Hospital A2
Brayford Way C1
Brayford Wharf East C1
Brayford Wharf North B1
Bruce Rd A2
Burton Rd A1
Bus Station (City) C2
Canwick Rd C2
Cardinal's Hat B2
Carline Rd B1
Castle B1
Castle St A1
Cathedral B2
Cathedral St B2
Cecil St A2
Chapel Lane A2
Cheviot St B3
Church Lane A2
City Hall B1
Clasketgate B2
Clayton Sports Gd A3
Coach Park C2
Collection, The B2
County Hospital (A&E) B3
County Hall B1
Courts C1
Cross St C2
Crown Courts B1
Curle Avenue A3
Danesgate B2
Drill Hall B2
Drury Lane B1
East Bight A2
East Gate A2
Eastcliff Rd B3
Eastgate B2
Egerton Rd A3
Ellis Windmill A1
Engine Shed, The C1
Exchequer Gate B2
Firth Rd C1
Flaxengate B2
Florence St B3
George St C3
Good Lane A2
Gray St A1
Great Northern Terrace C3
Greetwell Rd B3
Greetwellgate B3
Grove, The A3
Haffenden Rd A2
High St B2/C1
Hungate B2
James St A2
Jews House & Court B2
Kesteven St C2
Langworthgate A2
Lawn, The B1
Lee Rd A3
Library B2
Lincoln Central Station C2
Lincoln College B2
Lincolnshire Life A1
Lincoln University Technical Coll (UTC) B2
Lindum Rd B2
Lindum Sports Ground A3
Lindum Terrace B3
Liquorice Park B1
Mainwaring Rd A3
Manor Rd A2
Market C2
Massey Rd A3
Medieval Bishop's Palace B2
Mildmay St A1
Mill Rd A1
Millman Rd B3
Minster Yard B2
Monks Rd B3
Montague St B2
Mount St A1
Nettleham Rd A2
Newland B1
Newport A2
Newport Arch A2
Newport Cemetery A2
Northgate A2
Odeon C1
Orchard St B1
Oxford St C2
Park St B1
Pelham Bridge C2
Pelham St C2
Portland St C2
Post Office A1/B2/B3
Potter Gate B2
Priory Gate B2
Queensway A3
Rasen Lane A1
Ropewalk C1
Rosemary Lane B2
St Anne's Rd B3
St Benedict's C1
St Giles Avenue A3
St Mark's Shopping Centre C1
St Marks St C1
St Mary-le-Wigford C1
St Mary's St C2
St Nicholas St A2
St Rumbold's St B2
St Swithin's B2
Saltergate C1
Saxon St A1
Sewell Rd B3
Silver St B2
Sincil St C2
Spital St A2
Spring Hill B1
Stamp End C3
Steep Hill B2
Stonebow & Guildhall C2
Stonefield Avenue A2
Tentercroft St C1
Theatre Royal B2
Tritton Rd C1
Tritton Retail Park C1
Union Rd B1
University of Lincoln C1
Upper Lindum St B3
Upper Long Leys Rd A1
Usher B2
Vere St A2
Victoria St B1
Victoria Terrace B1
Vine St B3
Wake St A1
Waldeck St A1
Waterside North C2
Waterside Shopping Centre C2
Waterside South C2
West Parade B1
Westgate A2
Wigford Way C1
Williamson St A2
Wilson St A1
Winn St B3
Wragby Rd A3
Yarborough Rd A1

Liverpool 337

Abercromby Square C5
Addison St A3
Adelaide Rd B6
Ainsworth St B4
Albany Rd B6
Albert Edward Rd B6
Angela St C6
Anson St B4
Argyle St C3
Arrad St C4
Ashton St B5
Audley St A4
Back Leeds St A2
Basnett St B3
Bath St A1
Beacon, The B3
Beatles Story, The C2
Beckwith St C3
Bedford Close C5
Bedford St North C5
Bedford St South C5
Benson St C4
Berry St C4
Birkett St A4
Bixteth St B2
Blackburne Place C4
Bluecoat B3
Bold Place C4
Bold St C4
Bolton St B3
Bridport St B4
Bronte St B4
Brook St A1
Brownlow Hill B4/B5
Brownlow St B5
Brunswick Rd A5
Brunswick St B1
Bus Station C2
Butler Crescent A6
Byrom St A3
Caledonia St C4
Cambridge St C5
Camden St A4
Canada Boulevard B1
Canning Dock C2
Canterbury St A4
Cardwell St C6
Carver St A4
Cases St B3
Castle St B2
Catherine St C5
Cavern Club B3
Central Library A3
Chapel St B2
Charlotte St B3
Chatham Place C6
Chatham St C5
Cheapside B2
Chavasse Park C2
Chestnut St C5
Christian St A3
Church St B3
Clarence St B4
Clayton Square Shopping Centre B3
Coach Station A4
Cobden St A5
Cockspur St A2
College St C3
College St North A5
College St South A5
Colquitt St C4
Comus St A3
Concert St C3
Connaught Rd B6
Cook St B2
Copperas Hill B4
Cornwallis St C3
Covent Garden B2
Craven St A4
Cropper St B3
Crown St B5/C6
Cumberland St B2
Cunard Building B1
Dale St B2
Dansie St B4
Daulby St B5
Dawson St B3
Dental Hospital B5
Derby Square B2
Drury Lane B2
Duckinfield St B4
Duke St C3
Earle St A2
East St A2
Eaton St A2
Edgar St A3
Edge Lane B6
Edinburgh Rd A6
Edmund St B2
Elizabeth St B5
Elliot St B3
Empire Theatre B4
Empress Rd B6
Epstein Theatre B3
Epworth St A5
Erskine St A5
Everyman Theatre C5
Exchange St East B2
FACT C4
Falkland St A5
Falkner St C5/C6
Farnworth St A6
Fenwick St B2
Fielding St A6
Fire Station A4
Fleet St C3
Fraser St A4
Freemasons Row A2
Gardner Row A3
Gascoyne St A2
George St B2
Gibraltar Road A1
Gilbert St C3
Gildart St A4
Gill St B4
Goree B2
Gower St C2
Gradwell St C3
Great Crosshall St A3
Great George St C4
Great Howard St A1
Great Newton St B4
Greek St B4
Green Lane B4
Greenside A5
Greetham St C3
Gregson St A5
Grenville St C3
Grinfield St C6
Grove St C5
Guelph St A6
Hackins Hey B2
Haigh St A4
Hall Lane B6
Hanover St B3
Harbord St C6
Hardman St C4
Harker St A4
Hart St B4
Hatton Garden A2
Hawke St B4
Helsby St B6
Henry St C3
Highfield St A2
Highgate St B6
Hilbre St B4
Hope Place C4
Hope St C4
Hope University A5
Houghton St B3
Hunter St A3
Hutchinson St A6
Information Ctr B4/C2
Institute for the Performing Arts C4
International Slavery Museum C2
Irvine St B6
Irwell St B2
Islington A4
James St B2
James St Station B2
Jenkinson St A4
John Moores University A2/A3/A4/B4/C4
Johnson St A3
Jubilee Drive B6
Kempston St A4
Kensington A6
Kensington Gardens B6
Kensington St A6
Kent St C3
King Edward St A1
Kinglake St B6
Knight St C4
Lace St A3
Langsdale St A4
Law Courts C2
Leece St C4
Leeds St A2
Leopold Rd B6
Lime St B3
Lime St Station B4
Liver St C2
Liverpool Central Station B3
Liverpool Landing Stage B1
Liverpool Institute for Performing Arts (LIPA) C4
Liverpool ONE C2
Liverpool Wheel, The C2
London Rd A4/B4
Lord Nelson St B4
Lord St B2
Lovat St C6
Low Hill A5
Low Wood St A6
Lydia Ann St C3
M&S Bank Arena C2
Mansfield St A4
Marmaduke St B6
Marsden St A6
Martensen St B6
Marybone A3
Maryland St C4
Mason St B6
Mathew St B2
May St B4
Melville Place C6
Merseyside Maritime Museum C2
Metquarter B3
Metropolitan Cathedral (RC) B5
Midghall St A2
Molyneux Rd A6
Moor Place B4
Moorfields B2
Moorfields Station B2
Moss St A5
Mount Pleasant B4/B5
Mount St C4
Mount Vernon B6
Mulberry St C5
Municipal Buildings B2
Mus of Liverpool C2
Myrtle St C5
Naylor St A2
Nelson St C4
New Islington A4
New Quay B1
Newington St C3
North John St B2
North St A3
North View B6
Norton St A4
O2 Academy B4
Oakes St B5
Odeon B2
Old Hall St A1
Old Leeds St A2
Oldham Place C4
Oldham St C4
Olive St C6
Open Eye Gallery C2
Oriel St A2
Ormond St B2
Orphan St C6
Overbury St C6
Overton St B6
Oxford St C5
Paisley St A1
Pall Mall A2
Paradise St C3
Park Lane C3
Parker St B3
Parr St C3
Peach St B5
Pembroke Place B4
Pembroke St B5
Philharmonic Hall C5
Phythian Park A6
Pickop St A2
Pilgrim St C4
Pitt St C3
Playhouse Theatre B3
Pleasant St B4
Police HQ C2
Police Sta A4/A6/B4
Pomona St B4
Port of Liverpool Building B2
Post Office A2/A4/A5/B2/B3/B4/C4
Pownall St C2
Prescot St A5
Preston St B3
Princes Dock A1
Princes Gardens A2
Princes Jetty A1
Princes Parade B1
Princes St B2
Pythian St A6
Queen Square Bus Station B3
Queensland St C6
Queensway Tunnel (Docks exit) B1
Queensway Tunnel (Entrance) B3
Radio City B2
Ranelagh St B3
Redcross St B2
Renfrew St B6
Renshaw St B4
Richmond Row A4
Richmond St B3
Rigby St A2
Roberts St A1
Rock St B4
Rodney St C4
Rokeby St A4
Romily St A6
Roscoe Lane C4
Roscoe St C4
Rose Hill A3
Royal Albert Dock C2
Royal Court Theatre B3
Royal Liver Building B1
Royal Liverpool Hospital (A&E) B5
Royal Mail St B4
Rumford Place B2
Rumford St B2
Russell St B4
St Andrew St B4
St Anne St A4
St Georges Hall B3
St John's Centre B3
St John's Gardens B3
St John's Lane B3
St Joseph's Crescent A4
St Minishull St B5
St Nicholas Place B1
St Paul's Square A2
Salisbury St A4
Salthouse Dock C2
Salthouse Quay C2
Sandon St C5
Saxony Rd B6
Schomberg St A6
School Lane B2
Seel St C3
Seymour St B4
Shaw St A5
Shopmobility C2
Sidney Place C6
Sir Thomas St B3
Skelhorne St B4
Slater St C3
Smithdown Lane B6
Soho Square A4
Soho St A4
South John St B2
Springfield A4
Stafford St A4
Standish St A3
Stanley St B2
Strand St C2
Strand, The B2
Suffolk St C3
Sydney Jones Library C5
Tabley St C3
Tarleton St B3
Tate Liverpool Gallery C2
Teck St B6
Temple St B2
Titanic Memorial B1
Tithebarn St B2
Town Hall B2
Trowbridge St B4
Trueman St A3
Union St B2
Unity Theatre C4
University C5
University of Liverpool B5
Upper Baker St A6
Upper Duke St C4
Upper Frederick St C3
Vauxhall Rd A2
Vernon St B2
Victoria Gallery & Museum B5
Victoria St B2
Vine St C5
Wakefield St A4

Walker Art Gallery A3
Walker St A6
Wapping C2
Water St B1/B2
Waterloo Rd A1
Wavertree Rd B6
West Derby Rd A6
West Derby St B5
Western Approaches War Museum B2
Whitechapel B3
Whitley Gardens A5
William Brown St B3
William Henry St A4
Williamson Square B3
Williamson St B3
Williamson's Tunnels Heritage Centre ✦ C6
Women's Hospital C6
Wood St B3
World Museum, Liverpool A3
York St C3

Llandudno 337

Abbey Place B1
Abbey Rd B1
Adelphi St B3
Alexandra Rd C2
Anglesey Rd A1
Argyll Rd B3
Arvon Avenue A2
Atlee Close C3
Augusta St B3
Back Madoc St B2
Bodafon St B3
Bodhyfryd Rd A2
Bodnant Crescent C3
Bodnant Rd C3
Bridge Rd C2
Bryniau Rd C1
Builder St B3
Builder St West C2
Cabin Lift Cable Car ✦ A2
Camera Obscura ✦ A3
Caroline Rd B2
Chapel St A2
Charlton St B3
Church Crescent C1
Church Walks A2
Claremont Rd B2
Clement Avenue A2
Clifton Rd B2
Clonmel St B3
Coach Station B3
Conway Rd B3
Conwy Archive Service B2
Council St West C3
Cricket and Rec Gd B2
Cwlach Rd A2
Cwlach St A1
Cwm Howard Lane C3
Cwm Place C3
Cwm Rd C3
Dale Rd C1
Deganwy Avenue B2
Denness Place C2
Dinas Rd C2
Dolydd B1
Erol Place B2
Ewloe Drive C3
Fairways C2
Ffordd Dewi C3
Ffordd Dulyn C2
Ffordd Dwyfor C3
Ffordd Elisabeth C3
Ffordd Gwynedd C3
Ffordd Las C3
Ffordd Morfa C3
Ffordd Penrhyn C3
Ffordd Tudno C3
Ffordd yr Orsedd C3
Ffordd Ysbyty C2
Fire & Ambulance Sta B3
Garage St B3
George St A2
Gloddaeth Avenue B1
Gloddaeth St B2
Gogarth Rd B1
Great Orme Mines ✦ A1
Great Ormes Rd B1
Great Orme Tramway ✦ A2
Happy Valley A2
Happy Valley Rd A3
Haulfre Gardens A1
Herkomer Crescent C1
Hill Terrace A2
Home Front Mus B2
Hospice B1
Howard Rd B3
Information Centre B2
Invalids' Walk B1
James St B2
Jubilee St B3
King's Avenue C2
King's Rd C2
Knowles Rd C2
Lees Rd C2
Library B2
Llandudno A2
Llandudno (A&E) C2
Llandudno Station B3
Llandudno Football Gd C2
Llewelyn Avenue A2
Lloyd St B2
Lloyd St West B1
Llwynon Rd A1
Llys Maelgwn B1
Madoc St B2
Maelgwn Rd B2
Maes-y-Cwm C3
Maes-y-Orsedd C3
Maesdu Bridge C2
Maesdu Rd C2/C3
Marian Place C2
Marian Rd C2
Marine Drive (Toll) A3
Market St A2
Miniature Golf Course A1
Morfa Rd B1
Mostyn B3
Mostyn Broadway B3
Mostyn St B3
Mowbray Rd C2
New St A2
Norman Rd B3
North Parade A2
North Wales Golf Links C1
Old Bank, The A2
Old Rd A2
Oval, The B1
Oxford Rd B3
Parade, The B3
Parc Llandudno Retail Park B3
Pier ✦ A3
Plas Rd A2
Police Station B3
Post Office A2/B3
Promenade A3
Pyllau Rd A1
Rectory Lane A2
Rhuddlan Avenue C3
St Andrew's Avenue B2
St Andrew's Place B2
St Beuno's Rd A1
St David's Place B2
St David's Rd B2
St George's Place A3
St Mary's Rd B2
St Seriol's Rd B2
Salisbury Pass B1
Salisbury Rd B2
Somerset St B3
South Parade A2
Stephen St B3
Tabor Hill A2
Town Hall B2
Trinity Avenue B1
Trinity Crescent C1
Trinity Square B3
Tudno St A2
Ty-Coch Rd A2
Ty-Gwyn Rd A1/A2
Ty'n-y-Coed Rd A1
Vaughan St B3
Victoria Shopping Centre B3
Victoria A2
War Memorial ✦ A2
Werny Wylan C3
West Parade B1
Whiston Pass A2
Winllan Avenue C2
Wyddfyd Rd A2
York Rd A2

Llanelli 337

Alban Rd B3
Albert St B1
Als St B3
Amos St C1
Andrew St A3
Ann St C2
Annesley St B2
Arfryn Avenue A3
Avenue Cilfig, The A2
Belvedere Rd A1
Bigyn Park Terrace C3
Bigyn Rd C3
Bond Avenue C3
Brettenham St A1
Bridge St B2
Bryn Place C1
Bryn Rd C1
Bryn Terrace C1
Bryn-More Rd C1
Brynhyfryd Rd A2
Brynmelyn Avenue A3
Brynmor Rd B1
Burry St C1
Bus Station B2
Caersalem Terrace C2
Cambrian St C1
Caswell St C3
Cedric St B3
Cemetery A2
Chapman St A1
Charles Terrace C2
Church St B2
Clos Caer Elms A1
Clos Sant Paul C2
Coastal Link Rd B1/C1
Coldstream St B2
Coleshill Terrace B1
College Hill B3
College Square B3
Copperworks Rd C2
Coronation Rd C3
Corporation Avenue A3
Council Offices B2
Court B2
Cowell St B2
Cradock St C2
Craig Avenue C3
Cricket Ground A1
Derwent St A1
Dillwyn St C2
Druce St C1
Eastgate Leisure Complex ✦ B2
Elizabeth St B2
Emma St C2
Erw Rd B1
Felinfoel Rd A2
Fire Station A3
Firth Rd C3
Fron Terrace C3
Furnace United Rugby Football Ground A1
Gelli-On B2
George St C2
Gilbert Crescent A2
Gilbert Rd A2
Glanmor Rd C2
Glanmor Terrace C2
Glasfryn Terrace A3
Glenalla Rd B3
Glevering St B3
Goring Rd A2
Gorsedd Circle A2
Grant St C3
Graveyard C2
Great Western Close C2
Greenway St B1
Hall St B2
Harries Avenue A2
Hedley Terrace A2
Heol Elli B3
Heol Goffa A3
Heol Nant-y-Felin A3
Heol Siloh B2
Hick St C2
High St C1
Indoor Bowls Centre B1
Inkerman St B2
Island Place B2
James St B3
John St B2
King George Avenue B3
Lake View Close A2
Lakefield Place C1
Lakefield Rd C1
Langland Rd C3
Leisure Centre B1
Library B2
Llanelli House B2
Llanelli Parish Church B2
Llanelli Station C2
Llewellyn St C2
Lliedi Crescent A3
Lloyd St B2
Llys Alys B3
Llys Fran A3
Llysnewedd C1
Long Row A3
Maes Gors C2
Maesyrhaf A3
Mansel St C3
Marblehall Rd B3
Marborough Rd A2
Margam St C3
Marged St C2
Marine St C1
Mariners, The C1
Market B2
Market St B2
Marsh St C2
Martin Rd C3
Miles St A1
Mill Lane A3/B2
Mincing Lane B2
Murray St B2
Myn y Mor B1
Nathan St C1
Nelson Terrace C1
Nevill St C2
New Dock Rd C2
New Rd A1
New Zealand St A1
Odeon B2
Old Lodge C2
Old Rd A2
Paddock St C2
Palace Avenue B3
Parc Howard A2
Parc Howard Museum & Art Gallery A2
Park Crescent B1
Park St B2
Parkview Terrace B1
Pemberton St C2
Pembrey Rd A1
Peoples Park B1
Police Station B2
Post Office B2/C2
Pottery Place B3
Pottery St B3
Princess St B1
Prospect Place A2
Pryce St A1
Queen Mary's Walk C3
Queen Victoria Rd C1
Raby St B1
Railway Terrace C2
Ralph St B2
Ralph Terrace C1
Regalia Terrace B3
Rhydyrafon A3
Richard St B2
Robinson St B2
Roland Avenue A1
Russell St C3
St David's Close C1
St Elli Shopping Ctr B2
St Margaret's Drive A1
Spowart Avenue A1
Station Rd B2/C2
Stepney Place B2
Stepney St B2
Stewart St A1
Stradey Park Avenue A1
Sunny Hill A2
Superstore A2
Swansea Rd A3
Talbot St C3
Temple St B3
Thomas St A2
Tinopolos TV Studios ✦ B2
Toft Place A3
Town Hall B2
Traeth Ffordd C1
Trinity Rd C3
Trinity Terrace C2
Tunnel Rd B3
Tyisha Rd C3
Union Blgs A2
Upper Robinson St B2
Vauxhall Rd B2
Walter's Rd B3
Waun Lanyrafon B2
Waun Rd A3
Wern Rd B3
West End A2
Y Bwthyn C3
Zion Row B3

London 338

Abbey Orchard St E4
Abbey St E8
Abchurch Lane D7
Abingdon St E5
Achilles Way D3
Acton St B5
Addington St E5
Air St D4
Albany St B3
Albemarle St D4
Albert Embankment F5
Alberta St F6
Aldenham St A4
Alderney St F3
Aldersgate St C7
Aldford St D3
Aldgate ⊖ C8
Aldgate High St C8
Aldwych C5
Allsop Place B2
Alscot Rd E8
Amwell St B6
Angel ⊖ A6
Appold St C8
Argyle Square B5
Argyle St B5
Argyll St C4
Arnold Circus B8
Artillery Lane C8
Artillery Row E4
Ashbridge St B2
Association of Photographers Gallery B7
Baker St ⊖ B2
Baker St B2
Balaclava Rd F8
Balcombe St B2
Baldwin's Gardens C6
Balfour St F7
Baltic St B7
Bank ⊖ C7
Bank Museum C7
Bank of England C7
Bankside D7
Bankside Gallery D7
Banner St B7
Barbican ⊖ C7
Barbican Centre for Arts, The C7
Barbican Gallery C7
Basil St E2
Bastwick St B7
Bateman's Row B8
Bath St B7
Bath Terrace E7
Bayley St C4
Baylis Rd E6
Bayswater Rd D2
Beak St D4
Beauchamp Place E2
Bedford Row C5
Bedford Square C4
Bedford St D5
Bedford Way B4
Beech St C7
Belgrave Place E3
Belgrave Rd F4
Belgrave Square E3
Bell Lane C8
Belvedere Rd E5
Berkeley Square D3
Berkeley St D3
Bermondsey St E8
Bernard St B5
Berners Place C4
Berners St C4
Berwick St C4
Bessborough St F4
Bethnal Green Rd B8
Bevenden St B7
Bevis Marks C8
BFI (British Film Institute) D5
BFI London IMAX Cinema D6
Bidborough St B5
Binney St C3
Birdcage Walk E4
Bishopsgate C8
Black Prince Rd F5
Blackfriars ⊖ D6
Blackfriars Bridge D6
Blackfriars Rd E6
Blackfriars Passage D6
Blandford St C2
Blomfield St C7
Bloomsbury St C4
Bloomsbury Way C5
Bolton St D3
Bond St ⊖ C3
Borough ⊖ E7
Borough High St E7
Borough Rd E6
Boswell St C5
Bourne St F3
Bow St C5
Bowling Green Lane B6
Brad St D6
Brandon St F7
Bressenden Place E4
Brewer St D4
Brick St D3
Bridge St E5
Britannia Walk B7
British Film Institute (BFI) D5
British Library B4
British Museum C5
Britton St B6
Broad Sanctuary E4
Broadley St B2
Broadway E4
Brompton Rd E2
Brompton Square E2
Brook Drive F6
Brook St D3
Brown St C2
Brunswick Place B7
Brunswick Shopping Centre, The B5
Brunswick Square B5
Brushfield St C8
Bruton St D3
Bryanston St C2
BT Centre C7
Buckingham Gate E4
Buckingham Palace E4
Buckingham Palace Rd F3
Bunhill Row B7
Byward St D8
Cabinet War Rooms & Churchill Museum E4
Cadogan Lane E3
Cadogan Place E2
Cadogan Square F2
Cadogan St F2
Cale St F2
Caledonian Rd A5
Calshot St A5
Calthorpe St B5
Calvert Avenue B8
Cambridge Circus C4
Cambridge Square C2
Cambridge St F3
Camomile St C8
Cannon St D7
Cannon St ⊖ D7
Capel Manor College B3
Capland St B1
Carey St C5
Carlisle Lane E5
Carlisle Place E4
Carlton House Terrace D4
Carmelite St D6
Carnaby St C4
Carter Lane C6
Carthusian St C7
Cartwright Gardens B5
Castle Baynard St D6
Cavendish Place C3
Cavendish Square C3
Caxton Hall E4
Caxton St E4
Central St B7
Chalton St B4
Chancery Lane ⊖ C6
Chapel St C2
Chapel St E3
Charing Cross ⊖ D5
Charing Cross Rd C4
Charles II St D4
Charles Dickens Museum, The B5
Charles Square B7
Charles St D3
Charlotte Rd B8
Charlotte St C4
Chart St B7
Charterhouse Square C6
Charterhouse St C6
Chatham St F7
Cheapside C7
Chenies St C4
Chesham St E3
Chester Square F3
Chester Way F6
Chesterfield Hill D3
Cheval Place E2
Chiltern St C3
Chiswell St C7
Church St B2
City Garden Row A6
City Rd B7
City Thameslink C6
City University, The B6
Claremont Square A6
Clarendon St F3
Clarges St D3
Clerkenwell Close B6
Clerkenwell Green B6
Clerkenwell Rd B6
Cleveland St C4
Clifford St D4
Clink Prison Mus D7
Cliveden Place F3
Clock Museum C7
Club Row B8
Cockspur St D4
Coleman St C7
Columbia Rd B8
Commercial Rd C8
Commercial St C8
Compton St B6
Conduit St D3
Congreve St F8
Connaught Square C2
Connaught St C2
Constitution Hill E3
Copperfield St E6
Coptic St C5
Cornhill C7
Cornwall Rd D6
Coronet St B8
County St E7
Courtauld Gallery D5
Courtenay St F6
Covent Garden ⊖ D5
Covent Garden ✦ D5
Cowcross St C6
Cowper St B7
Crampton St F7
Cranbourn St D4
Craven St D5
Crawford Place C2
Crawford St C2
Creechurch Lane C8
Cricket Museum B1
Cromer St B5
Cromwell Rd F1
Crosby Row E7
Crucifix Lane E8
Cumberland Gate D2
Cumberland St F3
Cumberland Terrace A3
Cuming Museum F7
Curtain Rd B8
Curzon St D3
Cut, The E6
D'arblay St C4
Dante Rd F6
Davies St C3
Dean St C4
Deluxe Gallery B8
Denbigh Place F4
Denmark St C4
Dering St C3
Devonshire St C3
Diana, Princess of Wales Memorial Fountain ✦ D1
Diana, Princess of Wales Memorial Walk E4
Dingley Rd B7
Dorset St C2
Doughty St B5
Douglas St F4
Dover St D3
Downing St E5
Draycott Avenue F2
Draycott Place F2
Druid St E8
Drummond St B4
Drury Lane C5
Drysdale St B8
Duchess St C3
Dufferin St B7
Duke of Wellington Pl E3
Duke St C3/D3
Duke St Hill D7
Duke's Place C8
Duncannon St D5
Dunton Rd F8
East Rd B7
East St F7
Eastcastle St C4
Eastcheap D8
Eastman Dental Hospital B5
Eaton Gate F3
Eaton Place E3
Eaton Square E3
Eaton Terrace F3
Ebury Bridge F3
Ebury Bridge Rd F3
Eccleston Bridge F3
Eccleston Square F3
Eccleston St E3
Edgware Rd C2
Edgware Rd ⊖ C2
Egerton Gardens E2
Eldon St C7
Elephant & Castle F7
Elephant and Castle E6
Elephant Rd F7
Elizabeth Bridge F3
Elizabeth St F3
Elm Tree Rd B1
Elystan Place F2
Elystan St F2
Embankment ⊖ D5
Endell St C5
Endsleigh Place B4
Enid St E8
Ennismore Gardens E2
Erasmus St F4
Euston ⊖ B4
Euston Rd B4
Euston Square ⊖ B4
Evelina Children's Hospital E5
Eversholt St A4
Exhibition Rd E1
Exmouth Market B6
Fair St E8
Falmouth Rd E7
Fann St B7
Farringdon ⊖ C6
Farringdon Rd C6
Farringdon St C6
Featherstone St B7
Fenchurch St D8
Fenchurch St D8
Fetter Lane C6
Finsbury Circus C7
Finsbury Pavement C7
Finsbury Square B7
Fitzalan St F6
Fitzmaurice Place D3
Fleet St C6
Fleming Lab. Mus C1
Floral St D5
Florence Nightingale Museum E5
Folgate St C8
Fore St C7
Foster Lane C7
Foundling Mus, The B5
Francis St F4
Frazier St E6
Freemason's Hall C5
Friday St C7
Fulham Rd F1
Gainsford St E8
Garden Row E6
Gee St B7
Geological Museum E1
George Row E9
George St C2
Gerrard St D4
Gibson Rd F5
Giltspur St C6
Glasshouse St D4
Glasshouse Walk F5
Gloucester Place C2
Gloucester Square C1
Gloucester St F4
Golden Hinde D7
Golden Lane B7
Golden Square D4
Goodge St ⊖ C4
Goodge St C4
Gordon Hospital F4
Gordon Square B4
Goswell Rd B6
Gough St B5
Goulston St C8
Gower St B4
Gracechurch St D7
Grafton Way B4
Graham Terrace F3
Grange Rd E8
Grange Walk E8
Gray's Inn Rd B5
Great College St E5
Great Cumberland Pl C2
Great Dover St E7
Great Eastern St B8
Great Guildford St D7
Great Marlborough St C4
Great Ormond St B5
Great Ormond Street Children's Hosp B5
Great Percy St B5
Great Peter St E4
Great Portland St ⊖ B3
Great Portland St C3
Great Queen St C5
Great Russell St C4
Great Scotland Yard D5
Great Smith St E4
Great Suffolk St D6/E6
Great Titchfield St C4
Great Tower St D8
Great Windmill St D4
Greek St C4
Green Park ⊖ D4
Green St D3
Greencoat Place F4
Gresham St C7
Greville St B5/C6
Greycoat Hospital Sch E4
Greycoat Place E4
Grosvenor Crescent E3
Grosvenor Gardens E3
Grosvenor Place E3
Grosvenor Square D3
Grosvenor St D3
Grove End Rd B1
Guards Museum and Chapel E4
Guildhall Art Gallery C7
Guilford St B5
Guy's Hospital D7
Haberdasher St B7
Hackney Rd B8
Half Moon St D3
Halkin St E3
Hall PL B1
Hall St B6
Hallam St C3
Hamilton Close B1
Hampstead Rd B4
Hanover Square C3
Hans Crescent E2
Hans Rd E2
Hanway St C4
Hardwick St B6
Harewood Avenue B2
Harley St C3
Harper Rd E7
Harrington Rd F1
Harrison St B5
Harrowby St C2
Hasker St F2
Hastings St B5
Hatfields D6
Hay's Galleria D8
Hay's Mews D3
Hayles St F6
Haymarket D4
Hayward Gallery D5
Helmet Row B7
Herbrand St B5
Hercules Rd E5
Hertford St D3
Heygate St F7
High Holborn C5
Hill St D3
HMS Belfast D8
Hobart Place E3
Holborn ⊖ C5
Holborn C6
Holborn Viaduct C6
Holland St D6
Holmes Museum B2
Holywell Lane B8
Horse Guards' Rd D4
Horseferry Rd F4
Houndsditch C8
Houses of Parliament E5
Howland St C4
Hoxton Square B8
Hoxton St B8
Hugh St F3
Hunter St B5
Hunterian Museum C5
Hyde Park D2
Hyde Park Corner ⊖ E3
Hyde Park Crescent C2
Hyde Park St C2
Imperial Coll London E1
Imperial College Rd E1
Imperial War Mus E6
Information Centre D4, F3, C7
Inner Circle B3
Ironmonger Row B7
Jacob St E9
Jamaica Rd E8
James St C3
James St D5
Jermyn St D4
Jockey's Fields C5
John Carpenter St D6
John Fisher St D9
John Islip St F4
John St B5
Johnathan St F5
Judd St B5
Kennings Way F6
Kennington ⊖ F6
Kennington Lane F6
Kennington Park Rd F6
Kennington Rd E6/F6
Kensington Gardens D1
Kensington Gore E1
Kensington Rd E1
Keyworth St E6
King Charles St E5
King St D5
King William St C7
King's College London D5
King's Cross ⊖ A5
King's Cross Rd B5
King's Cross St Pancras ⊖ A5
King's Rd F2
Kingley St C4
Kingsland Rd B8
Kingsway C5
Kinnerton St E3
Kipling St E7
Knightsbridge ⊖ E2
Lamb St C8
Lamb's Conduit St C5
Lambeth Bridge F5
Lambeth High St F5
Lambeth North ⊖ E6
Lambeth Palace E5
Lambeth Palace Rd E5
Lambeth Rd E6
Lambeth Walk F5
Lancaster Gate ⊖ D1
Lancaster Place D5
Lancaster St E6
Lancaster Terrace D1
Langham Place C3
Lant St E7
Leadenhall St C8
Leake St E5
Leather Lane C6
Leathermarket St E8
Leicester Square ⊖ D4
Leicester St D4
Leonard St B7
Leroy St E8
Lever St B7
Lexington St D4
Lidlington Place A4
Lime St D8
Lincoln's Inn Fields C5
Lindsey St C6
Lisle St D4
Lisson Grove B1
Lisson St C2
Liverpool St C8
Liverpool St ⊖ C8
Lloyd Baker St B6
Lloyd Square B6
Lodge Rd B2
Lollard St F6
Lombard St C7
London Aquarium E5
London Bridge ⊖ D7
London Bridge Hospital D7
London City Hall D8
London Dungeon E5
London Guildhall Univ C7
London Rd E6
London St C1
London Transport Museum D5
London Wall C7
London Eye ✦ E5
Long Acre D5
Long Lane C6
Long Lane E7
Longford St B3
Lord's Cricket Gd (MCC & Middlesex CCC) B1
Lower Belgrave St E3
Lower Grosvenor Pl E3
Lower Marsh E6
Lower Sloane St F3
Lower Thames St D7
Lowndes St E3
Ludgate Circus C6
Ludgate Hill C6
Lupus St F4
Luxborough St C3
Lyall St E3
Macclesfield Rd B7
Madame Tussaud's ✦ B3
Maddox St D3
Malet St C4
Mall, The E4
Maltby St E8
Manchester Square C3
Manchester St C3
Manciple St E7
Mandela Way F8
Mandeville Place C3
Mansell St D8
Mansion House C7
Mansion House ⊖ D7
Maple St C4
Marble Arch ⊖ C2
Marble Arch D2
Marchmont St B5
Margaret St C4
Margery St B6
Mark Lane D8
Marlborough Rd D4
Marshall St C4
Marshalsea Rd E7
Marsham St E4
Marylebone ⊖ B2
Marylebone High St C3
Marylebone Lane C3
Marylebone Rd B3/C2
Marylebone St C3
Mecklenburgh Square B5
Middle Temple Lane C6
Middlesex St (Petticoat Lane) C8
Midland Rd A4
Millbank F5
Milner St F2
Minories C8
Monck St E4
Monkton St F6
Monmouth St C4
Montagu Place C2
Montagu Square C2
Montagu St C5
Montague Place C4
Montpelier St E2
Montpelier Walk E2
Monument ⊖ D7
Monument St D7
Monument, The ✦ D7
Moor Lane C7
Moorfields C7
Moorfields Eye Hospital B7
Moorgate C7
Moorgate ⊖ C7
Moreland St B6
Morley St E6
Mortimer St C4
Mossop St F2
Mount Pleasant B6
Mount St D3
Murray Grove A7
Mus of Gdn History E5
Museum of London C7
Museum St C5
Myddelton Square B6
Myddelton St B6
National Gallery D4
National Hospital B5
National Portrait Gallery D4
Natural History Museum E1
Neal St C5
Nelson's Column ✦ D5
Neville St F1
New Bond St C3/D3
New Bridge St C6
New Cavendish St C3
New Change C7
New Fetter Lane C6
New Inn Yard B8
New Kent Rd F7
New North Rd A7
New Oxford St C4
New Scotland Yard E5
New Square C5
Newburn St F5
Newgate St C6
Newington Butts F6
Newington Causeway E7
Newton St C5
Nile St B7
Noble St C7
Noel St C4
Norfolk Crescent C2
Norfolk Square C1
North Audley St D3
North Carriage Drive D2
North Crescent C4
North Ride D2
North Row D3
North Wharf Rd C1
Northampton Square B6
Northington St B5
Northumberland Ave D5
Norton Folgate C8
Nottingham Place C3
Old Bailey C6
Old Broad St C7
Old Brompton Rd F1
Old Compton St C4
Old County Hall E5
Old Gloucester St C5
Old Jamaica Rd E9
Old Kent Rd F8
Old King Edward St C7
Old Marylebone Rd C2
Old Montague St C9
Old Nichol St B8
Old Paradise St F5
Old Spitalfields Mkt C8
Old St B7
Old St ⊖ B7
Old Vic E6
Onslow Gardens F1
Onslow Square F1
Ontario St E6
Open Air Theatre B3
Operating Theatre Museum D7
Orange St D4
Orchard St C3
Ossulston St A4
Outer Circle B2
Ovington Square E2
Oxford Circus ⊖ C4
Oxford St C3/C4
Paddington ⊖ C1
Paddington St C3
Page's Walk E8
Palace St E4
Pall Mall D4
Pall Mall East D4
Pancras Rd A5
Panton St D4
Paris Garden D6
Park Crescent B3
Park Lane D3
Park Rd B2
Park St D3
Park St D7
Parker St C5
Parliament Square E5
Parliament St E5
Paternoster Square C6
Paul St B7
Pear Tree St B6
Pelham Crescent F2
Pelham St F1
Penfold St C2
Penton Place F6
Penton Rise B5
Penton St A6
Pentonville Rd A5/A6
Percival St B6
Petticoat Lane (Middlesex St) C8
Petty France E4
Phoenix Place B5
Phoenix Rd A4
Photo Gallery D4
Piccadilly D3
Piccadilly Circus ⊖ D4
Pilgrimage St E7
Pimlico ⊖ F4
Pimlico Rd F3

Pitfield St B8
Pollock's Toy Mus C4
Polygon Rd A4
Pont St E2
Porchester Place C2
Portland Place C3
Portman Mews C3
Portman Square C3
Portman St C2
Portugal St C5
Postal Mus, The B5
Poultry C7
Praed St C1
Primrose St C8
Prince Consort Rd E1
Prince's Gardens E1
Princes St C7
Procter St C5
Provost St B7
Quaker St B8
Queen Anne St C3
Queen Elizabeth Hall D5
Queen Elizabeth St E8
Queen Square B5
Queen St D7
Queen Street Place D7
Queen Victoria St D6
Queens Gallery E4
Queensberry Place F1
Quilter St B9
Radnor St B7
Rathbone Place C4
Rawlings St F2
Rawstorne St B6
Red Lion Square C5
Red Lion St C5
Redchurch St B8
Redcross Way D7
Reedworth St F6
Regency St F4
Regent Square B5
Regent St C4
Regent's Park B3
Richmond Terrace E5
Ridgmount St C4
Riley Rd E8
Rivington St B8
Robert St B3
Rochester Row F4
Rockingham St E7
Rodney Rd F7
Rolls Rd F8
Ropemaker St C7
Rosebery Avenue B6
Rossmore Rd B2
Rothsay St E8
Rotten Row E2
Roupell St D6
Royal Acad of Arts D4
Royal Academy of Dramatic Art (RADA) B4
Royal Acad of Music B3
Royal Albert Hall E1
Royal Artillery Memorial E2
Royal Brompton Hospital F1/F2
Royal Coll of Nursing C3
Royal Coll of Surgeons C5
Royal Festival Hall D5
Royal London Hospital for Integrated Medicine C5
Royal Marsden Hosp F1
Royal National Theatre D6
Royal National Throat, Nose and Ear Hosp B5
Royal Opera House D5
Rushworth St E6
Russell Square B4
Russell Square B5
Rutland Gate E2
Saatchi Gall F2
Sackville St D4
Sadlers Wells B6
Saffron Hill C6
St Alban's St D4
St Andrew St C6
St Barnabas St F3
St Bartholomew's Hospital C6
St Botolph St C8
St Bride St C6
St George's Circus E6
St George's Drive F4
St George's Rd E6
St George's Square F4
St Giles High St C4
St James's Palace D4
St James's Park E4
St James's St D4
St John St B6
St John's Wood Rd B1
St Margaret St E5
St Mark's Hospital B6
St Martin's Lane D5
St Martin's Le Grand C7
St Mary Axe C8
St Mary's Hospital C1
St Pancras International A5
St Paul's C7
St Paul's Cathedral C7
St Paul's Churchyard C6
St Thomas St D7
St Thomas' Hospital E5
Sale Place C2
Sancroft St F5
Savile Row D4
Savoy Place D5
Savoy St D5
School of Hygiene & Tropical Medicine C4
Science Museum E1
Scrutton St B8
Sekforde St B6
Serpentine Gallery E1
Serpentine Rd D2
Seven Dials C5
Seward St B6
Seymour Place C2
Seymour St C2
Shad Thames D8/E8
Shaftesbury Avenue D4
Shakespeare's Globe Theatre D7
Shepherd Market D3
Sherwood St D4
Shoe Lane C6
Shoreditch High St B8
Shoreditch High St B8
Shorts Gardens C5
Shouldham St C2
Shrek's Adventure E5
Sidmouth St B5
Silk St C7
Sir John Soane's Museum C5
Skinner St B6
Sloane Avenue F2
Sloane Square F2
Sloane Square F3
Sloane St E2
Snow Hill C6
Soho Square C4
Somerset House D5
South Audley St D3
South Carriage Drive E2
South Eaton Place F3
South Kensington F1
South Molton St C3
South Parade F1
South Place C7
South St D3
South Terrace F2
South Wharf Rd C1
Southampton Row C5
Southampton St D5
Southwark D6
Southwark Bridge D7
Southwark Bridge Rd D7
Southwark Cath D7
Southwark Park Rd F8
Southwark St D7
Spa Rd E8
Speakers' Corner D2
Spencer St B6
Spital Square C8
Spring St C1
Stamford St D6
Stanhope St B4
Stanhope Terrace D1
Stephenson Way B4
Stock Exchange C6
Stoney St D7
Strand C5
Strathearn Place D2
Stratton St D3
Sumner St D6
Sussex Gardens C1
Sussex Place C1
Sussex Square D1
Sussex St F3
Sutton's Way B7
Swan St E7
Swanfield St B8
Swinton St B5
Sydney Place F1
Sydney St F2
Tabard St E7
Tabernacle St B7
Tachbrook St F4
Tanner St E8
Tate Britain F5
Tate Modern D7
Tavistock Place B5
Tavistock Square B4
Tea & Coffee Mus D7
Temple D6
Temple Avenue D6
Temple Place D5
Terminus Place E3
Thayer St C3
Theobald's Rd C5
Thorney St F5
Threadneedle St C7
Throgmorton St C7
Thurloe Place F1
Thurloe Square F2
Tonbridge St B5
Tooley St D8
Torrington Place B4
Tothill St E4
Tottenham Court Rd B4
Tottenham Ct Rd C4
Tottenham St C4
Tower Bridge D8
Tower Bridge App D8
Tower Bridge Rd E8
Tower Hill D8
Tower Hill D8
Tower of London, The D8
Toynbee St C8
Trafalgar Square D4
Trinity Square D8
Trinity St E7
Trocadero Centre D4
Tudor St D6
Turin St B9
Turnmill St C6
Tyers St F5
Ufford St E6
Union St D6
University Coll Hosp B4
University College London (UCL) B4
University of London C4
Univ of Westminster C3
University St B4
Upper Belgrave St E3
Upper Berkeley St C2
Upper Brook St D3
Upper Grosvenor St D3
Upper Ground D6
Upper Montague St C2
Upper St Martin's La D5
Upper Thames St D7
Upper Wimpole St C3
Upper Woburn Place B4
Vauxhall Bridge Rd F4
Vauxhall St F5
Vere St C3
Vernon Place C5
Vestry St B7
Victoria E3
Victoria and Albert Museum E1
Victoria Coach Station F3
Victoria Embankment D5
Victoria Place Shopping Centre F3
Victoria St E4
Villiers St D5
Vincent Square F4
Vinopolis City of Wine D7
Virginia Rd B8
Wakley St B6
Walbrook C7
Walcot Square F6
Wallace Collection C3
Walnut Tree Walk F6
Walton St F2
Walworth Rd F7
Wardour St C4/D4
Warner St B6
Warren St B4
Warren St B4
Warwick Square F4
Warwick Way F3
Waterloo E6
Waterloo Bridge D5
Waterloo East D6
Waterloo Rd E6
Watling St C7
Webber St E6
Welbeck St C3
Wellington Arch E3
Wellington Mus E3
Wellington Rd B2
Wellington Row B9
Wells St C4
Wenlock St A7
Wentworth St C8
West Carriage Drive D2
West Smithfield C6
West Square E6
Westbourne St D1
Westbourne Terrace C1
Westminster E5
Westminster Abbey E5
Westminster Bridge E5
Westminster Bridge Rd E6
Westminster Cathedral (RC) E4
Westminster City Hall E4
Westminster Hall E5
Weymouth St C3
Wharf Rd A7
Wharton St B5
Whitcomb St D4
White Cube B8
White Lion Hill D6
White Lion St A6
Whitechapel Rd C9
Whitecross St B7
Whitefriars St C6
Whitehall D5
Whitehall Place D5
Wigmore Hall C3
Wigmore St C3
William IV St D5
Willow Walk F8
Wilmington Square B6
Wilson St C7
Wilton Crescent E3
Wilton Rd F4
Wimpole St C3
Winchester St F3
Wincott St F6
Windmill Walk D6
Woburn Place B5
Woburn Square B4
Wood St C7
Woodbridge St B6
Wootton St D6
Wormwood St C8
Worship St B7
Wren St B5
Wynyatt St B6
Young Vic E6
York Rd E5
York St C2
York Terrace East B3
York Terrace West B3
York Way A5

Luton 337

Adelaide St B1
Albert Rd C2
Alma St B2
Alton Rd C3
Anthony Gardens C1
Arthur St C2
Ashburnham Rd B1
Ashton Rd C2
Back St A2
Bailey St C3
Baker St C2
Biscot Rd A1
Bolton Rd B3
Boyle Close A2
Brantwood Rd B1
Bretts Mead C1
Bridge St B2
Brook St A1
Brunswick St A3
Burr St A3
Bury Park Rd A1
Bute St B2
Buxton Rd B2
Cambridge St C3
Cardiff Grove B1
Cardiff Rd B1
Cardigan St A2
Castle St B2/C2
Chapel St C2
Charles St A3
Chase St C2
Cheapside B2
Chequer St C3
Chiltern Rise C1
Church St B2/B3
Cinema A2
Cobden St A3
College A3
Collingdon St A1
Concorde Avenue A3
Corncastle Rd C1
Cowper St C2
Crawley Green Rd B3
Crawley Rd A1
Crescent Rd A3
Crescent Rise A3
Cromwell Rd A1
Cross St A2
Cross Way, The C1
Crown Court B2
Cumberland St B2
Cutenhoe Rd C3
Dallow Rd B1
Downs Rd B1
Dudley St A2
Duke St A2
Dumfries St B1
Dunstable Place B2
Dunstable Rd A1/B1
Edward St A3
Elizabeth St C2
Essex Close C3
Farley Hill C1
Flowers Way B2
Francis St A1
Frederick St A2
Galaxy Leisure Complex A2
George St B2
George St West B2
Gordon St B2
Grove Rd B1
Guildford St A2
Haddon Rd A3
Harcourt St C2
Hart Hill Drive A3
Hart Hill Lane A3
Hartley Rd A3
Hastings St B2
Hat Factory, The B2
Hatters Way A1
Havelock Rd A2
Hibbert St C2
High Town Rd A3
Highbury Rd A1
Hightown Community Sports & Arts Centre A3
Hillary Crescent C1
Hillborough Rd C1
Hitchin Rd A3
Holly St C2
Holm C1
Hucklesby Way A2
Hunts Close C1
Inkerman St A2
John St B2
Jubilee St A3
Kelvin Close C2
King St B2
Kingsland Rd C3
Larches, The A2
Latimer Rd C2
Lawn Gardens C2
Lea Rd B3
Library B2
Library Rd B2
Library Theatre B2
Liverpool Rd B1
London Rd C2
Luton Station A2
Lyndhurst Rd B1
Magistrates Court B2
Mall, The B2
Manchester St B2
Manor Rd B3
Manor Road Park B3
May St C3
Meyrick Avenue C1
Midland Rd A2
Mill St A2
Milton Rd B1
Moor St A1
Moor, The A1
Moorland Gardens A2
Moulton Rise A3
Napier Rd B1
New Bedford Rd A1
New Town St C2
North St A3
Old Bedford Rd A2
Old Orchard C2
Osbourne Rd C3
Oxen Rd A3
Park Square B2
Park St B3/C3
Park St West B2
Park Viaduct B3
Parkland Drive C1
Police Station B1
Pomfret Avenue A3
Pondwicks Rd B3
Post Office A1/B2
Power Court B3
Princess St B1
Red Rails C1
Regent St B2
Reginald St A2
Rothesay Rd B1
Russell Rise C1
Russell St C1
Ruthin Close C1
St Ann's Rd B3
St George's Square B2
St Mary's B3
St Marys Rd B3
St Paul's Rd C2
St Saviour's Crescent C1
Salisbury Rd B1
Seymour Avenue C3
Seymour Rd C3
Silver St B2
South Rd C2
Stanley St B1
Station Rd A2
Stockwood Crescent C2
Stockwood Park C1
Strathmore Avenue C2
Stuart St B2
Studley Rd A1
Surrey St C3
Sutherland Place C1
Tavistock St C2
Taylor St A3
Telford Way A1
Tennyson Rd C2
Tenzing Grove C1
Thistle Rd B3
Town Hall B2
Townsley Close C2
UK Centre for Carnival Arts B3
Union St B2
Univ of Bedfordshire B3
Upper George St B2
Vicarage St B3
Villa Rd A2
Waldeck Rd A1
Wardown House Mus & Gallery A2
Wellington St B1/B2
Wenlock St A2
Whitby Rd A1
Whitehill Avenue C1
William St A2
Wilsden Avenue C1
Windmill Rd B3
Windsor St C2
Winsdon Rd B1
York St A3

Macclesfield 337

108 Steps B2
Abbey Rd A1
Alton Drive A3
Armett St C1
Athey St B1
Bank St C3
Barber St C3
Barton St C1
Beech Lane A2
Beswick St B1
Black Lane A2
Black Rd C3
Blakelow Gardens C3
Blakelow Rd C3
Bond St B1/C1
Bread St C1
Bridge St B1
Brock St A2
Brocklehurst Avenue A3
Brook St B3
Brookfield Lane B3
Brough St West C1
Brown St C1
Brynton Rd A2
Buckley St C2
Bus Station B2
Buxton Rd B3
Byrons St C2
Canal St B3
Carlsbrook Avenue A3
Castle St B2
Catherine St B1
Cemetery A1
Chadwick Terrace A3
Chapel St C2
Charlotte St B2
Chester Rd B1
Chestergate B1
Christ Church B1
Churchill Way B2
Coare St A1
Commercial Rd B2
Conway Crescent A3
Copper St C3
Cottage St B1
Crematorium A1
Crew Avenue A1
Crompton Rd B1/C1
Cross St C2
Crossall St C1
Cumberland St A1/B1
Dale St B3
Duke St B2
Eastgate B3
Exchange St B2
Fence Avenue B3
Fence Ave Ind Est A3
Flint St B3
Foden St A2
Fountain St B3
Garden St A3
Gas Rd B2
Gateway Gallery B1
George St B2
Glegg St B3
Golf Course C3
Goodall St B3
Grange Rd C1
Great King St B1
Green St B3
Grosvenor Shopping Centre B2
Gunco Lane C3
Half St C2
Hallefield Rd B3
Hatton St C1
Hawthorn Way A3
Heapy St C3
Henderson St B1
Heritage Centre B2
Hibel Rd A2
High St C2
Hobson St C2
Hollins Rd C3
Hope St West B1
Horseshoe Drive B1
Hurdsfield Rd A3
Information Centre B2
James St C2
Jodrell St B3
John St C2
Jordangate A2
King Edward St B2
King George's Field C3
King St B2
King's School A1
Knight Pool C3
Knight St C3
Lansdowne St A3
Library B2
Lime Grove B3
Loney St B1
Longacre St B1
Lord St C2
Lowe St C2
Lowerfield Rd A3
Lyon St B1
Macclesfield College C1
Macclesfield Sta B2
MADS Little Theatre C2
Marina B3
Market B2
Market Place B2
Masons Lane A3
Mill Lane C2
Mill Rd C2
Mill St B2
Moran Rd C1
New Hall St A2
Newton St C1
Nicholson Avenue A3
Nicholson Close A3
Northgate Avenue A2
Old Mill Lane C2
Paradise Mill C2
Paradise St B1
Park Green B2
Park Lane C1
Park Rd C1
Park St C2
Park Vale Rd C1
Parr St B1
Peel St C2
Percyvale St A3
Peter St C1
Pickford St B2
Pierce St B1
Pinfold St B1
Pitt St C2
Police Station B2
Pool St C2
Poplar Rd C2
Post Office B2
Pownall St A2
Prestbury Rd A1/B1
Queen Victoria St B2
Queen's Avenue A3
Registrar B2
Retail Park C2
Richmond Hill C3
Riseley St B1
Roan Court B3
Roe St B2
Rowan Way A3
Ryle St C2
Ryle's Park Rd C1
St George's St C2
St Michael's B2
Samuel St B2
Saville St C3
Shaw St B1
Silk Rd, The A2/B2
Slater St C1
Snow Hill C3
South Park C1
Spring Gardens A2
Statham St C2
Station St A2
Steeple St A3
Sunderland St B2
Superstore A1/A2/C2
Swettenham St B3
Thistleton Close C2
Thorp St B2
Town Hall B2
Townley St B2
Treacle Market B2
Turnock St C3
Union Rd B3
Union St B2
Victoria Park B3
Vincent St C2
Waters Green B2
Waterside C2
West Bond St B1
West Park A1
West Park Museum A1
Westbrook Drive A1
Westminster Rd A1
Whalley Hayes B1
Windmill St C3
Withyfold Drive A2
York St B3

Maidstone 340

Albion Place B3
All Saints B2
Allen St A3
Amphitheatre C2
Archbishop's Palace B2
Bank St B2
Barker Rd C2
Barton Rd C3
Beaconsfield Rd C1
Bedford Place B1
Bishops Way B2
Bluett St A3
BMI The Somerfield Hospital A1
Bower Lane C1
Bower Mount Rd B1
Bower Place C1
Bower St B1
Boxley Rd A3
Brenchley Gardens A2
Brewer St A3
Broadway B2
Broadway Shopping Centre B2
Brunswick St C3
Buckland Hill A1
Buckland Rd B1
Bus Station B3
Campbell Rd C3
Church Rd C1
Church St B3
Cinema C2
Clifford Way C1/C2
College Avenue C2
College Rd C2
Collis Memorial Gdn C3
Cornwallis Rd B1
Corpus Christi Hall B2
Council Offices B3
County Hall A2
County Rd A3
Crompton Gardens C3
Crown & County Courts B2
Curzon Rd A3
Dixon Close C2
Douglas Rd C1
Earl St B2
Eccleston Rd C2
Fairmeadow B2
Fisher St A2
Florence Rd C1
Foley St A3
Foster St C3
Freedom Leisure Centre A1/A2
Fremlin Walk Shopping Centre B2
Gabriel's Hill B3
George St C3
Grecian St A3
Hardy St A3
Hart St C2
Hastings Rd C3
Hayle Rd C3
Hazlitt B2
Heathorn St A3
Hedley St A3
High St B2
HM Prison A3
Holland Rd A3
Hope St A2
Information Centre B2
James St A3
James Whatman Way A2
Jeffrey St A3
Kent County Council Offices A2
Kent History & Liby Ctr A2
King Edward Rd C2
King St B3
Kingsley Rd C3
Knightrider St B3
Launder Way C1
Lesley Place A1
Library B2
Little Buckland Ave A1
Lockmeadow Leisure Complex C2
London Rd B1
Lower Boxley Rd A2
Lower Fant Rd C1
Magistrates Court B3
Maidstone Barracks Station A1
Maidstone East Sta A2
Maidstone Museum & Bentlif Art Gall B2
Maidstone Utd FC A3
Maidstone West Sta B2
Mall, The B3
Market C2
Market Buildings B2
Marsham St B3
Medway St B2
Melville Rd C3
Mill St B2
Millennium Bridge C2
Mote Rd B3
Muir Rd C3
Old Tovil Rd C2
Palace Avenue B3
Perryfield St A2
Police Station B3
Post Office B2/C3
Priory Rd C3
Prospect Place C1
Pudding Lane B2
Queen Anne Rd B3
Queens Rd A1
Randall St A2
Rawdon Rd C3
Reginald Rd C1
Riverstage A1
Rock Place B1
Rocky Hill B1
Romney Place B3
Rose Yard B2
Rowland Close C1
Royal Engineers' Rd A2
Royal Star Arcade B2
St Annes Court B1
St Faith's St B2
St Luke's Rd A3
St Peter St B2
St Peter's Bridge B2
St Peter's Wharf Retail Park B2
St Philip's Avenue C3
Salisbury Rd A3
Sandling Rd A2
Scott St A2
Scrubs Lane B1
Sheal's Crescent C3
Somerfield Lane B1
Somerfield Rd B1
Staceys St A2
Station Rd A2
Superstore A1/B2/B3
Terrace Rd B1
Tonbridge Rd C1
Tovil Rd C2
Town Hall B2
Trinity Park B3
Tufton St B3
Tyrwhitt-Drake Museum of Carriages B2
Union St B3
Upper Fant Rd C1
Upper Stone St C3
Victoria St B1
Warwick Place B1
Wat Tyler Way B3
Waterloo St C3
Waterlow Rd A3
Week St B2
Well Rd A3
Westree Rd C1
Wharf Rd C1
Whatman Park A1
Wheeler St A3
Whitchurch Close B1
Woodville Rd C3
Wyatt St B3
Wyke Manor Rd B3

Manchester 337

Adair St B6
Addington St A5
Adelphi St A1
Advent Way B6
Albert Square B3
Albion St C3
Ancoats Grove B6
Ancoats Grove North B6
Angela St C2
Aquatics Centre C4
Ardwick Green North C5
Ardwick Green Park C5
Ardwick Green South C5
Arlington St A2
Artillery St B3
Arundel St C2
Atherton St B2
Atkinson St B3
Aytoun St B4
Back Piccadilly A4
Baird St B5
Balloon St A4
Bank Place A1
Baring St B5
Barrack St C1
Barrow St A1
Bendix St A5
Bengal St A5
Berry St C5
Blackfriars Rd A3
Blackfriars St A3
Blantyre St C2
Bloom St B4
Blossom St A5
Boad St B5
Bombay St B4
Booth St A3
Booth St B4
Bootle St B3
Brazennose St B3
Brewer St A5
Bridge St A3
Bridgewater Hall B3
Bridgewater Place A4
Bridgewater St B2
Brook St C4
Brotherton Drive A2
Brown St A3
Brown St B4
Brunswick St C6
Brydon Avenue C6
Buddhist Centre A4
Bury St A2
Bus & Coach Station B4
Bus Station B4
Butler St A6
Buxton St C5
Byrom St B3
Cable St A5
Cambridge St C3/C4
Camp St B3
Canal St B4
Cannon St A4
Cardroom Rd A6
Carruthers St A6
Castle St C2
Castlefield Arena B2
Cateaton St A3
Cathedral A3
Cathedral St A3
Cavendish St C4
Chapel St A1/A3
Chapeltown St B5
Charles St C4
Charlotte St B4
Chatham St B4
Chepstow St B3
Chester Rd C1/C2
Chester St C4
Chetham's School of Music A3
China Lane B5
Chippenham Rd A6
Chorlton Rd C2
Chorlton St B4
Church St A2
Church St A4
City Park A4
City Rd East C3
Civil Justice Centre B2
Cleminson St A2
Clowes St A3
College Land A3
Collier St B2
Commercial St C3
Conference Centre C4
Cooper St B4
Copperas St A4
Corn Exchange, The A4
Cornbrook C1
Cornell St A5
Corporation St A4
Cotter St C6
Cotton St A5
Cow Lane B1
Cross St B3
Crown Court B4
Crown St C2
Dalberg St C6
Dale St A4/B5
Dancehouse, The C4
Dantzic St A4
Dark Lane C6
Dawson St C2
Dean St A5
Deansgate A3/B3/C2
Deansgate Castlefield C3
Deansgate Station C3
Dolphin St C6
Downing St C5
Ducie St B5
Duke Place B2
Duke St B2
Durling St C6
East Ordsall Lane A2/B1
Edge St A4
Egerton St C2
Ellesmere St C1
Everard St C1
Everyman B2
Every St B6
Exchange Square A4
Factory, The B2
Fairfield St B5
Faulkner St B4
Fennel St A3
Fire Station A5
Ford St A2
Ford St C6
Fountain St B4
Frederick St A2
Gartside St B2
Gaythorne St A1
George Leigh St A5
George St B4
Gore St A2
Goulden St A5
Granby Row B4
Gravel Lane A3
Great St B6
Great Ancoats St A5
Great Bridgewater St B3
Great George St A1
Great Jackson St C2
Great Marlborough St C4
Great Northern Leisure Complex B3
Greengate A3
Grosvenor St C5
Gun St A5
Hall St B3
Hampson St B1
Hanover St A4
Hanworth Close C5
Hardman St B3
Harkness St C6
Harrison St B6
Hart St B4
Helmet St B6
Henry St A5
Heyrod St B6
High St A4
Higher Ardwick C6
Hilton St A4/A5
Holland St A6
HOME Entertainment Complex C3
Hood St A5
Hope St B1
Hope St B4
Houldsworth St A5
Hoyle St C6
Hulme Hall Rd C1
Hulme St A1
Hulme St C3
Hyde Rd C6
Islington Way A1
Information Centre B4
Irwell St A2
Jackson Crescent C2
Jackson's Row B3
James St A1
Jenner Close C2
Jersey St A5
John Dalton St B3
John Ryland's Liby B3
John St A2
Kennedy St B3
Kincardine Rd C5
King St A3
King St West A3
Law Courts B3
Laystall St B5
Lever St A5
Library B3
Linby St C2
Little Lever St A4
Liverpool Rd B2
Liverpool St B1
Lloyd St B3
Lockton Close C5
London Rd B5
Long Millgate A3
Longacre St B6
Loom St A5
Lower Byrom St B2
Lower Mosley St B3
Lower Moss Lane C2
Lower Ormond St C4
Loxford Lane C4
Luna St A5
Major St B4
Mamucium B2
Manchester Arndale A4
Manchester Art Gallery B4
Manchester Central Convention Complex B3
Manchester Metropolitan University (MMU) B4/C4
Manchester Piccadilly Station B5
Manchester Technology Centre C4
Mancunian Way C3

- Manor St C5
- Marble St A4
- Market St A2
- Market St A4
- Market St A4
- Marsden St A3
- Marshall St A5
- Mayan Avenue A2
- Medlock St C3
- Middlewood St B1
- Miller St A4
- Minshull St B4
- Mosley St A4
- Mount St B3
- Mulberry St B3
- Murray St A5
- Museum of Science & Industry (MOSI) B2
- Nathan Drive A2
- National Football Museum A4
- Naval St A5
- New Bailey St A2
- New Elm Rd B2
- New Islington A6
- New Islington Sta B6
- New Quay St B2
- New Union St A6
- Newton St A5
- Nicholas St B4
- North Western St C6
- Oak St A4
- Odeon A4/B3
- Old Mill St A6
- Oldfield Rd A1/C1
- Oldham Rd A5
- Oldham St A4
- Opera House B3
- Ordsall Lane C1
- Oxford Rd C4
- Oxford Rd C4
- Oxford St B4
- Paddock St C6
- Palace Theatre B4
- Pall Mall A3
- Palmerston St B6
- Parker St B4
- Peak St B5
- Penfield Close C5
- Peoples' History Museum B2
- Peru St A1
- Peter St B3
- Piccadilly A4
- Piccadilly B5
- Piccadilly Gardens B4
- Piercy St A6
- Poland St A5
- Police Museum A5
- Police Station B3/B5
- Pollard St B6
- Port St A5
- Portland St B4
- Portugal St East B5
- Post Office A2/A4/A5/B3/B4/C4
- Potato Wharf B2
- Princess St B3/C4
- Quay St A2
- Quay St B2
- Queen St B3
- Radium St A5
- Redhill St A5
- Regent Retail Park B1
- Regent Rd B1
- Rice St B2
- Richmond St B4
- River St C3
- Roby St B5
- Rodney St A6
- Rosamond St A2
- Royal Exchange A3
- Sackville St B4
- St Andrew's St B6
- St Ann St A3
- St Ann's A3
- St George's Avenue C1
- St James St B4
- St John St B3
- St John's Cath (RC) A2
- St Mary's B3
- St Mary's Gate A3
- St Mary's Parsonage A3
- St Peter's Square B3
- St Stephen St A2
- Salford Approach A3
- Salford Central A2
- Sheffield St B5
- Sherratt St A5
- Shopmobility A4
- Shudehill A4
- Shudehill A4
- Sidney St C4
- Silk St A5
- Silver St B4
- Skerry Close C5
- Snell St B6
- South King St B3
- Sparkle St B5
- Spear St A4
- Spring Gardens A4
- Stanley St B2
- Store St B5
- Superstore B1
- Swan St A4
- Tariff St B5
- Tatton St C1
- Temperance St B6/C6
- Thirsk St C6
- Thomas St A4
- Thompson St A5
- Tib Lane B3
- Tib St A4
- Town Hall (Manchester) B3
- Town Hall (Salford) A2
- Trafford St C3
- Travis St B5
- Trinity Way A2
- Turner St A4
- Union St C6
- University of Manchester (North Campus) C5
- University of Salford A1
- Upper Brook St C5
- Upper Cleminson St A1
- Upper Wharf St A1
- Urban Exchange A5
- Vesta St B6
- Victoria A4
- Victoria Station A4
- Wadesdon Rd C5
- Water St B2
- Watson St B3
- West Fleet St B1
- West King St A2
- West Mosley St B4
- Weybridge Rd A6
- Whitworth St B4
- Whitworth St West C3
- William St A2
- William St C6
- Wilmott St C3
- Windmill St B3
- Windsor Crescent A1
- Withy Grove A4
- Woden St C1
- Wood St B3
- Woodward St A6
- Worrall St C1
- Worsley St C2
- York St B4
- York St C2
- York St C4

Merthyr Tydfil Merthyr Tudful 340

- Aberdare Rd B2
- Abermorlais Terrace B2
- Alexandra Rd A3
- Alma St C3
- Arfryn Place C3
- Argyle St C3
- Avenue De Clichy C2
- Beacons Place Shopping Centre C2
- Bethesda St B2
- Bishops Grove A3
- Brecon Rd A1/B2
- Briarmead A3
- Bryn St C3
- Bryntirion Rd B3/C3
- Bus Station B2
- Cae Mari Dwn B3
- Caedraw Rd C2
- Castle Square A1
- Castle St B2
- Chapel C2
- Chapel Bank B1
- Church St B3
- Civic Centre B2
- Clos Penderyn B1
- Coedcae'r Court C3
- College Boulevard C2
- County and Crown Courts B2
- Court St C3
- Cromwell St B2
- Cyfarthfa Castle, Mus and Art Gallery A1
- Cyfarthfa Ind Est A1
- Cyfarthfa Park A1
- Cyfarthfa Retail Park B1
- Cyfarthfa Rd A1
- Dane St A2
- Dane Terrace A2
- Danyparc B3
- Darren View A3
- Dixon St B2
- Dyke St C3
- Dynevor St B2
- Elwyn Drive C3
- Fire Station B2
- Fothergill St B3
- Galonuchaf Rd A3
- Garth St B2
- Georgetown B2
- Grawen Terrace A2
- Grove Park A2
- Grove, The A2
- Gurnos Rd A2
- Gwaelodygarth Rd A2/A3
- Gwaunfarren Grove A3
- Gwaunfarren Rd A3
- Gwendoline St A3
- Hampton St C3
- Hanover St A2
- Heol S O Davies B1
- Heol-Gerrig B1
- High St A3/B2/B3/C2
- Highland View C3
- Howell Close B1
- Jackson's Bridge B2
- James St C3
- John St B3
- Joseph Parry's Cott B2
- Lancaster St A2
- Library B2
- Llewellyn St A2
- Llwyfen St B2
- Llwyn Berry B1
- Llwyn Dic Penderyn B1
- Llwyn-y-Gelynen C1
- Lower Thomas St B3
- Market C2
- Mary St C3
- Masonic St C2
- Merthyr Tydfil College B2
- Merthyr Town FC B3
- Merthyr Tydfil Leisure Centre C3
- Merthyr Tydfil Sta C3
- Meyrick Villas A2
- Miniature Railway A1
- Mount St A2
- Nantygwenith St B1
- Norman Terrace B2
- Oak Rd A2
- Old Cemetery B3
- Pandy Close A1
- Pantycelynen B1
- Parade, The B3
- Park Terrace B2
- Penlan View C2
- Penry St B2
- Pentwyn Villas A2
- Penyard Rd B3
- Penydarren Park A3
- Penydarren Rd B3
- Plymouth St C3
- Police Station C2
- Pont Marlais West B2
- Post Office B2
- Quarry Row B2
- Queen's Rd B3
- Rees St C3
- Rhydycar Link C2
- Riverside Park A1
- St David's B3
- St Tydfil's C2
- St Tydfil's Avenue C3
- St Tydfil's Square Shopping Centre C2
- Saxon St A2
- School of Nursing A2
- Seward St A3
- Shiloh Lane B3
- Stone Circles B3
- Stuart St A2
- Summerhill Place B3
- Superstore B3
- Swan St C2
- Swansea Rd B1
- Taff Glen View C3
- Taff Vale Court B3
- Theatre Soar B2
- Thomastown Park B3
- Tramroad Lane A3
- Tramroad Side B2
- Tramroad Side North B3
- Tramroad Side South C3
- Trevithick Gardens C3
- Trevithick St A3
- Tudor Terrace B2
- Twynyrodyn Rd C3
- Union St B3
- Upper Colliers Row B1
- Upper Thomas St B3
- Victoria St B2
- Vue C3
- Vulcan Rd B2
- Walk, The B2
- Warlow St C3
- Well St A2
- Welsh Assembly Government Offices C2
- Wern Lane C1
- Wern, The (Merthyr RFC) C2
- West Grove A2
- William St C3
- Yew St C3
- Ynysfach Engine Ho C2
- Ynysfach Rd C2

Middlesbrough 340

- Abingdon Rd C3
- Acklam Rd C1
- Albert Park C2
- Albert Rd B2
- Albert Terrace C2
- Ambulance Station C1
- Aubrey St C3
- Avenue, The C2
- Ayresome Gardens C2
- Ayresome Green Lane C1
- Ayresome St C2
- Barton Rd A1
- Bilsdale Rd C3
- Bishopton Rd C3
- Borough Rd B2/B3
- Bowes Rd A2
- Breckon Hill Rd B3
- Bridge St West B2
- Brighouse Rd A1
- Burlam Rd C1
- Bus Station B2
- Cannon Park B1
- Cannon Park Way B2
- Cannon St B1
- Captain Cook Square B2
- Carlow St C1
- Castle Way C3
- Chipchase Rd C2
- Cineworld B3
- Cleveland Centre B2
- Clive Rd C2
- Commercial St A2
- Corporation Rd B2
- Costa St C2
- Council Offices B3
- Crescent Rd C2
- Crescent, The C2
- Cumberland Rd C2
- Depot Rd A2
- Derwent St B2
- Devonshire Rd C2
- Diamond Rd B2
- Dock St B3
- Dorman Museum C2
- Douglas St B3
- Eastbourne Rd C2
- Eden Rd C3
- Fire Station A3
- Forty Foot Rd A2
- Gilkes St B2
- Gosford St A2
- Grange Rd B2
- Gresham Rd B2
- Harehills Rd C1
- Harford St C2
- Hartington Rd B2
- Haverton Hill Rd A1
- Hey Wood St B1
- Highfield Rd C3
- Hillstreet Centre B2
- Holwick Rd B1
- Hutton Rd C3
- Ironmasters Way B1
- Lambton Rd C3
- Lancaster Rd C2
- Lansdowne Rd C3
- Latham Rd C2
- Law Courts B2/B3
- Lees Rd B2
- Leeway B3
- Library B2/C2
- Linthorpe Cemetery C1
- Linthorpe Rd B2
- Lloyd St B2
- Longford St C2
- Longlands Rd C3
- Lower East St A3
- Lower Lake C3
- Macmillan Academy C1
- Maldon Rd C1
- Manor St B2
- Marsh St B2
- Marton Rd B3
- Middlesbrough By-Pass B2/C1
- Middlesbrough Coll B3
- Middlesbrough Dock B3
- Middlesbrough Leisure Park B3
- Middlesbrough Sta B2
- Middletown Park C2
- MIMA B3
- Mulgrave Rd C2
- Newport Bridge B1
- Newport Bridge Approach Rd B1
- Newport Rd B2
- North Ormesby Rd B3
- North Rd B2
- Northern Rd C1
- Outram St B2
- Oxford Rd C2
- Park Lane C2
- Park Rd North C2
- Park Rd South C2
- Park Vale Rd C3
- Parliament Rd B1
- Police Station A2
- Port Clarence Rd A3
- Portman St B2
- Post Office B3/C1/C2
- Princes Rd B2
- Python A2
- Riverside Park Rd A1
- Riverside Stadium (Middlesbrough FC) B3
- Rockliffe Rd C2
- Romaldkirk Rd B1
- Roman Rd C2
- Roseberry Rd C3
- St Barnabas' Rd C2
- St Paul's Rd B2
- Saltwells Rd B3
- Scott's Rd A3
- Seaton Carew Rd A3
- Shepherdson Way B3
- Shopmobility B2
- Snowdon Rd A2
- South West Ironmasters Park B1
- Southfield Rd B2
- Southwell Rd C2
- Springfield Rd C1
- Startforth Rd A2
- Stockton Rd C1
- Stockton St A2
- Superstore B2
- Surrey St C2
- Sycamore Rd C2
- Tax Offices B3
- Tees Viaduct C1
- Teessaurus Park A2
- Teesside Tertiary Coll C3
- Temenos B3
- Thornfield Rd C1
- Town Hall B2
- Transporter Bridge (Toll) A3
- Union St B2
- University of Teesside B2
- Upper Lake C2
- Valley Rd C3
- Ventnor Rd C2
- Victoria Rd B2
- Vulcan St A2
- Warwick St C2
- Wellesley Rd B3
- West Lane B1
- West Lane Hospital C1
- Westminster Rd C2
- Wilson St B2
- Windward Way B3
- Woodlands Rd B2
- York Rd C3

Milton Keynes 340

- Abbey Way A1
- Arbrook Avenue B1
- Armourer Drive A3
- Arncliffe Drive A1
- Avebury C2
- Avebury Boulevard C2
- Bankfield B3
- Bayard Avenue A2
- Belvedere A2
- Bishopstone A1
- Blundells Rd A1
- Boundary, The C3
- Boycott Avenue C2
- Bradwell Common Bvd B1
- Bradwell Rd C1
- Bramble Avenue A2
- Brearley Avenue C2
- Breckland A1
- Brill Place B1
- Burnham Drive B1
- Campbell Park B3
- Cantle Avenue A3
- Central Retail Park C1
- Century Avenue C2
- Chaffron Way C3
- Childs Way C1
- Christ the Cornerstone B2
- Cineworld B2
- Civic Offices B2
- Cleavers Avenue B2
- Colesbourne Drive A3
- Conniburrow Bvd B2
- Currier Drive A2
- Dansteed Way A2/A3/B1
- Deltic Avenue B1
- Downs Barn A2
- Downs Barn Bvd A3
- Eaglestone C3
- Eelbrook Avenue B1
- Elder Gate B1
- Evans Gate C2
- Fairford Crescent A3
- Falcon Avenue B3
- Fennel Drive A2
- Fishermead Boulevard C3
- Food Centre B3
- Fulwoods Drive C3
- Glazier Drive A2
- Glovers Lane A1
- Grafton Gate C1
- Grafton St A1/C2
- Gurnards Avenue B3
- Harrier Drive C3
- The Hub Leisure Quarter B2/C2
- Ibstone Avenue B1
- Langcliffe Drive A1
- Leisure Centre C3
- Leisure Plaza C1
- Leys Rd C1
- Library B2
- Linceslade Grove C1
- Linford Wood A2
- Magistrates Court B2
- Marlborough Gate B3
- Marlborough St A2/B3
- Mercers Drive A1
- Midsummer C2
- Midsummer Boulevard B2
- Midsummer Place B2
- Milton Keynes Central C1
- Milton Keynes Hospital (A&E) C3
- Monks Way A1
- Mullen Avenue A3
- Mullion Place C3
- National Film & Sci-Fi Museum B2
- Neath Hill A3
- North Elder C1
- North Grafton B1
- North Overgate A3
- North Row B2
- North Saxon B2
- North Secklow B2
- North Skeldon A3
- North Witan B1
- Oakley Gardens A3
- Odeon B2
- Oldbrook Boulevard C2
- Open-Air Theatre B3
- Overgate A3
- Overstreet A3
- Patriot Drive B1
- Pencarrow Place B3
- Penryn Avenue B3
- Perran Avenue C3
- Pitcher Lane C1
- Place Retail Park, The C1
- Police Station B2
- Portway B2
- Post Office A2/B2/B3
- Precedent Drive B1
- Quinton Drive B1
- Ramsons Avenue B2
- Retail Park C2
- Rockingham Drive A2
- Rooksley B1
- Saxon Gate B2
- Saxon St A1/C3
- Secklow Gate B2
- Shackleton Place C2
- Shopmobility B2
- Silbury Boulevard B2
- Skeldon A3
- South Enmore B3
- South Grafton C2
- South Row C2
- South Saxon C2
- South Secklow B3
- South Witan C2
- Springfield B3
- Stainton Drive A1/B1
- Stanton Wood A1
- Stantonbury A1
- Stantonbury Leisure Centre A1
- Strudwick Drive C2
- Sunrise Parkway A2
- Superstore C1/C2
- Theatre & Art Gallery B3
- theCentre:mk B2
- Tolcarne Avenue C3
- Towan Avenue C3
- Trueman Place C2
- Vauxhall A1
- Winterhill Retail Park C2
- Witan Gate B2
- Xscape B3

Newcastle upon Tyne 340

- Albert St B3
- Argyle St B3
- Back New Bridge St B3
- BALTIC Centre for Contemporary Art C3
- Barker St A3
- Barrack Rd B1
- Bath Lane B1
- Bessie Surtees House C2
- Bigg Market C2
- Biscuit Factory B3
- Black Gate C2
- Blackett St B2
- Blandford Square C1
- Boating Lake A1
- Boyd St B3
- Brandling Park A2
- Bus Station B2
- Buxton St B3
- Byron St A3
- Camden St B2
- Castle Keep C2
- Central C1
- Central Library B2
- Central Motorway B2
- Chester St A3
- Cineworld B1
- City Hall B2
- City Rd B3/C3
- City Walls C1
- Civic Centre A2
- Claremont Rd A1
- Clarence St B3
- Clarence Walk B3
- Clayton St C1/B1
- Clayton St West C1
- Close, The C2
- Coach Station C1
- College St B2
- Collingwood St C2
- Copland Terrace B3
- Coppice Way B3
- Corporation St B1
- Courts C3
- Crawhall Rd B3
- Dean St C2
- Dental Hospital A1
- Dinsdale Place A3
- Dinsdale Rd A3
- Discovery C1
- Doncaster Rd A3
- Durant Rd B2
- Eldon Square B1
- Eldon Square Shopping Centre B2
- Ellison Place B2
- Eskdale Terrace A2
- Eslington Terrace A2
- Exhibition Park A1
- Falconar St B3
- Fenkle St C1
- Forth Banks C1
- Forth St C1
- Gallowgate B1
- Gate, The B1
- Gateshead Millennium Bridge C3
- Gateshead Quays C3
- Gibson St B3
- Goldspink Lane A3
- Grainger Market B2
- Grainger St B2
- Grantham Rd A3
- Granville Rd A3
- Great North Children's Hospital A1
- Great North Museum: Hancock A2
- Grey St B2
- Groat Market C2
- Guildhall C2
- Hancock St A2
- Hanover St C2
- Hatton Gallery A1
- Hawks Rd C3
- Haymarket B2
- Heber St B1
- Helmsley Rd A3
- High Bridge B2
- High Level Bridge C2
- Hillgate C3
- Howard St B3
- Hutton Terrace A3
- Jesmond A2
- Jesmond Rd A2/A3
- John Dobson St B2
- Jubilee Rd B3
- Kelvin Grove A3
- Kensington Terrace A2
- Laing Gallery B2
- Lambton Rd A2
- Leazes Crescent B1
- Leazes Lane B1
- Leazes Park B1
- Leazes Park Rd B1
- Leazes Terrace B1
- Library A2
- Life Science Centre C1
- Live C2
- Low Friar St C1
- Manor Chare C2
- Manors B2
- Manors Station B2
- Market St B2
- Melbourne St B2
- Mill Rd C3
- Monument B2
- Monument Mall Shopping Centre B2
- Morpeth St A2
- Mosley St C2
- Napier St A3
- New Bridge St West B2/B3
- Newcastle Central Station C1
- Newcastle University A1
- Newgate St B1
- Newington Rd A3
- Northern Design Centre C3
- Northern Stage Theatre A2
- Northumberland Rd B2
- Northumberland St B2
- Northumbria University A2
- Northwest Radial Rd A1
- O2 Academy C1
- Oakwellgate C3
- Open University C3
- Orchard St C2
- Osborne Rd A2
- Osborne Terrace A3
- Pandon C3
- Pandon Bank B3
- Park Terrace A1
- Percy St B1
- Pilgrim St B2
- Pipewellgate C2
- Pitt St B1
- Plummer Tower A2
- Police Station C1
- Portland Rd A3/B3
- Portland Terrace A3
- Post Office B1/B2
- Pottery Lane C1
- Prudhoe Place B1
- Prudhoe St B1
- Quayside C2
- Queen Elizabeth II Bridge C2
- Queen Victoria Rd A1
- Richardson Rd A1
- Ridley Place B2
- Rock Terrace B3
- Rosedale Terrace A3
- Royal Victoria Infirmary A1
- Sage Gateshead C3
- St Andrew's St B1
- St James B1
- St James' Boulevard C1
- St James' Park (Newcastle Utd FC) B1
- St Mary's Heritage Centre C3
- St Mary's (RC) C1
- St Mary's Place B2
- St Nicholas C2
- St Nicholas St C2
- St Thomas' St B1
- Sandyford Rd A2/A3
- Shield St B3
- Shieldfield B3
- Shopmobility B1
- Side, The C2
- Simpson Terrace B3
- South Shore Rd C3
- South St C1
- Starbeck Avenue A3
- Stepney Rd B3
- Stoddart St B3
- Stowell St B1
- Strawberry Place B1
- Swing Bridge C2
- Temple St C1
- Terrace Place B1
- Theatre Royal B2
- Times Square C1
- Tower St B3
- Trinity House C2
- Tyne Bridge C2
- Tyne Bridges C2
- Tyne Theatre & Opera House C1
- Tyneside B2
- Victoria Square A2
- Warwick St A3
- Waterloo St C1
- Wellington St B1
- Westgate Rd C1/C2
- Windsor Terrace A2
- Worswick St B2
- Wretham Place B3

Newport Casnewydd 340

- Albert Terrace B1
- Allt-yr-Yn Avenue A1
- Alma St C2
- Ambulance Station C3
- Bailey St B2
- Barrack Hill A2
- Bath St A3
- Bedford Rd B3
- Belle Vue Lane C1
- Belle Vue Park C1
- Bishop St A3
- Blewitt St B1
- Bolt Close C3
- Bolt St C3
- Bond St A2
- Bosworth Drive A1
- Bridge St B1
- Bristol St A3
- Bryngwyn Rd B1
- Brynhyfryd Avenue C1
- Brynhyfryd Rd C1
- Bus Station B2
- Caerau Crescent C1
- Caerau Rd B1
- Caerleon Rd A3
- Capel Crescent C2
- Cardiff Rd C2
- Caroline St B3
- Castle (Remains) A2
- Cedar Rd B3
- Charles St B2
- Charlotte Drive C2
- Chepstow Rd A3
- Church Rd A3
- Cineworld B2
- Civic Centre B1
- Clarence Place A2
- Clifton Place B1
- Clifton Rd C1
- Clyffard Crescent B1
- Clytha Park Rd B1
- Clytha Square C2
- Coldra Rd C1
- Collier St A3
- Colne St B3
- Comfrey Close A1
- Commercial Rd C3
- Commercial St B2
- Corelli St A3
- Corn St B2
- Corporation Rd B3
- Coulson Close C2
- County Court A2
- Courts A1, B1
- Crawford St A3
- Cyril St B3
- Dean St A3
- Devon Place B1
- Dewsland Park Rd C2
- Dolman B2
- Dolphin St C3
- East Dock Rd C3
- East St B1
- East Usk Rd A3
- Ebbw Vale Wharf B3
- Emlyn St B2
- Enterprise Way C3
- Eton Rd B3
- Evans St A2
- Factory Rd A2
- Fields Rd B1
- Francis Drive C2
- Frederick St C3
- Friars Rd C1
- Friars Walk B2
- Gaer Lane C1
- George St C3
- George Street Bridge C3
- Godfrey Rd B1
- Gold Tops B1
- Gore St A3
- Gorsedd Circle C1
- Grafton Rd A3
- Graham St B1
- Granville St C3
- Harlequin Drive A1
- Harrow Rd B3
- Herbert Rd A3
- Herbert Walk C2
- Hereford St A3
- High St B2
- Hill St B2
- Hoskins St A2
- Information Centre B2
- Ivor St B2
- Jones St B1
- Junction Rd A3
- Keynshaw Avenue C2
- King St C2
- Kingsway B2
- Kingsway Centre B2
- Ledbury Drive A2
- Library A3
- Library, Museum & Art Gallery B2
- Liverpool Wharf B3
- Llanthewy Rd B1
- Llanvair Rd A3
- Locke St A2
- Lower Dock St C3
- Lucas St A2
- Manchester St A3
- Market B2
- Marlborough Rd B3
- Mellon St C3
- Mill St A2
- Morgan St A3
- Mountjoy Rd C2
- Newport Bridge A2
- Newport Centre B2
- Newport RFC B3
- Newport Station B2
- North St B2
- Oakfield Rd B1
- Park Square C2
- Police Station A3/C2
- Post Office B2/C3
- Power St A1
- Prince St A3
- Pugsley St A2
- Queen St C2
- Queen's Close A1
- Queen's Hill A1
- Queen's Hill Crescent A1
- Queensway B2
- Railway St B2
- Riverfront Theatre & Arts Centre, The B2
- Riverside A3
- Rodney Rd B2
- Royal Gwent (A&E) C2
- Rudry St A3
- Rugby Rd B3
- Ruperra Lane C3
- Ruperra St C3
- St Edmund St B1
- St Mark's Crescent A1
- St Mary St B1
- St Vincent Rd A3
- St Woolos C2
- St Woolos General (no A&E) C1
- St Woolos Rd B1
- School Lane B2
- Serpentine Rd B1
- Shaftesbury Park A2
- Sheaf Lane A3
- Skinner St B2
- Sorrel Drive A1
- South Market St C3
- Spencer Rd B1
- Stow Hill B2/C1/C2
- Stow Park Avenue C1
- Stow Park Drive C1
- TA Centre A1
- Talbot St B2
- Tennis Club A1
- Tregare St A3
- Trostrey St A3
- Tunnel Terrace B1
- Turner St A3
- University of Wales Newport City Campus B3
- Upper Dock St B2
- Usk St A3
- Usk Way B3/C3
- Victoria Crescent B1
- War Memorial A3
- Waterloo Rd C1
- West St B1
- Wharves B2
- Wheeler St A2
- Whitby Place A3
- Windsor Terrace B1
- York Place C1

Newquay 340

- Agar Rd B2
- Alma Place B1
- Ambulance Station B2
- Anthony Rd C1
- Atlantic Hotel A1
- Bank St B1
- Barrowfields A3
- Bay View Terrace B2
- Beach Rd B1
- Beachfield Avenue B1
- Beacon Rd A1
- Belmont Place A1
- Berry Rd B2
- Blue Reef Aquarium B1
- Boating Lake C2
- Bus Station B1
- Chapel Hill B1
- Chester Rd A3
- Cheviot Rd C1/C2
- Chichester Crescent C2
- Chynance Drive C1
- Chyverton Close C1
- Cliff Rd B2
- Coach Park B2
- Colvreath Rd A3
- Cornwall College Newquay B3
- Council Offices B1
- Crantock St B1
- Crescent, The B1
- Criggar Rocks A3
- Dale Close C3
- Dale Rd C3
- Dane Rd A1
- East St B2
- Edgcumbe Avenue B3
- Edgcumbe Gardens B3
- Eliot Gardens B3
- Elm Close C3
- Ennor's Rd B1
- Fernhill Rd B1
- Fire Station B1
- Fore St B1
- Gannel Rd C2
- Golf Driving Range B3
- Gover Lane B1
- Great Western Beach A2
- Grosvenor Avenue B2
- Harbour A1
- Hawkins Rd C2
- Headleigh Rd B2
- Hilgrove Rd A3/B3
- Holywell Rd B3
- Hope Terrace B1
- Huer's Hut, The A1
- Information Centre B1
- Island Crescent B2
- Jubilee St B1
- Kew Close C3
- Killacourt Cove A2
- King Edward Crescent A1
- Lanhenvor Avenue B2
- Library B1
- Lifeboat Station A1
- Lighthouse B1
- Linden Avenue C2
- Listry Rd C2
- Lusty Glaze Beach A3
- Lusty Glaze Rd A3
- Manor Rd B1
- Marcus Hill B2
- Mayfield Rd B2
- Meadowside C3
- Mellanvrane Lane C2
- Michell Avenue B2
- Miniature Golf Course C3
- Miniature Railway B3
- Mount Wise B1
- Mowhay Close C3
- Narrowcliff A3
- Newquay B2
- Newquay Hospital B2
- Newquay Town Football Ground B1
- Newquay Zoo B3
- North Pier A1
- North Quay Hill A1
- Oakleigh Terrace B2
- Pargolla Rd B2
- Pendragon Crescent C3
- Pengannel Close C1
- Penina Avenue C3
- Pirate's Quest B1
- Police Sta & Courts B2
- Post Office B1/B2
- Quarry Park Rd B3
- Rawley Lane C2
- Reeds Way B1
- Robartes Rd B2
- St Anne's Rd A3
- St Aubyn Crescent B3
- St George's Rd B1
- St John's Rd B1
- St Mary's Rd B1
- St Michael's B1
- St Michael's Rd B1
- St Thomas' Rd B2
- Seymour Avenue B2
- South Pier A1
- South Quay Hill A1
- Superstore B2
- Sweet Briar Crescent C3
- Sydney Rd A1
- Tolcarne Beach A2
- Tolcarne Point A2
- Tolcarne Rd B2
- Tor Rd B2
- Towan Beach A1
- Towan Blystra Rd B3
- Tower Rd A1
- Trebarwith Crescent B2
- Tredour Rd C2
- Treforda Rd C3
- Tregoss Rd B3
- Tregunnel Hill B1/C1
- Tregunnel Saltings C1
- Trelawney Rd B2
- Treloggan Lane C3

Treloggan Rd C3
Trembath Crescent C1
Trenance Avenue B2
Trenance Gardens B2
Trenance Lane C2
Trenance Leisure Park B3
Trenance Rd B2
Trenarth Rd B2
Treninnick Hill C3
Tretherras Rd B3
Trethewey Way C1
Trevemper Rd C2
Ulalia Rd B3
Vivian Close B2
Waterworld B3
Whitegate Rd B3
Wych Hazel Way C3

Newtown 340
Y Drenewydd

Ash Close A3
Back Lane B2
Baptist Chapel B2
Barn Lane A2
Bear Lanes Shopping Centre B2
Beech Close A2
Beechwood Drive A2
Brimmon Close C2
Brimmon Rd C2
Broad St B2
Bryn Bank A1
Bryn Close A2
Bryn Gardens A1
Bryn Lane A1/A2
Bryn Meadows A2
Bryn St A2
Bryn, The A1
Brynglais Avenue A2
Brynglais Close A2
Bus Station B2
Byrnwood Drive A1
Cambrian Bridge B3
Cambrian Gardens B2
Cambrian Way B2
Canal Rd A3
Castle Mound B2
Cedewain C1
Ceiriog C2
Cemetery A3
Church (Remains of) B2
Churchill Drive A3
Cledan B3
Colwyn B3
Commercial St A2
Council Offices B1
Crescent St A1
Cwm Llanfair A2
Dinas B2
Dolafon Rd B3
Dolerw Park B1
Dolfor Rd C1
Fairfield Drive A2
Ffordd Croesawdy B2
Fire Station C1
Frankwell St A2
Frolic St B2
Fron Lane A1
Garden Lane A2
Gas St B2
Glyndwr C1
Golwgydre Lane B2
Gorsedd Circle B1
Hafren C1
Halfpenny Bridge B2
High St B2
Hillside Avenue A3
Hoel Treowen C2
Kerry Rd B3
Ladywell Shopping Ctr B2
Library B1
Llanfair Rd A2
Llanidloes Rd C1
Llys Ifor A2
Lon Cerddyn B1
Lon Helyg C1
Lonesome Lane A3
Long Bridge A2
Lower Canal Rd B3
Maldwyn Leisure Ctr C1
Market B2
Market St B2
Milford Rd B1
Mill Close B2
Miniature Railway ✦ B1
Montgomery County Infirmary (Newtown) A2
Mwyn Fynydd A3
New Church St B2
New Rd B2
Newtown Bypass C3
Newtown Football Gd B1
Newtown Station B2
Oak Tree Avenue A3
Old Kerry Rd B2
Oldbarn Lane A2
Oriel Davies Gallery B2
Park Close B1
Park Lane B1
Park St B2
Park, The B1
Parklands B1
Pavillion Court C1
Plantation Lane C1
Police Station B1
Pont Brynfedw A2
Pool Rd B3
Poplar Rd A3
Post Office B2
Powys C1
Powys Theatre A2
Regent B2
Robert Owen House B1
Robert Owen Mus B2
Rugby Club A3
St David's B2
School Lane A2
Sheaf St B3
Short Bridge St B2
Stone St B2
Superstore B3/C1
Sycamore Drive A2
Textile Museum A2
Town Hall B2
Union St A2
Vastre Industrial Est B3
War Memorial B2
WHSmith Museum B2
Wynfields C1
Y Ffrydd A3

Northampton 340

78 Derngate B3
Abington Square B3
Abington St B3
Alcombe St A3
All Saints' B2
Ambush St B1
Angel St B2
Army Reserve Centre A3
Arundel St A2
Ash St A2
Auctioneers Way C2
Bailiff St A2
Barrack Rd A2
BBOB Rugby FC A1
Beaconsfield Terrace A3
Becket's Park C3
Bedford Rd B3
Billing Rd B3
Brecon St A1
Brewery C2
Bridge St C2
Broad St B2
Burns St A3
Bus Station B2
Campbell St A2
Castle (Site of) B2
Castle St B2
Cattle Market Rd C2
Central Museum & Art Gallery B2
Charles St A3
Cheyne Walk B3
Church Lane A2
Clare St A3
Cloutsham St A3
College St B2
Colwyn Rd A3
Cotton End C2
Countess Rd A1
County Hall B2
Court A2
Craven St A3
Crown & County Courts B3
Denmark Rd B3
Derngate B3
Doddridge Church B2
Drapery, The B2
Duke St A3
Dunster St A3
Earl St A3
Euston Rd C2
Fire Station A3
Foot Meadow B2
Gladstone Rd A1
Gold St B2
Grafton St A2
Gray St A3
Green St B1
Greenwood Rd B1
Greyfriars B2
Grosvenor Centre B2
Grove Rd A3
Guildhall B2
Hampton St A2
Harding Terrace A2
Hazelwood Rd B3
Herbert St B2
Hervey St A3
Hester St A2
Holy Sepulchre A2
Hood St A3
Horse Market B2
Hunter St A3
Information Centre B2
Kettering Rd A3
Kingswell St B2
Lady's Lane B2
Leicester St A2
Leslie Rd A2
Library B3
Lorne Rd A2
Lorry Park A1
Louise Rd A2
Lower Harding St A2
Lower Hester St A2
Lower Mounts B3
Lower Priory St A2
Main Rd C1
Marefair B2
Market Square B2
Marlboro Rd B1
Marriott St A2
Millers Meadow A1
Military Rd A3
Mounts Baths Leisure Centre A3
Nene Valley Retail Pk C1
New South Bridge Rd C2
Northampton General Hospital (A&E) B3
Northampton Marina C3
Northampton Sta B1
Northcote St A2
Nunn Mills Rd C3
Old Towcester Rd C2
Overstone Rd A3
Pembroke Rd A1
Penn Court C2
Police Station B3
Post Office A1/B3
Quorn Way A2
Ransome Rd C3
Regent Square A2
Ridings, The B3
Robert St A2
Royal & Derngate Theatres B3
St Andrew's Rd B1
St Andrew's St A2
St Edmund's Rd B3
St George's St A2
St Giles B3
St Giles St B3
St Giles' Terrace B3
St James Park Rd B1
St James Rd B1
St James Retail Park C1
St James' Mill Rd B1
St James' Mill Rd East C1
St Leonard's Rd C2
St Mary's St B2
St Michael's Rd A3
St Peter's B2
St Peter's Way Shopping Precinct B2
St Peter's Way B2
Salisbury St A2
Scarletwell St B2
Semilong Rd A2
Sheep St B2
Sol Central (Leisure Centre) B2
Somerset St A3
South Bridge C2
Southfield Avenue C2
Spencer Bridge Rd A1
Spencer Rd A3
Spring Gardens B3
Spring Lane B2
Superstore C2
Swan St B3
Tintern Avenue A1
Towcester Rd C2
Univ of Northampton (Waterside Campus) C3
Upper Bath St B2
Upper Mounts A2
Victoria Park A1
Victoria Promenade B2
Victoria Rd B3
Victoria St A2
Wellingborough Rd B3
West Bridge B1
York Rd B3

Norwich 341

Albion Way C3
All Saints Green C2
Anchor St A3
Anglia Square A2
Argyle St C3
Arts Centre B1
Ashby St C2
Assembly House B1
Bank Plain B2
Barker St A1
Barn Rd A1
Barrack St A3
Ber St C2
Bethel St B1
Bishop Bridge A3
Bishopbridge Rd A3
Bishopgate A3
Blackfriars St A2
Botolph St A2
Bracondale C3
Brazen Gate C2
Bridewell Museum B2
Brunswick Rd C1
Bull Close Rd A2
Bus Station C2
Calvert St A2
Cannell Green A3
Carrow Rd C3
Castle & Museum B2
Castle Mall B2
Castle Meadow B2
Cathedral ✝ B2
Cathedral (RC) ✝ B1
Cathedral Retail Park A1
Cattlemarket St B2
Chantry Place C1
Chantry Rd C1
Chapel Loke C2
Chapelfield East B1
Chapelfield Gardens B1
Chapelfield North B1
Chapelfield Rd B1
Cinema City B2
City Hall ✦ B1
City Rd C2
City Wall C1/C3
Close, The B2/B3
Colegate A2
Coslany St B1
Cow Hill B1
Cow Tower A3
Cowgate A2
Crown & Magistrates' Courts A2
Dragon Hall Heritage Centre C3
Duke St A1
Edward St A2
Elm Hill B2
Erpingham Gate ✦ B2
Fishergate A2
Forum, The B1
Foundry Bridge B3
Fye Bridge A2
Garden St C2
Gas Hill B3
Gentlemans Walk B2
Grapes Hill B1
Great Hospital Halls, The A3
Grove Avenue C1
Grove Rd C1
Guildhall ✦ B1
Gurney Rd A3
Hall Rd C2
Heathgate A3
Heigham St A1
Hollywood A2
Horn's Lane C2
Hungate Medieval Art ✦ B2
Ipswich Rd C1
ITV Anglia C3
James Stuart Gdns B3
King St B2
King St C3
Koblenz Avenue C3
Leisure Centre A3
Library B1
London St B2
Lower Clarence Rd B3
Maddermarket B1
Magdalen St A2
Mariners Lane C2
Market B2
Market Avenue B2
Mountergate B3
Mousehold St A3
Newmarket Rd C1
Norfolk St C1
Norwich City FC C3
Norwich Gallery B2
Norwich School ✦ B2
Norwich Station B3
Oak St A1
Odeon C3
Palace St A2
Pitt St A1
Playhouse B2
Police Station B1
Post Office A2/B2/B3/C1
Pottergate B1
Prince of Wales Rd B2
Princes St B2
Pull's Ferry ✦ B3
Puppet Theatre A2
Queen St B2
Queens Rd C2
Recorder Rd B3
Riverside Entertainment Centre C3
Riverside Leisure Ctr C3
Riverside Rd B3
Riverside Retail Park C3
Rosary Rd B3
Rose Lane B2
Rouen Rd C2
St Andrews St B2
St Augustines St A1
St Benedicts St B1
St Crispins Road A1
St Ethelbert's Gate ✦ B2
St Faiths Lane B3
St Georges St A2
St Giles St B1
St James Close A3
St Julians C2
St Leonards Rd B3
St Martin's Lane A1
St Peter Mancroft B2
St Peters St B1
St Stephens Rd C1
St Stephens St C1
Shopmobility C1
Silver Rd A2
Silver St A2
Southwell Rd C2
St. Andrew's & Blackfriars' Hall ✦ B2
Strangers' Hall B1
Superstore C2
Surrey St C2
Sussex St A1
Theatre Royal B1
Theatre St B1
Thorn Lane C2
Thorpe Rd B3
Tombland B2
Union St C1
Vauxhall St B1
Victoria St C1
Vue B2
Walpole St B1
Waterfront, The C3
Wensum St A2
Wessex St C1
Westwick St A1
Wherry Rd C3
Whitefriars A2
Willow Lane B1

Nottingham 341

Abbotsford Drive A3
Addison St A1
Albert Hall ✦ B1
Alfred St Central A3
Alfreton Rd B1
All Saints St A1
Annesley Grove A2
Arboretum A1
Arboretum St A1
Arthur St A1
Arts Theatre B3
Ashforth St A3
Balmoral Rd A1
Barker Gate B3
Bath St B3
BBC Nottingham C3
Beacon Hill Rise B3
Belgrave Rooms B1
Bellar Gate B3
Belward St B3
Brewhouse Yard C2
Broad Marsh Bus Sta C2
Broad St B3
Brook St B3
Burns St A1
Burton St B2
Bus Station A2
Canal St C2
Carlton St B3
Carrington St C2
Castle C2
Castle Boulevard C1
Castle Gate C2
Castle Meadow Rd C1
Castle Meadow Retail Pk C1
Castle Rd C2
Castle Wharf C2
Cavendish Rd East C1
Cemetery A1/B1
Chaucer St B1
Cheapside B2
Church Rd A3
City Link C3
City of Caves ✦ C2
Clarendon St B1
Cliff Rd C3
Clumber Rd East C1
Clumber St B2
College St B1
Collin St C2
Contemporary C3
Conway Close A2
Cornerhouse, The B2
Council House B2
Cranbrook St B3
Cranmer St A2
Cromwell St B1
Curzon St B3
Derby Rd B1
Dryden St A2
Exchange Centre, The B2
Fishpond Drive C1
Fletcher Gate B3
Forest Rd East A1
Forest Rd West A1
Friar Lane C2
Gedling Grove A1
Gedling St B3
George St B3
Gill St A2
Glasshouse St B2
Goldsmith St B2
Goose Gate B3
Great Freeman St A2
Guildhall B2
Hamilton Drive C1
Hampden St A1
Heathcote St B3
High Pavement C3
High School A1
HM Revenue & Customs C2
Holles Crescent C1
Hope Drive C1
Hungerhill Rd A3
Huntingdon Drive C1
Huntingdon St A2
Information Centre B2
Instow Rise A3
International Community Centre A2
Kent St B3
King St B2
Lace Market B3
Lace Mkt Theatre C3
Lamartine St B3
Leisure Centre C3
Lenton Rd C1
Lewis Close A3
Lincoln St B2
London Rd C3
Long Row B2
Low Pavement C2
Lower Parliament St B3
Magistrates' Court C2
Maid Marian Way B2
Mansfield Rd A2/B2
Middle Hill C2
Milton St B2
Mount St B2
National Ice Centre & Motorpoint Arena C3
National Justice Museum C3
Newcastle Drive B1
Newstead Grove A2
North Sherwood St A2
Nottingham Arena C3
Nottingham Cath ✝ B1
Nottingham College C3
Nottingham Station C3
Nottingham Trent University A2/B2
Old Market Square B2
Oliver St A1
Park Drive C1
Park Row C1
Park Terrace B1
Park Valley C1
Park, The C1
Peas Hill Rd A3
Peel St A1
Pelham St B2
Peveril Drive C1
Plantagenet St A3
Playhouse Theatre B1
Plumptre St C3
Police Station B1/B2
Poplar St C3
Portland Rd B1
Post Office B2
Queen's Rd C3
Raleigh St A1
Regent St B1
Rick St B3
Robin Hood St B3
Robin Hood Statue ✦ C2
Ropewalk, The B1
Royal Centre B2
Royal Children Inn C2
Royal Concert Hall B2
St Ann's Hill Rd A2
St Ann's Way A2
St Ann's Well Rd A3
St James' St B2
St Mark's St B3
St Mary's Rest Garden B3
St Mary's Gate B3
St Nicholas C2
St Peter's C2
St Peter's Gate B2
Salutation Inn C2
Shakespeare St B2
Shelton St A2
Shopmobility A2
South Parade B2
South Rd C1
South Sherwood St B2
Station Street C3
Stoney St B3
Talbot St B1
Tattershall Drive C1
Tennis Drive B1
Tennyson St A1
Theatre Royal B2
Trent St C3
Trent University B2
Union Rd B3
Upper Parliament St B2
Victoria Centre B2
Victoria Leisure Ctr B3
Victoria Park B3
Victoria St B2
Walter St A1
Warser Gate B3
Watkin St A2
Waverley St A1
Wheeler Gate B2
Wilford Rd C2
Wilford St C2
Wollaton St B1
Woodborough Rd A2
Woolpack Lane B3
Ye Old Trip to Jerusalem ✦ C2
York St A2

Oban 341

Aird's Crescent B2
Albany St B2
Albert Lane A2
Albert Rd A2
Alma Crescent B1
Ambulance Station C2
Angus Terrace C3
Ardconnel Rd A2
Ardconnel Terrace B2
Argyll Square B2
Argyll St B2
Atlantis Leisure Ctr A2
Bayview Rd A1
Benvoulin Rd A2
Bowling Green A2
Breadalbane St A2
Bus Station B2
Campbell St B2
College B2
Colonsay Terrace C3
Combie St B2
Corran Brae A1
Corran Esplanade A1/A2
Corran Halls, The A2
Court B2
Crannaig-a-Mhinisteir B1
Crannog Lane C2
Croft Avenue A2
Dalintart Drive C3
Dalriach Rd A2
Distillary ✦ B2
Drummore Rd C2
Duncraggan Rd A2
Dunollie Rd A2
Dunuaran Rd B1
Feochan Grove C3
Ferry Terminal B1
Gallanach Rd B1
George St A2
Glencruitten Drive C3
Glencruitten Rd B3
Glenmore Rd C1
Glenshellach Rd C1
Glenshellach Terrace B2
Hazeldean Crescent A3
High St B2
Hill St B2
Industrial Estate C2
Information Centre B2
Islay Rd C3
Jacob's Ladder ✦ B2
Jura Rd C3
Knipoch Place C3
Laurel Crescent A2
Laurel Rd A2/A3
Library B1
Lifeboat Station B1
Lighthouse Pier B1
Lismore Crescent A2
Lochavullin Drive B2
Lochavullin Rd C2
Lochside St B2
Longsdale Crescent A3
Longsdale Rd A2/A3
Longsdale Terrace A3
Lunga Rd C3
Lynn Rd C2
Market St B2
McCaig Rd C3
McCaig's Tower ✦ A2
Mill Lane C2
Miller Rd C2
Millpark Avenue C2
Millpark Rd C2
Mossfield Avenue B3
Mossfield Drive B3
Mossfield Stadium B3
Nant Drive C3
Nelson Rd C2
North Pier B2
Nursery Lane A2
Oban B2
Oban Phoenix A2
Police Station B2
Polvinister Rd B3
Post Office A2/B2
Pulpit Drive C1
Pulpit Hill C1
Pulpit Hill Viewpoint ✦ B1
Quarry Rd C2
Queen's Park Place B2
Railway Quay B1
Retail Park B2
Rockfield Rd B2
St Columba's ✝ A1
St John's ✝ A2
Scalpay Terrace C3
Shore St B1
Shuna Terrace C3
Sinclair Drive C2
Soroba Rd B2/C2
South Pier B1
Stevenson St B2
Tweedale St B2
Ulva Rd C2
Villa Rd B1
War & Peace A2

Oxford 341

Adelaide St A1
Albert St A1
All Souls (College) B2
Ashmolean Mus B2
Balliol (College) B2
Banbury Rd A2
Bate Collection of Musical Instruments C2
Beaumont St B1
Becket St B1
Blackhall Rd A2
Blue Boar St B2
Bodleian Library B2
Botanic Garden B3
Brasenose (College) B2
Brewer St C2
Broad St B2
Burton-Taylor Theatre B2
Bus Station B1
Canal St A1
Cardigan St A1
Carfax Tower B2
Castle B1
Castle St B1
Catte St B2
Cemetery C1
Christ Church (Coll) B2
Christ Church Cath ✝ C2
Christ Church Mdw C2
City of Oxford College C1
Clarendon Centre B2
Cornmarket St B2
Corpus Christi (Coll) B2
County Hall B1
Covered Market B2
Cowley Place C3
Cranham St A1
Cranham Terrace A1
Cricket Ground B1
Crown & County Courts C2
Deer Park B3
Exeter (College) B2
Fire Station B1
Folly Bridge C2
George St B1
Great Clarendon St A1
Harris Manchester (College) B2
Hart St A1
Hertford (College) B2
High St B3
Hollybush Row B1
Holywell St B2
Hythe Bridge St B1
Ice Rink C1
Jericho St A1
Jesus (College) B2
Jowett Walk B3
Juxon St A1
Keble (College) A2
Keble Rd A2
Library B2
Linacre (College) A3
Lincoln (College) B2
Little Clarendon St A1
Longwall St B3
Magdalen (College) B3
Magdalen Bridge B2
Magdalen St B2
Magistrate's Court C2
Manor Rd B3
Mansfield (College) A2
Mansfield Rd A3
Market B1
Marlborough Rd C2
Martyrs' Memorial ✦ B2
Merton (College) B3
Merton Field B3
Merton St B2
Mus of Modern Art B2
Museum of Oxford B2
Museum Rd A2
New College (College) B3
New Inn Hall St B2
New Rd B1
New Theatre B2
Norfolk St C1
Nuffield (College) B1
Observatory A1
Observatory St A1
Odeon B1/B2
Old Fire Station B1
Old Greyfriars St C2
Oriel (College) B2
Oxford Castle & Prison B1
Oxford Station B1
Oxford University Research Centres A1
Oxpens Rd C1
Paradise Square C1
Paradise St B1
Park End St B1
Parks Rd A2/B2
Pembroke (College) C2
Phoenix A1
Picture Gallery C2
Plantation Rd A1
Playhouse B2
Police Station C2
Post Office A1/B2
Pusey St B1
Queen's (College) B3
Queen's Lane B3
Radcliffe Camera B2
Rewley Rd B1
Richmond Rd A1
Rose Lane B3
Ruskin (College) B1
Said Business School B1
St Aldates C2
St Anne's (College) A1
St Antony's (College) A1
St Bernard's Rd A1
St Catherine's (Coll) B3
St Cross Building A3
St Cross Rd A3
St Edmund Hall (Coll) B3
St Giles St A2
St Hilda's (College) C3
St John St B2
St John's (College) B2
St Mary the Virgin B2
St Michael at the Northgate B2
St Peter's (College) B1
St Thomas St B1
Science Area A2
Science Museum B2
Sheldonian Theatre B2
Somerville (College) A1
South Parks Rd A2
Speedwell St C2
Sports Ground C3
Thames St C2
Town Hall B2
Trinity (College) B2
Turl St B2
University Coll (Coll) B3
Univ Natural History Mus & Pitt Rivers Mus A2
University Parks A2
Wadham (College) B2
Walton Crescent A1
Walton St A1
Western Rd C2
Westgate C2
Woodstock Rd A1
Worcester (College) B1

Perth 341

AK Bell Library B2
Abbot Crescent C1
Abbot St C1
Albany Terrace A1
Albert Monument A3
Alexandra St B2
Atholl St A2
Balhousie Avenue A2
Balhousie Castle & Black Watch Museum A2
Balhousie St A2
Ballantine Place A1
Barossa Place A2
Barossa St A2
Barrack St A2
Bell's Sports Centre A2
Bellwood B3
Blair St B1
Burn Park C1
Bus Station B2
Caledonian Rd B2
Canal Crescent B2
Canal St B3
Cavendish Avenue C1
Charles St B2
Charlotte Place A2
Charlotte St A3
Church St A1
City Hall B3
Club House C3
Clyde Place C1
Coach Park C3
Commercial St A3
Concert Hall ✦ B3
Council Chambers B3
County Place B2
Court B3
Craigie Place C2
Crieff Rd A1
Croft Park C2
Cross St B2
Darnhall Crescent C1
Darnhall Drive C1
Dewars Centre B1
Dundee Rd B3
Dunkeld Rd A1
Earl's Dykes B1
Edinburgh Rd C3
Elibank St B1
Fair Maid's House ✦ A3
Fergusson B3
Feus Rd A1
Fire Station A1
Foundary Lane A2
Friar St C1
George St B3
Glamis Place C1
Glasgow Rd B1
Glenearn Rd C2
Glover St B1/C1
Golf Course A2
Gowrie St A3
Gray St B1
Graybank Rd B1
Greyfriars Burial Gd B3
Hay St A2
High St B2/B3
Inchaffray St A1
Industrial/Retail Park B1
Information Centre B2
Isla Rd A3
James St B2
Keir St A3
King Edward St B3
King James VI Golf Course C3
King St B2
Kings Place C2
Kinnoull Causeway B2
Kinnoull St B2
Knowelea Place C1
Knowelea Terrace C1
Ladeside Bsns Centre A1
Leisure Pool B1
Leonard St B2
Lickley St B2
Lochie Brae A3
Long Causeway A1
Low St A2
Main St A3
Marshall Place C3
Melville St A2
Mill St B3
Milne St B2
Murray Crescent C1
Murray St B2
Needless Rd C1
New Rd B2
North Inch A3
North Methven St A2
Park Place C1
Perth B2
Perth Bridge A3
Perth Business Park B1
Perth Museum & Art Gallery B3
Perth Station C2
Pickletulllum Rd B1
Pitheavlis Crescent C1
Playhouse B2
Police Station A2
Pomarium St B2
Post Office B2/C2
Princes St B3
Priory Place C2
Queen St C1
Queen's Bridge B3
Riggs Rd B1
Riverside B3
Riverside Park B3
Rodney Gardens B3
Rose Terrace A2
St Catherine's Rd A1/A2
St Catherine's Retail Park A1
St John St B3
St John's Kirk B3
St John's Shopping Ctr B2
St Leonards Bridge C2
St Ninians Cathedral ✝ A2
Scott Monument C2
Scott St B2
Sheriff Court B3
Shore Rd C3
Skate Park C3
South Inch C2
South Inch Bsns Ctr C3
South Inch Park C2
South Inch View C2
South Methven St B2
South St B3
South William St B2
Stables, The A1
Stanners, The B3
Stormont St A2
Strathmore St A3
Stuart Avenue C1
Superstore B1/B2
Tay St B3
Union Lane A2
Victoria St B2
Watergate B3
Wellshill Cemetery A1
West Bridge St A3
West Mill St B2
Whitefriers Crescent B1
Whitefriers St B1
Wilson St C1
Windsor Terrace C1
Woodside Crescent C1
York Place B2
Young St C1

Peterborough 341

Athletics Arena B3
Bishop's Palace B2
Bishop's Rd B2/B3
Boongate A3
Bourges Boulevard A1
Bourges Retail Pk B1/B2
Bridge House (Council Offices) C2
Bridge St B2
Bright St A1
Broadway A2
Broadway A2
Brook St A2
Burghley Rd A2
Bus Station B2
Cavendish St A3
Charles St A3
Church St B2
Church Walk A2
Cobden Avenue A1
Cobden St A1
Cowgate B2
Craig St A2
Crawthorne Rd A2
Cromwell Rd A1
Dickens St A3
Eastfield Rd A3
Eastgate B3
East Station Road C2
Fire Station A1
Fletton Avenue C2
Frank Perkins Parkway C3
Geneva St A2
George St C1
Gladstone St A1
Glebe Rd C2
Gloucester Rd C3
Granby St B3
Grove St C1
Guildhall B2
Hadrians Court C3
Hawksbill Way C2
Henry St A2
Hereward Cross (shopping) B2

Hereward Rd B3
Information Centre B2
Jubilee St C1
Kent Rd B1
Key Theatre C2
Kirkwood Close B1
Lea Gardens B1
Library A2
Lincoln Rd A2
London Rd C2
Long Causeway B2
Lower Bridge St C2
Magistrates Court B2
Manor House St A2
Mayor's Walk A1
Midland Rd A1
Monument St A2
Morris St A3
Mus & Art Gallery B2
Nene Valley Railway C1
New Rd A2
New Rd C1
Northminster A2
Old Customs House C2
Oundle Rd C1
Padholme Rd A3
Palmerston Rd C1
Park Rd A2
Passport Office B2
Peterborough Cath B2
Peterborough Nene Valley C1
Peterborough Sta B1
Police Station B2
Post Office A3/B2
Priestgate B2
Queen's Walk C2
Queensgate Centre B2
Railworld Wildlife Haven C1
Regional Fitness & Swimming Centre B3
River Lane B1
Rivergate Shopping Centre B2
Riverside Mead C3
Russell St A1
St John's B2
St John's St A3
St Marks St A2
St Peter's Rd B2
Saxon Rd A3
Spital Bridge A1
Stagshaw Drive C3
Star Rd B3
Superstore B1
Thorpe Lea Rd B1
Thorpe Rd B1
Thorpe's Lea Rd B1
Tower St A2
Town Hall B2
Viersen Platz B2
Vineyard Rd B3
Wake Rd B3
Wellington St A3
Wentworth St B2
Westgate B2
Weston Homes Stadium (Peterborough United FC) The C2
Whalley St A3
Wharf Rd C1
Whitsed St A3
YMCA A3

Plymouth 341

Alma Rd A1
Anstis St B1
Armada Shopping Ctr B2
Armada St A3
Armada Way B2
Arts Centre B2
Athenaeum B1
Athenaeum St C1
Barbican C3
Barbican C3
Baring St A3
Bath St B1
Beaumont Park B3
Beaumont Rd B3
Black Friars Gin Distillery C2
Box, The B2
Breton Side B3
Coach Station B2
Castle St C3
Cathedral (RC) B1
Cecil St B1
Central Park A1
Central Park Avenue A2
Charles Church B3
Charles Cross B3
Charles St B2
Cineworld B2
Citadel Rd C2
Citadel Rd East C2
Civic Centre B2
Cliff Rd C1
Clifton Place A3
Cobourg St A2
College of Art B2
Continental Ferry Port B1
Cornwall St B2
Crescent, The B1
Dale Rd A2
Deptford Place A3
Derry Avenue A2
Derry's Cross B1
Drake Circus B2
Drake Circus Shopping Centre B2
Drake Statue C2
Eastlake St B2
Ebrington St B3
Elizabethan House C3
Elliot St C1
Endsleigh Place A2
Exeter St B3
Fire Station A3
Fish Quay C3
Gibbons St A3
Glen Park Avenue A2
Grand Parade C1
Great Western Rd C1
Greenbank Rd A3
Greenbank Terrace A3
Guildhall B2
Hampton St B3
Harwell St B1
Hill Park Crescent A3
Hoe Approach B2
Hoe Rd C2
Hoe, The C2
Hoegate St C2
Houndiscombe Rd A2
Information Centre C3
James St A2
Kensington Rd A3
King St B1
Lambhay Hill C3
Leigham St C1
Library B2
Lipson Rd A3/B3
Lockyer St C2
Lockyers Quay C3
Madeira Rd C2
Marina B3
Market B1
Market Avenue B1
Martin St B1
Mayflower St B2
Mayflower Stone & Steps C3
Mayflower C3
Merchant's House B2
Millbay Rd B1
National Marine Aquarium C3
Neswick St B1
New George St B2
New St C3
North Cross A2
North Hill A3
North Quay B2
North Rd East A2
North Rd West A1
North St B3
Notte St B2
Octagon, The B1
Octagon St B1
Pennycomequick A1
Pier St C1
Plymouth Naval Memorial C2
Plymouth Pavilions B1
Plymouth Station A2
Police Station B3
Post Office B2,C1,C3
Princess St B2
Promenade, The C2
Prysten House B2
Queen Anne's Battery Watersports Centre C3
Radford Rd C1
Regent St B3
Rope Walk C3
Royal Citadel C2
Royal Parade B2
Royal Theatre B2
Russell Place A1
St Andrew's B2
St Andrew's Cross B2
St Andrew's St B2
St Lawrence Rd A2
Saltash Rd A2
Shopmobility B2
Smeaton's Tower C2
Southern Terrace A3
Southside St C2
Stuart Rd A1
Sutherland Rd A2
Sutton Rd B3
Sydney St A1
Teats Hill Rd C3
Tothill Avenue B3
Union St B1
Univ of Plymouth A2
Vauxhall St B2/3
Victoria Park A1
Walker Terrace C1
West Hoe Rd C1
Western Approach B1
Whittington St A1
Wyndham St B1

Poole 341

Ambulance Station A3
Baiater Gardens C2
Baiter Park C3
Ballard Close C2
Ballard Rd C2
Bay Hog Lane B1
BMI The Harbour Hospital A3
Bridge Approach C1
Bus Station B2
Castle St B2
Catalina Drive B3
Chapel Lane B2
Church St B1
Cinnamon Lane B1
Colborne Close B3
Dear Hay Lane B2
Denmark Lane A3
Denmark Rd A3
Dolphin Centre B2
East St B2
Elizabeth Rd A3
Emerson Rd B2
Ferry Rd C1
Ferry Terminal C1
Fire Station A2
Freightliner Terminal C1
Furnell Rd B3
Garland Rd A3
Green Rd B2
Heckford Lane A3
Heckford Rd A3
High St B2
High St North A3
Hill St B2
Holes Bay Rd A1
Hospital (A&E) A3
Information Centre C2
Kingland Rd B3
Kingston Rd A3
Labrador Drive C3
Lagland St B2
Lander Close C3
Lighthouse, Poole Centre for the Arts B3
Longfleet Rd A3
Maple Rd A3
Market Close B2
Market St B2
Mount Pleasant Rd B3
New Harbour Rd C1
New Harbour Rd South C1
New Harbour Rd West C1
New Orchard B1
New Quay Rd C1
New St B2
Newfoundland Drive B2
North St B2
Old Lifeboat C2
Old Orchard B2
Parish Rd A3
Park Lake Rd B3
Parkstone Rd A3
Perry Gardens B2
Pitwines Close B2
Police Station A2
Poole Central Library B2
Poole Lifting Bridge C1
Poole Park B2
Poole Station A2
Poole Museum C1
Post Office B2
Quay, The C2
RNLI College B1
St John's Rd A3
St Margaret's Rd A2
St Mary's Maternity Unit A3
St Mary's Rd A3
Seldown Bridge B3
Seldown Lane B3
Seldown Rd B3
Serpentine Rd A2
Scaplen's Court C1
Shaftesbury Rd A3
Skinner St B2
Slipway B1
Stanley Rd C2
Sterte Avenue A2
Sterte Avenue West A1
Sterte Close A2
Sterte Esplanade A2
Sterte Rd A2
Strand St C2
Superstore B3
Swimming Pool B3
Taverner Close B3
Thames St B1
Towngate Bridge B2
Twin Sails Bridge B1
Vallis Close C3
Waldren Close B3
West Quay B1
West Quay Rd B1
West St B1
West View Rd A2
Whatleigh Close B2
Wimborne Rd A3

Portsmouth 341

Action Stations C1
Admiralty Rd A1
Alfred Rd A2
Anglesea Rd B2
Arundel St B3
Aspex B1
Bishop St A2
Broad St C1
Buckingham House C2
Burnaby Rd B2
Bus Station B1
Camber Dock C1
Cambridge Rd B2
Car Ferry to Isle of Wight B1
Cascades Shopping Centre A3
Castle Rd C3
Civic Offices B3
Clarence Pier C2
College St B1
Commercial Rd A3
Cottage Grove B3
Cross St A1
Cumberland St A2
Duisburg Way C2
Durham St A3
East St B1
Edinburgh Rd A2
Elm Grove C3
Emirates Spinnaker Tower B1
Governor's Grn C1
Great Southsea St C3
Green Rd B3
Greetham St B3
Grosvenor St B3
Groundlings A2
Grove Rd North C3
Grove Rd South C3
Guildhall B3
Guildhall Walk B3
Gunwharf Quays Designer Outlet B1
Gunwharf Rd B1
Hambrook St C2
Hampshire Terrace B2
Hanover St A1
Hard, The B1
High St C2
HM Naval Base A1
HMS Nelson (Royal Naval Barracks) A2
HMS Monitor M.33 A1
HMS Victory A1
HMS Warrior A1
Hovercraft Terminal C2
Hyde Park Rd B3
Information Ctr A1/B3
Isambard Brunel Rd B3
Isle of Wight Car Ferry Terminal B1
Kent Rd C3
Kent St A2
King St B3
King's Rd C3
King's Terrace C2
Lake Rd A3
Law Courts B3
Library B3
Long Curtain Rd C2
Marina B1
Market Way A3
Marmion Rd C3
Mary Rose A1
Middle St B3
Millennium Promenade Walk B1/C1
Museum Rd B2
National Museum of the Royal Navy A1
Naval Recreation Gd C2
Nightingale Rd C3
Norfolk St B3
North St A2
Osborne Rd C3
Paradise St A3
Park Rd B2
Passenger Catamaran to Isle of Wight B1
Passenger Ferry to Gosport B1
Pelham Rd C3
Pembroke Gardens C2
Pier Rd C2
Point Battery C1
Police Station B3
Portsmouth & Southsea Station A3
Portsmouth Harbour Station B1
Portsmouth Historic Dockyard A1
Portsmouth Museum & Art Gallery B2
Post Office A1/A3/B3
Queen St A1
Queen's Crescent C3
Ravelin Park B2
Register Office B2
Round Tower C1
Royal Garrison Church C1
St Edward's Rd C3
St George's Rd B2
St George's Square B1
St George's Way B2
St James's Rd B3
St James's St A2
St John's Cath (RC) A3
St Thomas's Cath C1
St Thomas's St B2
Shopmobility A3/B1
Somers Rd B3
Southsea Common C2
Southsea Terrace C2
Square Tower C1
Station St A3
Town Fortifications C1
Unicorn Rd A2
United Services Recreation Ground B2
University of Portsmouth A2/B2
Univ of Portsmouth B3
Upper Arundel St A3
Victoria Avenue C2
Victoria Park A2
Victory Gate A1
Vue B1
Warblington St B1
Western Parade C2
White Hart Rd C1
Winston Churchill Ave B3

Preston 342

Adelphi St A2
Anchor Court B3
Aqueduct St A1
Ardee Rd C1
Arthur St B2
Ashton St A1
Avenham Lane B3
Avenham Park C3
Avenham Rd B3
Avenham St B3
Bairstow St B3
Balderstone Rd C1
Beamont Drive A1
Beech St South C2
Bird St C1
Bow Lane B2
Brieryfield Rd A1
Broadgate C1
Brook St A2
Bus Station A3
Butler St B2
Cannon St B3
Carlton St A1
Chaddock St B3
Channel Way B1
Chapel St B3
Christ Church St B2
Christian Rd B2
Cold Bath St A2
Coleman Court C1
Connaught Rd C2
Corporation St A2/B2
County Hall B2
Cricket Ground C2
Croft St A1
Cross St B3
Crown Court A3
Crown St A3
East Cliff C3
East Cliff Rd B3
Edward St A2
Elizabeth St A3
Euston St B1
Fishergate B2/B3
Fishergate Hill B2
Fishergate Shopping Centre B2
Fitzroy St B1
Fleetwood St A1
Friargate A3
Fylde Rd A1/A2
Gerrard St B2
Glover's Court B3
Good St B2
Grafton St B2
Great George St A3
Great Shaw St A3
Greenbank St A2
Guild Way B1
Guild Hall & Charter B3
Guildhall St B3
Harrington St A2
Harris Museum B3
Hartington Rd B1
Hasset Close C2
Heatley St B2
Hind St C2
Information Centre B3
Kilruddery Rd C1
Lancashire Archives B2
Lancaster Rd A3/B3
Latham St B3
Lauderdale St C2
Lawson St A3
Leighton St A2
Leyland Rd C1
Library A1
Library B3
Liverpool Rd C1
Lodge St B2
Lune St B3
Magistrate's Court A3
Main Sprit West B3
Maresfield Rd C1
Market St West A3
Marsh Lane B1/B2
Maudland Bank A2
Maudland Rd A2
Meadow Court C2
Meath Rd C1
Miller Arcade B3
Miller Park C3
Moor Lane A3
Mount St B3
North Rd A3
North St A3
Northcote Rd B1
Old Milestones B1
Old Tram Rd C3
Pedder St A1/A2
Peel St A2
Penwortham Bridge C2
Penwortham New Bridge C1
Pitt St B2
Playhouse A3
Police Station A3
Portway B1
Post Office B3
Preston Station B2
Retail Park B2
Ribble Bank St B2
Ribble Viaduct C2
Ribblesdale Place B3
Ringway B3
River Parade C1
Riverside C2
St George's Shopping Centre B3
St Georges B3
St John's Minster B3
St Johns Shopping Ctr A3
St Mark's Rd A1
St Walburges A1
Salisbury Rd B1
Sessions House B3
Snow Hill A3
South End C2
South Meadow Lane C2
Spa Rd B1
Sports Ground C2
Strand Rd B1
Syke St B3
Talbot Rd B1
Taylor St C1
Tithebarn St A3
Town Hall B3
Tulketh Brow A1
University of Central Lancashire A2
Valley Rd C1
Victoria St A2
Walker St A3
Walton's Parade B2
Warwick St A3
Wellfield Bsns Park A1
Wellfield Rd A1
Wellington St A1
West Cliff C2
West Strand A1
Winckley Rd C1
Winckley Square B3
Wolseley Rd C2

Reading 342

Abbey Ruins B2
Abbey Square B2
Abbey St B2
Abbot's Walk B2
Acacia Rd C2
Addington Rd C3
Addison Rd A1
Allcroft Rd C3
Alpine St C2
Baker St B1
Berkeley Avenue C1
Bridge St B1
Brigham Rd A1
Broad St B1
Broad Street Mall B1
Carey St B1
Castle Hill C1
Castle St B1
Causeway, The A3
Caversham Rd A1
Christchurch Meadows A2
Civic Offices B1
Coley Hill C1
Coley Place C1
Craven Rd C3
Crown St C2
De Montfort Rd A1
Denmark Rd C3
Duke St B2
East St B2
Edgehill St C2
Eldon Rd B3
Eldon Terrace B3
Elgar Rd C1
Erleigh Rd C3
Field Rd C1
Fire Station A1
Fobney St B1
Forbury Gardens B2
Forbury Rd B2
Forbury Retail Park B2
Francis St C1
Friar St B1
Garrard St B1
Gas Works Rd B3
George St A2
Greyfriars B1
Grove, The B2
Gun St B1
Henry St C1
Hexagon Theatre, The B1
Hill's Meadow A2
Howard St B1
Inner Distribution Rd B1
Katesgrove Lane C1
Kenavon Drive B2
Kendrick Rd C2
King's Mdw Rec Gd A2
King's Rd B2
Library B2
London Rd C3
London St B2
Lynmouth Rd A1
Magistrate's Court B1
Market Place B2
Mill Lane B2
Mill Rd A2
Minster St B1
Morgan Rd C3
Mount Pleasant C2
Museum of English Rural Life (MERL) C3
Napier Rd A2
Newark St C2
Newport Rd A1
Oracle Shopping Centre, The B1
Orts Rd B3
Oxford Road B1
Pell St C1
Post Office B1
Queen Victoria St B1
Queen's Rd A2
Queen's Rd B2
Randolph Rd A1
Reading Bridge A2
Reading College B3
Reading Station A1
Redlands Rd C3
Riverside Museum B3
Rose Kiln Lane C1
Royal Berkshire Medical Museum C3
Royal Berks Hospital (A&E) C3
St Giles C2
St Laurence B2
St Mary's B1
St Mary's Butts B1
St Saviour's Rd C1
Send Rd A3
Sherman Rd C2
Sidmouth St B2
Silver St C2
South St B2
South St Arts Ctr B2
Southampton St C2
Station Rd B1
Superstore A3
Swansea Rd A1
Thames Lido A2
Tudor Road A1
University of Reading C3
Valpy St B2
Vastern Rd A1
Vue B2
Waldeck St C2
Watlington St B3
West St B1
Whitby Drive C3
Wolseley St C1
York Rd A1
Zinzan St B1

St Andrews 342

Abbey St B2
Abbey Walk B3
Abbotsford Crescent A1
Albany Park C3
Allan Robertson Drive C2
Ambulance Station C1
Anstruther Rd C3
Argyle St B1
Auld Burn Rd B2
Bassaguard Ind Est B1
Bell St B2
Blackfriars Chapel (Ruins) B2
Boase Avenue B2
Braid Crescent C3
Brewster Place C3
Bridge St B1
British Golf Mus A1
Broomfaulds Avenue C1
Bruce Embankment A1
Bruce St C2
Bus Station A1
Byre Theatre B2
Canongate C1
Cathedral and Priory (Ruins) B3
Cemetery B3
Chamberlain St C1
Church St B2
Churchill Crescent C2
City Rd A1
Claybraes C1
Cockshaugh Public Park B1
Cosmos Community Centre B3
Council Office A2
Crawford Gardens C1
Doubledykes Rd B1
Drumcarrow Rd C1
East Sands B3
East Scores A3
Fire Station C1
Forrest St C1
Fraser Avenue C1
Freddie Tait St C2
Gateway Centre A1
Glebe Rd B2
Golf Place A1
Grange Rd C3
Greenside Place B2
Greyfriars Gardens A2
Hamilton Avenue C2
Hepburn Gardens B1
Holy Trinity B2
Horseleys Park C1
Information Centre B2
Irvine Crescent C3
James Robb Avenue C1
James St B1
John Knox Rd C1
Kennedy Gardens B1
Kilrymont Close C3
Kilrymont Place C3
Kilrymont Rd C3
Kinburn Park B1
Kinkell Terrace C3
Kinnesburn Rd B2
Ladebraes Walk B2
Lady Buchan's Cave A3
Lamberton Place C1
Lamond Drive C2
Langlands Rd B2
Largo Rd C1
Learmonth Place C1
Library B2
Links Clubhouse A1
Links, The A1
Livingstone Crescent B2
Long Rocks A2
Madras College B2
Market St A2
Martyr's Monument A1
Murray Park A2
Murray Place A2
Mus of the Univ of St Andrews (MUSA) A2
Nelson St B2
New Course, The A1
New Picture House A2
North Castle St A3
North St A2
Old Course, The A1
Old Station Rd A1
Pends, The B3
Pilmour Links A1
Pipeland Rd B2/C2
Police Station A2/C1
Post Office B2
Preservation Trust B2
Priestden Park C3
Priestden Place C3
Priestden Rd C3
Queen's Gardens B2
Queen's Terrace B2
Roundhill Rd C2
Royal & Ancient Golf Club A1
St Andrews B1
St Andrews Aquarium A2
St Andrews Botanic Garden B1
St Andrews Castle (Ruins) & Visitor Centre A2
St Leonard's School B3
St Mary St B3
St Mary's College B2
St Nicholas St C3
St Rules Tower B3
St Salvator's College A2
Sandyhill Crescent C2
Sandyhill Rd C2
Scooniehill Rd C2
Scores, The A2
Shields Avenue C3
Shoolbraids C2
Shore, The B3
Sloan St B1
South St B2
Spottiswoode Gdns C1
Station Rd A1
Swilcen Bridge A1
Tom Morris Drive C2
Tom Stewart Lane C1
Town Hall B2
Union St A2
University Chapel A2
University Library A2
University of St Andrews A1
Viaduct Walk B1
War Memorial A3
Wardlaw Gardens B1
Warrack St C3
Watson Avenue B2
West Port B2
West Sands A1
Westview B2
Windmill Rd A1
Winram Place C1
Wishart Gardens C2
Woodburn Park B3
Woodburn Place B3
Woodburn Terrace B3
Younger Hall A2

Salisbury 342

Albany Rd A2
Arts Centre A3
Ashley Rd A1
Avon Approach A2
Ayleswade Rd C2
Bedwin St A2
Belle Vue A2
Bishops Walk B2
Blue Boar Row B2
Bourne Avenue A3
Bourne Hill A3
Britford Lane C2
Broad Walk C2
Brown St B2
Castle St A2
Catherine St B2
Chapter House B2
Church House B2
Churchfields Rd B1
Churchill Gardens C3
Churchill Way East B3
Churchill Way North A3
Churchill Way South C2
Churchill Way West A1
City Hall B2
Close Wall B2
Coldharbour Lane A1
College St A3
Council and Registry Offices A3
Court A1
Crane Bridge Rd B2
Crane St B2
Cricket Ground C1
Culver St South B3
De Vaux Place C2
Devizes Rd A1
Dews Rd B1
Elm Grove B3
Elm Grove Rd A3
Endless St A2
Estcourt Rd A3
Exeter St C2
Fairview Rd A3
Fire Station A1
Fisherton St A1
Folkestone Rd C1
Fowlers Hill B3
Fowlers Rd B3
Friary Lane B2
Friary, The B3
Gas Lane A1
Gigant St B3
Greencroft B3
Greencroft St A3
Guildhall B2
Hall of John Halle B2
Hamilton Rd A2
Harnham Mill B1
Harnham Rd C1/C2
High St B2
Ho of John A'Port B2
Information Centre B2
Kelsey Rd A3
King's Rd A2
Laverstock Rd B3
Library B2
London Rd A3
Lower St C1
Maltings, The B2
Manor Rd A3
Marsh Lane A1
Medieval Hall B2
Milford Hill B3
Milford St B3
Mill Rd B1
Mill Stream Approach A2
Mompesson House B2
New Bridge Rd C2
New Canal B2
New Harnham Rd C2
New St B2
North Canonry B2
North Gate B2
North Walk B2
Old Blandford Rd C1
Old Deanery B2
Old George Hall B2
Park St A3
Parsonage Green C1
Playhouse Theatre A2
Police Station A3
Post Office A2/B2
Poultry Cross B2
Queen Elizabeth Gdns B1
Queen's Rd A3
Rampart Rd B3
Rifles, The B2
St Ann St B2
St Ann's Gate B2
St Marks Rd A3
St Martins B3
St Paul's A1
St Paul's Rd A1
St Thomas B2
Salisbury Cathedral B2
Salisbury Cathedral Sch (Bishop's Palace) C2
Salisbury Mus, The B2
Salisbury Station A1
Salt Lane A3
Saxon Rd C1
Scots Lane A2
Shady Bower B3
Shopmobility B2
South Canonry C2
South Gate C2
Southampton Rd B2
Spire View A1
Sports Ground C3
Tollgate Rd B3
Town Path B1
Wain-a-Long Rd A3
Wessex Rd A3
West Walk C2
Wilton Rd A1
Wiltshire College B3
Winchester St B3
Windsor Rd A1
Wyndham Rd A2
YHA B3
York Rd A1

Scarborough 342

Aberdeen Walk B2
Albert Rd A2
Albion Rd C2
Auborough St B2
Balmoral Centre B2
Belle Vue St C1
Belmont Rd C2
Blenheim Terrace A2
Brunswick Shopping Centre B2
Castle Dykes B3
Castle Hill A3
Castle Rd B2
Castle Walls A3
Castlegate B3
Cemetery B1
Central Tramway B2
Coach Park B1
Columbus Ravine A1
Court B1
Crescent, The C2
Cricket Ground A1
Cross St B2
Crown Terrace C2
Dean Rd B1
Devonshire Drive A1
East Harbour B3
East Pier B3
Eastborough B2
Elmville Avenue B1
Esplanade C2
Falconers Rd B2
Falsgrave Rd C1
Fire Station B2
Foreshore Rd B2
Friargate B2
Gladstone Rd B1
Gladstone St B1
Hollywood Plaza A1
Holms, The A3
Hoxton Rd B1
King St B2
Library B2
Lifeboat Station B3
Londesborough Rd C1
Longwestgate B3
Marine Drive A3
Luna Park B3
Miniature Railway A1
Nelson St B1
Newborough B2
Nicolas St B2
North Marine Rd A1
North St B2
Northway B1
Old Harbour B3
Olympia Leisure B2
Peasholm Park A1
Peasholm Rd A1
Police Station B1
Post Office B2
Princess St B3
Prospect Rd B1
Queen St B2
Queen's Parade A2
Queen's Tower (Remains) A3
Ramshill Rd C2
Roman Signal Sta A3
Roscoe St C1
Rotunda Museum C2
Royal Albert Drive A2
Royal Albert Park A2
St Martin-on-the-Hill C2
St Martin's Avenue C2
St Mary's B3
St Thomas St B2
Sandside B3
Scarborough C1
Scarborough Art Gallery C2
Scarborough Bowls Centre A1
Scarborough Castle A3
Shopmobility C2
Somerset Terrace C2
South Cliff Lift C2
Spa Theatre, The C2
Spa, The C2
Stephen Joseph Theatre C1
Tennyson Avenue B1
Tollergate B2
Town Hall B2
Trafalgar Rd B1
Trafalgar Square A1
Trafalgar St West B1
Valley Bridge Parade C2
Valley Rd C1
Vernon Rd C2
Victoria Park Mount A1
Victoria Rd B1
West Pier B3
Westborough C1
Westover Rd C1
Westwood C1
Woodall Avenue A1
YMCA Theatre B2
York Place B2
Yorkshire Coast College (Westwood Campus) C1

Sheffield 342

Addy Drive A2
Addy St A2
Adelphi St A3
Albert Terrace Rd A3
Albion St A2
Aldred Rd A1
Allen St A4
Alma St A4
Angel St B5
Arundel Gate B5
Arundel St C4
Ashberry Rd A2
Ashdell Rd C1
Ashgate Rd C1
Athletics Centre B2
Attercliffe Rd A6
Bailey St B4
Ball St A4
Balm Green B4
Bank St B4
Barber Rd A2
Bard St B5
Barker's Pool B4
Bates St A1
Beech Hill Rd C1
Beet St B3
Bellefield St A3
Bernard Rd A6
Bernard St B6
Birkendale A2
Birkendale Rd A2
Birkendale View A1
Bishop St C4
Blackwell Place B6
Blake St A2
Blonk St A5
Bolsover St B2
Botanical Gardens ✿ C1
Bower Rd A1
Bradley St A1
Bramall Lane C4
Bramwell St A3
Bridge St A4/A5
Brighton Terrace Rd A1
Broad Lane B3
Broad St B6
Brocco St A3
Brook Hill B3
Broomfield Rd C1
Broomgrove Rd C2
Broomhall Place C3
Broomhall Rd C2
Broomhall St C3
Broomspring Lane C2
Brown St C5
Brunswick St B3
Burgess St B4
Burlington St A2
Burns Rd A2
Cadman St A6
Cambridge St B4
Campo Lane B4
Carver St B4
Castle Square B5
Castlegate A5
Cathedral B4
Cathedral (RC) ✝ B4
Cavendish St B3
Charles St C4
Charter Row C4
Children's Hospital B2
Church St B4
City Hall B4
City Hall B4
City Rd C6
Claremont Crescent B2
Claremont Place B2
Clarke St C3
Clarkegrove Rd C2
Clarkehouse Rd C1
Clarkson St B2
Cobden View Rd A1
Collegiate Crescent C2
Commercial St B5
Commonside A1
Conduit Rd B1
Cornish St A3
Corporation St A4
Cricket Inn Rd B6
Cromwell St A1
Crookes Rd B1
Crookes Valley Park B2
Crookes Valley Rd B2
Crookesmoor Rd A2
Crown Court A4
Crucible Theatre B5
Cutlers' Hall B4
Cutlers Gate A6
Daniel Hill A2
Dental Hospital B2
Derek Dooley Way A5
Devonshire Green B3
Devonshire St B3
Division St B4
Dorset St C2
Dover St A3
Duchess Rd C5
Duke St B5
Duncombe St A1
Durham Rd B2
Earl St C4
Earl Way C4
Ecclesall Rd C3
Edward St B3
Effingham Rd A6
Effingham St A6
Egerton St C3
Eldon St B3
Elmore Rd B1
Exchange St B5
Eyre St C4
Fargate B4
Farm Rd C5
Fawcett St A3
Filey St B3
Fir St A1
Fire Station C4
Fitzalan Square/ Ponds Forge B5
Fitzwater Rd C6
Fitzwilliam Gate C4
Fitzwilliam St B3
Flat St B5
Foley St A6
Foundry Climbing Ctr A4
Fulton Rd A1
Furnace Hill A4
Furnival Rd A5
Furnival Square C4
Furnival St C4
Garden St B3
Gell St B3
Gibraltar St A4
Glebe Rd B1
Glencoe Rd C6
Glossop Rd B2/B3/C1
Gloucester St C2
Government Offices C4
Granville Rd C6
Granville Rd / The Sheffield College C5
Graves Gallery B5
Green Lane A4
Hadfield St A1
Hanover St C3
Hanover Way C3
Harcourt Rd B1
Harmer Lane B5
Havelock St C2
Hawley St B4
Haymarket B5
Headford St C3
Heavygate Rd A1
Henry St A3
High St B4
Hodgson St C3
Holberry Gardens C2
Hollis Croft B4
Holly St B4
Hounsfield Rd B3
Howard Rd A1
Hoyle St A3
Hyde Park A6
Infirmary Rd A3
Infirmary Rd A3
Jericho St A3
Johnson St A5
Kelham Island Industrial Museum A4
Lawson Rd C1
Leadmill Rd C5
Leadmill St C5
Leadmill, The ✦ C5
Leamington St A1
Leavygreave Rd B3
Lee Croft B4
Leopold St B4
Leveson St A6
Library A2/B5/C1
Light, The C4
Lyceum Theatre B5
Malinda St A3
Maltravers St A5
Manor Oaks Rd B6
Mappin St B3
Marlborough Rd B1
Mary St C4
Matilda St C4
Matlock Rd A1
Meadow St A3
Melbourn Rd A1
Melbourne Avenue C1
Millennium Galleries B5
Milton St C3
Mitchell St B3
Mona Avenue A1
Mona Rd A1
Montgomery Terr Rd A3
Montgomery Theatre B4
Monument Grounds C6
Moor Oaks Rd B1
Moor, The C4
Moor Market C4
Moore St C3
Mowbray St A4
Mushroom Lane B2
National Emergency Service A4
National Videogame B5
Netherthorpe Rd B3
Netherthorpe Rd B3
Newbould Lane C1
Nile St C1
Norfolk Park Rd C6
Norfolk Rd C6
Norfolk St B4
North Church St B4
Northfield Rd A1
Northumberland Rd B1
Nursery St A5
O2 Academy B5
Oakholme Rd C1
Octagon B2
Odeon B5
Old St B6
Orch Sq Shopping Ctr B4
Oxford St A2
Paradise St B4
Park Lane C2
Park Square B5
Parker's Rd B1
Pearson Building (University) C2
Penistone Rd A3
Pinstone St B4
Pitt St B3
Police Station B5
Pond Hill B5
Pondorosa, The A2
Pond St B5
Ponds Forge International Sports Centre B5
Portobello St B3
Post Office A2/B3/B5/ C1/C3/C4/C6
Powell St A2
Queen St B4
Queen's Rd C5
Ramsey Rd B1
Red Hill B3
Redcar Rd B1
Regent St B3
Rockingham St B4
Roebuck Rd A2
Royal Hallamshire Hospital C2
Russell St A4
Rutland Park C1
St George's Close B3
St Mary's Gate C3
St Mary's Rd C4/C5
St Philip's Rd A3
Savile St A5
School Rd B1
Scotland St A4
Severn Rd B1
Shalesmoor A4
Shalesmoor A3
Sheaf St B5
Sheffield Cathedral ✝ B4
Sheffield Hallam Univ B5
Sheffield Ice Sports Ctr – Skate Central C5
Sheffield Institute of Arts B5
Sheffield Interchange B5
Sheffield Parkway A6
Sheffield Station ⇌ C5
Sheffield Sta/ Sheffield Hallam Univ B5
Sheffield University B2
Shepherd St A3
Shipton St A2
Shopmobility B3
Shoreham St C4
Showroom C5
Shrewsbury Rd C5
Sidney St C4
Site Gallery C5
Slinn St A1
Smithfield A4
Snig Hill A5
Snow Lane A4
Solly St B3
South Lane C4
South Street Park B5
Southbourne Rd C1
Spital Hill A5
Spital St A5
Spring Hill B1
Spring Hill Rd B1
Springvale Rd A1
Stafford Rd C6
Stafford St B6
Suffolk Rd C5
Summer St B2
Sunny Bank C3
Superstore A3/C3
Surrey St B4
Sussex St A6
Sutton St B3
Sydney Rd A2
Sylvester St C4
Talbot St B5
Taptonville Rd B1
Tenter St B4
Town Hall B4
Townend St A1
Townhead St B4
Trafalgar St B4
Tree Root Walk B2
Trinity St A4
Trippet Lane B4
Turner Mus of Glass B3
Union St B4
Univ Drama Studio B2
Univ of Sheffield B3
Upper Allen St A3
Upper Hanover St B3
Upperthorpe Rd A2/A3
Verdon St A5
Victoria Rd C2
Victoria St B3
Waingate B5
Watery St A3
Watson Rd C1
Wellesley Rd B2
Wellington St C3
West Bar A4
West Bar Green A4
West One Plaza B3
West St B3
West St B3
Westbourne Rd C1
Western Bank B2
Western Rd A1
Weston Park B2
Weston Park Hosp B2
Weston Park Mus B2
Weston St A2
Wharncliffe Rd C3
Whitham Rd B1
Wicker A5
Wilkinson St B2
William St C3
Winter Garden ✦ B4
Winter St B2
York St B4
Yorkshire Artspace C5
Young St C4

Shrewsbury 342

Abbey Foregate B3
Abbey Gardens B2
Abbey Lawn Bsns Park B3
Abbots House B2
Albert St A2
Alma St B1
Ashley St A3
Ashton Rd C1
Avondale Drive A3
Bage Way C3
Barker St B1
Beacall's Lane A2
Beeches Lane C2
Beehive Lane C1
Belle Vue Gardens C2
Belle Vue Rd C2
Belmont Bank C1
Berwick Avenue A1
Berwick Rd A1
Betton St C2
Bishop St B3
Bradford St B3
Bridge St B1
Burton St A3
Bus Station B2
Butcher Row B2
Butler Rd C1
Bynner St C2
Canon St B3
Canonbury C1
Castle Bsns Park, The A2
Castle Foregate A2
Castle Gates B2
Castle Walk B3
Castle St B2
Cathedral (RC) ✝ C1
Chester St A2
Cineworld C3
Claremont Bank B1
Claremont Hill B1
Cleveland St B3
Coleham Head B2
Coleham Pumping Station C2
College Hill B1
Corporation Lane A1
Coton Crescent A1
Coton Hill A2
Coton Mount A1
Crescent Lane C1
Crewe St A2
Cross Hill B1
Dana, The B2
Darwin Centre B2
Dingle, The ✿ B1
Dogpole B2
English Bridge B2
Fish St B2
Frankwell B1
Gateway Ctr, The A2
Gravel Hill Lane A1
Greenhous West Mid Showground A1
Greyfriars Rd C2
Hampton Rd A3
Haycock Way C3
High St B1
Hills Lane B1
Holywell St B3
Hunter St A1
Information Centre B1
Ireland's Mansion & Bear Steps B1
John St A3
Kennedy Rd C1
King St B3
Kingsland Bridge C1
Kingsland Bridge (toll) C1
Kingsland Rd C1
Library B2
Lime St C2
Longden Coleham C2
Longden Rd C1
Longner St B1
Luciefelde Rd C1
Mardol B1
Marine Terrace C2
Market B1
Monkmoor Rd B3
Moreton Crescent C2
Mount St A1
New Park Close A3
New Park Rd A2
New Park St A3
North St A2
Oakley St C1
Old Coleham C2
Old Market Hall B1
Old Potts Way C3
Par Shopping Ctr, The B2
Police Station B1
Post Office B1/B2/B3
Pride Hill B1
Pride Hill Centre B1
Priory Rd B1
Pritchard Way C3
Quarry Swimming & Fitness Centre, The B1
Queen St A3
Raby Crescent C2
Rad Brook C1
Rea Brook C3
Rea Brook Valley Country Park & Local Nature Reserve C3
Riverside B1
Roundhill Lane A1
St Alkmund's B2
St Chad's B1
St Chad's Terrace B1
St John's Hill B1
St Julians Friars C2
St Mary's B2
St Mary's St B2
Salters Lane C2
Scott St C3
Severn Theatre B1
Severn Bank A3
Severn St A2
Shrewsbury ⇌ B2
Shrewsbury Abbey B3
Shrewsbury High School C1
Shrewsbury Museum & Art Gall B1
Shrewsbury Prison Tours ✦ B2
Shrewsbury School ✦ C1
Shropshire Regimental Museum B2
Shropshire Wildlife Trust ✦ B3
Smithfield Rd B1
South Hermitage C1
Square, The B1
Superstore C3
Swan Hill B1
Sydney Avenue A3
Tankerville St B3
Tilbrook Drive A3
Town Walls C1
Trinity St C2
Underdale Rd B3
University Centre Shrewsbury (Guildhall) B1
Victoria Avenue B1
Victoria Quay B1
Victoria St B2
Welsh Bridge B1
Whitehall St B3
Wood St A2
Wyle Cop B2

Southampton 342

Above Bar St A2
Albert Rd North B3
Albert Rd South C3
Andersons Rd B3
Argyle Rd A2
Arundel Tower ✦ B1
Bargate, The ✦ B2
BBC South A1
Bedford Place A1
Belvidere Rd A3
Bernard St C2
Blechynden Terrace A1
Brinton's Rd A2
Britannia Rd A3
Briton St C2
Brunswick Place A2
Bugle St C1
Canute Rd C3
Castle Way C2
Catchcold Tower ✦ B1
Central Bridge C3
Central Rd C2
Channel Way C3
Chapel Rd B3
City Art Gallery A1
City College B3
City Cruise Terminal C1
Civic Centre A1
Civic Centre Rd A1
Coach Station B1
Commercial Rd A1
Cumberland Place A1
Cunard Rd C2
Derby Rd A3
Devonshire Rd A1
Dock Gate 4 C2
Dock Gate 8 B1
East Park (Andrew's Park) A2
East Park Terrace A2
East St B2
Endle St B3
European Way C2
Fire Station A2
Floating Bridge Rd C3
God's House Tower ✦ C2
Golden Grove A3
Graham Rd A2
Guildhall A1
Hanover Buildings B2
Harbour Lights C3
Harbour Parade B1
Hartington Rd A3
Havelock Rd A1
Henstead Rd A1
Herbert Walker Ave B1
High St B2
Hoglands Park B2
Holy Rood (Rems), Merchant Navy Memorial B2
Houndwell Park B2
Houndwell Place B2
Hythe Ferry C2
Isle of Wight Ferry Terminal C1
James St B3
Kingsway A2
Leisure World B1
Library A1
Lime St B2
London Rd A2
Marine Parade B3
Marlands Shopping Centre, The A1
Marsh Lane B2
Mayflower Meml ✦ C1
Mayflower Park C1
Mayflower Theatre, The A1
Medieval Merchant's House C1
Melbourne St B3
Morris Rd A1
National Oceanography Centre ✦ C3
Neptune Way C3
New Rd A2
Nichols Rd A3
North Front A2
Northam Rd A3
Ocean Dock C2
Ocean Village Marina C3
Ocean Way C3
Odeon B1
Ogle Rd B1
Old Northam Rd A2
Orchard Lane B2
Oxford Avenue A2
Oxford St C2
Palmerston Park A2
Palmerston Rd A2
Parsonage Rd A3
Peel St A3
Platform Rd C2
Polygon, The A1
Portland Terrace B1
Post Office B2
Pound Tree Rd B2
Quays Swimming & Diving Complex, The B1
Queen's Park C2
Queen's Peace Fountain ✦ A2
Queen's Terrace C2
Queensway B2
Radcliffe Rd A3
Rochester St A3
Royal Pier C1
Royal South Hants Hospital A2
St Andrew's Rd A2
St Mary's B3
St Mary St A2
St Mary's Leisure Ctr A2
St Mary's Place B2
St Mary's Rd A2
St Mary's Stadium (Southampton FC) A3
St Michael's C1
SeaCity Museum A1
Showcase Cinema de Lux B1
Solent Sky C3
South Front B2
Southampton Central Station ⇌ A1
Southampton Solent University A2
Terminus Terrace C2
Threefield Lane B2
Titanic Engineers' Memorial ✦ A2
Town Quay C1
Town Walls B2
Tudor House C1
Vincent's Walk B2
Westgate Hall C1
West Marlands Rd A1
West Park A1
West Park Rd A1
West Quay Rd B1
West Quay Retail Park B1
Western Esplanade B1
Westquay Shopping Centre B1
Westquay South B1
White Star Way C2
Winton St A2

Southend-on-Sea 343

Adventure Island ✦ C3
Albany Avenue A1
Albert Rd C3
Alexandra Rd C2
Alexandra St C2
Alexandra Yacht Club ✦ C2
Ashburnham Rd B2
Avenue Rd B1
Avenue Terrace B1
Balmoral Rd B1
Baltic Avenue B3
Baxter Avenue A2/B2
Beecroft Art Gallery B2
Bircham Rd A2
Boscombe Rd B3
Boston Avenue A1/B2
Bournemouth Park Rd A3
Browning Avenue A3
Bus Station C3
Byron Avenue A3
Cambridge Rd C1/C2
Canewdon Rd B1
Carnarvon Rd A2
Central Avenue A3
Central Museum B2
Chelmsford Avenue A1
Chichester Rd B2
Church Rd C3
Civic Centre A2
Clarence Rd C2
Clarence St C2
Cliff Avenue B1
Cliffs Pavilion C1
Clifftown Parade C2
Clifftown Rd C2
Colchester Rd A1
Coleman St B3
College Way B2
County Court B3
Cromer Rd B3
Crowborough Rd A2
Dryden Avenue A3
East St A2
Elmer Approach B2
Elmer Avenue B2
Forum, The B2
Gainsborough Drive A1
Gayton Rd A2
Glenhurst Rd A2
Gordon Place B2
Gordon Rd B2
Grainger Rd A2
Greyhound Way A3
Grove, The A3
Guildford Rd B3
Hamlet Court Rd B1
Hamlet Rd C1
Harcourt Avenue A1
Hartington Rd C3
Hastings Rd B3
Herbert Grove C3
Heygate Avenue C3
High St B2/C2
Information Centre C3
Kenway A2
Kilworth Avenue B3
Lancaster Gardens B3
London Rd B1
Lucy Rd C3
MacDonald Avenue A1
Magistrates' Court A2
Maldon Rd A2
Marine Avenue C1
Marine Parade C3
Marine Rd C1
Milton Rd B1
Milton St B2
Napier Avenue B2
North Avenue A3
North Rd A1/B1
Odeon B2
Osborne Rd B1
Park Crescent B1
Park Rd B1
Park St B1
Park Terrace B1
Pier Hill C3
Pleasant Rd C3
Police Station A2
Post Office B2/B3
Princes St B2
Queens Rd B2
Queensway B2/B3/C3
Radio Essex C2
Rayleigh Avenue A1
Redstock Rd A2
Rochford Avenue A1
Royal Mews C2
Royal Terrace C2
Royals Shopping Centre, The C3
Ruskin Avenue A3
St Ann's Rd B3
St Helen's Rd B1
St John's Rd B1
St Leonard's Rd C3
St Lukes Rd A3
St Vincent's Rd C1
Salisbury Avenue A1/B1
Scratton Rd C2
Shakespeare Drive A1
Shopmobility B2
Short St A2
South Avenue A3
Southchurch Rd B3
Southend Central ⇌ B2
Southend Pier Railway C3
Southend United FC A1
Southend Victoria ⇌ B2
Stanfield Rd A2
Stanley Rd C3
Sutton Rd A3/B3
Swanage Rd B3
Sweyne Avenue A1
Sycamore Grove A3
Tennyson Avenue A3
Tickfield Avenue A2
Tudor Rd A1
Tunbridge Rd A2
Tylers Avenue B3
Tyrrel Drive B3
University of Essex B2/C2
Vale Avenue A2
Victoria Avenue A2
Victoria Shopping Centre, The B2
Warrior Square B3
Wesley Rd C3
West Rd A1
West St A1
Westcliff Avenue C1
Westcliff Parade C1
Western Esplanade C1
Weston Rd C2
Whitegate Rd B3
Wilson Rd C1
Wimborne Rd B3
York Rd C3

Stirling 343

Abbey Rd A3
Abbotsford Place A3
Abercromby Place C1
Albert Halls B1
Albert Place B1
Alexandra Place A3
Allan Park C2
Ambulance Station A2
AMF Ten Pin Bowling ✦ B2
Argyll Avenue A3
Argyll's Lodging ✦ B1
Back O' Hill Ind Est A1
Back O' Hill Rd A1
Baker St B2
Ballengeich Pass A1
Balmoral Place B1
Barn Rd B1
Barnton St B2
Bastion, The ✦ C2
Bow St B1
Bruce St A2
Burghmuir Retail Park C2
Burghmuir Rd A2/B2/C2
Bus Station B2
Cambuskenneth Bridge A3
Castle Court B1
Causewayhead Rd A2
Cemetery A1
Changing Room, The B1
Church of the Holy Rude B1
Clarendon Place C1
Club House B1
Colquhoun St C3
Corn Exchange B2
Council Offices C2
Court B2
Cowane Centre A2
Cowane St A2
Cowane's Hospital B1
Crofthead Rd A1
Dean Crescent A3
Douglas St A2
Drip Rd A1
Drummond Lane C1
Drummond Place C1
Drummond Place Lane C1
Dumbarton Rd C2
Eastern Access Rd B2
Edward Avenue A3
Edward Rd A2
Forrest Rd A2
Fort A1
Forth Crescent B2
Forth St A2
Gladstone Place C1
Glebe Avenue C1
Glebe Crescent C1
Golf Course C1
Goosecroft Rd B2
Gowanhill A1
Greenwood Avenue B1
Harvey Wynd A1
Information Centre B1
Irvine Place B2
James St A2
John St B1
Kerse Rd C3
King's Knot ✦ B1
King's Park C1
King's Park Rd C1
Laurencecroft Rd A2
Leisure Pool B2
Library B2
Linden Avenue C2
Lovers Wk A2
Lower Back Walk B1
Lower Bridge St A2
Lower Castlehill A1
Mar Place B1
Meadow Place A3
Meadowforth Rd C3
Middlemuir Rd C3
Millar Place A3
Morris Terrace B2
Mote Hill A1
Murray Place B2
Nelson Place C2
Old Town Cemetery B1
Old Town Jail ✦ B1
Park Terrace C1
Phoenix Industrial Est C3
Players Rd C3
Port St C2
Post Office B2
Princes St B2
Queen St B2
Queen's Rd B1
Queenshaugh Drive A3
Ramsay Place A2
Riverside Drive A3
Ronald Place A1
Rosebery Place A2
Royal Gardens B1
Royal Gardens B1
St Mary's Wynd B1
St Ninian's Rd C2
Scott St A2
Seaforth Place B2
Shore Rd B2
Smith Art Gallery & Museum B1
Snowdon Place C1
Snowdon Place Lane C1
Spittal St B2
Springkerse Ind Est C3
Springkerse Rd C3
Stirling Arcade B2
Stirling Bsns Centre C2
Stirling Castle A1
Stirling County Rugby Football Club A3
Stirling Enterprise Pk B3
Stirling Old Bridge A2
Stirling Station ⇌ B2
Superstore A1/A2
Sutherland Avenue A3
TA Centre C3
Tannery Lane A2
Thistle Industrial Est C3
Thistles Shopping Centre, The B2
Tolbooth ✦ B1
Town Wall B1
Union St A2
Upper Back Walk B1
Upper Bridge St A1
Upper Castlehill B1
Upper Craigs C2
Victoria Place C1
Victoria Rd B1
Victoria Square B1/C1
Vue B2
Wallace St A2
Waverley Crescent A3
Wellgreen Rd C2
Windsor Place C1
YHA ▲ B1

Stoke 343

Ashford St A3
Avenue Rd A3
Aynsley Rd A2
Barnfield C1
Bath St C2
Beresford St A3
Bilton St C2
Boon Avenue C2
Booth St C2
Boothen Rd C2/C3
Boughey St C2
Boughey Rd B3
Brighton St B1
Campbell Rd C2
Carlton Rd B3
Cauldon Rd A3
Cemetery A2
Cemetery Rd A2
Chamberlain Avenue C1
Church (RC) B2
Church St C2
City Rd C3
Civic Centre & King's Hall B3
Cliff Vale Place A1
College Rd A3
Convent Close B2
Copeland St B2
Cornwallis St C3
Corporation St C2
Crowther St A3
Dominic St B1
Elenora St B2
Elgin St B2
Epworth St A3
Etruscan St A1
Film Theatre B3
Fleming Rd C2
Fletcher Rd C2
Floyd St B2
Foden St C2
Frank St C2
Franklin Rd C1
Frederick Avenue B1
Garden St C1
Garner St A1
Gerrard St B2
Glebe St B3
Greatbach Avenue B1
Hanley Park A3
Harris St B1
Hartshill Rd B1
Hayward St A2
Hide St B2
Higson Avenue B2
Hill St B2
Honeywall B2
Hunters Drive C1
Hunters Way C1
Keary St C2
Kingsway B2
Leek Rd B3
Library C2
Lime St C2
Liverpool Rd B2
London Rd C2
Lonsdale St C2
Lovatt St B2
Lytton St B3
Market C2
Newcastle Lane C1
Newlands St A2
Norfolk St A2
North St A1/B2
Northcote Avenue B2
Oldmill St C3
Oriel St B1
Oxford St B1
Penkhull New Rd C1
Penkhull St C1
Portmeirion Pottery ✦ C2
Post Office A3
Princes Rd B1
Pump St B2
Quarry Avenue B1
Quarry Rd B1
Queen Anne St A3
Queen's Rd C1
Queensway A1/B2/C3
Richmond St B1
Richmond St Park B1
Rothwell St C1
St Peter's B3
St Thomas Place C1
Scrivenor Rd A1
Seaford St A3
Selwyn St C3
Shelton New Rd A1
Shelton Old Rd B2
Sheppard St C2
Sir Stanley Matthews Sports Centre B3
Spark St C2
Spencer Rd B3
Spode Museum Heritage Centre B2
Spode St C2
Squires View B3
Staffordshire Univ B3
Station Rd B3
Stoke Business Park C3
Stoke Rd A2
Stoke-on-Trent Coll A3
Stoke-on-Trent Sta ⇌ B3
Sturgess St C2
Thistley Hough C1
Thornton Rd B3
Tolkien Way B1
Trent Valley Rd C1
Vale St B2
Villas, The C1
Watford St A3
Wellesley St A3
West Avenue B1
Westland St B1
Yeaman St C2
Yoxall Avenue B1

Stratford-upon-Avon 343

Albany Rd B1
Alcester Rd B1
Ambulance Station B1
Arden St B2
Avenue Farm A1
Ave Farm Ind Est A1
Avenue Rd A3
Baker Avenue A1
Bandstand C3
Benson Rd A3
Birmingham Rd A2
Boat Club B3
Borden Place C1
Bridge St B2
Bridgetown Rd C3
Bridgeway B3
Broad St C2
Broad Walk C2
Brookvale Rd C1
Brunel Way B1
Bull St C2
Butterfly Farm ✦ C3
Cemetery C1
Chapel Lane B2
Cherry Orchard C1
Chestnut Walk B2
Children's Playground C3
Church St C2
Civic Hall B2
Clarence Rd B1
Clopton Bridge ✦ B3

Clopton Rd A2
College B1
College Lane C2
College St C2
Community Sports Ctr B1
Council Offices (District) B2
Courtyard, The C2
Cox's Yard B3
Cricket Ground C3
Ely Gardens B2
Ely St B2
Evesham Rd C1
Fire Station B1
Foot Ferry C3
Fordham Avenue A2
Garrick Way C1
Gower Memorial B3
Great William St B2
Greenhill St B2
Greenway, The C2
Grove Rd B2
Guild St B2
Guildhall & School B2
Hall's Croft C2
Harvard House B2
Henley St B2
Hertford Rd C1
High St B2
Holton St C2
Holy Trinity C2
Information Centre B3
Jolyffe Park Rd A2
Kipling Rd C3
Library B2
Lodge Rd B1
Maidenhead Rd A3
Mansell St B2
Masons Court B2
Masons Rd A1
Maybird Shopping Pk A2
Maybrook Retail Park A2
Maybrook Rd A1
Mayfield Avenue A2
Meer St B2
Mill Lane C2
Moat House Hotel B3
Narrow Lane C2
Nash's Ho & New Pl B2
New St C2
Old Town C2
Orchard Way C1
Other Place, The C2
Paddock Lane C1
Park Rd A1
Payton St B2
Percy St A2
Police Station B2
Post Office B2
Recreation Ground C2
Regal Road A2
Rother St B2
Rowley Crescent A3
Royal Shakespeare Theatre B3
Ryland St C2
Saffron Meadow C2
St Andrew's Crescent B1
St Gregory's A3
St Gregory's Rd A3
St Mary's Rd A2
Sanctus Drive C2
Sanctus St C1
Sandfield Rd C2
Scholars Lane B2
Seven Meadows Rd C2
Shakespeare Institute C2
Shakespeare St B2
Shakespeare's Birthplace B2
Sheep St B2
Shelley Rd C3
Shipston Rd C3
Shottery Rd C1
Slingates Rd A2
Southern Lane C2
Station Rd B1
Stratford Healthcare B2
Stratford Hospital B2
Stratford Leisure Ctr B3
Stratford Sports Club B1
Stratford-upon-Avon Station B1
Swan Theatre B3
Swan's Nest Lane B3
Talbot Rd A2
Tiddington Rd B3
Timothy's Bridge Industrial Estate A1
Timothy's Bridge Rd A1
Town Hall & Council Offices B2
Town Square B2
Trinity Close C2
Tyler St B2
War Memorial Gdns B3
Warwick Rd B3
Waterside B3
Welcombe Rd A3
West St C2
Western Rd A2
Wharf Rd A2
Willows North, The B1
Willows, The B1
Wood St B2

Sunderland 343

Albion Place C2
Alliance Place B1
Argyle St C2
Ashwood St C1
Athenaeum St B2
Azalea Terrace C2
Beach St A1
Bedford St B2
Beechwood Terrace C1
Belvedere Rd C2
Blandford St B2
Borough Rd B3
Bridge Crescent B2
Bridge St B2
Bridges, The B2
Brooke St A2
Brougham St B2
Burdon Rd C2
Burn Park C1
Burn Park Rd C1
Burn Park Tech Park C1
Carol St B1
Charles St A3
Chester Rd C1
Chester Terrace B1
Church St A3
Civic Centre C2
Cork St B3
Coronation St B3
Cowan Terrace C2
Dame Dorothy St A2
Deptford Rd B1
Deptford Terrace A1
Derby St C2
Derwent St C2
Dock St A3
Dundas St A2
Durham Rd C1
Easington St A2
Egerton St C3
Empire B3
Empire Theatre B2
Farringdon Row B1
Fawcett St B2
Fire Station B1
Fox St C1
Foyle St B3
Frederick St B3
Hanover Place A1
Havelock Terrace C1
Hay St A2
Headworth Square B3
Hendon Rd B3
High St East B3
High St West B2/B3
Holmeside B2
Hylton Rd B1
John St B3
Kier Hardie Way A2
Lambton St B3
Laura St C3
Lawrence St B3
Library & Arts Centre B3
Lily St B1
Lime St B1
Livingstone Rd B2
Low Row B2
Magistrates' Court B2
Matamba Terrace B1
Millburn St B1
Millennium Way A2
Minster B2
Monkwearmouth Station Museum A2
Mowbray Park C3
Mowbray Rd C3
Murton St C3
National Glass Ctr A3
New Durham Rd C1
Newcastle Rd A2
Nile St B3
Norfolk St B3
North Bridge St A2
Northern Gallery for Contemporary Art (NGCA) B3
Otto Terrace C1
Park Lane C2
Park Lane C2
Park Rd C2
Paul's Rd B3
Peel St C3
Point, The B2
Police Station B2
Priestly Crescent A1
Queen St B2
Railway Row B1
Retail Park B1
Richmond St A2
Roker Avenue A2
Royalty Theatre C1
Royalty, The C1
Ryhope Rd C2
St Mary's Way B2
St Michael's Way B2
St Peter's A3
St Peter's A2
St Peter's Way A3
St Vincent St C3
Salem Rd C3
Salem St C3
Salisbury St C3
Sans St B3
Shopmobility B2
Silkworth Row B1
Southwick Rd A2
Stadium of Light (Sunderland AFC) A2
Stadium Way A2
Stobart St A2
Stockton Rd C2
Suffolk St C3
Sunderland B2
Sunderland Aquatic Centre A2
Sunderland College C2
Sunderland Mus B3
Sunderland St B3
Sunderland Station B2
Tatham St C3
Tavistock Place B3
Thelma St C1
Thomas St North A2
Thornholme Rd C1
Toward Rd C3
Transport Interchange C2
Trimdon St Way B1
Tunstall Rd C2
University C1
University Library C1
University of Sunderland (City Campus) B1
University of Sunderland (St Peter's Campus) A3
Univ of Sunderland (Sir Tom Cowie Campus) A3
Vaux Brewery Way A2
Villiers St B3
Villiers St South B3
Vine Place C2
Violet St B1
Walton Lane B3
Waterworks Rd B1
Wearmouth Bridge B2
West Sunniside B3
West Wear St B3
Westbourne Rd B1
Western Hill C1
Wharncliffe B1
Whickham St A3
White House Rd C3
Wilson St North A2
Winter Gardens C3
Wreath Quay A1

Swansea Abertawe 343

Adelaide St C3
Albert Row C3
Alexandra Rd B3
Argyle St C1
Baptist Well Place A2
Beach St C1
Belle Vue Way B3
Berw Rd A1
Berwick Terrace A2
Bond St C1
Brangwyn Concert Hall C1
Bridge St A3
Brooklands Terrace B1
Brunswick St C1
Bryn-Syfi Terrace A2
Bryn-y-Mor Rd C1
Bullins Lane B1
Burrows Rd C1
Bus Station C2
Bus/Rail link A3
Cadfan Rd A1
Cadrawd Rd A1
Caer St B3
Carig Crescent A1
Carlton Terrace B2
Carmarthen Rd A3
Castle Square B3
Castle St B3
Catherine St C1
Cinema C3
Civic Centre & Library C2
Clarence St C2
Colbourne Terrace A2
Constitution Hill B1
Court B3
Creidiol Rd A2
Cromwell St B2
Crown Courts C1
Duke St B1
Dunvant Place C2
Dyfatty Park A3
Dyfatty St A3
Dyfed Avenue A1
Dylan Thomas Ctr B3
Dylan Thomas Theatre C3
Eaton Crescent C1
Eigen Crescent A1
Elfed Rd A1
Emlyn Rd A1
Evans Terrace A3
Fairfield Terrace B1
Ffynone Drive B1
Ffynone Rd B1
Fire Station B3
Firm St A2
Fleet St C1
Francis St C1
Fullers Row B2
George St B2
Glamorgan St C2
Glynn Vivian Art Gallery B3
Gower Coll Swansea C1
Graig Terrace A3
Grand Theatre C2
Granogwen Rd A2
Guildhall C1
Guildhall Rd South C1
Gwent Rd A1
Gwynedd Avenue A1
Hafod St A3
Hanover St B1
Harcourt St B2
Harries St A2
Heathfield B2
Henrietta St B1
Hewson St B2
High St A3/B3
High View A2
Hill St A2
Historic Ships Berth C3
HM Prison C2
Islwyn Rd A1
King Edward's Rd C1
Kingsway, The B2
LC, The C3
Long Ridge A2
Madoc St C2
Mansel St B2
Maritime Quarter C3
Market B3
Mayhill Gardens B1
Mayhill Rd A1
Milton Terrace A2
Mission Gallery C3
Montpelier Terrace B1
Morfa Rd A3
Mount Pleasant B2
National Waterfront Museum C3
New Cut Rd A3
New St A3
Nicander Parade A2
Nicander Place A2
Nicholl St B2
Norfolk St B2
North Hill Rd A2
Northampton Lane B2
Observatory C3
Orchard St B3
Oxford St B2
Oystermouth Rd C1
Page St B2
Pant-y-Celyn Rd B1
Parc Tawe North B3
Parc Tawe Shopping & Leisure Centre B3
Patti Pavilion C1
Paxton St C2
Pen-y-Graig Rd A1
Penmaen Terrace B1
Phillips Parade C1
Picton Terrace B2
Plantasia B3
Plantasia B3
Police Station B2
Post Office A1/A2/C1/C2
Powys Avenue A1
Primrose St B2
Princess Way B3
Promenade B2
Pryder Gardens A1
Quadrant Shopping Centre C2
Quay Park B3
Rhianfa Lane B1
Rhondda St B2
Richardson St C2
Rodney St C1
Rose Hill B1
Rosehill Terrace B1
Russell St B1
St Helen's Avenue C1
St Helen's Crescent C1
St Helen's Rd C1
St James Gardens B1
St James's Crescent B1
St Mary's B3
Sea View Terrace A3
Singleton St C2
South Dock C3
Stanley Place B2
Strand B3
Swansea Castle B3
Swansea Metropolitan University B2
Swansea Museum C3
Swansea Station A3
Taliesyn Rd B1
Tan y Marian Rd A1
Tegid Rd A2
Teilo Crescent A1
Tenpin Bowling B3
Terrace Rd B1/B2
Tontine St A3
Townhill Rd A1
Tramshed, The C3
Trawler Rd C3
Union St B2
Upper Strand A3
Vernon St A3
Victoria Quay C3
Victoria Rd B3
Vincent St C1
Walter Rd B1
Watkin St A2
Waun-Wen Rd A2
Wellington St C2
Westbury St C1
Western St C1
Westway C2
William St C2
Wind St B3
Woodlands Terrace B1
YMCA B2
York St C3

Swindon 343

Albert St C3
Albion St C1
Alfred St A2
Alvescot Rd C3
Art Gallery & Mus C3
Ashford Rd C1
Aylesbury St A2
Bath Rd C2
Bathampton St B1
Bathurst Rd B3
Beatrice St A2
Beckhampton St B3
Bowood Rd C1
Bristol St B1
Broad St A3
Brunel Shopping Centre, The B2
Brunel Statue B2
Brunswick St C2
Bus Station B2
Cambria Bridge Rd B1
Cambria Place B1
Canal Walk B2
Carr St B1
Cemetery C1/C3
Chandler Close C3
Chapel C1
Chester St B1
Christ Church C3
Church Place B1
Cirencester Way A3
Clarence St B2
Clifton St C1
Cockleberry A2
Colbourne A3
Colbourne St A3
College St B2
Commercial Rd B2
Corporation St A2
Council Offices B3
County Cricket Gd A3
County Rd A3
Courts B2
Cricklade Street C3
Crombey St B1/C2
Cross St C2
Curtis St B1
Deacon St C1
Designer Outlet (Great Western) B1
Dixon St C2
Dover St C2
Dowling St C2
Drove Rd C3
Dryden St C1
Durham St C3
East St B1
Eastcott Hill C2
Eastcott Rd C2
Edgeware Rd B2
Edmund St C2
Elmina Rd A3
Emlyn Square B1
English Heritage National Monuments Record Centre B1
Euclid St B3
Exeter St B1
Fairview C1
Faringdon Rd B1
Farnsby St B1
Fire Station B3
Fleet St B2
Fleming Way B2/B3
Florence St A2
Gladstone St A3
Gooch St A2
Graham St A3
Great Western Way A1/A2
Groundwell Rd B3
Hawksworth Way A1
Haydon St A2
Henry St B2
Hillside Avenue C1
Holbrook Way B2
Hunt St C3
Hydro B1
Hythe Rd C2
Information Centre B2
Joseph St C1
Kent Rd C2
King William St C2
Kingshill Rd C1
Lansdown Rd C2
Lawn, The C3
Leicester St B3
Library B2
Lincoln St B3
Little London C3
London St B1
Magic B3
Maidstone Rd C2
Manchester Rd A3
Maxwell St B1
Milford St B2
Milton Rd B1
Morse St C2
Newcastle St B3
Newcombe Drive A1
Hawksworth Ind Est A1
Newhall St C2
North St C2
North Star A1
North Star Avenue A1
Northampton St B3
Nurseries, The C1
Oasis Leisure Centre A1
Ocotal Way A3
Okus Rd C1
Old Town C3
Oxford St B1
Parade, The B2
Park Lane B1
Park Lane B1
Park, The B1
Pembroke St C2
Plymouth St B3
Polaris Way A2
Police Station B2
Ponting St A2
Post Office B1/B2/C3
Poulton St A3
Princes St B2
Prospect Hill C2
Prospect Place C2
Queen St B2
Queen's Park C3
Radnor St C1
Read St C1
Reading St B1
Regent Circus C2
Regent St B2
Retail Park A2/A3/B3
Rosebery St A3
St Mark's B1
Salisbury St A3
Savernake St C2
Science & Technology Facilities Council HQ A2
Shelley St C1
Sheppard St B1
Shopmobility B2
South St C2
Southampton St B3
Spring Gardens B3
Stafford Street C2
Stanier St C2
Station Road A2
STEAM GWR B1
Swindon College A2
Swindon Rd C2
Swindon Station A2
Swindon Town Football Club A3
TA Centre B1
Tennyson St B1
Theobald St B1
Town Hall B2
Transfer Bridges A3
Union St C2
Upham Rd C3
Victoria Rd C3
Walcot Rd B3
War Memorial B2
Wells St B3
Western St C2
Westmorland Rd B3
Whalebridge B2
Whitehead St C1
Whitehouse Rd A2
William St C1
Wood St C3
Wyvern Theatre & Arts Centre B2
York Rd B3

Taunton 343

Addison Grove A1
Albemarle Rd A1
Alfred St B3
Alma St C2
Avenue, The A1
Bath Place C1
Belvedere Rd A1
Billet St B2
Billetfield C2
Birch Grove A1
Brewhouse Theatre B2
Bridge St B1
Bridgwater & Taunton Canal A2
Broadlands Rd C1
Burton Place C1
Bus Station B1
Canal Rd A2
Cann St C1
Canon St B2
Castle St B1
Cheddon Rd A2
Chip Lane A1
Clarence St B1
Cleveland St B1
Clifton Terrace A2
Coleridge Crescent C3
Compass Hill C1
Compton Close A2
Corporation St B1
Council Offices A1
County Walk Shopping Centre C2
Courtyard B2
Cranmer Rd B2
Crescent, The C1
Critchard Way B3
Cyril St A1
Deller's Wharf B1
Duke St B2
East Reach B3
East St B3
Eastbourne Rd B2
Eastleigh Rd C3
Eaton Crescent A2
Elm Grove A1
Elms Close A1
Fons George C1
Fore St B2
Fowler St A1
French Weir Rec Grd B1
Geoffrey Farrant Walk A2
Gray's Almshouses B2
Grays Rd B3
Greenway Avenue A1
Guildford Place C1
Hammet St B2
Haydon Rd B3
Heavitree Way A2
Herbert St A1
High St C2
Holway Avenue C3
Hugo St B3
Huish's Almshouses B2
Hurdle Way C2
Information Centre C2
Jubilee St A1
King's College C3
Kings Close C3
Laburnum St B2
Lambrook Rd B3
Lansdowne Rd A3
Leslie Avenue A1
Leycroft Rd B3
Library C2
Linden Grove A1
Magdalene St B2
Magistrates Court B1
Malvern Terrace A2
Market House B2
Mary St C2
Middle St B2
Mitre Court B3
Mount Nebo C1
Mount St C2
Mount, The C2
Mountway C2
Mus of Somerset B1
North St B2
Northfield Avenue B1
Northfield Rd B1
Northleigh Rd C3
Obridge Allotments A3
Obridge Lane A3
Obridge Rd A3
Obridge Viaduct A3
Orchard Shopping Ctr C2
Osborne Way C1
Park St C1
Paul St C2
Plais St A2
Playing Field C3
Police Station C1
Portland St B1
Post Office B1/B2
Priorswood Ind Est A3
Priorswood Rd A2
Priory Avenue B2
Priory Bridge Rd B2
Priory Fields Retail Pk A3
Priory Park A2
Priory Way A3
Queen St B3
Railway St A1
Records Office A2
Recreation Ground A1
Riverside Place B2
St Augustine St B2
St George's C2
St Georges Square C2
St James B2
St James St B2
St John's C1
St John's Rd B1
St Josephs Field C2
St Mary Magdalene's B2
Samuels Court A1
Shire Hall & Law Courts C1
Somerset County Cricket Ground B2
Somerset County Hall C1
Somerset Cricket B2
South Rd C3
South St C3
Staplegrove Rd B1
Station Approach A2
Station Rd A1
Stephen St B2
Superstore C2
Swimming Pool A1
Tancred St B2
Tangier Way B1
Tauntfield Close C3
Taunton Castle B1
Taunton Deane Cricket Club C2
Taunton Station A2
Thomas St A1
Toneway A3
Tower St B1
Trenchard Way A2
Trevor Smith Place C3
Trinity Bsns Centre C3
Trinity Rd C3
Trinity St B3
Trull Rd C1
Tudor House B2
Upper High St C1
Venture Way A3
Victoria Gate B3
Victoria Park B3
Victoria St B3
Viney St B3
Vivary Park Golf Club C2
Vivary Rd C1
War Memorial C1
Wellesley St A2
Wheatley Crescent A3
Whitehall A1
Wilfred Rd B3
William St A1
Wilton Church C1
Wilton Close C1
Wilton Grove C1
Wilton St C1
Winchester St B2
Winters Field B2
Wood St B1
Yarde Place B1

Telford 343

Alma Avenue C1
Amphitheatre C2
Bowling Alley B2
Brandsfarm Way C3
Brunel Rd B1
Bus Station B2
Buxton Rd C1
Central Park A2
Chelsea Gardens B2
Coach Central B2
Coachwell Close B1
Colliers Way A1
Courts B2
Dale Acre Way B3
Darliston C3
Deepdale B3
Deercote B2
Dinthill C3
Doddington C3
Dodmoor Grange C3
Downemead B3
Duffryn B3
Dunsheath B3
Euston Way A3
Eyton Mound C1
Eyton Rd C1
Forgegate A2
Grange Central B2
Hall Park Way B1
Hinkshay Rd C2
Hollinsworth Rd A2
Holyhead Rd A3
Housing Trust A1
Ice Rink B2
Information Centre B2
Ironmasters Way A2
Job Centre B1
Land Registry B1
Lawn Central B2
Lawnswood C1
Library B2
Malinsgate B1
Matlock Avenue C1
Moor Rd C1
Mount Rd C1
Odeon B2
Park Lane A1
Police Station B1
Post Office A2/B2/C1
Priorslee Avenue A3
Queen Elizabeth Ave C3
Queen Elizabeth Way B1
Queensway A2/B3
QEII Arena C2
Rampart Way A2
Randlay Avenue C3
Randlay Wood C3
Rhodes Avenue C1
Royal Way B1
St Leonards Rd B1
St Quentin Gate B2
Shifnal Rd A3
Silkin Way C2
Sixth Avenue A1
Southwater Leisure Complex B2
Southwater Way B1
Spout Lane C1
Spout Mound B1
Spout Way C1
Stafford Court B3
Stafford Park B3
Stirchley Avenue C3
Stone Row C1
Superstoore B1
Telford Bridge Retail Park A1
Telford Central Sta A3
Telford Centre, The B2
Telford Forge Shopping Park A1
Telford Hornets RFC C2
Telford International Centre C2
Telford Way A3
Third Avenue A2
Town Park C2
Town Park Visitor Ctr B2
Wellswood Avenue A2
West Centre Way B1
Withywood Drive C1
Wonderland C2
Woodhouse Central B2
Yates Way A1

Torquay 344

Abbey Rd B2
Alexandra Rd A2
Alpine Rd B3
AMF Bowling C3
Ash Hill Rd A2
Babbacombe Rd B3
Bampfylde Rd B1
Barton Rd A1
Beacon Quay C2
Belgrave Rd A1/B1
Belmont Rd A3
Berea Rd A3
Braddons Hill Rd East B3
Brewery Park A3
Bronshill Rd A2
Carlton Rd A3
Castle Circus A2
Castle Rd A2
Cavern Rd A3
Central B2
Chatsworth Rd A2
Chestnut Avenue B1
Church St A1
Coach Station A1
Corbyn Head C1
Croft Hill B1
Croft Rd B1
East St A1
Egerton Rd A3
Ellacombe Church Rd A3
Ellacombe Rd A2
Falkland Rd B1
Fleet St B2
Fleet Walk Shopping Centre B2
Grafton Rd B3
Grange Rd A3
Haldon Pier C2
Hatfield Rd A2
Highbury Rd A2
Higher Warberry Rd A3
Hillesdon Rd B3
Hoxton Rd A3
Hunsdon Rd B3
Information Centre B2
Inner Harbour C3
Kenwyn Rd A3
King's Drive, The B1
Laburnum St A1
Law Courts A2
Library A2
Lime Avenue B1
Living Coasts C3
Lower Warberry Rd B3
Lucius St B1
Lymington Rd A1
Magdalene Rd A1
Marina C2
Market Forum, The B2
Market St B2
Meadfoot Lane C3
Meadfoot Rd C3
Melville St B2
Middle Warberry Rd B3
Mill Lane A1
Montpellier Rd B3
Morgan Avenue A1
Museum Rd B3
Newton Rd A1
Oakhill Rd A1
Outer Harbour C2
Parkhill Rd C3
Pimlico B2
Police Station A1
Post Office A1/B2
Prince of Wales Steps C3
Princes Rd A3
Princes Rd East A3
Princes Rd West A3
Princess Gardens C2
Princess Pier C2
Princess Theatre C2
Rathmore Rd B1
Recreation Grd B1
Riviera International Centre B1
Rock End Avenue C3
Rock Rd B2
Rock Walk B2
Rosehill Rd A3
South West Coast Path C3
St Efride's Rd A1
St John's B3
St Luke's Rd B2
St Luke's Rd North B2
St Luke's Rd South B2
St Marychurch Rd A2
Scarborough Rd B1
Shedden Hill B2
South Pier C2
South St A1
Spanish Barn B1
Stitchill Rd B3
Strand B3
Sutherland Rd B3
Teignmouth Rd A1
Temperance St B2
Terrace, The B3
Thurlow Rd A1
Tor Bay B1
Tor Church Rd A1
Tor Hill Rd A1
Torbay Rd B2
Torquay Museum B3
Torquay Station C1
Torquay Tennis Club B1
Torre Abbey B1
Torre Abbey Meadows B1
Torre Abbey Sands B1
Torwood Gardens B3
Torwood St C3
Town Hall A2
Union Square Shopping Centre A2
Union St A1
Upton Hill A2
Upton Park A1
Upton Rd A1
Vanehill Rd C3
Vansittart Rd A1
Vaughan Parade C2
Victoria Parade C3
Victoria Rd A2
Warberry Rd West B2
Warren Rd B2
Windsor Rd A2/A3
Woodville Rd A3

Truro 344

Adelaide Ter B1
Agar Rd B3
Arch Hill C2
Arundell Place C2
Avenue, The A3
Avondale Rd B1
Back Quay B3
Barrack Lane C3
Barton Meadow A1
Benson Rd A2
Bishops Close A2
Bosvean Gardens B1
Bosvigo Gardens B1
Bosvigo Lane A1
Bosvigo Rd B2
Broad St A3
Burley Close C3
Bus Station B3
Calenick St B2
Campfield Hill B3
Carclew St B3
Carew Rd A2
Carey Park B2
Carlyon Rd A2
Carvoza Rd A3
Castle St B2
Cathedral View A2
Chainwalk Drive A2
Chapel Hill B1
Charles St B2
City Hall B3
City Rd B2
Coinage Hall B3
Comprigney Hill A1
Coosebean Lane A1
Copes Gardens A2
County Hall B1
Courtney Rd A2
Crescent Rd B1
Crescent Rise B1
Crescent, The B1
Daniell Court C2
Daniell Rd C2
Daniell St C2
Daubuz Close A2
Daubuz Moors Nature Reserve A3
Dobbs Lane B1
Edward St B2
Eliot Rd A2
Elm Court A3
Enys Close A1
Enys Rd A1
Fairmantle St B3
Falmouth Rd C2
Ferris Town B2
Fire Station B1
Frances St B2
George St B2
Green Close C2
Green Lane C1
Grenville Rd A2
Hall For Cornwall B3
Hendra Rd A2
Hendra Vean A1
High Cross B3
Higher Newham Lane C3
Higher Trehaverne A2
Hillcrest Avenue B1
Hospital B2
Hunkin Close A2
Hurland Rd C3
Infirmary Hill B2
James Place B3
Kenwyn Church Rd A1
Kenwyn Hill A1
Kenwyn Rd A2
Kenwyn St B2
Kerris Gardens A1
King St B3
Leats, The B2
Lemon Quay B3
Lemon St Gallery B3
Library B1/B3
Malpas Rd B3
Magistrates Court A3
Market B3
Merrifield Close B1
Mitchell Hill A3

Moresk Close A3
Moresk Rd A3
Morlaix Avenue C3
Nancemere Rd A3
Newham Bsns Park C3
Newham Industrial Est C3
Newham Rd C3
Northfield Drive C3
Oak Way A3
Palace's Terrace A3
Park View C2
Pendarves Rd A2
Plaza Cinema A3
Police Station A2/B3
Post Office B3
Prince's St B3
Pydar St A2
Quay St B3
Redannick Crescent C2
Redannick Lane B2
Richard Lander Monument C2
Richmond Hill B1
River St B2
Rosedale Rd A2
Royal Cornwall Mus B2
St Aubyn Rd C3
St Clement St B3
St George's Rd A1
Standing Cross B3
School Lane C2
Spires, The A2
Station Rd B1
Stokes Rd A2
Strangways Terrace C3
Tabernacle St B3
Trehaverne Lane A2
Tremayne Rd A2
Treseder's Gardens A3
Treworder Rd B1
Treyew Rd B1
Truro Cathedral B3
Truro Harbour Office B3
Truro Station B3
Union St B2
Upper School Lane C2
Victoria Gardens B2
Waterfall Gardens B2

Wick 344

Ackergill Crescent A2
Ackergill St A2
Albert St C2
Ambulance Station A2
Argyle Square C2
Assembly Rooms C2
Bank Row C2
Bankhead B1
Barons Well B2
Barrogill St C2
Bay View B3
Bexley Terrace C3
Bignold Park C2
Bowling Green C2
Breadalbane Terrace C2
Bridge of Wick B1
Bridge St B2
Brown Place C2
Burn St B2
Bus Station B1
Caithness General Hospital (A&E) B1
Cliff Rd B1
Coach Rd B2
Coastguard Station C3
Corner Crescent B3
Coronation St C1
Council Offices B2
Court B2
Crane Rock C3
Dempster St C2
Dunnet Avenue A2
Fire Station B2
Francis St C1
George St A1
Girnigoe St B2
Glamis Rd B2
Gowrie Place B1
Grant St C2
Green Rd B2
Gunns Terrace B3
Harbour Quay B2
Harbour Rd C3
Harbour Terrace C2
Harrow Hill C2
Henrietta St A2/B2
Heritage Museum C2
High St B2
Hill Avenue A2
Hillhead Rd B3
Hood St C1
Huddart St C2
Kenneth St C1
Kinnaird St C2
Kirk Hill B1
Langwell Crescent B3
Leishman Avenue B3
Leith Walk A2
Library B2
Liby & Swimming Pool C1
Lifeboat Station C3
Lighthouse C3
Lindsay Drive B3
Lindsay Place B3
Loch St C2
Louisburgh St B2
Lower Dunbar St C2
Macleay Lane B1
Macleod Rd B3
MacRae St C2
Martha Terrace B2
Miller Avenue B1
Miller Lane B1
Moray St C2
Mowat Place B3
Murchison St C3
Newton Avenue C1
Newton Rd C1
Nicolson St C3
North Highland Coll. B2
North River Pier B3
Northcote St C2
Owen Place A2
Police Station B1
Port Dunbar B3
Post Office B2/C2
Pulteney Distillery C2
River St B2
Robert St A1
Rutherford St C2
St John's Episcopal C2
Sandigoe Rd B3
Scalesburn B3
Seaforth Avenue C1
Shore Lane B2
Shore, The B2
Sinclair Drive B3
Sinclair Terrace C2
Smith Terrace C3
South Pier C3
South Quay C3
South Rd C1
South River Pier B3
Station Rd B1
Superstore A1/B1
Telford St B2
Thurso Rd B1
Thurso St B1
Town Hall B2
Union St B2
Upper Dunbar St C2
Vansittart St C3
Victoria Place B2
War Memorial A1
Well of Cairndhuna C3
Wellington Avenue C3
Wellington St C3
West Banks Avenue C1
West Banks Terrace C1
West Park C1
Whitehorse Park B2
Wick Harbour Bridge B2
Wick Industrial Estate A2
Wick Parish Church B1
Wick Station B1
Williamson St B2
Willowbank B2

Winchester 344

Andover Rd A2
Andover Rd Retail Pk A2
Archery Lane C2
Arthur Rd A2
Bar End Rd C3
Beaufort Rd C2
Beggar's Lane B3
Bereweeke Avenue A1
Bereweeke Rd A1
Boscobel Rd A2
Brassey Rd A2
Broadway B3
Brooks Shopping Centre, The B3
Bus Station B3
Butter Cross B2
Canon St C2
Castle Wall C2/C3
Cathedral C2
Cheriton Rd A1
Chesil St C3
Chesil Theatre C3
Christchurch Rd C1
City Mill B3
City Museum B2
City Rd B2
Clifton Rd B1
Clifton Terrace B2
Close Wall C2/C3
Coach Park A2
Colebrook St C3
College St C2
College Walk C3
Compton Rd C2
Council Offices C3
County Council Offices B2
Cranworth Rd A2
Cromwell Rd C1
Culver Rd C2
Discovery Centre B2
Domum Rd C3
Durngate Place B3
Eastgate St B3
East Hill C3
Edgar Rd C2
Egbert Rd A2
Elm Rd B1
Everyman C2
Fairfield Rd A1
Fire Station B3
Fordington Avenue B1
Fordington Rd A1
Friarsgate B3
Gordon Rd B3
Great Hall & Round Table, The B2
Greenhill Rd B1
Guildhall B3
Hatherley Rd A1
High St B2
Hillier Way A3
HM Prison B1
Hyde Abbey (Remains) A2
Hyde Abbey Rd B2
Hyde Close A2
Hyde St A2
Information Centre B3
Jane Austen's Ho C2
Jewry St B2
King Alfred Place A2
Kingsgate Arch C2
Kingsgate Park C2
Kingsgate Rd C2
Kingsgate St C2
Lankhills Rd A2
Law Courts B2
Library B2
Lower Brook St B3
Magdalen Hill B3
Market Lane B2
Mews Lane B1
Middle Brook St B2
Middle Rd B1
Military Museums B2
Milland Rd C3
Milverton Rd B1
Monks Rd A3
North Hill Close A2
North Walls B2
North Walls Rec Gnd A3
Nuns Rd A3
Oram's Arbour B1
Owens Rd A2
Parchment St B2
Park & Ride C3
Park Avenue B3
Playing Field A1
Police HQ B1
Portal Rd C3
Post Office B2/C1
Ranelagh Rd C1
Regimental Mus B2
River Park Leisure Ctr B3
Romans' Rd C2
Romsey Rd B1
Royal Hampshire County Hospital (A&E) B1
St Cross Rd C2
St George's St B2
St Giles Hill C3
St James Villas C2
St James' Lane B1
St James' Terrace B1
St John's B3
St John's St B3
St Michael's Rd C2
St Paul's Hill B1
St Peter St B2
St Swithun St C2
St Thomas St C2
Saxon Rd A2
School of Art B3
Sleepers Hill Rd C1
Southgate St B2
Sparkford Rd C1
Square, The B2
Staple Gardens B2
Station Rd B2
Step Terrace B1
Stockbridge Rd A1
Stuart Crescent C1
Sussex St B2
Swan Lane B2
Tanner St B3
Theatre Royal B2
Tower St B2
Union St B3
Univ of Southampton (Winchester School of Art) B3
Univ of Winchester (King Alfred Campus) C1
Upper Brook St B2
Wales St B3
Water Lane B3
Weirs, The C3
West End Terrace B1
Western Rd B1
Westgate B2
Wharf Hill C3
Winchester Station A2
Winnall Moors Wildlife Reserve A3
Wolvesey Castle C3
Worthy Lane A2
Worthy Rd A2

Windsor 344

Adelaide Square C3
Albany Rd C2
Albert St B1
Alexandra Gardens B2
Alexandra Rd C2
Alma Rd B2
Arthur Rd B2
Bachelors Acre B3
Barry Avenue B2
Beaumont Rd C2
Bexley St B1
Boat House B2
Brocas St B2
Brocas, The A2
Brook St C3
Bulkeley Avenue C1
Castle Hill B3
Charles St B2
Claremont Rd C2
Clarence Crescent B2
Clarence Rd B1
Clewer Court Rd B1
Coach Park B2
College Crescent C1
Cricket Ground C3
Dagmar Rd C2
Datchet Rd B3
Devereux Rd C2
Dorset Rd C2
Duke St B1
Elm Rd C1
Eton College A3
Eton College Natural History Museum A2
Eton Court A2
Eton Square A2
Eton Wick Rd A2
Farm Yard B3
Fire Station C2
Frances Rd C2
Frogmore Drive B3
Gloucester Place C3
Goslar Way C1
Goswell Hill B2
Goswell Rd B2
Green Lane C1
Grove Rd C2
Guildhall B3
Helena Rd C2
Helston Lane B1
High St A2/B3
Holy Trinity C2
Home Park, The A3/C3
Household Cavalry C2
Imperial Rd C1
Information Centre B2
Keats Lane A2
King Edward VII Ave A3
King Edward VII Hospital C2
King George V Memorial B3
King Stable St A2
King's Rd C3
Library A2/B2
Long Walk, The C3
Maidenhead Rd B1
Meadow Lane A2
Municipal Offices C3
Nell Gwynne's Ho B3
Osborne Rd C2
Oxford Rd B1
Park St B3
Peascod St B2
Police Station C2
Post Office A2/C1
Princess Margaret Hospital (private) C2
Old Court Art Space, The C2
Queen Elizabeth Bridge A1
Queen Victoria's Walk B3
Queen's Rd C2
River St B2
Romney Island A3
Romney Lock A3
Romney Lock Rd A3
Russell St C2
St George's Chapel B3
St John's B3
St John's Chapel A2
St Leonards Rd C2
St Mark's Rd C2
Sheet St C3
Shopmobility B2
South Meadow A2
South Meadow Lane A2
Springfield Rd C1
Stovell Rd B1
Sunbury Rd A2
Tangier Lane A2
Temple Rd C2
Thames St B3
Theatre Royal B3
Trinity Place C2
Vansittart Rd B1/C1
Victoria Barracks C2
Victoria St C2
Westmead C1
White Lilies Island A1
William St B2
Windsor & Eton Central B2
Windsor & Eton Riverside A3
Windsor Bridge B3
Windsor Castle B3
Windsor Leisure Ctr B1
Windsor Relief Rd A1
Windsor Royal Station Shopping Centre B2
Windsor Yards B2
York Avenue C1
York Rd C1

Wolverhampton 344

Albion St B3
Arena B2
Art Gallery B2
Ashland St C1
Austin St A1
Badger Drive A3
Bailey St B3
Bath Avenue B1
Bath Rd B1
Bell St C2
Berry St B3
Bilston Rd C3
Bilston St C3
Birmingham Canal A3
Bone Mill Lane A2
Brewery Rd B1
Bright St A1
Burton Crescent B3
Bus Station B3
Cambridge St A3
Camp St B2
Cannock Rd A3
Castle St C2
Chapel Ash C1
Cherry St C1
Chester St A1
Church Lane C2
Church St C2
Civic Centre B2
Civic Hall B2
Clarence Rd B2
Cleveland St C2
Clifton St C1
Coach Station B2
Compton Rd B1
Corn Hill B3
Coven St A3
Craddock St A1
Cross St North A2
Crown & County Courts C3
Crown St A2
Culwell St B3
Dale St C1
Darlington St C1
Devon Rd A1
Drummond St B2
Dudley Rd C2
Dudley St B2
Duke St C3
Dunkley St B1
Dunstall Avenue A2
Dunstall Hill A2
Dunstall Rd A1/A2
Evans St A1
Fawdry St A1
Field St B3
Fire Station C1
Fiveways A2
Fowler Playing Fields A3
Fox's Lane A2
Francis St A2
Fryer St B3
Gloucester St A1
Gordon St C3
Graiseley St C1
Grand B3
Grand Station B3
Granville St C3
Great Brickkiln St C1
Great Hampton St A1
Great Western St A2
Grimstone St B3
Harrow St A1
Hilton St A3
Hive Library The B2
Horseley Fields C3
Humber Rd C1
Jack Hayward Way A2
Jameson St A1
Jenner St C3
Kennedy Rd B3
Kimberley St C1
King St B2
Laburnum St C1
Lansdowne Rd B1
Leicester St A1
Lever St C3
Library C3
Lichfield St B2
Light House B3
Little's Lane B3
Lock St B3
Lord St C1
Lowe St A1
Maltings, The B2
Mander Centre C2
Mander St C1
Market C2
Market St B2
Maxwell Rd C3
Merridale St C1
Middlecross C3
Molineux St B2
Mostyn St A1
Newhampton Arts Centre B1
New Hampton Rd East A1
Nine Elms Lane A3
North Rd A2
Oaks Crescent C1
Oxley St A2
Paget St A1
Park Avenue B1
Park Road East A1
Park Road West B1
Paul St C2
Pelham St C1
Penn Rd C2
Piper's Row C3
Piper's Row C3
Pitt St C2
Police Station C3
Pool St C2
Poole St A3
Post Office A1/B2/B2/C2/C3
Powlett St C3
Queen St B2
Raby St C3
Railway Drive B3
Red Hill St A2
Red Lion St B2
Retreat St C1
Ring Rd B2
Royal, The C3
Rugby St A1
Russell St C1
St Andrew's B1
St David's B3
St George's C3
St George's Parade C2
St James St C3
St John's C2
St John's C2
St John's Retail Park C2
St John's Square C2
St Mark's C1
St Marks Rd C1
St Marks St C1
St Patrick's B2
St Peter's B2
St Peter's B2
Salisbury St C1
Salop St C2
School St C2
Sherwood St A2
Smestow St A3
Snow Hill C2
Springfield Rd A3
Stafford St A2/B2
Staveley Rd A1
Steelhouse Lane C3
Stephenson St C1
Stewart St C2
Sun St B3
Tempest St C2
Temple St C2
Tettenhall Rd B1
Thomas St C2
Thornley St B2
Tower St C2
University B2
Upper Zoar St C1
Vicarage Rd C3
Victoria St C2
Walpole St A1
Walsall St C3
Ward St C3
Warwick St C3
Water St A3
Waterloo Rd B2
Wednesfield Rd B3
West Park (not A&E) B1
West Park Swimming Pool B1
Wharf St C3
Whitmore Hill B2
Wolverhampton B3
Wolverhampton B3
Wolverhampton St George's C2
Wolverhampton Wanderers Football Gnd (Molineux) B2
Worcester St C2
Wulfrun Centre C2
Yarwell Close A3
York St C3
Zoar St C1

Worcester 344

Albany Terrace A1
Angel Place B2
Angel St B2
Ashcroft Rd A2
Athelstan Rd C3
Avenue, The C1
Back Lane North A1
Back Lane South A1
Barbourne Rd A2
Bath Rd C2
Battenhall Rd C3
Bridge St B2
Britannia Square A1
Broad St B2
Bromwich Lane C1
Bromwich Rd C1
Bromyard Rd C1
Bus Station B2
Butts, The B2
Carden St B3
Castle St A2
Cathedral C2
Cathedral Plaza B2
Charles St B3
Chequers Lane B1
Chestnut St A2
Chestnut Walk A2
Citizens' Advice Bureau B2
City Walls Rd B2
Cole Hill C3
College St C2
Commandery, The C3
Cripplegate Park B1
Croft Rd B1
Cromwell St B3
Cross, The B2
Crowngate Centre B2
Deansway B2
Diglis Parade C2
Diglis Rd C2
Edgar Tower C2
Farrier St A2
Foregate St B2
Fort Royal Hill C3
Fort Royal Park C3
Foundry St B3
Friar St C2
George St B3
Grand Stand Rd B1
Greenhill C3
Greyfriars B2
Guildhall B2
Henwick Rd B1
High St B2
Hill St B3
Hive, The B2
Huntingdon Hall B2
Hylton Rd B1
Information Centre B2
King Charles Place Shopping Centre C1
King's School C2
King's School Playing Field C2
Kleve Walk C2
Lansdowne Crescent A3
Lansdowne Rd A3
Lansdowne Walk A3
Laslett St A3
Little Chestnut St A2
Little London A2
London Rd C3
Lowell St A3
Lowesmoor B2
Lowesmoor Terrace A3
Lowesmoor Wharf A3
Magistrates Court A2
Midland Rd B3
Mill St C2
Moors Severn Terrace, The A1
Mus & Art Gallery A2
Museum of Royal Worcester C2
New Rd C1
New St B2
Northfield St A2
Odeon B2
Old Palace The C2
Padmore St B3
Park St C3
Pheasant St B3
Pitchcroft Racecourse A1
Police Station A2
Portland St C2
Post Office B2
Quay St B2
Queen St B2
Rainbow Hill A3
Recreation Ground A2
Reindeer Court B2
Rogers Hill A3
Sabrina Terrace A2
St Dunstan's Cre. C3
St John's C1
St Martin's Gate B3
St Martin's Quarter B3
St Oswald's Rd A2
St Paul's St B3
St Swithin's Church B2
St Wulstans Crescent C3
Sansome Walk A2
Severn St C2
Shambles, The B2
Shaw St B2
Shire Hall Crown Ct A2
Shrub Hill Rd B3
Shrub Hill Retail Park B3
Slingpool Walk C1
South Parade B2
Southfield St A2
Sports Centre A3
Stanley Rd B3
Swan, The A1
Swimming Pool A2
Tallow Hill B3
Tennis Walk A2
Tolladine Rd B3
Tudor House B2
Tybridge St B1
Tything, The A2
Univ of Worcester B2
Vincent Rd B3
Vue C2
Washington St A3
Woolhope Rd C3
Worcester Bridge B2
Worcester County Cricket Club C1
Worcester Foregate Street B2
Worcester Shrub Hill B3
Worcester Royal Grammar School A2
Wylds Lane C3

Wrexham Wrecsam 344

Abbot St B2
Acton Rd A3
Albert St C3
Alexandra Rd C1
Aran Rd A3
Barnfield C3
Bath Rd C2
Beeches, The A3
Beechley Rd C3
Belgrave Rd C2
Bellevue Park C2
Bellevue Rd C2
Belvedere Drive A1
Bennion's Rd C3
Berse Rd A1
Bersham Rd C1
Birch St C3
Bodhyfryd B3
Border Retail Park B3
Bradley Rd C2
Bright St B1
Bron-y-Nant B1
Brook St C2
Bryn-y-Cabanau Rd C3
Bury St C3
Bus Station B2
Butchers Market B3
Caia Rd C3
Cambrian Ind Est C3
Caxton Place B2
Cemetery C1
Centenary Rd C1
Central Retail Park B2
Chapel St C2
Charles St B3
Chester Rd A3
Chester St B3
Cilcen Grove A3
Citizens Advice Bureau B2
Cobden Rd B1
Council Offices B3
County B2
Crescent Rd B3
Crispin Lane A2
Croesnewyth Rd B1
Cross St A2
Cunliffe St A2
Derby Rd C3
Dolydd Rd B1
Duke St B2
Eagles Meadow C3
Earle St C2
East Avenue A2
Edward St C2
Egerton St B2
Empress Rd C1
Erddig Rd C2
Fairy Rd C2
Fire Station B2
Foster Rd A3
Foxwood Drive C1
Garden Rd A2
General Market B3
Gerald St B2
Gibson St C1
Glyndwr University Plas Coch Campus A1
Greenbank St C3
Greenfield A2
Grosvenor Rd B2
Grove Park B2
Grove Park Rd B3
Grove Rd A3
Guildhall B2
Haig Rd C3
Hampden Rd C2
Hazel Grove A3
Henblas St B3
High St B3
Hightown Rd C3
Hill St B2
Holt Rd B3
Holt St B3
Hope St B2
Huntroyde Avenue C3
Information Centre B3
Island Green Shopping Centre B2
Jobcentre Plus B2
Jubilee Rd B2
King St B2
Kingsmills Rd C3
Lambpit St B3
Law Courts B3
Lawson Close A3
Lawson Rd A3
Lea Rd C2
Library & Arts Centre B2
Lilac Way B1
Llys David Lord B1
Lorne St A2
Maesgwyn Rd B1
Maesydre Rd A3
Manley Rd B3
Market St B3
Mawddy Avenue A2
Mayville Avenue A2
Memorial Gallery B2
Memorial Hall B3
Mold Rd A1
Mount St C3
Neville Crescent A3
New Rd A2
North Wales Regional Tennis Centre A1
Oak Drive A3
Odeon C3
Park Avenue A3
Park St A2
Peel St C1
Pen y Bryn C2
Pentre Felin C2
Penymaes Avenue A3
Peoples Market B3
Percy St C2
Pines, The A3
Plas Coch Rd A1
Plas Coch Retail Park A1
Police Station B3
Poplar Rd C2
Post Office A2/B3/C3
Powell Rd B3
Poyser St C2
Price's Lane A2
Primose Way B1
Princess St C1
Queen St B3
Queens Square B2
Regent St B2
Rhosddu Rd A2/B2
Rhosnesni Lane A3
Rivulet Rd C3
Ruabon Rd C2
Ruthin Rd C1/C2
St Giles C3
St Giles Way C3
St James Court A2
St Mary's B2
Salisbury Rd C3
Salop Rd C3
Sontley Rd C2
Spring Rd A2
Stanley St C3
Stansty Rd A2
Station Approach B2
Studio B2
Superstore B3/C1
Talbot Rd C2
Techniquest Glyndŵr A2
Town Hill C2
Trevor St C2
Trinity St B2
Tuttle St C3
Vale Park A1
Vernon St B2
Vicarage Hill B2
Victoria Rd C2
Walnut St A2
War Memorial B3
Waterworld Leisure Centre B3
Watery Rd B1/B2
Wellington Rd C2
Westminster Drive A3
William Aston Hall A1
Windsor Rd A1
Wrecsam
Wrexham AFC A1
Wrexham Central B2
Wrexham General B2
Wrexham Maelor Hospital (A&E) B1
Wrexham Technology Park B1
Wynn Avenue A2
Yale College B3
Yale Grove A3
Yorke St C3

York 344

Aldwark B2
Barbican Rd C3
Bar Convent Living Heritage Centre C1
Barley Hall B2
Bishopgate St C2
Bishopshill Senior C2
Bishopthorpe Rd C2
Blossom St C1
Bootham A1
Bootham Crescent A1
Bootham Terrace A1
Bridge St B2
Brook St A2
Brownlow St A2
Burton Stone Lane A1
Castle Museum C2
Castlegate B2
Cemetery Rd C3
Cherry St C2
City Screen B2
City Wall A2/B1/C3
Clarence St A2
Clementhorpe C2
Clifford St B2
Clifford's Tower B2
Clifton A1
Coach park A2
Coney St B2
Coppergate Centre B2
Cromwell Rd C2
Crown Court C2
Davygate B2
Deanery Gardens A2
DIG B2
Dodsworth Avenue A3
Eboracum Way A3
Ebor Industrial Estate B3
Eldon St A2
Everyman C1
Fairfax House B2
Fire Station C3
Fishergate C3
Foss Islands Rd B3
Foss Islands Retail Pk B3
Fossbank A3
Garden St A2
George St C3
Gillygate A2
Goodramgate B2
Grand Opera House B2
Grosvenor Terrace A1
Guildhall B2
Hallfield Rd A3
Heslington Rd C3
Heworth Green A3
Holy Trinity B2
Hope St C3
Huntington Rd A3
Information Centre B2
James St B3
Jorvik Viking Ctr B2
Kent St C3
Lawrence St C3
Layerthorpe A3
Leeman Rd B1
Lendal B2
Lendal Bridge B1
Library A2/B1
Longfield Terrace A1
Lord Mayor's Walk A2
Lowther St A2
Mansion House B2
Margaret St C3
Marygate A1
Melbourne St C3
Merchant Adventurers' Hall B2
Merchant Taylors' Hall B2
Micklegate B1
Micklegate Bar C1
Monkgate A2
Moss St C1
Museum Gdns B1
Museum St B1
National Railway Museum B1
Navigation Rd B3
Newton Terrace C2
North Parade A1
North St B2
Nunnery Lane C1
Nunthorpe Rd C1
Ouse Bridge B2
Paragon St C3
Park Grove A3
Park St C1
Parliament St B2
Peasholme Green B3
Penley's Grove St A2
Piccadilly B2
Police Station B2
Post Office B1/B2/C3
Priory St B1
Queen Anne's Rd A1
Regimental Mus B2
Richard III Experience at Monk Bar A2
Roman Bath B2
Rowntree Park C2
St Andrewgate B2
St Benedict Rd C1
St John St A2
St Olave's Rd A1
St Peter's Grove A1
St Saviourgate B2
Scarcroft Hill C1
Scarcroft Rd C1
Shambles, The B2
Shopmobility B2
Skeldergate C2
Skeldergate Bridge C2
Station Rd B1
Stonebow, The B2
Stonegate B2
Superstore A3
Sycamore Terrace A1
Terry Avenue C2
Theatre Royal B2
Thorpe St C1
Toft Green B1
Tower St C2
Townend St A2
Treasurer's House A2
Trinity Lane B1
Undercroft Mus A2
Union Terrace A2
Victor St C2
Vine St C2
Walmgate B3
War Memorial B1
Wellington St C3
York Art Gallery A1
York Barbican C3
York Brewery B1
York Dungeon, The B2
York Minster A2
York St John Univ. A2
York Station B1

Index to road maps of Britain

Abbreviations used in the index

Aberdeen	Aberdeen City
Aberds	Aberdeenshire
Ald	Alderney
Anglesey	Isle of Anglesey
Angus	Angus
Argyll	Argyll and Bute
Bath	Bath and North East Somerset
BCP	Bournemouth, Christchurch and Poole
Bedford	Bedford
Blackburn	Blackburn with Darwen
Blackpool	Blackpool
Bl Gwent	Blaenau Gwent
Borders	Scottish Borders
Brack	Bracknell
Bridgend	Bridgend
Brighton	City of Brighton and Hove
Bristol	City and County of Bristol
Bucks	Buckinghamshire
Caerph	Caerphilly
Cambs	Cambridgeshire
Cardiff	Cardiff
Carms	Carmarthenshire
C Beds	Central Bedfordshire
Ceredig	Ceredigion
Ches E	Cheshire East
Ches W	Cheshire West and Chester
Clack	Clackmannanshire
Conwy	Conwy
Corn	Cornwall
Cumb	Cumbria
Darl	Darlington
Denb	Denbighshire
Derby	City of Derby
Derbys	Derbyshire
Devon	Devon
Dorset	Dorset
Dumfries	Dumfries and Galloway
Dundee	Dundee City
Durham	Durham
E Ayrs	East Ayrshire
Edin	City of Edinburgh
E Dunb	East Dunbartonshire
E Loth	East Lothian
E Renf	East Renfrewshire
Essex	Essex
E Sus	East Sussex
E Yorks	East Riding of Yorkshire
Falk	Falkirk
Fife	Fife
Flint	Flintshire
Glasgow	City of Glasgow
Glos	Gloucestershire
Gtr Man	Greater Manchester
Guern	Guernsey
Gwyn	Gwynedd
Halton	Halton
Hants	Hampshire
Hereford	Herefordshire
Herts	Hertfordshire
Highld	Highland
Hrtlpl	Hartlepool
Hull	Hull
Invclyd	Inverclyde
IoM	Isle of Man
IoW	Isle of Wight
Jersey	Jersey
Kent	Kent
Lancs	Lancashire
Leicester	City of Leicester
Leics	Leicestershire
Lincs	Lincolnshire
London	Greater London
Luton	Luton
Mbro	Middlesbrough
Medway	Medway
Mers	Merseyside
Midloth	Midlothian
M Keynes	Milton Keynes
Mon	Monmouthshire
Moray	Moray
M Tydf	Merthyr Tydfil
N Ayrs	North Ayrshire
Neath	Neath Port Talbot
NE Lincs	North East Lincolnshire
Newport	City and County of Newport
N Lanark	North Lanarkshire
N Lincs	North Lincolnshire
N Nhants	North Northamptonshire
Norf	Norfolk
Northumb	Northumberland
Nottingham	City of Nottingham
Notts	Nottinghamshire
N Som	North Somerset
N Yorks	North Yorkshire
Orkney	Orkney
Oxon	Oxfordshire
Pboro	Peterborough
Pembs	Pembrokeshire
Perth	Perth and Kinross
Plym	Plymouth
Powys	Powys
Ptsmth	Portsmouth
Reading	Reading
Redcar	Redcar and Cleveland
Renfs	Renfrewshire
Rhondda	Rhondda Cynon Taff
Rutland	Rutland
S Ayrs	South Ayrshire
Scilly	Scilly
S Glos	South Gloucestershire
Shetland	Shetland
Shrops	Shropshire
S Lanark	South Lanarkshire
Slough	Slough
Som	Somerset
Soton	Southampton
Southend	Southend-on-Sea
Staffs	Staffordshire
Stirling	Stirling
Stockton	Stockton-on-Tees
Stoke	Stoke-on-Trent
Suff	Suffolk
Sur	Surrey
Swansea	Swansea
Swindon	Swindon
S Yorks	South Yorkshire
T&W	Tyne and Wear
Telford	Telford and Wrekin
Thurrock	Thurrock
Torbay	Torbay
Torf	Torfaen
V Glam	The Vale of Glamorgan
Warks	Warwickshire
Warr	Warrington
W Berks	West Berkshire
W Dunb	West Dunbartonshire
Wilts	Wiltshire
Windsor	Windsor and Maidenhead
W Isles	Western Isles
W Loth	West Lothian
W Mid	West Midlands
W Nhants	West Northamptonshire
Wokingham	Wokingham
Worcs	Worcestershire
Wrex	Wrexham
W Sus	West Sussex
W Yorks	West Yorkshire
York	City of York

How to use the index

Example **Witham Friary** Som **45** E8

- grid square
- page number
- county or unitary authority

A

Aar–All

Aaron's Hill Sur 50 E3
Aaron's Town Cumb 240 E2
Abbas Combe Som 30 C2
Abberley Worcs 116 D5
Abberton Essex 89 B8
Worcs 117 G9
Abberwick Northumb 264 G4
Abbess End Essex 87 C9
Abbess Roding Essex 87 C9
Abbey Devon 27 E10
Abbeycwmhir Powys 113 C11
Abbey-cwm-hir Powys 113 C11
Abbeydale Glos 80 B5
S Yorks 186 E4
Abbeydale Park S Yorks 186 E4
Abbey Dore Hereford 97 E7
Abbey Field Essex 107 G9
Abbey Gate Kent 53 B9
Abbey Green Shrops 149 C10
Staffs 169 D7
Abbey Hey Gtr Man 184 B5
Abbeyhill Edin 280 G5
Abbey Hulton Stoke 168 F6
Abbey Mead Sur 66 F4
Abbey St Bathans
Borders 272 C5
Abbeystead Lancs 203 C7
Abbey Town Cumb 238 G5
Abbey Village Lancs 194 C6
Abbey Wood London 68 D3
Abbots Bickington Devon 24 E5
Abbots Bromley Staffs 151 E11
Abbotsbury Dorset 17 D7
Abbotsford W Sus 36 C4
Abbotsham Devon 24 B6
Abbotskerswell Devon 9 B7
Abbots Langley Herts 85 E9
Abbotsleigh Devon 8 F6
Abbots Leigh N Som 60 E4
Abbotsley Cambs 122 F4
Abbot's Meads Ches W 166 B5
Abbots Morton Worcs 117 F10
Abbots Ripton Cambs 122 B4
Abbots Salford Warks 117 G11
Abbotstone Hants 48 G5
Abbotswood Hants 32 C5
Sur 50 C4
Abbots Worthy Hants 48 G3
Abbotts Ann Hants 47 E10
Abcott Shrops 115 B7
Abdon Shrops 131 F11
Abdy S Yorks 186 B6
Aber Ceredig 93 B9
Aberaeron Ceredig 111 E9
Aberaman Rhondda 77 E8
Aberangell Gwyn 146 G6
Aber-Arad Carms 92 D6
Aberarder Highld 290 E6
Aberarder House Highld 300 G6
Aberarder Lodge Highld 291 E7
Aberargie Perth 286 F5
Aberarth Ceredig 111 E9
Aberavon Neath 57 C8
Aber-banc Ceredig 93 C7
Aberbargoed Caerph 77 E11
Aberbechan Powys 130 E2
Aberbeeg Bl Gwent 78 E2
Aberbran Powys 95 F9
Abercanaid M Tydf 77 E9
Abercarn Caerph 78 G2
Abercastle Pembs 91 E7
Abercegir Powys 128 C6
Aberchalder Highld 290 C5
Aberchirder Aberds 302 D6
Abercorn W Loth 279 F11
Aber Cowarch Gwyn 147 F7
Abercraf Powys 76 C4
Abercregan Neath 57 B11
Abercrombie Fife 287 G9
Abercwmboi Rhondda 77 F8
Abercych Pembs 92 C4
Abercynafon Powys 77 B9
Abercynffig = *Aberkenfig*
Bridgend 57 E11
Abercynon Rhondda 77 F9
Aberdalgie Perth 286 E4
Aberdâr = *Aberdare*
Rhondda 77 E7
Aberdare = *Aberdâr*
Rhondda 77 E7
Aberdaron Gwyn 144 D3
Aberdeen Aberdeen 293 C11
Aberdesach Gwyn 162 E6
Aberdour Fife 280 D3
Aberdovey = *Aberdyfi*
Gwyn 128 D2
Aberdulais Neath 76 E3
Aberdyfi = *Aberdovey*
Gwyn 128 D2
Aberedw Powys 95 B11
Abereiddy Pembs 90 E5
Abererch Gwyn 145 B7
Aberfan M Tydf 77 E9
Aberfeldy Perth 286 C2
Aberffraw Anglesey 162 B5
Aberffrwd Ceredig 112 B3
Mon 78 D5
Aberford W Yorks 206 F4
Aberfoyle Stirlinging 285 G9
Abergarw Bridgend 58 C2
Abergarwed Neath 76 E4
Abergavenny Mon 78 C3
Abergele Conwy 180 F6
Aber-Giâr Carms 93 C10
Abergorlech Carms 93 E11
Abergwaun = *Fishguard*
Pembs 91 D9
Abergwesyn Powys 113 G7
Abergwili Carms 93 G8
Abergwynant Gwyn 146 F3
Abergwynfi Neath 57 B11
Aber-gwynfi Neath 57 B11
Abergwyngregyn Gwyn 179 G11
Abergynolwyn Gwyn 128 B3
Aber-Hirnant Gwyn 147 C9
Aberhosan Powys 128 D6
Aberkenfig = *Abercynffig*
Bridgend 57 E11
Aberlady E Loth 281 E9
Aberlemno Angus 287 B9
Aberlerry Ceredig 128 E2
Aberllefenni Gwyn 128 B5
Aberllydan = *Broad Haven*
Pembs 72 C5
Aberllynfi = *Three Cocks*
Powys 96 D3
Abermagwr Ceredig 112 C3
Abermaw = *Barmouth*
Gwyn 146 F2
Abermeurig Ceredig 111 F11
Aber miwl = *Abermule*
Powys 130 E3
Abermorddu Flint 166 D4
Abermule = *Aber-miwl*
Powys 130 E3
Abernaint Powys 148 E2
Abernant Carms 92 G6
Powys 130 D3
Aber-nant Rhondda 77 E8
Abernethy Perth 286 F5
Abernyte Perth 286 D6
Aber-oer Wrex 166 F3
Aberogwr = *Ogmore by Sea*
V Glam 57 F11
Aberpennar = *Mountain Ash*
Rhondda 77 F8
Aberporth Ceredig 110 G5
Aber-Rhiwlech Gwyn 147 E8
Aberriw = *Berriew*
Powys 130 C3
Abersoch Gwyn 144 D6
Abersychan Torf 78 E3
Abertawe = *Swansea*
Swansea 56 C6
Aberteifi = *Cardigan*
Ceredig 92 B3
Aberthin V Glam 58 D4
Abertillery Bl Gwent 78 E2
Abertridwr Caerph 58 B6
Powys 147 F10
Abertrinant Gwyn 128 B2
Abertysswg Caerph 77 D10
Aberuchill Castle
Perth 285 E11
Aberuthven Perth 286 F3
Aber-Village Powys 96 G2
Aberyscir Powys 95 F9
Aberystwyth Ceredig 111 A11
Abhainn Suidhe
W Isles 305 H2
Abingdon-on-Thames
Oxon 83 F7
Abinger Common Sur 50 D6
Abinger Hammer Sur 50 D5
Abington S Lanark 259 E10
W Nhants 120 E5
Abington Pigotts Cambs 104 C6
Abington Vale
W Nhants 120 E5
Abingworth W Sus 35 D10
Ab Kettleby Leics 154 E4
Ab Lench Worcs 117 G10
Ablington Glos 81 D10
Wilts 47 D7
Abney Derbys 185 F11
Aboyne Aberds 293 D7
Abraham Heights Lancs 211 G9
Abram Gtr Man 194 G6
Abriachan Highld 300 F5
Abridge Essex 87 F7
Abronhill N Lanark 278 F5
Abshot Hants 33 F8
Abson S Glos 61 E8
Abthorpe W Nhants 102 B2
Abune-the-Hill Orkney 314 D2
Aby Lincs 190 F6
Acaster Malbis York 207 D7
Acaster Selby N Yorks 207 E7
Accrington Lancs 195 B9
Acha Argyll 275 B8
Argyll 288 D3
Achabraid Argyll 275 E9
Achachork Highld 298 E4
Achadh an Eas Highld 308 F6
Achad nan Darach
Highld 284 B4
Achadunan Argyll 284 F5
Achafolla Argyll 275 B8
Achagary Highld 308 D7
Achaglass Argyll 255 C8
Achahoish Argyll 275 F8
Achalader Perth 286 C5
Achallader Argyll 285 C7
Achalone Highld 310 D5
Acha Mor W Isles 304 F5
Achanalt Highld 300 C2
Achanamara Argyll 275 E8
Achandunie Highld 300 B6
Achanelid Argyll 275 E11
Ach'an Todhair Highld 290 F2
Achany Highld 309 J5
Achaphubuil Highld 290 F2
Acharacle Highld 289 C8
Acharn Highld 289 D9
Perth 285 C11
Acharole Highld 310 D6
Acharossan Argyll 275 F10
Acharry Muir Highld 309 K6
Achath Aberds 293 B9
Achavanich Highld 310 E5
Achavelgin Highld 301 D9
Achavraat Highld 301 E9
Achddu Carms 74 E6
Achdregnie Moray 302 G2
Achduart Highld 307 J5
Achentoul Highld 310 F2
Achfary Highld 306 F7
Achfrish Highld 309 H5
Achgarve Highld 307 K3
Achiemore Highld 308 C3
Highld 310 D2
A'Chill Highld 294 E4
Achiltibuie Highld 307 J5
Achina Highld 308 C7
Achinahuagh Highld 308 C5
Achindaul Highld 290 E3
Achindown Highld 301 E8
Achinduich Highld 309 J5
Achinduin Argyll 289 F10
Achingills Highld 310 C5
Achininver Highld 308 C5
Achintee Highld 290 F3
Highld 299 E9
Achintraid Highld 295 B10
Achlaven Argyll 289 F11
Achlean Highld 291 D10
Achleck Argyll 288 E6
Achlorachan Highld 300 D3
Achluachrach Highld 290 E4
Achlyness Highld 306 D7
Achmelvich Highld 307 G5
Achmore Highld 295 B10
Stirlinging 285 D9
Achnaba Argyll 275 E10
Argyll 289 F11
Achnabat Highld 300 F5
Achnabreck Argyll 275 D9
Achnacarnin Highld 306 F5
Achnacarry Highld 290 E3
Achnacloich Argyll 289 F11
Highld 295 E7
Achnaconeran Highld 290 B6
Achnacraig Argyll 288 E6
Achnacree Argyll 289 F11
Achnacree Bay Argyll 289 F11
Achnacroish Argyll 289 E10
Achnadrish Argyll 288 D6
Achnafalnich Argyll 284 E6
Achnagarron Highld 300 C6
Achnaha Highld 288 C6
Achnahanat Highld 309 K5
Achnahannet Highld 301 G9
Achnahard Argyll 288 G5
Achnairn Highld 309 H5
Achnaluachrach Highld 309 J6
Achnandarach Highld 295 B10
Achnanellan Highld 290 E2
Achnasaul Highld 290 E3
Achnasheen Highld 299 D11
Achnashelloch Argyll 275 D9
Achnavast Highld 310 C4
Achneigie Highld 299 B10
Achormlarie Highld 309 K6
Achorn Highld 310 F5
Achosnich Highld 288 C6
Achranich Highld 289 E9
Achreamie Highld 310 C4
Achriabhach Highld 290 G3
Achriesgill Highld 306 D7
Achrimsdale Highld 311 J3
Achtoty Highld 308 C6
Achurch N Nhants 137 G10
Achuvoldrach Highld 308 D5
Achvaich Highld 309 K7
Achvarasdal Highld 310 C3
Ackenthwaite Cumb 211 C10
Ackergill Highld 310 D7
Acklam Mbro 225 B9
N Yorks 216 G5
Ackleton Shrops 132 D5
Acklington Northumb 252 C6
Ackton W Yorks 198 C2
Ackworth Moor Top
W Yorks 198 D2
Acle Norf 161 G8
Acock's Green W Mid 134 G2
Acol Kent 71 F10
Acomb Northumb 241 D10
York 207 C7
Acre Gtr Man 196 F2
Lancs 195 C9
Acrefair Wrex 166 G3
Acres Nook Staffs 168 E4
Acre Street W Sus 21 B11
Acton Ches E 167 E10
Dorset 18 F5
London 67 C8
Shrops 130 G6
Staffs 168 G4
Suff 107 C7
Worcs 116 D6
Wrex 166 E4
Acton Beauchamp
Hereford 116 G3
Acton Bridge Ches W 183 F9
Acton Burnell Shrops 131 C10
Acton Green Hereford 116 G3
London 67 D8
Acton Pigott Shrops 131 C10
Acton Place Suff 107 B7
Acton Reynald Shrops 149 E10
Acton Round Shrops 132 D2
Acton Scott Shrops 131 F9
Acton Trussell Staffs 151 F8
Acton Turville S Glos 61 C10
Adabroc W Isles 304 B7
Adambrae W Loth 269 A10
Adam's Green Dorset 29 F8
Adbaston Staffs 150 D5
Adber Dorset 29 C9
Adbolton Notts 154 B2
Adderbury Oxon 101 D9
Adderley Shrops 150 B3
Adderley Green Stoke 168 G6
Adderstone Northumb 264 C4
Addiewell W Loth 269 C9
Addingham W Yorks 205 D7
Addingham Moorside
W Yorks 205 D7
Addington Bucks 102 F4
Corn 6 B5
Kent 53 B7
London 67 G11
Addinston Borders 271 E10
Addiscombe London 67 F10
Addlestone Sur 66 G5
Addlestonemoor Sur 66 F4
Addlethorpe Lincs 175 B8
Adel W Yorks 205 F11
Adeney Telford 150 F4
Adeyfield Herts 85 D9
Adfa Powys 129 C11
Adforton Hereford 115 C8
Adgestone IoW 21 D7
Adisham Kent 55 C8
Adlestrop Glos 100 F4
Adlingfleet E Yorks 199 C10
Adlington Ches E 184 E6
Lancs 194 E6
Adlington Park Lancs 194 E5
Admaston Staffs 151 E10
Telford 150 G2
Admington Warks 100 B4
Adpar Ceredig 92 C6
Adsborough Som 28 B3
Adscombe Som 43 F7
Adstock Bucks 102 E4
Adstone W Nhants 119 G11
Adswood Gtr Man 184 D5
Adversane W Sus 35 C9
Advie Highld 301 F11
Adwalton W Yorks 197 B8
Adwell Oxon 83 F11
Adwick le Street
S Yorks 198 F4
Adwick upon Dearne
S Yorks 198 G3
Adziel Aberds 303 D9
Ae Dumfries 247 F11
Ae Village Dumfries 247 F11
Affetside Gtr Man 195 E9
Affleck Aberds 303 G8
Affpuddle Dorset 18 C2
Affric Lodge Highld 299 G11
Afon Eitha Wrex 166 F3
Afon-wen Flint 181 G10
Afon Wen Gwyn 145 B8
Afton IoW 20 D2
Agar Nook Leics 153 G9
Agbrigg W Yorks 197 D10
Aggborough Worcs 116 B6
Agglethorpe N Yorks 213 B11
Aglionby Cumb 239 F10
Agneash IoM 192 D5
Aifft Denb 165 B10
Aigburth Mers 182 D5
Aiginis W Isles 304 E6
Aike E Yorks 209 D7
Aikenway Moray 302 E2
Aikerness Orkney 314 A4
Aikers Orkney 314 G4
Aiketgate Cumb 230 B5
Aikton Cumb 239 G7
Ailby Lincs 190 F6
Ailey Hereford 96 B6
Ailstone Warks 118 G4
Ailsworth Pboro 138 D2
Aimes Green Essex 86 E5
Ainderby Quernhow
N Yorks 215 C7
Ainderby Steeple
N Yorks 224 G6
Aingers Green Essex 108 G2
Ainley Top W Yorks 196 D6
Ainsdale Mers 193 E10
Ainsdale-on-Sea Mers 193 E9
Ainstable Cumb 230 B6
Ainsworth Gtr Man 195 E9
Ainthorpe N Yorks 226 D4
Aintree Mers 182 B5
Aird Argyll 275 C8
Dumfries 236 C2
Highld 299 B7
W Isles 296 F3
W Isles 304 E7
Airdachuilinn Highld 306 E7
Aird a Mhachair
W Isles 297 G3
Aird a' Mhulaidh
W Isles 305 G3
Aird Asaig W Isles 305 H3
Aird Dhail W Isles 304 B6
Airdens Highld 309 K6
Airdeny Argyll 289 G11
Aird Mhidhinis W Isles 297 L3
Aird Mhighe W Isles 296 C6
W Isles 305 J3
Aird Mhòr W Isles 297 G4
Aird Mhor W Isles 297 L3
Aird of Sleat Highld 295 E7
Airdrie N Lanark 268 B5
Airds of Kells Dumfries 237 B8
Aird Thunga W Isles 304 E6
Airdtorrisdale Highld 308 C6
Aird Uig W Isles 304 E2
Airedale W Yorks 198 B3
Aire View N Yorks 204 D5
Airidh a Bhruaich
W Isles 305 G4
Airieland Dumfries 237 D9
Airinis W Isles 304 E6
Airlie Angus 287 B7
Airlies Dumfries 236 D5
Airmyn E Yorks 199 B8
Airntully Perth 286 D4
Airor Highld 295 E9
Airth Falk 279 D7
Airthrey Castle
Stirlinging 278 B6
Airton N Yorks 204 B4
Airyhassen Dumfries 236 E5
Airy Hill N Yorks 227 D7
Airyligg Dumfries 236 C4
Aisby Lincs 155 B10
Lincs 188 C5
Aisgernis W Isles 297 J3
Aish Devon 8 C3
Devon 8 D6
Aisholt Som 43 F7
Aiskew N Yorks 214 B5
Aislaby N Yorks 216 B5
N Yorks 227 D7
Stockton 225 C8
Aisthorpe Lincs 188 E6
Aith Orkney 314 E2
Shetland 312 D8
Shetland 313 H5
Aithnen Powys 148 E4
Aithsetter Shetland 313 K6
Aitkenhead S Ayrs 245 B8
Aitnoch Highld 301 F9
Akeld Northumb 263 D11
Akeley Bucks 102 D4
Akenham Suff 108 B2
Albany T&W 243 F7
Albaston Corn 12 G4
Alberbury Shrops 149 G7
Albert Town Pembs 72 B6
Albert Village Leics 152 F6
Albourne W Sus 36 D3
Albourne Green W Sus 36 D3
Albrighton Shrops 132 C6
Shrops 149 F9
Albro Castle Ceredig 92 B3
Alburgh Norf 142 F5
Albury Herts 105 G8
Sur 50 D5
Albury End Herts 105 G8
Albury Heath Sur 50 D5
Albyfield Cumb 240 G2
Alby Hill Norf 160 C3
Alcaig Highld 300 D5
Alcaston Shrops 131 F9
Alcester Dorset 30 C5
Warks 117 F11
Alcester Lane's End
W Mid 133 G11
Alciston E Sus 23 D8
Alcombe Som 42 D3
Wilts 61 F10
Alconbury Cambs 122 B3
Alconbury Weald
Cambs 122 B4
Alconbury Weston
Cambs 122 B3
Aldbar Castle Angus 287 B9
Aldborough Norf 160 C3
N Yorks 215 F8
Aldborough Hatch
London 68 B3
Aldbourne Wilts 63 D9
Aldbrough E Yorks 209 F10
Aldbrough St John
N Yorks 224 C4
Aldbury Herts 85 C7
Aldcliffe Lancs 211 G9
Aldclune Perth 291 G11
Aldeburgh Suff 127 F9
Aldeby Norf 143 E8
Aldenham Herts 85 F10
Alderbrook E Sus 37 B8
Alderbury Wilts 31 B11
Aldercar Derbys 170 F6
Alderford Norf 160 F2
Alder Forest Gtr Man 184 B3
Alderholt Dorset 31 E10
Alderley Glos 80 G3
Alderley Edge Ches E 184 F4
Alderman's Green
W Mid 135 G7
Aldermaston W Berks 64 F5
Aldermaston Soke
W Berks 64 G6
Aldermaston Wharf
W Berks 64 F6
Alderminster Warks 100 B4
Aldermoor Soton 32 D5
Alder Moor Staffs 152 D4
Alderney BCP 18 C6
Alder Row Som 45 E9
Aldersbrook London 68 B2
Alder's End Hereford 98 C2
Aldersey Green Ches W 167 D7
Aldershawe Staffs 134 B2
Aldershot Hants 49 C11
Alderton Glos 99 E10
Shrops 149 E9
Suff 108 C6
Wilts 61 C10
W Nhants 102 B4
Alderton Fields Glos 99 E10
Alderwasley Derbys 170 E4
Aldfield N Yorks 214 F5
Aldford Ches W 166 D6
Aldgate Rutland 137 C9
Aldham Essex 107 F8
Suff 107 B10
Aldie Highld 309 L7
Aldingbourne W Sus 22 B6
Aldingham Cumb 210 E5
Aldington Kent 54 F5
Worcs 99 C11
Aldington Frith Kent 54 F4
Aldivalloch Moray 302 G3
Aldochlay Argyll 277 C7
Aldon Shrops 115 B8
Aldoth Cumb 229 B8
Aldourie Castle Highld 300 F6
Aldreth Cambs 123 C8
Aldridge W Mid 133 C11
Aldringham Suff 127 E8
Aldrington Brighton 36 F3
Aldsworth Glos 81 C11
Aldunie Moray 302 G3
Aldwark Derbys 170 D2
N Yorks 215 G9
Aldwarke S Yorks 186 C6
Aldwick W Sus 22 D6
Aldwincle N Nhants 137 G10
Aldworth W Berks 64 D5
Alehouseburn Aberds 302 C6
Alehousehill Aberds 303 G10
Ale Oak Shrops 130 G4
Alexandria W Dunb 277 F7
Aley Som 43 F7
Aley Green C Beds 85 B9
Alfardisworthy Devon 24 E3
Alfington Devon 15 B8
Alfold Sur 50 G4
Alfold Bars W Sus 50 G4
Alfold Crossways Sur 50 F4
Alford Aberds 293 B7
Lincs 191 F7
Som 44 G6
Alfred's Well Worcs 117 C8
Alfreton Derbys 170 D6
Alfrick Worcs 116 G4
Alfrick Pound Worcs 116 G4
Alfriston E Sus 23 E8
Algakirk Lincs 156 B5
Algaltraig Argyll 275 F11
Algarkirk Lincs 156 B5
Alhampton Som 44 G6
Aline Lodge W Isles 305 G3
Alisary Highld 289 B9
Alkborough N Lincs 199 C11
Alkerton Glos 80 D3
Oxon 101 C7
Alkham Kent 55 E9
Alkington Shrops 149 B10
Alkmonton Derbys 152 B3
Alkrington Garden Village
Gtr Man 195 G11
Alladale Lodge Highld 309 L4
Allaleigh Devon 8 E6
Allanaquoich Aberds 292 D3
Allanbank Borders 271 F10
N Lanark 268 D6
Allangrange Mains
Highld 300 D6
Allanshaugh Borders 271 F8
Allanshaws Borders 271 G9
Allanton Borders 273 E7
N Lanark 269 D7
S Lanark 268 E4
Allaston Glos 79 E10
Allathasdal W Isles 297 L2
Allbrook Hants 33 C7
All Cannings Wilts 62 G5
Allendale Town
Northumb 241 F8
Allen End Warks 134 D3
Allenheads Northumb 232 B3
Allensford Durham 242 G3
Allens Green Herts 87 B7
Allensmore Hereford 97 D9
Allenton Derby 153 C7
Allenwood Cumb 239 F11
Aller Devon 9 B7
Devon 27 F9
Dorset 30 G3
Som 28 B6
Allerby Cumb 229 D7
Allerford Som 27 B11
Som 42 D2
Aller Park Devon 9 B7
Allerston N Yorks 217 C7
Allerthorpe E Yorks 207 D11
Allerton Mers 182 D6
W Yorks 205 G8
Allerton Bywater
W Yorks 198 B2
Allerton Mauleverer
N Yorks 206 B4
Allesley W Mid 134 G6
Allestree Derby 152 B6
Allet Corn 4 F5
Allexton Leics 136 C6
Allgreave Ches E 169 B7
Allhallows Medway 69 D10
Allhallows-on-Sea
Medway 69 D10
Alligin Shuas Highld 299 D8
Allimore Green Staffs 151 F7
Allington Kent 53 B8
Lincs 172 G5
Wilts 47 F8
Wilts 61 D11
Wilts 62 G5
Allington Bar Wilts 61 E11
Allithwaite Cumb 211 D7
Alloa Clack 279 C7
Allonby Cumb 229 C7
Allostock Ches W 184 G2
Alloway S Ayrs 257 F8
Allowenshay Som 28 E5
All Saints Devon 28 G4
All Saints South Elmham
Suff 142 G6
Allscot Shrops 132 D4
Allscott Telford 150 G2
All Stretton Shrops 131 D9
Allt Carms 75 E9
Alltami Flint 166 B3
Alltbeithe Highld 290 C2
Alltchaorunn Highld 284 B5
Alltforgan Powys 147 E9
Alltmawr Powys 95 B11
Alltnacaillich Highld 308 E4
Allt-na-giubhsaich
Aberds 292 E4
Allt na h-Airbhe Highld 307 K6
Allt-nan-sùgh Highld 295 C11
Alltrech Argyll 289 F8
Alltsigh Highld 290 B6
Alltwalis Carms 93 E8
Alltwen Neath 76 E2
Alltyblaca Ceredig 93 B10
Allt-yr-yn Newport 59 B9

Allwood Green Suff 125 C10
Alma Notts 171 E7
Almagill Dumfries 238 B3
Almeley Hereford 114 G6
Almeley Wooton
Hereford 114 G6
Almer Dorset 18 B4
Almholme S Yorks 198 F5
Almington Staffs 150 C4
Alminstone Cross Devon 24 C4
Almondbank Perth 286 E4
Almondbury W Yorks 197 D7
Almondsbury S Glos 60 C6
Almondvale W Loth 269 B11
Almshouse Green Essex 106 E5
Alne N Yorks 215 F9
Alne End Warks 118 F2
Alne Hills Warks 118 E2
Alness Highld 300 C6
Alnessferry Highld 300 C6
Alne Station N Yorks 215 F10
Alnham Northumb 263 G11
Alnmouth Northumb 264 G6
Alnwick Northumb 264 G5
Alperton London 67 C7
Alphamstone Essex 107 D7
Alpheton Suff 125 G7
Alphington Devon 14 C4
Alpington Norf 142 C5
Alport Derbys 170 C2
Powys 130 D5
Alpraham Ches E 167 D9
Alresford Essex 107 G11
Alrewas Staffs 152 F3
Alsager Ches E 168 D3
Alsagers Bank Staffs 168 F4
Alscot Bucks 84 E4
Alsop en le Dale
Derbys 169 D11
Alston Cumb 231 B10
Devon 28 G4
Alstone Glos 99 E9
Glos 99 G8
Som 43 D10
Alstonefield Staffs 169 D10
Alston Sutton Som 44 C2
Alswear Devon 26 C2
Alt Gtr Man 196 G2
Altandhu Highld 307 H4
Altanduin Highld 311 G2
Altarnun Corn 11 E10
Altass Highld 309 J4
Altbough Hereford 97 E10
Altdargue Aberds 293 C7
Alterwall Highld 310 C6
Altham Lancs 203 G11
Alt Hill Gtr Man 196 G2
Althorne Essex 88 F6
Althorpe N Lincs 199 F10
Alticane S Ayrs 244 F6
Alticry Dumfries 236 D4
Altmore Windsor 65 D11
Altnabreac Station
Highld 310 E4
Altnacealgach Hotel
Highld 307 H7
Altnacraig Argyll 289 G10
Altnafeadh Highld 284 B6
Altnaharra Highld 308 F5
Altofts W Yorks 197 C11
Alton Derbys 170 C5
Hants 49 F8
Staffs 169 G9
Wilts 47 D7
Alton Barnes Wilts 62 G6
Altonhill E Ayrs 257 B10
Alton Pancras Dorset 30 G2
Alton Priors Wilts 62 G6
Altonside Moray 302 D2
Altour Highld 290 E4
Altrincham Gtr Man 184 D3
Altrua Highld 290 E4
Altskeith Stirling 285 G8
Altyre Ho Moray 301 D10
Alum Rock W Mid 134 F2
Alva Clack 279 B7
Alvanley Ches W 183 G7
Alvaston Derby 153 C7
Alvechurch Worcs 117 C10
Alvecote Warks 134 C4
Alvediston Wilts 31 C7
Alveley Shrops 132 G5
Alverdiscott Devon 25 B8
Alverstoke Hants 21 B8
Alverstone IoW 21 D7
Alverthorpe W Yorks 197 C10
Alverton Notts 172 G3
Alves Moray 301 C11
Alvescot Oxon 82 E3
Alveston S Glos 60 B6
Warks 118 F4
Alveston Down S Glos 60 B6
Alveston Hill Warks 118 G4
Alvie Highld 291 C10
Alvingham Lincs 190 C5
Alvington Glos 79 E10
Som 29 D8
Alwalton Cambs 138 D2
Alway Newport 59 B10
Alweston Dorset 29 E11
Alwington Devon 24 C6
Alwinton Northumb 251 B10
Alwoodley W Yorks 205 E11
Alwoodley Gates
W Yorks 206 E2
Alwoodley Park
W Yorks 205 E11
Alyth Perth 286 C6
Amalebra Corn 1 B5
Amalveor Corn 1 B5
Amatnatua Highld 309 K4
Am Baile W Isles 297 K3
Ambaston Derbys 153 C8
Ambergate Derbys 170 E4
Amber Hill Lincs 174 F2
Amberley Glos 80 E5
Hereford 97 B10
W Sus 35 E8
Amble Northumb 253 C7
Amblecote W Mid 133 F7
Ambler Thorn W Yorks 196 B5
Ambleside Cumb 221 E7
Ambleston Pembs 91 F10
Ambrosden Oxon 83 B10
Am Buth Argyll 289 G10
Amcotts N Lincs 199 E11
Amen Corner Brack 65 F10
Amersham Bucks 85 F7
Amersham Common
Bucks 85 F7
Amersham Old Town
Bucks 85 F7
Amersham on the Hill
Bucks 85 F7
Amerton Staffs 151 D9
Amesbury Bath 45 B7
Wilts 47 E7
Ameysford Dorset 31 G9
Amington Staffs 134 C4
Amisfield Dumfries 247 G11
Amlwch Anglesey 178 C6
Amlwch Port Anglesey 179 C7
Ammanford = Rhydaman
Carms 75 C10
Ammerham Som 28 F5
Amod Argyll 255 D8
Amotherby N Yorks 216 E4
Ampfield Hants 32 C6
Ampleforth N Yorks 215 D11
Ampney Crucis Glos 81 E9
Ampney St Mary Glos 81 E9
Ampney St Peter Glos 81 E9
Amport Hants 47 E9
Ampthill C Beds 103 D10
Ampton Suff 125 C7
Amroth Pembs 73 D11
Amulree Perth 286 D2
Amwell Herts 85 C11
Anagach Highld 301 G10
Anaheilt Highld 289 C10
Anancaun Highld 299 C10
An Caol Highld 298 D6
Ancarraig Highld 300 G4
Ancaster Lincs 173 G7
Anchor Shrops 130 G3
Anchorage Park Ptsmth 33 G11
Anchor Corner Norf 141 D10
Anchorsholme Blackpool 202 E2
Anchor Street Norf 160 E6
An Cnoc W Isles 304 E6
Ancoats Gtr Man 184 B5
Ancroft Northumb 273 F9
Ancroft Northmoor
Northumb 273 F9
Ancrum Borders 262 E4
Ancton W Sus 35 G7
Ancumtoun Orkney 314 A7
Anderby Lincs 191 F8
Anderby Creek Lincs 191 F8
Andersea Som 43 G10
Andersfield Som 43 G8
Anderson Dorset 18 B3
Anderton Ches W 183 F10
Corn 7 E8
Lancs 194 E6
Andertons Mill Lancs 194 E4
Andover Hants 47 D11
Andover Down Hants 47 D11
Andoversford Glos 81 B8
Andreas IoM 192 C5
Andwell Hants 49 C7
Anelog Gwyn 144 D3
Anerley London 67 F10
Anfield Mers 182 C5
Angarrack Corn 2 B3
Angarrick Corn 3 B7
Angelbank Shrops 115 B11
Angersleigh Som 27 D11
Angerton Cumb 238 F6
Angle Pembs 72 E5
An Gleann Ur W Isles 304 E6
Angmering W Sus 35 G9
Angram N Yorks 206 D6
N Yorks 223 F7
Anick Northumb 241 D11
Anie Stirling 285 F9
Ankerdine Hill Worcs 116 F4
Ankerville Highld 301 B8
Anlaby E Yorks 200 B4
Anlaby Park Hull 200 B5
An Leth Meadhanach
W Isles 297 K3
Anmer Norf 158 D4
Anmore Hants 33 E11
Annan Dumfries 238 D5
Annanside Cumb 210 B1
Annat Argyll 284 E4
Highld 290 D5
Highld 299 D8
Anna Valley Hants 47 E10
Annbank S Ayrs 257 E10
Annesley Notts 171 E8
Annesley Woodhouse
Notts 171 E7
Annfield Plain Durham 242 G5
Anniesland Glasgow 267 B10
Annifirth Shetland 313 J3
Annishader Highld 298 D4
Annis Hill Suff 143 F7
Annitsford T&W 243 C7
Annscroft Shrops 131 B9
Ann's Hill Hants 33 G9
Annwell Place Derbys 152 F6
Ansdell Lancs 193 B10
Ansells End Herts 85 B11
Ansford Som 44 G6
Ansley Warks 134 E5
Ansley Common Warks 134 E6
Anslow Staffs 152 D4
Anslow Gate Staffs 152 D3
Ansteadbrook Sur 50 G2
Anstey Herts 105 E8
Leics 135 B10
Anstruther Easter Fife 287 G9
Anstruther Wester Fife 287 G9
Ansty Hants 49 E8
Warks 135 G7
Wilts 31 B7
W Sus 36 C3
Ansty Coombe Wilts 31 B7
Ansty Cross Dorset 30 G3
Anthill Common Hants 33 E10
Anthony Corn 7 E7
Anthony's Cross Glos 98 G4
Anthorn Cumb 238 F5
Antingham Norf 160 C5
An t-Ob W Isles 296 C6
Anton's Gowt Lincs 174 F3
Antonshill Falk 279 E7
Antony Corn 7 E7
Antony Passage Corn 7 D8
Antrobus Ches W 183 F10
Anvil Green Kent 54 D6
Anvilles W Berks 63 F10
Anwick Lincs 173 E10
Anwoth Dumfries 237 D7
Aonachan Highld 290 E4
Aoradh Argyll 274 G3
Apedale Staffs 168 F4
Aperfield London 52 B2
Apes Dale Worcs 117 C9
Apes Hall Cambs 139 E11
Apethorpe N Nhants 137 D10
Apeton Staffs 151 F7
Apley Lincs 189 F10
Apley Forge Shrops 132 D4
Apperknowle Derbys 186 F5
Apperley Glos 99 F7
Apperley Bridge
W Yorks 205 F9
Apperley Dene
Northumb 242 F3
Appersett N Yorks 223 G7
Appin Argyll 289 E11
Appin House Argyll 289 E11
Appleby N Lincs 200 E3
Appleby-in-Westmorland
Cumb 231 G9
Appleby Magna Leics 134 B6
Appleby Parva Leics 134 B6
Applecross Highld 299 E7
Applecross Ho Highld 299 E7
Appledore Devon 27 E9
Devon 40 G3
Kent 39 B7
Appledore Heath Kent 54 G3
Appleford Oxon 83 G8
Applegarthtown
Dumfries 248 G4
Applehouse Hill Windsor 65 C10
Applemore Hants 32 F5
Appleshaw Hants 47 D10
Applethwaite Cumb 229 F11
Appleton Halton 183 D8
Oxon 82 E6
Appleton-le-Moors
N Yorks 216 B4
Appleton-le-Street
N Yorks 216 E4
Appleton Park Warr 183 E10
Appleton Roebuck
N Yorks 207 E7
Appleton Thorn Warr 183 E10
Appleton Wiske N Yorks 225 E7
Appletreehall Borders 262 F2
Appletreewick
N Yorks 213 G11
Appley IoW 21 C8
Som 27 C9
Appley Bridge Lancs 194 F4
Apse Heath IoW 21 E7
Apsey Green Suff 126 E5
Apsley Herts 85 D9
Apsley End C Beds 104 E2
Apuldram W Sus 22 C4
Aqueduct Telford 132 B3
Aquhythie Aberds 293 B9
Arabella Highld 301 B8
Arbeadie Aberds 293 D8
Arberth = Narberth
Pembs 73 C10
Arbirlot Angus 287 C10
Arboll Highld 311 L2
Arborfield Wokingham 65 F9
Arborfield Cross
Wokingham 65 F9
Arborfield Garrison
Wokingham 65 F9
Arbourthorne S Yorks 186 D5
Arbroath Angus 287 C10
Arbury Cambs 123 E8
Arbuthnott Aberds 293 F9
Archavandra Muir
Highld 309 K7
Archdeacon Newton
Darl 224 B5
Archenfield Hereford 96 C5
Archiestown Moray 302 E2
Archnalea Highld 289 C10
Arclid Ches E 168 C3
Arclid Green Ches E 168 C3
Ardachu Highld 309 J6
Ardailly Argyll 255 B7
Ardalanish Argyll 274 B4
Ardallie Aberds 303 F10
Ardalum Ho Argyll 288 F6
Ardamaleish Argyll 275 G11
Ardanaiseig Argyll 284 E4
Ardaneaskan Highld 295 B10
Ardanstur Argyll 275 B9
Ardargie House Hotel
Perth 286 F4
Ardarroch Highld 295 B10
Ardban Highld 295 B9
Ardbeg Argyll 254 C5
Argyll 276 E3
Ardcharnich Highld 307 L6
Ardchiavaig Argyll 274 B4
Ardchonnell Argyll 275 B10
Ardchronie Highld 309 L6
Ardchuilk Highld 300 F2
Ardchullarie More
Stirling 285 F9
Ardchyle Stirling 285 E9
Ardclach Highld 301 E9
Ard-dhubh Highld 299 E7
Arddleen Powys 148 F5
Ardechvie Highld 290 D3
Ardeley Herts 104 F6
Ardelve Highld 295 C10
Arden Argyll 277 E7
E Renf 267 D10
Ardencaple Ho Argyll 275 B8
Ardendrain Highld 300 F5
Arden Park Gtr Man 184 C6
Ardens Grafton Warks 118 G2
Ardentallen Argyll 289 G10
Ardentinny Argyll 276 D3
Ardentraive Argyll 275 F11
Ardeonaig Stirling 285 D10
Ardersier Highld 301 D7
Ardery Highld 289 C9
Ardessie Highld 307 L5
Ardfern Argyll 275 C9
Ardfernal Argyll 274 F6
Ardgartan Argyll 284 G6
Ardgay Highld 309 K5
Ardglassie Aberds 303 C10
Ardgour Highld 290 G2
Ardgye Moray 301 C11
Ardheslaig Highld 299 D7
Ardiecow Moray 302 C5
Ardinamir Argyll 275 B8
Ardindrean Highld 307 L6
Ardingly W Sus 36 B4
Ardington Oxon 64 B2
Ardington Wick Oxon 64 B2
Ardintoul Highld 295 C10
Ardlair Aberds 302 G5
Highld 299 B9
Ardlamey Argyll 255 C7
Ardlamont Ho Argyll 275 G10
Ardlawhill Aberds 303 C8
Ardleigh Essex 107 F11
Ardleigh Green London 68 B4
Ardleigh Heath Essex 107 E10
Ardler Perth 286 C6
Ardley Oxon 101 F10
Ardley End Essex 87 C8
Ardlui Argyll 285 F7
Ardlussa Argyll 275 E7
Ardmair Highld 307 K6
Ardmay Argyll 284 G6
Ardmenish Argyll 274 F6
Ardminish Argyll 255 C7
Ardmolich Highld 289 B9
Ardmore Argyll 289 G9
Highld 306 D7
Highld 309 L7
Ardnacross Argyll 289 E7
Ardnadam Argyll 276 F3
Ardnagowan Argyll 284 G4
Ardnagrask Highld 300 E5
Ardnarff Highld 295 B10
Ardnastang Highld 289 C10
Ardnave Argyll 274 F3
Ardneil N Ayrs 266 F3
Ardno Argyll 284 G5
Ardo Aberds 303 F8
Ardoch Argyll 277 F7
Perth 286 D4
Ardoch *continued*
Stirling 285 F9
Ardochy House Highld 290 C4
Ardo Ho Aberds 303 G9
Ardoyne Aberds 302 G6
Ardpatrick Argyll 275 G8
Ardpatrick Ho Argyll 255 B8
Ardpeaton Argyll 276 D4
Ardradnaig Perth 285 C11
Ardrishaig Argyll 275 E9
Ardross Fife 287 G9
Highld 300 B6
Ardrossan N Ayrs 266 G4
Ardross Castle Highld 300 B6
Ardshave Highld 309 K7
Ardsheal Highld 289 D11
Ardshealach Highld 289 C8
Ardskenish Argyll 274 D4
Ardsley S Yorks 197 F11
Ardslignish Highld 289 C7
Ardtalla Argyll 254 B5
Ardtalnaig Perth 285 D11
Ardtaraig Argyll 275 E11
Ardtoe Highld 289 B8
Ardtreck Highld 294 B5
Ardtrostan Perth 285 E10
Ardtur Argyll 289 E11
Arduaine Argyll 275 B8
Ardullie Highld 300 C5
Ardvannie Highld 309 L6
Ardvar Highld 306 F6
Ardvasar Highld 295 E8
Ardveich Stirling 285 E10
Ardverikie Highld 291 E7
Ardvorlich Perth 285 E10
Ardwell Dumfries 236 E3
Moray 302 F3
S Ayrs 244 E5
Ardwell Mains Dumfries 236 E3
Ardwick Gtr Man 184 B5
Areley Kings Worcs 116 C6
Arford Hants 49 F10
Argoed Caerph 77 F11
Powys 113 E9
Powys 130 E5
Shrops 130 G6
Shrops 148 E6
Argos Hill E Sus 37 B9
Arichamish Argyll 275 C10
Arichastlich Argyll 284 D6
Aridhglas Argyll 288 G5
Arileod Argyll 288 D3
Arinacrinachd Highld 299 D7
Arinagour Argyll 288 D4
Arineckaig Highld 299 E9
Arion Orkney 314 E2
Arisaig Highld 295 G8
Ariundle Highld 289 C10
Arivegaig Highld 289 C8
Arivoichallum Argyll 254 C4
Arkendale N Yorks 215 G7
Arkesden Essex 105 E9
Arkholme Lancs 211 E11
Arkleby Cumb 229 D8
Arkleton Dumfries 249 E9
Arkle Town N Yorks 223 E10
Arkley London 86 F2
Arksey S Yorks 198 F5
Arkwright Town Derbys 186 G6
Arle Glos 99 G8
Arlebrook Glos 80 D4
Arlecdon Cumb 219 B10
Arlescote Warks 101 B7
Arlesey C Beds 104 D3
Arleston Telford 150 G3
Arley Ches E 183 E11
Arley Green Ches E 183 E11
Arlingham Glos 80 C2
Arlington Devon 40 E6
E Sus 23 D8
Glos 81 D10
Arlington Beccott Devon 40 E6
Armadale Highld 308 C7
W Loth 269 B8
Armadale Castle Highld 295 E8
Armathwaite Cumb 230 B6
Armigers Essex 105 F11
Arminghall Norf 142 C5
Armitage Staffs 151 F11
Armitage Bridge
W Yorks 196 E6
Armley W Yorks 205 G11
Armscote Warks 100 C4
Armsdale Staffs 150 C5
Armshead Staffs 168 F6
Armston N Nhants 137 F11
Armthorpe S Yorks 198 F6
Arnabost Argyll 288 D4
Arnaby Cumb 210 C3
Arncliffe N Yorks 213 E8
Arncroach Fife 287 G9
Arndilly Ho Moray 302 E2
Arne Dorset 18 D5
Arnesby Leics 136 E2
Arngask Perth 286 F5
Arnisdale Highld 295 D10
Arnish Highld 298 E5
Arniston Midloth 270 C6
Arnol W Isles 304 D5
Arnold E Yorks 209 E8
Notts 171 F9
Arno's Vale Bristol 60 E6
Arnprior Stirling 278 C2
Arnside Cumb 211 D9
Aros Mains Argyll 289 E7
Arowry Wrex 149 B9
Arpafeelie Highld 300 D6
Arpinge Kent 55 F7
Arrad Foot Cumb 210 C6
Arram E Yorks 208 E6
Arrathorne N Yorks 224 G4
Arreton IoW 20 D6
Arrington Cambs 122 G6
Arrivain Argyll 284 D6
Arrochar Argyll 284 G6
Arrow Warks 117 F11
Arrowe Hill Mers 182 D3
Arrowfield Top Worcs 117 C10
Arrow Green Hereford 115 F8
Arrunden W Yorks 196 F6
Arscaig Highld 309 H5
Arscott Shrops 131 B8
Arthill Ches E 184 D2
Arthington W Yorks 205 E11
Arthingworth W Nhants 136 G5
Arthog Gwyn 146 G2
Arthrath Aberds 303 F9
Arthursdale W Yorks 206 F3
Arthurstone Perth 286 C6
Arthurville Highld 309 L7
Artington Sur 50 D3
Artrochie Aberds 303 F10
Arundel W Sus 35 F8
Arwick Orkney 314 D3
Aryhoulan Highld 290 G2
Asby Cumb 229 G7
Ascog Argyll 266 C2
Ascoil Highld 311 H2
Ascot Windsor 66 F2
Ascott Warks 100 E6
Ascott d'Oyley Oxon 82 B4
Ascott Earl Oxon 82 B3
Ascott-under-Wychwood
Oxon 82 B4
Asenby N Yorks 215 D7
Asfordby Leics 154 F4
Asfordby Hill Leics 154 F4
Asgarby Lincs 173 F10
Lincs 174 B4
Ash Devon 8 F6
Dorset 30 E5
Kent 55 B9
Kent 68 G5
Som 28 C3
Som 29 C7
Sur 49 C11
Ashaig Highld 295 C8
Ashansworth Hants 48 B2
Ashampstead W Berks 64 D5
Ashampstead Green
W Berks 64 D5
Ashbank Kent 53 C10
Ash Bank Staffs 168 F6
Ashbeer Som 42 F5
Ashbocking Suff 126 G3
Ashbourne Derbys 169 F11
Ashbrittle Som 27 C9
Ashbrook Shrops 131 E9
Ash Bullayne Devon 26 G3
Ashburnham Forge
E Sus 23 B11
Ashburton Devon 8 B5
Ashbury Devon 12 B6
Oxon 63 C9
Ashby N Lincs 200 F2
Ashby by Partney Lincs 174 B6
Ashby cum Fenby
NE Lincs 201 G9
Ashby de la Launde
Lincs 173 D9
Ashby-de-la-Zouch
Leics 153 F7
Ashby Folville Leics 154 G4
Ashby Hill NE Lincs 201 G8
Ashby Magna Leics 135 E11
Ashby Parva Leics 135 F10
Ashby Puerorum Lincs 190 G4
Ashby St Ledgers
W Nhants 119 D11
Ashby St Mary Norf 142 C6
Ashchurch Glos 99 E8
Ashcombe Devon 14 F4
Ashcombe Park N Som 59 G10
Ashcott Som 44 F2
Ashcott Corner Som 44 F2
Ashculme Devon 27 E10
Ashdon Essex 105 C11
Ashe Hants 48 D4
Asheldham Essex 89 E7
Ashen Essex 106 C4
Ashendon Bucks 84 C2
Asheridge Bucks 84 E6
Ashey IoW 21 D7
Ashfield Argyll 275 E8
Carms 94 F3
Hants 32 D5
Hereford 97 G11
Shrops 148 D6
Stirling 285 G11
Suff 126 E4
Ashfield Cum Thorpe
Suff 126 E4
Ashfield Green Suff 124 F5
Suff 126 C5
Ashfields Shrops 150 D4
Ashfold Crossways
W Sus 36 B2
Ashfold Side N Yorks 214 F2
Ashford Devon 8 F3
Devon 40 F4
Hants 31 E10
Kent 54 E4
Sur 66 E5
Ashford Bowdler
Shrops 115 C10
Ashford Carbonell
Shrops 115 C10
Ashford Common Sur 66 E5
Ashford Hill Hants 64 G5
Ashford in the Water
Derbys 185 G11
Ashgate Derbys 186 G5
Ashgill S Lanark 268 F5
Ash Green Sur 50 D2
Warks 134 F6
Ashgrove Bath 45 B8
Ash Grove Wrex 166 G5
Ash Hill Devon 14 G4
Ashiestiel Borders 261 B10
Ashill Devon 27 E9
Norf 141 C7
Som 28 D4
Ashingdon Essex 88 G5
Ashington BCP 18 B6
Northumb 253 F7
Som 29 C9
W Sus 35 D10
Ashington End Lincs 175 B8
Ashintully Castle Perth 292 G3
Ashkirk Borders 261 E11
Ashlett Hants 33 G7
Ashleworth Glos 98 F6
Ashley Cambs 124 E3
Ches E 184 E3
Devon 25 E10
Dorset 31 G10
Glos 80 G6
Hants 19 B11
Hants 47 G11
Kent 55 D10
N Nhants 136 E5
Staffs 150 B5
Wilts 61 F10
Ashley Dale Staffs 150 B5
Ashley Down Bristol 60 D5
Ashley Green Bucks 85 D7
Ashleyhay Derbys 170 E3
Ashley Heath Ches E 184 D3
Dorset 31 G10
Staffs 150 B4
Ashley Moor Hereford 115 D9
Ashley Park Sur 66 F6
Ash Magna Shrops 149 B11
Ashmanhaugh Norf 160 E6
Ashmansworth Hants 48 B2
Ashmansworthy Devon 24 D4
Ashmead Green Glos 80 F3
Ashmill Devon 12 B3
Ash Mill Devon 26 C3
Ash Moor Devon 26 D3
Ashmore Dorset 30 D6
Ashmore Green W Berks 64 F4
Ashmore Lake W Mid 133 D9
Ashmore Park W Mid 133 C9
Ashnashellach Lodge
Highld 299 E10
Ashopton Derbys 185 D11
Ashorne Warks 118 F6
Ashover Derbys 170 C4
Ashover Hay Derbys 170 C5
Ashow Warks 118 C6
Ash Parva Shrops 149 B11
Ashperton Hereford 98 C2
Ashprington Devon 8 D6
Ash Priors Som 27 B11
Ashreigney Devon 25 E10
Ashridge Court Devon 25 G11
Ash Street Suff 107 B10
Ashtead Sur 51 B7
Ash Thomas Devon 27 E8
Ashton Corn 2 D4
Hants 33 D9
Hereford 115 E10
Invclyd 276 F4
N Nhants 137 F11
Pboro 138 B2
Som 44 D2
W Nhants 102 B5
Ashton Common Wilts 45 B11
Ashton Gate Bristol 60 E5
Ashton Green E Sus 23 C7
Ashton Hayes Ches W 167 B8
Ashton Heath Halton 183 F9
Ashton-in-Makerfield
Gtr Man 183 B9
Ashton Keynes Wilts 81 G8
Ashton under Hill Worcs 99 D9
Ashton-under-Lyne
Gtr Man 184 B6
Ashton upon Mersey
Gtr Man 184 C3
Ashton Vale Bristol 60 E5
Ashurst Hants 32 E4
Kent 52 F4
Lancs 194 F3
W Sus 35 D11
Ashurst Bridge Hants 32 E4
Ashurst Wood W Sus 52 F2
Ashvale Bl Gwent 77 C10
Ash Vale Sur 49 C11
Ashwater Devon 12 B3
Ashwell Devon 14 G3
Herts 104 D5
Rutland 155 G7
Som 28 D5
Ashwell End Herts 104 C5
Ashwellthorpe Norf 142 D2
Ashwick Som 44 D6
Ashwicken Norf 158 F4
Ashwood Staffs 133 F7
Ashybank Borders 262 F2
Askam in Furness Cumb 210 D4
Askern S Yorks 198 E5
Askerswell Dorset 16 C6
Askerton Hill Lincs 172 F4
Askett Bucks 84 D4
Askham Cumb 230 G6
Notts 188 G2
Askham Bryan York 207 D7
Askham Richard York 206 D6
Asknish Argyll 275 D10
Askrigg N Yorks 223 G8
Askwith N Yorks 205 D9
Aslackby Lincs 155 C11
Aslacton Norf 142 E3
Aslockton Notts 154 B4
Asloun Aberds 293 B7
Asney Som 44 F3
Aspall Suff 126 D3
Aspatria Cumb 229 C8
Aspenden Herts 105 F7
Asperton Lincs 156 B5
Aspley Nottingham 171 G8
Staffs 150 C6
Aspley Guise C Beds 103 D8
Aspley Heath C Beds 103 D8
Warks 117 C11
Aspull Gtr Man 194 F6
Aspull Common
Gtr Man 183 B10
Assater Shetland 312 F4
Asselby E Yorks 199 B8
Asserby Lincs 191 F7
Asserby Turn Lincs 191 F7
Assington Suff 107 D8
Assington Green Suff 124 G5
Assynt Ho Highld 300 C5
Astbury Ches E 168 C4
Astcote W Nhants 120 G3
Asterby Lincs 190 F3
Asterley Shrops 131 B7
Asterton Shrops 131 E7
Asthall Oxon 82 C3
Asthall Leigh Oxon 82 C4
Astle Ches E 184 G4
Highld 309 K7
Astley Gtr Man 195 G8
Shrops 149 F10
Warks 134 F6
Worcs 116 D5
Astley Abbotts Shrops 132 D4
Astley Bridge Gtr Man 195 E8
Astley Cross Worcs 116 D6
Astley Green Gtr Man 184 B2
Astmoor Halton 183 E8
Aston Ches E 167 F10
Ches W 183 F9
Derbys 152 C3
Derbys 185 E11
Flint 166 B4
Hereford 115 C9
Hereford 115 E9
Herts 104 G5
Oxon 82 E4
Powys 130 E5
Shrops 132 E6
Shrops 149 D10
Staffs 151 E7
Staffs 168 G3
S Yorks 187 D7
Telford 132 B2
W Mid 133 F11
Wokingham 65 C9
Aston Abbotts Bucks 102 G6
Aston Bank Worcs 116 C2
Aston Botterell Shrops 132 G2
Aston-by-Stone Staffs 151 C8
Aston Cantlow Warks 118 F2
Aston Clinton Bucks 84 C5
Aston Crews Hereford 98 G3
Aston Cross Glos 99 E8
Aston End Herts 104 G5
Aston Eyre Shrops 132 E3
Aston Fields Worcs 117 D9
Aston Flamville Leics 135 E9
Aston Ingham Hereford 98 G3
Aston juxta Mondrum
Ches E 167 D11
Aston le Walls
W Nhants 119 G9
Aston Magna Glos 100 D3
Aston Munslow Shrops 131 F10
Aston on Carrant Glos 99 E8
Aston on Clun Shrops 131 G7
Aston-on-Trent Derbys 153 D8
Aston Pigott Shrops 130 B6
Aston Rogers Shrops 130 B6
Aston Rowant Oxon 84 F2
Aston Sandford Bucks 84 D3
Aston Somerville Worcs 99 D10
Aston Square Shrops 148 D6
Aston Subedge Glos 100 C2
Aston Tirrold Oxon 64 B5
Aston Upthorpe Oxon 64 B5
Astrop W Nhants 101 D10
Astrope Herts 84 C5
Astwick C Beds 104 D4
Astwith Derbys 170 C6
Astwood M Keynes 103 B9
Worcs 117 D8
Worcs 117 F7
Astwood Bank Worcs 117 E10
Aswarby Lincs 173 G9
Aswardby Lincs 190 G5
Atcham Shrops 131 B10
Atch Lench Worcs 117 G10
Athelhampton Dorset 17 C11
Athelington Suff 126 C4
Athelney Som 28 B4
Athelstaneford E Loth 281 F10
Atherfield Green IoW 20 F5
Atherington Devon 25 C9
W Sus 35 G8
Athersley North
S Yorks 197 F11
Athersley South
S Yorks 197 F11
Atherstone Som 28 D5
Warks 134 D6
Atherstone on Stour
Warks 118 G4
Atherton Gtr Man 195 G7
Athnamulloch Highld 299 G11
Athron Hall Perth 286 G4
Atley Hill N Yorks 224 E5
Atlow Derbys 170 F2
Attadale Highld 295 B11
Attadale Ho Highld 295 B11
Attenborough Notts 153 B10
Atterbury M Keynes 103 D7
Atterby Lincs 189 C7
Attercliffe S Yorks 186 D5
Atterley Shrops 132 D2
Atterton Leics 135 D7
Attleborough Norf 141 D10
Warks 135 E7
Attlebridge Norf 160 F2
Attleton Green Suff 124 G4
Atwick E Yorks 209 C9
Atworth Wilts 61 F11
Auberrow Hereford 97 B9
Aubourn Lincs 172 C6
Auch Argyll 285 D7
Auchagallon N Ayrs 255 D9
Auchallater Aberds 292 E3
Auchareoch N Ayrs 255 E10
Aucharnie Aberds 302 E6
Auchattie Aberds 293 D8
Auchavan Angus 292 G3
Auchbreck Moray 302 G2
Auchenback E Renf 267 D10
Auchenbainzie Dumfries 247 D8
Auchenblae Aberds 293 F9
Auchenbrack Dumfries 247 D7
Auchenbreck Argyll 255 C8
Argyll 275 E11
Auchencairn Dumfries 237 D9
Dumfries 247 G11
N Ayrs 256 D2
Auchencairn Ho
Dumfries 237 D10
Auchencar N Ayrs 255 D9
Auchencarroch W Dunb 277 E8
Auchencrosh S Ayrs 236 B3
Auchencrow Borders 273 C7
Auchendinny Midloth 270 C5
Auchengray S Lanark 269 E9
Auchenhalrig Moray 302 C3
Auchenharvie N Ayrs 266 G5
Auchenheath S Lanark 268 G6
Auchenhew N Ayrs 256 E2
Auchenlaich Stirling 285 G10
Auchenleck Dumfries 237 D9
Auchenlochan Argyll 275 F10
Auchenmalg Dumfries 236 D4
Auchenreoch E Dunb 278 F3
Auchensoul S Ayrs 245 E7
Auchentibber S Lanark 268 E3
Auchentiber N Ayrs 267 F7
Auchertyre Highld 295 C10
Auchessan Stirling 285 E8
Auchgourish Highld 291 B11
Auchinairn E Dunb 268 B2
Auchindrain Argyll 284 G4
Auchindrean Highld 307 L6
Auchininna Aberds 302 E6
Auchinleck Dumfries 236 B6
E Ayrs 258 E3
Auchinloch N Lanark 278 G3
Auchinner Perth 285 F10
Auchinraith S Lanark 268 D3
Auchinroath Moray 302 D2
Auchinstarry N Lanark 278 F4
Auchintoul Aberds 293 B7
Highld 309 K5
Auchiries Aberds 303 F10
Auchlee Aberds 293 D10
Auchleeks Ho Perth 291 G9
Auchleven Aberds 302 G6
Auchlinn Aberds 303 D7
Auchlochan S Lanark 259 B8
Auchlossan Aberds 293 C7
Auchlunachan Highld 307 L6
Auchlunies Aberds 293 D10
Auchlyne Stirling 285 E9
Auchmacoy Aberds 303 F9
Auchmair Moray 302 G3
Auchmantle Dumfries 236 C3
Auchmenzie Aberds 302 G5
Auchmillan E Ayrs 258 D2
Auchmithie Angus 287 C10
Auchmore Highld 300 D4
Auchmuirbridge Fife 286 G6
Auchmull Angus 293 F7
Auchnacraig Argyll 289 G9
Auchnacree Angus 292 G6
Auchnafree Perth 286 D2
Auchnagallin Highld 301 F10
Auchnagarron Argyll 275 E11
Auchnagatt Aberds 303 E9
Auchnaha Argyll 275 E10
Auchnahillin Highld 301 F7
Auchnarrow Moray 302 G2
Auchnashelloch Perth 285 F11
Auchnotteroch Dumfries 236 C1
Aucholzie Aberds 292 D5
Auchrannie Angus 286 B6
Auchroisk Highld 301 G10
Auchronie Angus 292 E6
Auchterarder Perth 286 F3
Auchteraw Highld 290 C5
Auchterderran Fife 280 B4
Auchterhouse Angus 287 D7
Auchtermuchty Fife 286 F6
Auchterneed Highld 300 D4
Auchtertool Fife 280 C4
Auchtertyre Moray 301 D11
Stirling 285 E7
Auchtubh Stirling 285 E9
Auckengill Highld 310 C7
Auckley S Yorks 199 G7
Audenshaw Gtr Man 184 B6
Audlem Ches E 167 G11
Audley Staffs 168 E3
Audley End Essex 105 D10
Essex 106 D6
Norf 142 G2
Suff 125 G7
Auds Aberds 302 C6
Aughertree Cumb 229 D11
Aughton E Yorks 207 F10
Lancs 193 F11
Lancs 211 F10
S Yorks 187 D7
Wilts 47 B8
Aughton Park Lancs 194 F2
Aukside Durham 232 F4
Auldearn Highld 301 D9
Aulden Hereford 115 G9
Auldgirth Dumfries 247 F10
Auldhame E Loth 281 E11
Auldhouse S Lanark 268 E2
Auldtown of Carnoustie
Aberds 302 E6
Ault a'chruinn Highld 295 C11
Aultanrynie Highld 308 F3
Aultbea Highld 307 L3
Aultdearg Highld 300 C2
Aultgrishan Highld 307 L2
Aultguish Inn Highld 300 B3
Ault Hucknall Derbys 171 B7
Aultibea Highld 311 G4
Aultiphurst Highld 310 C2
Aultivullin Highld 310 C2
Aultmore Highld 301 G10
Moray 302 D4
Aultnagoire Highld 300 G5
Aultnamain Inn Highld 309 L6
Aultnaslat Highld 290 C3
Aulton Aberds 302 G6
Aulton of Atherb Aberds 303 E9
Aultvaich Highld 300 E5
Aunby Lincs 155 G10
Aundorach Highld 291 B11
Aunk Devon 27 G8
Aunsby Lincs 155 B10
Auquhorthies Aberds 303 G8
Aust S Glos 60 B5
Austendike Lincs 156 E5
Austen Fen Lincs 190 C5
Austenwood Bucks 66 B3
Austerfield S Yorks 187 C11
Austerlands Gtr Man 196 F3
Austhorpe W Yorks 206 G3
Austrey Warks 134 B5
Austwick N Yorks 212 F5
Authorpe Lincs 190 E6
Authorpe Row Lincs 191 G8
Avebury Wilts 62 F6
Avebury Trusloe Wilts 62 F5
Aveley Thurrock 68 C5
Avening Glos 80 F5
Avening Green S Glos 80 G2
Averham Notts 172 E3
Avernish Highld 295 C10
Avery Hill London 68 E2
Aveton Gifford Devon 8 F3
Avielochan Highld 291 B11
Aviemore Highld 291 B10
Avington Hants 48 G4
W Berks 63 F11
Avoch Highld 301 D7
Avon Hants 19 B8
Wilts 62 D3
Avonbridge Falk 279 G8
Avoncliff Wilts 45 B10
Avon Dassett Warks 101 B8
Avonmouth Bristol 60 D4
Avonwick Devon 8 D4
Awbridge Hants 32 C4
Awhirk Dumfries 236 D2
Awkley S Glos 60 B5
Awliscombe Devon 27 G10
Awre Glos 80 D2
Awsworth Notts 171 G7
Axbridge Som 44 C2
Axford Hants 48 E6
Wilts 63 F8
Axmansford Hants 64 G5
Axminster Devon 15 B11
Axmouth Devon 15 C11
Axton Flint 181 E10
Axtown Devon 7 B10
Axwell Park T&W 242 E5
Aycliff Kent 55 E10
Aycliffe Durham 233 G11
Aydon Northumb 242 D2
Aykley Heads Durham 233 C11
Aylburton Glos 79 E10
Aylburton Common
Glos 79 E10
Ayle Northumb 231 B10
Aylesbeare Devon 14 C6
Aylesbury Bucks 84 C4
Aylesby NE Lincs 201 F8
Aylesford Kent 53 B8
Aylesham Kent 55 C8
Aylestone Leicester 135 C11
Aylestone Hill Hereford 97 C10
Aylestone Park
Leicester 135 C11
Aylmerton Norf 160 B3
Aylsham Norf 160 D3
Aylton Hereford 98 D3
Aylworth Glos 100 G2
Aymestrey Hereford 115 D8
Aynho W Nhants 101 E10
Ayot Green Herts 86 C2
Ayot St Lawrence Herts 85 B11
Ayot St Peter Herts 86 B2
Ayr S Ayrs 257 E8
Ayre of Atler Shetland 313 G6
Ayres Shetland 313 H5
Ayres End Herts 85 C11
Ayres of Selivoe
Shetland 313 J4
Ayres Quay T&W 243 F9
Aysgarth N Yorks 213 B10
Ayshford Devon 27 D8
Ayside Cumb 211 C7
Ayston Rutland 137 C7
Aythorpe Roding Essex 87 B9
Ayton Borders 273 C8
T&W 243 F7
Ayton Castle Borders 273 C8
Aywick Shetland 312 E7
Azerley N Yorks 214 E5

B

Babbacombe Torbay 9 B8
Babbington Notts 171 G7
Babbinswood Shrops 148 C6
Babbs Green Herts 86 B5
Babcary Som 29 B9
Babel Carms 94 D6
Babel Green Suff 106 B4
Babell Flint 181 G11
Babeny Devon 13 F9
Babingley Norf 158 D3
Babraham Cambs 123 G10
Babworth Notts 187 E11
Bac W Isles 304 D6

Bachau Anglesey 178 E6
Bache Shrops 131 G9
Bacheldre Powys 130 E4
Bachelor's Bump E Sus 38 E4
Bache Mill Shrops 131 F10
Bach-y-gwreiddyn
Swansea 75 E10
Backaland Orkney 314 C5
Backaskaill Orkney 314 A4
Backbarrow Cumb 211 C7
Backbower Gtr Man 185 C7
Backburn Aberds 293 D10
Backe Carms 74 B3
Backfolds Aberds 303 D10
Backford Ches W 182 G6
Backford Cross Ches W 182 G5
Backhill Aberds 303 F7
Aberds 303 F10
Backhill of Clackriach
Aberds 303 E9
Backhill of Fortree
Aberds 303 E9
Backhill of Trustach
Aberds 293 D8
Backies Highld 311 J2
Backlass Highld 310 D6
Highld 310 E4
Back Muir Fife 279 D11
Back of Keppoch Highld 295 G8
Back o' th' Brook Staffs 169 E9
Back Rogerton E Ayrs 258 E3
Back Street Suff 124 F4
Backwell N Som 60 F3
Backwell Common
N Som 60 F3
Backwell Green N Som 60 F3
Backworth T&W 243 C8
Bacon End Essex 87 B10
Baconend Green Essex 87 B10
Bacon's End W Mid 134 F3
Baconsthorpe Norf 160 B2
Bacton Hereford 97 E7
Norf 160 C6
Suff 125 D11
Bacton Green Norf 160 C6
Suff 125 D10
Bacup Lancs 195 C11
Badachonacher Highld 300 B6
Badachro Highld 299 B7
Badanloch Lodge Highld 308 F7
Badarach Highld 309 K5
Badavanich Highld 299 D11
Badbea Highld 307 K5
Badbury Swindon 63 C7
Badbury Wick Swindon 63 C7
Badby W Nhants 119 F11
Badcall Highld 306 D7
Badcaul Highld 307 K5
Baddeley Edge Stoke 168 E6
Baddeley Green Stoke 168 E6
Baddesley Clinton
Warks 118 C4
Baddesley Ensor Warks 134 D5
Baddidarach Highld 307 G5
Baddoch Aberds 292 E3
Baddock Highld 301 D7
Baddow Park Essex 88 E2
Badeach Moray 302 F2
Badenscallie Highld 307 J5
Badenscoth Aberds 303 F7
Badentoy Park Aberds 293 D11
Badenyon Aberds 292 B5
Badgall Corn 11 D10
Badgeney Cambs 139 D8
Badger Shrops 132 D5
Badgergate Stirling 278 B5
Badger's Hill Worcs 99 B10
Badger's Mount Kent 68 G3
Badger Street Som 28 D3
Badgeworth Glos 80 B6
Badgworth Som 43 C11
Badharlick Corn 11 D11
Badicaul Highld 295 C9
Badingham Suff 126 D6
Badintagairt Highld 309 H4
Badlesmere Kent 54 C4
Badlipster Highld 310 E6
Badluarach Highld 307 K4
Badminton S Glos 61 C10
Badnaban Highld 307 G5
Badnabay Highld 306 E7
Badnagie Highld 310 F5
Badninish Highld 309 K7
Badrallach Highld 307 K5
Badsey Worcs 99 C11
Badshalloch W Dunb 277 D9
Badshot Lea Sur 49 D11
Badsworth W Yorks 198 E3
Badwell Ash Suff 125 D9
Badwell Green Suff 125 D10
Badworthy Devon 8 C3
Bae Cinmel = Kinmel Bay
Conwy 181 E7
Bae Colwyn = Colwyn Bay
Conwy 180 F4
Bae Penrhyn = Penrhyn Bay
Conwy 180 E4
Baffins Ptsmth 33 G11
Bagber Dorset 30 E3
Bagby N Yorks 215 C9
Bagby Grange N Yorks 215 C9
Bag Enderby Lincs 190 G5
Bagendon Glos 81 D8
Bagginswood Shrops 132 G3
Baggrow Cumb 229 C9
Bàgha Chàise W Isles 296 D5
Bagh a Chaisteil
W Isles 297 M2
Bagham Kent 54 C5
Baghasdal W Isles 297 K3
Bagh Mor W Isles 296 F4
Bagh Shiarabhagh
W Isles 297 L3
Bagillt Flint 182 F2
Baginton Warks 118 C6
Baglan Neath 57 C8
Bagley Shrops 149 D8
Som 44 D3
W Yorks 205 F10
Bagley Green Som 27 D10
Bagley Marsh Shrops 149 D7
Bagmore Hants 49 E7
Bagnall Staffs 168 E6
Bagnor W Berks 64 F3
Bagpath Glos 80 E5
Glos 80 G4
Bagshaw Derbys 185 E9
Bagshot Sur 66 G2
Wilts 63 F10
Bagshot Heath Sur 66 G2
Bagslate Moor
Gtr Man 195 E11
Bagstone S Glos 61 B7
Bagthorpe Norf 158 C5
Notts 171 E7
Baguley Gtr Man 184 D4
Bagworth Leics 135 B8
Bagwyllydiart Hereford 97 F8
Bagwy Llydiart Hereford 97 F8
Bail Àrd Bhuirgh
W Isles 304 C6
Bailbrook Bath 61 F9
Baildon W Yorks 205 F9
Baildon Green W Yorks 205 F8
Baile W Isles 296 C5
Baile Ailein W Isles 304 F4
Baile a Mhanaich
W Isles 296 F3
Baile an Truiseil
W Isles 304 C5
Bailebeag Highld 291 B7
Baile Boidheach Argyll 275 F8
Baile Gharbhaidh
W Isles 297 G3
Baile Glas W Isles 296 F4
Baile Mhartainn
W Isles 296 D3
Baile Mhic Phail
W Isles 296 D4
Baile Mor Argyll 288 G4
W Isles 296 E3
Baile na Creige W Isles 297 L2
Baile nan Cailleach
W Isles 296 F3
Baile Raghaill W Isles 296 D3
Bailey Green Hants 33 B11
Baileyhead Cumb 240 B2
Bailiesward Aberds 302 F4
Bailiff Bridge W Yorks 196 C6
Baillieston Glasgow 268 C3
Bail' lochdrach W Isles 296 F4
Bailrigg Lancs 202 B5
Bail Uachdraich
W Isles 296 E4
Bail' Ur Tholastaidh
W Isles 304 D7
Bainbridge N Yorks 223 G8
Bainsford Falk 279 E7
Bainshole Aberds 302 F6
Bainton E Yorks 208 C5
Oxon 101 F11
Pboro 137 B11
Baintown Fife 287 G7
Bairnkine Borders 262 F5
Baker's Cross Kent 53 F9
Bakers End Herts 86 B5
Baker's Hill Glos 79 C9
Baker Street Thurrock 68 C6
Baker's Wood Bucks 66 B4
Bakesdown Corn 24 G2
Bakestone Moor Derbys 187 F8
Bakewell Derbys 170 B2
Bala = Y Bala Gwyn 147 B8
Balachroick Highld 291 C10
Balachuirn Highld 298 E5
Balance Hill Staffs 151 C11
Balavil Highld 291 C9
Balavoulin Perth 291 G10
Balbeg Highld 300 F4
Highld 300 G4
Balbeggie Perth 286 E5
Balbegno Castle Aberds 293 F8
Balbithan Aberds 293 B9
Balbithan Ho Aberds 293 B10
Balblair Highld 300 E5
Highld 301 C7
Highld 309 K5
Balby S Yorks 198 G5
Balcherry Highld 311 L2
Balchladich Highld 306 F5
Balchraggan Highld 300 E5
Highld 300 F5
Highld 300 G5
Balchrick Highld 306 D6
Balchrystie Fife 287 G8
Balcladaich Highld 300 G2
Balcombe W Sus 51 G10
Balcombe Lane W Sus 51 G10
Balcomie Fife 287 F10
Balcraggie Lodge Highld 310 F5
Balcurvie Fife 287 G7
Baldersby N Yorks 215 D7
Baldersby St James
N Yorks 215 D7
Balderstone Gtr Man 196 E2
Lancs 203 G8
Balderton Ches W 166 C5
Notts 172 E4
Baldhu Corn 4 G5
Baldingstone Gtr Man 195 E10
Baldinnie Fife 287 F8
Baldock Herts 104 E4
Baldon Row Oxon 83 E9
Baldoon Highld 300 B6
Baldovie Dundee 287 D8
Baldrine IoM 192 D5
Baldslow E Sus 38 E3
Baldwin IoM 192 D4
Baldwinholme Cumb 239 G8
Baldwin's Gate Staffs 168 G3
Baldwins Hill W Sus 51 F11
Bale Norf 159 B10
Balearn Aberds 303 D10
Balemartine Argyll 288 E1
Balephuil Argyll 288 E1
Balerno Edin 270 B3
Baleromindubh Argyll 274 D4
Balevullin Argyll 288 E1
Balfield Angus 293 G7
Balfour Orkney 314 E4
Balfour Mains Orkney 314 E4
Balfron Stirling 277 D10
Balfron Station Stirling 277 D10
Balgaveny Aberds 302 E6
Balgavies Angus 287 B9
Balgonar Fife 279 C10
Balgove Aberds 303 F8
Balgowan Highld 291 D8
Perth 286 E3
Balgown Highld 298 C3
Balgrennie Aberds 292 C6
Balgrochan E Dunb 278 F2
Balgy Highld 299 D8
Balhaldie Stirling 286 G2
Balhalgardy Aberds 303 G7
Balham London 67 E9
Balhary Perth 286 C6
Baliasta Shetland 312 C8
Baligill Highld 310 C2
Baligortan Argyll 288 E5
Baligrundle Argyll 289 E10
Balindore Argyll 289 F11
Balinoe Argyll 288 E1
Balintore Angus 286 B6
Highld 301 B8
Balintraid Highld 301 B7
Balintuim Aberds 292 E3
Balk N Yorks 215 C9
Balkeerie Angus 287 C7
Balkemback Angus 287 D7
Balk Field Notts 188 E2
Balkholme E Yorks 199 B9
Balkissock S Ayrs 244 G4
Ball Corn 10 G6
Shrops 148 D6
Ballabeg IoM 192 E3
Ballacannel IoM 192 D5
Ballachraggan Moray 301 E11
Ballachrochin Highld 301 F8
Ballachulish Highld 284 B4
Balladen Lancs 195 C10
Ballajora IoM 192 C5
Ballaleigh IoM 192 D4
Ballamodha IoM 192 E3
Ballantrae S Ayrs 244 G3
Ballaquine IoM 192 D5
Ballard's Ash Wilts 62 C5
Ballards Gore Essex 88 G6
Ballard's Green Warks 134 E5
Ballasalla IoM 192 C4
IoM 192 E3
Ballater Aberds 292 D5
Ballathie Perth 286 D5
Ballaugh IoM 192 C4
Ballaveare IoM 192 E4
Ballcorach Moray 301 G11
Ballechin Perth 286 B3
Balleich Stirling 277 B10
Balleigh Highld 309 L7
Ballencrieff E Loth 281 F9
Ballencrieff Toll
W Loth 279 G9
Ballentoul Perth 291 G10
Ball Green Stoke 168 E5
Ball Haye Green Staffs 169 D7
Ball Hill Devon 24 C3
Ball Hill Hants 64 G2
Ballidon Derbys 170 E2
Balliekine N Ayrs 255 D9
Balliemore Argyll 275 E11
Argyll 289 G10
Ballikinrain Stirling 277 D11
Ballimeanoch Argyll 284 F4
Ballimore Argyll 275 E10
Stirling 285 F9
Ballinaby Argyll 274 G3
Ballinbreich Fife 286 E6
Ballindean Perth 286 E6
Ballingdon Suff 107 C7
Ballingdon Bottom Herts 85 C8
Ballinger Bottom Bucks 84 E6
Ballinger Bottom (South)
Bucks 84 E6
Ballinger Common Bucks 84 E6
Ballingham Hereford 97 E11
Ballingham Hill Hereford 97 E11
Ballingry Fife 280 B3
Ballinlick Perth 286 C3
Ballinluig Perth 286 B3
Ballintean Highld 291 C10
Ballintuim Perth 286 B5
Balliveolan Argyll 289 E10
Balloch Angus 287 B7
Highld 301 E7
N Lanark 278 G4
W Dunb 277 E7
Ballochan Aberds 293 D7
Ballochearn Stirling 277 D11
Ballochford Moray 302 F3
Ballochmorrie S Ayrs 244 G6
Ball o'Ditton Halton 183 D7
Ballogie Aberds 293 D7
Balls Cross W Sus 35 B7
Balls Green Essex 107 G11
E Sus 52 F3
W Sus 35 C10
Ball's Green Glos 80 F5
Balls Hill W Mid 133 E9
Ballygown Argyll 288 E6
Ballygrant Argyll 274 G4
Ballygroggan Argyll 255 F7
Ballyhaugh Argyll 288 D3
Balmacara Highld 295 C10
Balmacara Square
Highld 295 C10
Balmaclellan Dumfries 237 B8
Balmacneil Perth 286 B3
Balmacqueen Highld 298 B4
Balmae Dumfries 237 E8
Balmaha Stirling 277 C8
Balmalcolm Fife 287 G7
Balmalloch N Lanark 278 F4
Balmeanach Argyll 288 F6
Argyll 289 E8
Highld 295 B7
Highld 298 E3
Highld 298 E5
Balmedie Aberds 293 B11
Balmer Shrops 149 C8
Balmer Heath Shrops 149 C8
Balmerino Fife 287 E7
Balmerlawn Hants 32 G4
Balmesh Dumfries 236 D3
Balmichael N Ayrs 255 D10
Balminnoch Dumfries 236 C4
Balmirmer Angus 287 D9
Balmoral Borders 261 B11
Balmore E Dunb 278 G2
Highld 298 E2
Highld 300 F3
Highld 301 E8
Perth 286 B3
Balmule Fife 280 D4
Balmullo Fife 287 E8
Balmungie Highld 301 D7
Balmurrie Dumfries 236 C4
Balnaboth Angus 292 G5
Balnabreich Moray 302 D3
Balnabruaich Highld 301 C7
Balnabruich Highld 311 G5
Balnacarn Highld 290 B4
Balnacoil Highld 311 H2
Balnacra Highld 299 E9
Balnacruie Highld 301 G9
Balnafoich Highld 300 F6
Balnagall Highld 311 L2
Balnagowan Aberds 293 C7
Balnagrantach Highld 300 F4
Balnaguard Perth 286 B3
Balnahanaid Perth 285 C10
Balnahard Argyll 274 D5
Argyll 288 F6
Balnain Highld 300 F4
Balnakeil Highld 308 C3
Balnakelly Aberds 293 B7
Balnaknock Highld 298 C4
Balnamoon Aberds 303 D9
Angus 293 G7
Balnapaling Highld 301 C7
Balne N Yorks 198 D5
Balnoon Corn 2 B2
Balochroy Argyll 255 B8
Balole Argyll 274 G4
Balone Fife 287 F8
Balornock Glasgow 268 B2
Balquharn Perth 286 D4
Balquhidder Stirling 285 E9
Balquhidder Station
Stirling 285 E9
Balquhindachy Aberds 303 E8
Balrownie Angus 293 G7
Balsall W Mid 118 B4
Balsall Common W Mid 118 B4
Balsall Heath W Mid 133 G11
Balsall Street W Mid 118 B4
Balsam Cambs 123 G11
Balscote Oxon 101 C7
Balscott Oxon 101 C7
Balsham Cambs 123 G11
Balsporran Cottages
Highld 291 F8
Balstonia Thurrock 69 C7
Baltasound Shetland 312 C8
Balterley Staffs 168 E3
Balterley Green Staffs 168 E3
Balterley Heath Staffs 168 E2
Baltersan Dumfries 236 C6
Balthangie Aberds 303 D8
Balthayock Perth 286 E5
Baltonsborough Som 44 G4
Balure Argyll 289 E11
Balvaird Highld 300 D5
Balvenie Moray 302 E3
Balvicar Argyll 275 B8
Balvraid Highld 295 D10
Highld 301 F8
Balwest Corn 2 C3
Bamber Bridge Lancs 194 B5
Bamber's Green Essex 105 G11
Bamburgh Northumb 264 C5
Bamff Perth 286 B6
Bamford Derbys 186 E2
Gtr Man 195 E11
Bamfurlong Glos 99 G8
Gtr Man 194 G5
Bampton Cumb 221 B10
Devon 27 C7
Oxon 82 E4
Bampton Grange Cumb 221 B10
Banavie Highld 290 F3
Banbury Oxon 101 C9
Bancffosfelen Carms 75 C7
Banchor Highld 301 E9
Banchory Aberds 293 D8
Banchory-Devenick
Aberds 293 C11
Bancycapel Carms 74 B6
Banc-y-Darren Ceredig 128 G3
Bancyfelin Carms 74 B4
Bancyffordd Carms 93 D8
Bandirran Perth 286 D6
Bandonhill London 67 G9
Bandrake Head Cumb 210 B6
Banff Aberds 302 C6
Bangor Gwyn 179 G9
Bangor is y coed = Bangor
on Dee Wrex 166 F5
Bangor on Dee = Bangor-is-
y-coed Wrex 166 F5
Bangors Corn 11 B10
Bangor Teifi Ceredig 93 C7
Banham Norf 141 F11
Bank Hants 32 F3
Bankend Dumfries 238 D2
Bank End Cumb 210 B3
Cumb 228 D6
Bank Fold Blackburn 195 C8
Bankfoot Perth 286 D4
Bankglen E Ayrs 258 G4
Bankhead Aberdeen 293 B10
Aberds 293 C8
Dumfries 236 C2
Falk 278 E6
S Lanark 269 G7
Bank Hey Blackburn 203 G9
Bank Houses Lancs 202 C4
Bankland Som 28 B4
Bank Lane Gtr Man 195 D9
Bank Newton N Yorks 204 C4
Banknock Falk 278 F5
Banks Cumb 240 E3
Lancs 193 C11
Orkney 314 C4
Bank's Green Worcs 117 D9
Bankshead Shrops 130 F6
Bankshill Dumfries 248 G5
Bankside Falk 279 E7
Bank Street Worcs 116 E2
Bank Top Gtr Man 195 E8
Lancs 194 F4
Stoke 168 E5
T&W 242 D4
W Yorks 196 C6
W Yorks 205 F9
Banners Gate W Mid 133 D11
Banningham Norf 160 D4
Banniskirk Ho Highld 310 D5
Banniskirk Mains Highld 310 D5
Bannister Green Essex 106 G3
Bannockburn Stirling 278 C5
Banns Corn 4 F4
Banstead Sur 51 B8
Bantam Grove W Yorks 197 B9
Bantaskin Falk 279 F7
Bantham Devon 8 G3
Banton N Lanark 278 F5
Banwell N Som 43 B11
Banyard's Green Suff 126 C5
Bapchild Kent 70 G2
Baptist End W Mid 133 F8
Bapton Wilts 46 F3
Barabhas W Isles 304 D5
Barabhas Iarach
W Isles 304 D5
Barabhas Uarach
W Isles 304 C5
Barachandroman Argyll 289 G8
Baramore Highld 289 B8
Barassie S Ayrs 257 C8
Baravullin Argyll 289 F10
Barbadoes Stirling 277 B11
Barbaraville Highld 301 B7
Barbauchlaw W Loth 269 B8
Barber Booth Derbys 185 E10
Barber Green Cumb 211 C7
Barber's Moor Lancs 194 D3
Barbican Plym 7 E9
Barbieston S Ayrs 257 F10
Barbon Cumb 212 C2
Barbourne Worcs 116 F6
Barbreck Ho Argyll 275 C9
Barbridge Ches E 167 D10
Barbrook Devon 41 D8
Barby W Nhants 119 C10
Barby Nortoft
W Nhants 119 C11
Barcaldine Argyll 289 E11
Barcelona Corn 6 E4
Barcheston Warks 100 D5
Barclose Cumb 239 E10
Barcombe E Sus 36 E6
Barcombe Cross E Sus 36 D6
Barcroft W Yorks 204 F6
Barden N Yorks 224 G2
Bardennoch Dumfries 246 E3
Barden Park Kent 52 D5
Barden Scale N Yorks 205 B7
Bardfield End Green
Essex 106 E2
Bardfield Saling Essex 106 F3
Bardister Shetland 312 F5
Bardnabeinne Highld 309 K7
Bardney Lincs 173 B10
Bardon Leics 153 G8
Bardon Mill Northumb 241 E7
Bardowie E Dunb 277 G11
Bardown E Sus 37 B11
Bardrainney Invclyd 276 G6
Bardrishaig Argyll 275 B8
Bardsea Cumb 210 E6
Bardsey W Yorks 206 E3
Bardsley Gtr Man 196 G2
Bardwell Suff 125 C8
Bare Lancs 211 G9
Bare Ash Som 43 F9
Bareless Northumb 263 B9
Bar End Hants 33 B7
Barepot Cumb 228 F6
Bareppa Corn 3 D7
Barfad Argyll 275 G9
Dumfries 236 C5
Barford Norf 142 B2
Sur 49 F11
Warks 118 E5
Barford St John Oxon 101 E8
Barford St Martin Wilts 46 G5
Barford St Michael
Oxon 101 E8
Barfrestone Kent 55 C9
Bargaly Dumfries 236 C6
Bargarran Renfs 277 G9
Bargate Derbys 170 F5
Bargeddie N Lanark 268 C4
Bargoed Caerph 77 F10
Bargrennan Dumfries 236 B5
Barham Cambs 122 B2
Kent 55 C8
Suff 126 G2
Barharrow Dumfries 237 D8
Barhill Dumfries 237 C10
Bar Hill Cambs 123 E7
Staffs 168 G3
Barholm Dumfries 237 D7
Lincs 155 G11
Barkby Leics 136 B2
Barkby Thorpe Leics 136 B2
Barkers Green Shrops 149 D10
Barkers Hill Wilts 30 B6
Barkestone-le-Vale
Leics 154 C5
Barkham Wokingham 65 F9
Barking London 68 C2
Suff 125 G11
Barking Riverside London 68 C3
Barkingside London 68 B2
Barking Tye Suff 125 G11
Barkisland W Yorks 196 D5
Barkla Shop Corn 4 E4
Barkston Lincs 172 G6
N Yorks 206 F5
Barkston Ash N Yorks 206 F5
Barkway Herts 105 D7
Barlake Som 45 D7
Barlanark Glasgow 268 C3
Barland Powys 114 E5
Barland Common
Swansea 56 D5
Barlaston Staffs 151 B7
Barlavington W Sus 35 D7
Barlborough Derbys 187 F7
Barlby N Yorks 207 G8
Barlestone Leics 135 B8
Barley Herts 105 D7
Lancs 204 E2
Barleycroft End Herts 105 F8
Barley End Bucks 85 C7
Barley Green Lancs 204 E2
Barley Mow T&W 243 G7
Barleythorpe Rutland 136 B6
Barling Essex 70 B2
Barlings Lincs 189 G9
Barlow Derbys 186 G4
N Yorks 198 B6
T&W 242 E5
Barlow Moor Gtr Man 184 C4
Barmby Moor E Yorks 207 D11
Barmby on the Marsh
E Yorks 199 B7
Barmer Norf 158 C6
Barming Heath Kent 53 B8
Barmolloch Argyll 275 D9
Bar Moor T&W 242 E4
Barmoor Castle
Northumb 263 B11
Barmoor Lane End
Northumb 264 B2
Barmouth = Abermaw
Gwyn 146 F2
Barmpton Darl 224 B6
Barmston E Yorks 209 B9
T&W 243 F8
Barmulloch Glasgow 268 B2
Barnaby Green Suff 127 B9
Barnacabber Argyll 276 D3
Barnack Pboro 137 B11
Barnacle Warks 135 G7
Barnaline Argyll 275 B10
Barnard Castle Durham 223 B11
Barnard Gate Oxon 82 C6
Barnardiston Suff 106 B4
Barnard's Green Worcs 98 B5
Barnardtown Newport 59 B10
Barnbarroch Dumfries 237 D10
Barnbow Carr W Yorks 206 F3
Barnburgh S Yorks 198 G3
Barnby Suff 143 F9
Barnby Dun S Yorks 198 F6
Barnby in the Willows
Notts 172 E5
Barnby Moor Notts 187 E11
Barncluith S Lanark 268 E4
Barndennoch Dumfries 247 F9
Barne Barton Plym 7 D8
Barnehurst London 68 D4
Barnes Cray London 68 D4
Barnes Hall S Yorks 186 B4
Barnes Street Kent 52 D6
Barnet London 86 F2
Barnetby le Wold
N Lincs 200 F5
Barnet Gate London 86 F2
Barnett Brook Ches E 167 G10
Barney Norf 159 C9
Barnfield Kent 54 D2
Barnfields Hereford 97 C9
Staffs 169 D7
Barnham Suff 125 B7
W Sus 35 G7
Barnham Broom Norf 141 B11
Barnhead Angus 287 B10
Barnhill Ches W 167 E7
Dundee 287 D8
Moray 301 D11
Barnhills Dumfries 236 B1
Barningham Durham 223 C11
Suff 125 B9
Barningham Green Norf 160 C2
Barnmoor Green Warks 118 E3
Barnoldby le Beck
NE Lincs 201 G8
Barnoldswick Lancs 204 D3
N Yorks 212 E3
Barns Borders 260 B6
Barnsbury London 67 C10
Barnsdale Rutland 137 B8
Barns Green W Sus 35 B10
Barnside W Yorks 197 F7
Barnsley Glos 81 D9
Shrops 132 E5
S Yorks 197 F10
Barnsole Kent 55 B9
Barnstaple Devon 40 G5
Barnston Essex 87 B10
Mers 182 E3
Barnstone Notts 154 B4
Barnt Green Worcs 117 C10
Barnton Ches W 183 F10
Edin 280 F3
Barnwell N Nhants 137 G10
Barnwell All Saints
N Nhants 137 G10
Barnwell St Andrew
N Nhants 137 F10
Barnwood Glos 80 B5
Barochreal Argyll 289 G10
Barons Cross Hereford 115 F9
Barr Highld 289 D8
S Ayrs 245 E7
Som 27 C11
Barra Castle Aberds 303 G7
Barrachan Dumfries 236 E5
Barrachnie Glasgow 268 C3
Barrack Aberds 303 E8
Barrack Hill Newport 59 B10
Barraer Dumfries 236 C5
Barraglom W Isles 304 E3
Barrahormid Argyll 275 E8
Barran Argyll 289 G10
Barranrioch Argyll 289 G10
Barrapol Argyll 288 E1
Barras Aberds 293 E10
Cumb 222 C6
Barrasford Northumb 241 C10
Barravullin Argyll 275 C9
Barregarrow IoM 192 D4
Barrets Green Ches E 167 D9
Barrhead E Renf 267 D9
Barrhill S Ayrs 244 G6
Barrington Cambs 105 B7
Som 28 D5
Barripper Corn 2 B4
Barrmill N Ayrs 267 E7
Barrock Highld 310 B6
Barrock Ho Highld 310 C6
Barrow Glos 99 G7
Lancs 203 F10
Rutland 155 F7
Shrops 132 C3
Som 44 E5
Suff 124 E5
S Yorks 186 B5
Barroway Drove Norf 139 C11
Barrow Bridge Gtr Man 195 E7
Barrowburn Northumb 263 G9
Barrowburn Northumb 263 G9
Barrowby Lincs 155 B7
Barrowcliff N Yorks 217 B10
Barrow Common N Som 60 F4
Barrowden Rutland 137 C8
Barrowford Lancs 204 F3
Barrow Green Kent 70 G3
Barrow Gurney N Som 60 F4
Barrow Hann N Lincs 200 C5
Barrow Haven N Lincs 200 C5
Barrowhill Kent 54 F6
Barrow Hill Derbys 186 F6
Dorset 18 B5
Barrow-in-Furness
Cumb 210 F4
Barrow Island Cumb 210 F3
Barrowmore Estate
Ches W 167 B7
Barrow Nook Lancs 194 G2
Barrows Green Ches E 167 D11
Cumb 211 B10
Notts 171 E7
Barrow's Green Mers 183 D8
Barrow Street Wilts 45 G10
Barrow upon Humber
N Lincs 200 C5
Barrow upon Soar
Leics 153 F11
Barrow upon Trent
Derbys 153 D7
Barrow Vale Bath 60 G6
Barrow Wake Glos 80 B6
Barry Angus 287 D9
V Glam 58 F6
Barry Dock V Glam 58 F6
Barry Island V Glam 58 F6
Barsby Leics 154 G3
Barsham Suff 143 F7
Barshare E Ayrs 258 F3
Barstable Essex 69 B8
Barston W Mid 118 B4
Bartestree Hereford 97 C11
Barthol Chapel Aberds 303 F8
Bartholomew Green
Essex 106 G4
Barthomley Ches E 168 E3
Bartington Ches W 183 F10
Bartley Hants 32 E4
Bartley Green W Mid 133 G10
Bartlow Cambs 105 B11
Barton Cambs 123 F8
Ches W 166 E6
Glos 80 B4
Glos 99 F11
IoW 20 D6
Lancs 193 F11
Lancs 202 F6
N Som 43 B11
N Yorks 224 D4
Oxon 83 D9
Torbay 9 B8
Warks 118 G2
Barton Abbey Oxon 101 G9
Barton Bendish Norf 140 B4
Barton Court Hereford 98 C4
Barton End Glos 80 F4
Barton Gate Devon 41 E7
Staffs 152 F3
Barton Green Staffs 152 F3
Barton Hartshorn Bucks 102 E2
Barton Hill Bristol 60 E6
N Yorks 216 G4
Barton in Fabis Notts 153 C10
Barton in the Beans
Leics 135 B7
Barton-le-Clay C Beds 103 E11
Barton-le-Street
N Yorks 216 E4
Barton-le-Willows
N Yorks 216 G4
Barton Mills Suff 124 C4
Barton on Sea Hants 19 C10
Barton on the Heath
Warks 100 E5
Barton St David Som 44 G4
Barton Seagrave
N Nhants 121 B7
Bartonsham Hereford 97 D10
Barton Stacey Hants 48 E2
Barton Town Devon 41 E7
Barton Turf Norf 161 E7
Barton Turn Staffs 152 F4
Barton-under-Needwood
Staffs 152 F3
Barton-upon-Humber
N Lincs 200 C4
Barton Upon Irwell
Gtr Man 184 B3
Barton Waterside
N Lincs 200 C4
Barugh S Yorks 197 F10
Barugh Green S Yorks 197 F10
Barway Cambs 123 B10
Barwell Leics 135 D8
London 67 G7
Barwick Devon 25 F9
Herts 86 B5
Som 29 E9
Barwick in Elmet
W Yorks 206 F3
Baschurch Shrops 149 E8
Bascote Warks 119 E8
Bascote Heath Warks 119 E7
Base Green Suff 125 E10
Basford Shrops 131 F7
Staffs 168 F5
Basford Green Staffs 169 E7
Bashall Eaves Lancs 203 E9
Bashley Hants 19 B10
Bashley Park Hants 19 B10
Basildon Essex 69 B8
Basingstoke Hants 48 C6
Baslow Derbys 186 G3
Bason Bridge Som 43 D10
Bassaleg Newport 59 B9
Bassenthwaite Cumb 229 E10
Bassett Soton 32 D6
S Yorks 186 E3
Bassett Green Soton 32 D6
Bassingbourn Cambs 104 C6
Bassingfield Notts 154 B2
Bassingham Lincs 172 C6
Bassingthorpe Lincs 155 D9
Bassus Green Herts 104 F6
Basta Shetland 312 D7
Basted Kent 52 B6
Baston Lincs 156 G2
Bastonford Worcs 116 G6
Bastwick Norf 161 F8
Baswich Staffs 151 E8
Baswick Steer E Yorks 209 D7
Batavaime Stirling 285 D8
Batch Som 43 B10
Batchcott Shrops 115 C9
Batchfields Hereford 98 B3
Batchley Worcs 117 D10
Batchworth Herts 85 G9
Batchworth Heath Herts 85 G9
Batcombe Dorset 29 G10
Som 45 F7
Bate Heath Ches E 183 F11
Bateman's Green
Worcs 117 B11
Bateman's Hill Pembs 73 E8
Batemoor S Yorks 186 E5
Batford Herts 85 B10
Bath Bath 61 F8
Bathampton Bath 61 F9
Bathealton Som 27 C9
Batheaston Bath 61 F9
Bathford Bath 61 F9
Bathgate W Loth 269 B9
Bathley Notts 172 D3
Bathpool Corn 11 G11
Som 28 B3
Bath Side Essex 108 E5
Bath Vale Ches E 168 C5
Bathville W Loth 269 B8
Bathway Som 44 C5
Bathwick Bath 61 F9
Batlers Green Herts 85 F11
Batley W Yorks 197 C8
Batley Carr W Yorks 197 C8
Batsford Glos 100 E3
Batson Devon 9 G9
Batsworthy Devon 26 D4
Batten's Green Som 28 D3
Battenton Green Worcs 116 D6
Battersby N Yorks 225 D11
Battersea London 67 D9
Battisborough Cross
Devon 7 F11
Battisford Suff 125 G11
Battisford Tye Suff 125 G10
Battle E Sus 38 D2
Powys 95 E10
Battledown Glos 99 G9
Battledown Cross Devon 25 F7
Battlefield Shrops 149 F10
Battle Hill T&W 243 D8
Battlesbridge Essex 88 G3
Battlescombe Glos 80 D6
Battlesden C Beds 103 F9
Battlesea Green Suff 126 B4
Battleton Som 26 B6
Battlies Green Suff 125 E7
Battram Leics 135 B8
Battramsley Hants 20 B2
Battramsley Cross Hants 20 B2
Batt's Corner Hants 49 E10
Battyeford W Yorks 197 C7
Batworthy Devon 13 D10
Bauds of Cullen Moray 302 C4
Baugh Argyll 288 E2
Baughton Worcs 99 C7
Baughurst Hants 48 B5
Baulking Oxon 82 G4
Baumber Lincs 190 G2
Baunton Glos 81 E8
Baverstock Wilts 46 G4
Bawburgh Norf 142 B3
Bawdeswell Norf 159 E10
Bawdrip Som 43 F10
Bawdsey Suff 108 C6
Bawsey Norf 158 F3
Bawtry S Yorks 187 C11
Baxenden Lancs 195 B9
Baxterley Warks 134 D5
Baxter's Green Suff 124 F5
Bay Dorset 30 B4
Highld 298 D2
Baybridge Hants 33 C8
Northumb 241 G11
Baycliff Cumb 210 E5
Baydon Wilts 63 D9
Bayford Herts 86 D4
Som 30 B2
Bay Gate Lancs 203 D11
Bay Horse Lancs 202 C5
Bayles Cumb 231 C10
Bayley's Hill Kent 52 C4
Baylham Suff 126 G2
Baylis Green Worcs 117 C11
Baynard's Green Oxon 101 F10
Baynhall Worcs 99 B7
Baysham Hereford 97 F11
Bayston Hill Shrops 131 B9
Bayswater London 67 C9
Baythorne End Essex 106 C4
Baythorpe Lincs 174 G2
Bayton Worcs 116 C3
Bayton Common Worcs 116 C4
Bay View Kent 70 E4
Bayworth Oxon 83 E8
Beach Highld 289 D9
S Glos 61 E8
Beachampton Bucks 102 D5
Beachamwell Norf 140 B5
Beachans Moray 301 E10
Beacharr Argyll 255 C7
Beachborough Kent 55 F7
Beach Hay Worcs 116 C4
Beachlands E Sus 23 E11
Beachley Glos 79 G9
Beacon Corn 2 B5
Devon 27 F11
Devon 28 F2
Beacon Down E Sus 37 C9
Beacon End Essex 107 G9
Beaconhill Northumb 243 B7
Beacon Hill Bath 61 F9
Bucks 84 G6
Cumb 210 E4
Dorset 18 C5
Essex 88 C5
Kent 53 G10
Notts 172 E4
Suff 108 B4
Sur 49 F11
Beacon Lough T&W 243 F7
Beacon's Bottom Bucks 84 F3
Beaconsfield Bucks 66 B2
Beaconside Staffs 151 E8
Beacrabhaic W Isles 305 J3
Beadlam N Yorks 216 C3
Beadlow C Beds 104 D2
Beadnell Northumb 264 D6
Beaford Devon 25 E9
Beal Northumb 273 G11
N Yorks 198 B4
Bealach Highld 289 D11
Bealach Maim Argyll 275 E10
Bealbury Corn 7 B7
Beal's Green Kent 53 G9
Bealsmill Corn 12 F3
Beambridge Shrops 131 F10
Beam Bridge Som 27 D10
Beam Hill Staffs 152 D4
Beamhurst Staffs 151 B11
Beamhurst Lane Staffs 151 B11
Beaminster Dorset 29 G7
Beamish Durham 242 G6
Beamond End Bucks 84 F6
Beamsley N Yorks 205 C7
Bean Kent 68 E5
Beanacre Wilts 62 F2
Beancross Falk 279 F8
Beanhill M Keynes 103 D7
Beanley Northumb 264 F3
Beansburn E Ayrs 257 B10
Beanthwaite Cumb 210 C4
Beaquoy Orkney 314 D3
Bear Cross BCP 19 B7
Beard Hill Som 44 E6
Beardly Batch Som 44 E6
Beardwood Blackburn 195 B7
Beare Devon 27 G7
Beare Green Sur 51 E7
Bearley Warks 118 E3
Bearley Cross Warks 118 E3
Bearnus Argyll 288 E5
Bearpark Durham 233 C10
Bearsbridge Northumb 241 F7
Bearsden E Dunb 277 G10
Bearsted Kent 53 B9
Bearstone Shrops 150 B4
Bearwood BCP 18 B6
Hereford 115 F7
W Mid 133 F10
Beasley Staffs 168 F4
Beattock Dumfries 248 C3
Beauchamp Roding
Essex 87 C9
Beauchief S Yorks 186 E4
Beauclerc Northumb 242 E2
Beaudesert Warks 118 D3
Beaufort Bl Gwent 77 C11
Beaufort Castle Highld 300 E5
Beaulieu Hants 32 G5
Beaulieu Park Essex 88 C2
Beaulieu Wood Dorset 30 F2
Beauly Highld 300 E5
Beaumaris Anglesey 179 F10
Beaumont Cumb 239 F8
Essex 108 G3
Windsor 66 E3
Beaumont Hill Darl 224 B5
Beaumont Leys
Leicester 135 B11
Beausale Warks 118 C4
Beauvale Notts 171 F8
Beauworth Hants 33 B9
Beavan's Hill Hereford 98 G3
Beaworthy Devon 12 B5
Beazley End Essex 106 F4
Bebington Mers 182 E4
Bebside Northumb 253 G7
Beccles Suff 143 E8
Becconsall Lancs 194 C2
Beck Bottom Cumb 210 C5
W Yorks 197 C10
Beckbury Shrops 132 C5
Beckces Cumb 230 F4
Beckenham London 67 F11
Beckermet Cumb 219 D10
Beckermonds N Yorks 213 C7
Beckery Som 44 F3
Beckett End Norf 140 D5
Beckfoot Cumb 220 E3
Cumb 229 B7
Beck Foot Cumb 222 F2
W Yorks 205 F8
Beckford Worcs 99 D9
Beckhampton Wilts 62 F5
Beck Head Cumb 211 C8
Beck Hole N Yorks 226 E6
Beck Houses Cumb 221 F11
Beckingham Lincs 172 E5
Notts 188 D3
Beckington Som 45 C10
Beckjay Shrops 115 B7
Beckley E Sus 38 C5
Hants 19 B10
Oxon 83 C9
Beckley Furnace E Sus 38 C4
Beck Row Suff 124 B3
Beckside Cumb 212 B2
Beck Side Cumb 210 C4
Cumb 211 C7
Beckton London 68 C2
Beckwith N Yorks 205 C11
Beckwithshaw N Yorks 205 C11
Becontree London 68 B3
Bedale N Yorks 214 B5
Bedburn Durham 233 E8
Bedchester Dorset 30 D5
Beddau Rhondda 58 B5
Beddgelert Gwyn 163 F9
Beddingham E Sus 36 F6
Beddington London 67 G10
Beddington Corner
London 67 F9
Bedfield Suff 126 D4
Bedford Bedford 121 G11
Gtr Man 183 B11
Bedford Park London 67 D8
Bedgebury Cross Kent 53 G8
Bedgrove Bucks 84 C4
Bedham W Sus 35 C8
Bedhampton Hants 22 B2

Bedingfield Suff 126 D3
Bedingham Green Norf 142 E5
Bedlam N Yorks 214 G5
Som 45 D9
Bedlam Street W Sus 36 D3
Bedlar's Green Essex 105 G10
Bedlington Northumb 253 G7
Bedlington Station
Northumb 253 G7
Bedlinog M Tydf 77 E9
Bedminster Bristol 60 E5
Bedminster Down Bristol 60 F5
Bedmond Herts 85 E9
Bednall Staffs 151 F9
Bednall Head Staffs 151 F9
Bedrule Borders 262 F4
Bedstone Shrops 115 B7
Bedwas Caerph 59 B7
Bedwell Herts 104 G4
Wrex 166 F5
Bedwellty Caerph 77 E11
Bedwellty Pits Bl Gwent 77 D11
Bedwlwyn Wrex 148 B4
Bedworth Warks 135 F7
Bedworth Heath Warks 134 F6
Bedworth Woodlands
Warks 134 F6
Bed-y-coedwr Gwyn 146 D4
Beeby Leics 136 B3
Beech Hants 49 F7
Staffs 151 B7
Beechcliff Staffs 151 B7
Beechcliffe W Yorks 205 E7
Beechen Cliff Bath 61 G9
Beech Hill Gtr Man 194 F5
W Berks 65 G7
Beechingstoke Wilts 46 B5
Beech Lanes W Mid 133 F10
Beechwood Halton 183 E8
Newport 59 B10
W Mid 118 B5
W Yorks 206 F2
Beecroft C Beds 103 G10
Beedon W Berks 64 D3
Beedon Hill W Berks 64 D3
Beeford E Yorks 209 C8
Beeley Derbys 170 B3
Beelsby NE Lincs 201 G8
Beenham W Berks 64 F5
Beenham's Heath
Windsor 65 D10
Beenham Stocks
W Berks 64 F5
Beeny Corn 11 C8
Beer Devon 15 D10
Som 44 G2
Beercrocombe Som 28 C4
Beer Hackett Dorset 29 E9
Beesands Devon 8 G6
Beesby Lincs 191 E7
Beeslack Midloth 270 C4
Beeson Devon 8 G6
Beeston C Beds 104 B3
Ches W 167 D8
Norf 159 F8
Notts 153 B10
W Yorks 205 G11
Beeston Hill W Yorks 205 G11
Beeston Park Side
W Yorks 197 B9
Beeston Regis Norf 177 E11
Beeston Royds
W Yorks 205 G11
Beeston St Lawrence
Norf 160 E6
Beeswing Dumfries 237 C10
Beetham Cumb 211 D9
Som 28 E3
Beetley Norf 159 F9
Beffcote Staffs 150 F6
Began Cardiff 59 C8
Begbroke Oxon 83 C7
Begdale Cambs 139 B9
Begelly Pembs 73 D10
Beggar Hill Essex 87 E10
Beggarington Hill
W Yorks 197 C9
Beggars Ash Hereford 98 D4
Beggars Bush W Sus 35 F11
Beggar's Bush Powys 114 E5
Beggars Pound V Glam 58 F4
Beggearn Huish Som 42 F4
Beguildy Powys 114 B3
Beighton Norf 143 B7
S Yorks 186 E6
Beighton Hill Derbys 170 E3
Beili-glas Mon 78 C4
Beitearsaig W Isles 305 G1
Beith N Ayrs 266 E6
Bekesbourne Kent 55 B7
Bekesbourne Hill Kent 55 B7
Belah Cumb 239 F9
Belan Powys 130 C4
Belaugh Norf 160 F5
Belbins Hants 32 C5
Belbroughton Worcs 117 B8
Belchalwell Dorset 30 F3
Belchalwell Street Dorset 30 F3
Belchamp Otten Essex 106 C6
Belchamp St Paul Essex 106 C5
Belchamp Walter Essex 106 C6
Belcher's Bar Leics 135 B8
Belchford Lincs 190 F3
Beleybridge Fife 287 F9
Belfield Gtr Man 196 E2
Belford Northumb 264 C4
Belgrano Conwy 181 F7
Belgrave Ches W 166 C5
Leicester 135 B11
Staffs 134 C4
Belgravia London 67 D9
Belhaven E Loth 282 F3
Belhelvie Aberds 293 B11
Belhinnie Aberds 302 G4
Bellabeg Aberds 292 B5
Bellamore S Ayrs 244 F6
Bellanoch Argyll 275 D8
Bellanrigg Borders 260 B6
Bellasize E Yorks 199 B10
Bellaty Angus 286 B6
Bell Bar Herts 86 D3
Bell Busk N Yorks 204 B4
Bell Common Essex 86 E6
Belleau Lincs 190 F6
Belle Eau Park Notts 171 D11
Belle Green S Yorks 197 F11
Bellehiglash Moray 301 F11
Belle Isle W Yorks 197 B10
Bell End Worcs 117 B8
Bellerby N Yorks 224 G2
Belle Vale Mers 182 D6
W Mid 133 G9
Bellever Devon 13 F9
Bellevue Worcs 117 C9
Belle Vue Cumb 229 E8
Cumb 239 F9
Gtr Man 184 B5
Shrops 149 G9
S Yorks 198 G5
Belle Vue *continued*
W Yorks 197 D10
Bellfield E Ayrs 257 B10
Bellfields Sur 50 C3
Bell Green London 67 E11
W Mid 135 G7
Bell Heath Worcs 117 B9
Bell Hill Hants 34 C2
Belliehill Angus 293 G7
Bellingdon Bucks 84 D6
Bellingham London 67 E11
Northumb 251 G8
Bellmount Norf 157 E10
Belloch Argyll 255 D7
Bellochantuy Argyll 255 D7
Bell o' th' Hill Ches W 167 F8
Bellsbank E Ayrs 245 C11
Bell's Close T&W 242 E5
Bell's Corner Suff 107 D9
Bellshill N Lanark 268 C4
Northumb 264 C4
Bellside N Lanark 268 D6
Bellsmyre W Dunb 277 F8
Bellspool Borders 260 B5
Bellsquarry W Loth 269 C10
Bells Yew Green E Sus 52 F6
Belluton Bath 60 G6
Bellyeoman Fife 280 D2
Belmaduthy Highld 300 D6
Belmesthorpe Rutland 155 G10
Belmont Blackburn 195 D7
Durham 234 C2
E Sus 38 E4
London 67 G9
London 85 G11
Oxon 63 B11
S Ayrs 257 E8
Shetland 312 C7
Belnacraig Aberds 292 B5
Belnagarrow Moray 302 E3
Belnie Lincs 156 C5
Belowda Corn 5 C9
Belper Derbys 170 F4
Belper Lane End Derbys 170 F4
Belph Derbys 187 F8
Belsay Northumb 242 B4
Belses Borders 262 D3
Belsford Devon 8 D5
Belsize Herts 85 E8
Belstead Suff 108 C2
Belston S Ayrs 257 E9
Belstone Devon 13 C8
Belstone Corner Devon 13 B8
Belthorn Blackburn 195 C8
Beltinge Kent 71 F7
Beltingham Northumb 241 E7
Beltoft N Lincs 199 F10
Belton Leics 153 E8
Lincs 155 B8
N Lincs 199 F9
Norf 143 C9
Belton in Rutland
Rutland 136 C6
Beltring Kent 53 D7
Belts of Collonach
Aberds 293 D8
Belvedere London 68 D3
W Loth 269 B9
Belvoir Leics 154 C6
Bembridge IoW 21 D8
Bemersyde Borders 262 C3
Bemerton Wilts 46 G6
Bemerton Heath Wilts 46 G6
Bempton E Yorks 218 E3
Benacre Suff 143 G10
Ben Alder Lodge Highld 291 F7
Ben Armine Lodge
Highld 309 H7
Benbuie Dumfries 246 D6
Ben Casgro W Isles 304 F6
Benchill Gtr Man 184 D4
Bencombe Glos 80 F3
Benderloch Argyll 289 F11
Bendish Herts 104 G3
Bendronaig Lodge
Highld 299 F10
Benenden Kent 53 G10
Benfield Dumfries 236 C5
Benfieldside Durham 242 G3
Bengal Pembs 91 E9
Bengate Norf 160 D6
Bengeo Herts 86 C4
Bengeworth Worcs 99 C10
Bengrove Glos 99 E9
Benhall Glos 99 G8
Benhall Green Suff 127 E7
Benhall Street Suff 127 E7
Benhilton London 67 F9
Benholm Aberds 293 G10
Beningbrough N Yorks 206 B6
Benington Herts 104 G5
Lincs 174 F5
Benington Sea End
Lincs 174 F6
Benllech Anglesey 179 E8
Benmore Argyll 276 E2
Stirling 285 E8
Benmore Lodge Argyll 289 F7
Highld 309 H3
Bennacott Corn 11 C11
Bennah Devon 14 E2
Bennan N Ayrs 255 E10
Bennane Lea S Ayrs 244 F3
Bennetland E Yorks 199 B10
Bennetsfield Highld 300 D6
Bennett End Bucks 84 F3
Bennetts End Herts 85 D9
Benniworth Lincs 190 E2
Benover Kent 53 D8
Ben Rhydding W Yorks 205 D8
Bensham T&W 242 E6
Benslie N Ayrs 266 G6
Benson Oxon 83 G10
Benston Shetland 313 H6
Bent Aberds 293 F8
Benter Som 44 D6
Bentfield Bury Essex 105 F9
Bentfield Green Essex 105 F10
Bentgate Gtr Man 196 E2
Bent Gate Lancs 195 C9
Benthall Northumb 264 D6
Shrops 132 C3
Bentham Glos 80 B6
Benthoul Aberdeen 293 C10
Bentilee Stoke 168 F6
Bentlass Pembs 73 E7
Bentlawnt Shrops 130 C6
Bentley Essex 87 F9
E Yorks 208 F6
Hants 49 E9
Suff 108 D2
S Yorks 198 F5
Warks 134 D5
W Mid 133 D9
Worcs 117 D9
Bentley Common Warks 134 D5
Bentley Heath Herts 86 F2
W Mid 118 B3
Bentley Rise S Yorks 198 G5
Benton Devon 41 F7
Benton Green W Mid 118 B5
Bentpath Dumfries 249 E8
Bents W Loth 269 C9
Bents Head W Yorks 205 F7
Bentwichen Devon 41 G8
Bentworth Hants 49 E7
Benvie Dundee 287 D7
Benville Dorset 29 G8
Benwell T&W 242 E6
Benwick Cambs 138 E6
Beobridge Shrops 132 E5
Beoley Worcs 117 D11
Beoraidbeg Highld 295 F8
Bepton W Sus 34 D5
Berden Essex 105 F9
Bere Alston Devon 7 B8
Berechurch Essex 107 G9
Bere Ferrers Devon 7 C9
Berefold Aberds 303 F9
Berepper Corn 2 E5
Bere Regis Dorset 18 C2
Bergh Apton Norf 142 C6
Berghers Hill Bucks 66 B2
Berhill Som 44 F2
Berinsfield Oxon 83 F9
Berkeley Glos 79 F11
Berkeley Heath Glos 79 F11
Berkeley Road Glos 80 E2
Berkeley Towers
Ches E 167 E11
Berkhamsted Herts 85 D7
Berkley Som 45 D10
Berkley Down Som 45 D9
Berkley Marsh Som 45 D10
Berkswell W Mid 118 B4
Bermondsey London 67 D10
Bermuda Warks 135 F7
Bernards Heath Herts 85 D11
Bernera Highld 295 C10
Berner's Cross Devon 25 F10
Berner's Hill E Sus 53 G8
Berners Roding Essex 87 D10
Bernice Argyll 276 C2
Bernisdale Highld 298 D4
Berrick Salome Oxon 83 G10
Berriedale Highld 311 G5
Berrier Cumb 230 F3
Berriew *=Aberriw*
Powys 130 C3
Berrington Northumb 273 G10
Shrops 131 B10
Worcs 115 D11
Berrington Green
Worcs 115 D11
Berriowbridge Corn 11 F11
Berrow Som 43 C10
Worcs 98 E5
Berrow Green Worcs 116 F4
Berry Swansea 56 D3
Berry Brow W Yorks 196 E6
Berry Cross Devon 25 E7
Berry Down Cross Devon 40 E5
Berryfield Wilts 61 G11
Berryfields Oxon 84 B3
Berrygate Hill E Yorks 201 C8
Berry Hill Glos 79 C9
Pembs 91 C11
Stoke 168 F6
Worcs 117 E7
Berryhillock Moray 302 C5
Berrylands London 67 F7
Berry Moor S Yorks 197 G9
Berrynarbor Devon 40 D5
Berry Pomeroy Devon 8 C6
Berrysbridge Devon 26 G6
Berry's Green London 52 B2
Bersham Wrex 166 F4
Berstane Orkney 314 E4
Berth-ddu Flint 166 B2
Berthengam Flint 181 F10
Berwick E Sus 23 D8
Kent 54 F6
S Glos 60 C5
Berwick Bassett Wilts 62 E5
Berwick Hill Northumb 242 B5
Berwick Hills Mbro 225 B10
Berwick St James Wilts 46 F5
Berwick St John Wilts 30 C6
Berwick St Leonard
Wilts 46 G2
Berwick-upon-Tweed
Northumb 273 E9
Berwick Wharf Shrops 149 G10
Berwyn Denb 165 G11
Bescaby Leics 154 D6
Bescar Lancs 193 E11
Bescot W Mid 133 D10
Besford Shrops 149 E11
Worcs 99 C8
Bessacarr S Yorks 198 G6
Bessels Green Kent 52 B4
Bessels Leigh Oxon 83 E7
Besses o' th' Barn
Gtr Man 195 F10
Bessingby E Yorks 218 F3
Bessingham Norf 160 B3
Best Beech Hill E Sus 52 G6
Besthorpe Norf 141 D11
Notts 172 C4
Bestwood Nottingham 171 G9
Bestwood Village Notts 171 F9
Beswick E Yorks 208 D6
Gtr Man 184 B5
Betchcott Shrops 131 D8
Betchton Heath Ches E 168 C3
Betchworth Sur 51 D8
Bethania Ceredig 111 E11
Gwyn 163 E10
Gwyn 164 F2
Bethany Corn 6 D6
Bethel Anglesey 178 G5
Corn 5 E10
Gwyn 147 B9
Gwyn 163 B8
Bethelnie Aberds 303 F7
Bethersden Kent 54 E2
Bethesda Gwyn 163 B10
Pembs 73 B9
Bethlehem Carms 94 F3
Bethnal Green London 67 C10
Betley Staffs 168 F3
Betley Common Staffs 168 F2
Betsham Kent 68 E6
Betteshanger Kent 55 C10
Bettiscombe Dorset 16 B3
Bettisfield Wrex 149 B9
Betton Shrops 130 C6
Shrops 150 B3
Betton Strange Shrops 131 B10
Bettws Bridgend 58 B2
Mon 78 B3
Newport 78 G3
Bettws Cedewain Powys 130 D2
Bettws Gwerfil Goch
Denb 165 F8
Bettws Ifan Ceredig 92 B6
Bettws Newydd Mon 78 D5
Bettws-y-crwyn Shrops 130 G4
Bettyhill Highld 308 C7
Betws Bridgend 57 D11
Carms 75 C10
Betws Bledrws Ceredig 111 G11
Betws-Garmon Gwyn 163 D8
Betws Ifan Ceredig 92 B6
Betws-y-Coed Conwy 164 D4
Betws-yn-Rhos Conwy 180 G6
Beulah Ceredig 92 B5
Powys 113 G8
Bevendean Brighton 36 F4
Bevercotes Notts 187 G11
Bevere Worcs 116 F6
Beverley E Yorks 208 F6
Beverston Glos 80 G5
Bevington Glos 79 F11
Bewaldeth Cumb 229 E10
Bewbush W Sus 51 F8
Bewcastle Cumb 240 C3
Bewdley Worcs 116 B5
Bewerley N Yorks 214 G3
Bewholme E Yorks 209 C9
Bewley Common Wilts 62 F2
Bewlie Borders 262 D3
Bewlie Mains Borders 262 D3
Bewsey Warr 183 D9
Bexfield Norf 159 D10
Bexhill E Sus 38 F2
Bexley London 68 E3
Bexleyheath London 68 D3
Bexleyhill W Sus 34 B6
Bexon Kent 53 B11
Bexwell Norf 140 C2
Beyton Suff 125 E8
Beyton Green Suff 125 E8
Bhalasaigh W Isles 304 E3
Bhaltos W Isles 304 E2
Bhatarsaigh W Isles 297 M2
Bhlàraidh Highld 290 B5
Bibstone S Glos 79 G11
Bibury Glos 81 D10
Bicester Oxon 101 G11
Bickenhall Som 28 D3
Bickenhill W Mid 134 G3
Bicker Lincs 156 B4
Bicker Bar Lincs 156 B4
Bicker Gauntlet Lincs 156 B4
Bickershaw Gtr Man 194 G6
Bickerstaffe Lancs 194 G2
Bickerton Ches E 167 E8
Devon 9 G11
N Yorks 206 C5
Bickford Staffs 151 G7
Bickham Som 42 E3
Bickingcott Devon 26 B3
Bickington Devon 13 G11
Devon 40 G4
Bickleigh Devon 7 C10
Devon 26 F6
Bickleton Devon 40 G4
Bickley Ches W 167 F8
London 68 F2
Worcs 116 C2
Bickley Moss Ches W 167 F8
Bickley Town Ches W 167 F8
Bickleywood Ches W 167 F8
Bickmarsh Warks 100 B2
Bicknacre Essex 88 E3
Bicknoller Som 42 F6
Bicknor Kent 53 B11
Bickton Hants 31 E11
Bicton Hereford 115 E9
Pembs 72 D4
Shrops 130 G5
Shrops 149 F8
Bicton Heath Shrops 149 G9
Bidborough Kent 52 E5
Bidden Hants 49 D8
Biddenden Kent 53 F11
Biddenden Green Kent 53 E11
Biddenham Bedford 103 B10
Biddestone Wilts 61 E11
Biddick T&W 243 F8
Biddick Hall T&W 243 E9
Biddisham Som 43 C11
Biddlesden Bucks 102 C2
Biddlestone Northumb 251 B11
Biddulph Staffs 168 D5
Biddulph Moor Staffs 168 D6
Bideford Devon 25 B7
Bidford-on-Avon Warks 118 G2
Bidlake Devon 12 D5
Bidston Mers 182 C3
Bidston Hill Mers 182 D3
Bidwell C Beds 103 G10
Bielby E Yorks 207 E11
Bieldside Aberdeen 293 C10
Bierley IoW 20 F6
W Yorks 205 G9
Bierton Bucks 84 B4
Bigbury Devon 8 F3
Bigbury-on-Sea Devon 8 G3
Bigby Lincs 200 F5
Bigfrith Windsor 65 C11
Biggar Cumb 210 F3
S Lanark 260 B2
Biggar Road N Lanark 268 C5
Biggin Derbys 169 D11
Derbys 170 F3
N Yorks 206 F6
Thurrock 69 D7
Biggings Shetland 313 G3
Biggin Hill London 52 B2
Biggleswade C Beds 104 C3
Bighouse Highld 310 C2
Bighton Hants 48 G6
Biglands Cumb 239 G7
Big Mancot Flint 166 B4
Bignall End Staffs 168 E4
Bignor W Sus 35 E7
Bigods Essex 106 G2
Bigram Stirling 285 G10
Bigrigg Cumb 219 C10
Big Sand Highld 299 B7
Bigswell Orkney 314 E3
Bigton Shetland 313 L5
Bilberry Corn 5 C10
Bilborough Nottingham 171 G8
Bilbrook Som 42 E4
Staffs 133 C7
Bilbrough N Yorks 206 D6
Bilbster Highld 310 D6
Bilby Notts 187 E10
Bildershaw Durham 233 G10
Bildeston Suff 107 B9
Billacombe Plym 7 E10
Billacott Corn 11 C11
Billericay Essex 87 G11
Billesdon Leics 136 C4
Billesley Warks 118 F2
W Mid 133 G11
Billesley Common
W Mid 133 G11
Billingborough Lincs 156 C2
Billinge Mers 194 G4
Billingford Norf 126 B3
Norf 159 E10
Billingham Stockton 234 G5
Billinghay Lincs 173 E11
Billingley S Yorks 198 G2
Billingshurst W Sus 35 B9
Billingsley Shrops 132 F4
Billington C Beds 103 G8
Lancs 203 F10
Staffs 151 E7
Billockby Norf 161 G8
Bill Quay T&W 243 E7
Billy Mill T&W 243 D8
Billy Row Durham 233 D9
Bilmarsh Shrops 149 D9
Bilsborrow Lancs 202 F6
Bilsby Lincs 191 F7
Bilsby Field Lincs 191 F7
Bilsdon Devon 14 C2
Bilsham W Sus 35 G7
Bilsington Kent 54 G4
Bilson Green Glos 79 C11
Bilsthorpe Notts 171 C10
Bilsthorpe Moor Notts 171 D11
Bilston Midloth 270 C5
W Mid 133 D9
Bilstone Leics 135 B7
Bilting Kent 54 D5
Bilton E Yorks 209 G9
Northumb 264 G6
N Yorks 206 B2
Warks 119 C9
Bilton Haggs N Yorks 206 D5
Bilton in Ainsty N Yorks 206 D5
Bimbister Orkney 314 E3
Binbrook Lincs 190 C2
Binchester Blocks
Durham 233 E10
Bincombe Dorset 17 E9
Som 43 F7
Bindal Highld 311 L3
Bindon Som 27 C10
Binegar Som 44 D6
Bines Green W Sus 35 D11
Binfield Brack 65 E10
Binfield Heath Oxon 65 D8
Bingfield Northumb 241 C11
Bingham Edin 280 G6
Notts 154 B4
Bingley W Yorks 205 F8
Bings Heath Shrops 149 F10
Binham Norf 159 B9
Binley Hants 48 C2
W Mid 119 B7
Binley Woods Warks 119 B7
Binnegar Dorset 18 D3
Binniehill Falk 279 G7
Binscombe Sur 50 D3
Binsey Oxon 83 D7
Binsoe N Yorks 214 D4
Binstead Hants 49 E9
IoW 21 C7
Binsted Hants 49 E9
W Sus 35 F7
Binton Warks 118 G2
Bintree Norf 159 E10
Binweston Shrops 130 C6
Birch Essex 88 B6
Gtr Man 195 F11
Birch Acre Worcs 117 C11
Birchall Hereford 98 D3
Staffs 169 E7
Bircham Newton Norf 158 C5
Bircham Tofts Norf 158 C5
Birchan Coppice Worcs 116 C6
Birchanger Essex 105 G10
Birch Berrow Worcs 116 E4
Birchburn N Ayrs 255 E10
Birch Cross Staffs 152 C2
Birchden E Sus 52 F4
Birchencliffe W Yorks 196 D6
Birchend Hereford 98 C3
Birchendale Staffs 151 B11
Bircher Hereford 115 D9
Birches Green W Mid 134 E2
Birches Head Stoke 168 F5
Birchett's Green E Sus 53 G7
Birchfield Highld 301 G9
W Mid 133 E11
Birch Green Essex 88 B6
Herts 86 C3
Lancs 194 F3
Worcs 99 B7
Birchgrove Cardiff 59 D7
E Sus 36 B6
Swansea 57 B8
Birchhall Corner Essex 107 E10
Birch Heath Ches W 167 C8
Birch Hill Brack 65 F11
Ches W 183 G8
Birchill Devon 28 G4
Birchills W Mid 133 D10
Birchington Kent 71 F9
Birchley Heath Warks 134 E5
Birchmoor Warks 134 C5
Birchmoor Green
C Beds 103 E8
Bircholt Forstal Kent 54 E5
Birchover Derbys 170 C2
Birch Vale Derbys 185 D8
Birchwood Herts 86 D2
Lincs 172 B6
Som 28 E2
Warr 183 C10
Birchy Hill Hants 19 B11
Bircotes Notts 187 C10
Birdbrook Essex 106 C4
Birdbush Wilts 30 C6
Birdfield Argyll 275 D10
Birdforth N Yorks 215 D9
Birdham W Sus 22 D4
Birdholme Derbys 170 B5
Birdingbury Warks 119 D8
Birdlip Glos 80 C6
Birdsall N Yorks 216 F6
Birds Edge W Yorks 197 F8
Birds End Suff 124 E5
Birdsgreen Shrops 132 F5
Birds Green Essex 87 D9
Birdsmoorgate Dorset 28 G5
Birdston E Dunb 278 F3
Bird Street Suff 125 G10
Birdwell S Yorks 197 G10
Birdwood Glos 80 B2
Birgham Borders 263 B7
Birichen Highld 309 K7
Birkacre Lancs 194 D5
Birkby Cumb 229 D7
N Yorks 224 E6
W Yorks 196 D6
Birkdale Mers 193 D10
Birkenbog Aberds 302 C5
Birkenhead Mers 182 D4
Birkenhills Aberds 303 E7
Birkenshaw N Lanark 268 C3
S Lanark 268 F5
W Yorks 197 B8
Birkenshaw Bottoms
W Yorks 197 B8
Birkenside Borders 271 G11
Birkett Mire Cumb 230 G2
Birkhall Aberds 292 D5
Birkhill Angus 287 D7
Borders 260 F6
Borders 271 G11
Birkholme Lincs 155 E9
Birkhouse W Yorks 197 C7
Birkin N Yorks 198 B4
Birks Cumb 222 G3
W Yorks 197 B9
Birkshaw Northumb 241 D7
Birley Hereford 115 G9
Birley Carr S Yorks 186 C4
Birley Edge S Yorks 186 C4
Birleyhay Derbys 186 E5
Birling Kent 69 G7
Northumb 252 B6
Birling Gap E Sus 23 F9
Birlingham Worcs 99 C8
Birmingham W Mid 133 F11
Birnam Perth 286 C4
Birniehill S Lanark 268 E2
Birse Aberds 293 D7
Birsemore Aberds 293 D7
Birstall Leics 135 B11
W Yorks 197 B8
Birstall Smithies
W Yorks 197 B8
Birstwith N Yorks 205 B10
Birthorpe Lincs 156 C2
Birtle Gtr Man 195 E10
Birtley Hereford 115 D7
Northumb 241 B9
Shrops 131 E9
T&W 243 F7
Birtley Green Sur 50 E4
Birtsmorton Worcs 98 D6
Birts Street Worcs 98 D5
Bisbrooke Rutland 137 D7
Biscathorpe Lincs 190 D2
Biscombe Som 27 E11
Biscot Luton 103 G11
Biscovey Corn 5 E11
Bisham Windsor 65 C10
Bishampton Worcs 117 G9
Bish Mill Devon 26 B2
Bishon Common Hereford 97 C8
Bishop Auckland
Durham 233 F10
Bishopbridge Lincs 189 C8
Bishopbriggs E Dunb 278 G2
Bishop Burton E Yorks 208 F5
Bishopdown Wilts 47 G7
Bishop Kinkell Highld 300 D5
Bishop Middleham
Durham 234 E2
Bishopmill Moray 302 C2
Bishop Monkton
N Yorks 214 F6
Bishop Norton Lincs 189 C7
Bishopsbourne Kent 55 C7
Bishops Cannings Wilts 62 G4
Bishop's Castle Shrops 130 F6
Bishop's Caundle Dorset 29 E11
Bishop's Cleeve Glos 99 F9
Bishop's Down Dorset 29 E11
Bishops Frome Hereford 98 B3
Bishopsgarth Stockton 234 G4
Bishopsgate Sur 66 E3
Bishops Green Essex 87 B5
Bishop's Green W Berks 64 G4
Bishop's Hull Som 28 C2
Bishop's Itchington
Warks 119 F7
Bishops Lydeard Som 27 B11
Bishop's Norton Glos 98 G6
Bishops Nympton Devon 26 C3
Bishop's Offley Staffs 150 D5
Bishop's Quay Corn 2 D6
Bishop's Stortford
Herts 105 G9
Bishop's Sutton Hants 48 G6
Bishop's Tachbrook
Warks 118 E6
Bishops Tawton Devon 40 G5
Bishopsteignton Devon 14 G4
Bishopstoke Hants 33 D7
Bishopston Bristol 60 D5
Swansea 56 D5
Bishopstone Bucks 84 C4
E Sus 23 E7
Hereford 97 C8
Kent 71 F8
Swindon 63 C8
Wilts 31 B9
Bishopstrow Wilts 45 E11
Bishop Sutton Bath 44 B5
Bishop's Waltham Hants 33 D9
Bishopswood Som 28 E3
Bishop's Wood Staffs 132 B6
Bishopsworth Bristol 60 F5
Bishop Thornton
N Yorks 214 G5
Bishopthorpe York 207 D7
Bishopton Darl 234 G3
Dumfries 236 E6
N Yorks 214 E6
Renfs 277 G8
Warks 118 F3
Bishopwearmouth T&W 243 F9
Bishop Wilton E Yorks 207 B11
Bishpool Newport 59 B10
Bishton Newport 59 B11
Staffs 151 E10
Bisley Glos 80 D6
Sur 50 B3
Bisley Camp Sur 50 B2
Bispham Blackpool 202 E2
Bispham Green Lancs 194 E3
Bissoe Corn 4 G5
Bissom Corn 3 C7
Bisterne Hants 31 G10
Bisterne Close Hants 32 G2
Bitchet Green Kent 52 C5
Bitchfield Lincs 155 D9
Bittadon Devon 40 E4
Bittaford Devon 8 D3
Bittering Norf 159 F8
Bitterley Shrops 115 B11
Bitterne Soton 33 E7
Bitterne Park Soton 32 E6
Bitterscote Staffs 134 C4
Bitteswell Leics 135 F10
Bittles Green Dorset 30 C5
Bitton S Glos 61 F7
Bix Oxon 65 B8
Bixter Shetland 313 H5
Blaby Leics 135 D11
Blackacre Dumfries 248 E2
Blackadder West
Borders 272 E6
Blackawton Devon 8 E6
Black Bank Cambs 139 F10
Warks 135 F7
Black Banks Darl 224 C5
Black Barn Lincs 157 D8
Blackbeck Cumb 219 D10
Blackbird Leys Oxon 83 E9
Blackborough Devon 27 F9
Norf 158 G3
Blackborough End Norf 158 G3
Black Bourton Oxon 82 E3
Blackboys E Sus 37 C8
Blackbraes Aberds 293 B10
Blackbrook Derbys 170 F4
Derbys 185 E9
Mers 183 B8
Staffs 150 B5
Sur 51 D7
Blackburn Aberds 293 B10
Aberds 302 F5
Blackburn 195 B7
Blackburn *continued*
S Yorks 186 C5
W Loth 269 B9
Black Callerton T&W 242 D5
Black Carr Norf 141 D11
Blackcastle Midloth 271 D8
Blackchambers Aberds 293 B9
Black Clauchrie S Ayrs 245 G7
Black Corner W Sus 51 F9
Black Corries Lodge
Highld 284 B6
Blackcraig Dumfries 246 G6
Blackcraigs Angus 293 E7
Black Crofts Argyll 289 F11
Black Cross Corn 5 C8
Black Dam Hants 48 C6
Blackden Heath Ches E 184 G3
Blackditch Oxon 82 D6
Blackdog Aberds 293 B11
Black Dog Devon 26 F4
Blackdown Dorset 28 G5
Hants 33 C8
Warks 118 D6
Blackdyke Cumb 238 G4
Blackdykes E Loth 281 E11
Blacker Hill S Yorks 197 G11
Blacketts Kent 70 F2
Blackfell T&W 243 F7
Blackfen London 68 E3
Blackfield Hants 32 G6
Blackford Cumb 239 E9
Dumfries 248 G4
Perth 286 G2
Shrops 131 G11
Som 29 B11
Som 42 D2
Som 44 D2
Blackford Bridge
Gtr Man 195 F10
Blackfordby Leics 152 F6
Blackfords Staffs 151 G9
Blackgang IoW 20 F5
Blackgate Angus 287 B8
Blackhall Aberds 293 D8
Edin 280 G4
Renfs 267 C9
Blackhall Colliery
Durham 234 D5
Blackhall Mill T&W 242 F4
Blackhall Rocks Durham 234 D5
Blackham E Sus 52 F3
Blackhaugh Borders 261 B10
Blackheath Essex 107 G10
London 67 D11
Suff 127 C8
Sur 50 D4
W Mid 133 F9
Blackheath Park London 68 D2
Black Heddon Northumb 242 B3
Blackhill Aberds 303 D10
Aberds 303 E10
Aberds 303 F10
Durham 242 G3
Hants 32 D4
Highld 298 D3
Black Hill W Yorks 204 E6
Blackhillock Moray 302 E4
Blackhills Highld 301 D9
Moray 302 D2
Swansea 56 C5
Blackhorse Devon 14 C5
S Glos 61 D7
Black Horse Drove
Cambs 139 E11
Blackjack Lincs 156 B5
Black Lake W Mid 133 E9
Blackland Wilts 62 F4
Blacklands E Sus 38 E4
Hereford 98 C2
Black Lane Gtr Man 195 F9
Blacklaw Aberds 302 D6
Blackleach Lancs 202 G5
Blackley Gtr Man 195 G11
W Yorks 196 D6
Blacklunans Perth 292 G3
Black Marsh Shrops 130 D6
Blackmarstone Hereford 97 D10
Blackmill Bridgend 58 B2
Blackminster Worcs 99 C11
Blackmoor Bath 60 G5
Gtr Man 195 G7
Hants 49 G9
N Som 60 G3
Som 27 D11
Black Moor Lancs 194 E3
W Yorks 205 F11
Blackmoorfoot W Yorks 196 E5
Blackmoor Gate Devon 41 E7
Blackmore Essex 87 E10
Shrops 130 B6
Blackmore End Essex 106 E4
Herts 85 B11
Worcs 98 C6
Black Mount Argyll 284 C6
Blackness Aberds 293 D8
E Sus 52 G4
Falk 279 F11
Blacknest Hants 49 E9
Windsor 66 F3
Blacknoll Dorset 18 D2
Black Notley Essex 106 G5
Blacko Lancs 204 E3
Blackoe Shrops 149 B10
Blackpark Dumfries 236 C5
Black Park Wrex 166 G4
Black Pill Swansea 56 C6
Blackpole Worcs 117 F7
Black Pole Lancs 202 F5
Blackpool Blackpool 202 F2
Devon 7 E11
Devon 9 F7
Devon 14 G2
Pembs 73 C9
Blackpool Gate Cumb 240 B2
Blackridge W Loth 269 B7
Blackrock Argyll 274 G4
Bath 60 F6
Mon 78 C2
Black Rock Brighton 36 G4
Corn 2 C5
Blackrod Gtr Man 194 E6
Blackshaw Dumfries 238 D2
Blackshaw Head
W Yorks 196 B3
Blackshaw Moor Staffs 169 D8
Blacksmith's Corner
Suff 108 C2
Blacksmith's Green Suff 126 D2
Blacksnape Blackburn 195 C8
Blackstone Worcs 116 C5
W Sus 36 D2
Black Street Suff 143 F10
Black Tar Pembs 73 D7
Blackthorn Oxon 83 B10
Blackthorpe Suff 125 E8
Blacktoft E Yorks 199 C10
Blacktop Aberdeen 293 C10
Black Torrington Devon 25 F7
Blacktown Newport 59 C9
Black Vein Caerph 78 G2
Blackwall Derbys 170 F3
Blackwall *continued*
London 67 C11
Blackwall Tunnel
London 67 C11
Blackwater BCP 19 B8
Corn 4 F4
Hants 49 B11
IoW 20 D6
Norf 159 E11
Som 28 D3
Blackwaterfoot N Ayrs 255 E9
Blackwater Lodge
Moray 302 G3
Blackweir Cardiff 59 D7
Blackwell Cumb 239 G10
Darl 224 C5
Derbys 170 D6
Derbys 185 G10
Devon 27 B8
Warks 100 C4
Worcs 117 C9
W Sus 51 F11
Blackwood Caerph 77 F11
S Lanark 268 G5
Warr 183 C10
Blackwood Hill Staffs 168 D6
Blacon Ches W 166 B5
Bladbean Kent 55 D7
Blades N Yorks 223 F9
Bladnoch Dumfries 236 D6
Bladon Oxon 82 C6
Blaenannerch Ceredig 92 B4
Blaenau Carms 75 C10
Flint 166 D2
Blaenau Dolwyddelan
Conwy 164 E2
Blaenau Ffestiniog
Gwyn 164 F2
Blaenau-Gwent Bl Gwent 78 E2
Blaenavon Torf 78 D3
Blaenbedw Fawr
Ceredig 111 G7
Blaencaerau Bridgend 57 C11
Blaencelyn Ceredig 111 G7
Blaen-Cil-Llech Ceredig 92 C6
Blaen Clydach Rhondda 77 G7
Blaencwm Rhondda 76 F6
Blaendulais *=Seven Sisters*
Neath 76 D4
Blaendyryn Powys 95 D8
Blaenffos Pembs 92 D3
Blaengarw Bridgend 76 G6
Blaengwrach Neath 76 D5
Blaengwynfi Neath 57 B11
Blaen-gwynfi Neath 57 B11
Blaenllechau Rhondda 77 F8
Blaen-pant Ceredig 92 C5
Blaenpennal Ceredig 112 E2
Blaenplwyf Ceredig 111 B11
Blaenporth Ceredig 92 B5
Blaenrhondda Rhondda 76 E6
Blaenwaun Carms 92 F4
Blaen-waun Carms 92 F4
Ceredig 111 G7
Blaen-y-coed Carms 92 F6
Blaenycwm Ceredig 112 B6
Blaen-y-cwm Bl Gwent 77 C10
Denb 147 C10
Gwyn 146 E4
Powys 147 E11
Blagdon N Som 44 B4
Torbay 9 C7
Blagdon Hill Som 28 D2
Blagill Cumb 231 B10
Blaguegate Lancs 194 F3
Blaich Highld 290 F2
Blain Highld 289 C8
Blaina Bl Gwent 78 D2
Blainacraig Ho Aberds 293 D7
Blair Fife 280 C6
Blair Atholl Perth 291 G10
Blairbeg N Ayrs 256 C2
Blairburn Fife 279 D9
Blairdaff Aberds 293 B8
Blair Drummond Stirling 278 B4
Blairdryne Aberds 293 D9
Blairglas Argyll 276 D6
Blairgorm Highld 301 G10
Blairgowrie Perth 286 C5
Blairhall Fife 279 D10
Blairhill N Lanark 268 B4
Blairingone Perth 279 B9
Blairland N Ayrs 266 F6
Blairlinn N Lanark 278 G5
Blairlogie Stirling 278 B6
Blairlomond Argyll 276 B3
Blairmore Argyll 276 E3
Highld 306 D6
Blairnamarrow Moray 292 B4
Blairquhosh Stirling 277 E10
Blair's Ferry Argyll 275 G10
Blairskaith E Dunb 277 F11
Blaisdon Glos 80 B2
Blaise Hamlet Bristol 60 D5
Blakebrook Worcs 116 B6
Blakedown Worcs 117 B7
Blake End Essex 106 G4
Blakelands M Keynes 103 C7
Blakelaw Borders 263 C7
T&W 242 D6
Blakeley Staffs 133 E7
Blakeley Lane Staffs 169 F7
Blakelow Ches E 167 E11
Blakemere Hereford 97 C7
Blakenall Heath
W Mid 133 C10
Blakeney Glos 79 D11
Norf 177 E8
Blakenhall Ches E 168 F2
W Mid 133 D8
Blakeshall Worcs 132 G6
Blakesley W Nhants 120 G2
Blanchland Northumb 241 G11
Blandford Camp Dorset 30 F6
Blandford Forum Dorset 30 F5
Blandford St Mary Dorset 30 F5
Bland Hill N Yorks 205 C10
Blandy Highld 308 D6
Blanefield Stirling 277 F11
Blanerne Borders 272 D6
Blank Bank Staffs 168 F4
Blankney Lincs 173 C9
Blantyre S Lanark 268 D3
Blar a'Chaorainn Highld 290 G3
Blaran Argyll 275 B9
Blarghour Argyll 275 B10
Blarmachfoldach Highld 290 G2
Blarnalearoch Highld 307 K6
Blasford Hill Essex 88 C2
Blashford Hants 31 F11
Blaston Leics 136 D6
Blatchbridge Som 45 D9
Blatherwycke N Nhants 137 D9
Blawith Cumb 210 B5
Blaxhall Suff 127 F7
Blaxton S Yorks 199 G7
Blaydon T&W 242 E5
Blaydon Burn T&W 242 E5
Blaydon Haughs T&W 242 E5
Bleach Green Cumb 219 B9
Suff 126 B4

Bleadney Som 44 D3
Bleadon N Som 43 B10
Bleak Acre Hereford 98 B2
Bleak Hall M Keynes 103 D7
Bleak Hey Nook
Gtr Man 196 F4
Bleak Hill Hants 31 E10
Blean Kent 70 G6
Bleasby Lincs 189 E10
Notts 172 F2
Bleasby Moor Lincs 189 E10
Bleasdale Lancs 203 D7
Bleatarn Cumb 222 C4
Blebocraigs Fife 287 F8
Bleddfa Powys 114 D4
Bledington Glos 100 G4
Bledlow Bucks 84 E3
Bledlow Ridge Bucks 84 F3
Bleet Wilts 45 B11
Blegbie E Loth 271 C9
Blegbury Devon 24 B2
Blencarn Cumb 231 E8
Blencogo Cumb 229 B9
Blendworth Hants 34 E2
Blenheim Oxon 83 D9
Oxon 83 E9
Blenheim Park Norf 158 C6
Blenkinsopp Hall
Northumb 240 E5
Blennerhasset Cumb 229 C9
Blervie Castle Moray 301 D10
Bletchingdon Oxon 83 B8
Bletchingley Sur 51 C10
Bletchley M Keynes 103 E7
Shrops 150 C2
Bletherston Pembs 91 G11
Bletsoe Bedford 121 F10
Blewbury Oxon 64 B4
Bliby Kent 54 F4
Blickling Norf 160 D3
Blidworth Notts 171 D9
Blidworth Bottoms
Notts 171 E9
Blidworth Dale Notts 171 E9
Blindburn Northumb 263 G8
Blindcrake Cumb 229 E8
Blindley Heath Sur 51 D11
Blindmoor Som 28 E3
Blingery Highld 310 E7
Blisland Corn 11 G8
Blissford Hants 31 E11
Bliss Gate Worcs 116 C4
Blisworth W Nhants 120 G4
Blithbury Staffs 151 E11
Blitterlees Cumb 238 G4
Blockley Glos 100 D3
Blofield Norf 142 B6
Blofield Heath Norf 160 G6
Blo' Norton Norf 125 B10
Bloodman's Corner
Suff 143 D10
Bloomfield Bath 45 B7
Bath 61 G8
Borders 262 E3
W Mid 133 E9
Bloomsbury London 67 C10
Blore Staffs 150 C4
Staffs 169 F10
Bloreheath Staffs 150 B4
Blossomfield W Mid 118 B2
Blount's Green Staffs 151 C11
Blowick Mers 193 D11
Blowinghouse Corn 4 E4
Bloxham Oxon 101 D8
Bloxholm Lincs 173 E9
Bloxwich W Mid 133 C9
Bloxworth Dorset 18 C3
Blubberhouses N Yorks 205 B9
Blue Anchor Corn 5 D8
Som 42 E4
Swansea 56 B4
Bluebell Telford 149 G11
Blue Bell Hill Kent 69 G8
Bluecairn Borders 271 G10
Blue Hill Herts 104 G5
Blue Row Essex 89 C8
Bluetown Kent 54 B2
Blue Town Kent 70 D2
Blue Vein Wilts 61 F10
Bluewater Kent 68 E5
Blughasary Highld 307 J6
Blundellsands Mers 182 B4
Blundeston Suff 143 D10
Blundies Staffs 132 F6
Blunham C Beds 122 G3
Blunsdon St Andrew
Swindon 62 B6
Bluntington Worcs 117 C7
Bluntisham Cambs 123 C7
Blunts Corn 6 C6
Blunt's Green Warks 118 D2
Blurton Stoke 168 G5
Blyborough Lincs 188 C6
Blyford Suff 127 B8
Blymhill Staffs 150 G6
Blymhill Lawns Staffs 150 G6
Blyth Borders 270 F2
Northumb 253 G8
Notts 187 D10
Blyth Bridge Borders 270 F2
Blythburgh Suff 127 B9
Blythe Borders 271 F11
Blythe Bridge Staffs 169 G7
Blythe Marsh Staffs 169 G7
Blyth End Warks 134 E4
Blythswood Renfs 267 B10
Blyton Lincs 188 C5
Boarhills Fife 287 F9
Boarhunt Hants 33 F10
Boarsgreave Lancs 195 C10
Boarshead E Sus 52 G4
Boars Hill Oxon 83 E7
Boarstall Bucks 83 C10
Boasley Cross Devon 12 C5
Boath Highld 300 B5
Boat of Garten Highld 291 B11
Bobbing Kent 69 F11
Bobbington Staffs 132 E6
Bobbingworth Essex 87 D8
Bobby Hill Suff 125 C10
Boblainy Highld 300 F4
Bocaddon Corn 6 D3
Bochastle Stirling 285 G10
Bockhanger Kent 54 E4
Bocking Essex 106 G5
Bocking Churchstreet
Essex 106 F5
Bocking's Elm Essex 89 B11
Bockleton Worcs 115 E11
Bockmer End Bucks 65 B10
Bocombe Devon 24 C5
Bodantionail Highld 299 B7
Boddam Aberds 303 E11
Shetland 313 M5
Bodden Som 44 E6
Boddington Glos 99 F7
Bodedern Anglesey 178 E4
Bodellick Corn 10 G5
Bodelva Corn 5 E11
Bodelwyddan Denb 181 F8
Bodenham Hereford 115 G10
Bodenham *continued*
Wilts 31 B11
Bodenham Bank Hereford 98 E2
Bodenham Moor
Hereford 115 G10
Bodermid Gwyn 144 D3
Bodewryd Anglesey 178 C5
Bodfari Denb 181 G9
Bodffordd Anglesey 178 F6
Bodham Norf 177 E10
Bodiam E Sus 38 B3
Bodicote Oxon 101 D9
Bodiechell Aberds 303 E7
Bodieve Corn 10 G5
Bodiggo Corn 5 D10
Bodilly Corn 2 C5
Bodinnick Corn 6 E2
Bodle Street Green
E Sus 23 C11
Bodley Devon 41 D7
Bodmin Corn 5 B11
Bodmiscombe Devon 27 F10
Bodney Norf 140 D6
Bodorgan Anglesey 162 B5
Bodsham Kent 54 D6
Boduan Gwyn 144 B6
Boduel Corn 6 C4
Bodwen Corn 5 C10
Bodymoor Heath Warks 134 D4
Bofarnel Corn 6 C2
Bogallan Highld 300 D6
Bogbrae Aberds 303 F10
Bogend Borders 272 F5
Notts 171 F7
S Ayrs 257 C9
Bogentory Aberds 293 C9
Boghall Midloth 270 B4
W Loth 269 B9
Boghead Aberds 293 D8
S Lanark 268 G5
Bogmoor Moray 302 C3
Bogniebrae Aberds 302 E5
Aberds 302 E6
Bognor Regis W Sus 22 D6
Bograxie Aberds 293 B9
Bogs Aberds 302 G5
Bogs Bank Borders 270 E3
Bogside N Lanark 268 E6
Bogthorn W Yorks 204 F6
Bogton Aberds 302 D6
Bogtown Aberds 302 C5
Bogue Dumfries 246 G4
Bohemia E Sus 38 E4
Wilts 32 D2
Bohenie Highld 290 E4
Bohetherick Corn 7 B8
Bohortha Corn 3 C9
Bohuntine Highld 290 E4
Bohuntinville Highld 290 E4
Boirseam W Isles 296 C6
Bojewyan Corn 1 C3
Bokiddick Corn 5 C11
Bolahaul Fm Carms 74 B6
Bolam Durham 233 G9
Northumb 252 G3
Bolam West Houses
Northumb 252 G3
Bolas Heath Telford 150 E3
Bolberry Devon 9 G8
Bold Heath Mers 183 D8
Boldmere W Mid 134 E2
Boldon T&W 243 E9
Boldon Colliery T&W 243 E8
Boldre Hants 20 B2
Boldron Durham 223 C10
Bole Notts 188 D3
Bolehall Staffs 134 C4
Bolehill Derbys 170 E3
Derbys 186 G6
S Yorks 186 E5
Bole Hill Derbys 186 G4
Bolenowe Corn 2 B5
Boleside Borders 261 C11
Boley Park Staffs 134 B2
Bolham Devon 27 E7
Notts 188 E2
Bolham Water Devon 27 E11
Bolholt Gtr Man 195 E9
Bolingey Corn 4 E5
Bolitho Corn 2 C5
Bollihope Durham 232 E6
Bollington Ches E 184 F6
Bollington Cross Ches E 184 F6
Bolney W Sus 36 C3
Bolnhurst Bedford 121 F11
Bolnore W Sus 36 C4
Bolshan Angus 287 B10
Bolsover Derbys 187 G7
Bolsterstone S Yorks 186 B3
Bolstone Hereford 97 E11
Boltby N Yorks 215 B9
Bolter End Bucks 84 G3
Bolton Cumb 231 G8
E Loth 281 G10
E Yorks 207 C11
Gtr Man 195 F8
Northumb 264 G4
W Yorks 205 F9
Bolton Abbey N Yorks 205 C7
Bolton Bridge N Yorks 205 C7
Bolton-by-Bowland
Lancs 203 D11
Boltonfellend Cumb 239 D11
Boltongate Cumb 229 C10
Bolton Green Lancs 194 D5
Bolton Houses Lancs 202 G4
Bolton-le-Sands Lancs 211 F9
Bolton Low Houses
Cumb 229 C10
Bolton New Houses
Cumb 229 C10
Bolton-on-Swale
N Yorks 224 F5
Bolton Percy N Yorks 206 E6
Bolton Town End Lancs 211 F9
Bolton upon Dearne
S Yorks 198 G3
Bolton Wood Lane
Cumb 229 C11
Bolton Woods W Yorks 205 F9
Boltshope Park Durham 232 B4
Bolventor Corn 11 F9
Bomarsund Northumb 253 G7
Bombie Dumfries 237 D9
Bomby Cumb 221 B10
Bomere Heath Shrops 149 F9
Bonaly Edin 270 B4
Bonar Bridge Highld 309 K6
Bonawe Argyll 284 D4
Bonby N Lincs 200 D4
Boncath Pembs 92 D4
Bonchester Bridge
Borders 262 G3
Bonchurch IoW 21 F7
Bondend Glos 80 B5
Bond End Staffs 152 F2
Bondleigh Devon 25 G11
Bondman Hays Leics 135 B9
Bonds Lancs 202 E5
Bondstones Devon 25 F9
Bonehill Devon 13 F10
Bonehill *continued*
Staffs 134 C3
Bo'ness Falk 279 E9
Bonhill W Dunb 277 F7
Boningale Shrops 132 C6
Bonjedward Borders 262 E5
Bonkle N Lanark 268 D6
Bonnavoulin Highld 289 D7
Bonning Gate Cumb 221 F9
Bonnington Borders 261 B7
Edin 270 B2
Kent 54 F5
Bonnybank Fife 287 G7
Bonnybridge Falk 278 E6
Bonnykelly Aberds 303 D8
Bonnyrigg and Lasswade
Midloth 270 B6
Bonnyton Aberds 302 F6
Angus 287 B10
Angus 287 D7
E Ayrs 257 B10
Bonsall Derbys 170 D3
Bonskeid House Perth 291 G10
Bonson Som 43 E8
Bont Mon 78 B5
Bontddu Gwyn 146 F3
Bont-Dolgadfan Powys 129 C7
Bont Fawr Carms 94 F4
Bont goch = *Elerch*
Ceredig 128 F3
Bonthorpe Lincs 191 G7
Bontnewydd Ceredig 112 D2
Gwyn 163 D7
Bont-newydd Conwy 181 G8
Bont Newydd Gwyn 146 E5
Gwyn 164 G2
Bontuchel Denb 165 D9
Bonvilston = *Tresimwn*
V Glam 58 E5
Bon-y-maen Swansea 57 B7
Boode Devon 40 F4
Booker Bucks 84 G4
Bookham Dorset 30 G2
Booleybank Shrops 149 D11
Boon Borders 271 F11
Boon Hill Staffs 168 E4
Boorley Green Hants 33 E8
Boosbeck Redcar 226 B3
Boose's Green Essex 106 E6
Boot Cumb 220 E3
Booth Staffs 151 D10
W Yorks 196 B4
Booth Bank Ches E 184 D2
Booth Bridge Lancs 204 D4
Boothby Graffoe Lincs 173 D7
Boothby Pagnell Lincs 155 C9
Boothen Stoke 168 G5
Boothferry E Yorks 199 B8
Boothgate Derbys 170 F5
Booth Green Ches E 184 E6
Boothroyd W Yorks 197 C8
Boothsdale Ches W 167 B8
Boothstown Gtr Man 195 G8
Boothtown W Yorks 196 B5
Boothville W Nhants 120 E5
Booth Wood W Yorks 196 D4
Bootle Cumb 210 B2
Mers 182 B4
Booton Norf 160 E2
Boots Green Ches W 184 G3
Boot Street Suff 108 B4
Booze N Yorks 223 E10
Boquhan Stirling 277 D10
Boquio Corn 2 C5
Boraston Shrops 116 D2
Boraston Dale Shrops 116 C2
Borden Kent 69 G11
W Sus 34 C4
Border Cumb 238 G5
Bordesley W Mid 133 F11
Bordesley Green W Mid 134 F2
Bordlands Borders 270 F3
Bordley N Yorks 213 G8
Bordon Hants 49 F10
Bordon Camp Hants 49 F9
Boreham Essex 88 D3
Wilts 45 E11
Boreham Street E Sus 23 C11
Borehamwood Herts 85 F11
Boreland Dumfries 236 C5
Dumfries 248 E5
Fife 280 C6
Stirling 285 D9
Boreland of Southwick
Dumfries 237 C11
Boreley Worcs 116 D6
Borestone Stirling 278 C5
Borgh W Isles 296 C5
W Isles 297 L2
Borghasdal W Isles 296 C6
Borghastan W Isles 304 D4
Borgie Highld 308 D6
Borgue Dumfries 237 E8
Highld 311 G5
Borley Essex 106 C6
Borley Green Essex 106 C6
Suff 125 E9
Bornais W Isles 297 J3
Bornesketaig Highld 298 B3
Borness Dumfries 237 E8
Borough Scilly 1 G3
Boroughbridge N Yorks 215 F7
Borough Green Kent 52 B6
Borough Marsh
Wokingham 65 D9
Borough Park Staffs 134 B4
Borough Post Som 28 C4
Borras Wrex 166 E4
Borras Head Wrex 166 E5
Borreraig Highld 296 F7
Borrobol Lodge Highld 311 G2
Borrodale Highld 297 G7
Borrohill Aberds 303 D9
Borrowash Derbys 153 C8
Borrowby N Yorks 215 B8
N Yorks 226 B5
Borrowdale Cumb 220 C5
Borrowfield Aberds 293 D10
Borrowston Highld 310 E7
Borrowstoun Mains
Falk 279 E9
Borstal Medway 69 F8
Borth = *Y Borth* Ceredig 128 E2
Borthwick Midloth 271 D7
Borthwickbrae Borders 261 G10
Borthwickshiels
Borders 261 F10
Borth-y-Gest Gwyn 145 B11
Borve Highld 298 E4
Borve Lodge W Isles 305 J2
Borwick Lancs 211 E10
Borwick Rails Cumb 210 D3
Bosavern Corn 1 C3
Bosbury Hereford 98 C3
Boscadjack Corn 2 C5
Boscastle Corn 11 C8
Boscean Corn 1 C3
Boscombe BCP 19 C8
Wilts 47 F8
Boscomoor Staffs 151 G8
Boscoppa Corn 5 E10
Boscreege Corn 2 C3
Bosham W Sus 22 C4
Bosham Hoe W Sus 22 C4
Bosherston Pembs 73 G7
Boskednan Corn 1 C4
Boskenna Corn 1 E4
Bosleake Corn 4 G3
Bosley Ches E 168 B6
Boslowick Corn 3 C7
Boslymon Corn 5 C11
Bosoughan Corn 5 C7
Bosporthennis Corn 1 B4
Bossall N Yorks 216 G4
Bossiney Corn 11 D7
Bossingham Kent 54 D6
Bossington Hants 47 G10
Kent 55 B8
Som 41 D11
Bostadh W Isles 304 D3
Bostock Green Ches W 167 B11
Boston Lincs 174 G4
Boston Long Hedges
Lincs 174 F5
Boston Spa W Yorks 206 D4
Boston West Lincs 174 F3
Boswednack Corn 1 B4
Boswin Corn 2 C5
Boswinger Corn 5 G9
Boswyn Corn 2 B5
Botallack Corn 1 C3
Botany Bay London 86 F3
Mon 79 E8
Botcherby Cumb 239 F10
Botcheston Leics 135 B9
Botesdale Suff 125 B10
Bothal Northumb 252 F6
Bothampstead W Berks 64 D4
Bothamsall Notts 187 G11
Bothel Cumb 229 D9
Bothenhampton Dorset 16 C5
Bothwell S Lanark 268 D4
Bothy Highld 290 F4
Botley Bucks 85 E7
Hants 33 E8
Oxon 83 D7
Botloe's Green Glos 98 F4
Botolph Claydon Bucks 102 G4
Botolphs W Sus 35 F11
Bottacks Highld 300 C4
Botternell Corn 11 G11
Bottesford Leics 154 B6
N Lincs 199 F11
Bottisham Cambs 123 E10
Bottlesford Wilts 46 B6
Bottom Boat W Yorks 197 C11
Bottomcraig Fife 287 E7
Bottom House Staffs 169 E8
Bottomley W Yorks 196 D5
Bottom of Hutton Lancs 194 B3
Bottom o' th' Moor
Gtr Man 195 E7
Bottom Pond Kent 53 B11
Bottoms Corn 1 E3
Bottreaux Mill Devon 26 B4
Bottrells Close Bucks 85 G7
Botts Green Warks 134 E4
Botusfleming Corn 7 C8
Botwnnog Gwyn 144 C5
Bough Beech Kent 52 D3
Boughrood Powys 96 D2
Boughrood Brest Powys 96 D2
Boughspring Glos 79 F9
Boughton Ches W 166 B6
Lincs 173 F10
Norf 140 C3
Notts 171 B11
W Nhants 120 D5
Boughton Aluph Kent 54 D4
Boughton Corner Kent 54 D4
Boughton Green Kent 53 C9
Boughton Heath
Ches W 166 B6
Boughton Lees Kent 54 D4
Boughton Malherbe
Kent 53 D11
Boughton Monchelsea
Kent 53 C9
Boughton Street Kent 54 B5
Bougton End C Beds 103 D9
Boulby Redcar 226 B5
Bould Oxon 100 G4
Boulden Shrops 131 F10
Boulder Clough
W Yorks 196 C4
Bouldnor IoW 20 D3
Bouldon Shrops 131 F10
Boulmer Northumb 265 G7
Boulsdon Glos 98 G4
Boulston Pembs 73 C7
Boultenstone Aberds 292 B6
Boultham Lincs 173 B7
Boultham Moor Lincs 173 B7
Boulton Derbys 153 C7
Boulton Moor Derbys 153 C7
Boundary Leics 152 F6
Staffs 169 G7
Boundstone Sur 49 E10
Bountis Thorne Devon 24 D5
Bourn Cambs 122 F6
Bournbrook W Mid 133 G10
Bourne Lincs 155 E11
N Som 44 B3
Bourne End Bedford 121 E10
Bucks 65 B11
C Beds 103 C9
Herts 85 D8
Bournemouth BCP 19 C7
Bournes Green Glos 80 E6
Southend 70 B2
Worcs 117 C8
Bourne Vale W Mid 133 D11
Bourne Valley BCP 19 C7
Bournheath Worcs 117 C9
Bournmoor Durham 243 G8
Bournside Glos 99 G8
Bournstream Glos 80 G2
Bournville W Mid 133 G10
Bourton Bucks 102 E4
Dorset 45 G9
N Som 59 G11
Oxon 63 B8
Shrops 131 D11
Wilts 62 G4
Bourton on Dunsmore
Warks 119 C8
Bourton-on-the-Hill
Glos 100 E3
Bourton-on-the-Water
Glos 100 G3
Bourtreehill N Ayrs 257 B8
Bousd Argyll 288 C4
Bousta Shetland 313 H4
Boustead Hill Cumb 239 F7
Bouth Cumb 210 B6
Bouthwaite N Yorks 214 E2
Bouts Worcs 117 F10
Bovain Stirling 285 D9
Boveney Bucks 66 D2
Boveridge Dorset 31 E9
Boverton V Glam 58 F3
Bovey Tracey Devon 14 F2
Bovingdon Herts 85 E8
Bovingdon Green Bucks 65 B10
Herts 85 E8
Bovinger Essex 87 D8
Bovington Camp Dorset 18 D2
Bow Borders 271 G9
Devon 8 D6
Devon 26 G2
Orkney 314 G3
Oxon 82 G4
Bowbank Durham 232 G4
Bowbeck Suff 125 B8
Bow Brickhill M Keynes 103 E8
Bowbridge Glos 80 E5
Bowbrook Shrops 149 G9
Bow Broom S Yorks 187 B7
Bowburn Durham 234 D2
Bowcombe IoW 20 D5
Bow Common London 67 C11
Bowd Devon 15 C8
Bowden Borders 262 C3
Devon 8 F6
Dorset 30 C3
Bowden Hill Wilts 62 F2
Bowdens Som 28 B6
Bowderdale Cumb 222 E3
Bowdon Gtr Man 184 D3
Bower Highld 310 C6
Northumb 251 G7
Bower Ashton Bristol 60 E5
Bowerchalke Wilts 31 C8
Bower Heath Herts 85 B10
Bowerhill Wilts 62 G2
Bower Hinton Som 29 D7
Bowerhope Borders 261 E7
Bower House Tye Suff 107 C9
Bowermadden Highld 310 C6
Bowers Staffs 150 B6
Bowers Gifford Essex 69 B9
Bowershall Fife 279 C11
Bowertower Highld 310 C6
Bowes Durham 223 C9
Bowes Park London 86 G4
Bowgreave Lancs 202 E5
Bowgreen Gtr Man 184 D3
Bowhill Borders 261 D10
Fife 280 B4
Bowhouse Dumfries 238 D2
Bowhousebog or Liquo
N Lanark 269 D7
Bowing Park Mers 182 D6
Bowismiln Borders 262 E2
Bowithick Corn 11 E9
Bowker's Green Lancs 194 G2
Bowland Bridge Cumb 211 B8
Bowldown Wilts 62 D2
Bowlee Gtr Man 195 F10
Bowlees Durham 232 F4
Bowler's Town E Sus 38 C6
Bowley Hereford 115 G10
Bowley Lane Hereford 98 C3
Bowley Town Hereford 115 G10
Bowlhead Green Sur 50 F2
Bowling W Dunb 277 G9
W Yorks 205 G9
Bowling Alley Hants 49 D9
Bowling Bank Wrex 166 F5
Bowling Green Corn 5 D10
Corn 12 G3
Glos 81 E8
Hants 19 B11
Shrops 150 D2
W Mid 133 F8
Worcs 116 G6
Bowlish Som 44 E6
Bowmans Kent 68 E4
Bowmanstead Cumb 220 F6
Bowmore Argyll 254 B4
Bowness-on-Solway
Cumb 238 E6
Bowness-on-Windermere
Cumb 221 F8
Bow of Fife Fife 287 F7
Bowridge Hill Dorset 30 B4
Bowrie-fauld Angus 287 C9
Bowsden Northumb 273 G9
Bowsey Hill Windsor 65 C10
Bowshank Borders 271 G9
Bowside Lodge Highld 310 C2
Bowston Cumb 221 F9
Bow Street Ceredig 128 G2
Norf 141 D10
Bowthorpe Norf 142 B3
Bowyer's Common Hants 34 B3
Box Glos 80 E5
Wilts 61 F10
Boxbush Glos 80 C2
Glos 98 G3
Box End Bedford 103 B10
Boxford Suff 107 C9
W Berks 64 E2
Boxgrove W Sus 22 B6
Box Hill Sur 51 C7
Wilts 61 F10
Boxley Kent 53 B9
Boxmoor Herts 85 D9
Box's Shop Corn 24 G2
Boxted Essex 107 E9
Suff 124 G6
Boxted Cross Essex 107 E10
Boxted Heath Essex 107 E10
Box Trees W Mid 118 C2
Boxwell Glos 80 G4
Boxworth Cambs 122 E6
Boxworth End Cambs 123 D7
Boyatt Wood Hants 32 C6
Boyden End Suff 124 F4
Boyden Gate Kent 71 F8
Boyland Common Norf 141 G11
Boylestone Derbys 152 B3
Boylestonfield Derbys 152 B3
Boyndie Aberds 302 C6
Boyn Hill Windsor 65 C11
Boynton E Yorks 218 F2
Boysack Angus 287 C9
Angus 287 C10
Boys Hill Dorset 29 E11
Boys Village V Glam 58 F4
Boythorpe Derbys 186 G5
Boyton Corn 12 C2
Suff 109 B7
Wilts 46 F3
Boyton Cross Essex 87 D10
Boyton End Essex 106 E2
Suff 106 C4
Bozeat N Nhants 121 F8
Bozen Green Herts 105 F8
Braaid IoM 192 E4
Braal Castle Highld 310 C5
Brabling Green Suff 126 E5
Brabourne Kent 54 E5
Brabourne Lees Kent 54 E5
Brabster Highld 310 C7
Bracadale Highld 294 B5
Bracara Highld 295 F9
Braceborough Lincs 155 G11
Bracebridge Lincs 173 B7
Bracebridge Heath
Lincs 173 B7
Bracebridge Low Fields
Lincs 173 B7
Braceby Lincs 155 B10
Bracewell Lancs 204 D3
Bracken Bank W Yorks 204 F6
Brackenber Cumb 222 B4
Brackenbottom N Yorks 212 E6
Brackenfield Derbys 170 D5
Brackenhall W Yorks 197 D7
Bracken Hill W Yorks 197 C7
Brackenlands Cumb 229 B11
Bracken Park W Yorks 206 E3
Brackenthwaite Cumb 229 B11
Cumb 229 G9
N Yorks 205 C11
Brackla = *Bragle*
Bridgend 58 D2
Bracklamore Aberds 303 D8
Bracklesham W Sus 22 D4
Brackletter Highld 290 E3
Brackley Argyll 255 C8
W Nhants 101 D11
Brackloch Highld 307 G6
Bracknell Brack 65 F11
Braco Perth 286 G2
Bracobrae Moray 302 D5
Braco Castle Perth 286 F2
Bracon N Lincs 199 F9
Bracon Ash Norf 142 D3
Braco Park Aberds 303 C9
Bracorina Highld 295 F9
Bradaford Devon 12 C3
Bradbourne Derbys 170 E2
Bradbury Durham 234 F2
Bradda IoM 192 F2
Bradden W Nhants 102 B2
Braddock Corn 6 C3
Braddocks Hay Staffs 168 D5
Bradeley Stoke 168 E5
Bradeley Green Ches E 167 G8
Bradenham Bucks 84 F4
Norf 141 B8
Bradenstoke Wilts 62 D4
Brades Village W Mid 133 E9
Bradfield Devon 27 F9
Essex 108 E2
Norf 160 C5
W Berks 64 E6
Bradfield Combust Suff 125 F7
Bradfield Green
Ches E 167 D11
Bradfield Heath Essex 108 F2
Bradfield St Clare Suff 125 F8
Bradfield St George
Suff 125 E8
Bradford Corn 11 F8
Derbys 170 C2
Devon 24 F6
Gtr Man 184 B5
Northumb 264 C5
W Yorks 205 G9
Bradford Abbas Dorset 29 E9
Bradford Leigh Wilts 61 G10
Bradford-on-Avon
Wilts 61 G10
Bradford-on-Tone Som 27 C11
Bradford Peverell Dorset 17 C9
Bradgate S Yorks 186 C6
Bradiford Devon 40 G5
Brading IoW 21 D8
Bradley Derbys 170 F2
Glos 80 G3
Hants 48 E6
NE Lincs 201 F8
Staffs 151 F7
W Mid 133 D8
Wrex 166 E4
W Yorks 197 C7
Bradley Cross Som 44 C3
Bradley Fold Gtr Man 195 F9
Bradley Green Ches W 167 F8
Glos 80 G2
Som 43 F9
Warks 134 C5
Worcs 117 E9
Bradley in the Moors
Staffs 169 G9
Bradley Mills W Yorks 197 D7
Bradley Mount Ches E 184 F6
Bradley Stoke S Glos 60 C6
Bradlow Hereford 98 D4
Bradmore Notts 153 C11
W Mid 133 D7
Bradney Shrops 132 D5
Som 43 F10
Bradninch Devon 27 G8
Bradnock's Marsh
W Mid 118 B4
Bradnop Staffs 169 D8
Bradnor Green Hereford 114 F5
Bradpole Dorset 16 C5
Bradshaw Gtr Man 195 E8
Staffs 168 D6
W Yorks 196 E5
W Yorks 205 G7
Bradstone Devon 12 E3
Bradville M Keynes 102 C6
Bradwall Green Ches E 168 C3
Bradway S Yorks 186 E4
Bradwell Derbys 185 E11
Devon 40 E3
Essex 106 G6
M Keynes 102 D6
Norf 143 C10
Staffs 168 F4
Bradwell Common
M Keynes 102 D6
Bradwell Grove Oxon 82 D2
Bradwell Hills Derbys 185 E11
Bradwell on Sea Essex 89 D8
Bradwell Waterside
Essex 89 D7
Bradworthy Devon 24 E4
Bradworthy Cross Devon 24 E4
Brae Dumfries 237 B10
Highld 307 L3
Highld 309 J4
Shetland 312 G5
Braeantra Highld 300 B5
Braebuster Orkney 314 F5
Braedownie Angus 292 F4
Braeface Falk 278 E5
Braefield Highld 300 F4
Braefindon Highld 300 D6
Braegrum Perth 286 E4
Braehead Dumfries 236 D6
Orkney 314 B4
Orkney 314 F5
S Ayrs 257 E8
S Lanark 259 C8
S Lanark 267 D11
S Lanark 269 E9
Stirling 278 C6
Braehead of Lunan
Angus 287 B10
Braehoulland Shetland 312 F4
Braehour Highld 310 D4
Braehungie Highld 310 F5
Braeintra Highld 295 B10
Braelangwell Lodge
Highld 309 K5
Braemar Aberds 292 D3
Braemore Highld 299 B11
Braemore *continued*
Highld 310 F4
Brae of Achnahaird
Highld 307 H5
Brae of Boquhapple
Stirling 285 G10
Braepark Edin 280 F3
Brae Roy Lodge Highld 290 D5
Braeside Invclyd 276 F4
Braes of Enzie Moray 302 D3
Braes of Ullapool Highld 307 K6
Braeswick Orkney 314 C6
Braevallich Argyll 275 C10
Braewick Shetland 312 F4
Shetland 313 H5
Brafferton Darl 233 G11
N Yorks 215 E8
Brafield-on-the-Green
W Nhants 120 F6
Bragar W Isles 304 D4
Bragbury End Herts 104 G5
Bragenham Bucks 103 F8
Bragle = *Brackla*
Bridgend 58 D2
Bragleenmore Argyll 289 G11
Braichmelyn Gwyn 163 B10
Braichyfedw Powys 129 E7
Braid Edin 280 G4
Braides Lancs 202 C4
Braidfauld Glasgow 268 C2
Braidley N Yorks 213 C10
Braids Argyll 255 C8
Braidwood S Lanark 268 F6
Braigh Chalasaigh
W Isles 296 D5
Braigo Argyll 274 G3
Brailsford Derbys 170 G3
Brailsford Green Derbys 170 G3
Braingortan Argyll 275 F11
Brain's Green Glos 79 D11
Brainshaugh Northumb 252 C6
Braintree Essex 106 G5
Braiseworth Suff 126 C2
Braishfield Hants 32 B5
Braiswick Essex 107 F9
Braithwaite Cumb 229 G10
S Yorks 198 E6
W Yorks 204 E6
Braithwell S Yorks 187 C8
Brakefield Green Norf 141 B10
Brakenhill W Yorks 198 D2
Bramber W Sus 35 E11
Bramblecombe Dorset 30 G3
Brambridge Hants 33 C7
Bramcote Notts 153 B10
Warks 135 F8
Bramcote Hills Notts 153 B10
Bramcote Mains Warks 135 F8
Bramdean Hants 33 B10
Bramerton Norf 142 C5
Bramfield Herts 86 B3
Suff 127 C7
Bramford Suff 108 B2
W Mid 133 E8
Bramhall Gtr Man 184 D5
Bramhall Moor Gtr Man 184 D6
Bramhall Park Gtr Man 184 D5
Bramham W Yorks 206 E4
Bramhope W Yorks 205 E11
Bramley Derbys 186 F6
Hants 48 B6
Sur 50 D4
S Yorks 187 C7
W Yorks 205 F10
Bramley Corner Hants 48 B6
Bramley Green Hants 49 B7
Bramley Head N Yorks 205 B8
Bramley Vale Derbys 171 B7
Bramling Kent 55 B8
Brampford Speke Devon 14 B4
Brampton Cambs 122 C4
Cumb 231 G9
Cumb 240 E2
Derbys 186 G5
Hereford 97 D8
Lincs 188 F4
Norf 160 E4
Suff 143 G8
S Yorks 198 G2
Brampton Abbotts
Hereford 98 F2
Brampton Ash N Nhants 136 F5
Brampton Bryan
Hereford 115 C7
Brampton en le Morthen
S Yorks 187 D7
Brampton Park Cambs 122 C4
Brampton Street Suff 143 G8
Bramshall Staffs 151 C11
Bramshaw Hants 32 D3
Bramshill Hants 65 G8
Bramshott Hants 49 G10
Bramwell Som 28 B6
Branatwatt Shetland 313 H4
Branault Highld 289 C7
Branbridges Kent 53 D7
Brancaster Norf 176 E3
Brancaster Staithe Norf 176 E3
Brancepeth Durham 233 D10
Branch End Northumb 242 E3
Branchill Moray 301 D10
Branchton Invclyd 276 F4
Brand End Lincs 174 F5
Branderburgh Moray 302 B2
Brandesburton E Yorks 209 D8
Brandeston Suff 126 E4
Brand Green Glos 98 F4
Hereford 98 C5
Brandhill Shrops 115 B8
Brandis Corner Devon 24 G6
Brandish Street Som 42 D2
Brandiston Norf 160 E2
Brandlingill Cumb 229 F8
Brandon Durham 233 D10
Lincs 172 F6
Northumb 264 F2
Suff 140 F5
Warks 119 B8
Brandon Bank Cambs 140 F2
Brandon Creek Norf 140 E2
Brandon Parva Norf 141 B11
Brandsby N Yorks 215 E11
Brands Hill Windsor 66 D4
Brandwood Shrops 149 D9
Brandwood End
W Mid 117 B11
Brandy Carr W Yorks 197 C10
Brandy Hole Essex 88 F4
Brandyquoy Orkney 314 G4
Brandy Wharf Lincs 189 B8
Brane Corn 1 D4
Bran End Essex 106 F3
Branksome BCP 18 C6
Darl 224 B5
Branksome Park BCP 19 C7
Bransbury Hants 48 E2
Bransby Lincs 188 F5
Branscombe Devon 15 D9
Bransford Worcs 116 G5
Bransgore Hants 19 B9
Branshill Clack 279 C7
Bransholme Hull 209 G8
Branson's Cross Worcs 117 C11
Branston Leics 154 D6
Lincs 173 B8
Staffs 152 E4
Branston Booths Lincs 173 B9
Branstone IoW 21 E7
Bransty Cumb 219 B9
Brant Broughton Lincs 172 E6
Brantham Suff 108 E2
Branthwaite Cumb 229 D11
Cumb 229 G7
Branthwaite Edge Cumb 229 G7
Brantingham E Yorks 200 B2
Branton Northumb 264 F2
S Yorks 198 G6
Branton Green N Yorks 215 G8
Branxholme Borders 261 G11
Branxholm Park
Borders 261 G11
Branxton Northumb 263 B9
Brascote Leics 135 C8
Brassey Green Ches W 167 C8
Brassington Derbys 170 E2
Brasted Kent 52 C3
Brasted Chart Kent 52 C3
Brathens Aberds 293 D8
Bratoft Lincs 175 B7
Brattle Kent 54 G2
Brattleby Lincs 188 E6
Bratton Som 42 D2
Telford 150 G2
Wilts 46 C2
Bratton Clovelly Devon 12 C5
Bratton Fleming Devon 40 F6
Bratton Seymour Som 29 B11
Braughing Herts 105 F7
Braughing Friars Herts 105 G8
Braulen Lodge Highld 300 F2
Braunston W Nhants 119 D10
Braunstone Leics 135 C11
Braunstone Town
Leicester 135 C11
Braunston-in-Rutland
Rutland 136 B6
Braunton Devon 40 F3
Brawby N Yorks 216 D4
Brawith N Yorks 225 D10
Brawl Highld 310 C2
Brawlbin Highld 310 D4
Bray Windsor 66 D2
Braybrooke N Nhants 136 G5
Braydon Side Wilts 62 B4
Brayford Devon 41 G7
Brayfordhill Devon 41 G7
Brays Grove Essex 87 D7
Bray Shop Corn 12 G2
Braystones Cumb 219 D10
Brayswick Worcs 98 B6
Braythorn N Yorks 205 D10
Brayton N Yorks 207 G8
Braytown Dorset 18 D2
Bray Wick Windsor 65 D11
Braywoodside Windsor 65 D11
Brazacott Corn 11 C11
Brazenhill Staffs 151 E7
Brea Corn 4 G3
Breach Bath 60 G6
Kent 69 F10
W Sus 22 B3
Breachacha Castle
Argyll 288 D3
Breachwood Green
Herts 104 G2
Breacleit W Isles 304 E3
Breaden Heath Shrops 149 B8
Breadsall Derbys 153 B7
Breadsall Hilltop Derby 153 B7
Breadstone Glos 80 E2
Bread Street Glos 80 D4
Breage Corn 2 D4
Breakachy Highld 300 E4
Brealeys Devon 25 D8
Bream Glos 79 D10
Breamore Hants 31 D11
Bream's Meend Glos 79 D9
Brean Som 43 B9
Breanais W Isles 304 F1
Brearley W Yorks 196 B4
Brearton N Yorks 214 G6
Breascleit W Isles 304 E4
Breaston Derbys 153 C9
Brechfa Carms 93 E10
Brechin Angus 293 G7
Breckan Orkney 314 F2
Breckles Norf 141 E9
Breck of Cruan Orkney 314 E3
Breckrey Highld 298 C5
Brecks S Yorks 187 C7
Brecon Powys 95 F10
Bredbury Gtr Man 184 C6
Bredbury Green
Gtr Man 184 C6
Brede E Sus 38 D4
Bredenbury Hereford 116 F2
Bredfield Suff 126 G5
Bredgar Kent 69 G11
Bredhurst Kent 69 G9
Bredicot Worcs 117 G8
Bredon Worcs 99 D8
Bredon's Hardwick
Worcs 99 D8
Bredon's Norton Worcs 99 D8
Bredwardine Hereford 96 C6
Breedon on the Hill
Leics 153 E8
Breeds Essex 87 C11
Breedy Butts Lancs 202 E2
Breibhig W Isles 297 M2
W Isles 304 E6
Breich W Loth 269 C9
Breightmet Gtr Man 195 F8
Breighton E Yorks 207 G10
Breinton Hereford 97 D9
Breinton Common
Hereford 97 C9
Breiwick Shetland 313 J6
Brelston Green Hereford 97 G11
Bremhill Wilts 62 E3
Bremhill Wick Wilts 62 E3
Bremirehoull Shetland 313 L6
Brenachoile Lodge
Stirling 285 G8
Brenchley Kent 53 E7
Brenchoillie Argyll 284 G4
Brendon Devon 24 E5
Devon 24 F5
Devon 41 D9
Brenkley T&W 242 B6
Brent Corn 6 E4
Brent Cross London 67 B8
Brent Eleigh Suff 107 B8
Brentford London 67 D7
Brentford End London 67 D7
Brentingby Leics 154 F5
Brent Knoll Som 43 C10
Brent Mill Devon 8 D3
Brent Pelham Herts 105 E8
Brentry Bristol 60 D5

Brentwood Essex 87 G9
Brenzett Kent 39 B8
Brenzett Green Kent 39 B8
Brereton Staffs 151 F11
Brereton Cross Staffs 151 F11
Brereton Green Ches E 168 C3
Brereton Heath Ches E 168 C4
Breretonhill Staffs 151 F11
Bressingham Norf 141 G11
Bressingham Common
Norf 141 G11
Bretby Derbys 152 E5
Bretford Warks 119 B8
Bretforton Worcs 99 C11
Bretherdale Head
Cumb 221 E11
Bretherton Lancs 194 C3
Brettabister Shetland 313 H6
Brettenham Norf 141 G8
Suff 125 G9
Bretton Derbys 186 F2
Flint 166 C5
Pboro 138 C3
Brewer's End Essex 105 G11
Brewers Green Norf 142 G2
Brewer Street Sur 51 C10
Brewlands Bridge
Angus 292 G3
Brewood Staffs 133 B7
Briach Moray 301 D10
Briants Puddle Dorset 18 C2
Briar Hill W Nhants 120 F4
Brick End Essex 105 F11
Brickendon Herts 86 D4
Bricket Wood Herts 85 E10
Brickfields Worcs 117 F7
Brickhill Bedford 121 G11
Brick Hill Sur 66 G3
Brick House End Essex 105 F9
Brickhouses Ches E 168 C3
Brick Houses S Yorks 186 E4
Brick-kiln End Notts 171 D9
Brickkiln Green Essex 106 E4
Bricklehampton Worcs 99 C9
Bride IoM 192 B5
Bridekirk Cumb 229 E8
Bridell Pembs 92 C3
Bridestowe Devon 12 D6
Brideswell Aberds 302 F5
Bridford Devon 14 D2
Bridfordmills Devon 14 D2
Bridge Corn 2 D6
Corn 4 G3
Kent 55 C7
Som 28 F5
Bridge Ball Devon 41 D8
Bridge End Bedford 121 G10
Cumb 230 B3
Devon 8 F3
Durham 232 D6
Essex 106 E3
Flint 166 D4
Hereford 98 B2
Lincs 156 B2
Northumb 241 D10
Northumb 241 E10
Oxon 83 G9
Bridge-End Shetland 313 K5
Bridge End Sur 50 B5
Warks 118 E5
Worcs 98 E6
Bridgefoot Aberds 292 C6
Angus 287 D7
Cumb 229 F7
Bridge Green Essex 105 D9
Norf 142 G2
Bridgehampton Som 29 C9
Bridge Hewick N Yorks 214 E6
Bridgehill Durham 242 G3
Bridge Ho Argyll 254 B4
Bridgeholm Green
Derbys 185 E8
Bridgehouse Gate
N Yorks 214 F3
Bridgelands Borders 261 C11
Bridgemary Hants 33 G9
Bridgemere Ches E 168 F2
Bridgemont Derbys 185 E8
Bridgend Aberds 293 B7
Aberds 302 F5
Angus 293 G7
Argyll 255 D8
Argyll 274 G4
Argyll 275 D9
Corn 6 D2
Cumb 221 C7
Devon 7 F11
Fife 287 F7
Glos 80 E4
Highld 300 D3
Invclyd 276 F5
Moray 302 F3
N Lanark 278 G3
Pembs 92 B3
W Loth 279 F10
Bridgend = Pen-y-Bont ar-ogwr Bridgend 58 C2
Bridgend of Lintrathen
Angus 286 B6
Bridgeness Falk 279 E10
Bridge of Alford Aberds 293 B7
Bridge of Allan Stirling 278 B5
Bridge of Avon Moray 301 F11
Moray 301 G11
Bridge of Awe Argyll 284 E4
Bridge of Balgie Perth 285 C9
Bridge of Cally Perth 286 B5
Bridge of Canny Aberds 293 D8
Bridge of Craigisla
Angus 286 B6
Bridge of Dee Dumfries 237 D9
Bridge of Don
Aberdeen 293 B11
Bridge of Dun Angus 287 B10
Bridge of Dye Aberds 293 E8
Bridge of Earn Perth 286 F5
Bridge of Ericht Perth 285 B9
Bridge of Feugh Aberds 293 D9
Bridge of Forss Highld 310 C4
Bridge of Gairn Aberds 292 D5
Bridge of Gaur Perth 285 B9
Bridge of Lyon Perth 285 C11
Bridge of Muchalls
Aberds 293 D10
Bridge of Muick Aberds 292 D5
Bridge of Oich Highld 290 C5
Bridge of Orchy Argyll 284 D6
Bridge of Waith Orkney 314 E2
Bridge of Walls
Shetland 313 H4
Bridge of Weir Renfs 267 B7
Bridge Reeve Devon 25 E11
Bridgerule Devon 24 G3
Bridges Corn 5 D10
Shrops 131 D7
Bridge Sollers Hereford 97 C8
Bridge Street Suff 107 B7
Bridgeton Glasgow 268 C2
Bridgetown Corn 12 D2
Bridgetown *continued*
Devon 8 C6
Som 42 G2
Staffs 133 B9
Bridge Town Warks 118 G4
Bridge Trafford Ches W 183 G7
Bridge Yate S Glos 61 E7
Bridgham Norf 141 F9
Bridgnorth Shrops 132 E4
Bridgtown Staffs 133 B9
Bridgwater Som 43 F10
Bridlington E Yorks 218 F3
Bridport Dorset 16 C5
Bridstow Hereford 97 G11
Brierfield Lancs 204 F2
Brierholme Carr
S Yorks 199 E7
Brierley Glos 79 B10
Hereford 115 F9
S Yorks 198 E2
Brierley Hill W Mid 133 F8
Brierton Hrtlpl 234 E5
Briery Cumb 229 G11
Briery Hill Bl Gwent 77 D11
Briestfield W Yorks 197 D8
Brigflatts Cumb 222 G2
Brigg N Lincs 200 F3
N Lincs 200 F4
Briggate Norf 160 D6
Briggswath N Yorks 227 D7
Brigham Cumb 229 E7
Cumb 229 E11
E Yorks 209 C7
Brighouse W Yorks 196 C6
Brighstone IoW 20 E4
Brightgate Derbys 170 D3
Brighthampton Oxon 82 E5
Brightholmlee S Yorks 186 B3
Brightley Devon 13 B7
Brightling E Sus 37 C11
Brightlingsea Essex 89 B9
Brighton Brighton 36 G4
Corn 5 E8
Brighton Hill Hants 48 D6
Brighton le Sands Mers 182 B4
Brightons Falk 279 F8
Brightside S Yorks 186 D5
Brightwalton W Berks 64 D2
Brightwalton Green
W Berks 64 D2
Brightwalton Holt
W Berks 64 D2
Brightwell Suff 108 C4
Brightwell Baldwin
Oxon 83 F11
Brightwell cum Sotwell
Oxon 83 G9
Brigmerston Wilts 47 D7
Brignall Durham 223 C11
Brig o'Turk Stirling 285 G9
Brigsley NE Lincs 201 G9
Brigsteer Cumb 211 B9
Brigstock N Nhants 137 F8
Brill Bucks 83 C11
Corn 2 D6
Brilley Hereford 96 B5
Brilley Mountain Powys 114 G5
Brimaston Pembs 91 G8
Brimfield Hereford 115 D10
Brimington Derbys 186 G6
Brimington Common
Derbys 186 G6
Brimley Devon 13 F11
Devon 28 G4
Brimpsfield Glos 80 C6
Brimps Hill Glos 79 B11
Brimpton W Berks 64 G5
Brimpton Common
W Berks 64 G5
Brims Orkney 314 H2
Brims Castle Highld 310 B4
Brimscombe Glos 80 E5
Brimsdown London 86 F5
Brimstage Mers 182 E4
Brinacory Highld 295 F9
Brincliffe S Yorks 186 D4
Brind E Yorks 207 G10
Brindham Som 44 E4
Brindister Shetland 313 H4
Shetland 313 K6
Brindle Lancs 194 C6
Brindle Heath Gtr Man 195 G10
Brindley Ches E 167 E9
Brindley Ford Stoke 168 E5
Brindwoodgate Derbys 186 F4
Brineton Staffs 150 G6
Bringewood Forge
Hereford 115 C9
Bringhurst Leics 136 E6
Bringsty Common
Hereford 116 F4
Brington Cambs 121 B11
Brinian Orkney 314 D4
Briningham Norf 159 C10
Brinkhill Lincs 190 G5
Brinkley Cambs 124 G2
Notts 172 E2
Brinkley Hill Hereford 97 E11
Brinklow M Keynes 103 D8
Warks 119 B8
Brinkworth Wilts 62 C4
Brinmore Highld 300 G6
Brinnington Gtr Man 184 C6
Brinscall Lancs 194 C6
Brinsea N Som 60 G2
Brinsford Staffs 133 B8
Brinsley Notts 171 F7
Brinsop Hereford 97 C8
Brinsop Common
Hereford 97 C8
Brinsworth S Yorks 186 D6
Brinsworthy Devon 41 G9
Brinton Norf 159 B10
Brisco Cumb 239 G10
Briscoe Cumb 219 C10
Briscoerigg N Yorks 205 C11
Brisley Norf 159 E8
Brislington Bristol 60 E6
Brissenden Green Kent 54 F2
Bristnall Fields W Mid 133 F9
Bristol Bristol 60 E5
Briston Norf 159 C11
Britain Bottom S Glos 61 B9
Britannia Lancs 195 C11
Britford Wilts 31 B11
Brithdir Caerph 77 E11
Ceredig 92 B6
Gwyn 146 F5
Brithem Bottom Devon 27 E8
British Torf 78 E3
Briton Ferry = Llansawel
Neath 57 C8
Britten's Bath 45 B7
Britwell Slough 66 C3
Britwell Salome Oxon 83 G11
Brixham Torbay 9 D8
Brixton Devon 7 E11
London 67 D10
Brixton Deverill Wilts 45 F11
Brixworth W Nhants 120 C4
Brize Norton Oxon 82 D4
Broad Alley Worcs 117 D7
Broad Blunsdon
Swindon 81 G11
Broadbottom Gtr Man 185 C7
Broadbridge W Sus 22 B4
Broadbridge Heath
W Sus 50 G6
Broadbury Devon 12 B5
Broadbush Swindon 81 G11
Broad Campden Glos 100 D3
Broad Carr W Yorks 196 D5
Broad Chalke Wilts 31 B8
Broad Clough Lancs 195 C11
Broadclyst Devon 14 B5
Broad Colney Herts 85 E11
Broad Common Worcs 117 D7
Broadfield Gtr Man 195 E10
Invclyd 276 G6
Lancs 194 C4
Lancs 195 B8
Pembs 73 E10
W Sus 51 G9
Broadford Highld 295 C8
Sur 50 D3
Broad Ford Kent 53 F8
Broadford Bridge W Sus 35 C9
Broadgate Hants 32 C6
Broadgrass Green Suff 125 E9
Broad Green Cambs 124 F3
C Beds 103 C9
Essex 105 D8
Essex 107 G7
London 67 F10
Mers 182 C6
Suff 124 F5
Suff 125 F11
Worcs 116 F5
Worcs 117 C9
Broadgreen Wood Herts 86 D4
Broadhalgh Gtr Man 195 E11
Broadham Green Sur 51 C11
Broadhaugh Borders 249 B10
Broadhaven Highld 310 D7
Broad Haven = Aberllydan
Pembs 72 C5
Broadheath Gtr Man 184 D3
Broad Heath Powys 114 E6
Staffs 151 D7
Worcs 116 D3
Broadhembury Devon 27 G10
Broadhempston Devon 8 B6
Broad Hill Cambs 123 B11
Broad Hinton Wilts 62 D6
Broadholm Derbys 170 F4
Broadholme Derbys 170 F5
Lincs 188 G5
Broad Ings E Yorks 208 C2
Broadland Row E Sus 38 D4
Broadlands Devon 14 G3
Broadlane Corn 2 C4
Broad Lane Corn 4 G3
Broad Lanes Shrops 132 F5
Broadlay Carms 74 D5
Broad Laying Hants 64 G2
Broad Layings Hants 64 G2
Broadley Lancs 195 D11
Moray 302 C3
Broadley Common Essex 86 D6
Broadleys Aberds 303 C8
Broad Marston Worcs 100 B2
Broadmayne Dorset 17 D10
Broad Meadow Staffs 168 F4
Broadmeadows
Borders 261 C10
Broadmere Hants 48 D6
Broadmoor Pembs 73 D9
Sur 50 D6
Broadmoor Common
Hereford 98 D2
Broadmore Green
Worcs 116 G6
Broadoak Dorset 16 B4
Glos 80 C2
Hants 33 E8
Shrops 149 F9
Wrex 166 D5
Broad Oak Carms 93 G11
Cumb 220 G2
Dorset 30 E3
E Sus 37 C10
E Sus 38 D4
Hants 49 C9
Hereford 97 G9
Kent 54 F4
Kent 71 G7
Mers 183 B8
Shrops 132 F5
Broadoak End Herts 86 C4
Broadoak Park Gtr Man 195 G9
Broad Parkham Devon 24 C5
Broadplat Oxon 65 C8
Broadrashes Moray 302 D4
Broadrock Glos 79 F8
Broadsands Torbay 9 D7
Broadsea Aberds 303 C9
Broad's Green Essex 87 C11
Wilts 62 F3
Broadshard Som 28 E6
Broadstairs Kent 71 F11
Broadstone BCP 18 B6
Kent 53 D11
Mon 79 E8
Shrops 131 F10
Broad Street E Sus 38 D5
Kent 53 B10
Kent 54 E6
Kent 55 E7
Medway 69 E9
Suff 107 C9
Wilts 46 B6
Broadstreet Common
Newport 59 C11
Broad Street Green
Essex 88 D5
Broad Tenterden Kent 53 G11
Broad Town Wilts 62 D5
Broadwas Worcs 116 F5
Broadwater Herts 104 G4
W Sus 35 G11
Broadwater Down Kent 52 F5
Broadwaters Worcs 116 B6
Broadwath Cumb 239 F11
Broadway Carms 74 D3
Carms 74 D5
Pembs 72 C5
Som 28 D4
Suff 127 B7
Worcs 99 D11
Broadway Lands
Hereford 97 E11
Broadwell Glos 79 C9
Glos 100 F4
Oxon 82 E3
Warks 119 D9
Broadwey Dorset 17 E9
Broadwindsor Dorset 28 G6
Broadwood Kelly Devon 25 F10
Broadwoodwidger Devon 12 D4
Brobury Hereford 96 C6
Brochel Highld 298 E5
Brochroy Argyll 284 D4
Brock Lancs 202 E6
Brockamin Worcs 116 G5
Brockbridge Hants 33 D10
Brockdish Norf 126 B4
Brockencote Worcs 117 C7
Brockenhurst Hants 32 G4
Brocketsbrae S Lanark 259 B8
Brockfield Devon 28 F4
Brockford Green Suff 126 D2
Brockford Street Suff 126 D2
Brockhall W Nhants 120 E2
Brockhall Village
Lancs 203 F10
Brockham Sur 51 D7
Brockham End Bath 61 F8
Brockham Park Sur 51 D8
Brockhampton Glos 99 F8
Glos 99 G10
Hants 22 B2
Hereford 97 E11
Brockhampton Green
Dorset 30 F2
Brockhill Borders 261 E9
Brock Hill Essex 88 F2
Brockholes W Yorks 197 E7
Brockhollands Glos 79 D10
Brockhurst Derbys 170 C4
Hants 33 G10
Warks 135 G9
Brocklebank Cumb 230 C2
Brocklehirst Dumfries 238 C3
Brocklesby Lincs 200 E6
Brockley London 67 E11
N Som 60 F3
Brockley Corner Suff 124 C6
Brockley Green Suff 106 B4
Suff 124 G6
Brockleymoor Cumb 230 D5
Brockloch Dumfries 246 D2
Brockmanton Hereford 115 F10
Brockmoor W Mid 133 F8
Brockscombe Devon 12 C5
Brock's Green Hants 64 G4
Brock's Watering Norf 142 E2
Brockton Shrops 130 C6
Shrops 130 F6
Shrops 131 E11
Shrops 132 C4
Staffs 150 C6
Telford 150 F4
Brockweir Glos 79 E8
Brockwell Som 42 E2
Brockwood Hants 33 B10
Brockworth Glos 80 B5
Brocton Corn 5 B10
Staffs 151 F9
Brodick N Ayrs 256 B2
Brodie Moray 301 D9
Brodiesord Aberds 302 C5
Brodsworth S Yorks 198 F4
Brogaig Highld 298 C4
Brogborough C Beds 103 D9
Broke Hall Suff 108 C3
Brokenborough Wilts 62 B2
Broken Cross Ches E 184 G5
Ches W 183 G11
Broken Green Herts 105 G8
Brokerswood Wilts 45 C10
Brokes N Yorks 224 F3
Brombil Neath 57 D9
Bromborough Mers 182 E4
Bromborough Pool
Mers 182 E4
Bromdon Shrops 132 G2
Brome Suff 126 B2
Bromesberrow Glos 98 E4
Bromesberrow Heath
Glos 98 E4
Brome Street Suff 126 B3
Bromeswell Suff 126 G6
Bromfield Cumb 229 B9
Shrops 115 B9
Bromford W Mid 134 E2
Bromham Bedford 121 G10
Wilts 62 F3
Bromley Herts 105 G8
London 67 C11
London 68 F2
Shrops 132 D4
Shrops 149 D8
S Yorks 186 B4
W Mid 133 F8
Bromley Common London 68 F2
Bromley Cross Essex 107 F11
Gtr Man 195 E8
Bromley Green Kent 54 F3
Bromley Hall Staffs 150 C5
Bromley Heath S Glos 61 D7
Bromley Park London 67 F11
Bromley Wood Staffs 152 E2
Bromlow Shrops 130 C6
Brompton London 67 D9
Medway 69 F9
N Yorks 217 C8
N Yorks 225 F7
Shrops 131 B10
Brompton-by-Sawdon
N Yorks 217 C8
Brompton-on-Swale
N Yorks 224 F4
Brompton Ralph Som 42 G5
Brompton Regis Som 42 G3
Bromsash Hereford 98 G2
Bromsberrow Heath Glos 98 E4
Bromsgrove Worcs 117 C9
Bromstead Common
Staffs 150 F6
Bromstead Heath Staffs 150 F6
Bromstone Kent 71 F11
Bromyard Hereford 116 G3
Bromyard Downs
Hereford 116 F3
Bronaber Gwyn 146 C4
Broncroft Shrops 131 F10
Brondesbury London 67 C8
Brondesbury Park London 67 C8
Broneirion Powys 129 F10
Brongest Ceredig 92 B6
Brongwyn Ceredig 92 C5
Bronington Wrex 149 B9
Bronllys Powys 96 D2
Bronnant Ceredig 112 D2
Bronwydd Ceredig 93 C7
Bronwydd Arms Carms 93 G8
Bronydd Powys 96 B4
Bronygarth Shrops 148 B5
Brook Carms 74 D3
Devon 12 G5
Devon 14 C2
Hants 32 B4
Hants 32 E3
IoW 20 E3
Kent 54 E5
Sur 50 D5
Sur 50 F2
Brook Bottom Gtr Man 185 D7
Gtr Man 196 G3
Lancs 202 E6
Brooke Norf 142 D5
Rutland 136 B6
Brookenby Lincs 190 B2
Brookend Glos 79 E11
Glos 79 F9
Oxon 100 G6
Brook End Bedford 121 E11
Cambs 121 C11
C Beds 104 B3
Herts 104 F6
M Keynes 103 C8
Wilts 61 C10
Worcs 99 B7
Brookfield Derbys 185 B8
Lancs 203 G7
Mbro 225 B9
Renfs 267 C8
Brookfoot W Yorks 196 C6
Brookgreen IoW 20 E3
Brook Green London 67 D8
Suff 125 F7
Brookhampton Oxon 83 F10
Shrops 131 E11
Som 29 B10
Brook Hill Hants 32 E3
Notts 153 C11
Brookhouse Blackburn 195 B7
Ches E 184 F6
Denb 165 B9
Lancs 211 G10
S Yorks 187 D8
W Yorks 196 B5
Brookhouse Green
Ches E 168 C4
Brookhouses Derbys 185 D8
Staffs 169 G7
Brookhurst Mers 182 E4
Brookland Kent 39 B7
Brooklands Dumfries 237 B10
Gtr Man 184 C3
Shrops 167 G8
Sur 66 G5
W Yorks 206 F2
Brookleigh Devon 14 B5
Brookmans Park Herts 86 E2
Brookpits W Sus 35 G8
Brook Place Sur 66 G3
Brookrow Shrops 116 C2
Brooks Corn 6 C3
Powys 130 D2
Brooksbottoms Gtr Man 195 D9
Brooksby Leics 154 F3
Brooks End Kent 71 F9
Brooks Green W Sus 35 C10
Brookside Brack 66 E2
Derbys 186 G5
Telford 132 B3
Brook Street Essex 87 G9
Kent 52 D5
Kent 54 G2
Suff 106 B6
W Sus 36 B4
Brookthorpe Glos 80 C4
Brookvale Halton 183 E8
Brookville Norf 140 D4
Brook Waters Wilts 30 C6
Brookwood Sur 50 B2
Broom C Beds 104 C3
Cumb 231 G9
Devon 28 G4
E Renf 267 D10
Pembs 73 D10
S Yorks 186 C5
Warks 117 G11
Broombank Worcs 116 C3
Broome Norf 143 E7
Shrops 131 D10
Shrops 131 G8
Worcs 117 B8
Broomedge Warr 184 D2
Broome Park Northumb 264 G4
Broomer's Corner
W Sus 35 C10
Broomershill W Sus 35 D9
Broomfield Aberds 303 F9
Cumb 230 B2
Essex 88 D2
Kent 53 C10
Kent 71 F7
Som 43 G8
Wilts 61 D11
Broomfields Shrops 149 F8
Broomfleet E Yorks 199 B11
Broom Green Norf 159 E9
Broomhall Ches E 167 F10
Windsor 66 F3
Broomhall Green
Ches E 167 F10
Broomham E Sus 23 C8
Broomhaugh Northumb 242 E2
Broomhill Borders 261 D11
Bristol 60 D6
Ches W 167 B7
Highld 301 G9
Kent 55 B8
Norf 140 C2
Northumb 252 C6
Notts 171 F8
S Yorks 198 G2
Broom Hill Bristol 60 E6
Dorset 31 G8
Durham 242 G4
London 68 F3
Suff 108 B5
Worcs 117 B8
Broomhill Bank Kent 52 E5
Broomholm Norf 160 C6
Broomhouse Glasgow 268 C3
Broomlands N Ayrs 257 B8
Broomley Northumb 242 E2
Broompark Durham 233 C10
Broomridge Stirling 278 C6
Broom's Barn Suff 124 D5
Broom's Green Glos 98 E4
Broomsgrove E Sus 38 E4
Broomsthorpe Norf 158 D6
Broom Street Kent 70 G4
Broomton Highld 301 B8
Broomy Hill Hereford 97 D9
Broomy Lodge Hants 32 E2
Broomyshaw Staffs 169 F9
Brora Highld 311 J3
Broseley Shrops 132 C3
Brotherhouse Bar Lincs 156 G5
Brotheridge Green
Worcs 98 C6
Brotherlee Durham 232 D4
Brotherstone Borders 262 B4
Brothertoft Lincs 174 F3
Brotherton N Yorks 198 B3
Brothybeck Cumb 230 C2
Brotton Redcar 226 B3
Broubster Highld 310 C4
Brough Cumb 222 C5
Derbys 185 E11
E Yorks 200 B2
Highld 310 B6
Notts 172 D4
Orkney 314 E3
Orkney 314 H4
Shetland 312 C7
Shetland 312 F6
Shetland 312 F7
Shetland 313 G7
Brough *continued*
Shetland 313 H6
Shetland 313 J7
Broughall Shrops 167 G9
Brough Lodge Shetland 312 D7
Brough Sowerby Cumb 222 C5
Broughton Borders 260 B4
Bucks 84 C4
Cambs 122 B5
Edin 280 F5
Flint 166 C4
Hants 47 G10
Lancs 202 F6
M Keynes 103 C7
N Lincs 200 F3
N Nhants 120 B6
N Yorks 204 C4
N Yorks 216 E5
Orkney 314 B4
Oxon 101 D8
Shrops 132 E6
Staffs 150 C5
V Glam 58 E2
Broughton Astley Leics 135 E10
Broughton Beck Cumb 210 C5
Broughton Common
N Lincs 200 E3
Wilts 61 G11
Broughton Cross Cumb 229 E7
Broughton Gifford Wilts 61 G11
Broughton Green Worcs 117 E9
Broughton Hackett
Worcs 117 G8
Broughton in Furness
Cumb 210 B4
Broughton Lodges Leics 154 E4
Broughton Mills Cumb 220 G4
Broughton Moor Cumb 228 E6
Broughton Park
Gtr Man 195 G10
Broughton Poggs Oxon 82 E2
Broughtown Orkney 314 B6
Broughty Ferry Dundee 287 D8
Brow Edge Cumb 211 C7
Browhouses Dumfries 239 D7
Browland Shetland 313 H4
Brown Bank N Yorks 205 C10
Brownber Cumb 222 D4
Brownbread Street
E Sus 23 B11
Brown Candover Hants 48 F5
Brownedge Ches E 168 C3
Brown Edge Lancs 193 E11
Mers 183 C8
Staffs 168 E6
Brownheath Devon 27 D10
Shrops 149 D9
Brown Heath Ches W 167 B7
Hants 33 D8
Brownheath Common
Worcs 117 E7
Brownhill Aberds 302 E6
Aberds 303 E8
Blackburn 203 G9
Shrops 149 E8
Brownhills Fife 287 F9
Shrops 150 B3
W Mid 133 B10
Brownieside Northumb 264 E5
Browninghill Green
Hants 48 B5
Brown Knowl Ches W 167 E7
Brown Lees Staffs 168 D5
Brownlow Ches E 168 C4
Mers 194 G4
Brownlow Fold Gtr Man 195 E8
Brownlow Heath
Ches E 168 C4
Brown Moor W Yorks 206 G3
Brownmuir Aberds 293 F9
Brown's Bank Ches E 167 G10
Brown's End Glos 98 E4
Brown's Green W Mid 133 E10
Brownshill Glos 80 E5
Brownshill Green
W Mid 134 G6
Brownside Lancs 204 G3
Brownsover Warks 119 B10
Brownston Devon 8 E3
Brown Street Suff 125 E11
Browns Wood M Keynes 103 D8
Browsburn N Lanark 268 C5
Browston Green Norf 143 C9
Browtop Cumb 229 G7
Broxa N Yorks 227 G8
Broxbourne Herts 86 D5
Broxburn E Loth 282 F3
W Loth 279 G11
Broxfield Northumb 264 F6
Broxholme Lincs 188 F6
Broxted Essex 105 F11
Broxton Ches W 167 E7
Broxtowe Nottingham 171 G8
Broxwood Hereford 115 G7
Broyle Side E Sus 23 C7
Brù W Isles 304 D5
Bruairnis W Isles 297 L3
Bruan Highld 310 F7
Bruar Lodge Perth 291 F10
Brucefield Fife 280 D2
Brucehill W Dunb 277 F7
Bruche Warr 183 D10
Brucklebog Aberds 293 D9
Bruera Ches W 166 C6
Bruern Abbey Oxon 100 G5
Bruichladdich Argyll 274 G3
Bruisyard Suff 126 D6
Brumby N Lincs 199 F11
Brunant Powys 130 B5
Brund Staffs 169 C10
Brundall Norf 142 B6
Brundish Norf 143 D7
Suff 126 D5
Brundish Street Suff 126 C5
Brundon Suff 107 C7
Brunery Highld 289 B9
Brunnion Corn 2 B2
Brunshaw Lancs 204 G3
Brunstane Edin 280 G6
Brunstock Cumb 239 F10
Brunswick Gtr Man 184 B4
Brunswick Park London 86 G3
Brunswick Village T&W 242 C6
Bruntcliffe W Yorks 197 B9
Brunt Hamersland
Shetland 313 H6
Brunthwaite W Yorks 205 D7
Bruntingthorpe Leics 136 F2
Brunton Fife 287 E7
Northumb 264 E6
Wilts 47 B8
Brushes Gtr Man 185 B7
Brushfield Derbys 185 G11
Brushford Devon 25 F11
Som 26 B6
Bruton Som 45 G7
Bryans Midloth 270 C6
Bryan's Green Worcs 117 D7
Bryanston Dorset 30 F5
Bryant's Bottom Bucks 84 F5
Brydekirk Dumfries 238 C5
Bryher Scilly 1 G3
Brymbo Conwy 180 G4
Wrex 166 E3
Brympton Som 29 D8
Brympton D'Evercy Som 29 D8
Bryn Caerph 77 F11
Carms 75 E8
Ches W 183 G10
Gtr Man 194 G5
Gwyn 179 G9
Neath 57 C10
Powys 130 C3
Rhondda 76 D6
Shrops 130 F5
Swansea 56 C4
Brynafan Ceredig 112 C4
Brynamman Carms 76 C2
Brynawel Caerph 77 G11
Brynberian Pembs 92 D2
Brynbryddan Neath 57 C9
Neath 57 C9
Bryn Bwbach Gwyn 146 B2
Bryncae Rhondda 58 C3
Rhondda 58 C3
Bryn Celyn Anglesey 179 F10
Flint 181 F11
Bryncethin Bridgend 58 C2
Bridgend 58 C2
Bryncir Gwyn 163 G7
Bryncoch Bridgend 58 C2
Bryn-coch Neath 57 B8
Bryn Common Flint 166 D3
Bryncroes Gwyn 144 C4
Bryncrug Gwyn 128 C2
Brynderwen Powys 130 D3
Bryndu Carms 75 D8
Bryn Du Anglesey 178 G4
Bryn Dulas Conwy 180 F6
Bryneglwys Denb 165 F10
Bryn Eglwys Gwyn 163 B10
Brynford Flint 181 G11
Bryn Gates Gtr Man 194 G5
Brynglas Newport 59 B10
Bryn-glas Conwy 164 B4
Brynglas Sta Gwyn 128 C2
Bryn Golau Rhondda 58 B3
Bryngwran Anglesey 178 F4
Bryngwyn Ceredig 92 B5
Mon 78 D5
Powys 96 B3
Brynhenllan Pembs 91 D10
Bryn-henllan Pembs 91 D10
Brynhoffnant Ceredig 110 G6
Bryniau Denb 181 E9
Bryning Lancs 194 B2
Brynithel Bl Gwent 78 E2
Bryn-Iwan Carms 92 E6
Brynllywarch Powys 130 F3
Brynmawr Bl Gwent 77 C11
Bryn-mawr Gwyn 144 C4
Bryn Mawr Powys 148 F5
Brynmenyn Bridgend 58 B2
Brynmill Swansea 56 C6
Brynmorfudd Conwy 164 C4
Bryn Myrddin Carms 93 G8
Brynna Rhondda 58 C3
Bryn-nantllech Conwy 164 B6
Brynnau Gwynion
Rhondda 58 C3
Bryn-newydd Denb 165 G11
Bryn Offa Wrex 166 F4
Brynore Shrops 149 B7
Bryn-penarth Powys 130 C2
Bryn Pen-y-lan Wrex 166 G4
Bryn Pydew Conwy 180 F4
Brynrefail Anglesey 179 D7
Gwyn 163 C9
Bryn Rhyd-yr-Arian
Conwy 165 B7
Bryn-rhys Conwy 180 F4
Brynsadler Rhondda 58 C4
Bryn Saith Marchog
Denb 165 E9
Brynsiencyn Anglesey 163 B7
Bryn Sion Gwyn 147 F7
Brynsworthy Devon 40 G4
Bryn Tanat Powys 148 E4
Brynteg Anglesey 179 E7
Ceredig 93 C9
Wrex 166 E4
Bryntirion Bridgend 57 E11
Bryn-y-cochin Shrops 149 B7
Bryn-y-gwenin Mon 78 B4
Bryn-y-maen Conwy 180 F4
Bryn-yr-Eos Wrex 166 G3
Bryn-yr-eryr Gwyn 162 F5
Bryn-yr-ogof Denb 165 D11
Buaile nam Bodach
W Isles 297 L3
Bualintur Highld 294 C6
Bualnaluib Highld 307 K3
Buarthmeini Gwyn 146 C6
Bubbenhall Warks 119 C7
Bubblewell Glos 80 E5
Bubnell Derbys 186 G2
Bubwith E Yorks 207 F10
Buccleuch Borders 261 G8
Buchanan Smithy
Stirling 277 D9
Buchanhaven Aberds 303 E11
Buchan Hill W Sus 51 G9
Buchanty Perth 286 E3
Buchley E Dunb 277 G11
Buchlyvie Stirling 277 C11
Buckabank Cumb 230 B3
Buckbury Worcs 98 E6
Buckden Cambs 122 D3
N Yorks 213 D8
Buckenham Norf 143 B7
Buckerell Devon 27 G10
Bucket Corner Hants 32 C6
Buckfast Devon 8 B4
Buckfastleigh Devon 8 B4
Buckham Dorset 29 G7
Buckhaven Fife 281 B7
Buck Hill Wilts 62 E3
Buckholm Borders 261 B11
Buckholt Mon 79 B8
Buckhorn Devon 12 B3
Buckhorn Weston Dorset 30 C3
Buckhurst Kent 53 E10
Buckhurst Hill Essex 86 G6
Buckie Moray 302 C4
Buckies Highld 310 C5
Buckingham Bucks 102 E3
Buckland Bucks 84 C5
Devon 8 G3
Devon 14 G3
Glos 99 D11
Hants 20 B2
Herts 105 E7
Kent 55 E10
Oxon 82 F4
Sur 51 C8
Buckland Brewer Devon 24 C6
Buckland Common Bucks 84 D6
Buckland Dinham Som 45 C9
Buckland Down Som 45 C8
Buckland End W Mid 134 F2
Buckland Filleigh Devon 25 F7
Buckland in the Moor
Devon 13 G10
Buckland Marsh Oxon 82 F4
Buckland Monachorum
Devon 7 B9
Buckland Newton
Dorset 29 F11
Buckland Ripers Dorset 17 E8
Bucklands Borders 262 F2
Buckland St Mary Som 28 E3
Buckland Valley Kent 55 E10
Bucklandwharf Bucks 84 C5
Bucklebury W Berks 64 E5
Bucklebury Alley
W Berks 64 E4
Bucklegate Lincs 156 B6
Buckleigh Devon 24 B6
Bucklerheads Angus 287 D8
Bucklers Hard Hants 20 B4
Bucklesham Suff 108 C4
Buckley = Bwcle Flint 166 C3
Buckley Green Warks 118 D3
Buckley Hill Mers 182 B4
Bucklow Hill Ches E 184 E2
Buckminster Leics 155 E7
Buckmoorend Bucks 84 E4
Bucknall Lincs 173 B11
Stoke 168 F6
Bucknell Oxon 101 F11
Shrops 115 C7
Buckoak Ches W 183 G8
Buckover S Glos 79 G11
Buckpool Moray 302 C4
W Mid 133 F7
Buckridge Worcs 116 C4
Bucksburn Aberdeen 293 C10
Buck's Cross Devon 24 C4
Bucks Green W Sus 50 G5
Buckshaw Village Lancs 194 C5
Bucks Hill Herts 85 E9
Bucks Horn Oak Hants 49 E10
Buckskin Hants 48 C6
Buck's Mills Devon 24 C5
Buckton E Yorks 218 E3
Hereford 115 C7
Northumb 264 B3
Buckton Vale Gtr Man 196 G3
Buckworth Cambs 122 B2
Budbrooke Warks 118 D5
Budby Notts 171 B10
Buddgbrake Shetland 312 B8
Buddileigh Staffs 168 F3
Budd's Titson Corn 24 G2
Bude Corn 24 F2
Budge's Shop Corn 6 D6
Budlake Devon 14 B5
Budle Northumb 264 B5
Budleigh Som 27 D11
Budleigh Salterton Devon 15 E7
Budlett's Common E Sus 37 C7
Budock Water Corn 3 C7
Budworth Heath
Ches W 183 F11
Buersil Head Gtr Man 196 E2
Buerton Ches E 167 G11
Buffler's Holt Bucks 102 D3
Bufton Leics 135 B8
Bugbrooke W Nhants 120 F3
Bugford Devon 40 E6
Bughtlin Edin 280 G3
Buglawton Ches E 168 C5
Bugle Corn 5 D10
Bugle Gate Worcs 116 D6
Bugley Dorset 30 C3
Wilts 45 E11
Bugthorpe E Yorks 207 B11
Building End Essex 105 D8
Buildwas Shrops 132 C2
Builth Road Powys 113 G10
Builth Wells Powys 113 G10
Buirgh W Isles 305 J2
Bulbourne Herts 84 C6
Bulbridge Wilts 46 G5
Bulby Lincs 155 D11
Bulcote Notts 171 G11
Buldoo Highld 310 C3
Bulford Wilts 47 E7
Bulford Camp Wilts 47 E7
Bulkeley Ches E 167 E8
Bulkeley Hall Shrops 168 G2
Bulkington Warks 135 F7
Wilts 46 B2
Bulkworthy Devon 24 E5
Bullamoor N Yorks 225 G7
Bull Bay = Porthllechog
Anglesey 178 C6
Bullbridge Derbys 170 E5
Bullbrook Brack 65 F11
Bulleign Kent 53 G11
Bullenhill Wilts 45 B11
Bullen's Green Herts 86 D2
Bulley Glos 80 B3
Bullgill Cumb 229 D7
Bull Hill Hants 20 B2
Bullhurst Hill Derbys 170 G3
Bullinghope Hereford 97 D10
Bullington Hants 48 E3
Lincs 189 F9
Bullo Glos 79 D11
Bullockstone Kent 71 F7
Bulls Cross London 86 F4
Bulls Green Som 45 D8
Bull's Green Herts 86 B3
Norf 143 E8
Bull's Hill Hereford 97 G11
Bullwood Argyll 276 G3
Bullyhole Bottom Mon 79 F7
Bulmer Essex 106 C6
N Yorks 216 F3
Bulmer Tye Essex 106 D6
Bulphan Thurrock 68 B6
Bulstrode Herts 85 E8
Bulthy Shrops 148 G6
Bulverhythe E Sus 38 F3
Bulwark Aberds 303 E9
Mon 79 G8
Bulwell Nottingham 171 F8
Bulwell Forest
Nottingham 171 F8
Bulwick Leics 136 F3
N Nhants 137 E9
Bumble's Green Essex 86 D6
Bumwell Hill Norf 142 E2
Bun Abhainn Eadarra
W Isles 305 H3
Bunacaimb Highld 295 G8
Bun a'Mhuillin W Isles 297 K3
Bunarkaig Highld 290 E3
Bunbury Ches E 167 D9
Bunbury Heath Ches E 167 D9
Bunce Common Sur 51 D8
Bunchrew Highld 300 E6
Bundalloch Highld 295 C10
Buness Shetland 312 C8
Bunessan Argyll 288 G5
Bungay Suff 142 F6
Bunkers Hill Gtr Man 184 D6
Oxon 83 B7
Bunker's Hill Cambs 139 B8
Lincs 174 E3

Bunker's Hill *continued*
Lincs 189 G7
Norf 142 B3
Suff 143 C10
Bunloit Highld 300 G5
Bun Loyne Highld 290 C4
Bunnahabhain Argyll 274 F5
Bunny Notts 153 D11
Bunny Hill Notts 153 D11
Bunree Highld 290 G2
Bunroy Highld 290 E4
Bunsley Bank Ches E 167 G11
Bunstead Hants 32 C6
Buntait Highld 300 F3
Buntingford Herts 105 F7
Bunting's Green Essex 106 E6
Bunwell Norf 142 E2
Bunwell Bottom Norf 142 D2
Buoltach Highld 310 F5
Burbage Derbys 185 G8
Leics 135 E8
Wilts 63 G8
Burcher Hereford 114 E6
Burchett's Green
Windsor 65 C10
Burcombe Wilts 46 G5
Burcot Oxon 83 F9
Worcs 117 C9
Burcote Shrops 132 D4
Burcott Bucks 84 B4
Bucks 103 G7
Som 44 D4
Burdiehouse Edin 270 B5
Burdon T&W 243 G9
Burdonshill V Glam 58 E6
Burdrop Oxon 101 D7
Bures Suff 107 E8
Bures Green Suff 107 D8
Burford Ches E 167 E10
Devon 24 C4
Oxon 82 C3
Shrops 115 D11
Som 44 E5
Burg Argyll 288 E5
Argyll 288 G6
Burgar Orkney 314 D3
Burgate Hants 31 D11
Suff 125 B11
Burgates Hants 34 B3
Burgedin Powys 148 G4
Burge End Herts 104 E2
Burgess Hill W Sus 36 D4
Burgh Suff 126 G4
Burgh by Sands Cumb 239 F8
Burgh Castle Norf 143 B9
Burghclere Hants 64 G3
Burghclere Common
Hants 64 G3
Burgh Common Norf 141 E11
Burghead Moray 301 C11
Burghfield W Berks 65 F7
Burghfield Common
W Berks 64 F6
Burghfield Hill W Berks 65 F7
Burgh Heath Sur 51 B8
Burgh Hill E Sus 23 C8
E Sus 38 B2
Burghill Hereford 97 C9
Burgh le Marsh Lincs 175 B8
Burgh Muir Aberds 293 B9
Aberds 303 G7
Burgh next Aylsham
Norf 160 D4
Burgh on Bain Lincs 190 D2
Burgh St Margaret
= *Fleggburgh* Norf 161 G8
Burgh St Peter Norf 143 E9
Burgh Stubbs Norf 159 C10
Burghwallis S Yorks 198 E4
Burgois Corn 10 G4
Burham Kent 69 G8
Burham Court Kent 69 G8
Buriton Hants 34 C2
Burland Ches E 167 E10
Burlawn Corn 10 G5
Burleigh Brack 65 E11
Glos 80 E5
Burlescombe Devon 27 D9
Burleston Dorset 17 C11
Burlestone Devon 8 F6
Burley Hants 32 G2
Rutland 155 G7
Shrops 131 G9
W Yorks 205 G11
Burley Beacon Hants 32 G2
Burleydam Ches E 167 G10
Burley Gate Hereford 97 B11
Burley in Wharfedale
W Yorks 205 D9
Burley Lawn Hants 32 G2
Burley Lodge Hants 32 F2
Burley Street Hants 32 G2
Burley Woodhead
W Yorks 205 E9
Burlinch Som 28 B3
Burlingham Green Norf 161 G7
Burlingjobb Powys 114 F5
Burlish Park Worcs 116 C6
Burlorne Tregoose Corn 5 B10
Burlow E Sus 23 B9
Burlton Shrops 149 D9
Burmantofts W Yorks 206 G2
Burmarsh Hereford 97 B10
Kent 54 G5
Burmington Warks 100 D5
Burn N Yorks 198 B5
Burnage Gtr Man 184 C5
Burnard's Ho Devon 24 G4
Burnaston Derbys 152 C5
Burnbank S Lanark 268 D4
Burn Bridge N Yorks 206 C2
Burnby E Yorks 208 D2
Burncross S Yorks 186 B4
Burndell W Sus 35 G7
Burnden Gtr Man 195 F8
Burnedge Gtr Man 196 E2
Burnend Aberds 303 E8
Burneside Cumb 221 F10
Burness Orkney 314 B6
Burneston N Yorks 214 B6
Burnett Bath 61 F7
Burnfoot Borders 261 G10
Borders 262 F2
Dumfries 239 C7
Dumfries 247 E11
E Ayrs 245 B10
N Lanark 268 B5
Perth 286 G3
Burngreave S Yorks 186 D5
Burnham Bucks 66 C2
N Lincs 200 D5
Burnham Deepdale
Norf 176 E4
Burnham Green Herts 86 B3
Burnham Market Norf 176 E4
Burnham Norton Norf 176 E4
Burnham-on-Crouch
Essex 88 F6
Burnham-on-Sea Som 43 D10
Burnham Overy Staithe
Norf 176 E4
Burnham Overy Town
Norf 176 E4
Burnham Thorpe Norf 176 E5
Burnhead Aberds 293 D10
Borders 262 F2
Dumfries 247 D9
Dumfries 247 G10
S Ayrs 244 C6
Burnhervie Aberds 293 B9
Burnhill Green Staffs 132 C5
Burnhope Durham 233 B9
Burnhouse N Ayrs 267 E7
Burnhouse Mains
Borders 271 F8
Burniere Corn 10 G5
Burniestrype Moray 302 C3
Burniston N Yorks 227 G10
Burnlee W Yorks 196 F6
Burnley Lancs 204 G2
Burnley Lane Lancs 204 G2
Burnley Wood Lancs 204 G2
Burnmouth Borders 273 C9
Burn Naze Lancs 202 E2
Burn of Cambus
Stirling 285 G11
Burnopfield Durham 242 F5
Burnrigg Cumb 239 F11
Burnsall N Yorks 213 G10
Burn's Green Herts 104 G6
Burnside Aberds 303 E8
Angus 287 B9
E Ayrs 258 G3
Fife 286 G5
Perth 286 E4
Shetland 312 F4
S Lanark 268 C2
T&W 243 G8
W Loth 279 G11
Burnside of Duntrune
Angus 287 D8
Burnstone Devon 24 C4
Burnswark Dumfries 238 B5
Burnt Ash Glos 80 E5
Burntcommon Sur 50 C4
Burntheath Derbys 152 C4
Burnt Heath Derbys 186 F2
Essex 107 F11
Burnt Hill W Berks 64 E5
Burnthouse Corn 3 B7
Burnt Houses Durham 233 G8
Burntisland Fife 280 D4
Burnt Mills Essex 88 G2
Burnt Oak E Sus 37 B8
London 86 G2
Burnton E Ayrs 245 B11
Burnt Tree W Mid 133 E9
Burnturk Fife 287 G7
Burntwood Staffs 133 B11
Burntwood Green
Staffs 133 B11
Burntwood Pentre Flint 166 C3
Burnt Yates N Yorks 214 G5
Burnworthy Som 27 D11
Burnwynd Edin 270 B2
Burpham Sur 50 C4
W Sus 35 F8
Burradon Northumb 251 B11
T&W 243 C7
Burrafirth Shetland 312 B8
Burraland Shetland 312 F5
Shetland 313 J4
Burras Corn 2 C5
Burrastow Shetland 313 J4
Burraton Corn 7 D8
Burraton Coombe Corn 7 D8
Burravoe Shetland 312 F7
Shetland 312 G5
Burray Village Orkney 314 G4
Burrelldales Aberds 303 F7
Burrells Cumb 222 B3
Burrelton Perth 286 D6
Burridge Devon 28 F4
Devon 40 F5
Hants 33 E8
Burrigill Highld 310 F6
Burrill N Yorks 214 B4
Burringham N Lincs 199 F10
Burrington Devon 25 D10
Hereford 115 C8
N Som 44 B3
Burrough End Cambs 124 F2
Burrough Green Cambs 124 F2
Burrough on the Hill
Leics 154 G5
Burroughs Grove Bucks 65 B11
Burroughston Orkney 314 D5
Burrow Devon 14 B5
Som 28 C6
Som 42 E2
Burrowbridge Som 43 G11
Burrow-bridge Som 28 B5
Burrowhill Sur 66 G3
Burrows Cross Sur 50 D5
Burrowsmoor Holt
Notts 172 G2
Burrsville Park Essex 89 B11
Burrswood Kent 52 F4
Burry Swansea 56 C3
Burry Green Swansea 56 C3
Burry Port = *Porth Tywyn*
Carms 74 E6
Burscott Devon 24 C4
Burscough Lancs 194 E2
Burscough Bridge Lancs 194 E2
Bursdon Devon 24 D3
Bursea E Yorks 208 G2
Burshill E Yorks 209 D7
Bursledon Hants 33 F7
Burslem Stoke 168 F5
Burstall Suff 107 C11
Burstallhill Suff 107 B11
Burstock Dorset 28 G6
Burston Devon 26 G2
Norf 142 G2
Staffs 151 C8
Burstow Sur 51 E10
Burstwick E Yorks 201 B8
Burtersett N Yorks 213 B7
Burtholme Cumb 240 E2
Burthorpe Suff 124 E5
Burthwaite Cumb 230 B4
Burtle Som 43 E11
Burtle Hill Som 43 E11
Burtoft Lincs 156 B5
Burton BCP 17 C9
BCP 19 C9
Ches W 167 C8
Ches W 182 G4
Lincs 189 G7
Northumb 264 C5
Pembs 73 D7
Som 29 E8
Som 43 E7
V Glam 58 F4
Wilts 45 G10
Wilts 61 D10
Wrex 166 D5
Burton Agnes E Yorks 218 G2
Burton Bradstock Dorset 16 D5
Burton Corner Lincs 174 F4
Burton Dassett Warks 119 G7
Burton End Cambs 106 B2
Essex 105 G10
Burton Ferry Pembs 73 D7
Burton Fleming
E Yorks 217 E11
Burton Green Essex 106 F6
W Mid 118 B5
Wrex 166 D4
Burton Hastings Warks 135 E8
Burton-in-Kendal
Cumb 211 D10
Burton in Lonsdale
N Yorks 212 E3
Burton Joyce Notts 171 G10
Burton Latimer
N Nhants 121 C8
Burton Lazars Leics 154 F5
Burton-le-Coggles
Lincs 155 D9
Burton Leonard
N Yorks 214 G6
Burton Manor Staffs 151 E8
Burton on the Wolds
Leics 153 E11
Burton Overy Leics 136 D3
Burton Pedwardine
Lincs 173 G10
Burton Pidsea E Yorks 209 G10
Burton Salmon N Yorks 198 B3
Burton Stather N Lincs 199 D11
Burton upon Stather
N Lincs 199 D11
Burton upon Trent
Staffs 152 E5
Burton Westwood
Shrops 132 D2
Burtonwood Warr 183 C9
Burwardsley Ches W 167 D8
Burwarton Shrops 132 F2
Burwash E Sus 37 C11
Burwash Common
E Sus 37 C10
Burwash Weald E Sus 37 C10
Burwell Cambs 123 D11
Lincs 190 F5
Burwen Anglesey 178 C6
Burwick Orkney 314 H4
Shetland 313 J5
Burwood Shrops 131 F9
Burwood Park Sur 66 G6
Bury Cambs 138 G5
Gtr Man 195 E10
Som 26 B6
W Sus 35 E8
Buryas Br Corn 1 D4
Burybank Staffs 151 B7
Bury End Bedford 121 G9
C Beds 104 E2
Worcs 99 D11
Bury Green Herts 86 E4
Herts 105 G8
Bury Hollow W Sus 35 E8
Bury Park Luton 103 G11
Bury St Edmunds Suff 125 E7
Bury's Bank W Berks 64 F3
Burythorpe N Yorks 216 G5
Busbiehill N Ayrs 257 B9
Busbridge Sur 50 E3
Busby E Renf 267 D11
Buscot Oxon 82 F2
Buscott Som 44 F2
Bush Aberds 293 G9
Corn 24 F2
Bush Bank Hereford 115 G9
Bushbury Sur 51 D7
W Mid 133 C8
Bushby Leics 136 C3
Bush Crathie Aberds 292 D4
Bush End Essex 87 B9
Bush Estate Norf 161 D8
Bushey Dorset 18 E5
Herts 85 G10
Bushey Ground Oxon 82 D4
Bushey Heath Herts 85 G11
Bushey Mead London 67 F8
Bushfield Cumb 249 G11
Bush Green Norf 141 D10
Norf 142 F4
Suff 125 F8
Bush Hill Park London 86 F4
Bushley Worcs 99 E7
Bushley Green Worcs 99 E7
Bushmead Bedford 122 E2
Bushmoor Shrops 131 F8
Bushton Wilts 62 D5
Bushy Common Norf 159 G9
Bushy Hill Sur 50 C4
Busk Cumb 231 C8
Gtr Man 196 F2
Buslingthorpe Lincs 189 D9
Bussage Glos 80 E5
Bussex Som 43 F11
Busta Shetland 312 G5
Bustard Green Essex 106 F2
Bustard's Green Norf 142 E3
Bustatoun Orkney 314 A7
Busveal Corn 4 G4
Butcher's Common Norf 160 E6
Butcher's Cross E Sus 37 B9
Butcombe N Som 60 G4
Butetown Cardiff 59 D7
Bute Town Caerph 77 D10
Butlane Head Shrops 149 G8
Butleigh Som 44 G4
Butleigh Wootton Som 44 G4
Butlersbank Shrops 149 E11
Butlers Cross Bucks 85 G7
Butler's Cross Bucks 84 D4
Butler's End Warks 134 G4
Butler's Hill Notts 171 F8
Butlers Marston Warks 118 G6
Butley Suff 127 G7
Butley High Corner Suff 109 B7
Butley Low Corner Suff 109 B7
Butley Town Ches E 184 F6
Butlocks Heath Hants 33 F7
Butter Bank Staffs 151 E7
Butterburn Cumb 240 C5
Buttercrambe N Yorks 207 B10
Butteriss Gate Corn 2 C6
Butterknowle Durham 233 F8
Butterleigh Devon 27 F7
Butterley Derbys 170 C4
Derbys 170 E6
Buttermere Cumb 220 B3
Wilts 63 G10
Butterrow Glos 80 E5
Butters Green Staffs 168 E4
Buttershaw W Yorks 196 B6
Butterstone Perth 286 C4
Butterton Staffs 168 G4
Staffs 169 D9
Butterwick Cumb 221 B10
Durham 234 F3
Lincs 174 G5
N Yorks 216 D4
N Yorks 217 E9
Butteryhaugh Northumb 250 E4
Butt Green Ches E 167 E11
Buttington Powys 130 B5
Butt Lane Staffs 168 E4
Buttonbridge Shrops 116 B4
Button Haugh Green
Suff 125 D9
Buttonoak Worcs 116 B5
Button's Green Suff 125 G8
Butts Devon 14 D2
Buttsash Hants 32 F6
Buttsbear Cross Corn 24 G3
Buttsbury Essex 87 F11
Butts Green Essex 105 E9
Butt's Green Essex 88 E3
Hants 32 B4
Buttsole Kent 55 C10
Butt Yeats Lancs 211 F11
Buxhall Suff 125 F10
Buxhall Fen Street
Suff 125 F10
Buxley Borders 272 E6
Buxted E Sus 37 C7
Buxton Derbys 185 G9
Norf 160 E4
Buxworth Derbys 185 E8
Bwcle = *Buckley* Flint 166 C3
Bwlch Flint 181 G11
Powys 96 G2
Bwlch-derwin Gwyn 163 F7
Bwlchgwyn Wrex 166 E3
Bwlch-Llan Ceredig 111 F11
Bwlchnewydd Carms 93 G7
Bwlch-newydd Carms 93 G7
Bwlchtocyn Gwyn 144 D6
Bwlch-y-cibau Powys 148 F3
Bwlch-y-cwm Cardiff 58 C6
Bwlchyddar Powys 148 E3
Bwlch-y-fadfa Ceredig 93 B8
Bwlch-y-ffridd Powys 129 D11
Bwlchygroes Pembs 92 D4
Bwlchyllyn Gwyn 163 D8
Bwlch-y-Plain Powys 114 B4
Bwlch-y-sarnau Powys 113 C10
Bybrook Kent 54 E4
Bycross Hereford 97 C7
Byeastwood Bridgend 58 C2
Byebush Aberds 303 F7
Bye Green Bucks 84 C5
Byerhope Northumb 232 B3
Byermoor T&W 242 F5
Byers Green Durham 233 E10
Byfield W Nhants 119 G10
Byfleet Sur 66 G5
Byford Hereford 97 C7
Byford Common Hereford 97 C7
Bygrave Herts 104 D5
Byker T&W 243 E7
Byland Abbey N Yorks 215 D10
Bylchau Conwy 165 C7
Byley Ches W 168 B2
Bynea Carms 56 B4
Byram N Yorks 198 B3
Byrness Northumb 251 C7
Bythorn Cambs 121 B11
Byton Hereford 115 E7
Byton Hand Hereford 115 E7
Bywell Northumb 242 E2
Byworth W Sus 35 C7

C

Cabbacott Devon 24 C6
Cabbage Hill Brack 65 E11
Cabharstadh W Isles 304 F5
Cabin Shrops 130 F6
Cablea Perth 286 D3
Cabourne Lincs 200 G6
Cabrach Argyll 274 G5
Moray 302 G3
Cabrich Highld 300 E5
Cabus Lancs 202 D5
Cackle Hill Lincs 157 D7
Cackleshaw W Yorks 204 F6
Cackle Street E Sus 23 B11
E Sus 37 B7
E Sus 38 D4
Cadbolt Highld 301 B8
Cadbury Devon 26 G6
Cadbury Barton Devon 25 D11
Cadbury Heath S Glos 61 E7
Cadder E Dunb 278 G2
Cadderlie Argyll 284 D4
Caddington C Beds 85 B9
Caddleton Argyll 275 B8
Caddonfoot Borders 261 C10
Caddonlee Borders 261 B10
Cadeby Leics 135 C8
S Yorks 198 G4
Cadeleigh Devon 26 F6
Cademuir Borders 260 B6
Cader Denb 165 C8
Cade Street E Sus 37 C10
Cadger Path Angus 287 B8
Cad Green Som 28 D4
Cadgwith Corn 2 G6
Cadham Fife 286 G6
Cadishead Gtr Man 184 C2
Cadle Swansea 56 B6
Cadley Lancs 202 G6
Wilts 47 C8
Wilts 63 F8
Cadmore End Bucks 84 G3
Cadnam Hants 32 E3
Cadney N Lincs 200 G4
Cadney Bank Wrex 149 C9
Cadole Flint 166 C2
Cadoxton V Glam 58 F6
Cadoxton-Juxta-Neath
Neath 57 B9
Cadshaw Blackburn 195 D8
Cadwell Herts 104 E3
Cadzow S Lanark 268 E4
Caehopkin Gwyn 163 C7
Cae Clyd Gwyn 164 G2
Cae-gors Carms 75 E9
Caehopkin Powys 76 C4
Caemorgan Ceredig 92 B3
Caenby Lincs 189 D8
Caenby Corner Lincs 189 D7
Caerau Bridgend 57 C11
Cardiff 58 D6
Caerau Park Newport 59 B9
Cae'r-bont Powys 76 C4
Cae'r-bryn Carms 75 C9
Caerdeon Gwyn 146 F2
Caer-Estyn Wrex 166 D4
Caerfarchell Pembs 90 F5
Caer-Farchell Pembs 90 F5
Caerffili = *Caerphilly*
Caerph 59 B7
Caerfyrddin = *Carmarthen*
Carms 93 G8
Caergeiliog Anglesey 178 F4
Caergwrle Flint 166 D4
Caergybi = *Holyhead*
Anglesey 178 E2
Caerhendy Neath 57 C9
Caerhun Gwyn 163 B9
Cae'r-Lan Powys 76 C4
Caerleon Newport 78 G4
Caer Llan Mon 79 D7
Caermead V Glam 58 F3
Caermeini Pembs 92 E2
Caernarfon Gwyn 163 C7
Caerphilly = *Caerffili*
Caerph 59 B7
Caersws Powys 129 E10
Caerwedros Ceredig 111 F7
Caerwent Mon 79 G7
Caerwent Brook Mon 60 B3
Caerwych Gwyn 146 B2
Caerwys Flint 181 G10
Caethle Gwyn 128 D2
Cage Green Kent 52 D5
Caggan Highld 291 B10
Caggle Street Mon 78 B5
Cailness Stirling 285 G7
Caim Anglesey 179 E10
Cainscross Glos 80 D4
Caio Carms 94 D3
Cairinis W Isles 296 E4
Cairisiadar W Isles 304 E2
Cairminis W Isles 296 C6
Cairnbaan Argyll 275 D9
Cairnbanno Ho Aberds 303 E8
Cairnborrow Aberds 302 E4
Cairnbrogie Aberds 303 G8
Cairnbulg Castle
Aberds 303 C10
Cairncross Angus 292 F6
Borders 273 C7
Cairnderry Dumfries 236 B5
Cairndow Argyll 284 F5
Cairness Aberds 303 C10
Cairneyhill Fife 279 D10
Cairnfield Ho Moray 302 C4
Cairngaan Dumfries 236 F3
Cairngarroch Dumfries 236 E2
Cairnhill Aberds 302 F6
Aberds 303 D7
N Lanark 268 C5
Cairnie Aberds 293 C10
Aberds 302 E4
Cairnlea S Ayrs 244 G6
Cairnleith Crofts Aberds 303 F9
Cairnmuir Aberds 303 C9
Cairnorrie Aberds 303 E8
Cairnpark Aberds 293 B10
Dumfries 247 D9
Cairnryan Dumfries 236 C2
Cairnton Orkney 314 F3
Cairston Orkney 314 E2
Caister-on-Sea Norf 161 G10
Caistor Lincs 200 G6
Caistor St Edmund Norf 142 C4
Caistron Northumb 251 C11
Caitha Bowland Borders 271 G9
Cakebole Worcs 117 C7
Calais Street Suff 107 D9
Calanais W Isles 304 E4
Calbost W Isles 305 G6
Calbourne IoW 20 D4
Calceby Lincs 190 F5
Calcoed Flint 181 G11
Calcot Glos 81 C9
W Berks 65 E7
Calcot Row W Berks 65 E7
Calcott Kent 71 G7
Shrops 149 G8
Calcott's Green Glos 80 B3
Calcutt N Yorks 206 B2
Wilts 81 G10
Caldback Shetland 312 C8
Caldbeck Cumb 230 D2
Caldbergh N Yorks 213 B11
Caldecote Cambs 122 F6
Cambs 138 F2
Herts 104 D4
Warks 135 E7
W Nhants 120 G3
Caldecote Hill Herts 85 G11
Caldecott N Nhants 121 D9
Oxon 83 F7
Rutland 137 E7
Caldecotte M Keynes 103 D7
Calder Cumb 219 E10
Calder Bridge Cumb 219 D10
Calderbrook Gtr Man 196 D2
Caldercruix N Lanark 268 B6
Calder Grove W Yorks 197 D10
Calder Hall Cumb 219 E10
Calder Mains Highld 310 D4
Caldermill S Lanark 268 G3
Caldermoor Gtr Man 196 D2
Calderstones Mers 182 D6
Calder Vale Lancs 202 D6
Calderwood S Lanark 268 D2
Caldhame Angus 287 C8
Caldicot = *Cil-y-coed*
Mon 60 B3
Caldmore W Mid 133 D10
Caldwell Derbys 152 F5
N Yorks 224 C3
Caldy Mers 182 D2
Caledrhydiau Ceredig 111 G9
Cale Green Gtr Man 184 D5
Calenick Corn 4 G6
Caleys Fields Worcs 100 C4
Calf Heath Staffs 133 B8
Calford Green Suff 106 B3
Calfsound Orkney 314 C5
Calgary Argyll 288 D5
Caliach Argyll 288 D5
Califer Moray 301 D10
California Cambs 139 G10
Falk 279 F8
Norf 161 G10
Suff 108 C3
W Mid 133 G10
Calke Derbys 153 E7
Callakille Highld 298 D6
Callaly Northumb 252 B3
Callander Stirling 285 G10
Callandrode Stirling 285 G10
Callands Warr 183 C9
Callaughton Shrops 132 D2
Callendar Park Falk 279 F7
Callert Ho Highld 290 G2
Callerton T&W 242 D5
Callerton Lane End
T&W 242 D5
Callestick Corn 4 E5
Calligarry Highld 295 E8
Callington Corn 7 B7
Callingwood Staffs 152 E3
Callow Derbys 170 E3
Hereford 97 E9
Callow End Worcs 98 B6
Callow Hill Mon 79 B8
Som 44 E4
Wilts 62 C4
Worcs 116 C4
Callow Marsh Hereford 98 B3
Callows Grave Worcs 115 D11
Calmore Hants 32 E4
Calmsden Glos 81 D8
Calne Wilts 62 E4
Calne Marsh Wilts 62 E4
Calow Derbys 186 G6
Calow Green Derbys 170 B6
Calrofold Ches E 184 G6
Calshot Hants 33 G7
Calstock Corn 7 B8
Calstone Wellington
Wilts 62 F4
Calthorpe Norf 160 C3
Oxon 101 D9
Calthwaite Cumb 230 C5
Calton Glasgow 268 C2
N Yorks 204 B4
Staffs 169 E10
Calton Lees Derbys 170 B3
Calvadnack Corn 2 B5
Calveley Ches E 167 D9
Calver Derbys 186 G2
Calverhall Shrops 150 B2
Calver Hill Hereford 97 B7
Calverleigh Devon 26 E6
Calverley W Yorks 205 F10
Calver Sough Derbys 186 F2
Calvert Bucks 102 G3
Calverton M Keynes 102 D5
Notts 171 F10
Calvine Perth 291 G10
Calvo Cumb 238 G4
Cam Glos 80 F3
Camaghael Highld 290 F3
Camas an Staca Argyll 274 G5
Camas-luinie Highld 295 C11
Camasnacroise Highld 289 D10
Camas Salach Highld 289 C8
Camastianavaig Highld 295 B7
Camasunary Highld 295 D7
Camault Muir Highld 300 E5
Camb Shetland 312 D7
Camber E Sus 39 D7
Camberley Sur 65 G11
Camberwell London 67 D10
Camblesforth N Yorks 199 B7
Cambo Northumb 252 F2
Cambois Northumb 253 G8
Camborne Corn 4 G3
Cambourne Cambs 122 F6
Cambridge Borders 271 F11
Cambs 123 F9
Glos 80 E3
W Yorks 205 D10
Cambridge Batch N Som 60 F4
Cambridge Town
Southend 70 C2
Cambrose Corn 4 F3
Cambus Clack 279 C7
Cambusavie Farm
Highld 309 K7
Cambusbarron Stirling 278 C5
Cambusdrenny Stirling 278 C5
Cambuskenneth Stirling 278 C6
Cambuslang S Lanark 268 D2
Cambusmore Lodge
Highld 309 K7
Cambusnethan
N Lanark 268 D6
Camden London 67 C9
Camden Hill Kent 53 F9
Camden Park Kent 52 F5
Cameley Bath 44 B6
Camelford Corn 11 E8
Camel Green Dorset 31 E10
Camelon Falk 279 E7
Camelsdale Sur 49 G11
Camer Kent 69 F7
Cameron Fife 280 B6
Cameron Bridge Fife 280 B6
Camerory Highld 301 F10
Camer's Green Worcs 98 D5
Camerton Bath 45 B7
Cumb 228 E6
E Yorks 201 B8
Camghouran Perth 285 B9
Cammachmore Aberds 293 D11
Cammeringham Lincs 188 E6
Camnant Powys 113 F11
Camoquhill Stirling 277 D10
Camore Highld 309 K7
Camp Lincs 172 E5
Campbeltown Argyll 255 E8
Camp Corner Oxon 83 E10
Camperdown T&W 243 C7
Camphill Derbys 185 F11
Camp Hill N Yorks 214 C6
Pembs 73 C10
Warks 134 E6
W Yorks 196 D5
Campion Hills Warks 118 D6
Campions Essex 87 C7
Cample Dumfries 247 E9
Campmuir Perth 286 D6
Campsall S Yorks 198 E4
Campsea Ashe Suff 126 F6
Camps End Cambs 106 C2
Campsey Ash Suff 126 F6
Campsfield Oxon 83 B7
Camps Heath Suff 143 E10
Campton C Beds 104 D2
Camptoun E Loth 281 F10
Camptown Borders 262 G5
Camp Town W Yorks 206 F2
Camquhart Argyll 275 E10
Camrose Pembs 91 G8
Camserney Perth 286 C2
Camster Highld 310 E6
Camuschoirk Highld 289 C9
Camuscross Highld 295 D8
Camusnagaul Highld 290 F2
Highld 307 L5
Camusrory Highld 295 F10
Camusteel Highld 299 E7
Camusterrach Highld 299 E7
Camusvrachan Perth 285 C10
Canada Hants 32 D3
Lincs 200 G6
Canadia E Sus 38 D2
Canal Foot Cumb 210 D6
Canal Side S Yorks 199 E7
Canbus Clack 279 C7
Candacraig Ho Aberds 292 B5
Candlesby Lincs 175 B7
Candle Street Suff 125 C10
Candy Mill S Lanark 269 G11
Cane End Oxon 65 D7
Caneheath E Sus 23 D9
Canewdon Essex 88 G5
Canford Bottom Dorset 31 G8
Canford Cliffs BCP 19 D7
Canford Heath BCP 18 C6
Canford Magna BCP 18 B6
Cangate Norf 160 F6
Canham's Green Suff 125 D11
Canholes Derbys 185 G8
Canisbay Highld 310 B7
Canklow S Yorks 186 C6
Canley W Mid 118 B6
Cann Dorset 30 C5
Cannalidgey Corn 5 B8
Cannard's Grave Som 44 E6
Cann Common Dorset 30 C5
Cannich Highld 300 F3
Cannington Som 43 F9
Canning Town London 68 C2
Cannock Staffs 133 B9
Cannock Wood Staffs 151 G10
Cannon's Green Essex 87 D9
Cannop Glos 79 C10
Canonbie Dumfries 239 B9
Canon Bridge Hereford 97 C8
Canonbury London 67 C10
Canon Frome Hereford 98 C3
Canon Pyon Hereford 97 B9
Canons Ashby
W Nhants 119 G11
Canonsgrove Som 28 C2
Canons Park London 85 G11
Canon's Town Corn 2 B2
Canterbury Kent 54 B6
Cantley Norf 143 C7
S Yorks 198 G6
Cantlop Shrops 131 B10
Canton Cardiff 59 D7
Cantraybruich Highld 301 E7
Cantraydoune Highld 301 E7
Cantraywood Highld 301 E7
Cantsfield Lancs 212 E2
Canvey Island Essex 69 C9
Canwick Lincs 173 B7
Canworthy Water Corn 11 C10
Caol Highld 290 F3
Caolas Argyll 288 E2
W Isles 297 M2
Caolas Fhlodaigh
W Isles 296 F4
Caolas Liubharsaigh
W Isles 297 G4
Caolas Scalpaigh
W Isles 305 J4
Caolas Stocinis W Isles 305 J3
Caol Ila Argyll 274 F5
Caolasnacon Highld 290 G3
Capel Carms 75 E8
Kent 52 E6
Sur 51 E7
Capel Bangor Ceredig 128 G3
Capel Betws Lleucu
Ceredig 112 F2
Capel Carmel Gwyn 144 D3
Capel Coch Anglesey 179 E7
Capel Cross Kent 53 E8
Capel Curig Conwy 164 D2
Capel Cynon Ceredig 93 B7
Capel Dewi Carms 93 G9
Ceredig 93 C9
Ceredig 128 G2
Capel Garmon Conwy 164 D4
Capel Green Suff 109 B7
Capel-gwyn Anglesey 178 F4
Capel Gwyn Carms 93 G9
Capel Gwynfe Carms 94 G4
Capel Hendre Carms 75 C9
Capel Hermon Gwyn 146 D4
Capel Isaac Carms 93 F11
Capel Iwan Carms 92 D5
Capel-le-Ferne Kent 55 F8
Capel Llanilltern Cardiff 58 C5
Capel Mawr Anglesey 178 G6
Capel Newydd = *Newchapel*
Pembs 92 D4
Capel Parc Anglesey 178 D6
Capel St Andrew Suff 109 B7
Capel St Mary Suff 107 D11
Capel Seion Carms 75 C8
Ceredig 112 B2
Capel Siloam Conwy 164 E4
Capel Tygwydd Ceredig 92 C5
Capel Uchaf Gwyn 162 F6
Capelulo Conwy 180 F2
Capel-y-ffin Powys 96 E5
Capel-y-graig Gwyn 163 B8
Capenhurst Ches W 182 G5
Capernwray Lancs 211 E10
Capheaton Northumb 252 G2
Capland Som 28 D4
Cappercleuch Borders 260 E6
Capplegill Dumfries 248 B4
Capstone Medway 69 F9
Captain Fold Gtr Man 195 E11
Capton Devon 8 E6
Som 42 F5
Caputh Perth 286 D4
Caradon Town Corn 11 G11
Carbis Corn 5 D10
Carbis Bay Corn 2 B2
Carbost Highld 294 B5
Highld 298 E4
Carbrain N Lanark 278 G5
Carbrook S Yorks 186 D5
Carbrooke Norf 141 C9
Carburton Notts 187 G10
Carcant Borders 271 E7
Carcary Angus 287 B10
Carclaze Corn 5 E10
Carclew Corn 3 B7
Car Colston Notts 172 G2
Carcroft S Yorks 198 E4
Cardenden Fife 280 C4
Cardeston Shrops 149 G7
Cardew Cumb 230 B2
Cardewlees Cumb 239 G8
Cardiff Cardiff 59 D7
Cardigan = *Aberteifi*
Ceredig 92 B3
Cardinal's Green Cambs 106 B2
Cardington Bedford 103 B11
Shrops 131 D10
Cardinham Corn 6 B2
Cardonald Glasgow 267 C10
Cardow Moray 301 E11
Cardrona Borders 261 B8
Cardross Argyll 276 F6
Cardurnock Cumb 238 F5
Careby Lincs 155 F10
Careston Angus 293 G7
Careston Castle Angus 287 B9
Care Village Leics 136 D4
Carew Pembs 73 E8
Carew Cheriton Pembs 73 E8
Carew Newton Pembs 73 E8
Carey Hereford 97 E11
Carey Park Corn 6 E4
Carfin N Lanark 268 D5
Carfrae E Loth 271 B11
Carfury Corn 1 C4
Cargate Common Norf 142 E2
Cargenbridge Dumfries 237 B11
Cargill Perth 286 D5
Cargo Cumb 239 F9
Cargo Fleet Mbro 234 G6
Cargreen Corn 7 C8
Carham Northumb 263 B8
Carhampton Som 42 E4
Carharrack Corn 4 G4
Carie Perth 285 B10
Perth 285 D10
Carines Corn 4 D5
Carisbrooke IoW 20 D5
Cark Cumb 211 D7
Carkeel Corn 7 C8
Carlabhagh W Isles 304 D4
Carland Cross Corn 5 E7
Carlbury N Yorks 224 B4
Carlby Lincs 155 G11
Carlecotes S Yorks 197 G7
Carleen Corn 2 C4
Carlenrig Borders 249 C9
Carlesmoor N Yorks 214 E3
Carleton Cumb 219 D10
Cumb 230 F6
Cumb 239 G10
Lancs 202 F2
N Yorks 204 D5
W Yorks 198 C3
Carleton Forehoe Norf 141 B11
Carleton Hall Cumb 219 F11
Carleton-in-Craven
N Yorks 204 D5
Carleton Rode Norf 142 E2
Carleton St Peter Norf 142 C6
Carley Hill T&W 243 F9
Carlidnack Corn 3 D7
Carlincraig Aberds 302 E6
Carlingcott Bath 45 B7
Carlinghow W Yorks 197 C8
Carlingwark Devon 27 E11
Carlin How Redcar 226 B4
Carlisle Cumb 239 F10
Carloggas Corn 5 B7
Corn 5 E9
Carloonan Argyll 284 F4
Carlops Borders 270 D3
Carlton Bedford 121 F9
Cambs 124 G2
Leics 135 C7
Notts 171 G10
N Yorks 198 C6
N Yorks 213 C11
N Yorks 216 B2
N Yorks 224 C3
Stockton 234 G3
Suff 127 E7
S Yorks 197 E11
W Yorks 197 B10
Carlton Colville Suff 143 F10
Carlton Curlieu Leics 136 D3
Carlton Green Cambs 124 G2
Carlton Husthwaite
N Yorks 215 D9
Carlton in Cleveland
N Yorks 225 E10
Carlton in Lindrick
Notts 187 E9
Carlton le Moorland
Lincs 172 D6
Carlton Miniott N Yorks 215 C7
Carlton on Trent Notts 172 C3
Carlton Purlieus
N Nhants 136 F6
Carlton Scroop Lincs 172 G6
Carluddon Corn 5 D10
Carluke S Lanark 268 E6
Carlyon Bay Corn 5 E11
Carmarthen = *Caerfyrddin*
Carms 93 G8
Carmel Anglesey 178 E5
Carms 75 B9
Flint 181 F11
Gwyn 163 E7
Powys 113 D11
Carmichael S Lanark 259 B10
Carminow Cross Corn 5 B11
Carmont Aberds 293 E10
Carmunnock Glasgow 268 D2
Carmyle Glasgow 268 C2
Carmyllie Angus 287 C9
Carnaby E Yorks 218 F2
Carnach Highld 299 G10
Highld 307 K5
W Isles 305 J4
Carnachy Highld 308 D7
Càrnais W Isles 304 E2
Càrnan W Isles 297 G3
Carn Arthen Corn 2 B5
Carnbahn Perth 285 C10
Carnbee Fife 287 G9
Carnbo Perth 286 G4
Carnbrea Corn 4 G3
Carn Brea Village Corn 4 G3
Carnbroe N Lanark 268 C4
Carndu Highld 295 C10
Carnduff S Lanark 268 F3
Carnduncan Argyll 274 G3
Carne Corn 3 B10
Corn 3 E7
Corn 5 D9
Carnebone Corn 2 C6
Carnedd Powys 129 E10
Carnetown Rhondda 77 G9
Carnforth Lancs 211 E9
Lancs 211 E10
Carnglas Swansea 56 C6
Carn-gorm Highld 295 C11
Carnhedryn Pembs 90 F6
Carnhedryn Uchaf Pembs 90 F5
Carnhell Green Corn 2 B4
Carnhot Corn 4 F4
Carnkie Corn 2 B5
Corn 2 C6
Carnkief Corn 4 E5
Carno Powys 129 D9
Carnoch Highld 300 D2
Highld 300 F3
Carnock Fife 279 D10
Carnon Downs Corn 4 G5
Carnousie Aberds 302 D6
Carnoustie Angus 287 D9
Carnsmerry Corn 5 D10
Carn Towan Corn 1 D3
Carntyne Glasgow 268 B2
Carnwadric E Renf 267 D10
Carnwath S Lanark 269 F9
Carnyorth Corn 1 C3
Caroe Corn 11 C9
Carol Green W Mid 118 B5
Carpalla Corn 5 E9
Carpenders Park Herts 85 G10
Carpenter's Hill Worcs 117 C11
Carperby N Yorks 213 B10
Carpley Green N Yorks 213 B8
Carr Gtr Man 195 D9
S Yorks 187 C8
Carradale Argyll 255 D9
Carragraich W Isles 305 J3
Carr Bank Cumb 211 D9
Carrbridge Highld 301 G9
Carrbrook Gtr Man 196 G3
Carr Cross Lancs 193 E11
Carreglefn Anglesey 178 D5
Carreg-wen Pembs 92 C4
Carreg y Garth Gwyn 163 B9
Carr Gate W Yorks 197 C10
Carr Green Gtr Man 184 D2
Carr Hill T&W 243 E7
Carrhouse Devon 26 F3
Carr Houses Mers 193 G10
Carrick Argyll 275 E10
Dumfries 237 D7
Fife 287 E8
Carrick Castle Argyll 276 C3
Carrick Ho Orkney 314 C5
Carriden Falk 279 E10
Carrington Gtr Man 184 C2
Lincs 174 E4
Midloth 270 C6
Nottingham 171 G9
Carrog Conwy 164 F3
Denb 165 G10
Carroch Dumfries 246 E5

Carrog Conwy 164 F3
Denb 165 G10
Carroglen Perth 285 E11
Carrol Highld 311 J2
Carron Falk 279 E7
Moray 302 E2
Carronbridge Dumfries 247 D9
Carron Bridge Stirling 278 E4
Carronshore Falk 279 E7
Carrot Angus 287 C8
Carroway Head Staffs 134 D3
Carrow Hill Mon 78 G6
Carrshield Northumb 232 B2
Carrutherstown
Dumfries 238 C4
Carr Vale Derbys 171 B7
Carrville Durham 234 C2
Carry Argyll 275 G10
Carsaig Argyll 275 E8
Argyll 289 G7
Carscreugh Dumfries 236 D4
Carsegowan Dumfries 236 D6
Carse Gray Angus 287 B8
Carse Ho Argyll 275 G8
Carseriggan Dumfries 236 C5
Carsethorn Dumfries 237 D11
Carshalton London 67 G9
Carshalton Beeches
London 67 G9
Carshalton on the Hill
London 67 G9
Carsington Derbys 170 E3
Carskiey Argyll 255 G7
Carsluith Dumfries 236 D6
Carsphairn Dumfries 246 E3
Carstairs S Lanark 269 F8
Carstairs Junction
S Lanark 269 F9
Carswell Marsh Oxon 82 F4
Cartbridge Sur 50 B4
Carterhaugh Borders 261 D10
Carter Knowle S Yorks 186 E4
Carter's Clay Hants 32 C4
Carter's Green Essex 87 C8
Carter's Hill Wokingham 65 F9
Carterspiece Glos 79 C9
Carterton Oxon 82 D3
Carterway Heads
Northumb 242 G2
Carthamartha Corn 12 F3
Carthew Corn 2 B5
Corn 5 D10
Carthorpe N Yorks 214 C6
Cartington Northumb 252 C2
Cartland S Lanark 269 F7
Cartledge Derbys 186 F4
Cartmel Cumb 211 D7
Cartmel Fell Cumb 211 B8
Cartsdyke Invclyd 276 F5
Cartworth W Yorks 196 F6
Carty Port Dumfries 236 C6
Carway Carms 75 D7
Carwinley Cumb 239 C10
Carwynnen Corn 2 B5
Cary Fitzpaine Som 29 B9
Carzantic Corn 12 E3
Carzield Dumfries 247 G11
Carzise Corn 2 C3
Cascob Powys 114 D4
Cashes Green Glos 80 D4
Cashlie Perth 285 C8
Cashmoor Dorset 31 E7
Cas Mael = *Puncheston*
Pembs 91 F10
Cassey Compton Glos 81 C9
Cassington Oxon 83 C7
Cassop Durham 234 D2
Castallack Corn 1 D5
Castell Conwy 164 B3
Denb 165 B10
Castellau Rhondda 58 B5
Castell-Howell Ceredig 93 B8
Castell nedd = *Neath*
Neath 57 B8
Castell Newydd Emlyn
= *Newcastle Emlyn*
Carms 92 C6
Castell-y-bwch Torf 78 G3
Castell-y-rhingyll Carms 75 C9
Casterton Cumb 212 D2
Castle Devon 28 G4
Som 27 B9
Castle Acre Norf 158 F6
Castle Ashby W Nhants 121 F7
Castle Bolton N Yorks 223 G10
Castle Bromwich W Mid 134 F2
Castle Bytham Lincs 155 F9
Castlebythe Pembs 91 F10
Castle Caereinion
Powys 130 B3
Castle Camps Cambs 106 C2
Castle Carlton Lincs 190 E5
Castle Carrock Cumb 240 F2
Castlecary N Lanark 278 F5
Castle Cary Som 44 G6
Castle Combe Wilts 61 D10
Castlecraig Highld 301 C8
Castle Craig Borders 270 G2
Castlecroft Staffs 133 D7
Castle Donington Leics 153 D8
Castle Douglas Dumfries 237 C9
Castle Eaton Swindon 81 F10
Castle Eden Durham 234 D4
Castle End Pboro 138 B2
Castlefairn Dumfries 246 F6
Castlefields Halton 183 E8
Castle Fields Shrops 149 G10
Castle Forbes Aberds 293 B8
Castleford W Yorks 198 B2
Castle Frome Hereford 98 B3
Castle Gate Corn 1 C5
Castlegreen Shrops 130 F6
Castle Green London 68 C3
Sur 66 G3
S Yorks 197 G9
Castle Gresley Derbys 152 F5
Castlehead Renfs 267 C9
Castle Heaton Northumb 273 G8
Castle Hedingham
Essex 106 D5
Castlehill Argyll 254 B4
Borders 260 B6
Highld 310 C5
S Ayrs 257 E9
W Dunb 277 F7
Castle Hill E Sus 37 B9
Gtr Man 184 C6
Kent 53 E7
Suff 108 B3
Worcs 116 F5
Castle Huntly Perth 287 E7
Castle Kennedy
Dumfries 236 D3
Castlemaddy Dumfries 246 F3
Castlemartin Pembs 72 F6
Castlemilk Dumfries 238 B5
Glasgow 268 D2
Castlemorris Pembs 91 E8
Castlemorton Worcs 98 D5
Castle O'er Dumfries 248 E6
Castlerigg Cumb 229 G11
Castle Rising Norf 158 E3
Castleside Durham 233 B7
Castle Street W Yorks 196 C3
Castle Stuart Highld 301 E7
Castlethorpe M Keynes 102 C6
N Lincs 200 F3
Castleton Angus 287 C7
Argyll 275 E9
Derbys 185 E11
Gtr Man 195 E11
Moray 301 G11
Newport 59 C9
N Yorks 226 D3
Castleton Village Highld 300 E6
Castle Toward Argyll 266 B2
Castletown Ches W 166 E6
Cumb 230 E6
Dorset 17 G9
Highld 301 E7
Highld 310 C5
IoM 192 F3
Staffs 151 E8
T&W 243 F9
Castle Town W Sus 36 E2
Castletump Glos 98 F4
Castle-upon-Alun
V Glam 58 E2
Castle Vale W Mid 134 E2
Castleweary Borders 249 C10
Castlewigg Dumfries 236 E6
Castley N Yorks 205 D11
Castling's Heath Suff 107 C9
Caston Norf 141 D9
Castor Pboro 138 D2
Caswell Swansea 56 D5
Catacol N Ayrs 255 C10
Cat Bank Cumb 220 F6
Catbrain S Glos 60 C5
Catbrook Mon 79 E8
Catch Flint 182 G2
Catchall Corn 1 D4
Catchems Corner
W Mid 118 B4
Catchems End Worcs 116 B5
Catchgate Durham 242 G5
Catchory Highld 310 D6
Catcleugh Northumb 250 C6
Catcliffe S Yorks 186 D6
Catcomb Wilts 62 D4
Catcott Som 43 F11
Caterham Sur 51 B10
Catfield Norf 161 E7
Catfirth Shetland 313 H6
Catford London 67 E11
Catforth Lancs 202 F5
Cathays Cardiff 59 D7
Cathays Park Cardiff 59 D7
Cathcart Glasgow 267 C11
Cathedine Powys 96 F2
Catherine-de-Barnes
W Mid 134 G3
Catherine Slack
W Yorks 196 B5
Catherington Hants 33 E11
Catherton Shrops 116 B3
Cat Hill S Yorks 197 F8
Cathiron Warks 119 B9
Catholes Cumb 222 G3
Cathpair Borders 271 F9
Catisfield Hants 33 F8
Catley Lane Head
Gtr Man 195 D11
Catley Southfield
Hereford 98 C3
Catlodge Highld 291 D8
Catlowdy Cumb 239 B11
Catmere End Essex 105 D9
Catmore W Berks 64 C3
Caton Devon 13 G11
Lancs 211 G10
Caton Green Lancs 211 F10
Catrine E Ayrs 258 D2
Cat's Ash Newport 78 G5
Cat's Common Norf 160 E6
Cats Edge Staffs 169 E7
Catsfield E Sus 38 E2
Catsfield Stream E Sus 38 E2
Catsgore Som 29 B8
Catsham Som 44 G5
Catshaw S Yorks 197 G8
Catshill W Mid 133 B11
Worcs 117 C9
Cat's Hill Cross Staffs 150 C6
Catslackburn Borders 261 D8
Catslip Oxon 65 B8
Catstree Shrops 132 D4
Cattadale Argyll 274 G4
Cattal N Yorks 206 C4
Cattawade Suff 108 E2
Cattedown Plym 7 E9
Catterall Lancs 202 E5
Catterick N Yorks 224 F4
Catterick Bridge
N Yorks 224 F4
Catterick Garrison
N Yorks 224 F3
Catterlen Cumb 230 E5
Catterline Aberds 293 F10
Catterton N Yorks 206 D6
Catteshall Sur 50 E3
Catthorpe Leics 119 B11
Cattistock Dorset 17 B7
Cattle End W Nhants 102 C3
Catton Northumb 241 F8
N Yorks 215 D7
Catwick E Yorks 209 D8
Catworth Cambs 121 C11
Caudle Green Glos 80 C6
Caudlesprings Norf 141 C8
Caulcott C Beds 103 C9
Oxon 101 G10
Cauld Borders 261 G11
Cauldcoats Holdings
Falk 279 F10
Cauldcots Angus 287 C10
Cauldhame Stirling 278 C2
Cauldmill Borders 262 G2
Cauldon Staffs 169 F9
Cauldon Lowe Staffs 169 F9
Cauldwells Aberds 303 D7
Caulkerbush Dumfries 237 D11
Caulside Dumfries 249 G10
Caundle Marsh Dorset 29 E11
Caunsall Worcs 132 G6
Caunton Notts 172 D2
Causeway Hants 33 E11
Hants 34 C2
Mon 60 B2
Causewayend S Lanark 260 B2
Causeway End Cumb 210 C6
Cumb 211 B9
Dumfries 236 C6
Essex 87 B11
Wilts 62 C4
Causeway Foot W Yorks 197 E7
W Yorks 205 G7
Causeway Green W Mid 133 F9
Causewayhead Cumb 238 G4
Stirling 278 B6
Causewaywood Shrops 131 D10
Causey Durham 242 F6
Causeyend Aberds 293 B11
Causey Park Bridge
Northumb 252 E5
Causeyton Aberds 293 B8
Caute Devon 24 E6
Cautley Cumb 222 G3
Cavendish Suff 106 B6
Cavendish Bridge Leics 153 D8
Cavenham Suff 124 D5
Cavers Carre Borders 262 D3
Caversfield Oxon 101 F11
Caversham Reading 65 E8
Caversham Heights
Reading 65 D8
Caverswall Staffs 169 G7
Cavil E Yorks 207 G11
Cawdor Highld 301 D8
Cawkeld E Yorks 208 C5
Cawkwell Lincs 190 F3
Cawood N Yorks 207 F7
Cawsand Corn 7 E8
Cawston Norf 160 E2
Warks 119 C9
Cawthorne N Yorks 216 B5
S Yorks 197 F9
Cawthorpe Lincs 155 E11
Cawton N Yorks 216 D2
Caxton Cambs 122 F6
Caynham Shrops 115 C11
Caythorpe Lincs 172 F6
Notts 171 F11
Cayton N Yorks 217 C11
Ceallan W Isles 296 F4
Ceann a Bhaigh W Isles 296 E3
Ceann a Bhàigh
W Isles 305 J4
Ceannacroc Lodge
Highld 290 B4
Ceann a Deas Loch
Baghasdail W Isles 297 K3
Ceann Shiphoirt
W Isles 305 G4
Ceann Tarabhaigh
W Isles 305 G4
Cearsiadair W Isles 304 F5
Ceathramh Meadhanach
W Isles 296 D4
Cefn Newport 59 B9
Powys 148 G5
Cefn Berain Conwy 165 B7
Cefn-brith Conwy 164 E6
Cefn-bryn-brain Carms 76 C2
Cefn-bychan Swansea 56 B4
Wrex 166 G3
Cefncaeau Carms 56 B4
Cefn Canol Powys 148 C4
Cefn-coch Conwy 164 B5
Cefn Coch Powys 129 C10
Powys 148 D2
Cefn-coed-y-cymmer
M Tydf 77 D9f
Cefn Cribbwr Bridgend 57 E11
Cefn Cross Bridgend 57 E11
Cefn-ddwysarn Gwyn 147 B9
Cefn Einion Shrops 130 F5
Cefneithin Carms 75 C9
Cefn-eurgain Flint 166 B2
Cefn Fforest Caerph 77 F11
Cefn Glas Bridgend 57 E11
Cefn Golau Bl Gwent 77 D10
Cefn-gorwydd Powys 95 B8
Cefn Hengoed Caerph 77 F10
Cefn-hengoed Swansea 57 B7
Cefn Llwyd Ceredig 128 G2
Cefn-mawr Wrex 166 G3
Cefnpennar Rhondda 77 E8
Cefn Rhigos Rhondda 76 D6
Cefn-y-bedd Flint 166 D4
Cefn-y-Crib Torf 78 F2
Cefn-y-Garth Swansea 76 E2
Cefn-y-pant Carms 92 F3
Cegidfa = *Guilsfield*
Powys 148 G4
Cei-bach Ceredig 111 F8
Ceinewydd = *New Quay*
Ceredig 111 F7
Ceint Anglesey 179 F7
Ceinws Powys 128 B5
Cellan Ceredig 94 B2
Cellarhead Staffs 169 F7
Cellarhill Kent 70 G3
Celyn-Mali Flint 165 B11
Cemaes Anglesey 178 C5
Cemmaes Powys 128 B6
Cemmaes Road
= *Glantwymyn* Powys 128 C6
Cenarth Carms 92 C5
Cenin Gwyn 163 F7
Central Invclyd 276 F5
Central Milton Keynes
M Keynes 102 D6
Ceos W Isles 304 F5
Ceres Fife 287 F8
Ceri = *Kerry* Powys 130 F2
Cerne Abbas Dorset 29 G11
Cerney Wick Glos 81 F9
Cerrigceinwen Anglesey 178 G6
Cerrig Llwydion Neath 57 C9
Cerrig-mân Anglesey 179 C7
Cerrigydrudion Conwy 165 F7
Cess Norf 161 F8
Cessford Borders 262 E6
Ceunant Gwyn 163 C8
Chaceley Glos 99 E7
Chaceley Hole Glos 98 E6
Chaceley Stock Glos 99 F7
Chacewater Corn 4 G4
Chackmore Bucks 102 D3
Chacombe W Nhants 101 C9
Chadbury Worcs 99 B10
Chadderton Gtr Man 196 F2
Chadderton Fold
Gtr Man 195 F11
Chaddesden Derby 153 B7
Chaddesley Corbett
Worcs 117 C7
Chaddlehanger Devon 12 F5
Chaddlewood Plym 7 D11
Chaddleworth W Berks 64 D2
Chadkirk Gtr Man 184 D6
Chadlington Oxon 100 G6
Chadshunt Warks 118 G6
Chadsmoor Staffs 151 G9
Chadstone W Nhants 121 F7
Chad Valley W Mid 133 F10
Chadwell Leics 154 E5
Shrops 150 G5
Chadwell End Bedford 121 D11
Chadwell Heath London 68 B3
Chadwell St Mary
Thurrock 68 D6
Chadwick Worcs 116 D6
Chadwick End W Mid 118 C4
Chadwick Green Mers 183 B8
Chaffcombe Som 28 E5
Chafford Hundred
Thurrock 68 D5
Chagford Devon 13 D10
Chailey E Sus 36 D5
Chainbridge Cambs 139 C8
Chain Bridge Lincs 174 G4
Chainhurst Kent 53 D8
Chalbury Dorset 31 F8
Chalbury Common Dorset 31 F8
Chaldon Sur 51 B10
Chaldon Herring or East
Chaldon Dorset 17 E11
Chale IoW 20 F5
Chale Green IoW 20 F5
Chalfont Common Bucks 85 G8
Chalfont Grove Bucks 85 G7
Chalfont St Giles Bucks 85 G7
Chalfont St Peter Bucks 85 G8
Chalford Glos 80 E5
Oxon 84 E2
Wilts 45 C11
Chalford Hill Glos 80 E5
Chalgrave C Beds 103 F10
Chalgrove Oxon 83 F10
Chalk Kent 69 E7
Chalk End Essex 87 C10
Chalkfoot Cumb 230 B2
Chalkhill Norf 141 C7
Chalkhouse Green Oxon 65 D8
Chalkshire Bucks 84 D4
Chalksole Kent 55 E9
Chalkway Som 28 F5
Chalkwell Kent 69 G11
Southend 69 B11
Challaborough Devon 8 G3
Challacombe Devon 41 E7
Challister Shetland 312 G7
Challoch Dumfries 236 C5
Challock Kent 54 C4
Chalmington Dorset 29 G9
Chalton C Beds 103 F10
Hants 34 D2
Chalvedon Essex 69 B8
Chalvey Slough 66 D3
Chalvington E Sus 23 D8
Chambercombe Devon 40 D4
Chamber's Green Kent 54 E2
Champson Devon 26 B4
Chance Inn Fife 287 F7
Chancery = *Rhydgaled*
Ceredig 111 B11
Chance's Pitch Hereford 98 C4
Chandler's Cross Herts 85 F9
Worcs 98 D5
Chandler's Ford Hants 32 C6
Chandlers Green Hants 49 B8
Channel's End Bedford 122 F2
Channel Tunnel Kent 55 F7
Channerwick Shetland 313 L6
Chantry Devon 25 C9
Som 45 D8
Suff 108 C2
Chapel Corn 4 C6
Cumb 229 E10
Fife 280 C5
Chapel Allerton Som 44 C2
W Yorks 206 F2
Chapel Amble Corn 10 F5
Chapel Brampton
W Nhants 120 D4
Chapel Chorlton Staffs 150 B6
Chapel Cleeve Som 42 E4
Chapel Cross E Sus 37 C10
Chapel End Bedford 103 B11
Bedford 122 F2
Cambs 138 G2
C Beds 103 C11
Ches E 167 G11
Essex 105 G11
N Nhants 138 F2
Warks 134 E6
Chapel-en-le-Frith
Derbys 185 E9
Chapel Field Gtr Man 195 F9
Norf 161 E7
Chapel Fields W Mid 118 B6
York 207 C7
Chapelgate Lincs 157 E8
Chapel Green Herts 104 D6
Warks 119 E9
Warks 134 F5
Chapel Haddlesey
N Yorks 198 B5
Chapelhall N Lanark 268 C5
Chapel Head Cambs 138 G6
Chapelhill Dumfries 248 E3
Highld 301 B8
N Ayrs 266 G4
Perth 286 D4
Perth 286 E3
Perth 286 E6
Chapel Hill Aberds 303 F10
Glos 79 E10
Lincs 174 E2
Mon 79 F8
N Yorks 206 D2
Chapel House Lancs 194 F3
Chapel Knapp Wilts 61 F11
Chapelknowe Dumfries 239 C8
Chapel Lawn Shrops 114 B6
Chapel-le-Dale
N Yorks 212 D4
Chapel Leigh Som 27 B10
Chapel Mains Borders 271 G11
Chapel Milton Derbys 185 E9
Chapel of Garioch
Aberds 303 G7
Chapel of Stoneywood
Aberdeen 293 B10
Chapel on Leader
Borders 271 G11
Chapel Outon Dumfries 236 E6
Chapel Plaister Wilts 61 F10
Chapel Row Essex 88 E3
E Sus 23 C10
W Berks 64 F5
Chapels Blackburn 195 C7
Cumb 210 C4
Chapel St Leonards
Lincs 191 G9
Chapel Stile Cumb 220 D6
Chapelthorpe W Yorks 197 D10
Chapelton Angus 287 C10
Devon 25 B9
Highld 291 B11
S Lanark 268 F3
Chapelton Row Dumfries 237 E8
Chapeltown Blackburn 195 D8
Moray 302 G2
S Yorks 186 B5
W Yorks 206 F2
Chapel Town Corn 5 D7
Chapman's Hill Worcs 117 B9
Chapmanslade Wilts 45 D10
Chapman's Town E Sus 23 B10
Chapmans Well Devon 12 C3
Chapmore End Herts 86 B4
Chappel Essex 107 F7
Charaton Cross Corn 6 B6
Charcott Kent 52 D4
Chard Som 28 F4
Chard Junction Dorset 28 G4
Chardleigh Green Som 28 E4
Chardstock Devon 28 G4
Charfield S Glos 80 G2
Charfield Green S Glos 80 G2
Charfield Hill S Glos 80 G2
Charford Worcs 117 D9
Chargrove Glos 80 B6
Charing Kent 54 D3
Charing Cross Dorset 31 E10
Charing Heath Kent 54 D2
Charing Hill Kent 54 C3
Charingworth Glos 100 D4
Charlbury Oxon 82 B5
Charlcombe Bath 61 F8
Charlcutt Wilts 62 D3
Charlecote Warks 118 F5
Charlemont W Mid 133 E10
Charles Devon 41 G7
Charles Bottom Devon 41 G7
Charlesfield Borders 262 D3
Dumfries 238 D5
Charleshill Sur 49 E11
Charleston Angus 287 C7
Renfs 267 C9
Charlestown Aberdeen 293 C11
Corn 5 E10
Derbys 185 C8
Dorset 17 F9
Fife 279 E11
Gtr Man 195 G10
Gtr Man 195 G11
Highld 299 B8
Highld 300 E6
W Yorks 196 B3
W Yorks 205 F9
Charlestown of Aberlour
Moray 302 E2
Charles Tye Suff 125 G10
Charlesworth Derbys 185 C8
Charleton Devon 8 G5
Charlinch Som 43 F8
Charlottetown Fife 286 F6
Charlton Hants 47 D11
Herts 104 F3
London 68 D2
Northumb 251 F8
Oxon 64 B2
Redcar 226 B2
Som 28 B3
Som 44 E6
Som 45 C7
Sur 66 F5
Telford 149 G11
Wilts 30 C6
Wilts 46 B6
Wilts 62 B3
W Nhants 101 D10
Worcs 99 B10
Worcs 116 C6
W Sus 34 E5
Charlton Abbots Glos 99 G10
Charlton Adam Som 29 B8
Charlton-All-Saints
Wilts 31 C11
Charltonbrook S Yorks 186 B4
Charlton Down Dorset 17 C9
Charlton Horethorne
Som 29 C11
Charlton Kings Glos 99 G9
Charlton Mackrell Som 29 B8
Charlton Marshall Dorset 30 G5
Charlton Musgrove Som 30 B2
Charlton on Otmoor
Oxon 83 B9
Charlton on the Hill
Dorset 30 G5
Charlton Park Glos 99 G9
Charlton St Peter Wilts 46 B6
Charlwood E Sus 51 G11
Hants 49 G7
Sur 51 E8
Charlynch Som 43 F8
Charminster BCP 19 C8
Dorset 17 C9
Charmouth Dorset 16 C3
Charnage Wilts 45 G10
Charndon Bucks 102 G3
Charnes Staffs 150 C5
Charney Bassett Oxon 82 G5
Charnock Green Lancs 194 D5
Charnock Hall S Yorks 186 E5
Charnock Richard
Lancs 194 D5
Charsfield Suff 126 F5
Chart Corner Kent 53 C9
Charter Alley Hants 48 B5
Charterhouse Som 44 B3
Chartershall Stirling 278 C6
Charterville Allotments
Oxon 82 C4
Chartham Kent 54 C6
Chartham Hatch Kent 54 B6
Chart Hill Kent 53 D9
Chartridge Bucks 84 E6
Chart Sutton Kent 53 D10
Charvil Wokingham 65 D9
Charwelton W Nhants 119 F10
Chase Cross London 87 G8
Chase End Street Worcs 98 D5
Chase Hill S Glos 61 B8
Chase Terrace Staffs 133 B10
Chasetown Staffs 133 B10
Chastleton Oxon 100 F4
Chasty Devon 24 G4
Chatburn Lancs 203 E11
Chatcull Staffs 150 C5
Chatford Shrops 131 B9
Chatham Caerph 59 B8
Medway 69 F9
Chatham Green Essex 88 B2
Chathill Northumb 264 D5
Chat Hill W Yorks 205 G8
Chatley Worcs 117 E7
Chattenden Medway 69 E9
Chatter End Essex 105 F9
Chatteris Cambs 139 F7
Chatterley Staffs 168 E4
Chattern Hill Sur 66 E5
Chatterton Lancs 195 D9
Chattisham Suff 107 C11
Chattle Hill Warks 134 E3
Chatto Borders 263 F7
Chatton Northumb 264 D3
Chaulden Herts 85 D8
Chaul End C Beds 103 G11
Chavel Shrops 149 G8
Chavenage Green Glos 80 F5
Chavey Down Brack 65 F11
Chawleigh Devon 26 E2
Chawley Oxon 83 E7
Chawson Worcs 117 E7
Chawston Bedford 122 F3
Chawton Hants 49 F8
Chaxhill Glos 80 C2
Chazey Heath Oxon 65 D7
Cheadle Gtr Man 184 D5
Staffs 169 G8
Cheadle Heath Gtr Man 184 D5
Cheadle Hulme Gtr Man 184 D5
Cheadle Park Staffs 169 G8
Cheam London 67 G8
Cheapside Herts 105 E8
Sur 50 B4
Windsor 66 F2
Chearsley Bucks 84 C2
Chebsey Staffs 151 D7
Checkendon Oxon 65 C7
Checkley Ches E 168 F2
Hereford 97 D11
Staffs 151 B10
Checkley Green Ches E 168 F2
Chedburgh Suff 124 F5
Cheddar Som 44 C3
Cheddington Bucks 84 B6
Cheddleton Staffs 169 E7
Cheddleton Heath
Staffs 169 E7
Cheddon Fitzpaine Som 28 B2
Chedglow Wilts 80 G6
Chedgrave Norf 143 D7
Chedington Dorset 29 F7
Chediston Suff 127 B7
Chediston Green Suff 127 B7
Chedworth Glos 81 C9
Chedworth Laines Glos 81 C8
Chedzoy Som 43 F10
Cheeklaw Borders 272 E5
Cheeseman's Green Kent 54 F4
Cheetam Hill Gtr Man 195 G10
Cheglinch Devon 40 E4
Chegworth Kent 53 C10
Cheldon Devon 26 E2
Chelfham Devon 40 F6
Chelford Ches E 184 G4
Chellaston Derby 153 C7
Chell Heath Stoke 168 E5
Chellington Bedford 121 F9
Chells Herts 104 F5
Chelmarsh Shrops 132 F4
Chelmer Village Essex 88 D2
Chelmick Shrops 131 E9
Chelmondiston Suff 108 D4
Chelmorton Derbys 169 B10
Chelmsford Essex 88 D2
Chelmsine Som 27 D11
Chelmsley Wood W Mid 134 F3
Chelsea London 67 D9
Chelsfield London 68 G3
Chelsham Sur 51 B11
Chelston Som 27 C11
Torbay 9 C7
Chelston Heathfield
Som 27 C11
Chelsworth Suff 107 B9
Chelsworth Common
Suff 107 B9
Cheltenham Glos 99 G8
Chelveston N Nhants 121 D9
Chelvey N Som 60 F3
Chelvey Batch N Som 60 F3
Chelwood Bath 60 G6
Chelwood Common
E Sus 36 B6
Chelwood Gate E Sus 36 B6
Chelworth Wilts 81 G7
Chelworth Lower Green
Wilts 81 G9
Chelworth Upper Green
Wilts 81 G9
Chelynch Som 45 E7
Chemistry Shrops 167 G8
Cheney Longville
Shrops 131 G8
Chenhalls Corn 2 B3
Chenies Bucks 85 F8
Cheny Longville Shrops 131 G8
Chepstow Mon 79 G8
Chequerbent Gtr Man 195 F7
Chequerfield W Yorks 198 C3
Chequers Corner Norf 139 B9
Chequertree Kent 54 F4
Cherhill Wilts 62 E4
Cherington Glos 80 F6
Warks 100 D5
Cheristow Devon 24 B3
Cheriton Devon 41 D8
Hants 33 B9
Kent 55 F7
Swansea 56 C3
Cheriton Bishop Devon 13 C11
Cheriton Cross Devon 13 C11
Cheriton Fitzpaine Devon 26 F5
Cheriton or Stackpole Elidor
Pembs 73 F7
Cherrington Telford 150 E3
Cherrybank Perth 286 E5
Cherry Burton E Yorks 208 E5
Cherry Green Essex 105 F11
Herts 105 F7
Cherry Hinton Cambs 123 F9
Cherry Orchard Shrops 149 G9
Worcs 117 G7
Cherry Tree Blackburn 195 B7
Gtr Man 185 C7
Cherrytree Hill Derby 153 B7
Cherry Willingham
Lincs 189 G8
Chertsey Sur 66 F4
Chertsey Meads Sur 66 F5
Cheselbourne Dorset 17 B11
Chesham Bucks 85 E7
Gtr Man 195 E10
Chesham Bois Bucks 85 F7
Cheshunt Herts 86 E5
Chesley Kent 69 G11
Cheslyn Hay Staffs 133 B9
Chessetts Wood Warks 118 C3
Chessington London 67 G7
Chessmount Bucks 85 E7
Chestall Staffs 151 G11
Chester Ches W 166 B6
Chesterblade Som 45 E7
Chesterfield Derbys 186 G5
Staffs 134 B2
Chesterhill Midloth 271 B7
Chesterhope Northumb 251 F9
Chesterknowes Borders 262 D2
Chester-le-Street
Durham 243 G7
Chester Moor Durham 233 B11
Chesters Borders 262 E4
Borders 262 G4
Chesterton Cambs 123 E9
Cambs 138 D2
Glos 81 E8
Oxon 101 G11
Shrops 132 D5
Staffs 168 F4
Warks 118 F6
Chesterton Green
Warks 118 F6
Chesterwood Northumb 241 D8
Chestfield Kent 70 F6
Chestnut Hill Cumb 229 G11
Chestnut Street Kent 69 G11
Cheston Devon 8 D3
Cheswardine Shrops 150 D4
Cheswell Telford 150 F4
Cheswick Northumb 273 F10
Cheswick Buildings
Northumb 273 F10
Cheswick Green W Mid 118 B2
Chetnole Dorset 29 F10
Chettiscombe Devon 27 E7
Chettisham Cambs 139 G10
Chettle Dorset 31 E7
Chetton Shrops 132 E3
Chetwode Bucks 102 F2
Chetwynd Aston Telford 150 F5
Cheveley Cambs 124 E3
Chevening Kent 52 B3
Cheverell's Green Herts 85 B9
Chevin End W Yorks 205 E9
Chevington Suff 124 F5
Chevithorne Devon 27 D7
Chew Magna Bath 60 G5
Chew Moor Gtr Man 195 F7
Chew Stoke Bath 60 G5
Chewton Keynsham Bath 61 F7
Chewton Mendip Som 44 C5
Cheylesmore W Mid 118 B6
Chichacott Devon 13 B8
Chicheley M Keynes 103 B8
Chichester W Sus 22 C5
Chickenley W Yorks 197 C9
Chickerell Dorset 17 E8
Chicklade Wilts 46 G2
Chickney Essex 105 F11
Chicksands C Beds 104 D2
Chicksgrove Wilts 46 G3
Chickward Hereford 114 G5
Chidden Hants 33 D11
Chiddingfold Sur 50 F3
Chiddingly E Sus 23 C8
Chiddingstone Kent 52 D3
Chiddingstone Causeway
Kent 52 D4
Chiddingstone Hoath
Kent 52 E3
Chideock Dorset 16 C4
Chidgley Som 42 F4
Chidham W Sus 22 C3
Chidswell W Yorks 197 C9
Chieveley W Berks 64 E3
Chignall St James
Essex 87 D11
Chignall Smealy Essex 87 C11
Chigwell Essex 86 G6
Chigwell Row Essex 87 G7
Chilbolton Hants 47 F11
Chilbolton Down Hants 48 F2
Chilbridge Dorset 31 G7
Chilcomb Hants 33 B8
Chilcombe Dorset 16 C6
Som 42 F6
Chilcompton Som 44 C6
Chilcote Leics 152 G5
Childerditch Essex 68 B6
Childerley Gate Cambs 123 F7
Childer Thornton
Ches W 182 F5
Child Okeford Dorset 30 E4
Childrey Oxon 63 B11
Childsbridge Kent 52 B5
Child's Ercall Shrops 150 E3
Child's Hill London 67 B8
Childswickham Worcs 99 D11
Childwall Mers 182 D6
Childwick Bury Herts 85 C10
Childwick Green Herts 85 C10
Chilfrome Dorset 17 B7
Chilgrove W Sus 34 E4
Chilham Kent 54 C5
Chilhampton Wilts 46 G5
Chilla Devon 24 G6
Chillaton Devon 12 E4
Chillenden Kent 55 C9
Chillerton IoW 20 E5
Chillesford Suff 127 G7
Chillingham Northumb 264 D3
Chillington Devon 8 G5
Som 28 E5
Chilmark Wilts 46 G3
Chilmington Green Kent 54 E3
Chilsham E Sus 23 C10
Chilson Oxon 82 B4
Som 28 G4
Chilson Common Som 28 G4
Chilsworthy Corn 12 G4
Devon 24 F4
Chiltern Green C Beds 85 B10
Chilthorne Domer Som 29 D8
Chiltington E Sus 36 D5
Chilton Bucks 83 C11
Durham 233 F11
Kent 71 G11
Oxon 64 B3
Suff 107 C7
Chilton Candover Hants 48 E5
Chilton Cantelo Som 29 C9
Chilton Foliat Wilts 63 E10
Chilton Lane Durham 234 E2
Chilton Moor T&W 234 B2
Chilton Polden Som 43 F11
Chilton Street Suff 106 B5
Chilton Trinity Som 43 F9
Chilvers Coton Warks 135 E7
Chilwell Notts 153 B10
Chilworth Hants 32 D6
Sur 50 D4
Chilworth Old Village
Hants 32 D6
Chimney Oxon 82 E5
Chimney-end Oxon 82 B4
Chimney Street Suff 106 B4
Chineham Hants 49 C7
Chingford London 86 G5
Chingford Green London 86 G5
Chingford Hatch London 86 G5
Chinley Derbys 185 E8
Chinley Head Derbys 185 E9
Chinnor Oxon 84 E3
Chipley Som 27 C10
Chipmans Platt Glos 80 D3
Chipnall Shrops 150 C4
Chippenhall Green Suff 126 B5
Chippenham Cambs 124 D3
Wilts 62 E2
Chipperfield Herts 85 E8
Chipping Herts 105 E7
Lancs 203 E8
Chipping Barnet London 86 F2
Chipping Campden
Glos 100 D3
Chipping Hill Essex 88 B4
Chipping Norton Oxon 100 F6
Chipping Ongar Essex 87 E8
Chipping Sodbury S Glos 61 C8
Chipping Warden
W Nhants 101 B9
Chipstable Som 27 B8
Chipstead Kent 52 B3
Sur 51 B9
Chirbury Shrops 130 D5
Chirk = *Y Waun* Wrex 148 B5
Chirk Bank Shrops 148 B5
Chirk Green Wrex 148 B5
Chirmorrie S Ayrs 236 B4
Chirnside Borders 273 D7
Chirnsidebridge
Borders 273 D7
Chirton T&W 243 D8
Wilts 46 B5
Chisbury Wilts 63 F9
Chiselborough Som 29 E7
Chiseldon Swindon 63 D7
Chiserley W Yorks 196 B4
Chislehampton Oxon 83 F9
Chislehurst London 68 E2
Chislehurst West London 68 E2
Chislet Kent 71 G8
Chislet Forstal Kent 71 G8
Chiswell Dorset 17 G9
Chiswell Green Herts 85 E10
Chiswick London 67 D8
Chiswick End Cambs 105 B7
Chisworth Derbys 185 C7
Chitcombe E Sus 38 C4
Chithurst W Sus 34 C4
Chittering Cambs 123 C9
Chitterley Devon 26 G6
Chitterne Wilts 46 E3
Chittlehamholt Devon 25 C11
Chittlehampton Devon 25 B10
Chittoe Wilts 62 F3
Chitts Hills Essex 107 F9
Chitty Kent 71 G8
Chivelstone Devon 9 G10
Chivenor Devon 40 G4
Chivery Bucks 84 D6
Chobham Sur 66 G3
Choicelee Borders 272 E4
Cholderton Wilts 47 E8
Cholesbury Bucks 84 D6
Chollerford Northumb 241 C10
Chollerton Northumb 241 C10
Cholmondeston
Ches E 167 C10
Cholsey Oxon 64 B5
Cholstrey Hereford 115 F9
Cholwell Bath 44 B6
Chop Gate N Yorks 225 F11
Choppington Northumb 253 G7
Chopwell T&W 242 F4
Chorley Ches E 167 E9
Lancs 194 D5
Shrops 132 G3
Staffs 151 G11
Chorley Common W Sus 34 B4
Chorleywood Herts 85 F8
Chorleywood Bottom
Herts 85 F8
Chorleywood West Herts 85 F8
Chorlton Ches E 168 E2
Chorlton-cum-Hardy
Gtr Man 184 C4
Chorlton Lane Ches W 167 F7
Choulton Shrops 131 F7
Chowdene T&W 243 F7
Chowley Ches W 167 D7
Chownes Mead W Sus 36 C4
Chreagain Highld 289 C10
Chrishall Essex 105 D8
Christchurch BCP 19 C9
Cambs 139 D9
Glos 79 C9
Newport 59 B10
Christian Malford Wilts 62 D3
Christleton Ches W 166 B6
Christmas Common Oxon 84 G2
Christon N Som 43 B11
Christon Bank Northumb 264 E6
Christow Devon 14 D2
Chryston N Lanark 278 G3
Chub Tor Devon 7 B10
Chuck Hatch E Sus 52 G3
Chudleigh Devon 14 F3
Chudleigh Knighton
Devon 14 F2
Chulmleigh Devon 25 E11
Chunal Derbys 185 C8
Church Lancs 195 B8
Churcham Glos 80 B3
Church Aston Telford 150 F4
Churchbank Shrops 114 B6
Church Brampton
W Nhants 120 D4
Churchbridge Corn 6 D4
Staffs 133 B9
Church Brough Cumb 222 C5
Church Broughton
Derbys 152 C4
Church Charwelton
W Nhants 119 F10
Church Clough Lancs 204 F3
Church Common Hants 34 B2
Church Coombe Corn 4 G3
Church Cove Corn 2 G6
Church Crookham
Hants 49 C10
Churchdown Glos 80 B5
Church Eaton Staffs 150 F6
Churchend Essex 89 G8
Essex 106 G2
Glos 80 D3
Reading 65 E7
S Glos 80 G2
Church End Bedford 122 F2
Bucks 84 B6
Bucks 84 D2
Cambs 121 C11
Cambs 123 C7
Cambs 123 D7
Cambs 138 G4
Cambs 139 B7
C Beds 85 B8
C Beds 103 E9
C Beds 103 G9
C Beds 104 D3
C Beds 122 G3
Essex 88 B2
Essex 105 C11
Essex 105 F11
Essex 106 F4
E Yorks 209 C7
Glos 80 D2
Glos 99 D7
Hants 49 B7
Herts 85 C10
Herts 85 F8
Herts 104 E5
Herts 105 G8
Lincs 156 C4
Lincs 190 B6
London 67 C8
London 86 G2
Norf 157 F10
Oxon 82 D5
Oxon 100 E6
Suff 108 D4
Sur 50 B5
Warks 134 E4
Warks 134 E5
Wilts 62 D4
W Mid 119 B7
Worcs 98 C6
Church Enstone Oxon 101 G7
Churches Green E Sus 23 B10
Church Fenton N Yorks 206 F6
Churchfield Hereford 98 B4
W Mid 133 E10
Churchfields Wilts 31 B10
Churchgate Herts 86 E4
Churchgate Street Essex 87 C7
Church Green Devon 15 B9

Church Green *continued*
Norf 141 E11
Church Gresley Derbys 152 F5
Church Hanborough
Oxon 82 C6
Church Hill Ches W 167 C10
Pembs 73 C7
Staffs 151 G10
W Mid 133 D9
Worcs 117 D11
Church Hougham Kent 55 E9
Church Houses N Yorks 226 F3
Churchill Devon 28 G4
Devon 40 E5
N Som 44 B2
Oxon 100 G5
Worcs 117 B7
Worcs 117 G8
Churchill Green N Som 60 G2
Churchinford Som 28 E2
Church Knowle Dorset 18 E4
Church Laneham Notts 188 F4
Church Langton Leics 136 E4
Church Lawford Warks 119 B8
Church Lawton Ches E 168 D4
Church Leigh Staffs 151 B10
Church Lench Worcs 117 G10
Church Mayfield Staffs 169 G11
Church Minshull
Ches E 167 C11
Churchmoor Rough
Shrops 131 F8
Church Norton W Sus 22 D5
Church Oakley Hants 48 C5
Churchover Warks 135 G10
Church Preen Shrops 131 D10
Church Pulverbatch
Shrops 131 C8
Churchstanton Som 27 E11
Churchstoke Powys 130 E5
Churchstow Devon 8 F4
Church Stowe W Nhants 120 F2
Church Street Essex 106 C5
Kent 69 E8
Church Stretton Shrops 131 E9
Churchton Pembs 73 D10
Churchtown Corn 11 F7
Cumb 230 C3
Derbys 170 C3
Devon 24 G3
Devon 41 E7
IoM 192 C5
Lancs 202 E5
Mers 193 D11
Shrops 130 F5
Som 42 F3
Church Town Corn 4 G3
Leics 153 F7
N Lincs 199 F9
Sur 51 C11
Church Village Rhondda 58 B5
Church Warsop Notts 171 B9
Church Westcote Glos 100 G4
Church Whitfield Kent 55 D10
Church Wilne Derbys 153 C8
Churchwood W Sus 35 D8
Churnet Grange Staffs 169 E7
Churnsike Lodge
Northumb 240 B5
Churscombe Torbay 9 C7
Churston Ferrers Torbay 9 D8
Churt Sur 49 F11
Churton Ches W 166 D6
Churwell W Yorks 197 B9
Chute Cadley Wilts 47 C10
Chute Standen Wilts 47 C10
Chwefforrdd Conwy 180 G4
Chwilog Gwyn 145 B8
Chwitffordd = *Whitford*
Flint 181 F10
Chyandour Corn 1 C5
Chyanvounder Corn 2 E5
Chycoose Corn 3 B8
Chynhale Corn 2 C4
Chynoweth Corn 2 C2
Chyvarloe Corn 2 E5
Cicelyford Mon 79 E8
Cilan Uchaf Gwyn 144 D5
Cilau Pembs 91 D8
Cilcain Flint 165 B11
Cilcennin Ceredig 111 E10
Cilcewydd Powys 130 C4
Cilfor Gwyn 146 B2
Cilfrew Neath 76 E3
Cilfynydd Rhondda 77 G9
Cilgerran Pembs 92 C3
Cilgwyn Carms 94 F4
Ceredig 92 C6
Gwyn 163 E7
Pembs 91 D11
Ciliau Aeron Ceredig 111 F9
Cill Amhlaidh W Isles 297 G3
Cill Donnain W Isles 297 J3
Cille Bhrighde W Isles 297 K3
Cill Eireabhagh W Isles 297 G4
Cille Pheadair W Isles 297 K3
Cilmaengwyn Neath 76 D2
Cilmery Powys 113 G10
Cilsan Carms 93 G11
Ciltalgarth Gwyn 164 G5
Ciltwrch Powys 96 C3
Cilybebyll Neath 76 E2
Cil y coed = *Caldicot*
Mon 60 B3
Cilycwm Carms 94 D5
Cimla Neath 57 B9
Cinderford Glos 79 C11
Cinderhill Derbys 170 F5
Nottingham 171 G8
Cinder Hill Gtr Man 195 F9
Kent 52 D4
W Mid 133 E8
W Sus 36 B5
Cinnamon Brow Warr 183 C10
Cippenham Slough 66 C2
Cippyn Pembs 92 B2
Circebost W Isles 304 E3
Cirencester Glos 81 E8
Ciribhig W Isles 304 D3
City London 67 C10
Powys 130 F4
V Glam 58 D3
City Dulas Anglesey 179 D7
Clabhach Argyll 288 D3
Clachaig Argyll 276 E2
Highld 292 B2
N Ayrs 255 E10
Clachan Argyll 255 B8
Argyll 275 B8
Argyll 284 F5
Argyll 289 E10
Highld 295 B7
Highld 298 C4
Highld 307 L6
W Isles 297 G3
Clachaneasy Dumfries 236 B5
Clachanmore Dumfries 236 E2
Clachan na Luib
W Isles 296 E4
Clachan of Campsie
E Dunb 278 F2
Clachan of Glendaruel
Argyll 275 E10
Clachan-Seil Argyll 275 B8
Clachan Strachur Argyll 284 G4
Clachbreck Argyll 275 F8
Clachnabrain Angus 292 G5
Clachtoll Highld 307 G5
Clackmannan Clack 279 C8
Clackmarras Moray 302 D2
Clacton-on-Sea Essex 89 B11
Cladach N Ayrs 256 B2
Cladach Chairinis
W Isles 296 F4
Cladach Chireboist
W Isles 296 E3
Claddach Argyll 254 B2
Claddach-knockline
W Isles 296 E3
Cladich Argyll 284 E4
Cladich Steading Argyll 284 E4
Cladswell Worcs 117 F10
Claggan Highld 289 E8
Highld 290 F3
Perth 285 D11
Claigan Highld 298 D2
Claines Worcs 117 F7
Clandown Bath 45 B7
Clanfield Hants 33 D11
Oxon 82 E3
Clanking Bucks 84 D4
Clanville Hants 47 D10
Som 44 G6
Wilts 62 D2
Claonaig Argyll 255 B9
Claonel Highld 309 J5
Clapgate Dorset 31 G8
Herts 105 G8
Clapham Bedford 121 G10
Devon 14 D3
London 67 D9
N Yorks 212 F4
W Sus 35 F9
Clapham Green
Bedford 121 G10
N Yorks 205 B10
Clapham Hill Kent 70 G6
Clapham Park London 67 E9
Clap Hill Kent 54 F5
Clapper Corn 10 G6
Clapper Hill Kent 53 F10
Clappers Borders 273 D8
Clappersgate Cumb 221 E7
Clapphoull Shetland 313 L6
Clapton Som 28 F6
Som 44 C6
W Berks 63 E11
Clapton in Gordano
N Som 60 E3
Clapton-on-the-Hill
Glos 81 B11
Clapton Park London 67 B11
Clapworthy Devon 25 C11
Clarach Ceredig 128 G2
Clarack Aberds 292 D6
Clara Vale T&W 242 E4
Clarbeston Pembs 91 G10
Clarbeston Road Pembs 91 G10
Clarborough Notts 188 E2
Clardon Highld 310 C5
Clare Oxon 83 F11
Suff 106 B5
Clarebrand Dumfries 237 C9
Claregate W Mid 133 C7
Claremont Park Sur 66 G6
Claremount W Yorks 196 B5
Clarencefield Dumfries 238 D3
Clarence Park N Som 59 G10
Clarendon Park
Leicester 135 C11
Clareston Pembs 73 C7
Clarilaw Borders 262 D3
Borders 262 F2
Clarken Green Hants 48 C5
Clark Green Ches E 184 F6
Clarksfield Gtr Man 196 G2
Clark's Green Sur 51 F7
Clark's Hill Lincs 157 E7
Clarkston E Renf 267 D11
N Lanark 268 B5
Clase Swansea 57 B7
Clashandorran Highld 300 E5
Clashcoig Highld 309 K6
Clasheddy Highld 308 C6
Clashgour Argyll 284 C6
Clashindarroch Aberds 302 F4
Clashmore Highld 306 F5
Highld 309 L7
Clashnessie Highld 306 F5
Clashnoir Moray 302 G2
Clate Shetland 313 G7
Clatford Wilts 63 F7
Clatford Oakcuts Hants 47 F10
Clathy Perth 286 F3
Clatt Aberds 302 G5
Clatter Powys 129 E9
Clatterford IoW 20 D5
Clatterford End Essex 87 C10
Essex 87 D9
Essex 87 E8
Clatterin Bridge Aberds 293 F8
Clatto Fife 287 F8
Clatworthy Som 42 G5
Clauchlands N Ayrs 256 C2
Claughton Lancs 202 E6
Lancs 211 F11
Mers 182 D4
Clavelshay Som 43 G9
Claverdon Warks 118 E3
Claverham N Som 60 F2
Claverhambury Essex 86 E6
Clavering Essex 105 E9
Claverley Shrops 132 E5
Claverton Bath 61 G9
Claverton Down Bath 61 G9
Clawdd-côch V Glam 58 D5
Clawdd-newydd Denb 165 E9
Clawdd Poncen Denb 165 G9
Clawthorpe Cumb 211 D10
Clawton Devon 12 B3
Claxby Lincs 189 C10
Lincs 191 G7
Claxby St Andrew Lincs 191 G7
Claxton Norf 142 C6
N Yorks 216 G3
Claybokie Aberds 292 D2
Claybrooke Magna Leics 135 F9
Claybrooke Parva Leics 135 F9
Clay Common Suff 143 G9
Clay Coton W Nhants 119 B11
Clay Cross Derbys 170 C5
Claydon Glos 99 E8
Oxon 119 G9
Suff 126 G2
Clay End Herts 104 F6
Claygate Dumfries 239 B9
Kent 52 C6
Kent 53 E8
Sur 67 G7
Claygate Cross Kent 52 B6
Clayhall Hants 21 B8
London 86 G6
Clayhanger Devon 27 C8
Som 28 E4
W Mid 133 C10
Clayhidon Devon 27 D11
Clayhill E Sus 38 C4
Hants 32 F4
Clay Hill Bristol 60 E6
London 86 F4
W Berks 64 E5
Clayhithe Cambs 123 E10
Clayholes Angus 287 D9
Clay Lake Lincs 156 E5
Clayland Stirling 277 D11
Clay Mills Derbys 152 D5
Clayock Highld 310 D5
Claypit Hill Cambs 123 G7
Claypits Devon 27 B7
Glos 80 D3
Kent 55 B9
Suff 140 G4
Claypole Lincs 172 F5
Clays End Bath 61 G8
Claythorpe Lincs 190 F6
Clayton Gtr Man 184 B5
Staffs 168 G5
S Yorks 198 F3
W Sus 36 E3
W Yorks 205 G8
Clayton Brook Lancs 194 C5
Clayton Green Lancs 194 C5
Clayton Heights
W Yorks 205 G8
Clayton-le-Dale Lancs 203 G9
Clayton-le-Moors
Lancs 203 G10
Clayton-le-Woods
Lancs 194 C5
Clayton West W Yorks 197 E9
Clayworth Notts 188 D2
Cleadale Highld 294 G6
Cleadon T&W 243 E9
Cleadon Park T&W 243 E9
Clearbrook Devon 7 B10
Clearwell Glos 79 D9
Newport 59 B9
Clearwood Wilts 45 D10
Cleasby N Yorks 224 C5
Cleat Orkney 314 B4
Orkney 314 H4
Cleatlam Durham 224 B2
Cleator Cumb 219 C10
Cleator Moor Cumb 219 B10
Cleave Devon 28 G2
Clebrig Highld 308 F5
Cleckheaton W Yorks 197 B7
Cleddon Mon 79 E8
Cleedownton Shrops 131 G11
Cleehill Shrops 115 B11
Cleekhimin N Lanark 268 D5
Cleemarsh Shrops 131 G11
Clee St Margaret
Shrops 131 G11
Cleestanton Shrops 115 B11
Cleethorpes NE Lincs 201 F10
Cleeton St Mary Shrops 116 B2
Cleeve Glos 80 C2
N Som 60 F3
Oxon 64 C6
Cleeve Hill Glos 99 F9
Cleeve Prior Worcs 99 B11
Cleghorn S Lanark 269 F8
Clegyrnant Powys 129 B8
Clehonger Hereford 97 D9
Cleirwy = *Clyro* Powys 96 C4
Cleish Perth 279 B11
Cleland N Lanark 268 D5
Clements End Glos 79 D9
Clement's End C Beds 85 B8
Clement Street Kent 68 E4
Clench Wilts 63 G7
Clench Common Wilts 63 F7
Clencher's Mill Hereford 98 D4
Clenchwarton Norf 157 E11
Clennell Northumb 251 B10
Clent Worcs 117 B8
Cleobury Mortimer
Shrops 116 B3
Cleobury North Shrops 132 F2
Cleongart Argyll 255 D7
Clephanton Highld 301 D8
Clerkenwater Corn 5 B11
Clerkenwell London 67 C10
Clerk Green W Yorks 197 C8
Clerklands Borders 262 E2
Clermiston Edin 280 G3
Clestrain Orkney 314 F3
Cleuch Head Borders 262 G3
Cleughbrae Dumfries 238 C3
Clevancy Wilts 62 D5
Clevans Renfs 267 B7
Clevedon N Som 60 E2
Cleveley Oxon 101 G7
Cleveleys Lancs 202 E2
Cleverton Wilts 62 B3
Clevis Bridgend 57 F10
Clewer Som 44 C2
Clewer Green Windsor 66 D2
Clewer New Town
Windsor 66 D3
Clewer Village Windsor 66 D3
Cley next the Sea Norf 177 E8
Cliaid W Isles 297 L2
Cliasmol W Isles 305 H2
Cliburn Cumb 231 G7
Click Mill Orkney 314 D3
Cliddesden Hants 48 D6
Cliff Derbys 185 D8
Warks 134 D4
Cliffburn Angus 287 C10
Cliffe Lancs 203 G10
Medway 69 D8
N Yorks 207 G9
N Yorks 224 B4
Cliff End E Sus 38 E5
W Yorks 196 D6
Cliffe Woods Medway 69 E8
Clifford Devon 24 C4
Hereford 96 B4
W Yorks 206 E4
Clifford Chambers
Warks 118 G3
Clifford's Mesne Glos 98 G4
Cliffs End Kent 71 G10
Clifftown Southend 69 B11
Clifton Bristol 60 E5
C Beds 104 D3
Ches W 183 F8
Cumb 230 F6
Derbys 169 G11
Devon 40 E5
Gtr Man 195 G9
Lancs 202 G5
Northumb 252 G6
Nottingham 153 C11
N Yorks 205 D9
Oxon 101 E9
Stirling 285 D7
S Yorks 186 C6
S Yorks 187 B8
Worcs 98 B6
W Yorks 197 C7
Clifton *continued*
York 207 C7
Clifton Campville Staffs 152 G5
Cliftoncote Borders 263 E8
Clifton Green Gtr Man 195 G9
Clifton Hampden Oxon 83 F8
Clifton Junction
Gtr Man 195 G9
Clifton Maybank Dorset 29 E9
Clifton Moor York 207 B7
Clifton Reynes
M Keynes 121 G8
Clifton upon Dunsmore
Warks 119 B10
Clifton upon Teme
Worcs 116 E4
Cliftonville Kent 71 E11
N Lanark 268 B4
Norf 160 B6
Climping W Sus 35 G8
Climpy S Lanark 269 D8
Clink Som 45 D9
Clinkham Wood Mers 183 B8
Clint N Yorks 205 B11
Clint Green Norf 159 G10
Clintmains Borders 262 C4
Clints N Yorks 224 E2
Cliobh W Isles 304 E2
Clipiau Gwyn 146 G6
Clippesby Norf 161 G8
Clippings Green Norf 159 G10
Clipsham Rutland 155 F9
Clipston Notts 154 C2
W Nhants 136 G4
Clipstone C Beds 103 F8
Clitheroe Lancs 203 E10
Cliuthar W Isles 305 J3
Clive Ches W 167 B11
Shrops 149 E10
Clive Green Ches W 167 C11
Clive Vale E Sus 38 E4
Clivocast Shetland 312 C8
Clixby Lincs 200 G6
Cloatley Wilts 81 G7
Cloatley End Wilts 81 G7
Clocaenog Denb 165 E9
Clochan Aberds 303 E9
Moray 302 C4
Clock Face Mers 183 C8
Clock House London 67 G9
Clockmill Borders 272 E5
Clock Mills Hereford 96 B5
Clodiau Powys 130 B4
Cloddymoss Moray 301 D9
Clodock Hereford 96 F6
Cloford Som 45 E8
Cloford Common Som 45 E8
Cloigyn Carms 74 C6
Clola Aberds 303 E10
Clophill C Beds 103 D11
Clopton N Nhants 137 G11
Suff 126 G4
Clopton Corner Suff 126 G4
Clopton Green Suff 124 G5
Suff 125 E9
Closeburn Dumfries 247 E9
Close Clark IoM 192 E3
Close House Durham 233 F10
Closworth Som 29 E9
Clothall Herts 104 E5
Clothall Common Herts 104 E5
Clotton Ches W 167 C8
Clotton Common
Ches W 167 C8
Cloudesley Bush Warks 135 F9
Clouds Hereford 97 D11
Cloud Side Staffs 168 C6
Clough Gtr Man 196 D2
Gtr Man 196 F2
W Yorks 196 E5
Clough Dene Durham 242 F5
Cloughfold Lancs 195 C10
Clough Foot W Yorks 196 C2
Clough Hall Staffs 168 E4
Clough Head W Yorks 196 C5
Cloughton N Yorks 227 G10
Cloughton Newlands
N Yorks 227 F10
Clounlaid Highld 289 D9
Clousta Shetland 313 H5
Clouston Orkney 314 E2
Clova Aberds 302 G4
Angus 292 F5
Clovelly Devon 24 C4
Clove Lodge Durham 223 B8
Clovenfords Borders 261 B10
Clovenstone Aberds 293 B9
Cloves Moray 301 C11
Clovullin Highld 290 G2
Clowance Wood Corn 2 C4
Clow Bridge Lancs 195 B10
Clowne Derbys 187 F7
Clows Top Worcs 116 C4
Cloy Wrex 166 G5
Cluanie Inn Highld 290 B2
Cluanie Lodge Highld 290 B2
Clubmoor Mers 182 C5
Clubworthy Corn 11 C11
Cluddley Telford 150 G2
Clun Shrops 130 G6
Clunbury Shrops 131 G7
Clunderwen Carms 73 B10
Clune Highld 301 D9
Highld 301 G7
Clunes Highld 290 E4
Clungunford Shrops 115 B7
Clunie Aberds 302 D6
Perth 286 C5
Clunton Shrops 130 G6
Cluny Fife 280 B4
Cluny Castle Aberds 293 B8
Highld 291 D8
Clutton Bath 44 B6
Ches W 167 E7
Clutton Hill Bath 44 B6
Clwt-grugoer Conwy 165 C7
Clwt-y-bont Gwyn 163 C9
Clydyfagwyr M Tydf 77 D8
Clydach Mon 78 C2
Swansea 75 E11
Clydach Terrace Powys 77 C11
Clydach Vale Rhondda 77 G7
Clydebank W Dunb 277 G9
Clyffe Pypard Wilts 62 D5
Clynder Argyll 276 E4
Clyne Neath 76 E4
Clynelish Highld 311 J2
Clynnog-fawr Gwyn 162 F6
Clyro = *Cleirwy* Powys 96 C4
Clyst Honiton Devon 14 C5
Clyst Hydon Devon 27 G8
Clyst St George Devon 14 D5
Clyst St Lawrence Devon 27 G8
Clyst St Mary Devon 14 C5
Cnip W Isles 304 E2
Cnoc Amhlaigh W Isles 304 E7
Cnoc an t-Solais
W Isles 304 D6
Cnocbreac Argyll 274 F5
Cnoc Fhionn Highld 295 D10
Cnoc Màiri W Isles 304 E6
Cnoc Rolum W Isles 296 F3
Cnwch-coch Ceredig 112 B3
Coachford Aberds 302 E4
Coad's Green Corn 11 F11
Coal Aston Derbys 186 F5
Coal Bank Darl 234 G3
Coalbrookdale Telford 132 C3
Coalbrookvale Bl Gwent 77 D11
Coalburn S Lanark 259 C8
Coalburns T&W 242 E4
Coalcleugh Northumb 232 B2
Coaley Glos 80 E3
Coaley Peak Glos 80 E3
Coalford Aberds 293 D10
Coalhall E Ayrs 257 F10
Coalhill Essex 88 F3
Coalmoor Telford 132 B3
Coalpit Field Warks 135 F7
Coalpit Heath S Glos 61 C7
Coalpit Hill Staffs 168 E4
Coal Pool W Mid 133 C10
Coalport Telford 132 C3
Coalsnaughton Clack 279 B8
Coaltown of Balgonie
Fife 280 B5
Coaltown of Wemyss
Fife 280 B6
Coalville Leics 153 G8
Coalway Glos 79 C9
Coanwood Northumb 240 F5
Coarsewell Devon 8 E4
Coat Som 29 C7
Coatbridge N Lanark 268 C4
Coatdyke N Lanark 268 C5
Coate Swindon 63 C7
Wilts 62 G4
Coates Cambs 138 D6
Glos 81 E7
Lancs 204 D3
Lincs 188 E6
Midloth 270 C4
Notts 188 E4
W Sus 35 D7
Coatham Redcar 235 F7
Coatham Mundeville
Darl 233 G11
Coatsgate Dumfries 248 B3
Cobairdy Aberds 302 E5
Cobbaton Devon 25 B10
Cobbler's Corner Worcs 116 F5
Cobbler's Green Norf 142 E5
Cobbler's Plain Mon 79 E7
Cobbs Warr 183 D10
Cobb's Cross Glos 98 E5
Cobbs Fenn Essex 106 E5
Cobby Syke N Yorks 205 B9
Coberley Glos 81 B7
Cobhall Common
Hereford 97 D9
Cobham Kent 69 F7
Sur 66 G6
Cobleland Stirling 277 B10
Cobler's Green Essex 87 B11
Cobley Dorset 31 C8
Cobley Hill Worcs 117 C10
Cobnash Hereford 115 E9
Cobridge Stoke 168 F5
Cobscot Shrops 150 B3
Coburty Aberds 303 C9
Cockadilly Glos 80 E4
Cock Alley Derbys 186 G6
Cock and End Suff 124 G4
Cockayne N Yorks 226 F2
Cockayne Hatley
C Beds 104 B5
Cock Bank Wrex 166 F5
Cock Bevington Warks 117 G11
Cock Bridge Aberds 292 C4
Cockburnspath Borders 282 G5
Cock Clarks Essex 88 E4
Cockden Lancs 204 G3
Cockenzie and Port Seton
E Loth 281 F8
Cocker Bar Lancs 194 C4
Cockerham Lancs 202 C5
Cockermouth Cumb 229 E8
Cockernhoe Herts 104 G2
Cockernhoe Green
Herts 104 G2
Cockersdale W Yorks 197 B8
Cockerton Darl 224 B5
Cockett Swansea 56 C6
Cocketty Aberds 293 F9
Cockfield Durham 233 G8
Suff 125 G8
Cockfosters London 86 F3
Cock Gate Hereford 115 D9
Cock Green Essex 87 B11
Cockhill Som 44 G6
Cock Hill N Yorks 206 B6
Cocking W Sus 34 D5
Cocking Causeway
W Sus 34 D5
Cockington Torbay 9 C7
Cocklake Som 44 D2
Cocklaw Northumb 241 C10
Cockleford Glos 81 C7
Cockley Beck Cumb 220 E4
Cockley Cley Norf 140 C5
Cockley Hill W Yorks 197 D7
Cock Marling E Sus 38 D5
Cocknowle Dorset 18 E4
Cockpole Green
Wokingham 65 C9
Cocks Corn 4 E5
Cocks Green Suff 125 F7
Cockshead Ceredig 112 F2
Cockshoot Hereford 97 D11
Cockshutford Shrops 131 F11
Cockshutt Shrops 132 G4
Shrops 149 D8
Cock Street Kent 53 C9
Suff 107 D9
Cockthorpe Norf 177 E7
Cockwells Corn 2 C2
Cockwood Devon 14 E5
Som 43 E8
Cockyard Derbys 185 F8
Hereford 97 E8
Codda Corn 11 F9
Coddenham Suff 126 G2
Coddenham Green Suff 126 F2
Coddington Ches W 167 D7
Hereford 98 C4
Notts 172 E4
Codford St Mary Wilts 46 F3
Codford St Peter Wilts 46 F3
Codicote Herts 86 B2
Codicote Bottom Herts 86 B2
Codmore Bucks 85 E7
Codmore Hill W Sus 35 C9
Codnor Derbys 170 F6
Codnor Breach Derbys 170 F6
Codnor Gate Derbys 170 E6
Codnor Park Derbys 170 E6
Codrington S Glos 61 D8
Codsall Staffs 133 C7
Codsall Wood Staffs 132 B6
Codsend Som 41 F11
Coedcae Bl Gwent 77 D11
Coedcae *continued*
Torf 78 D3
Coed Cwnwr Mon 78 F6
Coed Darcy Neath 76 F2
Coedely Rhondda 58 B4
Coed Eva Torf 78 G3
Coedkernew Newport 59 C9
Coed Llai = *Leeswood*
Flint 166 D3
Coed Mawr Gwyn 179 G9
Coed Morgan Mon 78 C5
Coedpoeth Wrex 166 E3
Coed-Talon Flint 166 D3
Coedway Powys 148 G6
Coed-y-bryn Ceredig 93 C7
Coed-y-caerau Newport 78 G5
Coed-y-fedw Mon 78 D6
Coed y Garth Ceredig 128 E3
Coed y go Shrops 148 D5
Coed-y-paen Mon 78 F4
Coed-y-parc Gwyn 163 B10
Coed-yr-ynys Powys 96 G3
Coed Ystumgwern
Gwyn 145 E11
Coed-y-wlad Powys 130 B4
Coelbren Powys 76 C4
Coffee Hall M Keynes 103 D7
Coffinswell Devon 9 B7
Cofton Devon 14 E5
Cofton Common
W Mid 117 B10
Cofton Hackett Worcs 117 B10
Cog V Glam 59 F7
Cogan V Glam 59 E7
Cogenhoe W Nhants 120 E6
Cogges Oxon 82 D5
Coggeshall Essex 106 G6
Coggeshall Hamlet
Essex 107 G7
Coggins Mill E Sus 37 B9
Coignafearn Lodge
Highld 291 B8
Coignascallan Highld 291 B9
Coig Peighinnean
W Isles 304 B7
Coig Peighinnean Bhuirgh
W Isles 304 C6
Coilacriech Aberds 292 D5
Coilantogle Stirling 285 G9
Coilessan Argyll 284 G6
Coilleag W Isles 297 K3
Coillemore Highld 300 B6
Coillore Highld 294 B5
Coirea-chrombe Stirling 285 G9
Coisley Hill S Yorks 186 E6
Coity Bridgend 58 C2
Cokenach Herts 105 D7
Cokhay Green Derbys 152 D5
Col W Isles 304 D6
Colaboll Highld 309 H5
Colan Corn 5 C7
Colaton Raleigh Devon 15 D7
Colbost Highld 298 E2
Colburn N Yorks 224 F3
Colby Cumb 231 G9
IoM 192 E3
Norf 160 C4
Colchester Essex 107 F10
Colchester Green Suff 125 F8
Colcot V Glam 58 F6
Cold Ash W Berks 64 F4
Cold Ashby W Nhants 120 B3
Cold Ash Hill Hants 49 G10
Cold Ashton S Glos 61 E9
Cold Aston Glos 81 B10
Coldbackie Highld 308 D6
Coldbeck Cumb 222 E4
Coldblow London 68 E4
Cold Blow Pembs 73 C10
Cold Brayfield
M Keynes 121 G8
Coldbrook Powys 96 D3
Cold Christmas Herts 86 B5
Cold Cotes N Yorks 212 E4
Coldean Brighton 36 F4
Coldeast Devon 14 G2
Coldeaton Derbys 169 D10
Cold Elm Glos 98 E6
Colden W Yorks 196 B3
Colden Common Hants 33 C7
Coldfair Green Suff 127 E8
Coldham Cambs 139 C8
Staffs 133 B7
Coldham's Common
Cambs 123 F9
Cold Hanworth Lincs 189 E8
Coldharbour Corn 4 F5
Devon 27 E9
Dorset 17 E9
Glos 79 E9
Kent 52 C5
London 68 D4
Sur 50 E6
Cold Harbour Dorset 18 D4
Herts 85 B10
Kent 69 G11
Lincs 155 C9
Oxon 64 D6
Wilts 45 B11
Wilts 45 D11
Windsor 65 D10
Cold Hatton Telford 150 E2
Cold Hatton Heath
Telford 150 E2
Cold Hesledon Durham 234 B4
Cold Hiendley W Yorks 197 E11
Cold Higham W Nhants 120 G3
Coldingham Borders 273 B8
Cold Inn Pembs 73 D10
Cold Kirby N Yorks 215 C10
Coldmeece Staffs 151 C7
Cold Moss Heath
Ches E 168 C3
Cold Newton Leics 136 B4
Cold Northcott Corn 11 D10
Cold Norton Essex 88 E4
Coldoch Stirling 278 B3
Cold Overton Leics 154 G6
Coldra Newport 59 B11
Coldrain Perth 286 G4
Coldred Kent 55 D9
Coldridge Devon 25 F11
Cold Row Lancs 202 E3
Coldstream Angus 287 D7
Borders 263 B8
Coldvreath Corn 5 D9
Coldwaltham W Sus 35 D8
Cold Well Staffs 151 G11
Coldwells Aberds 303 E11
Coldwells Croft Aberds 302 G5
Cole Som 45 G7
Colebatch Shrops 130 F6
Colebrook Devon 27 F8
Colebrooke Devon 13 B11
Coleburn Moray 302 D2
Coleby Lincs 173 C7
N Lincs 199 D11
Cole End Essex 105 D11
Warks 134 F3
Coleford Devon 26 G3
Glos 79 C9
Coleford *continued*
Som 45 D7
Coleford Water Som 42 G6
Colegate End Norf 142 F3
Cole Green Herts 86 C3
Herts 105 E8
Colehall W Mid 134 F2
Cole Henley Hants 48 C3
Colehill Dorset 31 G8
Coleman Green Herts 85 C11
Coleman's Hatch E Sus 52 G3
Colemere Shrops 149 C8
Colemore Hants 49 G8
Colemore Green Shrops 132 D4
Coleorton Leics 153 F8
Coleorton Moor Leics 153 F8
Cole Park London 67 E7
Colerne Wilts 61 E10
Colesbourne Glos 81 C7
Colesbrook Dorset 30 B4
Cole's Cross Dorset 28 G5
Colesden Bedford 122 F2
Coles Green Suff 107 C11
Worcs 116 G5
Cole's Green Suff 126 E5
Coleshill Bucks 85 F7
Oxon 82 G2
Warks 134 F4
Coles Meads Sur 51 C9
Colestocks Devon 27 G9
Colethrop Glos 80 C4
Coley Bath 44 B5
Reading 65 E8
W Yorks 196 B6
Colfin Dumfries 236 D2
Colgate W Sus 51 G8
Colgrain Argyll 276 E6
Colham Green London 66 C5
Colindale London 67 B8
Colinsburgh Fife 287 G8
Colinton Edin 270 B4
Colintraive Argyll 275 F11
Colkirk Norf 159 D8
Collace Perth 286 D6
Collafield Glos 79 C11
Collafirth Shetland 312 G6
Collam W Isles 305 J3
Collamoor Head Corn 11 C9
Collaton Devon 9 G9
Collaton St Mary Torbay 9 D7
College Milton S Lanark 268 D2
College of Roseisle
Moray 301 C11
College Park London 67 C8
College Town Brack 65 G11
Collennan S Ayrs 257 C8
Collessie Fife 286 F6
Colleton Mills Devon 25 D11
Collett's Br Norf 139 B9
Collett's Green Worcs 116 G6
Collier Row London 87 G8
Collier's End Herts 105 G7
Collier's Green E Sus 38 C3
Kent 53 F9
Colliers Hatch Essex 87 E8
Collier Street Kent 53 D8
Collier's Wood London 67 E9
Colliery Row T&W 234 B2
Collieston Aberds 303 G10
Collin Dumfries 238 B2
Collingbourne Ducis
Wilts 47 C8
Collingbourne Kingston
Wilts 47 B8
Collingham Notts 172 C4
W Yorks 206 D3
Collington Hereford 116 E2
Collingtree W Nhants 120 F5
Collingwood Northumb 243 B7
Collins End Oxon 65 D7
Collins Green Warr 183 C9
Worcs 116 F4
Colliepriest Devon 27 E7
Colliston Angus 287 C10
Colliton Devon 27 G9
Collycroft Warks 135 F7
Collyhurst Gtr Man 195 G11
Collynie Aberds 303 F8
Collyweston N Nhants 137 C9
Colmonell S Ayrs 244 F4
Colmslie Borders 262 B2
Colmsliehill Borders 271 G10
Colmworth Bedford 122 F2
Colnabaichin Aberds 292 C4
Colnbrook Slough 66 D4
Colne Cambs 123 B7
Lancs 204 E3
Colne Bridge W Yorks 197 C7
Colne Edge Lancs 204 E3
Colne Engaine Essex 107 E7
Colnefields Cambs 123 B7
Colney Norf 142 B3
Colney Hatch London 86 G3
Colney Heath Herts 86 D2
Colney Street Herts 85 E11
Coln Rogers Glos 81 D9
Coln St Aldwyns Glos 81 D10
Coln St Dennis Glos 81 C9
Cologin Argyll 289 G10
Colpitts Grange
Northumb 241 F11
Colpy Aberds 302 F6
Colquhar Borders 270 G6
Colscott Devon 24 E5
Colshaw Staffs 169 B8
Colsterdale N Yorks 214 C2
Colsterworth Lincs 155 E8
Colston E Dunb 268 B2
Pembs 91 F9
Colston Bassett Notts 154 C3
Colstrope Bucks 65 B9
Coltfield Moray 301 C11
Colt Hill Hants 49 C8
Colthouse Cumb 221 F7
Colthrop W Berks 64 F4
Coltishall Norf 160 F5
Coltness N Lanark 268 D6
Colton Cumb 210 B6
Norf 142 B2
N Yorks 206 E6
Staffs 151 E11
Suff 125 D7
W Yorks 206 G3
Colton Hills Staffs 133 D8
Colt Park Cumb 210 E5
Colt's Green S Glos 61 C8
Colt's Hill Kent 52 E6
Col Uarach W Isles 304 E6
Columbia T&W 243 F8
Columbjohn Devon 14 B5
Colva Powys 114 G4
Colvend Dumfries 237 D10
Colvister Shetland 312 D7
Colwall Hereford 98 C4
Colwall Green Hereford 98 C4
Colwall Stone Hereford 98 C5
Colwell IoW 20 D2
Northumb 241 B11
Colwich Staffs 151 E10
Colwick Notts 171 G10
Colwinston = *Tregolwyn*
V Glam 58 D2
Colworth W Sus 22 C6
Colwyn Bay = *Bae Colwyn*
Conwy 180 F4
Colychurch Bridgend 58 D2
Colyford Devon 15 C10
Colyton Devon 15 C10
Colzie Fife 286 F6
Combe Devon 7 E10
Devon 8 B4
Devon 9 G9
E Sus 37 B10
Hereford 114 E6
Oxon 82 B6
Som 28 B6
W Berks 63 G11
Combe Almer Dorset 18 B5
Combebow Devon 12 D5
Combe Common Sur 50 F3
Combe Down Bath 61 G9
Combe Fishacre Devon 8 C6
Combe Florey Som 43 G7
Combe Hay Bath 45 B8
Combeinteignhead
Devon 14 G4
Combe Martin Devon 40 D5
Combe Moor Hereford 115 E7
Combe Pafford Torbay 9 B8
Combe Raleigh Devon 27 G11
Comberbach Ches W 183 F10
Comberford Staffs 134 B3
Comberton Cambs 123 F7
Hereford 115 D9
Combe St Nicholas Som 28 E4
Combe Throop Som 30 C2
Combpyne Devon 15 C11
Combrew Devon 40 G4
Combridge Staffs 151 B11
Combrook Warks 118 G6
Combs Derbys 185 F8
Suff 125 F10
W Yorks 197 D8
Combs Ford Suff 125 F11
Combwich Som 43 E9
Comers Aberds 293 C8
Come-to-Good Corn 4 G6
Comeytrowe Som 28 C2
Comford Corn 2 B6
Comfort Corn 2 D6
Comhampton Worcs 116 D6
Comins Coch Ceredig 128 G2
Comiston Edin 270 B4
Comley Shrops 131 D9
Commercial End
Cambs 123 E11
Commins Denb 165 C10
Commins Capel Betws
Ceredig 112 F2
Commins Coch Powys 128 C6
Common Cefn-llwyn
Mon 78 G4
Commondale N Yorks 226 C3
Common Edge Blackpool 202 G2
Common End Cumb 228 G6
Derbys 170 C6
Common Hill Hereford 97 E11
Commonmoor Corn 6 B4
Common Moor Corn 6 B4
Common Platt Wilts 62 B6
Commonside Ches W 183 G8
Derbys 170 G2
Notts 171 D7
Common Side Ches W 167 B9
Derbys 170 F6
Derbys 186 F4
Commonwood Herts 85 E8
Shrops 149 D9
Wrex 166 E5
Common-y-coed Mon 60 B2
Comp Kent 52 B6
Compass Som 43 G9
Compstall Gtr Man 185 C7
Compton Derbys 169 F11
Devon 9 C7
Hants 32 B4
Hants 33 B7
Plym 7 D9
Staffs 132 G6
Sur 49 D11
Sur 50 D3
W Berks 64 D4
Wilts 46 C6
W Mid 133 D7
W Sus 34 E3
W Yorks 206 E3
Compton Abbas Dorset 30 D5
Compton Abdale Glos 81 B9
Compton Bassett Wilts 62 E4
Compton Beauchamp
Oxon 63 B9
Compton Bishop Som 43 B11
Compton Chamberlayne
Wilts 31 B8
Compton Common Bath 60 G6
Compton Dando Bath 60 G6
Compton Dundon Som 44 G3
Compton Durville Som 28 D6
Compton End Hants 33 B7
Compton Green Glos 98 F4
Compton Greenfield
S Glos 60 C5
Compton Martin Bath 44 B4
Compton Pauncefoot
Som 29 B10
Compton Valence Dorset 17 C7
Comrie Fife 279 D10
Highld 300 D4
Perth 285 C11
Perth 285 E11
Comrue Dumfries 248 F3
Conaglen House Highld 290 G2
Conanby S Yorks 187 B7
Conchra Argyll 275 E11
Highld 295 C10
Concord T&W 243 F8
Concraig Perth 286 F2
Concraigie Perth 286 C5
Conder Green Lancs 202 B5
Conderton Worcs 99 D9
Condicote Glos 100 F3
Condorrat N Lanark 278 G4
Condover Shrops 131 B9
Coney Hall London 67 G11
Coney Hill Glos 80 B5
Coneyhurst W Sus 35 C10
Coneysthorpe N Yorks 216 E4
Coneythorpe N Yorks 206 B3
Coney Weston Suff 125 B9
Conford Hants 49 G10
Congash Highld 301 G10
Congdon's Shop Corn 11 F11
Congeith Dumfries 237 C10
Congelow Kent 53 D7
Congerstone Leics 135 B7
Congham Norf 158 E4
Congleton Ches E 168 C5
Congleton Edge Ches E 168 C5
Congl-y-wal Gwyn 164 G2

Congresbury N Som 60 G2
Congreve Staffs 151 G8
Conham Bristol 60 E6
Conicavel Moray 301 D9
Coningsby Lincs 174 D2
Conington Cambs 122 D6
Cambs 138 F3
Conisbrough S Yorks 187 B8
Conisby Argyll 274 G3
Conisholme Lincs 190 B6
Coniston Cumb 220 F6
E Yorks 209 F9
Coniston Cold N Yorks 204 B4
Conistone N Yorks 213 F9
Conkwell Wilts 61 G9
Connage Moray 302 C4
Connah's Quay Flint 166 B3
Connel Argyll 289 F11
Connel Park E Ayrs 258 G4
Conniburrow M Keynes 103 D7
Connista Highld 298 B4
Connon Corn 6 C3
Connor Downs Corn 2 B3
Conock Wilts 46 B5
Conon Bridge Highld 300 D5
Conon House Highld 300 D5
Cononish Stirling 285 E7
Cononley N Yorks 204 D5
Cononley Woodside
N Yorks 204 D5
Cononsyth Angus 287 C9
Conordan Highld 295 B7
Conquermoor Heath
Telford 150 F3
Consall Staffs 169 F7
Consett Durham 242 G4
Constable Burton
N Yorks 224 G3
Constable Lee Lancs 195 C10
Constantine Corn 2 D6
Constantine Bay Corn 10 G3
Contin Highld 300 D4
Contlaw Aberdeen 293 C10
Conwy Conwy 180 F3
Conyer Kent 70 G3
Conyers Green Suff 125 D7
Cooden E Sus 38 F2
Cooil IoM 192 E4
Cookbury Devon 24 F6
Cookbury Wick Devon 24 F5
Cookham Windsor 65 B11
Cookham Dean Windsor 65 C11
Cookham Rise Windsor 65 C11
Cookhill Worcs 117 F11
Cookley Suff 126 B6
Worcs 132 G6
Cookley Green Oxon 83 G11
Cookney Aberds 293 D10
Cookridge W Yorks 205 E11
Cooksbridge E Sus 36 E6
Cooksey Corner Worcs 117 D8
Cooksey Green Worcs 117 D8
Cook's Green Essex 89 B11
Suff 125 G9
Cookshill Staffs 168 G6
Cooksland Corn 5 B11
Cooksmill Green Essex 87 D10
Cooksongreen Ches W 183 G9
Coolham W Sus 35 C10
Cooling Medway 69 D9
Coolinge Kent 55 F8
Cooling Street Medway 69 E8
Coombe Bucks 84 D4
Corn 4 G2
Corn 4 G5
Corn 4 G6
Corn 5 E9
Corn 6 C4
Corn 24 E2
Devon 14 G4
Devon 27 D8
Glos 80 G3
Hants 33 C11
Kent 55 B9
London 67 E8
Som 28 B3
Som 28 F6
Wilts 30 C5
Wilts 47 C7
Coombe Bissett Wilts 31 B10
Coombe Dingle Bristol 60 D5
Coombe Hill Glos 99 F7
Coombe Keynes Dorset 18 E2
Coombes W Sus 35 F11
Coombesdale Staffs 150 B6
Coombeswood W Mid 133 F9
Coomb Hill Kent 69 G7
Coombs End S Glos 61 C9
Coombses Som 28 F4
Coopersale Common
Essex 87 E7
Coopersale Street Essex 87 E7
Cooper's Corner Kent 52 D3
Cooper's Green E Sus 37 C7
Herts 85 D11
Cooper's Hill C Beds 103 D10
Sur 66 E3
Cooper Street Kent 55 B10
Cooper Turning
Gtr Man 194 F6
Cootham W Sus 35 E9
Copcut Worcs 117 E7
Copdock Suff 108 C2
Coped Hall Wilts 62 C5
Copenhagen Denb 165 B8
Copford Essex 107 G8
Copford Green Essex 107 G8
Copgrove N Yorks 214 G6
Copister Shetland 312 F6
Cople Bedford 104 B2
Copley Durham 233 F7
Gtr Man 185 B7
W Yorks 196 C5
Copley Hill W Yorks 197 B8
Coplow Dale Derbys 185 F11
Copmanthorpe York 207 D7
Copmere End Staffs 150 D6
Copnor Ptsmth 33 G11
Copp Lancs 202 F4
Coppathorne Corn 24 G2
Coppenhall Ches E 168 D2
Staffs 151 F8
Coppenhall Moss
Ches E 168 D2
Copperhouse Corn 2 B3
Coppice Gtr Man 196 G2
Coppicegate Shrops 132 G4
Coppingford Cambs 138 G3
Coppins Corner Kent 54 D2
Coppleham Som 42 G2
Copplestone Devon 26 G3
Coppull Lancs 194 E5
Coppull Moor Lancs 194 E5
Copsale W Sus 35 C11
Copse Hill London 67 E8
Copster Green Lancs 203 G9
Copster Hill Gtr Man 196 G2
Copston Magna Warks 135 F9
Cop Street Kent 55 B9
Copt Green Warks 118 D3
Copthall Green Essex 86 E6
Copt Heath W Mid 118 B3
Copt Hewick N Yorks 214 E6
Copthill Durham 232 C3
Copthorne Ches E 167 G11
Corn 11 C11
Shrops 149 G9
Sur 51 F10
Coptiviney Shrops 149 B8
Copt Oak Leics 153 G9
Copton Kent 54 B4
Copy's Green Norf 159 B8
Copythorne Hants 32 E4
Corbets Tey London 68 B5
Corbridge Northumb 241 E11
Corbriggs Derbys 170 B6
Corby N Nhants 137 F7
Corby Glen Lincs 155 E9
Corby Hill Cumb 239 F11
Cordon N Ayrs 256 C2
Cordwell Norf 142 E2
Coreley Shrops 116 C2
Cores End Bucks 66 B2
Corfe Som 28 D2
Corfe Castle Dorset 18 E5
Corfe Mullen Dorset 18 B5
Corfton Shrops 131 F9
Corfton Bache Shrops 131 F9
Corgarff Aberds 292 C4
Corgee Corn 5 C10
Corhampton Hants 33 C10
Corlae Dumfries 246 D5
Corlannau Neath 57 C9
Corley Warks 134 F6
Corley Ash Warks 134 F5
Corley Moor Warks 134 F5
Cornaa IoM 192 D5
Cornabus Argyll 254 C4
Cornaigbeg Argyll 288 E1
Cornaigmore Argyll 288 C4
Argyll 288 E1
Cornard Tye Suff 107 C8
Cornbank Midloth 270 C4
Cornbrook Shrops 116 B2
Corncatterach Aberds 302 F5
Cornel Conwy 164 C2
Corner Row Lancs 202 F4
Cornett Hereford 97 B11
Corney Cumb 220 G2
Cornforth Durham 234 E2
Cornharrow Dumfries 246 E5
Cornhill Aberds 302 D5
Powys 96 C2
Stoke 168 E5
Cornhill-on-Tweed
Northumb 263 B9
Cornholme W Yorks 196 B2
Cornish Hall End Essex 106 D3
Cornquoy Orkney 314 G5
Cornriggs Durham 232 C2
Cornsay Durham 233 C8
Cornsay Colliery
Durham 233 C9
Cornton Stirling 278 B5
Corntown Highld 300 D5
V Glam 58 D2
Cornwell Oxon 100 F5
Cornwood Devon 8 D2
Cornworthy Devon 8 D6
Corpach Highld 290 F2
Corpusty Norf 160 C2
Corran Highld 290 G2
Highld 295 E10
Corran a Chan Uachdaraich
Highld 295 C7
Corranbuie Argyll 275 G9
Corrany IoM 192 D5
Corrichoich Highld 311 G4
Corrie N Ayrs 255 C11
Corrie Common
Dumfries 248 F6
Corriecravie N Ayrs 255 E10
Corriecravie Moor
N Ayrs 255 E10
Corriedoo Dumfries 246 G5
Corriegarth Lodge
Highld 291 B7
Corriemoillie Highld 300 C3
Corriemulzie Lodge
Highld 309 K3
Corrievarkie Lodge
Perth 291 F7
Corrievorrie Highld 301 G7
Corrigall Orkney 314 E3
Corrimony Highld 300 F3
Corringham Lincs 188 C5
Thurrock 69 C8
Corris Gwyn 128 B5
Corris Uchaf Gwyn 128 B4
Corrour Highld 290 G5
Corrour Shooting Lodge
Highld 290 G6
Corrow Argyll 284 G5
Corry Highld 295 C8
Corrybrough Highld 301 G8
Corrydon Perth 292 G3
Corryghoil Argyll 284 E5
Corrykinloch Highld 309 G3
Corrylach Argyll 255 D8
Corrymuckloch Perth 286 D2
Corrynachenchy Argyll 289 E8
Corry of Ardnagrask
Highld 300 E5
Corsback Highld 310 B6
Corscombe Dorset 29 F8
Corse Aberds 302 E6
Glos 98 F5
Corse Lawn Worcs 98 E6
Corse of Kinnoir Aberds 302 E5
Corsewall Dumfries 236 C2
Corsham Wilts 61 E11
Corsindae Aberds 293 C8
Corsley Wilts 45 D10
Corsley Heath Wilts 45 D10
Corsock Dumfries 237 B9
Corston Bath 61 F7
Orkney 314 E3
Wilts 62 C2
Corstorphine Edin 280 G3
Cors-y-Gedol Gwyn 145 E11
Cortachy Angus 287 B7
Corton Suff 143 D10
Wilts 46 E2
Corton Denham Som 29 C10
Cortworth S Yorks 186 B6
Coruanan Lodge Highld 290 G2
Corunna W Isles 296 E4
Corvast Highld 309 K5
Corwen Denb 165 G9
Cory Devon 24 D5
Coryates Dorset 17 D8
Coryton Cardiff 58 C6
Devon 12 E5
Thurrock 69 C8
Còsag Highld 295 D10
Cosby Leics 135 E10
Coscote Oxon 64 B4
Coseley W Mid 133 E8
Cosford Warks 119 B9
Cosgrove W Nhants 102 C5
Cosham Ptsmth 33 F11
Cosheston Pembs 73 E8
Cosmeston V Glam 59 F7
Cosmore Dorset 29 F11
Cossall Notts 171 G7
Cossall Marsh Notts 171 G7
Cosses S Ayrs 244 G4
Cossington Leics 154 G2
Som 43 E11
Costa Orkney 314 D3
Costessey Norf 160 G3
Costessey Park Norf 160 G3
Costhorpe Notts 187 D9
Costislost Corn 10 G6
Costock Notts 153 D11
Coston Leics 154 E6
Norf 141 B11
Coswinsawsin Corn 2 B4
Cote Oxon 82 E4
Som 43 E10
W Sus 35 F10
Cotebrook Ches W 167 B9
Cotehill Cumb 239 G11
Cotes Cumb 211 B9
Leics 153 E11
Staffs 150 C6
Cotesbach Leics 135 G10
Cotes Heath Staffs 150 C6
Cotes Park Derbys 170 E6
Cotford St Lukes Som 27 B11
Cotgrave Notts 154 B2
Cothall Aberds 293 B10
Cotham Bristol 60 E5
Notts 172 F3
Cothelstone Som 43 G7
Cotheridge Worcs 116 G5
Cotherstone Durham 223 B10
Cothill Oxon 83 F7
Cotland Mon 79 E8
Cotleigh Devon 28 G2
Cotmanhay Derbys 171 G7
Cotmarsh Wilts 62 D5
Cotmaton Devon 15 D8
Coton Cambs 123 F8
Shrops 149 C10
Staffs 134 B3
Staffs 150 E6
Staffs 151 C9
W Nhants 120 C3
Coton Clanford Staffs 151 E7
Coton Hayes Staffs 151 C9
Coton Hill Shrops 149 G9
Staffs 151 C9
Coton in the Clay Staffs 152 D3
Coton in the Elms
Derbys 152 F4
Coton Park Derbys 152 F5
Cotonwood Shrops 149 B10
Staffs 150 E6
Cotswold Community
Wilts 81 F8
Cott Devon 8 C5
Cottam E Yorks 217 F9
Lancs 202 G6
Notts 188 F4
Cottartown Highld 301 F10
Cottenham Cambs 123 D8
Cottenham Park London 67 F8
Cotterdale N Yorks 222 G6
Cottered Herts 104 F6
Cotterhill Woods
S Yorks 187 E9
Cotteridge W Mid 117 B10
Cotterstock N Nhants 137 E10
Cottesbrooke W Nhants 120 C4
Cottesmore Rutland 155 G8
Cotteylands Devon 26 E6
Cottingham E Yorks 208 G6
N Nhants 136 E6
Cottingley W Yorks 205 F8
Cottisford Oxon 101 E11
Cotton Staffs 169 F9
Suff 125 D11
Cotton End Bedford 103 B11
W Nhants 120 F5
Cotton Stones W Yorks 196 C4
Cotton Tree Lancs 204 F4
Cottonworth Hants 47 F11
Cottown Aberds 293 B9
Aberds 302 G5
Aberds 303 E8
Cotts Devon 7 B8
Cottwood Devon 25 E10
Cotwall Telford 150 F2
Cotwalton Staffs 151 B8
Coubister Orkney 314 E3
Couch Green Hants 48 G4
Couch's Mill Corn 6 D2
Coughton Hereford 97 G11
Warks 117 E11
Coughton Fields Warks 117 F11
Cougie Highld 300 G2
Coulaghailtro Argyll 275 G8
Coulags Highld 299 E9
Coulby Newham Mbro 225 B10
Coulderton Cumb 219 D9
Couldoran Highld 299 E8
Couligartan Stirling 285 G8
Coulin Highld 299 D10
Coulin Lodge Highld 299 D10
Coull Aberds 293 C7
Argyll 274 G3
Coulmony Ho Highld 301 E9
Coulport Argyll 276 D4
Coulsdon London 51 B9
Coulshill Perth 286 G3
Coulston Wilts 46 C3
Coulter S Lanark 260 C2
Coultings Som 43 E8
Coulton N Yorks 216 E2
Coultra Fife 287 E7
Cound Shrops 131 C11
Coundlane Shrops 131 B11
Coundmoor Shrops 131 C11
Coundon Durham 233 F10
W Mid 134 G6
Coundongate Durham 233 F10
Coundon Grange
Durham 233 F10
Counters End Herts 85 D8
Countersett N Yorks 213 B8
Countess Wilts 47 E7
Countess Cross Essex 107 E7
Countess Wear Devon 14 D4
Countesthorpe Leics 135 D11
Countisbury Devon 41 D8
County Oak W Sus 51 F9
Coupar Angus Perth 286 C6
Coup Green Lancs 194 B5
Coupland Cumb 222 B4
Northumb 263 C10
Cour Argyll 255 C9
Courance Dumfries 248 E3
Coursley Som 42 G6
Court-at-Street Kent 54 F5
Court Barton Devon 14 D2
Court Colman Bridgend 57 E11
Court Corner Hants 48 B6
Courteenhall W Nhants 120 G5
Court Henry Carms 93 G11
Courthill Perth 286 C5
Court House Green
W Mid 135 G7
Courtsend Essex 89 G8
Courtway Som 43 G8
Cousland Midloth 271 B7
Cousley Wood E Sus 53 G7
Couston Argyll 275 F11
Cova Shetland 313 J5
Cove Argyll 276 E4
Borders 282 G5
Devon 27 D7
Hants 49 B11
Highld 307 K3
Cove Bay Aberdeen 293 C11
Cove Bottom Suff 127 B9
Covehithe Suff 143 G10
Coven Staffs 133 B8
Covender Hereford 98 C2
Coveney Cambs 139 G9
Covenham St Bartholomew
Lincs 190 C4
Covenham St Mary
Lincs 190 C4
Coven Heath Staffs 133 C8
Coven Lawn Staffs 133 B8
Coventry W Mid 118 B6
Coverack Corn 3 F7
Coverack Bridges Corn 2 C5
Coverham N Yorks 214 B2
Covesea Moray 301 B11
Covingham Swindon 63 B7
Covington Cambs 121 C11
S Lanark 259 B11
Cowan Bridge Lancs 212 D2
Cow Ark Lancs 203 D9
Cowbar Redcar 226 B5
Cowbeech E Sus 23 C10
Cowbeech Hill E Sus 23 C10
Cowbit Lincs 156 F5
Cowbog Aberds 303 D8
Cowbridge Lincs 174 F4
Som 42 E3
Cowbridge = *Y Bont-Faen*
V Glam 58 E3
Cowcliffe W Yorks 196 D6
Cowdale Derbys 185 G9
Cowden Kent 52 E3
Cowdenbeath Fife 280 C3
Cowdenburn Borders 270 E4
Cowen Head Cumb 221 F9
Cowers Lane Derbys 170 F4
Cowes IoW 20 B5
Cowesby N Yorks 215 B9
Cowesfield Green Wilts 32 C3
Cowfold W Sus 36 C2
Cowgill Cumb 212 B5
Cow Green Suff 125 D11
Cowgrove Dorset 18 B5
Cowhill Derbys 170 F5
S Glos 79 G10
Cow Hill Lancs 203 G7
Cowhorn Hill S Glos 61 E7
Cowie Aberds 293 E10
Stirling 278 D6
Cowlands Corn 4 G6
Cowleaze Corner Oxon 82 E4
Cowley Derbys 186 F4
Devon 14 B4
Glos 81 C7
London 66 C5
Oxon 83 E8
Cowleymoor Devon 27 E7
Cowley Peachy London 66 C5
Cowling Lancs 194 D5
N Yorks 204 E5
N Yorks 214 B4
Cowlinge Suff 124 G4
Cowlow Derbys 185 G9
Cowmes W Yorks 197 D7
Cowpe Lancs 195 C10
Cowpen Northumb 253 G7
Cowpen Bewley
Stockton 234 G5
Cowplain Hants 33 E11
Cow Roast Herts 85 C7
Cowshill Durham 232 C3
Cowslip Green N Som 60 G3
Cowstrandburn Fife 279 C10
Cowthorpe N Yorks 206 C4
Coxall Hereford 115 C7
Coxbank Ches E 167 G11
Coxbench Derbys 170 G5
Coxbridge Som 44 F4
Cox Common Suff 143 G8
Coxford Corn 11 B9
Norf 158 D6
Soton 32 D5
Coxgreen Staffs 132 F6
Cox Green Gtr Man 195 E8
Sur 50 G5
Windsor 65 D11
Coxheath Kent 53 C8
Coxhill Kent 55 D8
Cox Hill Corn 4 G4
Coxhoe Durham 234 D2
Coxley Som 44 E4
W Yorks 197 D9
Coxley Wick Som 44 E4
Coxlodge T&W 242 D6
Cox Moor Notts 171 D8
Coxpark Corn 12 G4
Coxtie Green Essex 87 F9
Coxwold N Yorks 215 D10
Coychurch Bridgend 58 D2
Coylton S Ayrs 257 E10
Coylumbridge Highld 291 B11
Coynach Aberds 292 C6
Coynachie Aberds 302 F4
Coytrahen Bridgend 57 D11
CoytrahÛn Bridgend 57 D11
Crabadon Devon 8 E5
Crabbet Park W Sus 51 F10
Crabble Kent 55 E9
Crabbs Cross Worcs 117 E10
Crabbs Green Herts 105 F9
Crabgate Norf 159 D11
Crab Orchard Dorset 31 F9
Crabtree Plym 7 D10
W Sus 36 B2
Crabtree Green Wrex 166 G4
Crackaig Argyll 274 G6
Crackenedge W Yorks 197 C8
Crackenthorpe Cumb 231 G9
Crackington Haven Corn 11 B8
Crackley Staffs 168 E4
Warks 118 C5
Crackleybank Shrops 150 G5
Crackpot N Yorks 223 F9
Crackthorn Corner
Suff 125 B10
Cracoe N Yorks 213 G9
Cracow Moss Ches E 168 F2
Staffs 168 F3
Craddock Devon 27 E9
Cradhlastadh W Isles 304 E2
Cradle Edge W Yorks 205 F7
Cradle End Herts 105 G9
Cradley Hereford 98 B4
W Mid 133 G8
Cradley Heath W Mid 133 F8
Cradoc Powys 95 E10
Crafthole Corn 7 E7
Crafton Bucks 84 B5
Crag Bank Lancs 211 E9
Crag Foot Lancs 211 E9
Craggan Highld 301 G10
Moray 301 F11
Stirling 285 E9
Cragganvallie Highld 300 F5
Craggenmore Moray 301 F11
Cragg Hill W Yorks 205 F10
Craggie Highld 301 F7
Highld 311 H2
Craggiemore Highld 309 J7
Cragg Vale W Yorks 196 C4
Craghead Durham 242 G6
Crahan Corn 2 C5
Crai Powys 95 G7
Craibstone Moray 302 D4
Craichie Angus 287 C9
Craig Dumfries 237 B8
Dumfries 237 C8
Highld 299 E10
Craiganor Lodge Perth 285 B10
Craig Berthlwyd M Tydf 77 F9
Craig Castle Aberds 302 G4
Craig-cefn-parc
Swansea 75 E11
Craigdallie Perth 286 E6
Craigdam Aberds 303 F8
Craigdarroch Dumfries 246 E6
Highld 300 D4
Craigdhu Highld 300 E4
Craig Douglas Borders 261 E7
Craigearn Aberds 293 B9
Craigellachie Moray 302 E2
Craigencallie Ho
Dumfries 237 B7
Craigencross Dumfries 236 C2
Craigend Borders 271 F9
Glasgow 268 B3
Perth 286 E3
Perth 286 E5
Stirling 278 D5
Craigendive Argyll 275 E11
Craigendoran Argyll 276 E6
Craigendowie Angus 293 G7
Craigends Renfs 267 B8
Craigens Argyll 274 G3
E Ayrs 258 F3
Craigentinny Edin 280 G5
Craigerne Borders 261 B7
Craighall Perth 286 C5
Craighat Stirling 277 E9
Craighead Fife 287 G10
Highld 301 C7
Craighill Aberds 303 E7
Craighlaw Mains
Dumfries 236 C5
Craighouse Argyll 274 G6
Craigie Aberds 293 B11
Dundee 287 D8
Perth 286 C5
Perth 286 E5
S Ayrs 257 C10
S Ayrs 257 E8
Craigiefield Orkney 314 E4
Craigiehall Edin 280 F3
Craigielaw E Loth 281 F9
Craigierig Borders 260 E6
Craigleith Edin 280 G4
Craig Llangiwg Neath 76 D2
Craig-llwyn Shrops 148 D4
Craiglockhart Edin 280 G4
Craig Lodge Argyll 275 G10
Craigmalloch E Ayrs 245 E11
Craigmaud Aberds 303 D8
Craigmill Stirling 278 B6
Craigmillar Edin 280 G5
Craigmore Argyll 266 B2
Craig-moston Aberds 293 F8
Craignant Shrops 148 B5
Craignell Dumfries 237 B7
Craigneuk N Lanark 268 C5
N Lanark 268 D5
Craignish Castle Argyll 275 C8
Craignure Argyll 289 F9
Craigo Angus 293 G8
Craigow Perth 286 G4
Craig Penllyn V Glam 58 D3
Craigrory Highld 300 E6
Craigrothie Fife 287 F7
Craigroy Moray 301 D11
Craigruie Stirling 285 E8
Craig's End Essex 106 D4
Craigsford Mains
Borders 262 B3
Craigshall Dumfries 237 D10
Craigshill W Loth 269 B11
Craigside Durham 233 D8
Craigston Castle Aberds 303 D7
Craigton Aberdeen 293 C10
Angus 287 B7
Angus 287 D9
Glasgow 267 C10
Highld 300 E6
Highld 309 H6
Highld 309 K6
Craigtown Highld 310 D2
Craig-y-don Conwy 180 E3
Craig-y-Duke Swansea 76 E2
Craig-y-nos Powys 76 B4
Craig-y-penrhyn
Ceredig 128 E3
Craig-y-Rhacca Caerph 59 B7
Craik Borders 249 B8
Crail Fife 287 G10
Crailing Borders 262 E5
Crailinghall Borders 262 E5
Crakaig Highld 311 H3
Crakehill N Yorks 215 E8
Crakemarsh Staffs 151 B11
Crambe N Yorks 216 G4
Crambeck N Yorks 216 F4
Cramhurst Sur 50 E2
Cramlington Northumb 243 B7
Cramond Edin 280 F3
Cramond Bridge Edin 280 F3
Crampmoor Hants 32 C5
Cranage Ches E 168 B3
Cranberry Staffs 150 B6
Cranborne Dorset 31 E9
Cranbourne Brack 66 E2
Hants 48 C6
Cranbrook Devon 14 B6
Kent 53 F9
London 68 B2
Cranbrook Common Kent 53 F9
Crane Moor S Yorks 197 G10
Crane's Corner Norf 159 G8
Cranfield C Beds 103 C9
Cranford Devon 24 C4
London 66 D6
Cranford St Andrew
N Nhants 121 B8
Cranford St John
N Nhants 121 B8
Cranham Glos 80 C5
London 68 B5
Cranhill Glasgow 268 B2
Warks 118 G2
Crank Mers 183 B8
Crank Wood Gtr Man 194 G6
Cranleigh Sur 50 F5
Cranley Suff 126 C3
Cranley Gardens London 67 B9
Cranmer Green Suff 125 C10
Cranmore IoW 20 D3
Som 45 E7
Cranna Aberds 302 D6
Crannich Argyll 289 E7
Crannoch Moray 302 D4
Cranoe Leics 136 D5
Cransford Suff 126 E6
Cranshaws Borders 272 C3
Cranstal IoM 192 B5
Cranswick E Yorks 208 C6
Crantock Corn 4 C5
Cranwell Lincs 173 F8
Cranwich Norf 140 E5
Cranworth Norf 141 C9
Craobh Haven Argyll 275 C8
Crapstone Devon 7 B10
Crarae Argyll 275 D10
Crask Highld 308 C7
Crask Inn Highld 309 G5
Craskins Aberds 293 C7
Crask of Aigas Highld 300 E4
Craster Northumb 265 F7
Craswall Hereford 96 D5
Crateford Shrops 132 F4
Staffs 133 B8
Cratfield Suff 126 B6
Crathes Aberds 293 D9
Crathie Aberds 292 D4
Highld 291 D7
Crathorne N Yorks 225 D8
Craven Arms Shrops 131 G8
Crawcrook T&W 242 E4
Crawford Lancs 194 G3
S Lanark 259 E11
Crawforddyke S Lanark 269 F7
Crawfordjohn S Lanark 259 E9
Crawick Dumfries 259 G7
Crawley Devon 28 F3
Hants 48 G2
Oxon 82 C4
W Sus 51 F9
Crawley Down W Sus 51 F10
Crawley End Essex 105 C8
Crawley Hill Sur 65 G11
Crawleyside Durham 232 C5
Crawshaw W Yorks 197 E8
Crawshawbooth Lancs 195 B10
Crawton Aberds 293 F10
Cray N Yorks 213 D8
Perth 292 G3
Crayford London 68 E4
Crayke N Yorks 215 E11
Craymere Beck Norf 159 C11
Crays Hill Essex 88 G2
Cray's Pond Oxon 64 C6
Crazies Hill Wokingham 65 C9
Creacombe Devon 26 D4
Creagan Argyll 289 E11
Creagan Sithe Argyll 284 G6
Creag Aoil Highld 290 F3
Creagastrom W Isles 297 G4
Creag Ghoraidh
W Isles 297 G3
Creaguaineach Lodge
Highld 290 G5
Creaksea Essex 88 F6
Creamore Bank Shrops 149 C10
Crean Corn 1 E3
Creaton W Nhants 120 C4
Creca Dumfries 238 C6
Credenhill Hereford 97 C9
Crediton Devon 26 G4
Creebridge Dumfries 236 C6
Creech Dorset 18 E4
Creech Bottom Dorset 18 E4
Creech Heathfield Som 28 B3
Creech St Michael Som 28 B3
Creed Corn 5 F8
Creediknowe Shetland 312 G7
Creegbrawse Corn 4 G4
Creekmoor BCP 18 C6
Creekmouth London 68 C3
Creeksea Essex 88 F6
Creeting Bottoms Suff 126 F2
Creeting St Mary Suff 125 F11
Creeton Lincs 155 E10
Creetown Dumfries 236 D6
Creggans Argyll 284 G4
Cregneash IoM 192 F2
Creg-ny-Baa IoM 192 D4
Cregrina Powys 114 G2
Creich Fife 287 E7
Creigau Mon 79 F7
Creighton Staffs 151 B11
Creigiau Cardiff 58 C5
Crelly Corn 2 C5
Cremyll Corn 7 E9
Crendell Dorset 31 E9
Crepkill Highld 298 E4
Creslow Bucks 102 G6
Cressage Shrops 131 C11
Cressbrook Derbys 185 G11
Cresselly Pembs 73 D9
Cressex Bucks 84 G4
Cress Green Glos 80 E3
Cressing Essex 106 G5
Cresswell Northumb 253 E7
Staffs 151 B9
Cresswell Quay Pembs 73 D9
Creswell Derbys 187 G8
Staffs 151 D7
Staffs 151 D8
Creswell Green Staffs 151 G11
Cretingham Suff 126 E4
Cretshengan Argyll 275 G8
Creunant = *Crynant*
Neath 76 E3
Crewe Ches E 168 D2
Ches W 166 E6
Crewe-by-Farndon
Ches W 166 E6
Crewgarth Cumb 231 E8
Crewgreen Powys 148 F6
Crewkerne Som 28 F6
Crews Hill London 86 F4
Crew's Hole Bristol 60 E6
Crewton Derby 153 C7
Crianlarich Stirling 285 E7
Cribbs Causeway S Glos 60 C5
Cribden Side Lancs 195 C9
Cribyn Ceredig 111 G10
Criccieth Gwyn 145 B9
Crich Derbys 170 E5
Crich Carr Derbys 170 E4
Crichie Aberds 303 E9
Crichton Midloth 271 C7
Crick Mon 79 G7
W Nhants 119 C11
Crickadarn Powys 95 C11
Cricket Hill Hants 65 G10
Cricket Malherbie Som 28 E5
Cricket St Thomas Som 28 F5
Crickham Som 44 D2
Crickheath Shrops 148 E5
Crickheath Wharf
Shrops 148 E5
Crickhowell Powys 78 B2
Cricklade Wilts 81 G10
Cricklewood London 67 B8
Crickmery Shrops 150 D3
Crick's Green Hereford 116 G2
Criddlestyle Hants 31 E11
Cridling Stubbs N Yorks 198 C4
Cridmore IoW 20 E5
Crieff Perth 286 E2
Criggan Corn 5 C10
Criggion Powys 148 F5
Crigglestone W Yorks 197 D10
Crimble Gtr Man 195 E11
Crimchard Som 28 F4
Crimdon Park Durham 234 D5
Crimond Aberds 303 D10
Crimonmogate Aberds 303 D10
Crimp Corn 24 D3
Crimplesham Norf 140 C3
Crimscote Warks 100 B4
Crinan Argyll 275 D8
Crinan Ferry Argyll 275 D8
Crindau Newport 59 B10
Crindledyke N Lanark 268 D6
Cringleford Norf 142 B3
Cringles W Yorks 204 D6
Cringletie Borders 270 G4
Crinow Pembs 73 C10
Cripple Corner Essex 107 E7
Cripplesease Corn 2 B2
Cripplestyle Dorset 31 E9
Cripp's Corner E Sus 38 C3
Crispie Argyll 275 F10
Crist Derbys 185 E8
Critchell's Green Hants 32 B3
Critchill Som 45 D9
Critchmere Sur 49 G11
Crit Hall Kent 53 G9
Crizeley Hereford 97 E8
Croanford Corn 10 G6
Croasdale Cumb 219 B11
Crobeag W Isles 304 F5
Crockenhill Kent 68 F4
Crocker End Oxon 65 B8
Crockerhill Hants 33 F9
W Sus 22 B6
Crockernwell Devon 13 C11
Crockers Devon 40 F5
Crocker's Ash Hereford 79 B8
Crockerton Wilts 45 E11
Crockerton Green Wilts 45 E11
Crocketford or Ninemile Bar
Dumfries 237 B10
Crockey Hill York 207 D8
Crockham Heath
W Berks 64 G2
Crockham Hill Kent 52 C2
Crockhurst Street Kent 52 E6
Crockleford Heath
Essex 107 F10
Crockleford Hill Essex 107 F10
Crockness Orkney 314 G3
Crock Street Som 28 E4
Croesau Bach Shrops 148 D4
Croeserw Neath 57 B11
Croes-goch Pembs 87 E11
Croes-Hywel Mon 78 C4
Croes-lan Ceredig 93 C7
Croes Llanfair Mon 78 D4
Croesor Gwyn 163 G10
Croespenmaen Caerph 77 F11
Croes-wian Flint 181 G10
Croesyceiliog Carms 74 B6
Torf 78 F4
Croes-y-mwyalch Torf 78 G4
Croes y pant Mon 78 E4
Croesywaun Gwyn 163 D8
Croft Hereford 115 D9
Leics 135 D10
Lincs 175 C8
Pembs 92 C3
Warr 183 C10
Croftamie Stirling 277 D9
Croftfoot S Lanark 268 C2
Crofthandy Corn 4 G4
Croftlands Cumb 210 D5
Croftmalloch W Loth 269 C8
Croft Mitchell Corn 2 B5
Croftmoraig Perth 285 C11
Croft of Tillymaud
Aberds 303 F11
Crofton Cumb 239 G8
London 68 F2
Wilts 63 G9
W Yorks 197 D11
Croft-on-Tees N Yorks 224 D5
Crofts Dumfries 237 B9
Crofts Bank Gtr Man 184 B3
Crofts of Benachielt
Highld 310 F5
Crofts of Haddo Aberds 303 F8
Crofts of Inverthernie
Aberds 303 E7
Crofts of Meikle Ardo
Aberds 303 E8
Crofty Swansea 56 B4
Croggan Argyll 289 G9
Croglin Cumb 231 B7
Croich Highld 309 K4
Croick Highld 310 D2
Croig Argyll 288 D5
Crois Dughaill W Isles 297 J3
Cromarty Highld 301 C7
Cromasaig Highld 299 C10
Crombie Fife 279 D10
Crombie Castle Aberds 302 D5
Cromblet Aberds 303 F7
Cromdale Highld 301 G10
Cromer Herts 104 F5
Norf 160 A4
Cromer-Hyde Herts 86 C2
Cromford Derbys 170 D3
Cromhall S Glos 79 G11
Cromhall Common
S Glos 61 B7
Cromor W Isles 304 F6
Crompton Fold Gtr Man 196 F2
Cromra Highld 291 D7
Cromwell Notts 172 C3
Cromwell Bottom
W Yorks 196 C6
Cronberry E Ayrs 258 E4
Crondall Hants 49 D9
Cronk-y-Voddy IoM 192 D4
Cronton Mers 183 D7
Crook Cumb 221 G9
Devon 27 G11
Durham 233 D9
Crookdake Cumb 229 C9
Crooke Gtr Man 194 F5
Crooked Billet London 67 E8
Crookedholm E Ayrs 257 B11
Crooked Soley Wilts 63 E10
Crooked Withies Dorset 31 F9
Crookes S Yorks 186 D4
Crookesmoor S Yorks 186 D4
Crookfur E Renf 267 D10
Crookgate Bank Durham 242 F5
Crookhall Durham 242 G4
Crookham Northumb 263 B10
W Berks 64 G4
Crookham Village Hants 49 C9
Crookhaugh Borders 260 D4
Crookhill T&W 242 E5
Crookhouse Borders 263 D7
Crooklands Cumb 211 C10
Crook of Devon Perth 286 G4
Crookston Glasgow 267 C10
Cropredy Oxon 101 B9
Cropston Leics 153 G11
Cropthorne Worcs 99 C9
Cropton N Yorks 216 B5
Cropwell Bishop Notts 154 B3
Cropwell Butler Notts 154 B3
Cros W Isles 304 B7
Crosben Highld 289 D9
Crosbost W Isles 304 F5
Crosby Cumb 229 D7
IoM 192 E4
Mers 182 B4
N Lincs 199 E11
Crosby Court N Yorks 225 G7
Crosby Garrett Cumb 222 D4
Crosby-on-Eden Cumb 239 F11
Crosby Ravensworth
Cumb 222 C2
Crosby Villa Cumb 229 D7
Croscombe Som 44 E5
Crosemere Shrops 149 D8
Crosland Edge W Yorks 196 E6
Crosland Hill W Yorks 196 E6
Crosland Moor W Yorks 196 D6
Croslands Park Cumb 210 E4
Cross Devon 40 F3
Devon 40 G6
Shrops 149 B7
Som 44 C2
Crossaig Argyll 255 B9
Crossal Highld 294 B6
Crossapol Argyll 288 E1
Cross Ash Mon 78 B6
Cross-at-Hand Kent 53 D9
Cross Bank Worcs 116 C4
Crossbrae Aberds 302 D6
Crossburn Falk 279 G7
Crossbush W Sus 35 F8
Crosscanonby Cumb 229 D7
Cross Coombe Corn 4 E4
Crosscrake Cumb 211 B10
Crossdale Street Norf 160 B4
Cross End Bedford 121 F11
Essex 107 E7
M Keynes 103 D8
Crossens Mers 193 D11
Crossflatts W Yorks 205 E8
Crossford Fife 279 D11
S Lanark 268 F6
Crossgate Lincs 156 D4
Orkney 314 E4
Staffs 151 B8
Cross Gate W Sus 35 E8
Crossgatehall E Loth 271 B7
Crossgates Cumb 229 G7
Fife 280 D2
N Yorks 217 C10
Powys 113 E11
Cross Gates W Yorks 205 F7
W Yorks 206 G3
Crossgill Cumb 231 C10
Lancs 211 G11
Crossgreen Shrops 149 F9
Cross Green Devon 12 D3
Staffs 133 B8
Suff 124 G6
Suff 125 F7
Suff 125 G9
Telford 150 G2
Warks 119 F7
W Yorks 206 G2
Crosshands Carms 92 G3
Cross Hands Carms 75 C9
Cross-hands Carms 92 G3
Cross Hands Pembs 73 C9
Cross Heath Staffs 168 F4
Crosshill E Ayrs 257 E11
Fife 280 B3
S Ayrs 245 B8
Cross Hill Corn 10 G6
Derbys 170 F6
Glos 79 F9
Cross Hills N Yorks 204 E6
Cross Holme N Yorks 225 F11
Crosshouse E Ayrs 257 B9
Cross Houses Shrops 131 B10
Shrops 132 E3
Crossings Cumb 240 B2
Cross in Hand E Sus 37 C9
Leics 135 G10
Cross Inn Carms 74 C3
Ceredig 111 E10
Ceredig 111 F7
Rhondda 58 C5
Crosskeys Caerph 78 G2
Cross Keys Kent 52 C4
Wilts 61 E11
Crosskirk Highld 310 B4
Crosslands Cumb 210 B6
Cross Lane Ches E 167 C11
Cross Lane Head Shrops 132 D4
Crosslanes Shrops 148 F6
Cross Lanes Corn 2 E5
Dorset 30 G3
N Yorks 215 F10
Oxon 65 D7
Wrex 166 F5
Crosslee Borders 261 F8
Renfs 267 B8
Crossley Hall W Yorks 205 G8
Cross Llyde Hereford 97 F8
Crossmichael Dumfries 237 C9
Crossmill E Renf 267 D10
Crossmoor Lancs 202 F4
Crossmount Perth 285 B11
Cross Oak Powys 96 G2
Cross of Jackston
Aberds 303 F7
Cross o' th' hands
Derbys 170 F3
Cross o' th' Hill Ches W 167 F7
Crosspost W Sus 36 C3
Crossroads Aberds 293 D9
E Ayrs 257 C11
Fife 281 B7
Cross Roads Devon 12 D5
W Yorks 204 F6
Cross Stone Aberds 303 G9
Cross Street Suff 126 B3
Crosston Angus 287 B9
Crosstown Corn 24 D2
V Glam 58 F4
Cross Town Ches E 184 F3
Crosswater Sur 49 F11
Crossway Hereford 98 E2
Mon 78 B6
Powys 113 F11
Crossway Green Mon 79 G8
Worcs 116 D6
Crossways Dorset 17 D11
Kent 68 D5
Mon 96 G6
S Glos 79 G11
Sur 49 F11

Crosswell =Ffynnongroes
Pembs. 92 D2
Crosswood Ceredig 112 C3
Crosthwaite Cumb 221 G8
Croston Lancs 194 D3
Crostwick Norf 160 F5
Crostwight Norf 160 D6
Crothair W Isles 304 E3
Crouch Kent 52 B6
Kent 54 B5
Crouch End London 67 B9
Crouchers W Sus 22 C4
Croucheston Wilts 31 B9
Crouch Hill Dorset 30 E2
Crouch House Green
Kent 52 D2
Croughly Moray 301 G11
Croughton W Nhants 101 E10
Crovie Aberds 303 C8
Crow Hants 31 G11
Crowan Corn 2 C4
Crowborough E Sus 52 G4
Staffs 168 D6
Crowborough Warren
E Sus 52 G4
Crowcombe Som 42 F6
Crowcroft Worcs 116 G5
Crowden Derbys 185 B9
Devon 12 B5
Crowder Park Devon 8 D4
Crowdhill Hants 33 C7
Crowdicote Derbys 169 B10
Crowdleham Kent 52 B5
Crowdon N Yorks 227 F9
Crow Edge S Yorks 197 G7
Crowell Oxon 84 F2
Crowell Hill Oxon 84 F3
Crowfield Suff 126 F2
W Nhants 102 C2
Crowgate Street Norf 160 E6
Crowgreaves Shrops 132 D4
Crow Green Essex 87 F9
Crowhill Gtr Man 184 B6
M Keynes 102 D6
Crow Hill Hereford 98 F2
Crowhole Derbys 186 F4
Crowhurst E Sus 38 E3
Sur 51 D11
Crowhurst Lane End
Sur 51 D11
Crowland Lincs 156 G4
Crowlas Corn 2 C2
Crowle N Lincs 199 E9
Worcs 117 F8
Crowle Green Worcs 117 F8
Crowle Hill N Lincs 199 E9
Crowle Park N Lincs 199 E9
Crowmarsh Gifford Oxon 64 B6
Crown Corner Suff 126 C5
Crown East Worcs 116 G6
Crow Nest W Yorks 205 F8
Crownfield Bucks 84 F4
Crownhill Plym 7 D9
Crown Hills Leicester 136 C2
Crownland Suff 125 D10
Crownpits Sur 50 E3
Crownthorpe Norf 141 C11
Crowntown Corn 2 C4
Crown Wood Brack 65 F11
Crows-an-wra Corn 1 D3
Crow's Green Essex 106 F3
Crowshill Norf 141 B8
Crowsley Oxon 65 D8
Crowsnest Shrops 131 C7
Crow's Nest Corn 6 B5
Crowther's Pool Powys 96 B4
Crowthorne Brack 65 G10
Crowton Ches W 183 G9
Crow Wood Halton 183 D8
Croxall Staffs 152 G3
Croxby Lincs 189 B11
Croxby Top Lincs 189 B11
Croxdale Durham 233 D11
Croxden Staffs 151 B11
Croxley Green Herts 85 F9
Croxteth Mers 182 B6
Croxton Cambs 122 E4
N Lincs 200 E5
Norf 141 F7
Norf 159 C9
Staffs 150 C5
Croxtonbank Staffs 150 C5
Croxton Green Ches E 167 E8
Croxton Kerrial Leics 154 D6
Croy Highld 301 E7
N Lanark 278 F4
Croyde Devon 40 F2
Croyde Bay Devon 40 F2
Croydon Cambs 104 B6
London 67 F10
Crozen Hereford 97 B11
Crubenbeg Highld 291 D8
Crubenmore Lodge
Highld 291 D8
Cruckmeole Shrops 131 B8
Cruckton Shrops 149 G8
Cruden Bay Aberds 303 F10
Crudgington Telford 150 F2
Crudie Aberds 303 D7
Crudwell Wilts 81 G7
Crug Powys 114 C3
Crugmeer Corn 10 F4
Crugybar Carms 94 D3
Cruise Hill Worcs 117 E10
Crulabhig W Isles 304 E3
Crumlin Caerph 78 F2
Crumplehorn Corn 6 E4
Crumpsall Gtr Man 195 G10
Crumpsbrook Shrops 116 B2
Crumpton Hill Worcs 98 B5
Crundale Kent 54 D5
Pembs 73 B7
Cruwys Morchard Devon 26 E5
Crux Easton Hants 48 B2
Cruxton Dorset 17 B8
Crwbin Carms 75 C7
Crya Orkney 314 F3
Cryers Hill Bucks 84 F5
Crymlyn Gwyn 179 G10
Crymych Pembs 92 E3
Crynant =Creunant
Neath 76 E3
Crynfryn Ceredig 111 E11
Cuaich Highld 291 E8
Cuaig Highld 299 D7
Cuan Argyll 275 B8
Cubbington Warks 118 D6
Cubeck N Yorks 213 B9
Cubert Corn 4 D5
Cubitt Town London 67 D11
Cubley S Yorks 197 G8
Cubley Common Derbys 152 B3
Cublington Bucks 102 G6
Hereford 97 D8
Cuckfield W Sus 36 B4
Cucklington Som 30 B3
Cuckney Notts 187 G9
Cuckold's Green Suff 143 G9
Wilts 46 B3
Cuckoo Green Suff 143 D10
Cuckoo Hill Notts 188 C2
Cuckoo's Corner Hants 49 E8
Wilts 46 B4
Cuckoo's Knob Wilts 63 G7
Cuckoo Tye Suff 107 C7
Cuckron Shetland 313 H6
Cucumber Corner Norf 143 B7
Cuddesdon Oxon 83 E10
Cuddington Bucks 84 C2
Ches W 183 G10
Cuddington Heath
Ches W 167 F7
Cuddy Hill Lancs 202 F5
Cudham London 52 B2
Cudlipptown Devon 12 F6
Cudliptown Devon 12 F6
Cudworth Som 28 E5
Sur 51 E8
S Yorks 197 F11
Cudworth Common
S Yorks 197 F11
Cuerden Green Lancs 194 C5
Cuerdley Cross Warr 183 D8
Cufaude Hants 48 B6
Cuffern Pembs 91 G7
Cuffley Herts 86 E4
Cuiashader W Isles 304 C7
Cuidhir W Isles 297 L2
Cuidhtinis W Isles 296 C6
Cuiken Midloth 270 C4
Cuilcheanna Ho Highld 290 G2
Cuin Argyll 288 D6
Culbo Highld 300 C6
Culbokie Highld 300 D6
Culburnie Highld 300 E4
Culcabock Highld 300 E6
Culcairn Highld 300 C6
Culcharry Highld 301 D8
Culcheth Warr 183 B11
Culcronchie Dumfries 237 C7
Cùl Doirlinn Highld 289 B8
Culdrain Aberds 302 F5
Culduie Highld 299 E7
Culeave Highld 309 K5
Culford Suff 124 D6
Culfordheath Suff 125 C7
Culfosie Aberds 293 C9
Culgaith Cumb 231 F8
Culham Oxon 83 F8
Culkein Highld 306 F5
Culkein Drumbeg Highld 306 F6
Culkerton Glos 80 F6
Cullachie Highld 301 G9
Cullen Moray 302 C5
Cullercoats T&W 243 C9
Cullicudden Highld 300 C6
Cullingworth W Yorks 205 F7
Cullipool Argyll 275 B8
Cullivoe Shetland 312 C7
Culloch Perth 285 F11
Culloden Highld 301 E7
Cullompton Devon 27 F8
Culmaily Highld 311 K2
Culmazie Dumfries 236 D5
Culm Davy Devon 27 D10
Culmer Sur 50 F2
Culmers Kent 70 G5
Culmington Shrops 131 G9
Culmore Stirling 278 B3
Culmstock Devon 27 E10
Culnacraig Highld 307 J5
Cul na h-Aird W Isles 305 H3
Culnaightrie Dumfries 237 D9
Culnaknock Highld 298 C5
Culnaneam Highld 294 C6
Culpho Suff 108 B4
Culrain Highld 309 K5
Culra Lodge Highld 291 F7
Culross Fife 279 D9
Culroy S Ayrs 257 G8
Culscadden Dumfries 236 E6
Culsh Aberds 292 D5
Aberds 303 E8
Culshabbin Dumfries 236 D5
Culswick Shetland 313 J4
Cultercullen Aberds 303 G9
Cults Aberdeen 293 C10
Aberds 302 F5
Dumfries 236 E6
Fife 287 G7
Culverlane Devon 8 C4
Culverstone Green Kent 68 G6
Culverthorpe Lincs 173 G8
Culworth W Nhants 101 B10
Culzie Lodge Highld 300 B5
Cumberlow Green Herts 104 E6
Cumbernauld N Lanark 278 G5
Cumbernauld Village
N Lanark 278 F5
Cumber's Bank Wrex 149 B8
Cumberworth Lincs 191 G8
Cumdivock Cumb 230 B2
Cumeragh Village Lancs 203 F7
Cuminestown Aberds 303 D8
Cumledge Borders 272 D5
Cumlewick Shetland 313 L6
Cumlodden Argyll 275 D11
Cumloden Dumfries 236 C6
Cummersdale Cumb 239 G9
Cummerton Aberds 303 C8
Cummertrees Dumfries 238 D4
Cummingston Moray 301 C11
Cumnock E Ayrs 258 E3
Cumnor Oxon 83 E7
Cumnor Hill Oxon 83 D7
Cumrew Cumb 240 G2
Cumwhinton Cumb 239 G10
Cumwhitton Cumb 240 G2
Cundall N Yorks 215 E8
Cundy Cross S Yorks 197 F11
Cundy Hos S Yorks 186 B4
Cunninghamhead
N Ayrs 267 G7
Cunnister Shetland 312 D7
Cupar Fife 287 F7
Cupar Muir Fife 287 F7
Cupernham Hants 32 C5
Cupid Green Herts 85 D9
Cupid's Hill Mon 97 F8
Curbar Derbys 186 G3
Curborough Staffs 152 G2
Curbridge Hants 33 E8
Oxon 82 D4
Curdridge Hants 33 E8
Curdworth Warks 134 E3
Curgurrell Corn 3 B9
Curin Highld 300 D3
Curland Som 28 D3
Curland Common Som 28 D3
Curlew Green Suff 127 D7
Curling Tye Green Essex 88 D4
Curload Som 28 B4
Currarie S Ayrs 244 E5
Currian Vale Corn 5 D9
Curridge W Berks 64 E3
Currie Edin 270 B3
Currock Cumb 239 G10
Curry Lane Corn 11 C11
Curry Mallet Som 28 C4
Curry Rivel Som 28 B5
Cursiter Orkney 314 E3
Curteis' Corner Kent 53 F11
Curtisden Green Kent 53 E8
Curtisknowle Devon 8 E4
Curtismill Green Essex 87 F8
Cury Corn 2 E5
Cusbay Orkney 314 C5
Cusgarne Corn 4 G5
Cushnie Aberds 303 C7
Cushuish Som 43 G7
Cusop Hereford 96 C4
Custards Hants 32 F3
Custom House London 68 C2
Cusveorth Coombe Corn 4 G5
Cusworth S Yorks 198 G4
Cutcloy Dumfries 236 F6
Cutcombe Som 42 F2
Cutgate Gtr Man 195 E11
Cuthill E Loth 281 G7
Cutiau Gwyn 146 F2
Cutlers Green Essex 105 E11
Cutler's Green Som 44 C5
Cutmadoc Corn 5 C11
Cutmere Corn 6 C6
Cutnall Green Worcs 117 D7
Cutsdean Glos 99 E11
Cutsyke W Yorks 198 C2
Cutteslowe Oxon 83 C8
Cutthorpe Derbys 186 G4
Cuttiford's Door Som 28 E4
Cutts Shetland 313 K6
Cuttybridge Pembs 72 B6
Cuttyhill Aberds 303 D10
Cuxham Oxon 83 F11
Cuxton Medway 69 F8
Cuxwold Lincs 201 G7
Cwm Bl Gwent 77 D11
Denb 181 F9
Neath 57 C10
Powys 129 D11
Powys 130 E5
Shrops 114 B6
Swansea 57 B7
Cwmafan Neath 57 C9
Cwmaman Rhondda 77 F8
Cwmann Carms 93 B11
Cwmavon Torf 78 D3
Cwmbach Carms 75 E7
Carms 92 F5
Powys 96 D3
Rhondda 77 E8
Cwmbâch Rhondda 77 E8
Cwmbach Llechrhyd
Powys 113 G10
Cwmbelan Powys 129 G8
Cwmbran Torf 78 G3
Cwmbrwyno Ceredig 128 G4
Cwm-byr Carms 94 E2
Cwm Capel Carms 75 E7
Cwmcarn Caerph 78 G2
Cwmcarvan Mon 79 D7
Cwm-celyn Bl Gwent 78 D2
Cwm-Cewydd Gwyn 147 G7
Cwmcoednerth Ceredig 92 B6
Cwm-cou Ceredig 92 C5
Cwmcrawnon Powys 77 B10
Cwmcych Carms 92 D5
Cwmdare Rhondda 77 E7
Cwm Dows Caerph 78 F2
Cwmdu Carms 94 E2
Powys 96 G3
Swansea 56 C6
Cwmduad Carms 93 E7
Cwm-Dulais Swansea 75 E10
Cwmdwr Carms 94 E4
Cwmerfyn Ceredig 128 G3
Cwmfelin Bridgend 57 D11
M Tydf 77 E9
Cwmfelin Boeth Carms 73 B11
Cwm felin fach Caerph 77 G11
Cwmfelin Mynach Carms 92 G4
Cwmffrwd Carms 74 B6
Cwm Ffrwd-oer Torf 78 E3
Cwm-Fields Torf 78 E3
Cwm Gelli Caerph 77 F11
Cwmgiedd Powys 76 C3
Cwmgors Neath 76 C2
Cwmgwili Carms 75 C9
Cwmgwrach Neath 76 E5
Cwm Gwyn Swansea 56 C6
Cwm Head Shrops 131 F8
Cwm-hesgen Gwyn 146 D5
Cwmhiraeth Carms 92 D6
Cwm-hwnt Rhondda 76 D6
Cwmifor Carms 94 F3
Cwm Irfon Powys 95 B7
Cwmisfael Carms 75 B7
Cwm-Llinau Powys 128 B6
Cwmllynfell Neath 76 C2
Cwm-mawr Carms 75 C8
Cwm-miles Carms 92 G3
Cwm Nant-gam
Bl Gwent 78 C2
Cwmnantyrodyn
Caerph 77 F11
Cwmorgan Pembs 92 E5
Cwmparc Rhondda 77 F7
Cwm-parc Rhondda 77 F7
Cwmpengraig Carms 92 D6
Cwm Penmachno
Conwy 164 F3
Cwmpennar Rhondda 77 E8
Cwm Plysgog Ceredig 92 C3
Cwmrhos Powys 96 G3
Cwmrhydyceirw
Swansea 57 B7
Cwmsychpant Ceredig 93 B9
Cwmsyfiog Caerph 77 E11
Cwmsymlog Ceredig 128 G4
Cwmtillery Bl Gwent 78 D2
Cwm-twrch Isaf Powys 76 C3
Cwm-twrch Uchaf
Powys 76 C3
Cwmwdig Water Pembs 90 E6
Cwmwysg Powys 95 F7
Cwm-y-glo Carms 75 C9
Gwyn 163 C8
Cwmynyscoy Torf 78 F3
Cwmyoy Mon 96 G5
Cwmystwyth Ceredig 112 C5
Cwrt Gwyn 128 C3
Cwrt-newydd Ceredig 93 B9
Cwrt-y-cadno Carms 94 C3
Cwrt-y-gollen Powys 78 B2
Cydweli =Kidwelly
Carms 74 D6
Cyffordd Llandudno
=Llandudno Junction
Conwy 180 F3
Cyffylliog Denb 165 D9
Cyfronydd Powys 130 B2
Cymau Flint 166 D3
Cymdda Bridgend 58 C2
Cymer Neath 57 B11
Cymmer Rhondda 77 G8
Cyncoed Cardiff 59 C7
Cynghordy Carms 94 C6
Cynheidre Carms 75 D7
Cynonville Neath 57 B10
Cyntwell Cardiff 58 D6
Cynwyd Denb 165 G9
Cynwyl Elfed Carms 93 F7
Cywarch Gwyn 147 F7

D

Daccombe Devon 9 B8
Dacre Cumb 230 F5
N Yorks 214 G3
Dacre Banks N Yorks 214 G3
Daddry Shield Durham 232 D3
Dadford Bucks 102 D3
Dadlington Leics 135 D8
Dafarn Faig Gwyn 163 F7
Dafen Carms 75 E8
Daffy Green Norf 141 B9
Dagdale Staffs 151 C11
Dagenham London 68 C3
Daggons Dorset 31 E10
Daglingworth Glos 81 D7
Dagnall Bucks 85 B7
Dagtail End Worcs 117 E10
Dagworth Suff 125 E10
Dail Beag W Isles 304 D4
Dail bho Dheas W Isles 304 B6
Dail bho Thuath
W Isles 304 B6
Daill Argyll 274 G4
Dailly S Ayrs 245 C7
Dail Mor W Isles 304 D4
Dainton Devon 9 B7
Dairsie or Osnaburgh
Fife 287 F8
Daisy Green Suff 125 D10
Suff 125 D11
Daisy Hill Gtr Man 195 G7
W Yorks 197 B9
W Yorks 205 G8
Daisy Nook Gtr Man 196 G2
Dalabrog W Isles 297 J3
Dalavich Argyll 275 B10
Dalbeattie Dumfries 237 C10
Dalbeg Highld 291 B8
Dalblair E Ayrs 258 F4
Dalbog Angus 293 F7
Dalbrack Stirling 285 G11
Dalbury Derbys 152 C5
Dalby IoM 192 E3
Lincs 190 G6
N Yorks 216 E2
Dalchalloch Perth 291 G9
Dalchalm Highld 311 J3
Dalchenna Argyll 284 G4
Dalchirach Moray 301 F11
Dalchonzie Perth 285 E11
Dalchork Highld 309 H5
Dalchreichart Highld 290 B4
Dalchruin Perth 285 F11
Dalderby Lincs 174 B2
Dale Cumb 230 C6
Gtr Man 196 F3
Pembs 72 D4
Shetland 312 G6
Dale Abbey Derbys 153 B8
Dalebank Derbys 170 C5
Dale Bottom Cumb 229 G11
Dale Brow Ches E 184 F6
Dale End Derbys 170 C2
N Yorks 204 D5
Dale Head Cumb 221 B8
Dale Hill E Sus 53 G7
E Sus 53 G8
Dalelia Highld 289 C9
Dale Moor Derbys 153 B8
Dale of Walls Shetland 313 H3
Dales Brow Gtr Man 195 G9
Dales Green Staffs 168 D5
Daless Highld 301 F8
Dalestie Moray 292 B3
Dalestorth Notts 171 C8
Dalfaber Highld 291 B11
Dalfoil Stirling 277 D11
Dalganachan Highld 310 E4
Dalgarven N Ayrs 266 F5
Dalgety Bay Fife 280 E3
Dalginross Perth 285 E11
Dalguise Perth 286 C3
Dalhalvaig Highld 310 D2
Dalham Suff 124 E4
Dalhastnie Angus 293 F7
Dalhenzean Perth 292 G3
Dalinlongart Argyll 276 E2
Dalkeith Midloth 270 B6
Dallam Warr 183 C9
Dallas Moray 301 D11
Dallas Lodge Moray 301 D11
Dallcharn Highld 308 D6
Dalleagles E Ayrs 258 G3
Dallicott Shrops 132 E5
Dallimores IoW 20 C6
Dallinghoo Suff 126 G5
Dallington E Sus 23 B11
W Nhants 120 E4
Dallow N Yorks 214 E3
Dalmadilly Aberds 293 B9
Dalmally Argyll 284 E5
Dalmarnock Glasgow 268 C2
Perth 286 C3
Dalmary Stirling 277 B10
Dalmellington E Ayrs 245 B11
Dalmeny Edin 280 F2
Dalmigavie Highld 291 B9
Dalmigavie Lodge
Highld 301 G7
Dalmilling S Ayrs 257 E9
Dalmore Highld 300 C6
Dalmuir W Dunb 277 G9
Dalnabreck Highld 289 C8
Dalnacardoch Lodge
Perth 291 F9
Dalnacroich Highld 300 D3
Dalnaglar Castle Perth 292 G3
Dalnahaitnach Highld 301 G8
Dalnamein Lodge Perth 291 G9
Dalnarrow Argyll 289 F9
Dalnaspidal Lodge
Perth 291 F8
Dalnavaid Perth 292 G2
Dalnavie Highld 300 B6
Dalnaw Dumfries 236 B5
Dalnawillan Lodge
Highld 310 E4
Dalness Highld 284 B5
Dalnessie Highld 309 H6
Dalqueich Perth 286 G4
Dalrannoch Argyll 289 E11
Dalreavoch Highld 309 J7
Dalriach Highld 301 F10
Dalrigh Stirling 285 E7
Dalry Edin 280 G4
N Ayrs 266 F5
Dalrymple E Ayrs 257 G9
Dalscote W Nhants 120 G3
Dalserf S Lanark 268 E6
Dalshannon N Lanark 278 G4
Dalston Cumb 239 G9
London 67 C10
Dalswinton Dumfries 247 F10
Dalton Cumb 211 D10
Dumfries 238 C4
Lancs 194 F3
Northumb 241 F10
Northumb 242 C4
Dalton continued
N Yorks 215 D8
N Yorks 224 D2
S Lanark 268 D3
S Yorks 187 C7
W Yorks 197 D7
Dalton-in-Furness
Cumb 210 E4
Dalton-le-Dale Durham 234 B4
Dalton Magna S Yorks 187 C7
Dalton-on-Tees
N Yorks 224 D5
Dalton Parva S Yorks 187 C7
Dalton Piercy Hrtlpl 234 E5
Dalveallan Highld 300 F6
Dalveich Stirling 285 E10
Dalvina Lo Highld 308 E6
Dalwey Telford 132 B3
Dalwhinnie Highld 291 E8
Dalwood Devon 28 G3
Dalwyne S Ayrs 245 D8
Damask Green Herts 104 F5
Damems W Yorks 204 F6
Damerham Hants 31 D10
Damery Glos 80 G2
Damgate Norf 143 B8
Norf 161 F9
Dam Green Norf 141 F11
Damhead Moray 301 D10
Dam Head W Yorks 196 B6
Damhead Holdings
Midloth 270 B5
Dam Mill Staffs 133 C7
Damnaglaur Dumfries 236 F3
Dam of Quoiggs Perth 286 G2
Damside Borders 270 F3
Dam Side Lancs 202 D4
Danaway Kent 69 G11
Danbury Essex 88 E3
Danbury Common Essex 88 E3
Danby N Yorks 226 D4
Danby Wiske N Yorks 224 F6
Dan Caerlan Rhondda 58 C5
Dancers Hill Herts 86 F2
Dancing Green Hereford 98 G2
Dandaleith Moray 302 E2
Danderhall Midloth 270 B6
Dandy Corner Suff 125 D11
Danebank Ches E 185 E7
Dane Bank Gtr Man 184 B6
Danebridge Ches E 169 B7
Dane End Herts 104 G6
Danegate E Sus 52 G5
Danehill E Sus 36 B6
Dane in Shaw Ches E 168 C5
Danemoor Green Norf 141 B11
Danesbury Herts 86 B2
Danesfield Bucks 65 C10
Danesford Shrops 132 E4
Daneshill Hants 49 C7
Danesmoor Derbys 170 C6
Danes Moss Ches E 184 G6
Dane Street Kent 54 C5
Daneway Glos 80 E6
Dangerous Corner
Gtr Man 195 G7
Lancs 194 E4
Daniel's Water Kent 54 E3
Danna na Cloiche Argyll 275 F7
Dannonchapel Corn 10 E6
Danskine E Loth 271 B11
Danthorpe E Yorks 209 G10
Danygraig Caerph 78 G2
Danzey Green Warks 118 D2
Dapple Heath Staffs 151 D10
Darby End W Mid 133 F9
Darby Green Hants 65 G10
Darbys Green Worcs 116 F4
Darby's Hill W Mid 133 F9
Darcy Lever Gtr Man 195 F8
Dardy Powys 78 B2
Darenth Kent 68 E5
Daresbury Halton 183 E9
Daresbury Delph Halton 183 E9
Darfield S Yorks 198 G2
Darfoulds Notts 187 F9
Dargate Kent 70 G5
Dargate Common Kent 70 G5
Dargavel Village Renfs 277 G8
Darite Corn 6 B5
Darkland Moray 302 C2
Darland Wrex 166 D5
Darlaston W Mid 133 D9
Darlaston Green W Mid 133 D9
Darley N Yorks 205 B10
Shrops 132 D3
Darley Abbey Derby 153 B7
Darley Bridge Derbys 170 C3
Darley Dale Derbys 170 C3
Darleyford Corn 11 G11
Darley Green Warks 118 C3
Darleyhall Herts 104 G2
Darley Head N Yorks 205 B9
Darley Hillside Derbys 170 C3
Darlingscott Warks 100 C4
Darlington Darl 224 C5
Darliston Shrops 149 C11
Darlton Notts 188 G3
Darmsden Suff 125 G11
Darnall S Yorks 186 D5
Darnaway Castle Moray 301 D9
Darnford Staffs 134 B2
Darnhall Ches W 167 C10
Darnhall Mains Borders 270 F4
Darn Hill Gtr Man 195 E10
Darnick Borders 262 C2
Darowen Powys 128 C6
Darra Aberds 303 E7
Darracott Devon 24 D2
Devon 40 F3
Darras Hall Northumb 242 C5
Darrington W Yorks 198 D3
Darrow Green Norf 142 F5
Darsham Suff 127 D8
Darshill Som 44 E6
Dartford Kent 68 E4
Dartford Crossing Kent 68 D5
Dartington Devon 8 C5
Dartmeet Devon 13 G9
Dartmouth Devon 9 E7
Dartmouth Park London 67 B9
Darton S Yorks 197 F10
Darvel E Ayrs 258 B3
Darvillshill Bucks 84 F4
Darwell Hole E Sus 23 B11
Darwen Blackburn 195 C7
Dassels Herts 105 F7
Datchet Windsor 66 D3
Datchet Common
Windsor 66 D3
Datchworth Herts 86 B3
Datchworth Green Herts 86 B3
Daubhill Gtr Man 195 F8
Daugh of Kinermony
Moray 302 E2
Dauntsey Wilts 62 C3
Dauntsey Lock Wilts 62 C3
Dava Moray 301 F10
Davenham Ches W 183 G11
Davenport Ches E 168 B4
Gtr Man 184 D5
Davenport Green
Ches E 184 F4
Gtr Man 184 D4
Daventry W Nhants 119 E11
Davidson's Mains Edin 280 F4
Davidston Highld 301 C7
Davidstow Corn 11 D9
David Street Kent 68 G6
David's Well Powys 113 B11
Davington Dumfries 248 C6
Kent 70 G4
Daviot Aberds 303 G7
Highld 301 F7
Davis's Town E Sus 23 B8
Davoch of Grange
Moray 302 D4
Davo Mains Aberds 293 F9
Davyhulme Gtr Man 184 B3
Daw Cross N Yorks 205 C11
Dawdon Durham 234 B4
Daw End W Mid 133 C10
Dawesgreen Sur 51 D8
Dawker Hill N Yorks 207 F7
Dawley Telford 132 B3
Dawley Bank Telford 132 B3
Dawlish Devon 14 F5
Dawlish Warren Devon 14 F5
Dawn Conwy 180 G5
Daw's Cross Essex 107 E7
Daw's Green Som 27 C11
Daws Heath Essex 69 B10
Dawshill Worcs 116 G6
Daw's House Corn 12 E2
Dawsmere Lincs 157 C8
Daybrook Notts 171 F9
Day Green Ches E 168 D3
Dayhills Staffs 151 C9
Dayhouse Bank Worcs 117 B9
Daylesford Glos 100 F4
Daywall Shrops 148 C5
Ddol Flint 181 G10
Ddôl Cownwy Powys 147 F10
Ddrydwy Anglesey 178 G5
Deacons Hill Herts 85 F11
Deadman's Cross
C Beds 104 C2
Deadman's Green
Staffs 151 B10
Deadwater Hants 49 F10
Northumb 250 D4
Deaf Hill Durham 234 D3
Deal Hall Essex 89 F8
Kent 55 C11
Dean Cumb 229 F7
Devon 8 C4
Devon 40 D6
Devon 40 E4
Devon 41 D8
Dorset 31 D7
Edin 280 G4
Hants 33 D9
Hants 48 G2
Lancs 195 B11
Oxon 100 G6
Som 45 E7
Dean Bank Durham 233 E11
Deanburnhaugh
Borders 261 G9
Dean Court Oxon 83 D7
Dean Cross Devon 40 E4
Deane Gtr Man 195 F7
Hants 48 C4
Deanend Dorset 31 D7
Dean Head S Yorks 197 G9
Deanich Lodge Highld 309 L3
Deanland Dorset 31 D7
Deanlane End W Sus 34 E2
Dean Lane Head
W Yorks 205 G7
Dean Park Renfs 267 B10
Dean Prior Devon 8 C4
Dean Row Ches E 184 E5
Deans W Loth 269 B10
Deans Bottom Kent 69 G11
Deanscales Cumb 229 F7
Deansgreen Ches E 183 D11
Dean's Green Warks 118 D2
Deanshanger W Nhants 102 D5
Deans Hill Kent 69 G11
Deanston Stirling 285 G11
Dean Street Kent 53 C8
Dearham Cumb 229 D7
Dearnley Gtr Man 196 D2
Debach Suff 126 G4
Debdale Gtr Man 184 B5
Debden Essex 86 F6
Essex 105 E11
Debden Cross Essex 105 E11
Debden Green Essex 86 F6
Essex 105 E11
De Beauvoir Town
London 67 C10
Debenham Suff 126 E3
Deblin's Green Worcs 98 B6
Dechmont W Loth 279 G10
Deckham T&W 243 E7
Deddington Oxon 101 E9
Dedham Essex 107 E11
Dedham Heath Essex 107 E11
Dedridge W Loth 269 B11
Dedworth Windsor 66 D2
Deebank Aberds 293 D8
Deecastle Aberds 292 D6
Deene N Nhants 137 E8
Deenethorpe N Nhants 137 E9
Deepcar S Yorks 186 B3
Deepclough Derbys 185 B8
Deepcut Sur 50 B2
Deepdale C Beds 104 B4
Cumb 212 C4
N Yorks 213 D7
Deepdene Sur 51 D7
Deepfields W Mid 133 E8
Deeping Gate Lincs 138 B2
Deeping St James Lincs 138 B3
Deeping St Nicholas
Lincs 156 F4
Deepthwaite Cumb 211 C10
Deepweir Mon 60 B3
Deerhill Moray 302 D4
Deerhurst Glos 99 F7
Deerhurst Walton Glos 99 F7
Deerland Pembs 73 C7
Deerness Orkney 314 F5
Deer's Green Essex 105 E9
Deerstones N Yorks 205 C7
Deerton Street Kent 70 G3
Defford Worcs 99 C8
Defynnog Powys 95 F8
Deganwy Conwy 180 F3
Degar V Glam 58 D4
Degibna Corn 2 D5
Deighton N Yorks 225 E7
W Yorks 197 D7
York 207 E8
Deiniolen Gwyn 163 C9
Deishar Highld 291 B11
Delabole Corn 11 E7
Delamere Ches W 167 B9
Delfour Highld 291 C10
Delfrigs Aberds 303 G9
Delliefure Highld 301 F10
Dell Lodge Highld 292 B2
Dell Quay W Sus 22 C4
Delly End Oxon 82 C5
Delnabo Moray 292 B3
Delnadamph Aberds 292 C4
Delnamer Angus 292 G3
Delph Gtr Man 196 F3
Delves Durham 233 B8
Delvine Perth 286 C5
Delvin End Essex 106 D5
Dembleby Lincs 155 B10
Demelza Corn 5 C9
Denaby Main S Yorks 187 B7
Denbeath Fife 281 B7
Denbigh Denb 165 B9
Denbury Devon 8 B6
Denby Derbys 170 F5
Denby Bottles Derbys 170 F5
Denby Common Derbys 170 F6
Denby Dale W Yorks 197 F8
Denchworth Oxon 82 G5
Dendron Cumb 210 E4
Denel End C Beds 103 D10
Denend Aberds 302 F6
Dene Park Kent 52 C5
Deneside Durham 234 B4
Denford N Nhants 121 B9
Staffs 169 E7
Dengie Essex 89 E7
Denham Bucks 66 B4
Bucks 102 G5
Suff 124 E5
Suff 126 C3
Denham Corner Suff 126 C3
Denham End Suff 124 E5
Denham Green Bucks 66 B4
Denham Street Suff 126 C3
Denhead Aberds 303 D9
Fife 287 F8
Denhead of Arbilot
Angus 287 C9
Denhead of Gray
Dundee 287 D7
Denholm Borders 262 F3
Denholme W Yorks 205 G7
Denholme Clough
W Yorks 205 G7
Denholme Edge
W Yorks 205 G7
Denholme Gate
W Yorks 205 G7
Denholmhill Borders 262 F3
Denio Gwyn 145 B7
Denmead Hants 33 E11
Denmore Aberdeen 293 B11
Denmoss Aberds 302 E6
Dennington Suff 126 D5
Dennington Corner Suff 126 D5
Dennington Hall Suff 126 D5
Dennistoun Glasgow 268 B2
Denny Falk 278 E6
Denny Bottom Kent 52 F5
Denny End Cambs 123 D9
Dennyloanhead Falk 278 E6
Denny Lodge Hants 32 F4
Dennystown W Dunb 277 F7
Denshaw Gtr Man 196 E3
Denside Aberds 293 D10
Densole Kent 55 E8
Denston Suff 124 G5
Denstone Staffs 169 G9
Denstroude Kent 70 G6
Dent Cumb 212 B4
Dent Bank Durham 232 F4
Denton Cambs 138 F2
Darl 224 B4
E Sus 23 E7
Gtr Man 184 B6
Kent 55 D8
Kent 69 E7
Lincs 155 C7
Norf 142 F5
N Yorks 205 D9
Oxon 83 E9
W Nhants 120 F6
Denton Burn T&W 242 D5
Denton Holme Cumb 239 G10
Denton's Green Mers 183 B7
Denver Norf 140 C2
Denvilles Hants 22 B2
Denwick Northumb 264 G6
Deopham Norf 141 C11
Deopham Green Norf 141 D10
Deopham Stalland
Norf 141 D10
Depden Suff 124 F5
Depden Green Suff 124 F5
Deppers Bridge Warks 119 F7
Deptford London 67 D11
T&W 243 F9
Wilts 46 F4
Derby Derbys 153 B7
Devon 40 G5
Derbyhaven IoM 192 F3
Derbyshire Hill Mers 183 C8
Dereham Norf 159 G9
Dergoals Dumfries 236 D4
Deri Caerph 77 E10
Derriford Plym 7 D9
Derril Devon 24 G4
Derringstone Kent 55 D8
Derrington Shrops 132 E2
Staffs 151 E7
Derriton Devon 24 G4
Derry Stirling 285 E10
Derrydaroch Stirling 285 E7
Derry Downs London 68 F3
Derry Fields Wilts 81 G8
Derryguaig Argyll 288 F6
Derry Hill Wilts 62 E3
Derry Lodge Aberds 292 D2
Derrythorpe N Lincs 199 F10
Dersingham Norf 158 C3
Dertfords Wilts 45 D10
Dervaig Argyll 288 D6
Derwen Bridgend 58 C2
Denb 165 E9
Derwenlas Powys 128 D4
Derwydd Carms 75 B10
Desborough N Nhants 136 G6
Desford Leics 135 C9
Deskryshiel Aberds 292 B6
Detchant Northumb 264 B3
Detling Kent 53 B9
Deuchar Angus 292 G6
Deuddwr Powys 148 F4
Deuxhill Shrops 132 F3
Devauden Mon 79 F7
Deveral Corn 2 B3
Devil's Bridge
=Pontarfynach
Ceredig 112 B4
Devitts Green Warks 134 E5
Devizes Wilts 62 G4
Devol Invclyd 276 G6
Devonport Plym 7 E9
Devonside Clack 279 B8
Devon Village Clack 279 B8
Devoran Corn 3 B7
Dewar Borders 270 F6
Dewartown Midloth 271 C7
Dewes Green Essex 105 E9
Dewlands Common
Dorset 31 F9
Dewlish Dorset 17 B11
Dewsbury W Yorks 197 C8
Dewsbury Moor
W Yorks 197 C8
Dewshall Court Hereford 97 E9
Dhoon IoM 192 D5
Dhoor IoM 192 C5
Dhowin IoM 192 B5
Dhustone Shrops 115 B11
Dial Green W Sus 34 B6
Dial Post W Sus 35 D11
Dibberford Dorset 29 G7
Dibden Hants 32 F6
Dibden Purlieu Hants 32 F6
Dickens Heath W Mid 118 B2
Dickleburgh Norf 142 G3
Dickleburgh Moor Norf 142 G3
Dickon Hills Lincs 174 D6
Didbrook Glos 99 E11
Didcot Oxon 64 B4
Diddington Cambs 122 D3
Diddlebury Shrops 131 F10
Diddywell Devon 25 B7
Didley Hereford 97 E9
Didling W Sus 34 D4
Didlington Norf 140 D5
Didmarton Glos 61 B10
Didsbury Gtr Man 184 C4
Didworthy Devon 8 C3
Diebidale Highld 309 L4
Digbeth W Mid 133 F11
Digby Lincs 173 E9
Digg Highld 298 C4
Diggle Gtr Man 196 F4
Diglis Worcs 116 G6
Digmoor Lancs 194 F3
Digswell Herts 86 B3
Digswell Park Herts 86 C2
Digswell Water Herts 86 C3
Dihewyd Ceredig 111 F9
Dilham Norf 160 D6
Dilhorne Staffs 169 G7
Dillarburn S Lanark 268 G6
Dill Hall Lancs 195 B8
Dillington Cambs 122 D2
Som 28 D5
Dilston Northumb 241 E11
Dilton Marsh Wilts 45 D11
Dilwyn Hereford 115 G8
Dimlands V Glam 58 F3
Dimmer Som 44 G6
Dimple Derbys 170 C3
Gtr Man 195 D8
Dimsdale Staffs 168 F4
Dimson Corn 12 G4
Dinas Carms 92 E5
Corn 10 G4
Gwyn 144 B5
Gwyn 163 D7
Dinas Cross Pembs 91 D10
Dinas Dinlle Gwyn 162 D6
Dinas-Mawddwy Gwyn 147 G7
Dinas Mawr Conwy 164 E4
Dinas Powys V Glam 59 E7
Dinbych y Pysgod =Tenby
Pembs 73 E10
Dinckley Lancs 203 F9
Dinder Som 44 E5
Dinedor Hereford 97 D10
Dinedor Cross Hereford 97 D10
Dines Green Worcs 116 F6
Dingestow Mon 79 C7
Dinghurst N Som 44 B2
Dingle Mers 182 D5
Dingleden Kent 53 G10
Dingleton Borders 262 C2
Dingley N Nhants 136 F5
Dingwall Highld 300 D5
Dinlabyre Borders 250 E2
Dinmael Conwy 165 G8
Dinnet Aberds 292 D6
Dinnington Som 28 E6
S Yorks 187 D8
T&W 242 C6
Dinorwic Gwyn 163 C9
Dinton Bucks 84 C3
Wilts 46 G4
Dinwoodie Mains
Dumfries 248 E4
Dinworthy Devon 24 D4
Dipford Som 28 C2
Dipley Hants 49 B8
Dippenhall Sur 49 D10
Dippertown Devon 12 E4
Dippin N Ayrs 256 E2
Dipple Devon 24 D4
Moray 302 D3
S Ayrs 244 C6
Diptford Devon 8 D4
Dipton Durham 242 G5
Diptonmill Northumb 241 E10
Dirdhu Highld 301 G10
Direcleit W Isles 305 J3
Dirleton E Loth 281 E10
Dirt Pot Northumb 232 B3
Discoed Powys 114 E5
Discove Som 45 G7
Diseworth Leics 153 E9
Dishes Orkney 314 D6
Dishforth N Yorks 215 E7
Dishley Leics 153 E10
Disley Ches E 185 E7
Diss Norf 126 B2
Disserth Powys 113 F10
Distington Cumb 228 G6
Ditchampton Wilts 46 G5
Ditcheat Som 44 F6
Ditchfield Bucks 84 G4
Ditchford Hill Worcs 100 D4
Ditchingham Norf 142 E6
Ditchling E Sus 36 D4
Ditherington Shrops 149 G10
Ditteridge Wilts 61 F10
Dittisham Devon 9 E7
Ditton Halton 183 D7
Kent 53 B8
Ditton Green Cambs 124 F3
Ditton Priors Shrops 132 F2
Dittons E Sus 23 E10
Divach Highld 300 G4
Divlyn Carms 94 D5
Dixton Glos 99 E9
Mon 79 C8
Dizzard Corn 11 B9
Dobcross Gtr Man 196 F3
Dobs Hill Flint 166 C4
Dobson's Bridge Shrops 149 C9
Dobwalls Corn 6 C4
Doccombe Devon 13 D11
Dochfour Ho Highld 300 F6
Dochgarroch Highld 300 E6
Dockeney Norf 143 E7
Dockenfield Sur 49 E10
Docker Lancs 211 E11
Docking Norf 158 B5
Docklow Hereford 115 F11

Dockray Cumb 230 G3
Dockroyd W Yorks 204 F6
Doc Penfro = *Pembroke Dock* Pembs 73 E7
Docton Devon 24 C2
Dodbrooke Devon 8 G4
Dodburn Borders 249 B11
Doddenham Worcs 116 F5
Doddinghurst Essex 87 F9
Doddington Cambs 139 E7
Kent 54 B2
Lincs 188 G6
Northumb 263 C11
Shrops 116 B2
Doddiscombsleigh Devon 14 D3
Doddshill Norf 158 C3
Doddycross Corn 6 C6
Dodford W Nhants 120 E2
Worcs 117 C8
Dodington S Glos 61 C9
Som 43 E7
Dodleston Ches W 166 C5
Dodmarsh Hereford 97 C11
Dodscott Devon 25 D8
Dods Leigh Staffs 151 C10
Dodworth S Yorks 197 F10
Dodworth Bottom
S Yorks 197 G10
Dodworth Green
S Yorks 197 G10
Doe Bank W Mid 134 D2
Doe Green Warr 183 D9
Doehole Derbys 170 D5
Doe Lea Derbys 171 B7
Doffcocker Gtr Man 195 E7
Dogdyke Lincs 174 D2
Dog & Gun Mers 182 B5
Dog Hill Gtr Man 196 F3
Dogingtree Estate
Staffs 151 G9
Dogley Lane W Yorks 197 E7
Dogmersfield Hants 49 C9
Dogridge Wilts 62 B5
Dogsthorpe Pboro 138 C3
Dog Village Devon 14 B5
Doirlinn Highld 289 D8
Dolanog Powys 147 G11
Dolau Powys 114 D2
Rhondda 58 C3
Dolbenmaen Gwyn 163 G8
Dole Ceredig 128 F2
Dolemeads Bath 61 G9
Doley Staffs 150 D4
Dolfach Powys 129 C8
Dol-ffanog Gwyn 146 G4
Dolfor Powys 130 F2
Dol-fôr Powys 128 B6
Dolgarrog Conwy 164 B3
Dolgellau Gwyn 146 F4
Dolgerdd Ceredig 111 G8
Dolgoch Gwyn 128 C3
Dolgran Carms 93 E8
Dolhelfa Powys 113 C8
Dolhendre Gwyn 147 C7
Doll Highld 311 J2
Dollar Clack 279 B9
Dolley Green Powys 114 D5
Dollis Hill London 67 B8
Dollwen Ceredig 128 G3
Dolphin Flint 181 G11
Dolphingstone E Loth 281 G7
Dolphinholme Lancs 202 C6
Dolphinston Borders 262 F5
Dolphinton S Lanark 270 F2
Dolton Devon 25 E9
Dolwen Conwy 180 G5
Powys 129 B9
Dolwyd Conwy 180 F4
Dolwyddelan Conwy 164 E2
Dôl-y-Bont Ceredig 128 F2
Dol-y-cannau Powys 96 B3
Dolydd Gwyn 163 D7
Dolyhir Powys 114 F4
Dolymelinau Powys 129 D11
Dolywern Wrex 148 B4
Domewood Sur 51 E10
Domgay Powys 148 F5
Dommett Som 28 E3
Doncaster S Yorks 198 G5
Doncaster Common
S Yorks 198 G6
Dones Green Ches W 183 F10
Donhead St Andrew
Wilts 30 C6
Donhead St Mary Wilts 30 C6
Donibristle Fife 280 D3
Doniford Som 42 E5
Donington Lincs 156 B4
Shrops 132 C6
Donington Eaudike
Lincs 156 B4
Donington le Heath
Leics 153 G8
Donington on Bain
Lincs 190 E2
Donington South Ing
Lincs 156 C4
Donisthorpe Leics 152 G6
Don Johns Essex 106 F6
Donkey Street Kent 54 G6
Donkey Town Sur 66 G2
Donna Nook Lincs 190 B6
Donnington Glos 100 F3
Hereford 98 E4
Shrops 131 B11
Telford 150 G4
W Berks 64 F3
W Sus 22 C5
Donnington Wood
Telford 150 G4
Donwell T&W 243 F7
Donyatt Som 28 E4
Doomsday Green
W Sus 35 B11
Doonfoot S Ayrs 257 F8
Dora's Green Hants 49 D10
Dorback Lodge Highld 292 B2
Dorcan Swindon 63 C7
Dorchester Dorset 17 C9
Oxon 83 G9
Dordale Worcs 117 C8
Dordon Warks 134 C5
Dore S Yorks 186 E4
Dores Highld 300 F5
Dorking Sur 51 D7
Dorking Tye Suff 107 D8
Dorley's Corner Suff 127 D7
Dormansland Sur 52 E2
Dormans Park Sur 51 E11
Dormanstown Redcar 235 G7
Dormer's Wells London 66 C6
Dormington Hereford 97 C11
Dormston Worcs 117 F9
Dorn Glos 100 E4
Dornal S Ayrs 236 B4
Dorney Bucks 66 D2
Dorney Reach Bucks 66 D2
Dorn Hill Worcs 100 E3
Dornie Highld 295 C10
Dornoch Highld 309 L7
Dornock Dumfries 238 D6
Dorrery Highld 310 D4
Dorridge W Mid 118 B3
Dorrington Lincs 173 E9
Shrops 131 C9
Dorsington Warks 100 B2
Dorstone Hereford 96 C6
Dorton Bucks 83 C11
Dorusduain Highld 295 C11
Doseley Telford 132 B3
Dosmuckeran Highld 300 C2
Dosthill Staffs 134 C4
Staffs 134 D4
Dothan Anglesey 178 G5
Dothill Telford 150 G2
Dottery Dorset 16 B5
Doublebois Corn 6 C3
Double Hill Bath 45 B8
Dougarie N Ayrs 255 D9
Doughton Glos 80 G5
Norf 159 D7
Douglas IoM 192 E4
S Lanark 259 C8
Douglas & Angus
Dundee 287 D8
Douglastown Angus 287 C8
Douglas Water S Lanark 259 B9
Douglas West S Lanark 259 C8
Doulting Som 44 E6
Dounby Orkney 314 D2
Doune Highld 291 C10
Highld 309 J4
Stirling 285 G11
Doune Park Aberds 303 C7
Douneside Aberds 292 C6
Dounie Argyll 275 D8
Highld 309 K5
Highld 309 L6
Dounreay Highld 310 C3
Doura N Ayrs 266 G6
Dousland Devon 7 B10
Dovaston Shrops 149 E7
Dovecot Mers 182 C6
Dovecothall Glasgow 267 D10
Dove Green Notts 171 E7
Dove Holes Derbys 185 F9
Dovenby Cumb 229 E7
Dovendale Lincs 190 E4
Dove Point Mers 182 C2
Dover Gtr Man 194 G6
Kent 55 E10
Dovercourt Essex 108 E5
Doverdale Worcs 117 D7
Doverhay Som 41 D11
Doveridge Derbys 152 C2
Doversgreen Sur 51 D9
Dowally Perth 286 C4
Dowanhill Glasgow 267 B11
Dowbridge Lancs 202 G4
Dowdeswell Glos 81 B7
Dowe Hill Norf 161 F10
Dowlais M Tydf 77 D10
Dowlais Top M Tydf 77 D9
Dowland Devon 25 E9
Dowles Worcs 116 B5
Dowlesgreen Wokingham 65 F10
Dowlish Ford Som 28 E5
Dowlish Wake Som 28 E5
Downall Green Gtr Man 194 G5
Down Ampney Glos 81 F10
Downan Moray 301 F11
S Ayrs 244 G3
Downcraig Ferry
N Ayrs 266 D3
Downderry Corn 6 E6
Downe London 68 G2
Downend Glos 80 F4
IoW 20 D6
S Glos 60 D6
W Berks 64 D3
Down End Som 43 E10
Downfield Dundee 287 D7
Down Field Cambs 124 C2
Downgate Corn 11 G11
Corn 12 G3
Down Hall Cumb 239 G7
Downham Essex 88 F2
Lancs 203 E11
London 67 E11
Northumb 263 C9
Downham Market Norf 140 C2
Down Hatherley Glos 99 G7
Downhead Som 29 B9
Som 45 D7
Downhead Park
M Keynes 103 C7
Downhill Corn 5 B7
Perth 286 D4
T&W 243 F9
Downholland Cross
Lancs 193 F11
Downholme N Yorks 224 F2
Downicary Devon 12 C3
Downies Aberds 293 D11
Downinney Corn 11 C10
Downley Bucks 84 G4
Down Park W Sus 51 F10
Downs V Glam 58 E6
Down St Mary Devon 26 G2
Downside C Beds 103 G10
E Sus 23 E9
N Som 60 F3
Som 44 D6
Sur 50 B6
Sur 51 B7
Down Street E Sus 36 C6
Down Thomas Devon 7 E10
Downton Hants 19 C11
Powys 114 E4
Shrops 149 G10
Wilts 31 C11
Downton on the Rock
Hereford 115 C8
Dowsby Lincs 156 D2
Dowsdale Lincs 156 G5
Dowslands Som 28 C2
Dowthwaitehead Cumb 230 G3
Doxey Staffs 151 E8
Doxford Park T&W 243 G9
Doynton S Glos 61 E8
Drabblegate Norf 160 D4
Draethen Newport 59 B8
Draffan S Lanark 268 F5
Dragley Beck Cumb 210 D5
Dragonby N Lincs 200 E2
Dragons Green W Sus 35 C10
Drakehouse S Yorks 186 E6
Drakeland Corner Devon 7 D11
Drakelow Worcs 132 G6
Drakemyre Aberds 303 F9
N Ayrs 266 E5
Drake's Broughton Worcs 99 B8
Drakes Cross Worcs 117 B11
Drakestone Green Suff 107 B9
Drakewalls Corn 12 G4
Draughton N Yorks 204 C6
W Nhants 120 B5
Drawbridge Corn 6 B3
Drax N Yorks 199 B7
Draycot Oxon 83 D10
Draycot Cerne Wilts 62 D2
Draycote Warks 119 C8
Draycot Fitz Payne Wilts 62 G6
Draycot Foliat Swindon 63 D7
Draycott Derbys 153 C8
Glos 80 E2
Glos 100 D3
Shrops 132 E6
Som 29 C8
Som 44 C3
Worcs 99 B7
Draycott in the Clay
Staffs 152 D3
Draycott in the Moors
Staffs 169 G7
Drayford Devon 26 E3
Drayton Leics 136 E6
Lincs 156 B4
Norf 160 G3
Oxon 83 G7
Oxon 101 C8
Ptsmth 33 F11
Som 28 C6
Som 29 D7
Warks 118 F3
W Nhants 119 E11
Worcs 117 B8
Drayton Bassett Staffs 134 C3
Drayton Beauchamp
Bucks 84 C6
Drayton Parslow Bucks 102 F6
Drayton St Leonard
Oxon 83 F10
Drebley N Yorks 205 B7
Dreemskerry IoM 192 C5
Dreenhill Pembs 72 C6
Drefach Carms 75 C8
Carms 92 G5
Carms 93 D7
Dre-fach Carms 75 B11
Ceredig 93 B10
Drefelin Carms 93 D7
Dreggie Highld 301 G10
Dreghorn Edin 270 B4
N Ayrs 257 B9
Dre-gôch Denb 165 B10
Drellingore Kent 55 E8
Drem E Loth 281 F10
Dresden Stoke 168 G6
Dreumasdal W Isles 297 H3
Drewsteignton Devon 13 C10
Driby Lincs 190 G5
Driffield E Yorks 208 B6
Glos 81 F9
Drift Corn 1 D4
Drigg Cumb 219 F11
Drighlington W Yorks 197 B8
Drimnin Highld 289 D7
Drimnin Ho Highld 289 D7
Drimpton Dorset 28 F6
Drimsynie Argyll 284 G5
Dringhoe E Yorks 209 C9
Dringhouses York 207 D7
Drinisiadar W Isles 305 J3
Drinkstone Suff 125 E9
Drinkstone Green Suff 125 E9
Drishaig Argyll 284 F5
Drissaig Argyll 275 B10
Drive End Dorset 29 F9
Driver's End Herts 86 B2
Drochedlie Aberds 302 C5
Drochil Borders 270 G3
Drointon Staffs 151 D10
Droitwich Spa Worcs 117 E7
Droman Highld 306 D6
Dromore Dumfries 237 C7
Dron Perth 286 F5
Dronfield Derbys 186 F5
Dronfield Woodhouse
Derbys 186 F4
Drongan E Ayrs 257 F10
Dronley Angus 287 D7
Droop Dorset 30 F3
Drope Cardiff 58 D6
Dropping Well S Yorks 186 C5
Droughduil Dumfries 236 D3
Droxford Hants 33 D10
Droylsden Gtr Man 184 B6
Drub W Yorks 197 B7
Druggers End Worcs 98 D5
Druid Denb 165 G8
Druidston Pembs 72 B5
Druim Highld 301 D9
Druimarbin Highld 290 F2
Druimavuic Argyll 284 C4
Druimdrishaig Argyll 275 F8
Druimindarroch Highld 295 G8
Druimkinnerras Highld 300 F4
Druimnacroish Argyll 288 E6
Druimsornaig Argyll 289 F9
Druimyeon More Argyll 255 B7
Drum Argyll 275 F10
Edin 270 B6
Perth 286 G4
Drumardoch Stirling 285 F10
Drumbeg Highld 306 F6
Drumblade Aberds 302 E5
Drumblair Aberds 302 E6
Drumbuie Dumfries 246 G3
Highld 295 B9
Drumburgh Cumb 239 F7
Drumburn Dumfries 237 C11
Drumchapel Glasgow 277 G10
Drumchardine Highld 300 E5
Drumchork Highld 307 L3
Drumclog S Lanark 258 B4
Drumdelgie Aberds 302 E4
Drumderfit Highld 300 D6
Drumdollo Aberds 302 F6
Drumeldrie Fife 287 G8
Drumelzier Borders 260 C4
Drumfearn Highld 295 D8
Drumgask Highld 291 D8
Drumgelloch N Lanark 268 B5
Drumgley Angus 287 B8
Drumgreen Angus 292 F6
Drumguish Highld 291 D9
Drumhead Aberds 293 B11
Drumin Moray 301 F11
Drumindorsair Highld 300 E4
Drumlasie Aberds 293 C8
Drumlean Stirling 285 G8
Drumlemble Argyll 255 F7
Drumliah Highld 309 K6
Drumligair Aberds 293 B11
Drumlithie Aberds 293 E9
Drumloist Stirling 285 G10
Drummersdale Lancs 193 E11
Drummick Perth 286 E3
Drummoddie Dumfries 236 E5
Drummond Highld 300 C6
Drummore Dumfries 236 F3
Drummuir Moray 302 E3
Drummuir Castle Moray 302 E3
Drumnadrochit Highld 300 G5
Drumnagorrach Moray 302 D5
Drumness Perth 286 F2
Drumoak Aberds 293 D9
Drumore Argyll 255 E8
Drumpark Dumfries 247 G9
Drumpellier N Lanark 268 B4
Drumphail Dumfries 236 C4
Drumrash Dumfries 237 B8
Drumrunie Highld 307 J6
Drumry W Dunb 277 G10
Drums Aberds 303 G9
Drumsallie Highld 289 B11
Drumsmittal Highld 300 E6
Drumstinchall
Dumfries 237 D10
Drumsturdy Angus 287 D8
Drumtochty Castle
Aberds 293 F8
Drumtroddan Dumfries 236 E5
Drumuie Highld 298 E4
Drumuillie Highld 301 G9
Drumvaich Stirling 285 G10
Drumwalt Dumfries 236 D5
Drumwhindle Aberds 303 F9
Drunkendub Angus 287 C10
Drury Flint 166 C3
Drurylane Norf 141 C8
Drury Lane Wrex 167 G7
Drury Square Norf 159 F8
Drybeck Cumb 222 B3
Drybridge Moray 302 C4
N Ayrs 257 B9
Drybrook Glos 79 B10
Dryburgh Borders 262 C3
Dryden Borders 261 E11
Dry Doddington Lincs 172 F4
Dry Drayton Cambs 123 E7
Dryhill Kent 52 B3
Dry Hill Hants 49 F7
Dryhope Borders 261 E7
Drylaw Edin 280 F4
Drym Corn 2 C4
Drymen Stirling 277 D9
Drymere Norf 140 B5
Drymuir Aberds 303 E9
Drynachan Lodge Highld 301 F8
Drynain Argyll 276 D3
Drynham Wilts 45 B11
Drynie Park Highld 300 D5
Drynoch Highld 294 B6
Dry Sandford Oxon 83 E7
Dryslwyn Carms 93 G11
Dry Street Essex 69 B7
Dryton Shrops 131 B11
Drywells Aberds 302 D6
Duag Bridge Highld 309 K3
Duartbeg Highld 306 F6
Duartmore Bridge
Highld 306 F6
Dubbs Cross Devon 12 C3
Dubford Aberds 303 C8
Dubhchladach Argyll 275 G9
Dublin Suff 126 D3
Dubton Angus 287 B9
Dubwath Cumb 229 E9
Duchally Highld 309 H3
Duchlage Argyll 276 D6
Duchrae Dumfries 246 G5
Duck Corner Suff 109 C7
Duck End Bedford 103 C11
Bedford 121 G9
Bucks 102 F5
Cambs 122 E4
Essex 105 G10
Essex 106 E3
Essex 106 F3
Duckend Green Essex 106 G4
Duckhole S Glos 79 G10
Duckington Ches W 167 E7
Ducklington Oxon 82 D5
Duckmanton Derbys 186 G6
Duck's Cross Bedford 122 F2
Ducks Island London 86 F2
Duckswich Worcs 98 D6
Dudbridge Glos 80 E4
Dudden Hill London 67 B8
Duddenhoe End Essex 105 D9
Duddingston Edin 280 G5
Duddington N Nhants 137 C9
Duddlestone Som 28 C2
Duddleswell E Sus 37 B7
Duddlewick Shrops 132 G3
Duddo Northumb 273 G8
Duddon Ches W 167 C8
Duddon Bridge Cumb 210 B3
Duddon Common
Ches W 167 B8
Dudleston Shrops 148 B6
Dudleston Grove Shrops 149 B7
Dudleston Heath (Criftins)
Shrops 149 B7
Dudley T&W 243 C7
W Mid 133 E8
Dudley Hill W Yorks 205 G9
Dudley Port W Mid 133 E9
Dudley's Fields W Mid 133 C9
Dudley Wood W Mid 133 F8
Dudlows Green Warr 183 E10
Dudsbury Dorset 19 B7
Dudswell Herts 85 D7
Dudwells Pembs 91 G8
Duerdon Devon 24 D4
Duffield Derbys 170 G4
Duffieldbank Derbys 170 G5
Duffryn Neath 57 B10
Newport 59 B9
Shrops 130 G4
Dufftown Moray 302 F3
Duffus Moray 301 C11
Dufton Cumb 231 F9
Duggleby N Yorks 217 F7
Duich Argyll 254 B4
Duiletter Argyll 284 D5
Duinish Perth 291 G8
Duirinish Highld 295 B9
Duisdalebeg Highld 295 D8
Duisdalemore Highld 295 D9
Duisky Highld 290 F2
Duke End Warks 134 F4
Dukesfield Northumb 241 F10
Dukestown Bl Gwent 77 C10
Dukinfield Gtr Man 184 B6
Dulas Anglesey 179 D7
Dulcote Som 44 E5
Dulford Devon 27 F9
Dull Perth 286 C2
Dullatur N Lanark 278 F4
Dullingham Cambs 124 F2
Dullingham Ley Cambs 124 F2
Dulnain Bridge Highld 301 G9
Duloch Fife 280 D2
Duloe Bedford 122 E3
Corn 6 D4
Dulsie Highld 301 E9
Dulverton Som 26 B6
Dulwich London 67 E10
Dulwich Village London 67 E10
Dumbarton W Dunb 277 F7
Dumbleton Glos 99 D10
Dumcrieff Dumfries 248 C4
Dumfries Dumfries 237 B11
Dumgoyne Stirling 277 E10
Dummer Hants 48 D5
Dumpford W Sus 34 C4
Dumpinghill Devon 24 F6
Dumpling Green Norf 159 G10
Dumplington Gtr Man 184 B3
Dumpton Kent 71 F11
Dun Angus 287 B10
Dunach Argyll 289 G10
Dunadd Argyll 275 D9
Dunain Ho Highld 300 E6
Dunalastair Perth 285 B11
Dunan Highld 295 C7
Dunans Argyll 275 D9
Argyll 275 D11
Dunball Som 43 E10
Dunbar E Loth 282 F3
Dunbeath Highld 311 G5
Dunbeg Argyll 289 F10
Dunblane Stirling 285 G11
Dunbog Fife 286 F6
Dunbridge Hants 32 B4
Duncansclett Shetland 313 K5
Duncanston Highld 300 D5
Duncanstone Aberds 302 G5
Dun Charlabhaigh
W Isles 304 D3
Dunchideock Devon 14 D3
Dunchurch Warks 119 C9
Duncombe Lancs 202 F6
Duncote W Nhants 120 G3
Duncow Dumfries 247 G11
Duncraggan Stirling 285 G9
Duncrievie Perth 286 G5
Duncroisk Stirling 285 D9
Duncton W Sus 35 D7
Dundas Ho Orkney 314 H4
Dundee Dundee 287 D8
Dundeugh Dumfries 246 F3
Dundon Som 44 G3
Dundonald Fife 280 C4
S Ayrs 257 C9
Dundon Hayes Som 44 G3
Dundonnell Highld 307 L5
Dundonnell Hotel Highld 307 L5
Dundonnell House
Highld 307 L6
Dundraw Cumb 229 B10
Dundreggan Highld 290 B5
Dundreggan Lodge
Highld 290 B5
Dundrennan Dumfries 237 E9
Dundridge Hants 33 D9
Dundry N Som 60 F5
Dundurn Perth 285 E11
Dundyvan N Lanark 268 C4
Dunecht Aberds 293 C9
Dunfermline Fife 279 D11
Dunfield Glos 81 F10
Dunford Bridge S Yorks 197 G7
Dungate Kent 54 B2
Dunge Wilts 45 C11
Dungeness Kent 39 D9
Dungworth S Yorks 186 D3
Dunham Notts 188 G4
Dunham-on-the-Hill
Ches W 183 G7
Dunham on Trent Notts 188 G4
Dunhampstead Worcs 117 E8
Dunhampton Worcs 116 D6
Dunham Town Gtr Man 184 D2
Dunham Woodhouses
Gtr Man 184 D2
Dunholme Lincs 189 F8
Dunino Fife 287 F9
Dunipace Falk 278 E6
Dunira Perth 285 E11
Dunkeld Perth 286 C4
Dunkerton Bath 45 B8
Dunkeswell Devon 27 F10
Dunkeswick N Yorks 206 D2
Dunkirk Cambs 139 F10
Ches W 182 G5
Kent 54 B5
Norf 160 D4
Nottingham 153 B11
S Glos 61 B9
Staffs 168 E4
Wilts 62 G3
Dunk's Green Kent 52 C6
Dunlappie Angus 293 G7
Dunley Hants 48 C3
Worcs 116 D5
Dunlichity Lodge Highld 300 F6
Dunlop E Ayrs 267 F8
Dunmaglass Lodge
Highld 300 G5
Dunmere Corn 5 B10
Dunmore Argyll 275 G8
Falk 279 D7
Highld 300 E5
Dunnerholme Cumb 210 D4
Dunnet Highld 310 B6
Dunnichen Angus 287 C9
Dunnikier Fife 280 C5
Dunninald Angus 287 B11
Dunning Perth 286 F4
Dunnington E Yorks 209 C9
Warks 117 G11
York 207 C9
Dunningwell Cumb 210 C3
Dunnockshaw Lancs 195 B10
Dunnose IoW 21 F7
Dunnsheath Shrops 149 F9
Dunn Street Kent 54 D3
Kent 69 G9
Dunollie Argyll 289 F10
Dunoon Argyll 276 F3
Dunragit Dumfries 236 D3
Dunrobin Mains Highld 311 J2
Dunrostan Argyll 275 E8
Duns Borders 272 E5
Dunsa Derbys 186 G2
Dunsby Lincs 156 D2
Dunscar Gtr Man 195 E8
Dunscore Dumfries 247 G9
Dunscroft S Yorks 199 F7
Dunsdale Redcar 226 B2
Dunsden Green Oxon 65 D8
Dunsfold Sur 50 F4
Dunsfold Common Sur 50 F4
Dunsfold Green Sur 50 F4
Dunsford Devon 14 D2
Sur 50 F4
Dunshalt Fife 286 F6
Dunshillock Aberds 303 E9
Dunsill Notts 171 C7
Dunsinnan Perth 286 D5
Dunskey Ho Dumfries 236 D2
Dunslea Corn 11 G11
Dunsley N Yorks 227 C7
Staffs 133 G7
Dunsmore Bucks 84 D5
Warks 119 B10
Dunsop Bridge Lancs 203 C9
Dunstable C Beds 103 G10
Dunstal Staffs 151 D11
Dunstall Staffs 152 E3
Dunstall Common Worcs 99 C7
Dunstall Green Suff 124 E4
Dunstall Hill W Mid 133 C8
Dunstan Northumb 265 F7
Dunstan Steads
Northumb 264 E6
Dunster Som 42 E3
Duns Tew Oxon 101 F9
Dunston Derbys 186 G5
Dunston *continued*
Lincs 173 C9
Norf 142 C4
Staffs 151 F8
T&W 242 E6
Dunstone Devon 7 E11
Devon 8 G5
Dunston Heath Staffs 151 F8
Dunston Hill T&W 242 E6
Dunsville S Yorks 198 F6
Dunswell E Yorks 209 F7
Dunsyre S Lanark 269 F11
Dunterton Devon 12 F3
Dunthrop Oxon 101 F7
Duntisbourne Abbots
Glos 81 D7
Duntisbourne Leer Glos 81 D7
Duntisbourne Rouse
Glos 81 D7
Duntish Dorset 29 F11
Duntocher W Dunb 277 G9
Dunton Bucks 102 G6
C Beds 104 C4
Norf 159 C7
Dunton Bassett Leics 135 E10
Dunton Green Kent 52 B4
Dunton Patch Norf 159 C7
Dunton Wayletts Essex 87 G11
Duntrune Castle Argyll 275 D8
Duntulm Highld 298 B4
Dunure S Ayrs 257 F7
Dunvant = *Dynfant*
Swansea 56 C5
Dunvegan Highld 298 E2
Dunveth Corn 10 G5
Dunwear Som 43 F10
Dunwich Suff 127 C9
Dunwood Staffs 168 D6
Dupplin Castle Perth 286 F4
Durdar Cumb 239 G10
Durgan Corn 3 D7
Durgates E Sus 52 G6
Durham Durham 233 C11
Durisdeer Dumfries 247 C9
Durisdeermill Dumfries 247 C9
Durkar W Yorks 197 D10
Durleigh Som 43 F9
Durleighmarsh W Sus 34 C3
Durley Hants 33 D8
Wilts 63 G8
Durley Street Hants 33 D8
Durlock Kent 55 B9
Durlow Common
Hereford 98 D2
Durn Gtr Man 196 D2
Durnamuck Highld 307 K5
Durness Highld 308 C4
Durnfield Som 29 C7
Durno Aberds 303 G7
Durns Town Hants 19 B11
Duror Highld 289 D11
Durran Argyll 275 C10
Highld 310 C5
Durrant Green Kent 53 F11
Durrants Hants 22 B2
Durrington Wilts 47 E7
W Sus 35 F10
Durrisdale Orkney 314 D3
Dursley Glos 80 F3
Wilts 45 C11
Dursley Cross Glos 98 G3
Durston Som 28 B3
Durweston Dorset 30 F5
Dury Shetland 313 G6
Duryard Devon 14 C4
Duston W Nhants 120 E4
Dutch Village Essex 69 C9
Duthil Highld 301 G9
Dutlas Powys 114 B4
Duton Hill Essex 106 F2
Dutson Corn 12 D2
Dutton Ches W 183 F9
Duxford Cambs 105 B9
Oxon 82 F5
Duxmoor Shrops 115 B8
Dwygyfylchi Conwy 180 F2
Dwyran Anglesey 162 B6
Dwyrhiw Powys 129 C11
Dyce Aberdeen 293 B10
Dyche Som 43 E7
Dye House Northumb 241 F10
Dyer's Common S Glos 60 C5
Dyer's Green Cambs 105 B7
Dyffryn Bridgend 57 C11
Carms 92 G6
Ceredig 110 G5
Pembs 91 D8
Dyffryn Ardudwy Gwyn 145 E11
Dyffryn-bern Ceredig 110 G5
Dyffryn Castell Ceredig 128 G5
Dyffryn Ceidrych Carms 94 F4
Dyffryn Cellwen Neath 76 D5
Dyke Lincs 156 E2
Moray 301 D9
Dykehead Angus 292 G5
N Lanark 269 D7
Stirling 277 B11
Dykelands Aberds 293 G9
Dykends Angus 286 B6
Dykeside Aberds 303 E7
Dykesmains N Ayrs 266 G5
Dylife Powys 129 E7
Dymchurch Kent 39 B9
Dymock Glos 98 E4
Dynfant = *Dunvant*
Swansea 56 C5
Dyrham S Glos 61 D8
Dysart Fife 280 C6
Dyserth Denb 181 F9

E

Eabost Highld 294 B5
Eabost West Highld 298 E3
Each End Kent 55 B10
Eachway Worcs 117 B9
Eachwick Northumb 242 C4
Eadar Dha Fhadhail
W Isles 304 E2
Eagland Hill Lancs 202 D4
Eagle Lincs 172 B5
Eagle Barnsdale Lincs 172 B5
Eagle Moor Lincs 172 B5
Eaglesfield Cumb 229 F7
Dumfries 238 C6
Eaglesham E Renf 267 E11
Eaglestone M Keynes 103 D7
Eaglethorpe N Nhants 137 E11
Eagle Tor Derbys 170 C2
Eagley Gtr Man 195 E8
Eairy IoM 192 E3
Eakley Lanes M Keynes 120 G6
Eakring Notts 171 C11
Ealand N Lincs 199 E9
Ealing London 67 C7
Eals Northumb 240 F5
Eamont Bridge Cumb 230 F6
Earby Lancs 204 D3
Earcroft Blackburn 195 C7
Eardington Shrops 132 E4
Eardisland Hereford 115 F8
Eardisley Hereford 96 B6
Eardiston Shrops 149 D7
Worcs 116 D3
Earith Cambs 123 C7
Earle Northumb 263 D11
Earlestown Mers 183 B9
Earley Wokingham 65 E9
Earlham Norf 142 B4
Earlish Highld 298 C3
Earls Barton N Nhants 121 E7
Earls Colne Essex 107 F7
Earl's Common Worcs 117 F9
Earl's Court London 67 D9
Earl's Croome Worcs 99 C7
Earlsdon W Mid 118 B6
Earl's Down E Sus 23 B10
Earlsferry Fife 281 B9
Earlsfield Lincs 155 B8
London 67 E9
Earlsford Aberds 303 F8
Earl's Green Suff 125 D10
Earlsheaton W Yorks 197 C9
Earl Shilton Leics 135 D9
Earlsmill Moray 301 D9
Earl Soham Suff 126 E4
Earl Sterndale Derbys 169 B9
Earlston Borders 262 B3
E Ayrs 257 B10
Earlstone Common
Hants 64 G3
Earl Stoneham Suff 126 F2
Earl Stonham Suff 126 F2
Earlstoun Dumfries 246 G4
Earlswood Mon 79 F7
Sur 51 D9
Warks 118 C2
Earnley W Sus 22 D4
Earnock S Lanark 268 E3
Earnshaw Bridge Lancs 194 C4
Earsairidh W Isles 297 M3
Earsdon T&W 243 C8
Earsham Norf 142 F6
Earsham Street Suff 126 B4
Earswick York 207 B8
Eartham W Sus 22 B6
Earthcott Green S Glos 61 B7
Easby N Yorks 224 E3
N Yorks 225 D11
Easdale Argyll 275 B8
Easebourne W Sus 34 C5
Easenhall Warks 119 B9
Eashing Sur 50 E2
Easington Bucks 83 C11
Durham 234 C4
E Yorks 201 D11
Lancs 203 C10
Northumb 264 C4
Oxon 83 F11
Oxon 101 D9
Redcar 226 B4
Easington Colliery
Durham 234 C4
Easington Lane T&W 234 B3
Easingwold N Yorks 215 F10
Easole Street Kent 55 C9
Eason's Green E Sus 23 B8
Eassie Angus 287 C7
East Aberthaw V Glam 58 F4
Eastacombe Devon 25 B8
Devon 25 C9
Eastacott Devon 25 C10
East Acton London 67 C8
East Adderbury Oxon 101 D9
East Allington Devon 8 F5
East Amat Highld 309 K4
East Anstey Devon 26 B5
East Anton Hants 47 D11
East Appleton N Yorks 224 F4
East Ardsley W Yorks 197 B10
East Ashling W Sus 22 B4
East Aston Hants 48 D2
East Auchronie Aberds 293 C10
East Ayton N Yorks 217 B9
East Bank Bl Gwent 78 D2
East Barkwith Lincs 189 E11
East Barming Kent 53 C8
East Barnby N Yorks 226 C6
East Barnet London 86 F3
East Barns E Loth 282 F4
East Barsham Norf 159 C8
East Barton Suff 125 D8
East Beach W Sus 22 E5
East Beckham Norf 177 E11
East Bedfont London 66 E5
East Bergholt Suff 107 D11
East Bierley W Yorks 197 B7
East Bilney Norf 159 F9
East Blackdene Durham 232 D3
East Blatchington E Sus 23 E7
East Bloxworth Dorset 18 C3
East Boldon T&W 243 E9
East Boldre Hants 32 G5
East Bonhard Perth 286 E5
Eastbourne Darl 224 C6
E Sus 23 F10
East Bower Som 43 F10
East Brent Som 43 C11
Eastbridge Suff 127 D9
East Bridgford Notts 171 G11
East Briscoe Durham 223 B9
Eastbrook Som 28 C2
V Glam 59 E7
East Buckland Devon 41 G7
East Budleigh Devon 15 E7
Eastburn E Yorks 208 B5
W Yorks 204 E6
Eastburn Br W Yorks 204 E6
East Burnham Bucks 66 C3
East Burrafirth Shetland 313 H5
East Burton Dorset 18 D2
Eastbury London 85 G9
W Berks 63 D10
East Butsfield Durham 233 B8
East Butterleigh Devon 27 F7
East Butterwick
N Lincs 199 F10
Eastby N Yorks 204 C6
East Cairnbeg Aberds 293 F9
East Calder W Loth 269 B11
East Carleton Norf 142 C3
East Carlton N Nhants 136 F6
W Yorks 205 E10
East Chaldon or Chaldon Herring Dorset 17 E11
East Challow Oxon 63 B11
East Charleton Devon 8 G5
East Chelborough Dorset 29 F9
East Chiltington E Sus 36 D5
East Chinnock Som 29 E7
East Chisenbury Wilts 46 C6
East Cholderton Hants 47 D9
Eastchurch Kent 70 E3
East Clandon Sur 50 C5
East Claydon Bucks 102 F4
East Clevedon N Som 60 E2
East Clyne Highld 311 J3
East Clyth Highld 310 F7
East Coker Som 29 E8
Eastcombe Glos 80 E5
East Combe Som 43 G7
East Common N Yorks 207 G8
East Compton Dorset 30 D5
Som 44 E6
East Cornworthy Devon 8 D6
Eastcote London 66 B6
W Mid 118 B3
W Nhants 120 G3
Eastcote Village London 66 B6
Eastcott Corn 24 D3
Wilts 46 B4
East Cottingwith
E Yorks 207 E10
Eastcotts Bedford 103 B11
Eastcourt Wilts 63 G8
Wilts 81 G7
East Cowes IoW 20 B6
East Cowick E Yorks 199 C7
East Cowton N Yorks 224 E6
East Cramlington
Northumb 243 B7
East Cranmore Som 45 E7
East Creech Dorset 18 E4
East Croachy Highld 300 G6
East Croftmore Highld 291 B11
East Curthwaite Cumb 230 B2
East Dean E Sus 23 F9
Glos 98 G3
Hants 32 B3
W Sus 34 E6
East Dene S Yorks 186 C6
East Denton T&W 242 D6
East Didsbury Gtr Man 184 C5
Eastdon Devon 14 F5
Eastdown Devon 8 F6
East Down Devon 40 E6
East Drayton Notts 188 F3
East Dulwich London 67 E10
East Dundry N Som 60 F5
East Ella Hull 200 B5
Eastend Essex 86 C6
Oxon 100 G6
East End Bedford 122 F2
Bucks 84 B4
C Beds 103 C9
Dorset 18 B5
Essex 89 D8
E Yorks 201 B9
E Yorks 209 B9
E Yorks 209 G9
Glos 81 E11
Hants 20 B3
Hants 33 C11
Hants 64 G2
Herts 105 F9
Kent 53 E11
Kent 53 F10
Kent 70 E3
M Keynes 103 C8
N Som 60 E3
Oxon 82 C5
Oxon 101 D9
Oxon 101 E7
S Glos 61 E9
Som 29 B10
Som 44 C5
Som 45 D7
Suff 108 E2
Suff 126 F3
East End Green Herts 86 C3
Easter Aberchalder
Highld 291 B7
Easter Ardross Highld 300 B6
Easter Balgedie Perth 286 G5
Easter Balmoral Aberds 292 D4
Easter Boleskine Highld 300 G5
Easter Brackland
Stirling 285 G10
Easter Brae Highld 300 C6
Easter Cardno Aberds 303 C9
Easter Compton S Glos 60 C5
Easter Cringate Stirling 278 D4
Easter Culfosie Aberds 293 C9
Easter Davoch Aberds 292 C6
Easter Earshaig
Dumfries 248 C2
Easter Ellister Argyll 254 B3
Easter Fearn Highld 309 L6
Easter Galcantray
Highld 301 E8
Eastergate W Sus 22 B6
Easterhouse Glasgow 268 B3
Easter Housebyres
Borders 262 B2
Easter Howgate Midloth 270 C4
Easter Howlaws Borders 272 G4
Easter Kinkell Highld 300 D5
Easter Knox Angus 287 D9
Easter Langlee Borders 262 B2
Easter Lednathie Angus 292 G5
Easter Milton Highld 301 D9
Easter Moniack Highld 300 E5
Eastern Green W Mid 134 G5
Easter Ord Aberdeen 293 C10
Easter Quarff Shetland 313 K6
Easter Rhynd Perth 286 F5
Easter Row Stirling 278 B5
Easterside Mbro 225 B10
Easter Silverford Aberds 303 C7
Easter Skeld Shetland 313 J5
Easter Softlaw Borders 263 C7
Easterton Wilts 46 C4
Easterton of Lenabo
Aberds 303 E10
Easterton Sands Wilts 46 B4
Eastertown Som 43 C10
Eastertown of Auchleuchries
Aberds 303 F10
Easter Tulloch Highld 291 B11
Easter Whyntie Aberds 302 C6
East Everleigh Wilts 47 C8
East Ewell Sur 67 G8
East Farleigh Kent 53 C8
East Farndon W Nhants 136 F4
East Fen Common
Cambs 124 C2
East Ferry Lincs 188 B4
Eastfield Borders 262 D2
Bristol 60 D5
N Lanark 269 C7
N Lanark 278 G4
Northumb 243 B7
N Yorks 217 C10
Pboro 138 D4
S Lanark 268 C2
S Yorks 197 G9
Eastfield Hall Northumb 252 B6
East Fields W Berks 64 F3
East Finchley London 67 B9
East Finglassie Fife 280 B5
East Firsby Lincs 189 D8
East Fleet Dorset 17 E8
East Fortune E Loth 281 F10
East Garforth W Yorks 206 G4
East Garston W Berks 63 D11
Eastgate Durham 232 D5
Norf 160 E2
Pboro 138 D4
East Gateshead T&W 243 E7
East Ginge Oxon 64 B2
East Gores Essex 107 G7
East Goscote Leics 154 G2

East Grafton Wilts 63 G9
East Grange Moray 301 C10
East Green Hants 49 E9
Suff 124 G3
Suff 127 D8
East Grimstead Wilts 32 B2
East Grinstead W Sus 51 F11
East Guldeford E Sus 38 C6
East Haddon W Nhants 120 D3
East Hagbourne Oxon 64 B4
Easthall Herts 104 G3
East Halton N Lincs 200 D6
Eastham Mers 182 E5
Worcs 116 D3
East Ham London 68 C2
Eastham Ferry Mers 182 E5
East Hampnett W Sus 22 B6
Easthampstead Brack 65 F11
Easthampton Hereford 115 E8
East Hanney Oxon 82 G6
East Hanningfield Essex 88 E3
East Hardwick W Yorks 198 D3
East Harling Norf 141 F9
East Harlsey N Yorks 225 F8
East Harnham Wilts 31 B10
East Harptree Bath 44 B5
East Hartford Northumb 243 B7
East Harting W Sus 34 D3
East Hatch Wilts 30 B6
East Hatley Cambs 122 G5
Easthaugh Norf 159 F11
East Hauxwell N Yorks 224 G3
East Haven Angus 287 D9
Eastheath Wokingham 65 F10
East Heckington Lincs 173 G11
East Hedleyhope
Durham 233 C9
East Helmsdale Highld 311 H4
East Hendred Oxon 64 B3
East Herringthorpe
S Yorks 187 C7
East Herrington T&W 243 G9
East Heslerton N Yorks 217 D8
East Hewish N Som 59 G11
East Hill Kent 68 G5
East Hoathly E Sus 23 B8
East Hogaland Shetland 313 K5
East Holme Dorset 18 D3
East Holton Dorset 18 C5
East Holywell Northumb 243 C8
Easthope Shrops 131 D11
Easthopewood Shrops 131 D11
East Horndon Essex 68 B6
Easthorpe Essex 107 G8
Leics 154 B6
Notts 172 E2
East Horrington Som 44 D5
East Horsley Sur 50 C5
East Horton Northumb 264 C2
Easthouse Shetland 313 J5
Easthouses Midloth 270 B6
East Howdon T&W 243 D8
East Howe BCP 19 B7
East Huntspill Som 43 E10
East Hyde C Beds 85 B10
East Ilkerton Devon 41 D8
East Ilsley W Berks 64 C3
Easting Orkney 314 A7
Eastington Devon 26 F2
Glos 80 D3
Glos 81 C10
East Keal Lincs 174 C5
East Kennett Wilts 62 F6
East Keswick W Yorks 206 E3
East Kilbride S Lanark 268 E2
East Kimber Devon 12 B5
East Kingston W Sus 35 G9
East Kirkby Lincs 174 C4
East Knapton N Yorks 217 D7
East Knighton Dorset 18 D2
East Knowstone Devon 26 C4
East Knoyle Wilts 45 G11
East Kyloe Northumb 264 B3
East Kyo Durham 242 G5
East Lambrook Som 28 D6
East Lamington Highld 301 B7
Eastland Gate Hants 33 E11
East Langdon Kent 55 D10
East Langton Leics 136 E4
East Langwell Highld 309 J7
East Lavant W Sus 22 B5
East Lavington W Sus 34 D6
East Law Northumb 242 G3
East Layton N Yorks 224 D3
Eastleach Martin Glos 82 D2
Eastleach Turville Glos 81 D11
East Leake Notts 153 D11
East Learmouth
Northumb 263 B9
Eastleigh Devon 25 B7
Hants 32 D6
East Leigh Devon 8 E3
Devon 25 F11
East Lexham Norf 159 F7
East Lilburn Northumb 264 E2
Eastling Kent 54 B3
East Linton E Loth 281 F11
East Liss Hants 34 B3
East Lockinge Oxon 64 B2
East Loftus Redcar 226 B4
East Looe Corn 6 E5
East Lound N Lincs 188 B3
East Lulworth Dorset 18 E3
East Lutton N Yorks 217 F8
East Lydeard Som 27 B11
East Lydford Som 44 G5
East Lyng Som 28 B4
East Mains Aberds 293 D8
Borders 271 F11
S Lanark 268 E2
East Malling Kent 53 B8
East Malling Heath Kent 53 B7
East March Angus 287 D8
East Marden W Sus 34 E4
East Markham Notts 188 G2
East Marsh NE Lincs 201 E9
East Martin Hants 31 D9
East Marton N Yorks 204 C4
East Melbury Dorset 30 C5
East Meon Hants 33 C11
East Mere Devon 27 D7
East Mersea Essex 89 C9
East Mey Highld 310 B7
East Molesey Sur 67 F7
Eastmoor Derbys 186 G4
Norf 140 C4
East Moor W Yorks 197 C10
East Moors Cardiff 59 D8
East Morden Dorset 18 B4
East Morton W Yorks 205 E7
East Moulsecoomb
Brighton 36 F4
East Ness N Yorks 216 D3
East Newton E Yorks 209 F11
N Yorks 216 D2
Eastney Ptsmth 21 B9
Eastnor Hereford 98 D4
East Norton Leics 136 C5
East Nynehead Som 27 C11
East Oakley Hants 48 C5
Eastoft N Lincs 199 D10
East Ogwell Devon 14 G2
Eastoke Hants 21 B10
Easton Bristol 60 E6
Cambs 122 C2
Cumb 239 C10
Cumb 239 F7
Devon 8 F3
Devon 13 D10
Dorset 17 G9
Hants 48 G4
IoW 20 D2
Lincs 155 D8
Norf 160 G2
Som 44 D4
Suff 126 F5
W Berks 64 E2
Wilts 61 E11
Easton Grey Wilts 61 B11
Easton in Gordano
N Som 60 D4
Easton Maudit N Nhants 121 F7
Easton on the Hill
N Nhants 137 C10
Easton Royal Wilts 63 G8
Easton Town Som 44 G5
Wilts 61 B11
East Orchard Dorset 30 D4
East Ord Northumb 273 E9
Eastover Som 43 F10
East Panson Devon 12 C3
Eastpark Dumfries 238 D2
East Parley BCP 19 B8
East Peckham Kent 53 D7
East Pennard Som 44 F5
East Perry Cambs 122 D3
East Portholland Corn 5 G9
East Portlemouth Devon 9 G9
East Prawle Devon 9 G10
East Preston W Sus 35 G9
East Pulham Dorset 30 F2
East Putford Devon 24 D5
East Quantoxhead Som 42 E6
East Rainton T&W 234 B2
East Ravendale NE Lincs 190 B2
East Raynham Norf 159 D7
Eastrea Cambs 138 D5
East Rhidorroch Lodge
Highld 307 K7
Eastriggs Dumfries 238 D6
East Rigton W Yorks 206 E3
Eastrington E Yorks 199 B9
Eastrip Wilts 61 E10
East Rolstone N Som 59 G11
Eastrop Hants 48 C6
East Rounton N Yorks 225 E8
East Row N Yorks 227 C7
East Rudham Norf 158 D6
East Runton Norf 177 E11
East Ruston Norf 160 D6
Eastry Kent 55 C10
East Saltoun E Loth 271 B9
East Sheen London 67 D8
East Sherford Devon 7 E11
East Skelston Dumfries 247 F8
East Sleekburn
Northumb 253 G7
East Somerton Norf 161 F9
East Stanley Durham 242 G6
East Stockwith Lincs 188 C3
East Stoke Dorset 18 D3
Notts 172 F3
Som 29 D7
East Stour Dorset 30 C4
East Stour Common
Dorset 30 C4
East Stourmouth Kent 71 G9
East Stowford Devon 25 B10
East Stratton Hants 48 F4
East Street Kent 55 B10
Som 44 F4
East Studdal Kent 55 D10
East Suisnish Highld 295 B7
East Taphouse Corn 6 C3
East-the-Water Devon 25 B7
East Third Borders 262 B4
East Thirston Northumb 252 D5
East Tilbury Thurrock 69 D7
East Tisted Hants 49 G8
East Torrington Lincs 189 E10
East Town Som 42 G6
Som 44 E6
Wilts 45 B11
East Trewent Pembs 73 F8
East Tuddenham Norf 159 G11
East Tuelmenna Corn 6 B4
East Tytherley Hants 32 B3
East Tytherton Wilts 62 E3
East Village Devon 26 F4
V Glam 58 E3
Eastville Bristol 60 E6
Lincs 174 D6
East Wall Shrops 131 E10
East Walton Norf 158 F4
East Water Som 44 C4
East Week Devon 13 C9
Eastwell Leics 154 D5
East Wellow Hants 32 C4
Eastwell Park Kent 54 D4
East Wemyss Fife 280 B6
East Whitburn W Loth 269 B9
Eastwick Herts 86 C6
Shetland 312 F5
East Wickham London 68 D3
East Williamston Pembs 73 E9
East Winch Norf 158 F3
East Winterslow Wilts 47 G8
East Wittering W Sus 21 B11
East Witton N Yorks 214 B2
Eastwood Hereford 98 C2
Notts 171 F7
Southend 69 B10
S Yorks 186 C6
W Yorks 196 B3
East Woodburn
Northumb 251 F10
Eastwood End Cambs 139 E8
Eastwood Hall Notts 171 F7
East Woodhay Hants 64 G2
East Woodlands Som 45 E9
East Worldham Hants 49 F8
East Worlington Devon 26 E3
East Worthing W Sus 35 G11
East Wretham Norf 141 E8
East Youlstone Devon 24 D3
Eathorpe Warks 119 D7
Eaton Ches E 168 B5
Ches W 167 C9
Hereford 115 F10
Leics 154 D5
Norf 142 B4
Notts 188 F2
Oxon 82 E6
Shrops 131 F7
Shrops 131 F10
Eaton Bishop Hereford 97 D8
Eaton Bray C Beds 103 G9
Eaton Constantine
Shrops 131 B11
Eaton Ford Cambs 122 E3
Eaton Green C Beds 103 G9
Eaton Hastings Oxon 82 F3
Eaton Mascott Shrops 131 B10
Eaton on Tern Shrops 150 E3
Eaton Socon Cambs 122 F3
Eaton upon Tern Shrops 150 E3
Eau Brink Norf 157 F11
Eau Withington
Hereford 97 C10
Eaves Green W Mid 134 G5
Eavestone N Yorks 214 F4
Ebberly Hill Devon 25 D9
Ebberston N Yorks 217 C7
Ebbesbourne Wake Wilts 31 C7
Ebblake Hants 31 F10
Ebbw Vale Bl Gwent 77 D11
Ebchester Durham 242 F4
Ebdon N Som 59 G11
Ebernoe W Sus 35 B7
Ebford Devon 14 D5
Ebley Glos 80 D4
Ebnal Ches W 167 F7
Ebnall Hereford 115 F9
Ebreywood Shrops 149 F10
Ebrington Glos 100 C3
Ecchinswell Hants 48 B4
Ecclaw Borders 272 B5
Ecclefechan Dumfries 238 C5
Eccle Riggs Cumb 210 B4
Eccles Borders 272 G5
Gtr Man 184 B3
Kent 69 G8
Ecclesall S Yorks 186 E4
Ecclesfield S Yorks 186 C5
Ecclesgreig Aberds 293 G9
Eccleshall Staffs 150 D6
Eccleshill W Yorks 205 F9
Ecclesmachan W Loth 279 G11
Eccles on Sea Norf 161 D8
Eccles Road Norf 141 E10
Eccleston Ches W 166 C6
Lancs 194 D4
Mers 183 B7
Eccleston Park Mers 183 C7
Eccliffe Dorset 30 B3
Eccup W Yorks 205 E11
Echt Aberds 293 C9
Eckford Borders 262 D6
Eckfordmoss Borders 262 D6
Eckington Derbys 186 F6
Worcs 99 C8
Eckington Corner E Sus 23 D8
Ecklands S Yorks 197 G8
Eckworthy Devon 24 D6
Ecton N Nhants 120 E6
Staffs 169 D9
Ecton Brook W Nhants 120 E6
Edale Derbys 185 D10
Edale End Derbys 185 D11
Edbrook Som 43 E8
Edburton W Sus 36 E2
Edderside Cumb 229 B7
Edderton Highld 309 L7
Eddington Kent 71 F7
W Berks 63 F10
Eddistone Devon 24 C3
Eddleston Borders 270 F4
Eddlewood S Lanark 268 E4
Edenbridge Kent 52 D2
Edenfield Lancs 195 D9
Edenhall Cumb 231 E7
Edenham Lincs 155 E11
Eden Mount Cumb 211 D8
Eden Park London 67 F11
Edensor Derbys 170 B2
Edentaggart Argyll 276 C6
Edenthorpe S Yorks 198 F6
Edentown Cumb 239 F9
Eden Vale Durham 234 D4
Wilts 45 C11
Ederline Argyll 275 C9
Edern Gwyn 144 B5
Edford Som 45 D7
Edgarley Som 44 F4
Edgbaston W Mid 133 G11
Edgcote W Nhants 101 B10
Edgcott Bucks 102 G3
Som 41 F10
Edgcumbe Corn 2 C6
Edge Glos 80 D4
Shrops 131 B7
Edgebolton Shrops 149 E11
Edge End Glos 79 C9
Lancs 203 G10
Edgefield Norf 159 C11
Edgefield Street Norf 159 C11
Edge Fold Blackburn 195 D8
Gtr Man 195 F8
Edge Green Ches W 167 E7
Gtr Man 183 B9
Norf 141 F10
Edgehill Warks 101 B7
Edge Hill Mers 182 C5
Warks 134 D4
Edgeley Gtr Man 184 D5
Edge Mount S Yorks 186 C3
Edgerley Shrops 148 F6
Edgerston Borders 262 G5
Edgerton W Yorks 196 D6
Edgeside Lancs 195 C10
Edgeworth Glos 80 D6
Edginswell Devon 9 B7
Edgiock Worcs 117 E10
Edgmond Telford 150 F4
Edgmond Marsh Telford 150 E4
Edgton Shrops 131 F7
Edgware London 85 G11
Edgwick W Mid 134 G6
Edgworth Blackburn 195 D8
Edham Borders 262 B6
Edial Staffs 133 B11
Edinample Stirling 285 E9
Edinbane Highld 298 D3
Edinburgh Edin 280 G5
Edinchip Stirling 285 E9
Edingale Staffs 152 G4
Edingight Ho Moray 302 D5
Edinglassie Ho Aberds 292 B5
Edingley Notts 171 D11
Edingthorpe Norf 160 C6
Edingthorpe Green Norf 160 C6
Edington Som 43 E11
Wilts 46 C2
Edingworth Som 43 C11
Edintore Moray 302 E4
Edistone Devon 24 C2
Edithmead Som 43 D10
Edith Weston Rutland 137 B8
Edlaston Derbys 169 G11
Edlesborough Bucks 85 B7
Edlingham Northumb 252 B4
Edlington Lincs 190 G2
Edmondsham Dorset 31 E9
Edmondsley Durham 233 B10
Edmondstown Rhondda 77 G8
Edmondthorpe Leics 155 F7
Edmonston S Lanark 269 G11
Edmonstone Orkney 314 D5
Edmonton Corn 10 G5
London 86 G4
Edmundbyers Durham 242 G2
Ednam Borders 262 B6
Ednaston Derbys 170 G2
Edney Common Essex 87 E11
Edradynate Perth 286 B2
Edrom Borders 272 D6
Edstaston Shrops 149 C10
Edstone Warks 118 E3
Edvin Loach Hereford 116 F3
Edwalton Notts 153 B11
Edwardstone Suff 107 C8
Edwardsville M Tydf 77 F9
Edwinsford Carms 94 E2
Edwinstowe Notts 171 B10
Edworth C Beds 104 C4
Edwyn Ralph Hereford 116 F2
Edzell Angus 293 G7
Efail-fôch Neath 57 B9
Efail Isaf Rhondda 58 C5
Efailnewydd Gwyn 145 B7
Efailwen Carms 92 F2
Efenechtyd Denb 165 D10
Effingham Sur 50 C6
Effirth Shetland 313 H5
Effledge Borders 262 F3
Efflinch Staffs 152 F3
Efford Devon 26 G5
Plym 7 D10
Egbury Hants 48 C2
Egdon Worcs 117 G8
Egerton Gtr Man 195 E8
Kent 54 D2
Egerton Forstal Kent 53 D11
Egerton Green Ches E 167 E8
Egford Som 45 D9
Eggbeare Corn 12 D2
Eggborough N Yorks 198 C5
Eggbuckland Plym 7 D10
Eggesford Station
Devon 25 E11
Eggington C Beds 103 F9
Egginton Derbys 152 D5
Egginton Common
Derbys 152 D5
Egglesburn Durham 232 G5
Egglescliffe Stockton 225 C8
Eggleston Durham 232 G5
Egham Sur 66 E4
Egham Hythe Sur 66 E4
Egham Wick Sur 66 E3
Egleton Rutland 137 B7
Eglingham Northumb 264 F4
Egloshayle Corn 10 G5
Egloskerry Corn 11 D11
Eglwysbach Conwy 180 G4
Eglwys-Brewis V Glam 58 F4
Eglwys Cross Wrex 167 G7
Eglwys Fach Ceredig 128 D3
Eglwyswen Pembs 92 D3
Eglwyswrw Pembs 92 D2
Egmanton Notts 172 B2
Egmere Norf 159 B8
Egremont Cumb 219 C10
Mers 182 C4
Egton N Yorks 226 D6
Egton Bridge N Yorks 226 D6
Egypt Bucks 66 B3
Hants 48 E3
W Berks 64 D2
W Yorks 205 G7
Eiden Highld 309 J7
Eight Ash Green Essex 107 F8
Eighton Banks T&W 243 F7
Eignaig Highld 289 E9
Eign Hill Hereford 97 D10
Eil Highld 291 B10
Eilanreach Highld 295 D10
Eildon Borders 262 C3
Eileanach Lodge Highld 300 C5
Eilean Anabaich
W Isles 305 H4
Eilean Darach Highld 307 L6
Eilean Shona Ho Highld 289 B8
Einacleite W Isles 304 F3
Einsiob = *Evenjobb*
Powys 114 E5
Eisgean W Isles 305 G5
Eisingrug Gwyn 146 C2
Elan Village Powys 113 D8
Elberton S Glos 60 B6
Elborough N Som 43 B11
Elbridge Shrops 149 E7
W Sus 22 C6
Elburton Plym 7 E10
Elcho Perth 286 E5
Elcock's Brook Worcs 117 E10
Elcombe Glos 80 F3
Swindon 62 C6
Elcot W Berks 63 F11
Eldene Swindon 63 C7
Eldernell Cambs 138 D6
Eldersfield Worcs 98 E6
Elderslie Renfs 267 C8
Elder Street Essex 105 E11
Eldon Durham 233 F10
Eldon Lane Durham 233 F10
Eldrick S Ayrs 245 G7
Eldroth N Yorks 212 F5
Eldwick W Yorks 205 E8
Elemore Vale T&W 234 B3
Elerch = *Bont-goch*
Ceredig 128 F3
Elfhowe Cumb 221 F9
Elford Northumb 264 C5
Staffs 152 G3
Elford Closes Cambs 123 C10
Elgin Moray 302 C2
Elgol Highld 295 D7
Elham Kent 55 E7
Elie Fife 287 G8
Elim Anglesey 178 D5
Eling Hants 32 E5
W Berks 64 D4
Elishader Highld 298 C5
Elishaw Northumb 251 D9
Elizafield Dumfries 238 C2
Elkesley Notts 187 F11
Elkington W Nhants 120 B2
Elkins Green Essex 87 E10
Elkstone Glos 81 C7
Ellacombe Torbay 9 C8
Ellan Highld 301 G8
Elland W Yorks 196 C6
Elland Lower Edge
W Yorks 196 C6
Elland Upper Edge
W Yorks 196 C6
Ellary Argyll 275 F8
Ellastone Staffs 169 G10
Ellel Lancs 202 B5
Ellemford Borders 272 C4
Ellenborough Cumb 228 D6
Ellenbrook Herts 86 D2
IoM 192 E4
Ellenglaze Corn 4 D5
Ellenhall Staffs 150 D6
Ellen's Green Sur 50 F5
Ellerbeck N Yorks 225 F8
Ellerburn N Yorks 216 C6
Ellerby N Yorks 226 C5
Ellerdine Telford 150 E2
Ellerdine Heath Telford 150 E2
Ellerhayes Devon 27 G7
Elleric Argyll 284 C4
Ellerker E Yorks 200 B2
Ellerton E Yorks 207 F10
N Yorks 224 F5
Shrops 150 D4
Ellesborough Bucks 84 D4
Ellesmere Shrops 149 C8
Ellesmere Park Gtr Man 184 B3
Ellesmere Port Ches W 182 F6
Ellicombe Som 42 E3
Ellingham Hants 31 F10
Norf 143 E7
Northumb 264 D5
Ellingstring N Yorks 214 C3
Ellington Cambs 122 C3
Northumb 253 E7
Ellington Thorpe Cambs 122 C3
Elliot Angus 287 D10
Elliots Green Som 45 D9
Elliot's Town Caerph 77 E10
Ellisfield Hants 48 D6
Elliston Borders 262 D3
Ellistown Leics 153 G8
Ellon Aberds 303 F9
Ellonby Cumb 230 D4
Ellough Suff 143 F8
Elloughton E Yorks 200 B2
Ellwood Glos 79 D9
Elm Cambs 139 B9
Elmbridge Glos 80 B5
Worcs 117 D8
Elm Corner Sur 50 B5
Elm Cross Wilts 62 D6
Elmdon Essex 105 D9
W Mid 134 G3
Elmdon Heath W Mid 134 G3
Elmer W Sus 35 G7
Elmers End London 67 F11
Elmers Green Lancs 194 F3
Elmers Marsh W Sus 34 B5
Elmesthorpe Leics 135 D9
Elmfield IoW 21 C8
Elm Hill Dorset 30 B4
Elmhurst Bucks 84 B4
Staffs 152 G2
Elmley Castle Worcs 99 C9
Elmley Lovett Worcs 117 D7
Elmore Glos 80 B3
Elmore Back Glos 80 B3
Elm Park London 68 B4
Elmscott Devon 24 C2
Elmsett Suff 107 B11
Elms Green Hereford 115 F10
Worcs 116 D4
Elmslack Lancs 211 D9
Elmstead Essex 107 F11
London 68 E2
Elmstead Heath Essex 107 G11
Elmstead Market
Essex 107 G11
Elmsted Kent 54 E6
Elmsthorpe Leics 135 D9
Elmstone Kent 71 G9
Elmstone Hardwicke
Glos 99 F8
Elmswell E Yorks 208 B5
Suff 125 E9
Elmton Derbys 187 G8
Elness Orkney 314 C6
Elphin Highld 307 H7
Elphinstone E Loth 281 G7
Elrick Aberds 293 C10
Elrig Dumfries 236 E5
Elrigbeag Argyll 284 F5
Elrington Northumb 241 E9
Elscar S Yorks 197 G11
Elsdon Hereford 114 G6
Northumb 251 E10
Elsecar S Yorks 186 B5
S Yorks 197 G11
Elsenham Essex 105 F10
Elsenham Sta Essex 105 F10
Elsfield Oxon 83 C8
Elsham N Lincs 200 E4
Elsing Norf 159 F11
Elslack N Yorks 204 D4
Elson Hants 33 G10
Shrops 149 B7
Elsrickle S Lanark 269 G11
Elstead Sur 50 E2
Elsted W Sus 34 D4
Elsthorpe Lincs 155 E11
Elstob Durham 234 G2
Elston Devon 26 G3
Notts 172 F3
Wilts 46 E5
Elstone Devon 25 D11
Elstow Bedford 103 B11
Elstree Herts 85 F11
Elstronwick E Yorks 209 G10
Elswick Lancs 202 F4
T&W 242 E6
Elswick Leys Lancs 202 F4
Elsworth Cambs 122 E6
Elterwater Cumb 220 E6
Eltham London 68 E2
Eltisley Cambs 122 F5
Elton Cambs 137 E11
Ches W 183 F7
Derbys 170 C2
Glos 80 C2
Gtr Man 195 E9
Hereford 115 C9
Notts 154 B5
Stockton 225 B8
Elton Green Ches W 183 G7
Elton's Marsh Hereford 97 C9
Eltringham Northumb 242 E3
Elvanfoot S Lanark 259 F11
Elvaston Derbys 153 C8
Elveden Suff 124 B6
Elvet Hill Durham 233 C11
Elvingston E Loth 281 G9
Elvington Kent 55 C9
York 207 D9
Elwell Devon 41 G7
Dorset 17 E9
Elwick Hrtlpl 234 E5
Northumb 264 B4
Elworth Ches E 168 C2
Elworthy Som 42 G5
Ely Cambs 139 G10
Cardiff 58 D6
Emberton M Keynes 103 B7
Embleton Cumb 229 E9
Durham 234 F4
Northumb 264 E6
Embo Highld 311 K2
Emborough Som 44 C6
Embo Street Highld 311 K2
Embsay N Yorks 204 C6
Emerson Park London 68 B4
Emerson's Green S Glos 61 D7
Emerson Valley
M Keynes 102 E6
Emery Down Hants 32 F3
Emley W Yorks 197 E8
Emmbrook Wokingham 65 F9
Emmer Green Reading 65 D8
Emmett Carr Derbys 187 F7
Emmington Oxon 84 E2
Emneth Norf 139 B9
Emneth Hungate Norf 139 B10
Emorsgate Norf 157 E10
Empingham Rutland 137 B8
Empshott Hants 49 G9
Empshott Green Hants 49 G8
Emscote Warks 118 D5
Emstrey Shrops 149 G10
Emsworth Hants 22 B2
Enborne W Berks 64 F2
Enborne Row W Berks 64 G2
Enchmarsh Shrops 131 D10
Enderby Leics 135 D10
Endmoor Cumb 211 C10
Endon Staffs 168 E6
Endon Bank Staffs 168 E6
Energlyn Caerph 58 B6
Enfield London 86 F4
Worcs 117 D10
Enfield Highway London 86 F5
Enfield Lock London 86 F5
Enfield Town London 86 F4
Enfield Wash London 86 F5
Enford Wilts 46 C6
Engamoor Shetland 313 H4
Engedi Anglesey 178 F5
Engine Common S Glos 61 C7
Englefield W Berks 64 E6
Englefield Green Sur 66 E3
Englesea-brook Ches E 168 E3
English Bicknor Glos 79 B9
Englishcombe Bath 61 G8
English Frankton
Shrops 149 D9
Engollan Corn 10 G3
Enham Alamein Hants 47 D11
Enis Devon 25 B9
Enisfirth Shetland 312 F5
Enmore Som 43 G8
Enmore Field Hereford 115 E9
Enmore Green Dorset 30 C5
Ennerdale Bridge
Cumb 219 B11
Enniscaven Corn 5 D9
Enoch Dumfries 247 C9
Enochdhu Perth 292 G2
Ensay Argyll 288 E5
Ensbury BCP 19 B7
Ensbury Park BCP 19 C7
Ensdon Shrops 149 F8
Ensis Devon 25 B9
Enslow Oxon 83 B7
Enstone Oxon 101 G7
Enterkinfoot Dumfries 247 C9
Enterpen N Yorks 225 D9
Enton Green Sur 50 E3
Enville Staffs 132 F6
Eolaigearraidh W Isles 297 L3
Eorabus Argyll 288 G5
Eoropaidh W Isles 304 B7
Epney Glos 80 C3
Epperstone Notts 171 F11
Epping Essex 87 E7
Epping Green Essex 86 D6
Herts 86 D3
Epping Upland Essex 86 E6
Eppleby N Yorks 224 C3
Eppleworth E Yorks 208 G6
Epsom Sur 67 G8
Epwell Oxon 101 C7
Epworth N Lincs 199 G9
Epworth Turbary
N Lincs 199 G9
Erbistock Wrex 166 G5
Erbusaig Highld 295 C9
Erchless Castle Highld 300 E4
Erdington W Mid 134 E2
Eredine Argyll 275 C10
Eriboll Highld 308 D4
Ericstane Dumfries 260 G3
Eridge Green E Sus 52 F5
Erines Argyll 275 F9
Eriswell Suff 124 B4
Erith London 68 D4
Erlestoke Wilts 46 C3
Ermine Lincs 189 G7
Ermington Devon 8 E2
Ernesettle Plym 7 D8
Erpingham Norf 160 C3
Erriottwood Kent 54 B2
Errogie Highld 300 G5
Errol Perth 286 E6
Errol Station Perth 286 E6
Erskine Renfs 277 G9
Erskine Bridge Renfs 277 G9
Ervie Dumfries 236 C2
Erwarton Suff 108 E4
Erwood Powys 95 C11
Eryholme N Yorks 224 D6
Eryrys Denb 166 D2
Escomb Durham 233 E9
Escott Som 42 F5
Escrick N Yorks 207 E8
Esgairdawe Carms 94 C2
Esgairgeiliog Powys 128 B5
Esgyryn Conwy 180 F4
Esh Durham 233 C9
Esher Sur 66 G6
Eshiels Borders 261 B7
Esholt W Yorks 205 E9
Eshott Northumb 252 D6
Eshton N Yorks 204 B4
Esh Winning Durham 233 C9
Eskadale Highld 300 F4
Eskbank Midloth 270 B6
Eskdale Green Cumb 220 E2
Eskdalemuir Dumfries 249 D7
Eske E Yorks 209 E7
Eskham Lincs 190 B5
Eskholme S Yorks 198 D6
Esknish Argyll 274 G4
Esk Valley N Yorks 226 E6
Eslington Park
Northumb 264 G2
Esperley Lane Ends
Durham 233 G8
Esprick Lancs 202 F4
Essendine Rutland 155 G10
Essendon Herts 86 D3
Essich Highld 300 F6
Essington Staffs 133 C9
Esslemont Aberds 303 G9
Eston Redcar 225 B11
Estover Plym 7 D10
Eswick Shetland 313 H6
Etal Northumb 263 B10
Etchilhampton Wilts 62 G4
Etchingham E Sus 38 B2
Etchinghill Kent 55 F7
Staffs 151 F10
Etchingwood E Sus 37 C8
Etherley Dene Durham 233 F9
Ethie Castle Angus 287 C10
Ethie Mains Angus 287 C10
Etling Green Norf 159 G10
Etloe Glos 79 D11
Eton Windsor 66 D3
Eton Wick Windsor 66 D2
Etruria Stoke 168 F5
Etsell Shrops 131 C7
Etterby Cumb 239 F9
Etteridge Highld 291 D8
Ettersgill Durham 232 F3
Ettiley Heath Ches E 168 C2
Ettingshall W Mid 133 D8
Ettingshall Park W Mid 133 D8
Ettington Warks 100 B5
Etton E Yorks 208 E5
Pboro 138 B2
Ettrick Borders 261 G7
Ettrickbridge Borders 261 E9
Ettrickdale Argyll 275 G11
Ettrickhill Borders 261 G7
Etwall Derbys 152 C5
Etwall Common Derbys 152 C5
Eudon Burnell Shrops 132 F3
Eudon George Shrops 132 F3
Euston Suff 125 B7
Euximoor Drove Cambs 139 D9
Euxton Lancs 194 D5
Evanstown Bridgend 58 B3
Evanton Highld 300 C6
Evedon Lincs 173 F9
Eve Hill W Mid 133 E8
Evelix Highld 309 K7
Evendine Hereford 98 C5
Evenjobb = *Einsiob*
Powys 114 E5
Evenley W Nhants 101 E11
Evenlode Glos 100 F4
Even Pits Hereford 97 D11
Even Swindon Swindon 62 B6
Evenwood Durham 233 G9
Evenwood Gate Durham 233 G9
Everbay Orkney 314 D6
Evercreech Som 44 F6
Everdon W Nhants 119 F11
Everingham E Yorks 208 E2
Everland Shetland 312 D8
Everleigh Wilts 47 C8
Everley N Yorks 217 B9
Eversholt C Beds 103 E9
Evershot Dorset 29 G9
Eversley Essex 69 B8
Hants 65 G9
Eversley Centre Hants 65 G9
Eversley Cross Hants 65 G9
Everthorpe E Yorks 208 G4
Everton C Beds 122 G4
Hants 19 C11
Mers 182 C5
Notts 187 C11
Evertown Dumfries 239 B9
Evesbatch Hereford 98 B3
Evesham Worcs 99 C10
Evington Kent 54 D6
Leicester 136 C2
Ewanrigg Cumb 228 D6
Ewden Village S Yorks 186 B3
Ewell Sur 67 G8
Ewell Minnis Kent 55 E9
Ewelme Oxon 83 G10
Ewen Glos 81 F8
Ewenny V Glam 58 D2
Ewerby Lincs 173 F10
Ewerby Thorpe Lincs 173 F10
Ewes Dumfries 249 E9
Ewesley Northumb 252 E3
Ewhurst Sur 50 E5
Ewhurst Green E Sus 38 C3
Sur 50 F5
Ewloe Flint 166 B4
Ewloe Green Flint 166 B3
Ewood Blackburn 195 B7
Ewood Bridge Lancs 195 C9
Eworthy Devon 12 C5
Ewshot Hants 49 D10
Ewyas Harold Hereford 97 F7
Exbourne Devon 25 G10
Exbury Hants 20 B4
Exceat E Sus 23 F8
Exebridge Devon 26 C6
Exelby N Yorks 214 B5
Exeter Devon 14 C4
Exford Som 41 F11
Exfords Green Shrops 131 B9
Exhall Warks 118 F2
Warks 135 F7
Exlade Street Oxon 65 C7
Exley W Yorks 196 C5
Exley Head W Yorks 204 F6
Exminster Devon 14 D4
Exmouth Devon 14 E6
Exnaboe Shetland 313 M5
Exning Suff 124 D2
Exted Kent 55 E7
Exton Devon 14 D5
Hants 33 C10
Rutland 155 G8
Som 42 G2
Exwick Devon 14 C4
Eyam Derbys 186 F2
Eydon W Nhants 119 G10
Eye Hereford 115 E9
Pboro 138 C4
Suff 126 C2
Eye Green Pboro 138 C4
Eyemouth Borders 273 C8
Eyeworth C Beds 104 B4
Eyhorne Street Kent 53 C10
Eyke Suff 126 G6
Eynesbury Cambs 122 F3
Eynort Highld 294 C5
Eynsford Kent 68 F4
Eynsham Oxon 82 D6
Eype Dorset 16 C5
Eyre Highld 295 B7
Highld 298 D4
Eyres Monsell
Leicester 135 D11
Eythorne Kent 55 D9
Eyton Hereford 115 E9
Shrops 131 F7
Shrops 149 G7
Wrex 166 G4
Eyton on Severn
Shrops 131 B11
Eyton upon the Weald
Moors Telford 150 G3

F

Faberstown Wilts 47 C9
Faccombe Hants 47 B11
Faceby N Yorks 225 E9
Fachell Gwyn 163 B8
Fachwen Gwyn 163 C9
Facit Lancs 195 D11
Fackley Notts 171 C7
Faddiley Ches E 167 E9
Faddonch Highld 295 C11
Fadmoor N Yorks 216 B3
Faerdre Swansea 75 E11
Fagley W Yorks 205 G9
Fagwyr Swansea 75 E11
Faichem Highld 290 C4
Faifley W Dunb 277 G10
Failand N Som 60 E4
Failford S Ayrs 257 D11
Failsworth Gtr Man 195 G11
Fain Highld 299 B11
Faindouran Lodge
Moray 292 C2
Fairbourne Gwyn 146 G2
Fairbourne Heath Kent 53 C11
Fairburn N Yorks 198 B3
Fairburn House Highld 300 D4
Fair Cross London 68 B3
Fairfield Clack 279 C7
Derbys 185 G9
Gtr Man 184 B6
Gtr Man 195 E10
Kent 39 B7
Mers 182 C5
Stockton 225 B8
Worcs 99 C10
Worcs 117 B8
Fairfield Park Bath 61 F9
Fairfields Glos 98 E4
Fairford Glos 81 E11
Fair Green Norf 158 F3
Fairhaven Lancs 193 B10
N Ayrs 255 C10
Fairhill S Lanark 268 E4
Fair Hill Cumb 230 E6
Fairlands Sur 50 C3
Fairlee IoW 20 C6
Fairlie N Ayrs 266 D4
Fairlight E Sus 38 E5
Fairlight Cove E Sus 38 E5
Fairlop London 87 G7
Fairmile BCP 19 C9
Devon 15 B7
Sur 66 G6
Fairmilehead Edin 270 B4
Fair Moor Northumb 252 F5
Fairoak Caerph 77 F11
Staffs 150 C5
Fair Oak Hants 33 D7
Hants 64 G5
Lancs 203 D8
Fair Oak Green Hants 65 G7
Fairseat Kent 68 G6
Fairstead Essex 88 B3
Norf 158 F2
Fairview Glos 99 G9
Fairwarp E Sus 37 B7
Fairwater Cardiff 58 D6
Torf 78 G3
Fairwood Wilts 45 C10
Fairy Cottage IoM 192 D5
Fairy Cross Devon 24 C6
Fakenham Norf 159 D8
Fakenham Magna Suff 125 B8
Fala Midloth 271 C8
Fala Dam Midloth 271 C8
Falahill Borders 271 D7
Falcon Hereford 98 E2
Falcon Lodge W Mid 134 D2
Falconwood London 68 D3
Falcutt W Nhants 101 C11
Faldingworth Lincs 189 E9
Faldonside Borders 262 C2
Falfield Fife 287 G8
S Glos 79 G11
Falkenham Suff 108 D5
Falkenham Sink Suff 108 D5
Falkirk Falk 279 F7
Falkland Fife 286 G6
Falla Borders 262 G6
Fallgate Derbys 170 C5
Fallin Stirling 278 C6
Fallinge Derbys 170 B3
Fallings Heath W Mid 133 D9
Fallowfield Gtr Man 184 C5
Fallside N Lanark 268 C4
Falmer E Sus 36 F5
Falmouth Corn 3 C8
Falnash Borders 249 B9
Falsgrave N Yorks 217 B10
Falside W Loth 269 B9
Falsidehill Borders 272 G3
Falstone Northumb 250 F6
Fanagmore Highld 306 E6
Fancott C Beds 103 F10
Fangdale Beck
N Yorks 225 G11
Fangfoss E Yorks 207 C11
Fanich Highld 311 J2
Fankerton Falk 278 E5
Fanmore Argyll 288 E6
Fanner's Green Essex 87 C11
Fannich Lodge Highld 300 C2
Fans Borders 272 G2
Fanshowe Ches E 184 G5
Fant Kent 53 B8
Faoilean Highld 295 C7
Far Arnside Cumb 211 D8
Far Bank S Yorks 198 E6
Far Banks Lancs 194 C2
Far Bletchley M Keynes 103 E7
Farcet Cambs 138 E4
Far Coton Leics 135 C7
Far Cotton W Nhants 120 F4
Farden Shrops 115 B11
Fareham Hants 33 F9
Far End Cumb 220 F6
Farewell Staffs 151 G11
Far Forest Worcs 116 C4
Farforth Lincs 190 F4
Far Green Glos 80 E3
Farhill Derbys 170 C5
Far Hoarcross Staffs 152 E2
Faringdon Oxon 82 F3
Farington Lancs 194 B4
Farington Moss Lancs 194 C4
Farlam Cumb 240 F3
Farlands Booth Derbys 185 D9
Farlary Highld 309 J7
Far Laund Derbys 170 F5
Farleigh N Som 60 F3
Sur 67 G11
Farleigh Court Sur 67 G11
Farleigh Green Kent 53 C8
Farleigh Hungerford
Som 45 B10
Farleigh Wallop Hants 48 D6
Farleigh Wick Wilts 61 G10
Farlesthorpe Lincs 191 G7
Farleton Cumb 211 C10
Lancs 211 F11
Farley Bristol 60 E2
Derbys 170 C3
Shrops 131 B7
Shrops 132 C2
Staffs 169 G9
Wilts 32 B2
Far Ley Staffs 132 D5
Farley Green Suff 124 G4
Sur 50 D5
Farley Hill Luton 103 G11
Wokingham 65 G8
Farleys End Glos 80 B3
Farlington N Yorks 216 F2
Ptsmth 33 F11
Farlow Shrops 132 G2
Farmborough Bath 61 G7
Farmbridge End Essex 87 C10
Farmcote Glos 99 F11

Farmcote continued
Shrops 132 E5
Farmington Glos 81 B10
Farmoor Oxon 82 D6
Far Moor Gtr Man 194 G4
Farms Common Corn 2 C5
Farmtown Moray 302 D5
Farm Town Leics 153 F7
Farnah Green Derbys 170 F4
Farnborough Hants 49 C11
London 68 G2
Warks 101 B8
W Berks 64 C2
Farnborough Green
Hants 49 B11
Farnborough Park
Hants 49 B11
Farnborough Street
Hants 49 B11
Farncombe Sur 50 E3
Farndish Bedford 121 E8
Farndon Ches W 166 E6
Notts 172 E3
Farnell Angus 287 B10
Farnham Dorset 31 D7
Essex 105 G9
N Yorks 215 G7
Suff 127 E7
Sur 49 D10
Farnham Common Bucks 66 C3
Farnham Green Essex 105 F9
Farnham Park Bucks 66 C3
Farnham Royal Bucks 66 C3
Farnhill N Yorks 204 D6
Farningham Kent 68 F4
Farnley N Yorks 205 D10
W Yorks 205 G11
Farnley Bank W Yorks 197 E7
Farnley Tyas W Yorks 197 E7
Farnsfield Notts 171 D10
Farnworth Gtr Man 195 F8
Halton 183 D8
Far Oakridge Glos 80 E6
Farr Highld 291 C10
Highld 300 F6
Highld 308 C7
Farraline Highld 300 G5
Farr House Highld 300 F6
Farringdon Devon 14 C6
T&W 243 G9
Farrington Dorset 30 D4
Farrington Gurney Bath 44 B6
Far Royds W Yorks 205 G11
Far Sawrey Cumb 221 F7
Farsley W Yorks 205 F10
Farsley Beck Bottom
W Yorks 205 F10
Farther Howegreen
Essex 88 E4
Farthing Corner
Medway 69 G10
Farthing Green Kent 53 D10
Farthinghoe W Nhants 101 D10
Farthingloe Kent 55 E9
Farthingstone W Nhants 120 F2
Far Thrupp Glos 80 E5
Fartown W Yorks 196 D6
Farway Devon 15 B9
Farway Marsh Devon 28 G4
Fasach Highld 297 G7
Fasag Highld 299 D8
Fascadale Highld 289 B7
Faslane Port Argyll 276 D4
Fasnacloich Argyll 284 C4
Fasnakyle Ho Highld 300 G3
Fassfern Highld 290 F2
Fatfield T&W 243 G8
Fattahead Aberds 302 D6
Faucheldean W Loth 279 G11
Faugh Cumb 240 G2
Faughill Borders 262 C2
Fauld Staffs 152 D3
Fauldhouse W Loth 269 C8
Fauldiehill Angus 287 D9
Fauldshope Borders 261 D10
Faulkbourne Essex 88 B3
Faulkland Som 45 C8
Fauls Shrops 149 C11
Faverdale Darl 224 B5
Faversham Kent 70 G4
Favillar Moray 302 F2
Fawdington N Yorks 215 E8
Fawdon Northumb 264 F2
T&W 242 D6
Fawfieldhead Staffs 169 C9
Fawkham Green Kent 68 F5
Fawler Oxon 63 B10
Oxon 82 B5
Fawley Bucks 65 B9
Hants 33 G7
W Berks 63 C11
Fawley Bottom Bucks 65 B8
Fawley Chapel Hereford 97 F11
Faxfleet E Yorks 199 C11
Faygate W Sus 51 G8
Fazakerley Mers 182 B5
Fazeley Staffs 134 C4
Feagour Highld 291 D7
Fearby N Yorks 214 C3
Fearn Highld 301 B8
Fearnan Perth 285 C11
Fearnbeg Highld 299 D7
Fearnhead Warr 183 C10
Fearn Lodge Highld 309 L6
Fearnmore Highld 299 C7
Fearn Station Highld 301 B8
Fearnville W Yorks 206 F2
Featherstone Staffs 133 B8
W Yorks 198 C2
Featherwood Northumb 251 C8
Feckenham Worcs 117 E10
Fedw Fawr Anglesey 179 E10
Feering Essex 107 G7
Feetham N Yorks 223 F9
Fegg Hayes Stoke 168 E5
Feith Mhor Highld 301 G8
Feizor N Yorks 212 F5
Felbridge Sur 51 F11
Felbrigg Norf 160 B4
Felcourt Sur 51 E11
Felden Herts 85 E8
Felderland Kent 55 B10
Feldy Ches E 183 F11
Felhampton Shrops 131 F8
Felin-Crai Powys 95 G7
Felindre Carms 75 C7
Carms 93 D7
Carms 93 G11
Carms 94 E3
Carms 94 F4
Ceredig 111 F10
Powys 96 D3
Powys 96 G3
Powys 130 C3
Powys 130 G3
Rhondda 58 C3
Swansea 75 E10
Felindre Farchog Pembs 92 D2
Felinfach Ceredig 111 F10
Felinfach continued
Powys 95 E11
Felinfoel Carms 75 E8
Felingwmisaf Carms 93 G10
Felingwmuchaf Carms 93 G10
Felin Newydd Carms 94 D3
Felin-newydd Powys 96 D2
Felin Newydd = New Mills
Powys 129 C11
Felin Puleston Wrex 166 F4
Felin-Wnda Ceredig 92 B6
Felinwynt Ceredig 110 G4
Felixkirk N Yorks 215 C9
Felixstowe Suff 108 E5
Felixstowe Ferry Suff 108 D6
Felkington Northumb 273 G8
Felkirk W Yorks 197 E11
Felldyke Cumb 219 B11
Fell End Cumb 222 F4
Fellgate T&W 243 E8
Felling T&W 243 E7
Felling Shore T&W 243 E7
Fell Lane W Yorks 204 E6
Fellside T&W 242 E5
Fell Side Cumb 230 D2
Felmersham Bedford 121 F9
Felmingham Norf 160 D5
Felmore Essex 69 B8
Felpham W Sus 35 H7
Felsham Suff 125 F8
Felsted Essex 106 G3
Feltham London 66 E6
Som 28 D2
Felthamhill London 66 E5
Felthorpe Norf 160 F3
Felton Hereford 97 B11
Northumb 252 C5
N Som 60 F4
Felton Butler Shrops 149 F7
Feltwell Norf 140 E4
Fenay Bridge W Yorks 197 D7
Fence Lancs 204 F2
Fence Houses T&W 243 G8
Fencott Oxon 83 B9
Fen Ditton Cambs 123 E9
Fen Drayton Cambs 122 D6
Fen End Lincs 156 E4
W Mid 118 B4
Fengate Norf 160 E3
Pboro 138 D4
Fenham Northumb 273 G11
T&W 242 D6
Fenhouses Lincs 174 G3
Feniscliffe Blackburn 195 B7
Feniscowles Blackburn 194 B6
Feniton Devon 15 B8
Fenlake Bedford 103 B11
Fenn Green Shrops 132 G5
Fennington Som 27 B11
Fenn's Bank Wrex 149 B10
Fenn Street Medway 69 D9
Fenny Bentley Derbys 169 E11
Fenny Bridges Devon 15 B8
Fenny Castle Som 44 E4
Fenny Compton Warks 119 G8
Fenny Drayton Leics 134 D6
Fenny Stratford
M Keynes 103 E7
Fenrother Northumb 252 E5
Fen Side Lincs 174 D4
Fenstanton Cambs 122 D6
Fenstead End Suff 124 G6
Fen Street Norf 141 G11
Suff 125 B9
Suff 125 E11
Fenton Cambs 122 B6
Cumb 240 F2
Lincs 172 E5
Lincs 188 F4
Northumb 263 C11
Stoke 168 G5
Fentonadle Corn 11 F7
Fenton Barns E Loth 281 E10
Fenton Low Stoke 168 F5
Fenton Pits Corn 5 C11
Fenton Town Northumb 263 C11
Fenwick E Ayrs 267 G9
Northumb 242 C3
Northumb 273 G11
S Yorks 198 D5
Feochaig Argyll 255 F8
Feock Corn 3 B8
Feolin Ferry Argyll 274 G5
Ferguslie Park Renfs 267 C9
Ferindonald Highld 295 E8
Feriniquarrie Highld 296 F7
Ferlochan Argyll 289 E11
Fern Angus 292 G6
Bucks 65 B11
Fern Bank Gtr Man 185 B7
Ferndale Kent 52 E5
Rhondda 77 F7
Ferndown Dorset 31 G9
Ferne Wilts 30 C6
Ferness Highld 301 E9
Ferney Green Cumb 221 F8
Fernham Oxon 82 G3
Fernhill Gtr Man 195 E10
Rhondda 77 F8
W Sus 51 E10
Fern Hill Suff 106 B6
Fernhill Gate Gtr Man 195 F7
Fernhill Heath Worcs 117 F7
Fernhurst W Sus 34 B5
Fernie Fife 287 F7
Ferniebrae Aberds 303 D9
Ferniegair S Lanark 268 E4
Ferniehirst Borders 271 G8
Fernilea Highld 294 B5
Fernilee Derbys 185 F8
Fernsplatt Corn 4 G5
Ferrensby N Yorks 215 G7
Ferring W Sus 35 G9
Ferrybridge W Yorks 198 C3
Ferryden Angus 287 B11
Ferryhill Aberdeen 293 C11
Durham 233 E11
Ferry Hill Cambs 139 G7
Ferryhill Station
Durham 234 E2
Ferry Point Highld 309 L7
Ferryside = Glan-y-Fferi
Carms 74 C5
Ferryton Highld 300 C6
Fersfield Norf 141 G11
Fersit Highld 290 F5
Feshiebridge Highld 291 C10
Fetcham Sur 50 B6
Fetterangus Aberds 303 D9
Fettercairn Aberds 293 F8
Fetterdale Fife 287 E8
Fettes Highld 300 D5
Fewcott Oxon 101 F10
Fewston N Yorks 205 C9
Fewston Bents N Yorks 205 C9
Ffairfach Carms 94 G2
Ffair-Rhos Ceredig 112 D4
Ffaldybrenin Carms 94 C2
Ffarmers Carms 94 C3
Ffawyddog Powys 78 B2
Ffodun = Forden Powys 130 C4
Ffont y gari = Font y gary
V Glam 58 F5
Fforddlas Powys 96 D4
Ffordd-las Denb 165 C10
Ffordd-y-Gyfraith
Bridgend 57 E11
Fforest Carms 75 E9
Fforest-fach Swansea 56 B6
Fforest Gôch Neath 76 E2
Ffostrasol Ceredig 93 B7
Ffos-y-ffin Ceredig 111 E8
Ffos-y-go Wrex 166 E4
Ffridd Powys 130 D3
Ffrith Wrex 166 D3
Ffrwd Gwyn 163 D7
Ffwl y mwn = Fonmon
V Glam 58 F4
Ffynnon Carms 74 B5
Ffynnon ddrain Carms 93 G8
Ffynnongroes = Crosswell
Pembs 92 D2
Ffynnon Gron Pembs 91 F8
Ffynnongroyw Flint 181 E10
Ffynnon Gynydd Powys 96 C3
Ffynnon-oer Ceredig 111 G10
Fickleshole Sur 67 G11
Fidden Argyll 288 G5
Fiddes Aberds 293 E10
Fiddington Glos 99 E8
Som 43 E8
Fiddington Sands Wilts 46 C4
Fiddleford Dorset 30 E4
Fiddler' Green Norf 141 D10
Fiddler's Ferry Mers 193 C11
Warr 183 D9
Fiddler's Green Glos 99 G8
Hereford 97 D11
Fiddlers Hamlet Essex 87 E7
Field Hereford 114 G6
Som 44 E6
Staffs 151 C10
Field Assarts Oxon 82 C4
Field Broughton Cumb 211 C7
Field Common Sur 66 F6
Field Dalling Norf 159 B10
Field Green Kent 38 B3
Field Head Leics 135 B9
Fields End Herts 85 D8
Field's Place Hereford 115 G8
Fifehead Magdalen
Dorset 30 C3
Fifehead Neville Dorset 30 E3
Fifehead St Quintin
Dorset 30 E3
Fife Keith Moray 302 D4
Fifield Oxon 82 B2
Wilts 46 C6
Windsor 66 D2
Fifield Bavant Wilts 31 B8
Figheldean Wilts 47 D7
Filands Wilts 62 B2
Filby Norf 161 G9
Filby Heath Norf 161 G9
Filchampstead Oxon 83 D7
Filey N Yorks 218 C2
Filgrave M Keynes 103 B7
Filham Devon 8 D2
Filkins Oxon 82 E2
Filleigh Devon 25 B11
Devon 26 E2
Fillingham Lincs 188 D6
Fillongley Warks 134 F5
Filmore Hill Hants 33 B11
Filton S Glos 60 D6
Filwood Park Bristol 60 F5
Fimber E Yorks 217 G7
Finavon Angus 287 B8
Finberry Kent 54 F4
Fincastle Ho Perth 291 G10
Finchairn Argyll 275 C10
Fincham Mers 182 C6
Norf 140 B3
Finchampstead
Wokingham 65 G9
Finchdean Hants 34 E2
Finchingfield Essex 106 E3
Finchley London 86 G3
Findern Derbys 152 C6
Findhorn Moray 301 C10
Findhorn Bridge Highld 301 G8
Findochty Moray 302 C4
Findo Gask Perth 286 E4
Findon Aberds 293 D11
W Sus 35 F10
Findon Mains Highld 300 C6
Findon Valley W Sus 35 F10
Findrack Ho Aberds 293 C8
Finedon N Nhants 121 C8
Fineglen Argyll 275 B10
Fine Street Hereford 96 D6
Fingal Street Suff 126 D4
Fingask Aberds 303 G7
Fingerpost Worcs 116 C4
Fingest Bucks 84 G3
Finghall N Yorks 214 B3
Fingland Cumb 239 F7
Dumfries 259 F7
Finglesham Kent 55 C10
Fingringhoe Essex 107 G10
Finham W Mid 118 B6
Finkle Street S Yorks 186 B4
Finlarig Stirling 285 D9
Finmere Oxon 102 E2
Finnart Perth 285 B9
Finney Green Ches E 184 E5
Staffs 168 F3
Finningham Suff 125 D11
Finningley S Yorks 187 B11
Finnygaud Aberds 302 D5
Finsbury London 67 C10
Finsbury Park London 67 B10
Finstall Worcs 117 D9
Finsthwaite Cumb 211 B7
Finstock Oxon 82 B5
Finstown Orkney 314 E3
Fintry Aberds 303 D7
Dundee 287 D8
Stirling 278 D2
Finwood Warks 118 D3
Finzean Aberds 293 D8
Finzean Ho Aberds 293 D7
Fionnphort Argyll 288 G5
Fionnsbhagh W Isles 296 C6
Firbank Cumb 222 G2
Firbeck S Yorks 187 D9
Firby N Yorks 214 B5
N Yorks 216 F4
Firemore Highld 307 L3
Firgrove Gtr Man 196 E2
Firkin Argyll 285 G7
Firle E Sus 23 D7
Firsby Lincs 175 C7
Firsdown Wilts 47 G8
Firs Lane Gtr Man 194 G6
First Coast Highld 307 K4
Firswood Gtr Man 184 B4
Firth Borders 262 E2
Firth Moor Darl 224 C6
Firth Park S Yorks 186 C5
Fir Toll Kent 54 E2
Fir Tree Durham 233 E8
Fir Vale S Yorks 186 C5
Firwood Fold Gtr Man 195 E8
Fishbourne IoW 21 C7
W Sus 22 C4
Fishburn Durham 234 E3
Fishcross Clack 279 B7
Fisherford Aberds 302 F6
Fishermead M Keynes 103 D7
Fisher Place Cumb 220 B6
Fisherrow E Loth 280 G6
Fishersgate Brighton 36 F3
Fishers Green Herts 104 F4
Fisher's Pond Hants 33 C7
Fisherstreet W Sus 50 G3
Fisherton Highld 301 D7
S Ayrs 257 F7
Fisherton de la Mere
Wilts 46 F4
Fisherwick Staffs 134 B3
Fishery Windsor 65 C11
Fishguard = Abergwaun
Pembs 91 D9
Fishlake S Yorks 199 E7
Fishleigh Devon 25 F8
Fishleigh Barton Devon 25 C9
Fishleigh Castle Devon 25 F8
Fishley Norf 161 G8
W Mid 133 C10
Fishmere End Lincs 156 B5
Fishponds Bristol 60 D6
Fishpool Glos 98 F3
Gtr Man 195 F10
N Yorks 205 D10
Fishpools Powys 114 D3
Fishtoft Lincs 174 G5
Fishtoft Drove Lincs 174 F4
Fishtown of Usan
Angus 287 B11
Fishwick Borders 273 E8
Lancs 194 B5
Fiskavaig Highld 294 B5
Fiskerton Lincs 189 G8
Notts 172 E2
Fitling E Yorks 209 G11
Fittleton Wilts 46 D6
Fittleworth W Sus 35 D8
Fitton End Cambs 157 G8
Fitton Hill Gtr Man 196 G2
Fitz Shrops 149 F8
Fitzhead Som 27 B10
Fitzwilliam W Yorks 198 D2
Fiunary Highld 289 E8
Five Acres Glos 79 C9
Five Ash Down E Sus 37 C7
Five Ashes E Sus 37 C9
Five Bells Som 42 E5
Five Bridges Hereford 98 B3
Fivecrosses Ches W 183 F8
Fivehead Som 28 C5
Five Houses IoW 20 D4
Five Lane Ends Lancs 202 C6
Fivelanes Corn 11 E10
Five Lanes Mon 78 G6
Five Oak Green Kent 52 D6
Five Oaks W Sus 35 B9
Five Roads Carms 75 D7
Five Ways Warks 118 D4
Five Wents Kent 53 C10
Fixby W Yorks 196 C6
Flackley Ash E Sus 38 C5
Flack's Green Essex 88 B3
Flackwell Heath Bucks 65 B11
Fladbury Worcs 99 B9
Fladbury Cross Worcs 99 B9
Fladda Shetland 312 E5
Fladdabister Shetland 313 K6
Flagg Derbys 169 B10
Flaggoners Green
Hereford 116 G2
Flamborough E Yorks 218 E4
Flamstead Herts 85 C9
Flamstead End Herts 86 E4
Flansham W Sus 35 G7
Flanshaw W Yorks 197 C10
Flappit Spring W Yorks 205 F7
Flasby N Yorks 204 B4
Flash Staffs 169 B8
Flashader Highld 298 D3
Flask Inn N Yorks 227 E8
Flathurst W Sus 35 C7
Flaunden Herts 85 E8
Flawborough Notts 172 G3
Flawith N Yorks 215 F9
Flax Bourton N Som 60 F4
Flaxby N Yorks 206 B3
Flaxholme Derbys 170 G4
Flaxlands Norf 142 E2
Flaxley Glos 79 B11
Flax Moss Lancs 195 C9
Flaxpool Som 42 F6
Flaxton N Yorks 216 G3
Fleckney Leics 136 E2
Flecknoe Warks 119 E10
Fledborough Notts 188 G4
Fleet Dorset 17 E8
Hants 22 C2
Hants 49 C10
Lincs 157 E7
Fleet Downs Kent 68 E5
Fleetend Hants 33 F8
Fleet Hargate Lincs 157 E7
Fleetlands Hants 33 G9
Fleets N Yorks 213 G9
Fleetville Herts 85 D11
Fleetwood Lancs 202 D2
Fleggburgh =
Burgh St Margaret Norf 161 G8
Fleming Field Durham 234 C3
Flemings Kent 55 B9
Flemingston V Glam 58 E4
Flemington S Lanark 268 D3
S Lanark 268 G4
Flempton Suff 124 D6
Fleoideabhagh W Isles 296 C6
Fletchersbridge Corn 6 B2
Fletcher's Green Kent 52 C4
Fletchertown Cumb 229 C10
Fletching E Sus 36 C6
Fletching Common
E Sus 36 C6
Fleuchary Highld 309 K7
Fleuchlang Dumfries 237 D8
Fleur-de-lis Caerph 77 F11
Flexbury Corn 24 F2
Flexford Hants 32 C6
Sur 50 D2
Flimby Cumb 228 E6
Flimwell E Sus 53 G8
Flint Flint 182 G2
Flint Cross Cambs 105 C8
Flintham Notts 172 F2
Flint Hill Durham 242 G5
Flint Mountain = Mynydd
Fflint Flint 182 G2
Flinton E Yorks 209 F10
Flint's Green W Mid 134 G5
Flintsham Hereford 114 F6
Flishinghurst Kent 53 F9
Flitcham Norf 158 D4
Flitholme Cumb 222 B5
Flitton C Beds 103 D11
Flitwick C Beds 103 D10
Flixborough N Lincs 199 D11
Flixborough Stather
N Lincs 199 E11
Flixton Gtr Man 184 C2
N Yorks 217 D10
Suff 142 F6
Flockton W Yorks 197 E8
Flockton Green
W Yorks 197 D8
Flockton Moor W Yorks 197 E8
Flodaigh W Isles 296 F4
Flodden Northumb 263 B10
Flodigarry Highld 298 B4
Floodgates Hereford 114 F5
Flood's Ferry Cambs 139 E7
Flood Street Hants 31 D10
Flookburgh Cumb 211 D7
Flordon Norf 142 D3
Flore W Nhants 120 E2
Florence Stoke 168 G6
Flotterton Northumb 251 C11
Flowers Bottom Bucks 84 F4
Flowers Green E Sus 23 C10
Flowery Field Gtr Man 184 B6
Flowton Suff 107 B11
Fluchter E Dunb 277 G11
Flugarth Shetland 313 G6
Flushdyke W Yorks 197 C9
Flush House W Yorks 196 F6
Flushing Aberds 303 E10
Corn 3 C8
Corn 3 D7
Flyford Flavell Worcs 117 G9
Foals Green Suff 126 C5
Fobbing Thurrock 69 C8
Fochabers Moray 302 D3
Fochriw Caerph 77 D10
Fockerby N Lincs 199 D10
Fodderletter Moray 301 G11
Fodderstone Gap Norf 140 B3
Fodderty Highld 300 D5
Foddington Som 29 B9
Foel Powys 147 G9
Foel-gastell Carms 75 C8
Foffarty Angus 287 C8
Foggathorpe E Yorks 207 F11
Foggbrook Gtr Man 184 D6
Fogo Borders 272 F5
Fogorig Borders 272 F5
Fogrigarth Shetland 313 H4
Fogwatt Moray 302 D2
Foindle Highld 306 E6
Folda Angus 292 G3
Fold Head Lancs 195 D11
Fold Hill Lincs 175 E7
Foldrings S Yorks 186 C3
Fole Staffs 151 B10
Foleshill W Mid 135 G7
Foley Park Worcs 116 B6
Folke Dorset 29 E11
Folkestone Kent 55 F8
Folkingham Lincs 155 C11
Folkington E Sus 23 E9
Folksworth Cambs 138 F2
Folkton N Yorks 217 D11
Folla Rule Aberds 303 F7
Folley Shrops 132 D5
Follifoot N Yorks 206 C2
Follingsby T&W 243 E8
Folly Dorset 30 G2
Pembs 91 G8
Folly Cross Devon 25 F7
Folly Gate Devon 13 B7
Folly Green Essex 106 F6
Fonmon = Ffwl-y-mwn
V Glam 58 F4
Fonston Corn 11 C10
Fonthill Bishop Wilts 46 G2
Fonthill Gifford Wilts 46 G2
Fontmell Magna Dorset 30 D5
Fontmell Parva Dorset 30 E4
Fontwell W Sus 35 F7
Font-y-gary = Ffont-y-gari
V Glam 58 F5
Foodieash Fife 287 F7
Foolow Derbys 185 F11
Footbridge Glos 99 F10
Footherley Staffs 134 C2
Footrid Worcs 116 C3
Foots Cray London 68 E3
Forbestown Aberds 292 B5
Force Forge Cumb 220 G6
Force Green Kent 52 B2
Force Mills Cumb 220 G6
Forcett N Yorks 224 C3
Ford Argyll 275 C9
Bucks 84 D3
Derbys 186 E6
Devon 8 E2
Devon 8 G4
Devon 24 C6
Devon 28 G2
Glos 99 F11
Hereford 115 F10
Kent 71 F8
Mers 182 B4
Northumb 263 B10
Pembs 91 F9
Plym 7 D9
Shrops 149 G8
Som 27 B9
Som 44 C5
Staffs 169 E9
Wilts 47 G7
Wilts 61 E10
W Sus 35 G7
Forda Devon 12 C6
Devon 40 F3
Fordbridge W Mid 134 F3
Fordcombe Kent 52 E4
Fordell Fife 280 D3
Forden = Ffodun Powys 130 C4
Ford End Essex 87 B11
Essex 105 E9
Forder Corn 7 D8
Forder Green Devon 8 B5
Ford Forge Northumb 263 B10
Fordgate Som 43 G10
Ford Green Lancs 202 D5
Stoke 168 E5
Fordham Cambs 124 C2
Essex 107 F8
Norf 140 D2
Fordham Heath Essex 107 F8
Ford Heath Shrops 149 G8
Ford Hill Northumb 263 B11
Fordhouses W Mid 133 C8
Fordingbridge Hants 31 E10
Fordington Lincs 190 G6
Fordley T&W 243 C7
Fordon E Yorks 217 D10
Fordoun Aberds 293 F9
Ford's Green E Sus 36 B6
Suff 125 D11
Fordstreet Essex 107 F8
Ford Street Som 27 D11
Fordton Devon 14 B2
Fordwater Devon 28 G4
Fordwells Oxon 82 C4
Fordwich Kent 55 B7
Fordyce Aberds 302 C5
Forebridge Staffs 151 E8
Foredale N Yorks 212 F6
Forehill S Ayrs 257 E8
Foreland Fields IoW 21 D9
Foreland Ho Argyll 274 G3
Foremark Derbys 152 D6
Forest Becks Lancs 203 C11
Forestburn Gate
Northumb 252 D3
Forest Coal Pit Mon 96 G5
Forestdale London 67 G11
Forestersea Moray 301 D11
Forest Gate Hants 33 E10
London 68 C2
Forest Green Glos 80 E4
Sur 50 E6
Forest Hall Cumb 221 E10
T&W 243 D7
Forest Head Cumb 240 F3
Forest Hill London 67 E11
Oxon 83 D9
Wilts 63 F8
Forest Holme Lancs 195 B10
Forest-in-Teesdale
Durham 232 F3
Forest Lane Head
N Yorks 206 B2
Forest Lodge Argyll 284 C6
Highld 292 B2
Perth 291 F11
Forest Mill Clack 279 C9
Forest Moor N Yorks 206 B2
Forestreet Devon 24 E5
Forest Row E Sus 52 G2
Forestside W Sus 34 E3
Forest Side IoW 20 D5
Forest Town Notts 171 C9
Forewoods Common
Wilts 61 G10
Forfar Angus 287 B8
Forgandenny Perth 286 F4
Forge Corn 4 F3
Powys 128 D5
Forge Hammer Torf 78 F3
Forge Side Torf 78 D2
Forgewood N Lanark 268 D4
Forgie Moray 302 D3
Forglen Ho Aberds 302 D6
Forgue Aberds 302 E6
Forhill Worcs 117 B11
Formby Mers 193 F10
Forncett End Norf 142 E2
Forncett St Mary Norf 142 E3
Forncett St Peter Norf 142 E3
Forneth Perth 286 C4
Fornham All Saints Suff 124 D6
Fornham St Genevieve
Suff 124 D6
Fornham St Martin Suff 125 D7
Fornighty Highld 301 D9
Forrabury Corn 11 C7
Forres Moray 301 D10
Forrestfield N Lanark 269 B7
Forrest Lodge Dumfries 246 F3
Forry's Green Essex 106 E5
Forsbrook Staffs 169 G7
Forse Highld 310 F6
Forse Ho Highld 310 F6
Forshaw Heath Warks 117 C11
Forsinain Highld 310 E3
Forsinard Highld 310 E2
Forsinard Station Highld 310 E2
Forstal Kent 53 B8
Forston Dorset 17 B9
Fort Augustus Highld 290 C5
Forteviot Perth 286 F4
Fort George Highld 301 D7
Forth S Lanark 269 E8
Forthampton Glos 99 E7
Forthay Glos 80 F2
Forth Road Bridge Edin 280 F2
Fortingall Perth 285 C11
Fortis Green London 67 B9
Fort Matilda Invclyd 276 F5
Forton Hants 33 G10
Hants 48 E2
Lancs 202 C5
Shrops 149 F8
Som 28 F4
Staffs 150 E5
Forton Heath Shrops 149 F8
Fortrie Aberds 302 E6
Aberds 303 D7
Fortrose Highld 301 D7
Fortuneswell Dorset 17 G9
Fort William Highld 290 F3
Forty Green Bucks 84 E3
Bucks 84 G6
Forty Hill London 86 F4
Forward Green Suff 125 F11
Forwood Glos 80 E5
Fosbury Wilts 47 B10
Foscot Oxon 100 G4
Foscote Bucks 102 D4
Wilts 61 D11
W Nhants 102 B3
Fosdyke Lincs 156 C6
Fosdyke Bridge Lincs 156 C6
Foss Perth 285 B11
Foss Cross Glos 81 D9
Fossebridge Glos 81 C9
Fostall Kent 70 G5
Fosten Green Kent 53 F10
Fosterhouses S Yorks 199 E7
Foster's Booth
W Nhants 120 G3
Foster's Green Worcs 117 D9
Foster Street Essex 87 D7
Foston Derbys 152 C3
Leics 136 D2
Lincs 172 G5
N Yorks 216 F3
Foston on the Wolds
E Yorks 209 B8
Fotherby Lincs 190 C4
Fothergill Cumb 228 E6
Fotheringhay N Nhants 137 E11
Foubister Orkney 314 F5
Foul Anchor Cambs 157 F9
Foulbridge Cumb 230 B4
Foulby W Yorks 197 D11
Foulden Borders 273 D8
Norf 140 D5
Foul End Warks 134 E4
Foulford Hants 31 F11
Foulis Castle Highld 300 C5
Foul Mile E Sus 23 B10
Foulride Green E Sus 23 E9
Foulridge Lancs 204 E3
Foulsham Norf 159 E10
Foundry Corn 2 B3
Foundry Hill Norf 159 D11
Fountain Bridgend 57 E11
Fountainhall Borders 271 F8
Four Ashes Bucks 84 F5
Staffs 132 F6
Staffs 133 B8
Suff 125 C10
W Mid 118 B3
Four Crosses Powys 129 B11
Four Crosses continued
Powys 148 F5
Staffs 133 B9
Wrex 166 E3
Four Elms Devon 28 F3
Kent 52 D3
Four Foot Som 44 G5
Four Forks Som 43 F8
Four Gates Gtr Man 194 F6
Four Gotes Cambs 157 F9
Four Houses Corner
W Berks 64 F6
Four Lane End S Yorks 197 G9
Four Lane Ends Derbys 170 D5
Fourlane Ends
Blackburn 195 B7
Ches W 167 C9
Gtr Man 195 E9
W Yorks 205 G8
Four Lanes Corn 2 B5
Fourlanes End Ches E 168 D4
Four Marks Hants 49 G7
Four Mile Bridge
Anglesey 178 F3
Four Mile Elm Glos 80 C4
Four Oaks E Sus 38 C5
Glos 98 F3
Kent 70 G3
W Mid 134 D2
W Mid 134 G4
Four Oaks Park W Mid 134 D2
Fourpenny Highld 311 K2
Four Points W Berks 64 D5
Four Pools Worcs 99 C10
Four Roads Carms 74 D6
IoM 192 F3
Fourstones Northumb 241 D9
Four Throws Kent 38 B3
Four Wantz Essex 87 C10
Four Wents Kent 53 F9
Fovant Wilts 31 B8
Foveran Aberds 303 G9
Fowey Corn 6 E2
Fowler's Plot Som 43 F10
Fowley Common Warr 183 B11
Fowlis Angus 287 D7
Fowlis Wester Perth 286 E3
Fowlmere Cambs 105 B8
Fownhope Hereford 97 E11
Foxash Estate Essex 107 E11
Foxbar Renfs 267 C9
Foxbury London 68 E2
Foxcombe Hill Oxon 83 E7
Fox Corner C Beds 103 F8
Sur 50 C3
Foxcote Glos 81 B8
Som 45 B8
Foxcotte Hants 47 D10
Foxdale IoM 192 E3
Foxdown Hants 48 C4
Foxearth Essex 106 C6
Foxendown Kent 69 F7
Foxfield Cumb 210 B4
Foxford W Mid 135 G7
Foxham Wilts 62 D3
Fox Hatch Essex 87 F9
Fox Hill Bath 61 G9
Hereford 98 B3
Foxhills Hants 32 E4
Foxhole Corn 5 E9
Norf 142 D4
Swansea 57 C7
Fox Hole Swansea 56 D5
Foxholes N Yorks 217 E10
Fox Holes Wilts 45 E11
Foxhunt Green E Sus 23 B8
Fox Lane Hants 49 B11
Foxley Hereford 97 B8
Norf 159 E10
Staffs 168 E3
Wilts 61 B11
Foxlydiate Worcs 117 D10
Fox Royd W Yorks 197 D8
Fox Street Essex 107 F10
Foxt Staffs 169 F8
Foxton Cambs 105 B8
Durham 234 F3
Leics 136 E4
N Yorks 225 F8
Foxup N Yorks 213 D7
Foxwist Green Ches W 167 B10
Foxwood Shrops 116 B2
Foy Hereford 97 F11
Foyers Highld 300 G4
Foynesfield Highld 301 D8
Fraddam Corn 2 C3
Fraddon Corn 5 D8
Fradley Staffs 152 G3
Fradley Junction Staffs 152 G2
Fradswell Staffs 151 C9
Fraisthorpe E Yorks 218 G3
Framfield E Sus 37 C7
Framingham Earl Norf 142 C5
Framingham Pigot Norf 142 C5
Framlingham Suff 126 E5
Frampton Dorset 17 B8
Lincs 156 B6
Frampton Cotterell
S Glos 61 C7
Frampton Court Glos 99 E10
Frampton End S Glos 61 C7
Frampton Mansell Glos 80 E6
Frampton on Severn
Glos 80 D2
Frampton West End
Lincs 174 G3
Framsden Suff 126 F3
Framwellgate Moor
Durham 233 C11
France Lynch Glos 80 E6
Franche Worcs 116 B6
Frandley Ches W 183 F10
Frankby Mers 182 D2
Frankfort Norf 160 E6
Franklands Gate
Hereford 97 B10
Frankley Worcs 133 G9
Frankley Green Worcs 133 G9
Frankley Hill Worcs 117 B9
Frank's Bridge Powys 114 F2
Frankton Warks 119 C8
Frankwell Shrops 149 G9
Frans Green Norf 160 G2
Frant E Sus 52 F5
Fraserburgh Aberds 303 C9
Frating Essex 107 G11
Frating Green Essex 107 G11
Fratton Ptsmth 21 B9
Freasley Warks 134 D4
Freathy Corn 7 E8
Frecheville S Yorks 186 E5
Freckenham Suff 124 C3
Freckleton Lancs 194 B2
Fredley Sur 51 C7
Freebirch Derbys 186 G4
Freeby Leics 154 E6
Freefolk Hants 48 D3
Freehay Staffs 169 G8
Freeland Oxon 82 C6
Renfs 267 B9
Freeland Corner Norf 160 F3
Freemantle Soton 32 E6
Freester Shetland 313 H6
Freethorpe Norf 143 B8
Free Town Gtr Man 195 E10
Freezy Water London 86 F5
Freiston Lincs 174 G5
Freiston Shore Lincs 174 G5
Fremington Devon 40 G4
N Yorks 223 F10
Frenchay S Glos 60 D6
Frenchbeer Devon 13 D9
Frenches Green Essex 106 G4
Frenchmoor Hants 32 B3
French Street Kent 52 C3
Frenchwood Lancs 194 B4
Frenich Stirling 285 G8
Frensham Sur 49 E10
Frenze Norf 142 G2
Fresgoe Highld 310 C3
Freshbrook Swindon 62 C6
Freshfield Mers 193 F9
Freshford Bath 61 G9
Freshwater IoW 20 D2
Freshwater Bay IoW 20 D2
Freshwater East Pembs 73 F8
Fressingfield Suff 126 B5
Freston Suff 108 D3
Freswick Highld 310 C7
Fretherne Glos 80 D2
Frettenham Norf 160 F4
Freuchie Fife 286 G6
Freuchies Angus 292 G4
Freystrop Pembs 73 C7
Friarn Som 43 F7
Friar Park W Mid 133 E10
Friars Cliff BCP 19 C9
Friar's Gate E Sus 52 G3
Friar's Hill E Sus 38 E5
Friarton Perth 286 E5
Friday Bridge Cambs 139 C9
Friday Hill London 86 G5
Friday Street E Sus 23 E10
Suff 126 G6
Suff 127 E7
Sur 50 D6
Fridaythorpe E Yorks 208 B3
Friendly W Yorks 196 C5
Friern Barnet London 86 G3
Friesland Argyll 288 D3
Friesthorpe Lincs 189 E9
Frieston Lincs 172 F6
Frieth Bucks 84 G3
Frieze Hill Som 28 B2
Friezeland Notts 171 E7
Frilford Oxon 82 F6
Frilford Heath Oxon 82 F6
Frilsham W Berks 64 E4
Frimley Sur 49 B11
Frimley Green Sur 49 B11
Frimley Ridge Sur 49 B11
Frindsbury Medway 69 E8
Fring Norf 158 C4
Fringford Oxon 102 F2
Friningham Kent 53 B10
Frinkle Green Essex 106 C4
Frinsted Kent 53 B11
Frinton-on-Sea Essex 108 G4
Friockheim Angus 287 C9
Friog Gwyn 146 G2
Frisby Leics 136 C4
Frisby on the Wreake
Leics 154 F3
Friskney Lincs 175 D7
Friskney Eaudyke Lincs 175 D7
Friskney Tofts Lincs 175 E7
Friston E Sus 23 F8
Suff 127 E8
Fritchley Derbys 170 E5
Frith Kent 54 B2
Fritham Hants 32 E2
Frith Bank Lincs 174 F4
Frith Common Worcs 116 D3
Frithelstock Devon 25 D7
Frithelstock Stone Devon 25 D7
Frithend Hants 49 F10
Frith-hill Bucks 84 E6
Frith Hill Sur 50 E3
Frithsden Herts 85 D8
Frithville Lincs 174 E4
Frittenden Kent 53 E10
Frittiscombe Devon 8 G6
Fritton Norf 142 E4
Norf 143 C9
Norf 161 F8
Fritwell Oxon 101 F10
Frizinghall W Yorks 205 F8
Frizington Cumb 219 B10
Frizzeler's Green Suff 124 E5
Frobost W Isles 297 J3
Frocester Glos 80 E3
Frochas Powys 148 G5
Frodesley Shrops 131 C10
Frodingham N Lincs 199 E11
Frodsham Ches W 183 F8
Frogden Borders 263 D7
Frog End Cambs 123 F10
Cambs 123 G8
Froggatt Derbys 186 F2
Froghall Staffs 169 F8
Frogham Hants 31 E11
Kent 55 C9
Froghole Kent 52 C2
Frogholt Kent 55 F7
Frogland Cross S Glos 60 C6
Frog Moor Swansea 56 C3
Frogmore Devon 8 G5
Hants 33 C11
Hants 49 B10
Herts 85 E11
Frognal S Ayrs 257 D8
Frognall Lincs 156 G3
Frogpool Corn 4 G5
Frog Pool Worcs 116 D5
Frogs' Green Essex 105 D11
Frogshail Norf 160 B5
Frogwell Corn 6 B6
Frolesworth Leics 135 E10
Frome Som 45 D9
Fromebridge Glos 80 D3
Fromefield Som 45 D9
Frome St Quintin Dorset 29 G9
Fromes Hill Hereford 98 B3
Fromington Hereford 97 B10
Fron Denb 165 B9
Gwyn 145 B7
Gwyn 163 D8
Powys 113 D11
Powys 129 C8
Powys 130 C4
Powys 130 D3
Shrops 148 B5
Fron-Bache Denb 166 G2
Froncysyllte Wrex 166 G3
Fron-dêg Wrex 166 F3
Frongoch Gwyn 147 B8
Fron Isaf Wrex 166 G3
Frost Devon 26 F3
Frostenden Suff 143 G9
Frostenden Corner Suff 143 G9
Frosterley Durham 232 D6
Frost Hill N Som 60 G2

Frostlane Hants 32 F6
Frost Row Norf 141 C10
Frotoft Orkney 314 D4
Froxfield C Beds 103 E9
Wilts 63 F9
Froxfield Green Hants 34 B2
Froyle Hants 49 E9
Fryern Hill Hants 32 C6
Fryerning Essex 87 E10
Fryerns Essex 69 B8
Fryton N Yorks 216 E3
Fugglestone St Peter
Wilts 46 G6
Fulbeck Lincs 172 E6
Northumb 252 F5
Fulbourn Cambs 123 F10
Fulbrook Oxon 82 C3
Fulflood Hants 33 B7
Fulford Som 28 B2
Staffs 151 B9
York 207 D8
Fulham London 67 D8
Fulking W Sus 36 E2
Fullabrook Devon 40 E4
Fullarton Glasgow 268 C2
N Ayrs 257 B8
Fuller's End Essex 105 F10
Fuller's Moor Ches W 167 E7
Fuller Street Essex 88 B2
Fullerton Hants 47 F11
Fulletby Lincs 190 G3
Fullshaw S Yorks 197 G8
Full Sutton E Yorks 207 B10
Fullwell Cross London 86 G6
Fullwood E Ayrs 267 E8
Gtr Man 196 F2
Fulmer Bucks 66 B3
Fulmodestone Norf 159 C9
Fulneck W Yorks 205 G10
Fulnetby Lincs 189 F9
Fulney Lincs 156 E5
Fulready Warks 100 B5
Fulshaw Park Ches E 184 E4
Fulstone W Yorks 197 F7
Fulstow Lincs 190 B4
Fulthorpe Stockton 234 G4
Fulwell Oxon 101 G7
T&W 243 F9
Fulwood Lancs 202 G6
Som 28 C2
S Yorks 186 D4
Fundenhall Norf 142 D3
Fundenhall Street Norf 142 D2
Funtington W Sus 22 B3
Funtley Hants 33 F9
Funtullich Perth 285 E11
Funzie Shetland 312 D8
Furley Devon 28 G3
Furnace Argyll 284 G4
Carms 74 E6
Carms 75 E8
Ceredig 128 D3
Highld 299 B9
Furnace End Warks 134 E4
Furnace Green W Sus 51 F9
Furnace Wood W Sus 51 F11
Furneaux Pelham Herts 105 F8
Furner's Green E Sus 36 B6
Furness Vale Derbys 185 E8
Furneux Pelham Herts 105 F8
Furnham Som 28 F4
Further Ford End Essex 105 E9
Further Quarter Kent 53 F11
Furtho W Nhants 102 C5
Furze Devon 25 B10
Furzebrook Dorset 18 E4
Furzedown Hants 32 B5
London 67 E9
Furzehill Devon 41 D8
Dorset 31 G8
Furze Hill Hants 31 E11
Furzeley Corner Hants 33 E11
Furze Platt Windsor 65 C11
Furzey Lodge Hants 32 G5
Furzley Hants 32 D3
Furzton M Keynes 102 D6
Fyfett Som 28 E2
Fyfield Essex 87 D9
Glos 82 E2
Hants 47 D9
Oxon 82 F6
Wilts 63 F7
Wilts 63 G7
Fylingthorpe N Yorks 227 D8
Fyning W Sus 34 C4
Fyvie Aberds 303 F7

G

Gabalfa Cardiff 59 D7
Gabhsann bho Dheas
W Isles 304 C6
Gabhsann bho Thuath
W Isles 304 C6
Gable Head Hants 21 B10
Gablon Highld 309 K7
Gabroc Hill E Ayrs 267 E9
Gadbrook Sur 51 D8
Gaddesby Leics 154 G3
Gadebridge Herts 85 D8
Gadfa Anglesey 179 D7
Gadfield Elm Worcs 98 E5
Gadlas Shrops 149 B7
Gadlys Rhondda 77 E7
Gadshill Kent 69 E8
Gaer Newport 59 B9
Powys 96 G3
Gaer-fawr Mon 78 F6
Gaerllwyd Mon 78 F6
Gaerwen Anglesey 179 G7
Gagingwell Oxon 101 F8
Gaick Lodge Highld 291 E9
Gailey Staffs 151 G8
Gailey Wharf Staffs 151 G8
Gainfield Oxon 82 F4
Gainford Durham 224 B3
Gain Hill Kent 53 D8
Gainsborough Lincs 188 C4
Suff 108 C3
Gainsford End Essex 106 D4
Gairletter Argyll 276 E3
Gairloch Highld 299 B8
Gairlochy Highld 290 E3
Gairney Bank Perth 280 B2
Gairnshiel Lodge
Aberds 292 C4
Gaisgill Cumb 222 D2
Gaitsgill Cumb 230 B3
Galadean Borders 271 G11
Galashiels Borders 261 B11
Galdlys Flint 182 G2
Gale Gtr Man 196 D2
Galgate Lancs 202 B5
Galhampton Som 29 B10
Gallaberry Dumfries 247 G11
Gallachoille Argyll 275 E8
Gallanach Argyll 288 C4
Argyll 289 G10
Highld 294 G6
Gallantry Bank Ches E 167 E8
Gallatown Fife 280 C5
Galley Common Warks 134 E6
Galleyend Essex 88 E2
Galley Hill Cambs 122 D6
Lincs 190 F6
Galleywood Essex 88 E2
Galligill Cumb 231 B11
Gallin Perth 285 C9
Gallovie Highld 291 E7
Gallowfauld Angus 287 C8
Gallowhill Glasgow 267 D11
Renfs 267 B9
Gallowhills Aberds 303 D10
Gallows Corner London 87 G8
Gallowsgreen Torf 78 D3
Gallows Green Essex 106 F2
Essex 107 F8
Staffs 169 G9
Worcs 117 E8
Gallows Inn Derbys 171 G7
Gallowstree Common
Oxon 65 C7
Galltair Highld 295 C10
Galltegfa Denb 165 D10
Gallt Melyd = *Meliden*
Denb 181 E9
Gallt-y-foel Gwyn 163 C9
Gallypot Street E Sus 52 F3
Galmington Som 28 C2
Galmisdale Highld 294 G6
Galmpton Devon 8 G3
Torbay 9 D7
Galon Uchaf M Tydf 77 D9
Galphay N Yorks 214 E5
Galston E Ayrs 258 B2
Galtrigill Highld 296 F7
Gam Corn 11 F7
Gamble Hill W Yorks 205 G11
Gamblesby Cumb 231 D8
Gamble's Green Essex 88 C3
Gamelsby Cumb 239 G7
Gamesley Derbys 185 C8
Gamlingay Cambs 122 G4
Gamlingay Cinques
Cambs 122 G4
Gamlingay Great Heath
Cambs 122 G4
Gammaton Devon 25 B7
Gammaton Moor Devon 25 C7
Gammersgill N Yorks 213 C11
Gamston Notts 154 B2
Notts 188 F2
Ganarew Hereford 79 B8
Ganavan Argyll 289 F10
Ganders Green Glos 98 G4
Gang Corn 6 B6
Ganllwyd Gwyn 146 E4
Gannetts Dorset 30 D3
Gannochy Angus 293 F7
Perth 286 E5
Gansclet Highld 310 E7
Ganstead E Yorks 209 G9
Ganthorpe N Yorks 216 E3
Ganton N Yorks 217 D9
Gants Hill London 68 B2
Ganwick Corner Herts 86 F3
Gaodhail Argyll 289 F8
Gappah Devon 14 F3
Garafad Highld 298 C4
Garamor Highld 295 F8
Garbat Highld 300 C4
Garbhallt Argyll 275 D11
Garboldisham Norf 141 G10
Garbole Highld 301 G7
Garden City Bl Gwent 77 D11
Flint 166 B4
Gardeners Green
Wokingham 65 F10
Gardenstown Aberds 303 C7
Garden Village Swansea 56 B5
S Yorks 186 B3
Wrex 166 E4
W Yorks 206 G4
Garderhouse Shetland 313 J5
Gardham E Yorks 208 E5
Gardie Shetland 312 D7
Gardin Shetland 312 G6
Gare Hill Som 45 E9
Garelochhead Argyll 276 C4
Garford Oxon 82 F6
Garforth W Yorks 206 G4
Gargrave N Yorks 204 C4
Gargunnock Stirling 278 C4
Garizim Conwy 179 F11
Garker Corn 5 E10
Garlandhayes Devon 27 D11
Garlands Cumb 239 G10
Garleffin S Ayrs 244 G3
Garlic Street Norf 142 G4
Garlieston Dumfries 236 E6
Garliford Devon 26 B3
Garlinge Kent 71 F10
Garlinge Green Kent 54 C6
Garlogie Aberds 293 C9
Garmelow Staffs 150 D5
Garmond Aberds 303 D8
Garmondsway Durham 234 E2
Garmony Argyll 289 E8
Garmouth Moray 302 C3
Garmston Shrops 132 B2
Garn Powys 130 G2
Garnant Carms 75 C11
Garndiffaith Torf 78 E3
Garndolbenmaen Gwyn 163 G7
Garnedd Conwy 164 E2
Garnett Bridge Cumb 221 F10
Garnetts Essex 87 B10
Garnfadryn Gwyn 144 C5
Garnkirk N Lanark 268 B3
Garnlydan Bl Gwent 77 C11
Garnsgate Lincs 157 E8
Garnswllt Swansea 75 D10
Garn-swllt Swansea 75 D10
Garn-yr-erw Torf 78 C2
Garrabost W Isles 304 E7
Garrachra Argyll 275 E11
Garra Eallabus Argyll 274 F3
Garralburn Moray 302 D4
Garraron Argyll 275 C9
Garras Corn 2 E6
Garreg Flint 181 F10
Gwyn 163 G10
Garrets Green W Mid 134 F2
Garrick Perth 286 F2
Garrigill Cumb 231 C10
Garrison Stirling 285 G7
Garriston N Yorks 224 G3
Garroch Dumfries 246 G3
Garrogie Lodge Highld 291 B7
Garros Highld 298 C4
Garrow Perth 286 C2
Garrowhill Glasgow 268 C3
Garrygualach Highld 290 C3
Garryhorn Dumfries 246 E2
Garsdale Cumb 212 B4
Garsdale Head Cumb 222 G5
Garsdon Wilts 62 B3
Garshall Green Staffs 151 C9
Garsington Oxon 83 E9
Garstang Lancs 202 D5
Garston Herts 85 F10
Garston *continued*
Mers 182 E6
Garswood Mers 183 B9
Gartachoil Stirling 277 C10
Gartbreck Argyll 254 B3
Gartcosh N Lanark 268 B3
Garth Bridgend 57 C11
Ceredig 128 G2
Flint 181 E10
Gwyn 179 G9
Newport 59 B9
Newport 78 G4
Perth 285 B11
Powys 95 B9
Powys 114 C5
Shetland 313 H4
Shetland 313 H6
Wrex 166 G3
Garthamlock Glasgow 268 B3
Garthbeg Highld 291 B7
Garthbrengy Powys 95 E10
Garthdee Aberdeen 293 C11
Gartheli Ceredig 111 F11
Garthmyl Powys 130 D3
Garthorpe Leics 154 E6
N Lincs 199 D11
Garth Owen Powys 130 E2
Garth Row Cumb 221 F10
Garth Trevor Wrex 166 G3
Gartlea N Lanark 268 C5
Gartloch Glasgow 268 B3
Gartly Aberds 302 F5
Gartmore Stirling 277 B10
Gartmore Ho Stirling 277 B10
Gartnagrenach Argyll 255 B8
Gartness N Lanark 268 C5
Stirling 277 D10
Gartocharn W Dunb 277 D8
Garton E Yorks 209 F11
Garton-on-the-Wolds
E Yorks 208 B5
Gartsherrie N Lanark 268 B4
Gartur Stirling 277 B11
Gartymore Highld 311 H4
Garvald E Loth 281 G11
Garvamore Highld 291 D7
Garvard Argyll 274 D4
Garvault Hotel Highld 308 F7
Garve Highld 300 C3
Garvestone Norf 141 B10
Garvock Aberds 293 F9
Invclyd 276 G5
Garvock Hill Fife 280 D2
Garway Hereford 97 G9
Garway Hill Hereford 97 F8
Gaskan Highld 289 B9
Gasper Wilts 45 G9
Gastard Wilts 61 F11
Gasthorpe Norf 141 G9
Gaston Green Essex 87 B7
Gatacre Park Shrops 132 F5
Gatcombe IoW 20 D5
Gateacre Mers 182 D6
Gatebeck Cumb 211 B10
Gate Burton Lincs 188 E4
Gateford Notts 187 E9
Gateford Common
Notts 187 E9
Gateforth N Yorks 198 B5
Gatehead E Ayrs 257 B9
Gate Helmsley N Yorks 207 B9
Gatehouse Northumb 251 F7
Gatehouse of Fleet
Dumfries 237 D8
Gatelawbridge
Dumfries 247 D10
Gateley Norf 159 E9
Gatenby N Yorks 214 B6
Gatesgarth Cumb 220 B3
Gateshead T&W 243 E7
Gatesheath Ches W 167 C7
Gateside Aberds 293 B8
Angus 287 C8
Dumfries 248 E4
E Renf 267 D9
Fife 286 G5
N Ayrs 267 E7
Shetland 312 F4
Gatewen Wrex 166 E4
Gatherley Devon 12 E3
Gathurst Gtr Man 194 F4
Gatlas Newport 78 G4
Gatley End Cambs 104 C5
Gtr Man 184 D4
Gatton Sur 51 C9
Gattonside Borders 262 B2
Gatwick Glos 80 C2
Gatwick Airport W Sus 51 E9
Gaufron Powys 113 D9
Gaulby Leics 136 C3
Gauldry Fife 287 E7
Gauntons Bank Ches E 167 F9
Gaunt's Common Dorset 31 F8
Gaunt's Earthcott S Glos 60 C6
Gaunt's End Essex 105 F10
Gautby Lincs 189 G11
Gavinton Borders 272 E5
Gawber S Yorks 197 F10
Gawcott Bucks 102 E3
Gawsworth Ches E 168 B5
Gawthorpe W Yorks 197 C9
W Yorks 197 D7
Gawthrop Cumb 212 B3
Gawthwaite Cumb 210 C5
Gay Bowers Essex 88 E3
Gaydon Warks 119 G7
Gayfield Orkney 314 A4
Gayhurst M Keynes 103 B7
Gayle N Yorks 213 B7
Gayles N Yorks 224 D2
Gay Street W Sus 35 C9
Gayton Mers 182 E3
Norf 158 F4
Staffs 151 D9
W Nhants 120 G4
Gayton Engine Lincs 191 D7
Gayton le Marsh Lincs 190 E6
Gayton le Wold Lincs 190 D2
Gayton Thorpe Norf 158 F4
Gaywood Norf 158 E2
Gaza Shetland 312 F5
Gazeley Suff 124 E4
Geanies House Highld 301 B8
Gearraidh Bhailteas
W Isles 297 J3
Gearraidh Bhaird
W Isles 304 F5
Gearraidh Dubh W Isles 296 F4
Gearraidh na h-Aibhne
W Isles 304 E4
Gearraidh na Monadh
W Isles 297 K3
Gearraidh Sheilidh
W Isles 297 J3
Geary Highld 298 C2
Geat Wolford Warks 100 E4
Geddes House Highld 301 D8
Gedding Suff 125 F9
Geddington N Nhants 137 G7
Gedgrave Hall Suff 109 B8
Gedintailor Highld 295 B7
Gedling Notts 171 G10
Gedney Lincs 157 E8
Gedney Broadgate Lincs 157 E8
Gedney Drove End
Lincs 157 D9
Gedney Dyke Lincs 157 D8
Gedney Hill Lincs 156 G6
Gee Cross Gtr Man 185 C7
Geeston Rutland 137 C9
Gegin Wrex 166 E3
Geilston Argyll 276 F6
Geinas Denb 165 B9
Geirinis W Isles 297 G3
Geise Highld 310 C5
Geisiadar W Isles 304 E3
Geldeston Norf 143 E7
Gell Conwy 164 B5
Gelli Pembs 73 B9
Rhondda 77 G7
Gellideg M Tydf 77 D8
Gellifor Denb 165 C10
Gelligaer Caerph 77 F10
Gelli-gaer Neath 57 C9
Gelligroes Caerph 77 G11
Gelli-hôf Caerph 77 F11
Gellilydan Gwyn 146 B3
Gellinud Neath 76 E2
Gellinudd Neath 76 E2
Gellyburn Perth 286 D4
Gellygron Neath 76 E2
Gellywen Carms 92 G5
Gelsmoor Leics 153 F8
Gelston Dumfries 237 D9
Lincs 172 G6
Gembling E Yorks 209 B8
Gemini Warr 183 C9
Gendros Swansea 56 B6
Genesis Green Suff 124 F4
Gentleshaw Staffs 151 G11
Geocrab W Isles 305 J3
Georgefield Dumfries 249 E7
George Green Bucks 66 C4
Georgeham Devon 40 F3
George Nympton Devon 26 C2
Georgetown Bl Gwent 77 D10
Georgia Corn 1 B5
Gergask Highld 291 D8
Gerlan Gwyn 163 B10
Germansweek Devon 12 C4
Germiston Glasgow 268 B2
Germoe Corn 2 D3
Gernon Bushes Essex 87 E7
Gerrans Corn 3 B9
Gerrard's Bromley
Staffs 150 C5
Gerrards Cross Bucks 66 B4
Gerrick Redcar 226 C4
Geseilfa Powys 129 E8
Gestingthorpe Essex 106 D6
Gesto Ho Highld 294 B5
Geuffordd Powys 148 G4
Geufron Denb 166 G2
Gibbet Hill Warks 135 G10
W Mid 118 C6
Gibb Hill Ches W 183 F10
Gibbshill Dumfries 237 B9
Gib Heath W Mid 133 F11
Gibraltar Bedford 103 B10
Bucks 84 C3
Kent 55 F8
Gibralter Oxon 83 B7
Gibshill Invclyd 276 G6
Gibsmere Notts 172 F2
Giddeahall Wilts 61 E11
Giddy Green Dorset 18 D2
Gidea Park London 68 B4
Gidleigh Devon 13 D9
Giffard Park M Keynes 103 C7
Giffnock E Renf 267 D11
Gifford E Loth 271 B10
Giffordland N Ayrs 266 F5
Giffordtown Fife 286 F6
Gigg Gtr Man 195 F10
Giggetty Staffs 133 E7
Giggleswick N Yorks 212 G6
Giggshill Sur 67 F7
Gignog Pembs 91 G7
Gilberdyke E Yorks 199 B10
Gilbert's Coombe Corn 4 G3
Gilbert's End Worcs 98 C6
Gilbert's Green Warks 118 C2
Gilbertstone W Mid 134 G2
Gilbert Street Hants 49 G7
Gilchriston E Loth 271 B9
Gilcrux Cumb 229 D8
Gildersome W Yorks 197 B8
Gildersome Street
W Yorks 197 B8
Gildingwells S Yorks 187 D9
Gilesgate Durham 233 C11
Gilesgate Moor
Durham 233 C11
Gileston V Glam 58 F4
Gilfach Caerph 77 F11
Hereford 96 E6
Gilfach Goch Rhondda 58 B3
Gilfachrheda Ceredig 111 F8
Gillarran Cumb 228 G6
Gill N Yorks 204 E5
Gillamoor N Yorks 216 B3
Gillan Corn 3 E7
Gillar's Green Mers 183 B7
Gillbank Cumb 221 F7
Gillbent Gtr Man 184 E5
Gillen Highld 298 D2
Gillesbie Dumfries 248 E5
Gilling East N Yorks 216 D2
Gillingham Dorset 30 B4
Medway 69 F9
Norf 143 E8
Gilling West N Yorks 224 D3
Gillmoss Mers 182 B6
Gillock Highld 310 D6
Gillow Heath Staffs 168 D5
Gills Highld 310 B7
Gill's Green Kent 53 G9
Gillway Staffs 134 C4
Gilmanscleuch Borders 261 E8
Gilmerton Edin 270 B5
Perth 286 E2
Gilmonby Durham 223 C9
Gilmorton Leics 135 F11
Gilmourton S Lanark 268 G3
Gilnow Gtr Man 195 F8
Gilroyd S Yorks 197 G10
Gilsland Northumb 240 D4
Gilsland Spa Cumb 240 D4
Gilson Warks 134 E3
Gilstead W Yorks 205 F8
Gilston Borders 271 D8
Herts 86 C6
Gilston Park Herts 86 C6
Giltbrook Notts 171 F7
Gilver's Lane Worcs 98 C6
Gilwell Park Essex 86 F5
Gimingham Norf 160 B5
Ginclough Ches E 185 F7
Ginger's Green E Sus 23 C10
Giosla W Isles 304 F3
Gipping Suff 125 E11
Gipsey Bridge Lincs 174 F3
Gipsy Row Suff 107 D11
Gipsyville Hull 200 B5
Gipton W Yorks 206 F2
Gipton Wood W Yorks 206 F2
Girdle Toll N Ayrs 266 G6
Girlington W Yorks 205 G8
Girlsta Shetland 313 H6
Girsby Lincs 190 D2
N Yorks 225 D7
Girt Som 29 C10
Girtford C Beds 104 B3
C Beds 122 G3
Girthon Dumfries 237 D8
Girton Cambs 123 E8
Notts 172 B4
Girvan S Ayrs 244 D5
Gisburn Lancs 204 D2
Gisleham Suff 143 F10
Gislingham Suff 125 C11
Gissing Norf 142 F2
Gittisham Devon 15 B8
Givons Grove Sur 51 C7
Glachavoil Argyll 275 F11
Glackmore Highld 300 D6
Glack of Midthird Moray 302 E3
Gladestry Powys 114 F4
Gladsmuir E Loth 281 G9
Glaichbea Highld 300 F5
Glais Swansea 76 E2
Glaisdale N Yorks 226 D5
Glame Highld 298 E5
Glamis Angus 287 C7
Glan Adda Gwyn 179 G9
Glanafon Pembs 73 B7
Glanaman Carms 75 C11
Glan-Conwy Conwy 164 E4
Glandford Norf 177 E8
Glan-Duar Carms 93 C10
Glandwr Caerph 78 E2
Pembs 92 F3
Glan-Dwyfach Gwyn 163 G7
Glandy Cross Carms 92 F2
Glandyfi Ceredig 128 D3
Glan Gors Anglesey 179 F7
Glangrwyney Powys 78 B2
Glanhanog Powys 129 D8
Glanmule Powys 130 E3
Glanrafon Ceredig 128 G2
Glanrhyd Gwyn 144 B5
Pembs 92 C2
Glan-rhyd Gwyn 163 D7
Powys 76 D3
Glantlees Northumb 252 B4
Glanton Northumb 264 G3
Glanton Pike Northumb 264 G3
Glan-traeth Anglesey 178 F3
Glantwymyn = *Cemmaes Road* Powys 128 C6
Glanvilles Wootton
Dorset 29 F11
Glanwern Ceredig 128 F2
Glanwydden Conwy 180 E4
Glan-y-don Flint 181 F11
Glan y Ffer = *Ferryside*
Carms 74 C5
Glan-y-llyn Rhondda 58 C6
Glan-y-môr Carms 74 C4
Glan-y-nant Caerph 77 F10
Powys 129 G8
Glan-yr-afon Anglesey 179 E10
Flint 181 E10
Gwyn 164 G6
Gwyn 165 G8
Shrops 148 E4
Glan-y-wern Gwyn 146 C2
Glapthorn N Nhants 137 E10
Glapwell Derbys 171 B7
Glas-allt Shiel Aberds 292 E4
Glasbury Powys 96 D3
Glaschoil Highld 301 F10
Glascoed Denb 181 G7
Mon 78 E4
Powys 129 F11
Powys 148 G2
Wrex 166 E3
Glascorrie Aberds 292 D5
Perth 286 E2
Glascote Staffs 134 C4
Glascwm Powys 114 G3
Glasdir Flint 181 E10
Glasdrum Argyll 284 C4
Glasfryn Conwy 164 E6
Glasgoed Ceredig 92 B6
Glasgoforest Aberds 293 B10
Glasgow Glasgow 267 B11
Glashvin Highld 298 C4
Glasinfryn Gwyn 163 B9
Glasllwch Newport 59 B9
Glasnacardoch Highld 295 F8
Glasnakille Highld 295 D7
Glasphein Highld 297 G7
Glaspwll Powys 128 D4
Glassburn Highld 300 F3
Glassenbury Kent 53 F8
Glasserton Dumfries 236 F6
Glassford S Lanark 268 F4
Glassgreen Moray 302 C2
Glasshoughton W Yorks 198 C2
Glasshouse Glos 98 G4
Glasshouse Hill Glos 98 G4
Glasshouses N Yorks 214 G3
Glasslie Fife 286 G6
Glasson Cumb 228 D6
Cumb 239 E7
Lancs 202 B4
Glassonby Cumb 231 D7
Glasterlaw Angus 287 B9
Glaston Rutland 137 C7
Glastonbury Som 44 F4
Glatton Cambs 138 F3
Glazebrook Warr 183 C11
Glazebury Warr 183 B11
Glazeley Shrops 132 F4
Gleadless S Yorks 186 E5
Gleadless Valley
S Yorks 186 E5
Gleadmoss Ches E 168 B4
Gleadsmoss Ches E 168 B4
Gleanhead Dumfries 245 G10
Gleann Tholàstaidh
W Isles 304 D7
Gleaston Cumb 210 E5
Glebe Hants 33 D9
Shetland 313 J6
T&W 243 F8
Glecknabae Argyll 275 G11
Gledhow W Yorks 206 F2
Gledrid Shrops 148 B5
Gleiniant Powys 129 E9
Glemsford Suff 106 B6
Glen Dumfries 237 B10
Dumfries 237 D7
Glenallachie Moray 302 E2
Glenalmond College
Perth 286 E3
Glenalmond Ho Perth 286 E3
Glenamachrie Argyll 289 G11
Glenample Stirling 285 E9
Glenancross Highld 295 F8
Glenapp Castle S Ayrs 244 G3
Glenaros Ho Argyll 289 E7
Glen Auldyn IoM 192 C5
Glenbarr Argyll 255 D7
Glenbeg Highld 289 C7
Highld 301 G10
Glen Bernisdale Highld 298 E4
Glenbervie Aberds 293 E9
Glenboig N Lanark 268 B4
Glenborrodale Highld 289 C8
Glenbranter Argyll 276 B2
Glenbreck Borders 260 E3
Glenbrein Lodge Highld 290 B6
Glenbrittle House
Highld 294 C6
Glenbrook Edin 270 B2
Glenbuchat Castle
Aberds 292 B5
Glenbuchat Lodge
Aberds 292 B5
Glenbuck E Ayrs 259 D7
Glenburn Renfs 267 C9
Glenbyre Argyll 289 G7
Glencalvie Lodge Highld 309 L4
Glencanisp Lodge
Highld 307 G6
Glencaple Dumfries 237 C11
Glencarron Lodge
Highld 299 D10
Glencarse Perth 286 E5
Glencassley Castle
Highld 309 J4
Glencat Aberds 293 D7
Glenceitlein Highld 284 C5
Glencoe Highld 284 B4
Glencraig Fife 280 B3
Glencripesdale Highld 289 D8
Glencrosh Dumfries 247 F7
Glendavan Ho Aberds 292 C6
Glendearg Borders 262 B2
Glendevon Perth 286 G3
Glendoebeg Highld 290 C6
Glendoe Lodge Highld 290 C6
Glendoick Perth 286 E6
Glendoll Lodge Angus 292 F4
Glendoune S Ayrs 244 D5
Glenduckie Fife 286 F6
Glendye Lodge Aberds 293 E8
Gleneagles Hotel Perth 286 F3
Gleneagles House Perth 286 G3
Glenearn Perth 286 F5
Glenegedale Argyll 254 B4
Glenelg Highld 295 D10
Glenernie Moray 301 E10
Glenfarg Perth 286 F5
Glenfarquhar Lodge
Aberds 293 E9
Glenferness House
Highld 301 E9
Glenfeshie Lodge
Highld 291 D10
Glenfiddich Lodge
Moray 302 F3
Glenfield Leics 135 B10
Glenfinnan Highld 295 G10
Glenfinnan Lodge
Highld 295 G11
Glenfintaig Ho Highld 290 E4
Glenfoot Perth 286 F5
Glenfyne Lodge Argyll 284 F6
Glengap Dumfries 237 D8
Glengarnock N Ayrs 266 E6
Glengolly Highld 310 C5
Glengorm Castle Argyll 288 D6
Glengoulandie Perth 285 B11
Glengrasco Highld 298 E4
Glenhead Farm Angus 292 G4
Glen Ho Borders 261 C7
Glenholt Plym 7 C10
Glenhoul Dumfries 246 F4
Glenhurich Highld 289 C10
Glenkerry Borders 261 G7
Glenkiln Dumfries 237 B10
Glenkindie Aberds 292 B6
Glenlair Dumfries 237 B9
Glenlatterach Moray 301 D11
Glenlee Dumfries 246 G4
Glenleigh Park E Sus 38 F2
Glenleraig Highld 306 F6
Glenlichorn Perth 285 F11
Glenlicht Ho Highld 290 B2
Glenlivet Moray 301 G11
Glenlochar Dumfries 237 C9
Glenlochsie Perth 292 F2
Glenlocksie Lodge
Perth 292 F2
Glenloig N Ayrs 255 D10
Glenlomond Perth 286 G5
Glenluce Dumfries 236 D4
Glenlussa Ho Argyll 255 E8
Glenmallan Argyll 276 B5
Glenmark Angus 292 E6
Glenmarkie Lodge
Angus 292 G4
Glenmarksie Highld 300 D3
Glenmavis N Lanark 268 B4
W Loth 269 B9
Glenmaye IoM 192 E3
Glenmayne Borders 261 C11
Glenmeanie Highld 300 D2
Glenmidge Dumfries 247 F9
Glenmoidart Ho Highld 289 B9
Glen Mona IoM 192 D5
Glen Mor Highld 295 B10
Glenmore Argyll 275 B9
Argyll 275 G11
Highld 298 E4
Glenmore Lodge
Highld 291 C11
Glenmoy Angus 292 G6
Glen Nevis House Highld 290 F3
Glennoe Argyll 284 D4
Glen of Newmill Moray 302 D4
Glenogil Angus 292 G6
Glenowen Pembs 73 D7
Glen Parva Leics 135 D11
Glenprosen Lodge
Angus 292 G4
Glenprosen Village
Angus 292 G5
Glenquaich Lodge
Perth 286 D2
Glenquiech Angus 292 G6
Glenquithlie Aberds 303 C8
Glenrath Borders 260 C6
Glenrazie Dumfries 236 C5
Glenreasdell Mains
Argyll 255 B9
Glenree N Ayrs 255 E10
Glenridding Cumb 221 B7
Glenrosa N Ayrs 256 B2
Glenrossal Highld 309 J4
Glenrothes Fife 286 G6
Glensanda Highld 289 E10
Glensaugh Aberds 293 F8
Glensburgh Falk 279 E8
Glenshero Lodge Highld 291 D7
Glenshoe Lodge Perth 292 G3
Glen Sluain Argyll 275 D11
Glenstockadale
Dumfries 236 C2
Glenstriven Argyll 275 F11
Glentaggart S Lanark 259 D8
Glen Tanar House
Aberds 292 D6
Glentarkie Perth 286 F5
Glenternie Borders 260 B6
Glentham Lincs 189 C8
Glentirranmuir Stirling 278 C3
Glenton Aberds 302 G6
Glentress Borders 261 B7
Glentromie Lodge
Highld 291 D9
Glen Trool Lodge
Dumfries 245 G10
Glentrool Village
Dumfries 236 B5
Glentruan IoM 192 B5
Glentruim House Highld 291 D8
Glentworth Lincs 188 D6
Glenuaig Lodge Highld 299 E11
Glenuig Highld 289 B8
Glenure Argyll 284 C4
Glenurquhart Highld 301 C7
Glen Vic Askil Highld 298 E3
Glenview Argyll 284 E5
Glen Village Falk 279 F7
Glen Vine IoM 192 E4
Glespin S Lanark 259 D8
Gletness Shetland 313 H6
Glewstone Hereford 97 G11
Glinton Pboro 138 B3
Globe Town London 67 C11
Glodwick Gtr Man 196 G2
Glogue Pembs 92 E4
Glooston Leics 136 D4
Glororum Northumb 264 C5
Glossop Derbys 185 C8
Gloster Hill Northumb 253 C7
Gloucester Glos 80 B4
Gloup Shetland 312 C7
Gloweth Corn 4 G5
Glusburn N Yorks 204 E6
Glutt Lodge Highld 310 F3
Glutton Bridge Staffs 169 B9
Gluvian Corn 5 C8
Glympton Oxon 101 G8
Glyn Mon 79 F7
Powys 129 F8
Glynarthen Ceredig 92 B6
Glynbrochan Powys 129 G8
Glyn Castle Neath 76 E4
Glyn-Ceiriog Wrex 148 B4
Glyncoch Rhondda 77 G9
Glyncoed Bl Gwent 77 C11
Glyncorrwg Neath 57 B11
Glyn-Cywarch Gwyn 146 C2
Glynde E Sus 23 D7
Glyndebourne E Sus 23 C7
Glyndyfrdwy Denb 165 G10
Glynedd = *Glyn neath*
Neath 76 D5
Glyne Gap E Sus 38 F3
Glyn Etwy Bl Gwent 77 D11
Glynhafren Powys 129 G7
Glynllan Bridgend 58 B2
Glynmorlas Shrops 148 B6
Glyn-neath = *Glynedd*
Neath 76 D5
Glynogwr Bridgend 58 B3
Glyntaff Rhondda 58 B5
Glyntawe Powys 76 B4
Gnosall Staffs 150 E6
Gnosall Heath Staffs 150 E6
Goadby Leics 136 D4
Goadby Marwood Leics 154 D5
Goatacre Wilts 62 D4
Goatham Green E Sus 38 C4
Goathill Dorset 29 D11
Goathland N Yorks 226 E6
Goathurst Som 43 G9
Goathurst Common Kent 52 C3
Goat Lees Kent 54 D4
Gobernuisgach Lodge
Highld 308 E4
Gobernuisgeach Highld 310 F3
Gobhaig W Isles 305 H2
Gobley Hole Hants 48 D6
Gobowen Shrops 148 C6
Godalming Sur 50 E3
Goddards Bucks 84 G3
Goddard's Corner Suff 126 D5
Goddard's Green Kent 53 G10
W Berks 65 F7
Goddards' Green W Sus 36 C3
Godden Green Kent 52 B5
Goddington London 68 F3
Godley Gtr Man 185 B7
Godleybrook Staffs 169 G7
Godley Hill Gtr Man 185 C7
Godleys Green E Sus 36 D5
Godmanchester Cambs 122 C4
Godmanstone Dorset 17 B9
Godmersham Kent 54 C5
Godney Som 44 E3
Godolphin Cross Corn 2 C4
Godre'r-graig Neath 76 D3
God's Blessing Green
Dorset 31 G8
Godshill Hants 31 E11
IoW 20 E6
Godstone Sur 51 C10
Godswinscroft Hants 19 B9
Godwell Devon 8 D2
Godwick Norf 159 E8
Godwinscroft Hants 19 B9
Goetre Mon 78 D4
Goferydd Anglesey 178 E2
Goff's Oak Herts 86 E4
Gogar Edin 280 G3
Goginan Ceredig 128 G3
Goirtean a'Chladaich
Highld 290 F2
Golan Gwyn 163 G8
Golant Corn 6 E2
Golberdon Corn 12 G2
Golborne Gtr Man 183 B10
Golcar W Yorks 196 D6
Golch Flint 181 F11
Goldcliff Newport 59 C11
Golden Balls Oxon 83 F9
Golden Cross E Sus 23 C8
E Sus 23 C10
Golden Green Kent 52 D6
Golden Grove Carms 75 B9
Goldenhill Stoke 168 E5
Golden Hill Bristol 60 D5
Hants 19 B11
Pembs 73 E7
Pembs 91 G9
Golden Park Devon 24 C2
Golden Pot Hants 49 E8
Golden Valley Derbys 170 E6
Glos 99 G8
Hereford 98 B3
Golder Field Hereford 115 E11
Golders Green London 67 B9
Goldfinch Bottom
W Berks 64 G4
Goldhanger Essex 88 D6
Gold Hill Dorset 30 E4
Norf 139 E10
Golding Shrops 132 C10
Goldington Bedford 121 G11
Goldsborough N Yorks 206 B3
N Yorks 226 C6
Gold's Cross Bath 60 G5
Golds Green W Mid 133 E9
Goldsithney Corn 2 C2
Goldstone Shrops 150 D4
Goldthorn Park W Mid 133 D8
Goldthorpe S Yorks 198 G3
Goldworthy Devon 24 C5
Golford Kent 53 F9
Golftyn Flint 182 G3
Golgotha Kent 55 D9
Gollanfield Highld 301 D8
Gollawater Corn 4 E5
Gollinglith Foot
N Yorks 214 C3
Golly Wrex 166 D4
Golsoncott Som 42 F4
Golspie Highld 311 J2
Golval Highld 310 C2
Golynos Torf 78 E3
Gomeldon Wilts 47 F7
Gomersal W Yorks 197 B8
Gometra Ho Argyll 288 E5
Gomshall Sur 50 D5
Gonalston Notts 171 F11
Gonamena Corn 11 G11
Gonerby Hill Foot Lincs 155 B8
Gonfirth Shetland 313 G5
Good Easter Essex 87 C10
Gooderstone Norf 140 C5
Goodleigh Devon 40 G6
Goodley Stock Kent 52 C2
Goodmanham E Yorks 208 E3
Goodmayes London 68 B3
Goodnestone Kent 55 C9
Kent 70 G4
Goodrich Hereford 79 B9
Goodrington Torbay 9 D7
Good's Green Worcs 132 G5
Goodshaw Lancs 195 B10
Goodshaw Chapel
Lancs 195 B10
Goodshaw Fold Lancs 195 B10
Goodstone Devon 13 G11
Goodwick = *Wdig* Pembs 91 D8
Goodworth Clatford
Hants 47 E11
Goodyers End Warks 134 F6
Goodyhills Cumb 229 B8
Goole E Yorks 199 C8
Goom's Hill Worcs 117 G10
Goonabarn Corn 5 E9
Goonbell Corn 4 F4
Goon Gumpas Corn 4 G4
Goonhavern Corn 4 E5
Goonhusband Corn 2 D5
Goonlaze Corn 2 B6
Goonown Corn 4 E4
Goonpiper Corn 3 B8
Goonvrea Corn 4 F4
Gooseberry Green Essex 87 F11
Goose Eye W Yorks 204 E6
Gooseford Devon 13 C9
Goose Green Cumb 211 C10
Essex 108 F2
Gtr Man 194 G5
Hants 32 F4
Herts 86 D5
Kent 52 C6
Kent 53 F10
Lancs 194 C3
Norf 142 F2
S Glos 61 C8
W Sus 34 C3
W Sus 35 D10
Gooseham Mill Devon 24 D2
Goosehill W Yorks 197 C11
Goose Hill Hants 64 G4
Goosehill Green Worcs 117 E8
Goosemoor Staffs 150 F6
Goosemoor Green
Staffs 151 G11
Goosenford Som 28 B2
Goose Pool Hereford 97 D9
Goosewell Devon 40 D5
Goosey Oxon 82 G5
Goosnargh Lancs 203 F7
Goostrey Ches E 184 G3
Gorbals Glasgow 267 C11
Gorcott Hill Warks 117 D11
Gord Shetland 313 L6
Gorddinog Conwy 179 G11
Gordon Borders 272 G2
Gordonbush Highld 311 J2
Gordonsburgh Moray 302 C4
Gordonstoun Moray 301 C11
Gordonstown Aberds 302 D5
Aberds 303 F7
Gore Dorset 29 D9
Kent 55 B10
Gorebridge Midloth 270 C6
Gore Cross Wilts 46 C4
Gore End Hants 64 G2
Gorefield Cambs 157 G8
Gorehill W Sus 35 C7
Gore Pit Essex 88 B5
Gore Street Kent 71 F9
Gorgie Edin 280 G4
Gorhambury Herts 85 D10
Goring Oxon 64 C6
Goring-by-Sea W Sus 35 G10
Goring Heath Oxon 65 D7
Gorleston-on-Sea
Norf 143 C10
Gornalwood W Mid 133 E8
Gorrachie Aberds 303 D7
Gorran Churchtown Corn 5 G9
Gorran Haven Corn 5 G10
Gorran High Lanes Corn 5 G9
Gorrenberry Borders 249 D11
Gorrig Ceredig 93 C8
Gorse Covert Warr 183 C11
Gorsedd Flint 181 F11
Gorse Hill Gtr Man 184 B4
Swindon 63 B7
Gorseinon Swansea 56 B5
Gorseness Orkney 314 E4
Gorsethorpe Notts 171 B9
Gorseybank Derbys 170 E3
Gorsgoch Ceredig 111 G9
Gorslas Carms 75 C9
Gorsley Glos 98 F3
Gorsley Common
Hereford 98 F3
Gorsley Ley Staffs 133 B11
Gorstage Ches W 183 G10
Gorstan Highld 300 C3
Gorstanvorran Highld 289 B10
Gorstella Ches W 166 C5
Gorsteyhill Ches E 168 E2
Gorst Hill Worcs 116 C4
Gorstyhill Staffs 168 E2
Gorsty Hill Staffs 151 D11
Gortan Argyll 274 G3
Gortantaoid Argyll 274 F4
Gortenacullish Highld 295 G8
Gorteneorn Highld 289 C8

Gortenfern Highld 289 C8
Gortinanane Argyll 255 C8
Gorton Gtr Man 184 B5
Gortonallister N Ayrs 256 D2
Gosbeck Suff 126 F3
Gosberton Lincs 156 C4
Gosberton Cheal Lincs 156 D4
Gosberton Clough Lincs 156 D3
Goscote W Mid 133 C10
Goseley Dale Derbys 152 E6
Gosfield Essex 106 F5
Gosford Hereford 115 D10
  Oxon 83 C7
Gosford Green W Mid 118 B6
Gosforth Cumb 219 E11
  T&W 242 D6
Gosforth Valley Derbys 186 F4
Gosland Green Suff 124 G5
Gosling Green Suff 107 C9
Gosmere Kent 54 B4
Gosmore Herts 104 F3
Gospel Ash Staffs 132 E6
Gospel End Village
  Staffs 133 E7
Gospel Green W Sus 50 G2
Gospel Oak London 67 B9
Gosport Hants 21 B8
  Hants 32 C5
Gossabrough Shetland 312 E7
Gossard's Green C Beds 103 C9
Gossington Glos 80 E2
Gossops Green W Sus 51 F9
Goswick Northumb 273 F11
Gotham Dorset 31 E9
  E Sus 38 F2
  Notts 153 C10
Gothelney Green Som 43 F9
Gotherington Glos 99 F9
Gothers Corn 5 D9
Gott Argyll 288 E2
  Shetland 313 J6
Gotton Som 28 B2
Goudhurst Kent 53 F8
Goukstone Moray 302 D4
Goulceby Lincs 190 F3
Goulton N Yorks 225 E9
Gourdas Aberds 303 E7
Gourdon Aberds 293 F10
Gourock Invclyd 276 F4
Govan Glasgow 267 B11
Govanhill Glasgow 267 C11
Gover Hill Kent 52 C6
Goverton Notts 172 E2
Goveton Devon 8 F5
Govilon Mon 78 C3
Gowanhill Aberds 303 C10
Gowanwell Aberds 303 E8
Gowdall E Yorks 198 C6
Gowerton = Tre-Gwyr
  Swansea 56 B5
Gowhole Derbys 185 E8
Gowkhall Fife 279 D11
Gowkthrapple N Lanark 268 E5
Gowthorpe E Yorks 207 C11
Goxhill E Yorks 209 E9
  N Lincs 200 C6
Goxhill Haven N Lincs 200 B6
Goybre Neath 57 D9
Goytre Neath 57 D9
Gozzard's Ford Oxon 83 F7
Grabhair W Isles 305 G5
Graby Lincs 155 D11
Gracca Corn 5 D10
Gracemount Edin 270 B5
Grade Corn 2 G6
Graffham W Sus 34 D6
Grafham Cambs 122 D3
  Sur 50 E4
Grafton Hereford 97 D9
  N Yorks 215 G8
  Oxon 82 E3
  Shrops 149 F8
  Worcs 99 D9
  Worcs 115 E11
Grafton Flyford Worcs 117 F9
Grafton Regis W Nhants 102 B5
Grafton Underwood
  N Nhants 137 G8
Grafty Green Kent 53 D11
Grahamston Falk 279 E7
Graianrhyd Denb 166 D2
Graig Carms 74 E6
  Conwy 180 G4
  Denb 181 G9
  Rhondda 58 B5
  Wrex 148 B4
Graig-Fawr Swansea 75 E10
Graig-fechan Denb 165 E10
Graig Felen Swansea 75 E11
Graig Penllyn V Glam 58 D3
Graig Trewyddfa Swansea 57 B7
Grain Medway 69 D11
Grains Bar Gtr Man 196 F3
Grainsby Lincs 190 B3
Grainthorpe Lincs 190 B5
Grainthorpe Fen Lincs 190 B5
Graiselound N Lincs 188 B3
Grampound Corn 5 F8
Grampound Road Corn 5 E8
Gramsdal W Isles 296 F4
Granborough Bucks 102 F5
Granby Notts 154 B5
Grandborough Warks 119 D9
Grandpont Oxon 83 D8
Grandtully Perth 286 B3
Grange Cumb 220 B5
  Dorset 31 G8
  E Ayrs 257 B10
  Fife 287 G8
  Halton 183 E8
  Lancs 203 G7
  Medway 69 F9
  Mers 182 D2
  NE Lincs 201 F9
  N Yorks 223 G8
  Perth 286 E6
  Warr 183 C10
Grange Crossroads
  Moray 302 D4
Grange Estate Dorset 31 G10
Grange Hall Moray 301 C10
Grange Hill Durham 233 F10
  Essex 86 G6
Grangemill Derbys 170 D2
Grange Moor W Yorks 197 D8
Grangemouth Falk 279 E8
Grangemuir Fife 287 G9
Grange of Cree
  Dumfries 236 D6
Grange of Lindores Fife 286 F6
Grange-over-Sands
  Cumb 211 D8
Grangepans Falk 279 E10
Grange Park London 86 F4
  Mers 183 C7
  Swindon 62 C6
  W Nhants 120 F5
Grangetown Cardiff 59 E7
  Redcar 235 G7
Grangetown continued
  T&W 243 G10
Grange Villa Durham 242 G6
Grange Village Glos 79 C11
Granish Highld 291 B11
Gransmoor E Yorks 209 B8
Gransmore Green
  Essex 106 G3
Granston = Treopert
  Pembs 91 E7
Grantchester Cambs 123 F8
Grantham Lincs 155 B8
Grantley N Yorks 214 F4
Grantley Hall N Yorks 214 F4
Grantlodge Aberds 293 B9
Granton Dumfries 248 B3
  Edin 280 F4
Grantown Aberds 302 D5
Grantown-on-Spey
  Highld 301 G10
Grantsfield Hereford 115 E10
Grantshouse Borders 272 B6
Grant Thorold NE Lincs 201 F9
Graplin Dumfries 237 E8
Grappenhall Warr 183 D10
Grasby Lincs 200 G5
Grasmere Cumb 220 D6
Grasscroft Gtr Man 196 G3
Grassendale Mers 182 D5
Grassgarth Cumb 221 F8
  Cumb 230 C2
Grass Green Essex 106 D4
Grassholme Durham 232 G4
Grassington N Yorks 213 G10
Grassmoor Derbys 170 B6
Grassthorpe Notts 172 B3
Grasswell T&W 243 G8
Grateley Hants 47 E9
Gratton Devon 24 E5
Gratwich Staffs 151 C10
Gravel Ches W 167 B11
Gravel Castle Kent 55 D8
Graveley Cambs 122 E4
  Herts 104 F4
Gravelhill Shrops 149 G9
Gravel Hill Bucks 85 G8
Gravel Hole Gtr Man 196 F2
  Shrops 149 B7
Gravelly Hill W Mid 134 E2
Gravels Shrops 130 D6
Gravelsbank Shrops 130 C6
Graven Shetland 312 F6
Graveney Kent 70 G5
Graven Hill Oxon 101 G11
Gravenhunger Moss
  Shrops 168 G2
Gravesend Herts 105 F8
  Kent 68 E6
Grayingham Lincs 188 B6
Grayrigg Cumb 221 F11
Grays Thurrock 68 D6
Grayshott Hants 49 F11
Grayson Green Cumb 228 F5
Grayswood Sur 50 G2
Graythorp Hrtlpl 234 F6
Grazeley Wokingham 65 F7
Grazeley Green W Berks 65 F7
Greagdhubh Lodge
  Highld 291 D8
Greamchary Highld 310 F2
Greasbrough S Yorks 186 B6
Greasby Mers 182 D3
Greasley Notts 171 F7
Great Abington Cambs 105 B10
Great Addington
  N Nhants 121 B9
Great Alne Warks 118 F2
Great Altcar Lancs 193 F10
Great Amwell Herts 86 C5
Great Asby Cumb 222 C3
Great Ashfield Suff 125 D9
Great Ashley Wilts 61 G10
Great Ayton N Yorks 225 C11
Great Baddow Essex 88 E2
Great Bardfield Essex 106 E3
Great Barford Bedford 122 G2
Great Barrington Glos 82 C2
Great Barrow Ches W 167 B7
Great Barton Suff 125 D7
Great Barugh N Yorks 216 D4
Great Bavington
  Northumb 251 G11
Great Bealings Suff 108 B4
Great Bedwyn Wilts 63 G9
Great Bentley Essex 108 G2
Great Berry Essex 69 B7
Great Billing W Nhants 120 E6
Great Bircham Norf 158 C5
Great Blakenham Suff 126 G2
Great Blencow Cumb 230 E5
Great Bolas Telford 150 E2
Great Bookham Sur 50 C6
Great Bosullow Corn 1 C4
Great Bourton Oxon 101 B9
Great Bowden Leics 136 F4
Great Bower Kent 54 C4
Great Bradley Suff 124 G3
Great Braxted Essex 88 C5
Great Bricett Suff 125 G10
Great Brickhill Bucks 103 E8
Great Bridge W Mid 133 E9
Great Bridgeford Staffs 151 D7
Great Brington
  W Nhants 120 D3
Great Bromley Essex 107 F11
Great Broughton Cumb 229 E7
  N Yorks 225 D10
Great Buckland Kent 69 G7
Great Budworth
  Ches W 183 F11
Great Burdon Darl 224 B6
Great Burgh Sur 51 B8
Great Burstead Essex 87 G11
Great Busby N Yorks 225 D10
Great Canfield Essex 87 B9
Great Carlton Lincs 190 D6
Great Casterton Rutland 137 B9
  Rutland 137 B10
Great Cellws Powys 113 E11
Great Chalfield Wilts 61 G11
Great Chart Kent 54 E3
Great Chatwell Staffs 150 G5
Great Chell Stoke 168 E5
Great Chesterford
  Essex 105 C10
Great Cheveney Kent 53 E8
Great Cheverell Wilts 46 C3
Great Chilton Durham 233 E11
Great Chishill Cambs 105 D8
Great Clacton Essex 89 B11
Great Claydons Essex 88 E3
Great Cliff W Yorks 197 D10
Great Clifton Cumb 228 F6
Great Coates NE Lincs 201 F8
Great Comberton Worcs 99 C9
Great Common Suff 143 F7
  W Sus 35 B8
Great Corby Cumb 239 G11
Great Cornard Suff 107 C7
Great Cowden E Yorks 209 E10
Great Coxwell Oxon 82 G3
Great Crakehall
  N Yorks 224 G4
Great Cransley
  N Nhants 120 B6
Great Cressingham
  Norf 141 C7
Great Crosby Mers 182 B4
Great Crosthwaite
  Cumb 229 G11
Great Cubley Derbys 152 B3
Great Dalby Leics 154 G4
Great Denham Bedford 103 B10
Great Doddington
  N Nhants 121 E7
Great Doward Hereford 79 B9
Great Dunham Norf 159 G7
Great Dunmow Essex 106 G2
Great Durnford Wilts 46 F6
Great Easton Essex 106 F2
  Leics 136 E6
Great Eccleston Lancs 202 E4
Great Edstone N Yorks 216 C4
Great Ellingham Norf 141 D10
Great Elm Som 45 D8
Great Eppleton T&W 234 B3
Greater Doward Hereford 79 B9
Great Eversden Cambs 123 G7
Great Fencote N Yorks 224 G5
Greatfield Wilts 62 B5
Great Finborough Suff 125 F10
Greatford Lincs 155 G11
Great Fransham Norf 159 G7
Great Gaddesden Herts 85 C8
Greatgap Bucks 84 B6
Greatgate Staffs 169 G9
Great Gate Staffs 169 G9
Great Gidding Cambs 138 G2
Great Givendale
  E Yorks 208 C2
Great Glemham Suff 126 E6
Great Glen Leics 136 D3
Great Gonerby Lincs 155 B7
Great Gransden Cambs 122 F5
Great Green Cambs 104 C5
  Norf 142 F5
  Suff 125 B11
  Suff 125 F8
  Suff 126 B2
Great Habton N Yorks 216 D5
Great Hale Lincs 173 G10
Great Hallingbury Essex 87 B8
Greatham Hants 49 G9
  Hrtlpl 234 F5
  W Sus 35 D8
Great Hampden Bucks 84 E4
Great Harrowden
  N Nhants 121 C7
Great Harwood Lancs 203 G10
Great Haseley Oxon 83 E10
Great Hatfield E Yorks 209 E9
Great Haywood Staffs 151 E9
  Staffs 151 E10
Great Heath W Mid 134 G6
Great Heck N Yorks 198 C5
Great Henny Essex 107 D7
Great Hinton Wilts 46 B2
Great Hivings Bucks 85 E7
Great Hockham Norf 141 E9
Great Holcombe Oxon 83 F10
Great Holland Essex 89 B12
Great Hollands Brack 65 F11
Great Holm M Keynes 102 D6
Great Honeyborough
  Pembs 73 D7
Great Horkesley Essex 107 E9
Great Hormead Herts 105 F7
Great Horton W Yorks 205 G8
Great Horwood Bucks 102 E5
Great Houghton
  S Yorks 198 F2
  W Nhants 120 F5
Great Howarth Gtr Man 196 D2
Great Hucklow Derbys 185 F11
Great Job's Cross Kent 38 B4
Great Kelk E Yorks 209 B8
Great Kendale E Yorks 217 G10
Great Kimble Bucks 84 D4
Great Kingshill Bucks 84 F5
Great Langton N Yorks 224 F5
Great Lea Common
  Reading 65 F8
Great Leighs Essex 88 B2
Great Lever Gtr Man 195 F8
Great Limber Lincs 200 F6
Great Linford M Keynes 103 C7
Great Livermere Suff 125 C7
Great Longstone Derbys 186 G2
Great Lumley Durham 233 B11
Great Lyth Shrops 131 B9
Great Malgraves Thurrock 69 C7
Great Malvern Worcs 98 B5
Great Maplestead Essex 106 E6
Great Marton Blackpool 202 F2
Great Marton Moss
  Blackpool 202 G2
Great Massingham Norf 158 E5
Great Melton Norf 142 B2
Great Milton Oxon 83 E10
Great Missenden Bucks 84 E5
Great Mitton Lancs 203 F10
Great Mongeham Kent 55 C10
Greatmoor Bucks 102 G4
Great Moor Gtr Man 184 D6
  Staffs 132 D6
Great Moulton Norf 142 E3
Great Munden Herts 105 G7
Great Musgrave Cumb 222 C5
Greatness Kent 52 B4
Great Ness Shrops 149 F7
Great Notley Essex 106 G4
Great Oak Mon 78 D5
Great Oakley Essex 108 F3
  N Nhants 137 F7
Great Offley Herts 104 F2
Great Ormside Cumb 222 B4
Great Orton Cumb 239 G8
Great Ouseburn
  N Yorks 215 G8
Great Oxendon
  W Nhants 136 G4
Great Oxney Green
  Essex 87 D11
Great Palgrave Norf 158 G6
Great Pardon Essex 86 D6
Great Pattenden Kent 53 E8
Great Paxton Cambs 122 E4
Great Plumpton Lancs 202 G3
Great Plumstead Norf 160 G6
Great Ponton Lincs 155 C8
Great Preston W Yorks 198 B2
Great Purston
  W Nhants 101 D10
Great Raveley Cambs 138 G5
Great Rissington Glos 81 B11
Great Rollright Oxon 100 E6
Great Ryburgh Norf 159 D9
Great Ryle Northumb 264 G2
Great Ryton Shrops 131 C9
Great Saling Essex 106 F4
Great Salkeld Cumb 231 D7
Great Sampford Essex 106 D2
Great Sankey Warr 183 D9
Great Saredon Staffs 133 B9
Great Saxham Suff 124 E5
Great Shefford W Berks 63 E11
Great Shelford Cambs 123 G9
Great Shoddesden Hants 47 D9
Great Smeaton N Yorks 224 E6
Great Snoring Norf 159 C8
Great Somerford Wilts 62 C3
Great Stainton Darl 234 G2
Great Stambridge Essex 88 G5
Great Staughton Cambs 122 E2
Great Steeping Lincs 174 C6
Great Stoke S Glos 60 C6
Great Stonar Kent 55 B10
Greatstone-on-Sea Kent 39 C9
Great Stretton Leics 136 C3
Great Strickland Cumb 231 G7
Great Stukeley Cambs 122 C4
Great Sturton Lincs 190 F2
Great Sutton Ches W 182 F5
  Shrops 131 G10
Great Swinburne
  Northumb 241 B10
Great Tew Oxon 101 F7
Great Tey Essex 107 F7
Great Thirkleby N Yorks 215 D9
Great Thurlow Suff 124 G3
Great Torrington Devon 25 D7
Great Tosson Northumb 252 C2
Great Totham Essex 88 C5
Great Tows Lincs 190 C2
Great Tree Corn 6 D5
Great Urswick Cumb 210 E5
Great Wakering Essex 70 B2
Great Waldingfield Suff 107 C8
Great Walsingham Norf 159 B8
Great Waltham Essex 87 C11
Great Warley Essex 87 G9
Great Washbourne Glos 99 E9
Great Weeke Devon 13 D10
Great Weldon N Nhants 137 F8
Great Welnetham Suff 125 F7
Great Wenham Suff 107 D11
Great Whittington
  Northumb 242 C2
Great Wigborough Essex 89 C7
Great Wilbraham
  Cambs 123 F10
Great Wilne Derbys 153 C8
Great Wishford Wilts 46 F5
Great Witchingham
  Norf 160 E2
Great Witcombe Glos 80 C6
Great Witley Worcs 116 D5
Great Wolford Warks 100 E4
Greatworth W Nhants 101 C11
Great Wratting Suff 106 B3
Great Wymondley Herts 104 F4
Great Wyrley Staffs 133 B9
Great Wytheford
  Shrops 149 F11
Great Yarmouth Norf 143 B10
Great Yeldham Essex 106 D5
Greave Gtr Man 184 C6
  Lancs 195 C11
Grebby Lincs 174 B6
Greeba IoM 192 D4
Green Denb 165 B9
  Pembs 73 E7
  Powys 130 E5
Greenacres Gtr Man 196 F2
Greenan Argyll 275 G11
Greenbank Ches W 183 G10
  Falk 279 F7
  Shetland 312 C7
Green Bank Cumb 211 C7
Green Bottom Corn 4 F5
  Glos 79 B11
Greenburn W Loth 269 C8
Green Close N Yorks 212 F4
Green Clough W Yorks 205 G7
Green Crize Hereford 97 D10
Greencroft Durham 242 G5
Green Cross Sur 49 F11
Greendale Ches E 184 F5
Greendikes Northumb 264 D3
Greendown Som 44 C5
Green Down Devon 28 G3
Greendykes Northumb 264 D3
Greenend N Lanark 268 C4
  Oxon 100 G6
Green End Bedford 103 B10
  Bedford 121 E11
  Bedford 122 E2
  Bedford 122 G2
  Bucks 84 F4
  Bucks 103 E8
  Cambs 122 C4
  Cambs 123 F7
  C Beds 103 D11
  Herts 85 D8
  Herts 104 E5
  Herts 104 E6
  Herts 105 F7
  Lancs 204 D4
  N Yorks 226 E6
  Warks 134 F5
Greenfaulds N Lanark 278 G5
Greenfield C Beds 103 E11
  Glasgow 268 C2
  Gtr Man 196 G3
  Highld 289 D11
  Highld 290 C4
  Oxon 84 G2
Greenfield = Maes-Glas
  Flint 181 F11
Greenfoot N Lanark 268 B4
Greenford London 66 C6
Greengairs N Lanark 278 G5
Greengarth Hall Cumb 219 E11
Greengate Gtr Man 196 D2
  Norf 159 F10
Green Gate Devon 27 D8
Greengates W Yorks 205 F9
Greengill Cumb 229 D8
Green Hailey Bucks 84 E4
Greenhalgh Lancs 202 F4
Greenhall S Lanark 268 D3
Greenham Dorset 28 G6
  Som 27 C9
  W Berks 64 F3
Green Hammerton
  N Yorks 206 B5
Greenhaugh Northumb 251 F7
Green Haworth Lancs 195 B9
Greenhead Borders 261 D11
  Dumfries 247 D9
  N Lanark 268 E6
  Northumb 240 D5
  Staffs 169 F7
Green Head Cumb 230 B3
Green Heath Staffs 151 G9
Greenheys Gtr Man 195 G8
Greenhill Dumfries 238 B4
  Durham 234 B3
  Falk 278 F6
  Hereford 98 B4
  Kent 71 F7
  Leics 153 G8
Greenhill continued
  London 67 B7
  S Yorks 186 E4
  Worcs 99 B10
  Worcs 116 B6
Green Hill Kent 53 C9
  Lincs 155 B8
  Wilts 62 B5
  W Yorks 206 F4
Greenhill Bank Shrops 149 B7
Greenhillocks Derbys 170 F6
Greenhills N Ayrs 267 E7
  S Lanark 268 E2
Greenhithe Kent 68 E5
Greenholm E Ayrs 258 B2
Greenholme Cumb 221 D11
Greenhouse Borders 262 E3
Greenhow N Yorks 214 G2
Greenhow Hill N Yorks 214 G2
Greenigoe Orkney 314 F4
Greenland Highld 310 C6
  S Yorks 186 D5
Greenland Mains Highld 310 C6
Greenlands Bucks 65 B9
  Worcs 117 D11
Green Lane Devon 13 F11
  Hereford 98 B2
  Powys 130 D3
  Warks 117 E11
  Warks 118 B6
Greenlaw Aberds 302 D6
  Borders 272 F4
Greenlaw Mains Midloth 270 C4
Greenlea Dumfries 238 B2
Greenley M Keynes 102 C6
Greenloaning Perth 286 G2
Greenlooms Ches W 167 C7
Greenman's Lane Wilts 62 C3
Greenmeadow Swindon 62 B6
  Torf 78 F3
Green Moor S Yorks 186 B3
Greenmount Gtr Man 195 E9
Greenmow Shetland 313 L6
Greenoak E Yorks 199 B10
Greenock Invclyd 276 F5
Greenock West Invclyd 276 F5
Greenodd Cumb 210 C6
Green Ore Som 44 C5
Green Parlour Bath 45 C8
Green Quarter Cumb 221 E9
Greenrigg W Loth 269 C8
Greenrow Cumb 238 G4
Greens Borders 249 F11
Green St Green London 68 G3
Greensforge Staffs 133 F7
Greensgate Norf 160 F2
Greenside Cumb 222 E4
  Derbys 186 F5
  Gtr Man 184 B6
  T&W 242 E4
  W Yorks 197 D7
Green Side W Yorks 197 E7
  W Yorks 205 G11
Greensidehill Northumb 263 F11
Greens Norton
  W Nhants 102 B3
Greensplat Corn 5 D9
Greenstead Essex 107 F10
Greenstead Green Essex 106 F6
Greensted Essex 87 E8
Greensted Green Essex 87 E8
Green Street Essex 87 F10
  E Sus 38 E3
  Glos 80 B5
  Glos 80 E3
  Herts 85 F11
  Herts 105 G9
  Worcs 99 B7
  Worcs 99 C7
  W Sus 35 C10
Greenstreet Green
  Suff 107 B10
Green Street Green Kent 68 E5
  London 68 G3
Green Tye Herts 86 B6
Greenway Hereford 98 E4
  Pembs 91 E11
  Som 27 B11
  V Glam 58 E5
  Worcs 116 C4
Greenwell Cumb 240 F2
Greenwells Borders 262 C3
Greenwich London 67 D11
  Suff 108 C3
  Wilts 46 G2
Greenwith Common Corn 4 G5
Greenwoods Essex 87 F11
Greeny Orkney 314 D2
Greep Highld 298 E2
Greet Glos 99 E10
  Kent 54 B2
Greete Shrops 115 C11
Greetham Lincs 190 G4
  Rutland 155 G8
Greetland W Yorks 196 C5
Greetland Wall Nook
  W Yorks 196 C5
Greetwell N Lincs 200 G2
Gregg Hall Cumb 221 G9
Gregson Lane Lancs 194 B5
Gregynog Powys 129 D11
Grèin W Isles 297 L2
Greinetobht W Isles 296 D4
Greinton Som 44 F2
Gremista Shetland 313 J6
Grenaby IoM 192 E3
Grendon N Nhants 121 E7
  Warks 134 C5
Grendon Bishop
  Hereford 115 F11
Grendon Common
  Warks 134 D5
Grendon Green
  Hereford 115 F11
Grendon Underwood
  Bucks 102 G3
Grenofen Devon 12 G5
Grenoside S Yorks 186 C4
Greosabhagh W Isles 305 J3
Gresford Wrex 166 E5
Gresham Norf 160 B3
Greshornish Highld 298 D3
Gressenhall Norf 159 F9
Gressingham Lancs 211 F11
Gresty Green Ches E 168 E2
Greta Bridge Durham 223 C11
Gretna Dumfries 239 D8
Gretna Green Dumfries 239 D8
Gretton Glos 99 E10
  N Nhants 137 E7
  Shrops 131 D10
Gretton Fields Glos 99 E10
Grewelthorpe N Yorks 214 D4
Greyfield Bath 44 B6
Greygarth N Yorks 214 E3
Grey Green N Lincs 199 F9
Greylake Som 43 G11
Greylake Fosse Som 44 F2
Greynor Carms 75 D9
Greynor-isaf Carms 75 D9
Greyrigg Dumfries 248 F3
Greys Green Oxon 65 C8
Greysouthen Cumb 229 F7
Greystead Northumb 251 F7
Greystoke Cumb 230 E4
Greystoke Gill Cumb 230 F4
Greystone Aberds 292 D6
  Aberds 302 F6
  Angus 287 C9
  Cumb 211 D10
  Dumfries 237 B11
Greystonegill N Yorks 212 F3
Greystones S Yorks 186 D4
  Warks 99 B11
Greytree Hereford 97 F11
Greywell Hants 49 C8
Griais W Isles 304 D6
Grianan W Isles 304 E6
Gribb Dorset 28 G5
Gribthorpe E Yorks 207 F11
Gridley Corner Devon 12 C3
Griff Warks 135 F7
Griffins Hill W Mid 133 G10
Griffithstown Torf 78 F3
Griffydam Leics 153 F8
Grigg Kent 53 E11
Griggs Green Hants 49 G10
Grillis Corn 2 B5
Grilstone Devon 26 C2
Grimbister Orkney 314 E3
Grimblethorpe Lincs 190 D2
Grimeford Village Lancs 194 E6
Grimes Hill Worcs 117 B11
Grimesthorpe S Yorks 186 C5
Grimethorpe S Yorks 198 F2
Griminis W Isles 296 D3
  W Isles 296 F3
Grimister Shetland 312 D6
Grimley Worcs 116 E6
Grimness Orkney 314 G4
Grimoldby Lincs 190 D5
Grimpo Shrops 149 D7
Grimsargh Lancs 203 G7
Grimsbury Oxon 101 C9
Grimsby NE Lincs 201 E9
Grimscote W Nhants 120 G3
Grimscott Corn 24 F3
Grimshaw Blackburn 195 C8
Grimshaw Green Lancs 194 E3
Grimsthorpe Lincs 155 E10
Grimston E Yorks 209 F11
  Leics 154 E3
  Norf 158 E4
  York 207 C8
Grimstone Dorset 17 C8
Grimstone End Suff 125 D8
Grinacombe Moor Devon 12 C4
Grindale E Yorks 218 E2
Grindigar Orkney 314 F5
Grindiscol Shetland 313 K6
Grindle Shrops 132 C5
Grindleford Derbys 186 F2
Grindleton Lancs 203 D11
Grindley Staffs 151 D10
Grindley Brook Shrops 167 G8
Grindlow Derbys 185 F11
Grindon Northumb 273 G8
  Staffs 169 E9
  Stockton 234 F3
  T&W 243 G9
Grindonmoor Gate
  Staffs 169 E9
Grindsbrook Booth
  Derbys 185 D10
Gringley on the Hill
  Notts 188 C2
Grinsdale Cumb 239 F9
Grinshill Shrops 149 E10
Grinstead Hill Suff 125 G11
Grinton N Yorks 223 F10
Griomasaigh W Isles 297 G4
Griomsidar W Isles 304 F5
Grisdale Cumb 222 G5
Grishipoll Argyll 288 D3
Grisling Common E Sus 36 C6
Gristhorpe N Yorks 217 C11
Griston Norf 141 D8
Gritley Orkney 314 F5
Grittenham Wilts 62 C4
Grittlesend Hereford 98 B4
Grittleton Wilts 61 C11
Grizebeck Cumb 210 C4
Grizedale Cumb 220 G6
Groam Highld 300 E5
Grobister Orkney 314 D6
Grobsness Shetland 313 G5
Groby Leics 135 B10
Groes Conwy 165 C8
  Neath 57 D9
Groes Efa Denb 165 B10
Groes-faen Rhondda 58 C5
Groes-fawr Denb 165 B10
Groesffordd Gwyn 144 B5
  Powys 95 F11
Groesffordd Marli Denb 181 G8
Groeslon Gwyn 163 C8
  Gwyn 163 D7
Groes-lwyd Mon 96 G6
  Powys 148 G4
Groespluan Powys 130 B4
Groes-wen Caerph 58 B6
Grogport Argyll 255 C9
Gromford Suff 127 F7
Gronant Flint 181 E9
Gronwen Shrops 148 D5
Groombridge E Sus 52 F4
Grosmont Mon 97 G8
  N Yorks 226 D6
Gross Green Warks 119 F7
Grotaig Highld 300 G4
Groton Suff 107 C9
Grotton Gtr Man 196 G3
Grougfoot Falk 279 F10
Grove Bucks 103 G8
  Dorset 17 G10
  Hereford 98 C2
  Kent 71 G8
  Notts 188 F2
  Oxon 82 G6
  Pembs 73 E7
Grove End Kent 69 G11
  Warks 100 D6
  Warks 134 D3
Grove Green Kent 53 B9
Grovehill E Yorks 208 F6
  Herts 85 D9
Grove Hill E Sus 23 C10
  Kent 71 G8
Grove Park London 67 D8
  London 68 E2
Groves Kent 55 B9
Grovesend Swansea 75 E9
Grove Town W Yorks 198 C3
Grove Vale W Mid 133 E10
Grubb Street Kent 68 F5
Grub Street Staffs 150 D5
Grudie Highld 300 C3
Gruids Highld 309 J5
Gruinard House Highld 307 K4
Gruinards Highld 309 K5
Grula Highld 294 C5
Gruline Argyll 289 E7
Gruline Ho Argyll 289 F7
Grumbeg Highld 308 F6
Grumbla Corn 1 D4
Grunasound Shetland 313 K5
Grundisburgh Suff 126 G4
Grunsagill Lancs 203 C11
Gruting Shetland 313 J4
Grutness Shetland 313 N6
Gryn Goch Gwyn 162 F6
Gualachulain Highld 284 C5
Gualin Ho Highld 308 D3
Guardbridge Fife 287 F8
Guard House W Yorks 204 E6
Guarlford Worcs 98 B6
Guay Perth 286 C4
Gubbion's Green Essex 88 B2
Gubblecote Herts 84 C6
Guesachan Highld 289 B10
Guestling Green E Sus 38 E5
Guestling Thorn E Sus 38 D4
Guestwick Norf 159 D11
Guestwick Green Norf 159 D11
Guide Blackburn 195 B8
Guide Bridge Gtr Man 184 B6
Guide Post Northumb 253 F7
Guilden Morden Cambs 104 C5
Guilden Sutton Ches W 166 B6
Guildford Sur 50 D3
Guildford Park Sur 50 D3
Guildiehaugh W Loth 269 B9
Guildtown Perth 286 D5
Guilford Pembs 73 D7
Guilsborough W Nhants 120 C3
Guilsfield = Cegidfa
  Powys 148 G4
Guilthwaite S Yorks 187 D7
Guilton Kent 55 B9
Guineaford Devon 40 F5
Guisachan Highld 300 G3
Guisborough Redcar 226 B2
Guiseley W Yorks 205 E9
Guist Norf 159 D9
Guith Orkney 314 C5
Guiting Power Glos 99 G11
Gulberwick Shetland 313 K6
Gullane E Loth 281 E9
Guller's End Worcs 99 D7
Gulling Green Suff 124 F6
Gullom Holme Cumb 231 F9
Gulval Corn 1 C5
Gulworthy Devon 12 G4
Gumfreston Pembs 73 E10
Gumley Leics 136 E3
Gummow's Shop Corn 5 D7
Gunby E Yorks 207 F10
  Lincs 155 E8
  Lincs 175 B7
Gundenham Som 27 C10
Gundleton Hants 48 G6
Gun Green Kent 53 G9
Gun Hill E Sus 23 C9
Gunn Devon 40 G6
Gunnersbury London 67 D7
Gunnerside N Yorks 223 F9
Gunnerton Northumb 241 C10
Gunness N Lincs 199 E10
Gunnislake Corn 12 G4
Gunnista Shetland 313 J7
Gunstone Staffs 133 C7
Guns Village W Mid 133 E9
Gunter's Bridge W Sus 35 C7
Gunthorpe Lincs 188 B4
  Norf 159 C10
  Notts 171 G11
  Pboro 138 C3
  Rutland 137 B7
Gunton Suff 143 D10
Gunville IoW 20 D5
Gunwalloe Corn 2 E5
Gunwalloe Fishing Cove
  Corn 2 E5
Gupworthy Som 42 F3
Gurnard IoW 20 B5
Gurnett Ches E 184 G6
Gurney Slade Som 44 D6
Gurnos M Tydf 77 D8
  Powys 76 D3
Gushmere Kent 54 B4
Gussage All Saints Dorset 31 E8
Gussage St Andrew
  Dorset 31 E7
Gussage St Michael
  Dorset 31 E7
Gustard Wood Herts 85 B11
Guston Kent 55 E10
Gutcher Shetland 312 D7
Guthram Gowt Lincs 156 E3
Guthrie Angus 287 B9
Guyhirn Cambs 139 C7
Guyhirn Gull Cambs 139 C7
Guy's Cliffe Warks 118 D5
Guy's Head Lincs 157 D9
Guy's Marsh Dorset 30 C4
Guyzance Northumb 252 C6
Gwaelod-y-garth Cardiff 58 C6
Gwaenysgor Flint 181 E9
Gwalchmai Anglesey 178 F5
Gwalchmai Uchaf
  Anglesey 178 F5
Gwallon Corn 2 C2
Gwastad Pembs 91 G10
Gwastadgoed Gwyn 145 G11
Gwastadnant Gwyn 163 D10
Gwaun-Cae-Gurwen
  Neath 76 C2
Gwaun-Leision Neath 76 C2
Gwavas Corn 2 D5
  Corn 2 E5
Gwbert Ceredig 92 B3
Gwedna Corn 2 C4
Gweek Corn 2 D6
Gwehelog Mon 78 E5
Gwenddwr Powys 95 C11
Gwennap Corn 2 B6
Gwenter Corn 2 F6
Gwernaffield-y-Waun
  Flint 166 C2
Gwernafon Powys 129 E8
Gwerneirin Powys 129 F10
  Powys 130 G3
Gwernesney Mon 78 E6
Gwernogle Carms 93 E10
Gwernol Denb 166 E2
Gwern y brenin Shrops 148 D6
Gwernydd Powys 129 C11
Gwernymynydd Flint 166 C2
Gwern-y-Steeple V Glam 58 D5
Gwersyllt Wrex 166 E4
Gwespyr Flint 181 E10
Gwills Corn 4 D6
Gwinear Corn 2 B3
Gwinear Downs Corn 2 C4
Gwithian Corn 2 A3
Gwredog Anglesey 178 D6
Gwrhay Caerph 77 F11
Gwyddelwern Denb 165 F9
Gwyddgrug Carms 93 D9
Gwynfryn Wrex 166 E3
Gwystre Powys 113 D11
Gwytherin Conwy 164 C5
Gyfelia Wrex 166 F4
Gyffin Conwy 180 F3
Gylen Park Argyll 289 G10
Gyre Orkney 314 F3
Gyrn Denb 165 D11
Gyrn-goch Gwyn 162 F6

H

Habberley Shrops 131 C7
  Worcs 116 B6
Habergham Lancs 204 G2
Habertoft Lincs 175 B8
Habin W Sus 34 C4
Habrough NE Lincs 200 E6
Haccombe Devon 14 G3
Haceby Lincs 155 B10
Hacheston Suff 126 F6
Hackbridge London 67 F9
Hackenthorpe S Yorks 186 E6
Hackford Norf 141 C11
Hackforth N Yorks 224 G4
Hack Green Ches E 167 F10
Hackland Orkney 314 D3
Hackleton W Nhants 120 F6
Hacklinge Kent 55 C10
Hackman's Gate Worcs 117 B7
Hackness N Yorks 227 G9
  Orkney 314 G3
  Som 43 D10
Hackney London 67 C10
Hackney Wick London 67 C11
Hackthorn Lincs 189 E7
  Wilts 47 D7
Hackthorpe Cumb 230 G6
Haclait W Isles 297 G4
Haconby Lincs 156 D2
Hacton London 68 B4
Haddacott Devon 25 C8
Hadden Borders 263 B7
Haddenham Bucks 84 D2
  Cambs 123 B9
Haddenham End Field
  Cambs 123 B9
Haddington E Loth 281 G10
  Lincs 172 C6
Haddiscoe Norf 143 D8
Haddoch Aberds 302 E5
Haddon Cambs 138 E2
  Ches E 169 B7
Hade Edge W Yorks 196 F6
Hademore Staffs 134 B3
Haden Cross W Mid 133 F9
Hadfield Derbys 185 B8
Hadham Cross Herts 86 B6
Hadham Ford Herts 105 G8
Hadleigh Essex 69 B10
  Suff 107 C10
Hadleigh Heath Suff 107 C9
Hadley London 86 F2
  Telford 150 G3
  Worcs 117 E7
Hadley Castle Telford 150 G3
Hadley End Staffs 152 E2
Hadley Wood London 86 F3
Hadlow Kent 52 D6
Hadlow Down E Sus 37 C8
Hadlow Stair Kent 52 D6
Hadnall Shrops 149 F10
Hadspen Som 45 G7
Hadstock Essex 105 C11
Hadston Northumb 253 D7
Hady Derbys 186 G5
Hadzor Worcs 117 E8
Haffenden Quarter Kent 53 E11
Hafod Swansea 57 C7
Hafod-Dinbych Conwy 164 E5
Hafod Grove Pembs 92 C2
Hafodiwan Ceredig 111 G7
Hafod-lom Conwy 180 G5
Hafod-y-Green Denb 181 G8
Hafodyrynys Bl Gwent 78 F2
Hag Fold Gtr Man 195 G7
Haggate Gtr Man 196 F2
  Lancs 204 F3
Haggbeck Cumb 239 C11
Haggersta Shetland 313 J5
Haggerston London 67 C10
  Northumb 273 G10
Haggington Hill Devon 40 D5
Haggrister Shetland 312 F5
Haggs Falk 278 F5
Haghill Glasgow 268 B2
Hagley Hereford 97 C11
  Worcs 133 G8
Hagloe Glos 79 D11
Hagmore Green Suff 107 D9
Hagnaby Lincs 174 C4
  Lincs 191 F7
Hagnaby Lock Lincs 174 D4
Hague Bar Derbys 185 D7
Hagworthingham Lincs 174 B4
Haigh Gtr Man 194 F6
  S Yorks 197 E9
Haigh Moor W Yorks 197 C9
Haighton Green Lancs 203 G7
Haighton Top Lancs 203 G7
Haile Cumb 219 D10
Hailes Glos 99 E10
Hailey Herts 86 C5
  Oxon 64 B6
  Oxon 82 C5
Hailsham E Sus 23 D9
Hailstone Hill Wilts 81 G9
Hail Weston Cambs 122 E3
Haimer Highld 310 C5
Haimwood Powys 148 F6
Hainault London 87 G7
Haine Kent 71 F11
Hainford Norf 160 F4
Hains Dorset 30 D3
Hainton Lincs 189 E11
Hainworth W Yorks 205 F7
Hainworth Shaw
  W Yorks 205 F7
Hairmyres S Lanark 268 E2
Haisthorpe E Yorks 218 G2
Hakeford Devon 40 F6
Hakin Pembs 72 D5
Halabezack Corn 2 C6
Halam Notts 171 E11
Halamanning Corn 2 C3
Halbeath Fife 280 D2
Halberton Devon 27 E8
Halcon Som 28 B3
Halcro Highld 310 C6
Haldens Herts 86 C2
Hale Cumb 211 D10
  Gtr Man 184 D3
  Halton 183 E7
  Hants 31 D11
  Kent 71 F9
  Medway 69 F9
  Som 30 B3
  Sur 49 D10
Hale Bank Halton 183 E7
Hale Barns Gtr Man 184 D3
Halecommon W Sus 34 C4
Hale Coombe N Som 44 B2
Hale End London 86 G5
Hale Green E Sus 23 C9

Hale Mills Corn 4 G5
Hale Nook Lancs 202 E3
Hales Norf 143 D7
  Staffs 150 C4
Hales Bank Hereford 116 G2
Halesfield Telford 132 C4
Halesgate Lincs 156 D6
Hales Green Derbys 169 G11
  Norf 143 D7
Halesowen W Mid 133 G9
Hales Park Worcs 116 B5
Hales Place Kent 54 B6
Hales Street Norf 142 F3
Hale Street Kent 53 D7
Hales Wood Hereford 98 E2
Halesworth Suff 127 B7
Halewood Mers 183 D7
Half Moon Village Devon 14 B3
Halford Shrops 131 G8
  Warks 100 B5
Halfpenny Cumb 211 B10
Halfpenny Furze Carms 74 C3
Halfpenny Green Staffs 132 E6
Halfway Carms 75 E8
  Carms 94 E2
  Carms 94 E6
  S Yorks 186 E6
  W Berks 64 F2
  Wilts 45 D11
Halfway Bridge W Sus 34 C6
Halfway House Shrops 148 G6
Halfway Houses
  Gtr Man 195 F9
  Kent 70 E2
Halfway Street Kent 55 D9
Halgabron Corn 11 D7
Halifax W Yorks 196 B5
Halkburn Borders 271 G9
Halket E Ayrs 267 E8
Halkirk Highld 310 D5
Halkyn = Helygain Flint 182 G2
Halkyn Mountain Flint 182 G2
Hallam Fields Derbys 153 B9
Halland E Sus 23 B8
Hallaton Leics 136 D5
Hallatrow Bath 44 B6
Hallbankgate Cumb 240 F3
Hall Bower W Yorks 196 E6
Hall Broom S Yorks 186 D3
Hall Cross Lancs 202 G4
Hall Dunnerdale Cumb 220 F4
Halleaths Dumfries 248 G3
Hallen S Glos 60 C5
Hallend Warks 118 D2
Hall End Bedford 103 B10
  C Beds 103 D11
  Lincs 174 E6
  S Glos 61 B8
  Warks 134 C5
Hallew Corn 5 D10
Hallfield Gate Derbys 170 D5
Hall Flat Worcs 117 C9
Hallgarth Durham 234 C2
Hall Garth York 207 C9
Hallglen Falk 279 F7
Hall Green Ches E 168 D4
  Essex 106 D5
  Lancs 194 C3
  Lancs 194 F4
  W Mid 133 E10
  W Mid 134 G2
  W Mid 135 G7
  Wrex 167 G7
  W Yorks 197 D10
Hall Grove Herts 89 C8
Halliburton Borders 261 B11
  Borders 272 F3
Hallin Highld 298 D2
Halling Medway 69 G8
Hallingbury Street
  Essex 87 B8
Hallington Lincs 190 D4
  Northumb 241 B11
Hall i' th' Wood Gtr Man 195 E8
Halliwell Gtr Man 195 E8
Hall of Clestrain Orkney 314 F2
Hall of Tankerness
  Orkney 314 F5
Hall of the Forest
  Shrops 130 G4
Hallon Shrops 132 D5
Hallonsford Shrops 132 D5
Halloughton Notts 171 E11
Hallow Worcs 116 F6
Hallowes Derbys 186 F5
Hallow Heath Worcs 116 F6
Hallowsgate Ches W 167 B8
Hallrule Borders 262 G3
Halls E Loth 282 G3
Hallsands Devon 9 G11
Hall Santon Cumb 220 E2
Hall's Cross E Sus 23 D11
Hallsford Bridge Essex 87 E9
Halls Green Essex 86 D6
Hall's Green Herts 104 F5
  Kent 52 D4
Hallspill Devon 25 C7
Hallthwaites Cumb 210 B3
Hall Waberthwaite
  Cumb 220 F2
Hallwood Green Glos 98 E3
Hallworthy Corn 11 D9
Hallyards Borders 260 B6
Hallyburton House
  Perth 286 D6
Hallyne Borders 270 G3
Halmer End Staffs 168 F3
Halmond's Frome
  Hereford 98 B3
Halmore Glos 79 E11
Halmyre Mains Borders 270 F3
Halnaker W Sus 22 B6
Halsall Lancs 193 E11
Halse Som 27 B10
  W Nhants 101 C11
Halsetown Corn 2 B2
Halsfordwood Devon 14 C3
Halsham E Yorks 201 B9
Halsinger Devon 40 F4
Halstead Essex 106 E6
  Kent 68 G3
  Leics 136 B4
Halstock Dorset 29 F8
Halsway Som 42 F6
Haltcliff Bridge Cumb 230 D3
Halterworth Hants 32 C5
Haltham Lincs 174 C2
Haltoft End Lincs 174 F5
Halton Bucks 84 C5
  Halton 183 E8
  Lancs 211 G10
  Northumb 241 D11
  Wrex 148 B6
  W Yorks 206 G2
Halton Barton Corn 7 B8
Halton Brook Halton 183 E8
Halton East N Yorks 204 C6
Halton Fenside Lincs 174 C6
Halton Gill N Yorks 213 D7
Halton Green Lancs 211 F10
Halton Holegate Lincs 174 B6
Halton Lea Gate
  Northumb 240 F5
Halton Moor W Yorks 206 G2
Halton Shields
  Northumb 242 D2
Halton View Halton 183 D8
Halton West N Yorks 204 C2
Haltwhistle Northumb 240 E6
Halvergate Norf 143 B8
Halvosso Corn 2 C6
Halwell Devon 8 E5
Halwill Devon 12 B4
Halwill Junction Devon 24 G6
Halwin Corn 2 C5
Ham Devon 28 G2
  Glos 79 F11
  Glos 99 G9
  Highld 310 B6
  Kent 55 C10
  London 67 E7
  Plym 7 D9
  Shetland 313 K1
  Som 27 C11
  Som 28 B3
  Som 28 E3
  Som 45 D7
  Wilts 63 G10
Hamar Shetland 312 F5
Hamarhill Orkney 314 C5
Hamars Shetland 313 G6
Hambleden Bucks 65 B9
Hambledon Hants 33 E10
  Sur 50 F3
Hamble-le-Rice Hants 33 F7
Hambleton Lancs 202 E3
  N Yorks 205 C7
  N Yorks 207 G7
Hambleton Moss Side
  Lancs 202 E3
Hambridge Som 28 C5
Hambrook S Glos 60 D6
  W Sus 22 B3
Ham Common Dorset 30 B4
Hameringham Lincs 174 B4
Hamerton Cambs 122 B2
Hametoun Shetland 313 K1
Ham Green Bucks 83 B11
  Hants 48 G2
  Hereford 98 C4
  Kent 38 B5
  Kent 69 F10
  N Som 60 D4
  Wilts 61 G11
  Worcs 117 E10
Ham Hill Kent 69 G8
Hamilton S Lanark 268 D3
Hamister Shetland 313 G7
Hamlet Dorset 29 F9
Hammer W Sus 49 G11
Hammer Bottom Hants 49 G11
Hammerfield Herts 85 D8
Hammerpot W Sus 35 F9
Hammersmith Derbys 170 E5
  London 67 D8
Hammerwich Staffs 133 B11
Hammerwood E Sus 52 F2
Hammill Kent 55 B9
Hammond Street Herts 86 E4
Hammoon Dorset 30 E4
Ham Moor Sur 66 G5
Hamnavoe Shetland 312 E4
  Shetland 312 E6
  Shetland 312 F6
  Shetland 313 K5
Hamnish Clifford
  Hereford 115 F10
Hamp Som 43 F10
Hampden Park E Sus 23 E10
Hampen Glos 81 B9
Hamperden End Essex 105 E11
Hamperley Shrops 131 F8
Hampers Green W Sus 35 C7
Hampeth Northumb 252 B5
Hampnett Glos 81 B10
Hampole S Yorks 198 E4
Hampreston Dorset 19 B7
Hampsfield Cumb 211 C8
Hampson Green Lancs 202 C5
Hampstead London 67 B9
Hampstead Garden Suburb
  London 67 B9
Hampstead Norreys
  W Berks 64 D4
Hampsthwaite N Yorks 205 B11
Hampton Kent 71 F7
  London 66 F6
  Shrops 132 F4
  Swindon 81 G11
  Worcs 99 C10
Hampton Bank Shrops 149 C9
Hampton Beech Shrops 130 B6
Hampton Bishop
  Hereford 97 D11
Hampton Fields Glos 80 F5
Hampton Gay Oxon 83 B7
Hampton Green Ches W 167 F8
  Glos 80 E5
Hampton Hargate Pboro 138 E3
Hampton Heath Ches W 167 F7
Hampton Hill London 66 E6
Hampton in Arden
  W Mid 134 G4
Hampton Loade Shrops 132 F5
Hampton Lovett Worcs 117 D7
Hampton Lucy Warks 118 F5
Hampton Magna Warks 118 D5
Hampton on the Hill
  Warks 118 E5
Hampton Park Hereford 97 D10
  Soton 32 D6
Hampton Poyle Oxon 83 B8
Hamptons Kent 52 C6
Hampton Vale Pboro 138 E3
Hampton Wick London 67 F7
Hamptworth Wilts 32 D2
Hamrow Norf 159 E8
Hamsey E Sus 36 E6
Hamsey Green London 51 B10
Hamshill Glos 80 E3
Hamstall Ridware Staffs 152 F2
Hamstead IoW 20 C4
  W Mid 133 E10
Hamstead Marshall
  W Berks 64 F2
Hamsterley Durham 233 E8
  Durham 242 F4
Hamstreet Kent 54 G4
Ham Street Som 44 G5
Hamworthy BCP 18 C5
Hanbury Staffs 152 D3
  Worcs 117 E9
Hanbury Woodend
  Staffs 152 D3
Hanby Lincs 155 C10
Hanchett Village Suff 106 B3
Hanchurch Staffs 168 G4
Handbridge Ches W 166 B6
Handcross W Sus 36 B3
Handforth Ches E 184 E5
Hand Green Ches W 167 C8
Handless Shrops 131 E7
Handley Ches W 167 D7
  Derbys 170 C5
Handley Green Essex 87 E11
Handsacre Staffs 151 F11
Handside Herts 86 C2
Handsworth S Yorks 186 D6
  W Mid 133 E10
Handsworth Wood
  W Mid 133 E11
Handy Cross Bucks 84 G5
  Devon 24 B6
  Som 42 G6
Hanford Dorset 30 E4
  Stoke 168 G5
Hangersley Hants 31 F11
Hanging Bank Kent 52 C3
Hanging Heaton
  W Yorks 197 C9
Hanging Houghton
  W Nhants 120 C5
Hanging Langford Wilts 46 F4
Hangingshaw Borders 261 C9
  Dumfries 248 F4
Hangleton Brighton 36 F3
  W Sus 35 G9
Hangsman Hill S Yorks 199 E7
Hanham S Glos 60 E6
Hanham Green S Glos 60 E6
Hankelow Ches E 167 F11
Hankerton Wilts 81 G7
Hankham E Sus 23 D10
Hanley Stoke 168 F5
Hanley Castle Worcs 98 C6
Hanley Child Worcs 116 E3
Hanley Swan Worcs 98 C6
Hanley William Worcs 116 D3
Hanlith N Yorks 213 G8
Hanmer Wrex 149 B9
Hannaford Devon 25 B10
Hannafore Corn 6 E5
Hannah Lincs 191 F8
Hanningfields Green
  Suff 125 G7
Hannington Hants 48 B4
  Swindon 81 G11
  W Nhants 120 C6
Hannington Wick
  Swindon 81 F11
Hanscombe End C Beds 104 E2
Hansel Devon 8 F6
Hansel Village S Ayrs 257 C9
Hansley Cross Staffs 169 G9
Hanslope M Keynes 102 B6
Hanthorpe Lincs 155 E11
Hanwell London 67 C7
  Oxon 101 C8
Hanwood Shrops 131 B8
Hanwood Bank Shrops 149 G8
Hanworth Brack 65 F11
  London 66 E6
  Norf 160 B3
Happendon S Lanark 259 C9
Happisburgh Norf 161 C7
Happisburgh Common
  Norf 161 D7
Hapsford Ches W 183 G7
  Som 45 D9
Hapton Lancs 203 G11
  Norf 142 D3
Hararden = Penarlâg
  Flint 166 B4
Harberton Devon 8 D5
Harbertonford Devon 8 D5
Harbledown Kent 54 B6
Harborne W Mid 133 G10
Harborough Magna
  Warks 119 B9
Harborough Parva
  Warks 119 B9
Harbottle Northumb 251 C10
Harbour Heights E Sus 36 G6
Harbourland Kent 53 B9
Harbourneford Devon 8 C4
Harbours Hill Worcs 117 D9
Harbour Village Pembs 91 D8
Harbridge Hants 31 E10
Harbridge Green Hants 31 E10
Harburn W Loth 269 C10
Harbury Warks 119 F7
Harby Leics 154 C4
  Notts 188 G5
Harcombe Devon 14 E3
  Devon 15 C9
Harcourt Corn 3 B8
Harcourt Hill Oxon 83 E7
Hardbreck Orkney 314 F4
Hardeicke Glos 80 C4
Harden S Yorks 197 G7
  W Mid 133 C10
  W Yorks 205 F7
Hardendale Cumb 221 C11
Hardenhuish Wilts 62 E2
Harden Park Ches E 184 F4
Hardgate Aberds 293 C9
  Dumfries 237 C10
  N Yorks 214 G5
  W Dunb 277 G10
Hardham W Sus 35 D8
Hardhorn Lancs 202 F3
Hardingham Norf 141 C10
Hardings Booth Staffs 169 C9
Hardingstone W Nhants 120 F5
Hardings Wood Staffs 168 E4
Hardington Som 45 C8
Hardington Mandeville
  Som 29 E8
Hardington Marsh Som 29 F8
Hardington Moor Som 29 E8
Hardiston Perth 279 B11
Hardisworthy Devon 24 C2
Hardley Hants 32 G6
Hardley Street Norf 143 C7
Hardmead M Keynes 103 B8
Hardrow N Yorks 223 G7
Hardstoft Derbys 170 C6
Hardstoft Common
  Derbys 170 C6
Hardway Hants 33 G10
  Som 45 G8
Hardwick Bucks 84 B4
  Cambs 122 D3
  Cambs 123 F7
  N Nhants 121 D7
  Norf 142 F4
  Norf 158 F2
  Oxon 82 D5
  Oxon 101 C8
  Oxon 101 F11
  Shrops 131 E7
  Stockton 234 G4
  S Yorks 187 D7
  W Mid 133 D11
Hardwicke Glos 80 C3
  Glos 99 F8
  Hereford 96 C5
Hardwick Green Worcs 98 E6
Hardwick Village Notts 187 F10
Hardy's Green Essex 107 G8
Hare Som 28 D3
Hare Appletree Lancs 202 B6
Hareby Lincs 174 B4
Harecroft W Yorks 205 F7
Hareden Lancs 203 C8
Hare Edge Derbys 186 G4
Harefield London 85 G9
  Soton 33 E7
Harefield Grove London 85 G9
Haregate Staffs 169 D7
Hare Green Essex 107 G11
Hare Hatch Wokingham 65 D10
Harehill Derbys 152 B3
Harehills W Yorks 206 G2
Harehope Borders 270 G4
  Northumb 264 E3
Harelaw Durham 242 G5
Hareleeshill S Lanark 268 E5
Hareplain Kent 53 F10
Haresceugh Cumb 231 C8
Harescombe Glos 80 C4
Haresfield Glos 80 C4
  Swindon 82 G2
Haresfinch Mers 183 B8
Hareshaw N Lanark 268 C6
Hareshaw Head
  Northumb 251 F9
Harestanes E Dunb 278 G3
Harestock Hants 48 G3
Hare Street Essex 86 D6
  Herts 104 F6
  Herts 105 F7
Harewood W Yorks 206 D2
Harewood End Hereford 97 F10
Harewood Hill W Yorks 204 F6
Harford Carms 94 C2
  Devon 8 D2
  Devon 40 G6
Hargate Norf 142 E2
Hargate Hill Derbys 185 C8
Hargatewall Derbys 185 F10
Hargrave Ches W 167 C7
  N Nhants 121 C10
  Suff 124 F5
Harker Cumb 239 E9
Harker Marsh Cumb 229 E7
Harkland Shetland 312 E6
Harknett's Gate Essex 86 D6
Harkstead Suff 108 E3
Harlaston Staffs 152 G4
Harlaw Ho Aberds 303 G7
Harlaxton Lincs 155 C7
Harlech Gwyn 145 C11
Harlequin Notts 154 B3
Harlescott Shrops 149 F10
Harlesden London 67 C8
Harlesthorpe Derbys 187 F7
Harleston Devon 8 F5
  Norf 142 G4
  Suff 125 F10
Harlestone W Nhants 120 E4
Harle Syke Lancs 204 F3
Harley Shrops 131 C11
  S Yorks 186 B5
Harleyholm S Lanark 259 B10
Harley Shute E Sus 38 F3
Harleywood Glos 80 F4
Harling Road Norf 141 F9
Harlington C Beds 103 E10
  London 66 D5
  S Yorks 198 G3
Harlosh Highld 298 E2
Harlow Essex 86 C6
Harlow Carr N Yorks 205 C11
Harlow Green T&W 243 F7
Harlow Hill Northumb 242 D3
  N Yorks 205 C11
Harlthorpe E Yorks 207 F10
Harlton Cambs 123 G7
Harlyn Corn 10 F3
Harman's Corner Kent 69 G11
Harman's Cross Dorset 18 E5
Harmans Water Brack 65 F11
Harmby N Yorks 214 B2
Harmer Green Herts 86 B3
Harmer Hill Shrops 149 E9
Harmondsworth London 66 D5
Harmston Lincs 173 C7
Harnage Shrops 131 C11
Harnham Northumb 242 B3
  Wilts 31 B10
  Wilts 31 B11
Harnhill Glos 81 E9
Harold Hill London 87 G8
Harold Park London 87 G9
Haroldston West Pembs 72 B5
Haroldswick Shetland 312 B8
Harold Wood London 87 G8
Harome N Yorks 216 C2
Harpenden Herts 85 C10
Harpenden Common
  Herts 85 C10
Harper Green Gtr Man 195 F8
Harperley Durham 242 G5
Harper's Gate Staffs 169 D7
Harper's Green Norf 159 E8
Harpford Devon 15 C7
Harpham E Yorks 217 G11
Harpley Norf 158 D5
  Worcs 116 E3
Harpole W Nhants 120 E3
Harpsdale Highld 310 D5
Harpsden Oxon 65 C9
Harpsden Bottom Oxon 65 C9
Harpswell Lincs 188 D6
Harpton Powys 114 F4
Harpurhey Gtr Man 195 G11
Harpur Hill Derbys 185 G9
Harraby Cumb 239 G10
Harracott Devon 25 B9
Harrapool Highld 295 C8
Harras Cumb 219 B9
Harraton T&W 243 G7
Harrier Shetland 313 J1
Harrietfield Perth 286 E3
Harrietsham Kent 53 C11
Harringay London 67 B10
Harrington Cumb 228 F5
  Lincs 190 G5
  N Nhants 136 G5
Harringworth N Nhants 137 D8
Harris Highld 294 F5
Harriseahead Staffs 168 D5
Harriston Cumb 229 C9
Harrogate N Yorks 206 C2
Harrold Bedford 121 F8
Harrop Dale Gtr Man 196 F4
Harrow Highld 310 B6
  London 67 B7
Harrowbarrow Corn 7 B7
Harrowbeer Devon 7 B10
Harrowby Lincs 155 B8
Harrowden Bedford 103 B11
Harrowgate Hill Darl 224 B5
Harrowgate Village
  Darl 224 B5
Harrow Green Suff 125 G7
Harrow Hill Glos 79 B10
Harrow on the Hill
  London 67 B7
Harrow Street Suff 107 D9
Harrow Weald London 85 G11
Harry Stoke S Glos 60 D6
Harston Cambs 123 G8
Harston *continued*
  Leics 154 C6
Harswell E Yorks 208 E2
Hart Hrtlpl 234 E5
Hartbarrow Cumb 221 G8
Hartburn Northumb 252 F3
  Stockton 225 B8
Hartcliffe Bristol 60 F5
Hart Common Gtr Man 194 F6
Hartest Suff 124 G6
Hartest Hill Suff 124 G6
Hartfield E Sus 52 F3
  Highld 299 E7
Hartford Cambs 122 C5
  Ches W 183 G10
  Som 27 B7
Hartfordbeach
  Ches W 183 G10
Hartfordbridge Hants 49 B9
Hartford End Essex 87 B11
Hartforth N Yorks 224 D3
Hartgrove Dorset 30 D4
Hartham Herts 86 C4
Harthill Ches W 167 D8
  N Lanark 269 C8
  S Yorks 187 E7
Hart Hill Luton 104 G2
Hartington Derbys 169 C10
Hartland Devon 24 C3
Hartle Worcs 117 B8
Hartlebury Shrops 132 D4
  Worcs 116 C6
Hartlebury Common
  Worcs 116 C6
Hartlepool Hrtlpl 234 E6
Hartley Cumb 222 D5
  Kent 53 G9
  Kent 68 F6
  Northumb 243 B8
  Plym 7 D9
Hartley Green Kent 68 F6
  Staffs 151 D9
Hartley Mauditt Hants 49 F8
Hartley Westpall Hants 49 B7
Hartley Wintney Hants 49 B9
Hartlington N Yorks 213 G10
Hartlip Kent 69 G10
Hartmoor Dorset 30 C3
Hartmount Highld 301 B7
Hartoft End N Yorks 226 G5
Harton N Yorks 216 G4
  Shrops 131 F9
  T&W 243 E9
Hartpury Glos 98 F5
Hartsgreen Shrops 132 G5
Hart's Green Suff 125 F7
Hartshead W Yorks 197 C7
Hartshead Green
  Gtr Man 196 G3
Hartshead Moor Side
  W Yorks 197 C7
Hartshead Moor Top
  W Yorks 197 B7
Hartshead Pike
  Gtr Man 196 G3
Hartshill Stoke 168 F5
  Warks 134 E6
Hart's Hill W Mid 133 F8
Hartshill Green Warks 134 E6
Hartshorne Derbys 152 E6
Hartsop Cumb 221 C8
Hart Station Hrtlpl 234 D5
Hartswell Som 27 B9
Hartwell Staffs 151 B8
  W Nhants 120 G5
Hartwith N Yorks 214 G4
Hartwood Lancs 194 D5
  N Lanark 268 D6
Hartwoodburn Borders 261 D11
Harvel Kent 68 G6
Harvest Hill W Mid 134 G5
Harvieston Stirling 277 D11
Harvills Hawthorn
  W Mid 133 E9
Harvington Worcs 99 B11
  Worcs 117 C7
Harvington Cross Worcs 99 B11
Harvington Hill Worcs 99 B10
Harwell Notts 187 C11
  Oxon 64 B3
Harwich Essex 108 E5
Harwood Durham 232 E2
  Gtr Man 195 E8
Harwood Dale N Yorks 227 F9
Harwood Lee Gtr Man 195 E8
Harwood on Teviot
  Borders 249 B10
Harworth Notts 187 C10
Hasbury W Mid 133 G9
Hascombe Sur 50 E3
Haselbech W Nhants 120 B4
Haselbury Plucknett Som 29 E7
Haseley Warks 118 D4
Haseley Green Warks 118 D4
Haseley Knob Warks 118 C4
Haselor Warks 118 F2
Hasfield Glos 98 F6
Hasguard Pembs 72 D5
Haskayne Lancs 193 F11
Hasketon Suff 126 G4
Hasland Derbys 170 B5
Haslemere Sur 50 G2
Haslingbourne W Sus 35 C7
Haslingden Lancs 195 C9
Haslingfield Cambs 123 G8
Haslington Ches E 168 D2
Hasluck's Green W Mid 118 B2
Hassall Ches E 168 D3
Hassall Green Ches E 168 D3
Hassell Street Kent 54 D5
Hassendean Borders 262 E2
Hassingham Norf 143 B7
Hassocks W Sus 36 D3
Hassop Derbys 186 G2
Haster Highld 310 D7
Hasthorpe Lincs 175 B7
Hastigrow Highld 310 C6
Hasting Hill T&W 243 G9
Hastingleigh Kent 54 E5
Hastings E Sus 38 F4
  Som 28 D4
Hastingwood Essex 87 D7
Hastoe Herts 84 D6
Haston Shrops 149 E10
Haswell Durham 234 C3
Haswell Moor Durham 234 C3
Haswell Plough Durham 234 C3
Haswellsykes Borders 260 B6
Hatch C Beds 104 B3
  Devon 8 F4
  Hants 49 C7
  Wilts 30 B6
Hatch Beauchamp Som 28 C4
Hatch Bottom Hants 33 E7
Hatch End Bedford 121 E11
  London 85 G10
Hatchet Gate Hants 32 G5
Hatchet Green Hants 31 D11
Hatch Farm Hill W Sus 34 B6
Hatch Green Som 28 D4
Hatching Green Herts 85 C10
Hatchmere Ches W 183 G9
Hatch Warren Hants 48 D6
Hatcliffe NE Lincs 201 G8
Hateley Heath W Mid 133 E10
Hatfield Hereford 115 F11
  Herts 86 D2
  S Yorks 199 F7
  Worcs 117 G7
Hatfield Broad Oak Essex 87 B8
Hatfield Chase S Yorks 199 E8
Hatfield Garden Village
  Herts 86 D2
Hatfield Heath Essex 87 B8
Hatfield Hyde Herts 86 C2
Hatfield Peverel Essex 88 C3
Hatfield Woodhouse
  S Yorks 199 F7
Hatford Oxon 82 G4
Hatherden Hants 47 C10
Hatherleigh Devon 25 G8
Hatherley Glos 99 G8
Hathern Leics 153 E9
Hatherop Glos 81 D11
Hathersage Derbys 186 E2
Hathersage Booths
  Derbys 186 E2
Hathershaw Gtr Man 196 G2
Hatherton Ches E 167 F11
  Staffs 151 G9
Hatley St George Cambs 122 G5
Hatston Orkney 314 E4
Hatt Corn 7 C7
Hatterseat Aberds 303 G9
Hattersley Gtr Man 185 C7
Hatt Hill Hants 32 B4
Hattingley Hants 48 F6
Hatton Aberds 303 F10
  Angus 287 D9
  Derbys 152 D4
  Lincs 189 F11
  London 66 D5
  Moray 301 D11
  Shrops 131 E9
  Warks 118 D4
  Warr 183 E9
Hattonburn Aberds 293 C9
Hatton Castle Aberds 303 E7
Hattoncrook Aberds 303 G8
Hatton Grange Shrops 132 C5
Hatton Heath Ches W 167 C7
Hatton Hill Sur 66 G2
Hattonknowe Borders 270 F4
Hatton of Fintray
  Aberds 293 B10
Hatton Park N Nhants 121 D7
Haugh E Ayrs 257 D11
  Gtr Man 196 E2
  Lincs 190 F6
Haugham Lincs 190 E4
Haugh-head Borders 261 B8
Haugh Head Northumb 264 D2
Haughland Orkney 314 E5
Haughley Suff 125 E10
Haughley Green Suff 125 E10
Haughley New Street
  Suff 125 E10
Haugh of Glass Moray 302 F4
Haugh of Kilnmaichlie
  Moray 301 F11
Haugh of Urr Dumfries 237 C10
Haughs of Clinterty
  Aberdeen 293 B10
Haughton Ches E 167 D9
  Notts 187 G11
  Powys 148 F6
  Shrops 132 B4
  Shrops 132 D3
  Shrops 149 D7
  Shrops 149 F11
  Staffs 151 E7
Haughton Castle
  Northumb 241 C10
Haughton Green
  Gtr Man 184 C6
Haughton Le Skerne
  Darl 224 B6
Haughurst Hill W Berks 64 G5
Haulkerton Aberds 293 F9
Haultwick Herts 104 G6
Haunn Argyll 288 E5
  W Isles 297 K3
Haunton Staffs 152 G4
Hauxton Cambs 123 G8
Havannah Ches E 168 C5
Havant Hants 22 B2
Haven Hereford 97 B11
  Hereford 115 G8
Haven Bank Lincs 174 E2
Haven Side E Yorks 201 B7
Havenstreet IoW 21 C7
Havercroft W Yorks 197 E11
Haverfordwest = Hwlffordd
  Pembs 73 B7
Haverhill Suff 106 B3
Haverigg Cumb 210 D3
Havering-atte-Bower
  London 87 G8
Haveringland Norf 160 E3
Haversham M Keynes 102 C6
Haverthwaite Cumb 210 C6
Haverton Hill Stockton 234 G5
Haviker Street Kent 53 D8
Havyatt Som 44 F4
Havyatt Green N Som 60 G3
Hawarden = Penarlâg
  Flint 166 B4
Hawbridge Worcs 99 B8
Hawbush Green Essex 106 G5
Hawcoat Cumb 210 E4
Hawcross Glos 98 E5
Hawddamor Gwyn 146 F3
Hawen Ceredig 92 B6
Hawes N Yorks 213 B7
Hawes' Green Norf 142 D4
Hawes Side Blackpool 202 G2
Hawford Worcs 116 E6
Hawgreen Shrops 150 D2
Hawick Borders 262 F2
Hawkchurch Devon 28 G4
Hawkcombe Som 41 D11
Hawkedon Suff 124 G5
Hawkenbury Kent 52 F5
  Kent 53 E10
Hawkeridge Wilts 45 C11
Hawkerland Devon 15 D7
Hawkersland Cross
  Hereford 97 B10
Hawkesbury S Glos 61 B9
  Warks 135 G7
Hawkesbury Upton
  S Glos 61 B9
Hawkes End W Mid 134 G6
Hawkesley W Mid 117 B10
Hawk Green Gtr Man 185 D7
Hawkhill Northumb 264 G6
Hawk Hill Cumb 228 F6
Hawkhope Northumb 250 F6
Hawkhurst Kent 53 G9
Hawkhurst Common
  E Sus 23 B8
Hawkinge Kent 55 F8
Hawkin's Hill Essex 106 E3
Hawkley Gtr Man 194 G5
  Hants 34 B2
Hawkridge Som 41 G11
Hawksdale Cumb 230 B3
Hawks Green Staffs 151 G9
Hawkshaw Blackburn 195 D9
Hawkshead Cumb 221 F7
Hawkshead Hill Cumb 220 F6
Hawks Hill Bucks 66 B2
Hawk's Hill Sur 51 B7
Hawksland S Lanark 259 B8
Hawkspur Green
  Essex 106 E3
Hawks Stones W Yorks 196 B2
Hawkswick N Yorks 213 E9
Hawksworth Notts 172 G3
  W Yorks 205 E9
  W Yorks 205 F11
Hawkwell Essex 88 G4
Hawley Hants 49 B11
  Kent 68 E4
Hawley Bottom Devon 28 G2
Hawley Lane Hants 49 B11
Hawling Glos 99 G11
Hawn Orkney 314 D4
Hawnby N Yorks 215 B10
Hawne W Mid 133 G9
Haworth W Yorks 204 F6
Haws Bank Cumb 220 F6
Hawstead Suff 125 F7
Hawstead Green Suff 125 F7
Hawthorn Durham 234 B4
  Hants 49 G7
  Rhondda 58 B6
  Wilts 61 F11
Hawthorn Corner Kent 71 F8
Hawthorn Hill Brack 65 E11
  Lincs 174 D2
Hawthorns Staffs 168 F4
Hawthorpe Lincs 155 D10
Hawton Notts 172 E3
Haxby York 207 B8
Haxey N Lincs 188 B3
  N Lincs 199 G9
Haxey Carr N Lincs 199 G9
Haxted Sur 52 D2
Haxton Wilts 46 D6
Hay Corn 10 G5
Haybridge Shrops 116 C2
  Som 44 D4
  Telford 150 G3
Hayden Glos 99 G8
Haydock Mers 183 B9
Haydon Bath 45 C7
  Dorset 29 D11
  Som 28 C3
  Som 44 D5
  Swindon 62 B6
Haydon Bridge
  Northumb 241 E8
Haydon Wick Swindon 62 B6
Haye Corn 7 B7
Haye Fm Corn 6 B6
Hayes London 66 C6
  London 68 F2
  Staffs 169 C9
Hayes End London 66 C5
Hayes Knoll Wilts 81 G10
Hayes Town London 66 C6
Hayfield Derbys 185 D8
  Fife 280 C5
Hay Field S Yorks 187 B10
Hayfield Green
  S Yorks 187 B11
Haygate Telford 150 G2
Haygrass Som 28 C2
Hay Green Essex 87 E10
  Herts 104 D6
  Norf 157 F10
Hayhill E Ayrs 257 F11
Hayhillock Angus 287 C9
Haylands IoW 21 C7
Hayle Corn 2 B3
Hayley Green W Mid 133 G8
Hay Mills W Mid 134 G2
Haymoor End Som 28 B4
Haymoor Green
  Ches E 167 E11
Hayne Devon 26 F5
Haynes C Beds 103 C11
Haynes Church End
  C Beds 103 C11
Haynes West End
  C Beds 103 C11
Hay-on-Wye Powys 96 C4
Hayscastle Pembs 91 F7
Hayscastle Cross Pembs 91 G8
Haysford Pembs 91 G8
Hayshead Angus 287 C10
Hayston E Dunb 278 G2
Haystoun Borders 261 B7
Hay Street Herts 105 F7
Haythorne Dorset 31 F8
Hayton Aberdeen 293 C11
  Cumb 229 C8
  Cumb 240 F2
  E Yorks 208 D2
  Notts 188 E2
Hayton's Bent Shrops 131 G10
Hayton Vale Devon 13 F11
Haytown Devon 24 E5
Haywards Heath W Sus 36 C4
Haywood S Lanark 269 E9
  S Yorks 198 E5
Haywood Oaks Notts 171 D10
Hazard's Green E Sus 23 C11
Hazelbank S Lanark 268 F6
Hazelbeach Pembs 72 E6
Hazelbury Bryan Dorset 30 F2
Hazeleigh Essex 88 E4
Hazel End Essex 105 G9
Hazeley Hants 49 B8
Hazeley Bottom Hants 49 B9
Hazeley Heath Hants 49 B9
Hazeley Lea Hants 49 B8
Hazelgrove Notts 171 F8
Hazel Grove Gtr Man 184 D6
Hazelhurst Gtr Man 195 D9
  Gtr Man 195 G9
  Gtr Man 196 G3
Hazelslack Cumb 211 D9
Hazelslade Staffs 151 G10
Hazel Street Kent 53 B11
  Kent 53 F7
Hazel Stub Suff 106 C3
Hazelton Glos 81 B9
Hazelton Walls Fife 287 E7
Hazelwood Derbys 170 F4
  Devon 8 E4
  London 68 G2
Hazlehead S Yorks 197 G7
Hazlemere Bucks 84 F5
Hazler Shrops 131 E9
Hazlerigg T&W 242 C6
Hazles Staffs 169 F8
Hazlescross Staffs 169 F8
Hazleton Glos 81 B9
Hazlewood N Yorks 205 C7
Hazon Northumb 252 C5
Heacham Norf 158 B3
Headbourne Worthy
  Hants 48 G3
Headbrook Hereford 114 F6
Headcorn Kent 53 E10
Headingley W Yorks 205 F11
Headington Oxon 83 D8
Headington Hill Oxon 83 D8
Headlam Durham 224 B3
Headless Cross Cumb 211 D7
  Worcs 117 D10
Headley Hants 49 F10
  Hants 64 G4
  Sur 51 C8
Headley Down Hants 49 F10
Headley Heath Worcs 117 B11
Headley Park Bristol 60 F5
Head of Muir Falk 278 E6
Headon Devon 24 G5
  Notts 188 F2
Heads S Lanark 268 F4
Headshaw Borders 261 E11
Heads Nook Cumb 239 F11
Headstone London 66 B6
Headwell Fife 279 D11
Heady Hill Gtr Man 195 E10
Heage Derbys 170 E5
Healaugh N Yorks 206 D5
  N Yorks 223 F10
Heald Green Gtr Man 184 D4
Healds Green Gtr Man 195 F11
Heale Devon 40 D6
  Som 28 B5
  Som 28 D2
  Som 45 E7
Healey Gtr Man 195 D11
  Northumb 242 F2
  N Yorks 214 C3
  W Yorks 197 C8
  W Yorks 197 D9
Healey Cote Northumb 252 C4
Healeyfield Durham 233 B7
Healey Hall Northumb 242 F2
Healing NE Lincs 201 E8
Heamoor Corn 1 C5
Heaning Cumb 221 F8
Heanish Argyll 288 E2
Heanor Derbys 170 F6
Heanor Gate Derbys 170 F6
Heanton Punchardon
  Devon 40 F4
Heap Bridge Gtr Man 195 E10
Heapham Lincs 188 D5
Hearn Hants 49 F10
Hearnden Green Kent 53 D10
Hearthstane Borders 260 D4
Hearthstone Derbys 170 D4
Hearts Delight Kent 69 G11
Heasley Mill Devon 41 G8
Heast Highld 295 D8
Heath Cardiff 59 D7
  Derbys 170 B6
  Halton 183 E8
Heath and Reach
  C Beds 103 F8
Heath Charnock Lancs 194 E5
Heath Common W Sus 35 E10
  W Yorks 197 D11
Heathcot Aberds 293 C10
Heathcote Derbys 169 C10
  Shrops 150 D3
  Warks 118 E6
Heath Cross Devon 13 B10
  Devon 14 C2
Heath End Bucks 84 F5
  Bucks 85 D7
  Derbys 153 E7
  Hants 64 G2
  Hants 64 G5
  S Glos 61 B7
  Sur 49 D10
  Warks 118 E4
  W Mid 133 C10
  W Sus 35 D7
Heather Leics 153 G7
Heathercombe Devon 13 E10
Heatherfield Highld 298 E4
Heather Row Hants 49 C8
Heatherside Sur 50 B2
Heatherwood Park
  Highld 311 K2
Heatherybanks Aberds 303 E7
Heathfield Cambs 105 B9
  Devon 14 F2
  E Sus 37 C9
  Glos 80 F2
  Hants 33 F9
  Lincs 189 C10
  N Yorks 214 F2
  S Ayrs 257 E9
  Som 27 B11
  Som 43 G7
Heathfield Village Oxon 83 B8
Heath Green Hants 48 F6
  Worcs 117 C11
Heathhall Dumfries 237 B11
Heath Hayes Staffs 151 G10
Heath Hill Shrops 150 G5
Heath House Som 44 D2
Heathlands Wokingham 65 F10
Heath Lanes Telford 150 E2
Heath Park London 68 B4
Heathrow Airport London 66 D5
Heath Side Kent 68 E4
Heathstock Devon 28 G2
Heathton Shrops 132 E6
Heathtop Derbys 152 C4
Heath Town W Mid 133 D8
Heathwaite Cumb 221 F8
  N Yorks 225 E9
Heatley Staffs 151 D11
  Warr 184 D2
Heaton Gtr Man 195 F7
  Lancs 211 G8
  Staffs 169 C7
  T&W 243 D7
  W Yorks 205 G8
Heaton Chapel Gtr Man 184 C5
Heaton Mersey Gtr Man 184 C5
Heaton Moor Gtr Man 184 C5
Heaton Norris Gtr Man 184 C5
Heaton Royds W Yorks 205 F8
Heaton's Bridge Lancs 194 E2
Heaton Shay W Yorks 205 F8
Heaven's Door Som 29 C10
Heaverham Kent 52 B5
Heaviley Gtr Man 184 D6
Heavitree Devon 14 C4
Hebburn T&W 243 E8
Hebburn Colliery T&W 243 D8
Hebburn New Town
  T&W 243 E8
Hebden N Yorks 213 G10
Hebden Bridge W Yorks 196 B3
Hebden Green Ches W 167 B10
Hebing End Herts 104 G6
Hebron Anglesey 179 E7
  Carms 92 F3
  Northumb 252 F5
Heck Dumfries 248 G3

Heckdyke N Lincs 188 B3
Heckfield Hants 65 G8
Heckfield Green Suff 126 B3
Heckfordbridge Essex 107 G8
Heckingham Norf 143 D7
Heckington Lincs 173 G10
Heckmondwike
W Yorks 197 C8
Heddington Wilts 62 F3
Heddington Wick Wilts 62 F3
Heddle Orkney 314 E3
Heddon Devon 25 B11
Heddon-on-the-Wall
Northumb 242 D4
Hedenham Norf 142 E6
Hedge End Dorset 30 F4
Hants 33 E7
Hedgehog Bridge Lincs 174 F3
Hedgerley Bucks 66 B3
Hedgerley Green Bucks 66 B3
Hedgerley Hill Bucks 66 B3
Hedging Som 28 B4
Hedley Hill Durham 233 C9
Hedley on the Hill
Northumb 242 F3
Hednesford Staffs 151 G9
Hedon E Yorks 201 B7
Hedsor Bucks 66 B2
Hedworth T&W 243 E8
Heelands M Keynes 102 D6
Heeley S Yorks 186 E5
Hegdon Hill Hereford 115 G11
Heggerscales Cumb 222 C6
Heggle Lane Cumb 230 D3
Heglibister Shetland 313 H5
Heighington Darl 233 G11
Lincs 173 B8
Heighley Staffs 168 F3
Height End Lancs 195 C9
Heightington Worcs 116 C5
Heights Gtr Man 196 F3
Heights of Brae Highld 300 C5
Heights of Kinlochewe
Highld 299 C10
Heilam Highld 308 C4
Heiton Borders 262 C6
Helbeck Cumb 222 B5
Hele Devon 12 C2
Devon 13 G10
Devon 27 G7
Devon 40 D4
Som 27 C11
Torbay 9 B8
Helebridge Corn 24 G2
Helensburgh Argyll 276 E5
Helford Corn 3 D7
Helford Passage Corn 3 D7
Helham Green Herts 86 B5
Helhoughton Norf 159 D7
Helions Bumpstead
Essex 106 C3
Hellaby S Yorks 187 C8
Helland Corn 11 G7
Som 28 C4
Hellandbridge Corn 11 G7
Hell Corner W Berks 63 G11
Hellesdon Norf 160 G4
Hellesveor Corn 2 A2
Hellidon W Nhants 119 F10
Hellifield N Yorks 204 B3
Hellifield Green
N Yorks 204 B3
Hellingly E Sus 23 C9
Hellington Norf 142 C6
Hellister Shetland 313 J5
Hellman's Cross Essex 87 B9
Helm Northumb 252 D5
N Yorks 223 G8
Helmburn Borders 261 E9
Helmdon W Nhants 101 C11
Helme W Yorks 196 E5
Helmingham Suff 126 F3
Helmington Row
Durham 233 D9
Helmsdale Highld 311 H4
Helmshore Lancs 195 C9
Helmside Cumb 212 B3
Helmsley N Yorks 216 C2
Helperby N Yorks 215 F8
Helperthorpe N Yorks 217 E9
Helpringham Lincs 173 G10
Helpston Pboro 138 B2
Helsby Ches W 183 F7
Helscott Corn 24 G2
Helsey Lincs 191 G8
Helston Corn 2 D5
Helstone Corn 11 E7
Helston Water Corn 4 G5
Helton Cumb 230 G6
Helwith Bridge N Yorks 212 F6
Helygain = Halkyn Flint 182 G2
Hemblington Norf 160 G6
Hemblington Corner
Norf 160 G6
Hembridge Som 44 F5
Hemel Hempstead Herts 85 D9
Hemerdon Devon 7 D11
Hemford Shrops 130 C6
Hem Heath Stoke 168 G5
Hemingbrough N Yorks 207 G9
Hemingby Lincs 190 G2
Hemingfield S Yorks 197 G11
Hemingford Abbots
Cambs 122 C5
Hemingford Grey
Cambs 122 C5
Hemingstone Suff 126 G3
Hemington Leics 153 D9
N Nhants 137 F11
Som 45 C8
Hemley Suff 108 C5
Hemlington Mbro 225 C10
Hemp Green Suff 127 D7
Hempholme E Yorks 209 C7
Hempnall Norf 142 E4
Hempnall Green Norf 142 E4
Hempriggs House
Highld 310 E7
Hemp's Green Essex 107 F8
Hempshill Vale Notts 171 G8
Hempstead Essex 106 D2
Medway 69 G9
Norf 160 B2
Norf 161 D8
Hempsted Glos 80 B4
Hempton Norf 159 D8
Oxon 101 E8
Hempton Wainhill Oxon 84 E3
Hemsby Norf 161 F9
Hemsted Kent 54 E6
Hemswell Lincs 188 C6
Hemswell Cliff Lincs 188 D6
Hemsworth Dorset 31 F7
S Yorks 186 E5
W Yorks 198 E2
Hemyock Devon 27 E10
Henaford Devon 24 D2
Hen Bentref Llandegfan
Anglesey 179 G9
Henbrook Worcs 117 D8
Henbury Bristol 60 D5
Ches E 184 G5
Dorset 18 B5
Hendomen Powys 130 D4
Hendon London 67 B8
T&W 243 F10
Hendra Corn 2 B6
Corn 2 C5
Corn 2 D3
Corn 2 F6
Corn 5 C9
Corn 5 D9
Corn 11 E7
Hendrabridge Corn 6 B5
Hendraburnick Corn 11 D8
Hendra Croft Corn 4 D5
Hendre Flint 165 B11
Gwyn 110 B2
Powys 129 D9
Hendre-ddu Conwy 164 B5
Hendredenny Park
Caerph 58 B6
Hendreforgan Rhondda 58 B3
Hendrerwydd Denb 165 C10
Hendrewen Swansea 75 D10
Hendy Carms 75 E9
Hendy-Gwyn Carms 74 B2
Hendy Gwyn = Whitland
Carms 73 B11
Hên-efail Denb 165 C9
Heneglwys Anglesey 178 F6
Hen-feddau fawr Pembs 92 E4
Henfield S Glos 61 D7
W Sus 36 D2
Henford Devon 12 C3
Henfords Marsh Wilts 45 E11
Henghurst Kent 54 F3
Hengoed Caerph 77 F10
Denb 165 D9
Powys 114 G4
Shrops 148 C5
Hengrave Norf 160 F2
Suff 124 D6
Hengrove Bristol 60 F6
Hengrove Park Bristol 60 F5
Henham Essex 105 F10
Heniarth Powys 130 B2
Henlade Som 28 C3
Henleaze Bristol 60 D5
Henley Dorset 29 G11
Glos 80 B6
Shrops 115 B10
Shrops 131 F9
Som 44 G2
Suff 126 G3
Wilts 47 B10
Wilts 61 F10
W Sus 34 B5
Henley Common W Sus 34 B5
Henley Green W Mid 135 G7
Henley-in-Arden Warks 118 D3
Henley-on-Thames Oxon 65 C9
Henley's Down E Sus 38 E2
Henley Street Kent 69 F7
Henllan Ceredig 93 C7
Denb 165 B8
Henllan Amgoed Carms 92 G3
Henlle Shrops 148 C6
Henllys Torf 78 G3
Henllys Vale Torf 78 G3
Henlow C Beds 104 D3
Hennock Devon 14 E2
Henny Street Essex 107 D7
Henryd Conwy 180 G3
Henry's Moat Pembs 91 F10
Hensall N Yorks 198 C5
Henshaw Northumb 241 E7
W Yorks 205 E10
Hensingham Cumb 219 B9
Hensington Oxon 83 B7
Henstead Suff 143 F9
Hensting Hants 33 C7
Henstridge Devon 40 E5
Som 30 D2
Henstridge Ash Som 30 C2
Henstridge Bowden
Som 29 C11
Henstridge Marsh Som 30 C2
Henton Oxon 84 E3
Som 44 D3
Henwood Corn 11 G11
Oxon 83 E7
Henwood Green Kent 52 E6
Heogan Shetland 313 J6
Heol-ddu Carms 75 E7
Swansea 56 B6
Heolgerrig M Tydf 77 D8
Heol-laethog Bridgend 58 C2
Heol-las Bridgend 58 C2
Swansea 57 B7
Heol Senni Powys 95 G8
Heol-y-gaer Powys 96 D3
Heol-y-mynydd V Glam 57 G11
Hepburn Northumb 264 E3
Hepple Northumb 251 C11
Hepscott Northumb 252 G6
Hepthorne Lane Derbys 170 C6
Heptonstall W Yorks 196 B3
Hepworth Suff 125 C9
W Yorks 197 F7
Herbrandston Pembs 72 D5
Hereford Hereford 97 C10
Heribusta Highld 298 B4
Heriot Borders 271 E7
Hermiston Edin 280 G3
Hermitage Borders 250 D2
Dorset 29 F10
W Berks 64 E4
W Sus 22 B3
Hermitage Green Mers 183 C10
Hermit Hill S Yorks 197 G10
Hermit Hole W Yorks 205 F7
Hermon Anglesey 162 B5
Carms 93 E7
Carms 94 F3
Pembs 92 E4
Herne Kent 71 F7
Herne Bay Kent 71 F7
Herne Common Kent 71 F7
Herne Hill London 67 E10
Herne Pound Kent 53 C7
Herner Devon 25 B9
Hernhill Kent 70 G5
Herniss Corn 2 C6
Herodsfoot Corn 6 C4
Heron Cross Stoke 168 G5
Heronden Kent 55 C9
Herongate Essex 87 G10
Heronsford S Ayrs 244 G4
Heronsgate Herts 85 G8
Heron's Ghyll E Sus 37 B7
Herons Green Bath 44 B5
Heronston Bridgend 58 D2
Herra Shetland 312 D8
Herriard Hants 49 D7
Herringfleet Suff 143 D9
Herring's Green
Bedford 103 C11
Herringswell Suff 124 C4
Herringthorpe S Yorks 186 C6
Hersden Kent 71 G8
Hersham Corn 24 F3
Sur 66 G6
Herstmonceux E Sus 23 C10
Herston Dorset 18 F6
Orkney 314 G4
Hertford Herts 86 C4
Hertford Heath Herts 86 C4
Hertingfordbury Herts 86 C4
Hesketh Bank Lancs 194 C2
Hesketh Lane Lancs 203 E8
Hesketh Moss Lancs 194 C2
Hesket Newmarket
Cumb 230 D2
Heskin Green Lancs 194 D4
Hesleden Durham 234 D4
Hesleyside Northumb 251 G8
Heslington York 207 C8
Hessay York 206 C6
Hessenford Corn 6 D6
Hessett Suff 125 E8
Hessle E Yorks 200 B4
W Yorks 198 D2
Hest Bank Lancs 211 F9
Hester's Way Glos 99 G8
Hestinsetter Shetland 313 J4
Heston London 66 D6
Hestwall Orkney 314 E2
Heswall Mers 182 E3
Hethe Oxon 101 F11
Hethel Norf 142 C3
Hethelpit Cross Glos 98 F5
Hethersett Norf 142 C3
Hethersgill Cumb 239 D11
Hetherside Cumb 239 D10
Hetherson Green
Ches W 167 F8
Hethpool Northumb 263 D9
Hett Durham 233 D11
Hetton N Yorks 204 B5
Hetton Downs T&W 234 B3
Hetton-le-Hill T&W 234 B3
Hetton-le-Hole T&W 234 B3
Hetton Steads Northumb 264 B2
Heugh Northumb 242 C3
Heugh-head Aberds 292 B5
Heveningham Suff 126 C6
Hever Kent 52 E3
Heversham Cumb 211 C9
Hevingham Norf 160 E3
Hewas Water Corn 5 F9
Hewelsfield Glos 79 E9
Hewelsfield Common
Glos 79 E8
Hewer Hill Cumb 230 D3
Hew Green N Yorks 205 B10
Hewish N Som 60 G2
Som 28 F6
Hewood Dorset 28 G5
Heworth T&W 243 E7
York 207 C8
Hexham Northumb 241 E10
Hextable Kent 68 E4
Hexthorpe S Yorks 198 G5
Hexton Herts 104 E2
Hexworthy Devon 13 G9
Hey Lancs 204 E3
Heybridge Essex 87 F10
Essex 88 D5
Heybridge Basin Essex 88 D5
Heybrook Bay Devon 7 F10
Heydon Cambs 105 C8
Norf 160 D2
Heydour Lincs 155 B10
Heyford Park Oxon 101 F10
Hey Green W Yorks 196 E4
Heyheads Gtr Man 196 G3
Hey Houses Lancs 193 B10
Heylipol Argyll 288 E1
Heylor Shetland 312 E4
Heyope Powys 114 C4
Heyrod Gtr Man 185 B7
Heysham Lancs 211 G8
Heyshaw N Yorks 214 G3
Heyshott W Sus 34 D5
Heyshott Green W Sus 34 D5
Heyside Gtr Man 196 F2
Heytesbury Wilts 46 E2
Heythrop Oxon 101 F7
Heywood Gtr Man 195 E11
Wilts 45 C11
Hibaldstow N Lincs 200 G3
Hibb's Green Suff 125 G7
Hickford Hill Essex 106 C5
Hickleton S Yorks 198 F3
Hickling Norf 161 E8
Notts 154 D3
Hickling Green Norf 161 E8
Hickling Heath Norf 161 E8
Hickling Pastures Notts 154 D3
Hickmans Green Kent 54 B5
Hicks Forstal Kent 71 G7
Hicks Gate Bath 60 F6
Hick's Mill Corn 4 G5
Hickstead W Sus 36 C3
Hidcote Bartrim Glos 100 C3
Hidcote Boyce Glos 100 C3
Hifnal Shrops 132 D4
Higginshaw Gtr Man 196 F2
High Ackworth W Yorks 198 D2
Higham Derbys 170 D5
Fife 286 F6
Kent 69 E8
Lancs 204 F2
Suff 107 D10
Suff 124 E4
S Yorks 197 F10
Higham Common
S Yorks 197 F10
Higham Dykes
Northumb 242 B4
Higham Ferrers
N Nhants 121 D9
Higham Gobion C Beds 104 E2
Higham Hill London 86 G5
Higham on the Hill
Leics 135 D7
Highampton Devon 25 G7
Highams Park London 86 G5
Higham Wood Kent 52 D5
High Angerton Northumb 252 F3
High Bankhill Cumb 231 C7
High Banton N Lanark 278 E4
High Barn Lincs 174 C5
High Barnes T&W 243 F9
High Barnet London 86 F2
High Beach Essex 86 F6
High Bentham N Yorks 212 F3
High Bickington Devon 25 C10
High Biggins Cumb 212 D2
High Birkwith N Yorks 212 D5
High Birstwith N Yorks 205 B10
High Blantyre S Lanark 268 D3
High Bonnybridge Falk 278 F6
High Bradfield S Yorks 186 C3
High Bradley N Yorks 204 D6
High Bray Devon 41 G7
Highbridge Cumb 230 C3
Hants 33 C7
Highld 290 E3
Som 43 D10
Highbridge *continued*
W Mid 133 C10
Highbrook W Sus 51 G11
High Brooms Kent 52 E5
High Brotheridge Glos 80 C5
High Bullen Devon 25 C8
Highburton W Yorks 197 E7
Highbury London 67 B10
Ptsmth 33 G11
Som 45 D7
Highbury Vale
Nottingham 171 G8
High Buston Northumb 252 B6
High Callerton
Northumb 242 C5
High Cark Cumb 211 C7
High Casterton Cumb 212 D2
High Catton E Yorks 207 C10
High Church Northumb 252 F5
Highclere Hants 64 G2
Highcliffe BCP 19 C10
Derbys 186 F2
High Cogges Oxon 82 D5
High Common Norf 141 B9
High Coniscliffe Darl 224 B4
High Crompton Gtr Man 196 F2
High Cross Cambs 123 F8
Corn 2 D6
E Sus 37 B9
Hants 34 B2
Herts 85 F10
Herts 86 B5
Newport 59 B9
Warks 118 D3
W Sus 36 D2
High Crosshill S Lanark 268 C2
High Cunsey Cumb 221 G7
High Dubmire T&W 234 B2
High Dyke Durham 232 F5
High Easter Essex 87 C10
High Eggborough
N Yorks 198 C5
High Eldrig Dumfries 236 C4
High Ellington N Yorks 214 C3
Higher Alham Som 45 E7
Higher Ansty Dorset 30 G3
Higher Ashton Devon 14 E3
Higher Audley Blackburn 195 B7
Higher Bal Corn 4 E4
Higher Ballam Lancs 202 G3
Higher Bartle Lancs 202 G6
Higher Bebington Mers 182 D4
Higher Berry End
C Beds 103 E9
Higher Blackley
Gtr Man 195 G10
Higher Boarshaw
Gtr Man 195 F11
Higher Bockhampton
Dorset 17 C10
Higher Bojewyan Corn 1 C3
Higher Boscaswell Corn 1 C3
Higher Brixham Torbay 9 D8
Higher Broughton
Gtr Man 195 G10
Higher Burrow Som 28 C6
Higher Burwardsley
Ches W 167 D8
High Ercall Telford 149 F11
Higher Chalmington
Dorset 29 G9
Higher Cheriton Devon 27 G10
Higher Chillington Som 28 E5
Higher Chisworth
Derbys 185 C7
Highercliff Corn 6 D4
Higher Clovelly Devon 24 C4
Higher Condurrow Corn 2 B5
Higher Crackington Corn 11 B9
Higher Cransworth Corn 5 B9
Higher Croft Blackburn 195 B7
Higher Denham Bucks 66 B4
Higher Dinting Derbys 185 C8
Higher Disley Ches E 185 E7
Higher Downs Corn 2 C3
Higher Durston Som 28 B3
Higher End Gtr Man 194 G4
Higher Folds Gtr Man 195 G7
Higherford Lancs 204 E3
Higher Gabwell Torbay 9 B8
Higher Green Gtr Man 195 G8
Higher Halstock Leigh
Dorset 29 F8
Higher Heysham Lancs 211 G8
Higher Hogshead
Lancs 195 C11
Higher Holton Som 29 B11
Higher Hurdsfield
Ches E 184 G6
Higher Kingcombe
Dorset 16 B6
Higher Kinnerton Flint 166 C4
Higher Land Corn 12 G3
Higher Marsh Som 30 C2
Higher Melcombe Dorset 30 G2
Higher Menadew Corn 5 D10
Higher Molland Devon 41 G8
Higher Muddiford Devon 40 F5
Higher Nyland Dorset 30 C2
Higher Penwortham
Lancs 194 B4
Higher Pertwood Wilts 45 F11
Higher Porthpean Corn 5 E10
Higher Poynton Ches E 184 E6
Higher Prestacott Devon 12 B3
Higher Rads End
C Beds 103 E9
Higher Ridge Shrops 149 C7
Higher Rocombe Barton
Devon 9 B8
Higher Row Dorset 31 G8
Higher Runcorn Halton 183 E8
Higher Sandford
Dorset 29 C10
Higher Shotton Flint 166 B4
Higher Shurlach
Ches W 183 G11
Higher Slade Devon 40 D4
Higher Street Som 42 E6
Higher Tale Devon 27 G9
Higher Tolcarne Corn 5 B7
Higher Totnell Dorset 29 F10
Highertown Corn 4 G6
Corn 11 E8
Higher Town Corn 5 C10
Scilly 1 F4
Som 42 D3
Higher Tremarcoombe
Corn 6 B5
Higher Vexford Som 42 F6
Higher Walreddon Devon 12 G5
Higher Walton Lancs 194 B5
Warr 183 D9
Higher Wambrook Som 28 F3
Higher Warcombe Devon 40 D3
Higher Weaver Devon 27 G9
Higher Whatcombe
Dorset 30 G4
Higher Wheelton Lancs 194 C6
Higher Whitley
Ches W 183 E10
Higher Wincham
Ches W 183 F11
Higher Woodsford
Dorset 17 D11
Higher Wraxall Dorset 29 G9
Higher Wych Ches W 167 G7
High Etherley Durham 233 F9
High Ferry Lincs 174 F5
Highfield E Yorks 207 F10
Glos 79 E10
Gtr Man 194 G5
Gtr Man 195 F8
Herts 85 D9
N Ayrs 266 E6
Oxon 101 G11
Soton 32 E6
S Yorks 186 D5
T&W 242 F4
High Field Lancs 203 C10
Highfields Cambs 123 F7
Derbys 170 B6
Essex 88 B5
Glos 80 F3
Leicester 136 C2
Northumb 273 E9
Staffs 151 E8
S Yorks 198 F4
High Flatts W Yorks 197 F8
High Forge Durham 242 G6
High Friarside Durham 242 F5
High Gallowhill E Dunb 278 G2
High Garrett Essex 106 F5
Highgate E Sus 52 G2
Kent 53 G9
London 67 B9
Powys 130 D2
S Yorks 198 G3
W Mid 133 F11
High Grange Durham 233 E9
High Grantley N Yorks 214 F4
High Green Cumb 221 E8
Norf 141 B8
Norf 142 B2
Norf 159 G8
Shrops 132 G4
Suff 125 E7
S Yorks 186 B4
Worcs 99 B7
W Yorks 197 E7
High Halden Kent 53 F11
High Halstow Medway 69 D9
High Ham Som 44 G2
High Handenhold
Durham 242 G6
High Harrington Cumb 228 F6
High Harrogate N Yorks 206 B2
High Haswell Durham 234 C3
High Hatton Shrops 150 E2
High Hauxley Northumb 253 C7
High Hawsker N Yorks 227 D8
High Heath Shrops 150 D3
W Mid 133 C10
High Hesket Cumb 230 C5
High Hesleden Durham 234 D5
High Hill Cumb 229 G11
High Houses Essex 87 C11
High Hoyland S Yorks 197 E9
High Hunsley E Yorks 208 F4
High Hurstwood E Sus 37 B7
High Hutton N Yorks 216 F5
High Ireby Cumb 229 D10
High Kelling Norf 177 E10
High Kilburn N Yorks 215 D10
High Lands Durham 233 F8
Highlane Ches E 168 B5
Derbys 186 E6
High Lane Gtr Man 185 D7
Worcs 116 E3
Highlanes Corn 10 G4
Staffs 150 C5
High Lanes Corn 2 B3
High Laver Essex 87 D8
Highlaws Cumb 229 B8
Highleadon Glos 98 G5
High Legh Ches E 184 E2
Highleigh W Sus 22 D4
High Leven Stockton 225 C8
Highley Shrops 132 G4
High Littleton Bath 44 B6
High Longthwaite
Cumb 229 B11
High Lorton Cumb 229 F9
High Marishes N Yorks 216 D6
High Marnham Notts 188 G4
High Melton S Yorks 198 G4
High Mickley Northumb 242 E3
High Mindork Dumfries 236 D5
Highmoor Cumb 229 B11
Oxon 65 B8
High Moor Derbys 187 E7
Lancs 194 E4
Highmoor Cross Oxon 65 C8
Highmoor Hill Mon 60 B3
High Moorsley T&W 234 B2
Highnam Glos 80 B3
Highnam Green Glos 98 G5
High Nash Glos 79 C9
High Newton Cumb 211 C8
High Newton-by-the-Sea
Northumb 264 D6
High Nibthwaite Cumb 210 B5
Highoak Norf 141 C11
High Oaks Cumb 222 G2
High Offley Staffs 150 D5
High Ongar Essex 87 E9
High Onn Staffs 150 F6
High Onn Wharf Staffs 150 F6
High Park Cumb 221 G10
Mers 193 D11
Highridge Bristol 60 F5
High Risby N Lincs 200 E2
Highroad Well Moor
W Yorks 196 B5
High Roding Essex 87 B10
High Rougham Suff 125 E8
High Row Cumb 230 D3
Cumb 230 G3
High Salvington W Sus 35 F10
High Scales Cumb 229 B9
High Sellafield Cumb 219 E10
High Shaw N Yorks 223 G7
High Shields T&W 243 D9
High Shincliffe Durham 233 C11
High Side Cumb 229 E10
High Southwick T&W 243 F9
High Spen T&W 242 F4
High Stakesby N Yorks 227 C7
Highstead Kent 71 F8
Highsted Kent 70 G2
High Stoop Durham 233 C8
Highstreet Kent 70 G5
High Street Corn 5 E9
Kent 53 G8
Pembs 73 B11
Suff 107 B7
Suff 127 C8
Suff 127 F8
Suff 143 G7
Highstreet Green Essex 106 E5
Sur 50 F3
High Street Green Suff 125 F10
High Sunderland
Borders 261 C11
Hightae Dumfries 238 B3
Highter's Heath W Mid 117 B11
High Throston Hrtlpl 234 E5
High Tirfergus Argyll 255 F7
Hightown Ches E 168 C5
Hants 31 G11
Mers 193 G10
Soton 33 E7
Wrex 166 F4
W Yorks 197 C7
High Town Luton 103 G11
Shrops 132 E4
Staffs 151 G9
Hightown Green Suff 125 F9
Hightown Heights
W Yorks 197 C7
High Toynton Lincs 174 B3
High Trewhitt Northumb 252 B2
High Urpeth Durham 242 G6
High Valleyfield Fife 279 D10
High Walton Cumb 219 C9
High Warden Northumb 241 D10
High Water Head Cumb 220 F6
Highway Corn 4 G4
Hereford 97 B9
Som 29 C7
Wilts 62 E4
Windsor 65 C11
Highweek Devon 14 G2
High Westwood Durham 242 F4
High Whinnow Cumb 239 G8
Highwood Devon 27 F10
Dorset 18 D3
Essex 87 E10
Hants 31 F11
Worcs 116 D3
Highwood Hill London 86 G2
High Woolaston Glos 79 F9
High Worsall N Yorks 225 D7
Highworth Swindon 82 G2
Highworthy Devon 24 F6
High Wray Cumb 221 F7
High Wych Herts 87 C7
High Wycombe Bucks 84 G5
Hilborough Norf 140 C6
Hilborough Ho Norf 140 C6
Hilcot Glos 81 B7
Hilcote Derbys 171 D7
Hilcot End Glos 81 E9
Hilcott Wilts 46 B6
Hildenborough Kent 52 D5
Hilden Park Kent 52 D5
Hildersham Cambs 105 B10
Hildersley Hereford 98 G2
Hilderstone Staffs 151 C8
Hilderthorpe E Yorks 218 F3
Hilfield Dorset 29 F10
Hilgay Norf 140 D2
Hill S Glos 79 G10
Warks 119 D9
W Mid 134 D2
Hillam N Yorks 198 B4
Hillbeck Cumb 222 B5
Hillblock Pembs 73 B8
Hillborough Kent 71 F8
Hill Bottom Oxon 64 D6
Hillbourne BCP 18 C6
Hillbrae Aberds 302 E6
Aberds 303 G7
Hill Brow W Sus 34 B3
Hillbutts Dorset 31 G7
Hill Chorlton Staffs 150 B5
Hillcliffe Warr 183 D10
Hillcliffane Derbys 170 F3
Hillcommon Som 27 B11
Hill Common Norf 161 E8
Hill Corner Som 45 D10
Hill Croome Worcs 99 C7
Hillcross Derbys 152 C6
Hill Dale Lancs 194 E3
Hill Deverill Wilts 45 E11
Hilldyke Lincs 174 F4
Hill Dyke Lincs 174 F4
Hillend Fife 280 E2
N Lanark 268 B6
N Som 43 B11
Shrops 132 E6
Swansea 56 C2
Hill End Durham 232 D6
Fife 279 B10
Glos 99 D8
London 85 G8
N Yorks 205 C7
Som 29 E8
Worcs 117 E8
Hillend Green Glos 98 F4
Hillersland Glos 79 C9
Hillerton Devon 13 B10
Hillesden Bucks 102 F3
Hillesden Hamlet Bucks 102 E3
Hillesley Glos 61 B9
Hillfarance Som 27 C11
Hillfarrance Som 27 C11
Hillfield Devon 8 E6
W Mid 118 B2
Hillfields S Glos 60 D6
W Mid 118 B6
Hillfoot Aberds 303 D9
W Yorks 205 G10
Hillfoot End C Beds 104 E2
Hill Furze Worcs 99 B9
Hill Gate Hereford 97 F9
Hillgreen W Berks 64 D3
Hill Green Essex 105 E9
Kent 69 G10
Hillgrove W Sus 34 B6
Hillhampton Hereford 97 B11
Hillhead Aberds 302 F5
Aberds 303 G8
Corn 5 C11
Devon 9 E8
E Ayrs 257 B10
S Ayrs 257 F10
Hill Head Hants 33 G8
Northumb 241 D10
Hillhead of Auchentumb
Aberds 303 D9
Hillhead of Blairy
Aberds 302 D6
Hillhead of Cocklaw
Aberds 303 E10
Hill Hoath Kent 52 E3
Hill Hook W Mid 134 C2
Hillhouse Borders 271 D10
Hill Houses Shrops 116 B2
Hilliard's Cross Staffs 152 G3
Hilliclay Highld 310 C5
Hillingdon London 66 C5
Hillingdon Heath London 66 C5
Hillington Glasgow 267 C10
Norf 158 D4
Hillis Corner IoW 20 C5
Hillmoor Devon 27 E10
Hillmorton Warks 119 C10
Hill Mountain Pembs 73 D7
Hillockhead Aberds 292 B6
Aberds 292 C5
Hillock Vale Lancs 195 B9
Hill of Beath Fife 280 C3
Hill of Drip Stirling 278 B5
Hill of Fearn Highld 301 B8
Hill of Keillor Angus 286 C6
Hill of Mountblairy
Aberds 302 D6
Hill of Overbrae Aberds 303 C8
Hill Park Hants 33 F9
Kent 52 B2
Hillpool Worcs 117 B7
Hillpound Hants 33 D9
Hill Ridware Staffs 151 F11
Hillsborough S Yorks 186 C4
Hillside Aberds 293 D11
Angus 293 G9
Devon 8 C4
Devon 27 F11
Hants 49 C9
Mers 193 E10
Orkney 314 D3
Orkney 314 G4
Shetland 313 G6
Shrops 131 F11
Wilts 81 G9
Hill Side Hants 34 B3
S Yorks 197 G8
Worcs 116 E5
W Yorks 197 D7
Hill Somersal Derbys 152 C2
Hills Town Derbys 171 B7
Hillstreet Hants 32 D4
Hill Street Kent 54 D6
Hillswick Shetland 312 F4
Hilltop Bl Gwent 77 D11
Bucks 85 E7
Derbys 170 C4
Hill Top Derbys 186 F5
Durham 232 G5
Durham 233 C10
Durham 242 G5
Gtr Man 195 G8
Hants 32 G6
Notts 171 F7
N Yorks 214 G3
N Yorks 214 G5
Staffs 133 B7
S Yorks 186 C5
S Yorks 186 D3
S Yorks 187 B7
S Yorks 197 F9
Warks 134 E5
Warks 135 E7
W Mid 133 E9
W Sus 34 C5
W Yorks 196 E5
W Yorks 197 D10
W Yorks 205 G7
W Yorks 205 G11
Hillview T&W 243 G9
Hill View Dorset 18 B5
Hillway IoW 21 D8
Hillwell Shetland 313 M5
Hill Wood W Mid 134 C2
Hill Wootton Warks 118 D6
Hillyfields Hants 32 D5
Hilmarton Wilts 62 D4
Hilperton Wilts 45 B11
Hilperton Marsh Wilts 45 B11
Hilsea Ptsmth 33 G11
Hilston E Yorks 209 G11
Hiltingbury Hants 32 C6
Hilton Aberds 303 F9
Borders 273 E7
Cambs 122 D5
Cumb 231 G10
Derbys 152 C4
Dorset 30 G3
Durham 233 G9
Highld 309 L7
Highld 311 L3
Shrops 132 D5
Staffs 133 B11
Stockton 225 C9
Hilton House Gtr Man 194 F6
Hilton Lodge Highld 300 G2
Hilton of Cadboll Highld 301 B8
Hilton Park Gtr Man 195 G10
Himbleton Worcs 117 F8
Himley Staffs 133 E7
Hincaster Cumb 211 C10
Hinchley Wood Sur 67 F7
Hinchliffe Mill W Yorks 196 F6
Hinchwick Glos 100 E2
Hinckley Leics 135 E8
Hinderclay Suff 125 B10
Hinderton Ches W 182 F4
Hinderwell N Yorks 226 B5
Hindford Shrops 148 C6
Hindhead Sur 49 F11
Hindle Fold Lancs 203 G10
Hindley Gtr Man 194 G6
Northumb 242 F2
Hindley Green Gtr Man 194 G6
Hindlip Worcs 117 F7
Hindolveston Norf 159 D10
Hindon Wilts 46 G2
Hindpool Cumb 210 F3
Hindringham Norf 159 B9
Hindsford Gtr Man 195 G7
Hingham Norf 141 C10
Hinstock Shrops 150 D3
Hintlesham Suff 107 C11
Hinton Glos 79 E11
Hants 19 B10
Hereford 96 D6
S Glos 61 D8
Shrops 131 B8
Som 29 C9
W Nhants 119 G10
Hinton Ampner Hants 33 B9
Hinton Blewett Bath 44 B5
Hinton Charterhouse
Bath 45 B9
Hinton Cross Worcs 99 C10
Hinton-in-the-Hedges
W Nhants 101 D11
Hinton Martell Dorset 31 F8
Hinton on the Green
Worcs 99 C10
Hinton Parva Dorset 31 G7
Swindon 63 C8
Hinton St George Som 28 E6
Hinton St Mary Dorset 30 D3
Hinton Waldrist Oxon 82 F5
Hints Shrops 116 C2
Staffs 134 C3
Hinwick Bedford 121 E8
Hinwood Shrops 131 B7
Hinxhill Kent 54 E5
Hinxton Cambs 105 B9
Hinxworth Herts 104 C4
Hipperholme W Yorks 196 B6
Hipplecote Worcs 116 F4
Hipsburn Northumb 264 G6
Hipswell N Yorks 224 F3
Hirael Gwyn 179 G9
Hiraeth Carms 92 G3
Hirn Aberds 293 C9
Hirnant Powys 147 E11
Hirst N Lanark 269 C7
Northumb 253 F7
Hirst Courtney N Yorks 198 C6
Hirwaen Denb 165 C10
Hirwaun Rhondda 77 D7
Hirwaun Common
Bridgend 58 C2
Hiscott Devon 25 B8
Hislop Borders 249 C9
Hismley Wilts 45 D11
Histon Cambs 123 E8
Hitcham Suff 125 G9
Hitchill Dumfries 238 D4
Hitchin Herts 104 F3
Hitchin Hill Herts 104 F3
Hitcombe Bottom Wilts 45 E10
Hither Green London 67 E11
Hittisleigh Devon 13 C10
Hittisleigh Barton Devon 13 B10
Hive E Yorks 208 G2
Hixon Staffs 151 D10
Hoaden Kent 55 B9
Hoar Cross Staffs 152 E2
Hoarwithy Hereford 97 F10
Hoath Kent 71 G8
Hoath Corner Kent 52 E3
Hobarris Shrops 114 B6
Hobbister Orkney 314 F3
Hobble End Staffs 133 B10
Hobbles Green Suff 124 G4
Hobbs Cross Essex 87 C7
Essex 87 F7
Hobbs Wall Bath 61 G7
Hob Hill Ches W 167 E7
Hobkirk Borders 262 G3
Hobroyd Derbys 185 C8
Hobson Durham 242 F5
Hoby Leics 154 F3
Hoccombe Som 27 B10
Hockenden London 68 F3
Hockerill Herts 105 G9
Hockering Norf 159 G11
Hockering Heath Norf 159 G11
Hockerton Notts 172 D2
Hockholler Som 27 C11
Hockholler Green Som 27 C11
Hockley Ches E 184 E6
Essex 88 G4
Kent 54 B3
Staffs 134 C4
W Mid 118 B5
Hockley Heath W Mid 118 C3
Hockliffe C Beds 103 F9
Hockwold cum Wilton
Norf 140 F4
Hockworthy Devon 27 D8
Hocombe Hants 32 C6
Hoddesdon Herts 86 D5
Hoddlesden Blackburn 195 C8
Hoddomcross Dumfries 238 C5
Hoddom Mains Dumfries 238 C5
Hoden Worcs 99 B11
Hodgefield Staffs 168 E6
Hodgehill Ches E 168 B4
W Mid 134 F2
Hodgeston Pembs 73 F8
Hodley Powys 130 E3
Hodnet Shrops 150 D2
Hodnetheath Shrops 150 D2
Hodsock Notts 187 D10
Hodsoll Street Kent 68 G6
Hodson Swindon 63 C7
Hodthorpe Derbys 187 F8
Hoe Hants 33 D9
Norf 159 F9
Sur 50 D5
Hoe Benham W Berks 64 F2
Hoe Gate Hants 33 E10
Hoff Cumb 222 B3
Hoffleet Stow Lincs 156 B4
Hogaland Shetland 312 F5
Hogben's Hill Kent 54 B4
Hogganfield Glasgow 268 B2
Hoggard's Green Suff 125 F7
Hoggeston Bucks 102 G6
Hoggington Wilts 45 B10
Hoggrill's End Warks 134 E4
Hogha Gearraidh
W Isles 296 D3
Hog Hatch Sur 49 D10
Hoghton Lancs 194 B6
Hoghton Bottoms Lancs 194 B6
Hogley Green W Yorks 196 F6
Hognaston Derbys 170 E2
Hogpits Bottom Herts 85 E8
Hogsthorpe Lincs 191 G8
Hogstock Dorset 31 F7
Holbeach Lincs 157 E7
Holbeach Bank Lincs 157 D7
Holbeach Clough Lincs 156 D6
Holbeach Drove Lincs 156 G6
Holbeache Worcs 116 B5
Holbeach Hurn Lincs 157 D7
Holbeach St Johns
Lincs 156 F6
Holbeach St Marks
Lincs 157 C7
Holbeach St Matthew
Lincs 157 C8
Holbeck Notts 187 G8
W Yorks 205 G11
Holbeck Woodhouse
Notts 187 G8
Holberrow Green
Worcs 117 F10
Holbeton Devon 8 E2
Holborn London 67 C10
Holborough Kent 69 G8
Holbrook Derbys 170 G5
Suff 108 D3
S Yorks 186 E6
Holbrook Common
S Glos 61 E7
Holbrook Moor Derbys 170 F5
Holbrooks W Mid 134 G6
Holburn Northumb 264 B2
Holbury Hants 32 G6
Holcombe Devon 14 G5
Gtr Man 195 D9
Som 45 D7
Holcombe Brook
Gtr Man 195 E9
Holcombe Rogus Devon 27 D9
Holcot W Nhants 120 D5
Holdbrook London 86 F5
Holden Lancs 203 D11
Holdenby W Nhants 120 D3
Holden Fold Gtr Man 196 F2
Holdenhurst BCP 19 B8
Holder's Green Essex 106 F2
Holders Hill London 86 G2
Holdfast Worcs 99 D7
Holdgate Shrops 131 F11
Holdingham Lincs 173 F9
Holditch Dorset 28 G4
Holdsworth W Yorks 196 B5
Holdworth S Yorks 186 C3
Hole Devon 24 D4
W Yorks 204 F6
Hole Bottom W Yorks 196 C2
Holefield Borders 263 C8
Holehills N Lanark 268 B5
Holehouse Derbys 185 C8
Holehouses Ches E 184 F2

Hole-in-the-Wall
Hereford 98 F2
Holemill Aberdeen 293 C10
Holemoor Devon 24 F6
Hole's Hole Devon 7 B8
Holestane Dumfries 247 D9
Holestone Derbys 170 C4
Hole Street W Sus 35 E10
Holewater Devon 41 F8
Holford Som 43 E7
Holgate York 207 C7
Holker Cumb 211 D7
Holkham Norf 176 E5
Hollacombe Devon 24 G5
Devon 26 G4
Hollacombe Hill Devon 7 E10
Holland Orkney 314 A4
Orkney 314 D6
Sur 52 C2
Holland Fen Lincs 174 F2
Holland Lees Lancs 194 F4
Holland-on-Sea Essex 89 B12
Hollands Som 29 D9
Hollandstoun Orkney 314 A7
Hollee Dumfries 239 D7
Hollesley Suff 109 C7
Hollicombe Torbay 9 C7
Hollies Common Staffs 150 E6
Hollinfare Warr 183 C11
Hollingbourne Kent 53 B10
Hollingbury Brighton 36 F4
Hollingdean Brighton 36 F4
Hollingdon Bucks 103 F7
Hollingrove E Sus 37 C11
Hollingthorpe W Yorks 197 D10
Hollington Derbys 152 B4
E Sus 38 E3
Hants 48 B2
Staffs 151 B11
Hollington Cross Hants 48 B2
Hollington Grove
Derbys 152 B4
Hollingwood Derbys 186 G6
Hollingworth Gtr Man 185 B8
Hollin Hall Lancs 204 F4
Hollin Park W Yorks 206 F2
Hollins Cumb 222 G3
Derbys 186 G4
Gtr Man 195 F8
Gtr Man 195 F10
Gtr Man 195 F11
Staffs 168 D6
Staffs 168 E4
Staffs 169 F7
Hollinsclough Staffs 169 B9
Hollins End S Yorks 186 E5
Hollinsgreen Ches E 168 C2
Hollins Green Warr 183 C11
Hollins Lane Lancs 202 C5
Shrops 149 B10
Hollinswood Telford 132 B4
Hollinthorpe W Yorks 206 G3
Hollinwood Gtr Man 196 G2
Shrops 149 B10
Hollis Green Devon 27 F9
Hollis Head Devon 27 G7
Hollocombe Devon 25 E10
Hollocombe Town
Devon 25 E10
Holloway Derbys 170 D4
Wilts 45 G11
Windsor 65 C10
Holloway Hill Sur 50 E3
Hollow Brook Bath 60 G5
Hollowell W Nhants 120 C3
Hollow Meadows
S Yorks 186 D2
Hollowmoor Heath
Ches W 167 B7
Hollow Oak Dorset 18 C2
Hollows Dumfries 239 B9
Hollow Street Kent 71 G8
Holly Bank W Mid 133 C11
Hollyberry End W Mid 134 G5
Holly Brook Som 44 D4
Hollybush Caerph 77 E11
E Ayrs 257 G9
Stoke 168 G5
Torf 78 G3
Worcs 98 D5
Holly Bush Wrex 166 G6
Hollybush Corner Bucks 66 B3
Suff 125 F8
Hollybushes Kent 54 B2
Hollybush Hill Bucks 66 C3
Essex 89 B10
Hollycroft Leics 135 E8
Holly Cross Windsor 65 C10
Holly End Norf 139 B9
Holly Green Bucks 84 E3
Worcs 99 C7
Holly Hill N Yorks 224 E3
Hollyhurst Shrops 131 D9
Warks 135 F7
Hollym E Yorks 201 B10
Hollywaste Shrops 116 B2
Hollywater Hants 49 G10
Hollywood Worcs 117 B11
Holmacott Devon 25 B8
Holman Clavel Som 28 D2
Holmbridge W Yorks 196 F6
Holmbury St Mary Sur 50 E6
Holmbush Corn 5 E10
Dorset 28 G5
Holmcroft Staffs 151 D8
Holme Cambs 138 F3
C Beds 104 C3
Cumb 211 D10
N Lincs 200 F2
Notts 172 D4
N Yorks 215 C7
W Yorks 196 F6
W Yorks 205 G9
Holmebridge Dorset 18 D3
Holme Chapel Lancs 195 B11
Holme Green C Beds 104 C3
N Yorks 207 E7
Wokingham 65 F10
Holme Hale Norf 141 B7
Holme Hill NE Lincs 201 F9
Holme Lacy Hereford 97 D11
Holme Lane Notts 154 B2
Holme Marsh Hereford 114 G6
Holme Mills Cumb 211 D10
Holme next the Sea
Norf 176 E2
Holme-on-Spalding-Moor
E Yorks 208 F2
Holme on the Wolds
E Yorks 208 D5
Holme Pierrepont Notts 154 B2
Holmer Hereford 97 C10
Holmer Green Bucks 84 F6
Holmes Lancs 194 D2
Holme St Cuthbert
Cumb 229 B8
Holmes Chapel Ches E 168 B3
Holmesdale Derbys 186 F5
Holmesfield Derbys 186 F4
Holme Slack Lancs 203 G7
Holmes's Hill E Sus 23 C8
Holmeswood Lancs 194 D2
Holmethorpe Sur 51 C9
Holmewood Derbys 170 B6
Holme Wood W Yorks 205 G9
Holmfield W Yorks 196 B5
Holmfirth W Yorks 196 F6
Holmhead Angus 293 F7
Dumfries 246 F6
E Ayrs 258 E3
Holmhill Dumfries 247 D9
Holmisdale Highld 297 G7
Holmley Common
Derbys 186 F5
Holmpton E Yorks 201 C11
Holmrook Cumb 219 F11
Holmsgarth Shetland 313 J6
Holmside Durham 233 B10
Holmsleigh Green Devon 28 G2
Holmston S Ayrs 257 E9
Holmwood Corner Sur 51 E7
Holmwrangle Cumb 230 B6
Holne Devon 8 B4
Holnest Dorset 29 E11
Holnicote Som 42 D2
Holsworthy Devon 24 G4
Holsworthy Beacon
Devon 24 F5
Holt Dorset 31 G8
Hants 49 C8
Mers 183 C7
Norf 159 B11
Wilts 61 G11
Worcs 116 E6
Wrex 166 E6
Holtby York 207 C9
Holt End Hants 49 F7
Worcs 117 D11
Holt Fleet Worcs 116 E6
Holt Green Lancs 193 G11
Holt Head W Yorks 196 E5
Holt Heath Dorset 31 G9
Worcs 116 E6
Holt Hill Kent 53 B8
Staffs 152 D2
Holton Oxon 83 D10
Som 29 B11
Suff 127 B7
Holton cum Beckering
Lincs 189 E10
Holton Heath Dorset 18 C4
Holton le Clay Lincs 201 G9
Holton le Moor Lincs 189 B9
Holton St Mary Suff 107 D11
Holt Park W Yorks 205 E11
Holt Pound Hants 49 E10
Holts Gtr Man 196 G3
Holtspur Bucks 84 G6
Holt Wood Dorset 31 F8
Holtye E Sus 52 F3
Holway Dorset 28 G5
Dorset 29 C10
Flint 181 F11
Som 28 C2
Holwell Dorset 30 E2
Herts 104 E3
Leics 154 E4
Oxon 82 D2
Som 45 D8
Holwellbury C Beds 104 E3
Holwick Durham 232 F4
Holworth Dorset 17 E11
Holybourne Hants 49 E8
Holy City Devon 28 G3
Holy Cross T&W 243 D8
Worcs 117 B8
Holyfield Essex 86 E5
Holyhead = Caergybi
Anglesey 178 E2
Holy Island Northumb 273 B11
Holylee Borders 261 B9
Holymoorside Derbys 170 B4
Holyport Windsor 65 D11
Holystone Northumb 251 C11
Holytown N Lanark 268 C5
Holy Vale Scilly 1 G4
Holywell Cambs 122 C6
C Beds 85 B8
Corn 4 D5
Dorset 29 G9
E Sus 23 F9
Glos 80 G3
Hereford 97 C7
Herts 85 F9
Northumb 243 C8
Som 29 E8
Warks 118 D3
Holywell = Treffynnon
Flint 181 F11
Holywell Green
W Yorks 196 D5
Holywell Lake Som 27 C10
Holywell Row Suff 124 B4
Holywood Dumfries 247 G10
Homedowns Glos 99 E8
Homer Shrops 132 C2
Homer Green Mers 193 G10
Homersfield Suff 142 F5
Homerton London 67 B11
Hom Green Hereford 97 G11
Homington Wilts 31 B10
Honeybourne Worcs 100 C2
Honeychurch Devon 25 G10
Honeydon Bedford 122 F2
Honey Hall N Som 60 G2
Honeyhill Wokingham 65 F10
Honey Hill Kent 70 G6
Honeystreet Wilts 62 G6
Honey Street Wilts 62 G6
Honey Tye Suff 107 D9
Honeywick C Beds 103 G9
Honicknowle Plym 7 D9
Honiley Warks 118 C4
Honing Norf 160 D6
Honingham Norf 160 G2
Honington Lincs 172 G6
Suff 125 C8
Warks 100 C5
Honiton Devon 27 G11
Honkley Wrex 166 D4
Honley W Yorks 196 E6
Honley Moor W Yorks 196 E6
Honnington Telford 150 F4
Honor Oak London 67 E11
Honor Oak Park London 67 E11
Honresfeld Gtr Man 196 D2
Hoo Kent 71 G9
Hoober S Yorks 186 B6
Hoobrook Worcs 116 C6
Hood Green S Yorks 197 G10
Hood Hill S Yorks 186 B5
Hood Manor Warr 183 D9
Hooe E Sus 23 D11
Plym 7 E10
Hooe Common E Sus 23 C11
Hoo End Herts 85 B11
Hoofield Ches W 167 C8
Hoo Green Ches E 184 E2
Hoohill Blackpool 202 F2
Hoo Hole W Yorks 196 B4
Hook Cambs 139 E8
Devon 28 F4
Hook *continued*
E Yorks 199 B9
Hants 33 F8
Hants 49 C8
London 67 G7
Pembs 73 C7
Wilts 62 C5
Hook-a-gate Shrops 131 B9
Hook Bank Worcs 98 C6
Hooke Dorset 16 B6
Hook End Essex 87 F9
Oxon 65 C7
W Mid 134 G4
Hooker Gate T&W 242 F4
Hookgate Staffs 150 B4
Hook Green Kent 53 F7
Kent 68 F6
Hook Heath Sur 50 B3
Hook Norton Oxon 101 E7
Hook Park Hants 33 G7
Hook's Cross Herts 104 G5
Hook Street Glos 79 F11
Wilts 62 C5
Hookway Devon 14 B3
Hookwood Sur 51 E9
Hoole Ches W 166 B6
Hoole Bank Ches W 166 B6
Hooley Sur 51 B9
Hooley Bridge Gtr Man 195 E11
Hooley Brow Gtr Man 195 E11
Hooley Hill Gtr Man 184 B6
Hoo Meavy Devon 7 B10
Hoop Mon 79 D8
Hoopers Pool Wilts 45 C10
Hoops Devon 24 C5
Hoo St Werburgh
Medway 69 E9
Hooton Ches W 182 F5
Hooton Levitt S Yorks 187 C8
Hooton Pagnell S Yorks 198 F3
Hooton Roberts S Yorks 187 B7
Hopcroft's Holt Oxon 101 F9
Hope Derbys 185 E11
Devon 9 G8
Highld 308 D4
Powys 130 B5
Shrops 130 C6
Staffs 169 D10
Hope = Yr Hôb Flint 166 D4
Hope Bagot Shrops 115 C11
Hopebeck Cumb 229 G9
Hope Bowdler Shrops 131 E9
Hopedale Staffs 169 D10
Hope End Green Essex 105 G11
Hope Green Ches E 184 E6
Hopeman Moray 301 C11
Hope Mansell Hereford 79 B10
Hope Park Shrops 130 C6
Hopesay Shrops 131 G7
Hopesgate Shrops 130 C6
Hope's Green Essex 69 B9
Hope's Rough Hereford 98 B2
Hopetown W Yorks 197 C11
Hope under Dinmore
Hereford 115 G10
Hopgoods Green
W Berks 64 F4
Hopkinstown Rhondda 77 G9
Hopley's Green Hereford 114 G6
Hopperton N Yorks 206 B4
Hop Pole Lincs 156 G3
Hopsford Warks 135 G8
Hopstone Shrops 132 E5
Hopton Derbys 170 E3
Shrops 149 D11
Shrops 149 E7
Staffs 151 D8
Suff 125 B9
Hoptonbank Shrops 116 B2
Hopton Cangeford
Shrops 131 G10
Hopton Castle Shrops 115 B7
Hoptongate Shrops 131 G10
Hoptonheath Shrops 115 B7
Hopton Heath Staffs 151 D9
Hopton on Sea Norf 143 D10
Hopton Wafers Shrops 116 B2
Hopwas Staffs 134 B3
Hopwood Gtr Man 195 F11
Worcs 117 B10
Hopworthy Devon 24 G4
Horam E Sus 23 B9
Horbling Lincs 156 B2
Horbury W Yorks 197 D9
Horbury Bridge
W Yorks 197 D9
Horbury Junction
W Yorks 197 D10
Horcott Glos 81 E11
Horden Durham 234 C4
Horderley Shrops 131 F8
Hordle Hants 19 B11
Hordley Shrops 149 C7
Horeb Carms 75 D7
Carms 93 F10
Ceredig 93 C7
Flint 166 D3
Horfield Bristol 60 D6
Horgabost W Isles 305 J2
Horham Suff 126 C4
Horkesley Heath Essex 107 F9
Horkstow N Lincs 200 D3
Horkstow Wolds
N Lincs 200 D3
Horley Oxon 101 C8
Sur 51 E9
Horn Ash Dorset 28 G5
Hornblotton Som 44 G5
Hornblotton Green Som 44 G5
Hornby Lancs 211 F11
N Yorks 224 G4
N Yorks 225 D7
Horncastle Lincs 174 B3
Reading 65 E7
Hornchurch London 68 B4
Horncliffe Northumb 273 F8
Horndean Borders 273 F7
Hants 34 E2
Horndon Devon 12 F6
Horndon on the Hill
Thurrock 69 C7
Horne Sur 51 E10
Horner Som 41 D11
Horne Row Essex 88 E3
Horner's Green Suff 107 C9
Hornestreet Essex 107 E10
Horney Common E Sus 37 B7
Horn Hill Som 43 E8
Hornick Corn 5 E9
Horniehaugh Angus 292 G6
Horning Norf 160 F6
Horninghold Leics 136 D6
Horninglow Staffs 152 D4
Horningsea Cambs 123 E9
Horningsham Wilts 45 E10
Horningtoft Norf 159 E8
Horningtops Corn 6 C5
Hornsbury Som 28 E4
Hornsby Cumb 240 G2
Horns Corner Kent 38 B2
Horns Cross Devon 24 C5
E Sus 38 C4
Hornsea E Yorks 209 D10
Hornsea Bridge
E Yorks 209 D10
Hornsea Burton
E Yorks 209 D10
Hornsey London 67 B10
Hornsey Vale London 67 B10
Horns Green Kent 52 B3
Horn Street Kent 55 F7
Kent 69 G7
Hornton Oxon 101 B7
Horpit Swindon 63 C8
Horrabridge Devon 7 B10
Horringer Suff 124 E6
Horringford IoW 20 D6
Horrocks Fold Gtr Man 195 E8
Horrocksford Lancs 203 E10
Horsalls Kent 53 C11
Horsebridge Devon 12 G4
Hants 47 G10
Shrops 131 B7
Horse Bridge Staffs 169 E7
Horsebrook Devon 8 D4
Staffs 151 G7
Horsecastle N Som 60 F2
Horsedown Wilts 61 D10
Horsedowns Corn 2 C4
Horsehay Telford 132 B3
Horseheath Cambs 106 B2
Horseholm Dumfries 238 C2
Horsehouse N Yorks 213 C10
Horseley Heath W Mid 133 E9
Horsell Sur 50 B3
Horsell Birch Sur 50 B3
Horseman's Green
Wrex 166 G6
Horseman Side Essex 87 F8
Horsemere Green W Sus 35 G7
Horsenden Bucks 84 E3
Horsepools Glos 80 C4
Horseway Cambs 139 F8
Horseway Head
Hereford 114 E6
Horsey Norf 161 E9
Som 43 F10
Horsey Corner Norf 161 E9
Horsey Down Wilts 81 G9
Horsford Norf 160 F3
Horsforth W Yorks 205 F10
Horsforth Woodside
W Yorks 205 F10
Horsham Worcs 116 F4
W Sus 51 G7
Horsham St Faith Norf 160 F4
Horshoe Green Kent 52 E3
Horsington Lincs 173 B11
Som 30 C2
Horsley Derbys 170 G5
Glos 80 F4
Northumb 242 D3
Northumb 251 D8
Horsley Cross Essex 108 F2
Horsleycross Street
Essex 108 F2
Horsleyhill Borders 262 F2
Horsley Hill T&W 243 D9
Horsleyhope Durham 233 B7
Horsleys Green Bucks 84 F3
Horsley Woodhouse
Derbys 170 G5
Horsmonden Kent 53 E7
Horspath Oxon 83 E9
Horstead Norf 160 F5
Horsted Green E Sus 23 B7
Horsted Keynes W Sus 36 B5
Horton Bucks 84 B6
Dorset 31 F8
Kent 54 B6
Lancs 204 C3
S Glos 61 C9
Shrops 149 D9
Som 28 E4
Staffs 168 D6
Swansea 56 D3
Telford 150 G3
Wilts 62 G5
Windsor 66 D4
W Nhants 120 G6
Horton Common Dorset 31 F9
Horton Cross Som 28 D4
Horton-cum-Studley
Oxon 83 C9
Horton Green Ches W 167 F7
Horton Heath Dorset 31 F9
Hants 33 D7
Horton in Ribblesdale
N Yorks 212 E6
Horton Kirby Kent 68 F5
Hortonlane Shrops 149 G8
Horton Wharf Bucks 84 B6
Hortonwood Telford 150 G3
Horwich Gtr Man 194 E6
Horwich End Derbys 185 E8
Horwood Devon 25 B8
Horwood Riding S Glos 61 B8
Hoscar Lancs 194 E3
Hose Leics 154 D4
Hoselaw Borders 263 C8
Hoses Cumb 220 G4
Hosey Hill Kent 52 C3
Hosh Perth 286 E2
Hosta W Isles 296 D3
Hoswick Shetland 313 L6
Hotham E Yorks 208 G3
Hothfield Kent 54 D3
Hotley Bottom Bucks 84 E5
Hoton Leics 153 E11
Hotwells Bristol 60 E5
Houbans Shetland 312 F5
Houbie Shetland 312 D8
Houdston S Ayrs 244 D5
Hough Argyll 288 E1
Ches E 168 E2
Ches E 184 F5
Hougham Lincs 172 G5
Hough Green Halton 183 D7
Hough-on-the-Hill
Lincs 172 F6
Hough Side W Yorks 205 G10
Houghton Cambs 122 C5
Cumb 239 F10
Hants 47 G10
Northumb 242 D4
Pembs 73 D7
W Sus 35 E8
Houghton Bank Darl 233 G10
Houghton Conquest
C Beds 103 C10
Houghton Green E Sus 38 C6
Warr 183 C10
Houghton-le-Side
Darl 233 G10
Houghton-le-Spring
T&W 234 B2
Houghton on the Hill
Leics 136 C3
Houghton Regis
C Beds 103 G10
Houghton St Giles Norf 159 B8
Houghwood Mers 194 G4
Houlland Shetland 312 B7
Shetland 312 F7
Shetland 313 H5
Shetland 313 J6
Houlsyke N Yorks 226 D4
Houlton Warwicks 119 C11
Hound Hants 33 F7
Hound Green Hants 49 B8
Hound Hill Dorset 31 G7
Houndmills Hants 48 C6
Houndscroft Glos 80 E5
Houndslow Borders 272 F2
Houndsmoor Som 27 B10
Houndstone Som 29 D8
Houndwood Borders 272 C6
Hounsdown Hants 32 E5
Hounsley Batch N Som 60 G4
Hounslow London 66 D6
Hounslow Green Essex 87 B11
Hounslow West London 66 D6
Hourston Orkney 314 E2
Housabister Shetland 313 H6
Housay Shetland 312 F8
Househill Highld 301 D8
House of Daviot Highld 301 E7
House of Glenmuick
Aberds 292 D5
Houses Hill W Yorks 197 D7
Housetter Shetland 312 E5
Housham Tye Essex 87 C8
Houss Shetland 313 K5
Houston Renfs 267 B8
Houstry Highld 310 F5
Houton Orkney 314 F3
Hove Brighton 36 G3
Hove Edge W Yorks 196 C6
Hoveringham Notts 171 F11
Hoveton Norf 160 F6
Hovingham N Yorks 216 D3
How Cumb 240 F2
Howbeck Bank Ches E 167 F11
Howbrook S Yorks 186 B4
How Caple Hereford 98 E2
Howden Borders 262 E5
E Yorks 199 B8
W Loth 269 B11
Howden Clough
W Yorks 197 B8
Howden-le-Wear
Durham 233 E9
Howdon T&W 243 D8
Howdon Pans T&W 243 D8
Howe Highld 310 C7
Norf 142 C5
N Yorks 214 C6
Howe Bridge Gtr Man 195 G7
Howegreen Essex 88 E4
Howe Green Essex 87 B8
Essex 88 E2
Warks 134 F6
Howell Lincs 173 F10
How End C Beds 103 C10
Howe of Teuchar
Aberds 303 E7
Howe Street Essex 87 C11
Essex 106 E3
Howey Powys 113 F11
Howford Borders 261 B8
Borders 261 E9
Howgate Cumb 228 G5
Midloth 270 D4
Howgill Cumb 222 F2
Lancs 204 D2
N Yorks 205 B7
How Green Kent 52 D3
How Hill Norf 161 F7
Howick Mon 79 F8
Northumb 265 F7
Howick Cross Lancs 194 B4
Howle Durham 233 F7
Telford 150 E3
Howleigh Som 28 D2
Howlett End Essex 105 E11
Howley Glos 80 G2
Som 28 F3
Warr 183 D10
Hownam Borders 263 F7
Hownam Mains Borders 263 E7
Howpasley Borders 249 B8
Howsen Worcs 116 G5
Howsham N Lincs 200 G4
N Yorks 216 G4
Howslack Dumfries 248 B3
Howtel Northumb 263 C9
Howt Green Kent 69 F11
Howton Hereford 97 F8
Howtown Cumb 221 B8
Howwood Renfs 267 C7
How Wood Herts 85 E10
Hoxne Suff 126 B3
Hoxton London 67 C10
Hoy Orkney 314 F2
Hoylake Mers 182 D2
Hoyland S Yorks 197 G11
Hoyland Common
S Yorks 197 G11
Hoylandswaine S Yorks 197 G9
Hoyle W Sus 34 D6
Hoyle Mill S Yorks 197 F11
Hubbard's Hill Kent 52 C4
Hubberholme N Yorks 213 D8
Hubberston Pembs 72 D5
Hubbersty Head Cumb 221 G8
Hubberton Green
W Yorks 196 C4
Hubbert's Bridge Lincs 174 G3
Huby N Yorks 205 D11
N Yorks 215 F11
Hucclecote Glos 80 B5
Hucking Kent 53 B10
Hucknall Notts 171 F8
Huddersfield W Yorks 196 D6
Huddington Worcs 117 F8
Huddisford Devon 24 D4
Huddlesford Staffs 134 B3
Hud Hey Lancs 195 C9
Hudnall Herts 85 C8
Hudnalls Glos 79 E8
Hudswell N Yorks 224 E3
Wilts 61 F11
Huggate E Yorks 208 B3
Hugglepit Devon 24 C4
Hugglescote Leics 153 G8
Hughenden Valley Bucks 84 F5
Hughley Shrops 131 D11
Hugh Mill Lancs 195 C10
Hugh Town Scilly 1 G4
Hugus Corn 4 G5
Huish Devon 25 B7
Devon 25 E8
Wilts 62 G6
Huish Champflower Som 27 B9
Huish Episcopi Som 28 B6
Huisinis W Isles 305 G1
Hulcote C Beds 103 D8
W Nhants 102 B4
Hulcott Bucks 84 B5
Hulland Derbys 170 F2
Hulland Moss Derbys 170 F3
Hulland Ward Derbys 170 F3
Hullavington Wilts 61 C11
Hullbridge Essex 88 G4
Hull End Derbys 185 E9
Hulme Gtr Man 184 B4
Staffs 168 F6
Warr 183 C10
Hulme End Staffs 169 D10
Hulme Walfield Ches E 168 B4
Hulseheath Ches E 184 E2
Hulverstone IoW 20 E3
Hulver Street Suff 143 F9
Humber Devon 14 G3
Hereford 115 F10
Humber Bridge N Lincs 200 C4
Humberston NE Lincs 201 F10
Humberstone Leicester 136 B2
Humberston Fitties
NE Lincs 201 F10
Humbie E Loth 271 C9
Humbledon T&W 243 F9
Humble Green Suff 107 B8
Humbleton E Yorks 209 G10
Northumb 263 D11
Humby Lincs 155 C10
Hume Borders 272 G4
Hummersknott Darl 224 C5
Humshaugh Northumb 241 C10
Huna Highld 310 B7
Huncoat Lancs 203 G11
Huncote Leics 135 D10
Hundalee Borders 262 F4
Hundall Derbys 186 F5
Hunderthwaite Durham 232 G5
Hunderton Hereford 97 D9
Hundleby Lincs 174 B5
Hundle Houses Lincs 174 E3
Hundleshope Borders 260 B6
Hundleton Pembs 73 E7
Hundon Suff 106 B4
Hundred Acres Hants 33 E9
Hundred End Lancs 194 C2
Hundred House Powys 114 G2
Hungarton Leics 136 B3
Hungate W Yorks 197 B11
Hungerford Hants 31 E11
Shrops 131 F10
Som 42 E4
W Berks 63 F10
Windsor 65 E10
Hungerford Green
W Berks 64 D5
Hungerford Newtown
W Berks 63 E11
Hunger Hill Gtr Man 195 F7
Lancs 194 E4
Hungershall Park Kent 52 F5
Hungerstone Hereford 97 D8
Hungerton Lincs 155 D7
Hungladder Highld 298 B3
Hungreyhatton Shrops 150 D3
Hunmanby N Yorks 217 D11
Hunmanby Moor
N Yorks 218 D2
Hunningham Warks 119 D7
Hunningham Hill Warks 119 D7
Hunnington Worcs 133 G9
Hunny Hill IoW 20 D5
Hunsdon Herts 86 C6
Hunsdonbury Herts 86 C6
Hunsingore N Yorks 206 C4
Hunslet W Yorks 206 G2
Hunslet Carr W Yorks 206 G2
Hunsonby Cumb 231 D7
Hunspow Highld 310 B6
Hunstanton Norf 175 G11
Hunstanworth Durham 232 B5
Hunsterson Ches E 167 F11
Hunston Suff 125 D9
W Sus 22 C5
Hunston Green Suff 125 D9
Hunstrete Bath 60 G6
Hunsworth W Yorks 197 B7
Hunt End Worcs 117 E10
Huntenhull Green Wilts 45 D10
Huntercombe End Oxon 65 B7
Hunters Forstal Kent 71 F7
Hunter's Quay Argyll 276 F3
Huntham Som 28 B4
Hunthill Lodge Angus 292 F6
Huntingdon Cambs 122 C4
Huntingfield Suff 126 C6
Huntingford Dorset 45 G10
S Glos 80 G2
Huntington Ches W 166 C6
E Loth 281 F9
Hereford 97 C9
Hereford 114 G5
Staffs 151 G9
Telford 132 B3
York 207 B8
Hunting-tower Perth 286 E4
Huntley Glos 80 B2
Staffs 169 G8
Huntly Aberds 302 F5
Huntlywood Borders 272 G2
Hunton Hants 48 F3
Kent 53 D8
N Yorks 224 G3
Hunton Bridge Herts 85 E9
Hunt's Corner Norf 141 F11
Huntscott Som 42 E2
Hunt's Cross Mers 182 D6
Hunts Green Warks 134 D3
Hunt's Green Bucks 84 E5
W Berks 64 E2
Huntsham Devon 27 C8
Huntshaw Devon 25 C8
Huntshaw Water Devon 25 C8
Hunts Hill Bucks 84 F4
Hunt's Lane Leics 135 C9
Huntspill Som 43 D10
Huntstile Som 43 G9
Huntworth Som 43 G10
Hunwick Durham 233 E9
Hunworth Norf 159 B11
Hurcott Som 28 D5
Som 29 B8
Worcs 117 B7
Hurdcott Wilts 47 G7
Hurdley Powys 130 E5
Hurdsfield Ches E 184 G6
Hurgill N Yorks 224 E3
Hurlet Glasgow 267 C10
Hurley Warks 134 D4
Windsor 65 C10
Hurley Bottom Windsor 65 C10
Hurley Common Warks 134 D4
Hurlford E Ayrs 257 B11
Hurliness Orkney 314 H2
Hurlston Lancs 194 E2
Hurlston Green Lancs 193 E11
Hurn BCP 19 B8
E Yorks 208 E6
Hurn's End Lincs 174 F6
Hursey Dorset 28 G6
Hursley Hants 32 B6
Hurst Cumb 230 C4
Dorset 17 C11
Gtr Man 196 G2
N Yorks 223 E10
Som 29 D7
Hurst *continued*
Wokingham 65 E9
Hurstbourne Priors
Hants 48 D2
Hurstbourne Tarrant
Hants 47 C11
Hurstead Gtr Man 196 D2
Hurst Green Essex 89 B9
E Sus 38 B2
Lancs 203 F9
Sur 51 C11
W Mid 133 F9
Hurst Hill W Mid 133 E8
Hurstley Hereford 97 B7
Hurst Park Sur 66 F6
Hurstpierpoint W Sus 36 D3
Hurst Wickham W Sus 36 D3
Hurstwood Lancs 204 G3
Hurtmore Sur 50 D3
Hurworth-on-Tees Darl 224 C6
Hurworth Place Darl 224 D5
Hury Durham 223 B9
Husabost Highld 298 D2
Husbands Bosworth
Leics 136 G2
Husbandtown Angus 287 D8
Husborne Crawley
C Beds 103 D9
Husthwaite N Yorks 215 D10
Hutcherleigh Devon 8 E5
Hutchesontown
Glasgow 267 C11
Hutchwns Bridgend 57 F10
Hut Green N Yorks 198 C5
Huthwaite Notts 171 D7
Hutlerburn Borders 261 E10
Huttock Top Lancs 195 C11
Huttoft Lincs 191 F8
Hutton Borders 273 E9
Cumb 230 F4
Essex 87 F10
E Yorks 208 C6
Lancs 194 B3
N Som 43 B11
Hutton Bonville N Yorks 224 E6
Hutton Buscel N Yorks 217 C9
Hutton Conyers N Yorks 214 E6
Hutton Cranswick
E Yorks 208 C6
Hutton End Cumb 230 D4
Hutton Gate Redcar 225 B11
Hutton Hang N Yorks 214 B3
Hutton Henry Durham 234 D4
Hutton-le-Hole
N Yorks 226 G4
Hutton Magna Durham 224 C2
Hutton Mount Essex 87 G10
Hutton Roof Cumb 211 D11
Cumb 230 E3
Hutton Rudby N Yorks 225 D9
Huttons Ambo N Yorks 216 F5
Hutton Sessay N Yorks 215 D9
Hutton Village Redcar 225 C11
Hutton Wandesley
N Yorks 206 C6
Huxham Devon 14 B4
Huxham Green Som 44 F5
Huxley Ches W 167 C8
Huxter Shetland 313 G7
Shetland 313 H3
Shetland 313 H5
Huxton Borders 273 B7
Huyton Mers 182 C6
Huyton Park Mers 182 C6
Huyton Quarry Mers 183 C7
Hwlffordd = Haverfordwest
Pembs 73 B7
Hycemoor Cumb 210 B1
Hyde Glos 80 E5
Glos 99 F11
Gtr Man 184 B6
Hants 31 E11
Hants 48 G3
Hereford 115 F9
Hyde Chase Essex 88 E4
Hyde End W Berks 64 G5
Hyde Heath Bucks 84 E6
Hyde Lea Staffs 151 E8
Hyde Park S Yorks 198 G5
Hydestile Sur 50 E3
Hylton Castle T&W 243 F9
Hylton Red House T&W 243 F9
Hyltons Crossways Norf 160 D4
Hyndburn Bridge
Lancs 203 G10
Hyndford Bridge
S Lanark 269 G8
Hyndhope Borders 261 E9
Hynish Argyll 288 F1
Hyssington Powys 130 E6
Hystfield Glos 79 F11
Hythe Hants 32 F6
Kent 55 G7
Som 44 C2
Sur 66 E4
Hythe End Windsor 66 E4
Hythie Aberds 303 D10
Hyton Cumb 210 B1

I

Iarsiadar W Isles 304 E3
Ibberton Dorset 30 F3
Ible Derbys 170 D2
Ibsley Hants 31 F11
Ibstock Leics 153 G8
Ibstone Bucks 84 G3
Ibthorpe Hants 47 C11
Ibworth Hants 48 C5
Icelton N Som 59 F11
Ichrachan Argyll 284 D4
Ickburgh Norf 140 E6
Ickenham London 66 B5
Ickenthwaite Cumb 210 B6
Ickford Bucks 83 D11
Ickham Kent 55 B8
Ickleford Herts 104 E3
Icklesham E Sus 38 D5
Ickleton Cambs 105 C9
Icklingham Suff 124 C5
Ickornshaw N Yorks 204 E5
Ickwell C Beds 104 B3
Ickwell Green C Beds 104 B3
Icomb Glos 100 G4
Icy Park Devon 8 F3
Idbury Oxon 82 B2
Iddesleigh Devon 25 F9
Ide Devon 14 C3
Ideford Devon 14 F3
Ide Hill Kent 52 C3
Iden E Sus 38 C6
Iden Green Kent 53 F8
Kent 53 G10
Idle W Yorks 205 F9
Idle Moor W Yorks 205 F9
Idless Corn 4 F6
Idlicote Warks 100 C5
Idmiston Wilts 47 F7
Idole Carms 74 B6
Idridgehay Derbys 170 F3
Idridgehay Green
Derbys 170 F3
Idrigill Highld 298 C3
Idstone Oxon 63 C9
Idvies Angus 287 C9
Iet-y-bwlch Carms 92 F3
Iffley Oxon 83 E8
Ifield W Sus 51 F8
Ifield Green W Sus 51 F9
Ifieldwood W Sus 51 F8
Ifold W Sus 50 G4
Iford BCP 19 C8
E Sus 36 F6
Ifton Heath Shrops 148 B6
Ightfield Shrops 149 B11
Ightfield Heath Shrops 149 B11
Ightham Kent 52 B5
Igtham Common Kent 52 B5
Iken Suff 127 F8
Ilam Staffs 169 E10
Ilchester Som 29 C8
Ilchester Mead Som 29 C8
Ilderton Northumb 264 E2
Ileden Kent 55 C8
Ilford London 68 B2
Som 28 D5
Ilfracombe Devon 40 D4
Ilkeston Derbys 171 G7
Ilketshall St Andrew
Suff 143 F7
Ilketshall St Lawrence
Suff 143 G7
Ilketshall St Margaret
Suff 142 F6
Ilkley W Yorks 205 D8
Illand Corn 11 F11
Illey W Mid 133 G9
Illidge Green Ches E 168 C3
Illington Norf 141 F8
Illingworth W Yorks 196 B5
Illogan Corn 4 G3
Illogan Highway Corn 4 G3
Illshaw Heath W Mid 118 C2
Illston on the Hill Leics 136 D4
Ilmer Bucks 84 D3
Ilmington Warks 100 C4
Ilminster Som 28 E5
Ilsington Devon 13 F11
Ilston Swansea 56 C5
Ilton N Yorks 214 D3
Som 28 D5
Imachar N Ayrs 255 C9
Imber Wilts 46 D3
Imeraval Argyll 254 C4
Immervoulin Stirling 285 F9
Immingham NE Lincs 201 E7
Impington Cambs 123 E8
Ince Ches W 183 F7
Ince Blundell Mers 193 G10
Ince in Makerfield
Gtr Man 194 G5
Inchbae Lodge Highld 300 C4
Inchbare Angus 293 G8
Inchberry Moray 302 D3
Inchbraoch Angus 287 B11
Inchbrook Glos 80 E4
Inchcape Highld 309 J6
Incheril Highld 299 C10
Inchgrundle Angus 292 F6
Inchina Highld 307 K4
Inchinnan Renfs 267 B9
Inchkinloch Highld 308 E5
Inchlaggan Highld 290 C3
Inchlumpie Highld 300 B5
Inchmore Highld 300 E3
Highld 300 E5
Inchnacardoch Hotel
Highld 290 B5
Inchnadamph Highld 307 G7
Inchock Angus 287 C10
Inch of Arnhall Aberds 293 F8
Inchree Highld 290 G2
Inchrory Moray 292 C3
Inchs Corn 5 C9
Inchture Perth 286 E6
Inchyra Perth 286 E5
Indian Queens Corn 5 D8
Inerval Argyll 254 C4
Ingatestone Essex 87 F11
Ingbirchworth S Yorks 197 F8
Ingerthorpe N Yorks 214 F5
Ingestre Staffs 151 E9
Ingham Lincs 188 E6
Norf 161 D7
Suff 125 C7
Ingham Corner Norf 161 D7
Ingleborough Norf 157 F9
Ingleby Derbys 152 D6
Lincs 188 F5
Ingleby Arncliffe
N Yorks 225 E8
Ingleby Barwick
Stockton 225 C9
Ingleby Cross N Yorks 225 E9
Ingleby Greenhow
N Yorks 225 D11
Ingleigh Green Devon 25 F10
Inglemire Hull 209 G7
Inglesbatch Bath 61 G8
Inglesham Swindon 82 F2
Ingleton Durham 233 G9
N Yorks 212 E3
Inglewhite Lancs 202 E6
Ingmanthorpe N Yorks 206 C4
Ingoe Northumb 242 C2
Ingol Lancs 202 G6
Ingoldisthorpe Norf 158 C3
Ingoldmells Lincs 175 B9
Ingoldsby Lincs 155 C10
Ingon Warks 118 F4
Ingram Northumb 264 F2
Ingrams Green W Sus 34 C4
Ingrave Essex 87 G10
Ingrow W Yorks 205 F7
Ings Cumb 221 F8
Ingst S Glos 60 B5
Ingthorpe Rutland 137 B9
Ingworth Norf 160 D3
Inham's End Cambs 138 D5
Inhurst Hants 64 G5
Inkberrow Worcs 117 F10
Inkerman Durham 233 D8
Inkersall Derbys 186 G6
Inkersall Green Derbys 186 G6
Inkford Worcs 117 C11
Inkpen W Berks 63 G11
Inkpen Common
W Berks 63 G11
Inkstack Highld 310 B6
Inlands W Sus 22 B3
Inmarsh Wilts 62 G2
Inn Cumb 221 D8
Innellan Argyll 276 G3
Inner Hope Devon 9 G8
Innerleithen Borders 261 B8
Innerleven Fife 287 G7
Innermessan Dumfries 236 C2
Innerwick E Loth 282 G4
Perth 285 C9

Innie Argyll 275 B9
Inninbeg Highld 289 E8
Innis Chonain Argyll 284 E5
Innistrynich Argyll 284 E5
Innox Hill Som 45 D9
Innsworth Glos 99 G7
Insch Aberds 302 G6
Insh Highld 291 C10
Inshegra Highld 306 D7
Inshore Highld 308 C3
Inskip Lancs 202 F5
Inskip Moss Side Lancs 202 F5
Instoneville S Yorks 198 E5
Instow Devon 40 G3
Insworke Corn 7 E8
Intack Blackburn 195 B8
Intake S Yorks 186 E5
S Yorks 198 G5
W Yorks 205 F10
Interfield Worcs 98 B5
Intwood Norf 142 C3
Inver Aberds 292 D4
Highld 311 L2
Perth 286 C4
Inverailort Highld 295 G9
Inveraldie Angus 287 D8
Inveralivaig Highld 298 E4
Inveralligin Highld 299 D8
Inverallochy Aberds 303 C10
Inveran Highld 299 B8
Highld 309 K5
Inveraray Argyll 284 G4
Inverarish Highld 295 B7
Inverarity Angus 287 C8
Inverarnan Stirling 285 F7
Inverasdale Highld 307 L3
Inverawe Ho Argyll 284 D4
Inverbeg Argyll 276 B6
Inverbervie Aberds 293 F10
Inverboyndie Aberds 302 C6
Inverbroom Highld 307 L6
Invercarron Mains
Highld 309 K5
Invercassley Highld 309 J4
Invercauld House
Aberds 292 D3
Inverchaolain Argyll 275 F11
Invercharnan Highld 284 C5
Inverchoran Highld 300 D2
Invercreran Argyll 284 C4
Inverdruie Highld 291 B11
Inverebrie Aberds 303 F9
Invereck Argyll 276 E2
Inverernan Ho Aberds 292 B5
Invereshie House
Highld 291 C10
Inveresk E Loth 280 G6
Inverey Aberds 292 E2
Inverfarigaig Highld 300 G5
Invergarry Highld 290 C5
Invergelder Aberds 292 D4
Invergeldie Perth 285 E11
Invergordon Highld 301 C7
Invergowrie Perth 287 D7
Inverguseran Highld 295 E9
Inverhadden Perth 285 B10
Inverhaggernie Stirling 285 E7
Inverharroch Moray 302 F3
Inverherive Stirling 285 E7
Inverie Highld 295 F9
Inverinan Argyll 275 B10
Inverinate Highld 295 C11
Inverkeilor Angus 287 C10
Inverkeithing Fife 280 E2
Inverkeithny Aberds 302 E6
Inverkip Invclyd 276 G4
Inverkirkaig Highld 307 H5
Inverlael Highld 307 L6
Inverleith Edin 280 F4
Inverliever Lodge Argyll 275 C9
Inverliver Argyll 284 D4
Inverlochlarig Stirling 285 F8
Inverlochy Argyll 284 E5
Highld 290 F3
Moray 301 G11
Inverlounin Argyll 276 B4
Inverlussa Argyll 275 E7
Inver Mallie Highld 290 E3
Invermark Lodge Angus 292 F6
Invermoidart Highld 289 B8
Invermoriston Highld 290 B6
Invernaver Highld 308 C7
Inverneill Argyll 275 E9
Inverness Highld 300 E6
Invernettie Aberds 303 E11
Invernoaden Argyll 276 B2
Inveronich Argyll 284 G6
Inveroran Hotel Argyll 284 C6
Inverpolly Lodge Highld 307 H5
Inverquharity Angus 287 B8
Inverquhomery Aberds 303 E10
Inverroy Highld 290 E4
Inversanda Highld 289 D11
Invershiel Highld 295 D11
Invershin Highld 309 K5
Invershore Highld 310 F6
Inversnaid Hotel Stirling 285 G7
Invertrossachs Stirling 285 G9
Inverugie Aberds 303 E11
Inveruglas Argyll 285 G7
Inveruglass Highld 291 C10
Inverurie Aberds 303 G7
Invervar Perth 285 C10
Inverythan Aberds 303 E7
Inwardleigh Devon 13 B7
Inwood Shrops 131 D9
Inworth Essex 88 B5
Iochdar W Isles 297 G3
Iping W Sus 34 C5
Ipplepen Devon 8 B6
Ipsden Oxon 64 B6
Ipsley Worcs 117 D11
Ipstones Staffs 169 F8
Ipswich Suff 108 C3
Irby Mers 182 E3
Irby in the Marsh Lincs 175 C7
Irby upon Humber
NE Lincs 201 G7
Irchester N Nhants 121 D8
Ireby Cumb 229 D10
Lancs 212 D3
Ireland C Beds 104 C2
Orkney 314 F3
Shetland 313 L5
Wilts 45 C10
Ireland's Cross Shrops 168 G2
Ireland Wood W Yorks 205 F11
Ireleth Cumb 210 D4
Ireshopeburn Durham 232 D3
Ireton Wood Derbys 170 F3
Irlam Gtr Man 184 C2
Irlams o' th' Height
Gtr Man 195 G9
Irnham Lincs 155 D10
Iron Acton S Glos 61 C7
Ironbridge Telford 132 C3
Iron Bridge Cambs 139 D9
Irons Cross Warks 117 G11
Irongray Dumfries 237 B11
Iron Lo Highld 299 G10
Ironmacannie Dumfries 237 B8
Irons Bottom Sur 51 D9
Ironside Aberds 303 D8
Ironville Derbys 170 E6
Irstead Norf 161 E7
Irstead Street Norf 161 F7
Irthington Cumb 239 E11
Irthlingborough
N Nhants 121 C8
Irton N Yorks 217 C10
Irvine N Ayrs 257 B8
Irwell Vale Lancs 195 C9
Isabella Pit Northumb 253 G8
Isallt Bach Anglesey 178 F3
Isauld Highld 310 C3
Isbister Orkney 314 D2
Orkney 314 E3
Shetland 312 D5
Shetland 313 G7
Isel Cumb 229 E9
Isfield E Sus 36 D6
Isham N Nhants 121 C7
Ishriff Argyll 289 F8
Isington Hants 49 E9
Island Carr N Lincs 200 F3
Islands Common Cambs 122 E3
Islay Ho Argyll 274 G4
Isle Abbotts Som 28 C5
Isle Brewers Som 28 C5
Isleham Cambs 124 C2
Isle of Axholme N Lincs 199 F9
Isle of Dogs London 67 D11
Isle of Man Dumfries 238 B2
Isle of Whithorn
Dumfries 236 F6
Isleornsay Highld 295 D9
Islesburgh Shetland 312 G5
Islesteps Dumfries 237 B11
Isleworth London 67 D7
Isley Walton Leics 153 D8
Islibhig W Isles 304 F1
Islington London 67 C10
Telford 150 E4
Islip N Nhants 121 B9
Oxon 83 C8
Isombridge Telford 150 G2
Istead Rise Kent 68 F6
Isycoed Wrex 166 E6
Itchen Soton 32 E6
Itchen Abbas Hants 48 G4
Itchen Stoke Hants 48 G5
Itchingfield W Sus 35 B10
Itchington S Glos 61 B7
Itteringham Norf 160 C2
Itteringham Common
Norf 160 D3
Itton Devon 13 B9
Mon 79 F7
Itton Common Mon 79 F7
Ivegill Cumb 230 C4
Ivelet N Yorks 223 F8
Iver Bucks 66 C4
Iver Heath Bucks 66 C4
Iverley Staffs 133 G7
Iveston Durham 242 G4
Ivinghoe Bucks 84 B6
Ivinghoe Aston Bucks 85 B7
Ivington Hereford 115 F9
Ivington Green Hereford 115 F9
Ivybridge Devon 8 D2
Ivy Chimneys Essex 86 E6
Ivychurch Kent 39 B8
Ivy Cross Dorset 30 C5
Ivy Hatch Kent 52 C5
Ivy Todd Norf 141 B7
Iwade Kent 69 F11
Iwerne Courtney or Shroton
Dorset 30 E5
Iwerne Minster Dorset 30 E5
Iwood N Som 60 G3
Ixworth Suff 125 C8
Ixworth Thorpe Suff 125 C8

J

Jackfield Telford 132 C3
Jack Green Lancs 194 B5
Jack Hayes Staffs 168 F6
Jack Hill N Yorks 205 C10
Jack in the Green Devon 14 B6
Jacksdale Notts 170 E6
Jack's Green Essex 105 G11
Glos 80 D5
Jack's Hatch Essex 86 D6
Jackson Bridge
W Yorks 197 F7
Jackstown Aberds 303 F7
Jacobstow Corn 11 B9
Jacobstowe Devon 25 G9
Jacobs Well Sur 50 C3
Jagger Green W Yorks 196 D5
Jameston Pembs 73 F9
Jamestown Dumfries 249 D8
Highld 300 D4
W Dunb 277 E7
Jamphlars Fife 280 B4
Janetstown Highld 310 C4
Janke's Green Essex 107 F8
Jarrow T&W 243 D8
Jarvis Brook E Sus 37 B8
Jasper's Green Essex 106 F4
Java Argyll 289 F9
Jawcraig Falk 278 F6
Jaw Hill W Yorks 197 C9
Jaywick Essex 89 C11
Jealott's Hill Brack 65 E11
Jeaniefield Borders 271 G10
Jedburgh Borders 262 E5
Jedurgh Borders 262 F5
Jeffreyston Pembs 73 D9
Jellyhill E Dunb 278 G2
Jemimaville Highld 301 C7
Jennetts Hill W Berks 64 E5
Jennyfield N Yorks 205 B11
Jericho Gtr Man 195 E10
Jersey Farm Herts 85 D11
Jersey Marine Neath 57 C8
Jerviswood S Lanark 269 F7
Jesmond T&W 243 D7
Jevington E Sus 23 E9
Jewell's Cross Corn 24 G3
Jingle Street Mon 79 C7
Jockey End Herts 85 C8
Jodrell Bank Ches E 184 G3
Johnby Cumb 230 E4
John O'Gaunt Leics 136 B4
John O'Gaunts
W Yorks 197 B11
John o'Groats Highld 310 B7
John's Cross E Sus 38 C2
Johnshaven Aberds 293 G9
Johnson Fold Gtr Man 195 E7
Johnson's Hillock
Lancs 194 C5
Johnson Street Norf 161 F7
Johnston Pembs 72 C6
Johnstone Renfs 267 C8
Johnstonebridge
Dumfries 248 E3
Johnstone Mains
Aberds 293 F9
Johnstown Carms 74 B6
Wrex 166 F4
Jolly's Bottom Corn 4 F5
Joppa Corn 2 B3
Edin 280 G6
S Ayrs 257 F10
Jordan Green Norf 159 E11
Jordanhill Glasgow 267 B10
Jordans Bucks 85 G7
Jordanston Pembs 91 E8
Jordanthorpe S Yorks 186 E5
Jordon S Yorks 186 C6
Joyford Glos 79 C9
Joy's Green Glos 79 B10
Jubilee Gtr Man 196 E2
Notts 170 E6
Jugbank Staffs 150 B5
Jump S Yorks 197 G11
Jumpers Common BCP 19 C8
Jumpers Green BCP 19 C8
Jumper's Town E Sus 52 G3
Junction N Yorks 204 D6
Juniper Northumb 241 F10
Juniper Green Edin 270 B3
Jurby East IoM 192 C4
Jurby West IoM 192 C4
Jurston Devon 13 E9
Jury's Gap E Sus 39 D7

K

Kaber Cumb 222 C5
Kaimend S Lanark 269 F9
Kaimes Edin 270 B5
Kaimrig End Borders 269 G11
Kalemouth Borders 262 D6
Kame Fife 287 G7
Kames Argyll 275 B9
Argyll 275 F10
E Ayrs 258 D5
Kates Hill W Mid 133 E9
Kea Corn 4 G6
Keadby N Lincs 199 E10
Keal Cotes Lincs 174 C5
Kearby Town End
N Yorks 206 D2
Kearnsey Kent 55 E9
Kearsley Gtr Man 195 F9
Kearstwick Cumb 212 C2
Kearton N Yorks 223 F9
Kearvaig Highld 306 B7
Keasden N Yorks 212 F4
Kebroyd W Yorks 196 C4
Keckwick Halton 183 E9
Keddington Lincs 190 D4
Keddington Corner
Lincs 190 D5
Kedington Suff 106 B4
Kedleston Derbys 170 G4
Kedslie Borders 271 G11
Keekle Cumb 219 B10
Keelars Tye Essex 107 G11
Keelby Lincs 201 E7
Keele Staffs 168 F4
Keeley Green Bedford 103 B10
Keelham W Yorks 205 G7
Keenley Northumb 241 F7
Keenthorne Som 43 F8
Keeres Green Essex 87 C9
Keeston Pembs 72 B6
Keevil Wilts 46 B2
Kegworth Leics 153 D9
Kehelland Corn 4 G2
Keig Aberds 293 B8
Keighley W Yorks 205 E7
Keil Highld 289 D11
Keilarsbrae Clack 279 C7
Keilhill Aberds 303 D7
Keillmore Argyll 275 E7
Keillor Perth 286 C6
Keillour Perth 286 E3
Keills Argyll 274 G5
Keils Argyll 274 G6
Keinton Mandeville Som 44 G4
Keir Mill Dumfries 247 E9
Keisby Lincs 155 D10
Keiss Highld 310 C7
Keistle Highld 298 D4
Keith Moray 302 D4
Keith Hall Aberds 303 G7
Keith Inch Aberds 303 E11
Keithock Angus 293 G8
Kelbrook Lancs 204 E4
Kelby Lincs 173 G8
Kelcliffe W Yorks 205 E9
Keld Cumb 221 C11
N Yorks 223 E7
Keldholme N Yorks 216 B4
Keld Houses N Yorks 214 G2
Kelfield N Lincs 199 G10
N Yorks 207 F7
Kelham Notts 172 D3
Kelhurn Argyll 276 F6
Kellacott Devon 12 D4
Kellamergh Lancs 194 B2
Kellan Argyll 289 E7
Kellas Angus 287 D8
Moray 301 D11
Kellaton Devon 9 G11
Kellaways Wilts 62 D3
Kelleth Cumb 222 D3
Kelleythorpe E Yorks 208 B5
E Yorks 208 B6
Kelling Norf 177 E9
Kellingley N Yorks 198 C4
Kellington N Yorks 198 C5
Kelloe Durham 234 D2
Kelloholm Dumfries 258 G6
Kells Cumb 219 B9
Kelly Corn 10 G6
Devon 12 E3
Kelly Bray Corn 12 G3
Kelmarsh W Nhants 120 B4
Kelmscott Oxon 82 F3
Kelsale Suff 127 D7
Kelsall Ches W 167 B8
Kelsall Hill Ches W 167 B8
Kelsay Argyll 254 B2
Kelshall Herts 104 D6
Kelsick Cumb 238 G5
Kelso Borders 262 C6
Kelstedge Derbys 170 C4
Kelstern Lincs 190 C3
Kelsterton Flint 182 G3
Kelston Bath 61 F8
Keltneyburn Perth 285 C11
Kelton Dumfries 237 B11
Durham 232 G4
Kelty Fife 280 C2
Keltybridge Fife 280 B2
Kelvedon Essex 88 B5
Kelvedon Hatch Essex 87 F9
Kelvin S Lanark 268 E2
Kelvindale Glasgow 267 B11
Kelvinside Glasgow 267 B11
Kelynack Corn 1 D3
Kemacott Devon 41 D7
Kemback Fife 287 F8
Kemberton Shrops 132 C4
Kemble Glos 81 F7
Kemble Wick Glos 81 F7
Kemerton Worcs 99 D8
Kemeys Commander
Mon 78 E4
Kemincham Ches E 168 B4
Kemnay Aberds 293 B9
Kempe's Corner Kent 54 D4
Kempie Highld 308 D4
Kempley Glos 98 F3
Kempley Green Glos 98 F3
Kempsey Worcs 99 B7
Kempsford Glos 81 F11
Kemps Green Warks 118 C2
Kempshott Hants 48 C6
Kempston Bedford 103 B10
Kempston Church End
Bedford 103 B10
Kempston Hardwick
Bedford 103 B10
Kempston West End
Bedford 103 B9
Kempton Shrops 131 G7
Kemp Town Brighton 36 G4
Kemsing Kent 52 B4
Kemsley Kent 70 F2
Kemsley Street Kent 69 G10
Kenardington Kent 54 G3
Kenchester Hereford 97 C8
Kencot Oxon 82 E3
Kendal Cumb 221 G10
Kendal End Worcs 117 C10
Kendleshire S Glos 61 D7
Kendon Caerph 77 F11
Kendoon Dumfries 246 F4
Kendray S Yorks 197 F11
Kenfig Bridgend 57 E10
Kenfig Hill Bridgend 57 E10
Kengharair Argyll 288 E6
Kenilworth Warks 118 C5
Kenknock Stirling 285 D8
Kenley London 51 B10
Shrops 131 C11
Kenmore Argyll 284 G4
Highld 299 D7
Perth 285 C11
Kenmure Dumfries 237 B8
Kenn Devon 14 D4
N Som 60 F2
Kennacley W Isles 305 J3
Kennacraig Argyll 275 G9
Kennards House Corn 11 E11
Kenneggy Corn 2 D3
Kenneggy Downs Corn 2 D3
Kennerleigh Devon 26 F4
Kennet Clack 279 C8
Kennet End Suff 124 D4
Kennethmont Aberds 302 G5
Kennett Cambs 124 D3
Kennford Devon 14 D4
Kenninghall Norf 141 F10
Kenninghall Heath
Norf 141 G10
Kennington Kent 54 E4
London 67 D10
Oxon 83 E8
Kenn Moor Gate N Som 60 F2
Kennoway Fife 287 G7
Kenny Som 28 D4
Kenny Hill Suff 124 B3
Kennythorpe N Yorks 216 F5
Kenovay Argyll 288 E1
Kensaleyre Highld 298 D4
Kensal Green London 67 C8
Kensal Rise London 67 C8
Kensal Town London 67 C8
Kensary Highld 310 E6
Kensington London 67 D9
Mers 182 C5
Kensworth C Beds 85 B8
Kentallen Highld 284 B4
Kentchurch Hereford 97 F8
Kentford Suff 124 D4
Kentisbeare Devon 27 F9
Kentisbury Devon 40 E6
Kentisbury Ford Devon 40 E6
Kentish Town London 67 C9
Kentmere Cumb 221 E9
Kenton Devon 14 E5
London 67 B7
Suff 126 D3
T&W 242 D6
Kenton Bankfoot T&W 242 D6
Kenton Bar T&W 242 D6
Kenton Corner Suff 126 D4
Kenton Green Glos 80 C3
Kentra Highld 289 C8
Kentrigg Cumb 221 G10
Kents Corn 11 B9
Kents Bank Cumb 211 D7
Kent's Green Glos 98 G4
Kents Hill M Keynes 103 D7
Kent's Oak Hants 32 C4
Kent Street E Sus 38 D3
Kent 53 C7
W Sus 36 C2
Kenwick Shrops 149 C8
Kenwick Park Shrops 149 D8
Kenwyn Corn 4 F6
Kenyon Warr 183 B10
Keoldale Highld 308 C3
Keonchulish Ho Highld 307 K6
Kepdowrie Stirling 277 C11
Kepnal Wilts 63 G7
Keppanach Highld 290 G2
Keppoch Highld 295 C11
Keprigan Argyll 255 F7
Kepwick N Yorks 225 G9
Kerchesters Borders 263 B7
Kerdiston Norf 159 E11
Keresforth Hill S Yorks 197 F10
Keresley W Mid 134 G6
Keresley Newlands
Warks 134 G6
Kerfield Borders 270 G5
Kerley Downs Corn 4 G5
Kernborough Devon 8 G5
Kerne Bridge Hereford 79 B9
Kernsary Highld 299 B8
Kerridge Ches E 184 F6
Kerridge-end Ches E 184 F6
Kerris Corn 1 D4
Kerry = Ceri Powys 130 F2
Kerrycroy Argyll 266 C2
Kerry Hill Staffs 168 F6
Kerrysdale Highld 299 B8
Kerry's Gate Hereford 97 E7
Kersal Gtr Man 195 G10
Kersall Notts 172 C2
Kersbrook Cross Corn 12 F2
Kerscott Devon 25 B10
Kersey Suff 107 C10
Kersey Tye Suff 107 C9
Kersey Upland Suff 107 C9
Kershopefoot Cumb 249 G11
Kersoe Worcs 99 D9
Kerswell Devon 27 F9
Kerswell Green Worcs 99 B7
Kerthen Wood Corn 2 C3
Kesgrave Suff 108 B4
Kessingland Suff 143 F10
Kessingland Beach
Suff 143 F10
Kessington E Dunb 277 G11
Kestle Corn 5 F9
Kestle Mill Corn 5 D7
Keston London 68 G2
Keston Mark London 68 F2
Keswick Cumb 229 G11
Norf 142 C4
Norf 161 C7
Kete Pembs 72 E4
Ketford Glos 98 E4
Ketley Telford 150 G3
Ketley Bank Telford 150 G3
Ketsby Lincs 190 F5
Kettering N Nhants 121 B7
Ketteringham Norf 142 C3
Kettins Perth 286 D6
Kettlebaston Suff 125 G9
Kettlebridge Fife 287 G7
Kettlebrook Staffs 134 C4
Kettleburgh Suff 126 E5
Kettle Corner Kent 53 C8
Kettle Green Herts 86 B6
Kettlehill Fife 287 G7
Kettleholm Dumfries 238 B4
Kettleness N Yorks 226 B6
Kettleshulme Ches E 185 F7
Kettleshume Ches E 185 F7
Kettlesing N Yorks 205 B10
Kettlesing Bottom
N Yorks 205 B10
Kettlesing Head
N Yorks 205 B10
Kettlestone Norf 159 C9
Kettlethorpe Lincs 188 F4
W Yorks 197 D10
Kettletoft Orkney 314 C6
Kettlewell N Yorks 213 E9
Ketton Rutland 137 C9
Kevingtown London 68 F3
Kew London 67 D7
Keward Som 44 E4
Kew Bridge London 67 D7
Kewstoke N Som 59 G10
Kexbrough S Yorks 197 F9
Kexby Lincs 188 D5
York 207 C10
Keybridge Corn 11 G7
Keycol Kent 69 G11
Keyford Som 45 D9
Key Green Ches E 168 C5
N Yorks 226 E6
Keyham Leics 136 B3
Keyhaven Hants 20 C2
Keyingham E Yorks 201 B8
Keymer W Sus 36 D4
Keynsham Bath 61 F7
Keysers Estate Essex 86 D5
Key's Green Kent 53 F7
Keysoe Bedford 121 E11
Keysoe Row Bedford 121 E11
Keyston Cambs 121 B10
Key Street Kent 69 G11
Keyworth Notts 154 C2
Khantore Aberds 292 D4
Kibbear Som 28 C2
Kibblesworth T&W 242 F6
Kibworth Beauchamp
Leics 136 E3
Kibworth Harcourt
Leics 136 E3
Kidbrooke London 68 D2
Kidburngill Cumb 229 G7
Kiddal Lane End
W Yorks 206 F4
Kiddemore Green Staffs 133 B7
Kidderminster Worcs 116 B6
Kiddington Oxon 101 G8
Kidd's Moor Norf 142 C2
Kidlington Oxon 83 C7
Kidmore End Oxon 65 D7
Kidnal Ches W 167 F7
Kidsdale Dumfries 236 F6
Kidsgrove Staffs 168 E4
Kidstones N Yorks 213 C9
Kidwelly = Cydweli
Carms 74 D6
Kiel Crofts Argyll 289 F11
Kielder Northumb 250 E4
Kierfiold Ho Orkney 314 E2
Kiff Green W Berks 64 F5
Kilbagie Fife 279 D8
Kilbarchan Renfs 267 C8
Kilbeg Highld 295 E8
Kilberry Argyll 275 G8
Kilbirnie N Ayrs 266 E6
Kilbowie W Dunb 277 G10
Kilbraur Highld 311 H2
Kilbride Argyll 254 C4
Argyll 275 D9
Argyll 289 G10
Argyll 289 G11
Highld 295 C7
Kilbridemore Argyll 275 D11
Kilbryde Castle Stirling 285 G11
Kilburn Angus 292 G5
Derbys 170 F5
London 67 C9
N Yorks 215 D10
Kilby Leics 136 D2
Kilby Bridge Leics 136 D2
Kilchamaig Argyll 275 G9
Kilchattan Argyll 274 D4
Kilchattan Bay Argyll 266 E2
Kilchenzie Argyll 255 E7
Kilcheran Argyll 289 F10
Kilchiaran Argyll 274 G3
Kilchoan Argyll 275 B8
Highld 288 C6
Kilchoman Argyll 274 G3
Kilchrenan Argyll 284 E4
Kilconquhar Fife 287 G8
Kilcot Glos 98 F3
Kilcoy Highld 300 D5
Kilcreggan Argyll 276 E4
Kildale N Yorks 226 D2
Kildalloig Argyll 255 F8
Kildary Highld 301 B7
Kildaton Ho Argyll 254 C5
Kildavanan Argyll 275 G11
Kildermorie Lodge
Highld 300 B5
Kildonan Dumfries 236 D2
Highld 298 D3
N Ayrs 256 E2
Kildonan Lodge Highld 311 G3
Kildonnan Highld 294 G6
Kildrum N Lanark 278 F5
Kildrummy Aberds 292 B6
Kildwick N Yorks 204 D6
Kilfinan Argyll 275 F10
Kilfinnan Highld 290 D4
Kilgetty Pembs 73 D10
Kilgour Fife 286 G6
Kilgrammie S Ayrs 245 C7
Kilgwrrwg Common Mon 79 F7
Kilhallon Corn 5 E11
Kilham E Yorks 217 G11
Northumb 263 C9
Kilkeddan Argyll 255 E8
Kilkenneth Argyll 288 E1
Kilkenny Glos 81 B8
Kilkerran Argyll 255 F8
Kilkhampton Corn 24 E3
Killamarsh Derbys 187 E7
Killaworgey Corn 5 C8
Killay Swansea 56 C6
Killbeg Argyll 289 E8
Killean Argyll 255 C7
Killearn Stirling 277 D10
Killegruer Argyll 255 D7
Killen Highld 300 D6
Killerby Darl 224 B3
Killichonan Perth 285 B9
Killiechoinich Argyll 289 G10
Killiechonate Highld 290 E4
Killiechronan Argyll 289 E7
Killiecrankie Perth 291 G11
Killiemor Argyll 288 F6
Killiemore House Argyll 288 G6
Killilan Highld 295 B11
Killimster Highld 310 D7
Killin Stirling 285 D9
Killinallan Argyll 274 F4
Killingbeck W Yorks 206 G2
Killinghall N Yorks 205 B11
Killington Cumb 212 B2
Devon 41 D7
Killingworth T&W 243 C7
Killingworth Moor T&W 243 C7
Killingworth Village
T&W 243 C7
Killin Lodge Highld 291 C7
Killivose Corn 2 B4
Killmahumaig Argyll 275 D8
Killochyett Borders 271 F9
Killocraw Argyll 255 D7
Killundine Highld 289 E7
Killylung Dumfries 247 G11
Kilmacolm Invclyd 267 B7
Kilmaha Argyll 275 C10
Kilmahog Stirling 285 G10
Kilmalieu Highld 289 D10
Kilmaluag Highld 298 B4
Kilmany Fife 287 E7
Kilmarie Highld 295 D7
Kilmarnock E Ayrs 257 B10
Kilmaron Castle Fife 287 F7
Kilmartin Argyll 275 D9
Kilmaurs E Ayrs 267 G8
Kilmelford Argyll 275 B9
Kilmeny Argyll 274 G4
Kilmersdon Som 45 C7
Kilmeston Hants 33 B9
Kilmichael Argyll 255 E7
Argyll 275 F10
Kilmichael Glassary
Argyll 275 D9
Kilmichael of Inverlussa
Argyll 275 E8
Kilmington Devon 15 B11
Wilts 45 F9
Kilmington Common
Wilts 45 F9
Kilmoluaig Argyll 288 E1
Kilmonivaig Highld 290 E3
Kilmorack Highld 300 E4
Kilmore Argyll 289 G10
Highld 295 E8
Kilmory Argyll 275 F8
Highld 289 B7
Highld 294 E5
N Ayrs 255 E10
Kilmory Lodge Argyll 275 C8
Kilmote Highld 311 H3
Kilmuir Highld 298 B3
Highld 298 E2
Highld 300 E6
Highld 301 B7
Kilmun Argyll 275 B10
Argyll 276 E3
Kilnave Argyll 274 F3
Kilncadzow S Lanark 269 F7
Kilndown Kent 53 G8
Kiln Green Hereford 79 B10
Wokingham 65 D10
Kilnhill Cumb 229 E10
Kilnhurst S Yorks 187 B7
Kilninian Argyll 288 E5
Kilninver Argyll 289 G10
Kiln Pit Hill Northumb 242 G2
Kilnsea E Yorks 201 D12
Kilnsey N Yorks 213 F9
Kilnwick E Yorks 208 D5
Kilnwick Percy E Yorks 208 C2
Kilnwood Vale W Sus 51 G8
Kiloran Argyll 274 D4
Kilpatrick N Ayrs 255 E10
Kilpeck Hereford 97 E8
Kilphedir Highld 311 H3
Kilpin E Yorks 199 B9
Kilpin Pike E Yorks 199 B9
Kilrenny Fife 287 G9
Kilsby W Nhants 119 C11
Kilspindie Perth 286 E6
Kilsyth N Lanark 278 F4
Kiltarlity Highld 300 E5
Kilton Notts 187 F9
Redcar 226 B4
Som 43 E7
Kilton Thorpe Redcar 226 B3
Kiltyrie Perth 285 D10
Kilvaxter Highld 298 C3
Kilve Som 43 E7
Kilvington Notts 172 G3
Kilwinning N Ayrs 266 G6
Kimberley Norf 141 C11
Notts 171 G8
Kimberworth S Yorks 186 C6
Kimberworth Park
S Yorks 186 C6
Kimblesworth Durham 233 B11
Kimble Wick Bucks 84 D4
Kimbolton Cambs 121 D11
Hereford 115 E10
Kimbridge Hants 32 B4
Kimcote Leics 135 F11
Kimmeridge Dorset 18 F4
Kimmerston Northumb 263 B11
Kimpton Hants 47 D9
Herts 85 B11
Kimworthy Devon 24 E4
Kinabus Argyll 254 C3
Kinbeachie Highld 300 C6
Kinbrace Highld 310 F2
Kinbuck Stirling 285 G11
Kincaidston S Ayrs 257 F9
Kincaple Fife 287 F8
Kincardine Fife 279 D8
Highld 309 L6
Kincardine Bridge Falk 279 D8
Kincardine O'Neil
Aberds 293 D7
Kinclaven Perth 286 D5
Kincorth Aberdeen 293 C11
Kincorth Ho Moray 301 C10
Kincraig Highld 291 C10
Kincraigie Perth 286 C3
Kindallachan Perth 286 C3
Kine Moor S Yorks 197 G9
Kineton Glos 99 F11
Warks 118 G6
Kineton Green W Mid 134 G2
Kinfauns Perth 286 E5
Kingairloch Highld 289 D10
Kingarth Argyll 255 B11
Kingates IoW 20 F6
Kingbeare Corn 11 G11
Kingcoed Mon 78 D6
Kingdown N Som 60 G4
King Edward Aberds 303 D7
Kingerby Lincs 189 C9
Kingfield Sur 50 B4
Kingford Devon 24 F3
Devon 25 D10
Kingham Oxon 100 G5
Kinghay Wilts 30 B5
Kingholm Quay
Dumfries 237 B11
Kinghorn Fife 280 D5
Kingie Highld 290 C3
Kinglassie Fife 280 B4
Kingledores Borders 260 D4
Kingoodie Perth 287 E7
King's Acre Hereford 97 C9
Kingsand Corn 7 E8
Kingsash Bucks 84 D5
Kingsbarns Fife 287 F9
Kingsbridge Devon 8 G4
Som 42 F3
King's Bromley Staffs 152 F2
Kingsbrook Oxfordshire 84 C4
Kingsburgh Highld 298 D3
Kingsbury London 67 B8
Warks 134 D4
Kingsbury Episcopi Som 28 C6
Kingsbury Regis Som 29 D11
King's Caple Hereford 97 F11
Kingscauseway Highld 301 B7
Kingscavil W Loth 279 F10
Kingsclere Hants 48 B4
Kingsclere Woodlands
Hants 64 G4
King's Cliffe N Nhants 137 D10
Kings Clipstone Notts 171 C10
Kingscote Glos 80 F4
Kingscott Devon 25 D8
King's Coughton Warks 117 F11
Kingscourt Glos 80 E4
Kingscross N Ayrs 256 D2
Kingsditch Glos 99 G8
Kingsdon Som 29 B8
Kingsdown Kent 54 B2
Kent 55 D11
Swindon 63 B7
Wilts 61 F10
King's Dyke Cambs 138 D4
Kingseat Fife 280 C2
Kingseathill Fife 280 D2
King's End Worcs 116 G6
Kingsett Devon 12 E6
Kingsey Bucks 84 D2
Kingsfield Hereford 97 B10
Kingsfold Lancs 194 B4
W Sus 51 F7
Kingsford Aberds 293 B7
E Ayrs 267 F8
Worcs 132 G6
Kingsforth N Lincs 200 D4
King's Furlong Hants 48 C6
Kingsgate Kent 71 E11
King's Green Glos 98 E5
Worcs 116 E5
Kingshall Green Suff 125 E8
Kingshall Street Suff 125 E8
Kingsheanton Devon 40 F5
King's Heath W Mid 133 G11
W Nhants 120 E4
Kings Hedges Cambs 123 E9
Kingshill Glos 80 F3
Swindon 62 C6
Kings Hill Glos 81 E8
King's Hill Kent 53 C7
W Mid 133 D9
Kingsholm Glos 80 B4
Kingshouse Hotel
Highld 284 B6
Kingshurst W Mid 134 F3
Kingside Hill Cumb 238 G5
Kingskerswell Devon 9 B7
Kingskettle Fife 287 G7
Kingsknowe Edin 280 G4
Kingsland Anglesey 178 E2
Hereford 115 E8
London 67 C10
Shrops 149 G9
Kings Langley Herts 85 E9
Kingsley Ches W 183 G9
Hants 49 F9
Staffs 169 F8
Kingsley Green W Sus 49 G11
Kingsley Holt Staffs 169 F8
Kingsley Moor Staffs 169 F7
Kingsley Park W Nhants 120 E5
Kingslow Shrops 132 D5
King's Lynn Norf 158 E2
King's Meaburn Cumb 231 G8
Kingsmead Hants 33 E9
Kingsmere Oxon 101 G11
King's Mills Derbys 153 D8
Wrex 166 F4
Kingsmoor Essex 86 D6
Kings Moss Mers 194 G4
Kingsmuir Angus 287 C8
Fife 287 G9
Kings Muir Borders 261 B7
King's Newnham Warks 119 B9
King's Newton Derbys 153 D7
Kingsnordley Shrops 132 F5
Kingsnorth Kent 54 F4
King's Norton Leics 136 C3
W Mid 117 B11
King's Nympton Devon 25 D11
King's Pyon Hereford 115 G8
Kings Ripton Cambs 122 B5
King's Somborne Hants 47 G11
King's Stag Dorset 30 E2
King's Stanley Glos 80 E4
King's Sutton W Nhants 101 D9
King's Tamerton Plym 7 D9
Kingstanding W Mid 133 E11
Kingsteignton Devon 14 G3
Kingsteps Highld 301 D9
King Sterndale Derbys 185 G9
King's Thorn Hereford 97 E10
Kingsthorpe W Nhants 120 E5
Kingsthorpe Hollow
W Nhants 120 E5
Kingston Cambs 122 F6
Devon 8 F2
Devon 15 D8
Dorset 18 F5
Dorset 30 F3
E Loth 281 E10
Gtr Man 184 B6
Hants 31 G11
IoW 20 E5
Kent 55 C7
M Keynes 103 D8
Moray 302 C3
Ptsmth 33 G11
Kingston *continued*
Suff 108 B5
Kingston Bagpuize Oxon 82 F6
Kingston Blount Oxon 84 F2
Kingston by Sea W Sus 36 G2
Kingston Deverill Wilts 45 F10
Kingstone Hereford 97 D8
Hereford 98 G2
Som 28 E5
Staffs 151 D11
S Yorks 197 F10
Kingstone Winslow Oxon 63 B9
Kingston Gorse W Sus 35 G9
Kingston Lisle Oxon 63 B10
Kingston Maurward
Dorset 17 C10
Kingston near Lewes
E Sus 36 F5
Kingston on Soar
Notts 153 D10
Kingston Park T&W 242 D6
Kingston Russell Dorset 17 C7
Kingston St Mary Som 28 B2
Kingston Seymour
N Som 60 F2
Kingston Stert Oxon 84 E2
Kingston upon Hull Hull 200 B5
Kingston upon Thames
London 67 F7
Kingston Vale London 67 E8
Kingstown Cumb 239 F9
King Street Essex 87 E9
King's Walden Herts 104 G3
Kingsway Bath 61 G8
Halton 183 D8
Kingswear Devon 9 E7
Kingswells Aberdeen 293 C10
Kingswinford W Mid 133 F7
Kingswood Bucks 83 B11
Essex 69 B8
Glos 80 G2
Hereford 114 G5
Herts 85 E10
Kent 53 C10
Powys 130 C4
S Glos 60 E6
Som 42 F6
Sur 51 B8
Warks 118 C3
Warr 183 C9
Kingswood Brook
Warks 118 C3
Kingswood Common
Staffs 132 C6
Worcs 116 D4
Kings Worthy Hants 48 G3
Kingthorpe Lincs 189 F10
Kington Hereford 114 F5
S Glos 79 G10
Worcs 117 F9
Kington Langley Wilts 62 D2
Kington Magna Dorset 30 C3
Kington St Michael Wilts 62 D2
Kingussie Highld 291 C9
Kingweston Som 44 G4
Kinhrive Highld 301 B7
Kininvie Ho Moray 302 E3
Kinkell Bridge Perth 286 F3
Kinknockie Aberds 303 E10
Aberds 303 G9
Kinkry Hill Cumb 240 B2
Kinlet Shrops 132 G4
Kinloch Fife 286 F6
Highld 289 D8
Highld 294 F5
Highld 295 D8
Highld 308 F3
Perth 286 C5
Perth 286 C6
Kinlochan Highld 289 C10
Kinlochard Stirling 285 G8
Kinlochbeoraid Highld 295 G10
Kinlochbervie Highld 306 D7
Kinloch Damph Highld 299 E8
Kinlocheil Highld 289 B11
Kinlochewe Highld 299 C10
Kinloch Hourn Highld 295 E11
Kinloch Laggan Highld 291 E7
Kinlochleven Highld 290 G3
Kinloch Lodge Highld 308 D5
Kinlochmoidart Highld 289 B9
Kinlochmorar Highld 295 F10
Kinlochmore Highld 290 G3
Kinloch Rannoch Perth 285 B10
Kinlochspelve Argyll 289 G8
Kinloid Highld 295 G8
Kinloss Moray 301 C10
Kinmel Bay = Bae Cinmel
Conwy 181 E7
Kinmuck Aberds 293 B10
Kinmundy Aberds 293 B10
Kinnadie Aberds 303 E9
Kinnaird Perth 286 B3
Perth 286 E6
Kinnaird Castle Angus 287 B10
Kinnauld Highld 309 J7
Kinneff Aberds 293 F10
Kinneil Falk 279 E9
Kinnelhead Dumfries 248 C2
Kinnell Angus 287 B10
Kinnerley Shrops 148 E6
Kinnersley Hereford 96 B6
Worcs 99 C7
Kinnerton Powys 114 E4
Kinnerton Green Flint 166 C4
Kinnesswood Perth 286 G5
Kinninvie Durham 233 G7
Kinnordy Angus 287 B7
Kinoulton Notts 154 C3
Kinross Perth 286 G5
Kinrossie Perth 286 D5
Kinsbourne Green Herts 85 B10
Kinsey Heath Ches E 167 G11
Kinsham Hereford 115 E7
Worcs 99 D8
Kinsley W Yorks 198 E2
Kinson BCP 19 B7
Kintallan Argyll 275 E8
Kintbury W Berks 63 F11
Kintessack Moray 301 C9
Kintillo Perth 286 F5
Kintocher Aberds 293 C7
Kinton Hereford 115 C8
Shrops 149 F7
Kintore Aberds 293 B9
Kintour Argyll 254 B5
Kintra Argyll 254 C4
Argyll 288 G5
Kintradwell Highld 311 J3
Kintraw Argyll 275 C9
Kinuachdrachd Argyll 275 D8
Kinveachy Highld 291 B11
Kinver Staffs 132 G6
Kinwalsey Warks 134 F5
Kip Hill Durham 242 G6
Kiplin N Yorks 224 F5
Kippax W Yorks 206 G4
Kippen Stirling 278 C3
Kippford or Scaur
Dumfries 237 D10
Kippilaw Borders 262 D2

Kippilaw Mains Borders 262 D2
Kipping's Cross Kent 52 F6
Kippington Kent 52 C4
Kirbister Orkney 314 D6
Orkney 314 E2
Orkney 314 F3
Kirbuster Orkney 314 D2
Kirby Bedon Norf 142 B5
Kirby Bellars Leics 154 F4
Kirby Cane Norf 143 E7
Kirby Corner W Mid 118 B5
Kirby Cross Essex 108 G4
Kirby Fields Leics 135 C10
Kirby Green Norf 143 E7
Kirby Grindalythe
N Yorks 217 F8
Kirby Hill N Yorks 215 F7
N Yorks 224 D2
Kirby Knowle N Yorks 215 B9
Kirby-le-Soken Essex 108 G4
Kirby Misperton
N Yorks 216 D5
Kirby Moor Cumb 240 E2
Kirby Muxloe Leics 135 C10
Kirby Row Norf 143 E7
Kirby Sigston N Yorks 225 G8
Kirby Underdale
E Yorks 208 B2
Kirby Wiske N Yorks 215 C7
Kirdford W Sus 35 B8
Kirk Highld 310 D6
Kirkabister Shetland 312 G6
Shetland 313 K6
Kirkandrews Dumfries 237 E8
Kirkandrews-on-Eden
Cumb 239 F9
Kirkapol Argyll 288 E2
Kirkbampton Cumb 239 F8
Kirkbean Dumfries 237 D11
Kirkborough Cumb 229 D7
Kirkbrae Orkney 314 B4
Kirk Bramwith S Yorks 198 E6
Kirkbride Cumb 238 F6
Kirkbridge N Yorks 224 G5
Kirkbuddo Angus 287 C9
Kirkburn Borders 261 B7
E Yorks 208 B5
Kirkburton W Yorks 197 E7
Kirkby Lincs 189 C9
Mers 182 B6
N Yorks 225 D10
Kirkby Fenside Lincs 174 C4
Kirkby Fleetham
N Yorks 224 G5
Kirkby Green Lincs 173 D9
Kirkby Hill N Yorks 215 F7
Kirkby in Ashfield
Notts 171 D8
Kirkby-in-Furness
Cumb 210 C4
Kirkby la Thorpe Lincs 173 F10
Kirkby Lonsdale Cumb 212 D2
Kirkby Malham N Yorks 213 G7
Kirkby Mallory Leics 135 C9
Kirkby Malzeard
N Yorks 214 E4
Kirkby Mills N Yorks 216 B4
Kirkbymoorside
N Yorks 216 B3
Kirkby on Bain Lincs 174 C2
Kirkby Overblow
N Yorks 206 D2
Kirkby Stephen Cumb 222 D5
Kirkby Thore Cumb 231 F8
Kirkby Underwood
Lincs 155 D11
Kirkby Wharfe N Yorks 206 E6
Kirkby Woodhouse
Notts 171 E7
Kirkcaldy Fife 280 C5
Kirkcambeck Cumb 240 D2
Kirkcarswell Dumfries 237 E9
Kirkcolm Dumfries 236 C2
Kirkconnel Dumfries 258 G6
Kirkconnell Dumfries 237 C11
Kirkcowan Dumfries 236 C5
Kirkcudbright Dumfries 237 D8
Kirkdale Mers 182 C4
Kirk Deighton N Yorks 206 C3
Kirk Ella E Yorks 200 B4
Kirkfieldbank S Lanark 269 G7
Kirkforthar Feus Fife 286 G6
Kirkgunzeon Dumfries 237 C10
Kirk Hallam Derbys 171 G7
Kirkham Lancs 202 G4
N Yorks 216 F4
Kirkhamgate W Yorks 197 C9
Kirk Hammerton
N Yorks 206 B5
Kirkhams Gtr Man 195 F10
Kirkharle Northumb 252 G2
Kirkheaton Northumb 242 B2
W Yorks 197 D7
Kirkhill Angus 293 G8
E Renf 267 D11
Highld 300 E5
Midloth 270 C4
Moray 302 F2
W Loth 279 G11
Kirkholt Gtr Man 195 E11
Kirkhope Borders 261 E9
Kirkhouse Borders 261 C8
Cumb 240 F3
Kirkiboll Highld 308 D5
Kirkibost Highld 295 D7
Kirkinch Angus 287 C7
Kirkinner Dumfries 236 D6
Kirkintilloch E Dunb 278 G3
Kirk Ireton Derbys 170 E3
Kirkland Cumb 219 B11
Cumb 229 B11
Cumb 231 E8
Dumfries 247 E8
Dumfries 258 G6
S Ayrs 244 E6
Kirkland Guards Cumb 229 C9
Kirk Langley Derbys 152 B5
Kirkleatham Redcar 235 G7
Kirklees Gtr Man 195 E9
Kirklevington Stockton 225 D8
Kirkley Suff 143 E10
Kirklington Notts 171 D11
N Yorks 214 C6
Kirklinton Cumb 239 D10
Kirkliston Edin 280 G2
Kirkmaiden Dumfries 236 F3
Kirk Merrington
Durham 233 E11
Kirkmichael Perth 286 B4
S Ayrs 245 B8
Kirk Michael IoM 192 C4
Kirkmichael Mains
Dumfries 248 F2
Kirkmuirhill S Lanark 268 G6
Kirknewton Northumb 263 C10
W Loth 270 B2
Kirkney Aberds 302 F5
Kirk of Shotts N Lanark 268 C6
Kirkoswald Cumb 231 C7
S Ayrs 244 B6
Kirkpatrick Dumfries 247 E10
Kirkpatrick Durham
Dumfries 237 B9
Kirkpatrick-Fleming
Dumfries 239 C7
Kirk Sandall S Yorks 198 F6
Kirksanton Cumb 210 C2
Kirkshaw N Lanark 268 C4
Kirk Smeaton N Yorks 198 D4
Kirkstall W Yorks 205 F11
Kirkstead Borders 261 E7
Lincs 173 C11
Kirkstile Aberds 302 F5
Kirkstyle Highld 310 B7
Kirkthorpe W Yorks 197 C11
Kirkton Aberds 302 E6
Aberds 302 G6
Angus 286 C6
Angus 287 C8
Angus 287 D8
Argyll 275 C8
Borders 262 G2
Dumfries 247 G11
Fife 280 D4
Fife 287 E7
Highld 295 C10
Highld 299 E9
Highld 301 D7
Highld 309 K7
Perth 286 F3
S Lanark 259 E10
Stirling 285 G9
W Loth 269 B10
Kirktonhill Borders 271 E9
W Dunb 277 G7
Kirkton Manor Borders 260 B6
Kirkton of Airlie Angus 287 B7
Kirkton of Auchterhouse
Angus 287 D7
Kirkton of Auchterless
Aberds 303 E7
Kirkton of Barevan
Highld 301 E8
Kirkton of Bourtie
Aberds 303 G8
Kirkton of Collace
Perth 286 D5
Kirkton of Craig Angus 287 B11
Kirkton of Culsalmond
Aberds 302 F6
Kirkton of Durris
Aberds 293 D9
Kirkton of Glenbuchat
Aberds 292 B5
Kirkton of Glenisla
Angus 292 G4
Kirkton of Kingoldrum
Angus 287 B7
Kirkton of Largo Fife 287 G8
Kirkton of Lethendy
Perth 286 C5
Kirkton of Logie Buchan
Aberds 303 G9
Kirkton of Maryculter
Aberds 293 D10
Kirkton of Menmuir
Angus 293 G7
Kirkton of Monikie
Angus 287 D9
Kirkton of Oyne Aberds 302 G6
Kirkton of Rayne
Aberds 302 G6
Kirkton of Skene
Aberds 293 C10
Kirkton of Tough
Aberds 293 B8
Kirktoun E Ayrs 267 G8
Kirktown Aberds 303 D10
Kirktown of Alvah
Aberds 302 C6
Kirktown of Deskford
Moray 302 C5
Kirktown of Fetteresso
Aberds 293 E10
Kirktown of Mortlach
Moray 302 F3
Kirktown of Slains
Aberds 303 G10
Kirkurd Borders 270 G2
Kirkwall Orkney 314 E4
Kirkwhelpington
Northumb 251 G11
Kirkwood Dumfries 238 B4
N Lanark 268 C4
Kirk Yetholm Borders 263 D8
Kirmington N Lincs 200 E6
Kirmond le Mire Lincs 189 C11
Kirn Argyll 276 F3
Kirriemuir Angus 287 B7
Kirstead Green Norf 142 D5
Kirtlebridge Dumfries 238 C6
Kirtleton Dumfries 249 G7
Kirtling Cambs 124 F3
Kirtling Green Cambs 124 F3
Kirtlington Oxon 83 B7
Kirtomy Highld 308 C7
Kirton Lincs 156 B6
Notts 171 B11
Suff 108 D5
Kirton Campus W Loth 269 B10
Kirton End Lincs 174 G3
Kirton Holme Lincs 174 G3
Kirton in Lindsey
N Lincs 188 B6
Kiskin Cumb 210 B1
Kislingbury W Nhants 120 F3
Kitbridge Devon 28 G4
Kitchenroyd W Yorks 197 F8
Kitebrook Warks 100 E4
Kite Green Warks 118 D3
Kite Hill IoW 21 C7
Kites Hardwick Warks 119 D9
Kit Hill Dorset 30 D4
Kitlye Glos 80 E5
Kit's Coty Kent 69 G8
Kitt Green Gtr Man 194 F5
Kittisford Som 27 C9
Kittle Swansea 56 D5
Kitts End Herts 86 F2
Kitt's Green W Mid 134 F3
Kitt's Moss Gtr Man 184 E5
Kittwhistle Dorset 28 G5
Kittybrewster Aberdeen 293 C11
Kitwell W Mid 133 G9
Kitwood Hants 49 G7
Kivernoll Hereford 97 E9
Kiveton Park S Yorks 187 E7
Knaith Lincs 188 E4
Knaith Park Lincs 188 D4
Knaphill Sur 50 B3
Knapp Hants 32 C6
Perth 286 D6
Som 28 B4
Wilts 31 B8
Knapp Hill Wilts 30 B5
Knapthorpe Notts 172 D2
Knaptoft Leics 136 F2
Knapton Norf 160 C6
York 207 C7
Knapton Green Hereford 115 G8
Knapwell Cambs 122 E6
Knaresborough N Yorks 206 B3
Knarsdale Northumb 240 G5
Knatts Valley Kent 68 G5
Knauchland Moray 302 D5
Knaven Aberds 303 E8
Knave's Ash Kent 71 G7
Knaves Green Suff 126 D2
Knavesmire York 207 D7
Knayton N Yorks 215 B8
Knebworth Herts 104 G5
Knedlington E Yorks 199 B8
Kneesall Notts 172 C2
Kneesworth Cambs 104 C6
Kneeton Notts 172 F2
Knelston Swansea 56 D3
Knenhall Staffs 151 B8
Knettishall Suff 141 G9
Knightacott Devon 41 F7
Knightcote Warks 119 G7
Knightcott N Som 43 B11
Knightley Staffs 150 D6
Knightley Dale Staffs 150 E6
Knighton BCP 18 B6
Devon 7 F10
Dorset 29 E10
Leicester 135 C11
Oxon 63 B9
Som 43 E7
Staffs 150 D4
Staffs 168 G2
Wilts 63 E9
Worcs 117 F10
Knighton = Tref-y-Clawdd
Powys 114 C5
Knighton Fields
Leicester 135 C11
Knighton on Teme
Worcs 116 C2
Knightor Corn 5 D10
Knightsbridge Glos 99 F7
London 67 D9
Knight's End Cambs 139 E8
Knights Enham Hants 47 D11
Knight's Hill London 67 E10
Knightsmill Corn 11 E7
Knightsridge W Loth 269 B10
Knightswood Glasgow 267 B10
Knightwick Worcs 116 F4
Knill Hereford 114 E5
Knipe Fold Cumb 220 F6
Knipoch Argyll 289 G10
Knipton Leics 154 C6
Knitsley Durham 233 B8
Kniveton Derbys 170 E2
Knocharthur Highld 309 J7
Knock Argyll 289 F7
Cumb 231 F9
Moray 302 D5
Knockally Highld 311 G5
Knockan Highld 307 H7
Knockandhu Moray 302 G2
Knockando Moray 301 E11
Knockando Ho Moray 302 E2
Knockandoo Highld 301 G7
Knockbain Highld 300 D6
Knockbreck Highld 298 C2
Knockbrex Dumfries 237 E7
Knockcarrach Highld 290 B6
Knockdee Highld 310 C5
Knockdolian S Ayrs 244 F4
Knockdow Argyll 276 G2
Knockdown Glos 61 B10
Knockenbaird Aberds 302 G6
Knockenkelly N Ayrs 256 D2
Knockentiber E Ayrs 257 B9
Knockerdown Derbys 170 E2
Knockespock Ho Aberds 302 G5
Knockfarrel Highld 300 D5
Knockglass Dumfries 236 D2
Knockhall Kent 68 E5
Knockhall Castle
Aberds 303 G9
Knockholt Kent 52 B3
Knockholt Pound Kent 52 B3
Knockie Lodge Highld 290 B6
Knockin Shrops 148 E6
Knockin Heath Shrops 149 E7
Knockinlaw E Ayrs 257 B10
Knockinnon Highld 310 F5
Knocklaw Northumb 252 C3
Knocklearn Dumfries 237 B9
Knocklearoch Argyll 274 G4
Knockmill Kent 68 G5
Knocknaha Argyll 255 F7
Knocknain Dumfries 236 C1
Knockothie Aberds 303 F9
Knockrome Argyll 274 F6
Knocksharry IoM 192 D3
Knockstapplemore
Argyll 255 F7
Knockvologan Argyll 274 B4
Knodishall Suff 127 E8
Knokan Argyll 288 G6
Knole Som 29 B7
Knollbury Mon 60 B2
Knoll Green Som 43 F8
Knolls Green Ches E 184 F4
Knoll Top N Yorks 214 F3
Knolton Wrex 149 B7
Knolton Bryn Wrex 149 B7
Knook Wilts 46 E2
Knossington Leics 136 B6
Knotbury Staffs 169 B8
Knott End-on-Sea
Lancs 202 D3
Knotting Bedford 121 E10
Knotting Green
Bedford 121 E10
Knottingley W Yorks 198 C4
Knott Lanes Gtr Man 196 G2
Knott Oak Som 28 E5
Knotts Cumb 230 G4
Lancs 203 C11
Knotty Ash Mers 182 C6
Knotty Corner Devon 24 B6
Knotty Green Bucks 84 G6
Knowbury Shrops 115 C11
Knowe Dumfries 236 B5
Shetland 313 G5
Knowefield Cumb 239 F10
Knowehead Aberds 293 C7
Aberds 302 D5
Dumfries 246 E4
Knowes E Loth 282 F2
Knowesgate Northumb 251 F11
Knowes of Elrick
Aberds 302 D6
Knoweton N Lanark 268 D5
Knowetop N Lanark 268 D5
Knowhead Aberds 303 D9
Knowl Bank Staffs 168 F3
Knowle Bristol 60 E6
Devon 15 E7
Devon 26 G3
Devon 27 F8
Devon 40 F3
Hants 33 F9
Shrops 115 C11
Som 43 F10
Wilts 63 G7
W Mid 118 B3
Knowle Fields Worcs 117 F10
Knowlegate Shrops 115 C11
Knowle Green Lancs 203 F8
Sur 66 E4
Knowle Grove W Mid 118 B3
Knowle Hill Sur 66 F3
Knowle Park W Yorks 205 E7
Knowle St Giles Som 28 E4
Knowlesands Shrops 132 E4
Knowles Hill Devon 14 G3
Knowl Green Essex 106 C5
Knowl Hill Windsor 65 D10
Knowlton Dorset 31 E8
Kent 55 C9
Knowl Wall Staffs 151 B7
Knowl Wood W Yorks 196 C2
Knowsley Mers 182 B6
Knowsthorpe W Yorks 206 G2
Knowstone Devon 26 C4
Knox Bridge Kent 53 E9
Knucklas Powys 114 C5
Knuston N Nhants 121 D8
Knutsford Ches E 184 F3
Knutton Staffs 168 F4
Knuzden Brook Lancs 195 B8
Knypersley Staffs 168 D5
Kraiknish Highld 294 C5
Krumlin W Yorks 196 D5
Kuggar Corn 2 F6
Kyleakin Highld 295 C9
Kyle of Lochalsh Highld 295 C9
Kylepark N Lanark 268 C3
Kylerhea Highld 295 C9
Kylesknoydart Highld 295 F10
Kylesku Highld 306 F7
Kylesmorar Highld 295 F10
Kylestrome Highld 306 F7
Kyllachy House Highld 301 G7
Kymin Hereford 97 B11
Mon 79 C8
Kynaston Hereford 97 E10
Shrops 149 E7
Kynnersley Telford 150 F3
Kyre Worcs 116 E2
Kyre Green Worcs 116 E2
Kyre Magna Worcs 116 E2
Kyre Park Worcs 116 E2
Kyrewood Worcs 116 D2

L

Labost W Isles 304 D4
Lacasaidh W Isles 304 F5
Lacasdal W Isles 304 E6
Laceby NE Lincs 201 F8
Laceby Acres NE Lincs 201 F8
Lacey Green Bucks 84 F4
Ches E 184 E4
Lach Dennis Ches W 184 G2
Lache Ches W 166 C5
Lackenby Redcar 225 B11
Lackford Suff 124 C5
Lacock Wilts 62 F2
Ladbroke Warks 119 F8
Laddenvean Corn 3 E7
Laddingford Kent 53 D7
Lade Kent 39 C9
Lade Bank Lincs 174 E5
Ladies Riggs N Yorks 214 F2
Ladmanlow Derbys 185 G8
Ladock Corn 5 E7
Ladwell Hants 32 C6
Lady Orkney 314 B6
Ladybank Fife 287 F7
Ladybrook Notts 171 C8
Ladyburn Invclyd 276 F6
Ladycross Corn 12 D2
Ladyes Hill Warks 118 C5
Lady Green Mers 193 G10
Lady Hall Cumb 210 B3
Lady Halton Shrops 115 B9
Lady House Gtr Man 196 E2
Ladykirk Borders 273 F7
Ladyoak Shrops 131 C7
Lady Park T&W 242 F6
Ladyridge Hereford 97 E11
Ladysford Aberds 303 C9
Lady's Green Suff 124 F5
Ladywell London 67 E11
Shrops 149 C9
W Loth 269 B10
Ladywood Telford 132 C3
W Mid 133 F11
Worcs 117 E7
Lady Wood W Yorks 206 F2
Laffak Mers 183 B8
Laga Highld 289 C8
Lagafater Lodge
Dumfries 236 B3
Lagalochan Argyll 275 B9
Lagavulin Argyll 254 C5
Lagg Argyll 274 F6
N Ayrs 255 E10
Laggan Argyll 254 B3
Highld 289 B9
Highld 290 D4
Highld 291 D8
S Ayrs 245 G7
Lagganlia Highld 291 C10
Laggan Lodge Argyll 289 G8
Lagganmullan Dumfries 237 D7
Lagganulva Argyll 288 E6
Lagness W Sus 22 C5
Laide Highld 307 K3
Laig Highld 294 G6
Laigh Carnduff S Lanark 268 F3
Laigh Fenwick E Ayrs 267 G9
Laigh Glengall S Ayrs 257 F8
Laighmuir E Ayrs 267 F9
Laighstonehall S Lanark 268 E4
Laindon Essex 69 B7
Lair Highld 299 E10
Perth 292 G3
Laira Plym 7 D10
Lairg Highld 309 J5
Lairg Lodge Highld 309 J5
Lairgmore Highld 300 F5
Lairg Muir Highld 309 J5
Laisterdyke W Yorks 205 G9
Laithes Cumb 230 E5
Laithkirk Durham 232 G5
Laity Moor Corn 4 F3
Lake BCP 18 C5
Devon 12 D6
Devon 24 B6
Devon 40 G5
IoW 21 E7
Wilts 46 F6
Lake End Bucks 66 D2
Lakenham Norf 142 B4
Lakenheath Suff 140 G4
Laker's Green Sur 50 F4
Lakesend Norf 139 D10
Lakeside Cumb 211 B7
Thurrock 68 D5
Worcs 117 D11
Laleham Sur 66 F5
Laleston = Trelales
Bridgend 57 F11
Lamanva Corn 3 C7
Lamarsh Essex 107 D7
Lamas Norf 160 E4
Lamb Corner Essex 107 E10
Lambden Borders 272 G4
Lamberden Kent 38 B4
Lamberhead Green
Gtr Man 194 G4
Lamberhurst Kent 53 F7
Lamberhurst Quarter
Kent 53 F7
Lamberton Borders 273 D9
Lambert's End W Mid 133 E9
Lambeth London 67 D10
Lambfair Green Suff 124 G4
Lambfoot Cumb 229 E9
Lambhill Glasgow 267 B11
Lambley Northumb 240 F5
Notts 171 F10
Lambourn W Berks 63 D10
Lambourne Corn 4 E5
Essex 87 F7
Lambourne End Essex 87 G7
Lambourn Woodlands
W Berks 63 D10
Lambridge Bath 61 F9
Lamb's Cross Kent 53 D9
Lambs Green W Sus 51 F8
Lambs' Green Dorset 18 B5
Lambston Pembs 72 B6
Lambton T&W 243 G7
Lamellion Corn 6 C4
Lamerton Devon 12 F5
Lamesley T&W 243 F7
Laminess Orkney 314 C6
Lamington Highld 301 B7
S Lanark 259 C11
Lamlash N Ayrs 256 C2
Lamledra Corn 5 G10
Lamloch Dumfries 246 D2
Lammack Blackburn 195 B7
Lamonby Cumb 230 D4
Lamorick Corn 5 C10
Lamorna Corn 1 E4
Lamorran Corn 5 G7
Lampardbrook Suff 126 E5
Lampeter = Llanbedr Pont
Steffan Ceredig 93 B11
Lampeter Velfrey Pembs 73 C11
Lamphey Pembs 73 E8
Lamplugh Cumb 229 G7
Lamport W Nhants 120 C5
Lampton London 66 D6
Lamyatt Som 45 F7
Lana Devon 12 B2
Devon 24 F4
Lanark S Lanark 269 G7
Lancaster Lancs 211 G9
Lanchester Durham 233 B9
Lancing W Sus 35 G11
Landbeach Cambs 123 D9
Landcross Devon 25 C7
Landerberry Aberds 293 C9
Landewednack Corn 2 G6
Landford Wilts 32 D3
Landford Manor Wilts 32 C3
Landfordwood Wilts 32 C3
Land Gate Gtr Man 194 G5
Landguard Manor IoW 21 E7
Landhill Devon 12 B4
Landican Mers 182 D3
Landimore Swansea 56 C3
Landkey Devon 40 G5
Landkey Newland Devon 40 G5
Landore Swansea 57 B7
Landport E Sus 36 E6
Ptsmth 33 G10
Landrake Corn 7 C7
Landscove Devon 8 B5
Landshipping Pembs 73 C8
Landshipping Quay
Pembs 73 C8
Landslow Green
Gtr Man 185 B7
Landulph Corn 7 C8
Landwade Suff 124 D2
Landywood Staffs 133 B9
Lane Corn 4 C6
Laneast Corn 11 E10
Lane Bottom Lancs 204 F3
W Yorks 205 F7
Lane End Bucks 84 G4
Lane-end Corn 5 B10
Lane End Cumb 220 G2
Derbys 170 C6
Devon 24 G6
Dorset 18 C3
Flint 166 C3
Glos 79 B10
Hants 33 B9
Hants 33 B11
IoW 21 D9
Kent 68 E5
Lancs 204 D3
Sur 49 E10
S Yorks 186 B5
Wilts 45 D10
W Yorks 204 F6
Lane Ends Ches E 168 D2
Ches E 185 E7
Cumb 210 C6
Derbys 152 C4
Gtr Man 185 C7
Lancs 194 D6
Lancs 203 C11
Lancs 203 G11
N Yorks 204 E5
Stoke 168 E5
W Yorks 205 F10
Lane Green Staffs 133 C7
Laneham Notts 188 F4
Lanehead Durham 232 C2
Northumb 251 F7
Lane Head Derbys 185 F11
Durham 224 C2
Gtr Man 183 B10
Pembs 73 E8
W Mid 133 C9
W Yorks 197 F7
Lane Heads Lancs 202 F4
Lanehouse Dorset 17 F9
Lanercost Cumb 240 E3
Lanescot Corn 5 D11
Lanesend Pembs 73 D9
Lanes End Bucks 84 D6
Lane's End Shrops 132 G2
Lanesfield W Mid 133 D8
Laneshaw Bridge Lancs 204 E4
Lane Side Lancs 195 C9
Laney Green Staffs 133 B9
Lanfach Caerph 78 F2
Langaford Devon 12 B4
Langage Devon 7 E11
Langal Highld 289 C9
Langaller Som 28 B3
Langar Notts 154 C4
Langbank Renfs 277 G7
Langbar N Yorks 205 C7
Langbaurgh N Yorks 225 C11
Langburnshiels Borders 250 C2
Langcliffe N Yorks 212 G6
Langdale Highld 308 E6
Langdale End N Yorks 227 G8
Langdon Corn 12 D2
Langdon Beck Durham 232 E3
Langdon Hills Essex 69 B7
Langdown Hants 32 F6
Langdyke Dumfries 238 C3
Fife 287 G7
Langenhoe Essex 89 B8
Langford C Beds 104 C3
Devon 14 B4
Devon 27 G8
Essex 88 D4
Notts 172 D4
Oxon 82 E2
Som 28 B2
Langford Budville Som 27 C10
Langford Green Devon 27 G8
N Som 44 B3
Langham Dorset 30 B3
Essex 107 E10
Norf 177 E8
Rutland 154 G6
Som 28 E4
Suff 125 C9
Langhaugh Borders 260 C6
Langho Lancs 203 G10
Langholm Dumfries 249 G9
Langholme N Lincs 188 B3
Langhope Borders 261 E10
Langland Swansea 56 D6
Langlee Borders 262 B2
Langleeford Northumb 263 E10
Langlee Mains Borders 262 B2
Langlees Falk 279 E7
Langley Ches E 184 G6
Derbys 170 F6
Essex 105 D8
Glos 99 F10
Gtr Man 195 F11
Hants 32 G6
Herts 104 G4
Kent 53 C10
Northumb 241 E8
Oxon 82 B4
Slough 66 D4
Som 27 B9
Warks 118 E3
W Mid 133 F9
W Sus 34 B4
Langley Burrell Wilts 62 D2
Langleybury Herts 85 E9
Langley Common
Derbys 152 B5
Wokingham 65 F9
Langley Corner Bucks 66 C4
Langley Green Derbys 152 B5
Essex 107 G7
Warks 118 E3
W Mid 133 F9
W Sus 51 F9
Langley Heath Kent 53 C10
Langley Marsh Som 27 B9
Langley Mill Derbys 170 F6
Langley Moor Durham 233 C11
Langley Park Durham 233 C10
Langley Street Norf 143 C7
Langley Vale Sur 51 B8
Langloan N Lanark 268 C4
Langney E Sus 23 E10
Langold Notts 187 D9
Langore Corn 12 D2
Langport Som 28 B6
Langrick Lincs 174 F3
Langrick Bridge Lincs 174 F3
Langridge Bath 61 F8
Langridge Ford Devon 25 C9
Langrigg Cumb 222 C5
Cumb 229 B9
Langrish Hants 34 C2
Langsett S Yorks 197 G8
Langshaw Borders 262 B2
Langside Glasgow 267 C11
Perth 285 F11
Langskaill Orkney 314 B4
Langstone Devon 13 E10
Hants 22 C2
Newport 78 G5
Langthorne N Yorks 224 G5
Langthorpe N Yorks 215 F7
Langthwaite N Yorks 223 E10
Langtoft E Yorks 217 F10
Lincs 156 G2
Langton Durham 224 B3
Lincs 174 B2
Lincs 190 G5
N Yorks 216 F5
Langton by Wragby
Lincs 189 F11
Langton Green Kent 52 F4
Suff 126 C2
Langton Herring Dorset 17 E8
Langton Long Blandford
Dorset 30 F5
Langton Matravers
Dorset 18 F6
Langtree Devon 25 D7
Langtree Week Devon 25 D7
Langwathby Cumb 231 E7
Langwell Ho Highld 311 G5
Langwell Lodge Highld 307 J6
Langwith Derbys 171 B8
Langwith Junction
Derbys 171 B8
Langworth Lincs 189 F9
Lanham Green Essex 106 G5
Lanivet Corn 5 C10
Lanjeth Corn 5 E9
Lanjew Corn 5 C9
Lank Corn 11 F7
Lanlivery Corn 5 D11
Lanner Corn 2 B6
Lanreath Corn 6 D3
Lanrick Stirling 285 G10
Lansallos Corn 6 E3
Lansbury Park Caerph 59 B7
Lansdown Bath 61 F8
Glos 99 G8
Lanstephan Corn 12 D2
Lanteglos Corn 11 E7
Lanteglos Highway Corn 6 E3
Lanton Borders 262 E4
Northumb 263 C10
Lantuel Corn 5 B9
Lantyan Corn 6 D2
Lapal W Mid 133 G9
Lapford Devon 26 F2
Lapford Cross Devon 26 F2
Laphroaig Argyll 254 C4
Lapley Staffs 151 G7
Lapworth Warks 118 C3
Larachbeg Highld 289 E8
Larbert Falk 279 E7
Larbreck Lancs 202 E4
Larches Lancs 202 G6
Larden Green Ches E 167 E9
Larg Highld 292 B2
Largie Aberds 302 F6
Largiebaan Argyll 255 F7
Largiemore Argyll 275 E10
Largoward Fife 287 G8
Largs N Ayrs 266 D4
Largue Aberds 302 E6
Largybeg N Ayrs 256 E3
Largymeanoch N Ayrs 256 E2
Largymore N Ayrs 256 E2
Larkfield Invclyd 276 F4
Kent 53 B8
W Yorks 205 F10
Larkhall Bath 61 F9
S Lanark 268 E5
Larkhill Wilts 46 E6
Lark Hill Gtr Man 195 G7
Larklands Derbys 171 G7
Larks' Hill Suff 108 B3
Larling Norf 141 F9
Larport Hereford 97 D11
Larrick Corn 12 F2
Larriston Borders 250 E2
Lartington Durham 223 B10
Lary Aberds 292 C5
Lasborough Glos 80 G4
Lasham Hants 49 E7
Lashenden Kent 53 E10
Lask Edge Staffs 168 D6
Lassington Glos 98 G5
Lassodie Fife 280 C2
Lastingham N Yorks 226 G4
Latcham Som 44 D2
Latchbrook Corn 7 D8
Latchford Herts 105 G7
Oxon 83 E11
Warr 183 D10
Latchingdon Essex 88 E5
Latchley Corn 12 G4
Latchmere Green Hants 64 G6
Latchmore Bank Essex 87 B7
Lately Common Warr 183 B11
Lathallan Mill Fife 287 G8
Lathbury M Keynes 103 B7
Latheron Highld 310 F5
Latheronwheel Highld 310 F5
Latheronwheel Ho
Highld 310 F5
Lathom Lancs 194 E3
Lathones Fife 287 G8
Latimer Bucks 85 F8
Latteridge S Glos 61 C7
Lattiford Som 29 B11
Lattinford Hill Suff 107 D11
Latton Wilts 81 F9
Latton Bush Essex 87 D7
Lauchintilly Aberds 293 B9
Laudale Ho Highld 289 D9
Lauder Borders 271 F10
Lauder Barns Borders 271 F10
Laugharne = Talacharn
Carms 74 C4
Laughern Hill Worcs 116 F5
Laughterton Lincs 188 F4
Laughton E Sus 23 C8
Leics 136 F3
Lincs 155 C11
Lincs 188 B4
Laughton Common
E Sus 23 C7
S Yorks 187 D8
Laughton en le Morthen
S Yorks 187 D8
Launcells Corn 24 F2
Launcells Cross Corn 24 F3
Launceston Corn 12 D2
Launcherley Som 44 E4
Laund Lancs 195 C10
Launton Oxon 102 G2
Laurencekirk Aberds 293 F9
Laurieston Dumfries 237 C8
Falk 279 F8
Lavendon M Keynes 121 G8
Lavenham Suff 107 B8
Laverackloch Moray 301 C11
Laverhay Dumfries 248 D4
Laverlaw Borders 261 B7
Laverley Som 44 F5
Lavernock V Glam 59 F7
Laversdale Cumb 239 E11
Laverstock Wilts 47 G7
Laverstoke Hants 48 D3
Laverton Glos 99 D11
N Yorks 214 E4
Som 45 C9
Lavington Sands Wilts 46 B4
Lavister Wrex 166 D5
Lavrean Corn 5 D10
Lawers Perth 285 D10
Perth 285 E11
Lawford Essex 107 E11
Som 42 F6
Lawford Heath Warks 119 C9
Lawhill Perth 286 F3
Law Hill S Lanark 268 E6
Lawhitton Corn 12 E3
Lawkland N Yorks 212 F5
Lawkland Green
N Yorks 212 F5
Lawley Telford 132 B3
Lawn Swindon 63 C7
Lawnhead Staffs 150 E6
Lawns W Yorks 197 C10
Lawnswood W Yorks 205 F11
Lawnt Denb 165 B8
Lawrence Hill Newport 59 B10
Lawrence Weston
Bristol 60 D4
Lawrenny Pembs 73 D8
Lawrenny Quay Pembs 73 D8
Lawshall Suff 125 G7
Lawshall Green Suff 125 G7
Lawton Hereford 115 F8
Shrops 131 G10
Lawton-gate Ches E 168 D4
Lawton Heath End
Ches E 168 D3
Laxey IoM 192 D5
Laxfield Suff 126 C5
Laxfirth Shetland 313 H6
Shetland 313 J6
Laxford Bridge Highld 306 E7
Laxo Shetland 313 G6
Laxobigging Shetland 312 F6
Laxton E Yorks 199 B9
N Nhants 137 D8
Notts 172 B2
Laycock W Yorks 204 E6
Layer Breton Essex 88 B6
Layer de la Haye Essex 89 B7
Layer Marney Essex 88 B6
Layerthorpe York 207 C8
Layham Suff 107 C10
Laymore Dorset 28 G5
Layters Green Bucks 85 G7
Laytham E Yorks 207 F10
Layton Blackpool 202 F2
Lazenby Redcar 225 B11
Lazonby Cumb 230 D6
Lea Derbys 170 D4
Hereford 98 G3
Lancs 202 G5
Lincs 188 D4
Shrops 131 B8
Shrops 131 F7
Wilts 62 B3
Lea Bridge London 67 B11
Leabrooks Derbys 170 E6
Lea by Backford
Ches W 182 G5
Leacainn W Isles 305 H3
Leac a Li W Isles 305 J3
Leachkin Highld 300 E6
Leacnasaide Highld 299 B7
Leadburn Midloth 270 D4
Leadendale Staffs 151 B8
Leadenham Lincs 173 E7
Leaden Roding Essex 87 C9
Leadgate Cumb 231 C10
Durham 242 G4
T&W 242 F4
Leadhills S Lanark 259 G9
Leadingcross Green
Kent 53 C11
Leadmill Derbys 186 E2
Flint 166 C2
Lea End Worcs 117 B10
Leafield Oxon 82 B4
Wilts 61 F11
Lea Forge Ches E 168 F2
Leagrave Luton 103 G10
Leagreen Hants 19 C11
Lea Green Mers 183 C8
Lea Hall W Mid 134 F2
Lea Heath Staffs 151 D10
Leake Lincs 174 F6
N Yorks 225 G8
Leake Commonside
Lincs 174 E5
Leake Fold Hill Lincs 174 E6
Lealholm N Yorks 226 D5
Lealholm Side N Yorks 226 D5
Lea Line Hereford 98 G3
Lealt Argyll 275 D7
Highld 298 C5
Leam Derbys 186 F2
Lea Marston Warks 134 E4
Leamington Hastings
Warks 119 D8
Leamoor Common
Shrops 131 F8
Leamore W Mid 133 C9
Leamside Durham 234 B2
Leanach Argyll 275 D11
Leanachan Highld 290 F4
Leanaig Highld 300 D5
Leapgate Worcs 116 C6
Leargybreck Argyll 274 F6
Lease Rigg N Yorks 226 E6
Leasey Bridge Herts 85 C11
Leasgill Cumb 211 C9
Leasingham Lincs 173 F9
Leasingthorne Durham 233 F11
Leason Swansea 56 C3
Leasowe Mers 182 C3
Leatherhead Sur 51 B7
Leatherhead Common
Sur 51 B7
Leathern Bottle Glos 80 E2
Leathley N Yorks 205 D10
Leaths Dumfries 237 C9
Leaton Shrops 149 F9
Telford 150 G2
Leaton Heath Shrops 149 F9
Lea Town Lancs 202 G5
Lea Valley Herts 85 B11
Leaveland Kent 54 C4
Leavenheath Suff 107 D9
Leavening N Yorks 216 G5
Leavesden Green Herts 85 E9
Leaves Green London 68 G2
Lea Yeat Cumb 212 B5
Leazes Durham 242 F5
Lebberston N Yorks 217 C11
Leburnick Corn 12 E3
Lechlade-on-Thames
Glos 82 F2
Leck Lancs 212 D2
Leckford Hants 47 F11
Leckfurin Highld 308 D7
Leckgruinart Argyll 274 G3
Leckhampstead Bucks 102 D4
W Berks 64 D2
Leckhampstead Thicket
W Berks 64 D2
Leckhampton Glos 80 B6
Leckie Highld 299 C10
Leckmelm Highld 307 K6
Leckuary Argyll 275 D9
Leckwith V Glam 59 E7
Leconfield E Yorks 208 E6
Ledaig Argyll 289 F11
Ledburn Bucks 103 G8
Ledbury Hereford 98 D4
Ledcharrie Stirling 285 E9
Leddington Glos 98 E3
Ledgemoor Hereford 115 G8
Ledgowan Highld 299 D11
Ledicot Hereford 115 E8
Ledmore Angus 293 G7
Highld 307 H7
Lednagullin Highld 308 C7
Ledsham Ches W 182 G5
W Yorks 198 B3
Ledston W Yorks 198 B2
Ledstone Devon 8 F4
Ledston Luck W Yorks 206 G4
Ledwell Oxon 101 F8
Lee Argyll 288 G6
Devon 40 D3
Devon 40 D5
Hants 32 D5
Lancs 203 B7
London 67 E11
Northumb 241 F10
Shrops 149 C8
Leeans Shetland 313 J5
Lee Bank W Mid 133 F11
Leebotten Shetland 313 L6
Leebotwood Shrops 131 D9
Lee Brockhurst Shrops 149 D10
Leece Cumb 210 F4
Lee Chapel Essex 69 B7
Leechpool Mon 60 B4
Lee Clump Bucks 84 E6
Lee Common Bucks 84 E6
Leeds Kent 53 C10
W Yorks 205 G11
Leedstown Corn 2 C4
Leeford Devon 41 D9
Lee Gate Bucks 84 D5
Leegomery Telford 150 G3
Lee Ground Hants 33 F8
Lee Head Derbys 185 C8
Leeholme Durham 233 E10
Leek Staffs 169 D7
Leekbrook Staffs 169 E7
Leek Wootton Warks 118 D5
Lee Mill Devon 8 D2
Leeming N Yorks 214 B5
W Yorks 204 G6
Leeming Bar N Yorks 224 G5
Leemings Lancs 203 D10
Lee Moor Devon 7 C11
W Yorks 197 B10
Lee-on-the-Solent
Hants 33 G9

Lee-over-Sands Essex.. 89 C10
Lees Derbys 152 B5
Gtr Man........ 196 G3
W Yorks........ 204 F6
Leesthorpe Leics 154 G5
Leeswood = Coed-Llai
Flint........ 166 D3
Leetown Perth........ 286 E6
Leftwich Ches W 183 G11
Legar Powys........ 78 B2
Legbourne Lincs....... 190 E5
Legburthwaite Cumb ... 220 B6
Legerwood Borders.... 271 G11
Leggatt Hill W Sus 34 C6
Legsby Lincs........ 189 D10
Leicester Leicester.... 135 C11
Leicester Forest East
Leics........ 135 C10
Leicester Grange Warks 135 E8
Leigh Devon 26 E2
Dorset 18 B6
Dorset 29 F10
Dorset 30 F3
Glos 99 F7
Gtr Man........ 195 G7
Kent 52 D4
Shrops 130 C6
Sur 51 D8
Wilts........ 81 G9
Worcs........ 116 G5
Leigham Plym 7 D10
Leigh Beck Essex...... 69 C10
Leigh Common Som 30 B2
Leigh Delamere Wilts... 61 D11
Leigh Green Kent 54 G2
Leighland Chapel Som.... 42 F4
Leigh-on-Sea Southend. 69 B10
Leigh Park Hants 22 B2
Leigh Sinton Worcs...... 116 G5
Leighswood W Mid...... 133 C11
Leighterton Glos 80 G4
Leighton N Yorks........ 214 D3
Shrops 132 B2
Som 45 E8
Leighton = Tre'r llai
Powys........ 130 B4
Leighton Bromswold
Cambs........ 122 B2
Leighton Buzzard
C Beds........ 103 F8
Leigh upon Mendip Som. 45 D7
Leigh Woods N Som...... 60 E5
Leinthall Earls Hereford. 115 D8
Leinthall Starkes
Hereford........ 115 D8
Leintwardine Hereford.. 115 C8
Leire Leics........ 135 E10
Leirinmore Highld 308 C4
Leiston Suff 127 E8
Leitfie Perth........ 286 C6
Leith Edin 280 F5
Leithenhall Dumfries.... 248 D4
Leitholm Borders 272 G5
Lelant Corn........ 2 B2
Lelant Downs Corn 2 B2
Lelley E Yorks 209 G10
Lem Hill Worcs 116 C4
Lemington T&W 242 E5
Lemmington Hall
Northumb........ 264 G4
Lempitlaw Borders....... 263 C7
Lemsford Herts........ 86 C2
Lenacre Cumb 212 B3
Lenborough Bucks....... 102 E3
Lenchwick Worcs........ 99 B10
Lendalfoot S Ayrs........ 244 F4
Lendrick Lodge Stirling . 285 G9
Lenham Kent 53 C11
Lenham Forstal Kent 54 C2
Lenham Heath Kent...... 54 D2
Lennel Borders 273 G7
Lennoxtown E Dunb...... 278 F2
Lent Bucks........ 66 C2
Lenten Pool Denb........ 165 B8
Lenton Lincs........ 155 C10
Nottingham........ 153 B11
Lenton Abbey
Nottingham 153 B10
Lentran Highld........ 300 E5
Lent Rise Bucks........ 66 C2
Lenwade Norf 159 F11
Leny Ho Stirling........ 285 G10
Lenzie E Dunb........ 278 G3
Lenziemill N Lanark 278 G5
Leoch Angus........ 287 D7
Leochel-Cushnie
Aberds 293 B7
Leominster Hereford..... 115 F9
Leomonsley Staffs....... 134 B2
Leonard Stanley Glos..... 80 E4
Leonardston Pembs 72 D6
Leorin Argyll........ 254 C4
Lepe Hants........ 20 B5
Lephin Highld........ 297 G7
Lephinchapel Argyll ... 275 D10
Lephinmore Argyll..... 275 D10
Leppington N Yorks 216 G5
Lepton W Yorks 197 D8
Lepton Edge W Yorks..... 197 D8
Lerigoligan Argyll........ 275 C9
Lerrocks Stirling....... 285 G11
Lerryn Corn........ 6 D2
Lerwick Shetland........ 313 J6
Lesbury Northumb 264 G6
Leschangie Aberds 293 B9
Le Skerne Haughton
Darl........ 224 B6
Leslie Aberds 302 G5
Fife........ 286 G6
Lesmahagow S Lanark... 259 B8
Lesnewth Corn 11 C8
Lessendrum Aberds..... 302 E5
Lessingham Norf 161 D7
Lessness Heath London .. 68 D3
Lessonhall Cumb 238 G6
Leswalt Dumfries........ 236 C2
Letchmore Heath Herts. 85 F11
Letchworth Garden City
Herts........ 104 E4
Letcombe Bassett Oxon. 63 B11
Letcombe Regis Oxon.... 63 B11
Letham Angus 287 C9
Falk........ 279 D7
Fife........ 287 F7
Perth........ 286 E4
Letham Grange Angus . 287 C10
Lethem Borders........ 250 B5
Lethen Ho Highld 301 D9
Lethenty Aberds 303 E8
Aberds 303 G7
Letheringham Suff 126 F5
Letheringsett Norf 159 B11
Lettaford Devon 13 E10
Lettan Orkney........ 314 B7
Letter Aberds........ 293 B9
Letterewe Highld 299 B9
Letterfearn Highld..... 295 C10
Letterfinlay Highld...... 290 D4
Lettermay Argyll........ 284 G5
Lettermorar Highld 295 G9
Lettermore Argyll........ 288 E6
Letters Highld 307 L6
Letterston = Treletert
Pembs........ 91 F8
Lettoch Highld........ 292 B2
Highld........ 301 F10
Moray........ 302 F3
Perth........ 291 G11
Letton Hereford........ 96 B6
Hereford........ 115 C7
Letton Green Norf 141 B9
Lett's Green Kent........ 52 B3
Letty Brongu Bridgend .. 57 D11
Letty Green Herts 86 C3
Letwell S Yorks........ 187 D9
Leuchars Fife........ 287 E8
Leuchars Ho Moray 302 C2
Leumrabhagh W Isles... 305 G5
Levalsa Meor Corn........ 5 F10
Levan Invclyd 276 F4
Levaneap Shetland 313 G6
Levedale Staffs 151 F7
Level of Mendalgief
Newport........ 59 B10
Level's Green Essex 105 G9
Leven E Yorks 209 D8
Fife........ 287 G7
Levencorroch N Ayrs..... 256 E2
Levenhall E Loth 281 G7
Levens Cumb 211 B9
Levens Green Herts...... 105 G7
Levenshulme Gtr Man... 184 C5
Leventhorpe W Yorks ... 205 G8
Levenwick Shetland...... 313 L6
Lever-Edge Gtr Man..... 195 F8
Leverington Cambs 157 G8
Leverington Common
Cambs........ 157 G8
Leverstock Green Herts . 85 D9
Leverton Lincs........ 174 F6
W Berks 63 E10
Leverton Highgate Lincs 174 F6
Leverton Lucasgate
Lincs 174 F6
Leverton Outgate Lincs. 174 F6
Levington Suff........ 108 D4
Levisham N Yorks 226 G6
Levishie Highld 290 B6
Lew Oxon........ 82 D4
Lewannick Corn 11 E11
Lewcombe Dorset 29 F9
Lewdown Devon 12 D4
Lewes E Sus 36 E6
Leweston Pembs........ 91 G8
Lewisham London........ 67 D11
Lewiston Highld........ 300 G5
Lewistown Bridgend...... 58 B2
Lewknor Oxon........ 84 F2
Leworthy Devon 24 G4
Devon........ 41 F7
Lewson Street Kent...... 70 G3
Lewth Lancs 202 F5
Lewthorn Cross Devon... 13 F11
Lewtrenchard Devon 12 D5
Lexden Essex........ 107 G9
Ley Aberds........ 293 B7
Corn 6 B3
Som 41 F10
Leybourne Kent 53 B7
Leyburn N Yorks........ 224 G2
Leycett Staffs........ 168 F3
Leyfields Staffs 134 B4
Ley Green Herts 104 G3
Ley Hey Park Gtr Man.... 185 D7
Leyhill Bucks 85 E7
S Glos........ 79 G11
Ley Hill W Mid........ 134 D2
Leyland Lancs 194 C4
Leylodge Aberds........ 293 B9
Leymoor W Yorks 196 D6
Leys Aberds........ 292 C6
Aberds 303 D10
Cumb 219 B11
Perth........ 286 D6
Staffs 169 F8
Leys Castle Highld 300 E6
Leysdown-on-Sea Kent... 70 E4
Leys Hill Hereford 79 B9
Leysmill Angus........ 287 C10
Leys of Cossans Angus.. 287 C7
Leysters Hereford....... 115 E11
Leysters Pole Hereford. 115 E11
Leyton London 67 B11
Leytonstone London 67 B11
Lezant Corn 12 F2
Lezerea Corn 2 C5
Leziate Norf........ 158 F3
Lhanbryde Moray........ 302 C2
Liatrie Highld 300 F2
Libanus Powys........ 95 F9
Libberton S Lanark...... 269 G9
Libbery Worcs........ 117 F9
Liberton Edin........ 270 B5
Liceasto W Isles 305 J3
Lichfield Staffs 134 B2
Lick Perth........ 286 B2
Lickey Worcs 117 B9
Lickey End Worcs........ 117 C9
Lickfold W Sus 34 B6
Lickhill Worcs 116 C6
Lickleyhead Castle
Aberds 302 G6
Liddaton Devon........ 12 E5
Liddel Orkney........ 314 H4
Liddesdale Highld........ 289 D9
Liddeston Pembs 72 D5
Liddington Swindon 63 C8
Liden Swindon 63 C7
Lidgate Suff 124 F4
Lidget S Yorks........ 199 G7
Lidget Green W Yorks ... 205 G8
Lidgett Notts 171 B10
Lidgett Park W Yorks.... 206 F2
Lidham Hill E Sus 38 D4
Lidlington C Beds 103 D9
Lidsey W Sus........ 22 C6
Lidsing Kent........ 69 G9
Lidstone Oxon 101 G7
Lieurary Highld 310 C4
Liff Angus 287 D7
Lifford W Mid 117 B11
Lifton Devon........ 12 D3
Liftondown Devon 12 D3
Lightcliffe W Yorks....... 196 B6
Lighteach Shrops 149 C10
Lightfoot Green Lancs... 202 G6
Lighthorne Warks 118 F6
Lighthorne Heath Warks 119 F7
Lighthorne Rough
Warks........ 118 F6
Lightmoor Telford........ 132 B3
Light Oaks Staffs 168 E6
Lightpill Glos........ 80 E4
Lightwater Sur 66 G2
Lightwood Shrops 132 E2
Shrops 150 D3
Staffs 169 G8
Stoke 168 G6
S Yorks 186 E5
Lightwood Green
Ches E........ 167 G10
Wrex........ 166 G5
Liglartrie S Ayrs 244 F6
Lilbourne W Nhants 119 B11
Lilburn Tower Northumb. 264 E2
Lilford Gtr Man........ 195 G7
Lillesdon Som 28 C4
Lilleshall Telford 150 F4
Lilley Herts........ 104 F2
W Berks 64 D2
Lilliesleaf Borders 262 E2
Lillingstone Dayrell
Bucks........ 102 D4
Lillingstone Lovell
Bucks........ 102 C4
Lillington Dorset........ 29 E10
Warks........ 118 D6
Lilliput BCP........ 18 C6
Lilstock Som 43 E7
Lilybank Invclyd 276 G6
Lilyhurst Shrops 150 G4
Lilyvale Kent........ 54 F5
Limbrick Lancs 194 D6
Limbury Luton 103 G11
Limebrook Hereford 115 D7
Limefield Gtr Man........ 195 E10
Limehouse London...... 67 C11
Limehurst Gtr Man 196 G2
Limekilnburn S Lanark .. 268 E4
Limekiln Field Derbys... 187 G7
Limekilns Fife........ 279 E11
Limerigg Falk........ 279 G7
Limerstone IoW........ 20 E4
Lime Side Gtr Man....... 196 G2
Limestone Brae
Northumb........ 231 B11
Lime Street Worcs 98 E6
Lime Tree Park W Mid... 118 B5
Limington Som........ 29 C8
Limpenhoe Norf........ 143 C7
Limpenhoe Hill Norf.... 143 C8
Limpers Hill Wilts 45 G10
Limpley Stoke Wilts 61 G9
Limpsfield Sur 52 C2
Limpsfield Chart Sur 52 C2
Limpsfield Common Sur. 52 C2
Linbriggs Northumb...... 251 B9
Linburn W Loth........ 270 B2
Linby Notts 171 E8
Linchmere W Sus 49 G11
Lincluden Dumfries 237 B11
Lincoln Lincs 189 G7
Lincomb Worcs 116 D6
Lincombe Devon........ 8 D4
Devon 40 D3
Lindale Cumb........ 211 C8
Lindal in Furness Cumb . 210 D5
Lindean Borders 261 C11
Linden Glos 80 B4
Lindfield W Sus 36 B4
Lindford Hants 49 F10
Lindifferon Fife 287 F7
Lindley N Yorks 205 D10
W Yorks........ 196 D6
Lindley Green N Yorks.. 205 D10
Lindores Fife........ 286 F6
Lindow End Ches E...... 184 F4
Lindrick Dale S Yorks.... 187 E8
Lindridge Worcs 116 D3
Lindsell Essex 106 F2
Lindsey Suff........ 107 C9
Lindsey Tye Suff 107 B9
Lindwell W Yorks........ 196 C5
Lineholt Worcs 116 D6
Lineholt Common
Worcs 116 D6
Liney Som 43 F11
Linfitts Gtr Man 196 F3
Linford Hants........ 31 F11
Thurrock........ 69 D7
Lingague IoM 192 E3
Lingards Wood W Yorks . 196 E5
Lingbob W Yorks 205 F7
Lingdale Redcar 226 B3
Lingen Hereford........ 115 D7
Lingfield Darl 224 C6
Sur 51 E11
Lingfield Common Sur... 51 E11
Lingley Green Warr..... 183 D9
Lingley Mere Warr..... 183 D10
Lingreabhagh W Isles... 296 C6
Lingwood Norf 143 B7
Linhope Borders 249 C10
Northumb........ 263 F11
Linicro Highld........ 298 C3
Link N Som........ 44 B3
Linkend Worcs........ 98 E6
Linkenholt Hants 47 B11
Linkhill Kent........ 38 B4
Linkinhorne Corn........ 12 G2
Linklater Orkney........ 314 H4
Linklet Orkney 314 A7
Linksness Orkney........ 314 E5
Orkney 314 F2
Linktown Fife........ 280 C5
Linley Shrops 131 E7
Shrops 132 D3
Linley Brook Shrops..... 132 D3
Linleygreen Shrops 132 D3
Linley Green Hereford... 116 G3
Linlithgow W Loth........ 279 F10
Linlithgow Bridge
W Loth........ 279 F9
Linndhu Ho Argyll........ 289 D7
Linneraineach Highld ... 307 J6
Linns Angus 292 F3
Linnshaw Gtr Man........ 195 G8
Linshiels Northumb...... 251 B9
Linsiadar W Isles 304 E4
Linsidemore Highld...... 309 K5
Linslade C Beds 103 F8
Linstead Parva Suff..... 126 B6
Linstock Cumb........ 239 F10
Linthorpe Mbro........ 225 B9
Linthurst Worcs 117 C9
Linthwaite W Yorks...... 196 E6
Lintlaw Borders........ 272 D6
Lintmill Moray........ 302 C5
Linton Borders........ 263 D7
Cambs 105 B11
Derbys 152 F5
Hereford........ 98 F3
Kent 53 D9
Northumb 253 E7
N Yorks 213 G9
W Yorks........ 206 D3
Linton Heath Derbys 152 F5
Linton Hill Hereford...... 98 G3
Linton-on-Ouse
N Yorks 215 G9
Lintridge Glos........ 98 E4
Lintz Durham 242 F5
Lintzford T&W........ 242 F4
Lintzgarth Durham....... 232 C4
Linwood Hants 31 F11
Lincs........ 189 D10
Renfs 267 C8
Lionacleit W Isles........ 297 G3
Lional W Isles........ 304 B7
Lions Green E Sus........ 23 B9
Liphook Hants........ 49 G10
Lipley Shrops 150 C4
Lippitts Hill Essex 86 F5
Liquo or Bowhousebog
N Lanark 269 D7
Liscard Mers 182 C4
Liscombe Som........ 41 G11
Liskeard Corn 6 C5
Liss Hants 34 B3
Lissett E Yorks 209 B8
Liss Forest Hants 34 B3
Lissington Lincs 189 E10
Lisson Grove London..... 67 C9
Listerdale S Yorks....... 187 C7
Listock Som 28 C4
Listoft Lincs 191 G8
Liston Essex........ 107 C7
Liston Garden Essex.... 106 B6
Lisvane Cardiff........ 59 C7
Liswerry Newport 59 B10
Litcham Norf 159 F7
Litchard Bridgend........ 58 C2
Litchborough W Nhants . 120 G2
Litchfield Hants 48 C3
Litherland Mers 182 B4
Litlington Cambs 104 C6
E Sus........ 23 E8
Litmarsh Hereford 97 B10
Little Abington Cambs . 105 B10
Little Addington
N Nhants 121 C9
Little Airmyn E Yorks 199 B8
Little Almshoe Herts.... 104 F3
Little Alne Warks 118 E2
Little Altcar Mers........ 193 F10
Little Ann Hants 47 E10
Little Arowry Wrex 167 G7
Little Asby Cumb........ 222 D3
Little Ashley Wilts 61 G10
Little Assynt Highld 307 G6
Little Aston Staffs 133 C11
Little Atherfield IoW..... 20 E5
Little Ayre Orkney........ 314 G3
Little-ayre Shetland...... 313 G5
Little Ayton N Yorks 225 C11
Little Baddow Essex 88 D3
Little Badminton S Glos . 61 C10
Little Ballinluig Perth... 286 B3
Little Bampton Cumb ... 239 F7
Little Bardfield Essex... 106 E3
Little Barford Bedford.. 122 F3
Little Barningham Norf. 160 C2
Little Barrington Glos ... 82 C2
Little Barrow Ches W.... 183 G7
Little Barugh N Yorks.... 216 D5
Little Bavington
Northumb........ 241 B11
Little Bayham E Sus...... 52 F6
Little Bealings Suff 108 B4
Littlebeck N Yorks........ 227 D7
Little Beckford Glos 99 E9
Little Bedwyn Wilts........ 63 F9
Little Bentley Essex...... 108 F2
Little Berkhamsted Herts 86 D3
Little Billing W Nhants... 120 E6
Little Billington C Beds.. 103 G8
Little Birch Hereford 97 E10
Little Bispham Blackpool 202 E2
Little Blakenham Suff .. 108 B2
Little Blencow Cumb..... 230 E5
Little Bloxwich W Mid.. 133 C10
Little Bognor W Sus...... 35 C8
Little Bolehill Derbys 170 E3
Little Bollington Ches E. 184 D2
Little Bolton Gtr Man.... 184 B3
Little Bookham Sur....... 50 C6
Littleborough Devon...... 26 E4
Gtr Man........ 196 D2
Notts........ 188 E4
Little Bosullow Corn 1 C4
Littlebourne Kent........ 55 B8
Little Bourton Oxon...... 101 C9
Little Bowden Leics...... 136 F4
Little Boys Heath Bucks.. 84 F6
Little Bradley Suff 124 G3
Little Braithwaite
Cumb........ 229 G10
Little Brampton Shrops . 131 G7
Little Braxted Essex 88 C4
Little Bray Devon 41 F7
Little Brechin Angus..... 293 G7
Littlebredy Dorset 17 D7
Little Brickhill
M Keynes........ 103 E8
Little Bridgeford Staffs . 151 D7
Little Brington
W Nhants 120 E3
Little Bristol S Glos 80 G2
Little Britain Warks...... 118 G2
Little Bromley Essex.... 107 F11
Little Bromwich W Mid.. 134 F2
Little Broughton Cumb.. 229 E7
Little Budworth Ches W.. 167 B9
Little Burstead Essex... 87 G11
Littlebury Essex 105 D10
Littlebury Green Essex . 105 D9
Little Bytham Lincs...... 155 F10
Little Cambridge Essex . 106 F2
Little Canfield Essex.... 105 G11
Little Canford BCP........ 18 B6
Little Carleton Lancs..... 202 F2
Little Carlton Lincs 190 D5
Notts........ 172 D3
Little Casterton
Rutland........ 137 B10
Little Catwick E Yorks ... 209 E8
Little Catworth Cambs .. 122 C2
Little Cawthorpe Lincs.. 190 E5
Little Chalfield Wilts..... 61 G11
Little Chalfont Bucks...... 85 F7
Little Chart Kent........ 54 D2
Little Chart Forstal Kent . 54 D3
Little Chell Stoke 168 E5
Little Chester Derby 153 B7
Little Chesterford
Essex........ 105 C10
Little Chesterton Oxon. 101 G11
Little Cheverell Wilts 46 C3
Little Chishill Cambs..... 105 D8
Little Clacton Essex 89 B11
Little Clanfield Oxon...... 82 E3
Little Clegg Gtr Man..... 196 E2
Little Clifton Cumb....... 229 F7
Little Coates NE Lincs ... 201 F8
Little Colp Aberds........ 303 E7
Little Comberton Worcs . 99 C9
Little Comfort Corn....... 12 E2
Little Common E Sus..... 38 F2
Lincs........ 156 D6
Shrops 115 B7
W Sus........ 34 C6
Little Compton Warks .. 100 E5
Little Corby Cumb....... 239 F11
Little Cornard Suff 107 D7
Littlecote Bucks 102 G6
Littlecott Wilts 46 C6
Little Cowarne Hereford. 116 G2
Little Coxwell Oxon 82 G3
Little Crakehall N Yorks . 224 G4
Little Cransley N Nhants. 120 B6
Little Crawley M Keynes . 103 B8
Little Creaton W Nhants . 120 C4
Little Creich Highld 309 L6
Little Cressingham Norf 141 D7
Little Crosby Mers....... 193 G10
Little Cubley Derbys 152 B3
Little Dalby Leics 154 G5
Little Dawley Telford 132 B3
Littledean Glos........ 79 C11
Littledean Hill Glos...... 79 C11
Little Dens Aberds 303 E10
Little Dewchurch
Hereford........ 97 E10
Little Ditton Cambs 124 F3
Little Doward Hereford.... 79 B8
Littledown BCP........ 19 C8
Hants........ 47 B10
Little Downham Cambs 139 G10
Little Drayton Shrops ... 150 C3
Little Driffield E Yorks... 208 B6
Little Drybrook Glos 79 D9
Little Dunham Norf...... 159 G7
Little Dunkeld Perth 286 C4
Little Dunmow Essex ... 106 G3
Little Durnford Wilts 46 G6
Little Eastbury Worcs... 116 F6
Little Easton Essex 106 G2
Little Eaton Derbys 170 G5
Little Eccleston Lancs .. 202 E4
Little Ellingham Norf .. 141 D10
Little End Cambs........ 122 F3
Essex........ 87 E8
E Yorks 208 F2
Little Everdon
W Nhants 119 F11
Little Eversden Cambs.. 123 G7
Little Faringdon Oxon..... 82 E2
Little Fencote N Yorks... 224 G5
Little Fenton N Yorks.... 206 F6
Littleferry Highld 311 K2
Littlefield NE Lincs 201 F9
Littlefield Common Sur.. 50 C3
Littlefield Green
Windsor 65 D11
Little Finborough Suff. 125 G10
Little Fransham Norf... 159 G8
Little Frith Kent........ 54 B2
Little Gaddesden Herts.. 85 C7
Littlegain Shrops 132 D5
Little Gidding Cambs.... 138 G2
Little Gight Aberds....... 303 F8
Little Glemham Suff..... 126 F6
Little Glenshee Perth... 286 D3
Little Gorsley Glos........ 98 F3
Little Gransden Cambs.. 122 F5
Little Green Cambs 104 B5
Notts........ 172 G2
Som 45 D8
Suff........ 125 C11
Wrex........ 167 G7
Little Grimsby Lincs..... 190 C4
Little Gringley Notts 188 E2
Little Gruinard Highld... 307 L4
Little Habton N Yorks.... 216 D4
Little Hadham Herts..... 105 G8
Little Hale Lincs 173 G10
Norf........ 141 B8
Little Hallam Derbys 171 G7
Little Hallingbury Essex . 87 B7
Littleham Devon........ 14 E6
Devon........ 24 C6
Little Hampden Bucks 84 E5
Littlehampton W Sus 35 G8
Little Haresfield Glos..... 80 D4
Little Harrowden
N Nhants........ 121 C7
Little Harwood
Blackburn........ 195 B7
Little Haseley Oxon...... 83 E10
Little Hatfield E Yorks... 209 E9
Little Hautbois Norf..... 160 E5
Little Haven Pembs 72 C5
W Sus........ 51 G7
Little Hay Staffs 134 C2
Little Hayfield Derbys... 185 D8
Little Haywood Staffs.. 151 E10
Little Heath Ches E..... 167 G11
Ches W........ 166 B6
Herts 85 D8
Herts........ 86 E3
London........ 68 B3
Staffs........ 151 F8
Sur........ 66 G6
W Berks 65 E7
W Mid........ 134 G6
Little Heck N Yorks...... 198 C5
Littlehempston Devon...... 8 C6
Little Henham Essex.... 105 E10
Little Henny Essex....... 107 D7
Little Herbert's Glos..... 81 B7
Little Hereford
Hereford........ 115 D11
Little Hill Hereford 97 F9
Som 28 E3
Little Holbury Hants 32 G6
Little Honeyborough
Pembs........ 73 D7
Little Hoole Moss Houses
Lancs........ 194 C3
Little Horkesley Essex.. 107 E9
Little Hormead Herts.... 105 F8
Little Horsted E Sus...... 23 B7
Little Horton Wilts........ 62 G4
W Yorks........ 205 G9
Little Horwood Bucks... 102 E5
Littlehoughton
Northumb........ 264 F6
Little Houghton
S Yorks........ 198 G2
W Nhants 120 F6
Little Hucklow Derbys . 185 F11
Little Hulton Gtr Man.... 195 G8
Little Humber E Yorks ... 201 C8
Little Hungerford
W Berks 64 E4
Little Ilford London........ 68 B2
Little Ingestre Staffs..... 151 E9
Little Inkberrow Worcs 117 F10
Little Irchester
N Nhants........ 121 D8
Little Keyford Som........ 45 D9
Little Kimble Bucks 84 D4
Little Kineton Warks 118 G6
Little Kingshill Bucks 84 F5
Little Knowles Green
Suff 124 F5
Little Langdale Cumb ... 220 E6
Little Langford Wilts...... 46 F4
Little Laver Essex........ 87 D8
Little Lawford Warks 119 B9
Little Layton Blackpool .. 202 F2
Little Leigh Ches W..... 183 F10
Little Leighs Essex........ 88 B2
Little Lepton W Yorks.... 197 E8
Little Leven E Yorks 209 D8
Little Lever Gtr Man..... 195 F9
Little Limber Lincs....... 200 E6
Little Linford M Keynes. 102 C6
Little Load Som........ 29 C7
Little London Bucks...... 83 C10
Bucks 84 D5
Little London continued
Cambs 139 D8
Essex 105 F9
Essex 106 D3
E Sus........ 23 B9
Glos 80 B2
Hants........ 47 D11
Hants........ 48 B6
Lincs........ 156 E4
Lincs........ 157 E8
Lincs........ 189 D10
Lincs........ 190 F4
Norf........ 140 D5
Norf........ 160 C2
Norf........ 160 C5
Norf........ 160 E3
Oxon........ 83 E8
Powys........ 129 F10
Shrops 131 F10
Som 44 D6
Suff........ 125 F10
Worcs........ 116 C2
W Yorks........ 205 F10
Little Longstone
Derbys 185 G11
Little Lynturk Aberds.... 293 B7
Little Lyth Shrops 131 B9
Little Madeley Staffs.... 168 F3
Little Malvern Worcs..... 98 C5
Little Mancot Flint....... 166 B4
Little Maplestead Essex 106 E6
Little Marcle Hereford.... 98 D3
Little Marlow Bucks...... 65 B11
Little Marsden Lancs ... 204 F3
Little Marsh Bucks....... 102 G3
Norf........ 159 B10
Wilts........ 45 B11
Little Marton Blackpool. 202 G2
Little Mascalls Essex 88 E2
Little Massingham Norf. 158 E5
Little Melton Norf 142 B3
Little Merthyr Hereford... 96 B5
Little Milford Pembs 73 C7
Littlemill Aberds........ 292 D5
E Ayrs........ 257 F11
Highld........ 301 D9
Northumb 264 F6
Little Mill Kent........ 53 D7
Mon........ 78 E4
Little Milton Newport 59 B11
Oxon........ 83 E10
Little Minster Oxon 82 C4
Little Missenden Bucks .. 84 F6
Little Mongeham Kent.. 55 C10
Littlemoor Derbys 170 C5
Dorset........ 17 E9
Little Moor Gtr Man...... 184 D6
Lancs 203 E10
Little Moor End Lancs... 195 B8
Littlemore Oxon 83 E8
Little Morrell Warks 118 F6
Littlemoss Gtr Man...... 184 B6
Little Mountain Flint..... 166 C3
Little Musgrave Cumb... 222 C5
Little Ness Shrops........ 149 F8
Little Neston Ches W.... 182 F3
Little Newcastle Pembs... 91 F9
Little Newsham Durham. 224 B2
Little Norlington E Sus.... 23 C7
Little Norton Som 29 D7
Little Oakley Essex 108 F4
N Nhants........ 137 F7
Little Odell Bedford 121 F9
Little Offley Herts 104 F2
Little Onn Staffs 150 F6
Little Ormside Cumb..... 222 B4
Little Orton Cumb........ 239 F9
Leics........ 134 B6
Little Ouse Norf 140 F2
Little Ouseburn N Yorks 215 G8
Littleover Derby 152 C6
Little Overton Wrex...... 166 G5
Little Oxney Green
Essex 87 D11
Little Packington Warks 134 G4
Little Parndon Essex..... 86 C6
Little Paxton Cambs 122 E3
Little Petherick Corn 10 G4
Little Pitlurg Moray...... 302 E4
Little Plumpton Lancs .. 202 G3
Little Plumstead Norf... 160 G6
Little Ponton Lincs...... 155 C8
Littleport Cambs........ 139 F11
Little Posbrook Hants 33 G8
Little Poulton Lancs 202 F3
Little Preston Kent 53 B8
W Yorks........ 206 G3
Littler Ches W.......... 167 B10
Little Raveley Cambs.... 122 B5
Little Reedness
E Yorks 199 C10
Little Reynoldston
Swansea........ 56 D3
Little Ribston N Yorks .. 206 C3
Little Rissington Glos... 81 B11
Little Rogart Highld 309 J7
Little Rollright Oxon 100 E5
Little Ryburgh Norf...... 159 D9
Little Ryle Northumb 264 G2
Little Ryton Shrops 131 C9
Little Salisbury Wilts 63 G7
Little Salkeld Cumb 231 D7
Little Sampford Essex .. 106 E3
Little Sandhurst Brack.. 65 G10
Little Saredon Staffs..... 133 B8
Little Saxham Suff 124 E5
Little Scatwell Highld... 300 D3
Little Scotland Gtr Man.. 194 E6
Little Sessay N Yorks 215 E9
Little Shelford Cambs... 123 G9
Little Shoddesden Hants. 47 D9
Little Shrewley Warks .. 118 D4
Little Shurdington Glos.. 80 B6
Little Silver Devon 26 F6
Devon 40 E4
Little Singleton Lancs... 202 F3
Little Skillymarno
Aberds 303 D9
Little Skipwith N Yorks.. 207 F9
Little Smeaton N Yorks.. 198 D4
N Yorks 224 E6
Little Snoring Norf 159 C9
Little Sodbury S Glos..... 61 C9
Little Sodbury End
S Glos........ 61 C8
Little Somborne Hants.. 47 G11
Little Somerford Wilts... 62 C3
Little Soudley Shrops ... 150 D4
Little Stainforth
N Yorks 212 F6
Little Stainton Darl 234 G2
Little Stanmore London . 85 G11
Little Stanney Ches W... 182 G6
Little Staughton Bedford 122 E2
Littlestead Green Oxon.. 65 D8
Little Steeping Lincs.... 174 C6
Little Stoke S Glos 60 C6
Staffs 151 C8
Littlestone-on-Sea Kent. 39 C9
Little Stonham Suff..... 126 E2
Little Stretton Leics 136 C3
Little Stretton continued
Shrops 131 E8
Little Strickland Cumb. 221 B11
Little Studley N Yorks ... 214 E6
Little Stukeley Cambs... 122 B4
Little Sugnall Staffs..... 150 C6
Little Sutton Ches W 182 F5
Lincs........ 157 E9
Shrops 131 G10
Little Swinburne
Northumb........ 241 B10
Little Tarrington Hereford 98 C2
Little Tew Oxon 101 F7
Little Tey Essex........ 107 G7
Little Thetford Cambs.. 123 B10
Little Thirkleby N Yorks . 215 D9
Little Thornage Norf... 159 B11
Little Thornton Lancs... 202 E3
Littlethorpe Leics 135 D10
N Yorks........ 214 F6
Little Thorpe Durham ... 234 C4
W Yorks........ 197 C7
Little Thurlow Suff 124 G3
Little Thurlow Green
Suff........ 124 G3
Little Thurrock Thurrock. 68 D6
Littleton Bath 60 G5
Ches W........ 166 B6
Dorset........ 30 G5
Hants........ 48 G3
Perth........ 286 D6
Som........ 44 G3
Sur 50 D3
Sur 66 F5
W Sus........ 62 G2
Littleton Common Sur.... 66 E5
Littleton Drew Wilts..... 61 C10
Littleton-on-Severn
S Glos........ 60 B5
Littleton Panell Wilts.... 46 C4
Littleton-upon-Severn
S Glos........ 79 G9
Little Torboll Highld..... 309 K7
Little Torrington Devon.. 25 D7
Little Totham Essex....... 88 C5
Little Toux Aberds 302 D5
Littletown Durham....... 234 C2
IoW........ 20 C6
W Yorks........ 197 C8
Little Town Cumb 220 B4
Lancs 203 F9
Warr........ 183 C10
Little Tring Herts 84 C6
Little Twycross Leics 134 B6
Little Urswick Cumb 210 E5
Little Vantage W Loth ... 270 C2
Little Wakering Essex...... 70 B2
Little Walden Essex.... 105 C10
Little Waldingfield Suff. 107 B8
Little Walsingham Norf. 159 B8
Little Waltham Essex 88 C2
Little Walton Warks...... 135 G9
Little Warley Essex 87 G10
Little Warton Warks 134 C5
Little Washbourne Glos.. 99 E9
Little Weighton E Yorks . 208 G5
Little Weldon N Nhants.. 137 F8
Little Welland Worcs..... 98 D6
Little Welnetham Suff .. 125 E7
Little Welton Lincs........ 190 D4
Little Wenham Suff 107 D11
Little Wenlock Telford .. 132 B2
Little Weston Som........ 29 B10
Little Whitehouse IoW .. 20 C5
Little Whittingham Green
Suff........ 126 B5
Littlewick Green
Windsor 65 D10
Little Wigborough Essex. 89 B7
Little Wilbraham
Cambs........ 123 F10
Littlewindsor Dorset...... 28 G6
Little Wisbeach Lincs ... 156 C2
Little Wishford Wilts 46 F5
Little Witcombe Glos 80 B6
Little Witley Worcs 116 E5
Little Wittenham Oxon... 83 G9
Little Wolford Warks.... 100 D5
Littlewood Staffs 133 B9
Little Wood Corner Bucks 84 E6
Littlewood Green
Warks........ 117 E11
Little Woolgarston
Dorset........ 18 E5
Littleworth Bedford.... 103 C11
Glos 80 E4
Glos 100 D2
Oxon........ 82 F4
Oxon........ 83 D9
Oxon........ 83 G10
Staffs 151 E8
Staffs 151 G10
S Yorks 187 B10
Warks........ 118 E4
Wilts........ 63 G7
Worcs........ 117 E9
Worcs........ 117 G7
W Sus 35 C11
Littleworth Common
Bucks........ 66 B2
Little Worthen Shrops .. 130 B6
Littleworth End Warks.. 134 D3
Little Wratting Suff....... 106 B3
Little Wymington
Bedford........ 121 D9
Little Wymondley Herts. 104 F4
Little Wyrley Staffs 133 B10
Little Wytheford
Shrops 149 F11
Little Yeldham Essex ... 106 D5
Littley Green Essex 87 B11
Litton Derbys 185 F11
N Yorks 213 E8
Som........ 44 C5
Litton Cheney Dorset 17 C7
Litton Mill Derbys...... 185 G11
Liurbost W Isles 304 F5
Livermead Torbay.......... 9 C8
Liverpool Mers 182 C4
Liverpool Airport Mers . 182 E6
Liversedge W Yorks 197 C8
Liverton Devon 14 F2
Redcar 226 B4
Liverton Mines Redcar.. 226 B4
Liverton Street Kent..... 53 C11
Livesey Street Kent 53 C8
Livingshayes Devon...... 27 G7
Livingston W Loth 269 B11
Livingston Village
W Loth........ 269 B10
Lix Toll Stirling 285 D9
Lixwm Flint........ 181 G11
Lizard Corn........ 2 G6
Llaingoch Anglesey 178 E2
Llaithddu Powys........ 129 G11
Llampha V Glam........ 58 D2
Llan Powys........ 129 C7
Llanaber Gwyn 146 F2
Llanaelhaearn Gwyn.... 162 G5
Llanafan Ceredig........ 112 C3
Llanafan-fawr Powys ... 113 F9
Llanallgo Anglesey 179 D7
Llananno Powys 113 C11
Llanarmon Gwyn 145 B8
Llanarmon Dyffryn Ceiriog
Wrex........ 148 C3
Llanarmon Mynydd-mawr
Powys........ 148 D2
Llanarmon-yn-Ial
Denb........ 165 D11
Llanarth Ceredig 111 F8
Mon 78 C5
Llanarthne Carms 93 G10
Llanasa Flint........ 181 E10
Llanbabo Anglesey 178 D5
Llanbad Rhondda........ 58 C3
Llanbadarn Fawr
Ceredig........ 128 G2
Llanbadarn Fynydd
Powys........ 114 B2
Llanbadarn-y-Garreg
Powys........ 96 B2
Llanbadoc Mon........ 78 E5
Llanbadrig Anglesey 178 C5
Llanbeder Newport 78 G5
Llanbedr Gwyn 145 D11
Powys........ 96 B2
Powys........ 96 G4
Llanbedr-Dyffryn-Clwyd
Denb........ 165 D10
Llanbedrgoch Anglesey . 179 E8
Llanbedrog Gwyn........ 144 C6
Llanbedr Pont Steffan
= Lampeter Ceredig...... 93 B11
Llanbedr-y-cennin
Conwy........ 164 B3
Llanberis Gwyn 163 C9
Llanbethery V Glam 58 F4
Llanbister Powys 114 C2
Llanblethian = Llanfleiddan
V Glam........ 58 E3
Llanboidy Carms........ 92 G4
Llanbradach Caerph 77 G10
Llanbrynmair Powys..... 129 C7
Llancadle = Llancatal
V Glam........ 58 F4
Llancaiach Caerph 77 F10
Llancarfan V Glam 58 E5
Llancatal = Llancadle
V Glam........ 58 F4
Llancayo Mon 78 E5
Llancloudy Hereford 97 G9
Llancowrid Powys 130 E3
Llancynfelyn Ceredig ... 128 E2
Llan-dafal Bl Gwent 77 E11
Llandaff Cardiff........ 59 D7
Llandaff North Cardiff ... 59 D7
Llandanwg Gwyn 145 D11
Llandarcy Neath........ 57 B8
Llandawke Carms........ 74 C3
Llanddaniel Fab
Anglesey........ 179 G7
Llanddarog Carms........ 75 B8
Llanddeiniol Ceredig ... 111 C11
Llanddeiniolen Gwyn ... 163 B8
Llandderfel Gwyn........ 147 B9
Llanddeusant Anglesey . 178 D4
Carms........ 94 G5
Llanddew Powys........ 95 E11
Llanddewi Swansea....... 56 D3
Llanddewi-Brefi Ceredig 112 F3
Llanddewi Fach Mon...... 78 F4
Llanddewi'r Cwm Powys 95 B10
Llanddewi Rhydderch
Mon........ 78 C5
Llanddewi Skirrid Mon .. 78 B4
Llanddewi Velfrey
Pembs........ 73 B10
Llanddewi Ystradenni
Powys........ 114 D2
Llanddoged Conwy 164 C4
Llanddona Anglesey...... 179 F9
Llanddowror Carms....... 74 C3
Llanddulas Conwy 180 F6
Llanddwywe Gwyn...... 145 E11
Llanddyfynan Anglesey.. 179 F8
Llandecwyn Gwyn 146 B2
Llandefaelog Powys 95 E10
Llandefaelog Fach
Powys........ 95 E10
Llandefaelog-tre'r-graig
Powys........ 96 F2
Llandefalle Powys 96 D2
Llandegai Gwyn 179 G9
Llandegfan Anglesey 179 G9
Llandegla Denb........ 165 E11
Llandegley Powys 114 E2
Llandegveth Mon........ 78 F4
Llandegwning Gwyn 144 C5
Llandeilo Carms 94 G2
Llandeilo Graban Powys 95 C11
Llandeilo'r Fan Powys 95 E7
Llandeloy Pembs........ 91 F7
Llandenny Mon 78 E6
Llandenny Walks Mon ... 78 E5
Llandevaud Newport...... 78 G6
Llandevenny Mon........ 60 B2
Llandewi Ystradenny
Powys........ 114 D2
Llandilo Pembs 92 F2
Llandilo-yr-ynys Carms.. 93 G9
Llandinabo Hereford 97 F10
Llandinam Powys....... 129 F10
Llandissilio Pembs........ 92 G2
Llandogo Mon........ 79 E8
Llandough V Glam........ 58 E3
V Glam 59 E7
Llandovery = Llanymddyfri
Carms........ 94 E5
Llandow = Llandw
V Glam........ 58 E2
Llandre Carms........ 94 C3
Ceredig........ 128 F2
Llandrillo Denb 147 B10
Llandrillo-yn-Rhôs
Conwy........ 180 E4
Llandrindod Wells
Powys........ 113 E11
Llandrinio Powys 148 F5
Llandruidion Pembs 90 G5
Llandudno Conwy....... 180 E3
Llandudno Junction
= Cyffordd Llandudno
Conwy........ 180 F3
Llandudoch = St Dogmaels
Pembs........ 92 B3
Llandw = Llandow
V Glam........ 58 E2
Llandwrog Gwyn........ 163 D7
Llandybie Carms........ 75 B10
Llandyfaelog Carms 74 C6
Llandyfan Carms........ 75 B10
Llandyfriog Ceredig...... 92 C6
Llandyfrydog Anglesey.. 178 D6
Llandygwydd Ceredig 92 C4
Llandynan Denb 165 F11
Llandyrnog Denb 165 B10
Llandysilio Powys........ 148 F5
Llandyssil Powys 130 D3
Llandysul Ceredig........ 93 C8
Llanedeyrn Cardiff........ 59 C8

Llanedi Carms 75 D9
Llanedwen Anglesey 163 B8
Llaneglwys Powys 95 D11
Llanegryn Gwyn 110 B2
Llanegwad Carms 93 G10
Llaneilian Anglesey 179 C7
Llanelian yn-Rhôs Conwy 180 F5
Llanelidan Denb 165 E10
Llanelieu Powys 96 E3
Llanellen Mon 78 C4
Llanelli Carms 56 B4
Llanelltyd Gwyn 146 F4
Llanelly Mon 78 C2
Llanelly Hill Mon 78 C2
Llanelwedd Powys 113 G10
Llanelwy = St Asaph Denb 181 G8
Llanenddwyn Gwyn 145 E11
Llanengan Gwyn 144 D5
Llanerch Powys 130 E6
Llanerch Emrys Powys 148 E4
Llanerchymedd Anglesey 178 E6
Llanerfyl Powys 129 B10
Llaneuddog Anglesey 179 D7
Llan eurgain = Northop Flint 166 B2
Llanfabon Caerph 77 G10
Llanfachraeth Anglesey 178 E4
Llanfachreth Gwyn 146 E5
Llanfaelog Anglesey 178 G4
Llanfaelrhys Gwyn 144 D4
Llanfaenor Mon 78 B6
Llanfaes Anglesey 179 F10
Powys 95 F10
Llanfaethlu Anglesey 178 D4
Llanfaglan Gwyn 163 C7
Llanfair Gwyn 145 D11
Llanfair Caereinion Powys 130 B2
Llanfair Clydogau Ceredig 112 G2
Llanfair-Dyffryn-Clwyd Denb 165 D10
Llanfairfechan Conwy 179 F11
Llanfair Kilgeddin Mon 78 D4
Llanfair Kilgheddin Mon 78 D4
Llanfair-Nant-Gwyn Pembs 92 D3
Llanfairpwll-gwyngyll Anglesey 179 G8
Llanfair Talhaiarn Conwy 180 G6
Llanfair Waterdine Shrops 114 B4
Llanfairyneubwll Anglesey 178 F3
Llanfairynghornwy Anglesey 178 C4
Llanfallteg Carms 73 B11
Llanfallteg West Carms 73 B10
Llanfaredd Powys 113 G11
Llanfarian Ceredig 111 B11
Llanfechain Powys 148 E3
Llanfechan Powys 113 G9
Llanfechell Anglesey 178 C5
Llanferres Denb 165 C11
Llan Ffestiniog Gwyn 164 G2
Llanfflewyn Anglesey 178 D5
Llanfigael Anglesey 178 E4
Llanfihangel-ar-arth Carms 93 D9
Llanfihangel-Crucorney Mon 96 G6
Llanfihangel Glyn Myfyr Conwy 165 F7
Llanfihangel-helygen Powys 113 E10
Llanfihangel Nant Bran Powys 95 E8
Llanfihangel-nant-Melan Powys 114 F3
Llanfihangel Rhydithon Powys 114 D3
Llanfihangel Rogiet Mon 60 B2
Llanfihangel Tal-y-llyn Powys 96 F2
Llanfihangel Tor y Mynydd Mon 79 E7
Llanfihangel-uwch-Gwili Carms 93 G9
Llanfihangel-y-Creuddyn Ceredig 112 B3
Llanfihangel-yng-Ngwynfa Powys 147 F11
Llanfihangel yn Nhowyn Anglesey 178 F4
Llanfihangel-y-pennant Gwyn 128 B3
Gwyn 163 F8
Llanfilo Powys 96 E2
Llanfleiddan = Llanblethian V Glam 58 E3
Llanfoist Mon 78 C3
Llanfor Gwyn 147 B8
Llanfrechfa Torf 78 G4
Llanfrothen Gwyn 163 G10
Llanfrynach Powys 95 F11
Llanfwrog Anglesey 178 E4
Denb 165 D10
Llanfyllin Powys 148 F2
Llanfynydd Carms 93 F11
Flint 166 D3
Llanfyrnach Pembs 92 E4
Llangadfan Powys 147 G10
Llangadog Carms 74 D6
Carms 94 F4
Llangadwaladr Anglesey 162 B5
Powys 148 C3
Llangaffo Anglesey 162 B6
Llangain Carms 74 B5
Llangammarch Wells Powys 95 B8
Llangan V Glam 58 D3
Llangarron Hereford 97 G10
Llangasty Talyllyn Powys 96 F2
Llangathen Carms 93 G11
Llangattock Powys 78 B2
Llangattock Lingoed Mon 97 G7
Llangattock nigh Usk Mon 78 D4
Llangattock-Vibon-Avel Mon 79 B7
Llangedwyn Powys 148 E3
Llangefni Anglesey 179 F7
Llangeinor Bridgend 58 B2
Llangeitho Ceredig 112 F2
Llangeler Carms 93 D7
Llangendeirne Carms 75 C7
Llangennech Carms 75 E9
Llangennith Swansea 56 C2
Llangenny Powys 78 B2
Llangernyw Conwy 164 B5
Llangeview Mon 78 E5
Llangewydd Court Bridgend 57 E11
Llangian Gwyn 144 D5
Llangloffan Pembs 91 E8
Llanglydwen Carms 92 F3
Llangoed Anglesey 179 F10
Llangoedmor Ceredig 92 B3
Llangollen Denb 166 G2
Llangolman Pembs 92 F2
Llangors Powys 96 F2
Llangorwen Ceredig 128 G2
Llangovan Mon 79 D7
Llangower Gwyn 147 C8
Llangrannog Ceredig 110 G6
Llangristiolus Anglesey 178 G6
Llangrove Hereford 79 B8
Llangua Mon 97 F7
Llangunllo Powys 114 C4
Llangunnor Carms 74 B6
Llangurig Powys 113 B8
Llangwm Conwy 165 G7
Mon 78 E6
Pembs 73 D7
Llangwnnadl Gwyn 144 C4
Llangwyfan Denb 165 B10
Llangwyfan-isaf Anglesey 162 B4
Llangwyllog Anglesey 178 F6
Llangwyryfon Ceredig 111 C11
Llangybi Ceredig 112 G2
Gwyn 162 G6
Mon 78 F5
Llangyfelach Swansea 56 B6
Llangyndeyrn Carms 75 C7
Llangynhafal Denb 165 C10
Llangynidr Powys 77 B11
Llangyniew Powys 130 B2
Llangynin Carms 74 B2
Llangynog Carms 74 B4
Powys 147 D11
Llangynwyd Bridgend 57 D11
Llanhamlach Powys 95 F11
Llanharan Rhondda 58 C4
Llanharry Rhondda 58 C4
Llanhennock Mon 78 G5
Llanhilleth Bl Gwent 78 E2
Llanhowel Pembs 90 F6
Llanidloes Powys 129 G9
Llaniestyn Gwyn 144 C5
Llanifyny Powys 129 G7
Llanigon Powys 96 D4
Llanilar Ceredig 112 C2
Llanilid Rhondda 58 C3
Llanilltud Fawr = Llantwit Major V Glam 58 F3
Llanio Ceredig 112 F2
Llanion Pembs 73 E7
Llanishen Cardiff 59 C7
Mon 79 E7
Llanllawddog Carms 93 F9
Llanllechid Gwyn 163 B10
Llanllowell Mon 78 F5
Llanllugan Powys 129 C11
Llanllwch Carms 74 B5
Llanllwchaiarn Powys 130 E2
Llanllwni Carms 93 D9
Llanllwyd Shrops 130 G3
Llanllyfni Gwyn 163 E7
Llanmadoc Swansea 56 C2
Llanmaes Cardiff 58 D6
V Glam 58 F3
Llanmartin Newport 59 B11
Llanmerwig Powys 130 E3
Llanmihangel V Glam 58 E3
Llan-mill Pembs 73 C10
Llanmiloe Carms 74 D3
Llanmorlais Swansea 56 C4
Llannefydd Conwy 181 G7
Llannerch-y-môr Flint 181 F11
Llannon Carms 75 D8
Llan-non = Llanon Ceredig 111 D10
Llannor Gwyn 145 B7
Llanon Pembs 90 E6
Llanon = Llan-non Ceredig 111 D10
Llanover Mon 78 D4
Llanpumsaint Carms 93 F8
Llanreath Pembs 73 E7
Llanreithan Pembs 91 F7
Llanrhaeadr Denb 165 C9
Llanrhaeadr-ym-Mochnant Powys 148 D2
Llanrhian Pembs 90 E6
Llanrhidian Swansea 56 C3
Llanrhos Conwy 180 E3
Llanrhyddlad Anglesey 178 D4
Llanrhystud Ceredig 111 D10
Llanrosser Hereford 96 D5
Llanrothal Hereford 79 B7
Llanrug Gwyn 163 C8
Llanrumney Cardiff 59 C8
Llanrwst Conwy 164 C4
Llansadurnen Carms 74 C3
Llansadwrn Anglesey 179 F9
Carms 94 E3
Llansaint Carms 74 D5
Llansamlet Swansea 57 B7
Llansanffraid Glan Conwy Conwy 180 F4
Llansannan Conwy 164 B6
Llansannor V Glam 58 D3
Llansantffraed Ceredig 111 D10
Powys 96 G2
Llansantffraed Cwmdeuddwr Powys 113 D9
Llansantffraed-in-Elwel Powys 113 G11
Llansantffraid-ym-Mechain Powys 148 E4
Llansawel Carms 94 D2
Llansawel = Briton Ferry Neath 57 C8
Llansilin Powys 148 D4
Llansoy Mon 78 E6
Llanspyddid Powys 95 F10
Llanstadwell Pembs 72 D6
Llansteffan Carms 74 C5
Llanstephan Powys 96 C2
Llantarnam Torf 78 G4
Llanteems Mon 96 G6
Llanteg Pembs 73 C11
Llanthony Mon 96 F5
Llantilio Crossenny Mon 78 C5
Llantilio Pertholey Mon 78 B4
Llantood Pembs 92 C3
Llantrisant Anglesey 178 E5
Mon 78 F5
Rhondda 58 C4
Llantrithyd V Glam 58 E4
Llantwit Neath 57 B9
Llantwit Fardre Rhondda 58 B5
Llantwit Major = Llanilltud Fawr V Glam 58 F3
Llanuwchllyn Gwyn 147 C7
Llanussyllt = Saundersfoot Pembs 73 E10
Llanvaches Newport 78 G6
Llanvair Discoed Mon 78 G6
Llanvapley Mon 78 C5
Llanvetherine Mon 78 B5
Llanveynoe Hereford 96 E6
Llanvihangel Crucorney Mon 96 G6
Llanvihangel Gobion Mon 78 D4
Llanvihangel-Ystern-Llewern Mon 78 C6
Llanwarne Hereford 97 F10
Llanwddyn Powys 147 F10
Llanwenarth Mon 78 C3
Llanwenog Ceredig 93 B9
Llanwern Newport 59 B11
Llanwinio Carms 92 F5
Llanwnda Gwyn 163 D7
Pembs 91 D8
Llanwnnen Ceredig 93 B10
Llanwnog Powys 129 E10
Llanwrda Carms 94 E4
Llanwrin Powys 128 C5
Llanwrthwl Powys 113 E9
Llanwrtud = Llanwrtyd Wells Powys 95 B7
Llanwrtyd Wells = Llanwrtud Powys 95 B7
Llanwyddelan Powys 129 C11
Llanyblodwel Shrops 148 E4
Llanybri Carms 74 C4
Llanybydder Carms 93 C10
Llanycefn Pembs 91 G11
Llanychaer Pembs 91 D9
Llanycil Gwyn 147 C8
Llanycrwys Carms 94 B2
Llanymawddwy Gwyn 147 F8
Llanymddyfri = Llandovery Carms 94 E5
Llanymynech Powys 148 E5
Llanynghenedl Anglesey 178 E4
Llanynys Denb 165 C10
Llan-y-pwll Wrex 166 E5
Llanyrafon Torf 78 G4
Llanyre Powys 113 E10
Llanystumdwy Gwyn 145 B9
Llanywern Powys 96 F2
Llawhaden Pembs 73 B9
Llawnt Shrops 148 C5
Llawrdref Bellaf Gwyn 144 D5
Llawr-y-glyn Powys 129 E8
Llay Wrex 166 D4
Llechcynfarwy Anglesey 178 E5
Llecheiddior Gwyn 163 G7
Llechfaen Powys 95 F11
Llechfraith Gwyn 146 F3
Llechryd Caerph 77 D10
Ceredig 92 C4
Llechrydau Powys 148 C4
Llechwedd Conwy 180 F3
Lledrod Ceredig 112 C2
Llenmerewig Powys 130 E3
Llethrid Swansea 56 C4
Llettyrychen Carms 75 E7
Llidiad Nenog Carms 93 D10
Llidiardau Gwyn 147 B7
Llidiart-y-parc Denb 165 G10
Llithfaen Gwyn 162 G5
Lloc Flint 181 F10
Llong Flint 166 C3
Llowes Powys 96 C3
Lloyney Powys 114 B4
Llugwy Powys 128 D4
Llundain-fach Ceredig 111 F11
Llwydarth Bridgend 57 C11
Llwydcoed Rhondda 77 E7
Llwyn Denb 165 C9
Shrops 130 G5
Llwyncelyn Ceredig 111 F8
Llwyndafydd Ceredig 111 F7
Llwynderw Powys 130 C4
Llwyn-derw Powys 129 G8
Llwyndrain Pembs 92 E5
Llwyn-du Mon 78 B3
Llwynduris Ceredig 92 C4
Llwyndyrys Gwyn 162 G5
Llwyneinion Wrex 166 F3
Llwyngwril Gwyn 110 B2
Llwynhendy Carms 56 B4
Llwyn-hendy Carms 56 B4
Llwynmawr Wrex 148 B4
Llwyn-on Village M Tydf 77 C8
Llwyn-Têg Carms 75 D9
Llwyn-y-brain Carms 73 C11
Llwyn-y-go Shrops 148 E6
Llwynygog Powys 129 E7
Llwyn-y-groes Ceredig 111 F11
Llwynypia Rhondda 77 G7
Llwyn-yr-hwrdd Pembs 92 E4
Llynclys Shrops 148 E5
Llynfaes Anglesey 178 F6
Llysfaen Conwy 180 F5
Llyswen Powys 96 D2
Llysworney V Glam 58 E3
Llys-y-frôn Pembs 91 G10
Llywel Powys 95 E7
Llywernog Ceredig 128 G4
Load Brook S Yorks 186 D3
Loan Falk 279 F9
Loandhu Highld 301 B8
Loanend Northumb 273 E8
Loanhead Aberds 302 D6
Midloth 270 B5
Perth 286 D5
Loanreoch Highld 300 B6
Loans S Ayrs 257 C8
Loansdean Northumb 252 G5
Loans of Tullich Highld 301 B8
Lobb Devon 40 F3
Lobhillcross Devon 12 D5
Lobley Hill T&W 242 E6
Lobthorpe Lincs 155 E9
Loch a Charnain W Isles 297 G4
Loch a' Ghainmhich W Isles 304 F4
Lochailort Highld 295 G9
Lochaline Highld 289 E8
Lochanhully Highld 301 G9
Lochans Dumfries 236 D2
Locharbriggs Dumfries 247 G11
Lochassynt Lodge Highld 307 G6
Lochavich Ho Argyll 275 B10
Lochawe Argyll 284 E5
Loch Baghasdail W Isles 297 K3
Lochbuie Argyll 289 G8
Lochbuie Ho Argyll 289 G8
Lochcallater Lodge Aberds 292 E3
Lochcarron Highld 295 B10
Loch Choire Lodge Highld 308 F6
Lochdhu Highld 310 E4
Lochdochart House Stirling 285 E8
Lochdon Argyll 289 F9
Lochdrum Highld 300 B2
Lochead Argyll 275 E11
Argyll 275 F8
Lochearnhead Stirling 285 E9
Lochee Dundee 287 D7
Loch Eil Highld 290 F2
Lochend Edin 280 G5
Highld 300 F5
Highld 310 C6
Lochend Ho Stirling 277 B11
Locherben Dumfries 247 D11
Lochetive Ho Highld 284 C5
Loch Euphoirt W Isles 296 E4
Lochfoot Dumfries 237 B10
Lochgair Argyll 275 D10
Lochgarthside Highld 291 B7
Lochgelly Fife 280 C3
Lochgilphead Argyll 275 E9
Lochgoilhead Argyll 284 G6
Loch Head Dumfries 236 E5
Dumfries 245 E11
Lochhill Moray 302 C2
Lochhussie Highld 300 D4
Lochinch Castle Dumfries 236 C3
Lochindorb Lodge Highld 301 F9
Lochinver Highld 307 G5
Lochlane Perth 286 E2
Lochletter Highld 300 G4
Loch Loyal Lodge Highld 308 E6
Lochluichart Highld 300 C3
Lochmaben Dumfries 248 G3
Lochmore Cottage Highld 310 E4
Lochmore Lodge Highld 306 F7
Loch nam Madadh W Isles 296 E5
Lochnell Ho Argyll 289 F10
Lochore Fife 280 B3
Lochorodale Argyll 255 F7
Lochportain W Isles 296 D5
Lochran Perth 280 B2
Lochranza N Ayrs 255 B10
Lochs Crofts Moray 302 C3
Loch Sgioport W Isles 297 H4
Lochside Aberds 293 G9
Highld 301 D8
Highld 308 D4
Highld 310 F2
S Ayrs 257 E8
Lochslin Highld 311 L2
Lochstack Lodge Highld 306 E7
Lochton Aberds 293 D9
Lochty Angus 293 G7
Fife 287 G9
Perth 286 E4
Lochuisge Highld 289 D9
Lochurr Dumfries 247 F7
Lochwinnoch Renfs 267 D7
Lochwood Dumfries 248 D3
Glasgow 268 B3
Lochyside Highld 290 F3
Lockengate Corn 5 C10
Lockerbie Dumfries 248 G4
Lockeridge Wilts 62 F6
Lockeridge Dene Wilts 62 F6
Lockerley Hants 32 B3
Lockhills Cumb 230 B6
Locking N Som 43 B11
Lockinge Oxon 64 B2
Locking Stumps Warr 183 C10
Lockington E Yorks 208 D5
Leics 153 D9
Lockleaze Bristol 60 D6
Lockleywood Shrops 150 D3
Locksbottom London 68 F2
Locksbrook Bath 61 G8
Locksgreen IoW 20 C4
Locks Heath Hants 33 F8
Lockton N Yorks 226 G6
Lockwood W Yorks 196 D6
Loddington Leics 136 C5
N Nhants 120 B6
Loddiswell Devon 8 F4
Loddon Norf 143 D7
Loddon Ingloss Norf 142 D6
Lode Cambs 123 E10
Lode Heath W Mid 134 G3
Loders Dorset 16 C5
Lodgebank Shrops 149 D11
Lodge Green N Yorks 223 F9
W Mid 134 G5
Lodge Hill Corn 6 C4
W Mid 133 G10
W Yorks 197 C9
Lodge Lees Kent 55 D8
Lodge Moor S Yorks 186 D3
Lodge Park Worcs 117 D10
Lodsworth W Sus 34 C6
Lodsworth Common W Sus 34 C6
Lodway Bristol 60 D4
Lofthouse N Yorks 214 E2
W Yorks 197 B10
Lofthouse Gate W Yorks 197 C10
Loftus Redcar 226 B4
Logan E Ayrs 258 E3
Loganlea W Loth 269 C9
Logan Mains Dumfries 236 E2
Loggerheads Denb 165 C11
Staffs 150 B4
Logie Angus 293 G8
Fife 287 E8
Moray 301 D10
Logiealmond Lodge Perth 286 D3
Logie Coldstone Aberds 292 C6
Logie Hill Highld 301 B7
Logie Newton Aberds 302 F6
Logie Pert Angus 293 G8
Logierait Perth 286 B3
Login Carms 92 G3
Logmore Green Sur 50 D6
Loidse Mhorsgail W Isles 304 F3
Lolworth Cambs 123 E7
Lomeshaye Lancs 204 F2
Lôn Gwyn 147 C7
Lonbain Highld 298 D6
Londesborough E Yorks 208 D3
London Apprentice Corn 5 E10
London Beach Kent 53 F11
London Colney Herts 85 E11
Londonderry N Yorks 214 B6
W Mid 133 F10
London End Cambs 121 D11
London Fields W Mid 133 E8
London Minstead Hants 32 E3
Londonthorpe Lincs 155 B9
Londubh Highld 307 L3
Lonemore Highld 299 B7
Highld 309 L7
Long Ashton N Som 60 E5
Long Bank Worcs 116 C5
Longbar N Ayrs 266 E6
Longbarn Warr 183 C10
Long Bennington Lincs 172 G4
Longbenton T&W 243 D7
Longborough Glos 100 F3
Long Bredy Dorset 17 C7
Longbridge Plym 7 D10
Warks 118 E4
W Mid 117 B10
Longbridge Deverill Wilts 45 E11
Longbridge Hayes Stoke 168 E5
Longbridgemuir Dumfries 238 D3
Long Buckby W Nhants 120 D2
Long Buckby Wharf W Nhants 120 D2
Longburgh Cumb 239 F8
Longburton Dorset 29 E11
Longcause Devon 8 C5
Long Clawson Leics 154 D4
Longcliffe Derbys 170 D2
Long Common Hants 33 E8
Long Compton Staffs 151 E7
Warks 100 E5
Longcot Oxon 82 G3
Long Crendon Bucks 83 D11
Long Crichel Dorset 31 E7
Longcroft Cumb 238 F6
Falk 278 F5
Longcross Devon 12 F4
Sur 66 F3
Long Cross Wilts 45 G9
Longdale Cumb 222 D2
Longdales Cumb 230 C6
Long Dean Wilts 61 D11
Longden Shrops 131 B8
Longden Common Shrops 131 C8
Long Ditton Sur 67 F7
Longdon Staffs 151 G11
Worcs 98 D6
Longdon Green Staffs 151 G11
Longdon Heath Worcs 98 D6
Longdon Hill End Worcs 98 D6
Longdon on Tern Telford 150 F2
Longdown Devon 14 C3
Longdowns Corn 2 C6
Long Drax N Yorks 199 B7
Longdrum Angus 292 G4
Long Duckmanton Derbys 186 G6
Long Eaton Derbys 153 C9
Longfield Kent 68 F6
Shetland 313 M5
Wilts 45 B11
Longfield Hill Kent 68 F6
Longfleet BCP 18 C6
Longford Derbys 152 B4
Glos 98 G6
Kent 52 B4
London 66 D4
Shrops 150 C2
Telford 150 F4
Warr 183 C10
W Mid 135 G7
Longfordlane Derbys 152 B4
Longforgan Perth 287 E7
Longformacus Borders 272 D3
Longframlington Northumb 252 C4
Long Gardens Essex 106 D6
Long Green Ches W 183 G7
Suff 125 B11
Worcs 98 E6
Longham Dorset 19 B7
Norf 159 F8
Long Hanborough Oxon 82 C6
Longhaven Aberds 303 F11
Longhedge Wilts 45 E10
Longhill Aberds 303 D9
Longhirst Northumb 252 F6
Longhope Glos 79 B11
Orkney 314 G3
Longhorsley Northumb 252 E4
Longhoughton Northumb 264 G6
Longhouse Bath 61 G8
Long Itchington Warks 119 D8
Long John's Hill Norf 142 B4
Longlands Cumb 229 D11
London 68 E2
Longlane Derbys 152 B5
W Berks 64 E3
Long Lane Telford 150 F2
Long Lawford Warks 119 B9
Long Lee W Yorks 205 E7
Longlevens Glos 99 G7
Longley W Yorks 196 C5
W Yorks 196 F6
Longley Estate S Yorks 186 C5
Longley Green Worcs 116 G4
Longleys Perth 286 C6
Long Load Som 29 C7
Longmanhill Aberds 303 C7
Long Marston Herts 84 B5
N Yorks 206 C6
Warks 100 B3
Long Marton Cumb 231 G9
Long Meadow Cambs 123 E10
Long Meadowend Shrops 131 G8
Long Melford Suff 107 B7
Longmoor Camp Hants 49 G9
Longmorn Moray 302 D2
Longmoss Ches E 184 G5
Long Newnton Glos 80 G6
Longnewton Borders 262 D3
Stockton 225 B7
Long Newton E Loth 271 C10
Longney Glos 80 C3
Longniddry E Loth 281 F8
Longnor Shrops 131 C9
Staffs 151 G7
Staffs 169 C9
Longnor Park Shrops 131 C9
Long Oak Shrops 149 E7
Longparish Hants 48 E2
Longpark Cumb 239 E10
E Ayrs 257 B10
Long Park Hants 48 G2
Longport Stoke 168 F5
Long Preston N Yorks 204 B2
Longridge Glos 80 D5
Lancs 203 F8
Staffs 151 F8
W Loth 269 C9
Longridge End Glos 98 G6
Longrigg N Lanark 278 G6
Longriggend N Lanark 278 G6
Long Riston E Yorks 209 E8
Longrock Corn 1 C5
Long Sandall S Yorks 198 F6
Longscales N Yorks 205 B10
Longsdon Staffs 169 E7
Longshaw Gtr Man 194 G4
Staffs 169 F9
Longside Aberds 303 E10
Longsight Gtr Man 184 B5
Long Sight Gtr Man 196 F2
Longslow Shrops 150 B3
Longsowerby Cumb 239 G9
Longstanton Cambs 123 D7
Longstock Hants 47 F11
Longstone Corn 2 B2
Corn 11 G7
Edin 280 G4
Pembs 73 D10
Som 28 B5
Longstowe Cambs 122 G6
Long Stratton Norf 142 E3
Longstreet Wilts 46 C6
Long Street M Keynes 102 B5
Long Sutton Hants 49 D8
Lincs 157 E8
Som 29 B7
Longthorpe Pboro 138 D3
Long Thurlow Suff 125 D10
Longthwaite Cumb 230 G4
Longton Lancs 194 B3
Stoke 168 G6
Longtown Cumb 239 D9
Hereford 96 F6
Longtownmail Orkney 314 F4
Longview Mers 182 C6
Longville in the Dale Shrops 131 E10
Longway Bank Derbys 170 E4
Longwell Green S Glos 61 E7
Long Whatton Leics 153 E9
Longwick Bucks 84 D3
Long Wittenham Oxon 83 G8
Longwitton Northumb 252 F3
Longwood Shrops 132 B2
W Yorks 196 D6
Longwood Edge W Yorks 196 D6
Longworth Oxon 82 F5
Longyester E Loth 271 B10
Lon-las Swansea 57 B8
Lonmay Aberds 303 D10
Lonmore Highld 298 E2
Looe Corn 6 E5
Looe Mills Corn 6 C4
Loose Kent 53 C9
Loosegate Lincs 156 D6
Loose Hill Kent 53 C9
Loosley Row Bucks 84 E4
Lopcombe Corner Wilts 47 F9
Lopen Som 28 E6
Lopen Head Som 28 E6
Loppergarth Cumb 210 D5
Loppington Shrops 149 D9
Lopwell Devon 7 C9
Lorbottle Northumb 252 B2
Lorbottle Hall Northumb 252 B2
Lordsbridge Norf 157 G11
Lord's Hill Soton 32 D5
Lordshill Common Sur 50 E4
Lordswood Soton 32 D6
Lords Wood Medway 69 G9
Lornty Perth 286 C5
Loscoe Derbys 170 F6
W Yorks 198 C2
Loscombe Dorset 16 B6
Losgaintir W Isles 305 J2
Lossiemouth Moray 302 B2
Lossit Argyll 254 B2
Lossit Lodge Argyll 274 G5
Lostford Shrops 150 C2
Lostock Gtr Man 195 F7
Lostock Gralam Ches W 183 F11
Lostock Green Ches W 183 G11
Lostock Hall Lancs 194 B4
Lostock Junction Gtr Man 195 F7
Lostwithiel Corn 6 D2
Loth Orkney 314 C6
Lothbeg Highld 311 H3
Lothersdale N Yorks 204 D5
Lothianbridge Midloth 270 C6
Lothmore Highld 311 H3
Lottisham Som 44 G5
Loudwater Bucks 84 G6
Herts 85 F9
Loughborough Leics 153 F10
Loughor Swansea 56 B5
Loughton Essex 86 F6
M Keynes 102 D6
Shrops 132 G2
Lound Lincs 155 F11
Notts 187 D11
Suff 143 D10
Loundsley Green Derbys 186 G5
Lount Leics 153 F7
Lour Angus 287 C8
Louth Lincs 190 D4
Lovat Highld 300 E5
Lovaton Devon 7 B10
Love Clough Lancs 195 B10
Lovedean Hants 33 E11
Love Green Bucks 66 C4
Lover Wilts 32 C2
Loversall S Yorks 187 B9
Loves Green Essex 87 E10
Lovesome Hill N Yorks 225 F7
Loveston Pembs 73 D9
Lovington Som 44 G5
Low Ackworth W Yorks 198 D3
Low Alwinton Northumb 251 B10
Low Angerton Northumb 252 G3
Lowbands Glos 98 E5
Low Barlings Lincs 189 G9
Low Barugh S Yorks 197 F10
Low Bentham N Yorks 212 F2
Low Biggins Cumb 212 D2
Low Blantyre S Lanark 268 D3
Low Borrowbridge Cumb 222 E2
Low Bradfield S Yorks 186 C3
Low Bradley N Yorks 204 D6
Low Braithwaite Cumb 230 C4
Low Bridge Wilts 62 E3
Lowbridge House Cumb 221 E10
Low Brunton Northumb 241 C10
Low Burnham N Lincs 199 G9
Low Burton N Yorks 214 C4
Low Buston Northumb 252 B6
Lowca Cumb 228 G5
Low Catton E Yorks 207 C10
Low Clanyard Dumfries 236 F3
Low Common Norf 142 E2
Low Compton Gtr Man 196 F2
Low Coniscliffe Darl 224 C5
Low Cotehill Cumb 239 G11
Low Coylton S Ayrs 257 F10
Low Crosby Cumb 239 F10
Lowcross Hill Ches W 167 E7
Low Dalby N Yorks 217 B7
Lowdham Notts 171 F11
Low Dinsdale Darl 224 C6
Lowe Shrops 149 C10
Lowedges S Yorks 186 E4
Lowe Hill Staffs 169 D7
Low Eighton T&W 243 F7
Low Ellington N Yorks 214 C4
Lower Achachenna Argyll 284 E4
Lower Aisholt Som 43 F8
Lower Allscot Shrops 132 D4
Lower Altofts W Yorks 197 C11
Lower Ambie Corn 10 G5
Lower Ansty Dorset 30 G3
Lower Ardtun Argyll 288 G5
Lower Arncott Oxon 83 B10
Lower Ashtead Sur 51 B7
Lower Ashton Devon 14 E2
Lower Assendon Oxon 65 C8
Lower Badcall Highld 306 E6
Lower Ballam Lancs 202 G3
Lower Bartle Lancs 202 G5
Lower Basildon W Berks 64 D6
Lower Bassingthorpe Lincs 155 D9
Lower Bearwood Hereford 115 F7
Lower Bebington Mers 182 E4
Lower Beeding W Sus 36 B2
Lower Benefield N Nhants 137 F9
Lower Bentley Worcs 117 D9
Lower Beobridge Shrops 132 E5
Lower Berry Hill Glos 79 C9
Lower Binton Warks 118 G2
Lower Birchwood Derbys 170 E6
Lower Bitchet Kent 52 C5
Lower Blandford St Mary Dorset 30 F5
Lower Blunsdon Swindon 81 G10
Lower Bobbingworth Green Essex 87 D8
Lower Bockhampton Dorset 17 C10
Lower Boddington W Nhants 119 G9
Lower Bodham Norf 160 B2
Lower Bodinnar Corn 1 C4
Lower Bois Bucks 85 E7
Lower Bordean Hants 33 C11
Lower Boscaswell Corn 1 C3
Lower Bourne Sur 49 E10
Lower Bradley W Mid 133 D9
Lower Brailes Warks 100 D6
Lower Breakish Highld 295 C8
Lower Bredbury Gtr Man 184 C6
Lower Breinton Hereford 97 D9
Lower Broadheath Worcs 116 F6
Lower Brook Hants 32 B4
Lower Broughton Gtr Man 184 B4
Lower Brynamman Neath 76 C2
Lower Brynn Corn 5 C9
Lower Buckenhill Hereford 98 E2
Lower Buckland Hants 20 B2
Lower Bullingham Hereford 97 D10
Lower Bullington Hants 48 E3
Lower Bunbury Ches E 167 D9
Lower Burgate Hants 31 D11
Lower Burrow Som 28 C6
Lower Burton Hereford 115 F8
Lower Bush Medway 69 F7
Lower Cadsden Bucks 84 E4
Lower Caldecote C Beds 104 B3
Lower Cam Glos 80 E2
Lower Canada N Som 43 B11
Lower Carden Ches W 167 E7
Lower Catesby W Nhants 119 F10
Lower Cator Devon 13 F9
Lower Caversham Reading 65 E8
Lower Chapel Powys 95 D10
Lower Chedworth Glos 81 C9
Lower Cheriton Devon 27 G10
Lower Chicksgrove Wilts 46 G3
Lower Chute Wilts 47 C10
Lower Clapton London 67 B11
Lower Clent Worcs 117 B8
Lower Clicker Corn 6 C5
Lower Clopton Warks 118 F3
Lower Common Hants 48 E6
Hants 65 G9
Mon 78 B2
Mon 78 E4
Shrops 131 B9
Lower Copthurst Lancs 194 C5
Lower Cotburn Aberds 303 D7
Lower Cousley Wood E Sus 53 G7
Lower Cox Street Kent 69 G10
Lower Cragabus Argyll 254 C4
Lower Creedy Devon 26 G4
Lower Croan Corn 10 G6
Lower Crossings Derbys 185 E8
Lower Cumberworth W Yorks 197 F8
Lower Daggons Hants 31 E9
Lower Darwen Blackburn 195 B7
Lower Dean Bedford 121 D11
Devon 8 C4
Lower Dell Highld 292 B2
Lower Denby W Yorks 197 F8
Lower Denzell Corn 5 B7
Lower Deuchries Aberds 302 D6
Lower Diabaig Highld 299 C7
Lower Dicker E Sus 23 C9
Lower Dinchope Shrops 131 G9
Lower Dowdeswell Glos 81 B8
Lower Down Shrops 130 G6
Lower Drift Corn 1 D4
Lower Dunsforth N Yorks 215 G8
Lower Durston Som 28 B3
Lower Earley Wokingham 65 E9
Lower East Carleton Norf 142 C3
Lower Eastern Green W Mid 118 B5
Lower Edmonton London 86 G4
Lower Egleton Hereford 98 B2
Lower Elkstone Staffs 169 D9
Lower Ellastone Staffs 169 G10
Lower End Bucks 83 D11
Bucks 102 E4
C Beds 103 D8
C Beds 103 G9
Glos 81 E7
N Nhants 121 E7
Oxon 82 B4
W Nhants 120 E6
W Nhants 120 G5
Lower Everleigh Wilts 47 C7
Lower Eythorne Kent 55 D9
Lower Failand N Som 60 E4
Lower Faintree Shrops 132 F3
Lower Falkenham Suff 108 D5
Lower Farringdon Hants 49 F8
Lower Feltham London 66 E5
Lower Fittleworth W Sus 35 D8
Lowerford Lancs 204 F3
Lower Forge Shrops 132 F4
Lower Foxdale IoM 192 E3
Lower Frankton Shrops 149 C7
Lower Freystrop Pembs 73 C7
Lower Froyle Hants 49 E9
Lower Gabwell Devon 9 B8
Lower Gledfield Highld 309 K5
Lower Godney Som 44 E3
Lower Goldstone Kent 71 G9
Lower Gornal W Mid 133 E8
Lower Grange W Yorks 205 G8
Lower Gravenhurst C Beds 104 D2
Lower Green Essex 88 E2
Essex 105 E8
Essex 106 E4
Lower Green *continued*
Gtr Man 184 B2
Herts 104 E3
Kent 52 E5
Kent 52 E6
Norf 159 B9
Staffs 133 B8
Suff 124 D4
Sur 66 F6
Warks 119 D10
W Berks 63 G11
Lower Grove Common Hereford 97 F11
Lower Hacheston Suff 126 F6
Lower Halistra Highld 298 D2
Lower Halliford Sur 66 F5
Lower Halstock Leigh Dorset 29 F8
Lower Halstow Kent 69 F11
Lower Hamswell S Glos 61 E8
Lower Hamworthy BCP 18 C6
Lower Hardres Kent 55 C7
Lower Hardwick Hereford 115 F8
Lower Harpton Powys 114 E5
Lower Hartlip Kent 69 G10
Lower Hartshay Derbys 170 E5
Lower Hartwell Bucks 84 C3
Lower Hatton Staffs 150 B6
Lower Hawthwaite Cumb 210 B4
Lower Haysden Kent 52 D5
Lower Hayton Shrops 131 G10
Lower Hazel S Glos 60 B6
Lower Heath Ches E 168 C5
Lower Hempriggs Moray 301 C11
Lower Heppington Kent 54 C6
Lower Hergest Hereford 114 F5
Lower Herne Kent 71 F7
Lower Heyford Oxon 101 G9
Lower Heysham Lancs 211 G8
Lower Higham Kent 69 E8
Lower Highmoor Oxon 65 B8
Lower Holbrook Suff 108 E3
Lower Holditch Dorset 28 G4
Lower Holloway London 67 B10
Lower Holwell Dorset 31 E9
Lower Hook Worcs 98 C6
Lower Hookner Devon 13 E10
Lower Hopton Shrops 149 E7
W Yorks 197 D7
Lower Hordley Shrops 149 D7
Lower Horncroft W Sus 35 D8
Lower Horsebridge E Sus 23 C9
Lowerhouse Ches E 184 F6
Lancs 204 G2
Lower House Halton 183 D8
Lower Houses W Yorks 197 D7
Lower Howsell Worcs 98 B5
Lower Illey Worcs 133 G9
Lower Island Kent 70 F6
Lower Kersal Gtr Man 195 G10
Lower Kilburn Derbys 170 F5
Lower Kilcott Glos 61 B9
Lower Killeyan Argyll 254 C3
Lower Kingcombe Dorset 17 B7
Lower Kingswood Sur 51 C8
Lower Kinnerton Ches W 166 C4
Lower Kinsham Hereford 115 E7
Lower Knapp Som 28 B4
Lower Knightley Staffs 150 E6
Lower Knowle Bristol 60 E5
Lower Langford N Som 60 G3
Lower Largo Fife 287 G8
Lower Layham Suff 107 C10
Lower Ledwyche Shrops 115 C10
Lower Leigh Staffs 151 B10
Lower Lemington Glos 100 E4
Lower Lenie Highld 300 G5
Lower Lode Glos 99 E7
Lower Lovacott Devon 25 B8
Lower Loxhore Devon 40 F6
Lower Lydbrook Glos 79 B9
Lower Lye Hereford 115 D8
Lower Machen Newport 59 B8
Lower Maes-coed Hereford 96 E6
Lower Mains Clack 279 B9
Lower Mannington Dorset 31 F9
Lower Marsh Som 30 C2
Lower Marston Som 45 E9
Lower Meend Glos 79 E9
Lower Menadue Corn 5 D10
Lower Merridge Som 43 G8
Lower Mickletown W Yorks 198 B2
Lower Middleton Cheney W Nhants 101 C10
Lower Midway Derbys 152 E6
Lower Mill Corn 3 B10
Lower Milovaig Highld 296 F7
Lower Milton Som 44 D4
Lower Moor Wilts 81 G8
Worcs 99 B9
Lower Morton S Glos 79 G10
Lower Mountain Flint 166 D4
Lower Nazeing Essex 86 D5
Lower Netchwood Shrops 132 E2
Lower Netherton Devon 14 G3
Lower New Inn Torf 78 F4
Lower Ninnes Corn 1 C5
Lower Nobut Staffs 151 C10
Lower North Dean Bucks 84 F5
Lower Norton Warks 118 E4
Lower Nyland Dorset 30 C2
Lower Ochrwyth Caerph 59 B8
Lower Odcombe Som 29 D8
Lower Oddington Glos 100 F4
Lower Ollach Highld 295 B7
Lower Padworth W Berks 64 F6
Lower Penarth V Glam 59 F7
Lower Penn Staffs 133 D7
Lower Pennington Hants 20 C2
Lower Penwortham Lancs 194 B4
Lower Peover Ches W 184 G2
Lower Pexhill Ches E 184 G5
Lower Pilsley Derbys 170 C6
Lower Pitkerrie Highld 311 L2
Lower Place Gtr Man 196 E2
London 67 C8
Lower Pollicott Bucks 84 C2
Lower Porthkerry V Glam 58 F5
Lower Porthpean Corn 5 E10
Lower Quinton Warks 100 B3
Lower Rabber Hereford 114 G5
Lower Race Torf 78 E3
Lower Radley Oxon 83 F8
Lower Rainham Medway 69 F10
Lower Ratley Hants 32 C4
Lower Raydon Suff 107 D10
Lower Rea Glos 80 B4

Lower Ridge Devon 28 G2
Shrops 148 C6
Lower Roadwater Som 42 F4
Lower Rochford Worcs 116 D2
Lower Rose Corn 4 E5
Lower Row Dorset 31 G8
Lower Sapey Worcs 116 E3
Lower Seagry Wilts 62 C3
Lower Sheering Essex 87 C7
Lower Shelton C Beds 103 C9
Lower Shiplake Oxon 65 D9
Lower Shuckburgh
Warks 119 E9
Lower Skelty Swansea 56 C6
Lower Slackstead Hants 32 B5
Lower Slade Devon 40 D4
Lower Slaughter Glos 100 G3
Lower Solva Pembs 87 G11
Lower Soothill W Yorks 197 C9
Lower Soudley Glos 79 D11
Lower Southfield
Hereford 98 C3
Lower Stanton St Quintin
Wilts 62 C2
Lower Stoke Medway 69 D10
W Mid 119 B7
Lower Stondon C Beds 104 D3
Lower Stone Glos 79 G11
Lower Stonnall Staffs 133 C11
Lower Stow Bedon Norf 141 E9
Lower Stratton Som 28 D6
Swindon 63 B7
Lower Street E Sus 38 E2
Norf 160 B5
Norf 160 C3
Norf 160 F6
Suff 108 E3
Suff 124 G5
Lower Strensham Worcs 99 C8
Lower Stretton Warr 183 E10
Lower Studley Wilts 45 B11
Lower Sundon C Beds 103 F10
Lower Swainswick Bath 61 F9
Lower Swanwick Hants 33 F7
Lower Swell Glos 100 F3
Lower Sydenham
London 67 E11
Lower Tadmarton Oxon 101 D8
Lower Tale Devon 27 G9
Lower Tasburgh Norf 142 D3
Lower Tean Staffs 151 B10
Lower Thorpe
W Nhants 101 B10
Lower Threapwood
Wrex 166 G6
Lower Thurlton Norf 143 D8
Lower Thurnham Lancs 202 C5
Lower Thurvaston
Derbys 152 B4
Lower Todding Hereford 115 B8
Lower Tote Highld 298 C5
Lowertown Corn 2 D5
Corn 5 C11
Devon 12 E5
Lower Town Devon 27 E8
Hereford 98 C2
Pembs 91 D9
Worcs 117 F7
W Yorks 204 G6
Lower Trebullett Corn 12 F2
Lower Tregunnon Corn 11 E10
Lower Treworrick Corn 6 B4
Lower Tuffley Glos 80 C4
Lower Turmer Hants 31 F10
Lower Twitchen Devon 24 D5
Lower Twydall Medway 69 F10
Lower Tysoe Warks 100 B6
Lower Upham Hants 33 D8
Lower Upnor Medway 69 E9
Lower Vexford Som 42 F6
Lower Wainhill Oxon 84 E3
Lower Walton Warr 183 D10
Lower Wanborough
Swindon 63 C8
Lower Weacombe Som 42 E6
Lower Weald M Keynes 102 D5
Lower Wear Devon 14 D4
Lower Weare Som 44 C2
Lower Weedon
W Nhants 120 F2
Lower Welson Hereford 114 G5
Lower Westholme Som 44 E5
Lower Westhouse
N Yorks 212 E3
Lower Westmancote
Worcs 99 D8
Lower Weston Bath 61 F8
Lower Whatcombe
Dorset 30 G4
Lower Whatley Som 45 D8
Lower Whitley Ches W 183 F10
Lower Wick Glos 80 F2
Worcs 116 G6
Lower Wield Hants 48 E6
Lower Willingdon E Sus 23 E9
Lower Winchendon or
Nether Winchendon
Bucks 84 C2
Lower Withington
Ches E 168 B4
Lower Wolverton Worcs 117 G8
Lower Woodend Aberds 293 B8
Bucks 65 B10
Lower Woodford Wilts 46 G6
Lower Woodley Corn 5 B10
Lower Woodside Herts 86 D2
Lower Woolston Som 29 B11
Lower Woon Corn 5 C10
Lower Wraxall Dorset 29 G9
Som 44 F6
Wilts 61 G10
Lower Wych Ches W 167 G7
Lower Wyche Worcs 98 C5
Lower Wyke W Yorks 197 B7
Lower Yelland Devon 40 G3
Lower Zeals Wilts 45 G9
Lowes Barn Durham 233 C11
Lowesby Leics 136 B4
Lowestoft Suff 143 E10
Loweswater Cumb 229 G8
Low Etherley Durham 233 F9
Low Fell T&W 243 F7
Lowfield S Yorks 186 D5
Lowfield Heath W Sus 51 E9
Low Fold W Yorks 205 F10
Lowford Hants 33 E7
Low Fulney Lincs 156 E5
Low Garth N Yorks 226 D4
Low Gate Northumb 241 E10
N Yorks 214 F5
Low Geltbridge Cumb 240 F2
Lowgill Cumb 222 F2
Lancs 212 G3
Low Grantley N Yorks 214 E4
Low Green N Yorks 205 B10
Suff 125 E7
W Yorks 205 F10
Low Greenside T&W 242 E4
Low Habberley Worcs 116 B6
Low Ham Som 28 B6
Low Hauxley Northumb 253 C7
Low Hawsker N Yorks 227 D8
Low Hesket Cumb 230 B5
Low Hesleyhurst
Northumb 252 D3
Low Hill W Mid 133 C8
Low Hutton N Yorks 216 F5
Lowick Cumb 210 B5
N Nhants 137 G9
Northumb 264 B2
Lowick Bridge Cumb 210 B5
Lowick Green Cumb 210 B5
Low Knipe Cumb 230 G6
Low Laithe N Yorks 214 G3
Low Laithes S Yorks 197 G11
Lowlands Torf 78 F3
Low Leighton Derbys 185 D8
Low Lorton Cumb 229 F9
Low Marishes N Yorks 216 D6
Low Marnham Notts 172 B4
Low Mill N Yorks 226 F3
Low Moor Lancs 203 E10
W Yorks 197 B7
Lowmoor Row Cumb 231 F8
Low Moorsley T&W 234 B2
Low Moresby Cumb 228 G5
Lowna N Yorks 226 G3
Low Newton Cumb 211 C8
Low Newton-by-the-Sea
Northumb 264 E6
Lownie Moor Angus 287 C8
Lowood Borders 262 B2
Low Prudhoe Northumb 242 E4
Low Risby N Lincs 200 E2
Low Row Cumb 229 C9
Cumb 240 E3
N Yorks 223 F9
Low Salchrie Dumfries 236 C2
Low Smerby Argyll 255 E8
Low Snaygill N Yorks 204 D5
Lowsonford Warks 118 D3
Low Street Norf 141 B10
Thurrock 69 D7
Low Tharston Norf 142 D3
Lowther Cumb 230 G6
Lowthertown Dumfries 238 D6
Lowtherville IoW 21 F7
Low Thornley T&W 242 E5
Lowthorpe E Yorks 217 G11
Lowton Gtr Man 183 B10
Som 27 D11
Lowton Common
Gtr Man 183 B10
Lowton Heath Gtr Man 183 B10
Lowton St Mary's
Gtr Man 183 B10
Low Torry Fife 279 D10
Low Town Shrops 132 E4
Low Toynton Lincs 190 G3
Low Valley S Yorks 198 G2
Low Valleyfield Fife 279 D10
Low Walton Cumb 219 C9
Low Waters S Lanark 268 E4
Low Westwood Durham 242 F4
Low Whinnow Cumb 239 G8
Low Whita N Yorks 223 F10
Low Wood Cumb 210 C6
Low Worsall N Yorks 225 C7
Low Wray Cumb 221 E7
Loxbeare Devon 26 D6
Loxford London 68 B2
Loxhill Sur 50 F4
Loxhore Devon 40 F6
Loxhore Cott Devon 40 F6
Loxley S Yorks 186 D4
Warks 118 G5
Loxley Green Staffs 151 C11
Loxter Hereford 98 C4
Loxton N Som 43 B11
Loxwood W Sus 50 G4
Loyter's Green Essex 87 C8
Loyterton Kent 70 G3
Lozells W Mid 133 F11
Lubachlaggan Highld 300 B3
Lubachoinnich Highld 309 K4
Lubberland Shrops 116 B2
Lubcroy Highld 309 J3
Lubenham Leics 136 F4
Lubinvullin Highld 308 C5
Lucas End Herts 86 E4
Lucas Green Lancs 194 C5
Sur 50 B2
Luccombe Som 42 E2
Luccombe Village IoW 21 F7
Lucker Northumb 264 C5
Luckett Corn 12 G3
Lucking Street Essex 106 E6
Luckington Wilts 61 C10
Lucklawhill Fife 287 E8
Luckwell Bridge Som 42 F2
Lucton Hereford 115 E8
Ludag W Isles 297 K3
Ludborough Lincs 190 B3
Ludbrook Devon 8 E3
Ludchurch Pembs 73 C10
Luddenden W Yorks 196 B4
Luddenden Foot
W Yorks 196 C4
Ludderburn Cumb 221 G8
Luddesdown Kent 69 F7
Luddington N Lincs 199 D10
Warks 118 G3
Luddington in the Brook
N Nhants 138 G2
Lude House Perth 291 G10
Ludford Lincs 190 D2
Shrops 115 C10
Ludgershall Bucks 83 B11
Wilts 47 C9
Ludgvan Corn 2 C2
Ludham Norf 161 F7
Ludlow Shrops 115 C10
Ludney Lincs 190 B5
Som 28 E5
Ludstock Hereford 98 D3
Ludstone Shrops 132 E6
Ludwell Wilts 30 C6
Ludworth Durham 234 C3
Luffenhall Herts 104 F5
Luffincott Devon 12 C2
Lufton Som 29 D8
Lugar E Ayrs 258 E3
Lugate Borders 271 G8
Luggate Burn E Loth 282 G2
Lugg Green Hereford 115 E9
Luggiebank N Lanark 278 G5
Lugsdale Halton 183 D8
Lugton E Ayrs 267 E8
Lugwardine Hereford 97 C11
Luib Highld 295 C7
Luibeilt Highld 290 G4
Lulham Hereford 97 C8
Lullenden Sur 52 E2
Lullington Derbys 152 G5
Som 45 C9
Lulsgate Bottom N Som 60 F4
Lulsley Worcs 116 F4
Lulworth Camp Dorset 18 E2
Lumb Lancs 195 C10
Lancs 195 D9
Lumb *continued*
W Yorks 196 C4
W Yorks 197 E7
Lumb Foot W Yorks 204 F6
Lumburn Devon 12 G5
Lumbutts W Yorks 196 C3
Lumby N Yorks 206 G5
Lumley W Sus 22 B3
Lumley Thicks Durham 243 G8
Lumloch E Dunb 268 B2
Lumphanan Aberds 293 C7
Lumphinnans Fife 280 C3
Lumsdaine Borders 273 B7
Lumsden Aberds 302 G4
Lunan Angus 287 B10
Lunanhead Angus 287 B8
Luncarty Perth 286 E4
Lund E Yorks 208 D5
N Yorks 207 G9
Shetland 312 C7
Lundal W Isles 304 E3
Lundavra Highld 290 G2
Lunderton Aberds 303 E11
Lundie Angus 286 D6
Highld 290 B3
Lundin Links Fife 287 G8
Lundwood S Yorks 197 F11
Lundy Green Norf 142 E4
Lunga Argyll 275 C8
Lunna Shetland 312 G6
Lunning Shetland 312 G7
Lunnister Shetland 312 F5
Lunnon Swansea 56 D4
Lunsford Kent 53 B7
Lunsford's Cross E Sus 38 E2
Lunt Mers 193 G10
Luntley Hereford 115 F7
Lunts Heath Halton 183 D8
Lupin Staffs 152 F2
Luppitt Devon 27 F11
Lupridge Devon 8 E4
Lupset W Yorks 197 D10
Lupton Cumb 211 C11
Lurg Aberds 293 C8
Lurgashall W Sus 34 B6
Lurignich Argyll 289 D11
Lurley Devon 26 E6
Lusby Lincs 174 B4
Lushcott Shrops 131 D11
Luson Devon 8 F2
Luss Argyll 277 C7
Lussagiven Argyll 275 E7
Lusta Highld 298 D2
Lustleigh Devon 13 E11
Lustleigh Cleave Devon 13 E11
Luston Hereford 115 E9
Lusty Som 45 G7
Luthermuir Aberds 293 G8
Luthrie Fife 287 F7
Lutley W Mid 133 G8
Luton Devon 14 F4
Devon 27 G9
Luton 103 G11
Medway 69 F9
Lutsford Devon 24 D3
Lutterworth Leics 135 G10
Lutton Devon 7 D11
Devon 8 C3
Lincs 157 D8
N Nhants 138 F2
Lutton Gowts Lincs 157 E8
Lutworthy Devon 26 D3
Luxborough Som 42 F3
Luxley Glos 98 G3
Luxted London 68 G2
Luxton Devon 28 E2
Luxulyan Corn 5 D11
Luzley Gtr Man 196 G3
Luzley Brook Gtr Man 196 F2
Lyatts Som 29 E8
Lybster Highld 310 F6
Lydbury North Shrops 131 F7
Lydcott Devon 41 F7
Lydd Kent 39 C8
Lydden Kent 55 D9
Kent 71 F11
Lyddington Rutland 137 D7
Lydd on Sea Kent 39 C9
Lyde Orkney 314 E3
Shrops 130 C6
Lydeard St Lawrence
Som 42 G6
Lyde Cross Hereford 97 C10
Lyde Green Hants 49 B8
S Glos 61 D7
Lydford Devon 12 E6
Lydford Fair Place Som 44 G5
Lydford-on-Fosse Som 44 G5
Lydgate Derbys 186 F4
Gtr Man 196 G3
W Yorks 196 B2
Lydham Shrops 130 E6
Lydiard Green Wilts 62 B5
Lydiard Millicent Wilts 62 B5
Lydiard Plain Wilts 62 B5
Lydiard Tregoze Swindon 62 C6
Lydiate Mers 193 G11
Lydiate Ash Worcs 117 B9
Lydlinch Dorset 30 E2
Lydmarsh Som 28 F5
Lydney Glos 79 E10
Lydstep Pembs 73 F9
Lye W Mid 133 G8
Lye Cross N Som 60 G3
Lye Green Bucks 85 E7
E Sus 52 G4
Warks 118 D3
Wilts 45 B10
Lye Head Worcs 116 C5
Lye Hole N Som 60 G4
Lyewood Common E Sus 52 F4
Lyford Oxon 82 G5
Lymbridge Green Kent 54 E6
Lyme Green Ches E 184 G6
Lyme Regis Dorset 16 C2
Lymiecleuch Borders 249 C9
Lyminge Kent 55 E7
Lymington Hants 20 B2
Lyminster W Sus 35 G8
Lymm Warr 183 D11
Lymore Hants 19 C11
Lympne Kent 54 F6
Lympsham Som 43 C10
Lympstone Devon 14 E5
Lynbridge Devon 41 D8
Lynch Hants 48 D4
Som 42 D2
Lynchat Highld 291 C9
Lynchgate Shrops 131 F7
Lynch Hill Hants 48 D3
Slough 66 C2
Lyndale Ho Highld 298 D3
Lyndhurst Hants 32 F4
Lyndon Rutland 137 C8
Lyndon Green W Mid 134 F2
Lyne Borders 270 G4
Sur 66 F4
Lyneal Shrops 149 C8
Lyneal Mill Shrops 149 C9
Lyneal Wood Shrops 149 C9
Lyne Down Hereford 98 E2
Lyneham Oxon 100 G5
Wilts 62 D4
Lynemore Highld 301 G10
Lynemouth Northumb 253 E7
Lyne of Gorthleck
Highld 300 G5
Lyne of Skene Aberds 293 B9
Lyness Orkney 314 G3
Lyne Station Borders 260 B6
Lynford Norf 140 E6
Lyng Norf 159 F11
Som 28 B4
Lyngate Norf 160 C5
Lyngford Som 28 B2
Lynmore Highld 301 F10
Lynmouth Devon 41 D8
Lynn Staffs 133 C11
Telford 150 F5
Lynnwood Borders 261 G11
Lynsore Bottom Kent 55 D7
Lynsted Kent 70 G2
Lynstone Corn 24 F2
Lynton Devon 41 D8
Lynwilg Highld 291 B10
Lynworth Glos 99 G9
Lyons T&W 234 B3
Lyon's Gate Dorset 29 F11
Lyon's Green Norf 159 G8
Lyonshall Hereford 114 F6
Lyons Hall Essex 88 B2
Lypiatt Glos 80 D6
Lyrabus Argyll 274 G3
Lytchett Matravers
Dorset 18 B4
Lytchett Minster Dorset 18 C5
Lyth Highld 310 C6
Lytham Lancs 193 B11
Lytham St Anne's
Lancs 193 B10
Lythbank Shrops 131 B9
Lythe N Yorks 226 C6
Lythes Orkney 314 H4
Lythmore Highld 310 C4

M

Maam Argyll 284 F5
Mabe Burnthouse Corn 3 C7
Mabie Dumfries 237 B11
Mabledon Kent 52 E5
Mablethorpe Lincs 191 D8
Macclesfield Ches E 184 G6
Macclesfield Forest
Ches E 185 G7
Macduff Aberds 303 C7
Mace Green Suff 108 C2
Machan S Lanark 268 E5
Macharioch Argyll 255 G8
Machen Caerph 59 B8
Machrie N Ayrs 255 D9
Machrie Hotel Argyll 254 C4
Machrihanish Argyll 255 E7
Machroes Gwyn 144 D6
Machynlleth Powys 128 C4
Machynys Carms 56 B4
Mackerel's Common
W Sus 35 B8
Mackerye End Herts 85 B11
Mackham Devon 27 F11
Mackney Oxon 64 B5
Mackside Borders 262 G4
Mackworth Derbys 152 B6
Macmerry E Loth 281 G8
Madderty Perth 286 E3
Maddington Wilts 46 E5
Maddiston Falk 279 F8
Maddox Moor Pembs 73 C7
Madehurst W Sus 35 E7
Madeley Staffs 168 G3
Telford 132 C3
Madeley Heath Staffs 168 F3
Worcs 117 B9
Madeley Park Staffs 168 G3
Madeleywood Telford 132 C3
Maders Corn 12 G2
Madford Devon 27 E10
Madingley Cambs 123 E7
Madjeston Dorset 30 B4
Madley Hereford 97 D8
Madresfield Worcs 98 B6
Madron Corn 1 C5
Maenaddwyn Anglesey 179 E7
Maenclochog Pembs 91 F11
Maendy V Glam 58 D4
Maenporth Corn 3 D7
Maentwrog Gwyn 163 G11
Maen-y-groes Ceredig 111 F7
Maer Corn 24 F2
Staffs 150 B5
Maerdy Carms 94 G2
Conwy 165 G8
Rhondda 77 F7
Maes-bangor Ceredig 128 G3
Maesbrook Shrops 148 E5
Maesbury Shrops 148 D6
Maesbury Marsh Shrops 148 D6
Maesgeirchen Gwyn 179 G9
Maes-glas Newport 59 B9
Maes Glas = Greenfield
Flint 181 F11
Maesgwyn-Isaf Powys 148 G3
Maeshafn Denb 166 C2
Maesllyn Ceredig 93 C7
Maes Llyn Ceredig 93 C7
Maesmynis Powys 95 B10
Maes Pennant Flint 181 F11
Maes-Treylow Powys 114 D5
Maesteg Bridgend 57 C10
Maesybont Carms 75 B9
Maesycoed Rhondda 58 B5
Maesycrugiau Carms 93 C9
Maesycwmmer Caerph 77 G11
Maes-y-dre Flint 166 C2
Maesygwartha Mon 78 C2
Maesymeillion Ceredig 93 B8
Maesypandy Powys 129 D9
Maesyrhandir Powys 129 E11
Magdalen Laver Essex 87 D8
Maggieknockater Moray 302 E3
Maggots End Essex 105 F9
Magham Down E Sus 23 C10
Maghull Mers 193 G11
Magor Mon 60 B2
Magpie Green Suff 125 B11
Mahaar Dumfries 236 B2
Maida Vale London 67 C9
Maidenbower W Sus 51 F9
Maiden Bradley Wilts 45 F10
Maidencombe Torbay 9 B8
Maidenhall Suff 108 C3
Maidenhead Windsor 65 C11
Maiden Head N Som 60 F5
Maidenhead Court
Windsor 66 C2
Maiden Law Durham 233 B9
Maiden Newton Dorset 17 B7
Maidenpark Falk 279 E9
Maidens S Ayrs 244 B6
Maidensgrave Suff 108 B5
Maiden's Green Brack 65 E11
Maidensgrove Oxon 65 B8
Maiden's Hall Northumb 252 D6
Maidenwell Corn 11 G8
Lincs 190 F4
Maiden Wells Pembs 73 F7
Maidford W Nhants 120 G2
Maids Moreton Bucks 102 D4
Maidstone Kent 53 B9
Maidwell W Nhants 120 B4
Mail Shetland 313 L6
Mailand Shetland 312 C8
Mailingsland Borders 270 G4
Main Powys 148 F3
Maindee Newport 59 B10
Maindy Cardiff 59 D7
Mainholm S Ayrs 257 E9
Mains Cumb 229 G7
Mainsforth Durham 234 E2
Mains of Airies Dumfries 236 C1
Mains of Allardice
Aberds 293 F10
Mains of Annochie
Aberds 303 E9
Mains of Ardestie
Angus 287 D9
Mains of Arnage Aberds 303 F9
Mains of Auchoynanie
Moray 302 E4
Mains of Baldoon
Dumfries 236 D6
Mains of Balhall Angus 293 G7
Mains of Ballindarg
Angus 287 B8
Mains of Balnakettle
Aberds 293 F8
Mains of Birness Aberds 303 F9
Mains of Blackhall
Aberds 303 G7
Mains of Burgie Moray 301 D10
Mains of Cairnbrogie
Aberds 303 G8
Mains of Cairnty Moray 302 D3
Mains of Clunas Highld 301 E8
Mains of Crichie Aberds 303 E9
Mains of Daltulich
Highld 301 E7
Mains of Dalvey Highld 301 F11
Mains of Dellavaird
Aberds 293 E9
Mains of Drum Aberds 293 D10
Mains of Edingight
Moray 302 D5
Mains of Fedderate
Aberds 303 E8
Mains of Flichity Highld 300 G6
Mains of Hatton Aberds 303 D9
Aberds 303 E7
Mains of Inkhorn Aberds 303 F9
Mains of Innerpeffray
Perth 286 F3
Mains of Kirktonhill
Aberds 293 G8
Mains of Laithers
Aberds 302 E6
Mains of Mayen Moray 302 E5
Mains of Melgund
Angus 287 B9
Mains of Taymouth
Perth 285 C11
Mains of Thornton
Aberds 293 F8
Mains of Towie Aberds 303 E7
Mains of Ulbster Highld 310 E7
Mains of Watten Highld 310 D6
Mainsriddle Dumfries 237 D11
Mainstone Shrops 130 F5
Maisemore Glos 98 G6
Maitland Park London 67 C9
Major's Green W Mid 118 B2
Makeney Derbys 170 G5
Malacleit W Isles 296 D3
Malborough Devon 9 G9
Malcoff Derbys 185 E9
Malden Rushett London 67 G7
Maldon Essex 88 D4
Malehurst Shrops 131 B7
Malham N Yorks 213 G8
Maligar Highld 298 C4
Malinbridge S Yorks 186 D4
Malinslee Telford 132 B3
Malkin's Bank Ches E 168 D3
Mallaig Highld 295 F8
Mallaig Bheag Highld 295 F8
Malleny Mills Edin 270 B3
Malling Stirling 285 G9
Mallows Green Essex 105 F9
Malltraeth Anglesey 162 B6
Mallwyd Gwyn 147 G7
Malmesbury Wilts 62 B2
Malmsmead Devon 41 D9
Malpas Ches W 167 F7
Corn 4 G6
Newport 78 G4
W Berks 64 E6
Malswick Glos 98 F4
Maltby Lincs 190 E4
Stockton 225 C9
S Yorks 187 C8
Maltby le Marsh Lincs 191 E7
Malting End Suff 124 G4
Malting Green Essex 107 G9
Maltings Angus 293 G9
Maltman's Hill Kent 54 E2
Malton N Yorks 216 E5
Malvern Common Worcs 98 C5
Malvern Link Worcs 98 B5
Malvern Wells Worcs 98 C5
Mambeg Argyll 276 D4
Mamble Worcs 116 C3
Mamhilad Mon 78 E4
Manaccan Corn 3 E7
Manadon Plym 7 D9
Manafon Powys 130 C2
Manais W Isles 296 C7
Manar Ho Aberds 303 G7
Manaton Devon 13 E11
Manby Lincs 190 D5
Mancetter Warks 134 D6
Manchester Gtr Man 184 B4
Manchester Airport
Gtr Man 184 D4
Mancot Flint 166 B4
Mancot Royal Flint 166 B4
Mandally Highld 290 C4
Manea Cambs 139 F9
Maney W Mid 134 D2
Manfield N Yorks 224 C4
Mangaster Shetland 312 F5
Mangotsfield S Glos 61 D7
Mangrove Green Herts 104 G2
Mangurstadh W Isles 304 E2
Manhay Corn 2 C5
Manian-fawr Pembs 92 B3
Mankinholes W Yorks 196 C3
Manley Ches W 183 G8
Devon 27 E7
Manley Common
Ches W 183 G8
Manmoel Caerph 77 E11
Man-moel Caerph 77 E11
Mannal Argyll 288 E1
Mannamead Plym 7 D9
Mannerston W Loth 279 F10
Manningford Abbots
Wilts 46 B6
Manningford Bohune
Wilts 46 B6
Manningford Bruce Wilts 46 B6
Manningham W Yorks 205 G9
Mannings Heath W Sus 36 B2
Mannington Dorset 31 F9
Manningtree Essex 107 E11
Mannofield Aberdeen 293 C11
Manor London 68 B2
Manorbier Pembs 73 F9
Manorbier Newton
Pembs 73 F8
Manor Bourne Devon 7 F9
Manordeilo Carms 94 F3
Manor Estate S Yorks 186 D5
Manorhill Borders 262 C5
Manor Hill Corner Lincs 157 F8
Manor House W Mid 135 G7
Manorowen Pembs 91 D8
Manor Park Bucks 84 C4
Ches W 167 B11
E Sus 37 C7
London 68 B2
Notts 153 C11
Slough 66 C3
S Yorks 186 D5
W Yorks 205 D9
Manor Parsley Corn 4 F4
Manor Royal W Sus 51 F9
Man's Cross Essex 106 D5
Mansegate Dumfries 247 G9
Manselfield Swansea 56 D5
Mansel Lacy Hereford 97 B8
Mansell Gamage
Hereford 97 C7
Manselton Swansea 57 B7
Mansergh Cumb 212 C2
Mansewood Glasgow 267 C11
Mansfield E Ayrs 258 G4
Notts 171 C8
Mansfield Woodhouse
Notts 171 C8
Manson Green Norf 141 C10
Mansriggs Cumb 210 C5
Manston Dorset 30 D4
Kent 71 F10
W Yorks 206 F3
Manswood Dorset 31 F7
Manthorpe Lincs 155 B8
Lincs 155 F11
Mantles Green Bucks 85 F7
Manton N Lincs 200 G2
Notts 187 F9
Rutland 137 C7
Wilts 63 F7
Manton Warren N Lincs 200 F2
Manuden Essex 105 F9
Manwood Green Essex 87 C8
Manywells Height
W Yorks 205 F7
Maperton Som 29 B11
Maplebeck Notts 172 C2
Maple Cross Herts 85 G8
Mapledurham Oxon 65 D7
Mapledurwell Hants 49 C7
Maple End Essex 105 D11
Maplehurst W Sus 35 C11
Maplescombe Kent 68 G5
Mapleton Derbys 169 F11
Mapperley Derbys 170 G6
Nottingham 171 G9
Mapperley Park
Nottingham 171 G9
Mapperton Dorset 16 B6
Dorset 18 B4
Mappleborough Green
Warks 117 D11
Mappleton E Yorks 209 E10
Mapplewell S Yorks 197 F10
Mappowder Dorset 30 F2
Maraig W Isles 305 H3
Marazanvose Corn 4 E6
Marazion Corn 2 C2
Marbhig W Isles 305 G6
Marbrack Dumfries 246 E3
Marbury Ches E 167 F9
March Cambs 139 D8
S Lanark 259 G11
Marcham Oxon 83 F7
Marchamley Shrops 149 D11
Marchamley Wood
Shrops 149 C11
Marchington Staffs 152 C2
Marchington Woodlands
Staffs 152 D2
Marchroes Gwyn 144 D6
Marchwiel Wrex 166 F5
Marchwood Hants 32 E5
Marcross V Glam 58 F2
Marden Hereford 97 B10
Kent 53 E8
T&W 243 C9
Wilts 46 B5
Marden Ash Essex 87 E9
Marden Beech Kent 53 E8
Marden's Hill E Sus 52 G3
Marden Thorn Kent 53 E9
Mardleybury Herts 86 B3
Mardu Shrops 130 G5
Mardy Mon 78 B4
Shrops 148 C5
Marefield Leics 136 B4
Mareham le Fen Lincs 174 C3
Mareham on the Hill
Lincs 174 B3
Marehay Derbys 170 F5
Marehill W Sus 35 D9
Maresfield E Sus 37 C7
Maresfield Park E Sus 37 C7
Marfleet Hull 200 B6
Marford Wrex 166 D5
Margam Neath 57 D9
Margaret Marsh Dorset 30 D4
Margaret Roding Essex 87 C9
Margaretting Essex 87 E11
Margaretting Tye Essex 87 E11
Margate Kent 71 E11
Margery Sur 51 C9
Margnaheglish N Ayrs 256 C2
Margreig Dumfries 237 B10
Margrove Park Redcar 226 B3
Marham Norf 158 G4
Marhamchurch Corn 24 G2
Marholm Pboro 138 C2
Marian Flint 181 F9
Marian Cwm Denb 181 F9
Mariandyrys Anglesey 179 E10
Marianglas Anglesey 179 E8
Mariansleigh Devon 26 C2
Marian y de = South Beach
Gwyn 145 C7
Marian y mor = West End
Gwyn 145 C7
Marine Town Kent 70 E2
Marionburgh Aberds 293 C9
Marishader Highld 298 C4
Marjoriebanks Dumfries 248 G3
Mark Dumfries 236 D3
Dumfries 237 C7
S Ayrs 236 B2
Som 43 D11
Markbeech Kent 52 E3
Markby Lincs 191 F7
Mark Causeway Som 43 D11
Mark Cross E Sus 23 C7
E Sus 52 G5
Markeaton Derbys 152 B6
Market Bosworth Leics 135 C8
Market Deeping Lincs 138 B2
Market Drayton Shrops 150 C3
Market Harborough
Leics 136 F4
Markethill Perth 286 D6
Market Lavington Wilts 46 C4
Market Overton Rutland 155 F7
Market Rasen Lincs 189 D10
Market Stainton Lincs 190 F2
Market Warsop Notts 171 B9
Market Weighton
E Yorks 208 E3
Market Weston Suff 125 B9
Markfield Leics 153 G9
Mark Hall North Essex 87 C7
Mark Hall South Essex 87 C7
Markham Caerph 77 E11
Markham Moor Notts 188 G2
Markinch Fife 286 G6
Markington N Yorks 214 F5
Markland Hill Gtr Man 195 F7
Markle E Loth 281 F11
Marksbury Bath 61 G7
Mark's Corner IoW 20 C5
Marks Gate London 87 G7
Marks Tey Essex 107 G8
Markyate Herts 85 B9
Marland Gtr Man 195 E11
Marlas Hereford 97 F8
Marl Bank Worcs 98 C5
Marlborough Wilts 63 F7
Marlbrook Hereford 115 G10
Worcs 117 C9
Marlcliff Warks 117 G11
Marldon Devon 9 C7
Marle Green E Sus 23 B9
Marle Hill Glos 99 G9
Marlesford Suff 126 F6
Marley Kent 55 C7
Kent 55 C10
Marley Green Ches E 167 F9
Marley Heights W Sus 49 G11
Marley Hill T&W 242 F6
Marley Pots T&W 243 F9
Marlingford Norf 142 B2
Mar Lodge Aberds 292 D2
Marloes Pembs 72 D3
Marlow Bucks 65 B10
Hereford 115 B8
Marlow Bottom Bucks 65 B11
Marlow Common Bucks 65 B10
Marlpit Hill Kent 52 D2
Marlpits E Sus 38 E2
Marlpool Derbys 170 F6
Marnhull Dorset 30 D3
Marnoch Aberds 302 D5
Marnock N Lanark 268 B4
Marple Gtr Man 185 D7
Marple Bridge Gtr Man 185 D7
Marpleridge Gtr Man 185 D7
Marr S Yorks 198 F4
Marrel Highld 311 H4
Marr Green Wilts 63 G8
Marrick N Yorks 223 F11
Marrister Shetland 313 G7
Marros Carms 74 D2
Marsden T&W 243 E9
W Yorks 196 E4
Marsden Height Lancs 204 F3
Marsett N Yorks 213 B8
Marsh Bucks 84 D4
Devon 28 E3
W Yorks 196 D6
W Yorks 204 F6
Marshall Meadows
Northumb 273 D9
Marshall's Cross Mers 183 C8
Marshall's Elm Som 44 G3
Marshall's Heath Herts 85 B11
Marshalsea Dorset 28 G5
Marshalswick Herts 85 D11
Marsham Norf 160 E3
Marshaw Lancs 203 C7
Marsh Baldon Oxon 83 F9
Marsh Benham W Berks 64 F2
Marshborough Kent 55 B10
Marshbrook Shrops 131 F8
Marshchapel Lincs 190 B5
Marsh Common S Glos 60 C5
Marsh End Worcs 98 D6
Marshfield Newport 59 C9
S Glos 61 E9
Marshfield Bank
Ches E 167 D11
Marshgate Corn 11 C9
Marsh Gate W Berks 63 F10
Marsh Gibbon Bucks 102 G2
Marsh Green Ches W 183 F8
Devon 14 C6
Gtr Man 194 F5
Kent 52 E2
Staffs 168 D5
Telford 150 G2
Marsh Houses Lancs 202 C5
Marshland St James
Norf 139 B10
Marsh Lane Derbys 186 F6
Glos 79 D9
Marsh Mills Som 43 F7
Marshmoor Herts 86 D2
Marshside Kent 71 F8
Mers 193 D11
Marsh Side Norf 176 E3
Marsh Street Som 42 E3
Marshwood Dorset 16 B3
Marske N Yorks 224 E2
Marske-by-the-Sea
Redcar 235 G8
Marston Ches W 183 F11
Hereford 115 F7
Lincs 172 G5
Oxon 83 D8
Staffs 150 G6
Staffs 151 D8
Warks 119 B8
Warks 134 E4
Wilts 46 B3
Marston Bigot Som 45 E9
Marston Doles Warks 119 F9
Marston Gate Som 45 D9
Marston Green W Mid 134 F3
Marston Hill Glos 81 F10
Marston Jabbett Warks 135 F7
Marston Magna Som 29 C9
Marston Meysey Wilts 81 F10
Marston Montgomery
Derbys 152 B2
Marston Moretaine
C Beds 103 C9
Marston on Dove
Derbys 152 D4
Marston St Lawrence
W Nhants 101 C10
Marston Stannett
Hereford 115 F11
Marston Trussell
W Nhants 136 F3
Marstow Hereford 79 B9
Marsworth Bucks 84 C6
Marten Wilts 47 B9
Marthall Ches E 184 F4
Martham Norf 161 F9
Marthwaite Cumb 222 G2
Martin Hants 31 D9
Kent 55 D10
Lincs 173 D10
Lincs 174 B2
Martindale Cumb 221 B8
Martin Dales Lincs 173 C11
Martin Drove End Hants 31 C9
Martinhoe Devon 41 D7
Martinhoe Cross Devon 41 D7
Martin Hussingtree
Worcs 117 E7
Martin Mill Kent 55 D10
Martin Moor Lincs 174 C2
Martinscroft Warr 183 D11
Martin's Moss Ches E 168 C4
Martinstown Dorset 17 D8
Martinstown or
Winterbourne St Martin
Dorset 17 D8
Martlesham Suff 108 B4
Martlesham Heath Suff 108 B4
Martletwy Pembs 73 C8
Martley Worcs 116 E5
Martock Som 29 D7
Marton Ches E 168 B5
Ches W 167 B10
Cumb 210 D4
E Yorks 209 F9
E Yorks 218 E4
Lincs 188 E4
Mbro 225 B10
N Yorks 215 G8
N Yorks 216 C4
Shrops 130 C5
Shrops 149 E8
Warks 119 D8
Marton Green Ches W 167 B10
Marton Grove Mbro 225 B9
Marton-in-the-Forest
N Yorks 215 F11
Marton-le-Moor
N Yorks 215 E7
Marton Moor Warks 119 D8
Marton Moss Side
Blackpool 202 G2
Martyr's Green Sur 50 B5
Martyr Worthy Hants 48 G4
Marwick Orkney 314 D2
Marwood Devon 40 F4
Marybank Highld 300 D4
Highld 301 B7
Maryburgh Highld 300 D5
Maryfield Aberds 293 D7
Corn 7 D8
Maryhill Glasgow 267 B11
Marykirk Aberds 293 G8
Maryland Mon 79 D8
Marylebone Gtr Man 194 F5
Marypark Moray 301 F11
Maryport Cumb 228 D6
Dumfries 236 F3
Mary Tavy Devon 12 F6
Maryton Angus 287 B7
Angus 287 B10
Marywell Aberds 293 D7
Aberds 293 D11
Angus 287 C10
Masbrough S Yorks 186 C6
Mascle Bridge Pembs 73 D7
Masham N Yorks 214 C4
Mashbury Essex 87 C11
Masongill N Yorks 212 D3
Masonhill S Ayrs 257 E9
Mastin Moor Derbys 187 F7
Mastrick Aberdeen 293 C10
Matchborough Worcs 117 D11
Matching Essex 87 C8
Matching Green Essex 87 C8
Matching Tye Essex 87 C8
Matfen Northumb 242 C2
Matfield Kent 53 E7
Mathern Mon 79 G8
Mathon Hereford 98 B4
Mathry Pembs 91 E7
Matlaske Norf 160 C3
Matley Gtr Man 185 B7
Matlock Derbys 170 C3
Matlock Bank Derbys 170 C3
Matlock Bath Derbys 170 D3
Matlock Bridge Derbys 170 D3
Matlock Cliff Derbys 170 D4
Matlock Dale Derbys 170 D3
Matshead Lancs 202 E6
Matson Glos 80 B4
Matterdale End Cumb 230 G3
Mattersey Notts 187 D11
Mattersey Thorpe
Notts 187 D11
Matthewsgreen
Wokingham 65 F10
Mattingley Hants 49 B8
Mattishall Norf 159 G11
Mattishall Burgh Norf 159 G11
Mauchline E Ayrs 257 D11
Maud Aberds 303 E9
Maudlin Corn 5 C11
Dorset 28 F5
W Sus 22 B5
Maudlin Cross Dorset 28 F5
Maugersbury Glos 100 F4
Maughold IoM 192 C5
Mauld Highld 300 F4
Maulden C Beds 103 D11
Maulds Meaburn Cumb 222 B2
Maunby N Yorks 215 B7
Maund Bryan Hereford 115 G11
Maundown Som 27 B9
Mauricewood Midloth 270 C4
Mautby Norf 161 G9
Mavesyn Ridware
Staffs 151 F11
Mavis Enderby Lincs 174 B5
Maviston Highld 301 D9
Mawbray Cumb 229 B7
Mawdesley Lancs 194 E3
Mawdlam Bridgend 57 E10
Mawgan Corn 2 D6
Mawgan Porth Corn 5 B7
Maw Green Ches E 168 D2
Mawla Corn 4 F4
Mawnan Corn 3 D7
Mawnan Smith Corn 3 D7
Mawsley N Nhants 120 B6
Mawson Green S Yorks 198 D6
Mawthorpe Lincs 191 G7
Maxey Pboro 138 B2
Maxstoke Warks 134 F4
Maxted Street Kent 54 E6

Maxton Borders 262 C4
Kent 55 E10
Maxwellheugh Borders 262 C6
Maxwelltown Dumfries 237 B11
Maxworthy Corn 11 C11
Mayals Swansea 56 C6
May Bank Staffs 168 F5
Maybole S Ayrs 257 G8
Maybury Sur 50 B4
Maybush Soton 32 E5
Mayer's Green W Mid 133 E10
Mayes Green Sur 50 F6
Mayeston Pembs 73 E8
Mayfair London 67 C9
Mayfield E Sus 37 B9
Midloth 271 C7
Northumb 243 B7
Staffs 169 F11
W Loth 269 B8
Mayford Sur 50 B3
Mayhill Swansea 56 C6
May Hill Mon 79 C8
May Hill Village Glos 98 G4
Mayland Essex 88 E6
Maylandsea Essex 88 E6
Maynard's Green E Sus 23 B9
Mayne Ho Moray 302 C2
Mayon Corn 1 D3
Maypole Kent 68 E4
Kent 71 G7
London 68 G3
Mon 79 B7
Scilly 1 G4
Maypole Green Essex 107 G9
Norf 143 D8
Suff 125 F8
Suff 126 D5
Mays Green Oxon 65 C8
May's Green N Som 59 G11
Sur 50 B5
Mayshill S Glos 61 C7
Maythorn S Yorks 197 F7
Maythorne Notts 171 D11
Maywick Shetland 313 L5
Mead Devon 13 G11
Devon 24 D2
Mead End Hants 19 B11
Hants 33 E11
Wilts 31 C8
Meadgate Bath 45 B7
Meadle Bucks 84 D4
Meadowbank Ches W 167 B11
Edin 280 G5
Meadowend Essex 106 C4
Meadowfield Durham 233 D10
Meadowfoot N Ayrs 266 F4
Meadow Green Hereford 116 F4
Meadow Hall S Yorks 186 C5
Meadow Head S Yorks 186 E4
Meadowley Shrops 132 E3
Meadowmill E Loth 281 G8
Meadows Nottingham 153 B11
Meadowtown Shrops 130 C6
Meads E Sus 23 F10
Meadside Oxon 83 G9
Mead Vale Sur 51 D9
Meadwell Devon 12 E4
Meaford Staffs 151 B7
Meagill N Yorks 205 B9
Mealabost W Isles 304 E6
Mealabost Bhuirgh
W Isles 304 C6
Mealasta W Isles 304 F1
Meal Bank Cumb 221 F10
Meal Hill W Yorks 197 F7
Mealrigg Cumb 229 B8
Mealsgate Cumb 229 C10
Meanwood W Yorks 205 F11
Mearbeck N Yorks 212 G6
Meare Som 44 E3
Meare Green Som 28 B4
Som 28 C3
Mearns Bath 45 B7
E Renf 267 D10
Mears Ashby N Nhants 120 D6
Measborough Dike
S Yorks 197 F11
Measham Leics 152 G6
Meath Green Sur 51 E9
Meathop Cumb 211 C8
Meaux E Yorks 209 F7
Meaver Corn 2 F5
Meavy Devon 7 B10
Medbourne Leics 136 E5
M Keynes 102 D6
Medburn Northumb 242 C4
Meddon Devon 24 D3
Meden Vale Notts 171 B9
Medhurst Row Kent 52 D3
Medlam Lincs 174 D4
Medlar Lancs 202 F4
Medlicott Shrops 131 E8
Medlyn Corn 2 C6
Medmenham Bucks 65 C10
Medomsley Durham 242 G4
Medstead Hants 49 F7
Meerbrook Staffs 169 C7
Meer Common Hereford 115 G7
Meer End W Mid 118 C4
Meerhay Dorset 29 G7
Meers Bridge Lincs 191 D7
Meersbrook S Yorks 186 E5
Meesden Herts 105 E8
Meeson Telford 150 E3
Meeson Heath Telford 150 E3
Meeth Devon 25 F8
Meethe Devon 25 C11
Meeting Green Suff 124 F4
Meeting House Hill
Norf 160 D6
Meggernie Castle Perth 285 C9
Meggethead Borders 260 E5
Meidrim Carms 92 G5
Meifod Denb 165 D8
Powys 148 G3
Meigle N Ayrs 266 B3
Perth 286 C6
Meikle Earnock
S Lanark 268 E4
Meikle Ferry Highld 309 L7
Meikle Forter Angus 292 G3
Meikle Gluich Highld 309 L6
Meikle Obney Perth 286 D4
Meikleour Perth 286 D5
Meikle Pinkerton
E Loth 282 F4
Meikle Strath Aberds 293 F8
Meikle Tarty Aberds 303 G9
Meikle Wartle Aberds 303 F7
Meinciau Carms 75 C7
Meir Stoke 168 G6
Meir Heath Staffs 168 G6
Melbourn Cambs 105 C7
Melbourne Derbys 153 D7
E Yorks 207 E11
S Lanark 269 G11
Melbury Abbas Dorset 30 D5
Melbury Bubb Dorset 29 F9
Melbury Osmond Dorset 29 F9
Melbury Sampford
Dorset 29 F9
Melby Shetland 313 H3
Melchbourne Bedford 121 D10
Melcombe Som 43 G9
Melcombe Bingham
Dorset 30 G3
Melcombe Regis Dorset 17 E9
Meldon Devon 13 C7
Northumb 252 G4
Meldreth Cambs 105 B7
Meldrum Ho Aberds 303 G8
Melfort Argyll 275 B9
Melgarve Highld 290 D6
Meliden = *Gallt Melyd*
Denb 181 E9
Melinbyrhedyn Powys 128 D6
Melin Caiach Caerph 77 F10
Melincourt Neath 76 E4
Melincryddan Neath 57 B8
Melinsey Corn 3 B10
Melin-y-coed Conwy 164 C4
Melin-y-ddôl Powys 129 B11
Melin-y-grug Powys 129 B11
Melin-y-Wig Denb 165 F8
Melkington Northumb 273 G7
Melkinthorpe Cumb 231 F7
Melkridge Northumb 240 E6
Melksham Wilts 62 G2
Melksham Forest Wilts 62 G2
Mellangaun Highld 307 L3
Mellangoose Corn 2 D5
Melldalloch Argyll 275 F10
Mell Green W Berks 64 D3
Mellguards Cumb 230 B4
Melling Lancs 211 E11
Mers 193 G11
Mellingey Corn 10 G4
Melling Mount Mers 194 G2
Mellis Suff 126 C2
Mellis Green Suff 125 C11
Mellon Charles Highld 307 K3
Mellon Udrigle Highld 307 K3
Mellor Gtr Man 185 D7
Lancs 203 G9
Mellor Brook Lancs 203 G8
Mells Som 45 D8
Suff 127 B8
Mells Green Som 45 D8
Melmerby Cumb 231 D8
N Yorks 213 B11
N Yorks 214 D6
Melon Green Suff 124 F6
Melplash Dorset 16 B5
Melrose Borders 262 C2
Melsetter Orkney 314 H2
Melsonby N Yorks 224 D3
Meltham W Yorks 196 E6
Meltham Mills W Yorks 196 E6
Melton E Yorks 200 B3
Suff 126 G5
Meltonby E Yorks 207 C11
Melton Constable Norf 159 C10
Melton Mowbray Leics 154 F5
Melton Ross N Lincs 200 E5
Melvaig Highld 307 L2
Melverley Shrops 148 F6
Melverley Green Shrops 148 F6
Melvich Highld 310 C2
Membland Devon 7 F11
Membury Devon 28 G3
Memsie Aberds 303 C9
Memus Angus 287 B8
Mena Corn 5 C10
Menabilly Corn 5 E11
Menadarva Corn 4 G2
Menagissey Corn 4 F4
Menai Bridge = *Porthaethwy*
Anglesey 179 G9
Mendham Suff 142 G5
Mendlesham Suff 126 D2
Mendlesham Green
Suff 125 E11
Menethorpe N Yorks 216 F5
Mengham Hants 21 B10
Menheniot Corn 6 C5
Menherion Corn 2 B6
Menithwood Worcs 116 D4
Menna Corn 5 E8
Mennock Dumfries 247 B8
Menston W Yorks 205 E9
Menstrie Clack 278 B6
Mentmore Bucks 84 B6
Menzion Borders 260 E3
Meoble Highld 295 G9
Meole Brace Shrops 149 G9
Meols Mers 182 C2
Meon Hants 33 G8
Meonstoke Hants 33 D10
Meopham Kent 68 F6
Meopham Green Kent 68 F6
Meopham Station Kent 68 F6
Mepal Cambs 139 G8
Meppershall C Beds 104 D2
Merbach Hereford 96 B6
Mercaton Derbys 170 G3
Merchant Fields
W Yorks 197 B7
Merchiston Edin 280 G4
Mere Ches E 184 E2
Wilts 45 G10
Mere Brow Lancs 194 D2
Mereclough Lancs 204 G3
Mere Green W Mid 134 D2
Worcs 117 E9
Merehead Wrex 149 B9
Mere Heath Ches W 183 G11
Meresborough Medway 69 G10
Mereside Blackpool 202 G2
Meretown Staffs 150 E5
Mereworth Kent 53 C7
Mergie Aberds 293 E9
Meriden Herts 85 F10
W Mid 134 G4
Merkadale Highld 294 B5
Merkland Dumfries 237 B9
N Ayrs 256 B2
S Ayrs 244 E6
Merkland Lodge Highld 309 G4
Merle Common Sur 52 D2
Merley BCP 18 B6
Merlin's Bridge Pembs 72 C6
Merlin's Cross Pembs 73 E7
Merridale W Mid 133 D7
Merridge Som 43 G8
Merrie Gardens IoW 21 E7
Merrifield Devon 8 F6
Devon 24 G3
Merrington Shrops 149 E9
Merrion Pembs 72 F6
Merriott Dorset 16 B6
Som 28 E6
Merriottsford Som 28 E6
Merritown BCP 19 B8
Merrivale Devon 12 F6
Hereford 98 G2
Merrow Sur 50 C4
Merrybent Darl 224 C4
Merry Field Hill Dorset 31 G8
Merry Hill Herts 85 G10
W Mid 133 D7
Merryhill Green
Wokingham 65 E9
Merrylee E Renf 267 D11
Merry Lees Leics 135 B9
Merrymeet Corn 6 B5
Merry Meeting Corn 11 G7
Merry Oak Soton 32 E6
Mersham Kent 54 F5
Merstham Sur 51 C9
Merston W Sus 22 C5
Merstone IoW 20 E6
Merther Corn 5 G7
Merther Lane Corn 5 G7
Merthyr Carms 93 G7
Merthyr Cynog Powys 95 D9
Merthyr-Dyfan V Glam 58 F6
Merthyr Mawr Bridgend 57 F11
Merthyr Tydfil M Tydf 77 D8
Merthyr Vale M Tydf 77 F9
Merton Devon 25 E8
London 67 E9
Norf 141 D8
Oxon 83 B9
Merton Park London 67 F9
Mervinslaw Borders 262 G5
Meshaw Devon 26 D3
Messing Essex 88 B5
Messingham N Lincs 199 G11
Mesty Croft W Mid 133 E9
Mesur-y-dorth Pembs 87 E11
Metal Bridge Durham 233 E11
Metfield Suff 142 G5
Metherell Corn 7 B8
Metheringham Lincs 173 C9
Methersgate Suff 108 B5
Methil Fife 281 B7
Methilhill Fife 281 B7
Methlem Gwyn 144 C3
Methley W Yorks 197 B11
Methley Junction
W Yorks 197 B11
Methley Lanes
W Yorks 197 B11
Methlick Aberds 303 F8
Methven Perth 286 E4
Methwold Norf 140 E4
Methwold Hythe Norf 140 E4
Mettingham Suff 143 F7
Metton Norf 160 B3
Mevagissey Corn 5 G10
Mewith Head N Yorks 212 F4
Mexborough S Yorks 187 B7
Mey Highld 310 B6
Meyrick Park BCP 19 C7
Meysey Hampton Glos 81 F10
Miabhag W Isles 305 H2
W Isles 305 J3
Miabhig W Isles 304 E2
Mial Highld 299 B7
Michaelchurch Hereford 97 F10
Michaelchurch Escley
Hereford 96 E6
Michaelchurch on Arrow
Powys 114 G4
Michaelston-le-Pit
V Glam 59 E7
Michaelston-y-Fedw
Newport 59 C8
Michaelstow Corn 11 F7
Michealston-super-Ely
Cardiff 58 D6
Michelcombe Devon 8 B3
Micheldever Hants 48 F4
Michelmersh Hants 32 B4
Mickfield Suff 126 E2
Micklebring S Yorks 187 C8
Mickleby N Yorks 226 C6
Micklefield Bucks 84 G5
W Yorks 206 G4
Micklefield Green Herts 85 F8
Mickleham Sur 51 C7
Micklehurst Gtr Man 196 G3
Mickleover Derby 152 C6
Micklethwaite Cumb 239 G7
W Yorks 205 E8
Mickleton Durham 232 G5
Glos 100 C3
Mickletown W Yorks 197 B11
Mickle Trafford Ches W 166 B6
Mickley Derbys 186 F4
N Yorks 214 D5
Shrops 150 C2
Mickley Green Suff 124 F6
Mickley Square
Northumb 242 E3
Midanbury Hants 33 E7
Mid Ardlaw Aberds 303 C9
Mid Auchinleck Invclyd 276 G6
Midbea Orkney 314 B4
Mid Beltie Aberds 293 C8
Mid Calder W Loth 269 B11
Mid Cloch Forbie
Aberds 303 D7
Mid Clyth Highld 310 F6
Middle Assendon Oxon 65 B8
Middle Aston Oxon 101 F9
Middle Balnald Perth 286 B4
Middle Barton Oxon 101 F8
Middle Bickenhill
W Mid 134 G4
Middlebie Dumfries 238 B6
Middle Bockhampton
BCP 19 B9
Middle Bourne Sur 49 E10
Middle Bridge N Som 60 D3
Middle Burnham Som 43 D10
Middle Cairncake
Aberds 303 E8
Middlecave N Yorks 216 E5
Middle Chinnock Som 29 E7
Middle Claydon Bucks 102 F4
Middlecliffe S Yorks 198 F2
Middlecott Devon 13 D10
Devon 24 F6
Devon 26 F3
Middle Crackington Corn 11 B9
Middlecroft Derbys 186 G6
Middle Drums Angus 287 B9
Middle Duntisbourne
Glos 81 D7
Middlefield Falk 279 E7
Middleforth Green
Lancs 194 B4
Middle Green Bucks 66 C4
Som 27 D10
Suff 124 D4
Middleham N Yorks 214 B2
Middle Handley Derbys 186 F6
Middle Harling Norf 141 F9
Middle Herrington T&W 243 G9
Middlehill Corn 6 B5
Wilts 61 F10
Middle Hill Pembs 73 C7
Staffs 133 B9
Middlehope Shrops 131 F9
Middle Kames Argyll 275 E10
Middle Littleton Worcs 99 B11
Middle Luxton Devon 28 E2
Middle Madeley Staffs 168 F3
Middle Maes-coed
Hereford 96 E6
Middlemarsh Dorset 29 F11
Middle Marwood Devon 40 F4
Middle Mayfield Staffs 169 G10
Middle Mill Pembs 87 F11
Middlemoor Devon 12 G5
Middlemuir Aberds 303 D9
Aberds 303 E8
Aberds 303 G9
Middleport Stoke 168 F5
Middle Quarter Kent 53 F11
Middle Rainton T&W 234 B2
Middle Rasen Lincs 189 D9
Middlerig Falk 279 F8
Middle Rigg Perth 286 G4
Middle Rocombe Devon 9 B8
Middlesbrough Mbro 234 G5
Middlesceugh Cumb 230 C4
Middleshaw Cumb 211 B11
Middle Side Durham 232 F4
Middlesmoor N Yorks 213 E11
Middle Stoford Som 27 C11
Middle Stoke Devon 13 G9
Medway 69 D10
W Mid 119 B7
Middlestone Durham 233 E11
Middlestone Moor
Durham 233 E10
Middle Stoughton Som 44 D2
Middlestown W Yorks 197 D9
Middle Strath W Loth 279 G8
Middle Street Glos 80 E3
Middle Taphouse Corn 6 C3
Middlethird Borders 272 G3
Middlethorpe York 207 D7
Middleton Aberds 293 B10
Argyll 288 E1
Cumb 212 B2
Derbys 169 C11
Derbys 170 D3
Essex 107 D7
Gtr Man 195 F11
Hants 48 E2
Hereford 115 D10
Hrtlpl 234 E6
IoW 20 D2
Lancs 202 B4
Midloth 271 D7
N Nhants 136 F6
Norf 158 F3
Northumb 252 F3
Northumb 264 B4
N Yorks 204 E5
N Yorks 205 D8
N Yorks 216 B5
Perth 286 C5
Perth 286 F2
Perth 286 G5
Shrops 115 B10
Shrops 130 D5
Shrops 148 D6
Suff 127 D8
Swansea 56 D2
Warks 134 D3
W Yorks 197 B10
Middleton Baggot
Shrops 132 E2
Middleton Cheney
W Nhants 101 C9
Middleton Green Staffs 151 B9
Middleton Hall
Northumb 263 D11
Middleton-in-Teesdale
Durham 232 F4
Middleton Junction
Gtr Man 195 G11
Middleton Moor Suff 127 D8
Middleton of Rora
Aberds 303 E10
Middleton One Row
Darl 225 C7
Middleton-on-Leven
N Yorks 225 D9
Middleton-on-Sea
W Sus 35 G7
Middleton on the Hill
Hereford 115 E10
Middleton-on-the-Wolds
E Yorks 208 D4
Middleton Place Cumb 219 G11
Middleton Priors
Shrops 132 E2
Middleton Quernhow
N Yorks 214 D6
Middleton St George
Darl 224 C6
Middleton Scriven
Shrops 132 F3
Middleton Stoney
Oxon 101 G10
Middleton Tyas N Yorks 224 D4
Middletown Cumb 219 D9
N Som 60 E3
Powys 148 G6
Warks 117 E11
Middle Town Scilly 1 F4
Middle Tysoe Warks 100 C6
Middle Wallop Hants 47 F9
Middle Weald M Keynes 102 D5
Middlewich Ches E 167 B11
Middlewick Wilts 61 E11
Middle Wick Glos 80 F2
Middle Winterslow Wilts 47 G8
Middlewood Ches E 184 E6
Corn 11 F11
S Yorks 186 C4
Middle Woodford Wilts 46 F6
Middlewood Green
Suff 125 E11
Middleyard Glos 80 E4
Middlezoy Som 43 G11
Middridge Durham 233 F11
Midelney Som 28 C6
Midfield Highld 308 C5
Midford Bath 61 G9
Midgard Borders 262 F3
Mid Garrary Dumfries 237 B7
Midge Hall Lancs 194 C4
Midgehole W Yorks 196 B3
Midgeholme Cumb 240 F4
Midgham W Berks 64 F5
Midgham Green W Berks 64 F5
Midgley W Yorks 196 B4
W Yorks 197 E9
Mid Holmwood Sur 51 D7
Midhopestones S Yorks 186 B2
Midhurst W Sus 34 C5
Mid Lambrook Som 28 D6
Midland Orkney 314 F3
Mid Lavant W Sus 22 B5
Midlem Borders 262 D2
Mid Letter Argyll 284 G4
Midlock S Lanark 259 E11
Mid Main Highld 300 F4
Midmar Aberds 293 C8
Midmuir Argyll 289 G11
Mid Murthat Dumfries 248 D3
Midpark Argyll 255 B11
Midplaugh Aberds 302 E5
Midsomer Norton Bath 45 C7
Midton Invclyd 276 F4
Midtown Highld 307 L3
Highld 308 C5
Midtown of Buchromb
Moray 302 E3
Midtown of Glass
Aberds 302 E4
Mid Urchany Highld 301 E8
Midville Lincs 174 D5
Mid Walls Shetland 313 H4
Midway Ches E 184 E6
Som 45 D7
Mid Yell Shetland 312 D7
Miekle Toux Aberds 302 D5
Migdale Highld 309 K6
Migvie Aberds 292 C6
Milarrochy Stirling 277 C8
Milber Devon 14 G3
Milborne Port Som 29 D11
Milborne St Andrew
Dorset 18 B2
Milborne Wick Som 29 C11
Milbourne Northumb 242 B4
Wilts 62 B2
Milburn Aberds 302 E5
Aberds 302 F6
Cumb 231 F9
Milbury Heath S Glos 79 G11
Milby N Yorks 215 F8
Milch Hill Essex 106 G4
Milcombe Corn 6 D4
Oxon 101 E8
Milden Suff 107 B9
Mildenhall Suff 124 C4
Wilts 63 F8
Milebrook Powys 114 C6
Milebush Kent 53 D9
Mile Cross Norf 160 G4
Mile Elm Wilts 62 F3
Mile End Cambs 140 G2
Devon 14 G2
Essex 107 F9
Glos 79 C9
London 67 C11
Suff 124 G6
Mileham Norf 159 F8
Mile Oak Brighton 36 F2
Kent 53 E7
Shrops 148 D6
Staffs 134 C3
Miles Green Staffs 168 F4
Sur 50 B3
Miles Hill W Yorks 205 F11
Milesmark Fife 279 D11
Miles Platting Gtr Man 184 B5
Mile's Green W Berks 64 F4
Mile Town Kent 70 E2
Milfield Northumb 263 C10
Milford Derbys 170 F5
Devon 24 C2
Powys 129 E11
Shrops 149 E8
Staffs 151 E9
Sur 50 E2
Wilts 31 B11
Milford Haven Pembs 72 D6
Milford on Sea Hants 19 C11
Milkhouse Water Wilts 63 G7
Milkieston Borders 270 F4
Milkwall Glos 79 D9
Milkwell Wilts 30 C6
Milland W Sus 34 B4
Millarston Renfs 267 C9
Millbank Aberds 303 E11
Highld 310 C5
Kent 71 F8
Mill Bank W Yorks 196 C4
Millbeck Cumb 229 F11
Millbounds Orkney 314 C5
Millbreck Aberds 303 E10
Millbridge Sur 49 E10
Millbrook C Beds 103 D10
Corn 7 E8
Devon 41 G9
Gtr Man 185 B7
Soton 32 E5
Mill Brow Gtr Man 185 D7
Millburn S Ayrs 257 D10
Millcombe Devon 8 F6
Mill Common Norf 142 C6
Suff 143 G8
Mill Corner E Sus 38 C4
Milldale Staffs 169 E10
Mill Dam N Yorks 212 F3
Millden Lodge Angus 293 F7
Milldens Angus 287 B9
Millend Glos 80 D3
Glos 80 F3
Mill End Bucks 65 C9
Cambs 124 F3
Glos 81 C10
Herts 85 G8
Herts 104 E6
Mill End Green Essex 106 F2
Millendreath Corn 6 E5
Millerhill Midloth 270 B6
Miller's Dale Derbys 185 G10
Miller's Green Derbys 170 E3
Essex 87 D9
Millersneuk E Dunb 278 G3
Millerston Glasgow 268 B2
Mill Farm Aberds 303 C8
Millfield Pboro 138 C3
T&W 243 F9
Millgate Lancs 195 D11
Norf 160 D3
Millgillhead Cumb 229 G7
Mill Green Cambs 106 B2
Essex 87 E10
Hants 64 G4
Herts 86 D2
Norf 142 G2
Shrops 150 D3
Suff 107 C9
Suff 125 F9
Suff 126 E2
W Mid 133 C11
Millhalf Hereford 96 B5
Millhall Kent 53 B8
Mill Hall Dumfries 237 E8
Millhayes Devon 27 E10
Devon 28 G2
Millhead Lancs 211 E9
Millheugh S Lanark 268 E5
Millhill Devon 12 G5
Mill Hill Blackburn 195 B7
Essex 88 G4
E Sus 23 D10
Glos 79 D10
Gtr Man 195 F8
Kent 55 C11
Lincs 175 B8
London 86 G2
Suff 125 G7
Mill Hills Suff 108 B5
Mill Hirst N Yorks 214 G3
Millhouse Argyll 275 F10
Cumb 230 D3
Millhousebridge
Dumfries 248 F4
Millhouse Green
S Yorks 197 G8
Millhouses S Yorks 186 E4
Millhouses *continued*
S Yorks 198 G2
Millikenpark Renfs 267 C8
Millin Cross Pembs 73 C7
Millington E Yorks 208 C2
Millington Green
Derbys 170 F3
Mill Lane Hants 49 C9
Mill Meads London 67 C11
Millmeece Staffs 150 C6
Millmoor Devon 27 E10
Millness Cumb 211 C10
Mill of Brydock Aberds 302 D6
Mill of Chon Stirling 285 G8
Mill of Haldane W Dunb 277 E8
Mill of Kingoodie
Aberds 303 G8
Mill of Lynebain Aberds 302 F4
Mill of Muiresk Aberds 302 E6
Mill of Rango Orkney 314 E2
Mill of Sterin Aberds 292 D5
Mill of Uras Aberds 293 E10
Millom Cumb 210 C3
Millook Corn 11 B9
Millow C Beds 104 C4
Mill Park Argyll 255 G8
Mill Place N Lincs 200 F3
Millpool Corn 2 C3
Corn 11 G8
Millport N Ayrs 266 E3
Millquarter Dumfries 246 G4
Mill Shaw W Yorks 205 G11
Mill Side Cumb 211 C8
Mill Street Kent 53 B7
Norf 159 F11
Suff 107 D9
Milltack Aberds 303 D7
Millthorpe Derbys 186 F4
Lincs 156 C2
Mill Throp BCP 19 B8
Millthrop Cumb 222 G3
Milltimber Aberdeen 293 C10
Milltown Aberds 292 C4
Corn 6 B2
Corn 6 D2
Derbys 170 C5
Devon 40 F5
Highld 301 E9
Milltown of Aberdalgie
Perth 286 E4
Milltown of Auchindoun
Moray 302 E3
Milltown of Craigston
Aberds 303 D7
Milltown of Edinvillie
Moray 302 E2
Milltown of Kildrummy
Aberds 292 B6
Milltown of Rothiemay
Moray 302 E5
Milltown of Towie
Aberds 292 B6
Millwall London 67 D11
Milnathort Perth 286 G5
Milner's Heath Ches W 167 C7
Milngavie E Dunb 277 G11
Milnquarter Falk 278 F6
Milnrow Gtr Man 196 E2
Milnsbridge W Yorks 196 D6
Milnshaw Lancs 195 B9
Milnthorpe Cumb 211 C9
W Yorks 197 D10
Milnwood N Lanark 268 D4
Milo Carms 75 B9
Milson Shrops 116 C2
Milstead Kent 54 B2
Milston Wilts 47 D7
Milthorpe W Nhants 101 B11
Milton Angus 287 C7
Angus 292 E6
Cambs 123 E9
Cumb 211 C10
Cumb 240 E3
Derbys 152 D6
Dumfries 236 D4
Dumfries 237 B10
Dumfries 247 G8
Fife 287 E8
Glasgow 267 B11
Highld 299 E7
Highld 300 D3
Highld 300 E5
Highld 300 F4
Highld 301 B7
Highld 301 E7
Highld 310 D7
Kent 69 E7
Moray 292 B3
Moray 302 C5
Notts 188 G2
N Som 59 G10
Oxon 83 G7
Oxon 101 E8
Pembs 73 E8
Perth 286 F3
Powys 114 G4
Ptsmth 21 B9
Som 29 C7
Stirling 285 G9
Stoke 168 E6
S Yorks 197 G11
W Dunb 277 G8
Wilts 45 G11
Milton Abbas Dorset 30 G4
Milton Bridge Midloth 270 C4
Milton Bryan C Beds 103 E9
Milton Clevedon Som 45 F7
Milton Coldwells Aberds 303 F9
Milton Combe Devon 7 B9
Milton Common Oxon 83 E11
Milton Coombe Devon 7 B8
Milton Damerel Devon 24 E5
Miltonduff Moray 301 C11
Milton End Glos 80 C2
Glos 81 E10
Milton Ernest Bedford 121 F10
Milton Green Ches W 167 D7
Devon 12 F4
Milton Heights Oxon 83 G7
Miltonhill Moray 301 C10
Milton Hill Devon 14 F4
Oxon 83 G7
Miltonise Dumfries 236 B3
Milton Keynes
M Keynes 103 D7
Milton Keynes Village
M Keynes 103 D7
Milton Lilbourne Wilts 63 G7
Milton Malsor W Nhants 120 F4
Milton Morenish Perth 285 D10
Milton of Auchinhove
Aberds 293 C7
Milton of Balgonie Fife 287 G7
Milton of Buchanan
Stirling 277 C8
Milton of Campfield
Aberds 293 C8
Milton of Campsie
E Dunb 278 F3
Milton of Corsindae
Aberds 293 C8
Milton of Cullerlie
Aberds 293 C9
Milton of Cultoquhey
Perth 286 E2
Milton of Cushnie
Aberds 293 B7
Milton of Dalcapon
Perth 286 B3
Milton of Drimmie
Perth 286 B5
Milton of Edradour
Perth 286 B3
Milton of Gollanfield
Highld 301 D7
Milton of Lesmore
Aberds 302 G4
Milton of Logie Aberds 292 C6
Milton of Machany
Perth 286 F3
Milton of Mathers
Aberds 293 G9
Milton of Murtle
Aberdeen 293 C10
Milton of Noth Aberds 302 G5
Milton of Tullich Aberds 292 D5
Milton on Stour Dorset 30 B3
Milton Regis Kent 70 F2
Milton Street E Sus 23 E8
Milton under Wychwood
Oxon 82 B3
Milverton Som 27 B10
Warks 118 D6
Milwich Staffs 151 C9
Milwr Flint 181 G11
Mimbridge Sur 66 G3
Minard Argyll 275 D10
Minard Castle Argyll 275 D10
Minchington Dorset 31 E7
Minchinhampton Glos 80 E5
Mindrum Northumb 263 C8
Minehead Som 42 D3
Minera Wrex 166 E3
Mineshope Corn 11 B9
Minety Wilts 81 G8
Minffordd Gwyn 145 B11
Gwyn 146 G4
Gwyn 179 G9
Mingarrypark Highld 289 C8
Mingoose Corn 4 F4
Miningsby Lincs 174 C4
Minions Corn 11 G11
Minishant S Ayrs 257 G8
Minllyn Gwyn 147 G7
Minnes Aberds 303 G9
Minngearraidh W Isles 297 J3
Minnigaff Dumfries 236 C6
Minnonie Aberds 303 C7
Minnow End Essex 88 C2
Minnygap Dumfries 248 D2
Minshull Vernon
Ches E 167 C11
Minskip N Yorks 215 G7
Minstead Hants 32 E3
Minsted W Sus 34 C5
Minster Kent 70 E3
Kent 71 G10
Minsterley Shrops 131 C7
Minster Lovell Oxon 82 C4
Minsterworth Glos 80 B3
Minterne Magna Dorset 29 G11
Minterne Parva Dorset 29 G11
Minting Lincs 189 G11
Mintlaw Aberds 303 E10
Minto Borders 262 E3
Minto Kames Borders 262 E3
Minton Shrops 131 E8
Mintsfeet Cumb 221 G10
Minwear Pembs 73 C8
Minworth W Mid 134 E3
Mirbister Orkney 314 E2
Mirehouse Cumb 219 B9
Mireland Highld 310 C7
Mirfield W Yorks 197 D8
Miserden Glos 80 D6
Misery Corner Norf 142 F5
Miskin Rhondda 58 C4
Rhondda 77 F8
Misselfore Wilts 31 C8
Misson Notts 187 C11
Misterton Leics 135 G11
Notts 188 C3
Som 29 F7
Misterton Soss Notts 188 B3
Mistley Essex 108 E2
Mistley Heath Essex 108 E2
Mitcham London 67 F9
Mitcheldean Glos 79 B11
Mitchell Corn 5 E7
Mitchell Hill Borders 260 C3
Mitchellslacks
Dumfries 247 D11
Mitchelston Borders 271 F9
Mitchel Troy Mon 79 C7
Mitcheltroy Common
Mon 79 D7
Mite Houses Cumb 219 F11
Mitford Northumb 252 F5
Mithian Corn 4 E4
Mithian Downs Corn 4 F4
Mitton Staffs 151 F7
Worcs 99 E8
Mixbury Oxon 102 E2
Mixenden W Yorks 196 B5
Mixtow Corn 6 E2
Moat Cumb 239 C10
Moats Tye Suff 125 F10
Mobberley Ches E 184 F3
Staffs 169 G8
Moblake Ches E 167 G11
Mobwell Bucks 84 E5
Moccas Hereford 97 C7
Mochdre Conwy 180 F4
Powys 129 F11
Mochrum Dumfries 236 E5
Mockbeggar Hants 31 F11
Kent 54 E6
Medway 69 E8
Mockerkin Cumb 229 G7
Moclett Orkney 314 B4
Modbury Devon 8 E3
Moddershall Staffs 151 B8
Model Village Derbys 187 G8
Warks 119 E8
Modest Corner Kent 52 E5
Moelfre Anglesey 179 D8
Conwy 181 G7
Powys 148 D3
Moel Tryfan Gwyn 163 D8
Moel-y-crio Flint 165 B11
Moffat Dumfries 248 B3
Moffat Mills N Lanark 268 C5
Mogador Sur 51 C8
Moggerhanger C Beds 104 B2
Mogworthy Devon 26 D5
Moira Leics 152 F6
Moity Powys 96 C3
Molash Kent 54 C4
Mol-chlach Highld 294 D6
Mold Flint 166 C2
Moldgreen W Yorks 197 D7
Molehill Green Essex 105 G11
Molehill Green *continued*
Essex 106 G4
Molescroft E Yorks 208 E6
Molesden Northumb 252 G4
Molesworth Cambs 121 B11
Molinnis Corn 5 D10
Moll Highld 295 B7
Molland Devon 26 B4
Mollington Ches W 182 G5
Oxon 101 B8
Mollinsburn N Lanark 278 G4
Monachty Ceredig 111 E10
Monachylemore Stirling 285 F8
Monar Lodge Highld 300 E2
Monaughty Powys 114 D4
Monboddo House
Aberds 293 F9
Mondaytown Shrops 130 B6
Mondynes Aberds 293 F9
Monemore Stirling 285 D9
Monevechadan Argyll 284 G5
Monewden Suff 126 F4
Moneyacres E Ayrs 267 E8
Moneydie Perth 286 E4
Moneyhill Herts 85 G8
Money Hill Leics 153 F7
Moneyrow Green
Windsor 65 D11
Moneystone Staffs 169 F9
Mongleath Corn 3 C7
Moniaive Dumfries 247 E7
Monifieth Angus 287 D8
Monikie Angus 287 D8
Monimail Fife 286 F6
Monington Pembs 92 C2
Monk Bretton S Yorks 197 F11
Monk End N Yorks 224 D5
Monken Hadley London 86 F3
Monkerton Devon 14 C5
Monk Fryston N Yorks 198 B4
Monk Hesleden Durham 234 D5
Monkhide Hereford 98 C2
Monkhill Cumb 239 F8
W Yorks 198 C3
Monkhopton Shrops 132 E2
Monkland Hereford 115 F9
Monkleigh Devon 25 C7
Monkmoor Shrops 149 G10
Monknash V Glam 58 E2
Monkokehampton Devon 25 F9
Monkscross Corn 12 G3
Monkseaton T&W 243 C8
Monks Eleigh Suff 107 B9
Monk's Gate W Sus 36 B2
Monks Heath Ches E 184 G4
Monk Sherborne Hants 48 B6
Monkshill Aberds 303 E7
Monks Hill Kent 53 E11
Monksilver Som 42 F5
Monks Kirby Warks 135 G9
Monk Soham Suff 126 D4
Monks Orchard London 67 F11
Monk's Park Wilts 61 F11
Monkspath W Mid 118 B2
Monks Risborough Bucks 84 E4
Monksthorpe Lincs 174 B6
Monkston Park
M Keynes 103 D7
Monk Street Essex 106 F2
Monkswood Midloth 270 C6
Mon 78 E4
W Yorks 206 F2
Monkton Devon 27 G11
Kent 71 G9
Pembs 73 E7
S Ayrs 257 D9
T&W 243 E8
V Glam 58 E2
Monkton Combe Bath 61 G9
Monkton Deverill Wilts 45 F11
Monkton Farleigh Wilts 61 F10
Monktonhall E Loth 280 G6
Monkton Heathfield Som 28 B3
Monkton Up Wimborne
Dorset 31 E8
Monkwearmouth T&W 243 F9
Monkwood Hants 49 G7
Monkwood Green
Worcs 116 E6
Monmarsh Hereford 97 B10
Monmore Green W Mid 133 D8
Monmouth = *Trefynwy*
Mon 79 C8
Monmouth Cap Mon 97 F7
Monnington on Wye
Hereford 97 C7
Monreith Dumfries 236 E5
Monreith Mains
Dumfries 236 E5
Montacute Som 29 D7
Montcliffe Gtr Man 195 E7
Montcoffer Ho Aberds 302 C6
Montford Argyll 266 C2
Shrops 149 G8
Montford Bridge Shrops 149 F8
Montgarrie Aberds 293 B7
Montgomery Powys 130 D4
Montgomery Lines
Hants 49 C11
Monton Gtr Man 184 B3
Montpelier Bristol 60 E5
Montrave Fife 287 G7
Montrose Angus 287 B11
Montsale Essex 89 F8
Monwode Lea Warks 134 E5
Monxton Hants 47 E10
Monyash Derbys 169 B11
Monymusk Aberds 293 B8
Monzie Perth 286 E2
Monzie Castle Perth 286 E2
Moodiesburn N Lanark 278 G3
Moolham Som 28 E5
Moon's Green Kent 38 B5
Moon's Moat Worcs 117 D11
Moonzie Fife 287 F7
Moor Som 28 D6
Mooradale Shetland 312 F6
Moor Allerton W Yorks 205 F11
Moorbath Dorset 16 C3
Moorby Lincs 174 C3
Moorclose Cumb 228 F5
Gtr Man 195 F11
Moor Common Bucks 84 G4
Moorcot Hereford 115 F7
Moor Crichel Dorset 31 F7
Moor Cross Devon 8 D2
Moordown BCP 19 C7
Moore Halton 183 E9
Moor Edge W Yorks 205 F7
Moorend Cumb 239 G8
Derbys 170 F2
Dumfries 239 C7
Glos 80 C5
Glos 80 E2
Gtr Man 185 D7
S Glos 61 D7
Moor End Bucks 84 G4
Cambs 105 B7
C Beds 103 G9

Moor End *continued*
Durham 234 C2
EYorks 208 F2
Glos 99 G9
Lancs 202 E3
NYorks 207 F7
NYorks 215 G7
SYorks 197 G9
Worcs 117 F8
WYorks 196 B5
WYorks 206 D4
York 207 B9
Moorend Cross Hereford 98 B4
Moor End Field N Yorks 215 F8
Moorends S Yorks 199 D7
Moorfield Derbys 185 C8
Moorgate Norf 160 C3
SYorks 186 C6
Moorgreen Hants 33 D7
Notts 171 F7
Moor Green Herts 104 F6
Staffs 169 G7
Wilts 61 F11
W Mid 133 G11
Moorhaigh Notts 171 C8
Moorhall Derbys 186 G4
Moor Hall W Mid 134 D2
Moorhampton Hereford 97 B7
Moorhaven Village Devon 8 D3
Moorhayne Devon 28 F2
Moorhead W Yorks 205 F8
Moor Head W Yorks 197 B8
WYorks 197 E8
Moorhey Gtr Man 196 G2
Moorhole S Yorks 186 E6
Moorhouse Cumb 239 F8
Cumb 239 G7
Notts 172 B3
SYorks 198 E3
Moorhouse Bank Sur 52 C2
Moorhouses Lincs 174 D3
Moorland or Northmoor
Green Som 43 G10
Moorledge Bath 60 G5
Moorlinch Som 43 F11
Moor Monkton N Yorks 206 B6
Moor Monkton Moor
NYorks 206 B6
Moor of Balvack Aberds 293 B8
Moor of Granary
Moray 301 D10
Moor of Ravenstone
Dumfries 236 E5
Moor Park Cumb 229 D7
Hereford 97 C9
Herts 85 G9
Sur 49 D11
Moor Row Cumb 219 C10
Cumb 229 B10
Moorsholm Redcar 226 C3
Moorside Ches W 182 F3
Dorset 30 D3
Durham 233 B7
Gtr Man 195 G9
Gtr Man 196 F3
WYorks 197 B8
WYorks 205 F10
Moor Side Lancs 202 F5
Lancs 202 G4
Lincs 174 D2
WYorks 197 B7
WYorks 204 F6
Moorstock Kent 54 F6
Moor Street Kent 69 F10
Moorswater Corn 6 C4
Moorthorpe W Yorks 198 E3
Moor Top W Yorks 197 C7
Moortown Devon 12 B2
Devon 12 G6
Devon 25 C8
Hants 31 G11
IoW 20 E4
Lincs 189 B9
Telford 150 F2
WYorks 206 F2
Morangie Highld 309 L7
Morar Highld 295 F8
Moravian Settlement
Derbys 153 B8
Môrawelon Anglesey 178 E3
Morayhill Highld 301 E7
Morborne Cambs 138 E2
Morchard Bishop Devon 26 F3
Morchard Road Devon 26 G3
Morcombelake Dorset 16 C4
Morcott Rutland 137 C8
Morda Shrops 148 D5
Morden Dorset 18 B4
London 67 F9
Morden Green Cambs 104 C5
Morden Park London 67 F8
Mordiford Hereford 97 D11
Mordington Holdings
Borders 273 D8
Mordon Durham 234 F2
More Shrops 130 E6
Morebath Devon 27 C7
Morebattle Borders 263 E7
Morecambe Lancs 211 G8
More Crichel Dorset 31 F7
Moredon Swindon 62 B6
Moredun Edin 270 B5
Morefield Highld 307 K6
Morehall Kent 55 F8
Morelaggan Argyll 284 G6
Moreleigh Devon 8 E5
Morenish Perth 285 D9
Moresby Cumb 228 G5
Moresby Parks Cumb 219 B9
Morestead Hants 33 B8
Moreton Dorset 18 D2
Essex 87 D8
Hereford 115 E10
Mers 182 C3
Oxon 82 E6
Oxon 83 E11
Staffs 150 F5
Staffs 152 D2
Moreton Corbet
Shrops 149 E11
Moretonhampstead
Devon 13 D11
Moreton-in-Marsh Glos 100 E4
Moreton Jeffries
Hereford 98 B2
Moreton Morrell Warks 118 F6
Moreton on Lugg
Hereford 97 B10
Moreton Paddox Warks 118 G6
Moreton Pinkney
W Nhants 101 B11
Moreton Say Shrops 150 C2
Moreton Valence Glos 80 D3
Moretonwood Shrops 150 C2
Morfa Carms 56 B4
Carms 75 C9
Ceredig 110 G6
Gwyn 144 C3
Morfa Bach Carms 74 C5
Morfa Bychan Gwyn 145 B10
Morfa Dinlle Gwyn 162 D6
Morfa Glas Neath 76 D5
Morfa Nefyn Gwyn 162 G3
Morfydd Denb 165 F10
Morganstown Cardiff 58 C6
Morgan's Vale Wilts 31 C11
Moriah Ceredig 112 B2
Mork Glos 79 D9
Morland Cumb 231 G7
Morley Ches E 184 E4
Derbys 170 G5
Durham 233 F8
WYorks 197 B9
Morley Green Ches E 184 E4
Morleymoor Derbys 170 G5
Morley Park Derbys 170 F5
Morley St Botolph
Norf 141 D11
Morley Smithy Derbys 170 G5
Mornick Corn 12 G2
Morningside Edin 280 G3
N Lanark 268 D6
Morningthorpe Norf 142 E4
Morpeth Northumb 252 F6
Morphie Aberds 293 G9
Morrey Staffs 152 F2
Morridge Side Staffs 169 E8
Morrilow Heath Staffs 151 B9
Morris Green Essex 106 E4
Morriston = *Treforys*
Swansea 57 B7
Morristown V Glam 59 E7
Morston Norf 177 E8
Mortehoe Devon 40 D3
Morthen S Yorks 187 D7
Mortimer W Berks 65 G7
Mortimer's Cross
Hereford 115 E8
Mortimer West End
Hants 64 G6
Mortlake London 67 D8
Mortomley S Yorks 186 B4
Morton Cumb 230 D4
Cumb 239 G9
Derbys 170 C6
IoW 21 D8
Lincs 155 E11
Lincs 172 C5
Lincs 188 C4
Norf 160 F2
Notts 172 E2
S Glos 79 G10
Shrops 148 E5
Morton Bagot Warks 118 E2
Morton Common
Shrops 148 E5
Morton Mains Dumfries 247 D9
Morton Mill Shrops 149 E11
Morton-on-Swale
NYorks 224 G6
Morton Spirt Warks 117 G10
Morton Tinmouth
Durham 233 G9
Morton Underhill
Worcs 117 F10
Morvah Corn 1 B4
Morval Corn 6 D5
Morven Lodge Aberds 292 C5
Morvich Highld 295 C11
Highld 309 J7
Morville Shrops 132 E3
Morville Heath Shrops 132 E3
Morwellham Quay Devon 7 B8
Morwenstow Corn 24 E2
Mosborough S Yorks 186 E6
Moscow E Ayrs 267 G9
Mose Shrops 132 E5
Mosedale Cumb 230 E3
Moseley W Mid 133 D8
W Mid 133 G11
Worcs 116 F6
Moses Gate Gtr Man 195 F8
Mosley Common
Gtr Man 195 G8
Moss Argyll 288 E1
Highld 289 C8
SYorks 198 E5
Wrex 166 E4
Mossat Aberds 292 B6
Mossbank Shetland 312 F6
Moss Bank Halton 183 D8
Mers 183 B8
Mossbay Cumb 228 F5
Mossblown S Ayrs 257 E10
Mossbrow Gtr Man 184 D2
Mossburnford Borders 262 F5
Mossdale Dumfries 237 B8
Mossedge Cumb 239 D11
Moss Edge Lancs 202 D4
Lancs 202 E4
Mossend N Lanark 268 C4
Moss End Brack 65 E11
Ches E 183 F11
Mosser Mains Cumb 229 F8
Mossfield Highld 300 B6
Mossgate Staffs 151 B8
Mossgiel E Ayrs 257 D11
Mosshouses Borders 262 B2
Moss Houses Ches E 184 G5
Mossley Ches E 168 C5
Gtr Man 196 G3
Mossley Brow Gtr Man 196 G3
Mossley Hill Mers 182 D5
Moss Nook Gtr Man 184 D4
Mers 183 C8
Moss of Barmuckity
Moray 302 C2
Moss of Meft Moray 302 C2
Mosspark Glasgow 267 C10
Moss Pit Staffs 151 E8
Moss Side Cumb 238 G5
Gtr Man 184 B4
Moss-side Highld 301 D8
Moss Side Lancs 193 B11
Lancs 194 C4
Lancs 202 G3
Mers 182 B6
Moss-side Moray 302 D5
Mosstodloch Moray 302 D3
Mosston Angus 287 C9
Mosstown Aberds 303 C10
Mossy Lea Lancs 194 E4
Mosterton Dorset 29 F7
Moston Ches E 168 C2
Ches W 182 G6
Gtr Man 195 G11
Shrops 149 D11
Moston Green Ches E 168 C2
Mostyn Flint 181 E11
Mostyn Quay Flint 181 E11
Motcombe Dorset 30 B5
Mothecombe Devon 8 F2
Motherby Cumb 230 F4
Motherwell N Lanark 268 D5
Motspur Park London 67 F8
Mottingham London 68 E2
Mottisfont Hants 32 B4
Mottistone IoW 20 E4
Mottram in Longdendale
Gtr Man 185 B7
Mottram Rise Gtr Man 185 B7
Mottram St Andrew
Ches E 184 F5
Mott's Green Essex 87 B8
Mott's Mill E Sus 52 F4
Mouldsworth Ches W 183 G8
Moulin Perth 286 B3
Moulsecoomb Brighton 36 F4
Moulsford Oxon 64 C5
Moulsham Essex 88 D2
Moulsoe M Keynes 103 C8
Moultavie Highld 300 B6
Moulton Ches W 167 B11
Lincs 156 E6
NYorks 224 E4
Suff 124 E3
V Glam 58 E5
W Nhants 120 D5
Moulton Chapel Lincs 156 F5
Moulton Eaugate Lincs 156 F6
Moulton Park W Nhants 120 E5
Moulton St Mary Norf 143 B7
Moulton Seas End Lincs 156 D6
Moulzie Angus 292 F4
Mounie Castle Aberds 303 G7
Mount Corn 4 D5
Corn 6 B2
Highld 301 E9
WYorks 196 D5
Mountain Anglesey 178 E2
WYorks 205 G7
Mountain Air Bl Gwent 77 D11
Mountain Ash = *Aberpennar*
Rhondda 77 F8
Mountain Bower Wilts 61 D10
Mountain Cross Borders 270 F2
Mountain Street Kent 54 C5
Mountain Water Pembs 91 G8
Mount Ambrose Corn 4 G4
Mount Ballan Mon 60 B3
Mount Batten Plym 7 E9
Mountbenger Borders 261 D8
Mountbengerburn
Borders 261 D8
Mountblow W Dunb 277 G9
Mount Bovers Essex 88 G4
Mount Bures Essex 107 E8
Mount Canisp Highld 301 B7
Mount Charles Corn 5 B10
Corn 5 E10
Mount Cowdown Wilts 47 C9
Mount End Essex 87 E7
Mount Ephraim E Sus 23 B7
Mounters Dorset 30 D3
Mountfield E Sus 38 C2
Mountgerald Highld 300 C5
Mount Gould Plym 7 D9
Mount Hawke Corn 4 F4
Mount Hermon Corn 2 F6
Sur 50 B4
Mount Hill S Glos 61 E7
Mountjoy Corn 5 C7
Mount Lane Devon 12 B3
Mountnessing Essex 87 F10
Mounton Mon 79 G8
Mount Pleasant Bucks 102 E3
Ches E 168 D4
Corn 5 C10
Derbys 152 D6
Derbys 152 F5
Derbys 170 F4
Devon 27 G11
Durham 233 E11
E Sus 23 E7
E Sus 36 D6
Flint 182 G2
Hants 19 B11
Kent 71 F10
London 85 G8
MTydf 77 F9
Neath 57 B9
Norf 141 E9
Pembs 73 D8
Shrops 149 G9
Stockton 234 G4
Stoke 168 G5
Suff 106 B4
T&W 243 E7
Warks 135 F7
Worcs 99 D10
Worcs 117 E10
WYorks 197 C8
Mount Sion Wrex 166 E3
Mount Skippett Oxon 82 B5
Mountsolie Aberds 303 D9
Mountsorrel Leics 153 F11
Mount Sorrel Wilts 31 C8
Mount Tabor W Yorks 196 B5
Mount Vernon Glasgow 268 C3
Mount Wise Corn 7 E9
Mousehill Sur 50 E2
Mousehole Corn 1 D5
Mousen Northumb 264 C4
Mousley End Warks 118 D4
Mouswald Dumfries 238 C3
Mouth Mill Devon 24 B3
Mowbreck Lancs 202 G4
Mow Cop Ches E 168 D5
Mowden Darl 224 B5
Essex 88 C3
Mowhaugh Borders 263 E8
Mowmacre Hill
Leicester 135 B11
Mowshurst Kent 52 D3
Mowsley Leics 136 F2
Moxby N Yorks 215 F11
Moxley W Mid 133 D9
Moy Argyll 255 E8
Highld 290 E6
Highld 301 F7
Moy Hall Highld 301 F7
Moy Ho Moray 301 C10
Moyles Court Hants 31 F11
Moylgrove = *Trewyddel*
Pembs 92 C2
Moy Lodge Highld 290 E6
Muasdale Argyll 255 C7
Muchalls Aberds 293 D11
Much Birch Hereford 97 E10
Much Cowardne Hereford 98 B2
Much Cowarne Hereford 98 B2
Much Dewchurch
Hereford 97 E9
Muchelney Som 28 C6
Muchelney Ham Som 28 C6
Much Hadham Herts 86 B5
Much Hoole Lancs 194 C3
Much Hoole Moss Houses
Lancs 194 C3
Much Hoole Town
Lancs 194 C3
Muchlarnick Corn 6 D4
Much Marcle Hereford 98 E3
Muchrachd Highld 300 F2
Much Wenlock Shrops 132 C2
Muckairn Argyll 289 F11
Muckernich Highld 300 D5
Mucking Thurrock 69 C7
Muckle Breck Shetland 312 G7
Muckleford Dorset 17 C8
Mucklestone Staffs 150 B4
Muckleton Norf 158 B6
Shrops 149 E11
Muckletown Aberds 302 G5
Muckley Shrops 132 D2
Muckley Corner Staffs 133 B11
Muckley Cross Shrops 132 D2
Muckton Lincs 190 E5
Muckton Bottom Lincs 190 E5
Mudale Highld 308 F5
Mudd Gtr Man 185 C7
Muddiford Devon 40 F5
Muddlebridge Devon 40 G4
Muddles Green E Sus 23 C8
Mudeford BCP 19 C9
Mudford Som 29 D9
Mudford Sock Som 29 D9
Mudgley Som 44 D2
Mugdock Stirling 277 F11
Mugeary Highld 294 B6
Mugginton Derbys 170 G3
Muggintonlane End
Derbys 170 G3
Muggleswick Durham 232 B6
Mugswell Sur 51 C9
Muie Highld 309 J6
Muir Aberds 292 E2
Muircleugh Borders 271 F10
Muirden Aberds 303 D7
Muirdrum Angus 287 D9
Muiredge Fife 281 B7
Muirend Glasgow 267 C11
Muirhead Angus 287 D7
Fife 286 G6
Fife 287 F8
N Lanark 268 B3
S Ayrs 257 C8
Muirhouse Edin 280 F4
N Lanark 268 D5
Muirhouselaw Borders 262 D4
Muirhouses Falk 279 E10
Muirkirk E Ayrs 258 D5
Muirmill Stirling 278 E4
Muir of Alford Aberds 293 B7
Muir of Fairburn Highld 300 D4
Muir of Fowlis Aberds 293 B7
Muir of Kinellar
Aberds 293 B10
Muir of Miltonduff
Moray 301 D11
Muir of Ord Highld 300 D5
Muir of Pert Angus 287 D8
Muirshearlich Highld 290 E3
Muirskie Aberds 293 D10
Muirtack Aberds 303 F9
Muirton Aberds 303 D7
Highld 301 C7
Perth 286 E5
Perth 286 F3
Muirton Mains Highld 300 D4
Muirton of Ardblair
Perth 286 C5
Muirton of Ballochy
Angus 293 G8
Muiryfold Aberds 303 D7
Muker N Yorks 223 F8
Mulbarton Norf 142 C3
Mulben Moray 302 D3
Mulberry Corn 5 B10
Mulfra Corn 1 C5
Mulindry Argyll 254 B4
Mulla Shetland 313 G6
Mullardoch House
Highld 300 F2
Mullenspond Hants 47 D9
Mullion Corn 2 F5
Mullion Cove Corn 2 F5
Mumbles Hill Swansea 56 D6
Mumby Lincs 191 G8
Mumps Gtr Man 196 F2
Mundale Moray 301 D10
Munderfield Row
Hereford 116 G2
Munderfield Stocks
Hereford 116 G2
Mundesley Norf 160 B6
Mundford Norf 140 E6
Mundham Norf 142 D6
Mundon Essex 88 E5
Mundurno Aberdeen 293 B11
Mundy Bois Kent 54 D2
Munerigie Highld 290 C4
Muness Shetland 312 C8
Mungasdale Highld 307 K4
Mungrisdale Cumb 230 E3
Munlochy Highld 300 D6
Munsary Cottage Highld 310 E6
Munsley Hereford 98 C3
Munslow Shrops 131 F10
Munstone Hereford 97 C10
Murch V Glam 59 E7
Murchington Devon 13 D9
Murcot Worcs 99 C11
Murcott Oxon 83 B9
Wilts 81 G7
Murdieston Stirling 278 B3
Murdishaw Halton 183 E9
Murieston W Loth 269 C11
Murkle Highld 310 C5
Murlaggan Highld 290 D2
Highld 290 E5
Murra Orkney 314 F2
Murrayfield Edin 280 G4
Murrayshall Perth 286 E5
Murraythwaite Dumfries 238 C4
Murrell Green Hants 49 B8
Murrell's End Glos 98 E4
Glos 98 G5
Murrion Shetland 312 F4
Murrow Cambs 139 B7
Mursley Bucks 102 F6
Murston Kent 70 G2
Murthill Angus 287 B8
Murthly Perth 286 D4
Murton Cumb 231 G10
Durham 234 B3
Northumb 273 F9
Swansea 56 D5
T&W 243 C8
York 207 C8
Murton Grange
NYorks 215 B10
Murtwell Devon 8 D5
Musbury Devon 15 C11
Muscliff BCP 19 B7
Muscoates N Yorks 216 C3
Muscott W Nhants 120 E2
Musdale Argyll 289 G11
Mushroom Green
W Mid 133 F8
Musselburgh E Loth 280 G6
Musselwick Pembs 72 D4
Mustard Hyrn Norf 161 F8
Muston Leics 154 B6
NYorks 217 D11
Mustow Green Worcs 117 C7
Muswell Hill London 86 G3
Mutehill Dumfries 237 E8
Mutford Suff 143 F9
Muthill Perth 286 F2
Mutley Plym 7 D9
Mutterton Devon 27 G8
Mutton Hall E Sus 37 C9
Muxton Telford 150 G4
Mwdwl-eithin Flint 181 F11
Mwynbwll Flint 165 B11
Mybster Highld 310 D5
Myddfai Carms 94 F5
Myddle Shrops 149 E9
Myddlewood Shrops 149 E9
Myddyn-fych Carms 75 C10
Mydroilyn Ceredig 111 F9
Myerscough Lancs 202 F5
Myerscough Smithy
Lancs 203 G8
Mylor Bridge Corn 3 B8
Mylor Churchtown Corn 3 B8
Mynachdy Cardiff 59 D7
Rhondda 77 F8
Mynachlog-ddu Pembs 92 E2
Mynd Shrops 115 C7
Myndd Llandegai Gwyn 163 B10
Myndtown Shrops 131 F7
Mynydd Bach Ceredig 112 B4
Mynydd-bach Mon 79 G7
Swansea 57 B7
Mynydd-bach-y-glo
Swansea 56 B6
Mynydd Bodafon
Anglesey 179 D7
Mynydd Fflint = *Flint*
Mountain Flint 182 G2
Mynydd Gilan Gwyn 144 E5
Mynydd-isa Flint 166 C3
Mynyddislwyn Caerph 77 G11
Mynydd-llan Flint 181 G11
Mynydd Marian Conwy 180 F5
Mynydd Mechell
Anglesey 178 D5
Mynyddygarreg Carms 74 D6
Mynytho Gwyn 144 C6
Myrebird Aberds 293 D9
Myrelandhorn Highld 310 D6
Myreside Perth 286 E6
Myrtle Hill Carms 94 E5
Mytchett Sur 49 B11
Mytchett Place Sur 49 C11
Mytholm W Yorks 196 B3
Mytholmes W Yorks 204 F6
Mytholmroyd W Yorks 196 B4
Mythop Lancs 202 G3
Mytice Aberds 302 F4
Myton Warks 118 E6
Myton Hall N Yorks 215 F8
Myton-on-Swale
N Yorks 215 F8
Mytton Shrops 149 F8

N

Naast Highld 307 L3
Nab Hill W Yorks 197 D7
Nab's Head Lancs 194 B6
Naburn York 207 D7
Nab Wood W Yorks 205 F8
Naccolt Kent 54 E4
Nackington Kent 55 C7
Nacton Suff 108 C4
Nadderwater Devon 14 C3
Nafferton E Yorks 209 B7
Na Gearrannan W Isles 304 D3
Nag's Head Glos 80 F5
Naid-y-march Flint 181 G11
Nailbridge Glos 79 B10
Nailsbourne Som 28 B2
Nailsea N Som 60 D3
Nailstone Leics 135 B8
Nailsworth Glos 80 F5
Nailwell Bath 61 G8
Nairn Highld 301 D8
Nalderswood Sur 51 D8
Nance Corn 4 G3
Nanceddan Corn 2 C2
Nancegollan Corn 2 C4
Nancemellin Corn 4 G2
Nancenoy Corn 2 D6
Nancledra Corn 1 B5
Nangreaves Lancs 195 D10
Nanhoron Gwyn 144 C5
Nanhyfer = *Nevern*
Pembs 91 D11
Nannau Gwyn 146 E4
Nannerch Flint 165 B11
Nanpantan Leics 153 F10
Nanpean Corn 5 D9
Nanquidno Corn 1 D3
Nanstallon Corn 5 B10
Nant Carms 74 B6
Denb 165 D11
Nant Alyn Flint 165 B11
Nant-ddu Powys 77 B8
Nanternis Ceredig 111 F7
Nantgaredig Carms 93 G9
Nantgarw Rhondda 58 B6
Nant-glas Powys 113 E9
Nantglyn Denb 165 C8
Nantgwyn Powys 113 B9
Nantithet Corn 2 E5
Nantlle Gwyn 163 E8
Nantmawr Shrops 148 E4
Nant Mawr Flint 166 C3
Nantmel Powys 113 D10
Nantmor Gwyn 163 F10
Nant Peris = *Old Llanberis*
Gwyn 163 D10
Nantserth Powys 113 C9
Nant Uchaf Denb 165 D8
Nantwich Ches E 167 E11
Nant-y-Bai Carms 94 C5
Nant-y-Bwch Bl Gwent 77 C10
Nant-y-cafn Neath 76 D4
Nantycaws Carms 75 B7
Nant y Caws Shrops 148 D5
Nant-y-ceisiad Caerph 59 B8
Nant-y-derry Mon 78 D4
Nant-y-felin Conwy 179 G11
Nant-y-ffin Carms 93 E11
Nantyffyllon Bridgend 57 C11
Nantyglo Bl Gwent 77 C11
Nant-y-gollen Shrops 148 D4
Nant-y-moel Bridgend 76 G6
Nant-y-pandy Conwy 179 G11
Nant-y-Rhiw Conwy 164 D4
Nantyronen Station
Ceredig 112 B3
Napchester Kent 55 D10
Naphill Bucks 84 F4
Napleton Worcs 99 B7
Napley Staffs 150 B4
Napley Heath Staffs 150 B4
Nappa N Yorks 204 C3
Nappa Scar N Yorks 223 G9
Napton on the Hill
Warks 119 E9
Narberth = *Arberth*
Pembs 73 C10
Narberth Bridge Pembs 73 C10
Narborough Leics 135 D10
Norf 158 G4
Narfords Som 28 F3
Narkurs Corn 6 D6
Narracott Devon 24 D5
Narrowgate Corner
Norf 161 F8
Nasareth Gwyn 163 E7
Naseby W Nhants 120 B3
Nash Bucks 102 E5
Hereford 114 E6
Kent 55 B9
London 68 G2
Newport 59 C10
Shrops 116 C2
Som 29 E8
Nashend Glos 80 D5
Nash End Worcs 132 G5
Nashes Green Hants 49 D7
Nash Lee Bucks 84 D4
Nash Mills Herts 85 E9
Nash Street E Sus 23 C8
Kent 68 F6
Nassington N Nhants 137 D11
Nastend Glos 80 D3
Nast Hyde Herts 86 D2
Nasty Herts 105 G7
Natcott Devon 24 C3
Nateby Cumb 222 D5
Lancs 202 E5
Nately Scures Hants 49 C8
Natland Cumb 211 B10
Natton Glos 99 E8
Naughton Suff 107 B10
Naunton Glos 100 G2
Worcs 99 D7
Naunton Beauchamp
Worcs 117 G9
Navant Hill W Sus 34 B6
Navenby Lincs 173 D7
Navestock Heath Essex 87 F8
Navestock Side Essex 87 F9
Navidale Highld 311 H4
Navity Highld 301 C7
Nawton N Yorks 216 C3
Nayland Suff 107 E9
Nazeing Essex 86 D6
Nazeing Gate Essex 86 D6
Nazeing Long Green
Essex 86 E6
Nazeing Mead Essex 86 D5
Neacroft Hants 19 B9
Nealhouse Cumb 239 G8
Neal's Green Warks 134 G6
Neames Forstal Kent 54 B5
Neap Shetland 313 H7
Near Hardcastle
NYorks 214 F2
Near Sawrey Cumb 221 F7
Nearton End Bucks 102 F6
Neasden London 67 B8
Neasham Darl 224 C6
Neat Enstone Oxon 101 G7
Neath = *Castell-nedd*
Neath 57 B8
Neath Abbey Neath 57 B8
Neatham Hants 49 E8
Neath Hill M Keynes 103 C7
Neatishead Norf 160 E6
Neat Marsh E Yorks 209 G9
Neaton Norf 141 C8
Nebo Anglesey 179 C7
Ceredig 111 D10
Conwy 164 D4
Gwyn 163 E7
Nebsworth Warks 100 C3
Nechells W Mid 133 F11
Necton Norf 141 B7
Nedd Highld 306 F6
Nedderton Northumb 252 G6
Nedge Hill Som 44 C5
Telford 132 B4
Nedging Suff 107 B9
Nedging Tye Suff 107 B10
Needham Norf 142 G4
Needham Green Essex 87 B9
Needham Market Suff 125 G11
Needham Street Suff 124 D4
Needingworth Cambs 122 C6
Needwood Staffs 152 E3
Neen Savage Shrops 116 B3
Neen Sollars Shrops 116 C3
Neenton Shrops 132 F2
Nefod Shrops 148 B6
Nefyn Gwyn 162 G4
Neighbourne Som 44 D6
Neight Hill Worcs 117 F8
Neilston E Renf 267 D9
Neinthirion Powys 129 B9
Neithrop Oxon 101 C8
Nelly Andrews Green
Powys 130 B5
Nelson Caerph 77 F10
Lancs 204 F3
Nelson Village Northumb 243 B7
Nemphlar S Lanark 269 G7
Nempnett Thrubwell
N Som 60 G4
Nene Terrace Lincs 138 B5
Nenthall Cumb 231 B11
Nenthead Cumb 231 C11
Nenthorn Borders 262 B5
Neopardy Devon 13 B11
Nepcote W Sus 35 F10
Nepgill Cumb 229 F7
Nep Town W Sus 36 D2
Nerabus Argyll 254 B3
Nercwys Flint 166 C2
Nerston S Lanark 268 D2
Nesbit Northumb 263 C11
Ness Ches W 182 F4
Orkney 314 C4
Nesscliffe Shrops 149 F7
Nessholt Ches W 182 F4
Nesstoun Orkney 314 A7
Neston Ches W 182 F3
Wilts 61 F11
Netchells Green
W Mid 133 F11
Netham Bristol 60 E6
Nethanfoot S Lanark 268 F6
Nether Alderley Ches E 184 F4
Netheravon Wilts 46 D6
Nether Blainslie
Borders 271 G10
Nether Booth Derbys 185 D10
Netherbrae Aberds 303 D7
Netherbrough Orkney 314 E3
Nether Broughton Leics 154 D3
Netherburn S Lanark 268 F6
Nether Burrow Lancs 212 D2
Nether Burrows Derbys 152 B5
Netherbury Dorset 16 B5
Netherby Cumb 239 C9
NYorks 206 D2
Nether Cassock
Dumfries 248 C6
Nether Cerne Dorset 17 B9
Nether Chanderhill
Derbys 186 G4
Netherclay Som 28 C3
Nether Compton Dorset 29 D9
Nethercote Oxon 101 C9
Warks 119 E10
Nethercott Devon 12 B3
Devon 40 F3
Oxon 101 G9
Som 42 G6
Nether Crimond Aberds 303 G8
Netherdale Shetland 313 H3
Nether Dalgliesh
Borders 249 B7
Nether Dallachy Moray 302 C3
Nether Edge S Yorks 186 E4
Netherend Glos 79 E9
Nether End Derbys 186 G3
Leics 154 G4
WYorks 197 F8
Nether Exe Devon 26 G6
Netherfield E Sus 38 D2
M Keynes 103 D7
Notts 171 G10
Nethergate Norf 159 D11
Nether Glasslaw Aberds 303 D8
Nether Hall Leicester 136 B2
Netherhampton Wilts 31 B10
Nether Handley Derbys 186 F6
Nether Handwick Angus 287 C7
Nether Haugh S Yorks 186 B6
Nether Headon Notts 188 F2
Nether Heage Derbys 170 E5
Nether Heyford
W Nhants 120 F3
Nether Hindhope
Borders 263 G7
Nether Horsburgh
Borders 261 B8
Nether Howecleuch
S Lanark 260 G2
Nether Kellet Lancs 211 F10
Nether Kidston Borders 270 G4
Nether Kinmundy
Aberds 303 E10
Nether Kirton E Renf 267 D9
Netherland Green
Staffs 152 C2
Nether Langwith Notts 187 G8
Netherlaw Dumfries 237 E9
Netherlay Dorset 28 F6
Nether Leask Aberds 303 F10
Netherlee E Renf 267 D11
Nether Lenshie Aberds 302 E6
Netherley Aberds 293 D10
Mers 182 D6
WYorks 196 E4
Nether Loads Derbys 170 B4
Nethermill Dumfries 248 F2
Nethermills Moray 302 D5
Nether Monynut
Borders 272 C4
Nether Moor Derbys 170 B5
Nethermuir Aberds 303 E9
Netherne on-the-Hill
Sur 51 B9
Netheroyd Hill W Yorks 196 D6
Nether Padley Derbys 186 F3
Nether Park Aberds 303 D10
Netherplace E Renf 267 D10
Nether Poppleton York 207 B7
Netherraw Borders 262 E3
Nether Row Cumb 230 D2
Nether Savock Aberds 303 E10
Netherseal Derbys 152 G5
Nether Shiels Borders 271 F8
Nether Silton N Yorks 225 G9
Nether Skyborry Shrops 114 C5
Nether Street Suff 125 E8
Netherstoke Dorset 29 F8
Nether Stowe Staffs 152 G2
Nether Stowey Som 43 F7
Nether Street Essex 87 C9
Herts 86 B6
Netherthird E Ayrs 258 F3
Netherthong W Yorks 196 F6
Netherthorpe Derbys 186 G6
SYorks 187 E8
Netherton Aberds 303 E8
Angus 287 B9
Ches W 183 F8
Corn 11 G11
Cumb 228 D6
Devon 14 G3
Glos 81 E11
Hants 47 B11
Hereford 97 F10
Mers 193 G11
N Lanark 268 E5
Northumb 251 B11
Oxon 82 F6
Perth 286 B5
Shrops 132 G4
Stirling 277 F11
W Mid 133 F8
Worcs 99 C9
WYorks 196 E6
WYorks 197 D9
Netherton of Lonmay
Aberds 303 C10
Nethertown Cumb 219 D9
Highld 310 B7
Lancs 203 F10
Staffs 152 F2
Nether Urquhart Fife 286 G5
Nether Wallop Hants 47 F10
Nether Warden
Northumb 241 D10
Nether Wasdale Cumb 220 E2
Nether Welton Cumb 230 B3
Nether Westcote Glos 100 G4
Nether Whitacre Warks 134 E4
Nether Winchendon or
Lower Winchendon
Bucks 84 C2
Netherwitton Northumb 252 E4
Netherwood E Ayrs 258 D5
Nether Worton Oxon 101 E8
Nether Yeadon
WYorks 205 E10
Nethy Bridge Highld 301 G10
Netley Hants 33 F7
Netley Hill Soton 33 E7
Netley Marsh Hants 32 E4
Nettacott Devon 14 B4
Netteswell Essex 87 C7
Nettlebed Oxon 65 B8
Nettlebridge Som 44 D6
Nettlecombe Dorset 16 B6
IoW 20 F6
Nettleden Herts 85 C8
Nettleham Lincs 189 F8
Nettlestead Kent 53 C7
Suff 107 B11
Nettlestead Green Kent 53 C7
Nettlestone IoW 21 C8
Nettlesworth Durham 233 B11
Nettleton Glos 80 C6
Lincs 200 G6
Wilts 61 D10
Nettleton Green Wilts 61 D10
Nettleton Hill W Yorks 196 D5
Nettleton Shrub Wilts 61 D10
Nettleton Top Lincs 189 B10
Netton Wilts 46 F6
Neuadd Carms 94 G3
Nevendon Essex 88 G2
Nevern = *Nanhyfer*
Pembs 91 D11
Nevilles Cross Durham 233 C11
New Abbey Dumfries 237 C11
New Aberdour Aberds 303 C8
New Addington London 67 G11
Newall W Yorks 205 D10
Newall Green Gtr Man 184 D4
New Alresford Hants 48 G5
New Alyth Perth 286 C6
Newark Orkney 314 B7
Pboro 138 C4
Newark-on-Trent Notts 172 E3
New Arley Warks 134 F5
New Arram E Yorks 208 E6
Newarthill N Lanark 268 D5
New Ash Green Kent 68 F6
New Balderton Notts 172 E4
Newball Lincs 189 F9
Newbarn Kent 55 F7
New Barn Kent 68 F6
New Barnet London 86 F3
New Barnetby N Lincs 200 E5
Newbarns Cumb 210 E4
New Barton N Nhants 121 E7
New Basford Nottingham 171 G9
Newbattle Midloth 270 B6
New Beaupre V Glam 58 E4
New Beckenham London 67 E11
New Bewick Northumb 264 E3
Newbie Dumfries 238 D5
Newbiggin Cumb 210 F5
Cumb 211 D11
Cumb 219 G11
Cumb 230 F5
Cumb 231 B7
Cumb 231 F8
Durham 232 B5
Durham 232 F4
Durham 233 B8
NYorks 213 B9
NYorks 223 G9
Newbiggin-by-the-Sea
Northumb 253 F8
Newbigging Aberds 303 G7
Angus 287 D8
Borders 262 F6
Edin 280 F2
S Lanark 269 F10
New-bigging Angus 286 C6
Newbiggings Orkney 314 B6
Newbiggin Hall Estate
T&W 242 D6
Newbiggin-on-Lune
Cumb 222 D4
New Bilton Warks 119 B9
Newbold Derbys 186 G5
Gtr Man 196 E2
Leics 136 B5
Leics 153 F8
Newbold Heath Leics 135 B8
Newbold on Avon
Warks 119 B9
Newbold on Stour
Warks 100 B4
Newbold Pacey Warks 118 F5
Newbolds W Mid 133 C8
Newbold Verdon Leics 135 C8
New Bolingbroke Lincs 174 D4
New Bolsover Derbys 187 G7
Newborough Pboro 138 B4
Staffs 152 D2
New Boston Mers 183 B9
New Botley Oxon 83 D7
Newbottle T&W 243 G8
W Nhants 101 D10
New Boultham Lincs 189 G7
Newbourne Suff 108 C5
New Bradwell M Keynes 102 C6
New Brancepeth
Durham 233 C10
Newbridge Bath 61 F8
Caerph 78 F2
Ceredig 111 F10
Corn 1 C4
Corn 4 G5
Corn 7 B7
Dumfries 237 B11
Edin 280 G2
E Sus 52 G3
Hants 32 D3
IoW 20 D4
Lancs 204 F3
NYorks 216 B6
Oxon 82 E6
Pembs 91 E8
Shrops 148 D6
W Mid 133 D7
Wrex 166 G3
New Bridge Wrex 166 G3
Newbridge Green Worcs 98 D6
Newbridge-on-Usk Mon 78 G5
Newbridge-on-Wye
Powys 113 F10
New Brighton Flint 166 B3
Mers 182 C4
Wrex 166 E3
W Sus 22 B3
WYorks 197 B9
WYorks 205 F8
New Brimington Derbys 186 G6
New Brinsley Notts 171 E7
New Brotton Redcar 235 G9
Newbrough Northumb 241 D9
New Broughton Wrex 166 E4
New Buckenham Norf 141 E11
Newbuildings Devon 26 G3
New Buildings Bath 45 B7
Dorset 18 E5
Newburgh Aberds 303 D9
Aberds 303 G9
Borders 261 F8
Fife 286 F6
Lancs 194 E3
Newburn T&W 242 D5
Newbury Kent 54 B2
W Berks 64 F3
Wilts 45 E10
New Bury Gtr Man 195 F8
Newbury Park London 68 B2
Newby Cumb 231 G7
Lancs 204 D2
NYorks 205 D11
NYorks 212 E4
NYorks 215 F7
NYorks 225 C10
NYorks 227 G10
Newby Bridge Cumb 211 B7
Newby Cote N Yorks 212 E4
Newby East Cumb 239 F11
Newby Head Cumb 231 G7
New Byth Aberds 303 D8
Newby West Cumb 239 G9
Newby Wiske N Yorks 215 B7
Newcastle Bridgend 58 D2
Mon 78 B6
Shrops 130 G4
Newcastle Emlyn = *Castell*
Newydd Emlyn Carms 92 C6
Newcastleton or Copshaw
Holm Borders 249 F11

Newcastle-under-Lyme
Staffs 168 F4
Newcastle upon Tyne
T&W 242 E6
New Catton Norf 160 G4
Newchapel Powys 129 G9
Staffs 168 E5
Sur 51 E11
Newchapel =*Capel Newydd*
Pembs 92 D4
New Charlton London 68 D2
New Cheltenham S Glos 61 E7
New Cheriton Hants 33 B9
Newchurch Bl Gwent 77 C11
Carms 93 G7
Hereford 115 G7
IoW 21 D7
Kent 54 G5
Lancs 195 C10
Mon 79 F7
Powys 114 G4
Staffs 152 E2
Newchurch in Pendle
Lancs 204 F2
New Clipstone Notts 171 C9
New Costessey Norf 160 G3
Newcott Devon 28 F2
New Coundon Durham 233 E10
New Cowper Cumb 229 B8
Newcraighall Edin 280 G6
New Crofton W Yorks 197 D11
New Cross Ceredig 112 B2
London 67 D11
Oxon 65 D9
Som 28 D6
New Cross Gate London 67 D11
New Cumnock E Ayrs 258 G4
New Deer Aberds 303 E8
New Delaval Northumb 243 B7
New Delph Gtr Man 196 F3
New Denham Bucks 66 C4
Newdigate Sur 51 E7
New Downs Corn 1 C3
Corn 4 E4
New Duston W Nhants 120 E4
New Earswick York 207 B8
New Eastwood Notts 171 F7
New Edlington S Yorks 187 B8
New Elgin Moray 302 C2
New Ellerby E Yorks 209 F9
Newell Green Brack 65 E11
New Eltham London 68 E2
New End Lincs 190 G2
Warks 118 E2
Worcs 117 F11
Newenden Kent 38 B4
New England Essex 106 C4
Lincs 175 D8
Pboro 138 C3
Som 28 E4
Newent Glos 98 F4
Newerne Glos 79 E10
New Farnley W Yorks 205 G10
New Ferry Mers 182 D4
Newfield Durham 233 E10
Durham 242 G6
Highld 301 B7
Stoke 168 E6
New Fletton Pboro 138 D3
Newford Scilly 1 G4
Newfound Hants 48 C5
New Fryston W Yorks 198 B3
Newgale Pembs 90 G6
New Galloway Dumfries 237 B8
Newgarth Orkney 314 E2
Newgate Lancs 194 F4
Norf 177 E9
Newgate Corner Norf 161 G8
Newgate Street Herts 86 D4
New Gilston Fife 287 G8
New Greens Herts 85 D10
New Grimsby Scilly 1 F3
New Ground Herts 85 C7
Newgrounds Hants 31 E11
Newhailes Edin 280 G6
New Hainford Norf 160 F4
Newhall Ches E 167 F10
Derbys 152 E5
Newhall Green Warks 134 F5
New Hall Hey Lancs 195 C10
Newhall House Highld 300 C6
Newhall Point Highld 301 C7
Newham Lincs 174 E3
Northumb 264 D5
New Hartley Northumb 243 B8
Newhaven Derbys 169 C11
Devon 24 C5
Edin 280 F5
E Sus 36 G6
New Haw Sur 66 G5
Newhay N Yorks 207 G9
New Headington Oxon 83 D9
New Heaton Northumb 273 G7
New Hedges Pembs 73 E10
New Herrington T&W 243 G8
Newhey Gtr Man 196 E2
Newhill Fife 286 F6
Perth 286 G5
S Yorks 186 B6
Newhills Aberdeen 293 C10
New Hinksey Oxon 83 E8
New Ho Durham 232 D3
New Holkham Norf 159 B7
New Holland N Lincs 200 C5
W Yorks 205 F7
Newholm N Yorks 227 C7
New Horwich Derbys 185 E8
New Houghton Derbys 171 B7
Norf 158 D5
Newhouse Borders 262 E2
N Lanark 268 C5
Shetland 313 G6
New House Kent 68 E6
Newhouses Borders 271 G10
New Houses Gtr Man 194 G5
N Yorks 212 E6
New Humberstone
Leicester 136 B2
New Hunwick Durham 233 E9
New Hutton Cumb 221 G11
New Hythe Kent 53 B8
Newick E Sus 36 C6
Newingreen Kent 54 F6
Newington Edin 280 G5
Kent 55 F7
Kent 69 G11
Kent 71 F11
London 67 D10
Notts 187 C11
Oxon 83 F10
Shrops 131 G8
Newington Bagpath Glos 80 G4
New Inn Carms 93 D9
Devon 24 F6
Mon 79 E7
Pembs 91 E11
Torf 78 F4
New Invention Shrops 114 B5
W Mid 133 C9
New Kelso Highld 299 E9
New Kingston Notts 153 D10
New Kyo Durham 242 G5
New Ladykirk Borders 273 F7
New Lanark S Lanark 269 G7
Newland Cumb 210 D6
E Yorks 199 B10
Glos 79 D9
Hull 209 G7
N Yorks 199 C7
Oxon 82 C5
Worcs 98 B5
Newland Bottom Cumb 210 C5
Newland Common
Worcs 117 E8
Newland Green Kent 54 D2
Newlandrig Midloth 271 C7
Newlands Borders 250 E2
Borders 262 E2
Cumb 229 G10
Cumb 230 D2
Derbys 170 F6
Dumfries 247 F11
Glasgow 267 C11
Highld 301 E7
Moray 302 D3
Northumb 242 F3
Notts 171 C9
Staffs 151 E11
Newlands Corner Sur 50 D4
Newlandsmuir S Lanark 268 E2
Newlands of Geise
Highld 310 C4
Newlands of Tynet
Moray 302 C3
Newlands Park Anglesey 178 E3
New Lane Lancs 194 E2
New Lane End Warr 183 B10
New Langholm Dumfries 249 G9
New Leake Lincs 174 D6
New Leeds Aberds 303 D9
Newliston Edin 280 G2
Fife 280 C5
New Lodge S Yorks 197 F10
New Longton Lancs 194 B4
Newlot Orkney 314 E5
New Lubbesthorpe
Leics 135 C10
New Luce Dumfries 236 C3
Newlyn Corn 1 D5
Newmachar Aberds 293 B10
Newmains N Lanark 268 D6
New Malden London 67 F8
Newman's End Essex 87 C8
Newman's Green Suff 107 C7
Newman's Place Hereford 96 B5
Newmarket Glos 80 F4
Suff 124 E2
W Isles 304 E6
New Marske Redcar 235 G8
New Marston Oxon 83 D8
New Marton Shrops 148 C6
New Micklefield
W Yorks 206 G4
Newmill Borders 261 G11
Corn 1 C5
Moray 302 D4
New Mill Aberds 293 E9
Borders 262 G2
Corn 1 C5
Corn 4 F6
Cumb 219 E11
Herts 84 C6
Wilts 63 G7
W Yorks 197 F7
Newmillerdam
W Yorks 197 D10
Newmill of Inshewan
Angus 292 G6
Newmills Corn 11 D11
Fife 279 D10
Highld 300 C6
New Mills Borders 271 F10
Ches E 184 E3
Corn 5 E7
Derbys 185 D7
Glos 79 E10
Hereford 98 D4
New Mills =*Felin Newydd*
Powys 129 C11
Newmills of Boyne
Aberds 302 D5
Newmiln Perth 286 D5
Newmilns E Ayrs 258 B2
New Milton Hants 19 B10
New Mistley Essex 108 E2
New Moat Pembs 91 F11
Newmore Highld 300 B6
Highld 300 D5
New Moston Gtr Man 195 G11
Newnes Shrops 149 C7
Newney Green Essex 87 D11
Newnham Cambs 123 F8
Glos 79 C11
Hants 49 C8
Herts 104 D4
Kent 54 B3
Warks 118 E3
W Nhants 119 F11
Newnham Bridge Worcs 116 D2
New Ollerton Notts 171 B11
New Oscott W Mid 133 E11
New Pale Ches W 183 G8
Newpark Fife 287 F8
New Park N Yorks 205 B11
New Parks Leicester 135 B11
New Passage S Glos 60 B4
New Pitsligo Aberds 303 D8
New Polzeath Corn 10 F4
Newpool Staffs 168 D5
Newport Corn 12 D2
Devon 40 G5
Dorset 18 C3
Essex 105 E10
E Yorks 208 G3
Glos 79 F11
Highld 311 G5
IoW 20 D6
Newport 59 B10
Norf 161 F10
Som 28 C4
Telford 150 F4
Newport =*Trefdraeth*
Pembs 91 D11
Newport-on-Tay Fife 287 E8
Newport Pagnell
M Keynes 103 C7
Newpound Common
W Sus 35 B9
Newquay Corn 4 C6
New Quay =*Ceinewydd*
Ceredig 111 F7
New Rackheath Norf 160 G5
New Radnor Powys 114 E4
New Rent Cumb 230 D5
New Ridley Northumb 242 F3
New Road Side N Yorks 204 E5
W Yorks 197 B7
New Romney Kent 39 C9
New Rossington
S Yorks 187 B10
New Row Ceredig 112 C4
Lancs 203 F8
New Row *continued*
N Yorks 226 C2
Newsam Green
W Yorks 206 G3
New Sarum Wilts 46 G6
New Sawley Derbys 153 C9
Newsbank Ches E 168 B4
New Scarbro W Yorks 205 G10
Newseat Aberds 303 E10
Aberds 303 F7
Newsells Herts 105 D7
Newsham Lancs 202 F6
Northumb 243 B8
N Yorks 215 C7
N Yorks 224 C2
New Sharlston
W Yorks 197 C11
Newsholme E Yorks 199 B8
Lancs 204 C2
W Yorks 204 F6
New Silksworth T&W 243 G9
New Skelton Redcar 226 B3
New Smithy Derbys 185 E9
Newsome W Yorks 196 E6
New Southgate London 86 G3
New Springs Gtr Man 194 F6
New Sprowston Norf 160 G4
New Stanton Derbys 153 B9
Newstead Borders 262 C3
Northumb 264 D5
Notts 171 E8
Staffs 168 G5
W Yorks 197 E11
New Stevenston
N Lanark 268 D5
New Street Kent 68 G6
Staffs 169 E9
Newstreet Lane Shrops 150 B2
New Swanage Dorset 18 E6
New Swannington Leics 153 F8
Newtake Devon 14 G3
New Thirsk N Yorks 215 C8
Newthorpe Notts 171 F7
N Yorks 206 G5
Newthorpe Common
Notts 171 F7
New Thundersley Essex 69 B9
Newtoft Lincs 189 D8
Newton Argyll 275 D11
Borders 262 E3
Borders 262 F2
Bridgend 57 F10
Cambs 105 B8
Cambs 157 G8
Cardiff 59 D8
C Beds 104 C4
Ches W 166 B6
Ches W 167 D8
Ches W 183 F8
Corn 5 C11
Cumb 210 E4
Derbys 170 D6
Dorset 30 E3
Dumfries 239 C7
Dumfries 248 E4
Gtr Man 185 B7
Hereford 96 C5
Hereford 96 E6
Hereford 115 D7
Hereford 115 G10
Highld 301 C7
Highld 301 E7
Highld 306 F7
Highld 310 E7
Lancs 202 F2
Lancs 202 G4
Lancs 203 C9
Lancs 211 E11
Lincs 155 B10
Mers 182 D2
Moray 301 C11
N Nhants 137 G7
Norf 158 F6
Northumb 242 E2
Notts 171 G11
Perth 286 D2
S Glos 79 G10
Shetland 312 E5
Shetland 313 K5
Shrops 132 D4
Shrops 149 C8
S Lanark 259 C10
S Lanark 268 C3
Som 42 F6
Staffs 151 D10
Suff 107 C8
Swansea 56 D6
S Yorks 198 G5
Warks 119 B10
Wilts 32 C2
W Loth 279 F11
W Mid 133 E10
Newton Abbot Devon 14 G3
Newtonairds Dumfries 247 G9
Newton Arlosh Cumb 238 F5
Newton Aycliffe
Durham 233 G11
Newton Bewley Hrtlpl 234 F5
Newton Blossomville
M Keynes 121 G8
Newton Bromswold
N Nhants 121 D9
Newton Burgoland
Leics 135 B7
Newton by Toft Lincs 189 D9
Newton Cross Pembs 91 F7
Newton Ferrers Devon 7 F10
Newton Flotman Norf 142 D4
Newtongrange Midloth 270 C6
Newton Green Mon 79 G8
Newton Hall Durham 233 B11
Northumb 242 D2
Newton Harcourt Leics 136 D2
Newton Heath
Gtr Man 195 G11
Newtonhill Aberds 293 D11
Highld 300 E5
Newton Hill W Yorks 197 C10
Newton Ho Aberds 302 G6
Newton Hurst Staffs 151 D11
Newtonia Ches E 167 B11
Newton Ketton Darl 234 G2
Newton Kyme N Yorks 206 E5
Newton-le-Willows
Mers 183 B9
N Yorks 214 B4
Newton Leyes Milton
Keynes 103 E7
Newton Longville
Bucks 102 E6
Newton Mearns
E Renf 267 D10
Newtonmill Angus 293 G8
Newtonmore Highld 291 D9
Newton Morrell
N Yorks 224 D4
Oxon 102 F2
Newton Mulgrave
N Yorks 226 B5
Newton of Ardtoe
Highld 289 B8
Newton of Balcanquhal
Perth 286 F5
Newton of Balcormo
Fife 287 G9
Newton of Falkland
Fife 286 G6
Newton of Mountblairy
Aberds 302 D6
Newton of Pitcairns
Perth 286 F4
Newton on Ayr S Ayrs 257 E8
Newton on Ouse
N Yorks 206 B6
Newton-on-Rawcliffe
N Yorks 226 G6
Newton on the Hill
Shrops 149 E9
Newton on the Moor
Northumb 252 B5
Newton on Trent Lincs 188 G4
Newton Park Argyll 266 B2
Mers 183 C9
Newton Peveril Dorset 18 B4
Newton Poppleford
Devon 15 D7
Newton Purcell Oxon 102 E2
Newton Regis Warks 134 B5
Newton Reigny Cumb 230 E5
Newton Rigg Cumb 230 E5
Newton St Boswells
Borders 262 C3
Newton St Cyres Devon 14 B3
Newton St Faith Norf 160 F4
Newton St Loe Bath 61 G8
Newton St Petrock Devon 24 E6
Newton Solney Derbys 152 D5
Newton Stacey Hants 48 E2
Newton Stewart
Dumfries 236 C6
Newton Tony Wilts 47 E8
Newton Tracey Devon 25 B8
Newton under Roseberry
Redcar 225 C11
Newton Underwood
Northumb 252 F4
Newton upon Derwent
E Yorks 207 D10
Newton Valence Hants 49 G8
Newton with Scales
Lancs 202 G4
Newton Wood Gtr Man 184 B6
New Totley S Yorks 186 F4
Newtown Argyll 284 G4
BCP 18 C6
Bl Gwent 77 C11
Bucks 85 E7
Caerph 78 G2
Cambs 121 D11
Ches E 184 E6
Ches W 183 F8
Corn 2 D3
Corn 11 F11
Cumb 229 B7
Cumb 239 F9
Cumb 240 E2
Derbys 185 E7
Devon 26 B3
Dorset 29 G7
Falk 279 E9
Glos 79 E11
Glos 80 D3
Glos 99 E8
Gtr Man 194 F5
Gtr Man 195 G9
Hants 21 B8
Hants 32 C4
Hants 32 E3
Hants 33 D8
Hants 33 E10
Hants 33 F7
Hants 49 F8
Hants 49 G10
Hants 64 G3
Hereford 97 E10
Hereford 98 C2
Highld 290 C5
IoM 192 E4
IoW 20 C4
Mers 183 B7
Norf 143 B10
Northumb 252 C2
Northumb 263 C11
Northumb 264 D2
Oxon 65 C9
Powys 130 E2
Rhondda 77 F9
Shrops 132 C2
Shrops 149 C9
Shrops 149 E8
Som 28 E3
Som 43 F9
Staffs 133 C9
Staffs 168 C6
Staffs 169 C9
Wilts 30 B6
Wilts 63 G10
W Mid 133 F11
Worcs 116 F5
Worcs 117 E7
New Town Bath 45 B9
Bath 60 G5
Dorset 30 C3
Dorset 30 D6
Dorset 31 D7
Dorset 31 F7
Edin 280 G4
Edin 280 G5
E Loth 281 G8
E Sus 37 C7
Glos 99 E10
Kent 53 B7
Kent 68 E4
Lancs 203 F8
Luton 103 G11
Medway 69 G8
Oxon 100 F5
Reading 65 E8
Shetland 312 E6
Som 29 D9
Som 29 D11
Som 44 D3
Soton 33 E7
Swindon 63 C7
T&W 234 B2
T&W 243 E8
W Berks 64 D6
Wilts 46 C6
Wilts 63 E9
W Mid 133 B11
W Mid 133 E9
W Sus 35 B11
W Yorks 198 C3
Newtown-in-St Martin
Corn 2 E6
Newtown Linford Leics 135 B10
Newtown St Boswells
Borders 262 C3
Newtown Unthank Leics 135 C9
New Tredegar Caerph 77 E10
New Trows S Lanark 259 B8
Newtyle Angus 286 C6
New Ulva Argyll 275 E8
New Village E Yorks 209 G7
S Yorks 198 F5
New Walsoken Cambs 139 B9
New Waltham NE Lincs 201 G9
New Well Powys 113 B11
New Wells Powys 130 D3
New Whittington Derbys 186 F5
New Wimpole Cambs 104 B6
New Winton E Loth 281 G8
New Woodhouses
Shrops 167 G9
New Works Telford 132 B3
New Wortley W Yorks 205 G11
New Yatt Oxon 82 C5
Newyears Green London 66 B5
New York Lincs 174 D2
N Yorks 214 G3
T&W 243 C8
New Zealand Wilts 62 D4
Nextend Hereford 114 F6
Neyland Pembs 73 D7
Niarbyl IoM 192 E3
Nib Heath Shrops 149 F8
Nibley Glos 79 D11
S Glos 61 C7
Nibley Green Glos 80 F2
Nibon Shetland 312 F5
Nicholashayne Devon 27 D10
Nicholaston Swansea 56 D4
Nidd N Yorks 214 G6
Niddrie Edin 280 G5
Nigg Aberdeen 293 C11
Highld 301 B8
Nigg Ferry Highld 301 C7
Nightcott Som 26 B5
Nilig Denb 165 D8
Nimble Nook Gtr Man 196 G2
Nimlet S Glos 61 E8
Nimmer Som 28 E4
Nine Ashes Essex 87 E9
Ninebanks Northumb 241 G7
Nine Elms London 67 D9
Swindon 62 B6
Nine Maidens Downs Corn 2 B5
Nine Mile Burn Midloth 270 D3
Nineveh Worcs 116 C3
Worcs 116 E2
Ninewells Glos 79 C9
Nine Wells Pembs 90 G5
Ninfield E Sus 38 E2
Ningwood IoW 20 D3
Ningwood Common IoW 20 D3
Ninnes Bridge Corn 2 B2
Nisbet Borders 262 D5
Nisthouse Orkney 314 E3
Shetland 313 G7
Nithbank Dumfries 247 D9
Niton IoW 20 F6
Nitshill Glasgow 267 C10
Noah's Arks Kent 52 B5
Noah's Green Worcs 117 E10
Noak Bridge Essex 87 G11
Noak Hill Essex 87 G11
London 87 G8
Nob End Gtr Man 195 F9
Nobland Green Herts 86 B5
Noblethorpe S Yorks 197 F9
Nobold Shrops 149 G9
Nobottle W Nhants 120 E3
Nob's Crook Hants 33 C7
Nocton Lincs 173 C9
Noctorum Mers 182 D3
Nodmore W Berks 64 D2
Noel Park London 86 G4
Nogdam End Norf 143 C7
Nog Tow Lancs 202 G6
Noke Oxon 83 C8
Noke Street Medway 69 E8
Nolton Pembs 72 B5
Nolton Haven Pembs 72 B5
No Man's Heath Ches W 167 F8
Warks 134 B5
Nomansland Devon 26 E4
Herts 85 C11
Wilts 32 D3
No Man's Land Corn 6 D5
Hants 33 B8
Noneley Shrops 149 D9
Noness Shetland 313 L6
Nonikiln Highld 300 B6
Nonington Kent 55 C9
Nook Cumb 211 C10
Noon Nick W Yorks 205 F8
Noonsbrough Shetland 313 H4
Noonsun Ches E 184 F4
Noonvares Corn 2 C3
Noranside Angus 292 G6
Norbiton London 67 F7
Norbreck Blackpool 202 E2
Norbridge Hereford 98 C4
Norbury Ches E 167 F9
Derbys 169 G10
London 67 F10
Shrops 131 E7
Staffs 150 E5
Norbury Common
Ches E 167 F9
Norbury Junction Staffs 150 E5
Norbury Moor Gtr Man 184 D6
Norby N Yorks 215 C8
Shetland 313 H3
Norchard Worcs 116 D6
Norcote Glos 81 E8
Norcott Brook Ches W 183 E10
Norcross Blackpool 202 E2
Nordelph Norf 139 C11
Nordelph Corner Norf 141 C10
Norden Dorset 18 E4
Gtr Man 195 E11
Norden Heath Dorset 18 E4
Nordley Shrops 132 D3
Norham Northumb 273 F8
Norham West Mains
Northumb 273 F8
Nork Sur 51 B8
Norland Town W Yorks 196 C5
Norleaze Wilts 45 C11
Norley Ches W 183 G9
Devon 25 G8
Norley Common Sur 50 E4
Norleywood Hants 20 B3
Norlington E Sus 36 E6
Normacot Stoke 168 G6
Normanby N Lincs 199 D11
N Yorks 216 C4
Redcar 225 B10
Normanby-by-Spital
Lincs 189 D7
Normanby by Stow
Lincs 188 E5
Normanby le Wold
Lincs 189 B10
Norman Cross Cambs 138 E3
Normandy Sur 50 C2
Norman Hill Glos 80 F3
Norman's Bay E Sus 23 D11
Norman's Green Devon 27 G9
Normanston Suff 143 E10
Normanton Derby 152 C6
Leics 172 G4
Normanton *continued*
Lincs 172 F6
Notts 172 E2
Rutland 137 B8
Wilts 46 E6
W Yorks 197 C11
Normanton le Heath
Leics 153 G7
Normanton on Soar
Notts 153 E10
Normanton-on-the-Wolds
Notts 154 C2
Normanton on Trent
Notts 172 B3
Normanton Spring
S Yorks 186 E6
Normanton Turville
Leics 135 D9
Normoss Lancs 202 F2
Norney Sur 50 E2
Norr W Yorks 205 F7
Norrington Common
Wilts 61 G11
Norris Green Corn 7 B8
Mers 182 C5
Norris Hill Leics 152 F6
Norristhorpe W Yorks 197 C8
Norseman Orkney 314 E3
Northacre Norf 141 D9
North Acton London 67 C8
Northall Bucks 103 G9
Northallerton N Yorks 225 G7
Northall Green Norf 159 G9
Northam Devon 24 B6
Soton 32 E6
Northampton W Nhants 120 E5
North Anston S Yorks 187 E8
North Ascot Brack 66 F2
North Aston Oxon 101 F9
Northaw Herts 86 E3
Northay Devon 28 G5
Som 28 E3
North Ayre Shetland 312 F6
North Baddesley Hants 32 D5
North Ballachulish
Highld 290 G2
North Barrow Som 29 B10
North Barsham Norf 159 C8
North Batsom Som 41 G10
Northbeck Lincs 173 G9
North Beer Corn 12 C2
North Benfleet Essex 69 B9
North Bersted W Sus 22 C6
North Berwick E Loth 281 D11
North Bitchburn Durham 233 E9
North Blyth Northumb 253 G8
North Boarhunt Hants 33 E10
North Bockhampton BCP 19 B9
Northborough Pboro 138 B3
Northbourne BCP 19 B7
Kent 55 C10
North Bovey Devon 13 E10
North Bradley Wilts 45 C11
North Brentor Devon 12 E5
North Brewham Som 45 F8
Northbridge Street
E Sus 38 C2
Northbrook Dorset 17 C11
Hants 33 D9
Hants 48 F4
Oxon 101 G9
Wilts 46 C4
North Brook End Cambs 104 C5
North Broomage Falk 279 E7
North Buckland Devon 40 E3
North Burlingham Norf 161 G7
North Cadbury Som 29 B10
North Cairn Dumfries 236 B1
North Camp Hants 49 C11
North Carlton Lincs 188 F6
Notts 187 E9
North Carrine Argyll 255 G7
North Cave E Yorks 208 G3
North Cerney Glos 81 D8
North Chailey E Sus 36 C5
Northchapel W Sus 35 B7
North Charford Wilts 31 D11
North Charlton
Northumb 264 E5
North Cheam London 67 F8
North Cheriton Som 29 B11
Northchurch Herts 85 D7
North Cliff E Yorks 209 D10
North Cliffe E Yorks 208 F3
North Clifton Notts 188 G4
North Close Durham 233 E11
North Cockerington
Lincs 190 C5
North Coker Som 29 E8
North Collafirth
Shetland 312 E5
North Common S Glos 61 E7
Suff 125 B9
North Connel Argyll 289 F11
North Cornelly Bridgend 57 E10
North Corner Corn 3 F7
S Glos 61 C7
North Corriegills
N Ayrs 256 C2
North Corry Highld 289 D10
Northcote Devon 27 G11
North Cotes Lincs 201 G11
Northcott Corn 24 F2
Devon 12 C2
Devon 27 E9
Devon 27 F10
North Country Corn 4 G3
Northcourt Oxon 83 F8
North Court Som 41 F11
North Cove Suff 143 F9
North Cowton N Yorks 224 E5
North Craigo Angus 293 G8
North Crawley
M Keynes 103 C8
North Cray London 68 E3
North Creake Norf 159 B7
North Curry Som 28 B4
North Dalton E Yorks 208 C4
North Darley Corn 11 G11
North Dawn Orkney 314 F4
North Deighton N Yorks 206 C3
North Denes Norf 161 G10
Northdown Kent 71 E11
North Dronley Angus 287 D7
North Drumachter Lodge
Highld 291 F8
North Duffield N Yorks 207 F9
Northdyke Orkney 314 D2
North Dykes Cumb 230 D6
North Eastling Kent 54 B3
Northedge Derbys 170 B5
North Elham Kent 55 E7
North Elkington Lincs 190 C3
North Elmham Norf 159 E9
North Elmsall W Yorks 198 E3
North Elmshall W Yorks 198 E3
North Elphinestone
E Loth 281 G7
Northend Bath 61 F9
Bucks 84 G2
Essex 89 E7
Northend *continued*
Essex 105 D10
Warks 119 G7
North End Bath 60 G6
Bedford 103 B9
Bedford 121 F10
Bucks 102 F4
Bucks 102 F6
Cumb 239 F8
Devon 27 D10
Dorset 30 B4
Durham 233 C11
Essex 87 B11
Essex 106 D5
E Yorks 209 C9
E Yorks 209 E9
E Yorks 209 G11
Hants 31 D10
Hants 33 B9
Hants 64 G2
Leics 153 F11
Lincs 174 G2
Lincs 189 B8
Lincs 190 C5
Lincs 190 D6
Lincs 191 D7
Lincs 201 G10
London 67 B9
London 68 D4
N Lincs 200 C6
Norf 141 E10
Northumb 252 C4
N Som 60 F2
Ptsmth 33 G11
Som 28 B3
Wilts 81 G8
W Sus 35 F10
W Sus 35 G7
W Sus 51 F11
Northenden Gtr Man 184 C4
Northern Moor Gtr Man 184 C4
North Erradale Highld 307 L2
North Evington
Leicester 136 C2
North Ewster N Lincs 199 G10
North Fambridge Essex 88 F5
North Fearns Highld 295 B7
North Featherstone
W Yorks 198 C2
North Feltham London 66 E6
North Feorline N Ayrs 255 E10
North Ferriby E Yorks 200 B3
Northfield Aberdeen 293 C11
Borders 262 D3
Borders 273 B8
Edin 280 G5
E Yorks 200 B4
Highld 301 B7
M Keynes 103 C7
N Nhants 137 E7
Som 43 F9
W Mid 117 B10
Northfields Hants 33 B7
Lincs 137 B10
North Finchley London 86 G3
Northfleet Kent 68 E6
Northfleet Green Kent 68 E6
North Flobbets Aberds 303 F7
North Frodingham
E Yorks 209 C8
Northgate Lincs 156 D3
Som 27 B9
W Sus 51 F9
North Gluss Shetland 312 F5
North Gorley Hants 31 E11
North Green Norf 141 B10
Norf 142 F4
Suff 126 B6
Suff 126 E6
Suff 127 D7
North Greetwell Lincs 189 G8
North Grimston N Yorks 216 F6
North Halley Orkney 314 F5
North Halling Medway 69 F8
North Harrow London 66 B6
North Hayling Hants 22 C2
North Hazelrigg
Northumb 264 C3
North Heasley Devon 41 G8
North Heath W Berks 64 E3
W Sus 35 C9
North Hill Corn 11 F11
North Hillingdon London 66 C5
North Hinksey Oxon 83 D7
North Hinksey Village
Oxon 83 D7
North Ho Shetland 313 J5
North Holmwood Sur 51 D7
North Houghton Hants 47 G10
Northhouse Borders 249 B10
North Howden E Yorks 207 G11
North Huish Devon 8 D4
North Hyde London 66 D6
North Hykeham Lincs 172 B6
North Hylton T&W 243 F8
Northiam E Sus 38 B4
Northill C Beds 104 B2
Northington Glos 80 D2
Hants 48 F5
North Kelsey Lincs 200 G4
North Kelsey Moor
Lincs 200 G5
North Kensington London 67 C8
North Kessock Highld 300 E6
North Killingholme
N Lincs 200 D6
North Kilvington
N Yorks 215 B8
North Kilworth Leics 136 G2
North Kingston Hants 31 G11
North Kirkton Aberds 303 D11
North Kiscadale N Ayrs 256 D2
North Kyme Lincs 173 E11
North Laggan Highld 290 D4
North Lancing W Sus 35 F11
North Landing E Yorks 218 E4
Northlands Lincs 174 E4
Northlea Durham 243 G10
Northleach Glos 81 C10
North Lee Bucks 84 D4
North Lees N Yorks 214 E6
Northleigh Devon 15 B9
Devon 40 G6
North Leigh Kent 54 D6
Oxon 82 C5
North Leverton with
Habblesthorpe Notts 188 E3
Northlew Devon 12 B6
North Littleton Worcs 99 B11
North Looe Sur 67 G8
North Lopham Norf 141 G10
North Luffenham
Rutland 137 C8
North Marden W Sus 34 D4
North Marston Bucks 102 G5
North Middleton
Midloth 271 D7
Northumb 264 E2
North Millbrex Aberds 303 E8
North Molton Devon 26 B2
Northmoor Devon 24 D4
Northmoor *continued*
Oxon 82 E6
Northmoor Corner Som 43 G10
Northmoor Green or
Moorland Som 43 G10
North Moreton Oxon 64 B5
North Mosstown
Aberds 303 D10
North Motherwell
N Lanark 268 D4
North Moulsecoomb
Brighton 36 F4
Northmuir Angus 287 B7
North Mundham W Sus 22 C5
North Muskham Notts 172 D3
North Newbald E Yorks 208 F4
North Newington Oxon 101 D8
North Newnton Wilts 46 B6
North Newton Som 43 G9
Northney Hants 22 C2
North Nibley Glos 80 F2
North Oakley Hants 48 C4
North Ockendon London 68 C5
Northolt London 66 C6
Northop =*Llan-eurgain*
Flint 166 B2
Northop Hall Flint 166 B3
North Ormesby Mbro 234 G6
North Ormsby Lincs 190 C3
Northorpe Lincs 155 F11
Lincs 156 B4
Lincs 188 B5
W Yorks 197 C8
North Otterington
N Yorks 215 B7
Northover Som 29 C8
Som 44 F3
North Owersby Lincs 189 C9
Northowram W Yorks 196 B6
Northpark Argyll 275 G11
North Perrott Som 29 F7
North Petherton Som 43 G9
North Petherwin Corn 11 D11
North Pickenham Norf 141 B7
North Piddle Worcs 117 G9
North Poorton Dorset 16 B6
Northport Dorset 18 D4
North Port Argyll 284 E4
North Poulner Hants 31 F11
Northpunds Shetland 313 L6
North Queensferry Fife 280 E2
North Radworthy Devon 41 G9
North Rauceby Lincs 173 F8
North Reddish Gtr Man 184 C5
Northrepps Norf 160 B4
North Reston Lincs 190 E5
North Rigton N Yorks 205 D11
North Ripley Hants 19 B9
North Rode Ches E 168 B5
North Roe Shetland 312 E5
North Row Cumb 229 E10
North Runcton Norf 158 F2
North Sandwick
Shetland 312 D7
North Scale Cumb 210 F3
North Scarle Lincs 172 B5
North Seaton Northumb 253 F7
North Seaton Colliery
Northumb 253 F7
North Sheen London 67 D7
North Shian Argyll 289 E11
North Shields T&W 243 D9
North Shoebury Southend 70 B2
North Shore Blackpool 202 F2
Northside Aberds 303 D8
Orkney 314 D2
North Side Cumb 228 F6
Pboro 138 D5
North Skelmanae
Aberds 303 D9
North Skelton Redcar 226 B3
North Somercotes Lincs 190 B6
North Stainley N Yorks 214 D5
North Stainmore Cumb 222 B6
North Stifford Thurrock 68 C6
North Stoke Bath 61 F8
Oxon 64 B6
W Sus 35 E8
North Stoneham Hants 32 D6
Northstowe Cambs 123 D8
North Street Hants 31 D11
Hants 48 G6
Kent 54 B4
Medway 69 E10
W Berks 64 E6
North Sunderland
Northumb 264 C6
North Synton Borders 261 E11
North Tamerton Corn 12 B2
North Tawton Devon 25 G11
North Thoresby Lincs 190 B3
North Tidworth Wilts 47 D8
North Togston Northumb 252 C6
Northton Aberds 293 C9
Northtown Orkney 314 G4
Shetland 313 M5
North Town Devon 25 F8
Hants 49 C11
Som 29 B10
Som 44 E5
Windsor 65 C11
North Tuddenham
Norf 159 G10
Northumberland Heath
London 68 D4
Northville Torf 78 F3
North Walbottle T&W 242 D5
North Walney Cumb 210 F3
North Walsham Norf 160 C5
North Waltham Hants 48 D5
North Warnborough
Hants 49 C8
North Water Bridge
Angus 293 G8
North Waterhayne Devon 28 F3
North Watford Herts 85 F10
North Watten Highld 310 D6
Northway Devon 24 C5
Glos 99 E8
Som 27 B10
Swansea 56 D5
North Weald Bassett
Essex 87 E7
North Weirs Hants 32 G3
North Wembley London 67 B7
North Weston N Som 60 D3
Oxon 83 D11
North Wheatley Notts 188 D3
North Whilborough Devon 9 B7
North Whiteley Moray 302 E4
Northwich Ches W 183 G11
Northwick S Glos 60 B5
Som 43 D11
Worcs 116 F6
North Wick Bath 60 F5
North Widcombe Bath 44 B5
North Willingham
Lincs 189 D11
North Wingfield Derbys 170 B6

North Witham Lincs ... 155 E8
Northwold Norf ... 140 D5
Northwood Derbys ... 170 C3
IoW ... 20 C5
Kent ... 71 F11
London ... 85 G9
Mers ... 182 B6
Shrops ... 149 C9
Staffs ... 168 G5
Stoke ... 168 F5
Northwood Green Glos ... 80 B2
Northwood Hills London ... 85 G9
North Woolwich London ... 68 D2
North Wootton Dorset ... 29 E11
Norf ... 158 E2
Som ... 44 E5
North Wraxall Wilts ... 61 D10
North Wroughton
Swindon ... 63 C7
Norton Devon ... 9 E7
Devon ... 24 B3
E Sus ... 23 E7
Glos ... 99 G7
Halton ... 183 E9
Herts ... 104 E4
IoW ... 20 D2
Mon ... 78 B6
Notts ... 187 G9
N Som ... 59 G10
Powys ... 114 D6
Shrops ... 131 B11
Shrops ... 131 G9
Shrops ... 132 C4
Stockton ... 234 G4
Suff ... 125 D9
Swansea ... 56 D3
Swansea ... 56 D6
S Yorks ... 186 E5
S Yorks ... 198 D4
Wilts ... 61 C11
W Mid ... 133 G7
W Nhants ... 120 E2
Worcs ... 99 B10
Worcs ... 117 G7
W Sus ... 22 B6
W Sus ... 22 D5
Norton Ash Kent ... 70 G3
Norton Bavant Wilts ... 46 E2
Norton Bridge Staffs ... 151 C7
Norton Canes Staffs ... 133 B10
Norton Canon Hereford ... 97 B7
Norton Corner Norf ... 159 D11
Norton Disney Lincs ... 172 D5
Norton East Staffs ... 133 B10
Norton Ferris Wilts ... 45 F9
Norton Fitzwarren Som ... 27 B11
Norton Green Herts ... 104 G4
IoW ... 20 D2
Staffs ... 168 E6
W Mid ... 118 C3
Norton Hawkfield Bath ... 60 G5
Norton Heath Essex ... 87 E10
Norton in Hales Shrops ... 150 B4
Norton-in-the-Moors
Stoke ... 168 E5
Norton-Juxta-Twycross
Leics ... 134 B6
Norton-le-Clay N Yorks ... 215 E8
Norton Lindsey Warks ... 118 E4
Norton Little Green
Suff ... 125 D9
Norton Malreward Bath ... 60 F6
Norton Mandeville Essex ... 87 E9
Norton-on-Derwent
N Yorks ... 216 E5
Norton St Philip Som ... 45 B9
Norton Subcourse Norf ... 143 D8
Norton sub Hamdon Som ... 29 D7
Norton's Wood N Som ... 60 E2
Norton Woodseats
S Yorks ... 186 E5
Norwell Notts ... 172 C3
Norwell Woodhouse
Notts ... 172 C2
Norwich Norf ... 142 B4
Norwick Shetland ... 312 B8
Norwood Derbys ... 187 E7
Dorset ... 29 F8
Norwood End Essex ... 87 D9
Norwood Green London ... 66 D6
W Yorks ... 196 B6
Norwood Hill Sur ... 51 E8
Norwood New Town
London ... 67 E10
Norwoodside Cambs ... 139 D8
Noseley Leics ... 136 D4
Noss Highld ... 310 D7
Shetland ... 313 M5
Noss Mayo Devon ... 7 F11
Nosterfield N Yorks ... 214 C5
Nosterfield End Cambs ... 106 C2
Nostie Highld ... 295 C10
Notgrove Glos ... 100 G2
Nottage Bridgend ... 57 F10
Notter Corn ... 7 C7
Nottingham Nottingham ... 153 B11
Notting Hill London ... 67 C8
Nottington Dorset ... 17 E9
Notton Wilts ... 62 F2
W Yorks ... 197 E10
Nounsley Essex ... 88 C3
Noutard's Green Worcs ... 116 D5
Novar House Highld ... 300 C6
Nova Scotia Ches W ... 167 B10
Novers Park Bristol ... 60 F5
Noverton Glos ... 99 G9
Nowton Suff ... 125 E7
Nox Shrops ... 149 G8
Noyadd Trefawr Ceredig ... 92 B5
Noyadd Wilym Ceredig ... 92 C4
Nuffield Oxon ... 65 B7
Nun Appleton N Yorks ... 207 F7
Nunburnholme E Yorks ... 208 D2
Nuncargate Notts ... 171 E8
Nunclose Cumb ... 230 B5
Nuneaton Warks ... 135 E7
Nuneham Courtenay
Oxon ... 83 F9
Nuney Green Oxon ... 65 D7
Nunhead London ... 67 D11
Nun Hills Lancs ... 195 C11
Nun Monkton N Yorks ... 206 B6
Nunney Som ... 45 D8
Nunney Catch Som ... 45 E8
Nunnington N Yorks ... 216 D3
Nunnykirk Northumb ... 252 E3
Nunsthorpe NE Lincs ... 201 F9
Nunthorpe Mbro ... 225 C10
York ... 207 C8
Nunton Wilts ... 31 B11
Nunwick N Yorks ... 214 E6
Nupdown S Glos ... 79 F10
Nupend Glos ... 80 D3
Glos ... 80 F4
Nup End Bucks ... 84 B5
Herts ... 86 B2
Nuper's Hatch Essex ... 87 G8
Nuppend Glos ... 79 E10
Nuptown Brack ... 65 E11
Nursling Hants ... 32 D5
Nursted Hants ... 34 C3
Nursteed Wilts ... 62 G4
Nurston V Glam ... 58 F5
Nurton Staffs ... 132 D6
Nurton Hill Staffs ... 132 D6
Nutbourne W Sus ... 22 B3
W Sus ... 35 D9
Nutbourne Common
W Sus ... 35 D9
Nutburn Hants ... 32 C5
Nutcombe Sur ... 49 G11
Nutfield Sur ... 51 C10
Nut Grove Mers ... 183 C7
Nuthall Notts ... 171 G8
Nuthampstead Herts ... 105 E8
Nuthurst Warks ... 118 C3
W Sus ... 35 B11
Nutley E Sus ... 36 B6
Hants ... 48 E6
Nuttall Gtr Man ... 195 D9
Nutwell S Yorks ... 198 G6
Nybster Highld ... 310 C7
Nye N Som ... 60 G2
Nyetimber W Sus ... 22 D5
Nyewood W Sus ... 34 C4
Nyland Som ... 44 C3
Nymet Rowland Devon ... 26 F2
Nymet Tracey Devon ... 26 G2
Nympsfield Glos ... 80 E4
Nynehead Som ... 27 C10
Nythe Som ... 44 G2
Swindon ... 63 B7
Nyton W Sus ... 22 B6

O

Oadby Leics ... 136 C2
Oad Street Kent ... 69 G11
Oakall Green Worcs ... 116 E6
Oakamoor Staffs ... 169 G9
Oakbank W Loth ... 269 B11
Oak Bank Gtr Man ... 195 F10
Oak Cross Devon ... 12 B6
Oakdale BCP ... 18 C6
Caerph ... 77 F11
N Yorks ... 205 B11
Oake Som ... 27 B11
Oake Green Som ... 27 B11
Oaken Staffs ... 133 C7
Oakenclough Lancs ... 202 D6
Oakengates Telford ... 150 G4
Oakenholt Flint ... 182 G3
Oakenshaw Durham ... 233 D10
Lancs ... 203 G10
W Yorks ... 197 B7
Oakerthorpe Derbys ... 170 E5
Oakes W Yorks ... 196 D6
Oakfield Herts ... 104 F3
IoW ... 21 C7
Torf ... 78 G4
Oakford Ceredig ... 111 F9
Devon ... 26 C6
Oakfordbridge Devon ... 26 C6
Oakgrove Ches E ... 168 B6
M Keynes ... 103 D7
Oakham Rutland ... 137 B7
W Mid ... 133 F9
Oakhanger Ches E ... 168 E3
Hants ... 49 F9
Oakhill Som ... 44 D6
W Sus ... 51 G7
Oak Hill Stoke ... 168 G5
Suff ... 109 B7
Oakhurst Kent ... 52 C4
Oakington Cambs ... 123 E8
Oaklands Carms ... 74 B6
Herts ... 86 B2
Powys ... 113 G10
Oakleigh Park London ... 86 G3
Oakle Street Glos ... 80 B3
Oakley BCP ... 18 B6
Bedford ... 121 G10
Bucks ... 83 C10
Fife ... 279 D10
Glos ... 99 G9
Hants ... 48 C5
Oxon ... 84 E3
Staffs ... 150 B4
Suff ... 126 B3
Oakley Court Oxon ... 64 B6
Oakley Green Windsor ... 66 D2
Oakley Park Powys ... 129 F9
Suff ... 126 B3
Oakley Wood Oxon ... 64 B6
Oakmere Ches W ... 167 B9
Oakridge Glos ... 80 E6
Hants ... 48 C6
Oakridge Lynch Glos ... 80 E6
Oaks Shrops ... 131 C8
Oaksey Wilts ... 81 G7
Oaks Green Derbys ... 152 C3
Oakshaw Ford Cumb ... 240 B2
Oakshott Hants ... 34 B2
Oaks in Charnwood
Leics ... 153 F9
Oakthorpe Leics ... 152 G6
Oak Tree Darl ... 225 C7
Oakwell W Yorks ... 197 B8
Oakwood Derby ... 153 B7
London ... 86 F3
Northumb ... 241 D10
Warr ... 183 C11
W Yorks ... 206 F2
Oakwoodhill Sur ... 50 F6
Oakworth W Yorks ... 204 F6
Oape Highld ... 309 J4
Oare Kent ... 70 G4
Som ... 41 D10
W Berks ... 64 E4
Wilts ... 63 G7
Oareford Som ... 41 D10
Oasby Lincs ... 155 B10
Oath Som ... 28 B5
Oathill Dorset ... 28 F6
Oathlaw Angus ... 287 B8
Oatlands Glasgow ... 267 C11
N Yorks ... 205 C11
Oatlands Park Sur ... 66 G5
Oban Argyll ... 289 G10
Highld ... 295 G10
W Isles ... 305 H3
Obley Shrops ... 114 B6
Oborne Dorset ... 29 D11
Obthorpe Lincs ... 155 F11
Obthorpe Lodge Lincs ... 156 F2
Occlestone Green
Ches W ... 167 C11
Occold Suff ... 126 C3
Ocean Village Soton ... 32 E6
Ochiltree E Ayrs ... 258 E2
Ochr-y-foel Denb ... 181 F9
Ochtermuthill Perth ... 286 F2
Ochtertyre Perth ... 286 E2
Ochtow Highld ... 309 J4
Ockbrook Derbys ... 153 B8
Ocker Hill W Mid ... 133 E9
Ockeridge Worcs ... 116 E5
Ockford Ridge Sur ... 50 E3
Ockham Sur ... 50 B5
Ockle Highld ... 289 B7
Ockley Sur ... 50 F6
Ocle Pychard Hereford ... 97 B11
Octon E Yorks ... 217 F10
Octon Cross Roads
E Yorks ... 217 F10
Odam Barton Devon ... 26 D2
Odcombe Som ... 29 D8
Odd Down Bath ... 61 G8
Oddendale Cumb ... 221 C11
Odder Lincs ... 188 G6
Oddingley Worcs ... 117 F8
Oddington Glos ... 100 F4
Oxon ... 83 C9
Odell Bedford ... 121 F9
Odham Devon ... 25 G7
Odie Orkney ... 314 D6
Odiham Hants ... 49 C8
Odsal W Yorks ... 197 B7
Odsey Cambs ... 104 D5
Odstock Wilts ... 31 B10
Odstone Leics ... 135 B7
Offchurch Warks ... 119 D7
Offenham Worcs ... 99 B11
Offenham Cross Worcs ... 99 B11
Offerton Gtr Man ... 184 D6
T&W ... 243 F8
Offerton Green Gtr Man ... 184 D6
Offham E Sus ... 36 E5
Kent ... 53 B7
W Sus ... 35 F8
Offleyhay Staffs ... 150 D5
Offleymarsh Staffs ... 150 D5
Offleyrock Staffs ... 150 D5
Offord Cluny Cambs ... 122 D4
Offord D'Arcy Cambs ... 122 D4
Offton Suff ... 107 B11
Offwell Devon ... 15 B9
Ogbourne Maizey Wilts ... 63 E7
Ogbourne St Andrew
Wilts ... 63 E7
Ogbourne St George
Wilts ... 63 E8
Ogden W Yorks ... 205 G7
Ogdens Hants ... 31 E11
Ogil Angus ... 292 G6
Ogle Northumb ... 242 B4
Ogmore V Glam ... 57 F11
Ogmore-by-Sea = Aberogwr
V Glam ... 57 F11
Ogmore Vale Bridgend ... 76 G6
Okeford Fitzpaine Dorset ... 30 E4
Okehampton Devon ... 13 B7
Okehampton Camp
Devon ... 13 C7
Oker Derbys ... 170 C3
Okewood Hill Sur ... 50 F6
Okle Green Glos ... 98 F5
Okraquoy Shetland ... 313 K6
Okus Swindon ... 62 C6
Olchard Devon ... 14 F3
Old W Nhants ... 120 C5
Old Aberdeen
Aberdeen ... 293 C11
Old Alresford Hants ... 48 G5
Oldany Highld ... 306 F6
Old Arley Warks ... 134 E5
Old Balornock Glasgow ... 268 B2
Old Basford Nottingham ... 171 G8
Old Basing Hants ... 49 C7
Old Belses Borders ... 262 E3
Oldberrow Warks ... 118 D2
Old Bewick Northumb ... 264 E3
Old Bexley London ... 68 E3
Old Blair Perth ... 291 G10
Old Bolingbroke Lincs ... 174 B4
Oldborough Devon ... 26 F3
Old Boston Mers ... 183 B9
Old Bramhope
W Yorks ... 205 E10
Old Brampton Derbys ... 186 G4
Old Bridge of Tilt
Perth ... 291 G10
Old Bridge of Urr
Dumfries ... 237 C9
Oldbrook M Keynes ... 103 D7
Old Buckenham Norf ... 141 E11
Old Burdon T&W ... 243 G9
Old Burghclere Hants ... 48 B3
Oldbury Kent ... 52 B5
Shrops ... 132 E4
Warks ... 134 E6
W Mid ... 133 F9
Oldbury Naite S Glos ... 79 G10
Oldbury-on-Severn
S Glos ... 79 G10
Oldbury on the Hill Glos ... 61 B10
Old Byland N Yorks ... 215 B11
Old Cambus Borders ... 272 B6
Old Cardinham Castle
Corn ... 6 B2
Old Carlisle Cumb ... 229 B11
Old Cassop Durham ... 234 D2
Oldcastle Mon ... 96 G6
Oldcastle Heath Ches W ... 167 F7
Old Castleton Borders ... 250 E2
Old Catton Norf ... 160 G4
Old Chalford Oxon ... 100 F6
Old Church Stoke
Powys ... 130 E5
Old Clee NE Lincs ... 201 F9
Old Cleeve Som ... 42 E4
Old Colwyn Conwy ... 180 F5
Old Coppice Shrops ... 131 B9
Old Corry Highld ... 295 C8
Oldcotes Notts ... 187 D9
Old Coulsdon London ... 51 B10
Old Country Hereford ... 98 C4
Old Craig Aberds ... 303 G9
Angus ... 292 G4
Oldcroft Glos ... 79 D10
Old Crombie Aberds ... 302 D5
Old Cryals Kent ... 53 E7
Old Cullen Moray ... 302 C5
Old Dailly S Ayrs ... 244 D6
Old Dalby Leics ... 154 E3
Old Dam Derbys ... 185 F10
Old Deer Aberds ... 303 E9
Old Denaby S Yorks ... 187 B7
Old Ditch Som ... 44 D4
Old Dolphin W Yorks ... 205 G8
Old Down S Glos ... 60 B6
Old Duffus Moray ... 301 C11
Old Edlington S Yorks ... 187 B8
Old Eldon Durham ... 233 F10
Old Ellerby E Yorks ... 209 F9
Oldend Glos ... 80 D3
Old Fallings W Mid ... 133 C8
Oldfallow Staffs ... 151 G9
Old Farm Park
M Keynes ... 103 D8
Old Felixstowe Suff ... 108 D6
Oldfield Cumb ... 229 F7
Shrops ... 132 F3
Worcs ... 116 E6
W Yorks ... 196 E6
W Yorks ... 204 F6
Old Field Shrops ... 115 B9
Oldfield Brow Gtr Man ... 184 D3
Oldfield Park Bath ... 61 G8
Old Fletton Pboro ... 138 D3
Old Fold T&W ... 243 E7
Oldford Som ... 45 C9
Old Ford London ... 67 C11
Old Forge Hereford ... 79 B9
Oldfurnace Staffs ... 169 G8
Old Furnace Torf ... 78 E3
Old Gate Lincs ... 157 E8
Old Glossop Derbys ... 185 C8
Old Goginan Ceredig ... 128 G3
Old Goole E Yorks ... 199 C8
Old Gore Hereford ... 98 F2
Old Graitney Dumfries ... 239 D8
Old Grimsby Scilly ... 1 F3
Oldhall Renfs ... 267 C10
Old Hall Powys ... 129 G8
Oldhall Green Suff ... 125 F7
Old Hall Green Herts ... 105 G7
Oldhall Ho Highld ... 310 D6
Old Hall Street Norf ... 160 C6
Oldham Gtr Man ... 196 F2
Oldham Edge Gtr Man ... 196 F2
Oldhamstocks E Loth ... 282 G4
Old Harlow Essex ... 87 C7
Old Hatfield Herts ... 86 D2
Old Heath Essex ... 107 G10
Old Heathfield E Sus ... 37 C9
Old Hill W Mid ... 133 F9
Old Hills Worcs ... 98 B6
Old Hunstanton Norf ... 175 G11
Oldhurst Cambs ... 122 B6
Old Hurst Cambs ... 122 B5
Old Hutton Cumb ... 211 B11
Oldington Shrops ... 132 D4
Old Johnstone Dumfries ... 248 D6
Old Kea Corn ... 4 G6
Old Kilpatrick W Dunb ... 277 G9
Old Kinnernie Aberds ... 293 C9
Old Knebworth Herts ... 104 G4
Oldland S Glos ... 61 E7
Oldland Common S Glos ... 61 E7
Old Langho Lancs ... 203 F10
Old Laxey IoM ... 192 D5
Old Leake Lincs ... 174 E6
Old Leckie Stirling ... 278 C3
Old Lindley W Yorks ... 196 D5
Old Linslade C Beds ... 103 F8
Old Llanberis = Nant Peris
Gwyn ... 163 D10
Old Malden London ... 67 F8
Old Malton N Yorks ... 216 E5
Old Marton Shrops ... 148 C6
Old Mead Essex ... 105 F10
Oldmeldrum Aberds ... 303 G8
Old Micklefield
W Yorks ... 206 G4
Old Mill Corn ... 12 G3
Old Milton Hants ... 19 C10
Old Milverton Warks ... 118 D5
Oldmixon N Som ... 43 B10
Old Monkland N Lanark ... 268 C4
Old Nenthorn Borders ... 262 B5
Old Netley Hants ... 33 F7
Old Neuadd Powys ... 129 F11
Old Newton Suff ... 125 E11
Old Oak Common London ... 67 C8
Old Park Corn ... 6 B4
Telford ... 132 B3
Old Passage S Glos ... 60 B5
Old Perton Staffs ... 133 D7
Old Philpstoun W Loth ... 279 F11
Old Polmont Falk ... 279 F8
Old Portsmouth Ptsmth ... 21 B8
Old Quarrington
Durham ... 234 D2
Old Radnor Powys ... 114 F5
Old Rattray Aberds ... 303 D10
Old Rayne Aberds ... 302 G6
Old Romney Kent ... 39 B8
Old Shirley Soton ... 32 E5
Oldshore Beg Highld ... 306 D6
Old Shoreham W Sus ... 36 F2
Oldshoremore Highld ... 306 D7
Old Snydale W Yorks ... 198 C2
Old Sodbury S Glos ... 61 C9
Old Somerby Lincs ... 155 C9
Oldstead N Yorks ... 215 C10
Old Stillington Stockton ... 234 G3
Old Storridge Common
Worcs ... 116 G4
Old Stratford W Nhants ... 102 C5
Old Struan Perth ... 291 G10
Old Swan Mers ... 182 C5
Old Swarland Northumb ... 252 C5
Old Swinford W Mid ... 133 G8
Old Tame Gtr Man ... 196 F3
Old Tebay Cumb ... 222 D2
Old Thirsk N Yorks ... 215 C8
Old Tinnis Borders ... 261 D9
Old Toll S Ayrs ... 257 E9
Oldtown Aberds ... 293 C7
Aberds ... 302 G5
Highld ... 309 L5
Old Town Cumb ... 211 C11
Cumb ... 230 C5
Edin ... 280 G5
E Sus ... 23 F9
E Sus ... 38 F2
E Sus ... 38 F4
E Yorks ... 218 F3
Herts ... 104 F4
Scilly ... 1 G4
Swindon ... 63 C7
W Yorks ... 196 B3
Oldtown of Ord Aberds ... 302 D6
Old Trafford Gtr Man ... 184 B4
Old Tree Kent ... 71 G8
Old Tupton Derbys ... 170 B5
Oldwalls Swansea ... 56 C3
Old Warden C Beds ... 104 C2
Old Warren Flint ... 166 C4
Oldway Swansea ... 56 D5
Torbay ... 9 C7
Old Way Som ... 28 D5
Oldways End Devon ... 26 B5
Old Weston Cambs ... 121 B11
Old Wharf Hereford ... 98 D4
Oldwhat Aberds ... 303 D8
Old Whittington Derbys ... 186 G5
Oldwich Lane W Mid ... 118 C4
Old Wick Highld ... 310 D7
Old Wimpole Cambs ... 122 G6
Old Windsor Windsor ... 66 E3
Old Wingate Durham ... 234 D3
Old Wives Lees Kent ... 54 C5
Old Woking Sur ... 50 B4
Old Wolverton
M Keynes ... 102 C6
Oldwood Worcs ... 115 D11
Old Woodhall Lincs ... 174 B2
Old Woodhouses
Shrops ... 167 G9
Old Woodstock Oxon ... 82 B6
Olgrinmore Highld ... 310 D4
Olive Green Staffs ... 152 F2
Oliver's Battery Hants ... 33 B7
Ollaberry Shetland ... 312 E5
Ollag W Isles ... 297 G3
Ollerbrook Booth
Derbys ... 185 D10
Ollerton Ches E ... 184 F3
Notts ... 171 B11
Ollerton *continued*
Shrops ... 150 D2
Ollerton Fold Lancs ... 194 C6
Ollerton Lane Shrops ... 150 D3
Olmarch Ceredig ... 112 F2
Olmstead Green Essex ... 106 C2
Olney M Keynes ... 121 G7
Olrig Ho Highld ... 310 C5
Olton W Mid ... 134 G2
Olveston S Glos ... 60 B6
Olwen Ceredig ... 93 B11
Ombersley Worcs ... 116 E6
Ompton Notts ... 171 B11
Omunsgarth Shetland ... 313 J5
Onchan IoM ... 192 E4
Onecote Staffs ... 169 D9
Onehouse Suff ... 125 F10
Onen Mon ... 78 C6
Onesacre S Yorks ... 186 C3
Ongar Hill Norf ... 157 E11
Ongar Street Hereford ... 115 D7
Onibury Shrops ... 115 B9
Onich Highld ... 290 G2
Onllwyn Neath ... 76 C4
Onneley Staffs ... 168 G3
Onslow Village Sur ... 50 D3
Onthank E Ayrs ... 267 G8
Onziebust Orkney ... 314 D4
Openshaw Gtr Man ... 184 B5
Openwoodgate Derbys ... 170 F5
Opinan Highld ... 299 B7
Highld ... 307 K3
Orange Lane Borders ... 272 G5
Orange Row Norf ... 157 E10
Orasaigh W Isles ... 305 G5
Orbiston N Lanark ... 268 D4
Orbliston Moray ... 302 D3
Orbost Highld ... 298 E2
Orby Lincs ... 175 B7
Orchard Hill Devon ... 24 B6
Orchard Leigh Bucks ... 85 E7
Orchard Portman Som ... 28 C2
Orcheston Wilts ... 46 D5
Orcop Hereford ... 97 F9
Orcop Hill Hereford ... 97 F9
Ord Highld ... 295 D8
Ordale Shetland ... 312 C8
Ordhead Aberds ... 293 B8
Ordie Aberds ... 292 C6
Ordiequish Moray ... 302 D3
Ordiqhill Aberds ... 302 D5
Ordley Northumb ... 241 F10
Ordsall Gtr Man ... 184 B4
Notts ... 187 E11
Ore E Sus ... 38 E4
Oreston Plym ... 7 E10
Oreton Shrops ... 132 G3
Orford Suff ... 109 B8
Warr ... 183 C10
Organford Dorset ... 18 C4
Orgreave Staffs ... 152 F3
S Yorks ... 186 D6
Oridge Street Glos ... 98 F5
Orlandon Pembs ... 72 D4
Orlestone Kent ... 54 G3
Orleton Hereford ... 115 D9
Worcs ... 116 D3
Orleton Common
Hereford ... 115 D9
Orlingbury N Nhants ... 121 C7
Ormacleit W Isles ... 297 H3
Ormathwaite Cumb ... 229 F11
Ormesby Redcar ... 225 B10
Ormesby St Margaret
Norf ... 161 G9
Ormesby St Michael
Norf ... 161 G9
Ormiclate Castle
W Isles ... 297 H3
Ormidale Lodge Argyll ... 275 F11
Ormiscaig Highld ... 307 K3
Ormiston Borders ... 262 G2
E Loth ... 271 B8
Ormsaigbeg Highld ... 288 C6
Ormsaigmore Highld ... 288 C6
Ormsary Argyll ... 275 F8
Ormsgill Cumb ... 210 E3
Ormskirk Lancs ... 194 F2
Ornsby Hill Durham ... 233 B9
Orpington London ... 68 F3
Orrell Gtr Man ... 194 F4
Mers ... 182 B4
Orrell Post Gtr Man ... 194 G4
Orrisdale IoM ... 192 C4
Orrock Fife ... 280 D4
Orroland Dumfries ... 237 E9
Orsett Thurrock ... 68 C6
Orsett Heath Thurrock ... 68 D6
Orslow Staffs ... 150 F6
Orston Notts ... 172 G3
Orthwaite Cumb ... 229 E11
Ortner Lancs ... 202 C6
Orton Cumb ... 222 D2
N Nhants ... 120 B6
Staffs ... 133 D7
Orton Brimbles Pboro ... 138 D3
Orton Goldhay Pboro ... 138 D3
Orton Longueville
Pboro ... 138 D3
Orton Malborne Pboro ... 138 D3
Orton-on-the-Hill Leics ... 134 C6
Orton Rigg Cumb ... 239 G8
Orton Southgate Pboro ... 138 E2
Orton Waterville Pboro ... 138 D3
Orton Wistow Pboro ... 138 D2
Orwell Cambs ... 123 G7
Osbaldeston Lancs ... 203 G8
Osbaldeston Green
Lancs ... 203 G8
Osbaldwick York ... 207 C8
Osbaston Leics ... 135 C8
Shrops ... 148 E6
Telford ... 149 F11
Osbaston Hollow Leics ... 135 B8
Osbournby Lincs ... 155 B11
Oscroft Ches W ... 167 B8
Ose Highld ... 298 E3
Osea Island Essex ... 88 D6
Osehill Green Dorset ... 29 F11
Osgathorpe Leics ... 153 F8
Osgodby Lincs ... 189 C9
N Yorks ... 207 G8
N Yorks ... 217 C11
Osgodby Common
N Yorks ... 207 F8
Osidge London ... 86 G3
Oskaig Highld ... 295 B7
Oskamull Argyll ... 288 E6
Osleston Derbys ... 152 B4
Osmaston Derby ... 153 C7
Derbys ... 170 G2
Osmington Dorset ... 17 E10
Osmington Mills Dorset ... 17 E10
Osmondthorpe W Yorks ... 206 G2
Osmotherley N Yorks ... 225 F9
Osney Oxon ... 83 D8
Ospisdale Highld ... 309 L7
Ospringe Kent ... 70 G4
Ossaborough Devon ... 40 E3
Ossemsley Hants ... 19 B10
Osset Spa W Yorks ... 197 D9
Ossett W Yorks ... 197 C9
Ossett Street Side
W Yorks ... 197 C9
Ossington Notts ... 172 C3
Ostend Essex ... 88 F6
Norf ... 161 C7
Osterley London ... 66 D6
Oswaldkirk N Yorks ... 216 D2
Oswaldtwistle Lancs ... 195 B8
Oswestry Shrops ... 148 D5
Otby Lincs ... 189 C10
Oteley Shrops ... 149 C8
Otford Kent ... 52 B4
Otham Kent ... 53 C9
Otham Hole Kent ... 53 C10
Otherton Staffs ... 151 G8
Othery Som ... 43 G11
Otley Suff ... 126 F4
W Yorks ... 205 D10
Otterbourne Hants ... 33 C7
Otterburn Northumb ... 251 E9
N Yorks ... 204 B3
Otterburn Camp
Northumb ... 251 D9
Otterden Place Kent ... 54 C2
Otter Ferry Argyll ... 275 E10
Otterford Som ... 28 E2
Otterham Corn ... 11 C9
Otterhampton Som ... 43 E8
Otterham Quay Kent ... 69 F10
Otterham Station Corn ... 11 D9
Otter Ho Argyll ... 275 F10
Ottershaw Sur ... 66 G4
Otterspool Mers ... 182 D5
Otterswick Shetland ... 312 E7
Otterton Devon ... 15 D7
Otterwood Hants ... 32 G6
Ottery St Mary Devon ... 15 B8
Ottinge Kent ... 55 E7
Ottringham E Yorks ... 201 C9
Oughterby Cumb ... 239 F7
Oughtershaw N Yorks ... 213 C7
Oughterside Cumb ... 229 C8
Oughtibridge S Yorks ... 186 C4
Oughtrington Warr ... 183 D11
Oulston N Yorks ... 215 E10
Oulton Cumb ... 238 G6
Norf ... 160 D2
Staffs ... 150 E5
Staffs ... 151 B8
Suff ... 143 D10
W Yorks ... 197 B11
Oulton Broad Suff ... 143 E10
Oultoncross Staffs ... 151 C8
Oulton Grange Staffs ... 151 B8
Oulton Heath Staffs ... 151 B8
Oulton Street Norf ... 160 D3
Oundle N Nhants ... 137 F10
Ounsdale Staffs ... 133 E7
Ousby Cumb ... 231 E8
Ousdale Highld ... 311 G4
Ousden Suff ... 124 F4
Ousefleet E Yorks ... 199 C10
Ousel Hole W Yorks ... 205 E8
Ouston Durham ... 243 G7
Northumb ... 241 G7
Northumb ... 242 C3
Outcast Cumb ... 210 D6
Out Elmstead Kent ... 55 C8
Outer Hope Devon ... 8 G3
Outertown Orkney ... 314 E2
Outgate Cumb ... 221 F7
Outhgill Cumb ... 222 E5
Outhill Warks ... 118 D2
Outhills Aberds ... 303 D10
Outlands Staffs ... 150 C5
Outlane W Yorks ... 196 D5
Outlane Moor W Yorks ... 196 D5
Outlet Village Ches W ... 182 G6
Outmarsh Wilts ... 61 G11
Out Newton E Yorks ... 201 C11
Out Rawcliffe Lancs ... 202 E4
Outwell Norf ... 139 C10
Outwick Hants ... 31 D10
Outwood Gtr Man ... 195 F9
Som ... 28 B4
Sur ... 51 D10
W Yorks ... 197 C10
Outwoods Leics ... 153 F8
Staffs ... 150 F5
Staffs ... 152 E4
Warks ... 134 G4
Ouzlewell Green
W Yorks ... 197 B10
Ovenden W Yorks ... 196 B5
Ovenscloss Borders ... 261 C11
Over Cambs ... 123 C7
Ches W ... 167 B10
Glos ... 80 B4
S Glos ... 60 C5
Overa Farm Stud Norf ... 141 F9
Overbister Orkney ... 314 B6
Over Burrow Lancs ... 212 D2
Over Burrows Derbys ... 152 B5
Overbury Worcs ... 99 D9
Overcombe Dorset ... 17 E9
Over Compton Dorset ... 29 D9
Overend W Mid ... 133 G9
Over End Cambs ... 137 E11
Derbys ... 186 G3
Overgreen Derbys ... 186 G4
Over Green W Mid ... 134 E3
Over Haddon Derbys ... 170 B2
Over Hulton Gtr Man ... 195 F7
Over Kellet Lancs ... 211 E10
Over Kiddington Oxon ... 101 G8
Over Knutsford Ches E ... 184 F3
Over Langshaw
Borders ... 271 G10
Overleigh Som ... 44 F3
Overley Staffs ... 152 F3
Overley Green Warks ... 117 F11
Over Monnow Mon ... 79 C8
Overmoor Staffs ... 169 F7
Over Norton Oxon ... 100 F6
Over Peover Ches E ... 184 G3
Overpool Ches W ... 182 F5
Overs Shrops ... 131 D7
Overscaig Hotel Highld ... 309 G4
Overseal Derbys ... 152 F5
Over Silton N Yorks ... 225 G9
Overslade Warks ... 119 C9
Oversland Kent ... 54 B5
Oversley Green Warks ... 117 F11
Overstone W Nhants ... 120 D6
Over Stowey Som ... 43 F7
Overstrand Norf ... 160 A4
Over Stratton Som ... 28 D6
Over Tabley Ches E ... 184 E2
Overthorpe W Nhants ... 101 C9
W Yorks ... 197 D8
Overton Aberdeen ... 293 B10
Aberds ... 293 B9
Ches W ... 183 F8
Dumfries ... 237 C11
Glos ... 80 C2
Hants ... 48 D4
Invclyd ... 276 G5
Lancs ... 202 B4
N Yorks ... 207 B7
Shrops ... 115 C10
Overton *continued*
Staffs ... 151 B10
Swansea ... 56 D3
W Yorks ... 197 D9
Overton = Owrtyn Wrex ... 166 G5
Overton Bridge Wrex ... 166 G5
Overtown Lancs ... 212 D2
N Lanark ... 268 E6
Swindon ... 63 D7
W Yorks ... 197 D11
Over Town Lancs ... 195 B11
Over Wallop Hants ... 47 F9
Over Whitacre Warks ... 134 E5
Over Worton Oxon ... 101 F8
Oving Bucks ... 102 G5
W Sus ... 22 C6
Ovingdean Brighton ... 36 G5
Ovingham Northumb ... 242 E3
Ovington Durham ... 224 C2
Essex ... 106 C5
Hants ... 48 G5
Norf ... 141 C8
Northumb ... 242 E3
Owen's Bank Staffs ... 152 D4
Ower Hants ... 32 D4
Owermoigne Dorset ... 17 D11
Owlbury Shrops ... 130 E6
Owlcotes Derbys ... 170 B6
Owl End Cambs ... 122 B4
Owler Bar Derbys ... 186 F3
Owlerton S Yorks ... 186 D4
Owlet W Yorks ... 205 F9
Owlpen Glos ... 80 F4
Owl's Green Suff ... 126 D5
Owlsmoor Brack ... 65 G11
Owlswick Bucks ... 84 D3
Owlthorpe S Yorks ... 186 E6
Owmby Lincs ... 200 G5
Owmby-by-Spital Lincs ... 189 D8
Ownham W Berks ... 64 E2
Owrtyn = Overton Wrex ... 166 G5
Owslebury Hants ... 33 C8
Owston Leics ... 136 B5
S Yorks ... 198 E5
Owston Ferry N Lincs ... 199 G10
Owstwick E Yorks ... 209 G11
Owthorne E Yorks ... 201 B10
Owthorpe Notts ... 154 C3
Owton Manor Hrtlpl ... 234 F5
Oxborough Norf ... 140 C4
Oxclose S Yorks ... 186 E6
T&W ... 243 F7
Oxcombe Lincs ... 190 F4
Oxcroft Derbys ... 187 G7
Oxcroft Estate Derbys ... 187 G7
Oxen End Essex ... 106 F3
Oxenhall Glos ... 98 F4
Oxenholme Cumb ... 211 B10
Oxenhope W Yorks ... 204 F6
Oxen Park Cumb ... 210 B6
Oxenpill Som ... 44 E2
Oxenton Glos ... 99 E9
Oxenwood Wilts ... 47 B10
Oxford Oxon ... 83 D8
Stoke ... 168 E5
Oxgang E Dunb ... 278 G3
Oxgangs Edin ... 270 B4
Oxhey Herts ... 85 F10
Oxhill Durham ... 242 G5
Warks ... 100 B6
Oxlease Herts ... 86 D2
Oxley W Mid ... 133 C8
Oxley Green Essex ... 88 C6
Oxley's Green E Sus ... 37 C11
Oxlode Cambs ... 139 F9
Oxnam Borders ... 262 F5
Oxnead Norf ... 160 E4
Oxshott Sur ... 66 G6
Oxspring S Yorks ... 197 G9
Oxted Sur ... 51 C11
Oxton Borders ... 271 E9
Mers ... 182 D3
Notts ... 171 E10
N Yorks ... 206 E6
Oxton Rakes Derbys ... 186 G4
Oxwich Swansea ... 56 D3
Oxwich Green Swansea ... 56 D3
Oxwick Norf ... 159 D8
Oykel Bridge Highld ... 309 J3
Oyne Aberds ... 302 G6
Oystermouth Swansea ... 56 D6
Ozleworth Glos ... 80 G3

P

Pabail Iarach W Isles ... 304 E7
Pabail Uarach W Isles ... 304 E7
Pabo Conwy ... 180 F4
Pace Gate N Yorks ... 205 C8
Pachesham Park Sur ... 51 B7
Packers Hill Dorset ... 30 E2
Packington Leics ... 153 G7
Packmoor Staffs ... 168 E5
Packmores Warks ... 118 D5
Packwood W Mid ... 118 C3
Packwood Gullet
W Mid ... 118 C3
Padanaram Angus ... 287 B8
Padbury Bucks ... 102 E4
Paddington London ... 67 C9
Warr ... 183 D10
Paddlesworth Kent ... 55 F7
Kent ... 69 G7
Paddock Kent ... 54 C3
W Yorks ... 196 D6
Paddockhaugh Moray ... 302 D2
Paddockhill Ches E ... 184 F4
Paddockhole Dumfries ... 248 G6
Paddock Wood Kent ... 53 E7
Paddolgreen Shrops ... 149 C10
Padfield Derbys ... 185 B8
Padgate Warr ... 183 D10
Padham's Green Essex ... 87 F10
Padiham Lancs ... 203 G11
Padney Cambs ... 123 C10
Padog Conwy ... 164 E4
Padside N Yorks ... 205 B9
Padside Green N Yorks ... 205 B9
Padson Devon ... 13 B7
Padstow Corn ... 10 F4
Padworth W Berks ... 64 F6
Padworth Common
Hants ... 64 G6
Paganhill Glos ... 80 D4
Page Bank Durham ... 233 D10
Page Moss Mers ... 182 C6
Page's Green Suff ... 126 D2
Pagham W Sus ... 22 D5
Paglesham Churchend
Essex ... 88 G6
Paglesham Eastend
Essex ... 88 G6
Paibeil W Isles ... 296 E3
Paible W Isles ... 305 J2
Paignton Torbay ... 9 C7
Pailton Warks ... 135 G9
Painleyhill Staffs ... 151 C10
Painscastle Powys ... 96 B3
Painshawfield Northumb ... 242 E3
Pains Hill Sur ... 52 C2
Painsthorpe E Yorks ... 208 B2
Painswick Glos ... 80 D5
Painter's Forstal Kent ... 54 B3
Painters Green Wrex ... 167 G8
Painter's Green Herts ... 86 B3
Painthorpe W Yorks ... 197 D10
Paintmoor Som ... 28 F4
Pairc Shiaboist W Isles ... 304 D4
Paisley Renfs ... 267 C9
Pakefield Suff ... 143 E10
Pakenham Suff ... 125 D8
Pale Gwyn ... 147 B9
Pale Green Essex ... 106 C3
Palehouse Common
E Sus ... 23 B7
Palestine Hants ... 47 E9
Paley Street Windsor ... 65 D11
Palfrey W Mid ... 133 D10
Palgowan Dumfries ... 245 G9
Palgrave Suff ... 126 B2
Pallaflat Cumb ... 219 C9
Pallington Dorset ... 17 C11
Pallion T&W ... 243 F9
Pallister Mbro ... 225 B10
Palmarsh Kent ... 54 G6
Palmer Moor Derbys ... 152 C2
Palmersbridge Corn ... 11 F9
Palmers Cross Staffs ... 133 C7
Sur ... 50 E4
Palmer's Flat Glos ... 79 D9
Palmers Green London ... 86 G4
Palmer's Green Kent ... 53 E7
Palmerstown V Glam ... 58 F6
Palmersville T&W ... 243 C7
Palmstead Kent ... 55 D7
Palnackie Dumfries ... 237 D10
Palnure Dumfries ... 236 C6
Palterton Derbys ... 171 B7
Pamber End Hants ... 48 B6
Pamber Green Hants ... 48 B6
Pamber Heath Hants ... 64 G6
Pamington Glos ... 99 E8
Pamphill Dorset ... 31 G7
Pampisford Cambs ... 105 B9
Pan IoW ... 20 D6
Orkney ... 314 G3
Panborough Som ... 44 D3
Panbride Angus ... 287 D9
Pancakehill Glos ... 81 C9
Pancrasweek Devon ... 24 F3
Pancross V Glam ... 58 F4
Pandy Gwyn ... 128 C2
Gwyn ... 146 F4
Gwyn ... 147 D7
Mon ... 96 G6
Powys ... 129 C8
Wrex ... 148 B3
Wrex ... 166 G6
Pandy'r Capel Denb ... 165 E9
Pandy Tudur Conwy ... 164 C5
Panfield Essex ... 106 F4
Pangbourne W Berks ... 64 D6
Panhall Fife ... 280 C6
Panks Bridge Hereford ... 98 B2
Pannal N Yorks ... 206 C2
Pannal Ash N Yorks ... 205 C11
Pannel's Ash Essex ... 106 C5
Panpunton Powys ... 114 C5
Panshanger Herts ... 86 C3
Pant Denb ... 166 E2
Flint ... 181 G10
Gwyn ... 144 C4
M Tydf ... 77 D9
Powys ... 129 C11
Shrops ... 148 E5
Wrex ... 166 D5
Wrex ... 166 F3
Pantasaph Flint ... 181 F11
Pantdu Neath ... 57 C9
Panteg Ceredig ... 111 E9
Torf ... 78 F4
Pantersbridge Corn ... 6 B3
Pant-glas Gwyn ... 163 F7
Pant-glâs Powys ... 128 D5
Pant-glas Shrops ... 148 C5
Pantgwyn Carms ... 93 F11
Ceredig ... 92 B4
Pant-lasau Swansea ... 57 B7
Pantmawr Cardiff ... 58 C6
Pant Mawr Powys ... 129 G7
Panton Lincs ... 189 F11
Pant-pastynog Denb ... 165 C8
Pantperthog Gwyn ... 128 C4
Pantside Caerph ... 78 F2
Pant-teg Carms ... 93 F9
Pant-y-Caws Carms ... 92 F3
Pant-y-crûg Ceredig ... 112 B3
Pant-y-dwr Powys ... 113 B9
Powys ... 113 C9
Pant-y-ffridd Powys ... 130 C3
Pantyffynnon Carms ... 75 C10
Pantygasseg Torf ... 78 F3
Pantymwyn Flint ... 165 C11
Pant-y-pyllau Bridgend ... 58 C2
Pant-yr-awel Bridgend ... 58 B2
Pant-y-Wacco Flint ... 181 F10
Panxworth Norf ... 161 G7
Papcastle Cumb ... 229 E8
Papermill Bank Shrops ... 149 D11
Papigoe Highld ... 310 D7
Papil Shetland ... 313 K5
Papley N Nhants ... 138 F2
Orkney ... 314 G4
Papple E Loth ... 281 G11
Papplewick Notts ... 171 E8
Papworth Everard
Cambs ... 122 E5
Papworth St Agnes
Cambs ... 122 E5
Papworth Village Settlement
Cambs ... 122 E5
Par Corn ... 5 E11
Paradise Glos ... 80 C5
Paradise Green Hereford ... 97 B10
Paramoor Corn ... 5 F9
Paramour Street Kent ... 71 G9
Parbold Lancs ... 194 E3
Parbrook Som ... 44 F5
W Sus ... 35 B9
Parc Gwyn ... 147 C7
Parc Erissey Corn ... 4 G3
Parc-hendy Swansea ... 56 B4
Parchey Som ... 43 F10
Parciau Anglesey ... 179 E7
Parcllyn Ceredig ... 110 G4
Parc Mawr Caerph ... 77 G10
Parc-Seymour Newport ... 78 G6
Parc-y-rhôs Carms ... 93 B11
Pardown Hants ... 48 D5
Pardshaw Cumb ... 229 G7
Pardshaw Hall Cumb ... 229 F8
Parham Suff ... 126 E6
Park Corn ... 10 G6
Devon ... 14 B2
Dumfries ... 247 E10
Som ... 44 G3
Swindon ... 63 C7
Park Barn Sur ... 50 C3
Park Bottom Corn ... 4 G3
Park Bridge Gtr Man ... 196 G2
Park Broom Cumb ... 239 F10

Park Close Lancs 204 E3
Park Corner Bath 45 B9
E Sus 23 C8
E Sus 52 F4
Oxon 65 B7
Windsor 65 C11
Parkend Glos 79 D10
Glos 80 C3
Park End Bedford 121 G9
Cambs 123 E11
Mbro 225 B10
Northumb 241 B9
Som 43 G7
Staffs 168 E3
Worcs 116 C5
Parkengear Corn 5 F8
Parker's Corner W Berks 64 E6
Parker's Green Herts 104 F6
Kent 52 D6
Parkeston Essex 108 E4
Parkfield Corn 6 B6
S Glos 61 D7
W Mid 133 D8
Parkfoot Falk 278 F6
Parkgate Ches E 184 G3
Ches W 182 F3
Cumb 229 B10
Dumfries 248 F2
Essex 87 B11
Kent 53 G11
Sur 51 E8
S Yorks 186 B6
Park Gate Dorset 30 F2
Hants 33 F8
Kent 55 D7
Suff 124 F4
Worcs 117 C8
W Yorks 197 E8
Park Green Essex 105 F9
Parkhall W Dunb 277 G9
Park Hall Shrops 148 C6
Parkham Devon 24 C5
Parkham Ash Devon 24 C5
Parkhead Cumb 230 C2
Glasgow 268 C2
S Yorks 186 E4
Park Head Cumb 231 C7
Derbys 170 E5
W Yorks 197 F7
Parkhill Aberds 303 E10
Invclyd 277 G7
Park Hill Glos 79 F9
Kent 54 G3
Mers 194 G3
Notts 171 E11
N Yorks 214 F6
S Yorks 186 D5
Parkhill Ho Aberds 293 B10
Parkhouse Mon 79 E7
Parkhouse Green
Derbys 170 C6
Parkhurst IoW 20 C5
Parklands W Yorks 206 F3
Park Lane Staffs 133 B7
Wrex 149 B8
Park Langley London 67 F11
Park Mains Renfs 277 G9
Parkmill Swansea 56 D4
Park Mill W Yorks 197 E9
Parkneuk Aberds 293 F9
Fife 279 D11
Park Royal London 67 C7
Parkside C Beds 103 G10
Cumb 219 B10
Durham 234 B4
N Lanark 268 D6
Staffs 151 D8
Wrex 166 D5
Parkstone BCP 18 C6
Park Street Herts 85 E10
W Sus 50 G6
Park Town Luton 103 G11
Oxon 83 D8
Park Village Northumb 240 E5
W Mid 133 C8
Park Villas W Yorks 206 F2
Parkway Hereford 98 D4
Som 29 C9
Park Wood Kent 53 C9
Medway 69 G10
Parkwood Springs
S Yorks 186 D4
Parley Cross Dorset 19 B7
Parley Green BCP 19 B7
Parliament Heath Suff 107 C9
Parlington W Yorks 206 F4
Parmoor Bucks 65 B9
Parnacott Devon 24 F4
Parney Heath Essex 107 E10
Parr Mers 183 C8
Parracombe Devon 41 E7
Parr Brow Gtr Man 195 G8
Parrog Pembs 91 D10
Parsley Hay Derbys 169 C10
Parslow's Hillock Bucks 84 E4
Parsonage Green Essex 88 D2
Parsonby Cumb 229 D8
Parson Cross S Yorks 186 C5
Parson Drove Cambs 139 B7
Parsons Green London 67 D9
Parson's Heath Essex 107 F10
Partick Glasgow 267 B11
Partington Gtr Man 184 C2
Partney Lincs 174 B6
Parton Cumb 228 G5
Cumb 239 G7
Dumfries 237 B8
Glos 99 G7
Hereford 96 B6
Partridge Green W Sus 35 D11
Partrishow Powys 96 G5
Parwich Derbys 169 E11
Pasford Staffs 132 D6
Passenham W Nhants 102 D5
Passfield Hants 49 G10
Passingford Bridge Essex 87 F8
Passmores Essex 86 D6
Paston Norf 160 C6
Pboro 138 C3
Paston Green Norf 160 C6
Pasturefields Staffs 151 D9
Patchacott Devon 12 B5
Patcham Brighton 36 F4
Patchetts Green Herts 85 F10
Patching W Sus 35 F9
Patchole Devon 40 E6
Patchway S Glos 60 C6
Pategill Cumb 230 F6
Pateley Bridge N Yorks 214 F3
Paternoster Heath Essex 88 C6
Pathe Som 43 G11
Pather N Lanark 268 E5
Pathfinder Village Devon 14 C2
Pathhead Aberds 293 G9
E Ayrs 258 G4
Fife 280 C5
Midloth 271 C7
Path Head T&W 242 E5
Pathlow Warks 118 F3
Path of Condie Perth 286 F4
Pathstruie Perth 286 F4
Patient End Herts 105 F8
Patmore Heath Herts 105 F8
Patna E Ayrs 257 G10
Patney Wilts 46 B5
Patrick IoM 192 D3
Patrick Brompton
N Yorks 224 G4
Patricroft Gtr Man 184 B3
Patrington E Yorks 201 C10
Patrington Haven
E Yorks 201 C10
Patrixbourne Kent 55 B7
Patsford Devon 40 F4
Patterdale Cumb 221 B7
Pattiesmuir Fife 279 E11
Pattingham Staffs 132 D6
Pattishall W Nhants 120 G3
Pattiswick Essex 106 G6
Patton Shrops 131 E11
Patton Bridge Cumb 221 F11
Paul Corn 1 D5
Paulerspury W Nhants 102 B4
Paull E Yorks 201 B7
Paul's Green Corn 2 C4
Paulsgrove Ptsmth 33 F10
Paulton Bath 45 B7
Paulville W Loth 269 B9
Pave Lane Telford 150 F5
Pavenham Bedford 121 F9
Pawlett Som 43 E10
Pawlett Hill Som 43 E9
Pawston Northumb 263 C9
Paxford Glos 100 D3
Paxton Borders 273 E8
Payden Street Kent 54 C2
Payhembury Devon 27 G9
Paynes Green Sur 50 F6
Paynter's Cross Corn 7 C7
Paynter's Lane End Corn 4 G3
Paythorne Lancs 204 C2
Payton Som 27 C10
Peacehaven E Sus 36 G6
Peacehaven Heights
E Sus 36 G6
Peacemarsh Dorset 30 B4
Peak Dale Derbys 185 F9
Peak Forest Derbys 185 F10
Peak Hill Lincs 156 F5
Peakirk Pboro 138 B3
Pean Hill Kent 70 G6
Pear Ash Som 45 G9
Pearsie Angus 287 B7
Pearson's Green Kent 53 E7
Peartree Herts 86 C2
Pear Tree Derby 153 C7
Peartree Green Essex 87 F9
Hereford 97 E11
Soton 32 E6
Sur 50 F3
Peas Acre W Yorks 205 E8
Peasedown St John Bath 45 B8
Peasehill Derbys 170 F6
Peaseland Green Norf 159 F11
Peasemore W Berks 64 D3
Peasenhall Suff 127 D7
Pease Pottage W Sus 51 G9
Peas Hill Cambs 139 D8
Peaslake Sur 50 E5
Peasley Cross Mers 183 C8
Peasmarsh E Sus 38 C5
Som 28 E4
Sur 50 D3
Peaston E Loth 271 B8
Peastonbank E Loth 271 B8
Peathill Aberds 303 C9
Peat Inn Fife 287 G8
Peatling Magna Leics 135 E11
Peatling Parva Leics 135 F11
Peaton Shrops 131 G10
Peatonstrand Shrops 131 G10
Peats Corner Suff 126 E3
Pebmarsh Essex 107 E7
Pebsham E Sus 38 F3
Pebworth Worcs 100 B2
Pecket Well W Yorks 196 B3
Peckforton Ches E 167 D8
Peckham London 67 D10
Peckham Bush Kent 53 D7
Peckingell Wilts 62 E2
Pecking Mill Som 44 F6
Peckleton Leics 135 C9
Pedair-ffordd Powys 148 E2
Pedham Norf 160 G6
Pedlars End Essex 87 D8
Pedlar's Rest Shrops 131 G9
Pedlinge Kent 54 F6
Pedmore W Mid 133 G8
Pednor Bottom Bucks 84 E6
Pednormead End Bucks 85 E7
Pedwell Som 44 F2
Peebles Borders 270 G5
Peel Borders 261 B10
IoM 192 D3
Lancs 202 G3
Peel Common Hants 33 G9
Peel Green Gtr Man 184 B2
Peel Hall Gtr Man 184 D4
Peel Hill Lancs 202 G3
Peel Park S Lanark 268 E2
Peene Kent 55 F7
Peening Quarter Kent 38 B5
Peggs Green Leics 153 F8
Pegsdon C Beds 104 E2
Pegswood Northumb 252 F6
Pegwell Kent 71 G11
Peinaha Highld 298 D4
Peinchorran Highld 295 B7
Peingown Highld 298 B4
Peinlich Highld 298 D4
Peinmore Highld 298 E4
Pelaw T&W 243 E7
Pelcomb Pembs 72 B6
Pelcomb Bridge Pembs 72 B6
Pelcomb Cross Pembs 72 B6
Peldon Essex 89 B7
Pelhamfield IoW 21 C7
Pell Green E Sus 52 G6
Pellon W Yorks 196 B5
Pelsall W Mid 133 C10
Pelsall Wood W Mid 133 C10
Pelton Durham 243 G7
Pelton Fell Durham 243 G7
Pelutho Cumb 229 B8
Pelynt Corn 6 D4
Pemberton Carms 75 E8
Gtr Man 194 G5
Pembles Cross Kent 53 D11
Pembre = Pembrey
Carms 74 E6
Pembrey = Pembre
Carms 74 E6
Pembridge Hereford 115 F7
Pembroke = Penfro
Pembs 73 E7
Pembroke Dock = Doc
Penfro Pembs 73 E7
Pembroke Ferry Pembs 73 E7
Pembury Kent 52 E6
Pempwell Corn 12 F3
Penallt Mon 79 C8
Pen-allt Hereford 97 F11
Penally = Penalun
Pembs 73 F10
Penalt Hereford 97 F11
Penalun = Penally
Pembs 73 F10
Penare Corn 5 G9
Penarlâg = Hawarden
Flint 166 B4
Penarron Powys 130 F2
Penarth V Glam 59 E7
Penarth Moors Cardiff 59 E7
Penbeagle Corn 2 B2
Penbedw Flint 165 B11
Pen-bedw Pembs 92 D4
Penberth Corn 1 E4
Penbidwal Mon 96 G6
Penbodlas Gwyn 144 C5
Pen-bont Rhydybeddau
Ceredig 128 G3
Penboyr Carms 93 D7
Penbryn Ceredig 110 G5
Pencader Carms 93 D8
Pencaenewydd Gwyn 162 G6
Pencaerau Neath 57 B8
Pen-caer-fenny Swansea 56 B4
Pencaitland E Loth 271 B8
Pencarnisiog Anglesey 178 G5
Pencarreg Carms 93 B10
Pencarrow Corn 11 E8
Penceiliogi Carms 75 E8
Pencelli Powys 95 F11
Pen-clawdd Swansea 56 B4
Pencoed Bridgend 58 C3
Pencombe Hereford 115 G11
Pen-common Powys 76 D6
Pencoyd Hereford 97 F10
Pencoys Corn 2 B5
Pencraig Anglesey 179 F7
Hereford 97 G11
Powys 147 D10
Pencroesoped Mon 78 D4
Pencuke Corn 11 C9
Pendas Fields W Yorks 206 F3
Pendeen Corn 1 C3
Pendeford W Mid 133 C7
Penderyn Rhondda 77 D7
Pendine = Pentwyn
Carms 74 D2
Pendlebury Gtr Man 195 G9
Pendleton Gtr Man 184 B4
Lancs 203 F11
Pendock Worcs 98 E5
Pendoggett Corn 10 F6
Pendomer Som 29 E8
Pendoylan V Glam 58 D5
Pendre Bridgend 58 C2
Gwyn 110 C2
Powys 95 F10
Penegoed Powys 128 C5
Penelewey Corn 4 G6
Penenden Heath Kent 53 B9
Penffordd Pembs 91 G11
Penffordd Lâs = Staylittle
Powys 129 E7
Penfro = Pembroke
Pembs 73 E7
Pengam Caerph 77 F11
Penge London 67 E11
Pengegon Corn 2 B5
Pengelly Corn 11 E7
Pengenffordd Powys 96 E3
Pengersick Corn 2 D3
Pen-gilfach Gwyn 163 C9
Pengold Corn 11 C8
Pengorffwysfa Anglesey 179 C7
Pengover Green Corn 6 B5
Pen-groes-oped Mon 78 D4
Penguithal Hereford 97 G10
Pengwern Denb 181 F8
Penhale Corn 2 F5
Corn 5 D8
Penhale Jakes Corn 2 D4
Penhallick Corn 3 F7
Corn 4 G3
Penhallow Corn 4 E5
Penhalurick Corn 2 B6
Penhalvean Corn 2 B6
Penhelig Gwyn 128 D2
Penhill Devon 40 G4
Swindon 63 B7
Penhow Newport 78 G6
Penhurst E Sus 23 B11
Peniarth Gwyn 128 B2
Penicuik Midloth 270 C4
Peniel Carms 93 G8
Denb 165 C8
Penifiler Highld 298 E4
Peninver Argyll 255 E8
Penisa'r Waun Gwyn 163 C9
Penistone S Yorks 197 G8
Penjerrick Corn 3 C7
Penketh Warr 183 D9
Penkhull Stoke 168 G5
Penkill S Ayrs 244 D6
Penknap Wilts 45 D11
Penkridge Staffs 151 G8
Pen-lan Swansea 56 B6
Pen-Lan-mabws Pembs 91 F7
Penleigh Wilts 45 C11
Penley Wrex 149 B8
Penllech Gwyn 144 C4
Penllergaer Swansea 56 B6
Penllwyn Caerph 77 F11
Ceredig 128 G3
Penllyn V Glam 58 D3
Pen-llyn Anglesey 178 E4
Pen-lon Anglesey 162 B6
Penmachno Conwy 164 E3
Penmaen Caerph 77 F11
Swansea 56 D4
Penmaenan Conwy 180 F2
Penmaenmawr Conwy 180 F2
Penmaenpool Gwyn 146 F3
Penmaen Rhôs Conwy 180 F5
Penmark V Glam 58 F5
Penmarth Corn 2 B6
Penmayne Corn 10 F4
Pen Mill Som 29 D9
Penmon Anglesey 179 E10
Penmore Mill Argyll 288 D6
Penmorfa Ceredig 110 G6
Gwyn 163 G8
Penmynydd Anglesey 179 G8
Penn Bucks 84 G6
W Mid 133 D7
Pennal Gwyn 128 C4
Pennan Aberds 303 C8
Pennance Corn 4 G4
Pennant Ceredig 111 E10
Conwy 164 D5
Denb 147 C10
Denb 165 E8
Powys 129 D7
Pennant Melangell
Powys 147 D10
Pennar Pembs 73 E7
Pennard Swansea 56 D5
Pennar Park Pembs 72 E6
Penn Bottom Bucks 84 G6
Pennerley Shrops 131 D7
Pennington Cumb 210 D5
Gtr Man 183 B11
Hants 20 C2
Pennington Green
Gtr Man 194 F6
Pennorth Powys 96 F2
Penn Street Bucks 84 F6
Pennsylvania Devon 14 C4
S Glos 61 E8
Penny Bridge Cumb 210 C6
Pennycross Argyll 289 G7
Plym 7 D9
Pennygate Norf 160 E6
Pennygown Argyll 289 E7
Penny Green Derbys 187 F8
Penny Hill Lincs 157 D7
W Yorks 196 D5
Pennylands Lancs 194 F3
Pennymoor Devon 26 E5
Pennypot Kent 54 G6
Penny's Green Norf 142 D3
Pennytinney Corn 10 F6
Pennywell T&W 243 F9
Pen-onn V Glam 58 F5
Penparc Ceredig 92 B4
Pembs 91 E7
Penparcau Ceredig 111 B11
Penpedairheol Caerph 77 F10
Mon 78 E4
Penpergym Mon 78 C4
Penperlleni Mon 78 E4
Penpethy Corn 11 D7
Penpillick Corn 5 D11
Penplas Carms 74 B5
Penpol Corn 3 B8
Penpoll Corn 6 E2
Penponds Corn 2 B4
Penpont Corn 11 G7
Dumfries 247 E8
Powys 95 F9
Penprysg Bridgend 58 C3
Penquit Devon 8 E2
Penrallt Gwyn 145 B7
Powys 129 F9
Penrherber Carms 92 D5
Penrhiw Caerph 78 G2
Penrhiwceiber Rhondda 77 F8
Pen-Rhiw-fawr Neath 76 C2
Penrhiwgarreg Bl Gwent 78 E2
Penrhiw-llan Ceredig 93 C7
Penrhiw-pal Ceredig 92 B6
Penrhiwtyn Neath 57 B8
Penrhos Anglesey 178 E3
Gwyn 144 C6
Hereford 114 F6
Penrhôs Mon 78 C6
Penrhos Mon 78 C6
Powys 76 C3
Pen-rhos Wrex 166 E3
Penrhosfeilw Anglesey 178 E2
Penrhos Garnedd Gwyn 179 G9
Penrhyd Lastra Anglesey 178 C6
Penrhyn Bay = Bae-Penrhyn
Conwy 180 E4
Penrhyn Castle Pembs 92 B2
Penrhyn-coch Ceredig 128 G2
Penrhyndeudraeth
Gwyn 146 B2
Penrhynside Conwy 180 E4
Penrhyn side Conwy 180 E4
Penrhys Rhondda 77 F8
Penrice Swansea 56 D3
Penrith Cumb 230 E6
Penrose Corn 10 G3
Corn 11 F7
Penrose Hill Corn 2 D4
Penruddock Cumb 230 F4
Penryn Corn 3 C7
Pensarn Carms 74 B6
Conwy 181 F7
Pen-sarn Gwyn 145 D11
Gwyn 162 G6
Pensax Worcs 116 D4
Pensby Mers 182 E3
Penselwood Som 45 G9
Pensford Bath 60 G6
Pensham Worcs 99 C8
Penshaw T&W 243 G8
Penshurst Kent 52 E4
Pensilva Corn 6 B5
Pensnett W Mid 133 F8
Penston E Loth 281 G8
Penstone Devon 26 G3
Penstraze Corn 4 F5
Pentewan Corn 5 F10
Pentiken Shrops 130 G4
Pentir Gwyn 163 B9
Pentire Corn 4 C5
Pentirvin Shrops 130 C6
Pentlepoir Pembs 73 D10
Pentlow Essex 106 B6
Pentlow Street Essex 106 B6
Pentney Norf 158 G4
Penton Corner Hants 47 D10
Penton Grafton Hants 47 D10
Penton Mewsey Hants 47 D10
Pentonville London 67 C10
Pentowin Carms 74 B3
Pentraeth Anglesey 179 F8
Pentrapeod Caerph 77 E11
Pentre Carms 75 C8
Denb 165 D10
Flint 165 C11
Flint 166 B4
Flint 166 C2
Flint 166 D2
Flint 182 G2
Powys 129 F11
Powys 130 B4
Powys 130 D2
Powys 130 E5
Powys 147 D11
Powys 148 G3
Rhondda 77 F7
Shrops 149 E7
Shrops 149 F7
Wrex 148 B2
Wrex 166 G3
Pentrebach Carms 94 E6
M Tydf 77 E9
Rhondda 58 B5
Swansea 75 D10
Pentre-bâch Ceredig 93 B11
Pentre-bach Powys 95 E8
Pentrebane Cardiff 58 D6
Pentrebeirdd Powys 148 G3
Pentre Berw Anglesey 179 G7
Pentre-bont Conwy 164 E2
Pentre Broughton Wrex 166 E4
Pentre Bychan Wrex 166 F4
Pentrecagal Carms 92 C6
Pentre-cefn Shrops 148 D4
Pentre-celyn Denb 165 E11
Powys 129 B7
Pentre-chwyth Swansea 57 B7
Pentre Cilgwyn Wrex 148 B4
Pentre-clawdd Shrops 148 C5
Pentre-coed Shrops 149 B7
Pentre-cwrt Carms 93 D7
Pentre Dolau-Honddu
Powys 95 C9
Pentredwr Denb 165 F11
Pentre-dwr Swansea 57 B7
Pentrefelin Anglesey 178 C6
Carms 93 G11
Ceredig 94 B2
Conwy 180 G4
Denb 166 G2
Gwyn 145 B10
Pentre-Ffwrndan Flint 182 G3
Pentrefoelas Conwy 164 E5
Pentref-y-groes Caerph 77 F11
Pentre-galar Pembs 92 E3
Pentregat Ceredig 111 G7
Pentre-Gwenlais Carms 75 B10
Pentre Gwynfryn Gwyn 145 D11
Pentre Halkyn Flint 182 G2
Pentreheyling Shrops 130 E4
Pentre Hodre Shrops 114 B6
Pentre Isaf Conwy 164 B5
Pentre Llanrhaeadr
Denb 165 C9
Pentre Llifior Powys 130 D2
Pentrellwyn Ceredig 93 C8
Pentre-llwyn-llwyd
Powys 113 G9
Pentre-llyn Ceredig 112 C2
Pentre-llyn cymmer
Conwy 165 E7
Pentre Maelor Wrex 166 F5
Pentre Meyrick V Glam 58 D3
Pentre-newydd Shrops 148 B5
Pentre-Piod Torf 78 E3
Pentre-Poeth Carms 75 E8
Newport 59 B9
Pentre'r beirdd Powys 148 G3
Pentre'r Felin Conwy 164 B4
Pentre'r-felin Denb 165 B10
Powys 95 E8
Pentre-rhew Ceredig 112 G3
Pentre-tafarn-y-fedw
Conwy 164 C4
Pentre-ty-gwyn Carms 94 D6
Pentreuchaf Gwyn 145 B7
Pentre-uchaf Conwy 180 F5
Pentrich Derbys 170 E5
Pentridge Dorset 31 D8
Pentrisil Pembs 91 E11
Pentwyn Caerph 77 E10
Cardiff 59 C8
Pen-twyn Caerph 78 E2
Pentwyn = Pendine
Carms 74 D2
Pen-twyn Carms 75 C9
Mon 79 D8
Torf 78 E3
Pentwyn Berthlwyd
Caerph 77 F10
Pentwyn-mawr Caerph 77 F11
Pentyrch Cardiff 58 C6
Penuchadre V Glam 57 G11
Pen-Uchar Plwyf Flint 181 G11
Penuwch Ceredig 111 E11
Penwartha Corn 4 E5
Penwartha Coombe Corn 4 E5
Penweathers Corn 4 G6
Penwithick Corn 5 D10
Penwood Hants 64 G2
Penwortham Lane
Lancs 194 B4
Penwyllt Powys 76 B5
Pen-y-Ball Top Flint 181 F11
Penybanc Carms 75 C10
Pen-y-banc Carms 93 G8
Carms 94 G2
Pen-y-bank Caerph 77 E10
Penybedd Carms 74 E6
Penybont Ceredig 128 F2
Powys 114 E2
Pen-y-Bont Bl Gwent 78 D2
Carms 92 F6
Gwyn 128 C4
Gwyn 146 D2
Powys 148 E4
Pen y Bont ar ogwr
= Bridgend Bridgend 58 C2
Penybontfawr Powys 147 E11
Penybryn Caerph 77 F10
Pen-y-Bryn Gwyn 145 B9
Gwyn 146 F3
Pembs 92 C3
Powys 130 C3
Shrops 148 B6
Wrex 166 G3
Pen-y-cae Bridgend 58 C2
Neath 57 D9
Powys 76 C4
Pen-y-cae-mawr Mon 78 F6
Penycaerau Gwyn 144 D3
Pen-y-cefn Flint 181 F10
Pen-y-clawdd Mon 79 D7
Pen-y-coed Shrops 148 E5
Pen-y-coedcae Rhondda 58 B5
Penycwm Pembs 90 G6
Pen-y-Darren M Tydf 77 D9
Penydre Swansea 75 E11
Pen-y-fai Bridgend 57 E11
Carms 75 E7
Pen-y-fan Carms 56 B4
Mon 79 D8
Penyfeidr Pembs 91 F7
Pen-y-felin Flint 165 B11
Penyffordd Flint 166 C4
Pen-y-ffordd Denb 181 F8
Flint 181 E10
Penyffridd Gwyn 163 D8
Pen y Foel Shrops 148 E5
Penygarn Torf 78 E3
Pen-y-garn Carms 93 E11
Ceredig 128 F2
Penygarnedd Powys 148 E2
Pen-y-garnedd
Anglesey 179 F8
Penygelli Powys 130 E2
Pen-y-gop Conwy 164 G6
Penygraig Rhondda 77 G7
Pen-y-graig Gwyn 144 C3
Penygraigwen Anglesey 178 D6
Penygroes Gwyn 163 E7
Pembs 92 D3
Pen-y-groes Carms 75 C9
Pen-y-groeslon Gwyn 144 C4
Pen-y-Gwryd Hotel
Gwyn 163 D11
Pen-y-lan Cardiff 59 D7
Newport 59 B9
V Glam 58 D3
Pen-y-maes Flint 181 F11
Pen-y-Myndd Carms 75 E7
Penymynydd Flint 166 C4
Pen-y-Park Hereford 96 C5
Penyraber Pembs 91 D9
Pen-yr-englyn Rhondda 76 F6
Penyrheol Caerph 58 B6
Swansea 56 B5
Torf 78 F3
Pen-yr-heol Bridgend 58 C2
Mon 78 C6
Pen-yr-Heolgerrig
M Tydf 77 D8
Pen-y-rhiw Rhondda 58 B5
Penysarn Anglesey 179 C7
Pen-y-stryt Denb 165 E11
Penywaun Rhondda 77 E7
Pen-y-wern Shrops 114 B6
Penzance Corn 1 C5
Peopleton Worcs 117 G8
Peover Heath Ches E 184 G3
Peper Harow Sur 50 E2
Peppercombe Devon 24 C5
Pepper Hill Som 43 F7
W Yorks 196 B6
Peppermoor Northumb 264 F6
Pepper's Green Essex 87 C10
Pepperstock C Beds 85 B9
Perceton N Ayrs 267 G7
Percie Aberds 293 D7
Percuil Corn 3 C9
Percyhorner Aberds 303 C9
Percy Main T&W 243 D8
Per-ffordd-llan Flint 181 F10
Perham Down Wilts 47 D9
Periton Som 42 D3
Perivale London 67 C7
Perkhill Aberds 293 C7
Perkinsville Durham 243 G7
Perlethorpe Notts 187 G11
Perranarworthal Corn 3 B7
Perrancoombe Corn 4 E5
Perran Downs Corn 2 C3
Perranporth Corn 4 E5
Perranuthnoe Corn 2 D2
Perranwell Corn 3 B7
Corn 4 E5
Perranwell Station Corn 3 B7
Perran Wharf Corn 3 B7
Perranzabuloe Corn 4 E5
Perrott's Brook Glos 81 D8
Perry Devon 26 F5
Kent 55 B9
W Mid 133 E11
Perry Barr W Mid 133 E11
Perry Beeches W Mid 133 E11
Perry Common W Mid 133 E11
Perry Crofts Staffs 134 C4
Perryfields Worcs 117 C8
Perryfoot Derbys 185 E10
Perry Green Essex 106 G6
Herts 86 B6
Som 43 F9
Wilts 62 B3
Perrymead Bath 61 G9
Perrystone Hill Hereford 98 F2
Perry Street Kent 68 E6
Som 28 F4
Perrywood Kent 54 B4
Pershall Staffs 150 C6
Pershore Worcs 99 B8
Pert Angus 293 G8
Pertenhall Bedford 121 D11
Perth Perth 286 E5
Perthcelyn Rhondda 77 F9
Perthy Shrops 149 C7
Perton Hereford 97 C11
Staffs 133 D7
Pertwood Wilts 45 F11
Pested Kent 54 C4
Peterborough Pboro 138 D3
Peterburn Highld 307 L2
Peterchurch Hereford 96 D6
Peterculter Aberdeen 293 C10
Peterhead Aberds 303 E11
Peterlee Durham 234 C4
Petersburn N Lanark 268 C5
Petersfield Hants 34 C2
Peter's Finger Devon 12 D3
Peter's Green Herts 85 B10
Petersham London 67 E7
Peters Marland Devon 25 E7
Peterstone Wentlooge
Newport 59 C9
Peterston-super-Ely
V Glam 58 D5
Peterstow Hereford 97 G11
Peter Tavy Devon 12 F6
Petertown Orkney 314 F3
Peterville Corn 4 E4
Petham Kent 54 C6
Petherwin Gate Corn 11 D11
Petrockstow Devon 25 F8
Petsoe End M Keynes 103 B7
Pett E Sus 38 E5
Pettaugh Suff 126 F3
Pett Bottom Kent 54 E6
Kent 55 C7
Petteridge Kent 53 E7
Pettinain S Lanark 269 G9
Pettings Kent 68 G6
Pettistree Suff 126 G5
Pett Level E Sus 38 E5
Petton Devon 27 C8
Shrops 149 D8
Petts Wood London 68 F2
Petty Aberds 303 F7
Pettycur Fife 280 D5
Petty France S Glos 61 B9
Pettymuick Aberds 303 G9
Pettywell Norf 159 E11
Petworth W Sus 35 C7
Pevensey E Sus 23 E10
Pevensey Bay E Sus 23 E11
Peverell Plym 7 D9
Pewsey Wilts 63 G7
Pewsey Wharf Wilts 63 G7
Pewterspear Warr 183 E10
Phantassie E Loth 281 F11
Pharisee Green Essex 106 G2
Pheasants Bucks 65 B9
Pheasant's Hill Bucks 65 B9
Pheasey W Mid 133 D11
Pheonix Green Hants 49 B9
Phepson Worcs 117 F8
Philadelphia T&W 243 G8
Philham Devon 24 C3
Philiphaugh Borders 261 D10
Phillack Corn 2 B3
Philleigh Corn 3 B9
Phillip's Town Caerph 77 E10
Philpot End Essex 87 B10
Philpstoun W Loth 279 F10
Phocle Green Hereford 98 F2
Phoenix Green Hants 49 B9
Phoenix Row Durham 233 F9
Phorp Moray 301 D10
Pibsbury Som 28 B6
Pibwrlwyd Carms 74 B6
Pica Cumb 228 G6
Piccadilly S Yorks 187 B7
Warks 134 D4
Piccadilly Corner Norf 142 F5
Piccotts End Herts 85 D9
Pickburn S Yorks 198 F4
Picken End Worcs 98 C6
Pickering N Yorks 216 C5
Pickering Nook Durham 242 F5
Picket Hill Hants 31 F11
Picket Piece Hants 47 D11
Picket Post Hants 31 F11
Pickford W Mid 134 G5
Pickford Green W Mid 134 G5
Pickhill N Yorks 214 C6
Picklenash Glos 98 F4
Picklescott Shrops 131 D8
Pickles Hill W Yorks 204 F6
Pickletillem Fife 287 E8
Pickley Green Gtr Man 195 G7
Pickmere Ches E 183 F11
Pickney Som 27 B11
Pickstock Telford 150 E4
Pickup Bank Blackburn 195 C8
Pickwell Devon 40 E3
Leics 154 G5
Pickwick Wilts 61 E11
Pickwood Scar W Yorks 196 C5
Pickworth Lincs 155 C10
Rutland 155 G9
Picton Ches W 182 G6
Flint 181 E10
N Yorks 225 D8
Pict's Hill Som 28 B6
Piddinghoe E Sus 36 G6
Piddington Bucks 84 G4
Oxon 83 B10
W Nhants 120 G6
Piddlehinton Dorset 17 B10
Piddletrenthide Dorset 17 B10
Pidley Cambs 122 B6
Pidney Dorset 30 F2
Piece Corn 2 B5
Piercebridge Darl 224 B4
Piercing Hill Essex 86 F6
Pierowall Orkney 314 B4
Piff's Elm Glos 99 F8
Pigdon Northumb 252 F5
Pightley Som 43 F8
Pig Oak Dorset 31 G8
Pigstye Green Essex 87 D10
Pikehall Derbys 169 D11
Pike End W Yorks 196 D4
Pike Hill Lancs 204 G3
Pike Law W Yorks 196 D4
Pikeshill Hants 32 F3
Pikestye Hereford 97 B10
Pilford Dorset 31 G8
Pilgrims Hatch Essex 87 F9
Pilham Lincs 188 C5
Pilhough Derbys 170 C3
Pill N Som 60 D4
Pembs 72 D6
Pillaton Corn 7 C7
Staffs 151 G8
Pillerton Hersey Warks 100 B6
Pillerton Priors Warks 100 B5
Pilleth Powys 114 D5
Pilley Glos 81 B7
Hants 20 B2
S Yorks 197 G10
Pilley Bailey Hants 20 B2
Pillgwenlly Newport 59 B10
Pilling Lancs 202 D4
Pilling Lane Lancs 202 D3
Pillmouth Devon 25 C7
Pillowell Glos 79 D10
Pillows Green Glos 98 F5
Pillwell Dorset 30 D3
Pilmuir Borders 261 G11
Pilning S Glos 60 B5
Pilrig Edin 280 F5
Pilsbury Derbys 169 C10
Pilsdon Dorset 16 B4
Pilsgate Pboro 137 B11
Pilsley Derbys 170 C6
Derbys 186 G2
Pilsley Green Derbys 170 C6
Pilson Green Norf 161 G7
Piltdown E Sus 36 C6
Pilton Devon 40 G5
Edin 280 F4
N Nhants 137 G10
Rutland 137 C8
Som 44 E5
Pilton Green Swansea 56 D2
Piltown Som 44 F5
Pimhole Gtr Man 195 E10
Pimlico Herts 85 D9
Lancs 203 E10
London 67 D9
W Nhants 102 C2
Pimperne Dorset 29 F9
Dorset 30 F6
Pinchbeck Lincs 156 D4
Pinchbeck Bars Lincs 156 D3
Pinchbeck West Lincs 156 E4
Pincheon Green
S Yorks 199 D7
Pinckney Green Wilts 61 G10
Pincock Lancs 194 D5
Pineham Kent 55 D10
M Keynes 103 C7
Pinehurst Swindon 63 B7
Pinfarthings Glos 80 E5
Pinfold Lancs 193 E11
Pinfold Hill S Yorks 197 G9
Pinfoldpond C Beds 103 E8
Pinford End Suff 124 F6
Pinged Carms 74 E6
Pingewood W Berks 65 F7
Pin Green Herts 104 F4
Pinhoe Devon 14 C5
Pinkett's Booth W Mid 134 G5
Pink Green Worcs 117 D11
Pinkie Braes E Loth 281 G7
Pinkney Wilts 61 B11
Pinkneys Green Windsor 65 C11
Pinksmoor Som 27 D10
Pinley W Mid 119 B7
Pinley Green Warks 118 D4
Pin Mill Suff 108 D4
Pinminnoch Dumfries 236 D2
S Ayrs 244 E5
Pinmore S Ayrs 244 E6
Pinmore Mains S Ayrs 244 E6
Pinnacles Essex 86 D6
Pinner London 66 B6
Pinner Green London 85 G10
Pinnerwood Park
London 85 G10
Pin's Green Worcs 98 B6
Pinsley Green Ches E 167 F9
Pinstones Shrops 131 F9
Pinvin Worcs 99 B9
Pinwall Leics 134 C6
Pinwherry S Ayrs 244 F5
Pinxton Derbys 171 E7
Pipe and Lyde Hereford 97 C10
Pipe Aston Hereford 115 C9
Pipe Gate Shrops 168 G2
Pipehill Staffs 133 B11
Pipehouse Bath 45 B9
Piperhall Argyll 266 D2
Piperhill Highld 301 D8
Pipe Ridware Staffs 151 F11
Piper's Ash Ches W 166 B6
Piper's End Worcs 98 E6
Piper's Hill Worcs 117 D9
Piper's Pool Corn 11 E11
Pipewell N Nhants 136 F6
Pippacott Devon 40 F4
Pippin Street Lancs 194 C5
Pipps Hill Essex 69 B7
Pipsden Kent 53 G9
Pipton Powys 96 D3
Pirbright Sur 50 B2
Pirbright Camp Sur 50 B2
Pirnmill N Ayrs 255 C9
Pirton Herts 104 E2
Worcs 99 B7
Pisgah Ceredig 112 B3
Stirling 285 G11
Pishill Oxon 65 B8
Pishill Bank Oxon 84 G2
Pismire Hill S Yorks 186 C5
Pistyll Gwyn 162 G4
Pit Mon 78 D5
Pitagowan Perth 291 G10
Pitblae Aberds 303 C9
Pitcairngreen Perth 286 E4
Pitcalnie Highld 301 B8
Pitcaple Aberds 303 G7
Pitchcombe Glos 80 D5
Pitchcott Bucks 102 G5
Pitcher's Green Suff 125 F8
Pitchford Shrops 131 C10
Pitch Green Bucks 84 E3
Pitch Place Sur 49 F11
Sur 50 C3
Pitcombe Som 45 G7
Pitcorthie Fife 280 D2
Fife 287 G9
Pitcot Som 45 D7
V Glam 57 G11
Pitcox E Loth 282 F2
Pitcur Perth 286 D6
Pitfancy Aberds 302 E5
Pitfichie Aberds 293 B8
Pitforthie Aberds 293 F10
Pitgair Aberds 303 D7
Pitgrudy Highld 309 K7
Pithmaduthy Highld 301 B7
Pitkennedy Angus 287 B9
Pitkevy Fife 286 G6
Pitkierie Fife 287 G9
Pitlessie Fife 287 G7
Pitlochry Perth 286 B3
Pitmachie Aberds 302 G6
Pitmain Highld 291 C9
Pitmedden Aberds 303 G8
Pitminster Som 28 D2
Pitmuies Angus 287 C9
Pitmunie Aberds 293 B8
Pitney Som 29 B7
Pitrocknie Perth 286 C6
Pitscottie Fife 287 F8
Pitsea Essex 69 B8
Pitses Gtr Man 196 G2
Pitsford W Nhants 120 D5
Pitsford Hill Som 42 G6
Pitsmoor S Yorks 186 D5
Pitstone Bucks 84 B6
Pitstone Green Bucks 84 B6
Pitstone Hill Bucks 85 C7
Pitt Hants 33 B7
Pittachar Perth 286 E2
Pitt Court Glos 80 F3
Pittendreich Moray 301 C11
Pittentrail Highld 309 J7
Pittenweem Fife 287 G9
Pitteuchar Fife 280 B5
Pittington Durham 234 C2
Pittodrie Aberds 302 G6
Pitton Swansea 56 D2
Wilts 47 G8
Pitts Hill Stoke 168 E5
Pittswood Kent 52 D6
Pittulie Aberds 303 C9
Pittville Glos 99 G9
Pityme Corn 10 F5
Pity Me Durham 233 B11
Pityoulish Highld 291 B11
Pixey Green Suff 126 B4
Pixham Sur 51 C7
Worcs 98 B6
Pixley Hereford 98 D3
Shrops 150 D3
Pizien Well Kent 53 C7
Place Newton N Yorks 217 E7
Plaidy Aberds 303 D7
Corn 6 E5
Plain-an-Gwarry Corn 4 G3
Plain Dealings Pembs 73 B9
Plains N Lanark 268 B5
Plainsfield Som 43 F7
Plain Spot Notts 171 E7
Plain Street Corn 10 F5
Plaish Shrops 131 D10
Plaistow London 68 C2
London 68 E2
W Sus 50 G4
Plaistow Green Essex 106 F6
Plaitford Wilts 32 D3
Plaitford Green Hants 32 C3
Plank Lane Gtr Man 194 G6
Plans Dumfries 238 D3
Plantation Bridge Cumb 221 F9
Plantationfoot Dumfries 248 E4
Plardiwick Staffs 150 E6
Plasau Shrops 149 E7
Plâs Berwyn Denb 165 G11
Plas-canol Gwyn 145 F11
Plas Coch Wrex 166 E4
Plas Dinam Powys 129 F10
Plas Gogerddan Ceredig 128 G2
Plashet London 68 C2
Plashett Carms 74 D3
Plasiolyn Powys 129 C11
Plas Llwyngwern Powys 128 C5
Plas Meredydd Powys 130 D3
Plas Nantyr Wrex 148 B3
Plasnewydd Powys 129 D9
Plaster's Green Bath 60 G4
Plastow Green Hants 64 G4
Plas-yn-Cefn Denb 181 G8
Platt Kent 52 B6
Platt Bridge Gtr Man 194 G6
Platt Lane Shrops 149 B10
Platts Common
S Yorks 197 G11
Platt's Heath Kent 53 C11
Plawsworth Durham 233 B11
Plaxtol Kent 52 C6
Playden E Sus 38 C6
Playford Suff 108 B4
Play Hatch Oxon 65 D8
Playing Place Corn 4 G6
Playley Green Glos 98 E5
Plealey Shrops 131 B8
Pleamore Cross Som 27 D10
Plean Stirling 278 D6
Pleasant Valley Pembs 73 D10
Pleasington Blackburn 194 B6
Pleasley Derbys 171 C8
Pleasleyhill Notts 171 C8
Pleck Dorset 30 D3
Dorset 30 E2
W Mid 133 D9
Pleckgate Blackburn 203 G9
Pleck or Little Ansty
Dorset 30 G3
Pledgdon Green Essex 105 F11
Pledwick W Yorks 197 D10
Plemstall Ches W 183 G7
Plenmeller Northumb 240 E6
Pleshey Essex 87 C11
Plockton Highld 295 B10

Plocrapol W Isles 305 J3
Plot Gate Som 44 G4
Plot Street Som 44 F5
Ploughfield Hereford 97 C7
Plough Hill Warks 134 E6
Plowden Shrops 131 F7
Ploxgreen Shrops 131 C7
Pluckley Kent 54 D2
Pluckley Thorne Kent 54 E2
Plucks Gutter Kent 71 G9
Plumbland Cumb 229 D9
Plumbley S Yorks 186 E6
Plumford Kent 54 B4
Plumley Ches E 184 F2
Plump Hill Glos 79 B11
Plumpton Cumb 230 D5
E Sus 36 E5
W Nhants 101 B11
Plumpton End
W Nhants 102 B4
Plumpton Foot Cumb 230 D5
Plumpton Green E Sus 36 D5
Plumpton Head Cumb 230 E6
Plumstead London 68 D3
Norf 160 C2
Plumstead Common
London 68 D3
Plumstead Green Norf 160 C2
Plumtree Notts 154 C2
Plumtree Green Kent 53 D10
Plumtree Park Notts 154 C2
Plungar Leics 154 C5
Plush Dorset 30 G2
Plusha Corn 11 E11
Plushabridge Corn 12 G2
Plusterwine Glos 79 F9
Plwmp Ceredig 111 G7
Plymouth Plym 7 E9
Plympton Plym 7 D10
Plymstock Plym 7 E10
Plymtree Devon 27 G9
Pobgreen Gtr Man 196 F4
Pochin Houses Caerph 77 E11
Pocket Nook Gtr Man 183 B10
Pockley N Yorks 216 B2
Pocklington E Yorks 208 D2
Pockthorpe
Norf 141 D8
Norf 158 D6
Norf 159 E10
Norf 159 F11
Pode Hole Lincs 156 E4
Podimore Som 29 C8
Podington Bedford 121 E8
Podmoor Worcs 117 C7
Podmore Norf 159 G9
Staffs 150 B5
Podsmead Glos 80 B4
Poffley End Oxon 82 C5
Pogmoor S Yorks 197 F10
Point Corn 3 B8
Point Clear Essex 89 C9
Pointon Lincs 156 C2
Pokesdown BCP 19 C8
Pol a Charra W Isles 297 K3
Polbae Dumfries 236 B4
Polbain Highld 307 H4
Polbathic Corn 7 D7
Polbeth W Loth 269 C10
Polborder Corn 7 C7
Polbrock Corn 5 B10
Polchar Highld 291 C10
Polebrook N Nhants 137 F11
Pole Elm Worcs 98 B6
Polegate E Sus 23 D9
Pole Moor W Yorks 196 D5
Poles Highld 309 K7
Polesden Lacey Sur 50 C6
Poleshill Som 27 C9
Pole's Hole Wilts 45 C10
Polesworth Warks 134 C5
Polgear Corn 2 B5
Polgigga Corn 1 E3
Polglass Highld 307 J5
Polgooth Corn 5 E9
Poling W Sus 35 G8
Poling Corner W Sus 35 F8
Polkerris Corn 5 E11
Polla Highld 308 D3
Polladras Corn 2 C4
Pollard Street Norf 160 C6
Pollhill Kent 53 C11
Poll Hill Mers 182 E3
Pollie Highld 309 H7
Pollington E Yorks 198 D6
Polliwilline Argyll 255 G8
Polloch Highld 289 C9
Pollok Glasgow 267 C10
Pollokshields Glasgow 267 C11
Polmadie Glasgow 267 C11
Polmarth Corn 2 B6
Polmassick Corn 5 F9
Polmear Corn 5 E11
Polmont Falk 279 F8
Polmorla Corn 10 G5
Polnessan E Ayrs 257 G11
Polnish Highld 295 G9
Polopit N Nhants 121 B10
Polpenwith Corn 2 D6
Polpeor Corn 2 B2
Polperro Corn 6 E4
Polruan Corn 6 E2
Polsham Som 44 E4
Polsloe Devon 14 C4
Polstead Suff 107 D9
Polstead Heath Suff 107 C9
Poltalloch Argyll 275 D9
Poltesco Corn 2 F6
Poltimore Devon 14 B5
Polton Midloth 270 C5
Polwarth Borders 272 E4
Polwheveral Corn 2 D6
Polyphant Corn 11 E11
Polzeath Corn 10 F4
Pomeroy Derbys 169 B10
Pomphlett Plym 7 E10
Ponciau Wrex 166 F3
Pond Close Som 27 B10
Ponde Powys 96 D2
Pondersbridge Cambs 138 E5
Ponders End London 86 F5
Pond Park Bucks 85 E7
Pond Street Essex 105 D9
Pondtail Hants 49 C10
Pondwell IoW 21 C8
Poniou Corn 1 B4
Ponjeravah Corn 2 D6
Ponsanooth Corn 3 B7
Ponsford Devon 27 F8
Ponsonby Cumb 219 D11
Ponsongath Corn 3 F7
Ponsworthy Devon 13 G10
Pont Corn 6 E2
Pont Aber Carms 94 G4
Pont Aber-Geirw Gwyn 146 D5
Pontamman Carms 75 C10
Pontantwn Carms 74 C6
Pontardawe Neath 76 E2
Pontarddulais Swansea 75 E9
Pontarfynach = *Devils Bridge* Ceredig 112 B4
Pont-ar-gothi Carms 93 G10
Pont ar Hydfer Powys 95 F7
Pont-ar-llechau Carms 94 G4
Pontarsais Carms 93 F8
Pontblyddyn Flint 166 C3
Pontbren Araeth Carms 94 G3
Pontbren Llwyd Rhondda 76 D6
Pontcanna Cardiff 59 D7
Pont Cyfyng Conwy 164 D2
Pont Cysyllte Wrex 166 G3
Pontdolgoch Powys 129 E10
Pont Dolydd Prysor
Gwyn 146 B4
Pontefract W Yorks 198 C3
Ponteland Northumb 242 C5
Ponterwyd Ceredig 128 G4
Pontesbury Shrops 131 B7
Pontesbury Hill Shrops 131 B7
Pontesford Shrops 131 B8
Pontfadog Wrex 148 B4
Pontfaen Pembs 91 E10
Pont-faen Powys 95 E9
Shrops 148 B5
Pont Fronwydd Gwyn 146 E6
Pont-gareg Pembs 92 C2
Pontgarreg Ceredig 110 G6
Ponthen Shrops 148 F6
Pont-Henri Carms 75 D7
Ponthir Torf 78 G4
Ponthirwaun Ceredig 92 B5
Pont Hwfa Anglesey 178 E2
Pontiago Pembs 91 D8
Pont iets = *Pontyates*
Carms 75 D7
Pontithel Powys 96 D3
Pontllanfraith Caerph 77 F11
Pontlliw Swansea 75 E10
Pont-Llogel Powys 147 F10
Pontllyfni Gwyn 162 E6
Pontlottyn Caerph 77 D10
Pontneddfechan Powys 76 D6
Pontnewydd Torf 78 F3
Pont-newydd Carms 74 D6
Flint 165 B11
Pontnewynydd Torf 78 E3
Pont Pen-y-benglog
Gwyn 163 C10
Pontrhydfendigaid
Ceredig 112 D4
Pont Rhydgaled Powys 128 G6
Pont Rhyd-goch
Conwy 163 C11
Pont-Rhyd-sarn Gwyn 147 D7
Pont Rhyd-y-berry
Powys 95 D9
Pont Rhyd-y-cyff
Bridgend 57 D11
Pontrhydyfen Neath 57 C9
Pont-rhyd-y-groes
Ceredig 112 C4
Pontrhydyrun Torf 78 F3
Pont-Rhythallt Gwyn 163 C8
Pontrilas Hereford 97 F7
Pontrobert Powys 148 G2
Pont-rug Gwyn 163 C8
Pont Senni = *Sennybridge*
Powys 95 F8
Ponts Green E Sus 23 B11
Pontshill Hereford 98 G2
Pont-siôn Ceredig 93 B8
Pont Siôn Norton
Rhondda 77 G9
Pontsticill M Tydf 77 C9
Pont-Walby Neath 76 D5
Pontwgan Conwy 180 G3
Pontyates = *Pont-iets*
Carms 75 D7
Pontyberem Carms 75 C8
Pont-y-blew Shrops 148 B6
Pontyclun Rhondda 58 C4
Pontycymer Bridgend 76 G6
Pontyglasier Pembs 92 D2
Pont-y-gwaith Rhondda 77 G8
Pontymister Caerph 78 G2
Pontymoel Torf 78 E3
Pont-y-pant Conwy 164 E3
Pont y Pennant Gwyn 147 E8
Pontypool Torf 78 E3
Pontypridd Rhondda 58 B5
Pont yr Afon-Gam
Gwyn 164 G2
Pont-yr-hafod Pembs 91 F8
Pont-y-rhyl Bridgend 58 B2
Pont-Ystrad Denb 165 C9
Pont-y-wal Powys 96 D2
Pontywaun Caerph 78 G2
Pooksgreen Hants 32 E5
Pool Corn 4 G3
W Yorks 205 D10
Poolbrook Worcs 98 C5
Poole BCP 18 C6
N Yorks 198 B3
Som 27 C10
Poole Keynes Glos 81 F8
Poolend Staffs 169 D7
Poolestown Dorset 30 D2
Poolewe Highld 307 L3
Pooley Bridge Cumb 230 G5
Pooley Street Norf 141 G11
Poolfold Staffs 168 D5
Poolhead Shrops 149 C9
Pool Head Hereford 115 G11
Pool Hey Lancs 193 D11
Poolhill Glos 98 F4
Poolmill Hereford 97 G11
Pool o' Muckhart Clack 286 G4
Pool Quay Powys 148 G5
Poolsbrook Derbys 186 G6
Poolside Moray 302 E4
Poolstock Gtr Man 194 G5
Pooltown Som 42 F3
Pootings Kent 52 D3
Pope Hill Pembs 72 C6
Pope's Hill Glos 79 C11
Popeswood Brack 65 F10
Popham Devon 41 G8
Hants 48 E5
Poplar London 67 C11
Poplar Grove Lincs 190 B6
Poplars Herts 104 G5
Popley Hants 48 C6
Porchester Nottingham 171 G9
Porchfield IoW 20 C4
Porin Highld 300 D3
Poringland Norf 142 C5
Porkellis Corn 2 C5
Porlock Som 41 D11
Porlockford Som 41 D11
Porlock Weir Som 41 D11
Portachoillan Argyll 255 B8
Port Allen Perth 286 E6
Port Ann Argyll 275 E10
Port Appin Argyll 289 E11
Port Arthur Shetland 313 K5
Portash Wilts 46 G3
Port Askaig Argyll 274 G5
Portavadie Argyll 275 G10
Port Bannatyne Argyll 275 G11
Port Brae Fife 280 C5
Port Bridge Devon 9 D7
Portbury N Som 60 D4
Port Carlisle Cumb 238 E6
Port Charlotte Argyll 254 B3
Portchester Hants 33 F10
Portclair Highld 290 B6
Port Clarence Stockton 234 G5
Port Dinorwic = *Y Felinheli*
Gwyn 163 B8
Port Driseach Argyll 275 F10
Port Dundas Glasgow 267 B11
Porteath Corn 10 F5
Port Edgar Edin 280 F2
Port Ellen Argyll 254 C4
Port Elphinstone Aberds 293 B9
Portencalzie Dumfries 236 B2
Portencross N Ayrs 266 F3
Porterfield Renfs 267 B9
Port Erin IoM 192 F2
Port Erroll Aberds 303 F10
Porter's End Herts 85 B11
Portesham Dorset 17 D8
Portessie Moray 302 C4
Port e Vullen IoM 192 C5
Port-Eynon Swansea 56 D3
Portfield Argyll 289 G9
Som 28 B6
W Sus 22 B5
Portfield Gate Pembs 72 B6
Portgate Devon 12 D4
Port Gaverne Corn 10 E6
Port Glasgow Invclyd 276 G6
Portgordon Moray 302 C3
Portgower Highld 311 H4
Porth Corn 4 C6
Rhondda 77 G8
Porthallow Corn 3 E7
Corn 6 E4
Porthcawl Bridgend 57 F10
Porth Colmon Gwyn 144 C3
Porthcothan Corn 10 G3
Porthcurno Corn 1 E3
Portheiddy Pembs 90 E6
Port Henderson Highld 299 B7
Porthgain Pembs 90 E6
Porthgwarra Corn 1 E3
Porthhallow Corn 3 E7
Porthill Shrops 149 G9
Staffs 168 F5
Port Hill Oxon 65 B7
Porthilly Corn 10 F4
Porth Kea Corn 4 G6
Porthkerry V Glam 58 F5
Porthleven Corn 2 D4
Porthllechog = *Bull Bay*
Anglesey 178 C6
Porthloo Scilly 1 G4
Porthmadog Gwyn 145 B11
Porthmeor Corn 1 B4
Porth Navas Corn 3 D7
Porthoustock Corn 3 E8
Porthpean Corn 5 E10
Porthtowan Corn 4 F3
Porth Tywyn = *Burry Port*
Carms 74 E6
Porth-y-felin Anglesey 178 E2
Porthyrhyd Carms 75 B8
Carms 94 D4
Porth-y-waen Shrops 148 E5
Portico Mers 183 C7
Portincaple Argyll 276 C4
Portington Devon 12 F4
E Yorks 207 G11
Portinnisherrich Argyll 275 B10
Portinscale Cumb 229 G11
Port Isaac Corn 10 E5
Portishead N Som 60 D3
Portkil Argyll 276 E5
Portknockie Moray 302 C4
Port Lamont Argyll 275 F11
Portland Som 44 F3
Portlethen Aberds 293 D11
Portlethen Village
Aberds 293 D11
Portlevorchy Highld 306 D7
Portling Dumfries 237 D10
Port Lion Pembs 73 D7
Portloe Corn 3 B10
Port Logan Dumfries 236 E2
Portlooe Corn 6 E4
Portmahomack Highld 311 L3
Port Mead Swansea 56 B6
Portmeirion Gwyn 145 B11
Portmellon Corn 5 G10
Port Mholair W Isles 304 E7
Port Mor Highld 288 B6
Portmore Hants 20 B2
Port Mulgrave N Yorks 226 B5
Portnacroish Argyll 289 E11
Portnahaven Argyll 254 B2
Portnalong Highld 294 B5
Portnaluchaig Highld 295 G8
Portnancon Highld 308 C4
Port Nan Giùran
W Isles 304 E7
Port nan Long W Isles 296 D4
Portnellan Stirling 285 E8
Stirling 285 F8
Port Nis W Isles 304 B7
Portobello Edin 280 G6
T&W 243 F7
W Mid 133 D9
W Yorks 197 D10
Port of Menteith Stirling 285 G9
Porton Wilts 47 F7
Portpatrick Dumfries 236 D2
Port Quin Corn 10 E5
Portrack Stockton 225 B9
Port Ramsay Argyll 289 E10
Portreath Corn 4 F3
Portree Highld 298 E4
Port St Mary IoM 192 F3
Portscatho Corn 3 B9
Portsea Ptsmth 33 G10
Portsea Island Ptsmth 33 G11
Portskerra Highld 310 C2
Portskewett Mon 60 B4
Portslade Brighton 36 F3
Portslade-by-Sea
Brighton 36 G3
Portslade Village
Brighton 36 F3
Portsmouth Ptsmth 21 B9
W Yorks 196 B2
Port Solent Ptsmth 33 F10
Portsonachan Argyll 284 E4
Portsoy Aberds 302 C5
Port Sunlight Mers 182 E4
Port Sutton Bridge
Lincs 157 E9
Portswood Soton 32 E6
Port Talbot Neath 57 D9
Porttanachy Moray 302 C3
Port Tennant Swansea 57 C7
Portuairk Highld 288 C6
Portvasgo Highld 308 C5
Portway Dorset 18 D2
Glos 98 E5
Hereford 97 B9
Hereford 97 D9
Som 28 B6
Portway *continued*
Som 44 F3
W Mid 133 F9
Worcs 117 C11
Port Wemyss Argyll 254 B2
Port William Dumfries 236 E5
Portwood Gtr Man 184 C6
Portwrinkle Corn 7 E7
Posenhall Shrops 132 C3
Poslingford Suff 106 B5
Posso Borders 260 C6
Postbridge Devon 13 F9
Postcombe Oxon 84 F2
Post Green Dorset 18 C5
Postling Kent 54 F6
Postlip Glos 99 F10
Post Mawr = *Synod Inn*
Ceredig 111 G8
Postwick Norf 142 B5
Potarch Aberds 293 D8
Potash Suff 108 D2
Potbridge Hants 49 C8
Pot Common Sur 50 E2
Potholm Dumfries 249 F9
Potmaily Highld 300 F4
Potman's Heath Kent 38 B5
Potsgrove C Beds 103 F9
Potten End Herts 85 D8
Potten Street Kent 71 F9
Potter Brompton
N Yorks 217 D9
Pottergate Street Norf 142 E3
Potterhanworth Lincs 173 B9
Potterhanworth Booths
Lincs 173 B9
Potter Heigham Norf 161 F8
Potter Hill Leics 154 E4
S Yorks 186 B4
Potterne Wilts 46 B3
Potterne Wick Wilts 46 B4
Potternewton W Yorks 206 F2
Potters Bar Herts 86 E3
Potters Brook Lancs 202 C5
Potters Corner Kent 54 E3
Potter's Cross Staffs 132 G6
Potters Crouch Herts 85 D10
Potter's Forstal Kent 53 D11
Potter's Green E Sus 37 C8
W Mid 135 G7
Pottersheath Herts 86 B2
Potters Hill N Som 60 F4
Potters Marston Leics 135 D9
Potter Somersal Derbys 152 B2
Potterspury W Nhants 102 C5
Potter Street Essex 87 D7
Potterton Aberds 293 B11
W Yorks 206 F4
Pottery Field W Yorks 206 G2
Potthorpe Norf 159 E8
Pottington Devon 40 G5
Potto N Yorks 225 E9
Potton C Beds 104 B4
Pott Row Norf 158 E4
Pott Shrigley Ches E 184 F6
Pouchen End Herts 85 D8
Poughill Corn 24 F2
Devon 26 F5
Poulner Hants 31 F11
Poulshot Wilts 46 B3
Poulton Ches W 166 D5
Glos 81 E10
Mers 182 C4
Mers 182 E4
Poulton-le-Fylde Lancs 202 F2
Pound Som 28 D6
Pound Bank Worcs 98 B5
Worcs 116 C4
Poundbury Dorset 17 C9
Poundffald Swansea 56 C5
Poundfield E Sus 52 G4
Poundford E Sus 37 C9
Poundgate E Sus 37 B7
Poundgreen Wokingham 65 F7
Pound Green E Sus 37 C8
Hants 48 B5
IoW 20 D2
Suff 124 G4
Worcs 116 B5
Pound Hill W Sus 51 F9
Poundland S Ayrs 244 F5
Poundon Bucks 102 F2
Poundsbridge Kent 52 E4
Poundsgate Devon 13 G10
Poundstock Corn 11 B10
Pound Street Hants 64 G3
Pounsley E Sus 37 C8
Poverest London 68 F3
Povey Cross Sur 51 E9
Powburn Northumb 264 F3
Powderham Devon 14 E5
Powder Mills Kent 52 D5
Powers Hall End Essex 88 B4
Powerstock Dorset 16 B6
Powfoot Dumfries 238 D4
Pow Green Hereford 98 C4
Powhill Cumb 238 F6
Powick Worcs 116 G6
Powler's Piece Devon 24 D5
Powmill Perth 279 B10
Pownall Park Ches E 184 E4
Powntley Copse Hants 49 E8
Poxwell Dorset 17 E10
Poyle Slough 66 D4
Poynings W Sus 36 E3
Poyntington Dorset 29 D11
Poynton Ches E 184 E6
Telford 149 F11
Poynton Green Telford 149 F11
Poyntzfield Highld 301 C7
Poyston Pembs 73 B7
Poyston Cross Pembs 73 B7
Poystreet Green Suff 125 F9
Praa Sands Corn 2 D3
Pratling Street Kent 53 B8
Pratt's Bottom London 68 G3
Praze Corn 2 B3
Praze-an-Beeble Corn 2 B4
Predannack Wollas Corn 2 F5
Prees Shrops 149 C11
Preesall Lancs 202 D3
Preesall Park Lancs 202 D3
Prees Green Shrops 149 C11
Preesgweene Shrops 148 B5
Prees Heath Shrops 149 B11
Preeshenlle Shrops 148 C6
Prees Higher Heath
Shrops 149 B11
Prees Lower Heath
Shrops 149 C11
Prees Wood Shrops 149 C11
Prenbrigog Flint 166 C3
Prendergast Pembs 73 B7
Pembs 90 G6
Prenderguest Borders 273 D8
Prendwick Northumb 264 G2
Pren-gwyn Ceredig 93 C8
Prenteg Gwyn 163 G9
Prenton Mers 182 D4
Prescot Mers 183 C7
Prescott Devon 27 E9
Glos 99 F9
Prescott *continued*
Shrops 132 G3
Shrops 149 E8
Presdales Herts 86 C5
Preshome Moray 302 C4
Press Derbys 170 B5
Pressen Northumb 263 B8
Prestatyn Denb 181 E9
Prestbury Ches E 184 F6
Glos 99 G9
Presteigne Powys 114 E6
Presthope Shrops 131 D11
Prestleigh Som 44 E6
Prestolee Gtr Man 195 F9
Preston Borders 272 D5
Brighton 36 F4
Devon 14 G3
Dorset 17 E10
E Loth 281 F11
E Loth 281 G10
E Yorks 209 G9
Glos 81 E8
Glos 98 E3
Herts 104 G3
Kent 70 G4
Kent 71 G8
Lancs 194 B4
London 67 B7
Northumb 264 D5
Rutland 137 C7
Shrops 149 G10
Torbay 9 C7
T&W 243 D8
Wilts 62 D4
Wilts 63 E9
Preston Bagot Warks 118 D3
Preston Bissett Bucks 102 F3
Preston Bowyer Som 27 B10
Preston Brockhurst
Shrops 149 E10
Preston Brook Halton 183 E9
Preston Candover Hants 48 E6
Preston Capes
W Nhants 119 G11
Preston Crowmarsh
Oxon 83 G10
Preston Deanery
W Nhants 120 F5
Prestonfield Edin 280 G5
Preston Fields Warks 118 D3
Preston Grange T&W 243 C8
Preston Green Warks 118 D3
Preston Gubbals Shrops 149 F9
Preston-le-Skerne
Durham 234 G2
Preston Marsh Hereford 97 B11
Prestonmill Dumfries 237 D11
Preston Montford
Shrops 149 G8
Preston on Stour Warks 118 G4
Preston-on-Tees
Stockton 225 B8
Preston on the Hill
Halton 183 E9
Preston on Wye Hereford 97 C7
Prestonpans E Loth 281 G7
Preston Pastures Worcs 100 B3
Preston Plucknett Som 29 D8
Preston St Mary Suff 125 G8
Preston-under-Scar
N Yorks 223 G11
Preston upon the Weald
Moors Telford 150 F3
Preston Wynne Hereford 97 B11
Prestwich Gtr Man 195 G10
Prestwick Northumb 242 C5
S Ayrs 257 D9
Prestwold Leics 153 E11
Prestwood Bucks 84 E5
Staffs 133 F7
Staffs 169 G10
Prey Heath Sur 50 B3
Price Town Bridgend 76 G6
Prickwillow Cambs 139 G11
Priddy Som 44 C4
Pride Park Derbys 153 B7
Priestacott Devon 24 F6
Priestcliffe Derbys 185 G10
Priestcliffe Ditch
Derbys 185 G10
Priest Down Bath 60 G6
Priestfield W Mid 133 D8
Worcs 98 C6
Priesthaugh Borders 249 C11
Priesthill Glasgow 267 C10
Priesthorpe W Yorks 205 F10
Priest Hutton Lancs 211 E10
Priestley Green
W Yorks 196 B6
Prieston Borders 262 D2
Priestside Dumfries 238 D4
Priestthorpe W Yorks 205 F8
Priest Weston Shrops 130 D5
Priestwood Brack 65 F11
Kent 69 G7
Priestwood Green Kent 69 G7
Primethorpe Leics 135 E10
Primrose T&W 243 E8
Primrose Corner Norf 160 G6
Primrose Green Norf 159 F11
Primrosehill Herts 85 E9
Primrose Hill Bath 61 F8
Lancs 193 F11
London 67 C9
W Mid 133 F8
Primrose Valley
N Yorks 218 D2
Primsland Worcs 117 E8
Prince Hill Ches E 168 G2
Prince Royd W Yorks 196 D6
Princes End W Mid 133 E9
Princes Gate Pembs 73 C10
Prince's Marsh Hants 34 B3
Princes Park Mers 182 D5
Princes Risborough
Bucks 84 E4
Princethorpe Warks 119 C8
Princetown Caerph 77 C10
Devon 13 G7
Prinsted W Sus 22 B3
Printstile Kent 52 E5
Prion Denb 165 C9
Prior Muir Fife 287 F9
Prior Park Northumb 273 E9
Prior Rigg Cumb 239 D11
Priors Frome Hereford 97 D11
Priors Halton Shrops 115 B9
Priors Hardwick Warks 119 F9
Priorslee Telford 150 G4
Priors Marston Warks 119 F9
Prior's Norton Glos 99 G7
Priors Park Glos 99 E7
Priorswood Som 28 B2
Priory Pembs 72 D6
Priory Green Suff 107 C8
Priory Heath Suff 108 C3
Priory Wood Hereford 96 B5
Prisk V Glam 58 D4
Pristacott Devon 25 B8
Priston Bath 61 G7
Pristow Green Norf 142 F2
Prittlewell Southend 69 B11
Privett Hants 21 B7
Hants 33 B11
Prixford Devon 40 F4
Probus Corn 5 F7
Proncy Highld 309 K7
Prospect Cumb 229 C8
Prospect Village Staffs 151 G10
Prospidnick Corn 2 C4
Provanmill Glasgow 268 B2
Prowse Devon 26 F4
Prudhoe Northumb 242 E3
Prussia Cove Corn 2 D3
Ptarmigan Lodge
Stirling 285 G7
Pubil Perth 285 C8
Publow Bath 60 G6
Puckeridge Herts 105 G7
Puckington Som 28 D5
Pucklechurch S Glos 61 D7
Pucknall Hants 32 B5
Puckrup Glos 99 D7
Puckshole Glos 80 D4
Puddaven Devon 8 C5
Puddinglake Ches W 168 B2
Pudding Pie Nook Lancs 202 F6
Puddington Ches W 182 G4
Devon 26 E4
Puddle Corn 5 D11
Puddlebridge Som 28 E4
Puddledock Kent 52 C3
Kent 68 E4
Norf 141 E11
Puddletown Dorset 17 C11
Pudleigh Som 28 E4
Pudleston Hereford 115 F11
Pudsey W Yorks 196 B2
W Yorks 205 G10
Pulborough W Sus 35 D8
Pulcree Dumfries 237 D7
Pule Hill W Yorks 196 B5
Puleston Telford 150 E4
Pulford Ches W 166 D5
Pulham Dorset 30 F2
Pulham Market Norf 142 F3
Pulham St Mary Norf 142 F4
Pullens Green S Glos 79 G10
Pulley Shrops 131 B9
Pullington Kent 53 G10
Pulloxhill C Beds 103 E11
Pulverbatch Shrops 131 C8
Pumpherston W Loth 269 B11
Pumsaint Carms 94 C3
Puncheston = *Cas-Mael*
Pembs 91 F10
Puncknowle Dorset 16 D6
Punnett's Town E Sus 37 C10
Purbrook Hants 33 F11
Purewell BCP 19 C9
Purfleet Thurrock 68 D5
Puriton Som 43 E10
Purleigh Essex 88 E4
Purley London 67 G10
Purley on Thames
W Berks 65 D7
Purlogue Shrops 114 B5
Purlpit Wilts 61 F11
Purls Bridge Cambs 139 F9
Purn N Som 43 B10
Purse Caundle Dorset 29 D11
Purslow Shrops 131 G7
Purston Jaglin W Yorks 198 D2
Purtington Som 28 F5
Purton Glos 79 E11
W Berks 64 D3
Wilts 62 B5
Purton Common Wilts 62 B5
Purton Stoke Wilts 81 G9
Purwell Herts 104 F4
Pury End W Nhants 102 B4
Pusey Oxon 82 F5
Putley Hereford 98 D2
Putley Common Hereford 98 D2
Putley Green Hereford 98 D2
Putloe Glos 80 D3
Putney London 67 D8
Putney Heath London 67 E8
Putney Vale London 67 E8
Putnoe Bedford 121 G11
Putsborough Devon 40 E3
Putson Hereford 97 D10
Puttenham Herts 84 C5
Sur 50 D2
Puttock End Essex 106 C6
Puttock's End Essex 87 B9
Putton Dorset 17 E9
Puxey Dorset 30 E3
Puxley W Nhants 102 C5
Puxton N Som 60 G2
Pwll Carms 75 E7
Powys 130 C3
Pwll-clai Flint 181 G11
Pwllcrochan Pembs 72 E6
Pwll-glas Denb 165 E10
Pwllgloyw Powys 95 E10
Pwllheli Gwyn 145 B7
Pwll-Mawr Cardiff 59 D8
Pwll-melyn Flint 181 G11
Pwllmeyric Mon 79 G8
Pwll-trap Carms 74 B3
Pwll-y-glaw Neath 57 C9
Pwllypant Caerph 59 B7
Pye Bridge Derbys 170 E6
Pyecombe W Sus 36 E3
Pye Corner Devon 14 B4
Kent 53 D11
Newport 59 B9
S Glos 60 B6
Pye Green Staffs 151 G9
Pye Hill Notts 170 E6
Pyewipe NE Lincs 201 E9
Pyle IoW 20 F5
Swansea 56 D5
Pyle = *Y Pîl* Bridgend 57 E10
Pylehill Hants 33 D7
Pyle Hill Sur 50 B3
Pyleigh Som 42 G6
Pylle Som 44 F6
Pymore or Pymoor
Cambs 139 F9
Pype Hayes W Mid 134 E2
Pyrford Sur 50 B4
Pyrford Green Sur 50 B4
Pyrford Village Sur 50 B4
Pyrland Som 28 B2
Pyrton Oxon 83 F11
Pytchley N Nhants 121 C7
Pyworthy Devon 24 G4

Q

Quabbs Shrops 130 G4
Quabrook E Sus 52 G2
Quadring Lincs 156 C4
Quadring Eaudike Lincs 156 C4
Quags Corner W Sus 34 C5
Quainton Bucks 84 B2
Quaker's Yard M Tydf 77 F9
Quaking Houses
Durham 242 G5
Quality Corner Cumb 219 B9
Quarhouse Glos 80 E5
Quarley Hants 47 E9
Quarmby W Yorks 196 D6
Quarndon Derbys 170 G4
Quarndon Common
Derbys 170 G4
Quarrelton Renfs 267 C8
Quarrendon Bucks 84 B4
Quarr Hill IoW 21 C7
Quarriers Village
Invclyd 267 B7
Quarrington Lincs 173 G9
Quarrington Hill
Durham 234 D2
Quarrybank Ches W 167 B8
Quarry Bank W Mid 133 F8
Quarryford E Loth 271 B11
Quarryhead Aberds 303 C9
Quarry Heath Staffs 151 G8
Quarryhill Highld 309 L7
Quarry Hill Staffs 134 C4
Quarrywood Moray 301 C11
Quarter S Lanark 268 E4
Quartley Devon 27 B7
Quatford Shrops 132 E4
Quatquoy Orkney 314 E3
Quatt Shrops 132 F5
Quebec Durham 233 C9
W Sus 34 C3
Quedgeley Glos 80 C4
Queen Adelaide Cambs 139 G11
Queenborough Kent 70 E2
Queen Camel Som 29 C9
Queen Charlton Bath 60 F6
Queen Dart Devon 26 D4
Queenhill Worcs 99 D7
Queen Oak Dorset 45 G9
Queen's Bower IoW 21 E7
Queensbury London 67 B7
W Yorks 205 G8
Queen's Corner W Sus 34 B5
Queensferry Edin 280 F2
Flint 166 B4
Queen's Head Shrops 148 D6
Queenslie Glasgow 268 B3
Queen's Park Bedford 103 B10
Blackburn 195 B7
Ches W 166 B6
Essex 87 F11
W Nhants 120 E5
Queenstown Blackpool 202 F2
Queen Street Kent 53 D7
Wilts 62 B4
Queensville Staffs 151 E8
Queenzieburn N Lanark 278 F3
Quemerford Wilts 62 F4
Quendale Shetland 313 M5
Quendon Essex 105 E10
Queniborough Leics 154 G2
Quenington Glos 81 E10
Quernmore Lancs 202 B6
Queslett W Mid 133 E11
Quethiock Corn 6 C6
Quhamm Shetland 312 G6
Quholm Orkney 314 E2
Quick Gtr Man 196 G3
Quick Edge Gtr Man 196 G3
Quicks Green W Berks 64 D5
Quidenham Norf 141 F10
Quidhampton Hants 48 C4
Wilts 46 G6
Quilquox Aberds 303 F9
Quina Brook Shrops 149 C10
Quinbury End W Nhants 120 G2
Quindry Orkney 314 G4
Quinton W Mid 133 G9
W Nhants 120 G5
Quintrell Downs Corn 5 C7
Quixhill Staffs 169 G10
Quoditch Devon 12 B4
Quoig Perth 286 E2
Quoisley Ches E 167 F8
Quoit Corn 5 C8
Quorndon or Quorn
Leics 153 F11
Quothquan S Lanark 259 B11
Quoyloo Orkney 314 D2
Quoynee Highld 310 D6
Quoyness Orkney 314 F2
Quoys Shetland 312 B8
Shetland 313 G6

R

Raasay Ho Highld 295 B7
Rabbit's Cross Kent 53 D9
Rableyheath Herts 86 B2
Raby Cumb 238 G5
Mers 182 F4
Racecourse Suff 108 C3
Racedown Hants 47 E9
Rachan Mill Borders 260 C4
Rachub Gwyn 163 B10
Rack End Oxon 82 E6
Rackenford Devon 26 D5
Rackham W Sus 35 E9
Rackheath Norf 160 G5
Rackley Som 43 C11
Racks Dumfries 238 C2
Rackwick Orkney 314 B4
Orkney 314 G2
Radbourne Derbys 152 B5
Radcliffe Gtr Man 195 F9
Northumb 253 C7
Radcliffe on Trent Notts 154 B2
Radclive Bucks 102 E3
Radcot Oxon 82 F3
Raddery Highld 301 D7
Raddington Som 27 B8
Raddon Devon 26 G6
Radernie Fife 287 G8
Radfall Kent 70 G6
Radfield Kent 70 G2
Radford Bath 45 B7
Nottingham 171 G9
Oxon 101 G8
W Mid 134 G6
Worcs 117 F10
Radfordbridge Oxon 101 G8
Radford Semele Warks 118 E6
Radipole Dorset 17 E9
Radlet Som 43 F8
Radlett Herts 85 F11
Radley Oxon 83 F8
Radley Green Essex 87 D10
Radley Park Oxon 83 F8
Radlith Shrops 131 B8
Radmanthwaite Notts 171 C8
Radmoor Shrops 150 E2
Radmore Green Ches E 167 D9
Radmore Wood Staffs 151 D11
Radnage Bucks 84 F3
Radnor Corn 4 G4
Radnor Park W Dunb 277 G9
Radstock Bath 45 C7
Radstone W Nhants 101 C11
Radway Warks 101 B7
Radway Green Ches E 168 E3
Radwell Bedford 121 F10
Radwell *continued*
Herts 104 D4
Radwinter Essex 106 D2
Radwinter End Essex 106 D2
Radyr Cardiff 58 C6
Raehills Dumfries 248 E3
Raera Argyll 289 G10
Rafborough Hants 49 B11
Rafford Moray 301 D10
Raga Shetland 312 D6
Ragdale Leics 154 F3
Ragdon Shrops 131 E9
Raggalds W Yorks 205 G7
Ragged Appleshaw
Hants 47 D10
Raginnis Corn 1 D5
Raglan Mon 78 D6
Ragmere Norf 141 E11
Ragnal Wilts 63 E10
Ragnall Notts 188 G4
Rahane Argyll 276 D4
Rahoy Highld 289 D8
Raigbeg Highld 301 G8
Rails S Yorks 186 D3
Rainbow Hill Worcs 117 F7
Rainford Mers 194 G3
Rainford Junction Mers 194 G3
Rainham London 68 C4
Medway 69 F10
Rainhill Mers 183 C7
Rainhill Stoops Mers 183 D8
Rainow Ches E 185 F7
Rainowlow Ches E 185 F7
Rain Shore Gtr Man 195 D11
Rainsough Gtr Man 195 G10
Rainton Dumfries 237 D8
N Yorks 215 D7
Rainton Bridge T&W 234 B2
Rainton Gate Durham 234 B2
Rainworth Notts 171 D9
Raisbeck Cumb 222 D2
Raise Cumb 231 B10
Rait Perth 286 E6
Raithby Lincs 190 E4
Raithby by Spilsby Lincs 174 B5
Rake W Sus 34 B4
Rake Common Hants 34 B3
Rake End Staffs 151 F11
Rake Head Lancs 195 C10
Rakes Dale Staffs 169 G9
Rakeway Staffs 169 G8
Rakewood Gtr Man 196 E2
Raleigh Devon 40 G5
Ralia Lodge Highld 291 D9
Rallt Swansea 56 C4
Ram Carms 93 B11
Ram Alley Wilts 63 G8
Ramasaig Highld 297 G7
Rame Corn 2 C6
Corn 7 F8
Rameldry Mill Bank
Fife 287 G7
Ram Hill S Glos 61 D7
Ram Lane Kent 54 D3
Ramnageo Shetland 312 C8
Rampisham Dorset 29 G9
Rampside Cumb 210 F4
Rampton Cambs 123 D8
Notts 188 F3
Ramsbottom Gtr Man 195 D9
Ramsburn Moray 302 D5
Ramsbury Wilts 63 E9
Ramscraigs Highld 311 G5
Ramsdean Hants 34 C2
Ramsdell Hants 48 B5
Ramsden London 68 F3
Oxon 82 B5
Worcs 99 B8
Ramsden Bellhouse
Essex 88 G2
Ramsden Heath Essex 88 F2
Ramsden Wood
W Yorks 196 C2
Ramsey Cambs 138 F5
Essex 108 E4
IoM 192 C5
Ramseycleuch Borders 261 G7
Ramsey Forty Foot
Cambs 138 F6
Ramsey Heights Cambs 138 F5
Ramsey Island Essex 89 D7
Ramsey Mereside
Cambs 138 F5
Ramsey St Mary's
Cambs 138 F5
Ramsgate Kent 71 G11
Ramsgill N Yorks 214 E2
Ramshaw Durham 232 B5
Durham 233 F8
Ramsholt Suff 108 C6
Ramshorn Staffs 169 F9
Ramsley Devon 13 C8
Ramslye Kent 52 F5
Ramsnest Common Sur 50 G2
Ranais W Isles 304 F6
Ranby Lincs 190 F2
Notts 187 E11
Rand Lincs 189 F10
Randwick Glos 80 D4
Ranfurly Renfs 267 C7
Rangag Highld 310 E5
Rangemore Staffs 152 E3
Rangeworthy S Glos 61 B7
Rankinston E Ayrs 257 G11
Rank's Green Essex 88 B3
Ranmoor S Yorks 186 D4
Ranmore Common Sur 50 C6
Rannerdale Cumb 220 B3
Rannoch Lodge Perth 285 B9
Rannoch Station Perth 285 B8
Ranochan Highld 295 G10
Ranskill Notts 187 D11
Ranton Staffs 151 E7
Ranton Green Staffs 150 E6
Ranworth Norf 161 G7
Rapkyns W Sus 50 G6
Raploch Stirling 278 C5
Rapness Orkney 314 B5
Rapps Som 28 D4
Rascal Moor E Yorks 208 F2
Rascarrel Dumfries 237 E9
Rashielee Renfs 277 G9
Rashiereive Aberds 303 G9
Rashwood Worcs 117 D8
Raskelf N Yorks 215 E9
Rassal Highld 299 E8
Rassau Bl Gwent 77 C11
Rastrick W Yorks 196 C6
Ratagan Highld 295 D11
Ratby Leics 135 B10
Ratcliff London 67 C11
Ratcliffe Culey Leics 134 D6
Ratcliffe on Soar Leics 153 D9
Ratcliffe on the Wreake
Leics 154 G2
Ratford Wilts 62 E3
Ratfyn Wilts 47 E7
Rathen Aberds 303 C10
Rathillet Fife 287 E7
Rathmell N Yorks 204 B2
Ratho Edin 280 G2

Ratho Station Edin. 280 G2
Rathven Moray 302 C4
Ratlake Hants 32 C6
Ratley Warks 101 B7
Ratling Kent 55 C8
Ratlinghope Shrops 131 D8
Ratsloe Devon 14 B5
Rattar Highld 310 B6
Ratten Row Cumb 230 B3
Cumb 230 C2
Lancs 202 E4
Norf 157 G10
Rattery Devon 8 C4
Rattlesden Suff 125 F9
Rattray Perth 286 C5
Raughton Cumb 230 B3
Raughton Head Cumb 230 B3
Raunds N Nhants 121 C9
Ravelston Edin 280 G4
Ravenfield S Yorks 187 B7
Ravenglass Cumb 219 F11
Ravenhead Mers 183 C8
Ravenhills Green Worcs 116 G4
Raveningham Norf 143 D7
Ravenscar N Yorks 227 E9
Ravenscliffe Stoke 168 E4
W Yorks 205 F9
Ravenscraig Invclyd 276 F5
Ravensdale IoM 192 C4
Ravensden Bedford 121 G11
Ravenseat N Yorks 223 E7
Raven's Green Essex 108 G2
Ravenshall Staffs 168 F3
Ravenshead Notts 171 E9
Ravensmoor Ches E 167 E10
Ravensthorpe Pboro 138 C3
W Nhants 120 C3
W Yorks 197 C8
Ravenstone Leics 153 G8
M Keynes 120 G6
Ravenstonedale Cumb 222 E4
Ravenstown Cumb 211 D7
Ravenstruther S Lanark 269 F8
Ravenswood Village Settlement Wokingham 65 G10
Ravensworth N Yorks 224 D2
Raw N Yorks 227 D8
Rawcliffe E Yorks 199 C7
York 207 C7
Rawcliffe Bridge
E Yorks 199 C7
Rawdon W Yorks 205 F10
Rawdon Carrs W Yorks 205 F10
Rawfolds W Yorks 197 C7
Rawgreen Northumb 241 F10
Raw Green S Yorks 197 F9
Rawmarsh S Yorks 186 B6
Rawnsley Staffs 151 G10
Rawreth Essex 88 G3
Rawreth Shot Essex 88 G3
Rawridge Devon 28 F2
Rawson Green Derbys 170 F5
Rawtenstall Lancs 195 C10
Rawthorpe W Yorks 197 D7
Rawyards N Lanark 268 B5
Raxton Aberds 303 F8
Raydon Suff 107 D11
Raygill N Yorks 204 D4
Raylees Northumb 251 E10
Rayleigh Essex 88 G4
Rayne Essex 106 G4
Rayners Lane London 66 B6
Raynes Park London 67 F8
Reabrook Shrops 131 C7
Reach Cambs 123 D11
Read Lancs 203 G11
Reader's Corner Essex 88 E2
Reading Reading 65 E8
Readings Glos 79 B10
Reading Street Kent 54 G2
Kent 71 F11
Readymoney Corn 6 E2
Ready Token Glos 81 E10
Reagill Cumb 222 B2
Rearquhar Highld 309 K7
Rearsby Leics 154 G3
Reasby Lincs 189 F9
Rease Heath Ches E 167 E10
Reaster Highld 310 C6
Reaulay Highld 299 D7
Reawick Shetland 313 J5
Reawla Corn 2 B4
Reay Highld 310 C3
Rechullin Highld 299 D8
Reculver Kent 71 F8
Red Ball Devon 27 D9
Redberth Pembs 73 E9
Redbourn Herts 85 C10
Redbournbury Herts 85 C10
Redbourne N Lincs 189 B7
N Lincs 200 G3
Redbridge Dorset 17 D11
London 68 B2
Soton 32 E5
Red Bridge Lancs 211 D9
Redbrook Mon 79 C8
Wrex 167 G8
Red Bull Ches E 168 D4
Staffs 150 B4
Redburn Highld 300 C5
Highld 301 E9
Northumb 241 E7
Redcar Redcar 235 G8
Redcastle Angus 287 B10
Highld 300 E5
Redcliff Bay N Som 60 D2
Redcroft Dumfries 237 B9
Redcross Worcs 117 C7
Red Dial Cumb 229 B11
Reddicap Heath W Mid 134 D2
Redding Falk 279 F8
Reddingmuirhead Falk 279 F8
Reddish Gtr Man 184 C5
Warr 183 D11
Redditch Worcs 117 D10
Rede Suff 124 F6
Redenhall Norf 142 G5
Redenham Hants 47 D10
Redesdale Camp
Northumb 251 D8
Redesmouth Northumb 251 G9
Redford Aberds 293 F9
Angus 287 C9
Dorset 29 F10
Durham 233 E7
W Sus 34 B5
Redfordgreen Borders 261 F9
Redgorton Perth 286 E4
Redgrave Suff 125 B10
Redheugh Angus 292 G6
Redhill Aberds 293 C9
Aberds 302 F6
Herts 104 E6
Notts 171 F9
N Som 60 G4
Shrops 131 B9
Shrops 150 G4
Staffs 150 D6
Sur 51 C9
Telford 150 G4
Red Hill BCP 19 B7
Red Hill continued
Hants 34 E2
Hereford 97 D10
Kent 53 C7
Leics 135 D10
Pembs 72 B6
Warks 118 F2
Worcs 117 G7
W Yorks 198 B2
Redhills Cumb 230 F6
Devon 14 C4
Redhouse Argyll 275 G9
Red House Common
E Sus 36 C5
Redhouses Argyll 274 G4
Redisham Suff 143 G8
Red Lake Telford 150 G3
Redland Bristol 60 D5
Orkney 314 D3
Redland End Bucks 84 E4
Redlands Dorset 17 E9
Som 44 G3
Swindon 81 G11
Redlane Som 28 E2
Redlingfield Suff 126 C3
Red Lodge Suff 124 C3
Red Lumb Gtr Man 195 D10
Redlynch Som 45 G8
Wilts 32 C2
Redmain Cumb 229 E8
Redmarley D'Abitot Glos 98 E5
Redmarshall Stockton 234 G3
Redmile Leics 154 B5
Redmire N Yorks 223 G10
Redmonsford Devon 24 D4
Redmoor Corn 5 C11
Redmoss Aberds 303 F8
Rednal Shrops 149 D7
W Mid 117 B10
Redpath Borders 262 B3
Red Pits Norf 159 D11
Redpoint Highld 299 C7
Red Post Corn 24 F3
Red Rail Hereford 97 F10
Red Rice Hants 47 E10
Red Rock Gtr Man 194 F5
Red Roses Carms 74 C2
Red Row Northumb 253 D7
Redruth Corn 4 G3
Red Scar Lancs 203 G7
Redscarhead Borders 270 G4
Redstocks Wilts 62 G2
Red Street Staffs 168 E4
Redtye Corn 5 C10
Redvales Gtr Man 195 F10
Red Wharf Bay Anglesey 179 E8
Redwick Newport 60 C2
S Glos 60 B4
Redwith Shrops 148 E6
Redworth Darl 233 G10
Reed Herts 105 D7
Reed End Herts 104 D6
Reedham Lincs 174 D2
Norf 143 C8
Reedley Lancs 204 F2
Reedness E Yorks 199 C9
Reed Point Lincs 174 E2
Reeds Beck Lincs 174 B2
Reedsford Northumb 263 C9
Reeds Holme Lancs 195 C10
Reedy Devon 14 D2
Reen Manor Corn 4 E5
Reepham Lincs 189 G8
Norf 159 E11
Reeth N Yorks 223 F10
Reeves Green W Mid 118 B5
Refail Powys 130 C3
Regaby IoM 192 C5
Regil Bath 60 G4
Regoul Highld 301 D8
Reiff Highld 307 H4
Reigate Sur 51 C9
Reigate Heath Sur 51 C8
Reighton N Yorks 218 D2
Reighton Gap N Yorks 218 D2
Reinigeadal W Isles 305 H4
Reisque Aberds 293 B10
Reiss Highld 310 D7
Rejerrah Corn 4 D5
Releath Corn 2 C5
Relubbus Corn 2 C3
Relugas Moray 301 E9
Remenham Wokingham 65 C9
Remenham Hill
Wokingham 65 C9
Remony Perth 285 C11
Rempstone Notts 153 E11
Remusaig Highld 309 J7
Rendcomb Glos 81 D8
Rendham Suff 126 E6
Rendlesham Suff 126 G6
Renfrew Renfs 267 B10
Renhold Bedford 121 G11
Renishaw Derbys 186 F6
Renmure Angus 287 B10
Rennington Northumb 264 F6
Renshaw Wood Shrops 132 B6
Renton W Dunb 277 F7
Renwick Cumb 231 C7
Repps Norf 161 F8
Repton Derbys 152 D6
Reraig Highld 295 C10
Reraig Cot Highld 295 B10
Rerwick Shetland 313 M5
Rescassa Corn 5 G9
Rescobie Angus 287 B9
Rescorla Corn 5 D10
Resipole Highld 289 C9
Reskadinnick Corn 4 G2
Resolfen = Resolven
Neath 76 E4
Resolis Highld 300 C6
Resolven = Resolfen
Neath 76 E4
Restalrig Edin 280 G5
Reston Borders 273 C7
Cumb 221 F9
Restronguet Passage Corn 3 B8
Restrop Wilts 62 B5
Resugga Green Corn 5 D10
Reswallie Angus 287 B9
Retallack Corn 5 B8
Retew Corn 5 D8
Retford Notts 188 E2
Retire Corn 5 C10
Rettendon Essex 88 F3
Rettendon Place Essex 88 F3
Revesby Lincs 174 C3
Revesby Bridge Lincs 174 C4
Revidge Blackburn 195 B7
Rew Devon 9 G9
Devon 13 G11
Dorset 29 F11
Rewe Devon 14 B4
Rew Street IoW 20 C5
Rexon Devon 12 D4
Rexon Cross Devon 12 D4
Reybridge Wilts 62 F2
Reydon Suff 127 B9
Reydon Smear Suff 127 B9
Reymerston Norf 141 B10
Reynalton Pembs 73 D9
Reynoldston Swansea 56 C3
Rezare Corn 12 F3
Rhadyr Mon 78 E5
Rhaeadr Gwy = Rhayader
Powys 113 D9
Rhandir Conwy 180 G4
Rhandirmwyn Carms 94 C5
Rhayader = Rhaeadr Gwy
Powys 113 D9
Rhedyn Gwyn 144 C5
Rhegreanoch Highld 307 H5
Rhemore Highld 289 D7
Rhencullen IoM 192 C4
Rhenetra Highld 298 D4
Rhes-y-cae Flint 181 G11
Rhewl Denb 165 C10
Denb 165 F11
Shrops 148 C6
Wrex 149 B7
Rhewl-fawr Flint 181 E10
Rhewl-Mostyn Flint 181 E11
Rhian Highld 309 H5
Rhicarn Highld 307 G5
Rhiconich Highld 306 D7
Rhicullen Highld 300 B6
Rhidorroch Ho Highld 307 K6
Rhiews Shrops 150 B2
Rhifail Highld 308 E7
Rhigolter Highld 308 D3
Rhigos Rhondda 76 D6
Rhilochan Highld 309 J7
Rhippinllwyd Ceredig 92 C5
Ceredig 110 G6
Highld 301 B8
Rhiroy Highld 307 L6
Rhitongue Highld 308 D6
Rhivichie Highld 306 D7
Rhiw Gwyn 144 D4
Rhiwabon = Ruabon
Wrex 166 G4
Rhiwbebyll Denb 165 B10
Rhiwbina Cardiff 59 C7
Rhiwbryfdir Gwyn 163 F11
Rhiwceiliog Bridgend 58 C3
Rhiwderin Newport 59 B9
Rhiwen Gwyn 163 C9
Rhiwfawr Neath 76 C2
Rhiwinder Rhondda 58 B4
Rhiwlas Gwyn 147 B8
Gwyn 163 B9
Powys 148 C3
Rhode Som 43 G9
Rhode Common Kent 54 B5
Rhodes Gtr Man 195 F11
Rhodesia Notts 187 F9
Rhodes Minnis Kent 55 E7
Rhodiad Pembs 90 F5
Rhondda Rhondda 77 F7
Rhonehouse or Kelton Hill
Dumfries 237 D9
Rhoose V Glam 58 F5
Rhos Carms 93 D7
Rhôs Denb 165 C10
Neath 76 E2
Rhos Powys 148 F5
Rhosaman Carms 76 C2
Rhosbeirio Anglesey 178 C5
Rhoscefnhir Anglesey 179 F8
Rhoscolyn Anglesey 178 F3
Rhôs Common Powys 148 F5
Rhoscrowther Pembs 72 E6
Rhosddu Wrex 166 E4
Rhos-ddû Gwyn 144 B5
Rhosdylluan Gwyn 147 D7
Rhosesmor Flint 166 B2
Rhosfach Pembs 92 F2
Rhos-fawr Gwyn 145 B7
Rhosgadfan Gwyn 163 D8
Rhosgoch Anglesey 178 D6
Powys 96 B3
Rhos-goch Powys 96 B3
Rhosgyll Gwyn 163 G7
Rhos Haminiog Ceredig 111 E10
Rhos-hill Pembs 92 C3
Rhoshirwaun Gwyn 144 D3
Rhos Isaf Gwyn 163 D7
Rhoslan Gwyn 163 G7
Rhoslefain Gwyn 110 B2
Rhosllanerchrugog
Wrex 166 F3
Rhôs Lligwy Anglesey 179 D7
Rhosmaen Carms 94 G2
Rhosmeirch Anglesey 179 F7
Rhosneigr Anglesey 178 G4
Rhosnesni Wrex 166 E5
Rhôs-on-Sea Conwy 180 E4
Rhosrobin Wrex 166 E4
Rhossili Swansea 56 D2
Rhosson Pembs 90 F4
Rhostrehwfa Anglesey 178 G6
Rhostryfan Gwyn 163 D7
Rhostyllen Wrex 166 F4
Rhoswiel Shrops 148 B5
Rhosybol Anglesey 178 D6
Rhos-y-brithdir Powys 148 E2
Rhosycaerau Pembs 91 D8
Rhosygadair Newydd
Ceredig 92 B4
Rhosygadfa Shrops 148 C6
Rhos-y-garth Ceredig 112 C2
Rhosygilwen Pembs 92 C4
Rhos-y-gwaliau Gwyn 147 C8
Rhos-y-llan Gwyn 144 B4
Rhos-y-Madoc Wrex 166 G4
Rhosymedre Wrex 166 G3
Rhos-y-meirch Powys 114 D5
Rhosyn-coch Carms 92 G5
Rhu Argyll 275 G9
Argyll 276 E5
Rhuallt Denb 181 F9
Rhubodach Argyll 275 F11
Rhuddall Heath Ches W 167 C9
Rhuddlan Ceredig 93 C9
Denb 181 F8
Rhue Highld 307 K5
Rhulen Powys 96 B2
Rhunahaorine Argyll 255 C8
Rhyd Ceredig 92 C5
Gwyn 163 G10
Powys 129 C9
Rhydaman = Ammanford
Carms 75 C10
Rhydargaeau Carms 93 F8
Rhydcymerau Carms 93 D11
Rhydd Worcs 98 B6
Rhyd-Ddu Gwyn 163 E9
Rhydd Green Worcs 98 B6
Rhydding Neath 57 B8
Rhydfudr Ceredig 111 D11
Rhydgaled Conwy 165 C7
Rhydgaled = Chancery
Ceredig 111 B11
Rhydlewis Ceredig 92 B6
Rhydlios Gwyn 144 C3
Rhydlydan Conwy 164 E5
Powys 129 E11
Rhydmoelddu Powys 113 B11
Rhydness Powys 96 C2
Rhydowen Carms 92 F3
Ceredig 93 B8
Rhyd-Rosser Ceredig 111 D11
Rhydspence Hereford 96 B4
Rhydtalog Flint 166 D2
Rhyd-uchaf Gwyn 147 B8
Rhydwen Gwyn 146 F4
Rhydwyn Anglesey 178 D4
Rhyd-y-Brown Pembs 91 G11
Rhyd-y-clafdy Gwyn 144 B6
Rhydycroesau Powys 148 C4
Rhyd-y-cwm Shrops 130 G3
Rhydyfelin Carms 92 D5
Ceredig 111 B11
Powys 129 E11
Rhondda 58 B5
Rhyd-y-foel Conwy 180 F6
Rhyd-y-fro Neath 76 D2
Rhydygele Pembs 91 G7
Rhyd-y-gwin Swansea 75 E11
Rhyd-y-gwystl Gwyn 145 B8
Rhydymain Gwyn 146 E6
Rhyd-y-meirch Mon 78 D4
Rhyd-y-meudwy Denb 165 E10
Rhydymwyn Flint 166 B2
Rhyd-y-pandy Swansea 75 E11
Rhyd-y-sarn Gwyn 163 G11
Rhydywrach Carms 73 B11
Rhyl Denb 181 E8
Rhymney Caerph 77 D10
Rhyn Wrex 148 B6
Rhynd Fife 287 E8
Perth 286 E5
Rhynie Aberds 302 G4
Highld 301 B8
Ribbesford Worcs 116 C5
Ribblehead N Yorks 212 D5
Ribble Head N Yorks 212 D5
Ribbleton Lancs 203 G7
Ribby Lancs 202 G4
Ribchester Lancs 203 F8
Riber Derbys 170 D4
Ribigill Highld 308 D5
Riby Lincs 201 F7
Riby Cross Roads Lincs 201 F7
Riccall N Yorks 207 F8
Riccarton E Ayrs 257 B10
Richards Castle
Hereford 115 D9
Richborough Port Kent 71 G10
Richings Park Bucks 66 D4
Richmond London 67 E7
N Yorks 224 E3
S Yorks 186 D6
Richmond Hill W Yorks 206 G2
Richmond's Green
Essex 106 F2
Rich's Holford Som 42 G6
Rickard's Down Devon 24 B6
Rickarton Aberds 293 E10
Rickerby Cumb 239 F10
Rickerscote Staffs 151 E8
Rickford N Som 44 B3
Rickinghall Suff 125 B10
Rickleton T&W 243 G7
Rickling Essex 105 E9
Rickling Green Essex 105 F10
Rickmansworth Herts 85 G9
Rickney E Sus 23 D10
Riddell Borders 262 E2
Riddings Derbys 170 E6
Riddlecombe Devon 25 E10
Riddlesden W Yorks 205 E7
Riddrie Glasgow 268 B2
Ridgacre W Mid 133 G10
Ridge Bath 44 B5
Dorset 18 D4
Hants 32 D4
Herts 86 E2
Lancs 211 G9
Som 28 F3
Wilts 46 G3
Ridgebourne Powys 113 E11
Ridge Common Hants 34 C2
Ridge Green Sur 51 D10
Ridgehill N Som 60 G4
Ridge Hill Gtr Man 185 B7
Ridge Lane Warks 134 E5
Ridgemarsh Herts 85 G8
Ridge Row Kent 55 E8
Ridgeway Bristol 60 D6
Derbys 170 E5
Derbys 186 E6
Kent 54 E5
Newport 59 B9
Pembs 73 D10
Som 45 D8
Staffs 168 E5
Ridgeway Cross Hereford 98 B4
Ridgeway Moor Derbys 186 E6
Ridgewell Essex 106 C4
Ridgewood E Sus 23 B7
Ridgmont C Beds 103 D9
Ridgway Shrops 131 F7
Sur 50 B4
Riding Gate Som 30 B2
Riding Mill Northumb 242 E2
Ridley Kent 68 G6
Northumb 241 E7
Ridley Stokoe Northumb 250 F6
Ridleywood Wrex 166 E6
Ridlington Norf 160 C6
Rutland 136 C6
Ridlington Street Norf 160 C6
Ridsdale Northumb 251 G10
Riechip Perth 286 C4
Riemore Perth 286 C4
Rienachait Highld 306 F5
Rievaulx N Yorks 215 B11
Riff Orkney 314 E4
Riffin Aberds 303 E7
Rifle Green Torf 78 D3
Rift House Hrtlpl 234 E5
Rigg Dumfries 239 D7
Riggend N Lanark 278 G5
Rigsby Lincs 190 F6
Rigside S Lanark 259 B9
Riley Green Lancs 194 B6
Rileyhill Staffs 152 F2
Rilla Mill Corn 11 G11
Rillaton Corn 11 G11
Rillington N Yorks 217 E7
Rimac Lincs 191 C7
Rimington Lancs 204 D2
Rimpton Som 29 C10
Rimswell E Yorks 201 B10
Rimswell Valley
E Yorks 201 B10
Rinaston Pembs 91 F9
Rindleford Shrops 132 D4
Ringasta Shetland 313 M5
Ringford Dumfries 237 D8
Ringing Hill Leics 153 F9
Ringinglow S Yorks 186 E3
Ringland Newport 59 B11
Norf 160 G2
Ringles Cross E Sus 37 C7
Ringlestone Kent 53 B9
Kent 53 C11
Ringley Gtr Man 195 F9
Ringmer E Sus 36 E6
Ringmore Devon 8 F3
Ring o' Bells Lancs 194 E3
Ringorm Moray 302 E2
Ring's End Cambs 139 C7
Ringsfield Suff 143 F8
Ringsfield Corner Suff 143 F8
Ringshall Herts 85 C7
Suff 125 G10
Ringshall Stocks Suff 125 G10
Ringstead N Nhants 121 B9
Norf 176 E2
Ringtail Green Essex 87 B11
Ringwood Hants 31 F11
Ringwould Kent 55 D11
Rinmore Aberds 292 B6
Rinnigill Orkney 314 G3
Rinsey Corn 2 D3
Rinsey Croft Corn 2 D4
Riof W Isles 304 E3
Ripe E Sus 23 C8
Ripley Derbys 170 E5
Hants 19 B9
N Yorks 214 G5
Sur 50 B5
Riplingham E Yorks 208 G5
Ripon N Yorks 214 E6
Ripper's Cross Kent 54 E3
Rippingale Lincs 155 D11
Ripple Kent 55 D10
Worcs 99 D7
Ripponden W Yorks 196 D4
Rireavach Highld 307 K5
Risabus Argyll 254 C4
Risbury Hereford 115 G10
Risby E Yorks 208 G6
Lincs 189 C10
Suff 124 D5
Risca Caerph 78 G2
Rise E Yorks 209 E9
Rise Carr Darl 224 B5
Riseden E Sus 52 G6
Kent 53 F8
Rise End Derbys 170 D3
Risegate Lincs 156 D4
Riseholme Lincs 189 F7
Risehow Cumb 228 E6
Riseley Bedford 121 E10
Wokingham 65 G8
Rise Park London 87 G8
Nottingham 171 F9
Rishangles Suff 126 D3
Rishton Lancs 203 G10
Rishworth W Yorks 196 D4
Rising Bridge Lancs 195 B9
Risingbrook Staffs 151 E8
Risinghurst Oxon 83 D9
Rising Sun Corn 12 G3
Risley Derbys 153 B9
Warr 183 C10
Risplith N Yorks 214 F4
Rispond Highld 308 C4
Rivar Wilts 63 G10
Rivenhall Essex 88 B4
Rivenhall End Essex 88 B4
River Kent 55 E9
W Sus 34 C6
River Bank Cambs 123 D10
Riverhead Kent 52 B4
Rivers' Corner Dorset 30 E3
Riverside Cardiff 59 D7
Plym 7 D8
Stirling 278 C6
Worcs 117 D10
Riverside Docklands
Lancs 194 B4
Riverton Devon 40 G6
Riverview Park Kent 69 E7
Rivington Lancs 194 E6
Rixon Dorset 30 E3
Rixton Warr 183 C11
Roach Bridge Lancs 194 B5
Roaches Gtr Man 196 G3
Roachill Devon 26 C4
Roade W Nhants 120 G5
Road Green Norf 142 E5
Roadhead Cumb 240 C2
Roadmeetings S Lanark 269 F7
Roadside Highld 310 C5
Roadside of Catterline
Aberds 293 F10
Roadside of Kinneff
Aberds 293 F10
Roadwater Som 42 F4
Road Weedon W Nhants 120 F2
Roag Highld 298 E2
Roa Island Cumb 210 G4
Roast Green Essex 105 E9
Roath Cardiff 59 D7
Roath Park Cardiff 59 D7
Roberton Borders 261 G10
S Lanark 259 D10
Robertsbridge E Sus 38 C2
Robertstown Moray 302 E2
Rhondda 77 E8
Roberttown W Yorks 197 C7
Robeston Back Pembs 73 B9
Robeston Cross Pembs 72 D5
Robeston Wathen Pembs 73 B9
Robeston West Pembs 72 D5
Robhurst Kent 54 G2
Robin Hill Staffs 168 D6
Robin Hood Derbys 186 G3
Lancs 194 E4
W Yorks 197 B10
Robinhood End Essex 106 D4
Robin Hood's Bay
N Yorks 227 D9
Robins W Sus 34 B4
Robinson's End Warks 134 E6
Roborough Devon 7 C10
Devon 25 D9
Rob Roy's House Argyll 284 F5
Robroyston Glasgow 268 B2
Roby Mers 182 C6
Roby Mill Lancs 194 F4
Rocester Staffs 152 B2
Roch Pembs 91 G7
Rochdale Gtr Man 195 E11
Roche Corn 5 C9
Roche Grange Staffs 169 C7
Rochester Medway 69 F8
Northumb 251 D8
Rochford Essex 88 G5
Worcs 116 D2
Roch Gate Pembs 91 G7
Rock Caerph 77 F11
Corn 10 F4
Devon 28 G3
Neath 57 C9
Northumb 264 E6
Som 28 C4
Worcs 116 C4
W Sus 35 E10
Rockbeare Devon 14 C6
Rockbourne Hants 31 D10
Rockcliffe Cumb 239 E9
Dumfries 237 D10
Flint 182 G3
Lancs 195 C11
Rockcliffe Cross Cumb 239 E8
Rock End Staffs 168 D5
Rock Ferry Mers 182 D4
Rockfield Highld 311 L3
Mon 79 C7
Rockford Devon 41 D9
Hants 31 F11
Rockgreen Shrops 115 B10
Rockhampton S Glos 79 G11
Rockhead Corn 11 E7
Rockhill Shrops 114 B5
Rockingham N Nhants 137 E7
Rockland All Saints
Norf 141 D9
Rockland St Mary Norf 142 C6
Rockland St Peter Norf 141 D9
Rockley Notts 188 G2
Wilts 63 E7
Rockley Ford Som 45 C8
Rockness Glos 80 F4
Rockrobin E Sus 52 G6
Rocksavage Halton 183 E8
Rocks Park E Sus 37 C7
Rockstowes Glos 80 F3
Rockville Argyll 276 C4
Rockwell End Bucks 65 B9
Rockwell Green Som 27 C10
Rocky Hill Scilly 1 G4
Rodbaston Staffs 151 G8
Rodborough Glos 80 E4
Rodbourne Swindon 62 C6
Wilts 62 C2
Rodbourne Bottom Wilts 62 C2
Rodbourne Cheney
Swindon 62 B6
Rodbridge Corner
Essex 107 C7
Rodd Hereford 114 E6
Roddam Northumb 264 E2
Rodden Dorset 17 E8
Rodd Hurst Hereford 114 E6
Roddymoor Durham 233 D9
Rode Som 45 C10
Rodeheath Ches E 168 B5
Rode Heath Ches E 168 D3
Rode Hill Som 45 C10
Roden Telford 149 F11
Rodford S Glos 61 C7
Rodgrove Som 30 C2
Rodhuish Som 42 F4
Rodington Telford 149 G11
Rodington Heath
Telford 149 G11
Rodley Glos 80 C2
W Yorks 205 F10
Rodmarton Glos 80 F6
Rodmell E Sus 36 F6
Rodmer Clough
W Yorks 196 B3
Rodmersham Kent 70 G2
Rodmersham Green Kent 70 G2
Rodney Stoke Som 44 C3
Rodsley Derbys 170 G2
Rodway Som 43 F9
Telford 150 F3
Rodwell Dorset 17 F9
Roebuck Low Gtr Man 196 F3
Roecliffe N Yorks 215 F7
Roe Cross Gtr Man 185 B7
Roedean Brighton 36 G4
Roe End Herts 85 B8
Roe Green Gtr Man 195 G9
Herts 86 D2
Herts 104 E6
Roehampton London 67 E8
Roe Lee Blackburn 203 G9
Roesound Shetland 312 G5
Roestock Herts 86 D2
Roffey W Sus 51 G7
Rogart Highld 309 J7
Rogart Station Highld 309 J7
Rogate W Sus 34 C4
Roger Ground Cumb 221 F7
Rogerstone Newport 59 B9
Rogerton S Lanark 268 D2
Roghadal W Isles 296 C6
Rogiet Mon 60 B3
Rogue's Alley Cambs 139 B7
Roke Oxon 83 G10
Rokemarsh Oxon 83 G10
Roker T&W 243 F10
Rollesby Norf 161 F8
Rolleston Leics 136 C4
Notts 172 E2
Rollestone S Yorks 186 E5
Wilts 46 E5
Rollestone Camp Wilts 46 E5
Rolleston-on-Dove
Staffs 152 D4
Rolls Mill Dorset 30 E3
Rolston E Yorks 209 D10
Rolstone N Som 59 G11
Rolvenden Kent 53 G10
Rolvenden Layne Kent 53 G11
Romaldkirk Durham 232 G5
Romanby N Yorks 225 G7
Roman Hill Suff 143 E10
Romannobridge Borders 270 F3
Romansleigh Devon 26 C2
Rome Angus 293 G7
Romesdal Highld 298 D4
Romford Dorset 31 F9
Kent 52 E6
London 68 B4
Romiley Gtr Man 184 C6
Romney Street Kent 68 G4
Rompa Shetland 313 L6
Romsey Hants 32 C5
Romsey Town Cambs 123 F9
Romsley Shrops 132 G5
Worcs 117 B9
Romsley Hill Worcs 117 B9
Ronachan Ho Argyll 255 B8
Ronague IoM 192 E3
Rondlay Telford 132 B4
Ronkswood Worcs 117 G7
Rood End W Mid 133 F10
Rookby Cumb 222 C6
Rook End Essex 105 E11
Rookhope Durham 232 C4
Rooking Cumb 221 B8
Rookley IoW 20 E6
Rookley Green IoW 20 E6
Rooks Bridge Som 43 C11
Rooksey Green Suff 125 G8
Rooks Hill Kent 52 C5
Rooksmoor Glos 80 E4
Rook's Nest Som 42 G5
Rook Street Wilts 45 G10
Rookwith N Yorks 214 B4
Rookwood W Sus 21 B11
Roos E Yorks 209 G11
Roose Cumb 210 F4
Roosebeck Cumb 210 F5
Roosecote Cumb 210 F4
Roost End Essex 106 C4
Rootham's Green
Bedford 122 F2
Rooting Street Kent 54 D3
Rootpark S Lanark 269 E9
Ropley Hants 48 G6
Ropley Dean Hants 48 G6
Ropley Soke Hants 49 G7
Ropsley Lincs 155 C9
Rora Aberds 303 D10
Rorandle Aberds 293 B8
Rorrington Shrops 130 C5
Rosarie Moray 302 E3
Roscroggan Corn 4 G3
Rose Corn 4 E5
Roseacre Kent 53 B9
Lancs 202 F4
Rose-an-Grouse Corn 2 B2
Rose Ash Devon 26 C3
Rosebank E Dunb 278 G3
S Lanark 268 F6
Rosebery Midloth 270 D6
Rosebrae Moray 301 C11
Rosebrough Northumb 264 D4
Rosebush Pembs 91 F11
Rosecare Corn 11 B9
Rosedale Herts 86 E4
Rosedale Abbey
N Yorks 226 F4
Roseden Northumb 264 E2
Rosedinnick Corn 5 B8
Rosedown Devon 24 C3
Rosefield Highld 301 D8
Rose Green Essex 107 F8
Suff 107 C9
Suff 107 D8
W Sus 22 D6
Rose Grove Lancs 204 G2
Rosehall Highld 309 J4
N Lanark 268 C4
Rosehaugh Mains
Highld 300 D6
Rosehearty Aberds 303 C9
Rosehill Blackburn 195 C8
Corn 4 E5
Corn 5 C10
Gtr Man 184 D3
London 67 F9
Pembs 72 B5
Shrops 150 C3
T&W 243 D8
Rose Hill Bucks 66 C2
Derbys 153 B7
E Sus 23 B7
Gtr Man 195 F8
Lancs 204 G2
Oxon 83 E8
Suff 108 C3
Sur 51 D7
Roseisle Moray 301 C11
Roseland Corn 6 C5
Roselands E Sus 23 E10
Rosemarket Pembs 73 D7
Rosemarkie Highld 301 D7
Rosemary Lane Devon 27 E11
Rosemelling Corn 5 D10
Rosemergy Corn 1 B4
Rosemount Perth 286 C5
Rosenannon Corn 5 B9
Rosenithon Corn 3 E8
Roser's Cross E Sus 37 C9
Rose Valley Pembs 73 E8
Rosevean Corn 5 D10
Rosevear Corn 2 E5
Roseville W Mid 133 E8
Rosevine Corn 3 B9
Rosewarne Corn 2 B4
Corn 4 G2
Rosewell Midloth 270 C5
Roseworth Stockton 234 G4
Roseworthy Corn 2 B4
Corn 4 F5
Roseworthy Barton Corn 2 B4
Rosgill Cumb 221 B10
Rosherville Kent 68 E6
Roshven Highld 289 B9
Roskear Croft Corn 4 G3
Roskhill Highld 298 E2
Roskill House Highld 300 D6
Roskorwell Corn 3 E7
Rosley Cumb 230 B2
Roslin Midloth 270 C5
Rosliston Derbys 152 F4
Rosneath Argyll 276 E5
Ross Borders 273 C9
Dumfries 237 E8
Northumb 264 B4
Perth 285 E11
Rossett Wrex 166 D5
Rossett Green N Yorks 206 C2
Ross Green Worcs 116 E5
Rossie Ochill Perth 286 F4
Rossie Priory Perth 286 D6
Rossington S Yorks 187 B10
Rosskeen Highld 300 C6
Rossland Renfs 277 G8
Rossmore BCP 19 C7
Ross-on-Wye Hereford 98 G2
Roster Highld 310 F6
Rostherne Ches E 184 E2
Rostholme S Yorks 198 F5
Rosthwaite Cumb 220 C5
Cumb 220 G4
Roston Derbys 169 G10
Rosudgeon Corn 2 D3
Rosyth Fife 280 E2
Rotchfords Essex 107 E8
Rotcombe Bath 44 B6
Rothbury Northumb 252 C3
Rotherbridge W Sus 35 C7
Rotherby Leics 154 F3
Rotherfield E Sus 37 B9
Rotherfield Greys Oxon 65 C8
Rotherfield Peppard
Oxon 65 C8
Rotherham S Yorks 186 C6
Rotherhithe London 67 D11
Rothersthorpe
W Nhants 120 F4
Rotherwas Hereford 97 D10
Rotherwick Hants 49 B8
Rothes Moray 302 E2
Rothesay Argyll 275 G11
Rothiebrisbane Aberds 303 F7
Rothiemay Crossroads
Moray 302 E5
Rothiemurchus Lodge
Highld 291 C11
Rothienorman Aberds 303 F7
Rothiesholm Orkney 314 D6
Rothley Leics 153 G11
Northumb 252 F2
Rothley Plain Leics 153 G11
Rothley Shield East
Northumb 252 E2
Rothmaise Aberds 302 F6
Rothwell Lincs 189 B11
N Nhants 136 G6
W Yorks 197 B10
Rothwell Haigh
W Yorks 197 B10
Rotsea E Yorks 209 C7
Rottal Angus 292 G5
Rotten End Essex 106 F4
Suff 127 D7
Rotten Green Hants 49 B9
Rotten Row W Berks 64 E5
W Mid 118 B3
Rottingdean Brighton 36 G5
Rottington Cumb 219 C9
Rotton Park W Mid 133 F10
Roud IoW 20 E6
Rougham Norf 158 E6
Suff 125 E8
Rougham Green Suff 125 E8
Rough Bank Gtr Man 196 E2
Roughbirchworth
S Yorks 197 G9
Roughburn Highld 290 E5
Rough Close Staffs 151 B8
Rough Common Kent 54 B6
Roughcote Staffs 168 G6
Rough Haugh Highld 308 E7
Rough Hay Staffs 152 E4
Roughlee Lancs 204 E2
Roughley W Mid 134 D2
Roughmoor Som 28 B2
Swindon 62 B6
Roughrigg N Lanark 278 G6
Roughsike Cumb 240 B2
Roughton Lincs 174 C2
Norf 160 B4
Shrops 132 E5
Roughton Moor Lincs 174 C2
Roughway Kent 52 C6
Round Bush Herts 85 F10
Roundbush Essex 88 E5
Roundbush Green Essex 87 C9
Round Green Luton 103 G11
Roundham Som 28 F6
Roundhay W Yorks 206 F2
Round Maple Suff 107 C9
Round Oak Shrops 131 G7
W Mid 133 F8
Round's Green W Mid 133 F9
Roundshaw London 67 G10
Round Spinney
W Nhants 120 D5
Roundstonefoot
Dumfries 248 B4
Round Street Kent 69 F7
Roundstreet Common
W Sus 35 B9
Roundswell Devon 40 G4
Roundthorn Gtr Man 184 D4
Roundthwaite Cumb 222 E2
Roundway Wilts 62 G4
Roundyhill Angus 287 B7
Rousdon Devon 15 C11
Rousham Oxon 101 G9
Rous Lench Worcs 117 G10
Routenburn N Ayrs 266 C3
Routh E Yorks 209 E7
Rout's Green Bucks 84 F3
Row Corn 11 F7
Cumb 211 B8
Cumb 231 E8
Rowanburn Dumfries 239 B10
Rowanfield Glos 99 G8
Rowardennan Stirling 277 B7
Rowarth Derbys 185 D8
Row Ash Hants 33 E8
Rowbarton Som 28 B2
Rowberrow Som 44 B3
Row Brow Cumb 229 D7
Rowde Wilts 62 G3
Rowden Devon 13 B8
N Yorks 205 B11
Rowe Head Cumb 210 D5
Rowen Conwy 180 G3
Rowfoot Northumb 240 E5
Rowford Som 28 B2
Row Green Essex 106 G4
Row Heath Essex 89 B10
Rowhedge Essex 107 G10
Rowhill Sur 66 G4
Rowhook W Sus 50 G6
Rowington Warks 118 D4
Rowington Green
Warks 118 D4
Rowland Derbys 186 G2
Rowlands Castle Hants 34 E2
Rowlands Gill T&W 242 F5
Rowland's Green
Hereford 98 D3
Rowledge Sur 49 E10
Rowlestone Hereford 97 F7
Rowley E Yorks 208 G5
Shrops 130 B6
Rowley Green London 86 F2
Rowley Hill W Yorks 197 E7
Rowley Park Staffs 151 E8
Rowley Regis W Mid 133 F9
Rowley's Green W Mid 134 G6
Rowling Kent 55 C9
Rowly Sur 50 E4
Rownall Staffs 169 F7
Rowner Hants 33 G9
Rowney Green Worcs 117 C10
Rownhams Hants 32 D5
Row-of-trees Ches E 184 F4
Rowrah Cumb 219 B11
Rowsham Bucks 84 B4
Rowsley Derbys 170 B3
Rowstock Oxon 64 B3
Rowston Lincs 173 D9
Rowthorne Derbys 171 C7
Rowton Ches W 166 C6
Shrops 149 G7
Telford 150 F2
Rowton Moor Ches W 166 C6
Row Town Sur 66 G4
Roxburgh Borders 262 C5
Roxburgh Mains
Borders 262 D5
Roxby N Lincs 200 D2
N Yorks 226 B5
Roxeth London 66 B6
Roxton Bedford 122 G3
Roxwell Essex 87 D10
Royal British Legion Village
Kent 53 B8
Royal Leamington Spa
Warks 118 D6
Royal Oak Darl 233 G10
Lancs 194 G2
N Yorks 218 D2
Royal's Green Ches E 167 G10
Royal Tunbridge Wells
= Tunbridge Wells Kent 52 F5
Royal Wootton Bassett
Wilts 62 C5
Roybridge Highld 290 E4
Royd S Yorks 197 G8
Roydhouse W Yorks 197 E8
Royd Moor S Yorks 197 G8
W Yorks 198 E2
Roydon Essex 86 D6
Norf 141 G11
Norf 158 E4
Roydon Hamlet Essex 86 D6
Royds Green W Yorks 197 B11
Royston Glasgow 268 B2
Herts 105 C7
S Yorks 197 E11
Royston Water Som 28 E2
Royton Gtr Man 196 F2
Ruabon = Rhiwabon
Wrex 166 G4

Ruaig Argyll 288 E2
Ruan High Lanes Corn 3 B10
Ruan Lanihorne Corn 5 G7
Ruan Major Corn 2 F6
Ruan Minor Corn 2 F6
Ruarach Highld 295 C11
Ruardean Glos 79 B10
Ruardean Hill Glos 79 B10
Ruardean Woodside
Glos 79 B10
Rubery Worcs 117 B9
Rubha Ghaisinis
W Isles 297 G4
Rubha Stoer Highld 306 F5
Ruchazie Glasgow 268 B3
Ruchill Glasgow 267 B11
Ruckcroft Cumb 230 C6
Ruckhall Hereford 97 D9
Ruckinge Kent 54 G4
Ruckland Lincs 190 F4
Rucklers Lane Herts 85 E9
Ruckley Shrops 131 C10
Rudbaxton Pembs 91 G9
Rudby N Yorks 225 D9
Ruddington Notts 153 C11
Ruddle Glos 79 C11
Rudford Glos 98 G5
Rudge Shrops 132 D6
Som 45 C10
Rudge Heath Shrops 132 D5
Rudgeway S Glos 60 B6
Rudgwick W Sus 50 G5
Rudhall Hereford 98 F2
Rudheath Ches W 183 G11
Rudheath Woods
Ches W 184 G2
Rudhja Garbh Argyll 289 E11
Rudley Green Essex 88 E4
Rudloe Wilts 61 E10
Rudry Caerph 59 B7
Rudston E Yorks 217 F11
Rudyard Staffs 169 D7
Ruewood Shrops 149 D9
Rufford Lancs 194 D3
Rufforth York 206 C6
Ruffs Notts 171 F8
Rugby Warks 119 B10
Rugeley Staffs 151 F10
Ruggin Som 27 D11
Ruglen S Ayrs 245 C7
Rugley Northumb 264 G5
Ruilick Highld 300 E5
Ruishton Som 28 C3
Ruisigearraidh W Isles 296 C5
Ruislip London 66 B5
Ruislip Common London 66 B5
Ruislip Gardens London 66 B5
Ruislip Manor London 66 B6
Ruiton W Mid 133 E8
Ruloe Ches W 183 G9
Rumach Highld 295 G8
Rumbling Bridge Perth 279 B10
Rumbow Cottages
Worcs 117 B8
Rumburgh Suff 142 G6
Rumbush W Mid 118 B2
Rumer Hill Staffs 133 B9
Rumford Corn 10 G3
Falk 279 F8
Rumney Cardiff 59 D8
Rumsam Devon 40 G5
Rumwell Som 27 C11
Runcorn Halton 183 E8
Runcton W Sus 22 C5
Runcton Holme Norf 140 B2
Rundlestone Devon 13 G7
Runfold Sur 49 D11
Runhall Norf 141 B11
Runham Norf 143 B10
Norf 161 G9
Runham Vauxhall Norf 143 B10
Running Hill Head
Gtr Man 196 F4
Runnington Som 27 C10
Running Waters Durham 234 C2
Runsell Green Essex 88 D3
Runshaw Moor Lancs 194 D4
Runswick Bay N Yorks 226 B6
Runwell Essex 88 G2
Ruscombe Glos 80 D4
Wokingham 65 D9
Ruscote Oxon 101 C8
Rushall Hereford 98 E2
Norf 142 G3
Wilts 46 B6
W Mid 133 C10
Rushbrooke Suff 125 E7
Rushbury Shrops 131 E10
Rushcombe Bottom BCP 18 B5
Rushden Herts 104 E6
N Nhants 121 D9
Rushenden Kent 70 E2
Rusher's Cross E Sus 37 B10
Rushey Mead Leicester 136 B2
Rushford Devon 12 F4
Norf 141 G8
Rushgreen Warr 183 D11
Rush Green Essex 89 B11
Herts 86 C5
Herts 104 G4
London 68 B4
Norf 141 B11
Rush-head Aberds 303 E8
Rush Hill Bath 61 G8
Rushington Hants 32 E5
Rushlake Green E Sus 23 B10
Rushland Cross Cumb 210 B6
Rushley Green Essex 106 D5
Rushmere C Beds 103 F8
Suff 143 F9
Rushmere St Andrew
Suff 108 B4
Rushmere Street Suff 108 B4
Rushmoor Sur 49 E11
Telford 150 G2
Rushmore Hants 33 E11
Rushmore Hill London 68 G3
Rushock Hereford 114 F6
Worcs 117 C7
Rusholme Gtr Man 184 B5
Rushton Ches W 167 C9
Dorset 18 D3
N Nhants 136 G6
N Yorks 217 C9
Shrops 132 B2
Rushton Spencer Staffs 168 C6
Rushwick Worcs 116 G6
Rushyford Durham 233 F11
Rushy Green E Sus 23 C7
Ruskie Stirling 285 G10
Ruskington Lincs 173 E9
Rusland Cumb 210 B6
Rusling End Herts 104 G4
Rusper W Sus 51 F8
Ruspidge Glos 79 C11
Russel Highld 299 E8
Russell Hill London 67 G10
Russell's Green E Sus 38 E2
Russell's Hall W Mid 133 F8
Russell's Water Oxon 65 B8
Russel's Green Suff 126 C5
Russ Hill Sur 51 E8
Rusthall Kent 52 F5
Rustington W Sus 35 G9
Ruston N Yorks 217 C9
Ruston Parva E Yorks 217 G11
Ruswarp N Yorks 227 D7
Ruthall Shrops 131 F11
Rutherford Borders 262 C4
Rutherglen S Lanark 268 C2
Ruthernbridge Corn 5 B10
Ruthin V Glam 58 D3
Ruthin =Ruthun Denb 165 D10
Ruthrieston Aberdeen 293 C11
Ruthun =Ruthin Denb 165 D10
Ruthven Aberds 302 E5
Angus 286 C6
Highld 291 D9
Highld 301 F8
Ruthven House Angus 287 C7
Ruthvoes Corn 5 C8
Ruthwaite Cumb 229 D10
Ruthwell Dumfries 238 D3
Ruxley London 68 E3
Ruxton Hereford 97 F11
Ruxton Green Hereford 79 B8
Ruyton-XI-Towns
Shrops 149 E7
Ryal Northumb 242 C2
Ryal Fold Blackburn 195 C7
Ryall Dorset 16 C4
Worcs 99 C7
Ryarsh Kent 53 B7
Rychraggan Highld 300 F4
Rydal Cumb 221 D7
Ryde IoW 21 C7
Rydens Sur 66 F6
Rydeshill Sur 50 C3
Rydon Devon 14 G3
Rye E Sus 38 C6
Ryebank Shrops 149 C10
Rye Common Hants 49 C9
Ryecroft S Yorks 186 B6
W Yorks 205 F7
Ryecroft Gate Staffs 168 C6
Ryeford Glos 80 E4
Rye Foreign E Sus 38 C5
Rye Harbour E Sus 38 D6
Ryehill E Yorks 201 B8
Ryeish Green Wokingham 65 F8
Ryelands Hereford 115 F9
Rye Park Herts 86 C5
Rye Street Worcs 98 D5
Ryeworth Glos 99 G9
Ryhall Rutland 155 G10
Ryhill W Yorks 197 E11
Ryhope T&W 243 G10
Rylah Derbys 171 B7
Rylands Notts 153 B10
Rylstone N Yorks 204 B5
Ryme Intrinseca Dorset 29 E9
Ryther N Yorks 207 F7
Ryton Glos 98 E4
N Yorks 216 D5
Shrops 132 C5
T&W 242 E5
Warks 135 F7
Ryton-on-Dunsmore
Warks 119 C7
Ryton Woodside T&W 242 E4

S

Sabden Lancs 203 F11
Sabine's Green Essex 87 F8
Sackers Green Suff 107 D8
Sacombe Herts 86 B4
Sacombe Green Herts 86 B4
Sacriston Durham 233 B10
Sadberge Darl 224 B6
Saddell Argyll 255 D8
Saddell Ho Argyll 255 D8
Saddington Leics 136 E3
Saddle Bow Norf 158 F2
Saddlescombe W Sus 36 E3
Saddle Street Dorset 28 G5
Sadgill Cumb 221 D9
Saffron's Cross
Hereford 115 G10
Saffron Walden Essex 105 D10
Sageston Pembs 73 E9
Saham Hills Norf 141 C8
Saham Toney Norf 141 C8
Saighdinis W Isles 296 E4
Saighton Ches W 166 C6
Sain Dunwyd =St Donats
V Glam 58 F2
St Abbs Borders 273 B8
St Abb's Haven Borders 273 B8
St Agnes Corn 4 E4
Scilly 1 H3
St Albans Herts 85 D10
St Allen Corn 4 E6
St Andrews Fife 287 F9
St Andrew's Major
V Glam 58 E6
St Andrew's Wood Devon 27 F9
St Annes Lancs 193 B10
St Anne's Park Bristol 60 E6
St Ann's Dumfries 248 E3
Nottingham 171 G9
St Ann's Chapel Corn 12 G4
Devon 8 F3
St Anthony Corn 3 C9
St Anthony-in-Meneage
Corn 3 D7
St Anthony's T&W 243 E7
St Anthony's Hill E Sus 23 E10
St Arvans Mon 79 F8
St Asaph =Llanelwy
Denb 181 G8
St Athan =Sain Tathon
V Glam 58 F4
Sain Tathon =St Athan
V Glam 58 F4
St Augustine's Kent 54 C6
St Austell Corn 5 E10
St Austins Hants 20 B2
St Bees Cumb 219 C9
St Blazey Corn 5 E11
St Blazey Gate Corn 5 E11
St Boswells Borders 262 C3
St Breock Corn 10 G5
St Breward Corn 11 F7
St Briavels Glos 79 E9
St Briavels Common Glos 79 E8
St Bride's Pembs 72 C4
St Brides Major =
Saint-y-Brid V Glam 57 G11
St Bride's Netherwent
Mon 60 B2
St Brides-super-Ely
V Glam 58 D5
St Brides Wentlooge
Newport 59 C9
Saintbridge Glos 80 B5
St Budeaux Plym 7 D8
Saintbury Glos 100 D2
St Buryan Corn 1 D4
St Catherine Bath 61 E9
St Catherine's Argyll 284 G5
St Catherine's Hill BCP 19 B8
St Chloe Glos 80 E4
St Clears =Sanclêr
Carms 74 B3
St Cleer Corn 6 B5
St Clement Corn 4 G6
St Clether Corn 11 E10
St Colmac Argyll 275 G11
St Columb Major Corn 5 C8
St Columb Minor Corn 4 C6
St Columb Road Corn 5 D8
St Combs Aberds 303 C10
St Cross Hants 33 B7
St Cross South Elmham
Suff 142 G5
St Cyrus Aberds 293 G9
St David's Perth 286 E3
St David's =Tyddewi
Pembs 90 F5
St Day Corn 4 G4
St Decumans Som 42 E5
St Dennis Corn 5 D9
St Denys Soton 32 E6
St Devereux Hereford 97 E8
St Dials Torf 78 G3
St Dogmaels =Llandudoch
Pembs 92 B3
St Dominick Corn 7 B8
St Donat's =Sain Dunwyd
V Glam 58 F2
St Edith's Wilts 62 G3
St Endellion Corn 10 F5
St Enoder Corn 5 D7
St Erme Corn 4 E6
St Erney Corn 7 D7
St Erth Corn 2 B3
St Erth Praze Corn 2 B3
St Ervan Corn 10 G3
St Eval Corn 5 B7
St Ewe Corn 5 F9
St Fagans Cardiff 58 D6
St Fergus Aberds 303 D10
St Fillans Perth 285 E10
St Florence Pembs 73 E9
St Gennys Corn 11 B8
St George Bristol 60 E6
Conwy 181 F7
St George in the East
London 67 C10
St Georges N Som 59 G11
St George's Gtr Man 184 B4
Telford 150 G4
V Glam 58 D5
St George's Hill Sur 66 G5
St George's Well Devon 27 F8
St Germans Corn 7 D7
St Giles Lincs 189 G7
London 67 C10
St Giles in the Wood
Devon 25 D8
St Giles on the Heath
Devon 12 C3
St Giles's Hill Hants 33 B7
St Gluvias Corn 3 C7
St Godwalds Worcs 117 D9
St Harmon Powys 113 C9
St Helena Warks 134 C5
St Helen Auckland
Durham 233 F9
St Helens Cumb 228 E6
IoW 21 D8
Mers 183 B8
St Helen's E Sus 38 E4
S Yorks 197 F11
St Helen's Wood E Sus 38 E4
St Helier London 67 F9
St Hilary Corn 2 C3
V Glam 58 E4
Saint Hill Devon 27 F9
W Sus 51 F11
St Ibbs Herts 104 F3
St Illtyd Bl Gwent 78 E2
St Ippollytts Herts 104 F3
St Ishmael's Pembs 72 D4
St Issey Corn 10 G4
St Ive Corn 6 B6
St Ive Cross Corn 6 B6
St Ives Cambs 122 C6
Corn 2 A2
Dorset 31 G10
St James Dorset 30 C5
London 67 C9
Norf 160 E5
St James's End
W Nhants 120 E4
St James South Elmham
Suff 142 G6
St Jidgey Corn 5 B8
St John Corn 7 E8
St Johns London 67 D11
Warks 118 C5
St John's E Sus 52 G4
IoM 192 D3
Kent 52 B4
Kent 52 E5
Sur 50 B3
Worcs 116 G6
W Yorks 206 F4
St John's Chapel Devon 25 B8
Durham 232 D3
St John's Fen End
Norf 157 G10
St John's Highway
Norf 157 G10
St John's Park IoW 21 C8
St John's Town of Dalry
Dumfries 246 G4
St John's Wells Aberds 303 F7
St John's Wood London 67 C9
St Judes IoM 192 C4
St Julians Herts 85 D10
Newport 59 B10
St Just Corn 1 C3
St Justinian Pembs 90 F4
St Just in Roseland Corn 3 B9
St Katharines Wilts 63 G9
St Katherine's Aberds 303 F7
St Keverne Corn 3 E7
St Kew Corn 10 F6
St Kew Highway Corn 10 F6
St Keyne Corn 6 C4
St Lawrence Corn 5 B10
Essex 89 E7
IoW 20 F6
Kent 71 F11
St Leonards Dorset 31 G10
E Sus 38 F3
S Lanark 268 E2
St Leonard's Bucks 84 D6
St Leonard's Street Kent 53 B7
St Levan Corn 1 E3
St Luke's Derby 152 B6
London 67 C10
St Lythans V Glam 58 E6
St Mabyn Corn 10 G6
St Madoes Perth 286 E5
St Margarets Herts 86 C5
London 67 E7
St Margaret's Hereford 97 E7
St Margaret's at Cliffe
Kent 55 E11
St Margaret's Hope
Orkney 314 G4
St Margaret South Elmham
Suff 142 G6
St Mark's Glos 99 G8
IoM 192 E3
St Martin Corn 2 E6
Corn 6 E5
St Martins Perth 286 D5
St Martin's Shrops 148 B6
St Martin's Moor Shrops 148 B6
St Mary Bourne Hants 48 C2
St Marychurch Torbay 9 B8
St Mary Church V Glam 58 E4
St Mary Cray London 68 F3
St Mary Hill V Glam 58 D3
St Mary Hoo Medway 69 D10
St Mary in the Marsh
Kent 39 B9
St Mary's Orkney 314 F4
St Mary's Bay Kent 39 B9
St Maughans Mon 79 B7
St Maughans Green Mon 79 B7
St Mawes Corn 3 C8
St Mawgan Corn 5 B7
St Mellion Corn 7 B7
St Mellons Cardiff 59 C8
St Merryn Corn 10 G3
St Mewan Corn 5 E9
St Michael Caerhays Corn 5 G9
St Michael Church Som 43 G10
St Michael Penkevil Corn 5 G7
St Michaels Kent 53 F11
Torbay 9 C7
Worcs 115 D11
St Michael's Hamlet
Mers 182 D5
St Michael's on Wyre
Lancs 202 E5
St Michael South Elmham
Suff 142 G6
St Minver Corn 10 F5
St Monans Fife 287 G9
St Neot Corn 6 B3
St Neots Cambs 122 E3
St Newlyn East Corn 4 D6
St Nicholas Herts 104 F5
Pembs 91 D7
V Glam 58 E5
St Nicholas at Wade Kent 71 F9
St Nicholas South Elmham
Suff 142 G6
St Nicolas Park Warks 135 E7
St Ninians Stirling 278 C5
St Olaves Norf 143 D9
St Osyth Essex 89 B10
St Osyth Heath Essex 89 B10
St Owens Cross
Hereford 97 G10
St Pancras London 67 C10
St Paul's Glos 80 B4
St Paul's Cray London 68 F3
St Paul's Walden Herts 104 G3
St Peters Kent 71 F11
St Peter's Glos 99 G8
T&W 243 E7
St Peter South Elmham
Suff 142 G6
St Peter The Great
Worcs 117 G7
St Petrox Pembs 73 F7
St Pinnock Corn 6 C4
St Quivox S Ayrs 257 E9
St Ruan Corn 2 F6
Saint's Hill Kent 52 E4
St Stephen Corn 5 E8
St Stephens Corn 7 D8
Herts 85 D10
St Stephen's Corn 12 D2
St Teath Corn 11 E7
St Thomas Devon 14 C4
Swansea 57 C7
St Tudy Corn 11 F7
St Twynnells Pembs 73 F7
St Veep Corn 6 E2
St Vigeans Angus 287 C10
St Vincent's Hamlet
Essex 87 G9
St Wenn Corn 5 C9
St Weonards Hereford 97 G9
St Winnow Corn 6 D2
Sainty Brid =St Brides
Major V Glam 57 G11
St y-Nyll V Glam 58 D5
Saith ffynnon Flint 181 F11
Salcombe Devon 9 G9
Salcombe Regis Devon 15 D9
Salcott-cum-Virley
Essex 88 C6
Salden Bucks 102 F6
Sale Gtr Man 184 C3
Saleby Lincs 191 F7
Sale Green Worcs 117 F8
Salehurst E Sus 38 C2
Salem Carms 94 F2
Ceredig 128 G3
Corn 4 G4
Salen Argyll 289 E7
Highld 289 C8
Salendine Nook
W Yorks 196 D6
Salenside Borders 261 E11
Salesbury Lancs 203 G9
Saleway Worcs 117 F8
Salford C Beds 103 D8
Gtr Man 184 B4
Oxon 100 F5
Salford Ford C Beds 103 D8
Salford Priors Warks 117 G11
Salfords Sur 51 D9
Salhouse Norf 160 G6
Saligo Argyll 274 G3
Salisbury Wilts 31 B10
Salkeld Dykes Cumb 230 D6
Sallachan Highld 289 C11
Sallachy Highld 295 B11
Highld 309 J5
Salle Norf 160 E2
Salmans Kent 52 E4
Salmonby Lincs 190 G4
Salmond's Muir Angus 287 D9
Salmonhutch Devon 14 B2
Salperton Glos 99 G11
Salperton Park Glos 81 B9
Salph End Bedford 121 G11
Salsburgh N Lanark 268 C6
Salt Staffs 151 D9
Salta Cumb 229 B7
Saltaire W Yorks 205 F8
Saltash Corn 7 D8
Saltburn Highld 301 C7
Saltburn-by-the-Sea
Redcar 235 G9
Saltby Leics 155 D7
Salt Coates Cumb 238 G5
Saltcoats Cumb 219 F11
E Loth 281 E9
N Ayrs 266 G4
Saltcotes Lancs 193 B11
Saltdean Brighton 36 G5
Salt End E Yorks 201 B7
Salter Lancs 212 G2
Salterbeck Cumb 228 F5
Salterforth Lancs 204 D3
Salters Heath Hants 48 B6
Saltershill Shrops 150 D2
Salters Lode Norf 139 C11
Salter Street W Mid 118 C2
Salterswall Ches W 167 B10
Salterton Wilts 46 F6
Saltfleet Lincs 191 C7
Saltfleetby All Saints
Lincs 191 C7
Saltfleetby St Clement
Lincs 191 C7
Saltfleetby St Peter
Lincs 190 D6
Saltford Bath 61 F7
Salt Hill Slough 66 C3
Salthouse Cumb 210 F4
Norf 177 E9
Saltley W Mid 133 F11
Saltmarsh Newport 59 C11
Saltmarshe E Yorks 199 C9
Saltness Orkney 314 G2
Shetland 313 J4
Saltney Flint 166 B5
Salton N Yorks 216 D4
Saltrens Devon 25 C7
Saltwell T&W 243 E7
Saltwick Northumb 242 B5
Saltwood Kent 55 F7
Salum Argyll 288 E2
Salvington W Sus 35 F10
Salwarpe Worcs 117 E7
Salwayash Dorset 16 B5
Sambourne Warks 117 E11
Wilts 45 E11
Sambrook Telford 150 E4
Samhla W Isles 296 E3
Samlesbury Lancs 203 G7
Samlesbury Bottoms
Lancs 194 B6
Sampford Arundel Som 27 D10
Sampford Brett Som 42 E5
Sampford Chapple
Devon 25 G10
Sampford Courtenay
Devon 25 G10
Sampford Moor Som 27 D10
Sampford Peverell Devon 27 E8
Sampford Spiney Devon 12 G6
Sampool Bridge Cumb 211 B9
Samuel's Corner Essex 70 B3
Samuelston E Loth 281 G9
Sanachan Highld 299 E8
Sanaigmore Argyll 274 F3
Sanclêr =St Clears
Carms 74 B3
Sancreed Corn 1 D4
Sancton E Yorks 208 F4
Sand Highld 307 K4
Shetland 313 J5
Som 44 D2
Sandaig Highld 295 E9
Sandal W Yorks 197 D10
Sandale Cumb 229 C10
Sandal Magna
W Yorks 197 D10
Sandavore Highld 294 G6
Sandbach Ches E 168 C3
Sandbach Heath Ches E 168 C3
Sandbank Argyll 276 E3
Sandbanks BCP 18 D6
Kent 70 G4
Sandborough Staffs 152 F2
Sandbraes Lincs 200 G6
Sandend Aberds 302 C5
Sanderstead London 67 G10
Sandfields Glos 99 G8
Neath 57 C8
Staffs 134 B2
Sandford Cumb 222 B4
Devon 26 G4
Dorset 18 D4
Hants 31 G11
IoW 20 E6
N Som 44 B2
Shrops 148 E6
Shrops 149 C11
S Lanark 268 G4
Worcs 99 B7
W Yorks 205 F11
Sandford Batch N Som 44 B2
Sandfordhill Aberds 303 E11
Sandford Hill Stoke 168 G6
Sandford on Thames
Oxon 83 E8
Sandford Orcas Dorset 29 C10
Sandford St Martin
Oxon 101 F8
Sandgate Kent 55 G7
Sand Gate Cumb 211 D7
Sandgreen Dumfries 237 D7
Sandhaven Aberds 303 C9
Argyll 276 E3
Sandhead Dumfries 236 E2
Sandhill Bucks 102 F4
Cambs 139 F11
S Yorks 198 F2
Sandhills Dorset 29 E11
Dorset 29 G9
Mers 182 C4
Oxon 83 D9
Sur 50 F2
W Yorks 206 F3
Sandhoe Northumb 241 D11
Sandhole Argyll 275 D11
Sand Hole E Yorks 208 F2
Sandholme E Yorks 208 G2
Lincs 156 B6
Sandhurst Brack 65 G10
Glos 98 G6
Kent 38 B3
Sandhurst Cross Kent 38 B3
Sandhutton N Yorks 215 C7
Sand Hutton N Yorks 207 B9
Sandiacre Derbys 153 B9
Sandilands Lincs 191 E8
S Lanark 259 B9
Sandiway Ches W 183 G10
Sandleheath Hants 31 E10
Sandling Kent 53 B9
Sandlow Green Ches E 168 B3
Sandness Shetland 313 H3
Sandon Essex 88 E2
Herts 104 E6
Staffs 151 C8
Sandonbank Staffs 151 D8
Sandown IoW 21 E7
Sandown Park Kent 52 E6
Sandpit Dorset 28 G6
Sandpits Glos 98 F6
Sandplace Corn 6 D5
Sandridge Herts 85 C11
Wilts 62 F2
Sandringham Norf 158 D3
Sands Bucks 84 G4
Sandsend N Yorks 227 C7
Sands End London 67 D9
Sandside Cumb 210 D6
Cumb 211 C9
Orkney 314 F2
Sand Side Cumb 210 C4
Lancs 202 C4
Sandside Ho Highld 310 C3
Sandsound Shetland 313 J5
Sandtoft N Lincs 199 F8
Sandvoe Shetland 312 D5
Sandway Kent 53 C11
Sandwell W Mid 133 F10
Sandwich Kent 55 B10
Sandwich Bay Estate
Kent 55 B11
Sandwick Cumb 221 B8
Orkney 314 H4
Shetland 313 L6
Sandwith Cumb 219 C9
Sandwith Newtown
Cumb 219 C9
Sandy Carms 75 E7
C Beds 104 B3
Sandybank Orkney 314 C5
Sandy Bank Lincs 174 E3
Sandy Carrs Durham 234 C3
Sandycroft Flint 166 B4
Sandy Cross E Sus 37 C9
Sur 49 D11
Sandy Down Hants 20 B2
Sandyford Dumfries 248 E6
Stoke 168 E5
Sandygate Devon 14 G3
IoM 192 C4
S Yorks 186 D4
Sandy Gate Devon 14 C5
Sandy Haven Pembs 72 D5
Sandyhills Dumfries 237 D10
Sandylake Corn 6 C2
Sandylands Lancs 211 G8
Som 27 C10
Sandylane Swansea 56 D5
Sandy Lane Wilts 62 F3
Wrex 166 G5
W Yorks 205 F8
Sandypark Devon 13 D10
Sandysike Cumb 239 D9
Sandy Way IoW 20 E5
Sangobeg Highld 308 C4
Sangomore Highld 308 C4
Sanham Green W Berks 63 F10
Sankey Bridges Warr 183 D9
Sankyns Green Worcs 116 E5
Sanna Highld 288 C6
Sanndabhaig W Isles 297 G4
W Isles 304 E6
Sannox N Ayrs 255 C11
Sanquhar Dumfries 247 B7
Sansaw Heath Shrops 149 E10
Santon Cumb 220 E2
N Lincs 200 E2
Santon Bridge Cumb 220 E2
Santon Downham Suff 140 F6
Sapcote Leics 135 E9
Sapey Bridge Worcs 116 F4
Sapey Common
Hereford 116 E4
Sapiston Suff 125 B8
Sapley Cambs 122 C4
Sapperton Derbys 152 C3
Glos 80 E6
Lincs 155 C10
Saracen's Head Lincs 156 D6
Sarclet Highld 310 E7
Sardis Carms 75 D9
Pembs 73 D10
Sarisbury Hants 33 F8
Sarn Bridgend 58 C2
Flint 181 F10
Powys 130 E4
Sarnau Carms 74 B4
Ceredig 110 G6
Gwyn 147 B9
Powys 95 E10
Powys 148 F4
Sarn Bach Gwyn 144 D6
Sarnesfield Hereford 115 G7
Sarn Meyllteyrn Gwyn 144 C4
Saron Carms 75 C10
Carms 93 D7
Denb 165 C8
Gwyn 163 B8
Gwyn 163 D7
Sarratt Herts 85 F8
Sarratt Bottom Herts 85 F8
Sarre Kent 71 G9
Sarsden Oxon 100 G5
Sarsden Halt Oxon 100 G5
Sarsgrum Highld 308 C3
Sasaig Highld 295 E8
Sascott Shrops 149 G8
Satley Durham 233 C8
Satmar Kent 55 F9
Satran Highld 294 B6
Satron N Yorks 223 F8
Satterleigh Devon 25 C11
Satterthwaite Cumb 220 G6
Satwell Oxon 65 C8
Sauchen Aberds 293 B8
Saucher Perth 286 D5
Sauchie Clack 279 C7
Sauchieburn Aberds 293 G8
Saughall Ches W 182 G5
Saughall Massie Mers 182 D3
Saughton Edin 280 G4
Saughtree Borders 250 D3
Saul Glos 80 D2
Saundby Notts 188 D3
Saundersfoot =Llanusyllt
Pembs 73 E10
Saunderton Bucks 84 E3
Saunderton Lee Bucks 84 F4
Saunton Devon 40 F3
Sausthorpe Lincs 174 B5
Saval Highld 309 J5
Savary Highld 289 E8
Saveock Corn 4 F5
Saverley Green Staffs 151 B9
Savile Park W Yorks 196 C5
Savile Town W Yorks 197 C8
Sawbridge Warks 119 D10
Sawbridgeworth Herts 87 B7
Sawdon N Yorks 217 B8
Sawley Derbys 153 C9
Lancs 203 D11
N Yorks 214 F4
Sawood W Yorks 204 G6
Sawston Cambs 105 B9
Sawtry Cambs 138 G3
Sawyers Hill Wilts 81 G8
Sawyer's Hill Som 27 C11
Saxby Leics 154 F6
Lincs 189 D8
W Sus 35 G7
Saxby All Saints N Lincs 200 D3
Saxelbye Leics 154 E4
Saxham Street Suff 125 E11
Saxilby Lincs 188 F5
Saxlingham Norf 159 B10
Saxlingham Green Norf 142 D4
Saxlingham Nethergate
Norf 142 D4
Saxlingham Thorpe
Norf 142 D4
Saxmundham Suff 127 E7
Saxondale Notts 154 B3
Saxon Street Cambs 124 F3
Saxtead Suff 126 D5
Saxtead Green Suff 126 E5
Saxtead Little Green
Suff 126 D5
Saxthorpe Norf 160 C2
Saxton N Yorks 206 F5
Sayers Common W Sus 36 D3
Scackleton N Yorks 216 E2
Scadabhagh W Isles 305 J3
Scaftworth Notts 187 C11
Scagglethorpe N Yorks 216 E6
Scaitcliffe Lancs 195 B9
Scaladal W Isles 305 G3
Scalan Moray 292 B4
Scalasaig Argyll 274 D4
Scalby E Yorks 199 B10
N Yorks 227 G10
Scald End Bedford 121 F10
Scaldwell W Nhants 120 C5
Scaleby Cumb 239 E11
Scalebyhill Cumb 239 E10
Scale Hall Lancs 211 G9
Scale Houses Cumb 231 B7
Scales Cumb 210 E5
Cumb 230 F2
Cumb 231 C7
Lancs 202 G5
Scalford Leics 154 E5
Scaling Redcar 226 C4
Scaliscro W Isles 304 F3
Scallasaig Highld 295 D10
Scallastle Argyll 289 F8
Scalloway Shetland 313 K6
Scalpay W Isles 305 J4
Scalpay Ho Highld 295 C8
Scalpsie Argyll 255 B11
Scamadale Highld 295 F9
Scamblesby Lincs 190 F3
Scamland E Yorks 207 E11
Scammadale Argyll 289 G10
Scamodale Highld 289 B10
Scampston N Yorks 217 D7
Scampton Lincs 189 F7
Scaniport Highld 300 F6
Scapa Orkney 314 F4
Scapegoat Hill W Yorks 196 D5
Scar Orkney 314 B6
Scarborough N Yorks 217 B10
Scarcewater Corn 5 E8
Scarcliffe Derbys 171 B7
Scarcroft W Yorks 206 E3
Scarcroft Hill W Yorks 206 E3
Scardroy Highld 300 D2
Scarff Shetland 312 E4
Scarfskerry Highld 310 B6
Scargill Durham 223 C11
Scar Head Cumb 220 G5
Scarinish Argyll 288 E2
Scarisbrick Lancs 193 E11
Scarness Cumb 229 E10
Scarning Norf 159 G9
Scarrington Notts 172 G2
Scarth Hill Lancs 194 F2
Scarthingwell N Yorks 206 F5
Scartho NE Lincs 201 F9
Scarvister Shetland 313 J5
Scarwell Orkney 314 D2
Scatness Shetland 313 M5
Scatraig Highld 301 F7
Scatwell Ho Highld 300 D3
Scawby N Lincs 200 F3
Scawsby S Yorks 198 G5
Scawthorpe S Yorks 198 F5
Scawton N Yorks 215 C10
Scayne's Hill W Sus 36 C5
Scethrog Powys 96 F2
Scholar Green Ches E 168 D4
Scholemoor W Yorks 205 G8
Scholes Gtr Man 194 F5
S Yorks 186 B5
W Yorks 197 B7
W Yorks 197 F7
W Yorks 204 F6
W Yorks 206 F3
Scholey Hill W Yorks 197 B11
School Aycliffe
Durham 233 G11
Schoolgreen Wokingham 65 F8
School Green Ches W 167 C10
Essex 106 E4
IoW 20 D2
W Yorks 205 G8
Schoolhill Aberds 293 D11
School House Dorset 28 G5
Sciberscross Highld 309 H7
Scilly Bank Cumb 219 B9
Scissett W Yorks 197 E8
Scleddau Pembs 91 E8
Scofton Notts 187 E10
Scole Norf 126 B2
Scole Common Norf 142 G2
Scolpaig W Isles 296 D3
Scone Perth 286 E5
Sconser Highld 295 B7
Scoonie Fife 287 G7
Scoor Argyll 274 B5
Scopwick Lincs 173 D9
Scoraig Highld 307 K5
Scorborough E Yorks 208 D6
Scorrier Corn 4 G4
Scorriton Devon 8 B4
Scorton Lancs 202 D6
N Yorks 224 E5
Sco Ruston Norf 160 E5
Scotbheinn W Isles 296 F4
Scotby Cumb 239 G10
Scotch Corner N Yorks 224 E4
Scotches Derbys 170 F4
Scotforth Lancs 202 B5
Scotgate W Yorks 196 E6
Scot Hay Staffs 168 F4
Scothern Lincs 189 F8
Scotland Leics 136 D3
Leics 153 E7
Lincs 155 C10
W Berks 64 F5
Scotland End Oxon 100 E6
Scotland Gate Northumb 253 G7
Scotlands W Mid 133 C8
Scotland Street Suff 107 D9
Scotlandwell Perth 286 G5
Scot Lane End Gtr Man 194 F6
Scotsburn Highld 301 B7
Scotscalder Station
Highld 310 D4
Scotscraig Fife 287 E8
Scots' Gap Northumb 252 F2
Scotston Aberds 293 F9
Perth 286 C3
Scotstoun Glasgow 267 B10
Scotstown Highld 289 C10
Scotswood T&W 242 E5
Windsor 66 F2
Scottas Highld 295 E9
Scotter Lincs 199 G11
Scotterthorpe Lincs 199 G11
Scottlethorpe Lincs 155 E11
Scotton Lincs 188 B5
N Yorks 206 B2
N Yorks 224 F3
Scottow Norf 160 E5
Scott Willoughby Lincs 155 B11
Scoughall E Loth 282 E2
Scoulag Argyll 266 D2
Scoulton Norf 141 C9
Scounslow Green
Staffs 151 D11
Scourie Highld 306 E6
Scourie More Highld 306 E6
Scousburgh Shetland 313 M5
Scout Dike S Yorks 197 G8
Scout Green Cumb 221 D11
Scouthead Gtr Man 196 F3
Scowles Glos 79 C9
Scrabster Highld 310 B4
Scraesburgh Borders 262 F5
Scrafield Lincs 174 B4
Scragged Oak Kent 69 G10
Scrainwood Northumb 251 B11
Scrane End Lincs 174 G5
Scrapsgate Kent 70 E2
Scraptoft Leics 136 B2
Scrapton Som 28 E3
Scratby Norf 161 F10
Scrayingham N Yorks 216 G4
Scredda Corn 5 E10
Scredington Lincs 173 G9
Screedy Som 27 B9
Scremby Lincs 174 B6
Scremerston Northumb 273 F10
Screveton Notts 172 G2
Scrivelsby Lincs 174 B3
Scriven N Yorks 206 B2
Scronkey Lancs 202 D4
Scrooby Notts 187 C11
Scropton Derbys 152 C3
Scrub Hill Lincs 174 D2
Scruton N Yorks 224 G5
Scrwgan Powys 148 E3
Scuddaborg Highld 298 C3
Scuggate Cumb 239 C10
Sculcoates Hull 209 G7
Sculthorpe Norf 159 C7
Scunthorpe N Lincs 199 E11
Scurlage Swansea 56 D3
Sea Som 28 E4
Seaborough Dorset 28 F6
Seabridge Staffs 168 G4
Seabrook Kent 55 G7
Seaburn T&W 243 F10
Seacombe Mers 182 C4
Seacox Heath Kent 53 G8
Seacroft Lincs 175 C9
W Yorks 206 F3
Seadyke Lincs 156 B6
Seafar N Lanark 278 G5
Seafield Highld 311 L3
Midloth 270 C5
S Ayrs 257 E8
W Loth 269 B10
Seaford E Sus 23 F7
Seaforth Mers 182 B4
Seagrave Leics 154 F2
Seagry Heath Wilts 62 C3
Seaham Durham 234 B4
Seahouses Northumb 264 C6
Seal Kent 52 B4
Sealand Flint 166 B5
Seale Sur 49 D11
Seamer N Yorks 217 C10
N Yorks 225 C9
Seamill N Ayrs 266 F4
Sea Mill Cumb 210 F5
Sea Mills Bristol 60 D5
Corn 10 G4
Sea Palling Norf 161 D8
Searby Lincs 200 F5
Seasalter Kent 70 F5
Seascale Cumb 219 E10
Seathorne Lincs 175 B9
Seathwaite Cumb 220 C4
Cumb 220 F4
Seatle Cumb 211 C7
Seatoller Cumb 220 C4
Seaton Corn 6 E6
Cumb 228 E6
Devon 15 C10
Durham 243 G9
E Yorks 209 D9
Kent 55 B8
Northumb 243 B8
Rutland 137 D8
Seaton Burn T&W 242 C6
Seaton Carew Hrtlpl 234 F6
Seaton Delaval
Northumb 243 B8
Seaton Ross E Yorks 207 E11
Seaton Sluice Northumb 243 B8
Seatown Aberds 302 C5
Aberds 303 D11
Dorset 16 C4
Seaureaugh Moor Corn 2 B6
Seave Green N Yorks 225 E11
Seaview IoW 21 C8
Seaville Cumb 238 G5
Seavington St Mary Som 28 E6
Seavington St Michael
Som 28 D6
Seawick Essex 89 C10
Sebastopol Torf 78 F3
Sebay Orkney 314 F5
Sebergham Cumb 230 C3
Sebiston Velzian Orkney 314 D2
Seckington Warks 134 B5
Second Coast Highld 307 K4
Second Drove Cambs 139 F10
Sedbergh Cumb 222 G3
Sedbury Glos 79 G8
Sedbusk N Yorks 223 G7
Seddington C Beds 104 B3
Sedgeberrow Worcs 99 D10
Sedgebrook Lincs 155 B7
Sedgefield Durham 234 F3
Sedgeford Norf 158 B4
Sedgehill Wilts 30 B5
Sedgemere W Mid 118 B4
Sedgley W Mid 133 E8
Sedgley Park Gtr Man 195 G10
Sedgwick Cumb 211 B10
Sedlescombe E Sus 38 D3
Sedlescombe Street
E Sus 38 D3
Sedrup Bucks 84 C3
Seed Kent 54 B2
Seed Lee Lancs 194 C5
Seedley Gtr Man 184 B4
Seend Wilts 62 G2
Seend Cleeve Wilts 62 G2
Seend Head Wilts 62 G2
Seer Green Bucks 85 G7
Seething Norf 142 D6
Seething Wells London 67 F7
Sefton Mers 193 G11
Segensworth Hants 33 F8
Seggat Aberds 303 E7
Seghill Northumb 243 C7
Seifton Shrops 131 G9

Seighford Staffs 151 D7
Seilebost W Isles 305 J2
Seion Gwyn 163 B8
Seisdon Staffs 132 E6
Seisiadar W Isles 304 E7
Selattyn Shrops 148 C5
Selborne Hants 49 G8
Selby N Yorks 207 G8
Selgrove Kent 54 B4
Selham W Sus 34 C6
Selhurst London 67 F10
Selkirk Borders 261 D11
Sellack Hereford 97 F11
Sellack Boat Hereford 97 F11
Sellafirth Shetland 312 D7
Sellan Corn 1 C4
Sellibister Orkney 314 B7
Sellick's Green Som 28 D2
Sellindge Kent 54 F6
Selling Kent 54 B4
Sells Green Wilts 62 G3
Selly Hill N Yorks 227 D7
Selly Oak W Mid 133 G10
Selly Park W Mid 133 G11
Selmeston E Sus 23 D8
Selsdon London 67 G10
Selsey W Sus 22 E5
Selsfield Common
W Sus 51 G10
Selside Cumb 221 F10
N Yorks 212 D5
Selsley Glos 80 E4
Selsmore Hants 21 B10
Selson Kent 55 B10
Selsted Kent 55 E8
Selston Notts 171 E7
Selston Common Notts 171 E7
Selston Green Notts 171 E7
Selwick Orkney 314 F2
Selworthy Som 42 D2
Semblister Shetland 313 H5
Semer Suff 107 B9
Sem Hill Wilts 30 B5
Semington Wilts 61 G11
Semley Wilts 30 B5
Sempringham Lincs 156 C2
Send Sur 50 B4
Send Grove Sur 50 C4
Send Marsh Sur 50 B4
Senghenydd Caerph 77 G10
Sennen Corn 1 D3
Sennen Cove Corn 1 D3
Sennybridge = *Pont Senni*
Powys 95 F8
Serlby Notts 187 D10
Serrington Wilts 46 F5
Sessay N Yorks 215 D9
Setchey Norf 158 G2
Setley Hants 32 G4
Seton E Loth 281 G8
Seton Mains E Loth 281 F8
Setter Shetland 312 E6
Shetland 313 H5
Shetland 313 J7
Shetland 313 L6
Settiscarth Orkney 314 E3
Settle N Yorks 212 G6
Settrington N Yorks 216 E6
Seven Ash Som 43 G7
Sevenhampton Glos 99 G10
Swindon 82 G2
Seven Kings London 68 B3
Sevenoaks Kent 52 C4
Sevenoaks Common
Kent 52 C4
Sevenoaks Weald Kent 52 C4
Seven Sisters = *Blaendulais*
Neath 76 D4
Seven Springs Glos 81 B7
Seven Star Green Essex 107 F8
Severn Beach S Glos 60 B4
Severnhampton Swindon 82 G2
Severn Stoke Worcs 99 C7
Sevick End Bedford 121 G11
Sevington Kent 54 E4
Sewards End Essex 105 D11
Sewardstone Essex 86 F5
Sewardstonebury Essex 86 F5
Sewell C Beds 103 G9
Sewerby E Yorks 218 F3
Seworgan Corn 2 C6
Sewstern Leics 155 E7
Sexhow N Yorks 225 D9
Sezincote Glos 100 E3
Sgarasta Mhor W Isles 305 J2
Sgiogarstaigh W Isles 304 B7
Sgiwen = *Skewen* Neath 57 B8
Shabbington Bucks 83 D11
Shab Hill Glos 80 B6
Shackerley Shrops 132 B6
Shackerstone Leics 135 B7
Shacklecross Derbys 153 C8
Shackleford Sur 50 D2
Shackleton W Yorks 196 B3
Shacklewell London 67 B10
Shacklford Sur 50 D2
Shade W Yorks 196 C2
Shadforth Durham 234 C2
Shadingfield Suff 143 G8
Shadoxhurst Kent 54 F3
Shadsworth Blackburn 195 B8
Shadwell Glos 80 F3
London 67 C11
Norf 141 G8
W Yorks 206 F2
Shaffalong Staffs 169 E7
Shaftenhoe End Herts 105 D8
Shaftesbury Dorset 30 C5
Shafton S Yorks 197 E11
Shafton Two Gates
S Yorks 197 E11
Shaggs Dorset 18 E3
Shakeford Shrops 150 D3
Shakerley Gtr Man 195 G7
Shakesfield Glos 98 E3
Shalbourne Wilts 63 G10
Shalcombe IoW 20 D3
Shalden Hants 49 E7
Shalden Green Hants 49 E7
Shaldon Devon 14 G4
Shalfleet IoW 20 D4
Shalford Essex 106 F4
Som 45 G8
Sur 50 D4
Shalford Green Essex 106 F4
Shalloch Moray 302 D3
Shallowford Devon 25 B11
Devon 41 E8
Staffs 151 D7
Shalmsford Street Kent 54 C5
Shalstone Bucks 102 D2
Shamley Green Sur 50 E4
Shandon Argyll 276 D5
Shandwick Highld 301 B8
Shangton Leics 136 D4
Shankhouse Northumb 243 B7
Shanklin IoW 21 E7
Shannochie N Ayrs 255 E10
Shannochill Stirling 277 B10
Shanquhar Aberds 302 F5
Shanwell Fife 287 E8
Shanzie Perth 286 B6
Shap Cumb 221 B11
Shapridge Glos 79 B11
Shapwick Dorset 30 G6
Som 44 F2
Sharcott Wilts 46 B6
Shard End W Mid 134 F3
Shardlow Derbys 153 C8
Shareshill Staffs 133 B8
Sharlston W Yorks 197 D11
Sharlston Common
W Yorks 197 D11
Sharmans Cross W Mid 118 B2
Sharnal Street Medway 69 E9
Sharnbrook Bedford 121 F9
Sharneyford Lancs 195 C11
Sharnford Leics 135 E9
Sharnhill Green Dorset 30 F2
Sharoe Green Lancs 202 G6
Sharow N Yorks 214 E6
Sharpenhoe C Beds 103 E11
Sharperton Northumb 251 C11
Sharples Gtr Man 195 E8
Sharpley Heath Staffs 151 B9
Sharpness Glos 79 E11
Sharpsbridge E Sus 36 C6
Sharp's Corner E Sus 23 B9
Sharpstone Bath 45 B9
Sharp Street Norf 161 E7
Sharpthorne W Sus 51 G11
Sharptor Corn 11 G11
Sharpway Gate Worcs 117 D9
Sharrington Norf 159 B10
Sharrow S Yorks 186 D4
Sharston Gtr Man 184 D4
Shatterford Worcs 132 G5
Shatterling Kent 55 B9
Shatton Derbys 185 E11
Shaugh Prior Devon 7 C10
Shavington Ches E 168 E2
Shaw Gtr Man 196 F2
Swindon 62 B6
W Berks 64 F3
Wilts 61 F11
W Yorks 204 F6
Shawbank Shrops 131 G9
Shawbirch Telford 150 G2
Shawbury Shrops 149 E11
Shawclough Gtr Man 195 E11
Shaw Common Glos 98 F3
Shawdon Hall Northumb 264 G3
Shawell Leics 135 G10
Shawfield Gtr Man 195 E11
Staffs 169 C9
Shawfield Head
N Yorks 205 C11
Shawford Hants 33 C7
Som 45 C9
Shawforth Lancs 195 C11
Shaw Green Herts 104 E5
Lancs 194 D4
N Yorks 205 C11
Shawhead Dumfries 237 B10
N Lanark 268 C4
Shaw Heath Ches E 184 F3
Gtr Man 184 D5
Shawhill Dumfries 238 D6
Shawlands Glasgow 267 C11
Shaw Lands S Yorks 197 F10
Shaw Mills N Yorks 214 G5
Shawsburn S Lanark 268 E5
Shaw Side Gtr Man 196 F2
Shawton S Lanark 268 F3
Shawtonhill S Lanark 268 F3
Shay Gate W Yorks 205 F8
Sheandow Moray 302 F2
Shear Cross Wilts 45 E11
Shearington Dumfries 238 D2
Shearsby Leics 136 E2
Shearston Som 43 G9
Shebbear Devon 24 F6
Shebdon Staffs 150 D5
Shebster Highld 310 C4
Sheddens E Renf 267 D11
Shedfield Hants 33 E9
Sheen Staffs 169 C10
Sheepbridge Derbys 186 G5
Sheepdrove W Berks 63 D10
Sheep Hill Durham 242 F5
Sheeplane C Beds 103 E8
Sheepridge Bucks 65 B11
W Yorks 197 D7
Sheepscar W Yorks 206 G2
Sheepscombe Glos 80 C5
Sheepstor Devon 7 B11
Sheepwash Devon 25 F7
Northumb 253 F7
Sheepway N Som 60 D3
Sheepy Magna Leics 134 C6
Sheepy Parva Leics 134 C6
Sheering Essex 87 C8
Sheerness Kent 70 E2
Sheerwater Sur 66 G4
Sheet Hants 34 C3
Shrops 115 C10
Sheets Heath Sur 50 B2
Sheffield Corn 1 D5
S Yorks 186 D5
Sheffield Bottom
W Berks 65 F7
Sheffield Green E Sus 36 C6
Sheffield Park S Yorks 186 D5
Shefford C Beds 104 D2
Shefford Woodlands
W Berks 63 E11
Sheigra Highld 306 C6
Sheildmuir N Lanark 268 D5
Sheinton Shrops 132 C2
Shelderton Shrops 115 B8
Sheldon Derbys 169 B11
Devon 27 F10
W Mid 134 G3
Sheldwich Kent 54 B4
Sheldwich Lees Kent 54 B4
Shelf Bridgend 58 C2
W Yorks 196 B6
Shelfanger Norf 142 G2
Shelfield Warks 118 E2
W Mid 133 C10
Shelfield Green Warks 118 E2
Shelfleys W Nhants 120 F4
Shelford Notts 171 G11
Warks 135 F8
Shell Worcs 117 F9
Shelland Suff 125 E10
Shellbrook Leics 152 F6
Shelley Essex 87 E9
Suff 107 D10
W Yorks 197 E8
Shelley Woodhouse
W Yorks 197 E8
Shell Green Halton 183 D8
Shellingford Oxon 82 G4
Shellow Bowells Essex 87 D10
Shellwood Cross Sur 51 D8
Shelsley Beauchamp
Worcs 116 E4
Shelsley Walsh Worcs 116 E4
Shelthorpe Leics 153 F10
Shelton Bedford 121 D10
Norf 142 E4
Shelton *continued*
Notts 172 G3
Shrops 149 G9
Stoke 168 F5
Shelton Green Norf 142 E4
Shelton Lock Derby 153 C7
Shelton under Harley
Staffs 150 B6
Shelve Shrops 130 D6
Shelvin Devon 27 G11
Shelvingford Kent 71 F8
Shelwick Hereford 97 C10
Shelwick Green
Hereford 97 C10
Shenfield Essex 87 G10
Shenington Oxon 101 C7
Shenley Herts 85 E11
Shenley Brook End
M Keynes 102 D6
Shenleybury Herts 85 E11
Shenley Church End
M Keynes 102 D6
Shenley Fields W Mid 133 G10
Shenley Lodge
M Keynes 102 D6
Shenley Wood
M Keynes 102 D6
Shenmore Hereford 97 D7
Shennanton Dumfries 236 C5
Shennanton Ho
Dumfries 236 C5
Shenstone Staffs 134 C2
Worcs 117 C7
Shenstone Woodend
Staffs 134 C2
Shenton Leics 135 C7
Shenval Highld 300 G4
Moray 302 G2
Shenvault Moray 301 E10
Shepeau Stow Lincs 156 G6
Shephall Herts 104 G5
Shepherd Hill W Yorks 197 C9
Shepherd's Bush London 67 C8
Shepherd's Gate Norf 157 F11
Shepherd's Green Oxon 65 C8
Shepherd's Hill Sur 50 G2
Shepherd's Patch Glos 80 E2
Shepherd's Port Norf 158 C3
Shepherdswell or
Sibertswold Kent 55 D9
Shepley W Yorks 197 F7
Shepperdine S Glos 79 F10
Shepperton Sur 66 F5
Shepperton Green Sur 66 F5
Shepreth Cambs 105 B7
Shepshed Leics 153 F9
Shepton Beauchamp
Som 28 D6
Shepton Mallet Som 44 E6
Shepton Montague Som 45 G7
Shepway Kent 53 C9
Sheraton Durham 234 D4
Sherberton Devon 13 G8
Sherborne Bath 44 B5
Dorset 29 D10
Glos 81 C11
Sherborne St John Hants 48 B6
Sherbourne Warks 118 E5
Sherbourne Street Suff 107 C9
Sherburn Durham 234 C2
N Yorks 217 D9
Sherburn Grange
Durham 234 C2
Sherburn Hill Durham 234 C2
Sherburn in Elmet
N Yorks 206 G5
Shere Sur 50 D5
Shereford Norf 159 D7
Sherfield English Hants 32 C3
Sherfield on Loddon
Hants 49 B7
Sherfin Lancs 195 B9
Sherford Devon 8 G5
Dorset 18 C4
Som 28 C2
Sheriffhales Shrops 150 G5
Sheriff Hill T&W 243 E7
Sheriff Hutton N Yorks 216 F3
Sheriff's Lench Worcs 99 B10
Sheringham Norf 177 E11
Sherington M Keynes 103 B7
Sheringwood Norf 177 E11
Shermanbury W Sus 36 D2
Shernal Green Worcs 117 E8
Shernborne Norf 158 C4
Sherrard's Green Worcs 98 B5
Sherrardspark Herts 86 C2
Sherriffhales Shrops 150 G5
Sherrington Wilts 46 F3
Sherston Wilts 61 B11
Sherwood Nottingham 171 G9
Sherwood Green Devon 25 C9
Sherwood Park Kent 52 E6
Shettleston Glasgow 268 C2
Shevington Gtr Man 194 F4
Shevington Moor
Gtr Man 194 E4
Shevington Vale
Gtr Man 194 F4
Sheviock Corn 7 D7
Shewalton N Ayrs 257 B8
Shibden Head W Yorks 196 B5
Shide IoW 20 D5
Shiel Aberds 292 B4
Shiel Bridge Highld 295 D11
Shieldaig Highld 299 B8
Highld 299 D8
Shieldhall Glasgow 267 B10
Shieldhill Dumfries 248 F2
Falk 279 F7
S Lanark 269 G10
Shield Row Durham 242 G6
Shielfoot Highld 289 C8
Shielhill Angus 287 B8
Invclyd 276 G4
Shifford Oxon 82 E5
Shifnal Shrops 132 B4
Shilbottle Northumb 252 B5
Shilbottle Grange
Northumb 252 B6
Shildon Durham 233 F10
Shillford E Renf 267 D8
Shillingford Devon 27 C7
Oxon 83 G9
Shillingford Abbot Devon 14 D4
Shillingford St George
Devon 14 D4
Shillingstone Dorset 30 E4
Shillington C Beds 104 E2
Shillmoor Northumb 251 B9
Shilton Oxon 82 D3
Warks 135 G8
Shilvington Northumb 252 G5
Shimpling Norf 142 G3
Suff 125 G7
Shimpling Street Suff 125 G7
Shincliffe Durham 233 C11
Shiney Row T&W 243 G8
Shinfield Wokingham 65 F8
Shingay Cambs 104 B6
Shingham Norf 140 C5
Shingle Street Suff 109 C7
Shinner's Bridge Devon 8 C5
Shinness Highld 309 H5
Shipbourne Kent 52 C5
Shipdham Norf 141 B9
Shipdham Airfield Norf 141 B9
Shipham Som 44 B2
Shiphay Torbay 9 B7
Shiplake Oxon 65 D9
Shiplake Bottom Oxon 65 C8
Shiplake Row Oxon 65 D9
Shiplate N Som 43 B11
Shiplaw Borders 270 F4
Shipley Derbys 170 G6
Northumb 264 F4
Shrops 132 D6
W Sus 35 C10
W Yorks 205 F8
Shipley Bridge Sur 51 E10
Shipley Common
Derbys 171 G7
Shipley Shiels Northumb 251 E7
Shipmeadow Suff 143 F7
Shipping Pembs 73 D10
Shippon Oxon 83 F7
Shipston-on-Stour
Warks 100 C5
Shipton Bucks 102 F5
Glos 81 B8
N Yorks 207 B7
Shrops 131 E11
Shipton Bellinger Hants 47 D8
Shipton Gorge Dorset 16 C5
Shipton Green W Sus 22 C4
Shipton Lee Bucks 102 G4
Shipton Moyne Glos 61 B11
Shipton Oliffe Glos 81 B8
Shipton on Cherwell
Oxon 83 B7
Shipton Solers Glos 81 B8
Shiptonthorpe E Yorks 208 E3
Shipton-under-Wychwood
Oxon 82 B3
Shirburn Oxon 83 F11
Shirdley Hill Lancs 193 E11
Shirebrook Derbys 171 B8
Shirecliffe S Yorks 186 C4
Shiregreen S Yorks 186 C5
Shirehampton Bristol 60 D4
Shiremoor T&W 243 C8
Shirenewton Mon 79 G7
Shire Oak W Mid 133 C11
Shireoaks Derbys 185 E9
Notts 187 E9
Shires Mill Fife 279 D10
Shirkoak Kent 54 F2
Shirland Derbys 170 D6
Shirlett Shrops 132 D3
Shirley Derbys 170 G2
Hants 19 B9
London 67 F11
Soton 32 E6
W Mid 118 B2
Shirley Heath W Mid 118 B2
Shirley holms Hants 19 B11
Shirley Warren Soton 32 E5
Shirl Heath Hereford 115 F8
Shirrell Heath Hants 33 E9
Shirwell Devon 40 F5
Shirwell Cross Devon 40 F5
Shiskine N Ayrs 255 E10
Shitterton Dorset 18 C2
Shobdon Hereford 115 E8
Shobley Hants 31 F11
Shobnall Staffs 152 E4
Shobrooke Devon 26 G5
Shoby Leics 154 F3
Shocklach Ches W 166 F6
Shocklach Green
Ches W 166 F6
Shoeburyness Southend 70 C2
Sholden Kent 55 C11
Sholing Soton 32 E6
Sholing Common Soton 33 E7
Sholver Gtr Man 196 F3
Shootash Hants 32 C4
Shooters Hill London 68 D2
Shootersway Herts 85 D7
Shoot Hill Shrops 149 G8
Shop Corn 10 G3
Corn 24 E2
Devon 24 E5
Shop Corner Suff 108 E4
Shopford Cumb 240 C3
Shopnoller Som 43 G7
Shopp Hill W Sus 34 B6
Shopwyke W Sus 22 B5
Shore Gtr Man 196 D2
W Yorks 196 B2
Shore Bottom Devon 28 G2
Shoreditch London 67 C10
Som 28 C2
Shoregill Cumb 222 E5
Shoreham Kent 68 G4
Shoreham Beach W Sus 36 G2
Shoreham-by-Sea
W Sus 36 F2
Shore Mill Highld 301 C7
Shoresdean Northumb 273 F9
Shores Green Oxon 82 D5
Shoreside Shetland 313 J4
Shoreswood Northumb 273 F8
Shoreton Highld 300 C6
Shorley Hants 33 B9
Shorncliffe Camp Kent 55 F7
Shorncote Glos 81 F8
Shorne Kent 69 E7
Shorne Ridgeway Kent 69 E7
Shorne West Kent 69 E7
Shortacombe Devon 12 D6
Shortacross Corn 6 D5
Shortbridge E Sus 37 C7
Short Cross W Mid 133 G9
Shortfield Common Sur 49 E10
Shortgate E Sus 23 B7
Short Green Norf 141 F11
Shorthampton Oxon 100 G6
Shortheath Hants 49 F9
Sur 49 E10
Short Heath Derbys 152 G6
W Mid 133 C9
W Mid 133 E11
Shorthill Shrops 131 B8
Shortlands London 67 F11
Shortlanesend Corn 4 F6
Shortlees E Ayrs 257 B10
Shortmoor Devon 28 G2
Dorset 29 G7
Shorton Torbay 9 C7
Shortroods Renfs 267 B9
Shortstanding Glos 79 C9
Shortstown Bedford 103 B11
Short Street Wilts 45 D10
Shortwood Glos 80 F4
S Glos 61 D7
Shorwell IoW 20 E5
Shoscombe Bath 45 B8
Shoscombe Vale Bath 45 B8
Shotatton Shrops 149 E7
Shotesham Norf 142 D5
Shotgate Essex 88 G3
Shotley N Nhants 137 D8
Suff 108 D4
Shotley Bridge Durham 242 G3
Shotleyfield Northumb 242 G3
Shotley Gate Suff 108 E4
Shottenden Kent 54 C4
Shottermill Sur 49 G11
Shottery Warks 118 G3
Shotteswell Warks 101 B8
Shottisham Suff 108 C6
Shottle Derbys 170 F4
Shottlegate Derbys 170 F4
Shotton Durham 234 D4
Durham 234 F3
Flint 166 B4
Northumb 242 B6
Northumb 263 C8
Shotton Colliery
Durham 234 C3
Shotts N Lanark 269 C7
Shotwick Ches W 182 G4
Shouldham Norf 140 B3
Shouldham Thorpe Norf 140 B3
Shoulton Worcs 116 F6
Shover's Green E Sus 53 G7
Shraleybrook Staffs 168 F3
Shrawardine Shrops 149 F8
Shrawley Worcs 116 E6
Shreding Green Bucks 66 C4
Shrewley Warks 118 D4
Shrewley Common
Warks 118 D4
Shrewsbury Shrops 149 G9
Shrewton Wilts 46 E5
Shripney W Sus 22 C6
Shrivenham Oxon 63 B8
Shropham Norf 141 E9
Shroton or Iwerne Courtney
Dorset 30 E5
Shrub End Essex 107 G9
Shrubs Hill Sur 66 F3
Shrutherhill S Lanark 268 F5
Shucknall Hereford 97 C11
Shudy Camps Cambs 106 C2
Shulishadermor Highld 298 E4
Shulista Highld 298 B4
Shuna Ho Argyll 275 C8
Shurdington Glos 80 B6
Shurlock Row Windsor 65 E10
Shurnock Worcs 117 E10
Shurrery Highld 310 D4
Shurrery Lodge Highld 310 D4
Shurton Som 43 E8
Shustoke Warks 134 E4
Shute Devon 15 B11
Devon 26 G5
Shute End Wilts 31 B11
Shutford Oxon 101 C7
Shut Heath Staffs 151 E7
Shuthonger Glos 99 D7
Shutlanger W Nhants 120 G4
Shutta Corn 6 E5
Shutt Green Staffs 133 B7
Shuttington Warks 134 B5
Shuttlesfield Kent 55 E7
Shuttlewood Derbys 187 G7
Shuttleworth Gtr Man 195 D10
Shutton Hereford 98 F3
Shwt Bridgend 57 D11
Siabost bho Dheas
W Isles 304 D4
Siabost bho Thuath
W Isles 304 D4
Siadar W Isles 304 C5
Siadar Iarach W Isles 304 C5
Siadar Uarach W Isles 304 C5
Sibbaldbie Dumfries 248 F4
Sibbertoft W Nhants 136 G3
Sibdon Carwood Shrops 131 G8
Sibford Ferris Oxon 101 D7
Sibford Gower Oxon 101 D7
Sible Hedingham Essex 106 E5
Sibley's Green Essex 106 F2
Sibsey Lincs 174 E5
Sibsey Fen Side Lincs 174 E4
Sibson Cambs 137 D11
Leics 135 C7
Sibster Highld 310 D7
Sibthorpe Notts 172 F3
Notts 188 G2
Sibton Suff 127 D7
Sibton Green Suff 127 C7
Sicklesmere Suff 125 E7
Sicklinghall N Yorks 206 D3
Sid Devon 15 D8
Sidbrook Som 28 B3
Sidbury Devon 15 C8
Shrops 132 F3
Sidcot N Som 44 B2
Sidcup London 68 E3
Siddal W Yorks 196 C6
Siddick Cumb 228 E6
Siddington Ches E 184 G4
Glos 81 F8
Siddington Heath
Ches E 184 G4
Sidemoor Worcs 117 C9
Side of the Moor
Gtr Man 195 E8
Sidestrand Norf 160 B5
Sideway Stoke 168 G5
Sidford Devon 15 C8
Sidlesham W Sus 22 D5
Sidlesham Common
W Sus 22 C5
Sidley E Sus 38 F2
Sidlow Sur 51 D9
Sidmouth Devon 15 D8
Sidway Staffs 150 B5
Sigford Devon 13 G11
Sigglesthorne E Yorks 209 D9
Sighthill Edin 280 G3
Glasgow 268 B2
Sigingstone = *Tresigin*
V Glam 58 E3
Signet Oxon 82 C2
Sigwells Som 29 C10
Silchester Hants 64 G6
Sildinis W Isles 305 G4
Sileby Leics 153 F11
Silecroft Cumb 210 C2
Silfield Norf 142 D2
Silford Devon 24 B6
Silian Ceredig 111 G11
Silkstead Hants 32 C6
Silkstone S Yorks 197 F9
Silkstone Common
S Yorks 197 G9
Silk Willoughby Lincs 173 G9
Silloth Cumb 238 G4
Sills Northumb 251 C8
Sillyearn Moray 302 D5
Siloh Carms 94 D4
Silpho N Yorks 227 G9
Silsden W Yorks 204 D6
Silsoe C Beds 103 D11
Silton Dorset 30 B3
Silverburn Midloth 270 C4
Silverdale Lancs 211 E9
Staffs 168 F4
Silverdale Green Lancs 211 E9
Silver End Essex 88 B4
W Mid 133 F8
Silvergate Norf 160 D3
Silver Green Norf 142 E5
Silverhill E Sus 38 E3
Silver Hill E Sus 38 B2
Silverhill Park E Sus 38 E4
Silver Knap Som 29 C11
Silverknowes Edin 280 F4
Silverley's Green Suff 126 B5
Silvermuir S Lanark 269 F8
Silverstone W Nhants 102 C3
Silver Street Glos 80 E3
Kent 69 G11
Som 27 C11
Som 44 G4
Worcs 117 B11
Silverton Devon 27 G7
W Dunb 277 F8
Silvertonhill S Lanark 268 E4
Silvertown London 68 D2
Silverwell Corn 4 F4
Silvington Shrops 116 B2
Silwick Shetland 313 J4
Sim Hill S Yorks 197 G9
Simister Gtr Man 195 F10
Simmondley Derbys 185 C8
Simm's Cross Halton 183 D8
Simm's Lane End Mers 194 G4
Simonburn Northumb 241 C9
Simonsbath Som 41 F9
Simonsburrow Devon 27 D10
Simonside T&W 243 E8
Simonstone Lancs 203 G11
N Yorks 223 G7
Simprim Borders 272 F6
Simpson M Keynes 103 D7
Pembs 72 B5
Simpson Cross Pembs 72 B5
Simpson Green W Yorks 205 F9
Sinclair's Hill Borders 272 E6
Sinclairston E Ayrs 257 F11
Sinclairtown Fife 280 C5
Sinderby N Yorks 214 C6
Sinderhope Northumb 241 G8
Sinderland Green
Gtr Man 184 C2
Sindlesham Wokingham 65 F9
Sinfin Derby 152 C6
Sinfin Moor Derby 153 C7
Singdean Borders 250 C3
Singleborough Bucks 102 E5
Single Hill Bath 45 B8
Singleton Lancs 202 F3
W Sus 34 E5
Singlewell Kent 69 E7
Singret Wrex 166 D4
Sinkhurst Green Kent 53 E10
Sinnahard Aberds 292 B6
Sinnington N Yorks 216 B4
Sinton Worcs 116 E6
Sinton Green Worcs 116 E6
Sion Hill Bath 61 F8
Sipson London 66 D5
Sirhowy Bl Gwent 77 C11
Sisland Norf 142 D6
Sissinghurst Kent 53 F9
Sisterpath Borders 272 F5
Siston S Glos 61 D7
Sithney Corn 2 D4
Sithney Common Corn 2 D4
Sithney Green Corn 2 D4
Sittingbourne Kent 70 G2
Six Ashes Staffs 132 F5
Six Bells Bl Gwent 78 E2
Sixhills Lincs 189 D11
Six Hills Leics 154 E2
Sixmile Kent 54 E6
Six Mile Bottom Cambs 123 F11
Sixpenny Handley Dorset 31 D7
Sizewell Suff 127 E9
Skaigh Devon 13 C8
Skail Highld 308 E7
Skaill Orkney 314 C4
Orkney 314 E2
Orkney 314 F5
Skares E Ayrs 258 F2
Skateraw E Loth 282 F4
Skaw Shetland 312 B8
Shetland 312 G7
Skeabost Highld 298 E4
Skeabrae Orkney 314 D2
Skeeby N Yorks 224 E4
Skeete Kent 54 E6
Skeffington Leics 136 C4
Skeffling E Yorks 201 D11
Skegby Notts 171 C7
Notts 188 G3
Skegness Lincs 175 C9
Skelberry Shetland 313 G6
Shetland 313 M5
Skelbo Highld 309 K7
Skelbo Street Highld 309 K7
Skelbrooke S Yorks 198 E4
Skeldyke Lincs 156 B6
Skelfhill Borders 249 C11
Skellingthorpe Lincs 188 G6
Skellister Shetland 313 H6
Skellorn Green Ches E 184 E6
Skellow S Yorks 198 E4
Skelmanthorpe W Yorks 197 E8
Skelmersdale Lancs 194 F3
Skelmonae Aberds 303 F8
Skelmorlie N Ayrs 266 B3
Skelmuir Aberds 303 E9
Skelpick Highld 308 D7
Skelton Cumb 230 D4
E Yorks 199 B9
N Yorks 223 E11
Redcar 226 B3
York 207 B7
Skelton-on-Ure
N Yorks 215 F7
Skelwick Orkney 314 B4
Skelwith Bridge Cumb 220 E6
Skendleby Lincs 174 B6
Skendleby Psalter Lincs 190 G6
Skene Ho Aberds 293 C9
Skenfrith Mon 97 G9
Skerne E Yorks 208 B6
Skerne Park Darl 224 C5
Skeroblingarry Argyll 255 E8
Skerray Highld 308 C6
Skerricha Highld 306 D7
Skerryford Pembs 72 C6
Skerton Lancs 211 G9
Sketchley Leics 135 E8
Sketty Swansea 56 C6
Skewen = *Sgiwen* Neath 57 B8
Skewes Corn 5 B9
Skewsby N Yorks 216 E2
Skeyton Norf 160 D4
Skeyton Corner Norf 160 D5
Skiag Bridge Highld 307 G7
Skibo Castle Highld 309 L7
Skidbrooke Lincs 190 C6
Skidbrooke North End
Lincs 190 B6
Skidby E Yorks 208 G6
Skilgate Som 27 B7
Skillington Lincs 155 D7
Skinburness Cumb 238 F4
Skinflats Falk 279 E8
Skinidin Highld 298 E2
Skinner's Bottom Corn 4 F4
Skinners Green W Berks 64 F2
Skinnet Highld 308 C5
Skinningrove Redcar 226 B4
Skipness Argyll 255 B9
Skippool Lancs 202 E3
Skiprigg Cumb 230 B3
Skipsea E Yorks 209 B9
Skipsea Brough E Yorks 209 C9
Skipton N Yorks 204 C5
Skipton-on-Swale
N Yorks 215 D7
Skipwith N Yorks 207 F9
Skirbeck Lincs 174 G4
Skirbeck Quarter Lincs 174 G4
Skirethorns N Yorks 213 G9
Skirlaugh E Yorks 209 F8
Skirling Borders 260 B3
Skirmett Bucks 65 B9
Skirpenbeck E Yorks 207 B10
Skirwith Cumb 231 E8
Skirza Highld 310 C7
Skitby Cumb 239 D10
Skitham Lancs 202 E4
Skittle Green Bucks 84 E3
Skulamus Highld 295 C8
Skullomie Highld 308 C6
Skyborry Green Shrops 114 C5
Skye Green Essex 107 G7
Skye of Curr Highld 301 G9
Skyfog Pembs 90 F6
Skyreholme N Yorks 213 G11
Slack Derbys 170 C4
W Yorks 196 B3
W Yorks 196 D5
Slackcote Gtr Man 196 F3
Slackhall Derbys 185 E9
Slackhead Moray 302 C4
Slack Head Cumb 211 D9
Slackholme End Lincs 191 G8
Slacks of Cairnbanno
Aberds 303 E8
Slad Glos 80 D5
Sladbrook Glos 98 F5
Slade Devon 27 F10
Devon 40 D4
Kent 54 C2
Pembs 72 B6
Slade End Oxon 83 G9
Slade Green London 68 D4
Slade Heath Staffs 133 B8
Slade Hooton S Yorks 187 D8
Sladen Green Hants 48 C2
Sladesbridge Corn 10 G6
Slades Green Worcs 99 E7
Slaggyford Northumb 240 G5
Slaidburn Lancs 203 C10
Slaithwaite W Yorks 196 E5
Slaley Derbys 170 D3
Northumb 241 F11
Slamannan Falk 279 G7
Slape Cross Som 43 F10
Slapewath Redcar 226 B2
Slapton Bucks 103 G8
Devon 8 G6
W Nhants 102 B2
Slateford Edin 280 G4
Slate Haugh Moray 302 C4
Slatepit Dale Derbys 170 B4
Slattocks Gtr Man 195 F11
Slaugham W Sus 36 B3
Slaughterbridge Corn 11 D8
Slaughterford Wilts 61 E10
Slaughter Hill Ches E 168 D2
Slawston Leics 136 E5
Slay Pits S Yorks 199 F7
Sleaford Hants 49 F10
Lincs 173 F9
Sleagill Cumb 221 B11
Sleap Shrops 149 D9
Sleapford Telford 150 F2
Sleapshyde Herts 86 D2
Sleastary Highld 309 K6
Slebech Pembs 73 B8
Sledge Green Worcs 98 E6
Sledmere E Yorks 217 G8
Sleeches Cross E Sus 52 G5
Sleepers Hill Hants 33 B7
Sleetbeck Cumb 240 B2
Sleet Moor Derbys 170 E6
Sleight Dorset 18 B5
Sleights N Yorks 227 D7
Slepe Dorset 18 C4
Sliabhna h-Airde
W Isles 296 F3
Slickly Highld 310 C6
Sliddery N Ayrs 255 E10
Slideslow Worcs 117 C9
Sligachan Hotel Highld 294 C6
Sligneach Argyll 288 G4
Sligrachan Argyll 276 C3
Slimbridge Glos 80 E2
Slindon Staffs 150 C6
W Sus 35 F7
Slinfold W Sus 50 G6
Sling Glos 79 D9
Gwyn 163 B10
Slingsby N Yorks 216 E3
Slioch Aberds 302 F5
Slip End C Beds 85 B9
Herts 104 D5
Slippery Ford W Yorks 204 E6
Slipton N Nhants 121 B9
Slitting Mill Staffs 151 F10
Slochd Highld 301 G8
Slockavullin Argyll 275 D9
Slogan Moray 302 E3
Sloley Norf 160 E5
Sloncombe Devon 13 D10
Sloothby Lincs 191 G7
Slough Slough 66 D3
Slough Green Som 28 C3
W Sus 36 B3
Slough Hill Suff 125 G7
Sluggan Highld 301 G8
Slumbay Highld 295 B10
Sly Corner Kent 54 G3
Slyfield Sur 50 C3
Slyne Lancs 211 F9
Smailholm Borders 262 B4
Smallbridge Gtr Man 196 D2
Smallbrook Devon 14 B3
Glos 79 E9
Smallburgh Norf 160 E6
Smallburn Aberds 303 E10
E Ayrs 258 D5
Smalldale Derbys 185 E11
Derbys 185 F9
Small Dole W Sus 36 E2
Small End Lincs 174 D6
Smalley Derbys 170 G6
Smalley Common
Derbys 170 G6
Smalley Green Derbys 170 G6
Smallfield Sur 51 E10
Smallford Herts 85 D11
Small Heath W Mid 134 F2
Smallholm Dumfries 238 B4
Small Hythe Kent 53 G11
Smallmarsh Devon 25 C10
Smallrice Staffs 151 C9
Smallridge Devon 28 G4
Smallshaw Gtr Man 196 G2
Smallthorne Stoke 168 E5
Small Way Som 44 G6
Smallwood Ches E 168 C4
Worcs 117 D10
Smallwood Green Suff 125 F8
Smallwood Hey Lancs 202 D3
Smallworth Norf 141 G10
Smannell Hants 47 D11
Smardale Cumb 222 D4
Smarden Kent 53 E11
Smarden Bell Kent 53 E11
Smart's Hill Kent 52 E4
Smaull Argyll 274 G3
Smeatharpe Devon 27 E11
Smeaton Fife 280 C5
Smeeth Kent 54 F5
Smeeton Westerby
Leics 136 E3
Smelthouses N Yorks 214 G3
Smercleit W Isles 297 K3
Smerral Highld 310 F5
Smestow Staffs 133 E7
Smethcott Shrops 131 D9
Smethwick W Mid 133 F10
Smethwick Green
Ches E 168 C4
Smirisary Highld 289 B8
Smisby Derbys 152 F6
Smite Hill Worcs 117 F7
Smithaleigh Devon 7 D11
Smithbrook W Sus 34 C6
Smith End Green Worcs 116 G5
Smithfield Cumb 239 D10
Smith Green Lancs 202 C5
Smithies S Yorks 197 F11
Smithincott Devon 27 E9
Smithley S Yorks 197 G11
Smith's End Herts 105 D8
Smiths Green Ches E 184 G4
Smith's Green Ches E 168 E3
Essex 105 G11
Essex 106 C3
Smithston Aberds 302 G5
Smithstown Highld 299 B7
Smithton Highld 301 E7
Smithwood Green Suff 125 G8
Smithy Bridge Gtr Man 196 D2
Smithy Gate Flint 181 F11
Smithy Green Ches E 184 G2
Gtr Man 184 D5
Smithy Houses Derbys 170 F5
Smithy Lane Ends Lancs 194 E2
Smock Alley W Sus 35 D9
Smockington Leics 135 F9
Smoky Row Bucks 84 D4
Smoogro Orkney 314 F3
Smug Oak Herts 85 E10
Smyrton S Ayrs 244 G4
Smythe's Green Essex 88 B6
Snagshall E Sus 38 C3
Snaigow House Perth 286 C4
Snailbeach Shrops 131 C7
Snails Hill Som 29 E7
Snailswell Herts 104 E3
Snailwell Cambs 124 D2
Snainton N Yorks 217 C8
Snaisgill Durham 232 F5
Snaith E Yorks 198 C6
Snape N Yorks 214 C5
Suff 127 F7
Snape Green Lancs 193 E11
Snape Hill Derbys 186 F5
S Yorks 198 G2
Snapper Devon 40 G5
Snaresbrook London 67 B11
Snarestone Leics 134 B6
Snarford Lincs 189 E9
Snargate Kent 39 B7
Snarraness Shetland 313 H4
Snatchwood Torf 78 E3
Snave Kent 39 B8
Sneachill Worcs 117 G8
Snead Powys 130 E6
Snead Common Worcs 116 D4
Sneads Green Worcs 117 D7
Sneath Common Norf 142 F3
Sneaton N Yorks 227 D8
Sneatonthorpe N Yorks 227 D8
Snedshill Telford 132 B4
Sneinton Nottingham 153 B11
Snelland Lincs 189 E9
Snelston Derbys 169 G11
Snetterton Norf 141 E9
Snettisham Norf 158 C3
Sneyd Green Stoke 168 F5
Sneyd Park Bristol 60 D5
Snibston Leics 153 G8
Snig's End Glos 98 F5
Snipeshill Kent 70 G2
Sniseabhal W Isles 297 H3
Snitter Northumb 252 C2
Snitterby Lincs 189 C7
Snitterfield Warks 118 F4
Snitterton Derbys 170 C3
Snitton Shrops 115 B11
Snittongate Shrops 115 B11
Snodhill Hereford 96 C6
Snodland Kent 69 G7
Snods Edge Northumb 242 G3
Snowden Hill S Yorks 197 G9
Snowdown Kent 55 C8
Snow End Herts 105 E8
Snow Hill Ches E 167 E10
W Yorks 197 C10
Snow Lea W Yorks 196 D5
Snowshill Glos 99 E11
Snow Street Norf 141 G11
Snydale W Yorks 198 D2
Soake Hants 33 E11
Soar Anglesey 178 G5
Carms 94 F2
Devon 9 G9
Gwyn 146 B2
Powys 95 E9
Soar-y-Mynydd Ceredig 112 G5
Soberton Hants 33 D10
Soberton Heath Hants 33 E10
Sockbridge Cumb 230 F6
Sockburn Darl 224 D6
Sockety Dorset 29 F7
Sodom Denb 181 G9
Shetland 313 G7
Wilts 62 C4
Sodylt Bank Shrops 148 B6
Soham Cambs 123 C11
Soham Cotes Cambs 123 B11
Soho London 67 C9
Som 45 D7
W Mid 133 F10
Solas W Isles 296 D4
Soldon Cross Devon 24 E4
Soldridge Hants 49 G7
Sole Street Kent 54 D5

Sole Street continued
Kent 69 F7
Solfach = Solva Pembs 90 G5
Solihull W Mid 118 B2
Solihull Lodge W Mid 117 B11
Sollers Dilwyn Hereford 115 F8
Sollers Hope Hereford 98 E2
Sollom Lancs 194 D3
Solva = Solfach Pembs 90 G5
Somerby Leics 154 G5
Lincs 200 F5
Somercotes Derbys 170 E6
Somerdale Bath 61 F7
Somerford BCP 19 C9
Ches E 168 B4
Staffs 133 B7
Somerford Keynes Glos 81 G8
Somerley W Sus 22 D4
Somerleyton Suff 143 D9
Somersal Herbert
Derbys 152 B2
Somersby Lincs 190 G4
Somersham Cambs 123 B7
Suff 107 B11
Somers Town London 67 C9
Ptsmth 21 B8
Somerton Newport 59 B10
Oxon 101 F9
Som 29 B7
Suff 124 G6
Somerton Hill Som 29 B7
Somerwood Shrops 149 G11
Sompting W Sus 35 G11
Sompting Abbotts
W Sus 35 F11
Sonning Wokingham 65 D9
Sonning Common Oxon 65 C8
Sonning Eye Oxon 65 D9
Sontley Wrex 166 F4
Sookholme Notts 171 B8
Sopley Hants 19 B9
Sopwell Herts 85 D11
Sopworth Wilts 61 B10
Sorbie Dumfries 236 E6
Sordale Highld 310 C5
Sorisdale Argyll 288 C4
Sorley Devon 8 F4
Sorn E Ayrs 258 D3
Sornhill E Ayrs 258 C2
Sortat Highld 310 C6
Sotby Lincs 190 F2
Sothall S Yorks 186 E6
Sots Hole Lincs 173 C10
Sotterley Suff 143 G9
Soudley Shrops 131 E9
Shrops 150 D4
Soughley S Yorks 197 G7
Soughton = Sychdyn
Flint 166 B2
Soulbury Bucks 103 F7
Soulby Cumb 222 C4
Cumb 230 F5
Souldern Oxon 101 E10
Souldrop Bedford 121 E9
Sound Ches E 167 F10
Shetland 313 H5
Shetland 313 J6
Sound Heath Ches E 167 F10
Soundwell S Glos 60 D6
Sourhope Borders 263 E8
Sourin Orkney 314 C4
Sourlie N Ayrs 266 G6
Sour Nook Cumb 230 C3
Sourton Devon 12 C6
Soutergate Cumb 210 C4
South Acre Norf 158 G6
South Acton London 67 D7
South Alkham Kent 55 E8
Southall London 66 C6
South Allington Devon 9 G10
South Alloa Falk 279 C7
Southam Cumb 219 C9
Glos 99 F9
Warks 119 E8
South Ambersham
W Sus 34 C6
Southampton Soton 32 E6
South Anston S Yorks 187 E8
South Ascot Windsor 66 F2
South Ashford Kent 54 E4
South Auchmachar
Aberds 303 E9
Southay Som 28 D6
South Baddesley Hants 20 B3
South Ballachulish
Highld 284 B4
South Balloch S Ayrs 245 D8
South Bank Redcar 234 G6
York 207 C7
South Barrow Som 29 B10
South Beach Northumb 243 B8
South Beach = Marian-y-de
Gwyn 145 C7
South Beddington
London 67 G9
South Benfleet Essex 69 B9
South Bents T&W 243 E10
South Bersted W Sus 22 C6
South Blainslie
Borders 271 G10
South Bockhampton BCP 19 B9
Southborough Kent 52 E5
London 67 F7
London 68 F2
Southbourne BCP 19 C8
W Sus 22 B3
South Bramwith
S Yorks 198 E6
South Brent Devon 8 D3
South Brewham Som 45 F8
South Bromley London 67 C11
Southbrook Wilts 45 G10
South Broomage Falk 279 E7
South Broomhill
Northumb 252 D6
Southburgh Norf 141 C9
South Burlingham Norf 143 B7
Southburn E Yorks 208 C5
South Cadbury Som 29 B10
South Cairn Dumfries 236 C1
South Carlton Lincs 189 F7
Notts 187 E9
South Carne Corn 11 E10
South Cave E Yorks 208 G4
South Cerney Glos 81 F8
South Chailey E Sus 36 D5
South Chard Som 28 F4
South Charlton
Northumb 264 E5
South Cheriton Som 29 C11
Southchurch Southend 70 B2
South Church Durham 233 F10
South Cliffe E Yorks 208 F3
South Clifton Notts 188 G4
South Clunes Highld 300 E5
South Cockerington
Lincs 190 D5
South Common Devon 28 G4
Southcoombe Oxon 100 F6
South Cornelly Bridgend 57 E10
South Corriegills
N Ayrs 256 C2
South Corrielaw
Dumfries 248 G5
Southcote Reading 65 E7
Southcott Corn 11 B9
Devon 24 D6
Wilts 47 B7
Southcourt Bucks 84 C4
South Cove Suff 143 G9
South Creagan Argyll 289 E11
South Creake Norf 159 B7
Southcrest Worcs 117 D10
South Crosland
W Yorks 196 E6
South Croxton Leics 154 G3
South Croydon London 67 G10
South Cuil Highld 298 C3
South Dalton E Yorks 208 D5
South Darenth Kent 68 F5
Southdean Borders 250 B4
Southdene Mers 182 B6
South Denes Norf 143 C10
Southdown Bath 61 G8
Corn 7 E8
South Down Hants 33 C7
Som 28 E2
South Duffield N Yorks 207 G9
South Dunn Highld 310 D5
South Earlswood Sur 51 D9
Southease E Sus 36 F6
South Elkington Lincs 190 D3
South Elmsall W Yorks 198 E3
South Elphinstone
E Loth 281 G7
Southend Argyll 255 G7
Bucks 65 B9
Glos 80 F2
London 67 E11
Oxon 83 E9
W Berks 64 D2
W Berks 64 E5
Wilts 63 E7
South End Bedford 103 B10
Bucks 103 F7
Cumb 210 G4
E Yorks 209 E9
Hants 31 D10
South-end Herts 86 B6
South End N Lincs 200 C6
Norf 141 E9
Southend-on-Sea
Southend 69 B11
Southerhouse Shetland 313 K5
Southerly Devon 12 D6
Southernby Cumb 230 D3
Southern Cross Brighton 36 F3
Southernden Kent 53 D11
Southerndown V Glam 57 G11
Southerness Dumfries 237 D11
Southern Green Herts 104 E6
South Erradale Highld 299 B7
Southery Norf 140 E2
Southey Green Essex 106 E5
South Fambridge Essex 88 F5
South Farnborough
Hants 49 C11
South Fawley W Berks 63 C11
South Ferriby N Lincs 200 C3
Southfield Northumb 243 B7
South Field E Yorks 200 B4
Windsor 66 D3
Southfields London 67 E9
Thurrock 69 C7
Southfleet Kent 68 E6
South Flobbets Aberds 303 F7
Southford IoW 20 F6
South Garth Shetland 312 D7
South Garvan Highld 289 B11
Southgate Ceredig 111 A11
London 86 G3
Norf 159 C7
Norf 160 E2
Swansea 56 D5
W Sus 51 F9
South Glendale W Isles 297 K3
South Gluss Shetland 312 F5
South Godstone Sur 51 D11
South Gorley Hants 31 E11
South Gosforth T&W 242 D6
South Green Essex 87 G11
Essex 89 B8
Kent 69 G11
Norf 157 F10
Norf 159 G11
Suff 126 B3
South Gyle Edin 280 G3
South-haa Shetland 312 E5
South Hackney London 67 C11
South Ham Hants 48 C6
South Hampstead London 67 C9
South Hanningfield Essex 88 F2
South Harefield London 66 B5
South Harrow London 66 B6
South Harting W Sus 34 D3
South Hatfield Herts 86 D2
South Hayling Hants 21 B10
South Hazelrigg
Northumb 264 C3
South Heath Bucks 84 E6
Essex 89 B10
South Heighton E Sus 23 E7
South-heog Shetland 312 E5
South Hetton Durham 234 B3
South Hiendley
W Yorks 197 E11
South Hill Corn 12 G2
N Som 43 B10
Pembs 72 C4
South Hinksey Oxon 83 E8
South Hole Devon 24 C2
South Holme N Yorks 216 D3
South Holmwood Sur 51 D7
South Hornchurch
London 68 C4
South Huish Devon 8 G3
South Hykeham Lincs 172 C6
South Hylton T&W 243 F9
Southill C Beds 104 C3
Dorset 17 E9
Southington Hants 48 D4
South Kelsey Lincs 189 B8
South Kensington London 67 D9
South Kessock Highld 300 E6
South Killingholme
N Lincs 201 D7
South Kilvington
N Yorks 215 C8
South Kilworth Leics 136 G2
South Kirkby W Yorks 198 E2
South Kirkton Aberds 293 C9
South Kiscadale N Ayrs 256 D2
South Knighton Devon 14 G2
Leicester 136 C2
South Kyme Lincs 173 F11
South Lambeth London 67 D10
South Lancing W Sus 35 G11
Southlands Dorset 17 F9
South Lane S Yorks 197 F9
Southleigh Devon 15 C10
South Leigh Oxon 82 D5
South Leverton Notts 188 E3
South Littleton Worcs 99 B11
South Lopham Norf 141 G10
South Luffenham
Rutland 137 C8
South Malling E Sus 36 E6
Southmarsh Som 45 G8
South Marston Swindon 63 B7
Southmead Bristol 60 D5
South Merstham Sur 51 C9
South Middleton
Northumb 263 E11
South Milford N Yorks 206 G5
South Millbrex Aberds 303 E8
South Milton Devon 8 G4
South Mimms Herts 86 E2
Southminster Essex 89 F7
South Molton Devon 26 B2
Southmoor Oxon 82 F5
South Moor Durham 242 G5
South Moreton Oxon 64 B5
South Mundham W Sus 22 C5
South Muskham Notts 172 D3
South Newbald E Yorks 208 F4
South Newbarns Cumb 210 F4
South Newington Oxon 101 E8
South Newsham
Northumb 243 B8
South Newton Wilts 46 G5
South Normanton
Derbys 170 D6
South Norwood London 67 F10
South Nutfield Sur 51 D10
South Ockendon Thurrock 68 C5
Southoe Cambs 122 E3
Southolt Suff 126 D3
South Ormsby Lincs 190 F5
Southorpe Pboro 137 C11
South Ossett W Yorks 197 D9
South Otterington
N Yorks 215 B7
Southover Dorset 17 C8
E Sus 36 F6
E Sus 37 B11
South Owersby Lincs 189 C9
Southowram W Yorks 196 C6
South Oxhey Herts 85 G10
South Park Sur 51 D8
South Pelaw Durham 243 G7
South Perrott Dorset 29 F7
South Petherton Som 28 D6
South Petherwin Corn 12 E2
South Pickenham Norf 141 C7
South Pill Corn 7 D8
South Pool Devon 8 G5
South Poorton Dorset 16 B6
Southport Mers 193 D10
South Port Argyll 284 E4
Southpunds Shetland 313 L6
South Quilquox Aberds 303 F8
South Radworthy Devon 41 G9
South Rauceby Lincs 173 F8
South Raynham Norf 159 E7
South Reddish Gtr Man 184 C5
Southrepps Norf 160 B5
South Reston Lincs 190 E6
Southrey Lincs 173 B10
Southrop Glos 81 E11
Oxon 101 E7
Southrope Hants 49 E7
South Ruislip London 66 B6
South Runcton Norf 140 B2
South Scarle Notts 172 C4
Southsea Ptsmth 21 B8
Wrex 166 E4
South Shian Argyll 289 E11
South Shields T&W 243 D9
South Shore Blackpool 202 G2
South Side Durham 233 F8
Orkney 314 D5
South Somercotes Lincs 190 C6
South Stainley N Yorks 214 G6
South Stainmore Cumb 222 C6
South Stanley Durham 242 G5
South Stifford Thurrock 68 D6
Southstoke Bath 61 G8
South Stoke Oxon 64 C6
W Sus 35 F8
South Stour Kent 54 F4
South Street E Sus 36 D5
Kent 54 B5
Kent 68 G6
Kent 69 G10
Kent 70 F6
London 52 B2
South Tawton Devon 13 C9
South Tehidy Corn 4 G3
South Thoresby Lincs 190 F6
South Tidworth Wilts 47 D8
South Tottenham
London 67 B10
Southtown Norf 143 B10
Orkney 314 G4
Som 28 D4
Som 44 F5
South Town Devon 14 E5
Hants 49 F7
South Twerton Bath 61 G8
South Ulverston Cumb 210 D6
South View Hants 48 C6
Southville Devon 8 G4
Torf 78 F3
South Voxter Shetland 313 G5
Southwaite Cumb 230 C4
South Walsham Norf 161 G7
Southwark London 67 D10
South Warnborough
Hants 49 D8
Southwater W Sus 35 B11
Southwater Street
W Sus 35 B11
Southway Plym 7 C9
Som 44 E4
South Weald Essex 87 G9
South Weirs Hants 32 G3
Southwell Dorset 17 G9
Notts 172 E2
South Weston Oxon 84 F2
South Wheatley Corn 11 C10
Notts 188 D3
South Whiteness
Shetland 313 J5
Southwick Hants 33 F10
N Nhants 137 E10
Som 43 D11
T&W 243 F9
Wilts 45 B10
W Sus 36 F2
South Widcombe Bath 44 B5
South Wigston Leics 135 D11
South Willesborough
Kent 54 E4
South Willingham
Lincs 189 E11
South Wimbledon London 67 E9
South Wingate Durham 234 E4
South Wingfield Derbys 170 D5
South Witham Lincs 155 F8
Southwold Suff 127 B10
South Wonford Devon 24 F5
South Wonston Hants 48 F3
Southwood Derbys 153 E7
Hants 49 B10
Norf 143 B7
Som 44 G5
Worcs 116 E4
South Woodford London 86 G6
South Woodham Ferrers
Essex 88 F4
South Wootton Norf 158 E2
South Wraxall Wilts 61 G10
South Yardley W Mid 134 G2
South Yarrows Highld 310 E7
South Yeo Devon 25 G8
South Zeal Devon 13 C9
Soval Lodge W Isles 304 F5
Sowber Gate N Yorks 215 B7
Sowerby N Yorks 215 C8
W Yorks 196 C4
Sowerby Bridge
W Yorks 196 C5
Sowerby Row Cumb 230 D3
Sower Carr Lancs 202 E3
Sowley Green Suff 124 G4
Sowood W Yorks 196 D5
Sowood Green W Yorks 196 D5
Sowton Devon 14 C5
Sowton Barton Devon 14 D2
Soyal Highld 309 K5
Soyland Town W Yorks 196 C4
Spacey Houses N Yorks 206 C2
Spa Common Norf 160 C5
Spalding Lincs 156 E4
Spaldington E Yorks 207 G11
Spaldwick Cambs 122 C2
Spalford Notts 172 B4
Spanby Lincs 155 B11
Spango Invclyd 276 G4
Spanish Green Hants 49 B7
Sparham Norf 159 F11
Sparhamhill Norf 159 F11
Spark Bridge Cumb 210 C6
Sparkbrook W Mid 133 G11
Sparkford Som 29 B10
Sparkhill W Mid 133 G11
Sparkwell Devon 7 D11
Sparl Shetland 312 G5
Sparnon Corn 1 E3
Sparnon Gate Corn 4 G3
Sparrow Green Norf 159 G9
Sparrow Hill Som 44 C2
Sparrowpit Derbys 185 E9
Sparrow's Green E Sus 52 G6
Sparsholt Hants 48 G2
Oxon 63 B10
Spartylea Northumb 232 B3
Spath Staffs 151 B11
Spaunton N Yorks 226 G4
Spaxton Som 43 F8
Spean Bridge Highld 290 E4
Spear Hill W Sus 35 D10
Spearywell Hants 32 B4
Speckington Som 29 C9
Speed Gate Kent 68 F5
Speedwell Bristol 60 E6
Speen Bucks 84 F4
W Berks 64 F3
Speeton N Yorks 218 E2
Speke Mers 182 E6
Speldhurst Kent 52 E5
Spellbrook Herts 87 B7
Spelsbury Oxon 101 G7
Spelter Bridgend 57 C11
Spen W Yorks 197 B7
Spencers Wood
Wokingham 65 F8
Spen Green Ches E 168 C4
Spennells Worcs 116 C6
Spennithorne N Yorks 214 B2
Spennymoor Durham 233 E11
Spernall Warks 117 E11
Spetchley Worcs 117 G7
Spetisbury Dorset 30 G6
Spexhall Suff 143 G7
Speybank Highld 291 C10
Spey Bay Moray 302 C3
Speybridge Highld 301 G10
Speyview Moray 302 E2
Spillardsford Aberds 303 D10
Spilsby Lincs 174 B6
Spindlestone Northumb 264 C5
Spinkhill Derbys 187 F7
Spinney Hill W Nhants 120 E5
Spinney Hills Leicester 136 C2
Spinningdale Highld 309 L6
Spion Kop Notts 171 B9
Spirthill Wilts 62 D3
Spital Mers 182 E4
Windsor 66 D3
Spitalbrook Herts 86 D5
Spitalfields London 67 C10
Spitalhill Derbys 169 F11
Spital Hill S Yorks 187 C10
Spital in the Street
Lincs 189 D7
Spital Tongues T&W 242 D6
Spithurst E Sus 36 D6
Spittal Dumfries 236 D5
E Loth 281 F9
E Yorks 207 C11
Highld 310 D5
Northumb 273 E10
Pembs 91 G9
Stirling 277 D10
Spittalfield Perth 286 C5
Spittal Houses S Yorks 186 B5
Spittal of Glenmuick
Aberds 292 E5
Spittal of Glenshee
Perth 292 F3
Spittlegate Lincs 155 C8
Spixworth Norf 160 F4
Splatt Corn 10 F4
Corn 11 D10
Devon 25 F10
Som 43 F8
Splayne's Green E Sus 36 C6
Splott Cardiff 59 D7
Spofforth N Yorks 206 C3
Spondon Derby 153 B8
Spon End W Mid 118 B6
Spon Green Flint 166 C3
Spooner Row Norf 141 D11
Spoonleygate Shrops 132 D6
Sporle Norf 158 G6
Spotland Bridge
Gtr Man 195 E11
Spott E Loth 282 F3
Spratton W Nhants 120 C4
Spreakley Sur 49 E10
Spreyton Devon 13 B9
Spriddlestone Devon 7 E10
Spridlington Lincs 189 E8
Sprig's Alley Oxon 84 F3
Springbank Glos 99 G8
Spring Bank Cumb 229 G10
Springboig Glasgow 268 C3
Springbourne BCP 19 C8
Springburn Glasgow 268 B2
Spring Cottage Leics 152 F6
Spring End N Yorks 223 F9
Springfield Argyll 275 F11
Caerph 77 F11
Dumfries 239 D8
Essex 88 D2
Fife 287 F7
Gtr Man 194 F5
Highld 300 C6
M Keynes 103 D7
Moray 301 D10
W Mid 133 D8
W Mid 133 F9
W Mid 133 G11
Springfields Stoke 168 G5
Spring Gardens Som 45 D9
Spring Green Lancs 204 E4
Spring Grove London 67 D7
Springhead Gtr Man 196 G3
Springhill E Renf 267 D10
IoW 20 B6
N Lanark 269 D7
Staffs 133 B11
Staffs 133 C9
Spring Hill Gtr Man 196 F2
Lancs 195 B8
W Mid 133 D7
Springholm Dumfries 237 C10
Springkell Dumfries 239 B7
Spring Park London 67 F11
Springside N Ayrs 257 B9
Springthorpe Lincs 188 D5
Spring Vale S Yorks 197 G9
Spring Valley IoM 192 E4
Springwell Essex 105 C10
T&W 243 F7
T&W 243 F9
Springwells Dumfries 248 E3
Sproatley E Yorks 209 G9
Sproston Green Ches W 168 B2
Sprotbrough S Yorks 198 G4
Sproughton Suff 108 C2
Sprouston Borders 263 B7
Sprowston Norf 160 G4
Sproxton Leics 155 E7
N Yorks 216 C2
Sprunston Cumb 230 B3
Spunhill Shrops 149 C8
Spurlands End Bucks 84 F5
Spurstow Ches E 167 D9
Spurtree Shrops 116 D2
Spynie Moray 302 C2
Spyway Dorset 16 C6
Square and Compass
Pembs 91 E7
Squires Gate Blackpool 202 G2
Sraid Ruadh Argyll 288 E1
Srannda W Isles 296 C6
Sronphadruig Lodge
Perth 291 F9
Stableford Shrops 132 D5
Staffs 150 B6
Stacey Bank S Yorks 186 C3
Stackhouse N Yorks 212 F6
Stackpole Pembs 73 F7
Stackpole Quay Pembs 73 F7
Stacksford Norf 141 E11
Stacksteads Lancs 195 C10
Stackyard Green Suff 107 B9
Staddiscombe Plym 7 E10
Staddlethorpe E Yorks 199 B10
Staddon Devon 24 C3
Devon 24 G5
Staden Derbys 185 G9
Stadhampton Oxon 83 F10
Stadhlaigearraidh
W Isles 297 H3
Stadmorslow Staffs 168 D5
Staffield Cumb 230 C6
Staffin Highld 298 C4
Stafford Staffs 151 E8
Stafford Park Telford 132 B4
Stafford's Corner Essex 89 B7
Stafford's Green Dorset 29 C10
Stagbatch Hereford 115 F9
Stagden Cross Essex 87 C10
Stagehall Borders 271 G9
Stagsden Bedford 103 B9
Stagsden West End
Bedford 103 B9
Stag's Head Devon 25 B11
Stain Highld 310 C7
Stainburn Cumb 228 F6
N Yorks 205 D10
Stainby Lincs 155 E8
Staincliffe W Yorks 197 C8
Staincross S Yorks 197 E10
Staindrop Durham 233 G8
Staines Green Herts 86 C3
Staines-upon-Thames
Sur 66 E4
Stainfield Lincs 155 D11
Lincs 189 G10
Stainforth N Yorks 212 F6
S Yorks 198 E6
Staining Lancs 202 F3
Stainland W Yorks 196 D5
Stainsacre N Yorks 227 D8
Stainsby Derbys 170 B6
Lincs 190 G4
Stainton Cumb 211 B10
Cumb 230 F5
Cumb 239 F9
Durham 223 B11
Mbro 225 C9
N Yorks 224 F2
S Yorks 187 C9
Stainton by Langworth
Lincs 189 F9
Staintondale N Yorks 227 F9
Stainton le Vale Lincs 189 C11
Stainton with Adgarley
Cumb 210 E5
Stair Cumb 229 G10
E Ayrs 257 E10
Stairfoot S Yorks 197 F11
Stairhaven Dumfries 236 D4
Staithes N Yorks 226 B5
Stakeford Northumb 253 F7
Stake Hill Gtr Man 195 F11
Stakenbridge Worcs 117 B7
Stake Pool Lancs 202 D4
Stalbridge Dorset 30 D2
Stalbridge Weston
Dorset 30 D2
Stalham Norf 161 D7
Stalham Green Norf 161 E7
Stalisfield Green Kent 54 C3
Stallen Dorset 29 D10
Stallingborough
NE Lincs 201 E7
Stalling Busk N Yorks 213 B8
Stallington Staffs 151 B8
Stalmine Lancs 202 D3
Stalmine Moss Side
Lancs 202 D3
Stalybridge Gtr Man 185 B7
Stambermill W Mid 133 G8
Stamborough Som 42 F4
Stambourne Essex 106 D4
Stambourne Green
Essex 106 D4
Stamford Lincs 137 B10
Stamford Bridge
Ches W 167 B7
E Yorks 207 B10
Stamfordham Northumb 242 C3
Stamford Hill London 67 B10
Stamperland E Renf 267 D11
Stamshaw Ptsmth 33 G10
Stanah Cumb 220 B6
Lancs 202 E3
Stanborough Herts 86 C2
Stanbridge C Beds 103 G9
Dorset 31 G8
Stanbridgeford C Beds 103 G9
Stanbrook Essex 106 F2
Worcs 98 B6
Stanbury W Yorks 204 F6
Stand Gtr Man 195 F9
N Lanark 268 B5
Standburn Falk 279 G8
Standeford Staffs 133 B8
Standen Kent 53 E11
Standen Hall Lancs 203 E10
Standen Street Kent 53 G10
Standerwick Som 45 C10
Standford Hants 49 G10
Standford Bridge
Telford 150 E4
Standingstone Cumb 229 B11
Cumb 229 E7
Standish Glos 80 D4
Gtr Man 194 E5
Standish Lower Ground
Gtr Man 194 F5
Standlake Oxon 82 E5
Standon Hants 32 B6
Herts 105 G7
Staffs 150 B6
Standon Green End
Herts 86 B5
Stane N Lanark 269 D7
Stanecastle N Ayrs 257 B8
Stanfield Norf 159 E8
Stoke 168 E5
Stanford C Beds 104 C3
Kent 54 F6
Norf 141 E7
Shrops 148 G6
Stanford Bishop
Hereford 116 G3
Stanford Bridge Worcs 116 D4
Stanford Dingley
W Berks 64 E5
Stanford End Wokingham 65 G8
Stanford Hills Notts 153 E10
Stanford in the Vale
Oxon 82 G4
Stanford-le-Hope
Thurrock 69 C7
Stanford on Avon
W Nhants 119 B11
Stanford on Soar Notts 153 E10
Stanford on Teme
Worcs 116 D4
Stanford Rivers Essex 87 E8
Stanfree Derbys 187 G7
Stanground Pboro 138 D4
Stanhill Lancs 195 B8
Stanhoe Norf 158 B6
Stanhope Borders 260 D4
Durham 232 D5
Kent 54 E3
Stanion N Nhants 137 F8
Stank Cumb 210 E4
Stanklyn Worcs 117 C7
Stanks W Yorks 206 F3
Stanley Derbys 170 G6
Durham 242 G5
Lancs 194 F3
Notts 171 C7
Perth 286 D5
Shrops 132 G3
Shrops 132 G5
Staffs 168 E6
Wilts 62 E3
W Yorks 197 C10
Stanley Common
Derbys 170 G6
Stanley Crook Durham 233 D9
Stanley Downton Glos 80 E4
Stanley Ferry W Yorks 197 C11
Stanley Gate Lancs 194 G2
Stanley Green BCP 18 C6
Ches E 184 E5
Shrops 149 B10
Stanley Hill Hereford 98 C3
Stanley Moor Staffs 168 E6
Stanley Pontlarge Glos 99 E9
Stanleytown Rhondda 77 G8
Stanlow Ches W 182 F6
Staffs 132 D5
Stanmer Brighton 36 F4
Stanmore Hants 33 B7
London 85 G11
Shrops 132 E4
W Berks 64 D3
Stanner Powys 114 F5
Stannergate Dundee 287 D8
Stannersburn Northumb 250 F6
Stanners Hill Sur 66 G3
Stanningfield Suff 125 F7
Stanningley W Yorks 205 G10
Stannington Northumb 242 B6
S Yorks 186 D4
Stanpit BCP 19 C9
Stansbatch Hereford 114 E6
Stansfield Suff 124 G5
Stanshope Staffs 169 E10
Stanstead Suff 106 B6
Stanstead Abbotts Herts 86 C5
Stansted Kent 68 G6
Stansted Airport Essex 105 G11
Stansted Mountfitchet
Essex 105 G10
Stanthorne Ches W 167 B11
Stanton Glos 99 E11
Mon 96 G6
Northumb 252 F4
Staffs 169 F10
Suff 125 C9
Stantonbury M Keynes 102 C6
Stanton by Bridge
Derbys 153 D7
Stanton-by-Dale Derbys 153 B9
Stanton Chare Suff 125 C9
Stanton Drew Bath 60 G5
Stanton Fitzwarren
Swindon 81 G11
Stanton Gate Notts 153 B9
Stanton Harcourt Oxon 82 D6
Stanton Hill Notts 171 C7
Stanton in Peak Derbys 170 C2
Stanton Lacy Shrops 115 B9
Stanton Lees Derbys 170 C3
Stanton Long Shrops 131 E11
Stanton-on-the-Wolds
Notts 154 C2
Stanton Prior Bath 61 G7
Stanton St Bernard Wilts 62 G5
Stanton St John Oxon 83 D9
Stanton St Quintin Wilts 62 D2
Stanton Street Suff 125 D9
Stanton under Bardon
Leics 153 G9
Stanton upon Hine Heath
Shrops 149 E11
Stanton Wick Bath 60 G6
Stantway Glos 80 C2
Stanwardine in the Fields
Shrops 149 E8
Stanwardine in the Wood
Shrops 149 D8
Stanway Essex 107 G8
Glos 99 E11
Stanway Green Essex 107 G9
Suff 126 C4
Stanwell Sur 66 E5
Stanwell Moor Sur 66 E4
Stanwick N Nhants 121 C9
Stanwick-St-John
N Yorks 224 C3
Stanwix Cumb 239 F10
Stanycliffe Gtr Man 195 F11
Stanydale Shetland 313 H4
Staoinebrig W Isles 297 H3
Stape N Yorks 226 G5
Stapehill Dorset 31 G9
Stapeley Ches E 167 F11
Stapenhill Staffs 152 E5
Staple Kent 55 B9
Som 42 E6
Staplecross E Sus 38 C3
Staple Cross Devon 27 C8
Staplefield W Sus 36 B3
Staple Fitzpaine Som 28 D3
Stapleford Cambs 123 G9
Herts 86 B4
Leics 154 F6
Lincs 172 D5
Notts 153 B9
Wilts 46 F5
Stapleford Abbotts Essex 87 G8
Stapleford Tawney Essex 87 F8
Staplegrove Som 28 B2
Staplehay Som 28 C2
Staple Hill S Glos 61 D7
Worcs 117 C9
Staplehurst Kent 53 E9
Staple Lawns Som 28 D3
Staplers IoW 20 D6
Staples Hill W Sus 35 B8
Staplestreet Kent 70 G5
Stapleton Bristol 60 D6
Cumb 240 C2
Hereford 114 D6
Leics 135 D8
N Yorks 198 D4
N Yorks 224 C5
Shrops 131 C9
Som 29 C7
Stapley Som 27 E11
Staploe Bedford 122 E2
Staplow Hereford 98 C3
Stapness Shetland 313 J4
Star Anglesey 179 G8
Fife 287 G7
Pembs 92 E4
Som 44 B2
Stara Orkney 314 D2
Starbeck N Yorks 206 B2
Starbotton N Yorks 213 E9
Starcross Devon 14 E5
Stareton Warks 118 C6
Stargate T&W 242 E5
Star Hill Mon 79 E7
Starkholmes Derbys 170 D4
Starling Gtr Man 195 E9
Starlings Green Essex 105 E9
Starr's Green E Sus 38 D3
Starston Norf 142 G4
Start Devon 8 G6
Startforth Durham 223 B10
Start Hill Essex 105 G10
Startley Wilts 62 C2
Startop's End Bucks 84 C6
Starveall S Glos 61 B9
Starvecrow Kent 52 D5
Statenborough Kent 55 B10
Statford St Andrew Suff 127 E7
Statham Warr 183 D11
Stathe Som 28 B5
Stathern Leics 154 C5
Station Hill Cumb 229 B11
Station Town Durham 234 D4
Statland Common
Norf 141 D10
Staughton Green Cambs 122 D2
Staughton Highway
Cambs 122 E2
Staughton Moor Cambs 122 E2
Staunton Glos 79 C8
Glos 98 F5
Staunton in the Vale
Notts 172 G4
Staunton on Arrow
Hereford 115 E7
Staunton on Wye
Hereford 97 B7
Staupes N Yorks 205 B10
Staveley Cumb 211 B7
Cumb 221 F9
Derbys 186 G6
N Yorks 215 G7
Staveley-in-Cartmel
Cumb 211 B7
Staverton Devon 8 C5
Glos 99 G7
Wilts 61 G11
W Nhants 119 E10
Staverton Bridge Glos 99 G7
Stawell Som 43 F11
Stawley Som 27 C9
Staxigoe Highld 310 D7
Staxton N Yorks 217 D10
Staylittle Ceredig 128 F2
Staylittle = Penffordd-Lâs
Powys 129 E7
Staynall Lancs 202 E3
Staythorpe Notts 172 E3
Stead W Yorks 205 D8
Steam Mills Glos 79 B10
Stean N Yorks 213 E11
Steanbow Som 44 F5
Stearsby N Yorks 216 E2
Steart Som 29 B9
Som 43 D9
Stebbing Essex 106 G3
Stebbing Green Essex 106 G3
Stechford W Mid 134 F2
Stede Quarter Kent 53 F11
Stedham W Sus 34 C5
Steel Northumb 241 F10
Northumb 251 G9
Steel Bank S Yorks 186 D4
Steel Cross E Sus 52 G4
Steelend Fife 279 C10
Steele Road Borders 250 E2
Steeleroad-end Borders 250 E2
Steel Green Cumb 210 D3
Steel Heath Shrops 149 B10
Steen's Bridge
Hereford 115 F10
Steep Hants 34 B2
Steephill IoW 21 F7
Steep Lane W Yorks 196 C4
Steeple Dorset 18 E4
Essex 88 E6
Steeple Ashton Wilts 46 B2
Steeple Aston Oxon 101 F9
Steeple Barton Oxon 101 G8
Steeple Bumpstead
Essex 106 C3
Steeple Claydon Bucks 102 F3
Steeple Gidding Cambs 138 G2
Steeple Langford Wilts 46 F4
Steeple Morden Cambs 104 C5
Steep Marsh Hants 34 B3
Steeraway Telford 132 B3
Steeton W Yorks 204 E6
Stein Highld 298 D2
Steinmanhill Aberds 303 E7
Stella T&W 242 E5
Stelling Minnis Kent 54 D6
Stelvio Newport 59 B9
Stembridge Som 28 C6
Swansea 56 C3
Stemster Highld 310 C5
Stemster Ho Highld 310 C5
Stenalees Corn 5 D10
Stenaquoy Orkney 314 C5
Stencoose Corn 4 F4
Stenhill Devon 27 E9
Stenhouse Dumfries 247 E8
Edin 280 G4
Stenhousemuir Falk 279 E7
Stenigot Lincs 190 E3
Stennack Corn 2 B5
Stenness Shetland 312 F4
Stenscholl Highld 298 C4
Stenso Orkney 314 D3
Stenson Derbys 152 D6
Stenton E Loth 282 G2
Fife 280 B5
Stentwood Devon 27 F10
Stenwith Lincs 154 B6
Stepaside Corn 5 F9
Pembs 73 D10
Powys 129 F11
Stepping Hill Gtr Man 184 D6
Steppingley C Beds 103 D10
Stepps N Lanark 268 B3
Sterndale Moor Derbys 169 B10
Sternfield Suff 127 E7
Sterridge Devon 40 D5
Stert Wilts 46 B4
Sterte BCP 18 C6
Stetchworth Cambs 124 F2
Stevenage Herts 104 G4
Steven's Crouch E Sus 38 D2
Stevenston N Ayrs 266 G5
Stevenstone Devon 25 D8
Steventon Hants 48 D4
Oxon 83 G7
Shrops 115 C10
Steventon End Essex 105 C11
Stevington Bedford 121 G9
Stewards Essex 87 D7
Steward's Green Essex 87 E7
Stewartby Bedford 103 C10
Stewarton Argyll 255 F7
E Ayrs 267 F8
Stewkley Bucks 103 F7
Stewkley Dean Bucks 102 F6
Stewley Som 28 D4
Stewton Lincs 190 D5
Steyne Cross IoW 21 D8
Steyning W Sus 35 E11
Steynton Pembs 72 D6
Stibb Corn 24 E2
Stibbard Norf 159 D9
Stibb Cross Devon 24 E6
Stibb Green Wilts 63 G8
Stibbington Cambs 137 D11
Stichill Borders 262 B6
Sticker Corn 5 E9
Stickford Lincs 174 D5
Stick Hill Kent 52 E3
Sticklepath Devon 13 C8
Devon 40 G5
Som 28 E4
Som 42 F4
Sticklinch Som 44 F5
Stickling Green Essex 105 E9
Stickney Lincs 174 D4
Stiffkey Norf 177 E7
Stifford's Bridge Hereford 98 B4
Stiff Street Kent 69 G11
Stileway Som 44 E3
Stillingfleet N Yorks 207 E7
Stillington N Yorks 215 F11
Stockton 234 G3
Stilton Cambs 138 F3
Stinchcombe Glos 80 F2
Stinsford Dorset 17 C10
Stiperstones Shrops 131 C7
Stirchley Telford 132 B4
W Mid 133 G11
Stirkoke Ho Highld 310 D7
Stirling Aberds 303 E11
Stirling 278 C5
Stirtloe Cambs 122 D3
Stirton N Yorks 204 C5
Stisted Essex 106 G5
Stitchcombe Wilts 63 F8
Stitchin's Hill Worcs 116 G5
Stithians Corn 2 B6
Stittenham Highld 300 B6
Stivichall W Mid 118 B6
Stixwould Lincs 173 B11
Stoak Ches W 182 G6
Stobhill Northumb 252 G6
Stobhillgate Northumb 252 F6
Stobieside S Lanark 258 B4
Stobo Borders 260 B5
Stoborough Dorset 18 D4
Stoborough Green
Dorset 18 D4
Stobs Castle Borders 250 B2
Stobshiel E Loth 271 C9
Stobswood Northumb 252 E6
Stock Essex 87 F11
Lancs 204 D3
N Som 60 G3
Stockbridge Hants 47 G11
S Yorks 198 F5
W Sus 22 C5
W Yorks 205 E7
Stockbridge Village
Mers 182 C6
Stockbury Kent 69 G10
Stockcross W Berks 64 F2
Stockend Glos 80 D4
Stocker's Head Kent 54 C3
Stockerston Leics 136 D6
Stockfield W Mid 134 G2
Stock Green Worcs 117 F9
Stockheath Hants 22 B2
Stock Hill Suff 125 D9
Stockholes Turbary
N Lincs 199 F9
Stockiemuir Stirling 277 E10
Stocking Hereford 98 E2
Stockingford Warks 134 E6
Stocking Green Essex 105 D11

Stocking Pelham Herts 105 F9
Stockland Devon 28 G2
Stockland Bristol Som 43 E8
Stockland Green Kent 52 E5
W Mid 133 E11
Stockleigh English Devon 26 F5
Stockleigh Pomeroy
Devon 26 G5
Stockley Wilts 62 F4
Stocklinch Som 28 D5
Stockport Gtr Man 184 C5
Stocksbridge S Yorks 186 B3
Stocksfield Northumb 242 E3
Stocks Green Kent 52 D5
Stockstreet Essex 106 G6
Stockton Hereford 115 E10
Norf 143 E7
Shrops 130 C5
Shrops 132 D4
Telford 150 F5
Warks 119 E8
Wilts 46 F3
Stockton Brook Staffs 168 E6
Stockton Heath Warr 183 D10
Stockton-on-Tees
Stockton 225 B8
Stockton on Teme
Worcs 116 D4
Stockton on the Forest
York 207 B9
Stocktonwood Shrops 130 C5
Stockwell Devon 27 G7
Glos 80 C6
London 67 D10
Stockwell End W Mid 133 C7
Stockwell Heath Staffs 151 E11
Stockwitch Cross Som 29 C9
Stockwood Bristol 60 F6
Dorset 29 F9
Stock Wood Worcs 117 F10
Stockwood Vale Bath 60 F6
Stodday Lancs 202 B5
Stodmarsh Kent 71 G8
Stody Norf 159 C11
Stoer Highld 307 G5
Stoford Som 29 E9
Wilts 46 F5
Stoford Water Devon 27 F9
Stogumber Som 42 F5
Stogursey Som 43 E8
Stoke Devon 24 C2
Hants 22 C2
Hants 48 C2
Medway 69 D10
Plym 7 D9
Suff 108 C3
W Mid 119 B7
Stoke Abbott Dorset 29 G7
Stoke Albany N Nhants 136 F6
Stoke Aldermoor
W Mid 119 B7
Stoke Ash Suff 126 C2
Stoke Bardolph Notts 171 G10
Stoke Bishop Bristol 60 D5
Stoke Bliss Worcs 116 E3
Stoke Bruerne
W Nhants 102 B4
Stoke by Clare Suff 106 C4
Stoke-by-Nayland Suff 107 D9
Stoke Canon Devon 14 B4
Stoke Charity Hants 48 F3
Stoke Climsland Corn 12 G3
Stoke Common Hants 33 C7
Stoke Cross Hereford 116 G2
Stoke D'Abernon Sur 50 B6
Stoke Doyle N Nhants 137 F10
Stoke Dry Rutland 137 D7
Stoke Edith Hereford 98 C2
Stoke End Warks 134 D3
Stoke Farthing Wilts 31 B9
Stoke Ferry Norf 140 D4
Stoke Fleming Devon 9 F7
Stokeford Dorset 18 D3
Stoke Gabriel Devon 8 D6
Stoke Gifford S Glos 60 D6
Stoke Golding Leics 135 D7
Stoke Goldington
M Keynes 102 B6
Stokegorse Shrops 131 G11
Stoke Green Bucks 66 C3
Stokeham Notts 188 F3
Stoke Hammond Bucks 103 F7
Stoke Heath Shrops 150 D3
W Mid 135 G7
Worcs 117 D8
Stoke Hill Devon 14 C4
Hereford 98 B2
Stoke Holy Cross Norf 142 C4
Stokeinteignhead Devon 14 G4
Stoke Lacy Hereford 98 B2
Stoke Lane Hereford 116 G2
Stoke Lyne Oxon 101 F11
Stoke Mandeville Bucks 84 C4
Stokenchurch Bucks 84 F3
Stoke Newington
London 67 B10
Stokenham Devon 8 G6
Stoke on Tern Shrops 150 D2
Stoke-on-Trent Stoke 168 F5
Stoke Orchard Glos 99 F8
Stoke Park Suff 108 C3
Stoke Poges Bucks 66 C3
Stoke Pound Worcs 117 D9
Stoke Prior Hereford 115 F10
Worcs 117 D8
Stoke Rivers Devon 40 F6
Stoke Rochford Lincs 155 D8
Stoke Row Oxon 65 C7
Stoke St Gregory Som 28 B4
Stoke St Mary Som 28 C3
Stoke St Michael Som 45 D7
Stoke St Milborough
Shrops 131 G11
Stokesay Shrops 131 G8
Stokesby Norf 161 G8
Stokesley N Yorks 225 D10
Stoke sub Hamdon Som 29 D7
Stoke Talmage Oxon 83 F11
Stoke Trister Som 30 B2
Stoke Wake Dorset 30 F3
Stoke Water Dorset 29 G7
Stoke Wharf Worcs 117 D9
Stokoe Northumb 250 F6
Stolford Som 43 D8
Stondon Massey Essex 87 E9
Stone Bucks 84 C3
Glos 79 F11
Kent 38 B6
Kent 68 E5
Som 44 G5
Staffs 151 C8
S Yorks 187 D9
Worcs 117 B7
Stonea Cambs 139 E9
Stoneacton Shrops 131 E10
Stone Allerton Som 44 C2
Ston Easton Som 44 C6
Stonebow Worcs 99 B8
Stonebridge Essex 70 B2
London 67 C8
Norf 141 E8
Stonebridge continued
N Som 43 B11
Sur 51 D7
W Mid 134 G4
Stone Bridge Corner
Pboro 138 C5
Stonebridge Green Kent 54 D2
Stonebroom Derbys 170 D6
Stonebyres Holdings
S Lanark 268 G6
Stone Chair W Yorks 196 B6
Stoneclough Gtr Man 195 F9
Stonecombe Devon 40 E6
Stone Cross E Sus 23 E10
E Sus 37 B8
E Sus 52 G6
Kent 52 F4
Kent 54 F4
Kent 55 B10
W Mid 133 E10
Stonecrouch Kent 53 G7
Stonedge Borders 250 B3
Stone-edge Batch
N Som 60 E3
Stoneferry Hull 209 G8
Stonefield Argyll 289 F11
S Lanark 268 D3
Staffs 151 C7
Stonefield Castle Hotel
Argyll 275 F9
Stonegate E Sus 37 B11
N Yorks 226 D5
Stonegrave N Yorks 216 D3
Stonegravels Derbys 186 G5
Stonehall Kent 55 D9
Worcs 99 B7
Stonehaugh Northumb 241 B7
Stonehaven Aberds 293 E10
Stone Head N Yorks 204 E4
Stone Heath Staffs 151 B9
Stonehill Sur 66 G4
Stone Hill Kent 54 D2
Kent 54 F5
S Glos 60 E6
S Yorks 199 F7
Stonehills Hants 33 G7
Stonehouse Aberds 303 F8
Glos 80 D4
Northumb 240 F5
Plym 7 E9
S Lanark 268 F5
Stone House Cumb 212 B5
Stonehouses Staffs 169 G7
Stone in Oxney Kent 38 B6
Stoneleigh London 67 G8
Warks 118 C6
Stoneley Green Ches E 167 E10
Stonely Cambs 122 D2
Stonepits Worcs 117 F10
Stonequarry W Sus 52 F2
Stone Raise Cumb 230 B4
Stoner Hill Hants 34 B2
Stonesby Leics 154 E6
Stonesfield Oxon 82 B5
Stones Green Essex 108 F3
Stone Street Kent 52 C5
Suff 107 D9
Suff 143 G7
Stonestreet Green Kent 54 F5
Stonethwaite Cumb 220 C5
Stoneton Warks 119 G9
Stonewells Moray 302 C2
Stonewood Kent 68 E5
Stoneyard Green
Hereford 98 C4
Stoneybank E Loth 280 G6
Stoneybreck Shetland 313 N2
Stoneyburn W Loth 269 C9
Stoneycombe Devon 9 B7
Stoneycroft Mers 182 C5
Stoney Cross Hants 32 E3
Stoneyfield Gtr Man 195 E11
Moray 301 D11
Stoneyford Derbys 170 F6
Devon 27 F8
Stoneygate Aberds 303 F10
Leicester 136 C2
Stoney Hill Worcs 117 C9
Stoneyhills Essex 88 F6
Stoneykirk Dumfries 236 D2
Stoneylane Shrops 115 B11
Stoney Middleton
Derbys 186 F2
Stoney Royd W Yorks 196 C5
Stoney Stanton Leics 135 E9
Stoney Stoke Som 45 G8
Stoney Stratton Som 45 F7
Stoney Stretton Shrops 131 B7
Stoneywood Aberdeen 293 B10
Falk 278 E5
Stonganess Shetland 312 C7
Stonham Aspal Suff 126 F2
Stonnall Staffs 133 C11
Stonor Oxon 65 B8
Stonton Wyville Leics 136 D4
Stony Batter Hants 32 B3
Stony Cross Devon 25 B8
Hereford 98 B4
Hereford 115 D10
Stony Dale Notts 172 G2
Stonyfield Highld 300 B6
Stonyford Hants 32 D4
Stony Gate T&W 243 G9
Stony Green Bucks 84 F5
Stony Heap Durham 242 G4
Stony Heath Hants 48 B5
Stony Houghton Derbys 171 B7
Stony Knaps Dorset 28 G5
Stonyland Devon 25 B8
Stony Littleton Bath 45 B8
Stonymarsh Hants 32 B4
Stony Stratford
M Keynes 102 C5
Stoodleigh Devon 26 D6
Stop-and-Call Pembs 91 D8
Stopes S Yorks 186 D3
Stopgate Devon 28 F2
Stopham W Sus 35 D8
Stopper Lane Lancs 204 D2
Stopsley Luton 104 G2
Stoptide Corn 10 F4
Stores Corner Suff 109 B7
Storeton Mers 182 E4
Storiths N Yorks 205 C7
Stormontfield Perth 286 E5
Stormore Wilts 45 D10
Stornoway W Isles 304 E6
Storridge Hereford 98 B4
Storrington W Sus 35 E9
Storrs Cumb 221 G7
S Yorks 186 D3
Storth Cumb 211 C9
Storwood E Yorks 207 E10
Stotfield Moray 302 B2
Stotfold C Beds 104 D4
Stottesdon Shrops 132 G3
Stoughton Leics 136 C2
Sur 50 C3
W Sus 34 E4
Stoughton Cross Som 44 D2
Stoul Highld 295 F9
Stoulton Worcs 99 B8
Stourbridge W Mid 133 G8
Stourpaine Dorset 30 F5
Stourport on Severn
Worcs 116 C6
Stour Provost Dorset 30 C3
Stour Row Dorset 30 C4
Stourton Staffs 133 F7
Warks 100 D5
Wilts 45 G9
W Yorks 206 G2
Stourton Caundle Dorset 30 D2
Stourton Hill Warks 100 D6
Stout Som 44 G2
Stove Orkney 314 C6
Shetland 313 L6
Stoven Suff 143 G8
Stow Borders 271 G9
Lincs 155 B11
Lincs 188 E5
Stow Bardolph Norf 140 B2
Stow Bedon Norf 141 D9
Stowbridge Norf 140 B2
Stow cum Quy Cambs 123 E10
Stowe Glos 79 D9
Hereford 96 B5
Lincs 156 G2
Shrops 114 C6
Staffs 152 G2
Stowe-by-Chartley
Staffs 151 D10
Stowe Green Glos 79 D9
Stowell Glos 81 C9
Som 29 C11
Stowey Bath 44 B5
Stowfield Hereford 79 B9
Stowford Devon 12 B4
Devon 12 D4
Devon 24 E3
Devon 25 B10
Devon 41 E7
Stowgate Lincs 156 G3
Stowlangtoft Suff 125 D9
Stow Lawn W Mid 133 D8
Stow Longa Cambs 122 C2
Stow Maries Essex 88 F4
Stowmarket Suff 125 F10
Stow-on-the-Wold
Glos 100 F3
Stow Park Newport 59 B10
Stowting Kent 54 E6
Stowting Common Kent 54 E6
Stowting Court Kent 54 E6
Stowupland Suff 125 F11
Straad Argyll 275 G11
Strachan Aberds 293 D8
Strachurmore Argyll 284 G5
Stradbroke Suff 126 C4
Stradishall Suff 124 G4
Stradsett Norf 140 C3
Stragglethorpe Lincs 172 E6
Straid S Ayrs 244 E4
Straight Soley Wilts 63 E10
Straith Dumfries 247 F8
Straiton Edin 270 B5
S Ayrs 245 C9
Straloch Aberds 303 G8
Perth 292 G2
Stramshall Staffs 151 B11
Strand Glos 80 C2
London 67 C10
Strands Cumb 210 C3
Strang IoM 192 E4
Strangeways Gtr Man 184 B4
Strangford Hereford 97 F11
Stranghow Redcar 226 B3
Strangways Wilts 46 E6
Stranog Aberds 293 D10
Stranraer Dumfries 236 C2
Strata Florida Ceredig 112 D4
Stratfield Mortimer
W Berks 65 G7
Stratfield Saye Hants 65 G7
Stratfield Turgis Hants 49 B7
Stratford C Beds 104 B3
Glos 99 D7
London 67 C11
Stratford Marsh London 67 C11
Stratford New Town
London 67 C11
Stratford St Andrew
Suff 127 E7
Stratford St Mary Suff 107 E10
Stratford Sub Castle
Wilts 46 G6
Stratford Tony Wilts 31 B9
Stratford-upon-Avon
Warks 118 F3
Strath Highld 299 B7
Highld 310 D6
Strathallan Castle Perth 286 F3
Strathan Highld 295 F11
Highld 307 G5
Highld 308 C5
Strathan Skerray Highld 308 C6
Strathaven S Lanark 268 G4
Strathavon Lo Moray 301 G11
Strathblane Stirling 277 F11
Strathcanaird Highld 307 J6
Strathcarron Highld 299 E9
Strathcoil Argyll 289 F8
Strathcoul Highld 310 D5
Strathdon Aberds 292 B5
Strathellie Aberds 303 C10
Strathgarve Lodge
Highld 300 C4
Strathkinness Fife 287 F8
Strathmashie House
Highld 291 D7
Strathmiglo Fife 286 F6
Strathmore Lodge
Highld 310 E5
Strathpeffer Highld 300 D4
Strathrannoch Highld 300 B3
Strathtay Perth 286 B3
Strathvaich Lodge
Highld 300 B3
Strathwhillan N Ayrs 256 B2
Strathy Highld 300 B6
Highld 310 C2
Strathyre Stirling 285 F9
Stratton Corn 24 F2
Dorset 17 C9
Glos 81 E8
Stratton Audley Oxon 102 F2
Stratton Chase Bucks 85 G7
Stratton-on-the-Fosse
Som 45 C7
Stratton St Margaret
Swindon 63 B7
Stratton St Michael
Norf 142 E4
Stratton Strawless Norf 160 E4
Stravithie Fife 287 F9
Strawberry Bank Cumb 211 B8
Strawberry Hill E Sus 52 F5
London 67 E7
W Yorks 198 C2
Streat E Sus 36 D5
Streatham London 67 E10
Streatham Hill London 67 E10
Streatham Park London 67 E9
Streatham Vale London 67 E9
Streatley C Beds 103 F11
W Berks 64 C5
Street Cumb 222 D2
Lancs 202 C6
N Yorks 226 E4
Som 28 F5
Som 44 F3
Street Ash Som 28 E3
Street Ashton Warks 135 G9
Street Dinas Shrops 148 B6
Street End Hants 33 D9
Kent 54 C6
W Sus 22 D5
Street Gate T&W 242 F6
Streethay Staffs 152 G2
Streethouse W Yorks 197 C11
Street Houses N Yorks 206 D6
Streetlam N Yorks 224 F6
Street Lane Derbys 170 F5
Streetly W Mid 133 D11
Street Lydan Wrex 149 B8
Streetly End Cambs 106 B2
Street of Kincardine
Highld 291 B11
Street on the Fosse Som 44 F6
Strefford Shrops 131 F8
Strelley Notts 171 G8
Strensall York 216 G2
Strensham Worcs 99 C8
Stretch Down Devon 26 E4
Stretcholt Som 43 E9
Strete Devon 8 F6
Stretford Gtr Man 184 C4
Hereford 115 F10
Stretford Court Hereford 115 F8
Strethall Essex 105 D9
Stretham Cambs 123 C10
Strettington W Sus 22 B5
Stretton Ches W 166 E6
Derbys 170 C5
Rutland 155 F8
Staffs 151 G7
Staffs 152 D5
Warr 183 E10
Stretton en le Field
Leics 152 G6
Stretton Grandison
Hereford 98 C2
Stretton-on-Dunsmore
Warks 119 C8
Stretton-on-Fosse
Warks 100 D4
Stretton Sugwas
Hereford 97 C9
Stretton under Fosse
Warks 135 G8
Stretton Westwood
Shrops 131 D11
Strichen Aberds 303 D9
Strines Gtr Man 185 D7
Stringston Som 43 E7
Strixton N Nhants 121 E8
Stroat Glos 79 F9
Strode N Som 60 G4
Strom Shetland 313 J5
Stromeferry Highld 295 B10
Stromemore Highld 295 B10
Stromness Orkney 314 F2
Stronaba Highld 290 E4
Stronachlachar Stirling 285 F8
Stronachullin Lodge
Argyll 275 F9
Stronchreggan Highld 290 F2
Stronchrubie Highld 307 H7
Strone Argyll 255 F7
Argyll 274 G6
Argyll 276 E3
Highld 290 E3
Highld 291 D9
Highld 300 G5
Invclyd 276 G5
Stronelairg Lodge
Highld 291 C7
Stroneskar Argyll 275 C9
Stronmachair Stirling 285 G8
Stronmilchan Argyll 284 E5
Stronord Dumfries 236 C6
Stronsaul Argyll 276 F2
Strontian Highld 289 C10
Stronvar Stirling 285 E9
Strood Kent 53 G11
Medway 69 F8
Strood Green Sur 51 D8
W Sus 35 C8
W Sus 50 G6
Strothers Dale
Northumb 241 F11
Stroud Glos 80 D4
Hants 34 C2
Sur 50 F2
Stroude Sur 66 F4
Strouden BCP 19 C8
Stroud Green Essex 88 G5
Glos 80 D4
London 67 B10
Stroul Argyll 276 E4
Stroupster Highld 310 C7
Stroxton Lincs 155 C8
Stroxworthy Devon 24 D4
Struan Highld 294 B5
Perth 291 G10
Strubby Lincs 191 E7
Structon's Heath Worcs 116 D5
Strugg's Hill Lincs 156 B5
Strumpshaw Norf 142 B6
Strutherhill S Lanark 268 F5
Struthers Fife 287 G7
Struy Highld 300 F3
Stryd Anglesey 178 E2
Stryd y Facsen Anglesey 178 E4
Stryt-issa Wrex 166 F3
Stuartfield Aberds 303 E9
Stubb Norf 161 E8
Stubbermere W Sus 22 B3
Stubber's Green
W Mid 133 C10
Stubbings Windsor 65 C10
Stubbing's Green Suff 125 C11
Stubbington Hants 33 G9
Stubbins Lancs 195 D9
Lancs 202 E6
Stubble Green Cumb 219 F11
Stubbles W Berks 64 D5
Stubbs Cross Kent 54 F3
Stubbs Green Norf 143 D7
Stubb's Green Norf 142 D5
Stubhampton Dorset 30 E6
Stub Place Cumb 219 G11
Stubshaw Cross
Gtr Man 194 G5
Stubton Lincs 172 F5
Stubwood Staffs 151 B11
Stuckgowan Argyll 285 G7
Stuckton Hants 31 E11
Studdal Kent 55 D10
Studd Hill Kent 71 F7
Studfold N Yorks 212 E6
Stud Green Ches E 168 C2
Windsor 65 D11
Studham C Beds 85 B8
Studland Dorset 18 E6
Studley Warks 117 E11
Wilts 62 E3
Studley Green Bucks 84 F4
Wilts 45 B10
Studley Roger N Yorks 214 E5
Studley Royal N Yorks 214 E5
Stump Cross Essex 105 C10
Stumps Cross Glos 99 E11
Stuntney Cambs 123 B11
Stunts Green E Sus 23 C10
Sturbridge Staffs 150 C6
Sturford Wilts 45 E10
Sturgate Lincs 188 D5
Sturmer Essex 106 C3
Sturminster Common
Dorset 30 E3
Sturminster Marshall
Dorset 31 G7
Sturminster Newton
Dorset 30 E3
Sturry Kent 71 G7
Sturton N Lincs 200 G3
Sturton by Stow Lincs 188 E5
Sturton le Steeple Notts 188 E3
Stuston Suff 126 B2
Stutton N Yorks 206 E5
Suff 108 E3
Styal Ches E 184 E4
Styants Bottom Kent 52 B5
Styhead Lancs 203 F9
Styrrup Notts 187 C10
Suainebost W Isles 304 B7
Suardail W Isles 304 E6
Succoth Aberds 302 F4
Argyll 284 G6
Suckley Worcs 116 G4
Suckley Green Worcs 116 G4
Suckley Knowl Worcs 116 G4
Sucksquoy Orkney 314 H4
Suckstead Green Essex 105 F11
Sudborough N Nhants 137 G9
Sudbourne Suff 127 G8
Sudbrook Lincs 173 G7
Mon 60 B4
Sudbrooke Lincs 189 F8
Sudbury Derbys 152 C3
London 67 C7
Suff 107 C7
Sudden Gtr Man 195 E11
Suddie Highld 300 D6
Sudgrove Glos 80 D6
Suffield Norf 160 C4
N Yorks 227 G9
Sugnall Staffs 150 C5
Sugwas Pool Hereford 97 C9
Suisnish Highld 295 D7
Suladale Highld 298 D3
Sulaisiadar W Isles 304 E7
Sulby IoM 192 C4
Sulgrave T&W 243 F8
W Nhants 101 B11
Sulham W Berks 64 E6
Sulhampstead W Berks 64 F6
Sulhampstead Abbots
W Berks 64 F6
Sulhampstead Bannister
Upper End W Berks 64 F6
Sulhamstead W Berks 64 F6
Sulland Orkney 314 B5
Sullington W Sus 35 E9
Sullington Warren
W Sus 35 E9
Sullom Shetland 312 F5
Sullom Voe Oil Terminal
Shetland 312 F5
Sully V Glam 59 F7
Sumburgh Shetland 313 N6
Summerbridge N Yorks 214 G4
Summer Bridge
N Yorks 214 G4
Summercourt Corn 5 D7
Summerfield Kent 55 B9
Norf 158 B5
Worcs 116 C6
Summerfield Park
W Mid 133 F10
Summergangs Hull 209 G8
Summer Heath Bucks 84 G2
Summerhill Newport 59 B10
Pembs 73 D11
Staffs 133 B11
Telford 150 F4
Worcs 116 B6
Wrex 166 E4
Summer Hill E Sus 23 D9
W Mid 133 E9
Summerhouse Darl 224 B4
Summerlands Cumb 211 B10
Som 29 D8
Summerleaze Mon 60 B2
Summerley Derbys 186 F5
Summerscales N Yorks 205 C8
Summersdale W Sus 22 B5
Summerseat Gtr Man 195 E9
Summerston Glasgow 277 G11
Summerstown Bucks 102 G3
London 67 E9
Summertown Oxon 83 D8
Summit Gtr Man 195 E10
Gtr Man 196 D2
Gtr Man 196 F2
Sunbrick Cumb 210 E5
Sunbury Common Sur 66 E5
Sunbury-on-Thames Sur 66 F6
Sundayshill S Glos 79 G11
Sundaywell Dumfries 247 G8
Sunderland Argyll 274 G3
Cumb 229 D9
Lancs 202 B4
T&W 243 F9
Sunderland Bridge
Durham 233 D11
Sundhope Borders 261 D8
Sundon Park Luton 103 F11
Sundridge Kent 52 B3
London 68 E2
Sun Green Gtr Man 185 B7
Sunhill Glos 81 E10
Sunipol Argyll 288 D5
Sunken Marsh Essex 69 C10
Sunk Island E Yorks 201 D9
Sunningdale Windsor 66 F3
Sunninghill Windsor 66 F2
Sunningwell Oxon 83 E7
Sunniside Durham 233 D8
T&W 242 F6
T&W 243 G8
Sunny Bank Gtr Man 195 F10
Sunny Bower Lancs 203 G10
Sunnybrow Durham 233 E9
Sunnyfields S Yorks 198 F4
Sunny Hill Derby 152 C6
Sunnyhurst Blackburn 195 C7
Sunnylaw Stirling 278 B5
Sunnymead Oxon 83 D8
Sunnymeads Windsor 66 D4
Sunnymede Essex 87 G11
Sunnyside S Yorks 187 C7
Sunnyside continued
W Sus 51 F11
Sunset Hereford 114 F6
Sunton Wilts 47 C8
Surbiton London 67 F7
Surby IoM 192 E3
Surfleet Lincs 156 D5
Surfleet Seas End Lincs 156 D5
Surlingham Norf 142 B6
Surrex Essex 107 G7
Suspension Bridge
Norf 139 E10
Sustead Norf 160 B3
Susworth Lincs 199 G10
Sutcombe Devon 24 E4
Sutcombemill Devon 24 E4
Sutherland Grove
Argyll 289 E11
Suton Norf 141 D11
Sutors of Cromarty
Highld 301 C8
Sutterby Lincs 190 G5
Sutterton Lincs 156 B5
Sutterton Dowdyke
Lincs 156 C5
Sutton Bucks 66 D4
Cambs 123 B8
C Beds 104 B4
Devon 8 G4
E Sus 23 F7
Kent 55 D10
Lincs 172 E5
London 67 G9
Mers 183 C8
Norf 161 E7
Notts 154 B5
Notts 187 E11
N Yorks 198 B3
Oxon 82 D6
Pboro 137 D11
Pembs 72 B6
Shrops 132 F4
Shrops 149 D7
Shrops 149 G10
Shrops 150 C3
Som 44 G6
Staffs 150 E5
Suff 108 B6
Sur 50 D5
S Yorks 198 E5
W Sus 35 D7
Sutton Abinger Sur 50 D6
Sutton at Hone Kent 68 E5
Sutton Bassett
N Nhants 136 E5
Sutton Benger Wilts 62 D2
Sutton Bingham Som 29 E8
Sutton Bonington
Notts 153 E10
Sutton Bridge Lincs 157 E9
Sutton Cheney Leics 135 C8
Sutton Coldfield W Mid 134 D2
Sutton Corner Lincs 157 D8
Sutton Courtenay Oxon 83 G8
Sutton Crosses Lincs 157 E8
Sutton Cum Lound
Notts 187 E11
Sutton End W Sus 35 D7
Sutton Forest Side
Notts 171 D8
Sutton Gault Cambs 123 B8
Sutton Green Ches W 182 F5
Sur 50 C4
Wrex 166 F6
Sutton Hall Shrops 132 C4
Sutton Heath Mers 183 C8
Sutton Hill Telford 132 C4
Sutton Holms Dorset 31 F9
Sutton Howgrave
N Yorks 214 D6
Sutton in Ashfield Notts 171 D7
Sutton-in-Craven
N Yorks 204 E6
Sutton Ings Hull 209 G8
Sutton in the Elms
Leics 135 E10
Sutton Lakes Hereford 97 B10
Sutton Lane Ends
Ches E 184 G6
Sutton Leach Mers 183 C8
Sutton Maddock Shrops 132 C4
Sutton Mallet Som 43 F11
Sutton Mandeville Wilts 31 B7
Sutton Manor Mers 183 C8
Sutton Marsh Hereford 97 C10
Sutton Mill N Yorks 204 E6
Sutton Montis Som 29 C10
Sutton on Hull Hull 209 G8
Sutton on Sea Lincs 191 E8
Sutton-on-the-Forest
N Yorks 215 G11
Sutton on the Hill
Derbys 152 C4
Sutton on Trent Notts 172 B3
Sutton Poyntz Dorset 17 E10
Sutton Row Wilts 31 B7
Sutton St Edmund Lincs 157 G7
Sutton St James Lincs 157 F7
Sutton St Michael
Hereford 97 B10
Sutton St Nicholas
Hereford 97 B10
Sutton Scarsdale
Derbys 170 B6
Sutton Scotney Hants 48 F3
Sutton Street Suff 108 C6
Sutton under Brailes
Warks 100 D6
Sutton-under-
Whitestonecliffe
N Yorks 215 C9
Sutton upon Derwent
E Yorks 207 D10
Sutton Valence Kent 53 D10
Sutton Veny Wilts 45 E11
Sutton Waldron Dorset 30 D5
Sutton Weaver Ches W 183 F8
Sutton Wick Bath 44 B5
Oxon 83 G7
Swaby Lincs 190 F5
Swadlincote Derbys 152 F6
Swaffham Norf 140 B6
Swaffham Bulbeck
Cambs 123 E11
Swaffham Prior Cambs 123 E11
Swafield Norf 160 C5
Swaile's Green E Sus 38 C3
Swainby N Yorks 225 E9
Swain House W Yorks 205 F9
Swainshill Hereford 97 C9
Swainsthorpe Norf 142 C4
Swainswick Bath 61 F9
Swaithe S Yorks 197 G11
Swalcliffe Oxon 101 D7
Swalecliffe Kent 70 F6
Swallow Lincs 201 G7
Swallow Beck Lincs 173 B7
Swallowcliffe Wilts 31 B7
Swallowfield Wokingham 65 G8
Swallowfields Devon 8 C5
Swallowhurst Cumb 220 G2
Swallownest S Yorks 187 E7
Swallows Cross Essex 87 F10
Swalwell T&W 242 E6
Swampton Hants 48 C2
Swanage Dorset 18 F6
Swanbach Ches E 167 G11
Swanbister Orkney 314 F3
Swanborough Swindon 81 G11
Swan Bottom Bucks 84 D6
Swanbourne Bucks 102 F6
Swanbridge V Glam 59 F7
Swan Green Ches W 184 G2
Suff 126 C5
Swanland E Yorks 200 B3
Swanley Glos 80 F2
Kent 68 F4
Swanley Bar Herts 86 E3
Swanley Village Kent 68 F4
Swanmore Hants 33 D9
IoW 21 C7
Swannay Orkney 314 D2
Swannington Leics 153 F8
Norf 160 F2
Swanpool Lincs 189 G7
Swanscombe Kent 68 E6
Swansea = Abertawe
Swansea 56 C6
Swanside Mers 182 C6
Swanston Edin 270 B4
Swan Street Essex 107 F7
Swanton Abbott Norf 160 D5
Swanton Hill Norf 160 D5
Swanton Morley Norf 159 F10
Swanton Novers Norf 159 C10
Swanton Street Kent 53 B11
Swan Village W Mid 133 E9
Swanwick Derbys 170 E6
Hants 33 F8
Swanwick Green Ches E 167 F9
Swarby Lincs 173 G8
Swarcliffe W Yorks 206 F3
Swardeston Norf 142 C4
Swarister Shetland 312 E7
Swarkestone Derbys 153 D7
Swarland Northumb 252 C5
Swarraton Hants 48 F5
Swartha W Yorks 205 D7
Swarthmoor Cumb 210 D5
Swartland Orkney 314 D2
Swathwick Derbys 170 B5
Swaton Lincs 156 B2
Swavesey Cambs 123 D7
Sway Hants 19 B11
Swayfield Lincs 155 E9
Swaythling Soton 32 D6
Sweet Green Worcs 116 E2
Sweetham Devon 14 B3
Sweethay Som 28 C2
Sweetholme Cumb 221 B11
Sweethouse Corn 5 C11
Sweets Corn 11 B9
Sweetshouse Corn 5 C11
Swefling Suff 126 E6
Swell Som 28 C5
Swelling Hill Hants 49 G7
Swepstone Leics 153 G7
Swerford Oxon 101 E7
Swettenham Ches E 168 B4
Swetton N Yorks 214 E3
Swffryd Caerph 78 F2
Swiftsden E Sus 38 B2
Swift's Green Kent 53 E11
Swilland Suff 126 G3
Swillbrook Lancs 202 G5
Swillington W Yorks 206 G3
Swillington Common
W Yorks 206 G3
Swimbridge Devon 25 B10
Swimbridge Newland
Devon 40 G6
Swinbrook Oxon 82 C3
Swincliffe N Yorks 205 B10
W Yorks 197 B8
Swincombe Devon 41 E7
Swinden N Yorks 204 C3
Swinderby Lincs 172 C5
Swindon Glos 99 G8
Staffs 133 E7
Swindon 63 C7
Swine E Yorks 209 F8
Swinefleet E Yorks 199 C9
Swineford S Glos 61 F7
Swineshead Bedford 121 D11
Lincs 174 G2
Swineshead Bridge
Lincs 174 G2
Swinethorpe Lincs 172 B5
Swiney Highld 310 F6
Swinford Leics 119 B11
Oxon 82 D6
Swingate Notts 171 G8
Swingbrow Cambs 139 F7
Swingfield Minnis Kent 55 E8
Swingfield Street Kent 55 E8
Swingleton Green Suff 107 B9
Swinhoe Northumb 264 D6
Swinhope Lincs 190 B2
Swining Shetland 312 G6
Swinister Shetland 312 E5
Shetland 313 L6
Swinithwaite N Yorks 213 B10
Swinmore Common
Hereford 98 C3
Swinnie Borders 262 F4
Swinnow Moor
W Yorks 205 G10
Swinscoe Staffs 169 F10
Swinside Cumb 229 G10
Swinside Townfoot
Borders 262 F6
Swinstead Lincs 155 E10
Swinton Borders 272 F6
Glasgow 268 C3
Gtr Man 195 G9
N Yorks 214 D4
N Yorks 216 E5
S Yorks 186 B6
Swinton Bridge S Yorks 187 B7
Swinton Hill Borders 272 F6
Swintonmill Borders 272 F6
Swinton Park Gtr Man 195 G9
Swiss Valley Carms 75 E8
Swithland Leics 153 G10
Swordale Highld 300 C5
Highld 309 K6
Swordland Highld 295 F9
Swordly Highld 308 C7
Sworton Heath Ches E 183 E11
Swyddffynnon Ceredig 112 D3
Swynnerton Staffs 151 B7
Swyre Dorset 16 D6
Sycamore Devon 28 F3
Sychdyn = Soughton
Flint 166 B2
Sychtyn Powys 129 B9
Sydallt Wrex 166 D4
Syde Glos 81 C7
Sydenham London 67 E11
Oxon 84 E2
Som 43 F10
Sydenham Damerel
Devon 12 F4
Syderstone Norf 158 C6
Sydling St Nicholas
Dorset 17 B8
Sydmonton Hants 48 B3
Sydney Ches E 168 D2
Syerston Notts 172 F2
Syke Gtr Man 195 D11
Sykehouse S Yorks 198 D6
Sykes Lancs 203 C8
Syleham Suff 126 B4
Sylen Carms 75 D8
Symbister Shetland 313 G7
Symington Borders 271 F8
S Ayrs 257 C9
S Lanark 259 B11
Symondsbury Dorset 16 C4
Symonds Green Herts 104 F4
Symonds Yat Hereford 79 B9
Synderford Dorset 28 G5
Synod Inn = Post Mawr
Ceredig 111 G8
Synton Borders 261 E11
Synton Mains Borders 261 E11
Synwell Glos 80 G3
Syre Highld 308 E6
Syreford Glos 99 G10
Syresham W Nhants 102 C2
Syster Highld 310 C6
Syston Leics 154 G2
Lincs 172 G6
Sytchampton Worcs 116 D6
Sytch Ho Green Shrops 132 E5
Sytch Lane Telford 150 E2
Sywell N Nhants 120 D6

T

Taagan Highld 299 C10
Tabley Hill Ches E 184 F2
Tabor Gwyn 146 F5
Tàbost W Isles 304 B7
Tabost W Isles 305 G5
Tachbrook Mallory
Warks 118 E6
Tacker Street Som 42 F4
Tackley Oxon 101 G9
Tacleit W Isles 304 E3
Tacolneston Norf 142 D2
Tadcaster N Yorks 206 E5
Tadden Dorset 31 G7
Taddington Derbys 185 G10
Glos 99 E11
Taddiport Devon 25 D7
Tadhill Som 45 D7
Tadley Hants 64 G6
Oxon 64 B4
Tadlow Cambs 104 B5
C Beds 104 B5
Tadmarton Oxon 101 D7
Tadnoll Dorset 17 D11
Tadwick Bath 61 E8
Tadworth Sur 51 B8
Tafarnau-bach
Bl Gwent 77 C10
Tafarn-y-bwlch Pembs 91 E11
Tafarn-y-gelyn Denb 165 C11
Taff Merthyr Garden Village
M Tydf 77 F10
Taff's Well Rhondda 58 C6
Tafolwern Powys 129 C7
Tai Conwy 164 C3
Taibach Neath 57 D9
Tai-bach Powys 148 D3
Taigh a Ghearraidh
W Isles 296 D3
Taigh Bhalaigh W Isles 296 D3
Tai-mawr Conwy 165 G7
Tai-morfa Gwyn 144 D5
Tain Highld 309 L7
Highld 310 C6
Tai-nant Wrex 166 F3
Tainlon Gwyn 162 E6
Tairbeart W Isles 305 H3
Tai'r-Bull Powys 95 F9
Tairgwaith Neath 76 C2
Tai'r-heol Caerph 77 G10
Tai'r-ysgol Swansea 57 B7
Tai-Ucha Denb 165 D8
Takeley Essex 105 G11
Takeley Street Essex 105 G10
Talacharn = Laugharne
Carms 74 C4
Talachddu Powys 95 E11
Talacre Flint 181 E10
Talardd Gwyn 147 D7
Talaton Devon 15 B7
Talbenny Pembs 72 C4
Talbot Green Rhondda 58 C4
Talbot Heath BCP 19 C7
Talbot's End S Glos 80 G2
Talbot Village BCP 19 C7
Talbot Woods BCP 19 C7
Tale Devon 27 G9
Talerddig Powys 129 C8
Talgarreg Ceredig 111 G8
Talgarth Powys 96 E3
Talgarth's Well Swansea 56 D2
Talisker Highld 294 B5
Talke Staffs 168 E4
Talke Pits Staffs 168 E4
Talkin Cumb 240 F3
Talladale Highld 299 B9
Talla Linnfoots Borders 260 E4
Tallaminnoch S Ayrs 245 D10
Talland Corn 6 E4
Tallarn Green Wrex 166 G6
Tallentire Cumb 229 D8
Talley Carms 94 E2
Tallington Lincs 137 B11
Talmine Highld 308 C5
Talog Carms 92 F6
Talsarn Carms 94 F5
Tal-sarn Ceredig 111 F10
Talsarnau Gwyn 146 B2
Talskiddy Corn 5 B8
Talwrn Anglesey 179 F7
Wrex 166 F3
Tal-y-bont Ceredig 128 F3
Conwy 164 B3
Gwyn 145 E11
Gwyn 179 G10
Talybont-on-Usk Powys 96 G2
Tal-y-cafn Conwy 180 G3
Tal-y-coed Mon 78 B6
Talygarn Rhondda 58 C4
Talyllyn Powys 96 F2
Tal-y-llyn Gwyn 128 B4
Talysarn Gwyn 163 E7
Tal-y-waenydd Gwyn 163 F11
Talywain Torf 78 E3
Tal-y-wern Powys 128 C6
Tamanabhagh W Isles 304 F2
Tame Bridge N Yorks 225 D10
Tamer Lane End
Gtr Man 194 G6
Tamerton Foliot Plym 7 C9

Tame Water Gtr Man 196 F3
Tamfourhill Falk 279 E7
Tamworth Staffs 134 C4
Tamworth Green Lincs 174 G5
Tancred N Yorks 206 B5
Tandem W Yorks 197 D7
Tanden Kent 54 F2
Tandlehill Renfs 267 C8
Tandridge Sur 51 C11
Tanerdy Carms 93 G8
Tanfield Durham 242 F5
Tanfield Lea Durham 242 G5
Tang N Yorks 205 B10
Tangasdal W Isles 297 M2
Tang Hall York 207 C8
Tangiers Pembs 73 B7
Tangley Hants 47 C10
Tanglwst Carms 92 E6
Tangmere W Sus 22 B6
Tangwick Shetland 312 F4
Tangy Argyll 255 E7
Tan Hills Durham 233 B11
Tan Hinon Powys 129 F7
Tanhouse Lancs 194 F3
Tanis Wilts 62 G3
Tankersley S Yorks 197 G10
Tankerton Kent 70 F6
Tanlan Flint 181 E10
Tan-lan Conwy 164 C3
Gwyn 163 G10
Tanlan Banks Flint 181 E10
Tannach Highld 310 E7
Tannachie Aberds 293 E9
Tannadice Angus 287 B8
Tanner's Green Worcs 117 C11
Tannington Suff 126 D4
Tannington Place Suff 126 D4
Tannochside N Lanark 268 C4
Tan Office Suff 126 E2
Tan Office Green Suff 124 F5
Tansley Derbys 170 D4
Tansley Hill W Mid 133 F9
Tansley Knoll Derbys 170 C4
Tansor N Nhants 137 E11
Tanterton Lancs 202 G6
Tantobie Durham 242 G5
Tanton N Yorks 225 C10
Tanwood Worcs 117 C8
Tanworth-in-Arden
Warks 118 C2
Tan-y-bwlch Gwyn 163 G11
Tanyfron Wrex 166 E3
Tan-y-fron Conwy 165 C7
Tan-y-graig Anglesey 179 F8
Gwyn 144 B6
Tanygrisiau Gwyn 163 F11
Tan-y-groes Ceredig 92 B5
Tan-y-mynydd Gwyn 144 C6
Tan-y-pistyll Powys 147 D11
Tan-yr-allt Denb 181 E9
Gwyn 163 E7
Tanyrhydiau Ceredig 112 D4
Tanysgafell Gwyn 163 B10
Taobh a Chaolais
W Isles 297 K3
Taobh a' Ghlinne
W Isles 305 G5
Taobh a Thuath Loch
Aineort W Isles 297 J3
Taobh a Tuath Loch
Baghasdail W Isles 297 J3
Taobh Siar W Isles 305 H3
Taobh Tuath W Isles 296 C5
Taplow Bucks 66 C2
Tapnage Hants 33 E9
Tapton Derbys 186 G5
Tapton Hill S Yorks 186 D4
Tarbat Ho Highld 301 B7
Tarbert Argyll 255 B7
Argyll 275 E7
Argyll 275 G9
Tarbet Argyll 285 G7
Highld 295 F9
Highld 306 E6
Tarbock Green Mers 183 D7
Tarbolton S Ayrs 257 D10
Tarbrax S Lanark 269 D10
Tardebigge Worcs 117 D10
Tardy Gate Lancs 194 B4
Tarfside Angus 292 F6
Tarland Aberds 292 C6
Tarleton Lancs 194 C3
Tarleton Moss Lancs 194 C2
Tarlogie Highld 309 L7
Tarlscough Lancs 194 E2
Tarlton Glos 81 F7
Tarn W Yorks 205 F9
Tarnbrook Lancs 203 B7
Tarnock Som 43 C11
Tarns Cumb 229 B8
Tarnside Cumb 221 G8
Tarporley Ches W 167 C9
Tarpots Essex 69 B9
Tarr Som 42 G6
Tarraby Cumb 239 F10
Tarrant Crawford
Dorset 30 G6
Tarrant Gunville Dorset 30 E6
Tarrant Hinton Dorset 30 E6
Tarrant Keyneston
Dorset 30 G6
Tarrant Launceston
Dorset 30 F6
Tarrant Monkton Dorset 30 F6
Tarrant Rawston Dorset 30 F6
Tarrant Rushton Dorset 30 F6
Tarrel Highld 311 L2
Tarring Neville E Sus 36 G6
Tarrington Hereford 98 C2
Tarrington Common
Hereford 98 D2
Tarryblake Ho Moray 302 E5
Tarsappie Perth 286 E5
Tarskavaig Highld 295 E7
Tarts Hill Shrops 149 B8
Tarves Aberds 303 F8
Tarvie Highld 300 D4
Perth 292 G2
Tarvin Ches W 167 B7
Tarvin Sands Ches W 167 B7
Tasburgh Norf 142 D4
Tasley Shrops 132 E3
Taston Oxon 101 G7
Tat Bank W Mid 133 F9
Tatenhill Staffs 152 E4
Tatenhill Common
Staffs 152 E3
Tathall End M Keynes 102 B6
Tatham Lancs 212 F2
Tathwell Lincs 190 E4
Tatling End Bucks 66 B4
Tatsfield Sur 52 B2
Tattenhall Ches W 167 D7
Tattenhoe M Keynes 102 E6
Tatterford Norf 159 D7
Tattersett Norf 158 C6
Tattershall Lincs 174 D2
Tattershall Bridge
Lincs 173 D11
Tattershall Thorpe
Lincs 174 D2
Tattingstone Suff 108 D2
Tattingstone White Horse
Suff 108 D2
Tattle Bank Warks 118 E3
Tatton Dale Ches E 184 E2
Tatworth Som 28 F4
Taunton Gtr Man 196 G2
Som 28 C2
Taverham Norf 160 G3
Taverners Green Essex 87 B9
Tavernspite Pembs 73 C11
Tavistock Devon 12 G5
Taw Green Devon 13 B9
Tawstock Devon 25 B9
Taxal Derbys 185 F8
Tay Bridge Dundee 287 E8
Tayinloan Argyll 255 C7
Taymouth Castle Perth 285 C11
Taynish Argyll 275 E8
Taynton Glos 98 G4
Oxon 82 C2
Taynuilt Argyll 284 D4
Tayport Fife 287 E8
Tayvallich Argyll 275 E8
Tea Green Herts 104 G2
Tealby Lincs 189 C11
Tealing Angus 287 D8
Teams T&W 242 E6
Team Valley T&W 242 E6
Teanford Staffs 169 G8
Teangue Highld 295 E8
Teanna Mhachair
W Isles 296 E3
Teasley Mead E Sus 52 F4
Tebay Cumb 222 E2
Tebworth C Beds 103 F9
Tedburn St Mary Devon 14 C2
Teddington Glos 99 E9
London 67 E7
Teddington Hands Worcs 99 E9
Tedsmore Shrops 149 D7
Tedstone Delamere
Hereford 116 F3
Tedstone Wafer
Hereford 116 F3
Teesville Redcar 225 B10
Teeton W Nhants 120 C3
Teffont Evias Wilts 46 G3
Teffont Magna Wilts 46 G3
Tegryn Pembs 92 E4
Teigh Rutland 155 F7
Teigncombe Devon 13 D9
Teigngrace Devon 14 G2
Teignmouth Devon 14 G4
Teign Village Devon 14 E2
Telford Telford 132 B3
Telham E Sus 38 E3
Tellisford Som 45 B10
Telscombe E Sus 36 G6
Telscombe Cliffs E Sus 36 G5
Templand Dumfries 248 F3
Temple Corn 11 G8
Glasgow 267 B10
Midloth 270 D6
Wilts 45 E10
Windsor 65 C10
Temple Balsall W Mid 118 B4
Temple Bar Carms 75 B9
Ceredig 111 G10
W Sus 22 B5
Templeborough
S Yorks 186 C6
Temple Cloud Bath 44 B6
Templecombe Som 30 C2
Temple Cowley Oxon 83 E8
Temple End Essex 106 C6
Suff 124 G3
Temple Ewell Kent 55 E9
Temple Fields Essex 87 C7
Temple Grafton Warks 118 G2
Temple Guiting Glos 99 F11
Templehall Fife 280 C5
Temple Herdewyke
Warks 119 G7
Temple Hill Kent 68 D5
Temple Hirst N Yorks 198 C6
Templeman's Ash Dorset 28 G6
Temple Normanton
Derbys 170 B6
Temple Sowerby Cumb 231 F8
Templeton Devon 26 E5
Pembs 73 C10
W Berks 63 F11
Templeton Bridge Devon 26 E5
Templetown Durham 242 G4
Tempsford C Beds 122 G3
Ten Acres W Mid 133 G11
Tenandry Perth 291 G11
Tenbury Wells Worcs 115 D11
Tenby = *Dinbych-y-Pysgod*
Pembs 73 E10
Tencreek Corn 6 E4
Tendring Essex 108 G2
Tendring Green Essex 108 F2
Tendring Heath Essex 108 F2
Ten Mile Bank Norf 140 D2
Tenston Orkney 314 E2
Tenterden Kent 53 G11
Terfyn Conwy 180 F6
Gwyn 163 C9
Terhill Som 43 G7
Terling Essex 88 B3
Ternhill Shrops 150 C2
Terpersie Castle Aberds 302 G5
Terras Corn 5 E8
Terregles Banks
Dumfries 237 B11
Terrible Down E Sus 23 B7
Terrick Bucks 84 D4
Terriers Bucks 84 G5
Terrington N Yorks 216 E3
Terrington St Clement
Norf 157 E10
Terrington St John
Norf 157 G10
Terryhorn Aberds 302 F4
Terry's Green Warks 118 C2
Terwick Common W Sus 34 C4
Teston Kent 53 C8
Testwood Hants 32 E5
Tetbury Glos 80 G5
Tetbury Upton Glos 80 F5
Tetchill Shrops 149 C7
Tetchwick Bucks 83 B11
Tetcott Devon 12 B2
Tetford Lincs 190 G4
Tetley N Lincs 199 E9
Tetney Lincs 201 G10
Tetney Lock Lincs 201 G10
Tetsworth Oxon 83 E11
Tettenhall W Mid 133 D7
Tettenhall Wood W Mid 133 D7
Tetworth Cambs 122 G4
Teuchan Aberds 303 F10
Teversal Notts 171 C7
Teversham Cambs 123 F9
Teviothead Borders 249 B10
Tewel Aberds 293 E10
Tewin Herts 86 C3
Tewin Wood Herts 86 B3
Tewitfield Lancs 211 E10
Tewkesbury Glos 99 E7
Teynham Kent 70 G3
Teynham Street Kent 70 G3
Thackley W Yorks 205 F9
Thackley End W Yorks 205 F9
Thackthwaite Cumb 229 G8
Thainston Aberds 293 F8
Thakeham W Sus 35 D10
Thame Oxon 84 D2
Thames Ditton Sur 67 F7
Thames Haven Thurrock 69 C8
Thames Head Glos 81 F7
Thamesmead London 68 C3
Thanington Kent 54 B6
Thankerton S Lanark 259 B11
Tharston Norf 142 E3
Thatcham W Berks 64 F4
Thatto Heath Mers 183 C8
Thaxted Essex 106 E2
The Aird Highld 298 D4
Theakston N Yorks 214 B6
Thealby N Lincs 199 D11
The Alders Staffs 134 C3
Theale Som 44 D3
W Berks 64 E6
The Arms Norf 141 D7
Thearne E Yorks 209 F7
The Bage Hereford 96 C5
The Balloch Perth 286 F2
The Bank Ches E 168 D4
The Banks Gtr Man 185 D7
Wilts 62 D4
The Barony Ches E 167 E11
Orkney 314 D2
Worcs 98 C6
The Barton Wilts 62 D5
The Batch S Glos 61 E7
The Beeches Glos 81 E8
The Bell Gtr Man 194 F4
The Bents Staffs 151 C10
Theberton Suff 127 D8
The Blythe Staffs 151 D10
The Bog Shrops 131 D7
The Borough Dorset 30 E2
London 67 D10
The Bourne Sur 49 E10
Worcs 117 F9
The Bows Stirling 285 G11
The Braes Highld 295 B7
The Brampton Staffs 168 F4
The Brand Leics 153 G10
The Bratch Staffs 133 E7
The Breck Orkney 314 F3
The Brents Kent 70 G4
The Bridge Dorset 30 E3
The Broad Hereford 115 E9
The Brook Suff 125 B11
The Brushes Derbys 186 F5
The Bryn Mon 78 D4
The Burf Worcs 116 D6
The Butts Hants 49 F8
Som 45 D9
The Camp Glos 80 D6
Herts 85 D11
The Cape Warks 118 D5
The Chart Kent 52 C3
The Chequer Wrex 167 G7
The Chuckery W Mid 133 D10
The City Bucks 84 F3
The Cleaver Hereford 97 F10
The Close W Sus 22 C5
The Colony Oxon 100 D6
The Common Bath 60 G6
Bucks 102 E5
Dorset 30 E3
Shrops 150 D3
Suff 108 B2
Swansea 56 C4
Wilts 47 G8
Wilts 61 G11
Wilts 62 C4
W Sus 51 G7
The Corner Kent 53 E8
Shrops 131 F8
The Cot Mon 79 F8
The Craigs Highld 309 K4
The Crofts E Yorks 218 E4
The Cronk IoM 192 C4
The Cross Hands Leics 134 C6
The Cwm Mon 79 G7
Theddingworth Leics 136 F3
Theddlethorpe All Saints
Lincs 191 D7
Theddlethorpe St Helen
Lincs 191 D7
The Dell Suff 143 D9
The Delves W Mid 133 D10
The Den N Ayrs 266 E6
The Dene Durham 242 G4
Hants 47 C11
The Down Kent 53 F7
Shrops 132 E3
The Downs Sur 50 F3
The Dunks Wrex 166 E4
The Eals Northumb 251 F7
The Eaves Glos 79 D10
The Fall W Yorks 197 B10
The Fence Glos 79 D8
The Flat Glos 80 B3
The Flatt Cumb 240 B3
The Flourish Derbys 153 B8
The Folly Herts 85 C11
S Glos 61 E8
The Fording Hereford 98 F3
The Forge Hereford 114 F6
The Forstal Kent 54 F4
The Forties Derbys 152 F6
The Four Alls Shrops 150 C3
The Fox Wilts 62 B6
The Foxholes Shrops 132 G2
The Frenches Hants 32 C4
The Frythe Herts 86 C2
The Garths Shetland 312 B8
The Gibb Wilts 61 D10
The Glack Borders 260 B6
The Gore Shrops 131 G11
The Grange Norf 160 E2
N Yorks 225 F11
The Green Cambs 122 D5
C Beds 85 B8
Cumb 210 C3
Cumb 211 D7
Essex 88 B3
Hants 32 B3
M Keynes 103 C7
Norf 141 C11
Norf 159 B11
Oxon 101 F9
Shrops 130 G6
S Yorks 197 G8
Warks 118 F4
Wilts 45 G11
W Nhants 102 C5
The Grove Dumfries 237 B11
Durham 242 G3
Herts 85 F9
Shrops 131 B7
Shrops 131 G8
Worcs 99 C7
The Gutter Derbys 170 F5
The Gutter *continued*
Worcs 117 B9
The Hacket S Glos 61 B7
The Hague Derbys 185 C8
The Hall Shetland 312 D8
The Hallands N Lincs 200 C5
The Ham Wilts 45 C11
The Handfords Staffs 151 E7
The Harbour Kent 53 D10
The Haven W Sus 50 G5
The Headland Hrtlpl 234 E6
The Heath Norf 159 D8
Norf 160 E3
Norf 160 E4
Staffs 151 C11
Suff 108 D2
The Hem Shrops 132 B4
The Hendre Mon 79 C7
The Herberts V Glam 58 E3
The Hermitage Cambs 123 C7
The High Essex 86 C6
The Highlands E Sus 38 F2
The Hill Cumb 210 C3
The Hobbins Shrops 132 E4
The Hollands Staffs 168 D6
The Hollies Notts 172 E4
The Holmes Derbys 153 B7
The Holt Wokingham 65 D10
The Hook Worcs 98 C6
The Hope Shrops 115 B10
The Howe Cumb 211 B9
IoM 192 F2
The Humbers Telford 150 G3
The Hundred Hereford 115 E10
The Hyde London 67 B8
Worcs 98 C6
The Hythe Essex 107 G10
The Inch Edin 280 G5
The Knab Swansea 56 D6
The Knap V Glam 58 F5
The Knapp Hereford 116 G3
S Glos 79 G11
The Knowle W Mid 133 F9
The Laches Staffs 133 B8
The Lake Dumfries 237 E8
The Lakes Worcs 116 B5
The Lawe T&W 243 D9
The Lawns E Yorks 208 G6
Thelbridge Barton Devon 26 E3
The Leacon Kent 54 G3
The Leath Shrops 131 F11
The Lee Bucks 84 E6
The Lees Kent 54 C4
The Leigh Glos 99 F7
The Leys Staffs 134 C4
The Lhen IoM 192 B4
The Ling Norf 142 D6
The Lings Norf 141 B10
S Yorks 199 F7
The Linleys Wilts 61 F11
Thelnetham Suff 125 B10
The Lunt W Mid 133 D9
Thelveton Norf 142 G3
Thelwall Warr 183 D10
The Manor W Sus 22 C4
The Marsh Ches E 168 C4
Hereford 115 F9
Powys 130 D6
Shrops 150 D3
Staffs 150 D6
Suff 125 B11
Suff 126 B2
Wilts 62 C5
Themelthorpe Norf 159 E11
The Middles Durham 242 G6
The Mint Hants 34 B3
The Moor Flint 166 B4
Kent 38 B3
The Moors Hereford 97 E10
The Mount Hants 64 G2
Reading 65 E8
The Mumbles = *Y Mwmbwls*
Swansea 56 D6
The Murray S Lanark 268 E2
The Mythe Glos 99 E7
The Nant Wrex 166 E3
The Narth Mon 79 D8
The Neuk Aberds 293 D9
Thenford W Nhants 101 C10
The Node Herts 104 G4
The Nook Shrops 149 C11
Shrops 150 E3
The North Mon 79 D8
Theobald's Green Wilts 62 F4
The Oval Bath 61 G8
The Park Glos 99 G8
The Parks S Yorks 198 F6
The Pitts Wilts 31 B9
The Platt Oxon 83 E9
The Pludds Glos 79 B10
The Point Devon 14 E5
The Pole of Itlaw
Aberds 302 D6
The Port of Felixstowe
Suff 108 E5
The Potteries Stoke 168 F5
The Pound Glos 98 E4
The Quarry Glos 80 F2
Shrops 149 G9
The Quarter Kent 53 E11
Kent 53 G11
The Rampings Worcs 99 E7
The Rectory Lincs 156 G2
The Reddings Glos 99 G8
Therfield Herts 104 D6
The Rhos Pembs 73 C8
The Rhydd Hereford 97 E9
The Riddle Hereford 115 E9
The Ridge Wilts 61 F11
The Ridges Wokingham 65 G10
The Ridgeway Herts 86 E3
The Riding Northumb 241 D10
The Riggs Borders 261 C8
The Rink Borders 261 C11
The Rise Windsor 66 F2
The Rock Telford 132 B3
The Rocks Kent 53 B8
S Glos 61 C8
The Roe Denb 181 G8
The Rookery Herts 85 G10
Staffs 168 D5
The Row Lancs 211 D9
The Rowe Staffs 150 B6
The Ryde Herts 86 D2
The Sands Sur 49 D11
The Scarr Glos 98 F4
The Shoe Wilts 61 E10
The Shruggs Staffs 151 C8
The Slack Durham 233 F8
The Slade W Berks 64 F4
The Smeeth Norf 157 G10
The Smithies Shrops 132 D3
The Spa Wilts 62 G2
The Spring Warks 118 C5
The Square Torf 78 F3
The Stocks Kent 38 B6
Wilts 62 G2
The Straits Hants 49 F9
W Mid 133 E8
The Strand Wilts 46 B2
The Swillett Herts 85 F8
The Sydnall Shrops 150 C3
Thetford Lincs 156 F2
Norf 141 G7
The Thrift Cambs 104 D6
The Throat Wokingham 65 F10
The Toft Staffs 151 F8
The Towans Corn 2 B3
The Town Scilly 1 F3
The Twittocks Glos 99 D7
The Tynings Glos 80 B6
The Vale W Mid 133 G11
The Valley Ches E 167 D11
Kent 54 C3
Leics 154 F4
Pembs 73 D10
The Vauld Hereford 97 B10
The Village Newport 78 G4
Windsor 66 E3
W Mid 133 F7
The Walshes Worcs 116 C6
The Warren Kent 54 E3
Wilts 63 F8
The Waterwheel Shrops 131 C7
The Weaven Hereford 97 E10
The Wells Sur 67 G7
The Wern Wrex 166 E3
The Willows NE Lincs 201 F8
The Wood Shrops 148 E6
Shrops 149 D9
The Woodlands Leics 136 D3
Suff 107 C11
Suff 108 D3
The Woods W Mid 133 D10
The Wrangle Bath 44 B4
The Wrythe London 67 F9
The Wyke Shrops 132 B4
The Wymm Hereford 97 B10
Theydon Bois Essex 86 F6
Theydon Garnon Essex 87 F7
Theydon Mount Essex 87 F7
The Yeld Shrops 131 G11
Thicket Mead Bath 45 B7
Thick Hollins W Yorks 196 E6
Thickthorn Hall Norf 142 B3
Thickwood Wilts 61 E10
Thimbleby Lincs 190 G2
N Yorks 225 F9
Thimble End W Mid 134 E2
Thinford Durham 233 E11
Thingley Wilts 61 E11
Thingwall Mers 182 E3
Thirdpart N Ayrs 266 F3
Thirlby N Yorks 215 C9
Thirlestane Borders 271 F11
Thirn N Yorks 214 B4
Thirsk N Yorks 215 C8
Thirtleby E Yorks 209 G9
Thistleton Lancs 202 F4
Rutland 155 F8
Thistley Green Essex 88 B2
Suff 124 B3
Thixendale N Yorks 216 G6
Thockrington Northumb 241 B11
Tholomas Drove Cambs 139 B7
Tholthorpe N Yorks 215 F9
Thomas Chapel Pembs 73 D10
Thomas Close Cumb 230 C4
Thomastown Aberds 302 F5
Rhondda 58 B4
Thompson Norf 141 D8
Thomshill Moray 302 D2
Thong Kent 69 E7
Thongsbridge W Yorks 196 F6
Thoralby N Yorks 213 B10
Thoresby Notts 187 G10
Thoresthorpe Lincs 191 F7
Thoresway Lincs 189 B11
Thorganby Lincs 190 B2
N Yorks 207 E9
Thorgill N Yorks 226 F4
Thorington Suff 127 C8
Thorington Street Suff 107 D10
Thorlby N Yorks 204 C5
Thorley Herts 87 B7
IoW 20 D3
Thorley Houses Herts 105 G9
Thorley Street Herts 87 B7
IoW 20 D3
Thormanby N Yorks 215 E9
Thorn Devon 13 D9
Powys 114 E5
Thornaby on Tees
Stockton 225 B9
Thornage Norf 159 B11
Thornborough Bucks 102 E4
N Yorks 214 D5
Thornbury Devon 24 F6
Hereford 116 F2
S Glos 79 G10
W Yorks 205 G9
Thornby Cumb 239 G7
W Nhants 120 B3
Thorncliff W Yorks 197 E8
Thorncliffe Staffs 169 D8
Thorncombe Dorset 28 G5
Dorset 30 G5
Thorncombe Street Sur 50 E4
Thorncote Green
C Beds 104 B3
Thorncross IoW 20 E4
Thorndon Suff 126 D2
Thorndon Cross Devon 12 C6
Thorne Corn 24 G2
S Yorks 199 E7
Thorne Coffin Som 29 D8
Thornehillhead Devon 24 D6
Thorne Moor Devon 12 D3
Thornend Wilts 62 D3
Thorner W Yorks 206 E3
Thornes Staffs 133 C11
W Yorks 197 D10
Thorne St Margaret Som 27 C9
Thorney Bucks 66 D4
Notts 188 G5
Pboro 138 C5
Som 28 C6
Thorney Close T&W 243 G9
Thorney Crofts E Yorks 201 C8
Thorney Green Suff 125 E11
Thorney Hill Hants 19 B9
Thorney Island W Sus 22 C3
Thorney Toll Pboro 138 C6
Thorneywood Notts 171 G9
Thornfalcon Som 28 C3
Thornford Dorset 29 E10
Thorngrafton Northumb 241 D7
Thorngrove Som 43 G11
Thorngumbald E Yorks 201 B8
Thornham Norf 176 E2
Thornham Fold
Gtr Man 195 F11
Thornham Magna Suff 126 C2
Thornham Parva Suff 126 C2
Thornhaugh Pboro 137 C11
Thornhill Cardiff 59 C7
Cumb 219 D10
Derbys 185 E11
Dumfries 247 D9
Soton 33 E7
Stirling 278 B3
Torf 78 F3
Thornhill *continued*
Wilts 62 D5
W Yorks 197 D9
Thorn Hill S Yorks 186 C6
Thornhill Edge W Yorks 197 D8
Thornhill Lees W Yorks 197 D8
Thornhill Park Hants 33 E7
Thornhills W Yorks 197 C7
Thornholme E Yorks 218 G2
Thornicombe Dorset 30 G5
Thornielee Borders 261 B10
Thornley Durham 233 D8
Durham 234 D3
Thornly Park Renfs 267 C9
Thornroan Aberds 303 F8
Thorns N Yorks 223 E7
Suff 124 F4
Thornseat S Yorks 186 C2
Thornsett Derbys 185 D8
Thorns Green Ches E 184 E3
Thornthwaite Cumb 229 F10
N Yorks 205 B9
Thornton Angus 287 C7
Bucks 102 D5
E Yorks 207 D11
Fife 280 B5
Lancs 202 E2
Leics 135 B9
Lincs 174 B2
Mbro 225 C9
Mers 193 G10
Northumb 273 F9
Pembs 72 D6
W Yorks 205 G8
Thornton Curtis N Lincs 200 D5
Thorntonhall S Lanark 267 D11
Thornton Heath London 67 F10
Thornton Hough Mers 182 E4
Thornton in Craven
N Yorks 204 D4
Thornton in Lonsdale
N Yorks 212 E3
Thornton-le-Beans
N Yorks 225 G7
Thornton-le-Clay
N Yorks 216 F3
Thornton-le-Dale
N Yorks 216 C6
Thornton le Moor Lincs 189 B9
Thornton-le-Moor
N Yorks 215 B7
Thornton-le-Moors
Ches W 182 G6
Thornton-le-Street
N Yorks 215 B8
Thorntonloch E Loth 282 G4
Thornton Park Northumb 273 F8
Thornton Rust N Yorks 213 B9
Thornton Steward
N Yorks 214 B3
Thornton Watlass
N Yorks 214 B4
Thornwood Common
Essex 87 D7
Thornydykes Borders 272 F2
Thoroton Notts 172 G3
Thorp Gtr Man 196 F2
Thorp Arch W Yorks 206 D4
Thorpe Cumb 230 F5
Derbys 169 E11
E Yorks 208 D5
Lincs 191 E7
Norf 143 D8
Notts 172 F3
N Yorks 213 G10
Sur 66 F4
Thorpe Abbotts Norf 126 B3
Thorpe Acre Leics 153 E10
Thorpe Arnold Leics 154 E5
Thorpe Audlin W Yorks 198 D3
Thorpe Bassett N Yorks 217 E7
Thorpe Bay Southend 70 B2
Thorpe by Water
Rutland 137 D7
Thorpe Common Suff 108 D5
Thorpe Constantine
Staffs 134 B5
Thorpe Culvert Lincs 175 C7
Thorpe Edge W Yorks 205 F9
Thorpe End Norf 160 G5
Thorpe Fendykes Lincs 175 C7
Thorpe Green Essex 108 G3
Lancs 194 C5
Suff 125 G8
Sur 66 F4
Thorpe Hamlet Norf 142 B4
Thorpe Hesley S Yorks 186 B5
Thorpe in Balne
S Yorks 198 E5
Thorpe in the Fallows
Lincs 188 E6
Thorpe Langton Leics 136 E4
Thorpe Larches Durham 234 F3
Thorpe Latimer Lincs 156 B2
Thorpe Lea Sur 66 E4
Thorpe-le-Soken Essex 108 G3
Thorpe le Street
E Yorks 208 E2
Thorpe le Vale Lincs 190 C2
Thorpe Malsor
N Nhants 120 B6
Thorpe Mandeville
W Nhants 101 B10
Thorpe Market Norf 160 B4
Thorpe Marriot Norf 160 F3
Thorpe Morieux Suff 125 G8
Thorpeness Suff 127 F9
Thorpe on the Hill Lincs 172 B6
W Yorks 197 B10
Thorpe Row Norf 141 B9
Thorpe St Andrew Norf 142 B5
Thorpe St Peter Lincs 175 C7
Thorpe Salvin S Yorks 187 E8
Thorpe Satchville Leics 154 G4
Thorpe Street Suff 125 B10
Thorpe Thewles
Stockton 234 G4
Thorpe Tilney Lincs 173 D10
Thorpe Underwood
N Nhants 136 G5
N Yorks 206 B5
Thorpe Waterville
N Nhants 137 G10
Thorpe Willoughby
N Yorks 207 G7
Thorpe Wood N Yorks 207 G7
Thorpland Norf 140 B2
Thorrington Essex 89 B9
Thorverton Devon 26 G6
Thoulstone Wilts 45 D10
Thrandeston Suff 126 B2
Thrapston N Nhants 121 B9
Thrashbush N Lanark 268 B5
Threapland Cumb 229 D9
N Yorks 213 G9
Threapwood Ches W 166 F6
Staffs 169 G8
Three Ashes Hants 64 G6
Hereford 97 G10
Shrops 115 B7
Three Ashes *continued*
Som 45 D7
Three Bridges Argyll 284 F4
Lincs 190 D6
W Sus 51 F9
Three Burrows Corn 4 F4
Three Chimneys Kent 53 F10
Three Cocked Hat Norf 143 D8
Three Cocks = *Aberllynfi*
Powys 96 D3
Three Crosses Swansea 56 C5
Three Cups Corner
E Sus 37 C10
Three Fingers Wrex 167 G7
Three Gates Dorset 29 F10
Threehammer Common
Norf 160 E6
Three Hammers Corn 11 D10
Three Holes Norf 139 C10
Three Holes Cross Corn 10 G6
Threekingham Lincs 155 B11
Three Leg Cross E Sus 53 G7
Three Legged Cross
Dorset 31 F9
Threelows Staffs 169 F9
Three Maypoles W Mid 118 B2
Three Mile Cross
Wokingham 65 F8
Threemilestone Corn 4 G5
Threemiletown W Loth 279 F11
Three Oaks E Sus 38 E4
Threepwood Borders 271 G10
Three Sisters Denb 165 C9
Threewaters Corn 5 B10
Threlkeld Cumb 230 F2
Threshers Bush Essex 87 D7
Threshfield N Yorks 213 G9
Thrigby Norf 161 G9
Thringarth Durham 232 G4
Thringstone Leics 153 F8
Thrintoft N Yorks 224 G6
Thriplow Cambs 105 B8
Throapham S Yorks 187 D8
Throckenholt Lincs 139 B7
Throcking Herts 104 E6
Throckley T&W 242 D5
Throckmorton Worcs 99 B9
Throop Dorset 18 C2
Throphill Northumb 252 F4
Thropton Northumb 252 C2
Throsk Stirling 279 C7
Througham Glos 80 D6
Throughgate Dumfries 247 G9
Throwleigh Devon 13 C9
Throwley Kent 54 B3
Throwley Forstal Kent 54 C3
Throxenby N Yorks 217 B10
Thrumpton Notts 153 C10
Notts 188 E2
Thrumster Highld 310 E7
Thrunton Northumb 264 G3
Thrupe Som 44 D6
Thrupp Glos 80 E5
Oxon 82 F3
Oxon 83 B7
Thruscross N Yorks 205 B9
Thrushelton Devon 12 D4
Thrussington Leics 154 F2
Thruxton Hants 47 D9
Hereford 97 E8
Thrybergh S Yorks 187 B7
Thulston Derbys 153 C8
Thunder Bridge
W Yorks 197 E7
Thundergay N Ayrs 255 C9
Thunder Hill Norf 161 F8
Thunder's Hill E Sus 23 C9
Thundersley Essex 69 B9
Thundridge Herts 86 B5
Thurcaston Leics 153 G11
Thurcroft S Yorks 187 D7
Thurdon Corn 24 E3
Thurgarton Norf 160 C3
Notts 171 F11
Thurgoland S Yorks 197 G9
Thurlaston Leics 135 D10
Warks 119 C9
Thurlbear Som 28 C3
Thurlby Lincs 156 F2
Lincs 172 C6
Lincs 191 F7
Thurleigh Bedford 121 F11
Thurlestone Devon 8 G3
Thurloxton Som 43 G9
Thurlstone S Yorks 197 G8
Thurlton Norf 143 D8
Thurlton Links Norf 143 D8
Thurlwood Ches E 168 D4
Thurmaston Leics 136 B2
Thurnby Leics 136 C2
Thurne Norf 161 F8
Thurnham Kent 53 B10
Lancs 202 C5
Thurning N Nhants 137 G11
Norf 159 D11
Thurnscoe S Yorks 198 F3
Thurnscoe East S Yorks 198 F3
Thursby Cumb 239 G8
Thursford Norf 159 C9
Thursford Green Norf 159 C9
Thursley Sur 50 F2
Thurso Highld 310 C5
Thurso East Highld 310 C5
Thurstaston Mers 182 E2
Thurston Suff 125 D8
Thurston Clough
Gtr Man 196 F3
Thurston End Suff 124 G5
Thurstonfield Cumb 239 F8
Thurstonland W Yorks 197 E7
Thurton Norf 142 C6
Thurvaston Derbys 152 B2
Derbys 152 B4
Thuxton Norf 141 B10
Thwaite N Yorks 223 F7
Suff 126 D2
Thwaite Flat Cumb 210 E4
Thwaite Head Cumb 220 G6
Thwaites W Yorks 205 E7
Thwaite St Mary Norf 142 E6
Thwaites Brow W Yorks 205 E7
Thwing E Yorks 217 E11
Tibbermore Perth 286 E4
Tibberton Glos 98 G5
Telford 150 E3
Worcs 117 F8
Tibenham Norf 142 F2
Tibshelf Derbys 170 C6
Tibshelf Wharf Notts 171 C7
Tibthorpe E Yorks 208 B5
Ticehurst E Sus 53 G7
Tichborne Hants 48 G5
Tickencote Rutland 137 B9
Tickenham N Som 60 E3
Ticket Wood Devon 8 G4
Tickford End M Keynes 103 C7
Tickhill S Yorks 187 C9
Ticklerton Shrops 131 E9
Tickmorend Glos 80 F4
Ticknall Derbys 153 E7
Tickton E Yorks 209 E7
Tidbury Green W Mid 117 B11
Tidcombe Wilts 47 B9
Tiddington Oxon 83 E11
Warks 118 F4
Tidebrook E Sus 37 B10
Tideford Corn 6 D6
Tideford Cross Corn 6 C6
Tidenham Glos 79 F9
Tidenham Chase Glos 79 F9
Tideswell Derbys 185 F11
Tidmarsh W Berks 64 E6
Tidmington Warks 100 D5
Tidnor Hereford 97 D11
Tidpit Hants 31 D9
Tidworth Wilts 47 D8
Tiers Cross Pembs 72 C6
Tiffield W Nhants 120 G3
Tifty Aberds 303 E7
Tigerton Angus 293 G7
Tigh-na-Blair Perth 285 F11
Tighnabruaich Argyll 275 F10
Tighnacachla Argyll 274 G3
Tighnafiline Highld 307 L3
Tighness Argyll 284 G6
Tigley Devon 8 C5
Tilbrook Cambs 121 D11
Tilbury Thurrock 68 D6
Tilbury Green Essex 106 C4
Tilbury Juxta Clare
Essex 106 C5
Tile Cross W Mid 134 F3
Tilegate Green Essex 87 D8
Tile Hill W Mid 118 B5
Tilehouse Green W Mid 118 B3
Tilehurst Reading 65 E7
Tilekiln Green Essex 105 G10
Tiley Dorset 29 F11
Tilford Sur 49 E11
Tilford Common Sur 49 E11
Tilford Reeds Sur 49 E11
Tilgate W Sus 51 G9
Tilgate Forest Row
W Sus 51 G9
Tilkey Essex 106 G6
Tilland Corn 6 C6
Tillathrowie Aberds 302 F4
Tillers' Green Glos 98 E3
Tilley Shrops 149 D10
Tilley Green Shrops 149 D10
Tillicoultry Clack 279 B8
Tillietudlem S Lanark 268 F6
Tillingham Essex 89 E7
Tillington Hereford 97 B9
Staffs 151 E8
W Sus 35 C7
Tillington Common
Hereford 97 B9
Tillislow Devon 12 C3
Tillworth Devon 28 G4
Tillyarblet Angus 293 G7
Tillybirloch Aberds 293 C8
Tillycorthie Aberds 303 G9
Tilly Down Hants 47 D10
Tillydrine Aberds 293 D8
Tillyfour Aberds 293 B7
Tillyfourie Aberds 293 B8
Tillygarmond Aberds 293 D8
Tillygreig Aberds 303 G8
Tillykerrie Aberds 303 G8
Tilly Lo Aberds 293 C7
Tillynaught Aberds 302 C5
Tilmanstone Kent 55 C10
Tilney All Saints Norf 157 F11
Tilney cum Islington
Norf 157 G11
Tilney Fen End Norf 157 G10
Tilney High End Norf 157 F11
Tilney St Lawrence
Norf 157 G10
Tilsdown Glos 80 F2
Tilshead Wilts 46 D4
Tilsmore E Sus 37 C9
Tilsop Shrops 116 C2
Tilstock Shrops 149 B10
Tilston Ches W 167 E7
Tilstone Bank Ches W 167 D9
Tilstone Fearnall
Ches W 167 C9
Tilsworth C Beds 103 G9
Tilton on the Hill Leics 136 B4
Tilts S Yorks 198 F5
Tiltups End Glos 80 F4
Tilty Essex 105 F11
Timberden Bottom Kent 68 G4
Timberhonger Worcs 117 C8
Timberland Lincs 173 D10
Timbersbrook Ches E 168 C5
Timberscombe Som 42 E3
Timble N Yorks 205 C9
Timbold Hill Kent 54 B2
Timbrelham Corn 12 E3
Timperley Gtr Man 184 D3
Timsbury Bath 45 B7
Hants 32 C4
Timsgearraidh W Isles 304 E2
Timworth Suff 125 D7
Timworth Green Suff 125 D7
Tincleton Dorset 17 C11
Tindale Cumb 240 F4
Tindale Crescent
Durham 233 F9
Tindon End Essex 106 E2
Tingewick Bucks 102 E3
Tingley W Yorks 197 B9
Tingon Shetland 312 E4
Tingrith C Beds 103 E10
Tingwall Orkney 314 D3
Tinhay Devon 12 E3
Tinkers End Bucks 102 F5
Tinshill W Yorks 205 F11
Tinsley S Yorks 186 C6
Tinsley Green W Sus 51 F9
Tintagel Corn 11 D7
Tintern Parva Mon 79 E8
Tintinhull Som 29 D8
Tintwistle Derbys 185 B8
Tinwald Dumfries 248 G2
Tinwell Rutland 137 B10
Tipner Ptsmth 33 G10
Tippacott Devon 41 D9
Tipper's Hill Warks 134 F5
Tipperty Aberds 302 C6
Aberds 303 G9
Tipple Cross Devon 12 D3
Tipps End Norf 139 D10
Tip's Cross Essex 87 E9
Tiptoe Hants 19 B11
Tipton W Mid 133 E8
Tipton Green W Mid 133 E9
Tipton St John Devon 15 C7
Tiptree Essex 88 B5
Tiptree Heath Essex 88 B5
Tirabad Powys 95 C7
Tiraghoil Argyll 288 G5
Tircanol Swansea 57 B7
Tirdeunaw Swansea 57 B7
Tirinie Perth 291 G10
Tirley Glos 98 F6
Tirley Knowle Glos 98 F6
Tiroran Argyll 288 G6

Tirphil Caerph 77 E10
Tirril Cumb 230 F6
Tirryside Highld 309 H5
Tir-y-berth Caerph 77 F11
Tir-y-dail Carms 75 C10
Tisbury Wilts 30 B6
Tisman's Common
W Sus 50 G5
Tissington Derbys 169 E11
Titchberry Devon 24 B2
Titchfield Hants 33 F8
Titchfield Common Hants 33 F8
Titchfield Park Hants 33 F8
Titchmarsh N Nhants 121 B10
Titchwell Norf 176 E3
Titcomb W Berks 63 F11
Tithby Notts 154 B3
Tithebarn Staffs 169 G9
Tithe Barn Hillock Mers 183 B9
Titley Hereford 114 E6
Titlington Northumb 264 F4
Titmore Green Herts 104 F4
Titsey Sur 52 C2
Titson Corn 24 G2
Tittenhurst Windsor 66 F3
Tittensor Staffs 151 B7
Tittenhill Shrops 131 G10
Tittle Row Windsor 65 C11
Tittleshall Norf 159 E7
Titton Worcs 116 D6
Titty Hill W Sus 34 B5
Tiverton Ches W 167 C9
Devon 27 E7
Tivetshall St Margaret
Norf 142 F3
Tivetshall St Mary Norf 142 F3
Tividale W Mid 133 E9
Tivington Som 42 D2
Tivington Knowle Som 42 E2
Tivoli Cumb 228 G5
Tivy Dale S Yorks 197 F9
Tixall Staffs 151 E9
Tixover Rutland 137 C9
Toab Orkney 314 F5
Shetland 313 M5
Toadmoor Derbys 170 E4
Toad Row Suff 143 F10
Tobermory Argyll 289 D7
Toberonochy Argyll 275 C8
Tobha Beag W Isles 296 D5
Tobha Mor W Isles 297 H3
Tobhtarol W Isles 304 E3
Tobson W Isles 304 E3
Toby's Hill Lincs 191 C7
Tocher Aberds 302 F6
Tockenham Wilts 62 D4
Tockenham Wick Wilts 62 C4
Tockholes Blackburn 195 C7
Tockington S Glos 60 B6
Tockwith N Yorks 206 C5
Todber Dorset 30 C4
Todding Hereford 115 B8
Toddington C Beds 103 F10
Glos 99 E10
W Sus 35 G8
Toddlehills Aberds 303 E10
Todd's Green Herts 104 F4
Todenham Glos 100 D4
Todhill Angus 287 D8
Todhills Cumb 239 E9
Durham 233 E10
Todlachie Aberds 293 B8
Todmorden W Yorks 196 C2
Todpool Corn 4 G4
Todrig Borders 261 F10
Todwick S Yorks 187 E7
Toft Cambs 123 F7
Lincs 155 F11
Shetland 312 F6
Warks 119 C9
Toft Hill Durham 233 F9
Lincs 174 C2
Toft Monks Norf 143 E8
Toft next Newton Lincs 189 D8
Toftrees Norf 159 D7
Tofts Highld 310 C7
Toftshaw W Yorks 197 B7
Toftwood Norf 159 G9
Togston Northumb 252 C6
Tokavaig Highld 295 D8
Tokers Green Oxon 65 D8
Tokyngton London 67 C7
Tolastadh a Chaolais
W Isles 304 E3
Tolastadh bho Thuath
W Isles 304 D7
Tolborough Corn 11 F9
Tolcarne Corn 2 B5
Corn 2 C5
Tolcarne Wartha Corn 2 B5
Toldish Corn 5 D8
Tolgus Mount Corn 4 G3
Tolhurst E Sus 53 G7
Tolladine Worcs 117 F7
Tolland Som 42 G6
Tollard Farnham Dorset 30 D6
Tollard Royal Wilts 30 D6
Toll Bar Mers 183 C7
Rutland 137 B10
S Yorks 198 F5
Tollbar End W Mid 119 B7
Toll End W Mid 133 E9
Tollerford Dorset 17 B7
Toller Fratrum Dorset 17 B7
Toller Porcorum Dorset 17 B7
Tollerton Notts 154 C2
N Yorks 215 G10
Toller Whelme Dorset 29 G8
Tollesbury Essex 89 C7
Tollesby Mbro 225 B10
Tolleshunt D'Arcy Essex 88 C6
Tolleshunt Knights Essex 88 C6
Tolleshunt Major Essex 88 C5
Tollie Highld 300 D5
Toll of Birness Aberds 303 F10
Tolm W Isles 304 E6
Tolmers Herts 86 E4
Tolpuddle Dorset 17 C11
Tolskithy Corn 4 G3
Tolvaddon Downs Corn 4 G3
Tolvah Highld 291 D10
Tolworth London 67 F7
Tomaknock Perth 286 E2
Tom an Fhuadain
W Isles 305 G5
Tomatin Highld 301 G8
Tombreck Highld 300 F6
Tombui Perth 286 B2
Tomchrasky Highld 290 B4
Tomdoun Highld 290 C3
Tomich Highld 300 B6
Highld 300 G3
Tomich House Highld 300 E5
Tomintoul Aberds 292 D3
Moray 292 B3
Tomlow Warks 119 E9
Tomnaven Moray 302 F4
Tomnavoulin Moray 302 G2
Tomperrow Corn 4 G5
Tompkin Staffs 168 E6
Tompset's Bank E Sus 52 G2
Tomsleibhe Argyll 289 F8
Tomthorn Derbys 185 F9
Ton Mon 78 F5
Ton Breigam V Glam 58 D3
Tonbridge Kent 52 D5
Tonderghie Dumfries 236 F6
Tondu Bridgend 57 E11
Tone Som 27 C10
Tonedale Som 27 C10
Tone Green Som 27 C11
Tong Kent 53 D10
Shrops 132 B5
W Yorks 205 G10
Tonge Leics 153 E8
Tonge Corner Kent 70 F2
Tonge Fold Gtr Man 195 F8
Tonge Moor Gtr Man 195 E8
Tong Forge Shrops 132 B5
Tong Green Kent 54 C3
Tongham Sur 49 D11
Tongland Dumfries 237 D8
Tong Norton Shrops 132 B5
Tong Park W Yorks 205 F9
Tong Street W Yorks 205 G9
Tongue Highld 308 D5
Tongue End Lincs 156 F3
Tongwell M Keynes 103 C7
Tongwynlais Cardiff 58 C6
Tonmawr Neath 57 B10
Tonna = *Tonnau* Neath 57 B9
Tonnau = *Tonna* Neath 57 B9
Ton-Pentre Rhondda 77 F7
Ton-teg Rhondda 58 B5
Tontine Lancs 194 G4
Tonwell Herts 86 B4
Tonypandy Rhondda 77 G7
Ton-y-pistyll Caerph 77 F11
Tonyrefail Rhondda 58 B4
Toot Baldon Oxon 83 E9
Toothill Hants 32 D5
Swindon 62 C6
W Yorks 196 C6
Toot Hill Essex 87 E8
Staffs 169 G9
Tooting Graveney London 67 E9
Topcliffe N Yorks 215 D8
W Yorks 197 B9
Topcroft Norf 142 E5
Topcroft Street Norf 142 E5
Top End Bedford 121 E10
Top Green Notts 172 F3
Topham S Yorks 198 D6
Topleigh W Sus 34 D6
Top Lock Gtr Man 194 F6
Top of Hebers Gtr Man 195 F11
Top o' th' Lane Lancs 194 C5
Top o' th' Meadows
Gtr Man 196 F3
Toppesfield Essex 106 D4
Toppings Gtr Man 195 E8
Toprow Norf 142 D3
Topsham Devon 14 D5
Top Valley Nottingham 171 F9
Torbeg N Ayrs 255 E10
Torboll Farm Highld 309 K7
Torbothie N Lanark 269 D7
Torbreck Highld 309 J7
Torbrex Stirling 278 C5
Torbryan Devon 8 B6
Torbush N Lanark 268 D6
Torcross Devon 8 G6
Torcroy Highld 291 D9
Tore Highld 300 D6
Torfrey Corn 6 E2
Torgyle Highld 290 B5
Torinturk Argyll 275 G9
Torkington Gtr Man 184 D6
Torksey Lincs 188 F4
Torlum W Isles 296 F3
Torlundy Highld 290 F3
Tormarton S Glos 61 D9
Tormisdale Argyll 254 B2
Tormitchell S Ayrs 244 E6
Tormore Highld 295 E8
N Ayrs 255 D9
Tornagrain Highld 301 E7
Tornahaish Aberds 292 C4
Tornapress Highld 299 E8
Tornaveen Aberds 293 C8
Torness Highld 300 G5
Toronto Durham 233 E9
Torpenhow Cumb 229 D10
Torphichen W Loth 279 G9
Torphin Edin 270 B4
Torphins Aberds 293 C8
Torpoint Corn 7 E8
Torquay Torbay 9 C8
Torquhan Borders 271 F8
Torr Devon 7 E11
Devon 8 C2
Torra Argyll 254 B4
Torran Argyll 275 C9
Highld 298 E5
Highld 301 B7
Torrance E Dunb 278 G2
Torrans Argyll 288 G6
Torranyard N Ayrs 267 G7
Torre Som 42 E4
Torbay 9 C8
Torridon Highld 299 D9
Torridon Ho Highld 299 D8
Torries Aberds 293 B8
Torrin Highld 295 C7
Torrisdale Highld 308 C6
Torrisdale Castle Argyll 255 D8
Torrisdale-Square
Argyll 255 D8
Torrish Highld 311 H3
Torrisholme Lancs 211 G9
Torroble Highld 309 J5
Torroy Highld 309 K5
Torrpark Corn 11 D10
Torry Aberdeen 293 C11
Aberds 302 F4
Torryburn Fife 279 D10
Torsonce Borders 271 G9
Torsonce Mains Borders 271 G9
Torterston Aberds 303 E10
Torthorwald Dumfries 238 B2
Tortington W Sus 35 F8
Torton Worcs 116 C6
Tortworth S Glos 80 G2
Torvaig Highld 298 E4
Torver Cumb 220 G5
Torwood Falk 278 E6
Torwoodlee Mains
Borders 261 B11
Torworth Notts 187 D11
Tosberry Devon 24 C3
Toscaig Highld 295 B9
Toseland Cambs 122 E4
Tosside N Yorks 203 B11
Tostock Suff 125 E9
Totaig Highld 295 C10
Highld 298 D2
Totardor Highld 294 B5
Tote Highld 298 E4
Totegan Highld 310 C2
Tote Hill Hants 32 C6
W Sus 34 C5
Totford Hants 48 F5
Totham Hill Essex 88 C5
Totham Plains Essex 88 C5
Tothill Lincs 190 E6
Tot Hill Hants 64 G3
Totland IoW 20 D2
Totley S Yorks 186 F4
Totley Brook S Yorks 186 E4
Totley Rise S Yorks 186 E4
Totmonslow Staffs 151 B9
Totnell Dorset 29 F10
Totnes Devon 8 C6
Totnor Hereford 97 E11
Toton Notts 153 C10
Totronald Argyll 288 D3
Totscore Highld 298 C3
Tottenham London 86 G4
Tottenham Hale London 67 B10
Tottenhill Norf 158 G2
Tottenhill Row Norf 158 G2
Totteridge Bucks 84 G5
London 86 G2
Totternhoe C Beds 103 G9
Totteroak S Glos 61 C8
Totterton Shrops 131 F7
Totties W Yorks 197 F7
Tottington Gtr Man 195 E9
Norf 141 D7
Tottlebank Cumb 210 C6
Tottleworth Lancs 203 G10
Totton Hants 32 E5
Touchen End Windsor 65 D11
Toulston N Yorks 206 E5
Toulton Som 43 G7
Toulvaddie Highld 311 L2
Tournaig Highld 307 L3
Toux Aberds 303 D9
Tovil Kent 53 C9
Towan Corn 10 G3
Towan Cross Corn 4 F4
Toward Argyll 266 B2
Towcester W Nhants 102 B3
Towednack Corn 1 B5
Towerage Bucks 84 G4
Tower End Norf 158 F3
Tower Hamlets Kent 55 E10
Towerhead N Som 44 B2
Tower Hill Ches E 184 F6
Devon 12 C3
Essex 108 E5
Herts 85 E8
Mers 194 G2
Sur 51 D7
W Mid 133 E11
W Sus 35 B11
Towersey Oxon 84 D2
Tow House Northumb 241 E7
Towie Aberds 292 B6
Aberds 302 G5
Aberds 303 C8
Towiemore Moray 302 E3
Tow Law Durham 233 D8
Town Barton Devon 14 C2
Townend Derbys 185 E9
Staffs 151 B9
W Dunb 277 F8
Town End Bucks 84 F3
Cambs 139 D8
Cumb 211 B7
Cumb 211 C8
Cumb 212 C2
Cumb 220 D6
Cumb 221 E8
Cumb 221 F7
Cumb 231 F8
Derbys 185 F11
E Yorks 207 C10
Mers 183 D7
W Yorks 196 D5
Townfield Durham 232 B5
Town Fields Ches W 167 B10
Towngate Cumb 230 B6
Lincs 156 G2
Town Green Gtr Man 183 B9
Lancs 194 F2
Norf 161 G7
Townhead Argyll 275 G11
Cumb 229 D7
Cumb 230 D6
Cumb 231 E8
Cumb 231 F8
Dumfries 237 E8
N Lanark 268 B4
Northumb 251 E9
S Ayrs 244 C6
S Yorks 186 E4
S Yorks 197 G7
Town Head Cumb 220 D6
Cumb 221 E8
Cumb 222 C2
Cumb 222 C3
Cumb 231 F7
Cumb 231 F8
Cumb 231 G8
Cumb 231 G9
Derbys 185 F11
N Yorks 204 B2
N Yorks 212 F5
Staffs 169 F8
W Yorks 204 D6
Townhead of Greenlaw
Dumfries 237 C9
Townhill Fife 280 D2
Swansea 56 C6
Townhill Park Hants 33 E7
Town Kelloe Durham 234 D3
Townlake Devon 12 G4
Town Lane Gtr Man 183 B11
Town Littleworth E Sus 36 D6
Town of Lowton Mers 183 B10
Town Park Telford 132 B3
Town Row E Sus 52 G5
Townsend Bath 44 B5
Bucks 84 D2
Devon 25 B10
Herts 85 D10
Oxon 63 B11
Pembs 72 D4
Som 44 C4
Stoke 168 F6
Wilts 46 B3
Wilts 46 B4
Towns End Hants 48 B5
Som 30 D2
Town's End Bucks 102 G2
Dorset 18 B3
Dorset 18 E5
Dorset 29 F9
Som 45 D7
Townsend Fold Lancs 195 C10
Townshend Corn 2 C3
Town Street Glos 98 F6
Townwell S Glos 79 G11
Town Yetholm Borders 263 D8
Towthorpe E Yorks 217 G8
York 207 B8
Towton N Yorks 206 F5
Towyn Conwy 181 F7
Toxteth Mers 182 D5
Toynton All Saints Lincs 174 C5
Toynton Fen Side Lincs 174 C5
Toynton St Peter Lincs 174 C6
Toy's Hill Kent 52 C3
Trabboch E Ayrs 257 E10
Traboe Corn 2 E6
Trabrown Borders 271 F10
Tracebridge Som 27 C9
Tradespark Highld 301 D8
Orkney 314 F4
Trafford Park Gtr Man 184 B3
Traigh Ho Highld 295 F8
Trallong Powys 95 F9
Trallwn Rhondda 77 G9
Swansea 57 B7
Tramagenna Corn 11 E7
Tram Inn Hereford 97 E9
Tranch Torf 78 E3
Tranent E Loth 281 G8
Tranmere Mers 182 D4
Trantlebeg Highld 310 D2
Trantlemore Highld 310 D2
Tranwell Northumb 252 G5
Trapp Carms 75 B11
Traprain E Loth 281 F11
Trap's Green Warks 118 D2
Trapshill W Berks 63 G11
Traquair Borders 261 C8
Trash Green W Berks 65 F7
Travellers' Rest Carms 74 B5
Trawden Lancs 204 F4
Trawscoed Powys 95 E11
Trawsfynydd Gwyn 146 B4
Trawsnant Ceredig 111 D11
Treadam Mon 78 B5
Treaddow Hereford 97 G10
Treal Corn 2 F6
Trealaw Rhondda 77 G8
Treales Lancs 202 G4
Trearddur Anglesey 178 F3
Treaslane Highld 298 D3
Treath Corn 3 D7
Treator Corn 10 F4
Tre-Aubrey V Glam 58 E4
Trebanog Rhondda 77 G8
Trebanos Neath 76 E2
Trebarber Corn 5 C7
Trebartha Corn 11 F11
Trebarwith Corn 11 D7
Trebarwith Strand Corn 10 D6
Trebeath Corn 11 D11
Tre-Beferad V Glam 58 F3
Trebell Green Corn 5 C11
Treberfydd Powys 96 F2
Trebetherick Corn 10 F4
Trebilcock Corn 5 C9
Treble's Holford Som 43 G7
Tre-boeth Swansea 57 B7
Treborough Som 42 F4
Trebudannon Corn 5 C7
Trebullett Corn 12 F2
Treburgett Corn 11 F7
Treburgie Corn 6 C4
Treburley Corn 12 F3
Treburrick Corn 10 G3
Trebyan Corn 5 C11
Trecastle Powys 95 F7
Trecenydd Caerph 58 B6
Trecott Devon 25 G10
Trecwn Pembs 91 E9
Trecynon Rhondda 77 E7
Tredannick Corn 10 G6
Tredaule Corn 11 E10
Tredavoe Corn 1 D5
Treddiog Pembs 91 F7
Tredegar Bl Gwent 77 D10
Trederwen Powys 148 F5
Tre-derwen Powys 148 F4
Tredethy Corn 11 G7
Tredington Glos 99 F8
Warks 100 C5
Tredinnick Corn 1 C4
Corn 5 D10
Corn 6 B3
Corn 6 D4
Corn 10 G4
Tredogan V Glam 58 F5
Tredomen Caerph 77 G10
Powys 96 E2
Tredown Devon 24 D2
Tredrizzick Corn 10 F5
Tredunnock Mon 78 G5
Tredustan Powys 96 E2
Tredworth Glos 80 B4
Treen Corn 1 B4
Corn 1 E3
Treesmill Corn 5 D11
Treeton S Yorks 186 D6
Trefaes Gwyn 144 C5
Trefanny Hill Corn 6 D4
Trefasser Pembs 91 D7
Trefdraeth Anglesey 178 G6
Trefdraeth = *Newport*
Pembs 91 D11
Trefecca Powys 96 E2
Trefechan Ceredig 111 A11
M Tydf 77 D8
Wrex 166 F3
Trefeglwys Powys 129 E9
Trefeitha Powys 96 E2
Trefenter Ceredig 112 D2
Treffgarne Pembs 91 G9
Treffynnon Pembs 90 F6
Treffynnon = *Holywell*
Flint 181 F11
Trefgarn Owen Pembs 91 F7
Trefil Bl Gwent 77 C10
Trefilan Ceredig 111 F11
Trefin = *Trevine* Pembs 90 E6
Treflach Shrops 148 D5
Trefnanney Powys 148 F4
Trefnant Denb 181 G9
Trefonen Shrops 148 D5
Trefor Anglesey 178 E5
Gwyn 162 F5
Treforda Corn 11 E7
Treforest Rhondda 58 B5
Treforgan Ceredig 92 B4
Tre-Forgan Neath 76 D3
Treforys = *Morriston*
Swansea 57 B7
Trefriw Conwy 164 C3
Trefrize Corn 12 F2
Tref y Clawdd = *Knighton*
Powys 114 C5
Trefynwy = *Monmouth*
Mon 79 C8
Tregada Corn 12 E2
Tregadgwith Corn 1 D4
Tregadillett Corn 12 E2
Tre-gagle Mon 79 D8
Tregaian Anglesey 178 F6
Tregajorran Corn 4 G3
Tregamere Corn 5 C8
Tregardock Corn 10 E6
Tregare Mon 78 C6
Tregarland Corn 6 D5
Tregarlandbridge Corn 6 D4
Tregarne Corn 3 E7
Tregaron Ceredig 112 F3
Tregarrick Mill Corn 6 D4
Tregarth Gwyn 163 B10
Tregath Gwyn 163 B10
Tregatillian Corn 5 C8
Tregatta Corn 11 D7
Tregavarah Corn 1 D4
Tregear Corn 5 E7
Tregeare Corn 11 D10
Tregeiriog Wrex 148 C3
Tregele Anglesey 178 C5
Tregellist Corn 10 F6
Tregeseal Corn 1 C3
Tregew Corn 3 C8
Tre-Gibbon Rhondda 77 E7
Tregidden Corn 3 E7
Treginnis Pembs 90 G4
Treglemais Pembs 90 F6
Tregole Corn 11 B9
Tregolls Corn 2 B6
Tregolwyn = *Colwinston*
V Glam 58 D2
Tregona Corn 5 B7
Tregonce Corn 10 G4
Tregonetha Corn 5 C9
Tregonna Corn 10 G4
Tregonning Corn 5 D7
Tregony Corn 5 G8
Tregoodwell Corn 11 E8
Tregorden Corn 10 G6
Tregorrick Corn 5 E10
Tregoss Corn 5 C9
Tregoyd Powys 96 D4
Tregoyd Mill Powys 96 D3
Tregreenwell Corn 11 E7
Tregrehan Mills Corn 5 E10
Tregroes Ceredig 93 C8
Tregullon Corn 5 C11
Tregunna Corn 10 G5
Tregurrian Corn 5 B7
Tregurtha Downs Corn 2 C2
Tre Gwyr = *Gowerton*
Swansea 56 B5
Tregyddulan Pembs 91 D7
Tregynon Powys 129 D11
Tre-gynwr Carms 74 B6
Trehafod Rhondda 77 G8
Trehafren Powys 129 E11
Trehan Corn 7 D8
Treharris M Tydf 77 F9
Trehemborne Corn 10 G3
Treherbert Rhondda 76 F6
Tre-hill V Glam 58 E5
Trehunist Corn 6 C6
Tre-Ifor Rhondda 77 D7
Trekeivesteps Corn 11 G10
Trekenner Corn 12 F2
Trekenning Corn 5 C8
Treknow Corn 11 D7
Trelales = *Laleston*
Bridgend 57 F11
Trelan Corn 2 F6
Tre-lan Flint 165 B11
Trelash Corn 11 C9
Trelassick Corn 5 E7
Trelawnyd Flint 181 F9
Trelech Carms 92 E5
Treleddyd-fawr Pembs 90 F5
Treleigh Corn 4 G4
Treletert = *Letterston*
Pembs 91 F8
Trelew Corn 3 B8
Trelewis M Tydf 77 F10
Treligga Corn 11 E7
Trelights Corn 10 F5
Trelill Corn 10 F6
Trelion Corn 5 E8
Treliske Corn 4 F6
Trelissick Corn 3 B8
Treliver Corn 5 B9
Trellech Mon 79 D8
Trelleck Grange Mon 79 E7
Trelogan Flint 181 E10
Treloquithack Corn 2 D5
Trelowia Corn 6 D5
Trelowth Corn 5 E9
Trelystan Powys 130 C5
Tremadog Gwyn 163 G9
Tremail Corn 11 D9
Tremain Ceredig 92 B4
Tremaine Corn 11 D10
Tremains Bridgend 58 D2
Tremar Corn 6 B5
Trematon Corn 7 D7
Trematon Castle Corn 7 D8
Tremayne Corn 2 B4
Trembraze Corn 6 B5
Tremedda Corn 1 B5
Tremeirchion Denb 181 G9
Tremethick Cross Corn 1 C4
Tremore Corn 5 C10
Tremorebridge Corn 5 C10
Tremorfa Cardiff 59 D8
Tre-Mostyn Flint 181 F10
Trenance Corn 4 C6
Corn 5 B7
Corn 5 C9
Corn 10 G4
Trenant Corn 6 B4
Corn 10 G5
Trenarren Corn 5 F10
Trenay Corn 6 B3
Trench Telford 150 G3
Trench Green Oxon 65 D7
Trench Wood Kent 52 D5
Trencreek Corn 4 C6
Trencrom Corn 2 B2
Trendeal Corn 5 E7
Trenear Corn 2 C5
Treneglos Corn 11 D10
Trenerth Corn 2 B4
Trenewan Corn 6 E3
Trengune Corn 11 C9
Trenhorne Corn 11 F11
Treningle Corn 5 B10
Treninnick Corn 4 C6
Trenoon Corn 2 F6
Trenoweth Corn 3 C7
Trent Dorset 29 D9
Trentham Stoke 168 G5
Trentishoe Devon 40 D6
Trentlock Derbys 153 C9
Trent Vale Stoke 168 G5
Trenwheal Corn 2 C4
Treoes V Glam 58 D2
Treopert = *Granston*
Pembs 91 E7
Treorchy = *Treorci*
Rhondda 77 F7
Treorci = *Treorchy*
Rhondda 77 F7
Treowen Caerph 78 F2
Powys 130 E2
Tre-pit V Glam 58 E2
Trequite Corn 10 F6
Tre'r-ddôl Ceredig 128 E3
Trerhyngyll V Glam 58 D4
Trerise Corn 2 F6
Trer Ilai = *Leighton*
Powys 130 B4
Trerose Corn 3 D7
Trerulefoot Corn 6 D6
Tresaith Ceredig 110 G5
Tresamble Corn 3 B7
Tresarrett Corn 11 G7
Tresavean Corn 2 B6
Tresawle Corn 5 F7
Tresawsen Corn 4 F5
Trescoll Corn 5 C10
Trescott Staffs 132 D6
Trescowe Corn 2 C3
Tresean Corn 4 D5
Tresevern Croft Corn 2 B6
Tresham Glos 80 G3
Tresigin = *Sigingstone*
V Glam 58 E3
Tresillian Corn 5 F7
Tresimwn = *Bonvilston*
V Glam 58 E5
Tresinney Corn 11 E8
Tresinwen Pembs 91 C7
Treskerby Corn 4 G4
Treskillard Corn 2 B5
Treskilling Corn 5 D10
Treskinnick Cross Corn 11 B10
Treslothan Corn 2 B5
Tresmeer Corn 11 D10
Tresowes Green Corn 2 D3
Tresoweshill Corn 2 D4
Tresparrett Corn 11 C8
Tresparrett Posts Corn 11 C8
Tressady Highld 309 J7
Tressait Perth 291 G10
Tresta Shetland 312 D8
Shetland 313 H5
Treswell Notts 188 F3
Treswithian Corn 4 G2
Treswithian Downs
Corn 4 G2
Tre-Taliesin Ceredig 128 E3
Trethellan Water Corn 2 B6
Trethevy Corn 11 D7
Trethewey Corn 1 E3
Trethillick Corn 10 F4
Trethomas Caerph 59 B7
Trethosa Corn 5 E8
Trethowel Corn 5 E10
Trethurgy Corn 5 D10
Tretio Pembs 90 F5
Tretire Hereford 97 G10
Tretower Powys 96 G3
Treuddyn Flint 166 D3
Trevadlock Corn 11 F11
Trevail Corn 4 D5
Trevalga Corn 11 D7
Trevalgan Corn 1 A5
Trevalyn Wrex 166 D5
Trevance Corn 10 G4
Trevanger Corn 10 F5
Trevanson Corn 10 G5
Trevarrack Corn 1 C5
Trevarren Corn 5 C8
Trevarrian Corn 4 B6
Trevarrick Corn 5 G9
Trevarth Corn 4 G4
Trevaughan Carms 73 B11
Carms 93 G7
Tre-vaughan Carms 93 G8
Treveal Corn 1 A5
Trevegean Corn 1 D3
Treveighan Corn 11 F7
Trevellas Corn 4 E4
Trevelmond Corn 6 C4
Trevelver Corn 10 G5
Trevemper Corn 4 D6
Treven Corn 11 D7
Trevena Corn 2 D4
Trevenen Corn 2 D5
Trevenen Bal Corn 2 D5
Trevening Corn 11 F7
Treveor Corn 5 G9
Treverbyn Corn 5 D10
Corn 6 B4
Treverva Corn 3 C7
Trevescan Corn 1 E3
Trevethin Torf 78 E3
Trevia Corn 11 E7
Trevigro Corn 6 B6
Trevilder Corn 10 G6
Trevilla Corn 3 B8
Trevilson Corn 4 D6
Trevine Corn 10 F5
Trevine = *Trefin* Pembs 90 E6
Treviscoe Corn 5 D8
Treviskey Corn 2 B6
Trevithal Corn 1 D5
Trevoll Corn 4 D6
Trevone Corn 10 F3
Trevor Wrex 166 G3
Trevorrick Corn 10 G4
Trevor Uchaf Denb 166 G2
Trevowah Corn 4 D5
Trevowhan Corn 1 B4
Trew Corn 2 D4
Trewalder Corn 11 E7
Trewarmett Corn 11 D7
Trewartha Corn 2 B2
Corn 3 B10
Trewassa Corn 11 D8
Treween Corn 11 E10
Trewellard Corn 1 C3
Trewen Corn 11 E7
Corn 11 E11
Mon 79 G7
Trewennack Corn 2 D5
Trewennan Corn 11 E7
Trewern Powys 148 G5
Trewetha Corn 10 E6
Trewethen Corn 10 F6
Trewethern Corn 10 F6
Trewey Corn 1 B5
Trewidland Corn 6 D5
Trewindle Corn 6 C2
Trewint Corn 6 C5
Corn 11 B9
Corn 11 E10
Trewithian Corn 3 B9
Trewithick Corn 11 D11
Trewollock Corn 5 G10
Trewoodloe Corn 12 G2
Trewoofe Corn 1 D4
Trewoon Corn 2 F5
Corn 5 E9
Treworga Corn 5 G7
Treworgan Common
Mon 78 D6
Treworlas Corn 3 B9
Treworld Corn 11 C8
Trewornan Corn 10 G5
Treworrick Corn 6 B4
Treworthal Corn 3 B9
Trewyddel = *Moylgrove*
Pembs 92 C2
Trewyn Devon 24 G4
Tre-wyn Mon 96 G6
Treyarnon Corn 10 G3
Treyford W Sus 34 D4
Trezaise Corn 5 D9
Trezelah Corn 1 C5
Triangle Glos 79 E8
Staffs 133 B11
W Yorks 196 C4
Trickett's Cross Dorset 31 G9
Triffleton Pembs 91 G9
Trillacott Corn 11 D11
Trimdon Durham 234 E3
Trimdon Colliery
Durham 234 D3
Trimdon Grange
Durham 234 D3
Trimingham Norf 160 B5
Trimley Lower Street
Suff 108 D5
Trimley St Martin Suff 108 D5
Trimley St Mary Suff 108 D5
Trimpley Worcs 116 B5
Trimsaran Carms 75 E7
Trims Green Herts 87 B7
Trimstone Devon 40 E3
Trinafour Perth 291 G9
Trinant Caerph 78 E2
Tring Herts 84 C6
Tringford Herts 84 C6
Tring Wharf Herts 84 C6
Trinity Angus 293 G8
Devon 27 F7
Edin 280 F4
Trinity Fields Staffs 151 D8
Trisant Ceredig 112 B4
Triscombe Som 43 F7
Trislaig Highld 290 F2
Trispen Corn 4 E6
Tritlington Northumb 252 E6
Troan Corn 5 C7
Trochry Perth 286 C3
Trodigal Argyll 255 E7
Troearhiwgwair
Bl Gwent 77 D11
Troedrhiwdalar Powys 113 G9
Troedrhiwffenyd Ceredig 93 C8
Troedrhiwfuwch Caerph 77 E10
Troedyraur Ceredig 92 B6
Troedyrhiw M Tydf 77 E9
Trofarth Conwy 180 G5
Trolliloes E Sus 23 C10
Tromode IoM 192 E4
Trondavoe Shetland 312 F5
Troon Corn 2 B5
S Ayrs 257 C8
Trooper's Inn Pembs 73 C7
Trosaraidh W Isles 297 K3
Trossachs Hotel Stirling 285 G9
Troston Suff 125 C7
Trostre Carms 56 B4
Trostrey Common Mon 78 E5
Troswell Corn 11 C11
Trotshill Worcs 117 F7
Trotten Marsh W Sus 34 B4
Trottiscliffe Kent 68 G6
Trotton W Sus 34 C4
Trough Gate Lancs 195 C11
Troutbeck Cumb 221 E8
Cumb 230 F3
Troutbeck Bridge Cumb 221 F8
Troway Derbys 186 F5
Trowbridge Cardiff 59 C8
Wilts 45 B11
Trowell Notts 153 B9
Trow Green Glos 79 D9
Trowle Common Wilts 45 B10
Trowley Bottom Herts 85 C9
Trows Borders 262 C5
Trowse Newton Norf 142 B4
Troydale W Yorks 205 G10
Troy Town Kent 52 D2
Kent 54 E5
Medway 69 F8
Truas Corn 11 D7
Trub Gtr Man 195 F11
Trudoxhill Som 45 E8
Trueman's Heath
Worcs 117 B11
True Street Devon 8 C6
Trull Som 28 C2
Trumaisgearraidh
W Isles 296 D4
Trumfleet S Yorks 198 E6
Trumpan Highld 298 C2
Trumpet Hereford 98 D3
Trumpington Cambs 123 F8
Trumpsgreen Sur 66 F3
Trunch Norf 160 C5
Trunnah Lancs 202 E2
Truro Corn 4 G6
Truscott Corn 12 D2
Trusham Devon 14 E3
Trusley Derbys 152 B5
Trussall Corn 2 D5
Trussell Corn 11 D10
Trusthorpe Lincs 191 E8
Truthan Corn 4 E6
Truthwall Corn 2 C2
Trwstllewelyn Powys 130 D3
Tryfil Anglesey 178 E6
Trysull Staffs 133 E7
Trythogga Corn 1 C5
Tubbs Mill Corn 5 G9
Tubney Oxon 82 F6
Tubslake Kent 53 G9
Tuckenhay Devon 8 D6
Tuckermarsh Devon 7 B8
Tuckerton Som 28 B3
Tuckhill Shrops 132 F5
Tuckingmill Corn 4 G3
Corn 11 F7
Wilts 30 B6
Tucking Mill Bath 61 G9
Tuckton BCP 19 C8
Tuddenham Suff 108 B3
Suff 124 C4
Tuddenham St Martin
Suff 108 B3
Tudeley Kent 52 D6
Tudeley Hale Kent 52 D6
Tudhay Devon 28 G4
Tudhoe Durham 233 D11
Tudhoe Grange
Durham 233 E11
Tudor Hill W Mid 134 D2
Tudorville Hereford 97 G11
Tudweiliog Gwyn 144 B4
Tuebrook Mers 182 C5
Tuesley Sur 50 E3
Tuesnoad Kent 54 E2
Tuffley Glos 80 C4
Tufnell Park London 67 B9
Tufton Hants 48 D3
Pembs 91 F10
Tugby Leics 136 C5
Tugford Shrops 131 F11
Tughall Northumb 264 D6
Tulchan Lodge Angus 292 F3
Tullecombe W Sus 34 B4
Tullibardine Perth 286 F3
Tullibody Clack 279 B7
Tullich Argyll 284 F4
Highld 299 E9
Highld 300 G6
Tullich Muir Highld 301 B7
Tulliemet Perth 286 B3
Tulloch Aberds 293 F9
Aberds 303 F8
Highld 290 E5
Perth 286 E4
Tulloch Castle Highld 300 C5
Tullochgorm Argyll 275 D10
Tulloch-gribban Highld 301 G9
Tullochroisk Perth 285 B11
Tullochvenus Aberds 293 C7
Tulloes Angus 287 C9
Tullybannocher Perth 285 E11
Tullybelton Perth 286 D4
Tullycross Stirling 277 D9
Tullyfergus Perth 286 C6
Tullymurdoch Perth 286 B5
Tullynessle Aberds 293 B7
Tulse Hill London 67 E10
Tumble = *Y Tymbl* Carms 75 C8
Tumbler's Green Essex 106 F6
Tumby Lincs 174 D2
Tumby Woodside Lincs 174 D3
Tummel Bridge Perth 285 B11
Tumpy Green Glos 80 E2
Tumpy Lakes Hereford 97 B10
Tunbridge Hill Medway 69 E10
Tunbridge Wells = *Royal Tunbridge Wells* Kent 52 F5
Tunga W Isles 304 E6
Tungate Norf 160 D5
Tunley Bath 45 B7
Glos 80 E6
Tunnel Hill Worcs 98 C6
Tunnel Pits N Lincs 199 G8
Tunshill Gtr Man 196 E2
Tunstall E Yorks 209 G12
Kent 69 G11
Lancs 212 E2
Norf 143 B8
N Yorks 224 F4
Staffs 150 D5
Stoke 168 E5
Suff 127 G7
T&W 243 G9
Tunstead Derbys 185 G10
Gtr Man 196 G4
Norf 160 E5
Tunworth Hants 49 D7
Tupsley Hereford 97 C10
Tupton Derbys 170 B5
Turbary Common BCP 19 C7
Turfdown Corn 5 B11
Turf Hill Gtr Man 196 E2
Turfholm S Lanark 259 B8
Turfmoor Devon 28 G3
Shrops 149 F7
Turgis Green Hants 49 B7
Turin Angus 287 B9
Turkdean Glos 81 B10
Turkey Island Hants 33 E9
W Sus 34 D3
Turkey Tump Hereford 97 F10
Tur Langton Leics 136 E4
Turleigh Wilts 61 G10
Turleygreen Shrops 132 F5
Turlin Moor BCP 18 C5
Turmer Hants 31 F10
Turn Lancs 195 D10
Turnalt Argyll 275 C9
Turnastone Hereford 97 D7
Turnberry S Ayrs 244 B6
Turnchapel Plym 7 E9
Turnditch Derbys 170 F3
Turner Green Lancs 203 G8
Turner's Green E Sus 23 B10
E Sus 52 G6
Warks 118 D3
W Berks 64 F4
Turners Hill W Sus 51 F10
Turners Puddle Dorset 18 C2
Turnerwood S Yorks 187 E8
Turnford Herts 86 E5
Turnhouse Edin 280 G3
Turnhurst Stoke 168 E5
Turnstead Milton
Derbys 185 E8
Turnworth Dorset 30 F4
Turrerich Perth 286 D2
Turriff Aberds 303 D7
Tursdale Durham 234 D2
Turton Bottoms
Blackburn 195 D8
Turves Cambs 138 D6
Turves Green W Mid 117 B10
Turvey Bedford 121 G8
Turville Bucks 84 G3
Turville Heath Bucks 84 G2
Turweston Bucks 102 D2
Tushielaw Borders 261 F8
Tutbury Staffs 152 D4
Tutnall Worcs 117 C9
Tutnalls Glos 79 E10
Tutshill Glos 79 G8
Tutt Hill Kent 54 D3
Tuttington Norf 160 D4
Tutts Clump W Berks 64 E5
Tutwell Corn 12 F3
Tuxford Notts 188 G2
Twatt Orkney 314 D2
Shetland 313 H5
Twechar E Dunb 278 F4
Tweedale Telford 132 C4
Tweeddaleburn Borders 270 E5
Tweedmouth Northumb 273 E9
Tweedsmuir Borders 260 E3
Twelve Heads Corn 4 G5
Twelve Oaks E Sus 37 C11
Twelvewoods Corn 6 B4
Twemlow Green Ches E 168 B3
Twenties Kent 71 F10
Twenty Lincs 156 E3
Twerton Bath 61 G8
Twickenham London 67 E7
Twigworth Glos 98 G6
Twineham W Sus 36 D3
Twineham Green W Sus 36 C3
Twinhoe Bath 45 B8
Twinstead Essex 107 D7
Twinstead Green Essex 106 D6
Twiss Green Warr 183 B11
Twist Devon 28 G3
Twiston Lancs 204 E2
Twitchen Devon 41 G9
Shrops 115 B7
Twitchen Mill Devon 41 G9
Twitham Kent 55 B9
Twitton Kent 52 B4
Two Bridges Devon 13 G8
Glos 79 D11
Two Burrows Corn 4 F4
Two Dales Derbys 170 C3
Two Gates Staffs 134 C4
Two Mile Ash M Keynes 102 D6
W Sus 35 B10
Two Mile Hill Bristol 60 E6
Two Mile Oak Cross Devon 8 B6
Two Mills Ches W 182 G5
Two Pots Devon 40 E4
Two Waters Herts 85 D9
Twr Anglesey 178 E2
Twycross Leics 134 C6
Twydall Medway 69 F9
Twyford Bucks 102 F3
Derbys 152 D6
Dorset 30 D5
Hants 33 C7
Leics 154 G4

Twyford *continued*
Lincs 155 E8
Norf 159 E10
Oxon 101 D9
Shrops 148 D6
Wokingham 65 D9
Worcs 99 B10
Twyford Common
Hereford 97 D10
Twyn-Allws Mon 78 C3
Twynholm Dumfries 237 D8
Twyning Glos 99 D7
Twyning Green Glos 99 D8
Twynllanan Carms 94 G5
Twynmynydd Carms 75 C11
Twyn Shôn-Ifan Caerph 77 G11
Twynyrodyn M Tydf 77 D9
Twyn-yr-odyn V Glam 58 E6
Twyn-y-Sheriff Mon 78 D6
Twywell N Nhants 121 B9
Tyberton Hereford 97 D7
Tyburn W Mid 134 E2
Tyby Norf 159 D11
Ty-coch Swansea 56 C6
Tycroes Carms 75 C10
Tycrwyn Powys 148 F2
Tyddewi = *St Davids*
Pembs 90 F5
Tydd Gote Lincs 157 F9
Tydd St Giles Cambs 157 F8
Tydd St Mary Lincs 157 F8
Tyddyn Powys 129 F9
Tyddyn Angharad Denb 165 F9
Tyddyn Dai Anglesey 178 C6
Tyddyn-mawr Gwyn 163 G9
Ty-draw Conwy 164 D5
Swansea 57 C7
Tye Hants 22 C2
Tye Common Essex 87 G11
Tyegate Green Norf 161 G7
Tye Green Essex 87 C10
Essex 87 D7
Essex 87 F11
Essex 105 D11
Essex 105 G10
Essex 106 G5
Tyersal W Yorks 205 G9
Ty-fry Mon 78 F6
Tyganol V Glam 58 E4
Ty-hen Carms 92 G6
Gwyn 144 C3
Ty-isaf Carms 56 B4
Tyla Mon 78 C2
Tylagwyn Bridgend 58 B2
Tyldesley Gtr Man 195 G7
Tyle Carms 94 F3
Tyle-garw Rhondda 58 C4
Tyler Hill Kent 70 G6
Tylers Causeway Herts 86 D3
Tylers Green Bucks 84 G6
Tyler's Green Essex 87 D8
Sur 51 C11
Tyler's Hill Bucks 85 E7
Ty Llwyn Bl Gwent 77 D11
Tylorstown Rhondda 77 F8
Tylwch Powys 129 G9
Ty-mawr Anglesey 179 D7
Ty Mawr Carms 93 C10
Ty-mawr Conwy 181 F7
Ty Mawr Cwm Conwy 164 F6
Tynant Rhondda 58 B5
Ty-nant Conwy 165 G7
Gwyn 147 D8
Tyncelyn Ceredig 112 E2
Tyndrum Stirling 285 D7
Tyne Dock T&W 243 D9
Tyneham Dorset 18 E3
Tynehead Midloth 271 D7
Tynemouth T&W 243 D9
Tyne Tunnel T&W 243 D8
Tynewydd Ceredig 92 B4
Neath 76 D4
Rhondda 76 F6
Ty-Newydd Ceredig 111 D10
Tyning Bath 45 B7
Tyninghame E Loth 282 F2
Tyn-lon Gwyn 163 D7
Tynron Dumfries 247 E8
Tyntesfield N Som 60 E4
Tyntetown Rhondda 77 F9
Ty'n-y-bryn Rhondda 58 B4
Tyn-y-celyn Wrex 148 B3
Tyn-y-coed Shrops 148 D4
Ty'n-y-coedcae Caerph 59 B7
Tyn-y-cwm Swansea 75 E10
Tynyfedw Conwy 165 B7
Tyn-y-fedwen Powys 148 C2
Ty'n-y-ffordd Denb 181 G8
Tyn-y-ffridd Powys 148 C2
Ty'n-y-garn Bridgend 57 E11
Tynygongl Anglesey 179 E8
Tynygraig Ceredig 112 D3
Ty'n-y-graig Powys 113 G10
Ty'n-y-groes Conwy 180 G3
Tyn-y-maes Gwyn 163 C10
Tyn-y-pwll Anglesey 178 D6
Ty'n-yr-eithin Ceredig 112 E3
Tynyrwtra Powys 129 F7
Tyrells End C Beds 103 E9
Tyrell's Wood Sur 51 B7
Ty'r-felin-isaf Conwy 164 C5
Ty Rhiw Rhondda 58 C6
Tyrie Aberds 303 C9
Tyringham M Keynes 103 B7
Tyseley W Mid 134 G2
Ty-Sign Caerph 78 G2
Tythecott Devon 24 D6
Tythegston Bridgend 57 F11
Tytherington Ches E 184 F6
S Glos 61 B7
Som 45 D9
Wilts 46 E2
Tytherleigh Devon 28 G4
Tytherton Lucas Wilts 62 E2
Tyttenhanger Herts 85 D11
Ty-uchaf Powys 147 E10
Tywardreath Corn 5 E11
Tywardreath Highway
Corn 5 D11
Tywyn Conwy 180 F3
Gwyn 110 C2

U

Uachdar W Isles 296 F3
Uags Highld 295 B9
Ubberley Stoke 168 F6
Ubbeston Green Suff 126 C6
Ubley Bath 44 B4
Uckerby N Yorks 224 E4
Uckfield E Sus 37 C7
Uckinghall Worcs 99 D7
Uckington Glos 99 G8
Shrops 131 B11
Uddingston S Lanark 268 C3
Uddington S Lanark 259 C9
Udimore E Sus 38 D5
Udley N Som 60 G3
Udny Green Aberds 303 G8
Udny Station Aberds 303 G9
Udston S Lanark 268 D3
Udstonhead S Lanark 268 F4
Uffcott Wilts 62 D6
Uffculme Devon 27 E9
Uffington Lincs 137 B11
Oxon 63 B10
Shrops 149 G10
Ufford Pboro 137 C11
Suff 126 G5
Ufton Warks 119 E7
Ufton Green W Berks 64 F6
Ufton Nervet W Berks 64 F6
Ugadale Argyll 255 E8
Ugborough Devon 8 D3
Ugford Wilts 46 G5
Uggeshall Suff 143 G8
Ugglebarnby N Yorks 227 D7
Ughill S Yorks 186 C3
Ugley Essex 105 F10
Ugley Green Essex 105 F10
Ugthorpe N Yorks 226 C5
Uidh W Isles 297 M2
Uig Argyll 276 E2
Argyll 288 D3
Highld 296 F7
Highld 298 C3
Uigen W Isles 304 E2
Uigshader Highld 298 E4
Uisken Argyll 274 B4
Ulaw Aberds 303 G9
Ulbster Highld 310 E7
Ulcat Row Cumb 230 G4
Ulceby Lincs 190 G6
N Lincs 200 E6
Ulceby Skitter N Lincs 200 E6
Ulcombe Kent 53 D10
Uldale Cumb 229 D10
Uley Glos 80 F3
Ulgham Northumb 252 E6
Ullapool Highld 307 K6
Ullcombe Devon 28 F2
Ullenhall Warks 118 D2
Ullenwood Glos 80 B6
Ulleskelf N Yorks 206 E6
Ullesthorpe Leics 135 F10
Ulley S Yorks 187 D7
Ullingswick Hereford 97 B11
Ullington Worcs 100 B2
Ullinish Highld 294 B5
Ullock Cumb 229 G7
Cumb 229 G10
Ulnes Walton Lancs 194 D4
Ulpha Cumb 220 G3
Ulrome E Yorks 209 B9
Ulshaw N Yorks 214 B2
Ulsta Shetland 312 E6
Ulva House Argyll 288 F6
Ulverley Green W Mid 134 G2
Ulverston Cumb 210 D5
Ulwell Dorset 18 E6
Umberleigh Devon 25 C10
Unapool Highld 306 F7
Unasary W Isles 297 J3
Under Bank W Yorks 196 F6
Underbarrow Cumb 221 G9
Undercliffe W Yorks 205 G9
Underdale Shrops 149 G10
Underdown Devon 14 D3
Underhill London 86 F3
Wilts 45 G11
Underhoull Shetland 312 C7
Underling Green Kent 53 D9
Underriver Kent 52 C5
Underriver Ho Kent 52 C5
Under the Wood Kent 71 F8
Under Tofts S Yorks 186 D4
Underton Shrops 132 E3
Underwood Newport 59 B11
Notts 171 E7
Pembs 73 C7
Plym 7 D10
Undley Suff 140 G3
Undy Mon 60 B2
Ungisiadar W Isles 304 F3
Unifirth Shetland 313 H4
Union Cottage Aberds 293 D10
Union Mills IoM 192 E4
Union Street E Sus 53 G8
United Downs Corn 4 G4
Unstone Derbys 186 F5
Unstone Green Derbys 186 F5
Unsworth Gtr Man 195 F10
Unthank Cumb 230 B3
Cumb 230 D5
Cumb 231 C8
Derbys 186 F4
Unthank End Cumb 230 D5
Upavon Wilts 46 C6
Up Cerne Dorset 29 G11
Upchurch Kent 69 F10
Upcott Devon 24 D2
Devon 25 F9
Devon 25 F11
Devon 40 F3
Hereford 114 G6
Som 27 C11
Upend Cambs 124 F3
Up End M Keynes 103 B8
Up Exe Devon 26 G6
Upgate Norf 160 F2
Upgate Street Norf 141 E11
Norf 142 E5
Up Green Hants 65 G9
Uphall Dorset 29 G9
W Loth 279 G11
Uphall Station W Loth 279 G11
Upham Devon 26 F5
Hants 33 C8
Uphampton Hereford 115 E7
Worcs 116 E6
Up Hatherley Glos 99 G8
Uphempston Devon 8 C6
Uphill N Som 43 B10
Uphill Manor N Som 43 B10
Up Holland Lancs 194 F4
Uplands Glos 80 D5
Swansea 56 C6
Uplawmoor E Renf 267 D8
Upleadon Glos 98 F5
Upleadon Court Glos 98 F5
Upleatham Redcar 226 B2
Uplees Kent 70 G3
Uploders Dorset 16 C6
Uplowman Devon 27 D8
Uplyme Devon 16 C2
Up Marden W Sus 34 E3
Upminster London 68 B5
Up Mudford Som 29 D9
Up Nately Hants 49 C7
Upnor Medway 69 E9
Upottery Devon 28 F2
Uppacott Devon 25 B9
Uppat Highld 311 J2
Uppend Essex 105 F9
Upper Affcot Shrops 131 F8
Upper Ardchronie
Highld 309 L6
Upper Ardgrain
Aberds 303 F9
Upper Ardroscadale
Argyll 275 G11
Upper Arley Worcs 132 G5
Upper Armley W Yorks 205 G11
Upper Arncott Oxon 83 B10
Upper Astley Shrops 149 F10
Upper Aston Shrops 132 E6
Upper Astrop
W Nhants 101 D10
Upper Badcall Highld 306 E6
Upper Bangor Gwyn 179 G9
Upper Basildon W Berks 64 D5
Upper Batley W Yorks 197 B8
Upper Battlefield
Shrops 149 F10
Upper Beeding W Sus 35 E11
Upper Benefield
N Nhants 137 F9
Upper Bentley Worcs 117 D9
Upper Bighouse Highld 310 D2
Upper Birchwood
Derbys 170 E6
Upper Blainslie
Borders 271 G10
Upper Boat Rhondda 58 B6
Upper Boddam Aberds 302 F6
Upper Boddington
W Nhants 119 G9
Upper Bogrow Highld 309 L7
Upper Bogside Moray 302 D2
Upper Bonchurch IoW 21 F7
Upper Booth Derbys 185 D10
Upper Borth Ceredig 128 F2
Upper Boyndlie Aberds 303 C9
Upper Brailes Warks 100 D6
Upper Brandon Parva
Norf 141 B10
Upper Breakish Highld 295 C8
Upper Breinton Hereford 97 C9
Upper Broadheath
Worcs 116 F6
Upper Brockholes
W Yorks 196 B5
Upper Broughton Notts 154 D3
Upper Broxwood
Hereford 115 G7
Upper Bruntingthorpe
Leics 136 F2
Upper Brynamman
Carms 76 C2
Upper Buckenhill
Hereford 97 E11
Upper Bucklebury
W Berks 64 F4
Upper Bullington Hants 48 E3
Upper Burgate Hants 31 D11
Upper Burnhaugh
Aberds 293 D10
Upper Bush Medway 69 F7
Upperby Cumb 239 G10
Upper Caldecote
C Beds 104 B3
Upper Cam Glos 80 F3
Upper Canada N Som 43 B11
Upper Canterton Hants 32 E3
Upper Catesby
W Nhants 119 F10
Upper Catshill Worcs 117 C9
Upper Chapel Powys 95 C10
Upper Cheddon Som 28 B2
Upper Chicksgrove Wilts 31 B7
Upper Church Village
Rhondda 58 B5
Upper Chute Wilts 47 C9
Upper Clapton London 67 B10
Upper Clatford Hants 47 E11
Upper Coberley Glos 81 B7
Upper College Shrops 149 C11
Upper Colwall Hereford 98 C5
Upper Common Hants 48 D6
Upper Cotburn Aberds 303 D7
Upper Cotton Staffs 169 F9
Upper Coullie Aberds 293 B9
Upper Cound Shrops 131 C11
Upper Coxley Som 44 E4
Upper Cudworth
S Yorks 197 F11
Upper Culphin Aberds 302 D6
Upper Cumberworth
W Yorks 197 F8
Upper Cwmbran Torf 78 F3
Upperdale Derbys 185 G11
Upper Dallachy Moray 302 C3
Upper Deal Kent 55 C11
Upper Dean Bedford 121 D10
Devon 8 C4
Upper Denby W Yorks 197 D8
W Yorks 197 F8
Upper Denton Cumb 240 D4
Upper Derraid Highld 301 F10
Upper Diabaig Highld 299 C8
Upper Dicker E Sus 23 D9
Upper Dinchope Shrops 131 G9
Upper Dormington
Hereford 97 D11
Upper Dounreay Highld 310 C4
Upper Dovercourt Essex 108 E4
Upper Dowdeswell Glos 81 B8
Upper Druimfin Argyll 289 D7
Upper Dunsforth
N Yorks 215 G8
Upper Dunsley Herts 84 C6
Upper Eashing Sur 50 E3
Upper Eastern Green
W Mid 134 G5
Upper Eathie Highld 301 C7
Upper Edmonton London 86 G4
Upper Egleton Hereford 98 C2
Upper Elkstone Staffs 169 D9
Upper Ellastone Staffs 169 G10
Upper Elmers End
London 67 F11
Upper End Derbys 185 F9
Glos 81 C10
Glos 81 D8
Leics 154 G4
Upper Enham Hants 47 D11
Upper Farmcote Shrops 132 E5
Upper Farringdon Hants 49 F8
Upper Feorlig Highld 298 E2
Upper Fivehead Som 28 C4
Upper Forge Shrops 132 F4
Upper Framilode Glos 80 C3
Upper Froyle Hants 49 E9
Upper Gambolds Worcs 117 D9
Upper Gills Highld 310 B7
Upper Glenfintaig
Highld 290 E4
Upper Godney Som 44 E3
Upper Goldstone Kent 71 G9
Upper Gornal W Mid 133 E8
Upper Gravenhurst
C Beds 104 D2
Upper Green Essex 105 E8
Mon 78 B5
Suff 124 E4
W Berks 63 G11
W Yorks 197 B9
Upper Grove Common
Hereford 97 F11
Upper Guist Norf 159 D10
Upper Hackney Derbys 170 C3
Upper Hale Sur 49 D10
Upper Halistra Highld 298 D2
Upper Halliford Sur 66 F5
Upper Halling Medway 69 G7
Upper Ham Worcs 99 D7
Upper Hambleton
Rutland 137 B8
Upper Hamnish
Hereford 115 F10
Upper Harbledown Kent 54 B6
Upper Hardres Court
Kent 55 C7
Upper Hardwick
Hereford 115 F8
Upper Hartfield E Sus 52 G3
Upper Hartshay Derbys 170 E5
Upper Haselor Worcs 99 C10
Upper Hatton Staffs 150 B6
Upper Haugh S Yorks 186 B6
Upper Hawkhillock
Aberds 303 F10
Upper Hayesden Kent 52 E5
Upper Hayton Shrops 131 G10
Upper Heath Shrops 131 F11
Upper Heaton W Yorks 197 D7
Upper Hellesdon Norf 160 G4
Upper Helmsley
N Yorks 207 B9
Upper Hengoed Shrops 148 C5
Upper Hergest Hereford 114 G5
Upper Heyford Oxon 101 F9
W Nhants 120 F3
Upper Hill Glos 79 F11
Hereford 115 G9
Upper Hindhope
Borders 251 B7
Upper Holloway London 67 B9
Upper Holton Suff 127 B8
Upper Hopton W Yorks 197 D7
Upper Horsebridge
E Sus 23 C9
Upper Howsell Worcs 98 B5
Upper Hoyland
S Yorks 197 G11
Upper Hulme Staffs 169 C8
Upper Ifold Sur 50 G4
Upper Inglesham Swindon 82 F2
Upper Inverbrough
Highld 301 F8
Upper Kergord Shetland 313 H6
Upper Kidston Borders 270 G4
Upper Kilcott Glos 61 B9
Upper Killay Swansea 56 C5
Upper Killeyan Argyll 254 C3
Upper Kinsham
Hereford 115 D7
Upper Knockando
Moray 301 E11
Upper Lambourn
W Berks 63 C10
Upper Landywood
Staffs 133 B9
Upper Langford N Som 44 B3
Upper Langwith Derbys 171 B8
Upper Layham Suff 107 C10
Upper Leigh Staffs 151 B10
Upper Lenie Highld 300 G5
Upper Littleton N Som 60 G5
Upper Loads Derbys 170 B4
Upper Lochton Aberds 293 D8
Upper Lode Worcs 99 E7
Upper Longdon Staffs 151 G11
Upper Longwood
Shrops 132 B2
Upper Ludstone Shrops 132 D6
Upper Lybster Highld 310 F6
Upper Lydbrook Glos 79 B10
Upper Lyde Hereford 97 C9
Upper Lye Hereford 115 D7
Upper Maes-coed
Hereford 96 D6
Upper Marsh W Yorks 204 F6
Upper Midhope S Yorks 186 B2
Upper Midway Derbys 152 E5
Uppermill Gtr Man 196 F3
Upper Milovaig Highld 297 G7
Upper Milton Oxon 82 B3
Som 44 D4
Upper Minety Wilts 81 G8
Upper Mitton Worcs 116 C6
Upper Moor Worcs 99 B9
Upper Moor Side
W Yorks 205 G10
Upper Morton S Glos 79 G11
Upper Nash Pembs 73 E8
Upper Netchwood
Shrops 132 E2
Upper Newbold Derbys 186 G5
Upper Nobut Staffs 151 B10
Upper North Dean Bucks 84 F4
Upper Norwood London 67 F10
W Sus 34 D6
Upper Obney Perth 286 D4
Upper Ochrwyth Caerph 59 B8
Upper Oddington Glos 100 F4
Upper Ollach Highld 295 B7
Upper Padley Derbys 186 F2
Upper Pickwick Wilts 61 E11
Upper Pollicott Bucks 84 C2
Upper Poppleton York 207 C7
Upper Port Highld 301 G10
Upper Postern Kent 52 D6
Upper Quinton Warks 100 B3
Upper Race Torf 78 F3
Upper Ratley Hants 32 C4
Upper Ridinghill
Aberds 303 D10
Upper Rissington Glos 82 B2
Upper Rochford Worcs 116 D2
Upper Rodmersham Kent 70 G2
Upper Sandaig Highld 295 D9
Upper Sanday Orkney 314 F5
Upper Sapey Hereford 116 E3
Upper Saxondale Notts 154 B3
Upper Seagry Wilts 62 C2
Upper Shelton C Beds 103 C9
Upper Sheringham
Norf 177 E10
Upper Shirley London 67 G11
Soton 32 E6
Upper Siddington Glos 81 F8
Upper Skelmorlie
N Ayrs 266 B4
Upper Slackstead Hants 32 B5
Upper Slaughter Glos 100 G3
Upper Solva Pembs 90 G5
Upper Soudley Glos 79 C11
Uppersound Shetland 313 J6
Upper Stanton Drew
Bath 60 G6
Upper Staploe Bedford 122 F2
Upper Stoke Norf 142 C5
W Mid 135 G7
Upper Stondon C Beds 104 D2
Upper Stowe W Nhants 120 F2
Upper Stratton Swindon 63 B7
Upper Street Hants 31 D11
Norf 142 G3
Norf 160 B5
Upper Street *continued*
Norf 160 E6
Norf 160 F6
Norf 161 F7
Suff 108 E2
Suff 124 G5
Suff 126 G2
Upper Strensham
Worcs 99 D8
Upper Studley Wilts 45 B10
Upper Sundon C Beds 103 F10
Upper Swainswick Bath 61 F9
Upper Swanmore Hants 33 D9
Upper Swell Glos 100 F3
Upper Sydenham
London 67 E10
Upper Tankersley
S Yorks 186 B4
Upper Tean Staffs 151 B10
Upperthong W Yorks 196 F6
Upperthorpe Derbys 187 E7
N Lincs 199 G9
Upper Threapwood
Ches W 166 F6
Upper Thurnham Lancs 202 C5
Upper Tillyrie Perth 286 G5
Upperton E Sus 23 E10
Oxon 83 G11
W Sus 35 C7
Upper Tooting London 67 E9
Upper Tote Highld 298 D5
Uppertown Derbys 170 C4
Highld 300 F4
Highld 310 B7
Northumb 241 C9
Orkney 314 G4
Upper Town Derbys 170 D3
Derbys 170 E2
Durham 233 D7
Hereford 97 B11
N Som 60 F4
Suff 125 D8
Wilts 62 D3
W Yorks 204 G6
Upper Treverward
Shrops 114 B5
Upper Tysoe Warks 100 C6
Upper Up Glos 81 F8
Upper Upham Wilts 63 D8
Upper Upnor Medway 69 E9
Upper Vobster Som 45 D8
Upper Walthamstow
London 67 B11
Upper Wardington
Oxon 101 B9
Upper Wardley W Sus 34 B4
Upper Weald M Keynes 102 D5
Upper Weedon
W Nhants 120 F2
Upper Welland Worcs 98 C5
Upper Wellingham
E Sus 36 E6
Upper Welson Hereford 114 G5
Upper Westholme Som 44 E5
Upper Weston Bath 61 F8
Upper Weybread Suff 126 B4
Upper Whiston S Yorks 187 D7
Upper Wick Glos 80 F2
Worcs 116 G6
Upper Wield Hants 48 F6
Upper Wigginton
Shrops 148 B6
Upper Winchendon
Bucks 84 C2
Upper Witton W Mid 133 E11
Upper Wolvercote Oxon 83 D7
Upper Wolverton
Worcs 117 G8
Upperwood Derbys 170 D3
Upper Woodend
Aberds 293 B8
Upper Woodford Wilts 46 F6
Upper Woolhampton
W Berks 64 F5
Upper Wootton Hants 48 C5
Upper Wraxall Wilts 61 E10
Upper Wyche Hereford 98 C5
Uppincott Devon 26 G5
Uppingham Rutland 137 D7
Uppington Dorset 31 F8
Shrops 132 B2
Upsall N Yorks 215 B9
Upsher Green Suff 107 C8
Upshire Essex 86 E6
Up Somborne Hants 47 G11
Upstreet Kent 71 G8
Up Sydling Dorset 29 G10
Upthorpe Glos 80 E3
Suff 125 C9
Upton Bucks 84 C3
Cambs 122 B3
Ches W 166 B6
Corn 11 G11
Corn 24 G2
Cumb 230 D2
Devon 8 G4
Devon 27 G9
Dorset 17 E10
Dorset 18 C5
E Yorks 209 C8
Hants 32 D5
Hants 47 B11
IoW 21 C7
Kent 71 F11
Leics 135 D7
Lincs 188 D5
London 68 C2
Mers 182 D3
Mers 183 D7
Norf 161 G7
Notts 172 E2
Notts 188 F2
Oxon 64 B4
Oxon 82 C2
Pboro 138 C2
Slough 66 D3
Som 27 B7
Som 29 B7
Warks 118 F2
Wilts 45 G11
W Nhants 120 E4
W Yorks 198 E3
Upton Bishop Hereford 98 F2
Upton Cheyney S Glos 61 F7
Upton Cressett Shrops 132 E3
Upton Crews Hereford 98 F2
Upton Cross Corn 11 G11
Upton End C Beds 104 E2
Upton Field Notts 172 E2
Upton Green Norf 161 G7
Upton Grey Hants 49 D7
Upton Heath Ches W 166 B6
Upton Hellions Devon 26 G4
Upton Lea Bucks 66 C3
Upton Lovell Wilts 46 E2
Upton Magna Shrops 149 G11
Upton Noble Som 45 F8
Upton Park London 68 C2
Upton Pyne Devon 14 B4
Upton Rocks Halton 183 D8
Upton St Leonards Glos 80 C5
Upton Scudamore Wilts 45 D11
Upton Snodsbury Worcs 117 G8
Upton upon Severn
Worcs 99 C7
Upton Warren Worcs 117 D8
Upwaltham W Sus 34 E6
Upware Cambs 123 C10
Upwell Norf 139 C9
Upwey Dorset 17 E9
Upwick Green Herts 105 G9
Upwood Cambs 138 G5
Uradale Shetland 313 K6
Urafirth Shetland 312 F5
Uragaig Argyll 274 D4
Urchfont Wilts 46 B4
Urdimarsh Hereford 97 B10
Ure Shetland 312 F4
Ure Bank N Yorks 214 E6
Urgashay Som 29 C9
Urgha W Isles 305 J3
Urgha Beag W Isles 305 H3
Urishay Common
Hereford 96 D6
Urlar Perth 286 C2
Urlay Nook Stockton 225 C7
Urmston Gtr Man 184 C3
Urpeth Durham 242 G6
Urquhart Highld 300 D5
Moray 302 C2
Urra N Yorks 225 E11
Urray Highld 300 D5
Ushaw Moor Durham 233 C10
Usk Mon 78 E5
Usselby Lincs 189 C9
Usworth T&W 243 F8
Utkinton Ches W 167 B8
Utley W Yorks 204 E6
Uton Devon 14 B2
Utterby Lincs 190 C4
Uttoxeter Staffs 151 C11
Uwchmynydd Gwyn 144 D3
Uxbridge London 66 C5
Uxbridge Moor London 66 C5
Uyea Shetland 312 D5
Uyeasound Shetland 312 C7
Uzmaston Pembs 73 C7

V

Vachelich Pembs 90 F5
Vadlure Shetland 313 J4
Vagg Som 29 D8
Vaila Hall Shetland 313 J4
Vaivoe Shetland 312 G7
Vale W Yorks 196 B2
Vale Down Devon 12 D6
Vale of Health London 67 B9
Valeswood Shrops 149 E7
Valley = *Y Fali* Anglesey 178 F3
Valleyfield Dumfries 237 D8
Valley Park Hants 32 C6
Valley Truckle Corn 11 E7
Valsgarth Shetland 312 B8
Valtos Highld 298 C5
Van Caerph 59 B7
Powys 129 F9
Vange Essex 69 B8
Vanlop Shetland 313 M5
Varchoel Powys 148 G4
Varfell Corn 2 C2
Varteg Torf 78 D3
Vassa Shetland 313 H6
Vastern Wilts 62 C5
Vatsetter Shetland 312 E7
Shetland 313 L5
Vatten Highld 298 E2
Vaul Argyll 288 E2
Vauxhall London 67 D10
Mers 182 C4
W Mid 133 F11
Vaynol Hall Gwyn 163 B8
Vaynor M Tydf 77 C8
Veensgarth Shetland 313 J6
Velator Devon 40 F3
Veldo Hereford 97 C11
Velindre Powys 96 D3
Vellanoweth Corn 2 C2
Vellow Som 42 F5
Velly Devon 24 C3
Veness Orkney 314 D5
Venn Devon 8 F4
Venngreen Devon 24 E5
Venn Green Devon 24 E5
Vennington Shrops 130 B6
Venn Ottery Devon 15 C7
Venn's Green Hereford 97 B10
Venny Tedburn Devon 14 B2
Venterdon Corn 12 G3
Vention Devon 40 E3
Ventnor IoW 21 F7
Venton Devon 7 D11
Ventongimps Corn 4 E5
Ventonleague Corn 2 B3
Venus Hill Herts 85 E8
Veraby Devon 26 B3
Vermentry Shetland 313 H5
Vernham Bank Hants 47 B10
Vernham Dean Hants 47 B10
Vernham Row Hants 47 B10
Vernham Street Hants 47 B11
Vernolds Common
Shrops 131 G9
Verwood Dorset 31 F9
Veryan Corn 3 B10
Veryan Green Corn 5 G8
Vicarage Devon 15 D10
Vicarscross Ches W 166 B6
Vickerstown Cumb 210 F3
Victoria Corn 5 C9
S Yorks 197 F7
Victoria Dock Village
Hull 200 B6
Victoria Park Bucks 84 C4
Victory Gardens
Renfs 267 B10
Vidlin Shetland 312 G6
Viewpark N Lanark 268 C4
Vigo W Mid 133 C10
Vigo Village Kent 68 G6
Vinegar Hill Mon 60 B2
Vinehall Street E Sus 38 C3
Vines Cross E Sus 23 B9
Viney Hill Glos 79 D11
Vinney Green S Glos 61 D7
Virginia Water Sur 66 F3
Virginstow Devon 12 C3
Viscar Corn 2 C6
Vobster Som 45 D8
Voe Shetland 312 E5
Shetland 313 G6
Vogue Corn 4 G4
Vole Som 43 D11
Vowchurch Hereford 97 D7
Vowchurch Common
Hereford 97 D7
Voxmoor Som 27 D10
Voxter Shetland 312 F5
Voy Orkney 314 E2
Vron Gate Shrops 130 B6
Vulcan Village Mers 183 C9

W

Waberthwaite Cumb 220 G2
Wackerfield Durham 233 G9
Wacton Hereford 116 F2
Norf 142 E3
Wacton Common Norf 142 F3
Wadbister Shetland 313 J6
Wadborough Worcs 99 B8
Wadbrook Devon 28 G4
Waddesdon Bucks 84 B2
Waddeton Devon 9 D7
Waddicar Mers 182 B5
Waddicombe Devon 26 B5
Waddingham Lincs 189 B7
Waddington Lancs 203 E10
Lincs 173 C7
Waddingworth Lincs 189 G11
Waddon Devon 14 F3
London 67 G10
Wadebridge Corn 10 G5
Wadeford Som 28 E4
Wade Hall Lancs 194 C4
Wadenhoe N Nhants 137 G10
Wades Green Ches E 167 C11
Wadesmill Herts 86 B5
Wadhurst E Sus 52 G6
Wadshelf Derbys 186 G4
Wadsley S Yorks 186 C4
Wadsley Bridge S Yorks 186 C4
Wadswick Wilts 61 F10
Wadwick Hants 48 C2
Wadworth S Yorks 187 B9
Waen Denb 165 B10
Denb 165 C7
Flint 181 G11
Powys 129 E9
Waen Aberwheeler
Denb 165 B9
Waen-fâch Powys 148 F4
Waen Goleugoed Denb 181 G9
Waen-pentir Gwyn 163 B9
Waen-wen Gwyn 163 B9
Wag Highld 311 G4
Wagbeach Shrops 131 C7
Wagg Som 28 B6
Waggersley Staffs 151 B7
Waggs Plot Devon 28 G4
Wainfelin Torf 78 E3
Wainfleet All Saints
Lincs 175 D7
Wainfleet Bank Lincs 175 D7
Wainfleet St Mary Lincs 175 D8
Wainfleet Tofts Lincs 175 D7
Wainford Norf 142 E6
Waingroves Derbys 170 F6
Wainhouse Corner Corn 11 B9
Wain Lee Staffs 168 D5
Wainscott Medway 69 E8
Wainstalls W Yorks 196 B4
Waitby Cumb 222 D5
Waithe Lincs 201 G9
Wakefield W Yorks 197 C10
Wake Green W Mid 133 G11
Wake Hill N Yorks 214 E3
Wake Lady Green
N Yorks 226 F3
Wakeley Herts 104 F6
Wakerley N Nhants 137 D9
Wakes Colne Essex 107 F7
Wakes Colne Green
Essex 107 E7
Walberswick Suff 127 C9
Walberton W Sus 35 F7
Walbottle T&W 242 D5
Walby Cumb 239 E10
Walcombe Som 44 D5
Walcot Bath 61 F9
Lincs 155 B11
N Lincs 199 C11
Oxon 82 B4
Shrops 130 F6
Swindon 63 C7
Telford 149 G11
Worcs 99 B8
Walcote Leics 135 G11
Warks 118 F2
Walcot Green Norf 142 G2
Walcott Lincs 173 D10
Norf 161 C7
Walden N Yorks 213 C10
Walden Head N Yorks 213 C9
Walden Stubbs N Yorks 198 D5
Waldersey Cambs 139 C8
Waldershaigh S Yorks 186 B3
Walderslade Medway 69 G9
Walderton W Sus 34 E3
Walditch Dorset 16 C5
Waldley Derbys 152 B2
Waldridge Durham 243 G7
Waldringfield Suff 108 C5
Waldringfield Heath
Suff 108 B5
Waldron E Sus 23 B8
Waldron Down E Sus 37 C8
Wales Som 29 C9
S Yorks 187 E7
Wales Bar S Yorks 187 E7
Walesby Lincs 189 C10
Notts 187 G11
Walesby Grange Lincs 189 C10
Wales End Suff 106 B5
Waleswood S Yorks 187 E7
Walford Hereford 97 G11
Hereford 115 C7
Shrops 149 E8
Som 28 B3
Staffs 150 C6
Walford Heath Shrops 149 F8
Walgherton Ches E 167 F11
Walgrave W Nhants 120 C6
Walham Glos 98 G6
Walham Green London 67 D9
Walhampton Hants 20 B2
Walkden Gtr Man 195 G8
Walker T&W 243 E7
Walker Barn Ches E 185 G7
Walkerburn Borders 261 B9
Walker Fold Lancs 203 E9
Walkeringham Notts 188 C3
Walkerith Lincs 188 C3
Walkern Herts 104 F5
Walker's Green Hereford 97 B10
Walker's Heath W Mid 117 B11
Walkerville N Yorks 224 F4
Walkford BCP 19 C10
Walkhampton Devon 7 B10
Walkington E Yorks 208 F5
Walkley S Yorks 186 D4
Walkmill Shrops 131 E7
Walk Mill Lancs 204 G3
Walkmills Shrops 131 D9
Wall Corn 2 B4
Northumb 241 D10
Staffs 134 B2
Wallacestone Falk 279 F8
Wallaceton Dumfries 247 F8
Wallacetown S Ayrs 245 C7
S Ayrs 257 E8
Shetland 313 H5
Wallands Park E Sus 36 E6
Wallasey Mers 182 C4
Wallbank Lancs 195 D11
Wall Bank Shrops 131 E10
Wallbrook W Mid 133 E8
Wallcrouch E Sus 53 G7
Wallend London 68 C2
Wall End Cumb 210 C4
Kent 71 G8
Waller's Green Hereford 98 D3
Walley's Green Ches E 167 C11
Wall Heath W Mid 133 F7
Wall Hill Gtr Man 196 F3
Wallingford Oxon 64 B6
Wallington Hants 33 F9
Herts 104 E5
London 67 G9
Wallington Heath
W Mid 133 C9
Wallingwells Notts 187 E9
Wallis Pembs 91 F10
Wallisdown BCP 19 C7
Walliswood Sur 50 F6
Wall Mead Bath 45 B7
Wall Nook Durham 233 B10
Wallow Green Glos 80 F4
Wallridge Northumb 242 B3
Walls Shetland 313 J4
Wallsend T&W 243 D7
Wallston V Glam 58 E6
Wallsuches Gtr Man 195 E7
Wallsworth Glos 98 G6
Wall under Heywood
Shrops 131 E10
Wallyford E Loth 281 G7
Walmer Kent 55 C11
Walmer Bridge Lancs 194 C3
Walmersley Gtr Man 195 E10
Walmgate Stray York 207 C8
Walmley W Mid 134 E2
Walmsgate Lincs 190 F5
Walnut Grove Perth 286 E5
Walnut Tree M Keynes 103 D7
Walnuttree Green Herts 105 G9
Walpole Som 43 E10
Suff 127 C7
Walpole Cross Keys
Norf 157 F10
Walpole Highway Norf 157 G10
Walpole Marsh Norf 157 F9
Walpole St Andrew
Norf 157 F10
Walpole St Peter Norf 157 F9
Walrow Som 43 D10
Walsal End W Mid 118 B4
Walsall W Mid 133 D10
Walsall Wood W Mid 133 C10
Walsden W Yorks 196 C2
Walsgrave on Sowe
W Mid 135 G7
Walsham le Willows
Suff 125 C9
Walshaw Gtr Man 195 E9
Walshford N Yorks 206 C4
Walsoken Cambs 157 G9
Walson Mon 97 G8
Walston S Lanark 269 F11
Walsworth Herts 104 E4
Walters Ash Bucks 84 F4
Walter's Green Kent 52 E4
Walterston V Glam 58 E5
Walterstone Hereford 96 F6
Waltham Kent 54 D6
NE Lincs 201 G9
Waltham Abbey Essex 86 E5
Waltham Chase Hants 33 D9
Waltham Cross Herts 86 E5
Waltham on the Wolds
Leics 154 D6
Waltham St Lawrence
Windsor 65 D10
Waltham's Cross Essex 106 E3
Walthamstow London 67 B11
Walton Bucks 84 C4
Cumb 240 E2
Derbys 170 B5
Leics 135 F11
Mers 182 C5
M Keynes 103 D7
Pboro 138 C3
Powys 114 F5
Shrops 115 B9
Som 44 F3
Staffs 151 C7
Staffs 151 D7
Suff 108 D5
Telford 149 F11
Warks 118 G5
W Yorks 197 D11
W Yorks 206 D4
Walton Cardiff Glos 99 E8
Walton Court Bucks 84 C4
Walton East Pembs 91 G10
Walton Elm Dorset 30 D3
Walton Grounds
W Nhants 101 E10
Walton Heath Hants 33 F10
Walton Highway Norf 157 G9
Walton in Gordano
N Som 60 E2
Walton-le-Dale Lancs 194 B5
Walton Manor Oxon 83 D8
Walton-on-Thames Sur 66 F6
Walton on the Hill
Staffs 151 E9
Sur 51 B8
Walton-on-the-Naze
Essex 108 G5
Walton on the Wolds
Leics 153 F11
Walton-on-Trent
Derbys 152 F4
Walton Pool Worcs 117 B8
Walton St Mary N Som 60 E2
Walton Summit Lancs 194 B5
Walton Warren Norf 158 F4
Walton West Pembs 72 C5
Walwen Flint 181 F10
Flint 181 G11
Flint 182 F2
Walwick Northumb 241 C10
Walworth Darl 224 B4
London 67 D10
Walworth Gate Darl 233 G10
Walwyn's Castle Pembs 72 C5
Wambrook Som 28 F3
Wampool Cumb 238 G6
Wanborough Sur 50 D2
Swindon 63 C8
Wandel Dyke S Lanark 259 D11
Wandle Park London 67 F10
Wandon End Herts 104 G2
Wandsworth London 67 E9
Wangford Suff 127 B9
Wanlip Leics 154 G2
Wanlockhead Dumfries 259 G9
Wannock E Sus 23 E9
Wansford E Yorks 209 B7
Pboro 137 D11
Wanshurst Green Kent 53 D9
Wanson Corn 24 G1

Wanstead London 68 B2
Wanstrow Som 45 E8
Wanswell Glos 79 E11
Wantage Oxon 63 B11
Wants Green Worcs 116 F5
Wapley S Glos 61 D8
Wappenbury Warks 119 D7
Wappenham W Nhants 102 B2
Wapping London 67 C10
Warbleton E Sus 23 B10
Warblington Hants 22 B2
Warborough Oxon 83 G9
Warboys Cambs 138 G6
Warbreck Blackpool 202 F2
Warbstow Corn 11 C10
Warbstow Cross Corn 11 C10
Warburton Gtr Man 184 D2
Warburton Green
Gtr Man 184 E3
Warcop Cumb 222 B4
Warden Kent 70 E4
Northumb 241 D10
Powys 114 E6
Ward End W Mid 134 F2
Warden Hill Glos 99 G8
Warden Point IoW 20 D2
Warden Street C Beds 104 C2
Ward Green Suff 125 E10
S Yorks 197 G10
Ward Green Cross
Lancs 203 F8
Wardhedges C Beds 103 D11
Wardhill Orkney 314 D6
Wardington Oxon 101 B9
Wardlaw Borders 261 F7
Wardle Ches E 167 D10
Gtr Man 196 D2
Wardle Bank Ches E 167 D10
Wardley Gtr Man 195 G9
Rutland 136 C6
T&W 243 E7
W Sus 34 B4
Wardlow Derbys 185 G11
Wardour Wilts 30 B6
Wardpark N Lanark 278 F5
Wardrobes Bucks 84 E4
Wardsend Ches E 184 E6
Wardy Hill Cambs 139 G9
Ware Herts 86 C5
Kent 71 G9
Wareham Dorset 18 D4
Warehorne Kent 54 G3
Warenford Northumb 264 D4
Waren Mill Northumb 264 C4
Warenton Northumb 264 C4
Wareside Herts 86 B5
Waresley Cambs 122 G4
Worcs 116 C6
Ware Street Kent 53 B9
Warfield Brack 65 E11
Warfleet Devon 9 E7
Wargate Lincs 156 C4
Wargrave Mers 183 C9
Wokingham 65 D9
Warham Hereford 97 D9
Norf 176 E6
Warhill Gtr Man 185 B7
Waring's Green W Mid 118 C2
Wark Northumb 241 B9
Northumb 263 B8
Wark Common
Northumb 263 B8
Warkleigh Devon 25 C10
Warkton N Nhants 121 B7
Warkworth Northumb 252 B6
W Nhants 101 C9
Warlaby N Yorks 224 G6
Warland W Yorks 196 C2
Warleggan Corn 6 B3
Warleigh Bath 61 G9
Warley Essex 87 G9
Warley Town W Yorks 196 B5
Warley Woods W Mid 133 F10
Warlingham Sur 51 B11
Warmbrook Derbys 170 E3
Warmfield W Yorks 197 C11
Warmingham Ches E 168 C2
Warminghurst W Sus 35 D10
Warmington N Nhants 137 E11
Warks 101 B8
Warminster Wilts 45 D11
Warminster Common
Wilts 45 E11
Warmlake Kent 53 C10
Warmley S Glos 61 E7
Warmley Hill S Glos 61 E7
Warmley Tower S Glos 61 E7
Warmonds Hill
N Nhants 121 D9
Warmsworth S Yorks 198 G4
Warmwell Dorset 17 D11
Warnborough Green
Hants 49 C8
Warndon Worcs 117 F7
Warners End Herts 85 D8
Warnford Hants 33 C10
Warnham W Sus 51 G7
Warningcamp W Sus 35 F8
Warninglid W Sus 36 B2
Warpsgrove Oxon 83 F10
Warren Ches E 184 G5
Dorset 18 C3
Pembs 72 F6
S Yorks 186 B5
Warrenby Redcar 235 F7
Warren Corner Hants 34 B2
Hants 49 D10
Warren Heath Suff 108 C4
Warren Row Windsor 65 C10
Warren's Green Herts 104 F5
Warren Street Kent 54 C2
Warrington M Keynes 121 G7
Warr 183 D10
Warriston Edin 280 F5
Warsash Hants 33 F7
Warsill N Yorks 214 F4
Warslow Staffs 169 D9
Warsop Vale Notts 171 B8
Warstock W Mid 117 B11
Warstone Staffs 133 B9
Warter E Yorks 208 C3
Warthermarske N Yorks 214 D4
Warthill N Yorks 207 B9
Wartle Aberds 293 C7
Wartling E Sus 23 D11
Wartnaby Leics 154 E4
Warton Lancs 194 B2
Lancs 211 E9
Northumb 252 C2
Warks 134 C5
Warton Bank Lancs 194 B2
Warwick Warks 118 E5
Warwick Bridge Cumb 239 F11
Warwick on Eden
Cumb 239 F11
Warwicksland Cumb 239 B10
Warwick Wold Sur 51 C10
Wasbister Orkney 314 C3
Wasdale Head Cumb 220 D3
Wash Derbys 185 E9
Washall Green Herts 105 E8
Washaway Corn 5 B10
Washbourne Devon 8 E5
Washbrook Som 44 C2
Suff 108 C2
Washbrook Street Suff 108 C2
Wash Common W Berks 64 G3
Wash Dyke Norf 157 F10
Washerwall Staffs 168 F6
Washfield Devon 26 D6
Washfold N Yorks 223 E11
Washford Som 42 E5
Worcs 117 D11
Washford Pyne Devon 26 E4
Washingborough Lincs 189 G8
Washingley Cambs 138 F2
Washington T&W 243 F8
W Sus 35 E10
Washington Village
T&W 243 F8
Washmere Green Suff 107 B8
Washpit W Yorks 196 F6
Wash Water W Berks 64 G3
Washwood Heath
W Mid 134 F2
Wasing W Berks 64 G5
Waskerley Durham 233 B7
Wasperton Warks 118 F5
Wasp Green Sur 51 D10
Wasps Nest Lincs 173 C9
Wass N Yorks 215 D11
Waste Green Warks 118 D4
Wastor Devon 8 F2
Watchet Som 42 E5
Watchfield Oxon 63 B8
Som 43 D10
Watchgate Cumb 221 F10
Watchhill Cumb 229 C9
Watch House Green
Essex 106 G3
Watchill Dumfries 238 D6
Dumfries 248 G3
Watcombe Torbay 9 B8
Watendlath Cumb 220 B5
Water Devon 13 E11
Lancs 195 B10
Waterbeach Cambs 123 D9
W Sus 22 B5
Waterbeck Dumfries 238 B6
Waterdale Herts 85 E10
Waterden Norf 159 B7
Waterditch Hants 19 B9
Water Eaton M Keynes 103 E7
Oxon 83 C8
Waterend Bucks 84 F3
Cumb 229 G8
Glos 80 C3
Herts 86 C2
Water End Bedford 104 B2
C Beds 103 D11
C Beds 104 B5
Essex 105 C11
E Yorks 207 F11
Herts 49 C7
Herts 85 C8
Herts 86 E2
Waterfall Staffs 169 E9
Waterfoot Argyll 255 D9
Cumb 230 G5
E Renf 267 D11
Lancs 195 C10
Waterford Hants 20 B2
Herts 86 C4
Water Fryston W Yorks 198 B3
Water Garth Nook Cumb 210 F3
Watergate Corn 6 E4
Corn 11 E8
Watergore Som 28 D6
Waterhales Essex 87 F8
Waterham Kent 70 G5
Waterhay Wilts 81 G9
Waterhead Angus 292 F6
Cumb 221 E7
Devon 8 F3
Dumfries 248 E5
Waterhead on Minnoch
S Ayrs 245 E9
Waterheads Borders 270 E4
Waterheath Norf 143 E8
Waterhouses Durham 233 C9
Staffs 169 E9
Water Houses N Yorks 213 F7
Wateringbury Kent 53 C7
Waterlane Glos 80 E6
Waterlip Som 45 E7
Waterloo BCP 18 C6
Blackburn 195 B7
Corn 11 G8
Derbys 170 C6
Gtr Man 196 G2
Highld 295 C8
Mers 182 B4
N Lanark 268 E6
Norf 126 B2
Norf 143 E8
Norf 160 F4
Pembs 73 E7
Perth 286 D4
Shrops 149 C9
Waterloo Park Mers 182 B4
Waterloo Port Gwyn 163 C7
Waterlooville Hants 33 F11
Waterman Quarter Kent 53 E10
Watermead Glos 80 B5
Watermeetings
S Lanark 259 G11
Watermill E Sus 38 E2
Watermillock Cumb 230 G4
Watermoor Glos 81 E8
Water Newton Cambs 138 D2
Water Orton Warks 134 E3
Waterperry Oxon 83 D10
Waterrow Som 27 B9
Watersfield W Sus 35 D8
Watersheddings
Gtr Man 196 F2
Waterside Aberds 292 B5
Aberds 303 G10
Blackburn 195 C8
Bucks 85 E7
Cumb 229 B10
Derbys 185 E8
E Ayrs 245 B10
E Ayrs 267 G9
E Dunb 278 G3
E Renf 267 D10
Sur 51 D11
S Yorks 199 E7
Telford 150 F2
Waterslack Lancs 211 D9
Water's Nook Gtr Man 195 F7
Waterstein Highld 297 G7
Waterstock Oxon 83 D10
Waterston Pembs 72 D6
Water Stratford Bucks 102 E3
Waters Upton Telford 150 F2
Waterthorpe S Yorks 186 E6
Waterton Aberds 303 F9
Bridgend 58 D2
Water Yeat Cumb 210 B5
Watford Herts 85 F10
W Nhants 120 D2
Watford Gap Staffs 134 C2
Watford Heath Herts 85 G10
Watford Park Caerph 58 B6
Wath Cumb 222 D3
N Yorks 214 D6
N Yorks 214 F2
N Yorks 216 D3
Wath Brow Cumb 219 C10
Watherston Borders 271 F8
Wath upon Dearne
S Yorks 198 G2
Watledge Glos 80 E4
Watley's End S Glos 61 C7
Watlington Norf 158 G2
Oxon 83 G11
Watnall Notts 171 F8
Watsness Shetland 313 H3
Watten Highld 310 D6
Wattisfield Suff 125 C10
Wattisham Suff 125 G10
Wattisham Stone Suff 125 G10
Wattlefield Norf 142 D2
Wattlesborough Heath
Shrops 149 G7
Watton E Yorks 208 C6
Norf 141 C8
Watton at Stone Herts 86 B4
Watton Green Norf 141 C8
Watton's Green Essex 87 F8
Wattston N Lanark 268 B5
Wattstown Rhondda 77 G8
Wattsville Caerph 78 G2
Wauchan Highld 295 G11
Waulkmill Lodge Orkney 314 F3
Waun Gwyn 163 C9
Powys 148 F4
Waunarlwydd Swansea 56 B6
Waun Beddau Pembs 90 F5
Waunclunda Carms 94 E3
Waunfawr Gwyn 163 D8
Waun Fawr Ceredig 128 G2
Waungilwen Carms 92 D6
Waungron Swansea 75 E9
Waunlwyd Bl Gwent 77 D11
Waun-Lwyd Bl Gwent 77 D11
Waun-y-clyn Carms 75 E7
Waun y Gilfach Bridgend 57 D10
Wavendon M Keynes 103 D8
Wavendon Gate
M Keynes 103 D8
Waverbridge Cumb 229 B10
Waverley S Yorks 186 D6
Waverton Ches W 167 C7
Cumb 229 B10
Wavertree Mers 182 D5
Wawcott W Berks 63 F11
Wawne E Yorks 209 F7
Waxham Norf 161 D8
Waxholme E Yorks 201 B10
Way Kent 71 F10
Waye Devon 13 G11
Wayend Street Hereford 98 D4
Wayfield Medway 69 F9
Wayford Som 28 F6
Waymills Shrops 167 G9
Wayne Green Mon 78 B6
Way's Green Ches W 167 B10
Waytown Devon 24 C5
Devon 40 G5
Way Village Devon 26 E5
Way Wick N Som 59 G11
Wdig = Goodwick Pembs 91 D8
Weachyburn Aberds 302 D6
Weacombe Som 42 E6
Weald Oxon 82 E4
Wealdstone London 67 B7
Wearde Corn 7 D8
Weardley W Yorks 205 E11
Weare Som 44 C2
Weare Giffard Devon 25 C7
Wearhead Durham 232 D3
Wearne Som 28 B6
Weasdale Cumb 222 E3
Weasenham All Saints
Norf 158 E6
Weasenham St Peter
Norf 159 E7
Weaste Gtr Man 184 B4
Weatherhill Sur 51 E10
Weatheroak Hill Worcs 117 C11
Weaverham Ches W 183 G10
Weavering Street Kent 53 B9
Weaverslake Staffs 152 F2
Weaverthorpe N Yorks 217 E9
Webbington Som 43 B11
Webheath Worcs 117 D10
Webscott Shrops 149 E9
Wecock Hants 33 E11
Wedderlairs Aberds 303 F8
Wedderlie Borders 272 E2
Weddington Kent 55 B9
Warks 135 E7
Wedhampton Wilts 46 B5
Wedmore Som 44 D2
Wednesbury W Mid 133 D9
Wednesbury Oak
W Mid 133 E9
Wednesfield W Mid 133 C8
Weecar Notts 172 B4
Weedon Bucks 84 B4
Weedon Bec W Nhants 120 F2
Weedon Lois W Nhants 102 B2
Weeford Staffs 134 C2
Week Devon 8 C5
Devon 12 E5
Devon 25 B9
Devon 26 D2
Weeke Devon 26 F3
Hants 48 G3
Week Green Corn 11 B10
Weekley N Nhants 137 G7
Weekmoor Som 27 B10
Weeks IoW 21 C7
Week St Mary Corn 11 B10
Weel E Yorks 209 F7
Weeley Essex 108 G2
Weeley Heath Essex 108 G3
Weelsby NE Lincs 201 F9
Weem Perth 286 C2
Weeping Cross Staffs 151 E8
Weethley Warks 117 F11
Weethley Bank Warks 117 G11
Weethley Gate Warks 117 G11
Weeting Norf 140 F5
Weeton E Yorks 201 C11
Lancs 202 G3
N Yorks 205 D11
Weetwood W Yorks 205 F11
Weetwood Common
Ches W 167 B8
Weetwood Hall
Northumb 264 D2
Weir Essex 69 B10
Lancs 195 B11
Weirbrook Shrops 148 E6
Weir Quay Devon 7 C8
Welborne Norf 159 G11
Welborne Common
Norf 141 B11
Welbourn Lincs 173 E7
Welburn N Yorks 216 C3
Welburn *continued*
N Yorks 216 F4
Welbury N Yorks 225 E7
Welby Lincs 155 B9
Welches Dam Cambs 139 F9
Welcombe Devon 24 D2
Weld Bank Lancs 194 D5
Weldon N Nhants 137 F8
Northumb 252 D4
Welford W Berks 64 E2
W Nhants 136 G2
Welford-on-Avon
Warks 118 G3
Welham Leics 136 E5
Notts 188 E2
Som 45 G7
Welhambridge
E Yorks 207 G11
Welham Green Herts 86 D2
Well Hants 49 D9
Lincs 190 G6
N Yorks 214 C5
Welland Worcs 98 C5
Welland Stone Worcs 98 D6
Wellbank Angus 287 D8
Well Bottom Dorset 30 D6
Wellbrook E Sus 37 B9
Welldale Dumfries 238 D5
Well End Bucks 65 B11
Herts 86 F2
Weller's Town Kent 52 E4
Wellesbourne Warks 118 F5
Well Green Gtr Man 184 D3
Wellheads Aberds 302 F4
Well Heads W Yorks 205 G7
Well Hill Kent 68 G3
Wellhouse W Berks 64 E4
W Yorks 196 E5
Welling London 68 D3
Wellingborough
N Nhants 121 D7
Wellingham Norf 159 E7
Wellingore Lincs 173 D7
Wellington Cumb 219 E11
Hereford 97 B9
Som 27 C10
Telford 150 G3
Wellington Heath
Hereford 98 C4
Wellington Hill W Yorks 206 F2
Wellisford Som 27 C9
Wellow Bath 45 B8
IoW 20 D3
NE Lincs 201 F9
Notts 171 B11
Wellow Wood Hants 32 C3
Well Place Oxon 65 B7
Wellpond Green Herts 105 G8
Wellroyd W Yorks 205 F10
Wells Som 44 D5
Wellsborough Leics 135 C7
Wells Green Ches E 167 E11
Wells-next-the-Sea
Norf 176 E6
Wellsprings Som 28 B2
Well Street Kent 53 B7
Wellstye Green Essex 87 B10
Wellswood Torbay 9 C8
Welltown Corn 6 B2
Well Town Devon 26 F6
Wellwood Fife 279 D11
Welney Norf 139 E10
Welsford Devon 24 C3
Welshampton Shrops 149 B8
Welsh Bicknor Hereford 79 B9
Welsh End Shrops 149 B10
Welsh Frankton Shrops 149 C7
Welsh Harp London 67 B8
Welsh Hook Pembs 91 F8
Welsh Newton Hereford 79 B7
Welsh Newton Common
Hereford 79 B8
Welshpool Powys 130 B4
Welsh St Donats V Glam 58 D4
Welshwood Park Essex 107 F10
Welstor Devon 13 G10
Welton Bath 45 C7
Cumb 230 C3
E Ayrs 258 D2
E Yorks 200 B3
Lincs 189 F8
W Nhants 119 D11
Welton Hill Lincs 189 E8
Welton le Marsh Lincs 175 B7
Welton le Wold Lincs 190 D3
Welwick E Yorks 201 C10
Welwyn Herts 86 B2
Welwyn Garden City
Herts 86 C2
Wem Shrops 149 D10
Wembdon Som 43 F9
Wembley London 67 B7
Wembley Park London 67 B7
Wembury Devon 7 F10
Wembworthy Devon 25 F11
Wemyss Bay Invclyd 266 B3
Wenallt Ceredig 112 C3
Gwyn 146 F4
Gwyn 165 G7
Wendens Ambo Essex 105 D10
Wendlebury Oxon 83 B9
Wendling Norf 159 G8
Wendover Bucks 84 D5
Wendover Dean Bucks 84 E5
Wendron Corn 2 C5
Wendy Cambs 104 B6
Wenfordbridge Corn 11 F7
Wenhaston Suff 127 B8
Wenhaston Black Heath
Suff 127 C8
Wennington Cambs 122 B4
Lancs 212 E2
London 68 C4
Wensley Derbys 170 C3
N Yorks 213 B11
Wentbridge W Yorks 198 D3
Wentnor Shrops 131 E7
Wentworth Cambs 123 B9
S Yorks 186 B5
Wenvoe V Glam 58 E6
Weobley Hereford 115 G8
Weobley Marsh
Hereford 115 G8
Weoley Castle W Mid 133 G10
Wepham W Sus 35 F8
Wepre Flint 166 B3
Wereham Norf 140 C3
Wereham Row Norf 140 C3
Wereton Staffs 168 E3
Wergs W Mid 133 C7
Wern Gwyn 145 B10
Powys 77 B10
Powys 147 G9
Powys 148 E5
Powys 148 G5
Shrops 148 C5
Swansea 56 C4
Wern ddu Shrops 148 D4
Werneth Gtr Man 196 G2
Werneth Low Gtr Man 185 C7
Wernffrwd Swansea 56 C4
Wern-Gifford Mon 96 G6
Wernlas Shrops 148 E6
Wern-olau Swansea 56 B5
Wernrheolydd Mon 78 C5
Wern Tarw Bridgend 58 C3
Wern-y-cwrt Mon 78 D5
Wern-y-gaer Flint 166 B2
Wernyrheolydd Mon 78 C5
Werrington Corn 12 D2
Pboro 138 C3
Staffs 168 F6
Wervin Ches W 182 G6
Wescoe Hill N Yorks 205 D11
Wesham Lancs 202 G4
Wessington Derbys 170 D5
West Aberthaw V Glam 58 F4
Westacott Devon 40 G5
West Acre Norf 158 F5
West Acton London 67 C7
West Adderbury Oxon 101 D9
West Allerdean
Northumb 273 F9
West Allotment T&W 243 C8
West Alvington Devon 8 G4
West Amesbury Wilts 46 E6
West Anstey Devon 26 B5
West Appleton N Yorks 224 G4
West Ardhu Argyll 288 D6
West Ardsley W Yorks 197 B9
West Ardwell Dumfries 236 E2
West Arthurlie E Renf 267 D9
West Ashby Lincs 190 G3
West Ashford Devon 40 F4
West Ashling W Sus 22 B4
West Ashton Wilts 45 B11
West Auckland Durham 233 F9
West Ayton N Yorks 217 C9
West Bagborough Som 43 G7
West Bank Bl Gwent 78 D2
Halton 183 E8
West Barkwith Lincs 189 E11
West Barnby N Yorks 226 C6
West Barnes London 67 F8
West Barns E Loth 282 F3
West Barsham Norf 159 C8
West Bay Dorset 16 C5
West Beckham Norf 160 B2
West Bedfont Sur 66 E5
West Benhar N Lanark 269 C7
Westbere Kent 71 G7
West Bergholt Essex 107 F9
West Bexington Dorset 16 D6
West Bilney Norf 158 F4
West Blackdene Durham 232 D3
West Blackdown Devon 12 E5
West Blatchington
Brighton 36 F3
West Bold Borders 261 B9
West Boldon T&W 243 E9
Westborough Lincs 172 G5
Westbourne BCP 19 C7
Suff 108 B2
W Sus 22 B3
Westbourne Green
London 67 C9
West Bourton Dorset 30 B3
West Bowling W Yorks 205 G9
West Bradford Lancs 203 E10
West Bradley Som 44 F5
West Bretton W Yorks 197 E9
West Bridgford Notts 153 B11
West Brompton London 67 D9
West Bromwich
W Mid 133 E10
Westbrook Hereford 96 C5
Kent 71 E10
Sur 50 E3
Warr 183 C9
W Berks 64 E2
Wilts 62 F3
Westbrook Green Norf 142 G2
Westbrook Hay Herts 85 D8
West Broughton Derbys 152 C2
West Buckland Devon 41 G7
Som 27 C11
Westburn S Lanark 268 C3
West Burnside Aberds 293 F8
West Burrafirth
Shetland 313 H4
West Burton N Yorks 213 B10
W Sus 35 E7
Westbury Bucks 102 D2
Shrops 131 B7
Wilts 45 C11
Westbury Leigh Wilts 45 C11
Westbury-on-Severn
Glos 80 C2
Westbury on Trym Bristol 60 D5
Westbury Park Bristol 60 D5
Westbury-sub-Mendip
Som 44 D4
West Butsfield Durham 233 C8
West Butterwick
N Lincs 199 F10
Westby Lancs 202 G3
Lincs 155 D9
West Byfleet Sur 66 G4
West Caister Norf 161 G10
West Calder W Loth 269 C10
West Camel Som 29 C9
West Carlton W Yorks 205 E10
West Carr Hull 209 G7
N Lincs 199 F8
West Chadsmoor Staffs 151 G9
West Challow Oxon 63 B11
West Charleton Devon 8 G5
West Chelborough Dorset 29 F8
West Chevington
Northumb 252 D6
West Chiltington W Sus 35 D9
West Chiltington Common
W Sus 35 D9
West Chinnock Som 29 E7
West Chirton T&W 243 D8
West Chisenbury Wilts 46 C6
West Clandon Sur 50 C4
West Cliff BCP 19 C7
N Yorks 227 C7
West Cliffe Kent 55 E10
Westcliff-on-Sea
Southend 69 B11
West Clyne Highld 311 J2
Highld 311 J2
West Clyth Highld 310 F6
Highld 310 F6
West Coker Som 29 E8
Westcombe Som 29 B7
Som 45 F7
West Common Hants 32 G6
West Compton Dorset 17 C7
Som 44 E5
West Cornforth Durham 234 E2
Westcot Oxon 63 B10
Westcote Glos 100 G4
Westcotes Leicester 135 C11
Westcott Bucks 84 B2
Devon 27 G8
Shrops 131 C8
Sur 50 D6
Westcott Barton Oxon 101 F8
Westcourt Wilts 63 G8
West Cowick E Yorks 199 C7
West Cranmore Som 45 E7
Westcroft M Keynes 102 E6
W Mid 133 C8
West Cross Kent 53 G10
Swansea 56 D6
West Crudwell Wilts 80 G6
West Cullery Aberds 293 C9
West Curry Corn 11 C11
West Curthwaite Cumb 230 B2
West Darlochan Argyll 255 E7
Westdean E Sus 23 F8
West Dean Wilts 32 B3
W Sus 34 E5
West Deeping Lincs 138 B2
West Denant Pembs 72 C6
Westdene Brighton 36 F3
West Denton T&W 242 D5
West Derby Mers 182 C5
West Dereham Norf 140 C3
West Didsbury Gtr Man 184 C4
West Down Devon 40 E4
Hants 47 F11
Westdown Camp Wilts 46 D4
Westdowns Corn 11 E7
West Downs Corn 5 C10
West Drayton London 66 D5
Notts 188 G2
West Dulwich London 67 E10
West Ealing London 67 C7
West Edge Derbys 170 C4
West Ella E Yorks 200 B4
Westend Oxon 100 G6
S Glos 79 G10
West End Bedford 121 E11
Bedford 121 G9
Brack 65 E11
Brack 66 G2
Caerph 78 F2
Cumb 239 F8
Dorset 30 G6
E Yorks 201 B9
E Yorks 208 G4
E Yorks 209 B9
E Yorks 209 G9
E Yorks 217 G11
Glos 80 F5
Hants 33 E7
Hants 33 F9
Hants 48 F6
Herts 86 D3
Kent 54 B2
Kent 71 F7
Lancs 195 B8
Lancs 211 G8
Leics 153 F8
Lincs 174 F5
Lincs 190 B5
Mon 78 F6
Norf 141 B8
Norf 161 G10
N Som 60 F3
N Yorks 205 B8
N Yorks 206 E6
N Yorks 207 F7
Oxon 64 B5
Oxon 82 E6
S Glos 61 B8
S Lanark 269 F9
Som 44 C5
Som 45 G7
Suff 143 G9
Sur 49 E10
Sur 66 G6
S Yorks 199 F7
Wilts 30 C6
Wilts 31 C7
Wilts 62 D3
Windsor 65 D10
Worcs 99 D11
W Sus 36 D2
W Yorks 197 B7
W Yorks 205 F10
West End = *Marian-y-mor*
Gwyn 145 C7
West End Green Hants 65 G7
Westend Town
Northumb 241 D7
West-end Town V Glam 58 F3
Westenhanger Kent 54 F6
Wester Aberchalder
Highld 300 G5
Wester Arboll Highld 311 L2
Wester Auchinloch
N Lanark 278 G3
Wester Auchnagallin
Highld 301 F10
Wester Balgedie Perth 286 G5
Wester Brae Highld 300 C6
Wester Broomhouse
E Loth 282 F3
Wester Craiglands
Highld 301 D7
Wester Culbeuchly
Aberds 302 C6
Westerdale Highld 310 D5
N Yorks 226 D3
Wester Dalvoult Highld 291 B11
Wester Dechmont
W Loth 269 B10
Wester Deloraine
Borders 261 E8
Wester Denoon Angus 287 C7
Wester Ellister Argyll 254 B2
Wester Essendy Perth 286 C5
Wester Essenside
Borders 261 E10
Wester Feddal Perth 286 G2
Westerfield Shetland 313 H5
Suff 108 B3
Wester Fintray Aberds 293 B10
Westerfolds Moray 301 C11
Wester Galgantray
Highld 301 E8
Westergate W Sus 22 C6
Wester Gospetry Fife 286 G5
Wester Gruinards
Highld 309 K5
Wester Hailes Edin 270 B4
Westerham Kent 52 C2
Westerhope T&W 242 D5
Wester Housebyres
Borders 262 B2
Wester Kershope
Borders 261 D9
Wester Lealty Highld 300 B6
Westerleigh S Glos 61 D8
Westerleigh Hill S Glos 61 D8
Wester Lix Stirling 285 E9
Wester Milton Highld 301 D9
Wester Mosshead
Aberds 302 F5
Western Bank Cumb 229 B10
Western Downs Staffs 151 E8
Western Heights Kent 55 E10
Western Hill Durham 233 C11
Western Park Leicester 135 C10
Wester Ord Aberds 293 C10
Wester Parkgate
Dumfries 248 F2
Wester Quarff Shetland 313 K6
Wester Skeld Shetland 313 J4
Wester Strath Highld 300 D6
Westerton Aberds 293 B9
Aberds 302 E5
Angus 287 B10
Durham 233 E10
Moray 302 D3
W Sus 22 B5
Westertown Aberds 303 F7
Wester Watten Highld 310 D6
Westerwick Shetland 313 J4
West Ewell Sur 67 G8
West Farleigh Kent 53 C8
West Farndon
W Nhants 119 G10
West Felton Shrops 148 D6
West Fenton E Loth 281 E9
West Ferry Dundee 287 D8
Westfield Bath 45 C7
Cumb 228 F5
E Sus 38 D4
Hants 21 B10
Hereford 98 B4
Highld 310 C4
N Lanark 278 G4
Norf 141 B9
Redcar 235 G7
Sur 50 B4
S Yorks 186 E6
W Loth 279 G8
W Yorks 197 C8
W Yorks 205 E9
West Field N Lincs 200 D6
York 207 C7
Westfields Dorset 30 F2
Hereford 97 C9
West Fields W Berks 64 F3
Westfields of Rattray
Perth 286 C5
Westfield Sole Kent 69 G9
West Firle E Sus 23 D7
West Fleetham
Northumb 264 D5
West Flodden
Northumb 263 C10
Westford Som 27 C10
West Garforth W Yorks 206 G3
Westgate Durham 232 D4
N Lincs 199 F9
Norf 176 E4
Norf 177 E7
Westgate Hill W Yorks 197 B8
Westgate on Sea Kent 71 E10
Westgate Street Norf 160 E3
West Ginge Oxon 64 B2
West Gorton Gtr Man 184 B5
West Grafton Wilts 63 G8
West Green Hants 49 B8
London 67 B10
S Yorks 197 F11
W Sus 51 F9
West Greenskares
Aberds 303 C7
West Grimstead Wilts 32 B2
West Grinstead W Sus 35 C11
West Haddlesey
N Yorks 198 B5
West Haddon W Nhants 120 C2
West Hagbourne Oxon 64 B4
West Hagley Worcs 133 G8
Westhall Aberds 302 G6
Suff 143 G8
West Hall Cumb 240 D3
West Hallam Derbys 170 G6
Westhall Hill Oxon 82 C3
West Halton N Lincs 200 C2
Westham Dorset 17 F9
E Sus 23 E10
Som 44 D2
West Ham Hants 48 C6
London 68 C2
Westhampnett W Sus 22 B5
West Hampstead London 67 B9
West Handley Derbys 186 F5
West Hanney Oxon 82 G6
West Hanningfield Essex 88 F2
West Hardwick
W Yorks 198 D2
West Harling Norf 141 G9
West Harlsey N Yorks 225 F8
West Harnham Wilts 31 B10
West Harptree Bath 44 B5
West Harrow London 66 B6
West Harting W Sus 34 C3
West Harton T&W 243 E9
West Hatch Som 28 C3
Wilts 30 B6
Westhay Som 44 E2
Westhead Lancs 194 F2
West Head Norf 139 B11
West Heath Ches E 168 C4
Hants 48 B5
Hants 49 B11
London 68 D3
W Mid 117 B10
West Helmsdale Highld 311 H4
West Hendon London 67 B8
West Hendred Oxon 64 B2
West Herrington T&W 243 G8
West Heslerton N Yorks 217 D8
West Hewish N Som 59 G11
Westhide Hereford 97 C11
Westhill Aberds 293 C10
E Yorks 209 F10
Highld 301 E7
West Hill Devon 15 C7
E Sus 38 E4
E Yorks 218 F3
London 67 E8
N Som 60 D3
Som 30 B2
Staffs 151 G9
Wilts 61 F11
W Sus 51 G10
West Hoathly W Sus 51 G11
West Holme Dorset 18 D3
West Holywell T&W 243 C8
Westhope Hereford 115 G9
Shrops 131 F9
West Horndon Essex 68 B6
Westhorp W Nhants 119 G10
Westhorpe Lincs 156 C4
Notts 171 E11
Suff 125 D10
West Horrington Som 44 D5
West Horsley Sur 50 C5
West Horton Northumb 264 C2
West Hougham Kent 55 E9
Westhoughton Gtr Man 195 F7
West Houlland Shetland 313 H4
Westhouse N Yorks 212 E3
Westhouses Derbys 170 D6
West Houses Lincs 174 E4
West Howe BCP 19 B7
West Howetown Som 42 G2
Westhumble Sur 51 C7
West Huntington York 207 B8
West Huntspill Som 43 E10
West Hurn BCP 19 B8
West Hyde Herts 85 G8
West Hynish Argyll 288 F1
West Hythe Kent 54 G6
West Ilkerton Devon 41 D8
West Ilsley W Berks 64 C3
Westing Shetland 312 C7
Westington Glos 100 D2
West Itchenor W Sus 22 C3
West Jesmond T&W 243 D7
West Keal Lincs 174 C5
West Kennett Wilts 62 F6
West Kensington London 67 D8
West Kilbride N Ayrs 266 F4
West Kilburn London 67 C8
West Kingsdown Kent 68 G5
West Kingston W Sus 35 G9
West Kington Wilts 61 D10
West Kington Wick
Wilts 61 D10
West Kinharrachie
Aberds 303 F9
West Kirby Mers 182 D2
West Kirkby Mers 182 D2
West Knapton N Yorks 217 D7
West Knighton Dorset 17 D10
West Knoyle Wilts 45 G11
West Kyloe Northumb 273 G11
West Kyo Durham 242 G5
Westlake Devon 8 E2
West Lambrook Som 28 D6
Westland Argyll 275 G11
Westland Green Herts 105 G8
Westlands Staffs 168 G4
Worcs 117 E7
West Langdon Kent 55 D10
West Langwell Highld 309 J6
West Lavington Wilts 46 C4
W Sus 34 C5
West Layton N Yorks 224 D2
Westlea Northumb 252 G6
Swindon 62 C6
West Lea Durham 234 B4
West Leake Notts 153 D10
West Learmouth
Northumb 263 B9
Westleigh Devon 25 B7
Devon 27 D9
Gtr Man 194 G6
West Leigh Devon 25 F11
Hants 22 B2
Som 42 G6
Westleton Suff 127 D8
West Lexham Norf 158 F6
Westley Shrops 131 B7
Suff 124 E6
Westley Heights Essex 69 B7
Westley Waterless
Cambs 124 F2
West Lilling N Yorks 216 F2
Westlington Bucks 84 C3
Westlinton Cumb 239 E9
West Linton Borders 270 E2
West Liss Hants 34 B3
West Littleton S Glos 61 D9
West Lockinge Oxon 64 B2
West Looe Corn 6 E5
West Luccombe Som 41 D11
West Lulworth Dorset 18 E2
West Lutton N Yorks 217 F8
West Lydford Som 44 G5
West Lydiatt Hereford 97 C11
West Lyn Devon 41 D8
West Lyng Som 28 B4
West Lynn Norf 158 E2
West Mains Borders 271 F11
S Lanark 268 E2
West Malling Kent 53 B7
West Malvern Worcs 98 B5
Westmancote Worcs 99 D8
West Marden W Sus 34 E3
West Marina E Sus 38 F3
West Markham Notts 188 G2
Westmarsh Kent 71 G9
West Marsh NE Lincs 201 E9
West Marton N Yorks 204 C3
West Mathers Aberds 293 G9
West Melbury Dorset 30 C5
West Melton S Yorks 198 G2
West Meon Hants 33 C10
West Meon Woodlands
Hants 33 B10
West Merkland Highld 308 F3
West Mersea Essex 89 C8
Westmeston E Sus 36 E4
Westmill Herts 104 E3
Herts 105 F7
West Milton Dorset 16 B6
Westminster London 67 D10
West Minster Kent 70 E2
West Molesey Sur 66 F6
West Monkseaton T&W 243 C8
West Monkton Som 28 B3
West Moor T&W 243 C7
Westmoor End Cumb 229 D8
West Moors Dorset 31 G9
West Morden Dorset 18 B4
West Morriston Borders 272 G2
West Morton W Yorks 205 E7
West Mudford Som 29 C9
Westmuir Angus 287 B7
West Muir Angus 293 G7
West Myreriggs Perth 286 C6
Westness Orkney 314 D3
West Ness N Yorks 216 D3
West Newham Northumb 242 B3
Westnewton Cumb 229 C8
Northumb 263 C10
West Newton E Yorks 209 F9
Norf 158 D3
Som 28 B3
West Norwood London 67 E10
Westoe T&W 243 D9
West Ogwell Devon 14 G2
Weston Bath 61 F8
Ches E 168 E2
Ches E 184 G5
Devon 15 D9
Devon 27 G10
Dorset 17 G9
Dorset 29 F8
Halton 183 E8
Hants 34 C2
Hereford 115 F7
Herts 104 E5
Lincs 156 D5
Notts 172 B3
N Yorks 205 D9
Pembs 73 C8
Shrops 114 C6
Shrops 131 E11
Shrops 148 D5
Shrops 149 D11
S Lanark 269 F10
Soton 32 E6
Staffs 151 D9
Suff 143 F8
W Berks 63 E11
W Nhants 101 B11
Weston Bampfylde
Som 29 C10

Weston Beggard
Hereford 97 C11
Westonbirt Glos 61 B11
Weston by Welland
N Nhants 136 E5
Weston Colley Hants 48 F4
Weston Colville Cambs 124 G2
Westoncommon Shrops 149 D8
Weston Common Soton 33 E7
Weston Corbett Hants 49 D7
Weston Coyney Stoke 168 G6
Weston Ditch Suff 124 B3
Weston Favell
W Nhants 120 E5
Weston Green Cambs 124 G2
Norf 160 G2
Sur 67 F7
Weston Heath Shrops 150 G5
Weston Hills Lincs 156 E5
Weston in Arden Warks 135 F7
Westoning C Beds 103 E10
Weston-in-Gordano
N Som 60 E2
Weston Jones Staffs 150 E5
Weston Longville Norf 160 F2
Weston Lullingfields
Shrops 149 E8
Weston Manor IoW 20 D2
Weston Mill Plym 7 D9
Weston-on-Avon
Warks 118 G3
Weston-on-the-Green
Oxon 83 B8
Weston-on-Trent
Derbys 153 D8
Weston Park Bath 61 F8
Weston Patrick Hants 49 D7
Weston Point Halton 183 E7
Weston Rhyn Shrops 148 B5
Weston-sub-Edge Glos 100 C2
Weston-super-Mare
N Som 59 G10
Weston Town Som 45 E8
Weston Turville Bucks 84 C5
Weston under Lizard
Staffs 150 G6
Weston under Penyard
Hereford 98 G2
Weston under Wetherley
Warks 119 D7
Weston Underwood
Derbys 170 G3
M Keynes 121 G7
Westonwharf Shrops 149 D8
Westonzoyland Som 43 G11
West Orchard Dorset 30 D4
West Overton Wilts 62 F6
Westow N Yorks 216 F5
Westowe Som 42 G6
Westown Devon 27 E10
Perth 286 E6
West Panson Devon 12 C2
West Park Hrtlpl 234 E5
Hull 200 B5
Mers 183 B7
T&W 243 D9
W Yorks 205 F11
West Parley Dorset 19 B7
West Pasture Durham 232 G4
West Peckham Kent 52 C6
West Pelton Durham 242 G6
West Pennard Som 44 F4
West Pentire Corn 4 C5
West Perry Cambs 122 D2
West Pontnewydd Torf 78 F3
West Poringland Norf 142 C5
West Porlock Som 41 D11
Westport Argyll 255 E7
Som 28 D5
West Portholland Corn 5 G9
West Porton Renfs 277 G8
West Pulham Dorset 30 F2
West Putford Devon 24 D5
West Quantoxhead Som 42 E6
Westquarter Falk 279 F8
Westra V Glam 58 E6
West Rainton Durham 234 B2
West Rasen Lincs 189 D9
West Ravendale
NE Lincs 190 B2
West Raynham Norf 159 D7
West Retford Notts 187 E11
Westridge Green
W Berks 64 D5
Westrigg W Loth 269 B8
Westrip Glos 80 D4
Westrop Wilts 61 E11
Westrop Green W Berks 64 E4
West Rounton N Yorks 225 E8
West Row Suff 124 B3
West Royd W Yorks 205 F9
West Rudham Norf 158 D6
West Ruislip London 66 B5
Westrum N Lincs 200 F4
West Runton Norf 177 E11
Westruther Borders 272 F2
Westry Cambs 139 D7
West Saltoun E Loth 271 B9
West Sandford Devon 26 G4
West Sandwick Shetland 312 E6
West Scholes W Yorks 205 G7
West Scrafton N Yorks 213 C11
West Shepton Som 44 E6
West Sherford Devon 7 E10
West Side Bl Gwent 77 D11
Orkney 314 C5
West Skelston Dumfries 247 F8
West Sleekburn
Northumb 253 G7
West Somerton Norf 161 F9
West Southbourne BCP 19 C8
West Stafford Dorset 17 D10
West Stockwith Notts 188 C3
West Stoke Devon 13 G9
Som 29 D7
W Sus 22 B4
West Stonesdale
N Yorks 223 E7
West Stoughton Som 44 D2
West Stour Dorset 30 C3
West Stourmouth Kent 71 G9
West Stow Suff 124 C6
West Stowell Wilts 62 G6
West Strathan Highld 308 C5
West Stratton Hants 48 E4
West Street Kent 54 C2
Kent 55 C10
Medway 69 D8
Suff 125 C9
West Tanfield N Yorks 214 D5
West Taphouse Corn 6 C3
West Tarbert Argyll 275 G9
West Tarring W Sus 35 G10
West Third Borders 262 B4
West Thirston Northumb 252 D5
West Thorney W Sus 22 C3
Westthorpe Derbys 187 F7
West Thurrock Thurrock 68 D5
West Tilbury Thurrock 69 D7
West Tisted Hants 33 B11
West Tofts Norf 140 E6
Perth 286 D5
West Tolgus Corn 4 G3
West Torrington Lincs 189 E10
West Town Bath 60 G4
Devon 14 B3
Devon 24 C4
Hants 21 B10
Hereford 115 E8
N Som 60 F3
Som 44 F4
W Sus 36 D3
West Tytherley Hants 32 B3
West Tytherton Wilts 62 E2
Westvale Mers 182 B6
West Vale W Yorks 196 C5
West View Hrtlpl 234 D5
West Village V Glam 58 E3
Westville Devon 8 G4
Notts 171 F8
West Walton Norf 157 G9
West Walton Highway
Norf 157 G9
Westward Cumb 229 C11
Westward Ho! Devon 24 B6
West Watergate Corn 6 E4
West Watford Herts 85 F10
Westweekmoor Devon 12 C4
Westwell Kent 54 D3
Oxon 82 D2
Westwell Leacon Kent 54 D3
West Wellow Hants 32 D3
Westwells Wilts 61 F11
West Wemyss Fife 280 C6
Westwick Cambs 123 D8
Durham 223 B11
Norf 160 D5
West Wick N Som 59 G11
West Wickham Cambs 106 B2
London 67 F11
Westwick Row Herts 85 D9
West Williamston Pembs 73 D8
West Willoughby Lincs 173 G7
West Winch Norf 158 F2
West Winterslow Wilts 47 G8
West Wittering W Sus 21 B11
West Witton N Yorks 213 B11
Westwood Devon 14 B6
Devon 14 E5
Kent 55 D7
Kent 71 F11
Notts 171 E7
Pboro 138 D3
S Lanark 268 E2
Wilts 45 B10
Wilts 46 G6
West Woodburn
Northumb 251 F9
West Woodhay W Berks 63 G11
Westwood Heath
W Mid 118 B5
West Woodlands Som 45 E9
Westwood Park Essex 107 E9
Gtr Man 184 B3
Westwoodside N Lincs 188 B3
West Worldham Hants 49 F8
West Worlington Devon 26 E3
West Worthing W Sus 35 G10
West Wratting Cambs 124 G2
West Wycombe Bucks 84 G4
West Wylam Northumb 242 E4
Westy Warr 183 D10
West Yatton Wilts 61 E11
West Yell Shetland 312 E6
West Yeo Som 43 G10
West Yoke Kent 68 F5
West Youlstone Corn 24 D3
Wetham Green Kent 69 F10
Wetheral Cumb 239 G11
Wetheral Plain Cumb 239 F11
Wetherby W Yorks 206 D4
Wetherden Suff 125 E10
Wetherden Upper Town
Suff 125 D10
Wetheringsett Suff 126 D2
Wethersfield Essex 106 E4
Wethersta Shetland 312 G5
Wetherup Street Suff 126 E2
Wetley Rocks Staffs 169 F7
Wetmore Staffs 152 E5
Wettenhall Ches E 167 C10
Wettenhall Green
Ches E 167 C10
Wettles Shrops 131 F8
Wetton Staffs 169 D10
Wetwang E Yorks 208 B4
Wetwood Staffs 150 C5
Wexcombe Wilts 47 B9
Wexham Street Bucks 66 C3
Weybourne Norf 177 E10
Sur 49 D11
Weybread Suff 142 G4
Weybridge Sur 66 G5
Weycroft Devon 16 B2
Weydale Highld 310 C5
Weyhill Hants 47 D10
Weymouth Dorset 17 F9
Weythel Powys 114 F4
Whaddon Bucks 102 E6
Cambs 104 B6
Glos 80 C4
Glos 99 G9
Wilts 31 B11
Wilts 61 G11
Whaddon Gap Cambs 104 B6
Whale Cumb 230 G6
Whaley Derbys 187 G8
Whaley Bridge Derbys 185 E8
Whaley Thorns Derbys 187 G8
Whaligoe Highld 310 E7
Whalley Lancs 203 F10
Whalley Banks Lancs 203 F10
Whalley Range Gtr Man 184 C4
Whalleys Lancs 194 F3
Whalton Northumb 252 G4
Wham N Yorks 212 G5
Whaplode Lincs 156 E6
Whaplode Drove Lincs 156 G6
Whaplode St Catherine
Lincs 156 E6
Wharf Warks 119 G8
Wharfe N Yorks 212 F5
Wharles Lancs 202 F4
Wharley End C Beds 103 C8
Wharmley Northumb 241 D9
Wharncliffe Side
S Yorks 186 C3
Wharram le Street
N Yorks 217 F7
Wharram Percy
N Yorks 217 G7
Wharton Ches W 167 B11
Hereford 115 F10
Lincs 188 C4
Wharton Green
Ches W 167 B11
Whashton N Yorks 224 D3
Whasset Cumb 211 C10
Whatcombe Dorset 30 G4
Whatcote Warks 100 C6
Whatcroft Ches W 167 B11
Whateley Staffs 134 D4
Whatfield Suff 107 B10
Whatley Som 28 F5
Som 45 D8
Whatlington E Sus 38 D3
Whatmore Shrops 116 C2
Whatsole Street Kent 54 E6
Whatstandwell Derbys 170 E4
Whatton Notts 154 B4
Whauphill Dumfries 236 E6
Whaw N Yorks 223 E9
Wheal Alfred Corn 2 B3
Wheal Baddon Corn 4 G5
Wheal Busy Corn 4 G4
Wheal Frances Corn 4 E5
Wheal Kitty Corn 4 E4
Wheal Rose Corn 4 G4
Wheatacre Norf 143 E9
Wheatcroft Derbys 170 D5
Wheatenhurst Glos 80 D3
Wheathall Shrops 131 C9
Wheathampstead Herts 85 C11
Wheathill Shrops 132 G2
Som 44 G5
Wheat Hold Hants 64 G5
Wheatley Devon 14 C4
Hants 49 E9
Oxon 83 D9
S Yorks 198 G5
W Yorks 196 B5
Wheatley Hill Durham 234 D3
Wheatley Hills S Yorks 198 G6
Wheatley Lane Lancs 204 F2
Wheatley Park S Yorks 198 F5
Wheaton Aston Staffs 151 G7
Wheddon Cross Som 42 F2
Wheedlemont Aberds 302 G4
Wheelbarrow Town Kent 55 D7
Wheeler End Bucks 84 G4
Wheelerstreet Sur 50 E2
Wheelock Ches E 168 D3
Wheelock Heath
Ches E 168 D2
Wheelton Lancs 194 C5
Lancs 194 C6
Lancs 194 D5
Lancs 194 D6
Wheen Angus 292 F5
Wheldale W Yorks 198 B3
Wheldrake York 207 D9
Whelford Glos 81 F11
Whelley Gtr Man 194 F5
Whelpley Hill Herts 85 E7
Whelpo Cumb 230 D2
Whelp Street Suff 107 B8
Whelston Flint 182 F2
Whempstead Herts 104 G6
Whenby N Yorks 216 F2
Whepstead Suff 124 F6
Wherry Town Corn 1 D5
Wherstead Suff 108 C3
Wherwell Hants 47 E11
Wheston Derbys 185 F10
Whetley Cross Dorset 29 G7
Whetsted Kent 53 D7
Whetstone Leics 135 D11
London 86 G3
Whettleton Shrops 131 G8
Whicham Cumb 210 C2
Whichford Warks 100 E6
Whickham T&W 242 E6
Whickham Fell T&W 242 F6
Whiddon Devon 40 F5
Whiddon Down Devon 13 C9
Whifflet N Lanark 268 C4
Whigstreet Angus 287 C8
Whilton W Nhants 120 E2
Whilton Locks
W Nhants 120 E2
Whimble Devon 24 G5
Whim Farm Borders 270 E4
Whimple Devon 14 B6
Whimpwell Green Norf 161 D7
Whinburgh Norf 141 B10
Whinfield Darl 224 B6
Whinhall N Lanark 268 B5
Whin Lane End Lancs 202 E3
Whinmoor W Yorks 206 F3
Whinney Hill Stockton 225 B7
S Yorks 187 C7
Whinnieliggate
Dumfries 237 D9
Whinnyfold Aberds 303 F10
Whinny Heights
Blackburn 195 B7
Whins of Milton Stirling 278 C5
Whins Wood W Yorks 205 F7
Whipcott Devon 27 D9
Whippendell Botton
Herts 85 E9
Whippingham IoW 20 C6
Whipsiderry Corn 4 C6
Whipsnade C Beds 85 B8
Whipton Devon 14 C5
Whirley Grove Ches E 184 F5
Whirlow S Yorks 186 E4
Whisby Lincs 172 B6
Whissendine Rutland 154 G6
Whissonsett Norf 159 E8
Whisterfield Ches E 184 G4
Whistlefield Argyll 276 C2
Argyll 276 C4
Whistley Green
Wokingham 65 E9
Whistlow Oxon 101 F9
Whiston Mers 183 C7
Staffs 151 G7
Staffs 169 F8
S Yorks 186 D6
W Nhants 120 E6
Whiston Cross Mers 183 C7
Shrops 132 C5
Whitacre Heath Warks 134 E4
Whitbarrow Village
Cumb 230 F4
Whitbeck Cumb 210 C2
Whitbourne Hereford 116 F4
Whitbourne Moor Wilts 45 D10
Whitburn T&W 243 E10
W Loth 269 C8
Whitburn Colliery
T&W 243 E10
Whitby Ches W 182 F5
N Yorks 227 C7
Whitbyheath Ches W 182 F5
Whitchurch Bath 60 F6
Bucks 102 G5
Cardiff 59 C7
Devon 12 G5
Hants 48 D3
Hereford 79 B9
Pembs 90 F5
Shrops 167 G8
Som 30 C2
Whitchurch Canonicorum
Dorset 16 B3
Whitchurch Hill Oxon 64 D6
Whitchurch-on-Thames
Oxon 64 D6
Whitcombe Dorset 17 D10
Whitcombe *continued*
Som 29 C10
Whitcot Shrops 131 E7
Whitcott Keysett Shrops 130 G5
Whiteacen Moray 302 E2
Whiteacre Kent 54 D6
Whiteacre Heath Warks 134 E4
Whiteash Green Essex 106 E5
White Ball Som 27 D9
Whitebirk Blackburn 195 B8
Whitebog Highld 301 C7
Whitebridge Highld 290 B6
Whitebrook Mon 79 D8
Whiteburn Borders 271 F11
Whitebushes Sur 51 D9
Whitecairn Dumfries 236 D4
Whitecairns Aberds 293 B11
Whitecastle S Lanark 269 G10
Whitechapel Lancs 203 E7
London 67 C10
Whitechurch Maund
Hereford 97 B11
Whitecleat Orkney 314 F5
Whitecliff Glos 79 C9
Whiteclosegate Cumb 239 F10
White Colne Essex 107 F7
White Coppice Lancs 194 D6
Whitecote W Yorks 205 F10
Whitecraig E Loth 281 G7
Whitecraigs E Renf 267 D11
Whitecroft Glos 79 D10
Whitecrook W Dunb 267 B10
Whitecross Corn 2 C2
Corn 6 E2
Corn 10 G5
Falk 279 F9
Som 28 C6
Staffs 151 E7
White Cross Bath 44 B5
Bath 44 B6
Corn 2 E5
Corn 5 D7
Hereford 97 C9
Som 43 D10
Wilts 45 G9
White Cross Hill Cambs 123 B9
White End Worcs 98 E5
Whiteface Highld 309 L7
Whitefarland N Ayrs 255 C9
Whitefaulds S Ayrs 245 B7
Whitefield Aberds 303 G7
Dorset 18 C4
Gtr Man 195 F10
Perth 286 D5
Som 27 B9
Whitefield Lane End
Mers 183 D7
Whiteflat E Ayrs 258 D2
Whiteford Aberds 303 G7
Whitegate Ches W 167 B10
White Gate Gtr Man 195 G11
Som 28 F4
White Grit Shrops 130 D6
Whitehall Blackburn 195 C7
Bristol 60 E6
Devon 27 E10
Devon 40 F4
Hants 49 C8
Herts 104 E6
W Sus 35 C10
White Hall Herts 104 G5
Whitehall Village
Orkney 314 D6
Whitehaven Cumb 219 B9
Shrops 148 E5
Whitehawk Brighton 36 G4
Whiteheath Gate W Mid 133 F9
Whitehill E Sus 37 B8
Hants 49 G9
Kent 54 B4
Midloth 271 B7
Moray 302 D5
S Lanark 268 D4
Staffs 168 E3
White Hill Bath 45 B8
Wilts 45 G10
W Yorks 204 E6
Whitehills Aberds 302 C6
S Lanark 268 E2
T&W 243 E7
White Hills W Nhants 120 E4
Whiteholme Blackpool 202 E2
Whitehough Derbys 185 E8
Whitehouse Aberds 293 B8
Argyll 275 G9
White House Suff 108 B2
Whitehouse Common
W Mid 134 D2
Whitehouse Green
W Berks 65 F7
White Houses Notts 188 F2
Whiteinch Glasgow 267 B10
Whitekirk E Loth 281 E10
White Kirkley Durham 233 D7
Whiteknights Reading 65 E8
Whiteknowes Aberds 293 C7
Whitelackington Som 28 D5
White Lackington
Dorset 17 B10
White Ladies Aston
Worcs 117 G8
Whitelaw S Lanark 268 G2
Whiteleaf Bucks 84 E4
Whiteleas T&W 243 E9
Whiteleaved Oak Glos 98 D5
Whitelee Borders 262 C3
Northumb 250 B6
White Lee W Yorks 197 B8
Whitelees S Ayrs 257 C9
White-le-Head Durham 242 G5
Whiteley Bank IoW 21 E7
Whiteley Green Ches E 184 F6
Whiteley Village Sur 66 G5
White Lund Lancs 211 G8
Whitelye Mon 79 E8
Whitemans Green W Sus 36 B4
White Mill Carms 93 G9
Whitemire Moray 301 D9
Whitemoor Corn 5 D9
Nottingham 171 G8
Warks 118 C5
White Moor Derbys 170 F5
Whitemore Staffs 168 C5
Whitenap Hants 32 C5
White Ness Shetland 313 J5
White Notley Essex 88 B3
White Oak Kent 68 F4
Whiteoak Green Oxon 82 C4
White Ox Mead Bath 45 B8
Whiteparish Wilts 32 C2
White Pit Lincs 190 F5
Whitepits Wilts 45 F10
White Post Kent 52 E4
Notts 171 D10
Whiterashes Aberds 303 G8
Whiterigg Borders 262 C3
Whiterock Bridgend 58 D2
White Rocks Hereford 97 G8
White Roding or White
Roothing Essex 87 C9
Whiterow Highld 310 E7
White's Green W Sus 34 B6
Whiteshill Glos 80 D4
S Glos 60 D6
Whiteside Northumb 240 D6
W Loth 269 B9
Whitesmith E Sus 23 C8
Whitespots Dumfries 247 F10
White Stake Lancs 194 B4
Whitestaunton Som 28 E3
Whitestone Aberds 293 D8
Devon 14 C3
Devon 40 D3
Warks 135 F7
White Stone Hereford 97 C11
Whitestones Aberds 303 D8
Whitestreet Green Suff 107 D9
Whitewall Common Mon 60 B2
Whitewall Corner
N Yorks 216 E5
White Waltham Windsor 65 D10
Whiteway Bath 61 G8
Dorset 18 E3
Glos 80 C6
Glos 80 F4
Whitewell Aberds 303 C9
Corn 11 E7
Highld 291 C11
Lancs 203 D9
Wrex 167 G7
Whitewell Bottom
Lancs 195 C10
Whiteworks Devon 13 G8
Whitfield Kent 55 D10
Northumb 241 F7
S Glos 79 G11
W Nhants 102 D2
Whitfield Court Sur 50 B3
Whitfield Hall Northumb 241 F7
Whitford Devon 15 B11
Whitford = Chwitffordd
Flint 181 F10
Whitgift E Yorks 199 C10
Whitgreave Staffs 151 D7
Whithaugh Borders 249 F11
Whithebeir Orkney 314 C5
Whithorn Dumfries 236 E6
Whiting Bay N Ayrs 256 D2
Whitington Norf 140 D4
Whitkirk W Yorks 206 G3
Whitland = Hendy-Gwyn
Carms 73 B11
Whitlaw Borders 271 F9
Whitleigh Plym 7 C9
Whitletts S Ayrs 257 E9
Whitley Gtr Man 194 F5
N Yorks 198 C5
Reading 65 E8
S Yorks 186 C4
Wilts 61 F11
W Mid 119 B7
Whitley Bay T&W 243 C9
Whitley Bridge N Yorks 198 C5
Whitley Chapel
Northumb 241 F10
Whitley Head W Yorks 204 E6
Whitley Heath Staffs 150 D6
Whitley Lower W Yorks 197 D8
Whitley Reed Ches W 183 E10
Whitley Row Kent 52 C3
Whitley Sands T&W 243 C9
Whitley Thorpe N Yorks 198 C5
Whitley Wood Reading 65 F8
Whitlock's End W Mid 118 B2
Whitminster Glos 80 D3
Whitmoor Devon 27 E9
Whitmore Dorset 31 F9
Staffs 168 G4
Whitmore Park W Mid 134 G6
Whitnage Devon 27 D8
Whitnash Warks 118 E6
Whitnell Som 43 F8
Whitney Bottom Som 28 E4
Whitney-on-Wye
Hereford 96 B5
Whitrigg Cumb 229 D10
Cumb 238 F6
Whitriggs Borders 262 F3
Whitsbury Hants 31 D10
Whitslaid Borders 271 G11
Whitsome Borders 273 E7
Whitsomehill Borders 273 F7
Whitson Newport 59 C11
Whitstable Kent 70 F6
Whitstone Corn 11 B11
Whittingham Northumb 264 G3
Whittingslow Shrops 131 F8
Whittington Glos 99 G10
Lancs 212 D2
Norf 140 D4
Shrops 148 C6
Staffs 133 G7
Staffs 134 B3
Staffs 150 C5
Warks 134 D5
Worcs 117 G7
Whittington Moor
Derbys 186 G5
Whittlebury W Nhants 102 C3
Whittleford Warks 134 E6
Whittle-le-Woods
Lancs 194 C5
Whittlesey Cambs 138 D5
Whittlesford Cambs 105 B9
Whittlestone Head
Blackburn 195 D8
Whitton Borders 263 E7
Hereford 115 C8
London 66 E6
N Lincs 200 C2
Northumb 252 C3
Powys 114 D5
Shrops 115 C11
Stockton 234 G3
Suff 108 B2
Whittonditch Wilts 63 E9
Whittonstall Northumb 242 F3
Whittytree Shrops 115 B8
Whitway Hants 48 B3
Whitwell Derbys 187 F8
Herts 104 G3
IoW 20 F6
N Yorks 224 F5
Rutland 137 B8
Whitwell-on-the-Hill
N Yorks 216 F4
Whitwell Street Norf 160 E2
Whitwick Leics 153 F8
Whitwood W Yorks 198 C2
Whitworth Lancs 195 D11
Whixall Shrops 149 C10
Whixley N Yorks 206 B4
Whoberley W Mid 118 B6
Wholeflats Falk 279 E8
Whome Orkney 314 G3
Whorlton Durham 224 C2
N Yorks 225 E9
Whydown E Sus 38 F2
Whygate Northumb 241 B7
Whyke W Sus 22 C5
Whyle Hereford 115 E11
Whyteleafe Sur 51 B10
Wibdon Glos 79 F9
Wibsey W Yorks 205 G8
Wibtoft Leics 135 F9
Wichenford Worcs 116 E5
Wichling Kent 54 B2
Wick BCP 19 C8
Devon 27 G11
Highld 310 D7
S Glos 61 E8
Shetland 313 K6
Som 28 B6
Som 43 C10
Som 43 E8
V Glam 58 E2
Wilts 31 C11
Worcs 99 B9
W Sus 35 G8
Wicken Cambs 123 C11
W Nhants 102 D4
Wicken Bonhunt Essex 105 E9
Wickenby Lincs 189 E9
Wicken Green Village
Norf 158 C6
Wick Episcopi Worcs 116 G6
Wickersley S Yorks 187 C7
Wicker Street Green
Suff 107 C9
Wickford Essex 88 G3
Wickham Hants 33 E9
W Berks 63 E11
Wickham Bishops Essex 88 C4
Wickhambreaux Kent 55 B8
Wickhambrook Suff 124 G4
Wickhamford Worcs 99 C11
Wickham Green Suff 125 D11
W Berks 63 E11
Wickham Heath W Berks 64 F2
Wickham Market Suff 126 F6
Wickhampton Norf 143 B8
Wickham St Paul Essex 106 D6
Wickham's Cross Som 44 G4
Wickham Skeith Suff 125 D11
Wickham Street Suff 124 G5
Suff 125 D11
Wick Hill Brack 65 F10
Kent 53 E10
Wokingham 65 G9
Wickhurst Kent 52 D4
Wicklane Bath 45 B7
Wicklewood Norf 141 C11
Wickmere Norf 160 C3
Wickridge Street Glos 98 F6
Wick Rocks S Glos 61 E8
Wick St Lawrence
N Som 59 F11
Wickstreet E Sus 23 D8
Wick Street Glos 80 D5
Wickwar S Glos 61 B8
Widbrook Wilts 45 B10
Widcombe Bath 61 G9
Widdington Essex 105 E10
Widdrington Northumb 253 D7
Widdrington Station
Northumb 252 E6
Widecombe in the Moor
Devon 13 F10
Widegates Corn 6 D5
Widemarsh Hereford 97 C10
Widemouth Bay Corn 24 G2
Wideopen T&W 242 C6
Widewall Orkney 314 G4
Widewell Plym 7 C9
Widford Essex 87 D11
Herts 86 B6
Widgham Green Cambs 124 F3
Widham Wilts 62 B5
Widley Hants 33 F11
Widmer End Bucks 84 F5
Widmerpool Notts 154 D2
Widmoor Bucks 66 B2
Widmore London 68 F2
Widnes Halton 183 D8
Widworthy Devon 15 B10
Wierton Kent 53 D9
Wig Powys 130 F2
Wigan Gtr Man 194 F5
Wiganthorpe N Yorks 216 E3
Wigbeth Dorset 31 F8
Wigborough Som 28 D6
Wig Fach Bridgend 57 F10
Wiggaton Devon 15 C8
Wiggenhall St Germans
Norf 157 G11
Wiggenhall St Mary
Magdalen Norf 157 G11
Wiggenhall St Mary the
Virgin Norf 157 G11
Wiggenhall St Peter
Norf 158 G2
Wiggens Green Essex 106 C3
Wiggington Staffs 134 B4
Wigginstall Staffs 169 C9
Wigginton Herts 84 C6
Oxon 101 E7
Shrops 148 B6
Staffs 134 B4
York 207 B7
Wigginton Bottom Herts 84 D6
Wigginton Heath Oxon 101 D7
Wigglesworth N Yorks 204 B2
Wiggonby Cumb 239 G7
Wiggonholt W Sus 35 D9
Wighill N Yorks 206 D5
Wighton Norf 159 B8
Wightwick Manor Staffs 133 D7
Wigley Derbys 186 G4
Hants 32 D4
Wigmarsh Shrops 149 D7
Wigmore Hereford 115 D8
Medway 69 G10
Wigsley Notts 188 G5
Wigsthorpe N Nhants 137 G10
Wigston Leics 136 D2
Wigston Magna Leics 136 D2
Wigston Parva Leics 135 F9
Wigthorpe Notts 187 E9
Wigtoft Lincs 156 B5
Wigton Cumb 229 B11
Wigtown Dumfries 236 D6
Wigtwizzle S Yorks 186 B2
Wike W Yorks 206 E2
Wike Well End S Yorks 199 E7
Wilbarston N Nhants 136 F6
Wilberfoss E Yorks 207 C10
Wilberlee W Yorks 196 E5
Wilburton Cambs 123 C9
Wilby N Nhants 121 D7
Norf 141 F10
Suff 126 C4
Wilcot Wilts 62 G6
Wilcott Shrops 149 F7
Wilcott Marsh Shrops 149 F7
Wilcove Corn 7 D8
Wilcrick Newport 60 B2
Wilday Green Derbys 186 G4
Wildboarclough Ches E 169 B7
Wilden Bedford 121 F11
Worcs 116 C6
Wildern Hants 33 E7
Wildernesse Kent 52 B4
Wilderspool Warr 183 D10
Wilderswood Gtr Man 194 E6
Wilde Street Suff 124 B4
Wildhern Hants 47 C11
Wildhill Herts 86 D3
Wildmanbridge
S Lanark 268 E6
Wild Mill Bridgend 58 C2
Wildmoor Hants 49 B7
Oxon 83 F7
Worcs 117 B9
Wildridings Brack 65 F11
Wildsworth Lincs 188 B4
Wildwood Staffs 151 E8
Wilford Nottingham 153 B11
Wilgate Green Kent 54 B3
Wilkesley Ches E 167 G10
Wilkhaven Highld 311 L3
Wilkieston W Loth 270 B2
Wilkinthroop Som 29 C11
Wilkin Throop Som 29 C11
Wilksby Lincs 174 C3
Willacy Lane End Lancs 202 F5
Willand Devon 27 E8
Som 27 E11
Willand Moor Devon 27 E8
Willard's Hill E Sus 38 C2
Willaston Ches E 167 E11
Ches W 182 F4
Shrops 149 B11
Willen M Keynes 103 C7
Willenhall W Mid 119 B7
W Mid 133 D9
Willerby E Yorks 208 G6
N Yorks 217 D10
Willersey Glos 100 D2
Willersley Hereford 96 B6
Willesborough Kent 54 E4
Willesborough Lees
Kent 54 E4
Willesden London 67 C8
Willesden Green London 67 C8
Willesley Leics 152 G6
Wilts 61 B11
Willett Som 42 G6
Willey Shrops 132 D3
Warks 135 G9
Willey Green Sur 50 C2
Willhayne Som 28 E4
Williamhope Borders 261 C10
Williamscott Oxon 101 B9
William's Green Suff 107 C9
Williamslee Borders 270 G6
Williamstown Rhondda 77 G8
Williamthorpe Derbys 170 B6
Willian Herts 104 E4
Willicote Pastures
Worcs 100 B3
Willingale Essex 87 D9
Willingcott Devon 40 E3
Willingdon E Sus 23 E9
Willingham Cambs 123 C8
Suff 143 G8
Willingham by Stow
Lincs 188 E5
Willingham Green
Cambs 124 G2
Willington Bedford 104 B2
Derbys 152 D5
Durham 233 D9
Kent 53 C9
T&W 243 D8
Warks 100 D5
Willington Corner
Ches W 167 B8
Willington Quay T&W 243 D8
Willisham Suff 125 G11
Willisham Tye Suff 125 G11
Willitoft E Yorks 207 F10
Williton Som 42 E5
Willoughbridge Staffs 168 G3
Willoughby Lincs 191 G7
Warks 119 D10
Willoughby Hills Lincs 174 F4
Willoughby-on-the-Wolds
Notts 154 D2
Willoughby Waterleys
Leics 135 E11
Willoughton Lincs 188 C6
Willowbank Bucks 66 B5
Willow Green Ches W 183 F10
Worcs 116 F5
Willow Holme Cumb 239 F9
Willows Gtr Man 195 F8
Willows Green Essex 88 B2
Willowtown Bl Gwent 77 C11
Will Row Lincs 191 D7
Willsbridge S Glos 61 E7
Willslock Staffs 151 C11
Willstone Shrops 131 D9
Willsworthy Devon 12 E6
Wilmcote Warks 118 F3
Wilmington Bath 61 G7
Devon 15 B10
E Sus 23 E8
Kent 68 E4
Wilmington Green E Sus 23 D8
Wilminstone Devon 12 F5
Wilmslow Ches E 184 E4
Wilmslow Park Ches E 184 E5
Wilnecote Staffs 134 C4
Wilney Green Norf 141 G11
Wilpshire Lancs 203 G9
Wilsden W Yorks 205 F7
Wilsden Hill W Yorks 205 F7
Wilsford Lincs 173 G8
Wilts 46 B6
Wilts 46 F6
Wilsham Devon 41 D9
Wilshaw W Yorks 196 F6
Wilsic S Yorks 187 B9
Wilsill N Yorks 214 G3
Wilsley Green Kent 53 F9
Wilsley Pound Kent 53 F9
Wilson Hants 49 F8
Wilson Hereford 97 G11
Leics 153 E8
Wilsontown S Lanark 269 D9
Wilstead Bedford 103 C11
Wilsthorpe Derbys 153 C9
Lincs 155 G11
Wilstone Herts 84 C6
Wilstone Green Herts 84 C6
Wilthorpe S Yorks 197 F10
Wilton Borders 261 G11
Cumb 219 C10
Hereford 97 G11
N Yorks 217 C7
Redcar 225 B11
Som 28 C2
Wilts 46 G5
Wilts 63 G9
Wilton Park Bucks 85 G7
Wiltown Devon 27 D11
Som 28 C5
Wimbish Essex 105 D11
Wimbish Green Essex 106 D2
Wimblebury Staffs 151 G10
Wimbledon London 67 E8
Wimble Hill Hants 49 D10
Wimblington Cambs 139 E8
Wimboldsley Ches W 167 C11
Wimbolds Trafford
Ches W 182 G6
Wimborne Minster
Dorset 18 B6
Wimborne St Giles
Dorset 31 E8
Wimbotsham Norf 140 B2
Wimpole Cambs 104 B6
Wimpson Soton 32 E5
Wimpstone Warks 100 B4
Wincanton Som 30 B2
Winceby Lincs 174 B4
Wincham Ches W 183 F11
Winchburgh W Loth 279 G11
Winchcombe Glos 99 F10
Winchelsea E Sus 38 D6
Winchelsea Beach E Sus 38 D6
Winchester Hants 33 B7
Winchestown Bl Gwent 77 C11
Winchet Hill Kent 53 E8
Winchfield Hants 49 C9
Winchfield Hurst Hants 49 C9
Winchmore Hill Bucks 84 G6
London 86 G4
Wincle Ches E 169 B7
Wincobank S Yorks 186 C5
Winder Cumb 219 B10
Windermere Cumb 221 F8
Winderton Warks 100 C6
Windhill Highld 300 E5
S Yorks 198 G3
W Yorks 205 F9
Wind Hill Cumb 210 E5
Pembs 73 F9
Windhouse Shetland 312 D6
Winding Wood W Berks 63 E11
Windle Hill Ches W 182 F4
Windlehurst Gtr Man 185 D7
Windlesham Sur 66 G2
Windley Derbys 170 F4
Windmill Corn 10 G3
Flint 181 G11
Flint 182 G2
Windmill Hill Bristol 60 E5
E Sus 23 C10
Halton 183 E9
Kent 69 F10
Som 28 D4
Worcs 99 B8
W Yorks 197 D11
Windrush Glos 81 C11
Windsor N Lincs 199 E9
Windsor 66 D3
Windsoredge Glos 80 E4
Windsor Green Suff 125 G7
Windwhistle Som 28 F5
Windy Arbor Mers 183 D7
Windy Arbour Warks 118 C5
Windydoors Borders 261 B10
Windygates Fife 287 G7
Windyharbour Ches E 184 G4
Windy Hill Wrex 166 E4
Windyknowe W Loth 269 B9
Windy Nook T&W 243 E7
Windywalls Borders 263 C7
Windy-Yett E Ayrs 267 E9
Wineham W Sus 36 C2
Winestead E Yorks 201 C9
Winewall Lancs 204 E4
Winfarthing Norf 142 F2
Winford IoW 21 E7
N Som 60 F4
Winforton Hereford 96 B5
Winfrith Newburgh
Dorset 18 E2
Wing Bucks 103 G7
Rutland 137 C7
Wingate Durham 234 D4
Wingates Gtr Man 195 F7
Northumb 252 D4
Wingerworth Derbys 170 B5
Wingfield C Beds 103 F10
Suff 126 B4
S Yorks 186 B6
Wilts 45 B10
Wingfield Green Suff 126 B4
Wingfield Park Derbys 170 E5
Wingham Kent 55 B8
Wingham Green Kent 55 B8
Wingham Well Kent 55 B8
Wingmore Kent 55 D7
Wingrave Bucks 84 B5
Winkburn Notts 172 D2
Winkfield Brack 66 E2
Winkfield Place Brack 66 E2
Winkfield Row Brack 65 E11
Winkhill Staffs 169 E9
Winkhurst Green Kent 52 D3
Winklebury Hants 48 C6
Winkleigh Devon 25 F10
Winksley N Yorks 214 E5
Winkton BCP 19 B9
Winlaton T&W 242 E5
Winlaton Mill T&W 242 E5
Winless Highld 310 D7
Winllan Powys 148 E4
Winmarleigh Lancs 202 D5
Winmarleigh Moss
Lancs 202 D4
Winnal Hereford 97 E9
Winnal Common Hereford 97 E9
Winnall Hants 33 B7
Worcs 116 D6
Winnard's Perch Corn 5 B8
Winnersh Wokingham 65 E9
Winnington Ches W 183 G10
Staffs 150 B4
Winnington Green
Shrops 148 G6
Winnothdale Staffs 169 G8
Winscales Cumb 228 F6
Winscombe N Som 44 B2
Winsdon Hill Luton 103 G11
Winsford Ches W 167 B10
Som 42 G2
Winsham Devon 40 F3
Som 28 F5
Winshill Staffs 152 E5
Winsh-wen Swansea 57 B7
Winsick Derbys 170 B6
Winskill Cumb 231 D7
Winslade Devon 24 D5
Hants 49 D7
Winsley N Yorks 214 G4
Wilts 61 G10
Winslow Bucks 102 F5
Winslow Mill Hereford 98 D2
Winson Glos 81 D9
Winson Green W Mid 133 F10
Winsor Hants 32 E4
Winstanley Gtr Man 194 G5
Winstanleys Gtr Man 194 F5
Winster Cumb 221 G8
Derbys 170 C2
Winston Durham 224 B2
Suff 126 E3
Winstone Glos 81 D7
Winston Green Suff 126 E3
Winswell Devon 25 E7
Winterborne Bassett
Wilts 62 E6
Winterborne Came
Dorset 17 D10

Winterborne Clenston
Dorset 30 G4
Winterborne Herringston
Dorset 17 D9
Winterborne Houghton
Dorset 30 G4
Winterborne Kingston
Dorset 18 B3
Winterborne Monkton
Wilts 62 E6
Winterborne Muston
Dorset 18 B3
Winterborne Stickland
Dorset 30 G4
Winterborne Tomson
Dorset 18 B3
Winterborne Whitechurch
Dorset 30 G4
Winterborne Zelston
Dorset 18 B3
Winterbourne Kent 54 B5
S Glos 60 C6
W Berks 64 E3
Winterbourne Abbas
Dorset 17 C8
Winterbourne Bassett
Wilts 62 E6
Winterbourne Dauntsey
Wilts 47 G7
Winterbourne Down
S Glos 61 D7
Winterbourne Earls Wilts 47 G7
Winterbourne Gunner
Wilts 47 F7
Winterbourne Monkton
Dorset 17 D9
Winterbourne Steepleton
Dorset 17 D8
Winterbourne Stoke
Wilts 46 E5
Winterbrook Oxon 64 B6
Winterburn N Yorks 204 B4
Winterfield Bath 45 B7
Winter Gardens Essex 69 C9
Winterhay Green Som 28 D5
Winterhead N Som 44 B2
Winteringham N Lincs 200 C2
Winterley Ches E 168 D2
Wintersett W Yorks 197 D11
Wintershill Hants 33 D8
Winterton N Lincs 200 D2
Winterton-on-Sea Norf 161 F9
Winter Well Som 28 C3
Winthorpe Lincs 175 B9
Notts 172 D4
Winton BCP 19 C7
Cumb 222 C5
E Sus 23 E8
Gtr Man 184 B3
N Yorks 225 F8
Wintringham N Yorks 217 E7
Winwick Cambs 138 G2
Warr 183 C10
W Nhants 120 C2
Winwick Quay Warr 183 C10
Winyard's Gap Dorset 29 F7
Winyates Worcs 117 D11
Winyates Green Worcs 117 D11
Wirksworth Derbys 170 E3
Wirksworth Moor
Derbys 170 E4
Wirswall Ches E 167 G8
Wisbech Cambs 139 B9
Wisbech St Mary Cambs 139 B8
Wisborough Green
W Sus 35 B8
Wiseton Notts 188 D2
Wishanger Glos 80 D6
Wishaw N Lanark 268 D5
Warks 134 E3
Wisley Sur 50 B5
Wispington Lincs 190 G2
Wissenden Kent 54 E2
Wissett Suff 127 B7
Wistanstow Shrops 131 F8
Wistanswick Shrops 150 D3
Wistaston Ches E 167 E11
Wistaston Green
Ches E 167 E11
Wiston Pembs 73 B8
S Lanark 259 C11
W Sus 35 E10
Wiston Mains S Lanark 259 C11
Wistow Cambs 138 G5
Leics 136 D2
N Yorks 207 F7
Wiswell Lancs 203 F10
Witcham Cambs 139 G9
Witchampton Dorset 31 F7
Witchford Cambs 123 B10
Witcombe Som 29 C7
Withacott Devon 24 D6
Witham Essex 88 C4
Witham Friary Som 45 E8
Witham on the Hill
Lincs 155 F11
Witham St Hughs Lincs 172 C5
Withcall Lincs 190 E3
Withdean Brighton 36 F4
Witherenden Hill E Sus 37 B10
Withergate Norf 160 D5
Witheridge Devon 26 E4
Witheridge Hill Oxon 65 C7
Witherley Leics 134 D6
Withermarsh Green
Suff 107 D10
Withern Lincs 190 E6
Withernsea E Yorks 201 B10
Withernwick E Yorks 209 E9
Withersdale Street Suff 142 G5
Withersdane Kent 54 D5
Withersfield Suff 106 B3
Witherslack Cumb 211 C8
Witherwack T&W 243 F9
Withial Som 44 F5
Withiel Corn 5 B9
Withiel Florey Som 42 G3
Withielgoose Corn 5 B10
Withielgoose Mills Corn 5 B10
Withington Glos 81 B8
Gtr Man 184 C5
Hereford 97 C11
Shrops 149 G11
Staffs 151 B10
Withington Green
Ches E 184 G4
Withington Marsh
Hereford 97 C11
Withleigh Devon 26 E6
Withnell Lancs 194 C6
Withnell Fold Lancs 194 C6
Withybed Green Worcs 117 C10
Withybrook Som 45 D7
Warks 135 G8
Withybush Pembs 73 B7
Withycombe Som 41 F11
Som 42 E4
Withycombe Raleigh
Devon 14 E6
Withyditch Bath 45 B8
Withyham E Sus 52 F3
Withy Mills Bath 45 B7
Withymoor Village
W Mid 133 F8
Withypool Som 41 F10
Withystakes Staffs 169 F7
Withywood Bristol 60 F5
Witley Sur 50 F2
Witnells End Worcs 132 G5
Witnesham Suff 126 G3
Witney Oxon 82 C5
Wittensford Hants 32 E3
Wittering Pboro 137 C11
Wittersham Kent 38 B5
Witton Angus 293 F7
Norf 142 B6
W Mid 133 E11
Worcs 117 E7
Witton Bridge Norf 160 C6
Witton Gilbert Durham 233 B10
Witton Hill Worcs 116 E5
Witton-le-Wear Durham 233 E8
Witton Park Durham 233 E9
Wiveliscombe Som 27 B9
Wivelrod Hants 49 F7
Wivelsfield E Sus 36 C4
Wivelsfield Green E Sus 36 C5
Wivenhoe Essex 107 G10
Wivenhoe Cross Essex 107 G10
Wiveton Norf 177 E8
Wix Essex 108 F3
Wixams Bedford 103 C10
Wixford Warks 117 G11
Wixhill Shrops 149 D11
Wixoe Suff 106 C4
Woburn C Beds 103 E8
Woburn Sands
M Keynes 103 D8
Wofferwood Common
Hereford 116 G3
Wokefield Park W Berks 65 F7
Woking Sur 50 B4
Wokingham Wokingham 65 F10
Wolborough Devon 14 G3
Woldhurst W Sus 22 C5
Woldingham Sur 51 B11
Woldingham Garden Village
Sur 51 B11
Wold Newton E Yorks 217 E10
NE Lincs 190 B2
Wolfclyde S Lanark 260 B2
Wolferd Green Norf 142 D5
Wolferlow Hereford 116 E3
Wolferton Norf 158 D3
Wolfhampcote Warks 119 D10
Wolfhill Perth 286 D5
Wolf's Castle Pembs 91 F9
Wolfsdale Pembs 91 G8
Wolfsdale Hill Pembs 91 G8
Woll Borders 261 E11
Wollaston N Nhants 121 E8
Shrops 148 G6
W Mid 133 G7
Wollaton Nottingham 153 B10
Wollerton Shrops 150 C2
Wollerton Wood Shrops 150 C2
Wollescote W Mid 133 G8
Wollrig Borders 261 E11
Wolsingham Durham 233 D7
Wolstanton Staffs 168 F5
Wolstenholme
Gtr Man 195 D11
Wolston Warks 119 B8
Wolsty Cumb 238 G4
Wolterton Norf 160 C3
Wolvercote Oxon 83 D7
Wolverham Ches W 182 F6
Wolverhampton W Mid 133 D8
Wolverley Shrops 149 C9
Worcs 116 B6
Wolverstone Devon 27 G10
Wolverton Hants 48 B5
Kent 55 E9
M Keynes 102 C6
Shrops 131 F9
Warks 118 E4
Wilts 45 G9
Wolverton Common
Hants 48 B5
Wolvesnewton Mon 79 F7
Wolvey Warks 135 F8
Wolvey Heath Warks 135 F8
Wolviston Stockton 234 F5
Womaston Powys 114 E5
Wombleton N Yorks 216 C3
Wombourne Staffs 133 E7
Wombridge Telford 150 G3
Wombwell S Yorks 197 G11
Womenswold Kent 55 C8
Womersley N Yorks 198 D4
Wonastow Mon 79 C7
Wonderstone N Som 43 B10
Wonersh Sur 50 D4
Wonford Devon 14 C4
Wonson Devon 13 D9
Wonston Dorset 30 F2
Hants 48 F3
Wooburn Bucks 66 B2
Wooburn Green Bucks 66 B2
Wood Pembs 91 G7
Som 28 D4
Woodacott Devon 24 F5
Woodacott Cross Devon 24 F5
Woodale N Yorks 213 D10
Woodbank Argyll 255 F7
Ches W 182 G5
Shrops 131 F11
Woodbastwick Norf 160 F6
Woodbeck Notts 188 F3
Wood Bevington
Warks 117 G11
Woodborough Notts 171 F10
Wilts 46 B6
Woodbridge Dorset 30 D5
Dorset 30 E2
Glos 81 C8
Northumb 253 F7
Suff 108 B5
Woodbridge Hill Sur 50 C3
Woodbridge Walk Suff 109 B7
Wood Burcote
W Nhants 102 B3
Woodburn Common
Bucks 66 B2
Woodburn Moor Bucks 84 G6
Woodbury Devon 14 D6
Woodbury Salterton
Devon 14 D6
Woodchester Glos 80 E4
Woodchurch Kent 54 G2
Mers 182 D3
Woodcock Wilts 45 E11
Woodcock Heath
Staffs 151 D11
Woodcock Hill Herts 85 G9
W Mid 133 G10
Woodcombe Som 42 D3
Woodcot Hants 33 G9
Woodcote London 67 G10
Oxon 64 C6
Sur 51 B8
Telford 150 F5
Woodcote Green London 67 G9
Worcs 117 C8
Woodcott Hants 48 C2
Woodcroft Glos 79 F8
Woodcutts Dorset 31 D7
Wood Dalling Norf 159 D11
Woodditton Cambs 124 F3
Woodeaton Oxon 83 C8
Wood Eaton Staffs 150 F6
Wooden Pembs 73 D10
Woodend Ches E 185 D7
Cumb 219 C10
Cumb 220 F3
Cumb 229 F10
Cumb 229 G7
Essex 87 C9
Fife 280 B4
Notts 171 C7
Staffs 152 D3
W Loth 279 F11
W Nhants 102 B2
W Sus 22 B4
Wood End Bedford 103 B10
Bedford 121 D11
Bedford 121 F11
Bucks 102 E5
C Beds 103 C9
Gtr Man 196 F2
Hereford 98 C2
Herts 104 F6
Warks 118 C2
Warks 134 D4
Warks 134 F5
Windsor 66 E2
W Mid 133 C8
W Mid 135 G7
Wood Enderby Lincs 174 C3
Woodend Green Essex 105 F11
W Nhants 102 B2
Wood End Green London 66 C5
Woodend Ho Argyll 275 G11
Woodfalls Wilts 31 C11
Woodfield Glos 80 F2
Oxon 101 G11
S Ayrs 257 E8
Wood Field Sur 51 B7
Woodford Corn 24 E2
Devon 8 E5
Glos 79 F11
Gtr Man 184 E5
London 86 G6
N Nhants 121 B9
Plym 7 D10
Som 42 F5
Som 44 E4
Woodford Bridge London 86 G6
Woodford Green London 86 G6
Woodford Halse
W Nhants 119 G10
Woodford Wells London 86 G6
Woodgate Devon 27 D10
Norf 159 F10
W Mid 133 G9
Worcs 117 D9
W Sus 22 C6
Wood Gate Staffs 152 D3
Woodgate Hill Gtr Man 195 E10
Woodgates End Essex 105 F11
Woodgates Green
Worcs 116 C2
Woodgate Valley
W Mid 133 G10
Woodgreen Hants 31 D11
Oxon 82 C5
Wood Green Essex 86 E6
London 86 G4
Norf 142 E4
W Mid 133 D9
Worcs 116 D6
Woodhall Herts 86 C2
Invclyd 276 G6
N Yorks 207 G9
N Yorks 223 G9
Wood Hall Essex 105 E9
Woodhall Hills
W Yorks 205 F10
Woodhall Spa Lincs 173 C11
Woodham Bucks 84 B2
Durham 233 F11
Sur 66 G4
Woodham Ferrers Essex 88 F3
Woodham Mortimer
Essex 88 E4
Woodham Walter Essex 88 D4
Woodhatch Sur 51 D9
Woodhaven Fife 287 E8
Wood Hayes W Mid 133 C8
Woodhead Aberds 303 F7
Woodheads Borders 271 F10
Woodhey Gtr Man 195 D9
Mers 182 D4
Woodhey Green Ches E 167 E9
Woodhill Essex 88 E3
N Som 60 D3
Shrops 132 G4
Som 28 B5
Woodhorn Northumb 253 F7
Woodhouse Cumb 211 C10
Cumb 219 B9
Hants 47 D11
Leics 153 F10
N Lincs 199 F9
S Yorks 186 D6
W Yorks 196 C6
W Yorks 197 C11
W Yorks 205 E7
W Yorks 205 F11
Wood House Lancs 203 C10
Woodhouse Down S Glos 60 B6
Woodhouse Eaves
Leics 153 G10
Woodhouse Green
Staffs 168 C6
Woodhouselee Midloth 270 C4
Woodhouselees
Dumfries 239 C9
Woodhouse Mill
S Yorks 186 D6
Woodhouse Park
Gtr Man 184 D4
Woodhouses Ches W 183 F8
Cumb 239 G8
Gtr Man 184 C3
Gtr Man 196 G2
Staffs 133 B11
Staffs 152 F3
Woodhurst Cambs 122 B6
Woodingdean Brighton 36 F5
Woodington Hants 32 C4
Woodkirk W Yorks 197 C9
Woodlake Dorset 18 C3
Woodland Cumb 210 B4
Devon 8 B5
Devon 8 D2
Durham 233 F7
Kent 54 E6
Woodland Head Devon 13 B11
Woodlands Aberdeen 293 B10
Aberds 293 D9
Aberds 303 G8
Dorset 31 F9
Dumfries 238 B3
Gtr Man 185 B7
Hants 32 E4
Highld 300 C5
Kent 68 G5
London 67 D7
N Yorks 206 C2
Som 43 E7
Som 44 F4
S Yorks 198 F4
Wokingham 65 C9
W Yorks 196 B5
Woodlands Common
Dorset 31 F9
Woodlands Park
Windsor 65 D11
Woodlands St Mary
W Berks 63 E10
Woodlane Shrops 150 D3
Staffs 152 E2
Wood Lane Shrops 149 C8
Staffs 168 E4
Wood Lanes Ches E 184 E6
Woodleigh Devon 8 F4
Woodlesford W Yorks 197 B11
Woodley Gtr Man 184 C6
Hants 32 C5
Wokingham 65 E9
Woodley Green
Wokingham 65 E9
Woodleys Oxon 82 B6
Woodlinkin Derbys 170 F6
Woodloes Park Warks 118 D5
Woodmancote Glos 80 F3
Glos 81 D8
Glos 99 F9
Worcs 99 C8
W Sus 22 B3
W Sus 36 E2
Woodmancott Hants 48 E5
Woodmansey E Yorks 209 F7
Woodmansgreen W Sus 34 B5
Woodmans Green E Sus 38 D3
Woodmansterne Sur 51 B9
Woodmill Staffs 152 E2
Woodminton Wilts 31 C8
Woodnesborough Kent 55 B10
Woodnewton N Nhants 137 E10
Woodnook Lancs 195 B9
Lincs 155 C8
Wood Norton Norf 159 D10
Worcs 99 B10
Woodplumpton Lancs 202 G6
Woodram Som 28 D2
Woodrising Norf 141 C9
Wood Road Gtr Man 195 E9
Woodrow Bucks 84 F6
Cumb 229 B10
Dorset 30 E3
Dorset 30 F2
Worcs 117 B7
Worcs 117 D11
Wood Row W Yorks 197 B11
Woods Hereford 96 B5
Woods Bank W Mid 133 D9
Wood's Corner E Sus 23 B11
Woodsden Kent 53 G9
Woodseats Derbys 185 C7
Wood Seats S Yorks 186 B4
Woodseaves Shrops 150 C3
Staffs 150 D5
Woodsend Pembs 72 C5
Wilts 63 D8
Woods End Gtr Man 184 B2
Woodsetton W Mid 133 E8
Woodsetts S Yorks 187 E9
Woodsfield Worcs 98 B6
Woodsfold Lancs 202 F5
Woodsford Dorset 17 C11
Wood's Green E Sus 52 G6
Woodside Aberdeen 293 C11
Aberds 303 E10
Bedford 121 G11
Brack 66 E2
C Beds 85 B9
Ches E 167 C10
Ches W 183 G8
Derbys 170 G5
Derbys 187 G7
Dumfries 238 B2
Durham 233 F9
Essex 87 E7
Fife 287 G8
Hants 20 C2
Herts 85 E10
Herts 86 D3
IoW 20 C6
London 67 F10
N Lincs 199 G8
Perth 286 D6
Shrops 130 G6
Telford 132 C3
W Mid 133 F8
W Yorks 196 B6
Woodside Green Essex 87 B8
Kent 54 C2
Woodside of Arbeadie
Aberds 293 D9
Woodside Park London 86 G3
Woods Moor Gtr Man 184 D6
Woodspeen W Berks 64 F2
Woodspring Priory
N Som 59 F10
Wood Stanway Glos 99 E11
Woodstock Kent 70 G2
Oxon 82 B6
Pembs 91 F10
Woodston Pboro 138 D3
Wood Street Norf 161 E7
Sur 50 C3
Wood Street Village Sur 50 C3
Woodthorpe Derbys 187 G7
Leics 153 F10
Lincs 190 E6
Notts 171 G9
York 207 D7
Woodton Norf 142 E5
Woodtown Devon 24 C6
Devon 25 B7
Woodvale Mers 193 E10
Woodville Derbys 152 F6
Dorset 30 C4
Woodville Feus Angus 287 C10
Woodwall Green Staffs 150 C5
Wood Walton Cambs 138 G4
Woodway Oxon 64 C4
Woodway Park W Mid 135 G7
Woodwell N Nhants 121 B9
Woodwick Orkney 314 D3
Woodworth Green
Ches E 167 D9
Woodyates Dorset 31 D8
Woody Bay Devon 41 D7
Woofferton Shrops 115 D10
Wookey Som 44 D4
Wookey Hole Som 44 D4
Wool Dorset 18 D2
Woolacombe Devon 40 E3
Woolage Green Kent 55 D8
Woolage Village Kent 55 C8
Woolaston Glos 79 F9
Woolaston Common Glos 79 E9
Woolaston Slade Glos 79 E9
Woolaston Woodside
Glos 79 E9
Woolavington Som 43 E10
Woolbeding W Sus 34 C5
Wooldale W Yorks 197 F7
Wooler Northumb 263 D11
Woolfall Heath Mers 182 C6
Woolfardisworthy Devon 26 F4
Woolfardisworthy or
Woolsery Devon 24 C4
Woolfold Gtr Man 195 E9
Woolfords Cottages
S Lanark 269 D10
Woolford's Water Dorset 29 F11
Woolgarston Dorset 18 E5
Woolgreaves W Yorks 197 D10
Woolhampton W Berks 64 F5
Woolhope Hereford 98 D2
Woolhope Cockshoot
Hereford 98 D2
Woolland Dorset 30 F3
Woollard Bath 60 G6
Woollaston Staffs 151 F7
Woollaton Devon 25 E7
Woollensbrook Herts 86 C5
Woolley Bath 61 F8
Cambs 122 C3
Corn 24 D3
Derbys 170 C5
Wilts 61 G10
W Yorks 197 E10
Woolley Bridge Gtr Man 185 B8
Woolley Green Wilts 61 G10
Windsor 65 C11
Woolmere Green Worcs 117 E9
Woolmer Green Herts 86 B3
Woolmer Hill Sur 49 G11
Woolmersdon Som 43 G9
Woolminstone Som 28 F6
Woolpack Corner Kent 53 F11
Woolpit Suff 125 E9
Woolpit Green Suff 125 E9
Woolpit Heath Suff 125 E9
Woolridge Glos 98 G6
Woolsbridge Dorset 31 F9
Woolscott Warks 119 D9
Woolsery or
Woolfardisworthy
Devon 24 C4
Woolsgrove Devon 26 G3
Woolsington T&W 242 D5
Woolstanwood Ches E 167 D11
Woolstaston Shrops 131 D9
Woolsthorpe Lincs 155 E8
Woolsthorpe by Belvoir
Lincs 154 C6
Woolsthorpe-by-
Colsterworth Lincs 155 E8
Woolston Corn 6 B5
Devon 8 G4
Shrops 131 F8
Shrops 148 E6
Som 29 B10
Som 42 F5
Soton 32 E6
Warr 183 D10
Woolstone Glos 99 E9
M Keynes 103 D7
Oxon 63 B9
Woolston Green Devon 8 B5
Woolton Mers 182 D6
Woolton Hill Hants 64 G2
Woolvers Hill N Som 59 G11
Woolverstone Suff 108 D3
Woolverton Som 45 C9
Woolwell Devon 7 C10
Woolwich London 68 D2
Woolwich Ferry London 68 D2
Woon Corn 5 D10
Woonton Hereford 115 E10
Hereford 115 G7
Wooperton Northumb 264 E2
Wooplaw Borders 271 G9
Woore Shrops 168 G2
Wooton Shrops 115 C11
Shrops 132 F5
Wootten Green Suff 126 C4
Wootton Bedford 103 B10
Hants 19 B10
Hereford 97 D11
Hereford 114 G6
IoW 20 C6
Kent 55 D8
N Lincs 200 D5
Oxon 82 B6
Oxon 83 E7
Shrops 115 B9
Shrops 148 D6
Staffs 150 D6
Staffs 169 F10
W Nhants 120 F5
Wootton Bourne End
Bedford 103 B9
Wootton Bridge IoW 20 C6
Wootton Broadmead
Bedford 103 C10
Wootton Common IoW 20 C6
Wootton Courtenay Som 42 E2
Wootton Fitzpaine Dorset 16 B3
Wootton Green C Beds 103 C9
W Mid 118 B4
Wootton Rivers Wilts 63 G7
Woottons Staffs 151 B11
Wootton St Lawrence
Hants 48 C5
Wootton Wawen Warks 118 E3
Worbarrow Dorset 18 F3
Worcester Worcs 117 F7
Worcester Park London 67 F8
Wordsley W Mid 133 F7
Wordwell Suff 124 C6
Worfield Shrops 132 D5
Worgret Dorset 18 D4
Work Orkney 314 E4
Workhouse Common
Norf 161 E7
Workhouse End Bedford 122 G2
Workhouse Green Suff 107 D8
Workhouse Hill Essex 107 E9
Workington Cumb 228 F5
Worksop Notts 187 F9
Worlaby Lincs 190 F4
N Lincs 200 E4
Worlds End Hants 33 E10
W Mid 134 G2
World's End Bucks 84 D5
London 86 F4
Suff 125 F9
W Sus 36 D4
Worle N Som 59 G11
Worlebury N Som 59 G10
Worleston Ches E 167 D11
Worley Glos 80 F4
Worlingham Suff 143 F8
Worlington Devon 40 G3
Suff 124 C3
Worlingworth Suff 126 D4
Wormadale Shetland 313 J5
Wormald Green
N Yorks 214 G6
Wormbridge Hereford 97 E8
Wormbridge Common
Hereford 97 E8
Wormegay Norf 158 G3
Wormelow Tump
Hereford 97 E9
Wormhill Derbys 185 G10
Wormingford Essex 107 E8
Worminghall Bucks 83 D10
Wormington Glos 99 D10
Worminster Som 44 E5
Wormiston Ho Fife 287 G10
Wormit Fife 287 E7
Wormleighton Warks 119 G8
Wormley Herts 86 D5
Sur 50 F2
Wormleybury Herts 86 D5
Wormley West End Herts 86 D4
Worms Ash Worcs 117 C8
Wormshill Kent 53 B11
Worms Hill Kent 53 F8
Wormsley Hereford 97 B8
Wornish Nook Ches E 168 B4
Worplesdon Sur 50 C3
Worrall S Yorks 186 C4
Worrall Hill Glos 79 C10
Worsbrough S Yorks 197 G11
Worsbrough Bridge
S Yorks 197 G11
Worsbrough Common
S Yorks 197 F10
Worsbrough Dale
S Yorks 197 G11
Worsham Oxon 82 C3
Worsley Gtr Man 195 G8
Worsley Hall Gtr Man 194 F5
Worsley Mesnes
Gtr Man 194 G5
Worstead Norf 160 D6
Worsthorne Lancs 204 G3
Worston Devon 7 E11
Lancs 203 E11
Worswell Devon 7 F10
Worten Kent 54 E3
Worth Kent 55 B10
Som 44 D4
W Sus 51 F9
Wortham Suff 125 B11
Worth Abbey W Sus 51 G10
Worthen Shrops 130 C6
Worthenbury Wrex 166 F6
Worthing Norf 159 F9
W Sus 35 G10
Worthington Leics 153 E8
Worth Matravers Dorset 18 F5
Worthy Som 41 D11
Worthybrook Mon 79 C7
Worting Hants 48 C6
Wortley Glos 80 G3
S Yorks 186 B4
W Yorks 205 G11
Worton N Yorks 223 G9
Oxon 83 C7
Wilts 46 B3
Wortwell Norf 142 G5
Wotherton Shrops 130 C5
Wothorpe Pboro 137 B10
Wotter Devon 7 C11
Wotton Glos 80 B4
Sur 50 D6
Wotton-under-Edge
Glos 80 G3
Wotton Underwood
Bucks 83 B11
Woughton on the Green
M Keynes 103 D7
Woughton Park
M Keynes 103 D7
Wouldham Kent 69 G8
Woundale Shrops 132 E5
Wrabness Essex 108 E3
Wraes Aberds 302 F5
Wrafton Devon 40 F3
Wragby Lincs 189 F10
W Yorks 198 D2
Wragholme Lincs 190 B5
Wramplingham Norf 142 B2
Wrangaton Devon 8 D3
Wrangbrook W Yorks 198 E3
Wrangham Aberds 302 F6
Wrangle Lincs 174 E6
Wrangle Bank Lincs 174 E6
Wrangle Lowgate Lincs 174 E6
Wrangle Low Ground
Lincs 174 E6
Wrangway Som 27 D10
Wrantage Som 28 C4
Wrawby N Lincs 200 F4
Wraxall Dorset 29 G9
N Som 60 E3
Som 44 F6
Wray Lancs 212 F2
Wray Common Sur 51 C9
Wraysbury Windsor 66 E4
Wrayton Lancs 212 E2
Wrea Green Lancs 202 G3
Wreaks End Cumb 210 B4
Wreath Som 28 F4
Wreay Cumb 230 B4
Cumb 230 G4
Wrecclesham Sur 49 D10
Wrekenton T&W 243 F7
Wrelton N Yorks 216 B5
Wrenbury Ches E 167 F9
Wrenbury cum Frith
Ches E 167 F9
Wrench Green N Yorks 217 B9
Wreningham Norf 142 D3
Wrentham Suff 143 G9
Wrenthorpe W Yorks 197 C10
Wrentnall Shrops 131 C8
Wressle E Yorks 207 G10
N Lincs 200 F3
Wrestlingworth C Beds 104 B5
Wretham Norf 141 F8
Wretton Norf 140 D3
Wrexham Wrex 166 E4
Wreyland Devon 13 E11
Wribbenhall Worcs 116 B5
Wrickton Shrops 132 F2
Wrightington Bar Lancs 194 E4
Wright's Green Essex 87 B8
Wrinehill Staffs 168 F3
Wringsdown Corn 12 D2
Wrington N Som 60 G3
Wrinkleberry Devon 24 C4
Writhlington Bath 45 C8
Writtle Essex 87 D11
Wrockwardine Telford 150 G2
Wrockwardine Wood
Telford 150 G4
Wroot N Lincs 199 G8
Wrose W Yorks 205 F9
Wrotham Kent 52 B6
Wrotham Heath Kent 52 B6
Wroughton Swindon 62 C6
Wroxall IoW 21 F7
Warks 118 C4
Wroxeter Shrops 131 B11
Wroxhall Warks 118 C4
Wroxham Norf 160 F6
Wroxton Oxon 101 C8
Wyaston Derbys 169 G11
Wyatt's Green Essex 87 F9
Wybers Wood NE Lincs 201 F8
Wyberton Lincs 174 G4
Wyboston Bedford 122 F3
Wybunbury Ches E 168 F2
Wychbold Worcs 117 D8
Wych Cross E Sus 52 G2
Wychnor Staffs 152 F3
Wychnor Bridges Staffs 152 F3
Wyck Hants 49 F9
Wyck Rissington Glos 100 G3
Wycliffe Durham 224 C2
Wycoller Lancs 204 F4
Wycomb Leics 154 E5
Wycombe Marsh Bucks 84 G5
Wyddial Herts 105 E7
Wydra N Yorks 205 C10
Wye Kent 54 D5
Wyebanks Kent 54 C2
Wyegate Green Glos 79 D9
Wyesham Mon 79 C8
Wyfordby Leics 154 F5
Wyke Dorset 30 B3
Shrops 132 C2
Sur 50 C2
W Yorks 197 B7
Wyke Champflower Som 45 G7
Wykeham Lincs 156 D5
N Yorks 216 D6
N Yorks 217 C9
Wyken Shrops 132 E5
W Mid 135 G7
Wyke Regis Dorset 17 F9
Wykey Shrops 149 E7
Wykin Leics 135 D8
Wylam Northumb 242 E4
Wylde Hereford 115 D9
Wylde Green W Mid 134 E2
Wyllie Caerph 77 G11
Wylye Wilts 46 F4
Wymans Brook Glos 99 G8
Wymbush M Keynes 102 D6
Wymering Ptsmth 33 F10
Wymeswold Leics 154 E2
Wymington Bedford 121 E9
Wymondham Leics 155 F7
Norf 142 C2
Wymondley Bury Herts 104 F4
Wymott Lancs 194 C4
Wyndham Bridgend 76 G6
Wyndham Park V Glam 58 D5
Wynds Point Hereford 98 C5
Wynford Eagle Dorset 17 B7
Wyng Orkney 314 G3
Wynn's Green Hereford 98 B2
Wynyard Village
Stockton 234 F4
Wyre Piddle Worcs 99 B9
Wysall Notts 154 D2
Wyson Hereford 115 D10
Wythall Worcs 117 B11
Wytham Oxon 83 D7
Wythburn Cumb 220 C6
Wythenshawe Gtr Man 184 D4
Wythop Mill Cumb 229 F9
Wyton Cambs 122 C5
E Yorks 209 G9
Wyverstone Suff 125 D10
Wyverstone Green
Suff 125 D10
Wyverstone Street
Suff 125 D10
Wyville Lincs 155 D7
Wyvis Lodge Highld 300 B4

Y

Yaddlethorpe N Lincs 199 F11
Yafford IoW 20 E4
Yafforth N Yorks 224 G6
Yair Borders 261 C11
Yalberton Torbay 9 D7
Yalding Kent 53 C7
Yanley N Som 60 F5
Yanworth Glos 81 C9
Yapham E Yorks 207 C11
Yapton W Sus 35 G7
Yarberry N Som 43 B11
Yarborough NE Lincs 201 F9
Yarbridge IoW 21 D8
Yarburgh Lincs 190 C5
Yarcombe Devon 28 F2
Yard Som 42 F5
Yarde Som 42 F5
Yardhurst Kent 54 E3
Yardley W Mid 134 F2
Yardley Gobion
W Nhants 102 C5
Yardley Hastings
W Nhants 121 F7
Yardley Wood W Mid 118 B2
Yardro Powys 114 F4
Yarford Som 28 B2
Yarhampton Worcs 116 D5
Yarhampton Cross
Worcs 116 D5
Yarkhill Hereford 98 C2
Yarlet Staffs 151 D8
Yarley Som 44 D4
Yarlington Som 29 B11
Yarlside Cumb 210 F4
Yarm Stockton 225 C8
Yarmouth IoW 20 D3
Yarnacott Devon 40 G6
Yarnbrook Wilts 45 C11
Yarnfield Staffs 151 C7
Yarningale Common
Warks 118 D3
Yarnscombe Devon 25 C9
Yarnton Oxon 83 C7
Yarpole Hereford 115 E9
Yarrow Borders 261 D9
Northumb 250 F6
Som 43 D11
Yarrow Feus Borders 261 D8
Yarrowford Borders 261 C10
Yarsop Hereford 97 B8
Yarwell N Nhants 137 D11
Yate S Glos 61 C8
Yateley Hants 65 G10
Yate Rocks S Glos 61 C8
Yatesbury Wilts 62 E5
Yattendon W Berks 64 E5
Yatton Hereford 115 D8
N Som 60 F2
Yatton Keynell Wilts 61 D11
Yaverland IoW 21 D8
Yawthorpe Lincs 188 C5
Yaxham Norf 159 G10
Yaxley Cambs 138 E3
Suff 126 C2
Yazor Hereford 97 B8
Y Bala = *Bala* Gwyn 147 B8
Y Bont Faen = *Cowbridge*
V Glam 58 E3
Y Borth = *Borth* Ceredig 128 E2
Yeabridge Som 28 D6
Yeading London 66 C6
Yeadon W Yorks 205 E10
Yealand Conyers Lancs 211 E10
Yealand Redmayne
Lancs 211 D10
Yealand Storrs Lancs 211 D9
Yealmbridge Devon 7 E11
Yealmpton Devon 7 E11
Yearby Redcar 235 G8
Yearngill Cumb 229 C8
Yearsley N Yorks 215 E11
Yeaton Shrops 149 F8
Yeaveley Derbys 169 G11
Yedingham N Yorks 217 D7
Yelden Bedford 121 D10
Yeldersley Hollies
Derbys 170 G2
Yeldon Bedford 121 D10
Yelford Oxon 82 E5
Yelland Devon 40 G3
Yelling Cambs 122 E5
Yelsted Kent 69 G10
Yelvertoft W Nhants 119 B11
Yelverton Devon 7 B10
Norf 142 C5
Yenston Som 30 C2
Yeoford Devon 13 B11
Yeolmbridge Corn 12 D2
Yeo Mill Devon 26 B4
Yeo Vale Devon 24 C6
Yeovil Som 29 D9
Yeovil Marsh Som 29 D8
Yeovilton Som 29 C8
Yerbeston Pembs 73 D9
Yesnaby Orkney 314 E2
Yetlington Northumb 252 B2
Yetminster Dorset 29 E9
Yett N Lanark 268 D5
Yettington Devon 15 D7
Yetts o' Muckhart Clack 286 G4
Yew Green Warks 118 D4
Yewhedges Kent 54 B3
Yew Tree Gtr Man 185 B7
W Mid 133 D10
Yewtree Cross Kent 55 E7
Y Fali = *Valley* Anglesey 178 F3
Y Felinheli = *Port Dinorwic*
Gwyn 163 B8
Y Ferwig Ceredig 92 B3
Y Ffôr Gwyn 145 B7
Y-Ffrith Denb 181 E8
Y Gors Ceredig 112 B2
Y Gribyn Powys 129 E8
Yieldshields S Lanark 269 E7
Yiewsley London 66 C5
Yinstay Orkney 314 E5
Y Mwmbwls = *The Mumbles*
Swansea 56 D6
Ynus-tawelog Swansea 75 D10
Ynys Gwyn 145 B11
Ynysboeth Rhondda 77 F9
Ynysddu Caerph 77 G11
Ynysforgan Swansea 57 B7
Ynysgyffiog Gwyn 146 G2
Ynyshir Rhondda 77 G8
Ynys-isaf Powys 76 C3
Ynyslas Ceredig 128 E2
Ynysmaerdy Neath 57 B8
Rhondda 58 C4
Ynysmeudwy Neath 76 D2
Neath 76 D2
Ynys Tachwedd Ceredig 128 E2
Ynystawe Swansea 75 E11
Ynyswen Powys 76 C4
Rhondda 77 F7
Ynysybwl Rhondda 77 G9
Ynysygwas Neath 57 C9
Yockenthwaite N Yorks 213 D8
Yockleton Shrops 149 G7
Yodercott Devon 27 E9
Yokefleet E Yorks 199 C10
Yoker W Dunb 267 B10
Yonder Bognie Aberds 302 E5
Yondertown Devon 7 D11
Yopps Green Kent 52 C6
York Lancs 203 G10
York 207 C7
Yorkletts Kent 70 G5
Yorkley Glos 79 D10
Yorkley Slade Glos 79 D10
York Town Sur 65 G11
Yorton Shrops 149 E10
Yorton Heath Shrops 149 E10
Yottenfews Cumb 219 D10
Youlgrave Derbys 170 C2
Youlstone Devon 24 D3
Youlthorpe E Yorks 207 B11
Youlton N Yorks 215 G9
Youngsbury Herts 86 B5
Young's End Essex 88 B2
Young Wood Lincs 189 G10
Yoxall Staffs 152 F2
Yoxford Suff 127 D7
Y Pîl = *Pyle* Bridgend 57 E10
Yr Hôb = *Hope* Flint 166 D4
Ysbyty Cynfyn Ceredig 112 B5
Ysbyty Ifan Conwy 164 F4
Ysbyty Ystwyth Ceredig 112 C4
Ysceifiog Flint 181 G11
Ysgeibion Denb 165 D9
Yspitty Carms 56 B5
Ystalyfera Neath 76 D3
Ystrad Rhondda 77 F7
Ystrad Aeron Ceredig 111 F10
Ystradfellte Powys 76 C6
Ystradffin Carms 94 B5
Ystradgynlais Powys 76 C3
Ystradmeurig Ceredig 112 D4
Ystrad-mynach Caerph 77 G10
Ystradowen Carms 76 C2
V Glam 58 D4
Ystrad Uchaf Powys 129 C11
Ystumtuen Ceredig 112 B4
Ythanbank Aberds 303 F9
Ythanwells Aberds 302 F6
Ythsie Aberds 303 F8
Y Tymbl = *Tumble* Carms 75 E8
Y Waun = *Chirk* Wrex 148 B5

Z

Zeal Monachorum Devon 26 G2
Zeals Wilts 45 G9
Zelah Corn 4 E6
Zennor Corn 1 B5
Zoar Corn 3 F7
Zouch Notts 153 E10

County and unitary authority boundaries

Ordnance Survey National Grid

The blue lines which divide the Navigator map pages into squares for indexing match the Ordnance Survey National Grid and correspond to the small squares on the boundary map below. Each side of a grid square measures 10km on the ground.

The National Grid 100-km square letters and kilometre values are indicated for the grid intersection at the outer corners of each page. For example, the intersection SE6090 at the upper right corner of page 215 is 60km East and 90km North of the south-west corner of National Grid square SE.

SE6090
North Yorkshire
SE
York
East Ric
of Yorks
West
Yorkshire
South
Yorkshire
90km
60km

A
60
90
SE
Baxton's
Wood

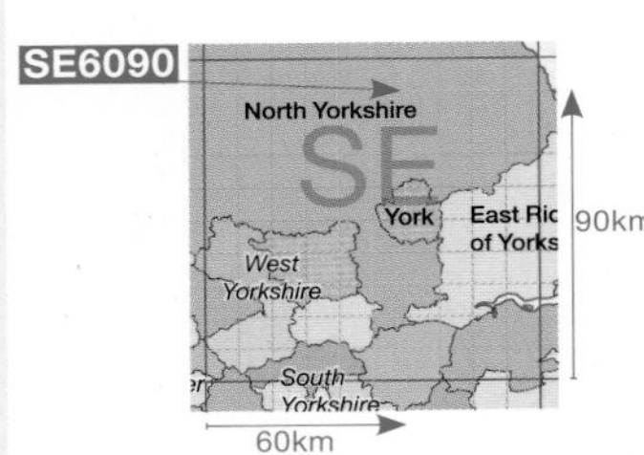

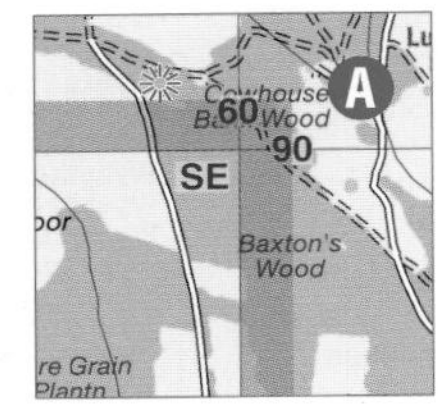

Using GPS with Navigator mapping

Since Navigator Britain is based on Ordnance Survey mapping, and rectified to the National Grid, it can be used with in-car or handheld GPS for locating identifiable waypoints such as road junctions, bridges, railways and farms, or assessing your position in relation to any of the features shown on the map.

On your receiver, choose British Grid as the location format and for map datum select Ordnance Survey (this may be described as Ord Srvy GB or similar, or more specifically as OSGB36). Your receiver will automatically convert the latitude/longitude co-ordinates transmitted by GPS into compatible National Grid data.

Positional accuracy of any particular feature is limited to 50–100m, due to the limitations of the original survey and the scale of Navigator mapping.

For further information see www.gps.gov.uk

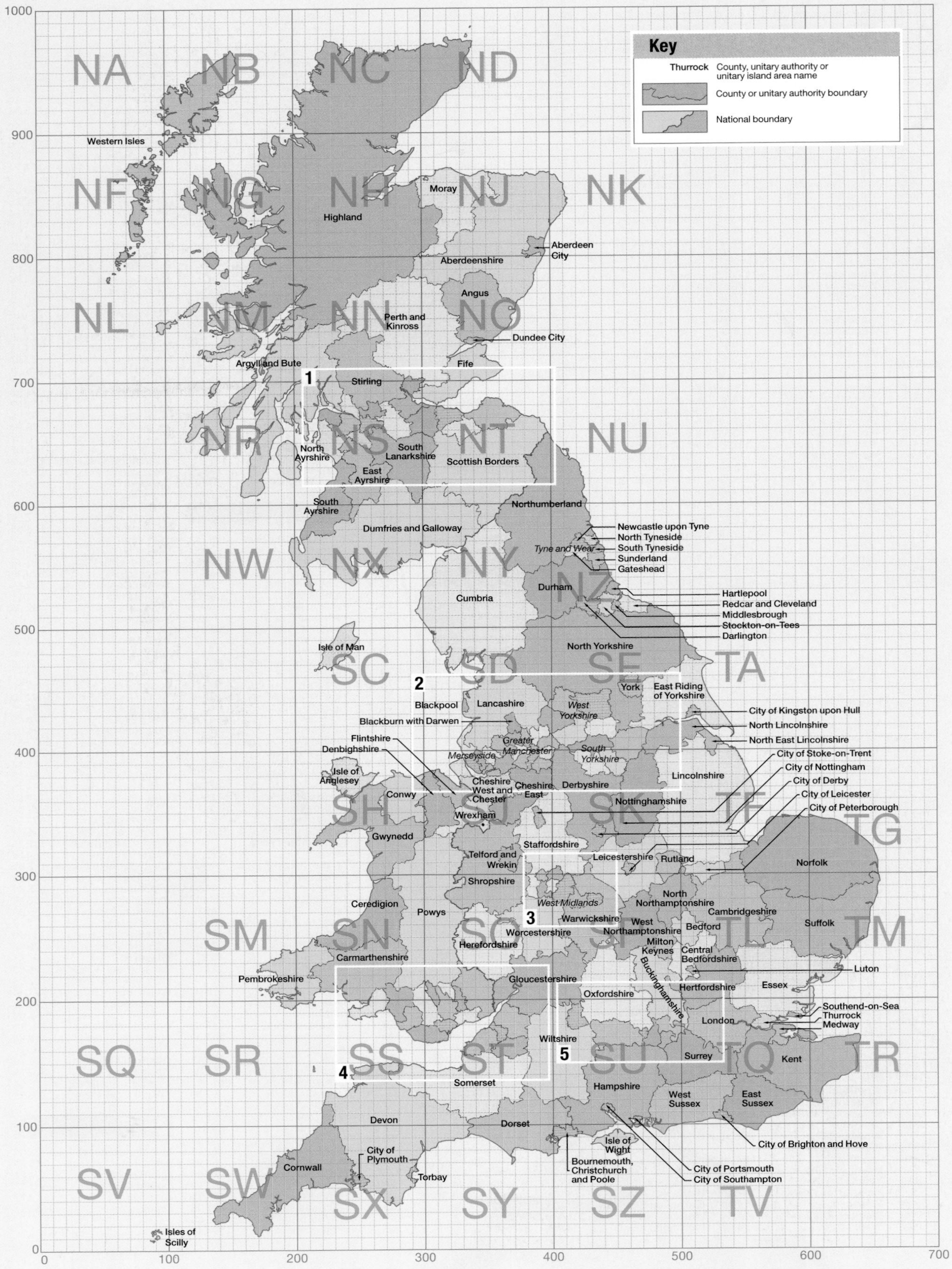

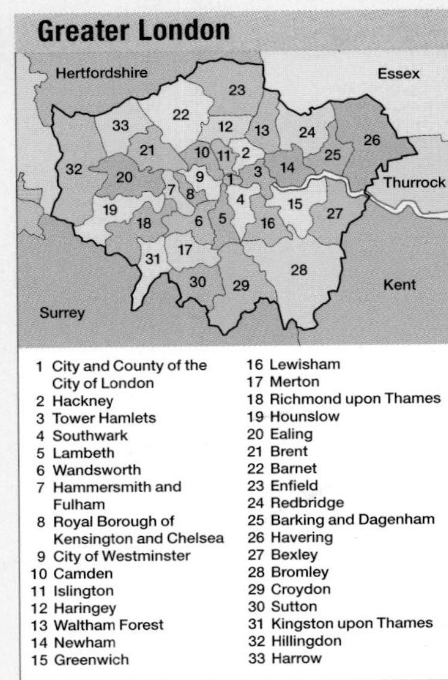

Key
Thurrock County, unitary authority or unitary island area name
County or unitary authority boundary
National boundary
NA NB NC ND NF NG NH NJ NK NL NM NN NO NR NS NT NU NW NX NY NZ SC SD SE TA SH SJ SK TF TG SM SN SO SP TL TM SQ SR SS ST SU TQ TR SV SW SX SY SZ TV
Western Isles
Highland
Moray
Aberdeenshire
Aberdeen City
Angus
Perth and Kinross
Dundee City
Argyll and Bute
Fife
Stirling
North Ayrshire
South Lanarkshire
East Ayrshire
Scottish Borders
South Ayrshire
Dumfries and Galloway
Northumberland
Newcastle upon Tyne
North Tyneside
South Tyneside
Tyne and Wear
Sunderland
Gateshead
Cumbria
Durham
Hartlepool
Redcar and Cleveland
Middlesbrough
Stockton-on-Tees
Darlington
Isle of Man
North Yorkshire
Blackpool
Lancashire
West Yorkshire
York
East Riding of Yorkshire
Blackburn with Darwen
City of Kingston upon Hull
North Lincolnshire
North East Lincolnshire
Flintshire
Denbighshire
Greater Manchester
Merseyside
South Yorkshire
City of Stoke-on-Trent
City of Nottingham
Isle of Anglesey
Cheshire West and Chester
Cheshire East
Derbyshire
Lincolnshire
City of Derby
City of Leicester
City of Peterborough
Conwy
Nottinghamshire
Wrexham
Gwynedd
Staffordshire
Telford and Wrekin
Leicestershire
Rutland
Norfolk
Shropshire
North Northamptonshire
West Midlands
Ceredigion
Powys
Warwickshire
Cambridgeshire
Suffolk
Worcestershire
West Northamptonshire
Bedford
Herefordshire
Milton Keynes
Central Bedfordshire
Carmarthenshire
Pembrokeshire
Gloucestershire
Luton
Buckinghamshire
Hertfordshire
Essex
Oxfordshire
Southend-on-Sea
Thurrock
Medway
London
Wiltshire
Surrey
Kent
Somerset
Hampshire
West Sussex
East Sussex
Devon
Dorset
City of Brighton and Hove
Isle of Wight
Cornwall
City of Plymouth
Torbay
Bournemouth, Christchurch and Poole
City of Portsmouth
City of Southampton
Isles of Scilly
1 2 3 4 5
0 100 200 300 400 500 600 700
1000 900 800 700 600 500 400 300 200 100 0

Greater London

Hertfordshire
Essex
Thurrock
Surrey
Kent
1 2 3 4 5 6 7 8 9 10 11 12 13 14 15 16 17 18 19 20 21 22 23 24 25 26 27 28 29 30 31 32 33

1 City and County of the City of London
2 Hackney
3 Tower Hamlets
4 Southwark
5 Lambeth
6 Wandsworth
7 Hammersmith and Fulham
8 Royal Borough of Kensington and Chelsea
9 City of Westminster
10 Camden
11 Islington
12 Haringey
13 Waltham Forest
14 Newham
15 Greenwich
16 Lewisham
17 Merton
18 Richmond upon Thames
19 Hounslow
20 Ealing
21 Brent
22 Barnet
23 Enfield
24 Redbridge
25 Barking and Dagenham
26 Havering
27 Bexley
28 Bromley
29 Croydon
30 Sutton
31 Kingston upon Thames
32 Hillingdon
33 Harrow

1 Central Scotland

East Dunbartonshire
West Dunbartonshire
Inverclyde
Falkirk
Clackmannanshire
East Lothian
Renfrewshire
East Renfrewshire
Glasgow City
North Lanarkshire
Midlothian
City of Edinburgh
West Lothian

2 Northern England

Rochdale
Bury
Salford
Bolton
Wigan
St Helens
Calderdale
Bradford
Kirklees
Leeds
Wakefield
Doncaster
Barnsley
Rotherham
Sheffield
Sefton
Wirral
Liverpool
Knowsley
Halton
Oldham
Tameside
Stockport
Manchester
Trafford
Warrington

3 West Midlands

City of Wolverhampton
Sandwell
Walsall
Coventry
Solihull
Birmingham
Dudley

4 South Wales and Bristol area

Caerphilly
Merthyr Tydfil
Rhondda, Cynon, Taff
Neath Port Talbot
Blaenau Gwent
Torfaen
Monmouthshire
Swansea
Bridgend
The Vale of Glamorgan
Cardiff
City and County of Newport
North Somerset
City and countyof Bristol
Bath and North-East Somerset
South Gloucestershire

5 Thames Valley

Slough
Windsor & Maidenhead
Reading
Swindon
Bracknell Forest
Wokingham
West Berkshire

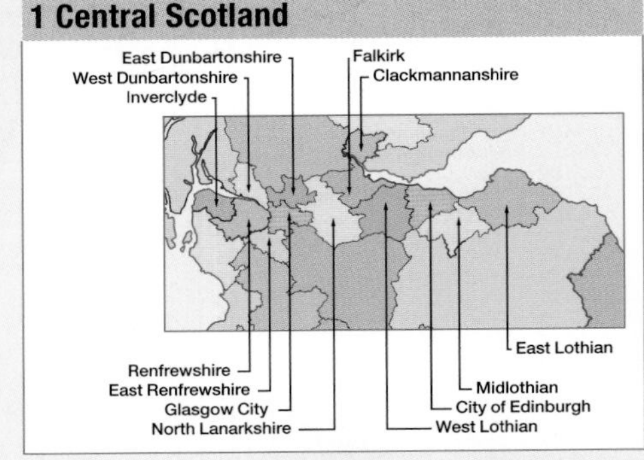

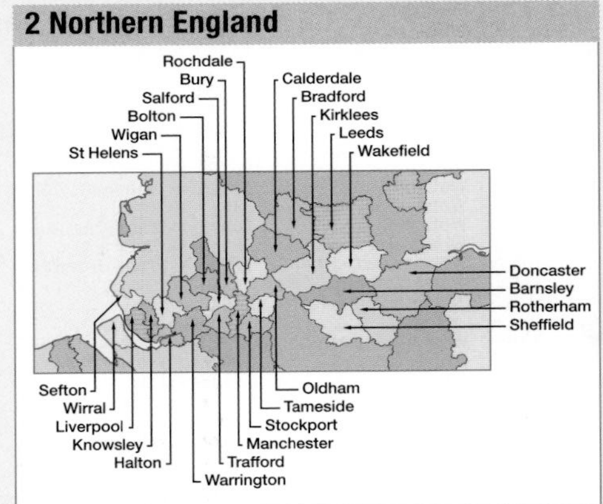

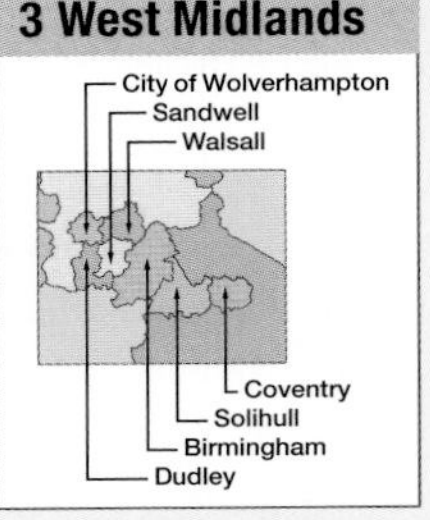

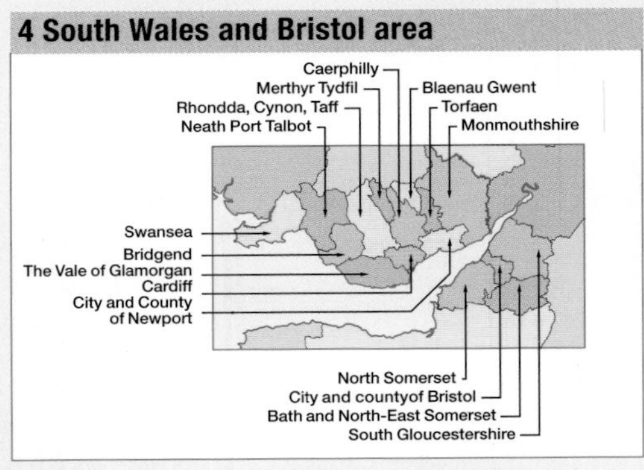

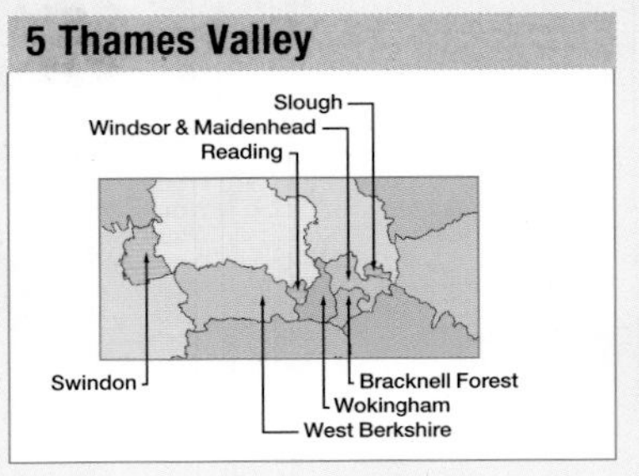